PATTERSON'S

AMERICAN EDUCATION

1995 Edition
VOLUME XCI

Editorial Staff
Managing Editor   Douglas Moody
Associate Editor   Wayne Moody
Assistant Editor   Michael McCreery
Assistant Editor   Rita Ostdick
Assistant Editor   James Thiessen

EDUCATIONAL DIRECTORIES INC.

Educational Directories Inc.
PO Box 199
Mount Prospect IL 60056-0199
(708) 459-0605

First edition published 1904. Ninety-first edition 1995

ISBN 0-910536-61-9
ISSN 0079-0230
Library of Congress Catalog Card Number: 04-012953

Printed in the United States of America

CONTENTS

How To Use This Directory   iv

Guide To Editorial Style   vii

Part I

    Secondary Schools Alphabetically By State   1

    United States Territorial Secondary Schools   510

    Catholic School Superintendents   517

    Lutheran School Superintendents   519

    Seventh-Day Adventists School Superintendents   520

    Educational Associations And Societies   521

Part II

    Patterson's SCHOOLS CLASSIFIED   525

    How To Use Patterson's SCHOOLS CLASSIFIED   526

    Index   819

HOW TO USE THIS DIRECTORY

Patterson's AMERICAN EDUCATION (published annually since 1904) is THE standard directory to secondary schools and is the first in a series of school directories published by Educational Directories Inc. Patterson's ELEMENTARY EDUCATION (published annually since 1989) is identical in format to Patterson's AMERICAN EDUCATION but is a directory to elementary schools; and Patterson's SCHOOLS CLASSIFIED (published annually since 1951) is the most comprehensive directory to post-secondary schools available. The three volumes combined fulfill the need for a single, systematized, comprehensive directory to our nation's schools from kindergarten through post-graduate studies.

Patterson's AMERICAN EDUCATION contains 12,000 public school districts, 30,000 public secondary schools, 3,000 private and Catholic secondary schools and more than 7,000 post-secondary schools in an easy to use and consistent format. It is an invaluable resource to anyone involved in education or educational research. School registrars, guidance counselors, principals, superintendents, directors of admissions, financial aid officers, schools of education, public libraries, government agencies, armed forces, and business people find it a welcome replacement for the multitude of other directories required for national coverage of our nation's school systems with their variation in size, content, format and publishing date.

One of the primary objectives of this directory is to make available the latest, most comprehensive information about secondary and post-secondary schools in a condensed and easily accessible format. Its general organization is geographical. Entries are arranged alphabetically, by state, then by community (post office) and then by school type. Each state begins with a listing of the officials in its Department of Education followed by the head of the State Board of Education. If a state has intermediate superintendents (a level of superintendent between the state superintendent of schools and the superintendents who actually supervise the schools) they appear in a table preceding the community listings. Community listings follow and include the community name, telephone area code, community population, county name, district name, total district student enrollment, the superintendent's name, address and telephone number followed by a listing of the district schools, showing their enrollment, grade range and the principal's name, address and telephone number. To avoid repetition, the name of the school is omitted when its name is the same as the community name. A district may be responsible for schools in more than one community. To achieve consistency, the district office is listed in the community in which it is located. A cross reference is provided to and from the schools of the district located in other communities.

A short line may appear at the end of the listing of public secondary schools. This line separates the public secondary schools from the private and Catholic secondary schools and the post-secondary schools located in the community. Private and Catholic school listings include their enrollment, grade range and the principal's name, address and telephone number. Post-secondary school listings include their name, address and type of school code. Please refer to page vii "Guide to Editorial Style" for an example of how these elements work together to provide an easy to use format.

Schools Listed

Patterson's AMERICAN EDUCATION lists the following types of schools

- **Middle Schools** teach any combination of grades two through eight.
- **Junior High Schools** teach any combination of grades not including one or twelve but including eight and nine.
- **Mid High Schools** teach nine but not eight or twelve.
- **Junior-Senior High Schools** teach any combination of grades not including one but including eight, nine and twelve.
- **High Schools** teach grades nine through twelve.
- **Senior High Schools** teach twelve but not nine.
- **K-12** teach grades one through twelve.
- **Vocational-Technical Programs**.

Included are:

- All graded State Approved public secondary schools.
- All graded Diocesan Catholic secondary schools.
- All graded Regionally Accredited private secondary schools.
- Non Regionally Accredited private secondary schools with more than 100 students.

Non graded, special education schools and other non-traditional secondary schools are not listed.

Patterson's ELEMENTARY EDUCATION lists Kindergarten Schools, Primary Schools, Elementary Schools, Middle Schools and K-12 Schools.

Addresses

Since the majority of our users view the directory as a source of mailing addresses rather than visiting addresses, it is editorial practice to list the official United States Postal Service mailing address whenever possible. When a school district chooses to route all of the mail for its schools through a central post office box, we follow its practice and provide the district address for each of its schools.

Enrollment/Population Codes

School and district student enrollments are shown by a code using the first digit in a series of digits to the right of the school or district name. Community populations are shown to the right of the community name. See page vi.

Grade Codes

The grade range for a school or district is identified by a code using a series of five digits to the right of the school enrollment code. The five digit code is easier to read than a twelve digit code and produces essentially the same result. The first digit in the series represents the first grade, the second digit the fifth grade, the third digit the eighth grade, the fourth digit the ninth grade, and the fifth digit the twelfth grade. If the digit is a "0" the school does not teach the indicated grade. If the digit is a "1" the school does teach the indicated grade. School systems follow a clearly defined organizational plan which is easy to identify using the code. For example, high schools which teach grades nine through twelve are identified by the code 00011. Senior high schools are identified by the code 00001 and Jr-Sr high schools by the code 00111. Vocational-Technical programs are identified by the code Vo Tech in the grade range field. See page vi.

ABBREVIATIONS

CCSD . . . . Community Consolidated School District
CESD . . . . Consolidated Elementary School District
CISD . . . . City Independent School District
CSD . . . . City School District
CUSD . . . . Community Unit School District
ECCSD . Elementary Community Consolidated School District
EHSD . . . . Elementary-High School District
ES . . . . Elementary School
ESD . . . . Elementary School District
EVD . . . . Exempted Village District
HSD . . . . High School District
IS . . . . Intermediate School
ISD . . . . Independent School District
JESD . . . . Joint Elementary School District
JHS . . . . Junior High School
JSD . . . . Joint School District
JSHS . . . . Junior-Senior High School
JUESD . . . . Joint Unified Elementary School District
JUHSD . . . . Joint Unified High School District
JUNESD . . . . . . Joint Union Elementary School District
JUNHSD . . . . Joint Union High School District

JUSD . . . . Joint Unified School District
JVSD . . . . Joint Vocational School District
K . . . . Kindergarten
MS . . . . Middle School
PS . . . . Primary School
RHSD . . . . Rural High School District
RISD . . . . Rural Independent School District
RSD . . . . Reorganized School District
S . . . . School
SAD . . . . School Administrative District
SD . . . . School District
SHS . . . . Senior High School
SSD . . . . Separate School District
UESD . . . . Unified Elementary School District
UFD . . . . Union Free District
UHSD . . . . Unified High School District
UNESD . . . . Union Elementary School District
UNHSD . . . . Union High School District
UNSD . . . . Union School District
USD . . . . Unified School District
Vo Tech . . . . Vocational-Technical

ENROLLMENT/POPULATION CODES

Code	From-To	Code	From-To
1	0-100	7	10,001-25,000
2	101-500	8	25,001-100,000
3	501-1,000	9	100,001-250,000
4	1,001-2,500	10	250,001-500,000
5	2,501-5,000	11	500,001-1,000,000
6	5,001-10,000	12	Over 1,000,000

GRADE CODES

A five digit code to the right of the school or district name indicates the grades taught.

0 = school does not teach the grade
1 = school does teach the grade
  Example: 00011 = (High School does not teach one through eight but does teach nine through twelve)

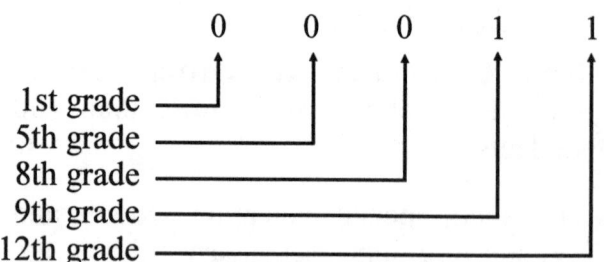

TYPE OF SCHOOL CODES

UC . . . . University/College
CC . . . . Community College/Junior College
CS . . . . Career School

HMS . . . . Home Study School
HND . . . . Handicapped School
HSP . . . . Hospital School

GUIDE TO EDITORIAL STYLE

Agate, AC 719, PC 1, Elbert
Agate SD 300 — 1-11111 / 764-2741
PO BOX 118   80101
James McDermott, supt.
S, PO BOX 118   80101 — 1-11111 / 764-2741
James McDermott, prin.

Aguilar, AC 719, PC 3, Las Animas
Aguilar RSD 6 — 2-11111 / 941-4614
PO BOX 567   81020
Lillian Stanton, supt.
JSHS, PO BOX 567   81020 — 1-00111 / 941-4640
Joan Crittenden, prin.

Akron, AC 303, PC 4, Washington
Akron SD R-1 — 2-11111 / 345-2268
PO BOX 429   80720
Delano Arnold, supt.
HS, 600 ELM AVE   80720 — 2-00011 / 345-2268
Charles Johnson, prin.

Alamosa, AC 719, PC 6, Alamosa
Alamosa SD RE-11J — 5-11111 / 589-6634
209 VICTORIA AVE   81101
Janet Makris, supt.
HS, 401 VICTORIA AVE   81101 — 3-00011 / 589-6696
Tim Snyder, prin.
Ortega MS, 1301 MAIN ST   81101 — 3-00100 / 589-6669
John Jordan, prin.

Adams State College   81102 — 4-UC / 824-6494

Anton, AC 303, PC 1, Washington
Arickaree SD R-2 — 2-11111 / 383-2202
12155 COUNTY RD NN   80801
Larry Stukey, supt.
Arickaree JSHS — 1-00111 / 383-2202
12155 COUNTY RD NN   80801
Larry Stukey, prin.

Antonito, AC 719, PC 3, Conejos
South Conejos SD RE-10 — 2-11111 / 376-5512
PO BOX 398   81120
Angelo Velasquez, supt.
HS, PO BOX 398   81120 — 2-00011 / 376-5463
Felix Gonzales, prin.
JHS, PO BOX 398   81120 — 1-00100 / 376-5468
Felix Gonzales, prin.

Arvada, AC 303, PC 8, Jefferson
Jefferson County SD R-1
Supt. — See Golden
SHS, 7951 W 65TH AVE   80004 — 4-00001 / 423-3830
James Melhouse, prin.
Arvada West SHS — 4-00001 / 422-2326
11325 ALLENDALE DR   80004
Ray Schneringer, prin.
Pomona HS — 4-00011 / 423-9092
8101 POMONA DR   80005
John Jost, prin.
JHS, 5751 BALSAM ST   80002 — 3-00110 / 423-1553
Ken Robke, prin.
Drake JHS — 3-00110 / 422-3471
12550 W 52ND AVE   80002
Gerald Neel, prin.
Moore MS — 3-00100 / 420-8641
8455 W 88TH AVE   80005
Ken Nakauchi, prin.
North Arvada JHS — 3-00100 / 421-2660
7285 PIERCE ST   80003
Jerry Owen, prin.
Oberon JHS, 7300 QUAIL ST   80005 — 3-00110 / 421-6776
Paul Mott, prin.

Faith Christian Academy — 3-11111 / 424-7310
6210 WARD RD   80004
(—), prin.
Maranatha Christian ES — 3-11111 / 431-5653
7180 OAK ST   80004 - (—), prin.

Aspen, AC 303, PC 6, Pitkin
Aspen SD 1 — 4-11111 / 925-3460
235 HIGH SCHOOL RD   81611
Tom Farrell, supt.
HS, 235 HIGH SCHOOL RD   81611 — 2-00011 / 925-2972
Bruce Lindberg, prin.
MS, 235 HIGH SCHOOL RD   81611 — 2-01100 / 925-6623
Michael Reeves, prin.

Ault, AC 303, PC 4, Weld
Ault-Highland SD RE-9 — 3-11111 / 834-1345
PO BOX 68   80610
Kenneth Frisbie, supt.
Highland HS, PO BOX 68   80610 — 2-00011 / 834-2816
Joann DeBus, prin.
Highland MS, PO BOX 68   80610 — 2-01100 / 834-2857
Roger McWilliams, prin.

Aurora, AC 303, PC 9, Arapahoe
Adams-Arapahoe SD 28J — 8-11111 / 344-8060
1085 PEORIA ST   80011
Victor Ross, supt.

• **State** — applicable to all addresses

• **City, area code, city population, county**
 City — Agate
 AC (area code) — 719
 PC (city population) — 1
   Refer to page vi for population codes.
 County — Elbert

• **School district name**
 Alamosa SD RE-11J
   Refer to page vi for abbreviations.

• **Name and address of superintendent**
 Address — 209 VICTORIA AVE
 City — Alamosa
 State — COLORADO
 Zip code — 81101
 Superintendent — Janet Makris

• **Student enrollment, grade range**
 Student enrollment — 2
 Grade range — 11111
   Refer to page vi for enrollment/ grade codes.

• **Telephone number**
 303-383-2202

• *Community schools — school, student enrollment, grade range, name, address and telephone number of principal. School name is omitted when its name is the same as the city name.*

• *If school district office is not located in this city, a cross reference will show office location.*
 Supt. — See Englewood

• *Post-secondary schools, private and Catholic secondary schools appear below a short line in the cities where they are located.*

• *Type of post-secondary school*
 Type of school — UC
   Refer to page vi for type of school codes.

Ault, AC 303, PC 4, Weld
Ault-Highland SD RE-9 — 3-11111 / 834-1345
PO BOX 68   80610
Kenneth Frisbie, supt.
Highland HS, PO BOX 68   80610 — 2-00011 / 834-2816
Joann DeBus, prin.
Highland MS, PO BOX 68   80610 — 2-01100 / 834-2857
Roger McWilliams, prin.

Aurora, AC 303, PC 9, Arapahoe
Adams-Arapahoe SD 28J — 8-11111 / 344-8060
1085 PEORIA ST   80011
Victor Ross, supt.
Central HS — 4-00011 / 340-1600
11700 E 11TH AVE   80010
Kenneth Lytwyniuk, prin.
Gateway HS — 4-00011 / 755-7160
1300 S SABLE BLVD   80012
Reinhold Mattes, prin.
Hinkley HS — 4-00011 / 340-1500
1250 CHAMBERS RD   80011
Stanley Pursley, prin.
Rangeview HS — 4-00011 / 695-6848
17599 E ILIFF AVE   80013
Marc Stine, prin.
Pickens Tech Ctr — Vo Tech / 344-4910
500 BUCKLEY RD   80011
Dale McCall, prin.
Aurora Hills MS — 3-00100 / 341-7450
1009 S UVALDA ST   80012
Harold Pyper, prin.
Columbia MS — 3-00100 / 690-6570
17600 E COLUMBIA AVE   80013
Harold Stevens, prin.
East MS, 1275 FRASER ST   80011 — 3-00100 / 340-0660
Nancy Pokorny, prin.
Mrachek MS — 4-00100 / 750-2836
1955 S TELLURIDE ST   80013
Charles Willsea, prin.
North MS — 3-00100 / 364-7411
12095 MONTVIEW BLVD   80010
Richard Rusak, prin.
South MS — 3-00100 / 364-7623
12310 E PARKVIEW DR   80011
Dan Colvin, prin.
West MS, 10100 E 13TH AVE   80010 — 3-00100 / 366-2671
John Basham, prin.

Cherry Creek SD 5
Supt. — See Englewood
Overland HS — 4-00011 / 696-3700
12400 E JEWELL AVE   80012
John Buckner, prin.
Smoky Hill HS — 4-00011 / 693-1700
16100 E SMOKY HILL RD   80015
Mary Jarvis, prin.
Eaglecrest JSHS — 4-00111 / 699-0408
5100 S PICADILLY ST   80015
Terry Conley, prin.
Horizon MS — 4-00100 / 693-4242
3981 S RESERVOIR RD   80013
Kathleen Smith, prin.
Laredo MS — 4-00100 / 693-1500
5000 S LAREDO ST   80015
Judith Hilton, prin.
Prairie MS — 4-00100 / 696-3750
12600 E JEWELL AVE   80012
Catherine Canny, prin.
Thunder Ridge MS — 3-00100 / 699-0408
5205 PICADILLY RD   80019
Terry Killin, prin.

Aurora Christian Academy — 2-11111 / 344-2530
11001 E ALAMEDA AVE   80012
(—), prin.
Colorado Career Academy — 2-CS / 690-6900
13790 E RICE PL   80015
Community College of Aurora — 4-CC / 360-4700
16000 E CENTRETECH PKY   80011
ITT Technical Institute — 3-CS / 695-1913
2121 S BLACKHAWK ST   80014
Parks Junior College — 2-CS / 367-2757
6 ABILENE ST   80011
Pickens Technical Center — CS / 344-4910
500 BUCKLEY RD   80011
Platt College — 2-CS / 369-5151
3100 S PARKER RD   80014
Regis Jesuit HS — 3-00011 / 699-1598
16300 E WEAVER PL   80016
James Knapp, prin.

Boulder, AC 303, PC 8, Boulder
Boulder Valley SD RE-2 — 7-11111 / 447-1010
PO BOX 9011   80301
Dean Damon, supt.

Naropa Institute — 2-UC / 444-0202
2130 ARAPAHOE AVE   80302

Part I

SECONDARY SCHOOLS

ALABAMA

STATE DEPARTMENT OF EDUCATION
Gordon Persons Building
50 N. Ripley St., Montgomery 36130
(205) 242-9700

State Superintendent of Education	Wayne Teague
Assistant State Superintendent Instructional Services	Charlie Williams
Assistant State Superintendent Admin. & Financial Services	Kenneth Wilson
Assistant State Superintendent General Administrative Services	William Rutherford
Assistant State Superintendent Professional Studies	Eddie Johnson

STATE BOARD OF EDUCATION
50 N. Ripley St., Montgomery 36130

President	Governor Jim Folsom

PUBLIC, PRIVATE AND CATHOLIC SECONDARY SCHOOLS

Abbeville, AC 205, PC 5, Henry
Henry County SD, PO BOX 635 36310 — 5-11111
Bill Davis, supt. — 585-2206
HS, PO BOX 519 36310 — 3-00011
Wiley Smith, prin. — 585-2065
MS, PO BOX 547 36310 — 2-00100
Danny Hooper, prin. — 585-2185
Other Schools – See Headland, Newville

Abbeville Christian Academy — 2-11111
PO BOX 9 36310 — 585-5100
Barbara Lindsey, prin.

Adamsville, AC 205, PC 5, Jefferson
Jefferson County SD
Supt. — See Birmingham
Minor SHS, 2285 MINOR PKY 35005 — 3-00001
C. Richard Humber, prin. — 798-3770
Bottonfield JHS — 3-00110
400 HILLCREST RD 35005 — 674-5605
James Pearson, prin.

Addison, AC 205, PC 3, Winston
Winston County SD
Supt. — See Double Springs
S, PO BOX 241 35540 — 3-11111
Olen Bolzle, prin. — 747-2286

Akron, AC 205, PC 2, Hale
Hale County SD
Supt. — See Greensboro
Akron Community JSHS East — 2-00111
PO BOX 38 35441 — 372-3787
Fredricka Waiters, prin.

Alabaster, AC 205, PC 7, Shelby
Shelby County SD
Supt. — See Columbiana
Thompson HS, 100 WARRIOR DR 35007 — 3-00011
James Elliott, prin. — 620-1000
Thompson MS, 36 6TH AVE SE 35007 — 3-00100
Jane Riley, prin. — 620-1050

Albertville, AC 205, PC 7, Marshall
Albertville CSD, PO BOX 1487 35950 — 5-11111
James Pratt, supt. — 891-1183
HS, 402 E MCCORD AVE 35950 — 3-00011
Frank Smith, prin. — 878-6580
Alabama Avenue MS — 3-00100
600 E ALABAMA AVE 35950 — 878-2341
Richard Denham, prin.

Alexander City, AC 205, PC 7, Tallapoosa
Alexander City CSD — 5-11111
PO BOX 1205 35010 — 234-5074
Paul Fanning, supt.
Russell HS, PO BOX 1029 35010 — 4-00011
David Dunaway, prin. — 234-8611
Alexander City Area Vo HS — Vo Tech
100 E COUNTRY CLUB DR 35010 — 234-8641
Joe Martin, prin.
MS, PO BOX 817 35010 — 3-00100
Jere Lawrence, prin. — 234-8660

Tallapoosa County SD
Supt. — See Dadeville
Horseshoe Bend S, RR 4 BOX 240A 35010 — 2-11111
James Peoples, prin. — 329-9110
Tallapoosa Area Vo HS — Vo Tech
100 JR COLLEGE DR 35010 — 234-8641
Joe Martin, prin.

Central Alabama Community College — 4-CC
PO BOX 699 35010 — 234-6346
Tallapoosa-Alexander City Vocational Ctr — 2-CS
100 E JUNIOR COLLEGE DR 35010

Alexandria, AC 205, PC 2, Calhoun
Calhoun County SD
Supt. — See Anniston
JSHS, PO BOX 180 36250 — 4-01111
Ronald Chambless, prin. — 820-4141

Aliceville, AC 205, PC 5, Pickens
Pickens County SD
Supt. — See Carrollton
JSHS, 300 EUTAW RD 35442 — 2-00111
Daniel Shakespear, prin. — 373-6378

Alpine, AC 205, PC 2, Talladega
Talladega County SD
Supt. — See Talladega
Winterboro S — 3-11111
22601 AL HIGHWAY 21 35014 — 362-9135
Don Moye, prin.
Pittard Area Vo HS — Vo Tech
22401 AL HIGHWAY 21 35014 — 362-3404
L. McMurphy, prin.

Pittard Area Vocational School — 2-CS
22401 AL HIGHWAY 21 35014

Andalusia, AC 205, PC 6, Covington
Andalusia CSD, 122 6TH AVE 36420 — 4-11111
David Brantley, supt. — 222-3186
HS, 701 E 3RD ST 36420 — 3-00011
Pete Kelley, prin. — 222-7569
MS, 1201 8TH AVE 36420 — 2-00100
Louie Fryer, prin. — 222-6542

Covington County SD — 5-11111
PO BOX 460 36420 — 222-7571
James Odom, supt.
Pleasant Home S, RR 7 BOX 10 36420 — 3-11111
James Garner, prin. — 222-1315
Straughn S, RR 10 BOX 310 36420 — 3-11111
John Thomasson, prin. — 222-2511
Other Schools – See Florala, Red Level

Lurleen B Wallace Junior College — 4-CC
PO BOX 1418 36420 — 222-6591

Anniston, AC 205, PC 8, Calhoun
Anniston CSD, PO BOX 1500 36202 — 5-11111
Paul Goodwin, supt. — 231-5000
HS, 1301 WOODSTOCK AVE 36201 — 4-00011
Ron Miller, prin. — 231-5010
MS, 4800 MCCLELLAN BLVD 36206 — 3-00100
Jacky Sparks, prin. — 231-5020

Calhoun County SD — 7-11111
PO BOX 2084 36202 — 236-7641
Jim Winn, supt.
Saks JSHS, 4401 SAKS RD 36206 — 3-00111
Edwin Henderson, prin. — 237-6381
Wellborn JSHS, 135 PINSON RD 36201 — 4-00111
Katrina Akers, prin. — 236-2652
White Plains S — 3-11111
250 WHITE PLAINS RD 36201 — 238-8548
Benny Character, prin.
Other Schools – See Alexandria, Jacksonville,
Ohatchee, Weaver

Ayers State Technical College — 2-CS
PO BOX 1647 36202 — 831-4540
Donoho S, 2501 HENRY RD 36201 — 3-11111
George Gorey, prin. — 237-5477
Gadsden Business College — 2-CS
PO BOX 1575 36202 — 237-7517
New World College of Business — 3-CS
1031 NOBLE ST 36201 — 236-7578

Arab, AC 205, PC 6, Marshall
Arab CSD, PO BOX O 35016 — 5-11111
James Cooley, supt. — 586-6011
HS, PO BOX 35016 — 3-00011
John Ingram, prin. — 586-6026
JHS, 125 OLD CULLMAN RD 35016 — 3-00100
Kerry Walker, prin. — 586-6074

Ardmore, AC 205, PC 4, Limestone
Limestone County SD
Supt. — See Athens
S, PO BOX 609 35739 — 3-11111
Ronnie Holt, prin. — 423-2685

Ariton, AC 205, PC 3, Dale
Dale County SD
Supt. — See Ozark
S, PO BOX 248 36311 — 2-11111
James Willis, prin. — 762-2371

Arley, AC 205, PC 2, Winston
Winston County SD
Supt. — See Double Springs
Meek S, PO BOX 126 35541 — 3-11111
Larry Reed, prin. — 384-5825

Ashford, AC 205, PC 4, Houston
Houston County SD
Supt. — See Dothan
JSHS, PO BOX S 36312 — 3-00111
Shirley McArdle, prin. — 899-5411
Houston Co. Area Vo Ctr — Vo Tech
PO BOX V 36312 — 899-3308
Donald Spivey, prin.

Ashford Academy — 2-11111
RR 3 BOX 604 36312 — 899-5905
Helen Dodson, prin.

Ashland, AC 205, PC 4, Clay
Clay County SD, PO BOX 278 36251 — 5-11111
James Fulbright, supt. — 354-5414
Clay County JSHS — 2-00111
PO BOX 160 36251 — 354-7510
Garey Reynolds, prin.
Other Schools – See Cragford, Lineville, Millerville

Ashville, AC 205, PC 4, St. Clair
Saint Clair County SD — 6-11111
PO BOX 248 35953 — 594-5693
Charles Ray, supt.
JSHS, PO BOX 717 35953 — 2-00111
Jerry Patterson, prin. — 594-7943
Eden Area Vo HS — Vo Tech
RR 2 BOX 248 35953 — 594-7055
John Hazelwood, prin.
Other Schools – See Moody, Odenville, Ragland,
Springville

John Pope Eden Area Vocational Center — 2-CS
RR 2 BOX 1855 35953 — 594-3461

Athens, AC 205, PC 7, Limestone
Athens CSD
  313 E WASHINGTON ST 35611 — 5-11111 / 233-6600
  Joe Anglin, supt.
  HS, PO BOX 109 35611 — 3-00011 / 233-6613
  Tee Jackson, prin.
  MS, 601 S CLINTON ST 35611 — 3-00100 / 233-6620
  Cecil Armstrong, supt.

Limestone County SD — 6-11111 / 232-5353
  300 N JEFFERSON ST 35611
  Don Osborne, supt.
  Clements S, RR 5 BOX 344 35611 — 3-11111 / 729-6564
  Mike Owens, prin.
  East Limestone S — 4-11111 / 232-5484
  RR 3 BOX 190 35611
  Jimmy Drake, prin.
  Limestone Co. Area Vo-Tech HS — Vo Tech / 232-4813
  505 E SANDERFER RD 35611
  Bob Hastings, prin.
  Other Schools – See Ardmore, Elkmont, Lester,
  Tanner

Athens Bible S, 507 HOFFMAN ST 35611 — 2-11111 / 232-3525
  Joseph Olson, prin.
Athens State College — 4-UC / 233-8164
  300 N BEATY ST 35611

Atmore, AC 205, PC 6, Escambia
Escambia County SD
Supt. — See Brewton
Escambia County HS — 3-00011 / 368-9181
  1215 S PRESLEY ST 36502
  Thomas Plash, prin.
Escambia County MS — 3-01100 / 368-9105
  PO BOX 1236 36504
  Herbert Payne, prin.

Atmore State Technical College — 3-CS / 368-8118
  PO BOX 1119 36504
Escambia Academy — 2-11111 / 368-2080
  RR 4 BOX 450 36502
  Michael Smith, prin.

Attalla, AC 205, PC 6, Etowah
Attalla CSD, 101 CASE AVE SE 35954 — 4-11111 / 538-8051
  James Crocker, supt.
Etowah HS, 316 JONES ST SE 35954 — 3-00011 / 538-8381
  Ernie Payne, prin.
Etowah MS, 429 4TH ST SW 35954 — 3-00100 / 538-9221
  Mike Brown, prin.

Etowah County SD
Supt. — See Gadsden
Etowah Co. Area Vo HS — Vo Tech / 538-3312
  105 BURKE AVE SE 35954
  Kathye Vance, prin.

Auburn, AC 205, PC 8, Lee
Auburn CSD, PO BOX 3270 36831 — 5-11111 / 887-2100
  Ed Richardson, supt.
HS, 405 S DEAN RD 36830 — 3-00011 / 887-2118
  Robert Dotson, prin.
JHS, 332 SAMFORD AVE 36830 — 3-00100 / 887-2120
  Clima White, prin.

Auburn University 36849 — 7-UC / 844-4080

Lee-Scott Academy — 2-11111 / 821-2430
  2307 E GLENN AVE 36830
  John Meals, prin.

Autaugaville, AC 205, PC 3, Autauga
Autauga County SD
Supt. — See Prattville
JSHS, PO BOX 99 36003 — 2-00111 / 365-8329
  Lorenzo Harrison, prin.

Bay Minette, AC 205, PC 6, Baldwin
Baldwin County SD — 7-11111 / 937-0308
  175 COURT SQ 36507
  J. Newton, supt.
Baldwin County HS, 1 TIGER DR 36507 — 4-00011 / 937-2341
  Walter Duck, prin.
North Baldwin Tech Ctr — Vo Tech / 937-6751
  505 W HURRICANE RD 36507
  Thomas Rhodes, prin.
MS, 600 BLACKBURN AVE 36507 — 3-00100 / 937-9243
  James Cox, prin.
Other Schools – See Daphne, Fairhope, Foley, Gulf
  Shores, Loxley, Robertsdale

James H Faulkner State Junior College — 5-CC / 937-9581
  1900 HIGHWAY 59 S 36507

Bayou La Batre, AC 205, PC 4, Mobile
Mobile County SD
Supt. — See Mobile
Alba JSHS, 288 S WINTZELL AVE 36509 — 4-00111 / 824-4134
  Lewis Lathan, prin.

Bear Creek, AC 205, PC 3, Marion
Marion County SD
Supt. — See Hamilton
Phillips JSHS, RR 1 BOX 3 35543 — 2-00111 / 486-3737
  Sonny Frix, prin.

Beatrice, AC 205, PC 2, Monroe
Monroe County SD
Supt. — See Monroeville
Shields JSHS, RR 1 BOX 29 36425 — 2-00111 / 789-2168
  Larry Woolfolk, prin.

Berry, AC 205, PC 4, Fayette
Fayette County SD
Supt. — See Fayette
JSHS, PO BOX 499 35546 — 2-00111 / 689-4467
  G. Traweek, prin.

Bessemer, AC 205, PC 8, Jefferson
Bessemer CSD, PO BOX 1230 35021 — 6-11111 / 481-9800
  Ernest Nicholson, supt.
Lanier HS, 100 HIGH SCHOOL DR 35023 — 4-00011 / 481-9836
  Michael Russell, prin.
Bessemer Area Vo HS — Vo Tech / 481-9842
  50 HIGH SCHOOL DR 35023
  Theodore Jones, prin.
Davis MS, 1224 CLARENDON AVE 35020 — 3-00100 / 481-9826
  Tolton Rosser, prin.

Jefferson County SD
Supt. — See Birmingham
Oak Grove S, 9180 LOCK 17 RD 35023 — 4-11111 / 491-1752
  Jack Hazelrig, prin.
Gilmore/Bell Vo Ctr — Vo Tech / 425-6172
  4933 BESSEMER JOHNS RD 35023
  J. Guyton, prin.

Bessemer Academy — 2-11111 / 428-6288
  1705 4TH AVE SW 35023
  Glennwood Mathis, prin.
Bessemer State Technical College — 3-CS / 428-6391
  PO BOX 308 35021

Billingsley, AC 205, PC 2, Autauga
Autauga County SD
Supt. — See Prattville
S, RR 1 36006 — 3-11111 / 755-1629
  Collier Hunt, prin.

Birmingham, AC 205, PC 10, Jefferson
Birmingham CSD — 8-11111 / 583-4600
  PO BOX 10007 35202
  Cleveland Hammonds, supt.
Alabama Fine Arts HS — 2-00011 / 252-9241
  820 18TH ST N 35203
  James Nelson, prin.
Carver HS, 3400 33RD TER N 35207 — 3-00011 / 849-3500
  Don Debrow, prin.
Ensley Magnet HS — 3-00011 / 783-6100
  2301 AVENUE J 35218
  Charles Warren, prin.
Huffman Magnet HS — 4-00011 / 853-6519
  950 OLD SPRINGVILLE RD 35215
  H. Henderson, prin.
Jackson-Olin HS — 3-00011 / 783-6115
  510 1TH STREET ENSLEY 35218
  Doris Willis, prin.
Parker HS, 900 4TH ST N 35204 — 4-00011 / 581-5100
  Ed Dansby, prin.
Phillips HS, 2316 7TH AVE N 35203 — 3-00011 / 581-5110
  Mallory Coats, prin.
Ramsay HS, 1800 13TH AVE S 35205 — 3-00011 / 581-5120
  Robert Atkins, prin.
Wenonah HS — 3-00011 / 929-8100
  2916 WILSON RD SW 35221
  Sidney Moore, prin.
West End HS — 4-00011 / 929-8110
  1840 PEARSON AVE SW 35211
  Alfred Cottrell, prin.
Woodlawn Magnet HS — 4-00011 / 599-8700
  5620 1ST AVE N 35212
  John Ippolito, prin.
Alabama Fine Arts JHS — 1-00000 / 252-9241
  820 18TH ST N 35203
  James Nelson, prin.
Arrington MS — 3-00100 / 929-8125
  2101 JEFFERSON AVE SW 35211
  Michael Wesley, prin.
Banks MS, 721 86TH ST S 35206 — 3-00100 / 838-7600
  Nancy Howard, prin.
Bush Magnet MS — 3-00100 / 783-6130
  1112 25TH STREET ENSLEY 35218
  Deborah Horn, prin.
Center Street MS — 2-00100 / 581-5130
  1832 CENTER WAY S 35205
  Gladys McGee, prin.
Glenn MS, 901 16TH ST W 35208 — 3-00100 / 783-6140
  Julian Todd, prin.
Green Acres MS — 2-00100 / 923-5959
  945 PINEVIEW RD 35228
  Carolyn Francisco, prin.
Hayes MS, 505 43RD ST N 35222 — 3-00100 / 599-8720
  (—), prin.
Hudson MS — 3-00100 / 849-3510
  3300 FL SHUTTLESWORTH DR 35207
  Errol Pharris, prin.
Huffman Magnet MS — 2-00100 / 838-7610
  517 HUFFMAN RD 35215
  Gloria Jemison, prin.
Jones Valley MS — 3-00100 / 929-8135
  2000 31ST ST SW 35221
  Barbara Wilder, prin.
Kirby MS, 1328 28TH ST N 35234 — 2-00100 / 581-5140
  Robert Hill, prin.
Lincoln MS, 901 9TH AVE N 35204 — 3-00100 / 581-5145
  Barb McDonald, prin.
Payne MS — 2-00100 / 783-6135
  1500 DANIEL PAYNE DR 35214
  Sylvia Pierce, prin.
Putnam Magnet MS — 2-00100 / 599-8730
  1757 MONTCLAIR RD 35210
  David Newell, prin.
Smith MS, 1124 FIVE MILE RD 35215 — 2-00100 / 853-5600
  Michael Curry, prin.

Washington MS, 115 4TH AVE S 35205 — 2-00100 / 581-5207
  Fred Shepherd, prin.
Wilkerson MS, 116 11TH CT W 35204 — 3-00100 / 581-5210
  Anita Skipwith, prin.
Other Schools – See Ensley

Hoover CSD
Supt. — See Hoover
Berry JSHS — 4-00111 / 822-1600
  2826 COLUMBIANA RD 35216
  Dennis Duncan, prin.
Simmons JHS — 3-00100 / 978-1590
  1575 PATTON CHAPEL RD 35226
  Carol Barber, prin.

Jefferson County SD — 8-11111 / 325-5207
  A-400 COURTHOUSE 35263
  Hugh Wright, supt.
Shades Valley HS — 3-00011 / 871-4628
  104 HERMOSA DR 35209
  Richard Lazenby, prin.
Erwin JSHS, 532 23RD AVE NW 35215 — 4-00111 / 853-2730
  Michael Burkett, prin.
Fultondale JSHS — 3-00111 / 631-5659
  900 N PINE HILL RD 35217
  John Harris, prin.
Dabbs Area Vo HS — Vo Tech / 956-3968
  5191 PINE WHISPERS DR 35210
  Robert Gregg, prin.
Gresham MS, 2650 GRESHAM DR 35243 — 3-00100 / 967-3248
  Ann Jones, prin.
Other Schools – See Adamsville, Bessemer, Brighton,
  Gardendale, Hueytown, Leeds, Mc Calla, Morris,
  Pinson, Pleasant Grove, Quinton, Trussville,
  Warrior

Shelby County SD
Supt. — See Columbiana
Oak Mountain MS — 2-00100 / 980-3660
  5650 CAHABA VALLEY RD 35242
  John Draper, prin.
Riverchase MS — 4-00100 / 733-6760
  853 WILLOW OAK DR 35244
  Charlotte Lusco, prin.

Altamont S — 2-01111 / 879-2006
  4801 ALTAMONT RD S 35222
  Martin Hames, prin.
Baptist Medical Centers — HSP / 322-9319
  PO BOX 830605 35283
Birmingham Southern College — 4-UC / 800-523-5793
  900 ARKADELPHIA RD 35254
Briarwood Christian HS — 2-00011 / 991-7544
  6255 CAHABA VALLEY RD 35242
  Gene Branham, prin.
Career Development Institute — 2-CS / 252-6396
  2233 4TH AVE N 35203
Carraway Methodist Medical Center — HSP / 226-6000
  1615 25TH ST N 35234
Herzing Institute — 3-CS / 933-8536
  1218 20TH ST S 35205
Highland, S, 4901 OLD LEEDS RD 35213 — 2-11111 / 956-9731
  Helen Possien, prin.
Holy Family HS, 2001 19TH ST 35218 — 2-00011 / 787-9937
  Phyllis Jones, prin.
Jefferson State Community College — 6-CC / 853-1200
  2601 CARSON RD 35215
John Carroll HS — 3-00011 / 940-2400
  PO BOX 19007 35219
  Lee Fisher, prin.
Lawson State Community College — 4-CC / 925-2515
  3060 WILSON RD SW 35221
Miles College — 3-UC / 923-2771
  PO BOX 3800 35208
Phillips Jr College/Southern Institute — 3-CC / 879-5100
  115 OFFICE PARK DR 35223
Rice College — 2-CS / 781-8600
  2116 BESSEMER RD 35208
Samford University — 6-UC / 800-888-7218
  800 LAKESHORE DR 35229
Shades Mountain Christian S — 3-11111 /
  2281 OLD TYLER RD 35226
  Sharon Berry, prin.
Southeastern Bible College — 2-UC / 800-749-8878
  3001 HIGHWAY 280 S 35243
University of Alabama at Birmingham — 7-UC / 934-8221
  UNIV STA 35294
University of Alabama Hospital — HSP / 934-5490
  619 19TH ST S 35233
Virginia College-Birmingham — 2-CS / 802-1200
  1900 28TH AVE S 35209
West Central Alabama Skills Center — 3-CS / 322-0504
  2112 11TH AVE S STE 201 35205

Blountsville, AC 205, PC 4, Blount
Blount County SD
Supt. — See Oneonta
Pennington JSHS, RR 1 BOX 10 35031 — 3-00111 / 429-4101
  Donnie Breaseale, prin.
Moore S, RR 3 BOX 592 35031 — 3-11111 / 466-7663
  Donald Harper, prin.

Boaz, AC 205, PC 6, Marshall
Etowah County SD
Supt. — See Gadsden
Sardis JSHS, 1420 CHURCH ST 35957 — 3-00111 / 593-5221
  Kirby Hubbard, prin.

Marshall County SD
Supt. — See Guntersville
HS, 907 BROWN ST 35957 — 3-00011 / 593-2401
  William Aaron, prin.

Boaz MS, 140 NEWT PARKER DR 35957 2-00100
Thomas Little, prin. 593-0799

Snead State Junior College 4-CC
220 N WALNUT ST 35957 593-5120

Boligee, AC 205, PC 2, Greene
Greene County SD
Supt. — See Eutaw
Paramount S, PO BOX 188 35443 3-11111
Cleophus Gaines, prin. 336-8557

Brantley, AC 205, PC 4, Crenshaw
Crenshaw County SD
Supt. — See Luverne
S, PO BOX 86 36009 3-11111
Elizabeth Sullivan, prin. 527-8879

Bremen, AC 205, PC 1, Cullman
Cullman County SD
Supt. — See Cullman
Cold Springs S, PO BOX 130 35033 3-11111
Edward Campbell, prin. 287-1787

Brewton, AC 205, PC 6, Escambia
Brewton CSD, PO BOX 59 36427 4-11111
Lynn Smith, supt. 867-8400
Miller HS, 1835 DOUGLAS AVE 36426 2-00011
Frank Cotton, prin. 867-8430
MS, 301 LILES BLVD 36426 2-01100
Vernon Baggett, prin. 867-8420

Escambia County SD 6-11111
PO BOX 307 36427 867-6251
Curtis Parker, supt.
Escambia-Brewton Area Vo HS Vo Tech
RR 6 BOX 164 36426 867-7829
Gail Davidson, prin.
Other Schools – See Atmore, East Brewton, Flomaton

Jefferson Davis State Junior College 4-CC
220 ALCO DR 36426 867-4832
Southern Normal HS 1-00111
PO BOX 408 36427 867-4831
Sherman Jones, prin.

Bridgeport, AC 205, PC 5, Jackson
Jackson County SD
Supt. — See Scottsboro
MS, 620 JACOBS AVE 35740 2-01100
Elizabeth Mountain, prin. 495-2967

Brighton, AC 205, PC 5, Jefferson
Jefferson County SD
Supt. — See Birmingham
S, 3400 BROWNS CIR 35020 2-11111
James Dudley, prin. 425-4021

Brilliant, AC 205, PC 3, Marion
Marion County SD
Supt. — See Hamilton
JSHS, PO BOX 195 35548 2-00111
George Wideman, prin. 465-2322

Brookwood, AC 205, PC 3, Tuscaloosa
Tuscaloosa County SD
Supt. — See Tuscaloosa
JSHS, 15981 HIGHWAY 216 35444 3-00111
Barry Sadler, prin. 553-3307

Brundidge, AC 205, PC 4, Pike
Pike County SD
Supt. — See Troy
Pike County JSHS, 552 S MAIN ST 36010 3-00111
Mark Bazzell, prin. 735-2389

Butler, AC 205, PC 4, Choctaw
Choctaw County SD 5-11111
PO BOX 839 36904 459-3031
Toreatha Johnson, supt.
Choctaw County HS 3-00011
201 ROGERS AVE 36904 459-2139
Vernon Underwood, prin.
Orr Area Vo HS Vo Tech
914A RIDERWOOD DR 36904 459-3711
Sarah Ray, prin.
Other Schools – See Silas

Patrician Academy 2-11111
911 S MULBERRY AVE 36904 459-3605
Jeanette Adams, prin.

Calera, AC 205, PC 4, Shelby
Shelby County SD
Supt. — See Columbiana
JSHS, PO BOX C 35040 2-00111
Daniel Goggins, prin. 668-3700

Camden, AC 205, PC 4, Wilcox
Wilcox County SD 5-11111
PO BOX 160 36726 682-4716
Arlester McBride, supt.
Wilcox Central HS 3-00011
PO BOX 1089 36726 682-9239
James Thomas, prin.
MS, PO BOX 698 36726 2-01100
C. D. McCall, prin. 682-4514

Camp Hill, AC 205, PC 4, Tallapoosa
Tallapoosa County SD
Supt. — See Dadeville
Bell S, PO BOX 457 36850 2-11111
Frank Holley, prin. 896-2865

Lyman Ward Military Academy 2-00111
PO BOX 547 36850 896-2907
Albert Hovey, prin.

Carbon Hill, AC 205, PC 4, Walker
Walker County SD
Supt. — See Jasper
HS, PO BOX 579 35549 2-00011
Bob Frost, prin. 924-8821

Carrollton, AC 205, PC 4, Pickens
Pickens County SD 5-11111
PO BOX 32 35447 367-2080
Ralph Smith, supt.
S, PO BOX 320 35447 3-11111
Howard Grayson, prin. 367-8152
Ladow Area Vo HS Vo Tech
RR 2 BOX 46 35447 367-8194
Percy Lee, prin.
Other Schools – See Aliceville, Gordo, Reform

Pickens Academy, RR 1 BOX 10M 35447 2-11111
Lynn Wright, prin. 367-8144

Cedar Bluff, AC 205, PC 4, Cherokee
Cherokee County SD
Supt. — See Centre
S, PO BOX 8 35959 3-11111
Bonida Scott, prin. 779-6211

Centre, AC 205, PC 5, Cherokee
Cherokee County SD 5-11111
130 E MAIN ST 35960 927-3362
H. Arnold, supt.
Cherokee County HS 3-00011
910 WARRIOR DR 35960 927-3625
Fred Reynolds, prin.
Cherokee Co. Area Vo HS Vo Tech
600 BAY SPRINGS RD 35960 927-5351
Ronald Rains, prin.
MS, 350 E MAIN ST 35960 2-00100
Linda Ray, prin. 927-5656
Other Schools – See Cedar Bluff, Gaylesville, Leesburg, Spring Garden

Centreville, AC 205, PC 5, Bibb
Bibb County SD 5-11111
103 SW DAVIDSON DR 35042 926-9881
Joe Elliot, supt.
Bibb County JSHS 4-00111
214 BIRMINGHAM RD 35042 926-9071
John Pratt, prin.
Other Schools – See West Blocton

Chatom, AC 205, PC 4, Washington
Washington County SD 5-11111
PO BOX 1359 36518 847-2401
Tillman Parnell, supt.
Washington County HS 2-00011
PO BOX 1329 36518 847-2851
Sidney Hinton, prin.
Washington Co. Area Vo Ctr Vo Tech
PO BOX 1298 36518 847-2040
Howard Daugherty, prin.
MS, PO BOX 1299 36518 2-00100
George Holcomb, prin. 847-2759
Other Schools – See Fruitdale, Leroy, Mc Intosh, Millry

Chelsea, AC 205, PC 4, Shelby
Shelby County SD
Supt. — See Columbiana
HS, PO BOX 639 35043 4-00011
Glen Frederick, prin. 678-2620
MS, PO BOX 600 35043 2-00100
Richard Conkle, prin. 678-2610

Cherokee, AC 205, PC 4, Colbert
Colbert County SD
Supt. — See Tuscumbia
Cherokee HS, RR 3 BOX 72 35616 2-00011
Bobby Ayers, prin. 359-4434
MS, PO BOX H 35616 2-01100
Nancy Parker, prin. 359-6432

Chickasaw, AC 205, PC 6, Mobile
Mobile County SD
Supt. — See Mobile
Clark MS, 12 12TH AVE 36611 3-01100
Ernestine Jackson, prin. 457-9236

Childersburg, AC 205, PC 5, Talladega
Talladega County SD
Supt. — See Talladega
HS, 421 4TH AVE SE 35044 3-00011
Dan Payant, prin. 378-6632
MS, 800 4TH ST SE 35044 3-01100
Marvin Rochelle, prin. 378-5592

Citronelle, AC 205, PC 5, Mobile
Mobile County SD
Supt. — See Mobile
HS, PO BOX 97 36522 3-00011
Charles Pettus, prin. 866-5557
MS, PO BOX 97 36522 3-00100
William Clark, prin. 866-2041

Clanton, AC 205, PC 6, Chilton
Chilton County SD 6-11111
1705 LAY DAM RD 35045 755-3190
Donald Hand, supt.
Chilton County HS, 1214 7TH ST S 35045 3-00011
Troy Mims, prin. 755-5135
Chilton Co. Vo-Tech HS Vo Tech
2829 4TH AVE N 35045 755-2997
Alton Culp, prin.

Adair MS, 102 1ST ST S 35045 3-01100
Frank Daniel, prin. 755-2480
Other Schools – See Jemison, Maplesville, Thorsby, Verbena

Clayton, AC 205, PC 4, Barbour
Barbour County SD 4-11111
PO BOX 429 36016 775-3453
Bob Baker, supt.
JSHS, CLAYTON BYPASS 36016 2-00111
Thomas Crossley, prin. 775-3545
Other Schools – See Louisville

Cleveland, AC 205, PC 3, Blount
Blount County SD
Supt. — See Oneonta
S, PO BOX 127 35049 3-11111
Ben Hayes, prin. 274-9915
Blount Co. Area Vo HS Vo Tech
PO BOX 125 35049 625-3424
Walter Self, prin.

Coffee Springs, AC 205, PC 2, Geneva
Geneva County SD
Supt. — See Geneva
S, PO BOX 68 36318 2-11111
John Williams, prin. 684-2752

Coffeeville, AC 205, PC 2, Clarke
Clarke County SD
Supt. — See Grove Hill
JSHS, PO BOX 128 36524 2-00111
Jerry Bumpers, prin. 276-3227

Collinsville, AC 205, PC 4, De Kalb
De Kalb County SD
Supt. — See Fort Payne
S, PO BOX 269 35961 3-11111
Samuel Clanton, prin. 524-2111

Columbia, AC 205, PC 3, Houston
Houston County SD
Supt. — See Dothan
Houston County S, PO BOX C 36319 3-11111
Eilene Dekle, prin. 696-2221

Columbiana, AC 205, PC 5, Shelby
Shelby County SD 7-11111
PO BOX 429 35051 669-5600
Norma Rogers, supt.
Shelby County HS 3-00011
101 WASHINGTON ST 35051 669-5640
Beverly Hall, prin.
School of Technology Vo Tech
701 HIGHWAY 70 35051 669-5620
Dan Acker, prin.
MS, 222 JOINERTOWN RD 35051 3-00100
Quida Mayfield, prin. 669-5650
Other Schools – See Alabaster, Birmingham, Calera, Chelsea, Montevallo, Pelham, Vincent

Cordova, AC 205, PC 5, Walker
Walker County SD
Supt. — See Jasper
HS 2-00011
600 MASSACHUSETTS AVE N 35550 483-7404
Tony Watkins, prin.
Bankhead MS, 500 SCHOOL RD 35550 2-01100
Steve Adkins, prin. 483-7245

Cottonwood, AC 205, PC 4, Houston
Houston County SD
Supt. — See Dothan
S, RR 1 BOX 700 36320 3-11111
John Tew, prin. 691-2587

Courtland, AC 205, PC 3, Lawrence
Lawrence County SD
Supt. — See Moulton
JSHS, 1205 TENNESSEE ST 35618 2-00111
Mylun White, prin. 637-2261

Cragford, AC 205, PC 2, Clay
Clay County SD
Supt. — See Ashland
Mellow Valley S, RR 1 36255 2-11111
James McCullers, prin. 354-2375

Crossville, AC 205, PC 4, De Kalb
De Kalb County SD
Supt. — See Fort Payne
S, PO BOX 38 35962 3-11111
Claud Cassidy, prin. 528-7858

Cullman, AC 205, PC 7, Cullman
Cullman County SD 6-11111
PO BOX 518 35056 734-2933
Felton Easterwood, supt.
Fairview S, 841 WELCOME RD 35055 4-11111
Keith Pattillo, prin. 796-5106
Good Hope S 4-11111
210 GOOD HOPE SCHOOL RD 35057 734-3807
Gene Raburn, prin.
West Point S 4-11111
4314 COUNTY ROAD 1141 35057 734-5375
Jan Farley, prin.
Cullman Co. Area Vo HS Vo Tech
17640 US HIGHWAY 31 35057 734-7740
Thomas Hancock, prin.
Other Schools – See Bremen, Hanceville, Holly Pond, Vinemont

Cullman CSD, PO BOX 887 35056 5-11111
Donald Dossey, supt. 734-2233
HS, 510 13TH ST NE 35055 3-00011
Leon Bentley, prin. 734-3923

Cullman City Area Vo HS — Vo Tech
PO BOX 887 35056 — 734-3923
Jerry Bishop, prin.
MS, 800 2ND AVE NE 35055 — 3-00100
Charlie Montgomery, prin. — 734-7959

St. Bernard Prep HS — 2-00011
101 ST BERNARD DR 35055 — 739-6682
Rev. Kevin McGrath, prin.

Dadeville, AC 205, PC 5, Tallapoosa
Tallapoosa County SD — 5-11111
COURTHOUSE 36853 — 825-1020
Mitchell Caldwell, supt.
JSHS, 611 E SOUTH ST 36853 — 3-00111
Jim Childers, prin. — 825-7848
Other Schools – See Alexander City, Camp Hill, Notasulga

Daleville, AC 205, PC 6, Dale
Daleville CSD — 4-11111
323 N DALEVILLE AVE 36322 — 598-2456
J. Moore, supt.
HS, 323 N DALEVILLE AVE 36322 — 2-00011
Mike Lindsey, prin. — 598-4461
MS, 323 N DALEVILLE AVE 36322 — 2-01100
Eddie Hill, prin. — 598-4463

Danville, AC 205, PC 2, Morgan
Lawrence County SD
Supt. — See Moulton
Speake S — 3-11111
6559 COUNTY ROAD 81 35619 — 974-9201
Charles Garner, prin.

Morgan County SD
Supt. — See Decatur
S, RR 2 35619 — 3-11111
Mitchell Owens, prin. — 773-9909

Daphne, AC 205, PC 7, Baldwin
Baldwin County SD
Supt. — See Bay Minette
HS, 300 E LAWSON RD 36526 — 3-00011
Timothy Reynolds, prin. — 626-3024
MS, 1000 MAIN ST 36526 — 3-00100
Ed Mitchell, prin. — 626-2845

Bayside Academy — 2-11111
PO BOX 130 36526
Rufus Bethea, prin.
United States Sports Academy — 2-UC
1 ACADEMY DR 36526 — 626-3303

Deatsville, AC 205, PC 2, Elmore
Elmore County SD
Supt. — See Wetumpka
Holtville JSHS — 3-00111
10425 HOLTVILLE RD 36022 — 569-3034
Don Oswald, prin.

Ingram State Technical Institute — 4-CS
PO BOX 209 36022 — 285-5177

Decatur, AC 205, PC 8, Morgan
Decatur CSD, 302 4TH AVE NE 35601 — 6-11111
Buddy Davis, supt. — 552-3000
Austin HS — 4-00011
1625 DANVILLE RD SW 35601 — 552-3060
Richard Pace, prin.
HS, 1011 PROSPECT DR SE 35601 — 3-00011
Timothy Lull, prin. — 552-3011
Austin Area Vo HS — Vo Tech
1625 DANVILLE RD SW 35601 — 552-3065
Richard Pace, prin.
Brookhaven MS — 4-00100
1302 5TH AVE SW 35601 — 552-3045
John Brandon, prin.
Cedar Ridge MS — 3-00100
2715 DANVILLE RD SW 35603 — 552-4622
Phillip Hastings, prin.
Oak Park MS, 1100 16TH AVE SE 35601 — 3-00100
Lawrence Walters, prin. — 552-3035
Morgan County SD — 6-11111
1325 POINT MALLARD PKY 35601 — 353-6442
Howard Morris, supt.
Other Schools – See Danville, Falkville, Somerville, Trinity

John C. Calhoun State Community College — 6-CC
PO BOX 2216 35602 — 306-2500

Demopolis, AC 205, PC 6, Marengo
Demopolis CSD, PO BOX 759 36732 — 4-11111
W. Hill, supt. — 289-1670
SHS, 607 HIGHWAY 80 W 36732 — 3-00011
H. Russell, prin. — 289-0294
JHS, 300 E PETTUS ST 36732 — 2-00110
Clarence Jackson, prin. — 289-4242

Marengo County SD
Supt. — See Linden
Essex S, RR 1 BOX 433 36732 — 2-11111
Flora Kennard, prin. — 289-3504

Demopolis Academy — 2-11111
1908 MAUVILLA DR 36732 — 289-0452
Larry Courtney, prin.

Dixon's Mills, AC 205, PC 2, Marengo
Marengo County SD
Supt. — See Linden

Marengo S, PO BOX 154 36736 — 3-11111
Douglas Marsh, prin. — 992-2395

Dora, AC 205, PC 4, Walker
Walker County SD
Supt. — See Jasper
HS, RR 5 BOX 42 35062 — 3-00011
Bob Erwin, prin. — 648-6863

Dothan, AC 205, PC 8, Houston
Dothan CSD, 500 DUSY ST 36301 — 7-11111
Don Musselman, supt. — 793-1397
HS, 1000 S OATES ST 36301 — 4-00011
James Woodham, prin. — 794-1400
Northview HS — 4-00011
3307 HIGHWAY 431 N 36303 — 794-1410
Philip Hardy, prin.
Dothan Area Vo Ctr — Vo Tech
3307 HIGHWAY 431 N 36303 — 794-1436
Jim McCarty, prin.
Beverlye MS, 427 S BEVERLY RD 36301 — 3-00100
James Daniels, prin. — 794-1432
Carver MS, 801 W NORTH ST 36303 — 3-00100
James Kelley, prin. — 794-1440
Girard MS, 600 GIRARD AVE 36303 — 3-00100
J. Roland, prin. — 794-1426
Honeysuckle MS — 3-00100
1407 HONEYSUCKLE RD 36301 — 794-1420
Sam Nichols, prin.

Houston County SD — 6-11111
PO BOX 1688 36302 — 792-8331
Kenneth Lord, supt.
Rehobeth S, RR 8 BOX 105 36301 — 4-11111
Donald Holman, prin. — 677-5153
Other Schools – See Ashford, Columbia, Cottonwood, Newton

Emmanuel Christian S — 2-11111
RR 15 BOX 8 36301 — 792-0935
Mark Redmond, prin.
Houston Academy — 2-11111
1001 BUENA VISTA DR 36303 — 794-4106
John O'Connell, prin.
Southeast Alabama Skills Center — 2-CS
PO BOX 6268 36302 — 793-2896
Troy State University — 4-UC
PO BOX 8368 36304 — 983-6556
Wallace College — 5-CC
RR 6 BOX 62 36303 — 983-3521

Double Springs, AC 205, PC 4, Winston
Winston County SD, PO BOX 9 35553 — 5-11111
Jackie Herron, supt. — 489-5018
Winston County JSHS — 2-00111
PO BOX 549 35553 — 489-5593
Frank Horsley, prin.
Winston Co. Tech Ctr — Vo Tech
PO BOX 146 35553 — 489-2121
B. Porter, prin.
Other Schools – See Addison, Arley, Lynn

Winston County Area Vocational Center — 1-CS
PO BOX 146 35553 — 489-2121

Douglas, AC 205, PC 2, Marshall
Marshall County SD
Supt. — See Guntersville
HS, PO BOX 300 35964 — 3-00011
Brenda Milner, prin. — 593-2810
MS, PO BOX 269 35964 — 2-01100
A. L. Bonds, prin. — 593-1240

East Brewton, AC 205, PC 5, Escambia
Escambia County SD
Supt. — See Brewton
Neal HS, PO BOX 2250 36427 — 2-00011
Phillip Ellis, prin. — 867-4225
Neal MS, PO BOX 2385 36427 — 2-01100
Michael Parker, prin. — 867-5035

Eclectic, AC 205, PC 4, Elmore
Elmore County SD
Supt. — See Wetumpka
Elmore County JSHS — 3-00111
PO BOX 690 36024 — 541-3662
Paul Sexton, prin.

Elba, AC 205, PC 5, Coffee
Coffee County SD — 4-11111
400 REDDOCK HILL RD 36323 — 897-5016
Clayton Bryant, supt.
Other Schools – See Jack, Kinston, New Brockton

Elba CSD, 101 TIGERS DR 36323 — 4-11111
Charles Pearce, supt. — 897-2801
JSHS, 103 TIGERS DR 36323 — 3-00111
Charles Clark, prin. — 897-2266
Elba Area Vo HS, 103 TIGERS DR 36323 — Vo Tech
Charles Clark, prin. — 897-2266

Elkmont, AC 205, PC 2, Limestone
Limestone County SD
Supt. — See Athens
Limestone County S — 3-11111
PO BOX 248 35620 — 732-4291
Steve Pettus, prin.

Ensley, AC 205, Jefferson
Birmingham CSD
Supt. — See Birmingham
Olin Vo HS, 1054 AVENUE F 35218 — Vo Tech
(—), prin. — 783-6126

Enterprise, AC 205, PC 7, Coffee
Enterprise CSD, 502 E WATTS ST 36330 — 6-11111
Thad Morgan, supt. — 347-9531
SHS, 502 E WATTS ST 36330 — 4-00001
David Carter, prin. — 347-2640
Dauphin JHS — 2-00110
1271 DAUPHIN STREET EXT 36330 — 347-1141
Perry Vickers, prin.
JHS, 110 E COLLEGE ST 36330 — 2-00110
Hinton Johns, prin. — 347-1733

Enterprise State Junior College — 4-CC
PO BOX 1300 36331 — 347-2623

Eufaula, AC 205, PC 7, Barbour
Eufaula CSD, 420 SANFORD AVE 36027 — 5-11111
Daniel Parker, supt. — 687-1100
HS, 300 LAKE RD 36027 — 3-00011
John Beasley, prin. — 687-1110
Moorer MS — 3-00100
101 SAINT FRANCIS RD 36027 — 687-1130
Vic Adkison, prin.

Lakeside S, 700 LAKE RD 36027 — 2-11111
Webster Reyner, prin. — 687-5748
Sparks State Technical College — 3-CS
PO BOX 580 36072 — 687-3543

Eutaw, AC 205, PC 4, Greene
Greene County SD — 4-11111
PO BOX 569 35462 — 372-3161
Charles Miles, supt.
JSHS, PO BOX 658 35462 — 3-00111
Eunice Outland, prin. — 372-3789
Kirksey Area Vo Ctr — Vo Tech
RR 1 BOX 336 35462 — 372-4636
J. J. Purter, prin.
Other Schools – See Boligee

Warrior Academy, PO BOX 268 35462 — 2-11111
Charles Adams, prin. — 372-3546

Evergreen, AC 205, PC 5, Conecuh
Conecuh County SD — 5-11111
PO BOX 548 36401 — 578-1752
William Coker, supt.
Hillcrest HS, 1989 JAGUAR DR 36401 — 3-00011
Ronnie Brogden, prin. — 578-1126
Conecuh Co. Area Vo Ctr — Vo Tech
1979 JAGUAR DR 36401 — 578-2218
John Ward, prin.
JHS, 204 N MAIN ST 36401 — 2-00100
Gloria Hartley, prin. — 578-2490

Reid State Technical College — 3-CS
PO BOX 588 36401 — 578-1313

Excel, AC 205, PC 3, Monroe
Monroe County SD
Supt. — See Monroeville
S, PO BOX 429 36439 — 3-11111
John Ross, prin. — 765-2351

Fairfield, AC 205, PC 7, Jefferson
Fairfield CSD, PO BOX 110 35064 — 4-11111
Simpson Berry, supt. — 780-6137
HS, 610 VALLEY RD 35064 — 3-00011
Alvin Washington, prin. — 785-5176
Fairfield Area Vo HS — Vo Tech
6405 AVENUE D 35064 — 783-6831
Thomas Pair, prin.
Forest Hills MS — 3-00100
7000 GRASSELLI RD 35064 — 783-6841
Harold Boykin, prin.

Fairhope, AC 205, PC 6, Baldwin
Baldwin County SD
Supt. — See Bay Minette
HS, 1 PIRATE DR 36532 — 4-00011
Andrew Schottgen, prin. — 928-8309
MS, 408 N SECTION ST 36532 — 3-00100
Barbara Cotton, prin. — 928-8309

Falkville, AC 205, PC 4, Morgan
Morgan County SD
Supt. — See Decatur
S, PO BOX 388 35622 — 3-11111
O. B. Owens, prin. — 784-5248

Fayette, AC 205, PC 5, Fayette
Fayette County SD — 5-11111
PO BOX 599 35555 — 932-4611
Jerry Lindsey, supt.
Fayette County HS — 3-00011
202 14TH CT NE 35555 — 932-6313
Radford Hester, prin.
Hubbertville S, RR 3 35555 — 2-11111
Bill Carothers, prin. — 487-2845
Fayette Co. Area Vo HS — Vo Tech
PO BOX 839 35555 — 932-5246
Ted Brock, prin.
Fayette MS, 418 3RD AVE NE 35555 — 2-00100
Ray Nelson, prin. — 932-7660
Other Schools – See Berry

Brewer State Junior College — 3-CC
2631 TEMPLE AVE N 35555 — 800-526-5755
Fayette Academy — 2-11111
622 20TH ST NW 35555 — 932-6722
Deborah Bynum, prin.

Flomaton, AC 205, PC 4, Escambia
Escambia County SD
Supt. — See Brewton
JSHS, RR 2 BOX 80T 36441 2-00111
K. Corbin, prin. 296-2627

Florala, AC 205, PC 4, Covington
Covington County SD
Supt. — See Andalusia
HS, PO BOX 218 36442 2-00011
Charles Stevenson, prin. 858-3765
Florala City MS, PO BOX 386 36442 2-00100
William Revell, prin. 858-3642

Florence, AC 205, PC 8, Lauderdale
Florence CSD, 541 RIVERVIEW DR 35630 6-11111
Edison Barney, supt. 766-3234
Bradshaw HS 3-00011
1201 BRADSHAW DR 35630 764-8821
Ronald Owens, prin.
Coffee HS, 648 N CHERRY ST 35630 3-00011
Gerald Johnson, prin. 764-7452
Burrell-Slater Area Vo HS Vo Tech
610 W COLLEGE ST 35630 766-7420
Robert Gunter, prin.

Lauderdale County SD 6-11111
PO BOX 278 35631 760-1300
William Walker, supt.
Central S, RR 4 BOX 241 35633 4-11111
Jerry Fulmer, prin. 764-2903
Rogers S, RR 1 BOX 300 35630 3-11111
William Carson, prin. 757-3106
Wilson S, RR 5 BOX 111 35630 4-11111
William Valentine, prin. 764-8470
Other Schools – See Killen, Lexington, Rogersville, Waterloo

International Bible College 2-UC
PO BOX IBC 35630 766-6610
Mars Hill Bible S 3-11111
698 COX CREEK PKY 35630 767-1203
Kenneth Barfield, prin.
Riverhill S, RR 11 BOX 47 35630 2-11111
Bettye Jeffery, prin. 766-5571
University of North Alabama 6-UC
UNIV STA 35632 760-4318

Foley, AC 205, PC 5, Baldwin
Baldwin County SD
Supt. — See Bay Minette
HS, 1 PRIDE PL 36535 4-00011
Lester Smith, prin. 943-2221
MS, 209 N PINE ST 36535 3-00100
Melvin Pettibone, prin. 943-1255

Fort Deposit, AC 205, PC 4, Lowndes
Lowndes County SD
Supt. — See Hayneville
Lowndes County MS, PO BOX P 36032 2-01100
Joseph Bedgood, prin. 227-4206

Fort Payne, AC 205, PC 7, De Kalb
De Kalb County SD 6-11111
PO BOX 777 35967 845-8575
Weldon Parrish, supt.
Other Schools – See Collinsville, Crossville, Fyffe, Geraldine, Ider, Rainsville, Sylvania, Valley Head

Fort Payne CSD, PO BOX 1029 35967 5-11111
Thomas McCormack, supt. 845-0915
HS, 201 45TH ST NE 35967 3-00011
Ronald Bell, prin. 845-0535
MS, 4910 MARTIN AVE NE 35967 3-01100
Quentin Benn, prin. 845-7501

Frisco City, AC 205, PC 4, Monroe
Monroe County SD
Supt. — See Monroeville
JSHS, PO BOX 70 36445 2-00111
Jane Bradley, prin. 267-3261

Fruitdale, AC 205, PC 2, Washington
Washington County SD
Supt. — See Chatom
S, PO BOX 488 36539 3-11111
Kelcey Lee, prin. 827-6655

Fyffe, AC 205, PC 4, De Kalb
De Kalb County SD
Supt. — See Fort Payne
S, PO BOX 7 35971 3-11111
Nelson Ellis, prin. 623-2116

Gadsden, AC 205, PC 8, Etowah
Etowah County SD 6-11111
3200 W MEIGHAN BLVD 35904 549-7577
Ralph Cain, supt.
Hokes Bluff HS 2-00011
1865 APPALACHIN RD 35903 492-1360
Mike Bailey, prin.
Southside HS 3-00011
2150 HIGHWAY 77 35901 442-2172
Rodney Thompson, prin.
Gaston S 3-11111
4550 US HIGHWAY 411 35901 547-8828
Jerry Stewart, prin.
Hokes Bluff MS, 5425 MAIN ST 35903 3-01100
H. Reeves, prin. 492-1963
Other Schools – See Attalla, Boaz, Glencoe, Rainbow City, Walnut Grove

Gadsden CSD, PO BOX 184 35999 6-11111
Fred Taylor, supt. 543-3512
HS, 607 S 12TH ST 35999 3-00011
Ed Miller, prin. 547-5446
Litchfield HS, 1109 HOKE ST 35903 2-00011
John Jacobs, prin. 492-3061
Sansom HS 3-00011
2210 W MEIGHAN BLVD 35904 546-3316
Jeppy Owens, prin.
Weaver Tech Ctr Vo Tech
1515 CAMPBELL AVE 35903 492-6441
James Gidley, prin.
Cory MS, 715 RALEY ST 35903 2-00100
Elaine Mayes, prin. 492-6793
Disque MS, 612 TRACY ST 35901 3-00100
Jackie Ragland, prin. 547-6341
Forrest MS 3-00100
2000 W MEIGHAN BLVD 35904 546-4992
Dock DeRamus, prin.

Coosa Christian S 2-11111
771 WHITES CHAPEL RD 35901 547-1841
C. Michael Davis, prin.
East Alabama Skills Center 2-CS
301 S 4TH ST 35901 549-8200
Gadsden Business College 2-CS
PO BOX 1544 35902 546-2863
Gadsden State Community College 5-CC
PO BOX 227 35902
Holy Name of Jesus Hospital HSP
MORAGNE PARK 35902 543-5200

Gardendale, AC 205, PC 6, Jefferson
Jefferson County SD
Supt. — See Birmingham
HS, 850 MOUNT OLIVE RD 35071 4-00011
Robin Thomas, prin. 631-5656
Bragg JHS, 840 ASH AVE 35071 3-00100
Carolyn Patrick, prin. 631-9551

Gaylesville, AC 205, PC 2, Cherokee
Cherokee County SD
Supt. — See Centre
S, PO BOX 8 35973 2-11111
Nancy Smith, prin. 422-3596

Geneva, AC 205, PC 5, Geneva
Geneva County SD 5-11111
PO BOX 250 36340 684-3686
Betty Faulk, supt.
Other Schools – See Coffee Springs, Hartford, Samson, Slocomb

Geneva CSD, 505 N CHEROKEE ST 36340 4-11111
Wynnton Melton, supt. 684-3256
HS, 505 N CHEROKEE ST 36340 3-00011
Wynnton Melton, prin. 684-9379
MS, 501 N CHEROKEE ST 36340 2-00100
Stephen Swann, prin. 684-6431

Georgiana, AC 205, PC 4, Butler
Butler County SD
Supt. — See Greenville
JSHS, PO BOX 680 36033 2-00111
Robert Wasden, prin. 376-9130

Geraldine, AC 205, PC 3, De Kalb
De Kalb County SD
Supt. — See Fort Payne
S, PO BOX 145 35974 3-11111
B. Morris, prin. 659-2142

Glencoe, AC 205, PC 5, Etowah
Etowah County SD
Supt. — See Gadsden
HS, 700 LONESOME BEND RD 35905 2-00011
Marion Smith, prin. 492-2250
MS, 1000 LONESOME BEND RD 35905 2-01100
Scarlett Farley, prin. 492-5627

Goodsprings, AC 205, PC 2, Walker
Walker County SD
Supt. — See Jasper
Martin S, PO BOX 157 35560 2-11111
Michael Banks, prin. 686-5580

Gordo, AC 205, PC 4, Pickens
Pickens County SD
Supt. — See Carrollton
JSHS, PO BOX C 35466 2-00111
Rufus Hayes, prin. 364-7353

Goshen, AC 205, PC 2, Pike
Pike County SD
Supt. — See Troy
JSHS, EAGLE CIR 36035 2-00111
Jane Thrash, prin. 484-3245

Grand Bay, AC 205, PC 5, Mobile
Mobile County SD
Supt. — See Mobile
Mobile County JSHS 3-00111
PO BOX 6 36541 – A. Stewart, prin. 865-6511

Grant, AC 205, PC 3, Marshall
Marshall County SD
Supt. — See Guntersville
Smith JSHS, 6077 MAIN ST 35747 2-00111
Richard Ferguson, prin. 728-4238

Greensboro, AC 205, PC 5, Hale
Hale County SD, PO BOX 360 36744 5-11111
Dan Butler, supt. 624-8836
Greensboro East S 4-11111
PO BOX 460 36744 624-4005
Larry Woods, prin.
Greensboro West S, PO BOX 40 36744 3-11111
Jack Clayton, prin. 624-7932
Hale Co. Area Vo HS Vo Tech
PO BOX 517 36744 624-3691
Joe Pearson, prin.
Other Schools – See Akron, Moundville, Newbern

Southern Academy 2-11111
407 COLLEGE ST 36744 624-8402
Paul Word, prin.

Greenville, AC 205, PC 6, Butler
Butler County SD 5-11111
215 SIMPSON ST 36037 382-2665
Jim Lawrence, supt.
HS, 211 SCHOOL HIGHLANDS RD 36037 3-00011
Roger Speed, prin. 382-2608
Butler Co. Area Vo HS Vo Tech
211 SCHOOL HIGHLANDS RD 36037 382-2608
Roger Speed, prin.
MS, 300 OVERLOOK RD 36037 3-01100
Gerald Benson, prin. 382-3450
Other Schools – See Georgiana, Mc Kenzie

Fort-Dale South Butler Academy 2-11111
PO BOX 777 36037 382-2606
Tom Bridges, prin.
Greenville Academy, 177 BYPASS 36037 2-11111
Clyde Stanford, prin. 382-3800

Grove Hill, AC 205, PC 4, Clarke
Clarke County SD, PO BOX 936 36451 5-11111
Gerald Stephens, supt. 275-3255
Clarke County HS 2-00011
PO BOX 937 36451 275-3368
James Counselman, prin.
Hall MS, PO BOX 458 36451 2-01100
Patricia Pugh, prin. 275-8993
Other Schools – See Coffeeville, Jackson

Guin, AC 205, PC 4, Marion
Marion County SD
Supt. — See Hamilton
Marion County JSHS 2-00111
PO BOX 549 35563 468-3377
Jim Atkinson, prin.

Gulf Shores, AC 205, PC 5, Baldwin
Baldwin County SD
Supt. — See Bay Minette
MS, PO BOX 3249 36547 2-01100
Pat Powell, prin. 968-8716

Guntersville, AC 205, PC 6, Marshall
Guntersville CSD, PO BOX 129 35976 4-11111
Harold Patterson, supt. 582-3159
HS, 14227 US HIGHWAY 431 35976 3-00011
James Irby, prin. 582-2046
Carlisle Park MS, 801 SUNSET DR 35976 2-00100
Dale Edwards, prin. 582-5182

Marshall County SD 6-11111
12380 US HIGHWAY 431 35976 582-3171
Charles Edmonds, supt.
Marshall Tech SHS Vo Tech
12312 US HIGHWAY 431 35976 582-5629
Frank Reed, prin.
Other Schools – See Boaz, Douglas, Grant

Gurley, AC 205, PC 4, Madison
Madison County SD
Supt. — See Huntsville
Madison County S 3-11111
PO BOX 158 35748 776-9264
Grad Goodson, prin.

Hackleburg, AC 205, PC 4, Marion
Marion County SD
Supt. — See Hamilton
JSHS, PO BOX 310 35564 2-00111
Max Ray, prin. 935-3223

Haleyville, AC 205, PC 5, Winston
Haleyville CSD, 2000 20TH ST 35565 4-11111
Dan Weaver, supt. 486-9231
JSHS, 1800 20TH ST 35565 3-00111
John Mullins, prin. 486-3122
Haleyville Area Vo HS Vo Tech
1900 20TH ST 35565 486-9481
Beverly Donaldson, prin.

Hamilton, AC 205, PC 6, Marion
Marion County SD 5-11111
PO BOX 189 35570 921-3192
David Sexton, supt.
HS, PO BOX 1508 35570 3-00011
Don Knight, prin. 921-3281
MS, PO BOX 1748 35570 3-01100
John Burrow, prin. 921-7030
Other Schools – See Bear Creek, Brilliant, Guin, Hackleburg

Bevill State Community College 2-CC
PO BOX 9 35570 921-3177

Hanceville, AC 205, PC 4, Cullman
Cullman County SD
Supt. — See Cullman
S, 801 COMMERCIAL ST SE 35077 4-11111
Robert Burgess, prin. 352-6111

Wallace State Community College 5-CC
PO BOX 2000 35077 352-6403

Hartford, AC 205, PC 4, Geneva
Geneva County SD
Supt. — See Geneva
Geneva County S, PO BOX 159 36344 3-11111
Mike Whitaker, prin. 588-2943

Hartselle, AC 205, PC 7, Morgan
Hartselle CSD   5-11111
  109 COLLEGE ST NW   35640   773-5419
  Lee Hartsell, supt.
HS, 904 SPARKMAN ST SW   35640   3-00011
  Jerry Reeves, prin.   773-5426
Hartselle Area Vo Ctr, BOOTH ST   35640   Vo Tech
  Jerry Reeves, prin.   773-4111
JHS, 130 PETAIN ST SW   35640   3-00100
  Frank Parker, prin.   773-6094

Hayden, AC 205, PC 2, Blount
Blount County SD
  Supt. — See Oneonta
JSHS, RR 1 BOX 5   35079   3-00111
  Larry Adams, prin.   647-0397

Hayneville, AC 205, PC 3, Lowndes
Lowndes County SD   5-11111
  PO BOX 755   36040   548-2131
  Eli Seaborn, supt.
Central JSHS, 49 MAIN ST   36040   3-00111
  William Walker, prin.   563-7311
Lowndes Co. Area Vo HS   Vo Tech
  189 MAIN ST   36040   563-7389
  Joe Thomas, prin.
MS, PO BOX 307   36040   2-01100
  Theresa Douglas, prin.   548-2184
Other Schools – See Fort Deposit, Letohatchee

Hazel Green, AC 205, PC 4, Madison
Madison County SD
  Supt. — See Huntsville
HS, 14290 HIGHWAY 231 431 N   35750   4-00011
  Jim Fondren, prin.   828-0764

Headland, AC 205, PC 5, Henry
Henry County SD
  Supt. — See Abbeville
HS, 8 SPORMAN ST   36345   2-00011
  Steve Williams, prin.   693-2442
MS, PO BOX 324   36345   2-00100
  George Davis, prin.   693-3764

Heflin, AC 205, PC 5, Cleburne
Cleburne County SD   4-11111
  406 VICKERY ST   36264   463-5624
  Robert Morton, supt.
Cleburne County JSHS   3-00111
  RR 4 BOX 24   36264   463-2012
  James Pirkle, prin.
Cleburne Co. Area Vo HS   Vo Tech
  RR 2 BOX 78A   36264 – Bill Ayers, prin. 748-2961
Other Schools – See Ranburne

Higdon, AC 205, PC 2, Jackson
Jackson County SD
  Supt. — See Scottsboro
North Sand Mountain S   3-11111
  PO BOX 128   35979   597-2111
  Ronald Shelton, prin.

Highland Home, AC 205, PC 2, Crenshaw
Crenshaw County SD
  Supt. — See Luverne
S, RR 1 BOX 199   36041   3-11111
  C. Richardson, prin.   537-4379

Holly Pond, AC 205, PC 3, Cullman
Cullman County SD
  Supt. — See Cullman
S, PO BOX 70   35083   3-11111
  Bill Lay, prin.   796-5169

Hollywood, AC 205, PC 3, Jackson
Jackson County SD
  Supt. — See Scottsboro
Jackson Co. Tech HS   Vo Tech
  RR 1 BOX 66   35752   574-6079
  Wendell Womack, prin.

Holt, AC 205, PC 5, Tuscaloosa
Tuscaloosa County SD
  Supt. — See Tuscaloosa
JSHS, 3801 ALABAMA AVE NE   35404   4-00111
  Richard Melendez, prin.   553-6703

Homewood, AC 205, PC 7, Jefferson
Homewood CSD   5-11111
  PO BOX 59366   35259   870-4203
  Byron Nelson, supt.
HS, 1901 LAKESHORE DR S   35209   3-00011
  Michael Hathorne, prin.   871-9663
MS, 1108 FRISCO ST   35209   3-00100
  John Dedrick, prin.   870-0878

Hoover, AC 205, PC 8, Jefferson
Hoover CSD   6-11111
  100 MUNICIPAL DR # 200   35216   985-2425
  Robert Bumpus, supt.
Other Schools – See Birmingham

Hope Hull, AC 205, PC 2, Montgomery

Hooper Academy   2-11111
  380 FISCHER RD   36043   288-5980
  Darrell Self, prin.

Hueytown, AC 205, PC 7, Jefferson
Jefferson County SD
  Supt. — See Birmingham
HS, 131 DABBS AVE   35023   3-00011
  B. Kaye Reach, prin.   491-3565
Pittman MS, 701 SUNRISE BLVD   35023   3-00100
  John Hudson, prin.   491-1070

Huntsville, AC 205, PC 9, Madison
Huntsville CSD, PO BOX 1256   35807   7-11111
  Ron Saunders, supt.   532-4640
Butler HS   4-00011
  3401 HOLMES AVE NW   35816   532-4920
  Tom Drake, prin.
Grissom HS   4-00011
  7901 BAILEY COVE RD SE   35802   650-4340
  Sidney Ingram, prin.
HS, 2304 BILLIE WATKINS ST SW   35801   4-00011
  William Smith, prin.   532-4870
Johnson HS, 6201 PUEBLO DR NW   35810   4-00011
  Evalyn Humphrey, prin.   851-4180
Lee HS, 606 FORREST CIR NE   35811   4-00011
  Tom Owen, prin.   532-4830
Huntsville Tech Ctr   Vo Tech
  2800 DRAKE AVE SW   35805   650-4450
  Warren Sadler, prin.
Challenger MS   2-00100
  13555 CHANEY THOMPSON RD SE   35803
  John Calvarese, prin.   650-4320
Chapman MS   3-00100
  2006 REUBEN DR NE   35811   532-4775
  Augustus Smith, prin.
Davis Hills MS   3-00100
  3221 MASTIN LAKE RD NW   35810   851-4110
  Wilbert Brown, prin.
MS, 817 ADAMS ST SE   35801   3-00100
  Sam Sullins, prin.   532-4755
Mountain Gap MS   3-00100
  821 MOUNTAIN GAP RD SE   35803   650-4400
  Robert Engle, prin.
Stone MS, 2620 CLINTON AVE W   35805   3-00100
  Alta Morrison, prin.   532-4628
Westlawn MS, 4217 9TH AVE SW   35805   3-00100
  Earline Pinckley, prin.   532-4767
White MS   3-00100
  4800 SPARKMAN DR NW   35810   851-4120
  Barry Carroll, prin.
Whitesburg MS   3-00100
  107 SANDERS RD SW   35802   650-4430
  James Puckett, prin.

Madison County SD   7-11111
  PO BOX 226   35804   532-3540
  Ralph Green, supt.
Madison Co. Tech Ctr   Vo Tech
  1275 JORDAN RD   35811   852-2170
  T. Birchfield, prin.
Other Schools – See Gurley, Hazel Green, Madison,
  New Hope, New Market, Toney

Drake State Technical College   3-CS
  3421 MERIDIAN ST N   35811   539-8161
Huntsville Hospital   HSP
  101 SIVLEY RD SW   35801   533-8123
Madison Academy   2-11111
  301 MAX LUTHER DR NW   35811   534-6631
  Morgan Outlaw, prin.
North Alabama Skills Center   2-CS
  PO BOX 3269   35810
Oakwood Academy   2-11111
  RURAL STATION BOX 108   35896   837-2804
  Jessie Bradley, prin.
Oakwood College   4-UC
  OAKWOOD RD NW   35896   837-1630
Phillips Junior College   3-CC
  4900 CORPORATE DR NW STE E   35805
     430-3377
Randolph S, 1005 DRAKE AVE SE   35802   3-11111
  George Edwards, prin.   881-1701
University of Alabama in Huntsville   6-UC
  PO BOX 1247   35899   895-6426
Virginia College   2-CS
  2800A BOB WALLACE AVE SW   35805   533-7387
Westminster Christian Academy   2-11111
  1400 EVANGEL DR NW   35816   837-7065
  James Redford, prin.

Ider, AC 205, PC 3, De Kalb
De Kalb County SD
  Supt. — See Fort Payne
S, PO BOX 127   35981   3-11111
  David Uptain, prin.   632-2302

Indian Springs, AC 205, PC 2, Shelby

Indian Springs S   2-00111
  190 WOODWARD DR   35124   988-3350
  Douglas Jennings, prin.

Irvington, AC 205, PC 3, Mobile
Mobile County SD
  Supt. — See Mobile
Bryant Vo Ctr, RR 2 BOX 480   36544   Vo Tech
  Paul Mallette, prin.   957-2845

Jack, AC 205, PC 1, Coffee
Coffee County SD
  Supt. — See Elba
Zion Chapel S, RR 1   36346   3-11111
  Robert Black, prin.   897-6275

Jackson, AC 205, PC 6, Clarke
Clarke County SD
  Supt. — See Grove Hill
HS, 324 STANLEY DR   36545   3-00011
  Robert Hagood, prin.   246-2571
MS, 235 COLLEGE AVE   36545   3-01100
  Bernice Johnson, prin.   246-3597

Jackson Academy, PO BOX 838   36545   2-11111
  Robert Gartman, prin.   246-5552

Jacksonville, AC 205, PC 7, Calhoun
Calhoun County SD
  Supt. — See Anniston
Pleasant Valley S   4-11111
  4141 PLEASANT VALLEY RD   36265   435-4828
  Wayne Wigley, prin.
Calhoun Co. Area Vo HS   Vo Tech
  1200 CHURCH AVE SE   36265   435-6235
  Mike Steifel, prin.

Jacksonville CSD, PO BOX 248   36265   4-11111
  Leonard Messer, supt.   782-5682
JSHS, 520 PELHAM RD N   36265   3-00111
  Mitchell McKay, prin.   782-5009

Jacksonville State University   6-UC
  700 PELHAM RD N   36265   782-5000

Jasper, AC 205, PC 7, Walker
Jasper CSD, PO BOX 500   35502   5-11111
  Bob Neighbors, supt.   384-6021
Walker HS, 1601 HIGHLAND AVE   35501   4-00011
  Ken Abbott, prin.   221-9277
Maddox MS, 1602 2ND AVE   35501   3-00100
  Glenda Crawford, prin.   384-3235

Walker County SD   6-11111
  PO BOX 311   35502   387-0555
  Maury Fowler, supt.
Curry HS, RR 13 BOX 65   35501   3-00011
  James Hubbert, prin.   384-3887
Walker Area Vo HS   Vo Tech
  1100 19TH ST E   35501   387-0561
  Ted Craven, prin.
Curry MS, RR 13 BOX 65A   35501   2-01100
  George Miller, prin.   384-3441
Other Schools – See Carbon Hill, Cordova, Dora,
  Goodsprings, Oakman, Parrish

Walker College   3-CC
  1411 INDIANA AVE   35501   800-777-0372

Jemison, AC 205, PC 4, Chilton
Chilton County SD
  Supt. — See Clanton
JSHS, 25195 US HIGHWAY 31   35085   3-00111
  Joe Mims, prin.   688-4528

Killen, AC 205, PC 4, Lauderdale
Lauderdale County SD
  Supt. — See Florence
Brooks JSHS, RR 4 BOX 428   35645   3-00111
  James Smith, prin.   757-2115
Thornton Area Vo HS   Vo Tech
  RR 1 BOX 400   35645   757-2101
  Connie Johnson, prin.

Kinston, AC 205, PC 3, Coffee
Coffee County SD
  Supt. — See Elba
S, PO BOX 158   36453   3-11111
  Jerry Barnes, prin.   565-3016

Lafayette, AC 205, PC 5, Chambers
Chambers County SD   6-11111
  PO BOX 408D   36862   864-9343
  Leonard Riley, supt.
HS, 214 1ST AVE SE   36862   2-00011
  Cornelius Reese, prin.   864-9881
Chambers Co. Area Vo Ctr   Vo Tech
  PO BOX 318   36862   864-8863
  Leonard Brown, prin.
Lafayette Southside MS   2-01100
  621 1ST ST SE   36862   864-8876
  Curtis Guy, prin.
Other Schools – See Valley

Chambers Academy   2-11111
  RR 3 BOX 166   36862   864-9852
  John Perry, prin.

Lanett, AC 205, PC 6, Chambers
Lanett CSD, PO BOX 329   36863   4-11111
  Rex Bryan, supt.   644-5900
HS, PO BOX 429   36863   2-00011
  Don Medders, prin.   644-5965
JHS, PO BOX 349   36863   2-00100
  Sanford Isom, prin.   644-5950

Springwood S, PO BOX 405   36863   2-11111
  Robert Steely, prin.   644-2191

Leeds, AC 205, PC 6, Jefferson
Jefferson County SD
  Supt. — See Birmingham
HS, 602 WHITMIRE ST   35094   2-00011
  Anna Vacca, prin.   699-6137
JHS, 1700 MOTON ST   35094   2-00100
  Homer Stewart, prin.   699-7711

Leesburg, AC 205, PC 2, Cherokee
Cherokee County SD
  Supt. — See Centre
Sand Rock S, RR 1 BOX 130   35983   3-11111
  James Hendon, prin.   523-3564

Leighton, AC 205, PC 3, Colbert
Colbert County SD
  Supt. — See Tuscumbia
Colbert County JSHS   2-00111
  PO BOX 429   35646   446-8214
  Everett Greenhill, prin.

Leroy, AC 205, PC 2, Washington
Washington County SD
Supt. — See Chatom
S, PO BOX 40 36548 3-11111
Cleophus Stephens, prin. 246-2000

Lester, AC 205, PC 1, Limestone
Limestone County SD
Supt. — See Athens
West Limestone S 3-11111
RR 1 BOX 99 35647 232-0100
Aubry Privett, prin.

Letohatchee, AC 205, PC 2, Lowndes
Lowndes County SD
Supt. — See Hayneville
Calhoun HS, RR 1 BOX 257 36047 2-00011
Willie Hill, prin. 227-4515

Lexington, AC 205, PC 3, Lauderdale
Lauderdale County SD
Supt. — See Florence
S, PO BOX 70 35648 3-11111
Patrick Brown, prin. 229-6622

Lincoln, AC 205, PC 5, Talladega
Talladega County SD
Supt. — See Talladega
HS, PO BOX 197 35096 3-00011
Ervin Romine, prin. 763-7459
Drew MS, 450 DREW AVE 35096 2-01100
James Coleman, prin. 763-7621

Linden, AC 205, PC 5, Marengo
Linden CSD, PO BOX 480609 36748 3-11111
Paul Whitcomb, supt. 295-8802
HS, PO BOX 480729 36748 2-00011
Charles Arledge, prin. 295-4287
Marengo Co. Vo HS Vo Tech
2450 E COATS AVE 36748 295-4237
Walter Davis, prin.
Austin JHS, PO BOX 480699 36748 2-00100
Mattie Richards-Herd, prin. 295-5378

Marengo County SD 4-11111
PO BOX 480339 36748 295-4123
Marcus Walters, supt.
Other Schools – See Demopolis, Dixon's Mills, Sweet Water, Thomaston

---

Marengo Academy 2-11111
2103 S MAIN ST 36748 295-4151
John Holley, prin.

Lineville, AC 205, PC 4, Clay
Clay County SD
Supt. — See Ashland
JSHS, PO BOX 278 36266 2-00111
Kermit Caldwell, prin. 396-2466
Clay Co. Area Vo Ctr Vo Tech
PO BOX 543 36266 396-2870
Richard Runyan, prin.

Livingston, AC 205, PC 5, Sumter
Sumter County SD, PO BOX 10 35470 5-11111
David Jones, supt. 652-9605
HS, PO BOX 40 35470 2-00011
Lula Larkins, prin. 652-2464
Sumter Co. Area Vo HS Vo Tech
PO BOX 1380 35470 652-9469
Alex Crawford, prin.
Other Schools – See York

Livingston University 4-UC
HWY 11 35470 652-9661

Loachapoka, AC 205, PC 2, Lee
Lee County SD
Supt. — See Opelika
S, PO BOX 187 36865 3-11111
Richard Harvey, prin. 887-8038

Locust Fork, AC 205, PC 2, Blount
Blount County SD
Supt. — See Oneonta
S, PO BOX 46 35097 3-11111
Gene Vinson, prin. 681-9032

Louisville, AC 205, PC 3, Barbour
Barbour County SD
Supt. — See Clayton
JSHS, PO BOX 37 36048 2-00111
Scarlette Abercrombie, prin. 266-5439

Dixie Academy, PO BOX 67 36048 2-11111
Sidney Grimes, prin. 266-5311

Lower Peach Tree, AC 205, PC 2, Wilcox
Monroe County SD
Supt. — See Monroeville
Monroe S 36751 2-11111
H. Williams, prin. 636-2032

Loxley, AC 205, PC 4, Baldwin
Baldwin County SD
Supt. — See Bay Minette
MS, PO BOX 38 36551 2-00100
Mike Dawkins, prin. 964-6231

Luverne, AC 205, PC 5, Crenshaw
Crenshaw County SD 5-11111
PO BOX 72 36049 335-6519
Samuel Carr, supt.
S, 200 1ST AVE 36049 4-11111
James Head, prin. 335-3331
Crenshaw Co. Area Vo HS Vo Tech
1406 S WOODFORD AVE 36049 335-3319
Trubie Strickland, prin.
Other Schools – See Brantley, Highland Home

Crenshaw Christian Academy 2-11111
RR 3 BOX 8S 36049 335-5749
Theresa Johnson, prin.

Lynn, AC 205, PC 3, Winston
Winston County SD
Supt. — See Double Springs
S, PO BOX 128 35575 2-11111
Ray Smoot, prin. 893-5471

Mc Calla, AC 205, PC 3, Jefferson
Jefferson County SD
Supt. — See Birmingham
McAdory S 4-11111
4800 MCADORY SCHOOL RD 35111 426-1237
Randy Fuller, prin.

Mc Intosh, AC 205, PC 2, Washington
Washington County SD
Supt. — See Chatom
JSHS, PO BOX 359 36553 2-00111
Warren Roberts, prin. 944-2441

Mc Kenzie, AC 205, PC 2, Butler
Butler County SD
Supt. — See Greenville
S, PO BOX 158 36456 2-11111
William Pritchett, prin. 374-2711

Madison, AC 205, PC 7, Madison
Madison County SD
Supt. — See Huntsville
Jones HS, 1304 HUGHES RD 35758 3-00011
Bill Broadway, prin. 837-8780
Liberty MS 3-01100
281 DOCK MURPHY DR 35758 430-0001
Dee Fowler, prin.

Maplesville, AC 205, PC 3, Chilton
Chilton County SD
Supt. — See Clanton
Isabella S 2-11111
11338 COUNTY ROAD 15 36750 755-3137
Martha Mims, prin.
S, PO BOX 146 36750 3-11111
George Walker, prin. 366-2991

Marbury, AC 205, PC 2, Autauga
Autauga County SD
Supt. — See Prattville
S, PO BOX A 36051 3-11111
William Hopper, prin. 755-2118

Marion, AC 205, PC 5, Perry
Perry County SD, PO BOX 900 36756 4-11111
John McCalpine, supt. 683-6528
HS, PO BOX 150 36756 3-00011
Bob Coley, prin. 683-4761
Marion Area Vo HS Vo Tech
101 HUBBARD DR 36756 683-9307
Bobby Coley, prin.
West Side MS, RR 1 BOX 265 36756 2-01100
Albert Nelson, prin. 683-8362
Other Schools – See Uniontown

Judson College 2-UC
PO BOX 120 36756 683-6161
Marion Military Institute 1-00011
1101 WASHINGTON ST 36756 683-2303
Joseph Fant, prin.
Marion Military Institute 2-CC
1101 WASHINGTON ST 36756 683-2305

Marion Junction, AC 205, PC 2, Dallas
Dallas County SD
Supt. — See Selma
Harrell MS 2-00100
700 COUNTY ROAD 206 36759 872-8304
Finis Sanders, prin.

Midfield, AC 205, PC 6, Jefferson
Midfield CSD 4-11111
417 PARKWOOD ST 35228 923-2262
Andy Rowell, supt.
HS, 1600 HIGH SCHOOL DR 35221 3-00011
Bill Sparks, prin. 923-2833
Midfield Area Vo HS Vo Tech
1600 HIGH SCHOOL DR 35221 923-9176
Bill Sparks, prin.
Rutledge MS, 1221 8TH ST 35228 3-01100
Herbert Alexander, prin. 780-8647

Midland City, AC 205, PC 4, Dale
Dale County SD
Supt. — See Ozark
Dale County HS, PO BOX J 36350 2-00011
Ronnie Jackson, prin. 983-3541

Millbrook, AC 205, PC 6, Elmore
Elmore County SD
Supt. — See Wetumpka
Stanhope-Elmore HS 3-00011
4300 MAIN ST 36054 285-4263
Ray Stringer, prin.
MS, 4228 CHAPMAN RD 36054 4-01100
Theodore Jackson, prin. 285-2100

Millerville, AC 205, PC 2, Clay
Clay County SD
Supt. — See Ashland
Graves JSHS, PO BOX 85 36267 2-00111
Raymond Camp, prin. 354-7564

Millport, AC 205, PC 4, Lamar
Lamar County SD
Supt. — See Vernon
South Lamar S, PO BOX 309 35576 3-11111
Terry Goodin, prin. 662-4411

Millry, AC 205, PC 3, Washington
Washington County SD
Supt. — See Chatom
S, PO BOX 65 36558 3-11111
R. Blackwell, prin. 846-2987

Mobile, AC 205, PC 9, Mobile
Mobile County SD 8-11111
PO BOX 1327 36633 690-8227
Paul Sousa, supt.
Davidson HS 4-00011
3900 PLEASANT VALLEY RD 36609 342-7156
Lewis Copeland, prin.
Le Flore HS, 700 DONALD ST 36617 4-00011
Fred Marshall, prin. 456-2806
Murphy HS, 100 S CARLEN ST 36606 4-00011
Linda Sparkman, prin. 479-4526
Rain HS 3-00011
3125 DAUPHIN ISLAND PKY 36605 479-0511
Thomas Reed, prin.
Shaw HS, 5960 ARLBERG ST 36608 4-00011
Albert Lowery, prin. 342-0850
Williamson HS, 1007 SWAN DR 36605 3-00011
Fred Green, prin. 471-2497
Baker JSHS, 8901 AIRPORT BLVD 36608 4-00111
John Sklopan, prin. 633-0330
Evans S, 100 N FLORIDA ST 36607 2-11111
Peter Kingsford, prin. 473-8831
Azalea MS 4-00100
3800 PLEASANT VALLEY RD 36609 342-5363
William Jessie, prin.
Chastang MS, 2800 BERKLEY AVE 36617 3-00100
Hilda Wilson, prin. 456-8416
Dunbar Creative/Perf Arts 2-01100
500 SAINT ANTHONY ST 36603 690-8255
Fred Sigler, prin.
Eanes MS, 1901 HURTEL ST 36605 3-00100
Zad Douglas, prin. 471-4341
Hillsdale MS, 6301 BILOXI AVE 36608 3-00100
Lebarron Byrd, prin. 342-3351
Phillips MS, 3255 OLD SHELL RD 36607 3-00100
Carolyn Taylor, prin. 471-4431
Pillans MS, 2051 MILITARY RD 36605 4-00100
Robert Shaw, prin. 478-6327
Scarborough MS 4-00100
1800 PHILLIPS LN 36618 344-6864
Vance Allen, prin.
Washington MS 3-00100
1961 ANDREWS ST 36617 471-2432
Eddie Butler, prin.
Other Schools – See Bayou La Batre, Chickasaw, Citronelle, Grand Bay, Irvington, Prichard, Saraland, Satsuma, Semmes, Theodore

---

Bishop State Community College 5-CC
351 N BROAD ST 36603 690-6419
Bishop State Community College 3-CS
925 DAUPHIN ISLAND PKY 36605 479-0003
CAPPS College 1-CS
3100 COTTAGE HILL RD # 500 36606 473-1393
Career Development Institute 2-CS
1060 SPRINGHILL AVE 36604
Carver State Technical College 2-CS
414 STANTON RD 36617 473-8692
Faith Academy 3-11111
8650 TANNER WILLIAMS RD 36608 649-1161
Tom Skelton, prin.
Government Street Christian S 2-11111
2157 GOVERNMENT ST 36606 473-2947
Donna Royal, prin.
McGill-Toolen HS 4-00011
1501 OLD SHELL RD 36604 432-0784
Rev. Shields, prin.
Mobile Christian S 3-11111
5900 COTTAGE HILL RD 36609 661-1613
Sharon Donaldson, prin.
Mobile Infirmary Medical Center HSP
PO BOX 2144 36652 431-4444
Phillips Junior College 2-CC
3446 DEMETROPOLIS RD 36693 666-9696
St. Paul's Episcopal S 4-11111
161 DOGWOOD LN 36608 342-6700
William Taylor, prin.
South Alabama Skills Center 2-CS
846 BUTLER DR # A 36693 661-0215
Southeast College of Technology 2-CS
828 DOWNTOWNER LOOP W 36609 343-8200
Spring Hill College 4-UC
4000 DAUPHIN ST 36608 460-2130
Ums Wright Prep S 4-11111
65 N MOBILE ST 36607 479-6551
Tony Havard, prin.
University of Mobile 4-UC
PO BOX 13220 36663 675-5990
University of South Alabama 7-UC
307 UNIVERSITY BLVD N 36688 460-6141

Monroeville, AC 205, PC 6, Monroe
Monroe County SD 6-11111
PO BOX 967 36461 575-2168
Sam Hollingsworth, supt.
Monroe County HS, TIGER DR 36460 3-00011
Pat Patterson, prin. 575-3258
Monroe Co. Area Vo HS, TIGER DR 36460 Vo Tech
C. Al Brown, prin. 575-4381

JHS, 315 YORK ST 36460   3-00100
Jimmy Lambert, prin.   575-4121
Other Schools – See Beatrice, Excel, Frisco City, Lower Peach Tree, Uriah

---

Alabama Southern Community College   4-CC
PO BOX 2000 36461   575-3156
Monroe Academy, PO BOX 927 36461   2-11111
David Walker, prin.   743-3932

Montevallo, AC 205, PC 5, Shelby
Shelby County SD
Supt. — See Columbiana
HS, 980 OAK ST 35115   2-00011
George Theodore, prin.   665-3800
MS, 195 SANFORD ST 35115   2-00010
John McClain, prin.   665-3810

Shelby Academy   2-11111
PO BOX 9178 35115   668-2299
Dewayne Kervin, prin.
University of Montevallo   5-UC
STATION 6001 35115   665-6000

Montgomery, AC 205, PC 9, Montgomery
Montgomery County SD   8-11111
PO BOX 1991 36102   269-3031
John Eberhart, supt.
Carver SHS   3-00001
2001 W FAIRVIEW AVE 36108   269-3636
Dwight Madison, prin.
Davis SHS, 3420 CARTER HILL RD 36111   4-00001
Elizabeth Armistead, prin.   269-3714
Lanier SHS, 1756 S COURT ST 36104   4-00001
Jimmie Adams, prin.   269-3726
Lee SHS, 225 ANN ST 36107   4-00001
James Bozeman, prin.   269-3742
Montgomery Area Vo Ctr   Vo Tech
1400 W 5TH ST 36106   269-3780
William Gary, prin.
Washington Area Vo Ctr   Vo Tech
607 S UNION ST 36104   269-3608
Marshall Green, prin.
Washington Area Vo Ctr   Vo Tech
632 S UNION ST 36104   269-3618
Marshall Green, prin.
Baldwin JHS   2-00110
410 S MCDONOUGH ST 36104   269-3870
Carolyn Hicks, prin.
Brewbaker JHS   4-00110
4425 BREWBAKER DR 36116   284-8008
Jim Barker, prin.
Capitol Heights JHS   4-00110
116 FEDERAL DR 36107   260-1000
Wallace Musick, prin.
Carver JHS   3-00110
2025 W FAIRVIEW AVE 36108   269-3640
Charles Everett, prin.
Cloverdale JHS   3-00110
1125 E FAIRVIEW AVE 36106   269-3647
Linda Wilson, prin.
Goodwyn JHS   3-00110
209 PERRY HILL RD 36109   260-1021
George Hammett, prin.
Houston Hill JHS, 215 HALL ST 36104   2-00110
Warren Davis, prin.   269-3694
McIntyre JHS, 1210 HUGH ST 36108   2-00110
John Wilson, prin.   269-3755
Other Schools – See Pike Road, Ramer

Alabama Christian Academy   3-11111
4700 WARES FERRY RD 36109   277-1985
Paul Anthony, prin.
Alabama State University   6-UC
PO BOX 271 36101   800-354-8865
Auburn University at Montgomery   6-UC
7300 UNIVERSITY DR 36117   244-3611
Baptist Medical Centers   HSP
2105 E SOUTH BLVD 36116   288-2100
Career Development Institute   2-CS
505 MONTGOMERY ST 36104
Central Alabama Skills Center   2-CS
PO BOX 240369 36124   242-5121
Coastal Training Institute   3-CS
5950 S MONTICELLO DR 36117
Community College of the Air Force   8-CC
130 W MAXWELL BLVD 36112   293-6436
Diesel Driving Academy   2-CS
3295 WETUMPKA HWY 36110
Draughons Junior College   3-CC
122 COMMERCE ST 36104   263-1013
Faulkner University   4-UC
5345 ATLANTA HWY 36109   272-5820
Green Gate S, 3265 MCGEHEE RD 36111   2-11111
Yvonna Richardson, prin.   281-3300
Humana Hospital   HSP
301 S RIPLEY ST 36104   269-8656
Huntingdon College   3-UC
1500 E FAIRVIEW AVE 36106   800-763-0313
Montgomery Academy   3-11111
3240 VAUGHN RD 36106   272-8210
Emerson Johnson, prin.
Montgomery Catholic HS   2-00011
5350 VAUGHN RD 36116   272-7220
Faustin Weber, prin.
Patterson State Technical College   3-CS
3920 TROY HWY 36116   284-9356
Prince Institute of Professional Studies   2-CS
7735 ATLANTA HWY 36117   271-1670

St. James S   4-11111
2005 N COUNTRY CLUB DR 36106   264-2416
John Bell, prin.
St. Jude HS   2-00011
2048 W FAIRVIEW AVE 36108   264-5376
Gerri Perry, prin.
Southern Christian University   1-UC
PO BOX 240240 36124   277-2277
Trenholm State Technical College   5-CS
1225 AIR BASE BLVD 36108   832-9000
Trinity Presbyterian S   3-11111
1700 E TRINITY BLVD 36106   277-0370
Brian Willett, prin.
Troy State University at Montgomery   4-UC
PO BOX 4419 36103   834-1400
Williams S, 2620 E 3RD ST 36107   2-11111
Kathleen Anderson, prin.   262-2671

Moody, AC 205, PC 5, St. Clair
Saint Clair County SD
Supt. — See Ashville
Moody JSHS   3-00111
600 HIGH SCHOOL DR 35004   640-5127
Randal Roberts, prin.

Morris, AC 205, PC 4, Jefferson
Jefferson County SD
Supt. — See Birmingham
Jordan JSHS   3-00111
8601 OLD HIGHWAY 31 35116   647-9811
James Trotter, prin.

Moulton, AC 205, PC 5, Lawrence
Lawrence County SD   6-11111
14131 MARKET ST 35650   905-2400
Patrick Graham, supt.
Lawrence County JSHS   3-00111
102 COLLEGE ST 35650   905-2440
Wayne Shelton, prin.
Lawrence Co. Vo-Tech HS   Vo Tech
PO BOX 606 35650   974-3751
Willard Terry, prin.
Other Schools – See Courtland, Danville, Mount Hope, Town Creek, Trinity

Moundville, AC 205, PC 4, Hale
Hale County SD
Supt. — See Greensboro
Hale County JSHS   2-00111
PO BOX 188 35474   371-2514
Dovel Rock, prin.

Mountain Brook, AC 205, PC 7, Jefferson
Mountain Brook CSD   5-11111
PO BOX 130040 35213   871-4608
Charles Mason, supt.
SHS, 3650 BETHUNE DR 35223   3-00001
Timmerman Norris, prin.   967-2090
JHS, 205 OVERBROOK RD 35213   3-00110
Garry Rickard, prin.   871-3516

Mount Hope, AC 205, PC 2, Lawrence
Lawrence County SD
Supt. — See Moulton
S, 8455 COUNTY ROAD 23 35651   2-11111
Tony Rutherford, prin.   905-2470

Munford, AC 205, PC 3, Talladega
Talladega County SD
Supt. — See Talladega
JSHS, PO BOX 529 36268   3-00111
Ken Brewer, prin.   358-4208

Muscle Shoals, AC 205, PC 6, Colbert
Muscle Shoals CSD   4-11111
PO BOX 2730 35662   389-2600
Martha Livingston, supt.
HS, 100 E TROJAN DR 35661   3-00011
Harry Smith, prin.   389-2640
Muscle Shoals Area Vo HS   Vo Tech
PO BOX 2186 35662   389-2660
Sylvia Coleman, prin.
Avalon MS, 1400 E AVALON AVE 35661   3-01100
H. Noah, prin.   389-2610

Shoals Community College   5-CC
PO BOX 2545 35662   381-2813

Newbern, AC 205, PC 2, Hale
Hale County SD
Supt. — See Greensboro
Sunshine S, RR 1 BOX 312 36765   2-11111
Herbert Pickens, prin.   624-8747

New Brockton, AC 205, PC 4, Coffee
Coffee County SD
Supt. — See Elba
JSHS, PO BOX 429 36351   2-00111
Stanley Walker, prin.   894-2350
Coffee Co. Area Vo HS   Vo Tech
PO BOX 160 36351   894-6748
Tom Moates, prin.

New Hope, AC 205, PC 4, Madison
Madison County SD
Supt. — See Huntsville
S, 5300 MAIN DR 35760   4-11111
Dennis Stephens, prin.   723-4225

New Market, AC 205, PC 4, Madison
Madison County SD
Supt. — See Huntsville
Buckhorn HS   3-00011
4123 WINCHESTER RD 35761   379-2123
Tom Ledbetter, prin.

Newton, AC 205, PC 4, Dale
Houston County SD
Supt. — See Dothan
Wicksburg S, RR 1 36352   3-11111
James Johnson, prin.   692-5549

Newville, AC 205, PC 3, Henry
Henry County SD
Supt. — See Abbeville
Newville Area Vo HS   Vo Tech
PO BOX 70 36353   889-4481
Napoleon Culver, prin.

Normal, AC 205, PC 5, Madison

Alabama A & M University   6-UC
PO BOX 908 35762   851-5245

Northport, AC 205, PC 7, Tuscaloosa
Tuscaloosa County SD
Supt. — See Tuscaloosa
Tuscaloosa County SHS   4-00001
2200 24TH ST 35476   339-5055
Ronald Lett, prin.
Northside JSHS   2-00111
12945 NORTHSIDE RD 35476   339-1750
David Patrick, prin.
Tuscaloosa Co. Area Vo HS   Vo Tech
2200 24TH ST 35476   339-5055
Ronald Lett, prin.
Northport JHS, 2300 26TH AVE 35476   3-00110
Octavia Miles, prin.   339-6641
Riverside JHS, 1400 3RD ST 35476   3-00110
James Davis, prin.   752-8515

American Christian Academy   2-11111
701 MRTN LTHER KING JR BLVD 35476
Dan Carden, prin.   758-2868

Notasulga, AC 205, PC 3, Macon
Macon County SD
Supt. — See Tuskegee
S, PO BOX 10 36866   3-11111
Robert Anderson, prin.   257-3510

Tallapoosa County SD
Supt. — See Dadeville
Reeltown S   3-11111
4085 ALABAMA HIGHWAY 120 36866
Sheldon Darnell, prin.   257-3784

Oakman, AC 205, PC 3, Walker
Walker County SD
Supt. — See Jasper
JSHS, PO BOX 286 35579   2-00111
Randy Woods, prin.   622-3381

Odenville, AC 205, PC 3, St. Clair
Saint Clair County SD
Supt. — See Ashville
St. Clair Co. S, BURGESS DR 35120   4-11111
Edward Moseley, prin.   629-6222

Ohatchee, AC 205, PC 4, Calhoun
Calhoun County SD
Supt. — See Anniston
S, 100 CHEROKEE TRL 36271   3-11111
Kenneth New, prin.   892-3270

Oneonta, AC 205, PC 5, Blount
Blount County SD   6-11111
PO BOX 578 35121   625-4102
J. Hazelrig, supt.
Appalachian S, RR 4 BOX 502 35121   3-11111
James Carr, prin.   274-9712
Other Schools – See Blountsville, Cleveland, Hayden, Locust Fork

Oneonta CSD, RR 1 BOX 14 35121   4-11111
Allen Jeffreys, supt.   625-4106
Oneonta City S, RR 1 BOX 14 35121   4-11111
Allen Jeffreys, prin.   625-3801

Opelika, AC 205, PC 7, Lee
Lee County SD, PO BOX 120 36803   6-11111
John Painter, supt.   745-9770
Beauregard S   4-11111
7343 AL HIGHWAY 51 36801   745-5916
Richard Brown, prin.
Sanford MS   2-01100
1500 LEE ROAD 11 36801   745-5023
James Sasser, prin.
Other Schools – See Loachapoka, Salem, Smiths, Valley

Opelika CSD, PO BOX 2469 36803   5-11111
J. Raley, supt.   745-9700
HS, 1701 LAFAYETTE PKY 36801   4-00011
Don Roberts, prin.   745-9715
Opelika City Area Vo Ctr 36802   Vo Tech
Don Roberts, prin.   745-9715
MS, 1206 DENSON DR 36801   4-00100
Mark Neighbors, prin.   745-9726

Opelika State Technical College   3-CS
PO BOX 2268 36803   745-6437

Opp, AC 205, PC 6, Covington
Opp CSD, PO BOX 428 36467   4-11111
Allen Miller, supt.   493-3173
HS, 502 N MALOY ST 36467   3-00011
Walter Pyron, prin.   493-4561
MS, 303 E STEWART AVE 36467   2-01100
Kenneth Short, prin.   493-6332

MacArthur State Technical College   3-CS
PO BOX 649 36467   493-3573

Orrville, AC 205, PC 2, Dallas
Dallas County SD
Supt. — See Selma
Keith HS   2-00011
1166 COUNTY ROAD 115 36767   875-4155
Willie Steele, prin.

Oxford, AC 205, PC 6, Calhoun
Oxford CSD, 310 E 2ND ST 36203   5-11111
John Toland, supt.   831-0243
JSHS, 915 STEWART ST 36203   4-00111
Louis Higgins, prin.   831-7507
Oxford Area Vo HS   Vo Tech
915 STEWART ST 36203   831-7505
Louis Higgins, prin.

Ozark, AC 205, PC 7, Dale
Dale County SD, PO BOX 948 36361   5-11111
Jerry Glover, supt.   774-2355
Other Schools – See Ariton, Midland City, Pinckard, Skipperville

Ozark CSD, PO BOX 788 36361   5-11111
John Moseley, supt.   774-5197
Carroll HS, 101 FOREST AVE 36360   4-00011
Larry Hicks, prin.   774-4915
Ozark Vo HS, FAUST AVE 36360   Vo Tech
Alice Parrish, prin.   774-4949
East Gate MS, RR 4 36360   2-01100
Sonny Raley, prin.   774-4910
Smith MS, 159 ENTERPRISE RD 36360   3-01100
James Jarmon, prin.   774-4913

Adams S, STUART TARTER RD 36360   2-11111
Celeste Sneed, prin.   774-5132
Alabama Aviation & Technical College   2-CS
PO BOX 1209 36361   774-5113

Parrish, AC 205, PC 4, Walker
Walker County SD
Supt. — See Jasper
JSHS, RR 1 BOX 116 35580   2-00011
George Harland, prin.   686-7701

Pelham, AC 205, PC 6, Shelby
Shelby County SD
Supt. — See Columbiana
HS, PO BOX 38 35124   4-00011
Tom Ferguson, prin.   620-1080

Pell City, AC 205, PC 6, St. Clair
Pell City CSD, 25 12TH ST S 35125   5-11111
Billy Pack, supt.   884-4440
HS, 1200 COGSWELL AVE 35125   3-00011
Tom Gilbert, prin.   338-2250
Duran JHS, 309 12TH ST S 35125   3-00100
Margaret Scott, prin.   338-2825

Phenix City, AC 205, PC 8, Russell
Phenix City SD, PO BOX 460 36868   5-11111
Thomas Davis, supt.   298-0534
Central HS, 2400 DOBBS DR 36867   3-00011
William Hayes, prin.   298-3626
South Girard JHS   3-00100
624 FONTAINE RD 36869   298-2527
Jeff Adams, prin.

Russell County SD   5-11111
PO BOX 400 36868   298-8791
T. Larry Thacker, supt.
Other Schools – See Seale

Chattahoochee Valley State Comm College   5-CC
2602 COLLEGE DR 36869   297-4981
Glenwood S, PO BOX 310 36868   2-11111
John Niblett, prin.   297-3614

Phil Campbell, AC 205, PC 4, Franklin
Franklin County SD
Supt. — See Russellville
S, PO BOX 849 35581   3-11111
Larry Whitfield, prin.   993-5311

Northwest Alabama Community College   4-CC
RR 3 BOX 77 35581   800-645-8967

Piedmont, AC 205, PC 6, Calhoun
Piedmont CSD, PO BOX 232 36272   4-11111
Hazel Kisor, supt.   447-8831
HS, PO BOX 272 36272   2-00011
Charles Bone, prin.   447-2829
MS, PO BOX 226 36272   2-00100
Betty Lou Lusk, prin.   447-6165

Pike Road, AC 205, PC 2, Montgomery
Montgomery County SD
Supt. — See Montgomery
Washington JHS   3-00110
696 GEORGIA WASHINGTON RD 36064   215-8290
Arthur McKnatt, prin.

Pinckard, AC 205, PC 3, Dale
Dale County SD
Supt. — See Ozark
South Dale JHS, PO BOX D 36371   2-00100
Robert Woodham, prin.   983-3077

Pinson, AC 205, PC 4, Jefferson
Jefferson County SD
Supt. — See Birmingham

Pinson Valley HS   3-00011
6895 HIGHWAY 75 35126   681-2640
Ronald Page, prin.
Rudd JHS   3-00100
4526 RUDD SCHOOL RD 35126   681-0684
Charles Smith, prin.

Pisgah, AC 205, PC 3, Jackson
Jackson County SD
Supt. — See Scottsboro
S, PO BOX 249 35765   3-11111
Bill Shelton, prin.   451-3241

Plantersville, AC 205, PC 3, Dallas
Dallas County SD
Supt. — See Selma
Dallas County JSHS   3-00111
PO BOX 145 36758   366-2232
William Griffin, prin.

Pleasant Grove, AC 205, PC 6, Jefferson
Jefferson County SD
Supt. — See Birmingham
JSHS, 805 7TH AVE 35127   3-00111
Terry Sanders, prin.   744-6911

Prattville, AC 205, PC 7, Autauga
Autauga County SD   6-11111
PO BOX 130 36067   365-5706
David Weedon, supt.
HS, PO BOX 9010 36067   4-00011
Roy Johnson, prin.   365-8804
Autauga Co. Area Vo HS   Vo Tech
PO BOX 249 36067   361-0258
Charles Riddle, prin.
JHS, PO BOX D 36067   3-00100
John Schremser, prin.   365-6697
Other Schools – See Autaugaville, Billingsley, Marbury

Autauga Academy   2-11111
PO BOX 608 36067   365-6665
Lawrence Raines, prin.

Prichard, AC 205, PC 8, Mobile
Mobile County SD
Supt. — See Mobile
Blount HS, 838 W MAIN ST 36610   3-00011
Alfred July, prin.   457-6682
Vigor HS, 913 N WILSON AVE 36610   4-00011
Thomas Langley, prin.   457-2341
Faulkner Vo-Tech HS   Vo Tech
33 W ELM ST 36610   452-3445
Herschell Wilson, prin.
Mobile County Training MS   2-00100
PO BOX 10097 36610   456-7608
Charles Sellers, prin.

Faulkner Area Vocational Center   2-CS
33 W ELM ST 36610   452-3445

Princeton, AC 205, PC 2, Jackson
Jackson County SD
Supt. — See Scottsboro
Paint Rock Valley S 35766   2-11111
Grant Barham, prin.   776-2628

Quinton, AC 205, PC 2, Walker
Jefferson County SD
Supt. — See Birmingham
West Jefferson S   2-11111
7000 W JEFFERSON RD 35130   674-6402
Ronald Cooper, prin.

Ragland, AC 205, PC 4, St. Clair
Saint Clair County SD
Supt. — See Ashville
S, PO BOX 610 35131   3-11111
Roger Pate, prin.   472-2123

Rainbow City, AC 205, PC 6, Etowah
Etowah County SD
Supt. — See Gadsden
Rainbow MS, 454 LUMBLEY RD 35906   2-00100
Harriet McMeekin, prin.   442-1095

Rainsville, AC 205, PC 5, De Kalb
De Kalb County SD
Supt. — See Fort Payne
Plainview S, PO BOX 469 35986   4-11111
Bob Gray, prin.   638-3510
De Kalb Vo HS, PO BOX 529 35986   Vo Tech
Conner Runyan, prin.   638-4421

Northeast Alabama State Junior College   4-CC
PO BOX 159 35986   228-6001

Ramer, AC 205, PC 2, Montgomery
Montgomery County SD
Supt. — See Montgomery
Montgomery County JSHS   2-00111
PO BOX 145 36069   562-3241
Lloyd Youngblood, prin.

Ranburne, AC 205, PC 2, Cleburne
Cleburne County SD
Supt. — See Heflin
JSHS, RR 1 BOX 2 36273   2-00111
Fred Lovvorn, prin.   568-3402

Red Bay, AC 205, PC 5, Franklin
Franklin County SD
Supt. — See Russellville
S, PO BOX 1518 35582   3-11111
Bob Forsythe, prin.   356-4408

Red Level, AC 205, PC 3, Covington
Covington County SD
Supt. — See Andalusia
S, PO BOX D 36474   3-11111
John Taylor, prin.   469-5315

Reform, AC 205, PC 4, Pickens
Pickens County SD
Supt. — See Carrollton
Pickens County JSHS   2-00111
PO BOX 1239 35481   375-2344
William James, prin.

Roanoke, AC 205, PC 6, Randolph
Roanoke CSD, PO BOX 312 36274   4-11111
Jerrell May, supt.   863-2628
Handley JSHS, PO BOX 312 36274   3-00111
James Nolen, prin.   863-6815
Other Schools – See Wedowee

Robertsdale, AC 205, PC 4, Baldwin
Baldwin County SD
Supt. — See Bay Minette
HS, PO BOX 69 36567   3-00011
John Falck, prin.   947-4154
South Baldwin Tech Ctr   Vo Tech
PO BOX 549 36567   947-5041
Brent Walters, prin.

Rockford, AC 205, PC 2, Coosa
Coosa County SD, PO BOX 37 35136   4-11111
Larry Hardman, supt.   377-4913
Central HS, RR 2 BOX 62 35136   3-00011
David Touart, prin.   377-4384
Coosa Co. Vo HS, RR 2 BOX 52 35136   Vo Tech
Steven Dyess, prin.   377-4678

Rogersville, AC 205, PC 4, Lauderdale
Lauderdale County SD
Supt. — See Florence
Lauderdale County S   3-11111
PO BOX 220 35652   247-3414
Ray Hester, prin.

Russellville, AC 205, PC 6, Franklin
Franklin County SD   5-11111
PO BOX 610 35653   332-1360
Hoyt Dillard, supt.
Belgreen S, RR 6 35653   2-11111
Ed Britton, prin.   332-1376
Franklin Co. Vo HS, RR 6 35653   Vo Tech
Orval Seay, prin.   332-2127
Other Schools – See Phil Campbell, Red Bay, Vina

Russellville CSD, PO BOX 880 35653   4-11111
Robert Clemmons, supt.   332-8440
HS, PO BOX 730 35653   3-00011
Louie Fryer, prin.   332-8460
MS, PO BOX 1213 35653   3-00100
Jerry Baker, prin.   332-8450

Salem, AC 205, PC 2, Lee
Lee County SD
Supt. — See Opelika
Wacoochee JHS, PO BOX 100 36874   2-00100
Herbert Williams, prin.   745-3062

Samson, AC 205, PC 4, Geneva
Geneva County SD
Supt. — See Geneva
S, 209 N BROAD ST 36477   3-11111
D. Wells, prin.   898-2371

Saraland, AC 205, PC 7, Mobile
Mobile County SD
Supt. — See Mobile
Adams MS, 401 BALDWIN RD 36571   3-00100
Frank Coleman, prin.   675-1880

Shiloh Christian S   3-11111
723 CLEVELAND RD 36571   675-3448
Charles Harvey, prin.

Satsuma, AC 205, PC 6, Mobile
Mobile County SD
Supt. — See Mobile
HS, PO BOX 487 36572   4-00011
L. Shoquist, prin.   675-0753

Satsuma Christian S   2-11111
PO BOX 557 36572   675-1280
Rose Fuller, prin.

Scottsboro, AC 205, PC 7, Jackson
Jackson County SD   6-11111
COURTHOUSE STE 20 35768   574-9200
W. Townson, supt.
Skyline S, RR 1 35768   3-11111
Wade Gentle, prin.   587-6561
Other Schools – See Bridgeport, Higdon, Hollywood, Pisgah, Princeton, Section, Stevenson, Woodville

Scottsboro CSD, 906 S SCOTT ST 35768   5-11111
Charles Carrick, supt.   259-4165
HS, 102 LEGION DR 35768   3-00011
James Holt, prin.   259-1818
JHS, 1601 JEFFERSON ST 35768   2-00100
Roy Durham, prin.   259-1204

Seale, AC 205, PC 2, Russell
Russell County SD
Supt. — See Phenix City
Russell County HS   2-00011
4699 HIGHWAY 431 36875   855-4378
Loyd Frey, prin.

Russell Area Vo HS — Vo Tech
US HIGHWAY 431 S 36875 — 855-4378
Jerry McKay, prin.
Russell County JHS — 2-00100
PO BOX 38 36875 — 855-4453
James Lowe, prin.

Section, AC 205, PC 3, Jackson
Jackson County SD
Supt. — See Scottsboro
S, PO BOX A 35771 — 3-11111
Bill Beavers, prin. — 228-6718

Selma, AC 205, PC 7, Dallas
Dallas County SD — 6-11111
PO BOX 1056 36702 — 875-3440
Marvin Warren, supt.
Southside JSHS — 3-00111
7975 US HIGHWAY 80 E 36701 — 872-8031
Ollis Grayson, prin.
Dallas Co. Area Vo HS — Vo Tech
1306 ROOSEVELT ST 36701 — 872-8031
Sam Gladden, prin.
Other Schools – See Marion Junction, Orrville, Plantersville

Selma CSD, PO BOX F 36702 — 6-11111
James Carter, supt. — 874-1600
HS, 2180 BROAD ST 36701 — 4-00011
Fred Reese, prin. — 874-1680
Selma Area Vo HS — Vo Tech
2180 BROAD ST 36701 — 874-1686
Fred Reese, prin.
Eastside JHS — 2-00100
400 WASHINGTON ST 36703 — 874-1670
Julia Scott, prin.
Westside MS — 3-00100
1701 SUMMERFIELD RD 36701 — 874-1675
Anna Sanner, prin.

Concordia College — 2-CC
PO BOX 1329 36702 — 874-5700
Meadowview Christian S — 3-11111
1512 OLD ORRVILLE RD 36701 — 872-8448
William Housley, prin.
Selma University — 2-UC
1501 LAPSLEY ST 36701 — 872-2533
Wallace State Community College — 4-CC
PO BOX 1049 36702

Semmes, AC 205, PC 4, Mobile
Mobile County SD
Supt. — See Mobile
Montgomery HS — 4-00011
4275 SNOW RD N 36575 — 649-0511
George Romano, prin.
MS, WOLF RD 36575 — 4-00100
Thomas Fletcher, prin. — 649-2430

Sheffield, AC 205, PC 7, Colbert
Sheffield CSD, 300 W 6TH ST 35660 — 4-11111
Roger Tomberlin, supt. — 383-0400
HS, 2800 E 19TH AVE 35660 — 2-00011
Neal Dansby, prin. — 383-6052
JHS, 1803 30TH ST 35660 — 2-00100
Otis Johnson, prin. — 386-5735

Silas, AC 205, PC 2, Choctaw
Choctaw County SD
Supt. — See Butler
Southern Choctaw HS — 2-00011
PO BOX 146 36919 — 542-9235
Roy Adams, prin.

Skipperville, AC 205, PC 1, Dale
Dale County SD
Supt. — See Ozark
Long S, RR 1 BOX 1 36374 — 3-11111
Bill Clark, prin. — 774-2380

Slocomb, AC 205, PC 4, Geneva
Geneva County SD
Supt. — See Geneva
S, PO BOX 380 36375 — 3-11111
Jerry Edgar, prin. — 886-2008
Geneva Co. Area Vo Ctr 36375 — Vo Tech
(—), prin. — 886-2792

Smiths, AC 205, PC 4, Lee
Lee County SD
Supt. — See Opelika
Smiths Station S, PO BOX 158 36877 — 4-01111
Larry Boswell, prin. — 298-0969

Somerville, AC 205, PC 2, Morgan
Morgan County SD
Supt. — See Decatur
Brewer HS, RR 2 BOX 149 35670 — 4-00011
Don Murphy, prin. — 778-8634
Brewer Vo HS, RR 2 BOX 149 35670 — Vo Tech
Andrew McCay, prin. — 778-8634

Spring Garden, AC 205, PC 2, Cherokee
Cherokee County SD
Supt. — See Centre
S, PO BOX 31 36275 — 2-11111
Joan Rogers, prin. — 447-7045

Springville, AC 205, PC 4, St. Clair
Saint Clair County SD
Supt. — See Ashville
S, PO BOX 1069 35146 — 3-11111
Ernest Bagley, prin. — 467-7833

Stevenson, AC 205, PC 4, Jackson
Jackson County SD
Supt. — See Scottsboro

North Jackson HS, PO BOX 848 35772 — 3-00011
Kenneth Harding, prin. — 437-2136
MS, PO BOX 527 35772 — 2-01100
Dianne Brooks, prin. — 437-2945

Sulligent, AC 205, PC 4, Lamar
Lamar County SD
Supt. — See Vernon
S, PO BOX 367 35586 — 4-11111
C. Elliott, prin. — 698-9254

Sumiton, AC 205, PC 5, Walker

Bevill State Community College — 4-CS
PO BOX 800 35148 — 648-3271

Sweet Water, AC 205, PC 2, Marengo
Marengo County SD
Supt. — See Linden
S, PO BOX 127 36782 — 3-11111
Anna McManus, prin. — 994-4263

Sylacauga, AC 205, PC 7, Talladega
Sylacauga CSD, PO BOX 1127 35150 — 4-11111
Joseph Morton, supt. — 245-5256
HS, PO BOX 88 35150 — 3-00011
John Carter, prin. — 249-8692
East Highland MS — 2-00100
PO BOX 450 35150 — 245-4376
Rozell Sims, prin.

Talladega County SD
Supt. — See Talladega
Comer S, 801 SEMINOLE AVE 35150 — 4-11111
Dwight Rayfield, prin. — 245-3111
Fayetteville S — 2-11111
170 W W AVERITTE DR 35150 — 245-4991
Dale Tankersley, prin.

Sylacauga Hospital — HSP
S MOBILE AVE 35150 — 249-5716

Sylvania, AC 205, PC 3, De Kalb
De Kalb County SD
Supt. — See Fort Payne
S, PO BOX 20 35988 — 3-11111
Gary Carlyle, prin. — 638-2030

Talladega, AC 205, PC 7, Talladega
Talladega County SD — 6-11111
PO BOX 887 35160 — 362-1401
L. Grissett, supt.
Talladega County Central JSHS — 3-00111
5104 HOWELLS COVE RD 35160 — 362-1797
John Stamps, prin.
Other Schools – See Alpine, Childersburg, Lincoln, Munford, Sylacauga

Talladega CSD, PO BOX 946 35160 — 5-11111
Charles Kearley, supt. — 362-2203
HS, PO BOX 1014 35160 — 4-00011
Sebron Harmon, prin. — 362-8240
Talladega Area Vo HS — Vo Tech
110 PICCADILLY CIR 35160 — 362-8242
John Jenkins, prin.
Ellis JHS, 414 ELM ST 35160 — 3-00100
Joyce Hutchinson, prin. — 362-4201

Alabama Institute for the Deaf and Blind — HND
PO BOX 698 35160
Talladega College — 3-UC
627 BATTLE ST W 35160 — 362-0206

Tallassee, AC 205, PC 6, Elmore
Tallassee CSD, 307 KING ST 36078 — 4-11111
Glen Baggett, supt. — 283-6864
JSHS, 502 BARNETT BLVD 36078 — 3-00111
Robert Johnson, prin. — 283-2187

Tanner, AC 205, PC 3, Limestone
Limestone County SD
Supt. — See Athens
S, RR 1 BOX 1 35671 — 3-11111
Harvey Craig, prin. — 232-0106

Tarrant City, AC 205, PC 6, Jefferson
Tarrant CSD, 1318 ALABAMA ST 35217 — 4-11111
Yancy Morris, supt. — 849-3700
HS, 830 JEFFERSON BLVD 35217 — 2-00011
Charles Richards, prin. — 849-0172
MS, 1425 E LAKE BLVD 35217 — 2-01100
Rodney Kennamer, prin. — 849-0168

Theodore, AC 205, PC 6, Mobile
Mobile County SD
Supt. — See Mobile
HS, 6201 SWEDETOWN RD 36582 — 4-00011
Richard Davis, prin. — 653-8121
MS, 5760 THEODORE DAWES RD 36582 — 4-00100
Barry Amacker, prin. — 653-9312

Thomaston, AC 205, PC 2, Marengo
Marengo County SD
Supt. — See Linden
Johnson S, PO BOX 67 36783 — 3-11111
Rayvell Smith, prin. — 627-3364

Thomasville, AC 205, PC 5, Clarke
Thomasville CSD, PO BOX 458 36784 — 4-11111
Theodore Cornelius, supt. — 636-9955
JSHS, 3001 GATES DR 36784 — 3-00111
Ted Cornelius, prin. — 636-4451

Thorsby, AC 205, PC 4, Chilton
Chilton County SD
Supt. — See Clanton

S, 54 OPPORTUNITY DR 35171 — 3-11111
Chris Davis, prin. — 646-3319

Toney, AC 205, PC 2, Madison
Madison County SD
Supt. — See Huntsville
Sparkman HS — 3-00011
2697 CARTERS GIN RD 35773 — 852-5800
Steve Holland, prin.

Town Creek, AC 205, PC 4, Lawrence
Lawrence County SD
Supt. — See Moulton
Hatton JSHS — 2-00111
6909 AL HIGHWAY 101 35672 — 685-3374
Larry Hancock, prin.
Hazlewood JSHS, PO BOX 819 35672 — 2-00111
John Yates, prin. — 685-2022

Toxey, AC 205, PC 2, Choctaw

South Choctaw Academy — 2-11111
PO BOX 160 36921 — 843-2426
M. Dempsey, prin.

Trinity, AC 205, PC 4, Morgan
Lawrence County SD
Supt. — See Moulton
East Lawrence JSHS — 3-00111
55 COUNTY ROAD 370 35673 — 905-2430
K. Thomaskutty, prin.

Morgan County SD
Supt. — See Decatur
West Morgan S, RR 2 BOX 218 35673 — 4-11111
Bill Simms, prin. — 353-5214

Troy, AC 205, PC 7, Pike
Pike County SD — 5-11111
109 E CHURCH ST 36081 — 566-1850
John Key, supt.
Other Schools – See Brundidge, Goshen

Troy CSD, PO BOX 529 36081 — 4-11111
John Vaughan, supt. — 566-3741
Henderson HS, PO BOX 1006 36081 — 3-00011
Lavon Cain, prin. — 566-3510
Troy-Pike Area Vo Ctr — Vo Tech
RR 6 BOX 285 36081 — 566-5395
Lowell Carter, prin.
Henderson MS, PO BOX 925 36081 — 3-00100
Amos Brown, prin. — 566-5770

Pike Liberal Arts S — 2-11111
PO BOX 329 36081 — 566-2023
DeLaney Kervin, prin.
Troy State University 36082 — 7-UC
670-3000

Trussville, AC 205, PC 6, Jefferson
Jefferson County SD
Supt. — See Birmingham
Hewitt-Trussville SHS — 4-00001
5275 TRUSSVILLE CLAY RD 35173 — 655-2132
Connie Williams, prin.
Hewitt-Trussville JHS — 3-00110
601 PARKWAY DR 35173 — 655-8888
Lawrence Carter, prin.

Tuscaloosa, AC 205, PC 8, Tuscaloosa
Tuscaloosa County SD — 7-11111
PO BOX 2568 35403 — 758-0411
Neil Hyche, supt.
Hillcrest HS, 300 PATRIOT PKY 35405 — 4-00011
Joyce Sellers, prin. — 758-6443
Hillcrest MS — 3-00100
401 HILLCREST SCHOOL RD 35405 — 391-3002
James Cain, prin.
Other Schools – See Brookwood, Holt, Northport

Tuscaloosa CSD, 1100 21ST ST E 35404 — 7-11111
Thomas Ingram, supt. — 759-3510
Central SHS East, 905 15TH ST 35401 — 4-00001
Richard Rhone, prin. — 759-3576
Tuscaloosa Center Technology — Vo Tech
1300 37TH ST E 35405 — 759-3648
Pat Edwards, prin.
Central Freshman HS West — 4-00010
1715 ML KING JR BLVD 35401 — 759-3720
Albert Wilson, prin.
Eastwood MS, 2301 14TH ST E 35404 — 3-00100
Rush Howard, prin. — 759-3612

Druid City Hospital — HSP
809 UNIVERSITY BLVD E 35401 — 759-7177
Fredd State Technical College — 3-CS
3401 ML KING JR BLVD 35401 — 752-9738
National Career College — 2-CS
1351 MCFARLAND BLVD E 35404 — 758-9091
Shelton State Community College — 4-CC
202 SKYLAND BLVD 35405 — 759-1541
Stillman College — 3-UC
PO BOX 1430 35403 — 800-841-5722
Tuscaloosa Academy — 2-11111
420 26TH ST E 35401 — 758-4462
Robert Dowda, prin.
University of Alabama — 7-UC
PO BOX 870132 35487 — 800-933-2262

Tuscumbia, AC 205, PC 6, Colbert
Colbert County SD, 116 W 5TH ST 35674 — 5-11111
Roger Moore, supt. — 386-8565
Colbert Heights JSHS — 3-00111
2000 WOODMONT DR 35674 — 383-7875
Gil Cleveland, prin.

Other Schools – See Cherokee, Leighton

Tuscumbia CSD, 300 E 7TH ST 35674 — 4-11111
  James Berry, supt. — 389-2900
  Deshler HS — 2-00011
    201 N COMMONS ST E 35674 — 389-2910
    William Hamilton, prin.
  Deshler Area Vo HS — Vo Tech
    PO BOX 149 35674 — 389-2912
    Royce Massey, prin.
  Northside MS, 600 N HIGH ST 35674 — 2-00100
    Larry Danley, prin. — 389-2920

Tuskegee, AC 205, PC 7, Macon
Macon County SD, PO BOX 90 36083 — 5-11111
  Norward Roussell, supt. — 727-1600
Other Schools – See Notasulga, Tuskegee Institute

Southern Vocational College — 1-CS
  PO BOX 688 36083

Tuskegee Institute, AC 205, Macon
Macon County SD
  Supt. — See Tuskegee
Washington S, PO BOX 1325 36087 — 2-00011
  Franklin Perry, prin. — 727-0073
Macon Co. Area Vo HS — Vo Tech
  PO BOX 1217 36087 — 727-4478
  Barbara Forrester, prin.
MS, PO BOX S 36088 — 3-00100
  John Stinson, prin. — 727-2580

Tuskegee University 36088 — 5-UC
  — 727-8500

Union Springs, AC 205, PC 5, Bullock
Bullock County SD — 4-11111
  PO BOX 231 36089 — 738-2860
  Feagin Johnson, supt.
Bullock County JSHS — 3-00111
  PO BOX 5108 36089 — 738-2198
  Ben Johnson, prin.
Bullock Co. Area Vo HS — Vo Tech
  303 E BLACKMAN AVE 36089 — 738-4370
  Thomas Sumpter, prin.

Bullock Memorial S — 2-11111
  PO BOX 31 36089 — 738-4782
  Philip Richardson, prin.

Uniontown, AC 205, PC 4, Perry
Perry County SD
  Supt. — See Marion
Hatch HS, PO BOX 709 36786 — 2-00011
  Walter Collins, prin. — 628-4061
MS, PO BOX 537 36786 — 2-01100
  Edwin Dial, prin. — 628-4331

Uriah, AC 205, PC 2, Monroe
Monroe County SD
  Supt. — See Monroeville
Blacksher S, PO BOX 68 36480 — 2-11111
  Ben Rhodes, prin. — 862-2130

Valley, AC 205, PC 6, Chambers
Chambers County SD
  Supt. — See Lafayette
HS, 501 US HIGHWAY 29 36854 — 3-00011
  P. Sikes, prin. — 756-4105
JHS, PO BOX 327 36854 — 2-00100
  Larry Newton, prin. — 756-3567

Lee County SD
  Supt. — See Opelika
Beulah S, 4848 LEE ROAD 270 36854 — 3-11111
  Jerry Southwell, prin. — 745-5010

Valley Head, AC 205, PC 3, De Kalb
De Kalb County SD
  Supt. — See Fort Payne
S, PO BOX 145 35989 — 3-11111
  Elaine Dobbs, prin. — 635-6228

Verbena, AC 205, PC 2, Chilton
Chilton County SD
  Supt. — See Clanton
S, PO BOX 128 36091 — 3-11111
  Joe Hopper, prin. — 755-1242

Vernon, AC 205, PC 4, Lamar
Lamar County SD — 5-11111
  PO BOX 1379 35592 — 695-7615
  Gerald Hughes, supt.
S, PO BOX 369 35592 — 4-11111
  John Boman, prin. — 695-7717
Lamar Co. Area Vo HS — Vo Tech
  RR 3 BOX 347 35592 — 695-7129
  James Hankins, prin.
Other Schools – See Millport, Sulligent

Vestavia Hills, AC 205, PC 7, Jefferson
Vestavia Hills CSD — 5-11111
  1204 MONTGOMERY HWY 35216 — 823-0295
  J. Smith, supt.
HS, 2235 LIME ROCK RD 35216 — 4-00011
  Michael Gross, prin. — 823-4444
Pizitz MS, 2020 PIZITZ DR 35216 — 3-00100
  David Miles, prin. — 823-0423

Vina, AC 205, PC 2, Franklin
Franklin County SD
  Supt. — See Russellville
S, PO BOX 36 35593 — 2-11111
  Jerry Parham, prin. — 356-4733

Vincent, AC 205, PC 4, Shelby
Shelby County SD
  Supt. — See Columbiana
JSHS, PO BOX 9 35178 — 2-00111
  Garry Adams, prin. — 672-1400

Vinemont, AC 205, PC 3, Cullman
Cullman County SD
  Supt. — See Cullman
S, PO BOX 189 35179 — 4-11111
  Huelee Adams, prin. — 734-0571

Wadley, AC 205, PC 3, Randolph
Randolph County SD
  Supt. — See Wedowee
S, PO BOX 49 36276 — 2-11111
  Robert Kirby, prin. — 395-2286

Southern Union State Junior College — 5-CC
  PO BOX 1000 36276 — 395-2211

Walnut Grove, AC 205, PC 3, Etowah
Etowah County SD
  Supt. — See Gadsden
West End JSHS, 4515 ELM ST 35990 — 2-00111
  Mitchell Thrasher, prin. — 589-6421

Warrior, AC 205, PC 5, Jefferson
Jefferson County SD
  Supt. — See Birmingham
Corner S — 3-11111
  10005 CORNER SCHOOL RD 35180 — 647-9711
  Eddie Bruce, prin.
S, 300 MONTGOMERY ST 35180 — 3-11111
  Jim Jett, prin. — 674-0566

Waterloo, AC 205, PC 2, Lauderdale
Lauderdale County SD
  Supt. — See Florence
S, PO BOX 68 35677 — 2-11111
  Roy Abston, prin. — 766-3100

Weaver, AC 205, PC 5, Calhoun
Calhoun County SD
  Supt. — See Anniston
JSHS, 917 CLAIRMONT DR 36277 — 3-00111
  Gene Bussey, prin. — 820-2110

Wedowee, AC 205, PC 3, Randolph
Randolph County SD — 4-11111
  PO BOX 288 36278 — 357-4611
  Jim McKay, supt.
Randolph County S — 3-11111
  PO BOX 696 36278 — 357-4751
  Hulond Humphries, prin.
Randolph-Roanoke Area Vo HS — Vo Tech
  PO BOX 127 36278 — 357-2839
  Robert Bugg, prin.
Other Schools – See Wadley, Woodland

Roanoke CSD
  Supt. — See Roanoke
Randolph Area Vo Ctr — Vo Tech
  PO BOX 127 36278 — 357-2839
  Robert Bugg, prin.

West Blocton, AC 205, PC 4, Bibb
Bibb County SD
  Supt. — See Centreville
JSHS, 100 SCHOOL ST 35184 — 3-00111
  Morris Moody, prin. — 938-9002
Bibb Co. Area Vo HS — Vo Tech
  RR 1 BOX 537 35184 — 938-7434
  Don Harmon, prin.

Wetumpka, AC 205, PC 5, Elmore
Elmore County SD — 6-11111
  PO BOX 617 36092 — 567-1200
  Roberta Pilcher, supt.
HS, 1251 COOSA RIVER PKY 36092 — 3-00011
  James Myers, prin. — 567-5158
Elmore Co. Area Vo HS — Vo Tech
  800 KELLY FITZPATRICK DR 36092 — 567-1219
  Howard Spivey, prin.
JHS, 409 N ALABAMA ST 36092 — 3-00100
  Tom Harris, prin. — 567-1248
Other Schools – See Deatsville, Eclectic, Millbrook

Winfield, AC 205, PC 5, Marion
Winfield CSD, PO BOX 70 35594 — 4-11111
  Dale Brasher, supt. — 487-4255
JSHS, PO BOX 70 35594 — 3-00111
  Stephen Brown, prin. — 487-6900
Winfield City Vo HS — Vo Tech
  PO BOX 70 35594 — 487-4251
  Butch Ivie, prin.

Woodland, AC 205, PC 2, Randolph
Randolph County SD
  Supt. — See Wedowee
S, PO BOX 157 36280 — 3-11111
  James McCord, prin. — 449-2315

Woodville, AC 205, PC 3, Jackson
Jackson County SD
  Supt. — See Scottsboro
S, RR 2 35776 — 3-11111
  Tony Baker, prin. — 776-2874

York, AC 205, PC 5, Sumter
Sumter County SD
  Supt. — See Livingston
Sumter County HS, PO BOX 70 36925 — 2-00011
  Ellis Levy, prin. — 392-4771

Sumter Academy — 2-11111
  RR 1 BOX 389 36925 — 392-5238
  Robert Magee, prin.

ALASKA

STATE DEPARTMENT OF EDUCATION
801 W. 10th St. #200, Juneau 99801
(907) 465-2800

Commissioner of Education	Gerald Covey
Deputy Commissioner	Mike Maher
Director Educational Program Support	Vince Barry
Director Vocational Rehabilitation	Keith Anderson
Director School Finance & Data Services	Duane Guiley
Director Administrative Services	Karen Rehfeld

STATE BOARD OF EDUCATION
801 W. 10th St., Juneau 99801

Chairperson   Patricia Norheim

PUBLIC, PRIVATE AND CATHOLIC SECONDARY SCHOOLS

Akhiok, AC 907, PC 1, Kodiak Island
Kodiak Island Borough SD
Supt. — See Kodiak
S, PO BOX 5049 99615 — 1-11111
Sonny Cook, prin. — 836-2223

Akiachak, AC 907, PC 2, Bethel
Yupiit SD, PO BOX 100 99551 — 2-11111
Leland Dishman, supt. — 825-4428
JSHS, PO BOX 100 99551 — 1-00111
Helen Eckelman, prin. — 825-4013
Other Schools – See Akiak, Tuluksak

Akiak, AC 907, PC 2, Bethel
Yupiit SD
Supt. — See Akiachak
HS, PO BOX 52227 99552 — 1-00011
Kevin Mutchelknaus, prin. — 765-7212

Akutan, AC 907, PC 3, Aleutians East
Aleutian East Borough SD
Supt. — See Sand Point
S, GENERAL DELIVERY 99553 — 1-11111
Donald Darling, prin. — 698-2205

Alakanuk, AC 907, PC 3, Wade Hampton
Lower Yukon SD
Supt. — See Mountain Village
S, PO BOX 9 99554 — 2-11111
John Kieckbusch, prin. — 238-3312

Ambler, AC 907, PC 2, Northwest Artic
Northwest Arctic SD
Supt. — See Kotzebue
S, GENERAL DELIVERY 99786 — 2-11111
Steven Cathers, prin. — 445-2154

Anaktuvuk Pass, AC 907, PC 2, North Slope
North Slope Borough SD
Supt. — See Barrow
Nunamiut S, PO BOX 21029 99721 — 1-11111
Steve Yates, prin. — 661-3226

Anchorage, AC 907, PC 9, Anchorage
Anchorage SD — 8-11111
PO BOX 196614 99519 — 333-9561
Robert Christal, supt.
Bartlett HS, 25500 MULDOON RD 99506 — 4-00011
Howard Hosken, prin. — 337-1585
Dimond HS, 2909 W 88TH AVE 99502 — 4-00011
Gail Opalinski, prin. — 243-1141
East HS, 4025 E 24TH AVE 99508 — 4-00011
Rita Holthouse, prin. — 263-1297
Service HS, 5577 ABBOTT RD 99507 — 4-00011
Marilyn Conaway, prin. — 346-2111
West HS, 1700 HILLCREST DR 99517 — 4-00011
Lance Bowie, prin. — 274-2502
Steller JSHS — 2-00111
2508 BLUEBERRY RD 99503 — 279-2541
Donald Shackelford, prin.
Central ABC JHS, 1405 E ST 99501 — 3-00100
Keith Taton, prin. — 272-2581
Clark JHS, 150 S BRAGAW ST 99508 — 3-00100
Lewis Sears, prin. — 277-4581
Hanshew JHS — 4-00100
10121 LAKE OTIS PKY 99507 — 349-1561
Joe Calderera, prin.
Mears JHS, 2700 W 100TH AVE 99515 — 4-00100
Beverley Bailey, prin. — 349-3332
Romig JHS, 2500 MINNESOTA DR 99503 — 3-00100
Sophia Dawson, prin. — 274-0541

Wendler JHS — 4-00100
2905 LAKE OTIS PKY 99508 — 277-3591
Kathleen Carmody, prin.
Other Schools – See Eagle River

Chugach SD, 165 E 56TH AVE # D 99518 — 2-11111
Robert Brown, supt. — 561-3666
Other Schools – See Chenega Bay, Cordova, Tatitlek, Whittier

———————————

Abbott Loop Christian S — 2-11111
2626 ABBOTT RD 99507 — 349-9641
Alaska Junior College — 2-CC
800 E DIMOND BLVD STE 3-350 99515
— 349-1905
Alaska Pacific University — 4-UC
4101 UNIVERSITY DR 99508 — 800-252-7528
Charter College — CS
2221 E NORTHERN LIGHTS BLVD 99508
— 277-1000
Grace Christian S — 2-11111
12407 PINTAIL ST 99516 — 345-4814
Muldoon Christian S — 2-11111
7041 DEBARR RD 99504 — 337-9495
Duane Fick, prin.
Travel Academy, The — 2-CS
1415 E TUDOR RD 99507 — 563-7575
University of Alaska — 6-UC
3211 PROVIDENCE DR 99508 — 786-1480

Anchor Point, AC 907, PC 3, Kenai Peninsula
Kenai Peninsula Borough SD
Supt. — See Soldotna
Nikolaevsk S, PO BOX 5129 99556 — 2-11111
Carlton Kuhns, prin. — 235-8972

Anderson, AC 907, PC 3, Yukon Koyukuk
Denali Borough SD
Supt. — See Healy
S, PO BOX 3120 99744 — 2-11111
Keith Gebhardt, prin. — 582-2700

Angoon, AC 907, PC 3, Skagway Yakutat
Chatham SD, PO BOX 109 99820 — 2-11111
Ed McLain, supt. — 788-3682
S, PO BOX 209 99820 — 2-11111
Mike Hull, prin. — 788-3262
Other Schools – See Gustavus, Juneau, Tenakee Springs

Aniak, AC 907, PC 3, Bethel
Kuspuk SD, PO BOX 49 99557 — 2-11111
Bobette Bush, supt. — 675-4250
JSHS, PO BOX 29 99557 — 1-00111
Robert Clift, prin. — 675-4330
Parent Regional Vo HS — Vo Tech
PO BOX 229 99557 — 675-4339
Robert Clift, prin.
Other Schools – See Crooked Creek, Kalskag, Red Devil, Sleetmute, Stony River

Anvik, AC 907, PC 1, Yukon Koyukuk
Iditarod Area SD
Supt. — See Mc Grath
Blackwell S, PO BOX 90 99558 — 1-11111
Vernold Yates, prin. — 663-6348

Arctic Village, AC 907, PC 1, Yukon Koyukuk
Yukon Flats SD
Supt. — See Fort Yukon
S, GENERAL DELIVERY 99722 — 1-11111
Paula Noel, prin. — 587-5211

Atka, AC 907, PC 1, Aleutians West
Aleutian Region SD
Supt. — See Unalaska
S, PO BOX 47050 99547 — 1-11111
John Concilus, prin. — 839-2210

Atmautluak, AC 907, PC 2, Bethel
Lower Kuskokwim SD
Supt. — See Bethel
Alexie Memorial S, PO BOX ATT 99559 — 1-11111
Kenneth Schneider, prin. — 553-5129

Atqasuk, AC 907, PC 2, North Slope
North Slope Borough SD
Supt. — See Barrow
Meade River S — 1-11111
GENERAL DELIVERY 99723 — 633-6315
John Havrilek, prin.

Barrow, AC 907, PC 5, North Slope
North Slope Borough SD — 4-11111
PO BOX 169 99723 — 852-5311
Patsy Aamodt, supt.
JSHS, PO BOX 8950 99723 — 2-00111
Guy Fisher, prin. — 852-8950
Hopson Memorial MS — 1-00100
PO BOX 3880 99723 — 852-3880
Peter Van Borkulo, prin.
Other Schools – See Anaktuvuk Pass, Atqasuk, Kaktovik, Nuiqsut, Point Hope, Point Lay, Wainwright

Beaver, AC 907, PC 2, Yukon Koyukuk
Yukon Flats SD
Supt. — See Fort Yukon
S, GENERAL DELIVERY 99724 — 1-11111
Peter Kores, prin. — 628-6313

Bethel, AC 907, PC 5, Bethel
Lower Kuskokwim SD — 5-11111
PO BOX 305 99559 — 543-4800
Sue Hare, supt.
Bethel Regional JSHS — 2-00111
PO BOX 700 99559 — 543-3957
Ronald Edwards, prin.
Other Schools – See Atmautluak, Chefornak, Eek, Goodnews Bay, Kasigluk, Kipnuk, Kongiganak, Kwethluk, Kwigillingok, Mekoryuk, Napakiak, Napaskiak, Newtok, Nightmute, Nunapitchuk, Oscarville, Quinhagak, Toksook Bay, Tuntutuliak, Tununak

———————————

Kuskokwim Community College — 2-CC
PO BOX 368 99559 — 543-4500

Bettles Field, AC 907, PC 1, Yukon Koyukuk
Yukon-Koyukuk SD
Supt. — See Fairbanks
Bettles S, GENERAL DELIVERY 99726 — 1-11111
George Nicholson, prin. — 692-5101

Big Lake, AC 907, PC 4, Matanuska Susitna
Matanuska-Susitna Borough SD
Supt. — See Palmer
Houston JSHS, PO BOX 52106 99652 — 3-00111
Max Whyte, prin. — 892-9250

Brevig Mission, AC 907, PC 2, Nome
Bering Strait SD
Supt. — See Unalakleet
S, GENERAL DELIVERY 99785 — 1-11111
Monica Dickens, prin. — 642-4021

Buckland, AC 907, PC 2, Northwest Artic
Northwest Arctic SD
  Supt. — See Kotzebue
S, GENERAL DELIVERY   99727   1-11111
  Donald Haile, prin.   494-2127

Cantwell, AC 907, PC 2, Yukon Koyukuk
Denali Borough SD
  Supt. — See Healy
S, PO BOX 29   99729   1-11111
  David Tash, prin.   768-2372

Chalkyitsik, AC 907, PC 1, Yukon Koyukuk
Yukon Flats SD
  Supt. — See Fort Yukon
S, GENERAL DELIVERY   99788   1-11111
  Margaret Fisher, prin.   848-8113

Chefornak, AC 907, PC 2, Bethel
Lower Kuskokwim SD
  Supt. — See Bethel
Chaptnquak S, PO BOX 50   99561   2-11111
  Howard Fuller, prin.   867-8700

Chenega Bay, AC 907, PC 1, Valdez Cordova
Chugach SD
  Supt. — See Anchorage
Chenega Bay Community S   1-11111
PO BOX 8030   99574   573-5123
  Glenn Miller, prin.

Chevak, AC 907, PC 3, Wade Hampton
Kashunamiut SD, 985 KSD WAY   99563   2-11111
  Al Weinberg, supt.   858-7713
S, 985 KSD WAY   99563   2-11111
  Henry Versnick, prin.   858-7712

Chignik, AC 907, PC 2, Lake & Peninsula
Lake & Peninsula SD
  Supt. — See King Salmon
Chignik Bay S   99564   1-11111
  Darrell Marshall, prin.   749-2213

Chignik Lagoon, AC 907, PC 1, Lake & Peninsula
Lake & Peninsula SD
  Supt. — See King Salmon
ES, GENERAL DELIVERY   99565   1-11111
  Jean Seaton, prin.   840-2210

Chignik Lake, AC 907, PC 2, Lake & Peninsula
Lake & Peninsula SD
  Supt. — See King Salmon
S, GENERAL DELIVERY   99564   1-11111
  Alex Hart, prin.   845-2210

Chistochina, AC 907, PC 1, Valdez Cordova
Copper River SD
  Supt. — See Glennallen
S, MILE 32 1/2 TOK HWY   99586   1-11111
  Laurie Coker, prin.   822-3854

Circle, AC 907, PC 1, Yukon Koyukuk
Yukon Flats SD
  Supt. — See Fort Yukon
S, GENERAL DELIVERY   99733   1-11111
  Georgia Gray, prin.   773-1250

Coffman Cove, AC 907, PC 2, Prince Wales Ketchikan
Southeast Island SD
  Supt. — See Ketchikan
Valentine S, PO BOX KCC   99950   1-11111
  Michael Williams, prin.   329-2244

Cold Bay, AC 907, PC 2, Aleutians East
Aleutian East Borough SD
  Supt. — See Sand Point
S, PO BOX 128   99571   1-11111
  Charles Beckley, prin.   532-2409
Nelson Lagoon S, PO BOX 19   99571   1-11111
  Linn Clawson, prin.   989-2225

Copper Center, AC 907, PC 2, Valdez Cordova
Copper River SD
  Supt. — See Glennallen
Kenny Lake HS   1-00111
HC 60 BOX 224   99573   822-3870
  George Hronkin, prin.

Cordova, AC 907, PC 4, Valdez Cordova
Chugach SD
  Supt. — See Anchorage
Icy Bay S, PO BOX 460   99574   1-11111
  Adele Bruns, prin.   424-3933

Cordova CSD, PO BOX 140   99574   2-11111
  Mike McHone, supt.   424-3267
JSHS, PO BOX 140   99574   2-00111
  Mike McHone, prin.   424-3266

Craig, AC 907, PC 4, Prince Wales Ketchikan
Craig CSD, PO BOX 800   99921   2-11111
  Martin Laster, supt.   826-3274
JSHS, PO BOX 800   99921   2-00111
  Robert Whicker, prin.   826-3274

Crooked Creek, AC 907, PC 2, Bethel
Kuspuk SD
  Supt. — See Aniak
John S, GENERAL DELIVERY   99575   1-11111
  Max Cole, prin.   432-2205

Deering, AC 907, PC 2, Northwest Artic
Northwest Arctic SD
  Supt. — See Kotzebue
S, GENERAL DELIVERY   99736   1-11111
  Dennis Hoyt, prin.   363-2121

Delta Junction, AC 907, PC 3, Southeast Fairbanks
Delta-Greely SD, PO BOX 527   99737   3-11111
  Leland Clune, supt.   895-4658

HS, PO BOX 1   99737   2-00011
  Sandra Hill, prin.   895-4696
Healy Lake S, PO BOX 527   99737   1-11111
  Dan Beck, prin.   895-4658
Ft. Greely JHS, PO BOX 647   99737   2-00100
  Gerald Clancy, prin.   896-3105

Dillingham, AC 907, PC 4, Dillingham
Dillingham CSD, PO BOX 170   99576   3-11111
  Donald Renfroe, supt.   842-5225
JSHS, PO BOX 170   99576   2-00111
  Barbara Dean, prin.   842-5221

Southwest Region SD   3-11111
PO BOX 90   99576   842-5288
  Don Evans, supt.
Other Schools – See Manokotak, New Stuyahok,
  Togiak

University of AK-Bristol Bay Campus   2-UC
PO BOX 1070   99576   842-5109

Diomede, AC 907, PC see Little Diomede
Bering Strait SD
  Supt. — See Unalakleet
S, GENERAL DELIVERY   99762   1-11111
  Owen Citrowske, prin.   686-3021

Dot Lake, AC 907, PC 1, Southeast Fairbanks
Alaska Gateway SD
  Supt. — See Tok
S, PO BOX 2276   99737   1-11111
  John Fremin, prin.   882-2663

Eagle, AC 907, PC 2, Southeast Fairbanks
Alaska Gateway SD
  Supt. — See Tok
Eagle Community S   1-11111
PO BOX 168   99738   547-2210
  Terry McMullin, prin.

Eagle River, AC 907, PC see Anchorage
Anchorage SD
  Supt. — See Anchorage
Chugiak JSHS, PO BOX 770218   99577   4-00111
  Jan Christensen, prin.   696-9600
Gruening JHS, 9601 LEE ST   99577   3-00100
  Robb Boyer, prin.   694-5554

Eagle River Christian Academy   2-11111
  10336 E EAGLE RIVER LOOP RD   99577   694-4602

Edna Bay, AC 907, PC 1, Prince Wales Ketchikan
Southeast Island SD
  Supt. — See Ketchikan
S, PO BOX EDB   99950   1-11111
  Mary Smart, prin.   225-9658

Eek, AC 907, PC 2, Bethel
Lower Kuskokwim SD
  Supt. — See Bethel
S, PO BOX 50   99578   1-11111
  John Mark, prin.   536-5229

Eielson A F B, AC 907, PC 6, Fairbanks North Star
Fairbanks-North Star Borough SD
  Supt. — See Fairbanks
Eielson JSHS   3-00111
  5271 INDUSTRIAL DR   99702   372-4265
  Larry Martin, prin.

Elim, AC 907, PC 2, Nome
Bering Strait SD
  Supt. — See Unalakleet
Aniguiin S, GENERAL DELIVERY   99739   1-11111
  James O'Leary, prin.   890-3021

Emmonak, AC 907, PC 3, Wade Hampton
Lower Yukon SD
  Supt. — See Mountain Village
S, GENERAL DELIVERY   99581   2-11111
  William Owens, prin.   949-1248

FPO AP, AC 907
Adak Region SD   3-11111
  PSC 486 BOX 1234   96506   592-3188
  Edward Gilley, supt.
Reeve JSHS   2-00111
  PSC 486 BOX 1234   96506   592-3204
  Steven Pautz, prin.

Fairbanks, AC 907, PC 8, Fairbanks North Star
Fairbanks-North Star Borough SD   7-11111
  520 5TH AVE   99701   452-2000
  Richard Cross, supt.
Lathrop HS, 901 AIRPORT WAY   99701   4-00011
  Jerry Hartsock, prin.   456-7794
West Valley HS, 3800 GEIST RD   99709   3-00011
  Mike Thibodeau, prin.   479-4221
Ryan MS, 951 AIRPORT WAY   99701   3-00100
  Sandy McGill, prin.   452-4751
Tanana JHS   3-00100
  600 TRAINOR GATE RD   99701   452-8145
  Ernie Manzie, prin.
Other Schools – See Eielson A F B, North Pole

Yukon-Koyukuk SD   3-11111
  PO BOX 80210   99708   474-9400
  Glenn Olson, prin.
Other Schools – See Bettles Field, Huslia, Kaltag,
  Manley Hot Springs, Minto, Nulato, Ruby

Yukon Flats SD
  Supt. — See Fort Yukon
Northern Lights S, PO BOX 539   99710   1-11111
  Mike Doppler, prin.   452-0400

Fairhill Christian S   2-11111
  101 CITY LIGHTS BLVD   99712   457-2167
Lighthouse Christian Academy   2-11111
  PO BOX 73560   99707   457-1283
Monroe Catholic JSHS   2-00111
  615 MONROE ST   99701   452-2044
  Kathleen Norris, prin.
University of Alaska   99775   6-UC
         474-7821

False Pass, AC 907, PC 1, Aleutians East
Aleutian East Borough SD
  Supt. — See Sand Point
S, PO BOX 30   99583   1-11111
  Lew Grimes, prin.   548-2224

Fort Yukon, AC 907, PC 3, Yukon Koyukuk
Yukon Flats SD, PO BOX 359   99740   2-11111
  Douglas Walker, supt.   662-2515
Other Schools – See Arctic Village, Beaver,
  Chalkyitsik, Circle, Fairbanks, Rampart, Venetie

Galena, AC 907, PC 3, Yukon Koyukuk
Galena CSD, PO BOX 299   99741   2-11111
  Darrell Johnson, supt.   656-1205
HS, PO BOX 299   99741   1-00011
  Patricia Hutcherson, prin.   656-1205

Gambell, AC 907, PC 3, Nome
Bering Strait SD
  Supt. — See Unalakleet
S, PO BOX 169   99742   2-11111
  Richard Bigelow, prin.   985-5229

Glennallen, AC 907, PC 2, Valdez Cordova
Copper River SD, PO BOX 108   99588   3-11111
  Reid Straabe, supt.   822-3234
JSHS, PO BOX 66   99588   2-00111
  Richard Lee, prin.   822-5286
Other Schools – See Chistochina, Copper Center

Alaska Bible College   1-UC
  PO BOX 289   99588   822-3201

Golovin, AC 907, PC 2, Nome
Bering Strait SD
  Supt. — See Unalakleet
Olson S, GENERAL DELIVERY   99762   1-11111
  Tim Whaling, prin.   779-3021

Goodnews Bay, AC 907, PC 2, Bethel
Lower Kuskokwim SD
  Supt. — See Bethel
Rocky Mountain S   1-11111
  GENERAL DELIVERY   99589   967-8213
  William Savage, prin.

Grayling, AC 907, PC 2, Yukon Koyukuk
Iditarod Area SD
  Supt. — See Mc Grath
David-Louis Memorial S   1-11111
  PO BOX 90   99590   453-5135
  Phyllis Kardos, prin.

Gustavus, AC 907, PC 2, Skagway Yakutat
Chatham SD
  Supt. — See Angoon
S, PO BOX 120   99826   1-11111
  Michael Opp, prin.   697-2248

Haines, AC 907, PC 4, Haines
Haines Borough SD   2-11111
  PO BOX 1289   99827   766-2644
  Nancy Billingsley, supt.
HS, PO BOX 1289   99827   2-00011
  Richard Hebhardt, prin.   766-2411
JHS, PO BOX 1289   99827   1-00100
  Bob Adkins, prin.   766-2811

Healy, AC 907, PC 2, Yukon Koyukuk
Denali Borough SD   2-11111
  PO BOX 280   99743   683-2278
  John Novak, supt.
Tri-Valley S, PO BOX 400   99743   2-11111
  Scott Iverson, prin.   683-2267
Other Schools – See Anderson, Cantwell

Hollis, AC 907, PC 2, Prince Wales Ketchikan
Southeast Island SD
  Supt. — See Ketchikan
S, PO BOX HYL   99950   1-11111
  Michael Spallato, prin.   530-9001

Holy Cross, AC 907, PC 2, Yukon Koyukuk
Iditarod Area SD
  Supt. — See Mc Grath
S, PO BOX 210   99602   1-11111
  Rodman Westor, prin.   476-7131

Homer, AC 907, PC 5, Kenai Peninsula
Kenai Peninsula Borough SD
  Supt. — See Soldotna
HS, 600 E FAIRVIEW AVE   99603   2-00011
  Richard Krieger, prin.   235-8186
JHS, 500 STERLING HWY   99603   2-00100
  Lincoln Saito, prin.   235-5291

Hoonah, AC 907, PC 3, Skagway Koyukuk
Hoonah CSD, PO BOX 157   99829   2-11111
  John Anttonen, supt.   945-3611
JSHS, PO BOX 157   99829   2-00111
  William Hutton, prin.   945-3613

Hooper Bay, AC 907, PC 3, Wade Hampton
Lower Yukon SD
  Supt. — See Mountain Village
S, GENERAL DELIVERY   99604   2-11111
  Quentin McCubrey, prin.   899-4415

Huslia, AC 907, PC 2, Yukon Koyukuk
Yukon-Koyukuk SD
  Supt. — See Fairbanks
Huntington S, PO BOX 110 99746   1-11111
  Joan Carrigan, prin.   829-2205

Hydaburg, AC 907, PC 2, Prince Wales Ketchikan
Hydaburg CSD, PO BOX 109 99922   2-11111
  Larry Schroeder, supt.   285-3491
JSHS, PO BOX 109 99922   1-00111
  Gloria Ingle, prin.   285-3591

Iliamna, AC 907, PC 1, Lake & Peninsula
Lake & Peninsula SD
  Supt. —- See King Salmon
Newhalen S 99606   1-11111
  Ken Eggleston, prin.   571-1211

Juneau, AC 907, PC 8, Juneau
Chatham SD
  Supt. — See Angoon
Cube Cove S, CUBE COVE #5 99850   1-11111
  Roger Hein, prin.   799-2244
Hobart Bay S, PO BOX HBH 99850   1-11111
  Mary Faulkner, prin.   673-2284

Juneau Borough SD   6-11111
  10014 CRAZY HORSE DR 99801   463-1700
  Robert VanSlyke, supt.
Juneau-Douglas HS   4-00011
  10014 CRAZY HORSE DR 99801   463-1900
  Ron Gleason, prin.
Drake MS   3-00100
  10014 CRAZY HORSE DR 99801   463-1899
  Charla Wright, prin.
Dryden MS   3-00100
  10014 CRAZY HORSE DR 99801   463-1850
  Lynn Divelbess, prin.

Sitka SD
  Supt. — See Sitka
Corner Bay Logging Camp S   1-11111
  CUBE COVE #99 99850   736-2324
  Jacquette Stout, prin.

Juneau Christian S   2-11111
  PO BOX 32000 99803   789-2179
University of Alaska Southeast   5-UC
  11120 GLACIER HWY 99801   789-4458

Kake, AC 907, PC 3, Wrangell Petersburg
Kake CSD, PO BOX 450 99830   2-11111
  Larry Stout, supt.   785-3741
JSHS, PO BOX 450 99830   1-00111
  Gonzalo DeLeon, prin.   785-3731

Kaktovik, AC 907, PC 2, North Slope
North Slope Borough SD
  Supt. — See Barrow
Kaveolook S, PO BOX 10 99747   1-11111
  Thomas Megown, prin.   640-6626

Kalskag, AC 907, PC 2, Bethel
Kuspuk SD
  Supt. — See Aniak
Morgan JSHS   1-00111
  GENERAL DELIVERY 99607   471-2288
  Ann Barton, prin.

Kaltag, AC 907, PC 2, Yukon Koyukuk
Yukon-Koyukuk SD
  Supt. — See Fairbanks
S, GENERAL DELIVERY 99748   1-11111
  Darrell Sanborn, prin.   534-2204

Kasigluk, AC 907, PC 2, Bethel
Lower Kuskokwim SD
  Supt. — See Bethel
Akiuk Memorial S   1-11111
  GENERAL DELIVERY 99609   477-6829
  Larry Ford, prin.
Akula S, GENERAL DELIVERY 99609   1-11111
  William Ferguson, prin.   477-6615

Kenai, AC 907, PC 6, Kenai Peninsula
Kenai Peninsula Borough SD
  Supt. — See Soldotna
Kenai Central HS   2-00011
  9583 KENAI SPUR HWY 99611   283-7524
  David Spence, prin.
JHS, 201 N TINKER LN 99611   2-00100
  Paul Sorenson, prin.   283-4896

Ketchikan, AC 907, PC 6, Ketchikan Gateway
Ketchikan Gateway Borough SD   5-11111
  PO BOX Z 99901   225-2118
  Richard Clevenger, supt.
HS, 2610 4TH AVE 99901   3-00011
  Don Pennington, prin.   225-9815
Revilla HS, 3131 BARANOF AVE 99901   1-00011
  Charley Jones, prin.   225-6681
Schoenbar JHS   2-00100
  217 SCHOENBAR RD 99901   225-5138
  Richard Clement, prin.

Southeast Island SD   2-11111
  PO BOX 8340 99901   225-9658
  Robert Weinstein, supt.
Craik Logging S, PO BOX 9813 99901   1-11111
  Phyllis Ulrich, prin.   225-9658
Gildersleeve S, PO BOX B 99901   1-11111
  Patricia McDonald, prin.   225-0678
Kasaan S, PO BOX KXA 99950   1-11111
  Jeffrey Boeskool, prin.   542-2217
LaBouchere Bay S, PO BOX WLB 99950   1-11111
  Kathleen Shirley, prin.   489-2215
Naukati S, PO BOX NKI 99950   1-11111
  Peter Kimzey, prin.   329-2222

Polk Inlet ES, PO BOX POQ 99950   1-11111
  Elizabeth Robbins, prin.   225-9658
Smith Cove S, PO BOX 9822 99901   1-11111
  Timothy Stathis, prin.   247-2410
Whale Pass S, PO BOX WWP 99950   1-11111
  James Baker, prin.   846-9001
Other Schools – See Coffman Cove, Edna Bay, Hollis,
  Meyers Chuck, Port Alexander, Rowan Bay,
  Thorne Bay

University of Alaska Southeast-Ketchikan   2-CC
  2600 7TH AVE 99901   225-6177

Kiana, AC 907, PC 2, Northwest Artic
Northwest Arctic SD
  Supt. — See Kotzebue
S, GENERAL DELIVERY 99749   2-11111
  Steven Jones, prin.   475-2168

King Cove, AC 907, PC 2, Aleutians East
Aleutian East Borough SD
  Supt. — See Sand Point
S, PO BOX 6 99612   2-11111
  Gerald Foldenauer, prin.   497-2354

King Salmon, AC 907, PC 3, Bristol Bay
Lake & Peninsula SD   3-11111
  PO BOX 498 99613   246-4280
  Frank Hill, supt.
Other Schools – See Chignik, Chignik Lagoon,
  Chignik Lake, Iliamna, Kokhanok, Levelock,
  Nondalton, Pedro Bay, Perryville, Pilot Point, Port
  Alsworth, Port Heiden

Kipnuk, AC 907, PC 2, Bethel
Lower Kuskokwim SD
  Supt. — See Bethel
S, GENERAL DELIVERY 99614   2-11111
  Robert Nelson, prin.   896-5011

Kivalina, AC 907, PC 2, Northwest Artic
Northwest Arctic SD
  Supt. — See Kotzebue
McQueen S, GENERAL DELIVERY 99750   1-11111
  Thomas Hanifan, prin.   645-2125

Klawock, AC 907, PC 3, Prince Wales Ketchikan
Klawock CSD, PO BOX 9 99925   2-11111
  Morris Ververs, supt.   755-2220
JSHS, PO BOX 9 99925   1-00111
  Blaine French, prin.   755-2220

Kodiak, AC 907, PC 6, Kodiak Island
Kodiak Island Borough SD   5-11111
  722 MILL BAY RD 99615   486-9220
  John Witteveen, supt.
Kodiak HS, 722 MILL BAY RD 99615   3-00011
  Larry LeDoux, prin.   486-9212
Big Sandy Lake S, PO BOX 509 99615   1-11111
  Dorothy Jordan, prin.   381-2033
Danger Bay S, PO BOX 2546 99615   1-11111
  Jolene Allen, prin.   379-1125
JHS, 722 MILL BAY RD 99615   3-00100
  Dennis Nicholson, prin.   486-9213
Other Schools – See Akhiok, Larsen Bay, Old Harbor,
  Ouzinkie, Port Lions

Kodiak Community College   3-CC
  PO BOX 946 99615   484-4161

Kokhanok, AC 907, PC 2, Lake & Peninsula
Lake & Peninsula SD
  Supt. — See King Salmon
S 99606   1-11111
  Sara Hornberger, prin.   282-2210

Kongiganak, AC 907, PC 2, Bethel
Lower Kuskokwim SD
  Supt. — See Bethel
Kiunya Memorial S   2-11111
  PO BOX 5109 99559   537-5126
  Ian Parks, prin.

Kotlik, AC 907, PC 2, Wade Hampton
Lower Yukon SD
  Supt. — See Mountain Village
S, PO BOX 20129 99620   2-11111
  Gerald Gates, prin.   899-4415

Kotzebue, AC 907, PC 5, Northwest Artic
Northwest Arctic SD   4-11111
  PO BOX 51 99752   442-3472
  Ed Gonion, supt.
HS, PO BOX 264 99752   2-00011
  Rolla Weber, prin.   442-3341
JHS, PO BOX 264 99752   1-00100
  Rolla Weber, prin.   442-3341
Other Schools – See Ambler, Buckland, Deering,
  Kiana, Kivalina, Noatak, Noorvik, Selawik,
  Shungnak

University of Alaska-Chuchi Campus   2-UC
  PO BOX 297 99752   442-3400

Koyuk, AC 907, PC 2, Nome
Bering Strait SD
  Supt. — See Unalakleet
Koyuk-Malemute S   1-11111
  GENERAL DELIVERY 99753   963-3021
  Tom Briscoe, prin.

Kwethluk, AC 907, PC 3, Bethel
Lower Kuskokwim SD
  Supt. — See Bethel
S, GENERAL DELIVERY 99621   2-11111
  Leslie Daenzer, prin.   757-6014

Kwigillingok, AC 907, PC 2, Bethel
Lower Kuskokwim SD
  Supt. — See Bethel
S, GENERAL DELIVERY 99622   1-11111
  Mary Fogerty-Samson, prin.   588-8629

Lake Minchumina, AC 907, PC 1, Yukon Koyukuk
Iditarod Area SD
  Supt. — See Mc Grath
Minchumina Community S   1-11111
  GENERAL DELIVERY 99757   674-3214
  Patrick Duffy, prin.

Larsen Bay, AC 907, PC 2, Kodiak Island
Kodiak Island Borough SD
  Supt. — See Kodiak
S, GENERAL DELIVERY 99624   1-11111
  Chip Lacey, prin.   847-2252

Levelock, AC 907, PC 2, Lake & Peninsula
Lake & Peninsula SD
  Supt. — See King Salmon
S, GENERAL DELIVERY 99625   1-11111
  Bob Dunton, prin.   287-3060

Manley Hot Springs, AC 907, PC 1, Yukon Koyukuk
Yukon-Koyukuk SD
  Supt. — See Fairbanks
Dart S, GENERAL DELIVERY 99756   1-11111
  Damaris Mortvedt, prin.   672-3202

Manokotak, AC 907, PC 2, Dillingham
Southwest Region SD
  Supt. — See Dillingham
S, GENERAL DELIVERY 99628   2-11111
  Charles Ward, prin.   289-1013

Marshall, AC 907, PC 2, Wade Hampton
Lower Yukon SD
  Supt. — See Mountain Village
S, GENERAL DELIVERY 99585   1-11111
  Roger Adams, prin.   679-6112

Mc Grath, AC 907, PC 3, Yukon Koyukuk
Iditarod Area SD, PO BOX 90 99627   2-11111
  John Monahan, supt.   524-3033
S, PO BOX 290 99627   2-11111
  Bartol Mwarey, prin.   524-3388
Other Schools – See Anvik, Grayling, Holy Cross,
  Lake Minchumina, Nikolai, Shageluk, Takotna

Mekoryuk, AC 907, PC 2, Bethel
Lower Kuskokwim SD
  Supt. — See Bethel
Nuniwaarmiut S   1-11111
  GENERAL DELIVERY 99630   827-8415
  Michael McGrath, prin.

Mentasta Lake, AC 907, PC 1, Valdez Cordova
Alaska Gateway SD
  Supt. — See Tok
S, GENERAL DELIVERY 99780   1-11111
  Dana Bartman, prin.   291-2327

Metlakatla, AC 907, PC 4, Prince Wales Ketchikan
Annette Island SD, PO BOX 7 99926   2-11111
  Robert Pratt, supt.   886-6332
HS, PO BOX 7 99926   2-00011
  James King, prin.   886-6000

Meyers Chuck, AC 907, PC 1, Prince Wales Ketchikan
Southeast Island SD
  Supt. — See Ketchikan
S 99903   1-00111
  David Greeley, prin.   946-1234

Minto, AC 907, PC 2, Yukon Koyukuk
Yukon-Koyukuk SD
  Supt. — See Fairbanks
S, GENERAL DELIVERY 99758   1-11111
  Todd Poage, prin.   798-7212

Mountain Village, AC 907, PC 3, Wade Hampton
Lower Yukon SD   4-11111
  PO BOX 32089 99632   591-2411
  John Gill, supt.
S, PO BOX 32105 99632   2-11111
  Richard Cuprak, prin.   591-2415
Other Schools – See Alakanuk, Emmonak, Hooper
  Bay, Kotlik, Marshall, Pilot Station, Pitkas Point,
  Russian Mission, Scammon Bay, Sheldon Point

Naknek, AC 907, PC 3, Bristol Bay
Bristol Bay Borough SD   2-11111
  PO BOX 169 99633   246-4225
  Richard Leath, supt.
Bristol Bay Consolidated JSHS   2-00111
  PO BOX 169 99633   246-4265
  Lou Matheson, prin.

Nanwalek, AC 907, PC 99, Kenai Peninsula
Kenai Peninsula Borough SD
  Supt. — See Soldotna
S 99603   1-11111
  Kathy Clark, prin.   281-2210

Napakiak, AC 907, PC 2, Bethel
Lower Kuskokwim SD
  Supt. — See Bethel
S, GENERAL DELIVERY 99634   2-11111
  Dana Barrington, prin.   589-2420

Napaskiak, AC 907, PC 2, Bethel
Lower Kuskokwim SD
  Supt. — See Bethel
Williams Memorial S   2-11111
  PO BOX 6089 99559   737-7212
  Michael Smith, prin.

Nenana, AC 907, PC 2, Yukon Koyukuk
Nenana CSD, PO BOX 10 99760 — 2-11111
Mary Boario, supt. — 832-5464
S, PO BOX 10 99760 — 2-11111
James McLean, prin. — 832-5464

New Stuyahok, AC 907, PC 2, Dillingham
Southwest Region SD
Supt. — See Dillingham
S, GENERAL DELIVERY 99636 — 1-11111
Rod Mebius, prin. — 693-3144

Newtok, AC 907, PC 2, Bethel
Lower Kuskokwim SD
Supt. — See Bethel
Ayaprun S, PO BOX WWT 99559 — 1-11111
Lawrence Ctibor, prin. — 237-2126

Nightmute, AC 907, PC 2, Bethel
Lower Kuskokwim SD
Supt. — See Bethel
S, GENERAL DELIVERY 99559 — 1-11111
Bain Robinson, prin. — 647-6313

Nikiski, AC 907, PC 5, Kenai Peninsula
Kenai Peninsula Borough SD
Supt. — See Soldotna
JSHS, PO BOX 10000 99635 — 2-00111
Robert Bellmore, prin. — 776-3456

Nikolai, AC 907, PC 2, Yukon Koyukuk
Iditarod Area SD
Supt. — See Mc Grath
Top of the Kuskokwim S — 1-11111
GENERAL DELIVERY 99627 — 293-2427
Pat Duffy, prin.

Ninilchik, AC 907, PC 2, Kenai Peninsula
Kenai Peninsula Borough SD
Supt. — See Soldotna
S, PO BOX 39010 99639 — 2-11111
Paul Kubena, prin. — 567-3301

Noatak, AC 907, PC 2, Northwest Artic
Northwest Arctic SD
Supt. — See Kotzebue
Napaaqtugmiut S — 2-11111
GENERAL DELIVERY 99761 — 485-2153
Bobbe Bluett, prin.

Nome, AC 907, PC 5, Nome
Nome CSD, PO BOX 131 99762 — 3-11111
Robert Kinna, supt. — 443-2231
Nome-Beltz JSHS, PO BOX 131 99762 — 2-00111
George Ihly, prin. — 443-5201

Northwest Community College — 2-CC
PO BOX 400 99762 — 443-2201

Nondalton, AC 907, PC 2, Lake & Peninsula
Lake & Peninsula SD
Supt. — See King Salmon
S, GENERAL DELIVERY 99640 — 1-11111
Terry Bentley, prin. — 294-2210

Noorvik, AC 907, PC 3, Northwest Artic
Northwest Arctic SD
Supt. — See Kotzebue
S, GENERAL DELIVERY 99763 — 2-11111
Mervin Finstad, prin. — 636-2178

North Pole, AC 907, PC 4, Fairbanks North Star
Fairbanks-North Star Borough SD
Supt. — See Fairbanks
HS, 601 W 8TH AVE 99705 — 3-00011
Terry Marquette, prin. — 488-3761
MS, 300 E 8TH AVE 99705 — 3-00100
Andre Layral, prin. — 488-2271

Northway, AC 907, PC 2, Southeast Fairbanks
Alaska Gateway SD
Supt. — See Tok
S, PO BOX 519 99764 — 1-11111
Bradford Heck, prin. — 778-2287

Nuiqsut, AC 907, PC 2, North Slope
North Slope Borough SD
Supt. — See Barrow
Nuiqsut Trapper S — 2-11111
GENERAL DELIVERY 99723 — 480-6712
Chuck Coons, prin.

Nulato, AC 907, PC 2, Yukon Koyukuk
Yukon-Koyukuk SD
Supt. — See Fairbanks
Demoski S, PO BOX 65029 99765 — 2-11111
Maurice McGinty, prin. — 898-2204

Nunapitchuk, AC 907, PC 2, Bethel
Lower Kuskokwim SD
Supt. — See Bethel
Tobeluk Memorial S — 2-11111
GENERAL DELIVERY 99641 — 527-5325
Rocke McFarland, prin.

Old Harbor, AC 907, PC 2, Kodiak Island
Kodiak Island Borough SD
Supt. — See Kodiak
S, PO BOX 49 99643 — 1-11111
Tom Shugak, prin. — 286-2213

Oscarville, AC 907, PC 1, Bethel
Lower Kuskokwim SD
Supt. — See Bethel
Qugcuun Memorial S — 1-11111
GENERAL DELIVERY 99695 — 737-7214
Raymond Thorson, prin.

Ouzinkie, AC 907, PC 2, Kodiak Island
Kodiak Island Borough SD
Supt. — See Kodiak
S, PO BOX 49 99644 — 1-11111
Dorothy Jordan, prin. — 680-2204

Palmer, AC 907, PC 5, Matanuska Susitna
Matanuska-Susitna Borough SD — 7-11111
125 W EVERGREEN AVE 99645 — 746-9200
Ell Sorenson, supt.
Colony HS, HC 1 BOX 6048 99645 — 3-00011
Rick Luthi, prin. — 745-9500
HS, 1170 W ARCTIC AVE 99645 — 3-00011
Patricia Chesbro, prin. — 745-3241
Glacier View S — 1-11111
HC 3 BOX 8454 99645 — 745-5122
Richard Tardiff, prin.
Skwentna S, PO BOX 17 99645 — 1-11111
Karen Flanagan, prin. — 733-2733
Colony MS, HC 1 BOX 6048 99645 — 3-00100
John Norman, prin. — 745-9536
MS, 1159 S CHUGACH ST 99645 — 3-00100
Lawrence Jacobson, prin. — 745-3812
Other Schools – See Big Lake, Talkeetna, Wasilla

Matanuska Christian S — 2-11111
12801 W ARTIC AVE 99645 — 745-2540
University of Alaska - Matanuska-Susitna — 4-UC
PO BOX 2889 99645 — 745-9705

Pedro Bay, AC 907, PC 1, Lake & Peninsula
Lake & Peninsula SD
Supt. — See King Salmon
S, GENERAL DELIVERY 99647 — 1-11111
Barbara Atwater, prin. — 850-2207

Pelican, AC 907, PC 2, Skagway Yakutat
Pelican CSD, PO BOX 90 99832 — 1-11111
Wyman Faircloth, supt. — 735-2236
S, PO BOX 90 99832 — 1-11111
Wyman Faircloth, prin. — 735-2236

Perryville, AC 907, PC 2, Lake & Peninsula
Lake & Peninsula SD
Supt. — See King Salmon
S, GENERAL DELIVERY 99648 — 1-11111
David Smith, prin. — 853-2210

Petersburg, AC 907, PC 5, Wrangell Petersburg
Petersburg CSD, PO BOX 289 99833 — 3-11111
Mary Francis, supt. — 772-4271
HS, PO BOX 289 99833 — 2-00011
Nancy Thomas, prin. — 772-3861
MS, PO BOX 289 99833 — 2-00100
Nancy Thomas, prin. — 772-3860

Pilot Point, AC 907, PC 1, Lake & Peninsula
Lake & Peninsula SD
Supt. — See King Salmon
S, GENERAL DELIVERY 99649 — 1-11111
Don Preston, prin. — 797-2210

Pilot Station, AC 907, PC 2, Wade Hampton
Lower Yukon SD
Supt. — See Mountain Village
S, PO BOX 5090 99650 — 2-11111
Jerry Gill, prin. — 549-3212

Pitkas Point, AC 907, PC 2, Wade Hampton
Lower Yukon SD
Supt. — See Mountain Village
S 99658 — 1-11111
Anthony Grenzy, prin. — 438-2413

Point Hope, AC 907, PC 3, North Slope
North Slope Borough SD
Supt. — See Barrow
Tikigaq S, PO BOX 148 99766 — 2-11111
Charles Mason, prin. — 368-2662

Point Lay, AC 907, PC 2, North Slope
North Slope Borough SD
Supt. — See Barrow
Cully S, GENERAL DELIVERY 99723 — 1-11111
Dale Hammond, prin. — 833-2312

Port Alexander, AC 907, PC 2, Wrangell Petersburg
Southeast Island SD
Supt. — See Ketchikan
S, PO BOX 8170 99836 — 1-11111
Donald Moss, prin. — 568-2205

Port Alsworth, AC 907, PC 1, Lake & Peninsula
Lake & Peninsula SD
Supt. — See King Salmon
S, GENERAL DELIVERY 99653 — 1-11111
Chris Eldridge, prin. — 781-2210

Port Heiden, AC 907, PC 2, Lake & Peninsula
Lake & Peninsula SD
Supt. — See King Salmon
S, GENERAL DELIVERY 99549 — 1-11111
Brett Bissell, prin. — 837-2210

Port Lions, AC 907, PC 2, Kodiak Island
Kodiak Island Borough SD
Supt. — See Kodiak
S, PO BOX 109 99550 — 1-11111
Bruce Johnson, prin. — 454-2237

Quinhagak, AC 907, PC 3, Bethel
Lower Kuskokwim SD
Supt. — See Bethel
Elitnaurviat S — 2-11111
GENERAL DELIVERY 99655 — 556-8628
Kenneth Groves, prin.

Rampart, AC 907, PC 1, Yukon Koyukuk
Yukon Flats SD
Supt. — See Fort Yukon
S, 199 RAMPART AVE 99701 — 1-11111
Steven Jacquier, prin. — 358-3112

Red Devil, AC 907, PC 1, Bethel
Kuspuk SD
Supt. — See Aniak
Willis S, GENERAL DELIVERY 99656 — 1-11111
Max Cole, prin. — 447-3213

Rowan Bay, AC 907, PC 2, Skagway
Southeast Island SD
Supt. — See Ketchikan
S, PO BOX RWB 99835 — 1-11111
Judith Jones, prin. — 785-6486

Ruby, AC 907, PC 2, Yukon Koyukuk
Yukon-Koyukuk SD
Supt. — See Fairbanks
Kangas S, PO BOX 68110 99768 — 1-11111
Richard Strick, prin. — 468-4465

Russian Mission, AC 907, PC 2, Wade Hampton
Lower Yukon SD
Supt. — See Mountain Village
S, PO BOX 90 99657 — 2-11111
Dan Gillen, prin. — 584-5126

Saint Mary's, AC 907, PC 2, Wade Hampton
Saint Mary's SD, PO BOX 171 99658 — 2-11111
Gary Greseth, supt. — 438-2311
Andreafski JSHS, PO BOX 171 99658 — 1-00111
Gary Greseth, prin. — 438-2834

Saint Michael, AC 907, PC 2, Nome
Bering Strait SD
Supt. — See Unalakleet
Andrews S, GENERAL DELIVERY 99659 — 2-11111
Tom Genne, prin. — 923-3041

Saint Paul Island, AC 907, PC 3, Aleutians West
Pribilof Islands SD, PO BOX 5 99660 — 2-11111
Mark Shellinger, supt. — 546-2222
S 99660 — 2-11111
Mark Shellinger, prin. — 546-2221

Sand Point, AC 907, PC 3, Aleutians East
Aleutian East Borough SD — 2-11111
PO BOX 429 99661 — 383-5222
Tom Ryan, supt.
S, PO BOX 269 99661 — 2-11111
William Biehl, prin. — 383-2393
Other Schools – See Akutan, Cold Bay, False Pass, King Cove

Savoonga, AC 907, PC 3, Nome
Bering Strait SD
Supt. — See Unalakleet
Kingeekuk Memorial S — 2-11111
GENERAL DELIVERY 99769 — 984-6811
Gene Ostwald, prin.

Scammon Bay, AC 907, PC 2, Wade Hampton
Lower Yukon SD
Supt. — See Mountain Village
S, GENERAL DELIVERY 99662 — 2-11111
William Foulk, prin. — 558-5312

Selawik, AC 907, PC 3, Northwest Artic
Northwest Arctic SD
Supt. — See Kotzebue
S, GENERAL DELIVERY 99770 — 2-11111
Leo Fiebiger, prin. — 484-2142

Seldovia, AC 907, PC 2, Kenai Peninsula
Kenai Peninsula Borough SD
Supt. — See Soldotna
English S, PO BOX 171 99663 — 1-11111
Mark Bergemann, prin. — 234-7616

Seward, AC 907, PC 5, Kenai Peninsula
Kenai Peninsula Borough SD
Supt. — See Soldotna
JSHS, PO BOX 227 99664 — 2-00111
Malcolm Fleming, prin. — 224-3351

Shageluk, AC 907, PC 2, Yukon Koyukuk
Iditarod Area SD
Supt. — See Mc Grath
Innoko River S, PO BOX 198 99665 — 1-11111
Howard Diamond, prin. — 473-8233

Shaktoolik, AC 907, PC 2, Nome
Bering Strait SD
Supt. — See Unalakleet
S, GENERAL DELIVERY 99771 — 1-11111
Richard Toymil, prin. — 955-3021

Sheldon Point, AC 907, PC 2, Wade Hampton
Lower Yukon SD
Supt. — See Mountain Village
S, GENERAL DELIVERY 99666 — 1-11111
Russell Johnston, prin. — 498-4112

Shishmaref, AC 907, PC 2, Nome
Bering Strait SD
Supt. — See Unalakleet
S, GENERAL DELIVERY 99772 — 2-11111
Carl Schwartz, prin. — 649-3021

Shungnak, AC 907, PC 2, Northwest Artic
Northwest Arctic SD
Supt. — See Kotzebue
S, GENERAL DELIVERY 99773 — 1-11111
John Bania, prin. — 437-2151

Sitka, AC 907, PC 6, Sitka
Mt. Edgecombe HSD 2-00011
 1330 SEWARD AVE 99835 966-2201
 Thomas Brown, supt.
Mt. Edgecumbe HS 2-00011
 1330 SEWARD AVE 99835 966-2201
 Bill Denkinger, prin.

Sitka SD, PO BOX 179 99835 4-11111
 John Holst, supt. 747-8622
 HS, 1000 LAKE ST 99835 2-00011
 LeRoy Demmert, prin. 747-3263
 False Island Logging Camp S 1-11111
  PO BOX FAK 99835 788-3512
 Kenneth Mann, prin.
 Blatchley MS 2-00100
  601 HALIBUT POINT RD 99835 747-8672
 Walter Clark, prin.
 Other Schools – See Juneau

 Sheldon Jackson College 2-UC
  801 LINCOLN ST 99835 747-5221
 University of Alaska SE - Sitka Campus 2-CC
  1332 SEWARD AVE 99835 747-6653

Skagway, AC 907, PC 3, Skagway Yakutat
Skagway CSD, PO BOX 497 99840 2-11111
 William Hopkins, supt. 983-2960
 S, PO BOX 497 99840 2-11111
 William Hopkins, prin. 983-2960

Sleetmute, AC 907, PC 2, Bethel
Kuspuk SD
 Supt. — See Aniak
 S, GENERAL DELIVERY 99668 1-11111
 Max Cole, prin. 449-4216

Soldotna, AC 907, PC 5, Kenai Peninsula
Kenai Peninsula Borough SD 6-11111
 144 N BINKLEY ST 99669 262-5846
 Robert Holmes, supt.
 Skyview HS, HC 2 BOX 301 99669 3-00011
 Marlene Byerly, prin. 262-7675
 HS, 425 W MARYDALE DR 99669 2-00011
 Ken Meacham, prin. 262-7411
 JHS, 426 W REDOUBT AVE 99669 3-00100
 Daryl Kellum, prin. 262-4344
 Other Schools – See Anchor Point, Homer, Kenai,
 Nanwalek, Nikiski, Ninilchik, Seldovia, Seward,
 Tyonek

 Kenai Peninsula Community College 3-CC
  34820 COLLEGE DR 99669 262-5801

Stebbins, AC 907, PC 2, Nome
Bering Strait SD
 Supt. — See Unalakleet
 Tukurngailnguq S 2-11111
 GENERAL DELIVERY 99671 934-3041
 Gurley Maurin, prin.

Stony River, AC 907, PC 1, Bethel
Kuspuk SD
 Supt. — See Aniak
 Michael S, GENERAL DELIVERY 99557 1-11111
 Max Cole, prin. 537-3226

Takotna, AC 907, PC 1, Yukon Koyukuk
Iditarod Area SD
 Supt. — See Mc Grath
 S, PO BOX 99675 1-11111
 Bartol Mwarey, prin. 298-2115

Talkeetna, AC 907, PC 2, Matanuska Susitna
Matanuska-Susitna Borough SD
 Supt. — See Palmer
 Susitna Valley JSHS 2-00111
 MILE 986 PARKS HWY 99676 733-2241
 Helen Oliver, prin.

Tanana, AC 907, PC 2, Yukon Koyukuk
Tanana CSD, PO BOX 89 99777 2-11111
 Ron DeLay, supt. 366-7203

Tanana City S, PO BOX 89 99777 2-11111
 Rod Pocock, prin. 366-7203

Tatitlek, AC 907, PC 2, Valdez Cordova
Chugach SD
 Supt. — See Anchorage
 Tatitlek Community S 1-11111
  PO BOX 167 99677 325-2252
 Linda Vickrey, prin.

Teller, AC 907, PC 2, Nome
Bering Strait SD
 Supt. — See Unalakleet
 Isabell S, GENERAL DELIVERY 99778 1-11111
 Patrick Crawford, prin. 642-3041

Tenakee Springs, AC 907, PC 1, Skagway Yakutat
Chatham SD
 Supt. — See Angoon
 S, PO BOX 62 99841 1-11111
 Arnold Strong, prin. 736-2204

Tetlin, AC 907, PC 1, Southeast Fairbanks
Alaska Gateway SD
 Supt. — See Tok
 S, GENERAL DELIVERY 99780 1-11111
 David McNeal, prin. 324-2104

Thorne Bay, AC 907, PC 3, Prince Wales Ketchikan
Southeast Island SD
 Supt. — See Ketchikan
 S, PO BOX 5 99950 2-11111
 Michael Walker, prin. 828-3921

Togiak, AC 907, PC 3, Dillingham
Southwest Region SD
 Supt. — See Dillingham
 S, GENERAL DELIVERY 99678 2-11111
 Bob Miller, prin. 493-5829

Tok, AC 907, PC 3, Southeast Fairbanks
Alaska Gateway SD 3-11111
 PO BOX 226 99780 883-5151
 Spike Jorgensen, supt.
 S, PO BOX 249 99780 2-11111
 Stephen Brown, prin. 883-5161
 Other Schools – See Dot Lake, Eagle, Mentasta Lake,
 Northway, Tetlin

Toksook Bay, AC 907, PC 2, Bethel
Lower Kuskokwim SD
 Supt. — See Bethel
 Nelson Island S 2-11111
 GENERAL DELIVERY 99559 427-7815
 Monte Nedrow, prin.

Tuluksak, AC 907, PC 2, Bethel
Yupiit SD
 Supt. — See Akiachak
 HS, PO BOX 115 99679 1-00011
 Freda Amhart, prin. 695-6112

Tuntutuliak, AC 907, PC 2, Bethel
Lower Kuskokwim SD
 Supt. — See Bethel
 Angapak Memorial S 1-11111
 GENERAL DELIVERY 99559 256-2415
 Linda Manwill, prin.

Tununak, AC 907, PC 2, Bethel
Lower Kuskokwim SD
 Supt. — See Bethel
 Albert Memorial S, PO BOX 49 99681 1-11111
 Donna Murphy, prin. 652-6827

Tyonek, AC 907, PC 2, Kenai Peninsula
Kenai Peninsula Borough SD
 Supt. — See Soldotna
 Bartlett S, PO BOX 82010 99682 1-11111
 Tamara Smid, prin. 583-2291

Unalakleet, AC 907, PC 3, Nome
Bering Strait SD, PO BOX 225 99684 4-11111
 David Bowling, supt. 624-3611
 S, GENERAL DELIVERY 99684 2-11111
 Janet Stout, prin. 624-3444

Other Schools – See Brevig Mission, Diomede, Elim,
Gambell, Golovin, Koyuk, Saint Michael,
Savoonga, Shaktoolik, Shishmaref, Stebbins,
Teller, Wales, White Mountain

Unalaska, AC 907, PC 5, Aleutians West
Aleutian Region SD 1-11111
 PO BOX 790 99685 581-3151
 Joseph Beckford, supt.
 Other Schools – See Atka

Unalaska CSD, PO BOX 260 99685 2-11111
 Joseph Beckford, supt. 581-1222
 JSHS, PO BOX 260 99685 2-00111
 Lesley Scharrer, prin. 581-1222

Valdez, AC 907, PC 5, Valdez Cordova
Valdez CSD, PO BOX 398 99686 3-11111
 Harry Rogers, supt. 835-4357
 HS, PO BOX 398 99686 2-00011
 Robert Collins, prin. 835-4767
 Gilson JHS, PO BOX 398 99686 2-00100
 Bill Bryson, prin. 835-2244

 Prince William Sound Community College 3-CC
  PO BOX 97 99686 835-2723

Venetie, AC 907, PC 2, Yukon Koyukuk
Yukon Flats SD
 Supt. — See Fort Yukon
 S, GENERAL DELIVERY 99781 1-11111
 Alan Saunddes, prin. 849-8415

Wainwright, AC 907, PC 2, North Slope
North Slope Borough SD
 Supt. — See Barrow
 Alak S, PO BOX 10 99782 2-11111
 Judy Houston, prin. 763-2541

Wales, AC 907, PC 2, Nome
Bering Strait SD
 Supt. — See Unalakleet
 Wales-Kingikmiut S 1-11111
  PO BOX 490 99783 664-3021
 Deborah Lenz, prin.

Wasilla, AC 907, PC 5, Matanuska Susitna
Matanuska-Susitna Borough SD
 Supt. — See Palmer
 HS, 701 BOGARD RD 99654 3-00011
 Dwight Probasco, prin. 376-5341
 Wasilla MS, 650 BOGARD RD 99654 3-00100
 Eric Henderson, prin. 376-5308

White Mountain, AC 907, PC 2, Nome
Bering Strait SD
 Supt. — See Unalakleet
 S, PO BOX 55 99784 1-11111
 Gary Crandall, prin. 638-3021

Whittier, AC 907, PC 2, Valdez Cordova
Chugach SD
 Supt. — See Anchorage
 Whittier Community S 1-11111
  PO BOX 638 99693 472-2575
 Joe Young, prin.

Wrangell, AC 907, PC 4, Wrangell Petersburg
Wrangell CSD, PO BOX 2319 99929 3-11111
 Linwood Laughy, supt. 874-2347
 HS, PO BOX 651 99929 2-00011
 Lyle Schwartz, prin. 874-3395
 Stikine MS, PO BOX 651 99929 2-00100
 Lyle Schwartz, prin. 874-3393

Yakutat, AC 907, PC 3, Skagway Yakutat
Yakutat CSD, PO BOX 429 99689 2-11111
 Larry Eklund, supt. 784-3317
 JSHS, PO BOX 429 99689 1-00111
 Larry Eklund, prin. 784-3317

ARIZONA

STATE DEPARTMENT OF EDUCATION
1535 W. Jefferson St., Phoenix 85007
(602) 542-4361

Superintendent of Public Instruction	C. Diane Bishop
Deputy Superintendent	Nancy Mendoza
Associate Superintendent Vocational Education	David Muehlbauer
Associate Superintendent Educational Services	Vacant
Associate Superintendent Support Services	Judy Richardson
Associate Superintendent Legislative & Special Programs	Gary Emanuel

STATE BOARD OF EDUCATION
1535 W. Jefferson St. #418, Phoenix 85007

Member   Ken Bennett

COUNTY SUPERINTENDENTS OF SCHOOLS

Apache County
James Tomchee   602-337-4364
PO BOX 548, Saint Johns 85936

Cochise County
Tom Campbell   602-432-9299
PO BOX 208, Bisbee 85603

Coconino County
Katharine Perko   602-779-6591
100 E BIRCH AVE, Flagstaff 86001

Gila County
Armida Bittner   602-425-3231
1400 E ASH ST, Globe 85501

Graham County
Max Hinton   602-428-2880
800 W MAIN ST, Safford 85546

Greenlee County
Jon Jensen   602-865-2822
PO BOX 1595, Clifton 85533

Lapaz County
Bruce Kulp   602-669-6183
PO BOX 1147, Parker 85344

Maricopa County
Lee Cook   602-254-7235
374 N 6TH AVE, Phoenix 85003

Mohave County
Keith Seaman   602-753-0747
809 E BEALE ST, Kingman 86401

Navajo County
B. Bennett   602-524-6161
PO BOX 668, Holbrook 86025

Pima County
Anita Lohr, 130 W CONGRESS ST   602-740-8451
Tucson 85701

Pinal County
Jack Harmon   602-868-6565
PO BOX 769, Florence 85232

Santa Cruz County
Roberto Conchola   602-761-7800
2100 N CONGRESS DR # 118
Nogales 85621

Yavapai County
Paul Street   602-771-3326
255 E GURLEY ST, Prescott 86301

Yuma County
Raymond Drysdale   602-329-2245
210 S 1ST AVE, Yuma 85364

PUBLIC, PRIVATE AND CATHOLIC SECONDARY SCHOOLS

Ajo, AC 602, PC 5, Pima
Ajo USD 15, PO BOX 68 85321   3-11111
    387-5619
    Alfredo Luna, supt.
HS, PO BOX 68 85321   2-00011
    Art Fenster, prin.   387-7603
JHS, PO BOX 68 85321   2-00100
    Art Fenster, prin.   387-7604

Apache Junction, AC 602, PC 7, Pinal
Apache Junction USD 43   5-11111
PO BOX 879 85217   982-1110
    William Wright, supt.
HS, 2525 S IRONWOOD DR 85220   4-00011
    Dudley Orr, prin.   982-1110
JHS, 801 E SOUTHERN AVE 85219   3-00100
    Gary Nine, prin.   982-1110

Central Arizona College   3-CC
273 E US HIGHWAY 60 85219   982-7261

Ash Fork, AC 602, PC 2, Yavapai
Ash Fork JUSD 31   2-11111
PO BOX 247 86320   637-2561
    Kenneth Tindall, supt.
HS, PO BOX 247 86320   1-00011
    Kenneth Tindall, prin.   637-2561

Avondale, AC 602, PC 7, Maricopa
Agua Fria UNHSD 216   4-00011
530 E RILEY DR 85323   932-4250
    John Durbin, supt.
Agua Fria Union HS   4-00011
530 E RILEY DR 85323   932-4250
    Carolyn Kennedy, prin.

Avondale ESD 44   5-11100
235 W WESTERN AVE 85323   932-0840
    Lee Peterson, supt.
JHS, 1406 N CENTRAL AVE 85323   3-00100
    George Tewksbury, prin.   932-2630

Bagdad, AC 602, PC 4, Yavapai
Bagdad USD 20, PO BOX 427 86321   3-11111
    Sylvester Krell, supt.   633-4101
HS, PO BOX 427 86321   2-00011
    Hubert Deglow, prin.   633-2201

Benson, AC 602, PC 5, Cochise
Benson ESD 9, PO BOX 2030 85602   3-11100
    Howard Lowe, supt.   586-2213

MS, PO BOX 2030 85602   2-01100
    Charles Young, prin.   586-2215

Benson UNHSD 9   2-00011
PO BOX 2030 85602   586-2214
    Howard Lowe, supt.
Benson Union HS   2-00011
PO BOX 2030 85602   586-2214
    Lou Burleson, prin.

Bisbee, AC 602, PC 6, Cochise
Bisbee USD 2, PO BOX G 85603   4-11111
    Herb Weissenfels, supt.   432-5381
HS, PO BOX G 85603   3-00011
    Larry Cummins, prin.   432-5714
Lowell MS, PO BOX G 85603   2-01100
    Michael May, prin.   432-5391

Black Canyon City, AC 602, PC 3, Yavapai
Canon ESD 50, PO BOX 89 85324   2-11100
    Gary Rathgeber, supt.   374-5588
Canon MS, PO BOX 89 85324   1-01100
    Vicki Elkins, prin.   374-5588

Bowie, AC 602, PC 3, Cochise
Bowie USD 14, PO BOX 157 85605   2-11111
    G. Zamudio, supt.   847-2545
HS, PO BOX 157 85605   1-00011
    (—), prin.   847-2545

Buckeye, AC 602, PC 6, Maricopa
Buckeye UNHSD 201   3-00011
902 E EASON AVE 85326   386-4423
    Vincent Vecchiarella, supt.
Buckeye Union HS   3-00011
902 E EASON AVE 85326   386-4423
    Don Davis, prin.

Bullhead City, AC 602, PC 7, Mohave
Bullhead City ESD 15   3-11100
1004 HANCOCK RD 86442   758-3961
    Douglas Lutz, supt.
JHS, 1004 HANCOCK RD 86442   3-00100
    F. Hoeprich, prin.   758-3921

Colorado River UNHSD 2   2-00011
2251 S HIGHWAY 95 86442   758-4477
    Michael Aylstock, supt.
Mohave HS   2-00011
2251 S HIGHWAY 95 86442   758-3916
    Robert Arends, prin.

Other Schools – See Mohave Valley

Camp Verde, AC 602, PC 6, Yavapai
Camp Verde USD 28   4-11111
PO BOX 728 86322   567-3382
    Phillip England, supt.
HS, PO BOX 728 86322   2-00011
    William Bean, prin.   567-6601
MS, PO BOX 728 86322   2-00100
    Benjamin Pareja, prin.   567-3993

Casa Grande, AC 602, PC 7, Pinal
Casa Grande ESD 4   5-11100
1460 N PINAL AVE 85222   836-2111
    Don Dermody, supt.
Casa Grande JHS   3-00100
300 W MCMURRAY BLVD 85222   836-7310
    Linda LaFontain, prin.

Casa Grande UNHSD 82   4-00011
616 E 10TH ST 85222   836-8532
    Scott McEuen, supt.
Casa Grande Union HS   4-00011
420 E FLORENCE BLVD 85222   836-8500
    James Cooper, prin.

Cashion, AC 602, PC 5, Maricopa
Littleton ESD 65, PO BOX 280 85329   4-11100
    Myrtle Combrink, supt.   936-3333
Underdown JHS, PO BOX 280 85329   2-00100
    Fred Fox, prin.   936-3316

Cave Creek, AC 602, PC 5, Maricopa
Cave Creek USD 93   4-11111
PO BOX 426 85331   488-9816
    David Alexander, supt.
Cactus Shadows HS   2-00011
33606 N 60TH ST 85331   488-9816
    Ed Wilkosz, prin.
Desert Arroyo MS   1-00100
33401 N 56TH ST 85331   488-9816
    William Wicevich, prin.

Chandler, AC 602, PC 8, Maricopa
Chandler USD 80   6-11111
1525 W FRYE RD 85224   786-7000
    Howard Conley, supt.
SHS, 350 N ARIZONA AVE 85224   4-00001
    Robert Caccamo, prin.   786-7140

18

Anderson JHS 3-00110
   1255 N DOBSON RD 85224 786-7170
   Gary Prosper, prin.
Bogle JHS 3-00100
   1600 W QUEEN CREEK RD 85248 786-5520
   Fred Coates, prin.
Willis JHS, 401 S MCQUEEN RD 85225 2-00110
   Fred De Prez, prin. 786-7180

East Valley Institute of Technology SD
   Supt. — See Mesa
EVIT Chandler Air S Vo Tech
   350 N ARIZONA AVE 85224 786-7140
   Robert Caccamo, prin.

Kyrene ESD 28
   Supt. — See Tempe
Kyrene Del Pueblo MS 3-00100
   360 S TWELVE OAKS BLVD 85284 496-4727
   Linda Kinnerup, prin.

Mesa USD 4
   Supt. — See Mesa
Hendrix JHS, 1550 W SUMMIT PL 85224 4-00110
   Susie Wissinger, prin. 345-0931

Seton Catholic HS 2-00011
   1150 N DOBSON RD 85224 963-1900
   Br. Daniel Casey, prin.

Chinle, AC 602, PC 6, Apache
Chinle USD 24, PO BOX 587 86503 5-11111
   Mary Ann Hunter, supt. 674-9400
HS, PO BOX 587 86503 4-00011
   Keith Crawley, prin. 674-9407
JHS, PO BOX 587 86503 2-00100
   Anthony Salandro, prin. 674-9405

Rough Rock Community S 2-11111
   PO BOX 217 86503 728-3311

Chino Valley, AC 602, PC 5, Yavapai
Chino Valley USD 51 3-11111
   PO BOX 225 86323 636-2458
   Ronald Minnich, supt.
Chino Valley HS, PO BOX 225 86323 2-00011
   Michael Henry, prin. 636-2298
Heritage MS, PO BOX 225 86323 2-01100
   Harold Tenney, prin. 636-4464

Clifton, AC 602, PC 5, Greenlee
Clifton USD 3, PO BOX 1567 85533 3-11111
   Luis Montoya, supt. 865-2752
HS, PO BOX 1567 85533 2-00011
   James Crinan, prin. 865-3262

Colorado City, AC 602, PC 4, Mohave
Colorado City USD 14 3-11111
   PO BOX 309 86021 875-2288
   Alvin Barlow, supt.
HS, PO BOX 309 86021 2-00011
   Lawrence Steed, prin. 875-2288
JHS, PO BOX 309 86021 2-00100
   Kimball Barlow, prin. 875-2288

Coolidge, AC 602, PC 6, Pinal
Coolidge USD 21 5-11111
   PO BOX 1499 85228 723-9349
   Carl Nuhn, supt.
HS, PO BOX 1499 85228 3-00011
   Sherrill Stephens, prin. 723-9326
McCray JHS, PO BOX 1499 85228 3-00100
   Ralph Brooks, prin. 723-9312

Central Arizona College 4-CC
   8470 N OVERFIELD RD 85228 426-4200

Cottonwood, AC 602, PC 6, Yavapai
Cottonwood-Oak Creek ESD 6 5-11100
   1 N WILLARD ST 86326 634-2288
   John Tavasci, supt.
MS, 1 N WILLARD ST 86326 2-00100
   Daniel Stephens, prin. 634-2231

Mingus UNHSD 4, 1801 E FIR ST 86326 4-00011
   Marvin Lamer, supt. 634-7531
Mingus Union HS, 1801 E FIR ST 86326 4-00011
   Marvin Lamer, supt. 634-7531

Dewey, AC 602, PC 3, Yavapai
Humboldt USD 22, PO BOX A 86327 4-11111
   Rod Cordes, supt. 772-9200
Bradshaw Mountain HS 3-00011
   PO BOX A 86327 775-4286
   Steven Harbeck, prin.
Bradshaw Mountain JHS 3-00100
   PO BOX A 86327 772-9200
   Craig Angalich, prin.

Douglas, AC 602, PC 7, Cochise
Douglas USD 27, PO BOX 1237 85608 5-11111
   Jesus Greer, supt. 364-2447
HS, 1500 15TH ST 85607 4-00011
   Mike Foster, prin. 364-3462
JHS, 842 12TH ST 85607 2-00100
   Clara La Forge, prin. 364-2461
Huber JHS 3-00100
   15TH ST & WASHINGTON 85607 364-2840
   Dale Kleck, prin.

Cochise College 4-CC
   RR 1 BOX 100 85607 364-7943

Duncan, AC 602, PC 3, Greenlee
Duncan USD 2, PO BOX 710 85534 3-11111
   Erwin Crotts, supt. 359-2472
HS, PO BOX 710 85534 2-00011
   J. Goodrum, prin. 359-2474

Elfrida, AC 602, PC 2, Cochise
Valley UNHSD 22 2-00011
   PO BOX 158 85610 – (—), supt. 642-3492
Valley Union HS, PO BOX 158 85610 2-00011
   G. Dale Mortenson, prin. 642-3492

El Mirage, AC 602, PC 6, Maricopa
Dysart USD 89 5-11111
   11405 N DYSART RD 85335 977-7281
   Frank Galas, supt.
Dysart HS, 11405 N DYSART RD 85335 2-00011
   Willard Bandes, prin. 583-5550
Dysart MS, 11405 N DYSART RD 85335 4-00100
   Joe Montes, prin. 583-5510

Eloy, AC 602, PC 6, Pinal
Eloy ESD 11 4-11100
   1011 N SUNSHINE BLVD 85231 466-7301
   Richard Carino, supt.
JHS 2-00100
   PHOENIX & SANTA CRUZ STS 85231 466-7171
   Dorothy Erdman, prin.

Santa Cruz Valley UNHSD 840 2-00011
   902 N MAIN ST 85231 466-7391
   William Sisco, supt.
Santa Cruz Valley HS 2-00011
   902 N MAIN ST 85231 466-7391
   Paul Young, prin.

Flagstaff, AC 602, PC 8, Coconino
Flagstaff USD 1 7-11111
   3285 SPARROW AVE 86004 527-6000
   Kent Matheson, supt.
Conconino HS, 1801 N IZABEL ST 86004 4-00011
   David Roth, prin. 773-8200
HS, 400 W ELM AVE 86001 4-00011
   Benny Bishop, prin. 773-8100
Sinagua HS, 3950 E BUTLER AVE 86004 3-00011
   Kirsten Hendricks, prin. 527-5500
East Flagstaff JHS 4-00100
   2410 E CEDAR AVE 86004 773-8250
   Bill Epperson, prin.
JHS, 755 N BONITO ST 86001 4-00100
   Homer Townsend, prin. 773-8150

Arizona Academy of Medical/Dental Asst. 1-CS
   2575 E 7TH AVE 86004 526-6359
Northern Arizona Institute of Technology 2-CS
   1120 W KAIBAB LN 86001 779-4532
Northern Arizona University 7-UC
   PO BOX 4092 86011 523-3232

Florence, AC 602, PC 6, Pinal
Florence USD 1, PO BOX 829 85232 4-11111
   Eric Kleinstiver, supt. 868-5812
HS, PO BOX 829 85232 2-00011
   Ed Segrave, prin. 868-5816
MS, PO BOX 829 85232 2-00100
   Phillip Verdugo, prin. 868-4095

Fort Defiance, AC 602, PC 5, Apache
Window Rock USD 8 5-11111
   PO BOX 559 86504 729-5705
   Floyd Ashley, supt.
Window Rock HS, PO BOX 559 86504 3-00011
   Charles Grant, prin. 729-5705
Tso Ho Tso MS, PO BOX 559 86504 3-00100
   Anna Watchman, prin. 729-5705

Fort Huachuca, AC 602, PC see Sierra Vista
Fort Huachuca Accommodation SD 00 4-11100
   PO BOX Q 85613 – Clark Stevens, supt. 458-5082
Smith MS, PO BOX Q 85613 2-00100
   George Pohlman, prin. 459-8892

Fort Thomas, AC 602, PC 2, Graham
Fort Thomas USD 7 2-11111
   PO BOX 28 85536 485-2427
   Jerry Hancock, supt.
JSHS, PO BOX 28 85536 2-00011
   Carter McEuen, prin. 485-2427

Fountain Hills, AC 602, PC 7, Maricopa
Fountain Hills USD 98 3-11111
   14260 N DEL CAMBRE AVE 85268 837-0690
   Walter Dunne, supt.
Fountain Hills JSHS 2-00011
   16000 E PALISADES BLVD 85268 837-7758
   Lenny Allsbrooks, prin.

Fredonia, AC 602, PC 4, Coconino
Fredonia-Moccasin USD 6 3-11111
   PO BOX 247 86022 643-7333
   Phillip Hardy, supt.
Fredonia-Moccasin HS 2-00011
   PO BOX 247 86022 643-7333
   Phillip Hardy, prin.

Gadsden, AC 602, PC 3, Yuma
Gadsden ESD 32, PO BOX 128 85336 4-11100
   Gary Hicks, supt. 627-2882
MS, PO BOX 128 85336 3-01100
   Charles Juenger, prin. 627-2239

Ganado, AC 602, PC 5, Apache
Ganado USD 20, PO BOX 1757 86505 5-11111
   Albert Yazzie, supt. 755-3436
HS, PO BOX 1757 86505 3-00011
   Tom Yazzie, prin. 755-3552

MS, PO BOX 1757 86505 2-00100
   Victor Benally, prin. 755-3436

Gila Bend, AC 602, PC 4, Maricopa
Gila Bend USD 24, PO BOX V 85337 3-11111
   Charles Landis, supt. 683-2225
HS, PO BOX V 85337 2-00011
   Stephen Marshall, prin. 683-2286

Gilbert, AC 602, PC 8, Maricopa
Gilbert USD 41, 140 S GILBERT RD 85296 6-11111
   Walter Delecki, supt. 892-0545
HS, 1101 E ELLIOT RD 85234 4-00011
   Charles Santa Cruz, prin. 497-0177
JHS, 1016 N BURK ST 85234 3-00100
   George Bowers, prin. 892-6908
Mesquite JHS 3-00100
   130 W MESQUITE ST 85233 926-1433
   Jill Bowers, prin.
Other Schools – See Higley

Glendale, AC 602, PC 9, Maricopa
Deer Valley USD 97
   Supt. — See Phoenix
Deer Valley HS 5-00011
   18424 N 51ST AVE 85308 866-5857
   Connie Harris, prin.
Deer Valley Vo-Tech Ctr Vo Tech
   18400 N 51ST AVE 85308 866-5889
   Barbara Daggett, prin.
Desert Sky MS 4-00100
   5130 W GROVERS AVE 85308 866-5825
   Janet Altersitz, prin.
Hillcrest MS, 22833 N 71ST AVE 85310 2-00100
   Carol Patterson, prin. 581-7970

Glendale ESD 40 6-11100
   7301 N 58TH AVE 85301 842-8100
   Richard Terbush, supt.
Challenger MS 3-00100
   6905 W MARYLAND AVE 85303 842-8314
   Steve Hodgson, prin.
Glendale Landmark MS 4-00100
   5730 W MYRTLE AVE 85301 842-8304
   Mary Metzger, prin.

Glendale UNHSD 205 7-00011
   7650 N 43RD AVE 85301 435-6000
   Dr. Gerald George, supt.
Apollo HS, 8045 N 47TH AVE 85302 4-00011
   Bob Thrasher, prin. 435-6300
HS, 6216 W GLENDALE AVE 85301 4-00011
   Margaret Dugan, prin. 435-6200
Independence HS 4-00011
   6602 N 75TH AVE 85303 435-6100
   Ron Gardner, prin.
Other Schools – See Phoenix

Peoria USD 11
   Supt. — See Peoria
Cactus HS 4-00011
   6330 W GREENWAY RD 85306 878-1038
   Rob DeSeelhorst, prin.
Ironwood HS 4-00011
   6051 W SWEETWATER AVE 85304 486-6400
   Marie Grey, prin.

American Graduate School Intrntnl. Mgmt. 4-UC
   15249 N 59TH AVE 85306 800-848-9084
Glendale Community College 6-CC
   6000 W OLIVE AVE 85302 435-3000
Maranatha Christian Academy 2-11111
   7101 N 55TH DR 85301 937-2975
NEC-Arizona Automotive Institute 4-CC
   6829 N 46TH AVE 85301 934-7273
Northwest Christian Academy 2-11111
   14240 N 43RD AVE 85306 978-2060

Globe, AC 602, PC 6, Gila
Globe USD 1, 501 E ASH ST 85501 5-11111
   Orval Nutting, supt. 425-3211
HS, 501 E ASH ST 85501 3-00011
   Jon Trotter, prin. 425-3211
MS, 501 E ASH ST 85501 2-00100
   Michael Minton, prin. 425-7105

Grand Canyon, AC 602, PC 4, Coconino
Grand Canyon USD 4 2-11111
   PO BOX 519 86023 638-2461
   John Vest, supt.
HS, PO BOX 519 86023 1-00011
   Loren Detwiler, prin. 638-2461

Heber, AC 602, PC 3, Navajo
Heber-Overgaard USD 6 2-11111
   PO BOX 547 85928 535-4667
   Franklin Greer, supt.
Mogollon JSHS, PO BOX 547 85928 2-00111
   Charles Beecroft, prin. 535-4238

Higley, AC 602, PC 2, Maricopa
Gilbert USD 41
   Supt. — See Gilbert
Highland HS 3-00011
   17901 E GUADALUPE RD 85236 813-0051
   Connie Honaker, prin.

Holbrook, AC 602, PC 5, Navajo
Holbrook USD 3, PO BOX 640 86025 4-11111
   Patrick Dallabetta, supt. 524-6144
HS, PO BOX 640 86025 3-00011
   Ben Wade, prin. 524-2815
JHS, PO BOX 640 86025 2-00100
   James Bell, prin. 524-3959

Northland Pioneer College — 4-CC
PO BOX 610 86025 — 524-1993

Joseph City, AC 602, PC 3, Navajo
Joseph City USD 2, PO BOX 8 86032 — 2-11111
(—), supt. — 288-3307
JSHS, PO BOX 8 86032 — 2-00111
Charles Foote, prin. — 288-3361

Kayenta, AC 602, PC 5, Navajo
Kayenta USD 27, PO BOX 337 86033 — 4-11111
Dr. Joseph Martin, supt. — 697-3251
Monument Valley HS — 3-00011
PO BOX 337 86033 — 697-2191
Sonny Franklin, prin.
MS, PO BOX 337 86033 — 3-00100
Donald Cochran, prin. — 697-2297

Kearny, AC 602, PC 4, Pinal
Ray USD 3, PO BOX 427 85237 — 4-11111
M. Cude, supt. — 363-5515
Ray HS, PO BOX 427 85237 — 2-00011
J. S. Castro, prin. — 363-5513
MS, PO BOX 427 85237 — 2-01100
Fred Howe, prin. — 363-5511

Kingman, AC 602, PC 7, Mohave
Kingman ESD 4 — 5-11100
3033 MCDONALD AVE 86401 — 753-5678
Carole Hartle, supt.
Golden Valley JHS — 3-00100
3404 SANTA MARIA RD 86413 — 565-9111
Robert Miller, prin.
JHS, 1969 DETROIT AVE 86401 — 3-00100
Sharyn Graf, prin. — 753-3588

Mohave UNHSD 30 — 4-00011
515 W BEALE ST 86401 — 753-6211
Michael Ford, supt.
SHS North, 4182 N BANK ST 86401 — 3-00001
Roger Fuss, prin. — 692-6480
JHS S, 400 GRANDVIEW AVE 86401 — 4-00011
Susan Chan, prin. — 753-6216

Manzanita Christian S — 2-11111
2040 GOLDEN AVE 86401 — 753-2307
Mohave Community College — 4-CC
1971 JAGERSON AVE 86401 — 757-4331

Lake Havasu City, AC 602, PC 7, Mohave
Lake Havasu USD 1 — 5-11111
2200 HAVASUPAI BLVD 86403 — 855-7861
Ray Lange, supt.
HS, 2675 PALO VERDE BLVD S 86403 — 4-00011
Margaret Metcalf, prin. — 855-4011
JHS, 98 SWANSON AVE 86403 — 3-00100
Philip Olmstead, prin. — 855-4066

Lakeside, AC 602, PC 3, Navajo
Blue Ridge USD 32 — 4-11111
PO BOX 885 85929 — 368-6126
Gordon Meredith, supt.
Blue Ridge HS, PO BOX 885 85929 — 3-00011
Kevin Bortin, prin. — 368-6328
Blue Ridge JHS, PO BOX 885 85929 — 2-00100
Nancy Dooley, prin. — 368-6377

Litchfield Park, AC 602, PC 5, Maricopa
Litchfield ESD 79 — 4-11100
553 E PLAZA CIR STE A 85340 — 257-3001
L. Heck, supt.
Western Sky MS — 2-00100
553 E PLAZA CIR # A 85340 — 935-0060
Ann Allison, prin.

Many Farms, AC 602, PC 4, Apache

Many Farms HS 86538 — 2-00011
Phil Hardy, prin.

Marana, AC 602, PC 4, Pima
Marana USD 6, 11279 W GRIER RD 85653 — 6-11111
Scott Foster, supt. — 682-3243
JHS, 11279 W GRIER RD 85653 — 3-00100
Bruce G. Dewey, prin. — 682-3243
Other Schools – See Tucson

Maricopa, AC 602, PC 4, Pinal
Maricopa USD 20, PO BOX 630 85239 — 3-11111
Robert Sanchez, supt. — 568-2293
HS, PO BOX 630 85239 — 2-00011
Bob Kilker, prin. — 568-9474
MS, PO BOX 630 85239 — 2-00100
Mathew Reese, prin. — 568-9474

Mayer, AC 602, PC 4, Yavapai
Mayer USD 43 — 2-11111
17300 E MULE DEER DR 86333 — 632-7834
Eli Casey, supt.
HS, 17300 E MULE DEER DR 86333 — 2-00011
David Perey, prin. — 632-7629

Orme S, HC 63 BOX 3040 86333 — 2-00111
Todd Horn, prin. — 632-7601

Mesa, AC 602, PC 10, Maricopa
East Valley Institute of Technology SD — 2-00011
200 S CENTER 85210 — 461-4104
Jack Shell, supt.
Other Schools – See Chandler, Scottsdale, Tempe

Mesa USD 4, 549 N STAPLEY DR 85203 — 8-11111
James Zaharis, supt. — 898-7700
Dobson SHS — 5-00001
1501 W GUADALUPE RD 85202 — 898-2900
Paul Walsh, prin.
SHS, 1630 E SOUTHERN AVE 85204 — 5-00001
Mary Jo Vecchiarelli, prin. — 898-5903
Mountain View SHS — 5-00001
2700 E BROWN RD 85213 — 898-4901
Craig Luketich, prin.
Red Mountain SHS — 2-00001
7301 E BROWN RD 85207 — 396-1800
Kenneth Salas, prin.
Westwood SHS, 945 W 8TH ST 85201 — 5-00001
Jack Joyce, prin. — 898-3900
Brimhall JHS — 2-00110
4949 E SOUTHERN AVE 85206 — 641-7747
Stephen Pierson, prin.
Carson JHS, 525 N WESTWOOD 85201 — 4-00110
Eldon Budge, prin. — 844-4505
Fremont JHS, 1001 N POWER RD 85205 — 4-00110
Ralph Stokes, prin. — 396-1700
Kino JHS, 848 N HORNE 85203 — 4-00110
Kirk Hansen, prin. — 835-1970
JHS, 828 E BROADWAY 85204 — 4-00110
Harold Crenshaw, prin. — 833-0080
Poston JHS, 2433 E ADOBE ST 85213 — 4-00110
Richard Wheeler, prin. — 835-1419
Powell JHS, 855 W 8TH AVE 85210 — 4-00110
Paul Mohr, prin. — 835-1437
Rhodes JHS, 1860 S LONGMORE 85202 — 4-00110
Linda Rottman, prin. — 839-9329
Shepherd JHS — 4-00110
1407 N ALTA MESA DR 85205 — 981-0983
Steve Smith, prin.
Other Schools – See Chandler

American Teller Schools — 2-CS
1819 S DOBSON RD 85202 — 730-8191
Apollo College — 2-CS
630 W SOUTHERN AVE 85210 — 831-6585
Arizona Inst. of Business & Technology — 2-CS
925 S GILBERT RD STE 201 85204 — 545-8755
AzTech Institute — 1-CS
941 S DOBSON RD STE 120 85202 — 898-9898
Denver Business College — 2-CS
1550 S ALMA SCHOOL RD # 100 85210 — 834-1000
Institute of Business-Medical Technology — 1-CS
20 E MAIN ST STE 600 85201 — 833-1028
Lamson Business College — 3-CC
1980 W MAIN ST STE 250 85201 — 898-7000
Mesa Community College — 6-CC
1833 W SOUTHERN AVE 85202 — 461-7000

Miami, AC 602, PC 4, Gila
Miami USD 40, PO BOX H 85539 — 4-11111
Stephen Blazevich, supt. — 425-3271
HS, PO BOX H 85539 — 3-00011
Robert Corley, prin. — 425-3271
Kornegay JHS, PO BOX H 85539 — 2-00110
David Pastor, prin. — 425-3271

Mohave Valley, AC 602, PC 3, Mohave
Colorado River UNHSD 2
Supt. — See Bullhead City
River Valley HS, 3000 E LAGUNA 86440 — 2-00011
Dennis Diehl, prin. — 768-2300

Mohave Valley ESD 16 — 5-11100
PO BOX 5070 86440 — 768-4538
Emmett Brown, supt.
JHS, PO BOX 5070 86440 — 2-00100
Craig Vallon, prin. — 768-9196

Morenci, AC 602, PC 4, Greenlee
Morenci USD 18 — 4-11111
PO BOX 1060 85540 — 865-2081
David Woodall, supt.
JSHS, PO BOX 1060 85540 — 2-00111
Lynne Nutall, prin. — 865-3631

Nogales, AC 602, PC 7, Santa Cruz
Nogales USD 1, 310 W PLUM ST 85621 — 6-11111
Raul Bejarano, supt. — 287-0800
HS, 1900 N APACHE BLVD 85621 — 4-00011
Marcelino Varona, prin. — 287-0900
Carpenter MS, 595 W KINO ST 85621 — 3-00100
Mary Matz, prin. — 287-0820
Pierson MS, 451 N ARROYO BLVD 85621 — 3-00100
Mark Valenzuela, prin. — 287-0830

Our Lady of Lourdes Academy — 2-00111
555 E PATAGONIA HWY 85621 — 287-5659
Sr. Luisa Valdez, prin.

Page, AC 602, PC 6, Coconino
Page USD 8, PO BOX 1927 86040 — 5-11111
Dan Dodds, supt. — 645-8801
HS, PO BOX 1927 86040 — 3-00011
Stacy Wadleigh, prin. — 645-4142
MS, PO BOX 1927 86040 — 3-00100
Roy Stringfellow, prin. — 645-8146

Paradise Valley, AC 602, PC 7, Maricopa

Modern Schools of America — 1-HMS
5301 N 37TH PL 85253

Parker, AC 602, PC 5, La Paz
Parker USD 27, PO BOX 1089 85344 — 4-11111
Harry Mackay, supt. — 669-9244

HS, PO BOX 1089 85344 — 3-00011
Duane Howard, prin. — 669-2202
Wallace MS, PO BOX 1089 85344 — 3-01100
Patrick Schlecht, prin. — 669-2141

Patagonia, AC 602, PC 3, Santa Cruz
Patagonia UNHSD 20 — 2-00111
PO BOX 254 85624 — 394-2203
Dennis Adams, supt.
Patagonia Union JSHS — 2-00111
PO BOX 254 85624 - (—), prin. — 394-2203

Payson, AC 602, PC 6, Gila
Payson USD 10, PO BOX 919 85547 — 5-11111
Russell Kinzer, supt. — 474-2463
HS, PO BOX 919 85547 — 3-00011
Philip Gille, prin. — 474-2233
JHS, PO BOX 919 85547 — 2-00100
Bill Lawson, prin. — 474-4511

Peoria, AC 602, PC 8, Maricopa
Peoria USD 11, PO BOX 39 85380 — 7-11111
Dr. Raymond S. Kellis, supt. — 486-6000
Centennial HS — 2-00011
14388 N 79TH AVE 85381 — 878-5612
Dave Moore, prin.
HS, 11200 N 83RD AVE 85345 — 4-00011
Jim Williams, prin. — 486-6300
Other Schools – See Glendale

Southwest Indian S — 2-00111
14202 N 73RD AVE 85381 — 979-6008

Phoenix, AC 602, PC 11, Maricopa
Alhambra ESD 68 — 6-11111
4510 N 37TH AVE 85019 — 246-5100
Carol Grosse, supt.
Andalucia Montebello MS — 2-01100
2636 W MONTEBELLO AVE 85017 — 336-2000
Ron Dickson, prin.
Granada East MS — 4-01100
3022 W CAMPBELL AVE 85017 — 246-5180
Frank Terbush, prin.
Simpson MS — 2-01100
2301 W MISSOURI AVE 85015 — 246-5020
Jesse Bass, prin.

Cartwright ESD 83 — 7-11100
3401 N 67TH AVE 85033 — 846-2800
William Dabb, supt.
Borman JHS, 3637 N 55TH AVE 85031 — 3-00100
Jack Kensler, prin. — 245-0110
Desert Sands JHS — 3-00100
6308 W CAMPBELL AVE 85033 — 846-1609
Ronald Poole, prin.
Estrella JHS, 3733 N 75TH AVE 85033 — 3-00100
John Woollums, prin. — 846-0914

Creighton ESD 14 — 5-11100
2702 E FLOWER ST 85016 — 381-6000
Donald Covey, supt.

Deer Valley USD 97 — 7-11111
20402 N 15TH AVE 85027 — 581-7700
Gerald Cuendet, supt.
Goldwater HS — 4-00011
2820 W ROSE GARDEN LN 85027 — 581-7838
Cheryl Ingram, prin.
Deer Valley MS — 4-00100
21100 N 27TH AVE 85027 — 581-7900
Pat Crisp, prin.
Other Schools – See Glendale

Fowler ESD 45, 1617 S 67TH AVE 85043 — 4-11100
Jack Null, supt. — 257-6230
Fowler MS — 3-01100
6707 W VAN BUREN ST 85043 — 257-6241
Kathleen Kaderlick, prin.

Glendale UNHSD 205
Supt. — See Glendale
Cortez HS, 8828 N 31ST AVE 85051 — 4-00011
Carolyn Sheley, prin. — 589-1500
Greenway HS — 4-00011
3930 W GREENWAY RD 85023 — 588-3500
Edward Murphy, prin.
Moon Valley HS — 4-00011
3625 W CACTUS RD 85029 — 588-4100
Melba Vallas, prin.
Sunnyslope HS — 4-00011
35 W DUNLAP AVE 85021 — 861-8560
James McElroy, prin.
Thunderbird HS — 4-00011
1750 W THUNDERBIRD RD 85023 — 866-6100
Jennifer Johnson, prin.
Washington HS — 4-00011
2217 W GLENDALE AVE 85021 — 864-3100
Sidney Bailey, prin.

Isaac ESD 5 — 6-11100
3348 W MCDOWELL RD 85009 — 484-4700
Herman Moya, supt.
Isaac JHS, 3402 W MCDOWELL RD 85009 — 4-00100
Mary Radcliffe, prin. — 484-4713

Kyrene ESD 28
Supt. — See Tempe
Akimel A-al MS — 2-00100
2720 E LIBERTY LN 85048 — 496-7415
Patricia Weegar, prin.
Kyrene Centennial MS — 2-00100
13808 S 36TH ST 85044 — 496-7400
Larry Pieratt, prin.

Madison ESD 38, 5601 N 16TH ST 85016 — 5-11100
  Robert Jones, supt. — 264-5951
Madison I MS, 5525 N 16TH ST 85016 — 3-01100
  Robert Chartier, prin. — 265-4793
Madison Meadows MS — 3-01100
  225 W OCOTILLO RD 85013 — 277-6221
  Phyllis Schwartz, prin.

Osborn ESD 8 — 5-11100
  1226 W OSBORN RD 85013 — 234-3366
  Wilma Basnett, supt.
Osborn MS — 2-00100
  1102 W HIGHLAND AVE 85013 — 234-2635
  Ali Rodgers, prin.

Paradise Valley USD 69 — 8-11111
  15002 N 32ND ST 85032 — 867-5100
  James Jurs, supt.
North Canyon HS — 4-00011
  1700 E UNION HILLS DR 85024 — 780-4205
  Robert Wright, prin.
Paradise Valley HS — 5-00011
  3950 E BELL RD 85032 — 867-5505
  Gary Damore, prin.
Polaris HS, 3950 E BELL RD 85032 — 4-00011
  Vern Vanalstine, prin. — 867-5580
Shadow Mountain HS — 5-00011
  2902 E SHEA BLVD 85028 — 867-5326
  David Silcox, prin.
Greenway MS, 3002 E NISBET RD 85032 — 3-00100
  Richard Buscher, prin. — 493-6300
Shea MS, 2728 E SHEA BLVD 85028 — 4-00100
  E. Dunn, prin. — 493-6020
Vista Verde MS — 2-00100
  2826 E GROVERS AVE 85032 — 493-6013
  E. Vanhorn, prin.
Other Schools – See Scottsdale

Phoenix ESD 1, 1817 N 7TH ST 85006 — 6-11100
  Patricia Williams, supt. — 257-3755
Phoenix Preparatory Academy — 3-00100
  735 E FILLMORE ST 85006 — 257-4844
  Ramon Leyba, prin.

Phoenix UNHSD 210 — 7-00011
  4502 N CENTRAL AVE 85012 — 271-3100
  Victor Herbert, supt.
Alhambra HS — 5-00011
  3839 W CAMELBACK RD 85019 — 271-2011
  John Hudson, prin.
Browne HS — 5-00011
  7402 W CATALINA DR 85033 — 271-2101
  Clinton Strickland, prin.
Camelback HS, 4612 N 28TH ST 85016 — 5-00011
  Harry Tolliver, prin. — 271-2281
Central HS, 4525 N CENTRAL AVE 85012 — 5-00011
  Greg Riccio, prin. — 271-2307
Hayden HS — 4-00011
  3333 W ROOSEVELT ST 85009 — 271-2402
  Kino Flores, prin.
Maryvale HS, 3415 N 59TH AVE 85033 — 4-00011
  Linda Golins, prin. — 271-2503
North HS, 1101 E THOMAS RD 85014 — 4-00011
  Nancy Kloss, prin. — 271-2705
South Mountain HS — 5-00011
  5401 S 7TH ST 85040 — 271-2884
  John Ewing, prin.
Metro Vo-Tech Inst — Vo Tech
  1900 W THOMAS RD 85015 — 271-2600
  Martin Hoeffel, prin.

Roosevelt ESD 66, 6000 S 7TH ST 85040 — 7-11100
  John Baracy, supt. — 243-4800
Greenfield MS, 7009 S 10TH ST 85040 — 3-01100
  Joe Pena, prin. — 232-4240
Julian S, 2149 E CARVER DR 85040 — 2-01100
  Gloria Henderson, prin. — 232-4950

Scottsdale USD 48 — 7-11111
  3811 N 44TH ST 85018 — 952-6100
  Duane Sheldon, supt.
Arcadia HS — 4-00011
  4703 E INDIAN SCHOOL RD 85018 — 952-6302
  J. Bruins, prin.
Ingleside MS, 5402 E OSBORN RD 85018 — 3-00100
  John Weimer, prin. — 852-2900
Other Schools – See Scottsdale

Tempe UNHSD 213
  Supt. — See Tempe
Mountain Pointe HS — 2-00011
  4201 E KNOX RD 85044 — 759-8449
  Harold Slemmer, prin.

Tolleson UNHSD 214
  Supt. — See Tolleson
Westview HS — 4-00011
  10850 W GARDEN LAKES PKY 85039 — 877-2438
  Stephan Knight, prin.

Washington ESD 6 — 7-11100
  8610 N 19TH AVE 85021 — 864-2600
  James Mitchell, supt.
Cholla MS, 3120 W CHOLLA ST 85029 — 3-00100
  Gary Batsell, prin. — 866-5151
Desert Foothills MS — 4-00100
  3333 W BANFF LN 85023 — 866-5155
  Kenneth Wamsley, prin.
Mountain Sky MS — 3-00100
  16225 N 7TH AVE 85023 — 866-5220
  David Stoeve, prin.
Palo Verde MS, 7502 N 39TH AVE 85051 — 4-00100
  Lyn Bailey, prin. — 866-5255

Royal Palm MS, 8520 N 19TH AVE 85021 — 4-00100
  Leonard Sweeney, prin. — 864-2883

Wilson ESD 7 — 3-11100
  3025 E FILLMORE ST 85008 — 275-8785
  Roger Romero, supt.
Wilson MS, 2929 E FILLMORE ST 85008 — 2-01100
  J. Thompson, prin. — 225-9242

Academy of Business College — 2-CC
  3320 W CHERYL DR STE 115 85051 — 942-4141
American Indian Bible College — 2-UC
  10020 N 15TH AVE 85021 — 800-933-3828
American Institute — 3-CS
  3443 N CENTRAL AVE STE 1800 85012 — 252-4986
American Institute of Technology — 2-CS
  440 S 54TH AVE 85043 — 233-2222
American Technical Center — 2-CS
  3116 E SHEA BLVD # 249 85028 — 245-0090
American Teller Schools — 2-CS
  635 W INDN SCHOL RD STE 201 85013 — 248-0885
Apollo College — 3-CC
  8503 N 27TH AVE 85051 — 864-1571
Apollo College — 2-CC
  7502 W THOMAS RD STE 6 85033 — 849-9000
Arizona College of the Bible — 2-UC
  2045 W NORTHERN AVE 85021 — 995-2670
Arizona Inst. of Business & Technology — 2-CS
  6049 N 43RD AVE 85019 — 242-6265
Arizona Inst. of Business & Technology — 2-CS
  4136 N 75TH AVE STE 211 85033 — 849-8208
Arizona Lutheran HS — 2-00011
  6036 S 27TH AVE 85041 — 268-8686
Bourgade Catholic HS — 2-00011
  4602 N 31ST AVE 85017 — 973-4000
  Sr. Mary Weisensel, prin.
Brophy College Prep HS — 4-00011
  4707 N CENTRAL AVE 85012 — 264-5291
  Fr. Growney, prin.
Bryman School — 2-CS
  4343 N 16TH ST 85016 — 274-4300
CAD Institute/The CAD Center — 2-CS
  4100 E BROADWAY RD 85040 — 800-658-5744
Conservatory/Recording Arts & Sciences — 2-CS
  1110 E MISSOURI AVE STE 530 85014 — 265-5566
DeVry Institute of Technology — 6-UC
  2149 W DUNLAP AVE 85021 — 870-9201
Garfield Girls S, 4820 N 7TH AVE 85013 — 2-00111
   — 274-7413
Gateway Community College — 4-CC
  108 N 40TH ST 85034 — 275-8500
Grace Christian S — 2-11111
  2940 W BETHANY HOME RD 85017 — 242-2010
Grand Canyon University — 4-UC
  3300 W CAMELBACK RD 85017 — 249-3300
High-Tech Institute — 2-CC
  1515 E INDIAN SCHOOL RD 85014 — 279-9700
ITT Technical Institute — 3-CC
  4837 E MCDOWELL RD 85008 — 231-0871
Lamson Junior College — 3-CC
  2701 W BETHANY HOME RD 85017 — 433-2000
Landmark Christian Academy — 2-11111
  7040 S 40TH ST 85040 — 268-1207
Laurel School — 2-HMS
  PO BOX 5338 85010
Long Medical Institute — 2-CS
  4126 N BLACK CANYON HWY 85017 — 279-9333
Metropolitan College of Court Reporting — 2-CC
  4640 E CACTUS RD STE 12 85040 — 955-5900
Motorcycle Mechanics Institute — 2-CS
  2844 W DEER VALLEY RD 85027 — 869-9644
Mundus Institute — 2-CS
  4745 N 7TH ST STE 100 85014 — 248-8548
Paradise Valley Community College — 4-CC
  18401 N 32ND ST 85032 — 493-2600
Phoenix Christian HS — 2-00111
  1751 W INDIAN SCHOOL RD 85015 — 265-4707
  James Wright, prin.
Phoenix College — 6-CC
  1202 W THOMAS RD 85013 — 285-7433
Phoenix Country Day S — 3-11111
  PO BOX 15087 85060 — 955-8200
Phoenix Indian HS, PO BOX 10 85001 — 4-00011
  Richard Christman, prin. — 241-2126
Refrigeration School — 3-CS
  4210 E WASHINGTON ST 85034 — 275-7133
Rice Aviation — 2-CS
  3201 E BROADWAY RD 85040 — 800-736-7014
Rio Salado Community College — 5-CC
  640 N 1ST AVE 85003 — 223-4000
Roberto-Venn School of Luthiery — 1-CS
  4011 S 16TH ST 85040 — 243-1179
St. Joseph's Hospital & Medical Center — HSP
  350 W THOMAS RD 85013 — 285-3101
St. Marys HS, 2525 N 3RD ST 85004 — 3-00011
  William Lehman, prin. — 254-6371
San Pablo S, 4001 N 30TH AVE 85016 — 2-00111
   — 956-9090
South Mountain Community College — 4-CC
  7050 S 24TH ST 85040 — 243-8000
Southwestern College — 2-UC
  2625 E CACTUS RD 85032 — 992-6101
Sterling School — 1-CS
  801 E INDIAN SCHOOL RD 85014 — 277-5276
TPI Schools Paralegal Institute — 2-HMS
  PO BOX 11408 85061 — 272-1855

Universal Technical Institute — 5-CC
  3121 W WELDON AVE 85017 — 264-4164
University of Phoenix — 6-UC
  4615 E ELWOOD ST 85040 — 966-9577
Valley Lutheran HS — 2-00011
  525 W COLTER ST 85013 — 230-1600
  Norman Brauer, prin.
Western Christian S — 2-11111
  3830 N 67TH AVE 85033
Western International University — 4-UC
  10202 N 19TH AVE 85021 — 943-2311
Western Truck School — 2-CS
  1835 S BLACK CANYON HWY # 1 85009 — 437-5303
Xavier College Prep HS — 3-00011
  4710 N 5TH ST 85012 — 277-3772
  Sr. Joan Fitzgerald, prin.

Pima, AC 602, PC 4, Graham
Pima USD 6, PO BOX 429 85543 — 3-11111
  Stan Smith, supt. — 485-2421
JSHS, PO BOX 429 85543 — 2-00011
  Neil DeWitt, prin. — 485-2421

Prescott, AC 602, PC 8, Yavapai
Prescott USD 1 — 6-11111
  146 S GRANITE ST 86303 — 445-5400
  Dr. James Howard, supt.
HS, 1050 RUTH ST 86301 — 4-00011
  Glen Treadaway, prin. — 445-2322
Granite Mountain MS — 2-00100
  1800 WILLIAMSON VALLEY RD 86301 — 445-5400
  Michael Harlan, prin.
Prescott Mile High MS — 3-00100
  300 S GRANITE ST 86303 — 445-5400
  Jay Collier, prin.

Arizona Academy of Medical/Dental Asst. — 1-CS
  1020 SANDRETTO DR # A 86301 — 778-4382
Embry-Riddle Aeronautical University — 4-UC
  3200 WILLOW CREEK RD 86301 — 800-442-3728
Prescott College — 3-UC
  220 GROVE AVE 86301 — 778-2090
Yavapai College — 5-CC
  1100 E SHELDON ST 86301 — 445-7300

Queen Creek, AC 602, PC 5, Maricopa
Queen Creek USD 95 — 3-11111
  20435 S ELLSWORTH RD 85242 — 987-9600
  Ralph Pomeroy, supt.
HS, 20435 S ELLSWORTH RD 85242 — 2-00011
  Michael Fleishman, prin. — 987-3078
MS, 20435 S ELLSWORTH RD 85242 — 2-00100
  Steve Chambers, prin. — 987-0023

Sacaton, AC 602, PC 4, Pinal
Sacaton ESD 18, PO BOX 98 85247 — 3-11100
  Jacob Garcia, supt. — 562-3339
MS, PO BOX 98 85247 — 2-01100
  Mary Malm, prin. — 562-3339

Safford, AC 602, PC 6, Graham
Safford USD 1, 734 W 11TH ST 85546 — 5-11111
  Mark Tregaskes, supt. — 428-2950
HS, 734 W 11TH ST 85546 — 3-00011
  John Bonefas, prin. — 428-5999
JHS, 734 W 11TH ST 85546 — 2-00100
  John Vail, prin. — 428-3447

Sahuarita, AC 602, PC 3, Pima
Sahuarita USD 30, PO BOX 26 85629 — 4-11111
  Donald Wright, supt. — 625-3502
HS, PO BOX 26 85629 — 3-00011
  William McNarie, prin. — 648-1160
JHS, PO BOX 26 85629 — 2-00100
  Charles Oldham, prin. — 625-4249

Saint David, AC 602, PC 4, Cochise
Saint David USD 21 — 2-11111
  PO BOX 70 85630 — 720-4492
  Dr. Ronald Nelson, supt.
HS, PO BOX 70 85630 — 2-00011
  Jackie Branning, prin. — 720-4781

Saint Johns, AC 602, PC 5, Apache
Saint Johns USD 1 — 4-11111
  PO BOX 3030 85936 — 337-2255
  Manuel Madrid, supt.
HS, PO BOX 429 85936 — 2-00011
  James McLarney, prin. — 337-2221
MS, PO BOX 3060 85936 — 2-01100
  Ken Crosby, prin. — 337-2132

Saint Michaels, AC 602, PC 3, Apache

St. Michaels Indian HS — 2-11111
  PO BOX 650 86511 — 871-4443

Salome, AC 602, PC 3, La Paz
Bicentennial UNHSD 76 — 2-00011
  PO BOX 519 85348 — 859-3453
  Thomas Overman, supt.
HS, PO BOX 519 85348 — 2-00011
  (—), prin. — 859-3453

San Carlos, AC 602, PC 5, Gila
San Carlos USD 20 — 3-11111
  PO BOX 207 85550 — 475-2315
  Leon Ben, supt.
HS, PO BOX 207 85550 — 2-00011
  Charles Bent, prin. — 475-2378

Sanders, AC 602, PC 3, Apache
Sanders USD 18, PO BOX 250 86512 — 3-11111
  Matthew Levario, supt. — 688-2703

Valley HS, PO BOX 250 86512   2-00011
Ted Goodluck, prin.   688-2703
JHS, PO BOX 250 86512   2-00100
Duane Noggle, prin.   688-2703

San Manuel, AC 602, PC 5, Pinal
Mammoth/San Manuel USD 8   4-1111
PO BOX 406 85631   385-2335
Claude Sanders, supt.
HS, PO BOX 406 85631   3-00011
James Donaldson, prin.   385-2335
Gardner MS, PO BOX 406 85631   2-00100
H. Lunt, prin.   385-2335

San Simon, AC 602, PC 2, Cochise
San Simon USD 18   2-11111
PO BOX 38 85632   845-2275
Michael Reed, supt.
HS, PO BOX 38 85632   1-00011
(—), prin.   845-2275

Scottsdale, AC 602, PC 9, Maricopa
East Valley Institute of Technology SD
Supt. — See Mesa
EVIT Scottsdale Vo-Tech Ctr   Vo Tech
2501 N 74TH ST 85257   990-4361
Sue Bradley, prin.

Paradise Valley USD 69
Supt. — See Phoenix
Horizon HS   5-00011
5601 E GREENWAY RD 85254   953-4104
John Stollar, prin.
Desert Shadows MS   3-00100
5858 E SWEETWATER AVE 85254   493-6000
William Cooper, prin.
Sunrise MS, 4960 E ACOMA DR 85254   3-00100
James Lee, prin.   493-6030

Scottsdale USD 48
Supt. — See Phoenix
Chaparral HS   4-00011
6935 E GOLD DUST AVE 85253   443-7011
Kim Greenawalt, prin.
Coronado HS, 2501 N 74TH ST 85257   4-00011
Donald Enz, prin.   990-4304
Saguaro HS, 6250 N 82ND ST 85250   5-00011
Herman Serignese, prin.   443-7114
Cocopah MS, 6615 E CHOLLA ST 85254   4-00100
Sam Merrill, prin.   443-7800
Mohave MS, 5520 N 86TH ST 85250   3-00100
Carol Erickson, prin.   423-3700
Mountainside MS   3-00100
11256 N 128TH ST 85259   451-3400
John Kriekard, prin.
Supai MS   3-00100
6720 E CONTINENTAL DR 85257   423-3720
Bob Burger, prin.

Devereux Center in Arizona   HND
6436 E SWEETWATER AVE 85254   998-2920
Judson S, PO BOX 1569 85252   2-11111
Dennis Gray, prin.   948-7731
Scottsdale Community College   5-CC
9000 E CHAPARRAL RD 85250   423-6000
Scottsdale Culinary Institute   2-CS
8100 E CAMELBACK RD 85251   990-3773
Thunderbird Adventist Academy   2-00011
7410 E SUTTON DR 85260   948-3300
Wright School of Architecture   1-UC
TALIESIN WEST 85261   860-2700

Sedona, AC 602, PC 6, Coconino

Verde Valley S   2-00011
3511 VERDE VALLEY SCHOOL RD 86351
Jonathan Ulsh, prin.   284-2272

Seligman, AC 602, PC 3, Yavapai
Seligman USD 40, PO BOX 278 86337   2-11111
John Kennedy, supt.   422-3233
HS, PO BOX 278 86337   2-00011
John Kennedy, prin.   422-3233

Sells, AC 602, PC 5, Pima
Indian Oasis-Baboquivari USD 40   4-11111
PO BOX 248 85634   383-2601
Michael Ryan, supt.
Baboquivari HS, PO BOX 248 85634   2-00011
Sharon Walker, prin.   383-2601
Baboquivari JHS, PO BOX 248 85634   2-00100
Sharon Walker, prin.   383-2601

Show Low, AC 602, PC 6, Navajo
Show Low USD 10   4-11111
1350 N CENTRAL AVE 85901   537-2682
Norlis McKay, supt.
HS, 1350 N CENTRAL AVE 85901   2-00011
Bruce Hopmeier, prin.   537-2901
JHS, 1350 N CENTRAL AVE 85901   2-00100
Norman Ehmke, prin.   537-5140

Sierra Vista, AC 602, PC 8, Cochise
Sierra Vista USD 68   6-11111
3555 E FRY BLVD 85635   458-4391
Jon Lokensgard, supt.
Buena HS, 3555 E FRY BLVD 85635   5-00011
Frances Miller, prin.   458-7880
MS, 3555 E FRY BLVD 85635   4-00100
Donald Rothery, prin.   458-0712

Shiloh Christian S   2-11111
200 N NORTH AVE 85635   459-2869

Snowflake, AC 602, PC 5, Navajo
Snowflake USD 5   5-11111
PO BOX 1100 85937   536-4156
Monty Harris, supt.
HS, PO BOX 1100 85937   3-00011
Ronald Squire, prin.   536-4154
JHS, PO BOX 1100 85937   2-00100
Jesse Hughes, prin.   536-2163

Somerton, AC 602, PC 6, Yuma
Somerton ESD 11, PO BOX E 85350   4-11100
Judith Bobbitt, supt.   627-8831
MS, PO BOX E 85350   2-00100
Mark Bastin, prin.   627-3580

Springerville, AC 602, PC 4, Apache
Round Valley USD 10   4-11111
PO BOX 610 85938   333-2632
Dr. Robert McKenzie, supt.
Round Valley HS, PO BOX 610 85938   3-00011
Don Roth, prin.   333-4315
Round Valley MS, PO BOX 610 85938   3-00100
Darwin Rhoton, prin.   333-4515

Superior, AC 602, PC 5, Pinal
Superior USD 15   3-11111
199 N LOBB AVE 85273   689-5291
Richard Krempasky, supt.
HS, 98 N HIGH SCHOOL AVE 85273   2-00011
James Ryan, prin.   689-5252
Roosevelt MS, 199 N LOBB AVE 85273   2-00100
Henry Diulus, prin.   689-5221

Teec Nos Pos, AC 602, PC 2, Apache
Red Mesa USD 27   3-11111
HC 6100 BOX 40 86514   656-3511
Jerald Wray, supt.
Red Mesa HS, HC 6100 BOX 40 86514   2-00011
Loren Joseph, prin.   656-3511

Tempe, AC 602, PC 9, Maricopa
East Valley Institute of Technology SD
Supt. — See Mesa
EVIT Tempe Auto S   Vo Tech
1730 S MILL AVE 85281   967-1661
Victor Sanchez, prin.

Kyrene ESD 28   6-11100
8700 S KYRENE RD 85284   496-4600
Bradley Barrett, supt.
Kyrene MS, 8700 S KYRENE RD 85284   3-00100
Susan Capuano, prin.   496-4666
Other Schools – See Chandler, Phoenix

Tempe ESD 3, PO BOX 27708 85285   7-11100
(—), supt.   730-7100
Connolly IS   1-00100
2002 E CONCORDA DR 85282   967-8933
Ronald Izzett, prin.
Fees IS, 1600 E WATSON DR 85283   3-00100
John Reinhold, prin.   897-6063
Gilliland IS, 1025 S BECK AVE 85281   1-00100
Lucinda Ishmael, prin.   966-7114
McKemy IS, 2250 S COLLEGE AVE 85282   3-00100
Robert Cleckner, prin.   921-9003

Tempe UNHSD 213   6-00011
500 W GUADALUPE RD 85283   839-0292
James Buchanan, supt.
Corona Del Sol HS   5-00011
1001 E KNOX RD 85284   752-8888
Eldon Mailes, prin.
Marcos De Niza HS   4-00011
6000 S LAKESHORE DR 85283   838-3200
Richard Riley, prin.
McClintock HS   4-00011
1830 E DEL RIO DR 85282   839-4222
Lavern Tarkington, prin.
HS, 1730 S MILL AVE 85281   3-00011
Victor Sanchez, prin.   967-1661
Other Schools – See Phoenix

Al Collins Graphic Design School   2-UC
1140 S PRIEST DR 85281   966-3000
Arizona State University   8-UC
1 ASU 85287   965-5606
Pima Medical Institute   2-CS
2300 E BROADWAY RD 85282   345-7777
Valley Christian HS   2-00011
1515 S INDIAN BEND RD 85281   967-4196

Thatcher, AC 602, PC 5, Graham
Thatcher USD 4, PO BOX 610 85552   4-11111
Max Peck, supt.   428-6381
HS, PO BOX 610 85552   2-00011
Ralph Smith, prin.   428-0482
MS, PO BOX 610 85552   2-00100
Phil Martin, prin.   428-0515

Eastern Arizona College   4-CC
3714 W CHURCH ST 85552   428-8322
New Life Christian S   2-11111
8TH & 1ST AVES 85552   428-3671

Tolleson, AC 602, PC 5, Maricopa
Tolleson ESD 17, PO BOX 278 85353   3-11100
Terry Barrett, supt.   936-9740
MS, 9401 W GARFIELD ST 85353   2-01100
Lara Ruben, prin.   936-9747

Tolleson UNHSD 214   4-00011
9419 W VAN BUREN ST 85353   247-4222
George Sisemore, supt.
Tolleson Union HS   4-00011
9419 W VAN BUREN ST 85353   936-1276
Cynthia Rudrud, prin.
Other Schools – See Phoenix

Tombstone, AC 602, PC 4, Cochise
Tombstone USD 1   4-11111
PO BOX 1000 85638   457-2217
David Hrach, supt.
HS, PO BOX 1000 85638   2-00011
Frank Bell, prin.   457-2215

Tsaile, AC 602, PC 1, Apache

Navajo Community College 86556   4-CC
724-3311

Tuba City, AC 602, PC 5, Coconino
Tuba City USD 15, PO BOX 67 86045   5-11111
Hector Tahu, supt.   283-4211
HS, PO BOX 67 86045   4-00011
George Lee, prin.   283-4211
JHS, PO BOX 67 86045   2-00100
William Eddings, prin.   283-4211

Tucson, AC 602, PC 10, Pima
Amphitheater USD 10   7-11111
701 W WETMORE RD 85705   292-4200
Rick Wilson, supt.
Amphitheater HS   5-00011
125 W YAVAPAI RD 85705   292-4550
Ramon Paz, prin.
Canyon Del Oro HS   4-00011
25 W CALLE CONCORDIA 85737   292-5900
Richard Evers, prin.
Amphitheater MS   4-00100
315 E PRINCE RD 85705   292-4501
Robert Smith, prin.
Cross MS, 1000 W CHAPALA DR 85704   3-00100
Deborah Clark, prin.   292-4520
La Cima MS   3-00100
5600 N LA CANADA DR 85704   292-4530
Don Bridges, prin.

Catalina Foothills USD 16   4-11111
2101 E RIVER RD 85718   299-6446
David Ackerman, supt.
Catalina Foothills HS   2-00011
4300 E SUNRISE DR 85718   577-5090
Darrell Higman, prin.
Esperero Canyon MS   2-00100
5801 N SABINO CANYON RD 85715   577-5330
Kathy Scheppe, prin.
Orange Grove MS   2-00100
1911 E ORANGE GROVE RD 85718   577-5315
Mary Scheetz, prin.

Flowing Wells USD 8   6-11111
1556 W PRINCE RD 85705   690-2200
J. Robert Hendricks, supt.
Flowing Wells HS   4-00011
3725 N FLOWING WELLS RD 85705   690-2254
Nicholas Clement, prin.
Flowing Wells JHS   4-00100
4545 N LA CHOLLA BLVD 85705   690-2301
Karyn Blair, prin.

Marana USD 6
Supt. — See Marana
Marana HS, 12000 W EMIGH RD 85743   2-00011
Larry Gray, prin.   682-4141
Mountain View HS   3-00011
3901 W LINDA VISTA BLVD 85741   744-0961
Lynn Edwards, prin.
Tortolita JHS, 4101 W HARDY RD 85741   3-00100
David Santa Maria, prin.   744-2393

Sunnyside USD 12   7-11111
2238 E GINTER RD 85706   741-2500
Ernest Fimbres, supt.
Desert View HS   4-00011
4101 E VALENCIA RD 85706   741-2467
Keith Lawson, prin.
Sunnyside HS, 1725 E BILBY RD 85706   4-00011
Raul Nido, prin.   741-2400
Apollo HS, 265 W NEBRASKA ST 85706   3-00100
Judson Jones, prin.   741-2642
Chaparral MS, 3700 E ALVORD RD 85706   3-00100
Norma Garcia, prin.   741-2649
Sierra MS   4-00100
5801 S DEL MORAL BLVD 85706   741-2656
Susan Masek, prin.

Tanque Verde USD 13   4-11110
4201 N MELPOMENE WAY 85749   749-5751
Lewis Sorensen, supt.
Gray JHS   2-00110
4201 N MELPOMENE WAY 85749   749-3838
Tracy Reimer, prin.

Tucson USD 1, PO BOX 40400 85717   8-11111
George Garcia, supt.   882-2400
Catalina HS, 3645 E PIMA ST 85716   4-00011
Ingrid Miller, prin.   881-3150
Cholla HS, 2001 E 22ND ST 85713   4-00011
Thomas Scarborough, prin.   628-2320
Palo Verde HS   4-00011
1302 S AVENIDA VEGA 85710   745-4700
Larry Williams, prin.
Pueblo HS, 3500 S 12TH AVE 85713   4-00011
Lorraine Richardson, prin.   628-2300

Rincon HS, 421 N ARCADIA AVE 85711   4-00011
    Ed Arriaga, prin.   745-4740
Sabino HS, 5000 N BOWES RD 85749   4-00011
    Carl Roberts, prin.   749-8025
Sahuaro HS, 545 N CAMINO SECO 85710   4-00011
    Joan Richardson, prin.   721-6320
Santa Rita HS   4-00011
    3951 S PANTANO RD 85730   721-6300
    Patricia Hale, prin.
Tucson Magnet HS   4-00011
    400 N 2ND AVE 85705   882-2480
    Henry Lujan, prin.
University HS   2-00011
    421 N ARCADIA AVE 85711   745-4760
    Rick Larson, prin.
Booth/Fickett Math/Science MS   3-00100
    7240 E CALLE ARTURO 85710   798-2574
    John Michel, prin.
Carson MS, 7777 E STELLA RD 85730   3-00100
    Carol Smith, prin.   798-2640
Dodge MS, 5831 E PIMA ST 85712   2-00100
    Jim Green, prin.   798-2006
Doolen MS   3-00100
    2400 N COUNTRY CLUB RD 85716   798-2530
    Sara Cortez, prin.
Gridley MS, 350 S HARRISON RD 85748   3-00100
    Betsy Hansen, prin.   798-2613
Hohokam MS   2-00100
    7400 S SETTLER AVE 85746   798-2845
    Judith Hokett, prin.
Magee MS   2-00100
    8300 E SPEEDWAY BLVD 85710   798-2583
    Cochelle Dubs, prin.
Mansfeld MS, 1300 E 6TH ST 85719   2-00100
    Arnie Adler, prin.   798-2743
Maxwell MS   3-00100
    2802 W ANKLAM RD 85745   798-2751
    Don Collier, prin.
Naylor MS   3-00100
    1701 S COLUMBUS BLVD 85711   798-2669
    Mike Schwanenberger, prin.
Pistor MS, 2840 W CANADA ST 85746   3-00100
    David Ross, prin.   798-2711
Safford Magnet MS   3-00100
    300 S 5TH AVE 85701   798-2782
    Peggy Schroder, prin.
Secrist MS   2-00100
    3400 S HOUGHTON RD 85730   798-2591
    Richard Gastellum, prin.
Townsend MS   2-00100
    2120 N BEVERLY AVE 85712   798-2560
    Roy Baker, prin.
Utterback Magnet MS   3-00100
    3233 S PINAL VIS 85713   798-2794
    Ross Sheard, prin.
Vail MS, 5350 E 16TH ST 85711   3-00100
    Kelly Langford, prin.   798-2686
Wakefield MS, 101 W 44TH ST 85713   2-00100
    Barbara Benton, prin.   798-2802

ABC Technical and Trade Schools   2-CC
    3761 E TECHNICAL DR 85713   748-1762
American Teller Schools   2-CS
    4023 E GRANT RD # A 85712   881-1541
Apollo College   2-CS
    3870 N ORACLE RD 85705   888-5885
AZ State School for the Deaf & Blind   HND
    PO BOX 5545 85703   770-3719
Chaparral Career College   3-CS
    4585 E SPEDWAY BLVD STE 204 85712
                                       327-6866
Desert Hills S   2-00111
    5245 N CAMINO DE OESTE 85745   882-7551
Desert Institute of the Healing Arts   2-CS
    639 N 6TH AVE 85705   882-0879

Fenster S of Southern Arizona   1-00011
    8500 E OCOTILLO DR 85715   749-3340
    Don Saffer, prin.
Golf Links Christian Academy   2-11111
    6902 E GOLF LINKS RD 85730   790-7082
Green Fields Country Day S   2-01111
    6000 N CAMINO DE LA TIERRA 85741 297-2288
Immaculate Heart HS   2-00011
    625 E MAGEE RD 85704   297-2851
    Sr. Luisa Sanchez, prin.
ITT Technical Institute   3-CC
    1840 E BENSON HWY 85714   294-2944
Lamson Business College   2-CS
    6367 E TANQUE VERDE RD #100 85715
                                       327-6851
Parks College   CC
    6992 E BROADWAY BLVD 85710   886-7979
Pima Community College   7-CC
    2202 W ANKLAM RD 85709   884-6047
Pima Medical Institute   1-CS
    3350 E GRANT RD 85716   326-1600
St. Gregory College Preparatory S   2-00111
    3231 N CRAYCROFT RD 85712   327-6395
    Donald Nickerson, prin.
St. Mary's Hospital   HSP
    1601 W SAINT MARYS RD 85745   622-5833
Salpointe Catholic HS   4-00011
    1545 E COPPER ST 85719   327-6581
    Fr. Leo McCarthy, prin.
Tucson College of Business   2-CS
    7310 E 22ND ST 85710   296-3261
University of Arizona 85721   8-UC
                                       621-2211
University of Arizona Medical Center   UC
    1501 N CAMPBELL AVE 85724
Vision Quest Learning Center   2-00011
    PO BOX 12948 85732

Tumacacori, AC 602, PC 2, Santa Cruz
Santa Cruz Valley USD 35   3-11100
    PO BOX 187 85640   281-8282
    Robert Brown, supt.
Calabasas MS, PO BOX 187 85640   2-00100
    Dan Fontes, prin.   281-8585

Vail, AC 602, PC 2, Pima
Vail ESD 20, PO BOX 800 85641   3-11100
    Calvin Baker, supt.   762-5181
Old Vail MS, PO BOX 800 85641   3-00100
    Debra D'Amore, prin.   762-5181

Wellton, AC 602, PC 4, Yuma
Antelope UNHSD 50   2-00011
    9168 S AVENUE 36 E 85356   785-3344
    Sidney Grande, supt.
Antelope Union HS   2-00011
    9168 S AVENUE 36 E 85356   785-3344
    Randy O'Donnell, prin.

West Sedona, AC 602, PC see Sedona

Oak Creek Ranch School   1-00111
    PO BOX NN 86340 – Jay Wick, prin. 634-5571

Whiteriver, AC 602, PC 4, Navajo
Whiteriver USD 20   4-11111
    PO BOX 190 85941   338-4842
    John Clark, supt.
Alchesay HS, PO BOX 190 85941   3-00011
    Tracy Carrington, prin.   338-4848
MS, PO BOX 190 85941   2-00100
    John Brach, prin.   338-4138

Wickenburg, AC 602, PC 5, Maricopa
Wickenburg USD 9   4-11111
    PO BOX 1418 85358   684-5556
    Patrick Schrader, supt.

HS, 251 S TEGNER ST 85390   3-00011
    Orin Fulton, prin.   684-2841
Vulture Peak MS   2-01100
    925 S VULTURE MINE RD 85390   684-7808
    Michael Helminski, prin.

Willcox, AC 602, PC 5, Cochise
Willcox USD 13   4-11111
    480 N BISBEE AVE 85643   384-4211
    Lynn Setterstedt-Jarrett, supt.
HS, 240 N BISBEE AVE 85643   2-00011
    Bob Nelson, prin.   384-4214
MS, 360 N BISBEE AVE 85643   2-01100
    J. Williams, prin.   384-4218

Williams, AC 602, PC 5, Coconino
Williams USD 2, 515 S 9TH ST 86046   3-11111
    Roger Short, supt.   635-4473
HS, 440 S 7TH ST 86046   2-00011
    Glen Hadlock, prin.   635-4474

Winkelman, AC 602, PC 3, Gila
Hayden/Winkelman USD 41   3-11111
    PO BOX 409 85292   356-7876
    Charles Lemley, supt.
Hayden HS, PO BOX 409 85292   2-00011
    David Lagunas, prin.   356-7876
Hambly JHS, PO BOX 409 85292   1-00100
    David Lagunas, prin.   356-7876

Winslow, AC 602, PC 6, Navajo
Winslow USD 1, PO BOX 580 86047   5-11111
    Gary Calhoun, supt.   289-3375
HS, PO BOX 580 86047   3-00011
    Paul Reynolds, prin.   289-3371
JHS, PO BOX 580 86047   2-00100
    Harvey Cassidy, prin.   289-3347

Young, AC 602, PC 3, Gila
Young ESD 5, PO BOX 390 85554   1-11111
    Sharon Friauf, supt.   462-3244
Young Teaching HS   1-00011
    PO BOX 390 85554   462-3244
    Sharon Friauf, prin.

Yuma, AC 602, PC 8, Yuma
Crane ESD 13, 4250 W 16TH ST 85364   5-11100
    Gary Knox, supt.   782-5183
Crane JHS, 3175 S 45TH AVE 85364   3-00100
    Robert Klee, prin.   726-0553

Yuma ESD 1, 450 W 6TH ST 85364   6-11100
    Thomas McCraley, supt.   782-6581
Fourth Avenue JHS   3-00100
    450 S 4TH AVE 85364   783-2193
    William Roberts, prin.
Gila Vista JHS   2-00100
    2245 S ARIZONA AVE 85364   782-5174
    Tom Tyree, prin.
Woodard JHS, 2250 S 8TH AVE 85364   3-00100
    Wes Vandenburg, prin.   782-6546

Yuma UNHSD 70   6-00011
    3150 S AVENUE A 85364   726-1733
    Perry Hill, supt.
Cibola HS, 4100 W 20TH ST 85364   2-00011
    Gary Wiersema, prin.   783-7837
Kofa HS, 3100 S AVENUE A 85364   5-00011
    George Voorhis, prin.   726-5750
HS, 400 S 6TH AVE 85364   5-00011
    Wes VanDenburg, prin.   782-1881

Arizona Western College   4-CC
    PO BOX 929 85366   726-1000

ARKANSAS

STATE DEPARTMENT OF EDUCATION
State Education Building
4 State Capitol Mall, Little Rock 72201
(501) 682-4475

Director of Education	Gene Wilhoit
Deputy Director of Education	John Fincher
Associate Director Federal Programs	Clarence Lovell
Associate Director Finance & Administration	Robert Shaver
Associate Director School Improvement	Emma Bass
Associate Director Human Resources	Clemetta Hood
Associate Director Special Education	Diane Sydoriak
Associate Director Accountability	Rodger Callahan

STATE BOARD OF EDUCATION
4 State Capitol Mall, Little Rock 72201

Chairperson   Elaine Scott

PUBLIC, PRIVATE AND CATHOLIC SECONDARY SCHOOLS

Alma, AC 501, PC 5, Crawford
Alma SD, PO BOX 2359 72921 — 4-11111
  Charles Dyer, supt. — 632-4791
HS, PO BOX 2139 72921 — 3-00011
  Jerry Valentine, prin. — 632-2162
MS, PO BOX 2229 72921 — 3-00100
  Ron Newton, prin. — 632-2168

Alpena, AC 501, PC 2, Boone
Alpena SD, PO BOX 270 72611 — 2-11111
  Norman Marvell, supt. — 437-2220
JSHS, PO BOX 270 72611 — 2-00111
  Richard Nance, prin. — 437-2220

Altheimer, AC 501, PC 3, Jefferson
USD, PO BOX N 72004 — 3-11111
  Cortez Smith, supt. — 766-8358
Altheimer-Sherrill JSHS — 2-00111
PO BOX N 72004 — 766-8248
  Robert McGhee, prin.

Altus, AC 501, PC 2, Franklin
Altus-Denning SD — 2-11111
PO BOX 339 72821 — 468-2231
  Shirley Little, supt.
Altus-Denning JSHS — 2-00111
PO BOX 339 72821 — 468-6111
  Terry Lusinger, prin.

Amity, AC 501, PC 3, Clark
Amity SD, PO BOX 67 71921 — 2-11111
  Bill Livingston, supt. — 342-5323
JSHS, PO BOX 67 71921 — 2-00111
  Deric Owens, prin. — 342-5323

Arkadelphia, AC 501, PC 7, Clark
Arkadelphia SD, 235 N 11TH ST 71923 — 4-11111
  Daniel Slay, supt. — 246-5564
SHS, HIGHWAY 8 71923 — 2-00001
  Troy Garlin, prin. — 246-7373
Goza JHS, 1305 CADDO ST 71923 — 3-00110
  Virginia Anderson, prin. — 246-4291

Henderson State University — 5-UC
1100 HENDERSON ST 71999 — 246-5511
Ouachita Baptist University — 4-UC
410 OUACHITA ST 71998 — 246-4531

Arkansas City, AC 501, PC 3, Desha
Arkansas City SD, PO BOX 248 71630 — 2-11111
  Gene Gregory, supt. — 877-2491
JSHS, PO BOX 248 71630 — 1-00111
  A. Hooks, prin. — 877-2474

Armorel, AC 501, PC 2, Mississippi
Armorel SD, PO BOX 99 72310 — 2-11111
  Kathy Lee, supt. — 763-6639
JSHS, PO BOX 99 72310 — 1-00111
  George Lawson, prin. — 763-6639

Ashdown, AC 501, PC 6, Little River
Ashdown SD, 511 N 2ND ST 71822 — 4-11111
  William Stringer, supt. — 898-3208
SHS, 751 RANKIN ST 71822 — 2-00001
  Judy Dowdy, prin. — 898-3562

JHS, 600 S ELLEN DR 71822 — 2-00110
  Sam Bray, prin. — 898-5138

Atkins, AC 501, PC 5, Pope
Atkins SD, 304 AVENUE 2 NW 72823 — 4-11111
  Alton Davidson, supt. — 641-7871
JSHS, 304 AVENUE 2 NW 72823 — 3-00111
  Robert Travis, prin. — 641-7871

Augusta, AC 501, PC 5, Woodruff
Augusta SD, 222 LOCUST ST 72006 — 3-11111
  Hershel Hooks, supt. — 347-2241
JSHS, 1011 MAIN ST 72006 — 2-00111
  Paul Morara, prin. — 347-2515

Bald Knob, AC 501, PC 5, White
Bald Knob SD, 103 W PARK AVE 72010 — 4-11111
  Jeff Heverling, supt. — 724-3361
JSHS, 103 W PARK AVE 72010 — 3-00111
  Dan Brackett, prin. — 724-3843

Barton, AC 501, PC 1, Phillips
Barton-Lexa SD, PO BOX 97 72312 — 3-11111
  Roy Kirkland, supt. — 572-7294
Barton JSHS, PO BOX 97 72312 — 2-00111
  David Bagley, prin. — 572-6867

Batesville, AC 501, PC 6, Independence
Batesville SD, 330 E COLLEGE ST 72501 — 4-11111
  Kenneth James, supt. — 793-6831
SHS, 1 SCHOOL RD 72501 — 3-00001
  Ron Coots, prin. — 793-6846
JHS, 2 SCHOOL RD 72501 — 3-00110
  Dan Yeager, prin. — 793-7533

Southside SD, 70 SCOTT DR 72501 — 3-11111
  Robert Calvery, supt. — 251-2341
Southside HS, 70 SCOTT DR 72501 — 2-00001
  Ted Hall, prin. — 251-2662
Southside MS, 70 SCOTT DR 72501 — 2-01100
  Tim Sisk, prin. — 251-2332

Arkansas College — 3-UC
2300 HIGHLAND RD 72501 — 800-423-2542
North Arkansas Community College — 1-CC
PO BOX 2404 72503 — 793-4919

Bauxite, AC 501, PC 2, Saline
Bauxite SD, PO BOX 345 72011 — 3-11111
  J. Ford, supt. — 557-5453
JSHS, PO BOX 345 72011 — 2-00111
  John Lowry, prin. — 557-5303

Bay, AC 501, PC 4, Craighead
Bay SD, PO BOX 39 72411 — 3-11111
  Forrest Jackson, supt. — 781-3711
Bay JSHS, PO BOX 39 72411 — 2-00111
  Jim Canada, prin. — 781-3772

Bearden, AC 501, PC 4, Ouachita
Bearden SD, PO BOX 195 71720 — 3-11111
  Don Cain, supt. — 687-2236
HS, PO BOX 195 71720 — 2-00011
  Charles Jones, prin. — 687-2913

MS, PO BOX 195 71720 — 2-01100
  Levenis Penix, prin. — 687-3503

Beebe, AC 501, PC 5, White
Beebe SD, 1201 W CENTER ST 72012 — 4-11111
  Floyd Lee Marshall, supt. — 882-5463
SHS, 1201 W CENTER ST 72012 — 2-00001
  Gary Washington, prin. — 882-3311
JHS, 1201 W CENTER ST 72012 — 2-00110
  Scott Embrey, prin. — 882-5487

Arkansas State University — 4-CC
PO BOX H 72012 — 882-6452

Bee Branch, AC 501, PC 2, Van Buren
South Side SD, RR 1 BOX 110 72013 — 2-11111
  Waco Sutterfield, supt. — 654-2633
Southside JSHS, RR 1 BOX 110 72013 — 2-00111
  Robert Stewart, prin. — 654-8113

Benton, AC 501, PC 7, Saline
Benton SD, PO BOX 939 72018 — 5-11111
  Frank Chenault, supt. — 778-4861
SHS, 211 N BORDER ST 72015 — 3-00001
  John Butler, prin. — 778-3288
JHS, 411 N BORDER ST 72015 — 3-00110
  Alan Tollett, prin. — 778-7698

Harmony Grove SD — 3-11111
2621 HIGHWAY 229 72015 — 778-6271
  Daniel Henley, supt.
Harmony Grove JSHS — 2-00111
2621 HIGHWAY 229 72015 — 776-2337
  William Gibbs, prin.

Bentonville, AC 501, PC 7, Benton
Bentonville SD, 400 NW 2ND ST 72712 — 5-11111
  Lewis Holloway, supt. — 271-1100
SHS, 402 TIGER BLVD 72712 — 3-00001
  Jim White, prin. — 271-1116
Walton JHS, 1501 CUB AVE 72712 — 3-00110
  Randy Mattingly, prin. — 271-1127

Bergman, AC 501, PC 2, Boone
Bergman SD, GENERAL DELIVERY 72615 — 3-11111
  Richard Holbert, supt. — 741-5213
JSHS, GENERAL DELIVERY 72615 — 2-00111
  Larry McKinney, prin. — 741-1414

Berryville, AC 501, PC 5, Carroll
Berryville SD, PO BOX 408 72616 — 4-11111
  Jack Leatherman, supt. — 423-3311
JSHS, PO BOX 408 72616 — 3-00111
  Everett Smith, prin. — 423-3312

Bigelow, AC 501, PC 2, Perry
East End SD, PO BOX B 72016 — 3-11111
  John Jordan, supt. — 759-2808
East End JSHS, PO BOX 164 72016 — 2-00111
  Mark Tyler, prin. — 759-2602

Biggers, AC 501, PC 2, Randolph
Biggers-Reyno SD, PO BOX 82 72413 — 2-11111
  J. Edington, supt. — 769-2480

Biggers-Reyno JSHS
PO BOX 82　72413
Randall Nicholson, prin.
2-00111
769-2480

Bismarck, AC 501, PC 2, Hot Spring
Bismark SD, RR 1 BOX 208　71929
James Guffey, supt.
3-11111
865-4888
JSHS, RR 1 BOX 208　71929
Ron Wright, prin.
2-00111
865-4541

Black Rock, AC 501, PC 3, Lawrence
Black Rock SD, PO BOX 240　72415
B. Maxwell, supt.
2-11111
878-6273
JSHS, PO BOX 240　72415
Mike Oldham, prin.
2-00111
878-6461

Blevins, AC 501, PC 2, Hempstead
Blevins SD, PO BOX 98　71825
Lavon Flaherty, supt.
2-11111
874-2801
JSHS, PO BOX 98　71825
Robert Davis, prin.
2-00111
874-2281

Blytheville, AC 501, PC 7, Mississippi
Blytheville SD, 200 S LAKE ST　72315
Frank Ladd, supt.
5-11111
762-2053
SHS, 600 N 10TH ST　72315
Tom Coleman, prin.
3-00001
762-2772
East JHS, 216 E MOULTRIE DR　72315
Idell Jenkins, prin.
2-00110
763-5924
West JHS, 700 CHICKASAWBA ST　72315
Leslie Tolley, prin.
3-00110
762-2983

Mississippi County Community College
PO BOX 1109　72316
4-CC
762-1020

Booneville, AC 501, PC 5, Logan
Booneville SD, PO BOX 88　72927
Stewart Scoggin, supt.
4-11111
675-3504
JSHS, 835 E 8TH ST　72927
Webster Watts, prin.
3-00111
675-3277

Bradford, AC 501, PC 3, White
Bradford SD, PO BOX 60　72020
Arthur Dunn, supt.
3-11111
344-2707
JSHS, PO BOX 60　72020
Donald Swiney, prin.
2-00111
344-2607

Bradley, AC 501, PC 3, Lafayette
Bradley SD, PO BOX 380　71826
Forrest Kyle, supt.
3-11111
894-3313
JSHS, PO BOX 380　71826
J. Gardenhire, prin.
2-00111
894-3316

Branch, AC 501, PC 2, Franklin
County Line SD, RR 1 BOX 105　72928
Kay Johnson, supt.
3-11111
635-2222
County Line JSHS
RR 1 BOX 105　72928
Jim Loyd, prin.
2-00111
635-2441

Briggsville, AC 501, PC 1, Yell
Fourche Valley SD
HC 69 BOX 138　72828
Jack O'Reilly, supt.
2-11111
299-4425
Fourche Valley JSHS
HC 69 BOX 138　72828
Ralph Edds, prin.
1-00111
299-4425

Brinkley, AC 501, PC 5, Monroe
Brinkley SD, PO BOX 807　72021
Bobbie Davis, supt.
4-11111
734-3761
JSHS, PO BOX 807　72021
Glen King, prin.
3-00111
734-3464

Brockwell, AC 501, PC 1, Izard
Izard County Consolidated SD
PO BOX 115　72517
Fred Walker, supt.
3-11111
258-7700
Izard County Consolidated JSHS
PO BOX 115　72517
Randy Willison, prin.
2-00111
258-7788

Brookland, AC 501, PC 3, Craighead
Brookland SD, PO BOX 35　72417
Bob Clark, supt.
3-11111
932-2080
JSHS, PO BOX 35　72417
Larry Nowlin, prin.
2-00111
932-8610

Bryant, AC 501, PC 6, Saline
Bryant SD, 200 NW 4TH ST　72022
Diana Julian, supt.
6-11111
847-2579
SHS, 200 NW 4TH ST　72022
Dan Spadoni, prin.
4-00001
847-3522
JHS, 200 NW 4TH ST　72022
Al Polsgrove, prin.
4-00110
847-8652

Cabot, AC 501, PC 6, Lonoke
Cabot SD, 404 N 2ND ST　72023
Larry Rogers, supt.
5-11111
843-3363
HS, 504 E LOCUST ST　72023
Jack Carrington, prin.
4-00011
843-3562
JHS, 38 PANTHER TRL　72023
Brooks Nash, prin.
3-00100
843-2788

Calico Rock, AC 501, PC 3, Izard
Calico Rock SD, PO BOX 240　72519
Paul Wilson, supt.
2-11111
297-8533
JSHS, PO BOX 240　72519
Mike Seay, prin.
2-00111
297-3745

Camden, AC 501, PC 7, Ouachita
Camden-Fairview SD
625 CLIFTON ST　71701
George Branch, supt.
4-11111
836-4193

Fairview SHS
2708 MOUNT HOLLY RD　71701
Paul Brewer, prin.
3-00001
231-5461
Fairview JHS
647 JEFFERSON DR NW　71701
Skip Redmond, prin.
2-00110
836-9361

Harmony Grove SD
401 OUACHITA ROAD 88　71701
Carlos Price, supt.
3-11111
574-0971
Harmony Grove JSHS
401 OUACHITA ROAD 88　71701
Harold Davidson, prin.
2-00111
574-0867

Caraway, AC 501, PC 4, Craighead
Riverside SD
Supt. — See Lake City
Riverside JSHS, PO BOX 699　72419
Gale Yates, prin.
2-00110
482-3327

Carlisle, AC 501, PC 4, Lonoke
Carlisle SD, PO BOX O　72024
Leon Miles, supt.
3-11111
552-3931
JSHS, PO BOX O　72024
Randall Carter, prin.
2-00111
552-3196

Carthage, AC 501, PC 2, Dallas
Carthage SD, PO BOX 16　71725
Randy King, supt.
2-11111
254-2231
JSHS, PO BOX 16　71725
Norma Bartel, prin.
1-00111
254-2231

Casa, AC 501, PC 2, Perry
Perry-Casa SD, PO BOX B　72025
Thomas McCormick, supt.
2-11111
233-6411
Perry-Casa JSHS, PO BOX B　72025
Sherry Holliman, prin.
1-00111
233-6214

Cave City, AC 501, PC 4, Sharp
Cave City SD, PO BOX 600　72521
David Green, supt.
3-11111
283-5391
JSHS, PO BOX 600　72521
Larry Brown, prin.
2-00111
283-5392

Cedarville, AC 501, PC 2, Crawford
Cedarville SD, PO BOX 97　72932
Melvin Landers, supt.
3-11111
474-7220
JSHS, PO BOX 97　72932
Glennis Cook, prin.
2-00111
474-7021

Center Ridge, AC 501, PC 2, Conway
Nemo Vista SD, RR 1 BOX 8　72027
Bill Jackson, supt.
2-11111
893-2925
Nemo Vista JSHS, RR 1 BOX 8　72027
Bill Jackson, prin.
2-00111
893-2811

Charleston, AC 501, PC 4, Franklin
Charleston SD, PO BOX 188　72933
Charles Harris, supt.
3-11111
965-7160
JSHS, PO BOX 188　72933
Ashley Whitman, prin.
2-00111
965-7150

Charlotte, AC 501, PC 1, Independence
Cord-Charlotte SD
225 SCHOOL RD　72522
Jerrell Lillard, supt.
2-11111
799-3704
Cord-Charlotte JSHS
225 SCHOOL RD　72522
Hirschel Jones, prin.
1-00111
799-3051

Cherry Valley, AC 501, PC 3, Cross
Cross County SD, PO BOX 158　72324
Charles Moore, supt.
3-11111
588-3338
Cross County JSHS
PO BOX 158　72324
Edith Fisher, prin.
2-00111
588-3337

Clarendon, AC 501, PC 4, Monroe
Clarendon SD, PO BOX 248　72029
Robert Stone, supt.
3-11111
747-3351
JSHS, PO BOX 248　72029
Dighton Ewan, prin.
2-00111
747-5255

Clarksville, AC 501, PC 6, Johnson
Clarksville SD, 1701 CLARK RD　72830
Dean Pitts, supt.
4-11111
754-8454
SHS, 1701 CLARK RD　72830
Mike Gunn, prin.
2-00001
754-2450
JHS, 1801 CLARK RD　72830
Tom Richardson, prin.
2-00110
754-6766

University of the Ozarks
415 N COLLEGE AVE　72830
3-UC
754-3839

Clinton, AC 501, PC 4, Van Buren
Alread SD, RR 3 BOX 173　72031
James McGaha, supt.
1-11111
745-5337
Alread JSHS, RR 3 BOX 173　72031
Bob Pack, prin.
1-00111
745-5337

Clinton SD, RR 6 BOX 98　72031
Truett Love, supt.
4-11111
745-2135
HS, RR 6 BOX 98　72031
Dwight Hutto, prin.
2-00011
745-4125
MS, RR 6 BOX 103-2　72031
Polly Johnson, prin.
2-01100
745-4744

Coal Hill, AC 501, PC 3, Johnson
Westside SD, PO BOX 189　72832
Jerry Smith, supt.
3-11111
497-1171
Westside JSHS, PO BOX 189　72832
Bolin Stewart, prin.
2-00111
497-1171

Concord, AC 501, PC 2, Cleburne
Concord SD, PO BOX 10　72523
Ed Bradberry, supt.
3-11111
668-3844

JSHS, PO BOX 358　72523
J. West, prin.
2-00111
668-3522

Conway, AC 501, PC 8, Faulkner
Conway SD, 2220 PRINCE ST　72032
Raymond Simon, supt.
5-11111
450-4800
SHS, 2300 PRINCE ST　72032
John Tyler, prin.
4-00001
450-4880
JHS, 1815 PRINCE ST　72032
Gerald Harrison, prin.
3-00110
450-4860

Central Baptist College
CBC STATION　72032
2-UC
329-6872
Hendrix College
1601 HARKRIDER ST　72032
4-UC
329-6811
St. Joseph HS, 1115 COLLEGE AVE　72032
Peter Stubbs, prin.
2-00111
329-5741
University of Central Arkansas
201 DONAGHEY AVE　72035
6-UC
329-2931

Corning, AC 501, PC 5, Clay
Corning SD, PO BOX 479　72422
Hollis Brown, supt.
4-11111
857-6818
JSHS, PO BOX 479　72422
Bob Miller, prin.
3-00111
857-3041

Cotter, AC 501, PC 3, Baxter
Cotter SD, PO BOX 70　72626
Robert Hackler, supt.
3-11111
435-6171
JSHS, PO BOX 70　72626
Charles Huddleston, prin.
2-00111
435-6323

Cotton Plant, AC 501, PC 4, Woodruff
Cotton Plant SD, PO BOX 40　72036
Randall James, supt.
2-11111
459-2081
JSHS, PO BOX 40　72036
W. Smith, prin.
2-00111
459-3471

Cove, AC 501, PC 2, Polk
Van Cove SD, PO BOX 69　71937
Jerry Shinn, supt.
2-11111
387-7961
Van-Cove JSHS, PO BOX 69　71937
Max Adcock, prin.
2-00111
387-2744

Crawfordsville, AC 501, PC 3, Crittenden
Crawfordsville SD, PO BOX 47　72327
Lois Croom, supt.
3-11111
823-5577
JSHS, PO BOX 46　72327
William Harden, prin.
2-00111
823-5533

Crossett, AC 501, PC 6, Ashley
Crossett SD, 301 W 9TH AVE　71635
Barbara Gates, supt.
5-11111
364-3112
SHS, 301 W 9TH AVE　71635
Roosevelt Early, prin.
3-00001
364-2625
Norman JHS, 301 W 9TH AVE　71635
Wendell Gibson, prin.
2-00110
364-4712

Cushman, AC 501, PC 2, Independence
Cushman SD, PO BOX 128　72526
Gary Anderson, supt.
2-11111
793-7266
JSHS, PO BOX 128　72526
Roger Ried, prin.
2-00111
793-6321

Danville, AC 501, PC 4, Yell
Danville SD, PO BOX 939　72833
Ted Lyons, supt.
3-11111
495-2333
JSHS, PO BOX 939　72833
Bradley Spikes, prin.
2-00111
495-2221

Dardanelle, AC 501, PC 5, Yell
Dardanelle SD, 209 CEDAR ST　72834
James Braden, supt.
4-11111
229-4111
HS, RR 2 BOX 1　72834
Marcia Lawrence, prin.
2-00111
229-4655
MS, RR 2 BOX 2　72834
Avis Cotton, prin.
2-00100
229-4550

Decatur, AC 501, PC 3, Benton
Decatur SD, PO BOX 97　72722
Joe Brown, supt.
2-11111
752-3986
JSHS, PO BOX 97　72722
Charles Waldrip, prin.
2-00111
752-3985

Deer, AC 501, PC 2, Newton
Deer SD, PO BOX 56　72628
Richard Denniston, supt.
2-11111
428-5433
JSHS, PO BOX 56　72628
Anthony Sweeney, prin.
2-00111
428-5288

Delaplaine, AC 501, PC 2, Greene
Delaplaine SD, PO BOX 68　72425
William Wilkinson, supt.
2-11111
249-3898
JSHS, PO BOX 68　72425
Donald Hardin, prin.
2-00111
249-3216

Delight, AC 501, PC 2, Pike
Delight SD, PO BOX 8　71940
Randy Hughes, supt.
2-11111
379-2214
JSHS, PO BOX 8　71940
David Combs, prin.
2-00111
379-2214

De Queen, AC 501, PC 5, Sevier
De Queen SD, PO BOX 950　71832
Bill Blackwood, supt.
4-11111
584-4312
HS, RR 4　71832
Merle Dickerson, prin.
2-00111
642-2426
MS, RR 4　71832
Tony Beltrani, prin.
2-00100
642-2428

Dermott, AC 501, PC 5, Chicot
Dermott SD, PO BOX 368　71638
Alton Gaston, supt.
4-11111
538-5264
SHS, PO BOX 368　71638
Archie Nimmer, prin.
2-00001
538-3291

JHS, PO BOX 368 71638 2-00110
Darrell Porter, prin. 538-3252

Des Arc, AC 501, PC 4, Prairie
Des Arc SD, RR 2 BOX A 72040 3-11111
Carroll Denton, supt. 256-4164
JSHS, RR 2 BOX A 72040 2-00111
Jerry Hinson, prin. 256-4166

De Valls Bluff, AC 501, PC 3, Prairie
De Valls Bluff SD, PO BOX 298 72041 2-11111
L. Gershner, supt. 998-2412
JSHS, PO BOX 298 72041 2-00111
Charles Eads, prin. 998-2361

De Witt, AC 501, PC 5, Arkansas
De Witt SD, 204 N JACKSON ST 72042 4-11111
Tom Cox, supt. 946-3576
HS, 204 N JACKSON ST 72042 2-00011
Tom Davis, prin. 946-4661
MS, 301 N JACKSON ST 72042 2-00100
Tim Walton, prin. 946-3708

Dierks, AC 501, PC 4, Howard
Dierks SD, PO BOX 124 71833 3-11111
Wayne Freppon, supt. 286-2191
JSHS, PO BOX 124 71833 2-00111
Gordon Allen, prin. 286-3234

Doddridge, AC 501, PC 2, Miller
Bright Star SD, RR 1 BOX 222 71834 2-11111
Leo Garrison, supt. 691-2800
Bright Star JSHS 2-00111
RR 1 BOX 222 71834 691-2342
Ted Brewer, prin.

Donaldson, AC 501, PC 2, Hot Spring
Ouachita SD, RR 1 BOX 32 71941 2-11111
Penny Ferguson, supt. 384-2318
Ouachita JSHS, RR 1 BOX 33 71941 2-00111
Betty Tidwell, prin. 384-2323

Dover, AC 501, PC 4, Pope
Dover SD, PO BOX 325 72837 3-11111
Richard Paul, supt. 331-2916
JSHS, PO BOX 325 72837 3-00111
Jamie Churchill, prin. 331-2120

Dumas, AC 501, PC 6, Desha
Dumas SD, PO BOX 8880 71639 4-11111
Don McHan, supt. 382-4571
SHS, PO BOX 8880 71639 3-00001
Mike Ratcliff, prin. 382-4151
JHS, PO BOX 8880 71639 3-00110
Carl Brewer, prin. 382-4476

Earle, AC 501, PC 5, Crittenden
Earle SD, PO BOX 637 72331 4-11111
Jack Crumbly, supt. 792-8486
JSHS, PO BOX 637 72331 2-00111
Rickey Nicks, prin. 792-8716

East Camden, AC 501, PC 3, Ouachita

Southern Arkansas University 3-CC
PO BOX 3048 71701 574-4500

Elaine, AC 501, PC 3, Phillips
Elaine SD, PO BOX 179 72333 3-11111
Kenneth Parker, supt. 827-6395
JSHS, PO BOX 419 72333 2-00111
Lucien Webster, prin. 827-6345

El Dorado, AC 501, PC 7, Union
El Dorado SD, 200 W OAK ST 71730 6-11111
Bob Watson, supt. 864-5001
HS, 501 TIMBERLANE DR 71730 3-00011
David Kellogg, prin. 864-5100
Barton SD, 400 W FAULKNER ST 71730 3-00011
Genevieve Fouse, prin. 864-5051
Rogers MS, 601 S QUAKER AVE 71730 3-00100
Nelson Post, prin. 864-5032

Parkers Chapel SD 3-11111
401 PARKERS CHAPEL RD 71730 862-4641
John Gross, supt.
Parkers Chapel JSHS 2-00111
401 PARKERS CHAPEL RD 71730 862-2360
P. Griffin, prin.

Union SD, 6049 MORO BAY HWY 71730 2-11111
Bruce Griffin, supt. 863-6671
Union JSHS 2-00111
6049 MORO BAY HWY 71730 863-8472
Eric Armour, prin.

Southern Arkansas University 2-CC
300 S WEST AVE 71730 862-8131
West Side Christian S 2-11111
2400 W HILLSBORO ST 71730 863-5636
Ray Smith, prin.

Elkins, AC 501, PC 3, Washington
Elkins SD, PO BOX 322 72727 3-11111
John Smith, supt. 643-2172
JSHS, PO BOX 322 72727 2-00111
Robert Allen, prin. 643-3381

Emerson, AC 501, PC 2, Columbia
Emerson SD, PO BOX 129 71740 2-11111
Arthur Pharr, supt. 547-2218
JSHS, PO BOX 100 71740 2-00111
Bobbie Stevens, prin. 547-2862

Emmet, AC 501, PC 2, Nevada
Emmet SD, PO BOX 334 71835 2-11111
Gene Ross, supt. 887-2319
JSHS, PO BOX 334 71835 1-00111
Frank Henson, prin. 887-2319

England, AC 501, PC 5, Lonoke
England SD, PO BOX 10 72046 4-11111
Jerome Wesson, supt. 842-2996
JSHS, PO BOX 10 72046 2-00111
James King, prin. 842-2031

Eudora, AC 501, PC 5, Chicot
Eudora SD, 111 N ARCHER ST 71640 4-11111
Frank Anthony, supt. 355-2546
HS, 111 N ARCHER ST 71640 2-00011
Glenn Ford, prin. 355-4451
JHS, 111 N ARCHER ST 71640 2-00100
James Maiden, prin. 355-4402

Eureka Springs, AC 501, PC 4, Carroll
Eureka Springs SD 3-11111
RR 4 BOX 591 72632 253-5999
Bill Meggenberg, supt.
JSHS, 44 KING ST 72632 2-00111
William Ernst, prin. 253-8875

Evening Shade, AC 501, PC 2, Sharp
Evening Shade SD 2-11111
PO BOX 240 72532 266-3590
John Walker, supt.
JSHS, PO BOX 240 72532 2-00111
Ben Adams, prin. 266-3391

Everton, AC 501, PC 2, Boone
Marion County SD 2-11111
RR 1 BOX 45 72633 427-5354
Estel Grigg, supt.
Bruno-Pyatt JSHS 2-00111
RR 1 BOX 45 72633 427-5227
Mark Sanders, prin.

Farmington, AC 501, PC 4, Washington
Farmington SD 4-11111
275 RHEAS MILL RD 72730 267-3434
Randall Lynch, supt.
JSHS, 275 RHEAS MILL RD 72730 2-00111
Vol Eads, prin. 267-3331

Fayetteville, AC 501, PC 8, Washington
Fayetteville SD, PO BOX 849 72702 6-11111
Winston Simpson, supt. 444-3000
SHS West Campus 3-00001
2550 OLD FARMINGTON RD 72701 444-3058
John Davidson, prin.
SHS East Campus, 1001 STONE ST 72701 4-00001
John Delap, prin. 444-3050
Ramay JHS, 401 S SANG AVE 72701 3-00110
Nich Tschepikow, prin. 444-3064
Woodland JHS, 1 E POPLAR ST 72703 3-00110
David Hunt, prin. 444-3067

Mission Boulevard Christian S 2-11111
2006 MISSION BLVD 72703 442-2565
Brad Jones, prin.
Remington College 2-CS
3348 N COLLEGE AVE 72703 442-2364
University of Arkansas 7-UC
1 UNIVERSITY OF ARK 72701 575-4148

Flippin, AC 501, PC 4, Marion
Flippin SD, PO BOX 239 72634 3-11111
George Lewis, supt. 453-2270
JSHS, PO BOX 239 72634 2-00111
John Carey, prin. 453-2233

Fordyce, AC 501, PC 5, Dallas
Fordyce SD, PO BOX 722 71742 4-11111
Jerry Bush, supt. 352-3005
HS, 1800 W COLLEGE ST 71742 2-00011
Bill Williams, prin. 352-2126
MS, 1800 W COLLEGE ST 71742 2-00100
Ted Ponder, prin. 352-7121

Foreman, AC 501, PC 4, Little River
Foreman SD, PO BOX 280 71836 3-11111
Sam Pickle, supt. 542-7211
JSHS, PO BOX 280 71836 2-00111
Pat Steele, prin. 542-7212

Forrest City, AC 501, PC 7, St. Francis
Forrest City SD, 334 GRAHAM ST 72335 6-11111
Emerson Hall, supt. 633-1485
HS, 467 VICTORIA ST 72335 4-00011
Oscar Collins, prin. 633-1464
MS, 1133 N DIVISION ST 72335 3-00100
Clarence Chambers, prin. 633-3230

East Arkansas Community College 72335 3-CC
633-4480

Fort Smith, AC 501, PC 8, Sebastian
Fort Smith SD, PO BOX 1948 72902 7-11111
Ben Gooden, supt. 785-2501
Northside SHS, 2301 N B ST 72901 4-00001
Bill Bardick, prin. 783-1171
Southside SHS, 4100 S GARY ST 72903 4-00001
Wayne Haver, prin. 646-7371
Chaffin JHS, 3025 MASSARD RD 72903 3-00110
Ralph Spencer, prin. 452-2226
Darby JHS, 616 N 14TH ST 72901 3-00110
Michael Heffley, prin. 783-4159
Kimmons JHS 3-00110
2201 S WALDRON RD 72903 785-2451
Dan Roberts, prin.

Ramsey JHS, 3201 JENNY LIND RD 72901 3-00110
Howard Pearson, prin. 783-5115

Ft. Smith Christian S 2-11111
4201 WINDSOR DR 72904 782-0282
Robert Wells, prin.
St. Edward School of Radiologic Tech. HSP
7301 ROGERS AVE 72903 484-6070
Sparks Regional Medical Center HSP
1311 S I ST 72901 441-5407
Trinity JHS 2-00110
1205 S ALBERT PIKE AVE 72903 782-2451
Sr. Betty Elmer, prin.
Westark Community College 5-CC
PO BOX 3649 72913 785-7004

Fouke, AC 501, PC 3, Miller
Fouke SD, PO BOX 20 71837 3-11111
Lynn Nix, supt. 653-4311
JSHS, PO BOX 20 71837 2-00111
Michael Hickey, prin. 653-4551

Fountain Hill, AC 501, PC 2, Ashley
Fountain Hill SD, PO BOX 147 71642 2-11111
Opal Crow, supt. 853-9277
JSHS, PO BOX 147 71642 1-00111
Elmer Sparks, prin. 853-5318

Gentry, AC 501, PC 4, Benton
Gentry SD, PO BOX 159 72734 3-11111
Randy Barrett, supt. 736-2253
HS, PO BOX 159 72734 2-00011
Ronald Biggs, prin. 736-2666
MS, PO BOX 159 72734 2-01100
Mickie Harris, prin. 736-2251

Ozark Adventist Academy 2-00011
RR 2 BOX 511 72734 736-2221
Richard Aldridge, prin.

Gillett, AC 501, PC 3, Arkansas
Gillett SD, PO BOX 179 72055 2-11111
Tom Wilson, supt. 548-2281
JSHS, PO BOX 179 72055 2-00111
Jon Howell, prin. 548-2316

Glenwood, AC 501, PC 4, Pike
Glenwood SD, PO BOX 27 71943 2-11111
Curtis Turner, supt. 356-2912
JSHS, PO BOX 27 71943 2-00111
Glen Minton, prin. 356-3612

Gosnell, AC 501, PC 5, Mississippi
Gosnell SD 4-11111
600 STATE HIGHWAY 181 72315 532-5611
Stan Williams, supt.
JSHS 2-00111
600 STATE HIGHWAY 181 72315 532-8311
Charles Yarbro, prin.

Gould, AC 501, PC 4, Lincoln
Gould SD, PO BOX 639 71643 2-11111
John Hickman, supt. 263-4715
JSHS, PO BOX 639 71643 2-00111
Gerald Works, prin. 263-4463

Grady, AC 501, PC 3, Lincoln
Grady SD, PO BOX 238 71644 2-11111
Paul Roberts, supt. 479-3351
JSHS, PO BOX 238 71644 2-00111
Howard Larry, prin. 479-3422

Gravette, AC 501, PC 4, Benton
Gravette SD, PO BOX 480 72736 4-11111
Paul Human, supt. 787-5268
HS, PO BOX 480 72736 2-00011
Ken Holland, prin. 787-5377
MS, PO BOX 480 72736 2-00100
Mitchell Wilber, prin. 787-5961

Greenbrier, AC 501, PC 4, Faulkner
Greenbrier SD, 4 SCHOOL DR 72058 4-11111
Bob New, supt. 679-4808
SHS, 72 GREEN VALLEY DR 72058 2-00001
James Floyd, prin. 679-4236
JHS, 10 SCHOOL DR 72058 2-00110
Mark Shaw, prin. 679-2113

Green Forest, AC 501, PC 4, Carroll
Green Forest SD, PO BOX 1950 72638 4-11111
James Johnston, supt. 438-5201
JSHS, PO BOX 1950 72638 2-00111
Carroll Allison, prin. 438-5203

Greenland, AC 501, PC 3, Washington
Greenland SD, PO BOX 57 72737 3-11111
Wesley Cannon, supt. 521-2366
JSHS, PO BOX 57 72737 2-00111
Ronald Brawner, prin. 521-2308

Greenwood, AC 501, PC 5, Sebastian
Greenwood SD, 444 E GARY ST 72936 4-11111
Bob Evans, supt. 996-4142
HS, 440 E GARY ST 72936 3-00011
Jerry Cecil, prin. 996-4141
Wells MS 3-00100
1211 RAYMOND E WELLS DR 72936 996-7440
Larry Bridges, prin.

Greers Ferry, AC 501, PC 3, Cleburne
West Side SD 2-11111
7295 GREERS FERRY RD 72067 825-6258
Gay Horton, supt.

West Side JSHS
7295 GREERS FERRY RD 72067 — 2-00111 / 825-7241
Gary Nipper, prin.

Gurdon, AC 501, PC 4, Clark
Gurdon SD, 314 SCHOOL ST 71743 — 3-11111 / 353-4454
Bobby Smithson, supt.
HS, 314 S 3RD ST 71743 — 2-00011 / 353-4311
Leonard Gills, prin.
MS, 504 S 5TH ST 71743 — 2-01100 / 353-4921
Jeff Alexander, prin.

Guy, AC 501, PC 2, Faulkner
Guy-Perkins SD, PO BOX 300 72061 — 2-11111 / 679-3507
Donald Rowlett, supt.
Guy-Perkins JSHS — 2-00111 / 679-3508
PO BOX 300 72061
Doug Carmack, prin.

Hackett, AC 501, PC 2, Sebastian
Hackett SD, PO BOX 188 72937 — 3-11111 / 638-8822
Raymond Massey, supt.
JSHS, PO BOX 188 72937 — 2-00111 / 638-8210
W. Mills, prin.

Hamburg, AC 501, PC 5, Ashley
Hamburg SD, 503 E LINCOLN ST 71646 — 4-11111 / 853-9851
Bobby Harper, supt.
SHS, 1109 S MAIN ST 71646 — 3-00001 / 853-9856
Max Dyson, prin.
JHS, 1109 CUB DR 71646 — 2-00110 / 853-2811
Carlton Lawrence, prin.

Hampton, AC 501, PC 4, Calhoun
Hampton SD, PO BOX 628 71744 — 3-11111 / 798-2229
Darrell Donaldson, supt.
JSHS, PO BOX 628 71744 — 2-00111 / 798-2742
William Anders, prin.

Hardy, AC 501, PC 3, Sharp
Highland SD, PO BOX 419 72542 — 4-11111 / 856-3273
Jack Kimbrell, supt.
Highland JSHS, PO BOX 419 72542 — 2-00111 / 856-3273
Ronnie Brogdon, prin.

Harrisburg, AC 501, PC 4, Poinsett
Harrisburg SD, PO BOX 47 72432 — 4-11111 / 578-2416
William Lackey, supt.
HS, PO BOX 47 72432 — 2-00011 / 578-2417
Danny Sample, prin.

Harrison, AC 501, PC 6, Boone
Harrison SD — 5-11111 / 743-2011
400 S SYCAMORE ST 72601
Charles Adair, supt.
SHS, 925 GOBLIN DR 72601 — 3-00001 / 741-8223
Terry Oswalt, prin.
JHS, 515 S PINE ST 72601 — 3-00110 / 741-3496
Roland Choate, prin.

North Arkansas Community College — 3-CC / 743-3000
420 PIONEER RIDGE DR 72601

Hartford, AC 501, PC 3, Sebastian
Hartford SD, PO BOX 489 72938 — 2-11111 / 639-2910
Larry Garland, supt.
JSHS, PO BOX 489 72938 — 2-00111 / 639-2239
Gary Walker, prin.

Hatfield, AC 501, PC 2, Polk
Hatfield SD, PO BOX 130 71945 — 2-11111 / 389-6534
James Regnier, supt.
JSHS, PO BOX 130 71945 — 2-00111 / 389-6164
Jerry Beth Alderman, prin.

Hattieville, AC 501, PC 2, Conway
Wonderview SD — 2-11111 / 354-0211
RR 1 BOX 219 72063
Ron Wilson, supt.
Wonderview JSHS — 2-00111 / 354-8668
RR 1 BOX 219 72063
Corky Haygood, prin.

Havana, AC 501, PC 2, Yell
Western Yell County SD — 2-11111 / 476-2836
PO BOX 214 72842
Robert Smalley, supt.
Western Yell County JSHS — 2-00111 / 476-2611
PO BOX 214 72842
Calvin Peters, prin.

Hazen, AC 501, PC 4, Prairie
Hazen SD, PO BOX 358 72064 — 3-11111 / 255-4549
Jerry Stone, supt.
JSHS, PO BOX 358 72064 — 2-00111 / 255-4546
James Hall, prin.

Heber Springs, AC 501, PC 6, Cleburne
Heber Springs SD — 4-11111 / 362-2451
800 W MOORE ST 72543
Richard Reavis, supt.
HS, 800 W MOORE ST 72543 — 2-00011 / 362-3141
Robert Martin, prin.
MS, 800 W MOORE ST 72543 — 2-00100 / 362-2488
Stanley Wildman, prin.

Hector, AC 501, PC 2, Pope
Hector SD, RR 1 BOX 24 72843 — 3-11111 / 284-2021
Randal Williams, supt.
JSHS, RR 1 BOX 24 72843 — 2-00111 / 284-3536
Glenn Johnston, prin.

Helena, AC 501, PC 6, Phillips
Helena-West Helena SD — 5-11111 / 338-8172
PO BOX 369 72342
Willis Williams, supt.
Other Schools – See West Helena

Lakeview SD, RR 1 BOX 221 72342 — 2-11111 / 827-6863
Leon Phillips, supt.
White JSHS, RR 1 BOX 221 72342 — 2-00111 / 827-3367
Eugene Johnson, prin.

Phillips County Community College — 4-CC / 338-6474
PO BOX 785 72342

Hermitage, AC 501, PC 3, Bradley
Hermitage SD, PO BOX 38 71647 — 3-11111 / 463-2246
Charles Scroggins, supt.
JSHS, PO BOX 38 71647 — 2-00111 / 463-2235
Dan Ebbs, prin.

Holly Grove, AC 501, PC 3, Monroe
Holly Grove SD, PO BOX 489 72069 — 2-11111 / 462-3397
Pamela Brown, supt.
JSHS, PO BOX 489 72069 — 2-00111 / 462-8856
Harry Mayo, prin.

Hope, AC 501, PC 6, Hempstead
Hope SD, 117 E 2ND ST 71801 — 5-11111 / 777-2251
Jim Jones, supt.
SHS, 1700 S MAIN ST 71801 — 3-00001 / 777-3451
Michael Brown, prin.
Yerger JHS, 500 E 9TH ST 71801 — 3-00110 / 777-5701
Larry Muldrew, prin.

Spring Hill SD, RR 1 BOX 834 71801 — 2-11111 / 777-8236
George Crews, supt.
Spring Hill JSHS — 2-00111 / 777-6087
RR 1 BOX 834 71801
J. Purtle, prin.

Horatio, AC 501, PC 3, Sevier
Horatio SD, PO BOX 435 71842 — 2-11111 / 832-2340
Pat Adcock, supt.
JSHS, PO BOX 435 71842 — 2-00111 / 832-2341
Robert France, prin.

Hot Springs National Park, AC 501, PC 8, Garland
Cutter-Morning Star SD — 3-11111 / 262-2414
2801 SPRING ST 71901
Carl Hughes, supt.
Cutter-Morning Star JSHS — 2-00111 / 262-1220
2801 SPRING ST 71901
R. Lyerly, prin.

Fountain Lake SD — 3-11111 / 623-5101
4207 PARK AVE 71901
Charles Clark, supt.
Fountain Lake JSHS — 2-00111 / 623-5101
4207 PARK AVE 71901
Larry Beckham, prin.

Hot Springs SD — 5-11111 / 624-3372
140 N BORDER TER 71901
Roy Rowe, supt.
HS, 701 EMORY ST 71913 — 3-00011 / 624-5286
Bill Stringer, prin.
MS, 700 MAIN ST 71913 — 3-00100 / 624-5228
Charles Butler, prin.

Lakeside SD, 2871 MALVERN AVE 71901 — 4-11111 / 262-1880
Steve Floyd, supt.
Lakeside SHS — 2-00001 / 262-1530
2871 MALVERN AVE 71901
J. Tarkington, prin.
Lakeside JHS — 3-00110 / 262-1316
2865 MALVERN AVE 71901
James Fotioo, prin.

Garland Co. Community College — 4-CC / 767-9371
1 COLLEGE DR 71913

Hoxie, AC 501, PC 5, Lawrence
Hoxie SD, PO BOX 40 72433 — 3-11111 / 886-2401
David Cook, supt.
JSHS, PO BOX 40 72433 — 2-00111 / 886-3612
Earl McDonald, prin.

Hughes, AC 501, PC 4, St. Francis
Hughes SD, PO BOX 9 72348 — 4-11111 / 339-2570
Randy Crowder, supt.
JSHS, PO BOX 9 72348 — 2-00111 / 339-2580
John Manning, prin.

Humnoke, AC 501, PC 2, Lonoke
Humnoke SD, PO BOX 57 72072 — 2-11111 / 275-3852
Paula Henderson, supt.
JSHS, PO BOX 57 72072 — 1-00111 / 275-3438
Roy Daniels, prin.

Humphrey, AC 501, PC 3, Arkansas
Humphrey SD, PO BOX 190 72073 — 2-11111 / 873-4326
Donald Henley, supt.
JSHS, PO BOX 190 72073 — 2-00111 / 873-4326
Charles Webster, prin.

Huntsville, AC 501, PC 4, Madison
Huntsville SD, PO BOX F 72740 — 4-11111 / 738-2011
Chester Woodruff, supt.
HS, PO BOX F 72740 — 2-00011 / 738-2500
Alvin Lievsay, prin.
MS, PO BOX G 72740 — 2-00100 / 738-6520
Shelby Sisemore, prin.

Huttig, AC 501, PC 3, Union
Huttig SD, PO BOX 408 71747 — 2-11111 / 943-2606
Bob Mathis, supt.
JSHS, PO BOX 408 71747 — 2-00111 / 943-2202
Johnny Sweet, prin.

Imboden, AC 501, PC 3, Lawrence
Sloan-Hendrix SD — 3-11111 / 869-2361
PO BOX 1080 72434
Michael Holland, supt.
Sloan-Hendrix JSHS — 2-00111 / 869-2361
PO BOX 1080 72434
Mitch Walton, prin.

Jacksonville, AC 501, PC 8, Pulaski
Pulaski Co. Special SD
Supt. — See Little Rock
SHS, 2400 LINDA LN 72076 — 4-00001 / 982-2128
James Johnson, prin.
North Pulaski SHS — 3-00001 / 982-9436
718 HARRIS RD 72076
Manuel Twillie, prin.
Jacksonville North JHS — 3-00110 / 982-9407
201 SHARP DR 72076
Troy Lowe, prin.
Jacksonville South JHS — 3-00110 / 982-1587
1320 SCHOOL DR 72076
Charles Green, prin.

Jasper, AC 501, PC 2, Newton
Jasper SD, PO BOX 446 72641 — 3-11111 / 446-2223
Tommy Stokes, supt.
JSHS, PO BOX 446 72641 — 2-00111 / 446-2223
Toby Hatfield, prin.

Jessieville, AC 501, PC 2, Garland
Jessieville SD, PO BOX 4 71949 — 3-11111 / 984-5381
George Foshee, supt.
JSHS, PO BOX 4 71949 — 2-00111 / 984-5011
Steve Wright, prin.

Jonesboro, AC 501, PC 8, Craighead
Jonesboro SD, 1307 FLINT ST 72401 — 5-11111 / 933-5800
Bill Beasley, supt.
SHS, 301 HURRICANE DR 72401 — 4-00001 / 935-2381
Cecil Province, prin.
Camp JHS — 3-00110 / 933-5820
1814 W NETTLETON AVE 72401
Jim Ellis, prin.
MacArthur JHS — 3-00110 / 933-5840
1615 WILKINS AVE 72401
Russell Clark, prin.

Nettleton SD, 4207 RACE ST 72401 — 4-11111 / 935-3381
John Sawyer, supt.
Nettleton HS, 2616 PROGRESS ST 72401 — 3-00011 / 932-4013
Dan Blalock, prin.
Nettleton JHS — 2-00110 / 932-8158
4203 CHIEFTIAN LN 72401
Clarence Higgins, prin.

Valley View SD — 3-11111 / 935-4602
2118 VALLEY VIEW DR 72401
Radius Baker, supt.
Valley View HS — 2-00011 / 932-3737
2118 VALLEY VIEW DR 72401
Weldon Parkinson, prin.

Westside Consolidated SD — 4-11111 / 935-7503
RR 4 BOX 104 72401
Grover Cooper, supt.
Westside JSHS, RR 4 BOX 104 72401 — 3-00111 / 935-7501
James Dunivan, prin.

South Central Career College — 2-CS / 972-6999
2311 E NETTLETON AVE # G 72401

Judsonia, AC 501, PC 4, White
Riverview SD
Supt. — See Kensett
JSHS, 916 JUDSON AVE 72081 — 2-00111 / 729-3371
Gene Sledge, prin.

White County Central SD — 2-11111 / 729-3992
3259 HIGHWAY 157 72081
Monty Betts, supt.
White County Central JSHS — 2-00111 / 729-3947
3259 HIGHWAY 157 72081
Jerry Lacy, prin.

Junction City, AC 501, PC 3, Union
Junction City SD, PO BOX 790 71749 — 3-11111 / 924-4575
Alvin Kelly, supt.
HS, PO BOX 790 71749 — 2-00011 / 924-4576
James Warnock, prin.

Kensett, AC 501, PC 4, White
Riverview SD — 3-11111 / 729-5451
701 W DANDRIDGE ST 72082
Eddie Wood, supt.
HS, PO BOX 419 72082 — 2-00111 / 742-3346
Tony Prothro, prin.
Other Schools – See Judsonia

Kingsland, AC 501, PC 2, Cleveland
Kingsland SD, RR 1 BOX 26 71652 — 2-11111 / 348-5335
L. Gene Franklin, supt.
JSHS, RR 1 BOX 26 71652 — 2-00111 / 348-5335
Sam Hartwick, prin.

Kingston, AC 501, PC 2, Madison
Kingston SD, PO BOX 149 72742 — 2-11111 / 665-2995
Edgar Morgan, supt.
JSHS, PO BOX 149 72742 — 2-00111 / 665-2835
Ron Austin, prin.

Kirby, AC 501, PC 2, Pike
Kirby SD, PO BOX 9 71950 — 2-11111 / 398-4212
Don Davis, supt.
JSHS, PO BOX 9 71950 — 2-00111 / 398-4211
Jackie Johnson, prin.

Lake City, AC 501, PC 4, Craighead
Riverside SD, PO BOX 178 72437   3-11111
  Darrell Shelton, supt.   237-4329
Riverside SHS, PO BOX 178 72437   2-00001
  Jim Cole, prin.   237-4328
Other Schools – See Caraway

Lake Village, AC 501, PC 5, Chicot
Lakeside SD   4-11111
  600 S LAKESHORE DR 71653   265-2285
  Joyce Vaught, supt.
Lakeside HS   2-00011
  600 S LAKESHORE DR 71653   265-2232
  Edward Briggs, prin.
Central MS   2-00100
  600 S LAKESHORE DR 71653   265-2284
  Ann Sikora, prin.

Lamar, AC 501, PC 3, Johnson
Lamar SD, PO BOX 208 72846   4-11111
  Joe Hickey, supt.   885-3907
JSHS, PO BOX 208 72846   2-00111
  Bill Elliot, prin.   885-3344

Lavaca, AC 501, PC 4, Sebastian
Lavaca SD, PO BOX 8 72941   3-11111
  Harvie Nichols, supt.   674-5611
JSHS, PO BOX 8 72941   2-00111
  Richard Abernathy, prin.   674-5612

Leachville, AC 501, PC 4, Mississippi
Buffalo Island Central SD
  Supt. — See Monette
Buffalo Island Central JHS   2-00110
  PO BOX 110 72438   539-6883
  Joe Jones, prin.

Lead Hill, AC 501, PC 2, Boone
Lead Hill SD, PO BOX 20 72644   2-11111
  Chuck Archer, supt.   436-5249
JSHS, PO BOX 20 72644   2-00111
  Pat Bailey, prin.   436-5677

Lepanto, AC 501, PC 4, Poinsett
East Poinsett County SD   3-11111
  502 MCCLELLAN ST 72354   475-2472
  Gerald Jennings, supt.
East Poinsett County SHS   2-00001
  502 MCCLELLAN ST 72354   475-2331
  Michael Pierce, prin.
Other Schools – See Tyronza

Leslie, AC 501, PC 2, Searcy
Leslie SD, PO BOX 220 72645   2-11111
  Roger Massey, supt.   447-2431
JSHS, PO BOX 220 72645   2-00111
  John Gray, prin.   447-2431

Lewisville, AC 501, PC 4, Lafayette
Lewisville SD, PO BOX 950 71845   3-11111
  Richard Capps, supt.   921-5500
JSHS, PO BOX 950 71845   2-00111
  Kenneth Lindsay, prin.   921-4275

Lincoln, AC 501, PC 4, Washington
Lincoln SD, PO BOX 479 72744   4-11111
  Frank Holman, supt.   824-3011
HS, PO BOX 479 72744   2-00011
  Ken Ramey, prin.   824-3013
MS, PO BOX 479 72744   2-00100
  James Gregory, prin.   824-3020

Little Rock, AC 501, PC 9, Pulaski
Little Rock SD   8-11111
  810 W MARKHAM ST 72201   324-2400
  Henry Williams, supt.
Central SHS, 1500 S PARK ST 72202   4-00001
  Rudolph Howard, prin.   324-2300
Fair SHS   3-00001
  13420 DAVID O DODD RD 72210   228-3100
  Al Niven, prin.
Hall SHS, 6700 H ST 72205   4-00001
  Victor Anderson, prin.   671-6200
McClellan Magnet SHS   4-00001
  9417 GEYER SPRINGS RD 72209   570-4100
  Jodie Carter, prin.
Parkview Magnet SHS   3-00001
  2501 BARROW RD 72204   228-3000
  Junious Babbs, prin.
Metropolitan Vo-Tech   Vo Tech
  7701 SCOTT HAMILTON DR 72209   565-8465
  Doyle Dillahunty, prin.
Cloverdale JHS   3-00110
  6300 HINKSON RD 72209   570-4085
  Gayle Bradford, prin.
Dunbar JHS, 1100 WRIGHT AVE 72206   3-00110
  Nancy Volsen, prin.   324-2440
Forest Heights JHS   3-00110
  5901 EVERGREEN DR 72205   671-6390
  Richard Maple, prin.
Henderson JHS, 401 BARROW RD 72205   3-00110
  Clell Watts, prin.   228-3050
Mann Magnet JHS   3-00110
  1000 E ROOSEVELT RD 72206   324-2450
  Marian Lacey, prin.
Pulaski Heights JHS   3-00110
  401 N PINE ST 72205   671-6250
  Ralph Hoffman, prin.
Southwest JHS   3-00110
  3301 S BRYANT ST 72204   570-4070
  Charity Smith, prin.
Other Schools – See Mabelvale

Pulaski Co. Special SD   7-11111
  PO BOX 8601 72216   490-2000
  Bob Lester, supt.
Mills SHS, 1205 E DIXON RD 72206   3-00001
  Bill Barnes, prin.   490-1477
Robinson SHS   3-00001
  21501 HIGHWAY 10 72212   868-5757
  Ed Shehane, prin.
Fuller JHS, 808 E DIXON RD 72206   3-00110
  Herbert Brooks, prin.   490-1503
Robinson JHS   2-00110
  21001 HIGHWAY 10 72212   868-5838
  Ray Bryan, prin.
Other Schools – See Jacksonville, North Little Rock, Sherwood

Arkansas Baptist College   2-UC
  1600 HIGH ST 72202   372-6883
Arkansas Baptist S   3-11111
  62 PLEASANT VALLEY DR 72212   227-7070
  Sam Tolleson, prin.
Arkansas School for the Blind   HND
  PO BOX 668 72203
Arkansas School for the Deaf   HND
  PO BOX 3811 72203
Baptist Schools of Allied Health   HSP
  11900 COLONEL GLENN RD 72210   223-7415
CARTI School of Radiation Therapy Tech   CS
  PO BOX 5210 72215   664-8573
Catholic HS, 6300 LEE AVE 72205   3-00011
  Fr. Tribou, prin.   664-3939
Eastern College of Health Vocations   2-CS
  6423 FORBING RD 72209   568-0211
ITT Technical Institute   2-CS
  4520 S UNIVERSITY AVE 72204   565-5550
Mount St. Mary Academy   3-00011
  3224 KAVANAUGH BLVD 72205   664-8006
  Sr. Deborah Troillett, prin.
NEC-College of Technology   4-CC
  9720 N RODNEY PARHAM RD 72207   224-8200
Philander Smith College   3-UC
  812 W 13TH ST 72202   375-9845
Pulaski Academy   4-11111
  12701 HINSON RD 72212   225-9320
  Arch McIntosh, prin.
Remington College   2-CS
  7601 SCOTT HAMILTON DR 72209   565-7000
SS. Joseph & Peter JHS   1-00100
  412 W 6TH ST 72201   534-7545
  Kim Bauman, prin.
St. Vincent Infirmary Medical Center   HSP
  2 SAINT VINCENT CIR 72205   660-3916
University of AR & VA Medical Center   2-HSP
  4300 W 7TH ST 72205   661-1202
University of Arkansas at Little Rock   6-UC
  2801 S UNIVERSITY AVE 72204   569-3200
University of Arkansas/Medical Sciences   4-UC
  4301 W MARKHAM ST 72205   686-5680

Lockesburg, AC 501, PC 3, Sevier
Lockesburg SD, PO BOX 88 71846   2-11111
  Warren Adcock, supt.   289-5161
JSHS, PO BOX 88 71846   2-00111
  Ed Boswell, prin.   289-2431

Lonoke, AC 501, PC 5, Lonoke
Lonoke SD, 411 W HOLLY ST 72086   4-11111
  Charles Knox, supt.   676-2042
SHS, 501 W ACADEMY ST 72086   2-00001
  George Davis, prin.   676-2476
JHS, 200 E LOCUST ST 72086   2-00110
  Danny Hazelwood, prin.   676-6670

Lynn, AC 501, PC 2, Lawrence
Lynn SD, PO BOX 338 72440   2-11111
  Gary Phillips, supt.   528-3462
JSHS, PO BOX 338 72440   2-00111
  David Davis, prin.   528-3766

Mabelvale, AC 501, PC see Little Rock
Little Rock SD
  Supt. — See Little Rock
JHS, PO BOX 187 72103   3-00110
  Walter Marshaleck, prin.   455-7400

Mc Crory, AC 501, PC 4, Woodruff
McCrory SD, PO BOX 427 72101   3-11111
  Charles Vondran, supt.   731-2535
JSHS, 510 N JACKSON 72101   2-00111
  Carroll Wilson, prin.   731-2851

Mc Gehee, AC 501, PC 5, Desha
Mc Gehee SD, PO BOX 767 71654   4-11111
  Barbara Wood, supt.   222-3670
JSHS, PO BOX 767 71654   3-00111
  Thomas Gathen, prin.   222-5026

Mc Neil, AC 501, PC 3, Columbia
Mc Neil SD, PO BOX 167 71752   2-11111
  James Berry, supt.   695-3500
JSHS, PO BOX 167 71752   2-00111
  Kiril Jones, prin.   695-3342

Mc Rae, AC 501, PC 3, White
McRae SD, PO BOX C 72102   2-11111
  Calvin Estes, supt.   726-3587
JSHS, PO BOX C 72102   2-00111
  Jeff Williams, prin.   726-3611

Magazine, AC 501, PC 3, Logan
Magazine SD, RR 1 BOX 112 72943   2-11111
  Allen Standridge, supt.   969-2566
Leftwich JSHS, RR 1 BOX 112 72943   2-00111
  James Isaacs, prin.   969-2640

Magnolia, AC 501, PC 7, Columbia
Magnolia SD, PO BOX 649 71753   5-11111
  Don McMahen, supt.   234-4933
SHS, PO BOX 649 71753   3-00001
  Jim Garrett, prin.   234-2610
JHS, 540 E NORTH ST 71753   3-00110
  Jerry Jones, prin.   234-2206

Walker SD, 655 HIGHWAY 79 S 71753   2-11111
  Darline Shepherd, supt.   234-5654
Walker JSHS, 655 HIGHWAY 79 S 71753   2-00111
  Lynnetta Roberts, prin.   234-4424

Southern Arkansas University   4-UC
  SAU BOX 1402 71753   235-4001

Malvern, AC 501, PC 6, Hot Spring
Glen Rose SD, RR 3 BOX 300 72104   3-11111
  Mike McNabb, supt.   332-3694
Glen Rose JSHS, RR 3 BOX 300 72104   2-00111
  Craig Fraiser, prin.   332-3520

Magnet Cove SD, PO BOX 1 72104   3-11111
  Harlan Buttrum, supt.   332-5468
Magnet Cove JSHS, PO BOX 1 72104   2-00111
  Basil Miller, prin.   332-5466

Malvern SD, 1517 S MAIN ST 72104   5-11111
  David Craig, supt.   332-7500
SHS, 525 E HIGHLAND AVE 72104   3-00001
  Steve Williams, prin.   332-6905
JHS, 1910 ROOSEVELT ST 72104   3-00110
  Gail McClure, prin.   332-7530

Mammoth Spring, AC 501, PC 4, Fulton
Mammoth Spring SD   2-11111
  PO BOX 370 72554   625-3612
  Fred Johnson, supt.
JSHS, PO BOX 370 72554   2-00111
  Jerry Elkins, prin.   625-7212

Manila, AC 501, PC 5, Mississippi
Manila SD, PO BOX 670 72442   3-11111
  Roland Wells, supt.   561-4419
JSHS, PO BOX 670 72442   2-00111
  Mike Chipman, prin.   561-4417

Mansfield, AC 501, PC 4, Sebastian
Mansfield SD, PO BOX 308 72944   3-11111
  Larry Austin, supt.   928-4006
JSHS, PO BOX 307 72944   2-00111
  William Wilson, prin.   928-4451

Marianna, AC 501, PC 6, Lee
Lee County SD 1   5-11111
  55 N CAROLINA ST 72360   295-7100
  James Davis, supt.
Lee HS, RR 2 BOX 16C 72360   3-00011
  Cecil Twillie, prin.   295-7130
Strong MS, 214 S ALABAMA ST 72360   3-00100
  Wayne Thompson, prin.   295-7140

Marion, AC 501, PC 5, Crittenden
Marion SD, 76 ELM ST 72364   4-11111
  Steve Singleton, supt.   739-5100
SHS, 1 PATRIOT DR 72364   3-00001
  Jerry Wood, prin.   739-5130
JHS, 2 PATRIOT DR 72364   2-00110
  John Heath, prin.   739-5140

Marked Tree, AC 501, PC 5, Poinsett
Marked Tree SD   3-11111
  406 SAINT FRANCIS ST 72365   358-2913
  Cliff Wishum, supt.
JSHS, 406 SAINT FRANCIS ST 72365   2-00111
  Jim DeLoach, prin.   358-2891

Marmaduke, AC 501, PC 4, Greene
Marmaduke SD   3-11111
  1010 GREYHOUND DR 72443   597-2723
  Jerry McIntosh, supt.
JSHS, 1010 GREYHOUND DR 72443   2-00111
  Don Purcell, prin.   597-2723

Marshall, AC 501, PC 4, Searcy
Marshall SD, PO BOX 310 72650   3-11111
  Lindsey Parks, supt.   448-3011
JSHS, PO BOX 310 72650   2-00111
  James Hendricks, prin.   448-3331

Marvell, AC 501, PC 4, Phillips
Marvell SD, PO BOX 126 72366   3-11111
  Ulicious Reed, supt.   829-2101
HS, PO BOX 126 72366   2-00011
  Daniel Kempf, prin.   829-2594
MS, PO BOX 126 72366   2-01100
  Ervin Smith, prin.   829-2106

Mayflower, AC 501, PC 4, Faulkner
Mayflower SD, PO BOX 127 72106   3-11111
  Phillip Bell, supt.   470-0506
JSHS, PO BOX 127 72106   2-00111
  Ron Hayes, prin.   470-0388

Maynard, AC 501, PC 2, Randolph
Maynard SD, PO BOX 499 72444   2-11111
  Harmon Seawel, supt.   647-2051
JSHS, PO BOX 499 72444   2-00111
  Dennis Bunch, prin.   647-2210

Melbourne, AC 501, PC 4, Izard
Melbourne SD, PO BOX 250 72556   2-11111
  Glen Billingsley, supt.   368-4500
JSHS, PO BOX 250 72556   2-00111
  Gerald Cooper, prin.   368-4500

Mena, AC 501, PC 6, Polk
Acorn SD, RR 3 BOX 450 71953 — 2-11111
John Thompson, supt. — 394-2348
Acorn JSHS, RR 3 BOX 450 71953 — 2-00111
W. Youngblood, prin. — 394-5544

Mena SD, 304 MENA ST 71953 — 4-11111
Wesley Berry, supt. — 394-1710
HS, 1220 MORROW ST 71953 — 3-00111
Quinton Taggert, prin. — 394-1144
MS, 304 MENA ST 71953 — 2-00100
Al Gathright, prin. — 394-2572

Rich Mountain Community College — 2-CC
601 BUSH ST 71953 — 394-5012

Mineral Springs, AC 501, PC 4, Howard
Mineral Springs SD — 2-11111
PO BOX 189 71851 — 287-4748
Dan Davis, supt.
JSHS, PO BOX 189 71851 — 2-00111
Dennis Meins, prin. — 287-4747

Monette, AC 501, PC 4, Craighead
Buffalo Island Central SD — 3-11111
PO BOX 730 72447 — 486-5411
George Holland, supt.
Buffalo Island Central SHS — 2-00001
PO BOX N 72447 – Homer Craig, prin. — 486-5512
Other Schools – See Leachville

Monticello, AC 501, PC 6, Drew
Drew Central SD, RR 4 BOX 10 71655 — 3-11111
Norman Hill, supt. — 367-5369
Drew Central JSHS — 2-00111
RR 4 BOX 10 71655 — 367-6076
Leeman Ngar, prin.

Monticello SD, 935 SCOGIN DR 71655 — 4-11111
Bobby Hibbard, supt. — 367-6862
SHS, 33 CLYDE ROSS DR 71655 — 2-00001
C. Hall, prin. — 367-3479
JHS, 212 CLYDE ROSS DR 71655 — 2-00110
Larry Johnston, prin. — 367-8517

University of Arkansas at Monticello — 4-UC
PO BOX 3596 71656 — 460-1020

Morrilton, AC 501, PC 6, Conway
South Conway SD — 5-11111
704 E CHURCH ST 72110 — 354-9400
Ray Fullerton, supt.
SHS, 701 E HARDING ST 72110 — 3-00001
Brian Bailey, prin. — 354-9430
JHS, 1400 POOR FARM RD 72110 — 3-00110
Bill Patterson, prin. — 354-9437

Sacred Heart S — 2-11111
106 N SAINT JOSEPH ST 72110 — 354-8113
Veo Condley, prin.

Mountainburg, AC 501, PC 2, Crawford
Mountainburg SD, PO BOX 15 72946 — 3-11111
James Bridges, supt. — 369-2121
JSHS, PO BOX 15 72946 — 2-00111
Jim Galloway, prin. — 369-2146

Mountain Home, AC 501, PC 6, Baxter
Mountain Home SD — 5-11111
1230 MAPLE ST 72653 — 425-1201
Roger Oge, supt.
SHS, 501 BOMBER BLVD 72653 — 3-00001
Randy Scarbrough, prin. — 425-1215
JHS, 2301 RODEO DR 72653 — 3-00110
Jan Gott, prin. — 425-1231

Mountain Pine, AC 501, PC 3, Garland
Mountain Pine SD, PO BOX 1 71956 — 3-11111
Don Bailey, supt. — 767-1540
JSHS, PO BOX 1 71956 — 2-00111
John Campbell, prin. — 767-6917

Mountain View, AC 501, PC 4, Stone
Mountain View SD — 4-11111
HC 71 BOX 159 72560 — 269-3443
Daniel Thomas, supt.
JSHS, HC 71 BOX 159 72560 — 2-00111
Mark Rector, prin. — 269-3943

Mount Holly, AC 501, PC 2, Union
Mount Holly SD, PO BOX 68 71758 — 2-11111
Winfred May, supt. — 554-2461
JSHS, PO BOX 68 71758 — 2-00111
Michael Morton, prin. — 554-2551

Mount Ida, AC 501, PC 3, Montgomery
Mount Ida SD, PO BOX 345 71957 — 3-11111
Barton Hunter, supt. — 867-2323
JSHS, PO BOX 345 71957 — 2-00111
E. Ramage, prin. — 867-4517

Mount Judea, AC 501, PC 1, Newton
Mount Judea SD, PO BOX 40 72655 — 2-11111
Ford Ewing, supt. — 434-5362
JSHS, PO BOX 40 72655 — 2-00111
Jether Raney, prin. — 434-5362

Mount Pleasant, AC 501, PC 2, Izard
Mount Pleasant SD — 2-11111
PO BOX 144 72561 — 346-5472
Jewel Caraway, supt.
JSHS, PO BOX 144 72561 — 2-00111
C. Johnson, prin. — 346-5481

Mount Vernon, AC 501, PC 2, Faulkner
Mt Vernon Enola SD — 2-11111
PO BOX 43 72111 — 849-2220
Roy Noblitt, supt.
Mt Vernon Enola JSHS — 1-00111
PO BOX 43 72111 — 849-2221
Bernard Bakker, prin.

Mulberry, AC 501, PC 4, Crawford
Mulberry SD, PO BOX D 72947 — 2-11111
Roger Benham, supt. — 997-1701
JSHS, PO BOX D 72947 — 2-00111
J. Rowland, prin. — 997-1363

Murfreesboro, AC 501, PC 4, Pike
Murfreesboro SD, PO BOX 339 71958 — 3-11111
Dave Holloway, supt. — 285-2201
JSHS, PO BOX 339 71958 — 2-00111
Mike Jackson, prin. — 285-3514

Nashville, AC 501, PC 5, Howard
Nashville SD 1, 600 N 4TH ST 71852 — 4-11111
Danny Howard, supt. — 845-3425
SHS — 2-00001
1301 MOUNT PLEASANT DR 71852 — 845-3261
Dennis Horn, prin.
JHS, 1000 N 8TH ST 71852 — 2-00110
Doug Graham, prin. — 845-3418

Newark, AC 501, PC 4, Independence
Newark SD, 1502 N HILL ST 72562 — 3-11111
Jerry Rose, supt. — 799-8691
JSHS, 1500 N HILL ST 72562 — 2-00111
George Green, prin. — 799-8691

Newport, AC 501, PC 6, Jackson
Newport SD, 406 WILKERSON DR 72112 — 4-11111
Steve Castleberry, supt. — 523-1328
HS, 406 WILKERSON DR 72112 — 3-00111
Floyd Parnell, prin. — 523-1321
JHS, 406 WILKERSON DR 72112 — 2-00100
Rick Rana, prin. — 523-1346

Norfork, AC 501, PC 2, Baxter
Norfork SD, HC 62 BOX 75 72658 — 2-11111
Lyndle McCurley, supt. — 499-7193
JSHS, HC 62 BOX 75 72658 — 2-00111
Bob Hulse, prin. — 499-7192

Norman, AC 501, PC 2, Montgomery
Caddo Hills SD, RR 1 BOX 249 71960 — 3-11111
John Bass, supt. — 356-3857
Caddo Hills JSHS — 2-00111
RR 1 BOX 249 71960 — 356-3857
Rick Green, prin.

Norphlet, AC 501, PC 3, Union
Norphlet SD, PO BOX E 71759 — 3-11111
Eddie Miller, supt. — 546-2781
JSHS, PO BOX E 71759 — 2-00111
Billy Joe Burson, prin. — 546-2512

North Little Rock, AC 501, PC 8, Pulaski
North Little Rock SD — 6-11111
PO BOX 687 72115 — 771-8000
James Smith, supt.
North Little Rock HS-Westside — 4-00001
101 W 22ND ST 72114 — 771-8100
Gregg Thompson, prin.
Lakewood MS — 3-00100
2300 LAKEVIEW RD 72116 — 771-8250
Ginny Wiseman, prin.
North Little Rock JHS-Eastside — 2-00010
2400 LAKEVIEW RD 72116 — 771-8200
Ken Kirspel, prin.
Ridgeroad MS, 4601 RIDGE RD 72116 — 3-00100
Arthur Tucker, prin. — 771-8155
Rose City MS, 5500 LYNCH DR 72117 — 2-00100
Kathy Cook, prin. — 945-1446

Pulaski Co. Special SD
Supt. — See Little Rock
Sylvan Hills SHS — 3-00001
484 BEAR PAW RD 72120 — 835-4411
Charles Ferriter, prin.
Oak Grove JSHS — 3-00111
10025 OAKLAND DR 72118 — 851-2212
Brenda Allen, prin.
Northwood JHS — 3-00110
10200 BAMBOO LN 72120 — 834-2950
Bob Reynolds, prin.

Abundant Life S — 2-11111
9200 SYLVAN HILLS HWY 72120 — 835-3120
Nora Yates, prin.
Central Arkansas Christian S — 3-11111
1 WINDSONG DR 72113 — 758-3160
Don Lee, prin.
Pulaski Vocational Technical School — CS
3000 W SCENIC DR 72118 — 771-1000
Shorter College — 2-CC
604 N LOCUST ST 72114 — 374-6305
South Central Career College — 3-CS
4500 W COMMERCIAL DR 72116 — 758-6800

Oark, AC 501, PC 2, Johnson
Oark SD, GENERAL DELIVERY 72852 — 2-11111
Bill Gilmore, supt. — 292-3353
JSHS, GENERAL DELIVERY 72852 — 1-00111
Jerry Bunch, prin. — 292-3337

Oden, AC 501, PC 2, Montgomery
Oden SD, PO BOX 150 71961 — 2-11111
Vernon Morrison, supt. — 326-4311
JSHS, PO BOX 150 71961 — 2-00111
William Edwards, prin. — 326-4311

Ola, AC 501, PC 4, Yell
Ola SD, PO BOX 279 72853 — 3-11111
Phillip Young, supt. — 489-5251
JSHS, PO BOX 279 72853 — 2-00111
Earl Jamison, prin. — 489-5713

Omaha, AC 501, PC 2, Boone
Omaha SD, PO BOX 480 72662 — 2-11111
David Land, supt. — 426-3366
JSHS, PO BOX 480 72662 — 2-00111
James Center, prin. — 426-3366

Osceola, AC 501, PC 6, Mississippi
Osceola SD, PO BOX 628 72370 — 4-11111
Carol Smith, supt. — 563-2561
SHS, PO BOX 628 72370 — 2-00001
Milton Washington, prin. — 563-2192
JHS, PO BOX 628 72370 — 2-00110
Howard McNeal, prin. — 563-2918

Ozark, AC 501, PC 5, Franklin
Ozark SD, PO BOX 135 72949 — 4-11111
Scott Stone, supt. — 667-4118
SHS, 1200 W SCHOOL ST 72949 — 2-00100
John Hoyt, prin. — 667-4116
JHS, 1301 WALDEN DR 72949 — 2-00110
James Ford, prin. — 667-4747

Pleasant View SD — 2-11111
RR 2 BOX 289 72949 — 997-8469
Gary Moon, supt.
Pleasant View JSHS — 2-00111
RR 2 BOX 289 72949 — 997-8469
Kerry Schneider, prin.

Arkansas Valley Voc. Tech. School — CS
PO BOX 506 72949 — 667-2117

Palestine, AC 501, PC 3, St. Francis
Palestine/Wheatley SD — 3-11111
PO BOX 790 72372 — 581-2646
Kenneth Turner, supt.
Palestine-Wheatley HS — 2-00011
PO BOX 790 72372 — 581-2425
Martha Moore, prin.

Pangburn, AC 501, PC 3, White
Pangburn SD, PO BOX 350 72121 — 3-11111
Jerome Browning, supt. — 728-4511
JSHS, PO BOX 350 72121 — 2-00111
Pat Rose, prin. — 728-3513

Paragould, AC 501, PC 7, Greene
Greene County Technical SD — 4-11111
5201 W KINGSHIGHWAY 72450 — 236-8182
Michael Cox, supt.
Greene County Technical HS — 3-00011
5201 W KINGSHIGHWAY 72450 — 239-8769
Dick Hefner, prin.
Greene County Technical JHS — 2-00100
5207 W KINGSHIGHWAY 72450 — 239-2147
Chester Key, prin.

Northeast Arkansas SD — 4-11111
631 W COURT ST 72450 — 239-2105
Lee Vent, supt.
Ridgecrest JSHS — 2-00111
1701 W COURT ST 72450 — 236-7744
John Shewmaker, prin.

Stanford SD — 2-11111
92 GREENE ROAD 654 72450 — 573-6688
Don Smith, supt.
Stanford JSHS — 2-00111
92 GREENE ROAD 654 72450 — 573-6551
Carol Eason, prin.

Crowley's Ridge College — 1-CC
100 COLLEGE DR 72450 — 800-264-1096
Crowleys Ridge Academy — 3-11111
626 ACADEMY DR 72450 — 236-6909
Scott Gatlin, prin.

Paris, AC 501, PC 5, Logan
Paris SD, 602 N 10TH ST 72855 — 4-11111
William Chambers, supt. — 963-3243
HS, 602 N 10TH ST 72855 — 2-00111
Elwood Brooks, prin. — 963-2247
MS, 2000 E WOOD ST 72855 — 2-00100
Larry Cozens, prin. — 963-6995

Parkin, AC 501, PC 4, Cross
Parkin SD, PO BOX 861 72373 — 3-11111
Joseph Whitby, supt. — 755-2742
JSHS, PO BOX 7 72373 — 2-00111
Jessie Bradford, prin. — 755-2791

Paron, AC 501, PC 2, Saline
Paron SD, 22265 HIGHWAY 9 72122 — 2-11111
Gerald Johnson, supt. — 594-5391
JSHS, 22265 HIGHWAY 9 72122 — 2-00111
David Smith, prin. — 594-5622

Pearcy, AC 501, PC 2, Garland
Lake Hamilton SD, 300 WOLF ST 71964 — 5-11111
Don Henson, supt. — 767-2306
Lake Hamilton SHS, 280 WOLF ST 71964 — 3-00001
Curtis Williams, prin. — 767-9311
Lake Hamilton JHS, 281 WOLF ST 71964 — 3-00110
Bud Walston, prin. — 767-2731

Pea Ridge, AC 501, PC 4, Benton
Pea Ridge SD, PO BOX 6 72751 — 3-11111
Marvin Higginbottom, supt. — 451-8181

JSHS, PO BOX 6 72751 — 2-00111
Jerry Endsley, prin. — 451-8182

Perryville, AC 501, PC 4, Perry
Perryville SD, 803 N ASH ST 72126 — 3-11111
Ernest Huff, supt. — 889-2327
JSHS, 803 N ASH ST 72126 — 2-00111
James Floyd, prin. — 889-2326

Piggott, AC 501, PC 5, Clay
Piggott SD, PO BOX 387 72454 — 3-11111
Leon Christenberry, supt. — 598-2572
HS, PO BOX 387 72454 — 2-00011
James Winberry, prin. — 598-3815
MS, PO BOX 387 72454 — 2-01100
Lendell Vennada, prin. — 598-3856

Pine Bluff, AC 501, PC 8, Jefferson
Dollarway SD — 4-11111
4900 DOLLARWAY RD 71602 — 534-7003
Maurice Horton, supt.
Dollarway SHS — 2-00001
4900 DOLLARWAY RD 71602 — 534-3878
Terry Julian, prin.
Dollarway JHS, 2602 FLUKER ST 71601 — 2-00110
O. Brown, prin. — 534-5243
Pine Bluff SD, PO BOX 7678 71611 — 6-11111
Willis Alderson, supt. — 543-4200
SHS, 711 W 11TH AVE 71601 — 4-00001
Andrew Tolbert, prin. — 543-4300
Robey JHS, 4101 S OLIVE ST 71603 — 3-00110
Kent Raymick, prin. — 543-4280

Watson Chapel SD — 5-11111
4100 CAMDEN RD 71603 — 879-0220
Charles Knight, supt.
Watson Chapel SHS — 3-00001
4000 CAMDEN RD 71603 — 879-3230
Gene Stewart, prin.
Watson Chapel JHS — 3-00110
3900 CAMDEN RD 71603 — 879-4420
Richard McLaughlin, prin.

Jefferson Regional Medical Center — HSP
1515 W 42ND AVE 71603 — 541-7850
South Central Career College — 2-CS
1614 BRENTWOOD DR 71601 — 535-6800
University of Arkansas at Pine Bluff — 5-UC
1200 UNIVERSITY DR 71601 — 541-6512

Plainview, AC 501, PC 3, Yell
Plainview-Rover SD — 2-11111
PO BOX 190 72857 — 272-4241
Jim Cunningham, supt.
Plainview-Rover JSHS — 2-00111
PO BOX 190 72857 — 272-4241
Jim Franks, prin.

Pleasant Plains, AC 501, PC 2, Independence
Midland SD, PO BOX 258 72568 — 3-11111
Richard Blevins, supt. — 345-2852
Midland JSHS, PO BOX 258 72568 — 2-00111
Frank Monroe, prin. — 345-2610

Pocahontas, AC 501, PC 6, Randolph
Pocahontas SD, 2300 N PARK ST 72455 — 4-11111
Marcus Van Camp, supt. — 892-4573
HS, 2312 STADIUM DR 72455 — 2-00011
Jerry Malone, prin. — 892-4573
JHS, 2405 N PARK ST 72455 — 3-01100
Bryon Busby, prin. — 892-4573

Black River Vocational Technical School — CS
PO BOX 468 72455 — 892-4565

Pottsville, AC 501, PC 3, Pope
Pottsville SD, PO BOX 70 72858 — 3-11111
Dain Duvall, supt. — 968-8101
JSHS, PO BOX 70 72858 — 2-00111
Gary Huggins, prin. — 968-6334

Poyen, AC 501, PC 2, Grant
Poyen SD, PO BOX 209 72128 — 2-11111
Jerry Newton, supt. — 332-2939
JSHS, PO BOX 209 72128 — 1-00110
Bob Daniel, prin. — 332-2939

Prairie Grove, AC 501, PC 4, Washington
Prairie Grove SD, 824 N MOCK ST 72753 — 4-11111
Tommy Tyler, supt. — 846-4213
SHS, 824 N MOCK ST 72753 — 2-00001
Roy Pearson, prin. — 846-4212
JHS, 824 N MOCK ST 72753 — 2-00110
Mike Luttrell, prin. — 846-4221

Prattsville, AC 501, PC 2, Grant
Prattsville SD, PO BOX 130 72129 — 2-11111
Jerry Franks, supt. — 699-4311
JSHS, PO BOX 130 72129 — 2-00111
Gary Shoptaw, prin. — 699-4311

Prescott, AC 501, PC 5, Nevada
Prescott SD, 762 MARTIN ST 71857 — 4-11111
Don Johnston, supt. — 887-3016
HS, 762 MARTIN ST 71857 — 2-00011
Ted Kirby, prin. — 887-3123
MS, 1030 E 5TH ST N 71857 — 2-01100
Donald Mitchell, prin. — 887-2521

Quitman, AC 501, PC 3, Cleburne
Quitman SD, PO BOX 178 72131 — 3-11111
J. McConnaughhay, supt. — 589-3156
JSHS, PO BOX 178 72131 — 2-00111
Michael Deal, prin. — 589-2554

Ravenden Springs, AC 501, PC 2, Randolph
Randolph County SD — 2-11111
5749 OAK RIDGE RD 72460 — 869-2479
Clifford Adams, supt.
Oak Ridge Central JSHS — 2-00111
5749 OAK RIDGE RD 72460 — 869-2479
Keith Evans, prin.

Rector, AC 501, PC 4, Clay
Clay County Central SD — 3-11111
PO BOX 367 72461 — 595-3151
Kelly Scobey, supt.
Clay County Central JSHS — 2-00111
PO BOX 367 72461 — 595-3357
Rob Louder, prin.

Redfield, AC 501, PC 4, Jefferson
White Hall SD
Supt. — See White Hall
JHS, PO BOX 350 72132 — 2-00110
James Kight, prin. — 397-2253

Rison, AC 501, PC 4, Cleveland
Rison SD, PO BOX 600 71665 — 3-11111
Reck Wallis, supt. — 325-6344
JSHS, PO BOX 600 71665 — 2-00111
John Johnson, prin. — 325-6241

Woodlawn SD, RR 2 BOX 56A 71665 — 2-11111
Max Watts, supt. — 357-8108
Woodlawn JSHS, RR 2 BOX 56A 71665 — 2-00111
David Williams, prin. — 357-8171

Rogers, AC 501, PC 7, Benton
Rogers SD, 220 S 5TH ST 72756 — 6-11111
Roland Smith, supt. — 636-3910
SHS, 1114 S 5TH ST 72756 — 4-00001
W. King, prin. — 636-2202
Elmwood JHS, 1600 N 13TH ST 72756 — 3-00110
Joe Bryant, prin. — 631-3600
Oakdale JHS — 3-00110
511 N DIXIELAND RD 72756 — 631-3615
Roger Brooks, prin.

Benton Co. Christian S — 2-11111
2005 S 12TH ST 72756 — 636-9186
Gorden Carlisle, prin.

Rohwer, AC 501, PC 1, Desha
Delta Special SD, PO BOX 41 71666 — 2-11111
Ronald Smead, supt. — 222-6031
Delta JSHS, PO BOX 41 71666 — 2-00111
William Bennett, prin. — 644-3800

Rose Bud, AC 501, PC 2, White
Rose Bud SD, 124 SCHOOL RD 72137 — 3-11111
Mark Willborg, supt. — 556-5815
JSHS, 124 SCHOOL RD 72137 — 2-00111
Ron Johnson, prin. — 556-5404

Rosston, AC 501, PC 2, Nevada
Nevada SD, PO BOX 50 71858 — 3-11111
Barney Kyzar, supt. — 871-2418
Nevada JSHS, PO BOX 50 71858 — 2-00111
Hardy Herrington, prin. — 871-2478

Russellville, AC 501, PC 7, Pope
Russellville SD, PO BOX 928 72811 — 5-11111
Danny Taylor, supt. — 968-1306
SHS, 2203 S KNOXVILLE AVE 72801 — 4-00001
Wesley White, prin. — 968-3151
Gardner JHS — 3-00110
1000 S ARKANSAS AVE 72801 — 968-1599
Dan Raines, prin.

Arkansas Tech University — 5-UC
215 W O ST 72801 — 968-0237

Saint Joe, AC 501, PC 2, Searcy
Saint Joe SD, PO BOX 69 72675 — 2-11111
John Szitar, supt. — 439-2213
JSHS, PO BOX 69 72675 — 1-00111
Stacy Richardson, prin. — 439-2213

Saint Paul, AC 501, PC 1, Madison
Saint Paul SD, PO BOX 125 72760 — 2-11111
Bill Schafer, supt. — 677-2411
JSHS, PO BOX 125 72760 — 2-00111
Dora Rogers, prin. — 677-2624

Salem, AC 501, PC 4, Fulton
Salem SD, 500 HIGH SCHOOL DR 72576 — 3-11111
Sam Casey, supt. — 895-2516
JSHS, 500 HIGH SCHOOL DR 72576 — 2-00111
Houston Case, prin. — 895-3293

Saratoga, AC 501, PC 2, Howard
Saratoga SD, PO BOX 90 71859 — 2-11111
Lewis Diggs, supt. — 388-9262
HS, PO BOX 90 71859 — 1-00011
James Stewart, prin. — 388-9262

Scotland, AC 501, PC 2, Van Buren
Scotland SD, PO BOX 4 72141 — 2-11111
Allen McDonald, supt. — 592-3413
JSHS, PO BOX 4 72141 — 1-00111
Rodney Haney, prin. — 592-3337

Scranton, AC 501, PC 2, Logan
Scranton SD, PO BOX 86 72863 — 2-11111
Bill Horne, supt. — 938-7121
JSHS, PO BOX 86 72863 — 2-00111
George Harrison, prin. — 938-7121

Searcy, AC 501, PC 7, White
Searcy SD, 801 N ELM ST 72143 — 5-11111
Tony Wood, supt. — 268-3517
SHS, 301 N ELLA ST 72143 — 3-00001
Bob Casteel, prin. — 268-8315
Ahlf JHS, 308 W VINE AVE 72143 — 2-00110
Mike Rippy, prin. — 268-3158

Harding Academy — 2-11111
PO BOX 775 72149 — 268-1515
Randy Lambeth, prin.
Harding University — 5-UC
900 E CENTER AVE 72149 — 279-4274

Sheridan, AC 501, PC 5, Grant
Sheridan SD, 400 N ROCK ST 72150 — 5-11111
David Robinson, supt. — 942-3135
SHS, 800 W VINE ST 72150 — 3-00001
Betty Cook, prin. — 942-3137
JHS, 500 N ROCK ST 72150 — 3-00110
Charles Tadlock, prin. — 942-3813

Sherwood, AC 501, PC 7, Pulaski
Pulaski Co. Special SD
Supt. — See Little Rock
Sylvan Hills JHS — 3-00110
401 DEE JAY HUDSON DR 72120 — 835-3740
Sue Clark, prin.

Shirley, AC 501, PC 2, Van Buren
Shirley SD, PO BOX 40 72153 — 3-11111
Bob Biggs, supt. — 723-8191
JSHS, PO BOX 40 72153 — 2-00111
Fred Ramsey, prin. — 723-8192

Siloam Springs, AC 501, PC 6, Benton
Siloam Springs SD — 4-11111
PO BOX 798 72761 — 524-3191
Randall Spear, supt.
SHS, 1500 W JEFFERSON ST 72761 — 2-00001
William Bergen, prin. — 524-5134
JHS, 1525 W TULSA ST 72761 — 2-00110
Grady Nichols, prin. — 524-6184

John Brown University — 3-UC
2000 W UNIVERSITY ST 72761 — 524-3131

Smackover, AC 501, PC 4, Union
Smackover SD, 1510 LISBON RD 71762 — 3-11111
Russell Johnson, supt. — 725-3132
JSHS, 505 W 7TH ST 71762 — 2-00111
Donald Smeltzer, prin. — 725-3101

Sparkman, AC 501, PC 3, Dallas
Sparkman SD, PO BOX 37 71763 — 2-11111
Jerry Moore, supt. — 678-2243
JSHS, PO BOX 37 71763 — 2-00111
Don Denton, prin. — 678-2242

Springdale, AC 501, PC 8, Washington
Springdale SD, 202 W EMMA AVE 72764 — 6-11111
Jim Rollins, supt. — 750-8800
SHS, 1103 W EMMA AVE 72764 — 4-00001
Don Love, prin. — 750-8832
Central JHS — 3-00110
2811 W HUNTSVILLE AVE 72762 — 750-8854
Nancy Roark, prin.
Southwest JHS, PRINCETON ST 72762 — 3-00110
Brice Wagner, prin. — 750-8849

Shiloh Christian S — 3-11111
1707 JOHNSON RD 72762 — 756-1140
Rod Goodsell, prin.

Stamps, AC 501, PC 4, Lafayette
Stamps SD, PO BOX 309 71860 — 3-11111
Glenn Fugatt, supt. — 533-2371
JSHS, PO BOX 309 71860 — 2-00111
Jimmy Allen, prin. — 533-4464

Star City, AC 501, PC 4, Lincoln
Star City SD, PO BOX 39 71667 — 4-11111
Dalda Womack, supt. — 628-4237
HS, PO BOX 39 71667 — 2-00011
Jim Moore, prin. — 628-4111
MS, PO BOX 39 71667 — 2-01100
Charlie Baggett, prin. — 628-5125

State University, AC 501, PC see Jonesboro

Arkansas State University — 6-UC
PO BOX 1630 72467 — 972-3024

Stephens, AC 501, PC 4, Ouachita
Stephens SD, PO BOX 427 71764 — 3-11111
Gary Kees, supt. — 786-5443
JSHS, PO BOX 427 71764 — 2-00111
John McWilliams, prin. — 786-5442

Strawberry, AC 501, PC 2, Lawrence
River Valley SD, PO BOX 50 72469 — 2-11111
Lynn Roe King, supt. — 528-3856
JSHS, PO BOX 50 72469 — 2-00111
Mike Smith, prin. — 528-3856

Strong, AC 501, PC 3, Union
Strong SD, PO BOX 735 71765 — 3-11111
Travis Wedgeworth, supt. — 797-7322
JSHS, PO BOX 735 71765 — 2-00111
Saul Lusk, prin. — 797-2312

Stuttgart, AC 501, PC 7, Arkansas
Stuttgart SD, PO BOX 928 72160 — 4-11111
Joe Williams, supt. — 673-3561

SHS, PO BOX 928 72160 — 3-00001
  Bill Hulsey, prin. — 673-3561
JHS, PO BOX 928 72160 — 2-00110
  Letroy Gathen, prin. — 673-3561

Subiaco, AC 501, PC 3, Logan

Subiaco Academy — 2-00011
  100 COLLEGE AVE 72865 — 934-4291
  David Hartz, prin.

Sulphur Rock, AC 501, PC 2, Independence
Sulphur Rock SD, PO BOX 98 72579 — 2-11111
  Dean Fugett, supt. — 799-3374
JSHS, PO BOX 98 72579 — 2-00111
  Dennis Martin, prin. — 799-8088

Swifton, AC 501, PC 3, Jackson
Swifton SD, PO BOX 99 72471 — 2-11111
  Richard Billingsley, supt. — 485-2381
JSHS, PO BOX 99 72471 — 2-00111
  Gene Goza, prin. — 485-2336

Taylor, AC 501, PC 3, Columbia
Taylor SD, 506 E PINE ST 71861 — 2-11111
  Jerry Camp, supt. — 694-2251
JSHS, 506 E PINE ST 71861 — 2-00111
  John Jandebeur, prin. — 694-2251

Texarkana, AC 501, PC 7, Miller
Genoa Central SD — 3-11111
  RR 7 BOX 518 75502 — 653-4343
  Gary Cobb, supt.
Genoa Central JSHS — 2-00111
  RR 7 BOX 518 75502 — 653-2272
  Albert Murphy, prin.

Texarkana SD, 3512 GRAND AVE 75502 — 6-11111
  Bobby Aldridge, supt. — 772-3371
Arkansas SHS — 4-00001
  1500 JEFFERSON AVE 75502 — 774-7641
  Russell Sapaugh, prin.
College Hill JHS, 1600 FOREST ST 75502 — 3-00110
  Lewis Thompson, prin. — 772-0281
North Heights JHS — 3-00110
  2118 E 35TH ST 75502 — 773-1091
  Marve Register, prin.

Timbo, AC 501, PC 1, Stone
Stone County SD, PO BOX 6 72680 — 2-11111
  Ronnie Lee, supt. — 746-4303
JSHS, PO BOX 6 72680 — 2-00111
  Tony Conley, prin. — 746-4303

Trumann, AC 501, PC 6, Poinsett
Trumann SD, 221 N PINE AVE 72472 — 4-11111
  Cecil Daves, supt. — 483-6444
JSHS, 221 N PINE AVE 72472 — 3-00111
  Joe Waleszonia, prin. — 483-5301

Tuckerman, AC 501, PC 4, Jackson
Jackson County SD — 3-11111
  PO BOX 1070 72473 — 349-2232
  Gene Fletcher, supt.
JSHS, PO BOX 1070 72473 — 2-00111
  Hugh Bruge, prin. — 349-2657

Turrell, AC 501, PC 3, Crittenden
Turrell SD, PO BOX 369 72384 — 3-11111
  M. McFatridge, supt. — 343-2533
JSHS, PO BOX 369 72384 — 2-00111
  Alfred Hogan, prin. — 343-2655

Tyronza, AC 501, PC 3, Poinsett
East Poinsett County SD
  Supt. — See Lepanto
East Poinsett County JHS — 2-00110
  RR 2 BOX 184 72386 — 487-2259
  Don Jones, prin.

Umpire, AC 501, PC 2, Howard
Umpire SD, PO BOX 60 71971 — 2-11111
  Charles McConnell, supt. — 583-2141
JSHS, PO BOX 60 71971 — 1-00111
  Linda Kitchens, prin. — 583-2141

Valley Springs, AC 501, PC 2, Boone
Valley Springs SD, PO BOX 86 72682 — 3-11111
  Roy Norvell, supt. — 429-5217
JSHS, PO BOX 86 72682 — 2-00111
  J. Collins, prin. — 429-5217

Van Buren, AC 501, PC 7, Crawford
Van Buren SD — 5-11111
  2221 E POINTER TRL 72956 — 474-7942
  Bill Mitchell, supt.
SHS, 2001 E POINTER TRL 72956 — 3-00001
  William Wyatt, prin. — 474-6821
Coleman JHS, 821 E POINTER TRL 72956 — 3-00110
  Edmond Brewer, prin. — 471-3160
Butterfield Trail JHS — 3-00110
  12TH & ELM STS 72956 — 474-6838
  Lonnie Myers, prin.

Vilonia, AC 501, PC 4, Faulkner
Vilonia SD, PO BOX 160 72173 — 4-11111
  Frank Mitchell, supt. — 796-3500
SHS, PO BOX 160 72173 — 3-00001
  Ed Sellers, prin. — 796-2111
JHS, PO BOX 160 72173 — 2-00110
  Jim Belote, prin. — 796-3912

Viola, AC 501, PC 2, Fulton
Viola SD, PO BOX 380 72583 — 2-11111
  Marvin Newton, supt. — 458-2323
JSHS, PO BOX 380 72583 — 2-00111
  Jerry Taylor, prin. — 458-2213

Waldo, AC 501, PC 4, Columbia
Waldo SD, PO BOX 367 71770 — 3-11111
  Richard Britt, supt. — 693-5731
JSHS, PO BOX 367 71770 — 2-00111
  Edgar Montgomery, prin. — 693-5825

Waldron, AC 501, PC 5, Scott
Waldron SD, PO BOX 1397 72958 — 4-11111
  Ray Morgan, supt. — 637-3179
HS, PO BOX 2410 72958 — 2-00011
  Robert Tutt, prin. — 637-3405
MS, RR 1 BOX 100A 72958 — 2-01100
  Randy Thrash, prin. — 637-4549

Walnut Ridge, AC 501, PC 5, Lawrence
Walnut Ridge SD, 508 E FREE ST 72476 — 3-11111
  Glen Murphy, supt. — 886-6634
HS, 508 E FREE ST 72476 — 2-00111
  Terry Belcher, prin. — 886-6623
MS, 508 E FREE ST 72476 — 2-01100
  Aaron Hosman, prin. — 886-6697

Williams Baptist College — 2-UC
  201 FULBRIGHT ST 72476 — 886-6741

Warren, AC 501, PC 6, Bradley
Warren SD, 803 N WALNUT ST 71671 — 4-11111
  Maxwell Williams, supt. — 226-6738
SHS, 803 N WALNUT ST 71671 — 2-00001
  Bruce Terry, prin. — 226-6736
JHS, 308 W PINE ST 71671 — 2-00110
  Glenetta Burks, prin. — 226-2366

Weiner, AC 501, PC 3, Poinsett
Weiner SD, PO BOX 408 72479 — 2-11111
  Charlotte Wright, supt. — 684-2253
JSHS, PO BOX 408 72479 — 2-00111
  Tom Knight, prin. — 684-2250

Western Grove, AC 501, PC 2, Newton
Western Grove SD — 2-11111
  300 SCHOOL ST 72685 — 429-5215
  Jack Robinson, supt.
JSHS, 300 SCHOOL ST 72685 — 2-00111
  Carlous Tennison, prin. — 429-5215

West Fork, AC 501, PC 4, Washington
West Fork SD, PO BOX 319 72774 — 2-11111
  John Selph, supt. — 839-2231
HS, PO BOX 319 72774 — 2-00011
  Roy Keyes, prin. — 839-3131
MS, PO BOX 319 72774 — 2-01100
  D. Mullins, prin. — 839-3342

West Helena, AC 501, PC 6, Phillips
Helena-West Helena SD
  Supt. — See Helena
Central HS, 1 SCHOOL ST 72390 — 4-00011
  Robert Thompson, prin. — 572-6744
Miller JHS, 898 HIGHWAY 49 72390 — 3-00100
  Bob Farrah, prin. — 572-3705

Desoto S, PO BOX 2807 72390 — 2-11111
  E. Morris, prin. — 572-6717

West Memphis, AC 501, PC 8, Crittenden
West Memphis SD — 6-11111
  PO BOX 826 72303 — 735-1915
  Bill Kissinger, supt.
SHS, 501 W BROADWAY ST 72301 — 4-00001
  Loutelious Holmes, prin. — 735-3660
East JHS, 1151 GOODWIN AVE 72301 — 2-00110
  Larry McCain, prin. — 735-2081
West JHS, 331 W BARTON AVE 72301 — 2-00110
  Bill Terwilliger, prin. — 735-3161
Wonder JHS, 1401 MADISON AVE 72301 — 3-00110
  Willie Harris, prin. — 735-8522

Health Care Training Institute — 2-CS
  222 N 6TH ST 72301
West Memphis Christian S — 2-11111
  PO BOX 2066 72303 — 735-0341
  Sam Jenkins, prin.

White Hall, AC 501, PC 5, Jefferson
White Hall SD — 5-11111
  1020 W HOLLAND AVE 71602 — 247-2002
  Jerry Lybrand, supt.
SHS, 700 BULLDOG DR 71602 — 3-00001
  Dan Young, prin. — 247-3255
JHS, 8106 DOLLARWAY RD 71602 — 3-00110
  James Pittillo, prin. — 247-2711
Other Schools – See Redfield

Wickes, AC 501, PC 3, Polk
Wickes SD, PO BOX C 71973 — 2-11111
  Michael Gray, supt. — 385-7101
JSHS, PO BOX C 71973 — 2-00111
  Jim Tankersley, prin. — 385-2366

Wilburn, AC 501, PC 2, Cleburne
Wilburn SD, PO BOX 1000 72179 — 2-11111
  Donald Sharp, supt. — 362-6107
JSHS, PO BOX 1000 72179 — 1-00111
  Oneta Williams, prin. — 362-6107

Williford, AC 501, PC 1, Sharp
Williford SD, PO BOX 137 72482 — 2-11111
  James McLeod, supt. — 966-4330
JSHS, PO BOX 137 72482 — 2-00111
  Roy Causbie, prin. — 966-4330

Wilson, AC 501, PC 4, Mississippi
South Mississippi County SD — 4-11111
  1700 W STATE HIGHWAY 14 72395 — 655-8633
  Harold Clemons, supt.
Rivercrest SHS — 2-00001
  1700 W STATE HIGHWAY 14 72395 — 655-8111
  Rogers Ford, prin.
Rivercrest JHS, 50 MAIN ST 72395 — 2-00110
  Larry James, prin. — 655-8421

Winslow, AC 501, PC 2, Washington
Winslow SD, PO BOX 140 72959 — 2-11111
  Danny Patrick, supt. — 634-2241
JSHS, PO BOX 140 72959 — 2-00111
  Mary Sallee, prin. — 634-7151

Witts Springs, AC 501, PC 1, Searcy
Witts Springs SD — 2-11111
  GENERAL DELIVERY 72686 — 496-2336
  Tim Passmore, supt.
JSHS, GENERAL DELIVERY 72686 — 2-00111
  (—), prin. — 496-2355

Wynne, AC 501, PC 6, Cross
Wynne SD, PO BOX 69 72396 — 5-11111
  Darrell Smith, supt. — 238-5000
HS, PO BOX 69 72396 — 3-00011
  Roy Hall, prin. — 238-5001
JHS, PO BOX 69 72396 — 3-00100
  Charles Cobb, prin. — 238-5040

Yellville, AC 501, PC 4, Marion
Yellville-Summit SD, RR 1 72687 — 3-11111
  Jerry Cunningham, supt. — 449-4061
Yellville-Summit HS, RR 1 72687 — 2-00011
  Jesse Bergeron, prin. — 449-4066
Yellville-Summit MS, RR 1 72687 — 2-00100
  John Dwyer, prin. — 449-6533

CALIFORNIA

STATE DEPARTMENT OF EDUCATION
721 Capitol Mall, Sacramento 95814
(916) 657-2451

Acting Superintendent of Public Instruction	William Dawson
Executive Deputy Superintendent	Robert La Liberte
Deputy Superintendent Management Services	Diane Kirkham
General Counsel Legal & Audits	Joseph Symkowick
Deputy Superintendent Curriculum & Instructional Leadership	Harvey Hunt
Deputy Superintendent Field Services	Robert Agee
Deputy Superintendent Governmental Policy	Joe Holsinger
Deputy Superintendent Specialized Programs	Shirley Thornton

STATE BOARD OF EDUCATION
721 Capitol Mall, Sacramento 95814

President   Marion McDowell

COUNTY SUPERINTENDENTS OF SCHOOLS

Alameda County
August Scornaienchi   510-887-0152
313 W WINTON AVE, Hayward 94544

Alpine County
James Parsons, 43 HAWKSIDE DR   916-694-2230
Markleeville 96120

Amador County
Kenneth Sherer   209-223-1750
217 REX AVE, Jackson 95642

Butte County
Jerry McGuire   916-538-7855
1859 BIRD ST, Oroville 95965

Calaveras County
Robert Bach   209-736-4662
PO BOX 760, Angels Camp 95222

Colusa County
JoAn Salzen   916-458-7601
146 7TH ST, Colusa 95932

Contra Costa County
Ronald Stewart   510-942-3388
77 SANTA BARBARA RD
Pleasant Hill 94523

Del Norte County
Gene Edinger   707-464-6141
301 W WASHINGTON BLVD
Crescent City 95531

El Dorado County
Ken Lowry   916-622-7130
6767 GREEN VALLEY RD
Placerville 95667

Fresno County
Peter Mehas, 1111 VAN NESS AVE   209-265-3000
Fresno 93721

Glenn County
Lloyd Hubbard   916-934-6575
525 W SYCAMORE ST
Willows 95988

Humboldt County
Louis Bucher   707-445-7000
901 MYRTLE AVE, Eureka 95501

Imperial County
Herbert Farrar, 1398 SPERBER RD   619-339-6464
El Centro 92243

Inyo County
Ken Baker   619-878-2426
PO BOX G, Independence 93526

Kern County
Kelly Blanton   805-398-3600
5801 SUNDALE AVE
Bakersfield 93309

Kings County
Gene Billingsley   209-584-1441
1144 W LACEY BLVD
Hanford 93230

Lake County
Judith Luchsinger   707-263-3080
1152 S MAIN ST, Lakeport 95453

Lassen County
William Gillaspie   916-257-2196
472-013 JOHNSTONVILLE RD N
Susanville 96130

Los Angeles County
Stuart Gothold   310-922-6111
9300 IMPERIAL HWY
Downey 90242

Madera County
Sally Frazier, 28123 AVENUE 14   209-673-6051
Madera 93638

Marin County
Byron Mauzy   415-472-4110
PO BOX 4925, San Rafael 94913

Mariposa County
William Pettus   209-966-3691
PO BOX 8, Mariposa 95338

Mendicino County
Jack Ward   707-463-4807
2240 EASTSIDE RD, Ukiah 95482

Merced County
Ronald Tiffee   209-385-8300
632 W 13TH ST, Merced 95340

Modoc County
Carol Harbaugh   916-233-7100
139 HENDERSON ST
Alturas 96101

Mono County
Edward Inwood   619-932-7311
PO BOX 477, Bridgeport 93517

Monterey County
William Barr   408-755-0300
PO BOX 80851, Salinas 93912

Napa County
Edgar Henderson   707-253-6800
1015 KAISER RD, Napa 94558

Nevada County
Harold Houser   916-272-7222
11745 MALTMAN DR
Grass Valley 95945

Orange County
John Dean   714-966-4000
PO BOX 9050, Costa Mesa 92628

Placer County
John Reinking   916-889-8020
360 NEVADA ST, Auburn 95603

Plumas County
William Cottini   916-283-6500
PO BOX 10330, Quincy 95971

Riverside County
Dale Holmes   909-788-6530
PO BOX 868, Riverside 92502

Sacramento County
David Meaney   916-228-2500
9738 LINCOLN VILLAGE DR
Sacramento 95827

San Benito County
James Lowry   408-637-5393
460 5TH ST, Hollister 95023

San Bernardino County
Barry Pulliam, 601 N E ST   909-387-4386
San Bernardino 92410

San Diego County
Harry Weinberg   619-292-3500
6401 LINDA VISTA RD
San Diego 92111

San Francisco County
Waldemar Rojas   415-241-6000
135 VAN NESS AVE
San Francisco 94102

San Joaquin County
Fred Wentworth   209-468-4800
PO BOX 213030, Stockton 95213

San Luis Obispo County
Linda Shephard, PO BOX 8105   805-543-7732
San Luis Obispo 93403

San Mateo County
Floyd Gonella   415-802-5300
101 TWIN DOLPHIN DR
Redwood City 94065

Santa Barbara County
William Cirone, PO BOX 6307   805-964-4711
Santa Barbara 93160

Santa Clara County
Colleen Wilcox, 100 SKYPORT DR   408-453-6500
San Jose 95110

Santa Cruz County
Diane Siri, 809 BAY AVE STE H   408-476-7140
Capitola 95010

Shasta County
Charles Menoher   916-225-0200
1644 MAGNOLIA AVE
Redding 96001

Sierra County
Michael Moore   916-993-4991
PO BOX 959, Loyalton 96118

Siskiyou County
Frank Tallerico   916-842-5751
609 S GOLD ST, Yreka 96097

Solano County
Wendall Kuykendall   707-421-6530
655 WASHINGTON ST
Fairfield 94533

Sonoma County
Marv Adams   707-524-2600
5340 SKYLANE BLVD
Santa Rosa 95403

Stanislaus County
Martin Petersen   209-525-4900
801 COUNTY CENTER THREE CT
Modesto 95355

Sutter County
John Boyd   916-741-5110
463 2ND ST, Yuba City 95991

Tehama County
Marvin Locke   916-527-5811
PO BOX 689, Red Bluff 96080

Trinity County
Donald Stewart   916-623-2861
PO BOX 1256, Weaverville 96093

Tulare County
Jim Vidak, 2637 W BURREL AVE   209-733-6300
Visalia 93291

Tuolumne County
Orville Millhollin   209-533-8710
175 FAIRVIEW LN, Sonora 95370

Ventura County
Charles Weis   805-652-7332
535 E MAIN ST, Ventura 93001

Yolo County
Elizabeth Zemmels   916-661-2724
175 WALNUT ST
Woodland 95695

Yuba County
Dennis Bissell   916-741-6231
938 14TH ST, Marysville 95901

PUBLIC, PRIVATE AND CATHOLIC SECONDARY SCHOOLS

Acton, AC 805, PC 4, Los Angeles
Acton-Agua Dulce UNESD 4-11100
PO BOX 68 93510 269-5999
Tom Brown, supt.
High Desert MS, PO BOX 68 93510 2-00100
Elizabeth Levering, prin. 269-0310

Adelanto, AC 619, PC 6, San Bernardino
Victor Valley UNHSD
Supt. — See Victorville
Adelanto MS 2-00100
18295 RACOON AVE 92301 246-4440
Gloria Garcia-Garza, prin.

Agoura Hills, AC 818, PC 7, Los Angeles
Las Virgenes USD
Supt. — See Calabasas
Agoura HS, 28545 DRIVER AVE 91301 4-00011
Michael Botsford, prin. 889-1262
Lindero Canyon MS 4-00100
5844 LARBOARD LN 91301 889-2134
Ronald Kaiser, prin.

Alameda, AC 510, PC 8, Alameda
Alameda City USD 6-11111
2200 CENTRAL AVE 94501 748-4000
Dennis Chaconas, supt.
HS, 2201 ENCINAL AVE 94501 4-00011
Betty Ruark, prin. 748-4022
Encinal HS, 210 CENTRAL AVE 94501 4-00011
Milton Werner, prin. 748-4023
Chipman MS, 401 PACIFIC AVE 94501 3-00100
Lynda Griebrok, prin. 748-4017
Lincoln MS 3-00100
1250 FERNSIDE BLVD 94501 748-4018
Michael Janvier, prin.
Wood MS, 420 GRAND ST 94501 3-00100
David Dierking, prin. 748-4015

California Sch. Professional Psychology 2-UC
1005 ATLANTIC AVE 94501 523-2300
College of Alameda 6-CC
555 ATLANTIC AVE 94501 522-7221
St. Josephs Notre Dame HS 3-00011
1011 CHESTNUT ST 94501 523-1526
Anthony Aiello, prin.

Alamo, AC 510, PC 6, Contra Costa
San Ramon Valley USD
Supt. — See Danville
Stone Valley MS 3-00100
3001 MIRANDA AVE 94507 837-3077
Jack Boterenbrood, prin.

Albany, AC 510, PC 7, Alameda
Albany City USD 5-11111
904 TALBOT AVE 94706 559-6500
J. Dale Hudson, supt.
HS, 603 KEY ROUTE BLVD 94706 3-00011
Virginia Behm, prin. 559-6550
MacGregor Vo HS Vo Tech
603 SAN GABRIEL AVE 94706 559-6570
Constance Hubbard, prin.
MS, 1000 JACKSON ST 94706 3-00100
Teresa Corpuz, prin. 559-6540

Alhambra, AC 818, PC 8, Los Angeles
Alhambra City SD 7-11111
PO BOX 110 91802 308-2200
Heber Meeks, supt.
HS, 101 S 2ND ST 91801 5-00011
Julie Hadden, prin. 308-2342
Keppel HS, 501 E HELLMAN AVE 91801 5-00011
Rudy Chavez, prin. 572-2242
Other Schools — See San Gabriel

California Sch. Professional Psychology 2-UC
1000 S FREMONT AVE 91803 284-2777
Ramona Secondary S 2-00111
1701 W RAMONA RD 91803 282-4151
Sr. Margaret Spiller, prin.

Aliso Viejo, AC 714, PC 6, Orange
Capistrano USD
Supt. — See San Juan Capistrano
Aliso Niguel JHS 4-00010
27652 LAGUNA HILLS DR 92656 831-5590
Denise Danne, prin.
MS, 111 PARK AVE 92656 2-00100
Cheryl Lampe, prin. 831-2622

La Monte Academie 2-11111
25182 EASTWING 92656 455-1270
Ann Sullivan, prin.

Alpaugh, AC 209, PC 3, Tulare
Alpaugh USD, PO BOX 9 93201 2-11111
Jeff Bauer, supt. 949-8413
JSHS, PO BOX 9 93201 2-00111
Jeff Bauer, prin. 949-8413

Alpine, AC 619, PC 6, San Diego
Alpine UNSD 4-11100
1323 ADMINISTRATION WAY 91901 445-3236
John Ancell, supt.
MacQueen MS 3-00100
8770 HARBISON CANYON RD 91901 445-3245
Pamela Lewis, prin.

Altadena, AC 818, PC 8, Los Angeles
Pasadena USD
Supt. — See Pasadena

Eliot MS, 2184 LAKE AVE 91001 3-00100
Delano Yarbrough, prin. 794-7121

Alta Loma, AC 909, PC see Cucamonga
Alta Loma ESD, PO BOX 370 91701 6-11100
Reed Montgomery, supt. 987-0766
JHS, PO BOX 370 91701 3-00100
James Dyer, prin. 987-4644
Vineyard JHS, PO BOX 370 91701 3-00100
Peter Watson, prin. 989-7664

Chaffey JUNHSD
Supt. — See Ontario
HS, 8880 BASELINE RD 91701 5-00011
Allen Martens, prin. 989-5511

Chaffey College 7-CC
5885 HAVEN AVE 91737 987-1737

Altaville, AC 209, PC see Angels Camp
Bret Harte UNHSD 3-00011
PO BOX 7000 95221 736-2507
Joseph Wilimek, supt.
Bret Harte Union HS 3-00011
PO BOX 208 95222 736-2507
Lloyd Gaspar, prin.
Other Schools — See Arnold, Copperopolis

Alturas, AC 916, PC 5, Modoc
Modoc JUSD, 906 W 4TH ST 96101 4-11111
Ronald Huebert, supt. 233-7203
Modoc HS, 900 N MAIN ST 96101 2-00011
Bob Larkins, prin. 233-7301
Modoc MS, 906 W 4TH ST 96101 2-00100
Robert Kuehl, prin. 233-7501

Anaheim, AC 714, PC 10, Orange
Anaheim UNHSD 7-00111
PO BOX 3520 92803 999-3511
Cynthia Grennan, supt.
HS, PO BOX 3520 92803 4-00011
Jack Weber, prin. 999-3717
Katella HS, PO BOX 3520 92803 4-00011
Gerald Glenn, prin. 999-3621
Loara HS, PO BOX 3520 92803 4-00011
Barry Escoe, prin. 999-3677
Magnolia HS, PO BOX 3520 92803 4-00011
David Steinle, prin. 220-4221
Savanna HS, PO BOX 3520 92803 4-00011
Mary Mejia, prin. 220-4262
Western HS, PO BOX 3520 92803 4-00011
Warren Stephenson, prin. 220-4040
Ball JHS, PO BOX 3520 92803 4-00100
Doug Munsey, prin. 999-3663
Brookhurst JHS, PO BOX 3520 92803 3-00100
Richard Lodyga, prin. 999-3613
Dale JHS, PO BOX 3520 92803 4-00100
Rob Montenegro, prin. 220-4210
Orangeview JHS, PO BOX 3520 92803 3-00100
Dave Loop, prin. 220-4205
South JHS, PO BOX 3520 92803 3-00100
Henry Frese, prin. 999-3667
Sycamore JHS, PO BOX 3520 92803 4-00100
Patricia Savage, prin. 999-3617
Other Schools — See Cypress, La Palma

Orange USD
Supt. — See Orange
Canyon HS, 220 S IMPERIAL HWY 92807 4-00011
Ralph Jameson, prin. 532-8000
El Rancho MS 3-00100
181 S DEL GIORGIO RD 92808 997-6238
Roger Duthoy, prin.

Placentia Yorba Linda USD
Supt. — See Placentia
Esperanza HS 4-00011
1830 N KELLOGG DR 92807 779-7870
George Allen, prin.

Associated Technical College 3-CS
1177 N MAGNOLIA AVE 92801 229-8785
California Career Schools 1-CS
392 W CERRITOS AVE 92805 635-6585
Computer Learning Center 2-CS
222 S HARBOR BLVD 92805 956-8060
ConCorde Career Institute 2-CS
1717 S BROOKHURST ST 92804 635-3450
Connelly HS, 2323 W BROADWAY 92804 2-00011
Trudee Christensen, prin. 776-1717
Fairmont Vo HS 3-01100
1557 W MABLE ST 92802 774-1052
David Jackson, prin.
Heritage Christian HS 1-01111
2530 W LA PALMA AVE 92801 255-9877
David Rader, prin.
Lutheran Bible Institute of California 2-UC
641 S WESTERN AVE 92804
Modern Technology School of X-Ray 2-CS
1232 E KATELLA AVE 92805 978-7702
NEC-Bryman Campus 3-CS
1120 N BROOKHURST ST 92801 778-6500
Orange County Business College 2-CS
2035 E BALL RD 92806 772-6941
Practical Schools 2-CS
900 E BALL RD 92806 535-6000
Servite HS 3-00011
1952 W LA PALMA AVE 92801 774-7575
Raymond Dunne, prin.

South Coast College of Court Reporting 2-CS
1380 S SANDERSON AVE 92806 635-6464
Southern CA College of Court Reporting 2-CS
1100 S CLAUDINA PL 92805 758-1500

Anderson, AC 916, PC 6, Shasta
Anderson UNHSD 4-00011
1471 FERRY ST 96007 365-2741
James Spence, supt.
HS, 1471 FERRY ST 96007 3-00011
Charles Bononi, prin. 365-2741
Other Schools — See Cottonwood

Cascade UNESD, 1645 MILL ST 96007 4-11100
Barry Reed, supt. 365-3392
MS, 1646 FERRY ST 96007 3-00100
Rene Lawson, prin. 365-7372

Happy Valley UNESD 3-11100
17480 PALM AVE 96007 357-2134
David Taylor, supt.
Happy Valley MS 2-01100
17480 PALM AVE 96007 357-2111
Robert Ferrera, prin.

Angwin, AC 707, PC 5, Napa

Pacific Union College 4-UC
1 ANGWIN AVE 94508 965-6234
Pacific Union Prep S 2-00011
MC KIBBIN HALL 94508 965-7272
Winston Dennis, prin.

Antioch, AC 510, PC 8, Contra Costa
Antioch USD, PO BOX 768 94509 7-11111
Alan Newell, supt. 706-4100
SHS, 700 W 18TH ST 94509 4-00001
Jeff Reich, prin. 706-5300
JHS, 1500 D ST 94509 4-00110
Donna Covey, prin. 706-5316
Park JHS, 1 SPARTAN WAY 94509 4-00110
Barbara Ewing, prin. 706-5314

Antioch Christian S 2-11111
640 E TREGALLAS RD 94509 757-1837
Timothy Hanford, prin.

Anza, AC 909, PC 2, Riverside
Hemet USD
Supt. — See Hemet
Hamilton S, 57550 MITCHELL RD 92539 3-11111
Walter Brubaker, prin. 763-1840

Apple Valley, AC 619, PC 8, San Bernardino
Apple Valley USD 7-11111
22974 BEAR VALLEY RD 92308 247-8001
J. Dean Hane, supt.
HS, 22974 BEAR VALLEY RD 92308 5-00011
Marilyn Cook, prin. 247-7206
JHS, 22974 BEAR VALLEY RD 92308 4-00100
Robert Turner, prin. 247-7267
Vista Campana MS 4-00100
22974 BEAR VALLEY RD 92308 242-7011
Virgil Barnes, prin.

Aptos, AC 408, PC 6, Santa Cruz
Pajaro Valley USD
Supt. — See Watsonville
HS, 7301 FREEDOM BLVD 95003 4-00011
Ron Severson, prin. 688-6565
JHS, PO BOX 367 95001 3-00100
Nancy Bilicich, prin. 688-3234

Cabrillo College 7-CC
6500 SOQUEL DR 95003 479-6100

Arbuckle, AC 916, PC 4, Colusa
Pierce JUSD, 940 WILDWOOD RD 95912 4-11111
Jim Lutz, supt. 476-2892
Pierce HS, 960 WILDWOOD RD 95912 2-00011
Carolyn Reiff, prin. 476-2277
Johnson JHS, 938 WILDWOOD RD 95912 2-00100
Ellen Armstrong, prin. 476-3261

Arcadia, AC 818, PC 8, Los Angeles
Arcadia USD, 234 CAMPUS DR 91007 6-11111
Terrence Towner, supt. 446-0131
Arcadia SHS, 234 CAMPUS DR 91007 4-00001
Dorothy Schneider, prin. 446-0131
Rancho HS, 234 CAMPUS DR 91007 1-00011
(—), prin. 447-2814
Dana JHS, 234 CAMPUS DR 91007 3-00110
Joseph Fox, prin. 447-1963
First Avenue JHS 3-00110
234 CAMPUS DR 91007 446-1668
Beverly Rodriguez, prin.
Foothills JHS, 234 CAMPUS DR 91007 3-00110
Aideen Honzay, prin. 303-7981

Dootson School of Trucking 2-CS
11625 CLARK ST 91006 303-1900
Rio Hondo Preparatory S 2-11111
PO BOX 118 91066 444-9531
Arlis Dowd, prin.

Arcata, AC 707, PC 7, Humboldt
Arcata ESD 3-11100
1125 16TH ST # 201 95521 822-0351
David Hochman, supt.
Sunny Brae MS 2-00100
1125 16TH ST # 201 95521 822-5988
Shari Westrick, prin.

Northern Humboldt UNHSD
  Supt. — See Mc Kinleyville
  HS, 1720 M ST 95521 — 3-00011
  Kim Kellenberg, prin. — 822-1731

Humboldt State University — 6-UC
  1 HARPS ST 95521 — 826-3011

Armona, AC 209, PC 5, Kings
  Armona UNESD, PO BOX 368 93202 — 4-11100
  Joe Looney, supt. — 583-5000
  Parkview MS, 11075 C ST 93202 — 2-01100
  Phil Holloway, prin. — 583-5020

Armona Union Academy — 2-11111
  PO BOX 397 93202 — 582-4468
  Sam Geli, prin.

Arnold, AC 209, PC 5, Calaveras
  Bret Harte UNHSD
  Supt. — See Altaville
  Arnold HS, PO BOX 780 95223 — 1-00011
  Timothy Miller, prin. — 795-4503

Arroyo Grande, AC 805, PC 7, San Luis Obispo
  Lucia Mar USD — 6-11111
  602 ORCHARD AVE 93420 — 473-4300
  Joseph Boeckx, supt.
  HS, 495 VALLEY RD 93420 — 4-00011
  Michael Sears, prin. — 473-4200
  Mesa MS, 2555 S HALCYON RD 93420 — 2-00100
  Robert Mistele, prin. — 473-4136
  Paulding MS — 3-00100
  600 CROWN HILL ST 93420 — 473-4100
  Gary Moore, prin.
  Other Schools — See Pismo Beach

Coastal Christian Academy — 2-11111
  1220 FARROLL AVE 93420 — 489-1213
  Marlin Miller, prin.

Artesia, AC 310, PC 7, Los Angeles
  ABC USD
  Supt. — See Cerritos
  Ross JHS, 17707 ELAINE AVE 90701 — 3-00100
  Harvey Hoyo, prin. — 924-8331

Arvin, AC 805, PC 6, Kern
  Arvin UNESD — 4-11100
  737 BEAR MOUNTAIN BLVD 93203 — 854-6500
  Michael McGuire, supt.
  Haven Drive MS — 3-00100
  737 BEAR MOUNTAIN BLVD 93203 — 854-6540
  Benjamin Paull, prin.

Kern HSD
  Supt. — See Bakersfield
  HS, PO BOX 518 93203 — 4-00011
  Jack Schulze, prin. — 854-5561

Atascadero, AC 805, PC 7, San Luis Obispo
  Atascadero USD — 6-11111
  5601 WEST MALL 93422 — 466-0393
  Judy Randazzo, supt.
  HS, 1 HIGH SCHOOL HILL RD 93422 — 4-00011
  James Stecher, prin. — 466-1705
  JHS, 6501 LEWIS AVE 93422 — 3-00100
  Chuck Wilbur, prin. — 466-2417

North County Christian S — 2-11111
  6225 ATASCADERO AVE 93422 — 466-4457
  Robert Willey, prin.

Atherton, AC 415, PC 6, San Mateo
  Menlo Park City ESD — 4-11100
  181 ENCINAL AVE 94027 — 321-7140
  Judy Rogers-Bianchi, supt.
  Other Schools — See Menlo Park

Sequoia UNHSD
  Supt. — See Redwood City
  Menlo-Atherton HS — 4-00011
  555 MIDDLEFIELD RD 94025 — 322-5311
  David Theis, prin.

Menlo College — 3-UC
  1000 EL CAMINO REAL 94027 — 323-6141
  Menlo S, 50 VALPARAISO AVE 94027 — 2-00111
  J. Anthony Paulus, prin. — 688-3863

Atwater, AC 209, PC 7, Merced
  Atwater ESD, 1601 GROVE AVE 95301 — 5-11100
  Sandra Lenker, supt. — 357-6100
  Mitchell IS, 1753 5TH ST 95301 — 3-00100
  Gayle Gallagher, prin. — 357-6124

Merced UNHSD
  Supt. — See Merced
  HS, PO BOX 835 95301 — 4-00011
  Larry Johnson, prin. — 357-6000

Merismos Christian S — 2-11111
  257 APPLEGATE RD 95301 — 357-0484
  Martin Comorosky, prin.

Auberry, AC 209, PC 4, Fresno
  Sierra USD, 31975 LODGE RD 93602 — 4-11111
  Don Witzansky, supt. — 855-3662
  Other Schools — See Prather, Tollhouse

Auburn, AC 916, PC 7, Placer
  Auburn UNESD, 471 MAIDU DR 95603 — 5-11100
  Edward Gilligan, supt. — 885-7242
  Cain MS, 150 PALM AVE 95603 — 3-00100
  Margie Bauman, prin. — 823-6106

Placer UNHSD, PO BOX 5048 95604 — 5-00011
  Randall Olson, supt. — 885-7986
  Placer HS, 275 ORANGE ST 95603 — 4-00011
  Tom Johnson, prin. — 885-4581
  Other Schools — See Colfax, Loomis

Forest Lake Christian S — 2-11111
  12515 COMBIE RD 95602 — 269-1535
  Jean Schoellerman, prin.

Avalon, AC 310, PC 5, Los Angeles
  Long Beach USD
  Supt. — See Long Beach
  JSHS, PO BOX 557 90704 — 2-00011
  Mark Ur, prin. — 510-0790

Avenal, AC 209, PC 6, Kings
  Reef-Sunset USD — 4-11111
  205 N PARK AVE 93204 — 386-9083
  Evelyn Bachelor, supt.
  HS, 601 E MARIPOSA ST 93204 — 2-00011
  Jake Colburn, prin. — 386-5253
  Reef-Sunset MS, 608 N 1ST AVE 93204 — 2-00100
  Frank Russell, prin. — 386-4128

Azusa, AC 818, PC 8, Los Angeles
  Azusa USD, PO BOX 500 91702 — 7-11111
  Rod Gaeta, supt. — 967-6211
  HS, PO BOX 500 91702 — 4-00011
  Joe Garcia, prin. — 969-3010
  Center MS, PO BOX 500 91702 — 3-00100
  Jon Blickenstaff, prin. — 969-1207
  Foothill MS, PO BOX 500 91702 — 3-00100
  Corey James, prin. — 334-0619
  Slauson MS, PO BOX 500 91702 — 3-00100
  Art Hiett, prin. — 969-9721
  Other Schools — See Covina

Azusa Pacific University — 4-UC
  PO BOX 7000 91702 — 969-3434

Baker, AC 619, PC 3, San Bernardino
  Baker Valley USD — 2-11111
  PO BOX 460 92309 — 733-4567
  Laverne Carlson, supt.
  SHS, PO BOX 460 92309 — 1-00001
  Laverne Carlson, prin. — 733-4387
  JHS, PO BOX 460 92309 — 1-00110
  Laverne Carlson, prin. — 733-4387

Bakersfield, AC 805, PC 9, Kern
  Bakersfield City ESD — 8-11100
  1300 BAKER ST 93305 — 631-4600
  Al Mijares, supt.
  Chipman JHS, 2905 EISSLER ST 93306 — 3-00100
  Jerry Tate, prin. — 631-5210
  Compton JHS, 3211 PICO AVE 93306 — 3-00100
  Don Londquist, prin. — 631-5230
  Curran JHS, 1116 LYMRIC WAY 93309 — 3-00100
  Hugh McGowan, prin. — 631-5240
  Emerson JHS, 801 4TH ST 93304 — 3-00100
  Donald Gill, prin. — 631-5260
  Sierra JHS, 3017 CENTER ST 93306 — 3-00100
  Al Capilla, prin. — 631-5470
  Stiern MS, 2551 MORNING DR 93306 — 4-00100
  Linda Mapes, prin. — 631-5480
  Washington JHS — 2-00100
  1101 NOBLE AVE 93305 — 631-5810
  Steve Castro, prin.

Beardsley ESD, 1001 ROBERTS LN 93308 — 4-11100
  Ken Chapman, supt. — 393-8550
  Beardsley JHS, 1001 ROBERTS LN 93308 — 2-00100
  Rocky Johnson, prin. — 392-9254

Edison ESD — 3-11100
  9600 EUCALYPTUS DR 93306 — 366-8625
  Barbara Clark, supt.
  Edison MS — 2-01100
  9600 EUCALYPTUS DR 93306 — 366-8216
  Ron Seckler, prin.

Fruitvale ESD — 4-11100
  2114 CALLOWAY DR 93312 — 589-3830
  Carl Olsen, supt.
  Fruitvale JHS — 2-00100
  2114 CALLOWAY DR 93312 — 589-3933
  John Hefner, prin.

Greenfield UNESD — 5-11100
  1624 FAIRVIEW RD 93307 — 832-2450
  Don Williams, supt.
  Greenfield JHS — 3-00100
  1624 FAIRVIEW RD 93307 — 832-4822
  Dwight Walsh, prin.

Kern HSD, 2000 24TH ST 93301 — 7-00011
  Tom Jones, supt. — 631-3100
  HS, 1241 G ST 93301 — 5-00011
  S. Bruce, prin. — 324-9841
  East Bakersfield HS — 4-00011
  2200 QUINCY DR 93306 — 871-7221
  John Gibson, prin.
  Foothill HS, 501 PARK DR 93306 — 4-00011
  Michael Ramos, prin. — 366-4491
  Highland HS — 4-00011
  2900 ROYAL SCOTS WAY 93306 — 872-2777
  Anne Scott, prin.
  North HS, 300 GALAXY AVE 93308 — 4-00011
  Bill Bimat, prin. — 399-3351
  South HS, 1101 PLANZ RD 93304 — 4-00011
  Elaine Jamison, prin. — 831-3680

Stockdale HS — 3-00011
  2800 BUENA VISTA RD 93311 — 665-2800
  Jeannine Thompson, prin.
  West HS, 1200 NEW STINE RD 93309 — 4-00011
  Don Cauthron, prin. — 832-2822
  Centennial JHS — 3-00010
  8601 HAGEMAN RD 93312 — 588-8601
  William Hatcher, prin.
  Other Schools — See Arvin, Lake Isabella, Shafter

Norris SD, 6940 CALLOWAY DR 93312 — 4-11100
  Alvin Sandrini, supt. — 399-7987
  Norris MS, 6940 CALLOWAY DR 93312 — 2-00100
  Steven Shelton, prin. — 399-5571

Panama-Buena Vista UNSD — 7-11100
  4200 ASHE RD 93313 — 831-8331
  Bill Williams, supt.
  Actis JHS — 3-00100
  2400 WESTHOLME BLVD 93309 — 833-1250
  Wayne Winter, prin.
  Tevis JHS — 3-00100
  3901 PIN OAK PARK BLVD 93311 — 831-8331
  Frances Seaman, prin.
  Thompson JHS, 4200 PLANZ RD 93309 — 3-00100
  Gabrielle Gladden, prin. — 832-8011

Rosedale UNESD — 4-11100
  2553 OLD FARM RD 93312 — 588-6000
  Gary Mullhofer, supt.
  Rosedale MS — 3-00100
  12463 ROSEDALE HWY 93312 — 588-6030
  Anne Colletta, prin.

Standard ESD — 5-11100
  1200 N CHESTER AVE 93308 — 392-2110
  Marty Butt, supt.
  Standard MS — 3-00100
  1200 N CHESTER AVE 93308 — 392-2130
  Tim Jones, prin.

Vineland ESD — 3-11100
  14713 WEEDPATCH HWY 93307 — 845-3713
  Stephen Greenfield, supt.
  Sunset MS, 8301 SUNSET BLVD 93307 — 2-01100
  Debra Hoff, prin. — 845-1320

Bakersfield Adventist Academy — 2-11111
  3333 BERNARD ST 93306 — 871-1591
  Samir Berbawy, prin.
Bakersfield College — 7-CC
  1801 PANORAMA DR 93305 — 395-4011
California State University — 5-UC
  9001 STOCKDALE HWY 93311 — 664-2011
Community Christian HS — 2-00011
  PO BOX 80775 93380 — 399-1750
  Wendell Meadows, prin.
Garces Memorial HS — 3-00011
  2800 LOMA LINDA DR 93305 — 327-2578
  Edwin Hearn, prin.
San Joaquin Valley College — 1-CC
  201 NEW STINE RD 93309 — 834-0126
Santa Barbara Business College — 2-CS
  211 S REAL RD 93309 — 322-3006
Western Truck School — 2-CS
  5801 STATE RD 93308 — 399-0701

Baldwin Park, AC 818, PC 8, Los Angeles
  Baldwin Park USD — 7-11111
  3699 HOLLY AVE 91706 — 962-3311
  Lawrence Kemper, supt.
  HS, 3900 PUENTE AVE 91706 — 4-00011
  Vernon Moyer, prin. — 960-5431
  Sierra Vista HS, 3600 FRAZIER ST 91706 — 4-00011
  Marilyn Ghirelli, prin. — 960-7741
  Holland JHS, 4733 LANDIS AVE 91706 — 3-00100
  Nancy Guest, prin. — 962-8412
  Jones JHS, 14250 MERCED AVE 91706 — 3-00100
  Marcus Beasley, prin. — 962-8312
  Olive JHS, 13701 OLIVE ST 91706 — 2-00100
  Morris Sawyer, prin. — 962-8416
  Santa Fe MS — 2-01100
  4650 BALDWIN PARK BLVD 91706 — 856-1525
  Gloria Orozco, prin.
  Sierra Vista JHS, 3600 FRAZIER ST 91706 — 3-00100
  Lilia Lopez, prin. — 962-1300

Baldwin Park Christian Baptist S — 2-11111
  13940 MERCED AVE 91706 — 337-8828
  T. Selvey, prin.

Ballico, AC 209, PC 2, Merced
  Ballico-Cressey ESD — 2-11100
  PO BOX 49 95303 — 632-5371
  Larry Naegeli, supt.
  MS, PO BOX 49 95303 — 2-01100
  Larry Naegeli, prin. — 632-5371

Banning, AC 909, PC 7, Riverside
  Banning USD — 5-11111
  161 W WILLIAMS ST 92220 — 922-0200
  Gloria Johnston, supt.
  HS, 100 W WESTWARD AVE 92220 — 4-00011
  Alex McConahay, prin. — 922-0285
  Coombs IS, 1151 W WILSON ST 92220 — 4-00100
  Kathy McNamara, prin. — 922-0268

Barstow, AC 619, PC 7, San Bernardino
  Barstow USD, 551 AVENUE H 92311 — 6-11111
  Joe Spaulding, supt. — 256-0611
  HS, 551 AVENUE H 92311 — 4-00011
  Jim Ostrander, prin. — 256-0611
  MS, 551 AVENUE H 92311 — 3-00100
  Dale Russell, prin. — 256-0611

Kennedy MS, 551 AVENUE H 92311   3-00100
   Everett McCullough, prin.   256-0611

Barstow Christian S   2-11111
   800 YUCCA AVE 92311   256-3556
   John Wilfong, prin.
Barstow College   4-CC
   2700 BARSTOW RD 92311   252-2411

Beaumont, AC 909, PC 6, Riverside
Beaumont USD, PO BOX 187 92223   5-11111
   John Wood, supt.   845-1631
HS, PO BOX 187 92223   3-00011
   Robert Jones, prin.   845-3171
Mountain View JHS   3-00100
   PO BOX 187 92223   845-1627
   Victor Kezer, prin.

Bell, AC 213, PC 8, Los Angeles
Los Angeles USD
   Supt. — See Los Angeles
HS, 4328 BELL AVE 90201   5-00011
   Melquiades Mares, prin.   560-1800

Bellflower, AC 310, PC 8, Los Angeles
Bellflower USD   7-11111
   16703 CLARK AVE 90706   866-9011
   Rebecca Turrentine, supt.
JSHS, 16703 CLARK AVE 90706   4-00111
   Don Ashton, prin.   920-1801
Other Schools – See Lakewood

St. John Bosco HS   3-00011
   13640 BELLFLOWER BLVD 90706   920-1734
   William Goodman, prin.

Bell Gardens, PC 8, Los Angeles
Montebello USD
   Supt. — See Montebello
HS, 6119 AGRA ST 90201   5-00011
   Margarita Rosette, prin.   213-773-3871
IS, 5841 LIVE OAK ST 90201   4-01100
   Louis Ayala, prin.   310-927-1319
Suva IS, 6660 SUVA ST 90201   4-01100
   Lary Weiss, prin.   310-927-2679

Belmont, AC 415, PC 7, San Mateo
Belmont ESD   4-11100
   2960 HALLMARK DR 94002   593-8203
   Carol Worthington, supt.
Ralston IS, 2675 RALSTON AVE 94002   3-00100
   Anne Campbell, prin.   591-5385

Sequoia UNHSD
   Supt. — See Redwood City
Carlmont HS, 1400 ALAMEDA 94002   4-00011
   Reuben Trinidad, prin.   595-0210

College of Notre Dame   3-UC
   1500 RALSTON AVE 94002   508-3607
Notre Dame HS   2-00011
   1540 RALSTON AVE 94002   595-1913
   Rita Gleason, prin.

Benicia, AC 707, PC 7, Solano
Benicia USD, 350 E K ST 94510   5-11111
   Annette O'Connor, supt.   747-8300
HS, 1101 MILITARY W 94510   4-00011
   Archie Kinney, prin.   747-8325
Liberty HS, 350 E K ST 94510   1-00011
   David Barnas, prin.   747-8323
MS, 1100 SOUTHAMPTON RD 94510   4-00100
   Carole Hiltman, prin.   747-8340

Berkeley, AC 510, PC 9, Alameda
Berkeley USD   6-11111
   2134 MRTN LTHER KING JR WAY 94704   644-6147
   LaVoneia Steele, supt.
HS, 2246 MILVIA ST 94704   4-00011
   Jim Henderson, prin.   644-6120
King JHS, 1781 ROSE ST 94703   3-00100
   Neil Smith, prin.   644-6280
Willard JHS, 2425 STUART ST 94705   3-00100
   Christine Lim, prin.   644-6330

American Baptist Seminary of the West   1-UC
   2606 DWIGHT WAY 94704   841-1905
Armstrong University   2-UC
   2222 HAROLD WAY 94704   848-2500
Arrowsmith Academy   2-00111
   2300 BANCROFT WAY 94704   540-0440
   Kenneth Yale, prin.
Church Divinity School of the Pacific   1-UC
   2451 RIDGE RD 94709   848-3282
Dominican School of Philosophy/Theology   1-UC
   2401 RIDGE RD 94709   849-2030
Franciscan School of Theology   1-UC
   1712 EUCLID AVE 94709   848-5232
Graduate Theological Union   2-UC
   2400 RIDGE RD 94709   649-2400
Jesuit School of Theology at Berkeley   2-UC
   1735 LE ROY AVE 94709   800-824-0122
Maybeck HS   2-00011
   2362 BANCROFT WAY 94704   841-8489
   Stanley Cardinet, prin.
New College Advanced Christian Studies   1-UC
   2600 DWIGHT WAY 94704   841-9386
Pacific Lutheran Theological Seminary   2-UC
   2770 MARIN AVE 94708   524-5264
Pacific School of Religion   2-UC
   1798 SCENIC AVE 94709   848-0528

St. Marys College HS   2-00011
   1294 ALBINA AVE 94706   526-9242
   James Borrelli, prin.
Starr King School for the Ministry   1-UC
   2441 LE CONTE AVE 94709   845-6232
University of California   8-UC
   110 SPROUL HALL 94720   642-6000
Vista Community College   5-CC
   2020 MILVIA ST 94704   841-8431
Wright Institute   2-UC
   2728 DURANT AVE 94704   841-9230

Beverly Hills, AC 310, PC 8, Los Angeles
Beverly Hills USD   5-11111
   255 S LASKY DR 90212   277-5900
   Sol Levine, supt.
HS, 241 S MORENO DR 90212   4-00011
   Ben Bushman, prin.   201-0661

Beverly Hills Prep S   2-00111
   9250 W OLYMPIC BLVD 90212   276-0151
   Violet Popovich, prin.

Bieber, AC 916, PC 3, Lassen
Big Valley JUSD, PO BOX 157 96009   2-11111
   Boyce McClain, supt.   294-5266
Big Valley HS, PO BOX 157 96009   2-00011
   Boyce McClain, prin.   294-5231
Big Valley IS, PO BOX 157 96009   2-01100
   Doe Brownfield, prin.   294-5214

Big Bear Lake, AC 909, PC 6, San Bernardino
Bear Valley USD   5-11111
   PO BOX 1529 92315   866-4631
   Rudy Macioge, supt.
Big Bear HS, PO BOX 1708 92315   3-00011
   Philip Hamilton, prin.   585-6892
MS, PO BOX 1607 92315   3-00100
   John Niederkorn, prin.   866-4634

Biggs, AC 916, PC 4, Butte
Biggs USD, PO BOX 397 95917   3-11111
   Wayne Boulding, supt.   868-1281
JSHS, PO BOX 397 95917   2-00111
   Robert McCarthy, prin.   868-5825

Big Pine, AC 619, PC 4, Inyo
Big Pine USD, PO BOX 908 93513   2-11111
   David Manship, supt.   938-2005
HS, PO BOX 908 93513   1-00011
   David Manship, prin.   938-2222

Bishop JUNHSD
   Supt. — See Bishop
Palisade Glacier SHS   1-00001
   PO BOX 938 93513   873-4275
   John Helmbold, prin.

Big Sur, PC 3, Monterey
Pacific USD   1-11111
   PACIFIC VLY # 1 93920   805-927-4507
   William Raebe, supt.
Pacific Valley S   1-11111
   PACIFIC VLY # 1 93920   805-927-4507
   William Raebe, prin.

Bishop, AC 619, PC 5, Inyo
Bishop JUNHSD   3-00011
   301 N FOWLER ST 93514   872-3680
   Rich Tucker, supt.
Bishop Union HS   3-00011
   301 N FOWLER ST 93514 – (—), prin.   873-4275
Other Schools – See Big Pine

Bishop UNESD, 800 W ELM ST 93514   4-11100
   Richard Anthony, supt.   872-1060
Home Street MS, 201 HOME ST 93514   3-00100
   Gail Koske, prin.   872-1381

Bloomington, AC 909, PC 7, San Bernardino
Colton JUSD
   Supt. — See Colton
HS, 10750 LAUREL AVE 92316   4-00011
   James Downs, prin.   876-4277
JHS, 18829 ORANGE ST 92316   3-00100
   Patricia Gupperton, prin.   876-4101
Harris JHS, 11150 ALDER AVE 92316   3-00100
   Thomas Barker, prin.   876-4251

Bloomington Christian S   2-11111
   9904 BLOOMINGTON AVE 92316   877-2810
   Nicholas MacKenzie, prin.

Blythe, AC 619, PC 6, Riverside
Palo Verde USD, 187 N 7TH ST 92225   5-11111
   Norman Guith, supt.   922-4164
Palo Verde HS   4-00011
   667 N LOVEKIN BLVD 92225   922-7148
   Michael Gilmore, prin.
MS, 825 N LOVEKIN BLVD 92225   3-00100
   Ricardo Medina, prin.   922-1300

Palo Verde College   3-CC
   811 W CHANSLOR WAY 92225   922-6168

Bonsall, AC 619, PC 4, San Diego
Bonsall UNESD   4-11100
   31505 OLD RIVER RD 92003   631-5200
   Steven Enoch, supt.
MS, PO BOX 3 92003   3-01100
   Kim Marshall, prin.   630-0672

Boonville, AC 707, PC 4, Mendocino
Anderson Valley USD   3-11111
   PO BOX 457 95415   895-3774
   Marlene Smeed, supt.
Anderson Valley JSHS   2-00111
   PO BOX 130 95415   895-3496
   J. Collins, prin.

Boron, AC 619, PC 4, Kern
Muroc JUSD
   Supt. — See North Edwards
JSHS, 26831 PROSPECT ST 93516   2-00111
   Michael Trownsell, prin.   762-5121

Borrego Springs, AC 619, PC 4, San Diego
Borrego Springs USD   2-11111
   PO BOX 235 92004   767-5357
   David West, supt.
JSHS, PO BOX 235 92004   2-00111
   David West, prin.   767-5335

Brawley, AC 619, PC 7, Imperial
Brawley ESD, 261 D ST 92227   5-11100
   John Anderson, supt.   344-2330
Worth JHS, 261 D ST 92227   3-00100
   Barbara Layaye, prin.   344-2153

Brawley UNHSD   4-00011
   480 N IMPERIAL AVE 92227   344-3560
   Roberto Casas, supt.
HS, 480 N IMPERIAL AVE 92227   4-00011
   Garth Isom, prin.   344-3560

Brea, AC 714, PC 8, Orange
Brea-Olinda USD, PO BOX 300 92622   6-11111
   Edgar Seal, supt.   990-7800
Brea-Olinda HS   4-00011
   789 WILDCAT WAY 92621   990-7850
   John Johnson, prin.
JHS, 400 N BREA BLVD 92621   3-00100
   Mike Condiff, prin.   990-7500

Brea School of Exceptional Children   HND
   875 N BREA BLVD 92621
Southern CA College of Business & Law   2-CS
   595 W LAMBERT RD 92621   256-8830

Brentwood, AC 510, PC 6, Contra Costa
Brentwood UNSD, 250 1ST ST 94513   4-11100
   J. Douglas Adams, supt.   634-1168
Hill MS, 140 BIRCH ST 94513   3-00100
   Jack England, prin.   634-3548

Liberty UNHSD, 20 OAK ST 94513   4-00011
   Phillip White, supt.   634-2166
La Paloma HS   2-00011
   6651 LONE TREE WAY 94513   634-2888
   Gerald Hardt, prin.
Liberty HS, 850 2ND ST 94513   4-00011
   Gene Clair, prin.   634-3521

Bridgeport, AC 619, PC 3, Mono
Eastern Sierra USD   3-11111
   PO BOX 575 93517   932-7443
   Rich Miller, supt.
Other Schools – See Coleville, Lee Vining

Bridgeville, AC 707, PC 2, Humboldt
Southern Trinity JUSD   2-11111
   HC BOX 156 95526   574-6237
   David Albee, supt.
Mt. Lassic HS, HC BOX 55 95526   1-00011
   David Albee, prin.   574-6239
Southern Trinity HS   1-00011
   HC BOX 155 95526   574-6239
   David Albee, prin.

Brisbane, AC 415, PC 5, San Mateo
Brisbane ESD, 1 SOLANO ST 94005   3-11100
   Steve Waterman, supt.   467-0550
Lipman IS, 1 SOLANO ST 94005   2-00100
   Ray Conti, prin.   467-9541

Broderick, AC 916, PC see Sacramento
Washington USD
   Supt. — See West Sacramento
Golden State MS, 1100 CARRIE ST 95605   4-00100
   Eileen Stewart, prin.   371-0173

Buena Park, AC 714, PC 8, Orange
Buena Park ESD   5-11100
   6885 ORANGETHORPE AVE 90620   522-8412
   Jack Townsend, supt.
JHS, 6931 ORANGETHORPE AVE 90620   3-00100
   Ronald Barry, prin.   522-8491

Fullerton JUNHSD
   Supt. — See Fullerton
HS, 8833 ACADEMY DR 90621   4-00011
   G. Triggs, prin.   870-3522

ITT Technical Institute   4-UC
   7100 KNOTT AVE 90620   523-9080

Burbank, AC 818, PC 8, Los Angeles
Burbank USD   7-11111
   330 N BUENA VISTA ST 91505   558-4600
   Arthur Pierce, supt.
HS, 902 N 3RD ST 91502   4-00011
   Keiko Hentell, prin.   558-4700
Burroughs HS   4-00011
   1920 W CLARK AVE 91506   558-4777
   Timothy Buchanan, prin.
MS, 3700 W JEFFRIES AVE 91505   3-00100
   Donna Coffey, prin.   558-4646

Jordan MS, 420 S MARIPOSA ST 91506   3-00100
  Mary Kljunak, prin.   558-4622
Muir MS, 1111 N KENNETH RD 91504   4-00100
  William Kuzma, prin.   558-5320

Bellarmine Jefferson HS   3-00011
  465 E OLIVE AVE 91501   842-2195
  Mary Rausch, prin.
Providence HS   2-00011
  511 S BUENA VISTA ST 91505   846-8141
  Sr. Lucille Dean, prin.
Woodbury University   3-UC
  7500 N GLENOAKS BLVD 91504   767-0888

Burlingame, AC 415, PC 8, San Mateo
Burlingame ESD   4-11100
  2303 TROUSDALE DR 94010   259-3800
  Robert Beuthel, supt.
Burlingame IS   3-00100
  1715 QUESADA WAY 94010   259-3830
  Robert Welch, prin.

San Mateo UNHSD
  Supt. — See San Mateo
HS, 400 CAROLAN AVE 94010   4-00011
  Lawrence Teshara, prin.   342-8971

Mercy HS, 2750 ADELINE DR 94010   2-00011
  Sr. Rosann Fraher, prin.   343-3631
Peninsula Hospital   HSP
  1783 EL CAMINO REAL 94010   696-5678

Burney, AC 916, PC 5, Shasta
Fall River JUSD
  Supt. — See Cassel
JSHS   2-00111
  37571 MOUNTAIN VIEW RD 96013   335-4576
  Cordell Angier, prin.

Byron, PC 3, Contra Costa
Byron UNESD   3-11100
  14401 BYRON HWY 94514   510-634-2128
  Charles Humbert, supt.
MS, 14401 BYRON HWY 94514   2-01100
  Bonnie Tilton, prin.   510-634-2128

Calabasas, AC 818, PC 3, Los Angeles
Las Virgenes USD   7-11111
  4111 LAS VIRGENES RD 91302   880-4000
  Albert Marley, supt.
HS, 22855 MULHOLLAND HWY 91302   4-00011
  Robert Sutton, prin.   888-0012
Wright MS   4-00100
  4029 LAS VIRGENES RD 91302   880-4614
  James Christianson, prin.
Other Schools – See Agoura Hills

Viewpoint S   2-11111
  23620 MULHOLLAND HWY 91302   340-2901
  Robert Dworkoski, prin.

Calexico, AC 619, PC 7, Imperial
Calexico USD, PO BOX 792 92232   6-11111
  Roberto Moreno, supt.   357-7351
HS, PO BOX 792 92232   4-00011
  Harry Pearson, prin.   357-7440
De Anza JHS, PO BOX 792 92232   4-00100
  Mickey Western, prin.   357-7425
Moreno JHS, 1202 KLOKE AVE 92231   3-00100
  Jorge Parra, prin.   357-7437

Calexico Mission Academy   2-11111
  601 E 1ST ST 92231   357-3711
  Ron Breingan, prin.
Vincent Memorial HS   2-00011
  525 SHERIDAN ST 92231   357-3461
  Sr. Margarita Gallardo, prin.

California City, AC 619, PC 6, Kern
Mojave USD
  Supt. — See Mojave
MS, 9736 REDWOOD BLVD 93505   2-00100
  Larry Adams, prin.   373-3241

Calimesa, AC 714, PC 5, Riverside

Mesa Grande Academy   2-11111
  975 FREMONT ST # A 92320   795-1112
  Robert Rice, prin.

Calipatria, AC 619, PC 5, Imperial
Calipatria USD, 601 W MAIN ST 92233   4-11111
  Jim Hanks, supt.   348-2892
HS, 601 W MAIN ST 92233   2-00011
  Dan Eddins, prin.   348-2254
Fremont MS, 601 W MAIN ST 92233   2-01100
  Pat Cook, prin.   348-2842

Calistoga, AC 707, PC 5, Napa
Calistoga JUSD, 1327 BERRY ST 94515   3-11111
  Jeff Johnson, supt.   942-4703
JSHS, 1608 LAKE ST 94515   2-00111
  Carol Ashford, prin.   942-6278

Heritage S, PO BOX 528 94515   2-11111
  Ronald Whitney, prin.   942-5133

Camarillo, AC 805, PC 8, Ventura
Oxnard UNHSD
  Supt. — See Oxnard
HS, 4660 MISSION OAKS BLVD 93012   4-00011
  Terry Tackett, prin.   389-6404

Pleasant Valley ESD   6-11100
  600 TEMPLE AVE 93010   482-2763
  Shirley Carpenter, supt.
Los Altos IS, 700 TEMPLE AVE 93010   3-00100
  Vincent Cavaliere, prin.   482-4656
Monte Vista IS, 888 LANTANA ST 93010   3-00100
  Stephen Hanke, prin.   482-8891

Cornerstone Christian S   2-11111
  1777 ARNEILL RD 93010   987-8621
  Ken Lee, prin.
St. John's Seminary   2-UC
  5012 SEMINARY RD 93012   482-2755
St. John's Seminary College   1-UC
  5118 SEMINARY RD 93012   482-2755

Cambria, AC 805, PC 6, San Luis Obispo
Cambria USD   3-11100
  2950 SANTA ROSA CREEK RD 93428   927-3880
  Vera Wallen, supt.
Santa Lucia MS   2-00100
  2850 SCHOOLHOUSE LN 93428   927-3693
  Denis deClercq, prin.

Coast UNHSD   2-00011
  2950 SANTA ROSA CREEK RD 93428   927-3880
  Vera Wallen, supt.
Coast HS   2-00011
  2950 SANTA ROSA CREEK RD 93428   927-3889
  Don Brinkman, prin.

Cameron Park, AC 916, PC 7, El Dorado
Buckeye UNESD
  Supt. — See Shingle Springs
Camerado Springs MS   3-00100
  2480 MERRYCHASE DR 95682   677-1658
  Margaret Stripe, prin.

Campbell, AC 408, PC 8, Santa Clara
Campbell UNESD, 155 N 3RD ST 95008   6-11100
  Marcia Plumleigh, supt.   364-4200
MS, 295 CHERRY LN 95008   3-01100
  Beverley Killmeyer, prin.   364-4222
Other Schools – See Los Gatos, San Jose

Campbell UNHSD
  Supt. — See San Jose
Westmont HS   4-00011
  4805 WESTMONT AVE 95008   378-1500
  Rhonda Farber, prin.

Phillips Junior College   3-CC
  1 W CAMPBELL AVE 95008   866-6666

Canoga Park, AC 818, PC see Los Angeles
Los Angeles USD
  Supt. — See Los Angeles
HS   4-00011
  6850 TOPANGA CANYON BLVD 91303   340-3221
  Larry Higgins, prin.
Columbus MS   4-00100
  22250 ELKWOOD ST 91304   348-5601
  Gail Hughes, prin.
Sutter JHS, 7330 WINNETKA AVE 91306   4-00100
  Carolyn Baker, prin.   341-6661

Chaminade Prep S   3-00011
  7500 CHAMINADE AVE 91304   347-8300
  Charles Potts, prin.
Coutin S   2-11111
  7119 OWENSMOUTH AVE 91303   992-0301
  Rick Pendleton, prin.
Faith Baptist S   4-11111
  7644 FARRALONE AVE 91304   340-6131
  Roland Rasmussen, prin.
Manoogian AGBU Marie S   3-11111
  6844 OAKDALE AVE 91306   883-2428
  Hagop Hagopian, prin.
West Valley Christian S   2-11111
  23834 HIGHLANDER RD 91307   884-4710
  Bernard Shaw, prin.

Canyon Country, AC 805, PC see Santa Clarita
William S. Hart UNHSD
  Supt. — See Santa Clarita
Canyon HS, 19300 NADAL ST 91351   4-00011
  Michael Allmandinger, prin.   252-6110
Sierra Vista JHS   4-00100
  19425 STILLMORE ST 91351   252-3113
  Jon Curwen, prin.

Santa Clarita Christian S   2-11111
  27249 LUTHER DR 91351   252-7371
  Lee Duncan, prin.

Capitola, AC 408, PC 7, Santa Cruz
Soquel UNESD   4-11100
  620 MONTEREY AVE 95010   475-8080
  Gayle Fairbanks-Carino, supt.
New Brighton MS   3-00100
  250 WASHBURN AVE 95010   475-6911
  Dave Schumaker, prin.

Carlsbad, AC 619, PC 8, San Diego
Carlsbad USD, 801 PINE AVE 92008   6-11111
  Susan Bentley, supt.   729-9291
HS, 801 PINE AVE 92008   4-00011
  William Dunmeyer, prin.   434-1726
Valley JHS, 801 PINE AVE 92008   4-00100
  Don Le May, prin.   434-0602

Army and Navy Academy   2-00111
  PO BOX 3000 92018   729-2385
  Jack Cargile, prin.

Carmel, AC 408, PC 5, Monterey
Carmel USD, PO BOX 222700 93922   4-11111
  Vance Baldwin, supt.   624-1546
HS, PO BOX 222780 93922   3-00011
  Marie Ishida, prin.   624-1821
MS, PO BOX 222740 93922   3-00100
  Karl Pallastrini, prin.   624-2785

Carmichael, AC 916, PC 8, Sacramento
San Juan USD, PO BOX 477 95609   8-11111
  George Jeffers, supt.   971-7700
Barrett MS, 4243 BARRETT RD 95608   3-00100
  Cheryl Magee, prin.   971-7842
Churchill JHS   3-00100
  4900 WHITNEY AVE 95608   971-7324
  Dave Cowles, prin.
Starr King MS   2-00100
  4848 COTTAGE WAY 95608   971-7320
  Martha Smith, prin.
Other Schools – See Citrus Heights, Fair Oaks,
  Orangevale, Sacramento

Jesuit HS, 1200 JACOB LN 95608   3-00011
  Fr. Nejasmich, prin.   482-6060
Sacramento Adventist Academy   2-11111
  5601 WINDING WAY 95608   481-2300
  Richard Carey, prin.
Victory Christian ES   2-11111
  3045 GARFIELD AVE 95608   488-6740
  Benjamin Potloff, prin.

Carpinteria, AC 805, PC 7, Santa Barbara
Carpinteria USD   5-11111
  1400 LINDEN AVE 93013   684-4511
  Pedro Garcia, supt.
HS, 4810 FOOTHILL RD 93013   3-00011
  David Goodfield, prin.   684-4107
MS, 5351 CARPINTERIA AVE 93013   3-00100
  Robin Sawaske, prin.   684-4544

Cate S, PO BOX 5005 93014   2-00011
  John McLeod, prin.   684-4127
Truck Marketing Institute   2-HMS
  PO BOX 5000 93014   684-5000

Carson, AC 310, PC 8, Los Angeles
Long Beach USD
  Supt. — See Long Beach
California Academy of Math & Science HS   2-00011
  1000 E VICTORIA ST 90747   516-4025
  Kathleen Clark, prin.

Los Angeles USD
  Supt. — See Los Angeles
SHS, 22328 MAIN ST 90745   4-00001
  Dhylan Lal, prin.   835-0181
Carnegie JHS, 21820 BONITA ST 90745   4-00110
  Earline Edwards, prin.   830-1330
Curtiss JHS, 1254 E HELMICK ST 90746   3-00110
  William Elkins, prin.   537-3551
White JHS, 22102 FIGUEROA ST 90745   4-00110
  Carolyn Bohm, prin.   328-7540

California State University   6-UC
  1000 E VICTORIA ST 90747   516-3300
Carson Christian S   2-11111
  651 E UNIVERSITY DR 90746   538-1031
  Irma Sykes, prin.
ITT Technical Institute   3-CC
  2035 E 223RD ST 90810   835-5595
Phillips Junior College   2-CC
  1 CIVIC PLAZA DR STE 110 90745   518-2600

Caruthers, AC 209, PC 4, Fresno
Caruthers UNHSD   2-00011
  PO BOX 545 93609   864-3224
  Edward Dorn, supt.
HS, PO BOX 545 93609   2-00011
  Edward Dorn, prin.   864-3224

Cassel, AC 916, PC 2, Shasta
Fall River JUSD, PO BOX 89 96016   4-11111
  Earnie Graham, supt.   335-4537
Other Schools – See Burney, Mc Arthur

Castaic, AC 805, PC 3, Los Angeles
Castaic UNSD   4-11100
  31616 RIDGE ROUTE RD 91384   257-0551
  Scott Brown, supt.
MS, 31634 RIDGE ROUTE RD 91384   2-00100
  Beverly Silsbee, prin.   257-0937

Castro Valley, AC 510, PC 8, Alameda
Castro Valley USD   6-11111
  PO BOX 2146 94546   537-3000
  Robert Fisher, supt.
HS, PO BOX 2146 94546   4-00011
  Tina Karp, prin.   537-5910
Canyon MS, PO BOX 2146 94546   4-00100
  Allen Honda, prin.   538-8833

Redwood Christian HS   2-00111
  19300 REDWOOD RD 94546   352-8330
  David Peterson, prin.
Shady Grove S   2-00111
  17467 ALMOND RD 94546   537-3088
  John Livergood, prin.

Castroville, AC 408, PC 6, Monterey
North Monterey County USD
  Supt. — See Moss Landing
North Monterey County HS   4-00011
  13990 CASTROVILLE BLVD 95012 633-5221
  Dennis Carroci, prin.
Gambetta MS   3-00100
  10301 SEYMOUR ST 95012 633-3391
  John Simpson, prin.

Cathedral City, AC 619, PC 8, Riverside
Palm Springs USD
  Supt. — See Palm Springs
HS, 69250 DINAH SHORE DR 92234 4-00011
  James Siegler, prin. 770-0100
Coffman MS, 34603 PLUMLEY RD 92234 4-00100
  Terri Loman, prin. 328-6565

Cedarville, AC 916, PC 3, Modoc
Surprise Valley JUSD 2-11111
  PO BOX 100 96104 279-6141
  Henry Bietz, supt.
Surprise Valley HS 1-00011
  470 LINCOLN ST 96104 279-6146
  Henry Bietz, prin.

Central Valley, AC 916, PC 5, Shasta
Gateway USD
  Supt. — See Redding
HS, 4066 LA MESA AVE 96019 4-00011
  Kathleen Wheeler, prin. 275-1543
IS, HARDENBROOK & MAIN 96019 2-00100
  Joe Brouillard, prin. 275-7020

Ceres, AC 209, PC 8, Stanislaus
Ceres USD, PO BOX 307 95307 6-11111
  Bruce Newlin, supt. 538-0141
HS, PO BOX 307 95307 4-00011
  Charles Edmonds, prin. 538-0130
Hensley JHS, PO BOX 307 95307 4-00100
  Karl Modgling, prin. 538-0158

Cerritos, AC 310, PC 8, Los Angeles
ABC USD 7-11111
  16700 NORWALK BLVD 90701 926-5566
  Larry Lucas, supt.
HS, 12500 183RD ST 90701 4-00011
  Gary Smuts, prin. 926-5566
Gahr HS, 11111 ARTESIA BLVD 90701 4-00011
  Nadine Barreto, prin. 926-5566
Whitney JSHS 3-00111
  16800 SHOEMAKER AVE 90701 926-5566
  Pauline Ferris, prin.
Carmenita JHS, 13435 166TH ST 90701 3-00100
  Kristen Powell, prin. 926-4405
Haskell JHS 3-00100
  11525 DEL AMO BLVD 90701 860-6529
  Paulette Fuller, prin.
Tetzlaff JHS 3-00100
  12351 DEL AMO BLVD 90701 865-9539
  Cameron Malotte, prin.
Other Schools – See Artesia, Hawaiian Gardens, Lakewood

Platt College 2-CS
  10900 183RD ST STE 290 90701 809-5100
Valley Christian HS 3-00011
  10818 ARTESIA BLVD 90701 860-0556
  Tim Holksema, prin.
Valley Christian JHS 2-00100
  18100 DUMONT AVE 90701 865-6519
  Robert Johnson, prin.

Chatsworth, AC 818, PC see Los Angeles
Los Angeles USD
  Supt. — See Los Angeles
HS, 10027 LURLINE AVE 91311 4-00011
  Donna Smith, prin. 341-6211
Aggeler Opportunity S Vo Tech
  21050 PLUMMER ST 91311 341-1232
  Robert Beck, prin.
Lawrence JHS, 10100 VARIEL AVE 91311 4-00100
  Anthony Ventresca, prin. 882-1214

Chaminade MS 3-00100
  19800 DEVONSHIRE ST 91311 363-8127
  Christine Hunter, prin.

Chester, AC 916, PC 4, Plumas
Plumas USD
  Supt. — See Quincy
JSHS, PO BOX 797 96020 2-00111
  Nick Nicholas, prin. 258-2126

Chico, AC 916, PC 8, Butte
Chico USD, 1163 E 7TH ST 95928 7-11111
  Robert Barbot, supt. 891-3000
HS, 901 THE ESPLANADE 95926 4-00011
  Roger Williams, prin. 891-3026
Pleasant Valley HS 4-00011
  1475 EAST AVE 95926 891-3050
  Robert Cranston, prin.
Bidwell JHS, 2376 NORTH AVE 95926 4-00100
  Paul Carras, prin. 891-3080
JHS, 280 MEMORIAL WAY 95926 3-00100
  Jeffrey Sloan, prin. 891-3066

California State University 95929 7-UC
  898-4636
Career West Academy 2-CS
  2505B ZANELLA WAY 95928 893-1388
Enloe Hospital 2-HSP
  1531 ESPLANADE 95926 891-7300

Chino, AC 909, PC 8, San Bernardino
Chino USD, 5130 RIVERSIDE DR 91710 7-11111
  Stephen Goldstone, supt. 628-1201
Ayala HS, 14255 PEYTON DR 91709 4-00011
  Glenna Ramsay, prin. 627-3848
HS, 5472 PARK PL 91710 4-00011
  Al Carr, prin. 627-7351
Lugo HS, 13400 PIPELINE AVE 91710 4-00011
  Ruperto Cisneros, prin. 591-3902
Canyon Hills JHS 3-00100
  2500 MADRUGADA DR 91709 464-9938
  Steve Simpkins, prin.
Magnolia JHS 4-00100
  13150 MOUNTAIN AVE 91710 627-9263
  Mark Goldbland, prin.
Ramona JHS, 4575 WALNUT AVE 91710 3-00100
  Jan Murphy, prin. 627-9144
Townsend JHS, 15359 ILEX DR 91709 3-00100
  Phil Hiatt, prin. 591-2161
Other Schools – See Ontario

Chowchilla, AC 209, PC 6, Madera
Alview-Dairyland UNESD 2-11100
  12861 AVENUE 18 1/2 93610 665-2394
  Jack Duren, supt.
Dairyland MS 2-01100
  12861 AVENUE 18 1/2 93610 665-2394
  Jack Duren, prin.

Chowchilla ESD, PO BOX 907 93610 4-11100
  Charles Jacobs, supt. 665-4421
Wilson MS, PO BOX 907 93610 2-00100
  Lee Brock, prin. 665-4421

Chowchilla UNHSD 3-00011
  805 HUMBOLDT AVE 93610 665-1331
  Ronald Moore, supt.
HS, 805 HUMBOLDT AVE 93610 3-00011
  Bob Green, prin. 665-1331

Chula Vista, AC 619, PC 9, San Diego
Sweetwater UNHSD 8-00111
  1130 5TH AVE 91911 691-5500
  John Rindone, supt.
SHS, 820 4TH AVE 91911 4-00001
  Robert Acuna, prin. 691-5765
Bonita Vista HS 4-00011
  751 OTAY LAKES RD 91913 691-5750
  Jeff Schaeffer, prin.
Castle Park HS, 1395 HILLTOP DR 91911 4-00011
  Earl Wiens, prin. 691-5600
Hilltop HS, 555 CLAIRE AVE 91910 4-00011
  William Demos, prin. 691-5640
Bonita Vista MS 4-00100
  650 OTAY LAKES RD 91910 691-5690
  Gerald LaRussa, prin.
Castle Park MS 4-00100
  160 QUINTARD ST 91911 – (—), prin. 691-5490
JHS, 415 5TH AVE 91910 4-00110
  Larry Perondi, prin. 691-5655
Eastlake JHS 4-00010
  1120 EASTLAKE PKY 91915 585-6287
  Marilyn Stenvall, prin.
Hilltop JHS, 44 E J ST 91910 4-00100
  Nancy Linen, prin. 691-5630
Other Schools – See Imperial Beach, National City, San Diego

Covenant Christian S 2-11111
  505 E NAPLES ST 91911 421-8822
  Mark Dolan, prin.
Pacific Coast College 2-CS
  1261 3RD AVE STE B 91911 691-0882
Southwestern College 7-CC
  900 OTAY LAKES RD 91910 421-6700

Citrus Heights, AC 916, PC 9, Sacramento
San Juan USD
  Supt. — See Carmichael
Mesa Verde HS, 7600 LAUPPE LN 95621 4-00011
  Linda Ferrick-Adams, prin. 971-5251
San Juan HS 4-00011
  7551 GREENBACK LN 95610 971-5112
  Roger Riley, prin.
Sylvan MS, 7137 AUBURN BLVD 95610 3-00100
  Kay McCarty, prin. 971-7873

National Career Education 2-CS
  6060 SUNRISE VISTA DR #3000 95610
  969-4900

City of Commerce, AC 213, Los Angeles

NEC-Sawyer Campus 4-CS
  5500 S EASTERN AVE 90040 724-1800
Systems Programming Development Inst 2-CS
  4900 TRIGGS ST 90022 261-8181

City of Industry, AC 818, PC 3, Los Angeles
Basset USD
  Supt. — See La Puente
Torch MS, 751 VINELAND AVE 91746 3-00100
  Susan Naeve, prin. 813-1882

Hacienda La Puente USD 7-11111
  PO BOX 60002 91716 333-2201
  Andrew Cazares, supt.
Workman HS, 16303 TEMPLE AVE 91744 4-00011
  Don White, prin. 855-3900
Other Schools – See Hacienda Heights, La Puente

Claremont, AC 909, PC 8, Los Angeles
Claremont USD 6-11111
  2080 N MOUNTAIN AVE 91711 398-0609
  Douglas Keeler, supt.
HS, 2080 N MOUNTAIN AVE 91711 4-00011
  Lonnie McConnell, prin. 624-9053
San Antonio HS 1-00011
  2080 N MOUNTAIN AVE 91711 398-0316
  Eric Andrew, prin.
El Roble IS 3-00100
  2080 N MOUNTAIN AVE 91711 398-0343
  Ralph Patterson, prin.

Claremont Graduate School 3-UC
  170 E 10TH ST 91711 621-8000
Claremont McKenna College 3-UC
  890 COLUMBIA AVE 91711 621-8111
Harvey Mudd College 3-UC
  260 E FOOTHILL BLVD 91711 621-8000
Pitzer College 3-UC
  1050 N MILLS AVE 91711 621-8000
Pomona College 4-UC
  333 N COLLEGE WAY 91711 621-8000
School of Theology at Claremont 2-UC
  1325 N COLLEGE AVE 91711 800-626-7821
Scripps College 3-UC
  1030 COLUMBIA AVE 91711 621-8178
The Webb S 3-00011
  1175 W BASELINE RD 91711 626-3587
  Susan Nelson, prin.
Vivian Webb S 2-00011
  1175 W BASELINE RD 91711 626-3587
  Susan Nelson, prin.
Webb School of California 2-00011
  1175 W BASELINE RD 91711 626-3587
  Susan Nelson, prin.

Clarksburg, AC 916, PC 2, Yolo
River Delta USD
  Supt. — See Rio Vista
Delta HS, PO BOX 100 95612 2-00011
  Sandra Fletcher, prin. 744-1714

Clayton, AC 510, PC 6, Contra Costa
Mt. Diablo USD
  Supt. — See Concord
Diablo View MS 2-00100
  300 DIABLO VIEW LN 94517 672-0898
  Marlene Sipes, prin.

Clearlake, AC 707, PC 7, Lake
Konocti USD, PO BOX 6630 95422 5-11111
  William Cornelison, supt. 994-6475
Konocti Adult S, PO BOX 6630 95422 1-00011
  Nancy Todd, prin. 994-6475
Oak Hill MS, PO BOX 920 95422 3-00100
  Bill MacDougall, prin. 994-6447
Other Schools – See Lower Lake

Cloverdale, AC 707, PC 5, Sonoma
Cloverdale USD, 97 SCHOOL ST 95425 4-11111
  Donald Sato, supt. 894-1920
HS, 509 N CLOVERDALE BLVD 95425 2-00011
  Dave Ashworth, prin. 894-1900
Washington Street MS 3-00100
  129 S WASHINGTON ST 95425 894-1940
  Marc Mager, prin.

Clovis, AC 209, PC 8, Fresno
Clovis USD, 1450 HERNDON AVE 93611 7-11111
  David Sawyer, supt. 297-4000
HS, 1055 FOWLER AVE 93611 5-00011
  Steve Weil, prin. 299-7211
Alta Sierra IS 4-00100
  380 W TEAGUE AVE 93611 297-8522
  Gary Giannoni, prin.
Buchanen IS 4-00100
  1560 MINNEWAWA AVE 93612 297-8522
  Randy Rowe, prin.
Clark IS, 902 5TH ST 93612 4-00100
  Hank Brown, prin. 299-6858
Other Schools – See Fresno

Valley Christian Academy 2-11111
  101 BARSTOW AVE 93612 299-2109
  Steven Sitter, prin.

Coachella, AC 619, PC 7, Riverside
Coachella Valley USD
  Supt. — See Thermal
Duke JHS, 85358 BAGDAD AVE 92236 3-00100
  Jerry Tripp, prin. 398-0139

Coalinga, AC 209, PC 6, Fresno
Coalinga/Huron JUSD 5-11111
  657 SUNSET ST 93210 935-7500
  C. Workman, supt.
HS, 657 SUNSET ST 93210 3-00011
  Ed Kreyenhagen, prin. 935-7520
JHS, 657 SUNSET ST 93210 3-00100
  Tomas Guajardo, prin. 935-7550

West Hills College 4-CC
  300 W CHERRY LN 93210 935-0801

Coleville, AC 916, PC 1, Mono
Eastern Sierra USD
  Supt. — See Bridgeport
JSHS, PO BOX 64 96107 2-00111
  Dave Wilson, prin. 495-2231

Colfax, AC 916, PC 4, Placer
Placer UNHSD
  Supt. — See Auburn

HS, 24995 BEN TAYLOR RD　95713　　3-00011
　Tom Spencer, prin.　　　　　　　346-2284

Colma, AC 415, PC 4, San Mateo
Jefferson ESD
　Supt. — See Daly City
Franklin IS, 700 STEWART AVE　94015　3-00100
　Thomas Zach, prin.　　　　　　　991-1202

Colton, AC 909, PC 8, San Bernardino
Colton JUSD, 1212 VALENCIA DR　92324　7-11111
　Herbert Fisher, supt.　　　　　　876-4227
HS, 777 W VALLEY BLVD　92324　　4-00011
　Fred Dischinger, prin.　　　　　　876-4261
JHS, 670 W LAUREL ST　92324　　3-00100
　Lansing Otis, prin.　　　　　　　876-4231
Other Schools – See Bloomington, Grand Terrace

———————————

MTI College　　　　　　　　　　2-CS
　760 VIA LATA STE 300　92324　　424-0123

Columbia, AC 209, PC 4, Tuolumne

———————————

Columbia College　　　　　　　　5-CC
　PO BOX 1849　95310　　　　　533-5100

Colusa, AC 916, PC 5, Colusa
Colusa USD, 745 10TH ST　95932　4-11111
　Jim Mark, supt.　　　　　　　　458-7791
HS, 901 COLUS AVE　95932　　　2-00011
　Robert Hulbert, prin.　　　　　　458-2156
Egling HS, 813 WEBSTER ST　95932　3-01100
　Ed Conrado, prin.　　　　　　　458-7631

Compton, PC 8, Los Angeles
Compton USD　　　　　　　　　8-11111
　604 S TAMARIND AVE　90220　310-639-4321
　Harold Cebrun, supt.
Centennial HS　　　　　　　　　4-00011
　2606 N CENTRAL AVE　90222　310-635-2715
　Jessie Jones, prin.
HS, 601 S ACACIA AVE　90220　　4-00011
　William Savant, prin.　　　　　310-635-3881
Dominguez HS　　　　　　　　　4-00011
　15301 S SAN JOSE AVE　90221　310-630-0142
　Fred Easter, prin.
Bunche MS　　　　　　　　　　3-00100
　12338 S MONA BLVD　90222　310-898-6010
　Eleanor Campbell, prin.
Davis MS, 621 W POPLAR ST　90220　4-00100
　Delores Davis-Holmes, prin.　310-898-6020
Enterprise MS　　　　　　　　　2-00100
　2600 W COMPTON BLVD　90220　310-898-6030
　Gipson Lyles, prin.
Roosevelt MS　　　　　　　　　3-00100
　1200 E ALONDRA BLVD　90221　310-898-6040
　Jim Marin, prin.
Walton MS　　　　　　　　　　3-00100
　900 W GREENLEAF BLVD　90220　310-898-6060
　Bettye Walker, prin.
Whaley MS　　　　　　　　　　3-00100
　14401 S GIBSON AVE　90221　310-898-6070
　Charles Littles, prin.
Willowbrook MS　　　　　　　　3-00100
　2601 N WILMINGTON AVE　90222　310-898-6080
　Melonka Turner, prin.
Other Schools – See Los Angeles

———————————

Compton Community College　　　5-CC
　1111 E ARTESIA BLVD　90221　310-637-2660
James Christian Academy　　　　2-11111
　1901 W REEVE ST　90220　　310-631-6235
　Dorothy Warren, prin.
Regina Caeli HS　　　　　　　　2-00011
　823 E COMPTON BLVD　90220　213-321-6152
　Sr. Greta Jupiter, prin.

Concord, AC 510, PC 9, Contra Costa
Mt. Diablo USD　　　　　　　　8-11111
　1936 CARLOTTA DR　94519　　682-8000
　Robert Baum, supt.
Clayton Valley HS　　　　　　　4-00011
　1101 ALBERTA WAY　94521　　682-7474
　Ray Schultz, prin.
HS, 4200 CONCORD BLVD　94521　4-00011
　Patricia Goodday, prin.　　　　687-2030
Mt. Diablo HS, 2450 GRANT ST　94520　4-00011
　Louis Suarez, prin.　　　　　　682-4030
Ygnacio Valley HS　　　　　　　4-00011
　755 OAK GROVE RD　94518　　685-8414
　Sheila Walker, prin.
El Dorado IS, 1750 WEST ST　94521　4-00100
　Jeff McCreary, prin.　　　　　682-5700
Glenbrook MS, 2351 OLIVERA RD　94520　3-00100
　Rob Stoker, prin.　　　　　　685-6835
Oak Grove MS, 2050 MINERT RD　94518　3-00100
　Audrey Wagman, prin.　　　　682-1843
Pine Hollow IS　　　　　　　　3-00100
　5522 PINE HOLLOW RD　94521　672-5444
　Marcie Brown, prin.
Other Schools – See Clayton, Pittsburg, Pleasant Hill,
　Walnut Creek

———————————

Carondelet HS, 1133 WINTON DR　94518　3-00011
　Sr. Kathleen Lang, prin.　　　686-5353
De La Salle HS, 1130 WINTON DR　94518　3-00011
　James Tschann, prin.　　　　686-3310
Heald Business College　　　　2-CC
　2150 JOHN GLENN DR # 100　94520　933-2436
Med-Help Training School　　　2-CS
　2702 CLAYTON RD STE 201　94519　682-2030

Navajo Aviation　　　　　　　　1-CS
　145 JOHN GLENN DR　94520　　685-1150

Copperopolis, AC 209, PC 3, Calaveras
Bret Harte UNHSD
　Supt. — See Altaville
Copper Cove HS, PO BOX 242　95228　1-00011
　Timothy Miller, prin.　　　　　785-4171

Corcoran, AC 209, PC 7, Kings
Corcoran JUSD　　　　　　　　5-11111
　1520 PATTERSON AVE　93212　992-3104
　Allan Asplund, supt.
HS, 1520 PATTERSON AVE　93212　3-00011
　Steve Bogan, prin.　　　　　　992-5061
Muir JHS, 1520 PATTERSON AVE　93212　3-00100
　Steven Brown, prin.　　　　　992-4167

Corning, AC 916, PC 6, Tehama
Corning UNESD, 1590 SOUTH ST　96021　4-11100
　Larry Phelps, supt.　　　　　824-7700
Maywood IS　　　　　　　　　3-00100
　1666 MARGUERITE AVE　96021　824-7730
　John Greene, prin.

Corning UNHSD　　　　　　　　3-00011
　643 BLACKBURN AVE　96021　824-5411
　Michael Henry, supt.
HS, 643 BLACKBURN AVE　96021　3-00011
　Michael Henry, prin.　　　　　824-5411

Corona, AC 909, PC 8, Riverside
Corona-Norco USD
　Supt. — See Norco
Centennial HS, 1820 RIMPAU AVE　91719　4-00011
　Dale Mitchell, prin.　　　　　736-6523
HS, 1150 W 10TH ST　91720　　4-00011
　Barb Falconer, prin.　　　　　736-3211
Buena Vista Vo HS　　　　　　Vo Tech
　300 S BUENA VISTA AVE　91720　736-3367
　Melanie Murphy-Corwin, prin.
Auburndale IS, 1255 RIVER RD　91720　3-00100
　Jonathan Greenburg, prin.　736-3231
Corona Fundamental IS　　　　3-00100
　1230 S MAIN ST　91720　　736-3321
　Bob McCall, prin.
Raney IS, 1010 W CITRON ST　91720　4-00100
　Sharon Stanton, prin.　　　　736-3221

———————————

Corona Christian S　　　　　　2-11111
　1901 W ONTARIO AVE　91720　734-5683
　Rev. Howard, prin.

Coronado, AC 619, PC 8, San Diego
Coronado USD, 555 D AVE　92118　4-11111
　David Blumenthal, supt.　　522-8900
HS, 650 D AVE　92118　　　　3-00011
　Jeffrey Davis, prin.　　　　　522-8907
MS, 911 7TH ST　92118　　　3-00100
　Gary Davidson, prin.　　　　522-8921

Costa Mesa, PC 8, Orange
Newport-Mesa USD
　Supt. — See Newport Beach
Estancia HS　　　　　　　　　4-00011
　2323 PLACENTIA AVE　92627　714-760-3410
　Frank Infusino, prin.
JSHS, 2650 FAIRVIEW RD　92626　4-00111
　Michael Murphy, prin.　714-556-3344
TeWinkle IS　　　　　　　　　3-00100
　3224 CALIFORNIA ST　92626　714-556-3433
　Mary Ann Ehret, prin.

———————————

Fashion Inst. of Design & Merchandising　2-CC
　3420 BRISTOL ST　92626　714-546-0930
Orange Coast College　　　　7-CC
　PO BOX 5005　92628　　714-432-0202
Southern California College　3-UC
　55 FAIR DR　92626　　　714-556-3610

Cotati, AC 707, PC 6, Sonoma
Cotati-Rohnert Park USD　　6-11111
　325 E COTATI AVE　94931　792-4720
　Walter Buster, supt.
MS, 216 E SCHOOL ST　94931　2-00100
　Rick Brewer, prin.　　　792-4790
Other Schools – See Rohnert Park

Cottonwood, AC 916, PC 4, Shasta
Anderson UNHSD
　Supt. — See Anderson
West Valley HS　　　　　　　3-00011
　3805 HAPPY VALLEY RD　96022　347-7171
　Richard Pangburn, prin.

Cottonwood UNESD　　　　　4-11100
　PO BOX 500　96022　　　347-3165
　Kenneth Osborn, supt.
West Cottonwood JHS　　　2-01100
　PO BOX 500　96022　　　347-3123
　Dale Hansen, prin.

Evergreen UNESD　　　　　3-11100
　19415 HOOKER CREEK RD　96022　347-3411
　Harley North, supt.
Evergreen MS　　　　　　　2-00100
　19435 NOLAND WAY　96022　347-3411
　Mike Leonard, prin.

Coulterville, AC 209, PC 3, Mariposa
Mariposa County USD
　Supt. — See Mariposa
HS, 5043 BROADWAY　95311　1-00011
　Kent Stoel, prin.　　　　966-3691

Covelo, AC 707, PC 4, Mendocino
Round Valley USD　　　　　2-11111
　PO BOX 276　95428　　　983-6171
　Sally Biggin, supt.
Round Valley HS, PO BOX 276　95428　2-00011
　Howard Chavez, prin.　　983-6174

Covina, AC 818, PC 8, Los Angeles
Azusa USD
　Supt. — See Azusa
Gladstone HS, 1340 N ENID AVE　91722　4-00011
　Albert Webb, prin.　　　334-0419

Charter Oak USD, PO BOX 9　91723　6-11111
　Susan Rainey, supt.　　966-8331
Charter Oak HS, PO BOX 9　91723　4-00011
　Sheila Richter, prin.　　915-5841
Royal Oak IS, PO BOX 9　91723　4-00100
　Bobbie Banderas, prin.　967-6354

Covina-Valley USD　　　　7-11111
　PO BOX 269　91723　　331-3371
　Jack Rankin, supt.
HS, PO BOX 269　91723　　4-00011
　Karl Major, prin.　　　331-3371
Northview HS, PO BOX 269　91723　4-00011
　Dave Samuelson, prin.　331-3371
Las Palmas IS, PO BOX 269　91723　3-00100
　Ronald Cytryn, prin.　967-2708
Sierra Vista IS, PO BOX 269　91723　3-00100
　Robert Shivers, prin.　967-2734
Other Schools – See West Covina

———————————

Western Christian HS　　　2-00011
　1115 E PUENTE AVE　91724　967-0733
　Jody DeGenaro, prin.

Crescent City, AC 707, PC 5, Del Norte
Del Norte County USD　　6-11111
　301 W WASHINGTON BLVD　95531　464-6141
　Gene Edinger, supt.
Del Norte HS　　　　　　　4-00011
　1301 EL DORADO ST　95531　464-0260
　Sherry Smith, prin.
Crescent Elk MS, 994 G ST　95531　3-00100
　Ruth Ross, prin.　　　464-0320

Crockett, AC 510, PC 5, Contra Costa
John Swett USD, 341 B ST　94525　4-11111
　Jon Frank, supt.　　　787-2355
Swett HS, 1098 POMONA AVE　94525　3-00011
　Lynne Palmer, prin.　787-1088
Carquinez MS　　　　　　　3-00100
　1099 POMONA AVE　94525　787-1081
　Arden Jones, prin.

Cucamonga, AC 909, PC 9, San Bernardino
Cucamonga ESD　　　　　　4-11100
　8776 ARCHIBALD AVE　91730　987-8942
　John Aycock, supt.
Rancho Cucamonga MS　　2-00100
　8776 ARCHIBALD AVE　91730　980-0969
　Lynne Kennedy, prin.

Culver City, AC 310, PC 8, Los Angeles
Culver City USD, 4034 IRVING PL　90232　5-11111
　C. Rethmeyer, supt.　842-4221
HS, 4401 ELENDA ST　90230　4-00011
　Laura Plasse, prin.　842-4200
MS, 4601 ELENDA ST　90230　4-00100
　Dennis Fox, prin.　　842-4200

———————————

Pepperdine University　　　3-UC
　400 CORPORATE POINTE　90230
West Los Angeles College　6-CC
　4800 FRESHMAN DR　90230　836-7110
Westside Preparatory S　　2-11111
　11450 PORT RD　90230　398-2222
　Les Birdsall, prin.

Cupertino, AC 408, PC 8, Santa Clara
Cupertino UNESD　　　　　7-11100
　10301 VISTA DR　95014　252-3000
　Patricia Lamson, supt.
Hyde JHS, 19325 BOLLINGER RD　95014　3-00100
　Marilyn Miller, prin.　252-6290
Kennedy JHS, 821 BUBB RD　95014　3-00100
　Larry Curb, prin.　　253-1525
Other Schools – See San Jose, Sunnyvale

Fremont UNHSD
　Supt. — See Sunnyvale
HS, 10100 FINCH AVE　95014　4-00011
　Barbara Nunes, prin.　366-7380
Homestead HS　　　　　　　4-00011
　21370 HOMESTEAD RD　95014　522-2500
　David Payne, prin.
Monta Vista HS　　　　　　4-00011
　21840 MCCLELLAN RD　95014　366-7600
　James Warren, prin.

———————————

Cogswell Polytechnical College　2-UC
　10420 BUBB RD　95014　252-5550
DeAnza College　　　　　　7-CC
　21250 STEVENS CREEK BLVD　95014　996-4760

Cypress, AC 714, PC 8, Orange
Anaheim UNHSD
　Supt. — See Anaheim
HS, 9801 VALLEY VIEW ST　90630　4-00011
　Elizabeth Jackman, prin.　220-4144
Lexington JHS　　　　　　　3-00100
　4351 ORANGE AVE　90630　220-4201
　Leroy Kellogg, prin.

Brethren JSHS — 2-00111
5172 ORANGE AVE 90630 — 952-1177
Barrett Luketic, prin.
Cypress College — 7-CC
9200 VALLEY VIEW ST 90630 — 826-2220

Daggett, AC 619, PC 3, San Bernardino
Silver Valley USD
Supt. — See Yermo
MS — 2-00100
HIGHWAY 66 AT PONNAY ST 92327 — 254-2715
James Swor, prin.

Daly City, AC 415, PC 8, San Mateo
Bayshore ESD, 1 MARTIN ST 94014 — 2-11100 / 467-5444
Winifred Kum, supt.
Robertson IS, 1 MARTIN ST 94014 — 2-01100 / 467-5443
Peggy Moore, prin.

Jefferson ESD, 101 LINCOLN AVE 94015 — 6-11100 / 991-1270
Joseph DiGeronimo, supt.
Pollicita MS, 550 E MARKET ST 94014 — 3-00100 / 991-1218
Steven Howe, prin.
Rivera IS, 1255 SOUTHGATE AVE 94015 — 2-00100 / 991-1225
Matteo Rizzo, prin.
Other Schools – See Colma

Jefferson UNHSD — 6-00011
699 SERRAMONTE BLVD # 100 94015
Robert Gross, supt. — 756-0300
Jefferson HS, 6996 MISSION ST 94014 — 4-00011 / 992-4050
Isaac McClanahan, prin.
Westmoor HS — 4-00011
131 WESTMOOR AVE 94015 — 756-3434
Gary Johnson, prin.
Serramonte JHS — 2-00010
699 SERRAMONTE BLVD 94015 — 992-9000
Judy Reagan, prin.
Other Schools – See Pacifica

Dana Point, AC 714, PC 8, Orange
Capistrano USD
Supt. — See San Juan Capistrano
Dana Hills HS — 4-00011
33333 GOLDEN LANTERN ST 92629 — 496-6666
Rickie Lundgren, prin.

Danville, AC 510, PC 8, Contra Costa
San Ramon Valley USD — 7-11111
699 OLD ORCHARD DR 94526 — 837-1511
John Duncan, supt.
Monte Vista HS — 4-00011
3131 STONE VALLEY RD 94526 — 820-2900
Robert Giannini, prin.
San Ramon Valley HS — 4-00011
140 LOVE LN 94526 — 837-0533
Patricia Wheeler, prin.
Los Cerros MS, 968 BLEMER RD 94526 — 3-00100 / 838-2900
Duff Danilovich, prin.
Wood IS, 600 EL CAPITAN DR 94526 — 3-00100 / 820-2922
Richard Boschetti, prin.
Other Schools – See Alamo, San Ramon

Athenian School — 2-00111
PO BOX 6000 94526 — 837-3221
Eleanor Dase, prin.

Davis, AC 916, PC 8, Yolo
Davis JUSD, 526 B ST 95616 — 6-11111 / 757-5300
Floyd Fenocchio, supt.
SHS, 315 W 14TH ST 95616 — 4-00001 / 757-5400
Howard Cohen, prin.
Emerson JHS — 3-00110
2121 CALAVARAS AVE 95616 — 757-5430
Sue Olds, prin.
Holmes JHS, 1220 DREXEL DR 95616 — 3-00110 / 757-5455
Mark Hagemann, prin.

D-Q University — 2-CC
PO BOX 409 95617 — 758-0470
University of California 95616 — 7-UC / 752-1011

Deep Springs, AC 619, PC 1, Inyo

Deep Springs College — 1-CC
HC 72 BOX 45001 VIA DYER NV 89010 — 872-2000

Delano, AC 805, PC 7, Kern
Delano JUNHSD — 4-00011
1747 PRINCETON ST 93215 — 725-4000
Sherrill Hufnagel, supt.
HS, 1331 CECIL AVE 93215 — 4-00011 / 725-4000
Shirley Martin, prin.

Delano UNESD, 1405 12TH AVE 93215 — 6-11100 / 721-5000
Milton Woolsey, supt.
Cecil Avenue JHS, 1405 12TH AVE 93215 — 4-00100 / 721-5030
Rose Marie Bans, prin.

Bakersfield College — 3-CC
1942 RANDOLPH ST 93215 — 725-4011

Delhi, AC 209, PC 5, Merced
Delhi ESD, PO BOX 338 95315 — 4-11100 / 668-6130
Kirk McCandless, supt.
El Capitan MS, PO BOX 338 95315 — 2-00100 / 668-6144
Chris Bayless, prin.

Denair, AC 209, PC 5, Stanislaus
Denair USD, PO BOX 368 95316 — 4-11111 / 632-7514
John Fitzgerald, supt.
HS, 3431 LESTER RD 95316 — 2-00011 / 632-9911
Alex Marshall, prin.

MS, 3460 LESTER RD 95316 — 2-01100 / 632-7585
Larry Hoyt, prin.

Diamond Bar, AC 909, PC 8, Los Angeles
Pomona USD
Supt. — See Pomona
Lorbeer JHS — 3-00100
501 DIAMOND BAR BLVD 91765 — 397-4527
Wayne Joseph, prin.
Walnut Valley USD
Supt. — See Walnut
HS, 21400 PATHFINDER RD 91765 — 4-00011 / 594-1405
Bob Corkrum, prin.
Chaparral MS — 4-00100
1405 SPRUCE TREE DR 91765 — 861-6227
Roger Skinner, prin.

Diamond Springs, AC 916, PC 5, El Dorado
El Dorado UNHSD — 6-00011
PO BOX 1450 95619 — 622-5081
David Murphy, supt.
Other Schools – See El Dorado Hills, Placerville, Shingle Springs

Diamond Springs Christian S — 2-11111
4253 FOWLER LN 95619 — 622-0559
Jack Runner, prin.

Dinuba, AC 209, PC 7, Tulare
Dinuba SD — 5-11111
1327 E EL MONTE WAY 93618 — 591-3650
Mark Fabrizio, supt.
HS, 1327 E EL MONTE WAY 93618 — 4-00011 / 591-4948
Ron Lyons, prin.
Washington IS — 3-00100
1327 E EL MONTE WAY 93618 — 591-7031
Thomas Ayers, prin.

Dixon, AC 916, PC 7, Solano
Dixon USD, 305 N ALMOND ST 95620 — 5-11111 / 678-5582
J. Gerry Laird, supt.
HS, 455 E A ST 95620 — 3-00011 / 678-2391
Marilys Tognetti, prin.
Jacobs IS, 200 N LINCOLN ST 95620 — 3-00100 / 678-9222
Gabriel Alvarado, prin.

Dorris, AC 916, PC 3, Siskiyou
Butte Valley USD, PO BOX 709 96023 — 2-11111 / 397-2131
Lindell Stanton, supt.
Butte Valley HS, PO BOX 728 96023 — 2-00011 / 397-4161
Thelma Kallstrom, prin.

Dos Palos, AC 209, PC 5, Merced
Dos Palos Oro Lomo JUSD — 5-11111
2041 ALMOND ST 93620 — 392-6101
Edward Butler, supt.
Dos Palos Joint Union HS — 3-00011
1701 E BLOSSOM ST 93620 — 392-2131
Ernie Wall, prin.
Bryant MS, 2041 ALMOND ST 93620 — 3-01100 / 392-6186
Brian Walker, prin.

Downey, AC 310, PC 8, Los Angeles
Downey USD — 7-11111
11627 BROOKSHIRE AVE 90241 — 904-3500
Ed Sussman, supt.
HS, 11627 BROOKSHIRE AVE 90241 — 4-00011 / 869-7301
Phil Jones, prin.
Warren HS — 4-00011
11627 BROOKSHIRE AVE 90241 — 869-7306
Edward Karcharik, prin.
East MS — 3-00100
11627 BROOKSHIRE AVE 90241 — 904-3586
Gary Hearty, prin.
Griffiths MS — 3-00100
11627 BROOKSHIRE AVE 90241 — 904-3580
Sara Cairns, prin.
South MS — 4-00100
11627 BROOKSHIRE AVE 90241 — 904-3572
Dale Lostetter, prin.
West MS — 3-00100
11627 BROOKSHIRE AVE 90241 — 904-3565
Gloria Widmann, prin.

Calvary Chapel Christian S — 3-11111
12808 WOODRUFF AVE 90242 — 803-6552
Scott Edwards, prin.
Pius X HS, 7851 GARDENDALE ST 90242 — 3-00011 / 861-2271
Michael Parmer, prin.

Downieville, AC 916, PC 3, Sierra
Sierra-Plumas JUSD, PO BOX E 95936 — 3-11111 / 289-3526
Michael Moore, supt.
JSHS, PO BOX B 95936 — 1-00111 / 289-3473
Lou Phillippi, prin.
Other Schools – See Loyalton, North San Juan

Duarte, AC 818, PC 7, Los Angeles
Duarte USD — 5-11111
1620 HUNTINGTON DR 91010 — 358-1191
Marcia McVey, supt.
HS, 1620 HUNTINGTON DR 91010 — 4-00011 / 358-1191
Al Scalise, prin.
Northview IS — 3-00100
1620 HUNTINGTON DR 91010 — 358-1191
Mary George, prin.

City of Hope Medical Center — HSP
1500 DUARTE RD 91010 — 359-8111

Dublin, AC 510, PC 7, Alameda
Dublin USD — 5-11111
7471 LARKDALE AVE 94568 — 828-2551
Vince Anaclerio, supt.
HS, 8151 VILLAGE PKY 94568 — 3-00011 / 833-3300
Mary Eversley, prin.
Wells MS, 6800 PENN DR 94568 — 3-00100 / 828-6227
James Hansen, prin.

Valley Christian HS — 2-00111
10800 DUBLIN BLVD 94568 — 828-4627
Andrew Fittinger, prin.

Dunsmuir, AC 916, PC 4, Siskiyou
Dunsmuir JUNHSD — 2-00011
5805 HIGH SCHOOL WAY 96025 — 235-4835
Robert Morris, supt.
HS, 5805 HIGH SCHOOL WAY 96025 — 2-00011 / 235-4835
Robert Morris, prin.

Durham, AC 916, PC 4, Butte
Durham USD, PO BOX 300 95938 — 4-11111 / 895-4675
Donald McNelis, supt.
HS, PO BOX 600 95938 — 2-00011 / 895-4680
Jim Gwyn, prin.
IS, PO BOX 310 95938 — 2-00100 / 895-4690
Steve Piluso, prin.

Earlimart, AC 805, PC 6, Tulare
Earlimart ESD, PO BOX 11970 93219 — 4-11100 / 849-2631
Sandra Torchia, supt.
MS, PO BOX 11970 93219 — 3-01100 / 849-2611
Gary Glover, prin.

East Palo Alto, AC 415, PC see Palo Alto
Ravenswood City ESD — 5-11100
2160 EUCLID AVE 94303 — 329-2800
Charlie Knight, supt.
McNair IS, 2033 PULGAS AVE 94303 — 2-01100 / 329-2888
Vera Clark, prin.
Other Schools – See Menlo Park

Edwards, AC 805, PC 6, Kern
Muroc JUSD
Supt. — See North Edwards
Desert HS, 1575 PAYNE AVE 93523 — 2-00011 / 258-4411
Tony Monetti, prin.
Payne Avenue MS — 2-00100
1577 PAYNE AVE 93523 — 258-4411
Mollie Graham, prin.

El Cajon, AC 619, PC 8, San Diego
Cajon Valley UNESD — 7-11100
PO BOX 1007 92022 — 588-3000
Dennis Smith, supt.
Cajon Valley IS — 3-00100
395 BALLANTYNE ST 92020 — 588-3092
Lisbeth Johnson, prin.
Emerald IS, 1221 EMERALD AVE 92020 — 3-00100 / 588-3097
Nancy Girvin, prin.
Greenfield IS — 3-00100
1495 GREENFIELD DR 92021 — 588-3103
Stephanie Troncone, prin.
Montgomery MS — 4-00100
1570 MELODY LN 92019 — 588-3107
Stephen Boyle, prin.

Grossmont UNHSD
Supt. — See La Mesa
El Cajon Valley HS — 4-00011
1035 E MADISON AVE 92021 — 579-5855
Frank Paredes, prin.
Granite Hills HS — 4-00011
1719 E MADISON AVE 92019 — 442-3463
Bob Avant, prin.
Valhalla HS, 1725 HILLSDALE RD 92019 — 4-00011 / 440-1501
Maria Theodore-Benedict, prin.

Christian Heritage College — 2-UC
2100 GREENFIELD DR 92019 — 800-676-2242
Christian HS — 3-00111
2100 GREENFIELD DR 92019 — 440-1531
Edward Giles, prin.
Cuyamaca College — 5-CC
2950 JAMACHA RD 92019 — 670-1980
Grossmont College — 7-CC
8800 GROSSMONT COLLEGE DR 92020 — 465-1700

El Centro, AC 619, PC 8, Imperial
Central UNHSD — 5-00011
1001 W BRIGHTON AVE 92243 — 352-2471
John Anderson, supt.
Central HS — 5-00011
1001 W BRIGHTON AVE 92243 — 352-2471
Barbara Oswalt, prin.

El Centro ESD — 6-11100
1256 BROADWAY ST 92243 — 352-5712
Everett Taylor, supt.
Kennedy MS, 900 N 6TH ST 92243 — 3-00100 / 352-0444
Sue Smith, prin.
Wilson JHS, 600 S WILSON ST 92243 — 3-00100 / 352-5341
JoAnn McDonald, prin.

El Cerrito, AC 510, PC 7, Contra Costa
West Contra Costa Usd
Supt. — See Richmond
HS, 540 ASHBURY AVE 94530 — 4-00011 / 525-0234
Paul Daniels, prin.
Portola JHS, 1021 NAVELLIER ST 94530 — 3-00100 / 524-0405
Abe Gonzales, prin.

El Dorado Hills, AC 916, PC 6, El Dorado
El Dorado UNHSD
Supt. — See Diamond Springs
Oak Ridge HS — 4-00011
1120 HARVARD WAY 95762 — 933-6980
James Fraysier, prin.

Rescue UNESD
Supt. — See Rescue
Marina Village MS 2-00100
1901 FRANCISCO DR 95762 933-3993
Joel Willen, prin.

Elk Creek, AC 916, PC 2, Glenn
Stoney Creek JUSD 2-11111
PO BOX 68 95939 968-5361
David Hansen, supt.
JSHS, PO BOX 68 95939 1-00111
David Hansen, prin. 968-5361

Elk Grove, AC 916, PC 7, Sacramento
Elk Grove USD 8-11111
8820 ELK GROVE BLVD 95624 686-7700
Robert Trigg, supt.
HS, 9800 ELK GROVE FLORIN RD 95624 5-00011
Paula Duncan, prin. 686-7741
Kerr MS, 8865 ELK GROVE BLVD 95624 4-00100
Arnold Adreani, prin. 686-7728
Other Schools – See Sacramento

El Monte, AC 818, PC 9, Los Angeles
El Monte UNHSD 6-00011
3537 JOHNSON AVE 91731 444-9005
David Sandell, supt.
Arroyo HS, 4921 CEDAR AVE 91732 4-00011
Jack Cline, prin. 444-9201
HS, 3048 TYLER AVE 91731 4-00011
Nick Salerno, prin. 444-7701
Mountain View HS 4-00011
2900 PARKWAY DR 91732 443-6181
Gloria Acosta-Araw, prin.
Other Schools – See Rosemead, South El Monte

Mountain View ESD 6-11100
2850 MOUNTAIN VIEW RD 91732 575-2151
Albert Gasparian, supt.
Kranz IS, 12460 FINEVIEW ST 91732 4-00100
Terry Tuchman, prin. 575-2190
Madrid MS, 3300 GILMAN RD 91732 3-00100
Steve Sherman, prin. 575-2020

El Segundo, AC 310, PC 7, Los Angeles
El Segundo USD 4-11111
641 SHELDON ST 90245 615-2650
William Manahan, supt.
HS, 641 SHELDON ST 90245 3-00011
William Watkins, prin. 615-2661
MS, 641 SHELDON ST 90245 2-00100
Megan Cassette, prin. 615-2690

El Sobrante, AC 510, PC 6, Contra Costa
West Contra Costa Usd
Supt. — See Richmond
Crespi JHS, 1121 ALLVIEW AVE 94803 4-00100
Robert Cone, prin. 223-8611

Calvary Christian Pentacostal Academy 2-11111
4892 SAN PABLO DAM RD 94803 222-3828
Susan Blankenchip, prin.

Elverta, AC 916, PC 3, Sacramento
Center USD, 8408 WATT AVE 95626 6-11111
Rex Fortune, supt. 338-6400
Center HS, 8306 WATT AVE 95626 4-00011
Claude Brock, prin. 338-6420
Center JHS, 8300 WATT AVE 95626 3-00100
Larry Brown, prin. 338-6450

Elverta JESD, 7900 ELOISE AVE 95626 2-11100
Fred Warchol, supt. 991-5400
Alpha IS, 8920 ELWYN AVE 95626 2-00100
Dianna Mangerich, prin. 991-4726

Emeryville, AC 510, PC 6, Alameda
Emery USD 3-11111
4727 SAN PABLO AVE 94608 655-6936
J. L. Handy, supt.
Emery JSHS, 1100 47TH ST 94608 2-00111
J. L. Handy, prin. 652-1056

Empire, AC 209, PC 4, Stanislaus
Empire UNESD
Supt. — See Modesto
Teel MS, PO BOX 1269 95319 4-00100
Herb Packer, prin. 526-0684

Encinitas, AC 619, PC 8, San Diego
San Dieguito UNHSD 6-00111
710 ENCINITAS BLVD 92024 753-6491
William Berrier, supt.
San Dieguito SHS 4-00001
710 ENCINITAS BLVD 92024 753-1121
Penny Cooper-Francisco, prin.
Sunset HS, 710 ENCINITAS BLVD 92024 2-00011
Roy Risner, prin. 753-3860
Dieguено JHS 4-00110
710 ENCINITAS BLVD 92024 944-1892
Mary Holloway, prin.
Oak Crest JHS 4-00110
710 ENCINITAS BLVD 92024 753-6241
Terry King, prin.
Other Schools – See San Diego, Solana Beach

Encino, AC 818, PC see Los Angeles

Crespi Carmelite HS 2-00011
5031 ALONZO AVE 91316 345-1672
Fr. Frederick Tillotson, prin.
Holy Martyrs S 2-01111
5300 WHITE OAK AVE 91316 784-6228
Vartkes Ghazarian, prin.

Landmark West S 2-01111
5461 LOUISE AVE 91316 986-5045
Richard Goldman, prin.

Escalon, AC 209, PC 5, San Joaquin
Escalon USD 5-11111
1520 YOSEMITE AVE 95320 838-3591
Bob Wallace, supt.
HS, 1520 YOSEMITE AVE 95320 3-00011
Dave Mantooth, prin. 838-7073
El Portal MS, 805 1ST ST 95320 3-00100
Jerry Emery, prin. 838-7095

Escondido, AC 619, PC 9, San Diego
Escondido UNESD 7-11100
1330 E GRAND AVE 92027 432-2400
Robert Fisher, supt.
Del Dios MS, 1330 E GRAND AVE 92027 4-00100
James Fitzpatrick, prin. 432-2439
Grant MS, 1330 E GRAND AVE 92027 4-00100
Julie Rich, prin. 432-2452
Hidden Valley MS 4-00100
1330 E GRAND AVE 92027 432-2457
Martha Law-Edwards, prin.

Escondido UNHSD 6-00011
302 N MIDWAY DR 92027 480-3000
Jane Gawronski, supt.
HS, 1535 N BROADWAY 92026 4-00011
Shirley Rehkopf, prin. 480-3030
Orange Glen HS 4-00011
2200 GLENRIDGE RD 92027 480-3070
Michael Wray, prin.
San Pasqual HS 4-00011
3300 BEAR VALLEY PKY S 92025 480-3100
Steve Spraker, prin.
Valley HS 2-00011
2801 BEAR VALLEY PKY S 92025 480-3130
Robert Clay, prin.

Calvin Christian HS 2-00011
2000 N BROADWAY 92026 489-2249
Jim Ouden, prin.
El Dorado College 2-CS
385 N ESCONDIDO BLVD 92025 743-2100
Escondido Adventist Academy 2-11111
1233 W 9TH AVE 92029 746-1800
Martha Havens, prin.
San Pasqual SDA Academy 2-11111
17701 SAN PASQUAL VALLEY RD 92025
Berit Von Pohle, prin. 747-1600
Westminster Theological Seminary 2-UC
1725 BEAR VALLEY PKY 92027 480-8474

Esparto, AC 916, PC 4, Yolo
Esparto USD, PO BOX 69 95627 3-11111
Jerry Elmore, supt. 787-3446
HS, PO BOX 69 95627 2-00011
Thomas McNicholas, prin. 787-3405

Etiwanda, AC 909, PC see Cucamonga
Chaffey JUNHSD
Supt. — See Ontario
HS, PO BOX 447 91739 4-00011
Doug Huckaby, prin. 899-2531
Etiwanda ESD, PO BOX 248 91739 5-11100
Gene Newton, supt. 899-2451
IS, PO BOX 248 91739 4-00100
Delores Lindsey, prin. 899-1701

Etna, AC 916, PC 3, Siskiyou
Etna UNHSD, 501 HOWELL AVE 96027 2-00111
Jeffrey Hamilton, prin. 467-3218
HS, PO BOX 340 96027 2-00011
David Tolson, prin. 467-3244
Other Schools – See Fort Jones

Eureka, AC 707, PC 8, Humboldt
Eureka City SD 6-11111
3200 WALFORD AVE 95503 441-2400
James Scott, supt.
HS, 1915 J ST 95501 4-00011
Greg Aslanian, prin. 441-2400
Winship JHS, 2500 CYPRESS ST 95503 2-00100
Hank Beck, prin. 441-2400
Zane JHS, 2155 S ST 95501 3-00100
Bob Steffen, prin. 441-2400

College of the Redwoods 6-CC
7351 TOMPKINS HILL RD 95501 445-6700
Eureka Nazarene S, 2039 E ST 95501 2-11111
Nancy Storment, prin. 442-4625
St. Bernard HS, 222 DOLLISON ST 95501 2-00011
Jeffrey Jacobs, prin. 443-2735

Exeter, AC 209, PC 6, Tulare
Exeter UNSD, 134 S E ST 93221 5-11111
Mike McLaughlin, supt. 592-9421
HS, 820 SAN JUAN AVE 93221 4-00011
Shirley Houser, prin. 592-2127
Wilson MS, 265 ALBERT AVE 93221 2-00100
Steve Van Zant, prin. 592-2144

Fairfax, AC 415, PC 6, Marin
Ross Valley SD
Supt. — See San Anselmo
White Hill IS, 101 GLEN DR 94930 2-00100
Bryce Farinacci, prin. 454-8390

Fairfield, AC 707, PC 8, Solano
Fairfield-Suisun USD 7-11111
1125 MISSOURI ST 94533 421-4000
Linda Erickson, supt.

Armijo HS, 824 WASHINGTON ST 94533 4-00011
Rae Lanpheir, prin. 422-7500
HS, 205 E ATLANTIC AVE 94533 4-00011
Reed McLaughlin, prin. 422-8672
Grange MS, 1975 BLOSSOM AVE 94533 3-00100
Richard Watson, prin. 421-4175
Sullivan MS, 2195 UNION AVE 94533 3-00100
Greg Hubbs, prin. 421-4115
Other Schools – See Suisun City

Fair Oaks, AC 916, PC 8, Sacramento
San Juan USD
Supt. — See Carmichael
Bella Vista HS 4-00011
8301 MADISON AVE 95628 971-5052
Jim Reidt, prin.
Del Campo HS, 4925 DEWEY DR 95628 4-00011
Lois Francimone, prin. 971-5664
Rogers MS, 4924 DEWEY DR 95628 3-00100
Monty Muller, prin. 971-7889

Sacramento Waldorf S 2-11111
3750 BANNISTER RD 95628 961-3900
Charles Blatchford, prin.

Fallbrook, AC 619, PC 7, San Diego
Fallbrook UNESD, PO BOX 698 92088 6-11100
Jennifer Jeffries, supt. 723-7000
Potter IS, PO BOX 698 92088 3-00100
Raye Clendening, prin. 723-7050

Fallbrook UNHSD 5-00011
PO BOX 368 92088 723-6332
Robert Thomas, supt.
HS, PO BOX 368 92088 4-00011
James Yahr, prin. 723-6300

Farmersville, AC 209, PC 6, Tulare
Farmersville ESD 4-11100
281 S FARMERSVILLE BLVD 93223 747-0776
Stan Halperin, supt.
JHS, 281 S FARMERSVILLE BLVD 93223 2-00100
Jeffrey Carlovsky, prin. 747-0764

Felton, AC 408, PC 6, Santa Cruz
San Lorenzo Valley USD 5-11111
6134 HIGHWAY 9 95018 335-4701
Robert Brickman, supt.
San Lorenzo Valley HS 4-00011
6134 HIGHWAY 9 95018 335-4425
Dave Weiss, prin.
San Lorenzo Valley JHS 3-00100
6134 HIGHWAY 9 95018 335-4452
Dan Cope, prin.

Ferndale, AC 707, PC 4, Humboldt
Ferndale UNHSD, 1231 MAIN ST 95536 2-00011
Charles Lakin, supt. 786-9505
HS, 1231 MAIN ST 95536 2-00011
Charles Lakin, prin. 786-9505

Fillmore, AC 805, PC 7, Ventura
Fillmore USD, PO BOX 697 93016 5-11111
David Haney, supt. 524-0280
HS, PO BOX 697 93016 3-00011
Lynn Johnson, prin. 524-1711
JHS, PO BOX 697 93016 2-00100
Peggy Glenn, prin. 524-2353

Firebaugh, AC 209, PC 5, Fresno
Firebaugh-Las Deltas USD 4-11111
1976 MORRIS KYLE DR 93622 659-1476
Violet Chuck, supt.
El Puente HS 1-00011
1976 MORRIS KYLE DR 93622 659-1204
Alfred Hansen, prin.
HS, 1976 MORRIS KYLE DR 93622 2-00011
William Waxman, prin. 659-1415
JHS, 1976 MORRIS KYLE DR 93622 2-00100
Patrick Holland, prin. 659-1481

Folsom, AC 916, PC 8, Sacramento
Folsom-Cordova USD 7-11111
125 E BIDWELL ST 95630 355-1100
Caroline Gonzalez, supt.
HS, 715 RILEY ST 95630 4-00011
Jill Solberg, prin. 985-3644
JHS, 500 BLUE RAVINE RD 95630 3-00100
Robert Mange, prin. 985-4466
Other Schools – See Rancho Cordova

Fontana, AC 909, PC 8, San Bernardino
Fontana USD, 9680 CITRUS AVE 92335 8-11111
Anthony Lardieri, supt. 357-5000
HS, 9453 CITRUS AVE 92335 5-00011
Kay Rager, prin. 357-5500
Fontana Miller HS 5-00011
6821 OLEANDER AVE 92336 357-5800
Michael Micallef, prin.
Alder MS, 7555 ALDER AVE 92336 4-00100
Lynette Forte, prin. 357-5330
Almeria MS, 7723 ALMERIA AVE 92336 4-00100
Brenda McGinniss, prin. 357-5350
MS, 8425 MANGO AVE 92335 4-00100
Dave Ackley, prin. 357-5370
Sequoia MS, 9452 HEMLOCK AVE 92335 4-00100
Lou Ann Archbold, prin. 357-5400
Southridge MS 4-00100
14500 LIVE OAK AVE 92337 357-5420
Gary Soto, prin.

Ambassador Christian S 2-11111
8405 N MAPLE AVE 92335 829-3108
L. Clark, prin.

Foresthill, AC 916, PC 4, Placer
Foresthill UNESD — 3-11100
  PO BOX 609 95631 — 367-2966
  Timothy Justus, supt.
Foresthill Divide MS — 2-00100
  22888 FORESTHILL RD 95631 — 367-3782
  Timothy Justus, prin.

Forestville, AC 707, PC 3, Sonoma
Analy UNHSD
  Supt. — See Sebastopol
El Molino HS, 7050 COVEY RD 95436 — 4-00011
  Frank Anderson, prin. — 887-3450

Fort Bragg, AC 707, PC 6, Mendocino
Fort Bragg USD — 5-11111
  312 S LINCOLN ST 95437 — 961-2850
  Anthony Sorci, supt.
HS, 300 DANA ST 95437 — 3-00011
  Judy Peterson, prin. — 961-2880
MS, 500 N HAROLD ST 95437 — 3-00100
  Linda Cohen, prin. — 961-2870

Fort Irwin, AC 619, PC see Barstow
Silver Valley USD
  Supt. — See Yermo
MS — 3-01100
  NATIONAL TRAINING CENTER 92310 — 386-1133
  Walter Maykulsky, prin.

Fort Jones, AC 916, PC 3, Siskiyou
Etna UNHSD
  Supt. — See Etna
Scott Valley JHS, PO BOX 607 96032 — 2-00110
  Mark Johnson, prin. — 468-5565

Fort Ord, AC 408, PC see Monterey
Monterey Peninsula USD
  Supt. — See Monterey
Seaside HS — 3-00011
  NOCHE BUENA ST AT FORD ORD 93941
  Bettye Lusk, prin. — 899-7033

Fortuna, AC 707, PC 6, Humboldt
Fortuna UNESD, 843 L ST 95540 — 3-11100
  Albert Keller, supt. — 725-2293
MS, 843 L ST 95540 — 2-01100
  Jack Persson, prin. — 725-3415

Fortuna UNHSD, 379 12TH ST 95540 — 3-00011
  Dennis Hanson, supt. — 725-4461
East HS, 392 16TH ST 95540 — 1-00011
  John Kassis, prin. — 725-1673
Fortuna Union HS, 379 12TH ST 95540 — 3-00011
  Dennis Hanson, prin. — 725-4461

Rohnerville ESD — 3-11100
  3850 ROHNERVILLE RD 95540 — 725-5197
  Kenneth Lytle, supt.
Thomas MS, 2800 THOMAS ST 95540 — 2-01100
  Anne Nicksic, prin. — 725-5197

Foster City, AC 415, PC 8, San Mateo
San Mateo-Foster City SD
  Supt. — See San Mateo
Bowditch MS, 1450 TARPON ST 94404 — 3-00100
  John Belforte, prin. — 312-7680

Fountain Valley, AC 714, PC 8, Orange
Fountain Valley ESD — 6-11100
  17210 OAK ST 92708 — 843-3200
  Ruben Ingram, supt.
Fulton MS, 8778 EL LAGO CIR 92708 — 3-00100
  Tom Markel, prin. — 375-2816
Masuda MS — 3-00100
  17415 LOS JARDINES W 92708 — 378-4250
  Don Keller, prin.
Other Schools – See Huntington Beach

Garden Grove USD
  Supt. — See Garden Grove
Los Amigos HS — 4-00011
  16566 NEWHOPE ST 92708 — 663-6288
  George Willson, prin.

Huntington Beach UNHSD
  Supt. — See Huntington Beach
HS, 17816 BUSHARD ST 92708 — 5-00011
  Gary Erbst, prin. — 962-3301

Ocean View ESD
  Supt. — See Huntington Beach
Vista View MS — 3-00100
  16250 HICKORY ST 92708 — 842-0626
  Barbara O'Connor, prin.

Coastline Community College — 7-CC
  11460 WARNER AVE 92708 — 546-7600
First Southern Baptist Christian S — 2-11111
  10350 ELLIS AVE 92708 — 962-6886
  Dale Hickey, prin.

Fowler, AC 209, PC 5, Fresno
Fowler USD, 658 E ADAMS AVE 93625 — 4-11111
  David Miller, supt. — 834-2591
HS, 701 E MAIN ST 93625 — 2-00011
  Doris Ostrand, prin. — 834-2564
Fremont MS — 2-01100
  306 E TUOLUMNE ST 93625 — 834-1691
  Ron Garcia, prin.

Fremont, AC 510, PC 9, Alameda
Fremont USD, PO BOX 5008 94537 — 8-11111
  Raphael Belluomini, supt. — 657-2350
American HS — 4-00011
  36300 FREMONT BLVD 94536 — 796-1776
  Darryl Stucker, prin.

Irvington HS, 41800 BLACOW RD 94538 — 4-00011
  Robert Gaskill, prin. — 656-5711
Kennedy HS, 39999 BLACOW RD 94538 — 4-00011
  Suzon Kornblum, prin. — 657-4070
Mission San Jose HS — 4-00011
  41717 PALM AVE 94539 — 657-3600
  Marcia Mathog, prin.
Washington HS — 4-00011
  38442 FREMONT BLVD 94536 — 794-8866
  Daryl Talken, prin.
Centerville JHS — 3-00100
  37720 FREMONT BLVD 94536 — 797-2072
  Garo Mirigian, prin.
Hopkins JHS, 600 DRISCOLL RD 94539 — 3-00100
  Tim Reichert, prin. — 656-3500
Horner JHS, 41365 CHAPEL WAY 94538 — 3-00100
  E. McCoy, prin. — 656-4000
Thornton JHS — 3-00100
  4357 THORNTON AVE 94536 — 793-9090
  Suzanne Smith, prin.
Walters JHS, 39600 LOGAN DR 94538 — 3-00100
  Marcella Smith, prin. — 656-7211

California School for the Blind — HND
  500 WALNUT AVE 94536
California School for the Deaf — HND
  39350 GALLAUDET DR 94538
Fremont Christian S — 4-11111
  4760 THORNTON AVE 94536 — 792-4700
  Larry Daugherty, prin.
Ohlone College — 6-CC
  PO BOX 3909 94539 — 659-6000
Santa Barbara Business College — 2-CS
  4333 HANSEN AVE 94536 — 793-4342
Sequoia Institute — 4-CS
  420 E WHITNEY PL 94539 — 800-248-8585
Silicon Valley College — 2-CS
  41350 CHRISTY ST 94538 — 623-9966

Fresno, AC 209, PC 10, Fresno
Central USD, 4605 N POLK AVE 93722 — 6-11111
  George Keledijian, supt. — 276-5200
Central HS — 4-00011
  2045 N DICKENSON AVE 93722 — 276-5276
  Dwight Miller, prin.
El Capitan MS — 3-00100
  4443 W WELDON AVE 93722 — 276-5270
  Douglas Perry, prin.

Clovis USD
  Supt. — See Clovis
Clovis West HS — 5-00011
  1070 E TEAGUE AVE 93720 — 431-6600
  Jerry MacDonald, prin.
Kastner IS, 7676 N 1ST ST 93720 — 4-00100
  Lynda Snauffer, prin. — 435-1620

Fresno USD, TULARE & M STS 93722 — 8-11111
  Charles McCully, supt. — 441-3000
Bullard SHS, 5445 N PALM AVE 93704 — 4-00011
  Richard McCleman, prin. — 441-3666
Hoover HS, 5550 N 1ST ST 93710 — 4-00011
  Carol Sarkisian Bonard, prin. — 441-3888
Duncan Polytechnical HS — 3-00011
  4330 E GARLAND AVE 93726 — 441-3304
  Carol Gaab, prin.
Edison HS — 4-00011
  540 E CALIFORNIA AVE 93706 — 441-3900
  Stanley McDonald, prin.
HS, 1839 N ECHO AVE 93704 — 5-00011
  John Marinovich, prin. — 441-3800
McLane HS, 2727 N CEDAR AVE 93703 — 5-00011
  Timothy Belcher, prin. — 441-3500
Roosevelt HS — 5-00011
  4250 E TULARE AVE 93702 — 441-3777
  Jane Hammaker, prin.
Ahwahnee MS — 3-00100
  1127 E ESCALON AVE 93710 — 441-3190
  Jim Hamilton, prin.
Cooper MS — 3-00100
  2277 W BELLAIRE WAY 93705 — 441-3193
  Dennis Sherard, prin.
Edison Computech MS — 3-00100
  555 E BELGRAVIA AVE 93706 — 441-3971
  Claudia Noakes, prin.
Ft. Miller MS — 3-00100
  1320 E DAKOTA AVE 93704 — 441-3196
  Julie Adams, prin.
Kings Canyon MS — 4-00100
  5117 E TULARE AVE 93727 — 441-3206
  Larry Powell, prin.
Scandinavian MS — 3-00100
  3216 N SIERRA VISTA AVE 93726 — 441-3144
  Jenna Reynolds, prin.
Sequoia MS — 4-00100
  4050 E HAMILTON AVE 93702 — 441-3210
  Gary Christensen, prin.
Tehipite MS, 630 N AUGUSTA ST 93701 — 3-00100
  Richard Shore, prin. — 441-3216
Tenaya MS, 1239 W MESA AVE 93711 — 3-00100
  Jeannette Phillips, prin. — 441-3220
Tioga MS, 3232 E FAIRMONT AVE 93726 — 3-00100
  Sam Gonzales, prin. — 441-3224
Wawona MS — 3-00100
  4524 N THORNE AVE 93704 — 441-3227
  Diane Parrish, prin.
Yosemite MS, 1292 N 9TH ST 93703 — 3-00100
  John Shropshire, prin. — 441-3230

Washington UNHSD — 4-00011
  6041 S ELM AVE 93706 — 485-8805
  William Griffin, supt.
Washington HS, 6041 S ELM AVE 93706 — 3-00011
  Columbus Craig, prin. — 485-8805

West Fresno ESD, 2888 S IVY AVE 93706 — 3-11100
  Joe Lee, supt. — 485-2272
West Fresno MS, 2888 S IVY AVE 93706 — 2-00100
  Errol Carter, prin. — 485-2013

California Sch. Professional Psychology — 2-UC
  1350 M ST 93721 — 486-8420
California State University — 7-UC
  SHAW & CEDAR AVE 93740 — 278-4240
Chestnut Avenue Baptist Academy — 2-11111
  1461 N CHESTNUT AVE 93703 — 251-5437
  Marcia Longwisch, prin.
Covenant Christian S — 2-11111
  4558 N MAPLE AVE 93726 — 292-5019
  Rev. Berry, prin.
Fresno Adventist Academy — 2-11111
  5397 E OLIVE AVE 93727 — 251-5548
  Steven McKeone, prin.
Fresno Christian S — 3-11111
  7280 N CEDAR AVE 93720 — 299-1695
  Tim Wilkins, prin.
Fresno City College — 7-CC
  1101 E UNIVERSITY AVE 93741 — 442-4600
Fresno Community Hospital/Medical Center — HSP
  PO BOX 1232 93715 — 442-3911
Fresno Institute of Technology — 2-CS
  1545 FULTON ST 93721 — 442-3574
Fresno Pacific College — 3-UC
  1717 S CHESTNUT AVE 93702 — 453-2000
Galen College Medical & Dental Assts. — 2-CS
  1325 N WISHON AVE 93728 — 264-9726
Heald 4 C's College — 2-CC
  255 W BULLARD AVE 93704 — 483-4222
Mennonite Brethren Biblical Seminary — 1-UC
  4824 E BUTLER AVE 93727 — 251-8628
Phillips Junior College — 2-CC
  2048 N FINE AVE 93727 — 453-1000
San Joaquin College of Law — 2-UC
  3385 E SHIELDS AVE 93726 — 225-4953
San Joaquin Memorial HS — 3-00011
  1406 N FRESNO ST 93703 — 268-9251
  Br. Albert Villagomez, prin.
San Joaquin Valley College — 2-CC
  3333 N BOND AVE 93726 — 229-7800
San Joaquin Valley College of Aeronautic — 2-CS
  4985 E ANDERSEN AVE 93727
Sierra Valley Business College — 2-CS
  4747 N 1ST ST # D 93726 — 222-0947
Truck Driving Academy — 2-CS
  5168 N BLYTHE AVE # 102 93722 — 276-5708
Truth Taberncle Christian Academy — 2-11111
  4411 N 1ST ST 93726 — 225-1027
  Vaughn Morton, prin.
Valley Childrens Hospital — HSP
  3151 N MILLBROOK AVE 93703 — 225-3000
West Coast Christian College — 2-CC
  6901 N MAPLE AVE 93710 — 299-7201
Western Truck School — 2-CS
  4565 N GOLDEN STATE BLVD 93722 — 276-1220

Fullerton, AC 714, PC 9, Orange
Fullerton ESD — 7-11100
  1401 W VALENCIA DR 92633 — 447-7400
  Duncan Johnson, supt.
Ladera Vista JHS — 3-00100
  1700 E WILSHIRE AVE 92631 — 447-7765
  (—), prin.
Nicholas JHS, 1100 W OLIVE AVE 92633 — 3-00100
  Mary Dalessi, prin. — 447-7775
Parks JHS — 3-00100
  1710 W ROSECRANS AVE 92633 — 447-7785
  Larry Beaver, prin.

Fullerton JUNHSD — 7-00011
  780 E BEECHWOOD AVE 92635 — 671-4331
  J. Jones, supt.
HS, 201 E CHAPMAN AVE 92632 — 4-00011
  Ed Shaw, prin. — 870-3720
Sunny Hills HS — 4-00011
  1801 W WARBURTON WAY 92633 — 870-3406
  George Giokaris, prin.
Troy HS, 2200 E DOROTHY LN 92631 — 4-00011
  Jerry Atkin, prin. — 870-3604
Other Schools – See Buena Park, La Habra

Biblical Christian College — 2-UC
  1601 W MALVERN AVE 92633 — 879-8626
California State University 92634 — 7-UC
   — 773-2011
Fullerton College — 7-CC
  321 E CHAPMAN AVE 92632 — 992-7000
Pacific Christian College — 2-UC
  2500 E NUTWOOD AVE 92631 — 879-3901
Rosary HS, 1340 N ACACIA AVE 92631 — 3-00111
  Trudy Mazzarella, prin. — 879-6302
Southern California College of Optometry — 2-UC
  2001 N ASSOCIATED RD 92631 — 870-7226
Western State University College of Law — 3-UC
  1111 N STATE COLLEGE BLVD 92631 — 738-1000

Galt, AC 209, PC 6, Sacramento
Galt JUENESD, 21 C ST 95632 — 4-11100
  Jeffrey Jennings, supt. — 745-2911
Greer MS, 248 W A ST 95632 — 3-00100
  June Gillis, prin. — 745-2641

Galt JUNHSD   4-00011
   145 N LINCOLN WAY   95632   745-3061
   Giannina Santangelo, supt.
   HS, 145 N LINCOLN WAY   95632   4-00011
    Luann Boone, prin.   745-3081

Garberville, AC 707, PC 4, Humboldt
   Southern Humbolt JUSD   4-11111
    PO BOX 129   95542   923-2789
    Clifton Anderson, supt.
   Other Schools – See Miranda

Gardena, AC 310, PC 8, Los Angeles
   Los Angeles USD
    Supt. — See Los Angeles
   HS, 1301 W 182ND ST   90248   4-00011
    John Howard, prin.   327-5900
   Peary JHS   4-00100
    1415 W GARDENA BLVD   90247   324-6606
    Louvonia Hall, prin.

   Junipero Serra HS   2-00011
    14830 VAN NESS AVE   90249   324-6675
    Arthur Hernandez, prin.

Garden Grove, AC 714, PC 9, Orange
   Garden Grove USD   8-11111
    10331 STANFORD AVE   92640   663-6000
    Ed Dundon, supt.
   Pacifica SHS   4-00001
    6851 LAMPSON AVE   92645   663-6515
    Michael Lombardi, prin.
   Bolsa Grande HS   4-00011
    9401 WESTMINSTER AVE   92644   663-6424
    Jim Morrison, prin.
   HS, 11271 STANFORD AVE   92640   4-00011
    Peg Mahfood, prin.   663-6115
   Rancho Alamitos HS   4-00011
    11351 DALE ST   92641   663-6415
    Thomas Robbins, prin.
   Santiago HS, 12342 TRASK AVE   92643   4-00011
    Donald Wise, prin.   663-6215
   Alamitos IS, 12381 DALE ST   92641   3-00100
    Kent Baird, prin.   663-6101
   Bell IS, 12345 SPRINGDALE ST   92645   3-00100
    James Monahan, prin.   663-6466
   Doig IS, 12752 TRASK AVE   92643   3-00100
    James Smith, prin.   663-6241
   Irvine IS, 10552 HAZARD AVE   92643   3-00100
    Ron Porter, prin.   663-6551
   Jordan IS, 9821 WOODBURY AVE   92644   3-00100
    Bill Langan, prin.   663-6124
   Ralston IS, 10851 LAMPSON AVE   92640   3-00100
    Denny Pace, prin.   663-6366
   Walton MS, 12181 BUARO ST   92640   3-00100
    Gerald Gereb, prin.   663-6040
   Other Schools – See Fountain Valley, Santa Ana, Westminster

   Orangewood Adventist Academy   2-11111
    13732 CLINTON ST   92643   534-4694
    Gordon Day, prin.
   Travel and Trade Career Institute   2-CS
    12541 BROOKHURST ST STE 100   92640
     636-2611

Garden Vall, AC 916, PC 3, El Dorado
   Black Oak Mine USD
    Supt. — See Georgetown
   Golden Sierra HS, PO BOX 175   95633   3-00011
    Teresa Gary, prin.   333-1280

Georgetown, AC 916, PC 4, El Dorado
   Black Oak Mine USD   4-11111
    PO BOX 349001   95634   333-4128
    Carol Dee, supt.
   Divide HS, PO BOX 349003   95634   1-00011
    Ruth Willen, prin.   333-1369
   Other Schools – See Garden Vall

Geyserville, AC 707, PC 3, Sonoma
   Geyserville USD, PO BOX 108   95441   2-11111
    Louis Schandler, supt.   433-3208
   Geyserville Educational Park HS   1-00011
    PO BOX 108   95441   433-3208
    Gail Tovani, prin.
   MS, PO BOX 108   95441   1-00100
    Gail Tovani, prin.   433-3208

Gilroy, AC 408, PC 8, Santa Clara
   Gilroy USD, 7810 ARROYO CIR   95020   6-11111
    Kenneth Noonan, supt.   847-2700
   HS, 7810 ARROYO CIR   95020   4-00011
    Ernest Zermeno, prin.   847-2424
   South Valley JHS   4-00100
    7810 ARROYO CIR   95020   847-2828
    Lucretia Peebles, prin.

   Gavilan Community College   5-CC
    5055 SANTA TERESA BLVD   95020   848-4712

Glendale, AC 818, PC 9, Los Angeles
   Glendale USD, 223 N JACKSON ST   91206   8-11111
    Rob Sanchis, supt.   241-3111
   SHS, 1440 E BROADWAY   91205   4-00011
    James Gibson, prin.   242-3161
   Hoover HS, 651 GLENWOOD RD   91202   5-00011
    Donald Duncan, prin.   242-6801
   Roosevelt MS   4-00110
    1017 S GLENDALE AVE   91205   242-6845
    Judith White, prin.
   Toll MS, 700 GLENWOOD RD   91202   4-00100
    Martin Pilgreen, prin.   244-8414

Wilson JHS, 1221 MONTEREY RD   91206   4-00110
   Neal Siegel, prin.   244-8145
Other Schools – See La Crescenta

Glendale Adventist Academy   3-11111
   700 KIMLIN DR   91206   244-8671
   Hal Hampton, prin.
Glendale Career College   1-CS
   1021 GRANDVIEW AVE   91201   243-1131
Glendale Community College   7-CC
   1500 N VERDUGO RD   91208   240-1000
Holy Family HS   2-00011
   400 E LOMITA AVE   91205   241-3178
   Jacqueline Kresal, prin.
Northwest College Medical Dental Assts.   2-CS
   124 S GLENDALE AVE   91205   242-0205

Glendora, AC 818, PC 8, Los Angeles
   Glendora USD   6-11111
    500 N LORAINE AVE   91741   963-1611
    Patrick Bushman, supt.
   HS, 1600 E FOOTHILL BLVD   91741   4-00011
    Kent Bechler, prin.   963-5731
   Goddard MS   3-00100
    859 E SIERRA MADRE AVE   91741   852-4500
    Ted McNevin, prin.
   Sandburg MS   3-00100
    819 W BENNETT AVE   91741   852-4530
    Bennett Conner, prin.

Citrus College   6-CC
   1000 W FOOTHILL BLVD   91741   963-0323
St. Lucy Priory HS   3-00011
   655 W SIERRA MADRE AVE   91741   335-3322
   Sr. Monica Collins, prin.

Goleta, AC 805, PC 8, Santa Barbara
   Santa Barbara SD
    Supt. — See Santa Barbara
   Dos Pueblos HS   4-00011
    7266 ALAMEDA AVE   93117   968-2541
    Michael Couch, prin.
   Goleta Valley JHS   3-00100
    6100 STOW CANYON RD   93117   967-3486
    Celia Ramos, prin.

Gonzales, AC 408, PC 5, Monterey
   Gonzales UNESD, PO BOX G   93926   4-11100
    Gordon Piffero, supt.   675-2727
   Fairview MS, PO BOX G   93926   3-01100
    John Ward, prin.   675-3704

   Gonzales UNHSD, PO BOX 939   93926   4-00011
    William Stratton, supt.   675-2495
   HS, PO BOX 939   93926   4-00011
    John Macias, prin.   675-2495

Granada Hills, AC 818, PC see Los Angeles
   Los Angeles USD
    Supt. — See Los Angeles
   HS, 10535 ZELZAH AVE   91344   5-00011
    Steve Quon, prin.   360-2361
   Kennedy HS, 11254 GOTHIC AVE   91344   4-00011
    Andreda Pruitt, prin.   368-3711
   Frost JHS, 12314 BRADFORD PL   91344   4-00100
    Jay Peterman, prin.   360-2146
   Henry MS, 17340 SAN JOSE ST   91344   4-00100
    Linda Lane, prin.   363-7401
   Porter JHS, 15960 KINGSBURY ST   91344   3-00110
    Sherry Breskin, prin.   891-1807

Grand Terrace, AC 909, PC 7, San Bernardino
   Colton JUSD
    Supt. — See Colton
   Terrace Hills JHS   3-00100
    22579 DE BERRY ST   92313   876-4256
    Kay Bunnell, prin.

Granite Bay, AC 916, PC 3, Placer
   Eureka UNESD, 5477 EUREKA RD   95746   4-11100
    Ronald Feist, supt.   791-4939
   Cavitt IS, 7200 FULLER DR   95746   3-00100
    Janet Schimpf, prin.   791-4152

Grass Valley, AC 916, PC 6, Nevada
   Grass Valley ESD   4-11100
    10840 GILMORE WAY   95945   273-4483
    John Burke, supt.
   Gilmore IS   3-00100
    10837 ROUGH AND READY HWY   95945
    Linda Breninger, prin.   273-8479

   Nevada JUNHSD, 11645 RIDGE RD   95945   5-00011
    Michael Barkhurst, supt.   273-3351
   Bear River HS   3-00011
    11130 MAGNOLIA RD   95949   268-3700
    Richard Werntz, prin.
   Nevada Union HS   4-00011
    11761 RIDGE RD   95945   273-4431
    Kurt Stenderup, prin.

   Pleasant Ridge UNESD   4-11100
    22580 KINGSTON LN   95949   268-2800
    James Meshwert, supt.
   Magnolia IS, 22431 KINGSTON LN   95949   3-00100
    David Rosenquist, prin.   268-2815

Greenfield, AC 408, PC 6, Monterey
   Greenfield UNESD, PO BOX 97   93927   4-11100
    Jeff Breslow, supt.   674-2840
   Vista Verde MS, PO BOX 2269   93927   3-00100
    Paul Griffin, prin.   674-1420

Greenville, AC 916, PC 4, Plumas
   Plumas USD
    Supt. — See Quincy
   JSHS, PO BOX 309   95947   2-00111
    Kest Porter, prin.   284-7197
   Wolf Creek MS, 430 MAIN ST   95947   2-00100
    Kest Porter, prin.   284-6631

Gridley, AC 916, PC 5, Butte
   Gridley UNESD   4-11100
    429 MAGNOLIA ST   95948   846-4721
    Stephen Fiss, supt.
   Sycamore MS   2-00100
    1125 SYCAMORE ST   95948   846-3636
    Dennis Wilson, prin.

   Gridley UNHSD   3-00011
    429 MAGNOLIA ST   95948   846-6249
    Stephen Fiss, supt.
   HS, 300 E SPRUCE ST   95948   3-00011
    Curtis Casey, prin.   846-4791

Groveland, AC 209, PC 2, Tuolumne
   Big Oak Flat-Groveland USD   3-11111
    PO BOX 1397   95321   962-5765
    Bea Lingenfelter, supt.
   Tioga HS, 19304 FERRETTI RD   95321   1-00011
    Bea Lingenfelter, supt.   962-4763
   Other Schools – See La Grange

Guadalupe, AC 805, PC 6, Santa Barbara
   Guadalupe UNESD   4-11100
    PO BOX 788   93434   343-2114
    Hugo Lara, supt.
   McKenzie JHS, PO BOX 788   93434   2-00100
    Susan Gerard, prin.   343-1951

Gustine, AC 209, PC 5, Merced
   Gustine USD, 286 5TH ST   95322   4-11111
    Frank Burk, supt.   854-3784
   HS, 501 NORTH AVE   95322   2-00011
    Audrey Musson, prin.   854-6414
   MS, 701 WALLIS AVE   95322   2-00100
    Dennis Shaw, prin.   854-6404

Hacienda Heights, AC 818, PC 8, Los Angeles
   Hacienda La Puente USD
    Supt. — See City of Industry
   Los Altos HS   4-00011
    15325 LOS ROBLES AVE   91745   333-4515
    Linda Harding, prin.
   Wilson HS   4-00011
    16455 WEDGEWORTH DR   91745   330-0621
    Barry Gross, prin.
   Cedarlane MS   2-00100
    16333 CEDARLANE DR   91745   855-3815
    Ken Quon, prin.
   Newton MS, 15616 NEWTON ST   91745   2-00100
    Gabe Parodi, prin.   855-3830
   Orange Grove MS   2-00100
    14505 ORANGE GROVE AVE   91745   855-3835
    Robert Dickey, prin.

Half Moon Bay, AC 415, PC 6, San Mateo
   Cabrillo USD, 498 KELLY AVE   94019   5-11111
    Jane Martin, supt.   712-7100
   HS, 498 KELLY AVE   94019   3-00011
    Raymond Eckert, prin.   712-7200
   Cunha IS, 498 KELLY AVE   94019   3-00100
    Randolph Chapin, prin.   712-7190

Hamilton City, AC 916, PC 4, Glenn
   Hamilton UNHSD   2-00011
    PO BOX 488   95951   826-3261
    Ray Odom, supt.
   Hamilton Union HS   2-00011
    PO BOX 488   95951   826-3261
    Ray Odom, prin.

Hanford, AC 209, PC 8, Kings
   Hanford ESD, PO BOX 1067   93232   5-11100
    Joe Simas, supt.   585-2265
   Wilson MS, PO BOX 1067   93232   3-00100
    Rebecca Presley, prin.   585-2334

   Hanford JUNHSD   4-00011
    120 E GRANGEVILLE BLVD   93230   582-4401
    Arthur Mayer, supt.
   Hanford HS East Campus   4-00011
    120 E GRANGEVILLE BLVD   93230   582-4407
    Gale Cluff, prin.
   Hanford HS West Campus   4-00011
    1150 W LACEY BLVD   93230   583-0157
    Bob Davis, prin.

   Lakeside UNESD   3-11100
    9100 JERSEY AVE   93230   582-2868
    Ron Madruga, supt.
   Lakeside MS, 9100 JERSEY AVE   93230   2-01100
    Kenneth Freed, prin.   582-2868

   Pioneer UNESD, 8810 14TH AVE   93230   3-11100
    Hugh Lee, supt.   584-8831
   Pioneer MS, 8810 14TH AVE   93230   2-01100
    John Webster, prin.   584-8831

Happy Camp, AC 916, PC 4, Siskiyou
   Siskiyou UNHSD
    Supt. — See Mount Shasta
   HS, 234 INDIAN CREEK ROAD   96039   2-00011
    Jay Clark, prin.   493-2697

Harbor City, AC 310, PC see Los Angeles
   Los Angeles USD
    Supt. — See Los Angeles

Narbonne HS   4-00001
   24300 WESTERN AVE   90710   326-0920
   Pat Donahoe, prin.

Hawaiian Gardens, AC 310, PC 7, Los Angeles
  ABC USD
   Supt. — See Cerritos
  Killingsworth JHS   3-00100
   21409 ELAINE AVE   90716   924-2309
   Stella Marquez, prin.

Hawthorne, PC 8, Los Angeles
  Centinela Valley UNHSD
   Supt. — See Lawndale
  HS   5-00011
   4859 W EL SEGUNDO BLVD   90250
   John Carter, prin.   310-970-1503

  Hawthorne ESD   6-11100
   4301 W 129TH ST   90250   310-676-2276
   Christa Metzger, supt.
  Hawthorne IS   3-00100
   4366 W 129TH ST   90250   310-676-0167
   Sharon Phillips, prin.
  Yukon IS   3-00100
   13838 YUKON AVE   90250   310-676-1908
   Steven Tabor, prin.

  Wiseburn ESD   4-11100
   13530 AVIATION BLVD   90250   310-643-3025
   Don Brann, supt.
  Dana MS   2-00100
   13500 AVIATION BLVD   90250   310-643-6165
   Kay Plush, prin.

Hayfork, AC 916, PC 5, Trinity
  Mountain Valley USD   3-11111
   PO BOX 339   96041   628-5265
   Marvin Stewart, supt.
  HS, PO BOX 10   96041   2-00011
   Robert Lowden, prin.   628-5261

Hayward, AC 510, PC 9, Alameda
  Hayward USD, PO BOX 5000   94540   7-11111
   K. Kobayashi, supt.   784-2600
  HS, PO BOX 5000   94540   4-00011
   Larry Ratto, prin.   582-0102
  Mt. Eden HS, PO BOX 5000   94540   4-00011
   John Davini, prin.   785-6000
  Tennyson HS, PO BOX 5000   94540   4-00011
   Gordon Pipkin, prin.   582-0707
  Harte IS, PO BOX 5000   94540   3-00100
   Susan Parker, prin.   886-5901
  King IS, PO BOX 5000   94540   3-00100
   Lea Lloyd, prin.   786-0955
  La Vista IS, PO BOX 5000   94540   3-00100
   Robert Costa, prin.   538-5905
  Ochoa IS, PO BOX 5000   94540   3-00100
   Nellie Richardson-Gardere, prin.   786-1265
  Winton IS, PO BOX 5000   94540   3-00100
   Chet Lloyd, prin.   538-8582

  American Heritage Christian S   2-11111
   425 GRESEL ST   94544   471-1010
   Keith Erickson, prin.
  California State University   6-UC
   25800 CARLOS BEE BLVD   94542   881-3000
  Chabot College   7-CC
   25555 HESPERIAN BLVD   94545   786-6600
  Heald Business College   2-CC
   777 SOUTHLAND DR STE 210   94545
      886-3101
  Heald Institute of Technology-Hayward   2-CC
   24301 SOUTHLAND DR STE 500   94545
      783-2100
  ITT Technical Institute   1-CS
   26239 EXECUTIVE PL   94545   785-8522
  Moreau HS, 27170 MISSION BLVD   94544   4-00011
   Patricia Geister, prin.   582-5851

Healdsburg, AC 707, PC 6, Sonoma
  Healdsburg SD   5-11111
   925 UNIVERSITY ST   95448   431-3401
   Lawrence Machi, supt.
  HS, 1024 PRINCE AVE   95448   4-00011
   Carolyn Kieser, prin.   431-3420
  JHS, 315 GRANT ST   95448   3-00100
   Stewart Fox, prin.   431-3410

  Rio Lindo Adventist Academy   2-00011
   3200 RIO LINDO AVE   95448   431-5100
   Dennis Plubell, prin.

Helendale, AC 619, PC 2, San Bernardino
  Helendale ESD, PO BOX 249   92342   3-11100
   David LaQuay, supt.   952-1180
  Riverview MS, PO BOX 249   92342   2-00100
   David LaQuay, prin.   952-1266

Hemet, AC 909, PC 8, Riverside
  Hemet USD   7-11111
   2350 W LATHAM AVE   92545   765-5100
   Jack McLaughlin, supt.
  Allesandro SHS   2-00001
   26866 SAN JACINTO ST   92543   765-5182
   James Smith, prin.
  HS, 41700 STETSON AVE   92544   4-00011
   Richard Glock, prin.   765-5150
  West Valley HS   4-00011
   831 E DEVONSHIRE AVE   92543   765-1600
   Carrol Doolittle, prin.
  Acacia MS, 1200 E ACACIA AVE   92543   4-00100
   Karen Doshier, prin.   765-1620
  Other Schools – See Anza

Baptist Christian S   2-11111
   26089 GIRARD ST   92544   658-3203
   Ronald Livesay, prin.

Herlong, AC 916, PC 4, Lassen
  Fort Sage USD, PO BOX 35   96113   3-11111
   Leonard Shipley, supt.   827-2129
  HS, PO BOX 97   96113   2-00011
   Margaret McNally, prin.   827-2101
  Render HS, PO BOX 910   96113   1-00011
   Dave Dutton, prin.   827-2949
  Fort Sage MS, PO BOX 35   96113   2-00100
   Gary Williams, prin.   827-2126

Hermosa Beach, AC 310, PC 7, Los Angeles
  Hermosa Beach City ESD   3-11100
   1645 VALLEY DR   90254   376-8961
   Gwen Gross, supt.
  Hermosa Valley MS   3-01100
   1645 VALLEY DR   90254   374-9682
   Deborah Frick, prin.

Hesperia, AC 619, PC 8, San Bernardino
  Hesperia USD, 9144 3RD AVE   92345   7-11111
   John Reed, supt.   244-9323
  HS, 9898 MAPLE AVE   92345   5-00011
   Barry Bettger, prin.   244-9898
  JHS, 10275 CYPRESS AVE   92345   4-00100
   Rob Challinor, prin.   244-9386
  Ranchero MS   3-00100
   17607 RANCHERO RD   92345   948-0175
   Mike Smith, prin.

  Hesperia Christian S   3-11111
   16775 OLIVE ST   92345   244-6164
   Mike Wilkerson, prin.

Highland, AC 909, PC 8, San Bernardino
  San Bernardino City USD
   Supt. — See San Bernardino
  San Andreas SHS   2-00001
   3232 PACIFIC ST   92346   862-5432
   Margaret Hill, prin.
  Serrano MS, 3131 PIEDMONT DR   92346   3-00100
   James Dilday, prin.   862-0230

Hillsborough, AC 415, PC 7, San Mateo
  Hillsborough CSD   4-11100
   300 EL CERRITO AVE   94010   342-5193
   Marilyn Loushin-Miller, supt.
  Crocker MS, 2600 RALSTON AVE   94010   2-00100
   Daniel Kreuzer, prin.   342-6331

  Crystal Springs Uplands S   2-00111
   400 UPLANDS DR   94010   342-4175
   Richard Drew, prin.

Hilmar, AC 209, PC 5, Merced
  Hilmar USD, 7807 LANDER AVE   95324   4-11111
   Tony Thornburg, supt.   667-5701
  HS, 7807 LANDER AVE   95324   3-00011
   Jack Mayer, prin.   667-5903
  MS, 7807 LANDER AVE   95324   2-00100
   Brenda Eisenhauer, prin.   632-8847

Hollister, AC 408, PC 7, San Benito
  Hollister ESD, 761 SOUTH ST   95023   5-11100
   Thomas Andrade, supt.   637-3781
  Rancho San Justo MS   3-00100
   1201 RANCHO DR   95023   637-1601
   Bernice Smith, prin.

  San Benito HSD   4-00011
   1220 MONTEREY ST   95023   637-5831
   Greg Hearn, supt.
  San Benito HS   4-00011
   1220 MONTEREY ST   95023   637-5831
   Bonnie McClung, prin.

Hollywood, AC 213, PC see Los Angeles
  Los Angeles USD
   Supt. — See Los Angeles
  Le Conte JHS   4-00110
   1316 N BRONSON AVE   90028   461-4741
   Carmen Terrazas, prin.

  Academy Pacific Business/Travel College   3-CS
   1777 VINE ST # 30   90028   462-3211
  Hollywood Scriptwriting Institute   1-HMS
   1605 N CAHUENGA BLVD # 216   90028
  Musicians Institute   2-CS
   1655 N MCCADDEN PL   90028   462-1384

Holtville, AC 619, PC 5, Imperial
  Holtville USD, 621 E 6TH ST   92250   4-11111
   Clifford Bernardi, supt.   356-2974
  HS, 755 OLIVE AVE   92250   2-00011
   Patricia Salcido, prin.   356-2926
  JHS, 800 BEALE AVE   92250   2-00100
   Joanne Singh, prin.   356-2811

Hoopa, AC 916, PC 3, Humboldt
  Klamath-Trinity JUSD   4-11111
   PO BOX 1308   95546   625-4221
   James Johnson, supt.
  Hoopa Valley HS   2-00011
   PO BOX 1308   95546   625-4218
   Doug Oliveira, prin.

Hughson, AC 209, PC 5, Stanislaus
  Hughson UNESD, PO BOX 189   95326   4-11100
   Carrolyn Nicholas, supt.   883-4428
  Ross MS, PO BOX 189   95326   2-00100
   Sue Smalling, prin.   883-4425

Hughson UNHSD, PO BOX 99   95326   3-00011
   Randall Heckman, supt.   883-0482
  HS, PO BOX 99   95326   3-00011
   Debra Davis, prin.   883-0469

Huntington Beach, AC 714, PC 9, Orange
  Fountain Valley ESD
   Supt. — See Fountain Valley
  Talbert MS, 9101 BRABHAM DR   92646   3-00100
   Carl Dane, prin.   378-4220

  Huntington Beach City ESD   6-11100
   PO BOX 71   92648   964-8888
   Duane Dishno, supt.
  Dwyer MS, PO BOX 71   92648   3-00100
   Ian Collins, prin.   536-7507
  Sowers MS, PO BOX 71   92648   4-00100
   Paul Morrow, prin.   962-7738

  Huntington Beach UNHSD   7-00011
   10251 YORKTOWN AVE   92646   964-3339
   David Hagen, supt.
  Edison HS, 21400 MAGNOLIA ST   92646   4-00011
   Brian Garland, prin.   962-1356
  HS, 1905 MAIN ST   92648   4-00011
   Jim Staunton, prin.   536-2514
  Marina HS   4-00011
   15871 SPRINGDALE ST   92649   893-6571
   Jim Keating, prin.
  Ocean View HS   4-00011
   17071 GOTHARD ST   92647   848-0656
   Carla Rush, prin.
  Other Schools – See Fountain Valley, Westminster

  Ocean View ESD   6-11100
   17200 PINEHURST LN   92647   847-2551
   James Tarwater, supt.
  Marine View MS   3-00100
   5682 TILBURG DR   92649   846-0624
   Janet Reece, prin.
  Mesa View MS, 17601 AVILLA LN   92647   3-00100
   Steve Johnson, prin.   842-6608
  Spring View MS   3-00100
   16662 TRUDY LN   92647   846-2891
   Robert Vouga, prin.
  Other Schools – See Fountain Valley

  Westminster ESD
   Supt. — See Westminster
  Stacy IS, 6311 LARCHWOOD DR   92647   3-00100
   Sheri Jones, prin.   894-7212

  Claremont HS   2-00111
   15461 SPRINGDALE ST   92649   379-5461
   Donna Connelly, prin.
  Golden West College   7-CC
   15744 GOLDENWEST ST   92647   892-7711
  Hope Christian Academy   2-11111
   14811 MONROE ST   92605   373-0742
   Deborah Haller, prin.
  Huntington College of Dental Technology   1-CS
   7466 EDINGER AVE   92647   841-9500
  Liberty Christian S   2-11111
   7661 WARNER AVE   92647   842-5992
   Clark Stephens, prin.

Huntington Park, AC 213, PC 8, Los Angeles
  Los Angeles USD
   Supt. — See Los Angeles
  HS, 6020 MILES AVE   90255   5-00011
   Antonio Garcia, prin.   583-3333
  Gage JHS, 2880 E GAGE AVE   90255   5-00100
   Joseph Caldera, prin.   587-5271
  Nimitz JHS   5-00100
   6021 CARMELITA AVE   90255   585-0957
   Guadalupe Simpson, prin.

  St. Matthias HS   2-00011
   6003 STAFFORD AVE   90255   587-2109
   Nancy Coonis, prin.

Idyllwild, AC 909, PC 4, Riverside

  Idyllwild School Of Music & the Arts   2-00011
   PO BOX 38   92549   659-2171
   William Lowman, prin.

Imperial, AC 619, PC 5, Imperial
  Imperial USD, 219 N E ST   92251   4-11111
   Frank Cranley, supt.   355-3200
  HS, 517 W BARIONI BLVD   92251   2-00011
   Cheryl Biagi, prin.   355-3220
  Wright IS, 515 W 10TH ST   92251   2-00100
   John Marshall, prin.   355-3240

  Imperial Valley College   5-CC
   PO BOX 158   92251   352-8320

Imperial Beach, AC 619, PC 8, San Diego
  Sweetwater UNHSD
   Supt. — See Chula Vista
  Mar Vista HS, 505 ELM AVE   91932   4-00011
   Gloria Samson, prin.   691-5400

Independence, AC 619, PC 4, Inyo
  Owens Valley USD, PO BOX E   93526   2-11111
   Joel Hampton, supt.   878-2405
  Owens Valley HS, PO BOX E   93526   1-00011
   (—), prin.   878-2405

Indio, AC 619, PC 8, Riverside
  Desert Sands USD   7-11111
   82879 US HIGHWAY 111   92201   775-3500
   Dolores Ballesteros, supt.

HS, 81750 AVENUE 46 92201   4-00011
  Rudy Ramirez, prin.   775-3800
MS, 81195 MILES AVE 92201   3-00100
  Robert Block, prin.   775-3800
Jefferson MS   3-00100
  83089 US HIGHWAY 111 92201   775-3500
  Harry Munoz, prin.
Wilson MS, 83501 DILLON AVE 92201   3-00100
  Michael Jimenez, prin.   775-3880
Other Schools – See La Quinta, Palm Desert

Christian School of the Desert   2-11111
  40700 YUCCA LN 92201   345-2848
  David Fulton, prin.

Inglewood, PC 9, Los Angeles
Inglewood USD   7-11111
  401 S INGLEWOOD AVE 90301   310-419-2500
  George McKenna, supt.
HS, 231 S GREVILLEA AVE 90301   4-00011
  Kenneth Crowe, prin.   310-419-2592
Morningside HS   4-00011
  10500 YUKON AVE 90303   310-419-0421
  Lisa Daniels, prin.
Crozier JHS   4-00100
  151 N GREVILLEA AVE 90301   310-419-2557
  Geraldine Martin, prin.
Monroe JHS   4-00100
  10711 S 10TH AVE 90303   310-419-2565
  Arnold Butler, prin.

Daniel Freeman Mem. Hospital   HSP
  333 N PRAIRIE AVE 90301   213-674-7050
Northrop-Rice Aviation Institute of Tech   2-CS
  8911 AVIATION BLVD 90301   310-337-4444
St. Marys Academy   2-00011
  701 GRACE AVE 90301   310-674-8470
  Sr. Nancy Munro, prin.
South Bay Lutheran HS   2-00011
  3600 W IMPERIAL HWY 90303   310-272-1101
  Norbert Huber, prin.
University of West Los Angeles   3-UC
  1155 W ARBOR VITAE ST 90301   310-215-3339

Ione, AC 209, PC 6, Amador
Amador County USD
  Supt. — See Jackson
Ione JHS 95640   2-00100
  Grant Sandro, prin.   274-2491

Irvine, AC 714, PC 9, Orange
Irvine USD, 5050 BARRANCA PKY 92714   7-11111
  David Brown, supt.   651-0444
HS, 4321 WALNUT AVE 92714   4-00011
  Gail Richards, prin.   552-4211
University HS, 4771 CAMPUS DR 92715   4-00011
  Leah Laule, prin.   854-7500
Woodbridge HS   4-00011
  2 MEADOWBROOK 92714   786-1104
  Greg Cops, prin.
Lakeside MS, 3 LEMONGRASS 92714   3-00100
  Tony Ferruzzo, prin.   559-1601
Rancho San Joaquin IS   3-00100
  4861 MICHELSON DR 92715   786-3005
  Judy Cunningham, prin.
Sierra Vista MS, 2 LIBERTY 92720   3-00100
  Jean Mylen, prin.   838-5440
Venado MS, 4 DEERFIELD AVE 92714   3-00100
  Bob Bruce, prin.   552-4771

Concordia University   4-UC
  1530 CONCORDIA 92715   800-229-1200
Irvine College of Business   2-CS
  16591 NOYES AVE 92714   863-1145
Irvine Valley College   5-CC
  5500 IRVINE CENTER DR 92720   559-9300
National Education Corporation   HMS
  18400 VON KARMAN AVE 92715
NEC-Bryman Campus   CS
  1732 REYNOLDS AVE 92714   261-7606
University of California 92717   7-UC
      856-6345
Western State University College of Law   2-UC
  16485 LAGUNA CANYON RD 92718

Jackson, AC 209, PC 5, Amador
Amador County USD   5-11111
  217 REX AVE 95642   223-1750
  Kenneth Sherer, supt.
Argonaut HS, 217 REX AVE 95642   3-00011
  J. Equinoa, prin.   223-2411
Jackson JHS, 217 REX AVE 95642   2-00100
  Rick Carder, prin.   223-1141
Other Schools – See Ione, Sutter Creek

Jamul, AC 619, PC 4, San Diego
Jamul-Dulzura UNESD   4-11100
  14581 LYONS VALLEY RD 91935   669-1400
  Thomas Bishop, supt.
Oak Grove MS   2-00100
  14545 LYONS VALLEY RD 91935   669-0591
  Gary Kehle, prin.

Joshua Tree, AC 619, PC 5, San Bernardino

College of the Desert   3-CC
  PO BOX 1398 92252   366-3791

Julian, AC 619, PC 4, San Diego
Julian UNESD, PO BOX 337 92036   3-11100
  Stephen Maddox, supt.   765-0661

Julian JHS, PO BOX 337 92036   2-00100
  Stephen Maddox, prin.   765-0575

Julian UNHSD, PO BOX 417 92036   2-00011
  Chet Francisco, supt.   765-0608
HS, PO BOX 417 92036   2-00011
  Bob Hamilton, prin.   765-0606

Kelseyville, AC 707, PC 5, Lake
Kelseyville USD, PO BOX 308 95451   4-11111
  Wally Holbrook, supt.   279-1511
HS, PO BOX 308 95451   3-00011
  David Butler, prin.   279-4923
Mountain Vista MS   3-00100
  PO BOX 308 95451   279-4060
  Enrico Frediani, prin.

Kentfield, AC 415, PC 6, Marin
Kentfield ESD   3-11100
  699 SIR FRANCIS DRAKE BLVD 94904   925-2230
  Robert Caine, supt.
Kent MS, 250 STADIUM WAY 94904   2-01100
  Nancy Schlobohm, prin.   925-2200

College of Marin   6-CC
  835 COLLEGE AVE 94904   457-8811
Marin Catholic HS   3-00011
  675 SIR FRANCIS DRAKE BLVD 94904   461-8844
  William Isetta, prin.

Kerman, AC 209, PC 6, Fresno
Kerman USD, 151 S 1ST ST 93630   5-11111
  John Burns, supt.   846-5383
HS, 205 S 1ST ST 93630   3-00011
  Dan Safreno, prin.   846-5383
MS, 601 S 1ST ST 93630   2-00100
  Barbara Avila, prin.   846-5383

King City, AC 408, PC 6, Monterey
King City JUNHSD   4-00011
  800 BROADWAY ST 93930   385-0606
  Joan King, supt.
HS, 720 BROADWAY ST 93930   4-00011
  Barry Lindaman, prin.   385-5461

King City UNESD   4-11100
  336 S VANDERHURST AVE 93930   385-1144
  Stephen Young, supt.
San Lorenzo MS, 415 PEARL ST 93930   3-00100
  L. Wayne Brown, prin.   385-5446

Kingsburg, AC 209, PC 6, Fresno
Kingsburg JUNESD   4-11100
  PO BOX 217 93631   897-2331
  Ron Allvin, supt.
Johnson JHS, PO BOX 217 93631   2-00100
  Shirley Willems, prin.   897-1091

Kingsburg JUNHSD   3-00011
  1900 18TH AVE 93631   897-5156
  Don Norrby, supt.
HS, 1900 18TH AVE 93631   3-00011
  Linda Clark, prin.   897-5156

La Canada-Flintridge, AC 818, PC 7, Los Angeles
La Canada USD, 5039 PALM DR 91011   5-11111
  James Davis, supt.   952-8300
La Canada JSHS   4-00111
  4463 OAK GROVE DR 91011   952-4200
  James Stratton, prin.

Delphi Academy   2-11111
  4490 CORNISHON AVE 91011   952-0909
  Maggie Reinhart, prin.
Flintridge Prep S   2-00111
  4543 CROWN AVE 91011   790-1178
  Peter Bachmann, prin.
Flintridge Sacred Heart Academy   2-00011
  440 SAINT KATHERINE DR 91011   792-6148
  Sr. Ramona Bascom, prin.
St. Francis HS   2-00011
  200 FOOTHILL BLVD 91011   790-0325
  Thomas Moran, prin.

La Crescenta, AC 818, PC 7, Los Angeles
Glendale USD
  Supt. — See Glendale
Crescenta Valley HS   4-00011
  4400 RAMSDELL AVE 91214   249-5871
  Kenneth Biermann, prin.
Rosemont JHS   3-00100
  4725 ROSEMONT AVE 91214   248-4224
  Lois Neil, prin.

Lafayette, AC 510, PC 7, Contra Costa
Acalanes UNHSD   5-00011
  1212 PLEASANT HILL RD 94549   935-2800
  James Perino, supt.
Acalanes HS   4-00011
  1200 PLEASANT HILL RD 94549   935-2600
  Leo Petty, prin.
Other Schools – See Moraga, Orinda, Walnut Creek

Lafayette ESD, PO BOX 1029 94549   5-11100
  James Martin, supt.   284-7011
Stanley IS, 3455 SCHOOL ST 94549   4-00100
  Camille Moore, prin.   283-6282

La Grange, AC 209, PC 2, Stanislaus
Big Oak Flat-Groveland USD
  Supt. — See Groveland
Don Pedro HS   1-00011
  3090 MERCED FALLS RD 95329   852-2864
  Bea Lingenfelter, prin.

Laguna Beach, AC 714, PC 7, Orange
Laguna Beach USD   4-11111
  550 BLUMONT ST 92651   497-7700
  Paul Possemato, supt.
HS, 625 PARK AVE 92651   3-00011
  Barbara Callard, prin.   497-7750
Thurston MS, 2100 PARK AVE 92651   3-00100
  Cheryl Baughn, prin.   497-7785

Art Institute of Southern California   2-UC
  2222 LAGUNA CANYON RD 92651   497-3309

Laguna Hills, AC 714, PC 7, Orange
Saddleback Valley USD
  Supt. — See Mission Viejo
HS, 25401 PASEO DE VALENCIA 92653   4-00011
  Wayne Mickaelian, prin.   770-5447

Laguna Niguel, AC 714, PC 8, Orange
Capistrano USD
  Supt. — See San Juan Capistrano
Niguel Hills MS   4-00100
  29070 PASEO ESCUELA 92677   831-3146
  James Henderson, prin.

La Habra, AC 310, PC 8, Orange
Fullerton JUNHSD
  Supt. — See Fullerton
La Habra HS   4-00011
  801 HIGHLANDER AVE 90631   905-0900
  Patricia Howell, prin.
Sonora HS, 401 S PALM ST 90631   4-00011
  Cynthia Ranii, prin.   905-9801

La Habra City ESD   5-11100
  PO BOX 307 90633   690-2300
  Richard Hermann, supt.
Imperial MS, PO BOX 307 90633   3-00100
  Betty Bidwell, prin.   690-2344
Washington MS, PO BOX 307 90633   3-00100
  Gary Mantey, prin.   690-2374

Painter Avenue Christian S   2-11111
  1301 S BEACH BLVD STE A 90631   947-5593
  Beverly Hernandez, prin.
Whittier Christian HS   3-00011
  2300 WORTH AVE 90631   694-3803
  William McKinley, prin.

La Jolla, AC 619, PC see San Diego
San Diego City USD
  Supt. — See San Diego
HS, 750 NAUTILUS ST 92037   4-00011
  J. Tarvin, prin.   454-3081
Muirlands JHS   3-00100
  1056 NAUTILUS ST 92037   459-4211
  Cassandra Countryman, prin.

Bishops S, 7607 LA JOLLA BLVD 92037   3-00111
  Michael Teitelman, prin.   459-4021
La Jolla Country Day S   3-11111
  9490 GENESEE AVE 92037   453-3440
  John Neiswender, prin.
Scripps Clinic & Research Foundation   HSP
  10666 N TORREY PINES RD 92037   455-9100
Scripps Memorial Hospital   HSP
  9888 GENESEE AVE 92037   457-6100
University of California   7-UC
  9450 GILMAN DR 92092   534-2230

Lake Arrowhead, AC 909, PC 6, San Bernardino
Rim of the World USD   6-11111
  PO BOX 430 92352   336-2031
  John Fitzpatrick, supt.
Rim of the World HS   4-00011
  PO BOX 430 92352   336-2038
  Joseph Kolmel, prin.
Henck IS, PO BOX 430 92352   3-00100
  David Cathalinat, prin.   336-0360

Lake Elsinore, AC 909, PC 7, Riverside
Lake Elsinore USD   7-11111
  545 CHANEY ST 92530   674-7731
  David Long, supt.
Elsinore HS, 21800 CANYON DR 92530   4-00011
  Jarvis Pahl, prin.   674-3194
Temescal Canyon HS   4-00011
  28755 EL TORO RD 92532   245-4484
  John Slatinsky, prin.
Elsinore JHS   3-00100
  1201 W GRAHAM AVE 92530   674-2118
  Cheryl Livengood, prin.
Terra Cotta JHS, 29251 ROBB RD 92530   4-00100
  Mike Sepulveda, prin.   674-0641

Lake Forest, AC 714, PC 3, Placer
Saddleback Valley USD
  Supt. — See Mission Viejo
El Toro HS, 25255 TOLEDO WAY 92630   4-00011
  Jack Clement, prin.   586-6333
Serrano IS, 24642 JERONIMO RD 92630   4-00100
  Cathy Kane, prin.   586-3221

Lake Isabella, AC 619, PC 5, Kern
Kern HSD
  Supt. — See Bakersfield
Kern Valley HS, PO BOX 1027 93240   3-00011
  Robert Dreiling, prin.   379-3997

Kernville UNESD 4-11100
PO BOX 3077 93240 379-3651
Christine Frazier, supt.
Wallace JHS 2-00100
3240 ERSKINE CREEK RD 93240 379-4646
Aileen DeLapp, prin.

Lakeport, AC 707, PC 5, Lake
Lakeport USD, 100 LANGE ST 95453 4-11111
Patrick Sayne, supt. 262-3000
Clear Lake HS, 100 LANGE ST 95453 3-00011
Donald Owens, prin. 263-3010
Terrace MS, 100 LANGE ST 95453 3-01100
Erin Smith-Hagberg, prin. 262-3007

Lakeside, AC 619, PC 8, San Diego
Grossmont UNHSD
Supt. — See La Mesa
El Capitan HS 4-00011
10410 ASHWOOD ST 92040 443-1081
Arthur Pegas, prin.

Lakeside UNESD, PO BOX 578 92040 5-11100
Jacquelyn Spacek, supt. 390-2600
Lakeside MS, PO BOX 578 92040 3-00100
Diana Adams, prin. 390-2636
Tierra Del Sol MS 3-00100
PO BOX 578 92040 390-2670
Barbara Sidote, prin.

Lakewood, AC 310, PC 8, Los Angeles
ABC USD
Supt. — See Cerritos
Artesia HS, 12108 DEL AMO BLVD 90715 4-00011
Yvonne Contreras, prin. 926-5566

Bellflower USD
Supt. — See Bellflower
Mayfair JSHS 4-00111
6000 WOODRUFF AVE 90713 925-9981
Sylvia McCune, prin.

Long Beach USD
Supt. — See Long Beach
HS, 4400 BRIERCREST AVE 90713 5-00011
Michael Escalante, prin. 425-1281
Hoover MS 4-00100
3501 COUNTRY CLUB DR 90712 421-1213
Gary Graves, prin.

St. Joseph HS 3-00011
5825 WOODRUFF AVE 90713 925-5073
Mary Mendoza, prin.
SW Longview Private S 2-11111
3508 FAIRMAN ST 90712 422-1582
Clarence Horton, prin.

La Mesa, AC 619, PC 8, San Diego
Grossmont UNHSD 7-00011
PO BOX 1043 91944 465-3131
Jo Ann Smith, supt.
Grossmont HS, PO BOX 1043 91944 4-00011
Stephen Laviree, prin. 460-5510
Helix HS, 7323 UNIVERSITY AVE 91941 4-00011
Douglas Smith, prin. 466-4194
Other Schools – See El Cajon, Lakeside, Santee, Spring Valley

La Mesa-Spring Valley ESD 7-11100
4750 DATE AVE 91941 668-5700
Warren Hogarth, supt.
MS, 4750 DATE AVE 91941 4-00100
Nancy Lander, prin. 668-5730
Parkway MS, 4750 DATE AVE 91941 4-00100
Frank Murphy, prin. 668-5810
Other Schools – See Spring Valley

Coleman College 4-UC
7380 PARKWAY DR 91942 465-3990
Grossmont District Hospital HSP
5555 GROSSMONT CENTER DR 91942 465-0711

La Mirada, PC 8, Los Angeles
Norwalk-La Mirada USD
Supt. — See Norwalk
HS, 13520 ADELFA DR 90638 4-00011
Howard Haas, prin. 310-868-0431
Benton MS 3-00100
15709 OLIVE BRANCH DR 90638 310-943-1553
Larry Lodwick, prin.
Hutchinson MS 3-00100
13900 ESTERO RD 90638 310-944-3268
Beverly Eien-Johnson, prin.

Biola University 5-UC
13800 BIOLA AVE 90639 213-903-6000

Lamont, AC 805, PC 7, Kern
Lamont ESD, 8201 PALM AVE 93241 5-11100
John Chavez, supt. 845-0751
Mountain View MS 3-00100
8201 PALM AVE 93241 845-2291
Paul Genoud, prin.

Lancaster, AC 805, PC 8, Los Angeles
Antelope Valley UNHSD 7-00011
44811 SIERRA HWY 93534 948-7655
Robert Girolamo, supt.
Antelope Valley HS 5-00011
44900 DIVISION ST 93535 948-8552
John Hutak, prin.
Other Schools – See Littlerock, Palmdale, Quartz Hill

Eastside UNESD 4-11100
6742 E AVENUE H 93535 946-2813
Charles Gastineau, supt.
Cole MS, 6742 E AVENUE H 93535 3-01100
Rebecca Pomerleau, prin. 946-1041

Lancaster ESD, 44711 CEDAR AVE 93534 7-11100
David Alvarez, supt. 948-4661
Park View IS, 44711 CEDAR AVE 93534 4-00100
R. Michael Dutton, prin. 942-0496
Piute IS, 44711 CEDAR AVE 93534 4-00100
E. Eugene Premer, prin. 942-9508

Westside UNESD 6-11100
46809 70TH ST W 93536 948-2669
George Reams, supt.
Other Schools – See Palmdale, Quartz Hill

Wilsona SD
Supt. — See Palmdale
Challenger MS, 41725 170TH ST E 93535 3-00100
Greg Gerard, prin. 264-1790

Antelope Valley Christian S 2-11111
3700 W AVENUE L 93536 943-0044
David Ralph, prin.
Antelope Valley College 6-CC
3041 W AVENUE K 93536 943-3241
Bethel Christian Baptist Academy 3-11111
3100 W AVENUE K 93536 943-2224
Rex Furman, prin.
Heritage Christian S 2-11111
44514 LONEOAK AVE 93534 945-4231
Susan Fernald, prin.
Lancaster Christian ES 2-11111
44339 BEECH AVE 93534 942-2137
Rosemary Staniforth, prin.
Paraclete HS, 42145 30TH ST W 93536 3-00011
Fr. William Caffrey, prin. 943-3255

La Palma, AC 714, PC 7, Orange
Anaheim UNHSD
Supt. — See Anaheim
Kennedy HS, 8281 WALKER ST 90623 4-00011
John Dahlem, prin. 220-4101
Walker JHS, 8132 WALKER ST 90623 3-00100
Barbara Ryan, prin. 220-4051

La Puente, AC 818, PC 8, Los Angeles
Basset USD, 904 WILLOW AVE 91746 6-11111
Linda Gonzales, supt. 918-3131
Bassett HS, 904 WILLOW AVE 91746 4-00011
Robert Nero, prin. 918-3331
Other Schools – See City of Industry

Hacienda La Puente USD
Supt. — See City of Industry
La Puenta HS 4-00011
15615 NELSON AVE 91744 336-1241
Stuart Reeder, prin.
Puente Hills HS 3-00011
15540 FAIRGROVE AVE 91744 855-3134
(—), prin.
Sierra Vista MS 2-00100
15801 SIERRA VISTA CT 91744 855-3840
Bob Twitchell, prin.
Sparks MS, 15100 GIORDANO ST 91744 3-00100
Irene Quinones, prin. 855-3845

Rowland USD
Supt. — See Rowland Heights
Nogales HS, 401 NOGALES ST 91744 5-00011
Ron Tyler, prin. 965-3437
Giano IS, 3223 S GIANO ST 91744 3-00100
Stephen Hansen, prin. 965-2461

Bishop Amat HS 4-00011
14301 FAIRGROVE AVE 91746 962-2495
Fr. Aidan Carroll, prin.
Fairgrove Adult School 2-CS
15540 FAIRGROVE AVE 91744 855-3139

La Quinta, AC 619, PC 7, Riverside
Desert Sands USD
Supt. — See Indio
MS, 79900 AVENIDA 50 92253 3-00100
Milton Jones, prin. 777-4220

Larkspur, AC 415, PC 7, Marin
Larkspur ESD 3-11100
18 MAGNOLIA AVE 94939 927-6960
Christopher Wilson, supt.
Hall MS, 200 DOHERTY DR 94939 2-00100
Jeffrey Plotnick, prin. 927-6978

Tamalpais UNHSD 5-00011
PO BOX 605 94977 924-1800
William Levinson, supt.
Redwood HS, 395 DOHERTY DR 94939 4-00011
Greg Duffey, prin. 924-6200
Other Schools – See Mill Valley, San Anselmo

La Selva Beach, AC 408, PC 4, Santa Cruz
Pajaro Valley USD
Supt. — See Watsonville
Renaissance SHS 2-00001
11 SPRING VALLEY RD 95076 728-6344
Gerald McGowan, prin.

Monterey Bay Academy 2-00011
783 SAN ANDREAS RD 95076 728-1481
Ted Winn, prin.

Laton, AC 209, PC 4, Fresno
Laton JUSD, PO BOX 248 93242 3-11111
David Vaughn, supt. 923-4369
HS, PO BOX 278 93242 2-00011
Larry Rowe, prin. 923-4849
Other Schools – See Selma

La Verne, AC 909, PC 8, Los Angeles
Bonita USD
Supt. — See San Dimas
Bonita HS, 3102 D ST 91750 4-00011
Bruce Cantley, prin. 593-4501
Ramona MS, 3490 RAMONA AVE 91750 4-00100
Karen Cline, prin. 394-3181

American Armenian International College 2-UC
1950 3RD ST 91750 593-0432
Calvary Baptist S 2-11111
2990 DAMIEN AVE 91750 593-4672
Edward Dial, prin.
Damien HS, 2280 BONITA AVE 91750 4-00011
Fr. Patrick Travers, prin. 596-1946
Lutheran HS, 3960 FRUIT ST 91750 2-00011
Donald Schulteis, prin. 593-4494
University of La Verne 5-UC
1950 3RD ST 91750 593-3511

Lawndale, AC 310, PC 8, Los Angeles
Centinela Valley UNHSD 6-00011
14901 INGLEWOOD AVE 90260 970-7700
Joseph Carrillo, supt.
Leuzinger HS 5-00011
4118 ROSECRANS AVE 90260 978-8500
Sonja Davis, prin.
Lloyde HS 2-00011
14901 INGLEWOOD AVE 90260 970-7762
Robert Cornner, prin.
Other Schools – See Hawthorne

Lawndale ESD, 4161 W 147TH ST 90260 5-11100
Joseph Condon, supt. 973-1300
Rogers IS, 4161 W 147TH ST 90260 3-00100
Martha Shaw, prin. 676-1197

Laytonville, AC 707, PC 4, Mendocino
Laytonville USD, PO BOX 868 95454 3-11111
Linda Tweto-Johnson, supt. 984-6414
HS, PO BOX 868 95454 2-00011
Mark Iacuaniello, prin. 984-6108

Lebec, AC 805, PC 3, Kern
El Tejon USD, PO BOX 876 93243 4-11100
Gary Fuller, supt. 248-6247
El Tejon MS, PO BOX 876 93243 2-01100
Dondreia Turk, prin. 248-6680

Lee Vining, AC 619, PC 3, Mono
Eastern Sierra USD
Supt. — See Bridgeport
JSHS, PO BOX 268 93541 1-00111
Gary Potter, prin. 647-6366

Leggett, AC 707, PC 3, Mendocino
Leggett Valley USD 2-11111
PO BOX 186 95585 925-6285
Hal Matthewson, supt.
Leggett Valley JSHS 1-00111
PO BOX 186 95585 925-6230
Hal Matthewson, prin.

Le Grand, AC 209, PC 4, Merced
Le Grand UNHSD, PO BOX 67 95333 3-00011
George Hinds, supt. 389-9400
Le Grand Union HS 2-00011
12961 E LE GRAND RD 95333 389-9400
Robert Enochs, prin.

Lemon Grove, AC 619, PC 7, San Diego
Lemon Grove ESD 5-11100
8025 LINCOLN ST 91945 589-5600
Joseph Farley, supt.
MS, 8025 LINCOLN ST 91945 3-00100
Nancy Merino, prin. 589-5628
Palm MS, 8025 LINCOLN ST 91945 3-00100
Barb Allen, prin. 589-5641

Lemoore, AC 209, PC 7, Kings
Central UNESD, PO BOX 1339 93245 4-11100
Carl Carlson, supt. 924-3405
Akers ES 3-10100
CORAL SEA & CONSTELLATION 93245
John Jones, prin. 998-5707

Lemoore UNESD, 100 VINE ST 93245 4-11100
Idanna Aaron, supt. 924-5621
Engvall MS, 100 VINE ST 93245 3-00100
Tom Lasek, prin. 924-5605

Lemoore UNHSD, 101 E BUSH ST 93245 4-00011
William Black, supt. 924-6610
HS, 101 E BUSH ST 93245 4-00011
Michael Cawley, prin. 924-6600

Kings Christian S, 900 E D ST 93245 2-11111
Duane Daniel, prin. 924-8301

Lennox, AC 310, PC 7, Los Angeles
Lennox ESD 6-11100
10319 FIRMONA AVE 90304 330-4950
Kenneth Moffett, supt.
MS, 10319 FIRMONA AVE 90304 4-00100
Larry Kennedy, prin. 330-4910

Lincoln, AC 916, PC 6, Placer
Western Placer USD, 630 6TH ST 95648 5-11111
Kenneth Sanders, supt. 645-6350

HS, 1081 7TH ST 95648 — 3-00011
Dale Pence, prin. — 645-6360
Edwards IS, 204 L ST 95648 — 3-00100
Barbara Farley, prin. — 645-6370

Linden, AC 209, PC 4, San Joaquin
Linden USD, 18527 E MAIN ST 95236 — 4-11111
Ronald Estes, supt. — 887-3894
HS, 18527 E MAIN ST 95236 — 3-00011
Tim Miller, prin. — 887-3073
Other Schools – See Stockton

Lindsay, AC 209, PC 6, Tulare
Lindsay USD — 5-11111
519 E HONOLULU ST 93247 — 562-5111
Ena Soflin, supt.
HS, 1701 E TULARE RD 93247 — 3-00011
Douglas Bugni, prin. — 562-5911
Garvey JHS, 340 N HARVARD AVE 93247 — 2-00100
Mike Salcido, prin. — 562-1311

Littlerock, AC 805, PC 4, Los Angeles
Antelope Valley UNHSD
Supt. — See Lancaster
Littlerock HS, 10833 E AVENUE R 93543 — 4-00011
Jeff Foster, prin. — 944-5209

Keppel UNESD
Supt. — See Pearblossom
Almondale MS, 9330 E AVENUE U 93543 — 3-00100
Rosaria Williams, prin. — 944-2152

Live Oak, AC 916, PC 7, Santa Cruz
Live Oak USD — 4-11111
2341 PENNINGTON RD 95953 — 695-2135
Sam Hill, supt.
HS, 2351 PENNINGTON RD 95953 — 2-00011
Michael Rupp, prin. — 695-2143
MS, 2082 PENNINGTON RD 95953 — 2-01100
Paulla McIntire, prin. — 695-2189

Livermore, PC 8, Alameda
Livermore Valley JUSD — 7-11111
685 E JACK LONDON BLVD 94550 — 510-606-3200
Joyce Mahdesian, supt.
Granada HS, 400 WALL ST 94550 — 4-00011
Jose Medeiros, prin. — 510-606-4800
HS, 600 MAPLE ST 94550 — 4-00011
Sheila Cooper, prin. — 510-606-4812
Christenson MS — 3-01100
5757 HAGGIN OAKS DR 94550 — 510-606-4702
Keith Cariveau, prin.
East Avenue MS — 3-00100
3951 EAST AVE 94550 — 510-606-4711
Michael Hazelhofer, prin.
Junction Avenue MS — 3-00100
298 JUNCTION AVE 94550 — 510-606-4720
Linda Maguire, prin.
Mendenhall MS — 3-00100
1701 EL PADRO DR 94550 — 510-606-4731
Robert See, prin.

Chabot College-Valley Campus — 3-CC
3033 COLLIER CANYON RD 94550
510-373-5800

Livingston, AC 209, PC 6, Merced
Livingston UNSD, 922 B ST 95334 — 4-11100
Harold Thompson, supt. — 394-3620
IS, 714 PRUSSO ST 95334 — 2-00100
Kathy Berkeley, prin. — 394-7953

Merced UNHSD
Supt. — See Merced
HS, 1616 3RD ST 95334 — 4-00011
Doug Creighton, prin. — 394-7961

Lodi, AC 209, PC 8, San Joaquin
Lodi USD, 1305 E VINE ST 95240 — 7-11111
Sam Swofford, supt. — 331-7000
HS, 3 S PACIFIC AVE 95242 — 4-00011
Kelly Staley, prin. — 331-7815
Tokay HS — 4-00011
1111 W CENTURY BLVD 95240 — 331-7990
Jacqueline Flowers, prin.
Senior MS, 945 S HAM LN 95242 — 3-00100
Jim Benevides, prin. — 331-7544
Other Schools – See Stockton, Woodbridge

Lodi Academy — 2-00011
1230 S CENTRAL AVE 95240 — 368-2781
Stanley Baldwin, prin.

Loma Linda, AC 714, PC 7, San Bernardino

Loma Linda Academy — 4-11111
10656 ANDERSON ST 92354 — 796-0161
Gayle Rhoads, prin.
Loma Linda University 92350 — 4-UC
824-4300

Lomita, AC 310, PC 7, Los Angeles
Los Angeles USD
Supt. — See Los Angeles
Fleming JHS, 25425 WALNUT ST 90717 — 4-00110
John Lade, prin. — 326-4242

Lompoc, AC 805, PC 8, Santa Barbara
Lompoc USD, PO BOX 8000 93438 — 7-11111
Barb Nelson, supt. — 736-2371
Cabrillo HS, PO BOX 8000 93438 — 4-00011
John Lemon, prin. — 733-4538
HS, PO BOX 8000 93438 — 4-00011
Ed Albright, prin. — 736-2371

Lompoc Valley MS — 4-00100
PO BOX 8000 93438 — 736-2371
Daniel Callahan, prin.
Other Schools – See Vandenberg AFB

Lone Pine, AC 619, PC 4, Inyo
Lone Pine USD, PO BOX 159 93545 — 2-11111
William Schmidt, supt. — 876-5579
HS, PO BOX 159 93545 — 2-00011
Donna Carson, prin. — 876-5577

Long Beach, AC 310, PC 10, Los Angeles
Long Beach USD — 8-11111
701 LOCUST AVE 90813 — 436-9931
Carl Cohn, supt.
Jordan HS, 6500 ATLANTIC AVE 90805 — 5-00011
Alta Cooke, prin. — 423-1471
Millikan SHS — 5-00011
2800 SNOWDEN AVE 90815 — 425-7441
Margie Godfrey, prin.
Polytechnic HS — 5-00011
1600 ATLANTIC AVE 90813 — 591-0581
H. Green, prin.
Wilson HS, 4400 E 10TH ST 90804 — 5-00011
Lawrence Burnight, prin. — 433-0481
Bancroft MS — 4-00100
5301 E CENTRALIA ST 90808 — 425-7461
Arlene Hayashida, prin.
Butler MS, 1400 E 20TH ST 90806 — 3-01100
Charlene Smith, prin. — 591-7477
DeMille MS — 4-00100
7025 E PARKCREST ST 90808 — 421-8424
Frederick Navarro, prin.
Franklin MS, 540 CERRITOS AVE 90802 — 4-00100
Melvin Collins, prin. — 435-4952
Hamilton MS, 1060 E 70TH ST 90805 — 4-00100
Ross Shickler, prin. — 602-0302
Hill MS, 1100 IROQUOIS AVE 90815 — 4-00100
Sue McKee, prin. — 598-7611
Hughes MS — 4-00100
3846 CALIFORNIA AVE 90807 — 595-0831
Daniel Woitovich, prin.
Jefferson MS, 750 EUCLID AVE 90804 — 4-00100
Susan Marumoto, prin. — 438-9904
Lindbergh MS — 4-00100
1022 E MARKET ST 90805 — 422-2845
Dennis Lyman, prin.
Marshall MS — 4-00100
5870 E WARDLOW RD 90808 — 429-7013
Adelmo Martinez, prin.
Rogers MS, 365 MONROVIA AVE 90803 — 3-00100
Patricia Lawrence, prin. — 434-7411
Stanford MS — 4-00100
5871 E LOS ARCOS ST 90815 — 594-9793
Judith Gutierrez, prin.
Stephens MS — 4-00100
1830 W COLUMBIA ST 90810 — 595-0841
John Bowles, prin.
Washington MS, 1450 CEDAR AVE 90813 — 3-00100
Shawn Ashley, prin. — 591-2434
Other Schools – See Avalon, Carson, Lakewood

Brooks College — 3-CC
4825 E PACIFIC COAST HWY 90804 — 597-6611
California Institute — 4-CS
4365 ATLANTIC AVE 90807 — 426-7031
California Paramedical & Tech. College — 2-CS
3745 N LONG BEACH BLVD 90807 — 595-6638
California State University — 7-UC
1250 N BELLFLOWER BLVD 90840 — 985-4111
Educorp Career College — 2-CS
230 E 3RD ST 90802 — 437-0501
First Baptist Church S — 2-11111
1000 PINE AVE 90813 — 432-8447
James Allen, prin.
Gethsemane Baptist S — 2-11111
6095 ORANGE AVE 90805 — 422-4206
Rev. Habrial, prin.
Long Beach City College — 7-CC
4901 E CARSON ST 90808 — 420-4111
NEC-Bryman Campus — 3-CS
5350 ATLANTIC AVE 90805 — 422-6007
St. Anthony HS, 620 OLIVE AVE 90802 — 3-00011
Irene Saumakian, prin. — 435-4496
St. Mary Medical Center — HSP
1050 LINDEN AVE 90813 — 491-9010
Travel and Trade Career Institute — 3-CS
3635 ATLANTIC AVE 90807 — 800-777-8824
UCC Vocational Center — 2-CS
1322 CORONADO AVE 90804 — 597-3798
Veterans Administration Medical Center — 2-HSP
5901 E 7TH ST 90822 — 494-5400

Loomis, AC 916, PC 6, Placer
Placer UNHSD
Supt. — See Auburn
Del Oro HS, 3301 TAYLOR RD 95650 — 4-00011
Tom Barry, prin. — 652-7243

Los Alamitos, AC 310, PC 7, Orange
Los Alamitos USD — 6-11111
10293 BLOOMFIELD ST 90720 — 430-1021
Michael Miller, supt.
Laurel HS — 2-00011
10291 BLOOMFIELD ST 90720 — 596-9212
David Bishop, prin.
HS, 3591 CERRITOS AVE 90720 — 4-00011
Carol Hart, prin. — 430-3511
McAuliffe MS — 4-00100
4112 CERRITOS AVE 90720 — 493-5428
Karen Lovelace, prin.

Los Altos, AC 415, PC 8, Santa Clara
Los Altos ESD — 5-11100
201 COVINGTON RD 94024 — 941-4010
Margaret Gratiot, supt.
Blach IS, 1120 COVINGTON RD 94024 — 2-00100
(—), prin. — 964-1196
Egan IS, 100 W PORTOLA AVE 94022 — 2-00100
Brenda Dyckman, prin. — 941-6174

Mountain View-Los Altos UNHSD
Supt. — See Mountain View
HS, 201 ALMOND AVE 94022 — 4-00011
David Brazer, prin. — 968-6571

Los Altos Hills, AC 415, PC 6, Santa Clara

Foothill College — 7-CC
12345 EL MONTE AVE 94022 — 960-4600
Pinewood S — 2-00111
26800 W FREMONT RD 94022 — 941-1532
Lynn Riches, prin.

Los Angeles, PC 12, Los Angeles
Compton USD
Supt. — See Compton
Vanguard USD — 2-00100
13305 S SAN PEDRO ST 90061 — 310-898-6050
Richard Banton, prin.

County Supt Programs — 3-00011
9300 E IMPERIAL HWY 90242 — 213-922-6111
Stuart Gothold, supt.
Los Angeles Co. HS of Art — 3-00011
5151 PASEO RANCHO CASTILLA 90032
Lupe Delgado, prin. — 213-224-3585

Los Angeles USD — 11-11111
450 N GRAND AVE 90012 — 213-625-6251
Sydney Thompson, supt.
Belmont HS, 1575 W 2ND ST 90026 — 5-00011
Augie Herrera, prin. — 213-250-0244
Bravo Medical Magnet HS — 4-00011
1200 CORNWELL ST 90033 — 213-342-0428
Rosa Hernandez, prin.
Crenshaw HS — 4-00011
5010 11TH AVE 90043 — 213-296-5370
Yvonne Noble, prin.
Dorsey HS — 4-00011
3537 FARMDALE AVE 90016 — 213-296-7120
Jerelene Wells, prin.
Downtown Business HS — 3-00011
1081 W TEMPLE ST 90012 — 213-625-4126
Ronney Sakoda, prin.
Eagle Rock JSHS — 4-00111
1750 YOSEMITE DR 90041 — 213-254-6891
Gloria Sierra, prin.
Fairfax HS — 4-00011
7850 MELROSE AVE 90046 — 213-651-5200
Michael O'Sullivan, prin.
Franklin SHS — 4-00011
820 N AVENUE 54 90042 — 213-254-7104
Charles Molina, prin.
Fremont HS — 5-00001
7676 S SAN PEDRO ST 90003 — 213-758-4141
John Haydel, prin.
Garfield SHS, 5101 E 6TH ST 90022 — 5-00001
Maria Tostado, prin. — 213-268-9361
Hamilton HS — 4-00011
2955 S ROBERTSON BLVD 90034 — 310-836-1602
Nina Russo, prin.
Hollywood SHS — 4-00001
1521 N HIGHLAND AVE 90028 — 213-461-3891
Jeanne Hon, prin.
Jefferson HS, 1319 E 41ST ST 90011 — 5-00011
Virginia Preciado, prin. — 213-232-2261
Jordan HS, 2265 E 103RD ST 90002 — 4-00011
Grace Strauther, prin. — 213-567-0531
King-Drew Medical Magnet HS — 2-00011
1750 E 118TH ST 90059 — 213-566-0420
Shirley Starke, prin.
LA S for Enriched Studies — 4-01111
5931 W 18TH ST 90035 — 213-938-1620
Marion Collins, prin.
Lincoln HS — 5-00011
3501 N BROADWAY 90031 — 213-223-4021
Lupe Sonnie, prin.
Locke HS, 325 E 111TH ST 90061 — 4-00011
Edward Robbs, prin. — 213-757-9381
HS, 4650 W OLYMPIC BLVD 90019 — 5-00011
Anne Falotico, prin. — 213-937-3210
Manual Arts SHS — 4-00001
4131 S VERMONT AVE 90037 — 213-232-1121
Robert Barner, prin.
Marshall HS, 3939 TRACY ST 90027 — 5-00011
Deborah Leidner, prin. — 213-660-1440
Roosevelt SHS — 5-00001
456 S MATHEWS ST 90033 — 213-268-7241
Henry Ronquillo, prin.
University HS — 4-00011
11800 TEXAS AVE 90025 — 310-478-9833
Jack Moscowitz, prin.
Venice HS — 4-00011
13000 VENICE BLVD 90066 — 310-306-7981
J. Jacobs, prin.
Washington Prep HS — 4-00011
10860 DENKER AVE 90047 — 213-757-9281
Marguerite LaMotte, prin.
Westchester HS — 4-00011
7400 W MANCHESTER AVE 90045
Eileen Banta, prin. — 310-670-4003
Wilson SHS — 4-00001
4500 MULTNOMAH ST 90032 — 213-223-1131
Ramon Castillo, prin.

East Los Angeles Occupational Center — Vo Tech
2100 MARENGO ST 90033 — 213-223-1283
Joe Tijerina, prin.
East Los Angeles Skills Center — Vo Tech
3921 SELIG PL 90031 — 213-227-0018
Pete Fernandez, prin.
Metropolitan Skills Center — Vo Tech
2801 W 6TH ST 90057 — 213-386-7269
J. McIntyre, prin.
Adams JHS, 151 W 30TH ST 90007 — 4-00110
Yolanda Smith, prin. — 213-744-1502
Audubon JHS — 4-00110
4120 11TH AVE 90008 — 213-299-2882
Travis Kiel, prin.
Bancroft JHS — 4-00110
929 N LAS PALMAS AVE 90038 — 213-464-3174
Willie Williams, prin.
Belvedere JHS — 4-00110
312 N RECORD AVE 90063 — 213-266-3730
David Gonzalez, prin.
Berendo JHS — 5-00100
1157 S BERENDO ST 90006 — 213-382-1343
Cecillia Duran, prin.
Bethune JHS, 155 W 69TH ST 90003 — 4-00110
Edith Morris, prin. — 213-971-3646
Burbank JHS — 4-00110
6460 N FIGUEROA ST 90042 — 213-255-0108
Eloisa Marquez, prin.
Burroughs JHS — 4-00110
600 S MCCADDEN PL 90005 — 213-938-9146
Earl Barner, prin.
Carver JHS — 4-00100
4410 MCKINLEY AVE 90011 — 213-233-3261
Lionel Riley, prin.
Clay JHS — 4-00100
12226 S WESTERN AVE 90047 — 213-757-4181
George Jones, prin.
Drew JHS — 4-00110
8511 COMPTON AVE 90001 — 213-583-6961
Joyce Brown, prin.
Edison JHS — 4-00110
6500 HOOPER AVE 90001 — 213-587-5108
Joe Santana, prin.
El Sereno JHS — 4-00110
2839 N EASTERN AVE 90032 — 213-223-2441
Antonio Delgado, prin.
Emerson JHS — 4-00100
1650 SELBY AVE 90024 — 310-475-8417
Charlotte Lerchenmuller, prin.
Foshay JHS — 4-00110
3751 S HARVARD BLVD 90018 — 213-735-0241
Howard Lappin, prin.
Gompers IS, 234 E 112TH ST 90061 — 4-00100
Robert Kinsella, prin. — 213-757-9211
Griffith JHS, 4765 E 4TH ST 90022 — 4-00110
Raul Salcido, prin. — 213-266-6106
Harte Prep IS — 4-00100
9301 S HOOVER ST 90044 — 213-757-9143
Catherine Sumpter, prin.
Hollenbeck JHS — 4-00110
2510 E 6TH ST 90023 — 213-268-0176
Evelyn Lucero, prin.
Irving JHS — 4-00100
3010 ESTARA AVE 90065 — 213-256-2123
Thelma Yoshi, prin.
King JHS — 4-00110
4201 FOUNTAIN AVE 90029 — 213-664-1176
Jerome Furey, prin.
Mann JHS — 4-00110
7001 S ST ANDREWS PL 90047 — 213-778-9450
Rosie Ollie, prin.
Marina Del Rey JHS — 3-00100
12500 BRADDOCK DR 90066 — 310-822-6788
Angela Reuser, prin.
Markham IS — 4-00100
1650 E 104TH ST 90002 — 213-564-6951
John Miller, prin.
Mt. Vernon JHS — 4-00110
4066 W 17TH ST 90019 — 213-733-2157
Leonard George, prin.
Muir JHS — 4-00110
5929 S VERMONT AVE 90044 — 213-971-4361
Willie Crittendon, prin.
Nightingale JHS — 4-00110
3311 N FIGUEROA ST 90065 — 213-221-2128
Jess Bojorquez, prin.
Palms JHS — 4-00100
10860 WOODBINE ST 90034 — 310-837-5236
Hugh Gottfried, prin.
Revere JHS — 3-00100
1450 ALLENFORD AVE 90049 — 310-451-5789
John Gaydowski, prin.
Stevenson JHS — 4-00110
725 S INDIANA ST 90023 — 213-262-4101
Edward Amarillas, prin.
Twain JHS — 3-00100
2224 WALGROVE AVE 90066 — 310-397-2125
Gwendolyn Doble, prin.
Virgil JHS — 5-00100
152 N VERMONT AVE 90004 — 213-388-0347
James Marshall, prin.
Webster JHS — 4-00110
11330 GRAHAM PL 90064 — 310-478-2041
Mary Voiles, prin.
Wright JHS, 6550 W 80TH ST 90045 — 4-00100
Virdell Twine, prin. — 310-670-5666

Other Schools – See Bell, Canoga Park, Carson, Chatsworth, Gardena, Granada Hills, Harbor City, Hollywood, Huntington Park, Lomita, Mission Hills, North Hollywood, Northridge, Pacific Palisades, Pacoima, Reseda, San Fernando, San Pedro, Sepulveda, Sherman Oaks, South Gate, Sunland, Sun Valley, Sylmar, Tarzana, Tujunga, Van Nuys, Wilmington, Woodland Hills

American Career College — 2-CS
4021 ROSEWOOD AVE 90004 — 213-383-2862
American College for the Applied Arts — 3-UC
1651 WESTWOOD BLVD 90024 — 310-470-2000
American Film Institute Center — 2-UC
2021 N WESTERN AVE 90027 — 213-856-7600
Apollo Training Academy — 2-11111
1404 N CATALINA ST 90027 — 213-661-6787
Vicky Owen, prin.
Arshag Dickranian Armenian S — 2-11111
1200 N CAHUENGA BLVD 90038 — 213-461-4377
Vartkes Kourouyan, prin.
Associated Technical College — 5-CS
1670 WESTWOOD BLVD 90017 — 213-484-2444
Bais Yaakov S for Girls — 2-00011
461 N LA BREA AVE 90036 — 213-938-3231
Rabbi Bursztyn, prin.
Bel-Air Preparatory S — 2-00111
8628 HOLLOWAY DR 90069 — 213-276-3068
Stephan Makoff, prin.
Bishop Mora Salesian HS — 2-00011
960 S SOTO ST 90023 — 213-261-7124
Manuel Villarreal, prin.
Brentwood JSHS — 2-00111
100 S BARRINGTON PL 90049 — 310-476-9633
Hunter Temple, prin.
Bryan College of Court Reporting — 3-CS
2511 BEVERLY BLVD 90057 — 213-484-8850
California State University — 7-UC
5151 PASEO RANCHO CASTILLA 90032 — 213-343-3000
California Tech University HS — 2-00001
1717 W CENTURY BLVD 90047 — 213-777-6656
Burl Ballentine, prin.
Cathedral HS — 2-00011
1253 BISHOP RD 90012 — 213-225-2438
Br. Michale Saggau, prin.
Cedars-Sinai Medical Center — HSP
8700 BEVERLY BLVD 90048 — 213-855-5334
Century Business College — 2-CS
3325 WILSHIRE BLVD 90010 — 213-383-1585
Children's Hospital of Los Angeles — HSP
4650 W SUNSET BLVD 90027 — 213-669-2301
Cleveland Chiropractic College of LA — 2-UC
590 N VERMONT AVE 90004 — 213-660-6166
Columbia College — 2-UC
925 N LA BREA AVE 90038 — 213-851-0550
Computer Learning Center — 4-CS
3130 WILSHIRE BLVD 90010 — 213-386-6311
Drew Medical Center — HSP
1621 E 120TH ST 90059 — 213-563-4987
Drew University — 2-UC
1621 E 120TH ST 90059 — 213-563-4800
Estelle Harman Actor's Workshop — 2-CS
522 N LA BREA AVE 90036 — 213-931-8137
Eubanks Conservatory of Music & Arts — 2-UC
4928 CRENSHAW BLVD 90043 — 213-291-7821
Fashion Inst. of Design & Merchandising — 4-CC
919 S GRAND AVE 90015 — 213-624-1200
Golden Day S — 2-11111
4508 CRENSHAW BLVD 90043 — 213-296-6280
Clark Parker, prin.
Halix Institute — 2-HMS
1543 W OLYIC BLVD #226 90015
Harvard Westlake S — 3-00111
700 N FARING RD 90077 — 213-274-7281
Thomas Hudnut, prin.
Hebrew Union College — 1-UC
3077 UNIVERSITY AVE 90007 — 213-749-3424
Hemphill Schools — 2-HMS
510 S ALVARADO ST 90057
Herzl S — 2-00111
1317 N CRSCENT HEIGHTS BLVD 90046
Sonia Berman, prin. — 213-654-8872
Holy Cross MS — 2-00100
104 W 47TH PL 90037 — 213-234-9023
Sr. Terese Flynn, prin.
Immaculate Heart HS — 3-00011
5515 FRANKLIN AVE 90028 — 213-461-3651
Sr. Ruth Murray, prin.
Immaculate Heart MS — 2-00100
5515 FRANKLIN AVE 90028 — 213-461-3651
Ann Phelps, prin.
Institute of Computer Technology — 3-CC
3200 WILSHIRE BLVD STE 400 90010 — 213-381-3333
John Tracy Clinic — 2-HMS
806 W ADAMS BLVD 90007
Leicester School — 2-CS
1106 W OLYMPIC BLVD 90015 — 213-746-7666
Le Lycee Francais de Los Angeles — 3-11111
3261 OVERLAND AVE 90034 — 310-836-3464
Raymond Kabbaz, prin.
Los Angeles Adventist Academy — 2-00011
846 E EL SEGUNDO BLVD 90059 — 213-321-2585
Virginia Thomas, prin.
Los Angeles City College — 7-CC
855 N VERMONT AVE 90029 — 213-669-4000
Los Angeles County USC Medical Center — HSP
1200 N STATE RD 90033

Los Angeles ORT Technical Institute — 2-CS
635 S HARVARD BLVD # 116 90005 — 213-387-4244
Los Angeles Southwest College — 5-CC
1600 W IMPERIAL HWY 90047 — 310-777-2225
Los Angeles Trade-Technical College — 7-CC
400 W WASHINGTON BLVD 90015 — 213-744-9500
Loyola HS — 4-00011
1901 VENICE BLVD 90006 — 213-381-5121
Fr. Robert Walsh, prin.
Loyola Marymount University — 6-UC
7101 W 80TH ST 90045 — 213-338-2700
Loyola Marymount University — 3-UC
PO BOX 15019 90015
Lycee International S — 2-11111
4155 RUSSELL AVE 90027 — 213-665-4526
Monique Mickus, prin.
Marlborough HS — 2-00111
250 S ROSSMORE AVE 90004 — 213-935-1147
Barbara Wagner, prin.
Marymount HS — 2-00011
10643 W SUNSET BLVD 90077 — 310-472-1205
Ann Gillick, prin.
Mt. St. Mary's College — 4-UC
12001 CHALON RD 90049 — 213-476-2237
Murphy HS — 2-00011
241 S DETROIT ST 90036 — 213-935-1161
Keith Murphy, prin.
NEC-Bryman Campus — 3-CS
1017 WILSHIRE BLVD 90017 — 213-481-1640
Notre Dame Academy For Girls — 2-00011
2851 OVERLAND AVE 90064 — 310-839-5289
Sr. Gina Blunck, prin.
Nova Institute of Health Technology — 2-CS
2400 S WESTERN AVE 90018 — 213-735-2222
Occidental College — 4-UC
1600 CAMPUS RD 90041 — 213-259-2500
Otis College of Art and Design — 3-UC
2401 WILSHIRE BLVD 90057 — 213-251-0505
Our Lady Loretta HS — 2-00011
2900 W PICO BLVD 90006 — 213-737-0012
Sharon Morano, prin.
Pacific Christian HS — 2-00111
625 COLEMAN AVE 90042 — 213-254-7161
Richard Riesen, prin.
Pacific Gateway College — 2-CS
3018 CARMEL ST 90065 — 818-247-9544
Pilgrim School — 3-11111
540 S COMMONWEALTH AVE 90020 — 213-385-7351
Nancy White, prin.
Pilibos Armenian S — 3-11111
1615 N ALEXANDRIA AVE 90027 — 213-668-2661
Annick Keshishian, prin.
Platt College — 3-CS
7470 N FIGUEROA ST 90041 — 213-258-8050
R.D. Colburn School of Performing Arts — 2-CS
3131 S FIGUEROA ST 90007 — 213-743-5252
Ribet Academy — 3-11111
2911 N SAN FERNANDO RD 90065 — 213-344-4330
Marie Jones, prin.
Sacred Heart HS — 2-00011
2111 GRIFFIN AVE 90031 — 213-225-2209
Sr. Reina Perea, prin.
St. Mary Magdalen MS — 2-01100
1223 S CORNING ST 90035 — 310-652-4723
Sr. Loretta O'Leary, prin.
St. Michael HS — 2-00011
1100 W MANCHESTER AVE 90044 — 213-751-1135
Sr. Lupe Solano, prin.
Southern California Inst. Architecture — 2-UC
5454 BEETHOVEN ST 90066 — 310-574-3625
Southwestern University School of Law — 4-UC
675 S WESTMORELAND AVE 90005 — 213-380-4800
SUTECH School of Voc/Tech Training — 2-CS
3427 E OLYMPIC BLVD 90023 — 213-262-3210
Technical Health Careers School — 2-CS
11603 S WESTERN AVE 90047 — 213-757-0273
UCLA Center for the Health Sciences — 1-UC
10833 LE CONTE AVE 90024 — 213-825-5654
University of California — 8-UC
405 HILGARD AVE 90024 — 213-825-4321
University of Judaism/Lee College — 2-UC
15600 MULHOLLAND DR 90077 — 310-476-9777
University of Southern California — 4-UC
12933 ERICKSON AVE 90242
University of Southern California — 7-UC
UNIV PARK 90089 — 213-740-2311
University of Southern California — 2-UC
HEALTH SCIENCE CAMPUS 90033 — 213-226-6501
Verbum Dei HS — 2-00011
11100 S CENTRAL AVE 90059 — 213-564-6651
Fr. Threatt, prin.
West Coast Talmudical Seminary S — 2-11111
7215 WARING AVE 90046 — 213-937-3763
Randall Rutschman, prin.
West Coast University — 4-UC
440 SHATTO PL 90020 — 213-487-4433
West Los Angeles Baptist S — 2-00111
1609 S BARRINGTON AVE 90025 — 310-826-8374
John Reynolds, prin.
West Los Angeles College — 1-CC
9700 S SEPULVEDA BLVD 90045 — 213-776-5264
West Los Angeles VA Medical Center — HSP
WILSHIRE & SAWTELLE BLVDS 90073 — 213-824-3132
Westview S — 2-00011
2000 STONER AVE 90025 — 310-478-5544
Judy Gordon, prin.

Whittier College 2-UC
5353 W 3RD ST 90020 213-938-3621
Windward S 2-00111
11350 PALMS BLVD 90066 310-391-7127
Thomas Gilder, prin.
Wise S 3-11111
15500 STEPHEN S WISE DR 90077
Metuka Benjamin, prin. 213-476-8561
Yeshiva Gedolah-Michael Diller HS 2-00011
5822 W 3RD ST 90036 213-938-2071
Aubrey Sher, prin.
Yeshiva Ohr Elchonon Chabad West Coast 2-11111
7215 WARING AVE 90046 213-937-3763
Rabbi Schochet, prin.
Yeshiva University HS 2-00011
9760 W PICO BLVD 90035 310-553-1575
Rabbi Tendler, prin.

Los Banos, AC 209, PC 7, Merced
Los Banos USD, 1717 S 11TH ST 93635 5-11111
R. Davis Cowles, supt. 826-3801
HS, 1966 S 11TH ST 93635 4-00011
Manuel Gastelo, prin. 826-6033
JHS, 659 K ST 93635 3-00100
Michael Villalta, prin. 826-0867

Merced College-Los Banos Campus 3-CC
16570 S MERCEY SPRINGS RD 93635 826-3431

Los Gatos, AC 408, PC 8, Santa Clara
Campbell UNESD
Supt. — See Campbell
Rolling Hills MS, 1585 MORE AVE 95030 3-01100
Jerry Davis, prin. 364-4235

Loma Prieta JUNESD 3-11100
23800 SUMMIT RD 95030 353-1101
Lee Tinder, supt.
English MS, 23800 SUMMIT RD 95030 2-00100
Gayle Shank, prin. 353-1123

Los Gatos-Saratoga JUNHSD 4-00011
17421 FARLEY RD W 95030 354-2520
Tod Likins, supt.
HS, 20 HIGH SCHOOL CT 95032 4-00011
Carlton Simonson, prin. 354-2730
Other Schools — See Saratoga

Los Gatos UNESD 4-11100
15766 POPPY LN 95030 395-5570
Stephen Benbow, supt.
Fisher MS, 17000 ROBERTS RD 95032 3-00100
Rob Lowry, prin. 356-2141

Los Molinos, AC 916, PC 4, Tehama
Los Molinos USD, PO BOX 609 96055 3-11100
A. Tolman, supt. 384-7900
HS, PO BOX 609 96055 2-00011
Darleen Barnard, prin. 384-7900

Los Nietos, AC 310, PC 6, Los Angeles
Los Nietos ESD, PO BOX 2405 90610 4-11100
Charles Menzies, supt. 692-0271
MS, 11425 RIVERA RD 90606 3-00100
Madeline Minear, prin. 695-0637

Los Olivos, AC 805, PC 2, Santa Barbara

Dunn S, PO BOX 98 93441 2-00111
Eric Ruoss, prin. 688-6471
Midland S, PO BOX 8 93441 1-00011
Dan Kunkle, prin. 688-5114

Los Osos, AC 805, PC 6, San Luis Obispo
San Luis Coastal USD
Supt. — See San Luis Obispo
MS, 1555 EL MORRO AVE 93402 2-00100
Greg Pruitt, prin. 528-5050

Lost Hills, AC 805, PC 4, Kern
Lost Hills UNESD 2-11100
PO BOX 158 93249 797-2626
John Bogie, supt.
MS, PO BOX 158 93249 2-01100
David Day, prin. 797-2633

Lower Lake, AC 707, PC 4, Lake
Konocti USD
Supt. — See Clearlake
HS, PO BOX 799 95457 3-00011
Lee Morine, prin. 994-6471

Loyalton, AC 916, PC 3, Sierra
Sierra-Plumas JUSD
Supt. — See Downieville
HS, PO BOX 37 96118 2-00011
Glenn Boehme, prin. 993-4454
IS, PO BOX 5 96118 1-00100
Michael Filippini, prin. 993-4186

Lucerne Valley, AC 619, PC 4, San Bernardino
Lucerne Valley UNSD 4-11100
10790 BARSTOW RD 92356 248-6108
Ron Peavy, supt.
Lucerne Valley JHS 2-00010
10790 BARSTOW RD 92356 248-7237
Emily Shoemaker, prin.
MS, 10790 BARSTOW RD 92356 2-00100
Joe Andreasen, prin. 248-7237

Lynwood, AC 310, PC 8, Los Angeles
Lynwood USD, 11321 BULLIS RD 90262 7-11111
Audrey Clarke, supt. 886-1600
HS, 12124 BULLIS RD 90262 5-00011
Mickey Cureton, prin. 603-1466

Hosler JHS, 11300 SPRUCE ST 90262 4-00100
(—), prin. 603-1447

Consolidated Welding School 2-CS
4343 E IMPERIAL HWY 90262 638-0418

Mc Arthur, AC 916, PC 3, Shasta
Fall River JUSD
Supt. — See Cassel
Fall River JSHS 2-00111
44215 WALNUT ST 96056 336-5515
Donald Sandberg, prin.

McCloud, AC 916, PC 4, Siskiyou
Siskiyou UNHSD
Supt. — See Mount Shasta
HS, PO BOX 1530 96057 1-00011
Michael Kern, prin. 964-2181

Mc Farland, AC 805, PC 6, Kern
McFarland USD, 601 2ND ST 93250 4-11111
James Perry, supt. 792-3081
HS, 259 W SHERWOOD AVE 93250 3-00011
Dave Bailey, prin. 792-3126
MS, 509 3RD PL 93250 3-00100
Earl Guinn, prin. 792-6090

Mc Kinleyville, AC 707, PC 7, Humboldt
Mc Kinleyville UNESD 4-11100
2275 CENTRAL AVE 95521 839-1549
Larry Georgianna, supt.
MS, 2285 CENTRAL AVE 95521 3-00100
Roy Fields, prin. 839-1508
Northern Humboldt UNHSD 4-00011
2755 MCKINLEYVILLE AVE 95521 839-4334
Bruce Griffith, supt.
HS, 1300 MURRAY RD 95521 3-00011
Brian Stephens, prin. 839-1518
Other Schools — See Arcata

Madera, AC 209, PC 8, Madera
Madera USD, 1902 HOWARD RD 93637 7-11111
Thomas Riley, supt. 675-4500
HS, 200 S L ST 93637 5-00011
Robert Peasley, prin. 675-4444
Jefferson JHS, 1407 SUNSET AVE 93637 4-00100
Joe Vived, prin. 673-9286

Malibu, AC 310, PC 7, Los Angeles
Santa Monica-Malibu USD
Supt. — See Santa Monica
Malibu Park MS 3-00110
30215 MORNING VIEW DR 90265 457-6801
Michael Matthews, prin.

Pepperdine University 6-UC
24255 PACIFIC COAST HWY 90263 456-4000

Mammoth Lakes, AC 619, PC 5, Mono
Mammoth USD, PO BOX 1320 93546 3-11111
Shalee Cunningham, supt. 934-6802
JSHS, PO BOX 1320 93546 2-00111
Robert Seevers, prin. 934-8541

Manhattan Beach, AC 310, PC 8, Los Angeles
Manhattan Beach USD 5-11111
1501 N REDONDO AVE 90266 546-3488
Gerald Davis, supt.
Mira Costa HS, 701 S PECK AVE 90266 4-00011
Darlene Gorey, prin. 318-7355
IS, 1501 N REDONDO AVE 90266 3-00100
Billie Jean Knight, prin. 546-3488

Manteca, AC 209, PC 8, San Joaquin
Manteca USD, PO BOX 32 95336 7-11111
Harold Hughes, supt. 825-3200
East Union HS, 1700 N UNION RD 95336 4-00011
Linda Frost, prin. 825-3125
HS, 450 E YOSEMITE AVE 95336 4-00011
William Jones, prin. 825-3150
Sierra HS, 1700 THOMAS ST 95337 3-00011
Frederick Arucan, prin. 825-3175

Maricopa, AC 805, PC 4, Kern
Maricopa USD 2-11111
955 STANISLAUS ST 93252 769-8231
Pamela Sanders, supt.
HS, 955 STANISLAUS ST 93252 2-00011
Dale Countryman, prin. 769-8234

Marina, AC 408, PC 8, Monterey
Monterey Peninsula USD
Supt. — See Monterey
Los Arboles MS 2-00100
294 HILLCREST AVE 93933 384-3550
Stan Cook, prin.

Marina Del Rey, AC 213, PC 6, Los Angeles

Antioch University 2-UC
4800 LINCOLN BLVD 90292 578-1080

Mariposa, AC 209, PC 4, Mariposa
Mariposa County USD 5-11111
PO BOX 8 95338 966-3691
William Pettus, supt.
Mariposa County HS 2-00011
PO BOX 127 95338 966-3663
Al Nocciolo, prin.
Spring Hill HS, PO BOX 5001 95338 2-00011
Richard Fox, prin. 966-2505
JHS, PO BOX 8 95338 2-00100
Judy Eppler, prin. 966-5272
Other Schools — See Coulterville, Yosemite Park

Martinez, AC 510, PC 8, Contra Costa
Martinez USD, 921 SUSANA ST 94553 5-11111
Patricia Crocker, supt. 313-0480
Alhambra HS, 150 E ST 94553 3-00011
Patrick Gemma, prin. 313-0440
JHS, COURT & WARREN STS 94553 3-00100
Michael Bowers, prin. 313-0414

Heald Institute of Technology 2-CC
2860 HOWE RD 94553 228-9000
VA Medical Center HSP
150 MUIR RD 94553 372-2000

Marysville, AC 916, PC 7, Yuba
Marysville JUSD, 1919 B ST 95901 6-11111
Peter Pillsbury, supt. 741-6000
HS, 12 E 18TH ST 95901 3-00011
Al Kinney, prin. 741-6180
Alicia IS, 1208 PASADO RD 95901 3-00100
Jack Stokes, prin. 741-6103
Foothill MS, 5351 FRUITLAND RD 95901 2-01100
Robert Wilkerson, prin. 741-6130
McKenney ST, 1904 HUSTON ST 95901 3-00100
Burke Adams, prin. 741-6187
Other Schools — See Olivehurst

Yuba College 7-CC
2088 N BEALE RD 95901 741-6700

Maxwell, AC 916, PC 3, Colusa
Maxwell USD, PO BOX 788 95955 2-11111
Wallace McCormick, supt. 438-2291
HS, PO BOX 788 95955 2-00011
Wallace McCormick, prin. 438-2291

Maywood, AC 213, PC 8, Los Angeles

Maywood Baptist Pilgrim S 2-11111
3759 E 57TH ST 90270 585-3167
Edward Arthurs, prin.

Meadow Vista, AC 916, PC 5, Placer
Placer Hills UNESD 4-11100
PO BOX 68 95722 878-2606
Ken Poulsen, supt.
Other Schools — See Weimar

Mendocino, AC 707, PC 4, Mendocino
Mendocino USD 3-11111
PO BOX 1154 95460 937-5868
Kenneth Matheson, supt.
HS, PO BOX 226 95460 2-00011
David Moss, prin. 937-5871
MS, PO BOX 226 95460 2-00100
John Stafford, prin. 937-0564

Mendota, AC 209, PC 6, Fresno
Mendota USD, 115 MCCABE AVE 93640 4-11111
Kulwant Singh Sidhu, supt. 655-4943
Mendota HS, 115 MCCABE AVE 93640 2-00011
Yvonne Healey, prin. 655-3246
McCabe JHS, 115 MCCABE AVE 93640 2-00100
Gilbert Rossette, prin. 655-4991

Menifee, AC 909, PC 99, Riverside
Menifee UNESD 5-11100
30205 MENIFEE RD 92584 672-1851
Glen Newman, supt.
Menifee Valley MS 4-00100
26255 GARBONI RD 92584 672-6400
Paul Drob, prin.

Menlo Park, AC 415, PC 8, San Mateo
Las Lomitas ESD 3-11100
1011 ALTSCHUL AVE 94025 854-2880
Charla Rolland, supt.
La Entrada MS, 2200 SHARON RD 94025 2-01100
Laurie Le Duc, prin. 854-3962

Menlo Park City ESD
Supt. — See Atherton
Hillview MS, 1100 ELDER AVE 94025 2-00100
Michael Moore, prin. 326-4341

Ravenswood City ESD
Supt. — See East Palo Alto
Menlo Oaks MS, 475 POPE ST 94025 2-01100
Clara Rice, prin. 329-2828

Sacred Heart Prep S 2-00011
150 VALPARAISO AVE 94027 322-1928
Richard Dioli, prin.
St. Patrick's Seminary 1-UC
320 MIDDLEFIELD RD 94025 325-5621

Merced, AC 209, PC 8, Merced
Merced City ESD, 444 W 23RD ST 95340 7-11100
Donald De Long, supt. 385-6600
Hoover IS, 800 E 26TH ST 95340 4-00100
Kathleen Crookham, prin. 385-6631
Rivera IS, 945 BUENA VISTA DR 95348 4-00100
Robert Wendel, prin. 385-6680
Tenaya IS, 760 W 8TH ST 95340 4-00100
Tom Parker, prin. 385-6687
Merced UNHSD, PO BOX 2147 95344 6-00111
Bill Tilley, supt. 385-6412
Merced North SHS 5-00011
PO BOX 2167 95344 385-6465
Gerald Hansen, prin.
Merced East Mid. HS 4-00010
PO BOX 2187 95344 385-6500
Ralph Swenson, prin.
Other Schools — See Atwater, Livingston

Merced College 6-CC
3600 M ST 95348 384-6000

Middletown, AC 707, PC 4, Lake
Middletown USD, PO BOX 338 95461 4-11111
Robert Slaby, supt. 987-3390
HS, PO BOX 338 95461 2-00011
Robert Slaby, prin. 987-2305
MS, PO BOX 338 95461 2-00100
JoAnn Rodriguez, prin. 987-2189

Millbrae, AC 415, PC 7, San Mateo
Millbrae ESD, 555 RICHMOND DR 94030 4-11100
Karen Philip, supt. 697-5693
Taylor MS, 850 TAYLOR BLVD 94030 3-00100
Sharon Fritz, prin. 697-4096

San Mateo UNHSD
Supt. — See San Mateo
Mills HS, 400 MURCHISON DR 94030 4-00011
Frank Seebode, prin. 697-3344

Mill Valley, AC 415, PC 7, Marin
Mill Valley ESD 4-11100
411 SYCAMORE AVE 94941 389-7700
John Harter, supt.
MS, 425 SYCAMORE AVE 94941 3-00100
Patricia Wool, prin. 389-7711

Tamalpais UNHSD
Supt. — See Larkspur
Tamalpais HS, 700 MILLER AVE 94941 3-00011
Frank Gold, prin. 388-3292

Golden Gate Baptist Theological Seminary 3-UC
STRAWBERRY POINT 94941 388-8080
North Bay Marin S, 70 LOMITA DR 94941 2-00111
Richard Curley, prin. 381-3003

Milpitas, AC 408, PC 8, Santa Clara
Milpitas USD 6-11111
1331 E CALAVERAS BLVD 95035 945-2300
John MacKay, supt.
HS, 1285 ESCUELA PKY 95035 4-00011
Charles Gary, prin. 945-5500
Rancho Milpitas MS 3-00100
1915 YELLOWSTONE AVE 95035 945-5561
Patricia Dell, prin.
Russell MS, 1500 ESCUELA PKY 95035 3-00100
Ellen Curtin, prin. 945-2312

Mira Loma, AC 909, PC 7, Riverside
Jurupa USD
Supt. — See Riverside
Jurupa Valley HS 4-00011
10551 BELLEGRAVE AVE 91752 360-2600
Alan Young, prin.

Miranda, AC 707, PC 2, Humboldt
Southern Humbolt JUSD
Supt. — See Garberville
South Fork HS, PO BOX 188 95553 2-00011
Jim Quast, prin. 943-3144
JHS, PO BOX 158 95553 2-00100
Harlan Tucker, prin. 943-3168

Mission Hills, AC 818, PC see Los Angeles
Los Angeles USD
Supt. — See Los Angeles
North Valley Occupational Center Vo Tech
11450 SHARP AVE 91345 365-9645
Gloria Martinez, prin.

Bishop Alemany HS 4-00011
15241 RINALDI ST 91345 365-3925
Fr. Milbauer, prin.
Our Lady Queen of Angels Seminary HS 2-00011
15101 SAN FRNND MSSION BLVD 91345
Fr. Martini, prin. 361-0187

Mission San Jose, AC 510, PC see Fremont

Queen of the Holy Rosary 2-CC
PO BOX 3908 94539 657-2468

Mission Viejo, AC 714, PC 8, Orange
Capistrano USD
Supt. — See San Juan Capistrano
Capistrano Valley HS 4-00011
26301 VIA ESCOLAR 92692 364-6100
Jessica Leadley, prin.

Saddleback Valley USD 8-11111
25631 DISENO DR 92691 586-1234
P. Hartman, supt.
HS, 25025 CHRISANTA DR 92691 4-00011
Robert Metz, prin. 837-7722
Silverado HS, 25632 DISENO DR 92691 2-00011
Barry Lietz, prin. 586-8800
La Paz IS, 25151 PRADERA DR 92691 4-00100
Ruth Lander, prin. 830-1720
Los Alisos IS, 25171 MOOR AVE 92691 3-00100
Jerry Ray, prin. 830-9700
Rancho Santa Margarita IS 3-00100
21931 ALMA ALDEA 92688 459-8253
Walter Otto, prin.
Trabuco Hills JHS 4-00010
27501 CORDOVA RD 92691 768-1934
William Brand, prin.
Other Schools – See Laguna Hills, Lake Forest

Futures HS 2-00111
26440 LA ALAMEDA # 350 92691 348-0608
Karen Bishop, prin.

Saddleback College 7-CC
28000 MARGUERITE PKY 92692 582-4500

Modesto, AC 209, PC 9, Stanislaus
Empire UNESD 5-11100
116 N MCCLURE RD 95357 521-2800
Robert Price, supt.
Other Schools – See Empire

Modesto CSD, 426 LOCUST ST 95351 8-11111
James Enochs, supt. 576-4090
Beyer HS, 1717 SYLVAN AVE 95355 4-00011
Chris Flesuras, prin. 576-4311
Davis HS, 1200 W RUMBLE RD 95350 4-00011
Carnell Edwards, prin. 576-4500
Downey HS, 1000 COFFEE RD 95355 4-00011
Joseph Gregori, prin. 576-4211
Johansen HS, 641 NORSEMAN DR 95357 4-00011
Bruce Urban, prin. 576-4702
HS, 18 H ST 95351 4-00011
David Cooper, prin. 576-4400
Hanshaw MS 3-00100
1725 LAS VEGAS ST 95358 576-4847
Charles Vidal, prin.
La Loma IS, 1800 ENCINA AVE 95354 3-00100
Lana Tuemmler, prin. 576-4627
Roosevelt IS, 1330 COLLEGE AVE 95350 3-00100
Fred Rich, prin. 576-4871
Twain IS, 707 S EMERALD AVE 95351 3-00100
Edward Parraz, prin. 576-4814

Stanislaus UNESD 5-11100
3601 CARVER RD 95356 529-9546
Andy Schindler, supt.
Prescott MS, 2243 W RUMBLE RD 95350 3-00100
Ken Narita, prin. 529-9892

Sylvan UNESD, 605 SYLVAN AVE 95350 6-11100
Michael Sibitz, supt. 524-9407
Somerset MS, 1037 FLOYD AVE 95350 3-00100
Sandra Ferguson, prin. 529-8350
Ustach MS, 2701 KODIAK DR 95355 4-00100
Barbara Shook, prin. 552-3000

Andon College at Modesto 2-CS
1314 H ST 95354 529-6011
Brethren Heritage S 2-11111
2524 FINNEY RD 95358 577-5584
Ivan Meador, prin.
Central Catholic HS 2-00011
200 S CARPENTER RD 95351 524-9611
Rex Wetzel, prin.
Galen College Medical & Dental Assts. 2-CS
1604 FORD AVE STE 10 95350 527-5084
Modesto Adventist Academy 2-00011
2036 E HATCH RD 95351 537-4521
Dann Dodd, prin.
Modesto Christian HS 2-01111
5755 SISK RD 95356 545-0771
Rev. Gary Miller, prin.
Modesto Junior College 7-CC
435 COLLEGE AVE 95397 575-6067
Valley Commercial College 2-CS
910 12TH ST 95354 578-0616
Western Truck School 2-CS
2316 NICKERSON DR 95358 531-9226

Mojave, AC 805, PC 5, Kern
Mojave USD, 3500 DOUGLAS AVE 93501 5-11111
E. Baldwin, supt. 824-4001
HS, 15732 O ST 93501 3-00011
Raymond Gary, prin. 824-4088
Joshua MS, 3200 PAT AVE 93501 2-00100
Mary Oleson, prin. 824-2411
Other Schools – See California City

Monrovia, AC 818, PC 8, Los Angeles
Monrovia USD 6-11111
325 E HUNTINGTON DR 91016 359-9181
Louise Taylor, supt.
HS, 845 W COLORADO BLVD 91016 4-00011
Lois Wurmbrand, prin. 359-5381
Clifton MS, 226 S IVY AVE 91016 3-00100
(—), prin. 359-3271
Santa Fe MS, 148 W DUARTE RD 91016 3-00100
Dreda Lutz, prin. 357-1137

Montclair, AC 909, PC 8, San Bernardino
Chaffey JUNHSD
Supt. — See Ontario
HS, 4725 BENITO ST 91763 4-00011
William Bertrand, prin. 621-6781

Ontario-Montclair ESD
Supt. — See Ontario
Serrano MS, 4725 SAN JOSE ST 91763 3-00100
Don Snell, prin. 624-0029
Vernon MS, 9775 VERNON AVE 91763 3-00100
Gary Whitcanack, prin. 624-5036

American Nanny College 2-CS
4650 ARROW HWY STE A10 91763 624-7711

Montebello, AC 213, PC 8, Los Angeles
Montebello USD 8-11111
123 S MONTEBELLO BLVD 90640 726-1225
Darline Robles, supt.
HS, 2100 W CLEVELAND AVE 90640 5-00011
Rodney Todd, prin. 728-0121
Schurr HS, 820 N WILCOX AVE 90640 5-00011
Terrance Devney, prin. 728-0471
Eastmont IS, 400 BRADSHAWE ST 90640 4-01100
Naomi Katayama, prin. 721-5133
La Merced IS 4-01100
215 E AVENIDA DE LA MERCED 90640
Stephen Stanton, prin. 722-7262
IS, 1600 W WHITTIER BLVD 90640 4-01100
Judi Peterson, prin. 721-5111
Other Schools – See Bell Gardens, Monterey Park

Cantwell HS 3-00011
329 N GARFIELD AVE 90640 887-2066
Merritt Hemenway, prin.

Monterey, AC 408, PC 8, Monterey
Monterey Peninsula USD 6-11111
PO BOX 1031 93942 649-1562
Bill DeBerry, supt.
HS, PO BOX 1031 93942 4-00011
Larry Snyder, prin. 649-1019
Colton MS, PO BOX 1031 93942 3-00100
Bess Halley, prin. 649-1951
Other Schools – See Fort Ord, Marina, Seaside

Monterey Institute of Intntnl. Studies 3-UC
425 VAN BUREN ST 93940 647-4100
Monterey Peninsula College 6-CC
980 FREMONT ST 93940 646-4010
Santa Catalina S 3-11111
1500 MARK THOMAS DR 93940 655-9300
Sr. Carlotta O'Donnell, prin.
York Episcopal HS, 9501 YORK RD 93940 2-00111
Richard Enemark, prin. 372-7338

Monterey Park, PC 8, Los Angeles
Montebello USD
Supt. — See Montebello
Macy IS, 2101 LUPINE AVE 91755 4-01100
Nicholas Monsour, prin. 213-722-0260

East Los Angeles College 7-CC
1301 AVENIDA CESAR CHAVEZ 91754
213-265-8650

Montgomery Creek, AC 916, PC 3, Shasta
Mountain UNESD 2-11100
PO BOX 368 96065 337-6214
Duncan Hobbs, supt.
MS, PO BOX 368 96065 1-01100
Duncan Hobbs, prin. 337-6214

Moorpark, AC 805, PC 8, Ventura
Moorpark USD, 30 FLORY AVE 93021 6-11111
Thomas Duffy, supt. 378-6300
Moorpark HS 4-00011
4500 TIERRA REJADA RD 93021 378-6305
Cary Dritz, prin.
Chaparral MS 4-00100
280 POINDEXTER AVE 93021 378-6302
Michael Berger, prin.

Moorpark College 6-CC
7075 CAMPUS RD 93021 378-1400

Moraga, AC 510, PC 7, Contra Costa
Acalanes UNHSD
Supt. — See Lafayette
Campolindo HS, 300 MORAGA RD 94556 3-00011
Tom Ehrhorn, prin. 376-5986

Moraga ESD, PO BOX 158 94556 4-11100
John Cooley, supt. 376-5943
IS, 1010 CAMINO PABLO 94556 3-00100
William Walters, prin. 376-7206

St. Mary's College of California 5-UC
PO BOX 4267 94575 631-4000

Moreno Valley, AC 909, PC 9, Riverside
Moreno Valley USD 8-11111
13911 PERRIS BLVD 92553 485-5600
Robert Lee, supt.
HS, 23300 COTTONWOOD AVE 92553 4-00011
Dean Olson, prin. 697-4300
Valley View HS, 13135 NASON ST 92555 5-00011
Joe Palomino, prin. 485-5720
Alessandro MS 3-00100
23309 DRACAEA AVE 92553 697-4286
Rhuenette Montle, prin.
Badger Springs MS 3-00100
24750 DELPHINIUM AVE 92553 485-5750
James Dutton, prin.
Canyon Springs Mid. HS 4-00010
23100 MANZANITA AVE 92557 485-5707
Edward Gilliam, prin.
Landmark MS 4-00100
15261 LEGENDARY DR 92555 485-5905
Patrick Kelleher, prin.
Mountain View MS 3-00100
13130 MORRISON ST 92555 485-5740
Mary Bruce, prin.
Palm MS, 11900 SLAWSON AVE 92557 3-00100
David Kuzmich, prin. 485-5920
Sunnymead MS 3-00100
12875 HEACOCK ST 92553 697-4260
Teri Atkinson, prin.
Vista Heights MS 4-00100
23049 OLD LAKE DR 92557 485-5816
Ernie Raugewitz, prin.

Val Verde SD
Supt. — See Perris
Rancho Verde HS   4-00011
  17750 LASSELLE ST 92551   485-6200
  Gretchen Wheelwright, prin.
Vista Verde MS   3-00100
  25777 KRAMERIA ST 92551   485-6270
  Alex Aitcheson, prin.

Morgan Hill, AC 408, PC 7, Santa Clara
Morgan Hill USD   6-11111
  15600 CONCORD CIR 95037   779-5272
  H. Crow, supt.
Live Oak SHS, 1505 E MAIN AVE 95037   4-00001
  John Almond, prin.   779-5210
Britton MS, 80 W CENTRAL AVE 95037   4-00110
  Barbara Mensch, prin.   779-5200
Other Schools – See San Jose

Morro Bay, AC 805, PC 6, San Luis Obispo
San Luis Coastal USD
Supt. — See San Luis Obispo
HS, 235 ATASCADERO RD 93442   3-00011
  Gregory Halfman, prin.   772-7327

Moss Landing, AC 408, PC 3, Monterey
North Monterey County USD   5-11111
  PO BOX 49 95039   633-4286
  Leo St. John, supt.
Other Schools – See Castroville, Watsonville

Mountain Center, AC 909, PC 99, Riverside

Morning Sky Residential School   HND
  PO BOX 408 92561

Mountain View, AC 415, PC 8, Santa Clara
Mountain View-Los Altos UNHSD   5-00011
  1299 BRYANT AVE 94040   940-4650
  Donald Phillips, supt.
HS, 3535 TRUMAN AVE 94040   4-00011
  Steve Hope, prin.   940-4600
Other Schools – See Los Altos

Mountain View ESD, 220 VIEW ST 94041   5-11100
  Patricia Bubenik, supt.   968-6565
Graham MS, 220 VIEW ST 94041   3-00100
  Gay Krause, prin.   965-9292

Whisman ESD   4-11100
  750 SAN PIERRE WAY # A 94043   903-6945
  Eve Bressler, supt.
Crittenden MS, 1701 ROCK ST 94043   3-01100
  James Lianides, prin.   903-6945

El Camino Hospital   HSP
  2500 GRANT RD 94040   968-8111
Mountain View Academy   2-00011
  360 S SHORELINE BLVD 94041   967-2324
  Milton Wheeler, prin.
St. Francis HS   4-00011
  1885 MIRAMONTE AVE 94040   968-1213
  James Bowler, prin.

Mount Shasta, AC 916, PC 5, Siskiyou
Mt. Shasta UNSD, 501 CEDAR ST 96067   4-11100
  Wilber Hawkins, supt.   926-6007
Sisson MS, 601 E ALMA ST 96067   2-01100
  Knute Momberg, prin.   926-3846

Siskiyou UNHSD   3-00011
  624 EVERITT MEMORIAL HWY 96067   926-3006
  Douglas DeBortoli, supt.
HS   2-00011
  710 EVERITT MEMORIAL HWY 96067   926-2614
  Gregg Gunkel, prin.
Other Schools – See Happy Camp, McCloud, Weed

Murrieta, AC 909, PC 2, Riverside
Murrieta Valley USD   5-11111
  26396 BECKMAN CT 92562   696-1600
  Tate Parker, supt.
Murrieta Valley HS   4-00011
  24105 WASHINGTON AVE 92562   696-1408
  Shelley Weston, prin.
Shivela Middle   4-00100
  24515 LINCOLN AVE 92562   696-1406
  Frank Passarella, prin.

Napa, AC 707, PC 8, Napa
Napa Valley USD   7-11111
  2425 JEFFERSON ST 94558   253-3511
  John Gyves, supt.
HS, 2475 JEFFERSON ST 94558   4-00011
  Lars Christensen, prin.   253-3711
Temescal HS   2-00011
  2447 OLD SONOMA RD 94558   253-3791
  Darlene Lance, prin.
Vintage HS, 1375 TROWER AVE 94558   4-00011
  (—), prin.   253-3601
Redwood MS, 3600 OXFORD ST 94558   4-00100
  Harrall Miller, prin.   253-3415
Silverado MS   4-00100
  1133 COOMBSVILLE RD 94558   253-3688
  David Wildman, prin.

Justin-Siena HS, 4026 MAHER ST 94558   2-00011
  Sr. Marion Irvine, prin.   255-0950
Napa Valley College   6-CC
  2277 NAPA VALLEJO HWY 94558   253-3000

National City, AC 619, PC 8, San Diego
Sweetwater UNHSD
Supt. — See Chula Vista

Sweetwater HS   4-00011
  2900 HIGHLAND AVE 91950   691-5730
  Louise Bach-Phipps, prin.
Granger JHS, 2101 GRANGER AVE 91950   4-00110
  Michael Johnson, prin.   691-5700
MS, 1701 D AVE 91950   3-00100
  Ernest Anastos, prin.   691-5710

Cabot College   3-CS
  41 E 12TH ST 91950   474-8017
California College for Health Sciences   2-CC
  222 W 24TH ST 91950   477-4800
San Diego Academy   3-11111
  2700 E 4TH ST 91950   267-9550
  Larry Kromann, prin.
Southport Christian Academy   2-11111
  142 E 16TH ST 91950   474-2834
  Ken Nichols, prin.

Needles, AC 619, PC 6, San Bernardino
Needles USD, 1900 ERIN DR 92363   4-11111
  Dennis Murray, supt.   326-3891
HS, 1900 ERIN DR 92363   2-00011
  Terry Brace, prin.   326-2191
MS, 1900 ERIN DR 92363   2-00100
  Joseph Brady, prin.   326-3895

Nevada City, AC 916, PC 5, Nevada
Nevada City SD   4-11100
  215 WASHINGTON ST 95959   265-1820
  Dennis Dobbs, supt.
Seven Hills IS, 700 HOOVER LN 95959   3-00100
  Lark Zachary, prin.   265-1840

Twin Ridges ESD   2-11100
  18847 OAK TREE RD 95959   292-4221
  Paul Alderete, supt.
Other Schools – See North San Juan

Woolman S, 13075 WOOLMAN LN 95959   1-00011
  Ted Menmuir, prin.   273-3183

Newark, AC 510, PC 8, Alameda
Newark USD, 5715 MUSICK AVE 94560   6-11111
  Gerald Trout, supt.   794-2141
Newark Memorial HS   4-00011
  39375 CEDAR BLVD 94560   794-2145
  Patricia Christa, prin.
JHS, 6201 LAFAYETTE AVE 94560   3-00100
  Gene Savage, prin.   794-2062

Newbury Park, AC 805, PC see Thousand Oaks
Conejo Valley USD
Supt. — See Thousand Oaks
HS, 456 N REINO RD 91320   4-00011
  Charles Eklund, prin.   498-3676
Sequoia IS, 2855 BORCHARD RD 91320   3-00100
  Max Beaman, prin.   498-3617

Newbury Park Adventist Academy   2-00011
  180 ACADEMY DR 91320   498-2191
  Harold Crook, prin.

New Cuyama, AC 805, PC 3, Santa Barbara
Cuyama JUSD, PO BOX 271 93254   2-11111
  Rowland King, supt.   766-2482
Cuyama Valley HS   1-00011
  PO BOX 271 93254   766-2293
  Ronald Barba, prin.

Newhall, AC 805, PC see Santa Clarita
William S. Hart UNHSD
Supt. — See Santa Clarita
Hart HS, 24825 NEWHALL AVE 91321   4-00011
  Laurence Strauss, prin.   259-7575
Placerita JHS   4-00100
  25015 NEWHALL AVE 91321   259-1551
  James Tanner, prin.

Master's College   3-UC
  PO BOX 221450 91322   259-3540

Newman, AC 209, PC 5, Stanislaus
Newman-Crows Landing USD   4-11111
  890 MAIN ST 95360   862-2933
  Ed Williams, supt.
Orestimba HS, 707 HARDIN RD 95360   2-00011
  (—), prin.   862-2916
Yolo IS, 907 R ST 95360   2-00100
  Francisco Santana, prin.   862-2984

Newport Beach, AC 714, PC 8, Orange
Newport-Mesa USD   7-11111
  PO BOX 1368 92659   760-3200
  Mac Bernd, supt.
Newport Harbor HS   4-00011
  PO BOX 1368 92659   760-3310
  Steve Pavich, prin.
Corona Del Mar JSHS   3-00111
  PO BOX 1368 92659   760-3320
  Tom Jacobson, prin.
Ensign IS, PO BOX 1368 92659   3-00100
  Scott Paulsen, prin.   760-3440
Other Schools – See Costa Mesa

Interior Designers Institute   2-UC
  1061 CAMELBACK ST 92660   675-4451
Platt College   2-CS
  3901 MACARTHUR BLVD STE 101 92660
     833-2300
Professional Career Centers   2-CS
  4041 MACARTHUR BLVD STE 210 92660

Nicolaus, AC 916, PC 2, Sutter
East Nicolaus JUNHSD   2-00011
  2454 NICOLAUS AVE 95659   656-2255
  Odette Ebersole, supt.
East Nicolaus HS   2-00011
  2454 NICOLAUS AVE 95659   656-2255
  Odette Ebersole, prin.

Norco, AC 909, PC 7, Riverside
Corona-Norco USD   7-11111
  2820 CLARK AVE 91760   736-5000
  Phillistine Rondo, supt.
HS, 2820 CLARK AVE 91760   4-00011
  Maggie Little, prin.   736-3241
IS, 2820 CLARK AVE 91760   3-00100
  Frank Ware, prin.   736-3206
Other Schools – See Corona

North Edwards, AC 619, PC 4, Kern
Muroc JUSD, PO BOX 833 93523   5-11111
  Gary Rice, supt.   769-4821
HS, PO BOX 833 93523   1-00011
  William Appleton, prin.   769-4179
Other Schools – See Boron, Edwards

North Highlands, AC 916, PC 8, Sacramento
Grant JUNHSD
Supt. — See Sacramento
Highlands HS, 6601 GUTHRIE ST 95660   4-00011
  Constance Farias, prin.   263-6485
Julio JHS, 6444 WALERGA RD 95660   3-00100
  Jeanne Akin, prin.   263-6477

North Hollywood, AC 818, PC see Los Angeles
Los Angeles USD
Supt. — See Los Angeles
SHS, 5231 COLFAX AVE 91601   4-00001
  Catherine Lum, prin.   769-8510
Madison JHS, 13000 HART ST 91605   4-00110
  Joanna Kunes, prin.   765-7796
Reed JHS, 4525 IRVINE AVE 91602   4-00110
  Lawrence Tash, prin.   762-0691

Belmont College Preparatory S   2-00111
  8234 AGNES AVE 91605   902-9831
  William Hanrahan, prin.
California Family Study Center   2-UC
  5433 LAUREL CANYON BLVD 91607   509-5959
Campbell Hall S   3-11111
  4533 LAUREL CANYON BLVD 91607   980-7280
  Rev. Thomas Clark, prin.
Concorde Career Institute   4-CS
  4150 LANKERSHIM BLVD 91602   766-8151
Harvard-Westlake S   4-00111
  3700 COLDWATER CANYON AVE 91604
  Thomas Hudnut, prin.   980-6692
Modern Technology School of X-Ray   2-CS
  6180 LAUREL CANYON BLVD # 1 91606
     763-2563
Oakwood S   2-11111
  11600 MAGNOLIA BLVD 91601   766-5177
  James Astman, prin.
Valley Torah HS   2-00011
  12003 RIVERSIDE DR 91607   984-1805
  Rabbi Stulberger, prin.

Northridge, AC 818, PC see Los Angeles
Los Angeles USD
Supt. — See Los Angeles
Holmes MS   3-00100
  9351 PASO ROBLES AVE 91325   886-3404
  Aaron Twombly, prin.
Nobel JHS, 9950 TAMPA AVE 91324   4-00100
  Ruth Jackson, prin.   349-4200
JHS, 17960 CHASE ST 91325   4-00100
  Beryl Ward, prin.   885-8253

California State University   7-UC
  18111 NORDHOFF ST 91330   885-1200
Highland Hall S   2-11111
  17100 SUPERIOR ST 91325   349-1394
  Erick Bluske, prin.
Phillips Junior College   2-UC
  8520 BALBOA BLVD 91325   895-2220
San Fernando Valley SDA Academy   2-11111
  17601 LASSEN ST 91325   349-1373
  Ronald Dasher, prin.

North San Juan, AC 916, PC 2, Nevada
Sierra-Plumas JUSD
Supt. — See Downieville
Pliocene Ridge JSHS   1-00011
  1999 RIDGE RD 95960   288-3247
  Debra Sandoval, prin.

Twin Ridges ESD
Supt. — See Nevada City
Grizzly Hill MS, PO BOX 529 95960   2-01100
  Brian Buckley, prin.   265-9052

Norwalk, AC 310, PC 8, Los Angeles
Little Lake City ESD
Supt. — See Santa Fe Springs
Lakeside JHS, 11000 KENNEY ST 90650   2-00100
  Sandra Sanders, prin.   868-9422

Norwalk-La Mirada USD   7-11111
  12820 PIONEER BLVD 90650   868-0431
  Robert Aguilar, supt.
Glenn HS   4-00011
  13520 SHOEMAKER AVE 90650   868-0431
  Bernard Samuels, prin.
HS, 11356 LEFFINGWELL RD 90650   4-00011
  Dwight Cosby, prin.   868-0431

Hargitt MS, 12940 FOSTER RD 90650 | 3-00100
Phyllis Pringle, prin. | 864-2593
Lampton MS | 3-00100
14716 ELMCROFT AVE 90650 | 868-0865
Edna Tobias, prin.
Waite MS | 3-00100
14320 NORWALK BLVD 90650 | 921-7981
Elaine Medina, prin.
Other Schools – See La Mirada

Baptist Christian S | 2-11111
12226 ALONDRA BLVD 90650 | 926-5541
Rev. Terry La Framboise, prin.
Cerritos College | 7-CC
11110 ALONDRA BLVD 90650 | 860-2451
Keystone Academy | 2-11111
14515 PIONEER BLVD 90650 | 929-1616
Philip Troutt, prin.
Pioneer Baptist S | 2-11111
11717 PIONEER BLVD 90650 | 863-5817
Gerald Mitchell, prin.

Novato, AC 415, PC 8, Marin
Novato USD, 1015 7TH ST 94945 | 6-11111
Joel Montero, supt. | 897-4201
HS, 625 ARTHUR ST 94947 | 4-00011
Jerry Kenney, prin. | 898-2125
San Marin HS, 15 SAN MARIN DR 94945 | 3-00011
Virginia Stewart, prin. | 898-2121
Hill MS, 720 DIABLO AVE 94947 | 3-00100
Mike Watenpaugh, prin. | 899-9300
San Jose MS, 1000 SUNSET PKY 94949 | 3-00100
Nancy Cooley, prin. | 883-7831
Sinaloa MS, 2045 VINEYARD RD 94947 | 3-00100
Richard Gerhardt, prin. | 897-2111

College of Marin | 4-CC
1800 IGNACIO BLVD 94949 | 883-2211

Nuevo, AC 909, PC 5, Riverside
Nuview UNSD | 4-11100
29780 LAKEVIEW AVE 92567 | 928-0066
Marcile Wright, supt.
Mountain Shadows MS | 2-00100
30401 RESERVOIR AVE 92567 | 928-3836
Vincent Ponce, prin.

Oakdale, AC 209, PC 7, Stanislaus
Oakdale JUNHSD, 168 S 3RD AVE 95361 | 4-00011
John Casey, supt. | 848-4884
HS, 739 W G ST 95361 | 4-00011
Steven Petsche, prin. | 847-3007
Other Schools – See Riverbank

Oakdale UNESD, 1235 E D ST 95361 | 5-11100
Kenneth Kennedy, supt. | 847-4226
JHS, 400 S MAAG AVE 95361 | 3-00100
Ken Meil, prin. | 847-2294

Oakhurst, AC 209, PC 5, Madera
Bass Lake SD, PO BOX 395 93644 | 4-11100
Angelo Pizelo, supt. | 683-6045
Oak Creek IS | 2-00100
40094 INDIAN SPRINGS RD 93644 | 683-6819
Sam Garamendi, prin.

Yosemite UNHSD | 4-00011
50200 ROAD 427 93644 | 683-8801
Angelo Pizelo, supt.
Yosemite HS | 3-00011
50200 ROAD 427 93644 | 683-4667
Bob Labelle, prin.

Oakland, AC 510, PC 10, Alameda
Oakland USD, 1025 2ND AVE 94606 | 8-11111
Richard Mesa, supt. | 836-8100
Fremont SHS | 4-00001
4610 FOOTHILL BLVD 94601 | 261-3240
Robert Duran, prin.
SHS, 1023 MACARTHUR BLVD 94610 | 4-00001
Joanne Grimm, prin. | 451-1208
Skyline SHS | 4-00001
12250 SKYLINE BLVD 94619 | 531-9161
Thomas Lorch, prin.
Castlemont HS | 4-00011
8601 MACARTHUR BLVD 94605 | 635-8600
Ellen Posey, prin.
Dewey HS, 3709 E 12TH ST 94601 | 2-00011
Charlene Lewis, prin. | 534-1721
McClymonds HS | 3-00011
2607 MYRTLE ST 94607 | 893-6569
Oliver Chambers, prin.
Oakland Technical HS | 4-00011
4351 BROADWAY 94611 | 658-5300
W. Ovid, prin.
Street Academy HS, 417 29TH ST 94609 | 2-00011
Patricia Williams-Myrick, prin. | 763-8845
Brewer JHS, 3748 13TH AVE 94610 | 3-00100
Ronald Solis, prin. | 530-4550
Carter MS, 4521 WEBSTER ST 94609 | 2-00100
George Jasper, prin. | 654-8936
Claremont MS | 3-00100
5750 COLLEGE AVE 94618 | 652-3931
Gail Hojo, prin.
Elmhurst MS, 1800 98TH AVE 94603 | 3-00100
Dorothy Spann, prin. | 562-5755
Foster MS, 2850 WEST ST 94608 | 2-01100
Mildred Gardner, prin. | 763-1178
Frick JHS, 2845 64TH AVE 94605 | 3-00110
Murphy Taylor, prin. | 562-6565
Harte JHS, 3700 COOLIDGE AVE 94602 | 4-00110
Mary Hamadeh, prin. | 482-5825

Havenscort JHS, 1390 66TH AVE 94621 | 3-00110
Clara Daniels, prin. | 562-7911
King Estates JHS | 3-00110
8251 FONTAINE ST 94605 | 569-1596
Lynn Dodd, prin.
Lowell MS, 991 14TH ST 94607 | 2-00100
Rosalyn Upshaw, prin. | 832-1436
Madison MS | 2-00100
400 CAPISTRANO DR 94603 | 568-5889
Rosa James, prin.
Montera JHS, 5555 ASCOT DR 94611 | 3-00110
Richard Adams, prin. | 531-0626
Roosevelt JHS, 1926 19TH AVE 94606 | 4-00110
Roberto Montez, prin. | 261-8516
Simmons JHS, 2101 35TH AVE 94601 | 4-00110
Sandra Shapiro, prin. | 534-0610
Westlake MS, 2629 HARRISON ST 94612 | 3-00110
DeLett Paul, prin. | 893-1045

Bishop O'Dowd HS | 4-00011
9500 STEARNS AVE 94605 | 577-9100
Fr. Ranalletti, prin.
California College of Arts & Crafts | 3-UC
5212 BROADWAY 94618 | 653-6522
College Preparatory S | 2-00011
6100 BROADWAY 94618 | 652-0111
Clinton Wilkins, prin.
Golden Gate Academy | 2-11111
3800 MOUNTAIN BLVD 94619 | 531-0110
Joyce Lee, prin.
Head-Royce S | 3-11111
4315 LINCOLN AVE 94602 | 531-1300
Paul Chapman, prin.
Heald Business College | 2-CC
1000 BROADWAY 94607 | 444-0201
Holy Names College | 3-UC
3500 MOUNTAIN BLVD 94619 | 436-1000
Holy Names HS | 2-00011
4660 HARBORD DR 94618 | 450-1110
Sr. Adele Hancock, prin.
Laney College | 6-CC
900 FALLON ST 94607 | 834-5740
Merritt College | 6-CC
12500 CAMPUS DR 94619 | 531-4911
Mills College | 3-UC
5000 MACARTHUR BLVD 94613 | 430-2255
NEC-Bryman Campus | 3-CS
1600 BROADWAY STE 201 94612 | 763-0800
Oakland College of Court Reporting | 2-CS
449 15TH ST STE 2 94612 | 287-5290
Patten Academy | 2-11111
2433 COOLIDGE AVE 94601 | 533-8300
Bebe Patten, prin.
Patten College | 3-UC
2433 COOLIDGE AVE 94601 | 533-8300
St. Andrew Mission Baptist S | 2-11111
2624 WEST ST 94612 | 465-8023
Robeth Lacy, prin.
St. Elizabeth HS, 1530 34TH AVE 94601 | 2-00011
Matilda Ignacio, prin. | 532-8947
Samuel Merritt College | 2-UC
370 HAWTHORNE AVE 94609 | 420-6011
Sierra Academy of Aeronautics | 1-CS
PO BOX 2429 94614 | 568-6100

Oakley, AC 510, PC 7, Contra Costa
Oakley UNESD, PO BOX 7 94561 | 5-11100
Frank Hengel, supt. | 625-0700
O'Hara Park MS, PO BOX 7 94561 | 3-00100
Glen Scrimger, prin. | 625-5060

Oak Park, AC 818, PC 4, Ventura
Oak Park USD, 5801 CONIFER ST 91301 | 4-11111
Marilyn Lippiatt, supt. | 707-7900
HS, 899 KANAN RD 91301 | 3-00011
Jeff Chancer, prin. | 707-7926
Medea Creek MS | 2-00100
1002 DOUBLETREE RD 91301 | 707-7922
Laurel Ford, prin.

Occidental, AC 707, PC 2, Sonoma
Harmony UNESD, PO BOX 279 95465 | 3-11100
Robert Maddux, supt. | 823-6220
Salmon Creek MS | 2-00100
1935 BOHEMIAN HWY 95465 | 874-1250
Paul Eelkema, prin.

Oceanside, AC 619, PC 9, San Diego
Oceanside City USD | 7-11111
2111 MISSION AVE 92054 | 757-2560
Steven Speach, supt.
El Camino HS | 4-00011
400 RANCHO DEL ORO DR 92057 | 757-8550
Mary Urelius, prin.
HS, 1ST & HORNE 92054 | 4-00011
Mary Gleisberg, prin. | 722-8201
Jefferson JHS, 823 ACACIA AVE 92054 | 4-00100
Linda Goldstein, prin. | 757-6060
Lincoln JHS | 4-00100
2000 CALIFORNIA ST 92054 | 757-0153
Pat Barnes, prin.

Vista USD
Supt. — See Vista
Roosevelt MS | 4-00100
850 SAGEWOOD DR 92057 | 726-8003
Vince Jewell, prin.

El Dorado College | 3-CS
2204 S EL CMNO REAL STE 104 92054 |
| 433-3660

Futures HS | 2-00111
2204 S EL CAMINO REAL 92054 | 721-7577
Karen Bishop, prin.
Mira Costa College | 6-CC
1 BARNARD DR 92056 | 757-2121

Ojai, AC 805, PC 6, Ventura
Ojai USD, PO BOX 878 93024 | 5-11111
Andrew Smidt, supt. | 640-4300
Nordhoff HS | 4-00011
1401 MARICOPA HWY 93023 | 640-4343
Michael Maez, prin.
Matilija JHS, 703 EL PASEO RD 93023 | 3-00100
James Berube, prin. | 640-4355

Happy Valley S, PO BOX 850 93024 | 1-00011
Dennis Rice, prin. | 646-4343
Oak Grove S, 220 W LOMITA AVE 93023 | 2-11111
Karen Hesli, prin. | 646-8236
Ojai Valley S, 723 EL PASEO RD 93023 | 2-11111
Michael Hermes, prin. | 646-1423
Thacher S, 5025 THACHER RD 93023 | 2-00011
Michael Mulligan, prin. | 646-4377
Villanova Prep S | 2-00011
12096 N VENTURA AVE 93023 | 646-1464
Leo Molitor, prin.

Olivehurst, AC 916, PC 6, Yuba
Marysville JUSD
Supt. — See Marysville
Lindhurst HS, 4446 OLIVE AVE 95961 | 4-00011
DeAnn Kamilos, prin. | 741-6150
Yuba Gardens IS, 1964 11TH AVE 95961 | 3-00100
(—), prin. | 741-6194

Olympic Valley, AC 916, PC 3, Placer

Squaw Valley Academy | 2-00011
PO BOX 2667 96146 | 583-1558
Donald Rees, prin.

Ontario, AC 909, PC 9, San Bernardino
Chaffey JUNHSD, 211 W 5TH ST 91762 | 7-00011
Dean Smothers, supt. | 988-8511
Chaffey HS, 1245 N EUCLID AVE 91762 | 5-00011
Glen England, prin. | 988-5560
HS, 901 W FRANCIS ST 91762 | 4-00011
David Martin, prin. | 988-7411
Other Schools – See Alta Loma, Etiwanda, Montclair,
Rancho Cucamonga

Chino USD
Supt. — See Chino
Woodcrest JHS | 2-00100
2725 S CAMPUS AVE 91761 | 923-3455
Adair Sattarfield, prin.

Mountain View ESD | 5-11100
2947A S TURNER AVE 91761 | 947-2992
Robert Cosgrove, supt.
Yokley JHS, 2947 S TURNER AVE 91761 | 3-00100
Bruce Perry, prin. | 947-6774

Ontario-Montclair ESD | 7-11100
950 W D ST 91762 – Frank Cosca, supt. | 983-9501
De Anza MS | 3-00100
1450 S SULTANA AVE 91761 | 986-8577
Ken Gabel, prin.
Imperial MS, 1450 E G ST 91764 | 3-00100
Sam Brown, prin. | 986-5838
Vina Danks MS, 1020 N VINE AVE 91762 | 3-00100
Jeanette Troesh, prin. | 983-2691
Other Schools – See Montclair

International Air Academy | 3-CS
2980 INLAND EMPIRE BLVD 91764 | 989-5222
Nova Institute of Health Technology | 1-CS
520 N EUCLID AVE 91762 | 984-5027
Ontario Christian HS | 2-00011
931 W PHILADELPHIA ST 91762 | 984-1756
Michael Van Hoven, prin.
Platt College | 2-CS
2920 INLAND EMPIRE BLVD # 1 91764 |
| 989-1187

Orange, AC 714, PC 9, Orange
Orange USD, PO BOX 11022 92668 | 8-11111
Marilyn Corey, supt. | 997-6100
El Modena HS, 3920 E SPRING ST 92669 | 4-00011
Nancy Murray, prin. | 997-6331
HS, 525 N SHAFFER ST 92667 | 4-00011
Robert Lewis, prin. | 997-6211
Portola MS, 270 N PALM DR 92668 | 3-00100
Dave Gunderson, prin. | 997-6361
Santiago MS | 3-00100
515 N RANCHO SANTIAGO BLVD 92669 |
Mary Ann Owsley, prin. | 997-6366
Yorba MS, 935 N CAMBRIDGE ST 92667 | 3-00100
Dennis Miller, prin. | 997-6161
Other Schools – See Anaheim, Villa Park

Chapman University | 6-UC
333 N GLASSELL ST 92666 | 997-6611
DTI Career Institute | 1-CS
1937 W CHAPMAN AVE STE 100 92668 |
| 937-3989
El Dorado S for the Gifted | 2-11111
4100 E WALNUT AVE 92669 | 633-4774
Glory Ludwick, prin.
Lutheran HS | 3-00011
2222 N SANTIAGO BLVD 92667 | 998-5151
Kenneth Ellwein, prin.

MTI College 1-CS
  2011 W CHAPMAN AVE STE 100 92668
      385-1132
St. Joseph Hospital HSP
  1100 W STEWART DR 92668 771-8111
S California Christian HS 2-00111
  8612 ORANGE OLIVE RD 92665 974-7766
  James Allen, prin.
University of California-Irvine Med. Ctr 2-UC
  101 CITY BLVD W 92668
West Coast University 3-UC
  550 S MAIN ST 92668

Orange Cove, AC 209, PC 6, Fresno
Kings Canyon JUSD
  Supt. — See Reedley
Citrus MS, 222 4TH ST 93646 2-00100
  Roger Trujillo, prin. 626-4541

Orangevale, AC 916, PC 8, Sacramento
San Juan USD
  Supt. — See Carmichael
Casa Roble Fundamental HS 4-00011
  9151 OAK AVE 95662 971-5452
  Jane Wise, prin.
Carnegie MS, 5820 ILLINOIS AVE 95662 4-00100
  Dave Ferencik, prin. 971-5623
Pasteur MS, 8935 ELM AVE 95662 3-00100
  Dennis Haggard, prin. 971-7891

Orcutt, AC 805, PC 4, Santa Barbara
Orcutt UNESD, PO BOX 2310 93457 5-11100
  Jack Garvin, supt. 937-6345
JHS, PO BOX 2310 93457 3-00100
  Ralph Tilton, prin. 937-6622
Other Schools – See Santa Maria

Orinda, AC 510, PC 7, Contra Costa
Acalanes UNHSD
  Supt. — See Lafayette
Miramonte HS 3-00011
  750 MORAGA WAY 94563 376-4423
  Robert Gilbert, prin.

Orinda UNESD, 8 ALTARINDA RD 94563 4-11100
  Richard Winefield, supt. 254-4901
IS, 80 IVY DR 94563 3-00100
  Lorraine Ritchie, prin. 376-4402

John F. Kennedy University 4-UC
  12 ALTARINDA RD 94563 254-0200
North Bay Orinda S 2-00111
  350 CAMINO PABLO 94563 254-7553
  Ronald Graydon, prin.

Orland, AC 916, PC 6, Glenn
Orland JSD, 1320 6TH ST 95963 4-11111
  Leeds Lacy, supt. 865-1200
HS, 1320 6TH ST 95963 3-00011
  Ed Changus, prin. 865-1210
Price IS, 1320 6TH ST 95963 2-00100
  David Fase, prin. 865-1225

Valley Oak Christian Academy 2-11111
  RR 3 BOX 3452A 95963 865-7173
  Vicki Stevens, prin.

Orosi, AC 209, PC 6, Tulare
Cutler-Orosi USD 5-11111
  41855 ROAD 128 93647 528-4763
  Eddie Ikard, supt.
HS, 41855 ROAD 128 93647 3-00011
  Tom Giampietro, prin. 528-4731
El Monte ES, 41465 ROAD 127 93647 3-10100
  Marvin Fillmore, prin. 528-3017

Oroville, AC 916, PC 7, Butte
Golden Feather UNESD 2-11100
  11696 NELSON BAR RD 95965 533-3833
  Saddie Nishitani, supt.
Concow MS 2-01100
  11679 NELSON BAR RD 95965 533-6033
  Sam Dresser, prin.

Oroville City ESD, 2795 YARD ST 95966 5-11100
  Donald Remley, supt. 533-0495
Central MS, 2795 YARD ST 95966 3-00100
  Lynne Vincent, prin. 533-0456

Oroville UNHSD 4-00011
  2211 WASHINGTON AVE 95966 538-2300
  John Porter, supt.
Las Plumas HS 4-00011
  2380 LAS PLUMAS AVE 95966 538-2310
  Lola Renda, prin.
HS, 1535 BRIDGE ST 95966 1-00011
  Dennis Doris, prin. 538-2320

Butte College 7-CC
  3536 BUTTE CAMPUS DR 95965 895-2511

Oxnard, AC 805, PC 9, Ventura
Hueneme ESD
  Supt. — See Port Hueneme
Blackstock MS, 701 E BARD RD 93033 3-00100
  Tom Haas, prin. 488-3644
Green MS, 3739 S C ST 93033 3-00100
  Deloris Carn, prin. 986-8750

Ocean View ESD, 2382 ETTING RD 93033 4-11100
  Don Hodes, supt. 488-4441
Ocean View JHS, 4300 OLDS RD 93033 3-00100
  Frank Samuels, prin. 488-6421

Oxnard ESD, 1051 S A ST 93030 7-11100
  Norman Brekke, supt. 487-3918
Fremont IS, 1051 S A ST 93030 4-00100
  Constance Sharp, prin. 487-3918
Haydock IS, 1051 S A ST 93030 4-00100
  Peter Nichols, prin. 487-3918
Nueva Vista IS, 1051 S A ST 93030 1-00100
  Richard Duarte, prin. 487-3918

Oxnard UNHSD, 309 S K ST 93030 7-00011
  Bill Studt, supt. 385-2500
Channel Islands HS 5-00011
  1400 RAIDERS WAY 93033 385-2756
  John Triolo, prin.
Hueneme HS, 500 W BARD RD 93033 4-00011
  Terry Taylor, prin. 385-2651
HS, 937 W 5TH ST 93030 4-00011
  Rick Rezins, prin. 385-2602
Rio Mesa HS, 545 CENTRAL AVE 93030 4-00011
  Eric Ortega, prin. 385-2724
Other Schools – See Camarillo

Rio ESD, 3300 CORTEZ ST 93030 5-11100
  Peter Rogalsky, supt. 485-3111
Rio Del Valle MS 2-00100
  3100 N ROSE AVE 93030 485-3119
  Rafael Perez, prin.

Oxnard College 6-CC
  4000 S ROSE AVE 93033 488-0911
St. John's Hospital HSP
  333 N F ST 93030 988-2500
Santa Clara HS, 2121 SAVIERS RD 93033 3-00011
  Sr. Anne Metcalf, prin. 483-9502
Sawyer College 3-CS
  2101 E GONZALES RD 93030 485-6000
Watterson College Pacific 4-CS
  815 N OXNARD BLVD 93030 656-5566

Pacifica, AC 415, PC 8, San Mateo
Jefferson UNHSD
  Supt. — See Daly City
Oceana HS, 401 PALOMA AVE 94044 2-00011
  Lois Jones, prin. 355-4131
Terra Nova HS 4-00011
  1450 TERRA NOVA BLVD 94044 359-3961
  Andrew McCarthy, prin.

Laguna Salada UNESD 5-11100
  375 REINA DEL MAR AVE 94044 359-1641
  Marc Liebman, supt.
Ortega MS 3-00100
  1283 TERRA NOVA BLVD 94044 359-3941
  Kitty Mindel, prin.
Other Schools – See San Bruno

Alma Heights Christian Academy 2-11111
  1030 LINDA MAR BLVD 94044 355-1935
  Joseph Gross, prin.

Pacific Grove, AC 408, PC 7, Monterey
Pacific Grove USD 4-11111
  555 SINEX AVE 93950 646-6520
  Joseph Jaconette, supt.
HS, 615 SUNSET DR 93950 3-00011
  Karl Black, prin. 646-6590
MS, 835 FOREST AVE 93950 2-00100
  Chris Whitmore, prin. 646-6566

Stanford University 3-UC
  HOPKINS MARINE STATION 93950

Pacific Palisades, AC 310, PC see Los Angeles
Los Angeles USD
  Supt. — See Los Angeles
Palisades HS, 15777 BOWDOIN ST 90272 4-00011
  Merle Price, prin. 454-0611

Pacoima, AC 818, PC see Los Angeles
Los Angeles USD
  Supt. — See Los Angeles
MacLay JHS, 12540 PIERCE ST 91331 4-00110
  Cecilia Costas, prin. 899-7492
JHS 4-00110
  9919 LAUREL CANYON BLVD 91331 899-5291
  Maria Wale, prin.

Palermo, AC 916, PC 6, Butte
Palermo UNSD 4-11100
  2261 ESPERANZA AVE 95968 533-4842
  Nancy Barnes, supt.
MS, 7350 BULLDOG WAY 95968 3-01100
  Sybil Janke, prin. 533-4708

Palmdale, AC 805, PC 8, Los Angeles
Antelope Valley UNHSD
  Supt. — See Lancaster
Highland HS, 39055 25TH ST W 93551 4-00011
  O. Clark, prin. 538-0304
HS, 2137 E AVENUE R 93550 5-00011
  Mary Bowman, prin. 273-3181

Palmdale ESD, 39139 10TH ST E 93550 7-11100
  Forrest McElroy, supt. 947-7191
Juniper IS 4-00100
  39066A PALM TREE WAY 93551 947-0181
  Esmeralda Mondragon, prin.
Mesa IS, 3243 E AVENUE R8 93550 4-00100
  David Millen, prin. 947-0188

Westside UNESD
  Supt. — See Lancaster
Hillview MS, 40525 PEONZA LN 93551 3-00100
  Paul Brunner, prin. 722-9993

Wilsona SD, 18050 E AVENUE O 93591 4-11100
  Chester Caldeira, supt. 264-1111
Other Schools – See Lancaster

Palm Desert, AC 619, PC 7, Riverside
Desert Sands USD
  Supt. — See Indio
HS, 43570 PHYLLIS JACKSON LN 92260 4-00011
  Raymond Hill, prin. 862-4300
MS, 74200 RUTLEDGE WAY 92260 4-00100
  Margaret Steen, prin. 862-4340

College of the Desert 7-CC
  43500 MONTEREY AVE 92260 346-8041
Institute Business & Medical Technology 2-CS
  75110 SAINT CHARLES PL # 10 92211
      776-5873

Palm Springs, AC 619, PC 8, Riverside
Palm Springs USD 7-11111
  333 S FARRELL DR 92262 327-1581
  William Diedrich, supt.
HS, 2248 E RAMON RD 92264 4-00011
  Richard Williams, prin. 778-0406
Cree MS, 1011 E VISTA CHINO 92262 4-00100
  Nancy Gravette, prin. 327-8471
Other Schools – See Cathedral City

Palo Alto, AC 415, PC 8, Santa Clara
Palo Alto USD 6-11111
  25 CHURCHILL AVE 94306 329-3700
  James Brown, supt.
Gunn HS, 780 ARASTRADERO RD 94306 4-00011
  Christopher Rich, prin. 354-8200
HS, 50 EMBARCADERO RD 94301 4-00011
  Sandra Pearson, prin. 329-3710
Jordan MS 3-00100
  750 N CALIFORNIA AVE 94303 494-8120
  Robert Alvares, prin.
Stanford MS, 480 E MEADOW DR 94306 3-00100
  Joy Addison, prin. 856-1713

Castilleja S, 1310 BRYANT ST 94301 2-00111
  James McManus, prin. 328-3160
Mid-Peninsula HS 2-00111
  870 N CALIFORNIA AVE 94303 493-5910
  Philip Bliss, prin.
Pacific Graduate School of Psychology 2-UC
  935 E MEADOW DR 94303 494-7477

Palo Cedro, AC 916, PC 4, Shasta
Junction ESD 3-11100
  9087 DESCHUTES RD 96073 547-3274
  David Hutt, supt.
Junction IS, 9019 DESCHUTES RD 96073 2-00100
  Tod Prouty, prin. 547-5494

Country Christian ES 2-11111
  21945 OLD FORTY FOUR DR 96073 547-5481
  Michael Neumeister, prin.

Palos Verdes Estates, AC 310, PC 7, Los Angeles
Palos Verdes Peninsula USD 6-11111
  3801 VIA LA SELVA 90274 378-9966
  Michael Caston, supt.
IS, 600 CLOYDEN RD 90274 4-00100
  Olivia LaBouff, prin. 378-8471
Other Schools – See Rancho Palos Verdes, Rolling Hills Estates

Rolling Hills Prep S 2-00111
  300 PASEO DEL MAR 90274 791-1101
  Keith Costello, prin.

Palos Verdes Peninsula, AC 310, PC see Rolling Hills Estates

Chadwick S, 26800 ACADEMY DR 90274 3-11111
  Jeffrey Moredock, prin. 377-1543

Panorama City, AC 818, Los Angeles

Catherine College 3-CS
  8155 VAN NUYS BLVD # 200 91402
      989-9000
Lycee International De Los Angeles 2-11111
  4155 RUSSELL AVE 91412 994-2961
  Monique Mickus, prin.

Paradise, AC 916, PC 8, Butte
Paradise USD 6-11111
  5665 RECREATION DR 95969 872-6400
  Richard Landess, supt.
HS, 5911 MAXWELL DR 95969 4-00011
  Richard Stout, prin. 872-6425
IS, 5657 RECREATION DR 95969 3-00100
  Carolyn Frederick, prin. 872-6465

Paradise Adventist S 2-11111
  5699 ACADEMY DR 95969 877-6540
  Jim Retzer, prin.

Paramount, AC 310, PC 8, Los Angeles
Paramount USD 7-11111
  15110 CALIFORNIA AVE 90723 602-6000
  Michele Lawrence, supt.
HS, 14429 DOWNEY AVE 90723 5-00011
  T. Sanders, prin. 602-6064
Alondra IS, 16200 DOWNEY AVE 90723 4-00100
  Massoud Golji, prin. 602-6930

Clearwater IS
14708 PARAMOUNT BLVD 90723
Ralph Anaya, prin.
4-00100
602-6920

Parlier, AC 209, PC 6, Fresno
Parlier USD
900 S NEWMARK AVE 93648
Fran Markham, supt.
4-11111
646-2731
HS, 900 S NEWMARK AVE 93648
David Austin, prin.
2-00011
646-3571
Martinez JHS
900 S NEWMARK AVE 93648
George Davila, prin.
2-00100
646-3527

Pasadena, AC 818, PC 9, Los Angeles
Pasadena USD
351 S HUDSON AVE 91101
Vera Vignes, supt.
7-11111
795-6981
Blair HS, 1201 S MARENGO AVE 91106
(—), prin.
4-00011
441-2201
Muir HS, 1905 LINCOLN AVE 91103
Gary Talbert, prin.
4-00011
798-7881
HS, 2925 E SIERRA MADRE BLVD 91107
Judy Codding, prin.
4-00011
798-8901
Marshall Fundamental JSHS
990 N ALLEN AVE 91104
Carrie Allen, prin.
4-00111
798-0713
Wilson MS, 300 MADRE ST 91107
(—), prin.
3-00100
449-7390
Other Schools – See Altadena

American Academy of Dramatic Arts/West
2550 PALOMA ST 91107
2-CC
798-0777
Art Center College of Design
1700 LIDA ST 91103
4-UC
396-2373
California Institute of Technology
1201 E CALIFORNIA BLVD 91125
4-UC
800-568-8324
Fuller Theological Seminary
135 N OAKLAND AVE 91182
4-UC
584-5200
Huntington Memorial Hospital
100 CONGRESS ST 91105
HSP
397-5000
Imperial S, 300 W GREEN ST 91129
Joseph Locke, prin.
2-11111
304-6070
La Salle HS
3880 E SIERRA MADRE BLVD 91107
Br. Philip Clarke, prin.
3-00100
351-8951
Living Way Christian Academy
2495 E MOUNTAIN ST 91104
Linda Thompson, prin.
2-11111
791-7295
Mayfield HS
500 BELLEFONTAINE ST 91105
Jeanne Holt, prin.
2-00011
682-2620
Northwest College Medical Dental Assts.
530 E UNION ST 91101
3-CS
796-5815
Pacific Oaks College
5 WESTMORELAND PL 91103
2-UC
397-1300
Pasadena City College
1570 E COLORADO BLVD 91106
7-CC
585-7547
Polytechnic S
1030 E CALIFORNIA BLVD 91106
Alexander Babcock, prin.
3-11111
792-2147
Watterson College
1165 E COLORADO BLVD 91106
4-CS
449-3990
Westridge S, 324 MADELINE DR 91105
Frances Scoble, prin.
2-01111
799-1153

Paso Robles, AC 805, PC 7, San Luis Obispo
Paso Robles SD, PO BOX 7010 93447
Julian Crocker, supt.
6-11111
238-2222
HS, PO BOX 7010 93447
Linda Janzen, prin.
4-00011
237-3333
Flamson MS, PO BOX 7010 93447
Greig Welch, prin.
4-00100
237-3350

Patterson, AC 209, PC 6, Stanislaus
Patterson JUSD, PO BOX 547 95363
Keith Daniel, supt.
5-11111
892-3700
HS, 200 N 7TH ST 95363
Vincent Rucobo, prin.
3-00011
892-3700
JHS, 201 N 9TH ST 95363
Ronald Hartman, prin.
2-00100
892-3700

Pearblossom, AC 805, PC 4, Los Angeles
Keppel UNESD, PO BOX 186 93553
Jean Fuller, supt.
5-11100
944-2155
Other Schools – See Littlerock

Pebble Beach, AC 408, PC 5, Monterey

Stevenson S, PO BOX 657 93953
Joseph Wandke, prin.
3-11111
624-1257

Penn Valley, AC 916, PC 4, Nevada
Pleasant Valley ESD
14685 PLEASANT VALLEY RD 95946
Wayne Padover, supt.
3-11100
432-7311
Pleasant Valley MS
14685 PLEASANT VALLEY RD 95946
William Krapfel, prin.
2-01100
432-7333

Perris, AC 909, PC 7, Riverside
Perris UNHSD, 1151 N A ST 92570
Stephen Teele, supt.
5-00111
943-6369
HS, 175 E NUEVO RD 92571
Carl Phillips, prin.
5-00111
657-2171
Pinacate MS, 1990 S A ST 92570
Harriet Williams, prin.
4-00100
943-6441

Val Verde SD, 975 MORGAN ST 92571
Leona Williams, supt.
6-11111
940-6100
Rivera MS, 21675 MARTIN ST 92570
(—), prin.
3-00100
940-6170
Other Schools – See Moreno Valley

Temple Christian S
745 N PERRIS BLVD 92571
Candy Stevens, prin.
2-11111
657-7326

Pescadero, AC 415, PC 3, San Mateo
La Honda-Pescadero USD
PO BOX 189 94060
Judith Frost, supt.
2-11111
879-0286
HS, 350 BUTANO CUTOFF RD 94060
Roger Yohe, prin.
1-00011
879-0274

Petaluma, AC 707, PC 8, Sonoma
Petaluma SD, 11 5TH ST 94952
Charles Cadman, supt.
6-11111
778-4604
Casa Grande HS
333 CASA GRANDE RD 94954
Michael Leuck, prin.
4-00011
778-4679
HS, 201 FAIR ST 94952
Frank Lynch, prin.
4-00011
778-4652
Kenilworth JHS
998 E WASHINGTON ST 94952
Susan Simon, prin.
3-00100
778-4714
JHS, 700 BANTAM WAY 94952
Gerald Lapinski, prin.
3-00100
778-4724

Columbia Pacific University
148 WILSON HILL RD 94952
1-HMS
800-227-0119
St. Vincent HS, PO BOX 517 94953
Edward Kavanaugh, prin.
2-00011
763-1032
Santa Rosa Junior College
20 KNOSS CONCOURSE 94952
3-CC
795-8038
World College West
PO BOX 481 94953
2-UC
765-4500

Phelan, AC 619, PC 2, San Bernardino
Snowline JUSD
PO BOX 296000 92329
Dan Steele, supt.
6-11111
868-5817
Chaparral HS, PO BOX 296000 92329
Gale George, prin.
1-00011
868-5400
Serrano HS, PO BOX 296000 92329
Bruce Moffitt, prin.
4-00011
868-3222
Pinon Mesa MS
PO BOX 296000 92329
Luke Ontiveros, prin.
4-00100
868-3126

Pico Rivera, AC 310, PC 8, Los Angeles
El Rancho USD
9333 LOCH LOMOND DR 90660
John Sherman, supt.
7-11111
942-1500
El Rancho HS
6501 PASSONS BLVD 90660
Dave Verdugo, prin.
5-00011
801-5295
Burke MS, 8101 ORANGE AVE 90660
Tom Cunningham, prin.
3-00100
801-5059
North Park MS, 4450 DURFEE AVE 90660
Robert Martinez, prin.
3-00100
801-5137
Rivera MS, 7200 CITRONELL AVE 90660
Manford Mainer, prin.
3-00100
801-5088

Armenian Mesrobian S
8110 PARAMOUNT BLVD 90660
David Ghoogasian, prin.
2-11111
723-3181
Southern California College Chiropractic
8420 BEVERLY RD 90660
2-UC
800-452-4476

Piedmont, AC 510, PC 7, Alameda
Piedmont City USD
760 MAGNOLIA AVE 94611
Gail Anderson, supt.
4-11111
420-3600
HS, 800 MAGNOLIA AVE 94611
Pam Bradford, prin.
3-00011
420-3626
MS, 740 MAGNOLIA AVE 94611
John Morrison, prin.
3-00100
420-3660

Pine Valley, AC 619, PC 4, San Diego
Mountain Empire USD
3291 BUCKMAN SPRINGS RD 91962
James Bloch, supt.
4-11111
445-8234
Mountain Empire HS
3305 BUCKMAN SPRINGS RD 91962
Mike Miller, prin.
3-00011
473-8601
Mountain Empire JHS
3305 BUCKMAN SPRINGS RD 91962
Anna Sullivan, prin.
2-00100
473-8601

Pinole, AC 510, PC 7, Contra Costa
West Contra Costa Usd
Supt. — See Richmond
Pinole Valley HS
2900 PINOLE VALLEY RD 94564
Doreen Covell, prin.
4-00011
758-4664
MS, 1575 MANN DR 94564
Shirley Calhoun, prin.
4-00100
724-4042

Pismo Beach, AC 805, PC 6, San Luis Obispo
Lucia Mar USD
Supt. — See Arroyo Grande
Judkins IS
680 WADSWORTH AVE 93449
Bryant Smith, prin.
3-00100
473-4130

Pittsburg, AC 510, PC 8, Contra Costa
Mt. Diablo USD
Supt. — See Concord
Riverview MS, 205 PACIFICA AVE 94565
Perry Julien, prin.
3-00100
458-3216

Pittsburg USD
2000 RAILROAD AVE 94565
Robert Newell, supt.
6-11111
432-4705
HS, 250 SCHOOL ST 94565
Jess Leber, prin.
4-00011
439-8261

Central JHS
1201 STONEMAN AVE 94565
Christopher Franklin, prin.
4-00100
439-9195
Hillview JHS, 333 YOSEMITE DR 94565
Peggy Holt, prin.
3-00100
432-2906

Christian Center S
1210 STONEMAN AVE 94565
Brenda Davidson, prin.
2-11111
439-2552
Los Medanos College
2700 E LELAND RD 94565
6-CC
798-3500

Placentia, AC 714, PC 8, Orange
Placentia Yorba Linda USD
1301 E ORANGETHORPE AVE 92670
James Fleming, supt.
7-11111
996-2550
El Dorado HS
1301 E ORANGETHORPE AVE 92670
Jo Ann Ball, prin.
4-00011
993-5350
Valencia HS
1301 E ORANGETHORPE AVE 92670
Joseph Quartucci, prin.
4-00011
996-4970
Kraemer JHS
1301 E ORANGETHORPE AVE 92670
Jerry Jertberg, prin.
3-00100
996-1551
Tuffree JHS
1301 E ORANGETHORPE AVE 92670
Larry Mauzey, prin.
3-00100
996-1881
Other Schools – See Anaheim, Yorba Linda

Placerville, AC 916, PC 6, El Dorado
El Dorado UNHSD
Supt. — See Diamond Springs
El Dorado HS, 561 CANAL ST 95667
Norman Menzie, prin.
4-00011
622-3634

Gold Oak UNESD
3171 PLEASANT VALLEY RD 95667
Bruce Hahn, supt.
4-11100
626-3150
Pleasant Valley MS
4120 PLEASANT VALLEY RD 95667
Margaret Lancina, prin.
2-00100
644-9620

Gold Trail UNSD
1575 OLD RANCH RD 95667
Steven Herrington, supt.
3-11100
626-3194
Gold Trail MS
889 COLD SPRINGS RD 95667
Don Schaefer, prin.
2-01100
622-6240

Mother Lode UNESD
3783 FORNI RD 95667
Carol Nordquist, supt.
4-11100
622-6464
Green MS, 3781 FORNI RD 95667
Maria Brugger, prin.
3-00100
622-4668

Placerville UNESD
1032 THOMPSON WAY 95667
Cynthia Simms, supt.
4-11100
622-7216
Markham MS, 2800 MOULTON DR 95667
Dax Bryson, prin.
2-00100
622-0403

Cosumnes River College
106 PLACERVILLE DR 95667
3-CC

Playa Del Rey, AC 310, PC see Venice

St. Bernard HS
9100 FALMOUTH AVE 90293
Fr. Brelsford, prin.
3-00011
823-4651

Pleasant Hill, AC 510, PC 8, Contra Costa
Mt. Diablo USD
Supt. — See Concord
College Park HS, 201 VIKING DR 94523
William Beemer, prin.
4-00011
682-7670
Sequoia MS, 265 BOYD RD 94523
Jim Durflinger, prin.
3-00100
934-8174
Valley View MS, 181 VIKING DR 94523
Walter Quinn, prin.
4-00100
686-6136

Diablo Valley College
321 GOLF CLUB RD 94523
7-CC
685-1230

Pleasanton, AC 510, PC 8, Alameda
Pleasanton USD
4665 BERNAL AVE 94566
Bill James, supt.
6-11111
462-5500
Amador Valley HS
1155 SANTA RITA RD 94566
Steve Dellanini, prin.
4-00011
846-2818
Foothill HS, 4375 FOOTHILL RD 94588
Iris Berke, prin.
4-00011
426-4243
Harvest Park IS
4900 VALLEY AVE 94566
Jerry Shelly, prin.
3-00100
426-4444
MS, 5001 CASE AVE 94566
Sally Rayhill, prin.
4-00100
426-4390

Point Arena, AC 707, PC 2, Mendocino
Point Arena JUNHSD
PO BOX 87 95468
Jerry Hart, supt.
2-00011
882-2803
HS, PO BOX 7 95468
Terry Hughey, prin.
2-00011
882-2134

Point Reyes Station, AC 415, PC 3, Marin
Shoreline USD
Supt. — See Tomales
West Marin MS, PO BOX 300 94956
Danielle Tarry, prin.
2-01100
663-1014

Pollock Pines, AC 916, PC 5, El Dorado
Pollock Pines ESD, 6181A PINE ST 95726
Elvin Peets, supt.
4-11100
644-5416

Sierra Ridge MS   3-01100
2700 AMBER TRL   95726   644-2031
Marilyn Gilbert, prin.

Pomona, AC 909, PC 9, Los Angeles
Pomona USD, PO BOX 2900   91769   8-11111
Irv Moskowitz, supt.   397-4700
Ganesha HS   4-00011
1151 GANESHA BLVD   91768   397-4404
Adlai Yarbrough, prin.
Garey HS   4-00011
321 W LEXINGTON AVE   91766   397-4451
Paul Breit, prin.
Park West HS, 1540 W 2ND ST   91766   3-00011
Michael Phillips, prin.   397-4485
HS, 475 BANGOR ST   91767   4-00011
Norman Fujimoto, prin.   397-4498
Emerson JHS, 635 LINCOLN AVE   91767   3-00100
Catherine Chamberlain, prin.   397-4516
Fremont JHS   4-00100
725 W FRANKLIN AVE   91766   397-4521
Gloria Marquez, prin.
Marshall JHS, 1921 ARROYO AVE   91768   3-00100
Isidore Cabrera, prin.   397-4532
Palomares JHS   3-00100
2211 N ORANGE GROVE AVE   91767   397-4539
Emma Lerew, prin.
Simons JHS   4-00100
900 E FRANKLIN AVE   91766   397-4544
Neil Romero, prin.
Other Schools – See Diamond Bar

California State Polytechnic University   7-UC
3801 W TEMPLE AVE   91768   869-7659
College of Osteopathic Medicine   2-UC
309 E POMONA MALL   91766   623-6116
DeVry Institute of Technology   4-UC
901 CORPORATE CENTER DR   91768   622-9800
Northwest College Medical Dental Assts.   3-CS
134 W HOLT AVE   91768   623-1552
Pomona Catholic HS   2-00011
533 W HOLT AVE   91768   623-5297
Sr. Mary Jimenez, prin.
Sawyer College   3-CS
1021 E HOLT AVE   91767   629-2534
Westech College   2-CS
500 W MISSION BLVD   91766   622-6486

Porterville, AC 209, PC 8, Tulare
Burton ESD   4-11100
264 N WESTWOOD ST   93257   781-8020
Gary Mekeel, supt.
Burton IS, 252 N WESTWOOD ST   93257   3-00100
Paul Sonksen, prin.   781-1658

Porterville SD, 589 W VINE AVE   93257   7-11111
Jacob Rankin, supt.   782-7000
Monache HS, 589 W VINE AVE   93257   4-00011
Charles McAninch, prin.   782-7152
HS, 589 W VINE AVE   93257   4-00011
Bill Cochran, prin.   782-7220
Bartlett IS, 589 W VINE AVE   93257   3-00100
Katherine Whitley, prin.   782-7100
Pioneer IS, 589 W VINE AVE   93257   3-00100
Don Erwin, prin.   782-7200

Porterville College   4-CC
100 E COLLEGE AVE   93257   781-3130

Port Hueneme, AC 805, PC 7, Ventura
Hueneme ESD   6-11100
205 N VENTURA RD   93041   488-3588
Ronald Rescigno, supt.
Other Schools – See Oxnard

Portola, AC 916, PC 4, Plumas
Plumas USD
Supt. – See Quincy
JSHS, 155 6TH ST   96122   2-00111
Rick Spears, prin.   832-4284

Portola Valley, AC 415, PC 5, San Mateo
Portola Valley ESD   3-11100
4575 ALPINE RD   94028   851-1777
James Shroyer, supt.
Corte Madera MS   2-00100
4575 ALPINE RD   94028   851-0409
Jim Shroyer, prin.

Woodside Priory S   2-00111
302 PORTOLA RD   94028   851-8221
Br. Joachim Froehlich, prin.

Potter Valley, AC 707, PC 4, Mendocino
Potter Valley Comm. USD   2-11111
PO BOX 219   95469   743-2101
Michael Warych, supt.
JSHS, PO BOX 219   95469   2-00111
Sharron Zoller, prin.   743-1142

Poway, AC 619, PC 8, San Diego
Poway USD   8-11111
13626 TWIN PEAKS RD   92064   748-0010
Robert Reeves, supt.
HS, 13626 TWIN PEAKS RD   92064   5-00011
Jerry Leininger, prin.   748-0245
Meadowbrook MS   4-00100
13626 TWIN PEAKS RD   92064   748-0802
William Adams, prin.
Twin Peaks MS   4-00100
13626 TWIN PEAKS RD   92064   748-5131
Stephen Halfaker, prin.
Other Schools – See San Diego

Prather, AC 209, PC 99, Fresno
Sierra USD
Supt. — See Auberry
Foothill MS, 29147 AUBERRY RD   93651   2-00100
Barbara Cowen, prin.   855-3551

Princeton, AC 916, PC 3, Colusa
Princeton JUSD, PO BOX 8   95970   2-11111
Michael vonKleist, supt.   439-2261
JSHS, PO BOX 8   95970   2-00111
Michael vonKleist, prin.   439-2261

Quartz Hill, AC 805, PC 6, Los Angeles
Antelope Valley UNHSD
Supt. — See Lancaster
HS, 6040 W AVENUE L   93536   4-00011
Susan Custer, prin.   943-3271

Westside UNESD
Supt. — See Lancaster
Walker MS   3-00100
5632 W AVENUE L8   93536   943-3258
Ronald Turner, prin.

Quincy, AC 916, PC 5, Plumas
Plumas USD, PO BOX 10330   95971   5-11111
Paul Hewitt, supt.   283-6500
JSHS, PO BOX 10440   95971   3-00111
Rebecca Calpe, prin.   283-3580
Other Schools – See Chester, Greenville, Portola

Feather River Community College   4-CC
PO BOX 11110   95971   283-0202

Ramona, AC 619, PC 7, San Diego
Ramona USD, 720 9TH ST   92065   6-11111
Judy Endeman, supt.   788-5000
Montecito HS, 720 9TH ST   92065   2-00011
Myron Bill, prin.   788-5070
HS, 1401 HANSON LN   92065   4-00011
Don Hagen, prin.   788-5015
Peirce MS, 1521 HANSON LN   92065   4-00011
Steve Levy, prin.   788-5050

Rancho Cordova, AC 916, PC 8, Sacramento
Folsom-Cordova USD
Supt. — See Folsom
Cordova HS, 2239 CHASE DR   95670   4-00011
Tom Nugent, prin.   362-1104
Mills JHS, 10439 COLOMA RD   95670   3-00100
Bill Tizzaro, prin.   363-6544
Mitchell JHS   3-00100
2100 ZINFANDEL DR   95670   635-8460
Robert Reed, prin.

Heald Business College   2-CC
2910 PROSPECT PARK DR   95670   638-1616

Rancho Cucamonga, AC 909, PC see Cucamonga
Central ESD   5-11100
10601 CHURCH ST STE 112   91730   989-8541
Sonja Yates, supt.
Cucamonga MS   3-00100
7611 HELLMAN AVE   91730   987-1788
Jeffrey Koenig, prin.
Musser MS   3-01100
11075 TERRA VISTA PKY   91730   980-1230
David Soden, prin.

Chaffey JUNHSD
Supt. — See Ontario
HS, 11801 LARK DR   91701   4-00011
Paul Ward, prin.   988-8511

Rancho Mirage, AC 619, PC 6, Riverside

Eisenhower Medical Center   HSP
39000 BOB HOPE DR   92270   340-3911
Palm Valley S, 35525 DAVALL DR   92270   2-11111
Michael Grella, prin.   328-0861

Rancho Palos Verdes, AC 310, PC 8, Los Angeles
Palos Verdes Peninsula USD
Supt. — See Palos Verdes Estates
Miraleste IS   3-00100
29323 PALOS VERDES DR E   90274   547-1103
Patrick Corwin, prin.

Marymount College   3-CC
30800 PALOS VERDES DR E   90274   377-5501

Rancho Santa Fe, AC 619, PC 5, San Diego
Rancho Sante Fe ESD   3-11100
PO BOX 809   92067   756-1141
R. Roger Rowe, supt.
MS, PO BOX 809   92067   2-00100
Glenda Sumida, prin.   756-1141

Fairbanks Country Day S   2-11111
PO BOX 8386   92067   756-0500
Christine Cornish, prin.
Golf Academy of San Diego   2-CS
PO BOX 3050   92067   756-2486

Red Bluff, AC 916, PC 7, Tehama
Antelope ESD   2-11100
22630 ANTELOPE BLVD   96080   527-1272
Patrick Sinclair, supt.
Berrendos ESD   2-00100
401 CHESTNUT AVE   96080   527-6700
Jack Salisbury, prin.

Red Bluff UNESD   4-11100
1755 AIRPORT BLVD   96080   527-7200
Jack Hansen, supt.
Vista MS, 1755 AIRPORT BLVD   96080   3-00100
William Lamp, prin.   527-7840

Red Bluff UNHSD   4-00011
PO BOX 1507   96080   529-8700
Mary Panucci, supt.
HS, 1260 UNION ST   96080   4-00011
Joseph Pelanconi, prin.   529-8710

Mercy HS, 233 RIVERSIDE WAY   96080   2-00011
Robert Teegarden, prin.   527-8313

Redding, AC 916, PC 8, Shasta
Enterprise ESD   5-11100
1155 MISTLETOE LN   96002   224-4100
Lee Jenkins, supt.
Parsons JHS, 750 HARTNELL AVE   96002   4-00100
Don Bagley, prin.   224-4190

Gateway USD   5-11111
4411 MOUNTAIN LAKES BLVD   96003   245-7900
Kenneth Matias, supt.
Buckeye JHS   2-01100
4411 MOUNTAIN LAKES BLVD   96003   225-0456
Roy Reddin, prin.
Other Schools – See Central Valley

Pacheco UNESD   3-11100
7433 PACHECO RD   96002   224-4589
Jim Weaver, supt.
Pacheco MS   3-01100
7430 CHURN CREEK RD   96002   224-4585
Kent Holtzclaw, prin.

Redding ESD, PO BOX 992418   96099   5-11100
William Kipp, supt.   225-0011
Sequoia MS, PO BOX 992418   96099   4-00100
Frank Adelman, prin.   225-0020

Shasta UNHSD, 1313 YUBA ST   96001   6-00011
Donald Demsher, supt.   241-3261
Enterprise HS   4-00011
3411 CHURN CREEK RD   96002   222-6601
Mike Stuart, prin.
Shasta HS, 2500 EUREKA WAY   96001   4-00011
Robert Embertson, prin.   241-4161
Foothill Mid HS   3-00100
2200 EUREKA WAY   96001   246-1700
Mike Martin, prin.

Grace Baptist S   2-11111
3782 CHURN CREEK RD   96002   222-2232
Stephan Roberts, prin.
Shasta College   6-CC
1065 OLD OREGON TRL N   96003   225-4600
Simpson College   2-UC
2211 COLLEGE VIEW DR   96003   222-6360

Redlands, AC 909, PC 8, San Bernardino
Redlands USD, PO BOX 3008   92373   7-11111
Ron Franklin, supt.   307-5300
SHS, 840 E CITRUS AVE   92374   5-00011
Tom Davis, prin.   307-5500
Cope MS, 1000 W CYPRESS AVE   92373   4-00100
Stephen Porterfield, prin.   307-5420
Moore MS   4-00110
1550 E HIGHLAND AVE   92374   307-5440
Marilyn Kemple, prin.
Redlands JHS   4-00010
501 E PENNSYLVANIA AVE   92374   307-5400
Doug Wells, prin.

Arrowhead Christian Academy   2-00111
105 TENNESSEE ST   92373   793-0601
Darrell Passwater, prin.
Calvary Chapel Christian S   2-11111
9700 ALABAMA ST   92374   793-4984
William Johnson, prin.
University of Redlands   5-UC
PO BOX 3080   92373   793-2121

Redondo Beach, AC 310, PC 8, Los Angeles
Redondo Beach Unified SD   6-11111
1401 INGLEWOOD AVE   90278   379-5449
Beverly Rohrer, supt.
Redondo Union HS   4-00011
631 VINCENT PARK   90277   397-5549
Robert Paulson, prin.
Adams MS   2-00100
1401 INGLEWOOD AVE   90278   798-8636
John Forthmann, prin.
Parras MS   2-00100
1401 INGLEWOOD AVE   90278   798-8616
Katherine Tellez, prin.

Coast Christian S, 525 EARLE LN   90278   2-11111
Nicolaus Colon, prin.   376-9577
South Bay Faith Academy   2-11111
101 S PACIFIC COAST HWY   90277   379-8242
Priscilla Miosi, prin.

Redwood City, AC 415, PC 8, San Mateo
Redwood City ESD   6-11100
815 ALLERTON ST   94063   365-1550
Ronald Crates, supt.
Kennedy MS, 815 ALLERTON ST   94063   3-00100
John Brand, prin.   365-4611
McKinley IS, 815 ALLERTON ST   94063   3-00100
Daniel Lairon, prin.   366-3827

Sequoia UNHSD, 480 JAMES AVE 94062 6-00011
Merle Fruehling, supt. 369-1411
Sequoia HS, 1201 BREWSTER AVE 94062 4-00011
Earl Walker, prin. 367-9780
Other Schools – See Atherton, Belmont, Woodside

Canada College 6-CC
4200 FARM HILL BLVD 94061 364-1212

Redwood Valley, AC 707, PC 4, Mendocino
Ukiah USD
Supt. — See Ukiah
MS, 700 E SCHOOL WAY 95470 2-01100
Jim Larson, prin. 485-8741

Reedley, AC 209, PC 7, Fresno
Kings Canyon JUSD 6-11111
675 W MANNING AVE 93654 637-1200
John Rogalsky, supt.
HS, 740 W NORTH AVE 93654 4-00011
Juan Garza, prin. 637-1200
Grant MS, 360 N EAST AVE 93654 3-00100
Bill Wachtel, prin. 637-1266
Navelencia MS 2-00100
22620 WAHTOKE AVE 93654 637-1251
Bob Yohn, prin.
Other Schools – See Orange Cove

Immanuel HS, 1128 S REED AVE 93654 2-00111
Ed Janzen, prin. 638-2529
Kings River Community College 5-CC
955 N REED AVE 93654 638-3641

Rescue, AC 916, PC 3, El Dorado
Rescue UNESD 5-11100
2390 BASS LAKE RD 95672 933-0129
Lorraine Garcy, supt.
Other Schools – See El Dorado Hills

Reseda, AC 818, PC see Los Angeles
Los Angeles USD
Supt. — See Los Angeles
Cleveland HS 4-00011
8140 VANALDEN AVE 91335 349-8410
Ida Windham, prin.
HS, 18230 KITTRIDGE ST 91335 4-00011
Robert Kladifko, prin. 342-6186

Trinity Lutheran JHS 2-00110
18425 KITTRIDGE ST 91335 342-7855
Jerad Romsa, prin.

Rialto, AC 909, PC 8, San Bernardino
Rialto USD, 182 E WALNUT AVE 92376 7-11111
Marlin Foxworth, supt. 820-7700
Eisenhower HS 5-00011
1321 N LILAC AVE 92376 820-7798
Edna Herring, prin.
HS, 595 S EUCALYPTUS AVE 92376 4-00011
Anna Rodriguez, prin. 820-6893
Frisbie MS 4-00100
1442 N EUCALYPTUS AVE 92376 820-7889
Shalimar Horsley, prin.
Kolb MS, 2351 N SPRUCE AVE 92377 4-00100
Mitchell Hovey, prin. 820-7849
MS, 324 N PALM AVE 92376 4-00100
Milt Lyles, prin. 820-7838

United States Truck Driving School 2-CS
924 W RIALTO AVE 92376 875-8000

Richmond, AC 510, PC 8, Contra Costa
West Contra Costa Usd 8-11111
1108 BISSELL AVE 94801 234-3825
Herbert Cole, supt.
De Anza HS 4-00011
5000 VALLEY VIEW RD 94803 223-3811
Ken Richter, prin.
Kennedy HS 3-00011
4300 CUTTING BLVD 94804 235-2291
Ted Abreu, prin.
HS, 1250 23RD ST 94804 4-00011
Albert Acuna, prin. 237-8770
Adams MS, 5000 PATTERSON CIR 94805 3-00100
Karen Hancox, prin. 235-5464
Other Schools – See El Cerrito, El Sobrante, Pinole, San Pablo

---

Dickinson-Warren Business College 2-CS
1001 S 57TH ST 94804 231-7555
La Cheim S, PO BOX 5000 94805 2-00011
David Neumann, prin. 525-6882
Salesian HS, 2851 SALESIAN AVE 94804 2-00011
Fr. John Itzaina, prin. 234-4434

Ridgecrest, AC 619, PC 8, Kern
Sierra Sands USD 6-11111
113 W FELSPAR AVE 93555 375-3363
Bruce Auld, supt.
Burroughs SHS, 500 FRENCH AVE 93555 4-00001
James Roulsten, prin. 375-4476
Monroe JHS, 340 W CHURCH AVE 93555 3-00110
Ken Bergevin, prin. 375-1301
Murray JHS, 921 E INYOKERN RD 93555 3-00110
John Hamlin, prin. 446-5525

Cerro Coso Community College 5-CC
3000 COLLEGE HEIGHTS BLVD 93555 375-5001
Immanuel Christian Baptist S 2-11111
201 W GRAAF AVE 93555 446-6114
Wayne Temple, prin.

Rio Dell, AC 707, PC 5, Humboldt
Rio Dell ESD, 95 CENTER ST 95562 2-11100
Steven Lowder, supt. 764-3783
MS, 95 CENTER ST 95562 2-01100
Eric Grantz, prin. 764-5694

Rio Linda, AC 916, PC 6, Sacramento
Grant JUNHSD
Supt. — See Sacramento
HS, 6309 DRY CREEK RD 95673 4-00011
Leo Burns, prin. 263-6466
JHS, 1101 G ST 95673 3-00100
Linda Jackson, prin. 263-6299

Rio Vista, AC 707, PC 5, Solano
River Delta USD 4-11111
445 MONTEZUMA ST 94571 374-6381
Dennis Grewer, supt.
HS, 410 S 4TH ST 94571 2-00011
Audrey Keebler, prin. 374-6336
River Delta Adult S 1-00011
445 MONTEZUMA ST 94571 374-5610
Ron Chaddick, prin.
Riverview MS, 525 S 2ND ST 94571 2-01100
Al Ramey, prin. 374-2345
Other Schools – See Clarksburg

Ripon, AC 209, PC 6, San Joaquin
Ripon USD, 304 N ACACIA AVE 95366 4-11111
Leo Zuber, supt. 599-2131
HS, 301 N ACACIA AVE 95366 3-00011
Tim Van Horn, prin. 599-4287

Ripon Christian S 3-11111
435 MAPLE AVE 95366 599-2155
Abel Geertsema, prin.

Riverbank, AC 209, PC 6, Stanislaus
Oakdale JUNHSD
Supt. — See Oakdale
HS, 6200 CLAUS RD 95367 3-00011
George Brown, prin. 869-1891

Riverbank SD, 3651 SANTA FE ST 95367 4-11100
Wayne Tierney, supt. 869-2539
Cardoza MS, 3525 SANTA FE ST 95367 3-00100
Joseph Galindo, prin. 869-2591

Riverdale, AC 209, PC 4, Fresno
Riverdale JUNESD 3-11100
PO BOX 338 93656 867-3589
James Brooks, supt.
MS, PO BOX 338 93656 2-01100
Liz Motta, prin. 867-3589

Riverdale JUNHSD 3-00011
PO BOX 726 93656 867-3562
Paul Klays, supt.
HS, PO BOX 726 93656 2-00011
Paul Klays, prin. 867-3562

Riverside, AC 909, PC 9, Riverside
Alvord USD, 10365 KELLER AVE 92505 7-11111
Barbara Poling, supt. 351-9367
La Sierra HS, 10365 KELLER AVE 92505 4-00011
Jack Menzia, prin. 351-9238
Norte Vista HS 4-00011
10365 KELLER AVE 92505 351-9201
Herbert Bice, prin.
Arizona IS, 10365 KELLER AVE 92505 4-00100
Wendel Tucker, prin. 351-9343
Loma Vista IS, 10365 KELLER AVE 92505 3-00100
Pam Weissman, prin. 351-9216
Wells IS, 10365 KELLER AVE 92505 3-00100
Richard Carr, prin. 351-9241

Jurupa USD, 3924 RIVERVIEW DR 92509 7-11111
Benita Roberts, supt. 360-2768
Rubidoux HS, 4250 OPAL ST 92509 4-00011
Don Vail, prin. 360-2821
Jurupa MS, 8700 GALENA ST 92509 4-00100
Walter Lancaster, prin. 360-2846
Mission MS, 5961 OSO LN 92509 4-00100
Donald Manzo, prin. 360-2842
Other Schools – See Mira Loma

Riverside USD, PO BOX 2800 92516 8-11111
Paul Houston, supt. 788-7134
Arlington HS, 2951 JACKSON ST 92503 4-00011
William Ermert, prin. 788-7240
North HS, 1550 3RD ST 92507 4-00011
Dale Kinnear, prin. 788-7311
Polytechnic HS 4-00011
5450 VICTORIA AVE 92506 788-7203
Stanley Conerly, prin.
Ramona HS 4-00011
7675 MAGNOLIA AVE 92504 788-7400
Gladys Walker, prin.
Central MS 3-00100
4795 MAGNOLIA AVE 92506 788-7282
John Casato, prin.
Chemawa MS 4-00100
8830 MAGNOLIA AVE 92503 788-7360
Georgia Renne, prin.
Gage MS, 6400 LINCOLN AVE 92506 4-00100
Barbara Carpenter, prin. 788-7350
Sierra MS, 4950 CENTRAL AVE 92504 3-00100
Robert Ortega, prin. 788-7501
University Heights MS 3-00100
1155 MASSACHUSETTS AVE 92507 788-7388
Diane Nussbaum, prin.

Bethel Christian S 2-11111
2425 VAN BUREN BLVD 92503 359-1123
David Just, prin.
California Baptist College 3-UC
8432 MAGNOLIA AVE 92504 689-5771
California Paramedical & Tech. College 2-CS
4550 LA SIERRA AVE 92505 687-9006
California School of Court Reporting 2-CS
3510 ADAMS ST 92504 359-0293
La Sierra Academy 3-11111
4900 GOLDEN AVE 92505 351-1445
Bud Moon, prin.
La Sierra University 4-UC
4700 PIERCE ST 92505 785-2022
Notre Dame HS 3-00011
7085 BROCKTON AVE 92506 369-2811
Stephen Krup, prin.
Phillips College 2-CS
4300 CENTRAL AVE 92506 787-9300
Riverside Christian HS 3-11111
3532 MONROE ST 92504 687-0077
Morris Lewis, prin.
Riverside City College 7-CC
4800 MAGNOLIA AVE 92506 684-3240
University of California 6-UC
PO BOX 112 92502 787-1012

Rocklin, AC 916, PC 7, Placer
Rocklin USD, 5035 MEYERS ST 95677 5-11111
John Anderson, supt. 624-2428
HS, 5301 VICTORY LN 95765 2-00011
Phillip Spears, prin. 632-1600
Spring View MS, 5040 5TH ST 95677 3-00100
David Pope, prin. 624-3381

Sierra College 6-CC
5000 ROCKLIN RD 95677 624-3333

Rohnert Park, AC 707, PC 8, Sonoma
Cotati-Rohnert Park USD
Supt. — See Cotati
Rancho Cotate HS 4-00011
5450 SNYDER LN 94928 792-4750
Penny Chennell, prin.
JHS, 7165 BURTON AVE 94928 3-00100
Rusty McManus, prin. 792-4800

Sonoma State University 6-UC
1801 E COTATI AVE 94928 664-2880

Rolling Hills Estates, AC 310, PC 6, Los Angeles
Palos Verdes Peninsula USD
Supt. — See Palos Verdes Estates
Palos Verdes Peninsula HS 5-00011
27118 SILVER SPUR RD 90274 377-4888
Kelly Johnson, prin.

Rosamond, AC 805, PC 6, Kern
Southern Kern USD, PO BOX CC 93560 5-11111
Michael Richardson, supt. 256-5000
HS, PO BOX CC 93560 3-00011
Richard Stockton, prin. 256-5020
Tropico MS, PO BOX CC 93560 3-00100
Richard Eubanks, prin. 256-5040

Rosemead, AC 818, PC 8, Los Angeles
El Monte UNHSD
Supt. — See El Monte
HS, 9063 MISSION DR 91770 4-00011
Denton Todd, prin. 286-3141

Garvey ESD, 2730 DEL MAR AVE 91770 6-11100
Anita Suazo, supt. 307-3400
Garvey IS, 2720 JACKSON AVE 91770 4-00100
(—), prin. 307-3385
Temple IS, 8470 FERN AVE 91770 2-00100
Chris Hunt, prin. 307-3360

Rosemead ESD 5-11100
3640 RIO HONDO AVE 91770 443-0173
Robert Hansen, supt.
Muscatel IS, 4201 IVAR AVE 91770 3-00100
Ronald Foland, prin. 287-1139

Don Bosco Technical Institute 3-00011
1151 SAN GABRIEL BLVD 91770 307-6500
Fr. Gergin, prin.
Don Bosco Technical Institute 2-CC
1151 SAN GABRIEL BLVD 91770 280-0451
NEC-Bryman Campus 3-CS
3505 HART AVE 91770 573-5470

Roseville, AC 916, PC 8, Placer
Roseville City ESD 6-11100
1000 DARLING WAY 95678 786-5090
Charles Pryor, supt.
Eich IS 4-00100
1509 SIERRA GARDENS DR 95661 783-5245
Ron Fischer, prin.

Roseville JUNHSD 5-00011
1750 CIRBY WAY 95661 786-2018
Robert Tomasini, supt.
Oakmont HS, 1710 CIRBY WAY 95661 4-00011
Don Genasci, prin. 782-3781
HS, 601 TAHOE AVE 95678 4-00011
John Montgomery, prin. 782-3753

Ross, AC 415, PC 4, Marin

Branson HS, PO BOX 887 94957 2-00011
Richard Fitzgerald, prin. 454-3612

Rowland Heights, AC 818, PC 8, Los Angeles
Rowland USD, PO BOX 8490 91748   7-11111
  Sharon Robison, supt.   965-2541
Rowland HS   4-00011
  2000 OTTERBEIN AVE 91748   965-3448
  Bill Weirich, prin.
Alvarado IS, 1901 DESIRE AVE 91748   4-00100
  Burl Hunt, prin.   964-2358
Other Schools – See La Puente, West Covina

Running Springs, AC 909, PC 4, San Bernardino

Cedu S, PO BOX 1176 92382   2-00111
  Timmothy Brace, prin.   867-2722

Sacramento, AC 916, PC 10, Sacramento
Elk Grove USD
  Supt. — See Elk Grove
Calvine HS   2-00011
  8333 VINTAGE PARK DR 95828   686-7760
  Dale Dodson, prin.
Daylor HS, 6131 ORANGE AVE 95823   2-00011
  (—), prin.   427-5428
Florin HS   4-00011
  7956 COTTONWOOD LN 95828   689-8600
  Odie Douglas, prin.
Rio Cazadero HS   2-00011
  7825 GRANDSTAFF DR 95823   422-3058
  Ron Rule, prin.
Valley HS, 6300 EHRHARDT AVE 95823   4-00011
  Frank Lucia, prin.   689-6500
Las Flores S, 5900 BAMFORD DR 95823   3-11111
  Donald Dodds, prin.   422-5604
Jackman MS, 7925 KENTWALL DR 95823   4-00100
  Terryl Summers, prin.   393-2352
Rutter MS   4-00100
  7350 PALMER HOUSE DR 95828   422-7590
  Bill Giachino, prin.

Grant JUNHSD, 1333 GRAND AVE 95838   7-00111
  James Rutter, supt.   263-6203
Foothill HS, 5000 MCCLOUD DR 95842   4-00011
  John Parks, prin.   263-6424
Grant Union HS   4-00011
  1400 GRAND AVE 95838   263-6355
  Wallace Dunn, prin.
Foothill Farms JHS   3-00100
  5001 DIABLO DR 95842   263-6440
  Carol Michael, prin.
King JHS, 3051 FAIRFIELD ST 95815   3-00100
  Willis Williams, prin.   263-6390
Rio Tierra JHS   3-00110
  3201 NORTHSTEAD DR 95833   263-6392
  Catherine Cooley, prin.
Other Schools – See North Highlands, Rio Linda

Natomas UNESD   5-11100
  1515 SPORTS DR STE 1 95834   641-3300
  General Davie, supt.
Natomas JHS, 3700 DEL PASO RD 95834   2-00100
  Deborah Keys, prin.   641-3333

Sacramento City USD   8-11111
  PO BOX 2271 95812   264-4300
  Charles Miura, supt.
Burbank HS, PO BOX 2271 95812   4-00011
  (—), prin.   433-5100
Johnson HS, PO BOX 2271 95812   4-00011
  Don Giusti, prin.   277-6400
Kennedy HS, PO BOX 2271 95812   4-00011
  (—), prin.   433-5200
McClatchy HS, PO BOX 2271 95812   4-00011
  William Dionisio, prin.   264-4400
HS, PO BOX 2271 95812   4-00011
  Mary Perez, prin.   277-6200
Skill & Business Ctr   Vo Tech
  PO BOX 2271 95812   277-6632
  Bob Honda, prin.
Bacon MS, PO BOX 2271 95812   3-00100
  Raymond Valdez, prin.   433-5000
Brannan MS, PO BOX 2271 95812   3-00100
  Barbara Chimento, prin.   264-4350
California MS, PO BOX 2271 95812   3-00100
  Robert Tafoya, prin.   264-4550
Carson MS, PO BOX 2271 95812   3-00100
  Greg Purcell, prin.   277-6750
Einstein MS, PO BOX 2271 95812   4-00100
  Rob Jones, prin.   228-5800
Goethe MS, PO BOX 2271 95812   3-00100
  Clyde Kidd, prin.   433-5400
Sutter MS, PO BOX 2271 95812   3-00100
  (—), prin.   264-4150
Wood MS, PO BOX 2271 95812   4-00100
  Nancy Pequeno, prin.   382-5900

San Juan USD
  Supt. — See Carmichael
El Camino HS   4-00011
  4300 EL CAMINO AVE 95821   971-7430
  Ernie Boone, prin.
Encina HS, 1400 BELL ST 95825   3-00011
  Tom Gemma, prin.   971-7538
Mira Loma HS, 4000 EDISON AVE 95821   4-00011
  Ed Marquez, prin.   971-7465
Rio Americano HS   4-00011
  4540 AMERICAN RIVER DR 95864   971-7494
  Ronald Uzelac, prin.
Arcade Fundamental MS   3-00100
  3500 EDISON AVE 95821   971-7300
  John Gabriel, prin.
Arden MS, 1640 WATT AVE 95864   3-00100
  Lynn Jacoby, prin.   971-7306

Salk Alternative MS   3-00100
  2950 HURLEY WAY 95864   971-7312
  Bill Hockenson, prin.

American River College   7-CC
  4700 COLLEGE OAK DR 95841   484-8011
CA Academy of Merchandising Art & Design   1-CS
  1333 HOWE AVE STE 208 95825   649-8168
California Nannie College   2-CS
  910 HOWE AVE 95825   921-2400
California State University   7-UC
  6000 J ST 95819   278-6011
Calvary Christian S   2-11111
  5051 47TH AVE 95824   393-3633
  Troy Fair, prin.
Capital Christian S   4-11111
  9470 MICRON AVE 95827   856-5600
  Ben Potloff, prin.
Christian Brothers HS   3-00011
  4315 MRTN LTHR KING JR BLVD 95820
  Dominick Puglisi, prin.   452-2876
Cosumnes River College   6-CC
  8401 CENTER PKY 95823   686-7300
Heald Institute of Technology-Sacramento   2-CC
  3737 MARCONI AVE 95821   972-0999
High-Tech Institute   2-CS
  1111 HOWE AVE 95825
ITT Technical Institute   3-CC
  9700 GOETHE RD 95827   366-3900
Lederwolff Culinary Academy   2-CS
  3300 STOCKTON BLVD 95820   456-7002
Loretto HS, 2360 EL CAMINO AVE 95821   2-00011
  Sr. Helen Timothy, prin.   482-7793
MTI-Western Business College   3-CS
  5221 MADISON AVE 95841   339-1500
NEC-Sawyer Campus   3-CS
  8475 JACKSON RD 95826   383-1909
Niles Bryant School   HMS
  3631 STOCKTON BLVD 95820
Radio Assoc. of Sacramento Medical Group   HSP
  1800 I ST 95814   444-0645
Sacramento City College   7-CC
  3835 FREEPORT BLVD 95822   449-7111
Sacramento Country S   2-11111
  2636 LATHAM DR 95864   481-8811
  Daniel White, prin.
Sacramento Medical Foundation Blood Bank   HSP
  1625 STOCKTON BLVD 95816   456-1500
St. Francis HS, 6051 M ST 95819   3-00011
  Sr. Catherine Sedgeman, prin.   452-3461
Sutter Community Hopitals   HSP
  2820 L ST 95816   733-8800
Truck Driving Academy   2-CS
  5711 FLORIN PERKINS RD 95828   381-2285
University of California-Davis   2-UC
  2315 STOCKTON BLVD 95817   453-3096
University of the Pacific   3-UC
  3200 5TH AVE 95817   739-7105
Western Career College   3-CS
  8909 FOLSOM BLVD 95826   361-1660

Saint Helena, AC 707, PC 5, Napa
St. Helena USD, 465 MAIN ST 94574   4-11111
  Emanuel Scrofani, supt.   967-2708
HS, 1401 GRAYSON AVE 94574   3-00011
  Len Casanega, prin.   967-2740
Stevenson IS, 1316 HILLVIEW PL 94574   2-00100
  Rich Svendsen, prin.   967-2725

Salinas, AC 408, PC 9, Monterey
Salinas UNHSD   6-00111
  431 W ALISAL ST 93901   753-4100
  Aurora Quevedo, supt.
Alisal HS, 777 WILLIAMS RD 93905   4-00011
  John Torres, prin.   753-4150
North Salinas HS, 55 KIP DR 93906   4-00011
  Derrell Kunnas, prin.   753-4230
HS, 726 S MAIN ST 93901   4-00011
  Rudy Herrera, prin.   753-4280
El Sausal MS, 1155 E ALISAL ST 93905   4-00100
  Abel Valdez, prin.   753-4180
Harden MS, 1561 MCKINNON ST 93906   4-00100
  Linda Harris, prin.   753-4900
Washington MS, 560 IVERSON ST 93901   4-00100
  Richard Jevons, prin.   753-4310

Santa Rita UNESD   4-11100
  57 RUSSELL RD 93906   443-7200
  Harold Blythe, supt.
Gavilan View MS   3-00100
  18250 VAN BUREN AVE 93906   443-7212
  Thomas Dietrich, prin.

Washington UNESD   3-11100
  43 SAN BENANCIO RD 93908   484-2166
  Jerry Tollefson, supt.
San Benancio MS   2-00100
  43 SAN BENANCIO RD 93908   484-1172
  Bonnie Tinder, prin.

Hartnell College   6-CC
  156 HOMESTEAD AVE 93901   755-6700
Heald Business College   2-CC
  PO BOX 3167 93912   757-1700
Notre Dame HS, 455 PALMA DR 93901   2-00011
  Roger Richter, prin.   757-5214
Palma HS, 919 IVERSON ST 93901   3-00111
  Br. Patrick Dunne, prin.   422-6391
Winham Street Christian Academy   2-11111
  526 CALIFORNIA ST 93901   758-0321
  Thomas Carvey, prin.

Salton City, AC 619, PC 3, Imperial
Coachella Valley USD
  Supt. — See Thermal
West Shores HS, PO BOX 162 92274   1-00011
      394-4331

San Andreas, AC 209, PC 4, Calaveras
Calaveras USD, PO BOX 788 95249   5-11111
  Jim Frost, supt.   754-3504
Calveras HS, PO BOX 607 95249   3-00011
  Ben Kolb, prin.   754-1811
Other Schools – See Valley Springs

San Anselmo, AC 415, PC 7, Marin
Ross Valley SD   4-11100
  46 GREEN VALLEY CT 94960   454-2162
  Frank Elliott, supt.
Other Schools – See Fairfax

Tamalpais UNHSD
  Supt. — See Larkspur
Drake HS   3-00011
  1327 SIR FRANCIS DRAKE BLVD 94960
  William Purcell, prin.   453-8770

San Domenico S   2-11111
  1500 BUTTERFIELD RD 94960   454-0200
  Linda Klett, prin.
San Francisco Theological Seminary   2-UC
  2 KENSINGTON RD 94960   258-6500

San Bernardino, AC 909, PC 9, San Bernardino
San Bernardino City USD   8-11111
  777 N F ST 92410   381-1100
  E. Neal Roberts, supt.
Cajon HS, 1200 W HILL DR 92407   4-00011
  Don Simpson, prin.   881-8120
Pacific HS, 1020 PACIFIC AVE 92404   4-00011
  Michael Davitt, prin.   384-0434
HS, 1850 N E ST 92405   4-00011
  Karen Craig, prin.   881-8217
San Gorgonio HS   4-00011
  2299 PACIFIC AVE 92404   862-1440
  Phil Haley, prin.
Sierra HS, 570 E 9TH ST 92410   2-00011
  James Alvarado, prin.   388-6478
Arrowview MS, 2299 N G ST 92405   4-00100
  Steve Perlut, prin.   881-8109
Curtis MS, 1472 E 6TH ST 92410   4-00100
  Susan Romo, prin.   388-6332
Del Vallejo MS   3-00100
  1855 E LYNWOOD DR 92404   882-8970
  Delfina Bryant, prin.
Golden Valley MS   4-00100
  3800 N WATERMAN AVE 92404   881-8168
  James Kissinger, prin.
King MS   3-00100
  1250 MEDICAL CENTER DR 92411   388-6350
  (—), prin.
Richardson Prep JHS, 455 S K ST 92410   3-00100
  Edith Krache, prin.   388-6438
Shandin Hills MS   4-00100
  4301 LITTLE MOUNTAIN DR 92407   880-6666
  Harold Volkommer, prin.
Other Schools – See Highland

American Technical College/Career Trng   CC
  191 S E ST 92401   885-3857
Aquinas HS, 2772 STERLING AVE 92404   2-00011
  Kenneth Johnson, prin.   886-4659
Associated Technical College   3-CS
  395 N E ST 92401   885-1888
California State University   6-UC
  5500 UNIVERSITY PKY 92407   880-5000
International School of Theology   1-UC
  PO BOX 5500 92412   886-7876
ITT Technical Institute   3-CC
  630 E BRIER DR # 150 92408   889-3800
NEC-Skadron Campus   4-CS
  825 E HOSPITALITY LN 92408   885-3896
San Bernardino County Medical Center   HSP
  24600 ARROWHEAD SPRINGS RD 92414
      387-8185
San Bernardino Valley College   7-CC
  701 S MOUNT VERNON AVE 92410   888-6511
United Health Careers Institute   3-CS
  570 W 4TH ST # 907 92401   884-8891

San Bruno, AC 415, PC 8, San Mateo
Laguna Salada UNESD
  Supt. — See Pacifica
Pacific Heights MS   2-00100
  3791 PACIFIC HEIGHTS BLVD 94066   355-6900
  Jim Leavitt, prin.

San Bruno Park ESD   5-11100
  500 ACACIA AVE 94066   244-0133
  Theresa Daem, supt.
Parkside IS, 1801 NILES AVE 94066   3-00100
  Judy Teague, prin.   244-0160

San Mateo UNHSD
  Supt. — See San Mateo
Capuchino HS   3-00011
  1501 MAGNOLIA AVE 94066   583-9977
  Gordon Young, prin.

Highlands Christian S   3-11111
  1900 MONTEREY DR 94066   873-4090
  Linda Packer, prin.
Skyline College   6-CC
  3300 COLLEGE DR 94066   355-7000

San Carlos, AC 415, PC 8, San Mateo
San Carlos ESD 4-11100
826 CHESTNUT ST 94070 593-7626
Don Shalvey, supt.
Central MS, 828 CHESTNUT ST 94070 3-00100
Jean Dehner, prin. 591-7197

Alpha Beacon Christian S 2-11111
750 DARTMOUTH AVE 94070 592-2811
Lillian Mark, prin.

San Clemente, AC 714, PC 8, Orange
Capistrano USD
Supt. — See San Juan Capistrano
HS, 700 E AVENIDA PICO 92673 4-00011
Christopher Cairns, prin. 492-4165
Shorecliffs JHS 3-00100
240 VIA SOCORRO 92672 498-1660
James Krembas, prin.

San Diego, AC 619, PC 12, San Diego
Poway USD
Supt. — See Poway
Mt. Carmel HS 4-00011
9550 CARMEL MOUNTAIN RD 92129 484-1180
Scott Fisher, prin.
Bernardo Heights MS 4-00100
12990 PASEO LUCIDO 92128 485-4850
Rich Helbling, prin.
Black Mountain MS 4-00100
9353 OVIEDO ST 92129 484-1300
Candace Toft, prin.
Rancho Bernardo JHS 4-00010
13010 PASEO LUCIDO 92128 485-4800
John Collins, prin.

San Diego City USD 9-11111
4100 NORMAL ST 92103 293-8686
Bertha Pendleton, supt.
Henry SHS 4-00001
6702 WANDERMERE DR 92120 286-7700
Mary Castleberry, prin.
SHS, 1405 PARK BLVD 92101 4-00001
Robert Amparan, prin. 525-7455
University City SHS 4-00001
6949 GENESEE AVE 92122 457-3040
Anne Bolton, prin.
Clairemont HS, 4150 UTE DR 92117 3-00011
Allan Peck, prin. 273-0201
Crawford HS, 4191 COLTS WAY 92115 4-00011
David Lemay, prin. 583-2500
Hoover HS, 4474 EL CAJON BLVD 92115 4-00011
Doris Alvarez, prin. 283-6281
Kearny HS 4-00011
7651 WELLINGTON WAY 92111 496-8370
Michael Lorch, prin.
Lincoln HS, 150 S 49TH ST 92113 3-00011
Virginia Foster, prin. 264-3171
Madison HS, 4833 DOLIVA DR 92117 4-00011
Russell Vowinkel, prin. 496-8410
Mira Mesa HS, 10510 REAGAN RD 92126 4-00011
James Vlassis, prin. 566-2262
Mission Bay HS 4-00011
2475 GRAND AVE 92109 273-1313
Maruta Gardner, prin.
Morse HS, 6905 SKYLINE DR 92114 5-00011
Shirley Peterson, prin. 262-0763
Point Loma HS 4-00011
2335 CHATSWORTH BLVD 92106 223-3121
Mary McNaughton, prin.
Scripps Ranch HS 4-00011
10410 TREENA ST 92131 621-9020
Barbara Brooks, prin.
Serra HS, 5156 SANTO RD 92124 4-00011
Laserik Saunders, prin. 496-8342
Gompers JSHS, 1005 47TH ST 92102 4-00111
Marie Thornton, prin. 263-2171
San Diego Arts HS, 2425 DUSK DR 92139 4-01111
Florence Johnson, prin. 470-0555
Bell JHS, 620 BRIARWOOD RD 92139 4-00110
Norman Kellner, prin. 479-7111
Challenger JHS 4-00100
10810 PARKDALE AVE 92126 586-7001
Samuel Wong, prin.
Correia JHS, 4302 VALETA ST 92107 3-00100
Ernest Calderon, prin. 222-0476
De Portola MS 3-00100
11010 CLAIREMONT MESA BLVD 92124
Robert Saunders, prin. 496-8080
Farb MS, 4880 LA CUENTA DR 92124 3-00100
Mary Gilliland, prin. 496-8090
Keiller MS, 7270 LISBON ST 92114 3-00100
Wendell Bass, prin. 263-9266
Kroc MS, 5050 CONRAD AVE 92117 3-00100
Barb Coates, prin. 496-8150
Lewis JHS 4-00110
5170 GREENBRIER AVE 92120 583-3233
Patricia Harris, prin.
Mann MS, 4345 54TH ST 92115 4-00100
Julie Elliott, prin. 582-8990
Marston MS 4-00100
3799 CLAIREMONT DR 92117 273-2030
Michele Marcus, prin.
Memorial JHS, 2850 LOGAN AVE 92113 4-00110
Antonio Alfaro, prin. 525-7400
Montgomery JHS, 2470 ULRIC ST 92111 4-00110
Ciprianita Powell, prin. 496-8330
O'Farrell Community MS 4-00100
6130 SKYLINE DR 92114 263-3009
Robert Stein, prin.

Pacific Beach MS 3-00100
4676 INGRAHAM ST 92109 273-9070
Charmaine Del Principe, prin.
Pershing JHS 3-00110
8204 SAN CARLOS DR 92119 465-3234
Dennis Brown, prin.
Roosevelt JHS, 3366 PARK BLVD 92103 4-00110
Michael Price, prin. 293-4450
Standley JHS 4-00110
6298 RADCLIFFE DR 92122 455-0550
Joene Bruhn, prin.
Taft JHS, 9191 GRAMERCY DR 92123 3-00100
William Vogel, prin. 496-8245
Wangenheim JHS 4-00100
9230 GOLD COAST DR 92126 578-1400
Delmer Evans, prin.
Wilson MS, 3838 ORANGE AVE 92105 4-00100
Beth Limoli, prin. 280-1661
Other Schools — See La Jolla

San Dieguito UNHSD
Supt. — See Encinitas
Torrey Pines HS 4-00011
3710 DEL MAR HEIGHTS RD 92130 755-0125
Simeon Greenstein, prin.

Sweetwater UNHSD
Supt. — See Chula Vista
Montgomery SHS 4-00001
3250 PALM AVE 92154 691-5675
Alan Sachrison, prin.
Southwest HS 4-00011
1685 HOLLISTER ST 92154 691-5465
Alan Goycochea, prin.
Mar Vista MS 4-00100
1267 THERMAL AVE 92154 691-5422
Victoria Kreiser, prin.
Montgomery JHS 4-00110
1051 PICADOR BLVD 92154 691-5440
Ramon Leyba, prin.
Southwest JHS, 2710 IRIS AVE 92154 4-00110
Ronald Williams, prin. 691-5455

Academy of Our Lady of Peace 3-00011
4860 OREGON ST 92116 297-2266
Sr. Dolores Anchondo, prin.
Advertising Arts College 2-UC
10025 MESA RIM RD 92121 546-0602
Associated Technical College 2-CS
1475 6TH AVE 92101 234-2181
California Sch. Professional Psychology 2-UC
6212 FERRIS SQ 92121 452-1664
California Western School of Law 3-UC
350 CEDAR ST 92101 239-0391
Century Schools 2-CC
2665 5TH AVE 92103 233-0184
Childrens Creative/Performing Arts Acad. 2-11111
4431 MOUNT HERBERT AVE 92117 279-4744
Janet Cherif, prin.
ConCorde Career Institute 2-CS
123 CAMINO DE LA REINA 92108 688-0800
Design Institute of San Diego 2-UC
8555 COMMERCE AVE 92121 566-1200
Edutek Professional College 2-CS
4560 ALVARADO CANYON RD 92120 582-1319
Edutek Professional Colleges 2-CS
5952 EL CAJON BLVD 92115 582-1319
Edutek Professional Colleges 3-CS
5952 EL CAJON BLVD 92115 582-1319
Edutek Professional Colleges 4-CS
1541 BROADWAY 92101 239-4138
Eldorado College 2-CS
2255 CAMINO DEL RIO S # 200 92108
294-9256
Fashion Careers of California 2-CS
1923 MORENA BLVD 92110 275-4700
Fashion Inst. of Design & Merchandising 2-CC
1010 2ND AVE STE 200 92101 235-4515
Foundation HS 2-00011
8912 CLAIREMONT MESA BLVD 92123
Anne Hill, prin. 299-1340
Futures in Education 2-HMS
1249 F ST 92101 235-4125
Horizon Christian ES 2-11111
5331 MOUNT ALIFAN DR 92111 277-4379
Nancy Friebel, prin.
ITT Technical Institute 3-UC
9680 GRANITE RIDGE DR 92123 571-8500
Kelsey-Jenney College 3-CC
201 A ST 92101 233-7418
Lutheran HS, 5310 ORANGE AVE 92115 2-00011
Ramon Wittig, prin. 287-7333
Marian HS, 1002 18TH ST 92154 2-00011
Audrey Tellers, prin. 423-2121
Maric College of Medical Careers 3-CS
7202 PRINCESS VIEW DR 92120 583-8232
National University 7-UC
4141 CAMINO DEL RIO S 92108 563-7100
National University School of Law 3-UC
3580 AERO CT 92123
New School of Architecture 2-UC
1249 F ST 92101 235-4100
North Park University 2-CS
3956 30TH ST 92104 297-3333
Parker S, 6501 LINDA VISTA RD 92111 3-11111
Jerral Miles, prin. 569-7900
Platt College 3-CS
6250 EL CAJON BLVD 92115 265-0107
Point Loma Nazarene College 4-UC
3900 LOMALAND DR 92106 221-2200

St. Augustine HS 3-00011
3266 NUTMEG ST 92104 282-2184
Fr. Sanders, prin.
San Diego City College 7-CC
1313 12TH AVE 92101 230-2400
San Diego Mesa College 7-CC
7250 MESA COLLEGE DR 92111 560-2600
San Diego Miramar College 6-CC
10440 BLACK MOUNTAIN RD 92126 693-6800
San Diego State University 8-UC
5300 CAMPANILE DR 92115 594-5200
Sarah Anthony S 2-11111
2801 MEADOW LARK DR 92123 297-1111
Sharp Memorial Hospital HSP
7901 FROST ST 92123 541-4000
Travel University International 2-CS
3655 RUFFIN RD STE 225 92123 292-9755
United States International University 5-UC
10455 POMERADO RD 92131 693-4772
University of San Diego 6-UC
5998 ALCALA PARK 92110 260-4506
University of San Diego HS 4-00011
5961 LINDA VISTA RD 92110 298-8277
Richard Kelly, prin.
Western State University College of Law 2-UC
2121 SAN DIEGO AVE 92110 297-9700
Western Truck School 2-CS
2425 MAR INDUSTRY DR 92121 229-8301

San Dimas, AC 909, PC 8, Los Angeles
Bonita USD, 115 W ALLEN AVE 91773 6-11111
Ron Raya, supt. 599-6787
HS, 115 W ALLEN AVE 91773 4-00011
Mary Breskin, prin. 599-6741
Lone Hill MS, 115 W ALLEN AVE 91773 3-00100
Marc Jackson, prin. 394-3175
Other Schools — See La Verne

L.I.F.E. Bible College 2-UC
1100 W COVINA BLVD 91773 800-356-0001

San Fernando, AC 818, PC 7, Los Angeles
Los Angeles USD
Supt. — See Los Angeles
SHS, 11133 OMELVENY AVE 91340 5-00001
Philip Saldivar, prin. 365-1121
JHS, 130 N BRAND BLVD 91340 4-00110
Mary Reza, prin. 361-0181

First Lutheran S 2-11111
777 N MACLAY AVE 91340 361-4800
Earl Reynolds, prin.
Sunland Christian S 2-11111
622 N MACLAY AVE 91340 898-0180
Terrence Neven, prin.

San Francisco, AC 415, PC 11, San Francisco
San Francisco USD 8-11111
135 VAN NESS AVE 94102 241-6000
Waldemar Rojas, supt.
Business & Commerce HHS 2-00001
350 BROADWAY 94133 291-7937
Carlos Cornejo, prin.
Lowell SHS 5-00001
1101 EUCALYPTUS DR 94132 759-2730
Paul Cheng, prin.
Twain SHS, 1541 12TH AVE 94122 2-00001
Evira Dundy, prin. 759-2760
Balboa HS, 1000 CAYUGA AVE 94112 4-00011
Juliet Montevirgin, prin. 469-4090
Burton HS, 45 CONKLING ST 94124 2-00011
Frenda Howell, prin. 695-5616
Downtown HS, 110 BARTLETT ST 94110 2-00011
Erma Cobb, prin. 695-5860
Galileo HS, 1055 BAY ST 94109 4-00011
John Quinn, prin. 749-3430
International Studies Academy 2-00011
693 VERMONT ST 94107 695-5866
Steve Hirabayashi, prin.
Lincoln HS, 2162 24TH AVE 94116 4-00011
Mae Gwen Chan, prin. 759-2700
McAteer HS, 555 PORTOLA DR 94131 4-00011
Joe Tolley, prin. 695-5700
Mission HS, 3750 18TH ST 94114 4-00011
Pat Aramendia, prin. 241-6240
Newcomer HS, 2340 JACKSON ST 94115 2-00011
Herb Chan, prin. 241-6584
O'Connell HS, 1920 41ST AVE 94116 3-00011
Gus Portocarrero, prin. 759-2724
School of the Arts 2-00011
700 FONT BLVD 94132 469-4027
Joseph Rosenblatt, prin.
Wallenberg Traditional HS 3-00011
40 VEGA ST 94115 749-3469
Mattie Walker, prin.
Washington HS, 600 32ND AVE 94121 5-00011
Al Vidal, prin. 750-8400
Wells HS, 1099 HAYES ST 94117 2-00011
Nancy Evangelho, prin. 241-6315
Wilson HS, 400 MANSELL ST 94134 4-00011
Jose Buenavista, prin. 469-4550
Aptos MS, 105 APTOS AVE 94127 3-00100
Lois Woods-Green, prin. 469-4520
Burbank MS 3-00100
325 LA GRANDE AVE 94112 469-4580
George Sloan, prin.
Denman MS, 241 ONEIDA AVE 94112 3-00100
Wilson Nacario, prin. 469-4535
Everett MS, 450 CHURCH ST 94114 3-00100
Lynette Porteous, prin. 241-6344

Francisco MS, 2190 POWELL ST 94133 — 3-00100
(—), prin. — 291-7900
Franklin MS, 1430 SCOTT ST 94115 — 3-00100
Diane Meltesen, prin. — 749-3476
Giannini MS, 3151 ORTEGA ST 94122 — 3-00100
Joseph Crivello, prin. — 759-2770
Hoover MS, 2290 14TH AVE 94116 — 4-00100
Ronald Pang, prin. — 759-2783
King Academic MS — 3-00100
350 GIRARD ST 94134 — 330-1500
James Taylor, prin.
Lick MS, 1220 NOE ST 94114 — 3-00100
Joan Hepperly, prin. — 695-5675
Mann MS, 3351 23RD ST 94110 — 3-00100
Richard Murphy, prin. — 695-5881
Marina MS, 3500 FILLMORE ST 94123 — 4-00100
Alyse Danis, prin. — 749-3495
Potrero Hill MS, 655 DE HARO ST 94107 — 3-00100
Ronald Cabral, prin. — 695-5905
Presidio MS, 450 30TH AVE 94121 — 3-00100
Benson Wong, prin. — 750-8435
Roosevelt MS — 3-00100
460 ARGUELLO BLVD 94118 — 750-8446
Charles Corsiglia, prin.
Visitacion Valley MS — 3-00100
450 RAYMOND AVE 94134 — 469-4590
Fannie Paegler, prin.

Academy of Art College — 2-UC
79 NEW MONTGOMERY ST 94105 — 274-2200
American Conservatory Theater — 1-UC
30 GRANT AVE 94108 — 834-3350
Antioch University — 2-UC
777 VALENCIA ST 94110
Archbishop Riordan HS — 3-00100
175 PHELAN AVE 94112 — 586-8200
Fr. Kenney, prin.
Bridgemont HS — 2-00011
501 CAMBRIDGE ST 94134 — 333-7600
Jonathan Jones, prin.
California College of Arts & Crafts — 2-UC
1700 17TH ST 94103 — 703-9500
California College of Podiatric Medicine — 2-UC
PO BOX 7855 94120 — 563-8070
California Culinary Academy — 3-CC
625 POLK ST 94102 — 771-3536
California Institute of Integral Studies — 2-UC
765 ASHBURY ST 94117 — 753-6100
California Sch. Professional Psychology — 4-UC
2749 HYDE ST 94109 — 346-4500
Children's Hospital of San Francisco — HSP
3700 CALIFORNIA ST 94118 — 387-8700
City College of San Francisco — 8-CC
50 PHELAN AVE 94112 — 239-3000
CollegeAmerica - San Francisco — 2-CS
814 MISSION ST STE 300 94103 — 882-4545
College for Recording Arts — 2-CS
665 HARRISON ST 94107 — 781-6306
Computer Learning Center — 4-CS
661 HOWARD ST 94105 — 495-0800
Convent HS, 2222 BROADWAY ST 94115 — 2-00011
Douglas Grant, prin. — 563-2900
Drew College Prep S — 2-00011
2901 CALIFORNIA ST 94115 — 346-4831
Samuel Cuddeback, prin.
Fashion Inst. of Design & Merchandising — 3-CC
55 STOCKTON ST 94108 — 433-6691
French American International S — 2-11111
220 BUCHANAN ST 94102 — 626-8564
Alain Weber, prin.
Golden Gate University — 5-UC
536 MISSION ST 94105 — 442-7000
Heald Business College — 2-CC
1453 MISSION ST 94103 — 673-5500
Heald Institute of Technology — 2-CC
250 EXECUTIVE PARK BLVD 94134 — 441-5555
Hebrew Academy of San Francisco — 2-11111
645 14TH AVE 94118 — 752-7490
Rabbi Lipner, prin.
Immaculate Conception Academy — 2-00011
3625 24TH ST 94110 — 824-2052
Sr. Carolyn McCormack, prin.
Lick-Wilmerding HS — 2-00011
755 OCEAN AVE 94112 — 333-4021
Albert Adams, prin.
Lincoln University — 2-UC
281 MASONIC AVE 94118 — 221-1212
Louise Salinger Academy of Fashion — 2-UC
101 JESSIE ST 94105 — 974-6666
Management College of San Francisco — 2-CS
1255 POST ST STE 450 94109 — 776-7244
Mercy HS, 3250 19TH AVE 94132 — 2-00011
Rosalind Crosby, prin. — 334-0525
NEC-Bryman Campus — 3-CS
731 MARKET ST 94103 — 777-2500
New College of California — 3-UC
50 FELL ST 94102 — 241-1300
Platt College — 2-CS
301 MISSION ST 94105 — 495-4000
Sacred Heart Prep HS — 4-00011
1100 ELLIS ST 94109 – Br. Brady, prin. — 775-6626
St. Ignatius College Prep — 4-00011
2001 37TH AVE 94116 — 731-7500
Fr. Prietto, prin.
St. Paul HS, 323 29TH ST 94131 — 2-00011
Sr. Maureen O'Brien, prin. — 648-0505
San Francisco Art Institute — 3-UC
800 CHESTNUT ST 94133 — 771-7020

San Francisco Christian S — 2-11111
25 WHITTIER ST 94112 — 586-1117
Rev. Allen, prin.
San Francisco Coll. of Mortuary Science — 1-CC
1598 DOLORES ST 94110 — 824-1313
San Francisco Conservatory of Music — 2-UC
1201 ORTEGA ST 94122 — 564-8086
San Francisco State University — 7-UC
1600 HOLLOWAY AVE 94132 — 338-1111
San Francisco University HS — 2-00011
3065 JACKSON ST 94115 — 346-8400
Peter Esty, prin.
Saybrook Institute — 2-UC
450 PACIFIC AVE FL 3 94133 — 433-9200
School of Communication Electronics — 2-CS
184 2ND ST 94105 — 896-0858
University of California — 5-UC
PARNASSUS AND 3RD AVE 94143 — 476-9000
University of CA Hastings College of Law — 4-UC
198 MCALLISTER ST 94102 — 565-4600
University of San Francisco — 6-UC
2130 FULTON ST 94117 — 666-6136
University of the Pacific — 3-UC
2155 WEBSTER ST 94115
Urban School of San Francisco — 2-00011
1563 PAGE ST 94117 — 626-2919
Mark Salkind, prin.
Voice Pentecost Christian S — 2-11111
1970 OCEAN AVE 94127 — 334-0105
John Nyquist, prin.
Woodside International S — 2-00111
1555 IRVING ST 94122 — 564-1063
John Edwards, prin.

San Gabriel, AC 818, PC 8, Los Angeles
Alhambra City SD
Supt. — See Alhambra
HS, 801 S RAMONA ST 91776 — 5-00011
Jack Mount, prin. — 308-2352

San Gabriel USD — 5-11100
102 E BROADWAY 91776 — 285-3111
Gary Goodson, supt.
Jefferson IS, 1440 LAFAYETTE ST 91776 — 3-00100
Berjouhi Koukeyan, prin. — 288-8812

San Gabriel Mission HS — 2-00011
254 S SANTA ANITA AVE 91776 — 282-3181
Frank Laurenzello, prin.
San Gabriel SDA Academy — 3-11111
8827 E BROADWAY 91776 — 444-7502
Lisa Bissell, prin.

Sanger, AC 209, PC 7, Fresno
Sanger USD, 1905 7TH ST 93657 — 6-11111
Robert Jones, supt. — 875-6521
HS, 1705 10TH ST 93657 — 4-00011
Fred Ratzlaff, prin. — 875-7121
Washington MS, 2207 9TH ST 93657 — 3-00100
Sherrey Bishop, prin. — 875-5561

San Jacinto, AC 909, PC 7, Riverside
San Jacinto USD, 600 E MAIN ST 92583 — 5-11111
Sandra Shackelford, supt. — 654-2785
HS, 500 IDYLLWILD DR 92583 — 3-00011
Ron White, prin. — 654-7374
Monte Vista MS — 3-00100
181 N RAMONA BLVD 92583 — 654-9361
Brian Jacobs, prin.

Mt. San Jacinto College — 5-CC
1499 N STATE ST 92583 — 654-8011

San Joaquin, AC 209, PC 4, Fresno
Golden Plains ESD
Supt. — See Tranquillity
El Portal HS, 21960 RAILROAD 93660 — 2-00011
(—), prin. — 693-2401

San Jose, AC 408, PC 11, Santa Clara
Alum Rock UNESD — 7-11100
2930 GAY AVE 95127 — 258-4923
Pedro Perales, supt.
Fischer MS, 1720 HOPKINS DR 95122 — 3-00100
Gregorio Gutierrez, prin. — 258-6244
George MS, 277 MAHONEY DR 95127 — 3-00100
James O'Berg, prin. — 259-2402
Mathson MS — 3-00100
2050 KAMMERER AVE 95116 — 251-3232
Lena Krinard, prin.
Ocala MS, 2800 OCALA AVE 95148 — 3-00100
Arthur Harris, prin. — 923-2800
Pala MS, 149 N WHITE RD 95127 — 3-00100
Kathy De Losa, prin. — 258-4996
Sheppard MS — 3-00100
480 ROUGH AND READY RD 95133 — 258-4323
Karen Kieselbach, prin.

Berryessa UNESD — 6-11100
1376 PIEDMONT RD 95132 — 923-1800
G. Wadley, supt.
Morrill MS, 1970 MORRILL AVE 95132 — 3-00100
Estella Quintanilla, prin. — 923-1930
Piedmont MS, 955 PIEDMONT RD 95132 — 3-00100
Frank Tom, prin. — 923-1945
Sierramont MS, 3155 KIMLEE DR 95132 — 3-00100
Ron Fairchild, prin. — 923-1955

Cambrian ESD, 4115 JACKSOL DR 95124 — 5-11100
Barry Groves, supt. — 377-2103
Price MS, 2650 NEW JERSEY AVE 95124 — 3-00100
Michael Demko, prin. — 377-2532

Campbell UNESD
Supt. — See Campbell
Monroe MS, 1055 S MONROE ST 95128 — 3-01100
Shelby Spain, prin. — 364-4232

Campbell UNHSD — 6-00011
3235 UNION AVE 95124 — 371-0960
Bruce Hauger, supt.
Del Mar HS, 3235 UNION AVE 95124 — 4-00011
Richard Robbins, prin. — 298-0260
Leigh HS, 3235 UNION AVE 95124 — 4-00011
James Russell, prin. — 377-4470
Other Schools – See Campbell, Saratoga

Cupertino UNESD
Supt. — See Cupertino
Miller JHS, 6151 RAINBOW DR 95129 — 3-00100
Steve Parker, prin. — 252-3755

East Side UNHSD — 7-00011
830 N CAPITOL AVE 95133 — 272-6400
Joe Coto, supt.
Hill HS, 3200 SENTER RD 95111 — 4-00011
Bill Kugler, prin. — 227-8800
Independence HS — 5-00011
1776 EDUCATIONAL PARK DR 95133 — 729-3911
John Sellarole, prin.
Lick HS, 57 N WHITE RD 95127 — 4-00011
Catherine Giammona, prin. — 729-3580
Mt. Pleasant HS — 4-00011
1750 S WHITE RD 95127 — 251-7820
Manny Morales, prin.
Oak Grove HS — 4-00011
285 BLOSSOM HILL RD 95123 — 225-9332
Karalee Roland, prin.
Overfelt HS — 4-00011
1835 CUNNINGHAM AVE 95122 — 259-0540
Elias Chamorro, prin.
Piedmont Hills HS — 4-00011
1377 PIEDMONT RD 95132 — 729-3950
Francisca Miranda, prin.
Santa Teresa HS, 6150 SNELL AVE 95123 — 4-00011
Mike Welch, prin. — 578-9100
Silver Creek HS — 4-00011
3434 SILVER CREEK RD 95121 — 274-1700
Rafael Renteria, prin.
Yerba Buena HS — 4-00011
1855 LUCRETIA AVE 95122 — 279-1500
Gary Zellner, prin.

Evergreen ESD, 3188 QUIMBY RD 95148 — 7-11100
James Smith, supt. — 270-6800
Chaboya MS, 3276 FOWLER RD 95135 — 3-00100
Bette Samdahl, prin. — 270-6900
LeyVa IS, 1865 MONROVIA DR 95122 — 3-00100
Cliff Black, prin. — 270-4992
Quimby Oak IS, 3190 QUIMBY RD 95148 — 4-00100
Phil Bond, prin. — 270-6735

Franklin-McKinley ESD — 7-11100
645 WOOL CREEK DR 95112 — 283-6000
Larry Aceves, supt.
Fair JHS, 1702 MCLAUGHLIN AVE 95122 — 4-00100
Laurence Holguin, prin. — 283-6400
Sylvandale JHS — 3-00100
653 SYLVANDALE AVE 95111 — 363-5700
Nancy McLaurin, prin.

Fremont UNHSD
Supt. — See Sunnyvale
Lynbrook HS — 4-00011
1280 JOHNSON AVE 95129 — 366-7700
Mike Hawkes, prin.

Moreland ESD — 5-11100
4710 CAMPBELL AVE 95130 — 379-1370
Jim Ritchie, supt.
Castro MS, 4600 STUDENT LN 95130 — 3-00100
Kate Ford, prin. — 379-3620
Rogers MS, 4835 DOYLE RD 95129 — 3-00100
Joe DiSalvo, prin. — 253-7262

Morgan Hill USD
Supt. — See Morgan Hill
Murphy MS — 4-00110
141 AVENIDA ESPANA 95139 — 281-1500
Donald Schaefer, prin.

Mt. Pleasant ESD — 5-11100
14265 STORY RD 95127 — 928-1200
Ida Jew, supt.
Boeger MS, 1944 FLINT AVE 95148 — 3-00100
Sandy Meyer, prin. — 928-1270

Oak Grove ESD — 7-11100
6578 SANTA TERESA BLVD 95119 — 227-8300
Tim Cuneo, supt.
Bernal IS — 3-00100
6610 SAN IGNACIO AVE 95119 — 578-5731
Henry Castaniada, prin.
Davis IS, 5035 EDENVIEW DR 95111 — 3-00100
Steve Anderson, prin. — 227-0616
Herman IS, 5955 BLOSSOM AVE 95123 — 3-00100
Oscar Donahue, prin. — 226-1886

San Jose USD, 1605 PARK AVE 95126 — 8-11111
Linda Murray, supt. — 998-6000
Broadway HS — 2-00011
1088 BROADWAY AVE 95125 — 998-6285
Kermit Hartley, prin.
Gunderson HS — 4-00011
622 GAUNDABERT LN 95136 — 998-6340
Arlando Smith, prin.
Leland HS, 6677 CAMDEN AVE 95120 — 4-00011
Don Bell, prin. — 998-6290

Lincoln HS, 555 DANA AVE 95126   4-00011
  Oreen Gernreich, prin.   998-6300
Pioneer HS   4-00011
  1290 BLOSSOM HILL RD 95118   998-6310
  Salvatore Cesario, prin.
San Jose HS Academy   3-00011
  275 N 24TH ST 95116   998-6320
  Basil Huffman, prin.
Willow Glen HS   4-00011
  2001 COTTLE AVE 95125   998-6330
  Mickey Long, prin.
Burnett MS, 850 N 2ND ST 95112   3-00100
  Michael O'Kane, prin.   998-6267
Castillero MS   4-00100
  6384 LEYLAND PARK DR 95120   998-6385
  Emerita Orta-Camilleri, prin.
Harte MS, 7050 BRET HARTE DR 95120   3-00100
  Joana Bregman, prin.   998-6270
Hoover MS, 1635 PARK AVE 95126   3-00100
  Patricia Gregory, prin.   998-6274
Markham MS, 2105 COTTLE AVE 95125   3-00100
  Mickey Long, prin.   998-6277
Muir MS, 1260 BRANHAM LN 95118   3-00100
  Cotine Weltzin, prin.   998-6281
Steinbeck MS, 820 STEINBECK DR 95123   4-00100
  Cecilia Espalin-Huffman, prin.   998-6395

Union ESD, 5175 UNION AVE 95124   5-11100
  Anthony Russo, supt.   377-8010
Dartmouth MS   3-00100
  5575 DARTMOUTH DR 95118   264-1122
  Carole Carlson, prin.
Union MS   3-00100
  2130 LOS GATOS ALMADEN RD 95124
  Martha Lux, prin.   371-0366

Archbishop Mitty HS   4-00011
  5000 MITTY WAY 95129   252-6610
  Timothy Brosnan, prin.
Aris Helicopters   1-CS
  1138 COLEMAN AVE 95110   998-3266
Bellarmine College Prep S   4-00011
  850 ELM ST 95126 – Fr. Reese, prin.   294-9224
Christian Community Academy   2-11111
  1523 MCLAUGHLIN AVE 95122   279-0846
  Ken Van Meter, prin.
Computer Learning Center   3-CS
  111 N MARKET ST STE 105 95113   271-3400
ConCorde Career Institute   2-CS
  1290 N 1ST ST 95112   441-6411
Evergreen Valley College   6-CC
  3095 YERBA BUENA RD 95135   274-7900
Heald Business College   2-CC
  684 EL PASEO DE SARATOGA 95130   370-2400
Heald Institute of Technology-San Jose   2-CC
  684 EL PASEO DE SARATOGA #A 95130
    295-8000
Liberty Baptist S, 2790 S KING RD 95122   3-11111
  Thomas Chaffin, prin.   274-5613
Masters Institute   1-CC
  50 AIRPORT PKY STE 8 95110   727-2955
National Hispanic University   2-CC
  135 E GISH RD STE 201 95112   441-2000
NEC-Bryman Campus   3-CS
  2015 NAGLEE AVE 95128   275-8800
NEC-San Jose Campus   2-CS
  1302 N 4TH ST 95112   452-8800
Notre Dame HS, 596 S 2ND ST 95112   2-00011
  Patricia Cain, prin.   294-1113
Palmer College of Chiropractic-West   3-UC
  90 E TASMAN DR 95134   944-6000
Presentation HS   3-00011
  2281 PLUMMER AVE 95125   264-1664
  Mary Miller, prin.
San Jose Christian College   2-UC
  PO BOX 1090 95108   293-9058
San Jose City College   7-CC
  2100 MOORPARK AVE 95128   298-2181
San Jose Medical Center   HSP
  675 E SANTA CLARA ST 95112   977-4535
San Jose State University   7-UC
  1 WASHINGTON SQ 95192   924-1000
Sawyer College   3-CS
  441 W TRIMBLE RD 95131   954-8200
Valley Christian HS   3-00011
  1570 BRANHAM LN 95118   377-5882

San Juan Capistrano, AC 714, PC 8, Orange
Capistrano USD   8-11111
  32972 CALLE PERFECTO 92675   489-7000
  James Fleming, supt.
Serra HS   2-00011
  31422 CAMINO CAPISTRANO 92675   489-7000
  Don Jeisy, prin.
Forster JHS   4-00100
  25601 CAMINO DEL AVION 92675   493-1133
  Patricia Boettcher, prin.
Other Schools – See Aliso Viejo, Dana Point, Laguna
  Niguel, Mission Viejo, San Clemente

Capistrano Valley Christian S   3-11111
  29352 EDGEWOOD RD 92675   493-5683
  Edward Carney, prin.
St. Margarets S   3-11111
  31641 LA NOVIA AVE 92675   661-0108
  Markham Campaigne, prin.
Santa Margarita HS   4-00011
  22062 ANTONIO PKY 92688   858-3350
  Msgr. Harris, prin.

San Leandro, AC 510, PC 8, Alameda
San Leandro USD   6-11111
  14735 JUNIPER ST 94579   667-3500
  Richard Tubbs, supt.
HS, 14735 JUNIPER ST 94579   4-00011
  Robert Oates, prin.   667-3540
Bancroft MS, 14735 JUNIPER ST 94579   3-00100
  Dennis Berger, prin.   667-3560
Muir MS, 14735 JUNIPER ST 94579   3-00100
  Ann Farias, prin.   667-3570

Chinese Christian S   3-11111
  750 FARGO AVE 94579   351-4957
  Katherine Dang, prin.
Western Career College   2-CS
  170 BAY FAIR MALL 94578   276-3888

San Lorenzo, AC 510, PC 7, Alameda
San Lorenzo USD, PO BOX 37 94580   6-11111
  Janis Duran, supt.   481-4600
Arroyo JSHS, PO BOX 37 94580   4-00111
  R. Michael Bowers, prin.   481-4662
JSHS, PO BOX 37 94580   4-00111
  Jerome Glenn, prin.   481-4627

Life Chiropractic College West   1-UC
  2005 VIA BARRETT 94580   276-9013

San Luis Obispo, AC 805, PC 8, San Luis Obispo
San Luis Coastal USD   6-11111
  1499 SAN LUIS DR 93401   543-2010
  Edwin Denton, supt.
HS, 1350 CALIFORNIA BLVD 93401   4-00011
  Mary Matakovich, prin.   544-5770
Laguna MS   3-00100
  11050 LOS OSOS VALLEY RD 93405   544-5555
  Richard Andrus, prin.
Other Schools – See Los Osos, Morro Bay

California Polytechnic State University   7-UC
  93407   756-1111
Central CA School Continuing Education   2-CS
  3195 MCMILLAN AVE STE F 93401   543-9123
Cuesta College   6-CC
  PO BOX J 93403   546-3101
Mission College Prep   2-00011
  682 PALM ST 93401   543-2131
  John Ruport, prin.

San Marcos, AC 619, PC 8, San Diego
San Marcos USD   7-11111
  1290 W SAN MARCOS BLVD 92069   744-4776
  Larry Maw, supt.
HS, 1615 W SAN MARCOS BLVD 92069   4-00011
  Robert Harman, prin.   744-5944
JHS, 650 W MISSION RD 92069   4-00100
  Susan Maki, prin.   744-1373

California State University   2-UC
  820 LOS VALLECITOS BLVD 92069   471-4100
Maric College of Medical Careers   2-CS
  1300 RANCHEROS DR 92069   747-1555
Palomar Community College   7-CC
  1140 W MISSION RD 92069   744-1150

San Marino, AC 818, PC 7, Los Angeles
San Marino USD, 1665 WEST DR 91108   5-11111
  Gary Richards, supt.   289-3691
HS, 2701 HUNTINGTON DR 91108   4-00011
  Don Banderas, prin.   304-1093
Huntington IS   3-00100
  1700 HUNTINGTON DR 91108   289-8948
  Loren Kleinrock, prin.

Southwestern Academy   2-11111
  2800 MONTEREY RD 91108   799-5010
  Kenneth Veronda, prin.

San Mateo, AC 415, PC 8, San Mateo
San Mateo-Foster City SD   6-11100
  PO BOX K 94402   312-7700
  Richard Damelio, supt.
Abbott MS, 600 36TH AVE 94403   3-00100
  Tom Harty, prin.   312-7600
Bayside MS, 2025 KEHOE AVE 94403   3-00100
  Toni-Sue Passantino, prin.   312-7660
Borel MS, 425 BARNESON AVE 94402   3-00100
  Clathel Zach, prin.   312-7670
Other Schools – See Foster City

San Mateo UNHSD   6-00011
  650 N DELAWARE ST 94401   348-8834
  Nicholas Gennaro, supt.
Aragon HS   4-00011
  900 ALAMEDA DE LAS PULGAS 94402
  Mark Avelar, prin.   342-7980
Hillsdale HS   4-00011
  3115 DEL MONTE ST 94403   574-7230
  Donald Leydig, prin.
HS, 506 N DELAWARE ST 94401   4-00011
  Charles Douglas, prin.   348-8050
Other Schools – See Burlingame, Millbrae, San Bruno

College of San Mateo   7-CC
  1700 W HILLSDALE BLVD 94402   574-6161
Junipero Serra HS   3-00011
  451 W 20TH AVE 94403   345-8207
  Michael Peterson, prin.

San Pablo, AC 510, PC 8, Contra Costa
West Contra Costa Usd
  Supt. – See Richmond

Helms MS, 2500 ROAD 20 94806   3-00100
  Linda La Nere, prin.   233-3988

Contra Costa College   6-CC
  2600 MISSION BELL DR 94806   235-7800

San Pedro, AC 310, PC see Los Angeles
Los Angeles USD
  Supt. — See Los Angeles
SHS, 1001 W 15TH ST 90731   4-00001
  Joe Viola, prin.   547-2491
Cooper Opportunity HS   Vo Tech
  2210 N TAPER AVE 90731   832-0376
  Warren Hockenbary, prin.
Dana JHS, 1501 S CABRILLO AVE 90731   4-00110
  Linda Lade, prin.   833-5235
Dodson JHS   4-00110
  28014 S MONTEREINA DR 90732   832-5342
  Peggy Selma, prin.

Mary Star of the Sea HS   2-00011
  810 W 8TH ST 90731   547-1138
  James Golden, prin.

San Rafael, AC 415, PC 8, Marin
Dixie ESD   4-11100
  380 NOVA ALBION WAY 94903   479-8881
  Larry Lyon, supt.
Miller Creek MS   2-00100
  2255 LAS GALLINAS AVE 94903   479-1660
  Linda Sheppard, prin.

San Rafael CSD   5-11111
  225 WOODLAND AVE 94901   485-2300
  Jeff Blackwell, supt.
HS, 185 MISSION AVE 94901   3-00011
  Bernard Llacuna, prin.   485-2330
Terra Linda HS   3-00011
  320 NOVA ALBION WAY 94903   485-2370
  Ann Link, prin.
Davidson MS   3-00100
  280 WOODLAND AVE 94901   485-2400
  Mary Buttler, prin.

Columbia Pacific University   6-HMS
  1415 3RD ST 94901   459-1650
Dominican College of San Rafael   3-UC
  50 ACACIA AVE 94901   457-4440
Marin Academy   2-00011
  1600 MISSION AVE 94901   453-4550
  Bruce Shaw, prin.

San Ramon, AC 510, PC 8, Contra Costa
San Ramon Valley USD
  Supt. — See Danville
California HS   4-00011
  9870 BROADMOOR DR 94583   828-9311
  (—), prin.
Pine Valley IS   3-00100
  3000 PINE VALLEY RD 94583   828-4360
  Jan Rowley, prin.

Santa Ana, AC 714, PC 10, Orange
Garden Grove USD
  Supt. — See Garden Grove
Fitz IS, 4600 W MCFADDEN AVE 92704   3-00100
  John Barriga, prin.   663-6351

Santa Ana USD, 1405 FRENCH ST 92701   8-11111
  Rudy Castruita, supt.   558-5501
Century HS, 1401 S GRAND AVE 92705   4-00011
  Thomas Reasin, prin.   568-7000
Saddleback HS   5-00011
  2802 S FLOWER ST 92707   241-6450
  Marylouise Ortega, prin.
HS, 520 W WALNUT ST 92701   5-00011
  Lewis Bratcher, prin.   567-4900
Valley HS   5-00011
  1801 S GREENVILLE ST 92704   241-6410
  Robert Nelson, prin.
Carr IS, 2120 W EDINGER AVE 92704   4-00100
  Vincent Tafolla, prin.   241-6430
Lathrop IS, 1111 S BROADWAY 92707   4-00100
  Greg Rankin, prin.   558-5701
MacArthur Fundamental IS   4-00100
  600 W ALTON AVE 92707   241-6515
  Jane Russo, prin.
McFadden IS, 2701 S RAITT ST 92704   4-00100
  Brenda McGaffigan, prin.   241-6525
Sierra IS, 1901 N MCCLAY ST 92701   4-00100
  Daniel Salcedo, prin.   558-5886
Spurgeon IS, 2701 W 5TH ST 92703   4-00100
  Cathy Makin, prin.   558-5586
Willard IS, 1342 N ROSS ST 92706   4-00100
  Robert Butcher, prin.   558-5731

Tustin USD
  Supt. — See Tustin
Foothill HS, 19251 DODGE AVE 92705   4-00011
  Janis Jones, prin.   730-7464
Hewes MS, 13232 HEWES AVE 92705   3-00100
  Regina Cain, prin.   730-7348

Bethel Baptist Church S   2-11111
  901 S EUCLID ST 92704   839-3600
  Terry Cantrell, prin.
California Coast University   3-UC
  700 N MAIN ST 92701   547-9625
California School of Court Reporting   2-CS
  1201 N MAIN ST 92701   541-6892

Calvary Chapel S — 4-11111
3800 S FAIRVIEW ST 92704 — 556-0965
David Rolph, prin.
Health Staff Training Institute — 2-CS
1505 E 17TH ST STE 122 92701 — 543-9828
Mater Dei HS — 4-00011
1202 W EDINGER AVE 92707 — 754-7711
Lyle Porter, prin.
Pacific Coast College — 3-CS
118 W 5TH ST 92701 — 558-8700
Pacific Travel School — 3-CS
2515 N MAIN ST 92701 — 543-9495
Rancho Santiago College — 8-CC
1530 W 17TH ST 92706 — 667-3000

Santa Barbara, AC 805, PC 8, Santa Barbara
Santa Barbara SD, 723 E COTA ST 93103 — 7-11111
Blas Garza, supt. — 963-4331
San Marcos HS, 723 E COTA ST 93103 — 4-00011
Robert Ferguson, prin. — 967-4581
HS, 723 E COTA ST 93103 — 4-00011
Andrew Hernandez, prin. — 966-9101
La Colina JHS, 723 E COTA ST 93103 — 3-00100
Robert Bowen, prin. — 967-4506
La Cumbre JHS, 723 E COTA ST 93103 — 4-00100
Nancy O'Leary, prin. — 687-0761
JHS, 723 E COTA ST 93103 — 3-00100
John Mendoza, prin. — 963-7751
Other Schools – See Goleta

Anacapa S — 2-00111
814 SANTA BARBARA ST 93101 — 965-0228
Gordon Sichi, prin.
Antioch University — 1-UC
801 GARDEN ST STE 101 93101 — 962-8179
Bishop Garcia Diego HS — 2-00011
4000 LA COLINA RD 93110 — 967-1266
Fr. Charles Hofschulte, prin.
Brooks Institute of Photography — 3-UC
801 ALSTON RD 93108 — 966-3888
Cancer Foundation of Santa Barbara — CS
PO BOX 837 93102 — 682-7300
Devereux Center in California — HND
PO BOX 1079 93102 — 800-359-7979
Fielding Institute — 3-UC
2112 SANTA BARBARA ST 93105 — 687-1099
Laguna Blanca S — 2-11111
4125 PALOMA DR 93110 — 687-2461
Arthur Merovick, prin.
Santa Barbara Business College — 2-CS
5266 HOLLISTER AVE 93111 — 967-9677
Santa Barbara City College — 7-CC
721 CLIFF DR 93109 — 965-0581
Santa Barbara Cottage & Gen. Hosp. — HSP
PO BOX 689 93102 — 569-7290
University of California 93106 — 7-UC
— 893-2485
Westmont College — 4-UC
955 LA PAZ RD 93108 — 565-6000

Santa Clara, AC 408, PC 8, Santa Clara
Santa Clara USD, PO BOX 397 95052 — 7-11111
Nicholas Gervase, supt. — 983-2000
HS, 3000 BENTON ST 95051 — 4-00011
Don Flohr, prin. — 985-5900
Wilcox HS, 3250 MONROE ST 95051 — 4-00011
Rod Adams, prin. — 554-6300
Buchser MS, 1111 BELLOMY ST 95050 — 4-00100
Marcia Skuse, prin. — 984-2900
Other Schools – See Sunnyvale

Institute for Business and Technology — 2-CS
2550 SCOTT BLVD 95050 — 727-1060
Mission College — 7-CC
3000 MISSION COLLEGE BLVD 95054 — 988-2200
St. Lawrence Academy — 2-00111
2000 SAINT LAWRENCE DR 95051 — 296-3002
Ronald Modeste, prin.
Santa Clara University 95053 — 6-UC
— 554-4764

Santa Clarita, AC 805, PC 9, Los Angeles
William S. Hart UNHSD — 7-00111
21515 REDVIEW DR 91350 — 259-0033
Walter Swanson, supt.
Other Schools – See Canyon Country, Newhall,
Saugus, Valencia

Santa Cruz, AC 408, PC 8, Santa Cruz
Live Oak ESD, 966 BOSTWICK LN 95062 — 4-11100
Rudy Carino, supt. — 475-6333
Del Mar MS, 1959 MERRILL ST 95062 — 3-00100
S. Nathan Cross, prin. — 475-6565

Santa Cruz CSD, 133 MISSION ST 95060 — 6-11111
David Sklarz, supt. — 429-3800
Harbor HS, 300 LA FONDA AVE 95062 — 4-00011
Ken Thomas, prin. — 429-3812
HS, 415 WALNUT AVE 95060 — 4-00011
Terry Pearman, prin. — 429-3959
Branciforte JHS, 315 POPLAR AVE 95062 — 3-00100
Roy Nelson, prin. — 429-3883
Mission Hill JHS, 425 KING ST 95060 — 3-00100
Ron Boleck, prin. — 429-3860
Other Schools – See Soquel

University of California-Santa Cruz 95064 — 6-UC
— 459-0111

Santa Fe Springs, AC 310, PC 7, Los Angeles
Little Lake City ESD — 5-11100
10515 PIONEER BLVD 90670 — 868-8241
Maria Ott, supt.
Lake Center JHS — 3-00100
10503 PIONEER BLVD 90670 — 868-4977
David Kommer, prin.
Other Schools – See Norwalk

Whittier UNHSD
Supt. — See Whittier
Santa Fe HS — 4-00011
10400 ORR AND DAY RD 90670 — 698-8121
Sandra Thorstenson, prin.

St. Paul HS — 4-00011
9635 GREENLEAF AVE 90670 — 698-6246
Fr. Gallagher, prin.

Santa Maria, AC 805, PC 8, Santa Barbara
Orcutt UNESD
Supt. — See Orcutt
Lakeview JHS, 3700 ORCUTT RD 93455 — 2-00100
Douglas Koel, prin. — 937-5586

Santa Maria-Bonita UNESD — 6-11100
708 S MILLER ST 93454 — 928-1783
Gail Tissier, supt.
El Camino MS — 3-00100
219 W EL CAMINO ST 93454 — 346-8573
Ray Blute, prin.
Fesler MS, 1100 E FESLER ST 93454 — 3-00100
Joanne Cameron, prin. — 346-8586

Santa Maria JUNHSD — 5-00011
829 S LINCOLN ST 93454 — 922-4573
Dean Reece, supt.
Righetti HS, 941 E FOSTER RD 93455 — 4-00011
Gerald Walsh, prin. — 937-2051
HS, 901 S BROADWAY 93454 — 4-00011
Jeff Hearn, prin. — 925-2567

Allan Hancock College — 6-CC
800 S COLLEGE DR 93454 — 922-6966
St. Joseph HS — 3-00011
4120 S BRADLEY RD 93455 — 937-2038
Fr. Thomas Elewaut, prin.
Santa Barbara Business College — 2-CS
303 PLAZA DR 93454 — 922-8256
Valley Christian Academy — 2-11111
2970 SANTA MARIA WAY 93455 — 937-6317
Charles Mason, prin.

Santa Monica, AC 310, PC 8, Los Angeles
Santa Monica-Malibu USD — 6-11111
1651 16TH ST 90404 — 450-8338
Neil Schmidt, supt.
HS, 601 PICO BLVD 90405 — 4-00011
Sylvia Rousseau, prin. — 395-3204
Adams MS, 2425 16TH ST 90405 — 3-00100
Jerry Kantor, prin. — 452-2326
Lincoln MS — 4-00100
1501 CALIFORNIA AVE 90403 — 393-9227
Ilene Straus, prin.
Other Schools – See Malibu

Concord HS — 2-00011
2121 CLOVERFIELD BLVD 90404 — 828-9443
Sonya Packer, prin.
Crossroads S, 1714 21ST ST 90404 — 3-11111
Paul Cumminc, prin. — 829-7391
Gemological Institute of America — 4-CS
1660 STEWART ST 90404 — 829-2991
Rand Graduate School — 1-UC
PO BOX 2138 90407 — 393-0111
St. John's Hospital & Health Center — HSP
1328 22ND ST 90404 — 829-8292
St. Monica HS — 3-00011
1030 LINCOLN BLVD 90403 — 394-3701
Sr. Cheryl Milner, prin.
Santa Monica College — 7-CC
1900 PICO BLVD 90405 — 450-5150

Santa Paula, AC 805, PC 8, Ventura
Briggs ESD — 2-11100
14438 W TELEGRAPH RD 93060 — 525-7151
Carol Vines, supt.
Briggs MS — 2-01100
14438 W TELEGRAPH RD 93060 — 525-7151
Carol Vines, supt.

Santa Paula ESD, PO BOX 710 93061 — 5-11100
David Phillips, supt. — 933-5342
Isbell MS, PO BOX 710 93061 — 3-00100
Arvid Brommers, prin. — 933-5329

Santa Paula UNHSD — 4-00011
500 E SANTA BARBARA ST 93060 — 525-0988
Robert Fisher, supt.
Santa Paula Union HS — 4-00011
404 N 6TH ST 93060 — 525-4406
Sandra Barbier, prin.

Thomas Aquinas College — 2-UC
10000 OJAI RD 93060 — 525-4417

Santa Rosa, AC 707, PC 9, Sonoma
Oak Grove UNESD, 5285 HALL RD 95401 — 3-11100
Robert Harper, supt. — 545-0171
Willowside MS, 5285 HALL RD 95401 — 2-01100
Loren Barker, prin. — 542-3322

Santa Rosa CSD, PO BOX 940 95402 — 7-11111
H. Lewis Alsobrook, supt. — 528-5181
Montgomery SHS — 4-00001
1250 HAHMAN DR 95405 — 528-5191
Cynthia Pilar, prin.
Piner HS, 1700 FULTON RD 95403 — 4-00011
Joseph Sewell, prin. — 528-5245
HS, 1235 MENDOCINO AVE 95401 — 4-00011
Michael Panas, prin. — 528-5291
Comstock JHS, 2750 W STEELE LN 95403 — 4-00110
Colleen Larson, prin. — 528-5266
Cook JHS, 2480 SEBASTOPOL RD 95407 — 4-00110
Carole Ellis, prin. — 528-5156
Rincon Valley JHS — 4-00110
950 MIDDLE RINCON RD 95409 — 528-5255
Jeannette Anglin, prin.
JHS, 500 E ST 95404 — 3-00110
Ron Campanile, prin. — 528-5281
Slater JHS, 3500 SONOMA AVE 95405 — 4-00110
Harry Arbios, prin. — 528-5241

Cardinal Newman HS — 2-00011
50 URSULINE RD 95403 — 546-6470
Thomas Beecher, prin.
Covenant Community S — 2-11111
1315 PACIFIC AVE 95404 — 528-8040
Ken McGrath, prin.
Empire College — 2-CS
3033 CLEVELAND AVE STE 107 95403
— 546-4000
Heald Business College — 2-CC
2425 MENDOCINO AVE 95403 — 525-1300
Redwood Junior Academy — 2-11111
385 MARK WEST SPRINGS RD 95404 — 545-1697
Ronald Williams, prin.
Rincon Valley Christian S — 2-11111
697 BENICIA DR 95409 — 539-1486
Patrick Clifford, prin.
Santa Rosa Junior College — 7-CC
1501 MENDOCINO AVE 95401 — 527-4443
Ursuline HS, 90 URSULINE RD 95403 — 2-00011
Sr. Margaret Johnson, prin. — 524-1130

Santa Ynez, AC 805, PC 5, Santa Barbara
Santa Ynez Valley UNHSD — 3-00011
PO BOX 398 93460 — 688-6487
Dean Anders, supt.
Santa Ynez Valley Union HS — 3-00011
PO BOX 398 93460 — 688-6487
Dean Anders, prin.

Santee, AC 619, PC 8, San Diego
Grossmont UNHSD
Supt. — See La Mesa
Santana HS — 4-00011
9915 N MAGNOLIA AVE 92071 — 448-5500
Terrie Pennock, prin.
West Hills Middle HS — 4-00010
8756 MAST BLVD 92071 — 562-0507
Bob Guess, prin.

San Ysidro, AC 619, PC see San Diego
San Ysidro ESD — 5-11100
4350 OTAY MESA RD 92173 — 428-4476
William O'Neill, supt.
MS, 4345 OTAY MESA RD 92173 — 3-00100
Manuel Paul, prin. — 428-5551

Saratoga, AC 408, PC 8, Santa Clara
Campbell UNHSD
Supt. — See San Jose
Prospect HS, 18900 PROSPECT RD 95070 — 4-00011
Bruce Samples, prin. — 253-1662
Los Gatos-Saratoga JUNHSD
Supt. — See Los Gatos
HS, 20300 HERRIMAN AVE 95070 — 3-00011
(—), prin. — 867-3411
Saratoga Union Elem SD — 4-11100
20460 FORREST HILLS DR 95070 — 867-3424
Mary Gardner, supt.
Redwood MS — 3-00100
13925 FRUITVALE AVE 95070 — 867-3042
Gail Wasserman, prin.

West Valley College — 7-CC
14000 FRUITVALE AVE 95070 — 867-2200

Saugus, AC 805, PC see Santa Clarita
William S. Hart UNHSD
Supt. — See Santa Clarita
HS, 21900 CENTURION WAY 91350 — 4-00011
Cheryl Brown, prin. — 297-3900

Sausalito, AC 415, PC 6, Marin
Sausalito ESD, 630 NEVADA ST 94965 — 2-11100
Patricia Blackwell-Davis, supt. — 332-3190
North Bay MS, 630 NEVADA ST 94965 — 1-01100
Peggy Hirsh, prin. — 332-3573

Scotts Valley, AC 408, PC 6, Santa Cruz
Scotts Valley UNESD — 4-11100
4444 SCTTS VALLEY DR STE 5B 95066
Andy La Couture, supt. — 438-1820
MS, 8 BEAN CREEK RD 95066 — 2-00100
Chris McGriff, prin. — 438-0610

Baymonte Christian ES — 2-11111
5000B GRANITE CREEK RD 95066 — 438-0100
Steve Patterson, prin.
Bethany Bible College — 2-UC
800 BETHANY DR 95066 — 438-3800

Seaside, AC 408, PC 8, Monterey
Monterey Peninsula USD
  Supt. — See Monterey
King MS, 1713 BROADWAY AVE 93955   3-00100
  Gwen Laster, prin.   899-7000

Sebastopol, AC 707, PC 6, Sonoma
Analy UNHSD, 6980 ANALY AVE 95472   4-00011
  John Hayes, supt.   824-6403
Analy HS, 6950 ANALY AVE 95472   4-00011
  Martin Webb, prin.   824-6436
Other Schools – See Forestville

Gravenstein UNESD   3-11100
  3840 TWIG AVE 95472   823-7008
  Joseph Carnation, supt.
Gravenstein ES, 3840 TWIG AVE 95472   2-10100
  Fred Cochran, prin.   823-5361

Sebastopol UNESD   4-11100
  7905 VALENTINE AVE 95472   829-4570
  Mike Carey, supt.
Brook Haven MS   2-00100
  7905 VALENTINE AVE 95472   829-4590
  James Pascoe, prin.

Twin Hills UNESD   3-11100
  700 WATERTROUGH RD 95472   823-0871
  Robert Perkins, supt.
Twin Hills MS   2-00100
  1685 WATERTROUGH RD 95472   823-7446
  Bob Hansen, prin.

Selma, AC 209, PC 7, Fresno
Laton JUSD
  Supt. — See Laton
Conejo MS, 4282 E CONEJO AVE 93662   2-00100
  Rich Wosnik, prin.   896-9225

Selma USD   6-11111
  3036 THOMPSON AVE 93662   896-6500
  Steve Bojorquez, supt.
HS, 3125 WRIGHT ST 93662   4-00011
  Gary Kinsey, prin.   896-6500
Heartland JSHS, 2269 SYLVIA ST 93662   1-00111
  Frank Hernandez, prin.   896-6500
Lincoln MS, 1239 NELSON BLVD 93662   3-00100
  Lucile Uzunovic, prin.   869-6500

Sepulveda, AC 818, PC see Los Angeles
Los Angeles USD
  Supt. — See Los Angeles
Monroe HS, 9229 HASKELL AVE 91343   5-00011
  Joan Elam, prin.   892-4311
JHS, 15330 PLUMMER ST 91343   4-00110
  Robert Reimann, prin.   892-3151

Centers of Learning S   2-11111
  8855 HASKELL AVE 91343   894-3213
  Debra Grill, prin.
Los Angeles Baptist HS   3-00111
  9825 WOODLEY AVE 91343   894-5742
  Gary Smidderks, prin.
North Hills Prep S   2-00111
  9433 SEPULVEDA BLVD 91343   894-8388
  Deborah Bayle, prin.
Veterans Administration Medical Center   HSP
  16111 PLUMMER ST 91343   891-7711

Shafter, AC 805, PC 6, Kern
Kern HSD
  Supt. — See Bakersfield
HS, 526 MANNEL AVE 93263   4-00011
  Charles Rekosh, prin.   746-4961

Richland-Lerdo UESD   5-11100
  331 N SHAFTER AVE 93263   746-3904
  Daniel Knapp, supt.
Richland JHS   2-00100
  331 N SHAFTER AVE 93263   746-3944
  Ronald Adams, prin.

Shandon, AC 805, PC 3, San Luis Obispo
Shandon JUSD, PO BOX 79 93461   2-11111
  Richard Summers, supt.   238-0286
HS, PO BOX 79 93461   1-00011
  Richard Summers, prin.   238-0286
JHS, PO BOX 79 93461   1-00100
  Richard Summers, prin.   238-0286

Sherman Oaks, AC 818, PC see Los Angeles
Los Angeles USD
  Supt. — See Los Angeles
Millikan JHS   4-00110
  5041 SUNNYSLOPE AVE 91423   788-5020
  David Almada, prin.

Buckley S   3-11111
  3900 STANSBURY AVE 91423   783-1610
  Walter Baumhoff, prin.
Los Angeles ORT Technical Institute   2-CS
  15130 VENTURA BLVD STE 250 91403
   788-7222
Notre Dame HS   4-00011
  13645 RIVERSIDE DR 91423   501-2300
  David Doyle, prin.

Shingle Springs, AC 916, PC 4, El Dorado
Buckeye UNESD, PO BOX 547 95682   5-11100
  Joyce Flanigan, supt.   677-2261
Other Schools – See Cameron Park

El Dorado UNHSD
  Supt. — See Diamond Springs
Ponderosa HS   4-00011
  3661 PONDEROSA RD 95682   622-5590
  David Sargent, prin.

Latrobe ESD, 7900 S SHINGLE RD 95682   2-11100
  Bonnie Allen, supt.   933-0423
Millers Hill MS   1-01100
  7900 S SHINGLE RD 95682   677-0260
  Bonnie Allen, prin.

Shoshone, AC 619, PC 2, Inyo
Death Valley USD   1-11111
  PO BOX 217 92384   852-4303
  Kenneth Smith, supt.
Death Valley HS, PO BOX 217 92384   1-00011
  Kenneth Smith, prin.   852-4394

Sierra Madre, AC 818, PC 7, Los Angeles

Alverno HS   2-00011
  200 N MICHILLINDA AVE 91024   355-3463
  Elizabeth Broome, prin.
Marantha HS, 160 N CANON AVE 91024   3-00011
  Stephen Allen, prin.   355-4242

Silverado, AC 714, PC 3, Orange

St. Michaels College Prep HS   1-00111
  19292 EL TORO RD 92676   858-0222
  Fr. Hubert Szanto, prin.

Simi Valley, AC 805, PC 9, Ventura
Simi Valley USD   7-11111
  875 COCHRAN ST 93065   520-6500
  Mary Wolford, supt.
Royal SHS, 1402 ROYAL AVE 93065   4-00001
  Michael McConahey, prin.   520-6875
SHS, 5400 COCHRAN ST 93063   4-00001
  Kathryn Scroggin, prin.   520-6850
Hillside JHS   4-00110
  2222 FITZGERALD RD 93065   520-6810
  (—), prin.
Sequoia JHS, 3570 COCHRAN ST 93063   4-00110
  Jan Britz, prin.   520-6800
Sinaloa JHS, 601 ROYAL AVE 93065   4-00110
  Pat Dews, prin.   520-6830
Valley View JHS, 3347 TAPO ST 93063   4-00110
  Don Gaudioso, prin.   520-6820

Simi Valley Adult Education   2-CS
  3192 E LOS ANGELES AVE 93065   527-4840

Snelling, AC 209, PC 2, Merced
Merced River UNESD   2-11100
  2241 TURLOCK RD 95369   722-4581
  Eldon Henderson, supt.
Other Schools – See Winton

Solana Beach, AC 619, PC 7, San Diego
San Dieguito UNHSD
  Supt. — See Encinitas
Warren JHS, 155 STEVENS AVE 92075   3-00100
  Marilyn Pugh, prin.   755-1558

Santa Fe Christian S   3-11111
  838 ACADEMY DR 92075   755-8900
  Garry Thornton, prin.

Soledad, AC 408, PC 6, Monterey
Soledad UNESD, PO BOX 186 93960   4-11100
  Richard Bray, supt.   678-3989
Main Street MS, 441 MAIN ST 93960   3-01100
  Marvin Silver, prin.   678-3923

Solvang, AC 805, PC 5, Santa Barbara
Solvang ESD, 565 ATTERDAG RD 93463   3-11100
  Scott Purdy, supt.   688-4810
MS, 565 ATTERDAG RD 93463   2-01100
  Scott Purdy, prin.   688-5112

Sonoma, AC 707, PC 6, Sonoma
Sonoma Valley USD   5-11111
  721 W NAPA ST 95476   935-6000
  Biefke Vos Saulino, supt.
Sonoma Valley HS   4-00011
  20000 BROADWAY 95476   935-6010
  Ralph Hahn, prin.
Altimira IS, 17805 ARNOLD DR 95476   4-00100
  Marilyn Kelly, prin.   935-6020

Hanna Boys HS   1-01111
  17000 ARNOLD DR 95476   996-6767
  Stephen Cederborg, prin.

Sonora, AC 209, PC 5, Tuolumne
Sonora UNHSD   4-00011
  251 BARRETTA ST 95370   533-8510
  Michael King, prin.
HS, 430 N WASHINGTON ST 95370   4-00011
  Jack Harris, prin.   532-5511

Soquel, AC 408, PC 6, Santa Cruz
Santa Cruz CSD
  Supt. — See Santa Cruz
HS, 401 OLD SAN JOSE RD 95073   4-00011
  Mary Lou Mendoza, prin.   429-3919

South El Monte, AC 818, PC 7, Los Angeles
El Monte UNHSD
  Supt. — See El Monte
JHS, 1001 DURFEE AVE 91733   4-00010
  Victor Chavez, prin.   442-0218

Valle Lindo ESD   4-11100
  1431 CENTRAL AVE 91733   580-0622
  Mary Labrucherie, supt.
Shively MS, 1431 CENTRAL AVE 91733   3-01100
  Wes Poutsma, prin.   580-0611

South Gate, PC 8, Los Angeles
Los Angeles USD
  Supt. — See Los Angeles
HS, 3351 FIRESTONE BLVD 90280   5-00011
  Raul Moreno, prin.   213-567-2333
JHS, 4100 FIRESTONE BLVD 90280   5-00100
  Peter Ferry, prin.   213-567-1431

Southeast Lutheran HS   2-00111
  8691 CALIFORNIA AVE 90280   213-563-2225
  Brent Baden, prin.

South Lake Tahoe, AC 916, PC 7, El Dorado
Lake Tahoe USD   6-11111
  PO BOX 14426 96151   541-2850
  Rich Fischer, supt.
HS, 1735 LAKE TAHOE BLVD 96150   4-00011
  William Murray, prin.   541-4111
MS, PO BOX 14426 96151   4-00100
  Rich Alexander, prin.   541-6404

Lake Tahoe Community College   4-CC
  PO BOX 14445 96151   541-4660

South Pasadena, AC 818, PC 7, Los Angeles
South Pasadena USD   5-11111
  1020 EL CENTRO ST 91030   441-5707
  Leslie Adelson, supt.
HS, 1401 FREMONT AVE 91030   4-00011
  Benjamin Ramirez, prin.   441-5731
MS, 1600 OAK ST 91030   3-00100
  Marsha Aguirre, prin.   441-5761

South San Francisco, AC 415, PC 8, San Mateo
South San Francisco USD   6-11111
  398 B ST 94080 – Richard Rigg, supt.   877-8700
El Camino HS, 398 B ST 94080   4-00011
  Diane Kline, prin.   877-8806
HS, 398 B ST 94080   4-00011
  Barb Olds, prin.   877-8754
Alta Loma MS, 398 B ST 94080   3-00100
  Bruce Grantham, prin.   877-8797
Parkway Heights MS, 398 B ST 94080   3-00100
  Richard Zaro, prin.   877-8788
Westborough MS, 398 B ST 94080   3-00100
  Philip White, prin.   877-8848

Spring Valley, AC 619, PC 8, San Diego
Grossmont UNHSD
  Supt. — See La Mesa
Monte Vista HS   4-00011
  3230 SWETWATER SPRINGS BLVD 91977
  Barbara Nowak, prin.   660-9902
Mt. Miguel HS   4-00011
  1800 SWEETWATER RD 91977   463-5551
  Brian Smith, prin.

La Mesa-Spring Valley ESD
  Supt. — See La Mesa
La Presa MS, 1001 LELAND ST 91977   4-00100
  Steven Coover, prin.   668-5720
MS, 3900 CONRAD DR 91977   4-00100
  Bill Yakubik, prin.   668-5750

United Training Institute   1-HMS
  PO BOX 715 91976

Stanford, AC 415, PC 7, Santa Clara

Stanford University   7-UC
  1 STANFORD UNIVERSITY 94305   723-2300

Stockton, AC 209, PC 9, San Joaquin
Lincoln USD, 2010 W SWAIN RD 95207   6-11111
  Lynne Rauch, supt.   953-8700
Lincoln HS   4-00011
  6844 ALEXANDRIA PL 95207   953-8920
  (—), prin.
Sierra MS, 6776 ALEXANDRIA PL 95207   3-00100
  Steve Schaumleffel, prin.   953-8748

Linden USD
  Supt. — See Linden
Waterloo MS, 7007 PEZZI RD 95215   2-01100
  Sue Rafferty, prin.   931-0818

Lodi USD
  Supt. — See Lodi
Bear Creek HS   4-00011
  10555 THORNTON RD 95209   953-8234
  Robert Vieth, prin.
Delta Sierra MS   3-00100
  2255 WAGNER HEIGHTS RD 95209   953-8510
  Debbie deGanna, prin.
Morada MS, 5001 EASTVIEW DR 95212   3-00100
  Karen Woznick, prin.   953-8491

Stockton City USD   8-11111
  701 N MADISON ST 95202   953-4050
  Mary Mend, supt.
Edison HS, 1425 S CENTER ST 95206   4-00011
  Merle Smart, prin.   953-4413
Franklin S   4-00011
  300 N GERTRUDE AVE 95215   953-4363
  Carl Toliver, prin.
Stagg HS, 1621 BROOKSIDE RD 95207   4-00011
  Rupert Asuncion, prin.   953-3053

Fremont MS, 2021 E FLORA ST 95205 — 4-00100
Margarita Wulftange, prin. — 953-4526
Hamilton MS, 2245 E 11TH ST 95206 — 4-00100
Edna Ramos, prin. — 953-4701
Marshall MS, 1141 LEVER BLVD 95206 — 4-00100
Richard Yescas, prin. — 953-4559
Webster MS — 4-00100
2725 MICHIGAN AVE 95204 —
Vernon Uyeda, prin. — 953-4579

Andon College at Stockton — 2-CS
1201 N EL DORADO ST 95202 — 462-8777
Brookside Christian S — 3-11111
2111 QUAIL LAKES DR 95207 — 473-8944
Dennis Gibson, prin.
Heald Business College — 2-CC
1776 W MARCH LN STE 330 95207 — 477-1114
Humphreys College — 2-UC
6650 INGLEWOOD AVE 95207 — 478-0800
MTI Business College of Stockton — 2-CS
6006 N EL DORADO ST 95207 — 957-3030
St. Mary HS, PO BOX 7247 95267 — 3-00011
Peter Morelli, prin. — 957-3340
San Joaquin Delta College — 7-CC
5151 PACIFIC AVE 95207 — 474-5051
San Joaquin General Hospital — HSP
PO BOX 1020 95201 — 468-6600
Stockton Christian S — 2-11111
9025 WEST LN 95210 — 957-3043
Percel Graves, prin.
University of the Pacific — 6-UC
3601 PACIFIC AVE 95211 — 946-2011
Western Truck School — 2-CS
1002 N BROADWAY AVE 95205 — 465-1191

Strathmore, AC 209, PC 4, Tulare
Strathmore UNHSD — 2-00011
PO BOX 37 93267 — 568-1731
Anneli Crawford, supt.
HS, PO BOX 37 93267 — 2-00011
Anneli Crawford, prin. — 568-1731

Studio City, AC 818, PC see North Hollywood

Los Angeles Business College — 2-CC
11012 VENTURA BLVD # 369 91604

Suisun City, AC 707, PC 7, Solano
Fairfield-Suisun USD
Supt. — See Fairfield
Crystal MS, 100 CORDELIA ST 94585 — 3-00100
Lois Campbell, prin. — 421-4135
Green Valley MS — 3-00100
3630 RITCHIE RD 94585 — 421-4185
John Rogers, prin.

Solano Community College — 6-CC
PO BOX 246 94585 — 864-7000

Sunland, AC 818, PC see Los Angeles
Los Angeles USD
Supt. — See Los Angeles
Mt. Gleason JHS — 4-00100
10965 MOUNT GLEASON AVE 91040 — 352-1466
Patricia Joe, prin.

Sunnyvale, AC 408, PC 9, Santa Clara
Cupertino UNESD
Supt. — See Cupertino
Cupertino JHS — 3-00100
1650 S BERNARDO AVE 94087 — 245-0303
Van Adams, prin.

Fremont UNHSD, PO BOX F 94087 — 6-00011
Betty Pacheco, supt. — 522-2200
Fremont HS, PO BOX F 94087 — 4-00011
Harry Bettencourt, prin. — 522-2400
Other Schools – See Cupertino, San Jose

Santa Clara USD
Supt. — See Santa Clara
Peterson MS, 1380 ROSALIA AVE 94087 — 4-00100
Bob Runyon, prin. — 720-1564

Sunnyvale ESD, PO BOX 3217 94088 — 6-11100
Benjamin Picard, supt. — 522-8200
MS, 1080 MANGO AVE 94087 — 4-00100
Thomas Sutkus, prin. — 522-8288

Sun Valley, AC 818, PC see Los Angeles
Los Angeles USD
Supt. — See Los Angeles
Francis Polytechnic SHS — 4-00001
12431 ROSCOE BLVD 91352 — 767-4860
Carolyn Burch, prin.
Byrd JHS, 9171 TELFAIR AVE 91352 — 4-00110
Gerald Horowitz, prin. — 767-9550
JHS, 7330 BAKMAN AVE 91352 — 4-00110
Emilio Garcia, prin. — 765-3010

Village Christian S — 4-11111
8930 VILLAGE AVE 91352 — 767-8382
Ronald Sipur, prin.

Susanville, AC 916, PC 6, Lassen
Lassen UNHSD — 4-00011
1324 CORNELL ST 96130 — 257-5134
Jane Maxwell, supt.
Lassen HS, 1110 MAIN ST 96130 — 3-00011
Jane Maxwell, prin. — 257-2141

Susanville ESD — 4-11100
940 HOSPITAL LN 96130 — 257-8200
Mark Evans, prin.
Diamond View MS — 2-00100
850 RICHMOND RD 96130 — 257-5144
Charles Spence, prin.

Lassen College — 4-CC
PO BOX 3000 96130 — 257-6181

Sutter, AC 916, PC 5, Sutter
Sutter UNHSD, PO BOX 498 95982 — 2-00011
Wayne Gadberry, supt. — 741-5161
HS, 2665 ACACIA AVE 95982 — 2-00011
Wayne Gadberry, prin. — 741-5161

Sutter Creek, AC 209, PC 4, Amador
Amador County USD
Supt. — See Jackson
Amador HS 95685 — 2-00011
Joe Garcia, prin. — 267-5244
Independence HS 95685 — 1-00011
William Miller, prin. — 267-5274

Sylmar, AC 818, PC see Los Angeles
Los Angeles USD
Supt. — See Los Angeles
SHS, 13050 BORDEN AVE 91342 — 4-00001
Linda Gutierrez-Ambro, prin. — 367-1971
Olive Vista JHS, 14600 TYLER ST 91342 — 4-00110
Charles Baldwin, prin. — 367-1071

First Lutheran JSHS — 2-00111
13361 GLENOAKS BLVD 91342 — 362-9223
William Stark, prin.
Hathaway S, PO BOX 923670 91392 — 2-11111
Brian Cahill, prin. — 896-2474
Los Angeles Lutheran HS — 2-00011
13570 ELDRIDGE AVE 91342 — 362-5861
Dale Wolfgram, prin.
Los Angeles Mission College — 5-CC
13356 ELDRIDGE AVE 91342 — 364-7600

Taft, AC 805, PC 6, Kern
Taft City ESD, 820 6TH ST 93268 — 4-11100
George Bury, supt. — 763-1521
Lincoln MS, 810 6TH ST 93268 — 3-00100
Linda LaMarre, prin. — 765-2127

Taft UNHSD, 701 7TH ST 93268 — 3-00011
Lynn Davies, supt. — 763-2300
Taft Union HS, 701 7TH ST 93268 — 3-00011
Donald Mills, prin. — 763-2334

Taft College — 4-CC
29 EMMONS PARK DR 93268 — 763-4282

Tahoe City, AC 916, PC 4, Placer
Tahoe-Truckee USD
Supt. — See Truckee
North Tahoe HS — 2-00011
2945 POLARIS RD 96145 — 583-6922
Donald Beno, prin.
North Tahoe IS, 2945 POLARIS RD 96145 — 2-00100
Bill Ellisen, prin. — 583-9387

Tarzana, AC 818, PC see Los Angeles
Los Angeles USD
Supt. — See Los Angeles
De Portola MS, 18720 LINNET ST 91356 — 4-00100
Richard Cord, prin. — 342-6173

Stoneridge Prep S — 2-00111
5955 LINDLEY AVE 91356 — 341-6543
Maria Arnold, prin.

Tehachapi, AC 805, PC 6, Kern
Tehachapi USD — 5-11111
400 S SNYDER AVE 93561 — 822-2100
D. Kent Ashworth, supt.
HS, 711 ANITA DR 93561 — 4-00011
Larry Yeghoian, prin. — 822-2100
Jacobsen JHS, 126 S SNYDER AVE 93561 — 3-00100
James Hollen, prin. — 822-2150

Temecula, AC 909, PC 8, Riverside
Temecula Valley USD — 6-11111
31350 RANCHO VISTA RD 92592 — 676-2661
Patricia Novotney, supt.
Temecula Valley HS — 4-00011
31555 RANCHO VISTA RD 92592 — 695-7300
John Parrott, prin.
Margarita MS — 4-00100
30600 MARGARITA RD 92591 — 695-7370
Richard Husband, prin.
MS, 42075 MEADOWS PKY 92592 — 4-00100
Karen Dubrule, prin. — 695-7350

Linfield S, 31950 PAUBA RD 92592 — 2-11111
James Adare, prin. — 676-8111

Temple City, AC 818, PC 8, Los Angeles
Temple City USD — 5-11111
9516 LONGDEN AVE 91780 — 285-2111
Clinton Taylor, supt.
HS, 9501 LEMON AVE 91780 — 4-00011
Ray Plutko, prin. — 285-2111
Oak Avenue IS, 6623 OAK AVE 91780 — 3-00100
Jeff Sweeney, prin. — 285-2111

Templeton, AC 805, PC 4, San Luis Obispo
Templeton USD — 4-11111
960 OLD COUNTY RD 93465 — 434-1445
Curtis Dubost, supt.

HS, 1200 S MAIN ST 93465 — 2-00011
Jim Fotinakes, prin. — 434-2844
Eagle Canyon HS — 1-00011
960 OLD COUNTY RD 93465 — 434-1445
Doug Nix, prin.
MS, 925 OLD COUNTY RD 93465 — 2-00100
Dean Smith, prin. — 434-1247

Thermal, AC 619, PC 3, Riverside
Coachella Valley USD — 6-11111
PO BOX 847 92274 — 399-5137
Stuart Greenfeld, supt.
Coachella Valley HS — 4-00011
83800 AIRPORT BLVD 92274 — 399-5183
Wayne Connell, prin.
Other Schools – See Coachella, Salton City

Thousand Oaks, AC 805, PC 9, Ventura
Conejo Valley USD — 7-11111
1400 E JANSS RD 91362 — 497-9511
Jerry Gross, supt.
HS, 2323 N MOORPARK RD 91360 — 4-00011
Keith Wilson, prin. — 495-7491
Colina IS, 1500 E HILLCREST DR 91362 — 3-00100
Michael Waters, prin. — 495-7429
Los Cerritos IS — 3-00100
2100 E AVNIDA DE LAS FLORES 91362
Jo Ann Yoos, prin. — 492-3538
Redwood IS — 3-00100
233 W GAINSBOROUGH RD 91360 — 497-7264
Richard Johnson, prin.
Other Schools – See Newbury Park, Westlake Village

California Lutheran University — 4-UC
60 OLSEN RD 91360 — 800-252-5884
Hillcrest Christian S — 2-11111
384 ERBES RD 91362 — 497-0954
Dan Peters, prin.
La Reina HS, 106 W JANSS RD 91360 — 3-00111
Sr. Lisa Megaffin, prin. — 495-6494

Tiburon, AC 415, PC 6, Marin
Reed UNESD, 277A KAREN WAY 94920 — 3-11100
Robert Kessler, supt. — 381-1281
Del Mar IS — 2-00100
105 AVENIDA MIRAFLORES 94920 — 435-1468
Sheila Puckett, prin.

Tollhouse, AC 209, PC 2, Fresno
Sierra USD
Supt. — See Auberry
Sierra HS, 33326 LODGE RD 93667 — 3-00011
Jerry Laird, prin. — 855-8311

Tomales, AC 707, PC 2, Marin
Shoreline USD, PO BOX 198 94971 — 3-11111
Stephen Davis, supt. — 878-2266
HS, PO BOX 198 94971 — 2-00011
James Patterson, prin. — 878-2286
Other Schools – See Point Reyes Station

Torrance, AC 310, PC 9, Los Angeles
Torrance USD — 7-11111
2335 PLAZA DEL AMO 90501 — 533-4200
Arnold Plank, supt.
North HS, 3620 W 182ND ST 90504 — 4-00011
Timothy Scully, prin. — 533-4412
South HS — 4-00011
4801 PACIFIC COAST HWY 90505 — 533-4352
John Schmidt, prin.
HS, 2200 W CARSON ST 90501 — 4-00011
Mary McCullough, prin. — 533-4395
West HS, 20410 VICTOR ST 90503 — 4-00011
William Bawden, prin. — 533-4299
Calle Mayor MS — 3-00100
4800 CALLE MAYOR 90505 — 533-4548
Marilou Ryder, prin.
Casimir MS, 17220 CASIMIR AVE 90504 — 2-00100
Richard Leibovitz, prin. — 533-4498
Hull MS, 2080 W 231ST ST 90501 — 3-00100
Victoria Estrada, prin. — 533-4516
Lynn MS, 5038 HALISON ST 90503 — 3-00100
Richard Long, prin. — 533-4495
Madrona MS — 3-00100
21364 MADRONA AVE 90503 — 533-4562
Kathryn Enloe, prin.
Magruder MS, 4100 W 185TH ST 90504 — 3-00100
Laurie Love, prin. — 533-4527

Bishop Montgomery HS — 4-00011
5430 TORRANCE BLVD 90503 — 540-2021
Br. Thomas Fahy, prin.
El Camino College — 7-CC
16007 CRENSHAW BLVD 90506 — 715-3111
Los Angeles Co. Harbor UCLA Medical Ctr. — HSP
1000 W CARSON ST 90502 — 533-2101
NEC-Bryman Campus — 2-CS
4212 ARTESIA BLVD 90504 — 542-6951

Tracy, AC 209, PC 8, San Joaquin
Tracy SD, 315 E 11TH ST 95376 — 6-11111
Ray Strong, supt. — 831-5000
HS, 315 E 11TH ST 95376 — 4-00011
James Franco, prin. — 831-5095
West JHS, 315 E 11TH ST 95376 — 3-00010
Robert Palous, prin. — 831-5430
Clover MS, 315 E 11TH ST 95376 — 3-00100
Denise Laven, prin. — 831-5240
Monte Vista MS, 315 E 11TH ST 95376 — 3-00100
Stephanie Germann, prin. — 831-5260
Williams MS, 315 E 11TH ST 95376 — 3-00100
Wayne Miller, prin. — 831-5289

Tranquillity, AC 209, PC 3, Fresno
Golden Plains ESD   4-11111
  PO BOX 520 93668   698-7217
  Daniel Grady, supt.
  HS, PO BOX 520 93668   3-00011
  Daniel Grady, supt.   698-7205
  Other Schools – See San Joaquin

Travis A F B, AC 707, PC see Fairfield
Travis USD, DE RONDE DR 94535   5-11111
  Robert McLennan, supt.   437-4604
  Vanden HS, DE RONDE DR 94535   3-00011
  Ronald Harden, prin.   437-8271
  Golden West IS, DE RONDE DR 94535   3-00100
  Paul Rose, prin.   437-8240

Trona, AC 619, PC 4, San Bernardino
Trona JUSD, 83600 TRONA RD 93562   3-11111
  Richard Fragale, supt.   372-4061
  JSHS, 83600 TRONA RD 93562   2-00111
  Don Lucas, prin.   372-4065

Truckee, AC 916, PC 5, Nevada
Tahoe-Truckee USD   5-11111
  11839 DONNER PASS RD 96161   587-3561
  Vincent Deveney, supt.
  Tahoe-Truckee JSHS   3-00111
  11839 DONNER PASS RD 96161   587-3574
  John Neary, prin.
  Other Schools – See Tahoe City

Tujunga, AC 818, PC see Los Angeles
Los Angeles USD
  Supt. — See Los Angeles
  Verdugo Hills HS   4-00011
  10625 PLAINVIEW AVE 91042   353-1171
  Gary Turner, prin.

Tulare, AC 209, PC 8, Tulare
Tulare City ESD   6-11100
  600 N CHERRY ST 93274   686-3335
  Bill Postlewaite, supt.
  Cherry Avenue MS   3-00100
  540 N CHERRY ST 93274   686-5735
  Mark Jensen, prin.
  Live Oak MS, 980 N LASPINA ST 93274   3-00100
  Loren Johnson, prin.   686-6138
  Mulcahy MS   3-00100
  1001 W SONORA AVE 93274   686-6033
  Bob James, prin.

Tulare JUNHSD   5-00011
  426 N BLACKSTONE ST 93274   688-2021
  Ned Kehrli, supt.
  HS, 755 E TULARE AVE 93274   4-00011
  Howard Berger, prin.   686-4761
  Tulare Western HS   4-00011
  824 W MAPLE AVE 93274   686-8751
  Roderick Hollingsworth, prin.
  Valley HS, 737 BARDSLEY AVE 93274   2-00011
  (—), prin.   686-8520

Tulelake, AC 916, PC 4, Siskiyou
Tulelake Basin JUSD   3-11111
  PO BOX 640 96134   667-2295
  Charles Binderup, supt.
  JSHS, PO BOX 640 96134   2-00111
  Douglas Smith, prin.   667-2292

Tuolumne, AC 209, PC 4, Tuolumne
Summerville UNHSD   3-00011
  17555 TUOLUMNE RD 95379   928-4228
  James Bailey, supt.
  Summerville HS   3-00011
  17555 TUOLUMNE RD 95379   928-4228
  James Bailey, prin.

Mother Lode Christian S   2-11111
  18393 GARDNER AVE 95379   928-4126
  Kyle Booth, prin.

Turlock, AC 209, PC 8, Stanislaus
Chatom UNESD   3-11100
  7201 CLAYTON RD 95380   634-2988
  Antonio Borba, supt.
  Chatom MS, 7201 CLAYTON RD 95380   2-01100
  Les Clements, prin.   634-2988

Turlock JSD, PO BOX 1105 95381   7-11111
  William Gibson, supt.   667-0632
  Roselawn HS   2-00011
  312 S ROSELAWN AVE 95380   634-9311
  Norma Grijalva, prin.
  HS, 1600 E CANAL DR 95380   5-00011
  Thomas Parker, prin.   667-2055
  JHS, 3951 N WALNUT RD 95382   4-00100
  Wray Haydock, prin.   667-0881

California State University   5-UC
  801 W MONTE VISTA AVE 95382   667-3122
Turlock Christian HS   2-00111
  PO BOX 944 95381   632-2337
  Donald Shapland, prin.

Tustin, AC 714, PC 8, Orange
Tustin USD, 300 S C ST 92680   7-11111
  David Andrews, supt.   730-7301
  HS, 300 S C ST 92680   4-00011
  Duffy Clark, prin.   730-7414
  Columbus Tustin MS, 300 S C ST 92680   3-00100
  Bob Boies, prin.   730-7352
  Currie MS, 300 S C ST 92680   3-00100
  Dan Brooks, prin.   730-7360
  Other Schools – See Santa Ana

Newbridge College   2-CS
  700 EL CAMINO REAL 92680   573-8787

Twentynine Palms, AC 619, PC 7, San Bernardino
Morongo USD, PO BOX 1209 92277   7-11111
  John Dempsey, supt.   367-9191
  HS, 72750 WILD CAT WAY 92277   3-00011
  Max Friedman, prin.   367-9591
  JHS, PO BOX 1209 92277   3-00100
  Jean Johnson, prin.   367-9507
  Other Schools – See Yucca Valley

Twin Peaks, AC 714, PC 4, San Bernardino

Calvary Chapel Christian S   2-11111
  101 GRANDVIEW 92391   337-3739
  Randall Leonard, prin.

Ukiah, AC 707, PC 7, Mendocino
Ukiah USD, 925 N STATE ST 95482   6-11111
  Charles Myers, supt.   463-5211
  HS, 1000 LOW GAP RD 95482   4-00011
  Philip Gary, prin.   463-5253
  Pomolita MS, 740 N SPRING ST 95482   4-00100
  Michael Lauletta, prin.   463-5224
  Other Schools – See Redwood Valley

Mendocino College   5-CC
  PO BOX 3000 95482   468-3100

Union City, AC 510, PC 8, Alameda
New Haven USD   7-11111
  34200 ALVARADO NILES RD 94587   471-1100
  Guy Emanuele, supt.
  Logan HS, 1800 H ST 94587   5-00011
  Dave Pava, prin.   471-2520
  Alvarado MS   4-01100
  31604 ALVARADO BLVD 94587   489-0700
  Kevin Brodehl, prin.
  Barnard-White MS   4-01100
  725 WHIPPLE RD 94587   471-5363
  Judy Silver, prin.
  New Haven MS   4-01100
  2801 HOP RANCH RD 94587   487-1700
  Gary Addiego, prin.

Western Truck School   2-CS
  2849 WHIPPLE RD # A 94587   800-929-1315

Upland, AC 909, PC 8, San Bernardino
Upland USD, PO BOX 1239 91785   7-11111
  Loren Sanchez, supt.   985-1864
  HS, PO BOX 1239 91785   5-00011
  Bert Raiche, prin.   949-7880
  Hillside JHS, PO BOX 1239 91785   2-00111
  Leila Minnis, prin.   949-8400
  Pioneer JHS, PO BOX 1239 91785   3-00100
  Roger Schulte, prin.   949-7770
  JHS, PO BOX 1239 91785   3-00100
  William Card, prin.   949-7810

Upper Lake, AC 707, PC 3, Lake
Upper Lake UNESD   3-11100
  PO BOX 36 95485   275-0223
  Richard Altimari, supt.
  MS, PO BOX 36 95485   2-00100
  Richard Altimari, prin.   275-0223

Upper Lake UNHSD, PO BOX 7 95485   2-00011
  Charles Zimmerman, supt.   275-2655
  HS, PO BOX 7 95485   2-00011
  Robert Lombard, prin.   275-2338

Vacaville, AC 707, PC 8, Solano
Vacaville USD, 751 SCHOOL ST 95688   7-11111
  Richard Jackson, supt.   453-6000
  HS, 100 W MONTE VISTA AVE 95688   4-00011
  Bob Thompson, prin.   453-6065
  Wood HS, 998 MARSHALL RD 95687   4-00011
  Michael Donnoe, prin.   453-6900
  Jepson MS, 580 ELDER ST 95688   3-00100
  Shereene Wilkerson, prin.   453-6280
  Vaca Pena MS, 200 KEITH WAY 95687   4-00100
  Cynthia Walker, prin.   453-6270

Vacaville Christian Academy   2-11111
  1117 DAVIS ST 95687   446-1776
  Karen Winter, prin.

Valencia, AC 805, PC see Santa Clarita
William S. Hart UNHSD
  Supt. — See Santa Clarita
  Learning Post HS   2-00011
  23007 DALBEY DR 91355   255-8338
  Judy Webber, prin.
  Arroyo Seco JHS   4-00100
  27171 VISTA DELGADO DR 91354   296-0991
  Jacqulyn Snyder, prin.

California Institute of the Arts   3-UC
  24700 MCBEAN PKY 91355   255-1050
College of the Canyons   5-CC
  26455 ROCKWELL CANYON RD 91355   259-7800

Vallejo, AC 707, PC 9, Solano
Vallejo City USD   7-11111
  211 VALLE VISTA AVE 94590   644-8921
  M. Dale Welsh, supt.
  Hogan SHS, 850 ROSEWOOD AVE 94591   4-00001
  Joseph Jones, prin.   552-3394
  SHS, 840 NEBRASKA ST 94590   4-00001
  William Dougherty, prin.   644-4021

Franklin JHS, 501 STARR AVE 94590   3-00110
  Linda Beckstrom, prin.   643-6489
Solano JHS   4-00110
  1025 CORCORAN AVE 94589   643-8641
  Phillip Saroyan, prin.
Springstowne JHS   4-00110
  2833 TENNESSEE ST 94591   643-8471
  Barb Armstrong, prin.
JHS, 1347 AMADOR ST 94590   4-00110
  Rich Changus, prin.   643-2341

California Maritime Academy   2-UC
  PO BOX 1392 94590   648-4200
Reignierd S   2-11111
  380 CONTRA COSTA ST 94590   644-0447
  Genevieve Reignierd, prin.
St. Patrick-St. Vincent HS   3-00011
  1500 BENICIA RD 94591   644-4425
  Sr. Sue Pixley, prin.

Valley Center, AC 619, PC 4, San Diego
Valley Center UNESD   4-11100
  28751 COLE GRADE RD 92082   749-0464
  Jeff Mulford, supt.
  MS, 28751 COLE GRADE RD 92082   3-00100
  Jim Zoll, prin.   749-8555

Valley Springs, AC 209, PC 3, Calaveras
Calaveras USD
  Supt. — See San Andreas
  Toyon MS   3-00100
  3412 DOUBLE SPRINGS RD 95252   754-4256
  William Hamilton, prin.

Vandenberg AFB, AC 805, PC 6, Santa Barbara
Lompoc USD
  Supt. — See Lompoc
  Vandenberg MS   4-00100
  1145 MOUNTAIN VIEW BLVD 93437   734-4391
  Jim Armstrong, prin.

Van Nuys, AC 818, PC see Los Angeles
Los Angeles USD
  Supt. — See Los Angeles
  Birmingham HS   5-00011
  17000 HAYNES ST 91406   881-1580
  Henry Gradillas, prin.
  Grant HS, 13000 OXNARD ST 91401   5-00011
  Eve Sherman, prin.   781-1400
  SHS, 6535 CEDROS AVE 91411   4-00001
  Robert Scharf, prin.   781-2371
  Fulton JHS, 7477 KESTER AVE 91405   4-00110
  Wayne Tyra, prin.   785-8624
  Mulholland JHS   4-00100
  17120 VANOWEN ST 91406   345-5446
  Alfredo Tarin, prin.
  JHS, 5435 VESPER AVE 91411   3-00110
  Lawrence Foster, prin.   785-5475

Ameritech Colleges   2-CS
  6843 LENNOX AVE 91405   901-7311
California Institute of Locksmithing   1-CS
  14721 OXNARD ST 91411   994-7426
Concorde Career Institute   2-CS
  6850 VAN NUYS BLVD 91405   780-5252
ITT Technical Institute   3-CC
  6723 VAN NUYS BLVD 91405   989-1177
Los Angeles Valley College   7-CC
  5800 FULTON AVE 91401   781-1200
Merit College   3-CS
  7101 SEPULVEDA BLVD 91405   988-6640
Montclair College Preparatory S   2-00111
  8071 SEPULVEDA BLVD 91402   787-5290
  Vernon Simpson, prin.
St. Genevieve HS   2-00011
  13967 ROSCOE BLVD 91402   894-6417
  Maria Castillo, prin.

Ventura, AC 805, PC 8, Ventura
Ventura USD   7-11111
  120 E SANTA CLARA ST 93001   641-5000
  Joseph Spirito, supt.
  Buena HS, 5670 TELEGRAPH RD 93003   4-00011
  Jaime Castellanos, prin.   641-5100
  HS, 2155 E MAIN ST 93001   4-00011
  Jerry Barshay, prin.   641-5116
  Anacapa MS, 100 S MILLS RD 93003   4-00100
  Charlotte McElroy, prin.   641-5135
  Balboa MS, 247 S HILL RD 93003   4-00100
  Henry Robertson, prin.   641-5145
  Cabrillo MS   3-00100
  1426 E SANTA CLARA ST 93001   641-5155
  Kristine Bergstrom, prin.
  De Anza MS, 2060 CAMERON ST 93001   3-00100
  David Myers, prin.   641-5165

St. Bonaventure HS   3-00011
  3167 TELEGRAPH RD 93003   648-6836
  Br. Paulinus Horkan, prin.
Ventura College   7-CC
  4667 TELEGRAPH RD 93003   642-3211

Victorville, AC 619, PC 8, San Bernardino
Victor Valley UNHSD   6-00111
  16350 MOJAVE DR 92392   955-3200
  Alvin Andrews, supt.
  Victor Valley HS   5-00011
  16500 MOJAVE DR 92392   955-3300
  Glenn Massengale, prin.
  Hook JHS, 15000 HOOK RD 92392   3-00100
  Mark LeBrun, prin.   955-3360

Victor Valley JHS   4-00100
  16925 FORREST AVE 92392   955-3400
  Kathleen Lento, prin.
Other Schools – See Adelanto

Victor Valley College   6-CC
  18422 BEAR VALLEY RD 92392   245-4271

Villa Park, AC 714, PC 6, Orange
Orange USD
  Supt. — See Orange
HS, 18042 TAFT AVE 92667   4-00011
  Daniel Burch, prin.   532-8020
Cerro Villa MS   3-00100
  17852 SERRANO AVE 92667   997-6251
  A. J. Roland, prin.

Visalia, AC 209, PC 8, Tulare
Visalia USD, 315 E ACEQUIA AVE 93291   7-11111
  Sharon Tucker, supt.   730-7551
Golden West HS   4-00011
  1717 N MCAULIFF ST 93292   730-7801
  Richard Doepker, prin.
Mt. Whitney HS   4-00011
  900 S CONYER ST 93277   730-7602
  Lynda Reddell, prin.
Redwood HS, 1001 W MAIN ST 93291   4-00011
  Janet Parker, prin.   730-7701
Divisadero MS   3-00100
  1200 S DIVISADERO ST 93277   730-7661
  Thomas Biscotti, prin.
Green Acres MS   4-00100
  1147 N MOONEY BLVD 93291   730-7671
  Geraldine Murphy, prin.
Valley Oak MS   4-00100
  2000 N LOVERS LN 93292   730-7681
  William Adams, prin.

Central Valley Christian S   2-11111
  5600 W TULARE AVE 93277   734-2684
  Merl Alons, prin.
College of the Sequoias   6-CC
  915 S MOONEY BLVD 93277   730-3700
Galen College Medical & Dental Assts.   2-CS
  3746 W MINERAL KING AVE # C 93291
     264-9726
San Joaquin Valley College   3-CC
  8400 W MINERAL KING AVE 93291   651-2500

Vista, AC 619, PC 8, San Diego
Vista USD, 1234 ARCADIA AVE 92084   7-11111
  Rene Townsend, supt.   726-2170
HS, 1234 ARCADIA AVE 92084   4-00011
  Rob Gira, prin.   726-5611
Lincoln MS, 1234 ARCADIA AVE 92084   4-00100
  Patricia Campbell, prin.   726-5766
Rancho Buena Vista Mid. HS   4-00100
  1234 ARCADIA AVE 92084   727-7284
  Alan Johnson, prin.
Washington MS   4-00100
  1234 ARCADIA AVE 92084   724-7115
  Stephanie Tarkington, prin.
Other Schools – See Oceanside

Maric College of Medical Careers   2-CS
  1593C E VISTA WAY 92084   758-8640
National University   3-UC
  2022 UNIVERSITY DR 92083   945-6100
Tri City Christian S   3-11111
  302 N EMERALD DR 92083   724-3016
  Robert Goode, prin.
Watterson College Pacific   2-CS
  2030 UNIVERSITY DR 92083   724-1500

Walnut, PC 8, Los Angeles
Walnut Valley USD   7-11111
  PO BOX 469 91788   909-595-1261
  Ronald Hockwalt, supt.
HS, 400 PIERRE RD 91789   4-00011
  Ken Gunn, prin.   909-594-1333
Suzanne MS   4-00100
  525 SUZANNE RD 91789   909-594-1657
  Bryan Cole, prin.
South Pointe MS   3-00100
  20671 LARKSTONE DR 91789   909-595-8171
  Marlene Tangeman, prin.
Other Schools – See Diamond Bar

Advance School of Driving   2-CS
  PO BOX 443 91788   714-595-2292
Christian Chapel ES   4-11111
  1920 BREA CANYON CUT OFF RD 91789
  Gerald Wheeler, prin.   909-598-9733
Mt. San Antonio College   8-CC
  1100 N GRAND AVE 91789   909-594-5611

Walnut Creek, AC 510, PC 8, Contra Costa
Acalanes UNHSD
  Supt. — See Lafayette
Las Lomas HS, 1460 S MAIN ST 94596   4-00011
  Patrick Lickiss, prin.   935-4110

Mt. Diablo USD
  Supt. — See Concord
Northgate HS   4-00011
  425 CASTLE ROCK RD 94598   938-0900
  Maurice Ghysels, prin.
Foothill MS, 2775 CEDRO LN 94598   4-00100
  Judy Kastely, prin.   939-8600

Walnut Creek ESD   5-11100
  960 YGNACIO VALLEY RD 94596   933-1500
  Kenneth Meinecke, supt.
IS, 2425 WALNUT BLVD 94596   3-00100
  Daniel Leary, prin.   933-7520

Berean Christian HS   2-00011
  245 EL DIVISADERO AVE 94598   945-6464
  Neil Sostrom, prin.
Contra Costa Christian HS   2-00011
  2721 LARKEY LN 94596   934-4964
  Nancy Edmiston, prin.

Wasco, AC 805, PC 7, Kern
Wasco UNESD   5-11100
  639 BROADWAY ST 93280   758-7100
  Gary Bray, supt.
Jefferson MS, 305 GRIFFITH AVE 93280   3-00100
  William Elliott, prin.   758-7140

Wasco UNHSD, PO BOX 250 93280   4-00011
  Thomas Blum, supt.   758-5324
HS, PO BOX 250 93280   4-00011
  Gerald Johnson, prin.   758-5324

Waterford, AC 209, PC 5, Stanislaus
Waterford ESD, PO BOX 270 95386   4-11100
  Allan Gordon, supt.   874-1809
MS, PO BOX 270 95386   3-01100
  Bob Bales, prin.   874-2382

Watsonville, AC 408, PC 8, Santa Cruz
North Monterey County USD
  Supt. — See Moss Landing
Moss Landing MS   3-00100
  1815 SALINAS RD 95076   633-5881
  Robert Mayeda, prin.

Pajaro Valley USD   7-11111
  165 BLACKBURN ST 95076   728-6230
  Anthony Avina, supt.
HS, 250 E BEACH ST 95076   4-00011
  Roger Mock, prin.   728-6390
Hall MS, 201 BREWINGTON AVE 95076   4-00100
  Murry Schekman, prin.   728-6270
Pajaro MS, 250 SALINAS RD 95076   3-00100
  Debra Kosaka, prin.   728-6238
Rolling Hills MS   4-00100
  130 HERMAN AVE 95076   728-6341
  Luis Carrillo, prin.
Other Schools – See Aptos, La Selva Beach

Monte Vista Christian S   3-11111
  2 SCHOOL WAY 95076   722-8178
  Donald Pearce, prin.

Weaverville, AC 916, PC 5, Trinity
Trinity UNHSD, PO BOX 1227 96093   2-00011
  Bill La Plante, supt.   623-6104
Alps View HS, PO BOX 1848 96093   1-00011
  Bill La Plante, prin.   623-4606
Trinity HS, PO BOX 1060 96093   2-00011
  Richard McCoy, prin.   623-6127

Weed, AC 916, PC 5, Siskiyou
Siskiyou UNHSD
  Supt. — See Mount Shasta
HS, 909 HILLSIDE DR 96094   2-00011
  Edith Edwards, prin.   938-4774

College of the Siskiyous   5-CC
  800 COLLEGE AVE 96094   938-4461

Weimar, AC 916, PC 3, Placer
Placer Hills UNESD
  Supt. — See Meadow Vista
Weimar Hills JHS, PO BOX 255 95736   3-01100
  Michael Bossi, prin.   637-4121

West Covina, PC 8, Los Angeles
Covina-Valley USD
  Supt. — See Covina
South Hills HS   4-00011
  645 S BARRANCA ST 91791   818-331-3371
  Judith North, prin.
Traweek IS   3-00100
  1941 E ROWLAND AVE 91791   818-331-0102
  Karl Major, prin.

Rowland USD
  Supt. — See Rowland Heights
Rincon IS   3-00100
  2800 E HOLLINGWORTH ST 91792
  Ray Warner, prin.   818-965-1696

West Covina USD   6-11111
  1717 W MERCED AVE 91790   818-338-8411
  John Costello, supt.
HS, 1609 E CAMERON AVE 91791   4-00011
  Ben Furuta, prin.   818-966-7571
Edgewood MS   4-00100
  1625 W DURNESS ST 91790   818-962-8665
  Doug Agatep, prin.

El Dorado College   3-CS
  1901 W PACIFIC AVE 91790   818-960-5173
ITT Technical Institute   4-UC
  1530 W CAMERON AVE 91790   818-960-8681
Northwest College Medical Dental Assts.   2-CS
  2121 W GARVEY AVE N 91790   818-962-3495
Watterson College-Pasadena   3-CS
  1422 S AZUSA AVE 91791   818-919-8701

Westlake Village, PC 6, Los Angeles
Conejo Valley USD
  Supt. — See Thousand Oaks
Westlake HS   4-00011
  100 LAKEVIEW CANYON RD 91362
  Curt Luft, prin.   805-497-6711

Westlake Institute of Technology   2-CS
  31826A VILLAGE CENTER RD 91361
     818-991-9992

Westminster, AC 714, PC 8, Orange
Garden Grove USD
  Supt. — See Garden Grove
La Quinta HS   4-00011
  10372 MCFADDEN AVE 92683   663-6315
  Michell Thomas, prin.
McGarvin IS, 9802 BISHOP PL 92683   3-00100
  Tom Holler, prin.   663-6218

Huntington Beach UNHSD
  Supt. — See Huntington Beach
Westminster HS   4-00011
  14325 GOLDENWEST ST 92683   893-1381
  Bonnie Maspero, prin.

Westminster ESD   6-11100
  14121 CEDARWOOD ST 92683   894-7311
  Gail Wickstrom, supt.
Johnson IS, 13603 EDWARDS ST 92683   3-00100
  (—), prin.   894-7244
Warner IS, 14171 NEWLAND ST 92683   3-00100
  Joan Read, prin.   894-7281
Other Schools – See Huntington Beach

Hebrew Academy   2-11111
  14401 WILLOW LN 92683   898-0051
  Barbara Heneghan, prin.

West Sacramento, AC 916, PC 8, Yolo
Washington USD   6-11111
  930 W ACRES RD 95691   371-9300
  Del Alberti, supt.
River City HS   4-00011
  1100 CLARENDON ST 95691   371-0700
  Stephen Vaczovsky, prin.
Other Schools – See Broderick

Western Truck School   2-CS
  PO BOX 980040 95798   372-6500

Westwood, AC 916, PC 4, Lassen
Westwood USD, PO BOX H 96137   3-11111
  Herold Sinclair, supt.   256-3235
JSHS, 4TH & GREENWOOD STS 96137   2-00111
  William Spalding, prin.   256-3235

Wheatland, AC 916, PC 4, Yuba
Wheatland ESD, PO BOX 818 95692   4-11100
  David Cole, supt.   633-3130
Bear River MS, PO BOX 818 95692   2-01100
  Joseph D'Andrea, prin.   633-3135

Wheatland UNHSD   2-00011
  1010 WHEATLAND RD 95692   633-3100
  Michael Edwards, supt.
Wheatland Union HS   2-00011
  1010 WHEATLAND RD 95692   633-3100
  Michael Edwards, prin.

Whitmore, AC 916, PC 1, Shasta

Cascade S, PO BOX 9 96096   2-00111
  Michael Allgood, prin.   472-3031

Whittier, AC 310, PC 8, Los Angeles
East Whittier City ESD   6-11100
  14535 WHITTIER BLVD 90605   698-0351
  Dorothy Fagan, supt.
East Whittier MS   3-00100
  14421 WHITTIER BLVD 90605   693-3766
  John Stoddard, prin.
Granada MS, 15337 LEMON DR 90604   3-00100
  Charles Royce, prin.   943-0283
Hillview MS, 10931 STAMY RD 90604   3-00100
  Kathy Grubbs, prin.   946-7446
Lowell JESD   5-11100
  11019 VALLEY HOME AVE 90603   943-0211
  Ronald Randolph, supt.
Rancho-Starbuck IS   3-00100
  11019 VALLEY HOME AVE 90603   943-0171
  Carl Lane, prin.
South Whittier ESD   5-11100
  PO BOX 3037 90605   944-6231
  Richard Graves, supt.
South Whittier IS   3-00100
  13243 LOS NIETOS RD 90605   944-0135
  David Morton, prin.

Whittier City ESD   6-11100
  7211 WHITTIER AVE 90602   698-9531
  Neal Avery, supt.
Dexter IS, 11532 FLORAL DR 90601   3-00100
  Donald Hoagland, prin.   695-2774
Edwards IS   3-00100
  6812 NORWALK BLVD 90606   695-2618
  (—), prin.

Whittier UNHSD   6-00011
  9401 PAINTER AVE 90605   698-8121
  Lee Eastwood, supt.
California HS, 9800 MILLS AVE 90604   4-00011
  Stephen Ball, prin.   698-8121

La Serna HS | | 4-00011
15301 YOUNGWOOD DR 90605 | | 698-8121
Leo Camalich, prin.
Pioneer HS, 10800 BEN AVON ST 90606 | | 4-00011
Patrick Mascorro, prin. | | 698-8121
HS, 12417 PHILADELPHIA ST 90601 | | 4-00011
Frederic Zimmerman, prin. | | 698-8121
Other Schools – See Santa Fe Springs

Los Angeles College of Chiropractic | | 4-UC
16200 AMBER VALLEY DR 90604 | | 800-221-5222
Nova Institute of Health Technology | | 2-CS
11416 WHITTIER BLVD 90601 | | 695-0771
Rio Hondo College | | 7-CC
3600 WORKMAN MILL RD 90601 | | 692-0921
Whittier Christian | | 2-00100
14625 KEESE DR 90604 | | 946-8888
Warner Peters, prin.
Whittier College | | 4-UC
13406 PHILADELPHIA ST 90601 | | 907-4238

Williams, AC 916, PC 4, Colusa
Williams USD, PO BOX 7 95987 | | 3-11111
Robert Dial, supt. | | 473-2550
JSHS, PO BOX 7 95987 | | 2-00111
Douglas Ash, prin. | | 473-5369

Willits, AC 707, PC 6, Mendocino
Willits USD | | 5-11111
48 W COMMERCIAL ST 95490 | | 459-5314
James Roberts, supt.
HS, 299 N MAIN ST 95490 | | 3-00011
G. MacDonald, prin. | | 459-5506
Baechtel Grove MS | | 3-00100
1150 MAGNOLIA ST 95490 | | 459-2417
Floyd Brandt, prin.

Willows, AC 916, PC 6, Glenn
Willows USD | | 4-11111
334 W SYCAMORE ST 95988 | | 934-6600
Gary Kemp, supt.
HS, 203 N MURDOCK AVE 95988 | | 2-00011
Preston Persky, prin. | | 934-6611
IS, 1145 W CEDAR ST 95988 | | 3-01100
Wayne Weatherford, prin. | | 934-6633

Butte College | | 3-CC
119 N BUTTE ST 95988 | | 895-2429

Wilmington, AC 310, PC see Los Angeles
Los Angeles USD
Supt. — See Los Angeles
Banning SHS, 1527 LAKME AVE 90744 | | 5-00001
Obelia Lamothe, prin. | | 549-7500
JHS, 1700 GULF AVE 90744 | | 4-00110
Ernest Tarango, prin. | | 518-1120

College of Oceaneering | | 2-CC
272 S FRIES AVE 90744 | | 834-2501
Los Angeles Harbor College | | 6-CC
1111 FIGUEROA PL 90744 | | 518-1000

Windsor, AC 707, PC 5, Sonoma
Windsor UNSD, 7650 BELL RD 95492 | | 4-11100
Ian Kirkpatrick, supt. | | 838-9444
MS, 7650 BELL RD 95492 | | 3-01100
Kenneth Moulton, prin. | | 838-6144

Winnetka, AC 818, PC see Los Angeles

NEC-Bryman Campus | | 2-CS
20835 SHERMAN WAY 91306 | | 887-7911

Winterhaven, AC 619, PC 3, Imperial
San Pasqual Valley USD | | 3-11111
676 BASE LINE RD 92283 | | 572-0222
Stewart Fisher, supt.

San Pasqual Valley HS | | 2-00011
676 BASE LINE RD 92283 | | 572-0222
Herbert Jagow, prin.
San Pasqual Valley MS | | 2-00100
676 BASE LINE RD 92283 | | 572-0222
Herbert Jagow, prin.

Winters, AC 916, PC 5, Yolo
Winters JUSD | | 4-11111
710 RAILROAD AVE 95694 | | 795-6100
Michael Roberts, supt.
HS, 101 GRANT AVE 95694 | | 2-00011
Mort Geivett, prin. | | 795-6140
MS, 425 ANDERSON AVE 95694 | | 2-00100
David Inns, prin. | | 795-6130

Winton, AC 209, PC 6, Merced
Merced River UNESD
Supt. — See Snelling
Washington MS | | 2-01100
4402 OAKDALE RD 95388 | | 358-5679
Eldon Henderson, prin.

Winton ESD, PO BOX 8 95388 | | 4-11100
Raymond Fitchett, supt. | | 357-6175
MS, PO BOX 1299 95388 | | 2-00100
Penny Rivero, prin. | | 357-6189

Woodbridge, AC 209, PC 5, San Joaquin
Lodi USD
Supt. — See Lodi
MS, PO BOX P 95258 | | 3-00100
(—), prin. | | 331-7575

Woodlake, AC 209, PC 6, Tulare
Woodlake UNSD | | 4-11111
300 W WHITNEY AVE 93286 | | 564-8081
Brian Vaccaro, supt.
HS, 400 W WHITNEY AVE 93286 | | 3-00011
Jennifer Earle, prin. | | 564-3307
Woodlake Valley MS | | 2-00100
497 N PALM ST 93286 | | 564-8061
Steve Tietjen, prin.

Woodland, AC 916, PC 8, Yolo
Woodland JUSD | | 6-11111
526 MARSHALL AVE 95695 | | 662-0201
Florentino Noriega, supt.
SHS, 21 N WEST ST 95695 | | 4-00001
Ben Flores, prin. | | 662-4678
Douglass JHS, 525 GRANADA DR 95695 | | 3-00110
Patrick McDougall, prin. | | 666-2191
Lee JHS, 520 WEST ST 95695 | | 4-00110
Barry Cooper, prin. | | 662-0251

Woodland Hills, AC 818, PC see Los Angeles
Los Angeles USD
Supt. — See Los Angeles
El Camino Real HS | | 5-00011
5440 VALLEY CIRCLE BLVD 91367 | | 888-8920
Martin King, prin.
Taft HS, 5461 WINNETKA AVE 91364 | | 5-00011
Ron Berz, prin. | | 348-7171
West Valley Occupational Center | | Vo Tech
6200 WINNETKA AVE 91367 | | 346-3540
Harlan Barbanell, prin.
Hale JHS, 23830 CALIFA ST 91364 | | 4-00100
C. Leighton, prin. | | 346-1851
Parkman JHS | | 4-00100
20800 BURBANK BLVD 91367 | | 348-8770
Michael Bennett, prin.

Los Angeles Pierce College | | 7-CC
6201 WINNETKA AVE 91371 | | 347-0551
Louisville HS | | 2-00011
22300 MULHOLLAND DR 91364 | | 346-8812
Sr. Myra McPartland, prin.

Woodside, AC 415, PC 6, San Mateo
Sequoia UNHSD
Supt. — See Redwood City
HS, 199 CHURCHILL AVE 94062 | | 4-00011
Gerald Baker, prin. | | 367-9750

Yermo, AC 619, PC 4, San Bernardino
Silver Valley USD | | 5-11111
PO BOX 847 92398 | | 254-2916
John Murphy, supt.
Silver Valley HS, PO BOX 847 92398 | | 3-00011
William Frey, prin. | | 254-2963
Other Schools – See Daggett, Fort Irwin

Yorba Linda, AC 714, PC 8, Orange
Placentia Yorba Linda USD
Supt. — See Placentia
Yorba JHS | | 4-00100
5350 FAIRMONT BLVD 92686 | | 970-0650
Richard Vouga, prin.
MS, 4777 CASA LOMA AVE 92686 | | 3-00100
Ken Lorge, prin. | | 528-7090

Yosemite Park, AC 209, PC 4, Mariposa
Mariposa County USD
Supt. — See Mariposa
HS, PO BOX 533 95389 | | 1-00011
Kent Stoel, prin. | | 966-3691

Yreka, AC 916, PC 6, Siskiyou
Yreka UNESD, 309 JACKSON ST 96097 | | 4-11100
Robert Singleton, supt. | | 842-1168
Jackson Street MS | | 3-01100
405 JACKSON ST 96097 | | 842-3561
Jonas Miller, prin.

Yreka UNHSD, 431 KNAPP ST 96097 | | 3-00011
William Mathews, supt. | | 842-2521
Discovery SHS | | 1-00001
504 W LENNOX ST 96097 | | 842-1659
James Beck, prin.
HS, PREECE WAY 96097 | | 3-00011
Lawrence Perry, prin. | | 842-6151

Yuba City, AC 916, PC 8, Sutter
Yuba City USD | | 7-11111
750 N PALORA AVE 95991 | | 741-5200
Lee Brittenham, supt.
HS, 850 B ST 95991 | | 4-00011
Frank Motta, prin. | | 741-5290
Gray Avenue IS, 808 GRAY AVE 95991 | | 3-00100
Alfonso Anaya, prin. | | 741-5240
Karperos MS | | 3-00100
1666 CARMINO DEL FLORES 95991 | | 741-5262
Cynthia DeLuz, prin.

Faith Christian S | | 2-11111
PO BOX 1690 95992 | | 674-3922
Jeff Christensen, prin.

Yucaipa, AC 909, PC 8, San Bernardino
Yucaipa-Calimesa JUSD | | 6-11111
12797 3RD ST 92399 | | 797-0174
Ronald Bennett, supt.
SHS, 33000 YUCAIPA BLVD 92399 | | 4-00001
Jan Button, prin. | | 797-0106
JHS, 12358 6TH ST 92399 | | 4-00110
Michael Likins, prin. | | 797-5181

Crafton Hills College | | 5-CC
11711 SAND CANYON RD 92399 | | 794-2161

Yucca Valley, AC 619, PC 7, San Bernardino
Morongo USD
Supt. — See Twentynine Palms
JSHS, 7600 SAGE AVE 92284 | | 4-00111
Doug Weller, prin. | | 365-3391
La Contenta JHS, PO BOX 910 92286 | | 3-00100
Kathleen Croy, prin. | | 228-1802

COLORADO

STATE DEPARTMENT OF EDUCATION
State Office Building
201 E. Colfax Ave., Denver 80203
(303) 866-6600

Commissioner of Education	William Randall
Deputy Commissioner	Richard Laughlin
Assistant Commissioner Public School Finance	Dan Stewart
Assistant Commissioner Educational Services	Arthur Ellis
Assistant Commissioner Adult Education	Nancy Bolt
Executive Director Federal Program Services	Betty Hinkle
Executive Director Special Services	Brian McNulty
Executive Director Management Services	Karen Stroup

STATE BOARD OF EDUCATION
201 E. Colfax Ave., Denver 80203

Chairperson   Sybil Downing

PUBLIC, PRIVATE AND CATHOLIC SECONDARY SCHOOLS

Agate, AC 719, PC 1, Elbert
Agate SD 300, PO BOX 118 80101 1-11111 764-2741
James McDermott, supt.
S, PO BOX 118 80101 1-11111 764-2741
James McDermott, supt.

Aguilar, AC 719, PC 3, Las Animas
Aguilar RSD 6, PO BOX 567 81020 2-11111 941-4614
Lillian Stanton, supt.
JSHS, PO BOX 567 81020 1-00111 941-4640
Joan Crittenden, prin.

Akron, AC 303, PC 4, Washington
Akron SD R-1, PO BOX 429 80720 2-11111 345-2268
Delano Arnold, supt.
HS, 600 ELM AVE 80720 2-00011 345-2268
Charles Johnson, prin.

Alamosa, AC 719, PC 6, Alamosa
Alamosa SD RE-11J 5-11111 589-6634
209 VICTORIA AVE 81101
Robert Osland, supt.
HS, 401 VICTORIA AVE 81101 3-00011 589-6696
Judith Baillie, prin.
Ortega MS, 1301 MAIN ST 81101 3-00100 589-6669
John Jordan, prin.

Adams State College 4-UC 800-824-6494
208 EDGEMONT BLVD 81102

Anton, AC 303, PC 1, Washington
Arickaree SD R-2 2-11111 383-2202
12155 COUNTY ROAD NN 80801
Larry Stukey, supt.
Arickaree JSHS 1-00111 383-2202
12155 COUNTY ROAD NN 80801
Larry Stukey, prin.

Antonito, AC 719, PC 3, Conejos
South Conejos SD RE-10 2-11111 376-5425
PO BOX 398 81120
Angelo Velasquez, supt.
HS, PO BOX 398 81120 2-00011 376-5468
Felix Gonzales, prin.
JHS, PO BOX 398 81120 1-00100 376-5468
Felix Gonzales, prin.

Arvada, AC 303, PC 8, Jefferson
Jefferson County SD R-1
Supt. — See Golden
HS, 7951 W 65TH AVE 80004 4-00011 423-3830
James Melhouse, prin.
Arvada West HS 4-00011 422-2326
11325 ALLENDALE DR 80004
Dale Anderson, prin.
Pomona HS, 8101 POMONA DR 80005 4-00011 423-9092
John Jost, prin.
JHS, 5751 BALSAM ST 80002 3-00100 423-1553
Ken Robke, prin.
Drake JHS, 12550 W 52ND AVE 80002 3-00100 422-3471
Russell Ramsey, prin.
Moore MS, 8455 W 88TH AVE 80005 3-00100 420-8641
Cynthia Fischer, prin.

North Arvada JHS 3-00100 421-2660
7285 PIERCE ST 80003
Jerry Owen, prin.
Oberon JHS, 7300 QUAIL ST 80005 3-00100 421-6776
Paul Mott, prin.

Faith Christian Academy 4-11111 424-7310
6210 WARD RD 80004
Maranatha Christian ES 3-11111 431-5653
7180 OAK ST 80004

Aspen, AC 303, PC 6, Pitkin
Aspen SD 1 4-11111 925-3460
235 HIGH SCHOOL RD 81611
Tom Farrell, supt.
HS, 235 HIGH SCHOOL RD 81611 2-00011 925-2972
Bruce Lindberg, prin.
MS, 235 HIGH SCHOOL RD 81611 2-01100 925-6623
Griff Smith, prin.

Ault, AC 303, PC 4, Weld
Ault-Highland SD RE-9 3-11111 834-1345
PO BOX 68 80610
Ronald Vandonselaar, supt.
Highland HS, PO BOX 68 80610 2-00011 834-2816
Jon Burnham, prin.
Highland MS, PO BOX 68 80610 2-01100 834-2820
Roger McWilliams, prin.

Aurora, AC 303, PC 9, Arapahoe
Adams-Arapahoe SD 28J 8-11111 344-8060
1085 PEORIA ST 80011
David Hartenbach, supt.
Central HS, 11700 E 11TH AVE 80010 4-00011 340-1600
Kenneth Lytwyniuk, prin.
Gateway HS, 1300 S SABLE BLVD 80012 4-00011 755-7160
Kenneth Vedra, prin.
Hinkley HS, 1250 CHAMBERS RD 80011 4-00011 340-1500
J. Nachazel, prin.
Rangeview HS, 17599 E ILIFF AVE 80013 4-00011 695-6848
Marc Stine, prin.
Pickens Tech Ctr Vo Tech 344-4910
500 BUCKLEY RD 80011
Dale McCall, prin.
Aurora Hills MS 3-00100 341-7450
1009 S UVALDA ST 80012
Harold Pyper, prin.
Columbia MS 3-00100 690-6570
17600 E COLUMBIA AVE 80013
Harold Stevens, prin.
East MS, 1275 FRASER ST 80011 3-00100 340-0660
Nancy Pokorny, prin.
Mrachek MS 4-00100 750-2836
1955 S TELLURIDE ST 80013
Charles Willsea, prin.
North MS 3-00100 364-7411
12095 MONTVIEW BLVD 80010
Richard Rusak, prin.
South MS, 12310 E PARKVIEW DR 80011 3-00100 364-7623
Dan Colvin, prin.
West MS, 10100 E 13TH AVE 80010 3-00100 366-2671
John Basham, prin.

Cherry Creek SD 5
Supt. — See Englewood
Eaglecrest HS 4-00011 699-0408
5100 S PICADILLY ST 80015
Terry Conley, prin.
Overland HS 4-00011 696-3700
12400 E JEWELL AVE 80012
John Buckner, prin.
Smoky Hill HS 4-00011 693-1700
16100 E SMOKY HILL RD 80015
Mary Jarvis, prin.
Horizon MS 4-00100 693-4242
3981 S RESERVOIR RD 80013
Gwen Sonnenburg, prin.
Laredo MS, 5000 S LAREDO ST 80015 4-00100 693-1500
Judith Hilton, prin.
Prairie MS, 12600 E JEWELL AVE 80012 4-00100 696-3750
Marlene Grueber, prin.
Thunder Ridge MS 3-00100 699-0408
5250 S PICADILLY ST 80015
Terry Killin, prin.

Aurora Christian Academy 2-11111 344-2530
11001 E ALAMEDA AVE 80012
Colorado Career Academy 2-CS 690-6900
13790 E RICE PL 80015
Community College of Aurora 4-CC 360-4700
16000 E CENTRETECH PKY 80011
ITT Technical Institute 3-UC 695-1913
2121 S BLACKHAWK ST 80014
Parks Junior College 2-CS 367-2757
6 ABILENE ST 80011
Pickens Technical Center CS 344-4910
500 BUCKLEY RD 80011
Platt College 2-CC 369-5151
3100 S PARKER RD 80014
Regis Jesuit HS 3-00011 699-1598
16300 E WEAVER PL 80016
Rick Sullivan, prin.

Bailey, AC 303, PC 2, Park
Platte Canyon SD 1 4-11111 838-7666
PO BOX 295 80421
Edwin Steinbrecher, supt.
Platte Canyon HS, PO BOX 295 80421 2-00011 838-4642
Susie Knupp, prin.
Fitzsimmons MS, PO BOX 295 80421 2-00100 838-2054
Richard Bryant, prin.

Basalt, AC 303, PC 4, Eagle
Roaring Fork SD RE-1
Supt. — See Glenwood Springs
HS, 51 SCHOOL ST 81621 2-00011 927-3121
Michael Costanzo, prin.

Bayfield, AC 303, PC 4, La Plata
Bayfield SD 10 JT-R 3-11111 884-2496
PO BOX 258 81122
Tom Brown, supt.
HS, PO BOX 258 81122 2-00011 884-9521
Jack Curran, prin.
MS, PO BOX 258 81122 2-00100 884-9592
Betty Yost, prin.

Bennett, AC 303, PC 4, Adams
Bennett SD 29J, 615 7TH ST 80102 — 3-11111
James Lathrop, supt. — 644-3234
HS, 610 7TH ST 80102 — 2-00011
Roger Ellis, prin. — 644-3234
MS, 510 7TH ST 80102 — 2-00100
Mark Purslow, prin. — 644-3234

Berthoud, AC 303, PC 5, Larimer
Thompson SD R-2J
Supt. — See Loveland
HS, 850 SPARTAN AVE 80513 — 3-00011
Leonard Sherman, prin. — 532-3743
Turner MS — 2-00100
950 MASSACHUSETTS AVE 80513 — 532-2661
Dennis Kuehl, prin.

Bethune, AC 719, PC 2, Kit Carson
Bethune SD R-5, PO BOX 127 80805 — 1-11111
James Poole, supt. — 346-7513
S, PO BOX 127 80805 — 1-11111
James Poole, prin. — 346-7513

Beulah, AC 719, PC 3, Pueblo
Pueblo County Rural SD 70
Supt. — See Pueblo
MS, 8734 SCHOOL HOUSE LN W 81023 — 1-00100
Mike Gregorich, prin. — 485-3127

Black Hawk, AC 303, PC 2, Gilpin
Gilpin County SD RE-1 — 2-11111
10595 HIGHWAY 119 80403 — 582-0625
Paul Coleman, supt.
Gilpin County S — 2-11111
10595 HIGHWAY 119 80403 — 582-3444
John Weishaar, prin.

Blanca, AC 719, PC 2, Costilla
Sierra Grande SD R-30 — 2-11111
RR 1 BOX 15 81123 — 379-3259
Lauren Bussey, supt.
Sierra Grande S, RR 1 BOX 15 81123 — 2-11111
Iva Gallegos, prin. — 379-3257

Boulder, AC 303, PC 8, Boulder
Boulder Valley SD RE-2 — 7-11111
PO BOX 9011 80301 — 447-1010
Dean Damon, supt.
HS, 1604 ARAPAHOE AVE 80302 — 4-00011
Jean Bonelli, prin. — 442-2430
Fairview HS — 4-00011
1515 GREENBRIAR BLVD 80303 — 499-7600
Donald Grove, prin.
New HS, 889 17TH ST 80302 — 3-00011
Rona Wilensky, prin. — 440-4459
Vocational Tech Ctr — Vo Tech
6600 ARAPAHOE RD 80303 — 447-5247
Donald Scheel, prin.
Base Line MS, 700 20TH ST 80302 — 2-00100
Fred Reichert, prin. — 443-1062
Burbank MS — 2-00100
290 MANHATTAN DR 80303 — 494-0335
Joette Donnelly, prin.
Casey MS, 2410 13TH ST 80304 — 3-00100
Dee Kehl, prin. — 442-5235
Centennial MS — 3-00100
2005 NORWOOD AVE 80304 — 443-3760
Gayla Lindquist, prin.
Platt MS, 6096 BASELINE RD 80303 — 3-00100
William Van Howe, prin. — 499-6800
Southern Hills MS, 1500 KNOX DR 80303 — 2-00100
Max McMillan, prin. — 494-2866
Other Schools — See Broomfield, Lafayette,
Louisville, Nederland

Boulder Valley Area Voc. Tech. Center — CS
6600 ARAPAHOE RD 80303 — 447-5247
Naropa Institute — 2-UC
2130 ARAPAHOE AVE 80302 — 444-0202
University of Colorado 80309 — 7-UC
492-8908

Branson, AC 719, PC 1, Las Animas
Branson RSD 82, PO BOX 128 81027 — 1-11111
Lester Mundy, supt. — 946-5531
JSHS, PO BOX 128 81027 — 1-00111
Lester Mundy, prin. — 946-5531

Briggsdale, AC 303, PC 1, Weld
Briggsdale SD RE-10 — 1-11111
PO BOX 125 80611 — 656-3417
Edward Schelhaas, supt.
JSHS, PO BOX 125 80611 — 1-00111
Edward Schelhaas, prin. — 656-3418

Brighton, AC 303, PC 7, Adams
Brighton SD 27J, 630 S 8TH AVE 80601 — 5-11111
John Meyer, supt. — 659-4820
HS, 270 S 8TH AVE 80601 — 4-00011
James Reitz, prin. — 659-4830
Overland Trail MS — 2-00100
445 N 19TH AVE 80601 — 659-3491
James Greule, prin.
Vikan MS, 879 JESSUP ST 80601 — 2-00100
Richard Veech, prin. — 659-1280

Northglenn-Thornton SD 12
Supt. — See Northglenn
Horizon SHS, 5321 E 136TH AVE 80601 — 4-00001
Dave Schmidt, prin. — 450-5227

Broomfield, AC 303, PC 7, Boulder
Boulder Valley SD RE-2
Supt. — See Boulder

HS, 1000 DAPHNE ST 80020 — 4-00011
Maria Goodloe, prin. — 466-7344
Broomfield Heights MS — 3-00100
1555 DAPHNE ST 80020 — 466-2387
Walt Grebing, prin.

Northglenn-Thornton SD 12
Supt. — See Northglenn
Westlake Village JHS — 4-00110
2800 W 135TH AVE 80020 — 469-1867
Margaret Claspell, prin.

Colorado Aero Tech — 4-CC
10851 W 120TH AVE 80021 — 800-888-3995

Brush, AC 303, PC 5, Morgan
Brush SD RE-2(J), PO BOX 585 80723 — 4-11111
Douglas Johnson, supt. — 842-5176
HS, PO BOX 585 80723 — 2-00011
Ron Prascher, prin. — 842-5171
MS, PO BOX 585 80723 — 2-00100
Tom Hill, prin. — 842-5035

High Plains Youth Center — 2-00111
901 INDUSTRIAL PARK RD 80723 — 842-5181

Buena Vista, AC 719, PC 4, Chaffee
Buena Vista SD R-31 — 3-11111
PO BOX 2027 81211 — 395-8656
D. Smith, supt.
HS, PO BOX 2027 81211 — 2-00011
Dennis Giese, prin. — 395-2487
McGinnis MS, PO BOX 2027 81211 — 2-00100
Daryl Nyquist, prin. — 395-8691

Burlington, AC 719, PC 5, Kit Carson
Burlington SD RE-6J — 3-11111
PO BOX 369 80807 — 346-8737
Red Mosier, supt.
HS, 380 MIKE LOUNGE DR 80807 — 2-00011
Jerry McVicker, prin. — 346-8455
MS, 2600 ROSE AVE 80807 — 2-01100
Ray Rhoades, prin. — 346-5440

Byers, AC 303, PC 4, Arapahoe
Byers SD 32J, PO BOX 420 80103 — 2-11111
George Sauter, supt. — 822-5292
HS, PO BOX 420 80103 — 1-00011
Michael Grandstaff, prin. — 822-5292

Calhan, AC 719, PC 3, El Paso
Calhan SD RJ-1, PO BOX 800 80808 — 2-11111
Richard Ullom, supt. — 347-2766
JSHS, PO BOX 800 80808 — 2-00111
Geary Cantrell, prin. — 347-2766

Ellicott SD 22 — 3-11111
350 N ELLICOTT HWY 80808 — 683-2328
Lionel Robertson, supt.
Ellicott JSHS — 2-00111
375 S ELLICOTT HWY 80808 — 683-2700
Dennis Carter, prin.

Campo, AC 719, PC 2, Baca
Campo SD RE-6, PO BOX 70 81029 — 1-11111
Leon Cummings, supt. — 787-2226
JSHS, PO BOX 70 81029 — 1-00111
Leon Cummings, prin. — 787-2226

Canon City, AC 719, PC 7, Fremont
Canon City SD RE-1 — 5-11111
101 N 14TH ST 81212 — 275-0691
Frank Cooper, supt.
HS, 1313 COLLEGE AVE 81212 — 4-00011
Ron Minty, prin. — 275-3351
MS, 1215 MAIN ST 81212 — 3-00100
Patti Schwab, prin. — 275-0652

St. Scholastica Academy — 1-00111
615 PIKE AVE 81212 — 275-7461
Sr. Benita Coffey, prin.

Carbondale, AC 303, PC 5, Garfield
Roaring Fork SD RE-1
Supt. — See Glenwood Springs
Roaring Fork HS — 2-00011
180 SNOWMASS DR 81623 — 963-3840
Patrick Henry, prin.
MS, 455 S 3RD ST 81623 — 2-01100
Leslie Sharp, prin. — 963-2240

Colorado Rocky Mountain S — 2-00011
1493 COUNTY ROAD 106 # X 81623 — 963-2562
Donald Reed, prin.

Castle Rock, AC 303, PC 6, Douglas
Douglas County SD RE-1 — 7-11111
620 WILCOX ST 80104 — 688-3195
Richard O'Connell, supt.
Douglas County HS — 4-00011
2842 FRONT ST 80104 — 688-3166
Edna Doherty, prin.
MS, 2693 FRONT ST 80104 — 3-00100
Gary Flynn, prin. — 688-3169
Other Schools — See Highlands Ranch, Parker

Cedaredge, AC 303, PC 4, Delta
Delta County SD 50(J)
Supt. — See Delta
HS, 2375 COTTONWOOD LN 81413 — 2-00011
Bill Kehmeier, prin. — 856-6882
MS, 360 N GRAND MESA DR 81413 — 2-01100
Jeanne Perry, prin. — 856-3118

Center, AC 719, PC 4, Saguache
Center SD 26Jt, PO BOX 730 81125 — 3-11111
Gary Kidd, supt. — 754-3442
HS, PO BOX 730 81125 — 2-00011
Herman Martinez, prin. — 754-2232
JHS, PO BOX 730 81125 — 1-00100
Herman Martinez, prin. — 754-2232

Cheraw, AC 719, PC 2, Otero
Cheraw SD 31, PO BOX 159 81030 — 2-11111
Johnie Dombaugh, supt. — 853-6655
S, PO BOX 159 81030 — 2-11111
Sheila Henry, prin. — 853-6655

Cheyenne Wells, AC 719, PC 4, Cheyenne
Cheyenne County SD RE-5 — 2-11111
PO BOX 577 80810 — 767-5866
Ken Bond, supt.
JSHS, PO BOX 577 80810 — 1-00111
Gary Wilson, prin. — 767-5612

Clifton, AC 303, PC 7, Mesa
Mesa County Valley SD 51
Supt. — See Grand Junction
Mt. Garfield MS, 3475 FRONT ST 81520 — 3-00100
Marilyn Conner, prin. — 464-0533

Collbran, AC 303, PC 2, Mesa
Plateau Valley SD 50 — 3-11111
RR 1 BOX 26 81624 — 487-3547
Craig Shafer, supt.
Grand Mesa HS, RR 1 BOX 26 81624 — 2-00011
John Henderson, prin. — 487-3576
Plateau Valley HS — 1-00110
RR 1 BOX 26 81624 — 487-3547
Jerry Schott, prin.

Colorado City, AC 719, PC 4, Pueblo
Pueblo County Rural SD 70
Supt. — See Pueblo
Craver MS, PO BOX 267 81002 — 2-00100
Gregg White, prin. — 676-3030

Colorado Springs, AC 719, PC 10, El Paso
Academy SD 20 — 7-11111
7610 N UNION BLVD 80920 — 598-2566
Janet Makris, supt.
Liberty HS — 4-00011
8720 SCARBOROUGH DR 80920 — 282-1000
Steve Morrison, prin.
Rampart HS, 8250 LEXINGTON DR 80920 — 4-00011
Mary Padgett, prin. — 594-9292
Challenger MS — 3-00100
10215 LEXINGTON DR 80920 — 598-1007
Peter Cicatelli, prin.
Eagleview MS — 3-00100
1325 VINDICATOR DR 80919 — 548-0316
Ross MaCaskill, prin.
Timberview MS — 4-00100
8680 SCARBOROUGH DR 80920 — 282-1144
William Shell, prin.
Other Schools — See USAF Academy

Cheyenne Mountain SD 12 — 5-11111
1118 W CHEYENNE RD 80906 — 475-6100
Harlan Else, supt.
Cheyenne Mountain SHS — 3-00001
1200 CRESTA RD 80906 — 475-6110
Allan Porter, prin.
Cheyenne Mountain JHS — 3-00110
1200 W CHEYENNE RD 80906 — 475-6120
Donald Wallace, prin.

Colorado Springs SD 11 — 8-11111
1115 N EL PASO ST 80903 — 520-2000
Kenneth Burnley, supt.
Coronado HS — 4-00011
1590 W FILLMORE ST 80904 — 520-2500
John Bushey, prin.
Doherty HS, 4525 BARNES RD 80917 — 4-00011
Larry Finnigsmier, prin. — 520-2600
Mitchell HS, 1205 POTTER DR 80909 — 4-00011
Delia Armstrong-Busby, prin. — 520-2700
Palmer HS, 301 N NEVADA AVE 80903 — 4-00011
Jay Engeln, prin. — 520-2800
Wasson HS, 2115 AFTON WAY 80909 — 4-00011
Jackie Provenzano, prin. — 520-2900
East JHS, 1600 N UNION BLVD 80909 — 3-00100
Harold Firestine, prin. — 520-2400
Emerson JHS — 3-00100
4220 E PIKES PEAK AVE 80909 — 520-2410
Jose Vela, prin.
Holmes JHS, 2455 MESA RD 80904 — 3-00100
Brenda Lebrasse, prin. — 520-2420
Irving JHS — 3-00100
1702 N MURRAY BLVD 80915 — 520-2430
Ralph Juarros, prin.
Mann JHS, 1001 E VAN BUREN ST 80907 — 3-00100
Ed Paulovich, prin. — 520-2440
North JHS, 612 E YAMPA ST 80903 — 3-00100
Gary Arthur, prin. — 520-2450
Russell JHS — 3-00100
3825 MONTEBELLO DR W 80918 — 520-2460
Newgene Ray, prin.
Sabin JHS, 3605 N CAREFREE CIR 80917 — 3-00100
Dennis Thruston, prin. — 520-2470
West JHS — 2-00100
1920 W PIKES PEAK AVE 80904 — 520-2480
Patricia Russell, prin.

Falcon SD 49
Supt. — See Falcon
Horizon MS, 1750 PIROS DR 80915 — 2-00100
Richens Smith, prin. — 574-7700

Hanover SD 28 1-11111
17050 S PEYTON HWY 80928 683-2247
Patrick Dawson, supt.
Hanover S, 17050 S PEYTON HWY 80928 1-11111
Tom Reiher, prin. 683-2247

Harrison SD 2 7-11111
1060 HARRISON RD 80906 576-8360
Tony Stansberry, supt.
Harrison HS, 2755 JANITELL RD 80906 4-00011
Pat Lofthus, prin. 576-8522
Sierra HS, 2250 JET WING DR 80916 4-00011
Robert Freehill, prin. 591-9400
Carmel MS 3-00100
1740 PEPPERWOOD DR 80910 597-6870
Richard Price, prin.
Gorman MS, 2883 S CIRCLE DR 80906 3-00100
Gary Strubel, prin. 576-8526
Panorama MS 3-00100
2145 S CHELTON RD 80916 591-2570
Criss Tausan, prin.

Widefield SD 3, 1820 MAIN ST 80911 6-11111
Gene Cosby, supt. 392-3481
Widefield SHS 4-00001
615 WIDEFIELD DR 80911 392-3427
Gary Wisler, prin.
Sproul JHS, 235 SUMAC DR 80911 3-00110
Mario Williams, prin. 392-3458
Watson JHS, 136 FONTAINE BLVD 80911 3-00110
Don Stanec, prin. 392-3418
Other Schools – See Fountain

Beth-El College of Nursing 2-UC
2790 N ACADEMY BLVD STE 200 80917
475-5170
Blair Junior College 4-CC
828 WOOTEN RD 80915 574-1082
Colorado College 4-UC
14 E CACHE LA POUDRE ST 80903 389-6000
Colorado School for the Deaf and Blind HND
33 N INSTITUTE ST 80903
Colorado Springs Christian S 4-11111
301 AUSTIN BLUFFS PKY 80918 599-3553
Colorado Springs S 2-11111
21 BROADMOOR AVE 80906 475-9747
Mary Flemke, prin.
Colorado Technical College 3-UC
4435 N CHESTNUT ST 80907 598-0200
Denver Academy of Court Reporting 2-CS
220 RUSKIN DR 80910 574-5010
Denver Paralegal Institute 2-CS
105 E VERMIJO AVE 80903 444-0190
Denver Technical College 2-UC
225 S UNION BLVD 80910 632-3000
Emery Aviation College CC
1245A AVIATION WAY 80916 591-9488
Evangelical Christian Academy 2-11111
2511 N LOGAN AVE 80907 634-7024
Fountain Valley S 2-00011
6155 FNTIN VALLEY SCHOOL RD 80911
Eric Waples, prin. 390-7035
Hilltop Christian S 2-11111
6915 PALMER PARK BLVD 80915 597-1880
Intermountain College 2-CS
4070 AUTUMN HGHTS DR UNIT B 80906
- -
Memorial Hospital HSP
1400 E BOULDER ST 80909 475-5000
National College 2-UC
2577 N CHELTON RD 80909 389-1486
Nazarene Bible College 2-UC
PO BOX 15749 80935 596-5110
Penrose Hospital HSP
2215 N CASCADE AVE 80907 630-5111
Pikes Peak Community College 6-CC
5675 S ACADEMY BLVD 80906 540-7551
PPI Health Careers School 2-CS
2345 N ACADEMY BLVD 80909 596-5900
St. Mary's HS, PO BOX 9210 80932 2-00011
Sr. Clarissa Tenbrink, prin. 635-7540
Technical Trades Institute 3-CC
2315 E PIKES PEAK AVE 80909 632-7626
United States Air Force Academy 80840 5-UC
472-4140
University of Colorado 5-UC
PO BOX 7150 80933 593-3119

Commerce City, AC 303, PC 7, Adams
Adams County SD 14 6-11111
4720 E 69TH AVE 80022 289-3950
George Starface, supt.
Adams City HS, 4625 E 68TH AVE 80022 4-00011
C. Thomas Budde, prin. 289-3111
Arnold JSHS, 6500 E 72ND AVE 80022 2-00111
Larry Nichols, prin. 289-2983
Adams City MS, 4451 E 72ND AVE 80022 3-00100
Karen Lewis, prin. 289-5881
Kearney MS, 6160 KEARNEY ST 80022 3-00100
Annette Sulzman, prin. 287-0261

Conifer, AC 303, PC 3, Jefferson
Jefferson County SD R-1
Supt. — See Golden
West Jefferson JHS 3-00110
9449 S BARNES AVE 80433 623-3551
Byron Tucker, prin.

Cortez, AC 303, PC 6, Montezuma
Montezuma-Cortez SD Re-1 5-11111
PO BOX R 81321 565-7282
Bill Thompson, supt.
Montezuma-Cortez HS, PO BOX R 81321 3-00011
Eugene Sparks, prin. 565-3722
MS, PO BOX R 81321 3-00100
Roger Braaten, prin. 565-7824

San Juan Basin AVTS 2-CS
PO BOX 970 81321 565-8457

Cotopaxi, AC 719, PC 2, Fremont
Cotopaxi SD RE-3 2-11111
PO BOX 385 81223 942-4131
Larry Coleman, supt.
JSHS, PO BOX 385 81223 2-00111
Geoffrey Gerk, prin. 942-4131

Craig, AC 303, PC 6, Moffat
Moffat County SD Re-1 5-11111
775 YAMPA AVE 81625 824-3268
Charles Grove, supt.
Moffat County HS, 900 FINLEY LN 81625 3-00011
Joel Sheridan, prin. 824-7036
MS, 915 YAMPA AVE 81625 3-01100
James Jordan, prin. 824-3289

Creede, AC 719, PC 2, Mineral
Creede Cons. SD 1 1-11111
PO BOX 429 81130 658-2220
James Boydston, supt.
JSHS, PO BOX 429 81130 1-00111
Buck Stroh, prin. 658-2220

Cripple Creek, AC 719, PC 3, Teller
Cripple Creek-Victor SD RE-1 2-11111
PO BOX 897 80813 689-2685
Donald McGill, supt.
Cripple Creek-Victor JSHS 2-00111
PO BOX 897 80813 689-2661
Cathy Pobega, prin.

De Beque, AC 303, PC 2, Mesa
De Beque SD 49Jt, PO BOX 70 81630 2-11111
Christina Rinehart, supt. 283-5597
JSHS, PO BOX 70 81630 1-00111
Ed Lundquist, prin. 283-5596

Deer Trail, AC 303, PC 2, Arapahoe
Deer Trail SD 26J, PO BOX 129 80105 2-11111
Stephen Beaber, supt. 769-4421
JSHS, PO BOX 129 80105 1-00111
Greg Swiatkowski, prin. 769-4421

Del Norte, AC 719, PC 4, Rio Grande
Del Norte SD C-7, PO BOX 159 81132 3-11111
Marlin Janas, supt. 657-4040
HS, PO BOX 159 81132 2-00011
Larry Barclay, prin. 657-4020
MS, PO BOX 159 81132 2-00100
Ken Bailey, prin. 657-4030

Delta, AC 303, PC 5, Delta
Delta County SD 50(J) 5-11111
765 2075 RD 81416 874-4438
Laddie Livingston, supt.
HS, 1400 PIONEER RD 81416 3-00011
Al Williams, prin. 874-8031
MS, 822 GRAND AVE 81416 3-01100
Earle Wise, prin. 874-8046
Other Schools – See Cedaredge, Hotchkiss, Paonia

Denver, AC 303, PC 10, Denver
Denver County SD 1 8-11111
900 GRANT ST 80203 764-3200
Evie Dennis, supt.
East HS, 1545 DETROIT ST 80206 4-00011
Pia Smith, prin. 394-8300
Jefferson HS, 3950 S HOLLY ST 80237 3-00011
David Strodtman, prin. 691-7000
Kennedy HS, 2855 S LAMAR ST 80227 4-00011
Bernadette Seick, prin. 763-4300
Lincoln HS 4-00011
2285 S FEDERAL BLVD 80219 727-5000
James Trevino, prin.
Manual HS, 1700 E 28TH AVE 80205 3-00011
Linda Transou, prin. 391-6300
Montbello HS 4-00011
5000 CROWN BLVD 80239 375-5700
Willard Smith, prin.
North HS, 2960 N SPEER BLVD 80211 4-00011
Joseph Sandoval, prin. 964-2700
South HS 4-00011
1700 E LOUISIANA AVE 80210 698-6100
George Diedrich, prin.
Washington HS 4-00011
655 S MONACO PKY 80224 394-8600
Vivian Johnston, prin.
West HS, 951 ELATI ST 80204 4-00011
Edward Cordova, prin. 620-5300
Griffith Opportunity S Vo Tech
1250 WELTON ST 80204 572-8218
Mary Ann Parthum, prin.
Thomas Career Ed Ctr Vo Tech
2650 ELIOT ST 80211 964-3000
Calvin Smith, prin.
Baker MS, 574 W 6TH AVE 80204 2-00100
Richard Jordan, prin. 629-6906
Cole MS, 3240 HUMBOLDT ST 80205 3-00100
Barbara Batey, prin. 296-8421
Gove MS, 4050 E 14TH AVE 80220 2-00100
Pauline McBeth, prin. 355-1676
Grant MS 3-00100
1751 S WASHINGTON ST 80210 722-4633
Farrell Howell, prin.
Hamilton MS 3-00100
8600 E DARTMOUTH AVE 80231 755-1267
Cheryl Betz, prin.
Henry MS, 3005 S GOLDEN WAY 80227 3-00100
Melanie Haas, prin. 989-2330
Hill MS, 451 CLERMONT ST 80220 3-00100
Madelyn Braverman, prin. 399-0254
Kepner MS, 911 S HAZEL CT 80219 3-00100
Arzelia Galvez, prin. 935-4601
King MS, 19535 E 46TH AVE 80249 4-00100
Leonard Miles, prin. 373-9870
Kunsmiller MS 3-00100
2250 S QUITMAN WAY 80219 934-5476
Moises Martinez, prin.
Lake MS, 1820 LOWELL BLVD 80204 3-00100
Gregory Tate, prin. 629-6902
Mann MS, 4130 NAVAJO ST 80211 3-00100
Martha Guevara, prin. 433-2553
Merrill MS, 1551 S MONROE ST 80210 3-00100
Richard Peacock, prin. 756-3621
Montessori MS, 1350 E 33RD AVE 80205 2-00100
(—), prin. 296-8412
Morey MS, 840 E 14TH AVE 80218 2-00100
Rhoda Imhoff, prin. 832-1139
Place MS 3-00100
7125 CHERRY CREEK NORTH DR 80224
Diane Dowell, prin. 758-6111
Rishel MS, 451 S TEJON ST 80223 3-00100
Irene Martinez-Jordan, prin. 777-4436
Skinner MS, 3435 W 40TH AVE 80211 3-00100
Gene Martinez, prin. 433-8851
Smiley MS, 2540 HOLLY ST 80207 3-00100
Beth Celva, prin. 399-0740

Mapleton SD 1, 591 E 80TH AVE 80229 5-11111
J. Tom Maes, supt. 288-6681
Dewey JHS, 7480 CONIFER RD 80221 2-00100
Cheryl Tufly, prin. 428-3523
York JHS, 9200 YORK ST 80229 3-00100
Cheryl Mull, prin. 287-5588
Other Schools – See Thornton

Northglenn-Thornton SD 12
Supt. — See Northglenn
Pecos JHS, 9450 PECOS ST 80221 3-00110
Larry Myres, prin. 428-4666

Westminster SD 50
Supt. — See Westminster
Ranum HS, 2401 W 80TH AVE 80221 4-00011
Dick Werpy, prin. 428-9577
Carpenter MS, 7001 LIPAN ST 80221 3-00100
Mark Whitney, prin. 428-8583
Clear Lake MS 3-00100
1940 ELMWOOD LN 80221 428-7526
Carol Proffitt, prin.
Hodgkins MS, 3475 W 67TH AVE 80221 3-00100
Peter Golden, prin. 428-7503

Academy of Floral Design 2-CS
837 ACOMA ST 80204 623-8855
Accelerated Schools Foundation 2-11111
2160 S COOK ST 80210 758-2003
Ernie Clore, prin.
American Diesel & Automotive College 2-CS
1002 S JASON ST 80223 778-6772
Barnes Business College 5-CS
150 SHERIDAN BLVD 80226 922-8454
Bel-Rea Institute of Animal Technology 2-CC
1681 S DAYTON ST 80231 800-950-8001
Beth Eden Baptist S 2-11111
2600 WADSWORTH BLVD 80215 232-2313
CollegeAmerica 2-CS
720 S COLORADO BLVD # 260 80222
691-9756
College for Financial Planning 6-UC
4695 S MONACO ST 80237 220-1200
Colorado Academy 3-11111
3800 S PIERCE ST 80235 986-1501
Christopher Babbs, prin.
Colorado Institute of Art 4-CC
200 E 9TH AVE 80203 800-275-2420
Community College of Denver 5-CC
1111 W COLFAX AVE 80204 556-2411
ConCorde Career Institute 3-CS
770 GRANT ST 80203 861-1151
Denver Academy, 1125 S RACE ST 80210 2-01111
777-5870
Denver Academy of Court Reporting 2-CS
7290 SAMUEL DR 80221 427-5292
Denver Automotive & Diesel College 3-CS
460 S LIPAN ST 80223 800-347-3232
Denver Business College 2-CS
7350 BROADWAY 80221 426-1000
Denver Christian S 2-00111
2135 S PEARL ST 80210 733-2421
Steve Ribbens, prin.
Denver Institute of Technology 4-CC
7350 BROADWAY 80221 650-5050
Denver Paralegal Institute 2-CS
1401 19TH ST 80202 800-848-0550
Denver Seminary 2-UC
PO BOX 10000 80250 761-2482
Denver Technical College 2-UC
925 S NIAGARA ST 80224 329-3000
Emily Griffith Opportunity School 1-CS
1250 WELTON ST 80204 572-8218
Heritage College of Health Careers 2-CS
12 LAKESIDE LN 80212 477-7240
HS, 901 LARIMER ST 80204 2-00011
893-6945

Holy Family HS, 4343 UTICA ST 80212 | 2-00011
Sr. Mary Lieb, supt. | 458-8822
Iliff School of Theology | 2-UC
2201 S UNIVERSITY BLVD 80210 | 800-678-3360
Interior Design Institute of Denver | 2-UC
6868 E JEWELL AVE 80224 | - -
Intermountain College | 2-CS
5801 W 44TH AVE 80212 | 455-9610
Lutheran HS | 2-00011
3201 W ARIZONA AVE 80219 | 934-2345
Kenneth Palmreuter, prin.
Machebeuf Catholic HS | 2-00011
1958 ELM ST 80220 | 322-1819
Elizabeth Mantelli, prin.
Metropolitan State College | 7-UC
PO BOX 173362 80217 | 556-3022
Mile Hi College | 3-CS
6464 W 14TH AVE 80214 | 233-7973
Mile High Adventist Academy | 2-11111
711 E YALE AVE 80210 | 744-1069
Mullen HS, 3601 S LOWELL BLVD 80236 | 3-00011
Vince Greco, prin. | 761-1764
National Academy of Nannies | 1-CS
1681 S DAYTON ST 80231 | 333-6264
National College | 2-UC
1325 S COLORADO BLVD # 100 80222 |
 | 758-6700
National Theatre Conservatory | 1-UC
1050 13TH ST 80204 | 893-4000
Parks College | 4-CC
9065 GRANT ST 80229 | 457-2757
Pima Medical Institute | 2-CS
7290 SAMUEL DR STE 200 80221 | 426-1800
Presbyterian Saint Luke's Center | HSP
601 E 19TH AVE 80203 | 839-6740
Presbyterian Saint Luke's Center | HSP
1719 E 19TH AVE # 27 80218 | 839-6485
Regis University | 5-UC
3333 REGIS BLVD 80221 | 458-4190
Rocky Mountain College of Art & Design | 2-UC
6875 E EVANS AVE 80224 | 800-888-2787
Rocky Mountain School of Meatcutting | 1-CS
790 W EVANS AVE 80223 | 722-1044
St. Anthony Hospital Systems | HSP
4231 W 16TH AVE 80204 | 629-4300
St. Thomas Seminary | 1-UC
1300 S STEELE ST 80210 | 722-4687
Teikyo Loretto Heights University | 3-UC
3001 S FEDERAL BLVD 80236 | 936-8441
University of Colorado at Denver | 6-UC
1200 LARIMER ST 80204 | 556-3279
University of Colorado Health Sciences | 4-UC
4200 E 9TH AVE 80262 | 270-7682
University of Denver | 6-UC
2199 S UNIVERSITY BLVD 80210 | 871-2111
University of Denver University College | 2-UC
2211 S JOSEPHINE ST 80208 | 871-3818
Yeshiva Toras Chaim Talmudic Seminary | 1-UC
1400 QUITMAN ST 80204 | 629-8200

Dolores, AC 303, PC 3, Montezuma
Dolores SD RE-4A | 3-11111
PO BOX 757 81323 | 882-7255
Greg Conway, supt.
HS, PO BOX 757 81323 | 2-00011
Greg Conway, prin. | 882-7288
JHS, PO BOX 757 81323 | 2-00100
Greg Conway, prin. | 882-7288

Dove Creek, AC 303, PC 3, Dolores
Dolores County SD RE 2 | 2-11111
PO BOX 459 81324 | 677-2522
Gary Hannah, supt.
Delores County HS | 2-00011
PO BOX 459 81324 – (—), prin. | 677-2237
Other Schools – See Egnar

Durango, AC 303, PC 7, La Plata
Durango SD 9-R, PO BOX 2467 81302 | 5-11111
Walt Jackson, supt. | 247-5411
HS, PO BOX 2467 81302 | 4-00011
Bob Wright, prin. | 259-1630
Miller MS, PO BOX 2467 81302 | 2-00100
Stan Dunlap, prin. | 247-1418
Smiley MS, PO BOX 2467 81302 | 3-00100
Norman Higgs, prin. | 247-9491

Colorado Timberline Academy | 1-00011
35554 HIGHWAY 550 81301 | 247-5898
Joseph Maceyak, prin.
Durango Air Service | 2-CS
1300 COUNTY ROAD 309 81301 | 247-5535
Fort Lewis College | 5-UC
1000 RIM DR 81301 | 247-7661

Eads, AC 719, PC 3, Kiowa
Eads SD RE-1, PO BOX 877 81036 | 2-11111
Gary Monter, supt. | 438-2218
HS, PO BOX 877 81036 | 1-00011
Gary Monter, prin. | 438-2214
JHS, PO BOX 877 81036 | 1-00100
David Adamson, prin. | 438-2216

Eagle, AC 303, PC 4, Eagle
Eagle County SD RE-50 | 5-11111
PO BOX 740 81631 | 328-6321
John Lange, supt.
Eagle Valley MS, PO BOX 1019 81631 | 2-00100
Gerald Santoro, prin. | 328-6224
Other Schools – See Gypsum, Minturn

Eaton, AC 303, PC 4, Weld
Eaton SD RE-2, PO BOX 8 80615 | 4-11111
Bill Powell, supt. | 454-3402
HS, PO BOX 8 80615 | 2-00011
Eugene Huser, prin. | 454-3374
MS, PO BOX 37 80615 | 2-01100
Ken Sudduth, prin. | 454-3358

Edgewater, AC 303, PC 5, Jefferson
Jefferson County SD R-1
Supt. — See Golden
Jefferson HS, 2305 PIERCE ST 80214 | 3-00011
Debbie Taylor, prin. | 238-1361

Egnar, AC 303, PC 1, San Miguel
Dolores County SD RE 2
Supt. — See Dove Creek
MS, PO BOX 247 81325 | 1-00100
Stephen Balloga, prin. | 677-2560

Elbert, AC 303, PC 2, Elbert
Elbert SD 200, PO BOX 38 80106 | 2-11111
Cindy Gross, supt. | 648-3013
JSHS, PO BOX 38 80106 | 1-00111
Jerry Wager, prin. | 648-3013

Elizabeth, AC 303, PC 3, Elbert
Elizabeth SD C-1, PO BOX 610 80107 | 4-11111
Dan McCormack, supt. | 646-4441
HS, PO BOX 660 80107 | 2-00011
Linda Fox, prin. | 646-4616
MS, PO BOX 369 80107 | 2-01100
Jim Eck, prin. | 646-4520

Englewood, AC 303, PC 8, Arapahoe
Cherry Creek SD 5 | 8-11111
4700 S YOSEMITE ST 80111 | 773-1184
Robert Tschirki, supt.
Cherry Creek HS | 5-00011
9300 E UNION AVE 80111 | 773-8920
Campus MS, 4785 S DAYTON ST 80111 | 4-00100
Nola Gill, prin. | 770-1150
Other Schools – See Aurora, Littleton

Englewood SD 1 | 5-11111
4101 S BANNOCK ST 80110 | 761-7050
Roscoe Davidson, supt.
HS, 3800 S LOGAN ST 80110 | 3-00011
Dennis Baker, prin. | 762-8630
Flood MS, 3695 S LINCOLN ST 80110 | 3-00100
Steven Cohen, prin. | 761-1226
Sinclair MS | 2-00100
300 W CHENANGO AVE 80110 | 781-7817
Robert Cady, prin.

Sheridan SD 2, PO BOX 1198 80150 | 4-11111
Kenneth Reiter, supt. | 761-8640
Sheridan HS, PO BOX 1198 80150 | 2-00011
Ken Bostdorff, prin. | 761-6307
Sheridan MS, PO BOX 1198 80150 | 2-00100
Paul Rochester, prin. | 789-1865

Kent Denver Country Day S | 3-00111
4000 E QUINCY AVE 80110 | 770-7660
Metro Christian S | 2-11111
6210 S YOSEMITE ST 80111 | 290-8491
St. Marys Girl Academy | 3-11111
4545 S UNIVERSITY BLVD 80110 | 762-8300
Mary Ann Surges, prin.
Swedish Medical Center | HSP
501 E HAMPDEN AVE 80110 | 788-6290
University of Phoenix | 2-UC
7800 E DORADO PL 80111 | 755-9090

Erie, AC 303, PC 4, Boulder
St. Vrain Valley SD RE-1J
Supt. — See Longmont
JSHS, PO BOX 67 80516 | 2-00111
William Davis, prin. | 828-3391

Estes Park, AC 303, PC 5, Larimer
Park SD R-3, PO BOX 1140 80517 | 4-11111
Bill Fears, supt. | 586-2361
Park HS, PO BOX 1140 80517 | 2-00011
Richard Kastendieck, prin. | 586-5321
MS, PO BOX 1140 80517 | 2-00100
Linda Gutsch, prin. | 586-4439

Evergreen, AC 303, PC 5, Jefferson
Jefferson County SD R-1
Supt. — See Golden
SHS, 5301 S OLIVE RD 80439 | 4-00001
John Vidal, prin. | 674-3341
JHS, 2052 HIGHWAY 74 80439 | 3-00110
Dan Patterson, prin. | 674-5536

Fairplay, AC 719, PC 2, Park
Park County SD RE-2 | 2-11111
PO BOX 189 80440 | 836-3114
William Granlund, supt.
South Park JSHS, PO BOX 189 80440 | 2-00111
Randy Hinson, prin. | 836-2007

Falcon, AC 719, PC 2, El Paso
Falcon SD 49 | 5-11111
10850 E WOODMEN RD 80831 | 495-3601
George Bolte, supt.
HS, 11110 STAPLETON DR N 80831 | 2-00011
Dean Palmer, prin. | 495-2261
MS, 11955 US HIGHWAY 24 80831 | 2-00100
Bill Noxon, prin. | 495-3661
Other Schools – See Colorado Springs

Flagler, AC 719, PC 3, Kit Carson
Arriba-Flagler SD C-20 | 2-11111
PO BOX 218 80815 | 765-4684
Mark Ricken, supt.
S, PO BOX 218 80815 | 2-11111
Fred Trimmer, prin. | 765-4684

Fleming, AC 303, PC 2, Logan
Frenchman SD RE-3 | 2-11111
506 N FREMONT ST 80728 | 265-2111
James Hess, supt.
HS, 506 N FREMONT ST 80728 | 1-00011
Patrick Dugan, prin. | 265-2022

Florence, AC 719, PC 5, Fremont
Florence SD RE-2, 403 W 5TH ST 81226 | 4-11111
Kathleen Graham, supt. | 784-6312
HS, 215 MAPLE ST 81226 | 3-00011
John Merriam, prin. | 784-6414

Fort Carson, AC 719, PC 7, El Paso
Fountain SD 8
Supt. — See Fountain
Carson MS, BLDG 6200 80913 | 2-00100
Richard Lirette, prin. | 382-8525

Fort Collins, AC 303, PC 8, Larimer
Poudre SD R-1 | 7-11111
2407 LA PORTE AVE 80521 | 482-7420
Don Unger, supt.
SHS, 1400 REMINGTON ST 80524 | 4-00001
John Brzeinski, prin. | 493-3110
Poudre SHS, 201 S IMPALA DR 80521 | 4-00001
Sandra Lundt, prin. | 484-1701
Rocky Mountain SHS | 4-00001
1300 W SWALLOW RD 80526 | 226-5626
Karen Dixon, prin.
Blevins JHS | 3-00110
2101 S TAFT HILL RD 80526 | 484-8350
Gerald Michels, prin.
Boltz JHS, 720 BOLTZ DR 80525 | 3-00110
Mike Walz, prin. | 226-3333
Lesher JHS, 1400 STOVER ST 80524 | 3-00110
Edwin Ginty, prin. | 484-0610
Lincoln JHS, 1600 LANCER DR 80521 | 3-00110
Phil Stewart, prin. | 484-3073
Webber JHS, 4201 SENECA ST 80526 | 3-00110
Sandra Bickel, prin. | 223-6698
Other Schools – See Laporte, Wellington

Choice City Christian S | 2-11111
608 E DRAKE RD 80525 | 484-3379
Colorado State University | 7-UC
102 ADMINISTRATION BLDG 80523 | 491-1101
Front Range Baptist Academy | 2-11111
625 W HARMONY RD 80526 | 223-2173
Front Range Community College | 5-CC
4616 S SHIELDS ST 80526 | 226-2500
Heritage Christian S | 2-11111
1500 ELLIS ST 80524 | 428-0868
Medical Careers Training Center | 2-CS
4020 S COLLEGE AVE 80525 | 223-2669
National Technological University | 4-UC
700 CENTRE AVE 80526 | 495-6405

Fort Lupton, AC 303, PC 6, Weld
Ft. Lupton SD RE-8 | 4-11111
301 REYNOLDS ST 80621 | 857-6291
Brent Mutsch, supt.
HS, 530 REYNOLDS ST 80621 | 3-00011
Scott Mader, prin. | 857-2713
IS, 201 S MCKINLEY AVE 80621 | 3-01100
Dan Vallez, prin. | 857-6205

Fort Morgan, AC 303, PC 6, Morgan
Ft. Morgan SD RE-3 | 5-11111
230 WALNUT ST 80701 | 867-5633
Robert Ash, supt.
HS, 709 E RIVERVIEW AVE 80701 | 3-00011
Ray Apking, prin. | 867-5648
MS, 300 DEUEL ST 80701 | 3-00100
Dan Bitner, prin. | 867-8253

Morgan Community College | 2-CC
17800 ROAD 20 80701 | 867-3081

Fountain, AC 719, PC 6, El Paso
Fountain SD 8 | 5-11111
425 W ALABAMA AVE 80817 | 382-5631
Dale Gasser, supt.
Fountain-Fort Carson HS | 3-00011
515 N SANTA FE AVE 80817 | 382-5653
Patrick Kane, prin.
Aragon MS, 211 S MAIN ST 80817 | 2-00100
William Weeks, prin. | 382-5635
Other Schools – See Fort Carson

Widefield SD 3
Supt. — See Colorado Springs
Janitell JHS | 3-00110
7636 FOUNTAIN MESA RD 80817 | 390-7867
Stan Richardson, prin.

Fowler, AC 719, PC 4, Otero
Fowler SD R-4J, PO BOX 218 81039 | 2-11111
Larry Vibber, supt. | 263-2424
HS, PO BOX 218 81039 | 2-00011
Al Lotrich, prin. | 263-4279
JHS, PO BOX 218 81039 | 1-00100
Al Lotrich, prin. | 263-4224

Frederick, AC 303, PC 3, Weld
St. Vrain Valley SD RE-1J
Supt. — See Longmont

JSHS, PO BOX 130 80530 — 2-00111
John Graueberger, prin. — 833-3533

Frisco, AC 303, PC 4, Summit
Summit SD RE-1, PO BOX 7 80443 — 4-11111
Nadine Johnson, supt. — 668-3011
Summit County HS, PO BOX 7 80443 — 2-00011
James Anastasio, prin. — 668-3522
Summit County MS, PO BOX 7 80443 — 2-00100
Wendy Moore, prin. — 668-5037

Fruita, AC 303, PC 5, Mesa
Mesa County Valley SD 51
Supt. — See Grand Junction
Fruita Monument HS, 1815 J RD 81521 — 4-00011
Mark Zipse, prin. — 858-3624
MS, 239 N MAPLE ST 81521 — 3-00100
Ralph Rangel, prin. — 858-3621

Gateway, AC 303, PC 2, Mesa
Mesa County Valley SD 51
Supt. — See Grand Junction
S, PO BOX 240 81522 — 1-11111
Charles Everett, prin. — 931-2276

Gilcrest, AC 303, PC 4, Weld
Gilcrest SD Re-1, PO BOX 157 80623 — 4-11111
Clifford Brookhart, supt. — 737-2403
Valley HS, PO BOX 156 80623 — 2-00011
Jerry Weiser, prin. — 737-2494
Other Schools – See La Salle, Platteville

Glenwood Springs, AC 303, PC 6, Garfield
Roaring Fork SD RE-1 — 5-11111
PO BOX 820 81602 — 945-6558
James Bader, supt.
HS, PO BOX 1700 81602 — 2-00011
Michael Wells, prin. — 945-5762
Roaring Fork Vo-Tech — Vo Tech
PO BOX 820 81602 — 945-5864
Charles Cloud, prin.
MS, PO BOX 250 81602 — 3-00100
Stan Johnson, prin. — 945-7192
Other Schools – See Basalt, Carbondale

Colorado Mountain College — 4-CC
PO BOX 10001 81602 — 945-8691

Golden, AC 303, PC 7, Jefferson
Jefferson County SD R-1 — 8-11111
1829 DENVER WEST DR 80401 — 273-6500
Lewis Finch, supt.
HS, 701 24TH ST 80401 — 4-00011
Judy Vance, prin. — 278-4494
Warren Occupational Tech Ctr — Vo Tech
13300 W ELLSWORTH AVE 80401 — 988-7470
Jane Wright, prin.
Bell MS, 1001 ULYSSES ST 80401 — 3-00100
Judy Cline, prin. — 279-6627
Other Schools – See Arvada, Conifer, Edgewater, Evergreen, Lakewood, Littleton, Westminster, Wheat Ridge

---

Colorado School of Mines — 4-UC
WEAVER TOWERS 1811 ELM ST 80401 — 273-3220
Red Rocks Community College — 4-CC
12600 W 6TH AVE 80401 — 988-6160

Granada, AC 719, PC 3, Prowers
Granada SD RE-1, PO BOX 259 81041 — 2-11111
Ian DeBono, supt. — 734-5492
JSHS, PO BOX 259 81041 — 1-00111
Ian Debono, prin. — 734-5492

Granby, AC 303, PC 3, Grand
East Grand SD 2, PO BOX 125 80446 — 4-11111
Gary Sibigtroth, supt. — 887-2581
Middle Park HS, PO BOX 130 80446 — 2-00011
Diana Kellner, prin. — 887-2104
East Grand MS, PO BOX 2210 80446 — 2-00100
(—), prin. — 887-3382

Grand Junction, AC 303, PC 8, Mesa
Mesa County Valley SD 51 — 7-11111
2115 GRAND AVE 81501 — 245-2422
Paul Rosier, supt.
Central HS, 3130 E 1/2 RD 81504 — 4-00011
William Lange, prin. — 434-7311
HS, 1400 N 5TH ST 81501 — 4-00011
Jerry Rose, prin. — 242-7496
Career Occupational Ed Ctr — Vo Tech
2935 NORTH AVE 81504 — 243-3142
Lee Searcy, prin.
Bookcliff MS — 3-00100
2935 ORCHARD AVE 81504 — 243-6350
Jim Haptonstall, prin.
East MS, 830 GUNNISON AVE 81501 — 2-00100
Sandra McGuire, prin. — 242-0512
Orchard Mesa MS — 3-00100
2736 UNAWEEP AVE 81503 — 242-5563
Tim Schlenvogt, prin.
Redlands MS, 2200 BROADWAY 81503 — 3-00100
J. Mills, prin. — 245-6084
West MS, 123 W ORCHARD AVE 81505 — 3-00100
Michael Henwood, prin. — 243-9040
Other Schools – See Clifton, Fruita, Gateway, Palisade

Cornerstone Christian S — 2-11111
PO BOX 88 81502 — 242-9078
Life Academy, 636 29 RD 81506 — 2-11111
242-9431
Mesa State College — 4-UC
PO BOX 2647 81502 — 241-1498
New Horizons Christian S — 2-11111
641 HORIZON DR 81506 — 243-2485
Technical Trades Institute — 2-CC
722 HORIZON DR 81506 — 245-8101

Greeley, AC 303, PC 8, Weld
Greeley SD 6, 811 15TH ST 80631 — 7-11111
John Pacheco, supt. — 352-1543
Greeley Central SHS — 4-00001
1515 14TH AVE 80631 — 352-9325
John Christensen, prin.
Greeley West SHS — 3-00001
2401 35TH AVE 80634 — 330-5303
Harold Alford, prin.
Evans JHS, 2900 15TH AVE 80631 — 3-00110
John Longtin, prin. — 353-5165
Heath JHS, 2223 16TH ST 80631 — 3-00110
Dale Krueger, prin. — 353-1750

Aims Community College — 5-CC
PO BOX 69 80632 — 330-8008
Dayspring Christian S — 2-11111
9TH AVE & 23RD ST 80631 — 353-7113
North Colorado Medical Center — HSP
1801 16TH ST 80631 — 352-4121
UNC Laboratory S, UNC CAMPUS 80639 — 3-11111
351-2321
University of Northern Colorado 80639 — 6-UC
351-2121

Greenwood Village, AC 303, PC 6, Englewood

Riverview Christian Academy — 2-11111
8081 E ORCHARD RD 80111 — 771-4042

Grover, AC 303, PC 2, Weld
Pawnee SD RE-12, PO BOX 38 80729 — 1-11111
Douglas Roe, supt. — 895-2222
Pawnee JSHS, PO BOX 38 80729 — 1-00111
Douglas Roe, prin. — 895-2222

Gunnison, AC 303, PC 5, Gunnison
Gunnison Watershed SD RE 1J — 4-11111
216 W GEORGIA AVE 81230 — 641-7760
Janice Johnson, supt.
HS, 800 W OHIO AVE 81230 — 2-00011
Steve Coleman, prin. — 641-7700
Ruland MS, 700 E VIRGINIA AVE 81230 — 2-00100
Robert Drexel, prin. — 641-7710

Western State College of Colorado — 4-UC
600 N ADAMS ST 81231 — 943-2119

Gypsum, AC 303, PC 4, Eagle
Eagle County SD RE-50
Supt. — See Eagle
Eagle Valley HS, PO BOX 188 81637 — 2-00011
Ivan Kershner, prin. — 524-7511

Haxtun, AC 303, PC 3, Phillips
Haxtun SD RE-2J, PO BOX 548 80731 — 2-11111
Jack Pendar, supt. — 774-6111
HS, PO BOX 548 80731 — 1-00011
Jack Pendar, prin. — 774-6111

Hayden, AC 303, PC 4, Routt
Hayden SD RE-1, PO BOX 70 81639 — 2-11111
Ken Brown, supt. — 276-3864
HS, PO BOX 70 81639 — 2-00011
Kevin Schott, prin. — 276-3761
MS, PO BOX 70 81639 — 2-00100
Kevin Schott, prin. — 276-3762

Henderson, AC 303, PC 3, Adams

National Training — 1-CS
9600 E 104TH AVE 80640

Highlands Ranch, AC 303, PC 5, Douglas
Douglas County SD RE-1
Supt. — See Castle Rock
HS, 9375 S CRESTHILL LN 80126 — 4-00011
Jim Wallendorf, prin. — 470-0700
Cresthill MS — 3-00100
9195 S CRESTHILL LN 80126 — 470-0300
Doug McFarland, prin.

Hoehne, AC 719, PC 2, Las Animas
Hoehne RSD 3, PO BOX 91 81046 — 2-11111
Jasper Butero, supt. — 846-4457
HS, PO BOX 91 81046 — 1-00011
Dan Evig, prin. — 846-4457
JHS, PO BOX 91 81046 — 1-00100
Dan Evig, prin. — 846-4457

Holly, AC 719, PC 3, Prowers
Holly SD RE-3, PO BOX 608 81047 — 2-11111
Lori Miller, supt. — 537-6616
JSHS, PO BOX 608 81047 — 2-00111
Bill Guarienti, prin. — 537-6512

Holyoke, AC 303, PC 4, Phillips
Holyoke SD RE-1J — 3-11111
435 S MORLAN AVE 80734 — 854-4049
Jeanne Howes, supt.
HS, 545 E HALE ST 80734 — 2-00011
Leland Morrison, prin. — 854-2284

Hotchkiss, AC 303, PC 3, Delta
Delta County SD 50(J)
Supt. — See Delta
HS, 3535 J 60 LN 81419 — 2-00011
John Jones, prin. — 872-3882
MS, PO BOX 60 81419 — 2-01100
Jim Kent, prin. — 872-3144

Hugo, AC 719, PC 3, Lincoln
Genoa-Hugo SD C113 — 2-11111
PO BOX 247 80821 — 743-2428
Dale Kanack, supt.
Genoa-Hugo JSHS — 2-00111
PO BOX 247 80821 — 743-2428
Charla Hannigan, prin.

Idaho Springs, AC 303, PC 4, Clear Creek
Clear Creek SD RE-1 — 4-11111
PO BOX 3399 80452 — 567-4467
John Klieforth, supt.
Clear Creek HS, PO BOX 3369 80452 — 2-00011
Walter Calinger, prin. — 567-4429
Clear Creek MS, PO BOX 3369 80452 — 2-00100
Michael Holmes, prin. — 567-4461

Idalia, AC 303, PC 2, Yuma
East Yuma County SD RJ-2
Supt. — See Wray
JSHS, PO BOX 40 80735 — 1-00111
Ken Fritz, prin. — 354-7298

Ignacio, AC 303, PC 3, La Plata
Ignacio SD 11 JT, PO BOX 460 81137 — 3-11111
Bob Gomez, supt. — 563-4521
HS, PO BOX 460 81137 — 2-00011
Ron Shaw, prin. — 563-9431
JHS, PO BOX 460 81137 — 2-00100
Ron Shaw, prin. — 563-4522

Iliff, AC 303, PC 2, Logan
Valley SD RE-1
Supt. — See Sterling
Caliche JSHS, RR 1 80736 — 2-00111
Fred Rasmussen, prin. — 522-8200

Joes, AC 303, PC 1, Yuma
West Yuma County SD RJ-1
Supt. — See Yuma
Liberty JSHS, PO BOX 112 80822 — 1-00111
Billie Vonderwahl, prin. — 358-4288

Johnstown, AC 303, PC 4, Weld
Johnstown-Milliken SD RE-5J — 4-11111
PO BOX G 80534 – Fred Palmer, supt. — 587-2336
Roosevelt HS, PO BOX G 80534 — 2-00011
John Bruce, prin. — 587-4633
Other Schools – See Milliken

Julesburg, AC 303, PC 4, Sedgwick
Julesburg SD RE-1 — 2-11111
PO BOX 359 80737 — 474-3365
James Howitt, supt.
HS, PO BOX 359 80737 — 2-00011
James Howitt, prin. — 474-3364

Karval, AC 719, PC 2, Lincoln
Karval SD RE-23, PO BOX 272 80823 — 1-11111
Richard Hoeppner, supt. — 446-5311
JSHS, PO BOX 272 80823 — 1-00111
Richard Hoeppner, prin. — 446-5311

Keenesburg, AC 303, PC 3, Weld
Keenesburg SD Re-3(J) — 4-11111
95 W BROADWAY 80643 — 732-4844
Dennis Disario, supt.
Weld Central JSHS — 3-00111
4977 COUNTY ROAD 59 80643 — 732-4254
Lou Predmore, prin.

Kersey, AC 303, PC 3, Weld
Platte Valley SD RE-7 — 3-11111
PO BOX 485 80644 — 352-6177
Glen Hanson, supt.
Platte Valley JSHS — 2-00111
PO BOX 487 80644 — 352-6168
Loyd Maskell, prin.

Kim, AC 719, PC 1, Las Animas
Kim RSD 88, PO BOX 100 81049 — 1-11111
Robert Hall, supt. — 643-5295
JSHS, PO BOX 100 81049 — 1-00111
Robert Hall, prin. — 643-5295

Kiowa, AC 303, PC 2, Elbert
Kiowa SD C-2, PO BOX 128 80117 — 2-11111
Hank Tschopp, supt. — 621-2220
JSHS, PO BOX 128 80117 — 1-00111
Carl Olkjer, prin. — 621-2115

Kit Carson, AC 719, PC 2, Cheyenne
Kit Carson SD R-1 — 2-11111
PO BOX 185 80825 — 962-3219
Ronald Kelton, supt.
S, PO BOX 185 80825 — 2-11111
Ronald Kelton, prin. — 962-3219

Kremmling, AC 303, PC 4, Grand
West Grand SD 1-JT — 3-11111
PO BOX 515 80459 — 724-3217
Joanne Ihrig, supt.
West Grand HS, PO BOX 515 80459 — 2-00011
Joe Shields, prin. — 724-3425
West Grand MS, PO BOX 515 80459 — 2-00100
Linda Ciminesi, prin. — 724-3489

Lafayette, AC 303, PC 7, Boulder
Boulder Valley SD RE-2
Supt. — See Boulder
Centaurus HS — 4-00011
10300 E SOUTH BOULDER RD 80026 — 665-9211
William Johnson, prin.
Angevine MS — 3-00100
1150 W SOUTH BOULDER RD 80026 — 665-5540
Annette Fante, prin.

Alexander Dawson S — 2-00111
4801 N 107TH ST 80026 — 665-6679
Barbara Connors, prin.

La Jara, AC 719, PC 3, Conejos
North Conejos SD RE-1J — 4-11111
PO BOX 72 81140 — 274-5174
Chris Martinez, supt.
Centauri HS — 2-00011
17891 STATE HIGHWAY 285 81140 — 274-5178
Kurt Cary, prin.
Centauri MS — 2-00100
17891 US HIGHWAY 285 81140 — 274-4301
Clinton Tucker, prin.

La Junta, AC 719, PC 6, Otero
East Otero SD R-1 — 4-11111
PO BOX 439 81050 — 384-8141
Suzanne Treece, supt.
HS, 1817 SMITHLAND AVE 81050 — 3-00011
Jim Sullivan, prin. — 384-4467
JHS, 901 SMITHLAND AVE 81050 — 2-00100
Ron Davis, prin. — 384-4371

Otero Junior College — 3-CC
1802 COLORADO AVE 81050 — 384-8721

Lakewood, AC 303, PC 9, Jefferson
Jefferson County SD R-1
Supt. — See Golden
Alameda HS — 3-00011
1255 S WADSWORTH BLVD 80232 — 985-4421
Ray Smith, prin.
Bear Creek HS, 3490 S KIPLING ST 80227 — 4-00011
Maran Doggett, prin. — 985-4444
Green Mountain HS — 4-00011
13175 W GREEN MOUNTAIN DR 80228
Carol Delockroy, prin. — 985-1591
HS, 9700 W 8TH AVE 80215 — 3-00011
Marcia Goldin, prin. — 238-0566
Carmody MS, 2050 S KIPLING ST 80227 — 4-00100
Patricia Termin, prin. — 985-8766
Creighton MS — 3-00100
75 INDEPENDENCE ST 80226 — 238-8523
Charles Horn, prin.
Dennison JHS — 2-00100
401 INDEPENDENCE ST 80226 — 233-4648
Lloyd Carlton, prin.
Dunstan MS, 1855 S WRIGHT ST 80228 — 3-00100
William Pereboom, prin. — 985-1545
O'Connell MS, 1275 S TELLER ST 80232 — 3-00100
Sue Brown, prin. — 986-4516

Christian Fellowship S — 2-11111
7350 W EASTMAN PL 80227 — 980-6622
Colorado Career Academy — 2-CS
95 S WADSWORTH BLVD 80226 — 234-0401
Colorado Christian University — 3-UC
180 S GARRISON ST 80226 — 238-5386
Colorado School of Trades — 2-CC
1575 HOYT ST 80215 — 233-4697
Silver State Baptist S — 2-11111
875 S SHERIDAN BLVD 80226 — 922-8850
Westland Christian Academy — 2-11111
430 S KIPLING ST 80226 — 985-1081

Lamar, AC 719, PC 6, Prowers
Lamar SD Re-2, 210 W PEARL ST 81052 — 4-11111
Bill Van Buskirk, supt. — 336-3251
HS, 1900 S 11TH ST 81052 — 3-00011
Eldon Elarton, prin. — 336-3488
MS, 104 W PARK ST 81052 — 2-00100
Bonnie Emrick, prin. — 336-7436

Lamar Community College — 3-CC
2401 S MAIN ST 81052 — 336-2248

Laporte, AC 303, PC 4, Larimer
Poudre SD R-1
Supt. — See Fort Collins
Cache La Poudre JHS — 2-00110
PO BOX 468 80535 — 482-6332
Edward Crockett, prin.

La Salle, AC 303, PC 4, Weld
Gilcrest SD Re-1
Supt. — See Gilcrest
North Valley MS, PO BOX 248 80645 — 2-00100
Walter Cooper, prin. — 284-5508

Las Animas, AC 719, PC 4, Bent
Las Animas SD RE-1 — 3-11111
1214 AMB THOMPSON BLVD 81054 — 456-0161
David Whitehead, supt.
HS, 300 GROVE AVE 81054 — 2-00011
James Lepich, prin. — 456-0211
MS, 1214 AMB THOMPSON BLVD 81054 — 2-00100
Jerry Nickell, prin. — 456-0228

La Veta, AC 719, PC 3, Huerfano
La Veta SD RE-2, PO BOX 85 81055 — 2-11111
Roger Brunelli, supt. — 742-3662
JSHS, PO BOX 85 81055 — 2-00111
Cary Dee Betts, prin. — 742-3662

Leadville, AC 719, PC 5, Lake
Lake County SD R-1 — 4-11111
PO BOX 977 80461 — 486-0160
James McCabe, supt.
Lake County HS, PO BOX 977 80461 — 2-00011
Robert Kent, prin. — 486-1566
Lake County IS, PO BOX 977 80461 — 3-01100
Rudy Malesich, prin. — 486-2564

Colorado Mountain College — 2-CC
901 US HIGHWAY 24 80461 — 800-621-8559

Limon, AC 719, PC 4, Lincoln
Limon SD RE-4J, PO BOX 249 80828 — 3-11111
Jerre Doss, supt. — 775-9052
JSHS, PO BOX 249 80828 — 2-00111
Scott Vratil, prin. — 775-2350

Littleton, AC 303, PC 8, Arapahoe
Cherry Creek SD 5
Supt. — See Englewood
West MS, 5151 S HOLLY ST 80121 — 4-00100
Steve Rogers, prin. — 771-3112
Jefferson County SD R-1
Supt. — See Golden
Chatfield HS, 7227 S SIMMS ST 80127 — 4-00011
Sally Blanchard, prin. — 972-0763
Columbine HS, 6201 S PIERCE ST 80123 — 4-00011
Ron Mitchell, prin. — 979-4700
Caryl MS — 3-00100
6509 W KEN CARYL AVE 80123 — 979-5150
James Deutsch, prin.
Deer Creek MS — 4-00100
9201 W COLUMBINE DR 80123 — 978-1662
Richard Myles, prin.
Littleton SD 6 — 7-11111
5776 S CROCKER ST 80120 — 347-3300
Cile Chavez, supt.
Arapahoe HS — 4-00011
2201 E DRY CREEK RD 80122 — 794-2641
Ron Booth, prin.
Heritage HS, 1401 W GEDDES AVE 80120 — 4-00011
James Ferguson, prin. — 795-1353
HS, 199 E LITTLETON BLVD 80121 — 4-00011
Timothy Westerberg, prin. — 798-2584
Euclid MS, 777 W EUCLID AVE 80120 — 3-00100
Aldis Sides, prin. — 794-4237
Goddard MS, 3800 W BERRY AVE 80123 — 3-00100
Sally Stanley, prin. — 798-2563
Newton MS — 3-00100
4001 E ARAPAHOE RD 80122 — 771-5540
James Sturgell, prin.
Powell MS, 8000 S CORONA WAY 80122 — 4-00100
Karen Briggs, prin. — 795-8822

Arapahoe Community College — 5-CC
PO BOX 9002 80160 — 794-1550

Longmont, AC 303, PC 8, Boulder
St. Vrain Valley SD RE-1J — 7-11111
395 S PRATT PKY 80501 — 776-6200
Fred Pierce, supt.
HS, 1040 SUNSET ST 80501 — 4-00011
Henry Aschenbrenner, prin. — 776-6014
Niwot HS, 8989 NIWOT RD 80503 — 3-00011
Mary White, prin. — 652-2550
Olde Columbine HS — 2-00011
1200 S SUNSET ST 80501 — 772-3333
Bill Blick, prin.
Skyline HS — 4-00011
600 E MOUNTAIN VIEW AVE 80501 — 651-0123
James Cook, prin.
St. Vrain Career Ctr — Vo Tech
1200 S SUNSET ST 80501 — 772-3333
Bill Blick, prin.
Heritage MS — 3-00100
233 E MOUNTAIN VIEW AVE 80501 — 772-7900
Karen Benge-Rosson, prin.
Longs Peak MS, 1500 14TH AVE 80501 — 3-00100
Manny Ortega, prin. — 776-5611
Sunset MS, 1300 S SUNSET ST 80501 — 3-00100
Peter Ross, prin. — 776-3963
Westview MS, 1651 AIRPORT RD 80503 — 3-00100
Robert Moderhak, prin. — 772-0832
Other Schools – See Erie, Frederick, Lyons, Mead

Faith Baptist S, 833 15TH AVE 80501 — 2-11111
776-5677

Louisville, AC 303, PC 7, Boulder
Boulder Valley SD RE-2
Supt. — See Boulder
MS, 1341 MAIN ST 80027 — 3-00100
Marsha McMillan, prin. — 666-6503

Loveland, AC 303, PC 8, Larimer
Thompson SD R-2J — 7-11111
535 DOUGLAS AVE 80537 — 669-3940
F. Saul, supt.
HS, 920 W 29TH ST 80538 — 4-00011
Jack Wilson, prin. — 667-5374
Thompson Valley HS — 4-00011
1669 EAGLE DR 80537 – Ben Hix, prin. — 669-0801
Ball MS, 2660 MONROE AVE 80538 — 3-00100
Joe Scaggs, prin. — 669-3550
Clark MS, 2605 CARLISLE DR 80537 — 3-00100
Charles Erickson, prin. — 667-7236
Reed MS, 370 W 4TH ST 80537 — 3-00100
Ken Bennett, prin. — 667-5136
Other Schools – See Berthoud

Champion Academy — 2-00011
300 42ND ST SW 80537 — 667-5592

Lyons, AC 303, PC 4, Boulder
St. Vrain Valley SD RE-1J
Supt. — See Longmont
JSHS, PO BOX 619 80540 — 2-00111
Mark Mills, prin. — 823-6631

Mc Clave, AC 719, PC 2, Bent
McClave SD RE-2, PO BOX 1 81057 — 2-11111
Ron Conrad, supt. — 829-4517
JSHS, PO BOX 1 81057 — 1-00111
Bushrod White, prin. — 829-4517

Mancos, AC 303, PC 3, Montezuma
Mancos SD RE-6, PO BOX 420 81328 — 3-11111
James Wilson, supt. — 533-7748
HS, PO BOX 420 81328 — 2-00011
Ray Carey, prin. — 533-7746
JHS, PO BOX 420 81328 — 1-00100
Ray Carey, prin. — 533-7746

Manitou Springs, AC 719, PC 5, El Paso
Manitou Springs SD 14 — 4-11111
701 DUCLO AVE 80829 — 685-1235
Gary Miller, supt.
HS, 401 EL MONTE PL 80829 — 2-00011
Larry Brown, prin. — 685-5413
MS, 415 EL MONTE PL 80829 — 2-00100
Keith Elsberry, prin. — 685-5453

Manzanola, AC 719, PC 2, Otero
Manzanola SD 3J, PO BOX 148 81058 — 2-11111
Ronald Allen, supt. — 462-5527
JSHS, PO BOX 148 81058 — 2-00111
Ted Kadlecek, prin. — 462-5528

Mead, AC 303, PC 2, Weld
St. Vrain Valley SD RE-1J
Supt. — See Longmont
MS, PO BOX 288 80542 — 2-00100
Keith Carmichael, prin. — 535-4447

Meeker, AC 303, PC 4, Rio Blanco
Meeker SD RE-1, PO BOX 1089 81641 — 3-11111
Karen Benner, supt. — 878-3701
HS, PO BOX 159 81641 — 2-00011
George Hertzke, prin. — 878-3631
Barone JHS, PO BOX 690 81641 — 2-00100
Michael Greek, prin. — 878-3625

Merino, AC 303, PC 2, Logan
Buffalo SD RE-4, PO BOX 198 80741 — 2-11111
Douglas Degroote, supt. — 522-7424
JSHS, 315 LEE 80741 — 2-00111
Dave Kautz, prin. — 522-7424

Milliken, AC 303, PC 4, Weld
Johnstown-Milliken SD RE-5J
Supt. — See Johnstown
MS, 66 IRENE AVE 80543 — 2-00100
Vaughn Griswold, prin. — 587-4341

Minturn, AC 303, PC 4, Eagle
Eagle County SD RE-50
Supt. — See Eagle
Battle Mountains HS — 2-00011
PO BOX 249 81645 — 949-4490
Erik Fredell, prin.
MS, PO BOX 280 81645 — 2-00100
Keith Thompson, prin. — 827-5721

Moffat, AC 719, PC 1, Saguache
Moffat SD 2, PO BOX 428 81143 — 2-11111
Thomas Rouse, supt. — 256-4710
S, PO BOX 428 81143 — 2-11111
Thomas Rouse, supt. — 256-4710

Monte Vista, AC 719, PC 5, Rio Grande
Monte Vista SD C-8 — 4-11111
345 PROSPECT AVE E 81144 — 852-5996
Timothy Snyder, supt.
HS, 349 PROSPECT AVE E 81144 — 2-00011
Paul Gabaldon, prin. — 852-3586
MS, 3720 SHERMAN AVE 81144 — 2-00100
Sarah Lucero, prin. — 852-5984

Sargent SD RE-33J — 2-11111
7090 N COUNTY ROAD 2 E 81144 — 852-4023
David Hamilton, supt.
Sargent JSHS — 2-00111
7090 N COUNTY ROAD 2 E 81144 — 852-4023
John Tillman, prin.

Montrose, AC 303, PC 6, Montrose
Montrose County SD RE-1J — 5-11111
PO BOX 219 81402 — 249-7726
Russell Stone, supt.
SHS, PO BOX 1626 81402 — 3-00001
Richard Hagan, prin. — 249-6636
Centennial JHS, PO BOX 219 81402 — 3-00110
Gary Rawls, prin. — 249-2576
Other Schools – See Olathe

Monument, AC 719, PC 4, El Paso
Lewis-Palmer SD 38, PO BOX B 80132 — 5-11111
Dallas Strawn, supt. — 481-2293
Lewis-Palmer HS, PO BOX B 80132 — 3-00011
Diane Burke, prin. — 488-2230
Lewis-Palmer MS, PO BOX B 80132 — 3-00100
Ted Belteau, prin. — 481-2006

Mosca, AC 719, PC 1, Alamosa
Sangre De Cristo SD RE-22J — 2-11111
PO BOX 145 81146 — 378-2321
Randy Bache, supt.
Sangre De Cristo JSHS — 2-00111
PO BOX 145 81146 — 378-2321
John Crowder, prin.

Naturita, AC 303, PC 2, Montrose
West End SD Re-2 — 2-11111
PO BOX 190 81422 — 865-2290
C. Curlin, supt.

MS, PO BOX 400 81422   1-00100
Wayne Hopewell, prin.   865-2204
Other Schools – See Nucla

Nederland, AC 303, PC 4, Boulder
Boulder Valley SD RE-2
Supt. — See Boulder
JSHS 80466   2-00111
Edward Ellis, prin.   447-5571

New Castle, AC 303, PC 3, Garfield
Garfield SD RE-2
Supt. — See Rifle
Riverside JHS, PO BOX 198 81647   2-00100
Charles Shupe, prin.   984-2372

New Raymer, AC 303, PC 1, Weld
Prairie SD RE-11, PO BOX 68 80742   2-11111
Robert Eaton, supt.   437-5386
Prairie JSHS, PO BOX 68 80742   1-00100
Robert Eaton, prin.   437-5386

Northglenn, AC 303, PC 8, Adams
Northglenn-Thornton SD 12   7-11111
11285 HIGHLINE DR 80233   451-1561
James Mitchell, supt.
SHS, 601 W 100TH PL 80221   4-00001
George McCulloch, prin.   451-1241
Huron JHS, 10900 HURON ST 80234   3-00100
Harry Odil, prin.   452-5471
Northeast JHS, 11700 IRMA DR 80233   3-00110
Curt Furness, prin.   452-1043
JHS, 1123 MURIEL DR 80233   3-00110
William Munsell, prin.   452-2921
Other Schools – See Brighton, Broomfield, Denver, Thornton

Norwood, AC 303, PC 2, San Miguel
Norwood SD R-2J, PO BOX 448 81423   2-11111
Roger Brainard, supt.   327-4712
HS, PO BOX 448 81423   1-00011
Lee Fleming, prin.   327-4336

Nucla, AC 303, PC 3, Montrose
West End SD Re-2
Supt. — See Naturita
HS, PO BOX 570 81424   2-00011
Phyllis Harrison, prin.   864-7350

Oak Creek, AC 303, PC 3, Routt
South Routt SD RE-3   2-11111
PO BOX 158 80467   736-2313
William Meek, supt.
Soroco HS, PO BOX 158 80467   2-00011
Richard Coleman, prin.   736-2531
Soroco JHS, PO BOX 158 80467   1-00100
Richard Coleman, prin.   736-8531

Olathe, AC 303, PC 4, Montrose
Montrose County SD RE-1J
Supt. — See Montrose
HS, PO BOX 280 81425   2-00011
B. Brown, prin.   323-5546
MS, PO BOX 294 81425   2-00100
Pat Myers, prin.   323-5521

Ordway, AC 719, PC 4, Crowley
Crowley County SD Re-1-J   3-11111
PO BOX 338 81063   267-3117
Gary Upchurch, supt.
Crowley County JSHS   2-00111
PO BOX 338 81063   267-3582
William Green, prin.

Otis, AC 303, PC 2, Washington
Lone Star SD 101   1-11111
44940 COUNTY ROAD 54 80743   848-2778
Wayne Laut, supt.
Lone Star JSHS   1-00111
44940 COUNTY ROAD 54 80743   848-2778
Wayne Laut, prin.

Otis SD R-3, PO BOX 401 80743   2-11111
Robert Rime, supt.   246-3413
JSHS, PO BOX 401 80743   1-00111
Robert Rime, prin.   246-3486

Ouray, AC 303, PC 3, Ouray
Ouray SD R-1, PO BOX N 81427   2-11111
Joe Cooper, supt.   325-4218
JSHS, PO BOX N 81427   2-00111
Ginny Ficco, prin.   325-4218

Ovid, AC 303, PC 2, Sedgwick
Platte Valley SD RE-3   2-11111
PO BOX 369 80744   463-5414
Keith Sommerfeld, supt.
Revere JSHS, PO BOX 369 80744   1-00111
James Engelkar, prin.   463-5477

Pagosa Springs, AC 303, PC 4, Archuleta
Archuleta County SD 50 Jt   4-11111
PO BOX 1498 81147   264-2228
Terry Alley, supt.
HS, PO BOX 1498 81147   2-00011
William Esterbrook, prin.   264-2232
MS, PO BOX 1498 81147   2-00100
Larry Lister, prin.   264-5988

Palisade, AC 303, PC 4, Mesa
Mesa County Valley SD 51
Supt. — See Grand Junction
HS, PO BOX 220 81526   3-00011
Lou Rollenhagen, prin.   464-5937

Paonia, AC 303, PC 4, Delta
Delta County SD 50(J)
Supt. — See Delta

HS, PO BOX 49 81428   2-00011
Don Valaer, prin.   527-4882
MS, PO BOX 10 81428   2-01100
Floyd Beard, prin.   527-4833

Parachute, AC 303, PC 3, Garfield
Garfield SD 16, PO BOX 68 81635   2-11111
John Pennington, supt.   285-7759
Grand Valley HS, PO BOX 68 81635   1-00011
John Miller, prin.   285-7561
St. John MS, PO BOX 68 81635   1-00100
Steve Sanchez, prin.   285-7834

Parker, AC 303, PC 6, Douglas
Douglas County SD RE-1
Supt. — See Castle Rock
Ponderosa HS   4-00011
7007 E BAYOU GULCH RD 80134   841-2770
William Larson, prin.
Parker Vista MS, 6651 E PINE LN 80134   3-00100
Roger Sieck, prin.   841-2656

Peetz, AC 303, PC 2, Logan
Plateau SD RE-5, PO BOX B 80747   2-11111
Roger Brenner, supt.   334-2435
JSHS, PO BOX B 80747   1-00111
Roger Brenner, prin.   334-2361

Peyton, AC 719, PC 2, El Paso
Peyton SD 23 Jt   2-11111
13990 BRADSHAW RD 80831   749-2330
Larry Mortensen, prin.
S, 13990 BRADSHAW RD 80831   2-11111
Katrina Robinson, prin.   749-2244

Pine, AC 303, PC 3, Jefferson

Pinewood S, 112 ROAD D 80470   2-11111
   838-4418

Platteville, AC 303, PC 2, Weld
Gilcrest SD Re-1
Supt. — See Gilcrest
South Valley MS, PO BOX 404 80651   2-00100
Bernie Martinez, prin.   785-2205

Pritchett, AC 719, PC 2, Baca
• Pritchett SD RE-3, PO BOX 7 81064   1-11111
Rosalie Bitner, supt.   523-4045
JSHS, PO BOX 7 81064   1-00111
Rosalie Bitner, prin.   523-4045

Pueblo, AC 719, PC 8, Pueblo
Pueblo County Rural SD 70   5-11111
24951 E US HIGHWAY 50 81006   542-0220
Michael Johnson, supt.
Pueblo County HS, 1050 35TH LN 81006   4-00011
Richard Amman, prin.   948-3352
Pleasant View MS   2-00100
23600 EVERETT RD 81006   542-7813
William Bregar, prin.
Vineland MS, 1132 36TH LN 81006   2-00100
Michael Mauro, prin.   948-3336
Other Schools – See Beulah, Colorado City, Pueblo West, Rye

Pueblo CSD 60, PO BOX 575 81002   7-11111
Henry Roman, supt.   549-7100
Centennial HS   4-00011
2525 MOUNTVIEW DR 81008   549-7335
Frank Latino, prin.
Central HS, 216 E ORMAN AVE 81004   4-00011
Sam Pantleo, prin.   549-7300
East HS, 9 MACNEIL RD 81001   4-00011
Jack Pecoraro, prin.   549-7222
South HS, 1801 HOLLYWOOD DR 81005   4-00011
Charles Rodriguez, prin.   549-7255
Corwin MS, 1500 LAKEVIEW AVE 81004   3-00100
Fred Ingo, prin.   546-4265
Freed MS, 715 W 20TH ST 81003   3-00100
Robert Panion, prin.   542-1253
Heaton MS, 6 ADAIR RD 81001   3-00100
Ralph Ray, prin.   542-1253
Pitts MS, 29 LEHIGH AVE 81005   3-00100
Lynda Quillen, prin.   561-4642
Risley MS, 620 N LA CROSSE AVE 81001   3-00100
Lee Roy Martinez, prin.   542-7148
Roncalli MS   3-00100
4202 W STATE HIGHWAY 78 81005
Frank Zerfas, prin.   564-0150

Park Hill Christian Academy   2-11111
1302 E 5TH ST 81001   544-6174
Parkview Episcopal Hospital   HSP
400 W 16TH ST 81003   584-4573
Pueblo College of Business & Technology   2-CS
330 LAKE AVE 81004   545-3100
Pueblo Community College   3-CC
900 W ORMAN AVE 81004   549-3325
United States Truck Driving School   2-CS
19825 WIGWAM RD 81008   382-3000
University of Southern Colorado   5-UC
2200 BONFORTE BLVD 81001   549-2306

Pueblo West, AC 719, PC 5, Pueblo
Pueblo County Rural SD 70
Supt. — See Pueblo
MS, 484 S MAHER DR 81007   2-00100
Rick Thielbar, prin.   547-3752

Rangely, AC 303, PC 4, Rio Blanco
Rangely SD RE-4, 402 W MAIN ST 81648   3-11111
Robert Mullen, supt.   675-2207
HS, 234 S JONES AVE 81648   2-00011
Chuck White, prin.   675-2253

MS, 550 RIVER RD 81648   2-00100
Jim Day, prin.   675-5021

Colorado Northwestern Community College   2-CC
500 KENNEDY DR 81648   800-562-1105

Ridgway, AC 303, PC 2, Ouray
Ridgway SD R-2, PO BOX 230 81432   2-11111
Robert Conder, supt.   626-5468
JSHS, PO BOX 230 81432   2-00111
Henry McCallum, prin.   626-5473

Rifle, AC 303, PC 5, Garfield
Garfield SD RE-2   5-11111
839 WHITERIVER AVE 81650   625-1595
Lennard Eckhardt, supt.
HS, 1350 PREFOUNTAINE AVE 81650   3-00011
John Burwell, prin.   625-1596
MS, 200 W 6TH ST 81650   2-00100
Ava Lanes, prin.   625-1776
Other Schools – See New Castle

Rocky Ford, AC 719, PC 5, Otero
Rocky Ford SD R-2, 601 S 8TH ST 81067   4-11111
Robert Collett, supt.   254-7423
HS, 601 S 8TH ST 81067   2-00011
Jeff Miller, prin.   254-7431
Jefferson MS, 601 S 8TH ST 81067   2-00100
Bob Brasher, prin.   254-7669

Rush, AC 719, PC 1, El Paso
Miami/Yoder SD 60 JT   2-11111
HC 82 BOX 3 80833   478-2186
Kathleen McRae, supt.
Miami/Yoder JSHS   1-00111
HC 82 BOX 3 80833   478-2186
Kathleen McRae, prin.

Rye, AC 719, PC 2, Pueblo
Pueblo County Rural SD 70
Supt. — See Pueblo
HS, PO BOX 10 81069   2-00011
Ron Ross, prin.   489-2271

Saguache, AC 719, PC 3, Saguache
Mountain Valley SD RE-1   2-11111
PO BOX 127 81149   655-2578
George Douglas, supt.
Mountain Valley S   2-11111
PO BOX 127 81149   655-2578
George Douglas, prin.

Salida, AC 719, PC 5, Chaffee
Salida SD R-32, PO BOX 70 81201   4-11111
Harvie Guest, supt.   539-4382
HS, PO BOX 70 81201   2-00011
James Ragan, prin.   539-2267
Kesner JHS, PO BOX 70 81201   2-00100
Calvin Reed, prin.   539-3556

Sanford, AC 719, PC 3, Conejos
Sanford SD 6J, PO BOX 39 81151   2-11111
Ron Simpson, supt.   274-5167
HS, PO BOX 39 81151   1-00011
Manuel Martinez, prin.   274-5167

San Luis, AC 719, PC 3, Costilla
Centennial SD R-1   2-11111
PO BOX 350 81152   672-3691
Robert Rael, supt.
Centennial HS, PO BOX 350 81152   2-00011
William Laird, prin.   672-3322
Centennial JHS, PO BOX 350 81152   1-00100
William Laird, prin.   672-3322

Seibert, AC 303, PC 2, Kit Carson
Hi-Plains SD R-23
Supt. — See Vona
Hi-Plains JSHS, PO BOX 116 80834   1-00111
Jim Smith, prin.   664-2616

Sheridan Lake, AC 719, PC 1, Kiowa
Plainview SD RE-2   2-11111
PO BOX 1268 81071   727-4361
Janet Palmer, supt.
Plainview S, PO BOX 1268 81071   2-11111
Janet Palmer, prin.   729-3331

Silverton, AC 303, PC 3, San Juan
Silverton SD 1, PO BOX 128 81433   2-11111
Dan Salfisberg, supt.   387-5543
JSHS, PO BOX 128 81433   1-00111
Dan Salfisberg, prin.   387-5543

Simla, AC 719, PC 2, Elbert
Big Sandy SD 100J, PO BOX 68 80835   2-11111
Leonard Hainley, supt.   541-2291
JSHS, PO BOX 68 80835   2-00111
Larry Reeves, prin.   541-2291

Springfield, AC 719, PC 4, Baca
Springfield SD RE-4   2-11111
389 TIPTON ST 81073   523-6654
Ron Masterson, supt.
HS, 389 TIPTON ST 81073   1-00011
Sharon Christie, prin.   523-6522
JHS, 389 TIPTON ST 81073   1-00100
Sharon Christie, prin.   523-6522

Steamboat Springs, AC 303, PC 6, Routt
Steamboat Springs SD RE-2   4-11111
PO BOX 774368 80477   879-1530
J. Aufderheide, supt.
HS, PO BOX 774368 80477   2-00011
Harlan Lear, prin.   879-1562

JHS, PO BOX 774368 80477   2-00100
Robert Harris, prin.   879-1058

Colorado Mountain College   3-CC
PO BOX 775288 80477   800-621-8559
Whiteman S   2-00011
42605 COUNTY ROAD 36 80487   879-1350
James Spillane, prin.

Sterling, AC 303, PC 7, Logan
Valley SD RE-1, PO BOX 910 80751   5-11111
W. Keith Christy, supt.   522-0792
HS, 400 W BROADWAY ST 80751   3-00011
Martin Foster, prin.   522-2944
MS, 1177 PAWNEE AVE 80751   3-00100
Keith Gentry, prin.   522-1041
Other Schools – See Iliff

Northeastern Junior College   4-CC
100 COLLEGE AVE 80751   522-6600

Strasburg, AC 303, PC 4, Adams
Strasburg SD 31J, PO BOX 207 80136   2-11111
Bruce Yoast, supt.   622-9211
JSHS, PO BOX 207 80136   2-00111
Joe Donahue, prin.   622-9211

Stratton, AC 719, PC 3, Kit Carson
Stratton SD R-4, PO BOX 266 80836   2-11111
William Callahan, supt.   348-5369
JSHS, PO BOX 266 80836   2-00111
Ron Hinz, prin.   348-5369

Swink, AC 719, PC 3, Otero
Swink SD 33, PO BOX 487 81077   2-11111
Randy Miller, supt.   384-8103
JSHS, PO BOX 487 81077   2-00111
Pat Lesar, prin.   384-8103

Telluride, AC 303, PC 4, San Miguel
Telluride SD R-1   2-11111
PO BOX 2280 81435   728-6617
Daniel Mangelsdorf, supt.
HS, PO BOX 187 81435   1-00011
Sandy McLaughlin, prin.   728-4377
MS, PO BOX 187 81435   1-00100
Sandy McLaughlin, prin.   728-4377

Thornton, AC 303, PC 8, Adams
Mapleton SD 1
Supt. — See Denver
Skyview HS, 8990 YORK ST 80229   4-00011
Jim Skeich, prin.   287-0285

Northglenn-Thornton SD 12
Supt. — See Northglenn
HS, 9351 WASHINGTON ST 80229   4-00011
R. Max Willsey, prin.   452-4800
Bollman Occupational Ctr   Vo Tech
9451 WASHINGTON ST 80229   451-1819
Dennis Kuretich, prin.
Thornton MS   3-00100
9451 HOFFMAN WAY 80229   289-2248
J. Albi, prin.

Colorado Assoc. of Paramedical Education   HSP
9191 GRANT ST 80229   451-7800

Trinidad, AC 719, PC 6, Las Animas
Trinidad SD 1   4-11111
240 N CONVENT ST 81082   846-3324
Victor Becco, supt.
HS, 816 WEST ST 81082   2-00011
Ed Achziger, prin.   846-2971
JHS, 614 PARK ST 81082   2-00100
Steve Dipaola, prin.   846-4411

Trinidad Catholic HS   1-00011
201 CHURCH ST 81082   846-7541
Joe Reorda, prin.
Trinidad State Junior College   4-CC
600 PROSPECT ST 81082   846-5541

USAF Academy, AC 719, PC 6, El Paso
Academy SD 20
Supt. — See Colorado Springs
Air Academy HS   4-00011
6910 CLARATON DR 80840   472-1295
Gregory Pierson, prin.

Vail, AC 303, PC 5, Eagle

Johnson & Wales University   2-CC
616 W LIONSHEAD CIR 81657   476-2993
Vail Mountain S   2-11111
3160 KATSOS RANCH RD 81657   476-3850

Vilas, AC 719, PC 2, Baca
Vilas SD RE-5, PO BOX 727 81087   1-11111
David Leadabrand, supt.   523-6738
JSHS, PO BOX 727 81087   1-00111
David Leadabrand, prin.   523-6738

Vona, AC 303, PC 2, Kit Carson
Hi-Plains SD R-23, PO BOX 8 80861   2-11111
Anthon Leon Sant, supt.   664-2636
Other Schools – See Seibert

Walden, AC 303, PC 3, Jackson
North Park SD R-1   2-11111
PO BOX 798 80480   723-4391
Harry Masinton, supt.
North Park JSHS, PO BOX 798 80480   2-00111
Derrol Almond, prin.   723-4392

Walsenburg, AC 719, PC 5, Huerfano
Huerfano SD RE-1, 611 W 7TH ST 81089   3-11111
Michael Hinnegan, supt.   738-1520
Mall HS, 335 W PINE ST 81089   2-00011
Patricia Deck, prin.   738-1610
MS, 415 WALSEN AVE 81089   2-00100
Patricia Deck, prin.   738-3083

Walsh, AC 719, PC 3, Baca
Walsh SD RE-1, PO BOX 68 81090   2-11111
Terry Cates, supt.   324-5632
JSHS, PO BOX 68 81090   2-00111
Roy Bezona, prin.   324-5221

Weldona, AC 303, PC 2, Morgan
Weldon Valley SD RE-20(J)   2-11111
911 NORTH AVE 80653   645-2411
Ronald Call, supt.
Weldon Valley S, 911 NORTH AVE 80653   2-11111
Ronald Call, prin.   645-2411

Wellington, AC 303, PC 4, Larimer
Poudre SD R-1
Supt. — See Fort Collins
JHS, PO BOX 440 80549   2-00110
Richard Kreutzer, prin.   568-3944

Westcliffe, AC 719, PC 2, Custer
Consolidated SD C-1   2-11111
PO BOX 730 81252   783-2357
Richard Wilson, prin.
Custer County Consolidated S   2-11111
PO BOX 730 81252   783-2291
Gary Frickell, prin.

Westminster, AC 303, PC 8, Adams
Jefferson County SD R-1
Supt. — See Golden
Standley Lake HS   4-00011
9300 W 104TH AVE 80021   465-1144
Jon Donaldson, prin.
Mandalay MS, 9651 PIERCE ST 80021   3-00100
Cynthia Stevenson, prin.   430-1021

Westminster SD 50   7-11111
4476 W 68TH AVE 80030   428-3511
Michael Massarotti, supt.
HS, 4276 W 68TH AVE 80030   4-00011
Chris Dittman, prin.   428-9541
Career Enrichment Park   Vo Tech
7300 LOWELL BLVD 80030   428-2600
Aarona Fugita, prin.
Shaw Heights MS   3-00100
8780 CIRCLE DR 80030   428-9533
Joe Laterra, prin.
Other Schools – See Denver

Belleview S, 3455 W 83RD AVE 80030   2-11111
   427-5459
Front Range Community College   5-CC
3645 W 112TH AVE 80030   466-8811

Weston, AC 719, PC 2, Las Animas
Primero RSD 2   2-11111
20200 STATE HIGHWAY 12 81091   868-2715
Nancy Degurse, supt.
Primero JSHS   1-00111
20200 STATE HIGHWAY 12 81091   868-2715
Nancy Degurse, prin.

Wheat Ridge, AC 303, PC 8, Jefferson
Jefferson County SD R-1
Supt. — See Golden
HS, 9505 W 32ND AVE 80033   4-00011
Dave Hendrickson, prin.   238-1281
Everitt MS, 3900 KIPLING ST 80033   3-00100
Richard Ransom, prin.   421-6910
MS, 7101 W 38TH AVE 80033   2-00100
Carl Schiele, prin.   424-4428

Lutheran Medical Center   HSP
8300 W 38TH AVE 80033   425-8416
United States Truck Driving School   2-CS
8150 W 48TH AVE 80033   800-727-7364

Wiggins, AC 303, PC 2, Morgan
Wiggins SD RE-50(J)   2-11111
PO BOX 128 80654   483-7762
Don Stratman, supt.
HS, PO BOX 128 80654   2-00011
Robert Sachs, prin.   483-7763
JHS, PO BOX 128 80654   1-00100
Robert Sachs, prin.   483-7761

Wiley, AC 719, PC 2, Prowers
Wiley SD RE-13 Jt   2-11111
PO BOX 247 81092   829-4806
Michael Clough, supt.
JSHS, PO BOX 247 81092   2-00111
Barbara Blake, prin.   829-4806

Windsor, AC 303, PC 6, Weld
Windsor SD RE-4, PO BOX 609 80550   4-11111
Brian Lessman, supt.   686-7411
HS, PO BOX 609 80550   2-00011
Kay Drake, prin.   686-7406
MS, PO BOX 609 80550   2-00100
Arlen Koehler, prin.   686-7496

Woodland Park, AC 719, PC 5, Teller
Woodland Park SD Re-2   5-11111
PO BOX 99 80866   687-6048
Fred Wall, supt.
HS, PO BOX 6820 80866   3-00011
Jim Taylor, prin.   687-9269
MS, PO BOX 6790 80866   3-00100
Stan Dodds, prin.   687-9257

Woodrow, AC 303, PC 1, Washington
Woodlin SD R-104   2-11111
HC 7 BOX 185 80757   386-2223
David Cockerham, supt.
Woodlin S, HC 7 BOX 185 80757   2-11111
Tom George, prin.   386-2223

Wray, AC 303, PC 4, Yuma
East Yuma County SD RJ-2   3-11111
PO BOX 157 80758   332-5764
Ken Fritz, supt.
HS, PO BOX 157 80758   2-00011
Jim Pagel, prin.   332-5758
Buchanan MS, PO BOX 157 80758   2-01100
Robert Selle, prin.   332-4723
Other Schools – See Idalia

Yoder, AC 719, PC 1, El Paso
Edison SD 54 Jt, 14550 EDISON RD 80864   1-11111
Patrick Dawson, supt.   478-2125
Edison S, 14550 EDISON RD 80864   1-11111
Patrick Dawson, prin.   478-2125

Yuma, AC 303, PC 5, Yuma
West Yuma County SD RJ-1   3-11111
PO BOX 327 80759   848-5831
Wayne Brown, supt.
HS, 1000 S ALBANY ST 80759   2-00011
Bruce Bennigsdorf, prin.   848-5488
Yuma MS, 500 S ELM ST 80759   2-01100
(—), prin.   848-2000
Other Schools – See Joes

CONNECTICUT

STATE DEPARTMENT OF EDUCATION
State Office Building
165 Capitol Ave., Hartford 06106
(203) 566-5497

Commissioner of Education	Vincent Ferrandino
Deputy Commissioner	Benjamin Dixon
Deputy Commissioner	Lorraine Aronson
Associate Commissioner Teaching & Learning	Betty Sternberg
Associate Commissioner Finance & Administrative Services	John Coroso
Associate Commissioner Educational Programs & Services	Theodore Sergi

STATE BOARD OF EDUCATION
165 Capitol Ave., Hartford 06106

Chairperson	Edgar Beckham

PUBLIC, PRIVATE AND CATHOLIC SECONDARY SCHOOLS

Ansonia, AC 203, PC 7, New Haven
Ansonia SD, 42 GROVE ST 06401 — 4-11111
Ruth Feinberg Connors, supt. — 736-9217
HS, 115 HOWARD AVE 06401 — 3-00011
William McAllister, prin. — 735-1877
Prendergast MS, 59 FINNEY ST 06401 — 3-01100
Jill Spanier, prin. — 735-8765
Willis MS, 85 CLIFTON AVE 06401 — 2-01100
John O'Brien, prin. — 735-9597

Vocational-Technical SD
Supt. — See Middletown
O'Brien Vo-Tech HS — Vo Tech
141 PRINDLE AVE 06401 — 735-9361
Ann Malafronte, prin.

Avon, AC 203, PC 4, Hartford
Avon SD, 34 SIMSBURY RD 06001 — 4-11111
Philip Streifer, supt. — 678-0482
HS, 510 W AVON RD 06001 — 3-00011
Michael Buckley, prin. — 673-2551
MS, 375 W AVON RD 06001 — 3-00100
Jerome Cramp, prin. — 673-3221

Avon Old Farms S — 2-00011
500 OLD FARMS RD 06001 — 673-3201
George Trautman, prin.

Baltic, AC 203, PC 4, New London

Academy of the Holy Family — 2-00011
54 W MAIN ST 06330 — 822-9272
Sr. Mary Patrick, prin.

Berlin, AC 203, PC 4, Hartford
Berlin SD, 240 KENSINGTON RD 06037 — 5-11111
Theodore Rokicki, supt. — 828-6581
HS, 139 PATTERSON WAY 06037 — 3-00011
Thomas Galvin, prin. — 828-6577
McGee MS, 899 NORTON RD 06037 — 3-00100
Guy Parillo, prin. — 828-0323

Bethany, AC 203, PC 4, New Haven
Regional SD 5
Supt. — See Woodbridge
Amity Regional JHS — 2-00110
190 LUKE HILL RD 06524 — 393-3102
Joseph Couture, prin.

Bethel, AC 203, PC 6, Fairfield
Bethel SD, PO BOX 253 06801 — 5-11111
Robert Gilchrest, supt. — 794-8601
HS, JUDD AVE 06801 — 3-00011
Robert Flanagan, prin. — 794-8624
MS, 600 WHITTLESEY DR 06801 — 3-00100
Emil Fusek, prin. — 794-8663

Bethlehem, AC 203, PC 4, Litchfield

Woodhall S, PO BOX 550 06751 — 1-00111
Jonathan Woodhall, prin. — 266-7788

Bloomfield, AC 203, PC 6, Hartford
Bloomfield SD — 5-11111
1133 BLUE HILLS AVE 06002 — 242-0791
Paul Copes, supt.
HS, 5 HUCKLEBERRY LN 06002 — 3-00011
M. McKinley, prin. — 242-5581
Arace MS, 390 PARK AVE 06002 — 3-01100
Marilyn Feldman, prin. — 242-0791

Bolton, AC 203, PC 2, Tolland
Bolton SD, 106 NOTCH RD 06043 — 3-11111
Richard Packman, supt. — 643-1569
HS, 72 BRANDY ST 06043 — 2-00011
Joseph Fleming, prin. — 643-2768

Branford, AC 203, PC 6, New Haven
Branford SD, 33 LAUREL ST 06405 — 5-11111
Bruce Storm, supt. — 488-7276
HS, 185 E MAIN ST 06405 — 3-00011
Edmund Higgins, prin. — 488-7291
IS, 185 DAMASCUS RD 06405 — 4-01100
Francis Walsh, prin. — 488-8317

Branford Hall Career Institute — 3-CS
9 BUSINESS PARK DR 06405 — 488-2525

Bridgeport, AC 203, PC 9, Fairfield
Bridgeport SD — 7-11111
45 LYON TER RM 303 06604 — 576-7301
James Connelly, supt.
Bassick HS, 1181 FAIRFIELD AVE 06605 — 3-00011
Joseph Rodriguez, prin. — 576-7350
Central HS, 1 LINCOLN BLVD 06606 — 4-00011
Andrew Karcich, prin. — 576-7377
Harding HS, 1734 CENTRAL AVE 06610 — 4-00011
Ed Goldstone, prin. — 576-7330
Cross MS, 1775 RESERVOIR AVE 06606 — 2-01100
Michele Bonney, prin. — 576-7553
Longfellow MS, 139 OCEAN TER 06605 — 3-01100
Jettie Tisdale, prin. — 576-8036

Vocational-Technical SD
Supt. — See Middletown
Bullard-Havens Vo-Tech HS — Vo Tech
500 PALISADE AVE 06610 — 579-6333
Joseph LaVorgna, prin.

Allstate Tractor Trailer Training School — 1-CS
2064 MAIN ST 06604 — 336-9567
Bridgeport Hospital — HSP
267 GRANT ST 06610 — 384-3464
Bridgeport Hospital — HSP
200 MILL HILL AVE 06610 — 384-3485
Butler Business School — 2-CS
2710 NORTH AVE 06604 — 333-3601
Housatonic Community College — 4-CC
510 BARNUM AVE 06608 — 579-6400
Kolbe Cathedral HS — 2-00011
33 CALHOUN PL 06604 — 335-2554
Jo Anne Jakab, prin.
St. Vincent's Medical Center — HSP
2800 MAIN ST 06606 — 576-5578
University of Bridgeport — 5-UC
126 PARK AVE 06604 — 576-4000

Bristol, AC 203, PC 8, Hartford
Bristol SD, PO BOX 450 06011 — 6-11111
Ed Maher, supt. — 584-7700
Bristol Central HS — 4-00011
480 WOLCOTT ST 06010 — 584-7732
Michael Ferry, prin.
Bristol Eastern HS, 632 KING ST 06010 — 4-00011
V. Everett Lyons, prin. — 584-7852
Chippins Hill MS — 3-00100
551 PEACEDALE ST 06010 — 584-3881
Ronald Stockman, prin.

Memorial Boulevard MS — 3-00100
70 MEMORIAL BLVD 06010 — 584-7882
Walter Ives, prin.
Northeast MS, 530 STEVENS ST 06010 — 2-00100
Frederick Mascola, prin. — 584-7839

St. Paul HS, 1001 STAFFORD AVE 06010 — 2-00111
Sr. Joan O'Connor, prin. — 584-0911

Brookfield, AC 203, PC 4, Fairfield
Brookfield SD, 100 POCONO RD 06804 — 5-11111
Michael Perrone, supt. — 775-7300
HS, 45 LONG MEADOW HILL RD 06804 — 3-00011
Thomas Smyth, prin. — 775-4583
Whisconier MS — 3-01100
17 W WHISCONIER RD 06804 — 775-6318
Richard Bellesheim, prin.

Brooklyn, AC 203, PC 4, Windham
Brooklyn SD, 119 GORMAN RD 06234 — 4-11100
Louise Berry, supt. — 774-9153
JHS, 119 GORMAN RD 06234 — 2-01100
Paul Carolan, prin. — 744-9153

Burlington, AC 203, PC 2, Hartford
Regional SD 10, 20 MILLS DR 06013 — 4-11111
Robert Goldman, supt. — 673-2538
Mills HS, 26 LYON RD 06013 — 3-00011
Anne O'Brien, prin. — 673-0423
Har-Bur MS, 26 LYON RD 06013 — 3-00100
Kenneth Platz, prin. — 673-6163

Canterbury, AC 203, PC 2, Windham
Canterbury SD, PO BOX 28 06331 — 3-11100
Robert Coffill, supt. — 546-6950
Baldwin MS — 2-01100
45 WESTMINSTER RD 06331 — 546-9421
Kathy LaFrancois, prin.

Central Village, AC 203, PC 4, Windham
Plainfield SD, PO BOX 705 06332 — 5-11111
David Marchesseault, supt. — 564-6403
Plainfield HS, 87 PUTNAM RD 06332 — 3-00011
Mark Nappi, prin. — 564-6417
Other Schools – See Plainfield

Chaplin, AC 203, PC 2, Windham
Regional SD 11, PO BOX 277 06235 — 2-00111
A. Wutzl, supt. — 455-9306
Parish Hill JSHS, PO BOX 275 06235 — 2-00111
Jan Skolnick, prin. — 455-9584

Cheshire, AC 203, PC 6, New Haven
Cheshire SD, 29 MAIN ST 06410 — 5-11111
Ralph Wallace, supt. — 250-2430
HS, 525 S MAIN ST 06410 — 4-00011
Paul Chesley, prin. — 272-5361
Dodd JHS, 100 PARK PL 06410 — 3-00100
Donald Wailonis, prin. — 272-3249

Cheshire Academy, 10 MAIN ST 06410 — 2-00111
John Hyslop, prin. — 272-5396

Clinton, AC 203, PC 5, Middlesex
Clinton SD, PO BOX 948 06413 — 4-11111
Vincent Mustaro, supt. — 669-5723
Morgan HS — 3-00011
27 KILLINGWORTH TPKE 06413 — 669-5701
William Barney, prin.
Eliot MS, 69 FAIRY DELL RD 06413 — 3-00100
Anthony Trainor, prin. — 669-5774

Colchester, AC 203, PC 5, New London
Colchester SD — 4-11111
  127 NORWICH AVE # 202 06415 — 537-7260
  Edward Favolise, supt.
Bacon Academy HS — 2-00011
  611 NORWICH AVE 06415 — 537-2378
  Robert Warren, prin.
Johnston MS, 360 NORWICH AVE 06415 — 2-00100
  Geraldine Andrew, prin. — 537-2313

Collinsville, AC 203, PC 5, Hartford
Canton SD, 39 DYER AVE 06022 — 4-11111
  David Quattropani, supt. — 693-7704
Canton JSHS, 76 SIMONDS AVE 06022 — 3-00111
  Nicholas Salvatore, prin. — 693-7707

Cornwall, AC 203, PC 2, Litchfield

Marvelwood S, PO BOX 98 06753 — 2-00011
  Mark Johnson, prin. — 672-6612

Coventry, AC 203, PC 5, Tolland
Coventry SD, 78 RIPLEY HILL RD 06238 — 4-11111
  Michael Malinowski, supt. — 742-7317
HS, 78 RIPLEY HILL RD 06238 — 2-00011
  Dennis Joy, prin. — 742-7346
Hale MS, 1776 MAIN ST 06238 — 3-01100
  Earle Bidwell, prin. — 742-7334

Cromwell, AC 203, PC 4, Middlesex
Cromwell SD — 4-11111
  9 MANN MEMORIAL DR 06416 — 635-5546
  James Gere, supt.
HS, 34 EVERGREEN RD 06416 — 2-00011
  James Gere, prin. — 635-5855
MS, 9 MANN MEMORIAL DR 06416 — 3-01100
  Harry Dumeer, prin. — 635-6061

Holy Apostles College — 2-UC
  33 PROSPECT HILL RD 06416 — 632-3000

Danbury, AC 203, PC 8, Fairfield
Danbury SD — 6-11111
  63 BEAVER BROOK RD 06810 — 797-4701
  Anthony Singe, supt.
HS, 43 CLAPBOARD RIDGE RD 06811 — 4-00011
  Elizabeth Feser, prin. — 797-4803
Broadview MS, 72 HOSPITAL AVE 06810 — 3-00100
  Willis Caterson, prin. — 797-4861
Rogers Park MS — 3-00100
  21 ROGERS PARK RD 06810 — 797-4881
  William Speilberg, prin.

Vocational-Technical SD
  Supt. — See Middletown
Abbott Vo-Tech HS — Vo Tech
  HAYESTOWN AVE 06810 — 797-4460
  Mario DiLorenzo, prin.

Danbury Hospital — HSP
  24 HOSPITAL AVE 06810 — 797-7000
Immaculate HS — 2-00011
  73 SOUTHERN BLVD 06810 — 744-1510
  Robert Gerwien, prin.
Western Connecticut State University — 5-UC
  181 WHITE ST 06810 — 797-4359
Wooster S, 55 RIDGEBURY RD 06810 — 2-00111
  John Effinger, prin. — 743-6311

Danielson, AC 203, PC 5, Windham
Killingly SD, PO BOX 210 06239 — 5-11111
  David Cressy, supt. — 774-9034
Killingly HS, 79 WESTFIELD AVE 06239 — 3-00011
  Catherine Sampson, prin. — 774-0841
Other Schools – See Dayville

Vocational-Technical SD
  Supt. — See Middletown
Ellis Vo-Tech HS, MAPLE ST 06239 — Vo Tech
  Ernest Gelinas, prin. — 774-8511

Quinebaug Valley Community College — 3-CC
  PO BOX 59 06239 — 774-1160

Darien, AC 203, PC 7, Fairfield
Darien SD, PO BOX 1167 06820 — 5-11111
  Eileen Gress, supt. — 656-7400
HS, 80 HIGH SCHOOL LN 06820 — 3-00011
  Bruce Hall, prin. — 655-3981
Middlesex MS — 3-00100
  204 HOLLOW TREE RIDGE RD 06820 — 655-2518
  Phillip Nelson, prin.

Dayville, AC 203, PC 4, Windham
Killingly SD
  Supt. — See Danielson
Killingly IS — 3-01100
  1599 UPPER MAPLE ST 06241 — 779-3523
  Jerre Filmore, prin.

Deep River, AC 203, PC 5, Middlesex
Regional SD 4, PO BOX 187 06417 — 3-00011
  John Proctor, supt. — 526-2417
Valley Regional HS — 2-00011
  179 KELSEY HILL RD 06417 — 526-5328
  Francis Baran, prin.
Winthrop JHS, WINTHROP ROAD 06417 — 2-00100
  Timothy Doyle, prin. — 526-9546

Derby, AC 203, PC 7, New Haven
Derby SD, PO BOX 373 06418 — 4-11111
  Nathan Chesler, supt. — 735-8701
HS, 8 NUTMEG AVE 06418 — 2-00011
  Charles DiCenso, prin. — 734-9293
MS, 8 NUTMEG AVE 06418 — 2-00100
  Charles DiCenso, prin. — 734-9293

Durham, AC 203, PC 5, Middlesex
Regional SD 13, 135A PICKETT LN 06422 — 4-11111
  William Breck, supt. — 349-3444
Coginchaug Regional HS — 2-00011
  135 PICKETT LN 06422 — 349-3491
  Michael Bower, prin.
Strong MS, 191 MAIN ST 06422 — 2-00100
  Laura Maniglia, prin. — 349-3495

Lake Grove School at Durham — 1-HND
  459R WALLINGFORD RD 06422 — 349-3467

East Granby, AC 203, PC 4, Hartford
East Granby SD, PO BOX 674 06026 — 3-11111
  A. T. Lederman, supt. — 653-6486
HS, 95 S MAIN ST 06026 — 2-00011
  Daniel Michael, prin. — 653-2541
MS, 95 S MAIN ST 06026 — 2-00100
  Daniel Michael, prin. — 653-2541

East Hampton, AC 203, PC 4, Middlesex
East Hampton SD, 94 MAIN ST 06424 — 4-11111
  John DeGennaro, supt. — 267-4466
HS, 39 N MAPLE ST 06424 — 2-00011
  Jane Baljevic, prin. — 267-2541
MS, 19 CHILDS RD 06424 — 2-00100
  Richard Huelsmann, prin. — 267-2533

East Hartford, AC 203, PC 8, Hartford
East Hartford SD, 31 SCHOOL ST 06108 — 6-11111
  Sam Leone, supt. — 282-3107
HS, 869 FORBES ST 06118 — 4-00011
  (—), prin. — 282-3203
MS, 777 BURNSIDE AVE 06108 — 3-00100
  James Fallon, prin. — 282-3179

Connecticut Business Institute — 2-CS
  809 MAIN ST 06108 — 291-2880
Data Institute — 2-CS
  745 BURNSIDE AVE 06108 — 528-4111

East Haven, AC 203, PC 8, New Haven
East Haven SD, 67 HUDSON ST 06512 — 5-11111
  Martin DeFelice, supt. — 468-3261
HS, 200 TYLER ST 06512 — 3-00011
  Norman DeMartino, prin. — 468-3267
Melillo MS, 67 HUDSON ST 06512 — 2-00100
  Arthur Martorella, prin. — 468-3229

East Lyme, AC 203, PC 4, New London
East Lyme SD, PO BOX 176 06333 — 5-11111
  John Reynolds, supt. — 739-3966
HS, PO BOX 210 06333 — 3-00011
  Gerald Mistretta, prin. — 739-6946
Other Schools – See Niantic

Easton, AC 203, PC 2, Fairfield
Easton SD, 215 CENTER RD 06612 — 3-11100
  G. Couillard, supt. — 261-2513
Keller MS, 360 SPORT HILL RD 06612 — 2-00100
  Frank Sippy, prin. — 268-8651

Redding SD, 215 CENTER RD 06612 — 4-11100
  G. Couillard, supt. — 261-2513
Other Schools – See West Redding

Regional SD 9, 215 CENTER RD 06612 — 3-00011
  G. Couillard, supt. — 261-2513
Other Schools – See West Redding

East Windsor, AC 203, PC 4, Hartford
East Windsor SD, 74 S MAIN ST 06088 — 4-11111
  Richard Teller, supt. — 623-3346
JSHS, 76 S MAIN ST 06088 — 3-00111
  Salvatore Saitta, prin. — 623-3361

Ellington, AC 203, PC 4, Tolland
Ellington SD, PO BOX 157 06029 — 4-11111
  Joseph Delucia, supt. — 872-8381
HS, 37 MAPLE ST 06029 — 3-00011
  M. Kouba, prin. — 872-8537
Other Schools – See Vernon-Rockville

Enfield, AC 203, PC 6, Hartford
Enfield SD, 27 SHAKER RD 06082 — 6-11111
  John Gallacher, supt. — 741-3551
HS, 1264 ENFIELD ST 06082 — 3-00011
  Joseph Gallucci, prin. — 741-3561
Fermi HS, 124 N MAPLE ST 06082 — 4-00011
  William Cutler, prin. — 763-2301
Kennedy MS, 155 RAFFIA RD 06082 — 4-00100
  Timothy Neville, prin. — 763-2368

Asnuntuck Community College — 3-CC
  170 ELM ST 06082 — 253-3010
Porter and Chester Institute — 2-CS
  138 WEYMOUTH RD 06082 — 800-870-6789

Fairfield, AC 203, PC 8, Fairfield
Fairfield SD, PO BOX 220 06430 — 6-11111
  Carol Harrington, supt. — 255-8371
HS, 755 MELVILLE AVE 06432 — 4-00011
  John Dodig, prin. — 255-8354
Fairfield Woods MS — 3-00100
  1115 FAIRFIELD WOODS RD 06432 — 255-8334
  Lynda Cox, prin.
Tomlinson MS — 3-00100
  240 UNQUOWA RD 06430 — 255-8336
  Margaret Fitzgerald, prin.

Bridgeport Engineering Institute — 2-UC
  785 UNQUOWA RD 06430 — 259-5717
Fairfield Prep S — 3-00011
  1073 N BENSON RD 06430 — 254-4000
  Fr. Arimond, prin.

Fairfield University — 5-UC
  25 N BENSON RD 06430 — 254-4000
Notre Dame HS — 3-00011
  220 JEFFERSON ST 06432 — 372-6521
  Armand Fabbri, prin.
Sacred Heart University — 4-UC
  5151 PARK AVE 06432 — 371-7900

Falls Village, AC 203, PC 3, Litchfield
Regional SD 1 — 2-00011
  WARREN TURNPIKE RD 06031 — 824-0855
  Marvin Maskovsky, supt.
Housatonic Valley Regional HS — 2-00011
  WARREN TURNPIKE RD 06031 — 824-5123
  John Mahoney, prin.

Farmington, AC 203, PC 5, Hartford
Farmington SD, 1 MONTIETH DR 06032 — 5-11111
  William Streich, supt. — 673-8268
HS, 10 MONTIETH DR 06032 — 3-00011
  Mark Cohan, prin. — 673-2514
Robbins MS, WOLF PIT RD 06032 — 3-00100
  James Aseltine, prin. — 677-2683

American Red Cross Blood Services — HSP
  209 FARMINGTON AVE 06032 — 678-2770
Miss Porter's S, 60 MAIN ST 06032 — 2-00011
  M. Ford, prin. — 677-1321
Tunxis Community College 06032 — 4-CC
  — 677-7701
University of Connecticut Health Center — 3-UC
  06032 — 679-2111

Gales Ferry, AC 203, PC 4, New London
Ledyard SD
  Supt. — See Ledyard
Ledyard MS, 1860 ROUTE 12 06335 — 2-00100
  Trent Alexopoulos, prin. — 464-0200

Glastonbury, AC 203, PC 6, Hartford
Glastonbury SD — 5-11111
  232 WILLIAMS ST E 06033 — 633-5231
  Jacqueline Jacoby, supt.
HS, 330 HUBBARD ST 06033 — 4-00011
  Alan Bookman, prin. — 633-5231
Welles MS, 1029 NEIPSIC RD 06033 — 3-00100
  Thomas Russo, prin. — 633-5231

Granby, AC 203, PC 4, Hartford
Granby SD, 11 N GRANBY RD 06035 — 4-11111
  John Burgess, supt. — 653-2583
Granby Memorial HS — 2-00011
  315 SALMON BROOK ST 06035 — 653-2531
  Robert Meyer, prin.
Granby Memorial MS — 2-00100
  321 SALMON BROOK ST 06035 — 653-2591
  Stanley Pestka, prin.

Greens Farms, AC 203, PC see Westport

Greens Farms Academy — 2-11111
  35 BEACHSIDE AVE 06436 — 255-1556
  James Coyle, prin.

Greenwich, AC 203, PC 8, Fairfield
Greenwich SD — 6-11111
  290 GREENWICH AVE 06830 — 625-7400
  John Whitner, supt.
HS, 10 HILLSIDE RD 06830 — 4-00011
  Eileen Petruzillo, prin. — 625-8000
Central MS, 9 INDIAN ROCK LN 06830 — 2-00100
  N. James Bulger, prin. — 661-8500
Western MS — 2-00100
  1 WESTERN JUNIOR HWY 06830 — 531-5700
  Don Strange, prin.
Other Schools – See Riverside

Brunswick School — 3-11111
  100 MAHER AVE 06830 — 869-0601
  Duncan Edwards, prin.
Connecticut Institute of Art — 1-CS
  581 W PUTNAM AVE 06830 — 869-4430
Convent of Sacred Heart S — 2-11111
  1177 KING ST 06831 — 531-6500
  Sr. Joan Magnetti, prin.
Greenwich Academy — 3-11111
  200 N MAPLE AVE 06830 — 869-4020
  Patricia Howard, prin.
Richmond College — 3-UC
  102 GREENWICH AVE 06830 — 800-727-2437

Groton, AC 203, PC 6, New London
Groton SD, PO BOX K 06340 — 6-11111
  George Reilly, supt. — 536-4957
Fitch HS — 4-00011
  101 GROTON LONG POINT RD 06340 — 445-7799
  John Murphy, prin.
Fitch MS, 61 FORT HILL RD 06340 — 3-00100
  Steven Durham, prin. — 445-9751
West Side MS — 2-00100
  250 BRANDEGEE AVE 06340 — 445-9779
  Robert Strouse, prin.
Other Schools – See Mystic

Vocational-Technical SD
  Supt. — See Middletown
Grasso Southeastern Vo-Tech HS — Vo Tech
  189 FORT HILL RD 06340 — 448-0220
  Susanna Girard, prin.

University of Connecticut — 2-UC
  AVERY POINT 06340
University of Connecticut 06340 — 2-CC
  — 446-1020

Guilford, AC 203, PC 5, New Haven
Guilford SD, PO BOX 367 06437 — 5-11111
 Thomas Giblin, supt. — 453-8200
HS, 605 NEW ENGLAND RD 06437 — 3-00011
 Barbara Truex, prin. — 453-2741
Adams MS, 200 CHURCH ST 06437 — 3-00100
 Judith Lawson, prin. — 453-2755

Hamden, AC 203, PC 8, New Haven
Hamden SD, 60 PUTNAM AVE 06517 — 6-11111
 David Shaw, supt. — 288-8473
HS, 2040 DIXWELL AVE 06514 — 4-00011
 Judith Philipi, prin. — 248-9311
Vocational Ctr — Vo Tech
 1255 SHEPARD AVE 06518 – (—), prin. — 288-5020
MS, 550 NEWHALL ST 06517 — 3-00100
 Charles Taylor, prin. — 777-5571

Vocational-Technical SD
 Supt. — See Middletown
Whitney Vo-Tech HS — Vo Tech
 71 JONES RD 06514 — 397-4031
 Cecil Robinson, prin.

Hamden Hall Country Day S — 3-1111
 1108 WHITNEY AVE 06517 — 865-6158
 James Maggart, prin.
Mt. Sacred Heart College — 1-CC
 265 BENHAM ST 06514 — 248-4225
Paier College of Art — 2-UC
 20 GORHAM AVE 06514 — 777-7319
Quinnipiac College — 4-UC
 275 MOUNT CARMEL AVE 06518 — 288-5251
Sacred Heart Academy — 2-00011
 265 BENHAM ST 06514 — 288-2309
 Sr. Carol Sansone, prin.
Stone Academy — 3-CS
 1315 DIXWELL AVE 06514 — 288-7474

Hartford, AC 203, PC 9, Hartford
Hartford SD, 249 HIGH ST 06103 — 8-11111
 T Haig, supt. — 722-8500
Bulkeley HS — 4-00011
 300 WETHERSFIELD AVE 06114 — 728-3300
 Anna Salamone-consoli, prin.
HS, 55 FOREST ST 06105 — 4-00011
 Amado Cruz, prin. — 278-5920
Weaver HS, 415 GRANBY ST 06112 — 4-00011
 Ed Davis, prin. — 243-9761
Fox MS, 305 GREENFIELD ST 06112 — 4-00100
 Jimmie Hill, prin. — 527-1871
Quirk MS, 85 EDWARDS ST 06120 — 4-00100
 Ismael Carreras, prin. — 247-9211
South MS, 215 SOUTH ST 06114 — 3-01100
 David Lawrence, prin. — 956-9607

Vocational-Technical SD
 Supt. — See Middletown
Prince Vo-Tech HS — Vo Tech
 500 BROOKFIELD ST 06106 — 246-8594
 Silas Shannon, prin.

Capital Community-Technical College — 3-CC
 401 FLATBUSH AVE 06106 — 527-4111
Connecticut Institute for the Blind — HND
 120 HOLCOMB ST 06112
Greater Hartford Community College — 4-CC
 61 WOODLAND ST 06105 — 549-4200
Hartford Camerata Conservatory — 1-CS
 834 ASYLUM AVE 06105 — 246-2588
Hartford College for Women — 2-CC
 1265 ASYLUM AVE 06105 — 236-1215
Hartford Graduate Center — 4-UC
 275 WINDSOR ST 06120 — 548-2400
Hartford Hospital — HSP
 PO BOX 5037 06102 — 545-2191
Hartford Secretarial School — 2-CS
 765 ASYLUM AVE 06105 — 522-2888
Hartford Seminary — 1-UC
 77 SHERMAN ST 06105 — 232-4451
Institute of Living Schools — 2-HND
 400 WASHINGTON ST 06106
Morse School of Business — 4-CS
 275 ASYLUM ST 06103 — 522-2261
Mt. Sinai Hospital — HSP
 500 BLUE HILLS AVE 06112 — 242-4431
St. Francis Hospital — HSP
 338 ASYLUM ST 06103 — 548-6001
School of the Hartford Ballet — 1-UC
 224 FARMINGTON AVE 06105
Trinity College — 4-UC
 300 SUMMIT ST 06106 — 297-2180
Watkinson S — 2-00111
 180 BLOOMFIELD AVE 06105 — 236-5618
 Charles Todd, prin.

Hebron, AC 203, PC 3, Tolland
Regional SD 8, 21 PENDLETON DR 06248 — 4-00011
 Herbert Pandiscio, supt. — 228-9417
RHAM HS, 67 RHAM RD 06248 — 3-00011
 Paula Schwartz, prin. — 228-9474
RHAM MS, RHAM RD 06248 — 2-00100
 Kristina Elias, prin. — 228-9423

Higganum, AC 203, PC 4, Middlesex
Regional SD 17, PO BOX 568 06441 — 4-11111
 Charles Sweetman, supt. — 345-0433
Haddam-Killingworth HS — 3-00011
 LITTLE CITY ROAD 06441 — 345-8541
 Richard Carmelich, prin.
Haddam-Killingworth MS — 2-00100
 LITTLE CITY ROAD 06441 — 345-8567
 Virginia Rebar, prin.

Jewett City, AC 203, PC 5, New London
Griswold SD, 305 SLATER AVE 06351 — 4-11111
 Edward Malvey, supt. — 376-7044
Griswold JSHS, 267 SLATER AVE 06351 — 3-00111
 Richard Foye, prin. — 376-7027

Kent, AC 203, PC 3, Litchfield

Kent School, PO BOX 2006 06757 — 3-00011
 Rev. Schell, prin. — 927-3501

Lakeville, AC 203, PC 4, Litchfield

Hotchkiss S, PO BOX 800 06039 — 3-00011
 Robert Oden, prin. — 435-2591

Lebanon, AC 203, PC 2, New London
Lebanon SD, PO BOX 166 06249 — 4-11111
 Albert Vertefeuille, supt. — 642-7795
Lyman Memorial HS — 2-00011
 917 EXETER RD 06249 — 642-7567
 James McKenna, prin.
MS, 891 EXETER RD 06249 — 2-01100
 Berthier Bosse, prin. — 642-4702

Ledyard, AC 203, PC 2, New London
Ledyard SD, 4 BLONDER PARK RD 06339 — 5-11111
 John Gillespie, supt. — 464-9255
HS, 24 GALLUP HILL RD 06339 — 4-00011
 William LaFleur, prin. — 464-9600
Other Schools – See Gales Ferry

Litchfield, AC 203, PC 4, Litchfield
Litchfield SD, PO BOX 110 06759 — 4-11111
 Robert Lindgren, supt. — 567-8701
Litchfield JSHS, PO BOX 110 06759 — 2-00111
 Suzanne D'Annolfo, prin. — 567-9471

Regional SD 6, 98 WAMOGO RD 06759 — 4-11111
 Timothy Breslin, supt. — 567-5493
Wamogo Regional JSHS 06759 — 2-00111
 Allen Fossbender, prin. — 567-8741

Connecticut Junior Republic — HND
 PO BOX 161 06759
Forman S, NORFOLK ROAD 06759 — 2-00011
 Peter Henry, prin. — 567-8712

Madison, AC 203, PC 4, New Haven
Madison SD, PO BOX 71 06443 — 5-11111
 H. Griffin, supt. — 245-7345
Hand HS, 302 GREEN HILL RD 06443 — 3-00011
 James Coyne, prin. — 245-7358
Brown MS, 980 DURHAM RD 06443 — 3-00100
 Jennifer Soloway, prin. — 421-3334

Manchester, AC 203, PC 8, Hartford
Manchester SD, 45 N SCHOOL ST 06040 — 6-11111
 James Kennedy, supt. — 647-3441
HS, 134 MIDDLE TPKE E 06040 — 4-00011
 James Spafford, prin. — 647-3526
Bennet MS, 1151 MAIN ST 06040 — 3-00100
 Marsha Gunther, prin. — 647-3575
Illing MS, 227 MIDDLE TPKE E 06040 — 3-00100
 Alan Beitman, prin. — 647-3400

Vocational-Technical SD
 Supt. — See Middletown
Cheney Vo-Tech HS — Vo Tech
 791 MIDDLE TPKE W 06040 — 649-5396
 Lewis Randall, prin.

East Catholic HS — 3-00011
 115 NEW STATE RD 06040 — 649-5336
 Peggy Siegmund, prin.
Manchester Community College — 5-CC
 PO BOX 1046 06045 — 646-4900
Manchester Memorial Hospital — HSP
 71 HAYNES ST 06040 — 646-1222

Meriden, AC 203, PC 8, New Haven
Meriden SD, 22 LIBERTY ST 06450 — 6-11111
 Gordon Bruno, supt. — 630-4171
Maloney HS, 121 GRAVEL ST 06450 — 4-00011
 Gladys Labas, prin. — 238-2334
Platt HS, 220 COE AVE 06451 — 3-00011
 John Goetz, prin. — 235-7963
Lincoln MS — 3-00100
 164 CENTENNIAL AVE 06451 — 238-2381
 John Lineen, prin.
Washington MS — 4-00100
 1225 N BROAD ST 06450 — 235-6606
 Shellie Pierce, prin.

Vocational-Technical SD
 Supt. — See Middletown
Wilcox Vo-Tech HS, OREGON RD 06451 — Vo Tech
 Andrew Jakab, prin. — 238-6260

Veterans Memorial Medical Center — HSP
 PO BOX 1009 06450 — 238-8270

Middlebury, AC 203, PC 5, New Haven
Regional SD 15, PO BOX 395 06762 — 5-11111
 Louis Esparo, supt. — 758-8258
Memorial MS, PO BOX 903 06762 — 2-01100
 Judith Dooling, prin. — 758-2496
Other Schools – See Southbury

Westover S, PO BOX 847 06762 — 2-00011
 Joseph Molder, prin. — 758-2423

Middletown, AC 203, PC 8, Middlesex
Middletown SD — 5-11111
 310 HUNTING HILL AVE 06457 — 638-1401
 David Larson, supt.

HS, 310 HUNTING HILL AVE 06457 — 3-00011
 Robert Kozacka, prin. — 347-8571
Wilson MS, 1 WILDERMAN WAY 06457 — 3-00100
 Frank Balisciano, prin. — 347-8594

Vocational-Technical SD — 6-00011
 25 INDUSTRIAL PARK RD 06457 — 638-4010
 Juan Lopez, supt.
Vinal Vo-Tech HS, 60 DANIELS ST 06457 — Vo Tech
 Thomas Scharrett, prin. — 344-7100
Other Schools – See Ansonia, Bridgeport, Danbury, Danielson, Groton, Hamden, Hartford, Manchester, Meriden, Milford, New Britain, Norwich, Stamford, Torrington, Waterbury, Willimantic

Mercy HS, 1740 RANDOLPH RD 06457 — 3-00011
 Sr. Mary McCarthy, prin. — 346-6659
Middlesex Community College — 4-CC
 100 TRAINING HILL RD 06457 — 344-3001
Wesleyan University 06459 — 5-UC
 — 347-9411
Wilcox College of Nursing — HSP
 28 CRESCENT ST 06457 — 344-6403
Xavier HS, 181 RANDOLPH RD 06457 — 3-00011
 Br. Harvey, prin. — 346-7735

Milford, AC 203, PC 8, New Haven
Milford SD, 70 W RIVER ST 06460 — 6-11111
 Mary Jo Kramer, supt. — 783-3401
Foran HS, 30 FORAN RD 06460 — 3-00011
 Anthony Albanese, prin. — 783-3501
Law HS, 20 LANSDALE AVE 06460 — 3-00011
 Jerold Wanosky, prin. — 783-3574
Harborside MS, HIGH ST 06460 — 2-00100
 Gary Cialfi, prin. — 783-3523
West Shore MS, 50 KAY AVE 06460 — 2-00100
 Gregory Baecker, prin. — 783-3553
Pumpkin Delight MS, 20 ART ST 06460 — 2-00100
 M. Martinez, prin. — 783-3531

Vocational-Technical SD
 Supt. — See Middletown
Platt Vo-Tech HS — Vo Tech
 600 ORANGE AVE 06460 — 783-5300
 Gale Tirrell, prin.

Academy of Our Lady of Mercy — 2-00011
 200 HIGH ST 06460 — 877-2786
 Ann Pratson, prin.

Monroe, AC 203, PC 3, Fairfield
Monroe SD, 375 MONROE TPKE 06468 — 5-11111
 Norman Michaud, supt. — 268-3914
Masuk HS, 1014 MONROE TPKE 06468 — 3-00011
 Peter Holst, prin. — 268-6201
Chalk Hill MS, 345 FAN HILL RD 06468 — 3-00100
 Anita Healy, prin. — 261-2530

Moodus, AC 203, PC 4, Middlesex
East Haddam SD, PO BOX 401 06469 — 4-11111
 Daniel Thompson, supt. — 873-1429
Hale-Ray JSHS, PO BOX 404 06469 — 2-00111
 Craig Edmondson, prin. — 873-8656

Mystic, AC 203, PC 5, New London
Groton SD
 Supt. — See Groton
Cutler MS, 160 FISHTOWN RD 06355 — 2-00100
 J. Sneider, prin. — 536-4918

Stonington SD
 Supt. — See Old Mystic
MS, RR 1 BOX 327 06355 — 2-01100
 Dennis Curran, prin. — 536-9613

Naugatuck, AC 203, PC 8, New Haven
Naugatuck SD, 380 CHURCH ST 06770 — 6-11111
 Alice Tufts, supt. — 723-4421
HS, 543 RUBBER AVE 06770 — 4-00011
 Richard Nabel, prin. — 723-0961
City Hill MS, 441 CITY HILL ST 06770 — 3-00100
 Jane Kessler, prin. — 729-8279
Hillside MS, 51 HILLSIDE AVE 06770 — 2-00100
 Brian Sullivan, prin. — 729-4625

New Britain, AC 203, PC 8, Hartford
New Britain SD, 1 LIBERTY SQ 06051 — 6-11111
 Paul Sequeira, supt. — 827-2204
HS, 110 MILL ST 06051 — 4-00011
 Evan Pitkoff, prin. — 225-6351
Pulaski MS — 3-00100
 757 FARMINGTON AVE 06053 — 225-7665
 Anna Marie Mistretta, prin.
Roosevelt MS, 40 GOODWIN ST 06051 — 3-00100
 Emmanuel Gluck, prin. — 224-9557
Slade MS, 183 STEELE ST 06052 — 3-00100
 Jeraldine Brown-Springer, prin. — 225-6395

Vocational-Technical SD
 Supt. — See Middletown
Goodwin Vo-Tech HS — Vo Tech
 735 SLATER RD 06053 — 827-7736
 John Tarnuzzer, prin.

Central Connecticut State University — 6-UC
 1615 STANLEY ST 06053 — 827-7116
Mary Immaculate Academy — 2-00011
 370 OSGOOD AVE 06053 — 229-1747
 Sr. Mary Rzasa, prin.
New Britain General Hospital — HSP
 100 GRAND ST 06052 — 224-5666
New England Technical Institute — 2-CS
 200 JOHN DOWNEY DR 06051 — 225-8641
St. Ann MS, 114 NORTH ST 06051 — 1-00100
 Sr. Regina Arena, prin. — 229-1929

St. Francis MS — 2-00100
30 PENDLETON RD 06053 — 225-8729
Sr. Marie Murphy, prin.
St. Thomas Aquinas HS — 2-00011
74 KELSEY ST 06051 — 225-7847
Judith Greco, prin.
Salter School — 2-CS
1 GROVE ST 06053 — 224-8838

New Canaan, AC 203, PC 7, Fairfield
New Canaan SD, 39 LOCUST AVE 06840 — 5-11111
Gary Richards, supt. — 966-9575
HS, 11 FARM RD 06840 — 3-00011
David Abbey, prin. — 966-9538
Saxe MS, 468 SOUTH AVE 06840 — 3-00100
Charles Terry, prin. — 966-5645

St. Luke's S, 377 N WILTON RD 06840 — 2-00111
Richard Whitcomb, prin. — 966-5612

New Fairfield, AC 203, PC 5, Fairfield
New Fairfield SD — 4-11111
3 BRUSH HILL RD 06812 — 796-1842
Rolfe Wenner, supt.
HS, 54 GILLOTTI RD 06812 — 3-00011
Owen McDonnell, prin. — 796-1803
MS, 54 GILLOTTI RD 06812 — 2-00100
James Rice, prin. — 796-1862

New Haven, AC 203, PC 9, New Haven
New Haven SD, 54 MEADOW ST 06519 — 7-11111
Reginald Mayo, supt. — 787-8888
Cross HS, 181 MITCHELL DR 06511 — 4-00011
Thomas Ragozzino, prin. — 787-8728
Hillhouse HS, 480 SHERMAN PKY 06511 — 3-00011
Lonnie Garris, prin. — 787-8484
Transitional HS — 2-00011
806 ORCHARD ST 06511 — 777-4830
Leroy Williams, prin.
Conte/Career Magnet HS — Vo Tech
21 WOOSTER PL 06511 — 787-8400
Charles Williams, prin.
Clemente MS — 3-01100
360 COLUMBUS AVE 06519 — 787-8886
Andrew Alberino, prin.
Fair Haven MS, 164 GRAND AVE 06513 — 3-01100
Joseph Montagna, prin. — 787-8430
Robinson MS, 150 FOURNIER ST 06511 — 2-01100
George Wells, prin. — 787-8770
Ross Arts MS, 185 BARNES AVE 06513 — 3-01100
Brenda Holland, prin. — 787-8974
Sheridan MS, 191 FOUNTAIN ST 06515 — 2-00100
Robert Canelli, prin. — 787-8828
Troup MS, 259 EDGEWOOD AVE 06511 — 3-01100
Richard Kaliszewski, prin. — 787-8854
West Hills Magnet MS — 2-01100
103 HALLOCK AVE 06519 — 787-8279
Janice Romo, prin.

Albertus Magnus College — 2-UC
700 PROSPECT ST 06511 — 773-8550
Berkeley Divinity School — 2-UC
363 SAINT RONAN ST 06511 — 432-6105
Connecticut Business Institute — 2-CS
984 CHAPEL ST 06510 — 562-8114
Connecticut School of Electronics — 3-CS
586 ELLA T GRASSO BLVD 06519 — 624-2121
Data Institute — 2-CS
109 CHURCH ST 06512 — 787-1990
Hopkins S, 986 FOREST RD 06515 — 3-00111
Thomas Rodd, prin. — 397-1001
St. Peter MS — 2-01100
10 SAINT PETERS AVE 06519 — 865-1421
Sr. Rosemarie Ryan, prin.
South Central Community College — 4-CC
60 SARGENT DR 06511 — 789-7071
Southern Connecticut State University — 6-UC
501 CRESCENT ST 06515 — 397-4000
Yale University — 7-UC
180 YORK ST 06511 — 432-4771
Yale University — 3-UC
382 CONGRESS AVE 06519 — 432-1900

Newington, AC 203, PC 8, Hartford
Newington SD, 131 CEDAR ST 06111 — 5-11111
Ernest Perlini, supt. — 666-5467
HS, 605 WILLARD AVE 06111 — 4-00011
Paul Hoey, prin. — 666-5611
Kellogg MS, 155 HARDING AVE 06111 — 2-00100
Amzie Brown, prin. — 666-5418
Wallace MS, 71 HALLERAN DR 06111 — 2-00100
Anne Giddings, prin. — 667-0861

Charter Oak State College — 3-UC
66 CEDAR ST 06111 — 666-4595
Connecticut Center for Massage Therapy — 2-CS
75 KITTS LN 06111 — 667-1886

New London, AC 203, PC 8, New London
New London SD — 5-11111
134 WILLIAMS ST 06320 — 447-1435
Rene Racette, supt.
HS, 490 JEFFERSON AVE 06320 — 3-00011
Louis Allen, prin. — 447-3231
JHS, 1 LINCOLN AVE 06320 — 2-00100
John Bassett, prin. — 447-3056

Connecticut College — 4-UC
270 MOHEGAN AVE 06320 — 439-2200
Lawrence & Memorial Hospitals — HSP
365 MONTAUK AVE 06320 — 442-0711

Mitchell College — 3-CC
437 PEQUOT AVE 06320 — 443-2811
Ridley-Lowell Business & Technical Inst — 2-CS
PO BOX 652 06320 — 443-7441
United States Coast Guard Academy — 3-UC
06320 — 444-8501
Williams S, 182 MOHEGAN AVE 06320 — 2-00111
Steven Danenberg, prin. — 443-5333

New Milford, AC 203, PC 6, Litchfield
New Milford SD, 50 EAST ST 06776 — 5-11111
Stephen Tracy, supt. — 355-8406
HS, 25 SUNNY VALLEY RD 06776 — 4-00011
Joanne Mendillo, prin. — 350-6647
Schaghticoke MS, 23 HIPP RD 06776 — 4-00100
Don Fiftal, prin. — 354-2204

Canterbury S, PO BOX 5000 06776 — 2-00011
Thomas Sheehy, prin. — 355-3103

Newtown, AC 203, PC 4, Fairfield
Newtown SD, 11 QUEEN ST 06470 — 5-11111
John Reed, supt. — 426-7621
MS, 11 QUEEN ST 06470 — 3-00100
Louis Villamana, prin. — 426-7638
Other Schools – See Sandy Hook

Niantic, AC 203, PC 5, New London
East Lyme SD
Supt. — See East Lyme
East Lyme HS, 25 SOCIETY RD 06357 — 3-00100
Jerome Belair, prin. — 739-4491

North Branford, AC 203, PC 6, New Haven
North Branford SD
Supt. — See Northford
HS, 49 CAPUTO RD 06471 — 3-00011
John De Caprio, prin. — 484-0421
IS, 675 FOXON RD 06471 — 3-00100
Nicholas Bauer, prin. — 484-2769

Northford, AC 203, PC 5, New Haven
North Branford SD — 4-11111
PO BOX 129 06472 — 484-0485
Donald McCarthy, supt.
Other Schools – See North Branford

North Grosvenordale, AC 203, PC 4, Windham
Thompson SD, 785 RIVERSIDE DR 06255 — 4-11111
Donald Hardy, supt. — 923-9581
Tourtellotte Memorial HS — 2-00011
785 RIVERSIDE DR 06255 — 923-9303
A. David Babbitt, prin.
Thompson MS, 785 RIVERSIDE DR 06255 — 2-01100
David Johnson, prin. — 923-9380

North Haven, AC 203, PC 7, New Haven
North Haven SD, 5 LINSLEY ST 06473 — 5-11111
Mary Jane Scarpellino, supt. — 239-2581
HS, 222 MAPLE AVE 06473 — 3-00011
Patricia Brozek, prin. — 239-1641
MS, 55 BAILEY RD 06473 — 3-00100
George Curry, prin. — 239-1683

Greater New Haven State Tech. College — 3-CC
88 BASSETT RD 06473 — 234-3300

North Stonington, AC 203, PC 2, New London
North Stonington SD — 3-11111
PO BOX 6001 06359 — 535-2800
Martin Gotowala, supt.
Wheeler JSHS, PO BOX 6001 06359 — 2-00111
Howard Sheldon, prin. — 535-0377

Norwalk, AC 203, PC 8, Fairfield
Norwalk SD, PO BOX 6001 06852 — 6-11111
Ralph Sloan, supt. — 854-4000
McMahon HS — 4-00011
300 HIGHLAND AVE 06854 — 852-9488
James Forcellina, prin.
HS, 55 CALVIN MURPHY DR 06851 — 4-00011
John Ramos, prin. — 838-4481
Briggs Vo-Tech HS — Vo Tech
350 MAIN AVE 06851 — 854-4000
John Henshall, prin.
Hale MS — 3-00100
STRAWBERRY HILL AVE 06851 — 854-4000
Joseph Cloherty, prin.
Ponus Ridge MS, 19 HUNTERS LN 06850 — 3-00100
Marie Iannazzi, prin. — 854-4000
Roton MS, 201 HIGHLAND AVE 06853 — 2-00100
Thomas Rietano, prin. — 854-4000
West Rocks MS, 81 W ROCKS RD 06851 — 3-00100
Margaret Kellher, prin. — 854-4000

Katharine Gibbs School — 3-CC
142 EAST AVE 06851 — 838-4173
Norwalk Community College — 4-CC
188 RICHARDS AVE 06854 — 853-2040
Norwalk Hospital — HSP
24 STEVENS ST 06850 — 852-2211
Norwalk State Technical College — 3-CC
181 RICHARDS AVE 06854 — 855-6600

Norwich, AC 203, PC 8, New London
Endowed & Incorporated Academies — 4-00011
305 BROADWAY 06360 — 887-2505
Mary Lou Bargnesi, supt.
Norwich Free Academy — 4-00011
305 BROADWAY 06360 — 887-2505
Mary Lou Bargnesi, prin.
Norwich SD, 23 MAHAN DR 06360 — 5-11111
Walt Juzwic, supt. — 823-4200
Norwich HS, MAHAN DR 06360 — 1-00011
Anthony Bauduccio, prin. — 823-4213

Kelly JHS, 15 MAHAN DR 06360 — 2-00100
Donald Steinman, prin. — 823-4211
Teachers Memorial JHS — 2-00100
15 TEACHERS DR 06360 — 823-4212
William Peckham, prin.

Vocational-Technical SD
Supt. — See Middletown
Norwich Vo-Tech HS — Vo Tech
590 NEW LONDON TPKE 06360 — 889-8453
Charles Salerno, prin.

Huntington Institute — 2-CS
193 BROADWAY 06360 — 886-0507
Mohegan Community College — 4-CC
21 MAHAN DR 06360 — 886-1931
Thames Valley State Technical College — 3-CC
574 NEW LONDON TPKE 06360 — 886-0177

Oakdale, AC 203, PC 3, New London
Montville SD — 5-11111
OLD COLCHESTER ROAD 06370 — 848-1228
Jacob Ludes, supt.
Montville HS — 3-00011
OLD COLCHESTER RD 06370 — 848-9208
William Farrington, prin.
Tyl MS, 166 CHESTERFIELD RD 06370 — 3-00100
Peter DeLisa, prin. — 848-2822

St. Thomas More S — 2-00111
85 COTTAGE RD 06370 — 859-1900
James Hanrahan, prin.

Oakville, AC 203, PC 6, Litchfield
Watertown SD
Supt. — See Watertown
Swift JHS, 250 COLONIAL ST 06779 — 3-00100
Carol Rector, prin. — 945-4830

Old Lyme, AC 203, PC 2, New London
Regional SD 18, 69 LYME ST 06371 — 4-11111
Jefferson Prestridge, supt. — 434-7238
Lyme-Old Lyme HS, 69 LYME ST 06371 — 2-00111
W. Brown, prin. — 434-1651
Lyme-Old Lyme MS, 53 LYME ST 06371 — 2-00100
Robert Chester, prin. — 434-2568

Old Mystic, AC 203, PC 3, New London
Stonington SD, PO BOX 479 06372 — 4-11111
Thomas Reale, supt. — 572-0506
Other Schools – See Mystic, Pawcatuck

Old Saybrook, AC 203, PC 4, Middlesex
Old Saybrook SD — 4-11111
50 SHEFFIELD ST 06475 — 395-3157
Salvatore Pascarella, supt.
HS, 1111 BOSTON POST RD 06475 — 2-00011
Thad Hasbrouck, prin. — 395-3175
MS, 60 SHEFFIELD ST 06475 — 3-01100
Michael Rafferty, prin. — 395-3168

Orange, AC 203, PC 7, New Haven
Regional SD 5
Supt. — See Woodbridge
Amity Regional JHS — 2-00110
100 OHMAN AVE 06477 — 397-9235
Robert Slie, prin.

Beth Chana-Hannah Academy — 2-11111
PO BOX 587 06477 — 795-5261
Rabbi Hecht, prin.

Oxford, AC 203, PC 4, New Haven
Oxford SD, 429 OXFORD RD 06478 — 4-11100
Michael Abdalla, supt. — 888-7754
Great Oak MS, 50 GREAT OAK RD 06478 — 2-00100
Frank Samulson, prin. — 888-4518

Pawcatuck, AC 203, PC 6, New London
Stonington SD
Supt. — See Old Mystic
Stonington HS, 176 S BROAD ST 06379 — 3-00011
Thomas Jones, prin. — 599-5781
MS, 100 FIELD ST 06379 — 2-01100
John Cross, prin. — 599-5696

Plainfield, AC 203, PC 5, Windham
Plainfield SD
Supt. — See Central Village
Plainfield Central MS — 3-00100
75 CANTERBURY RD 06374 — 564-6437
Mary Ann Dumas, prin.

Plainville, AC 203, PC 7, Hartford
Plainville SD — 4-11111
47 ROBERT HOLCOMB WAY 06062 — 793-3202
James Ritchie, supt.
HS, 47 ROBERT HOLCOMB WAY 06062 — 3-00011
Anthony Mosa, prin. — 793-3220
MS, 150 NORTHWEST DR 06062 — 2-00100
Paul Cavaliere, prin. — 793-3250

Plantsville, AC 203, PC 6, Hartford
Southington SD
Supt. — See Southington
Kennedy JHS, 1071 S MAIN ST 06479 — 3-00110
Robert Lasbury, prin. — 628-3274

Pomfret, AC 203, PC 3, Windham

Pomfret S 06258 — 2-00011
Bradford Hastings, prin. — 928-7731
Rectory ES, GENERAL DELIVERY 06258 — 2-01110
Thomas Army, prin. — 928-7759

Portland, AC 203, PC 6, Middlesex
Portland SD, PO BOX 231 06480 — 4-11111
LeRoy Dyer, supt. — 342-1640

HS, 95 HIGH ST 06480 — 2-00011
Donald Gates, prin. — 342-1720
MS, 314 MAIN ST 06480 — 2-00100
Margaret Downey, prin. — 342-1880

Preston, AC 203, PC 2, New London
Preston SD — 2-11110
56 SCHOOL HOUSE RD 06365 — 889-6098
Donald Holder, supt.
Preston Plains MS — 2-00100
1 ROUTE 164 06365 — 889-3831
Joseph Allegro, prin.

Prospect, AC 203, PC 6, New Haven
Regional SD 16, 30 COER RD 06712 — 4-11100
John Buck, supt. — 758-6671
Long River MS 06712 — 2-00100
Gary Gombar, prin. — 758-4421

Putnam, AC 203, PC 6, Windham
Putnam SD, 126 CHURCH ST 06260 — 4-11111
Louis Mager, supt. — 928-0533
HS, 152 WOODSTOCK AVE 06260 — 2-00011
Nelson King, prin. — 928-0525
MS, 35 WICKER ST 06260 — 2-00100
Matthew Carroll, prin. — 928-1014

Ridgefield, AC 203, PC 6, Fairfield
Ridgefield SD, PO BOX 629 06877 — 5-11111
Jeffrey Hanson, supt. — 544-9881
HS, 700 N SALEM RD 06877 — 3-00011
Joseph Ellis, prin. — 438-3785
East Ridge MS, 10 S RIDGE CT 06877 — 3-00100
Mary Gorman, prin. — 438-3744

Riverside, AC 203, PC 2, Fairfield
Greenwich SD
Supt. — See Greenwich
Eastern MS, 51 HENDRIE AVE 06878 — 2-00100
Benjamin Davenport, prin. — 637-1744

Rocky Hill, AC 203, PC 7, Hartford
Rocky Hill SD, 33 CHURCH ST 06067 — 4-11111
J. A. Vautour, supt. — 529-7796
HS, 50 CHAPIN AVE 06067 — 3-00011
Raymond Grasso, prin. — 529-2583
Griswold JHS, 144 BAILEY RD 06067 — 2-00100
Charles Stewart, prin. — 529-8201

Salisbury, AC 203, PC 4, Litchfield

Indian Mountain S — 2-01110
INDIAN MOUNTAIN RD 06039 — 435-0871
Dary Dunham, prin.
Salisbury S, 251 CANAAN RD 06068 — 2-00011
Richard Flood, prin. — 435-2531

Sandy Hook, AC 203, PC 4, Fairfield
Newtown SD
Supt. — See Newtown
Newtown HS, 12 BERKSHIRE RD 06482 — 3-00011
William Manfredonia, prin. — 426-7646

Seymour, AC 203, PC 7, New Haven
Seymour SD, 98 BANK ST 06483 — 4-11111
Eugene Coppola, supt. — 888-4565
HS, 2 BOTSFORD RD 06483 — 3-00011
Anthony LoPresti, prin. — 888-2561
MS, 25 PINE ST 06483 — 2-00100
Paul Porter, prin. — 888-4513

Shelton, AC 203, PC 8, Fairfield
Shelton SD, PO BOX 846 06484 — 6-11111
Leon Sylvester, supt. — 924-1023
HS, 120 MEADOW ST 06484 — 4-00011
Timothy Walsh, prin. — 924-9578
IS, 60 PERRY HILL RD 06484 — 4-00100
William Banfe, prin. — 924-1891

Simsbury, AC 203, PC 6, Hartford
Simsbury SD — 5-11111
933 HOPMEADOW ST 06070 — 651-3361
Joseph Townsley, supt.
HS, 34 FARMS VILLAGE RD 06070 — 4-00011
Dennis Carrithers, prin. — 658-0451
James Memorial MS — 3-00100
155 FIRETOWN RD 06070 — 651-3341
Michael Churilla, prin.

Ethel Walker S — 2-00011
230 BUSHY HILL RD 06070 — 658-4467
Margaret Bonz, prin.
Westminster S — 2-00011
995 HOPMEADOW ST 06070 — 658-4444
W. Cole, prin.

Somers, AC 203, PC 4, Tolland
Somers SD, 9TH DISTRICT RD 06071 — 4-11111
Paul Gagliarducci, supt. — 749-2279
HS, 9TH DISTRICT RD 06071 — 2-00011
Daniel Lynch, prin. — 749-0719
Avery MS, 9TH DISTRICT RD 06071 — 3-01100
Thomas Chilicki, prin. — 763-2073

New England Tractor Trailer Training — 3-CS
PO BOX 326 06071 — 749-0711

Southbury, AC 203, PC 5, New Haven
Regional SD 15
Supt. — See Middlebury
Pomperaug Regional HS — 3-00011
234 JUDD RD 06488 – John Voss, prin. — 262-3200
Rochambeau MS, 100 PETER RD 06488 — 3-01100
Aldro Jenks, prin. — 264-2711

Southington, AC 203, PC 8, Hartford
Southington SD, 49 BEECHER ST 06489 — 6-11111
Louis Saloom, supt. — 628-3202

SHS, 720 PLEASANT ST 06489 — 4-00001
Jerome Auclair, prin. — 628-3232
Depaolo JHS, 385 PLEASANT ST 06489 — 3-00110
Gerald Gingras, prin. — 628-3262
Other Schools – See Plantsville

Briarwood College — 2-CC
2279 MOUNT VERNON RD 06489 — 628-4751

South Kent, AC 203, PC 2, Litchfield

South Kent S, 40 BULLS RIDGE RD 06785 — 2-00011
Pedro Arango, prin. — 927-3539

South Windsor, AC 203, PC 7, Hartford
South Windsor SD, 1737 MAIN ST 06074 — 5-11111
Joseph Wood, supt. — 291-1200
HS, 161 NEVERS RD 06074 — 4-00011
Gregory Plunkett, prin. — 648-5000
Edwards MS, 100 ARNOLD WAY 06074 — 3-00100
Laura Boutilier, prin. — 648-5030

Stafford Springs, AC 203, PC 5, Tolland
Stafford SD, PO BOX 147 06076 — 4-11111
Wayne Senecal, supt. — 684-4211
Stafford HS, PO BOX 87 06076 — 2-00011
David Perry, prin. — 684-4233
Stafford MS, PO BOX 106 06076 — 2-00100
Joseph Matava, prin. — 684-2785

Stamford, AC 203, PC 9, Fairfield
Stamford SD, PO BOX 9310 06904 — 7-11111
Peter Horoschak, supt. — 977-4105
HS, 55 STRAWBERRY HILL AVE 06902 — 4-00011
Anthony Markosky, prin. — 977-4227
Westhill HS, 125 ROXBURY RD 06902 — 4-00011
H. Tucci, prin. — 977-4838
Cloonan MS, 11 W NORTH ST 06902 — 3-00100
Ethan Margolis, prin. — 977-4544
Dolan MS, 51 TOMS RD 06906 — 3-00100
Lynda Hautala, prin. — 977-4441
Turn-of-River MS, 117 VINE RD 06905 — 3-00100
Rodney Bass, prin. — 977-4284

Vocational-Technical SD
Supt. — See Middletown
Wright Vo-Tech HS — Vo Tech
PO BOX 1416 06904 — 324-7363
Daniel Kushman, prin.

Beth Benjamin Academy of Connecticut — 1-UC
132 PROSPECT ST 06901 — 325-4351
King & Low - H Thomas S — 3-11111
1450 NEWFIELD AVE 06905 — 322-3413
Elizabeth Cesare, prin.
Sacred Heart Academy — 2-00011
200 STRAWBERRY HILL AVE 06902 — 323-3173
Sr. Jeanne Paulella, prin.
St. Gabriel MS — 2-00100
948 NEWFIELD AVE 06905 — 322-7383
Michael Fettig, prin.
Stamford Hospital — HSP
PO BOX 9317 06904 — 325-7500
Trinity Catholic HS — 2-00011
926 NEWFIELD AVE 06905 — 322-3401
Sr. Ritamary Schulz, prin.
University of Connecticut — 2-CC
641 SCOFIELDTOWN RD 06903 — 322-3466
Westlawn School of Yacht Design — 1-HMS
733 SUMMER ST 06901

Storrs, AC 203, PC 7, Tolland
Mansfield SD — 4-11100
4 S EAGLEVILLE RD 06268 — 429-3350
Gordon Schimmel, supt.
Mansfield MS — 3-01100
205 SPRING HILL RD 06268 — 429-9341
Carole Iwanicki, prin.

Regional SD 19, 1235 STORRS RD 06268 — 3-00011
Robert Gaucher, supt. — 487-1862
Smith HS, 1235 STORRS RD 06268 — 3-00011
Mark Winzler, prin. — 487-0877

University of Connecticut 06268 — 7-UC — 486-2000

Stratford, AC 203, PC 8, Fairfield
Stratford SD, 1000 E BROADWAY 06497 — 6-11111
Raymond O'Connell, supt. — 385-4210
Bunnell HS, 1 BULLDOG BLVD 06497 — 3-00011
Edward Schuck, prin. — 385-4250
HS, 45 N PARADE ST 06497 — 3-00011
Raymond O'Connell, prin. — 385-4230
Flood MS, 490 CHAPEL ST 06497 — 2-00100
George Hames, prin. — 385-4280
Wooster MS, 150 LINCOLN ST 06497 — 3-00100
George Hames, prin. — 385-4275

Connecticut Business Institute — 3-CS
605 BROAD ST 06497 — 377-1775
Porter and Chester Institute — 3-CS
670 LORDSHIP BLVD 06497 — 375-4463

Suffield, AC 203, PC 4, Hartford
Suffield SD, 350 MOUNTAIN RD 06078 — 4-11111
Bernard Ellis, supt. — 668-3800
HS, 350 MOUNTAIN RD 06078 — 3-00011
Robert Pitocco, prin. — 668-3810
McAlister MS — 3-01100
260 MOUNTAIN RD 06078 — 668-3820
Ann Estes, prin.

St. Alphonsus College — 1-UC
1762 MAPLETON AVE 06078
Suffield Academy, 340 N MAIN ST 06078 — 2-00011
David Holmes, prin. — 668-7315

Terryville, AC 203, PC 6, Litchfield
Plymouth SD, 70 E MAIN ST 06786 — 4-11111
Allen Frazier, supt. — 589-2246
HS, 19 N MAIN ST 06786 — 2-00011
F. Wayne Ranhosky, prin. — 583-1607
Fisher MS, 75 N MAIN ST 06786 — 2-01100
Michael Buzzi, prin. — 583-1554

Thomaston, AC 203, PC 5, Litchfield
Thomaston SD, PO BOX 166 06787 — 4-11111
George Counter, supt. — 283-4796
HS, 140 BRANCH RD 06787 — 2-00011
Michael Piccirillo, prin. — 283-4381
MS, 49 THOMAS AVE 06787 — 2-01100
Robin Willink, prin. — 283-4341

Thompson, AC 203, PC 3, Windham

Marianapolis Prep S — 2-00011
PO BOX 368 06277 – Fr. Roth, prin. — 923-9565

Tolland, AC 203, PC 4, Tolland
Tolland SD, 51 TOLLAND GRN 06084 — 4-11111
John Vitale, supt. — 875-9682
HS, OLD CATHOLE RD 06084 — 3-00011
Michael Blake, prin. — 872-0561
MS, 96 OLD POST RD 06084 — 3-01100
Robert Lincoln, prin. — 875-2564

Torrington, AC 203, PC 8, Litchfield
Torrington SD, 355 MIGEON AVE 06790 — 5-11111
John Shine, supt. — 489-2327
HS, 50 MAJOR BESSE DR 06790 — 4-00011
Bruce Fox, prin. — 489-2294
Vogel-Wetmore MS — 4-00100
68 CHURCH ST 06790 — 489-2324
Anthony Distasio, prin.

Vocational-Technical SD
Supt. — See Middletown
Wolcott Vo-Tech HS — Vo Tech
75 OLIVER ST 06790 — 489-0261
William Perlotto, prin.

Trumbull, AC 203, PC 8, Fairfield
Trumbull SD, 6254 MAIN ST 06611 — 6-11111
Edwin Merritt, supt. — 261-3801
HS, 72 STROBEL RD 06611 — 4-00011
Robert McCarthy, prin. — 452-5150
Hillcrest MS — 3-00100
530 DANIELS FARM RD 06611 — 452-5190
Rosemary Seaman, prin.
Madison MS, 4630 MADISON AVE 06611 — 3-00100
Rob Gabriel, prin. — 452-5183

Christian Heritage S — 2-11111
575 WHITE PLAINS RD 06611 — 261-0230
Alan Brown, prin.
St. Joseph HS — 3-00011
2320 HUNTINGTON TPKE 06611 — 378-9378
Br. Burke, prin.

Uncasville, AC 203, PC 5, New London

St. Bernard HS — 2-00011
1593 NRWICH NEW LONDON TPKE 06382
Madeline Bergeron, prin. — 848-1271

Vernon-Rockville, AC 203, PC 8, Tolland
Ellington SD
Supt. — See Ellington
Ellington MS — 2-00100
46 MIDDLE BUTCHER RD 06066 — 875-2400
Barbara Ripa, prin.

Vernon SD, 30 PARK ST 06066 — 5-11111
Andrew Maneggia, supt. — 872-7361
Rockville HS — 4-00011
70 LOVELAND HILL RD 06066 — 872-7391
Alphonse Landroche, prin.
Vernon Center MS — 3-00100
777 HARTFORD TPKE 06066 — 872-0549
Dennis Beiu, prin.

Wallingford, AC 203, PC 8, New Haven
Wallingford SD — 6-11111
142 HOPE HILL RD 06492 — 949-6500
Joseph Cirasuolo, supt.
Hall HS, 106 POND HILL RD 06492 — 3-00011
Anthony Ruotolo, prin. — 294-5350
Sheehan HS, 142 HOPE HILL RD 06492 — 3-00011
Sean Meehan, prin. — 294-5900
Hammarskjold MS — 3-00100
106 POND HILL RD 06492 — 294-5340
Enrico Buccilli, prin.
Moran MS, 141 HOPE HILL RD 06492 — 3-00100
John Marriott, prin. — 949-0331

Choate Rosemary Hall S — 4-00011
PO BOX 788 06492 — 269-7722
Edward Shanahan, prin.

Washington, AC 203, PC 3, Litchfield
Regional SD 12
Supt. — See Washington Depot
Shepaug Valley HS — 2-00011
159 SOUTH ST 06793 — 868-7326
Eugene Horrigan, prin.
Shepaug Valley MS, SOUTH ST 06793 — 2-00100
Nancy Green, prin. — 868-7326

Swiss Hospitality Institute Cesar Ritz   2-CS
101 WYKEHAM RISE RD   06793   868-9555

Washington Depot, AC 203, PC 3, Litchfield
Regional SD 12, PO BOX 386   06794   3-11111
   Robert Nicoletti, supt.   868-7311
   Other Schools – See Washington

Devereux Center in Connecticut   HND
81 SABBADAY LN   06793   868-7377
Gunnery S, 99 GREEN HILL RD   06793   2-00011
   Susan Graham, prin.   868-7334

Waterbury, AC 203, PC 9, New Haven
Vocational-Technical SD
   Supt. — See Middletown
Kaynor Vo-Tech HS   Vo Tech
   43 TOMPKINS ST   06708   596-4302
   Georgia Smith-Jennings, prin.

Waterbury SD, 236 GRAND ST   06702   7-11111
   Joseph Sullivan, supt.   574-8004
Crosby HS, 300 PIERPONT RD   06705   4-00011
   Van Snyder, prin.   574-8061
Kennedy HS, 422 HIGHLAND AVE   06708   4-00011
   Louis Mazzaferro, prin.   574-8150
Wilby HS, 460 BUCKS HILL RD   06704   3-00011
   Francis Brennan, prin.   574-8100
North End MS   3-00100
   460 BUCKS HILL RD   06704   574-8099
   Joseph Cavanaugh, prin.
Wallace MS, 3465 E MAIN ST   06705   4-00100
   Michael Pace, prin.   574-8141
West Side MS, 483 CHASE PKY   06708   4-00100
   Martin Scully, prin.   574-8122

Data Institute   2-CS
101 PIERPONT RD   06705   756-5500
Holy Cross HS, 587 ORONOKE RD   06708   3-00011
   Timothy McDonald, prin.   757-9248
Industrial Management and Training   2-CS
   233 MILL ST   06706   753-7910
Mattatuck Community College   4-CC
   750 CHASE PKY   06708   575-0328
Sacred Heart HS, PO BOX 2120   06722   2-00011
   Richard Bishop, prin.   753-1605
St. Margaret's-McTernan School   2-11111
   585 CHASE PKY   06708   757-6640
   James Adams, prin.
St. Mary's Hospital   HSP
   41 JOHN ST   06708   574-6445
Teikyo Post University   4-UC
   PO BOX 2540   06723   755-0121
University of Connecticut   2-CC
   32 HILLSIDE AVE   06710   757-1231
Waterbury Hospital   HSP
   64 ROBBINS ST   06708   573-7334
Waterbury State Technical College   4-CC
   750 CHASE PKY   06708   575-8083

Waterford, AC 203, PC 5, New London
Waterford SD, 15 ROPE FERRY RD   06385   5-11111
   Randall Collins, supt.   444-5801
HS, 20 ROPE FERRY RD   06385   3-00011
   Michael Graner, prin.   442-9401
Clark Lane JHS, 105 CLARK LN   06385   2-00100
   Alfred Treidel, prin.   443-2837

Watertown, AC 203, PC 6, Litchfield
Watertown SD, 10 DEFOREST ST   06795   5-11111
   Dinoo Dastur, supt.   945-4801
HS, 324 FRENCH ST   06795   3-00011
   William Williams, prin.   945-4810
   Other Schools – See Oakville

Porter and Chester Institute   4-CS
320 SYLVAN LAKE RD   06779   274-9294
Taft S, 110 WOODBURY RD   06795   3-00011
   Lance Odden, prin.   274-2516

Westbrook, AC 203, PC 4, Middlesex
Westbrook SD   3-11111
   105 GOODSPEED DR   06498   399-6432
   Dalton Marks, supt.
HS, 156 MCVEAGH RD   06498   2-00011
   Carmen Marottolo, prin.   399-6214
MS, 866 BOSTON POST RD   06498   2-00100
   Philip House, prin.   399-9287

Oxford Academy, PO BOX P   06498   1-00111
   Philip Davis, prin.   399-6247

West Hartford, AC 203, PC 8, Hartford
West Hartford SD, 28 S MAIN ST   06107   6-11111
   John Battles, supt.   523-3500
Conard HS, 110 BERKSHIRE RD   06107   4-00011
   John Smith, prin.   521-1350
Hall HS, 975 N MAIN ST   06117   4-00011
   Elaine Bessette, prin.   232-4561
King Philip MS   3-00100
   100 KING PHILIP DR   06117   233-8236
   Paul Berkel, prin.

Sedgwick MS, 128 SEDGWICK RD   06107   3-00100
   Joan Kaiser, prin.   521-0610

American School for the Deaf   HND
   139 N MAIN ST   06107
Kingswood-Oxford S   3-00111
   170 KINGSWOOD RD   06119   233-9631
   Lee Levison, prin.
Northwest Catholic HS   2-00011
   29 WAMPANOAG DR   06117   236-4221
   Michael Griffin, prin.
St. Joseph College   3-UC
   1678 ASYLUM AVE   06117   232-4571
St. Timothy MS   2-00100
   225 KING PHILIP DR   06117   236-0614
   Robert DeBurro, prin.
University of Connecticut   2-CC
   1800 ASYLUM AVE   06117   241-4700
University of Hartford   6-UC
   200 BLOOMFIELD AVE   06117   768-4296

West Haven, AC 203, PC 8, New Haven
West Haven SD, 25 OGDEN ST   06516   6-11111
   John Onofrio, supt.   934-6631
HS, 1 CIRCLE ST   06516   4-00011
   Kenneth Henrici, prin.   932-5701
Bailey MS, 106 MORGAN LN   06516   2-00100
   David Shea, prin.   934-4985
Carrigan MS, 2 TETLOW ST   06516   3-00100
   Frank Raffone, prin.   934-4161

Baran Institute of Technology   2-CS
   15 KIMBERLY AVE   06516   934-7289
Notre Dame HS, 24 RICARDO ST   06516   3-00011
   Thomas Neagle, prin.   933-1673
Technical Careers Institute   4-CS
   11 KIMBERLY AVE   06516   932-2282
University of New Haven   5-UC
   300 ORANGE AVE   06516   932-7000

Weston, AC 203, PC 4, Fairfield
Weston SD, 135 SCHOOL RD   06883   4-11111
   K. Trigaux, supt.   221-3406
HS, 115 SCHOOL RD   06883   2-00011
   William Coan, prin.   222-2543
MS, 135 SCHOOL RD   06883   2-01100
   Richard Miller, prin.   222-2573

Westport, AC 203, PC 7, Fairfield
Westport SD, 110 MYRTLE AVE   06880   5-11111
   Paul Kelleher, supt.   227-8451
Staples HS, 70 NORTH AVE   06880   3-00011
   Gloria Rakovic, prin.   222-1209
Bedford MS, 170 RIVERSIDE AVE   06880   2-01100
   Glenn Hightower, prin.   227-8451
Coleytown MS, 255 NORTH AVE   06880   2-01100
   Daniel Christianson, prin.   227-8451

Connecticut Center for Massage Therapy   2-CS
   25 SYLVAN RD S   06880   221-7325

West Redding, AC 203, PC 2, Fairfield
Redding SD
   Supt. — See Easton
Read MS, ROUTE 53   06875   2-00100
   Dianne Otteson, prin.   938-2533

Regional SD 9
   Supt. — See Easton
Barlow HS   3-00011
   100 BLACK ROCK TPKE   06896   334-8003
   Nelson Quinby, prin.

Institute of Children's Literature   HMS
   93 LONG RIDGE RD   06896   800-243-9645
Long Ridge Writers Group   06896   HMS
   800-624-1476

West Simsbury, AC 203, PC 4, Hartford

Masters S, PO BOX 143   06092   2-11111
   Donald Steele, prin.   651-9361

West Willington, AC 203, PC 2, Tolland
Willington SD, 111 RIVER RD   06279   3-11100
   Michael McKee, supt.   429-3424
Hall Memorial MS, 111 RIVER RD   06279   2-01100
   Robert McGray, prin.   429-9391

Wethersfield, AC 203, PC 8, Hartford
Wethersfield SD, 51 WILLOW ST   06109   5-11111
   Richard Zanini, supt.   563-8181
HS, 411 WOLCOTT HILL RD   06109   3-00011
   Daniel Casey, prin.   563-8181
Deane MS   2-00100
   551 SILAS DEANE HWY   06109   563-3490
   Kenneth Edwards, prin.

Porter and Chester Institute   3-CS
   125 SILAS DEANE HWY   06109   529-2519

Willimantic, AC 203, PC 7, Windham
Vocational-Technical SD
   Supt. — See Middletown
Windham Vo-Tech HS   Vo Tech
   210 BIRCH ST   06226   456-3879
   Charles Wilt, prin.

Windham SD, 322 PROSPECT ST   06226   5-11111
   C. Patrick Proctor, supt.   423-8401
Windham HS, 355 HIGH ST   06226   3-00011
   Donald Berkowitz, prin.   423-8401
Kramer MS, 322 PROSPECT ST   06226   3-00100
   Ann Richardson, prin.   423-8401

Eastern Connecticut State University   5-UC
   83 WINDHAM ST   06226   456-5286
Windham Commmunity Memorial Hospital   HSP
   112 MANSFIELD AVE   06226   423-9201

Wilton, AC 203, PC 6, Fairfield
Wilton SD, PO BOX 277   06897   5-11111
   David Clune, supt.   762-3381
HS, 395 DANBURY RD   06897   3-00011
   John Sullivan, prin.   762-0381
Middlebrook MS   3-00100
   363 DANBURY RD   06897   762-8388
   Thomas Wiedenman, prin.

Windsor, AC 203, PC 7, Hartford
Windsor SD, PO BOX 10   06095   5-11111
   James Myers, supt.   688-3631
HS, 50 SAGE PARK RD   06095   4-00011
   Lawrence Shea, prin.   688-8334
Sage Park MS, 25 SAGE PARK RD   06095   3-00100
   William Sanders, prin.   688-6415

Baran Institute of Technology   2-CS
   611 DAY HILL RD   06095   688-3353
Loomis Chaffee S   3-00011
   4 BATCHELDER RD   06095   688-4934
   John Ratte, prin.
Technical Careers Institute   2-CS
   605 DAY HILL RD   06095   800-525-0415

Windsor Locks, AC 203, PC 7, Hartford
Windsor Locks SD, 50 CHURCH ST   06096   4-11111
   Lloyd Calvert, supt.   292-5000
HS, 58 S ELM ST   06096   2-00011
   Stephen Cullinan, prin.   292-5032
MS, 7 CENTER ST   06096   2-00100
   Carol Janssen, prin.   292-5012

Winsted, AC 203, PC 6, Litchfield
Endowed & Incorporated Academies   3-00011
   200 WILLIAMS AVE   06098   379-8521
   Robert Gazda, supt.
Gilbert S, 200 WILLIAMS AVE   06098   3-00011
   Robert Gazda, prin.   379-8521

Regional SD 7, PO BOX 656   06098   3-00111
   Robert Fish, supt.   379-1084
Northwestern Regional JSHS   3-00111
   7 CENTRAL AVE   06098   379-8525
   E. Llodra, prin.

Winchester SD, 338 MAIN ST   06098   4-11111
   David Bristol, supt.   379-0706
Pearson MS, 2 WETMORE AVE   06098   2-00100
   Gary Travers, prin.   379-7588

Northwestern Connecticut Comm. College   4-CC
   2 PARK PL   06098   379-8543

Wolcott, AC 203, PC 6, New Haven
Wolcott SD, 154 CENTER ST   06716   5-11111
   Thomas Jakubaitis, supt.   879-1484
HS, 457 BOUND LINE RD   06716   3-00011
   John Cook, prin.   879-1434
Alcott MS, 1490 WOODTICK RD   06716   3-00100
   Robert Gerace, prin.   879-2517

Woodbridge, AC 203, PC 6, New Haven
Regional SD 5, 25 NEWTON RD   06525   4-00111
   Stephen Gordon, supt.   397-4811
Amity Regional SHS   3-00001
   25 NEWTON RD   06525   397-4830
   Patricia Foley, prin.
   Other Schools – See Bethany, Orange

Woodbury, AC 203, PC 4, Litchfield
Regional SD 14, 129 MAIN ST N   06798   4-11111
   Joseph Sabatella, supt.   263-4339
Nonnewaug HS   3-00011
   5 MINORTOWN RD   06798   263-2186
   Rob Asman, prin.
MS, 67 WASHINGTON AVE   06798   2-00100
   John Keating, prin.   263-4306

Woodstock, AC 203, PC 2, Windham
Endowed & Incorporated Academies   3-00011
   ACADEMY RD   06281   928-6575
   William Troy, supt.
Woodstock Academy   3-00011
   ACADEMY RD   06281   928-6575
   William Troy, prin.

DELAWARE

STATE DEPARTMENT OF PUBLIC INSTRUCTION
Townsend Building
P.O. Box 1402, Dover 19903
(302) 736-4601

Superintendent of Public Instruction	Pascal Forgione
Deputy Superintendent	James Spartz
Assistant Superintendent Administrative Services	Jack Nichols
Associate Superintendent Standards & Curriculum	Bonnie Lesley
Associate Superintendent Assessments & Accountability	Marsha DeLain
Associate Superintendent Improvement & Assistance	Valerie Woodruff

STATE BOARD OF EDUCATION
P.O. Box 1402, Dover 19903

President   Paul Fine

PUBLIC, PRIVATE AND CATHOLIC SECONDARY SCHOOLS

Bear, AC 302, PC 4, New Castle

Caravel Academy	3-11111	
2801 DEL LAWS RD 19701	834-8938	
Carl Rice, prin.		

Bridgeville, AC 302, PC 4, Sussex
Woodbridge SD, PO BOX 427 19933 — 4-11111
Robert Sutton, supt. — 337-8296
Woodbridge HS, 307 S LAWS ST 19933 — 3-00011
Walter Gilefski, prin. — 337-8289
Woodbridge JHS — 2-00100
120 EDGEWOOD ST 19933 — 337-0533
Bayard Hendricks, prin.

Camden-Wyoming, AC 302, PC see Wyoming
Caesar Rodney SD — 6-11111
PO BOX 188 19934 — 697-2173
William Bach, supt.
Rodney HS, 239 OLD NORTH RD 19934 — 4-00011
David Robinson, prin. — 697-2161
Rodney JHS — 3-00100
25 E CAMDEN WYOMING AVE 19934 — 697-3203
Harold Roberts, prin.
Other Schools – See Dover

Claymont, AC 302, PC 7, New Castle
Brandywine SD — 7-11111
1000 PENNSYLVANIA AVE 19703 — 792-3800
Carl Smith, supt.
Other Schools – See Wilmington

Archmere Academy — 2-00011
3600 PHILADELPHIA PIKE 19703 — 798-6632
Fr. McLaughlin, prin.

Delaware City, AC 302, PC 4, New Castle
Colonial SD
Supt. — See New Castle
Gunning Bedford MS — 4-00100
PO BOX 560 19706 — 323-2870
Richard Farmer, prin.

Delmar, AC 302, PC 3, Sussex
Delmar SD, 300 N 8TH ST 19940 — 3-00111
Wayne Bastian, supt. — 846-9544
JSHS, 300 N 8TH ST 19940 — 3-00111
Jay Green, prin. — 846-9544

Dover, AC 302, PC 8, Kent
Caesar Rodney SD
Supt. — See Camden-Wyoming
Dover AFB MS — 2-00100
3100 HAWTHORNE DR 19901 — 674-3284
Charles Szvitich, prin.

Capital SD, 945 FOREST ST 19901 — 6-11111
Joseph Crossen, supt. — 672-1556
HS, 625 WALKER RD 19901 — 4-00011
William McGlumphy, prin. — 672-1526
Central MS, 0 DELAWARE AVE 19901 — 3-00100
Faith Newton, prin. — 672-1772

Polytech SD
Supt. — See Woodside
Polytech North HS — 2-00011
100 DENNYS RD 19901 — 674-5015
Dianne Sole, prin.

Delaware State College — 5-UC
1200 N DUPONT HWY 19901 — 739-4901
Delaware Technical & Community College — 4-CC
1832 N DUPONT HWY 19901 — 739-5321
Wesley College — 4-UC
120 N STATE ST 19901 — 739-2300

Felton, AC 302, PC 3, Kent
Lake Forest SD, RR 1 BOX 847-A 19943 — 5-11111
James VanSciver, supt. — 284-3020
Lake Forest HS, RR 1 BOX 847 19943 — 3-00011
(—), prin. — 284-9291
Other Schools – See Harrington

Frankford, AC 302, PC 3, Sussex
Indian River SD, RR 2 BOX 236 19945 — 6-11111
Charles Hudson, supt. — 436-1000
Indian River HS — 3-00011
RR 3 BOX 112 19945 — 732-3800
Lewis Patterson, prin.
Other Schools – See Georgetown, Millsboro,
Selbyville

Georgetown, AC 302, PC 5, Sussex
Indian River SD
Supt. — See Frankford
Sussex Central HS — 3-00011
301 W MARKET ST 19947 — 856-1900
John McCarthy, prin.

Sussex County Voc-Tech SD — 4-00011
PO BOX 351 19947 — 856-2541
George Frunzi, supt.
Sussex Tech High School — 3-00011
PO BOX 351 19947 — 856-0961
Patrick Savini, prin.

Delaware Technical & Community College — 5-CC
PO BOX 610 19947 — 856-5400

Greenville, AC 302, PC 3, New Castle
Red Clay Cons. SD
Supt. — See Wilmington
DuPont HS, 50 HILLSIDE RD 19807 — 4-00011
Susan Rash, prin. — 651-2626
DuPont MS, 3130 KENNETT PIKE 19807 — 4-00100
Harry Hinman, prin. — 651-2690

Harrington, AC 302, PC 4, Kent
Lake Forest SD
Supt. — See Felton
Chipman MS, 101 W CENTER ST 19952 — 4-00100
James Boyd, prin. — 398-8197

Hockessin, AC 302, PC 4, New Castle
Red Clay Cons. SD
Supt. — See Wilmington
DuPont MS — 3-00100
735 MEETING HOUSE RD 19707 — 239-3421
Robert Bartoli, prin.

Sanford S, PO BOX 888 19707 — 3-11111
Kristi Kerins, prin. — 239-5263
Wilmington Christian S — 1-11111
PO BOX 626 19707 — 239-2121
Sandy Outlar, prin.

Laurel, AC 302, PC 5, Sussex
Laurel SD, 815 S CENTRAL AVE 19956 — 4-11111
Heinz Retzlaff, supt. — 875-6100
HS, 1133 S CENTRAL AVE 19956 — 2-00011
Keith Duda, prin. — 875-6120
Laurel Central MS — 3-00100
801 S CENTRAL AVE 19956 — 875-6110
Donna Spedden, prin.

Lewes, AC 302, PC 4, Sussex
Cape Henlopen SD — 5-11111
1270 KINGS HWY 19958 — 645-6686
Suellen Skeen, supt.
Cape Henlopen HS — 3-00011
1250 KINGS HWY 19958 — 645-7711
Ronald Burrows, prin.
MS, 820 SAVANNAH RD 19958 — 2-01100
Gary Wray, prin. — 645-6288
Other Schools – See Milton

Beebe Medical Center School of Nursing — HSP
424 SAVANNAH RD 19958 — 645-3251

Middletown, AC 302, PC 5, New Castle
Appoquinimink SD
Supt. — See Odessa
HS, 504 S BROAD ST 19709 — 3-00011
William Cohee, prin. — 378-5000
Redding MS, 201 NEW ST 19709 — 3-00100
Mark Zawislak, prin. — 378-5030

St. Andrew's S — 2-00011
350 NOXONTOWN RD 19709 — 378-9511
Jonathan O'Brien, prin.

Milford, AC 302, PC 6, Kent
Milford SD, 906 LAKEVIEW AVE 19963 — 5-11111
Charles Moses, supt. — 422-1600
HS, 1019 N WALNUT ST 19963 — 3-00011
Robert Rescigno, prin. — 422-1610
MS, 612 LAKEVIEW AVE 19963 — 4-01100
Gary Annett, prin. — 422-1620

Millsboro, AC 302, PC 4, Sussex
Indian River SD
Supt. — See Frankford
Sussex Central MS — 3-00100
PO BOX 668 19966 — 934-3200
Robert Powell, prin.

Milton, AC 302, PC 4, Sussex
Cape Henlopen SD
Supt. — See Lewes
MS, 512 FEDERAL ST 19968 — 2-01100
William Howell, prin. — 684-8516

Newark, AC 302, PC 8, New Castle
Christina SD, 83 E MAIN ST 19711 — 7-11111
Iris Metts, supt. — 454-2000
Christiana HS — 4-00011
190 SALEM CHURCH RD 19713 — 454-2123
(—), prin.
Glasgow HS — 4-00011
1901 S COLLEGE AVE 19702 — 454-2381
Robert Anderson, prin.
HS, 750 E DELAWARE AVE 19711 — 4-00011
Francis Hagen, prin. — 454-2151
Gauger-Cobbs MS, 50 GENDER RD 19713 — 4-00100
John Vann, prin. — 454-2358

Kirk MS, 140 BRENNEN DR 19713 — 3-00100
Laverne Terry, prin. — 454-2164
Shue-Medill MS — 3-00100
1500 CAPITOL TRL 19711 — 454-2171
Robert Adams, prin.

New Castle County Voc-Tech SD
Supt. — See Wilmington
Hodgson Voc.-Tech. HS — 3-00011
2575 SUMMIT BRIDGE RD 19702 — 834-0990
Steven Godowsky, prin.

Delaware Technical & Community College — 6-CC
400 STANTON CHRISTIANA RD 19713
454-3917
University of Delaware 19711 — 7-UC
451-2000
USA Training Academy — 3-HMS
17 HAINES ST 19711

New Castle, AC 302, PC 5, New Castle
Colonial SD, 318 E BASIN RD 19720 — 6-11111
David Campbell, supt. — 323-2700
Penn HS, 713 E BASIN RD 19720 — 4-00011
William Roberts, prin. — 323-2801
MS, 903 DELAWARE ST 19720 — 3-00100
Ronald Meade, prin. — 323-2880
Read MS, 314 E BASIN RD 19720 — 3-00100
John Minker, prin. — 323-2760
Other Schools – See Delaware City

Dawn Training Institute — 1-CS
120 OLD CHURCHMANS RD 19720
800-323-9695
Wilmington College — 4-UC
320 N DUPONT HWY 19720 — 328-9401

Odessa, AC 302, PC 2, New Castle
Appoquinimink SD — 4-11111
PO BOX 4010 19730 — 378-5010
John Holton, supt.
Other Schools – See Middletown

Seaford, AC 302, PC 6, Sussex
Seaford SD, 1 DELAWARE PL 19973 — 5-11111
Russell Knorr, supt. — 629-4587
HS, 399 N MARKET ST 19973 — 3-00011
Richard Kapolka, prin. — 629-4525
MS, 500 E STEIN HWY 19973 — 3-00100
George Stone, prin. — 629-4586

Selbyville, AC 302, PC 4, Sussex
Indian River SD
Supt. — See Frankford
MS, PO BOX 230 19975 — 3-00100
Howard Gerken, prin. — 436-1020

Smyrna, AC 302, PC 6, Kent
Smyrna SD, 22 S MAIN ST 19977 — 5-11111
Wayne Barton, supt. — 653-8585
JSHS, 85 DUCK CREEK PKY 19977 — 3-00111
Alfred DiEmedio, prin. — 653-8581

Wilmington, AC 302, PC 8, New Castle
Brandywine SD
Supt. — See Claymont
Brandywine HS, 1400 FOULK RD 19803 — 3-00011
Donald Fantine, prin. — 479-1600
Concord HS, 2501 EBRIGHT RD 19810 — 4-00011
Ben Ellis, prin. — 475-3951
Mt. Pleasant HS — 3-00011
5201 WASHINGTON BLVD 19809 — 762-7125
Thomas Lapinski, prin.
Hanby JHS, 2523 BERWYN RD 19810 — 3-00100
James Bruton, prin. — 479-1631
Talley JHS, 1110 CYPRESS RD 19810 — 3-00100
Barry Bogden, prin. — 475-3976
New Castle County Voc-Tech SD — 5-00011
1417 NEWPORT RD 19804 — 995-8000
Dennis Loftus, supt.
Delcastle Technical HS — 4-00011
1417 NEWPORT RD 19804 — 995-8100
John Moyle, prin.
Howard Career Center HS — 3-00011
401 E 12TH ST 19801 — 571-5400
Henry Stenta, prin.
Other Schools – See Newark

Red Clay Cons. SD — 7-11111
1400 N WASHINGTON ST 19801 — 651-2600
Robert Simons, supt.
Dickinson HS — 3-00011
1801 MILLTOWN RD 19808 — 992-5500
Spencer Henry, prin.
McKean HS — 3-00011
301 MCKENNANS CHURCH RD 19808 — 992-5520
Craig Deidrick, prin.
HS, 100 N DUPONT RD 19807 — 3-00011
John Dohler, prin. — 651-2700
Conrad MS, 201 JACKSON AVE 19804 — 3-00100
Nancy Weaver, prin. — 992-5545

Skyline MS, 2900 SKYLINE DR 19808 — 3-00100
Lorelei Meanor, prin. — 454-3410
Stanton MS, 1800 LIMESTONE RD 19804 — 3-00100
Richard DiBlassio, prin. — 992-5540
Other Schools – See Greenville, Hockessin

Career Institute — 2-CS
711 N MARKET ST 19801 — 575-1400
Delaware Technical & Community College — 4-CC
333 N SHIPLEY ST 19801 — 571-5474
Goldey Beacom College — 4-UC
4701 LIMESTONE RD 19808 — 998-8814
Padua Academy — 3-00011
905 N BROOM ST 19806 — 421-3739
Sr. Ann Zwosta, prin.
St. Edmond's Academy — 2-01100
2120 VEALE RD 19810 — 475-5370
Br. Michael Smith, prin.
St. Elizabeth HS, 1500 CEDAR ST 19805 — 2-00011
Sr. Mary Hussey, prin. — 656-3369
St. Francis Hospital — HSP
701 N CLAYTON ST 19805 — 421-4801
St. Marks HS — 4-00011
2501 PIKE CREEK RD 19808 — 738-3300
Ronald Russo, prin.
Salesianum HS — 3-00011
1801 N BROOM ST 19802 — 654-2495
Fr. McGee, prin.
Star Technical Institute — 2-CS
631 W NEWPORT PIKE 19804 — 762-8324
Tatnall S, 1501 BARLEY MILL RD 19807 — 3-11111
Edward Lingenheld, prin. — 998-2292
Tower Hill S, 2813 W 17TH ST 19806 — 3-11111
Timothy Golding, prin. — 575-0550
Ursuline Academy — 3-11111
1106 PENNSYLVANIA AVE 19806 — 658-7158
Marie Beldyk, prin.
Widener University School of Law — 2-UC
PO BOX 7474 19803 — 478-5280
Wilmington Friends S — 3-11111
101 SCHOOL RD 19803 — 576-2900
Carol Ramsey, prin.

Woodside, AC 302, PC 2, Kent
Polytech SD, PO BOX 97 19980 — 3-00011
Jeff Adams, supt. — 697-2170
Polytech HS, PO BOX 97 19980 — 2-00011
Dianne Sole, prin. — 697-3255
Other Schools – See Dover

DISTRICT OF COLUMBIA

DISTRICT OF COLUMBIA PUBLIC SCHOOLS
415 12th St., N.W., Washington 20004
(202) 724-4222

Superintendent of Schools — Franklin Smith
Vice Superintendent — Kenneth Milner
Associate Superintendent — Constance Clark
Deputy Superintendent Administrative Services — Shelia Handy
Director of Personnel Services — James Daugherty

STATE BOARD OF EDUCATION
415 12th St., N.W., Washington 20004

President — Linda Moody

PUBLIC, PRIVATE AND CATHOLIC SECONDARY SCHOOLS

Washington, AC 202, PC 11, District of Columbia
District of Columbia SD — 8-11111
415 12TH ST NW 20004 — 724-4044
F. Dukes McKensie, supt.
Cardozo SHS — 3-00001
1300 CLIFTON ST NW 20009 — 673-7385
Bernard Lucas, prin.
Dunbar SHS — 3-00001
1301 NEW JERSEY AVE NW 20001 — 673-7233
Eva Rousseau, prin.
Phelps SHS, 704 26TH ST NE 20002 — 2-00001
Earnest Johnson, prin. — 724-4516
Senate Page SHS — 1-00001
1ST ST & INDEPENDNCE SE 20540 — 224-3926
Blanche Williams, prin.

Spingarn SHS — 3-00001
2500 BENNING RD NE 20002 — 724-4525
Elizabeth Smith, prin.
Woodson SHS, 5500 EADS ST NE 20019 — 4-00001
Lucile Christian, prin. — 724-4500
Anacostia HS, 1601 16TH ST SE 20020 — 3-00011
Zavolia Willis, prin. — 767-7040
Ballou HS, 3401 4TH ST SE 20032 — 4-00011
Richard Washington, prin. — 767-7071
Banneker HS, 800 EUCLID ST NW 20001 — 2-00011
Linette Adams, prin. — 673-7322
Bell Multi-Cultural HS — 3-00011
3145 HIATT PL NW 20010 — 673-7314
Maria Tukeva, prin.
Coolidge HS, 6315 5TH ST NW 20011 — 3-00011
Leonard Upson, prin. — 576-6143

DC Street Academy HS — 2-00011
10TH ST & MONROE STS NE 20017 — 576-7005
Reginald Elliott, prin.
Eastern HS — 4-00011
1700 E CAPITOL ST SE 20003 — 724-4805
Ralph Neal, prin.
Ellington HS of the Arts — 2-00011
3500 R ST NW 20007 — 282-0123
Carolyn Wilson, prin.
McKinley/Penn HS, 151 T ST NE 20002 — 3-00011
James Greene, prin. — 576-6011
Roosevelt HS, 4301 13TH ST NW 20011 — 3-00011
Robert Gill, prin. — 576-6130
Washington Dix Street Academy HS — 2-00011
6TH AND BRENTWOOD PKY NE 20002
Jerome Shelton, prin. — 724-4562

Wilson HS   4-00011
  3950 CHESAPEAKE ST NW   20016   282-0120
  Wilma Bonner, prin.
Backus JHS   2-00110
  5171 S DAKOTA AVE NE   20017   576-6110
  Ann Hilliard, prin.
Browne JHS, 850 26TH ST NE   20002   3-00110
  Cynthia Clark, prin.   724-4547
Deal JHS, 3815 FORT DR NW   20016   3-00110
  Reginald Moss, prin.   282-0100
Douglass JHS   2-00110
  2620 DOUGLASS RD SE   20020   767-7190
  Louise Buckner, prin.
Eliot JHS   2-00110
  1830 CONSTITUTION AVE NE   20002   724-4665
  Glennis Powell, prin.
Evans JHS   2-00110
  5600 E CAPITOL ST NE   20019   724-4727
  Zory Kenon, prin.
Francis JHS, 2425 N ST NW   20037   3-00110
  Courtney Fletcher, prin.   724-4841
Garnet-Patterson MS   2-00100
  10TH & U STS NW   20001   673-7329
  John Wood, prin.
Hardy MS   2-01100
  1550 FOXHALL RD NW   20007   282-0136
  Amanda Garnett, prin.
Hart JHS, 601 MISSISSIPPI AVE SE   20032   3-00110
  Evelyn Gainous, prin.   767-7077
Hine JHS, 335 8TH ST SE   20003   3-00110
  Princess Whitfield, prin.   724-4772
Jefferson JHS, 8TH AND H ST SW   20011   3-00110
  Vera White, prin.   724-4881
Johnson JHS, 1400 BRUCE PL SE   20020   3-00110
  Gwendolyn Paramore, prin.   767-7110
Kramer JHS, 1700 Q ST SE   20020   2-00110
  Raymond Poles, prin.   767-7080
Langley JHS, 101 T ST NE   20002   2-00110
  Tyrone Hopkins, prin.   576-6326
Lincoln JHS, 3101 16TH ST NW   20010   3-00110
  Roberto Butler, prin.   673-7345
MacFarland MS   2-00100
  4400 IOWA AVE NW   20011   576-6207
  Debra Nesmith, prin.
Miller JHS, 201 49TH ST NE   20019   2-00110
  Ronald Hasty, prin.   724-4611
Paul JHS, 5830 8TH ST NW   20011   3-00110
  Cecile Middleton, prin.   576-6190
Roper JHS, 4800 MEADE ST NE   20019   2-00110
  Helena Jones, prin.   724-4632
Shaw JHS   3-00110
  925 RHODE ISLAND AVE NW   20001   673-7203
  Percy Ellis, prin.
Sousa MS, 3650 ELY PL SE   20019   3-01100
  William Lipscomb, prin.   767-7020
Stuart-Hobson MS   2-01100
  4TH & E STS NE   20002   724-4758
  Helen Flagg, prin.
Taft JHS, 1800 PERRY ST NE   20018   2-00110
  James Howell, prin.   576-6101

Terrell JHS   2-00110
  1ST & PIERCE STS NW   20001   724-4898
  Vernon Baker, prin.

American University, The   7-UC
  4400 MASSACHUSETTS AVE NW   20016
                                           885-1000
Archbishop Carroll HS   3-00011
  4300 HAREWOOD RD NE   20017   529-0900
  Wilma Durham, prin.
Ardis School of Fashion Design   2-CS
  1728 CONNECTICUT AVE NW   20009   234-6537
Automation Academy   2-CS
  666 11TH ST NW STE 750   20001   638-6677
Barclay Career School   2-CS
  1511 K ST NW STE 200   20005   347-7200
Burke S, 2955 UPTON ST NW   20008   2-00111
  Jean Mooskin, prin.   362-8882
Catholic University of America   6-UC
  620 MICHIGAN AVE NE   20064   319-5000
Corcoran School of Art   2-UC
  500 17TH ST NW   20006   628-9484
De Sales School of Theology   1-UC
  721 LAWRENCE ST NE   20017   269-9412
Devereux Childrens Center of Washington   2-HND
  3050 R ST NW   20007   282-1200
District of Columbia School of Law   2-UC
  719 13TH ST NW   20005   727-5232
Dominican House of Studies   1-UC
  487 MICHIGAN AVE NE   20017   529-5300
Field S, 2126 WYOMING AVE NW   20008   2-00111
  Elizabeth Ely, prin.   232-0733
Gallaudet University   4-UC
  800 FLORIDA AVE NE   20002   651-5000
Georgetown Day S   4-11111
  4530 MACARTHUR BLVD NW   20007   333-7727
  Gladys Stern, prin.
Georgetown University   7-UC
  37TH AND O STS NW   20057   687-0100
Georgetown Visatation Prep HS   2-00011
  1524 35TH ST NW   20007   337-3350
  Daniel Kearns, prin.
George Washington University   20052   7-UC
                                           994-1000
Gonzaga College HS, 19 I ST NW   20001   3-00011
  Joseph Ciancaglini, prin.   842-1650
Howard University   7-UC
  2400 6TH ST NW   20059   636-6100
Howard University Divinity School   2-UC
  1400 SHEPHERD ST NE   20017   806-0500
Johns Hopkins University   2-UC
  1740 MASSACHUSETTS AVE NW   20036
Levine School of Music   2-CS
  1690 36TH ST NW   20007   337-2227
Maret S   2-11111
  3000 CATHEDRAL AVE NW   20068   939-8800
  Peter Sturtevant, prin.
McGraw-Hill Continuing Education Center   HMS
  4401 CONNECTICUT AVE NW   20008

Model Secondary School for the Deaf   HND
  KENDALL GREEN   20002
Mt. Vernon College   3-UC
  2100 FOXHALL RD NW   20007   625-4682
National Cathedral S   3-11111
  3609 WOODLEY RD NW   20016   537-6300
  Agnes Underwood, prin.
National Conservatory of Dramatic Arts   1-CS
  1556 WISCONSIN AVE NW   20007   333-2202
NEC-Capitol Hill Campus   3-CS
  810 1ST ST NE   20002   289-7700
Oakcrest HS, 4101 YUMA ST NW   20016   2-00111
  Barbara Falk, prin.   686-9736
Oblate College   1-UC
  391 MICHIGAN AVE NE   20017   529-6544
Our Lady of Perpetual Help ES   1-01100
  1604 MORRIS RD SE   20020   678-0211
  Sr. Elizabeth Semmelmayer, prin.
PTC Career Institute   2-CS
  529 14TH ST NW STE 350   20045   638-5300
St. Alban's S   3-01111
  MOUNT SAINT ALBAN   20016   537-6435
  Mark Mullins, prin.
St. Anselms Abbey S   2-00111
  4501 S DAKOTA AVE NE   20017   269-2350
  Fr. Weigand, prin.
St. Johns College HS   3-00111
  2607 MILITARY RD NW   20015   363-2316
  Br. Gallagher, prin.
Sidwell Friends S   2-01111
  3825 WISCONSIN AVE NW   20016   537-8150
  Robert Williams, prin.
Southeastern University   4-UC
  501 I ST SW   20024   488-8162
Strayer College   4-UC
  1025 15TH ST NW   20005   728-0355
Strayer College   3-CS
  6830 LAUREL ST NW   20012   722-8100
Trinity College   4-UC
  125 MICHIGAN AVE NE   20017   939-5000
University of the District of Columbia   4-UC
  1100 HARVARD ST NW   20009   673-7021
University of the District of Columbia   7-UC
  4200 CONNECTICUT AVE NW   20008   282-7300
University of the District of Columbia   4-UC
  800 MOUNT VERNON PL NW   20001   282-7300
Walter Reed Medical Center   HSP
  6825 16TH ST NW   20307   576-1100
Washington Conservatory of Music   2-CS
  PO BOX 5758   20016   320-2770
Washington Hospital Center   HSP
  110 IRVING ST NW   20010   877-6101
Washington Internationl S   3-11111
  3100 MACOMB ST NW   20008   364-1800
  Anne Pierce, prin.
Wesley Theological Seminary   2-UC
  4500 MASSACHUSETTS AVE NW   20016
                                           885-8600

FLORIDA

STATE DEPARTMENT OF EDUCATION
Florida Education Center
325 W. Gaines St., Tallahassee 32399
(904) 487-1785

Commissioner of Education	Betty Castor
Deputy Commissioner Planning, Budgeting & Management	William Golden
Deputy Commissioner Educational Facilities	H. James Schroeer
Deputy Commissioner Human Resource Development	Altha Manning
Deputy Commissioner Public Schools	Walter McCarroll

STATE BOARD OF EDUCATION
325 W. Gaines St., Tallahassee 32399

Chairperson	Governor Lawton Chiles

PUBLIC, PRIVATE AND CATHOLIC SECONDARY SCHOOLS

Alachua, AC 904, PC 5, Alachua
Alachua County SD
Supt. — See Gainesville
Santa Fe HS, RR 2 BOX 312 32615 3-00011
Ronald Nelson, prin. 462-1125
Mebane MS, RR 1 BOX 4 32615 3-00100
Charles Hall, prin. 462-1648

Altamonte Springs, AC 407, PC 8, Seminole
Seminole County SD
Supt. — See Sanford
Lake Brantley HS 5-00011
991 SAND LAKE RD 32714 862-1776
Darvin Boothe, prin.
Teague MS, 1100 SAND LAKE RD 32714 4-00100
Sidney Boyette, prin. 862-1519

Altamonte Christian S 2-11111
601 PALM SPRINGS DR 32701 831-0950
Gale Callaghan, prin.
Central Christian Academy 2-11111
536 E HIGHLAND ST 32701 332-6988
William Miller, prin.

Altha, AC 904, PC 2, Calhoun
Calhoun County SD
Supt. — See Blountstown
S, PO BOX 67 32421 2-11111
Harriett Peacock, prin. 762-3121

Alva, AC 813, PC 4, Lee
Lee County SD
Supt. — See Fort Myers
MS, 21219 N RIVER RD 33920 3-00100
Stephen Hutnik, prin. 728-2525

Apalachicola, AC 904, PC 5, Franklin
Franklin County SD 4-11111
155 AVENUE E 32320 653-8831
C. T. Ponder, supt.
JSHS, 190 14TH ST 32320 2-00111
Edward Dugger, prin. 653-8811
Other Schools – See Carrabelle

Apopka, AC 407, PC 7, Orange
Orange County SD
Supt. — See Orlando
HS, 555 MARTIN ST 32712 4-00011
Joseph Joyner, prin. 889-4194
MS, 425 N PARK AVE 32712 4-00100
Gary Preisser, prin. 886-0434

Forest Lake Academy 2-00011
3909 E SEMORAN BLVD 32703 862-8411
Robert Caskey, prin.

Arcadia, AC 813, PC 6, De Soto
De Soto County SD 5-11111
530 LASALONA AVE 33821 494-4222
Adrian Cline, supt.
DeSoto County HS 3-00011
1710 E GIBSON ST 33821 494-3434
William Turner, prin.
DeSoto MS, 420 E GIBSON ST 33821 3-00100
Robert Hrstka, prin. 494-4133

Atlantic Beach, AC 904, PC 7, Duval
Duval County SD
Supt. — See Jacksonville
Mayport MS, 2600 MAYPORT RD 32233 4-00100
Ron Davis, prin. 247-5977

Auburndale, AC 813, PC 6, Polk
Polk County SD
Supt. — See Bartow
HS, 1 BLOODHOUND TRL 33823 4-00011
William Londeree, prin. 967-4173
Stambaugh MS 4-00100
1226 N BARTOW RD 33823 965-5494
Gerald Winsett, prin.

Avon Park, AC 813, PC 6, Highlands
Highlands County SD
Supt. — See Sebring
HS, 700 E MAIN ST 33825 3-00011
Barbara Dean, prin. 452-4311
MS, 401 S LAKE AVE 33825 3-00100
Rodney Hollinger, prin. 452-4333

South Florida Community College 4-CC
600 W COLLEGE DR 33825 453-6661

Babson Park, AC 813, PC 4, Polk

Webber College 2-UC
PO BOX 96 33827 638-1431

Baker, AC 904, PC 3, Okaloosa
Okaloosa County SD
Supt. — See Fort Walton Beach
S, 1369 14TH ST 32531 4-11111
Tom Grandstaff, prin. 689-7279

Baldwin, AC 904, PC 4, Duval
Duval County SD
Supt. — See Jacksonville
JSHS, 291 MILL ST W 32234 3-00111
Jean Blevins, prin. 266-1200

Bartow, AC 813, PC 7, Polk
Polk County SD, PO BOX 391 33830 8-11111
John Stewart, supt. 534-0500

HS, 1270 S BROADWAY AVE 33830 3-00011
Ernest Cooper, prin. 534-7400
MS, 550 E CLOWER ST 33830 3-00100
Harry Williams, prin. 534-7415
Union Academy MS 2-00100
1195 E WABASH ST 33830 534-7435
Flora Haire, prin.
Other Schools – See Auburndale, Eaton Park, Fort
Meade, Frostproof, Haines City, Lakeland, Lake
Wales, Mulberry, Winter Haven

Bell, AC 904, PC 2, Gilchrist
Gilchrist County SD
Supt. — See Trenton
JSHS, PO BOX 130 32619 2-00111
James Longstreth, prin. 463-3232

Belle Glade, AC 407, PC 7, Palm Beach
Palm Beach County SD
Supt. — See West Palm Beach
Glades Central HS 3-00011
425 W CANAL ST N 33430 996-4945
Effie Grear, prin.
West Tech Ctr, 2625 NW 16TH ST 33430 Vo Tech
Shirley Maxson, prin. 996-4930
Lake Shore MS 4-00100
1101 SW AVENUE E 33430 996-4960
Richard Ramsey, prin.

Christian Day S 2-11111
17 NW AVENUE B 33430 996-5598
Kathy McReynolds, prin.
Glades Day S, 400 NE AVENUE L 33430 2-11111
Edward Sizemore, prin. 996-6769
West Technical Education Center 2-CS
2625 NW 16TH ST 33430 996-4930

Belleview, AC 904, PC 5, Marion
Marion County SD
Supt. — See Ocala
MS, 10500 SE 36TH AVE 34420 3-00100
Chuck Glanzer, prin. 347-2050

Blountstown, AC 904, PC 4, Calhoun
Calhoun County SD 4-11111
425 E CENTRAL AVE 32424 674-5927
Darryl Taylor, supt.
HS, 614 N MAIN ST 32424 2-00011
James Dunn, prin. 674-5724
MS, 611 MAYHAW DR 32424 2-00100
Michael Johnson, prin. 674-8234
Other Schools – See Altha

Boca Raton, AC 407, PC 8, Palm Beach
Palm Beach County SD
Supt. — See West Palm Beach
HS, 1501 NW 15TH ST 33486 4-00011
Norman Shearin, prin. 338-1400
Olympic Heights HS 4-00011
20101 LYONS RD 33434 852-6900
Jake Sello, prin.
Spanish River Community HS 5-00011
5100 JOG RD 33496 241-2200
Arthur Johnson, prin.
MS, 1251 NW 8TH ST 33486 4-00100
Dick Reed, prin. 338-1458
Loggers Run Community MS 4-00100
11584 W PALMETTO PARK RD 33428 241-2265
Juanita Lampi, prin.

Florida Atlantic University 6-UC
500 NW 20TH ST 33431 367-3000
Lynn University 4-UC
3601 N MILITARY TRL 33431 800-544-8035
Pope John Paul II HS 3-00011
4001 N MILITARY TRL 33431 994-8998
Fr. Foley, prin.
St. Andrews S, 3900 JOG RD 33434 3-00111
Rev. Andrews, prin. 483-8900
Southern Career Institute 2-HMS
PO BOX 2158 33427
West Boca Medical Center HSP
21644 STATE ROAD 7 33428 488-8000

Bonifay, AC 904, PC 5, Holmes
Holmes County SD 5-11111
211 W IOWA AVE 32425 547-9341
Jack Jones, supt.
Holmes County HS 3-00011
825 W HIGHWAY 90 32425 547-9000
James Lee, prin.
Bethlehem S, RR 3 BOX 385 32425 3-11111
Odell Paul, prin. 547-3621
MS, 401 MCLAUGHLIN AVE 32425 2-00100
Peggy Alderman, prin. 547-9460
Other Schools – See Graceville, Ponce De Leon

Bonita Springs, AC 813, PC 7, Lee
Lee County SD
Supt. — See Fort Myers
MS, 10140 W TERRY ST 33923 4-00100
William Lane, prin. 992-4422

Boynton Beach, AC 407, PC 8, Palm Beach
Palm Beach County SD
Supt. — See West Palm Beach
South Tech Ctr Vo Tech
1300 SW 30TH AVE 33426 369-7000
James Rascoe, prin.
Congress MS 4-00100
101 S CONGRESS AVE 33426 369-7072
Samuel Watson, prin.

McAuliffe MS 4-00100
6500 LE CHALET BLVD 33437 369-7060
Camille Dorman, prin.

Bethesda-Kennedy Hospital HSP
2815 S SEACREST BLVD 33435 737-7733
St. Vincent DePaul Regional Seminary 1-UC
10701 S MILITARY TRL 33436 732-4424
South Technical Education Center 4-CS
1300 SW 30TH AVE 33426 369-7000

Bradenton, AC 813, PC 8, Manatee
Manatee County SD 8-11111
215 MANATEE AVE W 34205 741-7200
Gene Witt, supt.
Bayshore HS, 5323 34TH ST W 34210 4-00011
Robert Stewart, prin. 751-7004
Manatee HS, 1000 32ND ST W 34205 4-00011
Patricia Lucas, prin. 746-7181
Southeast HS, 1200 37TH AVE E 34208 4-00011
Ralph Heath, prin. 741-3366
Manatee Area Vo-Tech Ctr Vo Tech
5603 34TH ST W 34210 – (—), prin. 751-7900
Braden River MS 3-00100
6201 RIVER CLUB BLVD 34202 751-7080
George Douglas, prin.
MS, 202 13TH AVE E 34208 4-00100
Lynette Edwards, prin. 741-3344
Harllee MS, 6423 9TH ST E 34203 3-00100
Charles King, prin. 751-7027
King MS, 600 75TH ST NW 34209 4-00100
Nancy Carson, prin. 741-3183
Sugg MS, 3801 59TH ST W 34209 4-00100
Judy Bills, prin. 741-3157
Other Schools – See Palmetto

Bradenton Academy 2-11111
6210 17TH AVE W 34209 792-7838
Murray Gerber, prin.
Bradenton Christian S 3-11111
3304 43RD ST W 34209 792-5454
Gerald Mitchell, prin.
Community Christian S 2-11111
5500 18TH ST E 34203 756-8748
Sam Coleman, prin.
Manatee Area Vocational-Technical Center 3-CS
5603 34TH ST W 34210 755-2641
Manatee Community College 6-CC
5840 26TH ST W 34207 755-1511
St. Stephen's Episcopal S 2-11111
315 41ST ST W 34209 746-2121
John Howard, prin.

Brandon, AC 813, PC 8, Hillsborough
Hillsborough County SD
Supt. — See Tampa
SHS, 1101 VICTORIA ST 33510 4-00001
Patrick Gregory, prin. 689-1254
Burns JHS, 600 BROOKER RD 33511 4-00110
Bill Pate, prin. 685-2398
Mann JHS, 409 E JERSEY AVE 33510 4-00110
Elizabeth Stelter, prin. 689-7111
McLane JHS, 306 N KNIGHTS AVE 33510 4-00110
John Alfano, prin. 689-7188

Grace Christian S, PO BOX 843 33509 2-11111
Robert Gustafson, prin. 689-8815
Tampa Bay Christian S 2-11111
3920 S KINGS AVE 33511 685-8336
Robert Bolles, prin.

Branford, AC 904, PC 3, Suwannee
Suwannee County SD
Supt. — See Live Oak
S, PO BOX 387 32008 3-11111
Mel McMullen, prin. 935-1231

Bristol, AC 904, PC 3, Liberty
Liberty County SD 4-11111
PO BOX 429 32321 643-2275
Robert Hill, supt.
Liberty County JSHS 2-00111
PO BOX 519 32321 643-2241
Tony Anderson, prin.

Bronson, AC 904, PC 3, Levy
Levy County SD, PO BOX 129 32621 5-11111
Paul Johnson, supt. 486-5231
JSHS, PO BOX 189 32621 2-00111
Michael McCaskill, prin. 486-5261
Other Schools – See Cedar Key, Chiefland, Williston

Brooksville, AC 904, PC 6, Hernando
Hernando County SD 7-11111
919 N BROAD ST 34601 796-6761
Harold Winkler, supt.
Central HS 4-00011
14075 KEN AUSTIN PKY 34613 596-9333
Carolyn Forbis, prin.
Hernando HS, 200 E KELLY ST 34601 4-00011
Elaine Sullivan, prin. 544-6425
Parrott MS, 19220 YOUTH DR 34601 4-00100
Marvin Gordon, prin. 544-6460
Powell MS, 4100 BARCLAY AVE 34609 3-00100
Clarence Wingrove, prin. 544-6465
West Hernando MS 4-00100
14325 KEN AUSTIN PKY 34613 597-0559
Dennis McGeehan, prin.
Other Schools – See Spring Hill

Hernando Christian Academy · 2-11111
7200 EMERSON RD   34601 · 796-0616
Roy Garner, prin.

Bunnell, AC 904, PC 4, Flagler
Flagler County SD · 5-11111
HIGHWAY 100 E   32110 · 437-7526
Donn Kaupke, supt.
Flagler-Palm Coast HS · 4-00011
PO BOX 488   32110 · 437-2474
Larry Hunsinger, prin.
Taylor MS, PO BOX 815   32110 · 4-00100
Scott Hunter, prin. · 445-4172

Bushnell, AC 904, PC 4, Sumter
Sumter County SD · 6-11111
202 N FLORIDA ST   33513 · 793-2315
Preston Morgan, supt.
South Sumter HS, 700 N MAIN ST   33513 · 3-00011
Robert Edwards, prin. · 793-3131
Other Schools – See Webster, Wildwood

Callahan, AC 904, PC 3, Nassau
Nassau County SD
Supt. — See Fernandina Beach
West Nassau County HS · 3-00011
300 BROWN ST S   32011 · 879-3461
John Ruis, prin.
MS, PO BOX 5001   32011 · 3-00100
Ben Rice, prin. · 879-3606

Cantonment, AC 904, PC 5, Escambia
Escambia County SD
Supt. — See Pensacola
Ransom MS · 4-00100
1000 W KINGSFIELD RD   32533 · 968-2145
Richard Harper, prin.

Cape Coral, AC 813, PC 8, Lee
Lee County SD
Supt. — See Fort Myers
HS · 4-00011
2300 SANTA BARBARA BLVD   33991 · 574-6766
Mary Gunter, prin.
Mariner HS · 4-00011
701 CHIQUITA BLVD N   33909 · 772-3324
Michael McNerney, prin.
Lee Co. Vo-Tech Ctr · Vo Tech
361 JUANITA BLVD   33909 · 574-4440
Susan Kasper, prin.
Caloosa MS · 3-00100
610 DEL PRADO BLVD S   33990 · 574-3232
Marilyn Strong, prin.
Gulf MS, 1809 SW 36TH TER   33914 · 4-00100
Douglas Santini, prin. · 549-0606
Trafalgar MS · 3-00100
2120 SW TRAFALGAR PKY   33991 · 283-2001
Alfred Willie, prin.

Carrabelle, AC 904, PC 4, Franklin
Franklin County SD
Supt. — See Apalachicola
S, PO BOX 549   32322 · 2-11111
(—), prin. · 697-3815

Casselberry, AC 407, PC 7, Seminole
Seminole County SD
Supt. — See Sanford
South Seminole MS · 4-00100
101 S WINTER PARK DR   32707 · 831-6808
Richard Mossman, prin.

Golf Academy of the South · 2-CS
307 DANESWOOD WAY   32707 · 699-1990

Cedar Key, AC 904, PC 3, Levy
Levy County SD
Supt. — See Bronson
S, PO BOX 369   32625 · 2-11111
Bob Hastings, prin. · 543-5223

Century, AC 904, PC 4, Escambia
Escambia County SD
Supt. — See Pensacola
HS, PO BOX 187   32535 · 2-00011
Richard Erwin, prin. · 256-3501
Carver MS, PO BOX 207   32535 · 2-00100
Robert Smith, prin. · 256-3788

Chattahoochee, AC 904, PC 5, Gadsden
Gadsden County SD
Supt. — See Quincy
JSHS, PO BOX 7   32324 · 2-00111
Joseph Pace, prin. · 663-4631

Chiefland, AC 904, PC 4, Levy
Levy County SD
Supt. — See Bronson
HS, 808 N MAIN ST   32626 · 2-00011
Terry Andrews, prin. · 493-6000
Chiefland MS, 811 NW 4TH DR   32626 · 2-00100
Mary Wells, prin. · 493-6025

Victory Christian S · 2-11111
PO BOX 40   32626 · 463-1473
Carl Cornwell, prin.

Chipley, AC 904, PC 5, Washington
Washington County SD · 5-11111
206 N 3RD ST   32428 · 638-6222
Bill Williams, supt.
HS, 200 N 2ND ST   32428 · 3-00011
Pat Williams, prin. · 638-6100

Washington-Holmes Vo-Tech Ctr · Vo Tech
209 HOYT ST   32428 · 638-1180
Gene Prough, prin.
Roulhac MS, 101 N PECAN ST   32428 · 2-00100
Calvin Stevenson, prin. · 638-6170
Other Schools – See Vernon

Washington Holmes Area Voc-Technical Ctr · 3-CS
757 HOYT ST   32428 · 638-1180

Citra, AC 904, PC 4, Marion
Marion County SD
Supt. — See Ocala
North Marion HS · 4-00011
151 W HIGHWAY 329   32113 · 620-7587
Walt Miller, prin.
North Marion MS · 3-00100
RR 1 BOX 1970   32113 · 620-7589
Scott Hackmyer, prin.

Clearwater, AC 813, PC 8, Pinellas
Pinellas County SD
Supt. — See Largo
HS, 540 S HERCULES AVE   34624 · 4-00011
Edward Evans, prin. · 442-7155
Countryside HS · 4-00011
3000 STATE ROAD 580   34621 · 725-7956
Lee Sullivan, prin.
Kennedy MS, 1660 PALMETTO ST   34615 · 4-00100
Charles Mock, prin. · 461-4888
Oak Grove MS · 3-00100
1370 S BELCHER RD   34624 · 531-0457
Edward Baldwin, prin.

Business Training Institute · 2-CS
21649 US 19 N #200   34625 · 791-7833
Clearwater Central Catholic HS · 3-00011
2750 HAINES BAYSHORE RD   34620 · 531-1449
Dion Horrigan, prin.
Clearwater Christian College · 2-UC
3400 GULF TO BAY BLVD   34619 · 726-1153
Lakeside Christian S · 2-11111
1897 SUNSET POINT RD   34625 · 461-3311
David Ray, prin.
National Aviation Academy · 2-CS
5770 ROOSEVELT BLVD STE 105   34620 · 531-2080
Pinellas Technical Education Center · 4-CS
6100 154TH AVE N   34620 · 531-3531
Tampa College-Pinellas · 1-UC
15064 US HIGHWAY 19 N   34624 · 530-9495

Clermont, AC 904, PC 6, Lake
Lake County SD
Supt. — See Tavares
Clermont HS, 301 EAST AVE   34711 · 3-00011
David Coggshall, prin. · 394-2100
JHS, 680 E HIGHLAND AVE   34711 · 3-00100
George Baker, prin. · 394-2123

Clewiston, AC 813, PC 6, Hendry
Hendry County SD
Supt. — See La Belle
HS, 1501 S FRANCISCO ST   33440 · 3-00011
John Chapman, prin. · 983-6165
MS, 601 W OSCEOLA AVE   33440 · 3-00100
John Sullivan, prin. · 983-9134

Cocoa, AC 407, PC 7, Brevard
Brevard County SD
Supt. — See Melbourne
HS, 2000 TIGER TRL   32926 · 4-00011
Richard Blake, prin. · 632-5300
Clearlake MS · 3-00100
1225 CLEARLAKE RD   32922 · 633-3660
Alice Graves, prin.
McNair Magnet MS · 2-00100
1 CHALLENGER DR   32922 · 633-3630
Neely Dunn, prin.

Bethel Christian Academy · 2-11111
PO BOX 3147   32922 · 727-2038
Wayne Guinn, prin.
Brevard Community College · 7-CC
1519 CLEARLAKE RD   32922 · 632-1111

Cocoa Beach, AC 407, PC 7, Brevard
Brevard County SD
Supt. — See Melbourne
HS, 1500 MINUTEMEN CSWY   32931 · 3-00011
Patricia Vann, prin. · 783-1776

Coconut Creek, AC 305, PC 8, Broward
Broward County SD
Supt. — See Fort Lauderdale
HS, 1400 NW 44TH AVE   33066 · 4-00011
Ron Wilhoit, prin. · 977-2100
Atlantic Vo Ctr · Vo Tech
4700 COCONUT CREEK PKY   33063 · 977-2000
Robert Crawford, prin.

Atlantic Vocational-Technical Center · 5-CS
4700 COCONUT CREEK PKY   33063 · 977-2000
Broward Community College-North Campus · 2-CC
1000 COCONUT CREEK BLVD   33066 · 972-9100

Coconut Grove, AC 305, PC see Miami
Dade County SD
Supt. — See Miami
Carver MS, 4901 LINCOLN DR   33133 · 3-00100
Samuel Gay, prin. · 444-7388

Cooper City, AC 305, PC 7, Broward
Broward County SD
Supt. — See Fort Lauderdale
HS, 9401 STIRLING RD   33328 · 4-00011
Sara Rogers, prin. · 680-7200
Pioneer MS, 5350 SW 90TH AVE   33328 · 4-00100
Thomas Wilson, prin. · 680-1100

Coral Gables, AC 305, PC 8, Dade
Dade County SD
Supt. — See Miami
HS, 450 BIRD RD   33146 · 5-00011
Mandy Offerle, prin. · 443-4871
Ponce De Leon MS · 3-00100
5801 AUGUSTO ST   33146 · 661-1611
Raymond Fontana, prin.

University of Miami · 7-UC
PO BOX 248006   33124 · 284-4323

Coral Springs, AC 305, PC 8, Broward
Broward County SD
Supt. — See Fort Lauderdale
HS, 7201 W SAMPLE RD   33065 · 4-00011
Bruce Wagar, prin. · 344-3400
Taravella HS · 4-00011
10600 RIVERSIDE DR   33071 · 344-2300
Ellen Huber, prin.
MS, 10300 WILES RD   33076 · 4-00100
Frances Vandiver, prin. · 344-5500
Forest Glen MS · 4-00100
6501 TURTLE RUN BLVD   33067 · 345-4970
David Goldstein, prin.
Ramblewood MS · 4-00100
8585 W ATLANTIC BLVD   33071 · 344-5555
James Flynn, prin.

Cottondale, AC 904, PC 3, Jackson
Jackson County SD
Supt. — See Marianna
JSHS, 2680 LEVY ST   32431 · 2-00111
Ken Daffin, prin. · 482-9821

Crawfordville, AC 904, PC 4, Wakulla
Wakulla County SD · 5-11111
PO BOX 100   32326 · 926-7131
Roger Stokley, supt.
Wakulla County HS · 3-00011
RR 2 BOX 4800   32327 · 926-7125
Andrea Carter, prin.
Wakulla MS, RR 2 BOX 4900   32327 · 3-00100
Robert Myhre, prin. · 926-7143

Crescent City, AC 904, PC 4, Putnam
Putnam County SD
Supt. — See Palatka
JSHS, RR 1 BOX 145   32112 · 2-00111
Michael Pegg, prin. · 698-1629

Crestview, AC 904, PC 6, Okaloosa
Okaloosa County SD
Supt. — See Fort Walton Beach
HS, 1300 N FERDON BLVD   32536 · 4-00011
Wayne Ansley, prin. · 689-7177
Crestview Vo-Tech Ctr · Vo Tech
1300 N FERDON BLVD   32536 · 689-7276
James Wise, prin.
Richbourg MS, 500 ALABAMA ST   32536 · 4-00100
John Ensor, prin. · 689-7229

Cross City, AC 904, PC 4, Dixie
Dixie County SD · 4-11111
PO BOX 5060   32628 · 498-3305
H. Allen Harden, supt.
Dixie County JSHS · 3-00111
PO BOX 890   32628 · 498-3394
Michael Whittington, prin.
Rains MS, PO BOX 2159   32628 · 2-00100
Mark Rains, prin. · 498-1994

Crystal River, AC 904, PC 5, Citrus
Citrus County SD
Supt. — See Inverness
HS, 1205 NE 8TH AVE   34428 · 3-00011
Craig Marlett, prin. · 795-4641
MS, 705 NE 3RD AVE   34428 · 3-00100
David Hickey, prin. · 795-2116

Dade City, AC 813, PC 6, Pasco
Pasco County SD
Supt. — See Land O'Lakes
Pasco Comprehensive HS · 4-00011
1204 HIGHWAY 52   33525 · 567-6721
Tina Tiede, prin.
Pasco MS, 505 S 14TH ST   33525 · 3-00100
Patrick Reedy, prin. · 567-5574

Pasco-Hernando Community College · 5-CC
2401 STATE HWY 41 N   33525 · 567-6701

Dania, AC 305, PC 7, Broward
Broward County SD
Supt. — See Fort Lauderdale
Olsen MS, 1301 SE 2ND AVE   33004 · 4-00100
James Vanover, prin. · 926-0950

Davie, AC 305, PC 8, Broward
Broward County SD
Supt. — See Fort Lauderdale
Nova HS, 3600 COLLEGE AVE   33314 · 4-00011
Steven Pomerantz, prin. · 370-1700
McFatter Vo-Tech Ctr · Vo Tech
6500 NOVA DR   33317 · 370-8324
Horace McLeod, prin.

Nova MS, 3602 COLLEGE AVE 33314   4-00100
   Steven Friedman, prin.   370-1755

McFatter Vocational-Technical Center   4-CS
   6500 NOVA DR 33317   370-8324

Daytona Beach, AC 904, PC 8, Volusia
Volusia County SD
   Supt. — See DeLand
   Mainland HS   4-00011
     125 S CLYDE MORRIS BLVD 32114   252-0401
     Tim Huth, prin.
   Seabreeze HS   4-00011
     2700 N OLEANDER AVE 32118   676-1400
     James Kirton, prin.
   Campbell MS, 601 S KEECH ST 32114   3-00100
     Stan Whitted, prin.   226-1800

Bethune-Cookman College   4-UC
   640 DR MARY MCLOD BTHN BLVD 32114
     800-448-0228
Daytona Beach Community College   6-CC
   PO BOX 2811 32120   255-8131
Embry-Riddle Aeronautical University   6-UC
   600 S CLYDE MORRIS BLVD 32114   239-6000
Father Lopez HS   2-00011
   960 MADISON AVE 32114   253-5213
   David Gonsalves, prin.
Halifax Medical Center   HSP
   PO BOX 2830 32120   254-4065
Phillips Junior College   2-CC
   1491 S NOVA RD 32114   255-1707
Phoenix College of Aeronautics   2-CC
   PO BOX 11706 32120   258-0703
Phoenix East Aviation   CS
   561 PEARL HARBOR DR 32114   258-0703
West Virginia Career College   CC
   1104 BEVILLE RD STE J 32114   255-0175
Wise Private S   2-11111
   250 POINCIANA AVE 32127   767-2113
   Rita Wise, prin.

Deerfield Beach, AC 305, PC 8, Broward
Broward County SD
   Supt. — See Fort Lauderdale
   HS, 910 SW 15TH ST 33441   4-00011
     Ronald Clodfelter, prin.   481-5600
   MS, 701 SE 6TH AVE 33441   3-00100
     Rayfield Henderson, prin.   481-5700

Americana Preparatory S   2-00111
   20 SW 12TH AVE 33442   421-8400
   Sam Sollenberger, prin.
Zion Lutheran Christian S   2-11111
   959 SE 6TH AVE 33441   421-3147
   David Rutherford, prin.

De Funiak Springs, AC 904, PC 6, Walton
Walton County SD   5-11111
   9 E SLOSS AVE 32433   892-3141
   Perry Rutherford, supt.
   Walton HS, RR 8 BOX 590 32433   3-00011
     Robert Fondren, prin.   892-7224
   Walton Co. Vo Ctr, 850 S 2ND ST 32433   Vo Tech
     Marilyn Holley, prin.   892-8105
   Walton MS, 105 GEORGIA ST 32433   3-00100
     (—), prin.   892-2102
   Other Schools – See Freeport, Paxton

DeLand, AC 904, PC 7, Volusia
Volusia County SD   8-11111
   PO BOX 2118 32721   734-7190
   Joan Kowal, supt.
   HS, 800 N HILL AVE 32724   4-00011
     Albert Bowie, prin.   738-8000
   MS, 1400 AQUARIUS AVE 32724   4-00100
     William Walden, prin.   738-8400
   Southwestern MS   2-00100
     605 W NEW HAMPSHIRE AVE 32720   734-7700
     Tyrone Presley, prin.
   Other Schools – See Daytona Beach, Deltona, Holly
     Hill, New Smyrna Beach, Ormond Beach, Pierson,
     Port Orange

Stetson University   5-UC
   401 N WOODLAND BLVD 32720   800-345-4280

Delray Beach, AC 407, PC 8, Palm Beach
Palm Beach County SD
   Supt. — See West Palm Beach
   Atlantic HS   4-00011
     2501 SEACREST BLVD 33444   243-1500
     Carole Shetler, prin.
   Carver MS, 301 SW 14TH AVE 33444   3-00100
     Paul Houlihan, prin.   243-1566

Deltona, AC 904, PC 7, Volusia
Volusia County SD
   Supt. — See DeLand
   Deltona HS   4-00011
     3233 HOWLAND BLVD 32725   789-9653
     Robert Moll, prin.
   MS, 250 ENTERPRISE RD 32725   4-00100
     Kathleen Reed, prin.   574-6626
   Galaxy MS, 2400 EUSTACE AVE 32725   4-00100
     Judith Barnhart, prin.   789-5544

Deltona Christian S   2-11111
   1200 PROVIDENCE BLVD 32725   574-1971
   Byron Herchenroder, prin.

Trinity Christian Academy   2-11111
   875 ELKCAM BLVD 32725   789-4515
   David Evans, prin.

Dunedin, AC 813, PC 8, Pinellas
Pinellas County SD
   Supt. — See Largo
   HS, 1651 PINEHURST RD 34698   4-00011
     Mildred Reed, prin.   469-4100
   Dunedin Highland MS   4-00100
     896 UNION ST 34698   734-9421
     Margaret Landers, prin.

Schiller International University   4-UC
   453 EDGEWATER DR 34698   736-5082

Dunnellon, AC 904, PC 4, Marion
Marion County SD
   Supt. — See Ocala
   HS, 10855 SW 180TH AVENUE RD 34432   3-00011
     James Yancey, prin.   489-3341
   MS, 11011 N WILLIAMS ST 34432   3-00100
     Lee Arnold, prin.   489-2395

Eaton Park, AC 813, PC 4, Polk
Polk County SD
   Supt. — See Bartow
   Traviss Vo-Tech Ctr   Vo Tech
     PO BOX 720 33840   499-2700
     Charles Paulk, prin.

Englewood, AC 813, PC 7, Sarasota
Charlotte County SD
   Supt. — See Port Charlotte
   Lemon Bay HS, 2201 PLACIDA RD 34224   3-00011
     William Strickland, prin.   629-4552

Heritage Christian S, 75 PINE ST 34223   2-11111
   John Meyer, prin.   474-5884

Estero, AC 813, PC 3, Lee
Lee County SD
   Supt. — See Fort Myers
   HS, 21900 RIVER RANCH RD 33928   4-00011
     Fred Bode, prin.   947-9400

Eustis, AC 904, PC 7, Lake
Lake County SD
   Supt. — See Tavares
   HS, 1300 E WASHINGTON AVE 32726   3-00011
     James Hollins, prin.   357-4147
   Lake Co Area Vo-Tech Ctr   Vo Tech
     2001 KURT ST 32726   357-8222
     Maxine Felts, prin.
   MS, 1801 BATES AVE 32726   3-00100
     Charles McDaniel, prin.   357-3368

Lake County Area Vocational-Tech. Center   4-CS
   2001 KURT ST 32726   357-8222

Everglades City, AC 813, PC 2, Collier
Collier County SD
   Supt. — See Naples
   Everglades S, SCHOOL DR 33929   2-11111
     Earl Hall, prin.   695-2561

Fernandina Beach, AC 904, PC 6, Nassau
Nassau County SD   6-11111
   1201 ATLANTIC AVE 32034   261-5761
   John Ruis, supt.
   HS, 435 CITRONA DR 32034   4-00011
     William Fryar, prin.   261-5713
   MS, 315 CITRONA DR 32034   3-00100
     (—), prin.   261-4461
   Other Schools – See Callahan, Hilliard, Yulee

Floral City, AC 904, PC 5, Citrus

New Testament Christian S   2-11111
   PO BOX 490 34436   726-0360
   Dennis Peeples, prin.

Fort Lauderdale, AC 305, PC 9, Broward
Broward County SD   9-11111
   600 SE 3RD AVE 33301   765-6000
   Virgil Morgan, supt.
   Dillard HS, 2501 NW 11TH ST 33311   4-00011
     Benjamin Williams, prin.   797-4800
   HS, 1600 NE 4TH AVE 33305   4-00011
     Jacquelyn Barber, prin.   765-6921
   Stranahan HS, 1800 SW 5TH PL 33312   4-00011
     Patricia Grimes, prin.   765-6832
   Western HS, 1200 SW 136TH AVE 33325   4-00011
     David Hogg, prin.   370-1600
   Everglades MS, 2400 NW 26TH ST 33311   3-00100
     William Lyons, prin.   497-1875
   New River MS   3-00100
     3100 RIVERLAND RD 33312   797-4500
     Edith Gooden-Gonzalez, prin.
   Parkway MS, 3600 NW 5TH CT 33311   4-00100
     Willie Dudley, prin.   797-4550
   Rogers MS, 700 SW 26TH ST 33315   3-00100
     Sterling DuPont, prin.   765-6893
   Sunrise MS, 1750 NE 14TH ST 33304   4-00100
     Roberta Insel, prin.   765-6785
   Tequesta Trace MS   4-00100
     1800 INDIAN TRCE 33326   384-5150
     Kim Flynn, prin.
   Other Schools – See Coconut Creek, Cooper City,
     Coral Springs, Dania, Davie, Deerfield Beach,
     Hallandale, Hollywood, Lauderdale Lakes,
     Lauderhill, Margate, Miramar, North Lauderdale,
     Oakland Park, Parkland, Pembroke Pines,
     Plantation, Pompano Beach, Sunrise

American Flyers College   2-CS
   5400 NW 21ST TER 33309   772-7500
Art Institute of Fort Lauderdale   4-UC
   1799 SE 17TH ST 33316   463-3000
ATI Career Training Center   2-CC
   2880 W CYPRESS CREEK RD 33309   973-4760
Atlantic Coast Institute   2-CS
   5225 W BROWARD BLVD 33317   581-2223
Broward Community College   7-CC
   225 E LAS OLAS BLVD 33301   475-6500
Cardinal Gibbons HS   4-00011
   4601 BAYVIEW DR 33308   491-2900
   Fr. Joseph Kershner, prin.
Career City College   2-CS
   1317 NE 4TH AVE 33304   764-4660
Fort Lauderdale Christian S   2-11111
   6330 NW 31ST AVE 33309   972-3444
   Denny Williams, prin.
Fort Lauderdale College   4-UC
   1040 BAYVIEW DR 33304   568-1600
Fort Lauderdale Preparatory S   2-11111
   3275 W OAKLAND PARK BLVD 33311   485-7500
   Anita Lonstein, prin.
ITT Technical Institute   2-CC
   3401 S UNIVERSITY DR 33328   476-9300
Keiser College of Technology   2-CC
   1500 NW 49TH ST 33309   776-4456
NEC-Bauder Campus   3-UC
   4801 N DIXIE HWY 33334   491-7171
Nova Southeastern University   6-UC
   3301 COLLEGE AVE 33314   800-541-6682
Pine Crest S, 1501 NE 62ND ST 33334   4-11111
   William McMillan, prin.   492-4100
RETS Technical Centers   2-CS
   3501 POWERLINE RD 33309   764-3432
St. Thomas Aquinas HS   4-00011
   2801 SW 12TH ST 33312   581-2127
   Sr. John Norton, prin.
School Of Nova University   4-11111
   3301 COLLEGE AVE 33314   476-1902
   James Byer, prin.
Westminster Academy   3-11111
   5620 NE 22ND AVE 33308   771-4600
   Kenneth Wackes, prin.

Fort Meade, AC 813, PC 5, Polk
Polk County SD
   Supt. — See Bartow
   JSHS, 700 EDGEWOOD DR N 33841   3-00111
     Joan Bailey, prin.   285-8174

Fort Myers, AC 813, PC 8, Lee
Lee County SD   8-11111
   2055 CENTRAL AVE 33901   334-1102
   James Adams, supt.
   Cypress Lake HS   4-00011
     6750 PANTHER LN 33919   481-2233
     Karl Engel, prin.
   HS, 2645 CORTEZ BLVD 33901   4-00011
     James Browder, prin.   334-2167
   Riverdale HS   4-00011
     2815 BUCKINGHAM RD 33905   694-4141
     Robert Durham, prin.
   Lee County Vo-Tech Ctr   Vo Tech
     3800 MICHIGAN AVE 33916   334-4544
     Ronald Pentiuk, prin.
   Cypress Lake MS   3-00100
     8901 CYPRESS LAKE DR 33919   481-1533
     Gayle Thompson, prin.
   Dunbar MS, 3800 EDISON AVE 33916   3-00100
     Charles Bell, prin.   334-1357
   MS, 3015 CENTRAL AVE 33901   3-00100
     Judi Hughes, prin.   936-1759
   Lee MS, 4203 BALLARD RD 33905   3-00100
     Ronald Davis, prin.   334-0158
   Three Oaks MS   3-00100
     18500 3 OAKS PKY 33912   267-5757
     Keith Lindahl, prin.
   Other Schools – See Alva, Bonita Springs, Cape
     Coral, Estero, Lehigh Acres, North Fort Myers

Bishop Verot HS   3-00011
   5598 SUNRISE DR 33919   936-6700
   Fr. Christopher Hudgin, prin.
Canterbury S, 8141 COLLEGE PKY 33919   2-11111
   Frank Romano, prin.   481-4323
Edison Community College   6-CC
   PO BOX 60210 33906   489-9300
Evangelical Christian S   3-11111
   8237 BEACON BLVD 33907   936-3319
   Douglas Dunn, prin.
International College   2-UC
   8695 COLLEGE PKY 33919   800-466-0019
Lee Co. Vocational-Technical School   4-CS
   3800 MICHIGAN AVE 33916   334-4544
Lee Memorial Hospital   HSP
   2776 CLEVELAND AVE 33901   334-5211
Radiation Therapy Regional Centers   2-CS
   7341 GLADIOLUS DR 33908   489-0380
Southwest Florida College of Business   2-CS
   1685 MEDICAL LN STE 200 33907   939-4766

Fort Pierce, AC 407, PC 8, St. Lucie
St. Lucie County SD   7-11111
   2909 DELAWARE AVE 34947   468-5000
   David Mosrie, supt.
   Ft. Pierce Central HS   4-00011
     1101 EDWARDS RD 34982   468-5888
     Gloria Johnson, prin.

Fort Pierce Westwood HS 4-00011
 1801 ANGLE RD 34947 468-5400
 Wayne Gent, prin.
Lincoln Park JSHS 4-00111
 1806 AVENUE I 34950 468-5474
 Elizabeth Lambertson, prin.
Forest Grove MS, 3201 S 25TH ST 34981 3-00100
 (—), prin. 468-5885
McCarty MS 4-00100
 1201 MISSISSIPPI AVE 34950 468-5700
 George Hill, prin.
Other Schools – See Port Saint Lucie

Indian River Community College 5-CC
 3209 VIRGINIA AVE 34981 468-4740
John Carroll HS 2-00011
 3402 DELAWARE AVE 34947 464-5200
 Clyde Russell, prin.
Webster College 2-CC
 2192 N US HIGHWAY 1 34946 464-7474

Fort Walton Beach, AC 904, PC 7, Okaloosa
Okaloosa County SD 8-11111
 120 LOWERY PL SE 32548 689-7100
 Bernadette Cover, supt.
Choctawhatchee HS 4-00011
 110 RACETRACK RD NW 32547 833-3614
 Richard Bounds, prin.
HS, 400 HOLLYWOOD BLVD SW 32548 4-00011
 Bob Walton, prin. 833-3300
Bay Area Vo-Tech Ctr Vo Tech
 1976 LEWIS TURNER BLVD 32547 833-3500
 Ed Baker, prin.
Bruner MS 4-00100
 322 HOLMES BLVD NW 32548 833-3266
 John Johnston, prin.
Pryor MS 3-00100
 201 RACETRACK RD NW 32547 833-3613
 Donna Hannah, prin.
Other Schools – See Baker, Crestview, Laurel Hill,
 Niceville, Shalimar, Valparaiso

Bay Area Vocational-Technical School 3-CS
 1976 LEWIS TURNER BLVD 32547 862-0167
Fort Walton Christian S 2-11111
 529 CLIFFORD ST 32547 862-1414
 Stanford Stone, prin.

Freeport, AC 904, PC 3, Walton
Walton County SD
 Supt. — See De Funiak Springs
JSHS, RR 3 BOX 1 32439 2-00111
 James Hicks, prin. 835-4212

Frostproof, AC 813, PC 5, Polk
Polk County SD
 Supt. — See Bartow
JSHS, 1000 N PALM AVE 33843 3-00111
 Max Linton, prin. 635-2221

Gainesville, AC 904, PC 8, Alachua
Alachua County SD 8-11111
 620 E UNIVERSITY AVE 32601 336-3300
 Robert Hughes, supt.
Buchholz HS, 5510 NW 27TH AVE 32606 4-00011
 Terry Stechmiller, prin. 336-2702
Eastside HS, 1201 SE 45TH TER 32641 4-00011
 Robert Schenck, prin. 336-2704
HS, 1900 NW 13TH ST 32609 4-00011
 W. Boyd, prin. 336-2707
Bishop MS, 1901 NE 9TH ST 32609 4-00100
 Carolyn Whitehead, prin. 336-2701
Ft. Clarke MS, 9301 NW 23RD AVE 32606 4-00100
 (—), prin. 332-8050
Lincoln MS, 1001 SE 12TH ST 32641 4-00100
 Virginia Childs, prin. 336-2711
Westwood MS 3-00100
 3215 NW 15TH AVE 32605 336-2718
 Michael Joyner, prin.
Other Schools – See Alachua, Hawthorne, High
 Springs, Newberry

Career City College 2-CC
 2400 SW 13TH ST 32608 335-4000
Heritage Christian S 2-11111
 3401 NW 34TH ST 32605 378-1395
 Alisa Epperson, prin.
Oak Hill S, 8009 SW 14TH AVE 32607 2-00111
 Michael Maher, prin. 332-3609
Santa Fe Community College 7-CC
 3000 NW 83RD ST 32606 395-5000
University of Florida 8-UC
 226 TIGERT HALL 32611 392-1365
Webster College 2-CC
 2002 NW 13TH ST 32609 375-8014

Gibsonton, AC 813, PC 5, Hillsborough
Hillsborough County SD
 Supt. — See Tampa
East Bay HS, 7710 BIG BEND RD 33534 4-00011
 J. Vince Thompson, prin. 671-5134
Eisenhower JHS 4-00100
 7620 BIG BEND RD 33534 671-5121
 John Owens, prin.

Glen Saint Mary, AC 904, PC 2, Baker
Baker County SD
 Supt. — See Macclenny
Baker County HS, 1 WILDCAT DR 32040 4-00011
 Rita Rhoden, prin. 259-6286

Gonzalez, AC 904, PC 6, Escambia
Escambia County SD
 Supt. — See Pensacola
Tate HS, PO BOX 68 32560 4-00011
 James May, prin. 968-9522

Goulds, AC 305, PC 6, Dade
Dade County SD
 Supt. — See Miami
Mays JHS 3-00100
 11700 HAINLIN MILL DR 33170 233-2300
 Robert Stinson, prin.

Graceville, AC 904, PC 5, Jackson
Holmes County SD
 Supt. — See Bonifay
Poplar Springs S, RR 2 BOX 88 32440 2-11111
 Jerry Dixon, prin. 263-6260

Jackson County SD
 Supt. — See Marianna
JSHS, 5539 BROWN ST 32440 3-00111
 (—), prin. 263-4451

Florida Baptist Theological College 2-UC
 5400 COLLEGE DR 32440 263-3261

Grand Ridge, AC 904, PC 3, Jackson
Jackson County SD
 Supt. — See Marianna
S, PO BOX 208 32442 3-11111
 John Hamilton, prin. 592-5161

Greenacres City, AC 407, PC 7, Palm Beach

Greenacres Christian Academy 2-11111
 400 JACKSON AVE 33463 965-0363
 Chadwick Donnally, prin.

Green Cove Springs, AC 904, PC 5, Clay
Clay County SD, 900 WALNUT ST 32043 7-11111
 Phyllis May, supt. 284-6510
Clay JSHS 3-00111
 2025 STATE ROAD 16 W 32043 284-6530
 David Owens, prin.
Other Schools – See Keystone Heights, Middleburg,
 Orange Park

National Training 2-CS
 STATE RT 209 32043 284-5785

Greensboro, AC 904, PC 3, Gadsden
Gadsden County SD
 Supt. — See Quincy
JSHS, PO BOX 10 32330 2-00111
 Charles Griffin, prin. 442-6126

Greenville, AC 904, PC 3, Madison
Madison County SD
 Supt. — See Madison
MS, PO BOX 428 32331 2-01100
 Nelson Cone, prin. 948-3201

Groveland, AC 904, PC 4, Lake
Lake County SD
 Supt. — See Tavares
MS, 205 E MAGNOLIA ST 34736 2-00100
 Cecil Gray, prin. 429-3322

Gulf Breeze, AC 904, PC 6, Santa Rosa
Santa Rosa County SD
 Supt. — See Milton
HS, 675 GULF BREEZE PKY 32561 4-00011
 (—), prin. 932-5388
MS, 649 GULF BREEZE PKY 32561 3-00100
 Anita Eilertsen, prin. 932-2261

Gulfport, AC 813, PC 7, Pinellas
Pinellas County SD
 Supt. — See Largo
Boca Ciega HS, 924 58TH ST S 33707 4-00011
 Barbara Paonessa, prin. 893-2780

Haines City, AC 813, PC 7, Polk
Polk County SD
 Supt. — See Bartow
HS, 2800 HORNET DR 33844 4-00011
 James Partain, prin. 422-6415
Boone MS, 225 S 22ND ST 33844 3-00100
 Eileen McDaniel, prin. 422-5956
Jenkins MS, 701 LEDWITH AVE 33844 3-00100
 Mike Condon, prin. 422-6481

Landmark Christian S 2-11111
 2020 E HINSON AVE 33844 422-2037
 Phil Pitts, prin.

Hallandale, AC 305, PC 8, Broward
Broward County SD
 Supt. — See Fort Lauderdale
HS, 720 NW 9TH AVE 33009 4-00011
 (—), prin. 457-2600

Miami Technical College 2-CS
 1001 N FEDERAL HWY 33009 769-3316

Havana, AC 904, PC 4, Gadsden
Gadsden County SD
 Supt. — See Quincy
Havana Northside HS 2-00011
 RR 2 BOX 75 32333 539-6437
 Nettie Black, prin.
MS, 420 E 6TH AVE 32333 2-00100
 Bettye Chatmon, prin. 539-6736

Gadsden Christian Academy 2-11111
 PO BOX 918 32333 539-5300
 Jacob Till, prin.

Hawthorne, AC 904, PC 4, Alachua
Alachua County SD
 Supt. — See Gainesville
JSHS, PO BOX 40 32640 3-00111
 Lamar Simmons, prin. 481-2417

Hialeah, AC 305, PC 9, Dade
Dade County SD
 Supt. — See Miami
SHS, 251 E 47TH ST 33013 5-00001
 Francis Wargo, prin. 822-1500
American HS 5-00011
 18350 NW 67TH AVE 33015 557-3770
 Robert Snyder, prin.
Hialeah-Miami Lakes HS 5-00011
 7977 W 12TH AVE 33014 823-1330
 Elliott Berman, prin.
Miami MacArthur North HS 2-00011
 13835 NW 97TH AVE 33016 826-1989
 Lawton Williams, prin.
Filer JHS, 531 W 29TH ST 33012 4-00110
 Thomas Shaw, prin. 822-6601
JHS, 6027 E 7TH AVE 33013 4-00110
 William Jones, prin. 681-3527
Marti JHS, 5701 W 24TH AVE 33016 4-00110
 Jose Enriquez, prin. 557-5931
Miami Lakes MS 4-00100
 6425 MIAMI LAKEWAY N 33014 557-3900
 James Cerra, prin.
Palm Springs JHS 4-00110
 1025 W 56TH ST 33012 821-2460
 Allan Bonilla, prin.

Automotive Transmission School 1-CS
 453 E OKEECHOBEE RD 33010 888-4898
Dade Christian S 4-11111
 6601 NW 167TH ST 33015 822-7690
 James Virtue, prin.
First Baptist S, 140 E 7TH ST 33010 2-11111
 Robert Partridge, prin. 888-9776
Florida National College 4-CC
 4206 W 12TH AVE 33012 821-3333
Hialeah Technical Center 2-CS
 1780 E 4TH AVE 33010 884-4387
Miami Lakes Technical Education Center 4-CC
 5780 NW 158TH ST 33014 557-4940
National School of Technology 2-CS
 4355 W 16TH AVE 33012 558-9500

Hialeah Gardens, AC 305, PC 6, Dade

Miami Union Academy 2-11111
 12051 W OKEECHOBEE RD 33016 821-8400
 Elisa Young, prin.

High Springs, AC 904, PC 5, Alachua
Alachua County SD
 Supt. — See Gainesville
Spring Hill MS, PO BOX 907 32643 2-01100
 Donald Lewis, prin. 454-2701

Hilliard, AC 904, PC 4, Nassau
Nassau County SD
 Supt. — See Fernandina Beach
JSHS, PO BOX 1199 32046 3-00111
 Edward Turvey, prin. 845-2171

Hobe Sound, AC 407, PC 7, Martin

Hobe Sound Bible College 2-UC
 PO BOX 1065 33475 546-5534
Hobe Sound Christian Academy 2-11111
 PO BOX 1065 33475 546-5534
 Clifford Churchill, prin.

Holly Hill, AC 904, PC 7, Volusia
Volusia County SD
 Supt. — See DeLand
MS, 1200 CENTER AVE 32117 3-00100
 Salvatore Campanella, prin. 252-0421

Hollywood, AC 305, PC 9, Broward
Broward County SD
 Supt. — See Fort Lauderdale
Hollywood Hills HS 4-00011
 5400 STIRLING RD 33021 985-5225
 Donald Cifra, prin.
McArthur HS 4-00011
 6501 HOLLYWOOD BLVD 33024 985-3150
 Sherry Clarke, prin.
South Broward HS 4-00011
 1901 N FEDERAL HWY 33020 926-0800
 Beverly James, prin.
Sheridan Vo Ctr Vo Tech
 5400 SHERIDAN ST 33021 985-3220
 Dan Boegli, prin.
Apollo MS, 6800 ARTHUR ST 33024 4-00100
 Janet Holt, prin. 985-3000
Attucks MS, 3500 N 22ND AVE 33020 3-00100
 Andrew Luciani, prin. 926-0900
Driftwood MS 4-00100
 2751 NW 70TH TER 33024 985-3100
 Frank Campana, prin.
McNicol MS, 1411 S 28TH AVE 33020 3-00100
 Jacob Greene, prin. 926-0975

Chaminade Madonna College Prep HS 3-00011
 500 E CHAMINADE DR 33021 989-5150
 Robert Minnaugh, prin.

Hollywood Christian S 3-11111
1708 N STATE ROAD 7 33021 966-2350
Larry Coy, prin.
Prospect Hall School of Business 3-CS
2620 HOLLYWOOD BLVD 33020 923-8100
Sheridan Hills Christian S 2-11111
3751 SHERIDAN ST 33021 966-7995
William Hewlett, prin.
Sheridan Vocational-Technical Center 4-CS
5400 SHERIDAN ST 33021 985-3220

Homestead, AC 305, PC 8, Dade
Dade County SD
Supt. — See Miami
HS, 2351 SE 12TH AVE 33034 4-00011
(—), prin. 245-7000
South Dade HS 4-00011
28401 SW 167TH AVE 33030 247-4244
Marian Link, prin.
Campbell Drive MS 4-00100
900 NE 23RD AVE 33033 248-7911
Gregory Zawyer, prin.
MS, 650 NW 2ND AVE 33030 4-00100
(—), prin. 247-4221
Redland MS, 16001 SW 248TH ST 33031 4-00100
Mona Jackson, prin. 247-6112

Hudson, AC 813, PC 6, Pasco
Pasco County SD
Supt. — See Land O'Lakes
HS, 14410 COBRA WAY 34669 4-00011
Arthur O'Donnell, prin. 863-1594
MS, 14540 COBRA WAY 34669 4-00100
Larry Albano, prin. 862-7676

Grace Christian School of Pasco 2-11111
9403 SCOT ST 34669 863-1825
Rev. Dean Pratt, prin.

Immokalee, AC 813, PC 7, Collier
Collier County SD
Supt. — See Naples
HS, 701 W IMMOKALEE DR 33934 3-00011
Gilbert Shely, prin. 657-3671
MS, 401 N 9TH ST 33934 4-00100
Cecilia Bates, prin. 657-3638

Indialantic, AC 407, PC 5, Brevard
Brevard County SD
Supt. — See Melbourne
Hoover JHS, 1 HAWK HAVEN DR 32903 3-00110
Dolores Gianelli, prin. 727-1611

Indiantown, AC 407, PC 5, Martin
Martin County SD
Supt. — See Stuart
MS, 16303 SW FARMS RD 34956 2-01100
David George, prin. 597-2146

Interlachen, AC 904, PC 4, Putnam
Putnam County SD
Supt. — See Palatka
HS, RR 1 BOX 10 32148 3-00011
Randolph Newland, prin. 684-2116
Price MS, RR 1 BOX 15 32148 3-00100
Howard Alred, prin. 684-2113

Inverness, AC 904, PC 6, Citrus
Citrus County SD 7-11111
1007 W MAIN ST 34450 726-1931
Carl Austin, supt.
Citrus HS 4-00011
600 W HIGHLAND BLVD 34452 726-2241
Edward Staten, prin.
Withlachoochee Vo Ctr Vo Tech
1201 W MAIN ST 34450 726-2430
Steven Kinard, prin.
MS, 1950 HIGHWAY 41 N 34450 4-00100
William Eldridge, prin. 726-1471
Other Schools – See Crystal River, Lecanto

Withlacoohee Technical Institute 3-CS
1201 W MAIN ST 34450 726-2430

Islamorada, AC 305, PC 4, Monroe

Island Christian S 2-11111
83400 OVERSEAS HWY 33036 664-4933
Rev. Hammon, prin.

Jacksonville, AC 904, PC 11, Duval
Duval County SD 9-11111
1701 PRUDENTIAL DR 32207 390-2000
Larry Zenke, supt.
Anderson HS of the Arts 3-00011
2445 SAN DIEGO RD 32207 346-5620
Jane Condon, prin.
Englewood HS, 4412 BARNES RD 32207 4-00011
Steve Hite, prin. 739-5212
First Coast HS 4-00011
590 DUVAL STATION RD 32218 757-0080
William Stone, prin.
Forrest HS, 5530 FIRESTONE RD 32244 4-00011
James Watson, prin. 573-1170
Jackson HS, 3816 N MAIN ST 32206 3-00011
Jack Shanklin, prin. 630-6950
Lee HS, 1200 S MCDUFF AVE 32205 3-00011
Ed Pratt-Dannals, prin. 381-3930
Mandarin HS 4-00011
4831 GREENLAND RD 32258 260-3911
Dalton Epting, prin.
Parker HS 4-00011
7301 PARKER SCHOOL RD 32211 720-1650
Jim Jaxon, prin.

Paxon HS, 3239 W 5TH ST 32254 3-00011
Milton Threadcraft, prin. 693-7583
Raines HS, 3663 RAINES AVE 32209 4-00011
Jim Johnson, prin. 924-3049
Ribault HS, 3701 WINTON DR 32208 4-00011
Earlene Lockett, prin. 924-3092
Sandalwood HS 4-00011
2750 JOHN PROM BLVD 32246 646-5100
Emory Trawick, prin.
White HS 4-00011
1700 OLD MIDDLEBURG RD 32210 693-7620
Ron Poppell, prin.
Wolfson HS, 7000 POWERS AVE 32217 4-00011
David White, prin. 739-5265
Stanton College Preparatory JSHS 4-00011
1149 W 13TH ST 32209 630-6760
Jim Williams, prin.
Grand Park Career Ctr Vo Tech
2335 W 18TH ST 32209 630-6895
Bobby McDuffie, prin.
Randolph Skill Ctr Vo Tech
1157 GOLFAIR BLVD 32209 924-3011
Nathaniel Davis, prin.
Southside Skill Ctr Vo Tech
2924 KNIGHTS LN E 32216 739-5235
Peggy Williams, prin.
Westside Skill Ctr Vo Tech
7450 WILSON BLVD 32210 573-1150
Jerry Gugel, prin.
Arlington MS 3-00100
8141 LONE STAR RD 32211 720-1680
Jordan Baker, prin.
Butler MS, 900 ACORN ST 32209 3-00100
Roy Mitchell, prin. 630-6900
Darnell-Cookman MS 3-00100
1701 N DAVIS ST 32209 630-6805
Mike Budd, prin.
Davis MS, 7050 MELVIN RD 32210 4-00100
Judy Silas, prin. 573-1060
DuPont MS, 2710 DUPONT AVE 32217 3-00100
William English, prin. 739-5200
Ft. Caroline MS 3-00100
3787 UNIVERSITY CLUB BLVD 32277 745-4927
Tim Ahearn, prin.
Gilbert MS, 1424 FRANKLIN ST 32206 3-00100
Ken Brockington, prin. 630-6700
Highlands MS 4-00100
10913 PINE ESTATES RD E 32218 696-8771
Bill Reynolds, prin.
Johnson MS, 1840 W 9TH ST 32209 3-00100
Mary Brown, prin. 630-6640
Kirby-Smith MS 3-00100
2034 HUBBARD ST 32206 630-6600
Elmora Atkins, prin.
Lake Shore MS 2-00100
2519 BAYVIEW RD 32210 381-7440
Frank Castellano, prin.
Land Mark MS 4-00100
101 KERNAN BLVD N 32225 221-7125
Lois Johnson, prin.
Landon MS, 1819 THACKER AVE 32207 2-00100
William Dutter, prin. 346-5650
Mandarin MS, 5100 HOOD RD 32257 4-00100
Walter Carr, prin. 292-0555
Northwestern MS 3-00100
2100 W 45TH ST 32209 924-3100
Theresa Hodge, prin.
Paxon MS, 3276 W 5TH ST 32254 4-00100
Quentin Messer, prin. 693-7600
Ribault MS 4-00100
3610 RIBAULT SCENIC DR 32208 924-3062
Dorothy Mitchell, prin.
Southside MS 3-00100
2948 KNIGHTS LN E 32216 739-5238
Peggy Williams, prin.
Stilwell MS, 7840 BURMA RD 32221 3-00100
Joe Fowler, prin. 693-7523
Stuart MS 3-00100
4815 WESCONNETT BLVD 32210 573-1000
Andrew Knight, prin.
Other Schools – See Atlantic Beach, Baldwin,
Jacksonville Beach, Neptune Beach

St. John's County SD
Supt. — See Saint Augustine
Switzerland Point MS 3-00100
777 GREENBRIAR RD 32259 287-2626
Bernard Scott, prin.

Baptist Medical Centers HSP
800 PRUDENTIAL DR 32207 393-2001
Bartram S 2-01111
2264 BARTRAM RD 32207
C. Bliss, prin.
Bishop Kenny HS 4-00011
PO BOX 5544 32247 398-7545
Jane Marnett, prin.
Bolles S, 7400 SAN JOSE BLVD 32217 4-11111
Harry DeMontmollin, prin. 733-9292
ConCorde Career Institute 3-CS
7960 ARLINGTON EXPY STE 120 32211
725-0525
Edward Waters College 3-UC
1658 KINGS RD 32209 355-3030
Episcopal HS 3-00111
4455 ATLANTIC BLVD 32207 396-5751
Dale Regan, prin.
First Coast Christian S 2-11111
7585 BLANDING BLVD 32244 777-3040
Bill Dougherty, prin.

Flagler Career Institute 2-CC
3225 UNIVERSITY BLVD S 32216 721-1622
Florida Community College 7-CC
501 W STATE ST 32202 632-3388
Florida Community College CC
101 W STATE ST 32202 633-8100
Florida Community College 4-CC
3939 ROOSEVELT BLVD 32205
Florida Community College 4-CC
4501 CAPPER RD 32218 766-6581
Florida Community College 4-CC
11901 BEACH BLVD 32246
Florida Technical College 2-CS
8711 LONE STAR RD 32211 724-2229
ITT Technical Institute 2-CC
6600 YOUNGERMAN CIR STE 10 32244
573-9100
Jacksonville University 4-UC
2800 UNIVERSITY BLVD N 32211 744-3950
Jones College 5-UC
5353 ARLINGTON EXPY 32211 743-1122
St. Vincent's Medical Center HSP
2708 SAINT JOHNS AVE 32205 387-7300
Southern Baptist Academy 2-11111
6415 N PEARL ST 32208 768-3877
Dan Hodges, prin.
Stenotype Inst. of Jacksonville Beach 1-CS
500 9TH AVE N 32250 246-7466
Trinity Christian Academy 4-11111
800 HAMMOND BLVD 32221 786-5320
Robert Gray, prin.
University Christian S 3-11111
5520 UNIVERSITY BLVD W 32216 737-6330
Patsy Spain, prin.
University Medical Center - Jacksonville HSP
655 W 8TH ST 32209 350-6899
University of North Florida 6-UC
4567 SAINT JOHNS BLUFF RD S 32224
646-2624
Victory Christian Academy 3-11111
10613 LEM TURNER RD 32218 764-7781
Judy England, prin.
Word of Life S, 8855 SANCHEZ RD 32217 2-11111
Rebecca Jordi, prin. 733-0300

Jacksonville Beach, AC 904, PC 7, Duval
Duval County SD
Supt. — See Jacksonville
Fletcher MS, 2000 3RD ST N 32250 4-00100
Bobby Powell, prin. 247-5929

Jasper, AC 904, PC 4, Hamilton
Hamilton County SD 4-11111
PO BOX 1059 32052 792-1228
Patricia Parks, supt.
Hamilton County HS 3-00011
RR 2 BOX 137 32052 792-1332
David Lauer, prin.
Hamilton Vo-Tech Ctr Vo Tech
RR 2 BOX 137 32052 792-2715
David Lauer, prin.
Hamilton MS, RR 4 BOX 177 32052 2-01100
Harry Pennington, prin. 792-1292

Jay, AC 904, PC 3, Santa Rosa
Santa Rosa County SD
Supt. — See Milton
JSHS, 700 S ALABAMA ST 32565 2-00011
Thomas Rowland, prin. 675-4507

Juno Beach, AC 407, PC 99, Palm Beach

Batt Learning Center 2-11111
205 US HIGHWAY 1 STE 202 33408
Judith Batt-Yarnell, prin. 625-2288

Jupiter, AC 407, PC 7, Palm Beach
Palm Beach County SD
Supt. — See West Palm Beach
HS, 500 MILITARY TRL 33458 5-00011
Joe Picklesimer, prin. 744-7900
MS, 15245 MILITARY TRL 33458 4-00100
Vera Garcia, prin. 744-7950

Jupiter Christian S 2-11111
PO BOX 967 33468 746-7800
Thomas Cathey, prin.

Keystone Heights, AC 904, PC 4, Clay
Clay County SD
Supt. — See Green Cove Springs
JSHS, 900 ORCHID AVE 32656 3-00111
Sheila Bridges, prin. 473-2761

Key West, AC 305, PC 7, Monroe
Monroe County SD 6-11111
PO BOX 1788 33041 296-6523
Robert Walker, supt.
HS, 2100 FLAGLER AVE 33040 4-00011
Bob Menendez, prin. 293-1510
Obryant MS, 1105 LEON ST 33040 3-00100
Frank Spoto, prin. 296-5628
Other Schools – See Marathon, Tavernier

Florida Keys Community College 4-CC
5901 COLLEGE RD 33040 296-9081

Kissimmee, AC 407, PC 8, Osceola
Osceola County SD 7-11111
817 BILL BECK BLVD 34744 870-4600
Chris Colombo, supt.

Gateway HS 4-00011
  93 PANTHER PAWS TRL 34744 933-1222
  David Williams, prin.
Osceola HS, 420 S THACKER AVE 34741 4-00011
  Charles Paradiso, prin. 846-5400
Beaumont MS 4-00100
  330 N BEAUMONT AVE 34741 846-4312
  Mike Smith, prin.
Denn John MS 4-00100
  2001 DENN JOHN LN 34744 846-2742
  Tom Tate, prin.
Neptune MS, 2727 NEPTUNE RD 34744 4-00100
  Rose Kish, prin. 846-6171
Parkway MS, 857 FLORIDA PKY 34743 3-00100
  Sylvia Evans, prin. 348-9446
Poinciana JHS 2-00010
  2300 S POINCIANA BLVD 34758 870-4860
  Michael Brizendine, prin.
Other Schools – See Saint Cloud

Florida Bible College 2-UC
  1701 S POINCIANA BLVD 34758 933-4500
Florida Christian College 2-UC
  1011 OSCEOLA BLVD 34744 847-8966
Southeastern Academy 3-HMS
  PO BOX 421768 34742 847-4444

La Belle, AC 813, PC 5, Hendry
Hendry County SD 6-11111
  PO BOX 1980 33935 675-5266
  Edward Upthegrove, supt.
HS, 4050 GARDEN RD 33935 3-00011
  R. Scott Cooper, prin. 675-2464
MS, PO BOX 1920 33935 3-00100
  James Allen, prin. 675-0213
Other Schools – See Clewiston

Lake Buena Vista, AC 407, PC 99, Marion
Orange County SD
  Supt. — See Orlando
Challenger Ctr Vo Tech
  5555 N CENTER DR 32830 824-4709
  Henry Wright, prin.

Lake Butler, AC 904, PC 4, Union
Union County SD, 55 SW 6TH ST 32054 4-11111
  Eugene Dukes, supt. 496-2045
Union County HS 2-00011
  1000 S LAKE AVE 32054 496-3040
  Donald Leech, prin.
MS, 150 SW 6TH ST 32054 3-01100
  Bobbie Whitehead, prin. 496-3046

Lake City, AC 904, PC 7, Columbia
Columbia County SD 6-11111
  PO BOX 1148 32056 755-8000
  Dianne Lane, supt.
Columbia SHS, PO BOX 1869 32056 4-00001
  Brian Jetter, prin. 755-8080
Columbia JHS North 3-00010
  PO BOX 1178 32056 755-8130
  Brian Jetter, prin.
MS, RR 10 BOX 1162 32025 4-00100
  Terry Huddleston, prin. 758-4800

Lake City Community College 5-CC
  RR 3 BOX 7 32055 752-1822

Lakeland, AC 813, PC 8, Polk
Polk County SD
  Supt. — See Bartow
Jenkins HS 3-00011
  6000 LAKELAND HIGHLANDS RD 33813
  Richard Lewis, prin. 648-3566
Kathleen HS 4-00011
  2600 CRUTCHFIELD RD 33805 688-5444
  Clint Wright, prin.
Lake Gibson HS 4-00011
  7007 N SOCRUM LOOP RD 33809 858-4436
  Ralph Gilchrest, prin.
HS, 726 HOLLINGSWORTH RD 33801 4-00011
  Carolyn Baldwin, prin. 499-2900
Crystal Lake MS 3-00100
  2410 N CRYSTAL LAKE DR 33801 499-2970
  Joel Whiddon, prin.
Kathleen MS 4-00100
  3627 KATHLEEN PNES 33809 853-6040
  Gary Spruce, prin.
Lake Gibson MS 4-00100
  6901 N SOCRUM LOOP RD 33809 858-1484
  Gwen Kessell, prin.
Lakeland Highlands MS 4-00100
  740 LAKE MIRIAM DR 33813 648-3500
  David Boyd, prin.
McKeel MS, 1810 W PARKER ST 33801 3-00100
  Jack Johnson, prin. 499-2818
Southwest MS, 2815 EDEN PKY 33803 3-00100
  Don Woods, prin. 499-2840

Evangel Christian S 1-11111
  777 CARPENTERS WAY 33809 859-1477
  David Revell, prin.
Florida Southern College 4-UC
  111 LAKE HOLLINGSWORTH DR 33801
  680-4111
Lakeland Christian S 3-11111
  1111 FOREST PARK ST 33803 688-2771
  Derek Keenan, prin.
Lakeland Regional Medical Center HSP
  1400 LAKELAND HILLS BLVD 33805 687-1100

Santa Fe Catholic HS 2-00111
  3110 US HIGHWAY 92 E 33801 665-4188
  Richard Bayhan, prin.
Southeastern College Assemblies of God 4-UC
  1000 LONGFELLOW BLVD 33801 665-4404
Tampa College-Lakeland 2-UC
  1200 US HIGHWAY 98 S 33801 686-1444
Temple Christian S 2-11111
  4210 LAKELAND HIGHLANDS RD 33813
  Vernon Hammond, prin. 646-5031
Traviss Vocational-Technical Center 3-CS
  3225 WINTER LAKE RD 33803 665-1220

Lake Mary, AC 407, PC 6, Seminole
Seminole County SD
  Supt. — See Sanford
HS 4-00011
  655 LONGWOOD LAKE MARY RD 32746
  Don Smith, prin. 323-2110
Greenwood Lakes MS 4-00100
  601 LAKE PARK DR 32746 321-7560
  Teddy Barker, prin.

Lake Placid, AC 813, PC 4, Highlands
Highlands County SD
  Supt. — See Sebring
HS, 202 GREEN DRAGON DR 33852 3-00011
  Roger Goddard, prin. 699-5010
MS, 201 S TANGERINE DR 33852 3-00100
  Thomas Knowles, prin. 699-5030

Lake Wales, AC 813, PC 6, Polk
Polk County SD
  Supt. — See Bartow
HS, 1009 N 6TH ST 33853 4-00011
  Keith Windham, prin. 678-4222
Roosevelt Vo Ctr, 115 E ST 33853 Vo Tech
  Harold Maready, prin. 678-4252
McLaughlin MS, 800 S 4TH ST 33853 4-00100
  Max Linton, prin. 678-4233

Vangaurd S 2-00111
  2249 N US HIGHWAY 27 33853 676-6091
  Harry Nelson, prin.
Warner Southern College 2-UC
  5301 US HIGHWAY 27 S 33853 800-949-7248

Lake Worth, AC 407, PC 8, Palm Beach
Palm Beach County SD
  Supt. — See West Palm Beach
HS, 1701 LAKE WORTH RD 33460 4-00011
  David Cantley, prin. 533-6300
Leonard HS, 4701 10TH AVE N 33463 4-00011
  Hugh Brady, prin. 641-1200
MS, 1300 BARNETT DR 33461 3-00100
  Sharon Walker, prin. 533-6350

Palm Beach Community College 7-CC
  4200 S CONGRESS AVE 33461 439-8207

Land O'Lakes, AC 813, PC 6, Pasco
Pasco County SD 8-11111
  7227 LAND O LAKES BLVD 34639 996-3600
  Thomas Weightman, supt.
HS, 20325 GATOR LN 34639 4-00011
  Albert Bashaw, prin. 996-3888
Pine View MS 3-00100
  5334 PARKWAY BLVD 34639 996-6080
  Max Ramos, prin.
Other Schools – See Dade City, Hudson, New Port
  Richey, Zephyrhills

Lantana, AC 407, PC 6, Palm Beach
Palm Beach County SD
  Supt. — See West Palm Beach
Santaluces Community HS 5-00011
  6880 LAWRENCE RD 33462 642-6200
  Glenn Heyward, prin.
MS, 1225 W DREW ST 33462 3-00100
  Kelly Brown, prin. 533-6380

Lake Worth Christian S 2-11111
  7592 HIGH RIDGE RD 33462 586-8216
  Larry Kooi, prin.

Largo, AC 813, PC 8, Pinellas
Pinellas County SD 8-11111
  PO BOX 2942 34649 586-1818
  Howard Hinesley, supt.
HS, 410 MISSOURI AVE N 34640 4-00011
  Barb Thornton, prin. 585-5606
Pinellas Park HS, 6305 118TH AVE 34643 4-00011
  Alec Liem, prin. 538-7410
Fitzgerald MS, 6410 118TH AVE 34643 4-00100
  Linda Tucker, prin. 541-2611
MS, 155 8TH AVE SE 34641 4-00100
  William Harris, prin. 584-2165
Other Schools – See Clearwater, Dunedin, Gulfport,
  Madeira Beach, Palm Harbor, Pinellas Park, Safety
  Harbor, Saint Petersburg, Seminole, Tarpon Springs

Lauderdale Lakes, AC 305, PC 8, Broward
Broward County SD
  Supt. — See Fort Lauderdale
Anderson HS, 3050 NW 41ST ST 33309 4-00011
  Thomas Geismar, prin. 497-3800
MS, 3911 NW 30TH AVE 33309 4-00100
  Jerutha Ford, prin. 497-3900

ConCorde Career Institute 2-CS
  4000 N STATE ROAD 7 33319 731-8880

Lauderhill, AC 305, PC 8, Broward
Broward County SD
  Supt. — See Fort Lauderdale
MS, 1901 NW 49TH AVE 33313 4-00100
  Moses Barnes, prin. 497-3950

Laurel Hill, AC 904, PC 3, Okaloosa
Okaloosa County SD
  Supt. — See Fort Walton Beach
S, PO BOX 188 32567 2-11111
  Grover Hicks, prin. 652-4111

Lecanto, AC 904, PC 4, Citrus
Citrus County SD
  Supt. — See Inverness
HS 4-00011
  3810 W EDUCATIONAL PATH 34461 746-2334
  Gary Foltz, prin.
MS 3-00100
  3800 W EDUCATIONAL PATH 34461 746-2050
  James Halcomb, prin.

Leesburg, AC 904, PC 7, Lake
Lake County SD
  Supt. — See Tavares
HS, 1401 W MEADOWS AVE 34748 4-00011
  James Polk, prin. 787-5047
Carver MS, 1200 BEECHER ST 34748 3-00100
  Ken Hollingsworth, prin. 787-7868
Oak Park MS, 2101 SOUTH ST 34748 3-00100
  Carolyn Samuel, prin. 787-3232

Career Training Institute 2-CS
  101 W MAIN ST 34748 326-5134
Lake-Sumter Community College 4-CC
  9501 US HIGHWAY 441 34788 365-3573

Lehigh Acres, AC 813, PC 7, Lee
Lee County SD
  Supt. — See Fort Myers
MS, 104 ARTHUR AVE 33936 3-00100
  Maryann Willie, prin. 369-6108

Live Oak, AC 904, PC 6, Suwannee
Suwannee County SD 6-11111
  224 PARSHLEY ST SW 32060 364-2600
  Charles Blalock, supt.
Suwannee HS, 1314 PINE AVE SW 32060 4-00011
  Frank Yanossy, prin. 364-2639
Suwannee-Hamilton Area Vo-Tech Ctr Vo Tech
  415 PINEWOOD DR SW 32060 364-2750
  Walter Boatright, prin.
Suwannee MS 4-00100
  1730 WALKER AVE SW 32060 364-2730
  Wyman Harvard, prin.
Other Schools – See Branford

Suwanee-Hamilton Area Voc.-Tech. Center 2-CS
  415 PINEWOOD DR SW 32060 362-2750

Longwood, AC 407, PC 7, Seminole
Seminole County SD
  Supt. — See Sanford
Lyman HS 4-00011
  1141 COUNTY ROAD 427 S 32750 831-5600
  Carlton Henley, prin.
Milwee MS 4-00100
  1725 COUNTY ROAD 427 S 32750 831-4122
  Eugene Petty, prin.
Rock Lake MS, 250 SLADE DR 32750 4-00100
  Paul Cave, prin. 767-5447

Lynn Haven, AC 904, PC 6, Bay
Bay County SD
  Supt. — See Panama City
Mosley HS, 501 MOSLEY DR 32444 4-00011
  Hugh Tucker, prin. 872-4400
Mowat MS 3-00100
  1903 W HIGHWAY 390 32444 265-2172
  Robert Hooper, prin.

Macclenny, AC 904, PC 5, Baker
Baker County SD 5-11111
  392 SOUTH BLVD E 32063 259-6251
  Tim Starling, supt.
Baker County MS 3-00100
  211 JONATHAN ST 32063 259-2226
  Glenn McKendree, prin.
Other Schools – See Glen Saint Mary

Madeira Beach, AC 813, PC 5, Pinellas
Pinellas County SD
  Supt. — See Largo
MS, 591 MADEIRA BEACH CSWY 33708 3-00100
  Brenda Poff, prin. 391-9747

Madison, AC 904, PC 5, Madison
Madison County SD 5-11111
  PO BOX 449 32341 973-4081
  Colleen Campbell, supt.
Madison County HS 3-00011
  RR 3 BOX 2300 32340 973-4173
  Lou Miller, prin.
MS, RR 1 BOX 225 32340 3-01100
  Ernest Washington, prin. 973-2208
Other Schools – See Greenville

North Florida Junior College 3-CC
  1002 TURNER DAVIS DR 32340 973-2288

Maitland, AC 407, PC 6, Orange
Orange County SD
  Supt. — See Orlando
MS, 1901 CHOCTAW TRL 32751 3-00100
  Kathleen Palmer, prin. 647-4432

ITT Technical Institute 2-UC
2600 LAKE LUCIEN DR STE 140 32751 660-2900
Orangewood Christian S 2-11111
1221 TRINITY WOODS LN 32751 339-0223
David Jacobs, prin.

Malone, AC 904, PC 3, Jackson
Jackson County SD
Supt. — See Marianna
S, PO BOX 68 32445 3-11111
Marvin Lassiter, prin. 482-9930

Marathon, AC 305, PC 6, Monroe
Monroe County SD
Supt. — See Key West
JSHS, 350 SOMBRERO BEACH RD 33050 3-00111
William Quinn, prin. 289-2480

Margate, AC 305, PC 8, Broward
Broward County SD
Supt. — See Fort Lauderdale
MS, 500 NW 65TH AVE 33063 4-00100
Harry Lacava, prin. 977-2277

Medical Arts Training Center 2-CS
441 S STATE ROAD 7 # 4 33068 800-334-6282

Marianna, AC 904, PC 6, Jackson
Jackson County SD 6-11111
2903 JEFFERSON ST 32446 482-1200
Lowell Centers, supt.
HS, 2979 DANIELS ST 32446 3-00011
Randy Free, prin. 482-9605
MS, 4144 SOUTH ST 32448 3-00100
Dianne Oswald, prin. 482-9609
Other Schools – See Cottondale, Graceville, Grand Ridge, Malone, Sneads

Chipola Junior College 4-CC
1200 COLLEGE ST 32446 526-2761

Mayo, AC 904, PC 3, Lafayette
LaFayette County SD 4-11111
RR 2 BOX 271 32066 294-1351
Randall Hewitt, supt.
LaFayette JSHS, RR 2 BOX 270 32066 3-00111
Richard Gardner, prin. 294-1701

Melbourne, AC 407, PC 8, Brevard
Brevard County SD 8-11111
2700 SAINT JOHNS ST 32940 631-1911
Abe Collinsworth, supt.
Eau Gallie SHS 4-00001
1400 COMMODORE BLVD 32935 242-6400
Thomas Sawyer, prin.
SHS, 74 BULLDOG BLVD 32901 4-00001
Don Beggs, prin. 952-5880
Palm Bay SHS, 1 PIRATE LN 32901 4-00001
Jane Chaney, prin. 952-5900
Central JHS, 250 W BREVARD DR 32935 4-00110
William Knowles, prin. 242-6440
Johnson JHS, 2155 CROTON RD 32935 4-00110
Brenda Blackburn, prin. 242-6430
Stone JHS 3-00110
1101 E UNIVERSITY BLVD 32901 723-0741
Betty Dunn, prin.
Other Schools – See Cocoa, Cocoa Beach, Indialantic, Merritt Island, Palm Bay, Rockledge, Satellite Beach, Titusville

Brevard Christian S 2-11111
1100 DORCHESTER AVE 32904 727-2038
Wayne Guinn, prin.
Business Training Institute CS
1900 EVANS RD STE 131 32904 724-0707
Central Catholic HS 2-00011
100 E FLORIDA AVE 32901 727-0793
Joseph Mancini, prin.
Devereux Hospital & Childrens Center-FL HND
8000 DEVEREUX DR 32940 242-9100
F.I.T. Aviation 1-CS
640 HARRY SUTTON RD 32901 727-0461
Florida Air Academy 2-00111
1950 ACADEMY DR 32901 723-3211
James Dwight, prin.
Florida Institute of Technology 5-UC
150 W UNIVERSITY BLVD 32901 800-888-4348
Keiser College of Technology 2-CC
701 S BABCOCK ST 32901 255-2255
New Covenant Christian S 2-11111
4028 S BABCOCK ST 32901 724-5433
Sandra Hancock, prin.
Phillips Junior College 3-CC
2401 N HARBOR CITY BLVD 32935 254-6459

Merritt Island, AC 407, PC 8, Brevard
Brevard County SD
Supt. — See Melbourne
SHS, 100 MUSTANG WAY 32953 4-00001
Henry Smith, prin. 454-1000
Edgewood JHS 3-00110
180 E MERRITT AVE 32953 454-1030
Ann Brush, prin.
Jefferson JHS 3-00110
1275 S COURTENAY PKY 32952 453-5154
Harry Nyquist, prin.

Merritt Island Christian S 3-11111
140 MAGNOLIA AVE 32952 453-2710
Rev. Bruce Borgan, prin.

Miami, AC 305, PC 10, Dade
Dade County SD 10-11111
1450 NE 2ND AVE 33132 995-1000
Octavio Visiedo, supt.
Braddock HS 5-00011
3601 SW 147TH AVE 33185 220-9400
Frederick Bertani, prin.
Miami Central HS 5-00011
1781 NW 95TH ST 33147 696-4161
Joseph Flannigan, prin.
Miami Coral Park HS 5-00011
8865 SW 16TH ST 33165 226-6565
William Machado, prin.
Miami Edison HS 5-00011
6161 NW 5TH CT 33127 751-7337
Willa Young, prin.
HS, 2450 SW 1ST ST 33135 5-00011
Diego Garcia, prin. 649-9800
Miami Jackson HS 5-00011
1751 NW 36TH ST 33142 634-2621
Freddie Woodson, prin.
Miami Killian HS 5-00011
10655 SW 97TH AVE 33176 271-3311
Patrick Snay, prin.
Miami MacArthur South HS 2-00011
11035 SW 84TH ST 33173 279-5422
Ransom Hill, prin.
Miami Norland HS 5-00011
1050 NW 195TH ST 33169 653-1416
Fridolin Damianos, prin.
Miami Northwestern HS 4-00011
7007 NW 12TH AVE 33150 836-0991
James Monroe, prin.
Miami Palmetto HS 4-00011
7460 SW 118TH ST 33156 235-1360
Leonard Glazer, prin.
Miami Southridge HS 5-00011
19355 SW 114TH AVE 33157 238-6110
Fred Rodgers, prin.
Miami Sunset HS 5-00011
13125 SW 72ND ST 33183 385-4255
Dennis Davis, prin.
South Miami HS 4-00011
6856 SW 53RD ST 33155 666-5871
Judy Weiner, prin.
Southwest Miami HS 5-00011
8855 SW 50TH TER 33165 274-0181
Ronald Ferrer, prin.
Baker Aviation S Vo Tech
3275 NW 42ND AVE 33142 871-3143
Doris Southern, prin.
Design & Architectural Magnet HS Vo Tech
4001 NE 2ND AVE 33137 573-7135
Jackie Hinchey-Sipes, prin.
Hopkins Tech Ctr Vo Tech
750 NW 20TH ST 33127 324-6070
John Leiva, prin.
Miami Agricultural S Vo Tech
10200 NW 17TH AVE 33147 696-6721
John McKinney, prin.
Miami Skill Ctr, 50 NW 14TH ST 33136 Vo Tech
Clifton Lewis, prin. 358-4925
South Dade Skill Ctr Vo Tech
28300 SW 152ND AVE 33033 247-7839
L. Todd, prin.
Turner Technical Arts HS Vo Tech
10151 NW 19TH AVE 33147 696-8324
John McKinney, prin.
Allapattah JHS, 1331 NW 46TH ST 33142 4-00100
Gloria Evans, prin. 634-9787
Arvida JHS, 10900 SW 127TH AVE 33186 4-00100
Gerald Dreyfuss, prin. 385-7144
Brownsville JHS 3-00110
4899 NW 24TH AVE 33142 633-1481
William Clark, prin.
Centennial MS 4-00100
8601 SW 212TH ST 33189 235-1581
Donald Hoecherl, prin.
Citrus Grove MS, 2153 NW 3RD ST 33125 4-00100
Janice Reincke, prin. 642-5055
Cutler Ridge JHS 4-00110
19400 SW 97TH AVE 33157 235-4761
John Moore, prin.
Dario MS, 350 NW 97TH AVE 33172 4-00100
Carmen Roses-Maristany, prin. 226-0179
Drew JHS, 1801 NW 60TH ST 33142 3-00100
Patricia Grimsley, prin. 633-6057
Glades MS, 9451 SW 64TH TER 33173 4-00100
Thomas Zelenak, prin. 271-3342
Hammocks MS 4-00100
9889 HAMMOCKS BLVD 33196 385-0896
Althea King, prin.
Jefferson MS, 525 NW 147TH ST 33168 3-00110
Allen Hindman, prin. 681-7481
Kinloch Park MS 4-00100
4340 NW 3RD ST 33126 445-5467
George Montada, prin.
Madison JHS, 3400 NW 87TH ST 33147 4-00100
Thelma Davis, prin. 836-2610
Mann MS, 8950 NW 2ND AVE 33150 4-00100
Bettie Campbell, prin. 757-9537
McMillan MS, 13100 SW 59TH ST 33183 4-00100
Stacey Jones, prin. 385-6877
Miami Edison MS 4-00100
6101 NW 2ND AVE 33127 754-4683
Ken Rogers, prin.
Norland MS, 1235 NW 192ND TER 33169 4-00100
Consuelo Dominguez, prin. 653-1210
Palmetto JHS, 7351 SW 128TH ST 33156 4-00110
Harold Blitman, prin. 238-3911
Richmond Heights MS 3-00100
15015 SW 103RD AVE 33176 238-2316
Willie Harris, prin.
Riviera MS, 10301 SW 48TH ST 33165 4-00100
Henry Pollack, prin. 226-4286
Rockway MS, 9393 SW 29TH TER 33165 3-00100
Jorge Sotolongo, prin. 221-8212
Shenandoah MS 3-00100
1950 SW 19TH ST 33145 856-8282
Lourdes Delgado, prin.
Southwood JHS 4-00110
16301 SW 80TH AVE 33157 251-5361
Robert Kaunski, prin.
Thomas MS, 13001 SW 26TH ST 33175 4-00100
Ollie Daniels, prin. 995-3800
Washington JHS 4-00110
1200 NW 6TH AVE 33136 324-8900
Charles Bethel, prin.
West Miami MS 3-00100
7525 CORAL WAY 33155 261-8383
Marta Becquer, prin.
Westview MS, 1901 NW 127TH ST 33167 4-00100
Darrell Berteaux, prin. 681-6647
Other Schools – See Coconut Grove, Coral Gables, Goulds, Hialeah, Homestead, Miami Beach, Miami Lakes, Miami Springs, North Miami, North Miami Beach, Opa-Locka, Perrine, South Miami

American Medical Training Institute 2-CS
7360 SW 167TH ST 33157 253-8028
Archbishop Curley-Notre Dame HS 3-00011
300 NE 50TH ST 33137 751-8367
Br. Richard De Maria, prin.
ATI Career Training Center 3-CS
1 NE 19TH ST 33132 573-1600
ATI Health Education Center 2-CS
1395 NW 167TH ST STE 200 33169 628-1000
Baker Aviation School 3-CS
3275 NW 42ND AVE 33142 871-3143
Belen Jesuit Prep HS 3-00111
500 SW 127TH AVE 33184 223-8600
Rev. Garcia, prin.
Brito Miami Private S 2-11111
2732 SW 32ND AVE 33133 448-1463
Antonio Brito, prin.
Calusa Preparatory S 2-11111
12515 SW 72ND ST 33183 596-3787
Linton Fowler, prin.
Caribbean Center for Advanced Studies 2-UC
8180 NW 36TH ST FL 2 33166 593-1223
Carrollton School 2-11111
3747 MAIN HWY 33133 446-5673
Sr. Ann Taylor, prin.
Chauffeurs Training School 2-CS
4101 NW 27TH AVE 33142 638-2200
Christopher Columbus HS 4-00011
3000 SW 87TH AVE 33165 223-5650
Br. Raymond Pasi, prin.
ConCorde Career Institute 2-CS
285 NW 199TH ST 33169 652-0055
Crown Business Institute 2-CS
1223 SW 4TH ST 33135 643-1600
Florida Christian S 3-11111
4200 SW 89TH AVE 33165 226-8152
Robert Andrews, prin.
Florida Computer and Business School 2-CS
8300 W FLAGLER ST # 200 33144 553-6065
Florida International University 7-UC
TAMIAMI TRL 33199 348-2363
Florida School of Business 4-CS
2990 NW 81ST TER 33147 696-6312
Garces Commercial College 2-CS
1301 SW 1ST ST 33135 643-1044
Greater Miami Academy 2-11111
500 NW 122ND AVE 33182 220-5955
Manuel Fuentes, prin.
Gulliver Prep S 3-00011
6575 SW 88TH ST 33156 666-7937
James Williams, prin.
Hi-Tech School of Miami 2-CS
10350 W FLAGLER ST 33174 221-3423
Holy Cross Academy 2-11111
12425 SW 72ND ST 33183 598-0009
Fr. Gregory Wendt, prin.
Hope Center HND
PO BOX 10789 33101 545-7572
International Fine Arts College 3-CC
1737 N BAYSHORE DR 33132 800-255-9023
Jackson Memorial Medical Center HSP
1611 NW 12TH AVE 33136 549-6641
La Luz Lincoln-Marti S 2-11111
904 SW 23RD AVE 33135 643-4888
Demetrio Perez, prin.
LaProgresiva Presbyterian S 2-11111
PO BOX 350866 33135 642-4755
Winston Sosa, prin.
La Salle HS, 3601 S MIAMI AVE 33133 2-00011
Fr. Angelucci, prin. 854-2334
Lindsey Hopkins Technical Education Ctr. 4-CS
750 NW 20TH ST 33127 324-6070
Martin College 2-CC
1901 NW 7TH ST 33125 541-8140
Miami Christian College 2-UC
PO BOX 19674 33101 953-1100
Miami Christian S 3-11111
200 NW 109TH AVE 33172 221-7754
Clifford Hanham, prin.
Miami Country Day S 3-11111
PO BOX 380608 33238 759-2843
John Knapp, prin.

Miami-Dade Community College 8-CC
 11011 SW 104TH ST 33176 347-7478
Miami-Dade Community College 2-CC
 11380 NW 27TH AVE 33167 237-1244
Miami-Dade Community College-Medical Ctr 3-CC
 950 NW 20TH ST 33127 347-4101
Miami Institute of Technology 3-CS
 1001 SW 1ST ST 33130 324-6781
Miami Job Corps Center 2-CS
 660 SW 3RD ST 33130 325-1276
Miami Technical College 2-CS
 8672 BIRD RD 33155 559-2062
Miami Technical College 2-CS
 7601 W FLAGLER ST 33144 263-9832
Miami Technical College 2-CS
 8546 BIRD RD 33155 220-1207
Morgan Vocational-Technical Institute 4-CS
 18180 SW 122ND AVE 33177 253-9920
NEC-Bauder Campus 2-CC
 7955 W 12TH ST STE 300 33126 477-0251
Northwest Christian Academy 2-11111
 951 NW 136TH ST 33168 685-8734
 Edward Rogers, prin.
Omni Technical School 2-CS
 1710 NW 7TH ST 33125 541-6200
Our Lady of Lourdes Academy 3-00011
 5525 SW 84TH ST 33143 667-1623
 Sr. Susan Kuk, prin.
Palmer Trinity HS 2-00111
 7900 SW 176TH ST 33157 251-2230
 Allen Adriance, prin.
Politechnical Institute of Florida 2-CS
 1405 SW 107TH AVE STE 201C 33174 226-8099
Ransom-Everglade S 3-00111
 3575 MAIN HWY 33133 460-8800
 John Cotton, prin.
St. Brendan HS 4-00011
 2950 SW 87TH AVE 33165 223-5181
 Fr. James McCreanor, prin.
St. John Vianney College Seminary 1-UC
 2900 SW 87TH AVE 33165 223-4561
St. Thomas University 4-UC
 16400 NW 32ND AVE 33054 800-367-9010
Scheck Hillel Community Day S 4-11111
 PO BOX 630 33163 931-2831
 Menachem Raab, prin.
SER-IBM Business Institute 2-CS
 42 NW 27TH AVE STE 421 33125 649-7500
Southern Technical Center 2-CS
 19151 S DIXIE HWY 33157 254-0995
University of Miami 2-UC
 4600 RICKENBACKER CSWY 33149
U.S. Schools 1-CS
 100 N PLAZA 33147 836-7424
Ward Stone College 2-CS
 9020 SW 137TH AVE FL 2 33186 386-9900
Westminister Christian S 3-11111
 6855 SW 152ND ST 33157 233-2030
 Gary Adams, prin.
Westwood Christian S 2-00111
 5801 SW 120TH AVE 33183 274-3380
 Marvin Gochenour, prin.

Miami Beach, AC 305, PC 8, Dade
Dade County SD
 Supt. — See Miami
HS, 2231 PRAIRIE AVE 33139 4-00011
 William Renuart, prin. 532-4515
Nautilus JHS 4-00100
 4301 N MICHIGAN AVE 33140 532-3481
 Martin Zigler, prin.

Beth Jacob S, 620 75TH ST 33141 2-00111
 Rabbi Ephraim Leizerson, prin. 865-0763
Hebrew Academy 2-11111
 2400 PINE TREE DR 33140 532-6421
 Raymond Bloom, prin.
Mt. Sinai Medical Center HSP
 4300 ALTON RD 33140 674-2222
Talmudic College of Florida 1-UC
 4014 CHASE AVE 33140 534-8444

Miami Lakes, AC 305, PC 7, Dade
Dade County SD
 Supt. — See Miami
Miami Lakes Tech Ctr Vo Tech
 5780 NW 158TH ST 33014 557-1100
 Noward Dean, prin.

Miami Shores, AC 305, PC 7, Dade

Barry University 5-UC
 11300 NE 2ND AVE 33161 899-3000

Miami Springs, AC 305, PC 7, Dade
Dade County SD
 Supt. — See Miami
HS, 751 DOVE AVE 33166 5-00011
 Charles Bales, prin. 885-3585
JHS 4-00100
 150 S ROYAL POINCIANA BLVD 33166
 Brenda Fuentes, prin. 888-6457

Middleburg, AC 904, PC 5, Clay
Clay County SD
 Supt. — See Green Cove Springs
SHS 4-00001
 3802 COUNTY ROAD 220 32068 282-9325
 Ira Strickland, prin.
Wilkinson JHS 4-00110
 5025 COUNTY ROAD 218 32068 282-5494
 Lucian Paulk, prin.

Milton, AC 904, PC 6, Santa Rosa
Santa Rosa County SD 7-11111
 603 CANAL ST 32570 623-3663
 Bennett Russell, supt.
HS, 103 STEWART ST NW 32570 4-00011
 Bill Helms, prin. 623-0341
Central JSHS, RR 6 BOX 230 32570 2-00111
 Radford Locklin, prin. 623-5754
Locklin Vo-Tech Ctr Vo Tech
 2216 BERRYHILL RD 32570 626-1918
 (—), prin.
Hobbs MS, 309 GLOVER LN 32570 3-00100
 Nancy Padgett, prin. 623-8152
King MS, 2499 STEWART ST NW 32570 3-00100
 Jack Taylor, prin. 623-4686
Other Schools – See Gulf Breeze, Jay, Navarre, Pace

Locklin Vocational-Technical Center 2-CS
 5330 BERRYHILL RD 32570 626-1918
Santa Rosa Christian S 2-11111
 PO BOX 643 32572 623-4671
 Robert Hobbs, prin.

Miramar, AC 305, PC 8, Broward
Broward County SD
 Supt. — See Fort Lauderdale
HS, 3601 SW 89TH AVE 33025 4-00011
 Robert Gillette, prin. 437-0600
Perry MS, 3400 SW 69TH AVE 33023 4-00100
 Linda Wilhoit, prin. 985-5400

Florida Bible Christian S 3-11111
 9300 PEMBROKE RD 33025 431-6770
 Edward Emery, prin.

Monticello, AC 904, PC 5, Jefferson
Jefferson County SD 4-11111
 1490 W WASHINGTON ST 32344 997-3562
 William McRae, supt.
Jefferson County HS 3-00011
 555 TIGER LN 32344 997-3555
 Kelly Kilpatrick, prin.
Howard MS, 1145 2ND ST 32344 3-01100
 Pink Hightower, prin. 997-2512

Aucilla Christian Academy 2-11111
 RR 1 BOX 56 32344 997-3597
 James Aman, prin.

Montverde, AC 407, PC 3, Lake

Montverde Academy 2-00111
 PO BOX 560097 34756 469-2561
 Walter Stephens, prin.

Moore Haven, AC 813, PC 4, Glades
Glades County SD 3-11111
 PO BOX 459 33471 946-0323
 Gary Clark, supt.
JSHS, PO BOX 99 33471 2-00111
 Bohdan Krawchuck, prin. 946-0811

Mount Dora, AC 904, PC 6, Lake
Lake County SD
 Supt. — See Tavares
HS, 700 N HIGHLAND ST 32757 3-00011
 Dorothy Carrier, prin. 383-2177
MS, 1250 GRANT AVE 32757 3-00100
 Claude Pennacchia, prin. 383-6101

Christian Home & Bible S 2-11111
 PO BOX 1017 32757 383-2155
 C. Stutzman, prin.

Mulberry, AC 813, PC 5, Polk
Polk County SD
 Supt. — See Bartow
HS, 1 NE 4TH CIR 33860 3-00011
 Steve Petrie, prin. 425-1148
JHS, 500 SE 9TH AVE 33860 2-00100
 Frank Satchel, prin. 425-3041

Spurgeon Baptist Bible College 1-UC
 4440 SPURGEON DR 33860

Naples, AC 813, PC 7, Collier
Collier County SD 7-11111
 3710 ESTEY AVE 33942 643-2700
 Robert Munz, supt.
Collier HS, 5600 COUGAR DR 33942 4-00011
 Paul Manley, prin. 597-8171
Lely HS, 324 LELY BLVD 33962 4-00011
 Michele Lugo, prin. 774-7224
HS, 1100 22ND AVE N 33940 4-00011
 Gary Brown, prin. 261-3538
Walker Vo-Tech Ctr Vo Tech
 3702 ESTEY AVE 33942 643-0919
 Charlotte Gore, prin.
East Naples MS, 4100 ESTEY AVE 33942 3-00100
 Robert Spano, prin. 643-3531
Golden Gate MS 4-00100
 2701 48TH TER SW 33999 455-3181
 Sharon Thompson, prin.
Gulfview MS, 709 3RD AVE S 33940 3-00100
 Gene Nara, prin. 262-2453
Oakridge MS 3-00100
 151 COUNTY ROAD 951 33999 353-6565
 Virgil Morar, prin.
Pine Ridge MS 3-00100
 1515 PINE RIDGE RD 33942 597-3136
 Ray Baker, prin.
Other Schools – See Everglades City, Immokalee

International College 2-UC
 2654 TAMIAMI TRL E 33962 774-4700
St. John Neumann HS 2-00011
 3000 53RD ST SW 33999 455-3044
 Br. Peter Zawot, prin.
Walker Vocational-Technical Center 4-CS
 3702 ESTEY AVE 33942 643-0919

Navarre, AC 904, PC 3, Santa Rosa
Santa Rosa County SD
 Supt. — See Milton
Holley-Navarre MS 2-00100
 1976 WILLIAMS CREEK DR 32566 434-0667
 George Dahlgren, prin.

Neptune Beach, AC 904, PC 6, Duval
Duval County SD
 Supt. — See Jacksonville
Fletcher HS, 700 SEAGATE AVE 32266 4-00011
 Larry Paulk, prin. 247-5905

Newberry, AC 904, PC 4, Alachua
Alachua County SD
 Supt. — See Gainesville
HS, PO BOX 339 32669 3-00011
 Wiley Dixon, prin. 472-2174
AA MS, 701 S MAIN ST 32669 3-00100
 Joan Longstreth, prin. 472-7022

New Port Richey, AC 813, PC 7, Pasco
Pasco County SD
 Supt. — See Land O'Lakes
Gulf HS, 5355 SCHOOL RD 34652 4-00011
 Cheryl Renneckar, prin. 842-8485
Ridgewood HS 4-00011
 7650 ORCHID LAKE RD 34653 847-3060
 Wendell Krinn, prin.
River Ridge JSHS 4-00111
 11646 TOWN CENTER RD 34654 836-4413
 Robert Dorn, prin.
Marchman Vo Ctr Vo Tech
 7825 CAMPUS DR 34653 842-7177
 Carole Pearson, prin.
Bayonet Point MS 4-00100
 11125 LITTLE RD 34654 863-1586
 Tom Rulison, prin.
Gulf MS, 6419 LOUISIANA AVE 34653 4-00100
 Richard Koop, prin. 842-5766

Pasco-Hernando Community College 2-CC
 10239 RIDGE RD 34654 847-2727
Trinity College of Florida 2-UC
 2430 TRINITY OAKS BLVD 34655 376-6911
Webster College 2-CC
 5623 US HIGHWAY 19 STE 300 34652
 849-4993

New Smyrna Beach, AC 904, PC 7, Volusia
Volusia County SD
 Supt. — See DeLand
New Smyrna Beach HS 4-00011
 100 BARRACUDA BLVD 32169 427-4155
 Kevin Tucker, prin.
New Smyrna Beach MS 4-00100
 1200 S MYRTLE AVE 32168 426-7450
 Joseph Reed, prin.

Niceville, AC 904, PC 7, Okaloosa
Okaloosa County SD
 Supt. — See Fort Walton Beach
HS, 800 JOHN SIMS PKY E 32578 4-00011
 David Morgan, prin. 833-4114
Ruckel MS, 201 PARTIN DR N 32578 4-00100
 Ginny Morgan, prin. 833-4142

Okaloosa-Walton Community College 5-CC
 100 COLLEGE BLVD E 32578 678-5111
Rocky Bayou Christian S 2-11111
 2101 PARTIN DR N 32578 678-7358
 Robert Grete, prin.

Nokomis, AC 813, PC 5, Sarasota
Sarasota County SD
 Supt. — See Sarasota
Laurel MS, 1900 LAUREL RD E 34275 3-00100
 William Hancock, prin. 486-2171

North Fort Myers, AC 813, PC 8, Lee
Lee County SD
 Supt. — See Fort Myers
HS, 5000 ORANGE GROVE BLVD 33903 4-00011
 Edmund Stickles, prin. 995-2117
Suncoast MS 4-00100
 1856 SUNCOAST LN 33917 997-2131
 Gilbert Nedwick, prin.

North Lauderdale, AC 305, PC 8, Broward
Broward County SD
 Supt. — See Fort Lauderdale
Silver Lake MS 4-00100
 7600 TAM OSHANTER BLVD 33068 726-7590
 Nick Gancitano, prin.

North Miami, AC 305, PC 8, Dade
Dade County SD
 Supt. — See Miami
SHS, 800 NE 137TH ST 33161 4-00001
 Craig Depriest, prin. 891-6590
JHS, 13105 NE 7TH AVE 33161 4-00110
 Freddie Pittman, prin. 891-5611

Florida International University 2-UC
 BISCAYNE BLVD AND 151ST ST 33181
 940-5625

Johnson & Wales University   2-CC
1701 NE 127TH ST   33181   892-7000
Miami Technical Institute   2-CS
14701 NW 7TH AVE   33168   688-8811

North Miami Beach, AC 305, PC 8, Dade
Dade County SD
Supt. — See Miami
SHS, 1247 NE 167TH ST   33162   5-00001
Patricia D'Alessio, prin.   949-8381
Highland Oaks JHS   4-00110
2375 NE 203RD ST   33180   932-3810
Jack Gilbert, prin.
Kennedy JHS, 1075 NE 167TH ST   33162   4-00110
Valerie Carrier, prin.   947-1451

National School of Technology   3-CS
16150 NE 17TH AVE   33162   949-9500
Southeastern University/Health Sciences   2-UC
1750 NE 168TH ST   33162   949-4000

North Palm Beach, AC 407, PC 7, Palm Beach

Benjamin S   3-11111
11000 ELLISON WILSON RD   33408   626-3747
Rod Kehl, prin.
QUALTEC Institute   2-CS
11760 US HIGHWAY 1 STE 500   33408

Oakland Park, AC 305, PC 8, Broward
Broward County SD
Supt. — See Fort Lauderdale
Northeast HS, 700 NE 56TH ST   33334   4-00011
Darcia Drago, prin.   928-0300
Rickards MS, 6000 NE 9TH AVE   33334   3-00100
Paulette McLane, prin.   928-1515

ATI Career Training Center   2-CS
3501 POWERLINE RD   33309   563-5899

Ocala, AC 904, PC 8, Marion
Marion County SD, 512 SE 3RD ST   34471   8-11111
John Smith, supt.   732-8041
Forest HS, 1614 SE FORT KING ST   34471   4-00011
Gary Miller, prin.   629-8711
Lake Weir HS   4-00011
10351 SE MARICAMP RD   34472   687-4040
Roddy Michele, prin.
Vanguard HS, 7 NW 28TH ST   34475   4-00011
Kenneth Vianello, prin.   629-8994
Fort King MS, 545 NE 17TH AVE   34470   3-00100
John Livingston, prin.   622-5186
Howard MS   3-00100
1108 NW MRTN LTHR KNG JR AV   34475
Clyde Folsom, prin.   732-8088
Osceola MS   4-00100
526 SE TUSCAWILLA AVE   34471   622-5171
Lynn Herrick, prin.
Other Schools – See Belleview, Citra, Dunnellon, Summerfield

Academy Biblical Character Development   2-11111
PO BOX 9093   34479   694-2223
Ivan Dobbins, prin.
Cambridge Academy   4-00111
8340 NW 47TH ST   34482   620-2717
Tanzee Nahas, prin.
Central Florida Community College   5-CC
PO BOX 1388   34478   237-2111
Marion Co. School Radiologic Technology   CS
438 SW 3RD ST   34474   629-7545
Ocala Christian Academy   3-11111
1714 SE 36TH AVE   34471   694-4178
Jesse Bloom, prin.
St. John Lutheran S   2-11111
1915 SE LAKE WEIR RD   34471   622-7275
Andrea Fischer, prin.
Webster College   2-CC
1530 SW 3RD AVE   34474   629-1941

Ocoee, AC 407, PC 7, Orange
Orange County SD
Supt. — See Orlando
MS, 400 S LAKEWOOD AVE   34761   4-00100
Jennifer Reeves, prin.   656-4133

Okeechobee, AC 813, PC 5, Okeechobee
Okeechobee County SD
100 SW 5TH AVE   34974   6-11111
Dan Mullins, supt.   763-3157
HS, 2800 HIGHWAY 441 N   34972   4-00011
Phoebe Raulerson, prin.   763-3191
Yearling MS, 925 NW 23RD LN   34972   3-00100
Sam Smith, prin.   763-2188

Opa-Locka, AC 305, PC 7, Dade
Dade County SD
Supt. — See Miami
Miami Carol City HS   5-00011
3422 NW 187TH ST   33056   621-5681
James Hunt, prin.
Carol City JHS   4-00100
3737 NW 188TH ST   33055   624-2652
Mary Henry, prin.
Lake Stevens JHS   4-00100
18484 NW 48TH PL   33055   620-1294
Norman Lindeblad, prin.
North Dade MS   3-00100
1840 NW 157TH ST   33054   624-8415
W. Robertson, prin.
Parkway JHS, 2349 NW 175TH ST   33056   4-00100
Robert Edwards, prin.   624-9613

Beacon Career Institute   2-CS
2900 NW 183RD ST   33056   620-4637
Florida Memorial College   4-UC
15800 NW 42ND AVE   33054   800-822-1362
Monsignor Edward Pace HS   3-00011
15600 NW 32ND AVE   33054   624-8534
Richard Perhla, prin.

Orange Park, AC 904, PC 6, Clay
Clay County SD
Supt. — See Green Cove Springs
SHS, 2300 KINGSLEY AVE   32073   4-00001
William Ward, prin.   272-8110
Lakeside JHS, 2750 MOODY AVE   32073   4-00110
Richard Ramsay, prin.   272-8666
JHS, 1500 GANO AVE   32073   3-00110
Stephanie Athens, prin.   278-2000
Ridgeview JHS   4-00110
466 MADISON AVE   32065   272-8124
Joanne Roberts, prin.

National Training   2-CS
PO BOX 1899   32067   272-4000
Orange Park Christian Academy   2-11111
1324 KINSLEY AVE   32073   269-0096
Stephen Weymouth, prin.
St. Johns Country Day S   3-11111
3100 DOCTORS LAKE DR   32073   264-9572
Stephan Russey, prin.

Orlando, AC 407, PC 9, Orange
Orange County SD
PO BOX 271   32802   9-11111
James Schott, supt.   849-3200
Boone HS, 2000 S MILLS AVE   32806   4-00011
Bruce Suther, prin.   898-5491
Colonial HS, 6100 OLEANDER DR   32807   5-00011
Everette Wright, prin.   277-5431
Cypress Creek HS   4-00011
1101 BEAR CROSSING DR   32824   859-0203
Joseph Worsham, prin.
Edgewater HS   4-00011
3100 EDGEWATER DR   32804   849-0130
Robert Williams, prin.
Evans HS, 4949 SILVER STAR RD   32808   5-00011
Dan Buckman, prin.   293-4900
Jones HS, 801 S RIO GRANDE AVE   32805   4-00011
Eddie Sneed, prin.   425-4681
Oak Ridge HS   5-00011
6000 WINEGARD RD   32809   855-2911
Dick Damron, prin.
Phillips HS   5-00011
6500 TURKEY LAKE RD   32819   352-4040
Larry Payne, prin.
University HS   4-00011
11501 EASTWOOD DR   32817   275-7627
Judy Cunningham, prin.
Orlando Vo-Tech Ctr   Vo Tech
301 W AMELIA ST   32801   425-2756
Joseph McCoy, prin.
Carver MS, 4500 COLUMBIA ST   32811   3-00100
Joseph Menchan, prin.   293-6541
Colonial 9th Grade Center   2-00010
7775 VALENCIA COLLEGE LN   32807   249-1002
Everette Wright, prin.
Conway MS, 4600 ANDERSON RD   32812   4-00100
Debora Graves, prin.   275-9263
Discovery MS   4-00100
11550 LOKANOTOSA TRL   32817   381-9970
Kathryn Blackburn, prin.
Evan 9th Grade Center   3-00010
2751 N APOPKA VINELAND RD   32818   296-6467
Joseph Saulsby, prin.
Howard MS, 800 E ROBINSON ST   32801   3-00100
Isom Rivers, prin.   425-2636
Jackson MS   4-00100
6000 STONEWALL JACKSON RD   32807
Lester Dabbs, prin.   275-1230
Lee MS, 1201 MAURY RD   32804   4-00100
Gary Schadow, prin.   843-1090
Liberty MS   4-00100
3405 S CHICKASAW TRL   32829   275-7610
Mary Bailey, prin.
Lockhart MS, 3411 DR LOVE RD   32810   4-00100
Otto Dickman, prin.   293-3655
Meadowbrook MS   4-00100
6000 NORTH LN   32808   295-8200
Lawrence Fox, prin.
Memorial MS, 2220 29TH ST   32805   4-00100
Prince Kelly, prin.   425-9016
Robinswood MS   4-00100
6305 BALBOA DR   32818   293-6000
Harriet Coleman, prin.
Southwest MS   4-00100
6450 DR PHILLIPS BLVD   32819   363-4822
John Meinecke, prin.
Union Park MS   3-00100
1844 WESTFALL DR   32817   277-4611
Glennis Terry, prin.
Walker MS, 150 AMIDON LN   32809   4-00100
Frances Cuddy, prin.   855-4016
Westridge MS   4-00100
3800 W OAK RIDGE RD   32809   351-5221
Ernest Bradley, prin.
Other Schools – See Apopka, Lake Buena Vista, Maitland, Ocoee, Winter Garden, Winter Park

Bishop Moore HS   3-00011
3901 EDGEWATER DR   32804   293-7561
Maureen Huntington, prin.

Career Training Institute   2-CS
2120 W COLONIAL DR   32804   843-3984
Central Florida Blood Bank   HSP
32 W GORE ST   32806   849-6100
Devereux Orlando Center   2-HND
6131 CHRISTIAN WAY   32808   296-5300
Downey Christian S   2-11111
PO BOX 677040   32867   275-0340
Joseph Zobel, prin.
Eastland Christian S   2-11111
6000 E COLONIAL DR   32807   277-5858
Dolores Green, prin.
Florida Hospital Medical Center   HSP
601 E ROLLINS ST   32803   896-6611
Florida Technical College   2-CS
1819 N SEMORAN BLVD   32807   678-5600
Heritage Prep S   2-11111
6000 W COLONIAL DR   32808   295-3086
Barbara Stewart, prin.
Lake Highland Prep S   4-11111
901 HIGHLAND AVE   32803   425-8688
Robert Mayfield, prin.
Luther HS   2-00111
550 N ECONLOCKHATCHEE TRL   32825   275-7750
Richard Wallace, prin.
Mid-Florida Tech. Institute   5-CS
2900 W OAK RIDGE RD   32809   855-5800
Motorcycle Mechanics Institute   2-CS
9751 DELEGATES DR   32837   240-2422
Orlando College - North   4-UC
5500 DIPLOMAT CIR   32810   628-5870
Orlando College - South   2-UC
2411 SAND LAKE RD   32809   841-1410
Orlando Regional Medical Center   HSP
1414 KUHL AVE   32806   841-5111
Orlando Vocational-Technical Center   4-CS
301 W AMELIA ST   32801   425-2756
Pine Castle Christian Academy   3-11111
731 FAIRLANE AVE   32809   438-2737
Nancy Boss, prin.
Pine Hills Christian Academy   2-11111
800 N PINE HILLS RD   32808   293-4571
Carl Swindell, prin.
Southern College   4-CC
5600 LAKE UNDERHILL RD   32807   273-1000
University of Central Florida   7-UC
PO BOX 25000   32816   823-3000
Valencia Community College   7-CC
PO BOX 3028   32802   299-5000
Valencia Community College East Campus   2-CC
701 N ECONLOCKHATCHEE TRL   32825
299-5000

Ormond Beach, AC 904, PC 8, Volusia
Volusia County SD
Supt. — See DeLand
MS, 151 DOMICILIO AVE   32174   4-00100
Roben Smith, prin.   676-1250

Calvary Christian Academy   2-11111
1687 W GRANADA BLVD   32174   672-2081
John Patterson, prin.
Harry Wendelstedt Umpire School   CS
88 S SAINT ANDREWS DR   32174   672-4879

Oviedo, AC 407, PC 7, Seminole
Seminole County SD
Supt. — See Sanford
HS, 601 KING ST   32765   4-00011
Wayne Epps, prin.   365-5671
Jackson Heights MS   4-00100
141 ACADEMY AVE   32765   365-3262
Michael Mizwicki, prin.
Tuskawilla MS   4-00100
1801 TUSKAWILLA RD   32765   678-2552
Gene Brewer, prin.

Pace, AC 904, PC 6, Santa Rosa
Santa Rosa County SD
Supt. — See Milton
HS, 4065 NORRIS RD   32571   4-00011
Frank Lay, prin.   994-5193
MS, 4085 NORRIS RD   32571   3-00100
Wanda Knowles, prin.   994-4013

Pahokee, AC 407, PC 6, Palm Beach
Palm Beach County SD
Supt. — See West Palm Beach
JSHS, 900 LARRIMORE RD   33476   3-00111
Grace Jones, prin.   924-6400

Palatka, AC 904, PC 7, Putnam
Putnam County SD, 200 S 7TH ST   32177   7-11111
Geri Melosh, supt.   329-0510
HS, 302 MELLON RD   32177   4-00011
John Murray, prin.   329-0579
Beasley MS, 1100 S 18TH ST   32177   3-00100
William Black, prin.   329-0569
Jenkins MS, 1100 N 19TH ST   32177   3-00100
Janet Cavuoti, prin.   329-0588
Other Schools – See Crescent City, Interlachen

St. Johns River Community College   4-CC
5001 SAINT JOHNS AVE   32177   328-1571

Palm Bay, AC 407, PC 8, Brevard
Brevard County SD
Supt. — See Melbourne
Southwest JHS   4-00110
451 ELDRON BLVD SE   32909   952-5800
Robert Petty, prin.

Palm Beach Gardens, AC 407, PC 7, Palm Beach
Palm Beach County SD
  Supt. — See West Palm Beach
Dwyer HS   3-00011
  13601 N MILITARY TRL 33410   625-7800
  Doug Long, prin.
HS, 4245 HOLLY DR 33410   4-00011
  Margaret Walton, prin.   694-7300
Duncan MS, 5150 117TH CT N 33418   4-00100
  Donald Rott, prin.   775-7215
Watkins MS   3-00100
  9480 MCARTHUR BLVD 33403   694-7375
  Bruce Mitchell, prin.

Palm City, AC 407, PC 5, Martin
Martin County SD
  Supt. — See Stuart
Hidden Oaks MS   3-00100
  2801 SW MARTIN HWY 34990   220-0034
  Shirley Granfield, prin.

Palm Coast, AC 904, PC 7, Flagler

FAA Center for Management Development   2-CS
  4500 PALM COAST PKY SE 32137   445-6381

Palmetto, AC 813, PC 6, Manatee
Manatee County SD
  Supt. — See Bradenton
HS, 1200 17TH ST W 34221   3-00011
  Jerry Cole, prin.   723-4848
Lincoln MS, 1400 1ST AVE E 34221   3-00100
  Ronald Hirst, prin.   723-4888

Palm Harbor, AC 813, PC 8, Pinellas
Pinellas County SD
  Supt. — See Largo
Carwise MS, 3301 BENTLEY DR 34684   3-00110
  John Leanes, prin.   588-6448
MS, 1800 TAMPA RD 34683   4-00100
  Pegoty Lopez, prin.   784-3984

Panama City, AC 904, PC 8, Bay
Bay County SD   7-11111
  1311 BALBOA AVE 32401   872-4100
  Stefanie Gall, supt.
Bay HS, 1200 HARRISON AVE 32401   4-00011
  Fred Goodwin, prin.   872-4600
Rutherford HS   4-00011
  1000 SCHOOL AVE 32401   872-4500
  Ernest Spiva, prin.
Haney Vo-Tech Ctr   Vo Tech
  3016 HIGHWAY 77 32405   769-2191
  Marion Riviere, prin.
Brown MS   3-00100
  5601 MERRITT BROWN RD 32404   872-4740
  Thomas Bowers, prin.
Everitt MS, 608 SCHOOL AVE 32401   3-00100
  David Creel, prin.   872-4790
Jinks MS, 600 W 11TH ST 32401   3-00100
  James McCallister, prin.   872-4695
Rosenwald MS, 1310 E 11TH ST 32401   3-00100
  Carol Love, prin.   872-4580
Surfside MS, 300 NAUTILUS ST 32413   4-01100
  Joel Creel, prin.   233-5380
Other Schools – See Lynn Haven

Covenant Christian S   2-11111
  2350 FRANKFORD AVE 32405   769-7448
  Jesse Bealor, prin.
Gulf Coast Community College   5-CC
  5230 W HIGHWAY 98 32401   769-1551
Haney Vocational-Technical Center   3-CS
  3016 HIGHWAY 77 32405   769-2191
Panama City Christian S   3-11111
  1104 BALBOA AVE 32401   769-2291
  Paul Williamson, prin.
Rock S, 2413 HARRIS AVE 32405   2-11111
  Steve Skinner, prin.   785-8334

Parkland, AC 305, PC 5, Broward
Broward County SD
  Supt. — See Fort Lauderdale
Douglas HS   4-00011
  5901 PINE ISLAND RD 33076   345-4900
  Michael Kinghorn, prin.

Paxton, AC 904, PC 3, Walton
Walton County SD
  Supt. — See De Funiak Springs
S, PO BOX 1168 32538   3-11111
  Virginia Pridgen, prin.   834-2111

Pembroke Pines, AC 305, PC 8, Broward
Broward County SD
  Supt. — See Fort Lauderdale
Pines MS, 200 N DOUGLAS RD 33024   4-00100
  Fran Bolden, prin.   437-0577
Young Resource Center MS   3-00100
  901 NW 129TH AVE 33028   437-0500
  Jim Davidson, prin.

Broward Community College-South Campus   2-CC
  7200 PINES BLVD 33024

Pensacola, AC 904, PC 8, Escambia
Escambia County SD   8-11111
  PO BOX 1470 32597   432-6121
  William Maloy, supt.
Escambia HS, 1310 N 65TH AVE 32506   4-00011
  Kenneth Sandiford, prin.   453-3221
HS, 500 W MAXWELL ST 32501   4-00011
  Horace Jones, prin.   433-8291

Pine Forest HS   4-00011
  2500 LONGLEAF DR 32526   944-1121
  Eula Largue, prin.
Washington HS   4-00011
  6000 COLLEGE PKY 32504   478-8134
  Eugene Pettis, prin.
Woodham HS, 150 E BURGESS RD 32503   4-00011
  Larry Rich, prin.   478-4020
Stone Area Vo-Tech Ctr   Vo Tech
  RR 10 BOX 530 32526   944-1424
  Robert Lindner, prin.
Bellview MS, 6201 MOBILE HWY 32526   4-00100
  Elizabeth Miller, prin.   944-0616
Brentwood MS, 201 HANCOCK LN 32503   3-00100
  Mary Fryman, prin.   494-5640
Brown-Barge MS   2-00100
  151 E FAIRFIELD DR 32503   444-2700
  Camille Barr, prin.
Brownsville MS, 1800 N KIRK ST 32505   3-00100
  Thomas Frazier, prin.   444-2400
Ferry Pass MS, 8355 YANCEY AVE 32514   4-00100
  Bill Fillingim, prin.   494-5650
Wedgewood MS   3-00100
  3420 W PINESTEAD RD 32505   494-5660
  Richard Messmer, prin.
Workman MS, 6299 LANIER DR 32504   4-00100
  Elvin McCorvey, prin.   494-5665
Other Schools – See Cantonment, Century, Gonzalez,
  Walnut Hill, Warrington

East Hill Christian S   2-11111
  1600 E MORENO ST 32503   432-2321
  William Wilson, prin.
Florida Institute of Ultrasound   1-CS
  8800 UNIVERSITY PKY STE 4A 32514   478-7300
George Stone Vocational Technical Center   3-CS
  2400 LONGLEAF DR 32526   944-1424
Gold Coast Christian Academy   2-11111
  3685 MULDOON RD 32526   453-3147
  Louis Lenso, prin.
Pensacola Catholic HS   2-00011
  3043 W SCOTT ST 32505   436-6400
  Sr. Kierstin Martin, prin.
Pensacola Christian College   2-UC
  PO BOX 18000 32523   478-8496
Pensacola Christian S   4-11111
  PO BOX 18000 32523   478-8480
  Arlin Horton, prin.
Pensacola Junior College   7-CC
  1000 COLLEGE BLVD 32504   484-1600
University of West Florida   6-UC
  11000 UNIVERSITY PKY 32514   474-2230

Perrine, AC 305, PC 7, Dade
Dade County SD
  Supt. — See Miami
Morgan Vo-Tech Inst   Vo Tech
  18180 SW 122ND AVE 33177   253-9920
  Fred Reed, prin.

Perry, AC 904, PC 6, Taylor
Taylor County SD   5-11111
  PO BOX 1603 32347   584-2009
  Elouise Gardiner, supt.
Taylor County HS   3-00011
  601 E LAFAYETTE ST 32347   584-7211
  James Sinor, prin.
Taylor Co. Vo-Tech Ctr   Vo Tech
  3233 S BYRON BUTLER PKY 32347   584-7603
  Bryant Russell, prin.
Taylor County JHS   2-00100
  318 N CLARK ST 32347   584-6426
  Tim Tripp, prin.

Pierson, AC 904, PC 5, Volusia
Volusia County SD
  Supt. — See DeLand
Taylor JSHS   3-00111
  100 E WASHINGTON AVE 32180   749-8700
  Peter Oatman, prin.

Pinellas Park, AC 813, PC 8, Pinellas
Pinellas County SD
  Supt. — See Largo
MS, 6940 70TH AVE 34665   3-00100
  Edward Douglas, prin.   546-3583

Pinellas Park Christian S   2-11111
  4981 78TH AVE 34665   546-9075
  William Slater, prin.

Plantation, AC 305, PC 8, Broward
Broward County SD
  Supt. — See Fort Lauderdale
HS, 6901 NW 16TH ST 33313   4-00011
  William Milano, prin.   797-4400
South Plantation HS   4-00011
  1300 SW 54TH AVE 33317   797-4600
  Paul Woodall, prin.
MS, 6600 W SUNRISE BLVD 33313   4-00100
  James Moller, prin.   797-4300
Seminole MS, 6200 SW 16TH ST 33317   4-00100
  Douglas Parrish, prin.   797-4350

American Academy   2-11111
  12200 W BROWARD BLVD 33325   473-0606
  William Laurie, prin.
American Heritage S   3-11111
  12200 W BROWARD BLVD 33325   472-0022
  William Laurie, prin.

Broward Christian S   2-11111
  1490 N FLAMINGO RD 33323   472-5750
  Ray Nichols, prin.

Plant City, AC 813, PC 7, Hillsborough
Hillsborough County SD
  Supt. — See Tampa
SHS, 1 RAIDER PL 33566   4-00001
  Douglas Erwin, prin.   754-1541
Tomlin JHS   4-00110
  501 N WOODROW WILSON ST 33567   754-2678
  William Maxwell, prin.
Turkey Creek JHS   4-00110
  5005 TURKEY CREEK RD 33567   737-1447
  Ron Frost, prin.

Hillsborough Community College   6-CC
  1206 N PARK RD 33566   757-2100
S & S Aircraft Flight Academy   1-CS
  PO BOX 1196 33564

Pompano Beach, AC 305, PC 8, Broward
Broward County SD
  Supt. — See Fort Lauderdale
Ely HS, 1201 NW 6TH AVE 33060   4-00011
  Hattie Giles, prin.   786-3600
Crystal Lake MS   4-00100
  3551 NE 3RD AVE 33064   786-3550
  Norbert Williams, prin.
MS, 310 NE 6TH ST 33060   4-00100
  Dan O'Keefe, prin.   786-7778

Highlands Christian Academy   3-11111
  501 NE 48TH ST 33064   421-1747
  Rev. Holland, prin.
Pompano Academy of Aeronautics   2-CS
  1006 NE 10TH ST 33060   800-545-7262
Ultrasound Diagnostic School   2-CS
  2760 E ATLANTIC BLVD 33062   942-6551

Ponce De Leon, AC 904, PC 2, Holmes
Holmes County SD
  Supt. — See Bonifay
JSHS, PO BOX 39 32455   2-00111
  Michael Anderson, prin.   836-4242

Ponte Vedra Beach, AC 904, PC 4, St. Johns
St. John's County SD
  Supt. — See Saint Augustine
Landrum MS, 230 LANDRUM LN 32082   2-00100
  Robert Allten, prin.   285-9080

Port Charlotte, AC 813, PC 8, Charlotte
Charlotte County SD   7-11111
  1445 PIATTI DR 33948   255-0808
  Robert Bedford, supt.
HS, 18200 TOLEDO BLADE BLVD 33948   4-00011
  Ellen Gray, prin.   625-9000
Charlotte Vo-Tech Ctr   Vo Tech
  18300 TOLEDO BLADE BLVD 33948   629-6819
  Roseann Samson, prin.
Murdock JHS   3-00100
  17325 MARINER WAY 33948   625-6677
  Louis Long, prin.
JHS, 23000 MIDWAY BLVD 33952   3-00100
  Clyde Hoff, prin.   625-5554
Other Schools – See Englewood, Punta Gorda,
  Rotonda West

Charlotte Vocational-Technical Center   3-CS
  18300 TOLEDO BLADE BLVD 33948   629-6819

Port Orange, AC 904, PC 8, Volusia
Volusia County SD
  Supt. — See DeLand
Spruce Creek HS, 801 TAYLOR RD 32127   4-00011
  Davin Hinson, prin.   756-7200
Silver Sands MS   4-00100
  1300 HERBERT ST 32119   322-7550
  Carol Kelley, prin.

Port Saint Joe, AC 904, PC 8, Gulf
Gulf County SD   4-11111
  CO COURTHOUSE 32456   229-8256
  B. Wilder, supt.
JSHS, 800 NILES RD 32456   3-00111
  Wesley Taylor, prin.   229-8251
Other Schools – See Wewahitchka

Faith Christian S, PO BOX 961 32456   2-11111
  Rev. Goebert, prin.   229-6707

Port Saint Lucie, AC 407, PC 4, St. Lucie
St. Lucie County SD
  Supt. — See Fort Pierce
HS, 1201 SE JAGUAR LN 34952   4-00011
  Charles Cuomo, prin.   337-6770
Northport MS   4-00100
  250 NW FLORESTA DR 34983   340-4700
  John Townsend, prin.
Southport MS   3-00100
  2420 SE MORNINGSIDE BLVD 34952   337-5900
  James Thomas, prin.

Princeton, AC 305, PC 6, Dade

Princeton Christian S   2-11111
  PO BOX 4299 33032   258-3107
  Charles Magsig, prin.

Punta Gorda, AC 813, PC 7, Charlotte
Charlotte County SD
  Supt. — See Port Charlotte

Charlotte HS, 1250 COOPER ST 33950   4-00011
   David Hulsey, prin.   639-2118
JHS, 825 CARMALITA ST 33950   3-00100
   Michael Bochenek, prin.   639-5188

Quincy, AC 904, PC 6, Gadsden
Gadsden County SD   6-11111
   PO BOX 1499 32353   627-9651
   Harold Henderson, supt.
Shanks HS, 1400 W KING ST 32351   4-00011
   Albert Wanton, prin.   875-8737
Gadsden Vo-Tech S   Vo Tech
   201 EXPERIMENT STATION RD 32351   627-7591
   Donald Mathews, prin.
Carter-Paramore MS   3-00100
   631 S STEWART ST 32351   627-6030
   Charles Fuller, prin.
Other Schools – See Chattahoochee, Greensboro, Havana

Munroe S, RR 5 BOX 35 32351   2-11111
   Les Jones, prin.   856-5500

Riverview, AC 813, PC 5, Hillsborough

Providence Christian S   2-11111
   5416 PROVIDENCE RD 33569   689-7127
   David Stockard, prin.

Riviera Beach, AC 407, PC 8, Palm Beach
Palm Beach County SD
   Supt. — See West Palm Beach
Suncoast HS, 600 W 28TH ST 33404   3-00011
   Kay Carnes, prin.   881-4675
North Tech Ctr, 7071 GARDEN RD 33404   Vo Tech
   Patricia Nugent, prin.   881-4600
Kennedy MS, 1901 AVENUE S 33404   3-00100
   Clifford Durden, prin.   881-4700

Greater Bethel Christian S   2-11111
   2800 AVENUE R 33404   842-1349
   Freida Hightower, prin.
North Technical Education Center   4-CS
   7071 GARDEN RD 33404   881-4600

Rockledge, AC 407, PC 7, Brevard
Brevard County SD
   Supt. — See Melbourne
HS, 220 RAIDER RD 32955   3-00011
   Thomas McIntyre, prin.   636-3711
Kennedy MS, 2100 FISKE BLVD S 32955   3-00100
   Robert Backus, prin.   633-3500

Rotonda West, AC 813, PC 5, Charlotte
Charlotte County SD
   Supt. — See Port Charlotte
Ainger JHS, 245 CONCORD RD 33947   3-00100
   Charles Sullivan, prin.   625-9600

Royal Palm Beach, AC 407, PC 7, Palm Beach
Palm Beach County SD
   Supt. — See West Palm Beach
Crestwood Community MS   4-00100
   64 SPARROW DR 33411   795-4943
   Brenda Montgomery, prin.

Ruskin, AC 813, PC 6, Hillsborough

First Baptist/Ruskin Christian S   2-11111
   820 COLLEGE AVE W 33570   645-6441
   William Taylor, prin.

Safety Harbor, AC 813, PC 7, Pinellas
Pinellas County SD
   Supt. — See Largo
MS, 125 7TH ST N 34695   4-00100
   Sally Barker, prin.   724-1400

Saint Augustine, AC 904, PC 7, St. Johns
St. John's County SD   7-11111
   40 ORANGE ST 32084   826-2000
   Gary Matthews, supt.
Nease HS, 10550 RAY RD 32095   4-00011
   William Mignon, prin.   824-7275
HS, 3205 VARELLA AVE 32095   4-00011
   Paula Steele, prin.   829-3471
St. Augustine Tech Ctr   Vo Tech
   2980 COLLINS AVE 32095   824-4401
   Steve Hand, prin.
Murray MS, 150 N HOLMES BLVD 32095   3-00100
   Harriette Coffee, prin.   824-6126
Sebastian MS   3-00100
   2955 LEWIS SPEEDWAY 32095   824-5548
   Ron Mickler, prin.
Other Schools – See Jacksonville, Ponte Vedra Beach

Flagler College   4-UC
   PO BOX 1027 32085   829-6481
Florida School for the Deaf and Blind   HND
   207 SAN MARCO AVE 32084
St. Augustine Technical Center   4-CS
   2980 COLLINS AVE 32095   824-4401
St. Joseph Academy   2-00011
   425 COLUMBUS ST 32095   824-0431
   Edward Locks, prin.

Saint Cloud, AC 407, PC 7, Osceola
Osceola County SD
   Supt. — See Kissimmee
HS, 2000 BULLDOG LN 34769   4-00011
   Tom Marcy, prin.   892-5106
MS, 1975 MICHIGAN AVE 34769   3-00100
   Gary Mogensen, prin.   892-5181

Saint Leo, PC 4, Pasco

St. Leo College   5-UC
   PO BOX 2008 33574   800-247-6559

Saint Petersburg, AC 813, PC 9, Pinellas
Pinellas County SD
   Supt. – See Largo
Gibbs HS, 850 34TH ST S 33711   4-00011
   Barb Shorter, prin.   893-5452
Hollins HS, 4940 62ND ST N 33709   4-00011
   John McLay, prin.   547-7876
Lakewood HS, 1400 54TH AVE S 33705   4-00011
   Walter Hall, prin.   893-2916
Northeast HS, 1717 54TH AVE N 33714   4-00011
   Michael Miller, prin.   570-3138
HS, 2501 5TH AVE N 33713   4-00011
   Barb Broughton, prin.   323-4100
Azalea MS, 7855 22ND AVE N 33710   3-00100
   Joann Andrews, prin.   345-0365
Bay Point MS, 2151 62ND AVE S 33712   4-00100
   Dennis Griffin, prin.   866-3121
Meadowlawn MS, 5900 16TH ST N 33703   3-00100
   J. Doug Gregory, prin.   527-7383
Riviera MS, 501 62ND AVE NE 33702   3-00100
   Carl Mostellar, prin.   526-9036
Sixteenth Street MS   4-00100
   701 16TH ST S 33705   822-2633
   Thomas Jones, prin.
Southside Fundamental MS   3-00100
   1701 10TH ST S 33705   896-3648
   Robert Jackson, prin.
Tyrone MS, 6421 22ND AVE N 33710   3-00100
   Victoria Desmond, prin.   384-6598

Admiral Farragut Academy   2-01111
   501 PARK ST N 33710   384-5501
   Edward Gilgenast, prin.
Bayfront Medical Center   HSP
   701 6TH ST S 33701   893-6604
Canterbury School of Florida   2-11111
   901 58TH AVE NE 33703   525-1419
   John Kenyon, prin.
Eckerd College   4-UC
   PO BOX 12560 33733   800-451-3212
Keswick Christian S   3-11111
   10101 54TH AVE N 33708   393-9100
   Donald Barber, prin.
Northside Christian S   3-11111
   7777 62ND AVE N 33709   541-7593
   Bruce Bucholtz, prin.
Pinellas Technical Education Center   5-CS
   901 34TH ST S 33711   327-3671
Poynter Institute for Media Studies   4-CS
   801 3RD ST S 33701   821-9494
St. Petersburg Catholic HS   2-00011
   6333 9TH AVE N 33710   344-4065
   Fr. Gabriel Zeis, prin.
St. Petersburg Junior College   7-CC
   PO BOX 13489 33733   341-3600
Shorecrest Prep S, 5101 1ST ST NE 33703   3-11111
   Mary Booker, prin.   522-2111
Stetson University   2-UC
   1401 61ST ST S 33707
University of South Florida 33701   2-UC
Van Dyck Institute of Tourism   2-CC
   1301 66TH ST N 33710   347-0074

Sanford, AC 407, PC 8, Seminole
Seminole County SD   8-11111
   1211 S MELLONVILLE AVE 32771   322-1252
   Paul Hagerty, supt.
Seminole HS   4-00011
   2701 RIDGEWOOD AVE 32773   322-4352
   Gretchen Schapker, prin.
Lakeview MS   3-00100
   100 LAKEVIEW AVE 32773   323-1610
   James Shupe, prin.
MS, 1700 S FRENCH AVE 32771   3-00100
   William Moore, prin.   322-3063
Other Schools – See Altamonte Springs, Casselberry, Lake Mary, Longwood, Oviedo, Winter Park, Winter Springs

Seminole Community College   6-CC
   100 WELDON BLVD 32773   323-1450
Seminole Trinity Christian S   2-11111
   801 W 22ND ST 32771   322-3942
   Gloria Rumler, prin.

Sarasota, AC 813, PC 8, Sarasota
Sarasota County SD   8-11111
   2418 HATTON ST 34237   953-5000
   Charles Fowler, supt.
Booker HS, 3201 N ORANGE AVE 34234   3-00011
   Janice Gibbs, prin.   355-2967
Riverview HS, 1 RAM WAY 34231   4-00011
   Arthur Williams, prin.   923-1484
HS, 1001 S TAMIAMI TRL 34236   4-00011
   Raymond Rainone, prin.   955-0181
Sarasota Co. Vo Ctr   Vo Tech
   4747 BENEVA RD 34233   924-1365
   Steve Harvey, prin.
Booker MS, 2250 MYRTLE ST 34234   3-00100
   Michael Mensch, prin.   359-5824
Brookside MS, 3636 S SHADE AVE 34239   4-00100
   Louis Robinson, prin.   361-6472
McIntosh MS, 701 MCINTOSH RD 34232   4-00100
   Robert Hageman, prin.   361-6520
MS, 1001 S SCHOOL AVE 34237   4-00100
   Allen Wilson, prin.   361-6464

Other Schools – See Nokomis, Venice

Cardinal Mooney HS   3-00011
   4171 FRUITVILLE RD 34232   371-4917
   Sr. Mary Haas, prin.
New College University of South Florida   4-UC
   5700 N TAMIAMI TRL 34243   359-4269
Ringling School of Art & Design   3-UC
   2700 N TAMIAMI TRL 34234   800-255-7695
Sarasota Christian S   2-11111
   5415 BAHIA VISTA ST 34232   371-6481
   Steven Ponchot, prin.
Sarasota Co. Vocational Technical Ctr.   4-CS
   4748 BENEVA RD 34233   924-1365
University of Sarasota   1-UC
   5250 17TH ST 34235   379-0404
West Florida Christian S   2-11111
   4311 WILKINSON RD 34233   921-6311
   David Bedell, prin.

Satellite Beach, AC 407, PC 6, Brevard
Brevard County SD
   Supt. — See Melbourne
Satelite SHS, 300 SCORPION CT 32937   4-00001
   Rita Galbraith, prin.   779-2000
Delaura JHS, 300 JACKSON AVE 32937   3-00110
   James Parker, prin.   773-7581

Sebastian, AC 407, PC 7, Indian River
Indian River County SD
   Supt. — See Vero Beach
Sebastian River JHS   3-00110
   9400 FELLSMERE RD 32958   589-8995
   Gregory Pearsaul, prin.

Sebring, AC 813, PC 6, Highlands
Highlands County SD   6-11111
   426 SCHOOL ST 33870   382-1121
   Richard Farmer, supt.
HS, 3514 KENILWORTH BLVD 33870   4-00011
   Dewayne Lemler, prin.   385-6176
MS, 500 E CENTER AVE 33870   4-00100
   David Spiegel, prin.   471-5444
Other Schools – See Avon Park, Lake Placid

Heartland Christian S   2-11111
   1160 PERSIMMON AVE 33870   385-6827
   Charles Scheihing, prin.

Seffner, AC 813, PC 3, Hillsborough
Hillsborough County SD
   Supt. — See Tampa
Armwood SHS   4-00011
   12000 E US HIGHWAY 92 33584   689-1217
   Evelyn Hughes, prin.

Seminole, AC 813, PC 6, Pinellas
Pinellas County SD
   Supt. — See Largo
Osceola HS, 9751 98TH ST 34647   4-00011
   Richard Misenti, prin.   393-8734
HS, 8401 131ST ST 34646   4-00011
   Richard Duncan, prin.   547-7536
Osceola MS, 9301 98TH ST 34647   3-00100
   Fred Ulrich, prin.   398-7408
MS, 8701 131ST ST 34646   4-00100
   Kate Herrington, prin.   393-8718

Shalimar, AC 904, PC 2, Okaloosa
Okaloosa County SD
   Supt. — See Fort Walton Beach
Meigs MS, 150 RICHBOURG AVE 32579   3-00100
   Robert Smith, prin.   833-4301

Sneads, AC 904, PC 4, Jackson
Jackson County SD
   Supt. — See Marianna
JSHS, PO BOX 219 32460   2-00111
   James Edwards, prin.   382-9007

South Daytona, AC 904, PC 7, Volusia

Warner Christian Academy   2-11111
   1730 S RIDGEWOOD AVE 32119   767-5451
   Russell Richards, prin.

South Miami, AC 305, PC 7, Dade
Dade County SD
   Supt. — See Miami
JHS, 6750 SW 60TH ST 33143   4-00110
   Rasamma Nyberg, prin.   661-3481

Jones College   2-CC
   5975 SUNSET DR STE 100 33143   669-9606

Spring Hill, PC 8, Hernando
Hernando County SD
   Supt. — See Brooksville
Springstead SHS   4-00001
   3300 MARINER BLVD 34609   904-683-2843
   Richard Fauble, prin.
Springstead West JHS   3-00010
   9412 FOX CHAPEL LN 34606   904-683-6368
   Richard Fauble, prin.

Starke, AC 904, PC 6, Bradford
Bradford County SD   5-11111
   582 N TEMPLE AVE 32091   964-6800
   Jo Ann Rowe, supt.
Bradford HS, 581 N TEMPLE AVE 32091   4-00011
   Steven McLeod, prin.   964-6800
Bradford Union Vo-Tech Ctr   Vo Tech
   609 N ORANGE ST 32091   964-6800
   James Ward, prin.

Bradford MS, 527 N ORANGE ST 32091 3-00100
Robert Paterson, prin. 964-6800

Stuart, AC 407, PC 7, Martin
Martin County SD 7-11111
500 E OCEAN BLVD 34994 287-6400
Frank Brogan, supt.
Martin County HS 4-00011
2801 S KANNER HWY 34994 287-0710
David Pentecost, prin.
South Fork HS 4-00011
10205 SW PRATT WHITNEY RD 34997 287-9810
Wanda Yarboro, prin.
Murray MS, 4400 SE MURRAY ST 34997 3-00100
Hank Salzler, prin. 287-4467
MS, 575 GEORGIA AVE 34994 4-00100
Don Wallen, prin. 287-4111
Other Schools – See Indiantown, Palm City

Chapman School of Seamanship 2-CS
4343 SE SAINT LUCIE BLVD 34997 800-225-2841

Summerfield, AC 904, PC 3, Marion
Marion County SD
Supt. — See Ocala
Lake Weir MS 4-00100
10220 SE SUNSET HARBOR RD 34491 288-4001
Jewett Springer, prin.

Sunrise, AC 305, PC 8, Broward
Broward County SD
Supt. — See Fort Lauderdale
Piper HS, 8000 NW 44TH ST 33351 4-00011
Robert Hankerson, prin. 572-1300
Bair MS, 9100 NW 21ST MNR 33322 4-00100
Greg Clark, prin. 572-1400
Westpine MS, 9393 NW 50TH ST 33351 3-00100
Kenneth Perkins, prin. 572-1350

Tallahassee, AC 904, PC 9, Leon
Leon County SD 8-11111
2757 W PENSACOLA ST 32304 487-7100
Bill Woolley, supt.
Godby HS, 1717 W THARPE ST 32303 4-00011
Merry McDaris, prin. 488-1325
Leon HS, 550 E TENNESSEE ST 32308 4-00011
Marvin Henderson, prin. 488-1971
Lincoln HS, 3838 TROJAN TRL 32311 4-00011
Bill Montford, prin. 487-2110
Rickards HS, 3013 JIM LEE RD 32301 4-00011
Bill Gesdorf, prin. 488-1783
Belle Vue MS 3-00100
2214 BELLEVUE WAY 32304 488-4467
Laura Hassler, prin.
Cobb MS, 915 HILLCREST ST 32308 3-00100
Edwin Bethea, prin. 488-3364
Deerlake MS, 9902 DEER LK W 32312 3-00100
Margarita Sasse, prin. 922-6545
Fairview MS, 3415 ZILLAH ST 32311 3-00100
Kae Ingram, prin. 488-6880
Griffin MS, 800 ALABAMA ST 32304 3-00100
Larry Carmichael, prin. 488-8436
Nims MS, 723 W ORANGE AVE 32310 3-00100
Henry Murphy, prin. 488-5960
Raa MS, 401 W THARPE ST 32303 3-00100
Norman Ingram, prin. 488-6287

Branell Institute 2-CS
1700 HALSTEAD BLVD STE 2-2 32308 668-0200
Florida A&M University 32307 6-UC
599-3000
Florida State University 8-UC
600 W COLLEGE AVE 32306 644-6200
Keiser College of Technology 2-CC
1605 E PLAZA DR 32308 942-9494
Lively Area Vocational Technical School 4-CS
500 APPLEYARD DR 32304 487-7401
MacLay Day S 3-11111
3737 N MERIDIAN RD 32312 893-2138
William Jablon, prin.
Marantha Christian Academy 2-11111
2532 W THARPE ST 32303 385-5920
Randolph Price, prin.
North Florida Christian S 4-11111
3000 N MERIDIAN RD 32312 385-7181
Tim Luther, prin.
Tallahassee Community College 6-CC
444 APPLEYARD DR 32304 488-9200
Tallahassee Memorial Hospital HSP
1300 MICCOSUKEE RD 32308 681-5385

Tampa, AC 813, PC 10, Hillsborough
Hillsborough County SD 9-11111
PO BOX 3408 33601 272-4000
Walter Sickles, supt.
Chamberlain SHS 4-00001
9401 NORTH BLVD 33612 932-6141
James Gatlin, prin.
Gaither SHS 4-00001
16200 N DALE MABRY HWY 33618 963-6284
Ronald Allen, prin.
Jefferson SHS 4-00001
4401 W CYPRESS ST 33607 872-5241
Arthur Smith, prin.
King SHS, 6815 N 56TH ST 33610 4-00001
Frank Scaglione, prin. 626-8111
Leto SHS, 4409 W SLIGH AVE 33614 4-00001
Virginia Massey, prin. 886-1741
Robinson SHS, 6311 S LOIS AVE 33616 3-00001
Sylvia Albritton, prin. 839-7250
Hillsborough HS 4-00011
5000 N CENTRAL AVE 33603 276-5620
Charles Holland, prin.
Plant HS, 2415 S HIMES AVE 33629 4-00011
James Hamilton, prin. 839-6461
Brewster Tech Ctr Vo Tech
2222 N TAMPA ST 33602 276-5448
Pete Labruzzo, prin.
Erwin Tech Ctr Vo Tech
2010 E HILLSBOROUGH AVE 33610 231-1800
Michael Donahue, prin.
Tampa Bay Area Vo-Tech Ctr Vo Tech
6410 ORIENT RD 33610 621-2441
James Carr, prin.
Tampa Bay Area Vo-Tech HS Vo Tech
6410 ORIENT RD 33610 621-2441
Robert Godwin, prin.
Adams JHS, 10201 NORTH BLVD 33612 4-00110
Kenneth Adum, prin. 933-5353
Buchanan JHS 4-00110
1001 W BEARSS AVE 33613 961-1286
Lee Cheshire, prin.
Coleman JHS 3-00100
1724 S MANHATTAN AVE 33629 289-8737
John Ward, prin.
Dowdell JHS 3-00110
1208 WISHING WELL WAY 33619 626-8131
Anthony Satchel, prin.
Hill JHS, 5200 EHRLICH RD 33624 4-00110
Mitchell Muley, prin. 963-2492
Madison JHS 3-00100
4444 W BAY VISTA AVE 33611 839-6321
John Marzolf, prin.
Middleton JHS, 4302 N 24TH ST 33610 3-00110
Dave Best, prin. 276-5608
Monroe JHS 3-00100
4716 W MONTGOMERY AVE 33616 839-5426
William Pent, prin.
Pierce JHS 3-00110
5511 N HESPERIDES ST 33614 884-2595
William Katz, prin.
Van Buren JHS, 8715 N 22ND ST 33604 3-00110
Gary Huskey, prin. 935-3131
Webb JHS, 6035 HANLEY RD 33634 4-00110
Angelina Ripple, prin. 884-3471
Wilson JHS, 1005 W SWANN AVE 33606 3-00110
Jackie Heard, prin. 276-5682
Other Schools – See Brandon, Gibsonton, Plant City, Seffner, Temple Terrace, Valrico

---

Academy of the Holy Names 3-11111
3319 BAYSHORE BLVD 33629 839-5371
Sr. Anne Turner, prin.
Bay Area Legal Academy 2-CS
3924 COCONUT PALM DR 33619 621-8074
Bayshore Christian S 2-11111
3909 S MACDILL AVE 33611 839-4297
Herman Valdes, prin.
Berkeley Prep S, 4811 KELLY RD 33615 3-11111
Joseph Merluzzi, prin. 885-1673
Brewster Vocational-Technical Center 2-CS
2222 N TAMPA ST 33602 273-9240
ConCorde Career Institute 2-CS
4202 W SPRUCE ST 33607 874-0094
Erwin Vocational Technical Center 3-CS
2010 E HILLSBOROUGH AVE 33610 238-8631
FL A&M University/University of South FL 2-UC
3702 SPECTRUM BLVD #180 33612 974-4031
Florida School of Business 3-CS
4817 N FLORIDA AVE 33603 239-3334
Florida Technical College 2-CS
4750 ADAMO DR 33605 247-1700
Harvest Time Christian S 2-11111
1511 S US HIGHWAY 301 33619 626-4600
Rev. Newberry, prin.
Hillsborough Baptist S 2-11111
4036A N FALKENBURG RD 33610 664-0737
Mary Draper, prin.
Hillsborough Community College 7-CC
PO BOX 31127 33631 253-7000
Hillsborough Community College 2-CC
1404 TECH BLVD 33619 253-7000
Hillsborough Community College 2-CC
PO BOX 30030 33630 253-7000
International Academy Merch. & Design 2-CC
211 S HOOVER BLVD 33609 286-8585
International Technical Institute 2-CS
PO BOX 11497 33680 621-3566
ITT Technical Institute 3-UC
4809 MEMORIAL HWY 33634 885-2244
Jesuit HS, 4701 N HIMES AVE 33614 3-00011
Thomas Mulryan, prin. 877-5344
Mary Help of Christians ES 2-00100
6400 E CHELSEA ST 33610 626-6191
Fr. Nazzaro, prin.
National Career Institute 2-CS
3910 N US HIGHWAY 301 # 200 33619 620-1446
NEC-Tampa Technical Institute 5-UC
2410 E BUSCH BLVD 33612 935-5700
Paralegal Careers 1-CS
1211 N WESTSHORE BLVD # 100 33607 289-6025
Riverhills Christian S 2-11111
8718 N 46TH ST 33617 985-2388
Willia Oppenheimer, prin.
St. Joseph's Hospital HSP
PO BOX 4227 33677 870-4020
Seminole Presbyterian S 3-11111
6101 N HABANA AVE 33614 872-6744
Jerry Mann, prin.
Southwest Florida Blood Bank HSP
PO BOX 2125 33601 876-5433
Suncoast School of Massage Therapy 2-CS
4910 W CYPRESS ST 33607 287-1099
Tampa Baptist Academy 3-11111
300 E SLIGH AVE 33604 238-3229
Barbara Bode, prin.
Tampa Catholic HS 3-00011
4630 N ROME AVE 33603 870-0860
Br. Myles Amend, prin.
Tampa College 2-UC
3924 COCONUT PALM DR 33619 621-0041
Tampa College 5-UC
3319 W HILLSBOROUGH AVE 33614 879-6000
Tampa General Hospital HSP
PO BOX 1289 33601 251-7985
Tampa Preparatory S 2-00111
625 NORTH BLVD 33606 251-8481
Susanna Grady, prin.
Temple Heights Christian S 3-11111
8406 N 46TH ST 33617 988-5143
Randy Hurst, prin.
Ultrasound Diagnostic School 2-CS
5804 BRECKENRIDGE PKY 33610 621-0072
University of South Florida 8-UC
4202 E FOWLER AVE 33620 974-3350
University of Tampa 4-UC
401 W KENNEDY BLVD 33606 800-733-4773
West Gate Christian S 2-11111
5121 KELLY RD 33615 884-5147
Charles Shaw, prin.

Tarpon Springs, AC 813, PC 7, Pinellas
Pinellas County SD
Supt. — See Largo
East Lake HS 4-00011
1300 SILVER EAGLE DR 34689 938-2451
Lisa Komarow, prin.
HS, 1411 GULF RD 34689 4-00011
John Nicely, prin. 937-5151
MS, 501 N FLORIDA AVE 34689 4-00100
Lawrence Goodbread, prin. 943-5511

St. Petersburg Junior College 6-CC
PO BOX 1284 34688

Tavares, AC 904, PC 6, Lake
Lake County SD 7-11111
210 W BURLEIGH BLVD 32778 343-3531
Thomas Sanders, supt.
HS, 603 N NEW HAMPSHIRE AVE 32778 3-00011
David Tucker, prin. 343-3007
MS, 13032 LANE PARK CUTOFF 32778 3-00100
Gary Nicholson, prin. 343-4545
Other Schools – See Clermont, Eustis, Groveland, Leesburg, Mount Dora, Umatilla

---

Tavares Christian S 2-11111
601 N BARROW AVE 32778 343-6892
Rev. Philip Symonds, prin.

Tavernier, AC 305, PC 4, Monroe
Monroe County SD
Supt. — See Key West
Coral Shores JSHS 3-00111
PO BOX 416 33070 853-3222
Penny Houser, prin.

Temple Terrace, AC 813, PC 7, Hillsborough
Hillsborough County SD
Supt. — See Tampa
Greco JHS, 6925 E FOWLER AVE 33617 4-00110
Pauline Crumpton, prin. 988-4126

Florida College 2-CC
119 N GLEN ARVEN AVE 33617 988-5131

Titusville, AC 407, PC 8, Brevard
Brevard County SD
Supt. — See Melbourne
Astronaut HS 4-00011
800 WAR EAGLE BLVD 32796 264-3000
Fred Bynum, prin.
HS, 150 TERRIER TRL N 32780 4-00011
Walter Christy, prin. 264-3100
Jackson MS 3-00100
1515 KNOX MCRAE DR 32780 269-1812
Clifford Estes, prin.
Madison MS, 3375 DAIRY RD 32796 3-00100
Robert Manning, prin. 264-3120

Trenton, AC 904, PC 4, Gilchrist
Gilchrist County SD 4-11111
PO BOX 67 32693 463-3200
Don Thomas, supt.
JSHS, PO BOX 7 32693 2-00111
William Slaughter, prin. 463-3210
Other Schools – See Bell

Umatilla, AC 904, PC 4, Lake
Lake County SD
Supt. — See Tavares
HS, 320 N TROWELL AVE 32784 3-00011
Melanie Young, prin. 669-3131
MS, 305 E LAKE ST 32784 2-00100
Mickey Marks, prin. 669-3171

Valparaiso, AC 904, PC 5, Okaloosa
Okaloosa County SD
Supt. — See Fort Walton Beach

Lewis MS, 281 MISSISSIPPI AVE 32580   3-00100
  Wayne McSheehy, prin.   833-4130

Valrico, AC 813, PC see Brandon
Hillsborough County SD
  Supt. — See Tampa
Bloomingdale SHS   4-00001
  1700 BLOOMINGDALE AVE 33594   684-6192
  Charles Harris, prin.

Venice, AC 813, PC 7, Sarasota
Sarasota County SD
  Supt. — See Sarasota
HS, 401 INDIAN AVE 34285   4-00011
  Dan Parrett, prin.   488-6726
Venice Area MS, 1900 CENTER RD 34292   4-00100
  Melida Barton, prin.   486-2100

Huffman Aviation International   1-CS
  400 AIRPORT AVE E 34285   484-3528

Vernon, AC 904, PC 3, Washington
Washington County SD
  Supt. — See Chipley
HS, PO BOX 606 32462   2-00011
  Ruth Mccrary, prin.   535-2046
Vernon MS, PO BOX 218 32462   2-00100
  Ruth Mccrary, prin.   535-2807

Vero Beach, AC 407, PC 7, Indian River
Indian River County SD   7-11111
  1990 25TH ST 32960   567-7165
  Gary Norris, supt.
SHS, 1707 16TH ST 32960   4-00001
  Douglas King, prin.   778-7000
JHS, 1507 19TH ST 32960   4-00110
  Marion Bass, prin.   567-2588
Other Schools — See Sebastian

FlightSafety International   2-CS
  PO BOX 32961   567-5178
St. Edward's S   3-11111
  1895 SAINT EDWARDS DR 32963   231-4136
  Peter Benedict, prin.

Walnut Hill, AC 904, PC 2, Escambia
Escambia County SD
  Supt. — See Pensacola
Ward JSHS   2-00111
  7650 HIGHWAY 97 32568   327-4283
  Garvin Wright, prin.

Warrington, AC 904, PC 7, Escambia
Escambia County SD
  Supt. — See Pensacola
MS, 450 S OLD CORRY FIELD RD 32507   4-00100
  Jan Williamson, prin.   453-7440

Wauchula, AC 813, PC 5, Hardee
Hardee County SD   5-11111
  1001 N 6TH AVE 33873   773-9058
  Derrel Bryan, supt.
Hardee HS, RR 1 BOX 420 33873   4-00011
  Richard Manning, prin.   773-3181
Hardee JHS, 200 S FLORIDA AVE 33873   4-00100
  Gary Moore, prin.   773-3147

Webster, AC 904, PC 3, Sumter
Sumter County SD
  Supt. — See Bushnell
South Sumter MS, RR 2 BOX 944P 33597   3-00100
  James Catlett, prin.   793-2232

West Palm Beach, AC 407, PC 8, Palm Beach
Palm Beach County SD   9-11111
  3340 FOREST HILL BLVD 33406   434-8200
  C. Uhlhorn, supt.
Forest Hill HS, 6901 PARKER AVE 33405   4-00011
  Carlos Rosello, prin.   540-2400
Palm Beach Lakes HS   5-00011
  3505 SHILOH DR 33407   640-5000
  Nathan Collins, prin.
Wellington HS   4-00011
  2101 GREENVIEW SHORES BLVD 33414
  Mona Jensen, prin.   795-4900
Bear Lakes MS   4-00100
  3505 SHENANDOAH RD 33409   640-5056
  Marcia Andrews, prin.

Conniston MS   3-00100
  673 CONNISTON RD 33405   687-7160
  Amelia Ostrosky, prin.
Davis MS, 1560 KIRK RD 33406   4-00100
  Sandra Jinks, prin.   641-1276
Omni MS, 5775 JOG RD 33496   3-00100
  Judith Klinek, prin.   241-2291
Roosevelt MS   2-00100
  1601 N TAMARIND AVE 33407   688-5250
  Joseph Littles, prin.
Wellington Landings Community MS   4-00100
  1100 AERO CLUB DR 33414   795-4975
  Joann Reynolds, prin.
Other Schools — See Belle Glade, Boca Raton, Boynton Beach, Delray Beach, Jupiter, Lake Worth, Lantana, Pahokee, Palm Beach Gardens, Riviera Beach, Royal Palm Beach

Berean Christian S   2-11111
  8350 OKEECHOBEE BLVD 33411   798-9300
  Daniel Burrell, prin.
Boyd Career School   2-CS
  2090 PALM BEACH LAKES BLVD 33409
      684-1222
Cardinal Newman HS   3-00011
  512 SPENCER DR 33409   683-6266
  Colleen Courtney, prin.
Career Center   2-CS
  1750 45TH ST # 204 33407   881-0220
Cooper Academy of Court Reporting   2-CS
  2247 PALM BEACH LAKES BLVD 33409
      640-6999
Engine Technical Institute   1-CS
  PO BOX 109600 33410   796-1077
Kings Academy, 4215 CHERRY RD 33409   4-11111
  Miles Loveland, prin.   686-4244
New England Institute of Technology   3-CC
  1126 53RD CT S 33407   842-8324
Northwood University   2-UC
  2600 N MILITARY TRL 33409   800-458-8325
Palm Beach Atlantic College   4-UC
  PO BOX 24708 33416   650-7700
Ross Technical Institute   2-CS
  1490 S MILITARY TRL STE 11 33415
      433-1288
St. Mary's Hospital   HSP
  901 45TH ST 33407   844-6300
South College   3-CC
  1760 N CONGRESS AVE 33409   697-9200
Summit Christian S   2-11111
  4900 SUMMIT BLVD 33415   686-8081
  David Frazier, prin.

Wewahitchka, AC 904, PC 4, Gulf
Gulf County SD
  Supt. — See Port Saint Joe
JSHS, PO BOX 130 32465   2-00111
  Larry Mathes, prin.   639-2228

Wildwood, AC 904, PC 5, Sumter
Sumter County SD
  Supt. — See Bushnell
HS, 700 HUEY ST 34785   3-00011
  Larry Ross, prin.   748-1314
MS, 200 CLEVELAND AVE 34785   2-00100
  Carl Maulin, prin.   748-1510

Williston, AC 904, PC 4, Levy
Levy County SD
  Supt. — See Bronson
HS, 427 W NOBLE AVE 32696   2-00011
  Rick Turner, prin.   486-4550
MS, 1345 NE 3RD AVE 32696   2-00100
  Judy Welborn, prin.   528-2941

Winter Garden, AC 407, PC 6, Orange
Orange County SD
  Supt. — See Orlando
West Orange HS   5-00011
  1625 BEULAH RD 34787   656-2424
  Sarah Jane Turner, prin.
Westside Vo-Tech Ctr   Vo Tech
  731 E STORY RD 34787   656-2851
  Walton Cobb, prin.
Lakeview MS, 1200 W BAY ST 34787   3-00100
  Michael Blasewitz, prin.   656-3044

Calvary Baptist Christian S   2-11111
  631 S DILLARD ST 34787   656-3001
  Ronald Lemp, prin.
Westside Vocational-Technical Center   4-CS
  955 E STORY RD 34787   656-2851

Winter Haven, AC 813, PC 7, Polk
Polk County SD
  Supt. — See Bartow
HS, 600 6TH ST SE 33880   4-00011
  Michael Tucker, prin.   291-5330
Ridge Vo-Tech Ctr   Vo Tech
  7700 STATE ROAD 544 33881   299-2512
  Carl Ray, prin.
Denison MS, 400 AVENUE A SE 33880   3-00100
  Robert Donaway, prin.   291-5353
Jewett MS, 601 AVENUE T NE 33881   3-00100
  Stephen White, prin.   291-5320
Westwood MS   3-00100
  3520 AVENUE J NW 33881   965-5484
  Anthony Greene, prin.

Polk Community College   5-CC
  999 AVENUE H NE 33881   297-1001
Ridge Vocational-Technical Center   4-CS
  7700 STATE ROAD 544 33881   422-6402

Winter Park, AC 407, PC 7, Orange
Orange County SD
  Supt. — See Orlando
HS, 2100 SUMMERFIELD RD 32792   4-00011
  Hugh Harris, prin.   644-6921
Glenridge MS   4-00100
  801 GLENRIDGE WAY 32789   644-2191
  Beth Provancha, prin.
Winter Park 9th Grade Center   3-00010
  528 HUNTINGTON AVE 32789   645-1155
  Hugh Harris, prin.

Seminole County SD
  Supt. — See Sanford
Lake Howell HS, 4200 DIKE RD 32792   4-00011
  (—), prin.   678-5565

Full Sail Center for the Recording Arts   2-CC
  3300 UNIVERSITY BLVD # 160 32792
      679-6333
Master's Academy   2-11111
  2315 WINTER GREEN BLVD 32792   678-8866
  Patrick Mennenga, prin.
Rollins College   5-UC
  PO BOX 2720 32790   646-2161
Trinity Prep S   3-00111
  5700 TRINITY PREP LN 32792   671-4140
  Joseph St. John, prin.
Winter Park Adult Vocational Center   5-CS
  901 W WEBSTER AVE 32789   647-6366

Winter Springs, AC 407, PC 7, Seminole
Seminole County SD
  Supt. — See Sanford
Indian Trails MS   3-00100
  550 TUSKAWILLA RD 32708   359-7533
  Bob Rainey, prin.

Yulee, AC 904, PC 6, Nassau
Nassau County SD
  Supt. — See Fernandina Beach
MS, PO BOX 68 32097   3-00100
  Marvin Davis, prin.   225-5116

Nassau Christian Academy   2-11111
  RR 2 BOX 705A 32097   261-4818
  Larry Montgomery, prin.

Zephyrhills, AC 813, PC 6, Pasco
Pasco County SD
  Supt. — See Land O'Lakes
HS, 6335 12TH ST 33540   4-00011
  Larry Robison, prin.   782-9551
Stewart MS, 38505 10TH AVE 33540   3-00100
  Bruce Baldwin, prin.   782-9574
Weightman MS, 30649 WELLS RD 33544   3-00100
  Katherine Piersall, prin.   929-2689

GEORGIA

STATE DEPARTMENT OF EDUCATION
2066 Twin Towers East, Atlanta 30334
(404) 656-2800

State Superintendent of Schools	Werner Rogers
Deputy Superintendent	Glenn Newsome
Associate Superintendent Administrative Services	Hall Rogers
Associate Superintendent Instructional Services	Peyton Williams
Associate Superintendent Special Services	Bill Gambill

STATE BOARD OF EDUCATION
2066 Twin Towers East, Atlanta 30334

Chairperson   Hollis Lathem

PUBLIC, PRIVATE AND CATHOLIC SECONDARY SCHOOLS

Abbeville, AC 912, PC 3, Wilcox
Wilcox County SD   31001   4-11111
  Larry Gibbs, supt.   467-2141
  Other Schools – See Rochelle

Acworth, AC 404, PC 5, Cobb

North Metro Technical Institute   2-CS
  5198 ROSS RD   30102   974-1855

Adairsville, AC 706, PC 4, Bartow
Bartow County SD
  Supt. — See Cartersville
HS, PO BOX 968   30103   3-00011
  Bob Rhinehart, prin.   773-3781
Adairsville MS   2-00100
  116 N FRANKLIN ST   30103   773-7164
  Joan Quijano, prin.

Adel, AC 912, PC 6, Cook
Cook County SD, PO BOX 152   31620   5-11111
  Larry Hunt, supt.   896-2294
Cook HS   3-00011
  1200 N HUTCHINSON AVE   31620   896-2213
  Paula Barker, prin.
Cook MS   3-00100
  310 N MARTIN LUTHER KING DR   31620
  Mary Ward, prin.   896-4541

Alamo, AC 912, PC 3, Wheeler
Wheeler County SD   4-11111
  PO BOX 427   30411   568-7198
  Ronny Clark, supt.
Wheeler County JSHS   2-00111
  PO BOX 425   30411   568-7166
  William Black, prin.

Albany, AC 912, PC 8, Dougherty
Dougherty County SD   7-11111
  PO BOX 1470   31702   431-1286
  William Gardner, supt.
HS, 801 W RESIDENCE AVE   31701   3-00011
  Gary Dorough, prin.   431-3300
Dougherty HS, 1800 PEARCE AVE   31705   4-00011
  Commodore Conyers, prin.   431-3310
Monroe HS, 900 LIPPITT DR   31701   4-00011
  Joseph Davis, prin.   431-3316
Westover HS   4-00011
  2600 PARTRIDGE DR   31707   431-3320
  Ralph Harper, prin.
MS, 1000 N JEFFERSON ST   31701   3-00100
  Ted Horton, prin.   431-3325
Dougherty MS, 1800 MASSEY DR   31705   3-00100
  Lawrence Medlin, prin.   431-3328
Highland MS   2-00100
  1001 HIGHLAND AVE   31701   431-3362
  Holly Thursby, prin.
King MS   2-00100
  2235 MRTN LUTHER KING JR DR   31701
  Freddie Powell, prin.   431-3342
Merry Acres MS   3-00100
  1601 FLORENCE DR   31707   431-3338
  Michael Manning, prin.
Radium Springs MS   3-00100
  2600 RADIUM SPRINGS RD   31705   431-3346
  James Ramsey, prin.
Southside MS, 1615 NEWTON RD   31701   3-00100
  Willie Edwards, prin.   431-3351

Albany State College   4-UC
  504 COLLEGE DR   31705   800-822-7267
Albany Technical Institute   3-CS
  1021 LOWE RD   31701   888-1320

Byne Memorial Baptist Church S   2-11111
  313 W SOCIETY AVE   31701   436-0173
Darton College   4-CC
  2400 GILLIONVILLE RD   31707   888-8740
Deerfield-Windsor Academy   3-11111
  2301 STUART AVE   31707   435-1301
  W. Henry, prin.
Meadows College of Business   3-CS
  832 S SLAPPEY BLVD   31701   883-1736
Sherwood Christian Academy   2-11111
  1203 7TH AVE   31707   888-2277
Turner Job Corps Center   4-CS
  2000 SCHILLING AVE   31705   431-1820

Alma, AC 912, PC 5, Bacon
Bacon County SD   4-11111
  601 N PIERCE ST   31510   632-7363
  John DeLoach, supt.
Bacon County HS   3-00011
  901 N PIERCE ST   31510   632-4414
  Phillip Murphy, prin.
Bacon Co MS, 901 N PIERCE ST   31510   2-00100
  Timothy Warnock, prin.   632-4662

Alpharetta, AC 404, PC 7, Fulton
Fulton County SD
  Supt. — See Atlanta
Chattahoochee HS   3-00011
  5230 TAYLOR RD   30202   740-7080
  Robert Burke, prin.
Milton HS, 86 SCHOOL DR   30201   4-00011
  L. Thomas, prin.   740-7000
Haynes Bridge MS   4-00100
  10665 HAYNES BRIDGE RD   30202   740-7030
  Gayle Giles, prin.
Holcomb Bridge MS   3-00100
  2700 HOLCOMB BRIDGE RD   30202   594-5280
  Vernon Alford, prin.
Taylor Road MS   3-00100
  5151 TAYLOR RD   30202   740-7090
  Hannah Martin, prin.

Americus, AC 912, PC 7, Sumter
Americus ISD, PO BOX 847   31709   5-11111
  Ronnie Williams, supt.   924-3605
HS, 805 HARROLD AVE   31709   4-00011
  Howard Hendley, prin.   924-3653
Staley MS, 915 N LEE ST   31709   3-00100
  Clyde McGrady, prin.   924-3168

Sumter County SD   4-11111
  PO BOX 967   31709   924-6949
  Robin Johnson, supt.
Sumter County HS   4-00011
  101 INDUSTRIAL BLVD   31709   924-5914
  Randall Stewart, prin.
Sumter Co MS   2-01100
  439 BUMPHEAD RD   31709   924-1010
  Carolyn Kerr, prin.

Georgia Southwestern College   4-UC
  800 WHEATLEY ST   31709   800-338-0082
Kings Academy   2-11111
  124 BRIARWOOD CIR   31709   924-5608
South Georgia Technical Institute   2-CS
  728 SOUTHERFIELD RD   31709   928-0283
Southland Academy   3-11111
  PO BOX 1127   31709   924-4406

Appling, AC 706, PC 3, Columbia
Columbia County SD   7-11111
  PO BOX 10   30802   541-0650
  Lynn Cadle, supt.

Other Schools – See Evans, Grovetown, Harlem

Ashburn, AC 912, PC 5, Turner
Turner County SD   4-11111
  PO BOX 609   31714   567-3338
  Jim Alberson, supt.
Turner County HS, 316 LAMAR ST   31714   3-00011
  Tom Day, prin.   567-4377
Turner County MS   2-00100
  1060 W WASHINGTON AVE   31714   567-3411
  Wayne Baxter, prin.

Athens, AC 706, PC 8, Clarke
Clarke County SD   7-11111
  PO BOX 1708   30603   546-7721
  John Balentine, supt.
Cedar Shoals HS   4-00011
  1300 CEDAR SHOALS DR   30605   546-5375
  Michael Stanton, prin.
Clarke Central HS   4-00011
  350 S MILLEDGE AVE   30605   357-5200
  Jim Willis, prin.
Burney-Harris-Lyons MS   3-00100
  440 DEARING EXT   30606   548-7208
  Barbara Mathis, prin.
Clarke MS, 1235 BAXTER ST   30606   3-00100
  Sharon Denero, prin.   543-6547
Hilsman MS   3-00100
  870 GAINES SCHOOL RD   30605   548-7281
  Pat Clifton, prin.

Athens Academy   3-11111
  PO BOX 6548   30604   549-9225
  William Smith, prin.
Athens Area Technical Institute   3-CC
  US HWY 29 N   30601   542-8050
Athens Christian S   3-11111
  1270 HIGHWAY 29 N   30601   549-7586
Prince Avenue Baptist Christian S   2-11111
  PO BOX 1112   30603   353-1993
University of Georgia   30602   8-UC
  542-2112

Atlanta, AC 404, PC 10, Fulton
Atlanta ISD, 210 PRYOR ST SW   30303   8-11111
  Lester Butts, supt.   827-8075
Archer HS, 2250 PERRY BLVD NW   30318   3-00011
  Eddie Henderson, prin.   792-5900
Carver HS   3-00011
  1275 CAPITOL AVE SW   30315   330-4108
  Norris Hogans, prin.
Crim HS, 256 CLIFTON ST SE   30317   3-00011
  Sherman Lofton, prin.   371-4881
Douglass HS   4-00011
  225 HIGHTOWER RD NW   30318   792-5925
  Samuel Hill, prin.
Fulton HS   3-00011
  2025 JONESBORO RD SE   30315   624-2016
  John Robinson, prin.
George HS, 800 HUTCHENS RD SE   30354   3-00011
  Bessie McLemore, prin.   362-5057
Grady HS   3-00011
  929 CHARLES ALLEN DR NE   30309   853-4000
  Vincent Murray, prin.
Harper HS, 3399 COLLIER DR NW   30331   4-00011
  Wallace Bibbs, prin.   699-4511
Mays HS   4-00011
  3450 BENJAMIN E MAYS DR SW   30331
  Ronald Brown, prin.   699-4537
North Atlanta HS   3-00011
  2890 N FULTON DR NE   30305   842-3108
  John Culbreath, prin.

Southside HS 4-00011
801 GLENWOOD AVE SE 30316 624-2064
William Shepherd, prin.
Therrell HS 4-00011
3099 PANTHER TRL SW 30311 346-2523
Alphonso Jones, prin.
Washington HS 4-00011
45 WHITEHOUSE DR SW 30314 752-0728
Robert Lowe, prin.
Bunche MS 3-00100
1925 NISKEY LAKE RD SW 30331 346-2503
Gloria Patterson, prin.
Coan MS 3-00100
1550 BOULEVARD DR NE 30317 371-4854
Gene Chandler, prin.
Inman MS, 774 VIRGINIA AVE NE 30306 3-00100
Barbara Naylor, prin. 853-4017
Kennedy MS 3-00100
225 JAMES P BRAWLEY DR NW 30314 330-4140
Charles Hawk, prin.
King MS, 582 CONNALLY ST SE 30312 3-00100
Rosa Hadley, prin. 330-4149
Long MS, 3200 LATONA DR SW 30354 3-00100
Leviticus Roberts, prin. 669-2257
Marshall MS 3-00100
1820 MARY DELL DR SE 30316 244-4300
Barbara Robinson, prin.
Parks MS, 1090 WINDSOR ST SW 30310 2-00100
Lewis Smith, prin. 752-0742
Price MS, 1670 CAPITOL AVE SE 30315 3-00100
Robert Hall, prin. 624-2028
Southwest MS 3-00100
3116 MAYO PL SW 30311 699-4533
Geraldine Williams, prin.
Sutton MS 3-00100
4360 POWERS FERRY RD NW 30327 256-6920
Hazel Hutcheson, prin.
Sylvan Hills MS 3-00100
1461 SYLVAN RD SW 30310 752-0711
John Goodlett, prin.
Turner MS 2-00100
98 ANDERSON AVE NW 30314 792-5931
Roy Hadley, prin.
Usher MS, 631 HARWELL RD NW 30318 2-00100
Harvenia Hill, prin. 699-4794
Walden MS, 320 IRWIN ST NE 30312 2-00100
Obadiah Jordan, prin. 330-4173
West Fulton MS 3-00100
1890 BANKHEAD HWY NW 30318 792-5944
Robert Bell, prin.

DeKalb County SD
Supt. — See Decatur
McNair SHS 3-00001
1804 BOULDERCREST RD SE 30316 241-5000
Gloria Hardiman, prin.
Cross Keys HS 3-00011
1626 N DRUID HILLS RD NE 30319 633-5141
E. Spencer, prin.
Druid Hills JSHS 4-00111
1798 HAYGOOD DR NE 30307 325-4755
Dewey Holbrook, prin.
Lakeside JSHS 4-00111
3801 BRIARCLIFF RD NE 30345 633-2631
Thomas Beuglas, prin.
Open Campus JSHS 3-00111
2415 N DRUID HILLS RD NE 30329 321-6989
William Hightower, prin.
Peachtree JHS 4-00110
4664 N PEACHTREE RD 30338 451-4613
George Moss, prin.

Fulton County SD 8-11111
786 CLEVELAND AVE SW 30315 768-3600
James Fox, supt.
North Springs HS 3-00011
7447 ROSWELL RD NE 30328 551-2490
Robert Lynch, prin.
Riverwood HS 4-00011
5900 HEARDS DR NW 30328 847-1980
Mary Chandler, prin.
Westlake HS, 2370 UNION RD SW 30331 3-00011
Michael Gray, prin. 346-6400
Ridgeview MS 3-00100
5340 TRIMBLE RD NE 30342 843-7710
Jan Barlow, prin.
Sandy Springs MS 3-00100
8750 COLONEL DR 30350 552-4970
Elizabeth Fogartie, prin.
Other Schools – See Alpharetta, College Park, East Point, Fairburn, Roswell, Union City

---

American College for the Applied Arts 4-UC
3330 PEACHTREE RD NE 30326 231-9000
American College in London 3-UC
3330 PEACHTREE RD NE 30326 231-9000
American Red Cross Blood Services HSP
1925 MONROE DR NE 30324 881-9800
Art Institute of Atlanta 4-CC
3376 PEACHTREE RD NE 30326 800-554-3346
Atlanta Area Technical Institute 6-CS
1560 STEWART AVE SW 30310 758-9451
Atlanta College-Medical/Dental Careers 2-CS
1400 W PEACHTREE ST NW 30309 249-8200
Atlanta College of Art 2-UC
1280 PEACHTREE ST NE 30309 800-832-2104
Atlanta Job Corps Center 3-CS
239 W LAKE AVE NW 30314 794-9512
Atlanta Metro College 4-CC
1630 STEWART AVE SW 30310 756-4000
Bauder Fashion College 3-CC
3500 PEACHTREE RD NE 30326 237-7573
Beulah Heights Bible College 2-UC
PO BOX 18145 30316 627-2681
Branell Institute 2-CS
1000 CRCL 75 PKY NW STE 100 30339 951-0051
Brown Coll. of Court Reporting & Bus. 2-CS
1100 SPRING ST NW # 20 30309 876-1227
Clark Atlanta University 5-UC
240 JAMES BRAWLEY DR SW 30314 880-8000
Crawford Long Hospital/Emory University 2-HSP
550 PEACHTREE ST NE 30308 686-2376
Draughons College 2-CS
1430 W PEACHTREE ST NW #101 30309 892-0814
Emory University 6-UC
1462 CLIFTON RD NE 30322 727-6123
Emory University Hospital UC
1364 CLIFTON RD NE 30322 727-4881
Galloway S 3-11111
215 W WIEUCA RD NW 30342 252-8389
Joseph Richardson, prin.
Georgia Baptist Medical Center HSP
300 BOULEVARD NE 30312 653-4795
Georgia Institute of Technology 7-UC
225 NORTH AVE NW 30332 894-4154
Georgia Medical Institute 1-CS
40 MARIETTA ST NW STE 1333 30303 525-3272
Georgia State University 7-UC
UNIVERSITY PLAZA 30303 651-2365
Grady Memorial Hospital HSP
80 BUTLER ST SE 30303 589-4252
Heiskell S 2-11111
3260 NORTHSIDE DR NW 30305 262-2233
Cyndie Heiskell, prin.
Holy Innocents Episcopal S 4-11111
805 MOUNT VERNON HWY NW 30327
Alice Malcolm, prin. 255-4026
Institute of Paper Science & Technology 1-UC
500 10TH ST NW 30318 853-9556
Interactive Learning Systems 2-CS
5600 ROSWELL RD NE 30342 843-0014
Interdenominational Theological Center 2-UC
671 BECKWITH ST SW 30314 527-7700
International S 3-11111
4820 LONG ISLAND DR NE 30342 843-3380
Alex Horsley, prin.
Lovett S 4-11111
4075 PACES FERRY RD NW 30327 262-3032
James Hendrix, prin.
Marist S 4-00111
3790 ASHFORD DUNWOODY RD NE 30319
Michael Maher, prin. 457-7201
Massey Business College 4-CC
120 RALPH MCGILL BLVD NE 30308 872-1900
Massey Institute 2-CS
5299 ROSWELL RD NE # 320 30342 256-3533
Masters Christian Academy 2-11111
1985 LA VISTA ROAD NE 30329 325-8540
Dan Carter, prin.
Mercer University in Atlanta 4-UC
3001 MERCER UNIVERSITY DR 30341 986-3200
Morehouse College 7-UC
830 WESTVIEW DR SW 30310 800-992-0642
Morehouse School of Medicine 2-UC
720 WESTVIEW DR SW 30310 681-2800
Morris Brown College 4-UC
643 MARTIN LUTHER KING JR D 30314 220-0270
NEC-Bryman Campus 3-CS
40 MARIETTA ST NW STE 8 30303 524-8800
Oglethorpe University 3-UC
4484 PEACHTREE RD NE 30319 233-6864
Pace Academy 3-11111
966 W PACES FERRY RD NW 30327 262-1345
George Kirkpatrick, prin.
Paideia S 3-11111
1509 PONCE DE LEON AVE NE 30307 377-3491
Phillips Junior College 2-CC
1400 W PEACHTREE ST NW 30309 249-8200
Portfolio Center 2-CS
125 BENNETT ST NW 30309 800-255-3169
PTC Career Institute 2-CS
44 BROAD ST NW 30303 681-1500
Quality Plus Business School 2-CS
1655 PEACHTREE ST NE # 450 30309 892-6669
St. Joseph's Hospital HSP
5665 PCHTREE DUNWOODY RD NE 30342 851-7120
St. Pius X Catholic HS 4-00011
2674 JOHNSON RD NE 30345 636-3023
Donald Sasso, prin.
Southeastern Center for the Arts 1-CS
1935 CLIFF VALLEY WAY NE 30329 633-1990
Spelman College 4-UC
350 SPELMAN LN SW 30314 800-241-3421
Ultrasound Diagnostic School 2-CS
13 CORP SQUARE OFFICE PARK 30329 248-9070
Westminister S 4-11111
1424 W PACES FERRY RD NW 30327 355-8673
Charles Breithaupst, prin.
Yeshiva HS, 3130 RAYMOND DR 30340 2-00111
Herbert Cohen, prin. 451-5299

Augusta, AC 706, PC 8, Richmond
Richmond County SD 8-11111
2083 HECKLE ST 30904 737-7200
John Strelec, supt.
Academy of Richmond County HS 4-00011
910 RUSSELL ST 30904 737-7152
Gerald Buckner, prin.
Butler Comprehensive HS 4-00011
2011 LUMPKIN RD 30906 796-4959
David Smith, prin.
Glenn Hills HS 4-00011
2840 GLENN HILLS DR 30906 796-4924
Charles Lamback, prin.
Johnson Health Professions HS 2-00011
1324 LANEY WALKER BLVD 30901 823-6933
Robetta McKenzie, prin.
Josey Comprehensive HS 3-00011
1701 15TH ST 30901 737-7360
Richard Johnson, prin.
Laney Comprehensive HS 3-00011
1339 LANEY WALKER BLVD 30901 823-6900
William Holmes, prin.
Westside HS, 1002 STELLING RD 30907 3-00011
Norman Griffin, prin. 868-4030
Davidson Fine Arts JSHS 3-01111
1114 TELFAIR ST 30901 823-6924
Beverly Barnhart, prin.
East Augusta MS 3-00100
320 KENTUCKY AVE 30901 823-6960
Eddie Robertson, prin.
Langford MS 3-00100
3019 WALTON WAY 30909 737-7301
David Smith, prin.
Murphey MS 3-00100
2610 MILLEDGEVILLE RD 30904 737-7350
Winnette Bradley, prin.
Sego MS, 3420 JULIA AVE 30906 3-00100
Kathryn Collins, prin. 796-4944
Tubman MS, 1740 WALTON WAY 30904 3-00100
Horace Larnback, prin. 737-7250
Tutt MS, 495 BOY SCOUT RD 30909 3-00100
William Watson, prin. 737-7288
Other Schools – See Hephzibah

Aquinas HS 2-00011
1920 HIGHLAND AVE 30904 736-5516
Fr. Fitzpatrick, prin.
Augusta Christian S 2-11111
PO BOX 11687 30907 863-2905
Augusta College 5-UC
2500 WALTON WAY 30904 737-1405
Augusta Preparatory S 1-11111
285 FLOWING WELLS RD 30907 863-2197
Randall Storms, prin.
Augusta Technical Institute 4-CC
3116 DEANS BRIDGE RD 30906 796-6900
Kerr Business College 3-CS
PO BOX 1986 30903 738-5046
Medical College of Georgia 4-UC
1120 15TH ST 30901 721-2725
Paine College 3-UC
1235 15TH ST 30901 800-476-7703
University Hospital 2-HSP
1350 WALTON WAY 30901 722-9011
Westminster Day S 3-11111
3067 WHEELER RD 30909 731-5260
Matthew Gossage, prin.

Austell, AC 404, PC 5, Cobb
Cobb County SD
Supt. — See Marietta
South Cobb HS, 1920 CLAY RD 30001 4-00011
Frank Croker, prin. 732-5682
Garrett MS 3-00100
5235 POWDER SPRINGS RD 30001 732-5628
Rose McNeese, prin.

Avondale Estates, AC 404, PC 4, De Kalb
DeKalb County SD
Supt. — See Decatur
Avondale JSHS 4-00111
1192 CLARENDON AVE 30002 289-6766
A. Kitchens, prin.

Bainbridge, AC 912, PC 7, Decatur
Decatur County SD 6-11111
PO BOX 1406 31717 248-2200
Glenn Keebler, supt.
HS, 1301 E COLLEGE ST 31717 4-00011
Don Connell, prin. 248-2230
Hutto MS 3-00100
1201 MRTN LUTHER KING JR DR 31717
Saint Thomas, prin. 248-2224
West Bainbridge MS 2-00100
1417 DOTHAN RD 31717 248-2206
Suzanne Bonifay, prin.

Bainbridge College 3-CC
HWY 84 E 31717 248-2500

Barnesville, AC 404, PC 5, Lamar
Lamar County SD
Supt. — See Milner
Lamar County Comprehensive HS 4-00011
1 TROJAN WAY 30204 358-1756
Dewaine Bell, prin.
Lamar County MS 2-00100
3 TROJAN WAY 30204 358-0193
Norma Greenwood, prin.

Gordon College 4-CC
419 COLLEGE DR 30204 358-5021

Baxley, AC 912, PC 5, Appling
Appling County SD　5-11111
RR 7 BOX 36　31513　367-8600
Ray Sellers, supt.
Appling County HS　4-00011
RR 7 BOX 45　31513　367-8610
Carlton Walton, prin.
Appling County JHS　3-00100
PO BOX 459　31513　367-8630
James Allen, prin.

Bellville, AC 912, PC 2, Evans

Pinewood Christian Academy　2-11111
PO BOX 7　30414　739-1272

Blackshear, AC 912, PC 5, Pierce
Pierce County SD, PO BOX 349　31516　5-11111
W. Strickland, supt.　449-2044
Pierce County JSHS　4-00111
RR 1 BOX 712A　31516　449-2055
Wes Bennett, prin.

Blairsville, AC 706, PC 3, Union
Union County SD, 10 HUGHES ST　30512　4-11111
Tom Stephens, supt.　745-2322
Union County HS　3-00011
446 WELBORNE ST　30512　745-2216
Jim Colwell, prin.
Union County MS　2-00100
448 WELBORNE ST　30512　745-2483
Bob Kelley, prin.
Other Schools – See Suches

Blakely, AC 912, PC 6, Early
Early County SD　5-11111
503 COLUMBIA ST　31723　723-4337
Richard Hall, supt.
Early County HS　3-00011
420 COLUMBIA ST　31723　723-3006
Ken Hall, prin.
Early County MS　3-00100
413 COLUMBIA ST　31723　723-3746
Betty Orange, prin.

Blue Ridge, AC 706, PC 4, Fannin
Fannin County SD　5-11111
PO BOX 606　30513　632-3771
Morgan Arp, supt.
Fannin Co HS, RR 3 BOX 3223　30513　3-00011
Douglas Davenport, prin.　632-2081
Fannin Co MS, RR 3 BOX 3330　30513　2-00100
Michael Ballew, prin.　632-6100

Bogart, AC 706, PC 4, Clarke

Interactive Learning Systems　3-CS
200 CLEVELAND RD STE 6　30622　548-9800

Bowdon, AC 404, PC 4, Carroll
Carroll County SD
Supt. — See Carrollton
HS, 504 W COLLEGE ST　30108　2-00011
Roger King, prin.　258-5408
MS, 233 KENT AVE　30108　2-01100
Debra Ivey, prin.　258-2161

Bremen, AC 404, PC 5, Haralson
Bremen ISD, 504 LAUREL ST　30110　4-11111
Dennis McBrayer, supt.　537-5508
HS, 504 GEORGIA AVE S　30110　2-00011
Roger Couch, prin.　537-2592
Sewell MS, 515 LAUREL ST　30110　2-00100
Anthony Wilkins, prin.　537-4874

Brooklet, AC 912, PC 4, Bulloch
Bulloch County SD
Supt. — See Statesboro
Southeast Bulloch JSHS　3-00111
PO BOX 68　30415　842-2131
Tom Bigwood, prin.

Brunswick, AC 912, PC 7, Glynn
Glynn County SD　7-11111
PO BOX 1677　31521　267-4100
L. E. McDowell, supt.
HS, 3920 HABERSHAM ST　31520　4-00011
Derrick Hulsey, prin.　267-4200
Glynn Academy HS　4-00011
PO BOX 1678　31521　267-4210
William Wood, prin.
Glynn MS, 901 GEORGE ST　31520　3-00100
H Ray Sharp, prin.　267-4150
Macon MS, 3885 ALTAMA AVE　31520　3-00100
Dawne Hudson, prin.　265-3337
Risley MS, 2900 ALBANY ST　31520　3-00100
Murray Miller, prin.　267-4160

Brunswick College　4-CC
3700 ALTAMA AVE　31520　264-7253

Buchanan, AC 706, PC 4, Haralson
Haralson County SD　5-11111
PO BOX 508　30113　646-3882
Melvin Reeves, supt.
MS, PO BOX 660　30113　2-01100
Joe Jones, prin.　646-5140
Other Schools – See Tallapoosa

Buena Vista, AC 912, PC 4, Marion
Marion County SD　4-11111
PO BOX 391　31803　649-2234
Herman Long, supt.
Tri-County JSHS, PO BOX 177　31803　3-00111
James Stapleton, prin.　649-7520

Buford, AC 404, PC 6, Gwinnett
Buford ISD　4-11111
70 WILEY DR STE 200　30518　945-2713
Beauty Baldwin, supt.
HS, 2750 SAWNEE AVE　30518　2-00011
Andy Henderson, prin.　945-6768
MS, 2200 HIGHWAY 13　30518　2-01100
Sue Morris, prin.　945-2094

Gwinnett County SD
Supt. — See Lawrenceville
Lanier MS, 918 BUFORD HWY　30518　3-00100
Charles Crawford, prin.　945-8419

Butler, AC 912, PC 4, Taylor
Taylor County SD　4-11111
PO BOX 1930　31006　862-5224
Wayne Smith, supt.
Taylor County JSHS　3-00111
PO BOX 1927　31006　862-3314
Bonnie Brannin, prin.

Byron, AC 912, PC 4, Peach
Peach County SD
Supt. — See Fort Valley
MS, PO BOX 1599　31008　3-00100
Terry Cheek, prin.　956-4999

Cairo, AC 912, PC 6, Grady
Grady County SD, PO BOX 300　31728　5-11111
Larry Rawlins, supt.　377-3701
HS, 455 5TH ST SE　31728　4-00011
Wayne Tootle, prin.　377-2222
Washington MS　3-00100
1277 BOOKER HILL BLVD SW　31728　377-2106
Ann Flowers, prin.

Calhoun, AC 706, PC 6, Gordon
Calhoun ISD, 700 W LINE ST　30701　4-11111
James Holloway, supt.　629-2900
HS, 315 S RIVER ST　30701　3-00011
Patricia Stokes, prin.　629-9213
MS, 504 OOTHCALOOGA ST　30701　3-00100
Brenda Erwin, prin.　629-3340

Gordon County SD　5-11111
PO BOX 127　30703　629-7366
Phil Robbins, supt.
Gordon Central HS　4-00011
335 WARRIOR PATH NE　30701　629-7391
Harold Hughes, prin.
Ashworth MS　2-00100
333 NEWTOWN RD NE　30701　625-9545
Faye Darby, prin.
Sonoraville East MS　2-00100
7300 HIGHWAY 53 EAST SE　30701　629-0793
Walter Walraven, prin.

Camilla, AC 912, PC 6, Mitchell
Mitchell County SD　5-11111
PO BOX 588　31730　336-2100
Bob Tabb, supt.
Mitchell-Baker JSHS　4-00111
RR 3 BOX 510　31730　336-0970
Kenneth Hubbard, prin.

Westwood S, PO BOX 528　31730　2-11111
336-7992

Canton, AC 404, PC 5, Cherokee
Cherokee County SD　7-11111
PO BOX 769　30114　479-1871
Corky Jones, supt.
Cherokee HS　4-00011
651 MARIETTA HWY　30114　479-4112
Rick Ingram, prin.
Sequoyah HS, 3349 HICKORY RD　30115　2-00011
Doe Kirkland, prin.　345-1474
Rusk MS, 3397 HICKORY RD　30115　3-00100
Joe Blackwell, prin.　345-2832
Teasley MS　3-00100
8871 KNOX BRIDGE HWY　30114　479-7077
Randy Martin, prin.
Other Schools – See Woodstock

Carnesville, AC 706, PC 3, Franklin
Franklin County SD　5-11111
PO BOX 99　30521　384-4554
Boyd Outz, supt.
Franklin County HS　3-00011
PO BOX 543　30521　384-4525
Jack Slaton, prin.
Franklin County MS　2-00100
PO BOX 544　30521　384-4581
Howard Mc Glennen, prin.

Carrollton, AC 404, PC 7, Carroll
Carroll County SD　6-11111
164 INDEPENDENCE DR　30116　832-3568
Leon Golden, supt.
Central HS, 113 CENTRAL RD　30116　4-00011
Scott Cowart, prin.　834-3386
Carroll County Vo HS　Vo Tech
1075 NEWNAN RD　30116　832-8380
Don Fussell, prin.
Central MS　3-00100
633 STRIPLING CHAPEL RD　30116　832-8114
Edna Herndon, prin.
Other Schools – See Bowdon, Mount Zion, Temple, Villa Rica

Carrollton ISD, PO BOX 740　30117　5-11111
Tom Upchurch, supt.　832-9633
HS, 202 TROJAN DR　30117　3-00011
Larry Harmon, prin.　834-7726

JHS, 510 STADIUM DR　30117　2-00100
Bill Waldrop, prin.　834-3378

Carroll Technical Institute　3-CS
997 S HIGHWAY 16　30116　836-6800
Oak Mountain Academy　2-11111
1575 S HIGHWAY 16　30116　834-6651
West Georgia College　30118　6-UC
836-6416

Cartersville, AC 404, PC 7, Bartow
Bartow County SD　6-11111
PO BOX 200007　30120　382-3813
Davis Nelson, supt.
Cass HS, 738 GRASSDALE RD NW　30120　4-00011
William Kiser, prin.　382-0230
Cass MS, 1653 CASSVILLE RD NW　30120　3-00100
Nettie Holt, prin.　386-2786
Other Schools – See Adairsville, Emerson

Cartersville ISD, 310 OLD MILL RD　30120　5-11111
Harold Barnett, supt.　382-5880
HS, 320 E CHURCH ST　30120　3-00011
J S Morgan, prin.　382-3200
MS, 315 ETOWAH DR　30120　3-00100
Barry Hester, prin.　382-3666

Cave Spring, AC 706, PC 3, Floyd

Georgia School for the Deaf　HND
PO BOX 99　30124

Cedartown, AC 404, PC 6, Polk
Polk County SD, PO BOX 128　30125　6-11111
Jim Carter, supt.　748-3821
HS, 167 FRANK LOTT DR　30125　3-00011
William Crick, prin.　748-0490
Cedar Hill MS　3-00100
402 E ELLAWOOD AVE　30125　748-4409
William Lundy, prin.
Purks MS, 330 WEST AVE　30125　2-00100
Clark Montgomery, prin.　748-4078
Other Schools – See Rockmart

Chamblee, AC 404, PC 6, De Kalb
DeKalb County SD
Supt. — See Decatur
JSHS　3-00111
3638 CHAMBLEE DUNWOODY RD　30341
Martha Reichrath, prin.　457-4323
Henderson JSHS　4-00111
2830 HENDERSON MILL RD NE　30341　939-3242
Bob Jordan, prin.
Occupational Ed Ctr Central　Vo Tech
3075 ALTON RD　30341　457-3393
Robert Burns, prin.

DeKalb Co. Occupational Education Center　2-CS
3075 ALTON RD　30341　457-3393

Chatsworth, AC 706, PC 5, Murray
Murray County SD, PO BOX 40　30705　5-11111
Mick McNeill, supt.　695-4531
Murray County HS　4-00011
1001 GREEN RD　30705　695-1414
Mike Davis, prin.
Bagley MS, 1004 GREEN RD　30705　3-00100
Daniel Harkleroad, prin.　695-1115
Gladden MS, 700 OLD ELLIJAY RD　30705　3-00100
John Payne, prin.　695-7448

Chickamauga, AC 706, PC 4, Walker
Chickamauga ISD, 105 LEE CIR　30707　4-11111
Paul Chambers, supt.　375-3183
Lee JSHS, 100 LEE CIR　30707　3-00111
Don Littleton, prin.　375-3181

Chula, AC 912, PC 2, Tift

Tiftarea Academy, PO BOX 10　31733　2-11111
382-0436

Clarkesville, AC 706, PC 4, Habersham
Habersham County SD　5-11111
PO BOX 467　30523　754-2118
Mrs Hooper, supt.
North Habersham MS　30523　2-00100
Bruce Forbes, prin.　754-2915
Other Schools – See Cornelia, Mount Airy

North Georgia Technical Institute　3-CS
PO BOX 65　30523　754-2131

Clarkston, AC 404, PC 6, De Kalb
DeKalb County SD
Supt. — See Decatur
JSHS, 618 N INDIAN CREEK DR　30021　4-00111
Charlie Henderson, prin.　292-8282

Atlanta Area School for the Deaf　HND
890 N INDIAN CREEK DR　30021
DeKalb Technical Institute　5-CC
495 N INDIAN CREEK DR　30021　297-9522

Claxton, AC 912, PC 4, Evans
Evans County SD, PO BOX 826　30417　4-11111
Durell Lynn, supt.　739-3544
JSHS, 102 N CLARK ST　30417　3-00111
Dewey Hulsey, prin.　739-3993

Clayton, AC 706, PC 4, Rabun
Rabun County SD, PO BOX 468　30525　4-11111
Roger Nicholas, supt.　746-5376
Other Schools – See Tiger

Cleveland, AC 706, PC 4, White
White County SD, 135 BROOK ST 30528 — 4-11111
  Raymond Collins, supt. — 865-2315
White County HS — 3-00011
  RR 5 BOX 5043 30528 — 865-2312
  Glenda Brooks, prin.
White County MS — 3-00100
  RR 5 BOX 5042 30528 — 865-4060
  W. Jenkins, prin.

Truett McConnell College 30528 — 4-CC
  865-2138

Cochran, AC 912, PC 5, Bleckley
Bleckley County SD — 4-11111
  PO BOX 516 31014 — 934-2821
  Donald Turknett, supt.
Bleckley County HS — 3-00011
  911 DYKES ST NE 31014 — 934-6258
  William Faircloth, prin.
Bleckley County MS, RR 3 31014 — 3-01100
  Charlotte Pipkin, prin. — 934-7270

Middle Georgia College 31014 — 4-CC
  934-3136

College Park, AC 404, PC 7, Fulton
Clayton County SD
  Supt. — See Jonesboro
North Clayton HS — 4-00011
  1525 NORMAN DR 30349 — 994-4035
  Leroy Rorie, prin.
North Clayton MS — 3-00100
  5517 W FAYETTEVILLE RD 30349 — 994-4025
  Gloria Duncan, prin.

Fulton County SD
  Supt. — See Atlanta
Banneker HS — 4-00011
  5935 FELDWOOD RD 30349 — 969-3410
  Hansell Gunn, prin.
Camp Creek MS — 3-00100
  4345 WELCOME ALL RD SW 30349 — 669-8030
  Minnie Miller, prin.
McNair MS, 2800 BURDETT RD 30349 — 3-00100
  Jessie Pottsdamer, prin. — 991-4160

Branell Institute — 2-CS
  4876 RIVERDALE RD # A 30337 — 997-1300
Mount Pisgah Christian S — 2-11111
  4140 STACKS RD 30349 — 761-8343
Woodward Academy — 4-11111
  PO BOX 87190 30337 — 765-8200
  David McCollum, prin.

Colquitt, AC 912, PC 4, Miller
Miller County SD, PO BOX 188 31737 — 4-11111
  Kelley Summers, supt. — 758-5592
Miller County JSHS 31737 — 2-00111
  Dave Richardson, prin. — 758-4130

Columbus, AC 706, PC 9, Muscogee
Muscogee County SD — 8-11111
  PO BOX 2427 31902 — 649-0500
  Robert Bushong, supt.
Carver HS, 3100 8TH ST 31906 — 3-00011
  Andrew Coleman, prin. — 649-0689
HS, 1700 CHEROKEE AVE 31906 — 4-00011
  Ronnie Shehane, prin. — 649-0701
Hardaway HS, 2901 COLLEGE DR 31906 — 4-00011
  Roger Hatcher, prin. — 649-0748
Jordan Vocational HS — 4-00011
  3200 HOWARD AVE 31904 — 649-0769
  William Screws, prin.
Kendrick HS — 4-00011
  6015 GEORGETOWN DR 31907 — 569-2532
  Gerald Carey, prin.
Shaw HS, 7601 SCHOMBURG RD 31909 — 4-00011
  Gordon Stallings, prin. — 569-2567
Spencer HS, 4340 VICTORY DR 31903 — 4-00011
  Joe Saulsbury, prin. — 685-7652
Arnold JHS, 2011 51ST ST 31904 — 3-00100
  Ruthie Hamlin, prin. — 649-0670
Baker MS, 1544 BENNING DR 31903 — 3-00100
  Marie DeRamus, prin. — 685-7600
Daniel MS, 1042 45TH ST 31904 — 2-00100
  Mark Williams, prin. — 649-0720
Eddy MS, 2100 S LUMPKIN RD 31903 — 3-00100
  Joseph Gosha, prin. — 685-7629
Fort MS, 2900 FLOYD ROAD 31907 — 3-00100
  David Shoemaker, prin. — 569-2517
Marshall MS, 1830 SHEPHERD DR 31906 — 2-00100
  Eddie Obleton, prin. — 649-0797
Richards MS — 3-00100
  2892 EDGEWOOD RD 31906 — 569-2554
  William Arrington, prin.
Rothschild MS, 1136 HUNT AVE 31907 — 3-00100
  Patricia Culpepper, prin. — 569-2563

Brookstone S — 3-11111
  440 BRADLEY PARK DR 31904 — 324-1392
  Robert Newton, prin.
Christian Heritage S — 2-11111
  3564 FOREST RD 31907 — 568-1251
Columbus College — 5-UC
  3600 ALGONQUIN DR 31907 — 568-2001
Columbus Technical Institute — 4-CC
  928 45TH ST 31907 — 649-1837
Meadows College of Business — 3-CC
  1170 BROWN AVE 31906 — 327-7668
Medical Center — HSP
  710 CENTER ST 31901 — 571-1200

Pacelli HS, 3556 TRINITY DR 31907 — 2-00011
  R. Fenchak, prin. — 561-8243

Commerce, AC 706, PC 5, Jackson
Commerce ISD, PO BOX 29 30529 — 4-11111
  Doc Elliot, supt. — 335-5500
HS, 272 LAKEVIEW DR 30529 — 2-00011
  D. Drew, prin. — 335-5942
MS, 325 LAKEVIEW DR 30529 — 2-00100
  Walker Davis, prin. — 335-5594

Conyers, AC 404, PC 6, Rockdale
Rockdale County SD — 6-11111
  PO BOX 1199 30207 — 860-4211
  Kathleen O'Neill, supt.
Heritage HS — 4-00011
  2400 GRANADE RD SW 30207 — 483-5428
  Michael Bochenko, prin.
Rockdale County HS — 4-00011
  1174 BULLDOG CIR NE 30207 — 483-8754
  William Silvey, prin.
MS, 335 SIGMAN RD NW 30207 — 4-00100
  Viki Dennard, prin. — 483-3371
Edwards MS — 4-00100
  2633 STANTON RD SE 30208 — 483-3255
  Kathy Garber, prin.
Memorial MS — 3-00100
  3205 UNDERWOOD RD SE 30208 — 922-0139
  Patty DeVane, prin.
Salem JHS — 3-00110
  3551 UNDERWOOD RD SE 30208 — 929-0176
  Robert Cresswell, prin.

Philadelphia Christian S — 2-11111
  2360 OLD COVINGTON HWY SW 30207
  483-4489

Cordele, AC 912, PC 7, Crisp
Crisp County SD, PO BOX 729 31015 — 5-11111
  J Vann Sikes, supt. — 276-3400
Crisp County HS — 4-00011
  1116 24TH AVE E 31015 — 276-3430
  Jay Brinson, prin.
Clark MS, 401 15TH ST N 31015 — 3-00100
  Sydney Brown, prin. — 276-3425

Crisp Academy — 2-11111
  150 CRISP ACADEMY DR 31015 — 273-6330

Cornelia, AC 706, PC 5, Habersham
Habersham County SD
  Supt. — See Clarkesville
South Habersham MS 30531 — 3-00100
  Larry Hill, prin. — 778-7121

Covington, AC 404, PC 7, Newton
Newton County SD — 6-11111
  PO BOX 1469 30209 — 787-1330
  E. Clamp, supt.
Newton County HS, 140 RAM DR 30209 — 4-00011
  Lowell Williamson, prin. — 787-2250
Cousins MS, 8134 GEIGER ST NW 30209 — 3-00100
  Wayne Mullins, prin. — 786-7311
Sharp MS, 3135 NEWTON DR NE 30209 — 3-00100
  Thomas Glanton, prin. — 787-3010

Cumming, AC 404, PC 5, Forsyth
Forsyth County SD — 6-11111
  101 SCHOOL ST 30130 — 887-2461
  Ina Fossett, supt.
Forsyth Central Comprehensive HS — 4-00011
  520 TRIBBLE GAP RD 30130 — 887-8151
  Kenny Foxx, prin.
South Forsyth HS — 3-00011
  585 PEACHTREE PKY 30131 — 781-2264
  Mike Weaver, prin.
North Forsyth MS — 2-00100
  3645 COAL MOUNTAIN DR 30130 — 889-0743
  Jackie West, prin.
Otwell MS, 135 ELM ST 30130 — 3-00100
  Judy Thornton, prin. — 887-5248
South Forsyth MS — 2-00100
  585 PEACHTREE PKY 30131 — 887-1837
  David Adams, prin.

Cuthbert, AC 912, PC 5, Randolph
Randolph County SD — 4-11111
  1208 ANDREW ST 31740 — 732-2641
  Kathryn Hardwick, supt.
Randolph-Clay JSHS — 3-00111
  RR 3 BOX 279 31740 — 732-2101
  Wesley Williams, prin.

Andrew College — 2-CC
  413 COLLEGE ST 31740 — 732-2171

Dacula, AC 404, PC 4, Gwinnett
Gwinnett County SD
  Supt. — See Lawrenceville
HS, 123 BROAD ST 30211 — 2-00011
  Dolford Layson, prin. — 963-6664
MS, 192 DACULA RD 30211 — 2-00100
  Betty Keene, prin. — 963-1110

Dahlonega, AC 706, PC 5, Lumpkin
Lumpkin County SD — 4-11111
  101 MOUNTAIN VIEW DR NE 30533 — 864-3611
  Gary Keith, supt.
Lumpkin County HS — 3-00011
  100 SCHOOL HILL RD NE 30533 — 864-2557
  Reggie Glaze, prin.
Lumpkin County MS — 3-00100
  200 SCHOOL HILL RD NE 30533 — 864-6180
  Richard Rentz, prin.

North Georgia College 30597 — 4-UC
  864-1800

Dallas, AC 404, PC 5, Paulding
Paulding County SD — 6-11111
  522 HARDEE ST 30132 — 443-8000
  Allene Magill, supt.
East Paulding HS — 3-00011
  6800 DRAGSTRIP RD 30132 — 445-5100
  David Magouyrk, prin.
Paulding County HS — 4-00011
  1155 VILLA RICA HWY 30132 — 443-8008
  Ricky Clemmons, prin.
East Paulding MS — 2-00100
  2351 HIRAM ACWORTH RD 30132 — 443-7000
  Ray Perren, prin.
Jones MS, 100 STADIUM DR 30132 — 3-00100
  Sam McClure, prin. — 443-8024
South Paulding MS — 2-00100
  1200 NEBO RD 30132 — 445-8500
  Don Rauscher, prin.

Dalton, AC 706, PC 7, Whitfield
Dalton ISD, PO BOX 1408 30722 — 5-11111
  Frank Thomason, supt. — 278-8766
HS, 1500 MANLEY ST 30720 — 4-00011
  John McMillian, prin. — 278-8757
Dalton S Health Occupations — Vo Tech
  1221 ELKWOOD DR 30720 — 278-8922
  Rubye Sane, prin.
JHS, 408 W CRAWFORD ST 30720 — 3-00100
  Don Amonett, prin. — 278-3903

Whitfield County SD — 6-11111
  PO BOX 2167 30722 — 278-8070
  Terry Cullifer, supt.
Southeast Whitfield County HS — 4-00011
  1954 RIVERBEND RD 30721 — 226-2753
  Mike Bryans, prin.
Eastbrook MS, 700 HILL RD 30721 — 3-00100
  William Russell, prin. — 278-6135
North Whitfield MS — 3-00100
  3264 CLEVELAND RD 30721 — 259-3381
  Richard Schoen, prin.
Valley Point MS, 3796 S DIXIE RD 30721 — 2-00100
  Nick Ownby, prin. — 277-9662
Other Schools – See Rocky Face, Tunnel Hill

Dalton College — 4-CC
  213 COLLEGE DR 30720 — 272-4436
Dalton Voc. School of Health Occupations — 2-CS
  1221 ELKWOOD DR 30720 — 278-8922

Damascus, AC 912, PC 2, Early

Southwest Georgia Academy — 2-11111
  RR 1 BOX 4 31741 — 725-4792

Danielsville, AC 706, PC 2, Madison
Madison County SD — 5-11111
  PO BOX 37 30633 — 795-2191
  Jim Perkins, supt.
Madison County HS, PO BOX 7 30633 — 3-00011
  Linda Holloman, prin. — 795-2197
Madison Co. MS, PO BOX 690 30633 — 3-00100
  Robert Harrison, prin. — 795-3341

Darien, AC 912, PC 4, McIntosh
McIntosh County SD — 4-11111
  PO BOX 495 31305 — 437-6645
  Hannah Tostensen, supt.
McIntosh County Academy — 3-00111
  PO BOX 535 31305 — 437-6691
  Charles Davis, prin.

Dawson, AC 912, PC 6, Terrell
Terrell County SD — 4-11111
  PO BOX 151 31742 — 995-4425
  Robert Aaron, supt.
Terrell JSHS — 3-00111
  488 CRAWFORD ST NE 31742 — 995-2544
  D. Pullum, prin.

Terrell Academy, PO BOX 312 31742 — 2-11111
  995-4242

Dawsonville, AC 706, PC 2, Dawson
Dawson County SD — 4-11111
  PO BOX 208 30534 — 265-3246
  Lloyd Harben, supt.
Dawson County HS — 2-00011
  PO BOX 129 30534 — 265-6555
  Kay Collins, prin.
Dawson County MS — 2-00100
  PO BOX 688 30534 — 265-2714
  Stan Worley, prin.

Decatur, AC 404, PC 7, De Kalb
Decatur ISD — 5-11111
  320 N MCDONOUGH ST 30030 — 370-4400
  Don Griffith, supt.
HS, 310 N MCDONOUGH ST 30030 — 2-00011
  William Funk, prin. — 370-4420
Renfroe MS, 220 W COLLEGE AVE 30030 — 2-00100
  Karen Eldridge, prin. — 370-4440

DeKalb County SD — 8-11111
  3770 N DECATUR RD 30032 — 297-2300
  Robert Freeman, supt.
Columbia JSHS — 4-00111
  2106 COLUMBIA DR 30032 — 284-8720
  Stanley Pritchett, prin.

Shamrock JSHS   4-00111
 3100 MOUNT OLIVE DR   30033   633-9235
 Anita Fay Smith, prin.
Southwest Dekalb JSHS   4-00111
 2863 KELLEY CHAPEL RD   30034   288-2461
 Michael Hall, prin.
Towers JSHS   4-00111
 3919 BROOKCREST CIR   30032   289-7166
 L. Glenn Lee, prin.
Occupational Ed Ctr South   Vo Tech
 3303 PANTHERSVILLE RD   30034   241-9400
 Larry Ladner, prin.
Chapel Hill JHS   3-00110
 3535 DOGWOOD FARM RD   30034   593-3109
 Clarence Callaway, prin.
McNair JHS   3-00110
 2190 WALLINGFORD DR   30032   241-5576
 Robert Stewart, prin.
Miller Grove JHS   4-00110
 2215 MILLER RD   30035   987-7470
 William Edwards, prin.
Other Schools – See Atlanta, Avondale Estates,
 Chamblee, Clarkston, Doraville, Dunwoody,
 Ellenwood, Lithonia, Stone Mountain, Tucker

Agnes Scott College   3-UC
 201 E COLLEGE AVE   30030   800-235-6602
Branell Institute   2-CS
 5255 SNPFNGER PARK DR # 120   30035
   593-1097
Cathedral Academy   2-11111
 4650 FLAT SHOALS PKY   30034   243-3656
Columbia Theological Seminary   2-UC
 701 S COLUMBIA DR   30030   378-8821
DeKalb College   7-CC
 3251 PANTHERSVILLE RD   30034   244-2240
DeKalb Co. Occupational Education Center   2-CS
 3303 PANTHERVILLE RD   30034
DeKalb Medical Center   HSP
 2701 N DECATUR RD   30033   297-5206
DeVry Institute of Technology   5-UC
 250 N ARCADIA AVE   30030   292-2645
Gupton-Jones College of Funeral Service   2-CC
 5141 SNAPFINGER WOODS DR   30035   593-2257
National Business Institute   2-CS
 243 W PONCE DE LEON AVE   30030   352-0800

Demorest, AC 706, PC 4, Habersham

Piedmont College   2-UC
 PO BOX 10   30535   800-277-7020

Dixie, AC 912, PC 2, Brooks

Westbrook S, PO BOX 100   31629   2-11111
   263-7843

Donalsonville, AC 912, PC 5, Seminole
Seminole County SD   4-11111
 800 S WOOLFORK AVE   31745   524-2433
 Jesse McLeod, supt.
Seminole County JSHS   3-00111
 800 S WOOLFORK AVE   31745   524-5135
 Louis Bonner, prin.

Doraville, AC 404, PC 6, De Kalb
DeKalb County SD
 Supt. — See Decatur
Sequoyah JHS, 3456 AZTEC RD   30340   4-00110
 Morris Clark, prin.   451-3821

Douglas, AC 912, PC 7, Coffee
Coffee County SD, PO BOX 959   31533   6-11111
 David Luke, supt.   384-2086
Coffee HS, 1303 S PETERSON AVE   31533   4-00011
 Leo Brooks, prin.   384-2094
Coffee MS, PO BOX 999   31533   3-00100
 Oscar Street, prin.   384-1342

Citizens Christian Academy   2-11111
 PO BOX 1064   31533   384-8862
South Georgia College   31533   4-CC
   800-342-6364

Douglasville, AC 404, PC 7, Douglas
Douglas County SD   7-11111
 PO BOX 1077   30133   920-4000
 Kathryn Shehane, supt.
Alexander Comp. HS   4-00011
 6500 ALEXANDER PKY   30135   920-4500
 Ray Mansfield, prin.
Douglas County Comprehensive HS   4-00011
 8705 CAMPBELLTON ST   30134   920-4400
 David Hill, prin.
Chapel Hill MS   3-00100
 3989 CHAPEL HILL RD   30135   920-4230
 Narvis McPherson, prin.
Chestnut Log MS, 2544 POPE RD   30135   3-00100
 Jeri Mansfield, prin.   920-4550
Fairplay MS   3-00100
 8311 HIGHWAY 166   30135   920-4200
 Vernon Hagen, prin.
Stewart MS, 8138 MALONE ST   30134   3-00100
 Michael Jones, prin.   920-4215
Other Schools – See Lithia Springs

Harvester Christian Academy   2-11111
 4241 CENTRAL CHURCH RD   30135   942-1583
Inner Harbor S   1-00111
 4685 DORSETT SHOALS RD   30135   942-2391
 Penny Honeycutt, prin.

Kings Way Christian S   2-11111
 6456 THE KINGS WAY   30135   949-0812

Dublin, AC 912, PC 7, Laurens
Dublin ISD, 207 SHAMROCK DR   31021   5-11111
 Charles Warnock, supt.   272-3440
HS, 1951 HILLCREST PKY   31021   3-00011
 Robert Waller, prin.   272-4727
JHS, 300 N CALHOUN ST   31021   3-00100
 Ernest Wade, prin.   272-8122

Laurens County SD   5-11111
 PO BOX 2128   31040   272-4767
 William Rowe, supt.
West Laurens HS   3-00011
 RR 5 BOX 138   31021   272-1155
 Cardon Dalley, prin.
East Laurens HS, RR 6   31021   3-00011
 Tryon Reynolds, prin.   272-3144
East Laurens MS, RR 2   31021   2-00100
 Steve Kyzer, prin.   272-1201
West Laurens MS, RR 5   31021   2-00100
 George Knight, prin.   272-8452

Heart of Georgia Technical Institute   2-CS
 560 PINEHALL RD   31021   275-6589
Trinity Christian HS   2-11111
 200 TRINITY RD   31021   272-7699

Duluth, AC 404, PC 6, Gwinnett
Gwinnett County SD
 Supt. — See Lawrenceville
HS, 3737 BROCK RD   30136   4-00011
 Ted Newman, prin.   476-5206
MS, 3057 S PEACHTREE ST   30136   3-01100
 John Ford, prin.   476-3372

Dunwoody, AC 404, PC 6, De Kalb
DeKalb County SD
 Supt. — See Decatur
SHS, 5035 VERMACK RD   30338   4-00001
 Jennie Springer, prin.   394-4442
Occupational Ed Ctr North   Vo Tech
 1995 WOMACK RD   30338   394-0321
 Frank Hall, prin.

Brandon Hall S   1-00111
 1701 BRANDON HALL DR   30350   394-8177
 Harrison Kimbrell, prin.
DeKalb Co. Occupational Education Center   2-CS
 1995 WOMACK RD   30338   297-2376

Eastanollee, AC 706, PC 2, Stephens
Stephens County SD
 Supt. — See Toccoa
Stephens County MS   30538   3-00100
 James Bellamy, prin.   779-2211

Eastman, AC 912, PC 6, Dodge
Dodge County SD   5-11111
 PO BOX 1029   31023   374-3783
 Charlotte Williams, supt.
Dodge County HS, RR 2   31023   3-00011
 Aubrey Corbitt, prin.   374-7711
Dodge County MS, HERMAN AVE   31023   2-00100
 John Jones, prin.   374-6492

East Point, AC 404, PC 8, Fulton
Fulton County SD
 Supt. — See Atlanta
Tri-Cities HS, 2575 HARRIS ST   30344   4-00011
 Hershel Robinson, prin.   669-8200
West MS, 2376 HEADLAND DR   30344   3-00100
 Sam Taylor, prin.   669-8130
Woodland MS   3-00100
 2816 BRIARWOOD BLVD   30344   346-6420
 Barbara Morrow, prin.

Atlanta Christian College   2-UC
 2605 BEN HILL RD   30344   761-8861
Colonial Hills Christian HS   2-11111
 2134 NEWNAN AVE   30344   758-7032

Eatonton, AC 706, PC 5, Putnam
Putnam County SD   4-11111
 304 W MARION ST   31024   485-5381
 Al Reeves, supt.
Putnam County HS   3-00011
 140 SPARTA HWY   31024   485-9971
 Jacob Bennekin, prin.
Putnam County MS   2-00100
 314 S WASHINGTON AVE   31024   485-8547
 Fabian Fain, prin.

Gatewood S, 139 PHILLIPS DR   31024   2-11111
   485-8231

Edison, AC 912, PC 4, Calhoun
Calhoun County SD
 Supt. — See Morgan
Calhoun County JSHS   3-00111
 PO BOX 366   31746   835-2435
 Larry Wilkerson, prin.

Elberton, AC 706, PC 6, Elbert
Elbert County SD, 50 LAUREL DR   30635   5-11111
 Frank Griffith, supt.   283-1904
Elbert County Comprehensive HS   3-00011
 600 JONES ST   30635   283-3680
 Timothy Wheeler, prin.
Elbert County MS   3-00100
 45 FOREST AVE   30635   283-2275
 Wallace Edwards, prin.

Ellenwood, AC 404, PC 2, Clayton
DeKalb County SD
 Supt. — See Decatur
Cedar Grove JSHS, 2360 RIVER RD   30049   3-00111
 Mary Ann Schrecengost, prin.   243-3770

Ellijay, AC 706, PC 4, Gilmer
Gilmer County SD   4-11111
 275 BOBCAT TRL   30540   276-5000
 Ben Arp, supt.
Gilmer HS, 500 S MAIN ST   30540   3-00011
 Alexander Rainey, prin.   276-5080
MS, 250 MCCUTCHEN ST   30540   3-00100
 Maxine Edwards, prin.   276-5030

Emerson, AC 404, PC 4, Bartow
Bartow County SD
 Supt. — See Cartersville
South Central MS   3-00100
 224 OLD OLD ALABAMA RD SE   30137   382-2120
 Becky Lee, prin.

Evans, AC 706, PC 7, Columbia
Columbia County SD
 Supt. — See Appling
HS, PO BOX 130   30809   4-00111
 Gene Sullivan, prin.   863-1198
Lakeside HS, 533 BLUE RIDGE DR   30809   4-00011
 Julius McAnally, prin.   863-0027
MS, PO BOX 129   30809   3-00100
 J. Wilcher, prin.   863-2275
Lakeside MS, 527 BLUE RIDGE DR   30809   3-00100
 Bruce Sliger, prin.   855-6900
Riverside MS   3-00100
 1095 FURYS FERRY RD   30809   868-3712
 Gloria Hamilton, prin.

Fairburn, AC 404, PC 5, Fulton
Fulton County SD
 Supt. — See Atlanta
Creekside HS, 7405 HERNDON RD   30213   4-00011
 Stephen Schyck, prin.   969-6070
Bear Creek MS   3-00100
 7415 HERNDON RD   30213   969-6080
 Tye Engram, prin.

Greater Atlanta Christian S   2-11111
 4500 RIDGE RD   30213   964-9871
 David Fincher, prin.
Landmark Christian S   2-00111
 50 BROAD ST   30213   306-0647

Fayetteville, AC 404, PC 6, Fayette
Fayette County SD   6-11111
 210 STONEWALL AVE   30214   460-3535
 Trigg Dalrymple, supt.
Fayette County HS   4-00011
 205 LAFAYETTE DR   30214   460-3540
 Gary Phillips, prin.
Fayette MS, 450 GRADY AVE   30214   4-00100
 Harry Sweatman, prin.   460-3550
Whitewater MS   2-00100
 1533 HIGHWAY 85 S   30214   460-3450
 Don Chaplin, prin.
Other Schools – See Peachtree City, Tyrone

Fayette Christian Academy   2-11111
 152 LONGVIEW RD   30214   461-3538

Fitzgerald, AC 912, PC 6, Ben Hill
Ben Hill County SD   4-11111
 PO BOX 5189   31750   423-3320
 Louis Harper, supt.
HS, BOX 389   31750   4-00011
 Ronnie Satterfield, prin.   423-2092
Ben Hill Co MS, PO BOX 190   31750   2-00100
 Lacy Frye, prin.   423-6525

Ben Hill Irwin Area Voc. Tech. Institute   3-CS
 PO BOX 1069   31750   468-7487

Flintstone, AC 706, PC 2, Walker
Walker County SD
 Supt. — See La Fayette
Chattanooga Valley MS   3-00100
 847 ALLGOOD RD   30725   820-0735
 Edward Combs, prin.

Folkston, AC 912, PC 4, Charlton
Charlton County SD, 500 S 3RD ST   31537   4-11111
 Jack Mullis, supt.   496-2596
Charlton County JSHS   3-00111
 500 N CROSS ST   31537   496-2501
 Michael Dean, prin.

Forest Park, AC 404, PC 7, Clayton
Clayton County SD
 Supt. — See Jonesboro
HS, 5452 PHILLIPS DR   30050   4-00011
 Margaret Manos, prin.   362-3890
Babb MS, 5500 REYNOLDS RD   30050   3-00100
 David Hawkins, prin.   362-3880
MS, 930 FINLEY DR   30050   3-00100
 Russ Keldorph, prin.   362-3840

Forsyth, AC 912, PC 5, Monroe
Monroe County SD   5-11111
 PO BOX 1308   31029   994-2031
 Charles Dumas, supt.
Persons HS   3-00011
 310 MONTPELIER AVE   31029   994-2812
 Mike Hickman, prin.

Monroe County MS
  RR 5 BOX 471 31029 — 3-00100 994-6186
  Cecil Porter, prin.

Monroe Academy, PO BOX 4 31029 — 2-11111 994-5986

Fort Oglethorpe, AC 706, PC 6, Catoosa
Catoosa County SD
  Supt. — See Ringgold
Lakeview-Fort Oglethorpe HS — 3-00011
  1001 BATTLEFIELD PKY 30742 — 866-0342
  Jack Sims, prin.

Fort Valley, AC 912, PC 6, Peach
Peach County SD — 5-11111
  PO BOX 1018 31030 — 825-5933
  H. Sheets, supt.
Peach County HS — 3-00011
  900 CAMPUS DR 31030 — 825-8258
  Frank Spearman, prin.
MS, 814 PEGGY DR 31030 — 4-00100
  Virginia Dixon, prin. — 825-2413
  Other Schools – See Byron

Fort Valley State College — 4-UC
  1005 STATE COLLEGE DR 31030 — 825-6307

Franklin, AC 706, PC 3, Heard
Heard County SD — 4-11111
  PO BOX 1330 30217 — 675-3320
  Benjamin Hyatt, supt.
Heard County JSHS, 545 MAIN ST 30217 — 3-00011
  Richard Carlisle, prin. — 675-3656

Franklin Springs, AC 404, PC 2, Franklin

Emmanuel College — 2-UC
  PO BOX 128 30639 — 245-7226

Gainesville, AC 404, PC 7, Hall
Gainesville ISD, 850 CENTURY PL 30501 — 5-11111
  Alan Zubay, supt. — 536-5275
HS, 830 CENTURY PL 30501 — 3-00011
  Wendell Christian, prin. — 536-4441
MS, 715 WOODSMILL RD 30501 — 3-00100
  Tom Ahr, prin. — 534-4237

Hall County SD — 7-11111
  711 GREEN ST NE STE 100 30501 — 534-1080
  H. Johnson, supt.
East Hall HS, 3534 E HALL RD 30507 — 3-00011
  William Sloan, prin. — 536-9921
Johnson HS — 4-00011
  3305 POPLAR SPRINGS RD 30507 — 536-2394
  William Ellis, prin.
North Hall HS — 4-00011
  4885 MOUNT VERNON RD 30506 — 983-7331
  John Corley, prin.
East Hall MS, 4120 E HALL RD 30507 — 2-00100
  Gary Stewart, prin. — 531-9457
North Hall MS, 4956 RILLA RD 30506 — 3-00100
  Michael Greavu, prin. — 983-9749
South Hall MS — 3-00100
  3515 POPLAR SPRINGS RD 30507 — 532-4416
  Charles McKinney, prin.
  Other Schools – See Oakwood

Brenau Academy — 1-00011
  1 CENTENNIAL CIR 30501 — 534-6140
  Frank Booth, prin.
Brenau College — 4-UC
  204 BOULEVARD 30501 — 534-6299
Gainesville College — 4-CC
  PO BOX 1358 30503 — 535-6241
Lakeview Academy — 2-11111
  796 LAKEVIEW DR 30501 — 532-4383
  H. Singleton, prin.
Riverside Military Academy — 1-00111
  1942 RIVERSIDE DR 30501 — 532-6251
  Charles Christopherson, prin.

Garden City, AC 912, PC 6, Chatham
Chatham County SD
  Supt. — See Savannah
Secondary Tech Ctr — Vo Tech
  101 WHEATHILL RD 31408 — 966-6866
  Don Frew, prin.
Mercer MS, 201 ROMMEL AVE 31408 — 3-00100
  Virginia Deloach, prin. — 966-6840

Gibson, AC 706, PC 3, Glascock
Glascock County SD — 2-11111
  PO BOX 205 30810 — 598-2291
  Anne Mein, supt.
Glascock County Cons. S — 2-11111
  PO BOX 35 30810 – (—), prin. — 598-2121

Glennville, AC 912, PC 5, Tattnall

Glenville Christian Academy — 2-11111
  PO BOX 706 30427 — 654-3034

Gray, AC 912, PC 4, Jones
Jones County SD, PO BOX 519 31032 — 5-11111
  Bill Mathews, supt. — 986-6580
Jones County HS, PO BOX 609 31032 — 3-00011
  John Trimnell, prin. — 986-5444
Califf MS, PO BOX 1419 31032 — 3-00100
  Lani Schewe, prin. — 986-3046

Greensboro, AC 706, PC 5, Greene
Greene County SD — 4-11111
  201 N MAIN ST 30642 — 453-7688
  Phil Brock, supt.
Greene-Taliaferro HS — 4-00011
  1002 S MAIN ST 30642 — 453-2271
  Sandra Driscoll, prin.
Greene-Taliaferro MS — 2-00100
  1002 S MAIN ST 30642 — 453-3308
  Gloria Raber, prin.

Greenville, AC 706, PC 4, Meriwether
Meriwether County SD — 5-11111
  PO BOX 70 30222 — 672-4297
  J Paul Abernathy, supt.
JSHS, PO BOX 340 30222 — 3-00111
  Charlie Glanton, prin. — 672-4930
  Other Schools – See Manchester

Griffin, AC 404, PC 7, Spalding
Griffin-Spalding County SD — 7-11111
  PO BOX N 30224 — 229-3700
  Eugene Kierbow, supt.
SHS, 1617 W POPLAR ST 30223 — 4-00001
  Larry White, prin. — 228-8641
Flynt Street MS, 1551 FLYNT ST 30223 — 3-00100
  John Goodrum, prin. — 229-3739
Kelsey Avenue MS — 3-00100
  200 KELSEY AVE 30223 — 229-3760
  Mike McLemore, prin.
Spalding JHS, 221 SPALDING DR 30223 — 3-00010
  Walter Pyron, prin. — 229-3734
Taylor Street MS — 4-00100
  234 E TAYLOR ST 30223 — 229-3727
  Tom Ison, prin.

Griffin Christian Academy — 2-11111
  2000 W MCINTOSH RD 30223 — 228-2307
Griffin Institute — 3-CS
  501 VARSITY RD 30223 — 228-7365

Grovetown, AC 706, PC 5, Columbia
Columbia County SD
  Supt. — See Appling
Columbia MS — 3-00100
  6000 COLUMBIA RD 30813 — 541-1252
  Donna Anderson, prin.

Hahira, AC 912, PC 4, Lowndes
Lowndes County SD
  Supt. — See Valdosta
MS, PO BOX 686 31632 — 3-00100
  Ann Rodgers, prin. — 245-2278

Hamilton, AC 706, PC 2, Harris
Harris County SD, PO BOX 388 31811 — 5-11111
  Tommy Lee, supt. — 628-4206
Harris County HS, PO BOX 448 31811 — 3-00011
  Kenneth Stephens, prin. — 628-4278
Harris Co-Carver MS — 3-00100
  PO BOX 408 31811 — 628-4951
  Arnold Jackson, prin.

Harlem, AC 706, PC 4, Columbia
Columbia County SD
  Supt. — See Appling
HS, PO BOX 699 30814 — 3-00011
  Barry Hemphill, prin. — 541-2736
MS, PO BOX 729 30814 — 3-00100
  Wayne Hardy, prin. — 541-2742

Hartwell, AC 706, PC 5, Hart
Hart County SD, PO BOX 696 30643 — 5-11111
  John Cleveland, supt. — 376-5141
Hart County HS, CAMPBELL DR 30643 — 3-00011
  Glorianne Patterson, prin. — 376-5461
Hart County MS, 560 POWELL RD 30643 — 3-00100
  Billy Shiflet, prin. — 376-5431

Hawkinsville, AC 912, PC 5, Pulaski
Pulaski County SD — 4-11111
  PO BOX 148 31036 — 892-9191
  Tony Portivent, supt.
JSHS, PO BOX 429 31036 — 3-00111
  Bonny Dixon, prin. — 783-2726

Hazlehurst, AC 912, PC 5, Jeff Davis
Jeff Davis County SD — 5-11111
  PO BOX 571 31539 — 375-6700
  G. C. Herrington, supt.
Jeff Davis HS, 310 BROXTON RD 31539 — 3-00011
  Ronald Dixon, prin. — 375-6760
Jeff Davis MS, PO BOX 1080 31539 — 3-00100
  James Phenis, prin. — 375-6750

Hephzibah, AC 706, PC 4, Richmond
Richmond County SD
  Supt. — See Augusta
Hephzibah Comprehensive HS — 4-00011
  PO BOX 310 30815 – R. Allen, prin. — 592-2089
MS, 2427 MIMS RD 30815 — 3-00100
  Chris Henry, prin. — 592-4534
Morgan Road MS — 3-00100
  3635 HIERS BLVD 30815 — 796-4992
  Vivian Pennamon, prin.
Spirit Creek MS — 3-00100
  4044 WINDSOR SPRING RD 30815 — 592-9445
  Virginia Bradshaw, prin.

Hiawassee, AC 706, PC 3, Towns
Towns County SD — 3-11111
  67 LAKEVIEW CIR STE C 30546 — 896-2279
  James Kimsey, supt.
Towns County Comprehensive S — 3-11111
  HIGHWAY 76 E 30546 – Jeff Ivey, prin. — 896-4131

Hinesville, AC 912, PC 7, Liberty
Liberty County SD — 6-11111
  110 S GAUSE ST 31313 — 876-2161
  Doris Thomson, supt.
Bradwell Institute HS — 4-00011
  100 PAFFORD ST 31313 — 876-6121
  Joan Hollingsworth, prin.
MS, 307 E WASHINGTON AVE 31313 — 4-00100
  Edmund Elmore, prin. — 876-8251
Liberty Co JHS, RR 1 BOX 40A 31313 — 2-00110
  Gene Nisbet, prin. — 876-4316

Hogansville, AC 706, PC 5, Troup
Troup County SD
  Supt. — See La Grange
JSHS, 611 E MAIN ST 30230 — 2-01111
  Stephanie Phillips, prin. — 812-7990

Homer, AC 706, PC 3, Banks
Banks County SD, PO BOX 248 30547 — 4-11111
  Dock Sisk, supt. — 677-2224
Banks County HS, PO BOX 277 30547 — 2-00011
  Bobby Whitlock, prin. — 677-2221
Banks County MS — 2-00100
  PO BOX 860 30547 — 677-2277
  Kay Rogers, prin.

Homerville, AC 912, PC 5, Clinch
Clinch County SD — 4-11111
  PO BOX 177 31634 — 487-5321
  Sterling Newton, supt.
Clinch County JSHS — 2-00111
  PO BOX 397 31634 — 487-5366
  Kay Hinson, prin.

Irwinton, AC 912, PC 3, Wilkinson
Wilkinson County SD — 4-11111
  PO BOX 206 31042 — 946-5521
  Marlene Tompkins, supt.
Wilkinson County HS — 3-00011
  PO BOX 547 31042 — 946-2441
  Kathy Culpepper, prin.
Wilkinson County MS — 2-00100
  PO BOX 527 31042 — 946-2541
  Willie Scott, prin.

Jackson, AC 404, PC 5, Butts
Butts County SD — 5-11111
  181 N MULBERRY ST 30233 — 775-8100
  Dennis Fordham, supt.
HS, 323 HARKNESS ST 30233 — 3-00011
  Johnnie Thompson, prin. — 775-8114
Henderson MS — 3-00100
  820 N MULBERRY ST 30233 — 775-8112
  George Tate, prin.

Jasper, AC 706, PC 4, Pickens
Pickens County SD — 4-11111
  488 STEGALL DR 30143 — 692-2532
  Kimsey Wood, supt.
Pickens HS, 670 W CHURCH ST 30143 — 3-00011
  Steve Sewell, prin. — 692-2463
Pickens Co. MS, 950 REFUGE RD 30143 — 3-00100
  Carl Adams, prin. — 692-2851

Pickens Technical Institute — 3-CS
  100 PICKENS TECHNICAL DR 30143 — 692-3411

Jefferson, AC 706, PC 5, Jackson
Jackson County SD — 5-11111
  PO BOX 279 30549 — 367-5151
  Sarah Greene, supt.
Jackson County Comprehensive HS — 3-00011
  PO BOX 159 30549 — 367-5003
  James Gurley, prin.
Jackson County MS — 2-00100
  PO BOX 339 30549 — 367-5267
  Shannon Adams, prin.

Jefferson ISD, PO BOX 507 30549 — 4-11111
  Donald Rooks, supt. — 367-9831
JSHS, PO BOX 507 30549 — 2-00111
  Arthur Wheaton, prin. — 367-9832

Jeffersonville, AC 912, PC 4, Twiggs
Twiggs County SD — 4-11111
  PO BOX 232 31044 — 945-3127
  C. W. Keily, supt.
Twiggs County Comprehensive JSHS — 2-00111
  100 WATSON DR 31044 — 945-3112
  Charles Lundy, prin.

Twiggs Academy — 2-11111
  RR 1 BOX 1825 31044 — 945-3175

Jesup, AC 912, PC 6, Wayne
Wayne County SD — 5-11111
  555 SUNSET BLVD 31545 — 427-1000
  Jerry Jones, supt.
Wayne County HS — 4-00011
  1355 W ORANGE ST 31545 — 427-1088
  Larry Cooper, prin.
Puckett MS, 475 DURRENCE RD 31545 — 3-00100
  Donald Westberry, prin. — 427-1061
Williams MS — 3-00100
  1175 S US HIGHWAY 301 31545 — 427-1025
  Tom Freeman, prin.

Jonesboro, AC 404, PC 5, Clayton
Clayton County SD, 120 SMITH ST 30236 — 7-11111
  Bob Livingston, supt. — 473-2700
HS, 7728 MOUNT ZION BLVD 30236 — 4-00011
  Grady Kilman, prin. — 473-2855

Mt. Zion HS
2535 MOUNT ZION PKY   30236   3-00011
Linda Jones, prin.   473-2940
MS, 137 SPRING ST   30236   3-00100
Gloria Adams, prin.   473-2805
Mundy's Mill MS   3-00100
1251 MUNDYS MILL RD   30236   473-2880
Nancy Wells, prin.
Pointe South MS   4-00100
626 FLINT RIVER RD   30236   473-2890
Dan Underwood, prin.
Other Schools – See College Park, Forest Park, Lovejoy, Morrow, Rex, Riverdale

Kennesaw, AC 404, PC 6, Cobb
Cobb County SD
Supt. — See Marietta
Harrison HS, 4500 DUE WEST RD   30144   3-00011
Dexter Mills, prin.   528-6638
North Cobb HS   4-00011
3400 HIGHWAY 293 N   30144   975-4261
Dale Gaddis, prin.
Awtrey MS, 3601 NOWLIN RD   30144   3-00100
Michael Johnson, prin.   975-4272
Lost Mountain MS   3-00100
700 OLD MOUNTAIN RD   30144   528-6627
Larry Cooper, prin.
Pine Mountain MS   4-00100
2720 PINE MOUNTAIN CIR   30144   528-6529
Henry Nettles, prin.

Devereux Center in Georgia   HND
1291 STANLEY RD   30144   800-342-3357
Shiloh Hills Christian S   2-11111
75 HAWKINS STORE RD   30144   926-7729

Kingsland, AC 912, PC 5, Camden
Camden County SD   5-11111
PO BOX 1329   31548   729-5687
David Rainer, supt.
Camden MS   3-00100
1300 MIDDLE SCHOOL DR   31548   729-3113
Gary Blount, prin.
Other Schools – See Saint Marys

La Fayette, AC 706, PC 6, Walker
Walker County SD, PO BOX 29   30728   7-11111
Truman Atkins, supt.   638-1240
HS, 301 N CHEROKEE ST   30728   3-00011
Gene Clonts, prin.   638-2342
MS, 1 ROADRUNNER BLVD   30728   3-00100
David Brothers, prin.   638-6440
Other Schools – See Flintstone, Rossville

La Grange, AC 706, PC 8, Troup
Troup County SD   5-11111
PO BOX 1228   30241   812-7900
J. Terry Jenkins, supt.
HS, PO BOX 820   30241   4-00011
Mickey McCoy, prin.   883-1590
Troup County Comprehensive HS   3-00011
1920 HAMILTON RD   30240   812-7957
Jim Kelly, prin.
Lees Crossing MS, 80 N KIGHT DR   30240   3-00100
Taryl Anderson, prin.   812-7943
Newman MS, 101 SHANNON DR   30240   2-00100
Larry Musick, prin.   883-1535
Whitesville Road MS   3-00100
1920 WHITESVILLE RD   30240   812-7968
Thomas Whatley, prin.
Other Schools – See Hogansville

Courts of Praise Christian S   2-11111
1904 HAMILTON RD   30240   884-3150
Kerr Business College   1-CS
PO BOX 976   30241   884-1751
La Grange Academy   2-11111
1501 VERNON ST   30240   882-8097
Martha Todd, prin.
La Grange College   3-UC
601 BROAD ST   30240   882-2911
West Georgia Technical Institute   2-CS
303 FORT DR   30240   882-2518

Lake City, AC 404, PC 5, Clayton

Lake City Christian S   2-11111
PO BOX 427   30260   363-8483

Lakeland, AC 912, PC 4, Lanier
Lanier County SD, PO BOX 158   31635   4-11111
L. Raymond Moore, supt.   482-3966
Lanier County JSHS   2-00111
PO BOX 277   31635   482-3868
Gene Sellars, prin.

Lawrenceville, AC 404, PC 7, Gwinnett
Gwinnett County SD   8-11111
PO BOX 343   30246   513-6600
George Thompson, supt.
Central Gwinnet HS   4-00011
564 W CROGAN ST   30245   963-8041
Wendell Jackson, prin.
Gwinnett Tech Inst   Vo Tech
1250 ATKINSON RD   30243   962-7580
Alvin Wilbanks, prin.
Gwinnett Vo Ctr   Vo Tech
990 MCELVANEY LN   30244   963-6838
Roy Bucks, prin.
Five Forks MS, 3250 RIVER DR   30244   4-00100
Ron Pennington, prin.   972-1506
MS, 723 HI HOPE RD   30243   4-00100
Joan Akin, prin.   963-6144

Richards MS, 600 HUSTON RD   30244   4-00100
Georgia Barnwell, prin.   995-7133
Sweetwater MS, 3500 CRUSE RD   30244   4-00100
Virginia Crowley, prin.   923-4131
Other Schools – See Buford, Dacula, Duluth, Lilburn, Lithonia, Norcross, Snellville, Suwanee

Gwinnett Technical Institute   5-CS
PO BOX 1505   30246   962-7580

Leesburg, AC 912, PC 4, Lee
Lee County SD, PO BOX 236   31763   5-11111
Robert Clay, supt.   759-6100
Lee County HS, 1 TROJAN WAY   31763   3-00011
William Sampson, prin.   759-6107
Lee County MS   3-00100
439 FIRETOWER RD   31763   759-6114
Mary O'Hearn, prin.

Lexington, AC 706, PC 2, Oglethorpe
Oglethorpe County SD   4-11111
PO BOX 190   30648   743-8128
Thomas Harris, supt.
Oglethorpe County HS   2-00111
RR 1 BOX 1060   30648   743-8124
Aubrey Finch, prin.
Oglethorpe County MS   2-00100
RR 1 BOX 1070   30648   743-8146
George Dougherty, prin.

Lilburn, AC 404, PC 6, Gwinnett
Gwinnett County SD
Supt. — See Lawrenceville
Berkmar HS   4-00011
405 PLEASANT HILL RD NW   30247   921-3636
Donna King, prin.
Parkview HS, 998 COLE RD SW   30247   4-00011
Don Spence, prin.   921-2874
MS   4-00100
4994 LAWRENCEVILLE HWY NW   30247
Mike Grzeskiewicz, prin.   921-1776
Trickum MS, 948 COLE RD SW   30247   4-00100
Mary Anne Charron, prin.   921-2705

Gwinnett College of Business   2-CS
4230 LWRNCVLL HWY NW STE 11   30247   381-7200
Killian Hill Christian S   2-11111
PO BOX 1455   30226   921-3224

Lincolnton, AC 706, PC 4, Lincoln
Lincoln County SD   4-11111
PO BOX 39   30817   359-3742
G. R. Edmunds, supt.
Lincoln County JSHS   3-00111
PO BOX 579   30817   359-3121
Joe Willis, prin.

Lindale, AC 706, PC 5, Floyd
Floyd County SD
Supt. — See Rome
Pepperell HS, 3 DRAGON DR   30147   3-00011
Stephen Johnston, prin.   236-1844
Pepperell MS   3-00100
200 HUGHES DAIRY RD   30147   236-1849
Ben Desper, prin.

Lithia Springs, AC 404, PC 7, Douglas
Douglas County SD
Supt. — See Douglasville
Lithia Springs Comprehensive HS   4-00011
2520 E COUNTY LINE RD   30057   732-2600
Larry Ruble, prin.
Turner MS, 7101 JUNIOR HIGH DR   30057   3-00100
John Bakelaar, prin.   732-2655

Lithonia, AC 404, PC 4, De Kalb
DeKalb County SD
Supt. — See Decatur
JSHS, 2451 RANDALL AVE   30058   4-00111
Byron Collier, prin.   482-8886
Salem JHS, 5333 SALEM RD   30038   2-00110
Dorothy Stroud, prin.   297-2300

Gwinnett County SD
Supt. — See Lawrenceville
Shiloh HS, 4210 SHILOH RD   30058   4-00011
Pat Mahon, prin.   972-8471
Shiloh MS, 4285 SHILOH RD   30058   4-00100
Valerie Clark, prin.   972-3224

Luther Rice Seminary   UC
3038 EVANS MILLS RD   30038   484-1204

Loganville, AC 404, PC 5, Walton
Walton County SD
Supt. — See Monroe
HS, 150 CLARK MCCULLERS DR   30249   3-00011
Ken Prichard, prin.   466-4892
MS, 152 CLARK MCCULLERS DR   30249   2-00100
Randy Bradberry, prin.   466-0713

Lookout Mountain, AC 404, PC 4, Walker

Covenant College   3-UC
SCENIC HWY   30750   820-1560

Louisville, AC 912, PC 4, Jefferson
Jefferson County SD   5-11111
PO BOX 449   30434   625-7626
Tucker Vaughn, supt.
JSHS, RR 3 BOX 432   30434   3-00111
Bill Kitterman, prin.   625-7764
Other Schools – See Wadley, Wrens

Thomas Jefferson Academy   2-11111
PO BOX 523   30434   625-8861

Lovejoy, AC 404, PC 3, Clayton
Clayton County SD
Supt. — See Jonesboro
HS, 1587 MCDONOUGH RD   30250   3-00011
Paul Robbins, prin.   473-2920
MS, 1588 LOVEJOY RD   30250   3-00100
Dan Colwell, prin.   473-2933

Ludowici, AC 912, PC 4, Long
Long County SD, PO BOX 428   31316   3-11111
Janet Watford, supt.   545-2367
Long County JSHS   2-00111
PO BOX 579   31316   545-2135
Perry West, prin.

Lumpkin, AC 912, PC 4, Stewart
Stewart County SD   4-11111
PO BOX 547   31815   838-4329
F. B. Wims, supt.
Stewart-Quitman HS   2-00011
PO BOX 706   31815   838-4301
Lindsey Haire, prin.
Stewart-Quitman MS   2-00100
PO BOX 706   31815   838-4532
John Morrison, prin.

Lyons, AC 912, PC 5, Toombs
Toombs County SD   4-11111
PO BOX 440   30436   526-3141
Kendall Brantley, supt.
Toombs County HS   3-00011
PO BOX 192   30436   526-6068
Jim Dupree, prin.
Toombs Co. MS, PO BOX 151   30436   2-00100
Sam Jones, prin.   526-8363

Toombs Christian S   2-11111
PO BOX 277   30436   526-8938

Mableton, AC 404, PC 7, Cobb
Cobb County SD
Supt. — See Marietta
Pebblebrook HS   3-00011
991 OLD ALABAMA RD   30059   732-5658
Kay Jackson, prin.
Floyd MS, 4803 FLOYD RD   30059   3-00100
James Snell, prin.   732-5619
Lindley MS   3-00100
1550 PEBBLEBROOK CIR   30059   732-5642
Marsha Elliott, prin.

Macon, AC 912, PC 9, Bibb
Bibb County SD, PO BOX 6157   31213   8-11111
Thomas Madison, supt.   741-8501
Central HS, 2155 NAPIER AVE   31204   4-00011
Leontine Espy, prin.   751-6770
Northeast HS   4-00011
1640 UPPER RIVER RD   31211   751-6787
(—), prin.
Southeast HS, 1070 ANTHONY RD   31204   3-00011
Vickie Scott, prin.   784-3120
Southwest HS   4-00011
1730 CANTERBURY RD   31206   788-8011
Columbus Watkins, prin.
Appling MS, 1210 SHURLING DR   31211   3-00100
Terry Sark, prin.   751-6758
Ballard Hudson MS   3-00100
1780 ANTHONY RD   31204   784-3153
Anita Robinson, prin.
McEvoy MS   3-00100
1751 WILLIAMSON RD   31206   784-3158
Charles Sheftall, prin.
Miller MS   4-00100
2241 MONTPELIER AVE   31204   751-6766
Martha Jones, prin.

Central Fellowshp Academy   2-11111
8460 HAWKINSVILLE RD   31206   788-6909
Covenant Academy   2-11111
595 WIMBISH RD   31210   471-0285
First Presbyterian Day S   3-11111
5671 CALVIN DR   31210   477-6506
Georgia Academy for the Blind   HND
2895 VINEVILLE AVE   31204
Gilead Christian Academy   2-11111
1931 ROCKY CREEK RD   31206   788-0606
Macon College   5-CC
COLLEGE STATION DR   31298   474-2800
Macon Technical Institute   3-CS
3300 MACON TECH DR   31206   781-0551
Macon Technical Institute   2-CS
940 FORSYTH ST   31201   781-0551
Medical Center of Central Georgia   HSP
777 HEMLOCK ST   31201   744-1451
Mercer University in Macon   5-UC
1400 COLEMAN AVE   31207   800-637-2378
Middle Georgia Christian S   2-01110
1686 WILLIAMSON RD   31206   788-0774
Mt. De Sales HS, PO BOX 6136   31213   3-00111
Sr. Mary Bayliss, prin.   746-2786
Southeastern School of Aeronautics   1-CS
HERBERT SMART AIRPORT   31201   800-423-7510
Stratford Academy   3-11111
6010 PEAKE RD   31297   477-8073
Henry Tift, prin.
Tatnall Square Academy   3-11111
760 LAKE CREST DR   31210   477-6760

Wesleyan College 2-UC
  4760 FORSYTH RD 31297 800-447-6610
Windsor Academy 2-11111
  4150 JONES RD 31206 781-1621

Madison, AC 706, PC 5, Morgan
Morgan County SD 5-11111
  1065 EAST AVE 30650 342-0752
  James Hagin, supt.
Morgan County HS 3-00011
  1231 COLLEGE DR 30650 342-2336
  Patrick McCullough, prin.
Morgan County MS, 920 PEARL ST 30650 4-00100
  Alfred Murray, prin. 342-0556

Manchester, AC 706, PC 5, Meriwether
Meriwether County SD
  Supt. — See Greenville
HS, 405 5TH AVE N 31816 2-00011
  Larry Keys, prin. 846-8445
MS 3-00100
  701 MRTIN LUTHER KING JR DR 31816
  Alfred Randolf, prin. 846-2846

Marietta, AC 404, PC 8, Cobb
Cobb County SD, PO BOX 1088 30061 8-11111
  Grace Calhoun, supt. 426-3300
Lassiter HS 4-00011
  2600 SHALLOWFORD RD 30066 591-6819
  James Wilson, prin.
Oakwood HS, 1560 JOYNER AVE 30060 2-00011
  Carla Northcutt, prin. 528-6510
Osborne HS, 2451 FAVOR RD 30060 4-00011
  Randy Dye, prin. 319-3791
Pope HS, 3001 HEMBREE RD NE 30062 4-00011
  Ronda Tighe, prin. 509-6077
Sprayberry HS 4-00011
  2525 SANDY PLAINS RD 30066 509-6111
  Paul Ross, prin.
Walton HS 4-00011
  1590 BILL MURDOCK RD 30062 509-6125
  Terry Poor, prin.
Wheeler HS, 375 HOLT RD 30068 4-00011
  Earl Holliday, prin. 509-6138
Daniell MS, 2900 SCOTT RD 30066 3-00100
  Michael Campbell, prin. 528-6520
Dickerson MS 4-00100
  855 WOODLAWN DR 30068 509-6007
  Carole Kell, prin.
Dodgen MS 4-00100
  1725 BILL MURDOCK RD 30062 509-6017
  Cathy Cochran, prin.
East Cobb MS, 380 HOLT RD 30068 4-00100
  Linda Starnes, prin. 509-6023
Hightower Trail MS 3-00100
  3905 POST OAK TRITT RD 30062 509-6201
  Steve Shelton, prin.
Mabry MS, 2700 JIMS RD 30066 3-00100
  Gerri Ray, prin. 591-6833
McCleskey MS 3-00100
  4080 MAYBREEZE RD 30066 591-6841
  Melba Fugitt, prin.
Simpson MS, 3340 TRICKUM RD 30066 3-00100
  Tony Melton, prin. 509-6103
Smitha MS 3-00100
  2025 POWDER SPRINGS RD 30064 528-6460
  Paula Smith, prin.
Other Schools – See Austell, Kennesaw, Mableton,
  Powder Springs, Smyrna

Marietta ISD, PO BOX 1265 30061 5-11111
  Ronald Galloway, supt. 422-3500
HS, 121 WINN ST 30064 4-00011
  (—), prin. 428-2631
MS, 340 AVIATION RD 30060 4-00100
  Robert Golden, prin. 422-0311

Chattahoochee Technical Institute 4-CC
  980 S COBB DR 30060 528-4545
Cumberland Christian Academy 2-11111
  3050 AUSTELL RD 30060 434-5487
Joseph Walker S, 700 COBB PKY N 30062 3-11111
  Donald Robertson, prin. 427-2689
Kennesaw State College 6-UC
  PO BOX 444 30061 423-6500
Kennestone Regional Medical Center HSP
  737 CHURCH ST 30060 426-2029
Life College 4-UC
  1269 BARCLAY CIR 30060 424-0554
Medix School 2-CS
  2480 WINDY HILL RD 30067 980-0002
Mt. Paran Christian S 2-11111
  1700 ALLGOOD RD 30062 578-0182
  Susan King, prin.
Southern College of Technology 5-UC
  1100 S MARIETTA PKY 30060 528-7281

Mc Donough, AC 404, PC 5, Henry
Henry County SD, PO BOX 479 30253 6-11111
  Gary Boehmer, supt. 957-6601
Henry County Comprehensive HS 4-00011
  401 E TOMLINSON ST 30253 957-3943
  Jackie Hammond, prin.
Eagle's Landing JSHS 2-00111
  301 TUNIS RD 30253 954-9515
  Ralph Lynch, prin.
Eagles Landing MS, 295 TUNIS RD 30253 2-00100
  Jim Isenberg, prin. 914-8189
Henry County JHS 4-00100
  166 HOLLY SMITH DR 30253 957-3945
  Randy Ford, prin.
Other Schools – See Stockbridge

Alliance Tractor Trailer Training Center 3-CS
  PO BOX 1008 30253 957-6401
Greater Atlanta Christian S 2-11111
  PO BOX 657 30253 957-2927

Mc Rae, AC 912, PC 5, Telfair
Telfair County SD 4-11111
  PO BOX 240 31055 868-5661
  Jerry Rogers, supt.
Telfair County HS 3-00011
  1900 S 3RD AVE 31055 863-6096
  Anthony McIver, prin.
Telfair County MS 2-00100
  101 HIGHWAY 280 W 31055 868-7465
  Carnell Wilson, prin.

Metter, AC 912, PC 5, Candler
Candler County SD 4-11111
  PO BOX 536 30439 685-5713
  James Wilcox, supt.
JSHS, 431 W VERTIA ST 30439 3-00111
  Rob Poole, prin. 685-2134

Milledgeville, AC 912, PC 7, Baldwin
Baldwin County SD 6-11111
  PO BOX 1188 31061 453-4176
  Hoyt Washington, supt.
Baldwin HS 4-00011
  155 GA HIGHWAY 49 W 31061 453-6429
  Rebecca Knowles, prin.
Baldwin MS, 151 S IRWIN ST 31061 3-00100
  Sam Hall, prin. 453-6433
Boddie MS 3-00100
  1340 ORCHARD HILL RD 31061 453-6400
  Harold Watson, prin.

Georgia College 5-UC
  231 W HANCOCK ST 31061 453-4458
Georgia Military College 2-CC
  201 E GREEN ST 31061 800-342-0413
Georgia Military S 2-00111
  201 E GREEN ST 31061 454-2700
John Milledge Academy 2-11111
  197 LOG CABIN RD NE 31061 452-5570

Millen, AC 912, PC 5, Jenkins
Jenkins County SD 4-11111
  PO BOX 660 30442 982-6000
  L. Batten, supt.
Jenkins County JSHS 2-00111
  117 E BARNEY AVE 30442 982-4791
  Hayward Cordy, prin.

Milner, AC 404, PC 2, Lamar
Lamar County SD, 103 BIRCH ST 30257 4-11111
  James Jenkins, supt. 358-1159
Other Schools – See Barnesville

Monroe, AC 404, PC 6, Walton
Walton County SD, 115 OAK ST 30655 6-11111
  Kenneth Cloud, supt. 267-6544
HS, 212 BRYANT RD 30655 3-00011
  Chris Quinn, prin. 267-7527
Carver MS, 1095 GOOD HOPE RD 30655 3-00100
  Anita Doster, prin. 267-6000
Other Schools – See Loganville

Walton Academy 2-11111
  PO BOX 1026 30655 267-7578
  William Nicholson, prin.

Montezuma, AC 912, PC 5, Macon
Macon County SD
  Supt. — See Oglethorpe
Macon County HS 3-00011
  611 VIENNA RD 31063 472-8579
  Carl Peaster, prin.
Douglass JSHS 2-00111
  425 WASHINGTON ST 31063 472-6644
  McArthur Brown, prin.

Monticello, AC 706, PC 4, Jasper
Jasper County SD 4-11111
  126 COURTHOUSE 30164 468-6350
  Julian Cope, supt.
Jasper County JSHS 3-00111
  1289 COLLEGE ST 31064 468-2227
  James Jordan, prin.

Piedmont Academy 2-11111
  PO BOX 231 31064 468-8818

Morgan, AC 912, PC 2, Calhoun
Calhoun County SD 4-11111
  PO BOX 38 31766 849-2765
  Corkin Cherubini, supt.
Other Schools – See Edison

Morrow, AC 404, PC 6, Clayton
Clayton County SD
  Supt. — See Jonesboro
HS, 2299 OLD REX MORROW RD 30260 4-00011
  Walter Pierce, prin. 362-3865
MS, 5968 MADDOX RD 30260 3-00100
  J. T. Brady, prin. 362-3860

Clayton Christian S 2-11111
  5900 REYNOLDS RD 30260 961-9300
Clayton State College 5-UC
  PO BOX 285 30260 961-3500

Moultrie, AC 912, PC 7, Colquitt
Colquitt County SD 6-11111
  PO BOX 1806 31776 985-1550
  Bill Mock, supt.
Colquitt County SHS 4-00001
  1800 PARK AVE SE 31768 890-6181
  Ed Turner, prin.
Colquitt County JHS 4-00110
  900 5TH ST SW 31768 890-6183
  Willie Williams, prin.

Moultrie Area Technical Institute 2-CS
  PO BOX 520 31776 985-2297

Mount Airy, AC 706, PC 3, Habersham
Habersham County SD
  Supt. — See Clarkesville
Habersham Central HS 3-00011
  RR 2 BOX 334 30563 778-7161
  James Jones, prin.

Central Heights Christian S 2-11111
  RR 2 BOX 339 30563 778-3360

Mount Berry, AC 706, PC 3, Floyd

Berry College 4-UC
  2277 MARTHA BERRY HWY NW 30165
  232-5374

Mount Vernon, AC 912, PC 4, Montgomery
Montgomery County SD 4-11111
  PO BOX 315 30445 583-2301
  Jim Poole, supt.
Montgomery County JSHS 3-00111
  DOBBINS ST 30445 583-2296
  Donald Elam, prin.

Brewton-Parker College 4-UC
  PO BOX 197 30445 583-2241

Mount Zion, AC 404, PC 3, Carroll
Carroll County SD
  Supt. — See Carrollton
JSHS, 132 EAGLE DR 30150 2-00111
  Lynn Huffstickler, prin. 834-6654

Nahunta, AC 912, PC 4, Brantley
Brantley County SD 4-11111
  PO BOX 613 31553 462-6176
  James Ferguson, supt.
Brantley County HS 3-00011
  PO BOX 1239 31553 462-5121
  Melton Callahan, prin.
Brantley MS, PO BOX 612 31553 2-00100
  Hymerick Thomas, prin. 462-7092

Nashville, AC 912, PC 5, Berrien
Berrien County SD 5-11111
  PO BOX 625 31639 686-2081
  Gerald Griffin, supt.
Berrien HS, 909 N DAVIS ST 31639 3-00011
  Wayne Strickland, prin. 686-7428
Berrien MS, 305 N ANN ST 31639 2-00100
  Louise Watson, prin. 686-2021

Newnan, AC 404, PC 7, Coweta
Coweta County SD 6-11111
  PO BOX 280 30264 254-2800
  Bob Welch, supt.
HS, 190 LAGRANGE ST 30263 4-00011
  Allen Wood, prin. 254-2880
Central MS, PO BOX 1803 30264 3-00100
  Eddie Lovett, prin. 254-2840
Evans MS, 1 EVANS DR 30263 3-00100
  Jerry Davis, prin. 254-2780
Fairmount Demonstration MS 2-01100
  FAIRMOUNT SCHOOL RD 30263 254-2870
  Sherry Warren, prin.
Other Schools – See Senoia, Sharpsburg

Heritage S, 2093 HIGHWAY 29 N 30263 2-11111
  Dennis Brown, prin. 253-9898

Norcross, AC 404, PC 6, Gwinnett
Gwinnett County SD
  Supt. — See Lawrenceville
Meadowcreek HS 4-00011
  4455 STEVE REYNOLDS BLVD 30093 381-9680
  Scott Smith, prin.
HS, 600 BEAVER RUIN RD 30071 4-00011
  Judy Rogers, prin. 448-3674
Pinckneyville MS 3-00100
  5440 W JONES BRIDGE RD 30092 263-0860
  Cynthia Loe, prin.
Summerour MS 3-00100
  585 MITCHELL RD 30071 448-3045
  Wanda Yeargin, prin.

Asher School of Business 2-CS
  100 PINNACLE WAY STE 110 30071
  368-0800
Greater Atlanta Christian S 4-11111
  PO BOX 4277 30091 923-9230
  David Fincher, prin.

Oakwood, AC 404, PC 4, Hall
Hall County SD
  Supt. — See Gainesville
West Hall HS, 5500 MCEVER RD 30566 4-00011
  Jack Pirkle, prin. 967-9826
West Hall MS, 5470 MCEVER RD 30566 3-00100
  Nelwyn Turk, prin. 967-4871

Lanier Technical Institute   3-CS
PO BOX 58   30566   531-6300

Ocilla, AC 912, PC 5, Irwin
Irwin County SD, PO BOX 225   31774   4-11111
   R. Gentry, supt.   468-7485
Irwin County HS   2-00011
   311 N ALMOND ST   31774   468-9421
   Bobby Griffin, prin.
Irwin County JHS   2-00100
   311 N ALMOND ST   31774   468-9421
   Jerry Yancey, prin.

Oglethorpe, AC 912, PC 4, Macon
Macon County SD   5-11111
   PO BOX 488   31068   472-8188
   Hosie Waters, supt.
Macon County JHS   2-00100
   PO BOX 487   31068   472-7045
   Annis Goddard, prin.
Other Schools – See Montezuma

Oxford, AC 404, PC 4, Newton

Oxford College of Emory University   3-CC
   30267   784-8888

Peachtree City, AC 404, PC 7, Fayette
Fayette County SD
   Supt. — See Fayetteville
McIntosh HS   4-00011
   201 WALT BANKS RD   30269   631-3232
   Stuart Bennett, prin.
Booth MS, 250 S PEACHTREE PKY   30269   3-00100
   Melvin Hunt, prin.   631-3240

Pearson, AC 912, PC 4, Atkinson
Atkinson County SD   4-11111
   PO BOX 608   31642   422-7373
   Edwin Davis, supt.
Atkinson County JSHS   2-00111
   PO BOX 248   31642   422-3267
   Mavis McKinnon, prin.

Pelham, AC 912, PC 5, Mitchell
Pelham ISD   4-11111
   188 W RAILROAD ST S   31779   294-8715
   James Parker, supt.
JSHS, 188 W RAILROAD ST S   31779   3-00111
   Herbert Houston, prin.   294-8623

Pembroke, AC 912, PC 4, Bryan
Bryan County SD, PO BOX 768   31321   4-11111
   Perry Bacon, supt.   653-4381
Byran County JSHS   3-00111
   PO BOX 278   31321   653-2881
   Don Carnley, prin.
Other Schools – See Richmond Hill

Perry, AC 912, PC 6, Houston
Houston County SD, PO BOX N   31069   7-11111
   Tony Hinnant, supt.   988-6200
HS, 1307 NORTH AVE   31069   3-00011
   Ronald Smith, prin.   988-6297
MS, SUNSHINE AVE   31069   2-00100
   Bob Pennington, prin.   988-6285
Other Schools – See Warner Robins

Westfield S, PO BOX 1241   31069   2-11111
   987-0547

Pinehurst, AC 912, PC 2, Dooly

Fullington Academy, PO BOX B   31070   2-11111
   645-3383

Portal, AC 912, PC 3, Bulloch
Bulloch County SD
   Supt. — See Statesboro
S, PO BOX 217   30450   2-10111
   Joanne Radcliffe, prin.   865-2640

Powder Springs, AC 404, PC 6, Cobb
Cobb County SD
   Supt. — See Marietta
McEachern HS   4-00011
   2400 NEW MACLAND RD   30073   439-4700
   Ralph Williams, prin.
Tapp MS, 3900 MACEDONIA RD   30073   4-00100
   Nancy McNeil, prin.   439-4730

Quitman, AC 912, PC 6, Brooks
Brooks County SD   5-11111
   PO BOX 511   31643   263-7531
   John Horton, supt.
Brooks County HS   3-00011
   PO BOX 512   31643   263-8923
   Donald Turner, prin.
Brooks County MS   2-00100
   PO BOX 271   31643   263-7521
   George Folsom, prin.

Rabun Gap, AC 706, PC 2, Rabun

Rabun Gap-Nacoochee S   2-00111
   HIGHWAY 441 N   30568   746-5736
   Stephen Boyce, prin.

Reidsville, AC 912, PC 4, Tattnall
Tattnall County SD   5-11111
   PO BOX 157   30453   557-4726
   Ron McCall, supt.
Tattnall Co. HS, RR 1 BOX 410   30453   2-00011
   Greg Maybin, prin.   557-4374

Rex, AC 404, PC 3, Clayton
Clayton County SD
   Supt. — See Jonesboro
Adamson MS, 3187 REX RD   30273   3-00100
Ronnie Blake, prin.   968-2925

Richmond Hill, AC 912, PC 5, Bryan
Bryan County SD
   Supt. — See Pembroke
JSHS, PO BOX 340   31324   3-00111
   Millie Morris, prin.   756-3361

Ringgold, AC 706, PC 4, Catoosa
Catoosa County SD   6-11111
   PO BOX 130   30736   965-2297
   Lee Sims, supt.
HS, 400 N SPARKS ST   30736   4-00011
   Richard Clark, prin.   935-2254
MS, 112 GYM ST   30736   3-00100
   Con Kellerhals, prin.   935-3381
Other Schools – See Fort Oglethorpe, Rossville

Riverdale, AC 404, PC 6, Clayton
Clayton County SD
   Supt. — See Jonesboro
HS, 160 ROBERTS DR   30274   4-00011
   Ed Scott, prin.   473-2905
MS, 400 ROBERTS DR   30274   4-00100
   Bobby Shephard, prin.   994-4045

Bible Baptist Christian S   2-11111
   91 VALLEY HILL ROAD   30274   478-6747

Roberta, AC 912, PC 3, Crawford
Crawford County SD   4-11111
   PO BOX 8   31078   836-3131
   C. Eugene Trammell, supt.
Crawford County Comprehensive HS   2-00011
   PO BOX 98   31078   836-3126
   David Hunt, prin.
Crawford County MS   2-00100
   PO BOX 335   31078   836-3181
   Michael Webb, prin.

Rochelle, AC 912, PC 4, Wilcox
Wilcox County SD
   Supt. — See Abbeville
Wilcox County JSHS   31079   2-00111
   Cary Clark, prin.   365-7231

Rockmart, AC 404, PC 5, Polk
Polk County SD
   Supt. — See Cedartown
HS, 316 N PIEDMONT AVE   30153   3-00011
   Byron Nx, prin.   684-5432
Elm Street MS   3-00100
   100 MORGAN VALLEY RD   30153   684-3151
   Jerry Buttrum, prin.

Rock Spring, AC 706, PC 2, Walker

Walker Technical Institute   3-CS
   265 BICENTENNIAL TRL   30739   764-1016

Rocky Face, AC 706, PC 4, Whitfield
Whitfield County SD
   Supt. — See Dalton
West Side MS   2-00100
   580 LAFAYETTE RD   30740   673-2611
   Ric Ayer, prin.

Rome, AC 706, PC 8, Floyd
Floyd County SD   6-11111
   600 RIVERSIDE PKY NE   30161   234-1031
   Jackie Collins, supt.
Coosa HS   3-00011
   4454 ALABAMA HWY NW   30165   236-1870
   Terry Lewis, prin.
Armuchee JSHS   3-00111
   4203 MARTHA BERRY HWY NW   30165
   Jody Puckett, prin.   236-1886
Model JSHS   3-00111
   3252 CALHOUN HWY NE   30161   236-1895
   Jerry Gatlin, prin.
Floyd Co. Technical HS   Vo Tech
   100 VOCATIONAL DR   30161   236-1860
   Kal Oravet, prin.
Coosa MS   3-00100
   5041 ALABAMA HWY NW   30165   236-1856
   Rob Puckett, prin.
Other Schools – See Lindale

Rome ISD, 508 E 2ND ST   30161   5-11111
   Larry Atwell, supt.   236-5050
HS   4-00011
   1000 VTRANS MEMORIAL HWY NE   30161
   Dennis Chamberlain, prin.   235-9653
MS   2-00100
   1020 VTRANS MEMORIAL HWY NE   30161
   Dennis Chamberlain, prin.   235-4695

Coosa Valley Technical Institute   2-CS
   112 HEMLOCK ST   30161   235-1142
Darlington S   3-11111
   1014 CAVE SPRING RD SW   30161   235-6051
   Bradford Gioia, prin.
Floyd College   4-CC
   PO BOX 1864   30162   295-6339
Floyd Medical Center   HSP
   PO BOX 233   30162   295-5500
Shorter College   3-UC
   315 SHORTER AVE   30165   800-868-6980

Rossville, AC 706, PC 5, Walker
Catoosa County SD
   Supt. — See Ringgold
Lakeview MS, 1200 CROSS ST   30741   3-00100
   Mike Lusk, prin.   866-1040

Walker County SD
   Supt. — See La Fayette
Ridgeland HS, RR 1 BOX 7   30741   4-00011
   Don Swafford, prin.   820-9361
MS, BRYAN ST   30741   3-00100
   Jim Fowler, prin.   866-2606

Roswell, AC 404, PC 8, Fulton
Fulton County SD
   Supt. — See Atlanta
HS, 11595 KING RD   30075   4-00011
   Jonathon Zachary, prin.   552-4500
Crabapple MS   4-00100
   10700 CRABAPPLE RD   30075   552-4520
   Janet Hopping, prin.

Howard S, 9415 WILLEO RD   30075   2-11111
   642-9644

Saint Marys, AC 912, PC 6, Camden
Camden County SD
   Supt. — See Kingsland
Camden County HS   4-00011
   2600 OSBORNE RD   31558   882-4351
   Marvin Whitley, prin.
Clark MS, 2900 MICKLER DR   31558   3-00100
   Joseph LaBelle, prin.   882-4373

Saint Simons Island, AC 912, PC 7, Glynn

Frederica Academy   2-11111
   200 HAMILTON RD   31522   638-9981
   W. Worthington, prin.

Sandersville, AC 912, PC 6, Washington
Washington County SD   5-11111
   PO BOX 716   31082   552-3981
   E. Tarver Averett, supt.
Washington County HS   3-00011
   PO BOX 1057   31082   552-2324
   Lamar Binion, prin.
Elder MS, PO BOX 816   31082   3-00100
   Bern Anderson, prin.   552-2007

Brentwood S, PO BOX 955   31082   3-11111
   552-5136
Houston Aeronautical College   2-CS
   RR 3 BOX 250   31082

Savannah, AC 912, PC 9, Chatham
Chatham County SD, 208 BULL ST   31401   8-11111
   Patrick Russo, supt.   651-7000
Beach HS, 3001 HOPKINS ST   31405   4-00011
   Ola Lewis, prin.   651-7335
Groves HS, 100 WHEATHILL RD   31408   3-00011
   Elijah McGraw, prin.   966-6820
Jenkins HS   4-00011
   1800 E DE RENNE AVE   31406   351-6318
   Frances Wong, prin.
Johnson HS, 3013 SHELL RD   31404   3-00011
   Robert Gilbert, prin.   351-6331
HS, 500 WASHINGTON AVE   31405   4-00011
   Marie Polite, prin.   651-7395
Windsor Forest HS   4-00011
   12419 LARGO DR   31419   921-3710
   Linda Herman, prin.
Bartlett MS   4-00100
   207 E MONTGOMERY CROSSROADS   31406
   Michael Stacey, prin.   921-3730
DeRenne MS, 3609 HOPKINS ST   31405   3-00100
   Bailey Walker, prin.   651-7350
Hubert MS, 768 GRANT ST   31401   3-00100
   Patricia DeVoe, prin.   651-7371
Myers MS, 2316 BREVARD CIR   31404   4-00100
   Cheryl Reynolds, prin.   351-6348
Scott MS, 402 MARKET ST   31408   3-00100
   Ray Pandtle, prin.   966-6851
Shuman MS, 415 GOEBEL AVE   31404   3-00100
   Roland James, prin.   651-7085
Tompkins MS, 151 HOWE ST   31408   3-00100
   Sam Manior, prin.   966-6868
Wilder MS, 1300 E 66TH ST   31404   3-00100
   Pamela Stevenson, prin.   351-6387
Other Schools – See Garden City

Armstrong State College   5-UC
   11935 ABERCORN ST   31419   800-633-2349
Benedictine Military S   2-00011
   6502 SEAWRIGHT DR   31406   356-3500
   Fr. Griffin, prin.
Bible Baptist S   2-11111
   4700 SKIDAWAY RD   31404   352-3067
Calvary Baptist Day S   3-11111
   4625 WATERS AVE   31404   351-2299
   Graham Lowe, prin.
Memorial Day S   2-11111
   6500 HABERSHAM ST   31405   352-4535
Pineland Christian S   2-11111
   4906 PINELAND DR   31405   238-5053
St. Andrew's School   2-11111
   PO BOX 30639   31410   897-4941
   Ray Stinson, prin.
St. Vincent Academy   2-00011
   207 E LIBERTY ST   31401   236-5508
   Sr. Mary Walsh, prin.

Savannah Christian S 3-11111
PO BOX 2848 31402 234-1653
George Charles, prin.
Savannah College of Art & Design 4-UC
342 BULL ST 31401 238-2483
Savannah Country Day S 3-11111
824 STILLWOOD DR 31419 925-8800
Paul Pressly, prin.
Savannah State College 31404 4-UC
356-2181
Savannah Technical Institute 4-CC
5717 WHITE BLUFF RD 31405 351-6362
South College 3-CC
709 MALL BLVD 31406 651-8100
South College 2-CC
1015 WHITAKER ST 31401 651-8133
Urban Christian Academy 2-11111
4560 ACL BLVD 31405 234-4710

Senoia, AC 404, PC 3, Coweta
Coweta County SD
Supt. — See Newnan
East Coweta MS 3-00100
6291 HIGHWAY 16 30276 599-6607
David Parrott, prin.

Sharpsburg, AC 404, PC 2, Coweta
Coweta County SD
Supt. — See Newnan
East Coweta HS 3-00011
400 MCCOLLUM SHARPSBURG RD 30277
John Boren, prin. 254-2850

Shellman, AC 912, PC 4, Randolph

Randolph Southern S 2-11111
PO BOX 287 31786 679-5324

Siloam, AC 706, PC 2, Greene

Nathaniel Green Academy 2-11111
PO BOX 109 30665 467-2147

Smyrna, AC 404, PC 8, Cobb
Cobb County SD
Supt. — See Marietta
Campbell HS, 3295 ATLANTA RD 30080 4-00011
Joe Boland, prin. 319-3726
Griffin MS 3-00100
4010 KING SPRINGS RD 30082 319-3744
Tom Higgins, prin.
Nash MS 3-00100
951 POWDER SPRINGS ST 30080 319-3776
Ellen Cohan, prin.

Snellville, AC 404, PC 7, Gwinnett
Gwinnett County SD
Supt. — See Lawrenceville
Brookwood HS 4-00011
1255 DOGWOOD RD 30278 972-7642
Emmett Lawson, prin.
South Gwinnett HS 4-00011
2288 E MAIN ST 30278 972-4840
Coley Krug, prin.
MS, 3155 PATE RD 30278 4-00100
Mike Moody, prin. 972-1530

Social Circle, AC 404, PC 5, Walton
Social Circle ISD, PO BOX 428 30279 3-11111
John Burks, supt. 464-2731
HS, PO BOX 1169 30279 2-00011
Robert Smith, prin. 464-2611
MS, PO BOX 1169 30279 2-00100
Bettye Ray, prin. 464-1932

Soperton, AC 912, PC 5, Treutlen
Treutlen County SD, 202 3RD ST 30457 4-11111
Gary Walden, supt. 529-4228
Treutlen JSHS, 1000 3RD ST 30457 2-00111
Robert Carroll, prin. 529-4536

Sparta, AC 706, PC 4, Hancock
Hancock County SD 4-11111
PO BOX 488 31087 444-6621
Marvin Lewis, supt.
Hancock Central JSHS 3-00111
RR 2 BOX 454C 31087 444-7009
W. Lusain, prin.

John Hancock Academy, PO BOX E 31087 2-11111
444-6470

Springfield, AC 912, PC 4, Effingham
Effingham County SD 5-11111
PO BOX 346 31329 754-6491
J. Michael Moore, supt.
Effingham County HS 4-00011
1589 GEORGIA HIGHWAY 119 S 31329
Harris Hinely, prin. 754-6404
Effingham County MS 4-00100
1290 GEORGIA HIGHWAY 119 S 31329
Franklin Goldwire, prin. 754-3332

Statenville, AC 912, PC 3, Echols
Echols County SD 3-11111
PO BOX 207 31648 559-5734
Mamie Pipkins, supt.
Echols County S 31648 3-11111
Emory Corbett, prin. 559-5413

Statesboro, AC 912, PC 7, Bulloch
Bulloch County SD 6-11111
500 NORTHSIDE DR E 30458 764-6201
Bill Bice, supt.
HS, 10 LESTER RD 30458 4-00011
Dennis Tipton, prin. 489-8751
James MS, 150 WILLIAMS RD 30458 3-00100
H. Tankersley, prin. 764-6091
Other Schools – See Brooklet, Portal

Bulloch Academy, RR 5 BOX 3 30458 2-11111
764-6297
Georgia Southern University 30460 7-UC
681-5531

Stillmore, AC 912, PC 3, Emanuel

Emanuel Academy, PO BOX 77 30464 2-11111
562-4405

Stockbridge, AC 404, PC 5, Henry
Henry County SD
Supt. — See Mc Donough
Stockbridge Comprehensive HS 4-00011
109 LEE ST 30281 474-8747
Melanie Jensen, prin.
JHS, 533 OLD CONYERS RD 30281 4-00100
Ralph Pack, prin. 474-5710

Mt. Vernon Christian S 2-11111
1738 FAIRVIEW RD 30281 474-1313

Stone Mountain, AC 404, PC 6, De Kalb
DeKalb County SD
Supt. — See Decatur
Redan SHS, 5247 REDAN RD 30088 5-00001
Percy Mack, prin. 469-1500
HS, 4555 CENTRAL DR 30083 4-00011
Sidney Lionberger, prin. 294-5413
Stone Mountain II MS 2-00100
5265 MIMOSA DR 30083 879-8764
Eleanor Finley, prin.

Forrest Hills Christian S 2-11111
6826 MEMORIAL DR 30083 469-3422
Stone Mountain Christian S 2-11111
PO BOX 509 30086 469-3431

Suches, AC 706, PC 2, Union
Union County SD
Supt. — See Blairsville
Woody Gap S 1-11111
3736 STATE HIGHWAY 60 30572 747-2401
George Burch, prin.

Summerville, AC 706, PC 6, Chattooga
Chattooga County SD 5-11111
PO BOX 30 30747 857-3447
Frank Stewart, supt.
Chattooga County HS 3-00011
PO BOX 30 30747 857-2402
David Jones, prin.
MS, HIGHWAY 100 30747 2-00100
Mitchell Williams, prin. 857-2444

Suwanee, AC 404, PC 4, Gwinnett
Gwinnett County SD
Supt. — See Lawrenceville
North Gwinnett HS 4-00011
20 LEVEL CREEK RD 30174 945-9558
Franklin Lewis, prin.

Swainsboro, AC 912, PC 6, Emanuel
Emanuel County SD 5-11111
PO BOX 130 30401 237-6674
Elizabeth Brown, supt.
HS, US HIGHWAY 1 S 30401 4-00011
Dessie Davis, prin. 237-2267
MS, 200 TIGER TRL 30401 3-00100
Marion Shaw, prin. 237-8047
Other Schools – See Twin City

East Georgia College 2-CC
237 THIGPEN DR 30401 237-7831
Swainsboro Technical Institute 3-CS
201 KITE RD 30401 237-6465

Sylvania, AC 912, PC 5, Screven
Screven County SD 5-11111
PO BOX 1668 30467 564-7114
Patricia Bazemore, supt.
Screven County HS 3-00011
PO BOX 1688 30467 564-7836
Rick Freeman, prin.
Central MS, 501 PINE ST 30467 3-00100
Arthur Freeland, prin. 564-7468

Sylvester, AC 912, PC 6, Worth
Worth County SD 5-11111
204A E FRANKLIN ST 31791 776-8600
Alan Kimbro, supt.
Worth County Comprehensive HS 3-00011
1206 N MONROE ST 31791 776-8625
Charles Prince, prin.
Worth County MS 3-00100
1305 N ISABELLA ST 31791 776-8620
Mance Daughtry, prin.

Talbotton, AC 706, PC 4, Talbot
Talbot County SD, PO BOX 515 31827 3-11111
John Terry, supt. 665-8528
Central S, PO BOX 308 31827 3-11111
Edward Barnwell, prin. 665-8577

Tallapoosa, AC 706, PC 5, Haralson
Haralson County SD
Supt. — See Buchanan
Haralson County Comprehensive HS 3-00011
PO BOX 547 30176 574-7647
Larry Olson, prin.
West Haralson MS 2-01100
PO BOX 246 30176 574-7060
Paul Dunn, prin.

Tallulah Falls, AC 404, PC 2, Habersham

Tallulah Falls S, PO BOX 10 30573 1-11111
Aaron Turner, prin. 754-3171

Temple, AC 404, PC 4, Carroll
Carroll County SD
Supt. — See Carrollton
JSHS, 589 SAGE ST 30179 2-01111
Denzil Rogers, prin. 562-3218

Thomaston, AC 706, PC 6, Upson
Thomaston-Upson County SD 4-11111
205 CIVIC CENTER DR 30286 647-9621
F. Bates, supt.
Upson-Lee HS, 101 HOLSTON DR 30286 3-00011
Angie Devivo, prin. 647-8171
Lee JHS, 319 S BETHEL ST 30286 2-01100
William Aplin, prin. 647-4291
Upson MS, 300 ADAMS ST 30286 3-00100
Jim Fowler, prin. 647-6256

Flint River Technical Institute 2-CS
PO BOX 1089 30286 647-9616

Thomasville, AC 912, PC 7, Thomas
Thomas County SD 5-11111
PO BOX 2300 31799 225-4380
Terrel Solana, supt.
Thomas County Central HS 4-00011
1500 US 84 BYPASS 31792 225-5050
Frank Delaney, prin.
Central MS, E PINETREE BLVD 31792 2-00100
Earl Williams, prin. 225-4394

Thomasville ISD 5-11111
915 E JACKSON ST 31792 225-2600
Fred Dorminy, supt.
HS, 315 S HANSELL ST 31792 3-00011
Jerry Studdard, prin. 225-2634
Thomasville Vo HS Vo Tech
PO BOX 1578 31799 225-2609
Lewis Brunner, prin.
MacIntyre Park MS 3-00100
117 GLENWOOD DR 31792 225-2628
Albert Copeland, prin.

Brookwood Academy 2-11111
100 CARDINAL RIDGE RD 31792 226-8070
Peter Mertz, prin.
Thomas College 2-UC
1501 MILLPOND RD 31792 226-1621
Thomas Technical Institute 2-CS
PO BOX 1578 31799 225-4094

Thomson, AC 706, PC 6, McDuffie
McDuffie County SD 5-11111
PO BOX 957 30824 595-1918
Ed Grisham, supt.
HS, PO BOX 1077 30824 4-00011
Bob Smith, prin. 595-9393
MS, 511 MAIN ST 30824 3-00100
Roy Sapough, prin. 595-3523

Briarwood Academy 2-11111
PO BOX 840 30824 595-5641

Tifton, AC 912, PC 7, Tift
Tift County SD, PO BOX 389 31793 6-11111
Frank King, supt. 386-6500
Tift County SHS, 700 W 8TH ST 31794 4-00001
O'Neal Bozeman, prin. 386-6540
Tift County JHS, RR 7 BOX 254 31794 4-00110
Ron Fritz, prin. 386-6545

Abraham Baldwin Agriculture College 5-CC
PO BOX 1 31793 386-3236
Moultrie Area Industrial-Technical Inst. 1-CS
314 E 14TH ST 31794 985-2297

Tiger, AC 706, PC 2, Rabun
Rabun County SD
Supt. — See Clayton
Rabun County JSHS 3-00111
RR 1 BOX 2335 30576 782-4526
Allen Fort, prin.

Toccoa, AC 706, PC 6, Stephens
Stephens County SD 5-11111
RR 1 BOX 75 30577 886-3783
Ed Mills, supt.
Stephens County HS 4-00011
RR 5 BOX 26 30577 886-6825
Ronald Keffer, prin.
Other Schools – See Eastanollee

Toccoa Falls, AC 404, PC 3, Stephens

Toccoa Falls College 3-UC
PO BOX 368 30577 886-6831

Trenton, AC 706, PC 4, Dade
Dade County SD, PO BOX 188 30752 4-11111
Charles Johnston, supt. 657-4361
Northwest Georgia HS 3-00011
RR 3 BOX 673A 30752 657-7517
Joy Odom, prin.

Dade MS, RR 3 BOX 94 30752   3-00100
  Gayle Gallaher, prin.   657-6491

Trion, AC 706, PC 4, Chattooga
  Trion ISD, PINE ST 30753   4-11111
    Bill Kinsy, supt.   734-2363
  JSHS, DALTON ST 30753   2-00111
    Clarence Blevins, prin.   734-7316

Tucker, AC 404, PC 8, De Kalb
  DeKalb County SD
    Supt. — See Decatur
  JSHS, 5036 LAVISTA RD 30084   4-00111
    Charles Buchanan, prin.   938-4471

Tunnel Hill, AC 706, PC 3, Whitfield
  Whitfield County SD
    Supt. — See Dalton
  Northwest Whitfield County HS   4-00011
    1651 TUNNEL HILL VARNELL RD 30755
    Linda Gilpatrick, prin.   673-6533

Twin City, AC 912, PC 4, Emanuel
  Emanuel County SD
    Supt. — See Swainsboro
  Emmanuel County JSHS   3-01111
    PO BOX 218 30471   763-2673
    David Price, prin.

Tyrone, AC 404, PC 5, Fayette
  Fayette County SD
    Supt. — See Fayetteville
  Sandy Creek HS, 360 JENKINS RD 30290   2-00011
    Wayne Robinson, prin.   969-2842
  Sandy Creek Evening S   2-00011
    360 JENKINS RD 30290   306-5994
    Bobbie Krause, prin.
  Flat Rock MS, 325 JENKINS RD 30290   2-00100
    Juliette Babb, prin.   969-2830

Union City, AC 404, PC 6, Fulton
  Fulton County SD
    Supt. — See Atlanta
  South Fulton Career Tech   Vo Tech
    4025 FLAT SHOALS RD 30291   969-3445
    Cynthia Lyon, prin.

Valdosta, AC 912, PC 8, Lowndes
  Lowndes County SD   6-11111
    PO BOX 1227 31698   245-2250
    John Baxter, supt.
  Lowndes HS   4-00011
    1112 N SAINT AUGUSTINE RD 31601   245-2260
    Michael Booker, prin.
  Lowndes MS, 506 COPELAND RD 31601   3-00100
    Fred Davis, prin.   245-2280
  Other Schools – See Hahira

  Valdosta ISD, PO BOX 5407 31603   6-11111
    Walter Altman, supt.   333-8500
  HS, 3101 N FORREST ST 31602   4-00011
    Bill Aldrich, prin.   333-8540
  JHS, 110 BURTON ST 31602   4-00100
    Tom Finland, prin.   333-8555

  Open Bible Christian HS   2-11111
    3014 N OAK STREET EXT 31602   244-6694
  Valdosta State College   6-UC
    PATTERSON ST 31698   333-5791
  Valdosta Technical Institute   3-CS
    4089 VAL TECH RD 31602   333-2100
  Valwood S, 1903 GORNTO RD 31602   2-11111
    242-8491

Vidalia, AC 912, PC 7, Toombs
  Vidalia ISD, 208 S COLLEGE ST 30474   5-11111
    Butch Mosely, supt.   537-3088
  HS, 1001 NORTH ST W 30474   3-00100
    Larry Cowart, prin.   537-7931

Vienna, AC 912, PC 5, Dooly
  Dooly County SD   5-11111
    202 E COTTON ST 31092   268-4761
    M. Hickerson, supt.
  Dooly County HS, 715 N 3RD ST 31092   3-00011
    Joe Ludlam, prin.   268-8181

Dooly County MS, 715 N 3RD ST 31092   2-00100
  Oneida Ingram, prin.   268-8179

Villa Rica, AC 404, PC 6, Carroll
  Carroll County SD
    Supt. — See Carrollton
  JSHS, 600 ROCKY BRANCH RD 30180   3-00111
    Lynn Jackson, prin.   459-5185

Wadley, AC 912, PC 4, Jefferson
  Jefferson County SD
    Supt. — See Louisville
  Wadley MS, PO BOX 969 30477   2-00100
    Barbara Jordan, prin.   252-5446

Waleska, AC 404, PC 3, Cherokee

  Reinhardt College   3-CC
    PO BOX 128 30183   479-1454

Warner Robins, AC 912, PC 8, Houston
  Houston County SD
    Supt. — See Perry
  Houston Co HS   2-00011
    920 HIGHWAY 96 31088   988-6340
    Sandra Neal, prin.
  Northside HS, 926 GREEN ST 31093   4-00011
    Edward Dyson, prin.   929-7858
  HS, 401 S DAVIS DR 31088   3-00011
    Marianne Melnick, prin.   929-7877
  Elberta Center JSHS   2-00111
    304 ELBERTA RD 31093   929-7898
    Dan Carpenter, prin.
  Northside MS, 500 JOHNSON RD 31093   3-00100
    Andrea Jordan, prin.   929-7845
  Rumble MS, 303 S DAVIS DR 31088   3-00100
    Frank Brown, prin.   929-7851
  Tabor MS, 920 GREEN ST 31093   3-00100
    James Snyder, prin.   929-7838
  MS, 425 MARY LN 31088   4-00100
    Larry Beck, prin.   929-7832
  Watson Center MS, DOVER DR 31098   2-00100
    Mike Rowland, prin.   929-7828

  Middle Georgia Technical Institute   3-CS
    1311 CORDER RD 31088   929-6800

Warrenton, AC 706, PC 4, Warren
  Warren County SD   4-11111
    PO BOX 228 30828   465-3383
    Robert Warren, supt.
  Warren County JSHS   2-00111
    PO BOX 192 30828   465-3742
    Charles Culver, prin.

Washington, AC 706, PC 5, Wilkes
  Wilkes County SD   4-11111
    PO BOX 279 30673   678-2718
    Jerry Robinson, prin.
  Washington-Wilkes Comprehensive HS   3-00011
    304 GORDON ST 30673   678-2426
    Keith Cowne, prin.
  Washington-Wilkes MS   2-00100
    304A GORDON ST 30673   678-7131
    Joyce Williams, prin.

Watkinsville, AC 706, PC 4, Oconee
  Oconee County SD   5-11111
    PO BOX 146 30677   769-5130
    Debra Harden, supt.
  Oconee County HS   3-00011
    PO BOX 534 30677   769-6655
    James Kahrs, prin.
  Oconee County MS   3-00100
    PO BOX 190 30677   769-3575
    Tom Odom, prin.

Waycross, AC 912, PC 7, Ware
  Ware County SD   5-11111
    PO BOX 1789 31502   283-8656
    B. Donald Dial, supt.
  Ware County HS   4-00011
    2301 CHEROKEE ST 31503   287-2351
    James Taylor, prin.
  HS, 700 CENTRAL AVE 31501   3-00011
    Patricia Mills, prin.   287-2388

Center JHS, 1301 BAILEY ST 31501   3-00100
  Robert Bussey, prin.   287-2333
Ware County JHS   3-00100
  1429 GORMAN RD 31503   287-2341
  Tony Adams, prin.

Okefenokee Technical Institute   2-CS
  1701 CARSWELL AVE 31503   283-2002
Waycross College   3-CC
  2001 FRANCIS ST 31503   285-6133

Waynesboro, AC 706, PC 6, Burke
  Burke County SD, PO BOX 908 30830   5-11111
    C. Douglas Day, supt.   554-5101
  Burke County Comprehensive HS   4-00011
    RR 2 BOX 51D 30830   554-6691
    Jack Willis, prin.
  Burke County MS, PO BOX 849 30830   3-00100
    Calvin Gill, prin.   554-3532

  Burke Academy, PO BOX 787 30830   2-11111
    554-4479

Weston, AC 912, PC 1, Webster

  Greenfield Academy   2-11111
    PO BOX 99 31832   828-2805

Winder, AC 404, PC 6, Barrow
  Barrow County SD   6-11111
    PO BOX 767 30680   867-4527
    Daniel Cromer, supt.
  Winder-Barrow HS   4-00011
    601 N 5TH AVE 30680   867-4519
    Randall Howell, prin.
  Russell MS, 211 W MIDLAND AVE 30680   3-00100
    Jerris Hayes, prin.   867-8181
  Winder-Barrow MS, 410 KING ST 30680   3-00100
    R. Wimberly, prin.   867-2116

Woodbury, AC 706, PC 4, Meriwether

  Flint River Academy   2-11111
    PO BOX 247 30293   553-2541
    Janne Bazemore, prin.

Woodstock, AC 404, PC 5, Cherokee
  Cherokee County SD
    Supt. — See Canton
  Etowah HS, 1895 EAGLE DR 30188   4-00011
    Bill Carpenter, prin.   926-4411
  Booth MS, 1899 EAGLE DR 30188   3-00100
    Phil Gramling, prin.   926-5707

Wrens, AC 404, PC 4, Jefferson
  Jefferson County SD
    Supt. — See Louisville
  JSHS, PO BOX 585 30833   3-00111
    Mickey Mauney, prin.   547-6580

Wrightsville, AC 912, PC 4, Johnson
  Johnson County SD   4-11111
    PO BOX 110 31096   864-3302
    Nick Holton, supt.
  Johnson County HS   2-00011
    210 TROJAN WAY 31096   864-2222
    C. Thomas, prin.
  Johnson Co MS   2-00100
    210 TROJAN WAY 31096   864-2222
    Curtis Dixon, prin.

Young Harris, AC 706, PC 3, Towns

  Young Harris College   2-CC
    PO BOX 98 30582   379-3111

Zebulon, AC 706, PC 4, Pike
  Pike County SD, PO BOX 386 30295   4-11111
    James Turpin, supt.   567-8489
  Pike County HS, PO BOX 819 30295   3-00111
    Darryl Dean, prin.   567-8770
  Pike County MS, PO BOX 405 30295   2-00100
    F. Pitts, prin.   567-3353

HAWAII

STATE DEPARTMENT OF EDUCATION
Queen Liliuokalani Building
P.O. Box 2360, Honolulu 96804
(808) 586-3232

Superintendent of Education	Charles Toguchi
Deputy Superintendent	Herman Aizawa
Assistant Superintendent Business Services	Alfred Suga
Assistant Superintendent Instructional Services	Mildred Higashi
Assistant Superintendent Information Services	Philip Bossert

STATE BOARD OF EDUCATION
P.O. Box 2360, Honolulu 96804

Chairperson	Debi Hartmann

PUBLIC, PRIVATE AND CATHOLIC SECONDARY SCHOOLS

Aiea, AC 808, PC 7, Honolulu
Central Oahu SD
Supt. — See Mililani
HS, 98-1276 ULUNE ST 96701 — 4-00011
  Gary Griffiths, prin. — 488-4964
IS, 99-600 KULAWEA ST 96701 — 3-00100
  Theodore Fisher, prin. — 488-8421

Ewa Beach, AC 808, PC 7, Honolulu
Leeward Oahu SD
Supt. — See Waipahu
Campbell HS, 91-980 NORTH RD 96706 — 4-00011
  Louis Vierra, prin. — 689-7902
Ilima IS — 4-00100
91-884 FORT WEAVER RD 96706 — 689-8375
  Merle Iwamasa, prin.

Lanakila Baptist HS — 2-00111
91-1235 RENTON RD 96706 — 681-3146
  John Shirota, prin.

Hana, AC 808, PC 3, Maui
Maui SD
Supt. — See Wailuku
S, PO BOX 128 96713 — 2-11111
  Patricia Eason, prin. — 248-8272

Hilo, AC 808, PC 8, Hawaii
Hawaii SD, PO BOX 4160 96720 — 8-11111
  Alan Garson, supt. — 933-4237
HS, 556 WAIANUENUE AVE 96720 — 4-00011
  Donna Saiki, prin. — 935-4881
Waiakea HS, 155 W KAWILI ST 96720 — 4-00011
  Danford Sakai, prin. — 935-5235
IS, 587 WAIANUENUE AVE 96720 — 3-00100
  (—), prin. — 935-9716
Waiakea IS, 200 W PUAINAKO ST 96720 — 4-00100
  Winston Towata, prin. — 959-3531
Other Schools – See Honokaa, Kailua-Kona, Kapaau,
Kealakekua, Laupahoehoe, Pahala, Pahoa

Hawaii Community College — 4-CC
1175 MANONO ST 96720 — 933-3311
St. Joseph HS, 1000 ULULANI ST 96720 — 2-00111
  Leroy Andrews, prin. — 935-4936
University of Hawaii at Hilo — 5-UC
523 W LANIKAULA ST 96720 — 933-3311

Honokaa, AC 808, PC 4, Hawaii
Hawaii SD
Supt. — See Hilo
S, PO BOX 239 96727 — 4-11111
  Gordon Kainoa, prin. — 775-7271

Honolulu, AC 808, PC 10, Honolulu
Central Oahu SD
Supt. — See Mililani
Moanalua HS, 2825 ALA ILIMA ST 96818 — 4-00011
  Jacqueline Heupel, prin. — 833-1836
Radford HS — 4-00011
4361 SALT LAKE BLVD 96818 — 422-2751
  Sharon Kauinana, prin.
Aliamanu IS — 4-00100
3271 SALT LAKE BLVD 96818 — 422-2791
  Charlene Matsuda, prin.
Moanalua IS, 1289 MAHIOLE ST 96819 — 3-00100
  Caroline Wong, prin. — 833-2921

Honolulu SD, 4967 KILAUEA AVE 96816 — 8-11111
  Ernesta Masagatani, supt. — 735-2438
Farrington HS, 1564 N KING ST 96817 — 4-00011
  Bernard Williams, prin. — 841-3331
Kaimuki HS, 2705 KAIMUKI AVE 96816 — 4-00011
  Thelma Nip, prin. — 732-7711
Kaiser HS — 4-00011
511 LUNALILO HOME RD 96825 — 395-7511
  Patricia Nekoba, prin.
Kalani HS — 4-00011
4680 KALANIANAOLE HWY 96821 — 373-2191
  Randiann Porras-Tang, prin.
McKinley HS, 1039 S KING ST 96814 — 4-00011
  Patricia Hamamoto, prin. — 536-1061
Roosevelt HS, 1120 NEHOA ST 96822 — 4-00011
  Charles Goo, prin. — 526-3131
Central IS, 1302 QUEEN EMMA ST 96813 — 3-00100
  Peter Uehara, prin. — 537-6594
Dole IS — 3-00100
1803 KAMEHAMEHA IV RD 96819 — 845-8541
  Geraldine Ichimura, prin.
Jarrett IS, 1903 PALOLO AVE 96816 — 2-00100
  Yoshiji Asami, prin. — 732-7728
Kaimuki IS, 631 18TH AVE 96816 — 3-00100
  Frank Fernandes, prin. — 734-2188
Kalakaua IS, 821 KALIHI ST 96819 — 3-00100
  Patricia Dang, prin. — 841-4591
Kawananakoa IS, 49 FUNCHAL ST 96813 — 3-00100
  Richard Anbe, prin. — 531-1644
Niu Valley IS — 3-00100
310 HALEMAUMAU ST 96821 — 373-2136
  Eric Heu, prin.
Stevenson IS, 1202 PROSPECT ST 96822 — 3-00100
  Cheryl Lippman, prin. — 537-3931
Washington IS, 1633 S KING ST 96826 — 3-00100
  Marsha Alegre, prin. — 941-2294

Academy of the Pacific HS — 2-01111
913 ALEWA DR 96817 — 595-6359
  Dorothy Douthit, prin.
Assets S, 1 OHANA NUI WAY 96818 — 2-11111
  Barrett McCandless, prin. — 423-1356
Chaminade University of Honolulu — 4-UC
3140 WAIALAE AVE 96816 — 735-4711
Damien Memorial HS — 3-00011
1401 HOUGHTAILING ST 96817 — 841-0195
  Br. Karl Walczak, prin.
Denver Business College — 2-CS
1916 YOUNG ST # 101 96826 — 942-1000
Hawaiian Mission Academy — 2-00011
1438 PENSACOLA ST 96822 — 536-2207
  Wayne Wentland, prin.
Hawaii Baptist Academy — 3-00111
2429 PALI HWY 96817 — 595-6301
  George Higa, prin.
Hawaii Business College — 3-CS
111 N KING ST 96817 — 524-4014
Hawaii Pacific University — 5-UC
1166 FORT STREET MALL 96813 — 544-0200
Hawaii School for the Deaf and the Blind — HND
3440 LEAHI AVE 96815
Heald Business College — 4-CC
1500 KAPIOLANI BLVD STE 202 96814 — 955-1500
Honolulu Community College — 5-CC
874 DILLINGHAM BLVD 96817 — 845-9225
Iolani S, 563 KAMOKU ST 96826 — 4-11111
  Thomas Miller, prin. — 949-5355

Japan-America Inst./Management Science — UC
6660 HAWAII KAI DR 96825 — 395-2314
Kamehameha S, 210 KONIG CIR 96817 — 5-11111
  Michael Chun, prin. — 842-8211
Kansai Gaidai Hawaii College — 2-CC
5257 KALANIANAOLE HWY 96821 — 377-5402
Kapiolani Community College — 6-CC
4303 DIAMOND HEAD RD 96816 — 734-9111
La Pietra School For Girls — 2-00111
2933 PONI MOI RD 96815 — 922-2744
  Scott Meiklejohn, prin.
Lutheran HS of Hawaii — 2-00011
1404 UNIVERSITY AVE 96822 — 949-5302
  Rev. Robert Meyer, prin.
Maryknoll HS — 3-00011
1402 PUNAHOU ST 96822 — 973-1888
  Andrew Corcoran, prin.
Medical Assisting School of Hawaii — 1-CS
1149 BETHEL ST STE 606 96813 — 524-3363
Mid-Pacific Institute — 4-00111
2445 KAALA ST 96822 — 973-5000
  Lester Cingcade, prin.
New York Technical Institute of Hawaii — 2-CS
1375 DILLINGHAM BLVD 96817 — 841-5827
Punahou Academy — 5-11111
1601 PUNAHOU ST 96822 — 944-5711
  Roderick McPhee, prin.
Sacred Hearts Academy — 2-00011
3255 WAIALAE AVE 96816 — 734-5058
  Betty White, prin.
St. Andrew's Priory S — 3-11111
224 QUEEN EMMA SQ 96813 — 532-6102
  Rev. David Kennedy, prin.
St. Francis HS, 2707 PAMOA RD 96822 — 2-00111
  Sr. Joan Souza, prin. — 988-4111
St. Francis Hospital — HSP
2230 LILIHA ST 96817 — 547-6480
St. Louis HS, 3140 WAIALAE AVE 96816 — 3-00111
  Burton Tomita, prin. — 739-7777
Travel Institute of the Pacific — 2-CS
1314 S KING ST STE 1164 96814 — 591-2708
Travel University International — 2-CS
1441 KPIOLANI BLVD STE 1414 96814 — 946-3355
University of Hawaii at Manoa — 7-UC
2500 CAMPUS RD 96822 — 956-8111
Varsity International S — 1-00111
2617 S KING ST STE 3D 96826 — 947-4430
  Judith Timbers, prin.

Hoolehua, AC 808, PC 2, Maui
Maui SD
Supt. — See Wailuku
Molokai JSHS, PO BOX 158 96729 — 3-00111
  William Rhyne, prin. — 567-6112

Kahuku, AC 808, PC 4, Honolulu
Windward Oahu SD
Supt. — See Kaneohe
JSHS, PO BOX 308 96731 — 4-00111
  Lea Albert, prin. — 293-9245

Kahului, AC 808, PC 7, Maui
Maui SD
Supt. — See Wailuku
Maui HS, 660 LONO AVE 96732 — 4-00011
  Michael Nakano, prin. — 877-7311
Maui Waena IS, 795 ONEHEE AVE 96732 — 3-00100
  Gwen Ueoka, prin. — 871-2553

Kaahumanu Hou S, 95 S KANE ST 96732   2-11111
  David Marocco, prin.   871-7311
Maui Community College   4-CC
  310 W KAAHUMANU AVE 96732   244-9181

Kailua, AC 808, PC 8, Honolulu
  Windward Oahu SD
    Supt. — See Kaneohe
  HS, 451 ULUMANU DR 96734   4-00011
    Mary Murakami, prin.   262-8151
  Kalaheo HS, 730 ILIAINA ST 96734   4-00011
    William Tam, prin.   254-3551
  IS, 145 S KAINALU DR 96734   3-00100
    Lorraine Henderson, prin.   261-1766

  Kailua Christian Academy   2-11111
    PO BOX 789 96734   261-7299
    Diana Abraham, prin.
  Redemption Academy   2-11111
    355 N KAINALU DR 96734   262-2341
    Adrien Yuen, prin.

Kailua-Kona, AC 808, PC 6, Hawaii
  Hawaii SD
    Supt. — See Hilo
  Kealakehe IS, 74-5062 ONIPAA ST 96740   3-00100
    Stanley Oka, prin.   329-2994

Kamuela, AC 808, PC 6, Hawaii

  Hawaii Prep Academy   3-11111
    PO BOX 428 96743   885-7321
    John Colson, prin.
  Parker S, PO BOX 429 96743   2-00111
    Pieper Toyama, prin.   885-7933

Kaneohe, AC 808, PC 8, Honolulu
  Windward Oahu SD   7-11111
    46-169 KAMEHAMEHA HWY 96744   247-6051
    John Sosa, supt.
  Castle HS   4-00011
    45-386 KANEOHE BAY DR 96744   235-4591
    Robert Ginlack, prin.
  King IS   3-00100
    46-155 KAMEHAMEHA HWY 96744   235-3605
    Cynthia Chun, prin.
  Other Schools – See Kahuku, Kailua

  Hawaii Pacific University   3-UC
    45-045 KAMEHAMEHA HWY 96744   235-3641
  Koolau Baptist Church Academy   2-11111
    45-633 KENEKE ST 96744   247-1377
    John Goodale, prin.
  Windward Community College   4-CC
    45-720 KEAAHALA RD 96744   235-0077

Kapaa, AC 808, PC 6, Kauai
  Kauai SD
    Supt. — See Lihue
  JSHS, 4695 MAILIHUNA RD 96746   4-00111
    Wayne Watanabe, prin.   822-4651

Kapaau, AC 808, PC 4, Hawaii
  Hawaii SD
    Supt. — See Hilo
  Kohala S, PO BOX 279 96755   4-11111
    Catherine Bratt, prin.   889-6221

Kealakekua, AC 808, PC 4, Hawaii
  Hawaii SD
    Supt. — See Hilo
  Konawaena JSHS, PO BOX 689 96750   4-00111
    Brian Nakashima, prin.   323-3808

Kihei, AC 808, PC 7, Maui
  Maui SD
    Supt. — See Wailuku
  Lokelani IS, 250 E LIPOA ST 96753   3-00100
    Marion Muller, prin.   874-5901

Lahaina, AC 808, PC 6, Maui
  Maui SD
    Supt. — See Wailuku
  Lahainaluna HS   3-00011
    980 LAHAINALUNA RD 96761   661-0313
    Henry Ariyoshi, prin.
  IS, 871 LAHAINALUNA RD 96761   3-00100
    Diane Dennis, prin.   667-6638

Laie, AC 808, PC 6, Honolulu

  Brigham Young University   4-UC
    55-220 KULANUI ST 96762   293-3700

Lanai City, AC 808, PC 4, Maui
  Maui SD
    Supt. — See Wailuku
  Lanai S, PO BOX 757 96763   3-11111
    Florentina Smith, prin.   565-7224

Laupahoehoe, AC 808, PC 3, Hawaii
  Hawaii SD
    Supt. — See Hilo
  S, PO BOX 189 96764   2-11111
    Jane Uyehara, prin.   962-6042

Lihue, AC 808, PC 6, Kauai
  Kauai SD, 3060 EIWA ST 96766   6-11111
    Shirley Akita, supt.   241-3493
  Kauai JSHS, 3577 LALA RD 96766   4-00111
    Linda Tanouye, prin.   245-2501
  Other Schools – See Kapaa, Waimea

  Kauai Community College   4-CC
    3-1901 KAUMUALII HWY 96766   245-8311

Makawao, AC 808, PC 6, Maui
  Maui SD
    Supt. — See Wailuku
  Kalama IS, 120 MAKANI RD 96768   4-00100
    Dennis Hokama, prin.   572-7719

  Seabury Hall S, 480 OLINDA RD 96768   2-00111
    Thomas Olverson, prin.   572-7235

Mililani, AC 808, PC 8, Honolulu
  Central Oahu SD   8-11111
    300 KAHELU AVE 96789   623-4328
    Robert Lee, supt.
  Mililani HS   4-00011
    95-1200 MEHEULA PKY 96789   623-5800
    Byron Yoshina, prin.
  Other Schools – See Aiea, Honolulu, Wahiawa, Waialua

  Hanalani S, 94-294 ANANIA DR 96789   2-11111
    Kermit Thompson, prin.   625-1692

Pahala, AC 808, PC 4, Hawaii
  Hawaii SD
    Supt. — See Hilo
  Ka'u S, PO BOX 100 96777   3-11111
    Josephine De Morales, prin.   928-8337

Pahoa, AC 808, PC 4, Hawaii
  Hawaii SD
    Supt. — See Hilo
  JSHS, 15-3038 PUNA RD 96778   3-00111
    Don Romero, prin.   965-8411

Pearl City, AC 808, PC 8, Honolulu
  Leeward Oahu SD
    Supt. — See Waipahu
  HS, 2100 HOOKIEKIE ST 96782   4-00011
    Gerald Suyama, prin.   455-9073
  Highlands IS   4-00100
    1460 HOOLAULEA ST 96782   455-4123
    Jane Himeda, prin.

  Leeward Community College   6-CC
    96-045 ALA IKE ST 96782   455-0011
  University of Hawaii   2-UC
    96-043 ALA IKE ST 96782   456-5921

Wahiawa, AC 808, PC 7, Honolulu
  Central Oahu SD
    Supt. — See Mililani
  Leilehua HS   4-00011
    1515 CALIFORNIA AVE 96786   622-4149
    Norman Minehira, prin.
  IS, 275 ROSE ST 96786   3-00100
    Roland Jenkins, prin.   622-1661
  Wheeler IS, 2 WHEELER AFB 96786   4-00100
    Roger Kim, prin.   622-1674

Waialua, AC 808, PC 5, Honolulu
  Central Oahu SD
    Supt. — See Mililani
  JSHS, 67-160 FARRINGTON HWY 96791   4-00111
    Tom Kurashige, prin.   637-5061

Waianae, AC 808, PC 6, Honolulu
  Leeward Oahu SD
    Supt. — See Waipahu
  HS, 85-251 FARRINGTON HWY 96792   4-00011
    Randal Tanaka, prin.   696-4244
  Nanakuli JSHS   4-00111
    89-980 NANAKULI AVE 96792   668-1568
    Alvin Nagasako, prin.
  IS, 85-626 FARRINGTON HWY 96792   4-00100
    David Stem, prin.   696-2922

  Maili Bible S, 87-138 GILIPAKE ST 96792   2-11111
    Larry Estrella, prin.   696-3038

Wailuku, AC 808, PC 7, Maui
  Maui SD, 54 S HIGH ST RM 4 96793   7-11111
    Ralph Murakami, supt.   243-5221
  Baldwin HS   4-00011
    1650 KAAHUMANU AVE 96793   244-3735
    Wallace Fujii, prin.
  Iao IS, 1910 KAOHU ST 96793   3-00100
    Elizabeth Ayson, prin.   244-4534
  Other Schools – See Hana, Hoolehua, Kahului, Kihei, Lahaina, Lanai City, Makawao

  St. Anthony HS   2-00111
    1618 LOWER MAIN ST 96793   244-4190
    Br. Dods, prin.

Waimea, AC 808, PC 4, Kauai
  Kauai SD
    Supt. — See Lihue
  HS, PO BOX 339 96796   3-00011
    Gary Kitabayashi, prin.   338-1717

Waipahu, AC 808, PC 8, Honolulu
  Leeward Oahu SD   8-11111
    94-299 FARRINGTON HWY 96797   678-4205
    Liberato Viduya, supt.
  HS, 94-1211 FARRINGTON HWY 96797   4-00011
    Milton Shishido, prin.   677-0741
  IS, 94-455 FARRINGTON HWY 96797   4-00100
    Gary Takaki, prin.   671-1702
  Other Schools – See Ewa Beach, Pearl City, Waianae

IDAHO

STATE DEPARTMENT OF EDUCATION
Len B. Jordan Office Building
650 W. State St., Boise 83720
(208) 334-3300

State Superintendent of Public Instruction	Jerry Evans
Deputy State Superintendent	August Hein
Associate Superintendent Finance & Administration	Robert Dutton
Associate Superintendent State-Federal Instructional Services	Darrell Loosle

STATE BOARD OF EDUCATION
650 W. State St. #307, Boise 83720

Executive Director	Rayburn Barton

PUBLIC, PRIVATE AND CATHOLIC SECONDARY SCHOOLS

Aberdeen, AC 208, PC 4, Bingham
Aberdeen SD 58, PO BOX 610 83210 — 3-11111
  John Condie, supt. — 397-4113
HS, PO BOX 610 83210 — 2-00011
  Grant Hansen, prin. — 397-4152

American Falls, AC 208, PC 5, Power
American Falls JSD 381 — 4-11111
  827 FORT HALL AVE 83211 — 226-5173
  Sheldon Kovarsky, supt.
HS, 254 TAYLOR ST 83211 — 3-00011
  Patrick Charlton, prin. — 226-2531
Thomas MS, 355 BANNOCK AVE 83211 — 3-01100
  Randy Jensen, prin. — 226-5203

Arco, AC 208, PC 4, Butte
Butte County JD 111 — 3-11111
  PO BOX 89 83213 — 527-8235
  Larry Vandel, supt.
Butte County HS — 2-00011
  250 S WATER ST 83213 — 527-8237
  Harald Jardine, prin.
Butte County MS — 2-00100
  120 S WATER ST 83213 — 527-3077
  Harald Jardine, prin.

Arimo, AC 208, PC 2, Bannock
Marsh Valley JSD 21 — 4-11111
  PO BOX 180 83214 — 254-3306
  Neal Hollingshead, supt.
Marsh Valley HS — 3-00011
  12655 S OLD HIGHWAY 91 83214 — 254-3711
  Greg Hunsaker, prin.
Marsh Valley MS — 2-00100
  12805 S OLD HIGHWAY 91 83214 — 254-3260
  Ron Jolley, prin.

Ashton, AC 208, PC 4, Fremont
Fremont County JSD 215
  Supt. — See Saint Anthony
North Fremont JSHS — 2-00111
  PO BOX 850 83420 — 652-7468
  Dick Seeley, prin.

Bancroft, AC 208, PC 2, Caribou
North Gem SD 149, PO BOX 70 83217 — 2-11111
  Robert Stevens, supt. — 648-7848
North Gem JSHS, 322 S MAIN ST 83217 — 2-00111
  Robert Stevens, prin. — 648-7848

Blackfoot, AC 208, PC 6, Bingham
Blackfoot SD 55, 270 E BRIDGE ST 83221 — 5-11111
  Steven Norton, supt. — 785-8800
HS, 870 S FISHER ST 83221 — 4-00011
  Dewane Wren, prin. — 785-8810
Mountain View MS — 4-00100
  645 MITCHELL LN 83221 — 785-8820
  Ron Reese, prin.

Snake River SD 52, 103 S 900 W 83221 — 5-11111
  Elzo White, supt. — 684-3001
Snake River HS — 3-00011
  922 W HIGHWAY 39 83221 — 684-3061
  Tracy Thompson, prin.
Snake River JHS — 2-00100
  918 W HIGHWAY 39 83221 — 684-3018
  Brian Jolley, prin.

Bliss, AC 208, PC 2, Gooding
Bliss JSD 234, E MAIN 83314 — 2-11111
  Michael Stefanic, supt. — 352-4445
S, 601 E US HIGHWAY 30 83314 — 2-11111
  Michael Stefanic, prin. — 352-4445

Boise, AC 208, PC 9, Ada
ISD of Boise City 1 — 8-11111
  1207 W FORT ST 83702 — 338-3400
  B. Parker, supt.
SHS, 1010 W WASHINGTON ST 83702 — 4-00001
  Blossom Turk, prin. — 338-3575
Borah SHS, 6001 CASSIA ST 83709 — 4-00001
  Douglas Standlee, prin. — 322-3855
Capital SHS, 8055 GODDARD RD 83704 — 4-00001
  Ron Arnold, prin. — 322-3875
East JHS — 4-00110
  415 WARM SPRINGS AVE 83712 — 338-3535
  Antonia Bicandi, prin.
Fairmont JHS, 2121 N COLE RD 83704 — 3-00110
  Judy Conner, prin. — 322-3835
Hillside JHS, 3536 HILL RD 83703 — 3-00110
  Julio Bilbao, prin. — 338-3545
Les Bois JHS, 701 E BOISE AVE 83706 — 3-00110
  Gary Slee, prin. — 338-3664
North JHS, 1105 N 13TH ST 83702 — 3-00110
  Kathy McCurdy, prin. — 338-3555
South JHS, 805 SHOSHONE ST 83705 — 4-00110
  Ron McNeley, prin. — 338-3565
West JHS, 711 N CURTIS RD 83706 — 3-00110
  Stan Holton, prin. — 322-3845

Meridian JSD 2
  Supt. — See Meridian
Lake Hazel MS — 4-00100
  11625 LA GRANGE ST 83709 — 362-3703
  Lee Mitchell, prin.

American Institute of Health Technology — 1-CS
  6600 EMERALD ST 83704 — 377-8080
Bishop Kelly HS — 3-00011
  7009 FRANKLIN RD 83709 — 375-6010
  David Lachiondo, prin.
Boise Bible College — 1-UC
  8695 MARIGOLD ST 83714 — 376-7731
Boise State University — 7-UC
  1910 UNIVERSITY DR 83725 — 800-824-7017
ITT Technical Institute — 3-CC
  950 LUSK ST 83706 — 344-8376
Maranatha Christian S — 2-11111
  12000 FAIRVIEW AVE 83704 — 377-0423
  Jerry Ternes, prin.
St. Alphonsus Regional Medical Center — HSP
  1055 N CURTIS RD 83706 — 378-2000
St. Luke's Hospital — HSP
  130 W BANNOCK ST 83702 — 386-2222

Bonners Ferry, AC 208, PC 4, Boundary
Boundary County SD 101 — 4-11111
  PO BOX 899 83805 — 267-3146
  Robert Singleton, supt.
HS, RR 4 BOX 6100 83805 — 3-00011
  Dan Meeker, prin. — 267-3149
Boundary County JHS — 2-00100
  PO BOX 899 83805 — 267-5852
  John Asher, prin.

Rocky Mountain Academy — 2-00011
  RR 1 83805 – Rob Speer, prin. — 267-7522

Bruneau, AC 208, PC 2, Owyhee
Bruneau-Grand View JSD 365
  Supt. — See Grand View
Rimrock JSHS, HC 85 BOX 184A 83604 — 2-00111
  Percy Christensen, prin. — 834-2260

Buhl, AC 208, PC 5, Twin Falls
Buhl JSD 412, 920 MAIN ST 83316 — 4-11111
  Eugene Pyles, supt. — 543-6436

HS, RR 5 BOX 5000 83316 — 2-00011
  Hy Schlieve, prin. — 543-8262
JHS, 216 7TH AVE N 83316 — 2-00100
  Mel Wiseman, prin. — 543-8292

Burley, AC 208, PC 6, Cassia
Cassia County JSD 151 — 6-11111
  237 E 19TH ST 83318 — 678-6600
  Everett Howard, supt.
SHS, 1 BOBCAT BLVD 83318 — 3-00001
  Robert Plotts, prin. — 678-6606
JHS, 700 W 16TH ST 83318 — 3-00110
  Dan Gillett, prin. — 678-6613
Other Schools – See Declo, Malta, Oakley

Caldwell, AC 208, PC 7, Canyon
Caldwell SD 132 — 5-11111
  1101 CLEVELAND BLVD 83605 — 455-3300
  Darrel Deide, supt.
SHS, 1100 WILLOW ST 83605 — 3-00001
  Warren Strong, prin. — 455-3304
Jefferson JHS, 3311 S 10TH AVE 83605 — 3-00110
  Holland Johnson, prin. — 455-3309

Vallivue SD 139 — 5-11111
  2423 S GEORGIA AVE 83605 — 454-0445
  Roy Rummler, supt.
Vallivue HS, 16412 S 10TH AVE 83605 — 3-00011
  Vaughn Heinrich, prin. — 454-9253
Vallivue JHS, 16358 S 10TH AVE 83605 — 3-00100
  James Robison, prin. — 454-1426

College of Idaho 83605 — 3-UC — 800-635-0434

Gem State Academy — 2-00011
  16115 MONTANA AVE 83605 — 459-1627
  John Gatchet, prin.

Cambridge, AC 208, PC 2, Washington
Cambridge JSD 432 — 2-11111
  PO BOX 39 83610 — 257-3211
  David Smith, supt.
JSHS, PO BOX 39 83610 — 2-00111
  Michael Woodman, prin. — 257-3311

Carey, AC 208, PC 3, Blaine
Blaine County SD 61
  Supt. — See Hailey
S, PO BOX 8 83320 — 2-11111
  Joni Cordell, prin. — 823-4391

Cascade, AC 208, PC 3, Valley
Cascade SD 422, PO BOX 291 83611 — 2-11111
  Eugene Novotny, supt. — 382-4227
JSHS, PO BOX 291 83611 — 2-00111
  William Leaf, prin. — 382-4227

Castleford, AC 208, PC 2, Twin Falls
Castleford JSD 417, 500 MAIN 83321 — 2-11111
  Kelly Murphey, supt. — 537-6511
HS, 500 MAIN 83321 — 2-11111
  Karen Garrison, prin. — 537-6511

Challis, AC 208, PC 4, Custer
Challis JSD 181, PO BOX 304 83226 — 3-11111
  John Brock, supt. — 879-4231
JSHS, PO BOX 304 83226 — 2-00111
  Glenn Johnson, prin. — 879-2255

Clark Fork, AC 208, PC 2, Bonner
Bonner County SD 82
  Supt. — See Sandpoint
JSHS, PO BOX 129 83811 — 2-00111
  Lewis Speelmon, prin. — 266-1131

109

Coeur D'Alene, AC 208, PC 7, Kootenai
Coeur D'Alene SD 271 — 6-11111
 311 N 10TH ST 83814 — 664-8241
 Douglas Cresswell, supt.
 HS, 5530 N 4TH ST 83814 — 4-00011
  Steve Casey, prin. — 667-4507
 Lake City HS, 6101 N RAMSEY RD 83814 — 2-00011
  John Brumley, prin. — 664-8241
 Canfield MS — 3-00100
  1800 E DALTON AVE 83814 — 664-9188
  James Lien, prin.
 Lakes MS, 15TH & HASTING AVE 83814 — 3-00100
  John House, prin. — 667-4544

North Idaho College — 5-CC
 1000 W GARDEN AVE 83814 — 769-3311

Cottonwood, AC 208, PC 3, Idaho
Cottonwood JSD 242 — 3-11111
 PO BOX 158 83522 — 962-3971
 Wesley Rash, supt.
 Prairie HS, PO BOX 540 83522 — 2-00011
  Wayne Montgomery, prin. — 962-3901
 Prairie MS, PO BOX 580 83522 — 2-01100
  Milton Baerlocher, prin. — 962-3521

Council, AC 208, PC 3, Adams
Council SD 13, PO BOX 468 83612 — 2-11111
 Keith Trappett, supt. — 253-4217
 JSHS, PO BOX 468 83612 — 2-00111
  Keith Trappett, prin. — 253-4297

Craigmont, AC 208, PC 3, Lewis
Highland JSD 305 — 2-11111
 PO BOX 127 83523 — 924-5211
 Dennis Carlson, supt.
 Highland JSHS, PO BOX 130 83523 — 2-00111
  Dennis Carlson, prin. — 924-5452

Culdesac, AC 208, PC 2, Nez Perce
Culdesac JSD 342, PO BOX 106 83524 — 2-11111
 Robert Bash, supt. — 843-5413
 S, PO BOX 106 83524 — 2-11111
  Loretta Stowers, prin. — 843-5413

Dayton, AC 208, PC 2, Franklin
West Side JSD 202, PO BOX 89 83232 — 3-11111
 Melvin Beutler, supt. — 747-3502
 West Side JSHS, PO BOX 89 83232 — 2-00111
  Elliot Larsen, prin. — 747-3411

Deary, AC 208, PC 3, Latah
Whitepine JSD 286
 Supt. — See Troy
 JSHS, PO BOX 9 83823 — 2-01111
  Ray Ireland, prin. — 877-1151

Declo, AC 208, PC 2, Cassia
Cassia County JSD 151
 Supt. — See Burley
 JSHS, 208 E MAIN 83323 — 2-00111
  Michael Matthews, prin. — 654-2030

Dietrich, AC 208, PC 2, Lincoln
Dietrich SD 314, PO BOX 428 83324 — 2-11111
 James Harshfield, supt. — 544-2158
 S, PO BOX 428 83324 — 2-11111
  James Harshfield, prin. — 544-2158

Donnelly, AC 208, PC 2, Valley
Mc Call-Donnelly SD 421
 Supt. — See Mc Call
 Mc Call-Donnelly JHS — 2-00100
  PO BOX 369 83615 — 325-8552
  Michael Howard, prin.

Driggs, AC 208, PC 3, Teton
Teton County SD 401
 Supt. — See Tetonia
 Teton HS, PO BOX 754 83422 — 2-00011
  Blaine McInelly, prin. — 354-2952
 Teton MS, PO BOX 529 83422 — 2-00100
  Craig Kunz, prin. — 354-2971

Dubois, AC 208, PC 2, Clark
Clark County SD 161 — 2-11111
 PO BOX 237 83423 — 374-5215
 Delbert McFadden, supt.
 Clark County JSHS — 1-00111
  PO BOX 237 83423 — 374-5215
  Delbert McFadden, prin.

Emmett, AC 208, PC 5, Gem
Emmett JSD 221, PO BOX 427 83617 — 5-11111
 Albert Vaughn, supt. — 365-6301
 HS, 721 W 12TH ST 83617 — 3-00011
  Duane Horning, prin. — 365-6323
 MS, 301 E 4TH ST 83617 — 3-01100
  Juanita Eaton, prin. — 365-2921

Fairfield, AC 208, PC 2, Camas
Camas County SD 121 — 2-11111
 PO BOX 370 83327 — 764-2472
 Larry McNutt, supt.
 Camas County HS — 1-00011
  PO BOX 370 83327 — 764-2472
  Larry McNutt, prin.

Filer, AC 208, PC 4, Twin Falls
Filer SD 413, PO BOX X 83328 — 4-11111
 William Feusahrens, supt. — 326-5981
 HS, PO BOX C 83328 — 2-00011
  Joseph Hendrickson, prin. — 326-5945
 MS, PO BOX H 83328 — 2-00100
  Gregory Lanting, prin. — 326-5906

Firth, AC 208, PC 2, Bingham
Firth SD 59, PO BOX 69 83236 — 4-11111
 John Tucker, supt. — 346-6811
 HS, PO BOX 247 83236 — 2-00011
  Michael Kress, prin. — 346-6811
 Gibbs MS, PO BOX 247 83236 — 2-00100
  Wayne Simmons, prin. — 346-6811

Fruitland, AC 208, PC 4, Payette
Fruitland SD 373, PO BOX 387 83619 — 4-11111
 Clark Adamson, supt. — 452-3595
 HS, PO BOX 387 83619 — 2-00011
  Mike Knee, prin. — 452-4411
 MS, PO BOX 387 83619 — 2-00100
  Melynda Gissel, prin. — 452-3350

Garden Valley, AC 208, PC 2, Boise
Garden Valley SD 71 83622 — 2-11111
 Clark Gardner, supt. — 462-3756
 JSHS 83622 — 2-00111
  Clark Gardner, prin. — 462-3756

Genesee, AC 208, PC 3, Latah
Genesee JSD 282, PO BOX 98 83832 — 2-11111
 John Eikum, supt. — 285-1161
 JSHS, PO BOX 98 83832 — 2-00111
  Dave Neumann, prin. — 285-1162

Glenns Ferry, AC 208, PC 4, Elmore
Glenns Ferry JSD 192 — 3-11111
 PO BOX 850 83623 — 366-7436
 Will Spalding, supt.
 JSHS, PO BOX 850 83623 — 2-00111
  Lendell Penner, prin. — 366-7434

Gooding, AC 208, PC 5, Gooding
Gooding JSD 231, 507 IDAHO ST 83330 — 4-11111
 Henry Kilmer, supt. — 934-4321
 HS, 1050 7TH AVE W 83330 — 2-00011
  Dennis Osman, prin. — 934-4831
 Frahm JHS, 830 MAIN ST 83330 — 2-00100
  Richard Thompson, prin. — 934-8443

Idaho State School for the Deaf/Blind — HND
 202 14TH AVE E 83330

Grace, AC 208, PC 3, Caribou
Grace JSD 148, PO BOX 328 83241 — 3-11111
 Bart Simmons, supt. — 425-3984
 HS, PO BOX 348 83241 — 2-00011
  Norma Harris, prin. — 425-3731
 JHS, PO BOX 348 83241 — 2-00100
  Barbara Lloyd, prin. — 425-3449

Grand View, AC 208, PC 2, Owyhee
Bruneau-Grand View JSD 365 — 3-11111
 PO BOX 310 83624 — 834-2253
 Ralph Hatch, supt.
 Other Schools — See Bruneau

Grangeville, AC 208, PC 5, Idaho
Grangeville JSD 241 — 4-11111
 PO BOX 430 83530 — 983-0990
 Al Arnzen, supt.
 HS, 910 S D ST 83530 — 2-00011
  Judy Leuck, prin. — 983-0580
 Other Schools — See Kooskia, Riggins

Greenleaf, AC 208, PC 3, Canyon

Greenleaf Friends Academy — 2-11111
 PO BOX 368 83626 — 459-6346
 Don Harvey, prin.

Hagerman, AC 208, PC 3, Gooding
Hagerman JSD 233 — 2-11111
 PO BOX 236 83332 — 837-4777
 Ronald Worrell, supt.
 JSHS, PO BOX 236 83332 — 2-00111
  Wayne Ills, prin. — 837-4572

Hailey, AC 208, PC 5, Blaine
Blaine County SD 61 — 5-11111
 PO BOX 1008 83333 — 788-2296
 Phillip Homer, supt.
 Wood River HS, PO BOX 948 83333 — 3-00011
  William Resko, prin. — 788-3481
 Wood River MS, PO BOX 1088 83333 — 2-00100
  Charles Turner, prin. — 788-3523
 Other Schools — See Carey

Hansen, AC 208, PC 3, Twin Falls
Hansen SD 415, PO BOX 250 83334 — 2-11111
 Richard Smith, supt. — 423-5593
 HS, PO BOX 250 83334 — 2-00011
  James Clark, prin. — 423-5593
 JHS, PO BOX 250 83334 — 1-00100
  James Clark, prin. — 423-5593

Harrison, AC 208, PC 2, Kootenai
Kootenai SD 274, HC 1 BOX 25 83833 — 2-11111
 Ronald Hill, supt. — 689-3631
 Kootenai JSHS, HC 1 BOX 25 83833 — 2-00111
  John Barnes, prin. — 689-3311

Hazelton, AC 208, PC 2, Jerome
Valley SD 262, 882 VALLEY RD 83335 — 2-11111
 Arlyn Bodily, supt. — 829-5333
 Valley JSHS, 882 VALLEY RD 83335 — 2-00111
  Dale Tilley, prin. — 829-5353

Homedale, AC 208, PC 4, Owyhee
Homedale JSD 370 — 4-11111
 203 E IDAHO AVE 83628 — 337-4611
 Richard Peters, supt.

 JSHS, 203 E IDAHO AVE 83628 — 2-00111
  Nolan Taggart, prin. — 337-4613

Horseshoe Bend, AC 208, PC 3, Boise
Horseshoe Bend SD 73 — 2-11111
 PO BOX 116 83629 — 793-2225
 Evelyn Cairns, supt.
 JSHS, PO BOX 116 83629 — 2-00111
  Michael Oke, prin. — 793-2225

Idaho Falls, AC 208, PC 8, Bonneville
Bonneville JSD 93 — 6-11111
 3497 N AMMON RD 83401 — 525-4400
 Thomas Campbell, supt.
 Bonneville HS, 3165 E IONA RD 83401 — 4-00011
  Dean Welker, prin. — 525-4406
 Hillcrest HS, 2800 OWEN ST 83406 — 4-00011
  Gary Higley, prin. — 525-4429
 Rocky Mountain MS — 3-00100
  3443 E IONA RD 83401 — 525-4403
  William Berrett, prin.
 Sandcreek MS, 2955 OWEN ST 83406 — 3-00100
  James Prince, prin. — 525-4416

Idaho Falls SD 91 — 7-11111
 690 JOHN ADAMS PKY 83401 — 525-7500
 T. Mattocks, supt.
 SHS, 601 S HOLMES AVE 83401 — 4-00001
  Steve Holtom, prin. — 525-7740
 Skyline SHS, 1767 BLUE SKY DR 83402 — 4-00001
  Lewis Gourley, prin. — 525-7770
 Eagle Rock JHS — 3-00110
  2020 PANCHERI DR 83402 — 525-7700
  Ken Piippo, prin.
 Gale JHS, 955 GARFIELD ST 83401 — 3-00110
  Randall Hurley, prin. — 525-7720
 Taylorview JHS — 3-00110
  350 CASTLEROCK 83404 — 524-7850
  Doris Backstrom, prin.

Eastern Idaho Technical College — 2-CS
 2299 E 17TH ST 83404 — 524-3000

Jerome, AC 208, PC 6, Jerome
Jerome JSD 261, 107 3RD AVE W 83338 — 5-11111
 Jim Cobble, supt. — 324-2392
 HS, 4 N 100 E 83338 — 3-00011
  Carrol Matthews, prin. — 324-8137
 MS, 116 3RD AVE W 83338 — 2-00100
  Craig Ainsworth, prin. — 324-8134

Kamiah, AC 208, PC 4, Lewis
Kamiah JSD 304, PO BOX 877 83536 — 3-11111
 Norman Winters, supt. — 935-2991
 JSHS, PO BOX 877 83536 — 2-00111
  William LaMunyan, prin. — 935-2662

Kellogg, AC 208, PC 5, Shoshone
Kellogg JSD 391 — 4-11111
 800 BUNKER AVE 83837 — 784-1348
 Larry Curry, supt.
 HS, 2 JACOBS GULCH RD 83837 — 2-00011
  Lawrence Wier, prin. — 784-1371
 MS, 800 BUNKER AVE 83837 — 2-00100
  Gregory Godwin, prin. — 784-1311

Kendrick, AC 208, PC 2, Latah
Kendrick SD 283 — 2-11111
 2001 HIGHWAY 3 83537 — 289-4211
 L. Taylor, supt.
 JSHS, 2001 HIGHWAY 3 83537 — 2-00111
  Gale Vallem, prin. — 289-4202

Ketchum, AC 208, PC 5, Blaine

Community S, PO BOX 2118 83340 — 2-11111
 Jon Maksik, prin. — 622-3955

Kimberly, AC 208, PC 4, Twin Falls
Kimberly SD 414, PO BOX 615 83341 — 4-11111
 John Garner, supt. — 423-4179
 HS, PO BOX O 83341 — 2-00111
  Ralph Campbell, prin. — 423-5541
 MS, PO BOX O 83341 — 2-00100
  Neal Miller, prin. — 423-4679

Kooskia, AC 208, PC 3, Idaho
Grangeville JSD 241
 Supt. — See Grangeville
 Clearwater Valley HS — 2-00011
  HIGHWAY 12 83539 — 926-4511
  Dave Snodgrass, prin.

Kuna, AC 208, PC 4, Ada
Kuna JSD 3, 610 N SCHOOL AVE 83634 — 4-11111
 Edwin Marshall, supt. — 922-1000
 HS, 1360 BOISE ST 83634 — 3-00011
  Jay Hummel, prin. — 922-1002
 JHS, 441 E PORTER RD 83634 — 2-00100
  Steven Snider, prin. — 922-1005

Lapwai, AC 208, PC 3, Nez Perce
Lapwai SD 341, PO BOX 247 83540 — 3-11111
 Dennis Kachelmier, supt. — 843-2622
 JSHS, 404 S MAIN 83540 — 2-00111
  Bryan Samuels, prin. — 843-2241

Leadore, AC 208, PC 1, Lemhi
South Lemhi SD 292 — 2-11111
 PO BOX 119 83464 — 768-2441
 Melvin Skeen, supt.
 S, PO BOX 119 83464 — 2-11111
  Melvin Skeen, prin. — 768-2441

Lewiston, AC 208, PC 8, Nez Perce
Lewiston ISD 1, 3317 12TH ST 83501 5-11111
  Joy Rapp, supt. 746-2337
SHS, 1114 9TH AVE 83501 4-00001
  James Wilund, prin. 743-5557
Jenifer JHS, 1213 16TH ST 83501 3-00110
  Robert Donaldson, prin. 743-8589
Sacajawea JHS, 3610 12TH ST 83501 3-00110
  Steve McRae, prin. 743-9436

Lewis Clark State College 4-UC
  500 8TH AVE 83501 799-5272
Shiloh S, 3215 ECHO HILLS DR 83501 2-11111
  Donald Craber, prin. 746-4542

Mc Call, AC 208, PC 4, Valley
Mc Call-Donnelly SD 421 4-11111
  PO BOX 944 83638 634-2161
  Robert Schmitt, supt.
Mc Call-Donnelly HS 2-00011
  PO BOX 967 83638 634-2218
  Douglas Flaming, prin.
  Other Schools – See Donnelly

Mackay, AC 208, PC 3, Custer
MacKay JSD 182, PO BOX 390 83251 2-11111
  Doran Parkins, supt. 588-2262
JSHS, 400 SPRUCE ST 83251 2-00111
  Doran Parkins, prin. 588-2262

Malad City, AC 208, PC 4, Oneida
Oneida County SD 351 4-11111
  250 W 400 N 83252 766-2255
  Lynn Schow, supt.
JSHS, 181 JENKINS AVE 83252 2-00111
  Jerry Esplin, prin. 766-4728

Malta, AC 208, PC 2, Cassia
Cassia County JSD 151
  Supt. — See Burley
Raft River HS, 68 TROJAN DR 83342 2-00011
  Patricia Lundquist, prin. 645-2220

Marsing, AC 208, PC 3, Owyhee
Marsing JSD 363, PO BOX 340 83639 3-11111
  Joe Whitten, supt. 896-4111
HS, PO BOX 340 83639 2-00011
  Darrel Pantalone, prin. 896-4112
IS, PO BOX 340 83639 2-01100
  Luis Gutierrez, prin. 896-4753

Melba, AC 208, PC 2, Canyon
Melba JSD 136, PO BOX 185 83641 3-11111
  Joe James, supt. 495-1141
JSHS, PO BOX 185 83641 2-00111
  Jim Potter, prin. 495-2221

Meridian, AC 208, PC 6, Ada
Meridian JSD 2 7-11111
  911 N MERIDIAN RD 83642 888-6701
  Bob Haley, supt.
Centennial HS 4-00011
  4600 E MCMILLAN RD 83642 939-1404
  Rex Johnson, prin.
HS, 1900 W PINE AVE 83642 4-00011
  Terry Kluever, prin. 888-4905
MS, 1507 W 8TH ST 83642 4-00100
  Bev Bradford, prin. 888-3002
Scott MS, 3400 E MCMILLAN RD 83642 4-00100
  Karen Ritchie, prin. 939-2101
  Other Schools – See Boise

Middleton, AC 208, PC 4, Canyon
Middleton SD 134, 5 S 3RD AVE W 83644 4-11111
  James Garrett, supt. 585-3027
HS, 511 W MAIN ST 83644 3-00011
  Jim Freeman, prin. 585-6657
MS, 200 S 4TH AVE W 83644 2-00100
  Allen Lake, prin. 585-3251

Midvale, AC 208, PC 2, Washington
Midvale SD 433 2-11111
  BRIDGE & SCHOOL ST 83645 355-2234
  John Meek, supt.
JSHS, BRIDGE & SCHOOL ST 83645 1-00111
  Jim Warren, prin. 355-2234

Montpelier, AC 208, PC 5, Bear Lake
Bear Lake County SD 33
  Supt. — See Paris
Bear Lake HS, 330 BOISE ST 83254 3-00011
  Glay Homer, prin. 847-0294
Bear Lake MS 2-00100
  633 WASHINGTON ST 83254 847-2255
  Ron Echols, prin.

Moscow, AC 208, PC 7, Latah
Moscow SD 281, 410 E 3RD ST 83843 5-11111
  Jack Hill, supt. 882-1120
SHS, 402 E 5TH ST 83843 3-00001
  K. Albright, prin. 882-2591
JHS, 1410 E D ST 83843 3-00110
  Alan Lee, prin. 882-3577

University of Idaho 83843 7-UC
  885-6326

Mountain Home, AC 208, PC 6, Elmore
Mountain Home SD 193 5-11111
  PO BOX 1390 83647 587-2580
  Harry Light, supt.
SHS, 300 S 11TH E 83647 3-00001
  Douglas Johnson, prin. 587-2570
JHS, 550 E JACKSON ST # D 83647 3-00110
  William Trueba, prin. 587-2590

Other Schools – See Mountain Home AFB

Mountain Home AFB, AC 208, PC 6, Elmore
Mountain Home SD 193
  Supt. — See Mountain Home
Stephensen MS, 300 MAIN ST 83648 2-00110
  Tim McMurtrey, prin. 832-4601

Mullan, AC 208, PC 3, Shoshone
Mullan SD 392, PO BOX 71 83846 2-11111
  Robin Stanley, supt. 744-1118
JSHS, PO BOX 71 83846 2-00111
  Tom Durbin, prin. 744-1126

Murtaugh, AC 208, PC 2, Twin Falls
Murtaugh JSD 418 2-11111
  PO BOX 117 83344 432-5551
  Michael Chesley, supt.
HS, PO BOX 117 83344 1-00011
  Michael Chesley, prin. 432-5451
MS, PO BOX 117 83344 1-00100
  Michael Chesley, prin. 432-5451

Nampa, AC 208, PC 8, Canyon
Nampa SD 131, 619 S CANYON ST 83686 6-11111
  Steven Schmitz, supt. 465-2700
SHS, 203 LAKE LOWELL AVE 83686 4-00001
  Shirley Vendrell, prin. 465-2760
South JHS 3-00110
  229 W GREENHURST RD 83686 465-2747
  Nancy Vandeventer, prin.
West JHS 3-00110
  806 CENTRAL MIDLAND BLVD 83651 465-2752
  Robert Gearheart, prin.

Nampa Christian S, PO BOX G 83653 2-11111
  Wesley Fulwood, prin. 466-8451
Northwest Nazarene College 4-UC
  623 HOLLY ST 83686 800-662-4968

New Meadows, AC 208, PC 3, Adams
Meadows Valley SD 11, PO BOX F 83654 2-11111
  Ronald Cummings, supt. 347-2411
Meadows Valley JSHS, PO BOX F 83654 2-00111
  Ronald Cummings, prin. 347-2118

New Plymouth, AC 208, PC 4, Payette
New Plymouth SD 372 3-11111
  PO BOX 50 83655 278-5740
  Frederick DiazGranados, supt.
HS, PO BOX 50 83655 2-00011
  Arlo Decker, prin. 278-5311
MS, PO BOX 50 83655 2-00100
  Arlo Decker, prin. 278-5311

Nezperce, AC 208, PC 2, Lewis
Nezperce JSD 302 2-11111
  PO BOX 279 83543 937-2551
  James McPherson, supt.
JSHS, PO BOX 279 83543 1-00111
  Renee Forsman, prin. 937-2551

Notus, AC 208, PC 2, Canyon
Notus JSD 135, PO BOX 256 83656 2-11111
  Robert Larsen, supt. 459-4633
HS, PO BOX 256 83656 2-00011
  Harold Wesche, prin. 459-4633

Oakley, AC 208, PC 3, Cassia
Cassia County JSD 151
  Supt. — See Burley
JSHS, 105 N ACADEMY 83346 2-00111
  J. Smith, prin. 862-3328

Orofino, AC 208, PC 5, Clearwater
Orofino JSD 171, PO BOX 789 83544 4-11111
  Alan Felgenhauer, supt. 476-5593
HS, 300 DUNLAP RD 83544 2-00011
  Simon Wilson, prin. 476-5557
JHS, PO BOX 706 83544 2-00100
  Eugene Hobbs, prin. 476-4613
  Other Schools – See Pierce, Weippe

Osburn, AC 208, PC 4, Shoshone
Wallace SD 393
  Supt. — See Wallace
Silver Hills MS, PO BOX 948 83849 2-00100
  John Cuthbert, prin. 556-1556

Paris, AC 208, PC 3, Bear Lake
Bear Lake County SD 33 4-11111
  PO BOX 300 83261 945-2891
  Ronald Wolff, supt.
  Other Schools – See Montpelier

Parma, AC 208, PC 4, Canyon
Parma SD 137, PO BOX 246 83660 3-11111
  Judith Nielsen, supt. 722-5115
HS, PO BOX 246 83660 2-00011
  Barb Russell, prin. 722-6116
MS, PO BOX 246 83660 2-00100
  Dominic Iaderosa, prin. 722-6311

Paul, AC 208, PC 3, Minidoka
Minidoka County JSD 331
  Supt. — See Rupert
West Minico JHS 3-00110
  RR 2 BOX 2081 83347 438-5018
  Gary Stears, prin.

Payette, AC 208, PC 6, Payette
Payette JSD 371, PO BOX 349 83661 4-11111
  Richard Dillon, supt. 642-9366
HS, 1500 7TH AVE S 83661 2-00011
  Henry Hudgens, prin. 642-3327
McCain MS, 1215 CENTER AVE 83661 2-00100
  Willie Sullivan, prin. 642-4122

Pierce, AC 208, PC 3, Clearwater
Orofino JSD 171
  Supt. — See Orofino
JHS, HC 64 BOX 52 83546 1-00100
  Doug Smith, prin. 464-2741

Plummer, AC 208, PC 3, Benewah
Plummer/Worley SD 44 3-11111
  PO BOX 130 83851 686-1621
  Robert Lukes, supt.
Lakeside HS, PO BOX 408 83851 2-00011
  Lonnie Winters, prin. 686-1937
Lakeside MS, PO BOX 209 83851 2-00100
  William Pogge, prin. 686-1627

Pocatello, AC 208, PC 8, Bannock
Pocatello SD 25, PO BOX 1390 83204 7-11111
  David Peck, supt. 232-3563
Highland SHS, 1800 BENCH RD 83201 4-00001
  Jeff Taylor, prin. 237-1300
SHS, 325 N ARTHUR AVE 83204 4-00001
  Carole McWilliam, prin. 233-2056
Alameda JHS 3-00110
  845 MCKINLEY AVE 83201 232-7119
  Gene Soderquist, prin.
Franklin JHS, 2271 E TERRY ST 83201 3-00110
  Bill Watkins, prin. 233-5590
Hawthorne JHS 3-00110
  1025 W ELDREDGE RD 83201 237-1680
  Gail Siemen, prin.
Irving JHS, 911 N GRANT AVE 83204 3-00110
  Frank Thomas, prin. 232-3039

Idaho State University 6-UC
  PO BOX 8270 83209 800-888-4784

Post Falls, AC 208, PC 6, Kootenai
Post Falls SD 273, PO BOX 40 83854 5-11111
  Kathryn Canfield-Davis, supt. 773-1658
HS, PO BOX 40 83854 3-00011
  Warren Toney, prin. 773-5411
JHS, PO BOX 40 83854 3-00100
  William Ramich, prin. 773-7554

Falls Christian Academy 2-11111
  1885 E HORSEHAVEN AVE 83854 773-7168
  Joe Williams, prin.

Potlatch, AC 208, PC 3, Latah
Potlatch SD 285, RR 2 BOX 1A 83855 3-11111
  Donald Armstrong, supt. 875-0327
JSHS, RR 2 BOX 1A 83855 2-00111
  Patrick Valliant, prin. 875-1231

Preston, AC 208, PC 5, Franklin
Preston JSD 201, 120 E 2ND S 83263 4-11111
  Orson Bowler, supt. 852-0283
HS, 151 E 2ND S 83263 3-00011
  Alfred Koch, prin. 852-0280
Jefferson JHS 2-00110
  1ST SOUTH & 1ST EAST STS 83263 852-0751
  John Palmer, prin.

Priest River, AC 208, PC 4, Bonner
Bonner County SD 82
  Supt. — See Sandpoint
Priest River Lamanna HS 2-00011
  PO BOX 549 83856 448-1211
  John Schwartz, prin.
JHS, PO BOX 519 83856 2-00100
  Richard Dacessio, prin. 448-1118

Rathdrum, AC 208, PC 4, Kootenai
Lakeland SD 272, PO BOX 39 83858 5-11111
  Robert Jones, supt. 687-0431
Lakeland SHS, PO BOX 69 83858 3-00001
  Charles Kinsey, prin. 687-0181
Lakeland JHS, PO BOX 98 83858 3-00110
  Georgeanne Griffith, prin. 687-0661

Rexburg, AC 208, PC 7, Madison
Madison SD 321, PO BOX 830 83440 5-11111
  Brent Orr, supt. 359-3300
Madison HS, 134 MADISON AVE 83440 4-00011
  Lane Hemming, prin. 359-3305
Madison JHS, 60 W MAIN ST 83440 3-00110
  Ronella Widdison, prin. 359-3310

Aero Technicians 1-CS
  PO BOX 7 83440 356-4446
  Ricks College 83460 6-CC
  356-1020

Richfield, AC 208, PC 2, Lincoln
Richfield SD 316, PO BOX E 83349 2-11111
  Larry Tinker, supt. 487-2790
S, PO BOX E 83349 2-11111
  Larry Tinker, prin. 487-2790

Rigby, AC 208, PC 5, Jefferson
Jefferson County JSD 251 5-11111
  201 IDAHO AVE 83442 745-6693
  Elwood Wilson, supt.
SHS, 290 N 3800 E 83442 3-00001
  Jack Wilcock, prin. 745-7704
JHS, 125 N 1ST W 83442 3-00110
  Kay Woodfield, prin. 745-6674

Riggins, AC 208, PC 2, Idaho
Grangeville JSD 241
  Supt. — See Grangeville
Salmon River JSHS, HIGH ST 83549 2-00111
  Marvin Anderson, prin. 628-3431

Ririe, AC 208, PC 3, Jefferson
Ririe JSD 252, PO BOX 508   83443 — 3-11111 / 538-7482
  Thales Johnson, supt.
JSHS, PO BOX 568   83443 — 2-00111 / 538-7311
  Roy Smith, prin.

Rockland, AC 208, PC 2, Power
Rockland SD 382, PO BOX 119   83271 — 2-11111 / 548-2231
  James Woodworth, supt.
S, PO BOX 119   83271 — 2-11111 / 548-2231
  Dan Ralphs, prin.

Rupert, AC 208, PC 6, Minidoka
Minidoka County JSD 331 — 6-11111 / 436-4727
  633 FREMONT ST   83350
  Michael Bishop, supt.
Minico SHS, RR 2 BOX 348   83350 — 4-00001 / 436-4721
  Stephen Hubsmith, prin.
East Minico JHS, 1815 H ST   83350 — 3-00110 / 436-3178
  David Borden, prin.
Other Schools – See Paul

Saint Anthony, AC 208, PC 5, Fremont
Fremont County JSD 215 — 5-11111 / 624-7542
  147 N 2ND W   83445
  Gary Larson, supt.
South Fremont HS, 550 N 1ST W   83445 — 3-00011 / 624-3416
  Grant Bischoff, prin.
South Fremont JHS, 226 W 3RD N   83445 — 2-00100 / 624-7880
  Sam Christiansen, prin.
Other Schools – See Ashton

Saint Maries, AC 208, PC 4, Benewah
Saint Maries JSD 41 — 4-11111 / 245-2579
  PO BOX 384   83861
  Dave Cox, supt.
HS, RR 3 BOX 33B   83861 — 2-00011 / 245-2142
  Jerry Bayley, prin.
MS, 1315 W JEFFERSON AVE   83861 — 2-00100 / 245-3495
  Ken Tams, prin.

Salmon, AC 208, PC 5, Lemhi
Salmon SD 291, PO BOX 790   83467 — 4-11111 / 756-4271
  Candis Donicht, supt.
HS, PO BOX 790   83467 — 2-00011 / 756-2415
  Sharyl Allen, prin.
JHS, PO BOX 790   83467 — 2-00100 / 756-2207
  Candis Donicht, prin.

Sandpoint, AC 208, PC 6, Bonner
Bonner County SD 82 — 6-11111 / 263-2184
  815 W PINE ST   83864
  Gary Barton, supt.
HS, 410 S DIVISION ST   83864 — 4-00011 / 263-3034
  A. Woolnough, prin.

JHS, 310 S DIVISION ST   83864 — 3-00100 / 265-4169
  Marcie Polin, prin.
Other Schools – See Clark Fork, Priest River

Shelley, AC 208, PC 5, Bingham
Shelley JSD 60 — 4-11111 / 357-3411
  545 SEMINARY AVE   83274
  Robert Lisonbee, supt.
SHS, 570 W FIR ST   83274 — 2-00001 / 357-7400
  Charlotte Arnold, prin.
JHS, 200 E FIR ST   83274 — 2-00110 / 357-5623
  Laron Shumway, prin.

Shoshone, AC 208, PC 4, Lincoln
Shoshone JSD 312, PO BOX 2D   83352 — 2-11111 / 886-2338
  Max Excell, supt.
JSHS, PO BOX 2D   83352 — 2-00111 / 886-2381
  Ben Christiansen, prin.

Soda Springs, AC 208, PC 5, Caribou
Soda Springs JSD 150 — 4-11111 / 547-3371
  PO BOX 947   83276
  Lawrence Rigby, supt.
HS, 3RD E 1ST N   83276 — 2-00011 / 547-4308
  Laird Jenkins, prin.
JHS, 250 E 2ND S   83276 — 2-00100 / 547-4922
  (—), prin.

Sugar City, AC 208, PC 4, Madison
Sugar-Salem JSD 322 — 4-11111 / 356-8802
  PO BOX 150   83448
  Thomas Morley, supt.
Sugar-Salem HS, PO BOX 240   83448 — 2-00011 / 356-0274
  J. Archibald, prin.
Sugar-Salem JHS, PO BOX 180   83448 — 2-00100 / 356-4437
  Lance Lindley, prin.

Terreton, AC 208, PC 2, Jefferson
West Jefferson SD 253 — 3-11111
  1272 E 1500 N   83450 – R. Palmer, supt. 663-4542
West Jefferson HS, 1260 E 1500 N   83450 — 2-00011 / 663-4390
  Ben Speelman, prin.

Tetonia, AC 208, PC 2, Teton
Teton County SD 401 — 3-11111 / 456-2287
  PO BOX 129   83452
  Gordon Woolley, supt.
Other Schools – See Driggs

Troy, AC 208, PC 3, Latah
Whitepine JSD 286 — 3-11111 / 835-3791
  PO BOX 280   83871
  Harold Ott, supt.
JSHS, PO BOX 280   83871 — 2-00111 / 835-2361
  O. Van Thomas, prin.
Other Schools – See Deary

Twin Falls, AC 208, PC 8, Twin Falls
Twin Falls SD 411 — 6-11111 / 733-6900
  201 MAIN AVE W   83301
  Terrell Donicht, supt.
SHS, 1615 FILER AVE E   83301 — 4-00001 / 733-6551
  Carl Snow, prin.
O'Leary JHS — 3-00110 / 733-2155
  2350 ELIZABETH BLVD   83301
  Wiley Dobbs, prin.
Stuart JHS, 644 CASWELL AVE W   83301 — 3-00110 / 733-4875
  Dale Thornsberry, prin.

College of Southern Idaho — 5-CC
  PO BOX 1238   83303 — 733-9554
Twin Falls Christian Academy — 2-11111
  798 EASTLAND DR N   83301 — 733-1452
  Brent Walker, prin.

Wallace, AC 208, PC 4, Shoshone
Wallace SD 393, PO BOX 500   83873 — 3-11111 / 753-4515
  Frank Bertino, supt.
HS, PO BOX 500   83873 — 2-00011 / 753-5315
  Ron McCracken, prin.
Wallace Vo S, 3RD & RIVER   83873 — Vo Tech / 556-1531
  Pete Martinez, prin.
Other Schools – See Osburn

Weippe, AC 208, PC 3, Clearwater
Orofino JSD 171
  Supt. — See Orofino
Timberline HS — 2-00011 / 435-4411
  1150 HIGHWAY 11   83553
  Richard Price, prin.
MS, 214 S 1ST ST E   83553 — 1-00100 / 435-4112
  Dale Durkee, prin.

Weiser, AC 208, PC 5, Washington
Weiser SD 431, 925 PIONEER RD   83672 — 4-11111 / 549-0616
  James Reed, supt.
HS, 690 W INDIANHEAD RD   83672 — 3-00011 / 549-2595
  Randy Powell, prin.
JHS, 320 E GALLOWAY ST   83672 — 2-00100 / 549-2620
  Larry Goto, prin.

Wendell, AC 208, PC 4, Gooding
Wendell SD 232, PO BOX 300   83355 — 3-11111 / 536-2418
  Larry Manly, supt.
JSHS, PO BOX 30   83355 — 2-00111 / 536-5531
  Roy Parton, prin.

Wilder, AC 208, PC 4, Canyon
Wilder SD 133, PO BOX 488   83676 — 2-11111 / 482-6228
  Bedford Boston, supt.
JSHS, PO BOX 488   83676 — 2-00111 / 482-6229
  Richard Seibold, prin.

ILLINOIS

STATE DEPARTMENT OF EDUCATION
100 N. 1st St., Springfield 62777
(217) 782-2221

Superintendent of Education — Joseph Spagnolo

Executive Deputy Superintendent — Vacant

Associate Superintendent Specialized Programs — Gail Lieberman

Associate Superintendent Finance & Support Service — Karol Richardson

Associate Superintendent Programs & Accountabilty — Mary Jayne Broncato

ILLINOIS STATE BOARD OF EDUCATION
100 N. 1st St., Springfield 62777

Chairperson — Michael Skarr

REGIONAL SUPERINTENDENTS OF SCHOOLS

Adams/Pike Region
  Steven Oelklaus — 217-223-6300
  237 N 6TH ST, Quincy 62301
Alexander/Johnson/Massac/Pulaski/Union
  Jerry Johnson — 618-634-2292
  RR 1 BOX 53C, Ullin 62992
Bond/Effingham/Fayette Region
  Delbert Maroon — 618-283-5011
  300 S 7TH ST, Vandalia 62471
Boone/Winnebago Region
  Richard Fairgrieves — 815-636-3060
  300 HEART BLVD
  Loves Park 61111

Brown/Cass/Schuyler Region
  Gene Ralston — 217-323-5559
  121 E 2ND ST, Beardstown 62618
Bureau Region
  Larry Marsh — 815-872-4281
  COURTHOUSE, Princeton 61356
Calhoun/Greene/Jersey Region
  James Frazier — 618-498-5541
  PO BOX 409, Jerseyville 62052
Carroll/JoDaviess Region
  John B. Lang — 815-777-2362
  330 N BENCH ST, Galena 61036

Champaign/Ford Region
  Martin Barrett — 217-893-3219
  200 S FREDRICK ST
  Rantoul 61866
Christian/Montgomery Region
  Thomas Rigdon — 217-824-4730
  PO BOX 766, Taylorville 62568
Clark/Coles/Cmbrlnd/Edgr/Moultrie/Shelby
  Rose Shepherd — 217-348-0151
  PO BOX 350, Charleston 61920
Clay/Jasper Richland Region
  Sam White — 618-392-4631
  103 W MAIN ST, Olney 62450

Clinton/Washington Region
Larry Wolfe, 810B FRANKLIN ST   618-594-2432
Carlyle 62231
Cook Region
Lloyd Lehman   312-443-6350
50 W WASHINGTON ST RM 402
Chicago 60602
Crawford/Lawrence Region
Roger Lewis, PO BOX 866   618-943-3522
Lawrenceville 62439
DeKalb Region
Thomas Weber   815-895-3096
245 W EXCHANGE ST # 2
Sycamore 60178
Dewitt/McLean Region
Donald Robinson, PO BOX 3125   309-888-5120
Bloomington 61702
Douglas/Piatt Region
Charles Edmundson   217-578-2824
125 N MAIN ST, Atwood 61913
Dupage Region
Berardo Desimone   708-682-7150
421 N COUNTY FARM RD
Wheaton 60187
Edwards/Wabash/Wayne/White Region
Kermit Braddock   618-847-3151
PO BOX 277, Fairfield 62837
Franklin Region
Barry Kohl   618-438-9711
202 W MAIN ST, Benton 62812
Fulton Region
Gary Grzanich   309-547-3041
PO BOX 307, Lewistown 61542
Gallatin/Hardin/Pope/Saline Region
John Wilson   618-253-5581
112 N GUM ST, Harrisburg 62946
Grundy/Kendall Region
Richard Krase   815-942-9024
1320 UNION ST, Morris 60450
Hamilton/Jefferson Region
Paul Cross, 900 BROADWAY ST   618-244-8040
Mount Vernon 62864
Hancock/McDonough Region
Robert Baumann   309-837-4821
130 1/2 S LAFAYETTE ST
Macomb 61455
Henderson/Mercer/Warren Region
Roger Birkhead   309-734-6822
200 W BROADWAY
Monmouth 61462

Henry/Stark Region
Ronald Hewitt   309-937-2465
PO BOX 5, Cambridge 61238
Iroquois Region
Donald Deany   815-432-6976
550 S 10TH ST, Watseka 60970
Jackson/Perry Region
Donald Brewer, 1001 WALNUT ST   618-687-7290
Murphysboro 62966
Kane Region
Clem Mejia, 719 S BATAVIA AVE   708-232-5955
Geneva 60134
Kankakee Region
Alan Lemon   815-937-2950
189 E COURT ST STE 400
Kankakee 60901
Knox Region
Raymond Franson   309-343-9151
PO BOX 430, Galesburg 61402
Lake Region
Edward Conwa   708-360-6313
18 N COUNTY ST # A-904
Waukegan 60085
LaSalle Region
William Novotney   815-434-0780
119 W MADISON ST
Ottawa 61350
Lee Region
Thomas Coffey   815-288-4405
COURTHOUSE, Dixon 61021
Livingston Region
Paul Studnicki   815-844-3189
310 E TORRANCE AVE
Pontiac 61764
Logan/Mason/Menard Region
George Janet, 12 COURT HOUSE   217-732-8388
Lincoln 62656
Macon Region
David Cooprider   217-424-3404
2240 E GEDDES AVE
Decatur 62526
Macoupin Region
Russell Massinelli   217-854-4016
220 N BROAD ST
Carlinville 62626
Madison Region
Harold Briggs   618-692-6200
PO BOX 600, Edwardsville 62025
Marion Region
Sam Nall, 200 E SCHWARTZ ST   618-548-3885
Salem 62881

Marshall/Putnam/Woodford Region
Iner Anderson   815-925-7381
PO BOX 289, Hennepin 61327
McHenry Region
Leslie Hellemann   815-334-4475
2200 N SEMINARY AVE
Woodstock 60098
Monroe/Randolph Region
Faye Hughes   618-282-6244
PO BOX 165, Red Bud 62278
Morgan/Scott Region
Paul Keller, 345 W STATE ST   217-243-1804
Jacksonville 62650
Ogle Region
Earl Gray   815-732-3201
PO BOX 196, Oregon 61061
Peoria Region
Gerald Brookhart   309-672-6906
COUNTY COURTHOUSE RM 503
Peoria 61602
Rock Island Region
Joseph Vermeire, 1504 3RD AVE   309-786-4451
Rock Island 61201
St. Clair Region
Martha O'Malley   618-397-8930
500 WILSHIRE DR
Belleville 62223
Sangamon Region
Harold Vose   217-753-6620
200 S 9TH ST STE 303
Springfield 62701
Stephenson Region
William Kested   815-235-8262
15 N GALENA AVE
Freeport 61032
Tazewell Region
Solie Myers   309-477-2290
PO BOX 699, Pekin 61555
Vermilion Region
Richard Weller   217-431-2668
RR 1 BOX 12D, Danville 61832
Whiteside Region
Gary Steinert   815-772-5104
200 E KNOX ST, Morrison 61270
Will Region
Frank Desiderio   815-740-8360
302 N CHICAGO ST, Joliet 60431
Williamson Region
Dale Reach, 200 W JEFFERSON ST   618-997-1301
Marion 62959

PUBLIC, PRIVATE AND CATHOLIC SECONDARY SCHOOLS

Abingdon, AC 309, PC 5, Knox
Abingdon CUSD 217   4-11111
201 W LOWER ST 61410   462-2301
Dale Miller, supt.
HS, 600 W MARTIN ST 61410   2-00011
Richard Greer, prin.   462-2338
JHS, 202 W SNYDER ST 61410   2-00100
Donald Smith, prin.   462-2336

Addison, AC 708, PC 8, Du Page
Addison SD 4   5-11100
222 JF KENNEDY DR 60101   628-2500
Larry Weck, supt.
Indian Trail JHS   4-00100
222 JF KENNEDY DR 60101   628-2514
Susan Liechti, prin.

DuPage HSD 88
Supt. — See Villa Park
Addison Trail HS   4-00011
213 N LOMBARD RD 60101   628-3302
Neil Codell, prin.

DeVry Institute of Technology   5-UC
1221 N SWIFT RD 60101   953-2000
Driscoll Catholic HS   2-00011
555 N LOMBARD RD 60101   543-6310
Rod Molek, prin.

Albion, AC 618, PC 4, Edwards
Edwards County CUSD 1   4-11111
106 W MAIN ST 62806   445-2814
Clifford Jones, supt.
Edwards County HS   2-00011
361 W MAIN ST 62806   445-2326
Terry Moreland, prin.

Aledo, AC 309, PC 5, Mercer
Aledo CUSD 201, 402 E MAIN ST 61231   4-11111
N. Kendall Pottorff, supt.   582-2238
HS, 1500 S COLLEGE AVE 61231   2-00011
Larry Stinson, prin.   582-2223
JHS, 205 N COLLEGE AVE 61231   2-00100
Glen Braden, prin.   582-2441

Alexis, AC 309, PC 3, Warren
Alexis CUSD 400, PO BOX 599 61412   2-11111
John Elder, supt.   482-3344
HS, PO BOX 599 61412   2-00011
John Elder, prin.   482-3333
JHS, PO BOX 599 61412   1-00100
John Elder, prin.   482-3333

Algonquin, AC 708, PC 7, McHenry
Dundee CUSD 300
Supt. — See Carpentersville
Jacobs HS, 11111 RANDALL RD 60102   4-00011
Linda Koerber, prin.   658-2501

MS, 500 LONGWOOD DR 60102   3-00100
Robert Whitehouse, prin.   658-2545

Alsip, AC 708, PC 7, Cook
Alsip-Hazelgreen-Oaklawn SD 126   4-11100
11900 S KOSTNER AVE 60658   389-1900
William Boucek, supt.
Prairie JHS   2-00100
11910 S KOSTNER AVE 60658   371-3080
Harold Hansen, supt.
Atwood Heights SD 125
Supt. — See Oak Lawn
Hamlin MS   2-00100
12150 S HAMLIN AVE 60658   597-1550
Mark Flood, prin.

Altamont, AC 618, PC 4, Effingham
Altamont CUSD 10   3-11111
116 N MAIN ST 62411   483-6195
Bernard May, supt.
HS, 7 S EWING ST 62411   2-00011
Eugene Logue, prin.   483-6194

Alton, AC 618, PC 8, Madison
Alton CUSD 11, PO BOX 9028 62002   6-11111
David VanWinkle, supt.   474-2600
HS, 2200 COLLEGE AVE 62002   4-00011
Thomas Thompson, prin.   474-2700
East MS   3-00100
1035 WASHINGTON AVE 62002   463-2131
L. Darlene Fearheiley, prin.
West MS, 1513 STATE ST 62002   3-00100
Sandra Bolen, prin.   463-2134
Other Schools — See Godfrey

Marquette HS, 219 E 4TH ST 62002   2-00011
John Rogers, prin.   463-0580
Mississippi Valley Christian S   2-11111
2009 SEMINARY ST 62002   462-1071
Elwood Heisey, prin.

Amboy, AC 815, PC 4, Lee
Amboy CUSD 272   4-11111
11 E HAWLEY ST 61310   857-3632
Terry Salem, supt.
HS, 11 E HAWLEY ST 61310   2-00011
Kevin Holland, prin.   857-3632
JHS, 140 APPLETON AVE 61310   2-01100
Donald Wyzgowski, prin.   857-3528

Anna, AC 618, PC 5, Union
Anna-Jonesboro Community HSD 81   3-00011
608 S MAIN ST 62906   833-8421
Robert Brutcher, supt.
Anna-Jonesboro HS   3-00011
608 S MAIN ST 62906   833-8502
James Smith, prin.

Anna CCSD 37, 301 S GREEN ST 62906   3-11100
Manul Goins, supt.   833-6812
JHS, 301 S GREEN ST 62906   2-00100
Duane Hileman, prin.   833-6415

Annawan, AC 309, PC 3, Henry
Annawan CUSD 226   3-11111
501 W SOUTH ST 61234   935-6781
Ronald Tuisl, supt.
HS, 501 W SOUTH ST 61234   2-00011
Richard Vankerrebroeck, prin.   935-6781

Antioch, AC 708, PC 6, Lake
Antioch CCSD 34   4-11100
850 HIGHVIEW DR 60002   395-0712
Donald Skidmore, supt.
Antioch MS, 800 HIGHVIEW DR 60002   3-00100
Deborah Kerr-Carpenter, prin.   395-1905
Antioch Community HSD 117   4-00011
1133 MAIN ST 60002   395-1421
Robert Schley, supt.
Antioch Community HS   4-00011
1133 MAIN ST 60002   395-1421
Michael Radakovich, prin.

Arcola, AC 217, PC 5, Douglas
Arcola CUSD 306   3-11111
351 W WASHINGTON ST 61910   268-4963
Malcolm Fox, supt.
JSHS, 351 W WASHINGTON ST 61910   2-00111
Steven Fink, prin.   268-4962

Argenta, AC 217, PC 3, Macon
Argenta-Oreana CUSD 1   4-11111
500 N MAIN ST 62501   795-4448
Robert Verdun, supt.
Argenta-Oreana HS   2-00011
500 N MAIN ST 62501   795-4822
David Bottom, prin.
Other Schools — See Oreana

Arlington Heights, AC 708, PC 8, Cook
Arlington Heights SD 25   5-11100
301 W SOUTH ST 60005   398-4200
Dorothy Weber, supt.
South MS, 314 S HIGHLAND AVE 60005   3-00100
Sherry Dunn, prin.   398-4248
Thomas MS, 303 E THOMAS ST 60004   3-00100
Charles Crissey, prin.   398-4260

Community Consolidated SD 59   6-11100
2123 S ARLINGTON HEIGHTS RD 60005
Robert Howard, supt.   593-4300
Other Schools — See Des Plaines, Elk Grove Village,
Mount Prospect

Township HSD 214   7-00011
  2121 S GOEBBERT RD 60005   437-4600
  Stephen Berry, supt.
Hersey HS, 1900 E THOMAS ST 60004   4-00011
  Don Kersemeier, prin.   259-8500
Other Schools – See Buffalo Grove, Elk Grove
  Village, Mount Prospect, Rolling Meadows,
  Wheeling

Northwest Community Hospital   HSP
  800 W CENTRAL RD 60005   259-1000
St. Viator HS, 1213 E OAKTON ST 60004   3-00011
  Walter Bowman, prin.   392-4050

Armstrong, AC 217, PC 2, Vermilion
Armstrong Twp. HSD 225   1-00011
  PO BOX 37 61812   569-2122
  Michael Stagliano, supt.
HS, PO BOX 37 61812   1-00011
  Michael Stagliano, supt.   569-2122

Arthur, AC 217, PC 4, Moultrie
Arthur CUSD 305   3-11111
  301 E COLUMBIA ST 61911   543-2511
  Allen Froman, supt.
HS, 301 E COLUMBIA ST 61911   2-00011
  Edgar Coller, prin.   543-2146
JHS, 301 E COLUMBIA ST 61911   1-00100
  Edgar Coller, prin.   543-2146

Ashland, AC 217, PC 4, Cass
Ashland-Chandlerville CUSD 262   3-11111
  PO BOX 260 62612   476-8112
  Ronald Blakely, supt.
Ashland-Chandlerville HS   2-00011
  PO BOX 260 62612   476-3312
  Dan Williams, prin.
JHS, PO BOX 260 62612   1-00100
  Dan Williams, prin.   476-3312
Other Schools – See Chandlerville

Ashton, AC 815, PC 4, Lee
Ashton CUSD 275   2-11111
  PO BOX 329 61006   453-7461
  George Taubenheim, supt.
HS, PO BOX 329 61006   2-00011
  John Zick, prin.   453-7461
MS, PO BOX 329 61006   2-01100
  John Zick, prin.   453-7461

Assumption, AC 217, PC 4, Christian
Central A & M SD   3-11111
  105 N COLLEGE ST 62510   226-4042
  Mark Gregory, supt.
Central A & M MS   2-00100
  404 COLEGROVE ST 62510   226-4241
  Marsha Parr, prin.
Other Schools – See Moweaqua

Astoria, AC 309, PC 4, Fulton
Astoria CUSD 1, PO BOX 487 61501   2-11111
  Ralph Marshall, supt.   329-2111
HS, PO BOX 487 61501   2-00011
  Nancy Kunzeman, prin.   329-2156
JHS, PO BOX 487 61501   2-00100
  Marte Griffin, prin.   329-2158

Athens, AC 217, PC 4, Menard
Athens CUSD 213   3-11111
  1 WARRIOR WAY 62613   636-8761
  Jeffrey Storm, supt.
JSHS, RR 1 BOX 11 62613   2-00011
  Ron Schwabe, prin.   636-8314

Atwood, AC 217, PC 4, Piatt
Atwood-Hammond CUSD 39   2-11111
  PO BOX 890 61913   578-3111
  Darrell Fulton, supt.
Atwood-Hammond HS   2-00011
  222 W MAGNOLIA ST 61913   578-2226
  Richard Shelby, prin.

Auburn, AC 217, PC 5, Sangamon
Auburn CUSD 10   4-11111
  606 W NORTH ST 62615   438-6164
  James Doglio, supt.
HS, 511 N 7TH ST 62615   2-00011
  Roland Creed, prin.   438-6817
JHS, 601 N 7TH ST 62615   2-00100
  Anton Cerveny, prin.   438-6919

Augusta, AC 217, PC 3, Hancock
Southeastern CUSD 337
  Supt. – See Bowen
Southeastern HS, PO BOX 236 62311   2-00011
  Michael Fray, prin.   392-2125

Aurora, AC 708, PC 8, Kane
Aurora East Unit SD 131   6-11111
  417 5TH ST 60505   844-5550
  Charles Ponquinette, supt.
Aurora East HS, 779 5TH AVE 60505   4-00011
  Jerome Roberts, prin.   898-0962
Cowherd MS   3-00100
  441 N FARNSWORTH AVE 60505   978-3760
  Stacy Onak, prin.
Simmons MS, 1130 SHEFFER RD 60505   3-00100
  Charles Maveus, prin.   898-8965
Waldo JHS, 56 JACKSON ST 60505   3-00100
  Bruce Weirich, prin.   898-8820

Aurora West Unit SD 129   6-11111
  80 S RIVER ST 60506   844-4431
  Sherry Eagle, supt.
West HS, 1201 W NEW YORK ST 60506   4-00011
  Mark McDonald, prin.   844-4600

Jefferson MS, 1151 PLUM ST 60506   3-00100
  C. Randall, prin.   844-4535
Washington MS   3-00100
  123 S CONSTITUTION DR 60506   844-4545
  Rose Gonzales-Pinnick, prin.

Illinois Math & Science Academy SD   2-00001
  1500 SULLIVAN RD 60506   801-6037
  Stephanie Marshall, supt.
Illinois Math & Science Academy   2-00001
  1500 SULLIVAN RD 60506   801-6037
  John Court, prin.
Indian Prairie CUSD 204
  Supt. – See Naperville
Waubonsie Valley HS   4-00011
  2590 ROUTE 34 60504   851-7900
  Gary Elmen, prin.
Granger MS   2-00100
  1305 LONG GROVE DR 60504   978-3450
  Adam Paikai, prin.

Aurora Central Catholic HS   2-00011
  157 N ROOT ST 60505   898-8806
  Robert Stewart, prin.
Aurora Christian S   3-11111
  14 BLACKHAWK AVE 60506   892-1551
  Paul House, prin.
Aurora University   4-UC
  347 S GLADSTONE AVE 60506   892-6431
Marmion Military Academy   2-00011
  1000 BUTTERFIELD RD 60504   897-6936
  Fr. Basil Yender, prin.
Rosary HS, 901 N EDGELAWN DR 60506   2-00011
  Sr. Francene Harbauer, prin.   896-0831

Avon, AC 309, PC 3, Fulton
Avon CUSD 176, PO BOX 400 61415   2-11111
  Henry Bonner, supt.   465-3708
HS, 320 E WOODS ST 61415   2-00011
  Bart Arthur, prin.   465-3621
JHS, 320 E WOODS ST 61415   2-00100
  Bart Arthur, prin.   465-3621

Barrington, AC 708, PC 6, Lake
Barrington CUSD 220   6-11111
  310 JAMES ST 60010   381-6300
  Fred Vorlop, supt.
HS, 616 W MAIN ST 60010   4-00011
  Edward Deyoung, prin.   381-1400
MS, 215 EASTERN AVE 60010   3-00100
  (—), prin.   381-0464
Barrington MS, 40 E DUNDEE RD 60010   3-00100
  Don Thompson, prin.   304-3990

Barry, AC 217, PC 4, Pike
Barry CUSD 1   2-11111
  401 MCDONOUGH ST 62312   335-2211
  C. Michael Kovachevich, supt.
HS, 401 MCDONOUGH ST 62312   2-00011
  R. Davenport, prin.   335-2323
JHS, 401 MCDONOUGH ST 62312   1-00100
  R. Davenport, prin.   335-2323

Barstow, AC 309, PC 2, Rock Island
Carbon Cliff-Barstow SD 36
  Supt. – See Carbon Cliff
Aldrin JHS, PO BOX 140 61236   1-00100
  Harold Roggendorf, prin.   496-2683

Bartonville, AC 309, PC 6, Peoria
Limestone Community HSD 310   4-00011
  4201 AIRPORT RD 61607   697-6271
  R. Scott Russell, supt.
Limestone HS, 4201 AIRPORT RD 61607   4-00011
  Bill Beach, prin.   697-6271

Oak Grove SD 68   2-11100
  4812 W PFEIFFER RD 61607   697-3367
  Stephen Heath, prin.
Oak Grove West JHS   2-00100
  6018 W LANCASTER RD 61607   697-0621
  Marc Devore, prin.

Batavia, AC 708, PC 7, Kane
Batavia Unit SD 101   5-11111
  12 W WILSON ST 60510   879-4645
  Edward Cave, supt.
HS, 1200 MAIN ST 60510   4-00011
  David Booth, prin.   879-4601
MS, 1501 S RADDANT RD 60510   3-00100
  Harold Wolff, prin.   879-4620

Beardstown, AC 217, PC 6, Cass
Beardstown CUSD 15   4-11111
  101 E 15TH ST 62618   323-3099
  Charles Waggoner, supt.
HS, 200 E 15TH ST 62618   2-00011
  Mary Castro, prin.   323-3665
JHS, 200 E 15TH ST 62618   2-00100
  Mary Castro, prin.   323-4005

Beckemeyer, AC 618, PC 4, Clinton
Breese SD 12
  Supt. – See Breese
MS, GENERAL DELIVERY 62219   2-01100
  David Timmermann, prin.   227-8242

Beecher, AC 708, PC 4, Will
Beecher CUSD 200U   3-11111
  538 MILLER ST 60401   946-2266
  Raymond Laporte, supt.
HS, 538 MILLER ST 60401   2-00011
  Patricia Hahto, prin.   946-2266

Beecher City, AC 618, PC 2, Effingham
Beecher City CUSD 20   2-11111
  PO BOX 98 62414   487-5100
  Joseph Stokes, supt.
JSHS, PO BOX 97 62414   2-00111
  J. T. Brachbill, prin.   487-5117

Belleville, AC 618, PC 8, St. Clair
Belle Valley SD 119   4-11100
  1901 MASCOUTAH AVE 62220   234-3445
  William Phillips, supt.
Belle Valley MS South   2-01100
  1901 MASCOUTAH AVE 62220   234-7723
  Robert Buscher, prin.
Belleville SD 118, 105 W A ST 62220   5-11100
  Ronald Riegel, supt.   233-2830
Central JHS, 200 S ILLINOIS ST 62220   2-00100
  Richard Binder, prin.   233-5377
West JHS   2-00100
  820 ROYAL HEIGHTS RD 62223   234-8200
  Bill Porzukowiak, prin.

Belleville Twp. HSD 201   5-00011
  2600 W MAIN ST 62223   233-5070
  Leo Hefner, supt.
HS East, 2555 WEST BLVD 62221   4-00011
  H. Fred Curtis, prin.   235-3300
HS West, 2600 W MAIN ST 62223   4-00011
  Phillip Silsby, prin.   233-5070

Harmony Emge SD 175   3-11100
  7401 WESTCHESTER DR 62223   397-8444
  Stan Burcham, supt.
Emge JHS   2-01100
  7401 WESTCHESTER DR 62223   397-6557
  Jack Ackermann, prin.

Althoff Catholic HS   3-00011
  5401 W MAIN ST 62223   235-1100
  Sr. Jan Renz, prin.
Belleville Area College   6-CC
  2500 CARLYLE RD 62221   235-2700
Governor French Academy   2-11111
  219 W MAIN ST 62220   233-7542
  Phillip Paeltz, prin.
St. Elizabeth Hospital   HSP
  211 S 3RD ST 62220   234-2120

Bellwood, AC 708, PC 7, Cook
Bellwood SD 88
  Supt. – See Stone Park
Roosevelt JHS, 2501 OAK ST 60104   3-00100
  Vinston Birdin, prin.   544-3318

Belvidere, AC 815, PC 7, Boone
Belvidere CUSD 100   5-11111
  1201 5TH AVE 61008   544-0301
  Frank Evans, supt.
HS, 1500 EAST AVE 61008   4-00011
  Jerry Fisher, prin.   547-6345
JHS, 919 E 6TH ST 61008   3-00100
  Frank Bell, prin.   544-3175

Calvary Baptist Christian S   2-11111
  1637 7TH AVE 61008   544-2998
  Rich Eckelbarger, prin.

Bement, AC 217, PC 4, Piatt
Bement CUSD 5   2-11111
  201 S CHAMPAIGN ST 61813   678-2111
  Darrell Stevens, supt.
HS, 201 S CHAMPAIGN ST 61813   2-00011
  Nyle Waters, prin.   678-8230
MS, 201 S CHAMPAIGN ST 61813   2-00100
  Darrell Stevens, prin.   678-4341

Bensenville, AC 708, PC 7, Du Page
Bensenville SD 2, 119 E GREEN ST 60106   4-11100
  Cesare Caldarelli, supt.   766-5940
Blackhawk JHS   2-00100
  250 S CHURCH RD 60106   766-2601
  Robert Barr, prin.

Fenton Community HSD 100   4-00011
  1000 W GREEN ST 60106   860-6257
  John Meredith, supt.
Fenton HS, 1000 W GREEN ST 60106   4-00011
  Alf Logan, prin.   766-2500

Environmental Technical Institute   2-CS
  1054 E IRVING PARK RD 60106   350-9100

Benson, AC 309, PC 2, Woodford
Roanoke-Benson CUSD 60
  Supt. – See Roanoke
Roanoke-Benson JHS   2-01100
  131 REITER ST 61516   394-2233
  Mark Zotz, prin.

Benton, AC 618, PC 6, Franklin
Benton CCSD 47   4-11100
  308 E CHURCH ST 62812   439-3136
  Allan Patton, supt.
Benton MS, 1000 FORREST ST 62812   3-01100
  Ronald Knox, prin.   438-4011
Benton Consolidated HSD 103   3-00011
  511 E MAIN ST 62812   439-3103
  John O'Dell, supt.
Benton Cons. HS, 511 E MAIN ST 62812   3-00011
  Gary Messersmith, prin.   439-3103

Berkeley, AC 708, PC 6, Cook
Berkeley SD 87 4-11100
5400 SAINT CHARLES RD 60163 547-3050
Joseph Palermo, supt.
MacArthur MS, 1310 N WOLF RD 60163 2-00100
Ron Paul, prin. 547-3085
Other Schools – See Northlake

Berwyn, AC 708, PC 8, Cook
Berwyn North SD 98 4-11100
1427 OAK PARK AVE 60402 484-6200
John Bevan, supt.
Lincoln JHS, 6432 16TH ST 60402 2-00100
Roberta Nash, prin. 795-2475

Berwyn South SD 100 4-11100
3105 CLINTON AVE 60402 749-3050
Dr. Gary M. Smit, supt.
Hiawatha MS, 6539 26TH ST 60402 2-01100
James McElwee, prin. 795-2327

J. S. Morton HSD 201
Supt. — See Cicero
Morton West HS, 2400 HOME AVE 60402 4-00011
Donald Ciner, prin. 656-2300

Bethalto, AC 618, PC 6, Madison
Bethalto CUSD 8 5-11111
322 E CENTRAL ST 62010 377-7200
Dale Dickerson, supt.
Civic Memorial HS 3-00011
200 SCHOOL ST 62010 377-7220
J. Willard Wallace, prin.
Trimpe JHS, 910 2ND ST 62010 2-00100
Harold Earnhart, prin. 377-7240

Bethany, AC 217, PC 4, Moultrie
Bethany CUSD 301 2-11111
PO BOX 97 61914 665-3232
Marilyn Bayley, supt.
JSHS, PO BOX 97 61914 2-00111
Allan Manhart, prin. 665-3631

Biggsville, AC 309, PC 2, Henderson
Union CUSD 115, RR 1 BOX 72 61418 3-11111
Dean Irlbeck, supt. 627-2371
Union HS, RR 1 BOX 72 61418 2-00011
Ray Goff, prin. 627-2377

Bismarck, AC 217, PC 3, Vermilion
Bismarck CUSD 1 3-11111
PO BOX 350 61814 759-7261
Timothy Musgrave, supt.
Bismarck-Henning HS 2-00011
PO BOX 350 61814 759-7291
Ronald Winkler, prin.
Bismarck-Henning JHS 2-01100
PO BOX 350 61814 759-7301
Earl Lindsey, prin.

Bloomingdale, AC 708, PC 7, Du Page
Bloomingdale SD 13 4-11100
181 S BLOOMINGDALE RD 60108 893-9590
Jerome Gordon, supt.
Westfield JHS 3-00100
149 FAIRFIELD WAY 60108 529-6211
Charles Swangren, prin.

Community Consolidated SD 93
Supt. — See Carol Stream
Stratford JHS, PO BOX 251 60108 3-00100
Robert Ballenger, prin. 980-9898

Bloomington, AC 309, PC 8, McLean
Bloomington SD 87 6-11111
PO BOX 249 61702 827-6031
Leonard Roberts, supt.
HS, 1202 E LOCUST ST 61701 4-00011
Robert Elliott, prin. 828-5201
JHS, 901 N COLTON AVE 61701 4-00100
Susan Silvey, prin. 827-0086

American College of Technology 1-CS
1300 W WASHINGTON ST 61701 800-593-5151
Central Catholic HS 2-00011
712 N CENTER ST 61701 827-5373
Joy Allen, prin.
Holy Trinity S 2-01100
705 N ROOSEVELT AVE 61701 282-7151
Edward Heineman, prin.
Illinois Wesleyan University 4-UC
PO BOX 2900 61702 556-3031
Mennonite College of Nursing 2-UC
804 N EAST ST 61701 829-0715

Blue Island, AC 708, PC 7, Cook
Blue Island SD 130 5-11100
12300 GREENWOOD AVE 60406 385-6800
Barbara Mackey, supt.
Kerr MS, 12915 MAPLE AVE 60406 3-00100
Marlene Talaski, prin. 385-6800
Other Schools – See Crestwood

Community HSD 218
Supt. — See Oak Lawn
Eisenhower HS 4-00011
12700 SACRAMENTO AVE 60406 597-6300
James Messaglia, prin.

Environmental Technical Institute 2-CS
13010 DIVISION ST 60406 385-0707

Blue Mound, AC 217, PC 4, Macon
Blue Mound-Boody CUSD 10 2-11111
PO BOX 320 62513 692-2148
Kermit Harden, supt.
HS, PO BOX 320 62513 2-00011
Gordon Eckols, prin. 692-2147

Bluffs, AC 217, PC 3, Scott
Scott-Morgan CUSD 2 2-11111
PO BOX 230 62621 754-3714
Robert Rogers, supt.
HS, PO BOX 230 62621 2-00011
Michael Davies, prin. 754-3815
JHS, PO BOX 230 62621 1-00100
Michael Davies, prin. 754-3815

Bluford, AC 618, PC 3, Jefferson
Webber Twp. HSD 204 2-00011
PO BOX 110 62814 732-6121
Dale Colwell, supt.
Webber Twp. HS, PO BOX 110 62814 2-00011
Dale Colwell, prin. 732-6121

Bolingbrook, AC 708, PC 8, Will
Valley View CUSD 365-U
Supt. — See Romeoville
HS, 350 BLAIR LN 60440 4-00011
Kenneth Sorrick, prin. 759-6400
Addams MS, 905 LILY CACHE LN 60440 3-00100
Otha Lang, prin. 759-7200
Humphrey MS 3-00100
777 FALCONRIDGE WAY 60440 972-9240
Ronald Krause, prin.
Ward MS, 200 RECREATION DR 60440 3-00100
William Zielke, prin. 972-9200

Bourbonnais, AC 815, PC 7, Kankakee
Bourbonnais SD 53 4-11100
281 W JOHN CASEY RD 60914 939-2574
John Alumbaugh, supt.
JHS, 200 W JOHN CASEY RD 60914 3-00100
Richard Campbell, prin. 937-4471

Bowen, AC 217, PC 2, Hancock
Southeastern CUSD 337 3-11111
PO BOX 247 62316 842-5236
Terry Robertson, supt.
Southeastern JHS, PO BOX 247 62316 2-00100
Terry Robertson, prin. 842-5236
Other Schools – See Augusta

Bradford, AC 309, PC 3, Stark
Bradford CUSD 1, 345 SILVER ST 61421 2-11111
David Messersmith, supt. 897-4611
HS, 115 HIGH ST 61421 2-00011
Judith Warthen, prin. 897-8169

Bradley, AC 815, PC 7, Kankakee
Bradley-Bourbonnais Community HSD 307 4-00011
701 W NORTH ST 60915 937-3715
Donald Turner, supt.
Bradley-Bourbonnais Community HS 4-00011
701 W NORTH ST 60915 937-3703
Keith Baldwin, prin.

Bradley SD 61, 200 STATE ST 60915 4-11100
L. Trumble, supt. 933-3371
Bradley Central MS 3-01100
235 N MICHIGAN AVE 60915 939-3564
Wayne Sneed, prin.

Braidwood, AC 815, PC 5, Will
Reed-Custer CUSD 255U 4-11111
255 COMET DR 60408 458-2307
A. Hendricks, supt.
Reed-Custer HS, 249 COMET DR 60408 2-00011
William Freemen, prin. 458-2166
Reed-Custer JHS, 307 COMET DR 60408 2-00100
Thomas Greene, prin. 458-2868

Breese, AC 618, PC 5, Clinton
Breese SD 12, 1100 N 7TH ST 62230 3-11100
Jerry Williams, supt. 526-7128
Other Schools – See Beckemeyer

Central Community HSD 71 2-00011
7740 OLD US HIGHWAY 50 62230 526-4578
Robert Astroth, supt.
Central Community HS 2-00011
7740 OLD US HIGHWAY 50 62230 526-4578
James Groff, prin.

Mater Dei HS, 205 MATER DEI DR 62230 3-00011
Curt Winter, prin. 526-7216

Bridgeport, AC 618, PC 4, Lawrence
Red Hill CUSD 10, 1250 JUDY AVE 62417 4-11111
Gary Glosser, supt. 945-2061
Red Hill HS, 908 CHURCH ST 62417 2-00011
Harry Rice, prin. 945-8221

Brimfield, AC 309, PC 3, Peoria
Brimfield CUSD 309 3-11111
323 W CLINTON ST 61517 446-3378
Bill Hunter, supt.
HS, PO BOX 307 61517 2-00011
Bill Hunter, prin. 446-3349

Broadlands, AC 217, PC 2, Champaign
Heritage CUSD 8
Supt. — See Homer
Heritage HS, PO BOX 260 61816 2-00011
Lyle Rigdon, prin. 834-3392

Brookfield, AC 708, PC 7, Cook
Brookfield SD 95 3-11100
3524 MAPLE AVE 60513 485-0606
Herbert Hageman, supt.
Gross MS, 3525 MAPLE AVE 60513 2-01100
Joseph Majchrowicz, prin. 485-0600

Brownstown, AC 618, PC 3, Fayette
Brownstown CUSD 201 2-11111
421 S COLLEGE AVE 62418 427-3355
Harlan Newbold, supt.
HS, 421 S COLLEGE AVE 62418 2-00011
Betty Jones, prin. 427-3839
JHS, 421 S COLLEGE AVE 62418 1-00100
Betty Jones, prin. 427-3839

Brussels, AC 618, PC 2, Calhoun
Brussels CUSD 42 2-11111
PO BOX 128 62013 883-2131
David McAfee, supt.
Brussels HS, PO BOX 128 62013 1-00011
Michael Siemer, prin. 883-2131

Buda, AC 309, PC 3, Bureau
Western CUSD 306
Supt. — See Sheffield
Western HS, STEWART ST 61314 2-00011
Tom Dobrich, prin. 895-3101
Western JHS, STEWART ST 61314 2-00100
Tom Dobrich, prin. 895-3273

Buffalo, AC 217, PC 3, Sangamon
Tri-City CUSD 1, PO BOX 290 62515 3-11111
Thomas Wolf, supt. 364-4811
Tri-City HS, PO BOX 290 62515 2-00011
Daniel Lucey, prin. 364-4530
Tri-City JHS, PO BOX 290 62515 2-00100
Daniel Lucey, prin. 364-4530

Buffalo Grove, AC 708, PC 8, Cook
Aptakisic-Tripp CCSD 102 4-11100
1231 WEILAND RD 60089 634-1358
C. Parks, supt.
Aptakisic JHS, 1231 WEILAND RD 60089 3-00100
Barry Brodsky, prin. 634-5300

Kildeer Countryside SD 96 5-11100
1050 IVY HALL LN 60089 459-4260
David Willard, supt.
Twin Groves MS-Rand 3-00100
2600 N BUFFALO GROVE 60089 465-8946
Barbara Hutton, prin.

Township HSD 214
Supt. — See Arlington Heights
HS, 1100 W DUNDEE RD 60089 4-00011
Carter Burns, prin. 541-5400

Wheeling CCSD 21
Supt. — See Wheeling
Cooper JHS 3-00100
1050 PLUM GROVE CIR 60089 520-2750
Wendy Billington, prin.

Bunker Hill, AC 618, PC 4, Macoupin
Bunker Hill CUSD 8 3-11111
504 E WARREN ST 62014 585-3116
Elden Duelm, supt.
HS, 314 S MEISSNER ST 62014 2-00011
Terry Dilliard, prin. 585-3232
Meissner MS, 504 E WARREN ST 62014 2-01100
Harold Wilkinson, prin. 585-4464

Burbank, AC 708, PC 8, Cook
Reavis Twp. HSD 220 4-00011
7698 AUSTIN AVE 60459 599-7200
W. Morrissey, supt.
Reavis HS, 7698 AUSTIN AVE 60459 4-00011
Clyde Rode, prin. 599-7200

Queen of Peace HS 4-00011
7659 LINDER AVE 60459 458-7600
Patricia Fitzgerald, prin.
St. Laurence HS, 5556 W 77TH ST 60459 4-00011
Br. Arthur Arndt, prin. 458-6900

Burlington, AC 708, PC 2, Kane
Central CUSD 301 4-11111
PO BOX 396 60109 464-6005
Gary Jewel, supt.
Central HS, PO BOX 68 60109 2-00011
Robert Barwa, prin. 464-6030
Central JHS, PO BOX 396 60109 2-01100
Robert Warski, prin. 464-6000

Burr Ridge, AC 708, PC 6, Du Page
CCSD 180, 15W451 91ST ST 60521 3-11100
Terry Tamblyn, supt. 325-5454
Palisades MS, 15W451 91ST ST 60521 2-00100
Roger Sanders, prin. 325-5454

Gower SD 62 3-11100
7941 S MADISON ST 60521 986-5383
Dr. Edward Vanmeir, supt.
Gower MS, 7941 S MADISON ST 60521 2-01100
William Snyder, prin. 323-8275

Bushnell, AC 309, PC 5, McDonough
Bushnell-Prairie City CUSD 170 3-11111
845 WALNUT ST 61422 772-9461
F. Lynn Hartweger, supt.
Bushnell-Prairie City HS 2-00011
845 WALNUT ST 61422 772-2113
Jerry Merrick, prin.
Bushnell-Prairie City JHS 2-00100
847 WALNUT ST 61422 772-3123
Raymond Krey, prin.

Byron, AC 815, PC 4, Ogle
Byron CUSD 226, PO BOX 911 61010 4-11111
William Young, supt. 234-5491
HS, PO BOX 911 61010 2-00011
Gary Hassler, prin. 234-5491

MS, PO BOX 397 61010 — 2-00100 / 234-5491
Frank Conry, prin.

Cahokia, AC 618, PC 7, St. Clair
Cahokia CUSD 187
1700 JEROME LN 62206 — 5-11111 / 332-3700
Elmer Kirchoff, supt.
HS, 800 RANGE LN 62206 — 4-00011 / 332-3730
Lawrence Taylor, prin.
Wirth JHS, 1900 MOUSETTE LN 62206 — 3-00100 / 332-3722
Ed Wolf, prin.

Parks College of St. Louis University — 4-UC / 337-7500
500 FALLING SPRINGS RD 62206

Cairo, AC 618, PC 5, Alexander
Cairo Unit SD 1, 303 34TH ST 62914 — 4-11111 / 734-4102
Elton Crim, supt.
HS, 4201 SYCAMORE ST 62914 — 2-00011 / 734-2187
Sandra McKinley, prin.
JHS, 2403 WALNUT ST 62914 — 2-00100 / 734-0300
Lonnie Henderson, prin.

Calumet City, AC 708, PC 8, Cook
Calumet City SD 155
MEMORIAL & SUPERIOR 60409 — 3-11100 / 862-7665
James Rajchel, supt.
Wentworth JHS
528 SUPERIOR AVE 60409 — 2-01100 / 862-0750
Gregory O'Rourke, prin.

Dolton SD 149
Supt. — See Dolton
Dirkson MS, 1650 PULASKI RD 60409 — 3-00100 / 868-2340
Raymond Wielgos, prin.

Hoover-Schrum Memorial SD 157 — 3-11100 / 862-4236
165TH & GORDON AVE 60409
Robert Schneider, supt.
Schrum Memorial MS
1502 GORDON AVE 60409 — 2-01100 / 862-4236
Michael Wierzbicki, prin.

Thornton Fractional Twp. HSD 215 — 4-00011 / 418-1906
1601 WENTWORTH AVE 60409
Kenneth Olsen, supt.
Thornton Fractional North HS — 4-00011 / 418-1910
755 PULASKI RD 60409
Douglas Long, prin.
Center for Science & Technology — Vo Tech / 418-1908
135 167TH ST 60409
Theodore Sanders, prin.
Other Schools – See Lansing

Calumet Park, AC 708, PC 6, Cook
Calumet Public SD 132 — 4-11100 / 388-8920
1440 W VERMONT AVE 60643
Willie Mack, supt.
Calumet MS — 2-01100 / 388-8820
1440 W VERMONT AVE 60643
Herman Vallo, prin.

Cambridge, AC 309, PC 4, Henry
Cambridge CUSD 227 — 3-11111 / 937-2069
300 S WEST ST 61238
William Schehl, supt.
Cambridge Community HS — 2-00011 / 937-2051
300 S WEST ST 61238
Dan Caras, prin.
JHS, 300 S WEST ST 61238 — 2-00100 / 937-2051
Dan Caras, prin.

Campbell Hill, AC 618, PC 2, Jackson
Trico CUSD 176, PO BOX 220 62916 — 4-11111 / 426-3391
James Davis, supt.
Trico HS, PO BOX 220 62916 — 2-00011 / 426-3722
Robert Koehn, prin.
Trico JHS, PO BOX 220 62916 — 2-00100 / 426-3117
Clarence Schorn, prin.

Camp Point, AC 217, PC 4, Adams
Camp Point CUSD 3, RR 1 62320 — 3-11111 / 593-7116
R. A. Scheiter, supt.
Central HS, RR 1 BOX 163A 62320 — 2-00011 / 593-7731
William Bucklew, prin.
Central JHS, RR 1 62320 — 2-00100 / 593-7731
Robert Bergman, prin.

Canton, AC 309, PC 7, Fulton
Canton Union SD 66 — 5-11111 / 647-9411
20 W WALNUT ST 61520
Paul Vonderhaar, supt.
HS, 1001 N MAIN ST 61520 — 3-00011 / 647-1820
Robert Hobart, prin.
Ingersoll JHS, 1605 E ASH ST 61520 — 3-01100 / 647-6951
Phillip Murphy, prin.

Graham Hospital — HSP / 647-5240
210 W WALNUT ST 61520
Spoon River College — 4-CC / 647-4645
RR 1 61520

Carbon Cliff, AC 309, PC 4, Rock Island
Carbon Cliff-Barstow SD 36 — 2-11100 / 496-2683
PO BOX 280 61239
Harold Roggendorf, supt.
Other Schools – See Barstow

Carbondale, AC 618, PC 8, Jackson
Carbondale Community HSD 165 — 4-00011 / 457-3371
300 N SPRINGER ST 62901
Margaret Hollis, supt.
Carbondale SHS — 3-00011 / 457-3371
200 N SPRINGER ST 62901
Russell Clover, prin.

Carbondale HS East — 2-00011 / 457-3378
1301 E WALNUT ST 62901
John Helmick, prin.

Carbondale ESD 95 — 4-11100 / 457-3591
PO BOX 968 62903
Larry Jacober, supt.
Lincoln JHS — 2-00100 / 457-2174
501 S WASHINGTON ST 62901
Larry Barnett, prin.

Southern Illinois University 62901 — 7-UC / 453-2341

Carlinville, AC 217, PC 6, Macoupin
Carlinville CUSD 1 — 4-11111 / 854-9823
812 W MAIN ST 62626
Randolph Tinder, supt.
HS, 829 W MAIN ST 62626 — 2-00011 / 854-3104
Richard Spohr, prin.
JHS, 110 ILLINOIS AVE 62626 — 2-00100 / 854-3106
Richard Nicholson, prin.

Blackburn College — 2-UC / 854-3231
700 COLLEGE AVE 62626

Carlyle, AC 618, PC 5, Clinton
Carlyle CUSD 1, 1400 13TH ST 62231 — 4-11111 / 594-8283
Ann Duncan, supt.
HS, 1461 12TH ST 62231 — 2-00011 / 594-2453
Patrick Sullivan, prin.
ES, 951 6TH ST 62231 — 3-10100 / 594-3766
Bill Kolmer, prin.

Carmi, AC 618, PC 6, White
Carmi-White County CUSD 5 — 4-11111 / 382-2341
301 W MAIN ST 62821
Robert Kidd, supt.
Carmi-White County HS — 2-00011 / 382-4661
800 W MAIN ST 62821
David Johnson, prin.
Carmi White Co. MS — 2-00100 / 382-4631
201 W MAIN ST 62821
Arthur Saunders, prin.

Carol Stream, AC 708, PC 8, Du Page
Community Consolidated SD 93 — 5-11100 / 462-8900
PO BOX 88093 60188
John Dibuono, supt.
Other Schools – See Bloomingdale

Glenbard Twp. HSD 87
Supt. — See Glen Ellyn
Glenbard North HS, 990 KUHN RD 60188 — 4-00011 / 653-7000
Margaret Atchison, prin.

Carpentersville, AC 708, PC 7, Kane
Dundee CUSD 300 — 7-11111 / 426-1300
300 CLEVELAND AVE 60110
Norman Wetzel, supt.
Dundee-Crown HS — 4-00011 / 426-1415
1500 KINGS RD 60110
James Wilbrandt, prin.
MS, 100 CLEVELAND AVE 60110 — 4-00100 / 426-1380
Russell Ballard, prin.
Other Schools – See Algonquin, Dundee, Hampshire

Carrier Mills, AC 618, PC 4, Saline
Carrier Mills-Stonefort CUSD 2 — 3-11111 / 994-2392
U S ROUTE 45 62917
Ernest Felty, supt.
HS, U S ROUTE 45 62917 — 2-00011 / 994-2392
Joseph Rodocker, prin.

Carrollton, AC 217, PC 5, Greene
Carrollton CUSD 1, 702 5TH ST 62016 — 3-11111 / 942-5314
Michael Barry, supt.
HS, 950 3RD ST 62016 — 2-00011 / 942-6913
Steven Amizich, prin.

Carterville, AC 618, PC 5, Williamson
Carterville CUSD 5 — 4-11111 / 985-4826
306 VIRGINIA AVE 62918
R. Dawson, supt.
HS, 816 S DIVISION ST 62918 — 2-00011 / 985-2940
Thomas Newton, prin.
JHS, 116 SCHOOL ST 62918 — 2-00100 / 985-6411
Chris Rigdon, prin.

John A. Logan College — 5-CC / 985-3741
RR 2 62918

Carthage, AC 217, PC 5, Hancock
Carthage CUSD 338 — 3-11111 / 357-3922
210 S ADAMS ST 62321
Marvin Boyer, supt.
HS, 600 MILLER ST 62321 — 2-00011 / 357-2136
Ralph Grimm, prin.
JHS, 600 MILLER ST 62321 — 2-00100 / 357-2136
Ralph Grimm, prin.

Cary, AC 708, PC 7, McHenry
Cary CCSD 26, 15 S 2ND ST 60013 — 5-11100 / 639-7788
Richard Fluck, supt.
JHS, 233 E ORIOLE TRL 60013 — 3-00100 / 639-2148
Robert Lipinski, prin.

Community HSD 155
Supt. — See Crystal Lake
Cary-Grove Community HS — 4-00011 / 639-3825
35 W 3 OAKS RD 60013
Catherine Green, prin.

Casey, AC 217, PC 5, Clark
Casey-Westfield CUSD 4C — 4-11111 / 932-2184
PO BOX 100 62420
James Koss, supt.
Casey-Westfield HS — 2-00011 / 932-2175
306 E EDGAR AVE 62420
Richard Yandell, prin.
Casey-Westfield JHS — 2-00100 / 932-2175
306 E EDGAR AVE 62420
Richard Yandell, prin.

Catlin, AC 217, PC 4, Vermilion
Catlin CUSD 5, PO BOX 323 61817 — 3-11111 / 427-2116
Wayne Scarlett, supt.
HS, PO BOX 323 61817 — 2-00011 / 427-5331
Wayne Scarlett, prin.

Centralia, AC 618, PC 7, Marion
Centralia SD 135, 400 S ELM ST 62801 — 4-11100 / 532-1907
Dan Griffin, supt.
JHS, 900 S PINE ST 62801 — 3-00100 / 533-7130
Donald Bretsch, prin.

Centralia Twp. HSD 200 — 4-00011 / 532-7391
1000 E 3RD ST 62801
Don Stanton, supt.
HS, 1000 E 3RD ST 62801 — 4-00011 / 532-7391
Edward Wainscott, prin.

Kaskaskia College — 4-CC / 532-1981
27210 COLLEGE RD 62801

Cerro Gordo, AC 217, PC 4, Piatt
Cerro Gordo CUSD 100 — 3-11111 / 763-5221
PO BOX 79 61818
Raymond Lauk, supt.
HS, PO BOX 79 61818 — 2-00011 / 763-2711
Gilbert Jones, prin.
JHS, PO BOX 79 61818 — 2-00100 / 763-6411
George Stanhope, prin.

Chadwick, AC 815, PC 3, Carroll
Chadwick-Milledgeville CUSD 399
Supt. — See Milledgeville
JHS, RR 2 BOX 15 61014 — 2-00100 / 684-5191
Gary Johnson, prin.

Champaign, AC 217, PC 8, Champaign
Champaign CUSD 4 — 6-11111 / 351-3838
703 S NEW ST 61820
Timothy Hyland, supt.
Centennial HS, 913 CRESCENT DR 61821 — 4-00011 / 351-3951
Al Davis, prin.
Central HS — 4-00011 / 351-3914
610 W UNIVERSITY AVE 61820
Joseph Wojtena, prin.
Edison MS, 306 W GREEN ST 61820 — 3-00100 / 351-3771
Frederick McNary, prin.
Franklin MS, 817 N HARRIS AVE 61820 — 3-00100 / 351-3819
U S Davidson, prin.
Jefferson MS, 1115 CRESCENT DR 61821 — 3-00100 / 351-3790
Martha Sierra-Perry, prin.

Judah Christian S — 2-11111 / 359-1701
908 N PROSPECT AVE 61820
Douglas Quine, prin.
Parkland College — 5-CC / 800-346-8089
2400 W BRADLEY AVE 61821

Chandlerville, AC 217, PC 3, Cass
Ashland-Chandlerville CUSD 262
Supt. — See Ashland
JHS, PO BOX 380 62627 — 2-00100 / 458-2224
B. Dillow, prin.

Channahon, AC 815, PC 5, Will
Channahon SD 17 — 4-11100 / 467-4315
24920 S SAGE ST 60410
Richard Dombrowski, supt.
JHS, 24150 S MINOOKA RD 60410 — 2-00100 / 467-4313
Tom Lesniak, prin.

Charleston, AC 217, PC 7, Coles
Charleston CUSD 1 — 5-11111 / 345-2106
410 W POLK AVE 61920
William Hill, supt.
HS, 1603 LINCOLN AVE 61920 — 3-00011 / 345-2196
Dean Tucker, prin.
JHS, 910 SMITH DR 61920 — 3-00100 / 345-2193
Tom Everett, prin.

Eastern Illinois University 61920 — 7-UC / 581-2011

Chatham, AC 217, PC 6, Sangamon
Ball Chatham CUSD 5 — 5-11111 / 483-2416
201 W MULBERRY ST 62629
Donald Kauerauf, supt.
Glenwood HS, RR 1 BOX 65A 62629 — 3-00011 / 483-2424
Michael Collins, prin.
Glenwood JHS, RR 1 BOX 66A 62629 — 3-00100 / 483-2481
Rick Taylor, prin.

Chenoa, AC 815, PC 4, McLean
Chenoa CUSD 9, 200 S 3RD AVE 61726 — 3-11111 / 945-7214
Alfred Smith, supt.
HS, DIVISION ST 61726 — 2-00011 / 945-2361
John Frattinger, prin.

Chester, AC 618, PC 6, Randolph
Chester CUSD 139 — 4-11111 / 826-4509
1901 SWANWICK ST 62233
Randy Dunn, supt.
HS, 1901 SWANWICK ST 62233 — 2-00011 / 826-2302
John Pearson, prin.

Chicago, AC 312, PC 12, Cook

City of Chicago SD 299 — 10-11111
  1819 W PERSHING RD 60609 — 535-8000
  Argie Johnson, supt.
Amundsen HS — 4-00011
  5110 N DAMEN AVE 60625 — 534-2320
  Edward Klunk, prin.
Austin HS, 231 N PINE AVE 60644 — 4-00011
  Decalvin Hughes, prin. — 534-6300
Bogan HS, 3939 W 79TH ST 60652 — 4-00011
  Joseph Rega, prin. — 535-2180
Bowen HS, 2710 E 89TH ST 60617 — 4-00011
  Gloria Walker, prin. — 535-6000
Calumet HS, 8131 S MAY ST 60620 — 3-00011
  Tam Hill, prin. — 535-3500
Carver Area HS — 3-00011
  13100 S DOTY AVE 60627 — 535-5250
  Willie Richie, prin.
Chicago HS for Agricultural Science — 2-00011
  3807 W 111TH ST 60655 — 535-2500
  Barbara Valerious, prin.
Chicago Vocational HS — 4-00011
  2100 E 87TH ST 60617 — 535-6100
  Betty Despenza-Green, prin.
Clemente Community Academy HS — 4-00011
  1147 N WESTERN AVE 60622 — 534-4000
  Lou Geraldi, prin.
Collins HS — 4-00011
  1313 S SACRAMENTO DR 60623 — 534-1500
  Clement Smith, prin.
Corliss HS, 821 E 103RD ST 60628 — 4-00011
  Edith Davis, prin. — 535-5115
Crane HS — 3-00011
  2245 W JACKSON BLVD 60612 — 534-7550
  Melver Scott, prin.
Cregier Vocational HS — 2-00011
  2040 W ADAMS ST 60612 — 534-7490
  Alfred Clark, prin.
Curie Metro HS — 5-00011
  4959 S ARCHER AVE 60632 — 535-2100
  Walter Pilditch, prin.
Dunbar Vocational HS — 4-00011
  3000 S KING DR 60616 — 534-9000
  Floyd Banks, prin.
Dusable HS, 4934 S WABASH AVE 60615 — 4-00011
  Charles Mingo, prin. — 535-1100
Englewood HS — 4-00011
  6201 S STEWART AVE 60621 — 535-3600
  Warner Birts, prin.
Farragut Career Academy HS — 4-00011
  2345 S CHRISTIANA AVE 60623 — 534-1300
  Edward Guerra, prin.
Fenger HS, 11220 S WALLACE ST 60628 — 4-00011
  Linda Layne, prin. — 535-5430
Flower Vocational HS — 3-00011
  3545 W FULTON BLVD 60624 — 534-6755
  Dorothy Williams, prin.
Forman HS — 4-00011
  3235 N LECLAIRE AVE 60641 — 534-3400
  John Garvey, prin.
Gage Park HS — 4-00011
  5630 S ROCKWELL ST 60629 — 535-9230
  Audrey Donaldson, prin.
Harlan Community Academy HS — 3-00011
  9652 S MICHIGAN AVE 60628 — 535-5400
  Barbara Edwards, prin.
Harper HS, 6520 S WOOD ST 60636 — 4-00011
  Richard Parker, prin. — 535-9150
Hirsch Metro HS — 3-00011
  7740 S INGLESIDE AVE 60619 — 535-3100
  Lonnie Jones, prin.
Hubbard HS, 6200 S HAMLIN AVE 60629 — 4-00011
  Charles Vietzen, prin. — 535-2200
Hyde Park Career Academy HS — 4-00011
  6220 S STONY ISLAND AVE 60637 — 535-0880
  Weldon Beverly, prin.
Jones Metropolitan HS — 3-00011
  606 S STATE ST 60605 — 534-8600
  Cozette Buckney, prin.
Juarez HS, 2150 S LAFLIN ST 60608 — 4-00011
  Jose Rodriguez, prin. — 534-7030
Julian HS, 10330 S ELIZABETH ST 60643 — 4-00011
  Willie Crittendon, prin. — 535-5170
Kelly HS — 4-00011
  4136 S CALIFORNIA AVE 60632 — 535-4900
  John Gelsomino, prin.
Kelvyn Park HS — 4-00011
  4343 W WRIGHTWOOD AVE 60639 — 534-4200
  Betzaida Figueroa, prin.
Kennedy HS, 6325 W 56TH ST 60638 — 4-00011
  Eva Nickolich, prin. — 535-2325
Kenwood Academy JSHS — 4-00111
  5015 S BLACKSTONE AVE 60615 — 535-1350
  Beverly LaCoste, prin.
King HS, 4445 S DREXEL BLVD 60653 — 4-00011
  Richard Smith, prin. — 535-1180
Lake View HS — 4-00011
  4015 N ASHLAND AVE 60613 — 534-5440
  Donna Macey, prin.
Lane Tech HS — 5-00011
  2501 W ADDISON ST 60618 — 534-5400
  David Schlichting, prin.
Lincoln Park HS — 4-00011
  2001 N ORCHARD ST 60614 — 534-8130
  Janis Todd, prin.
Lindblom Tech HS — 3-00011
  6130 S WOLCOTT AVE 60636 — 535-9300
  Cheryl Rutherford, prin.
Manley HS, 2935 W POLK ST 60612 — 3-00011
  Katherine Flanagan, prin. — 534-6900

Marshall Metro HS — 4-00011
  3250 W ADAMS ST 60624 — 534-6455
  Steve Newton, prin.
Mather HS, 5835 N LINCOLN AVE 60659 — 4-00011
  Arthur Cervinka, prin. — 534-2350
Morgan Park JSHS — 4-00111
  1744 W PRYOR AVE 60643 — 535-2550
  Charles Alexander, prin.
Near North Career Magnet HS — 3-00011
  1450 N LARRABEE ST 60610 — 534-8330
  Faye Grays, prin.
Orr Community Academy HS — 4-00011
  730 N PULASKI RD 60624 — 534-6500
  Cynthia Felton, prin.
Phillips Academy HS — 4-00011
  244 E PERSHING RD 60653 — 535-1603
  Juanita Tucker, prin.
Prosser Vocational HS — 4-00011
  2148 N LONG AVE 60639 — 534-3200
  Noreen Nagle, prin.
Richards Vocational HS — 3-00011
  5009 S LAFLIN ST 60609 — 535-4945
  Patrick Noonan, prin.
Robeson HS — 4-00011
  6835 S NORMAL BLVD 60621 — 535-3800
  Jacqueline Simmons, prin.
Roosevelt HS — 4-00011
  3436 W WILSON AVE 60625 — 534-5000
  Rafael Sanchez, prin.
Schurz HS — 5-00011
  3601 N MILWAUKEE AVE 60641 — 534-3420
  Sharon Bender, prin.
Senn Metropolitan Academy — 4-00011
  5900 N GLENWOOD AVE 60660 — 534-2365
  Christine Clayton, prin.
Simeon Vocational HS — 4-00011
  8235 S VINCENNES AVE 60620 — 535-3200
  Patricia Graham, prin.
South Shore HS — 4-00011
  7529 S CONSTANCE AVE 60649 — 535-6180
  Ed Washington, prin.
Steinmetz HS — 4-00011
  3030 N MOBILE AVE 60634 — 534-3030
  Constantine Kiamos, prin.
Sullivan JSHS — 4-00111
  6631 N BOSWORTH AVE 60626 — 534-2000
  Patricia Anderson, prin.
Taft HS, 6545 W HURLBUT ST 60631 — 4-00011
  William Watts, prin. — 534-1000
Tilden HS, 4747 S UNION AVE 60609 — 4-00011
  Hazel Steward, prin. — 535-1625
Von Steuben Metro HS — 4-00011
  5039 N KIMBALL AVE 60625 — 534-5100
  Harold Kiehm, prin.
Washington HS, 3535 E 114TH ST 60617 — 4-00011
  Reginald Brown, prin. — 535-5725
Wells Community Academy HS — 4-00011
  936 N ASHLAND AVE 60622 — 534-7010
  Carmen Martinez, prin.
Westinghouse Vocational HS — 4-00011
  3301 W FRANKLIN BLVD 60624 — 534-6400
  Stanton Payne, prin.
Young Magnet JSHS — 4-00111
  211 S LAFLIN ST 60607 — 534-7500
  Powhaten Collins, prin.
Morton Career Academy — Vo Tech
  431 N TROY ST 60612 — 534-6791
  Ana Marie Higginbotham, prin.
Albany Park Academy — 2-00100
  5039 N KIMBALL AVE 60625 — 534-5108
  Mary Lasher, prin.
Anderson Community Academy — 3-00100
  6315 S CLAREMONT AVE 60636 — 535-9070
  Helen Johnson, prin.
Arai MS, 900 W WILSON AVE 60640 — 3-00100
  Michele Krieger, prin. — 534-2610
Black Magnet IS — 2-01100
  9101 S EUCLID AVE 60617 — 535-6390
  Joyce Bristow, prin.
Burns MS — 4-01100
  2524 S CENTRAL PARK AVE 60623 — 534-1620
  Olga Villalba, prin.
Carver MS, 801 E 133RD PL 60627 — 3-01100
  Naomi Kilpatrick, prin. — 535-5656
Clark MS, 5101 W HARRISON ST 60644 — 3-00100
  Marietta Beverly, prin. — 534-6250
Daley East Branch MS — 2-00100
  4946 S PAULINA ST 60609 — 535-9219
  Steven Hara, prin.
De La Cruz MS, 2317 W 23RD 60608 — 2-00100
  Miguel Trujillo, prin. — 535-4585
Doolittle IS, 535 E 35TH ST 60616 — 2-01100
  Elisha Walker, prin. — 535-1040
Douglass MS, 543 N WALLER AVE 60644 — 3-00100
  Betty Smith, prin. — 534-6176
Dyett MS, 555 E 51ST ST 60615 — 3-00100
  Yvonne Minor, prin. — 535-1825
Evergreen Academy — 2-00100
  3737 S PAULINA ST 60609 — 535-4836
  Jerome Laz, prin.
Gompers MS, 12302 S STATE ST 60628 — 3-01100
  Blondean Davis, prin. — 535-5475
Hedges MS, 1954 W 48TH ST 60609 — 2-00100
  Armando Almendarez, prin. — 535-4680
Hope Community Academy — 3-01100
  5515 S LOWE AVE 60621 — 535-3160
  Joseph Lee, prin.
Irving Park MS — 2-00100
  3815 N KEDVALE AVE 60641 — 534-3750
  Carmen Sanchez, prin.

Lewis Branch MS — 2-01100
  5035 W NORTH AVE 60639 — 534-3370
  Pamela Dukes, prin.
Lowell MS, 3320 W HIRSCH ST 60651 — 3-01100
  Wilfredo Ortiz, prin. — 534-4300
Madero MS, 2832 W 24TH BLVD 60623 — 2-00100
  Rosa Ramirez, prin. — 534-1841
Marshall MS — 3-00100
  3900 N LAWNDALE AVE 60618 — 534-5200
  Sharon Hayes, prin.
Medill IS, 1326 W 14TH PL 60608 — 2-01100
  James Malles, prin. — 534-7760
Mitchell MS, 2233 W OHIO ST 60612 — 2-01100
  Deanna Rattner, prin. — 534-7655
Moos MS — 3-01100
  1711 N CALIFORNIA AVE 60647 — 534-4340
  Alice Peters, prin.
Piccolo MS, 1040 N KEELER AVE 60651 — 3-00100
  Thomas Stewart, prin. — 534-4565
Raster MS — 3-01100
  6936 S HERMITAGE AVE 60636 — 535-9144
  Earl Jeffrey, prin.
Schiller MS, 640 W SCOTT ST 60610 — 2-01100
  Marshall Taylor, prin. — 534-8490
Sullivan MS — 2-01100
  8255 S HOUSTON AVE 60617 — 535-6585
  Robert Esenberg, prin.
Tonti Branch MS — 2-00100
  4950 S LAPORTE AVE 60638 — 535-2000
  Maria Howell, prin.
Wirth Experimental JHS — 2-00100
  4959 S BLACKSTONE AVE 60615 — 535-1410
  James Johnson, prin.
Woodson North MS — 2-01100
  4414 S EVANS AVE 60653 — 535-1290
  William Taylor, prin.
Linne ES — 3-10100
  3221 N SACRAMENTO AVE 60618 — 534-5262
  Charles Giglio, prin.

Academy of Our Lady — 2-00011
  1309 W 95TH ST 60643 — 445-2300
  Sr. Miriam Cummings, prin.
Academy of the Sacred Heart/Hardey — 2-11111
  6250 N SHERIDAN RD 60660 — 262-4446
  Sr. Carol Campbell, prin.
Adler School of Professional Psychology — 2-UC
  65 E WACKER PL 60601 — 201-5900
American Academy of Art — 4-CC
  332 S MICHIGAN AVE FL 3 60604 — 939-3883
American Conservatory of Music, The — 2-UC
  16 N WABASH AVE 60602 — 263-4161
American Floral Art School — 2-CS
  529 S WABASH AVE # 600 60605 — 922-9328
American Medical Record Association — 2-HMS
  919 N MICHIGAN AVE # 1400 60611
American School — 2-HMS
  850 E 58TH ST 60637 — 947-3300
Archbishop Quigley HS — 2-00011
  103 E CHESTNUT ST 60611 — 787-9343
  Fr. John Daley, prin.
Archbishop Weber HS — 2-00011
  5252 W PALMER AVE 60639 — 637-7500
  Fr. Rog, prin.
Automotive Technical Institute — 1-CS
  5567 N ELSTON AVE 60630 — 792-8300
Bridgeport Catholic MS — 2-00100
  1040 W 32ND PL 60608 — 927-1041
  H. Barrientos, prin.
Brother Rice HS — 4-00011
  10001 S PULASKI RD 60642 — 779-3410
  Br. Michael Segvich, prin.
Cathedral HS, 751 N STATE ST 60610 — 2-00011
  John Callum, prin. — 642-8965
Catholic Theological Union — 2-UC
  5401 S CORNELL AVE 60615 — 324-8000
Chicago Academy for the Arts — 2-00011
  1010 W CHICAGO AVE 60622 — 421-0202
  Richard Odell, prin.
Chicago City-Wide College — 5-CC
  226 W JACKSON BLVD 60606 — 641-2595
Chicago College of Commerce — 6-CC
  11 E ADAMS ST 60603 — 236-3312
Chicago College of Osteopathic Medicine — 2-UC
  5200 S ELLIS AVE 60615 — 947-3000
Chicago Sch. of Professional Psychology — 2-UC
  806 S PLYMOUTH CT 60605 — 786-9443
Chicago S D A Academy — 2-11111
  7008 S MICHIGAN AVE 60637 — 873-3005
  Judith Fisher, prin.
Chicago State University — 5-UC
  9501 S KING DR 60628 — 995-2400
Chicago Theological Seminary — 2-UC
  5757 S UNIVERSITY AVE 60637 — 752-5757
College of Office Technology — 2-CS
  1514 W DIVISION ST # 2 60622 — 278-0042
Columbia College — 6-UC
  600 S MICHIGAN AVE 60605 — 663-1600
Computer Learning Center — 3-CS
  200 S MICHIGAN AVE LBBY 3 60604
  — 427-2700
Cook County Hospital — HSP
  1825 W HARRISON ST 60612 — 633-8533
Cooking & Hospitality Inst. of Chicago — 2-CS
  361 W CHESTNUT ST 60610 — 944-2725
Coyne American Institute — 2-CS
  1235 W FULLERTON AVE 60614 — 935-2520
De La Salle Institute — 3-00011
  3455 S WABASH AVE 60616 — 842-7355
  James Gay, prin.

De Paul University 7-UC
1 E JACKSON BLVD 60604 362-8850
De Paul University 6-UC
2323 N SEMINARY AVE 60614
DeVry Institute of Technology 3-UC
3300 N CAMPBELL AVE 60618 929-6550
East-West University 2-UC
816 S MICHIGAN AVE 60605 939-0111
Francis Parker S 3-11111
330 W WEBSTER AVE 60614 549-0172
Timothy Burns, prin.
Good Counsel HS 3-00011
3900 W PETERSON AVE 60659 478-3655
Sr. Mary Knipple, prin.
Gordon Technical HS 4-00011
3633 N CALIFORNIA AVE 60618 539-3600
Casimir Kozlik, prin.
Hales Franciscan HS 2-00011
4930 S COTTAGE GROVE AVE 60615 285-8400
Joseph Moffa, prin.
Harold Washington College 5-CC
30 E LAKE ST 60601 781-9430
Harrington Institute of Interior Design 2-UC
410 S MICHIGAN AVE 60605 939-4975
Harry S. Truman College 5-CC
1145 W WILSON AVE 60640 989-6125
Harvard S, 4731 S ELLIS AVE 60615 2-11111
Stephanie Clark, prin. 624-0394
Holy Cross Hospital HSP
2701 W 68TH ST 60629 471-5501
Holy Name Cathedral S 1-01100
751 N STATE ST 60610 337-3889
Margaret Grace, prin.
Holy Trinity HS 2-00011
1443 W DIVISION ST 60622 278-4212
Br. Kenneth Haders, prin.
Ida Crown Jewish Academy 2-00111
2828 W PRATT BLVD 60645 973-1450
Rabbi Michael Myers, prin.
IIT Kent College of Law 3-UC
77 S WACKER DR 60606
Illinois College of Optometry 3-UC
3241 S MICHIGAN AVE 60616 225-1700
Illinois Institute of Technology 5-UC
3300 S FEDERAL ST 60616 567-3001
Illinois Medical Training Center 3-CS
162 N STATE ST 60601 782-2061
Illinois School/Professional Psychology 2-UC
220 S STATE ST 60604 341-6500
Institute for Clinical Social Work 1-UC
30 N MICHIGAN AVE 60602 726-8480
International Academy Merch. & Design 4-CC
1 N STATE ST STE 400 60602 541-3910
John Marshall Law School 4-UC
315 S PLYMOUTH CT 60604 427-2737
Josephinum HS 2-00011
1501 N OAKLEY BLVD 60622 276-1261
Sr. Bonnie Kearny, prin.
Keller Graduate School of Management 4-UC
10 S RIVERSIDE PLZ 60606 454-0880
Kennedy-King College 4-CC
6800 S WENTWORTH AVE 60621 962-3200
Lake Forest Graduate Sch. of Management 2-UC
230 S LA SALLE ST 60604 435-5330
Latin School of Chicago 3-11111
59 W NORTH BLVD 60610 573-4500
Frank Hogan, prin.
Leo HS, 7901 S SANGAMON ST 60620 2-00011
Robert Foster, prin. 224-9600
Lexington Inst. of Hostpitality Careers 1-CC
10840 S WESTERN AVE 60643 779-3800
Liberty School Christian S 2-11111
6207 S UNIVERSITY AVE 60637 643-0123
James May, prin.
LifeSource HSP
1255 N GREENVIEW AVE 60622 298-9660
Louis A. Weiss Memorial Hospital HSP
4646 N MARINE DR 60640 878-8700
Lourdes HS, 4034 W 56TH ST 60629 3-00011
Mary Iannucilli, prin. 581-2555
Loyola University 2-UC
6525 N SHERIDAN RD 60626
Loyola University - Mundelein College 3-UC
6525 N SHERIDAN RD 60626 262-8100
Loyola University of Chicago 7-UC
820 N MICHIGAN AVE 60611 915-6402
Lutheran School of Theology at Chicago 2-UC
1100 E 55TH ST 60615 753-0700
Luther HS North 2-00011
5700 W BERTEAU AVE 60634 286-3600
Stephen Kurek, prin.
Luther HS South, 3130 W 87TH ST 60652 2-00011
Melvin Schroeder, prin. 737-1416
MacCormac Junior College 2-CC
506 S WABASH AVE 60605 922-1884
Madonna HS 2-00011
4055 W BELMONT AVE 60641 282-2552
Sr. Carol Schommer, prin.
Malcolm X College 3-CC
1900 W VAN BUREN ST 60612 942-3000
Maranatha Christian Academy 2-11111
115 W 108TH ST 60628 264-7702
Betty Millsap, prin.
Maria HS 4-00011
6727 S CALIFORNIA AVE 60629 925-8686
Barbara McKee, prin.
Marist HS, 4200 W 115TH ST 60655 4-00011
Br. Lawrence Lavallee, prin. 881-6360
McCormick Theological Seminary 2-UC
5555 S WOODLAWN AVE 60637 947-6300

Meadville/Lombard Theological School 1-UC
5701 S WOODLAWN AVE 60637 753-4065
Medical Careers Institute 2-CS
116 S MICHIGAN AVE 60603 782-9804
Michael Reese Hospital & Medical Center HSP
LAKESHORE DR AT 31ST ST 60616 791-3769
Midwestern Christian Academy 2-11111
3465 N CICERO AVE 60641 685-1106
Vernon Lee, prin.
Montay College 2-CC
3750 W PETERSON AVE 60659 539-1919
Moody Bible Institute 4-UC
820 N LA SALLE DR 60610 329-4000
Morgan Park Academy 2-11111
2153 W 111TH ST 60643 881-6700
David Jones, prin.
Mother McAuley Liberal Arts HS 4-00011
3737 W 99TH ST 60642 881-6500
Sr. Corrine Raven, prin.
Mt. Carmel HS 3-00011
6410 S DANTE AVE 60637 324-1020
Fr. Andres, prin.
Native American Educational Services 1-UC
2838 W PETERSON AVE 60659 761-5000
NEC-Bryman Campus 2-CS
17 N STATE ST STE 1800 60602 368-4911
Northeastern Illinois University 6-UC
5500 N SAINT LOUIS AVE 60625 583-4050
North Park Coll. & Theological Seminary 3-UC
3225 W FOSTER AVE 60625 509-2330
Northwestern Business College 4-CC
4829 N LIPPS AVE 60630 777-4220
Northwestern University 3-UC
303 E CHICAGO AVE 60611
Notre Dame HS 3-00011
3000 N MANGO AVE 60634 622-9494
John Balderman, prin.
Olive-Harvey College 4-CC
10001 S WOODLAWN AVE 60628 568-3700
Our Lady of Tepeyac HS 2-00011
2228 S WHIPPLE ST 60623 522-0023
Sr. Kathryn Wojcik, prin.
Pathfinder School 2-CS
19 E 21ST ST 60616 842-7272
PBS Training Center 2-CS
529 S WABASH AVE FL 2 60605 427-9006
Providence-St. Mel HS 3-00111
119 S CENTRAL PARK BLVD 60624 722-4600
Paul Adams, prin.
PTC Career Institute 2-CS
11 E ADAMS ST STE 400 60603 922-2005
Ravenswood Hospital Medical Center HSP
4550 N WINCHESTER AVE 60640 878-4300
Ray College of Design 3-UC
401 N WABASH AVE 60611 280-3500
Resurrection HS 4-00011
7500 W TALCOTT AVE 60631 775-6616
Therese Fenney, prin.
Richard J. Daley College 5-CC
7500 S PULASKI RD 60652 735-3000
Robert Morris College 4-UC
180 N LA SALLE ST 60601 836-4888
Roosevelt University 5-UC
430 S MICHIGAN AVE 60605 341-3500
Rush Presbyterian St. Lukes Medical Ctr. HSP
1753 W CONGRESS PKY 60612 942-5474
Rush University 4-UC
1653 W CONGRESS PKY 60612 942-5474
Sacred Heart HS 2-00011
6250 N SHERIDAN RD 60660 262-4446
Sr. Sarah Brennan, prin.
St. Augustine College 4-CC
1333 W ARGYLE ST 60640 878-8756
St. Barbara HS 2-00011
2867 S THROOP ST 60608 842-0042
Diane Rzasa, prin.
St. Benedict HS 2-00011
3900 N LEAVITT ST 60618 539-0066
Fr. Heidenrich, prin.
St. Francis De Sales HS 3-00011
10155 S EWING AVE 60617 731-7272
Walter Schultz, prin.
St. Gregory HS 2-00011
1677 W BRYN MAWR AVE 60660 907-2100
Thomas Bearden, prin.
St. Ignatius College Prep HS 4-00011
1076 W ROOSEVELT RD 60608 421-5900
James Lalley, prin.
St. Joseph HS 2-00011
4831 S HERMITAGE AVE 60609 927-3886
Rick Ruhl, prin.
St. Martin De Porres 2-00011
250 E 111TH ST 60628 995-3700
Charlene Szumilas, prin.
St. Mary of Providence School HND
4200 N AUSTIN AVE 60634
St. Patrick HS 3-00011
5900 W BELMONT AVE 60634 282-8844
Joseph Schmidt, prin.
St. Rita HS, 7740 S WESTERN AVE 60620 4-00011
Joseph Bamberger, prin. 925-6600
St. Scholastica HS 2-00011
7416 N RIDGE BLVD 60645 764-5715
Antonia Bouillette, prin.
St. Xavier College 4-UC
3700 W 103RD ST 60655 779-3300
Scholl College of Podiatric Medicine 2-UC
1001 N DEARBORN ST 60610 280-2940
School of the Art Institute of Chicago 4-UC
37 S WABASH AVE 60603 889-5136

South Chicago Community Hospital HSP
2320 E 93RD ST 60617 978-2000
Spertus College of Judaica 2-UC
618 S MICHIGAN AVE 60605 922-9012
Tabernacle Christian Academy 3-11111
1233 W 109TH PL 60643 445-3007
Rev. Booker, prin.
Taylor Business Institute 3-CS
36 S STATE ST STE 800 60603 236-6400
Telshe Yeshiva-Chicago 2-UC
3535 W FOSTER AVE 60625 463-7738
Tyler School of Secretarial Sciences 2-CS
8030 S KEDZIE AVE 60652 436-5050
University of Chicago 7-UC
5801 S ELLIS AVE 60637 702-8001
University of Chicago Lab S 4-11111
1362 E 59TH ST 60637 702-9450
Lucinda Katz, prin.
University of Illinois at Chicago 7-UC
PO BOX 5220 60680 996-3000
VanderCook College of Music 1-UC
3209 S MICHIGAN AVE 60616 225-6288
Wilbur Wright College North 5-CC
4300 N NARRAGANSETT AVE 60634 794-3182

Chicago Heights, AC 708, PC 8, Cook
Bloom Twp. HSD 206 5-00011
100 W 10TH ST 60411 755-7010
Richard Felicetti, supt.
Bloom HS, 101 W 10TH ST 60411 4-00011
Frank Nardi, prin. 755-1122
Bloom Trail HS 4-00011
22331 COTTAGE GROVE AVE 60411 758-7000
Gerald Lauritsen, prin.

Chicago Heights SD 170 5-11100
30 W 16TH ST 60411 756-4165
William McGee, supt.
Washington JHS, 25 W 16TH PL 60411 2-00100
Michael Stabile, prin. 756-4841

Marian Catholic HS 4-00011
666 ASHLAND AVE 60411 755-7565
Sr. Mary McCaughey, prin.
Prairie State College 4-CC
PO BOX 487 60411 756-3110

Chicago Ridge, AC 708, PC 7, Cook
Chicago Ridge SD 127-5 4-11100
10835 LOMBARD AVE 60415 636-2000
Bruce Lane, supt.
Finley JHS, 10835 LOMBARD AVE 60415 2-00100
Michael Backer, prin. 636-2005

Chillicothe, AC 309, PC 6, Peoria
Illinois Valley Central Unit SD 321 4-11111
PO BOX 298 61523 274-5418
Larry Williams, supt.
Illinois Valley Central HS 3-00011
1300 W SYCAMORE ST 61523 274-5481
Steve Garrison, prin.
JHS, 914 W TRUITT 61523 2-01100
Richard Greene, prin. 274-6266

Chrisman, AC 217, PC 4, Edgar
Edgar County CUSD 6 2-11111
RR 2 BOX 1A 61924 269-2513
Leo Sherman, supt.
HS, RR 2 BOX 1A 61924 2-00011
Roger Lawson, prin. 269-2823

Christopher, AC 618, PC 5, Franklin
Christopher Community HSD 38 2-00011
901 W ERNESTINE AVE 62822 724-9461
Richard Cook, supt.
Christopher Comm. HS 2-00011
901 W ERNESTINE AVE 62822 724-9461
Richard Cook, prin.

Cicero, AC 708, PC 8, Cook
J. S. Morton HSD 201 6-00011
2423 S AUSTIN BLVD 60650 656-2300
Robert Giles, supt.
Morton East HS 5-00011
2423 S AUSTIN BLVD 60650 656-2300
Cynthia Baranowski, prin.
Other Schools – See Berwyn

Morton College 4-CC
3801 S CENTRAL AVE 60650 656-8000

Cisne, AC 618, PC 3, Wayne
North Wayne CUSD 200 3-11111
PO BOX 235 62823 673-2151
Joyce Carson, supt.
Cisne HS, PO BOX 70 62823 2-00011
Randy Smith, prin. 673-2154
MS, PO BOX 69 62823 2-01100
Joyce Carson, prin. 673-2156

Cissna Park, AC 815, PC 3, Iroquois
Cissna Park CUSD 6, PO BOX 1 60924 2-11111
Daniel Heinold, supt. 457-2171
HS, PO BOX 1 60924 2-00011
Jeffrey Maurer, prin. 457-2171
JHS, PO BOX 1 60924 1-00100
Jeffrey Maurer, prin. 457-2171

Clarendon Hills, AC 708, PC 6, Du Page
Maercker SD 60 4-11100
5800 HOLMES AVE 60514 323-2086
David Lundeen, supt.
Westview Hills MS, 630 65TH ST 60514 2-00100
Greg Ostrowski, prin. 963-1450

Clay City, AC 618, PC 3, Clay
Clay City CUSD 10 — 2-11111
  PO BOX 542 62824 — 676-1431
  Jack Dunker, supt.
Clay City HS, PO BOX 405 62824 — 2-00011
  Jack Dunker, prin. — 676-1522
JHS, PO BOX 545 62824 — 2-00100
  Cecil Cochran, prin. — 676-1521

Clifton, AC 815, PC 4, Iroquois
Central CUSD 4, PO BOX 637 60927 — 4-11111
  Richard Bukowski, supt. — 694-2231
Central HS — 2-00011
  3100 N CENTRAL HIGH SCH RD 60927 — 694-2321
  Arlyn Rabideau, prin.
Nash JHS — 2-00100
  3100 N CENTRAL HIGH SCH RD 60927 — 694-2323
  Jerome Pankey, prin.

Clinton, AC 217, PC 6, De Witt
Clinton CUSD 15 — 4-11111
  115 W JOHNSON ST 61727 — 935-8321
  Gary Archey, supt.
HS, 1200 STATE ROUTE 54 W 61727 — 3-00011
  Jerry Bauersachs, prin. — 935-8337
JHS, 401 N CENTER ST 61727 — 3-00100
  Larry Bethard, prin. — 935-2103

Coal City, AC 815, PC 5, Grundy
Coal City CUSD 1 — 4-11111
  100 S BAIMA ST 60416 — 634-2287
  Jerry Arthur, supt.
HS, 655 W DIVISION ST 60416 — 2-00011
  Michael Throneburg, prin. — 634-2396
MS, 305 E DIVISION ST 60416 — 3-01100
  James Micetich, prin. — 634-2182

Cobden, AC 618, PC 4, Union
Cobden Unit SD 17 — 3-11111
  413 N APPLEKNOCKER ST 62920 — 893-2313
  John Gardner, supt.
HS, 413 N APPLEKNOCKER ST 62920 — 2-00011
  Robert Schluter, prin. — 893-4031
JHS, 413 N APPLEKNOCKER ST 62920 — 1-00100
  Robert Schluter, prin. — 893-4031

Colchester, AC 309, PC 4, McDonough
Colchester CUSD 180 — 3-11111
  204 S HUN ST 62326 — 776-3180
  James Taylor, supt.
HS, 600 S HUN ST 62326 — 2-00011
  Patricia Leezer, prin. — 776-3220
JHS, PO BOX 356 62326 — 1-00100
  Patricia Leezer, prin. — 776-3220

Colfax, AC 309, PC 3, McLean
Ridgeview CUSD 19 — 3-11111
  RR 2 BOX 49A 61728 — 723-5111
  Donald Hahn, supt.
Ridgeview HS, RR 2 BOX 49A 61728 — 2-00011
  C. Winn, prin. — 723-2951
Ridgeview JHS, RR 2 BOX 49A 61728 — 2-00100
  C. Winn, prin. — 723-2951

Collinsville, AC 618, PC 7, Madison
Collinsville CUSD 10 — 6-11111
  201 W CLAY ST 62234 — 346-6350
  John Renfro, supt.
HS, 2201 S MORRISON AVE 62234 — 4-00011
  Ron Ganschinietz, prin. — 346-6320
North JHS, 1841 VANDALIA ST 62234 — 3-00100
  John Denton, prin. — 346-6311

Columbia, AC 618, PC 6, Monroe
Columbia CUSD 4 — 4-11111
  100 PARKVIEW DR 62236 — 281-4772
  Jack Turner, supt.
HS, 100 PARKVIEW DR 62236 — 2-00011
  Dennis Patton, prin. — 281-5147
MS, 113 S RAPP AVE 62236 — 2-00100
  Roger Chamberlain, prin. — 281-4993

Concord, AC 217, PC 2, Morgan
Triopia CUSD 27, RR 1 BOX 141A 62631 — 2-11111
  Larry Armstrong, supt. — 457-2283
Triopia JSHS, RR 1 BOX 141A 62631 — 2-00111
  Larry Armstrong, prin. — 457-2281

Coulterville, AC 618, PC 3, Randolph
Coulterville Unit SD 1 — 2-11111
  PO BOX 386 62237 — 758-2338
  Ronald Mazander, supt.
HS, PO BOX 386 62237 — 1-00011
  Les Oyler, prin. — 758-2338
JHS, PO BOX 386 62237 — 1-00100
  Les Oyler, prin. — 758-2338

Country Club Hills, AC 708, PC 7, Cook
Bremen Community HSD 228
  Supt. — See Midlothian
Hillcrest HS — 4-00011
  17401 CRAWFORD AVE 60478 — 799-7000
  Gwendolyn Lee, prin.
Country Club Hills SD 160 — 4-11100
  4411 185TH ST 60478 — 957-6200
  Edward L. Chartraw, supt.
Southwood JHS, 18635 LEE ST 60478 — 3-01100
  Hugh Jackson, prin. — 957-6240

Cowden, AC 217, PC 3, Shelby
Cowden-Herrick Community HSD 188 — 2-00011
  PO BOX 188 62422 — 783-2126
  Lenard Defend, supt.

Cowden-Herrick HS — 2-00011
  PO BOX 188 62422 — 783-2125
  Larry Renshaw, prin.

Crescent City, AC 815, PC 3, Iroquois
Crescent-Iroquois Community SD 252 — 1-00011
  PO BOX 190 60928 — 683-2141
  Gregory Laplante, supt.
Crescent-Iroquois HS — 1-00011
  PO BOX 10 60928 — 683-2161
  Kathleen Redeker, prin.

Crest Hill, AC 815, PC 7, Will
Chaney-Monge SD 88 — 2-11100
  400 ELSIE AVE 60435 — 722-6673
  August Tomac, supt.
Monge JHS, 400 ELSIE AVE 60435 — 2-00100
  Cathleen Davis, prin. — 722-6673

Crestwood, AC 708, PC 7, Cook
Blue Island SD 130
  Supt. — See Blue Island
Hale MS, 5220 135TH ST 60445 — 2-00100
  Michael Korsak, prin. — 385-6690

Crete, AC 708, PC 6, Will
Crete-Monee CUSD 201U — 5-11111
  1742 S DIXIE HWY 60417 — 672-2670
  Steve Humphrey, supt.
Crete-Monee HS — 4-00011
  760 W EXCHANGE ST 60417 — 672-2800
  Printiss Lea, prin.
Crete-Monee JHS — 3-00100
  1500 SANGAMON ST 60417 — 672-2700
  J. Crawford, prin.

Creve Coeur, AC 309, PC 6, Tazewell
Creve Coeur SD 76 — 3-11100
  300 N HIGHLAND AVE 61611 — 698-3600
  Dean Peyton, supt.
Parkview JHS — 2-01100
  800 GROVELAND ST 61611 — 698-3610
  Don Bockler, prin.

Crystal Lake, AC 815, PC 7, McHenry
Community HSD 155 — 5-00011
  1 S VIRGINIA ST 60014 — 455-8500
  Joseph Saban, supt.
Crystal Lake Central HS — 4-00011
  45 W FRANKLIN ST 60014 — 459-2505
  John Mackie, prin.
Crystal Lake South HS — 4-00011
  1200 MCHENRY AVE 60014 — 455-3860
  Lawrence O'Meara, prin.
Other Schools – See Cary

Crystal Lake CCSD 47 — 6-11100
  221 LIBERTY DR 60014 — 459-6070
  Richard Bernotas, supt.
Lundahl JHS, 560 NASH RD 60014 — 4-00100
  Richard Carlstedt, prin. — 459-5971
North JHS, 170 N OAK ST 60014 — 3-00100
  Dennis Rasmussen, prin. — 459-9210

McHenry County College — 4-CC
  6200 NORTHWEST HWY RM 415 60014 — 455-3700

Cuba, AC 309, PC 4, Fulton
Fulton County CUSD 3 — 3-11111
  669 E MAIN ST 61427 — 785-5021
  Charles Fleming, supt.
HS, 652 E MAIN ST 61427 — 2-00011
  Douglas Foster, prin. — 785-5023
JHS, PO BOX 50 61427 — 2-01100
  Daryle Coleman, prin. — 785-5023

Cullom, AC 815, PC 3, Livingston
Tri-Point CUSD 6-J
  Supt. — See Kempton
Tri-Point HS, PO BOX 316 60929 — 2-00011
  Mary Kneiss, prin. — 253-6299

Dakota, AC 815, PC 3, Stephenson
Dakota CUSD 201 — 3-11111
  PO BOX 128 61018 — 449-2832
  James Fields, supt.
HS, PO BOX 128 61018 — 2-00011
  Debra Keith, prin. — 449-2812
JHS, PO BOX 128 61018 — 2-00100
  Debra Keith, prin. — 449-2812

Dallas City, AC 217, PC 4, Hancock
Dallas City CUSD 336 — 2-11111
  203 E 4TH ST 62330 — 852-3203
  Robert Clifton, supt.
HS, 203 E 4TH ST 62330 — 2-00011
  Don Brent, prin. — 852-3202

Danville, AC 217, PC 8, Vermilion
Community Unit SD 76
  Supt. — See Fithian
Newtown MS, RR 1 BOX 226A 61832 — 2-00011
  Michael Waters, prin. — 443-2883

Danville CCSD 118 — 6-11111
  516 N JACKSON ST 61832 — 431-5406
  David Fields, supt.
HS, 202 E FAIRCHILD ST 61832 — 4-00011
  Ellen Russell, prin. — 431-5461
North Ridge MS — 3-00100
  1619 N JACKSON ST 61832 — 431-5505
  Phillip Smith, prin.
South View MS, 133 E 9TH ST 61832 — 3-00100
  George Schildt, prin. — 431-5500

Danville Area Community College — 4-CC
  2000 E MAIN ST 61832 — 443-1811
Schlarman HS — 2-00011
  2112 N VERMILION ST 61832 — 442-2725
  James Monfredini, prin.
United Samaritans Medical Center — HSP
  812 N LOGAN AVE 61832 — 443-5238

Darien, AC 708, PC 7, Du Page
Cass SD 63, 8502 BAILEY RD 60561 — 3-11100
  Robert Leli, supt. — 985-2000
Cass JHS, 8502 BAILEY RD 60561 — 2-01100
  Harry Bohn, prin. — 985-1900

Darien SD 61, 7414 S CASS AVE 60561 — 4-11100
  John Nothacker, supt. — 968-7505
Eisenhower JHS, 1410 75TH ST 60561 — 2-00100
  Joseph Pederson, prin. — 964-5200

Hinsdale Twp. HSD 86
  Supt. — See Hinsdale
Hinsdale Twp. HS-South — 4-00011
  7401 CLARENDON HILLS RD 60561 — 887-1730
  Joseph Dalpiaz, prin.

Decatur, AC 217, PC 8, Macon
Decatur SD 61 — 7-11111
  101 W CERRO GORDO ST 62523 — 424-3000
  Roy Ragsdale, supt.
HS, 1 EDUCATIONAL PARK 62526 — 4-00011
  J. Foster, prin. — 424-3256
Eisenhower HS, 1200 S 16TH ST 62521 — 4-00011
  Anthony Harris, prin. — 424-3100
MacArthur HS — 4-00011
  1155 N FAIRVIEW AVE 62522 — 424-3156
  Gary Hunt, prin.
Jefferson MS — 3-00100
  4735 E CANTRELL ST 62521 — 424-3190
  Shirley Shaw, prin.
Mound MS, 3789 N WATER ST 62526 — 3-00100
  David Geibel, prin. — 424-3113
Roosevelt MS, 701 W GRAND AVE 62522 — 3-00100
  Mary Wortman, prin. — 424-3215

Decatur Christian S — 2-11111
  3770 N WATER ST 62526 — 877-5636
  Randall Thacker, prin.
Decatur Memorial Hospital — HSP
  2300 N EDWARD ST 62526 — 876-8121
Millikin University — 4-UC
  1184 W MAIN ST 62522 — 800-373-7733
Richland Community College — 4-CC
  1 COLLEGE PARK 62521 — 875-7200
St. Theresa HS, 2710 N WATER ST 62526 — 2-00011
  Lowell Brosamer, prin. — 875-2431

Deerfield, AC 708, PC 7, Lake
Deerfield SD 109 — 4-11100
  517 DEERFIELD RD 60015 — 945-1844
  Glenn McGee, supt.
Caruso JHS — 2-00100
  1801 MONTGOMERY RD 60015 — 945-8430
  Alvin Cohen, prin.
Shepard JHS, 440 GROVE AVE 60015 — 2-00100
  Jay Monier, prin. — 948-0620
Township HSD 113
  Supt. — See Highland Park
HS, 1959 WAUKEGAN RD 60015 — 4-00011
  John Scornavacco, prin. — 432-6510

Trinity College — 3-UC
  2077 HALF DAY RD 60015 — 948-8980
Trinity Evangelical Divinity School — 3-UC
  2065 HALF DAY RD 60015 — 800-345-8337

Deer Grove, AC 815, PC 1, Whiteside
Tampico CUSD 4
  Supt. — See Tampico
Hahanaman MS, PO BOX 68 61243 — 1-00100
  James Hochstatter, prin. — 438-5353

De Kalb, AC 815, PC 8, De Kalb
De Kalb CUSD 428, 901 S 4TH ST 60115 — 5-11111
  Robert Williams, supt. — 754-2350
HS, 1515 S 4TH ST 60115 — 4-00011
  Jerome Dunbar, prin. — 754-2100
Huntley MS, 821 S 7TH ST 60115 — 3-00100
  William Sanders, prin. — 754-2241

Northern Illinois University 60115 — 7-UC
   — 753-1271

De Land, AC 217, PC 2, Piatt
Deland-Weldon CUSD 57, RR 1 61839 — 2-11111
  Larry Baker, supt. — 736-2311
Deland-Weldon HS — 1-00011
  RR 1 BOX 47 61839 — 664-3314
  Larry Baker, prin.
Other Schools – See Weldon

Delavan, AC 309, PC 4, Tazewell
Delavan CUSD 703 — 3-11111
  907 LOCUST ST 61734 — 244-8283
  Richard Dutton, supt.
HS, 907 LOCUST ST 61734 — 2-00011
  Lawrence Carlton, prin. — 244-8285
JHS, 907 LOCUST ST 61734 — 1-00100
  Linda Brown, prin. — 244-8283

Depue, AC 815, PC 4, Bureau
DePue Unit SD 103 — 2-11111
  PO BOX 675 61322 — 447-2608
  Lindell Croft, supt.

HS, 204 PLEASANT DR   61322 | 2-00011
Terry Nelson, prin. | 447-2324

Des Plaines, AC 708, PC 8, Cook
Community Consolidated SD 59
Supt. — See Arlington Heights
Friendship JHS | 3-00100
550 ELIZABETH LN   60018 | 593-4350
Richard Jenness, prin.

Des Plaines CCSD 62 | 5-11100
777 E ALGONQUIN RD   60016 | 824-1136
(—), supt.
Algonquin JHS | 2-00100
767 E ALGONQUIN RD   60016 | 824-1205
Raymond Gunn, prin.
Chippewa JHS, 123 N 8TH AVE   60016 | 2-00100
John Pacay, prin. | 824-1503
Iroquois JHS, 1836 E TOUHY AVE   60018 | 2-00100
Jay Matthiesen, prin. | 824-1308

Maine Twp. HSD 207
Supt. — See Park Ridge
Maine West HS, 1755 S WOLF RD   60018 | 4-00011
James Coburn, prin. | 827-6176

Oakton Community College | 6-CC
1600 E GOLF RD   60016 | 635-1600

Dieterich, AC 217, PC 3, Effingham
Dieterich CUSD 30 | 3-11111
PO BOX 187   62424 | 925-5248
Bill McClain, supt.
JSHS, PO BOX 187   62424 | 2-00111
Daniel Sarver, prin. | 925-5247

Divernon, AC 217, PC 4, Sangamon
Divernon CUSD 13 | 2-11111
PO BOX 20   62530 | 628-3414
Lantz Stein, supt.
HS, PO BOX 20   62530 | 1-00011
Donald Beard, prin. | 628-3414

Dixon, AC 815, PC 7, Lee
Dixon Unit SD 170 | 5-11111
1335 FRANKLIN GROVE RD   61021 | 284-7722
Gerald Mitchell, supt.
HS, 300 LINCOLN STATUE DR   61021 | 3-00011
Mike Brunick, prin. | 284-7723
Madison MS, 620 DIVISION ST   61021 | 3-00100
Robert Wasson, prin. | 284-7725

Faith Christian S | 2-11111
7571 S RIDGE RD   61021 | 652-4806
James German, prin.
Jack Mabley Development Center | HND
1120 WASHINGTON AVE   61021 | 288-8300
Sauk Valley Community College | 4-CC
RR 1   61021 | 288-5511

Dolton, AC 708, PC 7, Cook
Dolton SD 148, PO BOX 160   60419 | 4-11100
Dorothea Fitzgerald, supt. | 841-2290
Lincoln JHS, 14151 LINCOLN AVE   60419 | 2-00100
Judy Broucek, prin. | 849-1318
Roosevelt JHS | 2-00100
14600 LA SALLE ST   60419 | 849-0881
Joseph Schissler, prin.

Dolton SD 149 | 5-11100
15141 DORCHESTER AVE   60419 | 841-9504
James Cunneen, supt.
Other Schools – See Calumet City

Thornton Twp. HSD 205
Supt. — See Harvey
Thornridge HS | 4-00011
15000 COTTAGE GROVE AVE   60419 | 841-5180
Barbara Palmer, prin.

Dongola, AC 618, PC 3, Union
Dongola Unit SD 66 | 2-11111
PO BOX 190   62926 | 827-3841
Steve Karraker, supt.
HS, RR 1 BOX 190   62926 | 2-00011
Richard Gray, prin. | 827-3524
JHS, RR 1 BOX 190   62926 | 1-00100
Richard Gray, prin. | 827-3524

Donovan, AC 815, PC 2, Iroquois
Donovan CUSD 3, PO BOX 186   60931 | 2-11111
Stewart Hammel, supt. | 486-7395
JSHS, PO BOX 186   60931 | 2-00111
Steve Binnchette, prin. | 486-7395

Downers Grove, AC 708, PC 8, Du Page
Center Cass SD 66 | 4-11100
300 MANNING RD   60516 | 971-3344
Richard Motuelle, supt.
Lakeview JHS | 2-00100
701 PLAINFIELD RD   60516 | 985-2700
William Ward, prin.

Community HSD 99 | 5-00011
6301 SPRINGSIDE AVE   60516 | 719-5400
David Eblen, supt.
Downers Grove North HS | 4-00011
4436 MAIN ST   60515 | 852-0400
James Freese, prin.
Downers Grove South HS | 5-00011
1436 NORFOLK ST   60516 | 852-0600
Craig Zeck, prin.

Downers Grove SD 58 | 6-11100
1860 63RD ST   60516 | 719-5800
Roger Garvelink, supt.
Herrick JHS | 2-00100
4435 MIDDAUGH AVE   60515 | 719-5810
Robert Paolicchi, prin.
O'Neill MS, 635 59TH ST   60516 | 3-00100
Richard Russell, prin. | 719-5815

Chicago College of Osteopathic Medicine | 2-UC
555 31ST ST   60515 | 971-6080
Marquette Manor Baptist Academy | 2-11111
333 75TH ST   60516 – Ron Allen, prin. | 964-5363

Downs, AC 309, PC 3, McLean
Tri-Valley CUSD 3 | 3-11111
PO BOX 195   61736 | 378-2351
Louie Boward, supt.
Tri-Valley HS, PO BOX 138   61736 | 2-00011
Dennis Moll, prin. | 378-2911
Tri-Valley JHS, PO BOX 138   61736 | 2-00100
Dennis Moll, prin. | 378-2911

Dundee, AC 708, PC 5, Kane
Dundee CUSD 300
Supt. — See Carpentersville
MS | 3-00100
37W450 STATE ROUTE 72   60118 | 426-1485
Walter Hay, prin.

Dunlap, AC 309, PC 3, Peoria
Dunlap CUSD 323 | 4-11111
PO BOX 408   61525 | 243-7716
William Collier, supt.
HS, PO BOX 275   61525 | 3-00011
S. Cassady, prin. | 243-7751
Pioneer JHS, PO BOX 248   61525 | 2-00100
Harvey Varness, prin. | 243-7778

Dupo, AC 618, PC 5, St. Clair
Dupo CUSD 196, 600 LOUISA AVE   62239 | 4-11111
George Taubenheim, supt. | 286-3812
HS, 600 LOUISA AVE   62239 | 2-00011
William Reynolds, prin. | 286-3214
JHS, 600 LOUISA AVE   62239 | 2-00100
William Reynolds, prin. | 286-3214

Du Quoin, AC 618, PC 6, Perry
Duquoin CUSD 300 | 4-11111
31 S MULBERRY ST   62832 | 542-3856
Tom Bock, supt.
HS, 500 E SOUTH ST   62832 | 3-00011
Gary Kelly, prin. | 542-4744
Ward MS, 120 E SPRING ST   62832 | 3-01100
Leon Longshore, prin. | 542-2646

Durand, AC 815, PC 4, Winnebago
Durand CUSD 322 | 3-11111
PO BOX 398   61024 | 248-2171
Lori Zbikowski, supt.
HS, PO BOX 398   61024 | 2-00011
Don Lamm, prin. | 248-2171
JHS, PO BOX 398   61024 | 2-00100
Donald Lamm, prin. | 248-2171

Dwight, AC 815, PC 5, Livingston
Dwight Twp. HSD 230 | 2-00011
801 S FRANKLIN ST   60420 | 584-2950
Larry Copes, supt.
HS, 801 S FRANKLIN ST   60420 | 2-00011
Robert Landgrebe, prin. | 584-2904

Earlville, AC 815, PC 4, La Salle
Earlville CUSD 9, PO BOX 539   60518 | 3-11111
Ronald Rood, supt. | 246-8361
HS, PO BOX 539   60518 | 2-00011
Larry Imel, prin. | 246-8361

East Alton, AC 618, PC 6, Madison
East Alton SD 13 | 4-11100
210 E SAINT LOUIS AVE   62024 | 254-0691
Michael Gray, supt.
MS, 1000 3RD ST   62024 | 2-00100
Clyde McGill, prin. | 254-0531

East Dubuque, AC 815, PC 4, Jo Daviess
East Dubuque Unit SD 119 | 3-11111
200 PARKLANE DR   61025 | 747-3188
Donald Kussmaul, supt.
HS, 200 PARKLANE DR   61025 | 2-00011
Michael Garrity, prin. | 747-3188

East Moline, AC 309, PC 7, Rock Island
East Moline SD 37, 836 17TH AVE   61244 | 5-11100
Garry Rudish, supt. | 755-4533
Glenview MS, 3210 7TH ST   61244 | 4-01100
Linda Kresser, prin. | 755-1919

United Twp. HSD 30 | 4-00011
1275 42ND AVE   61244 | 752-1611
R. Craig Whitlock, prin.
United Twp. HS, 1275 42ND AVE   61244 | 4-00011
Gordon Cornelius, prin. | 752-1633

East Moline Christian S | 2-11111
900 46TH AVE   61244 | 796-1485
Rev. Patrick, prin.

Easton, AC 309, PC 2, Mason
Illini Central CUSD 189
Supt. — See Mason City
Illini Central MS, PO BOX 80   62633 | 2-00100
James Winkelman, prin. | 562-7251

East Peoria, AC 309, PC 7, Tazewell
East Peoria Community HSD 309 | 4-00011
1401 E WASHINGTON ST   61611 | 694-8300
Gordon Johnson, supt.
HS, 1401 E WASHINGTON ST   61611 | 4-00011
Jeanne Williamson, prin. | 694-8300

East Peoria SD 86 | 4-11100
601 TAYLOR ST   61611 | 699-7228
Dan McCormick, supt.
Central JHS, 601 TAYLOR ST   61611 | 3-00100
Steve Hutton, prin. | 699-2716

Illinois Central College | 6-CC
1 COLLEGE DR   61635 | 694-5431

East Saint Louis, AC 618, PC 8, St. Clair
East St. Louis SD 189 | 7-11111
1005 STATE ST   62201 | 583-8200
Leroy Ducksworth, supt.
SHS, 4901 STATE ST   62205 | 4-00001
Samuel Morgan, prin. | 583-8400
East St. Louis-Lincoln SHS | 4-00001
1211 BOND AVE   62201 | 583-8405
John Bailey, prin.
Clark JHS, 3310 STATE ST   62205 | 3-00110
Leroy Howell, prin. | 583-8412
Hughes-Quinn/Rock JHS | 3-00110
10TH & OHIO AVE   62201 | 583-8421
Fonzy Coleman, prin.
King JHS, 7000 RIDGE AVE   62203 | 3-00110
Joe Lewis, prin. | 398-3166
Lansdowne JHS | 3-00110
3939 CASEYVILLE AVE   62204 | 583-8418
Cornelius Perry, prin.

State Community College East St. Louis | 3-CC
601 JAMES R THOMPSON BLVD   62201
| 583-2500

Edinburg, AC 217, PC 3, Christian
Edinburg CUSD 4 | 2-11111
100 E MARTIN ST   62531 | 623-5603
Robert Bondurant, supt.
HS, 100 E MARTIN ST   62531 | 2-00011
Dale Farr, prin. | 623-5733
JHS, 100 E MARTIN ST   62531 | 1-00100
Dale Farr, prin. | 623-5733

Edwardsville, AC 618, PC 7, Madison
Edwardsville CUSD 7 | 6-11111
708 SAINT LOUIS ST   62025 | 656-1182
Robert Stuart, supt.
HS, 145 WEST ST   62025 | 4-00011
Elizabeth Lewin, prin. | 656-7100
JHS, 59 S STATE   62025 | 3-00100
Ron Goff, prin. | 656-0485

Metro East Lutheran HS | 2-00011
6305 CENTER GROVE RD   62025 | 656-0043
Sigmund Bohnet, prin.
Southern Illinois University   62026 | 6-UC
| 692-2475

Effingham, AC 217, PC 7, Effingham
Effingham CUSD 40 | 5-11111
1000 W GROVE AVE   62401 | 342-2163
Donald Roberts, supt.
HS, 600 S HENRIETTA ST   62401 | 3-00011
Russell Marvel, prin. | 342-2174
Central MS, RR 1 BOX 9   62401 | 3-01100
Michael Schmitz, prin. | 536-5171

St. Anthony HS | 2-00011
304 E ROADWAY AVE   62401 | 342-6969
David Bartlett, prin.

Eldorado, AC 618, PC 5, Saline
Eldorado CUSD 4 | 4-11111
1040 WASHINGTON ST   62930 | 273-6394
Gary Siebert, supt.
HS, 2200 ILLINOIS AVE   62930 | 2-00011
Carroll Phelps, prin. | 273-2881
JHS, 1907 1ST ST   62930 | 2-00100
Rickey Cox, prin. | 273-8056

Elgin, AC 708, PC 8, Kane
Elgin Unit SD 46, 4 S GIFFORD ST   60120 | 8-11111
Marvin Edwards, supt. | 888-5000
HS, 1200 MAROON DR   60120 | 5-00100
Larry Nemmers, prin. | 888-5100
Larkin HS, 1475 LARKIN AVE   60123 | 4-00011
Renate Matthaeus, prin. | 888-5200
Central Secondary Work Exp | Vo Tech
46 S GIFFORD ST   60120 | 888-5343
Camille Peck, prin.
Abbott MS, 949 VAN ST   60123 | 3-00100
Greg Schneider, prin. | 888-5160
Ellis MS, 225 S LIBERTY ST   60120 | 2-00100
James Feuerborn, prin. | 888-5151
Kimball MS | 3-00100
451 N MCLEAN BLVD   60123 | 888-5290
David Covey, prin.
Larsen MS, 665 DUNDEE AVE   60120 | 3-00100
Ronald O'Neal, prin. | 888-5250
Other Schools – See Streamwood

Elgin Academy, 350 PARK ST   60120 | 2-11111
Seldon Edwards, prin. | 695-0300
Elgin Community College | 5-CC
1700 SPARTAN DR   60123 | 697-1000

Judson College   3-UC
1151 N STATE ST 60123   695-2500
St. Edward Central Catholic HS   3-00011
335 LOCUST ST 60123   741-7535
Jacqueline Hyzy, prin.
St. Joseph Hospital   HSP
77 N AIRLITE ST 60123   695-3200

Elizabeth, AC 815, PC 3, Jo Daviess
River Ridge CUSD 210   3-11111
PO BOX 489 61028   858-2219
Phillip Reasor, supt.
River Ridge HS, PO BOX 489 61028   2-00011
Dan Todd, prin.   858-2219
Other Schools – See Hanover

Elizabethtown, AC 618, PC 2, Hardin
Hardin County CUSD 1   3-11111
PO BOX 218 62931   287-2411
Neal Cole, supt.
Hardin Co. HS, RR 2 62931   2-00011
Don Joyner, prin.   287-2141
Hardin Co. JHS, RR 2 62931   2-00100
Jim Stunson, prin.   287-2141

Elk Grove Village, AC 708, PC 8, Cook
Community Consolidated SD 59
Supt. — See Arlington Heights
Grove JHS   3-00100
777 W ELK GROVE BLVD 60007   593-4367
Walter Hamann, prin.

Schaumburg CCSD 54
Supt. — See Schaumburg
Mead JHS   3-00100
1765 BIESTERFIELD RD 60007   307-2100
Robert Wolfeen, prin.

Township HSD 214
Supt. — See Arlington Heights
HS, 500 W ELK GROVE BLVD 60007   4-00011
Raymond Broderick, prin.   439-4800

Elkville, AC 618, PC 3, Jackson
Elverado CUSD 196, 114 S 8TH ST 62932   3-11111
William Valerius, supt.   568-1321
Elverado HS, 514 S 6TH ST 62932   2-00011
James Piper, prin.   568-1104
Other Schools – See Vergennes

Elmhurst, AC 708, PC 8, Du Page
Elmhurst SD 205, 145 ARTHUR ST 60126   6-11111
Joan Raymond, supt.   834-4530
York Community HS   4-00011
355 W SAINT CHARLES RD 60126   617-2400
James Nelson, prin.
Bryan JHS   2-00100
111 W BUTTERFIELD RD 60126   617-2350
Richard Stahl, prin.
Churchville JHS   2-00100
155 VICTORY PKY 60126   832-8682
Dennis Hatt, prin.
Sandburg JHS   2-00100
345 E SAINT CHARLES RD 60126   834-4534
George Jacobs, prin.

Elmhurst College   4-UC
190 PROSPECT AVE 60126   617-3100
Immaculate Conception HS   3-00011
217 COTTAGE HILL AVE 60126   530-3460
Frederick Shannon, prin.
Timothy Christian HS   2-00011
1061 PROSPECT AVE 60126   833-7575
Dan Van Prooyen, prin.
Timothy Christian JHS   2-00100
188 N BUTTERFIELD RD 60126   833-4617
William Lodewyk, prin.

Elmwood, AC 309, PC 4, Peoria
Elmwood CUSD 322   3-11111
301 W BUTTERNUT 61529   742-8464
Margaret Noe, supt.
HS, 301 W BUTTERNUT 61529   2-00011
Mike Conver, prin.   742-2851
JHS, 301 W BUTTERNUT 61529   2-00100
Mike Conver, prin.   742-2851

Elmwood Park, AC 708, PC 7, Cook
Elmwood Park CUSD 401   4-11111
8201 W FULLERTON AVE 60635   452-7272
J. S. Broncato, supt.
HS, 8201 W FULLERTON AVE 60635   3-00011
Paul Swanstrom, prin.   452-7272
Elm JHS, 7607 W CORTLAND ST 60635   2-00100
Sam Vaccaro, prin.   452-3550

El Paso, AC 309, PC 5, Woodford
El Paso CUSD 375   3-11111
PO BOX 115 61738   527-4410
James Miller, supt.
HS, 600 N ELM ST 61738   2-00011
Randall Vincent, prin.   527-4415
Centennial MS, 135 W 5TH ST 61738   2-01100
Donald Juricka, prin.   527-4435

Elsah, AC 618, PC 3, Jersey

Principia College 62028   3-UC
374-2131

Erie, AC 309, PC 4, Whiteside
Erie CUSD 1, RR 2 BOX 86 61250   3-11111
Earle Mailand, supt.   659-2239
HS, 616 6TH ST 61250   2-00011
Carol Duffy, prin.   659-2401

MS, 500 5TH AVE 61250   2-01100
Ronald Vail, prin.   659-2481

Eureka, AC 309, PC 5, Woodford
Eureka CUSD 140   4-11111
200 W CRUGER AVE 61530   467-3737
Randy Crump, supt.
HS, 200 W CRUGER AVE 61530   2-00011
Leonard Savage, prin.   467-2361
MS, 2005 S MAIN ST 61530   3-01100
Ed Steinbeck, prin.   467-3771

Eureka College   2-UC
300 E COLLEGE AVE 61530   467-3721

Evanston, AC 708, PC 8, Cook
Evanston CCSD 65   6-11100
1314 RIDGE AVE 60201   492-5986
Joseph Pollack, supt.
Chute MS, 1400 OAKTON ST 60202   3-00100
Edward Pate, prin.   492-7892
Haven MS, 2417 PRAIRIE AVE 60201   3-00100
Sally Julian, prin.   492-7886
Nichols MS, 800 GREENLEAF ST 60202   3-00100
Barbara Hiller, prin.   492-7881

Evanston Twp. HSD 202   5-00011
1600 DODGE AVE 60201   492-3856
Allan Alson, supt.
Evanston Twp. HS   5-00011
1600 DODGE AVE 60201   492-3856
Allan Alson, prin.

Garrett Evangelical Theological Seminary   2-UC
2121 SHERIDAN RD 60201   866-3901
Kendall College   2-UC
2408 ORRINGTON AVE 60201   866-1300
National-Louis University   6-UC
2840 SHERIDAN RD 60201   475-1100
Northwestern University   7-UC
2001 SHERIDAN RD 60208   491-3741
Roycemore S, 640 LINCOLN ST 60201   2-11111
Joseph Becker, prin.   866-6055
St. Francis Hospital   HSP
355 RIDGE AVE 60202   866-5810
Seabury-Western Theological Seminary   1-UC
2122 SHERIDAN RD 60201   328-9300

Evansville, AC 618, PC 3, Randolph
Sparta CUSD 140
Supt. — See Sparta
MS, 701 OAK ST 62242   1-01100
Meredith McGuire, prin.   853-4411

Evergreen Park, AC 708, PC 7, Cook
Evergreen Park Community HSD 231   3-00011
9901 S KEDZIE AVE 60642   424-7400
Michael Johnson, supt.
HS, 9901 S KEDZIE AVE 60642   3-00011
Charles Horn, prin.   424-7400

Evergreen Park ESD 124   4-11100
9400 S SAWYER AVE 60642   423-0950
James Cross, supt.
Central JHS, 9400 S SAWYER AVE 60642   2-00100
Margaret Longo, prin.   424-0148

Fairbury, AC 815, PC 5, Livingston
Prairie Central CUSD 8
Supt. — See Forrest
Prairie Central HS, 411 N 7TH ST 61739   3-00011
Daniel Schmitt, prin.   692-2355

Fairfield, AC 618, PC 6, Wayne
Fairfield Community HSD 225   3-00011
300 W KING ST 62837   842-2649
Donald Warkins, supt.
Fairfield Community HS   3-00011
300 W KING ST 62837   842-2649
Rena Talbert, prin.

Fairfield SD 112, 806 N 1ST ST 62837   3-11100
Hank Hanneken, supt.   842-6501
Center Street MS   2-01100
200 W CENTER ST 62837   842-2679
Michael Simpson, prin.

Frontier Community College   4-CC
RR 1 62837

Fairview Heights, AC 618, PC 7, St. Clair
Grant CCSD 110   3-11100
10110 LINCOLN TRL 62208   398-5577
Kenneth Perkins, supt.
Grant JHS, 10110 LINCOLN TRL 62208   2-01100
Jane Knight, prin.   397-2764

Pontiac-West Holliday SD 105   3-11100
400 ASHLAND PL 62208   233-6004
Robert Stuckey, supt.
Pontiac JHS, 400 ASHLAND PL 62208   2-00100
Robert Stuckey, prin.   233-2320

Farina, AC 618, PC 3, Fayette
South Central CUSD 401
Supt. — See Kinmundy
South Central HS, PO BOX 250 62838   2-00011
Lindell Roberts, prin.   245-3363

Farmer City, AC 309, PC 4, De Witt
Blue Ridge CUSD 18   3-11111
309 N JOHN ST 61842   928-9141
Richard Leahy, supt.
Blue Ridge HS, 411 N JOHN ST 61842   2-00011
Ron Conner, prin.   928-2622

Other Schools – See Mansfield

Farmington, AC 309, PC 5, Fulton
Farmington Central CUSD 265
Supt. — See Trivoli
HS, 568 E VERNON ST 61531   3-00011
Gary Schultz, prin.   245-2466
Chapman MS, 322 E FORT ST 61531   2-01100
John Patterson, prin.   245-2913

Findlay, AC 217, PC 3, Shelby
Findlay CUSD 2, 206 N MAIN ST 62534   2-11111
Ron Hash, supt.   756-8522
HS, 501 N DIVISION 62534   1-00011
Larry Bradford, prin.   756-8521
JHS, 501 W DIVISION 62534   1-00100
Larry Bradford, prin.   756-8521

Fisher, AC 217, PC 4, Champaign
Fisher CUSD 1, PO BOX 700 61843   3-11111
Sam McGrew, supt.   897-6125
JSHS, PO BOX 670 61843   2-00111
Roger Roberts, prin.   897-1225

Fithian, AC 217, PC 3, Vermilion
Community Unit SD 76   4-11111
RR 2 BOX 52A 61844   354-4355
James McNellis, supt.
Oakwood HS, RR 2 BOX 52B 61844   2-00011
Glenn Keever, prin.   354-2358
Other Schools – See Danville

Flanagan, AC 815, PC 3, Livingston
Flanagan CUSD 4, PO BOX 367 61740   2-11111
William Braksick, supt.   796-2233
HS 61740   2-00011
Charles Snook, prin.   796-2291

Flora, AC 618, PC 6, Clay
Flora CUSD 35, 509 S LOCUST ST 62839   4-11111
Gerald Hearring, supt.   662-2412
HS, 600 S LOCUST ST 62839   2-00011
Harry Penry, prin.   662-8316
JHS, RR 1 BOX 188 62839   2-00100
Charles Martin, prin.   662-8394

Flossmoor, AC 708, PC 6, Cook
Flossmoor SD 161   4-11100
2810 SCHOOL ST 60422   798-2651
L. Thomas Moore, supt.
Parker JHS, 2810 SCHOOL ST 60422   3-00100
Donald Kistler, prin.   798-0641

Homewood-Flossmoor Community HSD 233   4-00011
999 KEDZIE AVE 60422   799-3000
Laura Murray, supt.
Homewood-Flossmoor HS   4-00011
999 KEDZIE AVE 60422   799-3000
Laura Murray, prin.

Ford Heights, AC 708, PC 5, Cook
Ford Heights SD 169   3-11100
910 WOODLAWN AVE 60411   758-1370
Constance Shorter, supt.
Cottage Grove MS   2-00100
800 E LINCOLN HWY 60411   758-1400
Patricia Joseph, prin.

Forest Park, AC 708, PC 7, Cook
Forest Park SD 91   4-11100
939 BELOIT AVE 60130   366-5700
Joseph Scolire, supt.
MS, 925 BELOIT AVE 60130   2-00100
John Ericksen, prin.   366-5703

Forrest, AC 815, PC 4, Livingston
Prairie Central CUSD 8   4-11111
312 N CENTER ST 61741   657-8237
Calvin Jackson, supt.
Prairie Central JHS   2-00100
312 N CENTER ST 61741   657-8238
Leeon Carrico, prin.
Other Schools – See Fairbury

Forreston, AC 815, PC 4, Ogle
Forrestville Valley CUSD 221   4-11111
PO BOX 665 61030   938-2301
Michael Sass, supt.
HS, PO BOX 665 61030   2-00011
Richard Corpus, prin.   938-2175

Fox Lake, AC 708, PC 6, Lake
Fox Lake Grade SD 114   3-11100
17 FOREST AVE 60020   587-8275
Arthur Smejkal, supt.
Stanton MS   2-01100
101 HAWTHORNE LN 60020   587-2535
William Lomas, prin.

Grant Community HSD 124   3-00011
285 E GRAND AVE 60020   587-2561
Donald Klusendorf, supt.
Grant Community HS   3-00011
285 E GRAND AVE 60020   587-2561
John Vierke, prin.

Fox River Grove, AC 708, PC 5, McHenry
Fox River Grove CSD 3   3-11100
401 ORCHARD ST 60021   516-5100
Robert Stanger, supt.
JHS, 401 ORCHARD ST 60021   2-00100
Jacqueline Krause, prin.   516-5105

Frankfort, AC 815, PC 6, Will
Frankfort CCSD 157C   4-11100
110 OREGON ST 60423   469-5922
Joann Desmond, supt.

JHS, 22265 S 80TH AVE 60423   2-00100
John Loecke, prin.   469-4474

Lincoln-Way Community HSD 210
Supt. — See New Lenox
Lincoln-Way East Mid. HS   3-00010
201 COLORADO AVE 60423   469-9645
Joseph Davis, prin.

Summit Hill SD 161, RR 3 60423   4-11100
Julian Rogus, supt.   469-9103
Summit Hill JHS   2-00100
20130 S ROSEWOOD DR 60423   469-4330
Richard Carter, prin.

Franklin, AC 217, PC 3, Morgan
Franklin CUSD 1, 110 STATE ST 62638   2-11111
Fred Roberts, supt.   478-3011
HS, 110 STATE ST 62638   2-00111
Ross Myers, prin.   675-2395
JHS, 110 STATE ST 62638   2-00100
Ross Myers, prin.   675-2395

Franklin Grove, AC 815, PC 3, Lee
Lee Center CUSD 271
Supt. — See Paw Paw
Franklin Center JSHS   2-00111
PO BOX 188 61031   456-2323
Melvin Barron, prin.

Franklin Park, AC 708, PC 7, Cook
Franklin Park SD 84   4-11100
9750 FULLERTON AVE 60131   455-4230
Dan Pietrini, supt.
Hester JHS, 2836 GUSTAVE ST 60131   2-00100
Richard Hrejsa, prin.   455-2150

Leyden Community HSD 212   5-00011
3400 ROSE ST 60131   451-3000
Jack Schoenholtz, supt.
East Leyden HS, 3400 ROSE ST 60131   4-00011
George Shaffer, prin.   451-3025
Other Schools — See Northlake

Mannheim SD 83   5-11100
10401 GRAND AVE 60131   455-4413
John Ludolph, supt.
Other Schools — See Melrose Park

Freeburg, AC 618, PC 5, St. Clair
Freeburg Community HSD 77   3-00011
401 S MONROE ST 62243   539-5533
Steven Fannin, supt.
HS, 401 S MONROE ST 62243   3-00011
T. Truman, prin.   539-5533

Freeport, AC 815, PC 8, Stephenson
Freeport SD 145, PO BOX 387 61032   5-11111
Richard Olson, supt.   232-0308
HS, 701 W MOSELEY ST 61032   4-00011
Steve Fager, prin.   232-0400
JHS, W EMPIRE ST 61032   3-00100
Scott Wiley, prin.   232-0500

Aquin Central Catholic HS   2-00111
1419 S GALENA AVE 61032   235-3154
Joseph Steepleton, prin.
Highland Community College   4-CC
2998 W PEARL CITY RD 61032   235-6121

Fulton, AC 815, PC 5, Whiteside
River Bend CUSD 2, 415 12TH ST 61252   4-11111
Kent Hammer, supt.   589-2711
HS, 1207 12TH ST 61252   2-00011
Emmett Aubry, prin.   589-3511
JHS, 415 12TH ST 61252   2-00100
Nina Pifer, prin.   589-2611

Gages Lake, AC 708, PC 6, Lake
Woodland CCSD 50   5-11100
17370 W GAGES LAKE RD 60030   816-2532
Dennis Conti, supt.
Woodland MS   3-00100
17371 W GAGES LAKE RD 60030   362-3514
Donald Bradley, prin.

Galatia, AC 618, PC 3, Saline
Galatia CUSD 1, RR 2 BOX 168 62935   2-11111
William Cross, supt.   268-6371
HS, RR 1 BOX 27A 62935   2-00111
James Eatherly, prin.   268-4194
JHS, RR 1 62935   1-00100
James Eatherly, prin.   268-4194

Galena, AC 815, PC 5, Jo Daviess
Galena Unit SD 120   4-11111
1206 FRANKLIN ST 61036   777-0917
Kenneth Hupp, supt.
HS, 1206 FRANKLIN ST 61036   2-00011
Charles Slagley, prin.   777-0917
MS, 1230 FRANKLIN ST 61036   2-01100
Dale Henze, prin.   777-2413

Galesburg, AC 309, PC 8, Knox
Galesburg CUSD 205   6-11111
PO BOX 1206 61402   343-1151
William Abel, supt.
HS, 1125 W FREMONT ST 61401   4-00011
John Browning, prin.   343-4146
Churchill JHS, 905 MAPLE AVE 61401   3-00100
Richard Qualls, prin.   342-3129
Lombard JHS, 1220 E KNOX ST 61401   3-00100
Henry Hamann, prin.   342-9171

Bethany Christian Academy   2-11111
590 S ACADEMY ST 61401   342-3132
Kenneth Ilg, prin.
Carl Sandburg College   4-CC
2232 S LAKE STOREY RD 61401   344-2518
Knox College 61401   3-UC
   343-0112

Galva, AC 309, PC 5, Henry
Galva CUSD 224   3-11111
224 MORGAN RD 61434   932-2108
William Owens, supt.
JSHS, N CENTER AVE 61434   2-00111
Steve Johnson, prin.   932-2151

Gardner, AC 815, PC 4, Grundy
Gardner-South Wilmington Twp. HSD 73   2-00011
500 MAIN ST 60424   237-2176
Roger Clemmons, supt.
Gardner-South Wilmington Twp. HS   2-00011
500 MAIN ST 60424   237-2176
Daniel Jerbi, prin.

Geneseo, AC 309, PC 6, Henry
Geneseo CUSD 228   5-11111
209 S COLLEGE AVE 61254   944-2159
Harold Ford, supt.
Darnall HS, 700 N STATE ST 61254   3-00011
Ted McAvoy, prin.   944-4674
JHS, 115 W PEARL ST 61254   2-00100
Gary Zummallen, prin.   944-2151

Geneva, AC 708, PC 7, Kane
Geneva CUSD 304   5-11111
400 MCKINLEY AVE 60134   232-0678
John Murphy, supt.
Geneva Community HS   3-00011
415 LOGAN AVE 60134   232-7500
Craig Collins, prin.
Coultrap MS, 1113 PEYTON ST 60134   3-00100
Sandy Randall, prin.   232-2022

Genoa, AC 815, PC 5, De Kalb
Genoa-Kingston CUSD 424   4-11111
941 W MAIN ST 60135   784-6222
Gregory Sawka, supt.
Genoa-Kingston HS   2-00011
941 W MAIN ST 60135   784-5111
Don Billington, prin.
MS, 602 E HILL ST 60135   2-00100
Martha Jurkowski, prin.   784-5222

Georgetown, AC 217, PC 5, Vermilion
Georgetown-Ridge Farm CUSD 4   4-11111
400 W WEST ST 61846   662-8488
Robert Delmotte, supt.
Georgetown-Ridge Farm HS   2-00011
500 W MULBERRY ST 61846   662-6716
James Kelly, prin.
Miller JHS, 414 W WEST ST 61846   2-00100
(—), prin.   662-6606

Gibson City, AC 217, PC 5, Ford
Gibson City-Melvin-Sibley CUSD 1   3-11111
217 E 17TH ST 60936   784-8296
Richard Berg, supt.
GCMS HS, 815 N CHURCH ST 60936   2-00011
James Miglin, prin.   784-4292
Other Schools — See Melvin

Gillespie, AC 217, PC 5, Macoupin
Gillespie CUSD 7, 510 W ELM ST 62033   4-11111
Donald Mulch, supt.   839-2464
HS, 612 BROADWAY ST 62033   2-00011
Robert Fulton, prin.   839-2114
JHS, 412 OREGON ST 62033   2-00100
Kyle Hlafka, prin.   839-2116

Gilman, AC 815, PC 4, Iroquois
Iroquois West CUSD 10   3-11111
PO BOX 67 60938   265-4642
Frank Meyer, supt.
Iroquois West HS, PO BOX 67 60938   2-00011
Richard Brutcher, prin.   265-4229
Other Schools — See Onarga

Girard, AC 217, PC 4, Macoupin
Girard CUSD 3, 525 N 3RD ST 62640   3-11111
Chuck Langley, supt.   627-2915
HS, 525 N 3RD ST 62640   2-00011
Mark Keller, prin.   627-2136

Glasford, AC 309, PC 4, Peoria
Illini Bluffs CUSD 327, RR 1 61533   3-11111
Steven Mitchell, supt.   389-2231
Illini Bluffs HS, PO BOX 320 61533   2-00011
Dennis Brown, prin.   389-5681
MS, PO BOX 155 61533   2-01100
Dan Patterson, prin.   389-3451

Glencoe, AC 708, PC 6, Cook
Glencoe SD 35   4-11100
620 GREENWOOD AVE 60022   835-2100
Phillip Price, supt.
Central JHS   2-01100
620 GREENWOOD AVE 60022   835-2660
Nelson Armour, prin.

Glendale Heights, AC 708, PC 8, Du Page
Marquardt SD 15   5-11100
1890 GLEN ELLYN RD 60139   858-1166
Lawrence Golden, supt.
Marquardt MS   2-00100
1912 GLEN ELLYN RD 60139   858-3850
James Sayers, prin.

Queen Bee SD 16   4-11100
1560 BLOOMINGDALE RD 60139   260-6100
James White, supt.
Glenside MS   3-00100
1560 BLOOMINGDALE RD 60139   260-6112
Jacqueline Wolff, prin.

Universal Technical Institute   2-CS
601 REGENCY DR 60139   529-2662

Glen Ellyn, AC 708, PC 7, Du Page
Glenbard Twp. HSD 87   6-00011
800 ROOSEVELT RD 60137   469-9100
Robert Stevens, supt.
Glenbard South HS   4-00011
23W200 BUTTERFIELD RD 60137   469-6500
Peter Abruzzo, prin.
Glenbard West HS   4-00011
670 CRESCENT BLVD 60137   469-8600
Sue Bridge, prin.
Other Schools — See Carol Stream, Lombard

Glen Ellyn CCSD 89   5-11100
789 SHEEHAN AVE 60137   469-8900
Paul Zaccarine, supt.
Glen Crest JHS   3-00100
725 SHEEHAN AVE 60137   469-5220
Leonard Lindgren, prin.

Glen Ellyn SD 41, 793 N MAIN ST 60137   5-11100
P. Irwin, supt.   790-6406
Hadley JHS, 240 HAWTHORNE ST 60137   3-00100
Kenneth Stellon, prin.   790-6450

College of DuPage   7-CC
425 22ND ST 60137   858-2800
Midwest College of Engineering   1-UC
600 S LAMBERT RD 60137

Glenview, AC 708, PC 8, Cook
Glenview CCSD 34   5-11100
1401 GREENWOOD RD 60025   998-5000
W. J. Attea, supt.
Springman JHS   3-00100
2701 CENTRAL RD 60025   998-5020
Barbara Tucker, prin.

Northfield Twp. HSD 225   5-00011
1835 LANDWEHR RD 60025   998-6100
Jean McGrew, supt.
Glenbrook South HS   4-00011
4000 W LAKE AVE 60025   729-2000
William Schreiner, prin.
Other Schools — See Northbrook

Glenwood, AC 708, PC 6, Cook
Brookwood SD 167   4-11100
201 E GLENWOOD DYER RD 60425   758-5190
Kenneth Peterson, supt.
Brookwood JHS   2-00100
201 S GREENWOOD AVE 60425   758-5252
Stephen Racz, prin.

Glenwood School for Boys   2-01100
18700 S HALSTED ST 60425   754-0175
Rich Batterham, prin.

Godfrey, AC 618, PC 6, Madison
Alton CUSD 11
Supt. — See Alton
North MS, 5600 GODFREY RD 62035   2-00100
Thomas Gunning, prin.   463-2171

Lewis & Clark Community College   5-CC
5800 GODFREY RD 62035   466-3411

Golconda, AC 618, PC 3, Pope
Pope Co. CUSD 1   3-11111
RR 2 BOX 22 62938   683-2301
Terry Pearcy, supt.
Pope County HS, RR 2 BOX 22 62938   2-00011
Michael Irwin, prin.   683-3071

Goreville, AC 618, PC 3, Johnson
Goreville CUSD 1, PO BOX 210 62939   2-11111
Phillip Jones, supt.   995-2692
Goreville Twp JHS   2-00111
PO BOX 210 62939 – (—), prin.   995-2692

Granite City, AC 618, PC 8, Madison
Granite City CUSD 9   6-11111
1947 ADAMS ST 62040   451-5800
Steve Balen, supt.
HS, 3101 MADISON AVE 62040   4-00011
David Painter, prin.   451-5808
Coolidge JHS, 3231 NAMEOKI RD 62040   3-00100
James Jeffries, prin.   451-5826
Grigsby JHS, 3801 CARGILL RD 62040   3-00100
Ken Spalding, prin.   931-5544

Sanford-Brown Business College   2-CS
3237 W CHAIN OF ROCKS RD 62040   931-0300

Grant Park, AC 815, PC 4, Kankakee
Grant Park CUSD 6   2-11111
421 W HAMBLETON ST 60940   465-6013
Edward Butler, supt.
HS, 421 W HAMBLETON ST 60940   2-00011
Michael Nelson, prin.   465-2181

Granville, AC 815, PC 4, Putnam
Putnam County CUSD 535   4-11111
PO BOX 607 61326   339-2238
Frances Karanovich, supt.

Putnam County HS 2-00011
PO BOX 341 61326 339-6514
Joseph Massino, prin.
Other Schools – See Mc Nabb

Grayslake, AC 708, PC 6, Lake
Grayslake CCSD 46 4-11100
440 BARRON BLVD 60030 223-0065
Joan Hochschild, supt.
MS, 440 BARRON BLVD 60030 3-00100
Charles Davis, prin. 223-3680

Grayslake Community HSD 127 3-00011
400 N LAKE ST 60030 223-8621
Ray Novak, supt.
HS, 400 N LAKE ST 60030 3-00011
Elizabeth McDonald, prin. 223-8621

College of Lake County 6-CC
19351 W WASHINGTON ST 60030 223-6601

Grayville, AC 618, PC 4, White
Grayville CUSD 1 2-11111
728 W NORTH ST 62844 375-6521
Lillian Phillips, supt.
HS, 728 W NORTH ST 62844 2-00011
Lillian Phillips, prin. 375-7114

Greenfield, AC 217, PC 4, Greene
Greenfield CUSD 10, 502 EAST ST 62044 3-11111
Charles Barber, supt. 368-2219
HS, 502 EAST ST 62044 2-00011
Charles Barber, prin. 368-2219

Greenview, AC 217, PC 3, Menard
Greenview CUSD 200 2-11111
PO BOX 320 62642 968-2295
Robert Turk, supt.
HS, PO BOX 320 62642 1-00011
David Roberts, prin. 968-2295
JHS, PO BOX 320 62642 1-00100
David Roberts, prin. 968-2295

Greenville, AC 618, PC 5, Bond
Bond County CUSD 2 4-11111
1008 N HENA ST 62246 664-0170
Philip Pogue, supt.
HS, 1 VANDALIA RD 62246 3-00011
Donald Dillon, prin. 664-1370
JHS, 513 E BEAUMONT AVE 62246 2-00100
Hugh Westbrook, prin. 664-1226

Greenville College 3-UC
315 E COLLEGE AVE 62246 664-1840

Gridley, AC 309, PC 4, McLean
Gridley CUSD 10, PO BOX 958 61744 2-11111
Gene Cwick, supt. 747-3057
HS, PO BOX 989 61744 2-00011
William James, prin. 747-2156
JHS, PO BOX 958 61744 1-00100
Alan Beckman, prin. 747-2360

Griggsville, AC 217, PC 4, Pike
Griggsville CUSD 4 2-11111
PO BOX 439 62340 833-2352
Mike Mauzy, supt.
HS, STANFORD & LIBERTY 62340 1-00011
Pat Callahan, prin. 833-2352
JHS, STANFORD & LIBERTY 62340 1-00100
Pat Callahan, prin. 833-2353

Gurnee, AC 708, PC 7, Lake
Gurnee SD 56 4-11100
900 KILBOURNE RD 60031 336-0800
Wayne Schurter, supt.
Viking JHS, 4460 GRAND AVE 60031 2-00100
Marie Shinners, prin. 336-2108

Warren Twp. HSD 121 4-00011
500 N OPLAINE RD 60031 662-1400
Patrick McMahon, supt.
Warren Twp. HS 4-00011
500 N OPLAINE RD 60031 662-1400
Philip Roffman, prin.

Hamilton, AC 217, PC 5, Hancock
Hamilton CCSD 328 3-11111
270 N 10TH ST 62341 847-3315
Diane Robertson, supt.
HS, 1100 KEOKUK ST 62341 2-00011
Dennis Wright, prin. 847-3313
MS, 270 N 10TH ST 62341 2-00100
Sue Knight, prin. 847-3314

Hampshire, AC 708, PC 4, Kane
Dundee CUSD 300
Supt. — See Carpentersville
HS, 560 S STATE ST 60140 2-00011
Leigh Gilbert, prin. 683-2522
MS, 560 S STATE ST 60140 2-00100
Leigh Gilbert, prin. 683-2522

Hanna City, AC 309, PC 4, Peoria
Farmington Central CUSD 265
Supt. — See Trivoli
Logan City MS, 412 S EDEN RD 61536 2-01100
John Small, prin. 565-7115

Hanover, AC 815, PC 3, Jo Daviess
River Ridge CUSD 210
Supt. — See Elizabeth
River Ridge MS, PO BOX 25 61041 2-00100
James Spielman, prin. 591-3316

Hanover Park, AC 708, PC 8, Cook
Keeneyville SD 20 4-11100
5540 E ARLINGTON DR 60103 894-2250
Robert Snyder, supt.
Spring Wood JHS 3-00100
5540 E ARLINGTON DR 60103 893-8900
Daniel Brace, prin.

Hardin, AC 618, PC 4, Calhoun
Calhoun CUSD 40 3-11111
PO BOX 387 62047 576-2722
Terry Strauch, supt.
Calhoun HS, PO BOX 387 62047 2-00011
Terry Strauch, prin. 576-2229
Other Schools – See Kampsville

Harrisburg, AC 618, PC 6, Saline
Harrisburg CUSD 3, 40 S MAIN ST 62946 4-11111
John Hill, supt. 253-7637
HS, 333 W COLLEGE ST 62946 3-00011
Jim Collins, prin. 253-7635
Malan JHS, 124 S WEBSTER ST 62946 2-00100
Edward Bradley, prin. 253-7108

Southeastern Illinois College 4-CC
RR 4 BOX 510 62946 252-4411

Hartsburg, AC 217, PC 2, Logan
Hartsburg-Emden CUSD 21 2-11111
400 W FRONT ST 62643 642-5244
John Mizell, supt.
Hartsburg-Emden JSHS 2-01111
RR 1 BOX 2 62643 642-5244
Ronald Black, prin.

Harvard, AC 815, PC 6, McHenry
Harvard CUSD 50 4-11111
1101 N JEFFERSON ST 60033 943-4022
Richard Crosby, supt.
HS, 1103 N JEFFERSON ST 60033 3-00011
Steven Schultz, prin. 943-6461
JHS, 1301 GARFIELD ST 60033 2-00100
Frank Shields, prin. 943-6466

Harvey, AC 708, PC 8, Cook
Harvey SD 152 5-11100
15147 MYRTLE AVE 60426 333-0300
Sharon Hamilton, supt.
Brooks JHS, 14741 WALLACE ST 60426 3-00100
Jerry Jordan, prin. 333-6390

Thornton Twp. HSD 205 6-00011
15100 BROADWAY AVE 60426 596-1000
Richard Taylor, supt.
Thornton Twp. HS 5-00011
15100 BROADWAY AVE 60426 596-1000
William O'Neal, prin.
Other Schools – See Dolton, South Holland

West Harvey-Dixmoor SD 147 4-11100
155TH PLACE & HOYNE 60426 339-9500
Samuel Rhone, supt.
Parks MS, 14700 ROBEY AVE 60426 3-00100
Winston Johnson, prin. 371-9575

Havana, AC 309, PC 5, Mason
Havana CUSD 126 4-11111
500 S MCKINLEY ST 62644 543-3384
Jack Wagoner, supt.
HS, 500 S MCKINLEY ST 62644 2-00011
Robert Emme, prin. 543-3337
JHS, 700 E LAUREL AVE 62644 2-01100
Larry Bequeaith, prin. 543-6677

Hazel Crest, AC 708, PC 7, Cook
Hazel Crest SD 152-5 4-11100
1910 170TH ST 60429 335-0790
Alex Boyd, supt.
Palm MS 2-01100
170TH & DIXIE HIGHWAY 60429 335-4013
Jeanette Shivers, prin.
Woodland MS 2-01100
169TH & WESTERN AVE 60429 335-1995
Margie Gladney, prin.

Prairie-Hills ESD 144 5-11100
PO BOX 233 60429 – (—), supt. 210-2888
Other Schools – See Markham

Hebron, AC 815, PC 3, McHenry
Alden Hebron SD 19 2-11111
9604 ILLINOIS ST 60034 648-2886
Roger Damrow, supt.
Alden-Hebron HS 2-00011
9604 ILLINOIS ST 60034 648-2442
Janet Booth, prin.
Alden-Hebron JHS 2-00100
9604 ILLINOIS ST 60034 648-2442
Janet Booth, prin.

Henry, AC 309, PC 5, Marshall
Henry-Senachwine CUSD 5 3-11111
1023 COLLEGE ST 61537 364-3614
Rick Stoecker, supt.
Henry-Senachwine Consolidated HS 2-00011
1023 COLLEGE ST 61537 364-2829
Jerry Peterson, prin.

Herrin, AC 618, PC 7, Williamson
Herrin CUSD 4, 700 N 10TH ST 62948 4-11111
David Hindman, supt. 988-8024
HS, 700 N 10TH ST 62948 3-00011
Edwin Tresnak, prin. 942-6606
JHS, 700 S 14TH ST 62948 2-00100
Deborah Payne, prin. 942-5603

Herscher, AC 815, PC 4, Kankakee
Herscher CUSD 2, PO BOX 504 60941 4-11111
Lawrence Jacobsen, supt. 426-2162
HS, PO BOX 504 60941 3-00011
Clifford West, prin. 426-2103

Heyworth, AC 309, PC 4, McLean
Heyworth CUSD 4, 200 E MAIN ST 61745 3-11111
Roger Little, supt. 473-3727
HS, 308 W CLEVELAND 61745 2-00011
Mike Lynch, prin. 473-2322

Hickory Hills, AC 708, PC 7, Cook
North Palos SD 117 4-11100
9045 S 88TH AVE 60457 598-5500
Tom Kostes, supt.
Conrady JHS 3-00100
97TH & ROBERTS ROAD 60457 598-5500
Ronald Kanzulak, prin.

Northwestern Business College 2-CC
8020 W 87TH ST 60457 430-0990

Highland, AC 618, PC 6, Madison
Highland CUSD 5 5-11111
1800 LINDENTHAL ST 62249 654-2106
James Burgett, supt.
HS, 12760 TROXLER AVE 62249 3-00011
Fred Singleton, prin. 654-2106
JHS, 1600 LINDENTHAL ST 62249 2-00100
Rick Acuncius, prin. 654-2106

Woodridge Business Institute 2-CS
1310 MERCANTILE DR 62249 654-2539

Highland Park, AC 708, PC 8, Lake
North Shore SD 108 4-11100
530 RED OAK LN 60035 831-4370
Darrell Lund, supt.
Edgewood MS 3-00100
929 EDGEWOOD RD 60035 432-3858
Gregory Mullen, prin.
Elm Place MS 2-01100
2031 SHERIDAN RD 60035 432-9217
Daniel Kornblut, prin.
Northwood JHS, 945 NORTH AVE 60035 2-00100
David Johnson, prin. 432-4770

Township HSD 113 5-00011
1040 PARK AVE W 60035 432-6510
James Warren, supt.
HS, 433 VINE AVE 60035 4-00011
Jane Gard, prin. 926-9230
Other Schools – See Deerfield

Hillsboro, AC 217, PC 5, Montgomery
Hillsboro CUSD 3 4-11111
1311 VANDALIA RD 62049 532-2942
Les Dollinger, supt.
HS, 522 E TREMONT ST 62049 3-00011
Larry Ackerman, prin. 532-2841
JHS, 909 ROUNTREE ST 62049 2-00100
Mike Gaither, prin. 532-3742

Hillside, AC 708, PC 6, Cook
Proviso Twp. HSD 209
Supt. — See Maywood
Proviso West HS 4-00011
4701 HARRISON ST 60162 449-6400
Thomas Jandris, prin.

Hillside Academy 2-11111
431 N HILLSIDE AVE 60162 449-1310
Mary Bullock, prin.

Hinckley, AC 815, PC 4, De Kalb
Hinkley-Big Rock CUSD 429 3-11111
PO BOX 1210 60520 286-7133
Glen Littlefield, supt.
Hinckley-Big Rock HS 2-00011
PO BOX 1210 60520 286-3291
Roland Thompson, prin.

Hines, AC 708, Cook

Edward Hines Veterans Admin. Hospital HSP
5TH AVE & ROOSEVELT ROAD 60141 343-7200

Hinsdale, AC 708, PC 7, Du Page
Hinsdale CCSD 181 5-11100
5905 S COUNTY LINE RD 60521 887-1070
David Hendrix, supt.
MS, 100 S GARFIELD AVE 60521 3-00100
Walter Kistenfeger, prin. 887-1370

Hinsdale Twp. HSD 86 5-00011
200 55TH AND GRANT ST 60521 655-6100
John Thorson, supt.
Hinsdale Central HS 4-00011
200 55TH AND GRANT ST 60521 887-1340
Roger Miller, prin.
Other Schools – See Darien

Hinsdale Sanitarium & Hospital HSP
120 N OAK ST 60521 887-2415

Hoffman Estates, AC 708, PC 8, Cook
Schaumburg CCSD 54
Supt. — See Schaumburg
Eisenhower JHS, 800 HASSELL RD 60195 3-00100
James Muir, prin. 885-6760

Township HSD 211
Supt. — See Palatine
Conant HS, 700 E COUGAR TRL 60194   4-00011
   William Perry, prin.   885-4366
HS, 1100 W HIGGINS RD 60195   4-00011
   Dennis Garber, prin.   882-8000

ITT Technical Institute   2-CC
   375 W HIGGINS RD 60195   519-9300

Homer, AC 217, PC 4, Champaign
Heritage CUSD 8, 512 W 1ST ST 61849   3-11111
   Oris Bunn, supt.   896-2041
Heritage JHS, 512 W 1ST ST 61849   2-00100
   Judith Pacey, prin.   896-2421
Other Schools – See Broadlands

Homewood, AC 708, PC 7, Cook
Homewood SD 153   4-11100
   18205 ABERDEEN ST 60430   799-5661
   H. James Mahan, supt.
Hart JHS, 18211 ABERDEEN ST 60430   3-00100
   Richard Dervin, prin.   799-5544

Hoopeston, AC 217, PC 6, Vermilion
Hoopeston Area CUSD 11   4-11111
   615 E ORANGE ST 60942   283-6668
   Donald Dean, supt.
Hoopeston Area HS   3-00011
   615 E ORANGE ST 60942   283-6662
   Mark Conolly, prin.
Hoopeston Area JHS   2-00100
   615 E ORANGE ST 60942   283-6664
   Larry Hill, prin.

Hopkins Park, AC 815, PC 3, Kankakee
Pembroke CCSD 259, PO BOX AA 60944   3-11100
   Billy Mitchell, supt.   944-8168
Smith MS, PO BOX AG 60944   2-01100
   Robert Turner, prin.   944-5219

Hume, AC 217, PC 2, Edgar
Shiloh SD 2, RR 1 BOX 100 61932   2-11111
   Leo Sherman, supt.   887-2366
Shiloh HS, RR 1 BOX 100 61932   2-00011
   Philip Schumaker, prin.   887-2364

Huntley, AC 708, PC 4, McHenry
Huntley Consolidated SD 158   3-11111
   12017 MILL ST 60142   669-5248
   Robert Bunt, supt.
HS, 12015 MILL ST 60142   2-00011
   Gene Goeglein, prin.   669-5171

Hutsonville, AC 618, PC 3, Crawford
Hutsonville CUSD 1   2-11111
   W CLOVER ST 62433   563-4912
   Robert Chinn, supt.
HS, W CLOVER ST 62433   2-00011
   Robert McMillen, prin.   563-4913

Illiopolis, AC 217, PC 3, Sangamon
Illiopolis CUSD 12   2-11111
   PO BOX 240 62539   486-2241
   James Francis, supt.
HS, PO BOX 240 62539   1-00011
   Bill Dethrow, prin.   486-2241
JHS, PO BOX 240 62539   1-00100
   Bill Dethrow, prin.   486-2241

Ina, AC 618, PC 2, Jefferson

Rend Lake College   4-CC
   RR 1 62846   437-5321

Industry, AC 309, PC 3, McDonough
Industry CUSD 165   2-11111
   PO BOX 207 61440   254-3560
   Thomas Phelps, supt.
HS, PO BOX 207 61440   1-00011
   Sherri Zimmerman, prin.   254-3360

Ingleside, AC 708, PC see Fox Lake
Big Hollow SD 38   2-11100
   34699 N US HIGHWAY 12 60041   587-2632
   Ron Pazanin, supt.
Big Hollow MS   2-00100
   34643 N US HIGHWAY 12 60041   587-6800
   Katrina Heden, prin.
Gavin SD 37   3-11100
   25775 W ROUTE 134 60041   546-9913
   J. Michael Maloney, supt.
Gavin South JHS   2-00100
   25775 W STATE ROUTE 134 60041   546-9337
   Robert Bein, prin.

Itasca, AC 708, PC 6, Du Page
Itasca SD 10   3-11100
   400 E IRVING PARK RD 60143   773-1232
   Glennon Acksel, supt.
Peacock JHS, 301 E NORTH ST 60143   2-00100
   E. Anthony Degrazia, prin.   773-0335

National Safety Council   2-HMS
   1121 SPRING LAKE DR # 558 60143

Jacksonville, AC 217, PC 7, Morgan
Jacksonville SD 117   5-11111
   516 JORDAN ST 62650   243-9411
   Robert Freeman, supt.
HS, 1211 N DIAMOND ST 62650   4-00011
   Thomas Young, prin.   243-4384
Turner JHS, 664 LINCOLN AVE 62650   3-00100
   Paul Belobrajdic, prin.   243-3383

Heartland School of Business   2-CS
   211 W STATE ST STE 204 62650   243-9001
Illinois College   3-UC
   1101 W COLLEGE AVE 62650   245-3000
Illinois School for the Deaf   HND
   125 S WEBSTER ST 62650
Illinois School for Visually Impaired   HND
   658 E STATE ST 62650
MacMurray College   4-UC
   447 E COLLEGE AVE 62650   479-7000
Routt HS, 500 E COLLEGE AVE 62650   2-00011
   David Miller, prin.   243-8563
Westfair Christian Academy   2-11111
   14 CLARK DR 62650   243-7100
   Randy Cooper, prin.

Jerseyville, AC 618, PC 6, Jersey
Jerseyville CUSD 100   5-11111
   100 LINCOLN AVE 62052   498-5561
   Donald Snyders, supt.
Jersey Community HS   3-00011
   801 N STATE ST 62052   498-5521
   George Church, prin.
Illini JHS, 1101 S LIBERTY ST 62052   3-00100
   Thomas Frazier, prin.   498-5527

Johnston City, AC 618, PC 5, Williamson
Johnston City CUSD 1   4-11111
   1103 MONROE AVE 62951   983-8021
   John Metzger, supt.
HS, 1500 JEFFERSON AVE 62951   2-00011
   Robert Dobraski, prin.   983-8638

Joliet, AC 815, PC 8, Will
Joliet SD 86, 420 N RAYNOR AVE 60435   6-11100
   Louise Coleman, supt.   740-3196
Dirksen JHS, 203 S MIDLAND AVE 60436   3-00100
   Charles Kransberger, prin.   729-1566
Gompers JHS   3-00100
   1501 COPPERFIELD AVE 60432   727-5276
   Charles Kollross, prin.
Hufford JHS, 1125 N LARKIN AVE 60435   3-00100
   James Poch, prin.   725-3540
Washington JHS   3-00100
   402 RICHARDS ST 60433   727-5271
   Louis Nichols, prin.

Joliet Twp. HSD 204   5-00011
   201 E JEFFERSON ST 60432   727-6970
   Charles Baird, supt.
Joliet Central HS   4-00011
   201 E JEFFERSON ST 60432   727-6740
   James Maloney, prin.
Joliet West HS   4-00011
   401 N LARKIN AVE 60435   727-6940
   Richard Samlin, prin.

Troy CCSD 30 C   4-11100
   3077 W JEFFERSON ST STE 203 60435   725-8307
   Clair Swan, supt.
Troy JHS, 3077 W JEFFERSON ST 60435   3-01100
   Teri Wilson, prin.   725-6210

College of Saint Francis   4-UC
   500 WILCOX ST 60435   740-3369
Joliet Catholic Academy   3-00011
   1200 N LARKIN AVE 60435   741-0500
   Fr. Bernhard Bauerle, prin.
Joliet Junior College   6-CC
   1216 HOUBOLT DR 60436   729-9020
Marantha Christian S   2-11111
   1801 MAPLE RD 60432   726-3921
   Faith Baker, prin.
Ridgewood Baptist Academy   2-11111
   1968 HILLCREST RD 60433   726-2121
   David Rifenberick, prin.
St. Joseph College of Nursing   1-UC
   290 SPRINGFIELD AVE 60435   741-7382

Joppa, AC 618, PC 2, Massac
Joppa-Maple Grove CUSD 38   2-11111
   PO BOX 10 62953 – Ron Gray, supt.   543-7589
JSHS, PO BOX 10 62953   2-00111
   Steve Webb, prin.   543-7589

Joy, AC 309, PC 2, Mercer
Westmer CUSD 203   3-11111
   PO BOX 436 61260 – (—), supt.   584-4173
Westmer HS, PO BOX 436 61260   2-00011
   David Johnson, prin.   584-4174
Westmer JHS, PO BOX 436 61260   2-00100
   David Johnson, prin.   584-4174

Junction, AC 618, PC 2, Gallatin
Gallatin CUSD 7   4-11111
   RR 1 BOX 159 62954   272-3821
   Andy Hopson, supt.
Gallatin HS, RR 1 BOX 159 62954   2-00011
   Mike Phelps, prin.   272-5141
Gallatin JHS, RR 1 BOX 159 62954   2-00100
   David Disney, prin.   272-7341

Justice, AC 708, PC 7, Cook
Indian Springs SD 109   5-11100
   8001 S 82ND AVE 60458   496-8700
   Charles Thier, supt.
Wilkins JHS, 8001 S 82ND AVE 60458   3-00100
   Patrick Kurivial, prin.   496-8708

Kampsville, AC 618, PC 2, Calhoun
Calhoun CUSD 40
Supt. — See Hardin
Calhoun MS, PO BOX 336 62053   2-00100
   Michael Roth, prin.   653-4612

Kankakee, AC 815, PC 8, Kankakee
Kankakee SD 111   6-11111
   240 WARREN AVE 60901   933-0700
   Kay Green, supt.
HS, 1200 W JEFFERY ST 60901   4-00011
   Linda Yonke, prin.   933-0740
JHS, 2250 E CRESTWOOD ST 60901   3-00100
   Ronald Jones, prin.   933-0730

Bishop McNamara HS   2-00011
   BROOKMONT BLVD 60901   923-7413
   Fr. Lewandowski, prin.
Grace Baptist Academy   2-11111
   2499 WALDRON RD 60901   939-4579
   Gregory Rukes, prin.
Kankakee Community College   4-CC
   PO BOX 888 60901   933-0211
Marycrest College   1-CS
   280 E MERCHANT ST 60901   932-8724
Olivet Nazarene University 60901   4-UC
      939-5203

Kansas, AC 217, PC 3, Edgar
Kansas CUSD 3, PO BOX 350 61933   2-11111
   Lawrence Hanner, supt.   948-5174
HS, PO BOX 350 61933   2-00011
   Don Morgan, prin.   948-5175

Kempton, AC 815, PC 2, Ford
Tri-Point CUSD 6-J   3-11111
   PO BOX 128 60946   253-6299
   Wayne Blunier, supt.
Other Schools – See Cullom

Kewanee, AC 309, PC 7, Henry
Kewanee CUSD 229, 210 LYLE ST 61443   4-11111
   J. L. Golby, supt.   853-3341
HS, 1211 E 3RD ST 61443   3-00011
   Marvin Damron, prin.   853-3341

Wethersfield CUSD 230   3-11111
   439 WILLARD ST 61443   853-4860
   Gary Harrison, supt.
Wethersfield JSHS   2-00111
   439 WILLARD ST 61443   853-4205
   Thomas Buck, prin.

Black Hawk College   3-CC
   PO BOX 489 61443

Kincaid, AC 217, PC 4, Christian
South Fork SD 14, PO BOX 20 62540   2-11111
   Douglas Wilson, supt.   237-4333
South Fork JSHS, PO BOX 20 62540   2-00111
   Ronald Logan, prin.   237-4333

Kinderhook, AC 217, PC 2, Pike
West Pike CUSD 2   2-11111
   PO BOX 189 62345   432-8324
   Roger Hannel, supt.
West Pike HS, PO BOX 189 62345   1-00011
   Thomas Leahy, prin.   432-8324
West Pike JHS, CHANEY AVE 62345   1-00100
   Thomas Leahy, prin.   432-8324

Kinmundy, AC 618, PC 3, Marion
South Central CUSD 401   3-11111
   PO BOX 189 62854   547-3414
   William Walters, supt.
South Central MS, PO BOX 189 62854   2-00100
   Steve Laur, supt.   547-7734
Other Schools – See Farina

Kirkland, AC 815, PC 4, De Kalb
Hiawatha CUSD 426   3-11111
   PO BOX 428 60146   522-6676
   Kenneth Brooks, supt.
Hiawatha HS, PO BOX 428 60146   2-00011
   Grover Stevens, prin.   522-3335

Knoxville, AC 309, PC 5, Knox
Knoxville CUSD 202   4-11111
   600 E MAIN ST 61448   289-2328
   James Wenstom, supt.
HS, 600 E MAIN ST 61448   2-00011
   James Dunnan, prin.   289-2324
JHS, 701 MILL ST 61448   2-01100
   Debra Galbreath, prin.   289-4126

Lafox, AC 708, PC 2, Kane

Broadview Academy   2-00011
   PO BOX 307 60147   232-7441
   William Ruby, prin.

La Grange, AC 708, PC 7, Cook
La Grange Highlands SD 106   3-11100
   1750 W PLAINFIELD RD 60525   246-3085
   Elise Grimes, supt.
Highlands MS   2-00100
   1850 W PLAINFIELD RD 60525   579-6890
   H. Arthur Grundke, prin.

La Grange SD 102
Supt. — See La Grange Park
Park JHS, 325 N PARK RD 60525   3-00100
   James Battle, prin.   482-9300

La Grange SD 105   3-11100
   1001 S SPRING AVE 60525   482-2700
   Edward Olds, supt.
Gurrie JHS, 1001 S SPRING AVE 60525   2-00100
   James Ewing, prin.   482-2720

Lyons Twp. HSD 204 — 5-00011
100 S BRAINARD AVE   60525 — 579-6300
Dennis Kelly, supt.
Lyons Twp. SHS North — 4-00001
100 S BRAINARD AVE   60525 — 579-6300
Dolores Fittanto, prin.
Other Schools – See Western Springs

Pleasantdale SD 107 — 3-11110
7450 WOLF RD   60525 — 784-2013
Alice Ericksen, supt.
Pleasantdale North MS — 2-01100
7450 WOLF RD   60525 — 246-3210
John Peterson, prin.

La Grange Park, AC 708, PC 7, Cook
La Grange SD 102, 333 N PARK RD   60525 — 4-11100
Glenn Gustafson, supt. — 482-2400
Other Schools – See La Grange

Nazareth Academy — 3-00011
1209 W OGDEN AVE   60525 — 354-0061
Sr. Jacqueline Schmitz, prin.

La Harpe, AC 217, PC 4, Hancock
La Harpe CUSD 335, RR 1 BOX A   61450 — 2-11111
Steven Breckon, supt. — 659-7739
HS, RR 1 BOX A   61450 — 2-00011
Charles Apt, prin. — 659-3713
JHS, RR 1 BOX A   61450 — 2-00100
Gary Eddington, prin. — 659-7923

Lake Bluff, AC 708, PC 6, Lake
Lake Bluff ESD 65 — 3-11100
121 E SHERIDAN PL   60044 — 234-9400
Mark Vanclay, supt.
JHS, 31 E SHERIDAN PL   60044 — 2-00100
Kathleen O'Hara, prin. — 234-9407

Lake Forest, AC 708, PC 7, Lake
Lake Forest Community HSD 115 — 4-00011
1285 N MCKINLEY RD   60045 — 234-3600
Robert Kessler, supt.
HS, 1285 N MCKINLEY RD   60045 — 4-00011
Marilyn Howell, prin. — 234-3600

Lake Forest SD 67 — 4-11100
95 W DEERPATH RD   60045 — 234-6010
Arthur Jones, supt.
Deer Path JHS — 3-00100
155 W DEERPATH RD   60045 — 234-6010
Gary Kreischer, prin.

Lincolnshire-Prairieview SD 103 — 4-11100
1370 RIVERWOODS RD   60045 — 295-4030
Scott Guziec, supt.
Wright MS — 2-00100
1370 RIVERWOODS RD   60045 — 295-1560
Darryl Handcock, prin.

Barat College — 3-UC
700 E WESTLEIGH RD   60045 — 234-3000
Grove School — HND
40 E OLD MILL RD   60045
Lake Forest Academy — 2-00011
1500 W KENNEDY RD   60045 — 234-3210
Mary Hodgkins, prin.
Lake Forest College — 4-UC
555 N SHERIDAN RD   60045 — 234-3100
Lake Forest Graduate Sch. of Management — 2-UC
280 N SHERIDAN RD   60045 — 234-5080
Woodlands Academy — 2-00011
760 E WESTLEIGH RD   60045 — 234-4300
Sr. Claude Demoustier, prin.

Lake Villa, AC 708, PC 5, Lake
Lake Villa CCSD 41 — 4-11100
131 MCKINLEY AVE   60046 — 356-2385
Alan Simon, supt.
IS, 133 MCKINLEY AVE   60046 — 3-00100
Glenn Camp, prin. — 356-2118

Lake Zurich, AC 708, PC 7, Lake
Lake Zurich CUSD 95 — 5-11111
66 CHURCH ST   60047 — 438-2831
Edward Cox, supt.
HS, 300 CHURCH ST   60047 — 4-00011
Wayne Erck, prin. — 438-5155
MS North Campus — 3-00100
100 CHURCH ST   60047 — 438-2361
Philip Zarob, prin.
MS South Campus — 2-00100
435 W CUBA RD   60047 — 540-0003
William Ristow, prin.

La Moille, AC 815, PC 3, Bureau
La Moille CUSD 303 — 2-11111
PO BOX 470   61330 — 638-2018
Gerald Donahue, supt.
HS, PO BOX 470   61330 — 2-00011
Dennis Thompson, prin. — 638-2144
Allen MS, PO BOX 470   61330 — 2-01100
Gerald Donahue, prin. — 638-2233

Lanark, AC 815, PC 4, Carroll
Eastland CUSD 308 — 3-11111
200 S SCHOOL ST   61046 — 493-6301
Robert Colborn, supt.
Eastland HS, 500 S SCHOOL DR   61046 — 2-00011
Don Siegmund, supt. — 493-6341
Other Schools – See Shannon

Lansing, AC 708, PC 8, Cook
Lansing SD 158, 2721 RIDGE RD   60438 — 4-11100
W. H. Simpson, supt. — 474-6700

Memorial JHS, 2721 RIDGE RD   60438 — 3-00100
James Shrader, prin. — 474-2383
Sunnybrook SD 171 — 4-11100
19266 BURNHAM AVE   60438 — 895-0750
John Lucy, supt.
Heritage MS — 3-01100
19250 BURNHAM AVE   60438 — 895-0790
Dennis Soustek, prin.

Thornton Fractional Twp. HSD 215
Supt. — See Calumet City
Thornton Fractional South HS — 4-00011
18500 BURNHAM AVE   60438 — 418-1920
James Spivey, prin.

Illiana Christian HS — 3-00011
2261 INDIANA AVE   60438 — 474-0515
William Finley, prin.

La Salle, AC 815, PC 6, La Salle
La Salle-Peru Twp HSD 120 — 4-00011
541 CHARTRES ST   61301 — 223-1721
Robert Pomije, supt.
La Salle-Peru Twp HS — 4-00011
541 CHARTRES ST   61301 — 223-1721
Bruce Bauer, prin.

La Salle ESD 122 — 3-11100
1165 SAINT VINCENTS AVE   61301 — 223-0786
Al Humpage, supt.
Lincoln JHS — 2-00100
1165 SAINT VINCENTS AVE   61301 — 223-0933
Gerald Affelt, prin.

Lasalle-Peru Christian S — 2-11111
200 24TH ST   61301 — 223-1037
Lloyd Streeter, prin.

Lawrenceville, AC 618, PC 5, Lawrence
Lawrence County CUSD 20 — 4-11111
1802 CEDAR ST   62439 — 943-2326
Michael Weaver, supt.
HS, 503 8TH ST   62439 — 2-00011
Jon Frohock, prin. — 943-3389
Park View JHS, 1802 CEDAR ST   62439 — 2-00100
Douglas Slover, prin. — 943-2327

Lebanon, AC 618, PC 5, St. Clair
Lebanon CUSD 9 — 3-11111
200 W SCHUETZ ST   62254 — 537-4611
Charles Rohn, supt.
HS, 200 W SCHUETZ ST   62254 — 2-00011
Betty Gabryshak, prin. — 537-4423

McKendree College — 3-UC
701 COLLEGE RD   62254 — 537-4481

Leland, AC 815, PC 3, La Salle
Leland CUSD 1, 370 N MAIN ST   60531 — 2-11111
James Doolin, supt. — 495-3821
HS, 370 N MAIN ST   60531 — 2-00011
Randall Dwyer, prin. — 495-3231

Lemont, AC 708, PC 6, Cook
Lemont-Bromberek SD 113A — 4-11100
1130 KIM PL   60439 — 257-2286
C. Thomas Reiter, supt.
Central MS, 410 MCCARTHY RD   60439 — 2-00100
Thomas Lenhardt, prin. — 257-5476

Lemont Twp. HSD 210 — 3-00011
800 PORTER ST   60439 — 257-5838
Thomas Madden, supt.
Lemont Twp. HS, 800 PORTER ST   60439 — 2-00011
Thomas Trengove, prin. — 257-5838

Mt. Assissi Academy — 2-00011
13860 MAIN ST   60439 — 257-7844
Sr. Thomasine Novakovich, prin.

Lena, AC 815, PC 5, Stephenson
Lena-Winslow CUSD 202 — 4-11100
517 FREMONT ST   61048 — 369-4527
David Morrison, supt.
Lena-Winslow HS — 2-00011
516 FREMONT ST   61048 — 369-4548
Larry Maaske, prin.
Lena-Winslow JHS — 2-00100
517 FREMONT ST   61048 — 369-4991
David Morrison, prin.

Le Roy, AC 309, PC 5, McLean
Le Roy CUSD 2, 600 E PINE ST   61752 — 3-11111
Richard Schuler, supt. — 962-4211
HS, 505 E CENTER ST   61752 — 2-00011
Mike Company, prin. — 962-2911
JHS, 505 E CENTER ST   61752 — 2-00100
Mike Company, prin. — 962-2911

Lewistown, AC 309, PC 5, Fulton
Lewistown Community HSD 341 — 2-00011
PO BOX 37   61542 — 547-2288
Richard Well, supt.
Lewistown Community HS — 2-00011
PO BOX 37   61542 — 547-2288
Richard Well, prin.

Lewistown SD 141 — 3-11100
315 S ILLINOIS ST   61542 — 547-2259
Dennis Smith, supt.
Central MS, 401 E AVENUE L   61542 — 2-01100
William Timmons, prin. — 547-2231

Lexington, AC 309, PC 4, McLean
Lexington CUSD 7, PO BOX 67   61753 — 3-11111
Brent McArdle, supt. — 365-4141
HS, PO BOX 67   61753 — 2-00011
Michael Hawkins, prin. — 365-2711
JHS, PO BOX 67   61753 — 1-00100
John Coffey, prin. — 365-2741

Liberty, AC 217, PC 3, Adams
Liberty CUSD 2, PO BOX 199   62347 — 3-11111
Hobson Bale, supt. — 645-3433
HS, PO BOX 199   62347 — 2-00011
Lee Hoffman, prin. — 645-3389

Libertyville, AC 708, PC 7, Lake
Libertyville Community HSD 128 — 4-00011
708 W PARK AVE   60048 — 367-3159
Donald Gossett, supt.
SHS, 708 W PARK AVE   60048 — 4-00001
Wilber Booker, prin. — 367-3100
Brainerd Mid. HS — 3-00010
416 W PARK AVE   60048 — 367-3130
Wilber Booker, prin.

Libertyville SD 70, 1441 LAKE ST   60048 — 4-11100
Mark Friedman, supt. — 362-8393
Highland JHS — 3-00100
310 W ROCKLAND RD   60048 — 362-9020
Paul Kremaku, prin.

Lincoln, AC 217, PC 7, Logan
Lincoln Community HSD 404 — 3-00011
1000 PRIMM RD   62656 — 732-4131
Jerry Overby, supt.
Lincoln Community HS — 3-00011
1000 PRIMM RD   62656 — 732-4131
Fred Plese, prin.

Lincoln ESD 27, 100 S MAPLE ST   62656 — 4-11100
Lester Plotner, supt. — 732-2522
JHS, 208 BROADWAY ST   62656 — 2-00100
Wilbur Williams, prin. — 732-3535

Lincoln Christian College — 2-UC
100 CAMPUS VIEW DR   62656 — 732-3168
Lincoln College — 3-CC
300 KEOKUK ST   62656 — 732-3155

Lincolnshire, AC 708, PC 5, Lake
Adlai E. Stevenson SD 125
Supt. — See Prairie View
Stevenson HS — 4-00011
16070 W STATE ROUTE 22   60069 — 634-4000
Timothy Berkey, prin.

Lincolnwood, AC 708, PC 7, Cook
Lincolnwood SD 74 — 4-11100
6950 NE PRAIRIE RD   60645 — 675-8234
John Cahill, supt.
Lincoln Hall MS — 3-01100
6855 N CRAWFORD AVE   60646 — 675-8240
Mary Lou Johns, prin.

Lisle, AC 708, PC 7, Du Page
Lisle CUSD 202 — 4-11111
5211 CENTER AVE   60532 — 971-4050
Carlin Nalley, supt.
HS, 1800 SHORT ST   60532 — 2-00011
Ronald Logeman, prin. — 971-4370
JHS, 5207 CENTER AVE   60532 — 2-00100
Roger Wanic, prin. — 971-4350

Naperville CUSD 203
Supt. — See Naperville
Kennedy JHS — 3-00100
2929 GREEN TRAILS DR   60532 — 420-3220
Russell Bryan, prin.

Benet Academy, 2200 MAPLE AVE   60532 — 4-00011
Ernest Stark, prin. — 969-6550
Illinois Benedictine College — 4-UC
5700 COLLEGE RD   60532 — 960-1500

Litchfield, AC 217, PC 6, Montgomery
Litchfield CUSD 12 — 4-11111
1702 N STATE ST   62056 — 324-2157
David Elson, supt.
HS, 1705 N STATE ST   62056 — 2-00011
Dennis Canny, prin. — 324-3955
JHS, 1701 N STATE ST   62056 — 2-00100
Don Williams, prin. — 324-4668

Livingston, AC 618, PC 3, Madison
Livingston CCSD 4 — 2-11111
PO BOX 400   62058 — 637-2130
L. William Fever, supt.
JSHS, PO BOX 400   62058 — 1-00111
Tom Luenemann, prin. — 637-2130

Lockport, PC 6, Will
Fairmont SD 89 — 2-11100
745 GREEN GARDEN PL   60441 — 815-726-6156
Paul Rundio, supt.
Fairmont JHS — 2-01100
735 GREEN GARDEN PL   60441 — 815-726-5263
Dorothy Gee, prin.

Homer CCSD 33C — 5-11100
15733 S BELL RD   60441 — 708-301-3034
Edward Karns, supt.
Homer JHS, 15711 S BELL RD   60441 — 3-00100
Frank Fagan, prin. — 708-301-5500

Lockport Twp. HSD 205 — 4-00011
1323 E 7TH ST 60441 — 815-834-4400
Christopher Ward, supt.
Lockport Twp. SHS Central — 3-00001
1222 S JEFFERSON ST 60441 — 815-834-4340
Garry Raymond, prin.
Lockport Twp. Mid. HS East — 4-00010
1333 E 7TH ST 60441 — 815-834-4440
Robert Meader, prin.

Milne-Kelvin Grove SD 91 — 3-11100
808 ADAMS ST 60441 — 815-838-0737
James Stott, supt.
Kelvin Grove JHS — 2-00100
808 ADAMS ST 60441 — 815-838-0737
James Stott, prin.

Will County SD 92 — 4-11100
708 N STATE ST 60441 — 815-838-8031
John Tarter, supt.
Ludwig MS, 710 N STATE ST 60441 — 3-01100
William Barney, prin. — 815-838-8020

Cave Technical Institute — 4-CS
2842 S STATE ST 60441 — 815-727-1576

Lombard, AC 708, PC 8, Du Page
Glenbard Twp. HSD 87
Supt. — See Glen Ellyn
Glenbard East HS — 4-00011
1014 S MAIN ST 60148 — 627-9250
Paul Hadley, prin.

Lombard SD 44 — 5-11100
150 W MADISON ST 60148 — 620-3700
Gordon Wendlandt, supt.
Glenn Westlake MS — 3-00100
1514 S MAIN ST 60148 — 620-3785
Kim Perkins, prin.

Connecticut School of Broadcasting — 2-CS
200 W 22ND ST STE 202 60148 — 916-1700
Montini Catholic HS — 2-00011
19W070 16TH ST 60148 — 627-6930
Br. Thomas Harding, prin.
National College of Chiropractic — 3-UC
200 E ROOSEVELT RD 60148 — 629-2000
Northern Baptist Theological Seminary — 2-UC
660 E BUTTERFIELD RD 60148 — 620-2101

London Mills, AC 309, PC 2, Fulton
Spoon River Valley CUSD 4 — 3-11111
RR 1 BOX 55 61544 — 778-2204
David Ford, supt.
Spoon River Valley HS — 2-00011
RR 1 BOX 55 61544 — 778-2201
Larry Kernagis, prin.
Spoon River Valley JHS — 1-00100
RR 1 BOX 55 61544 — 778-2201
Larry Kernagis, prin.

Louisville, AC 618, PC 4, Clay
North Clay CUSD 25 — 3-11111
PO BOX 220 62858 — 665-3358
Ray Green, supt.
North Clay Comm. HS — 2-00011
PO BOX 220 62858 — 665-3102
Wilson Ford, prin.
North Clay JHS, PO BOX 279 62858 — 2-00100
Don Carlyle, prin. — 665-3393

Lovejoy, AC 618, PC 4, St. Clair
Brooklyn Unit SD 188 — 2-11111
800 MADISON ST 62059 — 271-1014
Carl Jason, supt.
HS, 800 MADISON ST 62059 — 1-00011
Robert Isom, prin. — 271-1014
JHS, 800 MADISON ST 62059 — 1-00100
(—), prin. — 271-1014

Loves Park, AC 815, PC 7, Winnebago
Harlem Unit SD 122 — 6-11111
PO BOX 2021 61130 — 654-4500
Donald Parker, supt.
Harlem JHS, 735 WINDSOR RD 61111 — 4-00110
James McClurg, prin. — 654-4510
Other Schools – See Machesney Park

Lovington, AC 217, PC 4, Moultrie
Lovington CUSD 303 — 2-11111
PO BOX 560 61937 — 873-4310
Richard Nelson, supt.
HS, PO BOX 530 61937 — 2-00011
Judy Uphoff, prin. — 873-4316

Machesney Park, AC 815, PC 7, Winnebago
Harlem Unit SD 122
Supt. — See Loves Park
Harlem SHS, 1 HUSKIE CIRCLE 61115 — 4-00001
Nelson Pyle, prin. — 654-4511

Mackinaw, AC 309, PC 4, Tazewell
Deer Creek-Mackinaw CUSD 701 — 3-11111
PO BOX 110 61755 — 359-4421
Ken Cox, supt.
Deer Creek-Mackinaw HS — 2-00011
PO BOX 110 61755 — 359-4421
Robin Houchin, prin.
Deer Creek Mackinaw ES — 2-10100
PO BOX 80 61755 — 359-4321
Dallas Davis, prin.

Macomb, AC 309, PC 7, McDonough
Macomb CUSD 185 — 4-11111
323 W WASHINGTON ST 61455 — 833-4161
Larry Roth, supt.
JSHS, 1525 S JOHNSON ST 61455 — 4-00011
Michael Sartore, prin. — 837-2331

McDonough District Hospital — HSP
525 E GRANT ST 61455 — 833-4101
Western Illinois University — 7-UC
900 W ADAMS ST 61455 — 295-1414

Macon, AC 217, PC 4, Macon
Macon CUSD 5, 728 S WALL ST 62544 — 3-11111
Roger Mitchell, supt. — 764-5251
HS, 728 S WALL ST 62544 — 2-00011
C. Loveall, prin. — 764-5233
MS, 728 S WALL ST 62544 — 2-00100
George Warnick, prin. — 764-5421

Madison, AC 618, PC 5, Madison
Madison CUSD 12, 1707 4TH ST 62060 — 4-11111
Daniel Kostencki, supt. — 877-1712
HS, 600 FARRISH ST 62060 — 2-00011
Robert Mehelic, prin. — 876-7010
MS, 1003 FARRISH ST 62060 — 2-01100
Raelynn Parks, prin. — 876-6409

Mahomet, AC 217, PC 5, Champaign
Mahomet-Seymour CUSD 3 — 4-11111
PO BOX 229 61853 — 586-2161
F. Leon Rodgers, supt.
Mahomet-Seymour HS — 3-00011
PO BOX 1098 61853 — 586-4962
John Harland, prin.
Mahomet-Seymour JHS — 3-00100
PO BOX 560 61853 — 586-4415
Del Ryan, prin.

Kishwaukee College — 4-CC
21193 MALTA RD 60150 — 825-2086

Manito, AC 309, PC 4, Mason
Midwest Central CUSD 191 — 4-11111
1010 S WASHINGTON ST 61546 — 968-6868
Michael Risen, supt.
Midwest Central HS — 2-00011
910 S WASHINGTON ST 61546 — 968-6766
Kathryn Cihlar, prin.
Midwest Central JHS — 2-00100
350 SOUTHMOOR ST 61546 — 968-6464
Scott Kuffel, prin.

Manlius, AC 815, PC 2, Bureau
Manlius CUSD 305 — 2-11111
PO BOX 289 61338 — 445-2592
Daryl McManus, supt.
HS, W MAPLE ST 61338 — 1-00011
Donna Luallen, prin. — 445-2842

Mansfield, AC 217, PC 3, Piatt
Blue Ridge CUSD 18
Supt. — See Farmer City
Blue Ridge JHS — 2-00100
247 MCKINLEY ST 61854 – (—), prin. — 489-5201

Manteno, AC 815, PC 5, Kankakee
Manteno CUSD 5 — 4-11111
250 N POPLAR ST 60950 — 468-8442
Dale Adams, supt.
HS, 443 N MAPLE ST 60950 — 2-00011
Anthony Plese, prin. — 468-8115
JHS, 250 N POPLAR ST 60950 — 2-01100
David Nelson, prin. — 468-8016

Maple Park, AC 708, PC 3, Kane
Kaneland CUSD 302 — 4-11111
47W326 KESLINGER RD 60151 — 365-5109
Dennis Dunton, supt.
Kaneland HS — 3-00011
47W326 KESLINGER RD 60151 — 365-5100
Ralph Heatherington, prin.
Kaneland MS — 2-00100
47W326 KESLINGER RD 60151 — 365-5100
Robert Woodrick, prin.

Marengo, AC 815, PC 5, McHenry
Marengo-Union CCSD 165 — 3-11100
539 LOCUST ST 60152 – Jim Cox, supt. — 568-8323
Locust MS, 539 LOCUST ST 60152 — 3-01100
Elizabeth Sullivan, prin. — 568-7632

Marengo Community HSD 154 — 2-00011
816 E GRANT HWY 60152 — 568-6511
Robert Seaver, supt.
HS, 816 E GRANT HWY 60152 — 2-00011
Jerry Trickett, prin. — 568-6511

Marion, AC 618, PC 7, Williamson
Crab Orchard CUSD 3 — 2-11111
RR 2 BOX 307 62959 — 982-2181
Dee Ozment, supt.
Crab Orchard HS — 2-00011
RR 2 BOX 307 62959 — 982-2181
Howard Stephens, prin.

Marion CUSD 2 — 5-11111
1410 W HENDRICKSON ST 62959 — 993-2321
Thomas Oates, supt.
HS, 1501 S CARBON ST 62959 — 4-00011
Albert Anderson, prin. — 993-8196
JHS, 1501 W MAIN ST 62959 — 3-00100
Kenneth McAnelly, prin. — 997-1317

Marissa, AC 618, PC 4, St. Clair
Marissa CUSD 40 — 3-11111
300 SCHOOL VIEW DR 62257 — 295-2313
Paul Tockstein, supt.
JSHS, 300 SCHOOL VIEW DR 62257 — 2-00111
Steve Harsy, prin. — 295-2393

Markham, AC 708, PC 7, Cook
Prairie-Hills ESD 144
Supt. — See Hazel Crest
Prairie-Hills JHS, 3035 W 153RD 60426 — 3-00100
Diedrus Underwood, prin. — 210-2860

Maroa, AC 217, PC 4, Macon
Maroa-Forsyth CUSD 2 — 3-11111
PO BOX 110 61756 — 794-3488
Stephen Stenger, supt.
Maroa-Forsyth HS — 2-00011
PO BOX 110 61756 — 794-3463
Jeffrey Holmes, prin.
Maroa-Forsyth JHS — 2-00100
PO BOX 110 61756 — 794-5115
Jeffrey Holmes, prin.

Marshall, AC 217, PC 5, Clark
Marshall CUSD 2C — 4-11111
PO BOX 160 62441 — 826-5912
Russel Ross, supt.
HS, 806 N 6TH ST 62441 — 2-00011
Ken Reed, prin. — 826-2395
JHS, 806 N 6TH ST 62441 — 2-00100
James Cooper, prin. — 826-2812

Martinsville, AC 217, PC 4, Clark
Martinsville CUSD 3C, PO BOX K 62442 — 2-11111
M. Cerra, supt. — 382-4321
HS, PO BOX K 62442 — 2-00011
Kim Hawkins, prin. — 382-4132
JHS, PO BOX K 62442 — 1-00100
Kim Hawkins, prin. — 382-4132

Mascoutah, AC 618, PC 6, St. Clair
Mascoutah CUSD 19 — 5-11111
720 W HARNETT ST 62258 — 566-7414
Victor Van Dyne, supt.
HS, 1313 W MAIN ST 62258 — 3-00011
Conrad Dean, prin. — 566-8523
JHS, 846 N 6TH ST 62258 — 2-00100
Raimonds Zvirbulis, prin. — 566-2305

Mason City, AC 217, PC 4, Mason
Illini Central CUSD 189 — 3-11111
208 N WEST ST 62664 — 482-5180
Randolph Harhausen, supt.
Illini Central HS, 208 N WEST ST 62664 — 2-00011
David Russell, prin. — 482-3252
Other Schools – See Easton

Matteson, AC 708, PC 7, Cook
Matteson ESD 162
Supt. — See Park Forest
Huth JHS, 3718 213TH PL 60443 — 3-00100
Ernestine Foster, prin. — 748-0470

ITT Technical Institute — 2-CS
600 HOLIDAY PLAZA DR 60443

Mattoon, AC 217, PC 7, Coles
Matoon CUSD 2, 100 N 22ND ST 61938 — 5-11111
Earnest Smith, supt. — 235-5446
HS, 2521 WALNUT AVE 61938 — 4-00011
Kirk Salmela, prin. — 234-6415
JHS, 1200 S 9TH ST 61938 — 3-00100
John Swick, prin. — 234-8859

Lake Land College — 5-CC
5001 LAKELAND BLVD 61938 — 235-3131

Maywood, AC 708, PC 8, Cook
Proviso Twp. HSD 209 — 5-00011
807 S 1ST AVE 60153 — 344-7000
Eric Eversley, supt.
Proviso East HS, 807 S 1ST AVE 60153 — 4-00011
Diane Dyer-Dawson, prin. — 344-7000
Other Schools – See Hillside

Foster G. McGaw Hospital — HSP
2160 S 1ST AVE 60153 — 216-8939
Loyola University — 3-UC
2160 S 1ST AVE 60153

Mazon, AC 815, PC 3, Grundy
Mazon-Verona-Kinsman ESD 2C — 2-11100
PO BOX 365 60444 — 448-2200
Ray Garritano, supt.
Mazon-Verona-Kinsman MS — 2-01100
PO BOX 365 60444 — 448-2127
Gary Fechter, prin.

Mc Henry, AC 815, PC 7, McHenry
Johnsburg CUSD 12 — 4-11111
2117 W CHURCH AVE 60050 — 385-6916
Robert Gough, supt.
Johnsburg HS — 3-00011
2002 W RINGWOOD RD 60050 — 385-9233
W. Dill, prin.

Johnsburg JHS — 3-00100
2117 W CHURCH AVE 60050 — 385-6210
Roger Kriewaldt, prin.

Mc Henry CCSD 15 — 5-11100
3926 MAIN ST 60050 — 385-7210
William Dodds, supt.
JHS, 3711 W KANE AVE 60050 — 3-00100 / 385-2522
Oscar Sola, prin.
Parkland JHS — 3-00100
1802 N RINGWOOD RD 60050 — 385-8810
William Burke, prin.

Mc Henry Community HSD 156 — 4-00011
3926 MAIN ST 60050 — 385-7900
Robert Swartzloff, supt.
Mc Henry HS-East — 3-00011
1012 N GREEN ST 60050 — 385-1145
Thomas Carl, prin.
Mc Henry HS-West — 3-00011
4724 W CRYSTAL LAKE RD 60050 — 385-7077
O. Gregory Johnson, prin.

Mc Leansboro, AC 618, PC 5, Hamilton
Hamilton County CUSD 10 — 4-11111
PO BOX 369 62859 — 643-2328
Lonnie Hughes, supt.
HS, 200 JERRY SLOAN ST 62859 — 2-00011 / 643-2328
Vince Mitchell, prin.
Hamilton County JHS — 2-00100
501 E RANDOLPH ST 62859 — 643-2328
Martin Cox, prin.

Mc Nabb, AC 815, PC 2, Putnam
Putnam County CUSD 535
Supt. — See Granville
Putnam Co. JHS, RR 1 BOX 15 61335 — 2-00100 / 882-2116
Gilbert Tonozzi, prin.

Media, AC 309, PC 2, Henderson
Southern CUSD 120
Supt. — See Stronghurst
Southern JHS, PO BOX 841 61460 — 2-01100 / 924-1441
Wendell Torrance, prin.

Melrose Park, AC 708, PC 7, Cook
Mannheim SD 83
Supt. — See Franklin Park
Mannheim JHS — 3-00100
2600 HYDE PARK AVE 60164 — 455-5020
Marilyn Finesilver, prin.

Walther Lutheran HS — 2-00011
900 CHICAGO AVE 60160 — 344-0404
Kevin Dunning, prin.

Melvin, AC 217, PC 2, Ford
Gibson City-Melvin-Sibley CUSD 1
Supt. — See Gibson City
GCMS MS, 300 N CENTER 60952 — 2-00100 / 388-7724
Michael Bleich, prin.

Mendon, AC 217, PC 3, Adams
Mendon CUSD 4, 380 COLLINS ST 62351 — 3-11111 / 936-2111
Gerhard Jung, supt.
Unity HS, PO BOX 218 62351 — 2-00011 / 936-2116
Doug Bryson, prin.
Unity MS, PO BOX 218 62351 — 2-00100 / 936-2727
Jan Galbraith, prin.

Mendota, AC 815, PC 6, La Salle
Mendota CCSD 289 — 4-11100
1806 GUILES AVE 61342 — 539-7631
Michael Castiglia, supt.
Northbrook MS, 1804 GUILES AVE 61342 — 2-00100 / 539-6237
Ernest Egnstrom, prin.

Mendota Twp. HSD 280 — 3-00011
302 16TH ST 61342 — 539-7446
Michael Duffy, supt.
Mendota Twp. HS, 302 16TH ST 61342 — 3-00011 / 539-7446
Robert Cooper, prin.

Meredosia, AC 217, PC 4, Morgan
Meredosia-Chambersburg CUSD 11 — 2-11111
PO BOX 440 62665 — 584-1744
William Estes, supt.
Meredosia-Chambersburg HS — 1-00011
PO BOX 440 62665 – (—), prin. — 584-1291
Meredosia-Chambersburg JHS — 1-00100
PO BOX 440 62665 – (—), prin. — 584-1291

Metamora, AC 309, PC 5, Woodford
Germantown Hills SD 69 — 3-11100
110 FANDEL RD 61548 — 383-2121
Joe Stieglitz, supt.
Germantown Hills JHS — 2-01100
103 WARRIOR WAY 61548 — 383-4121
J. Michael Dougherty, prin.

Metamora Twp. HSD 122 — 3-00011
101 W MADISON 61548 — 367-4151
Kenneth Maurer, supt.
HS, 101 W MADISON 61548 — 3-00011 / 367-4151
Greg Christy, prin.

Metropolis, AC 618, PC 6, Massac
Massac Unit SD 1, PO BOX 530 62960 — 4-11111 / 524-9376
Don Smith, supt.
Massac County HS — 3-00011
RR 2 BOX 506 62960 — 524-3440
Sidney Sexton, prin.
JHS, 1004 CATHERINE ST 62960 — 2-00100 / 524-2645
Lynne Lech, prin.

Middletown, AC 217, PC 2, Logan
New Holland-Middletown ESD 88 — 2-11100
PO BOX 187 62666 — 445-2421
James Gray, supt.
New Holland-Middletown MS — 2-01100
PO BOX 187 62666 — 445-2656
James Gray, prin.

Midlothian, AC 708, PC 7, Cook
Bremen Community HSD 228 — 5-00011
15233 PULASKI RD 60445 — 389-1175
James Riordan, supt.
Bremen HS, 15203 PULASKI RD 60445 — 3-00011 / 371-3600
Vita Meyer, prin.
Other Schools – See Country Club Hills, Oak Forest, Tinley Park

Milford, AC 815, PC 4, Iroquois
Milford Twp. HSD 233 — 2-00011
PO BOX 257 60953 — 889-4184
William Pearch, supt.
Milford Twp. HS, PO BOX 257 60953 — 2-00011 / 889-4184
Michael Gibson, prin.

Millbrook, AC 708, PC 2, Kendall
Newark CCSD 66
Supt. — See Newark
MS, 8411 FOX RIVER RD 60536 — 2-00100 / 553-5435
Debra Kurns, prin.

Milledgeville, AC 815, PC 4, Carroll
Chadwick-Milledgeville CUSD 399 — 3-11111
PO BOX 609 61051 — 225-7141
Terry Bowers, supt.
HS, PO BOX 609 61051 — 2-00011 / 225-7141
Galen Wirth, prin.
Other Schools – See Chadwick

Minonk, AC 309, PC 4, Woodford
Fieldcrest CUSD 6 — 4-11111
435 MAPLE AVE 61760 — 432-2177
Gerald Christensen, supt.
Fieldcrest HS, 435 MAPLE AVE 61760 — 2-00011 / 432-2828
Lorin Stevens, prin.
Other Schools – See Toluca, Wenona

Minooka, AC 815, PC 5, Grundy
Minooka CCSD 201 — 3-11100
PO BOX 519 60447 — 467-2261
Thomas Allen, supt.
JHS, PO BOX 519 60447 — 2-00100 / 467-2136
Sam Martin, prin.

Minooka Community HSD 111 — 3-00011
PO BOX 489 60447 — 467-2147
James Naylor, supt.
Minooka Community HS — 3-00011
PO BOX 489 60447 — 467-2147
Steven Thomas, prin.

Mokena, AC 708, PC 6, Will
Mokena SD 159, 11331 195TH ST 60448 — 4-11100 / 479-3100
Roger Reardon, supt.
JHS, 11331 195TH ST 60448 — 2-00100 / 479-3130
Gary Bradbury, prin.

Moline, AC 309, PC 8, Rock Island
Moline Unit SD 40 — 6-11111
1619 11TH AVE 61265 — 757-3500
Gilbert Walmsley, supt.
HS, 3600 23RD AVE 61265 — 4-00011 / 757-3545
Ken Schwab, prin.
Deere JHS, 2035 11TH ST 61265 — 3-00100 / 757-3535
Burdette Ringquist, prin.
Wilson JHS, 1301 48TH ST 61265 — 3-00100 / 757-3530
Clyde Storbeck, prin.

Black Hawk College — 5-CC
6600 34TH AVE 61265 — 796-1311
Commonwealth Business College — 2-CS
1527 47TH AVE 61265 — 762-2100
Temple Christian Academy — 2-11111
2305 7TH AVE 61265 — 764-1302
Bill Olmstead, prin.
United Medical Center — 1-HSP
501 10TH AVE 61265 — 757-2910

Momence, AC 815, PC 5, Kankakee
Momence CUSD 1 — 4-11111
415 N DIXIE HWY 60954 — 472-3500
Edward Allen, supt.
HS, 101 N FRANKLIN ST 60954 — 2-00011 / 472-6477
Joseph Ciaccio, prin.
JHS, 801 W 2ND ST 60954 — 2-01100 / 472-4184
Kenneth Fox, prin.

Monmouth, AC 309, PC 6, Warren
Monmouth Unit SD 38 — 4-11111
325 S 11TH ST 61462 — 734-4712
Donald Jenkins, supt.
HS, 325 W 1ST AVE 61462 — 3-00011 / 734-5118
Gary Collins, prin.
Central JHS, 401 E 2ND AVE 61462 — 2-00100 / 734-6426
Donald Daily, prin.

Warren CUSD 222, RR 1 61462 — 2-11111 / 734-9411
William Rees, supt.
Warren JSHS, RR 1 61462 — 2-00011 / 734-9411
John Van Kirk, prin.

Yorkwood CUSD 225 — 3-11111
RR 3 BOX 108 61462 — 734-8514
Daniel Whitsitt, supt.
Yorkwood HS, RR 3 61462 — 2-00011 / 734-8511
Lyman Schar, prin.

Yorkwood JHS, RR 3 61462 — 1-00100
Lyman Schar, prin. — 734-8511

Monmouth College — 3-UC
700 E BROADWAY 61462 — 457-2127

Monticello, AC 217, PC 5, Piatt
Monticello CUSD 25 — 4-11111
100 W JEFFERSON ST 61856 — 762-8511
P. David Schmink, supt.
HS, 101 E WILLIAM ST 61856 — 2-00011 / 762-8511
Fred Erickson, prin.
Washington MS — 2-01100
100 W JEFFERSON ST 61856 — 762-8511
Gerry Eckerty, prin.

Morris, AC 815, PC 7, Grundy
Morris Community HSD 101 — 3-00011
1000 UNION ST 60450 — 942-1184
Lawrence Zitkus, supt.
HS, 1000 UNION ST 60450 — 3-00011 / 942-1294
Greg Eaton, prin.

Morris SD 54, 519 FRANKLIN ST 60450 — 4-11100 / 942-0056
Michael Wright, supt.
Shabbona MS, 725 SCHOOL ST 60450 — 2-00100 / 942-3605
Charles Aubry, prin.

Nettle Creek CCSD 24 C — 1-11100
8820 SCOTT SCHOOL RD 60450 — 942-0511
David Walle, supt.
Nettle Creek MS — 1-01100
8820 SCOTT SCHOOL RD 60450 — 942-0511
David Walle, prin.

Morrison, AC 815, PC 5, Whiteside
Morrison CUSD 6 — 4-11111
643 GENESEE AVE 61270 — 772-4071
John Van Pelt, supt.
HS, 643 GENESEE AVE 61270 — 2-00011 / 772-4071
A. Robert Goff, prin.
JHS, 305 E WINFIELD ST 61270 — 2-00100 / 772-7264
James Blakemore, prin.

Morrison Institute of Technology — 2-CC
701 PORTLAND AVE 61270 — 772-7218

Morrisonville, AC 217, PC 4, Christian
Morrisonville CUSD 1 — 2-11111
PO BOX 13 62546 — 526-4431
Jerry Wesley, supt.
HS, PO BOX 13 62546 — 2-00011 / 526-4432
Jerry Birkey, prin.
JHS, PO BOX 13 62546 — 1-00100 / 526-4432
Jerry Birkey, prin.

Morton, AC 309, PC 7, Tazewell
Morton CUSD 709 — 5-11111
235 E JACKSON ST 61550 — 263-2581
Norman Durflinger, supt.
HS, 350 N ILLINOIS AVE 61550 — 3-00011 / 266-7182
Ron Patterson, prin.
JHS, 225 E JACKSON ST 61550 — 2-00100 / 266-6522
J. Michael Fuoss, prin.

Morton Grove, AC 708, PC 7, Cook
Golf ESD 67 — 2-11100
9401 WAUKEGAN RD 60053 — 966-8200
Linda Marks, supt.
Golf MS, 9401 WAUKEGAN RD 60053 — 2-01100 / 965-3740
Linda Marks, prin.

Mounds, AC 618, PC 4, Pulaski
Meridian CUSD 101 — 4-11111
RR 1 BOX 540 62964 — 342-6776
O. J. Thompson, supt.
Meridian JSHS, RR 1 BOX 600 62964 — 2-00111 / 342-6778
Larry Spain, prin.

Mount Carmel, AC 618, PC 6, Wabash
Wabash CUSD 348 — 4-11111
218 W 13TH ST 62863 — 262-4181
Larry Bradfield, supt.
HS, 201 N PEAR ST 62863 — 3-00011 / 262-5104
Sandra Ward, prin.
North MS, 1300 WALNUT ST 62863 — 3-01100 / 263-3876
Glenn Decker, prin.

Wabash Valley College — 4-CC
2222 COLLEGE DR 62863

Mount Carroll, AC 815, PC 4, Carroll
Mt. Carroll CUSD 304 — 3-11111
300 S MAIN ST 61053 — 244-2055
Paul Tobin, supt.
HS, 300 S MAIN ST 61053 — 2-00011 / 244-2055
(—), prin.
JHS, 300 S MAIN ST 61053 — 2-00100 / 244-2055
(—), prin.

Mount Morris, AC 815, PC 5, Ogle
Mt. Morris CUSD 261 — 3-11111
105 W BRAYTON RD 61054 — 734-6032
Joel McFadden, supt.
JSHS, 105 W BRAYTON RD 61054 — 2-00111 / 734-4825
Leo Marshall, prin.

Mount Olive, AC 217, PC 4, Macoupin
Mt. Olive CUSD 5 — 3-11111
804 W MAIN ST 62069 — 999-7831
Art McCormick, supt.
HS, 804 W MAIN ST 62069 — 2-00011 / 999-4231
Roger Kratochvil, prin.

Mount Prospect, AC 708, PC 8, Cook
Community Consolidated SD 59
Supt. — See Arlington Heights
Holmes JHS 3-00100
1900 W LONNQUIST BLVD 60056 593-4390
Russel Haak, prin.

Mt. Prospect SD 57 4-11100
701 W GREGORY ST 60056 394-7300
Thomas Many, supt.
Lincoln JHS, 700 W LINCOLN ST 60056 2-00100
Karen Uhren, prin. 394-7350

River Trails SD 26 4-11100
1900 E KENSINGTON RD 60056 297-4120
Thomas Rich, supt.
River Trails JHS, 1000 N WOLF RD 60056 3-01100
Mary Jordan, prin. 298-1750

Township HSD 214
Supt. — See Arlington Heights
Prospect HS 4-00011
801 W KENSINGTON RD 60056 255-9700
John Ashenfelter, prin.

Mount Pulaski, AC 217, PC 4, Logan
Mt. Pulaski CUSD 23 3-11111
119 N GARDEN ST 62548 792-5117
Dennis Burnett, supt.
HS, 206 S SPRING ST 62548 2-00011
Joseph Zimmerman, prin. 792-3209

Mount Sterling, AC 217, PC 4, Brown
Brown County CUSD 1 3-11111
214 E NORTH ST 62353 773-3350
Stephen Shuda, supt.
Brown Co. HS, PO BOX 152 62353 2-00011
Stephen Shuda, prin. 773-3345

Mount Vernon, AC 618, PC 7, Jefferson
Mt. Vernon SD 80 4-11100
PO BOX 767 62864 244-8080
Lawrence Loveall, supt.
Casey JHS, 1829 BROADWAY ST 62864 2-00100
Dwain Baldridge, prin. 244-8060

Mt. Vernon Twp. HSD 201 4-00011
320 S 7TH ST 62864 244-3700
John Garrett, supt.
HS, 320 S 7TH ST 62864 4-00011
James Shifflet, prin. 244-3700

Mount Zion, AC 217, PC 5, Macon
Mt. Zion CUSD 3, 455 ELM ST 62549 4-11111
Kenneth Hendricksen, supt. 864-2366
HS, 305 S HENDERSON ST 62549 3-00011
Gregory Bradley, prin. 864-2363
JHS, 315 S HENDERSON ST 62549 2-00100
Junius Futrell, prin. 864-2369

Moweaqua, AC 217, PC 4, Shelby
Central A & M SD
Supt. — See Assumption
Central A & M HS, 229 E PINE ST 62550 2-00011
Randall Grigg, prin. 768-3866

Mulberry Grove, AC 618, PC 3, Bond
Mulberry Grove CUSD 1 2-11111
RR 2 BOX 327 62262 326-8812
Robert Bankston, supt.
HS, RR 2 BOX 327 62262 2-00011
Robert Bankston, prin. 326-8221
JHS, RR 2 BOX 327 62262 1-00100
Robert Bankston, prin. 326-8221

Mundelein, AC 708, PC 7, Lake
Diamond Lake SD 76 3-11100
500 ACORN LN 60060 566-9221
Philip Simons, supt.
West Oak MS, 500 ACORN LN 60060 2-01100
Gary Clair, prin. 566-9220

Mundelein Consolidated HSD 120 4-00011
1350 W HAWLEY ST 60060 949-2242
Linda Hanson, supt.
Mundelein Cons. HS 4-00011
1350 W HAWLEY ST 60060 949-2200
John Davis, prin.

Mundelein ESD 75 4-11100
200 W MAPLE AVE 60060 949-2701
Richard Lanaghan, supt.
Sandburg MS, 855 W HAWLEY ST 60060 2-01100
Glen Schlichting, prin. 949-2707

Carmel HS, 1 CARMEL PKY 60060 4-00011
Sr. Diane O'Donnell, prin. 566-3000
University of St. Mary of the Lake 60060 2-UC
566-6401

Murphysboro, AC 618, PC 6, Jackson
Murphysboro CUSD 186 5-11111
819 WALNUT ST 62966 684-3781
Michael Mugge, supt.
HS, 1601 BLACKWOOD DR 62966 3-00011
Philip Trapani, prin. 687-2336
JHS, 2125 SPRUCE ST 62966 3-00100
George Starkweather, prin. 684-3041

Naperville, AC 708, PC 8, Du Page
Indian Prairie CUSD 204 6-11111
PO BOX 3990 60567 851-6161
Thomas Scullen, supt.
Gregory MS 4-00100
2621 SPRINGDALE CIR 60564 416-0600
Greg Fischer, prin.
Hill MS, 1836 BROOKDALE RD 60563 4-00100
Michael Raczak, prin. 369-6767
Other Schools – See Aurora

Naperville CUSD 203 7-11111
203 W HILLSIDE RD 60540 420-6300
Donald Weber, supt.
Naperville Central HS 4-00011
440 AURORA AVE 60540 420-6422
Thomas Paulsen, prin.
Naperville North HS 4-00011
899 N MILL ST 60563 420-6484
Bruce Cameron, prin.
Jefferson JHS, 1525 N LOOMIS ST 60563 3-00100
Paul Schmidt, prin. 420-6363
Lincoln JHS, 1320 OLYMPUS DR 60565 3-00100
Robert Raynett, prin. 420-6370
Madison JHS, 1000 RIVER OAK DR 60565 3-00100
Jerry Virgo, prin. 420-6400
Washington JHS 3-00100
201 N WASHINGTON ST 60540 420-6390
Terry Crandall, prin.
Other Schools – See Lisle

Krejci Academy 2-11111
619 E FRANKLIN AVE 60540 355-6870
Patti Boheme, prin.
North Central College 4-UC
30 N BRAINARD ST 60540 420-3400

Nashville, AC 618, PC 5, Washington
Nashville CCSD 49 3-11100
750 E GORMAN ST 62263 327-3055
Thomas Dahncke, supt.
MS, 750 E GORMAN ST 62263 2-01100
Don Miller, prin. 327-3055

Nashville Community HSD 99 2-00011
1300 S MILL ST 62263 327-8286
James Hill, supt.
Nashville Comm. HS 2-00011
1300 S MILL ST 62263 327-8286
John Cruser, prin.

Nauvoo, AC 217, PC 4, Hancock
Nauvoo-Colusa CUSD 325 2-11111
PO BOX 308 62354 453-6385
Kenneth Nudd, supt.
Nauvoo-Colusa HS 2-00011
HIGHWAY 96 N 62354 453-2231
Ronald Yockey, prin.
Nauvoo-Colusa JHS 1-00100
HIGHWAY 96 N 62354 453-2231
Ronald Yockey, prin.

St. Mary's Academy for Girls 1-00011
PO BOX 158 62354 453-6619
Sr. Phyllis McMurray, prin.

Neoga, AC 217, PC 4, Cumberland
Neoga CUSD 3, PO BOX 280 62447 3-11111
Bill Steichmann, supt. 895-2201
HS, PO BOX 280 62447 2-00011
David Carpenter, prin. 895-2205
JHS, PO BOX 280 62447 2-00100
David Carpenter, prin. 895-2205

Neponset, AC 309, PC 3, Bureau
Neponset CCSD 307, 201 W MAIN 61345 2-11111
W. Turner, supt. 594-2307
HS, 109 HARLAN ST 61345 1-00011
Willy Hewitt, prin. 594-2396

Newark, AC 815, PC 3, Kendall
Newark CCSD 66 2-11100
503 CHICAGO RD 60541 695-5143
Mary Wells, supt.
Other Schools – See Millbrook

Newark Community HSD 18 2-00011
PO BOX 4 60541 695-5164
Andrew Bertram, supt.
Newark Community HS 2-00011
PO BOX 4 60541 695-5164
Andrew Bertram, prin.

New Athens, AC 618, PC 4, St. Clair
New Athens CUSD 60 3-11111
501 HANFT ST 62264 475-2174
John Ingalls, supt.
HS, 501 HANFT ST 62264 2-00011
Paul Berowski, prin. 475-2173
JHS, 501 HANFT ST 62264 2-00100
George Lawrence, prin. 475-2172

New Berlin, AC 217, PC 3, Sangamon
CUSD 16, PO BOX 230 62670 3-11111
J. Gregory Reynolds, supt. 488-6111
HS, PO BOX 230 62670 2-00011
Larry Mahan, prin. 488-6411
JHS, PO BOX 230 62670 1-00100
Larry Mahan, prin. 488-6012

New Lenox, AC 815, PC 6, Will
Lincoln-Way Community HSD 210 5-00011
1801 E LINCOLN HWY 60451 485-7600
Lawrence Wyllie, supt.
Lincoln-Way Central HS 4-00011
1801 E LINCOLN HWY 60451 485-7600
Gerald Pius, prin.
Other Schools – See Frankfort

New Lenox SD 122 5-11100
809 N CEDAR RD 60451 485-2169
Alex Martino, supt.
Oster-Oakview JHS 3-00100
809 N CEDAR RD 60451 485-2125
Del Bitter, prin.

Providence Catholic HS 4-00011
1800 W LINCOLN HWY 60451 485-2136
Fr. McGrath, prin.

Newman, AC 217, PC 3, Douglas
Newman CUSD 303 2-11111
PO BOX 500 61942 837-2475
Charles White, supt.
HS, PO BOX 349 61942 2-00011
Dana Hales, prin. 837-2488

Newton, AC 618, PC 5, Jasper
Jasper County CUSD 1 4-11111
609 S LAFAYETTE ST 62448 783-8459
Joseph Wakeley, supt.
Newton Community HS 3-00011
101 W END AVE 62448 783-2303
Troy Hickey, prin.
Newton Central JHS 2-00100
100 MAXWELL ST 62448 783-8464
Jay Hart, prin.
Other Schools – See Sainte Marie, Wheeler

Niantic, AC 217, PC 3, Macon
Niantic-Harristown CUSD 6 3-11111
398 N ILLINOIS ST 62551 668-2338
David Bills, supt.
Niantic-Harristown HS 2-00011
398 N ILLINOIS ST 62551 668-2392
Bob Brady, prin.
Niantic-Harristown JHS 2-00100
398 N ILLINOIS ST 62551 668-2221
Ronald Jump, prin.

Niles, AC 708, PC 8, Cook
East Maine SD 63
Supt. — See Des Plaines
Gemini JHS 3-00100
8955 N GREENWOOD AVE 60714 827-1181
Patricia Johnson, prin.

Niles ESD 71 2-11100
6935 W TOUHY AVE 60714 647-9752
Eugene Zalewski, supt.
Culver MS, 6921 W OAKTON ST 60714 2-01100
Thomas Ray, prin. 966-9280

Niles College of Loyola University 3-UC
7135 N HARLEM AVE 60714
Northridge Preparatory S 2-00111
8108 W GOLF RD 60714 966-0084
Gerard Shepherd, prin.
Notre Dame HS 3-00011
7655 W DEMPSTER ST 60714 965-2900
Fr. Kenneth Molinaro, prin.
Willows Academy 2-00111
8200 W GREENDALE AVE 60714 692-5630
Marie Keenley, prin.

Noble, AC 618, PC 3, Richland
West Richland CUSD 2 3-11111
300 E NORTH AVE 62868 723-2334
Kern Doerner, supt.
West Richland HS 2-00011
300 E NORTH AVE 62868 723-2335
Harold Ash, prin.
West Richland JHS 1-00100
300 E NORTH AVE 62868 723-2335
Harold Ash, prin.

Nokomis, AC 217, PC 5, Montgomery
Nokomis CUSD 22, PO BOX 40 62075 3-11111
Joe Murphy, supt. 563-7311
JSHS, PO BOX 220 62075 2-00111
Robert Davis, prin. 563-2014

Normal, AC 309, PC 8, McLean
Board of Regents SD 3-11111
500 GREGORY ST 61761 438-8542
Michael Surma, supt.
University HS, 500 GREGORY ST 61761 3-00011
Steven Charton, prin. 438-8346

McLean Co. Unit SD 5 6-11111
1809 W HOVEY AVE 61761 452-4476
Robert Malito, supt.
Normal Community SHS 4-00001
303 KINGSLEY ST 61761 452-4461
Alan Chapman, prin.
Chiddix JHS, 300 S WALNUT ST 61761 3-00110
Jim Braksick, prin. 452-1191
Parkside JHS, 101 N PARKSIDE RD 61761 3-00110
Jerry Crabtree, prin. 452-8321

Bloomington-Normal School of Radiography HSP
900 FRANKLIN AVE 61761 452-2834
Calvary Baptist Academy 2-11111
PO BOX 587 61761 452-7912
Dwight Vanderboegh, prin.
Illinois State University 7-UC
212 N SCHOOL ST 61761 438-5677

Norridge, AC 708, PC 7, Cook
Ridgewood Community HSD 234 3-00011
7500 W MONTROSE AVE 60634 456-5880
Allen Schau, supt.

Ridgewood Community HS — 3-00011
7500 W MONTROSE AVE 60634 — 456-5880
Harold London, prin.

Lincoln Technical Institute — 4-CS
7320 W AGATITE AVE 60656 — 625-1535

Norris City, AC 618, PC 4, White
Norris City-Omaha-Enfield CUSD 3 — 3-11111
EAST ST 62869 – James Price, supt. — 378-3222
Norris City-Omaha-Enfield JSHS — 2-00111
RR 1 62869 — 378-3312
Michael Rosselli, prin.

Northbrook, AC 708, PC 8, Cook
Northbrook/Glenview SD 30 — 4-11100
2374 SHERMER RD 60062 — 498-4190
Harry Rossi, supt.
Maple JHS, 2370 SHERMER RD 60062 — 2-00100
Steven Waitz, prin. — 272-0964

Northbrook ESD 27 — 4-11100
1250 SANDERS RD 60062 — 498-2610
David Kroeze, supt.
Wood Oaks JHS — 3-00100
1250 SANDERS RD 60062 — 272-1900
R. K. Wilhite, prin.

Northbrook School Dist 28 — 4-11100
1475 MAPLE AVE 60062 — 498-7900
James Kucienski, supt.
JHS, 1475 MAPLE AVE 60062 — 2-00100
Gordon Hood, prin. — 498-7920

Northfield Twp. HSD 225
Supt. — See Glenview
Glenbrook North HS — 4-00011
2300 SHERMER RD 60062 — 272-6400
Michael McClellan, prin.

West Northfield SD 31 — 3-11100
3131 TECHNY RD 60062 — 272-6880
Paul Kimmelman, supt.
Field JHS, 2055 LANDWEHR RD 60062 — 2-00100
Frances McTague, prin. — 272-6884

Napoleon Hill Foundation — 2-HMS
1440 PADDOCK DR 60062

North Chicago, AC 708, PC 8, Lake
North Chicago SD 187 — 5-11111
2000 LEWIS AVE 60064 — 689-8150
Eleanor Jackson, supt.
North Chicago Community HS — 3-00011
1717 17TH ST 60064 — 578-7400
Jimmy Dew, prin.
Katzenmaier MS — 2-00100
1829 KENNEDY DR 60064 — 689-6330
Michael Penich, prin.
Novak-King MS — 2-00100
1500 KEMBLE AVE 60064 — 689-6336
Curtis Dorsey, prin.

University of Health Sciences — 3-UC
3333 GREEN BAY RD 60064 — 578-3000

Northfield, AC 708, PC 5, Cook
Sunset Ridge SD 29 — 2-11100
525 SUNSET RIDGE RD 60093 — 446-6383
Dr. Howard Bultinck, supt.
Sunset Ridge MS — 2-01100
525 SUNSET RIDGE RD 60093 — 446-6383
Howard Bultinck, prin.

St. Louise de Marillac HS — 2-00011
315 WAUKEGAN RD 60093 — 446-9106
Sr. Ann Butler, prin.

Northlake, AC 708, PC 7, Cook
Berkeley SD 87
Supt. — See Berkeley
Northlake MS — 2-01100
202 S LAKEWOOD AVE 60164 — 547-3095
James Quilty, prin.

Leyden Community HSD 212
Supt. — See Franklin Park
West Leyden HS — 4-00011
1000 N WOLF RD 60164 — 451-3000
James Macintyre, prin.

Oak Brook, AC 708, PC 6, Du Page
Butler SD 53, 2801 YORK RD 60521 — 3-11100
Robert Lee, supt. — 573-2887
Butler JHS, 2801 YORK RD 60521 — 2-00100
Dennis Lonstine, prin. — 573-2760

Bethany Theological Seminary — 1-UC
18W600 BUTTERFIELD RD 60521 — 620-2200

Oakbrook Terrace, AC 708, PC 4, Du Page

DeVry Inc. — 4-UC
1 TOWER LN STE 1000 60181 — 571-7700

Oak Forest, AC 708, PC 8, Cook
Arbor Park SD 145 — 4-11100
15901 FOREST AVE 60452 — 687-8040
James Upchurch, supt.
Arbor Park MS, 15900 OAK AVE 60452 — 3-01100
Thomas Savick, prin. — 687-5330

Bremen Community HSD 228
Supt. — See Midlothian
HS, 15201 CENTRAL AVE 60452 — 4-00011
Edward Roberts, prin. — 687-0500

Forest Ridge SD 142 — 4-11100
14950 LARAMIE AVE 60452 — 687-3334
T. Buell, supt.
Kerkstra MS — 3-00100
14950 LARAMIE AVE 60452 — 687-2860
Edward Young, prin.

Oak Forest Christian Academy — 2-11111
5217 149TH ST 60452 — 687-1510
Samuel Dalton, prin.

Oakland, AC 217, PC 3, Coles
Oakland CUSD 5, PO BOX 218 61943 — 2-11111
Norman Tracy, supt. — 346-2555
HS, PO BOX 376 61943 — 2-00011
Thomas Gardner, prin. — 346-2118

Oak Lawn, AC 708, PC 8, Cook
Atwood Heights SD 125 — 3-11100
4300 W 108TH PL 60453 — 371-0080
Samuel Rizzo, supt.
Other Schools – See Alsip

Community HSD 218 — 5-00011
10701 KILPATRICK AVE 60453 — 424-2000
Jerry Petersen, supt.
Richards HS — 4-00011
10601 CENTRAL AVE 60453 — 499-2550
Dan McAllister, prin.
Other Schools – See Blue Island, Palos Heights

Oak Lawn-Hometown SD 123 — 4-11100
4201 W 93RD ST 60453 — 423-0150
Dirk Manson, supt.
McGugan JHS, 5220 W 105TH ST 60453 — 3-00100
James Paziotopoulos, prin. — 499-6400

Oak Lawn Community HSD 229 — 4-00011
9400 SOUTHWEST HIGHWAY 60453 — 424-5200
Dominick Frigo, supt.
Oak Lawn Community HS — 4-00011
10701 KILPATRICK AVE 60453 — 424-5200
Les Luka, prin.

Ridgeland SD 122 — 4-11100
6500 W 95TH ST 60453 — 599-5550
Donald Johnson, supt.
Simmons MS, 6450 W 95TH ST 60453 — 2-00100
Douglas Freehauf, prin. — 599-8540

Christ Hospital — HSP
4440 W 95TH ST 60453 — 857-5001
Fox College of Executive/Legal Assts. — 2-CS
4201 W 93RD ST 60453 — 636-7700
Lincoln Technical Institute — 2-CS
8920 S CICERO AVE 60453 — 423-9000
NEC-Bryman Campus — 2-CS
4101 W 95TH ST 60453 — 423-0911
Southside Baptist S — 2-11111
5345 W 99TH ST 60453 — 425-3435
Robert Burckart, prin.

Oak Park, AC 708, PC 8, Cook
Oak Park-River Forest SD 200 — 5-00011
201 N SCOVILLE AVE 60302 — 383-0700
Donald Offermann, supt.
Oak Park-River Forest HS — 5-00011
201 N SCOVILLE AVE 60302 — 383-0700
Donald Offermann, prin.

Oak Park ESD 97 — 6-11100
970 MADISON ST 60302 — 524-3000
John Fagan, supt.
Emerson JHS — 3-00100
916 WASHINGTON BLVD 60302 — 524-3050
Glada Vaughn, prin.
Julian JHS — 3-00100
416 S RIDGELAND AVE 60302 — 524-3040
Benjamin Williams, prin.

Fenwick HS for Boys — 3-00011
505 WASHINGTON BLVD 60302 — 386-0127
James Quaid, prin.
West Suburban College of Nursing — 2-UC
1 ERIE CT 60302 — 383-6200

Oblong, AC 618, PC 4, Crawford
Oblong CUSD 4, PO BOX 40 62449 — 3-11111
Allen Price, supt. — 592-3933
HS, 700 S RANGE ST 62449 — 2-00011
Fritz Wheeler, prin. — 592-4235

Odin, AC 618, PC 4, Marion
Odin Community HSD 700 — 1-00011
PO BOX 188 62870 — 775-8266
Tom Smith, supt.
HS, PO BOX 188 62870 — 1-00011
David Wilson, prin. — 775-8266

O'Fallon, AC 618, PC 7, St. Clair
O'Fallon CCSD 90 — 4-11100
707 N SMILEY ST 62269 — 632-3666
George Halsey, supt.
Schaefer JHS, 505 S CHERRY ST 62269 — 3-00100
Allen Scharf, prin. — 632-3621

O'Fallon Twp. HSD 203 — 4-00011
600 S SMILEY ST 62269 — 632-3507
Tom Bradley, supt.
HS, 600 S SMILEY ST 62269 — 4-00011
Robert Bellina, prin. — 632-3507

Oglesby, AC 815, PC 5, La Salle
Oglesby ESD 125 — 2-11100
212 W WALNUT ST 61348 — 883-3517
James Boyle, supt.
Washington MS — 2-01100
212 W WALNUT ST 61348 — 883-3517
Robert Meehan, prin.

Illinois Valley Community College — 4-CC
RR 1 61348 — 224-2720

Ohio, AC 815, PC 2, Bureau
Ohio Community HSD 505 — 1-00011
103 MEMORIAL ST 61349 — 376-4414
Frank Dagne, supt.
Ohio Community HS — 1-00011
105 MEMORIAL ST 61349 — 376-2934
John Scherrer, prin.

Okawville, AC 618, PC 4, Washington
West Washington County CUSD 10 — 3-11111
PO BOX 46 62271 — 243-6454
Dan Jansen, supt.
JSHS, PO BOX 127 62271 — 2-00111
Richard Williams, prin. — 243-5201

Olney, AC 618, PC 6, Richland
East Richland CUSD 1 — 4-11111
1200 E LAUREL ST 62450 — 395-2324
Ed Armstrong, supt.
East Richland HS — 3-00011
1200 E LAUREL ST 62450 — 393-2191
George Toler, prin.
East Richland MS, 1099 N VAN ST 62450 — 3-00100
Gary Kallenbach, prin. — 395-4372

Olney Central College — 4-CC
305 NORTHWEST ST 62450

Olympia Fields, AC 708, PC 5, Cook
Rich Twp. HSD 227 — 5-00011
20290 GOVERNORS HWY 60461 — 747-2600
Duwayne Carnes, supt.
Rich Central HS, 3600 203RD ST 60461 — 4-00011
Larry Tandy, prin. — 748-6070
Other Schools – See Park Forest, Richton Park

Onarga, AC 815, PC 4, Iroquois
Iroquois West CUSD 10
Supt. — See Gilman
Iroquois West MS — 2-00100
303 N EVERGREEN ST 60955 — 268-4355
Mary Decker, prin.

Oneida, AC 309, PC 3, Knox
ROWVA CUSD 208 — 3-11111
PO BOX 69 61467 — 483-3711
Vincent Laird, supt.
ROWVA HS, PO BOX 69 61467 — 2-00011
Gary Buckingham, prin. — 483-6371
ROWVA JHS, PO BOX 69 61467 — 2-00100
Jerry Daniels, prin. — 483-2803

Opdyke, AC 618, PC 2, Jefferson
Opdyke-Belle-Rive CCSD 5 — 2-11100
RR 1 62872 – Ron O'Daniell, supt. — 756-2492
MS, RR 1 62872 — 2-01100
Ron O'Daniell, prin. — 756-2492

Orangeville, AC 815, PC 2, Stephenson
Orangeville CUSD 203 — 2-11111
PO BOX 430 61060 — 789-4450
Lawrence Eggleston, supt.
Orangeville HS, PO BOX 430 61060 — 2-00011
John Wheatley, prin. — 789-4289
JHS, 210 S ORANGE ST 61060 — 1-00100
John Wheatley, prin. — 789-4289

Oreana, AC 217, PC 3, Macon
Argenta-Oreana CUSD 1
Supt. — See Argenta
Argenta-Oreana MS — 2-00100
400 W SOUTH ST 62554 — 468-2121
Judy Brown, prin.

Oregon, AC 815, PC 5, Ogle
Oregon CUSD 220 — 4-11111
PO BOX 220 61061 – V. Scott, supt. — 732-2186
HS, 210 S 10TH ST 61061 — 2-00011
Michael Persenaire, prin. — 732-6241
JHS, 210 S 10TH ST 61061 — 2-00100
Ronald Jacobs, prin. — 732-3366

Orion, AC 309, PC 4, Henry
Orion CUSD 223, 900 12TH ST 61273 — 4-11111
Frank Young, supt. — 526-3388
HS, 1100 13TH ST 61273 — 2-00011
Larry Miller, prin. — 526-3361
MS, 802 12TH ST 61273 — 2-00100
Wesley Wells, prin. — 526-3392

Orland Park, AC 708, PC 8, Cook
Consolidated HSD 230 — 6-00011
15100 94TH AVE 60462 — 349-5750
Ronald Barnes, supt.
Sandburg HS — 5-00011
13300 LA GRANGE RD 60462 — 361-4600
Arthur Newbrough, prin.
Other Schools – See Palos Hills, Tinley Park

Orland Park SD 135 — 6-11100
  9401 151ST ST 60462 — 349-5700
  Thomas Pauley, supt.
  Jerling MS, 8851 151ST ST 60462 — 3-00100
  James Leib, prin. — 349-5380
  JHS, 14855 WEST AVE 60462 — 3-00100
  Peter Yuska, prin. — 349-5319

Robert Morris College — 2-CC
  43 ORLAND SQUARE DR 60462 — 460-8000

Oswego, AC 708, PC 5, Kendall
Oswego CUSD 308 — 5-11111
  PO BOX 729 60543 — 554-3447
  Karl Plank, supt.
  HS, PO BOX 729 60543 — 4-00011
  Daryl Thompson, prin. — 554-8871
  Thompson JHS, PO BOX 729 60543 — 3-00100
  Frederick La Chance, prin. — 554-9000
  Traugher JHS, PO BOX 729 60543 — 2-00100
  Gerner Anderson, prin. — 554-3444

Ottawa, AC 815, PC 7, La Salle
Ottawa ESD 141, 320 W MAIN ST 61350 — 4-11100
  Ronald Marino, supt. — 433-1133
  Shephard JHS — 3-00100
  701 E MCKINLEY RD 61350 — 434-7925
  Michael Bannister, prin.

Ottawa Twp. HSD 140 — 4-00011
  211 E MAIN ST 61350 — 433-1323
  Michael Clinch, supt.
  Ottawa Twp. HS, 211 E MAIN ST 61350 — 4-00011
  Thomas Jobst, prin. — 433-1323

Marquette HS, 1000 PAUL ST 61350 — 2-00011
  Joan Jobst, prin. — 433-0125

Palatine, AC 708, PC 8, Cook
Palatine CCSD 15 — 7-11100
  580 N 1ST BANK DR 60067 — 934-2770
  John Conyers, supt.
  Sundling JHS, 1100 N SMITH ST 60067 — 3-00100
  Mary Ross, prin. — 934-2830
  Winston Park JHS — 2-00100
  900 E PALATINE RD 60067 — 934-2863
  John Myers, prin.
  Other Schools – See Rolling Meadows

Township HSD 211 — 7-00011
  1750 S ROSELLE RD 60067 — 359-3300
  Gerald Chapman, supt.
  Fremd HS, 1000 S QUENTIN RD 60067 — 4-00011
  Thomas Howard, prin. — 358-6222
  HS, 1111 N ROHLWING RD 60067 — 4-00011
  Nancy Robb, prin. — 991-2600
  Other Schools – See Hoffman Estates, Schaumburg

William Rainey Harper College — 6-CC
  1200 W ALGONQUIN RD 60067 — 397-3000

Palestine, AC 618, PC 4, Crawford
Palestine CUSD 3, PO BOX 217 62451 — 3-11111
  Jerry Zachary, supt. — 586-2713
  HS, RR 1 BOX 256 62451 — 2-00011
  Don Osburn, prin. — 586-2712

Palmyra, AC 217, PC 3, Macoupin
Northwestern CUSD 2 — 2-11111
  RR 1 BOX 8A 62674 — 436-2210
  E. Kent Tuttle, supt.
  Northwestern HS, RR 1 BOX 8 62674 — 2-00011
  Daniel Daugherty, prin. — 436-2011
  Northwestern JHS, RR 1 BOX 8 62674 — 1-00100
  Daniel Daugherty, prin. — 436-2011

Palos Heights, AC 708, PC 7, Cook
Community HSD 218
  Supt. — See Oak Lawn
  Shepard HS — 4-00011
  13049 S RIDGELAND AVE 60463 — 597-6300
  Wayne Rabold, prin.

Palos Heights SD 128 — 3-11100
  6610 W HIGHLAND DR 60463 — 448-0060
  Ted Struck, supt.
  Independence JHS — 2-00100
  6610 W HIGHLAND DR 60463 — 448-0737
  James Willms, prin.

Chicago Christian HS — 2-00011
  12001 S OAK PARK AVE 60463 — 388-7650
  Carol De Jong, prin.
Trinity Christian College — 3-UC
  6601 W COLLEGE DR 60463 — 597-3000

Palos Hills, AC 708, PC 7, Cook
Consolidated HSD 230
  Supt. — See Orland Park
  Stagg HS, 8015 W 111TH ST 60465 — 4-00011
  Ross Cucio, prin. — 974-3300

Moraine Valley Community College — 6-CC
  10900 S 88TH AVE 60465 — 974-4300

Palos Park, AC 708, PC 5, Cook
Palos CCSD 118 — 4-11100
  8800 W 119TH ST 60464 — 448-4800
  Robert Piwko, supt.
  Palos South JHS — 3-00100
  131ST ST & 82ND AVE 60464 — 448-5971
  Michael Stritch, prin.

Pana, AC 217, PC 6, Christian
Pana CUSD 8, 14 E MAIN ST 62557 — 4-11111
  Barry Heaton, supt. — 562-3976
  Pana High School, 201 W 8TH ST 62557 — 2-00011
  John Pastor, prin. — 562-3931
  JHS, 407 S POPLAR ST 62557 — 2-00100
  James Dunseth, prin. — 562-2214

Paris, AC 217, PC 6, Edgar
Paris-Union SD 95, 414 S MAIN ST 61944 — 4-11111
  Sam McGowen, supt. — 465-8448
  HS, 309 S MAIN ST 61944 — 3-00011
  Steven Sabens, prin. — 466-1175
  Mayo MS, 310 E WOOD ST 61944 — 2-00100
  Joseph Creedon, prin. — 466-3050

Paris CUSD 4, PO BOX 160 61944 — 3-11100
  Verne Bear, supt. — 465-5391
  Crestwood JHS, PO BOX 160 61944 — 2-00100
  Alan Zuber, prin. — 465-5391

Park Forest, AC 708, PC 7, Cook
Matteson ESD 162 — 4-11100
  210 ILLINOIS ST 60466 — 748-0100
  Sandra Schmutzler, supt.
  Other Schools – See Matteson

Park Forest SD 163 — 4-11100
  242 S ORCHARD DR 60466 — 748-7050
  Donna Jemilo, supt.
  Forest Trail JHS, 215 WILSON ST 60466 — 3-00100
  Lorrie Reed, prin. — 481-2920

Rich Twp. HSD 227
  Supt. — See Olympia Fields
  Rich East Campus HS — 4-00011
  300 SAUK TRL 60466 — 748-5800
  Brian Barry, prin.

Park Ridge, AC 708, PC 8, Cook
Maine Twp. HSD 207 — 6-00011
  1131 S DEE RD 60068 — 696-3600
  James Elliott, supt.
  Maine East HS — 4-00011
  2601 DEMPSTER ST 60068 — 825-4484
  Carol Grenier, prin.
  Maine South HS, 1111 S DEE RD 60068 — 4-00011
  Thomas Cachur, prin. — 825-7711
  Other Schools – See Des Plaines

Park Ridge CCSD 64 — 5-11100
  164 S PROSPECT AVE 60068 — 318-4300
  Arlene Rieger, supt.
  Lincoln JHS, 200 S LINCOLN AVE 60068 — 3-00100
  Jim Blouch, prin. — 318-4215

Patoka, AC 618, PC 3, Marion
Patoka CUSD 100 — 2-11111
  1220 KINOKA RD 62875 — 432-5200
  Robert Raver, supt.
  HS, 1220 KINOKA RD 62875 — 1-00011
  Norma Borgmann, prin. — 432-5440
  JHS, 1220 KINOKA RD 62875 — 1-00100
  Norma Borgmann, prin. — 432-5200

Pawnee, AC 217, PC 4, Sangamon
Pawnee CUSD 11 — 3-11111
  PO BOX 1040 62558 — 625-2471
  Donald Burton, supt.
  HS, PO BOX 1040 62558 — 2-00011
  Randall Rader, prin. — 625-2471
  JHS, PO BOX 1040 62558 — 2-00100
  John Stahly, prin. — 625-2231

Paw Paw, AC 815, PC 3, Lee
Lee Center CUSD 271 — 3-11111
  PO BOX 508 61353 — 627-2841
  Charles McChesney, supt.
  JSHS, PO BOX 37 61353 — 2-00111
  Judith Prielipp, prin. — 627-2671
  Other Schools – See Franklin Grove

Paxton, AC 217, PC 5, Ford
Paxton-Buckley-Loda CUSD 10 — 4-11111
  PO BOX 50 60957 — 379-3314
  William Koenecke, supt.
  Paxton-Buckley-Loda HS — 2-00011
  700 W ORLEANS ST 60957 — 379-4331
  James Flaherty, prin.
  Paxton-Buckley-Loda JHS — 2-00100
  341 E CENTER ST 60957 — 379-4422
  Gerald Martin, prin.

Payson, AC 217, PC 4, Adams
Payson CUSD 1, 406 W STATE ST 62360 — 3-11111
  Clifford Arbogast, supt. — 656-3323
  Seymour JSHS — 2-00111
  420 W BRAINARD AVE 62360 — 656-3355
  Terry Morse, prin.

Pearl City, AC 815, PC 3, Stephenson
Pearl City CUSD 200 — 3-11111
  P O BOX 239 61062 — 443-2715
  John Pyfer, supt.
  HS, PO BOX 239 61062 — 2-00011
  Michael Parrott, prin. — 443-2715
  JHS, PO BOX 239 61062 — 1-00100
  Michael Parrott, prin. — 443-2715

Pecatonica, AC 815, PC 4, Winnebago
Pecatonica CUSD 321 — 3-11111
  PO BOX 419 61063 — 239-1639
  Michael Reeves, supt.
  HS, PO BOX 419 61063 — 2-00011
  Thomas Hoffman, prin. — 239-2611

Pekin, AC 309, PC 8, Tazewell
North Pekin & Marquette Hts. SD 102 — 3-11100
  PO BOX 187 61555 — 382-2172
  John Closen, supt.
  Georgetown MS, 51 YATES RD 61554 — 2-00100
  Patrick Callahan, prin. — 382-3456

Pekin Community HSD 303 — 4-00011
  1903 COURT ST 61554 — 347-4101
  Jack Wilt, supt.
  SHS East Campus — 4-00001
  1903 COURT ST 61554 — 347-4101
  Fred Vogt, prin.
  Mid HS West Campus — 4-00010
  207 N 9TH ST 61554 — 347-4101
  Timothy Ruwe, prin.

Pekin SD 108 — 5-11100
  501 WASHINGTON ST 61554 — 346-3151
  Jerry Parker, supt.
  Broadmoor JHS — 2-00100
  501 MAYWOOD AVE 61554 — 347-7008
  Charles Bowen, prin.
  Edison JHS, 1400 EARL ST 61554 — 2-00100
  David Engstrand, prin. — 346-2154

Faith Baptist Christian S — 2-11111
  1501 HOWARD CT 61554 — 347-6178
  Jerry Bond, prin.

Peoria, AC 309, PC 9, Peoria
Norwood ESD 63 — 2-11100
  6521 W FARMINGTON RD 61604 — 676-3523
  James Thomas, supt.
  Norwood MS — 2-01100
  6521 W FARMINGTON RD 61604 — 676-3523
  James Thomas, prin.
Peoria SD 150 — 7-11111
  3202 N WISCONSIN AVE 61603 — 672-6767
  John Strand, supt.
  Manual HS, 811 S GRISWOLD ST 61605 — 4-00011
  Sanford Farkash, prin. — 672-6605
  HS, 1615 N NORTH ST 61604 — 4-00011
  Richard Greene, prin. — 672-6630
  Richwoods HS — 4-00011
  6301 N UNIVERSITY ST 61614 — 693-4400
  James McCormick, prin.
  Woodruff HS — 4-00011
  1800 NE PERRY AVE 61603 — 672-6665
  David Barnwell, prin.
  Bills MS — 2-01100
  6001 N FROSTWOOD PKY 61615 — 693-4437
  Robert Bethel, prin.
  Blaine-Sumner MS — 2-01100
  919 S MATTHEW ST 61605 — 672-6504
  James Ulrich, prin.
  Columbia MS — 2-01100
  2612 N BOOTZ AVE 61604 — 672-6508
  Stewart Regnier, prin.
  Coolidge MS — 2-01100
  2708 W ROHMANN AVE 61604 — 672-6506
  Robert Sorensen, prin.
  Lindbergh MS — 2-01100
  6327 N SHERIDAN RD 61614 — 693-4427
  James Troy, prin.
  Longfellow MS — 2-00100
  1606 NE PERRY AVE 61603 — 672-6542
  Ronald Hayes, prin.
  Loucks MS — 2-01100
  2503 N UNIVERSITY ST 61604 — 672-6544
  Otto Geist, prin.
  Rolling Acres MS — 2-01100
  5617 N MERRIMAC AVE 61614 — 693-4422
  Adrian Hinton, prin.
  Sterling MS — 2-01100
  2315 N STERLING AVE 61604 — 672-6557
  Neil Wicker, prin.
  Trewyn MS — 3-01100
  1419 S FOLKERS AVE 61605 — 672-6500
  Timothy Delinski, prin.
  Von Steuben MS — 2-01100
  801 E FORREST HILL AVE 61603 — 672-6561
  David Obergfel, prin.
  Washington MS — 2-01100
  3706 N GRAND BLVD 61614 — 672-6563
  John Garrett, prin.
  White MS, 304 E ILLINOIS AVE 61603 — 2-01100
  Charles Siebel, prin. — 672-6567

Pleasant Valley SD 62 — 2-11100
  4607 W ELWOOD ST 61604 — 673-2494
  Terry Deppert, supt.
  Pleasant Valley MS — 2-01100
  4623 W RED BUD DR 61604 — 673-6750
  Todd Ricketts, prin.

Bradley University — 6-UC
  1501 W BRADLEY AVE 61625 — 676-7611
Father Sweeney S — 2-01100
  401 NE MADISON AVE FL 2 61603 — 637-6305
  Joan Wojcikewych, prin.
Methodist Medical Center of Illinois — HSP
  221 NE GLEN OAK AVE 61603 — 672-5515
Midstate College — 2-CC
  244 SW JEFFERSON AVE 61602 — 673-6365
Peoria Christian S — 3-11111
  3506 N CALIFORNIA AVE 61603 — 686-4500
  Lawrence Campbell, prin.
Peoria Notre Dame HS — 3-00011
  5105 N SHERIDAN RD 61614 — 691-8741
  Ronald Dwyer, prin.

St. Francis Medical Center | HSP
530 NE GLEN OAK AVE 61637 | 655-2000
St. Francis Medical Ctr. Coll of Nursing | 2-UC
211 NE GREENLEAF ST 61603 | 655-2596
University of Illinois | 4-UC
PO BOX 1649 61656

Peoria Heights, AC 309, PC 6, Peoria
Peoria Hts. CUSD 325 | 3-11111
1316 E KELLY AVE 61614 | 686-8800
Roger Bergia, supt.
HS, 508 E GLEN AVE 61614 | 2-00011
Tom Gamboe, prin. | 686-8803

Peotone, AC 708, PC 5, Will
Peotone CUSD 207U | 4-11111
PO BOX 399 60468 | 258-3246
Allen Hall, supt.
HS, PO BOX 399 60468 | 2-00011
Joseph Lacognata, prin. | 258-3236
JHS, PO BOX 399 60468 | 2-00100
Greg Oliver, prin. | 258-3246

Perry, AC 217, PC 2, Pike
Perry Community HSD 172 | 1-00011
PO BOX 98 62362 | 236-9161
James McCain, supt.
HS, PO BOX 98 62362 | 1-00011
Henry Walton, prin. | 236-9161

Peru, AC 815, PC 6, La Salle
Peru ESD 124, PO BOX 404 61354 | 3-11100
John Jacobson, supt. | 223-0486
Peru-Washington JHS | 2-00100
1313 ROCK ST 61354 | 223-0301
Marilyn Ponzer, prin.

Peru Catholic JHS, 1305 6TH ST 61354 | 2-01100
Mary Shisler, prin. | 223-8222
St. Bede Academy | 2-00011
50 SAINT BEDE DR 61354 | 223-3140
Rev. Ronald Margherio, prin.

Petersburg, AC 217, PC 4, Menard
Porta CUSD 202, PO BOX 202 62675 | 4-11111
Dan Wright, supt. | 632-3216
Porta JSHS, PO BOX 202 62675 | 2-00111
Ken Schwengel, prin. | 632-3216
Porta JHS, PO BOX 202 62675 | 2-00100
Ken Schwenger, prin. | 632-3216

Phoenix, AC 708, PC 4, Cook
South Holland SD 151
Supt. — See South Holland
Coolidge JHS, 15500 7TH AVE 60426 | 2-00100
Douglas Hamilton, prin. | 339-5300

Piasa, AC 618, PC 2, Macoupin
Southwestern CUSD 9 | 4-11111
PO BOX 99 62079 | 729-3221
Daniel Clasby, supt.
Southwestern HS, PO BOX 308 62079 | 3-00011
William Mills, prin. | 729-3211
Southwestern JHS | 2-00100
PO BOX 308 62079 | 729-3217
Charles Keene, prin.

Pinckneyville, AC 618, PC 5, Perry
Pinckneyville Community HSD 101 | 3-00011
600 E WATER ST 62274 | 357-2243
M. Brewer, supt.
HS, 600 E WATER ST 62274 | 3-00011
Craig Hiatt, prin. | 357-3843

Pinckneyville SD 50 | 3-11100
301 W MULBERRY ST 62274 | 357-5161
George Edwards, supt.
JHS, 700 E WATER ST 62274 | 2-01100
Lewis Schweizer, prin. | 357-2724

Pittsfield, AC 217, PC 5, Pike
Pikeland CUSD 10 | 4-11111
PO BOX 515 62363 | 285-2147
Delbert Scranton, supt.
HS, 201 E HIGBEE ST 62363 | 2-00011
Andrew Carmitchel, prin. | 285-6888
Pittsfield-Higbee MS | 2-01100
380 W ADAMS ST 62363 | 285-6965
Lee Hoffman, prin.

Plainfield, AC 815, PC 5, Will
Plainfield SD 202 | 5-11111
500 FORT BEGGS DR 60544 | 439-3240
David Stanfield, supt.
HS, 611 W PLAZA DR 60544 | 4-00011
Edward Wardzala, prin. | 436-3200
Indian Trail JHS | 3-00100
1005 N EASTERN AVE 60544 | 436-6128
George Capps, prin.

Plano, AC 708, PC 6, Kendall
Plano CUSD 88, 804 S HALE ST 60545 | 4-11111
William Woody, supt. | 552-8978
HS, 804 S HALE ST 60545 | 2-00011
Mike Nadeau, prin. | 552-3178
JHS, W ABE ST 60545 | 2-00100
Mike Nadeau, prin. | 552-3178

Pleasant Hill, AC 217, PC 4, Pike
Pleasant Hill CUSD 3 | 2-11111
PO BOX 207 62366 | 734-2311
Donald Peebles, supt.
HS, PO BOX 207 62366 | 2-00011
James Heafner, prin. | 734-2311

Pleasant Plains, AC 217, PC 3, Sangamon
Pleasant Plains CUSD 8 | 4-11111
PO BOX 320 62677 | 626-1041
Dennis White, supt.
HS, PO BOX 320 62677 | 2-00011
Ronald Sczurko, prin. | 626-1044
MS, PO BOX 320 62677 | 2-00100
John Marsaglia, prin. | 626-1044

Polo, AC 815, PC 5, Ogle
Polo CUSD 222, PO BOX 305 61064 | 3-11111
Donald Hay, supt. | 946-3815
Polo Community HS | 2-00011
PO BOX 305 61064 | 946-3314
James Brady, prin.
Polo Aplington MS | 2-01100
610 E MASON ST 61064 | 946-2519
Donna Gericke, prin.

Pontiac, AC 815, PC 7, Livingston
Pontiac CCSD 429 | 4-11100
117 W LIVINGSTON ST 61764 | 844-5632
Richard Freehill, supt.
JHS, 600 N MORROW ST 61764 | 2-00100
Mark Enright, prin. | 842-4343

Pontiac Twp. HSD 90 | 3-00011
1100 E INDIANA AVE 61764 | 844-6113
Dr. Ronald Yates, supt.
HS, 1100 E INDIANA AVE 61764 | 3-00011
Richard Defauw, prin. | 844-6113

Poplar Grove, AC 815, PC 3, Boone
North Boone CUSD 200 | 3-11111
PO BOX 399 61065 | 765-3322
Calvin Owens, supt.
North Boone HS | 2-00011
17641 POPLAR GROVE RD 61065 | 765-3311
Karen Severn, prin.

Port Byron, AC 309, PC 4, Rock Island
Riverdale 100 | 4-11111
9624 256TH ST N 61275 | 523-3184
Dennis Rucker, supt.
Riverdale HS, 9622 256TH ST N 61275 | 2-00011
Merredith Peterson, prin. | 523-3181
Riverdale JHS, 9822 256TH ST N 61275 | 2-00100
James Boyd, prin. | 523-3131

Posen, AC 708, PC 5, Cook
Posen-Robbins ESD 143-5 | 4-11100
14025 HARRISON AVE 60469 | 388-7200
Leotis Swopes, supt.
Gordon JHS | 2-00100
14100 HARRISON AVE 60469 | 388-7200
John Caracci, prin.
Other Schools – See Robbins

Potomac, AC 217, PC 3, Vermilion
Potomac CUSD 10 | 2-11111
7915 US ROUTE 136 61865 | 987-6155
Bob Dupriest, supt.
HS, 7915 US ROUTE 136 61865 | 1-00011
George Hughbanks, prin. | 987-6651
Potomac JHS | 1-00100
7915 US ROUTE 136 61865 | 987-6651
George Hughbanks, prin.

Prairie View, AC 708, PC 3, Lake
Adlai E. Stevenson SD 125 | 4-00011
16010 W HIGHWAY 22 60069 | 634-4000
Richard DuFour, supt.
Other Schools – See Lincolnshire

Princeton, AC 815, PC 6, Bureau
Princeton ESD 115 | 4-11100
725 W PUTNAM ST 61356 | 875-3162
James White, supt.
Logan JHS, 302 W CENTRAL AVE 61356 | 2-00100
Judson Lusher, prin. | 875-6415

Princeton Twp. HSD 500 | 3-00011
103 S EUCLID AVE 61356 | 875-3308
Carl Cherrie, supt.
HS, 103 S EUCLID AVE 61356 | 3-00011
Stephen Matthews, prin. | 875-3308

Princeville, AC 309, PC 4, Peoria
Princeville CUSD 326 | 3-11111
PO BOX 368 61559 | 385-4644
Robert Dawson, supt.
HS, 302 CORDIS AVE 61559 | 2-10011
Terry Milt, prin. | 385-4717
MS, 602 N TOWN AVE 61559 | 2-01100
Kyle Ganson, prin. | 385-4923

Prophetstown, AC 815, PC 4, Whiteside
Prophetstown-Lyndon CUSD 3 | 3-11111
310 W RIVERSIDE DR 61277 | 537-5101
Leroy Hooks, supt.
HS, 310 W RIVERSIDE DR 61277 | 2-00011
Don Fisher, prin. | 537-5161
Lyndon JHS, 310 W RIVERSIDE DR 61277 | 2-00100
Don Fisher, prin. | 537-5162

Prospect Heights, AC 708, PC 7, Cook
Prospect Heights SD 23 | 4-11100
700 N SCHOENBECK RD 60070 | 870-3850
Ronald Bearwald, supt.
Macarthur JHS | 3-00100
700 N SCHOENBECK RD 60070 | 870-3878
Philip Arenstein, prin.

Quincy, AC 217, PC 8, Adams
Quincy SD 172, 1444 MAINE ST 62301 | 6-11111
George Meyer, supt. | 223-8700

SHS, 3322 MAINE ST 62301 | 4-00001
Edward Harris, prin. | 224-3770
JHS, 100 S 14TH ST 62301 | 4-00110
Lynn Sprick, prin. | 222-3073

Blessing Hospital | 2-HSP
1005 BROADWAY 62301 | 223-5811
Blessing Hospital | 1-UC
BROADWAY AT 11TH 62301 | 223-5811
Calvary Academy, 1825 STATE ST 62301 | 2-11111
Brian Mayfield, prin. | 222-4412
Gem City College | 3-CC
700 STATE ST 62301 | 222-0391
John Wood Community College | 4-CC
150 S 48TH ST 62301 | 224-6500
Quincy College | 4-UC
1800 COLLEGE AVE 62301 | 228-5270
Quincy Notre Dame HS | 2-00011
1400 S 11TH ST 62301 | 223-2479
Sr. Mary Bender, prin.
Quincy Technical Schools | 2-CS
501 N 3RD ST 62301 | 800-438-5621
St. Mary Hospital | HSP
1415 VERMONT ST 62301 | 223-1200

Ramsey, AC 618, PC 3, Fayette
Ramsey CUSD 204, 716 W 6TH ST 62080 | 3-11111
James Bush, supt. | 423-2335
HS, 716 W 6TH ST 62080 | 2-00011
Deborah Philpot, prin. | 423-2333

Rantoul, AC 217, PC 7, Champaign
Rantoul CSD 137 | 4-11100
400 E WABASH AVE 61866 | 893-4171
David D. Glisson, supt.
Eater JHS, 400 E WABASH AVE 61866 | 2-00100
Terry Sheppard, prin. | 892-2115

Rantoul Twp. HSD 193 | 3-00011
200 S SHELDON ST 61866 | 892-2151
Gail Conley, supt.
Rantoul Twp. HS | 3-00011
200 S SHELDON ST 61866 | 892-2151
Gail Conley, prin.

Raymond, AC 217, PC 3, Montgomery
Panhandle CUSD 2 | 3-11111
317 E BROAD ST 62560 | 229-4215
Dennis Healy, supt.
Lincolnwood HS, PO BOX 110 62560 | 2-00011
Randy Blecha, prin. | 229-4237
Lincolnwood JHS, PO BOX 110 62560 | 2-00100
Randy Blecha, prin. | 229-4237

Red Bud, AC 618, PC 5, Randolph
Red Bud CUSD 132 | 4-11111
815 LOCUST ST 62278 | 282-3507
Wayne Collmeyer, supt.
HS, 815 LOCUST ST 62278 | 3-00011
Richard Hargrave, prin. | 282-3826

Richmond, AC 815, PC 4, McHenry
Richmond-Burton Community HSD 157 | 2-00011
10006 N MAIN ST 60071 | 678-4525
Dr. Ronald Erdmann, supt.
Richmond-Burton HS | 2-00011
10006 N MAIN ST 60071 | 678-4525
Louis Ramirez, prin.

Richton Park, AC 708, PC 7, Cook
Rich Twp. HSD 227
Supt. — See Olympia Fields
Rich South Campus HS | 4-00011
5000 SAUK TRL 60471 | 747-5500
Kenneth Reczkiewicz, prin.

River Forest, AC 708, PC 7, Cook
River Forest SD 90, 7776 LAKE ST 60305 | 4-11100
Tyra Manning, supt. | 771-8282
Roosevelt JHS, 7560 OAK AVE 60305 | 2-01100
Gary Niehaus, prin. | 366-9230

Concordia University | 4-UC
7400 AUGUSTA ST 60305 | 209-3004
Rosary College | 4-UC
7900 DIVISION ST 60305 | 366-2490
Trinity HS, 7574 DIVISION ST 60305 | 3-00011
Sr. Jeanne Bessette, prin. | 771-8383

River Grove, AC 708, PC 6, Cook

Holy Cross HS, 3000 N 80TH AVE 60171 | 3-00011
Br. Charles Drevon, prin. | 456-5110
Mother Guerin HS | 3-00011
8001 W BELMONT AVE 60171 | 453-6233
Sr. Jeanette Hagelskamp, prin.
Triton College | 6-CC
2000 N 5TH AVE 60171 | 456-0300

Riverside, AC 708, PC 6, Cook
Riverside-Brookfield Twp. HSD 208 | 3-00011
FIRST & RIDGEWOOD AVE 60546 | 442-7500
Charles Klingsporn, supt.
Riverside-Brookfield Twp. HS | 3-00011
FIRST & RIDGEWOOD AVE 60546 | 442-7500
Leslie Wilson, prin.

Riverside SD 96 | 3-11100
63 WOODSIDE RD 60546 | 447-5007
David Bonnette, supt.
Hauser JHS, 65 WOODSIDE RD 60546 | 2-00100
Michael Polite, prin. | 447-3896

Riverton, AC 217, PC 5, Sangamon
Riverton CUSD 14 4-11111
1014 E LINCOLN ST 62561 629-6009
Thomas Veihman, supt.
HS, 841 N 3RD 62561 2-00011
Gary Smith, prin. 629-6003
MS, PO BOX 530 62561 2-01100
Patricia Keating, prin. 629-6002

Roanoke, AC 309, PC 4, Woodford
Roanoke-Benson CUSD 60 3-11111
202 W HIGH ST 61561 923-8921
Lynn Curtis, supt.
Roanoke-Benson HS 2-00011
208 W HIGH ST 61561 923-8401
Dan Bertrand, prin.
Other Schools – See Benson

Robbins, AC 708, PC 6, Cook
Posen-Robbins ESD 143-5
Supt. — See Posen
Kellar JHS, 14125 S LYDIA AVE 60472 2-01100
(—), prin. 388-7200

Robinson, AC 618, PC 6, Crawford
Robinson CUSD 2 4-11111
PO BOX 254 62454 544-7511
Beverly Turkal, supt.
HS, 2000 N CROSS ST 62454 3-00011
Bruce Brotzman, prin. 544-9510
Nuttall MS, 400 W RUSTIC ST 62454 2-00100
Rodney Stewart, prin. 544-8618

Lincoln Trail College 4-CC
RR 3 62454

Rochelle, AC 815, PC 6, Ogle
Rochelle CCSD 231, 444 N 8TH ST 61068 4-11100
Dr. Joe Thiele, supt. 562-6363
JHS, 111 SCHOOL AVE 61068 2-00100
Kevin Zilm, prin. 562-7997

Rochelle Twp. HSD 212 3-00011
1070 N 7TH ST 61068 562-4161
Douglas Creason, supt.
Rochelle Twp. HS, 1070 N 7TH ST 61068 3-00011
Terry Roderick, prin. 562-4161

Rochester, AC 217, PC 5, Sangamon
Rochester CUSD 3A, ROUTE 29 W 62563 4-11111
Jack Taylor, supt. 498-9761
HS, ROUTE 29 W 62563 2-00011
Thomas Bertrand, prin. 498-9761
JHS, ROUTE 29 W 62563 2-00100
Timothy Katzmark, prin. 498-9761

Rock Falls, AC 815, PC 6, Whiteside
Rock Falls SD 13, 602 4TH AVE 61071 4-11100
Jack Etnyre, supt. 626-2604
MS, 1701 12TH AVE 61071 2-01100
Jeffrey Brown, prin. 626-2626

Rock Falls Twp. HSD 301 3-00011
101 12TH AVE 61071 625-3886
Dr. Jesse James, supt.
Rock Falls Twp. HS 3-00011
101 12TH AVE 61071 625-3886
Richard Kulupka, prin.

Rockford, AC 815, PC 9, Winnebago
Rockford SD 205 8-11111
201 S MADISON ST 61104 966-3000
William Bowen, supt.
Auburn HS, 5110 AUBURN ST 61101 4-00011
Ann Anderson, prin. 966-3300
Guilford HS 4-00011
5620 SPRING CREEK RD 61114 654-4870
Patricia Davis, prin.
Jefferson HS 4-00011
4145 SAMUELSON RD 61109 874-9536
David Johnson, prin.
Rockford East HS 4-00011
2929 CHARLES ST 61108 229-2100
Sam Parkinson, prin.
Eisenhower MS 3-00100
3525 SPRING CREEK RD 61107 229-2450
Yolanda Simmons, prin.
Flinn MS, 2525 OHIO PKY 61108 3-00100
John Paulsgrove, prin. 229-2800
Lincoln MS, 1500 CHARLES ST 61104 3-00100
Michael Burkhard, prin. 229-2400
West MS, 1900 N ROCKTON AVE 61103 4-01100
Michael Golden, prin. 966-3200

Berean Baptist Christian S 2-11111
5626 SAFFORD RD 61101 962-4841
George Stille, prin.
Boylan Central Catholic HS 4-00011
4000 SAINT FRANCIS DR 61103 877-2513
Sr. M. Anthony Marelli, prin.
Christian Life Center S 3-11111
5950 SPRING CREEK RD 61114 877-8000
Jeanne Mayo, prin.
Faith Center Academy 2-11111
4000 PRAIRIE RD 61102 964-7000
John Van Scoy, prin.
Keith Country Day S, 1 JACOBY PL 61107 2-11111
Ted Sanford, prin. 399-8823
Lutheran HS, 3411 N ALPINE RD 61114 2-01111
Donald Kortze, prin. 877-9551
North Love Christian S 2-11111
5301 E RIVERSIDE BLVD 61114 877-6021
Doug Thomas, prin.
Rockford Business College 3-CS
730 N CHURCH ST 61103 965-8616
Rockford College 3-UC
5050 E STATE ST 61108 226-4000
Rockford Lutheran HS 2-00011
3411 N ALPINE RD 61114 877-9551
C. Wilson, prin.
Rockford Memorial Hospital HSP
2400 N ROCKTON AVE 61103 968-6861
Rock Valley College 5-CC
3301 N MULFORD RD 61114 654-4260
St. Anthony Medical Center HSP
5666 E STATE ST 61108 395-5087
Swedish-American Hospital HSP
1400 CHARLES ST 61104 968-4400

Rock Island, AC 309, PC 8, Rock Island
Rock Island SD 41, 541 21ST ST 61201 6-11111
Charles Dyson, supt. 793-5900
HS, 1400 25TH AVE 61201 4-00011
Nathanial Anderson, prin. 793-5950
Vocational Improvement Program Vo Tech
2103 5TH AVE 61201 786-7414
James Davis, prin.
Edison JHS, 4141 9TH ST 61201 2-00100
Mary Meier, prin. 793-5920
Washington JHS, 3300 18TH AVE 61201 3-00100
Peter Nyman, prin. 793-5915

Alleman HS, 1103 40TH ST 61201 3-00011
Colin Letendre, prin. 786-7793
Augustana College 4-UC
639 38TH ST 61201 794-7208
Franciscan Medical Center HSP
2701 17TH ST 61201 793-2228

Rockton, AC 815, PC 5, Winnebago
Hononegah-Community HSD 207 4-00011
307 SALEM ST 61072 624-8951
Thomas Fegley, supt.
Hononegah HS, 307 SALEM ST 61072 4-00011
Richard Beck, prin. 624-8951

Rockton SD 140 4-11100
1050 E UNION ST 61072 624-2611
David Martin, supt.
Mack MS, 1050 E UNION ST 61072 2-01100
Peter Rehnberg, prin. 624-2611

Rolling Meadows, AC 708, PC 7, Cook
Palatine CCSD 15
Supt. — See Palatine
Plum Grove JHS 3-00100
2600 PLUM GROVE RD 60008 934-2902
Larry Fleming, prin.
Sandburg JHS, 2600 MARTIN LN 60008 3-00100
Barbara Karll, prin. 253-3555

Township HSD 214
Supt. — See Arlington Heights
HS, 2901 W CENTRAL RD 60008 4-00011
Jack Elliott, prin. 259-9640

Romeoville, AC 815, PC 7, Will
Valley View CUSD 365-U 7-11111
755 LUTHER DR 60441 886-2700
Dr. Harry Hayes, supt.
HS, 100 N INDEPENDENCE BLVD 60441 4-00011
David Carlson, prin. 886-1800
Martinez MS, 590 BELMONT DR 60441 3-00100
Nick Friend, prin. 886-6100
Other Schools – See Bolingbrook

Lewis University 5-UC
RT 53 60441 838-0500

Roodhouse, AC 217, PC 4, Greene
North Greene CUSD 3
Supt. — See White Hall
North Greene JHS 2-00100
403 W NORTH ST 62082 589-4623
Robert Pinkerton, prin.

Roscoe, AC 815, PC 4, Winnebago
Kinnikinnick CCSD 131 4-11100
5410 PINE LN 61073 623-2837
Robert Lauber, supt.
Kinnikinnick MS, 5410 PINE LN 61073 3-00100
Rod Sargeant, prin. 623-2166

Roselle, AC 708, PC 7, Du Page
Lake Park Community HSD 108 4-00011
600 MEDINAH RD 60172 529-4500
David Smith, supt.
Lake Park SHS-West 4-00001
500 W BRYN MAWR AVE 60172 529-4500
August Pasquini, prin.
Lake Park Freshman HS-East 4-00010
600 MEDINAH RD 60172 529-4500
Jerry Blew, prin.

Medinah SD 11 3-11100
700 E GRANVILLE AVE 60172 893-3737
L. Mitchell Bers, supt.
Medinah MS 2-00100
700 E GRANVILLE AVE 60172 893-3838
Richard Ganek, prin.

Roselle SD 12, 100 E WALNUT ST 60172 3-11100
Dennis O'Connell, supt. 529-2091
MS, 500 S PARK ST 60172 2-01100
John Rhodes, prin. 529-1600

Fox Valley Lutheran Academy 1-00011
300 RODENBURG RD 60193 377-0767
Janet Zimdahl, prin.

Roseville, AC 309, PC 4, Warren
Roseville CUSD 200 2-11111
RR 1 BOX AA1 61473 426-2157
Marilyn Yokel, supt.
HS, 200 W GOSSETT ST 61473 2-00011
Bruce Hall, prin. 426-2682

Rossville, AC 217, PC 4, Vermilion
Rossville-Alvin CUSD 7 2-11111
350 N CHICAGO ST 60963 748-6600
James O'Donley, supt.
Rossville-Alvin HS 2-00011
350 N CHICAGO ST 60963 748-6600
James O'Donley, prin.

Round Lake, AC 708, PC 5, Lake
Round Lake Area SD 116 6-11111
316 S ROSEDALE CT 60073 546-5522
Mary Davis, supt.
HS, 1 PANTHER BLVD 60073 4-00011
James Briscoe, prin. 546-2128
Magee MS 3-00100
500 N CEDAR LAKE RD 60073 546-2115
F. Harford, prin.

Roxana, AC 618, PC 4, Madison
Roxana CUSD 1 4-11111
401 CHAFFER AVE 62084 254-7544
Charles Conner, supt.
HS, 401 CHAFFER AVE 62084 3-00011
James Herndon, prin. 254-7553
JHS, 401 CHAFFER AVE 62084 2-00100
James Ciccarelli, prin. 254-7561

Royal, AC 217, PC 2, Champaign
Prairieview CCSD 192 2-11100
PO BOX 27 61871 583-3300
Don Walker, supt.
Other Schools – See Thomasboro

Rushville, AC 217, PC 5, Schuyler
Schuyler County CUSD 1 4-11111
215 W WASHINGTON ST 62681 322-4311
Ralph Marshall, supt.
HS, 730 N CONGRESS ST 62681 2-00011
John Bambrick, prin. 322-4316
JHS, 290 N MONROE ST 62681 2-01100
William Bavery, prin. 322-6746

Saint Anne, AC 815, PC 4, Kankakee
Saint Anne Community HSD 302 2-00011
PO BOX 630 60964 427-8214
William Trompeter, supt.
Saint Anne Comm. HS 2-00011
PO BOX 630 60964 427-8141
Genova Singleton, prin.

Saint Charles, AC 708, PC 7, Kane
St. Charles CUSD 303 6-11111
PO BOX 188 60174 377-4802
John Vanko, supt.
HS, 1020 DUNHAM RD 60174 5-00011
Francis Kostel, prin. 584-1100
Haines JHS, 305 S 9TH ST 60174 3-00100
Robert Lindahl, prin. 377-4825
Thompson JHS, 705 W MAIN ST 60174 4-00100
Kurt Anderson, prin. 377-4872

Saint Elmo, AC 618, PC 4, Fayette
St. Elmo CUSD 202 2-11111
1200 N WALNUT ST 62458 829-3264
Gerold Boice, supt.
HS, 300 W 12TH ST 62458 2-00011
Bruce Edwards, prin. 829-3227
JHS, 300 W 12TH ST 62458 1-00100
Bruce Edwards, prin. 829-3227

Sainte Marie, AC 618, PC 2, Jasper
Jasper County CUSD 1
Supt. — See Newton
East JHS, PO BOX 157 62459 2-01100
Ed Mitchell, prin. 455-3219

Saint Jacob, AC 618, PC 3, Madison
Triad CUSD 2 5-11111
9539 US HIGHWAY 40 62281 644-3771
William Hyten, supt.
Triad HS 3-00011
9539 US HIGHWAY 40 62281 644-5511
Richard Mason, prin.
Other Schools – See Troy

Saint Joseph, AC 217, PC 4, Champaign
St. Joseph-Ogden Community HSD 305 2-00011
PO BOX 890 61873 469-2586
Lynn Strack, supt.
St. Joseph-Ogden HS 2-00011
PO BOX 890 61873 469-2332
Lynn Strack, prin.

St. Joseph CCSD 169 3-11100
PO BOX 409 61873 469-7677
Gerald Meznarich, supt.
JHS, 409 S 5TH ST 61873 2-00100
Randy Hird, prin. 469-2291

Salem, AC 618, PC 6, Marion
Salem Community HSD 600 3-00011
1200 N BROADWAY 62881 548-0727
Robert Dunn, supt.

Salem Community HS   3-00011
1200 N BROADWAY 62881   548-0727
Charles Lewis, prin.

Salem SD 111, 315 S MAPLE ST 62881   4-11100
Galen Brant, supt.   548-7700
Salem Franklin Park JHS   3-01100
1325 N FRANKLIN ST 62881   548-7704
Barney Bruce, prin.

Selmaville CCSD 10   2-11100
2100 W MAIN ST 62881   548-2416
Vernon Shook, supt.
Selmaville South MS   2-01100
3185 SELMAVILLE RD 62881   548-0806
Earl Sullens, prin.

Sandoval, AC 618, PC 4, Marion
Sandoval CUSD 501   3-11111
859 W MISSOURI AVE 62882   247-3361
Melvin Wood, supt.
HS, 859 W MISSOURI AVE 62882   2-00011
Richard Rich, prin.   247-3361
JHS, 859 W MISSOURI AVE 62882   1-00100
Richard Rich, prin.   247-3361

Sandwich, AC 815, PC 6, De Kalb
Sandwich CUSD 430   4-11111
720 WELLS ST 60548   786-2187
Mary Summers, supt.
Sandwich Community HS   3-00100
515 LIONS RD 60548   786-2157
Gary Close, prin.
Dummer JHS, 422 WELLS ST 60548   2-00100
Richard Rutkowski, prin.   786-2138

Sauk Village, AC 708, PC 6, Cook
Community Consolidated SD 168   4-11100
1825 215TH PL 60411   758-1610
Thomas Ryan, supt.
Rickover JHS   3-00100
22151 TORRENCE AVE 60411   758-1900
Gwendolyn DeVries, prin.

Savanna, AC 815, PC 5, Carroll
Savanna CUSD 300, 18 ADAMS ST 61074   3-11111
Paul Seymour, supt.   273-3450
HS, 500 CRAIGMOOR ST 61074   2-00011
William Wright, prin.   273-7715
Savanna JHS, 500 CRAIGMOOR ST 61074   2-00100
Greg Stott, prin.   273-7715

Scales Mound, AC 815, PC 2, Jo Daviess
Scales Mound CUSD 211   2-11111
PO BOX 191 61075   845-2215
Ken Schablowsky, supt.
HS, PO BOX 191 61075   1-00011
Richard Crandall, prin.   845-2215
JHS, PO BOX 191 61075   1-00100
Richard Crandall, prin.   845-2215

Schaumburg, AC 708, PC 8, Cook
Schaumburg CCSD 54   7-11100
524 E SCHAUMBURG RD 60194   885-6700
William Kritzmire, supt.
Addams JHS   4-00100
700 S SPRINGINSGUTH RD 60193   307-2110
William Litwitz, prin.
Frost JHS, 320 W WISE RD 60193   3-00100
Daniel Farinosi, prin.   307-2120
Other Schools – See Elk Grove Village, Hoffman
Estates

Township HSD 211
Supt. — See Palatine
HS, 1100 W SCHAUMBURG RD 60194   4-00011
Jack Gaza, prin.   882-5200

Lake Forest Graduate Sch. of Management   2-UC
1295 E ALGONQUIN RD 60196   576-1212
Ray College of Design   2-UC
1051 PERIMETER DR 60173   619-3450
Schaumburg Christian S   3-11111
200 N ROSELLE RD 60194   885-3230
Rev. McQueary, prin.

Schiller Park, AC 708, PC 7, Cook
Schiller Park SD 81   4-11100
4050 WAGNER AVE 60176   671-1816
Drew Starsiak, supt.
Lincoln MS, 4050 WAGNER AVE 60176   2-00100
Barry Ekman, prin.   678-2916

Sciota, AC 309, PC 1, McDonough
Northwest CUSD 175   2-11111
18575 E 800TH ST 61475   456-3500
Gail Lester, supt.
Northwestern HS   2-00011
18575 E 800TH ST 61475   456-3750
Judith Lane, prin.
Northwestern JHS   1-00100
18575 E 800TH ST 61475   456-3750
Judith Lane, prin.

Seneca, AC 815, PC 4, La Salle
Seneca Twp. HSD 160   2-00011
PO BOX 20 61360   357-8761
Harlen Cotter, supt.
HS, PO BOX 20 61360   2-00011
Harlen Cotter, prin.   357-8761

Serena, AC 815, PC 2, La Salle
Community Unit SD 2   3-11111
PO BOX 107 60549   496-2850
Michael Schneider, supt.

Serena Comm. HS   2-00011
PO BOX 107 60549   496-2361
Pat Watkins, prin.

Sesser, AC 618, PC 4, Franklin
Sesser-Valier CUSD 196   3-11111
RR 1 BOX 465 62884   625-5105
David Thomas, supt.
Sesser-Valier HS   2-00011
RR 1 BOX 465 62884   625-5105
David Thomas, prin.
Sesser-Valier JHS   2-00100
RR 1 BOX 465 62884   625-2581
Carroll Kelly, prin.

Shabbona, AC 815, PC 3, De Kalb
Indian Creek CUSD   3-11111
506 S SHABBONA RD 60550   824-2197
James Hicks, supt.
Indian Creek JSHS   2-00111
506 S SHABBONA RD 60550   824-2197
James Hicks, prin.
Other Schools – See Waterman

Shannon, AC 815, PC 3, Carroll
Eastland CUSD 308
Supt. — See Lanark
Eastland JHS   2-00100
7-11 W COOK BOX 46 61078   864-2300
John Rogers, prin.

Sheffield, AC 815, PC 3, Bureau
Western CUSD 306, EAST ST 61361   2-11111
Mike Mercer, supt.   454-2503
Other Schools – See Buda

Shelbyville, AC 217, PC 5, Shelby
Shelbyville CUSD 4   4-11111
1001 W NORTH 6TH ST 62565   774-4626
Guy Parr, supt.
HS, 1001 W NORTH 6TH ST 62565   2-00011
James Lewis, prin.   774-3926
Moulton MS   3-01100
1101 W NORTH 6TH ST 62565   774-2169
Stuart Hott, prin.

Sparks College   2-CS
131 S MORGAN ST 62565   774-5112

Sheldon, AC 815, PC 4, Iroquois
Sheldon CUSD 5   2-11111
150 S RANDOLPH ST 60966   429-3317
Darrell Sy, supt.
HS, 150 S RANDOLPH ST 60966   1-00011
Mike Schmidt, prin.   429-3397

Sherrard, AC 309, PC 3, Mercer
Sherrard SD 200
Supt. — See Viola
HS, 4701 176TH AVE 61281   3-00011
Harry Hunt, prin.   593-2175
JHS, 4701 176TH AVE 61281   2-00100
Harry Hunt, prin.   593-2175

Sidell, AC 217, PC 3, Vermilion
Jamaica CUSD 12   2-11111
7087 N 600 EAST RD 61876   288-9306
Robert Yeazel, supt.
Jamaica HS, 7087 N 600 EAST RD 61876   2-00011
Robert Yeazel, prin.   288-9392
Jamaica JHS, 7087 N 600 EAST RD 61876   2-00100
Sharron Clayburn, prin.   288-9394

Silvis, AC 309, PC 6, Rock Island
Silvis SD 34, 1305 5TH AVE 61282   3-11100
Rene Noppe, supt.   792-9325
JHS, 1305 5TH AVE 61282   2-00100
Larry Brewer, prin.   792-3511

Skokie, AC 708, PC 8, Cook
Niles Twp. Community HSD 219   5-00011
7700 GROSS POINT RD 60077   673-6822
Errol Frank, supt.
Niles North HS   4-00011
9800 LAWLER AVE 60077   673-6900
Donald Childs, prin.
Niles West HS, 5701 OAKTON ST 60077   4-00011
Jean Rutherford, prin.   966-3800

Skokie SD 68, 9440 KENTON AVE 60076   4-11100
Thomas Kersten, supt.   676-9000
Old Orchard JHS   3-00100
9310 KENTON AVE 60076   676-9010
Gerald Gregory, prin.

Skokie SD 69, 5050 MADISON ST 60077   4-11100
Allan Maier, supt.   675-7666
Lincoln MS, 7839 LINCOLN AVE 60077   2-00011
Cecelia Aitken, prin.   676-3545

Skokie SD 73-5   3-11100
8000 E PRAIRIE RD 60076   673-1220
Vickie Markavitch, supt.
McCracken MS   2-01100
8000 E PRAIRIE RD 60076   673-1220
Vicki Gunther, prin.

Hebrew Theological College   1-UC
7135 CARPENTER RD 60077   267-9800
Knowledge Systems Institute   1-UC
3420 MAIN ST 60077   679-3135
Rabbi Fasman Yeshiva HS   1-00011
7135 CARPENTER RD 60077   267-9800
Rabbi Isenberg, prin.

Somonauk, AC 815, PC 4, De Kalb
Somonauk CUSD 432   3-11111
PO BOX 278 60552   498-2315
Emmert Dannenberg, supt.
HS, PO BOX 278 60552   2-00011
Glenn Posmer, prin.   498-2314

South Beloit, AC 815, PC 5, Winnebago
South Beloit CUSD 320   3-11111
850 HAYES AVE 61080   389-3478
Frank Miller, supt.
JSHS, 840 BLACKHAWK BLVD 61080   2-00111
Joel Green, prin.   389-1421

South Holland, AC 708, PC 7, Cook
South Holland SD 150   3-11100
848 E 170TH ST 60473   339-4240
Harry Agabedis, supt.
McKinley JHS, 848 E 170TH ST 60473   2-01100
William Kolloway, prin.   339-8500

South Holland SD 151   4-11100
320 E 161ST PL 60473   339-1516
Janice Potter, supt.
Other Schools – See Phoenix

Thornton Twp. HSD 205
Supt. — See Harvey
Thornwood HS   4-00011
17101 S PARK AVE 60473   339-7800
Gary Catalani, prin.

Seton Academy, 16100 SETON DR 60473   2-00011
Roberta Felker, prin.   333-6300
South Suburban College of Cook County   5-CC
15800 STATE ST 60473   596-2000

Sparland, AC 309, PC 2, Marshall
Sparland CUSD 3   2-11111
RR 1 BOX 43 61565   469-5701
Ken Williamson, supt.
HS, RR 1 BOX 43 61565   1-00011
Thomas Urban, prin.   469-3131
JHS, RR 1 61565   1-00100
Thomas Urban, prin.   469-3301

Sparta, AC 618, PC 5, Randolph
Sparta CUSD 140   4-11111
123 W COLLEGE ST 62286   443-3622
Robert Bulthaus, supt.
HS, 205 W HOOD ST 62286   3-00011
Douglas McFarland, prin.   443-4341
Sparta-Lincoln MS   3-01100
200 N SAINT LOUIS ST 62286   443-5331
Francesca Vallo, prin.
Other Schools – See Evansville

Springfield, AC 217, PC 9, Sangamon
Springfield SD 186   7-11111
1900 W MONROE ST 62704   525-3002
Robert Hill, supt.
Lanphier HS, 1300 N 11TH ST 62702   4-00011
Chuck Flamini, prin.   525-3080
HS, 101 S LEWIS ST 62704   4-00011
William Scheffler, prin.   525-3100
Springfield Southeast HS   4-00011
2350 E ASH ST 62703   525-3130
Gary Sullivan, prin.
Franklin MS   3-00100
1200 OUTER PARK DR 62704   525-3164
Lyle Wind, prin.
Grant MS, 1800 W MONROE ST 62704   3-00100
Richard Cheaney, prin.   525-3170
Washington MS   3-00100
2300 E JACKSON ST 62703   525-3182
Jack Joyner, prin.

Brown's Business College   2-CS
601 N BRUNS LN 62702   787-8797
Calvary Academy   2-11111
1730 W JEFFERSON ST 62702   546-5987
Donna Squires, prin.
Lincoln Land Community College   5-CC
SHEPHERD ROAD 62794   786-2268
Lutheran HS   2-00011
3500 W WASHINGTON ST 62707   546-6363
Ralph Nitz, prin.
Robert Morris College   2-CC
3101 MONTVALE DR 62704   793-2500
Sacred Heart-Griffin HS   3-00011
1200 W WASHINGTON ST 62702   787-1595
Sr. Kathleen Tait, prin.
St. John's Hospital   HSP
800 E CARPENTER 62769   544-6464
Sangamon State University   5-UC
SHEPHERD ROAD 62794   786-6600
Southern Illinois University   2-UC
PO BOX 3926 62708
Springfield College in Illinois   2-CC
1500 N 5TH ST 62702   525-1420
Ursuline Academy, 1400 N 5TH ST 62702   2-00011
Karen Anderson, prin.   523-5169

Spring Valley, AC 815, PC 6, Bureau
Hall Twp. HSD 502   2-00011
800 W ERIE ST 61362   664-2100
Sherwood Dees, supt.
Hall HS, 800 W ERIE ST 61362   2-00011
Daniel Cekay, prin.   664-2100

Stanford, AC 309, PC 3, McLean
Olympia CUSD 16   4-11111
RR 1 BOX 150 61774   379-6011
Carol Struck, supt.

Olympia HS, RR 1 BOX 149 61774 3-00011 / 379-5911
Andrew Cooney, prin.
Olympia MS, RR 1 BOX 149 61774 2-00100 / 349-5941
Kathryn Riddle, prin.

Staunton, AC 618, PC 5, Macoupin
Staunton CUSD 6 4-11111 / 635-3838
801 N DENEEN ST 62088
Victor Buehler, supt.
HS, 801 N DENEEN ST 62088 2-00011 / 635-3838
Jack Milan, prin.
JHS, 801 N DENEEN ST 62088 2-00100 / 635-3838
Mark Skertich, prin.

Steeleville, AC 618, PC 4, Randolph
Steeleville CUSD 138 2-11111 / 965-3432
701 S SPARTA ST 62288
Donald Badgley, supt.
HS, 701 S SPARTA ST 62288 2-00011 / 965-3432
Verlin Lorenz, prin.

Steger, AC 708, PC 6, Cook
Steger SD 194, 3753 PARK AVE 60475 4-11100 / 755-0022
Jon Nebor, supt.
Central JHS, 19 W 33RD ST 60475 2-00100 / 755-0021
Donald Moke, prin.

Sterling, AC 815, PC 7, Whiteside
Sterling CUSD 5, 1800 6TH AVE 61081 5-11111 / 625-3620
Richard Zion, supt.
HS, 1608 4TH AVE 61081 4-00011 / 625-6800
Thomas Gericke, prin.
Challand JHS, 1700 6TH AVE 61081 3-00100 / 626-3300
Brad Hawk, prin.

Newman Central Catholic HS 2-00111 / 625-0500
1101 W 23RD ST 61081
Donald Loftus, prin.
Sterling Christian S 2-11111 / 625-0309
PO BOX 1040 61081
Mike Day, prin.

Stillman Valley, AC 815, PC 3, Ogle
Meridian CUSD 223 4-11111 / 645-2606
PO BOX 89 61084
Kent Johansen, supt.
HS, PO BOX 89 61084 2-00011 / 645-2606
Robert Prusator, prin.
Meridian JHS, PO BOX 89 61084 2-00100 / 645-2277
Jack Powell, prin.

Stockton, AC 815, PC 4, Jo Daviess
Stockton CUSD 206 3-11111 / 947-3391
236 N PEARL ST 61085
Marvin Maaske, supt.
HS, 540 N RUSH ST 61085 2-00011 / 947-3323
William King, prin.
MS, 500 N RUSH ST 61085 2-00100 / 947-3702
William King, prin.

Stone Park, AC 708, PC 5, Cook
Bellwood SD 88 5-11100 / 344-9344
1801 N 36TH AVE 60165
Anthony Torres, supt.
Other Schools – See Bellwood

Strasburg, AC 217, PC 2, Shelby
Stewardson-Strasburg CUSD 5A 2-11111 / 682-3355
PO BOX 67 62465
Barbara Roberts, supt.
Stewardson-Strasburg HS 2-00011 / 682-3355
RR 1 BOX 67 62465
Nik Groothuis, prin.

Streamwood, AC 708, PC 8, Kane
Elgin Unit SD 46
Supt. — See Elgin
HS, 701 W SCHAUMBURG RD 60107 4-00011 / 213-5500
Glen Lose, prin.
Canton MS, 1100 SUNSET CIR 60107 4-00100 / 213-5525
Richard Wiggall, prin.
Tefft MS, 1100 SHIRLEY AVE 60107 3-00100 / 213-5540
Keith Sack, prin.

Streator, AC 815, PC 7, La Salle
Streator ESD 44 4-11100 / 672-2926
1520 N BLOOMINGTON ST 61364
Richard M. Peters, supt.
Northlawn JHS, 202 E 1ST ST 61364 3-00100 / 672-4558
Charles Irwin, prin.

Streator Twp. HSD 40 3-00011 / 672-0545
600 N JEFFERSON ST 61364
Henry Boer, supt.
Streator Twp. HS 3-00011 / 672-0545
600 N JEFFERSON ST 61364
John Gregg, prin.

Streator Woodland CUSD 5 3-11111 / 672-5974
RR 2 61364
Lawrence Sebby, supt.
Woodland JSHS, RR 2 61364 2-00111 / 672-2900
William Donath, prin.

Stronghurst, AC 309, PC 3, Henderson
Southern CUSD 120 2-11111 / 924-1461
PO BOX 179 61480
Wendell Torrance, supt.
Southern HS, PO BOX 179 61480 2-00011 / 924-1781
Richard Clifton, prin.
Other Schools – See Media

Sugar Grove, AC 708, PC 4, Kane

Waubonsee Community College 5-CC / 466-4811
RURAL ROUTE 47 60554

Sullivan, AC 217, PC 5, Moultrie
Sullivan CUSD 300 4-11111 / 728-8341
725 N MAIN ST 61951
Richard Voltz, supt.
HS, 725 N MAIN ST 61951 2-00011 / 728-8311
Daniel Hoefler, prin.
MS, 713 N MAIN ST 61951 3-01100 / 782-8381
Kirby Rodgers, prin.

Summit-Argo, AC 708, PC 6, Cook
Argo Community HSD 217 4-00011 / 728-3200
7329 W 63RD ST 60501
Frank Basile, supt.
Argo Comm. HS, 7329 W 63RD ST 60501 4-00011 / 728-3200
Frank Stout, prin.
Summit SD 104 4-11100 / 458-0505
60TH ST & 74TH AVE 60501
Kevin Cronin, supt.
Graves JHS, 6021 S 74TH AVE 60501 2-00100 / 458-7590
Dennis Lewis, prin.

Sycamore, AC 815, PC 6, De Kalb
Sycamore CUSD 427 5-11111 / 895-4431
245 W EXCHANGE ST 60178
Robert Hammon, supt.
HS, 555 ALBERT AVE 60178 3-00011 / 895-9132
Jeff Welcker, prin.
JHS, 150 MAPLEWOOD DR 60178 3-00100 / 895-9174
Jeffrey Clapsaddle, prin.

Table Grove, AC 309, PC 2, Fulton
V I T CUSD 2, RR 1 BOX 7 61482 2-11111 / 758-5138
James Hermes, supt.
V I T HS, RR 1 BOX 6 61482 2-00011 / 758-5136
F. Marshall, prin.
V I T JHS, RR 1 BOX 6 61482 1-00100 / 758-5136
F. Marshall, prin.

Tamms, AC 618, PC 3, Alexander
Egyptian CUSD 5, RR 1 BOX SD 62988 3-11111 / 776-5251
Michael Corzine, supt.
Egyptian HS, RR 1 62988 2-00011 / 776-5251
Lonny Jones, prin.
Egyptian JHS, RR 1 62988 2-00100 / 776-5251
Lonny Jones, prin.

Tampico, AC 815, PC 3, Whiteside
Tampico CUSD 4, PO BOX 437 61283 2-11111 / 438-2160
Larry Wilcoxen, supt.
HS, PO BOX 188 61283 2-00011 / 438-3085
James Hochstatter, prin.
Other Schools – See Deer Grove

Taylor Ridge, AC 309, PC 2, Rock Island
Rockridge CUSD 300 4-11111 / 795-1167
14110 134TH AVE W 61284
Dick Stoltz, supt.
Rockridge HS 2-00011 / 795-1736
14110 134TH AVE W 61284
Lewis Betts, prin.
Rockridge JHS 2-00100 / 795-1172
14110 134TH AVE W 61284
Clayton Naylor, prin.

Taylorville, AC 217, PC 7, Christian
Taylorville CUSD 3 5-11111 / 824-4951
101 E ADAMS ST 62568
Richard Wilson, supt.
HS, 815 W SPRINGFIELD RD 62568 3-00011 / 824-2268
(—), prin.
JHS, 120 E BIDWELL ST 62568 3-00100 / 824-4924
Bernadette Salisbury, prin.

Teutopolis, AC 217, PC 4, Effingham
Teutopolis CUSD 50 4-11111 / 857-3535
PO BOX 607 62467
Robert Shanks, supt.
HS, 801 W MAIN ST 62467 2-00011 / 857-3139
Robert Bothwell, prin.

Thomasboro, AC 217, PC 4, Champaign
Prairieview CCSD 192
Supt. — See Royal
Flatville JHS, RR 1 BOX 146B 61878 1-01100 / 694-4122
Lee Shores, prin.

Thompsonville, AC 618, PC 3, Franklin
Thompsonville Community HSD 112 2-00011 / 627-2301
304 SHAWNEETOWN RD 62890
Karla Lee, supt.
HS, 304 SHAWNEETOWN RD 62890 2-00011 / 627-2301
Kim Kaytor, prin.

Thomson, AC 815, PC 3, Carroll
Thomson CUSD 301 2-11111 / 259-2735
RR 1 BOX 1 61285
David Wongstrom, supt.
HS, RR 1 BOX 1 61285 2-00011 / 259-2735
William Gengenback, prin.

Tinley Park, AC 708, PC 8, Cook
Bremen Community HSD 228
Supt. — See Midlothian
HS, 6111 175TH ST 60477 4-00011 / 532-1900
John McGraw, prin.

Consolidated HSD 230
Supt. — See Orland Park
Andrew SE, 9001 171ST ST 60477 4-00011 / 532-7300
Arlene See, prin.

Kirby SD 140, PO BOX 98 60477 5-11100 / 532-6462
Arnold Drzonek, supt.
Grissom JHS, 17000 80TH AVE 60477 3-00100 / 429-3030
Phillip Scully, prin.

Prairie View JHS, 8500 175TH ST 60477 2-00100 / 532-6462
Fred Schafer, prin.

Tinley Park Community SD 146 4-11100 / 614-4500
17316 OAK PARK AVE 60477
Robert Procunier, supt.
Central JHS, 17248 67TH AVE 60477 3-00100 / 614-4510
Larry Anderson, prin.

Tiskilwa, AC 815, PC 3, Bureau
Tiskilwa CUSD 300 2-11111 / 646-4211
PO BOX 329 61368
James Whitmore, supt.
HS, PO BOX 269 61368 2-00011 / 646-4661
Ronald Lamour, prin.

Toledo, AC 217, PC 4, Cumberland
Cumberland CUSD 77 4-11111 / 923-3132
RR 1 BOX 182 62468
Joseph Trimmer, supt.
Cumberland HS, RR 1 BOX 182 62468 2-00011 / 923-3133
Richard Manuell, prin.
Cumberland JHS 2-00100 / 923-3135
RR 1 BOX 182 62468
Gary Calvert, prin.

Tolono, AC 217, PC 5, Champaign
Tolono CUSD 7 4-11111 / 485-6510
408 S CENTRAL ST 61880
David Newell, supt.
Unity HS, PO BOX Q 61880 2-00011 / 485-6230
Don Akers, prin.
Unity JHS, PO BOX T 61880 2-00100 / 485-6735
Thomas Talbott, prin.

Toluca, AC 815, PC 4, Marshall
Fieldcrest CUSD 6
Supt. — See Minonk
Fieldcrest MS, 306 N MAPLE ST 61369 2-00100 / 452-2318
Kenneth Baker, prin.

Toulon, AC 309, PC 4, Stark
Stark County CUSD 1 4-11111 / 286-7171
PO BOX 659 61483
Robert Mueller, supt.
Stark County SHS 2-00001 / 286-4451
PO BOX 419 61483
Stephen Bell, prin.
Other Schools – See Wyoming

Tower Hill, AC 217, PC 3, Shelby
Tower Hill Community HSD 185 1-00011 / 567-3161
PO BOX 157 62571
Odus Cheek, supt.
HS, PO BOX 157 62571 1-00011 / 567-3121
William Geiger, prin.

Tremont, AC 309, PC 4, Tazewell
Tremont CUSD 702 3-11111 / 925-3461
PO BOX 167 61568
Brock Butts, supt.
HS, PO BOX 167 61568 2-00011 / 925-2051
Steven Epperson, prin.
JHS, PO BOX 167 61568 2-00100 / 925-3823
Rodger Page, prin.

Trenton, AC 618, PC 4, Clinton
Wesclin CUSD 3, ROUTE 160 S 62293 4-11111 / 224-7341
Daniel Meyer, supt.
Wesclin HS, RR 2 BOX 123B 62293 2-00011 / 224-7341
Robert Wutzler, prin.
Wesclin JHS, RR 2 BOX 123B 62293 2-00100 / 224-7355
Terry Shute, prin.

Trivoli, AC 309, PC 2, Peoria
Farmington Central CUSD 265 4-11111 / 362-2424
PO BOX 68 61569
Harold Palishen, supt.
Other Schools – See Farmington, Hanna City

Troy, AC 618, PC 6, Madison
Triad CUSD 2
Supt. — See Saint Jacob
Triad MS-Molden 3-00100 / 667-6441
209 N DEWEY ST 62294
Max Pigg, prin.

Tunnel Hill, AC 618, PC 1, Johnson
New Simpson Hill Consolidated SD 32 2-11100 / 658-9066
PO BOX 142 62991
Dr. Terry Elms, supt.
New Burnside Center MS 2-01100 / 777-2731
P O BOX 142 62991
Robert Gorman, prin.

Tuscola, AC 217, PC 5, Douglas
Tuscola CUSD 301 4-11111 / 253-4241
409 S PRAIRIE ST 61953
James Voyles, supt.
HS, 500 S PRAIRIE ST 61953 2-00011 / 253-2377
James Damler, prin.
East Prairie JHS, 409 S PRAIRIE ST 61953 2-01100 / 253-2828
William Englehardt, prin.

Ullin, AC 618, PC 2, Pulaski
Century CUSD 100, PO BOX 41B 62992 3-11111 / 845-3518
Bob McIntosh, supt.
Century HS, PO BOX 41B 62992 2-00011 / 845-3518
Robert Cross, prin.
Century JHS, PO BOX 41B 62992 1-00100 / 845-3518
Robert Cross, prin.

Shawnee Community College 4-CC / 634-2242
SHAWNEE COLLEGE ROAD 62992

University Park, AC 708, PC 6, Will

Governors State University		4-UC
1 UNIVERSITY PKY 60466		534-5000

Urbana, AC 217, PC 8, Champaign

Board of Trustees SD		2-00011
1212 W SPRINGFIELD AVE 61801		333-2870
Russell Ames, supt.		
University of Illinois HS		2-00011
1212 W SPRINGFIELD AVE 61801		333-2870
Joel Crames, prin.		
Urbana SD 116, PO BOX 3039 61801		6-11111
Eugene Amberg, supt.		384-3636
HS, 1002 S RACE ST 61801		4-00011
Ronald Gerrietts, prin.		384-3524
MS, 1201 S VINE ST 61801		4-00100
John Prinz, prin.		384-3687
University of Illinois		8-UC
506 S WRIGHT ST 61801		333-6290

Valmeyer, AC 618, PC 3, Monroe

Valmeyer CUSD 3		3-11111
603 W MAIN ST 62295		939-5100
H. Baum, supt.		
HS, 603 W MAIN ST 62295		2-00011
James Pflasterer, prin.		935-2777
JHS, 603 W MAIN ST 62295		2-00100
James Pflasterer, prin.		939-5102

Vandalia, AC 618, PC 6, Fayette

Vandalia CUSD 203		4-11111
1109 N 8TH ST 62471		283-4525
Larry Bennett, supt.		
Vandalia Community HS		2-00011
1109 N 8TH ST 62471		283-5155
Darrell Gummert, prin.		
JHS, 1017 W FLETCHER ST 62471		2-00100
William Ladage, prin.		283-5151

Varna, AC 309, PC 2, Marshall

Mid County CUSD 4, RR 1 61375		3-11111
Arthur Urbanski, supt.		463-2309
Mid-County HS, RR 1 BOX 170 61375		2-00011
T. Bayler, prin.		463-2095
Mid-County JHS, RR 1 61375		2-00100
T. Bayler, prin.		463-2095

Venice, AC 618, PC 5, Madison

Venice CUSD 3, 700 BROADWAY 62090		2-11111
John Rush, supt.		451-7953
HS, 700 BROADWAY 62090		2-00011
Louis Williams, prin.		452-5348

Vergennes, AC 618, PC 2, Jackson

Elverado CUSD 196		
Supt. — See Elkville		
Elverado JHS, PO BOX 35 62994		2-00100
Nate Geiger, prin.		684-3527

Vernon Hills, AC 708, PC 7, Lake

Hawthorn CCSD 73		5-11100
201 HAWTHORN PKY 60061		367-3226
Edward Noyes, supt.		
Hawthorn JHS		3-00100
201 HAWTHORN PKY 60061		367-3220
Erwin Einhorn, prin.		

Vienna, AC 618, PC 4, Johnson

Vienna HSD 13-3 62995		2-00011
Marleis Lauterjung, supt.		658-4461
HS, PO BOX 397 62995		2-00011
Marleis Lauterjung, prin.		658-3011

Villa Grove, AC 217, PC 5, Douglas

Villa Grove CUSD 302		3-11111
700 N SYCAMORE ST 61956		832-2261
David Kuetemeyer, supt.		
HS, 700 N SYCAMORE ST 61956		2-00011
Bob Doan, prin.		832-2321
JHS, 700 N SYCAMORE ST 61956		2-00100
Danny Powell, prin.		832-2261

Villa Park, AC 708, PC 7, Du Page

DuPage HSD 88		5-00011
101 W HIGHRIDGE RD 60181		530-3981
Robert Lopatka, supt.		
Willowbrook HS		4-00011
1250 S ARDMORE AVE 60181		530-3439
Richard Chamberlain, prin.		
Other Schools – See Addison		
Salt Creek SD 48		3-11100
1110 S VILLA AVE 60181		279-8400
Maud Hall, supt.		
Albright MS, 1110 S VILLA AVE 60181		2-01100
Alan Church, prin.		279-6160
Villa Park SD 45		5-11100
255 W VERMONT ST 60181		530-6200
Barbara Devlin, supt.		
Jackson JHS, 301 W JACKSON ST 60181		3-00100
Brooks Young, prin.		530-6240
Jefferson JHS		2-00100
255 W VERMONT ST 60181		530-6230
David Voypick, prin.		

Viola, AC 309, PC 3, Mercer

Sherrard CUSD 200		4-11111
PO BOX 528 61486		596-2974
William Heitman, supt.		
Other Schools – See Sherrard		

Virden, AC 217, PC 5, Macoupin

Virden CUSD 4		4-11111
231 W FORTUNE ST 62690		965-4226
James Kirbach, supt.		
HS, 231 W FORTUNE ST 62690		2-00011
David Bruna, prin.		965-4127
JHS, 231 W FORTUNE ST 62690		2-00100
Ronald Graham, prin.		965-3942

Virginia, AC 217, PC 4, Cass

Virginia CUSD 64		2-11111
651 S MORGAN ST 62691		452-3085
Robert Clancy, supt.		
HS, 651 S MORGAN ST 62691		2-00011
Jerry Meyer, prin.		452-3087
JHS, 651 S MORGAN ST 62691		1-00100
Jerry Meyer, prin.		452-3087

Walnut, AC 815, PC 4, Bureau

Walnut Community HSD 508		2-00011
PO BOX 487 61376		379-2434
William Mattingly, supt.		
Walnut Community HS		2-00011
PO BOX 487 61376		379-2434
William Mattingly, prin.		

Waltonville, AC 618, PC 2, Jefferson

Waltonville CUSD 1		2-11111
RR 1 BOX 39 62894		279-7211
James Jenkins, supt.		
HS, RR 1 62894		2-00011
James Jenkins, prin.		279-7211

Wapella, AC 217, PC 3, De Witt

Wapella CUSD 5, PO BOX 127 61777		2-11111
Thomas Long, supt.		935-9112
HS, PO BOX 127 61777		1-00011
Thomas Long, prin.		935-2517
JHS, PO BOX 127 61777		1-00100
Thomas Long, prin.		935-2517

Warren, AC 815, PC 4, Jo Daviess

Warren CUSD 205		3-11111
PO BOX 428 61087		745-2653
Charles Norland, supt.		
HS, PO BOX 428 61087		2-00011
James Nielsen, prin.		745-2641
JHS, PO BOX 428 61087		1-00100
James Nielsen, prin.		745-2641

Warrensburg, AC 217, PC 4, Macon

Warrensburg-Latham CUSD 11		4-11111
PO BOX 199 62573		672-3514
Michael Alexander, supt.		
Warrensburg-Latham HS		2-00011
PO BOX 409 62573		672-3531
Phillip Shelton, prin.		

Warsaw, AC 217, PC 4, Hancock

Warsaw CUSD 316, 340 S 11TH ST 62379		3-11111	
Wayne Riesen, supt.		256-4282	
JSHS, 340 S 11TH ST 62379		2-00011	
Tom Bertucci, prin.		256-4281	

Washburn, AC 309, PC 4, Woodford

Lowpoint-Washburn CUSD 21		3-11111
508 E WALNUT ST 61570		248-7522
Thomas Wagner, supt.		
Lowpoint-Washburn HS		2-00011
508 E WALNUT ST 61570		248-7521
Richard James, prin.		
Lowpoint-Washburn JHS		2-00100
508 E WALNUT ST 61570		248-7521
Richard James, prin.		

Washington, AC 309, PC 7, Tazewell

District 50 Schools		3-11100
304 E ALMOND DR 61571		745-8914
Roger Stevens, supt.		
Manor MS, 100 SCHOOL ST 61571		2-01100
(—), prin.		745-3121
Washington Community HSD 308		4-00011
115 BONDURANT ST 61571		444-3167
Richard Longbucco, supt.		
Washington Comm. HS		4-00011
115 BONDURANT ST 61571		444-3167
Richard Longbucco, prin.		
Washington SD 52		3-11100
303 JACKSON ST 61571		444-3321
Ken Webb, supt.		
MS, 105 S SPRUCE ST 61571		2-00100
Ken Gisleson, prin.		444-3361

Waterloo, AC 618, PC 6, Monroe

Waterloo CUSD 5, 200 ROGER ST 62298		4-11111
Bill Taylor, supt.		939-3453
HS, 200 BELLEFONTAINE DR 62298		3-00011
Gary Gordon, prin.		939-3455
JHS, 200 BELLEFONTAINE DR 62298		2-00100
Edward Gardner, prin.		939-3457
Gibault Catholic HS		2-00011
501 COLUMBIA AVE 62298		939-3883
Dan Brueggeman, prin.		

Waterman, AC 815, PC 4, De Kalb

Indian Creek CUSD		
Supt. — See Shabbona		
Indian Creek MS, 425 S ELM ST 60556		1-00100
Jeanne Radecki, prin.		264-7712

Watseka, AC 815, PC 6, Iroquois

Iroquois County CUSD 9		4-11111
109 S 2ND ST 60970		432-4931
Martin Getty, supt.		

Watseka Community HS		2-00011
138 S BELMONT AVE 60970		432-2486
Roger Eddy, prin.		
Raymond MS, W MULBERRY ST 60970		2-00100
Carl Mooi, prin.		432-2115

Wauconda, AC 708, PC 6, Lake

Wauconda CUSD 118		5-11111
555 N MAIN ST 60084		526-7690
H. Darrell Dick, supt.		
Wauconda Community HS		3-00011
555 N MAIN ST 60084		526-6611
John Rayburn, prin.		
JHS, 215 SLOCUM LAKE RD 60084		3-00100
Christine Golden, prin.		526-2122

Waukegan, AC 708, PC 8, Lake

Waukegan CUSD 60		7-11111
1201 N SHERIDAN RD 60085		336-3100
Alan Brown, supt.		
HS, 2325 BROOKSIDE AVE 60085		5-00011
Brian Ali, prin.		360-5621
Career Academy		Vo Tech
1020 GLEN ROCK AVE 60085		360-5540
Bryan Wright, prin.		
Abbott MS		3-00100
1319 WASHINGTON ST 60085		360-5487
Rita Melius, prin.		
Benny MS		3-00100
1401 MONTESANO AVE 60087		360-5460
Gary Calsyn, prin.		
Jefferson MS, 600 S LEWIS AVE 60085		3-00100
Allan Mismash, prin.		360-5473
Webster MS, 930 NEW YORK ST 60085		3-00100
Eugene Head, prin.		360-5484
Lake County Baptist S		2-11111
1550 W YORKHOUSE RD 60087		623-7600
Dorland Abernathy, prin.		
Lake Shore Catholic School		2-01100
510 10TH ST 60085		623-4070
Mary Liddy, prin.		
Shimer College		1-UC
PO BOX A500 60079		623-8400

Waverly, AC 217, PC 4, Morgan

Waverly CUSD 6		2-11111
201 N MILLER ST 62692		435-2211
Patricia Tucker-Ladd, supt.		
HS, 201 N MILLER ST 62692		1-00011
W. Gary Stritzel, prin.		435-2211

Wayne City, AC 618, PC 4, Wayne

Wayne City CUSD 100		3-11111
PO BOX 476 62895		895-2152
Donald Sutton, supt.		
HS, PO BOX 447 62895		2-00011
David Beehn, prin.		895-2313
MS, PO BOX 536 62895		2-01100
Donald Sutton, prin.		895-2022

Weldon, AC 217, PC 2, De Witt

Deland-Weldon CUSD 57		
Supt. — See De Land		
Deland-Weldon MS, RR 1 61882		1-00100
Robert Jennings, prin.		736-2401

Wenona, AC 815, PC 3, Marshall

Fieldcrest CUSD 6		
Supt. — See Minonk		
Fieldcrest MS, 102 W ELM ST 61377		2-00100
William Seifort, prin.		853-4331

Westchester, AC 708, PC 7, Cook

Westchester SD 92-5		3-11100
9981 CANTERBURY ST 60154		450-2700
Thomas Cusack, supt.		
MS, 1620 NORFOLK AVE 60154		2-00100
L. Meyers, prin.		450-2735
Immaculate Heart of Mary HS		3-00011
10900 W CERMAK RD 60154		562-3115
Catherine Karl, prin.		
St. Joseph HS		3-00011
1840 MAYFAIR AVE 60154		562-4433
Anthony Quattrochi, prin.		

West Chicago, AC 708, PC 7, Du Page

Benjamin SD 25		4-11100
28W250 SAINT CHARLES RD 60185		231-3852
Rob Sabitino, supt.		
Benjamin MS		2-01100
28W300 SAINT CHARLES RD 60185		293-5080
Greg Kane, prin.		
Community HSD 94		4-00011
326 JOLIET ST 60185		231-0880
Joel Morris, supt.		
Community HS, 326 JOLIET ST 60185		4-00011
Alan Jones, prin.		231-0880
West Chicago SD 33		5-11100
312 E FOREST AVE 60185		293-6000
John Hennig, supt.		
JHS, 238 E HAZEL ST 60185		3-00100
David Burton, prin.		293-6060
Wheaton Christian HS		2-00011
900 PRINCE CROSSING RD 60185		231-0727
David Roth, prin.		

Western Springs, AC 708, PC 7, Cook

Lyons Twp. HSD 204
Supt. — See La Grange

Lyons Twp. HS South 4-00010
4900 GILBERT AVE 60558 579-6505
Lila Sullivan, prin.

Western Springs SD 101 3-11100
4335 HOWARD AVE 60558 246-3700
Dr. Donald E. Barnes, supt.
McClure JHS, 4225 WOLF RD 60558 2-00100
William Stelter, prin. 246-7590

West Frankfort, AC 618, PC 6, Franklin
West Frankfort CUSD 168 4-11111
PO BOX 425 62896 937-2421
Ronald Davis, supt.
Frankfort HS, 601 E MAIN ST 62896 3-00011
David Lee, prin. 932-3126
Central JHS, 1500 E 9TH ST 62896 2-00100
Linda Varis, prin. 937-2444

Westmont, AC 708, PC 7, Du Page
Westmont CUSD 201 4-11111
200 N LINDEN ST 60559 969-7741
Donald Wold, supt.
HS, 909 OAKWOOD DR 60559 3-00011
Joseph Sabatino, prin. 654-3043
JHS, 944 OAKWOOD DR 60559 2-00100
Keith Becker, prin. 654-2188

Westville, AC 217, PC 5, Vermilion
Westville CUSD 2 4-11111
125 W ELLSWORTH ST 61883 267-3141
Larry Huber, supt.
HS, 918 N STATE ST 61883 2-00011
Jay Hall, prin. 267-2183
JHS, 412 MOSES AVE 61883 2-00100
Andrew Weathers, prin. 267-2185

Wheaton, AC 708, PC 8, Du Page
Community Unit SD 200 7-11111
130 W PARK AVE 60187 682-2002
E. Travis, supt.
Wheaton North HS 4-00011
701 W THOMAS RD 60187 682-2140
Attila Weninger, prin.
Wheaton/Warrenville South HS 4-00011
1993 TIGER TRL 60187 682-2123
Charles Baker, prin.
Edison MS 3-00100
1125 S WHEATON AVE 60187 682-2050
Lawrence Fox, prin.
Franklin MS, 211 E FRANKLIN ST 60187 3-00100
Dennis Rosy, prin. 682-2060
Hubble MS, 603 S MAIN ST 60187 3-00100
(—), prin. 682-2160
Monroe MS 3-00100
1855 MANCHESTER RD 60187 682-2285
Rodney Rich, prin.

St. Francis HS 3-00011
2130 W ROOSEVELT RD 60187 668-5800
Michael Rice, prin.
Wheaton College 4-UC
501 COLLEGE AVE 60187 752-5000

Wheeler, AC 618, PC 2, Jasper
Jasper County CUSD 1
Supt. — See Newton
West JHS, RR 1 62479 2-01100
Andy Pullen, prin. 783-3697

Wheeling, AC 708, PC 8, Cook
Township HSD 214
Supt. — See Arlington Heights
HS, 900 S ELMHURST RD 60090 4-00011
Elizabeth Ennis, prin. 537-6500

Wheeling CCSD 21 6-11100
999 W DUNDEE RD 60090 537-8270
Bud Descarpentrie, supt.
Holmes JHS, 221 S WOLF RD 60090 3-00100
Thomas Torcheldo, prin. 520-2790
Other Schools – See Buffalo Grove

Worsham College of Mortuary Science 2-CS
495 NORTHGATE PKY 60090 808-8444

White Hall, AC 217, PC 5, Greene
North Greene CUSD 3 4-11111
528 N MAIN ST 62092 374-2842
Donald Peck, supt.
North Greene HS, 546 N MAIN ST 62092 2-00011
Donald Aubry, prin. 374-2131
Other Schools – See Roodhouse

Williamsfield, AC 309, PC 3, Knox
Williamsfield CUSD 210 61489 2-11111
James Kutkat, supt. 639-2219
HS, 300 KENTUCKY AVE 61489 1-00011
Richard Putnam, prin. 639-2216
MS, KENTUCKY AVE 61489 1-00100
Richard Putnam, prin. 639-2216

Williamsville, AC 217, PC 4, Sangamon
Williamsville CUSD 15 4-11111
PO BOX 469 62693 566-2014
Richard Hadfield, supt.
HS, PO BOX 469 62693 2-00011
Rich Spenn, prin. 566-3361
JHS, PO BOX 469 62693 2-00100
Rod McQuality, prin. 566-3600

Wilmette, AC 708, PC 8, Cook
Avoca SD 37, 2921 ILLINOIS RD 60091 3-11100
John Sloan, supt. 251-3587
Murphy MS, 2921 ILLINOIS RD 60091 2-00100
Don Reed, prin. 251-3617

New Trier Twp. HSD 203 5-00011
3013 ILLINOIS RD 60091 446-7000
Henry Bangser, supt.
Other Schools – See Winnetka

Wilmette SD 39, 615 LOCUST RD 60091 5-11100
Sam Mikaelian, supt. 256-2450
JHS, 620 LOCUST RD 60091 3-00100
William Melsheimer, prin. 256-7280

Loyola Academy 4-00011
1100 LARAMIE AVE 60091 256-1100
Bernard Bouillette, prin.
Loyola University Mallinckrodt Campus 2-UC
1041 RIDGE RD 60091 256-1094
Regina Dominican HS 2-00011
701 LOCUST RD 60091 256-7660
Sr. Marilee Ewing, prin.

Wilmington, AC 815, PC 5, Will
Wilmington CUSD 209U 4-11111
715 S JOLIET ST 60481 476-2594
Russ White, supt.
HS, 715 S JOLIET ST 60481 2-00011
Alan Fox, prin. 476-2846
Stevens MS, 221 RYAN ST 60481 2-00100
Leonard Sokoloff, prin. 476-2189

Winchester, AC 217, PC 4, Scott
Winchester CUSD 1, 149 S ELM ST 62694 3-11111
Rex Eddy, supt. 742-3175
HS, 200 W CROSS ST 62694 2-00011
Lantz Stein, prin. 742-3151

Windsor, AC 217, PC 4, Shelby
Windsor CUSD 1, PO BOX 200 61957 2-11111
Dwight Mayberry, supt. 459-2922
HS, 1424 MINNESOTA AVE 61957 1-00011
Dwight Mayberry, prin. 459-2636
JHS, 1424 MINNESOTA AVE 61957 1-00100
Dwight Mayberry, prin. 459-2636

Winfield, AC 708, PC 6, Du Page
Winfield SD 34 3-11100
0S150 WINFIELD RD 60190 260-2380
Calvin Roesner, supt.
MS, 0S150 PARK ST 60190 2-01100
Joe McHaley, prin. 668-6052

Central Du Page Hospital HSP
0N025 WINFIELD RD 60190 682-1600

Winnebago, AC 815, PC 4, Winnebago
Winnebago CUSD 323 4-11111
PO BOX 98 61088 335-2456
John Bevan, supt.
HS, PO BOX 516 61088 2-00011
Catherine Finch, prin. 335-2336
McNair MS, PO BOX 577 61088 2-00100
James Burns, prin. 335-2364

Winnetka, AC 708, PC 7, Cook
New Trier Twp. HSD 203
Supt. — See Wilmette
New Trier Twp. HS 5-00011
385 WINNETKA AVE 60093 446-7000
Dianna Lindsay, prin.

Winnetka SD 36, 1235 OAK ST 60093 4-11100
Dr. Donald S. Monroe, supt. 446-9400
Carleton-Washburne JHS 3-00100
515 HIBBARD RD 60093 446-9400
William Meuer, prin.

Hadley School for the Blind HND
700 ELM ST 60093
Music Center of the North Shore 4-CS
300 GREEN BAY RD 60093
North Shore Country Day S 2-11111
310 GREEN BAY RD 60093 446-0674
Julia Hall, prin.

Winthrop Harbor, AC 708, PC 6, Lake
Winthrop Harbor SD 1 3-11100
2309 9TH ST 60096 746-1471
Dr. Kenneth Anton, supt.
Westfield JHS, 2309 9TH ST 60096 2-01100
Terry Scherman, prin. 872-5438

Witt, AC 217, PC 3, Montgomery
Witt Unit SD 66, PO BOX 447 62094 2-11111
Walter Buchele, supt. 594-2232
HS, PO BOX 447 62094 1-00011
Ernest Petray, prin. 594-2231
JHS, PO BOX 447 62094 1-00100
Ernest Petray, prin. 594-2231

Wolf Lake, AC 618, PC 2, Union
Shawnee CUSD 84 3-11111
PO BOX 128 62998 833-5709
Wilmer Nall, supt.
Shawnee HS, PO BOX 128 62998 2-00011
John Phillippe, prin. 833-5307
Shawnee JHS, PO BOX 128 62998 1-00100
John Phillippe, prin. 833-5307

Wood Dale, AC 708, PC 7, Du Page
Wood Dale SD 7 4-11100
543 N WOOD DALE RD 60191 595-9510
Michael Smoot, supt.
JHS, 6N655 WOOD DALE RD 60191 2-00100
Lorenz Hartwig, prin. 766-6210

Woodhull, AC 309, PC 3, Henry
Alwood CUSD 225 3-11111
PO BOX 428 61490 334-2719
H. Wayne French, supt.

Alwood JSHS, PO BOX 308 61490 2-00111
David Berg, prin. 334-2102

Woodlawn, AC 618, PC 3, Jefferson
Woodlawn Community HSD 205 2-00011
PO BOX 268 62898 735-2631
Richard Small, supt.
Woodlawn Community HS 2-00011
PO BOX 268 62898 735-2631
Richard Small, prin.

Woodridge, AC 708, PC 8, Du Page
Woodridge SD 68 5-11100
7925 JANES AVE 60517 985-7925
Allen McCowan, supt.
Jefferson JHS, 7200 JANES AVE 60517 3-00100
Laura Jordan, prin. 852-8010

Wood River, AC 618, PC 7, Madison
East Alton-Wood River Community HSD 14 3-00011
777 N WOOD RIVER AVE 62095 254-3151
Thomas Parker, supt.
East Alton-Wood River HS 3-00011
777 N WOOD RIVER AVE 62095 254-3151
Thomas Parker, prin.

Wood River-Hartford ESD 15 3-11100
501 E LORENA AVE 62095 254-0607
W. C. Viniard, supt.
Lewis-Clark JHS 2-00100
501 E LORENA AVE 62095 254-4355
Sue Rives, prin.

Woodstock, AC 815, PC 7, McHenry
Woodstock CUSD 200 5-11111
501 W SOUTH ST 60098 337-5406
Joseph Hentges, supt.
HS, 501 W SOUTH ST 60098 4-00011
Jocelyn Booth, prin. 338-4370
Northwood MS 2-00100
2121 N SEMINARY AVE 60098 338-4900
Peter Anderson, prin.
Olson MS, 720 W JUDD ST 60098 3-00100
Don Deller, prin. 338-0473

Marian Central Catholic HS 2-00011
1001 MCHENRY AVE 60098 338-4220
John Burke, prin.

Worth, AC 708, PC 7, Cook
Worth SD 127 4-11100
111TH AND OAK PARK AVE 60482 448-2800
Eugene O'Donnell, supt.
JHS 2-00100
112TH AND NEW ENGLAND AVE 60482
Celeste Nelson, prin. 448-2800

Wyanet, AC 815, PC 4, Bureau
Wyanet Community HSD 510 1-00011
PO BOX 371 61379 – (—), supt. 699-2251
Wyanet Community HS 1-00011
PO BOX 371 61379 – (—), prin. 699-2251

Wyoming, AC 309, PC 4, Stark
Stark County CUSD 1
Supt. — See Toulon
Stark County JHS 2-00110
401 N GALENA AVE 61491 695-5191
Terry Hull, prin.

Yorkville, AC 708, PC 5, Kendall
Yorkville CUSD 115 4-11111
507 W KENDALL DR STE 4 60560 553-4382
Thomas Engler, supt.
HS, 702 GAME FARM RD 60560 3-00011
Frank Babich, prin. 553-4380
Circle Center JHS, 901 MILL ST 60560 2-00100
Douglas Trumble, prin. 553-4385

Zeigler, AC 618, PC 4, Franklin
Zeigler-Royalton CUSD 188 3-11111
PO BOX 38 62999 596-5841
George Connor, supt.
Ziegler-Royalton HS 2-00011
PO BOX 38 62999 596-5841
George Connor, prin.
Zeigler-Royalton JHS 2-00100
PO BOX 87 62999 596-2121
Mickey Stafko, prin.

Zion, AC 708, PC 7, Lake
Beach Park CCSD 3 4-11100
11315 W WADSWORTH RD 60099 623-9300
Lewis Edwards, supt.
Murphy JHS 2-00100
11315 W WADSWORTH RD 60099 623-9300
Scott Murphy, prin.

Zion-Benton Twp. HSD 126 4-00011
3901 21ST ST 60099 – David Cox, supt. 746-1202
Zion-Benton HS, 3901 21ST ST 60099 4-00011
David Cox, prin. 746-1202

Zion ESD, 2200 BETHESDA BLVD 60099 5-11100
Barbara Christiansen, supt. 872-5455
Central JHS, 1716 27TH ST 60099 3-00100
Jim Taylor, prin. 746-1431

Waukegan Christian S 2-11111
1630 23RD ST 60099 872-3553
Gary Arnold, prin.
Zion Christian S 2-11111
1828 HEBRON AVE 60099 872-4088
Valerie Burnette, prin.

INDIANA

STATE DEPARTMENT OF EDUCATION
State House
200 W. Washington St. #229, Indianapolis 46204
(317) 232-6610

Superintendent of Public Instruction	Suellen Reed
Deputy Superintendent	Robert Dalton
Senior Officer Administration & Finanical Management	Erwin Pump
Senior Officer Community Relations & Special Populations	Marcella Taylor
Senior Officer School Improvement & Performance	Phyllis Usher
Senior Officer Assessment, Research & Information Tech	J. Stephen Grimes

STATE BOARD OF EDUCATION
200 W. Washington St. #229, Indianapolis 46204

Chairperson	Suellen Reed

PUBLIC, PRIVATE AND CATHOLIC SECONDARY SCHOOLS

Albion, AC 219, PC 4, Noble
Central Noble Community SD — 4-11111
  200 E MAIN ST 46701 — 636-2175
  Earl Richter, supt.
Central Noble HS — 2-00011
  302 COUGAR CT 46701 — 636-2117
  Richard Gregg, prin.
Central Noble MS — 2-00100
  401 E HIGHLAND ST 46701 — 636-2279
  Joel Moore, prin.

Alexandria, AC 317, PC 6, Madison
Alexandria Community SD — 4-11111
  PO BOX 240 46001 — 724-4496
  John McFarren, supt.
Alexandria-Monroe HS — 3-00011
  1 BURDEN CT 46001 — 724-4414
  David Wood, prin.
MS, 308 W 11TH ST 46001 — 2-00100
  Timothy Fihe, prin. — 724-4166

Anderson, AC 317, PC 8, Madison
Anderson Community SD — 7-11111
  30 W 11TH ST 46016 — 641-2000
  Jane Kendrick, supt.
HS, 1301 LINCOLN ST 46016 — 4-00011
  Horace Chadbourne, prin. — 641-2069
Highland HS, 2108 E 200 N 46012 — 4-00011
  Lennon Brown, prin. — 641-2059
Madison Heights HS — 4-00011
  4610 MADISON AVE 46013 — 641-2037
  James Sutton, prin.
Anderson Area Vo-Tech — Vo Tech
  325 W 38TH ST 46013 — 641-2121
  Richard Dickerson, prin.
East Side MS, 2300 LINDBERG RD 46012 — 3-00100
  Lucinda McCord, prin. — 641-2047
North Side MS — 3-00100
  1815 INDIANA AVE 46012 — 641-2055
  Lee Richardson-Pate, prin.
South Side MS, 101 W 29TH ST 46016 — 3-00100
  Bruce King, prin. — 641-2051

West Central Community SD — 4-11111
  4956 W 300 N 46011 — 643-7444
  George Dickinson, supt.
Other Schools – See Frankton, Lapel

Anderson University — 4-UC
  1100 E 5TH ST 46012 — 649-9071
Indiana Business College — 2-CS
  1320 E 53RD ST # 106 46013 — 644-7514
Indiana Christian Academy — 2-11111
  432 W 300 N 46012 — 643-7884
  William Newton, prin.
Liberty Christian S — 2-11111
  2323 COLUMBUS AVE 46016 — 644-7773
  Joyce Hazen, prin.

Angola, AC 219, PC 6, Steuben
Metro SD of Steuben County — 5-11111
  400 S MARTHA ST 46703 — 665-2854
  Oren Skinner, supt.
HS, 755 S 100 E 46703 — 3-00011
  Rex Bolinger, prin. — 665-2186
MS, 575 E US HIGHWAY 20 46703 — 3-00100
  William Church, prin. — 665-9581

Tri-State University 46703 — 4-UC
  — 665-4100

Arcadia, AC 317, PC 4, Hamilton
Hamilton Heights SD — 4-11111
  PO BOX 469 46030 — 984-3538
  Wayne Kitch, supt.
Hamilton Heights HS — 3-00011
  PO BOX 379 46030 — 984-3551
  Tony Cook, prin.
Hamilton Heights MS — 3-01100
  PO BOX 609 46030 — 984-3588
  Chris Walton, prin.

Argos, AC 219, PC 4, Marshall
Argos Community SD — 3-11111
  410 N 1ST ST 46501 — 892-5139
  Ted Chittum, supt.
Argos Community JSHS — 2-00111
  500 YEARICK ST 46501 — 892-5137
  Richard Dehne, prin.

Attica, AC 317, PC 5, Fountain
Attica Consolidated SD — 3-11111
  205 S COLLEGE ST 47918 — 762-3236
  William Lake, supt.
JSHS, 211 E SYCAMORE ST 47918 — 2-00111
  Roy Jones, prin. — 762-6105

Auburn, AC 219, PC 6, De Kalb

Lakewood Park Christian Academy — 2-11111
  5555 COUNTY ROAD 29 46706 — 925-1393
  Mark Wever, prin.

Aurora, AC 812, PC 5, Dearborn
South Dearborn Community SD — 5-11111
  408 GREEN BLVD 47001 — 926-2090
  G. Platt, supt.
South Dearborn HS — 3-00011
  5770 HIGHLANDER DR N 47001 — 926-3772
  Marvin Duerstock, prin.
MS, 404 GREEN BLVD 47001 — 2-01100
  David Chalk, prin. — 926-2141

Austin, AC 812, PC 5, Scott
Scott County SD 1, PO BOX 9 47102 — 4-11111
  Berley Goodin, supt. — 794-8750
HS, 401 S HIGHWAY 31 47102 — 2-00011
  Sherman Smith, prin. — 794-8730
MS, 401 S HIGHWAY 31 47102 — 2-00100
  David Deaton, prin. — 794-8740

Bainbridge, AC 317, PC 3, Putnam
North Putnam Community SD — 4-11111
  PO BOX 169 46105 — 522-6218
  James Bates, supt.
Other Schools – See Roachdale

Batesville, AC 812, PC 5, Ripley
Batesville Community SD — 4-11111
  PO BOX 121 47006 — 934-2194
  James Freeland, supt.
HS, 1 BULLDOG BLVD W 47006 — 3-00011
  Fred Sagester, prin. — 934-4384
MS, 201 N MULBERRY ST 47006 — 2-00100
  Vivian Whitaker, prin. — 934-5175

Battle Ground, AC 317, PC 3, Tippecanoe
Tippecanoe SD
  Supt. — See Lafayette
MS, 511 MAIN ST 47920 — 2-00100
  Harold May, prin. — 567-2122

Bedford, AC 812, PC 7, Lawrence
North Lawrence Community SD — 6-11111
  PO BOX 729 47421 — 279-3521
  Dennis Turner, supt.
Bedford-North Lawrence HS — 4-00011
  RR 13 BOX 439 47421 — 279-9756
  Stan Glenn, prin.
North Lawrence Vo-Tech Ctr — Vo Tech
  HWY 58 EAST BOYD LANE 47421 — 279-3561
  Dave Embree, prin.
JHS, 1501 N ST 47421 — 3-00100
  Jim Pounds, prin. — 279-9781

Beech Grove, AC 317, PC 7, Marion
Beech Grove CSD, PO BOX 219 46107 — 4-11111
  Bradley Showalter, supt. — 788-4481
HS, 5330 HORNET AVE 46107 — 3-00011
  Gerald Yentes, prin. — 786-1447
MS, 1248 BUFFALO ST 46107 — 2-00100
  Samuel Merl, prin. — 784-6649

St. Francis Hospital Center — HSP
  1600 ALBANY ST 46107 — 783-8220

Berne, AC 219, PC 5, Adams
South Adams SD — 4-11111
  1027 US HIGHWAY 27 S 46711 — 589-3133
  Larry Leistner, supt.
South Adams JSHS — 3-00111
  1000 PARKWAY ST 46711 — 589-3131
  Larry Piety, prin.

Bicknell, AC 812, PC 5, Knox
North Knox SD, PO BOX 187 47512 — 4-11111
  Timothy Weaver, supt. — 735-4434
North Knox HS, PO BOX 187 47512 — 3-00111
  Donald DeBoer, prin. — 735-2990

Bloomfield, AC 812, PC 5, Greene
Bloomfield SD, PO BOX 266 47424 — 4-11111
  Jeff Abbott, supt. — 384-4507
HS, PO BOX 266 47424 — 2-00011
  W. Mattox, prin. — 384-4550
JHS, PO BOX 266 47424 — 2-00100
  Ralph Raper, prin. — 384-3020

Eastern SD of Greene County — 4-11111
  RR 4 BOX 623 47424 — 825-5621
  Keith Spurgeon, supt.
Eastern District JSHS — 3-00111
  RR 4 BOX 623 47424 — 825-5621
  Paul Hunt, prin.

Bloomington, AC 812, PC 8, Monroe
Monroe County Community SD — 7-11111
  315 S NORTH DR 47401 — 330-7700
  Jack Bowman, supt.
Bloomington HS North — 4-00011
  3901 N KINSER PIKE 47404 — 330-7724
  Dennis Martin, prin.
Bloomington HS South — 4-00011
  1965 S WALNUT ST 47401 — 330-7714
  Mike Riggle, prin.

Hoosier Hills Area Vo S — Vo Tech
3901 N KINSER PIKE 47404 — 330-7730
Edward Brown, prin.
Batchelor MS — 3-00100
900 W GORDON PIKE 47403 — 330-7763
Dale Glenn, prin.
Tri-North MS, 1000 W 15TH ST 47404 — 3-00100
Mike Walsh, prin. — 330-7745

Harmony S, PO BOX 1787 47402 — 2-11111
Steve Bonchek, prin. — 334-8349
Indiana University — 8-UC
300 N JORDAN AVE 47406 — 885-4602

Bluffton, AC 219, PC 6, Wells
Metro SD of Bluffton-Harrison — 4-11111
628 S BENNETT ST 46714 — 824-2620
Gary McMillen, supt.
HS, 428 S OAK ST 46714 — 2-00011
Frank O'Shea, prin. — 824-3724
Bluffton-Harrison MS — 3-01100
1500 STOGDILL RD 46714 — 824-3536
Joe Ogden, prin.

Boone Grove, AC 219, PC 2, Porter
Porter Township SD
Supt. — See Valparaiso
JSHS, 325 W 550 S 46302 — 3-00111
Timothy Holcomb, prin. — 464-4828

Boonville, AC 812, PC 6, Warrick
Warrick County SD — 6-11111
PO BOX 809 47601 — 897-0400
James Martin, supt.
HS, PO BOX 649 47601 — 3-00011
James Duffy, prin. — 897-4701
JHS, 555 N YANKEETOWN RD 47601 — 3-00100
Robert Lindley, prin. — 897-1420
Other Schools – See Lynnville, Newburgh

Borden, AC 812, PC 2, Clark
West Clark Community SD
Supt. — See Sellersburg
JSHS, 301 WEST ST 47106 — 2-00111
Ben Ruckle, prin. — 967-2087

Bourbon, AC 219, PC 4, Marshall
Triton SD, 100 TRITON DR 46504 — 4-11111
Rex Roth, supt. — 342-2255
Triton JSHS, 300 TRITON DR 46504 — 2-00111
Alice Neal, prin. — 342-6505

Brazil, AC 812, PC 6, Clay
Clay Community SD
Supt. — See Knightsville
Northview HS, 1 KNIGHT DR 47834 — 4-00011
Kirk Freeman, prin. — 448-2661
North Clay JHS, RR 13 BOX 48 47834 — 3-00100
Jerry Morgan, prin. — 448-1530

Bremen, AC 219, PC 5, Marshall
Bremen Public SD — 4-11111
512 W GRANT ST 46506 — 546-3929
Richard Kline, supt.
HS, 511 W GRANT ST 46506 — 2-00011
Don Harrison, prin. — 546-3511

Brookville, AC 317, PC 5, Franklin
Franklin County Community SD — 5-11111
PO BOX 1 47012 — 647-4128
W. Glentzer, supt.
Franklin County HS — 3-00011
10156 OXFORD PIKE 47012 — 647-4101
Ken Saxon, prin.
MS, 1010 FRANKLIN AVE 47012 — 2-00100
Gary Frost, prin. — 647-2644

Brownsburg, AC 317, PC 6, Hendricks
Brownsburg Community SD — 5-11111
225 S SCHOOL ST 46112 — 852-5726
Dr. Robert Herrold, supt.
HS, 1000 S ODELL ST 46112 — 4-00011
James Land, prin. — 852-2258
JHS, 320 STADIUM DR 46112 — 3-00100
Carol DeBoy, prin. — 852-3143

Bethesda Christian S — 2-11111
7950 N COUNTY ROAD 650 E 46112 — 852-3101
Charles Wilkins, prin.

Brownstown, AC 812, PC 5, Jackson
Brownstown Central Community SD — 4-11111
500 N ELM ST 47220 — 358-4271
Donal Neal, supt.
Brownstown Central HS — 3-00011
500 N ELM ST 47220 — 358-3453
Gerald Rose, prin.
Brownstown Central MS — 2-00100
520 W WALNUT ST 47220 — 358-4947
Bill Day, prin.

Bunker Hill, AC 317, PC 4, Miami
Maconaquah SD, RR 1 BOX 28A 46914 — 4-11111
Ronald Wilson, supt. — 689-9131
Maconaquah HS, RR 1 BOX 30 46914 — 3-00011
William Russ, prin. — 689-9127
Maconaquah MS, RR 1 BOX 30B 46914 — 3-00100
Steven Walther, prin. — 689-9102

Butler, AC 219, PC 5, De Kalb
DeKalb County Eastern Community SD — 4-11111
300 E WASHINGTON ST 46721 — 868-2125
Charles Hampel, supt.
Eastside JSHS, 603 E GREEN ST 46721 — 3-00111
Arlyn Reinhard, prin. — 868-2186

Cambridge City, AC 317, PC 4, Wayne
Western Wayne SD — 4-11111
PO BOX 109 47327 — 478-3261
Lynn Sheets, supt.
Lincoln JSHS — 3-00111
215 E PARKWAY DR 47327 — 478-5916
Darrell Durham, prin.

Campbellsburg, AC 812, PC 3, Washington
West Washington SD, RR 2 47108 — 4-11111
Ben Jennings, supt. — 755-4872
West Washington JSHS, RR 2 47108 — 3-00111
William Rector, prin. — 755-4996

Cannelton, AC 812, PC 4, Perry
Cannelton CSD — 2-11111
3RD & TAYLOR STS 47520 — 547-7741
Larry Moore, supt.
JSHS, 3RD & TAYLOR STS 47520 — 2-00111
Dale McNeely, prin. — 547-3296

Carmel, AC 317, PC 8, Hamilton
Carmel-Clay SD, 5201 E 131ST ST 46033 — 6-11111
R. S. Tegarden, supt. — 844-9961
SHS, 520 E MAIN ST 46032 — 4-00001
William Duke, prin. — 846-7721
JHS, 300 S GUILFORD RD 46032 — 4-00110
Charles Scott, prin. — 846-7331
Clay JHS, 5150 E 126TH ST 46033 — 4-00110
Steve Dillon, prin. — 844-7251

Cayuga, AC 317, PC 4, Vermillion
North Vermillion Community SD — 4-11111
RR 1 BOX 191 47928 — 492-4033
Jeff Baer, supt.
North Vermillion JSHS — 2-00111
RR 1 BOX 191 47928 — 492-3364
Oren Sutherlin, prin.

Cedar Lake, AC 219, PC 6, Lake
Hanover Community SD — 4-11111
PO BOX 645 46303 — 374-5546
Robert Leturgez, supt.
Hanover Central JSHS — 3-00111
10120 W 133RD AVE 46303 — 374-7371
Joseph Fetty, prin.

Centerville, AC 317, PC 4, Wayne
Centerville-Abington Community SD — 4-11111
115 W SOUTH ST 47330 — 855-3475
Brian Smith, supt.
HS, WILLOW GROVE ROAD 47330 — 3-00011
Philip Stevenson, prin. — 855-3481
JHS, 200 W SCHOOL ST 47330 — 2-00100
Brad Atkinson, prin. — 855-5113

Chalmers, AC 219, PC 3, White
Frontier SD, PO BOX 809 47929 — 3-11111
Norris Nierste, supt. — 984-5009
Frontier HS, PO BOX 128 47929 — 2-00011
Douglas Lesley, prin. — 984-5437

Charlestown, AC 812, PC 6, Clark
Greater Clark County SD
Supt. — See Jeffersonville
HS, 1 PIRATE PL 47111 — 3-00011
George Marshall, prin. — 256-3328
MS, 8804 HIGH JACKSON RD 47111 — 3-00100
James Williams, prin. — 256-6363

Charlottesville, AC 317, PC 2, Hancock
Eastern Hancock County Community SD — 4-11111
10370 E 250 N 46117 — 326-2268
Terry Russell, supt.
Eastern Hancock JSHS — 3-00111
10320 E 250 N 46117 — 936-5595
Mike Hanna, prin.

Chesterton, AC 219, PC 6, Porter
Duneland SD, 700 W PORTER AVE 46304 — 6-11111
Ken Payne, supt. — 926-1104
HS, 651 W MORGAN AVE 46304 — 4-00011
Jan Bergeson, prin. — 926-2151
Liberty MS, 50 W 900 N 46304 — 3-00100
Verne Ash, prin. — 926-2272
Westchester MS, 1050 S 5TH ST 46304 — 3-00100
James Ton, prin. — 926-2173

Fairhaven Baptist Academy — 2-11111
86 E OAK HILL RD 46304 — 926-6636
Bruce Snyder, prin.

Churubusco, AC 219, PC 4, Whitley
Smith-Green Community SD — 4-11111
222 W TULLEY ST 46723 — 693-2007
Howard Hull, supt.
JSHS, 1 EAGLE DR 46723 — 3-00111
Steve Doepker, prin. — 693-2131

Cicero, AC 317, PC 5, Hamilton

Indiana Academy — 2-00011
24815 STATE ROUTE 19 46034 — 984-3575
Nick Minder, prin.

Clarksville, AC 812, PC 7, Clark
Clarksville Community SD — 4-11111
200 ETTELS LN 47129 — 282-7753
Bill Conley, supt.
HS, 800 HIGH SCHOOL DR 47129 — 2-00011
Paul Love, prin. — 282-8231
MS, 101 ETTELS LN 47129 — 2-00100
Thomas Rose, prin. — 282-8235

Our Lady of Providence HS — 3-00111
707 W HIGHWAY 131 47129 — 945-2538
Gerald Wilkinson, prin.

Clay City, AC 812, PC 3, Clay
Clay Community SD
Supt. — See Knightsville
JSHS, 601 LANKFORD ST 47841 — 2-00111
Paul Sinders, prin. — 939-2154

Clayton, AC 317, PC 3, Hendricks
Mill Creek Community SD — 4-11111
PO BOX F 46118 — 539-6573
Brad Valentine, supt.
Cascade HS, PO BOX H 46118 — 2-00011
John Spoonmore, prin. — 539-6545
Cascade JHS, PO BOX K 46118 — 2-00100
Dorothy Crawley, prin. — 539-2045

Clinton, AC 317, PC 6, Vermillion
South Vermillion Community SD — 4-11111
PO BOX 387 47842 — 832-2426
Larry Carlson, supt.
South Vermillion HS, RR 1 47842 — 3-00011
Mark Kirby, prin. — 832-3551
South Vermillion MS — 2-00100
358 MULBERRY ST 47842 — 832-7727
Denver Kennett, prin.

Cloverdale, AC 317, PC 4, Putnam
Cloverdale Community SD — 4-11111
RR 3 BOX 1A 46120 — 795-4664
Steven Wittenauer, supt.
JSHS, RR 3 BOX 1A 46120 — 3-00111
Joe McNary, prin. — 795-4203
Other Schools – See Greencastle

Columbia City, AC 219, PC 6, Whitley
Whitley County Consolidated SD — 5-11111
400 N WHITLEY ST 46725 — 244-5772
Larry Stinson, supt.
Columbia City HS — 4-00011
600 N WHITLEY ST 46725 — 244-6136
James Isaacs, prin.
Marshall MS, 111 N WALNUT ST 46725 — 2-01100
Dan Mullett, prin. — 244-5771

Columbus, AC 812, PC 8, Bartholomew
Bartholomew Consolidated SD — 7-11111
2650 HOME AVE 47201 — 376-4220
C. Steven Snider, supt.
Columbus East HS — 4-00011
230 S MARR RD 47201 — 376-4369
Philip Houston, prin.
Columbus North HS — 4-00011
1400 25TH ST 47201 — 376-4432
Bill McCaa, prin.
Central MS, 725 7TH ST 47201 — 3-00100
David Edds, prin. — 376-4287
Northside MS, 1400 27TH ST 47201 — 3-00100
Gary McBride, prin. — 376-4405

Indiana Business College — 1-CS
PO BOX 1906 47202 — 342-1000
Ivy Tech Columbus — 4-CC
4475 CENTRAL AVE 47203 — 372-9925

Connersville, AC 317, PC 7, Fayette
Fayette County SD — 5-11111
1401 SPARTAN DR 47331 — 825-2178
Gerald Knorr, supt.
HS, 1100 SPARTAN DR 47331 — 4-00011
Stephen Kaiser, prin. — 825-1151
Connersville Area Vo S — Vo Tech
1300 SPARTAN DRIVE 47331 — 825-0521
Robert Hoffman, prin.
JHS, 1900 N GRAND AVE 47331 — 3-00100
Henry Hilton, prin. — 825-1139

Temple Christian S — 2-11111
PO BOX 246 47331 — 825-5196
Charles Utt, prin.

Converse, AC 317, PC 4, Miami
Oak Hill United SD — 4-11111
PO BOX 550 46919 — 395-3341
William Carnes, supt.
Oak Hill HS — 3-00011
7756 W DELPHI PIKE 27 46919 — 384-4381
Larry Stoner, prin.
Oak Hill JHS — 2-00100
7760 W DELPHI PIKE 27 46919 — 384-4381
Michael Costlow, prin.

Corydon, AC 812, PC 5, Harrison
South Harrison Community SD — 5-11111
121 HIGH SCHOOL RD 47112 — 738-2168
Kenneth Kidd, supt.
Corydon Central HS — 3-00011
375 COUNTRY CLUB RD 47112 — 738-4181
Thomas Book, prin.
MS, 100 HIGH SCHOOL RD 47112 — 2-00100
Mark Eastridge, prin. — 738-5750
Other Schools – See Elizabeth

Covington, AC 317, PC 5, Fountain
Covington Community SD — 4-11111
PO BOX 225 47932 — 793-4877
Bret Lewis, supt.
Covington Community HS — 2-00011
1017 6TH ST 47932 — 793-2287
Rick Snodgrass, prin.
MS, 514 RAILROAD ST 47932 — 2-00100
Leonard Orr, prin. — 793-4451

Crawfordsville, AC 317, PC 7, Montgomery
Crawfordsville Community SD 4-11111
  PO BOX 272 47933 362-2342
  John Coomer, supt.
  HS, 1 ATHIAN DR 47933 3-00011
    Charles Fiedler, prin. 362-2340
  Tuttle MS, 612 S ELM ST 47933 3-00100
    Don Fine, prin. 362-2992

North Montgomery Community SD
  Supt. — See Linden
  North Montgomery HS 3-00011
    5945 US HIGHWAY 231 N 47933 362-5140
    Frank Knuckles, prin.
  Northridge MS, 25 W 575 N 47933 2-00100
    Wes Hammond, prin. 364-1071

South Montgomery Community SD
  Supt. — See New Market
  Southmont HS, RR 2 47933 3-00011
    Mike Hallas, prin. 866-0350
  Southmont JHS, RR 2 47933 2-00100
    Stephen House, prin. 866-0350

Wabash College 3-UC
  301 W WABASH AVE 47933 362-1400

Crothersville, AC 812, PC 4, Jackson
Crothersville Community SD 3-11111
  109 N PRESTON ST 47229 793-2601
  Kim Thurston, supt.
  JSHS, 109 N PRESTON ST 47229 2-00111
    Francis Schill, prin. 793-2051

Crown Point, AC 219, PC 7, Lake
Crown Point Community SD 6-11111
  200 E NORTH ST 46307 663-3371
  Charles Skurka, supt.
  HS, 400 W JOLIET ST 46307 4-00011
    Robert Onda, prin. 663-4885
  Taft JHS, 1000 S MAIN ST 46307 3-00100
    David Sykes, prin. 663-1507

Hyles-Anderson College 2-UC
  8400 BURR ST 46307

Culver, AC 219, PC 4, Marshall
Culver Community SD 4-11111
  PO BOX 231 46511 842-3364
  William Mills, supt.
  Culver Community JSHS 3-00111
  701 SCHOOL ST 46511 842-3391
    Bradley Schuldt, prin.

Culver Military Academy & Summer Camps 3-00011
  1300 ACADEMY RD 46511 842-3311
  Alexander Nagy, prin.

Dale, AC 812, PC 4, Spencer
North Spencer County SD 4-11111
  PO BOX 316 47523 937-2400
  Ron Etienne, supt.
  Other Schools – See Lincoln City

Daleville, AC 317, PC 4, Delaware
Daleville Community SD 3-11111
  8700 S BRONCO DR 47334 378-3329
  Robert Ferguson, supt.
  JSHS, 8400 S BRONCO DR 47334 2-00111
    William Willetts, prin. 378-3371

Danville, AC 317, PC 5, Hendricks
Danville Community SD 4-11111
  PO BOX 389 46122 745-2212
  Bob Carnal, supt.
  Danville Community HS 3-00011
  100 WESTVIEW DR 46122 745-6431
    Peter Davis, prin.
  JHS, 49 N WAYNE ST 46122 2-00100
    James Disney, prin. 745-5491

Decatur, AC 219, PC 6, Adams
North Adams Community SD 5-11111
  PO BOX 191 46733 724-7146
  Ken Springer, supt.
  Bellmont HS 3-00011
  1000 E NORTH ADAMS DR 46733 724-7121
    Ronald Bittner, prin.
  Bellmont JHS, 1200 ADAMS ST 46733 3-00100
    Craig Anderson, prin. 724-3137

Reppert School of Auctioneering 1-CS
  PO BOX 189 46733 724-3804

Delphi, AC 317, PC 5, Carroll
Delphi Community SD 4-11111
  501 ARMORY RD 46923 564-2100
  John Williams, supt.
  Delphi Community HS 2-00011
  501 ARMORY RD 46923 564-3481
    Robert Handlin, prin.
  Delphi Community MS 2-00100
  501 ARMORY RD 46923 564-3411
    Robert Duke, prin.

Denver, AC 317, PC 3, Miami
North Miami Community SD 4-11111
  PO BOX 218 46926 985-3891
  Stephen Wise, supt.
  North Miami JSHS 3-00011
  RR 1 BOX 138B 46926 985-2931
    Richard Stuffle, prin.

Donaldson, AC 219, PC 2, Marshall

Ancilla Domini College 46513 3-CC 936-8898

Dubois, AC 812, PC 3, Dubois
Northeast Dubois County SD 4-11111
  PO BOX 158 47527 678-2781
  Richard Kerby, supt.
  Northeast Dubois HS 2-00011
  PO BOX 249 47527 678-2251
    James Wahl, prin.
  MS, 4550 N 4TH ST 47527 2-01100
    Keith Wortinger, prin. 678-2181

Dugger, AC 812, PC 3, Sullivan
Northeast SD
  Supt. — See Hymera
  Union JSHS, RR 1 BOX 177 47848 2-00111
    F. Thomas Risinger, prin. 648-2729

Dunkirk, AC 219, PC 5, Jay
Jay SD
  Supt. — See Portland
  West Jay Co. JHS 2-00100
  140 E HIGHLAND AVE 47336 768-7648
    Kevin McClung, prin.

Dyer, AC 219, PC 7, Lake
Lake Central SD
  Supt. — See Saint John
  Kahler MS, 452 ELM ST 46311 3-00100
    Jean Wease, prin. 865-3535

East Chicago, AC 219, PC 8, Lake
East Chicago SD 6-11111
  210 E COLUMBUS DR 46312 391-4100
  James Cogan, supt.
  East Chicago Central HS 4-00011
  1100 W COLUMBUS DR 46312 391-4000
    John Flores, prin.
  De La Garza Career Ctr Vo Tech
  410 E COLUMBUS DR 46312 391-4200
    Nick Ranich, prin.
  Block JHS, 2700 CARDINAL DR 46312 3-00100
    Diane Zych, prin. 391-4084
  West Side JHS 3-00100
  4001 INDIANAPOLIS BLVD 46312 391-4068
    Lloyd Booth, prin.

Edinburgh, AC 812, PC 5, Johnson
Edinburgh Community SD 3-11111
  202 KEELEY ST 46124 526-2681
  Dwight Beall, supt.
  Edinburgh Community JSHS 2-00111
  300 KEELEY ST 46124 526-5501
    Bruce Gaylor, prin.

Elizabeth, AC 812, PC 2, Harrison
South Harrison Community SD
  Supt. — See Corydon
  South Central JSHS 2-00111
  6675 E HIGHWAY 11 SE 47117 969-2941
    James Pressner, prin.

Elkhart, AC 219, PC 8, Elkhart
Baugo Community SD 4-11111
  29125 COUNTY ROAD 22 46517 293-8583
  Jerry Cook, supt.
  Jimtown HS 2-00011
  59021 COUNTY ROAD 3 46517 295-2343
    Floyd Trosper, prin.
  Jimtown JHS 2-00100
  58903 COUNTY ROAD 3 46517 294-6586
    H. Thomas Hixon, prin.

Concord Community SD 5-11111
  59040 MINUTEMAN WAY 46517 875-5161
  Larry Shomber, supt.
  Concord Community HS 4-00011
  59117 MINUTEMAN WAY 46517 875-6524
    Robert Sutton, prin.
  Concord JHS 3-00100
  24050 COUNTY ROAD 20 46517 875-5122
    Kevin Caird, prin.

Elkhart Community SD 7-11111
  2720 CALIFORNIA RD 46514 262-5500
  Frederick Bechtold, supt.
  Elkhart Central HS 4-00011
  1 BLAZER BLVD 46516 295-4700
    Robert Million, prin.
  Elkhart Memorial HS 4-00011
  2608 CALIFORNIA RD 46514 262-5600
    Carolyn Cook, prin.
  Elkhart Area Career Ctr Vo Tech
  2424 CALIFORNIA RD 46514 262-5650
    Clyde Riley, prin.
  Moran MS, 200 W LUSHER AVE 46517 3-00100
    Ned North, prin. 295-4805
  North Side MS 3-00100
  300 LAWRENCE ST 46514 262-5570
    Joyce Carver, prin.
  West Side MS 3-00100
  101 S NAPPANEE ST 46514 295-4815
    Levar Johnson, prin.

Associated Mennonite Biblical Seminaries 2-UC
  3003 BENHAM AVE 46517 295-3726

Ellettsville, AC 812, PC 5, Monroe
Richland-Bean Blossom Community SD 5-11111
  EDGEWOOD DRIVE 47429 876-7100
  C. Craig Glenn, supt.
  Edgewood HS 3-00011
  601 EDGEWOOD DR 47429 876-2277
    Willard Cazzell, prin.
  Edgewood JHS, PO BOX 277 47429 3-00100
    Phillip Rambo, prin. 876-2005

Elnora, AC 812, PC 3, Daviess
North Daviess County Community SD 4-11111
  RR 1 47529 – Jess Harty, supt. 636-7654
  North Daviess JSHS, RR 1 47529 3-00111
    William Beleslin, prin. 636-7307

Elwood, AC 317, PC 6, Madison
Elwood Community SD 4-11111
  1306 N ANDERSON ST 46036 552-9861
  Richard Merritt, supt.
  Elwood Community HS 3-00011
  1137 N 19TH ST 46036 552-9854
    Gordon Paquin, prin.
  Hinds Vocational S Vo Tech
  1105 N 19TH ST 46036 552-9881
    Wilbur Watson, prin.
  Elwood Community MS 3-00100
  1207 N 19TH ST 46036 552-7378
    Stephen Stanton, prin.

Eminence, AC 317, PC 2, Morgan
Eminence Consolidated SD 2-11111
  PO BOX 105 46125 996-3011
  James Petersen, supt.
  JSHS, HIGHWAY 42 N 46125 2-00111
    Gordon Werremeyer, prin. 528-2221

Evansville, AC 812, PC 9, Vanderburgh
Evansville-Vanderburgh SD 7-11111
  1 SE 9TH ST 47708 465-8477
  Phil Schoffstall, supt.
  Bosse HS 3-00011
  1300 WASHINGTON AVE 47714 477-1661
    Robert Adams, prin.
  Central HS, 5400 N 1ST AVE 47710 4-00011
    Thomas Sisk, prin. 465-8292
  Harrison HS, 211 FIELDING RD 47715 4-00011
    Walter Lewis, prin. 477-1046
  North HS, 2319 STRINGTOWN RD 47711 4-00011
    James Sharp, prin. 465-8283
  Reitz HS, FOREST HILLS 47712 4-00011
    Christine Settle, prin. 465-8206
  Evans MS, 837 TULIP AVE 47711 3-00100
    Sharron Mattingly, prin. 465-8330
  Glenwood MS 2-00100
  901 SWEETSER AVE 47713 465-8242
    Andrew Guarino, prin.
  Harwood MS, 3013 N 1ST AVE 47710 2-00100
    Ron Clayton, prin. 465-8316
  Helfrich Park MS 3-00100
  2603 W MARYLAND ST 47712 465-8246
    Daniel Ulrich, prin.
  McGary MS, 1535 JOYCE AVE 47714 3-00100
    William Miller, prin. 476-3035
  Oak Hill MS, 7700 OAK HILL RD 47711 3-00100
    Kenneth Wempe, prin. 867-6426
  Perry Heights MS 3-00100
  5800 HOGUE RD 47712 465-8326
    Charles Goodman, prin.
  Plaza Park MS 3-00100
  7301 LINCOLN AVE 47715 476-4971
    Shirley King, prin.
  Thomkins MS, 1300 W MILL RD 47710 3-00100
    Terry Yunker, prin. 465-8323
  Washington MS 2-00100
  1801 WASHINGTON AVE 47714 477-8983
    Norman Van Winkle, prin.

Evansville Day S 2-11111
  3400 N GREEN RIVER RD 47715 476-3039
  Lee Hensley, prin.
Indiana Business College 2-CS
  4601 THEATRE DR 47715 476-6000
ITT Technical Institute 3-CC
  5115 OAK GROVE RD 47715 479-1441
Ivy Tech Southwest 4-CC
  3501 N 1ST AVE 47710 426-2865
Mater Dei HS 3-00011
  1300 HARMONY WAY 47720 426-2258
  Herb Neighbors, prin.
Reitz Memorial HS 3-00011
  1500 LINCOLN AVE 47714 476-4973
  Gerry Adams, prin.
St. Mary's Medical Center HSP
  3700 WASHINGTON AVE 47750 479-4444
University of Evansville 6-UC
  1800 LINCOLN AVE 47722 800-423-8633
University of Southern Indiana 5-UC
  8600 UNIVERSITY BLVD 47712 464-1756
Welborn Baptist Hospital HSP
  401 SE 6TH ST 47713 426-8264
Westside Catholic JHS 2-00100
  2031 W MICHIGAN ST 47712 422-1014
  Donna McGinness, prin.

Fairland, AC 317, PC 4, Shelby
Northwestern Consolidated SD 4-11111
  4920 W 600 N 46126 835-7461
  Ted Thompson, supt.
  Triton Central HS, 4774 W 600 N 46126 2-00011
    David Shaffer, prin. 835-3000
  Triton MS, 4740 W 600 N 46126 3-01100
    Douglas Jaggers, prin. 835-3006

Fairmount, AC 317, PC 5, Grant
Madison-Grant United SD 4-11111
120 S MAIN ST 46928 948-4143
Robert Huff, supt.
Madison-Grant HS 3-00011
11700 S E 00 W 46928 948-4141
Larry Martin, prin.
Madison-Grant JHS 2-00100
11640 S E 00 W 46928 948-5132
Richard Hindman, prin.

Farmersburg, AC 812, PC 4, Sullivan
Northeast SD
Supt. — See Hymera
North Central HS 2-00011
RR 1 BOX 242 47850 397-2132
David Scott, prin.

Ferdinand, AC 812, PC 4, Dubois
Southeast Dubois County SD 4-11111
244 W 13TH ST 47532 367-1653
William Rohl, supt.
Forest Park JSHS 3-00111
1440 MICHIGAN ST 47532 367-1831
James Hagedorn, prin.

Marian Heights Academy 2-00011
812 E 10TH ST 47532 367-1431
Richard Mathena, prin.

Fishers, AC 317, PC 6, Hamilton
Hamilton Southeastern SD 5-11111
13327 CUMBERLAND RD 46038 594-4100
Charles Leonard, supt.
Hamilton Southeastern HS 4-00011
13910 E 126TH ST 46038 594-4190
Richard Hogue, prin.
Hamilton Southeastern JHS 4-00100
12001 OLIO RD 46038 594-4120
Roger Norris, prin.

Flora, AC 219, PC 4, Carroll
Carroll Consolidated SD 4-11111
2 S 3RD ST 46929 967-4113
Robert Foreman, supt.
Carroll JSHS, RR 1 46929 3-00111
Daniel Ronk, prin. 967-4157

Floyds Knobs, AC 812, PC 3, Floyd
New Albany-Floyd County Consolidated SD
Supt. — See New Albany
Floyd Central JSHS 4-00111
6575 OLD VINCENNES RD 47119 923-8811
Donald Sakel, prin.

Fort Branch, AC 812, PC 4, Gibson
South Gibson SD, 204 W VINE ST 47648 4-11111
Michael Green, supt. 753-4230
Gibson Southern HS 3-00011
RR 1 BOX 496 47648 753-3011
Wendell McCandless, prin.

Fortville, AC 317, PC 5, Hancock
Mt. Vernon Community SD 4-11111
1776 W STATE ROAD 234 46040 485-3100
Larry Yazel, supt.
Mt. Vernon HS, 8112 N 200 W 46040 3-00011
Darrell Thomas, prin. 485-3131
Mt. Vernon MS 3-00100
1862 W STATE ROAD 234 46040 485-3160
Dan Johnson, prin.

Fort Wayne, AC 219, PC 9, Allen
East Allen County SD
Supt. — See New Haven
Harding HS, 6501 WAYNE TRCE 46816 3-00011
Bill Griffith, prin. 447-1547
Village Woods MS 3-00100
2700 E MAPLEGROVE AVE 46806 447-5165
Neal Brown, prin.

Fort Wayne Community SD 8-11111
1200 S CLINTON ST 46802 425-7200
William Coats, supt.
Elmhurst HS 3-00011
3829 SANDPOINT RD 46809 425-7510
Thomas Gordon, prin.
North Side HS 4-00011
475 E STATE BLVD 46805 425-7530
Richard Gardner, prin.
Northrop HS 4-00011
7001 COLDWATER RD 46825 425-7550
Timon Kendall, prin.
Snider HS, 4600 FAIRLAWN PASS 46815 4-00011
Dennis McClurg, prin. 425-7570
South Side HS 4-00011
3601 S CALHOUN ST 46807 425-7610
Jennifer Manth, prin.
Wayne HS, 9100 WINCHESTER RD 46819 4-00011
Thomas Dohrmann, prin. 425-7630
FWCS Regional Vo S Vo Tech
1200 BARR ST 46802 425-7661
Lindy Betancourt, prin.
Blackhawk MS 3-00100
7200 E STATE BLVD 46815 425-7313
Timothy Matthias, prin.
Geyer MS, 420 E PAULDING RD 46816 3-00100
Nancy Schram, prin. 425-7343
Jefferson MS 3-00100
5303 WHEELOCK RD 46835 425-7374
Edward Innis, prin.
Kekionga MS, 2929 ENGLE RD 46809 3-00100
Larry Johnson, prin. 425-7378
Lakeside MS, 2100 LAKE AVE 46805 3-00100
James Tallman, prin. 425-7382
Lane MS, 4901 VANCE AVE 46815 3-00100
Kenneth Howe, prin. 425-7386
Memorial Park MS 3-00100
2200 MAUMEE AVE 46803 425-7410
Nick Karanovich, prin.
Miami MS, 8100 AMHERST DR 46819 3-00100
Charles Green, prin. 425-7414
Northwood MS 3-00100
1201 E WASHINGTON CENTER RD 46825
Henrietta Howell, prin. 425-7424
Portage MS, 3521 TAYLOR ST 46802 3-00100
Patricia Tharp, prin. 425-7431
Shawnee MS, 1000 E COOK RD 46825 3-00100
Thomas Duff, prin. 425-7447

Metro SD of Southwest Allen County 5-11111
4824 HOMESTEAD RD 46804 434-2421
Dave Hales, supt.
Homestead HS 4-00011
4310 HOMESTEAD RD 46804 434-2525
(—), prin.
Summit MS 3-00100
4509 HOMESTEAD RD 46804 432-4723
Jim Leinker, prin.
Woodside MS 4-00100
4312 HOMESTEAD RD 46804 434-2459
Terry Hippensteel, prin.

Northwest Allen County SD 5-11111
13119 COLDWATER RD 46845 637-3155
Steven Yager, supt.
Carroll HS, 3701 CARROLL RD 46818 3-00011
John Sayers, prin. 637-3161
Carroll JHS, 3905 CARROLL RD 46818 3-00100
Mark Seele, prin. 637-5159

Bishop Dwenger HS 3-00011
1300 E WASHINGTON CENTER RD 46825
John Gaughan, prin. 483-1108
Bishop Luers HS 2-00011
333 E PAULDING RD 46816 456-1261
Norm Glismann, prin.
Blackhawk Christian S 2-11111
7321 E STATE BLVD 46815 493-7476
Steven Longbrake, prin.
Canterbury S, 3210 SMITH RD 46804 3-11111
Jonathan Hancock, prin. 436-0746
Concordia Lutheran HS 3-00011
1601 SAINT JOE RIVER DR 46805 483-1102
David Widenhofer, prin.
Concordia Theological Seminary 2-UC
6600 N CLINTON ST 46825 481-2100
Indiana Institute of Technology 3-UC
1600 E WASHINGTON BLVD 46803 422-5561
Indiana U-Purdue U at Fort Wayne 6-UC
2101 E COLISEUM BLVD 46805 481-6103
International Business College 3-CC
3811 ILLINOIS RD 46804 432-8702
ITT Technical Institute 4-UC
4919 COLDWATER RD 46825 484-4107
Ivy Tech Northeast 4-CC
3800 N ANTHONY BLVD 46805 482-9171
Lutheran College of Health Professions 2-UC
535 HOME AVE 46807 458-2451
Michiana College 2-CC
4807 ILLINOIS RD 46804 800-743-2447
Parkview Memorial Hospital 2-HSP
2200 RANDALLIA DR 46805 484-6636
St. Francis College 3-UC
2701 SPRING ST 46808 434-3229
St. Joseph Medical Center 2-HSP
700 BROADWAY 46802 425-3000
Taylor University 2-UC
1025 W RUDISILL BLVD 46807 456-2111

Fountain City, AC 317, PC 3, Wayne
Northeastern Wayne SD 4-11111
PO BOX 406 47341 847-2821
Stephen Bailey, supt.
Northeastern JSHS 3-00111
7295 N US HIGHWAY 27 47341 847-2591
Charlie McCoy, prin.

Fowler, AC 317, PC 4, Benton
Benton Community SD 4-11111
PO BOX 512 47944 884-0850
Glenn Krueger, supt.
Other Schools – See Oxford

Francesville, AC 219, PC 3, Pulaski
West Central SD 4-11111
117 E MONTGOMERY ST 47946 567-9161
Roger Dickinson, supt.
West Central JSHS 2-00111
RR 2 BOX 15 47946 567-9119
Charles Mellon, prin.

Frankfort, AC 317, PC 7, Clinton
Clinton Prairie SD 4-11111
4431 W STATE ROAD 28 46041 659-1339
Charles Fink, supt.
Clinton Prairie JSHS 2-00111
2400 S COUNTY ROAD 450 W 46041 659-3305
Myron Chezem, prin.

Frankfort Community SD 5-11111
50 S MAISH RD 46041 654-5585
Joe Dixon, supt.
HS, 1 S MAISH RD 46041 3-00011
John Milholland, prin. 654-8545
MS, 329 N MAISH RD 46041 3-00100
Jim Platt, prin. 659-3321

Franklin, AC 317, PC 7, Johnson
Franklin Community SD 5-11111
998 GRIZZLY CUB DR 46131 738-5800
Delbert Jarman, supt.
Franklin Community HS 3-00011
625 GRIZZLY CUB DR 46131 738-5700
Walter Vanderbush, prin.
Custer Baker MS 3-00100
101 W STATE ROAD 44 46131 738-5840
Pam Millikan, prin.

Franklin College 3-UC
501 E MONROE ST 46131 738-8000

Frankton, AC 317, PC 4, Madison
West Central Community SD
Supt. — See Anderson
JSHS, 610 CLYDE ST 46044 3-00111
Stan Warner, prin. 754-7879

Fremont, AC 219, PC 4, Steuben
Fremont Community SD 4-11111
PO BOX 665 46737 495-5005
Barry Worl, supt.
HS, PO BOX 665 46737 2-00011
Gary Baker, prin. 495-9876
MS, PO BOX E 46737 2-01100
Karen Shepherd, prin. 495-6100

French Lick, AC 812, PC 4, Orange
Springs Valley Community SD 4-11111
101 LARRY BIRD BLVD 47432 936-4474
Dennis Weikert, supt.
Springs Valley Comm. JSHS 2-00111
101 LARRY BIRD BLVD 47432 936-9984
Larry Pritchett, prin.

Fulton, AC 219, PC 2, Fulton
Caston SD, PO BOX 8 46931 3-11111
Paul Baker, supt. 857-2035
Caston JSHS, PO BOX 128 46931 2-00111
James Hanna, prin. 857-3505

Garrett, AC 219, PC 6, De Kalb
Garrett-Keyser-Butler Community SD 4-11111
801 E HOUSTON ST 46738 357-3185
Alan Middleton, supt.
JSHS, 801 E HOUSTON ST 46738 3-00111
Roger Weimer, prin. 357-4114

Gary, AC 219, PC 9, Lake
Gary Community SD 7-11111
620 E 10TH PL 46402 886-6400
James Hawkins, supt.
Mann HS, 524 GARFIELD ST 46404 4-00011
Max Wolverton, prin. 886-1445
Roosevelt HS, 730 W 25TH AVE 46407 4-00011
William Reese, prin. 881-1500
Wallace HS, 415 W 45TH AVE 46408 4-00011
Marion Williams, prin. 980-6305
Westside HS, 900 GERRY ST 46406 4-00011
Donald Love, prin. 977-2100
Wirt HS, 210 N GRAND BLVD 46403 4-00011
Louise Robertson, prin. 938-1161
Emerson JSHS, 716 E 7TH AVE 46402 2-00111
Geraldine Wheaton, prin. 886-6555
Gary Tech Ctr, 1800 E 35TH AVE 46409 Vo Tech
Jerome Hurt, prin. 962-7571
Bailly MS, 4621 GEORGIA ST 46409 3-00100
Van Hambrick, prin. 980-6326
Beckman MS, 1430 W 23RD AVE 46407 3-00100
Clifton Gooden, prin. 977-2119
Dunbar-Pulaski MS 3-00100
1867 GEORGIA ST 46407 886-6581
Eugenia Sacopulos, prin.
Edison MS, 5400 W 5TH AVE 46406 3-00100
Richard Oppman, prin. 977-2132
Kennedy-King MS 3-00100
301 N PARKE ST 46403 938-1750
Mary Ward, prin.
Tolleston MS, 2700 W 19TH AVE 46404 4-00100
Howard King, prin. 977-2145

Lake Ridge SD, 6111 W RIDGE RD 46408 5-11111
Robert Beach, supt. 838-1819
Calumet HS, 3900 CALHOUN ST 46408 3-00011
Leroy Miller, prin. 838-6990
Lake Ridge MS, 3601 W 41ST AVE 46408 3-00100
Robert Mastej, prin. 980-0730

Indiana University Northwest 5-UC
3400 BROADWAY 46408 980-6700
Ivy Tech Northwest 4-CC
1440 E 35TH AVE 46409 981-1111

Gas City, AC 317, PC 6, Grant
Mississinewa Community SD 4-11111
424 W MAIN ST 46933 674-8528
Robert Bothwell, supt.
Mississinewa HS 3-00011
205 E NORTH H ST 46933 674-2248
Mike Powell, prin.
Baskett MS, 125 N BROADWAY 46933 3-00100
Terry Talbott, prin. 674-8536

Gaston, AC 317, PC 3, Delaware
Harrison-Washington Community SD 4-11111
10290 N COUNTY ROAD 600 W 47342 358-4006
Walter Harrison, supt.
Wes-Del HS 2-00011
10000 N COUNTY ROAD 600 W 47342 358-4091
Richard Johnson, prin.

Wes-Del MS 2-00100
10100 N COUNTY ROAD 600 W 47342 358-3349
William Bower, prin.

Goshen, AC 219, PC 7, Elkhart
Fairfield Community SD 4-11111
67315 COUNTY ROAD 31 46526 831-2188
Orville Bose, supt.
Fairfield JSHS 3-00111
67530 US HIGHWAY 33 46526 831-2184
Harold Seamon, prin.

Goshen Community SD 5-11111
721 E MADISON ST 46526 533-8631
Ken Blad, supt.
HS, 1 REDSKIN RD 46526 4-00011
Tom Tumey, prin. 533-8651
MS, 63682 COUNTY ROAD 21 46526 4-00100
Don Weirich, prin. 533-0391

Bethany Christian HS 2-00011
2904 S MAIN ST 46526 534-2567
William Hooley, prin.
Goshen College 4-UC
1700 S MAIN ST 46526 535-7000

Granger, AC 219, PC 4, St. Joseph

Davenport College of Business 2-CC
7121 GRAPE RD 46530 277-8447

Greencastle, AC 317, PC 6, Putnam
Cloverdale Community SD
Supt. — See Cloverdale
Putnam County Area Vo S Vo Tech
PO BOX 628 46135 653-3515
Thomas Garrison, prin.

Greencastle Community SD 4-11111
PO BOX 480 46135 – P. Renz, supt. 653-9771
HS, 910 E WASHINGTON ST 46135 3-00100
Robert Harbison, prin. 653-9711
MS, 400 FIRST ST 46135 2-00100
Ken Moran, prin. 653-9774

South Putnam Community SD 4-11111
RR 2 BOX 134 46135 653-3119
Earl Williams, supt.
South Putnam JSHS 3-00111
RR 2 BOX 278 46135 653-3148
Harvey Chiles, prin.

DePauw University 4-UC
313 S LOCUST ST 46135 658-4800

Greenfield, AC 317, PC 7, Hancock
Greenfield-Central Community SD 5-11111
1E W SOUTH ST 46140 462-4434
Gary Clinkenbeard, supt.
Greenfield-Central HS 4-00011
810 N BROADWAY ST 46140 462-9211
Robert Albano, prin.
JHS, 204 W PARK AVE 46140 2-00100
James Saunders, prin. 462-6827
Other Schools – See Maxwell

Hancock Memorial Hospital HSP
801 N STATE ST 46140 462-0457

Greensburg, AC 812, PC 6, Decatur
Decatur County Community SD 4-11111
1645 W STATE RD 46 47240 663-4595
Edward Kasamis, supt.
North Decatur JSHS 3-00111
3172 N STATE RD 3 47240 663-4204
Donel Criswell, prin.
South Decatur JSHS 3-00111
8885 S STATE RD 3 47240 591-3330
John Duncan, prin.

Greensburg Community SD 4-11111
504 E CENTRAL AVE 47240 663-4774
Arthur Turner, supt.
Greensburg Community HS 3-00011
1000 E CENTRAL AVE 47240 663-7176
Stephen Dickerson, prin.
Greensburg Community JHS 2-00100
505 E CENTRAL AVE 47240 663-7523
Richard Revalee, prin.

Greentown, AC 317, PC 4, Howard
Eastern-Howard Community SD 4-11111
220 S MERIDIAN ST 46936 628-3391
Lindan Hill, supt.
Eastern JSHS 3-00111
421 S HARRISON ST 46936 628-3333
Stephen Healy, prin.

Greenwood, AC 317, PC 8, Johnson
Center Grove Community SD 6-11111
2929 S MORGANTOWN RD 46143 881-9326
Denney French, supt.
Center Grove HS 4-00011
2717 S MORGANTOWN RD 46143 881-0581
Steve Davis, prin.
Center Grove MS 3-00100
4900 W STONES CROSSING RD 46143 882-9391
James Halik, prin.

Central Nine Career Center SD 1-00000
PO BOX 710 46142 888-4401
Nick Banos, supt.
Central Nine Career Center Vo Tech
PO BOX 710 46142 888-4401
Larry Fosler, prin.

Greenwood Community SD 5-11111
PO BOX 218 46142 889-4060
Robert Brenton, supt.
Greenwood Community HS 3-00011
615 W SMITH VALLEY RD 46142 889-4000
Robert Taylor, prin.
MS, 523 S MADISON AVE 46142 3-00100
Joseph DiPietro, prin. 889-4040

Aristotle College/Medical & Dental Tech. 2-CS
PO BOX 8 46142 888-4019

Griffith, AC 219, PC 7, Lake
Griffith Public SD 5-11111
132 N BROAD ST 46319 924-4250
Robert Kurtz, supt.
SHS, 600 N WIGGS ST 46319 3-00001
Samuel Cox, prin. 924-4281
JHS, 600 N RAYMOND ST 46319 3-00110
Terry Crowe, prin. 924-4280

Hagerstown, AC 317, PC 4, Wayne
Nettle Creek SD 4-11111
297 E NORTH MARKET ST 47346 489-4543
R. Howe, supt.
JSHS, 700 BAKER RD 47346 3-00111
Mark Childs, prin. 489-4511

Hamilton, AC 219, PC 3, Steuben
Hamilton Community SD 3-11111
901 S WAYNE ST 46742 488-2513
A. Gary Nordmann, supt.
Hamilton Community JSHS 2-00111
903 S WAYNE ST 46742 488-2161
Garst Haughey, prin.

Hamlet, AC 219, PC 3, Starke
Oregon-Davis SD, PO BOX 65 46532 3-11111
William Rentschler, supt. 867-2111
Oregon-Davis JSHS, 5990 N 750 E 46532 2-00111
Richard Kapiszka, prin. 867-2481

Hammond, AC 219, PC 8, Lake
Hammond CSD, 41 WILLIAMS ST 46320 7-11111
David Dickson, supt. 933-2400
HS, 5926 CALUMET AVE 46320 4-00011
Cassel White, prin. 933-2442
Morton HS, 6915 GRAND AVE 46323 4-00011
Theresa Mayerik, prin. 989-7316
Gavit JSHS, 1670 175TH ST 46324 4-00111
Chuck Hall, prin. 989-7328
Area Career Ctr, 5727 SOHL AVE 46320 Vo Tech
John Jandura, prin. 933-2428
Scott MS, 3635 173RD ST 46323 3-00100
Frank Lentvorsky, prin. 989-7340
Other Schools – See Whiting

Aristotle College/Medical & Dental Tech. 2-CS
5255 HOHMAN AVE 46320 931-1954
Bishop Noll Institute 3-00011
1519 HOFFMAN ST 46327 932-9058
Susan Lapeer, prin.
Hammond Baptist City S 2-11111
700 SIBLEY ST 46320 931-2237
David Douglass, prin.
Heritage Christian S 2-11111
7350 KENNEDY AVE 46323 845-4306
Greg Miller, prin.
Purdue University 6-UC
2233 171ST ST 46323 989-2203
St. Margaret Hospital HSP
5454 HOHMAN AVE 46320 932-2300
Sawyer College 3-CS
6040 HOHMAN AVE 46320 931-0436

Hanover, AC 812, PC 5, Jefferson
Southwestern-Jefferson County Cons. SD 4-11111
239 S MAIN CROSS ST 47243 866-6250
Patrick Leahey, supt.
Southwestern JSHS 3-00111
167 S MAIN CROSS ST 47243 866-6230
Donald Stephens, prin.

Hanover College 47243 4-UC
866-7000

Hardinsburg, AC 812, Orange
South Central Area Vocational SD 1-00000
7607 E COUNTY ROAD 523 S 47125 472-3885
George Rode, supt.
South Central Area Vo S Vo Tech
7607 E COUNTY ROAD 523 S 47125 472-3885
George Rode, prin.

Hartford City, AC 317, PC 6, Blackford
Blackford County SD 4-11111
1515 N MONROE ST 47348 348-7550
Joseph Wolfe, supt.
Blackford HS 3-00011
2392 N STATE ROAD 3 47348 348-7560
John Hill, prin.
MS, 820 W VAN CLEVE ST 47348 2-01100
Michael Parks, prin. 348-7590
Other Schools – See Montpelier

Hebron, AC 219, PC 5, Porter
Metro SD of Boone Township 4-11111
307 S MAIN ST 46341 996-2171
James Risk, supt.
JSHS, 307 S MAIN ST 46341 2-00111
James Rose, prin. 996-2171

Henryville, AC 812, PC 4, Clark
West Clark Community SD
Supt. — See Sellersburg
JSHS, 213 N FERGUSON ST 47126 2-00111
Fred Finch, prin. 294-1455

Highland, AC 219, PC 7, Lake
Highland SD, 9145 KENNEDY AVE 46322 5-11111
Philip Cartwright, supt. 922-5605
Highland HS, 9135 ERIE ST 46322 4-00011
Renner Ventling, prin. 922-5610
JHS, 2941 41ST ST 46322 3-00100
Beth Copenhaver, prin. 922-5620

Hobart, AC 219, PC 7, Lake
City of Hobart SD, 32 E 7TH ST 46342 5-11111
Mark Dartt, supt. 942-8885
HS, 36 E 8TH ST 46342 4-00011
William Cope, prin. 942-8521
MS, 705 E 4TH ST 46342 3-00100
Joanne Schafer, prin. 942-8541

River Forest CSD 4-11111
3334 MICHIGAN ST 46342 962-2909
Gerald MCcullum, supt.
River Forest HS 2-00011
3300 INDIANA ST 46342 962-7551
Jack Ford, prin.
River Forest JHS 2-00100
3300 INDIANA ST 46342 962-7811
Robert Marszalek, prin.

Calumet Baptist S 2-00111
PO BOX 807 46342 947-7270
Donald Callahan, prin.
College of Court Reporting 2-CS
111 W 10TH ST STE 111 46342 942-1459
St. Mary Medical Center HSP
1500 S LAKE PARK AVE 46342 881-8000

Hope, AC 812, PC 4, Bartholomew
Flat Rock-Hawcreek SD 4-11111
PO BOX 34 47246 546-4922
Glen Keller, supt.
Hauser JSHS, PO BOX 24 47246 2-00111
Eugene Genth, prin. 546-4421

Howe, AC 219, PC 3, Lagrange

Howe Military S 2-00011
31 ACADEMY PLACE 46746 562-2131
Richard Piper, prin.

Huntingburg, AC 812, PC 6, Dubois
Southwest Dubois County SD 4-11111
PO BOX 238 47542 – (—), supt. 683-3971
Southridge HS 2-00011
1110 S US HIGHWAY 231 47542 683-2272
Eugene Keusch, prin.
Southridge MS 2-00100
1112 S US HIGHWAY 231 47542 683-3372
Al Mihajlovits, prin.

Huntington, AC 219, PC 7, Huntington
Huntington County Community SD 6-11111
1360 WARREN RD 46750 356-7812
Max Spaulding, supt.
Huntington North HS 4-00011
450 MCGAHN ST 46750 356-6104
Van Bailey, prin.
Crestview MS, 929 GUILFORD ST 46750 3-00100
Donald Bradley, prin. 356-6210
Riverview MS 3-00100
2465 WATERWORKS RD 46750 356-0910
Marvin Tudor, prin.

Huntington College 3-UC
2303 COLLEGE AVE 46750 356-6000

Hymera, AC 812, PC 3, Sullivan
Northeast SD, PO BOX 493 47855 4-11111
Richard Walters, supt. 383-5761
Other Schools – See Dugger, Farmersburg

Indianapolis, AC 317, PC 11, Marion
Avon Community SD 5-11111
13013 ROCKVILLE RD 46234 272-2920
Richard Helton, supt.
Avon HS, 13013 ROCKVILLE RD 46234 3-00011
James Newcomer, prin. 272-2586
Avon MS, 13013 ROCKVILLE RD 46234 3-00100
David Leach, prin. 272-0128

Franklin Township Community SD 5-11111
6141 S FRANKLIN RD 46259 862-2411
E.B. Carver, supt.
Franklin Central HS 4-00011
6215 S FRANKLIN RD 46259 862-6646
Tom Potts, prin.
Franklin Twp. MS 4-00100
6019 S FRANKLIN RD 46259 862-2446
Leland Thompson, prin.

Indianapolis SD 8-11111
120 E WALNUT ST 46204 226-4411
Shirl Gilbert, supt.
Arlington HS 4-00011
4825 N ARLINGTON AVE 46226 226-4006
Jacqueline Greenwood, prin.
Arsenal Technical HS 4-00011
1500 E MICHIGAN ST 46201 226-4009
June Collins-Rimmer, prin.

Broad Ripple HS 4-00011
1115 BROAD RIPPLE AVE 46220 226-4005
Larry McCloud, prin.
Howe HS, 4900 JULIAN AVE 46201 4-00011
Madora Waker, prin. 226-4008
Manual HS, 2405 MADISON AVE 46225 4-00011
Sarah Bogard, prin. 226-4004
Northwest HS, 5525 W 34TH ST 46224 4-00011
Nancy Sutton, prin. 226-4001
Washington HS 4-00011
2215 W WASHINGTON ST 46222 226-4003
Alonzo Walker, prin.
Arlington Woods MS 2-00100
5801 E 30TH ST 46218 226-4299
Diane Pillow, prin.
Attucks JHS 3-00100
1140 DR MRTN LUTHER KING ST 46202
Annie Hayes, prin. 226-4007
Buck MS, 2701 N DEVON AVE 46219 3-00100
Roberta Bowers, prin. 226-4294
Coleman MS, 1740 E 30TH ST 46218 3-00100
William Wheatley, prin. 226-4110
Donnan MS, 1202 E TROY AVE 46203 3-00100
Margaret Crawford, prin. 226-4272
Douglass MS, 2020 DAWSON ST 46203 3-00100
Janet Hill, prin. 226-4219
Edison MS 3-00100
777 S WHITE RIVER PARKWAY 46221 226-4247
Amanda Hodges, prin.
Farrington MS, 4326 PATRICIA ST 46222 3-00100
Sherry Eggers, prin. 226-4261
Forest Manor MS, 4501 E 32ND ST 46218 3-00100
Terry Ogle, prin. 226-4363
Gambold MS, 3725 N KIEL AVE 46224 3-00100
Steven Padgett, prin. 226-4108
Harshman MS, 1501 E 10TH ST 46201 3-00100
Marcia Capuano, prin. 226-4101
Longfellow MS, 510 LAUREL ST 46203 3-00100
James Whisler, prin. 226-4228
McFarland MS 2-00100
3200 E RAYMOND ST 46203 226-4112
Karen Dailey, prin.
Marshall JHS, 10101 E 38TH ST 46236 4-00100
Concetta Raimondi, prin. 226-4002
Shortridge JHS 4-00100
3401 N MERIDIAN ST 46208 226-4010
Barbara Gillenwaters, prin.
Sidener MS 2-00100
2424 KESSLER BLVARD EAST DR 46220
Juanita Hardiman, prin. 226-4259

Metro SD of Decatur Township 6-11111
7523 S MOORESVILLE RD 46221 856-5265
Gerald Montgomery, supt.
Decatur Central HS 4-00011
5251 KENTUCKY AVE 46221 856-5288
Paul Kaiser, prin.
Decatur MS 4-00100
5108 S HIGH SCHOOL RD 46221 856-5274
John Taylor, prin.

Metro SD of Lawrence Township 7-11111
7601 E 56TH ST 46226 546-4921
Percy Clark, supt.
Lawrence Central HS 5-00011
7300 E 56TH ST 46226 545-5301
Caroline Hanna, prin.
Lawrence North HS 4-00011
7802 HAGUE RD 46256 849-9455
Allen Essig, prin.
Belzer MS, 7555 E 56TH ST 46226 4-00100
Steven Stults, prin. 545-7411
Craig MS, 6501 SUNNYSIDE RD 46236 4-00100
William Gavaghan, prin. 823-6805
Fall Creek Valley MS 3-00100
9701 E 63RD ST 46236 – (—), prin. 823-5490

Metro SD of Perry Township 7-11111
1130 E EPLER AVE 46227 780-4202
Douglas Williams, supt.
Meridian HS 4-00011
401 W MERIDIAN SCHOOL RD 46217 865-2650
James Head, prin.
Southport HS, 971 E BANTA RD 46227 4-00011
Lloyd Bodie, prin. 780-4317
Keystone MS 4-00100
5715 S KEYSTONE AVE 46227 780-4303
Haldon Cole, prin.
Meridian MS 4-00100
8040 S MERIDIAN ST 46217 865-2704
Morris Beck, prin.

Metro SD of Pike Township 6-11111
6901 ZIONSVILLE RD 46268 293-0393
Eric Witherspoon, supt.
Pike HS, 6701 ZIONSVILLE RD 46268 4-00011
Ron Furniss, prin. 291-5250
Guion Creek MS, 4401 W 52ND ST 46254 3-00100
Timothy Smith, prin. 293-4549
Lincoln MS, 5555 W 71ST ST 46268 3-00100
John Maloy, prin. 291-9499

Metro SD of Warren Township 6-11111
9301 E 18TH ST 46229 898-5935
Don Pennington, supt.
Warren Central SHS 4-00001
9500 E 16TH ST 46229 898-6133
Robert Albano, prin.
Walker Career Ctr, 9651 E 21ST ST 46229 Vo Tech
Timothy Armstrong, prin. 899-2000
Creston JHS, 10925 PROSPECT ST 46239 4-00110
Theresia Wynns, prin. 894-8883

Stonybrook JHS 4-00110
11300 STONY BROOK DR 46229 894-2744
Jack Washburn, prin.

Metro SD of Washington Township 6-11111
3801 E 79TH ST 46240 845-9400
Eugene White, supt.
North Central HS, 1801 E 86TH ST 46240 5-00011
James Jones, prin. 259-5301
Everett Light Career Ctr Vo Tech
1901 E 86TH ST 46240 259-5265
Eldon Horton, prin.
Eastwood MS, 4401 E 62ND ST 46220 3-00100
Gary Washburn, prin. 259-5401
Northview MS 3-00100
8401 WESTFIELD RD 46240 259-5421
Rudolph Wilson, prin.
Westlane MS, 1301 W 73RD ST 46260 3-00100
Steve Keith, prin. 259-5412

Metro SD of Wayne Township 7-11111
1220 S HIGH SCHOOL RD 46241 243-8251
Edward Bowes, supt.
Davis SHS 4-00001
1200 N GIRLS SCHOOL RD 46214 244-7691
James Mifflin, prin.
Davis JHS 3-00110
1155 S HIGH SCHOOL RD 46241 244-2438
David Shull, prin.
Fulton JHS, 7320 W 10TH ST 46214 4-00110
Steven Stephanoff, prin. 241-9285
South Wayne JHS 3-00110
4901 GADSDEN ST 46241 247-6265
Al Holok, prin.

Aristotle College/Medical & Dental Tech. 2-CS
5245 SOUTH US 31 46227 784-5400
Baptist Academy 2-11111
2565 VILLA AVE 46203 788-1587
Mark Dybwad, prin.
Bishop Chatard HS 3-00011
5885 CRITTENDEN AVE 46220 251-1451
Joseph Umile, prin.
Brebeuf Prep S, 2801 W 86TH ST 46268 3-00011
Fr. Stoeger, prin. 872-7050
Bristol University 2-UC
5920 CASTLEWAY WEST DR #102 46250
845-0882
Butler University 5-UC
4600 SUNSET AVE 46208 283-9900
Cardinal Ritter HS 2-00111
3360 W 30TH ST 46222 924-4333
Frank Velikan, prin.
Cathedral HS, 5225 E 56TH ST 46226 3-00011
Fr. Kelly, prin. 542-1481
Christian Theological Seminary 2-UC
1000 W 42ND ST 46208 924-1331
Colonial Christian S 2-11111
8140 UNION CHAPEL RD 46240 253-0649
Brian Washburn, prin.
Community Hospital of Indianapolis HSP
1500 N RITTER AVE 46219 355-5529
DePauw University 2-UC
1812 N CAPITOL AVE 46202
Eagledale Christian S 2-11111
4950 W 34TH ST 46224 291-4783
Warren Dafoe, prin.
Eliza Hendricks HS 2-01111
2596 N GIRLS SCHOOL RD 46214 244-3387
Doug Sinclair, prin.
Heritage Christian S 3-11111
6401 E 75TH ST 46250 849-3441
Timothy Hillen, prin.
Indiana Business College 3-CS
802 N MERIDIAN ST 46204 800-999-9229
Indiana Business College - Medical 2-CS
5460 VICTORY DR STE 100 46203 783-5100
Indiana School for the Deaf HND
1200 E 42ND ST 46205 924-4374
Indiana State School for the Blind HND
7725 N COLLEGE AVE 46240
Indiana U-Purdue U at Indianapolis 7-UC
355 LANSING ST 46202 264-4417
Indiana Vocational Technical College 5-CC
PO BOX 1763 46206 921-4860
International Business College 2-CC
7205 SHADELAND STATION WAY 46256
841-6400
ITT Technical Institute 4-CC
9511 ANGOLA CT 46268 875-8640
Ivy Tech Central Indiana 5-CC
1 W 26TH ST 46208 921-4882
Lincoln Technical Institute 4-CC
1201 STADIUM DR 46202 632-5553
Lutheran HS, PO BOX 39121 46239 2-00011
Richard Block, prin. 787-5474
Marian College 4-UC
3200 COLD SPRING RD 46222 929-0237
Martin University 2-UC
PO BOX 18567 46218 543-3250
Methodist Hospital of Indiana HSP
PO BOX 1367 46206 929-5470
Park-Tudor S 3-11111
7200 N COLLEGE AVE 46240 254-2700
Jim Leffler, prin.
Professional Careers Institute 3-CS
2611 WATERFRONT PKY 46214 299-6001
Roncalli HS, 3300 PRAGUE RD 46227 3-00011
Joe Hollowell, prin. 787-8277
St. Vincent Hospital HSP
2001 W 86TH ST 46260 871-3399

Scecina Memorial HS 3-00011
5000 NOWLAND AVE 46201 356-6377
Larry Neidlinger, prin.
University of Indianapolis 4-UC
1400 E HANNA AVE 46227 788-3211

Jasonville, AC 812, PC 4, Greene
Metro SD Shakamak 4-11111
RR 2 BOX 42 47438 665-3550
Donovan Wells, supt.
Shakamak JSHS, RR 2 BOX 42 47438 2-00111
Bill Ringo, prin. 665-2074

Jasper, AC 812, PC 7, Dubois
Greater Jasper Consolidated SD 5-11111
1520 SAINT CHARLES ST 47546 482-1801
Don Noblitt, supt.
HS, 1600 SAINT CHARLES ST 47546 3-00011
Larry Riggs, prin. 482-6050
MS, 340 W 6TH ST 47546 3-00100
M. L. Martin, prin. 482-6454

Jeffersonville, AC 812, PC 7, Clark
Greater Clark County SD 7-11111
2710 E HIGHWAY 62 47130 283-0701
Justin Roberts, supt.
HS, 2315 ALLISON LN 47130 4-00011
Ward Weber, prin. 282-6601
Parkview MS 3-00100
1600 BRIGMAN AVE 47130 288-4844
Michael Ehringer, prin.
River Valley MS 3-00100
2220 NEW ALBANY CHRLSTWN RD 47130
Dick Klemens, prin. 288-4848
Other Schools – See Charlestown, New Washington

Mid-America College of Funeral Service 2-CC
3111 HAMBURG PIKE 47130 800-221-6158

Kendallville, AC 219, PC 6, Noble
East Noble SD, 702 DOWLING ST 46755 5-11111
Rodger Smith, supt. 347-2502
East Noble HS, 901 GARDEN ST 46755 4-00011
Richard Anderson, prin. 347-2032
Kendallville Central MS 3-00100
401 E DIAMOND ST 46755 347-0100
Dwight Craft, prin.

Kentland, AC 219, PC 4, Newton
South Newton SD, 110 N 3RD ST 47951 4-11111
Howard Bloss, supt. 474-5184
South Newton JSHS, RR 1 47951 3-00111
Harry Basan, prin. 474-5167

Knightstown, AC 317, PC 4, Henry
Beard Memorial SD 4-11111
345 N ADAMS ST 46148 345-5101
Hal Jester, supt.
JSHS, 1 PANTHER TRL 46148 3-00111
Michael Brown, prin. 345-5153

Knightsville, AC 812, PC 3, Clay
Clay Community SD 5-11111
PO BOX 169 47857 443-4461
Thomas Rohr, supt.
Other Schools – See Brazil, Clay City

Knox, AC 219, PC 5, Starke
Knox Community SD 4-11111
2 REDSKIN TRL 46534 772-3712
Allen Bourff, supt.
Knox Community HS 3-00011
1 REDSKIN TRL 46534 772-6295
Stephen Sailor, prin.
Knox Community MS 3-00100
901 S MAIN ST 46534 772-4351
Charles James, prin.

Kokomo, AC 317, PC 8, Howard
Kokomo-Center Township Consolidated SD 6-11111
PO BOX 2188 46904 455-8000
Roger Thornton, supt.
Kokomo SHS South 4-00001
2501 S BERKLEY RD 46902 455-8040
Harold Canady, prin.
Kokomo Area Career Ctr Vo Tech
303 E SUPERIOR ST 46901 457-9151
William Heck, prin.
Kokomo JHS-Downtown 4-00110
303 E SUPERIOR ST 46901 454-7000
Harold Canady, prin.

Northwestern SD, 4154 W 350 N 46901 4-11111
Pat Mark, supt. 459-0701
Northwestern HS, 3431 N 400 W 46901 3-00011
Ryan Snoddy, prin. 457-8101
Northwestern JHS, 3431 N 400 W 46901 2-00100
Edward Burkhalter, prin. 457-8101

Taylor Community SD 4-11111
3750 E 300 S 46902 453-3035
Damon Peigh, supt.
Taylor JSHS, 3794 E 300 S 46902 3-00111
William Bozell, prin. 453-1101

Indiana University at Kokomo 4-UC
PO BOX 9003 46904 455-9225
Ivy Tech Kokomo 3-CC
1815 E MORGAN ST 46901 459-0561
Kokomo Christian S 2-11111
PO BOX 2798 46904 455-1447
Don Criss, prin.
St. Joseph Hospital & Health Center HSP
1907 W SYCAMORE ST 46901 456-5308

Kouts, AC 219, PC 4, Porter
East Porter Co. SD
Supt. — See Valparaiso
JSHS, PO BOX 348 46347 — 2-00111
Paul Rommelmann, prin. — 766-2231

La Crosse, AC 219, PC 3, La Porte
Dewey Township SD
Supt. — See La Porte
S, PO BOX 360 46348 — 2-11111
Michael McBride, prin. — 754-2321

Lafayette, AC 317, PC 8, Tippecanoe
Lafayette SD, 2300 CASON ST 47904 — 6-11111
Robert Myers, supt. — 449-3200
Jefferson HS, 1801 S 18TH ST 47905 — 4-00011
Dennis Blind, prin. — 449-3400
Sunnyside MS, 2500 CASON ST 47904 — 3-00100
John Forville, prin. — 449-3500
Tecumseh MS, 2101 S 18TH ST 47905 — 3-00100
Dennis Cahill, prin. — 449-3600

Tippecanoe SD, 21 ELSTON RD 47905 — 6-11111
Rich Wood, supt. — 474-2481
McCutcheon HS — 4-00011
4951 STATE RD 43 S 47905 — 474-1488
Medarda Bauer, prin.
East Tipp MS, 7501 E 300 N 47905 — 2-00100
John Shoaf, prin. — 589-3566
Southwestern MS, 2100 W 800 S 47905 — 2-00100
John Christopher, prin. — 538-3025
Wainwright MS, 7501 E 700 S 47905 — 2-00100
Richard Watts, prin. — 523-2151
Other Schools – See Battle Ground, West Lafayette

Central Catholic HS — 2-00111
2410 S 9TH ST 47905 — 474-2496
David Worland, prin.
Indiana Business College — 2-CS
1170 S CREASY LN 47905 — 447-9550
Ivy Tech Lafayette — 3-CC
PO BOX 6299 47903 — 477-9138
St. Elizabeth Hospital — HSP
PO BOX 7501 47903 — 423-6408

Lagrange, AC 219, PC 4, Lagrange
Lakeland SD, 200 S CHERRY ST 46761 — 4-11111
William Walz, supt. — 463-7101
Lakeland HS, 805 E 075 N 46761 — 3-00011
Garry DeRossett, prin. — 463-2149
Lakeland JHS, 1055 E 075 N 46761 — 2-00100
Everitt Billingsley, prin. — 463-7447

Prairie Heights Community SD — 4-11111
305 S 1150 E 46761 — 351-3214
Robert Slavens, supt.
Prairie Heights HS, 245 S 1150 E 46761 — 2-00011
Kenneth Workman, prin. — 351-3214
Prairie Heights MS, 395 S 1150 E 46761 — 3-01100
Brenda Rummell, prin. — 351-3214

Lake Station, AC 219, PC 7, Lake
Lake Station Community SD — 4-11111
2500 PIKE ST 46405 — 962-1159
Charles Costa, supt.
Edison JSHS, 3304 PARKSIDE AVE 46405 — 3-00011
Jeffery Jones, prin. — 962-8531

Lakeville, AC 219, PC 3, St. Joseph
Union-North United SD — 4-11111
PO BOX 429 46536 — 784-8141
David Pruis, supt.
Laville JSHS — 3-00111
69969 US HIGHWAY 31 46536 — 784-3151
Nancy Hipskind, prin.

Lanesville, AC 812, PC 3, Harrison
Lanesville Community SD — 3-11111
PO BOX 171 47136 — 952-2555
Carl Uesseler, supt.
JSHS, PO BOX 171 47136 — 2-00111
Carl Uesseler, prin. — 952-2555

Lapel, AC 317, PC 4, Madison
West Central Community SD
Supt. — See Anderson
JSHS, 2883 S STATE ROAD 13 46051 — 2-00111
Larry Galliher, prin. — 534-3136

La Porte, AC 219, PC 7, La Porte
Dewey Township SD — 2-11111
500 MONROE ST 46350 — 326-6808
Roger Luekens, supt.
Other Schools – See La Crosse

La Porte Community SD — 6-11111
1921 A ST 46350 — 362-7056
Peggy Ondrovich, supt.
HS, 602 F ST 46350 — 4-00011
Greg Handel, prin. — 362-3102
Boston MS, 1000 HARRISON ST 46350 — 3-00100
Fay Iorio, prin. — 362-6930
Kesling MS, 306 E 18TH ST 46350 — 3-00100
James Rubush, prin. — 362-7507

New Durham Township SD — 3-11111
500 MONROE ST 46350 — 326-6808
Roger Luekens, supt.
Other Schools – See Westville

Commonwealth Business College — 2-CS
8995 N STATE ROAD 39 46350 — 362-3338

Larwill, AC 219, PC 2, Kosciusko
Whitko Community SD
Supt. — See Pierceton
Whitko MS — 3-00100
710 N STATE ROAD 5 46764 — 327-3603
Mark Skiles, prin.

Lawrenceburg, AC 812, PC 5, Dearborn
Lawrenceburg Community SD — 4-11111
1 STADIUM LN 47025 — 537-7200
T. R. Ellis, supt.
HS, 100 TIGER BLVD 47025 — 3-00011
Anthony Dietrich, prin. — 537-7219
Greendale MS, 200 TIGER BLVD 47025 — 2-00100
W. Kuebler, prin. — 537-7259

Lebanon, AC 317, PC 7, Boone
Lebanon Community SD — 5-11111
404 N MERIDIAN ST 46052 — 482-0380
David Hutton, supt.
HS, 510 ESSEX DR 46052 — 3-00011
William Jensen, prin. — 482-0400
MS, 1800 N GRANT ST 46052 — 3-00100
Kenneth Hull, prin. — 482-3400

Leo, AC 219, PC 4, Allen
East Allen County SD
Supt. — See New Haven
JSHS, 14600 AMSTUTZ RD 46765 — 3-00111
Herbert Stuelpe, prin. — 627-3671

Leopold, AC 812, PC 2, Perry
Perry Central Community SD — 4-11111
HIGHWAY 37 47551 — 843-5576
Larry Feldmeyer, supt.
Perry Central JSHS — 3-00111
HIGHWAY 37 47551 — 843-5122
Joseph LaGrange, prin.

Liberty, AC 317, PC 4, Union
Union County SD — 4-11111
107 S LAYMAN ST 47353 — 458-5783
Todd Rudnick, supt.
Union County HS — 3-00011
410 E UNION ST 47353 — 458-5136
Steven Bryant, prin.
MS, 402 E UNION ST 47353 — 2-00100
Edward Ritter, prin. — 458-6358

Ligonier, AC 219, PC 5, Noble
West Noble SD — 4-11111
5094 N US HIGHWAY 33 46767 — 894-3191
Bruce Hippensteel, supt.
West Noble HS — 3-00011
5094 N US HIGHWAY 33 46767 — 894-3191
Roger Schermerhorn, prin.
West Noble MS — 2-00100
5194 N US HIGHWAY 33 46767 — 894-3196
Robert Wechter, prin.

Lincoln City, AC 812, PC 2, Spencer
North Spencer County SD
Supt. — See Dale
Heritage Hills JSHS — 4-00111
PO BOX 1776 47552 — 937-4472
Al Logsdon, prin.

Linden, AC 317, PC 3, Montgomery
North Montgomery Community SD — 4-11111
PO BOX 70 47955 — 339-7262
Gren LeFebvre, supt.
Other Schools – See Crawfordsville

Linton, AC 812, PC 6, Greene
Linton-Stockton SD — 4-11111
801 1ST ST NE 47441 — 847-6020
Earlene Holland, supt.
Linton-Stockton HS, 10 H ST NE 47441 — 2-00011
Nicholas Karazsia, prin. — 847-6024
Linton-Stockton JHS, 109 I ST NW 47441 — 2-00100
Daniel Phillips, prin. — 847-6022

Lizton, AC 317, PC 2, Hendricks
North West Hendricks SD — 4-11111
PO BOX 70 46149 — 994-5315
Larry Rambis, supt.
Tri-West JSHS, PO BOX 10 46149 — 3-00111
Ronald Ward, prin. — 994-5101

Logansport, AC 219, PC 7, Cass
Logansport Community SD — 5-11111
2829 GEORGE ST 46947 — 722-2911
Steve Kain, supt.
Logansport Community HS — 4-00011
1 BERRY LN 46947 — 753-0441
Gordan Newlin, prin.
El-Tip-Wa Area Vo S — Vo Tech
721 N 6TH ST 46947 — 722-3811
Don Grostefon, prin.
Columbia MS, 1300 N 3RD ST 46947 — 2-00100
Kay Scott, prin. — 753-3797
Lincoln MS, 2901 USHER ST 46947 — 2-00100
George Hainje, prin. — 753-7115

Loogootee, AC 812, PC 5, Martin
Loogootee Community SD — 4-11111
PO BOX 282 47553 — 295-2595
Larry Weitkamp, supt.
JSHS, 201 BROOKS AVE 47553 — 3-00111
John Strader, prin. — 295-3254

Lowell, AC 219, PC 6, Lake
Tri-Creek SD, 690 S BURR ST 46356 — 6-11111
Donald Yeoman, supt. — 696-6661
HS, 2051 E COMMERCIAL AVE 46356 — 3-00011
Mark Gould, prin. — 696-7733

MS, 200 W OAKLEY AVE 46356 — 3-00100
Rondal Black, prin. — 696-7701

Lynn, AC 317, PC 4, Randolph
Randolph Southern SD — 3-11111
PO BOX 385 47355 — 874-1181
Philip Dubbs, supt.
Randolph Southern JSHS — 2-00111
PO BOX 305 47355 — 874-2541
Larry Marker, prin.

Lynnville, AC 812, PC 3, Warrick
Warrick County SD
Supt. — See Boonville
Tecumseh JSHS, PO BOX 67 47619 — 2-00111
Thomas Welch, prin. — 922-3608

Madison, AC 812, PC 7, Jefferson
Madison Consolidated SD — 5-11111
PO BOX 99 47250 — 273-8511
Homer Lawson, supt.
Madison Consolidated SHS — 3-00001
743 CLIFTY DR 47250 — 265-6672
Roger Gallatin, prin.
Madison Consolidated JHS — 3-00110
701 8TH ST 47250 — 265-6756
Larry Cummins, prin.

Ivy Tech Southeast — 2-CC
HWY 62 & IVY TECH DR 47250 — 265-2580
King's Daughter's Hospital — HSP
PO BOX 447 47250 — 265-5211
Shawe Memorial HS — 2-00111
201 W STATE ST 47250 — 273-2150
Rita King, prin.

Marengo, AC 812, PC 3, Crawford
Crawford County Community SD — 4-11111
PO BOX 366 47140 — 365-2135
Lynn Blinzinger, supt.
Crawford County JSHS — 3-00111
PO BOX 387 47140 — 365-2125
Allen Benny, prin.

Marion, AC 317, PC 8, Grant
Eastbrook Community SD — 4-11111
560 S 900 E 46953 – Dennis Fox, supt. — 664-0624
Eastbrook HS, 560 S 900 E 46953 — 3-00011
Don Deemer, prin. — 664-1214
Eastbrook JHS, 560 S 900 E 46953 — 2-00100
Robert Shipley, prin. — 664-1214

Marion Community SD — 6-11111
PO BOX 2020 46952 — 662-2546
Shirley Smalley, supt.
HS, 750 W 26TH ST 46953 — 4-00011
Marjorie Record, prin. — 664-9051
Tucker Area Vo-Tech Ctr — Vo Tech
107 S PENNSYLVANIA ST 46952 — 664-9091
Jerry Whitton, prin.
Jones MS — 3-01100
100 N PENNSYLVANIA ST 46952 — 662-3935
Richard Persinger, prin.
Justice MS, 720 N MILLER AVE 46952 — 3-01100
Daryl Unnasch, prin. — 664-0507
McCulloch MS — 3-01100
3528 S WASHINGTON ST 46953 — 674-6917
Joselyn Whitticker, prin.

Indiana Business College — 2-CS
830 N MILLER AVE 46952 — 662-7497
Indiana Wesleyan University — 4-UC
4201 S WASHINGTON ST 46953 — 677-2100
Lakeview Christian S — 2-11111
PO BOX 10 46952 — 674-7715
Mike Chivalette, prin.

Marshall, AC 317, PC 2, Parke
Turkey Run Community SD — 3-11111
RR 1 BOX 333 47859 — 597-2245
Dale Deplanty, supt.
Turkey Run JSHS — 2-00111
RR 1 BOX 333 47859 — 597-2242
Ward Fritzen, prin.

Martinsville, AC 317, PC 7, Morgan
Metro SD of Martinsville — 6-11111
PO BOX 1416 46151 — 342-6641
James Auter, supt.
HS, 1360 E GRAY ST 46151 — 4-00011
Blake Ress, prin. — 342-5571
Martinsville East MS — 3-00100
1459 E COLUMBUS ST 46151 — 342-6675
David Gordon, prin.
Martinsville West MS — 3-00100
109 E GARFIELD AVE 46151 — 342-6628
Randy Taylor, prin.

Tabernacle Christian S — 2-11111
2189 BURTON LN 46151 — 342-0501
Don Nations, prin.

Maxwell, AC 317, PC 2, Hancock
Greenfield-Central Community SD
Supt. — See Greenfield
MS, 102 N MAIN ST 46154 — 2-00100
Howard Mandel, prin. — 326-3121

Medora, AC 812, PC 3, Jackson
Medora Community SD — 2-11111
PO BOX 369 47260 — 966-2210
James Gabbard, supt.
JSHS, PO BOX 248 47260 — 2-00111
James Stewart, prin. — 966-2201

Mentone, AC 219, PC 3, Kosciusko
Tippecanoe Valley SD — 4-11111
  PO BOX 338 46539 — 353-7741
  Karen Boling, supt.
Tippecanoe Valley HS — 3-00011
  PO BOX 38 46539 — 353-7031
  Charles Mills, prin.

Merrillville, AC 219, PC 8, Lake
Merrillville Community SD — 6-11111
  6701 DELAWARE ST 46410 — 736-4830
  Robert Schrenker, supt.
HS, 276 E 68TH PL 46410 — 4-00011
  Daniel Rapacz, prin. — 738-2390
Harrison MS, 1400 W 61ST AVE 46410 — 3-00100
  Larry Martin, prin. — 980-0571
Pierce MS, 199 E 70TH PL 46410 — 3-00100
  Gerald Niemeyer, prin. — 736-4837

Andrean HS, 5959 BROADWAY 46410 — 3-00011
  Fr. Cerretto, prin. — 887-5281
Commonwealth Business College — 3-CS
  4200 W LINCOLN HWY 46410 — 769-3321
Davenport College of Business — 3-CC
  8200 GEORGIA ST 46410 — 769-5556
Sawyer College — 3-CS
  3803 E LINCOLN HWY 46410 — 800-964-0218

Michigan City, AC 219, PC 8, La Porte
Michigan City Area SD — 6-11111
  408 S CARROLL AVE 46360 — 873-2000
  Nathaniel Clay, supt.
Elston HS, 317 DETROIT ST 46360 — 4-00011
  Tim Bietry, prin. — 873-2035
Rogers HS, 8466 PAHS RD 46360 — 4-00011
  Carmine Gentile, prin. — 873-2051
Barker JHS, 319 E BARKER AVE 46360 — 3-00100
  Nick Sweigart, prin. — 873-2057
Krueger JHS — 3-00100
  2001 SPRINGLAND AVE 46360 — 873-2061
  Kirk Rogers, prin.

Lakeshore Medical Lab Training Programs — CS
  402 FRANKLIN ST 46360 — 872-7032
Marquette HS, 306 W 10TH ST 46360 — 2-00011
  Dr. Richard Dornbos, prin. — 873-1325

Michigantown, AC 317, PC 2, Clinton
Clinton Central SD — 4-11111
  PO BOX 118 46057 — 249-2515
  Robert Brinson, supt.
Clinton Central JSHS — 3-00111
  PO BOX 178 46057 — 249-2255
  Ralph Walker, prin.

Middlebury, AC 219, PC 4, Elkhart
Middlebury Community SD — 5-11111
  57853 NORTHRIDGE DR 46540 — 825-9425
  Rex Baker, supt.
Northridge HS — 3-00011
  57697 NORTHRIDGE DR UNIT 1 46540
  James Lichtenberger, prin. — 825-2142
Heritage MS — 3-00100
  57697 NORTHRIDGE DR UNIT 2 46540
  Mitch Miller, prin. — 825-9531

Middletown, AC 317, PC 4, Henry
Shenandoah SD — 4-11111
  5100 N RAIDER RD 47356 — 354-2266
  Don Davenport, supt.
Shenandoah HS — 2-00011
  7354 W STATE ROAD 36 47356 — 354-6640
  Steve Telfer, prin.
Shenandoah MS — 2-00100
  5156 N RAIDER RD 47356 — 354-6638
  Michael Andrews, prin.

Milan, AC 812, PC 4, Ripley
Milan Community SD — 4-11111
  PO BOX 278 47031 — 654-2365
  Douglas Rose, supt.
JSHS, PO BOX 307 47031 — 2-00111
  Michael Horton, prin. — 654-3096

Milford, AC 219, PC 4, Kosciusko
Wawasee Community SD
  Supt. — See Syracuse
JHS, PO BOX 548 46542 — 2-00100
  Cynthia Kaiser, prin. — 658-9444

Mishawaka, AC 219, PC 8, St. Joseph
City of Mishawaka SD — 6-11111
  1402 S MAIN ST 46544 — 258-3000
  Stella Batagiannis, supt.
HS, 1202 LINCOLN WAY E 46544 — 4-00011
  Joseph Trimboli, prin. — 258-3010
Young MS, 1801 N MAIN ST 46545 — 2-00100
  John Ferrettie, prin. — 258-3020

Penn-Harris-Madison SD — 6-11111
  55900 BITTERSWEET RD 46545 — 259-7941
  Robert MacNaughton, supt.
Penn HS — 4-00011
  56100 BITTERSWEET RD 46545 — 259-7961
  Eugene Sweeney, prin.
Grissom MS, 13881 KERN RD 46544 — 3-00100
  Don Quimby, prin. — 633-4061
Schmucker MS — 4-00100
  56045 BITTERSWEET RD 46545 — 259-5661
  John Borland, prin.

Bethel College — 3-UC
  1001 W MCKINLEY AVE 46545 — 259-8511

Marian HS, 1311 S LOGAN ST 46544 — 2-00011
  Peter O'Rourke, prin. — 259-5257

Mitchell, AC 812, PC 5, Lawrence
Mitchell Community SD — 4-11111
  441 N 8TH ST 47446 — 849-4481
  James Oswalt, supt.
HS, 1000 W BISHOP BLVD 47446 — 3-00011
  Steve Phillips, prin. — 849-3663
JHS, 1000 W BISHOP BLVD 47446 — 2-00100
  David Branneman, prin. — 849-3747

Modoc, AC 317, PC 2, Randolph
Union SD, RR 1 47358 — 3-11111
  James Danner, supt. — 853-5464
Union JSHS, RR 1 47358 — 2-00111
  Richard Trapp, prin. — 853-5421

Monon, AC 219, PC 4, White
North White SD, PO BOX 656 47959 — 4-11111
  John Heath, supt. — 253-6618
North White JSHS — 2-00111
  PO BOX 1060 47959 — 253-6638
  Steven Schetzsle, prin.

Monroe, AC 219, PC 3, Adams
Adams Central Community SD — 4-11111
  222 W WASHINGTON ST 46772 — 692-6151
  Larry Rausch, supt.
Adams Central HS — 2-00111
  222 W WASHINGTON ST 46772 — 692-6151
  Donald Rush, prin.
Adams Central MS — 2-00100
  222 W WASHINGTON ST 46772 — 692-6151
  Niel Potter, prin.

Monroe City, AC 812, PC 3, Knox
South Knox SD, PO BOX 388 47557 — 4-11111
  Robert Ellis, supt. — 726-4440
Other Schools – See Vincennes

Monroeville, AC 219, PC 4, Allen
East Allen County SD
  Supt. — See New Haven
Heritage JSHS — 3-00111
  13608 MONROEVILLE RD 46773 — 623-6114
  Robert Herber, prin.

Monrovia, AC 317, PC 3, Morgan
Monroe-Gregg SD, PO BOX 468 46157 — 4-11111
  Mike Turner, supt. — 996-3720
JSHS, PO BOX 468 46157 — 3-00111
  Denis Ward, prin. — 996-2259

Montezuma, AC 317, PC 4, Parke
Southwest Parke Community SD — 4-11111
  RR 1 BOX 71B 47862 — 569-2073
  Joseph Koval, supt.
Riverton Parke JSHS — 2-00111
  RR 1 BOX 71A 47862 — 569-2046
  Michael Chobanov, prin.

Montgomery, AC 812, PC 2, Daviess
Barr-Reeve Community SD — 3-11111
  PO BOX 97 47558 — 486-3220
  Joe Woods, supt.
Barr-Reeve JSHS, PO BOX 128 47558 — 2-00111
  Jack Schmeltz, prin. — 486-3265

Monticello, AC 219, PC 6, White
Twin Lakes SD, 565 S MAIN ST 47960 — 5-11111
  Rodney Rich, supt. — 583-7211
Twin Lakes HS, 300 S 3RD ST 47960 — 3-00011
  Kevin Caress, prin. — 583-7108
Roosevelt MS — 3-00100
  721 W BROADWAY ST 47960 — 583-5552
  Patrick McTaggart, prin.

Montpelier, AC 317, PC 4, Blackford
Blackford County SD
  Supt. — See Hartford City
MS, 107 E MONROE ST 47359 — 2-01100
  (—), prin. — 728-2402

Mooresville, AC 317, PC 6, Morgan
Mooresville Consolidated SD — 5-11111
  320 N INDIANA ST 46158 — 831-0950
  Gary Myers, supt.
HS, 550 N INDIANA ST 46158 — 4-00011
  William Overholser, prin. — 831-9203
Hadley JHS, 200 W CARLISLE ST 46158 — 3-00100
  Curtis Freeman, prin. — 831-9208

Morocco, AC 219, PC 4, Newton
North Newton SD, PO BOX 8 47963 — 4-11111
  Larry Hanna, supt. — 285-2228
North Newton JSHS — 3-00111
  RR 2 BOX 111 47963 — 285-2252
  Gene Bell, prin.

Morristown, AC 317, PC 3, Shelby
Shelby Eastern SD
  Supt. — See Shelbyville
JSHS, PO BOX 247 46161 — 2-00111
  Paul Parker, prin. — 763-1221

Mount Summit, AC 317, PC 2, Henry
Blue River Valley SD — 3-11111
  PO BOX 217 47361 — 836-4816
  Gerald Bolton, supt.
Blue River Valley JSHS — 2-00111
  PO BOX 158 47361 — 836-4811
  Stephen Welsh, prin.

Mount Vernon, AC 812, PC 6, Posey
Metro SD of Mt. Vernon — 5-11111
  1000 W 4TH ST 47620 — 838-4471
  Melvin Levin, supt.

HS, 700 HARRIETT ST 47620 — 3-00011
  G. Donald Goerlitz, prin. — 838-4356
JHS, 701 TILE FACTORY RD 47620 — 3-00100
  Jerry Funkhouser, prin. — 833-2077

Muncie, AC 317, PC 8, Delaware
Cowan Community SD — 3-11111
  1000 W COUNTY ROAD 600 S 47302 — 289-4866
  Larry John, supt.
Cowan JSHS — 2-00111
  9401 S NOTTINGHAM ST 47302 — 289-7128
  Phillip Gardner, prin.
Delaware Community SD — 5-11111
  7821 N STATE ROAD 3 47303 — 284-5074
  Marlin Creasy, supt.
Delta HS — 3-00011
  3400 E STATE ROAD 28 47303 — 288-5597
  Randy Harris, prin.
Delta MS — 3-00100
  9800 N WILLIAMSON RD 47303 — 747-0869
  Thomas Gourley, prin.

Muncie Community SD — 6-11111
  2501 N OAKWOOD AVE 47304 — 747-5205
  Sam Abram, supt.
Muncie Central HS — 4-00011
  801 N WALNUT ST 47305 — 747-5260
  Joe Kinnett, prin.
Southside HS, 1601 E 26TH ST 47302 — 4-00011
  John Robbins, prin. — 747-5320
Muncie Area Career Ctr — Vo Tech
  2500 N ELGIN ST 47303 — 747-5250
  Susan Koebcke, prin.
Northside MS — 3-00100
  2400 N BETHEL AVE 47304 — 747-5290
  Charles Childers, prin.
Wilson MS, 2000 S FRANKLIN ST 47302 — 3-00100
  Michael Tolle, prin. — 747-5370

University Schools — 3-11111
  WAGONER HALL BALL STA 47306 — 285-7455
  Philip Borders, prin.
IN Academy for Science Math & Humanities — 2-00001
  WAGONER HALL-BALL STA 47306 — 285-7455
  Philip Borders, prin.
Burris Lab S — 3-11111
  2000 W UNIVERSITY AVE 47306 — 285-8600
  Vicki Vaughn, prin.

Ball Memorial Hospital — HSP
  2401 W UNIVERSITY AVE 47303 — 747-3393
Ball State University — 7-UC
  2000 W UNIVERSITY AVE 47306 — 285-5555
Heritage Hall, 6401 W RIVER RD 47304 — 2-11111
  Dennis Ice, prin. — 289-6371
Indiana Business College — 2-CS
  1809 N WALNUT ST 47303 — 288-8681
Ivy Tech East Central — 3-CC
  PO BOX 3100 47307 — 289-2291

Munster, AC 219, PC 7, Lake
Town of Munster SD — 5-11111
  8616 COLUMBIA AVE 46321 — 836-9111
  William Pfister, supt.
HS, 8808 COLUMBIA AVE 46321 — 4-00011
  Kevin McCaffrey, prin. — 836-3200
Wright MS, 8650 COLUMBIA AVE 46321 — 3-00100
  Don Guske, prin. — 836-6260

Nappanee, AC 219, PC 6, Elkhart
Wa-Nee Community SD — 5-11111
  1300 N MAIN ST 46550 — 773-3131
  Jerry Lelle, supt.
Northwood HS, 2101 N MAIN ST 46550 — 3-00011
  Louis Bonocorsi, prin. — 773-4127
MS, 755 E VAN BUREN ST 46550 — 2-00100
  George Roelandts, prin. — 773-7788
Other Schools – See Wakarusa

United Christian S — 2-11111
  29522 COUNTY ROAD 52 46550 — 773-7505
  Brandon Mullet, prin.

Nashville, AC 812, PC 3, Brown
Brown County SD, PO BOX 38 47448 — 4-11111
  I. Lewis, supt. — 988-6601
Brown County HS, PO BOX 68 47448 — 3-00011
  Wayne Wackowski, prin. — 988-6606
Brown County JHS — 2-00100
  PO BOX 578 47448 — 988-6605
  Rollin Goodpaster, prin.

New Albany, AC 812, PC 8, Floyd
New Albany-Floyd County Consolidated SD — 7-11111
  PO BOX 1087 47151 — 949-4200
  Edward Adams, supt.
SHS, 1020 VINCENNES ST 47150 — 4-00001
  Stephen Sipes, prin. — 949-4272
Prosser Vo Ctr — Vo Tech
  4202 CHARLESTOWN RD 47150 — 949-4266
  Stephen Cunningham, prin.
Hazelwood JHS — 3-00110
  1 HAZELWOOD AVE 47150 — 949-4280
  Maxwell White, prin.
Scribner JHS — 3-00110
  910 OLD VINCENNES RD 47150 — 949-4283
  Teresa Perkins, prin.
Other Schools – See Floyds Knobs

Graceland Christian S — 2-11111
  3600 KAMER MILLER RD 47150 — 944-6448
  Glenn Riggs, prin.

Indiana University Southeast 5-UC
4201 GRANT LINE RD 47150 941-2200

Newburgh, AC 812, PC 5, Warrick
Warrick County SD
Supt. — See Boonville
Castle HS 4-00011
3344 STATE ROUTE 261 47630 853-3331
Cecil Raymond, prin.
Castle JHS 3-00100
2800 HIGHWAY 261 47630 853-7347
Joe Loge, prin.

New Carlisle, AC 219, PC 4, St. Joseph
New Prairie United SD 4-11111
5329 N COUGAR RD 46552 654-7273
Doris Gramble, supt.
New Prairie HS 3-00011
5333 N COUGAR RD 46552 654-7271
Charles Stephans, prin.
New Prairie JHS 2-00100
5331 N COUGAR RD 46552 654-3070
Karlye Green, prin.

New Castle, AC 317, PC 7, Henry
New Castle Community SD 5-11111
522 ELLIOTT AVE 47362 521-7201
Larry Williams, supt.
New Castle Chrysler SHS 3-00001
801 PARKVIEW DR 47362 529-5212
John Newby, prin.
New Castle Area Vo S Vo Tech
1407 WALNUT ST 47362 521-7226
Beverly Hankenhoff, prin.
Parkview JHS, 601 PARKVIEW DR 47362 3-00110
Robert Crowe, prin. 521-7230

New Harmony, AC 812, PC 3, Posey
New Harmony Town & Twp. Consolidated SD 2-11111
PO BOX 396 47631 682-4661
Scott Turney, supt.
S, PO BOX 396 47631 2-11111
Fred Frayser, prin. 682-4401

New Haven, AC 219, PC 6, Allen
East Allen County SD 6-11111
1240 US HIGHWAY 30 E 46774 493-3761
James Gland, supt.
HS, 1300 GREEN RD 46774 3-00011
Robert Rohrbacher, prin. 493-3761
MS, 900 PROSPECT AVE 46774 3-00100
David Jones, prin. 493-3761
Other Schools – See Fort Wayne, Leo, Monroeville,
Woodburn

New Market, AC 317, PC 3, Montgomery
South Montgomery Community SD 4-11111
PO BOX 8 47965 866-0203
Rob Tandy, supt.
Other Schools – See Crawfordsville

New Palestine, AC 317, PC 3, Hancock
Southern Hancock County Community SD 4-11111
PO BOX 508 46163 861-4463
Betty Poindexter, supt.
HS, PO BOX 448 46163 3-00011
William Jones, prin. 861-4417
Doe Creek MS, PO BOX 478 46163 3-00100
James Snapp, prin. 861-4487

New Washington, AC 812, PC 3, Clark
Greater Clark County SD
Supt. — See Jeffersonville
JSHS, PO BOX 100 47162 2-00011
Dale Crafton, prin. 293-3368

Noblesville, AC 317, PC 7, Hamilton
Noblesville SD, 1775 FIELD DR 46060 6-11111
John Ellis, supt. 773-3171
HS, 300 N 17TH ST 46060 4-00011
John Ford, prin. 773-4680
JHS, 1625 FIELD DR 46060 4-00100
Libbie Conner, prin. 773-0782

North Judson, AC 219, PC 4, Starke
North Judson-San Pierre SD 4-11111
960 CAMPBELL DR 46366 896-2155
Judith Weitgenant, supt.
North Judson-San Pierre HS 2-00011
900 CAMPBELL DR 46366 896-2158
William Auker, prin.
JHS, 950 CAMPBELL DR 46366 2-00100
Jerome Jernas, prin. 896-2167

North Manchester, AC 219, PC 6, Wabash
Manchester Community SD 4-11111
PO BOX 308 46962 982-7518
Connie Curry, supt.
Manchester HS, 1 SQUIRE DR 46962 3-00011
James Smith, prin. 982-2196
Manchester JHS, 404 W 9TH ST 46962 2-00100
Kate Shimer, prin. 982-8602

Manchester College 4-UC
604 E COLLEGE AVE 46962 982-5000

North Vernon, AC 812, PC 6, Jennings
Jennings County SD, 34 MAIN ST 47265 5-11111
Phyllis Amick, supt. 346-4483
Jennings County HS 4-00011
800 W WALNUT ST 47265 346-5588
Steve Riordan, prin.
Jennings County MS 3-00100
820 W WALNUT ST 47265 346-4940
Roger Dean, prin.

Notre Dame, AC 219, PC 7, St. Joseph

Holy Cross College 2-CC
PO BOX 308 46556 233-6813
St. Mary's College 4-UC
46 MADELIVA 46556 284-4603
University of Notre Dame 7-UC
302 ADMINISTRATION BLDG 46556 239-5000

Oakland City, AC 812, PC 5, Gibson
East Gibson SD 4-11111
943 S FRANKLIN ST 47660 749-4755
Dale McCuiston, supt.
Wood Memorial HS 2-00011
943 S FRANKLIN ST 47660 749-4757
Roger Benson, prin.

Oakland City College 3-UC
143 N LUCRETIA ST 47660 749-1213

Oldenburg, AC 812, PC 3, Franklin

Academy of the Immaculate Conception 2-00011
MAIN ST 47036 934-4440
Frances Romweber, prin.

Orleans, AC 812, PC 4, Orange
Orleans Community SD 3-11111
173 W MARLEY ST 47452 865-2688
Earl Pfettscher, supt.
JSHS, 585 N EISENHOWER ST 47452 2-00111
Kenneth Hoffman, prin. 865-2994

Osgood, AC 812, PC 4, Ripley
Jac-Cen-Del Community SD 3-11111
4586 N US HIGHWAY 421 47037 689-4114
Stephen Gookins, supt.
Jac-Cen-Del JSHS 2-00111
4586 N US HIGHWAY 421 47037 689-4643
John Ward, prin.

Ossian, AC 219, PC 4, Wells
Northern Wells Community SD 5-11111
PO BOX 386 46777 622-4125
Michael Sailsbery, supt.
Norwell HS 3-00011
1100 E US HIGHWAY 224 46777 543-2213
Gary Drill, prin.
Norwell MS 3-00100
1100 E US HIGHWAY 224 46777 543-2218
William Denney, prin.

Oxford, AC 317, PC 4, Benton
Benton Community SD
Supt. — See Fowler
Benton Central JSHS, 4241 E 300 S 47971 4-00011
Michael Sipe, prin. 884-1600

Paoli, AC 812, PC 5, Orange
Paoli Community SD 4-11111
501 S ELM ST 47454 723-4717
Alva Sibbitt, supt.
JSHS, 501 S ELM ST 47454 3-00111
James Babcock, prin. 723-3905

Parker City, AC 317, PC 4, Randolph
Monroe Central SD, RR 1 BOX 17A 47368 4-11111
Timothy Long, supt. 468-6868
Monroe Central JSHS 3-00111
RR 1 BOX 17A 47368 468-7545
Kellie Stephen, prin.

Pekin, AC 812, PC 4, Washington
East Washington SD 4-11111
RR 2 BOX E2 47165 967-3926
H. Butler, supt.
Eastern HS, RR 2 BOX E3 47165 2-00011
James Feist, prin. 967-3931
East Washington MS 2-00100
RR 2 BOX E5 47165 967-5000
David Bailey, prin.

Pendleton, AC 317, PC 4, Madison
South Madison Community SD 5-11111
201 S EAST ST 46064 778-2152
Reggie Laconi, supt.
Pendleton Heights HS 4-00011
1 ARABIAN WAY 46064 778-2161
Loran Skinner, prin.
Pendleton Heights MS 3-00100
301 S EAST ST 46064 778-2139
Terry Auker, prin.

Peru, AC 317, PC 7, Miami
Peru Community SD 5-11111
2 1/2 N BROADWAY 46970 473-3081
Thomas McKaig, supt.
HS, 401 N BROADWAY 46970 3-00011
Leonard McIntire, prin. 472-3301
JHS, 30 DANIEL ST 46970 2-00100
Jerry Harshman, prin. 473-3084

Petersburg, AC 812, PC 4, Pike
Pike County SD, PO BOX 66 47567 4-11111
Mark Ransford, supt. 354-8731
Pike Central JSHS, RR 3 47567 4-00111
Rick Fears, prin. 354-8478

Pierceton, AC 219, PC 4, Kosciusko
Whitko Community SD 4-11111
PO BOX 114 46562 594-2658
John Hill, supt.
Other Schools – See Larwill, South Whitley

Plainfield, AC 317, PC 7, Hendricks
Plainfield Community SD 5-11111
985 LONGFELLOW DR 46168 839-2578
Jerry Holifield, supt.
HS, 709 STAFFORD RD 46168 3-00011
William Wakefield, prin. 839-7711
Plainfield Community MS 3-00100
401 ELM DR 46168 838-3966
Jerry Goldsberry, prin.

Charlton Indiana Boys S 2-00011
PO BOX 211 46168 839-7751
David Weaver, prin.

Plymouth, AC 219, PC 6, Marshall
Plymouth Community SD 5-11111
701 BERKLEY ST 46563 936-3115
Danny Bates, supt.
HS, 1 BIG RED DR 46563 3-00011
Larry Pinkerton, prin. 936-2178
Lincoln JHS, 220 N LIBERTY ST 46563 3-00100
John McNeil, prin. 936-3113

Poneto, AC 317, PC 2, Wells
Southern Wells Community SD 3-11111
9120 S 300 W 46781 728-5537
Mike Bushong, supt.
Southern Wells JSHS 2-00111
9120 S 300 W 46781 728-5534
James Schwarzkopf, prin.

Portage, AC 219, PC 8, Porter
Portage Township SD 6-11111
6240 US HIGHWAY 6 46368 762-6511
Donald Bivens, supt.
HS, 6450 US HIGHWAY 6 46368 5-00011
Forrest Rhode, prin. 762-6511
Fegely MS, 5384 STONE AVE 46368 3-00110
Terrance Levenda, prin. 762-6511
Willowcreek MS 4-00100
5962 CENTRAL AVE 46368 762-6511
Gerald Dixon, prin.

Portage Christian S 2-11111
PO BOX 28 46368 762-9531

Portland, AC 219, PC 6, Jay
Jay SD, 404 E ARCH ST 47371 5-11111
George Gilbert, supt. 726-9341
Jay County HS, RR 2 47371 4-00011
Joanne Gibson, prin. 726-9306
East Jay County JHS 2-00100
227 E WATER ST 47371 726-9371
John Minch, prin.
Other Schools – See Dunkirk

Poseyville, AC 812, PC 4, Posey
Metro SD of North Posey County 4-11111
PO BOX 279 47633 874-2243
B. Brenton, supt.
North Posey HS 3-00011
5418 HIGH SCHOOL RD 47633 673-4242
John Wood, prin.
North Posey JHS 2-00100
5394 HIGH SCHOOL RD 47633 673-4244
Kevin Sergesketter, prin.

Princeton, AC 812, PC 6, Gibson
North Gibson SD, RR 4 BOX 49 47670 4-11111
Keith Stewart, supt. 385-4851
Princeton Community HS 3-00011
RR 4 BOX 49 47670 385-2591
Lawrence Ramsey, prin.
Princeton Community MS 3-00100
410 E STATE ST 47670 385-2020
Jack Woods, prin.

Ramsey, AC 812, PC 2, Harrison
North Harrison Community SD 4-11111
PO BOX 8 47166 347-2407
Monty Schneider, supt.
North Harrison HS, PO BOX 37 47166 3-00011
Charlie Davis, prin. 347-3148
North Harrison MS, PO BOX 7 47166 2-00100
Jon Howerton, prin. 347-2421

Rensselaer, AC 219, PC 6, Jasper
Rensselaer Central SD 4-11111
605 W GROVE ST 47978 866-7822
Mitchell Ockermann, supt.
Rensselaer Central HS 3-00011
1204 E GRACE ST 47978 866-5175
David Day, prin.
MS, 1106 E LEOPOLD ST 47978 2-00100
Gordon Lewis, prin. 866-4661

St. Joseph's College 4-UC
PO BOX 890 47978 866-6171

Richmond, AC 317, PC 8, Wayne
Richmond Community SD 6-11111
300 HUB ETCHISON PKY 47374 973-3300
Ray Golarz, supt.
HS, 380 HUB ETCHISON PKY 47374 4-00011
John Lebo, prin. 973-3300
Hibberd MS, 900 S L ST 47374 2-00100
Dixie Robinson, prin. 973-3414
Test MS, 33 S 22ND ST 47374 3-00100
Don Warner, prin. 973-3300
Worth MS, 222 NW 7TH ST 47374 3-00100
Marla Stevens, prin. 973-3300

Earlham College
801 NATIONAL RD W   47374   4-UC
983-1200
Indiana University East
2325 CHESTER BLVD   47374   4-UC
966-8261
Ivy Tech Whitewater
2325 CHESTER BLVD   47374   3-CC
966-2656
Reid Memorial Hospital
1401 CHESTER BLVD   47374   HSP
983-3122

Rising Sun, AC 812, PC 4, Ohio
Rising Sun-Ohio County Community SD   4-11111
210 S HENRIETTA ST   47040   438-2655
Stephen Patz, supt.
HS, 210 S HENRIETTA ST   47040   2-00011
Kenneth McIntosh, prin.   438-2652

Roachdale, AC 317, PC 3, Putnam
North Putnam Community SD
Supt. — See Bainbridge
North Putnam JSHS   3-00111
RR 2 BOX 206   46172   522-1867
Alan Zerkel, prin.

Rochester, AC 219, PC 6, Fulton
Rochester Community SD   4-11111
PO BOX 108   46975   223-2159
R. Poffenbarger, supt.
Rochester Community HS   3-00011
PO BOX 108   46975   223-2176
Dennis Eller, prin.
Rochester Community MS   3-00100
PO BOX 108   46975   223-2280
Richard Cole, prin.

Rockport, AC 812, PC 4, Spencer
South Spencer County SD   4-11111
PO BOX 26   47635   649-2591
Gerald York, supt.
South Spencer HS, RR 1   47635   3-00011
Donald Metzger, prin.   649-9157
South Spencer MS   2-00100
RR 1 BOX 266   47635   649-2203
Teresa Schroeder, prin.

Rockville, AC 317, PC 5, Parke
Rockville Community SD   3-11111
602 HOWARD AVE   47872   569-5582
Richard Schelsky, supt.
JSHS, 506 N BEADLE ST   47872   2-00111
John Peitrzak, prin.   569-5686

Rossville, AC 317, PC 4, Clinton
Rossville Consolidated SD   46065   3-11111
Charles Whitlock, supt.   379-2990
JSHS   46065   2-00111
Ken Steeb, prin.   379-2551

Royal Center, AC 219, PC 3, Cass
Pioneer Regional SD   4-11111
115 S CHICAGO ST   46978   643-2605
Alan Miller, supt.
Pioneer JSHS   3-00111
US HIGHWAY 35   46978   643-3145
E. Pierson, prin.

Rushville, AC 317, PC 6, Rush
Rush Co. SD, 330 W 8TH ST   46173   5-11111
Edwin Lyskowinsky, supt.   932-4186
Rushville Consolidated HS   3-00011
1231 N PARK BLVD   46173   932-3901
Fred Smith, prin.
Rush MS, 1601 N PARK RD   46173   2-00100
Carole Storch, prin.   932-2968

Russiaville, AC 317, PC 3, Howard
Western SD, 600 W 2600 S   46979   4-11111
J. O. Interim, supt.   883-5576
Western JSHS, 600 W 2606 S   46979   3-00111
Charles Wolf, prin.   883-5541

Saint John, AC 219, PC 5, Lake
Lake Central SD   6-11111
8260 WICKER AVE   46373   365-8507
Thomas Roman, supt.
Lake Central HS   4-00011
8400 WICKER AVE   46373   365-8551
Jerry Newell, prin.
Other Schools – See Dyer, Schererville

Saint Leon, AC 812, PC 2, Dearborn
Sunman-Dearborn Community SD
Supt. — See Sunman
East Central HS, 1 TROJAN PL   47012   4-00011
James Helms, prin.   576-4811
Sunman-Dearborn MS   3-01100
8356 SCHUMAN RD   47012   576-3500
James Tucker, prin.

Saint Mary-of-the-Woods, AC 812, PC 3, Vigo

St. Mary-of-the-Woods College   3-UC
1 ST MARY OF WOODS COLL   47876
800-926-7692

Saint Meinrad, AC 812, PC 3, Spencer

St. Meinrad College   2-UC
ARCHABBEY   47577   357-6611
St. Meinrad School of Theology   47577   2-UC
357-6611

Salem, AC 812, PC 6, Washington
Salem Community SD   4-11111
500 N HARRISON ST   47167   883-4437
Lee Gold, supt.

HS, 700 N HARRISON ST   47167   3-00011
Max Bedwell, prin.   883-3904
MS, 1001 N HARRISON ST   47167   3-00100
Charles Hunt, prin.   883-3808

Schererville, AC 219, PC 7, Lake
Lake Central SD
Supt. — See Saint John
Grimmer MS, 225 W 77TH AVE   46375   3-00100
Ken Miller, prin.   865-6985

Hammond Baptist S   3-11111
134 W JOLIET ST   46375   322-5400
Robert Auclair, prin.

Scottsburg, AC 812, PC 6, Scott
Scott County SD 2   5-11111
375 E MCCLAIN AVE   47170   752-8921
William Riggs, supt.
HS, 500 S GARDNER ST   47170   3-00011
Curtis Wilson, prin.   752-8927
English MS, 145 S 3RD ST   47170   3-00100
Jerry Judd, prin.   752-8926

Sellersburg, AC 812, PC 6, Clark
West Clark Community SD   5-11111
601 RENZ AVE   47172   246-3375
Terry Smith, supt.
Silver Creek HS, 557 RENZ AVE   47172   3-00011
Michael Crabtree, prin.   246-3391
Silver Creek JHS   2-00100
495 N INDIANA AVE   47172   246-4421
Reid Bailey, prin.
Other Schools – See Borden, Henryville

Ivy Tech Southcentral   3-CC
8204 HIGHWAY 31 W   47172   246-3301

Selma, AC 317, PC 3, Delaware
Liberty-Perry Community SD   4-11111
PO BOX 337   47383   282-5615
Rich Amick, supt.
Wapahani HS   2-00011
10401 E COUNTY ROAD 167 S   47383   289-7323
Ronald Mayes, prin.
MS   2-00100
10501 E COUNTY ROAD 167 S   47383   288-7242
Donald Black, prin.

Seymour, AC 812, PC 7, Jackson
Seymour Community SD   5-11111
1638 S WALNUT ST   47274   522-3340
Robert Mahan, supt.
HS, 1350 W 2ND ST   47274   4-00011
James McCormick, prin.   522-4384
MS, 920 N OBRIEN ST   47274   3-00100
Timothy Lavery, prin.   522-5453

Sharpsville, AC 317, PC 3, Tipton
Northern Comm. Tipton County SD   4-11111
RR 2   46068 – Harry Day, supt.   963-2585
Tri Central JSHS, RR 2   46068   3-00111
Robert Blessing, prin.   963-2560

Shelbyville, AC 317, PC 7, Shelby
Shelby Eastern SD, 2451 N 600 E   46176   4-11111
John Jameson, supt.   544-2246
Other Schools – See Morristown, Waldron

Shelbyville Central SD   5-11111
54 W BROADWAY ST   46176   392-2505
James Peck, supt.
HS, 2003 S MILLER ST   46176   4-00011
Jamie Orem, prin.   398-9731
Blue River Career Ctr   Vo Tech
789 ST JOSEPH ST   46176   392-4191
Robert Hobbs, prin.
MS, 1200 W MCKAY RD   46176   3-00100
Michael Osha, prin.   392-2551

Southwestern Cons. Shelby County SD   3-11111
3406 W 600 S   46176   729-5746
James Compton, supt.
Southwestern JSHS, 3406 W 600 S   46176   2-00111
Donald Mitchell, prin.   729-5122

Sheridan, AC 317, PC 4, Hamilton
Marion-Adams SD, 509 E 4TH ST   46069   4-11111
Wayne Long, supt.   758-4172
Marion-Adams JSHS   3-00111
24185 HINESLEY RD   46069   758-4431
Allen Youmans, prin.

Shoals, AC 812, PC 3, Martin
Shoals Community SD   3-11111
RR 2 BOX 1   47581   247-2060
William Schad, supt.
Shoals Community JSHS   2-00111
RR 2 BOX 1   47581   247-2090
Stan Mosier, prin.

South Bend, AC 219, PC 9, St. Joseph
South Bend Community SD   7-11111
635 S MAIN ST   46601   282-4000
Virginia Calvin, supt.
Adams HS   4-00011
808 S TWYCKENHAM DR   46615   288-4655
Richard Phebus, prin.
Clay HS, 19131 DARDEN RD   46637   4-00011
Joann Ollman, prin.   272-3400
LaSalle HS, 2701 ELWOOD AVE   46628   4-00011
John Randall, prin.   234-1083
Riley HS, 405 E EWING AVE   46613   4-00011
George McCullough, prin.   289-5573

Washington HS   4-00011
4747 W WASHINGTON ST   46619   287-1026
Dave Kaser, prin.
Clay MS, 52900 LILY RD   46637   3-00100
James Knight, prin.   272-2405
Dickinson MS   3-00100
4404 ELWOOD AVE   46628   287-7245
Ron Johnson, prin.
Edison MS   3-00100
2701 EISENHOWER AVE   46615   233-9397
Patricia O'Connor, prin.
Jackson MS, 5001 MIAMI ST   46614   3-00100
Sharon Hurt, prin.   291-2354
Navarre MS, 4702 FORD ST   46619   3-00100
Robert Orlowski, prin.   289-7765

Christian Center S   2-11111
530 E IRELAND RD   46614   291-3292
Vicki Smith, prin.
Community Baptist Christian S   2-11111
5717 MIAMI ST   46614   291-3620
Keith Hutchison, prin.
Grace Baptist Church S   2-11111
19637 DUBOIS AVE   46637   272-2040
Dan Thomas, prin.
Indiana University at South Bend   5-UC
PO BOX 7111   46634   237-4181
Ivy Tech Northcentral   4-CC
1534 W SAMPLE ST   46619   289-7001
Memorial Hospital   HSP
615 N MICHIGAN ST   46601   284-7115
Michiana College   3-CC
1030 E JEFFERSON BLVD   46617   800-743-2447
St. Joseph HS   3-00011
1441 N MICHIGAN ST   46617   233-6137
Barbara Jemielity, prin.
Trinity S   2-00111
107 S GREENLAWN AVE   46617   287-5590
Deborah Mixell, prin.

South Whitley, AC 219, PC 4, Whitley
Whitko Community SD
Supt. — See Pierceton
Whitko HS, 1 BIG BLUE AVE   46787   3-00011
Tim Holcomb, prin.   723-5146

Speedway, AC 317, PC 7, Marion
Speedway City SD   4-11111
5335 W 25TH ST   46224   244-0236
N. Wagner, supt.
HS, 5357 W 25TH ST   46224   2-00011
John Bainbridge, prin.   244-7238
JHS, 5151 W 14TH ST   46224   2-00100
Donald Ross, prin.   244-3359

Spencer, AC 812, PC 5, Owen
Spencer-Owen Community SD   5-11111
205 E HILLSIDE AVE   47460   829-2233
Charles Pettit, supt.
Owen Valley Community HS   3-00011
RR 4 BOX 13   47460   829-2266
Daniel Cunningham, prin.
Owen Valley MS, RR 4 BOX 12   47460   3-00100
Jeff Sherfield, prin.   829-2249

Spiceland, AC 317, PC 3, Henry
South Henry SD   3-11111
6449 S CEMETERY DR   47385   987-7882
Alan Tasson, supt.
Other Schools – See Straughn

Straughn, AC 317, PC 2, Henry
South Henry SD
Supt. — See Spiceland
Tri JSHS   2-00111
6972 S STATE ROAD 103   47387   987-7988
Michael Newport, prin.

Sullivan, AC 812, PC 5, Sullivan
Southwest SD, 31 N COURT ST   47882   4-11111
Jerry Miller, supt.   268-6311
HS, 902 N SECTION ST   47882   3-00011
Ed Chickadaunce, prin.   268-6301
JHS, 820 N SECTION ST   47882   2-00100
Robert Street, prin.   268-4000

Sunman, AC 812, PC 3, Ripley
Sunman-Dearborn Community SD   5-11111
PO BOX 210   47041   623-2291
John Armbruster, supt.
Other Schools – See Saint Leon

Switz City, AC 812, PC 2, Greene
White River Valley SD   4-11111
PO BOX 1470   47465   659-1424
Stephen Campbell, supt.
White River Valley HS   2-00011
PO BOX 1470   47465   659-2286
Michael Douglass, prin.

Syracuse, AC 219, PC 5, Kosciusko
Wawasee Community SD   5-11111
12659 N SYRACUSE WEBSTER RD   46567
Henry Smith, supt.   457-3188
Wawasee HS, 1 WARRIOR PATH   46567   3-00011
Nyle Fox, prin.   457-3147
Wawasee MS   3-00100
9850 N STATE ROAD 13   46567   457-8839
Mikel Russell, prin.
Other Schools – See Milford

Tell City, AC 812, PC 6, Perry
Tell City-Troy Township SD   4-11111
837 17TH ST   47586   547-3300
Marion Chapman, supt.

HS, 900 12TH ST 47586 — 3-00011
  Dan Freed, prin. — 547-3131
JHS, 3400 TELL STREET RD 47586 — 3-00100
  Gary Stath, prin. — 547-3748

Terre Haute, AC 812, PC 8, Vigo
Vigo County SD, PO BOX 4331 47804 — 7-11111
  Charles Clark, supt. — 462-4216
Terre Haute North Vigo HS — 4-00011
  3434 MAPLE AVE 47804 — 462-4312
  C. Lisby, prin.
Terre Haute South Vigo HS — 4-00011
  3737 S 7TH ST 47802 — 462-4252
  David Cundiff, prin.
Honey Creek JHS — 3-00100
  6601 S CARLISLE ST 47802 — 462-4372
  Carlos Aballi, prin.
Otter Creek JHS — 3-00100
  4801 N LAFAYETTE ST 47805 — 462-4391
  Monica Hawkins, prin.
Rose JHS, 1275 3RD AVE 47807 — 3-00100
  Daniel Tanoos, prin. — 462-4474
Scott JHS, 2000 S 9TH ST 47802 — 2-00100
  Sandra Kelley, prin. — 462-4381
Wilson JHS, 301 S 25TH ST 47803 — 3-00100
  Sharon Pitts, prin. — 462-4396
Other Schools – See West Terre Haute

Father Gibault S — 2-00111
  5901 DIXIE BEE RD 47802 — 299-1156
  William Smith, prin.
Indiana Business College — 2-CS
  3175 S 3RD PL 47802 — 232-4458
Indiana State University — 6-UC
  217 N 6TH ST 47809 — 237-6311
Ivy Tech Wabash Valley — 4-CC
  7377 S DIXIE BEE ROAD 47802 — 299-1121
Rose-Hulman Institute of Technology — 4-UC
  5500 WABASH AVE 47803 — 877-1511
Terre Haute Christian S — 2-11111
  2500 MARGARET AVE 47802 — 238-2541
  Charles Rawsthorne, prin.

Thorntown, AC 317, PC 4, Boone
Western Boone County Community SD — 4-11111
  RR 2 BOX 58 46071 — 482-6333
  Albert Long, supt.
Western Boone JSHS, RR 2 46071 — 3-00111
  Michael Gearheart, prin. — 482-6143

Tipton, AC 317, PC 5, Tipton
Tipton Community SD — 4-11111
  221 N MAIN ST 46072 — 675-2147
  Barbara Erwin, supt.
HS, 619 S MAIN ST 46072 — 3-00011
  David Howenstine, prin. — 675-7431
MS, 817 S MAIN ST 46072 — 3-00100
  Stephen VanHorn, prin. — 675-7521

Topeka, AC 219, PC 3, Lagrange
Westview SD, 1545 S 600 W 46571 — 4-11111
  David Myers, supt. — 768-4404
Westview JSHS, 1635 S 600 W 46571 — 3-00111
  Stanley Shopa, prin. — 768-4146

Trafalgar, AC 317, PC 3, Johnson
Ninevah-Hensley-Jackson United SD — 4-11111
  PO BOX 160 46181 — 878-2100
  David Griffith, supt.
Indian Creek HS, RR 3 BOX 64 46181 — 2-00011
  Sandra Hillman, prin. — 878-2110
Indian Creek MS, RR 3 BOX 63 46181 — 2-00100
  Mike Bodine, prin. — 878-2130

Union City, AC 317, PC 5, Randolph
Randolph Eastern SD — 4-11111
  907 N PLUM ST 47390 — 964-4994
  William Smith, supt.
Union City Community HS — 2-00011
  603 N WALNUT ST 47390 — 964-4840
  Janet Caudle, prin.
West Side MS, 310 N WALNUT ST 47390 — 2-01100
  Daniel Noel, prin. — 964-4830

Union Mills, AC 219, PC 2, La Porte
South Central Community SD — 3-11111
  9808 S 600 W 46382 — 767-2263
  David Geise, supt.
South Central JSHS, 9808 S 600 W 46382 — 2-00111
  John Arnett, prin. — 767-2266

Upland, AC 317, PC 5, Grant

Taylor University — 4-UC
  500 W READE AVE 46989 — 998-5208

Valparaiso, AC 219, PC 7, Porter
East Porter Co. SD — 4-11111
  507 CAMPBELL ST 46383 — 462-5841
  Joseph Clune, supt.
Morgan Twp. JSHS — 2-00111
  209 S STATE ROAD 49 46383 — 462-5883
  Curtis Casbon, prin.
Washington Twp. JSHS — 2-00111
  383 E STATE ROAD 2 46383 — 464-3597
  Lonnie Steele, prin.
Other Schools – See Kouts

Porter Township SD, 248 S 500 W 46383 — 4-11111
  Leroy Webdell, supt. — 477-4933
Other Schools – See Boone Grove

Union Township SD
  Supt. — See Wheeler
Wheeler JSHS, 587 W 300 N 46383 — 3-00111
  Don Alkire, prin. — 759-2561
Valparaiso Community SD — 6-11111
  405 CAMPBELL ST 46383 — 531-3000
  Michael Benway, supt.
HS, 2727 CAMPBELL ST 46383 — 4-00011
  David Bess, prin. — 531-3070
Porter County Career Ctr — Vo Tech
  1005 FRANKLIN ST 46383 — 531-3170
  Kathy Spears, prin.
Franklin MS, 605 CAMPBELL ST 46383 — 3-00100
  Glenn Gambel, prin. — 531-3020
Jefferson MS — 3-00100
  1600 ROOSEVELT RD 46383 — 531-3140
  Paul Knauff, prin.

Ivy Tech Valparaiso — 3-CC
  2401 VALLEY DR 46383 — 464-8514
Porter Memorial Hospital — HSP
  814 LAPORTE AVE 46383 — 465-4600
South Haven Christian S — 2-11111
  780 JUNIPER RD 46383 — 759-5313
  Stephen Bensing, prin.
Valparaiso Technical Institute — 2-CS
  1 CENTER ST 46383 — 462-2191
Valparaiso University 46383 — 5-UC
  464-5115

Veedersburg, AC 317, PC 4, Fountain
Southeast Fountain SD — 4-11111
  RR 2 BOX 10A 47987 — 294-2254
  Robert Baker, supt.
Fountain Central JSHS, RR 2 47987 — 3-00111
  Larry Sager, prin. — 294-2206

Versailles, AC 812, PC 4, Ripley
Southeastern Career SD — 1-00000
  PO BOX 156 47042 – O. Pitts, supt. — 689-5253
Southeastern Career Ctr — Vo Tech
  PO BOX 156 47042 — 689-5253
  James Rogers, prin.

South Ripley Community SD — 4-11111
  PO BOX 690 47042 — 689-6282
  Stanley Nay, supt.
South Ripley JSHS — 3-00111
  PO BOX 218 47042 — 689-5303
  Theodore Ahaus, prin.

Vevay, AC 812, PC 4, Switzerland
Switzerland County SD — 4-11111
  305 W SEMINARY ST 47043 — 427-2611
  Perry Glancy, supt.
Switzerland County JSHS — 3-00111
  1020 W MAIN ST 47043 — 427-2626
  John Thomas, prin.

Vincennes, AC 812, PC 7, Knox
South Knox SD
  Supt. — See Monroe City
South Knox HS, RR 3 BOX 80 47591 — 2-00011
  Clyde Leonard, prin. — 726-4450
South Knox MS, RR 3 BOX 80 47591 — 2-00100
  William Amers, prin. — 726-4425

Vincennes Community SD — 5-11111
  PO BOX 1267 47591 — 882-4844
  Dennis Brooks, supt.
Lincoln HS, PO BOX 216 47591 — 3-00011
  James Pittman, prin. — 882-8480
Clark MS, 500 BUNTIN ST 47591 — 3-00100
  Paul Couchenour, prin. — 882-5172

Good Samaritan Hospital — HSP
  520 S 7TH ST 47591 — 885-3195
Indiana Business College — 2-CS
  1431 WILLOW ST 47591 — 882-2550
Rivet HS, 210 BARNETT ST 47591 — 2-00111
  Sr. Ann Mause, prin. — 882-6501
Vincennes University — 6-CC
  1002 N 1ST ST 47591 — 882-3350

Wabash, AC 219, PC 7, Wabash
Heartland Career Center SD — 1-00000
  PO BOX 606 46992 — 563-7481
  Neal Pedro, supt.
Heartland Career Ctr — Vo Tech
  PO BOX 606 46992 — 563-7481
  Robert Plunkett, prin.

Metro SD of Wabash County — 5-11111
  282 N WABASH ST 46992 — 563-7438
  David Herbert, supt.
Northfield JSHS, 154 E 200 N 46992 — 3-00111
  William Neale, prin. — 563-3522
Southwood JSHS — 3-00111
  564 E STATE ROAD 124 46992 — 563-2157
  Tom Mitchell, prin.
Whites JSHS, 5233 S 50 E 46992 — 2-00111
  Lewis Curless, prin. — 563-1158
Wabash CSD, PO BOX 744 46992 — 4-11111
  Randy Greene, supt. — 563-2151
HS, 580 N MIAMI ST 46992 — 3-00011
  Stephen Eikenberry, prin. — 563-4131
MS, 150 COLERAIN ST 46992 — 2-00100
  Jan Roland, prin. — 563-4137

Emmanuel Christian S — 2-11111
  4652 S 100 W 46992 — 563-3009
  Douglass Phillips, prin.

Wakarusa, AC 219, PC 4, Elkhart
Wa-Nee Community SD
  Supt. — See Nappanee
MS, PO BOX 367 46573 — 2-00100
  Carl Wesolek, prin. — 862-2710

Waldron, AC 317, PC 3, Shelby
Shelby Eastern SD
  Supt. — See Shelbyville
JSHS, PO BOX 128 46182 — 2-00111
  James Jaros, prin. — 525-6822

Walkerton, AC 219, PC 4, St. Joseph
John Glenn SD — 4-11111
  506 ROOSEVELT RD 46574 — 586-3129
  David McKee, supt.
Glenn HS, 100 JOHN GLENN DR 46574 — 3-00011
  Michael Shuler, prin. — 586-3195
Urey MS, 406 ADAMS ST 46574 — 2-00100
  Richard Reese, prin. — 586-3184

Walton, AC 219, PC 4, Cass
Southeastern SD, PO BOX 320 46994 — 4-11111
  Harry Cords, supt. — 626-2525
Cass JSHS, PO BOX 410 46994 — 3-00111
  William Isaacs, prin. — 626-2511

Warsaw, AC 219, PC 7, Kosciusko
Warsaw Community SD — 6-11111
  PO BOX 288 46581 — 267-3238
  Lee Harman, supt.
Warsaw Community HS — 4-00011
  1 TIGER LN 46580 — 267-5174
  Paul Crousore, prin.
Edgewood MS, 900 S UNION ST 46580 — 2-00100
  Gerald Chabot, prin. — 267-5828
Lakeview MS, 848 E SMITH ST 46580 — 3-00100
  Carolyn Mock, prin. — 269-7211

Washington, AC 812, PC 7, Daviess
Twin Rivers Vo SD — 1-00000
  301 E SOUTH ST 47501 — 254-1189
  Melvin Wood, supt.
Twin Rivers Vo S — Vo Tech
  301 E SOUTH ST 47501 — 254-1189
  Melvin Wood, prin.
Washington Community SD — 4-11111
  301 E SOUTH ST 47501 — 254-5536
  Tom Miller, supt.
HS, 608 E WALNUT ST 47501 — 3-00011
  Bruce Hatton, prin. — 254-3860
JHS, 210 NE 6TH ST 47501 — 2-00100
  Gary Twomey, prin. — 254-2682

Washington Catholic HS — 2-00011
  201 NE 2ND ST 47501 — 254-2050
  Dennis Bradley, prin.
Washington MS, 200 W MAIN ST 47501 — 2-00100
  Dennis Bradley, prin. — 254-2355

Waterloo, AC 219, PC 4, De Kalb
DeKalb County Central United SD — 5-11111
  PO BOX 420 46793 — 925-3914
  Keith Perry, supt.
DeKalb HS — 4-00011
  3424 COUNTY ROAD 427 46793 — 925-2363
  Dale Hummer, prin.
DeKalb MS — 3-00100
  3338 COUNTY ROAD 427 46793 — 925-0053
  Thomas Sanborn, prin.

Westfield, AC 317, PC 5, Hamilton
Westfield-Washington SD — 4-11111
  322 W MAIN ST 46074 — 896-2841
  Jeffrey Heier, supt.
Westfield-Washington HS — 2-00011
  326 W MAIN ST 46074 — 896-2841
  James Pantos, prin.
MS, 328 W MAIN ST 46074 — 3-01100
  Steve Psikula, prin. — 896-2841

West Lafayette, AC 317, PC 8, Tippecanoe
Tippecanoe SD
  Supt. — See Lafayette
Harrison HS, 5701 N 50 W 47906 — 4-00011
  James Garver, prin. — 463-3511
Klondike MS, 3307 KLONDIKE RD 47906 — 2-00100
  Anthony Guth, prin. — 463-2544
West Lafayette Community SD — 4-11111
  1130 N SALISBURY ST 47906 — 743-9631
  Thomas Fihe, supt.
HS, 1105 N GRANT ST 47906 — 3-00011
  Anne Koivo, prin. — 743-9502
JHS, GRANT AND LESLIE 47906 — 2-00100
  Anne Koivo, prin. — 743-1021

Purdue University — 8-UC
  SCHLEMAN HALL 47907 — 494-4600

West Lebanon, AC 317, PC 3, Warren
Metro SD of Warren County
  Supt. — See Williamsport
Seeger Memorial JSHS, RR 1 47991 — 3-00111
  Gary Kiger, prin. — 893-4445

West Terre Haute, AC 812, PC 4, Vigo
Vigo County SD
  Supt. — See Terre Haute
West Vigo HS — 3-00011
  4590 W SARAH MYERS DR 47885 — 462-4282
  James Jackson, prin.
West Vigo MS — 2-00100
  4750 W SARAH MYERS DR 47885 — 462-4361
  Gene Lowe, prin.

Westville, AC 219, PC 6, La Porte
New Durham Township SD
  Supt. — See La Porte
  JSHS, VALPARAISO ST 46391   2-00111
    Judy Williamson, prin.   785-2531

Purdue University   4-UC
  1401 S US HIGHWAY 421 46391   785-5200

Wheatfield, AC 219, PC 3, Jasper
Kankakee Valley SD   5-11111
  PO BOX 278 46392   987-4711
  Iran Floyd, supt.
Kankakee Valley HS   3-00011
  RR 3 BOX 182 46392   956-3143
  Dale Osburn, prin.
Kankakee Valley MS   3-00100
  RR 3 BOX 182 46392   956-3143
  Wayne Crawford, prin.

Wheeler, AC 219, PC 3, Porter
Union Township SD   4-11111
  PO BOX 246 46393   759-2531
  Stephen Hewlett, supt.
Other Schools – See Valparaiso

Whiteland, AC 317, PC 4, Johnson
Clark-Pleasant Community SD   4-11111
  50 CENTER ST 46184   535-7579
  Rex Sager, supt.
Whiteland Community High School   3-00011
  300 MAIN ST 46184   535-7562
  Robert Smith, prin.
Clark Pleasant MS, 222 TRACY ST 46184   3-00100
  Anne West, prin.   535-7121

Whiting, AC 219, PC 6, Lake
Hammond CSD
  Supt. — See Hammond

Clark JSHS, 1921 DAVIS AVE 46394   4-00111
  Aletta Hicks, prin.   659-3522

Whiting CSD, 1500 CENTER ST 46394   3-11111
  Gerald Novak, supt.   659-0656
JSHS, 1751 OLIVER ST 46394   2-00111
  Ronald Blake, prin.   659-0255

Calumet College   3-UC
  2400 NEW YORK AVE 46394   473-7770

Williamsport, AC 317, PC 4, Warren
Metro SD of Warren County   4-11111
  101 N MONROE ST 47993   762-3364
  Roy Stroud, supt.
Other Schools – See West Lebanon

Winamac, AC 219, PC 4, Pulaski
Eastern Pulaski Community SD   4-11111
  711 SCHOOL DR 46996   946-4010
  Robert Klitzman, supt.
Winamac Community HS   2-00011
  715 SCHOOL DR 46996   946-6151
  Wayne Showalter, prin.
Winamac Community MS   2-00100
  715 SCHOOL DR 46996   946-6525
  Linda Leasure, prin.

Winchester, AC 317, PC 6, Randolph
Randolph Central SD   4-11111
  PO BOX 27 47394   584-1401
  Charles Bragg, supt.
Winchester Community HS   3-00011
  700 N UNION ST 47394   584-8201
  David Gibson, prin.
Driver MS, RR 3 BOX 45 47394   2-00100
  Thomas Osborn, prin.   584-4671

Winona Lake, AC 219, PC 5, Kosciusko

Grace College   3-UC
  200 SEMINARY DR 46590   372-5101
Grace Theological Seminary 46590   1-UC
     372-5100

Wolcott, AC 219, PC 3, White
Tri-County SD, RR 2 BOX 73A 47995   3-11111
  Fred Minnick, supt.   279-2418
Tri-County JSHS, RR 1 BOX 130A 47995   2-00111
  Wayne Pearl, prin.   279-2105

Woodburn, AC 219, PC 4, Allen
East Allen County SD
  Supt. — See New Haven
Woodlan JSHS   3-00111
  17215 WOODBURN RD 46797   632-4203
  Philip Kurtz, prin.

Yorktown, AC 317, PC 5, Delaware
Mt. Pleasant Township Community SD   4-11111
  8800 W SMITH ST 47396   759-8230
  Jerome Secttor, supt.
HS, 8800 W SMITH ST 47396   3-00011
  James Mervilde, prin.   759-7706
MS, 8800 W SMITH ST 47396   2-00100
  David Uptgraff, prin.   759-6785

Zionsville, AC 317, PC 6, Boone
Eagle-Union Community SD   5-11111
  690 BEECH ST 46077   873-2858
  John McKinney, supt.
Zionsville Community HS   3-00011
  1000 WHITESTOWN RD 46077   873-3355
  Russell Hodgkin, prin.
MS, 900 WHITESTOWN RD 46077   3-00100
  Suzanne Wetherald, prin.   873-2426

IOWA

STATE DEPARTMENT OF PUBLIC INSTRUCTION
Grimes State Office Building
E. 14th & Grand Sts., Des Moines 50319
(515) 281-5294

Acting Director of Education	Ted Stilwill
Administrator Elementary & Secondary Education	Ted Stilwill
Administrator Educational Services	Sue Donielson
Administrator Vocational Rehabilitation Services	Margaret Knudsen
Administrator Financial & Information Services	Leland Tack

STATE BOARD OF EDUCATION
E. 14th & Grand Sts., Des Moines 50319

President   Ron McGauvran

AREA EDUCATION AGENCIES

Keystone AEA
  Donald Mueller   319-245-1480
  RR 2 BOX 19, Elkader 52043
Northern Trails AEA
  Dale Jensen   515-357-6125
  PO BOX M, Clear Lake 50428
Lakeland AEA
  Albert Wood, HWY 18 & 2ND ST   712-424-3211
  Cylinder 50528
AEA.4
  J. Hayden, 102 S MAIN AVE   712-722-4378
  Sioux Center 51250
Arrowhead AEA
  Don Ambroson   515-576-7434
  PO BOX 1399, Fort Dodge 50501

AEA 6
  R. Ploeger, 909 S 12TH ST   515-753-3564
  Marshalltown 50158
AEA 7
  R. C. Dickinson   319-273-8200
  3712 CEDAR HEIGHTS DR
  Cedar Falls 50613
Mississippi Bend AEA
  Glen Pelecky   319-359-1371
  729 21ST ST, Bettendorf 52722
Grant Wood AEA
  Ron Fielder, 4401 6TH ST SW   319-399-6700
  Cedar Rapids 52404
Heartland AEA
  Wayne Rand   515-270-9030
  6500 CORPORATE DR
  Johnston 50131

Western Hills AEA
  Bruce Hopkins   712-274-6000
  1520 MORNINGSIDE AVE
  Sioux City 51106
Loess Hills AEA
  James Blietz, PO BOX 1109   712-366-0503
  Council Bluffs 51502
Green Valley AEA
  Bob Steele, 1405 N LINCOLN ST   515-782-8443
  Creston 50801
Southern Prairie AEA
  D. G. Roseberry   515-682-8591
  900 TERMINAL AVE
  Ottumwa 52501
Great River AEA
  Robert Bonta   319-753-6561
  PO BOX 1065, Burlington 52601

PUBLIC, PRIVATE AND CATHOLIC SECONDARY SCHOOLS

Ackley, AC 515, PC 4, Hardin
Ackley-Geneva Community SD — 3-11111
511 STATE ST 50601 — 847-2611
Kirk Nelson, supt.
Ackley-Geneva JSHS — 2-00111
4TH & HARDIN 50601 — 847-2633
Steve Vanderpol, prin.

Adair, AC 515, PC 3, Adair
Adair-Casey Community SD — 2-11111
RR 2 BOX 107 50002 — 746-2241
Roger Myers, supt.
Adair-Casey JSHS 50002 — 2-00111
Terry Hutchings, prin. — 746-2241

Adel, AC 515, PC 5, Dallas
Adel-De Soto-Minburn Community SD — 4-11111
801 S 8TH ST 50003 — 993-4283
Tim Hoffman, supt.
Adel-De Soto-Minburn HS — 2-00011
801 S 8TH ST 50003 — 993-4584
Greg Detimmerman, prin.
Adel-De Soto-Minburn MS — 2-00100
215 N 11TH ST 50003 — 993-4778
William Kimber, prin.

Afton, AC 515, PC 3, Union
East Union Community SD — 3-11111
1000 EAGLE DR 50830 — 347-5215
Richard Turner, supt.
East Union JSHS, 1000 EAGLE DR 50830 — 2-00111
James Walter, prin. — 347-8421

Akron, AC 712, PC 4, Plymouth
Akron Westfield Community SD — 3-11111
KERR DRIVE 51001 — 568-2616
William Hellirich, supt.
Akron Westfield HS, KERR DRIVE 51001 — 2-00011
Bruce Michalsky, prin. — 568-2020
Akron Westfield MS, KERR DRIVE 51001 — 2-01100
Marian Rasmussen, prin. — 568-3322

Albert City, AC 712, PC 3, Buena Vista
Albert City-Truesdale Community SD — 2-11111
PO BOX 98 50510 — 843-5551
William Hullinger, supt.
Albert City-Truesdale JSHS — 2-00111
PO BOX 98 50510 — 843-5551
Charles Woodworth, prin.

Albia, AC 515, PC 5, Monroe
Albia Community SD — 4-11111
120 BENTON AVE E 52531 — 932-5165
David Sextro, supt.
HS, 503 B AVE E 52531 — 2-00011
Kenneth Walker, prin. — 932-2161
MS, 222 N 2ND ST 52531 — 2-01100
Phillip Brock, prin. — 932-2116

Alburnett, AC 319, PC 2, Linn
Alburnett Community SD 52202 — 3-11111
Robert Rampulla, supt. — 842-2261
JSHS 52202 — 2-00111
Raymond Cull, prin. — 842-2263

Alden, AC 515, PC 3, Hardin
Alden Community SD — 2-11111
PO BOX 48 50006 — 859-3395
James Jess, supt.
Alden Community JSHS — 2-00111
PO BOX 48 50006 — 859-3394
Michael Niece, prin.

Algona, AC 515, PC 6, Kossuth
Algona Community SD — 4-11111
200 N PHILLIPS ST 50511 — 295-3528
Harold Prior, supt.
HS, 600 S HALE ST 50511 — 2-00011
Douglas Kennedy, prin. — 295-7207
Laing MS, 213 S HARLAN ST 50511 — 2-00100
Gregory Stewart, prin. — 295-9447

Garrigan HS, 1224 N MCCOY ST 50511 — 2-00011
Eugene Meister, prin. — 295-3521

Alleman, AC 515, PC 2, Polk
North Polk Community SD — 3-11111
PO BOX 69 50007 — 685-3014
George Cain, supt.
North Polk JSHS, PO BOX 69 50007 — 2-00111
Gary Fjelland, prin. — 685-3528

Allison, AC 319, PC 4, Butler
Allison-Bristow Community SD — 2-11111
513 BIRCH 50602 — 267-2205
Warren Davison, supt.
Allison-Bristow JSHS — 2-00111
PO BOX 428 50602 — 267-2552
Daniel Moore, prin.

Alta, AC 712, PC 4, Buena Vista
Alta Community SD — 3-11111
101 W 5TH ST 51002 — 284-1010
Thomas Narak, supt.
JSHS, 101 W 5TH ST 51002 — 2-00111
R. Mueller, prin. — 284-1331

Alton, AC 712, PC 4, Sioux
Floyd Valley Community SD
Supt. — See Orange City
MS, 1108 5TH AVE 51003 — 2-00100
Terry Tomke, prin. — 756-4128

Ames, AC 515, PC 8, Story
Ames Community SD — 5-11111
120 S KELLOGG AVE 50010 — 232-3400
Ronald Rice, supt.
HS, 1921 RIDGEWOOD AVE 50010 — 4-00011
Charles Achter, prin. — 232-8440
MS, 321 STATE AVE 50014 — 3-00100
John Kinley, prin. — 292-8200

Iowa State University 50011 — 7-UC
294-2042

Anamosa, AC 319, PC 6, Jones
Anamosa Community SD — 4-11111
200 S GARNAVILLO ST 52205 — 462-4321
Randall McMaulley, supt.
HS, SADIE ST 52205 — 2-00011
Andrew Ward, prin. — 462-3594
MS, 200 S GARNAVILLO ST 52205 — 2-01100
Walter Fortney, prin. — 462-3553

Andrew, AC 319, PC 2, Jackson
Andrew Community SD — 2-11111
PO BOX 130 52030 — 672-3221
David Pappone, supt.
JSHS, PO BOX 130 52030 — 2-00111
Robert Baxter, prin. — 672-3221

Anita, AC 712, PC 4, Cass
Anita Community SD — 2-11111
PO BOX 337 50020 — 762-3231
Craig Artist, supt.
JSHS, PO BOX 337 50020 — 2-00111
Richard Kluver, prin. — 762-3231

Ankeny, AC 515, PC 7, Polk
Ankeny Community SD — 5-11111
PO BOX 189 50021 — 965-9600
Ben Norman, supt.
HS, 1302 N ANKENY BLVD 50021 — 4-00011
Gary Ratigan, prin. — 965-9630
Parkview MS — 3-00100
105 NW PLEASANT ST 50021 — 965-9640
Scott Osborn, prin.

Des Moines Area Community College — 6-CC
2006 S ANKENY BLVD 50021 — 964-6260
Faith Baptist Bible College & Seminary — 2-UC
1900 NW 4TH ST 50021 — 800-352-0147

Anthon, AC 712, PC 3, Woodbury
Anthon-Oto Community SD — 2-11111
110 W DIVISION ST 51004 — 373-5246
Dennis Johnson, supt.
Anthon-Oto JSHS — 2-00111
110 W DIVISION ST 51004 — 373-5244
Darrell Kirstine, prin.

Aplington, AC 319, PC 4, Butler
Aplington Community SD — 2-11100
215 10TH ST 50604 — 347-2394
Virgil Goodrich, supt.
Aplington/Parkersburg MS — 2-00100
215 10TH ST 50604 — 347-6621
Christine Day, prin.

Arlington, AC 319, PC 99, Fayette
Starmont Community SD — 3-11111
3202 40TH ST 50606 — 933-4598
Gary Stumberg, supt.
Starmont HS, 3202 40TH ST 50606 — 2-00011
Thomas Emerson, prin. — 933-2219
Starmont MS, 3202 40TH ST 50606 — 2-01100
Del Brouwer, prin. — 933-4902

Armstrong, AC 712, PC 4, Emmet
Armstrong-Ringsted Community SD — 3-11111
PO BOX 75 50514 — 864-3550
Charles Missman, supt.
Armstrong-Ringsted HS — 2-00011
PO BOX 75 50514 — 864-3542
Donald Gerlach, prin.
Other Schools – See Ringsted

Arthur, AC 712, PC 2, Ida
Odebolt-Arthur Community SD
Supt. — See Odebolt
Odebolt-Arthur MS 51431 — 2-00100
Rodger Miller, prin. — 367-2247

Atlantic, AC 712, PC 6, Cass
Atlantic Community SD — 4-11111
1100 LINN ST 50022 — 243-4252
Kenneth Fossen, supt.
HS, 1100 LINN ST 50022 — 2-00011
Roger Herring, prin. — 243-5358
Schuler JHS, 1100 LINN ST 50022 — 2-00100
Gere Huebner, prin. — 243-1330

Audubon, AC 712, PC 5, Audubon
Audubon Community SD — 3-11111
800 3RD AVE 50025 — 563-2607
Quentin Reifenrath, supt.
JSHS, 800 3RD AVE 50025 — 2-00111
Robert Lowe, prin. — 563-2607

Aurelia, AC 712, PC 4, Cherokee
Aurelia Community SD — 2-11111
3RD & ASH ST 51005 — 434-2284
Marlin Lode, supt.
JSHS, 3RD & ASH ST 51005 — 2-01111
Jack Johnson, prin. — 434-5595

Avoca, AC 712, PC 4, Pottawattamie
Hancock-Avoca Community School District — 2-11011
300 GRANT ST 51521 — 343-6304
Rodney Montang, supt.
HS, 300 GRANT ST 51521 — 2-00011
Ned Cox, prin. — 343-6304

Barnum, AC 515, PC 2, Webster
Manson Northwest Webster Community SD
Supt. — See Manson
Manson-Northwest Webster MS — 2-00100
303 PIERCE ST 50518 — 542-3212
Robert Cordes, prin.

Battle Creek, AC 712, PC 3, Ida
Battle Creek Community SD — 2-11100
600 CHESTNUT ST 51006 — 365-4354
Todd Wennerstrom, supt.
MS, 600 CHESTNUT ST 51006 — 1-00100
Steven McDermott, prin. — 365-4754

Baxter, AC 515, PC 3, Jasper
Baxter Community SD — 2-11111
PO BOX 189 50028 — 227-3102
Neil Seales, supt.
JSHS, PO BOX 189 50028 — 2-00111
Donna Deines, prin. — 227-3103

Bayard, AC 712, PC 3, Guthrie
Coon Rapids-Bayard Community SD
Supt. — See Coon Rapids
Coon Rapids-Bayard MS — 2-01100
PO BOX 309 50029 — 651-2686
Terris Vitzthum, prin.

Bedford, AC 712, PC 4, Taylor
Bedford Community SD — 3-11111
1006 ILLINOIS ST 50833 — 523-2656
Joe Drake, supt.
Bedford Community JSHS — 2-00111
1006 ILLINOIS ST 50833 — 523-2114
Mike Stanley, prin.

Belle Plaine, AC 319, PC 5, Benton
Belle Plaine Community SD — 3-11111
807 16TH ST 52208 — 444-3611
Richard Hobart, supt.
HS, 610 13TH AVE 52208 — 2-00011
John Long, prin. — 444-3720
Lincoln JHS, 1511 9TH AVE 52208 — 2-00100
John Long, prin. — 444-3631

Bellevue, AC 319, PC 4, Jackson
Bellevue Community SD — 3-11111
PO BOX 46 52031 — 872-4001
C. Hammann, supt.
JSHS, PO BOX 46 52031 — 2-00111
Gary Feuerbach, prin. — 872-4001

Marquette HS, 502 FRANKLIN ST 52031 — 2-00011
James Squiers, prin. — 872-3356

Belmond, AC 515, PC 5, Wright
Belmond Community SD — 3-11011
411 10TH AVE NE 50421 — 444-3930
Donald Cleveland, supt.
Belmond/Klemme Community HS — 2-00011
411 10TH AVE NE 50421 — 444-3930
Stephen Hennesy, prin.

Bennett, AC 319, PC 2, Cedar
Bennett Community SD, PO BOX D 52721 — 2-11111
Thomas Wirtz, supt. — 893-2226
JSHS, PO BOX D 52721 — 2-00111
Paul Olson, prin. — 893-2228

Bettendorf, AC 319, PC 8, Scott
Bettendorf Community SD — 5-11111
3311 CENTRAL AVE 52722 — 359-3681
Michael Coury, supt.
HS, 3333 18TH ST 52722 — 4-00011
Thomas Castle, prin. — 332-7001
MS, 2030 MIDDLE RD 52722 — 4-00100
Stacie Rissmann-Joyce, prin. — 359-3686

Scott Community College — 4-CC
500 BELMONT RD 52722 — 322-5015

Blairsburg, AC 515, PC 2, Hamilton
Northeast Hamilton Community SD — 2-11111
50034 – Harvey Hindley, supt. — 325-6202
Northeast Hamilton HS 50034 — 2-00111
Dennis Peters, prin. — 325-6234
Northeast Hamilton MS 50034 — 2-01100
Dennis Peters, prin. — 325-6234

Blakesburg, AC 515, PC 2, Wapello
Blakesburg Community SD 52536 — 2-11100
Connie Maxson, supt. — 938-2233
MS, PO BOX 68 52536 — 2-01100
David Wilmer, prin. — 938-2203

Bloomfield, AC 515, PC 5, Davis
Davis County Community SD — 4-11111
200 W LOCUST ST 52537 — 664-2200
Arvid Goettsche, supt.
Davis Co. Community HS — 3-00011
106 N EAST ST 52537 — 664-2200
Rob Pickard, prin.
Davis Co. MS, 500 E NORTH ST 52537 — 2-01100
Michael Bumgarner, prin. — 664-2200

Bode, AC 515, PC 2, Humboldt
Twin Rivers Community SD   2-11011
    PO BOX 153   50519   379-1645
    William Crumbaugh, supt.
Twin Rivers HS, PO BOX 153   50519   2-00011
    Don Hasenkamp, prin.   379-1526

Bonaparte, AC 319, PC 2, Van Buren
Harmony Community SD   3-11111
    PO BOX 130   52620   592-3600
    Alan Marshall, supt.
Other Schools – See Farmington

Bondurant, AC 515, PC 4, Polk
Bondurant-Farrar Community SD   3-11111
    3RD & GARFIELD   50035   967-7819
    Roger Ohde, supt.
Bondurant-Farrar JSHS   2-00011
    4TH & GARFIELD   50035   967-3711
    R. Moore, prin.

Boone, AC 515, PC 7, Boone
Boone Community SD, 500 7TH ST   50036   4-11111
    Donald Hansen, supt.   433-0750
HS, 500 7TH ST   50036   3-00011
    David Kapfer, prin.   433-0890
JHS, 500 7TH ST   50036   2-00100
    David Kapfer, prin.   433-0890

Des Moines Area Community College   4-CC
    1125 HANCOCK DR   50036   432-7203

Britt, AC 515, PC 4, Hancock
Britt Community SD   3-11011
    420 9TH AVE SW   50423   843-3863
    Ted Runyan, supt.
West Hancock HS   2-00011
    420 9TH AVE SW   50423   843-3864
    Jack Fisher, prin.

Brooklyn, AC 515, PC 4, Poweshiek
Brooklyn-Guernsey-Malcom Community SD   3-11111
    52211 – Maurice McDonald, supt.   522-7058
Brooklyn-Guernsey-Malcom JSHS   52211   2-00111
    Duane Munson, prin.   522-7058

Buffalo Center, AC 515, PC 4, Winnebago
Buffalo Center-Rake-Lakota Community SD   2-11011
    111 3RD AVE NW   50424   562-2921
    Ronald Pilgrim, supt.
North Iowa HS, 111 3RD AVE NW   50424   2-00011
    Kenneth Williams, prin.   562-2525

Burlington, AC 319, PC 8, Des Moines
Burlington Community SD   6-11111
    1429 WEST AVE   52601   753-6791
    James Mitchell, supt.
Burlington Community HS   4-00011
    421 TERRACE DR   52601   753-2211
    Berry Crist, prin.
Madison MS, 2132 MADISON AVE   52601   2-00100
    John Smull, prin.   753-6253
Mann MS, 811 WHITE ST   52601   2-00100
    Frances Disselhorst, prin.   753-5161
Oak Street MS, 903 OAK ST   52601   2-00100
    Robert Cameron, prin.   753-6773

Notre Dame HS   2-00011
    702 S ROOSEVELT AVE   52601   754-8431
    Sr. Celine Schumacher, prin.

Burnside, AC 515, PC 2, Webster
Southeast Webster Community SD   3-11111
    GENERAL DELIVERY   50521   359-2235
    Allan Lyons, supt.
Southeast Webster HS   2-00011
    GENERAL DELIVERY   50521   359-2235
    Ralph Johnson, prin.
Other Schools – See Dayton

Bussey, AC 515, PC 2, Marion
Twin Cedars Community SD   3-11111
    PO BOX 73   50044   944-5241
    Larry Fudge, supt.
Twin Cedars JSHS, RR 1   50044   2-00111
    Richard Heck, prin.   944-5243

Calmar, AC 319, PC 4, Winneshiek
South Winneshiek Community SD   3-11111
    PO BOX 430   52132   562-3269
    Russell Green, supt.
South Winneshiek HS   2-00011
    PO BOX 430   52132   562-3226
    David Ziesmer, prin.
Other Schools – See Ossian

Northeast Iowa Technical Institute   4-CC
    PO BOX 400   52132   562-3263

Camanche, AC 319, PC 5, Clinton
Camanche Community SD   4-11111
    PO BOX 160   52730   259-3000
    Larry Dennis, supt.
HS, PO BOX 160   52730   2-00011
    James Pearson, prin.   259-3008
MS, PO BOX 160   52730   2-01100
    Gary Cross, prin.   259-3014

Cantril, AC 319, PC 2, Van Buren
Fox Valley Community SD   2-11111
    SECOND & SUMMER   52542   397-2374
    William Mertens, supt.
Other Schools – See Milton

Carlisle, AC 515, PC 5, Warren
Carlisle Community SD   4-11111
    430 SCHOOL ST   50047   989-3589
    Ben Halupnik, supt.
JSHS, 430 SCHOOL ST   50047   3-00111
    Leroy Powell, prin.   989-0831

Carroll, AC 712, PC 6, Carroll
Carroll Community SD   4-11111
    2809 N GRANT RD   51401   792-5540
    Dale Proctor, supt.
HS, 2809 N GRANT RD   51401   2-00011
    Gary Currie, prin.   792-5542
MS, 1026 N ADAMS ST   51401   2-01100
    Steven Schulz, prin.   792-5543

Des Moines Area Community College   3-CC
    906 N GRANT RD   51401   792-1755
Kuemper HS, 109 S CLARK ST   51401   3-00011
    Keith Guy, prin.   792-3596

Carson, AC 712, PC 3, Pottawattamie
Riverside Community SD   3-11111
    PO BOX 218   51525   484-2212
    David Thomas, supt.
Riverside Community MS   2-00100
    PO BOX 218   51525   484-2291
    Richard Graves, prin.
Other Schools – See Oakland

Cascade, AC 319, PC 4, Dubuque
Western Dubuque Community SD
    Supt. — See Farley
Cascade JSHS   2-00111
    505 JOHNSON ST NW   52033   852-3201
    James O'Meara, prin.

Cedar Falls, AC 319, PC 8, Black Hawk
Cedar Falls Community SD   6-11111
    1002 W 1ST ST   50613   277-8800
    Daniel Smith, supt.
SHS, 1015 DIVISION ST   50613   4-00001
    Dean Dreyer, prin.   277-3100
Holmes JHS, 505 HOLMES DR   50613   3-00110
    Lee Mickey, prin.   277-7830
Peet JHS, 525 E SEERLEY BLVD   50613   3-00110
    Mark Farland, prin.   266-2657

American Institute of Commerce   2-CS
    2302 W 1ST ST   50613   277-0200
University of Northern Iowa   50614   7-UC
    273-2566

Cedar Rapids, AC 319, PC 9, Linn
Cedar Rapids Community SD   7-11111
    346 2ND AVE SW   52404   398-2000
    Steve Chambliss, supt.
Jefferson HS, 1243 20TH ST SW   52404   4-00011
    Robert Tesar, prin.   398-2435
Kennedy HS, 4545 WENIG RD NE   52402   4-00011
    Gregory Reed, prin.   398-2251
Metro HS, 1212 7TH ST SE   52401   3-00011
    Mary Wilcynski, prin.   398-2193
Washington HS   4-00011
    2205 FOREST DR SE   52403   398-2161
    Ralph Plagman, prin.
Franklin MS, 300 20TH ST NE   52402   3-00100
    Fred Althoff, prin.   398-2452
Harding MS, 4801 GOLF ST NE   52402   3-00100
    Sandra Ledford, prin.   398-2254
McKinley MS, 620 10TH ST SE   52403   3-00100
    Tom Van Deest, prin.   398-2348
Roosevelt MS, 300 13TH ST NW   52405   3-00100
    Carolyn Hack, prin.   398-2153
Taft MS, 5200 E AVE NW   52405   3-00100
    Alinda Hakanson, prin.   398-2243

College Community SD   5-11111
    401 76TH AVE SW   52404   848-5201
    Mick Starcevich, supt.
Prairie HS, 401 76TH AVE SW   52404   3-00011
    Kenneth Steine, prin.   848-5340
Prairie JHS, 401 76TH AVE SW   52404   3-00100
    David Crisman, prin.   848-5310

Coe College   4-UC
    1220 1ST AVE NE   52402   399-8686
Hamilton Business College   2-CS
    1924 D ST SW   52404   363-0481
Kirkwood Community College   6-CC
    PO BOX 2068   52406   398-5517
La Salle HS, 3700 1ST AVE NW   52405   2-00011
    Kerry Giongobbi, prin.   396-7791
Mt. Mercy College   4-UC
    1330 ELMHURST DR NE   52402   363-8213
Regis HS, 735 PRAIRIE DR NE   52402   2-00011
    Jeff Henderson, prin.   365-6991
St. Luke's Hospital   HSP
    1026 A AVE NE   52402   369-7204

Center Point, AC 319, PC 4, Linn
Center Point-Urbana Community SD   3-11111
    PO BOX 296   52213   849-2262
    Richard Whitehead, supt.
Center Point-Urbana HS   2-00011
    613 SUMMIT ST   52213   849-1102
    David Hanneman, prin.
Other Schools – See Urbana

Centerville, AC 515, PC 6, Appanoose
Centerville Community SD   4-11111
    PO BOX 370   52544   856-0601
    Marvin Judkins, supt.

HS, 600 HIGH ST   52544   3-00011
    Rick Hilbert, prin.   856-0610
Howar JHS, 11TH & TERRY   52544   2-00100
    Bruce Karpen, prin.   856-0629

Indian Hills Community College   2-CC
    721 N 1ST ST   52544   856-2143

Central City, AC 319, PC 4, Linn
Central City Community SD   3-11111
    400 BARBER ST   52214   438-6183
    David Hoyt, supt.
HS, 400 BARBER ST   52214   2-00011
    Kirk Ketelsen, prin.   438-6182
MS, 400 BARBER ST   52214   2-00100
    Kirk Ketelsen, prin.   438-6181

Chariton, AC 515, PC 5, Lucas
Chariton Community SD   4-11111
    315 S 7TH ST   50049   774-5967
    Dan Jansen, supt.
HS, 501 N GRAND ST   50049   2-00011
    Bernard Stephenson, prin.   774-5066
JHS, 1300 N 16TH   50049   2-00100
    Randy Hawk, prin.   774-5114

Charles City, AC 515, PC 6, Floyd
Charles City Community SD   4-11111
    500 N GRAND AVE   50616   228-3557
    Thomas Williams, supt.
SHS, SALSBURY & OWEN DRIVE   50616   3-00001
    Lyle Sprout, prin.   228-1112
JHS, 500 N GRAND AVE   50616   2-00110
    Ron Hoffman, prin.   228-3255

Charter Oak, AC 712, PC 2, Crawford
Charter Oak-Ute Community SD   2-11111
    321 MAIN ST   51439   678-3325
    Roger Friedrichsen, supt.
Charter Oak-Ute HS   51439   1-00011
    (—), prin.   678-3325
Charter Oak-Ute JHS   1-00100
    321 MAIN ST   51439 – (—), prin.   885-2261

Cherokee, AC 712, PC 6, Cherokee
Cherokee Community SD   4-11111
    PO BOX 801   51012   225-5721
    Jerry Kjeraard, supt.
Washington HS, PO BOX 801   51012   2-00011
    Clayton Courtright, prin.   225-2541
Wilson MS, PO BOX 801   51012   2-01100
    Larry Weede, prin.   225-3836

Western Iowa Technical Community College   2-CC
    724 N 1ST ST   51012

Churdan, AC 515, PC 2, Greene
Paton-Churdan Community SD   2-11111
    PO BOX 157   50050   389-3111
    Oran Teut, supt.
Paton-Churdan JSHS   2-00111
    PO BOX 157   50050   389-3111
    Chet Wisniewski, prin.

Clarence, AC 319, PC 3, Cedar
Clarence-Lowden Community SD   2-11111
    400 BALL ST   52216   452-3511
    Richard Bachman, supt.
JSHS, PO BOX 310   52216   2-00111
    John Hlubek, prin.   452-3179

Clarinda, AC 712, PC 6, Page
Clarinda Community SD   4-11111
    114 E GARFIELD ST   51632   542-5165
    James Poole, supt.
HS, 100 N CARDINAL DR   51632   2-00011
    Robin Spears, prin.   542-5167
MS, 16TH & GRANT   51632   2-00100
    Paul Hunnold, prin.   542-2132

Iowa Western Community College   3-CC
    923 E WASHINGTON ST   51632   542-5117

Clarion, AC 515, PC 5, Wright
Clarion-Goldfield Community SD   3-11111
    3RD AVE NE   50525   532-2648
    Robert Olson, supt.
HS, 1151 WILLOW DR   50525   2-00011
    Darrell Determann, prin.   532-2895
MS, 3RD AVE NE   50525   2-00100
    Kurt Wiethorn, prin.   532-2412

Clarksville, AC 319, PC 4, Butler
Clarksville Community SD   2-11111
    PO BOX 689   50619   278-4560
    Michael Haluska, supt.
JSHS, PO BOX 689   50619   2-00111
    Robert Saathoff, prin.   278-4273

Clear Lake, AC 515, PC 6, Cerro Gordo
Clear Lake Community SD   4-11111
    125 N 20TH ST   50428   357-2181
    Stephen Voelz, supt.
HS, 125 N 20TH ST   50428   2-00011
    Robert Huntington, prin.   357-5235
JHS, 1601 3RD AVE N   50428   2-00100
    Robert Mondt, prin.   357-6114

Cleghorn, AC 712, PC 2, Cherokee
Marcus-Meriden-Cleghorn Community SD   3-11111
    PO BOX 97   51014   376-4171
    Frank Ashmore, supt.
Meriden-Cleghorn MS   2-00100
    PO BOX 97   51014 – (—), prin.   436-2244
Other Schools – See Marcus

Clinton, AC 319, PC 8, Clinton
Clinton Community SD | 6-11111
600 S 4TH ST 52732 | 243-9600
Bennett Trochlil, supt.
HS, 817 8TH AVE S 52732 | 4-00011
Larry Howe, prin. | 243-7540
Lyons MS, 2810 N 4TH ST 52732 | 2-00100
James Moore, prin. | 242-7858
Washington MS, 751 2ND AVE S 52732 | 3-00100
Thomas Streba, prin. | 242-7936

Clinton Community College | 4-CC
1000 LINCOLN BLVD 52732 | 322-5015
Mater Dei HS, 525 8TH AVE S 52732 | 2-00111
James Anderson, prin. | 242-1663
Mt. St. Clare College | 2-UC
400 N BLUFF BLVD 52732 | 242-4023

Coggon, AC 319, PC 3, Linn
North Linn Community SD | 3-11111
3033 LYNX DR 52218 | 224-3291
Harold Pruin, supt.
North Linn HS, 3033 LYNX DR 52218 | 2-00011
Frank Shekleton, prin. | 224-3291
Other Schools – See Troy Mills

Colfax, AC 515, PC 4, Jasper
Colfax-Mingo Community SD | 3-11111
20 W BROADWAY ST 50054 | 674-3646
Bonnie Baum, supt.
Colfax-Mingo MS | 2-00011
204 N LEAGUE RD 50054 | 674-4459
David Morgan, prin.
Other Schools – See Mingo

College Springs, AC 712, PC 2, Page
South Page Community SD | 2-11111
PO BOX 98 51637 | 582-3212
Randy Moffit, supt.
South Page JSHS, PO BOX 98 51637 | 2-00111
Blaine Maher, prin. | 582-3211

Collins, AC 515, PC 2, Story
Collins-Maxwell Community SD
Supt. — See Maxwell
Collins-Maxwell MS 50055 | 2-01100
Scott Cakerice, prin. | 385-2446

Colo, AC 515, PC 3, Story
Colo-Nesco Comm SD | 3-11111
PO BOX 136 50056 | 377-2284
Gary Pillman, supt.
HS, PO BOX 215 50056 | 2-00011
Steven Bukrow, prin. | 377-2282
Other Schools – See Zearing

Columbus Junction, AC 319, PC 4, Louisa
Columbus Community SD | 3-11111
1004 COLTON ST 52738 | 728-2911
John Currie, supt.
Columbus Community HS | 2-00011
1004 COLTON ST 52738 | 728-2231
John Della Vedova, prin.
JHS, 1004 COLTON ST 52738 | 1-00100
John Della Vedova, prin. | 728-2231

Conrad, AC 515, PC 3, Grundy
BCLUW Community SD | 3-11111
PO BOX 670 50621 | 366-2819
Fran Morrow, supt.
BCLUW HS, PO BOX 670 50621 | 2-00011
Dan Hargrave, prin. | 366-2810
Other Schools – See Union

Coon Rapids, AC 712, PC 4, Carroll
Coon Rapids-Bayard Community SD | 3-11111
PO BOX 297 50058 | 684-2207
Kurt Kaiser, supt.
Coon Rapids-Bayard HS | 2-00011
PO BOX 297 50058 | 684-2208
Darrell Bartling, prin.
Other Schools – See Bayard

Coralville, AC 319, PC 7, Johnson
Iowa City Community SD
Supt. — See Iowa City
Northwest JHS, 1507 8TH ST 52241 | 3-00100
Bryce Hansen, prin. | 339-6827

Corning, AC 515, PC 4, Adams
Corning Community SD | 3-11111
904 8TH ST 50841 | 322-4242
Donna Henningsen, supt.
HS, 904 8TH ST 50841 | 2-00011
Fred Hepburn, prin. | 322-4245
JHS, 10TH & WASHINGTON 50841 | 2-00100
Fred Shearer, prin. | 322-3213

Correctionville, AC 712, PC 3, Woodbury
Eastwood Community SD | 2-11011
512 5TH ST 51016 | 372-4420
Richard Caldwell, supt.
River Valley HS, 512 5TH ST 51016 | 2-00011
Robert Tushla, prin. | 372-4656

Corwith, AC 515, PC 2, Hancock
Corwith-Wesley Community SD | 2-11011
PO BOX 127 50430 | 583-2304
Don West, supt.
Corwith-Wesley HS | 1-00011
PO BOX 127 50430 | 583-2304
Jeff Kruse, prin.

Corydon, AC 515, PC 4, Wayne
Wayne Community SD | 3-11111
102 N DEKALB ST 50060 | 872-2184
Jerry Hoffman, supt.
Wayne Community HS | 2-00011
PO BOX 151 50060 | 872-2184
Larry Boer, prin.
Wayne Community JHS | 2-00100
102 N DEKALB ST 50060 | 872-2184
David Phillips, prin.

Council Bluffs, AC 712, PC 8, Pottawattamie
Council Bluffs Community SD | 7-11111
12 SCOTT ST 51503 | 328-6418
Richard Christie, supt.
Jefferson HS, 2501 W BROADWAY 51501 | 4-00011
Roger Hamilton, prin. | 328-6493
Lincoln HS, 1205 BONHAM ST 51503 | 4-00011
James Lake, prin. | 328-6481
Tucker Ctr Vo Ed, 815 N 18TH ST 51501 | Vo Tech
Steve Hardiman, prin. | 328-6408
Kirn JHS, 100 NORTH AVE 51503 | 3-00100
Larry Dechant, prin. | 328-6454
Wilson JHS, 715 N 21ST ST 51501 | 3-00100
Melanie Shellberg, prin. | 328-6476

Lewis Central Community SD | 5-11111
1600 E SOUTH OMAHA BRDGE RD 51503
Leland Wise, supt. | 366-8202
Lewis Central HS | 3-00011
2000 HIGHWAY 275 51503 | 366-8222
James Hamilton, prin.
Lewis Central MS | 3-00100
2000 HIGHWAY 275 51503 | 366-8251
Dan Meyer, prin.

Iowa School for the Deaf 51501 | HND
Iowa Western Community College | 4-CC
2700 COLLEGE RD 51503 | 325-3201
Jennie Edmundson Memorial Hospital | HSP
933 E PIERCE ST 51503 | 328-6100
Loess Hills Christian S | 2-11111
2755 AVENUE N 51501 | 322-5817
Gary Ray, prin.
St. Albert JSHS | 2-00111
400 GLEASON AVE 51503 | 328-2316
Marilyn Wandersee, prin.

Cresco, AC 319, PC 5, Howard
Howard-Winneshiek Community SD | 4-11111
1000 SCHROEDER DR 52136 | 547-2762
Donald Pettengill, supt.
Crestwood HS | 2-00011
1000 SCHROEDER DR 52136 | 547-2764
Charles Miller, prin.
JHS, 1000 4TH AVE E 52136 | 2-00100
John Westling, prin. | 547-2300

Creston, AC 515, PC 6, Union
Creston Community SD | 4-11111
619 N MAPLE ST 50801 | 782-7028
Gerald Cowell, supt.
HS, PO BOX 386 50801 | 3-00011
Christopher Duree, prin. | 782-2116
Jones JHS, 801 N ELM ST 50801 | 2-00100
Kenneth Williams, prin. | 782-2129

Southwestern Community College | 3-CC
1501 W TOWNLINE ST 50801 | 782-7081

Crystal Lake, AC 515, PC 2, Hancock
Woden-Crystal Lake Community SD
Supt. — See Woden
Woden-Crystal Lake JSHS | 1-00111
PO BOX 130 50432 | 565-3322
Tom Nugent, prin.

Dallas Center, AC 515, PC 4, Dallas
Dallas Center-Grimes Community SD | 4-11111
PO BOX 512 50063 | 992-3866
Dennis Bishop, supt.
Dallas Center-Grimes Community HS | 2-00011
PO BOX 512 50063 | 992-3832
Richard Adkins, prin.
Other Schools – See Grimes

Danbury, AC 712, PC 2, Woodbury
Maple Valley Community SD
Supt. — See Mapleton
Maple Valley JHS, 304 EAST ST 51019 | 1-00100
Sandra Boerner, prin. | 883-2402

Danville, AC 319, PC 3, Des Moines
Danville Community SD | 3-11111
415 S MAIN ST 52623 | 392-4223
Ronald Bickford, supt.
JSHS 52623 | 2-00111
Connie Merschbrook, prin. | 392-4222

Davenport, AC 319, PC 8, Scott
Davenport Community SD | 7-11111
1001 N HARRISON ST 52803 | 323-9951
Peter Flynn, supt.
Central SHS, 1120 N MAIN ST 52803 | 3-00001
Paul Massman, prin. | 323-9951
North SHS, 626 W 53RD ST 52806 | 3-00001
James Andrews, prin. | 388-9881
West SHS, 3505 W LOCUST ST 52804 | 4-00001
James Blanche, prin. | 386-5500
Northwest Ed Ctr | Vo Tech
2406 N MARQUETTE ST 52804 | 326-5072
Patricia McCoy, prin.
Smart JHS, 1934 W 5TH ST 52802 | 3-00110
Bruce Potts, prin. | 323-1837

Sudlow JHS, 1414 E LOCUST ST 52803 | 3-00110
Clarenca Simmons, prin. | 326-3502
Williams JHS | 3-00110
3040 N DIVISION ST 52804 | 391-6550
Ralph Wahl, prin.
Wood JHS, 5701 N DIVISION ST 52806 | 3-00110
Paul Smith, prin. | 391-6350
Young JHS, 1709 N HARRISON ST 52803 | 3-00110
Barbara Macdowall, prin. | 326-4432
Other Schools – See Walcott

American Institute of Commerce | 4-CC
1801 E KIMBERLY RD 52807 | 355-3500
Assumption HS | 3-00011
1020 W CENTRAL PARK AVE 52804 | 326-5313
Thomas Sunderbruch, prin.
Hamilton Technical College | 3-UC
1011 E 53RD ST 52807 | 386-3570
Palmer College of Chiropractic | 4-UC
1000 BRADY ST 52803 | 326-9600
St. Ambrose University | 4-UC
518 W LOCUST ST 52803 | 383-8800
Teikyo Marycrest University | 3-UC
1607 W 12TH ST 52804 | 800-728-9705

Dayton, AC 515, PC 3, Webster
Southeast Webster Community SD
Supt. — See Burnside
Southeast Webster MS | 1-00100
PO BOX 26 50530 | 547-2314
Ralph Johnson, prin.

Decorah, AC 319, PC 6, Winneshiek
Decorah Community SD | 4-11111
510 WINNEBAGO ST 52101 | 382-4208
Kenneth Jensen, supt.
HS, 100 E CLAIBORNE DR 52101 | 2-00011
Leroy Kopriva, prin. | 382-3643
MS, 210 VERNON ST 52101 | 2-00100
Oliver Lybeck, prin. | 382-8427

North Wineshiek Community SD | 2-11111
RR 3 52101 – Richard Moore, supt. | 735-5411
North Winneshiek JSHS, RR 3 52101 | 2-00111
Linda Hartman, prin. | 735-5411

Luther College | 4-UC
700 COLLEGE DR 52101 | 387-2000

Delhi, AC 319, PC 2, Delaware
Maquoketa Valley Community SD | 3-11111
PO BOX 186 52223 | 922-2091
Robert Vittengl, supt.
Maquoketa Valley HS | 2-00011
PO BOX 186 52223 | 922-2091
John Mitts, prin.

Denison, AC 712, PC 6, Crawford
Denison Community SD | 4-11111
819 N 16TH ST 51442 | 263-2176
John Finnessy, supt.
HS, 819 N 16TH ST 51442 | 3-00011
Steve Westerberg, prin. | 263-3101
MS, 1515 BROADWAY 51442 | 2-00100
Larry Bandy, prin. | 263-9393

Denver, AC 319, PC 4, Bremer
Denver Community SD | 3-11111
PO BOX 384 50622 | 984-6323
Robert Conway, supt.
HS, PO BOX 384 50622 | 2-00011
Kevin Fiene, prin. | 984-5639
MS, PO BOX 384 50622 | 2-00100
Joann Butler, prin. | 984-6041

Des Moines, AC 515, PC 9, Polk
Des Moines Community SD | 8-11111
1800 GRAND AVE 50309 | 242-7911
Gary Wegenke, supt.
East HS, 815 E 13TH ST 50316 | 4-00011
Jerry Stillwell, prin. | 242-7788
Hoover HS, 4800 AURORA AVE 50310 | 3-00011
William McCollaugh, prin. | 242-7300
Lincoln HS, 2600 SW 9TH ST 50315 | 4-00011
Thomas Drake, prin. | 242-7500
North HS, 501 HOLCOMB AVE 50313 | 3-00011
Joan Roberts, prin. | 242-7200
Roosevelt HS, 4419 CENTER ST 50312 | 4-00011
Gerald Conley, prin. | 242-7272
Brody MS, 2501 PARK AVE 50321 | 3-00100
Connie Cook, prin. | 244-7129
Callanan MS, 3010 CENTER ST 50312 | 3-00100
Barbara Mullahey, prin. | 255-3147
Goodrell MS, 3300 E 29TH ST 50317 | 3-00100
Larry Martindale, prin. | 265-6051
Harding MS, 203 E EUCLID AVE 50313 | 3-00100
Mike Loffredo, prin. | 244-9189
Hiatt MS, 1214 E 15TH ST 50316 | 2-00100
Gary Eyerly, prin. | 242-7774
Hoyt MS, 2700 E 42ND ST 50317 | 3-00100
Betty Hyde, prin. | 265-7395
McCombs MS, 201 SW 80TH AVE 50320 | 3-00100
John Barrett, prin. | 287-2565
Meredith MS | 3-00100
4827 MADISON AVE 50310 | 242-7250
Robert Wells, prin.
Merrill MS, 5301 GRAND AVE 50312 | 3-00100
Paul Devin, prin. | 274-3441
Weeks MS, 901 PARK AVE 50315 | 3-00100
Wendell Miskimins, prin. | 288-6755

Saydel Consolidated SD   4-11111
5401 NW 2ND ST 50313   288-8557
Randall Clegg, supt.
Saydel HS, 5601 NE 7TH ST 50313   2-00011
Phillip Speece, prin.   262-9325
Woodside MS, 5810 NE 14TH ST 50313   2-00100
Lee McCarty, prin.   265-3451

West Des Moines Community SD
Supt. — See West Des Moines
Indian Hills JHS   2-00100
9401 INDIAN HILLS DR 50325   226-2811
William Wilson, prin.

American Institute of Business   4-CC
2500 FLEUR DR 50321   244-4221
Des Moines Area Community College   4-CC
1107 7TH ST 50314
Des Moines Christian S   2-11111
4801 FRANKLIN AVE 50310   274-3893
Daniel Henderson, prin.
Drake University   6-UC
2507 E UNIVERSITY AVE 50317   271-2191
Grand View College   4-UC
1200 GRANDVIEW AVE 50316   263-2800
Hamilton Business College   2-CS
2300 EUCLID AVE 50310   279-0253
Iowa Methodist Medical Center   HSP
1200 PLEASANT ST 50309   283-5891
Iowa Methodist School of Nursing   HSP
1117 PLEASANT ST 50309   241-6333
Mercy Hospital   HSP
400 UNIVERSITY AVE 50314   247-3180
University of Osteopathic Medicine   4-UC
3200 GRAND AVE 50312   271-1650

De Witt, AC 319, PC 5, Clinton
Central Clinton Community SD   4-11111
923 4TH AVE E 52742   659-0700
John Klotz, supt.
Central HS, 425 E 11TH ST 52742   2-00011
Joseph Utter, prin.   659-0715
Central JHS, 1010 4TH AVE E 52742   2-00100
Delbert Gilbert, prin.   659-0735

Diagonal, AC 515, PC 2, Ringgold
Diagonal Community SD   2-11111
PO BOX 94 50845   734-5331
Roger Godfrey, supt.
JSHS, PO BOX 94 50845   1-00111
Larry Tepley, prin.   734-5331

Dike, AC 319, PC 3, Grundy
Dike Community SD   3-11011
330 MAIN ST 50624   989-2552
Donald Gunderson, supt.
Dike-New Hartford HS   2-00011
330 MAIN ST 50624   989-2485
Michael Williams, prin.

Donnellson, AC 319, PC 3, Lee
Central Lee Community SD   4-11111
2642 HIGHWAY 218 52625   835-9510
Leland Morrison, supt.
Central HS   2-00011
2642 HIGHWAY 218 52625   835-5121
Robert Lamb, prin.
Central Lee JHS   2-00100
2642 HIGHWAY 218 52625   835-5139
Richard Denly, prin.

Dow City, AC 712, PC 2, Crawford
Dow City-Arion Community SD   2-11100
212 SCHOOL ST 51528   674-3248
Paul Tedesco, supt.
Dow City-Arion JHS   2-00100
212 SCHOOL ST 51528   674-3248
John Nielsen, prin.

Dows, AC 515, PC 3, Wright
Dows Community SD   2-11111
RR 2 BOX 2A 50071   852-4163
Tom Haller, supt.
JSHS, RR 2 BOX 2A 50071   2-00111
Robin Wagner, prin.   852-4162

Dubuque, AC 319, PC 8, Dubuque
Dubuque Community SD   6-11111
2300 CHANEY RD 52001   588-5100
Diana Lam, supt.
HS, 1800 CLARKE DR 52001   4-00011
Larry Mitchell, prin.   588-5220
Hempstead HS   4-00011
3715 PENNSYLVANIA AVE 52002   588-5160
Donald Moody, prin.
Jefferson JHS   3-00100
1105 ALTHAUSER AVE 52001   588-8360
Duane Frick, prin.
Jones JHS, 1090 ALTA VISTA ST 52001   3-00100
Elizabeth Hogan, prin.   588-8370
Washington JHS   3-00100
51 N GRANDVIEW AVE 52001   588-8380
Arthur Roling, prin.

Clarke College   3-UC
1550 CLARKE DR 52001   588-6300
Emmaus Bible College   2-UC
2570 ASBURY RD 52001   588-8000
Loras College   4-UC
1450 ALTA VISTA ST 52001   588-7103
University of Dubuque   3-UC
2000 UNIVERSITY AVE 52001   589-3223

University of Dubuque Theological Sem.   2-UC
2000 UNIVERSITY AVE 52001   589-3000
Wahlert HS, 2005 KANE ST 52001   3-00011
Donald Miller, prin.   583-9771
Wartburg Theological Seminary   2-UC
333 WARTBURG PL 52003   589-0200

Dumont, AC 515, PC 3, Butler
Dumont Community SD   2-11100
PO BOX 425 50625   857-3201
Dale Mulford, supt.
MS, 512 2ND STREET 50625   1-00100
Charles Bonjour, prin.   857-3201

Dunkerton, AC 319, PC 3, Black Hawk
Dunkerton Community SD   3-11111
509 S CANFIELD ST 50626   822-4295
Onalee Oaks, supt.
JSHS, 509 S CANFIELD ST 50626   2-00111
Dennis Modlin, prin.   822-4295

Dunlap, AC 712, PC 4, Harrison
Dunlap Community SD   2-11011
1102 IOWA ST 51529   643-2251
Paul Tedesco, supt.
HS, 1102 IOWA ST 51529   2-00011
James Altwegg, prin.   643-2258

Durant, AC 319, PC 4, Cedar
Durant Community SD   3-11111
408 7TH ST 52747   785-4432
James Wagner, supt.
HS, 408 7TH ST 52747   2-00011
Steve Reinert, prin.   785-4431
MS, 408 7TH ST 52747   2-01100
Steven Callison, prin.   785-4433

Dyersville, AC 319, PC 5, Dubuque

Beckman HS, 1325 9TH ST SE 52040   3-00111
Br. Betzold, prin.   875-7188

Dysart, AC 319, PC 4, Tama
Union Community SD
Supt. — See La Porte City
Union MS, 505 WEST 52224   2-00100
Lorraine Tressler, prin.   476-5100

Eagle Grove, AC 515, PC 5, Wright
Eagle Grove Community SD   3-11111
315 N IOWA AVE 50533   448-4749
John Nicholls, supt.
HS, 315 N IOWA AVE 50533   2-00011
Raymond Roseland, prin.   448-5143
Blue MS, 1015 NW 2ND ST 50533   2-01100
Susan Alborn'Yilek, prin.   448-4767

Iowa Central Community College   2-CC
316 NW 3RD ST 50533   448-4723

Earlham, AC 515, PC 4, Madison
Earlham Community SD   2-11111
PO BOX 430 50072   758-2235
Paul Hopp, supt.
HS, PO BOX 430 50072   2-00011
James McCraken, prin.   758-2214
MS, PO BOX 430 50072   2-00100
William Crilly, prin.   758-2213

Earling, AC 712, PC 2, Shelby

St. Joseph S, PO BOX 227 51530   2-01100
Sr. Linda Zahner, prin.   747-3081

Early, AC 712, PC 3, Sac
Schaller-Crestland Community SD
Supt. — See Schaller
Shaller-Crestland HS 50535   2-00011
Dennis Mozer, prin.   273-5192

Eddyville, AC 515, PC 4, Wapello
Eddyville Community SD   3-11111
103 N FRONT ST 52553   969-4226
Connie Maxson, supt.
JSHS 52553   2-00111
(—), prin.   969-4288

Edgewood, AC 319, PC 3, Delaware
Edgewood-Colesburg Community SD   3-11111
403 W UNION 52042   928-6411
William Brandt, supt.
Edgewood-Colesburg JSHS 52042   2-00111
Bruce West, prin.   928-6412

Eldon, AC 515, PC 4, Wapello
Cardinal Community SD   3-11111
PO BOX 275 52554 – Al Carr, supt.   652-7531
Cardinal JSHS, PO BOX 275 52554   2-00111
Terry Roberts, prin.   652-7531

Eldora, AC 515, PC 5, Hardin
Eldora-New Providence Community SD   3-11111
1100 10TH ST 50627   858-5631
Ingvert Appel, supt.
Eldora-New Providence HS   2-00011
1800 24TH ST 50627   858-3421
James Knaak, prin.
Other Schools – See New Providence

Eldridge, AC 319, PC 5, Scott
North Scott Community SD   5-11111
251 E IOWA ST 52748   285-4819
Pascal Deluca, supt.
North Scott HS, 200 S 1ST ST 52748   3-00011
Linda McClurg, prin.   285-9631

North Scott JHS, 502 S 5TH ST 52748   2-00100
David Griffin, prin.   285-8272

Elgin, AC 319, PC 3, Fayette
Valley Community SD   3-11111
23493 CANOE RD 52141   426-5501
William Brandt, supt.
Valley JSHS, 23493 CANOE RD 52141   2-00111
Bill Maske, prin.   426-5551

Elkader, AC 319, PC 4, Clayton
Central Community SD 52043   3-11111
Darwin Winke, supt.   245-1751
Central Community JSHS 52043   2-00111
Donald Grove, prin.   245-1750

Elk Horn, AC 712, PC 3, Shelby
Elk Horn-Kimballton Community SD   2-11111
51531 – J. Allan Hjelle, supt.   764-4616
Elk Horn-Kimballton JSHS 51531   1-00111
Randall Nichols, prin.   764-4606

Emmetsburg, AC 712, PC 5, Palo Alto
Emmetsburg Community SD   3-11111
1601 GRAND AVE 50536   852-3201
George Maurer, supt.
HS, 2ND & KING ST 50536   2-00011
Lenord Bruce, prin.   852-2966
MS, 10TH & PALMER 50536   2-01100
Dean Newlon, prin.   852-3312

Iowa Lakes Community College   4-CC
3200 COLLEGE DR 50536   852-3554

Epworth, AC 319, PC 4, Dubuque
Western Dubuque Community SD
Supt. — See Farley
Western Dubuque HS, 5TH AVE W 52045   3-00011
Art Huinker, prin.   876-3620

Divine Word College Seminary   1-UC
1 S CENTER AVE 52045   876-3353

Essex, AC 712, PC 3, Page
Essex Community SD   2-11111
PO BOX 299 51638   379-3117
Russell Hilker, supt.
JSHS, PO BOX 299 51638   2-00111
Angel Melendez, prin.   379-3115

Estherville, AC 712, PC 6, Emmet
Estherville Community SD   4-11111
301 N 6TH ST 51334   362-2692
William Hutchinson, supt.
HS, 1520 CENTRAL AVE 51334   2-00011
Chris Kjar, prin.   362-2659
MS, 321 N 6TH ST 51334   3-01100
Allen Steen, prin.   362-2335

Iowa Lakes Community College   5-CC
300 S 18TH ST 51334   362-2601

Everly, AC 712, PC 3, Clay
Clay Central/Everly Community SD   2-11111
PO BOX 110 51338   834-2227
David Holmquist, supt.
Clay Central/Everly HS   2-00011
PO BOX 110 51338   834-2227
Kevin Vickery, prin.
Other Schools – See Royal

Exira, AC 712, PC 3, Audubon
Exira Community SD   2-11111
PO BOX 335 50076   268-5555
Otto Faaborg, supt.
JSHS, PO BOX 335 50076   2-00111
Jerry Kuper, prin.   268-5318

Fairbank, AC 319, PC 4, Buchanan
Wapsie Valley Community SD   3-11111
2535 VIKING AVE 50629   638-6711
David Owens, supt.
Wapsie Valley HS   2-00011
2535 VIKING AVE 50629   638-6711
Gregory Harter, prin.
Other Schools – See Oran

Fairfield, AC 515, PC 6, Jefferson
Fairfield Community SD   4-11111
605 E BROADWAY AVE 52556   472-2655
John Kelley, supt.
HS, 605 E BROADWAY AVE 52556   3-00011
Ralph Messerli, prin.   472-2059
MS, 404 W FILLMORE AVE 52556   2-00100
Steven Triplett, prin.   472-5019

Maharishi International University   3-UC
RR 1 52556   472-5031

Farley, AC 319, PC 4, Dubuque
Western Dubuque Community SD   4-11111
PO BOX 279 52046   744-3885
Harold Knutsen, supt.
Other Schools – See Cascade, Epworth

Farmington, AC 319, PC 3, Van Buren
Harmony Community SD
Supt. — See Bonaparte
Harmony HS, RR 1 52626   2-00011
David Stammeyer, prin.   592-3192
Harmony MS, RR 2 52626   2-01100
Daniel Vogeler, prin.   878-3532

Farnhamville, AC 515, PC 2, Calhoun
Prairie Valley Community SD
Supt. — See Gowrie

Prairie Valley MS, RR 1 50538   2-00100   544-3226
William Jesse, prin.

Farragut, AC 712, PC 2, Fremont
Farragut Community SD   2-11111
PO BOX 36 51639   385-8131
Jack Hoenshel, supt.
JSHS 51639   2-00111
Dan Parks, prin.   385-8131

Fayette, AC 319, PC 4, Fayette

Upper Iowa University   4-UC
PO BOX 1857 52142   425-5200

Fenton, AC 515, PC 2, Kossuth
Sentral Community SD   2-11111
PO BOX 109 50539   889-2261
Dennis Tassell, supt.
Sentral JSHS, PO BOX 109 50539   2-00111
Randy Martin, prin.   889-2261

Fonda, AC 712, PC 3, Pocahontas
Newell-Fonda Community SD
Supt. — See Newell
Newell-Fonda MS   1-00100
3RD AND HOWARD STS 50540   288-4445
Randall Nielsen, prin.

Fontanelle, AC 515, PC 3, Adair
Bridgewater-Fontanelle Community SD   2-11111
PO BOX 158 50846   745-2671
Fred Whipple, supt.
Bridgewater-Fontanelle JSHS   2-00111
PO BOX 158 50846   745-2291
James Wood, prin.

Forest City, AC 515, PC 5, Winnebago
Forest City Community SD   4-11111
810 W K ST 50436   582-2323
Wayne Sesker, supt.
HS, 206 W SCHOOL ST 50436   2-00011
Larry Holstad, prin.   582-2324
MS, 216 W SCHOOL ST 50436   2-00100
Lee Hinkley, prin.   582-4772

Waldorf College   3-CC
106 S 6TH ST 50436   800-292-1903

Fort Dodge, AC 515, PC 8, Webster
Fort Dodge Community SD   5-11111
104 S 17TH ST 50501   576-1161
David Haggard, supt.
HS, 819 N 25TH ST 50501   4-00011
Richard Clark, prin.   955-1770
Phillips MS, 1015 5TH AVE N 50501   3-00100
Gary Reiners, prin.   576-3168

Iowa Central Community College   3-CC
330 AVENUE M 50501   576-7201
Sacred Heart JHS, 214 S 13TH ST 50501   2-00100
Ursula Candon, prin.   576-0563
St. Edmond HS, 501 N 22ND ST 50501   2-00011
Allan Eckelman, prin.   955-5850

Fort Madison, AC 319, PC 7, Lee
Fort Madison Community SD   5-11111
PO BOX 1423 52627   372-7252
Tony Spencer, supt.
HS, 2000 AVENUE B 52627   3-00011
Larry Shiley, prin.   372-1862
JHS, 1801 AVENUE G 52627   2-00100
Gordon Roxberg, prin.   372-4687

Aquinas JSHS, 2600 AVENUE A 52627   2-00111
George Boyle, prin.   372-2486

Fredericksburg, AC 319, PC 4, Chickasaw
Fredericksburg Community SD   2-11111
401 E HIGH ST 50630   237-5364
Joseph Starcevich, supt.
JSHS, MAIN ST 50630   2-00111
James Hotz, prin.   237-5334

Fremont, AC 515, PC 3, Mahaska
Fremont Community SD   2-11100
PO BOX 69 52561   933-4211
Robert McCurdy, supt.
MS, PO BOX 69 52561   1-00100
Monte Montgomery, prin.   933-4211

Galva, AC 712, PC 2, Ida
Galva-Holstein Community SD
Supt. — See Holstein
Galva-Holstein MS 51020   2-01100
Dennis Ohde, prin.   282-4213

Garden Grove, AC 515, PC 2, Decatur
Mormon Trail Community SD
Supt. — See Humeston
Mormon Trail JSHS   2-00111
PO BOX 177 50103   443-3425
Stephen Burr, prin.

Garnavillo, AC 319, PC 3, Clayton
Garnavillo Community SD   2-11111
PO BOX 17 52049   964-2321
James Whalen, supt.
JSHS, PO BOX 17 52049   2-00111
David Kuehl, prin.   964-2321

Garner, AC 515, PC 5, Hancock
Garner-Hayfield Community SD   3-11111
PO BOX 449 50438   923-2718
Dennis Bahr, supt.

Garner-Hayfield HS   2-00011
PO BOX 449 50438   923-2632
Paul Schoneman, prin.
Garner-Hayfield MS   2-01100
PO BOX 449 50438   923-2809
Beckey Hacker, prin.

Garwin, AC 515, PC 3, Tama
GMG Community SD   2-11111
306 PARK ST 50632   499-2005
Richard Hessenius, supt.
GMG JSHS, 306 PARK ST 50632   2-00111
Gary Sinclair, prin.   499-2005

George, AC 712, PC 4, Lyon
George Community SD   2-11011
500 E INDIANA AVE 51237   475-3311
Jerry Nichols, supt.
George-Little Rock HS   2-00011
500 E INDIANA AVE 51237 – (—), prin.   475-3311

Gilbert, AC 515, PC 3, Story
Gilbert Community SD   3-11111
103 MATHEWS DR 50105   232-3740
Douglas Williams, supt.
JSHS, 103 MATHEWS DR 50105   2-00111
James Quarnstrom, prin.   232-3738

Gilbertville, AC 319, PC 3, Black Hawk

Don Bosco HS, 405 16TH AVE 50634   2-00011
Michael Kavars, prin.   296-1692

Gilman, AC 515, PC 3, Marshall
East Marshall Community SD   3-11111
PO BOX 159 50106   498-7481
Doyle Scott, supt.
East Marshall MS, PO BOX 159 50106   2-01100
Steve Beecher, prin.   498-7483
Other Schools – See Le Grand

Gilmore City, AC 515, PC 3, Humboldt
Gilmore City-Bradgate Community SD   2-11100
402 SE E AVE 50541   373-6619
William Crumbaugh, supt.
Twin River Valley MS   2-00100
402 SE E AVE 50541   373-6124
Ronald Bollmeyer, prin.

Gladbrook, AC 515, PC 3, Tama
Gladbrook Community SD   2-11100
PO BOX 370 50635   473-2840
Lawrence McNabb, supt.
Gladbrook-Reinbeck MS   2-00100
PO BOX 370 50635   473-2842
Charles Earp, prin.

Glenwood, AC 712, PC 5, Mills
Glenwood Community SD   4-11111
801 S VINE ST 51534   527-9034
Thomas Rubel, supt.
HS, RR 2 BOX 102 51534   3-00011
Robert Bye, prin.   527-4897
MS, 811 S VINE ST 51534   2-00100
Russell Finken, prin.   527-4887

Glidden, AC 712, PC 4, Carroll
Glidden-Ralston Community SD   2-11111
PO BOX B 51443 – Dale Johnson, supt.   659-3411
Glidden-Ralston JSHS 51443   2-00111
Bryan Stearns, prin.   659-2205

Goose Lake, AC 319, PC 2, Clinton
Northeast Community SD 52750   3-11111
Gordon Cook, supt.   577-2449
Northeast JSHS 52750   2-00111
Robert Paul, prin.   577-2249

Gowrie, AC 515, PC 4, Webster
Prairie Valley Community SD   3-11111
1005 RIDDLE ST 50543   352-3173
Richard Wede, supt.
Prairie Valley HS, 1005 RIDDLE ST 50543   2-00011
Mike Dick, prin.   352-3142
Other Schools – See Farnhamville

Graettinger, AC 712, PC 3, Palo Alto
Graettinger Community SD 51342   2-11111
George Maurer, supt.   859-3286
HS 51342   2-00011
James Towell, prin.   859-3286
MS 51342   1-00100
James Towell, prin.   859-3286

Grafton, AC 515, PC 2, Worth
St. Ansgar Community SD
Supt. — See Saint Ansgar
MS 50440   2-01100
Emmett Tyler, prin.   748-2211

Grand Junction, AC 515, PC 3, Greene
East Greene Community SD   2-11111
PO BOX 377 50107   738-5741
Jack Anderson, supt.
JSHS, 405 12TH ST S 50107   2-00111
Ron McNeil, prin.   738-5721

Granville, AC 712, PC 2, Sioux

Spalding HS, PO BOX 146 51022   1-00011
Joe Mueting, prin.   727-3451

Greene, AC 515, PC 4, Butler
Greene Community SD   2-11111
208 N 4TH ST 50636   823-5523
Steve Ward, supt.
JSHS, 208 N 4TH ST 50636   2-00111
Michael Haluska, prin.   823-5631

Greenfield, AC 515, PC 4, Adair
Greenfield Community SD   3-11111
410 NW 2ND ST 50849   743-6127
Frederich Whipple, supt.
JSHS, 410 NW 2ND ST 50849   2-00111
Ray Leto, prin.   743-6141

Grimes, AC 515, PC 5, Polk
Dallas Center-Grimes Community SD
Supt. — See Dallas Center
Dallas Center-Grimes JHS   2-00100
410 N MAIN ST 50111   986-3651
Jerry Crosser, prin.

Grinnell, AC 515, PC 6, Poweshiek
Grinnell-Newburg Community SD   4-11111
927 4TH AVE 50112   236-2700
Clement Bodensteiner, supt.
Grinnell Community HS   2-00011
1333 SUNSET ST 50112   236-2720
David Stoakes, prin.
MS, EAST ST & GARFIELD AVE 50112   3-01100
Michael Fitzgerald, prin.   236-2750

Grinnell College   4-UC
PO BOX 805 50112   269-3000

Griswold, AC 712, PC 4, Cass
Griswold Community SD   3-11111
PO BOX 280 51535   778-2152
Philip Rink, supt.
JSHS, PO BOX 280 51535   2-00111
Lorene Dykstra, prin.   778-2154

Grundy Center, AC 319, PC 4, Grundy
Grundy Center Community SD   3-11111
1301 12TH ST 50638   824-5418
Robert Crouse, supt.
JSHS, 1006 M AVE 50638   2-00111
Harold Dole, prin.   824-5449

Guthrie Center, AC 515, PC 4, Guthrie
Guthrie Center Community SD   3-11111
700 STATE ST 50115   747-3521
Leonard Snyder, supt.
HS, 700 STATE ST 50115   2-00011
Kent Mutchler, prin.   747-2236
JHS, 700 STATE ST 50115   2-00100
Richard Friedrich, prin.   747-3842

Guttenberg, AC 319, PC 4, Clayton
Guttenberg Community SD   3-11111
131 S RIVER PARK DR 52052   252-2341
James Pasut, supt.
Guttenberg Community HS   2-00011
131 S RIVER PARK DR 52052   252-2341
James Whalen, prin.

Hamburg, AC 712, PC 4, Fremont
Hamburg Community SD, 105 E ST 51640   2-11111
Leo Humphrey, supt.   382-1063
JSHS, 105 E ST 51640   2-00111
J. Wolf, prin.   382-2703

Hampton, AC 515, PC 5, Franklin
Hampton Community SD   4-11111
PO BOX 336 50441   456-2175
Mark Wittmer, supt.
Hampton Community HS   2-00011
PO BOX 336 50441   456-4893
Berry Johnson, prin.
MS, PO BOX 336 50441   2-00100
Neal Nelson, prin.   456-4735

Harlan, AC 712, PC 6, Shelby
Harlan Community SD   4-11111
2102 DURANT ST 51537   755-2152
Roy Baker, supt.
Harlan Community HS   3-00011
2102 DURANT ST 51537   755-3101
Kent Klinkefus, prin.
MS, 70 S BALDWIN 51537   2-00100
Fred Maharry, prin.   755-3196

Hartley, AC 712, PC 4, O'Brien
Hartley-Melvin-Sanborn Community SD   3-11111
600 3RD ST NW 51346   728-2022
Steve Litts, supt.
Hartley-Melvin-Sanborn HS   2-00011
600 3RD ST NW 51346   728-2022
Dennis Frey, prin.
Other Schools – See Sanborn

Hastings, AC 712, PC 2, Mills
Nishna Valley Community SD   2-11111
RR 1 BOX 80B 51540   624-8696
William Reents, supt.
Nishna Valley JSHS   2-00111
RR 1 BOX 80B 51540   624-8696
Jeffrey Schumacher, prin.

Hawarden, AC 712, PC 4, Sioux
West Sioux Community SD   3-11111
1300 AVENUE P 51023   552-1461
Neil Moritz, supt.
West Sioux HS, 1300 AVENUE P 51023   2-00011
David Looysen, prin.   552-1181
West Sioux MS   2-00100
1130 CENTRAL AVE 51023   552-1022
Marlin Hansen, prin.

Hinton, AC 712, PC 3, Plymouth
Hinton Community SD   3-11111
PO BOX 128 51024   947-4329
Marvin Boehme, supt.

HS 51024   2-00011
  Earl Oleson, prin.   947-4328
MS 51024   2-00100
  Earl Oleson, prin.   947-4428

Holstein, AC 712, PC 4, Ida
Galva-Holstein Community SD   3-11111
  PO BOX 320 51025   368-4353
  Marlin Lode, supt.
Galva-Holstein HS, CIRCLE DRIVE 51025   2-00011
  Jan Brandhorst, prin.   368-2641
Other Schools – See Galva

Hubbard, AC 515, PC 3, Hardin
Hubbard-Radcliffe Community SD   3-11111
  PO BOX 129 50122   864-2211
  R Kelley Rogers, supt.
Hubbard-Radcliffe HS   2-00011
  PO BOX 129 50122   864-2211
  Richard Muller, prin.
Other Schools – See Radcliffe

Hudson, AC 319, PC 4, Black Hawk
Hudson Community SD   3-11111
  245 S WASHINGTON 50643   988-3233
  Martin Lucas, supt.
JSHS, 136 S WASHINGTON 50643   2-00111
  Gary Van Hemert, prin.   988-4137

Hull, AC 712, PC 4, Sioux
Boyden-Hull Community SD   3-11111
  801 1ST ST 51239   439-2711
  Craig Anderson, supt.
Boyden-Hull JSHS, 801 1ST ST 51239   2-00111
  Marjorie Wagner, prin.   439-2440

Western Christian HS   2-00011
  PO BOX 658 51239   439-1013
  Marian Vansoelen, prin.

Humboldt, AC 515, PC 5, Humboldt
Humboldt Community SD   4-11111
  900 SUMNER AVE 50548   332-1330
  Carl Mattes, supt.
SHS, HIGHWAY 169 S 50548   2-00001
  David Staver, prin.   332-1430
JHS, 210 TAFT ST N 50548   2-00110
  Robert Pattee, prin.   332-2812

Humeston, AC 515, PC 3, Wayne
Mormon Trail Community SD   2-11111
  PO BOX 156 50123   877-2521
  Tom Spear, supt.
Other Schools – See Garden Grove

Huxley, AC 515, PC 4, Story
Ballard Community SD   4-11111
  315 N MAIN AVE 50124 – (—), supt.   597-2811
Ballard Community SHS   2-00001
  PO BOX 307 50124   597-2971
  Steven Hornung, prin.
Ballard Community JHS   2-00110
  PO BOX 307 50124   597-2977
  Larry Shaeffer, prin.

Ida Grove, AC 712, PC 4, Ida
Ida Grove Community SD   3-11011
  900 JOHN MONTGOMERY DR 51445   364-3371
  Dean Collopy, supt.
HS, 900 JOHN MONTGOMERY DR 51445   2-00011
  Michael Andrews, prin.   364-3371

Independence, AC 319, PC 6, Buchanan
Independence Community SD   4-11111
  PO BOX 900 50644   334-2538
  Stan Slessor, supt.
HS, PO BOX 900 50644   3-00011
  Dale Greimann, prin.   334-6093
MS, PO BOX 900 50644   2-00100
  Meredith Miller, prin.   334-7166

Indianola, AC 515, PC 7, Warren
Indianola Community SD   5-11111
  1304 E 2ND AVE 50125   961-8477
  Harold Hulleman, supt.
SHS, 1304 E 1ST AVE 50125   3-00001
  Ann Shaw, prin.   961-6278
JHS, 1304 E 1ST AVE 50125   3-00110
  Robert Newsom, prin.   961-7475

Simpson College   4-UC
  PO BOX 708 50125   961-1611

Inwood, AC 712, PC 3, Lyon
West Lyon Community SD   3-11111
  HWY 182 N 51240   753-4917
  Ralph Herring, supt.
West Lyon HS, HWY 182 N 51240   2-00011
  James Van Steenwyk, prin.   753-4917
West Lyon JHS, HWY 182 N 51240   2-00100
  James Van Steenwyk, prin.   753-4917

Iowa City, AC 319, PC 8, Johnson
Iowa City Community SD   6-11111
  509 S DUBUQUE ST 52240   339-6800
  Barbara Grohe, supt.
HS, 1900 MORNINGSIDE DR 52245   4-00011
  Howard Vernon, prin.   339-6811
West HS, 2901 MELROSE AVE 52246   3-00011
  Jerry Arganbright, prin.   339-6817
Southeast JHS   3-00100
  2501 BRADFORD DR 52240   339-6823
  Frank Ward, prin.
Other Schools – See Coralville

Regina JSHS   2-00111
  2150 ROCHESTER AVE 52245   338-5436
  Brian Corkery, prin.
University of Iowa 52242   7-UC
      335-3549

Iowa Falls, AC 515, PC 6, Hardin
Iowa Falls Community SD   4-11111
  PO BOX 670 50126   648-2535
  Steven Schmit, supt.
HS, 1903 TAYLOR AVE 50126   2-00011
  John Robbins, prin.   648-2509
Riverbend MS, 1124 UNION ST 50126   2-00100
  Victor Amundson, prin.   648-2551

Ellsworth Community College   3-CC
  1100 COLLEGE AVE 50126   800-322-9235

Irwin, AC 712, PC 2, Shelby
IKM Community SD   3-11111
  PO BOX 217 51446   782-3127
  Dave Sextro, supt.
IKM MS, PO BOX 217 51446   2-01100
  Cyndi Morgan, prin.   782-3126
Other Schools – See Manilla

Jackson Junction, AC 319, PC 1, Winneshiek
Turkey Valley Community SD   3-11111
  3219 STATE HIGHWAY 24 52150   776-6011
  Gary Holst, supt.
Turkey Valley JSHS   2-00111
  PO BOX 30 52150   776-6011
  Ken Winter, prin.

Janesville, AC 319, PC 3, Bremer
Janesville Consolidated SD   2-11111
  PO BOX 478 50647   987-2581
  Randy Achenbach, supt.
JSHS, PO BOX 478 50647   2-00111
  Robert McCormack, prin.   987-2581

Jefferson, AC 515, PC 5, Greene
Jefferson-Scranton SD   4-11111
  MADISON & ELM 50129   386-4168
  Robert Schmidt, supt.
HS, 100 E SUNSET RD 50129   2-00011
  Gerald Waugh, prin.   386-2188
MS, 203 W HARRISON ST 50129   2-00100
  Thomas Yepsen, prin.   386-8126

Jesup, AC 319, PC 4, Buchanan
Jesup Community SD   3-11111
  531 PROSPECT ST 50648   827-1700
  Michael Krumm, supt.
HS, 531 PROSPECT ST 50648   2-00011
  Leland Jesse, prin.   827-1700
MS, 531 PROSPECT ST 50648   2-00100
  Leland Jesse, prin.   827-1700

Jewell, AC 515, PC 4, Hamilton
South Hamilton Community SD   3-11111
  PO BOX 100 50130   827-5479
  Richard Textor, supt.
South Hamilton JSHS   2-01111
  315 DIVISION ST 50130   827-5418
  Steve Gray, prin.

Johnston, AC 515, PC 5, Polk
Johnston Community SD   5-11111
  PO BOX 10 50131   278-0470
  K. Richard Sundblad, supt.
HS, PO BOX 10 50131   3-00011
  Thomas Downs, prin.   278-0449
MS, PO BOX 10 50131   3-01100
  Steven Fey, prin.   278-0476

Kalona, AC 319, PC 4, Washington
Mid-Prairie Community SD
  Supt. — See Wellman
Mid-Prairie JHS, PO BOX 1204 52247   2-00110
  Ray Schrepfer, prin.   656-2241

Iowa Mennonite HS   2-00011
  1421 540TH ST SW 52247   656-2073
  Wilbur Yoder, prin.

Kanawha, AC 515, PC 3, Hancock
Kanawha Community SD   2-11100
  PO BOX 130 50447   762-3215
  Ted Runyan, supt.
West Hancock JHS   2-00100
  PO BOX 130 50447   762-3261
  Larry Peppers, prin.

Keokuk, AC 319, PC 7, Lee
Keokuk Community SD   5-11111
  727 WASHINGTON ST 52632   524-1402
  David Scala, supt.
HS, 2285 MIDDLE RD 52632   3-00011
  T. Wemette, prin.   524-2542
MS, 14TH & MAIN ST 52632   3-00100
  Richard Elliott, prin.   524-3737

Cardinal Stritch S   2-00111
  2981 PLANK RD 52632   524-5450
  Jack Turner, prin.
Southeastern Community College   2-CC
  PO BOX 27 52632   524-3221

Keosauqua, AC 319, PC 4, Van Buren
Van Buren Community SD   3-11111
  PO BOX 39C 52565 – Ed Looney, supt.   293-3334

Van Buren Community JSHS   2-00111
  PO BOX 39C 52565   293-3183
  Richard Johnson, prin.

Keota, AC 515, PC 4, Keokuk
Keota Community SD   2-11111
  N ELLIS AVE 52248   636-2189
  Keith Sasseen, supt.
JSHS, N ELLIS AVE 52248   2-00111
  Leland Roegner, prin.   636-3491

Kingsley, AC 712, PC 4, Plymouth
Kingsley-Pierson Community SD   3-11111
  PO BOX 426 51028   378-2861
  Robert Bahl, supt.
HS, 90 VALLEY DR 51028   2-00011
  Mike Sherwood, prin.   378-2861
Other Schools – See Pierson

Klemme, AC 515, PC 3, Hancock
Klemme Community SD   2-10100
  PO BOX 249 50449   587-2153
  Don Cleveland, supt.
Klemme/Belmond JHS   2-00100
  PO BOX 249 50449   587-2620
  Gary Schwartz, prin.

Knoxville, AC 515, PC 6, Marion
Knoxville Community SD   4-11111
  1214 W JACKSON ST 50138   842-6552
  Randy Flack, supt.
SHS, 102 N LINCOLN ST 50138   2-00001
  James Dyer, prin.   842-2173
McGowen JHS, 308 W MARION ST 50138   2-00110
  Michael Spolar, prin.   842-3315

Lake City, AC 712, PC 4, Calhoun
Southern Cal Community SD   3-11111
  709 W MAIN ST 51449   464-7210
  Vernard Keerbs, supt.
Southern Cal HS, 709 W MAIN ST 51449   2-00011
  Walter Block, prin.   464-7211
Other Schools – See Lohrville

Lake Mills, AC 515, PC 4, Winnebago
Lake Mills Community SD   3-11111
  102 S 4TH AVE E 50450   592-0881
  Dale Sorenson, supt.
HS, 102 S 4TH AVE E 50450   2-00011
  James Bryant, prin.   592-0893
MS, 102 S 4TH AVE E 50450   2-00100
  Donald Borey, prin.   592-0893

Lake Park, AC 712, PC 3, Dickinson
Harris-Lake Park Community SD   2-11111
  PO BOX 8 51347   832-3640
  Gerald Bradley, supt.
Harris-Lake Park JSHS   2-00111
  PO BOX 8 51347   832-3616
  Gary Richardson, prin.

Lake View, AC 712, PC 4, Sac
Lake View-Auburn Community SD   2-10011
  PO BOX 110 51450   657-2817
  Patrick Morgan, supt.
Lake View-Auburn HS   2-00011
  PO BOX 110 51450   657-2816
  Daniel Buenz, prin.

Lamoni, AC 515, PC 4, Decatur
Lamoni Community SD   2-11111
  202 N WALNUT ST 50140   784-3342
  Sue Payne, supt.
HS, 202 N WALNUT ST 50140   2-00011
  Burnice McLaurin, prin.   784-3351
MS, 202 N WALNUT ST 50140   1-00100
  Larry Dusanek, prin.   784-7299

Graceland College 50140   4-UC
      784-5000

Lansing, AC 319, PC 4, Allamakee
Eastern Allamakee Community SD   3-11111
  696 MAIN ST 52151   538-4202
  John Grampovnik, supt.
Kee HS, 569 CENTER ST 52151   2-00011
  Jon Nordaas, prin.   538-4201
MS, 696 MAIN ST 52151   2-01100
  James Hanson, prin.   538-4118

La Porte City, AC 319, PC 4, Black Hawk
Union Community SD   4-11111
  200 ADAMS ST 50651   342-2674
  Ronald Crooks, supt.
Union HS, 200 ADAMS ST 50651   2-00011
  Neil Mullen, prin.   342-2697
Other Schools – See Dysart

Latimer, AC 515, PC 2, Franklin
Cal Community SD   2-11111
  PO BOX 459 50452   579-6087
  James Jess, supt.
Cal Community JSHS   2-00111
  PO BOX 459 50452   579-6086
  Homer Mileham, prin.

Laurens, AC 712, PC 4, Pocahontas
Laurens-Marathon Community SD   3-11111
  300 W GARFIELD ST 50554   845-4508
  Delmer Hofer, supt.
Laurens-Marathon HS   2-00011
  300 W GARFIELD ST 50554   845-4508
  Ron Day, prin.
Laurens-Marathon MS   2-00100
  300 W GARFIELD ST 50554   845-4508
  Dan Braunschweig, prin.

Lawton, AC 712, PC 2, Woodbury
Lawton-Bronson Community SD   3-11111
PO BOX 128   51030   944-5183
Dale Black, supt.
JSHS, PO BOX 128   51030   2-00111
Thomas Judkins, prin.   944-5181

Le Grand, AC 515, PC 3, Marshall
East Marshall Community SD
Supt. — See Gilman
East Marshall HS   2-00011
201 N FRANKLIN   50142   479-2785
Kyle Chaska, prin.

Le Mars, AC 712, PC 6, Plymouth
Le Mars Community SD   4-11111
921 3RD AVE SW   51031   546-4155
Roy Messerol'e, supt.
HS, 921 3RD AVE SW   51031   2-00011
James Patera, prin.   546-4153
MS, 977 3RD AVE SW   51031   3-00100
John Mandernach, prin.   546-7022

Gehlen S, 709 PLYMOUTH ST NE   51031   3-11111
Fr. Schrad, prin.   546-5126
Teikyo Westmar University   3-UC
1002 3RD AVE SE   51031   546-7081

Lenox, AC 515, PC 4, Taylor
Lenox Community SD   3-11111
600 S LOCUST ST   50851   333-2244
Pamela Rockwood, supt.
JSHS, 600 S LOCUST ST   50851   2-00111
Paul Oliphant, prin.   333-2244

Leon, AC 515, PC 4, Decatur
Central Decatur Community SD   3-11111
1201 NE POPLAR ST   50144   446-4818
Tom Spear, supt.
Central Decatur JSHS   2-00111
1201 NE POPLAR ST   50144   446-4816
Gary Battles, prin.

Letts, AC 319, PC 2, Louisa
Louisa-Muscatine Community SD   4-11111
14354 170TH ST   52754   726-3421
Mike Kortemeyer, supt.
Louisa-Muscatine JSHS   2-00111
14354 170TH ST   52754   726-3421
Roger Roskins, prin.

Liberty Center, AC 515, PC 2, Warren
Southeast Warren Community SD   3-11111
1621 TYLER ST   50145   466-3332
Thomas Behounek, supt.
Southeast Warren JSHS   2-00111
1621 TYLER ST   50145   466-3331
John Monroe, prin.

Lineville, AC 515, PC 2, Wayne
Lineville-Clio Community SD   2-11111
PO BOX 98   50147   876-5345
Eldon Cowles, supt.
Lineville-Clio JSHS   1-00111
PO BOX 98   50147   876-5345
Juanita Suhr, prin.

Linn Grove, AC 712, PC 2, Buena Vista
Sioux Central Community SD
Supt. — See Sioux Rapids
Sioux Central JHS   51033   2-00100
Richard Muller, prin.   296-3227

Lisbon, AC 319, PC 4, Linn
Lisbon Community SD   2-11111
PO BOX 839   52253   455-2075
David Bradley, supt.
HS, PO BOX 839   52253   2-00011
W. Chris Hanken, prin.   455-2106
MS, PO BOX 839   52253   1-00100
George Karam, prin.   455-2659

Little Rock, AC 712, PC 2, Lyon
Little Rock Community SD   2-11100
PO BOX 247   51243   479-2771
Jerry Nichols, supt.
George-Little Rock JHS   1-00100
PO BOX 247   51243   479-2246
Vincent Schaefer, prin.

Logan, AC 712, PC 4, Harrison
Logan-Magnolia Community SD   3-11111
1200 N 2ND AVE   51546   644-2250
Edwin Gambs, supt.
Logan-Magnolia JSHS   2-00111
1200 N 2ND AVE   51546   644-2250
Joe Bride, prin.

Lohrville, AC 712, PC 2, Calhoun
Southern Cal Community SD
Supt. — See Lake City
Southern Cal MS, PO BOX 276   51453   2-00100
Lois Irwin, prin.   465-3425

Lone Tree, AC 319, PC 3, Johnson
Lone Tree Community SD   2-11111
PO BOX 520   52755   629-4212
John Savage, supt.
JSHS, 303 S DEVOES ST   52755   2-00111
Stephen Ratzlaff, prin.   629-4610

Lost Nation, AC 319, PC 2, Clinton
Midland Community SD
Supt. — See Wyoming
MS, 100 WINTER   52254   2-00100
(—), prin.   678-2142

Lytton, AC 712, PC 2, Calhoun
Rockwell City-Lytton Community SD
Supt. — See Rockwell City
Rockwell City/Lytton MS   1-00100
PO BOX 175   50561   466-2223
Gary Willett, prin.

Mc Gregor, AC 319, PC 3, Clayton
Mar-Mac Community SD   52157   2-11100
John Stanton, supt.   873-3462
Mar-Mac MS   52157   1-00100
Larry Cox, prin.   873-3463

Madrid, AC 515, PC 4, Boone
Madrid Community SD   3-11111
599 N KENNEDY AVE   50156   795-3241
Marion Romitti, supt.
HS, 599 N KENNEDY AVE   50156   2-00011
Barry Green, prin.   795-3240
JHS, 599 N KENNEDY AVE   50156   1-00100
Berry Green, prin.   795-3240

Mallard, AC 712, PC 2, Palo Alto
Mallard Community SD   2-11100
PO BOX 326   50562   425-3451
Ronald Dobson, supt.
MS, PO BOX 326   50562   1-01100
Ronald Larson, prin.   425-3452

Malvern, AC 712, PC 4, Mills
Malvern Community SD   2-11111
RR 2 BOX 21   51551   624-8700
William Reents, supt.
JSHS, RR 2 BOX 21   51551   2-00111
Timothy Peterson, prin.   624-8645

Manchester, AC 319, PC 6, Delaware
West Delaware County Community SD   4-11111
601 NEW ST   52057   927-3515
Steve Swanson, supt.
West Delaware HS, 701 NEW ST   52057   3-00011
Roger Hanson, prin.   927-5002
West Delaware MS   3-01100
1101 DOCTOR ST   52057   927-5004
Galen Reinsmoen, prin.

Manilla, AC 712, PC 3, Crawford
IKM Community SD
Supt. — See Irwin
Irwin-Kirkman-Manilla HS   2-00011
PO BOX 580   51454   654-9385
William Miller, prin.

Manly, AC 515, PC 4, Worth
North Central Community SD   3-11111
105 S EAST ST   50456   454-2211
Bruce Burton, supt.
North Central JSHS   2-00111
105 S EAST ST   50456   454-2208
S. Brackey-Alborn-Yilek, prin.

Manning, AC 712, PC 4, Carroll
Manning Community SD   3-11111
209 10TH ST   51455   653-3771
Wayne Curlile, supt.
JSHS, 209 10TH ST   51455   2-00111
Don Ringgenberg, prin.   653-3781

Manson, AC 712, PC 4, Calhoun
Manson Northwest Webster Community SD   3-11111
1227 16TH ST   50563   469-2202
David Walkup, supt.
Manson-Northwest Webster HS   2-00011
1601 15TH ST   50563   469-2245
Rollie Wiebers, prin.
Other Schools – See Barnum

Mapleton, AC 712, PC 4, Monona
Maple Valley Community SD   3-11111
410 S 6TH ST   51034 – D. Webner, supt.   882-1315
Maple Valley HS, 410 S 6TH ST   51034   2-00111
Steve Oberg, prin.   882-1317
Other Schools – See Danbury

Maquoketa, AC 319, PC 6, Jackson
Maquoketa Community SD   4-11111
607 W SUMMIT ST   52060   652-4984
Richard Drey, supt.
HS, 600 WASHINGTON ST   52060   3-00011
Richard Wold, prin.   652-2451
MS, 200 E LOCUST ST   52060   2-00011
Lynn Disney, prin.   652-4956

Marcus, AC 712, PC 4, Cherokee
Marcus-Meriden-Cleghorn Community SD
Supt. — See Cleghorn
Marcus Community HS   2-00011
PO BOX 667   51035 – (—), prin.   376-4172

Marengo, AC 319, PC 4, Iowa
Iowa Valley Community SD   3-11111
359 E HILTON ST   52301   642-7714
Lyle Kooiker, supt.
Iowa Valley JSHS   2-00111
359 E HILTON ST   52301   642-3332
Dennis Dougherty, prin.

Marion, AC 319, PC 7, Linn
Linn-Mar Community SD   5-11111
3333 10TH ST   52302   377-7373
Joseph Pacha, supt.
Linn-Mar HS, 3333 10TH ST   52302   3-00011
Dale Monroe, prin.   377-7373
Linn-Mar JHS, 3333 10TH ST   52302   2-00100
John Corkery, prin.   377-7373

Marion ISD, PO BOX 606   52302   4-11111
William Jacobson, supt.   377-4691
JSHS, 675 S 15TH ST   52302   2-00111
Larry Twachtmann, prin.   377-9891

Marshalltown, AC 515, PC 8, Marshall
Marshalltown Community SD   5-11111
317 COLUMBUS DR   50158   754-1000
Stephen Williams, supt.
HS, 1602 S 2ND AVE   50158   4-00011
Jerry Stephen, prin.   754-1130
Anson MS, S 3RD AVE   50158   2-00100
Fred Wills, prin.   754-1090
Miller MS, 125 S 11TH ST   50158   3-00100
Burton Clement, prin.   754-1110

Marshalltown Community College   3-CC
PO BOX 536   50158   752-7106

Martensdale, AC 515, PC 2, Warren
Martensdale-St. Mary's Community SD   3-11111
PO BOX 187   50160   764-2466
Tom Scheldahl, supt.
Martensdale-St. Mary's JSHS   2-00111
PO BOX 187   50160   764-2486
Karlos McClure, prin.

Mason City, AC 515, PC 8, Cerro Gordo
Mason City Community SD   5-11111
1515 S PENNSYLVANIA AVE   50401   421-4400
David Darnell, supt.
HS, 1700 4TH ST SE   50401   4-00011
Joyce Judas, prin.   421-4436
Adams MS, 29 S ILLINOIS AVE   50401   3-00100
Stephen Pottratz, prin.   421-4420
Roosevelt MS, 303 15TH ST SE   50401   3-00100
Robert Boone, prin.   421-4423

Hamilton Business College   2-CS
100 1ST ST NW   50401   800-274-2530
Newman S, 2445 19TH ST SW   50401   3-11111
Don Greenlee, prin.   423-6939
North Iowa Area Community College   4-CC
500 COLLEGE DR   50401   423-1264
St. Joseph Mercy Hospital   HSP
84 BEAUMONT DR   50401   424-7722
World Wide College of Auctioneering   1-CS
PO BOX 949   50402   423-5242

Massena, AC 712, PC 2, Cass
C & M Community SD   2-11111
PO BOX 7   50853   779-2211
Leroy Ortman, supt.
C & M JSHS, PO BOX 7   50853   2-00111
Randy Peters, prin.   779-2212

Maxwell, AC 515, PC 3, Story
Collins-Maxwell Community SD   2-11111
PO BOX 207   50161   387-1115
Patrick Sullivan, supt.
Collins-Maxwell HS   50161   2-00011
Donald Peterson, prin.   387-1115
Other Schools – See Collins

Maynard, AC 319, PC 3, Fayette
West Central Community SD   50655   2-11111
P. Whitlatch, supt.   637-2284
West Central JSHS   50655   2-00111
Daniel Buenz, prin.   637-2284

Mediapolis, AC 319, PC 4, Des Moines
Mediapolis Community SD   4-11111
725 N NORTHFIELD ST   52637   394-3237
Bill Newman, supt.
HS, 725 N NORTHFIELD ST   52637   2-00011
Phillip Speece, prin.   394-3101
JHS, 725 N NORTHFIELD ST   52637   2-00100
James Devore, prin.   394-3101

Melcher, AC 515, PC 4, Marion
Melcher-Dallas Community SD   2-11111
PO BOX 489   50163   947-2321
Charles Stalker, supt.
Melcher-Dallas HS   2-00011
PO BOX 158   50163 – (—), prin.   947-3731
Melcher-Dallas JHS   1-00100
PO BOX 158   50163 – (—), prin.   947-3731

Middle Amana, AC 319, PC 2, Iowa
Amana Community SD   2-11100
PO BOX 70   52307   622-3255
Craig Okerberg, supt.
Amana-Clear Creek MS   2-00100
PO BOX 70   52307   622-3255
Mike Hooley, prin.

Miles, AC 319, PC 2, Jackson
East Central Community SD   3-11111
PO BOX 367   52064   682-7510
James House, supt.
East Central Community HS   2-00011
PO BOX 367   52064   682-7510
Warren Amman, prin.
Other Schools – See Sabula

Milford, AC 712, PC 4, Dickinson
Okoboji Community SD   3-11111
PO BOX 147   51351   338-4757
Marvin Anderson, supt.
Okoboji HS, PO BOX 147   51351   2-00011
Larry Traughber, prin.   338-2446
Okoboji MS, PO BOX 147   51351   2-01100
David Dorenkamp, prin.   332-5641

Milton, AC 515, PC 3, Van Buren
Fox Valley Community SD
Supt. — See Cantril
Fox Valley JSHS, 202 N UNION ST 52570 1-00111
Robert Rongstad, prin. 656-4976

Mingo, AC 515, PC 2, Jasper
Colfax-Mingo Community SD
Supt. — See Colfax
Colfax-Mingo MS, MOHAWK DR 50168 2-00100
Homer Terpstra, prin. 363-4282

Missouri Valley, AC 712, PC 5, Harrison
Missouri Valley Community SD 4-11111
711 E SUPERIOR ST 51555 642-2706
Ken Northrup, supt.
HS, 605 LINCOLN HWY 51555 2-00011
Roger Clausen, prin. 642-4149
MS, 711 E SUPERIOR ST 51555 2-01100
Frank Smith, prin. 642-2707

Mondamin, AC 712, PC 2, Harrison
West Harrison Community SD 51557 2-11111
Robert Raymer, supt. 646-2991
West Harrison JSHS 51557 2-00111
Edwin Daugherty, prin. 646-2231

Monona, AC 319, PC 4, Clayton
M-F-L Community SD, PO BOX D 52159 3-11011
John Stanton, supt. 539-2031
MFL-Mar-Mac HS, PO BOX D 52159 2-00011
Jay Pedersen, prin. 539-2031

Monroe, AC 515, PC 4, Jasper
PCM Community SD
Supt. — See Prairie City
PCM HS, HIGHWAY 163 50170 2-00011
Ron Young, prin. 259-2315

Montezuma, AC 515, PC 4, Poweshiek
Montezuma Community SD 3-11111
504 N 4TH ST 50171 623-5121
Lewis Lundy, supt.
SHS 50171 2-00001
Darrell Brand, prin. 623-5121
JHS 50171 2-00110
Tom Erickson, prin. 623-5129

Monticello, AC 319, PC 5, Jones
Monticello Community SD 4-11111
711 N MAPLE ST 52310 465-5963
Timothy Dose, supt.
HS, 217 S MAPLE ST 52310 2-00011
Keith Stamp, prin. 465-3575
MS, 217 S MAPLE ST 52310 2-00100
Daniel Lock, prin. 465-3575

Moorhead, AC 712, PC 2, Monona
East Monona Community SD 2-11111
PO BOX 8 51558 886-5232
Roger Friedrichsen, supt.
East Monona JSHS, PO BOX 8 51558 2-00111
Wallace Welander, prin. 886-5232

Moravia, AC 515, PC 3, Appanoose
Moravia Community SD 2-11111
5150 N TROSSELL ST 52571 724-3240
Joseph Graves, supt.
JSHS, 515 N TROSSELL ST 52571 2-00111
Fredrick Probasco, prin. 724-3241

Moulton, AC 515, PC 3, Appanoose
Moulton-Udell Community SD 2-11111
305 E 8TH ST 52572 642-3665
Ronald Bethards, supt.
Moulton-Udell JSHS 2-00111
305 E 8TH ST 52572 642-8131
Ken McKenna, prin.

Mount Ayr, AC 515, PC 4, Ringgold
Mount Ayr Community SD 3-11111
1001 E COLUMBUS ST 50854 464-0500
Philip Burmeister, supt.
JSHS, 1001 E COLUMBUS ST 50854 2-00111
Carroll Taylor, prin. 464-0510

Mount Pleasant, AC 319, PC 6, Henry
Mt. Pleasant Community SD 4-11111
202 N MAIN ST 52641 385-7750
John Roederer, supt.
SHS, 307 E MONROE ST 52641 2-00001
Thomas Lowe, prin. 385-7700
JHS, 400 N ADAMS ST 52641 2-00110
Ross Opsal, prin. 385-7730

Iowa Wesleyan College 3-UC
601 N MAIN ST 52641 385-8021

Mount Vernon, AC 319, PC 5, Linn
Mt. Vernon Community SD 4-11111
525 PALISADES RD 52314 895-8845
Adrian Ringold, supt.
HS, 525 PALISADES RD 52314 2-00011
Thomas Madson, prin. 895-8843
MS, 221 1ST ST E 52314 2-00100
Thomas Lass, prin. 895-6254

Cornell College 4-UC
600 1ST ST W 52314 800-747-1112

Moville, AC 712, PC 4, Woodbury
Woodbury Central Community SD 51039 3-11111
Thomas Cooper, supt. 873-3128
Woodbury Central HS, PO BOX AJ 51039 2-00011
Dean Von Bergen, prin. 873-3128
Woodbury Central MS, PO BOX AJ 51039 2-01100
Robert Jensen, prin. 873-3128

Murray, AC 515, PC 3, Clarke
Murray Community SD 2-11111
PO BOX 187 50174 447-2517
Lynn Padellford, supt.
JSHS, PO BOX 187 50174 2-00111
Gerald Brown, prin. 477-2517

Muscatine, AC 319, PC 7, Muscatine
Muscatine Community SD 6-11111
1403 PARK AVE 52761 263-7223
Janyce Myers, supt.
HS, 2705 CEDAR ST 52761 4-00011
(—), prin. 263-6141
Central MS, 901 CEDAR ST 52761 3-00100
Marvin Koopman, prin. 263-7784
West MS, 600 KINDLER AVE 52761 3-00100
Ronald Axel, prin. 263-0411

Muscatine Community College 4-CC
152 COLORADO ST 52761 322-5015

Nashua, AC 515, PC 4, Chickasaw
Nashua Community SD 3-11011
612 GREELEY ST 50658 435-4835
Linda Johanningmeier, supt.
Nashua Plainfield HS 2-00011
612 GREELEY ST 50658 435-4166
Terry Christie, prin.

Neola, AC 712, PC 3, Pottawattamie
Tri-Center Community SD 3-11111
PO BOX 217A 51559 485-2257
Edward Rastovski, supt.
Tri-Center HS, PO BOX 217A 51559 2-00011
Brett Nanninga, prin. 485-2258
Tri-Center JHS, PO BOX 217A 51559 2-00100
Jay Bellar, prin. 455-2257

Nevada, AC 515, PC 6, Story
Nevada Community SD 4-11111
1035 15TH ST 50201 382-2783
Kenneth Shaw, supt.
HS, 1001 15TH ST 50201 2-00011
Raphael Murray, prin. 382-3521
MS, 1035 15TH ST 50201 2-01100
James Walker, prin. 382-2751

Newell, AC 712, PC 4, Buena Vista
Newell-Fonda Community SD 2-11111
205 S CLARK ST 50568 272-3325
Merle Boerner, supt.
Newell-Fonda HS 2-00011
205 S CLARK ST 50568 272-3325
Phillip Casey, prin.
Other Schools – See Fonda

New Hampton, AC 515, PC 5, Chickasaw
New Hampton Community SD 4-11111
710 W MAIN ST 50659 394-2134
Robert Longmuir, supt.
HS, 710 W MAIN ST 50659 2-00011
John Anderson, prin. 394-2144
MS, 206 W MAIN ST 50659 2-00100
Larry Plumb, prin. 394-2259

New Hartford, AC 319, PC 3, Butler
New Hartford Community SD 2-11100
508 BEAVER 50660 983-2207
Don Gunderson, supt.
New Hartford-Dike JHS 2-00100
508 BEAVER 50660 983-2206
Robert Weber, prin.

New London, AC 319, PC 4, Henry
New London Community SD 3-11111
PO BOX 97 52645 367-0512
Vincent Smith, supt.
JSHS, PO BOX 97 52645 2-00111
Charles Lorber, prin. 367-0500

New Providence, AC 515, PC 2, Hardin
Eldora-New Providence Community SD
Supt. — See Eldora
Eldora-New Providence MS 2-01100
12TH ST AND 12TH AVE 50206 858-2599
Richard Keith, prin.

New Sharon, AC 515, PC 4, Mahaska
North Mahaska Community SD 3-11111
PO BOX 89 50207 637-2295
Merrill Knight, supt.
North Mahaska JSHS 2-00111
PO BOX 89 50207 637-4187
Bruce Johnson, prin.

Newton, AC 515, PC 7, Jasper
Newton Community SD 5-11111
807 S 6TH AVE W 50208 792-5809
Philip Hintz, supt.
HS, 800 E 4TH ST S 50208 4-00011
Gary Kirchhoff, prin. 792-5797
Berg JHS, 1900 N 5TH AVE E 50208 3-00100
David Gallaher, prin. 792-7741

New Virginia, AC 515, PC 2, Warren
Interstate 35 Community SD
Supt. — See Truro
Interstate 35 JHS, 117 BROADWAY 50210 2-00100
Robin Norris, prin. 449-3319

Nora Springs, AC 515, PC 4, Floyd
Nora Springs-Rock Falls Community SD 3-11111
509 N IOWA AVE 50458 749-5301
Clark Dey, supt.
Nora Springs-Rock Falls JSHS 2-00111
509 N IOWA AVE 50458 749-5301
R. Lowery, prin.

North English, AC 319, PC 3, Iowa
English Valleys Community SD 2-11111
PO BOX 490 52316 664-3634
Alan Jensen, supt.
English Valleys JSHS 2-00111
PO BOX 490 52316 664-3632
Gerry Beeler, prin.

Northwood, AC 515, PC 4, Worth
Northwood-Kensett Community SD 3-11111
1210 1ST AVE N 50459 324-2021
Jerry McIntire, supt.
Northwood-Kensett JSHS 2-00111
607 7TH ST N 50459 – John Lee, prin. 324-2142

Norwalk, AC 515, PC 6, Warren
Norwalk Community SD 4-11111
906 SCHOOL AVE 50211 981-0676
Dewitt Jones, supt.
HS, 1201 NORTH AVE 50211 3-00011
Gregory Anderson, prin. 981-4201
MS, 1412 NORTH AVE 50211 2-00100
Elaine Smith, prin. 981-0435

Oakland, AC 712, PC 4, Pottawattamie
Riverside Community SD
Supt. — See Carson
Riverside Community HS 2-00011
501 OAKLAND AVE 51560 – (—), prin. 482-6464

Odebolt, AC 712, PC 4, Sac
Odebolt-Arthur Community SD 2-11111
600 MAPLE 51458 – Dick Profit, supt. 668-2289
Odebolt-Arthur HS, 600 MAPLE 51458 2-00011
Larry Leinbaugh, prin. 668-2827
Other Schools – See Arthur

Oelwein, AC 319, PC 6, Fayette
Oelwein Community SD 4-11111
307 8TH AVE SE 50662 283-3536
Eldon Pyle, supt.
HS, 315 8TH AVE SE 50662 2-00011
Dominic Grasso, prin. 283-2731
JHS, 300 12TH AVE SE 50662 2-00100
John Youngblut, prin. 283-3015

Ogden, AC 515, PC 4, Boone
Ogden Community SD 3-11111
PO BOX 250 50212 275-2894
Raymond Gaul, supt.
HS, PO BOX 250 50212 2-00011
Stanley Friesen, prin. 275-4034
North MS, PO BOX 250 50212 2-01100
Gary Paulsen, prin. 275-2912

Olin, AC 319, PC 3, Jones
Olin Consolidated SD 2-10011
PO BOX 9 52320 484-2155
Marvin Ryan, supt.
HS, PO BOX 9 52320 2-00011
Paul Sundholm, prin. 484-2170

Onawa, AC 712, PC 5, Monona
West Monona Community SD 3-11111
1314 15TH ST 51040 423-2043
Robert Jackson, supt.
West Monana JSHS, 1314 15TH ST 51040 2-00111
Daniel Stehn, prin. 423-2453

Oran, AC 319, PC 2, Fayette
Wapsie Valley Community SD
Supt. — See Fairbank
Wapsie Valley JHS, PO BOX 8 50664 2-00100
Colby Withers, prin. 638-5211

Orange City, AC 712, PC 5, Sioux
Floyd Valley Community SD 3-11100
PO BOX 229 51041 737-4873
Rod Wilbeck, supt.
Other Schools – See Alton

Maurice-Orange City Community SD 3-11011
PO BOX 229 51041 737-4873
Rod Wilbeck, supt.
Maurice-Orange City/Floyd Valley HS 2-00011
615 8TH ST SE 51041 737-4871
P. Aykens, prin.

Northwestern College 4-UC
101 7TH ST SW 51041 737-4821
Unity Christian HS 2-00011
216 MICHIGAN AVE SW 51041 737-4114
Glenn Vos, prin.

Orient, AC 515, PC 2, Adair
Orient-Macksburg Community SD 50858 2-11111
Bill Cox, supt. 337-5061
Orient-Macksburg JSHS 50858 1-00111
Steven Lane, prin. 337-5061

Osage, AC 515, PC 5, Mitchell
Osage Community SD 4-11111
820 SAWYER DR 50461 732-5381
Dean Meier, supt.
HS, 820 SAWYER DR 50461 2-00011
Steve Nicholson, prin. 732-3102
MS, 820 SAWYER DR 50461 2-00100
Ross Grafft, prin. 732-3127

Osceola, AC 515, PC 5, Clarke
Clarke Community SD 4-10111
PO BOX 535 50213 342-4969
Steve Waterman, supt.

Clarke Community HS | 2-00011
800 N JACKSON ST   50213 | 342-6505
Mike Ashton, prin.
Clarke JHS, 800 N JACKSON ST   50213 | 2-00100
Mike Ashton, prin. | 342-6505

Oskaloosa, AC 515, PC 7, Mahaska
Oskaloosa Community SD | 5-11111
A AVE E & N MARKET ST   52577 | 673-8345
Harold Westra, supt.
SHS, 1800 N 3RD ST   52577 | 3-00001
Terry Eagen, prin. | 673-3407
JHS, 1704 N 3RD ST   52577 | 3-00110
Lowell Lenarz, prin. | 673-8308

William Penn College | 3-UC
201 TRUEBLOOD AVE   52577 | 800-779-7366

Ossian, AC 319, PC 3, Winneshiek
South Winneshiek Community SD
Supt. — See Calmar
South Winneshiek MS | 2-00100
PO BOX 298   52161 | 532-9365
Charles Ehler, prin.

Ottumwa, AC 515, PC 7, Wapello
Ottumwa Community SD | 5-11111
422 MCCARROLL DR   52501 | 684-6596
Joseph Scalzo, supt.
HS, 501 E 2ND ST   52501 | 4-00011
B. Kuntz, prin. | 683-4444
Evans JHS, 812 CHESTER AVE   52501 | 3-00100
Patricia Magwire, prin. | 684-6511

Indian Hills Community College | 4-CC
525 GRANDVIEW AVE   52501 | 683-5111

Oxford, AC 319, PC 3, Johnson
Clear Creek Community SD | 3-11011
PO BOX 487   52322 | 628-4510
Craig Okerberg, supt.
Other Schools – See Tiffin

Oxford Junction, AC 319, PC 3, Jones
Oxford Junction Consolidated SD   52323 | 2-11100
Dale Crozier, supt. | 486-2091
Olin-Oxford Junction MS   52323 | 1-00100
Dorance Hefte, prin. | 486-2721

Packwood, AC 319, PC 2, Jefferson
Pekin Community SD, RR 1   52580 | 3-11111
David Arnold, supt. | 695-3707
Pekin Community JSHS, RR 1   52580 | 2-00111
Joe Morgan, prin. | 695-3705

Palmer, AC 712, PC 2, Pocahontas
Pomeroy-Palmer Community SD
Supt. — See Pomeroy
Palmer-Pomeroy MS | 1-01100
HENRIETTA AVE   50571 | 359-7713
Wally Parman, prin.

Panora, AC 515, PC 4, Guthrie
Panorama Community SD | 3-11111
PO BOX 39   50216 | 755-2317
William Weddingfeld, supt.
Panorama HS, PO BOX 39   50216 | 2-00011
Louis McCrea, prin. | 755-2317
Panorama MS, PO BOX 39   50216 | 2-00100
Louis McCrea, prin. | 755-2317

Parkersburg, AC 319, PC 4, Butler
Parkersburg Community SD | 3-11011
610 N JOHNSON ST   50665 | 346-1012
Virgil Goodrich, supt.
Aplington-Parkersburg HS | 2-00011
610 N JOHNSON ST   50665 | 346-1571
Ned Sellers, prin.

Paullina, AC 712, PC 4, O'Brien
South O'Brien Community SD | 3-11111
PO BOX 638   51046 | 448-3452
Michael Davis, supt.
South O'Brien HS | 2-00011
PO BOX 638   51046 | 448-3454
Gary Nichol, prin.
Other Schools – See Primghar

Pella, AC 515, PC 6, Marion
Pella Community SD | 4-11111
210 UNIVERSITY ST   50219 | 628-1111
Orville Dunkin, supt.
HS, 212 E UNIVERSITY ST   50219 | 2-00011
Mark Lee, prin. | 628-3870
MS, 612 E 13TH ST   50219 | 2-00100
Donald Roehr, prin. | 628-4784

Central College | 4-UC
812 UNIVERSITY ST   50219 | 628-9000
Pella Christian HS | 2-00011
604 JEFFERSON ST   50219 | 628-4440
Clyde Rinsema, prin.

Peosta, AC 319, PC 2, Dubuque

Northeast Iowa Technical Institute | 2-CC
RR 1   52068 | 556-5110

Perry, AC 515, PC 6, Dallas
Perry Community SD | 4-11111
1219 WARFORD ST   50220 | 465-4656
Richard Staver, supt.
HS, 1200 18TH ST   50220 | 2-00011
Eugene Brady, prin. | 465-3503

MS, 2023 WILLIS AVE   50220 | 2-00100
Arthur Pixler, prin. | 465-3531

Pierson, AC 712, PC 2, Woodbury
Kingsley-Pierson Community SD
Supt. — See Kingsley
JHS   51048 | 2-00100
Stewart Goslinga, prin. | 375-5939

Plainfield, AC 319, PC 2, Bremer
Plainfield Community SD | 2-11100
PO BOX 38   50666 | 276-4451
Linda Johanningmeier, supt.
Nasha-Plainfield MS | 2-00100
PO BOX 38   50666 | 276-4451
Ron Reusche, prin.

Pleasant Valley, AC 319, PC 3, Scott
Pleasant Valley Community SD | 5-11111
PO BOX 332   52767 | 332-5550
Dale Barber, supt.
HS, PO BOX 332   52767 | 3-00011
James Spelhaug, prin. | 332-5151
Black Hawk JHS, PO BOX 332   52767 | 2-00100
Larry Brown, prin. | 289-4507

Pleasantville, AC 515, PC 4, Marion
Pleasantville Community SD | 3-11111
415 JONES ST   50225 | 848-0555
Charles Stalker, supt.
JSHS, 415 W JONES ST   50225 | 2-00011
David Isgrig, prin. | 848-0541

Pocahontas, AC 712, PC 4, Pocahontas
Pocahontas Area SD | 3-11111
201 1ST AVE SW   50574 | 335-4311
Dennis Pierce, supt.
Pocahontas Area HS | 2-00011
205 2ND AVE NW   50574 | 335-4848
Grant Stimson, prin.
Other Schools – See Rolfe

Pomeroy, AC 712, PC 3, Calhoun
Pomeroy-Palmer Community SD | 2-11111
202 E HARRISON ST   50575 | 468-2268
R. Skinner, supt.
HS, 202 E HARRISON ST   50575 | 2-00011
Tom McDonald, prin. | 468-2268
Other Schools – See Palmer

Postville, AC 319, PC 4, Allamakee
Postville Community SD | 3-11111
312 W POST   52162 – John Selk, supt. | 864-7651
Mott HS, 312 W POST   52162 | 2-00011
Dennis White, prin. | 864-7652

Prairie City, AC 515, PC 4, Jasper
PCM Community SD | 4-11111
PO BOX 490   50228 | 994-2685
Jim Matre, supt.
PCM MS, 405 PLAINSMEN RD   50228 | 2-00100
Robert Buyert, prin. | 994-2686
Other Schools – See Monroe

Preston, AC 319, PC 4, Jackson
Preston Community SD | 2-11111
PO BOX 10   52069 | 689-5822
James House, supt.
JSHS, PO BOX 10   52069 | 2-00111
David Miller, prin. | 689-4221

Primghar, AC 712, PC 3, O'Brien
South O'Brien Community SD
Supt. — See Paullina
South O'Brien JHS, PO BOX P   51245 | 2-00100
Richard Partiow, prin. | 757-3755

Quimby, AC 712, PC 2, Cherokee
Willow Community SD | 2-11100
PO BOX 188   51049 | 445-2232
Richard Caldwell, supt.
Willow Community MS   51049 | 2-00100
Robert Schelp, prin. | 445-2231

Radcliffe, AC 515, PC 3, Hardin
Hubbard-Radcliffe Community SD
Supt. — See Hubbard
Radcliffe-Hubbard MS | 2-00100
PO BOX 278   50230 | 899-2112
Edmund Frangenberg, prin.

Redfield, AC 515, PC 3, Dallas
Dexfield Community SD | 2-11100
1104 GRANT   50233 | 833-2331
Dean Turner, supt.
Dexfield JSHS, 1104 GRANT   50233 | 2-00111
Leonard Griffith, prin. | 833-2331

Red Oak, AC 712, PC 6, Montgomery
Red Oak Community SD | 4-11111
408 COOLBAUGH ST   51566 | 623-4888
Robert Cardoni, supt.
HS, 2011 N 8TH ST   51566 | 2-00011
Martin Pennock, prin. | 623-4971
JHS, 308 E CORNING ST # A   51566 | 2-00100
(—), prin. | 623-2563

Powell Sch. for the Mentally Handicapped | HND
1005 N 7TH ST   51566

Reinbeck, AC 319, PC 4, Grundy
Reinbeck Community SD | 2-11100
600 BLACKHAWK ST   50669 | 345-2712
Lawrence McNabb, supt.
Gladbrook-Reinbeck HS   50669 | 2-00011
Leroy Schultz, prin. | 345-2921

Remsen, AC 712, PC 4, Plymouth
Remson-Union Community SD | 2-11111
511 ROOSEVELT   51050 | 786-1101
Willis Hoff, supt.
Remson-Union HS | 2-00011
511 ROOSEVELT   51050 | 786-1101
Delos Schumacher, prin.
Remson-Union JHS | 1-00100
511 ROOSEVELT ST   51050 | 786-1101
Delos Schumacher, prin.

St. Marys HS, 523 MADISON ST   51050 | 2-00011
Fr. Craig Collison, prin. | 786-1433

Riceville, AC 515, PC 3, Howard
Riceville Community SD   50466 | 3-11011
Norman Kolberg, supt. | 985-2288
HS   50466 | 2-00011
Larry Abel, prin. | 985-2281

Ringsted, AC 712, PC 2, Emmet
Armstrong-Ringsted Community SD
Supt. — See Armstrong
Armstrong-Ringsted MS | 2-01100
PO BOX 218   50578 | 866-0191
Dennis Hoyer, prin.

Riverside, AC 319, PC 3, Washington
Highland Community SD | 3-11111
PO BOX B   52327 | 648-3822
Ira Cunningham, supt.
Highland HS, PO BOX B   52327 | 2-00011
Terry Bowton, prin. | 648-2891
Highland JHS, PO BOX B   52327 | 1-00100
Terry Bowton, prin. | 648-2891

Rockford, AC 515, PC 3, Floyd
Rudd-Rockford-Marble Rock Community SD | 3-11111
50468 – Steve Ward, supt. | 756-3610
JSHS   50468 | 2-00111
Carl Bishop, prin. | 756-3813

Rock Rapids, AC 712, PC 5, Lyon
Central Lyon Community SD | 3-11111
1105 S STORY ST   51246 | 472-4041
Albert Van Overmeer, supt.
Central Lyon HS | 2-00011
400 S 7TH AVE W   51246 | 472-4051
Larry Gearhart, prin.
Central Lyon MS | 2-00100
1105 S STORY ST   51246 | 472-4041
Lance Olson, prin.

Rock Valley, AC 712, PC 5, Sioux
Rock Valley Community SD | 3-11111
1712 20TH AVE   51247 | 476-2125
Les Douma, supt.
JSHS, 1712 20TH AVE   51247 | 2-00111
Everett Jensen, prin. | 476-2701

Rockwell, AC 515, PC 4, Cerro Gordo
Rockwell-Swaledale Community SD | 2-11111
50469 – Fred Muth, supt. | 822-3233
Rockwell-Swaledale JSHS   50469 | 2-00111
Richard Herrig, prin. | 822-3234

Rockwell City, AC 712, PC 4, Calhoun
Rockwell City-Lytton Community SD | 3-11111
1000 TONAWANDA ST   50579 | 297-7341
Dwayne Cross, supt.
Rockwell City/Lytton HS | 2-00011
1000 TONAWANDA ST   50579 | 297-8111
Charles Kuester, prin.
Other Schools – See Lytton

Roland, AC 515, PC 4, Story
Roland-Story Community SD
Supt. — See Story City
Roland-Story MS, 220 N MAIN ST   50236 | 2-01100
David Hemphill, prin. | 388-4348

Rolfe, AC 712, PC 3, Pocahontas
Pocahontas Area SD
Supt. — See Pocahontas
MS   50581 | 1-00100
Fred Muth, prin. | 848-3881

Royal, AC 712, PC 2, Clay
Clay Central/Everly Community SD
Supt. — See Everly
Clay Central/Everly MS | 2-00100
PO BOX 155   51357 | 933-2241
Marlin Gustin, prin.

Runnells, AC 515, PC 2, Polk
Southeast Polk Community SD | 5-11111
8379 NE UNIVERSITY AVE   50237 | 967-4294
Joseph Drips, supt.
Southeast Polk HS | 3-00011
8325 NE UNIVERSITY AVE   50237 | 967-6631
William Orcutt, prin.
Southeast Polk JHS | 3-00100
8301 NE UNIVERSITY AVE   50237 | 967-5509
Ray Svendson, prin.

Russell, AC 515, PC 3, Lucas
Russell Community SD | 2-11111
PO BOX 487   50238 | 535-2404
Robert McCurdy, supt.
JSHS, PO BOX 487   50238 | 1-00110
David Lockridge, prin. | 535-6105

Ruthven, AC 712, PC 3, Palo Alto
Ruthven-Ayrshire Community SD | 2-11111
PO BOX 159   51358 | 837-5211
Ron Sadler, supt.

Ruthven-Ayrshire JSHS   2-00111
  PO BOX 159   51358   837-5212
  Ervin Rowlands, prin.

Sabula, AC 319, PC 3, Jackson
East Central Community SD
  Supt. — See Miles
  MS   52070   2-00100
  Carl Kueter, prin.   687-2427

Sac City, AC 712, PC 4, Sac
Sac Community SD, S 16TH ST   50583   3-11111
  Jerry McMullen, supt.   662-7030
  Sac JSHS, 300 S 11TH ST   50583   2-00111
  Ernest Gottfried, prin.   662-3259

Saint Ansgar, AC 515, PC 4, Mitchell
St. Ansgar Community SD   3-11111
  206 E 8TH ST   50472   736-4681
  James Woodward, supt.
  HS, 206 E 8TH ST   50472   2-00011
  Emmett Tyler, prin.   736-4720
  Other Schools – See Grafton

Sanborn, AC 712, PC 4, O'Brien
Hartley-Melvin-Sanborn Community SD
  Supt. — See Hartley
  Hartley-Melvin-Sanborn MS   2-00100
  105 W 5TH   51248   729-3281
  Gerald Cummins, prin.

Schaller, AC 712, PC 3, Sac
Schaller-Crestland Community SD   3-11111
  300 S BERWICK   51053   275-4267
  Alan Meyer, supt.
  Other Schools – See Early

Schleswig, AC 712, PC 3, Crawford
Schleswig Community SD   2-11111
  PO BOX 250   51461   676-3313
  John Finnessy, supt.
  JSHS, PO BOX 250   51461   2-01100
  Duane Goode, prin.   676-3312

Sergeant Bluff, AC 712, PC 5, Woodbury
Sergeant Bluff-Luton Community SD   4-11111
  PO BOX 97   51054   943-4338
  Charles Scott, supt.
  Sergeant Bluff-Luton HS   2-00011
  PO BOX 97   51054   943-5561
  Ron Olien, prin.
  Sergeant Bluff-Luton MS   2-01100
  PO BOX 97   51054   943-4235
  Ron Brandl, prin.

Seymour, AC 515, PC 3, Wayne
Seymour Community SD   2-11111
  PARK AND MAIN STREET   52590   898-2291
  Richard Guess, supt.
  JSHS, PARK AND MAIN STREET   52590   2-00111
  Timothy Gilson, prin.   898-2291

Sheffield, AC 515, PC 4, Franklin
Sheffield-Chapin Community SD   50475   2-11011
  Clifford Cameron, supt.   892-4159
  Sheffield-Chapin HS   50475   2-00011
  Richard Helmer, prin.   892-4461

Shelby, AC 712, PC 3, Shelby
Shelby Community SD   2-11100
  304 WESTERN AVE   51570   544-2240
  Rod Montang, supt.
  JHS, PO BOX 309   51570   1-00100
  Richard Brockman, prin.   544-2240

Sheldon, AC 712, PC 5, O'Brien
Sheldon Community SD   4-11111
  1700 E 4TH ST   51201   324-2501
  Michael Teigland, supt.
  HS, 1700 E 4TH ST   51201   2-00011
  Robert Vander Plaats, prin.   324-2501
  MS, 727 6TH AVE   51201   2-01100
  Carl Turner, prin.   324-4346

Northwest Iowa Community College   2-CC
  603 W PARK ST   51201   324-5061

Shenandoah, AC 712, PC 6, Page
Shenandoah Community SD   4-11111
  616 W THOMAS AVE   51601   246-1581
  Joseph Kirchoff, supt.
  HS, 1000 MUSTANG DR   51601   2-00011
  Ronald Lottridge, prin.   246-4727
  MS, 101 W SUMMIT AVE   51601   2-01100
  Richard Cuva, prin.   246-2520

Sibley, AC 712, PC 5, Osceola
Sibley-Ocheyedan Community SD   4-11111
  120 11TH AVE NE   51249   754-2533
  Michael Rogers, supt.
  HS, 120 11TH AVE NE   51249   2-00011
  Jeff Zwagerman, prin.   754-3601
  Central MS, 120 11TH AVE NE   51249   2-01100
  Wayne Miller, prin.   754-2542

Sidney, AC 712, PC 4, Fremont
Sidney Community SD   2-11111
  PO BOX 609   51652   374-2141
  Eugene Hess, supt.
  JSHS, PO BOX 609   51652   2-00111
  Duane Ridnour, prin.   374-2141

Sigourney, AC 515, PC 4, Keokuk
Sigourney Community SD   3-11111
  107 W MARION ST   52591   622-2025
  Keith Sasseen, supt.

JSHS, RR 2   52591   2-00111
  Jerry Miletich, prin.   622-2010

Sioux Center, AC 712, PC 6, Sioux
Sioux Center Community SD   3-11111
  550 9TH ST NE   51250   722-2981
  Rick Melmer, supt.
  HS, 550 9TH ST NE   51250   2-00011
  Ken Wiersma, prin.   722-2981
  JHS, 550 9TH ST NE   51250   2-00100
  Ken Wiersma, prin.   722-2981

Dordt College   4-UC
  498 4TH AVE NE   51250   722-6000

Sioux City, AC 712, PC 8, Woodbury
Sioux City Community SD   7-11111
  1221 PIERCE ST   51105   279-6667
  James Austin, supt.
  East HS, 5011 MAYHEW AVE   51106   4-00011
  Richard Lilly, prin.   274-4000
  North HS, 4200 CHEYENNE BLVD   51104   4-00011
  Richard Bathurst, prin.   239-7001
  West HS, 2001 CASSELMAN ST   51103   3-00011
  James Deignan, prin.   279-6772
  East MS   4-00100
  1720 MORNINGSIDE AVE   51106   279-6800
  James Gaul, prin.
  Hoover MS   3-00100
  3601 COUNTRY CLUB BLVD   51104   279-6804
  Roger Wendt, prin.
  West MS, 1211 W 5TH ST   51103   3-00100
  Michael McTaggart, prin.   279-6813
  Wilson MS, 1010 IOWA ST   51105   3-00100
  Peter Hathaway, prin.   279-6816

Bishop Heelan HS   3-00011
  1021 DOUGLAS ST   51105   252-0573
  Fr. Avise, prin.
Briar Cliff College   3-UC
  3303 REBECCA ST   51104   279-5400
Holy Family MS Epiphany Center   2-00100
  1000 DOUGLAS ST   51105   252-3181
  Sr. Marge Ehlers, prin.
Marion Health Center   HSP
  624 JONES ST   51105   279-2018
Morningside College   4-UC
  1501 MORNINGSIDE AVE   51106   274-5000
St. Luke's Regional Medical Center   HSP
  2720 STONE PARK BLVD   51104   279-3172
Western Iowa Technical Community College   4-CC
  PO BOX 265   51102   274-6400

Sioux Rapids, AC 712, PC 3, Buena Vista
Sioux Central Community SD   3-11111
  505 ELM ST   50585 – Lee Burns, supt.   283-2571
  Sioux Central HS, 505 ELM ST   50585   2-00011
  Morris Johnson, prin.   283-2571
  Other Schools – See Linn Grove

Sloan, AC 712, PC 3, Woodbury
Westwood Community SD   3-11111
  PO BOX AD   51055   428-3355
  Leonard Grasso, supt.
  Westwood JSHS, PO BOX AD   51055   2-00111
  Gary Schrage, prin.   428-3303

Solon, AC 319, PC 4, Johnson
Solon Community SD, 403 S IOWA   52333   3-11111
  Kirk Rentschler, supt.   644-3401
  JSHS   52333   2-00111
  L. Meister, prin.   644-3401

Spencer, AC 712, PC 7, Clay
Spencer Community SD   4-11111
  800 E 3RD ST   51301   262-8950
  Glen Lohman, supt.
  HS, PO BOX 7188   51301   3-00011
  Gerald Vandyke, prin.   262-1742
  MS, 104 E 4TH ST   51301   2-00100
  Tom Conley, prin.   262-3345

Spencer College   2-CS
  PO BOX 5065   51301   800-383-7290

Spirit Lake, AC 712, PC 5, Dickinson
Spirit Lake Community SD   4-11111
  900 20TH ST   51360   336-2820
  Harold Overmann, supt.
  HS, 2700 HILL AVE   51360   2-00011
  Sheryl Hall, prin.   336-3707
  MS, 609 28TH ST   51360   2-01100
  Nancy Winter, prin.   336-1370

Springville, AC 319, PC 4, Linn
Springville Community SD   2-11111
  PO BOX 18   52336   854-6197
  Gary Biles, supt.
  JSHS, PO BOX 18   52336   2-00111
  Russell Adams, prin.   854-6196

Stanton, AC 712, PC 3, Montgomery
Stanton Community SD   51573   2-11111
  Judson Ashley, supt.   829-2162
  JSHS   51573   2-00111
  Gary Stephens, prin.   829-2162

Stanwood, AC 319, PC 3, Cedar
Lincoln Community SD   3-11111
  PO BOX 247   52337   945-3358
  Richard Bachman, supt.
  Lincoln JSHS, PO BOX 247   52337   2-00111
  Louis Grimm, prin.   945-3341

State Center, AC 515, PC 4, Marshall
West Marshall Community SD   3-11111
  PO BOX 670   50247   483-2660
  Dwight Pierson, supt.
  West Marshall HS   50247   2-00011
  Michael Anthony, prin.   483-2136
  West Marshall MS   50247   2-00100
  William Large, prin.   483-2165

Steamboat Rock, AC 515, PC 2, Hardin
Wellsburg/Steamboat Rock Community SD
  Supt. — See Wellsburg
  Wellsburg/Steamboat Rock MS   2-01100
  306 W MARKET   50672   868-2225
  Robert Hutchcroft, prin.

Storm Lake, AC 712, PC 6, Buena Vista
Storm Lake Community SD   4-11111
  419 LAKE AVE   50588   732-8060
  Bill Kruse, supt.
  HS, 621 TORNADO DR   50588   2-00011
  Michael Hanna, prin.   732-8065
  MS, 1811 HYLAND ST   50588   2-01100
  Ronald Bryan, prin.   732-8069

Buena Vista College   4-UC
  610 W 4TH ST   50588   749-2103
Iowa Central Community College   2-CC
  916 RUSSELL ST   50588   732-2991
St. Mary HS, 304 SENECA ST   50588   1-00011
  Fr. Van Haaften, prin.   732-4166

Story City, AC 515, PC 5, Story
Roland-Story Community SD   4-11111
  1009 STORY ST   50248   733-4301
  Dale Henricks, supt.
  Roland-Story HS, 1009 STORY ST   50248   2-00011
  Roger Pohlman, prin.   733-4329
  Other Schools – See Roland

Stuart, AC 515, PC 4, Guthrie
Stuart-Menlo Community SD   3-11111
  N 2ND & MAIN   50250   523-2187
  Larry Nulph, supt.
  Stuart-Menlo HS, N 2ND & MAIN   50250   2-00011
  Wayne O'Brien, prin.   523-1313
  Stuart-Menlo MS   50250   2-01100
  Wayne O'Brien, prin.   523-1313

Sully, AC 515, PC 3, Jasper
Lynnville-Sully Community SD   3-11111
  PO BOX 218   50251   594-4445
  Randall Betz, supt.
  Lynnville-Sully HS   50251   2-00011
  Rhonna Fiihr, prin.   594-3721
  Lynnville-Sully MS   50251   2-00100
  Rhonna Fiihr, prin.   594-2968

Sumner, AC 319, PC 4, Bremer
Sumner Community SD   3-11111
  PO BOX 178   50674   578-3425
  Don Miller, supt.
  JSHS, PO BOX 178   50674   2-00111
  Darwin Propes, prin.   578-3342

Swea City, AC 515, PC 3, Kossuth
North Kossuth Community SD   2-11111
  PO BOX B   50590 – Robert Pilcher, supt.   272-4102
  North Kossuth HS   2-00011
  PO BOX 567   50590   272-4361
  James Dyer, prin.
  North Kossuth MS   50590   1-01100
  Stephen Roman, prin.   272-4361

Tabor, AC 712, PC 3, Fremont
Fremont-Mills Community SD   3-11111
  PO BOX 310   51653   629-2325
  Robert Abbott, supt.
  Fremont-Mills JSHS   2-00111
  PO BOX 310   51653   629-2325
  Randell Botts, prin.

Tama, AC 515, PC 5, Tama
South Tama County Community SD   4-11111
  1702 HARDING ST   52339   484-4811
  Clarence Lippert, supt.
  South Tama County HS   2-00011
  1715 HARDING ST   52339   484-4345
  John Legg, prin.
  Other Schools – See Toledo

Terril, AC 712, PC 2, Dickinson
Terril Community SD   2-11111
  PO BOX 128   51364   853-6111
  Rodger Ritchie, supt.
  JSHS, PO BOX 128   51364   2-00111
  Orville Lewis, prin.   853-6112

Thompson, AC 515, PC 2, Winnebago
Thompson Community SD   2-11100
  4TH AND JACKSON   50478   584-2231
  C. R. Adams, supt.
  MS   50478   1-00100
  Lynn Hansen, prin.   584-2231

Thornburg, AC 515, PC 1, Keokuk
Tri-County Community SD   2-11111
  PO BOX 368   50255   634-2408
  Alan Jensen, supt.
  Tri-County HS   2-00011
  GENERAL DELIVERY   50255   634-2636
  Max Wolf, prin.
  Tri-County JHS   1-00100
  GENERAL DELIVERY   50255   634-2636
  Max Wolf, prin.

Thornton, AC 515, PC 2, Cerro Gordo
Meservey-Thornton Community SD 2-11100
PO BOX 150 50479 998-2315
Leroy Scharnhorst, supt.
Meservey-Thornton MS 2-00100
212 ELM ST 50479 998-2315
Leroy Scharnhorst, prin.

Tiffin, AC 319, PC 2, Johnson
Clear Creek Community SD
Supt. — See Oxford
Clear Creek HS, PO BOX 199 52340 2-00011
Thomas McAreavy, prin. 645-2361

Tipton, AC 319, PC 5, Cedar
Tipton Community SD 3-11111
400 E 6TH ST 52772 886-6121
Jeffory Corkery, supt.
JSHS, 400 E 6TH ST 52772 2-00111
Chris Habben, prin. 886-6027

Titonka, AC 515, PC 3, Kossuth
Titonka Consolidated SD 2-11100
PO BOX 287 50480 928-2717
Don West, supt.
MS, PO BOX 287 50480 2-00100
(—), prin. 928-2720

Toledo, AC 515, PC 4, Tama
South Tama County Community SD
Supt. — See Tama
South Tama County MS 2-00100
201 S GREEN ST 52342 484-4121
Les Koch, prin.

Traer, AC 319, PC 4, Tama
North Tama County Community SD 3-11111
605 WALNUT ST 50675 478-2265
Gary Croskrey, supt.
North Tama JSHS 2-00111
605 WALNUT ST 50675 478-2911
Thomas McDermott, prin.

Treynor, AC 712, PC 3, Pottawattamie
Treynor Community SD 2-11111
PO BOX 369 51575 487-3414
L. L. Haack, supt.
JSHS, GENERAL DELIVERY 51575 2-00111
Thomas Vint, prin. 487-3804

Tripoli, AC 319, PC 4, Bremer
Tripoli Community SD 3-11111
209 8TH AVE SW 50676 882-4201
Roger Ahrens, supt.
JSHS 50676 2-00111
Randall Stanek, prin. 882-4202

Troy Mills, AC 319, PC 2, Linn
North Linn Community SD
Supt. — See Coggon
North Linn JHS 2-00100
3255 OSCEOLA ST 52344 224-3411
Frank Shekleton, prin.

Truro, AC 515, PC 2, Madison
Interstate 35 Community SD 3-11111
PO BOX 98 50257 765-4291
Don Brichacek, supt.
Interstate 35 HS, PO BOX 98 50257 2-00011
Richard Magnuson, prin. 765-4818
Other Schools – See New Virginia

Underwood, AC 712, PC 3, Pottawattamie
Underwood Community SD 3-11111
PO BOX 130 51576 566-2332
Cynthia Hollinger, supt.
HS, PO BOX 130 51576 2-00011
Thomas Dannen, prin. 566-2703
MS, PO BOX 130 51576 2-00100
Thomas Dannen, prin. 566-2332

Union, AC 515, PC 2, Hardin
BCLUW Community SD
Supt. — See Conrad
BCLUW MS, PO BOX A 50258 2-01100
Gerald Gade, prin. 486-5371

University Park, AC 515, PC 3, Mahaska

Vennard College 2-UC
PO BOX 29 52595 673-8391

Urbana, AC 319, PC 3, Benton
Center Point-Urbana Community SD
Supt. — See Center Point
Urbana Center Point MS 2-01100
PO BOX 246 52345 443-2426
Melinda Krumm, prin.

Urbandale, AC 515, PC 7, Polk
Urbandale Community SD 5-11111
7101 AIRLINE AVE 50322 253-2300
Thomas Davis, supt.
HS, 7111 AURORA AVE 50322 3-00011
Robert Stouffer, prin. 253-2322
MS, 7701 AURORA AVE 50322 3-00100
Diana Bourisaw, prin. 253-2312

Van Horne, AC 319, PC 3, Benton
Benton Community SD 4-11111
PO BOX 70 52346 228-8241
Steven Wehr, supt.
Benton Community HS 2-00011
400 1ST STREET 52346 228-8701
Gary Zittergruen, prin.
Benton Community MS 2-00100
400 1ST STREET 52346 228-8701
Timothy Means, prin.

Van Meter, AC 515, PC 3, Dallas
Van Meter Community SD 2-11111
PO BOX 257 50261 996-2221
Craig Cochran, supt.
JSHS, PO BOX 257 50261 2-00111
Jack Rockwell, prin. 996-2221

Ventura, AC 515, PC 3, Cerro Gordo
Ventura Community SD 2-11111
PO BOX 18 50482 829-4484
Gary Schichtl, supt.
JSHS, PO BOX 18 50482 2-00111
Tom Fey, prin. 829-4484

Victor, AC 319, PC 3, Iowa
H-L-V Community SD, PO BOX B 52347 2-11111
William Lynch, supt. 647-2161
H-L-V JSHS, PO BOX B 52347 2-00111
Donald Lewis, prin. 647-2161

Villisca, AC 712, PC 4, Montgomery
Villisca Community SD 2-11111
205 S 4TH AVE 50864 826-2542
Robert Busch, supt.
Villisca Community JSHS 2-00111
205 S 4TH AVE 50864 826-2552
Lee Haidsiak, prin.

Vinton, AC 319, PC 6, Benton
Vinton-Shellsburg Community SD 4-11111
810 W 9TH ST 52349 472-4728
Patricia McClure, supt.
Washington HS, 212 W 15TH ST 52349 2-00011
Terry Christiansen, prin. 472-4721
Tilford MS, 308 E 13TH ST 52349 2-00100
David Strudthoff, prin. 472-4736

Iowa Braille and Sight Saving School HND
52349

Walcott, AC 319, PC 4, Scott
Davenport Community SD
Supt. — See Davenport
JHS, 545 E JAMES ST 52773 2-00110
Joseph Kussatz, prin. 284-6795

Wall Lake, AC 712, PC 3, Sac
Wall Lake Community SD 2-01100
206 BOYER ST 51466 664-2627
Patrick Morgan, supt.
Wall Lake View Auburn MS 1-00100
206 BOYER ST 51466 664-2431
Larry Faust, prin.

Walnut, AC 712, PC 3, Pottawattamie
Walnut Community SD 2-11111
PO BOX 528 51577 784-2251
Warren Winterhof, supt.
JSHS, PO BOX 528 51577 1-00111
Walter Aeckerle, prin. 784-3615

Wapello, AC 319, PC 4, Louisa
Wapello Community SD 3-11111
445 N CEDAR ST 52653 523-3641
Larry Anderson, supt.
HS, 501 BUCHANAN AVE 52653 2-00011
William Hamilton, prin. 523-3241
JHS, 501 BUCHANAN AVE 52653 2-00100
William Hamilton, prin. 523-8131

Washington, AC 319, PC 6, Washington
Washington Community SD 4-11111
PO BOX 926 52353 653-6543
Kim Kreinbring, supt.
SHS, PO BOX 271 52353 2-00001
Francis Johnston, prin. 653-2143
JHS, 1111 S AVENUE B 52353 2-00110
Maynard Lust, prin. 653-5414

Waterloo, AC 319, PC 8, Black Hawk
Waterloo Community SD 7-11111
1516 WASHINGTON ST 50702 291-4800
James Kimmet, supt.
East HS, 214 HIGH ST 50703 4-00011
Augusta Clark, prin. 291-4829
West HS, 501 E RIDGEWAY AVE 50702 4-00011
Barbara Corson, prin. 291-4885
Central IS, 1350 KATOSKI DR 50701 3-00100
Lloyd Applegate, prin. 291-4823
Hoover IS, 630 HILLCREST RD 50701 3-00100
Nancy Zimmerman, prin. 291-4851
Logan IS, 1515 LOGAN AVE 50703 3-00100
Ray Jorgensen, prin. 291-4864
West IS, 1115 W 5TH ST 50702 3-00100
Roger Anderson, prin. 291-4892

Allen Memorial Hospital HSP
1825 LOGAN AVE 50703 235-3649
Columbus HS, 3231 W 9TH ST 50702 3-00011
Michael Palmer, prin. 233-3358
Covenant Medical Center HSP
3421 W 9TH ST 50702 236-4111
Hawkeye Community College 4-CC
1501 E ORANGE RD 50701 296-2320
Walnut Ridge Baptist Academy 2-11111
1307 W RIDGEWAY AVE 50701 235-9309
Timothy Wilhite, prin.

Waukee, AC 515, PC 5, Dallas
Waukee Community SD 4-11111
905 WARRIOR LN 50263 987-5161
Clair Eason, supt.
HS, 905 WARRIOR LN 50263 2-00011
Bernard Van Roekel, prin. 987-5163
MS, 4TH & LOCUST 50263 2-01100
James Nass, prin. 987-5177

Waukon, AC 319, PC 5, Allamakee
Allamakee Community SD 4-11111
1105 3RD AVE NW 52172 568-3409
Wayne Burk, supt.
SHS, 1105 3RD AVE NW 52172 2-00001
John Dotson, prin. 568-3466
JHS, 107 5TH ST NW 52172 2-00110
Rupert Cabellero, prin. 568-6321

Waverly, AC 319, PC 6, Bremer
Waverly-Shell Rock Community SD 4-11111
215 3RD ST NW 50677 352-3630
Michael Book, supt.
Waverly-Shell Rock HS 3-00011
1400 4TH AVE SW 50677 352-2087
Al Dorenkamp, prin.
Waverly-Shell Rock JHS 2-00100
215 3RD ST NW 50677 352-3632
Richard Jensen, prin.

Wartburg College 4-UC
PO BOX 1003 50677 352-8450

Wayland, AC 319, PC 3, Henry
Waco Community SD 3-11111
PO BOX 158 52654 256-6200
Laverne Hueholt, supt.
Waco JSHS, PO BOX 158 52654 2-00111
Linda Uthe, prin. 256-6200

Webster City, AC 515, PC 6, Hamilton
Webster City Community SD 4-11111
825 BEACH ST 50595 832-9200
Dennis Bahr, supt.
HS, 1001 LYNX AVE 50595 3-00011
Daniel Conrad, prin. 832-9210
MS, 740 BANK ST 50595 2-00100
J. Grove, prin. 832-9220

Iowa Central Community College 2-CC
1725 BEACH ST 50595 832-1632

Wellman, AC 319, PC 4, Washington
Mid-Prairie Community SD 4-11111
PO BOX 150 52356 646-6093
Rose Dillard, supt.
Mid-Prairie SHS, PO BOX 150 52356 2-00001
Stephen Williams, prin. 646-6091
Other Schools – See Kalona

Wellsburg, AC 515, PC 3, Grundy
Wellsburg/Steamboat Rock Community SD 2-11111
609 S MONROE 50680 869-3732
Neil Okones, supt.
Wellsburg/Steamboat Rock HS 2-00011
609 S MONROE 50680 869-5121
Michael Milligan, prin.
Other Schools – See Steamboat Rock

West Bend, AC 515, PC 3, Palo Alto
West Bend Community SD 2-11011
PO BOX 247 50597 887-7821
Ronald Dobson, supt.
West Bend-Mallard HS 2-00011
PO BOX 247 50597 887-7831
Lindsey Beecher, prin.

West Branch, AC 319, PC 4, Cedar
West Branch Community SD 3-11111
PO BOX 637 52358 643-7213
James Behle, supt.
HS, PO BOX 637 52358 2-00011
Ed Hauth, prin. 643-7216
West Branch MS, PO BOX 637 52358 2-00100
Gwen Cumberland-Schaeffer, prin. 643-5324

West Burlington, AC 319, PC 5, Des Moines
West Burlington ISD 3-11111
211 RAMSEY ST 52655 752-8747
James Sleister, supt.
HS, 408 W VAN WEISS BLVD 52655 2-00011
Robert Bowen, prin. 754-6567
MS, 211 RAMSEY ST 52655 2-01100
Glen McCollum, prin. 754-5538

Southeastern Community College 4-CC
PO BOX F 52655 752-2731

West Des Moines, AC 515, PC 8, Polk
West Des Moines Community SD 6-11111
1101 5TH ST 50265 226-2700
Dale Grabinski, supt.
Valley HS, 1140 35TH ST 50266 4-00011
Robert Brooks, prin. 226-2600
Stilwell JHS, 1601 VINE ST 50265 3-00100
Les Aasheim, prin. 226-2770
Other Schools – See Des Moines

Dowling HS, 1400 BUFFALO RD 50265 4-00011
James Dowdle, prin. 225-3000
NEC-National Institute of Technology 3-CC
1119 5TH ST 50265 223-1486

West Liberty, AC 319, PC 5, Muscatine
West Liberty Community SD 4-11111
823 N ELM ST 52776 627-2116
W. Lee Hoover, supt.
JSHS, 113 E 7TH ST 52776 2-00111
Thomas O'Toole, prin. 627-2115

West Point, AC 319, PC 4, Lee

Marquette JSHS, 413 AVENUE C 52656 — 2-00111 / 837-6131
Daniel Kieler, prin.

Westside, AC 712, PC 2, Crawford
AR-WE-VA Community SD — 2-11111 / 663-4311
PO BOX 108 51467
Robert W. Neilsen, supt.
JSHS, 108 CLINTON ST 51467 — 2-00111 / 663-4312
David Wyckoff, prin.

West Union, AC 319, PC 4, Fayette
North Fayette County Community SD — 4-11111 / 422-3851
PO BOX 73 52175
Ron O'Kones, supt.
North Fayette HS, PO BOX 73 52175 — 2-00011 / 422-3852
Steve Story, prin.

Wheatland, AC 319, PC 3, Clinton
Calamus/Wheatland Community SD — 3-11111 / 374-1292
PO BOX 278 52777
Charles Freese, supt.
Calamus/Wheatland JSHS — 2-00111 / 374-1292
PO BOX 278 52777
Joan Anderson, prin.

Whiting, AC 712, PC 3, Monona
Whiting Community SD — 2-11111 / 458-2468
606 WEST ST 51063
Gary Funkhouser, supt.
JSHS, 606 WEST ST 51063 — 1-00111 / 458-2473
Richard Atkins, prin.

Williamsburg, AC 319, PC 4, Iowa
Williamsburg Community SD — 3-11111 / 668-1059
PO BOX 120 52361
William Thompson, supt.
JSHS, 810 W WALNUT 52361 — 2-00111 / 668-1050
Steven Johns, prin.

Wilton, AC 319, PC 5, Muscatine
Wilton Community SD — 3-11111 / 732-2035
PO BOX 3001 52778
Steven Colby, supt.
HS, 1000 CYPRESS ST 52778 — 2-00011 / 732-2629
Tom Corrick, prin.

Winfield, AC 319, PC 4, Henry
Winfield-Mt. Union Community SD — 3-11111 / 257-7700
PO BOX E 52659 – Carl Reno, supt.
Winfield-Mt. Union JSHS — 2-00111 / 257-7701
PO BOX E 52659 – Mike Hardy, prin.

Winterset, AC 515, PC 5, Madison
Winterset Community SD — 4-11111 / 462-2718
PO BOX 30 50273
Richard Wiederhold, supt.
HS, 624 HUSKY DR 50273 — 2-00011 / 462-3320
Kevin Crawford, prin.
MS, 110 W WASHINGTON ST 50273 — 2-00100 / 462-3010
Molly Clark, prin.

Winthrop, AC 319, PC 3, Buchanan
East Buchanan Community SD — 3-11111 / 935-3367
414 5TH ST N 50682
Dwaine Hoffman, supt.
East Buchanan HS, 414 5TH ST N 50682 — 2-00011 / 935-3367
Gary Janssen, prin.
East Buchanan JHS, 414 5TH ST N 50682 — 2-00100 / 935-3367
Gary Janssen, prin.

Woden, AC 515, PC 2, Hancock
Woden-Crystal Lake Community SD — 2-11111 / 926-5312
PO BOX 135 50484
Wayne Sesker, supt.
Other Schools – See Crystal Lake

Woodbine, AC 712, PC 4, Harrison
Woodbine Community SD — 3-11111 / 647-2411
501 WEARE ST 51579
William Tyne, supt.
HS, 501 WEARE ST 51579 — 2-00011 / 647-2227
Larry Lambert, prin.

Woodward, AC 515, PC 4, Dallas
Woodward-Granger Community SD — 3-11111 / 438-2115
306 W 3RD ST 50276
Dale Weeks, supt.
Woodward-Granger HS — 2-00011 / 438-2021
306 W 3RD ST 50276
Larry Blaker, prin.
Woodward-Granger MS — 2-00100 / 438-2021
306 W 3RD ST 50276
Larry Blaker, prin.

Wyoming, AC 319, PC 3, Jones
Midland Community SD 52362 — 3-11111 / 488-2292
Paul Grumley, supt.
Midland Community HS 52362 — 2-00111 / 488-2292
Gary Mohl, prin.
Other Schools – See Lost Nation

Zearing, AC 515, PC 3, Story
Colo-Nesco Comm SD
Supt. — See Colo
Nesco MS, 407 S CENTER ST 50278 — 2-00100 / 487-7411
Duane Newton, prin.

KANSAS

STATE DEPARTMENT OF EDUCATION
Kansas State Education Building
120 SE 10th Ave., Topeka 66612
(913) 296-3201

Commissioner of Education   Lee Droegemueller

Assistant Commissioner   Sharon Freden

Deputy Commissioner Fiscal Services & Quality Control   Dale Dennis

Assistant Commissioner   Ferman Marsh

STATE BOARD OF EDUCATION
120 SE 10th Ave., Topeka 66612

Chairperson   Paul Adams

PUBLIC, PRIVATE AND CATHOLIC SECONDARY SCHOOLS

Abilene, AC 913, PC 6, Dickinson
Abilene USD 435, PO BOX 639 67410 — 4-11111 / 263-2630
William Neuenswander, supt.
HS, 1300 N CEDAR ST 67410 — 2-00011 / 263-1260
Myron Graber, prin.
MS, 500 NW 14TH ST 67410 — 2-00100 / 263-1471
Stephen Groninga, prin.

Agra, AC 913, PC 2, Phillips
Eastern Heights USD 324 — 2-11111 / 638-2244
PO BOX 209 67621
Charles Hennen, supt.
Eastern Heights JSHS — 1-00111 / 638-2244
PO BOX 209 67621
Charles Hennen, prin.

Albert, AC 316, PC 2, Barton
Otis-Bison USD 403 — 2-11111 / 923-4661
RR 1 BOX 76A 67511
Steve Neely, supt.
Other Schools – See Bison, Otis

Allen, AC 316, PC 2, Lyon
North Lyon County USD 251
Supt. — See Americus
Northern Hts. HS, RR 1 66833 — 2-00011 / 528-3521
Steven Mollach, prin.

Alma, AC 913, PC 3, Wabaunsee
Mill Creek Valley USD 329 — 3-11111 / 765-3394
PO BOX 157 66401
Michael Wilson, supt.

Wabaunsee HS, PO BOX 218 66401 — 2-00011 / 765-3523
Bob Baier, prin.

Almena, AC 913, PC 2, Norton
Northern Valley USD 212 — 2-11111 / 669-2445
512 BRYANT ST 67622
LeeRoy Schuckman, supt.
Northern Valley HS — 1-00011 / 669-2445
PO BOX 217 67622
LeeRoy Schuckman, prin.
Other Schools – See Long Island

Altamont, AC 316, PC 4, Labette
Labette County USD 506 — 4-11111 / 784-5326
PO BOX 188 67330
L. Curran, supt.
Labette County HS — 3-00011 / 784-5329
PO BOX 407 67330
Robert Holtzman, prin.

Alton, AC 913, PC 2, Osborne
Osborne County USD 392
Supt. — See Osborne
Alton-Osborne JHS — 1-00100 / 984-2216
PO BOX 65 67623 – Pat Call, prin.

Altoona, AC 316, PC 2, Wilson
Altoona-Midway USD 387
Supt. — See Buffalo
Altoona-Midway MS 66710 — 1-00100 / 568-5725
Lonnie Bratcher, prin.

Americus, AC 316, PC 3, Lyon
North Lyon County USD 251 — 3-11111 / 443-5116
PO BOX 527 66835
Marvin Selby, supt.
Other Schools – See Allen

Andale, AC 316, PC 3, Sedgwick
Renwick USD 267, PO BOX 68 67001 — 4-11111 / 445-2165
Tom Mercer, supt.
HS, PO BOX 28 67001 — 2-00011 / 445-2521
Fred Spexarth, prin.
Other Schools – See Garden Plain

Andover, AC 316, PC 5, Butler
Andover USD 385 — 4-11111 / 733-5017
PO BOX 248 67002
Harry Austin, supt.
HS, 1744 N ANDOVER ROAD 67002 — 3-00011 / 733-1335
John Gasper, prin.
MS, 1747 N ANDOVER ROAD 67002 — 2-00100 / 733-5061
Robert Palmer, prin.

Anthony, AC 316, PC 5, Harper
Anthony-Harper USD 361 — 4-11111 / 842-5183
PO BOX 486 67003
Don Gasper, supt.
Chaparral HS, RR 1 67003 — 2-00011 / 842-5155
Sam High, prin.

Argonia, AC 316, PC 3, Sumner
Argonia USD 359, 503 N PINE ST 67004 — 2-11111 / 435-6311
William Muckenthaler, supt.

JSHS, 503 N PINE ST 67004   2-00111 / 435-6611
  Mark Walker, prin.

Arkansas City, AC 316, PC 7, Cowley
Arkansas City USD 470   5-11111 / 442-4190
  PO BOX 1028 67005
  Jean Snell, supt.
HS, 1200 W RADIO LN 67005   3-00011 / 442-4230
  Michael Clagg, prin.
MS, 400 E KANSAS AVE 67005   3-00100 / 442-1800
  Jean Hollingsworth, prin.

Cowley County Community College   4-CC / 442-0430
  PO BOX 1147 67005

Arma, AC 316, PC 4, Crawford
Northeast USD 246   3-11111 / 347-4116
  PO BOX 669 66712
  Bill Biggs, supt.
Northeast HS, PO BOX 669 66712   2-00111 / 347-4115
  John Underwood, prin.

Ashland, AC 316, PC 4, Clark
Ashland USD 220   2-11111 / 635-2220
  PO BOX 187 67831
  Dale Moody, supt.
JSHS, PO BOX 187 67831   1-00011 / 635-2814
  Don Plinsky, prin.

Atchison, AC 913, PC 7, Atchison
Atchison USD 409   4-11111 / 367-4384
  605 KANSAS AVE 66002
  Michael Pomarico, supt.
SHS, 1500 RILEY ST 66002   2-00001 / 367-4162
  LeBaron Baptista, prin.
JHS, 301 N 5TH ST 66002   3-00110 / 367-5363
  Charles Hays, prin.

Atchison Catholic MS   2-01100 / 367-3503
  201 DIVISION ST 66002
  Donna McCloskey, prin.
Benedictine College   3-UC / 367-5340
  1020 N 2ND ST 66002
Maur Hill Prep S, 1000 GREEN ST 66002   2-00011 / 367-5482
  Mark Watson, prin.
Mt. St. Scholastica Academy   2-00011 / 367-1334
  810 R ST 66002
  Sr. Dorthy Wolters, prin.

Attica, AC 316, PC 3, Harper
Attica USD 511, PO BOX 415 67009   2-11111 / 254-7661
  James Harrod, supt.
HS, PO BOX 415 67009   1-00011 / 254-7915
  Bill Smith, prin.

Atwood, AC 913, PC 4, Rawlins
Atwood USD 318, 410 MAIN ST 67730   2-11111 / 626-3236
  James Finn, supt.
HS, 100 N 8TH ST 67730   2-00011 / 626-3289
  William Hall, prin.

Augusta, AC 316, PC 6, Butler
Augusta USD 402   4-11111 / 775-5484
  301 W KELLY AVE 67010
  Jim Markos, supt.
HS, 2020 OHIO ST 67010   3-00011 / 775-5461
  Doug Wilson, prin.
MS, 903 STATE ST 67010   3-00100 / 775-6383
  Robert McCalla, prin.

Axtell, AC 913, PC 2, Marshall
Axtell USD 488, PO BOX N 66403   2-11111 / 736-2304
  David Gailey, supt.
HS, PO BOX Q 66403   1-00011 / 736-2237
  Rodney Moyer, prin.
MS, PO BOX Q 66403   1-00100 / 736-2237
  Rodney Moyer, prin.
Other Schools – See Bern

Baileyville, AC 913, PC 2, Nemaha
B & B USD 451, 301 NEMAHA ST 66404   2-11111 / 336-6661
  Allen Pokorny, supt.
Baileyville-St. Benedict JSHS   1-00111 / 336-6631
  301 NEMAHA ST 66404
  David Perry, prin.

Baldwin City, AC 913, PC 5, Douglas
Baldwin City USD 348   4-11111 / 594-2721
  PO BOX 67 66006
  John Nuspl, supt.
Baldwin HS, PO BOX 67 66006   2-00011 / 594-2725
  Joe Gresnick, prin.
Baldwin MS, PO BOX 67 66006   2-00100 / 594-2448
  Cryss Brunner, prin.

Baker University   4-UC / 594-6451
  8TH & GROVE ST 66006

Barnes, AC 913, PC 2, Washington
Barnes USD 223, PO BOX 188 66933   2-11111 / 763-4231
  Jack Bittner, supt.
Other Schools – See Hanover, Linn

Basehor, AC 913, PC 4, Leavenworth
Basehor-Linwood USD 458   4-11111 / 724-1396
  PO BOX 282 66007 – Ed Sink, supt.
Basehor-Linwood HS   2-00011 / 724-2266
  2108 N 155TH ST 66007
  Donald Swartz, prin.
Other Schools – See Linwood

Baxter Springs, AC 316, PC 5, Cherokee
Baxter Springs USD 508   3-11111 / 856-2375
  1520 CLEVELAND AVE 66713
  James Harris, supt.

HS, 100 MILITARY AVE 66713   2-00011 / 856-3366
  Tim Burns, prin.
MS, 1520 CLEVELAND AVE 66713   2-00100 / 856-3355
  Gary Krokroskia, prin.

Bazine, AC 913, PC 2, Ness
Bazine USD 304, PO BOX 218 67516   2-11111 / 398-2535
  Robert Briggs, supt.
HS, PO BOX 218 67516   1-00011 / 398-2535
  Robert Briggs, prin.

Belle Plaine, AC 316, PC 4, Sumner
Belle Plaine USD 357   3-11111 / 488-2288
  PO BOX 760 67013
  Lonn Poage, supt.
HS, 820 N MERCHANT 67013   2-00011 / 488-2421
  Stanley Slaven, prin.
MS, 700 N MERCHANT 67013   2-00100 / 488-2222
  Randy Rivers, prin.

Belleville, AC 913, PC 5, Republic
Belleville USD 427   3-11111 / 527-5621
  PO BOX 469 66935
  Dale Rawson, supt.
HS, PO BOX 469 66935   2-00011 / 527-2281
  Edward Fuhrman, prin.
Belleville West MS   2-01100 / 527-5669
  PO BOX 469 66935
  Larry Cates, prin.

Beloit, AC 913, PC 5, Mitchell
Beloit USD 273, PO BOX 547 67420   3-11111 / 738-3261
  Greg Renter, supt.
JSHS, PO BOX 606 67420   2-00111 / 738-3593
  Larry Andersen, prin.

North Central KS Area Voc-Tech School   2-CS / 738-2276
  PO BOX 507 67420
St. Johns HS, 209 S CHERRY ST 67420   1-00011 / 738-2942
  Bertha Johnson, prin.

Bennington, AC 913, PC 3, Ottawa
Twin Valley USD 240   2-11111 / 488-3325
  PO BOX 38 67422
  Larry Geil, supt.
HS, PO BOX 8 67422   1-00011 / 488-3321
  Marvin Cain, prin.
Other Schools – See Tescott

Bern, AC 913, PC 2, Nemaha
Axtell USD 488
  Supt. — See Axtell
HS, PO BOX 144 66408   1-00011 / 336-3031
  Orville Walker, prin.

Bird City, AC 913, PC 2, Cheyenne
Cheylin USD 103, PO BOX 28 67731   2-11111 / 734-2341
  Richard Cain, supt.
Cheylin West HS, PO BOX 28 67731   1-00011 / 734-2341
  Richard Cain, prin.
Cheylin West MS, PO BOX 28 67731   1-00100 / 734-2341
  Richard Cain, prin.

Bison, AC 316, PC 2, Rush
Otis-Bison USD 403
  Supt. — See Albert
Otis-Bison JHS 67520   1-00100 / 356-2611
  Wayne Lindsey, prin.

Blue Rapids, AC 913, PC 4, Marshall
Valley Heights USD 498
  Supt. — See Waterville
Valley Heights JSHS   2-00111 / 363-2508
  508 CHESTNUT ST 66411
  John Bergkamp, prin.

Bonner Springs, AC 913, PC 6, Wyandotte
Bonner Springs USD 204   4-11111 / 422-5600
  PO BOX 435 66012
  James Shepherd, supt.
SHS, PO BOX 216 66012   2-00001 / 422-5121
  Don Stokesbury, prin.
Pioneer JHS, PO BOX 336 66012   3-00110 / 422-5115
  William Allen, prin.

Brewster, AC 913, PC 2, Thomas
Brewster USD 314   2-11111 / 694-2236
  PO BOX 220 67732
  Ralph Foster, supt.
HS, PO BOX 220 67732   1-00011 / 694-2236
  Ralph Foster, prin.

Brookville, AC 913, PC 2, Saline
Ell-Saline USD 307
  Supt. — See Salina
Ell-Saline HS, 414 E ANDERSON 67425   2-00011 / 225-6633
  Grady Sewell, prin.
Ell-Saline MS, 414 E ANDERSON 67425   1-00100 / 225-6633
  Grady Sewell, prin.

Bucklin, AC 316, PC 3, Ford
Bucklin USD 459, PO BOX 8 67834   2-11111 / 826-3828
  Terry Marshall, supt.
HS, PO BOX 8 67834   2-00011 / 826-3241
  John Jones, prin.

Buffalo, AC 316, PC 2, Wilson
Altoona-Midway USD 387   2-11111 / 537-7721
  RR 1 BOX 45A 66717
  James Jerome, supt.
Altoona-Midway HS   2-00011 / 537-7711
  RR 1 BOX 45 66717
  Frank Kennedy, prin.
Other Schools – See Altoona

Buhler, AC 316, PC 4, Reno
Buhler USD 313, PO BOX 320 67522   4-11111 / 543-2258
  Jack Parker, supt.
HS, PO BOX 350 67522   3-00011 / 543-2255
  David Coe, prin.
Other Schools – See Hutchinson

Burden, AC 316, PC 3, Cowley
Central USD 462, PO BOX 128 67019   2-11111 / 438-2218
  Dean McGrath, supt.
Central JSHS 67019   2-00111 / 438-2215
  Greg Cartwright, prin.

Burlingame, AC 316, PC 4, Osage
Burlingame USD 454   2-11111 / 654-3328
  303 S DACOTAH ST 66413
  Jerry Will, supt.
HS, 303 S DACOTAH ST 66413   2-00011 / 654-3315
  Andy Metsker, prin.
Lincoln MS, 303 S DACOTAH ST 66413   2-01100 / 654-3393
  Dallas Scothorn, prin.

Burlington, AC 316, PC 5, Coffey
Burlington USD 244, 200 S 6TH ST 66839   3-11111 / 364-8478
  Larry Clark, supt.
HS, 830 CROSS ST 66839   2-00011 / 364-8672
  Dan Mueller, prin.
MS, 720 CROSS ST 66839   2-00100 / 364-2156
  William Scott, prin.

Burr Oak, AC 913, PC 2, Jewell
White Rock USD 104
  Supt. — See Esbon
White Rock HS, PO BOX 345 66936   1-00011 / 647-6361
  Douglas McNichols, prin.

Burrton, AC 316, PC 3, Harvey
Burrton USD 369, PO BOX 448 67020   2-11111 / 463-3840
  Dean Weaver, supt.
HS, PO BOX 448 67020   1-00011 / 463-3820
  Steve Neill, prin.

Bushton, AC 316, PC 2, Rice
Lorraine USD 328
  Supt. — See Lorraine
Quivira Heights HS   1-00011 / 526-3597
  500 S MAIN ST 67427
  Lloyd Holmes, prin.

Caldwell, AC 316, PC 4, Sumner
Caldwell USD 360, 22 N WEBB ST 67022   2-11111 / 845-2511
  D. Monson, supt.
JSHS, 31 N OSAGE ST 67022   2-00111 / 845-2514
  Robert Foster, prin.

Caney, AC 316, PC 4, Montgomery
Caney Valley USD 436   3-11111 / 879-2115
  109 W 4TH AVE 67333
  Harold Howard, supt.
Caney Valley JSHS, RR 1 BOX 67A 67333   2-00111 / 879-2191
  Les VanWinkle, prin.

Canton, AC 316, PC 3, McPherson
Canton-Galva USD 419   2-11111 / 628-4901
  PO BOX 317 67428
  David Grove, supt.
HS, PO BOX 275 67428   2-00011 / 628-4401
  Terry Stratman, prin.
Other Schools – See Galva

Carbondale, AC 913, PC 4, Osage
Santa Fe Trail USD 434   4-11111 / 836-7656
  RR 1 BOX 434 66414
  Ted Jones, supt.
Santa Fe Trail HS   2-00011 / 665-7161
  RR 1 BOX 434 66414
  Steve Johnston, prin.
Other Schools – See Overbrook

Cawker City, AC 913, PC 3, Mitchell
Waconda USD 272   3-11111 / 781-4328
  PO BOX 326 67430
  Daniel Newman, supt.
Waconda East HS, PO BOX 46 67430   1-00011 / 781-4911
  Stephen Heide, prin.
Other Schools – See Downs

Cedar Vale, AC 316, PC 3, Chautauqua
Cedar Vale USD 285   2-11111 / 758-2265
  PO BOX 458 67024
  Mark Torkelson, supt.
JSHS, PO BOX 458 67024   1-00111 / 758-2791
  Mark Torkelson, prin.

Centralia, AC 913, PC 2, Nemaha
Vermillion USD 380
  Supt. — See Vermillion
JSHS 66415   2-00111 / 857-3324
  David Zumbahlen, prin.

Chanute, AC 316, PC 6, Neosho
Chanute USD 413   4-11111 / 431-4650
  410 S EVERGREEN ST 66720
  Dr. Marvin Johnson, supt.
SHS, 400 S HIGHLAND ST 66720   3-00001 / 431-2210
  James Day, prin.
Royster JHS, 400 W MAIN ST 66720   2-00110 / 431-3280
  Ron Spire, prin.

Neosho County Community College   3-CC / 431-2820
  1000 S ALLEN AVE 66720

Chapman, AC 913, PC 4, Dickinson
Chapman USD 473   4-11111 / 922-6521
  PO BOX 249 67431
  Robert King, supt.

HS, 400 W 4TH 67431 — 2-00011
Richard Hall, prin. — 922-6561
JHS, 622 N MARSHALL 67431 — 2-00100
John Sanborn, prin. — 922-6555

Chase, AC 316, PC 3, Rice
Chase USD 401, PO BOX 366 67524 — 2-11111
Dean Schultz, supt. — 938-2913
HS, PO BOX 366 67524 — 1-00011
Mike Nulton, prin. — 938-2923
Other Schools – See Raymond

Cheney, AC 316, PC 4, Sedgwick
Cheney USD 268, PO BOX 529 67025 — 3-11111
Don Wells, supt. — 542-3512
JSHS, 100 W 6TH 67025 — 2-00111
Ronald Traxson, prin. — 542-3113

Cherokee, AC 316, PC 3, Crawford
Cherokee USD 247 — 3-11111
PO BOX 270 66724 — 457-8350
Thomas Woolbright, supt.
Southeast HS, PO BOX 277 66724 — 2-00011
Bradley Reed, prin. — 457-8365

Cherryvale, AC 316, PC 4, Montgomery
Cherryvale USD 447 — 3-11111
618 E 4TH ST 67335 — 336-2137
Aubury Schultz, supt.
HS, 700 S CARSON ST 67335 — 2-00011
Steven Pegram, prin. — 336-2167
MS, 426 E 4TH ST 67335 — 1-00100
Gordon McBride, prin. — 336-2181

Chetopa, AC 316, PC 4, Labette
Chetopa USD 505, RR 1 BOX 5 67336 — 2-11111
Ken Schnautz, supt. — 236-7244
JSHS, RR 1 BOX 5 67336 — 2-00111
John Presnall, prin. — 236-7244

Cimarron, AC 316, PC 4, Gray
Cimarron-Ensign USD 102 — 3-11111
PO BOX 489 67835 — 855-7743
Duane Rankin, supt.
JSHS, PO BOX 489 67835 — 2-00111
Rudy Louis, prin. — 855-3323

Claflin, AC 316, PC 3, Barton
Claflin USD 354, PO BOX 346 67525 — 2-11111
William Wilson, supt. — 587-3878
HS, PO BOX 348 67525 — 1-00111
Landell Barton, prin. — 587-3801

Clay Center, AC 913, PC 5, Clay
Clay Center USD 379 — 4-11111
PO BOX 97 67432 — 632-3176
Charles Mansfield, supt.
HS, 1630 9TH ST 67432 — 2-00011
Brian Harris, prin. — 632-2131
Other Schools – See Wakefield

Clearwater, AC 316, PC 4, Sedgwick
Clearwater USD 264 — 4-11111
PO BOX 248 67026 — 584-2091
Gary Reynolds, supt.
HS, 801 E ROSS ST 67026 — 2-00011
Keith Pauly, prin. — 584-2361
MS, 140 S 4TH ST 67026 — 2-00100
Fred Marten, prin. — 584-2036

Clifton, AC 913, PC 3, Washington
Clifton-Clyde USD 224, PO BOX A 66937 — 2-11111
Mike Killian, supt. — 455-3313
Clifton-Clyde MS, PO BOX B 66937 — 1-00100
Ross Knitter, prin. — 455-3324
Other Schools – See Clyde

Clyde, AC 913, PC 3, Cloud
Clifton-Clyde USD 224
Supt. — See Clifton
Clifton-Clyde HS, 616 N HIGH ST 66938 — 2-00011
Glenn Walker, prin. — 446-3444

Coffeyville, AC 316, PC 7, Montgomery
Coffeyville USD 445 — 5-11111
PO BOX 968 67337 — 252-6800
Larry Thomas, supt.
Field Kindley Memorial HS — 3-00011
1110 W 8TH ST 67337 — 252-6810
Ron Childress, prin.
Roosevelt MS, 1000 W 8TH ST 67337 — 2-00100
Joe Vacca, prin. — 252-6820

Coffeyville Community College — 4-CC
402 W 11TH ST 67337 — 251-7700

Colby, AC 913, PC 6, Thomas
Colby USD 315 — 4-11111
210 S RANGE AVE 67701 — 462-3941
R. Combs, supt.
HS, 710 W 3RD ST 67701 — 2-00011
Lee Leiker, prin. — 462-3377
MS, 750 W 3RD ST 67701 — 2-00100
Robb Ross, prin. — 462-3968

Colby Community College — 4-CC
1255 S RANGE AVE 67701 — 462-3984

Coldwater, AC 316, PC 3, Comanche
Comanche County USD 300 — 2-11111
PO BOX 721 67029 — 582-2181
J. Chadwick, supt.
JSHS, 600 N LEAVENWORTH 67029 — 2-00111
Keith Custer, prin. — 582-2158
Other Schools – See Protection

Colony, AC 316, PC 2, Anderson
Crest USD 479
Supt. — See Kincaid
Crest HS, PO BOX 325 66015 — 2-00011
Ray Funk, prin. — 852-3521

Columbus, AC 316, PC 5, Cherokee
Columbus USD 493 — 4-11111
PO BOX 21 66725 — 429-3661
Larry Reynolds, supt.
HS, 500 W MAPLE ST 66725 — 2-00011
Don Derrick, prin. — 429-3821
Central MS — 2-01100
850 S HIGHSCHOOL AVE 66725 — 429-3943
Robert Wells, prin.

Concordia, AC 913, PC 6, Cloud
Concordia USD 333 — 4-11111
217 W 7TH ST 66901 — 243-3518
Larry Nelson, supt.
JSHS, 436 W 10TH ST 66901 — 3-00111
Bruce Petersen, prin. — 243-2452

Cloud County Community College — 4-CC
PO BOX 1002 66901 — 243-1435

Conway Springs, AC 316, PC 4, Sumner
Conway Springs USD 356 — 2-11111
PO BOX 218 67031 — 456-2961
David Scraper, supt.
HS, PO BOX 650 67031 — 2-00011
Joseph Bono, prin. — 456-2963
MS, PO BOX 128 67031 — 2-00100
Darren Kinyon, prin. — 456-2965

Copeland, AC 316, PC 2, Gray
Copeland USD 476 — 2-11111
PO BOX 156 67837 — 668-5565
Patty Faircloth, supt.
HS, PO BOX 156 67837 — 1-00011
Patty Faircloth, prin. — 668-5565
South Gray JHS, PO BOX 156 67837 — 1-00100
Patty Faircloth, prin. — 668-5565

Cottonwood Falls, AC 316, PC 3, Chase
Chase County USD 284 — 3-11111
PO BOX 569 66845 — 273-6303
Rick Weiss, supt.
Chase County HS 66845 — 2-00011
Alva VanEtten, prin. — 273-6354
Other Schools – See Strong City

Council Grove, AC 316, PC 4, Morris
Morris County USD 417 — 4-11111
17 WOOD ST 66846 – Jim Selby, supt. — 767-5192
HS, 129 HOCKADAY ST 66846 — 2-00011
Dennis Delay, prin. — 767-5149

Courtland, AC 913, PC 2, Republic
Pike Valley USD 426
Supt. — See Scandia
Pike Valley JHS, PO BOX 320 66939 — 1-00100
Stanley Estes, prin. — 374-4221

Cuba, AC 913, PC 2, Republic
Hillcrest USD 455 — 2-11111
PO BOX 167 66940 — 729-3816
Darrell Genereux, supt.
Hillcrest HS, PO BOX 167 66940 — 1-00011
Bill Hagerman, prin. — 729-3333

Cunningham, AC 316, PC 3, Kingman
Cunningham USD 332 — 2-11111
PO BOX 67 67035 — 298-3271
Melvin Ormiston, supt.
HS, PO BOX 98 67035 — 1-00011
Bob Stackhouse, prin. — 298-2473

Deerfield, AC 316, PC 3, Kearny
Deerfield USD 216 — 2-11111
PO BOX 274 67838 — 426-8516
David Bilderback, supt.
JSHS, PO BOX 274 67838 — 2-00111
Kent Tarrant, prin. — 426-8401

Denton, AC 913, PC 2, Doniphan
Midway USD 433, RR 1 BOX 30B 66017 — 2-11111
George McAfee, supt. — 359-6526
Midway JSHS, RR 1 BOX 30B 66017 — 1-00111
Daryl Moore, prin. — 359-6526

Derby, AC 316, PC 7, Sedgwick
Derby USD 260 — 6-11111
120 E WASHINGTON ST 67037 — 788-8410
Melva Owens, supt.
HS, 801 E MADISON AVE 67037 — 4-00011
Jerry Singer, prin. — 788-8500
MS, 715 E MADISON AVE 67037 — 3-00100
Ron Brown, prin. — 788-8580

De Soto, AC 913, PC 4, Johnson
De Soto USD 232, PO BOX 449 66018 — 4-11111
Marilyn Layman, supt. — 585-1141
SHS, PO BOX 469 66018 — 2-00001
Joseph Novak, prin. — 585-1143
JHS, PO BOX 509 66018 — 2-00110
William Gilhaus, prin. — 585-1186

Dexter, AC 316, PC 2, Cowley
Dexter USD 471, PO BOX 97 67038 — 2-11111
Max Logsdon, supt. — 876-5415
JSHS, PO BOX 97 67038 — 1-00111
Max Logsdon, prin. — 876-5415

Dighton, AC 316, PC 4, Lane
Dighton USD 482, PO BOX 878 67839 — 2-11111
Ron Musselwhite, supt. — 397-2835

HS, PO BOX 939 67839 — 2-00011
Roger Timken, prin. — 397-5333
MS, PO BOX 1029 67839 — 2-01100
John Levin, prin. — 397-5319

Dodge City, AC 316, PC 7, Ford
Dodge City USD 443 — 5-11111
PO BOX 460 67801 — 227-1620
Gene Young, supt.
SHS, 1601 1ST AVE 67801 — 4-00001
Dwayne Colvin, prin. — 227-1611
JHS, 2000 6TH AVE 67801 — 3-00110
William Hatfield, prin. — 227-1610

Dodge City Community College — 4-CC
2501 N 14TH AVE 67801 — 225-1321

Douglass, AC 316, PC 4, Butler
Douglass USD 396 — 3-11111
PO BOX 158 67039 — 746-2183
Marvin Sisk, supt.
HS, PO BOX 158 67039 — 2-00011
James Keller, prin. — 746-2195

Downs, AC 913, PC 4, Osborne
Waconda USD 272
Supt. — See Cawker City
HS, PO BOX 247 67437 — 1-00011
Steve Heide, prin. — 454-3332

Easton, AC 913, PC 2, Leavenworth
Easton USD 449 — 3-11111
32502 EASTON RD 66020 — 651-9740
Charles Wilson, supt.
Pleasant Ridge HS — 2-00011
32500 EASTON RD 66020 — 651-5556
Ronald Alsop, prin.
Easton-Salt Creek MS — 2-00100
PO BOX 259 66020 — 773-5556
Alan Beck, prin.

Effingham, AC 913, PC 3, Atchison
Atchison County Community USD 377 — 3-11111
RR 1 BOX 37 66023 — 833-5050
L. Williams, supt.
Atchison Co. Community HS 66023 — 2-00011
Wally Autem, prin. — 833-2240
Atchison Co. Community MS 66023 — 2-01100
Charles Bain, prin. — 833-4420

Elbing, AC 316, PC 2, Butler

Berean Academy, PO BOX 67 67041 — 2-00011
James Thiessen, prin. — 799-2211

El Dorado, AC 316, PC 7, Butler
Circle USD 375
Supt. — See Towanda
Oil Hill MS, 2700 W 6TH AVE 67042 — 2-01100
Don Coffman, prin. — 321-9515

El Dorado USD 490 — 4-11111
1518 W 6TH AVE 67042 — 321-2780
John Heim, supt.
HS, 401 MCCOLLUM RD 67042 — 3-00011
Kenneth Petz, prin. — 321-3721
JHS, 500 W CENTRAL AVE 67042 — 3-00100
Merle Patterson, prin. — 321-5717

Butler County Community College — 4-CC
901 S HAVERHILL RD 67042 — 321-5083

Elkhart, AC 316, PC 4, Morton
Elkhart USD 218, PO BOX 999 67950 — 3-11111
Philip Johnston, supt. — 697-2195
HS, PO BOX 999 67950 — 2-00011
Don Simmons, prin. — 697-2193
MS, PO BOX 999 67950 — 2-01100
Gil Endicott, prin. — 697-2197

Ellinwood, AC 316, PC 4, Barton
Ellinwood USD 355 — 3-11111
PO BOX 368 67526 — 564-3226
Terry McGreevy, supt.
HS, PO BOX 368 67526 — 2-00011
Don Caffee, prin. — 564-3136
JHS, PO BOX 368 67526 — 1-00100
Don Caffee, prin. — 564-3136

Ellis, AC 913, PC 4, Ellis
Ellis USD 388, PO BOX 256 67637 — 2-11111
Clair Beecher, supt. — 726-4281
HS, 1706 MONROE ST 67637 — 2-00011
Reggie Romine, prin. — 726-3151

Ellsworth, AC 913, PC 4, Ellsworth
Ellsworth USD 327 — 3-11111
PO BOX 306 67439 — 472-5561
Kent Garhart, supt.
HS, PO BOX 46 67439 — 2-00011
David South, prin. — 472-4471
Other Schools – See Kanopolis

Elwood, AC 913, PC 4, Doniphan
Elwood USD 486, PO BOX 368 66024 — 2-11111
William Allen, supt. — 365-6735
HS, PO BOX 368 66024 — 1-00011
Patrick McKernan, prin. — 365-6735

Emporia, AC 316, PC 8, Lyon
Emporia USD 253 — 5-11111
PO BOX 1008 66801 — 341-2200
Richard Gregory, supt.
HS, 3302 W 18TH AVE 66801 — 4-00011
Jerry Baumgardner, prin. — 341-2365

MS, 2300 GRAPHIC ARTS RD 66801   4-00100
 J. Bastin, prin.   341-2335
Lowther MS North
 216 W 6TH AVE 66801   4-00100
 Gary Smith, prin.   341-2350

Emporia State University   6-UC
 1200 COMMERCIAL ST 66801   343-1200
Newman Hospital   HSP
 1127 CHESTNUT ST 66801   343-6800

Erie, AC 316, PC 4, Neosho
Erie-St. Paul USD 101   4-11111
 PO BOX 137 66733   244-3264
 Paul Bingle, supt.
 HS 66733   2-00011
 Roy Bishop, prin.   244-3287
 JHS, PO BOX 18 66733   2-00100
 Gary Snawder, prin.   244-5161
 Other Schools – See Saint Paul, Thayer

Esbon, AC 913, PC 2, Jewell
White Rock USD 104   2-11111
 PO BOX 19 66941   725-3222
 Dana Randel, supt.
 White Rock MS, PO BOX 139 66941   1-00100
 Dana Randel, prin.   725-3444
 Other Schools – See Burr Oak

Eskridge, AC 913, PC 3, Wabaunsee
Wabaunsee East USD 330   3-11111
 PO BOX 158 66423   449-2282
 Glen Hughes, supt.
 Mission Valley HS 66423   2-00011
 Michael Mikos, prin.   449-2297

Eudora, AC 913, PC 5, Douglas
Eudora USD 491, PO BOX 500 66025   3-11111
 Dan Bloom, supt.   542-2191
 HS, PO BOX A 66025   2-00011
 Charlie Watts, prin.   542-2115

Eureka, AC 316, PC 5, Greenwood
Eureka USD 389, 106 W 6TH ST 67045   3-11111
 Leon Attebery, supt.   583-5588
 HS, RR 2 BOX 250 67045   2-00011
 Dotson Bradbury, prin.   583-7428
 JHS, RR 2 BOX 250 67045   2-00100
 Raymond Leo Davis, prin.   583-7428

Everest, AC 913, PC 2, Brown
South Brown County USD 430
 Supt. — See Horton
 MS, PO BOX 226 66424   2-01100
 James Kepple, prin.   548-7536

Florence, AC 316, PC 3, Marion
Marion USD 408
 Supt. — See Marion
 MS, 701 W 7TH ST 66851   1-00100
 Tod Gordon, prin.   878-4471

Fort Leavenworth, AC 913, PC see Leavenworth
Ft. Leavenworth USD 207   4-11110
 GRANT AVE 66027   651-7373
 Tom Devlin, supt.
 Patton JHS 66027   2-00110
 Milton Wade, prin.   651-7371

Fort Riley, AC 913, PC see Junction City
Geary Co. USD 475
 Supt. — See Junction City
 JHS, 4020 1ST DIVISION RD 66442   3-00110
 Leland Sharpe, prin.   784-4475

Fort Scott, AC 316, PC 6, Bourbon
Ft. Scott USD 234   4-11111
 5TH & MAIN STS 66701   223-0800
 Bill Sailors, supt.
 HS, 1005 S MAIN ST 66701   3-00011
 Jim Robins, prin.   223-0600
 MS, 412 S NATIONAL AVE 66701   3-00100
 Bill Madison, prin.   223-3262

Fort Scott Community College   4-CC
 2108 HORTON ST 66701   223-2700

Fowler, AC 316, PC 3, Meade
Fowler USD 225, PO BOX 170 67844   2-11111
 Lawrence Goslin, supt.   646-5661
 HS, 801 MAIN 67844   1-00011
 Robert Scheiv, prin.   646-5221

Frankfort, AC 913, PC 3, Marshall
Vermillion USD 380
 Supt. — See Vermillion
 JSHS, 604 N KANSAS AVE 66427   2-00111
 Bruce Custer, prin.   292-4486

Fredonia, AC 316, PC 5, Wilson
Fredonia USD 484   3-11111
 PO BOX 539 66736   378-4177
 B. F. Parker, supt.
 HS, 916 ROBINSON ST 66736   2-00011
 Eugene Haydock, prin.   378-4172
 MS, 203 N 8TH ST 66736   2-00100
 Robert Graham, prin.   378-4167

Frontenac, AC 316, PC 5, Crawford
Frontenac USD 249   3-11111
 200 E LANYON ST 66763   231-7551
 Gregory Hafner, supt.
 JSHS, 201 S CRAWFORD ST 66763   2-00111
 Joe Martin, prin.   231-7550

Galena, AC 316, PC 5, Cherokee
Galena USD 499, 702 E 7TH ST 66739   3-11111
 James Christman, supt.   783-2324
 HS, 8TH & LINCOLN 66739   2-00011
 Randy McDaniel, prin.   783-1905

Galva, AC 913, PC 3, McPherson
Canton-Galva USD 419
 Supt. — See Canton
 MS, PO BOX 96 67443   1-00100
 Patricia Fells, prin.   654-3321

Garden City, AC 316, PC 7, Finney
Garden City USD 457   6-11111
 1205 FLEMING ST 67846   276-5112
 Milton Pippenger, supt.
 SHS, 1412 N MAIN ST 67846   4-00001
 Richard Patton, prin.   276-5170
 Henderson JHS, 2406 FLEMING ST 67846   3-00110
 Steve Ternes, prin.   276-5210
 Hubert JHS, 1205 A ST 67846   3-00110
 Duane Weisz, prin.   276-5200

Garden City Community College   4-CC
 801 CAMPUS DR 67846   276-7611

Garden Plain, AC 316, PC 3, Sedgwick
Renwick USD 267
 Supt. — See Andale
 JSHS, PO BOX 128 67050   2-00111
 Floyd Farris, prin.   535-2272

Gardner, AC 913, PC 5, Johnson
Gardner-Edgerton-Antioch USD 231   4-11111
 PO BOX 97 66030   884-7102
 Gary George, supt.
 Gardner-Edgerton HS   2-00011
 318 E WASHINGTON ST 66030   884-7101
 Ronald Mersch, prin.
 Nike MS   2-00100
 I-35 AT GARDNER-ANTIOCH RD 66030
 Jim Cathey, prin.   884-7756

Garnett, AC 913, PC 5, Anderson
Garnett USD 365, PO BOX 328 66032   4-11111
 Ken Woods, supt.   448-6155
 Anderson County HS   2-00011
 PO BOX 426 66032   448-3115
 Roger Welborn, prin.

Girard, AC 316, PC 5, Crawford
Girard USD 248   4-11111
 401 N SUMMIT ST 66743   724-4325
 John Battitori, supt.
 HS, 401 N SUMMIT ST 66743   2-00011
 Jack Leake, prin.   724-4326
 MS, 401 N SUMMIT ST 66743   2-00100
 Gary Pernot, prin.   724-4114

Glasco, AC 913, PC 3, Cloud
Southern Cloud USD 334   2-11111
 PO BOX 227 67445   568-2247
 Curtis Norris, supt.
 HS, PO BOX 158 67445   1-00011
 Curtis Norris, prin.   568-2291
 Other Schools – See Miltonvale

Goddard, AC 316, PC 4, Sedgwick
Goddard USD 265   4-11111
 PO BOX 249 67052   794-2267
 Charles Edmonds, supt.
 SHS, 301 S MAIN 67052   3-00001
 Ernest Plagge, prin.   794-2261
 JHS, 335 N WALNUT 67052   3-00110
 Jill Hackett, prin.   794-2211

Goessel, AC 913, PC 3, Marion
Goessel USD 411, PO BOX 68 67053   2-11111
 Carl Thieszen, supt.   367-8118
 HS, PO BOX 6 67053   1-00011
 Chester Roberts, prin.   367-2242

Goodland, AC 913, PC 5, Sherman
Goodland USD 352   4-11111
 PO BOX 509 67735   899-2397
 Jack Hobbs, supt.
 HS, PO BOX 509 67735   2-00011
 Bill Steiner, prin.   899-5656
 Grant JHS, PO BOX 509 67735   2-00100
 James Mull, prin.   899-7561

Grainfield, AC 913, PC 2, Gove
Wheatland USD 292
 Supt. — See Park
 Wheatland JSHS, PO BOX 149 67737   2-00111
 Dallas Lee, prin.   673-4223

Great Bend, AC 316, PC 7, Barton
Great Bend USD 428   5-11111
 201 S PATTON RD 67530   793-1500
 Clay Guthmiller, supt.
 SHS, 2027 MORTON ST 67530   3-00001
 Michael Hester, prin.   793-1521
 MS, 1919 HARRISON ST 67530   3-00110
 John Thissen, prin.   793-1510

Barton County Community College   4-CC
 RR 3 BOX 136Z 67530   792-2701

Greensburg, AC 316, PC 4, Kiowa
Greensburg USD 422   2-11111
 401 S OAK ST 67054   723-2145
 Gary Goodheart, supt.
 HS, 420 S MAIN 67054   2-00011
 Michael Ronen, prin.   723-2164

Gridley, AC 316, PC 2, Coffey
Le Roy-Gridley USD 245
 Supt. — See Le Roy
 HS, PO BOX 426 66852   1-00011
 James Ochs, prin.   836-2151

Grinnell, AC 913, PC 2, Gove
Grinnell USD 291, PO BOX 68 67738   2-11111
 Robert Martin, supt.   824-3277
 HS, PO BOX 68 67738   1-00011
 Kenneth Tidball, prin.   824-3277
 MS, PO BOX 126 67738   1-01100
 Robert Martin, prin.   824-3296

Gypsum, AC 913, PC 2, Saline
Southeast of Saline USD 306   3-11111
 5056 E HIGHWAY K4 67448   536-4291
 Robert Goodwin, supt.
 Southeast Saline JSHS   2-00111
 5056 E HIGHWAY K4 67448   536-4286
 Richard Harlan, prin.

Haddam, AC 913, PC 2, Washington
North Central USD 221   2-11111
 RR 1 BOX 122 66944   778-2564
 Ron Meitler, supt.
 Other Schools – See Morrowville

Halstead, AC 316, PC 4, Harvey
Halstead USD 440, 520 W 6TH ST 67056   3-11111
 Earl Guiot, supt.   835-2641
 HS, 520 W 6TH ST 67056   2-00011
 Orvin Kuhlmann, prin.   835-2682

Hamilton, AC 316, PC 2, Greenwood
Hamilton USD 390   2-11111
 HC 1 BOX 5 66853   678-3321
 Ralph Bradley, supt.
 HS, HC 1 BOX 5 66853   1-00011
 Cris Leonard, prin.   678-3651

Hanover, AC 913, PC 3, Washington
Barnes USD 223
 Supt. — See Barnes
 HS 66945   2-00011
 Paul Schultz, prin.   337-2281

Hanston, AC 316, PC 2, Hodgeman
Hanston USD 228   2-11111
 PO BOX 219 67849   623-2641
 Woody Gibbons, supt.
 JSHS, PO BOX 219 67849   1-00111
 N. Zimmer, prin.   623-2611

Hardtner, AC 316, PC 2, Barber
South Barber County USD 255
 Supt. — See Kiowa
 South Barber MS   1-00100
 301 E CENTRAL AVE 67057   296-4415
 Wesley Rader, prin.

Hartford, AC 316, PC 3, Lyon
Southern Lyon County USD 252   3-11111
 PO BOX 278 66854   392-5519
 Dennis Versch, supt.
 HS, PO BOX 218 66854   1-00011
 John Enos, prin.   392-5515
 Other Schools – See Olpe

Haven, AC 316, PC 4, Reno
Haven USD 312, PO BOX 130 67543   4-11111
 Harold Voth, supt.   465-7727
 HS, 400 E 5TH 67543   2-00111
 Richard White, prin.   465-2585
 MS, 320 N EMPORIA 67543   2-00100
 Brian Boston, prin.   465-2587

Haviland, AC 316, PC 3, Kiowa
Haviland USD 474   2-11111
 PO BOX 243 67059   862-5256
 Larry Wade, supt.
 HS, PO BOX 243 67059   1-00011
 Ken Coover, prin.   862-5217

Barclay College   1-UC
 PO BOX 288 67059   862-5252

Hays, AC 913, PC 7, Ellis
Hays USD 489, 323 W 12TH ST 67601   5-11111
 Fred Kaufman, supt.   623-2400
 HS, 2300 E 13TH ST 67601   3-00011
 Theresa Davidson, prin.   623-2600
 Felton MS, 101 E 29TH ST 67601   2-00100
 Monte Selby, prin.   623-2450
 Kennedy MS, 1309 FORT ST 67601   3-00100
 Eric Harfmann, prin.   623-2470

Barton County Community College   1-CC
 2210 CANTERBURY DR 67601   625-3984
Fort Hays State University   5-UC
 600 PARK ST 67601   628-5880
Thomas More Marion HS   2-00011
 1701 HALL ST 67601   625-6577
 Joseph Dente, prin.

Haysville, AC 316, PC 6, Sedgwick
Haysville USD 261   5-11111
 1745 W GRAND AVE 67060   524-0831
 Lynn Stevens, supt.
 JHS, 900 W GRAND AVE 67060   3-00100
 Larry Weatherbie, prin.   524-3233
 Other Schools – See Wichita

Healy, AC 316, PC 2, Lane
Healy USD 468, RR 1 BOX 53A 67850   2-11111
 Jennie Mills, supt.   398-2248

JSHS, RR 1 BOX 53A 67850   1-00111
Jennie Mills, prin.   398-2248

Herington, AC 913, PC 5, Dickinson
Herington USD 487   3-11111
  19 N BROADWAY 67449   258-2263
  Thomas Vernon, supt.
HS, RR 1 BOX 6 67449   2-00011
  Brady Burton, prin.   258-2261
MS, 2 S A ST 67449   2-00100
  Lola Lowen, prin.   258-2448

Herndon, AC 913, PC 2, Rawlins
Herndon USD 317, PO BOX 68 67739   1-11111
  Gordon Tope, supt.   322-5311
JSHS, PO BOX 68 67739   1-00111
  Gordon Tope, prin.   322-5311

Hesston, AC 316, PC 5, Harvey
Hesston USD 460   3-11111
  PO BOX 2000 67062   327-4931
  Gary Price, supt.
HS, PO BOX 2000 67062   2-00011
  Marvin Estes, prin.   327-7122
MS, PO BOX 2000 67062   2-01100
  Janice Strecker, prin.   327-7111

Hesston College   3-CC
  PO BOX 3000 67062   327-8233

Hiawatha, AC 913, PC 5, Brown
Hiawatha USD 415   4-11111
  PO BOX 398 66434   742-2266
  John Severin, supt.
HS, 600 REDSKIN DR 66434   2-00011
  B. Pennel, prin.   742-3312
Other Schools – See Robinson

Highland, AC 913, PC 3, Doniphan
Highland USD 425, PO BOX 8 66035   2-11111
  Jan Collins, supt.   442-3286
HS, PO BOX 8 66035   1-00011
  Cheryl Rasmussen, prin.   442-3286

Highland Community College   3-CC
  PO BOX 68 66035   442-3236

Hill City, AC 913, PC 4, Graham
Hill City USD 281   3-11111
  PO BOX 309 67642   674-2135
  Thomas Heiman, supt.
HS, 804 W HILL ST 67642   2-00011
  Galen Schmitz, prin.   674-2117
Longfellow MS, 203 N 2ND AVE 67642   2-00100
  John Deuk, prin.   674-3451

Hillsboro, AC 316, PC 5, Marion
Durham-Hillsboro-Lehigh USD 410   3-11111
  812 E A ST 67063   947-3184
  Gordon Mohn, supt.
HS, 500 E GRAND AVE 67063   2-00011
  Glen Suppes, prin.   947-3991
MS, GRAND & JEFFERSON 67063   2-00100
  Evan Yoder, prin.   947-3297

Tabor College   2-UC
  400 S JEFFERSON ST 67063   947-3121

Hoisington, AC 316, PC 5, Barton
Hoisington USD 431   3-11111
  106 N MAIN ST 67544   653-4134
  Randall Evans, supt.
HS, 218 E 7TH ST 67544   2-00011
  Richard Roda, prin.   653-2141
MS, 360 W 11TH ST 67544   2-00100
  Dean Andereck, prin.   653-4951

Holcomb, AC 316, PC 4, Finney
Holcomb USD 363, PO BOX 8 67851   3-11111
  Ernest Nordberg, supt.   277-2629
HS 67851   2-00011
  Dean Katt, prin.   277-2063
MS 67851   2-00100
  Dave Novack, prin.   277-2699

Holton, AC 913, PC 5, Jackson
Holton USD 336   4-11111
  515 PENNSYLVANIA AVE 66436   364-3650
  Jerry Fuqua, supt.
HS, 901 NEW YORK AVE 66436   2-00011
  Ron Folk, prin.   364-2181
JHS, 900 IOWA AVE 66436   2-00100
  Mark Wilson, prin.   364-2441

North Jackson USD 335, RR 3 66436   2-11111
  Dan Stockstill, supt.   364-2194
Jackson Hts. HS, RR 3 66436   2-00011
  Jack Sheldon, prin.   364-2195

Holyrood, AC 913, PC 2, Ellsworth
Lorraine USD 328
  Supt. — See Lorraine
Quivira Heights MS   1-00100
  PO BOX 148 67450   252-3666
  Kenneth Parks, prin.

Hope, AC 913, PC 2, Dickinson
Rural Vista USD 481   2-11111
  PO BOX 217 67451   366-7215
  Gerald McClure, supt.
HS, PO BOX 218 67451   1-00011
  Randal Bagby, prin.   366-7221
Other Schools – See White City

Horton, AC 913, PC 4, Brown
South Brown County USD 430   3-11111
  114 W 8TH ST 66439   486-2611
  Ronald Lantaff, supt.
HS, 114 1ST AVE E 66439   2-00011
  Keith Burgat, prin.   486-2151
Other Schools – See Everest

Howard, AC 316, PC 3, Elk
West Elk USD 282   2-11111
  PO BOX 607 67349   374-2113
  Jim Davenport, supt.
West Elk JSHS 67349   2-00111
  Dennis Murray, prin.   374-2147

Hoxie, AC 913, PC 4, Sheridan
Hoxie USD 412, PO BOX 348 67740   3-11111
  Don Hague, supt.   675-3258
HS 67740   2-00011
  Roger Morris, prin.   675-3286

Hoyt, AC 913, PC 2, Jackson
Royal Valley USD 337
  Supt. — See Mayetta
Royal Valley HS, PO BOX 128 66440   2-00011
  James Pendarvis, prin.   986-6251

Hugoton, AC 316, PC 5, Stevens
Hugoton USD 210, 205 E 6TH ST 67951   4-11111
  Nelson Bryant, supt.   544-4397
HS, 215 W 11TH ST 67951   2-00011
  Dale Honeck, prin.   544-4311
MS, 115 W 11TH ST 67951   2-00100
  Loretta Kerr, prin.   544-4341

Humboldt, AC 316, PC 4, Allen
Humboldt USD 258   3-11111
  910 NEW YORK ST 66748   473-3121
  Gary Church, supt.
HS, 1011 BRIDGE ST 66748   2-00011
  Floyd Woods, prin.   473-2251
Zillah MS, RR 1 BOX 92 66748   2-00100
  Warren Isaac, prin.   473-3348

Hutchinson, AC 316, PC 8, Reno
Buhler USD 313
  Supt. — See Buhler
Prairie Hills MS   2-00100
  3200 LUCILLE DR 67502   662-6027
  E. Williams, prin.

Hutchinson USD 308   6-11111
  PO BOX 1908 67504   665-4400
  W. L. Hawver, supt.
HS, 1401 N SEVERANCE ST 67501   4-00011
  Mike Wortman, prin.   665-4500
Liberty MS, 200 W 14TH AVE 67501   2-00100
  Lila Fritschen, prin.   665-4700
Sherman MS, 210 E AVENUE A 67501   2-00100
  Jim Woods, prin.   665-4800

Nickerson USD 309   4-11111
  4501 W 4TH AVE 67501   663-7141
  Ron Clifton, supt.
North Reno MS   2-01100
  1616 WILSHIRE DR 67501   662-4573
  Al Disney, prin.
Other Schools – See Nickerson

Central Christian S   2-11111
  1910 E 30TH AVE 67502   663-2174
  Larry Mitchell, prin.
Hutchinson Community College   4-CC
  1300 N PLUM ST 67501   665-3500
Trinity HS, 1400 E 17TH AVE 67501   2-00111
  Richard Robl, prin.   662-5800

Independence, AC 316, PC 6, Montgomery
Independence USD 446   4-11111
  PO BOX 487 67301   332-1800
  L. Charles Mock, supt.
HS, 1301 N 10TH ST 67301   3-00011
  Joanne Brookshier, prin.   332-1815
MS, 300 W LOCUST ST 67301   3-00100
  Orlin Milner, prin.   332-1836

Independence Community College   4-CC
  PO BOX 708 67301   331-4100

Ingalls, AC 316, PC 2, Gray
Ingalls USD 477, PO BOX 99 67853   2-11111
  John O'Brien, supt.   335-5136
HS 67853   1-00011
  James Hardy, prin.   335-5136

Inman, AC 316, PC 4, McPherson
Inman USD 448, PO BOX 129 67546   2-11111
  Richard Erickson, supt.   585-6424
JSHS, 404 S MAIN 67546   2-00111
  Mike Hull, prin.   585-6441

Iola, AC 316, PC 6, Allen
Iola USD 257, 402 E JACKSON ST 66749   4-11111
  Wes Dreyer, supt.   365-4700
SHS, 300 E JACKSON ST 66749   3-00001
  Keith King, prin.   365-4715
JHS, 600 EAST ST 66749   2-00110
  Don Wilmoth, prin.   365-4785

Allen County Community College   3-CC
  1801 N COTTONWOOD ST 66749   365-5116

Jennings, AC 913, PC 2, Decatur
Prairie Heights USD 295   2-11111
  PO BOX 160 67643   678-2413
  Larry Johnson, supt.
HS, PO BOX 160 67643   1-00011
  Larry Johnson, prin.   678-2414

Jetmore, AC 316, PC 3, Hodgeman
Jetmore USD 227, PO BOX 127 67854   2-11111
  Duane Steele, supt.   357-8301
HS, PO BOX 127 67854   1-00011
  Duane Steele, prin.   357-8378

Jewell, AC 913, PC 3, Jewell
Jewell USD 279, PO BOX 20 66949   2-11111
  Ron Alford, supt.   428-3217
HS 66949   1-00011
  Roger Antle, prin.   428-3233
Other Schools – See Randall

Johnson, AC 316, PC 4, Stanton
Stanton County USD 452   3-11111
  PO BOX C 67855   492-6226
  Roger Pickering, supt.
HS, PO BOX C 67855   2-00011
  Jerry Cullen, prin.   492-6284
Stanton County MS, PO BOX C 67855   1-00100
  Jack LaFay, prin.   492-2223

Junction City, AC 913, PC 7, Geary
Geary Co. USD 475   6-11111
  PO BOX 370 66441   238-6184
  Mary Devin, supt.
SHS, 824 N EISENHOWER DR 66441   4-00001
  Gregory Springston, prin.   238-3185
JHS, 300 W 9TH ST 66441   3-00110
  Ferrell Miller, prin.   238-5171
Other Schools – See Fort Riley

Barton County Community College   1-CC
  PO BOX 223 66441   762-5045
St. Xaviers HS   2-00111
  200 N WASHINGTON ST 66441   238-2841
  James Hemenway, prin.

Kanopolis, AC 913, PC 3, Ellsworth
Ellsworth USD 327
  Supt. — See Ellsworth
MS, PO BOX 37 67454   2-01100
  Robert Brock, prin.   472-4477

Kansas City, AC 913, PC 9, Wyandotte
Kansas City USD 500   7-11111
  625 MINNESOTA AVE 66101   551-3200
  Jim Hensley, supt.
Harmon HS, 2400 STEELE RD 66106   4-00011
  Larry Englebrick, prin.   722-7300
Schlagle HS, 2214 N 59TH ST 66104   3-00011
  Carol Levar, prin.   596-5300
Washington HS   4-00011
  7340 LEAVENWORTH RD 66109   596-5400
  Bruce Thezan, prin.
Wyandotte HS   4-00011
  2501 MINNESOTA AVE 66102   551-3400
  Jeff Stewart, prin.
Sumner Academy/Arts & Sciences   3-00111
  800 OAKLAND AVE 66101   551-3300
  Connie Moritz, prin.
Career Learning Ctr   Vo Tech
  3016 N 9TH ST 66101   551-3635
  Frank Burris, prin.
Argentine MS, 2200 RUBY AVE 66106   3-00100
  Glenn Schoenfish, prin.   722-7350
Arrowhead MS, 1715 N 82ND ST 66112   3-00100
  James Tinsley, prin.   596-5450
Central MS, 925 IVANDALE ST 66101   3-00100
  James Antos, prin.   551-3450
Coronado MS, 1735 N 64TH TER 66102   3-00100
  Karl Baxley, prin.   596-5850
Eisenhower MS, 2901 N 72ND ST 66109   3-00100
  Stanley Jasinskas, prin.   596-5350
Northwest MS, 2400 N 18TH ST 66104   2-00100
  Leslie Brown, prin.   551-3350
Rosedale MS   3-00100
  3600 SPRINGFIELD ST 66103   722-7450
  James Maier, prin.
West MS, 2600 N 44TH ST 66104   3-00100
  Steven Gering, prin.   596-5750

Piper-Kansas City USD 203   4-11111
  12036 LEAVENWORTH RD 66109   721-2088
  Sandra Terril, supt.
Piper HS, 4400 N 107TH ST 66109   2-00011
  Dale Graham, prin.   721-2100
Piper MS, 4420 N 107TH ST 66109   2-00100
  Laurence Breedlove, prin.   721-1144

Turner-Kansas City USD 202   5-11111
  1800 S 55TH ST 66106   287-7500
  Robert Hale, supt.
Turner SHS, 1312 S 55TH ST 66106   3-00001
  Joseph Snyder, prin.   287-6700
Pierson JHS, 1800 S 55TH ST 66106   3-00110
  William Haas, prin.   287-6900

Bethany Medical Center   HSP
  51 N 12TH ST 66102   281-8703
Bishop Ward HS, 708 N 18TH ST 66102   2-00011
  Timothy Hannon, prin.   371-1201
Central Baptist Theological Seminary   2-UC
  741 N 31ST ST 66102   800-677-2287
Donnelly College   2-CC
  608 N 18TH ST 66102   621-6070

Kansas City Kansas Community College 5-CC
7250 STATE AVE 66112 334-1100
Kansas State Sch./Visually Handicapped HND
1100 STATE AVE 66102
St. John the Baptist MS 1-01100
420 BARNETT AVE 66101 321-0649
Mary Staley, prin.
University of Kansas Medical Center 4-UC
3901 RAINBOW BLVD 66160 588-1619

Kensington, AC 913, PC 3, Smith
West Smith County USD 238 2-11111
PO BOX 188 66951 476-2218
Warren Barnell, supt.
HS, PO BOX 188 66951 2-00011
Tom Croston, prin. 476-2217

Kincaid, AC 316, PC 2, Anderson
Crest USD 479, PO BOX 68 66039 2-11111
Larry Wittmer, supt. 439-5330
Crest East MS, PO BOX 68 66039 2-01100
Gail Dunbar, prin. 439-5313
Other Schools – See Colony

Kingman, AC 316, PC 5, Kingman
Kingman USD 331 4-11111
PO BOX 416 67068 532-3134
Steven Davies, supt.
HS, 260 W KANSAS AVE 67068 2-00011
Gary Sechrist, prin. 532-3136
Other Schools – See Norwich

Kinsley, AC 316, PC 4, Edwards
Kinsley-Offerle USD 347 2-11111
110 E 1ST ST 67547 – John Dunn, supt. 659-3646
HS, 716 COLONY AVE 67547 2-00011
Harvey Swager, prin. 659-2126
Other Schools – See Offerle

Kiowa, AC 316, PC 4, Barber
South Barber County USD 255 2-11111
PO BOX 124 67070 825-4115
Glen Piper, supt.
South Barber HS, 1220 N 8TH ST 67070 2-00011
Ronald Holmes, prin. 825-4214
Other Schools – See Hardtner

Kismet, AC 316, PC 2, Seward
Kismet-Plains USD 483
Supt. — See Plains
Southwestern Heights HS 2-00011
RR 1 BOX 24A 67859 563-7292
Vernon Welch, prin.

La Crosse, AC 913, PC 4, Rush
La Crosse USD 395 2-11111
PO BOX 778 67548 222-2505
Dennis Wilson, supt.
HS, PO BOX 810 67548 2-00011
William Shimeall, prin. 222-2528
McCracken MS 67556 1-00100
Melvin Barnett, prin. 394-2248

La Cygne, AC 913, PC 4, Linn
Prairie View USD 362 3-11111
RR 2 BOX 92A 66040 – Joe Smith, supt. 757-2677
Prairie View JSHS 2-00111
RR 2 BOX 92 66040 757-4447
Daniel Stwalley, prin.

Lakin, AC 316, PC 4, Kearny
Lakin USD 215 3-11111
500 W KINGMAN AVE 67860 355-6761
Ernest McClain, supt.
HS, 407 N CAMPBELL ST 67860 2-00011
Jack Hulsey, prin. 355-6411
MS, 500 W KINGMAN AVE 67860 2-00100
Vernon Dietz, prin. 355-6973

Langdon, AC 316, PC 1, Reno
Fairfield USD 310 2-11111
PO BOX 127 67583 596-2152
Larry Combs, supt.
Fairfield HS 2-00011
16115 S LANGDON RD 67583 596-2481
Greg Markowitz, prin.
Fairfield MS 2-00100
16115 S LANGDON RD 67583 596-2615
Larry Geist, prin.

Lansing, AC 913, PC 6, Leavenworth
Lansing USD 469 4-11111
613 HOLIDAY PLZ 66043 727-1100
Richard Flores, supt.
HS, 220 LION LN 66043 3-00011
Wilbur Barnes, prin. 727-3357
MS, 300 OLIVE ST 66043 2-00100
Bart Altenbernb, prin. 727-1197

Larned, AC 316, PC 5, Pawnee
Ft. Larned USD 495, 120 E 6TH ST 67550 4-11111
Ronald White, supt. 285-3185
HS, 815 CORSE AVE 67550 2-00011
Jeffry Felton, prin. 285-2151
MS, 1023 SANTA FE ST 67550 2-00100
Tom Renshaw, prin. 285-3119
Other Schools – See Pawnee Rock

Lawrence, AC 913, PC 8, Douglas
Lawrence USD 497 6-11111
3705 CLINTON PKY 66047 832-5000
Al Azinger, supt.
SHS, 1901 LOUISIANA ST 66046 4-00001
Bradford Tate, prin. 842-6222

Lawrence Central JHS 3-00110
1400 MASSACHUSETTS ST 66044 832-5400
Dan Jaimes, prin.
Lawrence South JHS 3-00110
2734 LOUISIANA ST 66046 832-5450
Randall Weseman, prin.
Lawrence West JHS 3-00110
2700 HARVARD RD 66049 832-5500
Michael Lowe, prin.

Center for Training in Bus. & Industry 2-CS
2211 SILICON DR 66046 841-9640
Haskell Indian Junior College 3-CC
155 INDIAN AVE RM 1305 66046 749-8450
University of Kansas 66045 8-UC
864-2700

Leavenworth, AC 913, PC 8, Leavenworth
Leavenworth USD 453 5-11111
200 N 4TH ST 66048 684-1400
Richard Branstrator, supt.
SHS, 2012 10TH AVE 66048 4-00001
Jim Van Maanen, prin. 684-1550
Leavenworth East JHS 2-00110
400 CHESTNUT ST 66048 684-1530
Sheri Gentzler, prin.
Leavenworth West JHS 2-00110
1901 SPRUCE ST 66048 684-1520
Kerry O'Brien, prin.

Immaculata HS, 600 SHAWNEE ST 66048 2-00011
Sr. Rita Smith, prin. 682-3900
St. Mary College 3-UC
4100 S 4TH ST 66048 682-5151

Leawood, AC 913, PC 7, Johnson
Blue Valley USD 229
Supt. — See Overland Park
MS, 2410 W 123RD ST 66209 3-00100
Jim Gill, prin. 345-7400

Lebo, AC 316, PC 3, Coffey
Lebo-Waverly USD 243
Supt. — See Waverly
HS, PO BOX 45 66856 1-00011
Richard Barnaby, prin. 256-6341

Lenexa, AC 913, PC 8, Johnson

Wright Business School 2-CS
9500 MARSHALL DR 66215 492-2888

Lenora, AC 913, PC 2, Norton
West Solomon Valley USD 213 2-11111
PO BOX 98 67645 567-4350
Lelia Hall, supt.
HS, PO BOX 98 67645 1-00011
Lelia Hall, prin. 567-4235

Leon, AC 316, PC 3, Butler
Bluestem USD 205, PO BOX 8 67074 3-11111
Gary McEachern, supt. 742-3261
Bluestem HS, PO BOX 338 67074 2-00011
Dale Harper, prin. 742-3281
Bluestem JHS, RR 1 BOX 3A 67074 2-01100
Ron Wrampe, prin. 742-3263

Leoti, AC 316, PC 4, Wichita
Leoti USD 467, PO BOX 967 67861 3-11111
Harold Vestal, supt. 375-4677
Wichita County HS, PO BOX K 67861 2-00011
Randy Steinle, prin. 375-2213
Wichita County MS 2-00100
PO BOX 908 67861 375-2219
John Johnston, prin.

Le Roy, AC 316, PC 3, Coffey
Le Roy-Gridley USD 245 2-11111
PO BOX 278 66857 964-2212
Harvey Watson, supt.
HS, PO BOX 188 66857 1-00011
John Hetzel, prin. 964-2217
Other Schools – See Gridley

Lewis, AC 316, PC 2, Edwards
Lewis USD 502, PO BOX 97 67552 2-11111
William Stapleton, supt. 324-5547
HS, PO BOX 97 67552 1-00011
William Stapleton, prin. 324-5541

Liberal, AC 316, PC 7, Seward
Liberal USD 480, PO BOX 949 67905 5-11111
Harvey Ludwick, supt. 626-3800
HS, 1611 W 2ND ST 67901 3-00011
Jim Maskus, prin. 626-3802
South JHS, 950 S GRANT AVE 67901 2-00100
Curtis Beer, prin. 626-3803
West JHS, 500 N WESTERN AVE 67901 2-00100
Darin Headrick, prin. 626-3804

Liberal Area Voc./Tech. School 2-CS
PO BOX 1599 67905 626-3819
Seward County Community College 3-CC
PO BOX 1137 67905 624-1951

Lincoln, AC 913, PC 4, Lincoln
Lincoln USD 298, PO BOX 289 67455 2-11111
Bradley Killen, supt. 524-4436
JSHS, 700 S 4TH ST 67455 2-00111
Bob Finger, prin. 524-4193

Lindsborg, AC 913, PC 5, McPherson
Lindsborg USD 400 3-11111
126 S MAIN ST 67456 227-2981
Marlin Berry, supt.
Smoky Valley HS 2-00011
401 N CEDAR ST 67456 227-2909
Larry Nelson, prin.

Bethany College 3-UC
421 N 1ST ST 67456 227-3311

Linn, AC 913, PC 2, Washington
Barnes USD 223
Supt. — See Barnes
HS 66953 1-00011
Steve Joonas, prin. 348-5531

Linwood, AC 913, PC 2, Leavenworth
Basehor-Linwood USD 458
Supt. — See Basehor
Basehor-Linwood MS 2-00100
PO BOX 1 66052 724-2323
Michael Boyd, prin.

Little River, AC 316, PC 2, Rice
Little River USD 444 2-11111
PO BOX 218 67457 897-6325
Darrel Kellerman, supt.
HS, PO BOX 8 67457 2-00011
Jerry Cook, prin. 897-6201

Logan, AC 913, PC 3, Phillips
Logan USD 326, PO BOX 98 67646 2-11111
Earl Loyd, supt. 689-7595
HS, PO BOX 98 67646 1-00011
Charles Dougherty, prin. 689-7574

Long Island, AC 913, PC 2, Phillips
Northern Valley USD 212
Supt. — See Almena
MS, PO BOX 98 67647 1-01100
Dwight Vallin, prin. 854-7681

Longton, AC 316, PC 2, Elk
Elk Valley USD 283 2-11111
PO BOX 87 67352 642-2811
Roger Rankin, supt.
JSHS, PO BOX 87 67352 1-00111
Mike Miller, prin. 642-2215

Lorraine, AC 913, PC 2, Ellsworth
Lorraine USD 328 3-11111
PO BOX 109 67459 472-5241
Norman Linton, supt.
Other Schools – See Bushton, Holyrood, Wilson

Lost Springs, AC 913, PC 2, Marion
Centre USD 397, PO BOX 38 66859 2-11111
Demitry Evancho, supt. 983-4304
Centre JSHS, RR 1 BOX 106 66859 2-00111
Donald Karr, prin. 983-4321

Louisburg, AC 913, PC 4, Miami
Louisburg USD 416 4-11111
PO BOX 550 66053 837-2944
James Knox, supt.
JSHS, 505 AMITY ST 66053 2-00011
Don Meek, prin. 837-2941

Lucas, AC 913, PC 2, Russell
Russell County USD 407
Supt. — See Russell
Lucas-Luray HS 67648 1-00011
Phillip Riedel, prin. 525-6244

Lyndon, AC 913, PC 3, Osage
Lyndon USD 421, PO BOX 488 66451 2-11111
Tom Bishard, supt. 828-4413
HS 66451 2-00011
Dan Fulton, prin. 828-4911

Lyons, AC 316, PC 5, Rice
Lyons USD 405, 510 EAST AVE S 67554 3-11111
Larry Frisbie, supt. 257-5196
HS, 601 E AMERICAN RD 67554 2-00011
Rob Wedel, prin. 257-5114
MS, 401 S DOUGLAS AVE 67554 2-00100
Jon Utech, prin. 257-3961

Macksville, AC 316, PC 2, Stafford
Macksville USD 351 2-11111
PO BOX 487 67557 348-3415
Jack Miller, supt.
HS, PO BOX 307 67557 1-00011
Gerald Bowman, prin. 348-2475

Mc Louth, AC 913, PC 3, Jefferson
Mc Louth USD 342 3-11111
PO BOX 40 66054 796-6121
Robert Behrens, supt.
HS, PO BOX 40 66054 2-00011
Nancy Albrecht, prin. 796-6122

Mc Pherson, AC 316, PC 7, McPherson
Mc Pherson USD 418 5-11111
PO BOX 1147 67460 241-9400
Robert Shannon, supt.
HS, 801 E 1ST ST 67460 3-00011
William Parker, prin. 241-9500
MS, 700 E ELIZABETH ST 67460 3-00100
Merry Wade, prin. 241-9450

Central College 2-UC
1200 S MAIN ST 67460 241-0723
McPherson College 2-UC
1600 E EUCLID ST 67460 241-0731

Madison, AC 316, PC 3, Greenwood
Madison-Virgil USD 386 — 2-11111
PO BOX 398 66860 — 437-2910
John Glover, supt.
HS, 1500 SW BOULEVARD 66860 — 1-00011
Tom Foerschler, prin. — 437-2912

Maize, AC 316, PC 4, Sedgwick
Maize USD 266, 201 S PARK ST 67101 — 5-11111
Joe Hickey, supt. — 722-0614
HS, 4600 N MAIZE RD 67101 — 3-00011
Ken Rickard, prin. — 722-0441
IS, 304 E CENTRAL ST 67101 — 3-00100
Terry Gurss, prin. — 722-0421

Manhattan, AC 913, PC 8, Riley
Manhattan USD 383 — 6-11111
2031 POYNTZ AVE 66502 — 587-2000
Dan Yunk, supt.
HS, 2100 POYNTZ AVE 66502 — 4-00011
James Rezac, prin. — 587-2100
MS, 901 POYNTZ AVE 66502 — 4-00100
Marvin Marsh, prin. — 587-2150

American Institute of Baking — 2-CS
1213 BAKERS WAY 66502 — 537-4750
Kansas State University — 7-UC
ANDERSON HALL 110 66506 — 532-6222
Manhattan Christian College — 2-UC
1415 ANDERSON AVE 66502 — 539-3571

Mankato, AC 913, PC 4, Jewell
Mankato USD 278 — 2-11111
PO BOX 308 66956 — 378-3102
Rod Dietz, supt.
JSHS, PO BOX 308 66956 — 2-00111
Harold Terpening, prin. — 378-3126

Marion, AC 316, PC 4, Marion
Marion USD 408, 601 E MAIN ST 66861 — 3-11111
Doug Huxman, supt. — 382-2117
HS, 701 E MAIN ST 66861 — 2-00011
Jim Giesbrecht, prin. — 382-2168
Other Schools – See Florence

Marysville, AC 913, PC 5, Marshall
Marysville USD 364 — 4-11111
1011 WALNUT ST 66508 — 562-5308
William Oborny, supt.
HS, 1111 WALNUT ST 66508 — 2-00011
Ralph Wilkerson, prin. — 562-5386
JHS, 1005 WALNUT ST 66508 — 2-00100
Ralph Wilkerson, prin. — 562-5356

Mayetta, AC 913, PC 2, Jackson
Royal Valley USD 337 — 3-11111
PO BOX 117 66509 — 966-2246
Marceta Reilly, supt.
Royal Valley MS, PO BOX 155 66509 — 2-00100
Edward DeKeyser, prin. — 966-2251
Other Schools – See Hoyt

Meade, AC 316, PC 4, Meade
Meade USD 226, PO BOX 400 67864 — 2-11111
Dave Easterday, supt. — 873-2081
HS, PO BOX 400 67864 — 2-00011
Ron Keller, prin. — 873-2981

Medicine Lodge, AC 316, PC 4, Barber
Barber County North USD 254 — 3-11111
PO BOX 288 67104 — 886-3370
Daryl Johnson, supt.
HS, PO BOX D 67104 — 2-00011
Milton Moore, prin. — 886-5668
MS, 1ST & MAIN 67104 — 2-01100
Pat Simmons, prin. — 886-5644

Melvern, AC 913, PC 2, Osage
Marais Des Cygnes Valley USD 456 — 2-11111
PO BOX 158 66510 – Jim Irey, supt. — 549-3521
Marais Des Cygnes HS 66510 — 2-00011
Tom Conway, prin. — 549-3313
Other Schools – See Quenemo

Meriden, AC 913, PC 3, Jefferson
Jefferson West USD 340 — 3-11111
PO BOX 267 66512 — 484-3444
William Majors, supt.
Jefferson West HS 66512 — 2-00011
Angelo Cocolis, prin. — 484-3331
Other Schools – See Ozawkie

Miltonvale, AC 913, PC 2, Cloud
Southern Cloud USD 334
Supt. — See Glasco
HS, PO BOX 394 67466 — 1-00111
Kim Maschmann, prin. — 427-3250

Minneapolis, AC 913, PC 4, Ottawa
North Ottawa County USD 239 — 3-11111
PO BOX A 67467 – Ron Brown, supt. — 392-2167
HS, 602 WOODLAND AVE 67467 — 2-00011
Milt Dougherty, prin. — 392-2113

Minneola, AC 316, PC 3, Clark
Minneola USD 219 — 2-11111
PO BOX 157 67865 — 885-4372
Eddie L. Goble, supt.
HS, PO BOX 157 67865 — 1-00011
Jeff Freeborn, prin. — 885-4611

Montezuma, AC 316, PC 3, Gray
Montezuma USD 371 — 2-11111
PO BOX 355 67867 — 846-2293
George Smirl, supt.
South Gray JSHS, PO BOX 355 67867 — 1-00011
George Smirl, prin. — 846-2281

Moran, AC 316, PC 3, Allen
Marmaton Valley USD 256 — 2-11111
RR 1 BOX 35 66755 — 237-4250
Ernie Price, supt.
Marmaton Valley HS — 1-00011
RR 1 BOX 35 66755 — 237-4251
Larry Anderson, prin.

Morland, AC 913, PC 2, Graham
West Graham-Morland USD 280 — 2-11111
PO BOX 226 67650 — 627-5481
Gary Akers, supt.
HS, PO BOX 128 67650 — 1-00011
Gary Akers, prin. — 627-3285

Morrowville, AC 316, PC 2, Washington
North Central USD 221
Supt. — See Haddam
North Central HS 66958 — 1-00011
Harold Boggs, prin. — 265-3585

Moscow, AC 316, PC 2, Stevens
Moscow USD 209 — 2-11111
PO BOX 158 67952 — 598-2205
William Grimes, supt.
HS, PO BOX 158 67952 — 1-00011
Larry Philippi, prin. — 598-2250

Mound City, AC 913, PC 3, Linn
Jayhawk USD 346 — 3-11111
PO BOX 278 66056 — 795-2247
Gary Wimmer, supt.
Jayhawk-Linn JSHS, PO BOX D 66056 — 2-00111
R. Harvey, prin. — 795-2224

Moundridge, AC 316, PC 4, McPherson
Moundridge USD 423, PO BOX K 67107 — 2-11111
Terry Schmidt, supt. — 345-8611
HS, PO BOX 610 67107 — 2-00011
Bill Nelson, prin. — 345-2816
MS, PO BOX 607 67107 — 2-01100
Brenda Randel, prin. — 345-2826

Mullinville, AC 316, PC 2, Kiowa
Mullinville USD 424 — 2-11100
PO BOX 6 67109 — 548-2521
Robert Minchew, supt.
HS, PO BOX 6 67109 — 1-00100
Charles Atkinson, prin. — 548-2217

Mulvane, AC 316, PC 5, Sedgwick
Mulvane USD 263 — 4-11111
PO BOX 129 67110 — 777-1102
Dean Parks, supt.
SHS, 915 WESTVIEW DR 67110 — 2-00001
James Burkhart, prin. — 777-1183
JHS, 628 E MULVANE ST 67110 — 2-00110
Jerry Quigley, prin. — 777-1155

Natoma, AC 913, PC 2, Osborne
Paradise USD 399 — 2-11111
PO BOX 100 67651 — 885-4749
Emery Hart, supt.
JSHS, PO BOX 100 67651 — 1-00111
Lesta Jaggers, prin. — 885-4749

Neodesha, AC 316, PC 5, Wilson
Neodesha USD 461 — 3-11111
522 WISCONSIN ST 66757 — 325-2610
Jerry Webster, supt.
JSHS, 1009 N 8TH ST 66757 — 2-00111
Tom Davis, prin. — 325-3015

Ness City, AC 913, PC 4, Ness
Ness City USD 303 — 2-11111
414 E CHESTNUT ST 67560 — 798-2210
Roy Keller, supt.
HS, 200 N 5TH ST 67560 — 2-00011
David Zlab, prin. — 798-3991

Newton, AC 316, PC 7, Harvey
Newton USD 373, PO BOX 307 67114 — 5-11111
Willis Heck, supt. — 284-6200
HS, 900 W 12TH ST 67114 — 4-00011
William Harrington, prin. — 284-6280
Chisholm MS, 900 E 1ST ST 67114 — 2-01100
Kathleen Perkins, prin. — 284-6260
Santa Fe MS — 3-01100
130 W BROADWAY ST 67114 — 284-6270
Gordon Stineman, prin.

Nickerson, AC 316, PC 4, Reno
Nickerson USD 309
Supt. — See Hutchinson
HS, PO BOX 67 67561 — 2-00011
Gary Graber, prin. — 669-0197

North Newton, AC 316, PC 4, Harvey

Bethel College — 3-UC
300 E 27TH ST 67117 — 283-2500

Norton, AC 913, PC 5, Norton
Norton USD 211 — 3-11111
105 E WAVERLY ST 67654 — 877-3386
Patrick Terry, supt.
Norton Community HS — 2-00011
513 W WILBERFORCE ST 67654 — 877-3338
Larry Stull, prin.
JHS, 706 JONES AVE 67654 — 2-00100
Greg Mann, prin. — 877-5851

Nortonville, AC 913, PC 3, Jefferson
Jefferson County North USD 339
Supt. — See Winchester

Jefferson County North MS — 2-01100
PO BOX 298 66060 — 886-3870
Scott Slava, prin.

Norwich, AC 316, PC 2, Kingman
Kingman USD 331
Supt. — See Kingman
HS 67118 — 1-00011
Lanny Hower, prin. — 478-2235

Oakley, AC 913, PC 4, Logan
Oakley USD 274, 208 E 2ND ST 67748 — 3-11111
Donald Marchant, supt. — 672-4588
HS, 118 W 7TH ST 67748 — 2-00011
A. Clement, prin. — 672-3241
MS, 611 CENTER AVE 67748 — 2-00100
Donna Workman, prin. — 672-3620

Oberlin, AC 913, PC 4, Decatur
Oberlin USD 294 — 3-11111
131 E COMMERCIAL ST 67749 — 475-3805
Wayne Steinert, supt.
Decatur Community JSHS — 2-00111
605 E COMMERCIAL ST 67749 — 475-2231
Gordon Matson, prin.

Offerle, AC 316, PC 2, Edwards
Kinsley-Offerle USD 347
Supt. — See Kinsley
MS, PO BOX 130 67563 — 2-01100
Duane Adams, prin. — 659-2866

Olathe, AC 913, PC 8, Johnson
Olathe USD 233, PO BOX 2000 66051 — 7-11111
Ron Wimmer, supt. — 780-7000
Olathe East SHS — 3-00001
14545 W 127TH ST 66062 — 780-7120
Karl Krawitz, prin.
Olathe North SHS — 3-00001
600 E PRAIRIE ST 66061 — 780-7140
Charles Nichols, prin.
Olathe South SHS — 4-00001
1640 E 151ST ST 66062 — 780-7160
Lowell Ghosey, prin.
Indian Trail JHS, 1440 E 151ST ST 66062 — 3-00110
Nancy Keith, prin. — 780-7230
Frontier Trail JHS — 3-00110
15300 W 143RD ST 66062 — 780-7210
Stan Smith, prin.
Oregon Trail JHS — 3-00110
1800 W DENNIS AVE 66061 — 780-7250
Jim Houghton, prin.
Pioneer Trail JHS — 3-00110
15500 W 127TH ST 66062 — 780-7270
James Laird, prin.
Santa Fe Trail JHS — 3-00110
1100 N RIDGEVIEW RD 66061 — 780-7290
Philip Clark, prin.

Kansas School for the Deaf — HND
450 E PARK ST 66061
Mid-America Nazarene College — 4-UC
PO BOX 1776 66051 — 782-3750

Olpe, AC 316, PC 2, Lyon
Southern Lyon County USD 252
Supt. — See Hartford
HS, PO BOX 206 66865 — 1-00011
Mike Dougherty, prin. — 475-3223

Onaga, AC 913, PC 3, Pottawatomie
Onaga-Havensville-Wheaton USD 322 — 2-11111
PO BOX 60 66521 — 889-4614
James Weixelman, supt.
HS, 500 HIGH ST 66521 — 2-00011
John Pavlovich, prin. — 889-4251

Osage City, AC 913, PC 5, Osage
Osage City USD 420, 520 MAIN ST 66523 — 3-11111
Dale Lilly, supt. — 528-3176
HS, 420 S 5TH ST 66523 — 2-00011
David Carriger, prin. — 528-3172

Osawatomie, AC 913, PC 5, Miami
Osawatomie USD 367 — 3-11111
12TH AND TROJAN DR 66064 — 755-4172
H. Dean, supt.
HS, 1200 TROJAN DR 66064 — 2-00011
H. Dean, prin. — 755-2191
MS, 428 PACIFIC AVE 66064 — 2-00100
Randy Madden, prin. — 755-4155

Osborne, AC 913, PC 4, Osborne
Osborne County USD 392 — 2-11111
PO BOX 209 67473 — 346-2145
Joseph Clouse, supt.
HS, 219 N 2ND ST 67473 — 2-00011
Ron Sturgeon, prin. — 346-2143
Other Schools – See Alton

Oskaloosa, AC 913, PC 4, Jefferson
Oskaloosa USD 341 — 3-11111
PO BOX 345 66066 — 863-2539
James White, supt.
HS, PO BOX 345 66066 — 2-00011
Mark Conwell, prin. — 863-2281
MS, PO BOX 345 66066 — 2-00100
Paula Burnetta, prin. — 863-3237

Oswego, AC 316, PC 4, Labette
Oswego USD 504, PO BOX 129 67356 — 2-11111
Terry Karlin, supt. — 795-2126
HS, 410 KANSAS ST 67356 — 2-00011
Jerry Graham, prin. — 795-2125
MS, 208 IOWA ST 67356 — 1-00100
Cynthia Farris, prin. — 795-4724

Otis, AC 316, PC 2, Rush
Otis-Bison USD 403
  Supt. — See Albert
Otis-Bison HS 67565   2-00011
  Mark Goodheart, prin.   387-2337

Ottawa, AC 913, PC 7, Franklin
Ottawa USD 290, 420 S MAIN ST 66067   4-11111
  Don Duncan, supt.   242-3750
HS, 1120 S ASH ST 66067   3-00011
  Gary Mavity, prin.   242-4176
East Central Vo Coop Ottawa   Vo Tech
  908 W 11TH ST 66067 – (—), prin.   242-5955
JHS, 502 S MAIN ST 66067   3-00100
  Margaret Betterton, prin.   242-3237

Ottawa University   3-UC
  1001 S CEDAR ST 66067   242-5200

Overbrook, AC 913, PC 3, Osage
Santa Fe Trail USD 434
  Supt. — See Carbondale
MS, PO BOX 324 66524   2-01100
  Loren Rohloff, prin.   665-7615

Overland Park, AC 913, PC 9, Johnson
Blue Valley USD 229   6-11111
  PO BOX 23901 66223   681-4000
  David Benson, supt.
Blue Valley North HS   4-00011
  12200 LAMAR AVE 66209   345-7300
  Elizabeth Sanders, prin.
Blue Valley Northwest HS   3-00011
  13260 SWITZER RD 66213   681-7000
  Russ Kokoruda, prin.
Blue Valley MS   3-00100
  7500 W 149TH TER 66223   681-4150
  Richard Seipel, prin.
Harmony MS, 10101 W 141ST ST 66221   2-00100
  Glenda Moehleman, prin.   681-4800
Overland Trail MS   3-00100
  6201 W 133RD ST 66209   681-4400
  Kathleen Currence, prin.
Oxford MS, 12500 SWITZER RD 66213   3-00100
  Robert Wilson, prin.   681-4175
Other Schools – See Leawood, Stilwell

Johnson County Community College   6-CC
  12345 COLLEGE BLVD 66210   469-8500
Kansas City College & Bible School   1-UC
  7401 METCALF AVE 66204   722-0272
St. Thomas Aquinas HS   3-00011
  11411 PFLUMM RD 66215   345-1411
  Blake Mulvany, prin.

Oxford, AC 316, PC 4, Sumner
Oxford USD 358, PO BOX 937 67119   2-11111
  A. O. George, supt.   455-2227
HS, PO BOX 970 67119   2-00011
  Rich Hayes, prin.   455-2410

Ozawkie, AC 913, PC 2, Jefferson
Jefferson West USD 340
  Supt. — See Meriden
Jefferson West MS 66070   2-00100
  Terry Stanton, prin.   876-2110

Palco, AC 913, PC 2, Rooks
Palco USD 269, PO BOX 21 67657   2-11111
  Timothy Shafer, supt.   737-4635
HS, PO BOX 29 67657   1-00011
  Joan Friend, prin.   737-4645
Damar MS, PO BOX 38 67657   1-00100
  Joan Friend, prin.   839-4265

Paola, AC 913, PC 5, Miami
Paola USD 368, PO BOX 268 66071   4-11111
  William Cleary, supt.   294-3646
HS, PO BOX 268 66071   2-00011
  Dan Locke, prin.   294-4367
MS, PO BOX 268 66071   2-00100
  Olin McCool, prin.   294-3726

Park, AC 913, PC 2, Gove
Quinter USD 293, PO BOX 28 67751   2-11111
  Larry Lysell, supt.   673-4213
Other Schools – See Quinter

Wheatland USD 292   2-11111
  PO BOX 28 67751   673-4213
  Larry Lysell, supt.
Other Schools – See Grainfield

Parsons, AC 316, PC 7, Labette
Parsons 503   4-11111
  PO BOX 1056 67357   421-5950
  John Hetlinger, supt.
HS, 3030 MORTON AVE 67357   3-00011
  George Tignor, prin.   421-3660
MS, 2719 MAIN ST 67357   2-00100
  Timothy Fox, prin.   421-4190

Labette Community College   4-CC
  200 S 14TH ST 67357   421-6700

Pawnee Rock, AC 316, PC 2, Barton
Ft. Larned USD 495
  Supt. — See Larned
MS 67567   1-00100
  Lyle Parks, prin.   982-4327

Peabody, AC 316, PC 4, Marion
Peabody-Burns USD 398   2-11111
  506 N ELM ST 66866   983-2198
  Robert Herbig, supt.

HS, 900 N WALNUT ST 66866   2-00011
  John Ireland, prin.   983-2196
MS, 900 N WALNUT ST 66866   1-00100
  John Ireland, prin.   983-2196

Perry, AC 913, PC 3, Jefferson
Perry USD 343, PO BOX 29 66073   3-11111
  Henry Murphy, supt.   597-5138
Perry-Lecompton HS 66073   2-00011
  Ann Starlin-Horner, prin.   597-5124
MS 66073   2-00100
  Eric Hyler, prin.   597-5159

Phillipsburg, AC 913, PC 5, Phillips
Phillipsburg USD 325   3-11111
  240 S 7TH ST 67661 – Rob Little, supt.   543-5281
HS, 410 S 7TH ST 67661   2-00011
  David Roberts, prin.   543-5251
MS, 647 7TH ST 67661   2-01100
  Robert McVicker, prin.   543-5114

Pittsburg, AC 316, PC 7, Crawford
Pittsburg USD 250, PO BOX 75 66762   5-11111
  Dan Neunswander, supt.   235-3100
HS, 1978 E 4TH ST 66762   3-00011
  Steve Parsons, prin.   235-3200
MS, 1310 N BROADWAY ST 66762   3-00100
  Blaine Babb, prin.   235-3240

Colgan HS, PO BOX 266 66762   2-00011
  Patrick Forbes, prin.   231-4690
Pittsburg State University   5-UC
  1701 S BROADWAY ST 66762   231-7000

Plains, AC 316, PC 3, Meade
Kismet-Plains USD 483   3-11111
  PO BOX 517 67869   563-7292
  D. J. Miller, supt.
Other Schools – See Kismet

Plainville, AC 913, PC 4, Rooks
Plainville USD 270   2-11111
  111 W MILL ST 67663   434-4678
  J. D. Brunnemer, supt.
HS, 202 SE 3RD ST 67663   2-00011
  Dennis Stout, prin.   434-4547

Pleasanton, AC 913, PC 4, Linn
Pleasanton USD 344   2-11111
  PO BOX 480 66075   352-8534
  Bob Cole, supt.
HS 66075   2-00011
  John Maples, prin.   352-8701

Pomona, AC 913, PC 3, Franklin
West Franklin USD 287   3-11111
  PO BOX 38 66076   566-3396
  James Cain, supt.
HS, PO BOX A 66076   2-00011
  Terry Adams, prin.   566-3392
Other Schools – See Williamsburg

Pratt, AC 316, PC 6, Pratt
Pratt USD 382   4-11111
  401 N NINNESCAH ST 67124   672-6418
  Howard E. Gray, supt.
HS, 401 S HAMILTON ST 67124   2-00011
  Jim Menze, prin.   672-6416
Liberty MS, 300 S IUKA ST 67124   2-00100
  Rich McCall, prin.   672-5529
Skyline USD 438   2-11111
  RR 2 BOX 138 67124   672-5651
  A. Boland, supt.
Skyline HS, RR 2 BOX 138 67124   2-00011
  Scott Sheldon, prin.   672-5651

Pratt Community College   3-CC
  HWY 61 67124   672-5641

Pretty Prairie, AC 316, PC 3, Reno
Pretty Prairie USD 311   2-11111
  PO BOX 218 67570   459-6241
  David Brax, supt.
HS, PO BOX 326 67570   1-00011
  George Leary, prin.   459-6313
MS, PO BOX 326 67570   1-00100
  Bradley Wade, prin.   459-6313

Protection, AC 316, PC 3, Comanche
Comanche County USD 300
  Supt. — See Coldwater
HS, 210 S JEFFERSON 67127   1-00011
  Phillip Keidel, prin.   622-4545

Quenemo, AC 913, PC 2, Osage
Marais Des Cygnes Valley USD 456
  Supt. — See Melvern
Marais Des Cygnes MS 66528   1-00100
  Jerry Ewing, prin.   759-3512

Quinter, AC 913, PC 3, Gove
Quinter USD 293
  Supt. — See Park
JSHS, PO BOX 459 67752   2-00111
  Fred Irwin, prin.   754-3660

Randall, AC 913, PC 1, Jewell
Jewell USD 279
  Supt. — See Jewell
MS 66963   1-01100
  Ron Alford, prin.   739-2216

Randolph, AC 913, PC 2, Riley
Blue Valley USD 384   2-11111
  PO BOX 98 66554   293-5256
  Dennis Cox, supt.

Blue Valley HS 66554   1-00011
  Terry McCarty, prin.   293-5255
MS, PO BOX 98 66554   2-01100
  Dennis Cox, prin.   293-5256

Ransom, AC 913, PC 2, Ness
Smoky Hill USD 302   2-11111
  PO BOX 248 67572   731-2434
  Ralph Kenworthy, supt.
JSHS, PO BOX 248 67572   1-00111
  Mike Kastle, prin.   731-2352

Raymond, AC 316, PC 2, Rice
Chase USD 401
  Supt. — See Chase
MS 67573   1-00100
  Ralph Renfro, prin.   534-2305

Rexford, AC 913, PC 2, Thomas
Golden Plains USD 316
  Supt. — See Selden
Golden Plains HS, PO BOX 100 67753   1-00011
  William Leggett, prin.   687-3265
Golden Plains JHS   1-00100
  PO BOX 100 67753   687-3265
  William Leggett, prin.

Richmond, AC 913, PC 3, Franklin
Central Heights USD 288   3-11111
  3521 ELLIS RD 66080   869-3455
  Henry Huddleston, supt.
Central Heights JSHS   2-00111
  3521 ELLIS RD 66080   869-3555
  Charles Gash, prin.

Riley, AC 913, PC 3, Riley
Riley County USD 378   3-11111
  PO BOX 326 66531   485-2818
  Rob Winter, supt.
Riley County HS, PO BOX 38 66531   2-00011
  Craig Neuenswander, prin.   485-2892

Riverton, AC 316, PC 3, Cherokee
Riverton USD 404   3-11111
  PO BOX 290 66770   848-3386
  Bill Sweeten, supt.
HS, PO BOX 290 66770   2-00011
  Dennis Burke, prin.   848-3388

Robinson, AC 913, PC 2, Brown
Hiawatha USD 415
  Supt. — See Hiawatha
JHS 66532   2-01100
  Steven Adams, prin.   544-6523

Rolla, AC 316, PC 2, Morton
Rolla USD 217, PO BOX 167 67954   2-11111
  Walter Hays, supt.   593-4344
HS, PO BOX 167 67954   1-00011
  Robert Sondergaard, prin.   593-4345

Rosalia, AC 316, PC 2, Butler
Flinthills USD 492   2-11111
  PO BOX 188 67132   476-2215
  John Watson, supt.
Flinthills HS 67132   1-00011
  Doug Curtright, prin.   476-2215

Rose Hill, AC 316, PC 4, Butler
Rose Hill USD 394   4-11111
  315 S ROSE HILL RD 67133   776-3300
  Michael Rooney, supt.
HS, 315 S ROSE HILL RD 67133   2-00011
  Allen Roth, prin.   776-3360
MS, 315 S ROSE HILL RD 67133   2-01100
  Marietta Gray, prin.   776-3320

Rossville, AC 913, PC 4, Shawnee
Kaw Valley USD 321
  Supt. — See Saint Marys
HS, PO BOX 68 66533   2-00011
  John Johnson, prin.   584-6193

Rozel, AC 316, PC 2, Pawnee
Pawnee Heights USD 496   2-11111
  PO BOX 98 67574   527-4212
  Glen Davis, supt.
Pawnee Heights HS   1-00011
  PO BOX 97 67574   527-4211
  Raymond Patterson, prin.

Russell, AC 913, PC 5, Russell
Russell County USD 407   4-11111
  802 N MAIN ST 67665   483-2173
  Don Degenhardt, supt.
HS, 565 E STATE ST 67665   2-00011
  Bill Brown, prin.   483-5631
Ruppenthal JHS, 400 N ELM ST 67665   2-01100
  Rick Riffel, prin.   483-3174
Other Schools – See Lucas

Sabetha, AC 913, PC 4, Nemaha
Sabetha USD 441   4-11111
  107 OREGON ST 66534   284-2175
  Von C. Lauer, supt.
HS, 1011 S US HIGHWAY 75 66534   2-00011
  Dennis Stones, prin.   284-2155
MS, 751 BLUE JAY DR 66534   2-00100
  Terry L. Duntz, prin.   284-2151
Other Schools – See Wetmore

Saint Francis, AC 913, PC 4, Cheyenne
St. Francis USD 297   2-11111
  PO BOX 605 67756   332-2282
  Carl Werner, supt.
JSHS, 100 COLLEGE ST 67756   2-00111
  Ward Cassidy, prin.   332-2153

Saint George, AC 913, PC 2, Pottawatomie
Pottawatomie West USD 323
  Supt. — See Westmoreland
  Rock Creek JSHS, 9355 FLUSH RD 66535 2-00111
    Don Grover, prin. 494-8591

Saint John, AC 316, PC 4, Stafford
St. John-Hudson USD 350 2-11111
  406 N MONROE ST 67576 549-3564
  James Wells, supt.
  JSHS, 505 N BROADWAY ST 67576 2-00111
    Duane Channell, prin. 549-3277

Saint Marys, AC 913, PC 4, Pottawatomie
Kaw Valley USD 321 4-11111
  PO BOX 160 66536 437-2254
  George Brown, supt.
  HS, 601 E LASLEY ST 66536 2-00011
    L. Jackson, prin. 437-6257
  Other Schools – See Rossville

Saint Paul, AC 316, PC 3, Neosho
Erie-St. Paul USD 101
  Supt. — See Erie
  HS 66771 1-00011
    Paul Bingle, prin. 449-2245

Salina, AC 913, PC 8, Saline
Ell-Saline USD 307 2-11111
  1757 N HALSTEAD RD 67401 827-1121
  Bernard White, supt.
  Other Schools – See Brookville

Salina USD 305, PO BOX 797 67402 6-11111
  Andy Tompkins, supt. 826-4700
  Salina Central HS 4-00011
  650 E CRAWFORD ST 67401 826-4751
    Stephen Williams, prin.
  Salina South HS 3-00011
  730 MAGNOLIA RD 67401 826-4766
    Jane Botz, prin.
  Roosevelt/Lincoln JHS 3-00100
  210 W MULBERRY ST 67401 826-4785
    Stan Lauer, prin.
  Salina South MS, 2040 S 4TH ST 67401 3-00100
    Clay Thompson, prin. 826-4776

Brown Mackie College 3-CC
  126 S SANTA FE AVE 67401 825-5422
Kansas State University College of Tech 2-CC
  2409 SCANLAN AVE 67401 826-2600
Kansas Wesleyan University 3-UC
  100 E CLAFLIN AVE 67401 827-5541
Sacred Heart HS, 230 E CLOUD ST 67401 2-00111
  Nick Compagnone, prin. 827-4422
St. Johns Military S 2-01111
  PO BOX 827 67402 823-7231
  Kenneth Faerber, prin.

Satanta, AC 316, PC 4, Haskell
Satanta USD 507, PO BOX 279 67870 2-11111
  George Anshutz, supt. 649-2234
  JSHS, PO BOX 69 67870 2-00011
    Sue Curtis-Lee, prin. 649-2611

Scandia, AC 913, PC 2, Republic
Pike Valley USD 426 2-11111
  PO BOX 291 66966 335-2206
  Richard Ahlvers, supt.
  Pike Valley HS, PO BOX 339 66966 1-00011
    Dale Haug, prin. 335-2294
  Other Schools – See Courtland

Scott City, AC 316, PC 5, Scott
Scott County USD 466 4-11111
  PO BOX 249 67871 872-7231
  James Thompson, supt.
  HS, 712 MAIN ST 67871 2-00011
    Sam Rawdon, prin. 872-5385
  MS, 809 W 9TH ST 67871 2-01100
    Neal George, prin. 872-3110

Sedan, AC 316, PC 4, Chautauqua
Chautauqua County USD 286 3-11111
  416 E ELM ST 67361 725-3187
  Michael Pond, supt.
  HS, 416 E ELM ST 67361 2-00011
    George Blevins, prin. 725-3186

Sedgwick, AC 316, PC 4, Harvey
Sedgwick USD 439, PO BOX K 67135 2-11111
  Cloyce Spradling, supt. 772-5783
  HS, PO BOX K 67135 2-00011
    Max Craft, prin. 772-5155

Selden, AC 913, PC 2, Sheridan
Golden Plains USD 316 2-11111
  PO BOX 199 67757 386-4560
  William Leggett, supt.
  Other Schools – See Rexford

Seneca, AC 913, PC 4, Nemaha
Nemaha Valley USD 442 3-11111
  PO BOX 150 66538 336-6101
  Louis Holaday, supt.
  Nemaha Valley HS 2-00011
  214 N 11TH ST 66538 336-3557
    Duane Osborne, prin.

Sharon Springs, AC 913, PC 3, Wallace
Wallace County USD 241 2-11111
  PO BOX 580 67758 852-4252
  Fred Staker, supt.
  Wallace County HS 1-00011
  PO BOX 550 67758 852-4240
    Aaron Feist, prin.

Shawnee Mission, AC 913, PC see Merriam
Shawnee Mission USD 512 8-11111
  7235 ANTIOCH RD 66204 831-1900
  Marjorie Kaplan, supt.
  Shawnee Mission East HS 4-00011
  7500 MISSION RD 66208 967-7800
    Marlin Stanberry, prin.
  Shawnee Mission North HS 4-00011
  7401 JOHNSON DR 66202 789-3700
    Blanche Banks, prin.
  Shawnee Mission Northwest HS 4-00011
  12701 W 67TH ST 66216 962-3100
    Frank Mermoud, prin.
  Shawnee Mission South HS 4-00011
  5800 W 107TH ST 66207 967-7700
    Corky Jacobs, prin.
  Shawnee Mission West HS 4-00011
  8800 W 85TH ST 66212 967-7900
    John Krueger, prin.
  Antioch MS, 8200 W 71ST ST 66204 3-00100
    Kevin Peters, prin. 789-3600
  Hocker Grove MS 3-00100
  10400 JOHNSON DR 66203 789-3500
    John Niska, prin.
  Indian Hills MS 2-00100
  6400 MISSION RD 66208 789-3450
    Jim Wink, prin.
  Indian Woods MS 3-00100
  9700 WOODSON DR 66207 967-7750
    Larry King, prin.
  Mission Valley MS 3-00100
  8500 MISSION RD 66206 967-7950
    Charlotte Sands, prin.
  Trailridge MS, 7500 QUIVIRA RD 66216 3-00100
    Mary Fugate, prin. 962-3200
  Westridge MS, 9300 NIEMAN RD 66214 3-00100
    Rob Winter, prin. 752-2800

Bishop Miege HS 3-00011
  5041 REINHARDT DR 66205 262-2700
  Joseph Passantino, prin.

Silver Lake, AC 913, PC 4, Shawnee
Silver Lake USD 372 3-11111
  PO BOX 39 66539 582-4026
  Robert Albers, supt.
  HS, PO BOX 39 66539 2-00011
    Larry Winter, prin. 582-4639

Smith Center, AC 913, PC 4, Smith
Smith Center USD 237 3-11111
  PO BOX 329 66967 282-6665
  Mike Philpot, supt.
  JSHS, PO BOX 329 66967 2-00111
    Jim Kuhn, prin. 282-6600

Solomon, AC 913, PC 3, Dickinson
Solomon USD 393 2-11111
  PO BOX 247 67480 655-2541
  John McFarland, supt.
  JSHS, 400 N WALNUT ST 67480 2-00111
    Bernard Girrard, prin. 655-2551

South Haven, AC 316, PC 2, Sumner
South Haven USD 509 2-11111
  PO BOX 229 67140 892-5216
  James Sutton, supt.
  HS, PO BOX 229 67140 2-00011
    Rich Austin, prin. 892-5215

Spearville, AC 316, PC 3, Ford
Spearville USD 381 2-11111
  PO BOX 338 67876 385-2676
  James Koftan, supt.
  JSHS, PO BOX 158 67876 2-00111
    Ralph Blevins, prin. 385-2631

Spring Hill, AC 913, PC 4, Johnson
Spring Hill USD 230 4-11111
  PO BOX 346 66083 592-7200
  Barton Goering, supt.
  HS, 300 W SOUTH ST 66083 2-00011
    Charles Coblentz, prin. 592-7299
  MS, 300 S WEBSTER ST 66083 2-01100
    Stephen Fleer, prin. 592-7288

Stafford, AC 316, PC 4, Stafford
Stafford USD 349, PO BOX 400 67578 2-11111
  Dennis Boepple, supt. 234-5243
  HS, PO BOX 370 67578 2-00011
    Kevin Case, prin. 234-5248

Sterling, AC 316, PC 4, Rice
Sterling USD 376, PO BOX 188 67579 3-11111
  C. W. Deel, supt. 278-3621
  HS, 308 E WASHINGTON AVE 67579 2-00011
    Mike Neal, prin. 278-2171

Sterling College 67579 2-UC
    278-2173

Stilwell, AC 913, PC 2, Johnson
Blue Valley USD 229
  Supt. — See Overland Park
  Blue Valley HS, 6001 W 159TH ST 66085 4-00011
    Marsha Barrett, prin. 681-4200

Stockton, AC 913, PC 4, Rooks
Stockton USD 271, 211 MAIN ST 67669 2-11111
  James Deines, supt. 425-6367
  HS, 105 N CYPRESS ST 67669 2-00011
    Michael Stegman, prin. 425-6784

Strong City, AC 316, PC 3, Chase
Chase County USD 284
  Supt. — See Cottonwood Falls
  Chase County MS 66869 1-00100
    Jerry Perrin, prin. 273-6676

Sublette, AC 316, PC 4, Haskell
Sublette USD 374, PO BOX 670 67877 3-11111
  Gerald Marshall, supt. 675-2277
  HS, PO BOX 460 67877 2-00011
    Mike Simmons, prin. 675-2232
  MS, PO BOX 490 67877 1-00100
    Mike Simmons, prin. 675-8504

Sylvan Grove, AC 913, PC 2, Lincoln
Sylvan Grove USD 299 2-11111
  PO BOX 308 67481 526-7175
  Jude Stecklein, supt.
  Sylvan Unified JSHS 2-00111
  PO BOX 308 67481 526-7175
    Stan Labertew, prin.

Syracuse, AC 316, PC 4, Hamilton
Syracuse USD 494 2-11111
  PO BOX 966 67878 384-7872
  Roy Piper, supt.
  JSHS, PO BOX 966 67878 2-00111
    G. Clark, prin. 384-5296

Tecumseh, AC 913, PC 3, Shawnee
Shawnee Heights USD 450 5-11111
  4401 SE SHAWNEE HEIGHTS RD 66542
  Steve McClure, supt. 379-0584
  Shawnee Heights SHS 2-00001
  4201 SE SHAWNEE HEIGHTS RD 66542
    John Waugh, prin. 379-0751
  Shawnee Heights HS 3-00010
  4141 SE SHAWNEE HEIGHTS RD 66542
    Warren Watson, prin. 379-0532
  Shawnee Heights JHS 3-00100
  4335 SE SHAWNEE HEIGHTS RD 66542
    Gerald Tilley, prin. 379-0545

Tescott, AC 913, PC 2, Ottawa
Twin Valley USD 240
  Supt. — See Bennington
  HS, PO BOX 196 67484 1-00011
    John Krajicek, prin. 283-4385

Thayer, AC 316, PC 2, Neosho
Erie-St. Paul USD 101
  Supt. — See Erie
  HS, PO BOX 278 66776 1-00011
    Marvin Francisco, prin. 839-5203

Tipton, AC 913, PC 2, Mitchell

Tipton Catholic HS 1-00011
  PO BOX 146 67485 373-5835
  Galen Schmidtberger, prin.

Tonganoxie, AC 913, PC 4, Leavenworth
Tonganoxie USD 464 4-11111
  PO BOX 199 66086 845-2153
  Ron Burgess, supt.
  SHS, PO BOX 179 66086 2-00001
    Lee Smith, prin. 845-3332
  JHS, PO BOX 980 66086 2-00110
    Marvin Pine, prin. 845-2627

Topeka, AC 913, PC 9, Shawnee
Auburn-Washburn USD 437 5-11111
  5928 SW 53RD ST 66610 862-0419
  Howard Shuler, supt.
  Washburn HS, 5900 SW 61ST ST 66619 4-00011
    William Edwards, prin. 862-0958
  Washburn MS, 5620 SW 61ST ST 66619 3-00100
    David Reese, prin. 862-1490

Seaman USD 345 5-11111
  901 NW LYMAN RD 66608 233-3045
  Kent Hurn, supt.
  Seaman SHS 3-00001
  4850 NW ROCHESTER RD 66617 286-1100
    Don Pierce, prin.
  Logan JHS, 1124 NW LYMAN RD 66608 2-00110
    Charles Sodergren, prin. 232-8200
  Northern Hills JHS 2-00110
  5620 NW TOPEKA BLVD 66617 246-1472
    William Adams, prin.

Topeka USD 501, 624 SW 24TH ST 66611 7-11111
  Jeff Weaver, supt. 233-0313
  Highland Park HS 3-00011
  2424 SE CALIFORNIA AVE 66605 266-7616
    Susan Rogers, prin.
  HS, 800 SW 10TH AVE 66612 4-00011
    Ned Nusbaum, prin. 232-0483
  Topeka West HS 4-00011
  2001 SW FAIRLAWN RD 66604 272-1643
    Rob McFrazier, prin.
  Chase MS, 2250 NE STATE ST 66616 2-00100
    Ernie Hodison, prin. 234-8631
  Eisenhower MS 3-00100
  3305 SE MINNESOTA AVE 66605 266-9345
    Gerald Meier, prin.
  French MS, 5257 SW 33RD ST 66614 3-00100
    Wagner VanVlack, prin. 272-2676
  Jardine MS, 2600 SW 33RD ST 66611 3-00100
    Ralph Clark, prin. 266-7874
  Landon MS 3-00100
  731 SW FAIRLAWN RD 66606 272-3931
    Patty Pressman, prin.
  Robinson MS, 1125 SW 14TH ST 66604 3-00100
    Judy Reiners, prin. 235-2371

Baker University School of Nursing | 2-UC
1500 W 10TH ST 66604 | 354-5853
Bryan Travel College | 2-CS
1527 SW FAIRLAWN RD 66604 | 272-0899
Hayden HS, 401 SW GAGE BLVD 66606 | 2-00011
Urban Langer, prin. | 272-5210
Shawnee County Youth Center | 2-11111
1440 NW 25TH ST 66618 | 233-6459
Claude Tidwell, prin.
Topeka School of Medical Technology | CS
1915 SW 6TH AVE # 207 66606 | 295-8933
Topeka Technical College | 2-CS
1620 NW GAGE BLVD 66618 | 232-5858
Washburn University of Topeka | 5-UC
1700 SW COLLEGE AVE 66621 | 295-6300

Towanda, AC 316, PC 4, Butler
Circle USD 375, PO BOX 9 67144 | 4-11111
John Gahagan, supt. | 536-2577
Circle HS, PO BOX 159 67144 | 2-00011
William Dunlap, prin. | 536-2277
Other Schools – See El Dorado

Tribune, AC 316, PC 3, Greeley
Greeley County USD 200 | 2-11111
PO BOX 580 67879 | 376-4211
Orrin Oppliger, supt.
Greeley County JSHS | 2-00111
PO BOX 580 67879 | 376-4265
Bruce Bolen, prin.

Troy, AC 913, PC 4, Doniphan
Troy USD 429, PO BOX 585 66087 | 2-11111
Randy Freeman, supt. | 985-3950
HS 66087 | 2-00011
Elizabeth Reust, prin. | 985-3533

Udall, AC 316, PC 3, Cowley
Udall USD 463, 303 S SEYMOUR 67146 | 2-11111
Robert Van Arsdale, supt. | 782-3355
JSHS 67146 | 2-00111
John Hart, prin. | 782-3623

Ulysses, AC 316, PC 6, Grant
Ulysses USD 214 | 4-11111
111 S BAUGHMAN ST 67880 | 356-3655
Philip Knight, supt.
HS, 501 N MCCALL ST 67880 | 2-00011
Kevin Burr, prin. | 356-1380
Kepley MS, 113 N COLORADO ST 67880 | 2-00100
Stephen Wolf, prin. | 356-3125

Uniontown, AC 316, PC 2, Bourbon
Uniontown USD 235 | 2-11111
PO BOX 70 66779 | 756-4302
James Lambert, supt.
HS 66779 | 2-00011
Tracey Smith, prin. | 756-4301

Utica, AC 913, PC 2, Ness
Nes Tre La Go USD 301 | 1-11111
PO BOX 128 67584 | 391-2281
Nellie Schriock, supt.
HS, PO BOX 128 67584 | 1-00011
Nellie Schriock, prin. | 391-2281

Valley Center, AC 316, PC 5, Sedgwick
Valley Center USD 262 | 4-11111
PO BOX 157 67147 | 755-7100
Ron Ballard, supt.
HS, 800 N MERIDIAN ST 67147 | 3-00011
Howard Moon, prin. | 755-7130
JHS, 737 N MERIDIAN ST 67147 | 3-00100
Brad Rahe, prin. | 755-7160

Valley Falls, AC 913, PC 4, Jefferson
Valley Falls USD 338 | 2-11111
PO BOX 190 66088 | 945-3259
John Burke, supt.
HS 66088 | 2-00011
David Dubois, prin. | 945-3229

Vermillion, AC 913, PC 2, Marshall
Vermillion USD 380 | 3-11111
PO BOX 107 66544 | 382-6216
Jim Barrett, supt.
Other Schools – See Centralia, Frankfort

Victoria, AC 913, PC 4, Ellis
Victoria USD 432, PO BOX 157 67671 | 2-11111
Bruce Ward, supt. | 735-9212
HS, PO BOX 8 67671 | 2-00011
Mike Kreller, prin. | 735-9211

Wa Keeney, AC 913, PC 4, Trego
Wa Keeney USD 208 | 3-11111
PO BOX 68 67672 | 743-2145
Dan Thornton, supt.
Trego Community HS | 2-00011
1200 RUSSELL AVE 67672 | 743-2061
Brad Starnes, prin.

Wakefield, AC 913, PC 3, Clay
Clay Center USD 379
Supt. — See Clay Center
HS 67487 | 1-00011
Lynn Wait, prin. | 461-5437

Wamego, AC 913, PC 5, Pottawatomie
Wamego USD 320 | 4-11111
510 W US HIGHWAY 24 66547 | 456-7643
Norris Wika, supt.
HS, 801 LINCOLN ST 66547 | 2-00011
Gene Willich, prin. | 456-2214
JHS, 1701 KAW VALLEY RD 66547 | 2-00100
Larry Doll, prin. | 456-7682

Washington, AC 913, PC 4, Washington
Washington USD 222 | 2-11111
PO BOX 275 66968 | 325-2261
Roger Baskerville, supt.
JSHS 66968 | 2-00111
Rob Hassler, prin. | 325-2261

Waterville, AC 913, PC 3, Marshall
Valley Heights USD 498 | 2-11111
PO BOX 89 66548 | 363-2398
David Walters, supt.
Other Schools – See Blue Rapids

Wathena, AC 913, PC 4, Doniphan
Wathena USD 406, PO BOX 38 66090 | 3-11111
Kay Schultz, supt. | 989-4427
HS, PO BOX 38 66090 | 2-00011
Thomas Alstrom, prin. | 989-4426

Waverly, AC 913, PC 3, Coffey
Lebo-Waverly USD 243 | 3-11111
PO BOX 457 66871 | 733-2651
Ted Vannocker, supt.
HS, PO BOX 8 66871 | 1-00011
Larry Rapp, prin. | 733-2561
Other Schools – See Lebo

Wellington, AC 316, PC 6, Sumner
Wellington USD 353 | 4-11111
PO BOX 648 67152 | 326-4300
Ronald Fagan, supt.
SHS, 605 N A ST 67152 | 2-00001
Merlyn Elder, prin. | 326-4310
JHS, 311 N A ST 67152 | 3-00110
Mel Coates, prin. | 326-4320

Wellsville, AC 913, PC 4, Franklin
Wellsville USD 289 | 3-11111
PO BOX 537 66092 | 883-2388
Donovan Williams, supt.
JSHS, PO BOX 537 66092 | 2-00111
George Stewart, prin. | 883-2057

Weskan, AC 913, PC 2, Wallace
Weskan USD 242, PO BOX 155 67762 | 2-11111
Allaire Homburg, supt. | 943-5423
HS, PO BOX 155 67762 | 1-00011
Allaire Homburg, prin. | 943-5423

Westmoreland, AC 913, PC 3, Pottawatomie
Pottawatomie West USD 323 | 3-11111
PO BOX 70 66549 | 457-3732
Richard Doll, supt.
Other Schools – See Saint George

Wetmore, AC 913, PC 2, Nemaha
Sabetha USD 441
Supt. — See Sabetha
HS, PO BOX AB 66550 | 1-00011
Paul Alexander, prin. | 866-2860

White City, AC 913, PC 3, Morris
Rural Vista USD 481
Supt. — See Hope
HS, PO BOX 8 66872 | 1-00011
Mary Lawrenz, prin. | 349-2211

Whitewater, AC 316, PC 3, Butler
Remington-Whitewater USD 206 | 3-11111
RR 1 67154 – John McDonald, supt. | 799-2115
Remington HS, RR 1 67154 | 2-00011
Tom Ostrander, prin. | 799-2123

Wichita, AC 316, PC 10, Sedgwick
Haysville USD 261
Supt. — See Haysville
Haysville Campus HS | 3-00011
2100 W 55TH ST S 67217 | 524-3281
Kirk Pope, prin.

Wichita USD 259 | 8-11111
217 N WATER ST 67202 | 833-4003
Larry Vaughn, supt.
Wichita East HS | 4-00011
2301 E DOUGLAS AVE 67211 | 833-2550
Katie McHenry, prin.
Wichita Heights HS | 4-00011
5301 N HILLSIDE ST 67219 | 833-4500
Mark Christian, prin.
Wichita North HS | 4-00011
1437 ROCHESTER ST 67203 | 833-3000
Ralph Teran, prin.
Wichita Northwest HS | 4-00011
1220 N TYLER RD 67212 | 833-3300
Charles McLean, prin.
Wichita South HS | 4-00011
701 W 33RD ST S 67217 | 833-3800
Carolyn Bridges, prin.
Wichita Southeast HS | 4-00011
903 S EDGEMOOR ST 67218 | 833-2700
Barbara Mohney, prin.
Wichita West HS, 820 S OSAGE ST 67213 | 4-00011
Mark Evans, prin. | 833-3600
Central Vo Bldg | Vo Tech
324 N EMPORIA ST 67202 | 833-4320
Doyle Wilcox, prin.
Schweiter Technical HS | Vo Tech
1400 GEORGE WASHINGTON DR 67211
Joseph McIntyre, prin. | 833-2990
Trans Educational Center | Vo Tech
4141 N SENECA ST 67204 | 833-3290
Joseph McIntyre, prin.
Vo-Tech Center, 301 S GROVE ST 67211 | Vo Tech
Tom Dixon, prin. | 833-2460
Allison JHS, 221 N SENECA ST 67213 | 3-00100
Rosemary Hood, prin. | 833-3660

Brooks Magnet MS | 3-00100
3802 E 27TH ST N 67220 | 833-2345
Brenda Moore, prin.
Coleman MS | 3-00100
1544 N GOVERNEOUR RD 67206 | 833-2690
Kathy Wilson, prin.
Curtis MS, 1031 S EDGEMOOR ST 67218 | 3-00100
Glenda Richardson, prin. | 833-2760
Hadley MS, 1101 DOUGHERTY ST 67212 | 3-00100
Maurice Ediger, prin. | 833-3515
Hamilton MS | 2-00100
1407 S BROADWAY ST 67211 | 833-3680
Dwight Jones, prin.
Jardine MS, 3550 ROSS PKY 67210 | 3-00100
Cheryl Mcfarthing, prin. | 833-2945
Marshall MS, 1510 PAYNE ST 67203 | 3-00100
Gerald Lewis, prin. | 833-3100
Mayberry Magnet MS | 3-00100
207 S SHERIDAN ST 67213 | 833-3500
Linda Wilson, prin.
Mead MS, 2601 E SKINNER ST 67211 | 3-00100
Diana Raugust, prin. | 833-2970
Pleasant Valley MS | 3-00100
2220 W 29TH ST N 67204 | 833-3200
Marlene Brown, prin.
Robinson MS, 328 N OLIVER ST 67208 | 3-00100
Kathryn Busch, prin. | 833-2600
Truesdell MS, 2464 S GLENN ST 67217 | 4-00100
James Sowers, prin. | 833-3900
Wilbur MS, 340 N TYLER RD 67212 | 3-00100
Cherie Crain, prin. | 833-3435

Amtech Institute | 3-CS
4011 E 31ST ST S 67210 | 682-6548
Aviation Education Center | 1-CS
2021 S EISENHOWER ST 67209 | 833-3595
Bishop Carroll HS | 3-00011
8101 W CENTRAL AVE 67212 | 722-2390
David Wessling, prin.
Bryan Institute | 2-CS
1004 S OLIVER ST 67218 | 685-2284
Climate Control Institute | 2-CS
3030 N HILLSIDE ST 67219 | 686-7355
Friends University | 4-UC
2100 W UNIVERSITY ST 67213 | 261-5800
HCA Wesley Medical Center | HSP
550 N HILLSIDE ST 67214 | 688-2065
Kansas Newman College | 3-UC
3100 MCCORMICK ST 67213 | 942-4291
Kapaun Mt. Carmel HS | 3-00011
8506 E CENTRAL AVE 67206 | 634-0315
Charles Chevalier, prin.
St. Francis Regional Medical Center | HSP
929 N SAINT FRANCIS ST 67214 | 268-5102
St. Joseph Medical Center | HSP
3600 E HARRY ST 67218 | 689-5300
Southern Technical College | 2-CS
2015 S MERIDIAN ST 67213 | 942-7733
Wichita Area Vocational Technical School | 2-CS
217 N WATER ST 67202 | 833-4455
Wichita Business College | 2-CS
501 E PAWNEE ST STE 515 67211 | 263-1261
Wichita State University | 7-UC
1845 FAIRMOUNT ST 67260 | 689-3001
Wichita Technical Institute | 2-CS
942 S WEST ST 67213 | 943-2241

Williamsburg, AC 913, PC 2, Franklin
West Franklin USD 287
Supt. — See Pomona
HS, PO BOX 7 66095 | 1-00011
Max Turner, prin. | 746-5777

Wilson, AC 913, PC 3, Ellsworth
Lorraine USD 328
Supt. — See Lorraine
HS, PO BOX 220 67490 | 1-00011
Maurice Strecker, prin. | 658-2202
MS, PO BOX 220 67490 | 1-00100
Maurice Strecker, prin. | 658-2202

Winchester, AC 913, PC 3, Jefferson
Jefferson County North USD 339 | 3-11111
PO BOX Q 66097 | 774-2000
Robert Shanks, supt.
Jefferson County North HS | 2-00011
PO BOX D 66097 | 774-8515
Jonathan Brown, prin.
Other Schools – See Nortonville

Winfield, AC 316, PC 7, Cowley
Winfield USD 465 | 5-11111
920 MILLINGTON ST 67156 | 221-5100
William Medley, supt.
HS, 300 VIKING BLVD 67156 | 3-00011
Jim Ratzlaff, prin. | 221-5160
MS, 400 E 9TH AVE 67156 | 3-00100
Dan Flummerfelt, prin. | 221-5130

Southwestern College | 3-UC
100 COLLEGE ST 67156 | 221-8236

Winona, AC 913, PC 2, Logan
Triplains USD 275, PO BOX 97 67764 | 2-11111
Ashley Anderson, supt. | 846-7869
HS, PO BOX 97 67764 | 1-00011
Ashley Anderson, prin. | 846-7869

Yates Center, AC 316, PC 4, Woodson
Yates Center USD 366 | 3-11111
PO BOX 160 66783 | 625-3205
Billy Norris, supt.
HS, PO BOX 160 66783 | 2-00011
Jerome Hudson, prin. | 625-2352

KENTUCKY

STATE DEPARTMENT OF EDUCATION
Capital Plaza Tower
500 Mero St., Frankfort 40601
(502) 564-4770

Commissioner of Education — Thomas Boysen

Deputy Commissioner Management Support Services — Randy Kimbrough

Deputy Commissioner Learning Results Services — Edward Reidy

Deputy Commissioner Learning Support Services — Lois Adams-Rodgers

STATE BOARD OF EDUCATION
500 Mero St. 1st Fl., Frankfort 40601

Chairperson — Joseph Kelly

PUBLIC, PRIVATE AND CATHOLIC SECONDARY SCHOOLS

Adairville, AC 502, PC 3, Logan
Logan County SD
Supt. — See Russellville
MS, PO BOX 277 42202 — 2-00100
Patricia Lindauer, prin. — 539-7711

Albany, AC 606, PC 4, Clinton
Clinton County SD — 4-11111
PO BOX 416 42602 — 387-6480
James Carver, supt.
Clinton County HS, RR 3 42602 — 3-00011
David Warinner, prin. — 387-5569
Clinton County MS, RR 3 42602 — 2-01100
Eddie Starnes, prin. — 387-6466

Alexandria, AC 606, PC 6, Campbell
Campbell County SD — 5-11111
101 ORCHARD LN 41001 — 635-2173
Ron McCormick, supt.
Campbell County HS — 4-00011
8000 ALEXANDRIA PIKE 41001 — 635-4161
Glen Ravenscraft, prin.
Reiley MS — 3-00100
4930 US HIGHWAY 27 41001 — 635-2118
Michael Henry, prin.
Other Schools – See Cold Spring

Bishop Brossart HS, 4 GROVE ST 41001 — 2-00011
Thomas Seither, prin. — 635-2108

Anchorage, AC 502, PC 4, Jefferson
Anchorage ISD, 11400 RIDGE RD 40223 — 2-11110
Robert Wynkoop, supt. — 245-8927
Anchorage 9th Grade Center — 1-00100
11400 RIDGE RD 40223 — 245-2121
Teresa Myers, prin.
MS, 11400 RIDGE RD 40223 — 2-00100
Teresa Myers, prin. — 245-2121

Ashland, AC 606, PC 7, Boyd
Ashland ISD, 1420 CENTRAL AVE 41101 — 5-11111
Kathleen Al-Rubaiy, supt. — 327-2706
Blazer HS, 1500 BLAZER BLVD 41102 — 4-00011
Janice Ledford, prin. — 327-2700
Verity MS, 2600 KANSAS ST 41101 — 3-00100
Herb Conley, prin. — 329-9777

Boyd County SD — 5-11111
1104 BOB MCCULLOUGH DR 41102 — 928-4141
Dan Branham, supt.
Boyd County SHS — 4-00011
12307 MIDLAND TRAIL RD 41102 — 928-6473
Brice Thornbury, prin.
Boyd County Vo HS — Vo Tech
12300 MIDLAND TRAIL RD 41102 — 928-6431
Philip Salisbury, prin.
Boyd County MS — 4-00100
1226 SUMMITT RD 41102 — 928-9547
Mickey Rice, prin.

Fairview ISD, 2127 MAIN ST W 41102 — 3-11111
Paul Reliford, supt. — 324-3877
Fairview JSHS, 2123 MAIN ST W 41102 — 2-00111
Robert Morrison, prin. — 324-9226

Ashland Community College — 5-CC
1400 COLLEGE DR 41101 — 329-2999
Kentucky Tech Ashland State Voc-Tech Sch — 4-CS
4818 ROBERTS DR 41102 — 928-6427
King's Daughter's Hospital — HSP
PO BOX 151 41105 — 327-4000

Rose Hill Christian S — 2-11111
1001 WINSLOW RD 41102 — 329-1957
Keith McKim, prin.

Auburn, AC 502, PC 4, Logan
Logan County SD
Supt. — See Russellville
MS, PO BOX 7 42206 — 2-00100
Michael Hurt, prin. — 542-6689
Chandlers MS — 2-00100
7815 CHANDLERS RD 42206 — 542-4139
James Thompson, prin.

Augusta, AC 606, PC 4, Bracken
Augusta ISD, 207 BRACKEN ST 41002 — 2-11111
Larry Kelsch, supt. — 756-2545
JSHS, 207 BRACKEN ST 41002 — 2-00111
Harold Johnson, prin. — 756-2105

Barbourville, AC 606, PC 5, Knox
Barbourville ISD, PO BOX 520 40906 — 3-11111
James Davis, supt. — 546-3120
JSHS, SCHOOL ST 40906 — 2-00111
Larry Warren, prin. — 546-3129

Knox County SD, PO BOX 700 40906 — 6-11111
J. Hampton, supt. — 546-3157
Knox Central HS, 311 N MAIN ST 40906 — 4-00011
Robert Messer, prin. — 546-9253
Other Schools – See Corbin

Union College — 3-UC
310 COLLEGE ST 40906 — 800-489-8646

Bardstown, AC 502, PC 6, Nelson
Bardstown ISD, 308 N 5TH ST 40004 — 4-11111
Robert Smotherman, supt. — 348-1650
HS, 400 N 5TH ST 40004 — 2-00011
Thomas Hamilton, prin. — 348-1673
MS, 410 N 5TH ST 40004 — 3-01100
J. Traw, prin. — 348-1680

Nelson County SD — 5-11111
1200 CARDINAL DR # 310 40004 — 349-7000
Victor Johnson, supt.
Nelson County HS — 4-00011
1070 BLOOMFIELD RD 40004 — 349-7010
Brady Link, prin.
Old Kentucky Home MS — 2-00100
221 E MUIR AVE 40004 — 349-7040
Bill Peterson, prin.
Other Schools – See Bloomfield, New Haven

Bethlehem HS — 2-00011
309 W STEPHEN FOSTER AVE 40004 — 348-8594
Sr. Margaret Willis, prin.

Bardwell, AC 502, PC 3, Carlisle
Carlisle County SD, RR 1 42023 — 3-11111
Robert Watson, supt. — 628-5476
Carlisle County HS — 2-00011
RR 1 BOX 238 42023 — 628-3119
Dana Rohrer, prin.
Carlisle County MS — 2-00100
RR 1 BOX 239 42023 — 628-5414
Dana Rohrer, prin.

Barlow, AC 502, PC 3, Ballard
Ballard County SD, RR 1 42024 — 4-11111
John Evans, supt. — 665-5197
Ballard Memorial HS, RR 1 42024 — 2-00011
Sam Workman, prin. — 665-5151

Ballard Vo S, RR 1 42024 — Vo Tech
Donald Wells, prin. — 665-5112
Ballard County MS, RR 1 42024 — 2-00100
Donna Wear, prin. — 665-5153

Beattyville, AC 606, PC 4, Lee
Lee County SD, PO BOX 668 41311 — 4-11111
Glenn Wilson, supt. — 464-5000
Lee County HS, PO BOX 97 41311 — 2-00011
Sam Watkins, prin. — 464-5005
Lee County MS, PO BOX N 41311 — 2-00100
Tom Cockerham, prin. — 464-5010

Bedford, AC 502, PC 3, Trimble
Trimble County SD — 4-11111
PO BOX 275 40006 — 255-3201
J. Sachleben, supt.
Trimble County HS, RR 2 BOX 5A 40006 — 2-00011
Garrett Bowling, prin. — 255-7781
Trimble County MS — 2-00100
RR 2 BOX 90A 40006 — 255-7361
Dale Vincent, prin.

Belfry, AC 606, PC 3, Pike
Pike County SD
Supt. — See Pikeville
HS, PO BOX 160 41514 — 3-00011
Frank Welch, prin. — 353-7239

Bellevue, AC 606, PC 6, Campbell
Bellevue ISD, 215 CENTER ST 41073 — 3-11111
William Dosch, supt. — 261-2108
JSHS, 201 CENTER ST 41073 — 2-00111
Michael Foulks, prin. — 261-2980

Benton, AC 502, PC 5, Marshall
Marshall County SD — 5-11111
RR 7 BOX 102 42025 — 527-8628
Kenneth Shadowen, supt.
Marshall County HS — 4-00011
RR 7 BOX 100B 42025 — 527-1453
Gene Brooks, prin.
Marshall County Area Vo Ed Ctr — Vo Tech
RR 7 BOX 100A 42025 — 527-8648
James Cothran, prin.
MS, 1100 JOE CREASON DR 42025 — 2-00100
Gerald Jones, prin. — 527-9091
South Marshall MS — 2-00100
RR 1 BOX 94 42025 — 527-3828
Darrell Morgan, prin.
Other Schools – See Calvert City

Berea, AC 606, PC 6, Madison
Berea ISD, 3 PIRATE PKY 40403 — 3-11111
Rudy Thomas, supt. — 986-8446
Berea Community HS — 2-00011
1 PIRATE PKY 40403 — 986-4911
Will Bondurant, prin.
Berea Community MS — 2-00100
1 PIRATE PKY 40403 — 986-4911
Will Bondurant, prin.

Madison County SD
Supt. — See Richmond
Madison Southern HS — 3-00011
213 GLADES RD 40403 — 986-8424
Jesse Ward, prin.
Foley MS, 211 GLADES RD 40403 — 3-00100
H. Broaddus, prin. — 986-8473

Berea College 40404 — 4-UC
986-9341

Betsy Layne, AC 606, PC 3, Floyd
Floyd County SD
Supt. — See Prestonsburg
HS, PO BOX 437 41605 — 3-00011
Alan Osborne, prin. — 478-9138

Beverly, AC 606, PC 1, Bell

Red Bird S, HC 69 BOX 710 40913 — 2-11111
598-2416

Bloomfield, AC 502, PC 3, Nelson
Nelson County SD
Supt. — See Bardstown
MS, 100 HILL ST 40008 — 2-01100
L. Cheek, prin. — 252-8383

Booneville, AC 606, PC 2, Owsley
Owsley County SD — 4-11111
PO BOX 340 41314 — 593-6363
E. Rasner, supt.
Owsley County JSHS — 2-00111
PO BOX 707 41314 — 593-5185
Earl Jackson, prin.

Bowling Green, AC 502, PC 8, Warren
Bowling Green ISD — 5-11111
1211 CENTER ST 42101 — 781-2254
Joel Brown, supt.
HS, 1801 ROCKINGHAM LN 42104 — 3-00011
Fred Carter, prin. — 842-1674
MS, 1141 CENTER ST 42101 — 2-00100
John Napier, prin. — 781-4585

Warren County SD — 6-11111
806 KENTON ST 42101 — 781-5150
Leonard McCoy, supt.
Greenwood HS — 4-00011
5065 SCOTTSVILLE RD 42104 — 842-3627
Peggy Cowles, prin.
Warren Central HS — 3-00011
559 MORGANTOWN RD 42101 — 842-7302
David Crowe, prin.
Warren East HS — 3-00011
6867 LOUISVILLE RD 42101 — 781-1277
Aaron Milliken, prin.
Drakes Creek MS — 3-00100
704 CYPRESSWOOD WAY 42104 — 843-0165
Bonnie Beck, prin.
Moss MS — 3-00100
2565 RUSSELLVILLE RD 42101 — 843-0166
Harry Dye, prin.
Warren East MS — 2-00100
7031 LOUISVILLE RD 42101 — 843-0181
Harold Cowles, prin.

Anchored Christian S — 2-11111
1000 ROSELAWN WAY 42104 — 781-9077
Martha Vaught, prin.
Draughons Junior College — 2-CS
2424 AIRWAY CT 42103 — 843-6750
Kentucky Tech Bowling Green Voc-Tech Sch — 4-CS
1845 LOOP DR 42101 — 843-5467
Western Kentucky University — 7-UC
1526 RUSSELLVILLE RD 42101 — 745-2551

Brandenburg, AC 502, PC 4, Meade
Meade County SD — 5-11111
PO BOX 337 40108 — 422-3366
David Wilson, supt.
Meade County HS — 4-00011
938 OLD STATE RD 40108 — 422-4931
Vernon Wilson, prin.
Stuart Pepper MS — 3-00100
615 OLD EKRON RD 40108 — 422-3363
Clayton Cornett, prin.

Brooksville, AC 606, PC 3, Bracken
Bracken County SD — 4-11111
PO BOX 26 41004 — 735-2523
Howard Hall, supt.
Bracken County HS — 2-00011
PO BOX 128 41004 — 735-3153
Robert Barr, prin.
Bracken County MS, RR 1 BOX 4A 41004 — 2-01100
Gary Clayton, prin. — 735-3425

Brownsville, AC 502, PC 3, Edmonson
Edmonson County SD — 4-11111
PO BOX 129 42210 — 597-2101
D. Webb, supt.
Edmonson County HS — 3-00011
220 HIGH SCHOOL RD 42210 — 597-2151
Bill Clemmons, prin.
Edmonson County MS — 2-00100
PO BOX 98 42210 — 597-2932
Jeffrey Stice, prin.

Buckhorn, AC 606, PC 2, Perry
Perry County SD
Supt. — See Hazard
HS 41721 — 2-00011
Dennis Wooten, prin. — 398-7176

Buckner, AC 502, PC 2, Oldham
Oldham County SD
Supt. — See La Grange
Oldham County HS — 4-00011
PO BOX 187 40010 — 222-9461
Martha Sammons, prin.
Oldham County MS — 3-00100
PO BOX 157 40010 — 222-1451
Norman Brown, prin.

Burgin, AC 606, PC 4, Mercer
Burgin ISD, PO BOX B 40310 — 2-11111
Charles Scott, supt. — 748-4000
JSHS, PO BOX B 40310 — 2-00111
Orin Simmerman, prin. — 748-5282

Burkesville, AC 502, PC 4, Cumberland
Cumberland County SD — 4-11111
PO BOX 420 42717 — 864-3377
Gary Lee, supt.
Cumberland County HS — 2-00011
PO BOX 380 42717 — 864-3451
Ronnie Skipworth, prin.
Cumberland County MS — 2-00100
PO BOX 70 42717 — 864-5818
Jimmie Radford, prin.

Burna, AC 502, PC 2, Livingston
Livingston County SD
Supt. — See Smithland
Livingston County MS — 2-00100
PO BOX 109 42028 — 988-3263
Elbert Wilson, prin.

Cadiz, AC 502, PC 4, Trigg
Trigg County SD, PO BOX 31 42211 — 4-11111
Jim Wallace, supt. — 522-6075
Trigg County HS, PO BOX 501A 42211 — 3-00011
Edward Postel, prin. — 522-2200
Trigg County MS, PO BOX 504A 42211 — 2-00100
Ben Burkeen, prin. — 522-2210

Calhoun, AC 502, PC 3, McLean
McLean County SD — 4-11111
PO BOX 245 42327 — 273-5257
R. Devine, supt.
McLean County HS — 3-00011
PO BOX 70 42327 — 273-5278
Earl Melloy, prin.

Calvert City, AC 502, PC 5, Marshall
Marshall County SD
Supt. — See Benton
North Marshall MS — 3-00100
RR 2 BOX 385 42029 — 395-7108
Donna Perry, prin.

Campbellsville, AC 502, PC 6, Taylor
Campbellsville ISD — 4-11111
136 S COLUMBIA AVE 42718 — 465-4162
David Fryrear, supt.
HS, 230 W MAIN ST 42718 — 2-00011
Charles Vaughn, prin. — 465-8774
MS, 315 ROBERTS RD 42718 — 2-01100
Marion Hall, prin. — 465-5121

Taylor County SD — 4-11111
1209 E BROADWAY ST 42718 — 465-5371
Gary Seaborne, supt.
Taylor County HS — 3-00011
310 INGRAM AVE 42718 — 465-4431
Donald Skaggs, prin.
Taylor County MS — 2-00100
1207 E BROADWAY ST 42718 — 465-2877
Cherry Harvey, prin.

Campbellsville College — 3-UC
200 W COLLEGE ST 42718 — 465-8158

Campton, AC 606, PC 2, Wolfe
Wolfe County SD, PO BOX 160 41301 — 4-11111
James Lacy, supt. — 668-3155
Wolfe County HS, JOHNSON ST 41301 — 2-00011
Charles Tapley, prin. — 668-3106
Wolfe County MS, JOHNSON ST 41301 — 2-00100
Edwina Staab, prin. — 668-7862

Carlisle, AC 606, PC 4, Nicholas
Nicholas County SD — 4-11111
395 W MAIN ST 40311 — 289-3770
Cebert Gilbert, supt.
Nicholas County HS — 2-00011
318 SCHOOL DR 40311 — 289-3780
Greg Reid, prin.

Carrollton, AC 502, PC 5, Carroll
Carroll County SD, PO BOX 90 41008 — 4-11111
Woody Barwick, supt. — 732-7070
Carroll County HS — 2-00011
1706 HIGHLAND AVE 41008 — 732-7075
William Cord, prin.
Carroll County MS, 408 5TH ST 41008 — 2-00100
John Jones, prin. — 732-7080

Cave City, AC 502, PC 4, Barren
Caverna ISD, PO BOX 428 42127 — 4-11111
Larry Burke, supt. — 773-2530
Other Schools – See Horse Cave

Cecilia, AC 502, PC 3, Hardin
Hardin County SD
Supt. — See Elizabethtown
Central Hardin SHS — 4-00001
3040 LEITCHFIELD RD 42724 — 737-6833
Dale Campbell, prin.
West Hardin JHS — 3-00110
10471 LEITCHFIELD RD 42724 — 862-3924
Dan McCamish, prin.

Clinton, AC 502, PC 4, Hickman
Hickman County SD, RR 3 42031 — 3-11111
Charles Cooper, supt. — 653-2341
Hickman County JSHS — 2-00111
301 CRESAP ST 42031 — 653-4044
Phillip Rudolph, prin.

Cloverport, AC 502, PC 4, Breckinridge
Cloverport ISD, PO BOX 217 40111 — 2-11111
J. Scaggs, supt. — 788-3910
Fraize JSHS, 101 4TH ST 40111 — 2-00111
Thomas Belcher, prin. — 788-3388

Cold Spring, AC 606, PC 5, Campbell
Campbell County SD
Supt. — See Alexandria
Cline MS — 2-00100
20 E ALEXANDRIA PIKE 41076 — 781-4544
(—), prin.

Columbia, AC 502, PC 5, Adair
Adair County SD — 4-11111
1312 GREENSBURG ST 42728 — 384-2476
Kermit Grider, supt.
Adair County HS — 3-00011
1312 GREENSBURG ST 42728 — 384-2751
George Critz, prin.
Adair MS, 1312 GREENSBURG ST 42728 — 3-01100
Richie Coomer, prin. — 384-3341

Lindsey Wilson College — 4-UC
210 LINDSEY WILSON ST 42728 — 800-982-0332

Corbin, AC 606, PC 6, Whitley
Corbin ISD, 108 E CENTER ST 40701 — 4-11111
Ed McNeel, supt. — 528-1303
HS, 1901 SNYDER ST 40701 — 3-00011
Ronald Dunlevy, prin. — 528-3902
MS, 700 S KENTUCKY AVE 40701 — 3-00100
Darrell Tremaine, prin. — 523-3619

Knox County SD
Supt. — See Barbourville
Lynn Camp JSHS — 3-00111
BARBOURVILLE HIGHWAY 40701 — 528-5429
Michael Jones, prin.

St. Camillus Academy — 2-11111
709 E CENTER ST 40701 — 528-5077
Sr. Margaret Maag, prin.

Covington, AC 606, PC 8, Kenton
Covington ISD, 25 E 7TH ST 41011 — 6-11111
James Biggs, supt. — 292-5800
Holmes HS, 2500 MADISON AVE 41014 — 4-00011
Richard Howard, prin. — 292-5841
Chapman Vo Ed Ctr — Vo Tech
25TH & MADISON 41014 — 291-5911
Terry Mann, prin.
Holmes JHS, 2500 MADISON AVE 41014 — 3-00100
Richard Poe, prin. — 292-5837

Kenton County SD
Supt. — See Erlanger
Scott HS — 4-00011
5400 OLD TAYLOR MILL RD 41015 — 356-3146
(—), prin.

Calvary Christian S — 2-11111
5955 TAYLOR MILL RD 41015 — 356-9201
David Phillips, prin.
Covington Catholic HS — 2-00011
1600 DIXIE HWY 41011 — 431-5351
Lawrence Stall, prin.
Covington Latin HS, 21 E 11TH ST 41011 — 2-00111
Robert Larcher, prin. — 291-7044
Holy Cross HS, 3617 CHURCH ST 41015 — 2-00011
William Goller, prin. — 431-1335
Kentucky Tech Northern KY State Voc-Tech — 5-CS
1025 AMSTERDAM RD 41011 — 431-2700
Notre Dame Academy — 3-00011
1600 HILTON DR 41011 — 261-4300
Sr. Rita Geoppinger, prin.
Southwestern College of Business — 2-CS
2929 DIXIE HWY 41017 — 341-6633
Thomas More College — 4-UC
2771 TURKEYFOOT RD 41017 — 341-5800
Villa Madonna Academy — 2-11111
2500 AMSTERDAM RD 41017 — 331-6333
Sr. Victoria Eisenman, prin.

Crestwood, AC 502, PC 4, Oldham
Oldham County SD
Supt. — See La Grange
South Oldham HS — 4-00011
PO BOX 549 40014 — 241-6681
Joe McWilliams, prin.
South Oldham MS — 3-00100
6403 W HIGHWAY 146 40014 — 241-0320
W. Denny, prin.

Cumberland, AC 606, PC 5, Harlan
Harlan County SD
Supt. — See Harlan
HS, 600 SWIMLAND RD 40823 — 2-00011
Ed Clem, prin. — 589-4625
ES, 716 SCHOOL RD 40823 — 2-01100
Ruth Lewis, prin. — 589-4512

Southeast Community College — 4-CC
300 COLLEGE RD 40823 — 589-2145

Cynthiana, AC 606, PC 6, Harrison
Harrison County SD — 5-11111
RR 7 BOX 158 41031 — 234-7110
Roy Woodward, supt.
Harrison County HS — 3-00011
550 WEBSTER AVE 41031 — 234-7117
Joyce Clifford, prin.

Harrison County MS   3-00100
  550 WEBSTER AVE   41031   234-7123
  Robert Ogden, prin.

Danville, AC 606, PC 7, Boyle
Boyle County SD, PO BOX 520   40423   5-11111
  Tom Mills, supt.   236-6634
Boyle County HS   3-00011
  1637 PERRYVILLE RD   40422   236-5047
  Thomas Brown, prin.
Boyle County MS   3-00100
  1651 PERRYVILLE RD   40422   236-4212
  Roger Meek, prin.

Danville ISD, 359 PROCTOR ST   40422   4-11111
  Bill Grimes, supt.   238-1300
HS, 203 E LEXINGTON AVE   40422   3-00011
  Robert Rowland, prin.   238-1308
Danville Bate MS   2-00100
  470 STANFORD AVE   40422   238-1305
  David Davis, prin.

Centre College   3-UC
  600 W WALNUT ST   40422   236-5211
Kentucky College of Business   2-CC
  115 E LEXINGTON AVE   40422   236-6991
Kentucky School for the Deaf   HND
  S 2ND ST   40422

Dawson Springs, AC 502, PC 5, Hopkins
Dawson Springs ISD, 316 ELI ST   42408   2-11111
  Dan Brown, supt.   797-3811
S, 317 ELI ST   42408   2-11111
  Philip Back, prin.   797-2957

Hopkins County SD
  Supt. – See Madisonville
Charleston MS   1-00100
  3560 CHARLESTON RD   42408   825-6135
  Ben Finley, prin.
Dalton MS, 4335 DALTON RD   42408   1-00100
  Darrell Allen, prin.   825-6137

Dayton, AC 606, PC 6, Campbell
Dayton ISD, 999 VINE ST   41074   4-11111
  Jack Moreland, supt.   491-6565
JSHS, 200 JACKSON ST   41074   3-00111
  George Johns, prin.   261-4357

Dixon, AC 502, PC 3, Webster
Webster County SD   4-11111
  PO BOX 420   42409   639-5083
  Jerry Ralston, supt.
Webster County HS   3-00011
  PO BOX 400   42409   639-5092
  Lonnie Burgett, prin.

Dry Ridge, AC 606, PC 4, Grant
Grant County SD
  Supt. – See Williamstown
Grant County HS, US 25   41035   3-00011
  Larry Davis, prin.   824-7161
Grant County MS, 255 SCHOOL ST   41035   3-00100
  Ronald Livingood, prin.   824-4461

Earlington, AC 502, PC 4, Hopkins
Hopkins County SD
  Supt. – See Madisonville
MS, 299 W THOMPSON ST   42410   2-00100
  Richard Stanley, prin.   825-6154

Eastern, AC 606, PC 2, Floyd
Floyd County SD
  Supt. – See Prestonsburg
Allen Central HS, PO BOX 139   41622   3-00011
  John Sword, prin.   358-9543

Eddyville, AC 502, PC 4, Lyon
Lyon County SD, PO BOX 674   42038   3-11111
  Larry Lock, supt.   388-9715
Lyon County HS, PO BOX 400   42038   2-00011
  Bud Nichols, prin.   388-2296
Lyon County MS, PO BOX 400   42038   2-00100
  Carroll Wadlington, prin.   388-4484

Edgewood, AC 606, PC 6, Kenton

St. Elizabeth Medical Center   HSP
  1 MEDICAL VILLAGE DR   41017   344-2111

Edmonton, AC 502, PC 4, Metcalfe
Metcalfe County SD   4-11111
  PO BOX 119   42129   432-3171
  Charles Roberts, supt.
Metcalfe County HS   42129   2-00011
  Gary Richardson, prin.   432-2481

Elizabethtown, AC 502, PC 7, Hardin
Elizabethtown ISD   4-11111
  PO BOX 605   42702   765-6146
  David Thompson, supt.
HS, 620 N MULBERRY ST   42701   3-00011
  Phillip Owen, prin.   769-3381
Stone JHS, MORNINGSIDE DRIVE   42701   2-00100
  Robert Hilton, prin.   769-6343

Hardin County SD, 110 S MAIN ST   42701   7-11111
  Lois Gray, supt.   769-8800
Bluegrass JHS   3-00110
  170 W A JENKINS RD   42701   765-2658
  David Reed, prin.
Other Schools – See Cecilia, Glendale, Radcliff, Vine
  Grove

Elizabethtown Community College   4-CC
  600 COLLEGE STREET RD   42701   769-1632
Kentucky Tech Elizabthtwn State Voc-Tec   3-CS
  505 UNIVERSITY DR   42701   765-2104

Elkhorn City, AC 606, PC 3, Pike
Pike County SD
  Supt. – See Pikeville
HS, 551 RUSSELL ST   41522   2-00011
  James Hawkins, prin.   754-9098

Elkton, AC 502, PC 4, Todd
Todd County SD, 806 S MAIN ST   42220   4-11111
  Floyd Hines, supt.   265-2436
Todd County Central HS   3-00011
  806 S MAIN ST   42220   265-2506
  Arthur Douglas, prin.
Todd County MS, 515 W MAIN ST   42220   2-00100
  Bruce Gray, prin.   265-2511

Eminence, AC 502, PC 4, Henry
Eminence ISD, PO BOX 146   40019   3-11111
  David Baird, supt.   845-4788
HS, 254 W BROADWAY ST   40019   2-00011
  Kenneth Gray, prin.   845-5427
Eminence MS   2-01100
  254 W BROADWAY ST   40019   845-5427
  Steve Frommeyer, prin.

Erlanger, AC 606, PC 7, Kenton
Erlanger-Elsmere ISD   4-11111
  500 GRAVES AVE   41018   727-2009
  Harold Ensor, supt.
Lloyd HS, 450 BARTLETT ST   41018   3-00011
  William Steiden, prin.   727-1555
Tichenor MS, 305 BARTLETT ST   41018   3-00100
  Lucy Riffle, prin.   727-2255

Kenton County SD   7-11111
  20 KENTON LANDS RD   41018   344-8888
  Neil Stiegelmeyer, supt.
Other Schools – See Covington, Fort Mitchell,
  Independence, Taylor Mill

St. Henry HS, 3837 DIXIE HWY   41018   2-00011
  David Otte, prin.   342-7522

Evarts, AC 606, PC 4, Harlan
Harlan County SD
  Supt. – See Harlan
JSHS, PO BOX 9   40828   3-00111
  Wallace Napier, prin.   837-2502

Fairdale, AC 502, PC 5, Jefferson
Jefferson County SD
  Supt. – See Louisville
HS, 1001 FAIRDALE RD   40118   4-00011
  Marilyn Hohmann, prin.   473-8248

Falmouth, AC 606, PC 4, Pendleton
Pendleton County SD, RR 5   41040   4-11111
  Owen Collins, supt.   654-6911
Pendleton County HS, RR 5   41040   3-00011
  Steve Craig, prin.   654-3355
Pendleton County MS   2-00100
  506 CHAPEL ST   41040   654-3325
  George Tackett, prin.

Fedscreek, AC 606, PC 2, Pike
Pike County SD
  Supt. – See Pikeville
JSHS, 120 FEDSCREEK RD   41524   2-00111
  Leslie Rowe, prin.   835-2286

Fern Creek, AC 502, PC 6, Jefferson
Jefferson County SD
  Supt. – See Louisville
HS, 9115 FERN CREEK RD   40291   4-00011
  John Sizemore, prin.   473-8251

Flemingsburg, AC 606, PC 5, Fleming
Fleming County SD   4-11111
  211 W WATER ST   41041   845-5851
  David Barnett, supt.
Fleming County HS, RR 2   41041   3-00011
  Robert Hall, prin.   845-6601
Simons MS, 242 W WATER ST   41041   2-00100
  Alice Rosenberg, prin.   845-9331

Florence, AC 606, PC 7, Boone
Boone County SD   6-11111
  8330 US HIGHWAY 42   41042   282-2157
  Ted Wetekamp, supt.
Boone County HS   4-00011
  7056 BURLINGTON PIKE   41042   283-2795
  William Baker, prin.
Jones MS, 8000 SPRUCE DR   41042   3-00100
  Tom Hummel, prin.   371-4916
Ockerman MS   3-00100
  8300 US HIGHWAY 42   41042   371-8656
  Melvyn Carroll, prin.
Other Schools – See Hebron, Union

Heritage Academy, 7216 US 42   41042   2-11111
  Howard Davis, prin.   525-0213
Kentucky Career Institue   2-CS
  PO BOX 143   41022   371-9393
Kentucky College of Business   2-CC
  7627 TANNERS LN   41042   525-6510

Fort Campbell, PC 7, Christian
Ft. Campbell Dependent SD   4-11111
  77 TEXAS AVE   42223 – (—), supt.   502-439-1927

HS, 1101 OHIO AVE   42223   3-00011
  J. Stewart, prin.   615-431-5056
Mahaffey MS   2-00100
  585 S CAROLINA AVE   42223   502-439-3792
  Suzanne Jones, prin.
Wassom MS   2-00100
  3066 FORREST AVE   42223   502-439-1832
  Carolyn Dove, prin.

Fort Knox, AC 502, PC 7, Hardin
Ft. Knox Dependent SD   4-11111
  7474 MISSISSIPPI ST   40121   624-7853
  Robert Burrow, supt.
HS, 7501 MISSOURI ST   40121   3-00011
  Charles Meyer, prin.   624-6647
Scott MS, 7474 MISSISSIPPI ST   40121   2-00100
  Robert Brown, prin.   624-2236

Embry Riddle Aeronautical University   4-UC
  PO BOX 130   40121   942-0625
Sullivan College   2-CC
  N IROQUOIS BLDG 6683   40121   942-8503

Fort Mitchell, AC 606, PC 6, Kenton
Beechwood ISD   3-11111
  50 BEECHWOOD RD   41017   331-3250
  Gary Branson, supt.
Beechwood JSHS   2-00111
  54 BEECHWOOD RD   41017   331-1220
  Carl Hicks, prin.

Kenton County SD
  Supt. – See Erlanger
Dixie Heights HS   4-00011
  3010 DIXIE HWY   41017   341-7650
  Margaret Morrissey, prin.
Turkey Foot MS   3-00100
  3230 TURKEYFOOT RD   41017   341-0216
  (—), prin.

Southern Ohio College   3-CC
  309 BUTTERMILK PIKE   41017   341-5627

Fort Thomas, AC 606, PC 7, Campbell
Ft. Thomas ISD   4-11111
  2356 MEMORIAL PKY   41075   781-3333
  Fred Williams, supt.
Highlands JSHS   4-00111
  2400 MEMORIAL PKY   41075   781-3333
  George Frakes, prin.

Frankfort, AC 502, PC 8, Franklin
Frankfort ISD, 315 STEELE ST   40601   3-11111
  Michael Oder, supt.   875-8661
HS, 328 SHELBY ST   40601   2-00011
  Larry Montgomery, prin.   875-8655

Franklin County SD   6-11111
  916 E MAIN ST   40601   695-6700
  Paul Rice, supt.
Franklin County HS   3-00011
  1100 E MAIN ST   40601   695-6750
  James Shrock, prin.
Western Hills HS   3-00011
  100 DOCTORS DR   40601   875-2900
  Mike McKenzie, prin.
Franklin County Vo Ed Ctr   Vo Tech
  1106 E MAIN ST   40601   695-6790
  Scott McBrayer, prin.
Bondurant MS   3-00100
  300 BONDURANT DR   40601   875-8440
  Huston Wells, prin.
Elkhorn MS, 1060 E MAIN ST   40601   3-00100
  David Simpson, prin.   695-6740

Kentucky State University   4-UC
  400 E MAIN ST   40601   227-6813

Franklin, AC 502, PC 6, Simpson
Simpson County SD   5-11111
  PO BOX 467   42135   586-8877
  Gary Pack, supt.
Franklin Simpson HS   3-00011
  PO BOX 389   42135   586-3273
  Frank Cardwell, prin.
Franklin Simpson MS   2-00100
  PO BOX 637   42135   586-4401
  Eddie Copas, prin.

Frenchburg, AC 606, PC 3, Menifee
Menifee County SD   3-11111
  PO BOX 118   40322   768-2171
  Richard Ratliff, supt.
Menifee County JSHS   2-00111
  HC 69 BOX 340   40322   768-2141
  Elaine Brown, prin.

Fulton, AC 502, PC 5, Fulton
Fulton ISD, 313 MAIN ST   42041   3-11111
  Larry Salmon, supt.   472-1553
Fulton City HS   2-00011
  STEPHEN BEALE DR   42041   472-1741
  Ward Bushart, prin.

Georgetown, AC 502, PC 7, Scott
Scott County SD, PO BOX 561   40324   5-11111
  Dallas Blankenship, supt.   863-3663
Scott County HS   4-00011
  1036 LONG LICK PIKE   40324   863-3663
  Bill Jones, prin.
MS, 200 CLAY AVE   40324   3-00100
  Gregory Figgs, prin.   863-3805

Scott County MS | 3-00100
1072 LONG LICK PIKE 40324 | 863-3663
Patrick Lair, prin.

Georgetown College | 4-UC
400 E COLLEGE ST 40324 | 863-8009

Glasgow, AC 502, PC 7, Barren
Barren County SD | 5-11111
PO BOX 379 42142 | 651-3787
Charles Campbell, supt.
Barren County HS | 3-00011
507 TROJAN TRAIL RD 42141 | 651-6315
Glenn Flanders, prin.

Glasgow ISD, PO BOX 1239 42142 | 4-11011
L. Tennant, supt. | 651-6757
HS, 1601 COLUMBIA AVE 42141 | 3-00011
James Nelson, prin. | 651-8801

Glendale, AC 502, PC 2, Hardin
Hardin County SD
Supt. — See Elizabethtown
East Hardin JHS, 129 COLLEGE ST 42740 | 3-00110
Paul Connelly, prin. | 369-7370

Grayson, AC 606, PC 5, Carter
Carter County SD | 5-11111
228 CAROL MALONE 41143 | 474-6696
Ross Julson, supt.
East Carter County SHS, RR 1 41143 | 3-00001
Harlan Fleming, prin. | 474-5714
East Carter JHS | 3-00110
520 ROBERT AND MARY ST 41143 | 474-6696
George Steele, prin.
Other Schools – See Olive Hill

Kentucky Christian College | 3-UC
617 N CAROL MALONE BLVD 41143 | 474-6613

Greensburg, AC 502, PC 4, Green
Green County SD, PO BOX 369 42743 | 4-11111
M. Lowe, supt. | 932-5231
Green County HS, PO BOX 227 42743 | 3-00011
J. Weaver, prin. | 932-7481
Green County MS, PO BOX 176 42743 | 2-00100
James Mills, prin. | 932-7773

Greenup, AC 606, PC 4, Greenup
Greenup County SD | 5-11111
3449 OLD DAM CT 41144 | 473-9819
Ronald Gullett, supt.
Greenup County HS | 4-00011
4011 OHIO RIVER RD 41144 | 473-9812
James Thoroughman, prin.
Other Schools – See South Shore, Wurtland

Greenville, AC 502, PC 5, Muhlenberg
Muhlenberg County SD | 6-11111
PO BOX 167 42345 | 338-2871
Harry Loy, supt.
Muhlenberg North HS | 3-00011
501 STATE ROUTE 189 BYP 42345 | 338-0040
Denny Vincent, prin.
Muhlenberg South HS | 3-00011
RR 4 BOX 151 42345 | 338-9404
Jerry Oates, prin.
Muhlenberg South MS | 2-00100
100 PAXTON DR 42345 | 338-4650
Deborah Houghland, prin.
Other Schools – See Powderly

Hardinsburg, AC 502, PC 4, Breckinridge
Breckinridge County SD | 5-11111
PO BOX 148 40143 | 756-2186
Huston Dehaven, supt.
Other Schools – See Harned

Harlan, AC 606, PC 5, Harlan
Harlan County SD | 6-11111
102 BALL PARK RD 40831 | 573-4330
Michael Eberbaugh, supt.
Cawood HS, 91 BALL PARK RD 40831 | 3-00011
William Lee, prin. | 573-5029
Other Schools – See Cumberland, Evarts

Harlan ISD, 420 E CLOVER ST 40831 | 3-11111
Jerry Austin, supt. | 573-8700
JSHS, 420 E CENTRAL ST 40831 | 3-01111
David Johnson, prin. | 573-8750

Harned, AC 502, PC 2, Breckinridge
Breckinridge County SD
Supt. — See Hardinsburg
Breckinridge County HS | 3-00011
RR 1 BOX 130 40144 | 756-2149
Robert Cox, prin.

Harrodsburg, AC 606, PC 6, Mercer
Harrodsburg ISD | 3-11111
E LEXINGTON ST 40330 | 734-8400
H. Snodgrass, supt.
HS, 371 E LEXINGTON ST 40330 | 2-00011
Kearney Lykins, prin. | 734-8420
MS, E LEXINGTON ST 40330 | 2-00100
Richard Webb, prin. | 734-8415

Mercer County SD | 4-11111
PO BOX 287 40330 | 734-4365
Norman Poynter, supt.
Mercer County JSHS | 3-00111
937 MOBERLY RD 40330 | 734-3394
James Gash, prin.

King MS, 1101 MOBERLY RD 40330 | 3-01100
John Gumm, prin. | 734-2766

Hartford, AC 502, PC 5, Ohio
Ohio County SD, PO BOX 70 42347 | 5-11111
Grover Canty, supt. | 298-3249
Ohio County HS | 4-00011
1400 US HIGHWAY 231 S 42347 | 274-3366
Fred Harper, prin.
Ohio County MS | 2-00100
1400 US HIGHWAY 231 S 42347 | 274-7893
Ruth Fields, prin.

Hawesville, AC 502, PC 3, Hancock
Hancock County SD | 4-11111
RR 2 BOX 154B 42348 | 927-6914
Charles Crotzer, supt.
Other Schools – See Lewisport

Hazard, AC 606, PC 6, Perry
Hazard ISD, 325 BROADWAY ST 41701 | 4-11111
Fred Stidham, supt. | 436-3911
HS, HIGHWAY 15 S 41701 | 2-00011
Jimmie Cornett, prin. | 436-3711
Eversole MS, 601 BROADWAY ST 41701 | 3-01100
Nancy Sutton, prin. | 436-4721

Knott County SD
Supt. — See Hindman
Cordia HS, RR 2 BOX 265 41701 | 2-00011
Bobby Smith, prin. | 785-4457

Perry County SD, 315 PARK AVE 41701 | 6-11111
K. Colwell, supt. | 439-5814
Napier HS, PO BOX 899 41702 | 3-00011
Richard Russell, prin. | 439-1519
Other Schools – See Buckhorn, Jeff

Hazard Community College | 4-CC
1 COMMUNITY COLLEGE DR 41701 | 436-5721
Kentucky Tech Hazard State Voc-Tech Sch | 4-CS
101 VO TECH DR 41701 | 436-3101

Hebron, AC 606, PC 4, Boone
Boone County SD
Supt. — See Florence
Conner HS, PO BOX 36 41048 | 4-00011
Ralph Rollins, prin. | 689-7884
Conner MS, PO BOX 86 41048 | 3-00100
Michael Hibbett, prin. | 689-7616

Henderson, AC 502, PC 8, Henderson
Henderson County SD | 6-11111
1805 2ND ST 42420 | 826-9578
Gayle Ecton, supt.
Henderson County SHS | 4-00001
2424 ZION RD 42420 | 827-2506
Howard Crittenden, prin.
Henderson County North JHS | 3-00110
1707 2ND ST 42420 – Scott Long, prin. | 826-7280
Henderson County South JHS | 3-00110
800 S ALVES ST 42420 | 826-9568
David Jordan, prin.

Henderson Community College | 3-CC
2660 S GREEN ST 42420 | 827-1867

Hickman, AC 502, PC 5, Fulton
Fulton County SD, PO BOX 50 42050 | 3-11111
Charles Terrett, supt. | 236-3923
Fulton County JSHS, RR 4 42050 | 2-00111
Larry Gardner, prin. | 236-3904

Highland Heights, AC 606, PC 5, Campbell

Northern Kentucky University | 6-UC
LOUIE B NUNN DR 41076 | 572-5100

Hi Hat, AC 606, PC 2, Floyd
Floyd County SD
Supt. — See Prestonsburg
South Floyd HS, PO BOX 310 41636 | 3-00011
Terry Stewart, prin. | 452-9600

Hindman, AC 606, PC 3, Knott
Knott County SD, PO BOX 869 41822 | 5-11111
Harold Combs, supt. | 785-3153
Knott County Central HS | 3-00011
PO BOX 819 41822 | 785-3166
James Reynolds, prin.
Other Schools – See Hazard

Hodgenville, AC 502, PC 5, Larue
Larue County SD, PO BOX 39 42748 | 4-11111
Roger Truitt, supt. | 358-4111
Larue County HS | 3-00011
911 S LINCOLN BLVD 42748 | 358-3195
Philippe Eason, prin.
Larue County MS | 2-00100
911 S LINCOLN BLVD 42748 | 358-3196
Barbara Haynes, prin.

Hopkinsville, AC 502, PC 8, Christian
Christian County SD | 6-11111
PO BOX 609 42241 | 887-1300
Kirby Hall, supt.
Christian County HS | 4-00011
220 GLASS AVE 42240 | 887-1100
W. Kay Lancaster, prin.
HS, 430 KOFFMAN DR 42240 | 4-00011
Harold Wood, prin. | 887-1200
Christian County MS | 3-00100
210 GLASS AVE 42240 | 887-1130
Thomas Hickey, prin.

MS, 434 KOFFMAN DR 42240 | 3-00100
Linda Ledford, prin. | 887-1230
North Drive MS, 831 NORTH DR 42240 | 3-00100
Robert Roach, prin. | 887-1250

CareerCom Junior College of Business | 3-CC
1102 S VIRGINIA ST 42240 | 886-1302
Hopkinsville Community College | 4-CC
PO BOX 2100 42241 | 886-3921
University Heights Academy | 2-11111
PO BOX 1070 42241 | 886-0254
Marvin Denison, prin.

Horse Cave, AC 502, PC 4, Hart
Caverna ISD
Supt. — See Cave City
Caverna JSHS, RR 2 42749 | 2-00111
Kenneth Henderson, prin. | 773-2828

Hyden, AC 606, PC 2, Leslie
Leslie County SD, PO BOX 949 41749 | 5-11111
Richard Bowling, supt. | 672-2397
Leslie County HS, PO BOX 970 41749 | 3-00011
O. Shepherd, prin. | 672-2337
Leslie County MS | 2-00100
GENERAL DELIVERY 41749 | 672-5580
Anthony Little, prin.

Independence, AC 606, PC 7, Kenton
Kenton County SD
Supt. — See Erlanger
Kenton HS, 5545 MADISON PIKE 41051 | 4-00011
Michael Tolliver, prin. | 356-3541
Twenhofel MS | 3-00100
6955 TAYLOR MILL RD 41051 | 356-5559
Ronald Schneider, prin.

Inez, AC 606, PC 3, Martin
Martin County SD | 5-11111
PO BOX 366 41224 | 298-3572
William Slone, supt.
Clark HS, HC 63 BOX 810 41224 | 3-00011
John Haney, prin. | 298-3591
MS, PO BOX 1308 41224 | 2-00100
Thomas Dials, prin. | 298-3264
Other Schools – See Warfield

Irvine, AC 606, PC 5, Estill
Estill County SD, PO BOX 391 40336 | 5-11111
Roger Kirby, supt. | 723-2181
Estill County HS, PO BOX 119 40336 | 3-00011
Stephen Garrett, prin. | 723-3337
Estill County MS, PO BOX 529 40336 | 2-00100
Clayton Justice, prin. | 723-5136

Jackson, AC 606, PC 4, Breathitt
Breathitt County SD | 5-11111
PO BOX 750 41339 | 666-2491
Hargus Rogers, supt.
Breathitt County HS | 3-00011
406 COURT ST 41339 | 666-7511
Paul Herald, prin.
Sebastian MS, PO BOX 788 41339 | 2-00100
Carl McIntosh, prin. | 666-8894

Jackson ISD, 938 HIGHLAND AVE 41339 | 2-11111
O. Collins, supt. | 666-4979
JSHS, 938 HIGHLAND AVE 41339 | 2-00111
Robert DeHoag, prin. | 666-5164

Lees College | 2-CC
601 JEFFERSON AVE 41339 | 666-7521

Jamestown, AC 502, PC 4, Russell
Russell County SD | 5-11111
PO BOX 260 42629 | 343-3191
S. Stephens, supt.
Other Schools – See Russell Springs

Jeff, AC 606, PC 3, Perry
Perry County SD
Supt. — See Hazard
Combs Memorial HS | 3-00011
PO BOX 159 41751 | 436-6811
Everett Noe, prin.

Jeffersontown, AC 502, PC 7, Jefferson
Jefferson County SD
Supt. — See Louisville
HS, 9600 OLD SIX MILE LN 40299 | 4-00011
Harold Russell, prin. | 473-8275

Jenkins, AC 606, PC 5, Letcher
Jenkins ISD, PO BOX 74 41537 | 3-11111
Bill Caudill, supt. | 832-2183
HS, PO BOX 552 41537 | 2-00011
Homer Brown, prin. | 832-2184
MS, PO BOX 552 41537 | 2-00100
Regennia Morrow, prin. | 832-4778

La Grange, AC 502, PC 5, Oldham
Oldham County SD | 6-11111
PO BOX 207 40031 | 222-8880
Blake Haselton, supt.
Other Schools – See Buckner, Crestwood

Lancaster, AC 606, PC 5, Garrard
Garrard County SD | 4-11111
322 W MAPLE AVE 40444 | 792-3018
William Wesley, supt.
Garrard County HS | 3-00011
304 W MAPLE AVE 40444 | 792-2146
Marshall Norton, prin.

Garrard MS, 324 W MAPLE AVE 40444   2-00100
Randy Hughes, prin.   792-2108

Lawrenceburg, AC 502, PC 6, Anderson
Anderson County SD   5-11111
103 N MAIN ST 40342   839-3406
Ronald Fentress, supt.
Anderson County HS   3-00011
750 W BROADWAY ST 40342   839-5118
Larry Barnett, prin.
Anderson County MS   3-00100
126 N MAIN ST 40342   839-9261
Larry Basham, prin.

Lebanon, AC 502, PC 6, Marion
Marion County SD   5-11111
223 N SPALDING AVE 40033   692-3721
Happy Osborne, supt.
Marion County HS, RR 3 40033   3-00011
Gwen Nelson, prin.   692-6066
MS, 235 N SPALDING AVE 40033   2-00100
David Hogan, prin.   692-3441
St. Charles MS   2-00100
1155 HIGHWAY 327 40033   692-4578
Judy Gaddie, prin.

Leitchfield, AC 502, PC 5, Grayson
Grayson County SD   5-11111
PO BOX 4009 42755   259-4011
Craig Bangtson, supt.
Grayson County HS   4-00011
240 HIGH SCHOOL RD 42754   259-4078
Arnold Hack, prin.
Grayson County Vo Ed Ctr   Vo Tech
120 HIGH SCHOOL RD 42754   259-3195
Morris Craig, prin.
Grayson County MS, 726 MILL ST 42754   3-00100
R. Gary Gibson, prin.   259-4175

Letcher, AC 606, PC 2, Letcher
Letcher County SD
Supt. — See Whitesburg
HS 41832   2-00011
Sherrill Slone, prin.   633-2524

Lewisburg, AC 502, PC 3, Logan
Logan County SD
Supt. — See Russellville
MS, STACKER ST 42256   2-00100
Darrell Dooley, prin.   755-4823

Lewisport, AC 502, PC 4, Hancock
Hancock County SD
Supt. — See Hawesville
Hancock County HS, RR 1 42351   3-00011
Robert Kerrick, prin.   927-6953
Hancock County MS, RR 1 42351   2-00100
Dale Gray, prin.   927-6712

Lexington, AC 606, PC 9, Fayette
Fayette County SD   8-11111
701 E MAIN ST 40502   281-0100
Ronald Walton, supt.
Bryan Station HS   4-00011
1866 EDGEWORTH DR 40505   299-9212
Donna George, prin.
Clay HS, 2100 FONTAINE RD 40502   4-00011
Michael Courtney, prin.   269-3326
Dunbar HS   4-00011
1600 MAN O WAR BLVD 40513   224-3140
Jon Akers, prin.
Fayette Co. HS   2-00011
400 LAFAYETTE PKY 40503   281-0350
Lewis Hughley, prin.
Lafayette HS, 401 REED LN 40503   4-00011
Thurmas Reynolds, prin.   281-0306
Tates Creek HS   4-00011
1107 CENTRE PKY 40517   272-1512
Kenneth Cox, prin.
Eastside Ctr for Applied Technology   Vo Tech
2208 LIBERTY RD 40509   252-4464
Woodrow Wilson, prin.
Southside Vo Ctr   Vo Tech
1784 HARRODSBURG RD 40504   278-0470
Mark Williams, prin.
Beaumont MS   3-00100
2080 GEORGIAN WAY 40504   277-0359
Russell Behanan, prin.
Bryan Station MS   3-00100
1865 WICKLAND DR 40505   299-4317
Thomas Jones, prin.
Clark MS, 3341 CLAYS MILL RD 40503   3-00100
Jack Musgrave, prin.   223-7683
Crawford MS   3-00100
1813 CHARLESTON DR 40505   299-2213
Deborah Tronzo, prin.
Leestown MS   3-00100
2010 LEESTOWN RD 40511   254-9223
Rafael Cordoves, prin.
Morton MS   3-00100
1225 TATES CREEK RD 40502   266-3281
Jack Lyons, prin.
Southern MS   3-00100
400 WILSON DOWNING RD 40517   272-5313
William Partin, prin.
Tates Creek MS   4-00100
1105 CENTRE PKY 40517   272-3452
David Shepard, prin.
Traditional Magnet MS   3-00100
350 N LIMESTONE ST 40508   252-8166
Michael Carr, prin.
Winburn MS, 1060 WINBURN DR 40511   3-00100
Virgil Covington, prin.   299-7711

Blue Grass Baptist S   2-11111
1330 RED RIVER DR 40517   272-1217
Greg Waltermire, prin.
Computer School, The   2-CS
820 LANE ALLEN RD 40504   276-1929
Fugazzi College   2-CC
406 LAFAYETTE AVE 40502   266-0401
Kentucky College of Business   3-CC
628 E MAIN ST 40508   253-0621
Kentucky Tech Central KY State Voc-Tech   4-CS
150 VO TECH RD 40510   255-8501
Lexington Catholic HS   2-00011
2250 CLAYS MILL RD 40503   277-7183
James Taylor, prin.
Lexington Christian Academy   2-00111
PO BOX 23160 40523   223-8822
Roy Chase, prin.
Lexington Community College   5-CC
OSWALD BLDG COOPER 40506   257-4872
Lexington Electronics Institute   2-CS
3340 HOLWYN RD 40503   223-3310
Lexington Theological Seminary   2-UC
631 S LIMESTONE ST 40508   252-0361
Pathology and Cytology Laboratories   2-CS
290 BIG RUN RD 40503   278-9513
St. Joseph's Hospital   HSP
1400 HARRODSBURG RD 40504   278-3436
Sayre S, 194 N LIMESTONE ST 40507   2-11111
William Heim, prin.   254-1361
Sullivan College   3-CC
2659 REGENCY RD 40503   276-4357
Transylvania University   4-UC
300 N BROADWAY ST 40508   800-872-6798
University of Kentucky 40506   7-UC
   257-9000

Liberty, AC 606, PC 4, Casey
Casey County SD, RR 1 BOX 21 42539   5-11111
Wendell Emerson, supt.   787-6941
Casey County HS, RR 4 42539   3-00011
James Beeler, prin.   787-6151
Casey County MS, RR 4 BOX 50A 42539   2-00100
Glenda Myers, prin.   787-6769

London, AC 606, PC 6, Laurel
Laurel County SD   6-11111
275 S LAUREL RD 40741   864-5114
Joe McKnight, supt.
North Laurel HS   4-00011
1300 E DANIEL BOONE PKY 40741   877-1712
Gregory Smith, prin.
South Laurel HS   4-00011
201 S LAUREL RD 40741   864-7371
Roger Marchum, prin.
South Laurel MS   4-00100
223 S LAUREL RD 40741   878-9300
Ora Cobb, prin.
North Laurel MS   4-00100
101 JOHNSON RD 40741   878-2290
Mike Cox, prin.

Kentucky Tech Laurel Co State Voc-Tech   2-CS
1711 N MAIN ST 40741   - -
Sue Bennett College   2-CC
101 COLLEGE ST 40741   864-2238

Lost Creek, AC 606, PC 2, Breathitt

Riverside Christian S 41348   2-11111
Doran Hostetler, prin.   666-2359

Louisa, AC 606, PC 4, Lawrence
Lawrence County SD   5-11111
PO BOX 607 41230   638-9671
Ed Michael, supt.
Lawrence County HS   3-00011
PO BOX 60 41230   638-9676
Richard Lyon, prin.
MS, PO BOX 567 41230   3-01100
William Sparks, prin.   638-4574

Louisville, AC 502, PC 10, Jefferson
Jefferson County SD   8-11111
PO BOX 34020 40232   473-3251
Stephen Daeschner, supt.
Atherton HS, 3000 DUNDEE RD 40205   4-00011
Janice Fish, prin.   473-8202
Ballard HS   4-00011
6000 BROWNSBORO RD 40222   473-8206
Alexandra Allen, prin.
Butler HS, 2222 CRUMS LN 40216   4-00011
Kenneth Frick, prin.   473-8220
Central HS   4-00011
1130 W CHESTNUT ST 40203   473-8226
Harold Fenderson, prin.
Doss HS   4-00011
7601 SAINT ANDRWS CHURCH RD 40214
Gordon Milby, prin.   473-8239
Dupont Manual HS, 120 W LEE ST 40208   4-00011
Beverly Keepers, prin.   473-8241
Iroquois HS, 4615 TAYLOR BLVD 40215   4-00011
Beverly Jasmin, prin.   473-8269
Jefferson County HS   3-00011
911 S BROOK ST 40203   473-3173
Louis Tsioropoulos, prin.
Male HS, 4409 PRESTON HWY 40213   4-00011
Joseph Burks, prin.   368-5831
Moore HS, 6415 OUTER LOOP 40228   4-00011
Warren Shelton, prin.   473-8304
Seneca HS, 3510 GOLDSMITH LN 40220   4-00011
John Locke, prin.   473-8323

Shawnee HS, 4018 W MARKET ST 40212   3-00011
John Huggins, prin.   473-8326
Southern HS   4-00011
8620 PRESTON HWY 40219   473-8330
Steve Stallings, prin.
Waggener HS   3-00011
330 S HUBBARDS LN 40207   473-8340
Nina Hopper, prin.
Western HS, 2501 ROCKFORD LN 40216   4-00011
Lucian Yates, prin.   473-8344
Buechel Metro. JSHS   2-00111
1960 BASHFORD MANOR LN 40218   473-8316
Maurice Risner, prin.
Youth Performing Arts JSHS   2-00111
1517 S 2ND ST 40208   473-8355
Beverly Keepers, prin.
Brown S, 546 S 1ST ST 40202   3-11111
Lenora Hay, prin.   473-8216
Ahrens Vo HS, 546 S 1ST ST 40202   Vo Tech
David Schalk, prin.   473-8201
Detrich Vo Ed Ctr, 1900 S 7TH ST 40208   Vo Tech
Patricia Jarrett, prin.   473-8237
Barret MS, 2561 GRINSTEAD DR 40206   3-00100
Don Matlock, prin.   473-8207
Bruce MS, 3307 E INDIAN TRL 40213   3-00100
Linda Compton, prin.   473-8219
Carrithers MS   3-00100
4320 BILLTOWN RD 40299   473-8224
Ann Goins, prin.
Conway MS, 6300 TERRY RD 40258   3-00100
Dennis Boswell, prin.   473-8233
Highland MS, 1700 NORRIS PL 40205   3-00100
Robert Knight, prin.   473-8266
Iroquois MS   3-00100
5650 SOUTHERN PKY 40214   473-8270
Cheryl Demarsh, prin.
Jefferson County Traditional MS   3-00100
1418 MORTON AVE 40204   473-8272
Bob Zachery, prin.
Jefferson MS   4-00100
4401 RANGELAND RD 40219   473-8273
Mary Hardin, prin.
Johnson MS, 2509 WILSON AVE 40210   3-00100
Norvel Martin, prin.   473-8277
Kammerer MS   3-00100
7315 WESBORO RD 40222   473-8279
Nancy Weber, prin.
Knight MS, 9803 BLUE LICK RD 40229   3-00100
Susan Freepartner, prin.   473-8287
Lassiter MS   3-00100
8200 CANDLEWORTH DR 40214   473-8288
Fred Harbison, prin.
Meyzeek MS, 828 S JACKSON ST 40203   4-00100
Deborah Baker, prin.   473-8299
Myers MS, 2815 KLONDIKE LN 40218   3-00100
Larry McKeehan, prin.   473-8305
Newburg MS, 5008 E INDIAN TRL 40218   3-00100
Nancy Hottman, prin.   473-8306
Noe MS, 121 W LEE ST 40208   4-00100
Ronnie Cratcher, prin.   473-8307
Southern MS   4-00100
4530 BELLEVUE AVE 40215   473-8331
George Clemmons, prin.
Western MS, 2201 W MAIN ST 40212   3-00100
Mary Jaeger, prin.   473-8345
Westport MS   4-00100
8100 WESTPORT RD 40222   473-8346
James Stone, prin.
Williams MS   3-00100
2415 ROCKFORD LN 40216   473-8242
Judith Birkhead, prin.
Other Schools – See Fairdale, Fern Creek,
Jeffersontown, Middletown, Pleasure Ridge Park,
Valley Station

Assumption HS, 2170 TYLER LN 40205   3-00011
Karen Russ, prin.   458-9551
Bellarmine College   4-UC
2001 NEWBURG RD 40205   800-535-1133
Brown Cancer Center   1-HSP
529 S JACKSON ST 40202   588-6905
Christian Academy of Louisville   2-11111
3110 ROCK CREEK DR 40207   897-3372
Carole Marra, prin.
College of Merchandising Design   2-CC
3901 ATKINSON DR 40218   456-6653
DeSales HS, 425 KENWOOD DR 40214   2-00011
David Winkler, prin.   368-6519
Evangel Christian S   2-11111
5400 MINORS LN 40219   968-7744
Roger Hoagland, prin.
Highview Baptist S   3-11111
7711 FEGENBUSH LN 40228   239-2509
William Maggard, prin.
Holy Cross HS, 5144 DIXIE HWY 40216   2-00011
Terry Crawley, prin.   447-4363
Holy Rosary Academy   2-00011
4801 SOUTHSIDE DR 40214   366-4561
Karen Juliano, prin.
ITT Technical Institute   2-CS
10509 TIMBERWOOD CIR 40223
Jefferson Community College   6-CC
109 E BROADWAY ST 40202   584-0181
Kentucky College of Business   2-CC
3950 DIXIE HWY 40216   447-7665
Kentucky Country Day S   3-11111
4100 SPRINGDALE RD 40241   423-0440
Jonathan Brougham, prin.
Kentucky School for the Blind   HND
1867 FRANKFORT AVE 40206

Kentucky Tech Jefferson State Voc-Tech   4-CS
727 W CHESTNUT ST 40203
Louisville Collegiate S   3-11111
2427 GLENMARY AVE 40204   451-5330
Frederick Hill, prin.
Louisville Presbyterian Theological Sem.   2-UC
1044 ALTA VISTA RD 40205   895-3411
Louisville Technical Institute   3-CC
3901 ATKINSON DR 40218   456-6509
Maryhurst HS, 1015 DORSEY LN 40223   1-00011
Melinda Stricklen, prin.   245-1576
Mercy Academy   2-00011
1176 E BROADWAY ST 40204   584-4273
Mary Boyce, prin.
Merton Acadmey   2-01100
6010 PRESTON HWY 40219   969-5462
Rosemary Newton, prin.
NEC-College of Technology   4-CC
300 HIGH RISE DR 40213   966-5555
Northside Christian S   2-11111
2214 BANK ST 40212   778-1113
Sidney Main, prin.
Portland Christian S   2-11111
2500 PORTLAND AVE 40212   778-6114
Donald Rucker, prin.
Presentation Academy   2-00011
861 S 4TH ST 40203   583-5935
Sr. Stephanie Warren, prin.
RETS Electronic Institute   4-CC
4146 OUTER LOOP 40219   968-7191
Sacred Heart Academy   3-00011
3175 LEXINGTON RD 40206   897-6097
Sr. Maureen Field, prin.
St. Anthony Medical Center   HSP
1313 SAINT ANTHONY PL 40204   587-1161
St. Francis HS   2-00011
233 W BROADWAY ST 40202   585-2057
Thomas Pike, prin.
Saint Xavier HS   4-00011
1609 POPLAR LEVEL RD 40217   637-4712
Perry Sangalli, prin.
Southern Baptist Theological Seminary   4-UC
2825 LEXINGTON RD 40280   897-4011
Spalding University   3-UC
851 S 4TH ST 40203   585-9911
Spencerian College   2-CS
PO BOX 16418 40256   447-1000
Sullivan College   4-CC
PO BOX 33 40201   800-844-1354
Trinity HS   4-00011
4011 SHELBYVILLE RD 40207   895-9427
Peter Flaig, prin.
University of Louisville   7-UC
2301 S 3RD ST 40292   588-5555
Ursuline-Pitt S, 2117 PAYNE ST 40206   1-11111
Sarah Heuel, prin.   895-7488
Walden S, 4238 WESTPORT RD 40207   2-11111
Linda Van Houten, prin.   893-0433

Ludlow, AC 606, PC 5, Kenton
Ludlow ISD, 525 ELM ST 41016   4-11111
Jon Draud, supt.   261-8210
JSHS, 515 ELM ST 41016   2-00111
Charles Holloway, prin.   261-8211

Mc Kee, AC 606, PC 3, Jackson
Jackson County SD   4-11111
PO BOX 217 40447   287-7181
Justin Minnehan, supt.
Jackson County HS   3-00011
PO BOX 427 40447   287-7155
Betty Bond, prin.
Jackson County MS   3-00100
PO BOX 1329 40447   287-8351
Gene Lake, prin.

Madisonville, AC 502, PC 7, Hopkins
Hopkins County SD   6-11111
PO BOX 509 42431   825-6000
John McClearn, supt.
Madisonville North Hopkins HS   4-00011
4515 HANSON RD 42431   825-6017
James Stevens, prin.
Browning Springs MS 42431   3-00100
Paul Armstrong, prin.   825-6006
Other Schools – See Dawson Springs, Earlington, Nebo, Nortonville

Grace Baptist Christian S   2-11111
735 LENIN RD 42431   322-3381
Lawrence Richardson, prin.
Kentucky Tech Madisonville State Vo-Tech   3-CS
100 SCHOOL ST 42431   825-6546
Madisonville Community College   4-CC
2000 COLLEGE DR 42431   821-2250

Manchester, AC 606, PC 4, Clay
Clay County SD   5-11111
128 RICHMOND RD 40962   598-2168
Charles White, supt.
Clay County HS, RR 7 BOX 44 40962   4-00011
Douglas Adams, prin.   598-3737
Clay County MS   3-00100
239 RICHMOND RD 40962   598-1810
Albert Webb, prin.

Marion, AC 502, PC 5, Crittenden
Crittenden County SD   4-11111
PO BOX 362 42064   965-3525
Dennis Lacy, supt.

Crittenden County HS   2-00011
PO BOX 311 42064   965-2248
Randy Congdon, prin.
Crittenden County MS   2-00100
RR 2 BOX 655 42064   965-5221
Jerry Thurman, prin.

Martin, AC 606, PC 3, Floyd

Piarist S, PO BOX 870 41649   1-00011
Fr. Carroll, prin.   285-3950

Mayfield, AC 502, PC 6, Graves
Graves County SD, 1007 CUBA RD 42066   5-11111
Bob Miller, supt.   247-2656
Graves County HS, RR 8 42066   4-00011
Jerald Ellington, prin.   247-6242

Mayfield ISD, 709 S 8TH ST 42066   4-11111
Don Sparks, supt.   247-3868
HS, 700 DOUTHITT ST 42066   2-00011
Joe Smith, prin.   247-4461
MS, S 7TH ST 42066   2-00100
James Almand, prin.   247-7521

Mid-Continent Baptist Bible College   1-UC
PO BOX 7010 42066   247-8521
Northside Baptist Christian S   2-11111
611 W LOCKRIDGE ST 42066   247-0516
Barbara Hopper, prin.

Maysville, AC 606, PC 6, Mason
Mason County SD, PO BOX 99 41056   5-11111
Felici Felice, supt.   564-5563
Mason County HS   3-00011
1320 US HIGHWAY 68 41056   564-3393
Duane Lambert, prin.
Mason County MS   3-00100
420 CHENAULT DR 41056   564-6748
Ronald Ishmael, prin.

Maysville Community College 41056   3-CC
759-7141
St. Patrick S, 318 LIMESTONE ST 41056   2-11111
Fr. Berscheid, prin.   564-5949

Middlesboro, AC 606, PC 7, Bell
Middlesboro ISD, 220 N 20TH ST 40965   4-11111
Dwight Henn, supt.   248-9411
HS, 4400 CUMBERLAND AVE 40965   3-00011
Darryl Wilder, prin.   248-9430
MS, 4004 CUMBERLAND AVE 40965   2-00100
Larry Davis, prin.   248-9420

Middletown, AC 502, PC 6, Jefferson
Jefferson County SD
Supt. — See Louisville
Eastern HS   4-00011
12400 OLD SHELBYVILLE RD 40243   473-8243
James Sexton, prin.
Crosby MS, 303 GATEHOUSE LN 40243   3-00100
Sherry Howard, prin.   473-8235

Midway, AC 606, PC 4, Woodford

Midway College   3-UC
512 E STEPHENS ST 40347   800-755-0031

Millersburg, AC 606, PC 3, Bourbon

Millersburg Military Institute   1-00011
PO BOX 278 40348   484-3352
Edward Allin, prin.

Monticello, AC 606, PC 6, Wayne
Monticello ISD, 135 CAVE ST 42633   3-11111
Kay Smith, supt.   348-5311
HS, 135 CAVE ST 42633   2-00011
Harold Van Hook, prin.   348-5312

Wayne County SD   5-11111
PO BOX 437 42633   348-8484
David Gover, supt.
Wayne County HS, RR 4 BOX 2 42633   3-00011
George Horton, prin.   348-5575
Wayne County MS, PO BOX 5 42633   2-00100
Obie Bates, prin.   348-6691

Morehead, AC 606, PC 6, Rowan
Rowan County SD, 121 E 2ND ST 40351   5-11111
Kenneth Bland, supt.   784-8928
Rowan County HS, 100 VIKING DR 40351   3-00011
Bill Buelterman, prin.   784-8956
Rowan County MS, W SUN ST 40351   3-00100
Herbert Ramey, prin.   784-8911

Kentucky Tech Rowan State Voc-Tech Sch   3-CS
PO BOX 1098 40351   783-1538
Morehead State University   6-UC
150 UNIVERSITY BLVD 40351   783-2000

Morganfield, AC 502, PC 5, Union
Union County SD, 510 S MART ST 42437   5-11111
David Holland, supt.   389-1694
Union County HS   3-00011
4464 US HIGHWAY 60 W 42437   389-1454
Michael Thomas, prin.
Union County MS   3-00100
4465 US HIGHWAY 60 W 42437   389-0224
James Dickens, prin.

Clements Job Corps Center   3-CS
2302 US HIGHWAY 60 E 42437   389-2419

Morgantown, AC 502, PC 4, Butler
Butler County SD, PO BOX 339 42261   4-11111
James Carver, supt.   526-5624
Butler County HS, PO BOX 248 42261   3-00011
Kenneth Reed, prin.   526-2204
Butler County MS, PO BOX 10 42261   3-00100
Larry Watkins, prin.   526-5647

Mount Olivet, AC 606, PC 2, Robertson
Robertson County SD   2-11111
PO BOX 108 41064   724-5431
George Kirk, supt.
Deming JSHS, PO BOX 168 41064   2-00111
Chuck Brown, prin.   724-5421

Mount Sterling, AC 606, PC 6, Montgomery
Montgomery County SD   5-11111
640 WOODFORD DR 40353   497-8760
Richard Hughes, supt.
Montgomery County HS   4-00011
724 WOODFORD DR 40353   497-8765
John Radjunas, prin.
Montgomery County MS   3-00100
3570 INDIAN MOUND DR 40353   497-8770
James Robinson, prin.

Mount Vernon, AC 606, PC 5, Rockcastle
Rockcastle County SD   5-11111
245 RICHMOND ST 40456   256-2125
Bige Towery, supt.
Rockcastle County HS   3-00011
PO BOX 1410 40456   256-4816
Ronnie Cash, prin.

Mount Washington, AC 502, PC 6, Bullitt
Bullitt County SD
Supt. — See Shepherdsville
Bullitt East HS, PO BOX 69 40047   3-00011
Ted Pearce, prin.   538-7322
MS, 269 WATER ST 40047   3-00100
Deborah Atherton, prin.   538-4227

Munfordville, AC 502, PC 4, Hart
Hart County SD, PO BOX 68 42765   4-11111
Robert Nash, supt.   524-2631
Hart County JSHS   3-00111
1014 S DIXIE HWY 42765   524-9341
Charles Wuertzer, prin.

Murray, AC 502, PC 7, Calloway
Calloway County SD   5-11111
PO BOX 800 42071 – J. Rose, supt.   753-3033
Calloway County HS   3-00011
2108 COLLEGE FARM RD 42071   753-5479
Jerry Ainley, prin.
Calloway County MS   3-00100
2108A COLLEGE FARM RD 42071   753-4182
Marilyn Willis, prin.

Murray ISD, 814 POPLAR ST 42071   4-11111
W. Franklin, supt.   753-4363
HS, 501 DORAN RD 42071   2-00011
Willis Wells, prin.   753-5202
MS, 801 MAIN ST 42071   2-01100
Pat Seiber, prin.   753-5125

Murray State University 42071   6-UC
800-272-4678

Nebo, AC 502, PC 2, Hopkins
Hopkins County SD
Supt. — See Madisonville
West Hopkins HS   2-00011
2700 RABBIT RIDGE RD 42441   825-6130
Mike Duncan, prin.
MS, 100 S BERNARD ST 42441   2-00100
Euel Darnall, prin.   825-6133

Neon, AC 606, PC see Fleming-Neon
Letcher County SD
Supt. — See Whitesburg
Fleming Neon HS, PO BOX 367 41840   2-00011
David Jones, prin.   855-7597
Fleming Neon MS   2-01100
PO BOX 425 41840   855-7864
Dannie Caudill, prin.

New Castle, AC 502, PC 3, Henry
Henry County SD, PO BOX 299 40050   4-11111
Garnett Twyman, supt.   845-7270
Henry County HS, PO BOX 229 40050   3-00011
Darrell Treece, prin.   845-2888
Henry County MS   2-00100
PO BOX 267 40050   845-2348
Jerry Harris, prin.

New Haven, AC 502, PC 3, Nelson
Nelson County SD
Supt. — See Bardstown
MS, 489 HIGH ST 40051   2-01100
William Broaddus, prin.   549-3164

Newport, AC 606, PC 7, Campbell
Newport ISD, 301 E 8TH ST 41071   5-11111
Dan Sullivan, supt.   292-3004
HS, 900 E 6TH ST 41071   3-00011
Wanda Griffith, prin.   292-3023
MS, 30 W 8TH ST 41071   2-00100
Henley McIntosh, prin.   292-3017

Holy Spirit JHS | 1-00100
10 CHESAPEAKE AVE 41071 | 292-0487
Sr. Juanita Nadicksbernd, prin.
Newport Catholic HS | 2-00011
13 CAROTHERS RD 41071 | 292-0001
Carl Foster, prin.

Nicholasville, AC 606, PC 7, Jessamine
Jessamine County SD | 6-11111
501 E MAPLE ST 40356 | 885-4179
Lawrence Allen, supt.
Jessamine County HS | 4-00011
2101 WILMORE RD 40356 | 887-2421
Robert Korwatch, prin.
Jessamine County MS | 4-00100
851 WILMORE RD 40356 | 885-5561
Becke Cleaver, prin.

Nortonville, AC 502, PC 4, Hopkins
Hopkins County SD
Supt. — See Madisonville
South Hopkins HS | 3-00011
PO BOX 1611 42442 | 825-6125
Lanny Woodward, prin.
South Hopkins MS | 2-00100
PO BOX 1610 42442 | 825-6140
Daryl Herring, prin.

Olive Hill, AC 606, PC 4, Carter
Carter County SD
Supt. — See Grayson
West Carter County SHS | 2-00001
PO BOX 479 41164 | 286-2481
Gloria Sparks, prin.
Carter County Vo S | Vo Tech
RR 5 BOX 366 41164 | 286-4022
Harold Walker, prin.
West Carter County JHS | 3-00110
PO BOX 910 41164 | 286-5354
Phillip Barker, prin.

Olmstead, AC 502, PC 2, Logan
Logan County SD
Supt. — See Russellville
MS, 1170 OLMSTEAD RD 42265 | 2-00100
Mark Bennett, prin. | 726-3811

Oneida, AC 606, PC 3, Clay

Oneida Baptist Institute | 3-11111
PO BOX 67 40972 | 847-4111
Joann Seymore, prin.

Owensboro, AC 502, PC 8, Daviess
Daviess County SD | 6-11111
PO BOX 1510 42302 | 685-3161
Ed Allen, supt.
Apollo HS, 2280 TAMARACK RD 42301 | 4-00011
Bob Combs, prin. | 685-3121
Daviess County HS | 4-00011
4255 NEW HARTFORD RD 42303 | 684-5285
Waymond Morris, prin.
Daviess County MS | 4-00100
1415 E 4TH ST 42303 | 684-9632
Mike Robinson, prin.
Burns MS, 4610 GOETZ DR 42301 | 4-00100
Mike Clark, prin. | 685-5191
Owensboro ISD, PO BOX 746 42302 | 5-11111
Bill Chandler, supt. | 686-1000
HS, 1800 FREDERICA ST 42301 | 3-00011
Larry Moore, prin. | 686-1110
MS, 1300 BOOTH AVE 42301 | 4-00100
Joseph Conway, prin. | 686-1130

Brescia College | 3-UC
717 FREDERICA ST 42301 | 800-264-1234
Good Shepherd Christian S | 2-11111
PO BOX 1099 42302 | 683-3223
Marian Turley, prin.
Kentucky Tech Owensboro Voc-Tech School | 4-CS
PO BOX 1677 42302
Kentucky Wesleyan College | 3-UC
3000 FREDERICA ST 42301 | 926-3111
Owensboro Catholic HS | 3-00011
1524 W PARRISH AVE 42301 | 684-3215
Harold Staples, prin.
Owensboro Catholic MS | 2-00100
2540 CHRISTIE PL 42301 | 683-0480
James Duffy, prin.
Owensboro Community College | 4-CC
4800 NEW HARTFORD RD 42303 | 686-4400
Owensboro-Daviess Co. Hospital | HSP
PO BOX 570 42302 | 688-2100
Owensboro Junior College of Business | 3-CC
1515 E 18TH ST 42303 | 926-4040

Owenton, AC 502, PC 4, Owen
Owen County SD | 4-11111
1600 HIGHWAY 22 E 40359 | 484-3934
Bonita Burns, supt.
Owen County HS | 3-00011
2060 HIGHWAY 22 E 40359 | 484-5509
Jerry Sebastian, prin.
Bowling MS, 1960 HIGHWAY 22 E 40359 | 2-00100
Jo Wallace, prin. | 484-5701

Owingsville, AC 606, PC 4, Bath
Bath County SD, PO BOX 409 40360 | 4-11111
Bill Morgan, supt. | 674-6314
Bath County HS, CHENAULT DR 40360 | 3-00011
Arnie Isaacs, prin. | 674-6325

Bath Co. MS, 423 W MAIN ST 40360 | 3-01100
Lonnie Vice, prin. | 874-8165

Paducah, AC 502, PC 8, McCracken
McCracken County SD | 6-11111
260 BLEICH RD 42003 | 554-6800
Clinton Kirk, supt.
Lone Oak HS, 225 COLLEGE AVE 42001 | 3-00011
Wallace Adams, prin. | 554-6820
Reidland HS | 3-00011
5349 OLD BENTON RD 42003 | 898-2441
Wayne Ezell, prin.
Lone Oak MS | 3-00100
300 CUMBERLAND AVE 42001 | 554-6830
Cliff Owen, prin.
Reidland MS | 3-00100
5347 OLD BENTON RD 42003 | 898-3533
James Mitchell, prin.
Other Schools – See West Paducah

Paducah ISD, PO BOX 2550 42002 | 5-11111
Walt Bromenschenkel, supt. | 444-5606
Paducah Tilghman HS | 3-00011
2400 WASHINGTON ST 42003 | 444-5650
Les Bivens, prin.
MS, 342 LONE OAK RD 42001 | 3-00100
Terry Waltman, prin. | 444-5710

Institute of Electronic Technology | 2-CC
509 S 30TH ST 42001 | 444-9676
Kentucky Tech West KY State Voc-Tech Sch | 4-CS
PO BOX 7769 42002
Lourdes Hospital | HSP
1530 LONE OAK RD 42003 | 444-2101
Paducah Community College | 4-CC
PO BOX 7380 42002 | 554-9200
St. Mary JSHS, 1243 ELMDALE RD 42003 | 2-00111
Michael Collins, prin. | 442-1681

Paintsville, AC 606, PC 5, Johnson
Johnson County SD | 5-11111
253 N MAYO TRL 41240 | 789-2530
Frank Hamilton, supt.
Johnson Central HS | 4-00011
257 N MAYO TRL 41240 | 789-2500
Thomas Swartz, prin.

Paintsville ISD, 305 2ND ST 41240 | 3-11111
Leon Burchett, supt. | 789-2654
HS, 225 2ND ST 41240 | 2-00011
Grayson Boyd, prin. | 789-2656
MS, 225 2ND ST 41240 | 2-00100
Grayson Boyd, prin. | 789-2656

Kentucky Tech Mayo State Voc-Tech School | 4-CS
513 3RD ST 41240 | 789-5321

Paris, AC 606, PC 6, Bourbon
Bourbon County SD | 5-11111
3343 LEXINGTON RD 40361 | 987-2180
Larry Powers, supt.
Bourbon County HS | 3-00011
3343 LEXINGTON RD 40361 | 987-2185
Jack Tucker, prin.
Bourbon County MS | 3-00100
3343 LEXINGTON RD 40361 | 987-2189
Carol Christian, prin.

Paris ISD, 301 W 7TH ST 40361 | 4-11111
Tod Williams, supt. | 987-2160
HS, 302 W 7TH ST 40361 | 2-00011
Homer Goins, prin. | 987-2168
Southside MS, 1481 S MAIN ST 40361 | 2-00100
M. Rupp, prin. | 987-2166

Phelps, AC 606, PC 4, Pike
Pike County SD
Supt. — See Pikeville
JSHS, PO BOX 131 41553 | 3-00111
Elizabeth Compton, prin. | 456-3482

Pikeville, AC 606, PC 6, Pike
Pike County SD, PO BOX 3097 41502 | 7-11111
Reo Johns, supt. | 432-7700
Pike County Central HS | 3-00011
100 WINNERS CIRCLE DR 41501 | 432-4352
Roger Johnson, prin.
Shelby Valley HS | 3-00011
100 WILDCAT DR 41501 | 639-0033
Jerry Meade, prin.
Millard JSHS, 440 MILLARD HWY 41501 | 3-00111
Robert Wright, prin. | 432-3380
Other Schools – See Belfry, Elkhorn City, Fedscreek, Phelps, Virgie

Pikeville ISD, PO BOX 2010 41502 | 4-11111
John Waddell, supt. | 432-8161
JSHS, CHAMPIONSHIP DR 41501 | 3-00111
Howard Wallen, prin. | 432-0185

Kentucky College of Business | 2-CC
198 S MAYO TRL 41501 | 432-5477
Methodist Hospital of Kentucky | HSP
911 S BYPASS RD 41501 | 437-3500
Pikeville College | 3-UC
214 SYCAMORE ST 41501 | 432-9200

Pine Knot, AC 606, PC 4, McCreary
McCreary County SD
Supt. — See Stearns
MS, PO BOX 187 42635 | 2-00100
Ray Ball, prin. | 354-2511

Pineville, AC 606, PC 4, Bell
Bell County SD, PO BOX 340 40977 | 5-11111
Pearl Lefevers, supt. | 337-7051
Bell County HS, RR 1 40977 | 4-00011
George Thompson, supt. | 337-7061
Bell County MS, RR 1 BOX 87C 40977 | 3-00100
Doug Ramsey, prin. | 337-3104
Pineville ISD | 3-11111
401 W VIRGINIA AVE 40977 | 337-2361
Diana Lincks, supt.
JSHS, 401 W VIRGINIA AVE 40977 | 2-00111
Thomas Kelemen, prin. | 337-2361

Clear Creek Baptist Bible College | 2-UC
300 CLEAR CREEK RD 40977 | 337-3196

Pippa Passes, AC 606, PC 2, Knott

Alice Lloyd College | 3-UC
PURPOSE RD 41844 | 368-2101
Buchanan S, PURPOSE RD 41844 | 2-11111
Otis Balkcom, prin. | 368-2324

Pleasure Ridge Park, AC 502, PC 7, Jefferson
Jefferson County SD
Supt. — See Louisville
Pleasure Ridge Park HS | 4-00011
5901 GREENWOOD RD 40258 | 473-8311
Charles Miller, prin.

Powdery, AC 502, PC 3, Muhlenberg
Muhlenberg County SD
Supt. — See Greenville
Muhlenberg North MS | 2-00100
PO BOX 31 42367 | 338-3550
Clyde Stovall, prin.

Prestonsburg, AC 606, PC 5, Floyd
Floyd County SD | 6-11111
69 N ARNOLD AVE 41653 | 886-2354
Steve Towler, supt.
HS, N LAKE DRIVE 41653 | 3-00011
Karen Trivette, prin. | 886-2252
Adams MS, 1040 S LAKE DR 41653 | 3-00100
Janice Allen, prin. | 886-2671
Other Schools – See Betsy Layne, Eastern, Hi Hat

Perkins Job Corps Center | 2-CS
BOX G-11 GOBLE ROBERTS RD 41653
Prestonburg Community College | 4-CC
1 BERT T COMBS DR 41653 | 886-3863

Princeton, AC 502, PC 6, Caldwell
Caldwell County SD | 4-11111
PO BOX 229 42445 | 365-6601
Robert Rogers, supt.
Caldwell County HS | 3-00011
350 BECKNER LN 42445 | 365-3531
John Hina, prin.
Caldwell County MS | 3-00100
440 BECKNER LN 42445 | 365-9566
David Franklin, prin.

Providence, AC 502, PC 5, Webster
Providence ISD, 310 W MAIN ST 42450 | 3-11111
Keith Shoulders, supt. | 667-7007
HS, CEDAR ST 42450 | 2-00011
A. Edwards, prin. | 667-7065

Raceland, AC 606, PC 4, Greenup
Raceland ISD, 550 RAMS BLVD 41169 | 3-11111
Charles Sammons, supt. | 836-2144
JSHS, 500 RAMS BLVD 41169 | 2-00011
John Stephens, prin. | 836-8221

Radcliff, AC 502, PC 7, Hardin
Hardin County SD
Supt. — See Elizabethtown
North Hardin HS | 4-00011
801 S LOGSDON PKY 40160 | 351-3167
Kim Shaw, prin.
Radcliff MS, 1145 S DIXIE BLVD 40160 | 3-01100
Steve Brown, prin. | 351-1171

Richmond, AC 606, PC 7, Madison
Madison County SD | 6-11111
PO BOX 768 40476 | 624-4500
Shannon Johnson, supt.
Madison Central HS | 4-00011
705 N 2ND ST 40475 | 624-4505
William Fultz, prin.
Model Laboratory HS | 2-00011
EASTERN KY UNIVERSITY 40475 | 622-3766
Bruce Bonar, prin.
Moores MS, 1143 BEREA RD 40475 | 3-00100
Juanita Cox, prin. | 624-4545
Madison MS, 101 SUMMIT ST 40475 | 3-00100
Douglas Roberts, prin. | 624-4550
Model Laboratory MS | 2-00100
EASTERN KY UNIVERSITY 40475 | 622-3766
Bruce Bonar, prin.
Other Schools – See Berea

Eastern Kentucky University | 7-UC
521 LANCASTER AVE 40475 | 800-262-7493
Kentucky College of Business | 2-CC
139 S KILLARNEY LN 40475 | 623-8956

Russell, AC 606, PC 5, Greenup
Russell ISD, 409 BELFONTE ST 41169 | 5-11111
Ronnie Back, supt. | 836-9679

HS, 709 RED DEVIL LN 41169   3-00011 / 836-9658
Elizabeth Trabandt, prin.
MS, 707 RED DEVIL LN 41169   3-00100 / 836-8135
Scott Grosse, prin.

Russell Springs, AC 502, PC 4, Russell
Russell County SD
Supt. — See Jamestown
Russell County SHS   3-00001 / 866-3341
2166 S HIGHWAY 127 42642
Patricia Rippetoe, prin.
Russell County JHS   3-00110 / 866-2224
2258 S HIGHWAY 127 42642
Vernie McGagha, prin.

Russellville, AC 502, PC 6, Logan
Logan County SD, PO BOX 417 42276   5-11111 / 726-2436
H. Marksberry, supt.
Logan County HS   3-00011 / 726-8454
2200 BOWLING GREEN RD 42276
Bob Nylin, prin.
Other Schools – See Adairville, Auburn, Lewisburg, Olmstead

Russellville ISD   4-11111 / 726-8405
355 S SUMMER ST 42276
Gary Rye, supt.
HS, 1101 W 9TH ST 42276   2-00011 / 726-8421
Joseph Meguiar, prin.
MS, 210 E 7TH ST 42276   2-01100 / 726-8428
Fredia Baker, prin.

Saint Catharine, AC 606, PC 3, Washington

St. Catharine College   2-CC / 336-9303
HWY 150 40061

Salyersville, AC 606, PC 4, Magoffin
Magoffin County SD   5-11111 / 349-6117
PO BOX 109 41465
Ray Hammers, supt.
Magoffin County HS   3-00011 / 349-2011
201 HORNET DR 41465
Owen Barnett, prin.
Whitaker MS, HORNET RD 41465   3-00100 / 349-5190
Jacqueline Howard, prin.

Sandy Hook, AC 606, PC 3, Elliott
Elliott County SD, PO BOX 767 41171   4-11111 / 738-5117
E. Binion, supt.
Elliot County JSHS   3-00111 / 738-5225
PO BOX 168 41171
Dwight Johnson, prin.

Scottsville, AC 502, PC 5, Allen
Allen County SD   5-11111 / 237-3181
238 BOWLING GREEN RD 42164
J. Weaver, supt.
Allen County HS, PO BOX 127 42164   3-00011 / 622-4119
David Young, prin.
Allen County Vo Ed Ctr   Vo Tech / 622-4711
HWY 231 42164 – Jim Young, prin.
Bazzell MS   3-00100 / 622-7140
201 NEW GALLATIN RD 42164
Tom Keen, prin.

Shelbyville, AC 502, PC 6, Shelby
Shelby County SD   5-11111 / 633-2375
PO BOX 159 40066
Leon Mooneyhan, supt.
Shelby County HS, PO BOX 69 40066   4-00011 / 633-2344
Walter Hawkins, prin.
Shelby County East MS   3-00100 / 633-1478
600 ROCKET LN 40065
Carolyn Chesher, prin.
Shelby County West MS   3-00100 / 633-4869
1155 MAIN ST 40065
Lynn Swigert, prin.

Living Waters Christian S   2-11111 / 633-0734
5425 FRANKFORT RD 40065
Kent Sullivan, prin.

Shepherdsville, AC 502, PC 5, Bullitt
Bullitt County SD   6-11111 / 543-2271
1040 HIGHWAY 44 E 40165
George Valentine, supt.
Bullitt Central HS   4-00011 / 543-7021
1330 HIGHWAY 44 E 40165
Barbara Elliott, prin.
North Bullitt HS   3-00011 / 957-2186
3200 E HEBRON LN 40165
Dwight Hoskins, prin.
Riverview HS, 325 E 2ND ST 40165   2-00011 / 543-8300
Lonnie Dawson, prin.
Bernheim MS, 700 AUDUBON DR 40165   3-00100 / 543-7614
Joe Mills, prin.
Bullitt Lick MS   2-00100 / 543-6806
555 W BLUE LICK RD 40165
Glenn Gray, prin.
Hebron MS, 3300 E HEBRON LN 40165   3-00100 / 957-3540
John Rowland, prin.
Other Schools – See Mount Washington

Silver Grove, AC 606, PC 4, Campbell
Silver Grove ISD, 3RD ST 41085   2-11111 / 441-3873
Michael King, supt.
JSHS, 3RD & 4 MILE PK 41085   2-00111 / 441-3873
Ernie Matthews, prin.

Smithland, AC 502, PC 2, Livingston
Livingston County SD   4-11111 / 928-2111
PO BOX 219 42081
Lee Jones, supt.
Livingston Central HS   2-00011 / 928-2065
PO BOX 367 42081
John Counts, prin.
Other Schools – See Burna

Somerset, AC 606, PC 7, Pulaski
Pulaski County SD, PO BOX P 42502   6-11111 / 679-1123
Bert Minton, supt.
Pulaski County HS   4-00011 / 679-1574
511 E UNIVERSITY DR 42501
Michael Hicks, prin.
Southwestern Pulaski County HS   4-00011 / 678-9000
1765 WTLO RD 42501
G. Roberts, prin.
Northern MS, 350 OAKLEAF LN 42501   3-00100 / 678-5230
David Cothron, prin.
Southern MS   3-00100 / 679-6855
200 ENTERPRISE DR 42501
Bob Anderson, prin.

Somerset ISD, 305 COLLEGE ST 42501   4-11111 / 679-4451
Conley Manning, supt.
HS, COLLEGE ST 42501   3-00011 / 678-4721
Charles Eckler, prin.
Meece MS, 210 BARNETT ST 42501   2-00100 / 678-5821
Jack Keeney, prin.

Kentucky Tech Somerset Area Voc-Tech Sch   3-CS / 679-4303
230 AIRPORT RD 42501
Somerset Community College   4-CC / 679-8501
808 MONTICELLO ST 42501

South Shore, AC 606, PC 4, Greenup
Greenup County SD
Supt. — See Greenup
McKell MS, RR 1 BOX 245 41175   3-01100 / 932-3221
John Younce, prin.

Springfield, AC 606, PC 5, Washington
Washington County SD   4-11111 / 336-5470
PO BOX 192 40069
Jack Waff, supt.
Washington County JSHS   3-00111 / 336-5475
LINCOLN PARK ROAD 40069
William Hardin, prin.

Stanford, AC 606, PC 5, Lincoln
Lincoln County SD   5-11111 / 365-2124
PO BOX 265 40484
Bruce Johnson, supt.
Lincoln County HS   4-00011 / 365-9111
US HIGHWAY 27 40484
Larry Morgan, prin.
Lincoln County MS   3-00100 / 365-2124
US HIGHWAY 27 S 40484
Larry Woods, prin.

Stanton, AC 606, PC 5, Powell
Powell County SD   5-11111 / 663-3300
PO BOX 430 40380
James Potts, supt.
Powell County HS   3-00011 / 663-3320
PO BOX 488 40380
Lonnie Morris, prin.
Powell County MS   3-00100 / 663-3308
PO BOX 400 40380
Bill Rose, prin.

Stearns, AC 606, PC 4, McCreary
McCreary County SD   5-11111 / 376-2591
HC 69 BOX 24 42647
Eddie Brown, supt.
McCreary Central HS   3-00011 / 376-5051
RR 2 BOX 10A 42647
Bob Nelson, prin.
Other Schools – See Pine Knot, Whitley City

Taylor Mill, AC 606, PC 6, Kenton
Kenton County SD
Supt. — See Erlanger
Woodland MS   3-00100 / 356-7300
5399 OLD TAYLOR MILL RD 41015
Gary Jackson, prin.

Taylorsville, AC 502, PC 3, Spencer
Spencer County SD   4-11111 / 477-3250
PO BOX 339 40071
Bill Stout, supt.
Spencer County JSHS   3-00111 / 477-3255
PO BOX 849 40071
Murrell Lawson, prin.

Tollesboro, AC 606, PC 3, Lewis
Lewis County SD
Supt. — See Vanceburg
JSHS, PO BOX 1 41189   2-00111 / 798-2541
Jim Staton, prin.

Tompkinsville, AC 502, PC 5, Monroe
Monroe County SD   4-11111 / 487-5456
PO BOX 518 42167
James Graves, supt.
Monroe County HS   3-00011 / 487-6217
PO BOX 400 42167
Prentice Stanford, prin.
Monroe County MS   3-00100 / 487-9624
OLD MULKEY RD 42167
Larry Moore, prin.

Union, AC 606, PC 4, Boone
Boone County SD
Supt. — See Florence
Ryle JSHS   4-00111 / 384-3320
10379 US HIGHWAY 42 41091
Randall Cooper, prin.

Valley Station, AC 502, PC 7, Jefferson
Jefferson County SD
Supt. — See Louisville
Valley JSHS, 10200 DIXIE HWY 40272   4-00111 / 473-8339
Terry Shinkle, prin.
Frost MS, 13700 SANDRAY BLVD 40272   3-00100 / 473-8256
Joseph Vibbert, prin.
Stuart MS   4-00100 / 473-8334
4603 VALLEY STATION RD 40272
Stuart Watts, prin.

Beth Haven Christian S   2-11111 / 937-3516
5515 JOHNSONTOWN RD 40272
Roland Brown, prin.

Vanceburg, AC 606, PC 4, Lewis
Lewis County SD, PO BOX 159 41179   5-11111 / 796-2811
Michael Forman, supt.
Lewis County SHS, PO BOX 99 41179   2-00001 / 796-2823
John Cordle, prin.
Meade Vo Ed Ctr, PO BOX 130 41179   Vo Tech / 796-6106
Douglas Applegate, prin.
Lewis County JHS, PO BOX 69 41179   3-00110 / 796-6228
Jonna Bertram, prin.
Other Schools – See Tollesboro

Vancleve, AC 606, PC 2, Breathitt

Kentucky Mountain Bible College   2-CC / 666-5000
PO BOX 10 41385
Mt. Carmel HS, PO BOX 2 41385   2-11111 / 666-5008
Daniel Kinnell, prin.

Versailles, AC 606, PC 6, Woodford
Woodford County SD   5-11111 / 873-4701
131 MAPLE ST 40383
Jim Jackson, supt.
Woodford County HS   4-00011 / 873-5434
180 FRANKFORT ST 40383
Peter Lefaivre, prin.
Woodford County MS   3-00100 / 873-4721
130 MAPLE ST 40383
Roy Chapman, prin.

Vine Grove, AC 502, PC 5, Hardin
Hardin County SD
Supt. — See Elizabethtown
Alton MS   3-01100 / 877-2135
100 COUNTRY CLUB RD 40175
Gary King, prin.

Virgie, AC 606, PC 3, Pike
Pike County SD
Supt. — See Pikeville
MS, PO BOX 310 41572   2-00100 / 639-2774
Phillip Johnson, prin.

Walton, AC 606, PC 4, Boone
Walton-Verona ISD   3-11111 / 485-4181
PO BOX 167 41094
Robert Storer, supt.
Walton-Verona JSHS   2-00111 / 485-7721
35 HIGH SCHOOL RD 41094
William Boyle, prin.

Warfield, AC 606, PC 2, Martin
Martin County SD
Supt. — See Inez
MS, PO BOX 378 41267   2-00100 / 395-5900
Jack Cornette, prin.

Warsaw, AC 606, PC 4, Gallatin
Gallatin County SD, 110 W MAIN 41095   4-11111 / 567-2828
James Palm, supt.
Gallatin County HS   2-00011 / 567-5041
PO BOX 146 41095
Joe Payne, prin.
Gallatin County MS   2-00100 / 567-5791
PO BOX 149 41095
Debbie Foltz, prin.

West Liberty, AC 606, PC 4, Morgan
Morgan County SD   4-11111 / 743-3205
PO BOX 489 41472
James Earl Reed, supt.
Morgan County HS   3-00011 / 743-3705
PO BOX 606 41472
John Johnston, prin.
Morgan County MS   3-01100 / 743-7520
PO BOX 580 41472
Helen Pennington, prin.

West Paducah, AC 502, PC 2, McCracken
McCracken County SD
Supt. — See Paducah
Heath HS   3-00011 / 488-3126
4330 METROPOLIS LAKE RD 42086
Bill Bond, prin.
Heath MS   2-00100 / 488-3128
4330 METROPOLIS LAKE RD 42086
Vernon Edwards, prin.

Whitesburg, AC 606, PC 4, Letcher
Letcher County SD   5-11111 / 633-4455
PO BOX 788 41858
Jack Burkich, supt.

HS, 202 COLLEGE DR 41858   3-00011
 Edwin Holbrook, prin.   633-2339
MS, PARK ST 41858   2-00100
 Raymond Thomas, prin.   633-2761
 Other Schools – See Letcher, Neon

Whitesville, AC 502, PC 3, Daviess

Trinity HS   2-00011
 10510 MAIN CROSS ST 42378   233-5533
 John Calhoun, prin.

Whitley City, AC 606, PC 4, McCreary
McCreary County SD
 Supt. — See Stearns
MS, PO BOX 520 42653   2-00100
 Donald Douglas, prin.   376-5081

Williamsburg, AC 606, PC 6, Whitley
Whitley County SD, 116 N 4TH ST 40769   5-11111
 Lonnie Anderson, supt.   549-7000
Whitley County HS   4-00011
 350 BLEVARD OF CHAMPIONS RD 40769
 Kenneth Powell, prin.   549-7025

Whitley County MS   3-00100
 351 BLEVARD OF CHAMPIONS RD 40769
 Gary Perkins, prin.   549-7070

Williamsburg ISD, 1000 MAIN ST 40769   3-11111
 James Simpson, supt.   549-6047
JSHS, 1000 MAIN ST 40769   2-00111
 Jerry Hodges, prin.   549-6046

Cumberland College   4-UC
 6178 COLLEGE STATION DR 40769
  800-343-1609

Williamstown, AC 606, PC 5, Grant
Grant County SD, PO BOX 369 41097   5-11111
 James Gardner, supt.   824-3323
 Other Schools – See Dry Ridge

Williamstown ISD   3-11111
 300 HELTON ST 41097   824-7144
 Joe Gold, supt.
JSHS, 300 HELTON ST 41097   2-00111
 Mark Cooper, prin.   824-4421

Wilmore, AC 606, PC 5, Jessamine

Asbury College   4-UC
 1 MACKLEM DR 40390   858-3511
Asbury Theological Seminary   3-UC
 204 N LEXINGTON AVE 40390   800-227-2879

Winchester, AC 606, PC 7, Clark
Clark County SD   6-11111
 1600 W LEXINGTON AVE 40391   744-4545
 Donald Pace, supt.
Clark HS, 620 BOONE AVE 40391   4-00011
 Guy Strong, prin.   744-6111
Clark MS, 1 EDUCATIONAL PLZ 40391   3-00100
 Conard Young, prin.   744-0427
Conkwright MS   2-00100
 360 MOUNT STERLING RD 40391   744-8433
 Russell Bradt, prin.

Wurtland, AC 606, PC 4, Greenup
Greenup County SD
 Supt. — See Greenup
MS, 700 CENTER ST 41144   2-00100
 Roger Dillon, prin.   836-1023

LOUISIANA

STATE DEPARTMENT OF EDUCATION
P.O. Box 94064, Baton Rouge 70804
(504) 342-3602

Superintendent of Education	Raymond Arveson
Deputy Superintendent Education	Charles Smith
Deputy Superintendent Management & Finance	Marlyn Langley
Assistant Superintendent Research & Development	Mari Ann Fowler
Assistant Superintendent Educational Support Programs	Gayle Neal
Assistant Superintendent Vocational Education	Chris Strother
Assistant Superintendent Academic Programs	Moselle Dearbone
Assistant Superintendent Special Education Services	Leon Borne

STATE BOARD OF EDUCATION
P.O. Box 94064, Baton Rouge 70804

Executive Director   Carole Wallin

PUBLIC, PRIVATE AND CATHOLIC SECONDARY SCHOOLS

Abbeville, AC 318, PC 7, Vermilion
Vermilion Parish SD   6-11111
 PO BOX 520 70511   898-5766
 Daniel Dartez, supt.
HS, 1305 SENIOR HIGH DR 70510   3-00011
 Clarence Moss, prin.   893-1874
Williams MS, 1105 PRAIRIE AVE 70510   3-00100
 Jared Mula, prin.   893-3943
 Other Schools – See Erath, Gueydan, Kaplan, Maurice

Gulf Area Technical Institute   2-CS
 PO BOX 878 70511   893-4984
Vermillion Catholic HS   2-00011
 425 PARK AVE 70510   893-6636
 George Laird, prin.

Abita Springs, AC 504, PC 4, St. Tammany
St. Tammany Parish SD
 Supt. — See Covington
JHS, PO BOX 217 70420   2-01110
 Margaret Sharp, prin.   892-2070

Albany, AC 504, PC 3, Livingston
Livingston Parish SD
 Supt. — See Livingston
HS, PO BOX 1090 70711   2-00011
 Arthur Perkins, prin.   567-9319
MS, PO BOX 1210 70711   2-01100
 Janice Bernard, prin.   567-5231

Alexandria, AC 318, PC 8, Rapides
Rapides Parish SD   7-11111
 PO BOX 1230 71309   487-0888
 E. Nichols, supt.
HS, 800 OLA ST 71303   4-00011
 Aubrey Sanders, prin.   448-8234

Bolton HS, 2101 VANCE AVE 71301   4-00011
 Ron Akins, prin.   448-3628
Peabody Magnet HS   3-00011
 PO BOX 1151 71309   448-3457
 Dennis Frazier, prin.
JHS, 122 MARYLAND AVE 71301   3-00100
 Richard Ducote, prin.   445-5343
Brame JHS, 4800 DAWN ST 71301   3-00100
 Donald Holloway, prin.   443-3688
Jones Street JHS, PO BOX 2030 71309   2-00100
 Michael Vercher, prin.   445-6241
Kelso-Twin Cities JHS   1-00100
 4515 NEW YORK AVE 71302   442-6936
 Clifton Cowan, prin.
 Other Schools – See Buckeye, Elmer, Glenmora,
 Lecompte, Lena, Pineville, Tioga

Alexandria Regional Technical Institute   2-CS
 PO BOX 5698 71307   487-5443
Holy Savior Menard HS   2-00111
 4603 COLISEUM BLVD 71303   445-8233
 Sr. Janez Schonfeld, prin.
Louisiana Institute of Technology   2-CS
 3349 MASONIC DR 71301   442-1864
Louisiana State University at Alexandria   4-CC
 8100 HIGHWAY 71 S 71302   473-6413
Rapides General Hospital   2-HSP
 PO BOX 30101 71301   473-3100

Amite, AC 504, PC 5, Tangipahoa
Tangipahoa Parish SD   7-11111
 PO BOX 457 70422   748-7153
 Ted Cason, supt.
HS, 400 S LAUREL ST 70422   3-00011
 Ora Finn, prin.   748-9301

West Side MS, 409 W OAK ST 70422   3-01100
 Robert Williamson, prin.   748-9073
 Other Schools – See Hammond, Independence,
 Kentwood, Loranger, Ponchatoula, Tickfaw

Oak Forest Academy   2-11111
 600 WALNUT ST 70422   748-4222
 David Bass, prin.

Anacoco, AC 318, PC 3, Vernon
Vernon Parish SD
 Supt. — See Leesville
JSHS, PO BOX 230 71403   2-00111
 Norman Beason, prin.   239-3039

Angie, AC 504, PC 2, Washington
Washington Parish SD
 Supt. — See Franklinton
JHS, 64433 DIXON ST 70426   2-00100
 James Kennedy, prin.   986-3105

Arabi, AC 504, PC 6, St. Bernard
St. Bernard Parish SD
 Supt. — See Chalmette
Arabi Park MS   3-00100
 6801 N ROCHEBLAVE ST 70032   279-4424
 Kathleen Gonzales, prin.

Arcadia, AC 318, PC 5, Bienville
Bienville Parish SD   5-11111
 PO BOX 418 71001   263-9416
 William Britt, supt.
JSHS, 1700 DANIEL ST 71001   2-00111
 James Tilley, prin.   263-2264
 Other Schools – See Bienville, Castor, Gibsland,
 Ringgold, Saline

Arnaudville, AC 318, PC 4, St. Landry
St. Landry Parish SD
  Supt. — See Opelousas
  Beau Chene HS, RR 3 BOX 166 70512   3-00011
    Ronnie Daigle, prin.   662-5815

Athens, AC 318, PC 2, Claiborne
Claiborne Parish SD
  Supt. — See Homer
  S, RR 1 BOX 129A 71003   2-11111
    Bertrand Heckel, prin.   258-3241

  Mount Olive Christian S   2-11111
    RR 1 BOX 89 71003
    D. Carpenter, prin.   258-5661

Atlanta, AC 318, PC 2, Winn
Winn Parish SD
  Supt. — See Winnfield
  S, RR 1 BOX 38 71404   2-11111
    Archie Chandler, prin.   628-4613

Avondale, AC 504, PC 6, Jefferson
Jefferson Parish SD
  Supt. — See Harvey
  Ford JHS, 435 S JAMIE BLVD 70094   3-00110
    Curtis London, prin.   436-2474

Baker, AC 504, PC 7, East Baton Rouge
East Baton Rouge Parish SD
  Supt. — See Baton Rouge
  HS, 3200 GROOM RD 70714   4-00011
    Harry Ingalls, prin.   775-1259
  MS, 5903 GROOM RD 70714   3-00100
    Sherman Dyer, prin.   775-9750

  Bethany Christian S   2-11111
    13855 PLANK RD 70714   774-0133
    Matthew Avery, prin.
  Central Private S   3-11111
    12801 CENTERRA CT 70714   261-3341
    James Gardner, prin.

Basile, AC 318, PC 4, Evangeline
Evangeline Parish SD
  Supt. — See Ville Platte
  JSHS, PO BOX 666 70515   2-01111
    Johnny Jeans, prin.   432-5012

Baskin, AC 318, PC 2, Franklin
Franklin Parish SD
  Supt. — See Winnsboro
  S, PO BOX 698 71219   2-11111
    Madge Wilson, prin.   248-2381

Bastrop, AC 318, PC 7, Morehouse
Morehouse Parish SD
  PO BOX 872 71221   6-11111
    Michael Faulk, supt.   281-5784
  HS, 402 HIGHLAND AVE 71220   4-00011
    Rick Van Loon, prin.   281-0194
  MS, PO BOX 1021 71221   3-00100
    Hamp Lenoir, prin.   281-0776
  Other Schools – See Mer Rouge

  Bastrop Technical Institute   2-CS
    PO BOX 1120 71221   283-0836
  Prairie View Academy   2-11111
    9942 EDWIN ST 71220   281-7044
    James Brent, prin.

Baton Rouge, AC 504, PC 9, East Baton Rouge
East Baton Rouge Parish SD   8-11111
  PO BOX 2950 70821   922-5618
    Dr. Bernard Weiss, supt.
  HS, 2825 GOVERNMENT ST 70806   4-00011
    Lois Anne Sumrall, prin.   383-0520
  Belaire HS, 12121 TAMS DR 70815   4-00011
    Shelton Watts, prin.   272-1860
  Broadmoor HS   4-00011
    10100 GOODWOOD BLVD 70815   926-1420
    W. Bozant, prin.
  Capitol HS, 1000 N 23RD ST 70802   4-00011
    Lloyd Norwood, prin.   383-0353
  Central HS   4-00011
    10200 E BROOKSIDE DR 70818   261-3438
    Glen Gentry, prin.
  Glen Oaks HS   4-00011
    6650 CEDAR GROVE DR 70812   356-4306
    Kenneth Payne, prin.
  Istrouma HS   4-00011
    3730 WINBOURNE AVE 70805   355-7701
    Elisha Jackson, prin.
  Lee HS, 1105 LEE DR 70808   4-00011
    Jack Stokeld, prin.   383-7744
  McKinley HS   4-00011
    800 E MCKINLEY ST 70802   344-7696
    Charlie Thomas, prin.
  Scotlandville Magnet HS   4-00011
    9870 SCOTLAND AVE 70807   775-3715
    Freddie Williams, prin.
  Tara HS, 9002 WHITEHALL AVE 70806   4-00011
    Gary Blocker, prin.   927-6100
  Woodlawn HS   4-00011
    14939 TIGER BEND RD 70817   293-1200
    Paul Loup, prin.
  Southern University Lab School   2-11111
    PO BOX 9414 70813   771-3490
    Mattie Faye Spears, prin.
  University Lab School   3-11111
    LOUISIANA STATE UNIV 70803   388-3221
    James Fox, prin.

Arlington Vo Ctr   Vo Tech
  807 DEAN LEE DR 70820   766-8188
  Gwen Bruton, prin.
Broadmoor MS, 1225 SHARP RD 70815   3-00100
  George Williams, prin.   272-0540
Capitol MS   3-00100
  4200 GUS YOUNG AVE 70802   344-7956
  Ollie Brown, prin.
Central MS, 11526 SULLIVAN RD 70818   3-00100
  Earl Phillips, prin.   261-2237
Crestworth MS, 10650 AVENUE F 70807   3-00100
  James Williams, prin.   775-6845
Glasgow MS   3-00100
  1676 GLASGOW AVE 70808   925-2942
  Daniel Landry, prin.
Glen Oaks MS   3-00100
  5300 MONARCH AVE 70811   357-3790
  Derrell Hill, prin.
Istrouma Magnet MS   4-00100
  2500 ERIE ST 70805   357-6464
  Mary Blunschi, prin.
Kenilworth MS, 7600 BOONE AVE 70808   3-00100
  Gerard Scallan, prin.   766-8111
McKinley Magnet MS   4-00100
  1557 MCCALOP ST 70802   388-0089
  Josie Williams, prin.
Park Forest MS, 3760 ALETHA DR 70814   3-00100
  Sherry Berry, prin.   275-6650
Prescott MS, 4055 PRESCOTT RD 70805   4-00100
  Anna Bernard, prin.   357-6481
Scotlandville MS   2-00100
  9147 ELMGROVE GARDEN DR 70807   775-1688
  Willie Phillips, prin.
Sherwood MS   3-00100
  1020 MARLBROOK DR 70815   272-3090
  Darryl Morris, prin.
Southeast MS   3-00100
  15000 S HARRELLS FERRY RD 70816   293-5930
  Richard Day, prin.
Westdale MS, 5650 CLAYCUT RD 70806   3-00100
  M. Pitts, prin.   924-1308
Other Schools – See Baker, Zachary

Special School District 1   3-00000
  PO BOX 94064 70804   342-1508
  Leonard Hayes, supt.

Baton Rouge General Medical Center   HSP
  PO BOX 2511 70821   387-7623
Baton Rouge School of Computers   3-CC
  9255 INTERLINE AVE 70809   923-2525
Baton Rouge Technical Institute   2-CS
  3250 N ACADIAN THRUWAY E 70805   359-9201
Bishop Sullivan HS   3-00011
  17521 MONITOR AVE 70817   753-9782
  Joseph Scimeca, prin.
Camelot Career College   2-CS
  2618 WOODDALE BLVD 70805   928-3005
Catholic HS   3-00111
  855 HEARTHSTONE DR 70806   383-0397
  Gregory Brandao, prin.
Chapel Trafton S   2-11111
  11111 ROY EMERSON DR 70810   767-7097
  Kenneth Worsham, prin.
Christian Life Academy   3-11111
  2037 QUAIL DR 70808   769-6760
  Larry Perdue, prin.
Commercial College of Baton Rouge   4-CS
  5677 FLORIDA BLVD STE 210 70806
    927-3470
Culinary Arts Institute of Louisiana   2-CS
  427 LAFAYETTE ST 70802   343-6233
Delta Junior College   4-CC
  7290 EXCHANGE PL 70806   927-7780
Diesel Driving Academy   1-CS
  8136 AIRLINE HWY 70815
Divine Guidance S   2-11111
  3617 LANIER DR 70814   926-9722
  Glenda Colbert, prin.
Domestic Health Care Institute   2-CS
  4826 JAMESTOWN AVE 70808   925-5312
Earl K. Long Memorial Hospital   HSP
  5825 AIRLINE HWY 70805   358-1002
Episcopal HS   3-01111
  3200 WOODLAND RIDGE BLVD 70816   753-3180
  Paul Hancock, prin.
Family Christian Academy   2-11111
  9119 WORLD MINISTRY AVE 70810   768-2838
  William Wheeler, prin.
Hosanna Christian Academy   2-11111
  8850 GOODWOOD BLVD 70806   926-4800
  David Patterson, prin.
Insurance Achievement   1-HMS
  7330 HIGHLAND RD 70808
International Technical Institute   2-CC
  13944 AIRLINE HWY 70817   752-4233
Jimmy Swaggart Bible College & Seminary   2-UC
  PO BOX 38000 70828
Louisiana Art Institute   2-CS
  7380 EXCHANGE PL 70806   928-7770
Louisiana School/Visually Impaired   HND
  PO BOX 4328 70821
Louisiana State School for the Deaf   HND
  PO BOX 3074 70821
Louisiana State University & A & M Coll.   8-UC
  LOUISIANA STATE UNIV 70803   388-1175
Our Lady of the Lake Medical Center   HSP
  5000 HENNESSY BLVD 70808   769-7799
Parkview Baptist S   4-11111
  PO BOX 45212 70895   293-2820
  Alexander Ward, prin.

Redemptorist HS   2-00111
  4000 SAINT GERARD AVE 70805   357-0936
  John Fabre, prin.
Runnels S   2-11111
  17255 S HARRELLS FERRY RD 70816   751-5712
  L. Runnels, prin.
St. Isadore MS, 6380 HOOPER RD 70811   2-00100
  Mary Kelly, prin.   355-6730
St. Josephs Academy   3-00011
  3015 BROUSSARD ST 70808   383-7207
  Sr. Judith Brun, prin.
Southern University A&M College   6-UC
  SOUTHERN UNIVERSITY 70813   771-2430
Starkey Academy, 10510 JOOR RD 70818   2-11111
  Carol Haar, prin.   261-1390
Temple Christian S   2-11111
  7513 PRESCOTT RD 70812   356-3242
  Bob Burnett, prin.

Bell City, AC 318, PC 2, Calcasieu
Calcasieu Parish SD
  Supt. — See Lake Charles
  S, PO BOX 100 70630   2-11111
    Roy Blanchette, prin.   622-3210

Belle Chasse, AC 504, PC 6, Plaquemines
Plaquemines Parish SD
  Supt. — See Port Sulphur
  S, 8346 HIGHWAY 23 70037   4-10011
    Sara Lott, prin.   394-2810
  MS, 13476 HIGHWAY 23 70037   2-01100
    Monica Wertz, prin.   656-2315

Belle Rose, AC 504, PC 3, Assumption
Assumption Parish SD
  Supt. — See Napoleonville
  MS, PO BOX 129 70341   2-01100
    Harding Anderson, prin.   473-8917

Benton, AC 318, PC 4, Bossier
Bossier Parish SD
  PO BOX 2000 71006   7-11111
    W. Lewis, supt.   965-2281
  JSHS, PO BOX 719 71006   3-00111
    Kent Seabaugh, prin.   965-2346
  Other Schools – See Bossier City, Elm Grove,
    Haughton, Plain Dealing, Princeton

Bernice, AC 318, PC 4, Union
Union Parish SD
  Supt. — See Farmerville
  S, PO BOX 570 71222   2-10011
    Robert Harkins, prin.   285-7606

Berwick, AC 504, PC 5, St. Mary
St. Mary Parish SD
  Supt. — See Centerville
  HS, 700 PATTIE DR 70342   2-00011
    Ludness Henry, prin.   384-8450
  JHS, 3010 HIGHWAY 182 70342   2-00100
    Stanley Beaubouef, prin.   384-5665

Bienville, AC 318, PC 2, Bienville
Bienville Parish SD
  Supt. — See Arcadia
  S, PO BOX 106 71008   2-11111
    Charles Cage, prin.   385-7591

Bogalusa, AC 504, PC 7, Washington
Bogalusa City SD, PO BOX 310 70429   5-11111
  Sue Magee-Tullos, supt.   735-1392
  HS, PO BOX 580 70429   4-00011
    Gary Magee, prin.   735-8161
  JHS, 1403 NORTH AVE 70427   3-00100
    James Raborn, prin.   732-3706

  Sullivan Technical Institute   2-CS
    1710 SULLIVAN DR 70427   732-6640

Boothville, AC 504, PC 5, Plaquemines
Plaquemines Parish SD
  Supt. — See Port Sulphur
  Boothville-Venice S   3-11111
    40139 HIGHWAY 23 70038   534-7520
    Laverne Duncan, prin.

Bossier City, AC 318, PC 8, Bossier
Bossier Parish SD
  Supt. — See Benton
  Airline HS, 2801 AIRLINE DR 71111   4-00011
    D. C. Machen, prin.   746-3558
  Bossier HS, 700 COLEMAN AVE 71111   3-00011
    Richard Concilio, prin.   222-9424
  Parkway HS, 4301 PANTHER DR 71112   3-00011
    Bettye McCauley, prin.   746-1430
  Bossier Career Ctr, 1518 COX ST 71111   Vo Tech
    Jesse Coleman, prin.   742-0809
  Cope MS, 4814 SHED RD 71111   2-00100
    Timothy Gilbert, prin.   742-1730
  Greenacres MS, 2220 AIRLINE DR 71111   3-00100
    Clay Bohanan, prin.   746-2635
  Rusheon JHS   3-00100
    2401 OLD MINDEN RD 71112   746-8106
    Wayne Earp, prin.

  Bossier Parish Community College   4-CC
    2719 AIRLINE DR 71111   746-9851
  Coastal College   2-CS
    5520 INDUSTRIAL DRIVE EXT 71112

Bourg, AC 504, PC 4, Terrebonne
Terrebonne Parish SD
  Supt. — See Houma

South Terrebone HS   4-00011
PO BOX 640   70343   868-7850
Gerald Picou, prin.

Boutte, AC 504, PC 4, St. Charles
St. Charles Parish SD
  Supt. — See Luling
Hahnville HS, 200 TIGER DR   70039   4-00011
Bobby Stephenson, prin.   758-7537

Braithwaite, AC 504, PC 1, Plaquemines
Plaquemines Parish SD
  Supt. — See Port Sulphur
Phoenix S   2-11111
  13073 HIGHWAY 15   70040   333-4573
  John Barthelemy, prin.

Lynn Oaks S, 1 LYNN OAKS DR   70040   2-11111
Carol Nunez, prin.   682-3171

Breaux Bridge, AC 318, PC 6, St. Martin
St. Martin Parish SD
  Supt. — See Saint Martinville
HS   3-00011
  1015 BRUX BRIDGE SR HIGH RD   70517
  Ronnie Dore, prin.   332-3131
JHS, 100 MARTIN ST   70517   2-00100
John Beazley, prin.   332-2844

Broussard, AC 318, PC 5, Lafayette
Lafayette Parish SD
  Supt. — See Lafayette
MS, 1325 S MORGAN AVE   70518   3-01100
Jim Rabalais, prin.   837-9031

Brusly, AC 504, PC 4, West Baton Rouge
West Baton Rouge Parish SD
  Supt. — See Port Allen
HS, 630 FRONTAGE RD   70719   2-00011
Frank Hannan, prin.   749-2815
MS, 601 N KIRKLAND ST   70719   3-01100
Jerry Lowe, prin.   749-3123

Buckeye, AC 318, PC 1, Rapides
Rapides Parish SD
  Supt. — See Alexandria
JSHS, GENERAL DELIVERY   71328   3-00111
Clark Yates, prin.   466-5678

Bunkie, AC 318, PC 6, Avoyelles
Avoyelles Parish SD
  Supt. — See Marksville
HS, RR 1 BOX 3   71322   3-00011
Thomas Roy, prin.   346-6216
MS, PO BOX 470   71322   3-00100
Leon Holts, prin.   346-7227

Buras, AC 504, PC 5, Plaquemines
Plaquemines Parish SD
  Supt. — See Port Sulphur
S, 35655 HIGHWAY 11   70041   4-11011
Stanley Gaudet, prin.   657-9435
MS, 34158 HIGHWAY 11   70041   2-00100
Carmen Ingraham, prin.   657-7721

Cade, AC 318, PC 2, St. Martin

Episcopal S of Acadiana   2-00111
PO BOX 380   70519   365-1416
Hiram Goza, prin.

Calhoun, AC 318, PC 2, Ouachita
Ouachita Parish SD
  Supt. — See Monroe
Calhoun MS, PO BOX 30   71225   2-00100
Don Coker, prin.   644-2616

Calvin, AC 318, PC 2, Winn
Winn Parish SD
  Supt. — See Winnfield
S, PO BOX 80   71410   2-11111
Lanis Carpenter, prin.   727-8784

Cameron, AC 318, PC 4, Cameron
Cameron Parish SD, PO BOX W   70631   4-11111
Thomas McCall, supt.   775-5784
Johnson Bayou S   2-11111
  HC 69 BOX 232   70631   569-2138
  Charles Vining, prin.
Other Schools – See Creole, Hackberry, Lake Charles

Campti, AC 318, PC 3, Natchitoches
Natchitoches Parish SD
  Supt. — See Natchitoches
Lakeview JSHS, PO BOX 200   71411   3-00111
James Guin, prin.   476-3360

Carencro, AC 318, PC 6, Lafayette
Lafayette Parish SD
  Supt. — See Lafayette
MS, 4301 SAINT JOSEPH ST   70520   3-01100
William Butcher, prin.   896-6127

Castor, AC 318, PC 2, Bienville
Bienville Parish SD
  Supt. — See Arcadia
S, PO BOX 69   71016   2-11111
Danny Gour, prin.   544-7271

Cecilia, AC 318, PC 3, St. Martin
St. Martin Parish SD
  Supt. — See Saint Martinville
HS, PO BOX 360   70521   3-00011
Eric Castille, prin.   667-6145
JHS, PO BOX 129   70521   2-00100
Joseph Jarreau, prin.   667-6226

Centerville, AC 318, PC 3, St. Mary
St. Mary Parish SD   7-11111
  PO BOX 170   70522   836-9661
  Steve Gauthier, supt.
S, PO BOX 59   70522   3-11111
  Robert McDonald, prin.   836-5103
Other Schools – See Berwick, Franklin, Morgan City, Patterson

Chalmette, AC 504, PC 8, St. Bernard
St. Bernard Parish SD   6-11111
  67 E CHALMETTE CIR   70043   271-2533
  Daniel Daste, supt.
HS, 1100 E JUDGE PEREZ DR   70043   3-00011
  Wayne Warner, prin.   271-4506
Jackson Fundamental HS   4-00011
  201 8TH ST   70043 – Kathy Boyd, prin.   279-5238
MS, 75 E CHALMETTE CIR   70043   3-00100
  Sam Boyd, prin.   271-3414
Other Schools – See Arabi, Meraux, Saint Bernard

Nunez Community College   4-CS
  3700 LA FONTAINE ST   70043   278-7440
St. Bernard Parish Community College   3-CC
  2500 PALMISANO BLVD   70043   277-1142

Chataignier, AC 318, PC 2, Evangeline
Evangeline Parish SD
  Supt. — See Ville Platte
JSHS, PO BOX 189   70524   2-01111
  Warren Young, prin.   885-3173

Chatham, AC 318, PC 3, Jackson
Jackson Parish SD
  Supt. — See Jonesboro
JSHS, PO BOX 37   71226   2-00111
  Terry Hayden, prin.   249-2115

Chauvin, AC 504, PC 5, Terrebonne
Terrebonne Parish SD
  Supt. — See Houma
Lacache MS   3-01100
  5266 HIGHWAY 56   70344   594-3945
  Mark Trosclair, prin.

Choudrant, AC 318, PC 3, Lincoln
Lincoln Parish SD
  Supt. — See Ruston
JSHS, PO BOX 220   71227   2-00111
  Ronald Crawford, prin.   768-2542

Church Point, AC 318, PC 5, Acadia
Acadia Parish SD
  Supt. — See Crowley
HS, 305 E LOUGARRE ST   70525   3-00011
  Ronald Doguet, prin.   684-5472
MS   2-01100
  340 W MARTIN LUTHER KING DR   70525
  C. Michael Doughty, prin.   684-6381

Clinton, AC 504, PC 4, East Feliciana
East Feliciana Parish SD   5-11111
  PO BOX 397   70722   683-8277
  Perry Spears, supt.
HS, PO BOX 426   70722   2-00011
  John Harris, prin.   683-3321
MS, 12126 LIBERTY ST   70722   2-01100
  James Sensley, prin.   683-5267
Other Schools – See Jackson

Silliman Institute, PO BOX 946   70722   2-11111
H. Polk, prin.   683-5383

Colfax, AC 318, PC 4, Grant
Grant Parish SD, PO BOX 208   71417   5-11111
James Lemoine, supt.   627-3274
Other Schools – See Dry Prong, Georgetown, Montgomery

Columbia, AC 318, PC 2, Caldwell
Caldwell Parish SD   4-11111
  PO BOX 1019   71418   649-2689
  James Turner, supt.
Caldwell Parish HS   3-00011
  102 SCHOOL LOOP   71418   649-2750
  Marshall Davis, prin.
Caldwell Parish JHS   2-00100
  103 SCHOOL LOOP   71418   649-2340
  Don Davis, prin.

Converse, AC 318, PC 2, Sabine
Sabine Parish SD
  Supt. — See Many
S, PO BOX 10   71419   2-11111
  Larry Patrick, prin.   567-2673

Cottonport, AC 318, PC 5, Avoyelles

Avoyelles Technical Institute   2-CS
PO BOX 307   71327   876-2401

Cotton Valley, AC 318, PC 4, Webster
Webster Parish SD
  Supt. — See Minden
S, PO BOX 457   71018   3-11111
Dan Stanford, prin.   832-4769

Coushatta, AC 318, PC 4, Red River
Red River Parish SD   4-11111
  PO BOX 350   71019   932-4081
  Wiley Cole, supt.
HS, 915 E CARROL ST   71019   2-00011
  Laurine Adcock, prin.   932-4913
Martin S, RR 2 BOX 2340   71019   2-11111
  Kathy Thomas, prin.   932-5663

Springville JHS, RR 5 BOX 563   71019   2-01100
Luther Myers, prin.   932-5265
Other Schools – See Hall Summit

Covington, AC 504, PC 6, St. Tammany
St. Tammany Parish SD   8-11111
  PO BOX 940   70434   892-2276
  Terry Bankston, supt.
SHS, 838   70434   4-00001
  Catherine Boesch, prin.   892-3422
Pitcher JHS   3-00110
  415 S JEFFERSON AVE   70433   892-3021
  Nancy Woods, prin.
Other Schools – See Abita Springs, Folsom, Lacombe, Madisonville, Mandeville, Pearl River, Slidell

Delta Junior College   2-CC
100 COVINGTON CTR STE 30   70433
   892-5332
Northlake Christian S   2-11111
70104 WOLVERINE DR   70433   892-2683
  Michael Cagley, prin.
St. Pauls S, PO BOX 928   70434   3-00111
Br. Billiard, prin.   892-3200
St. Scholastica Academy   2-00111
122 S MASSACHUSETTS ST   70433   892-2540
  Marguerite Celestin, prin.

Creole, AC 318, PC 2, Cameron
Cameron Parish SD
  Supt. — See Cameron
South Cameron JSHS   2-00111
  PO BOX 10   70632   542-4628
  Dennis Batts, prin.

Crowley, AC 318, PC 7, Acadia
Acadia Parish SD, PO BOX 309   70527   7-11111
Bob Stringer, supt.   783-3664
HS, RR 2 BOX 300   70526   3-00011
  Eric Stutes, prin.   783-5313
MS, 401 W NORTHERN AVE   70526   3-00100
  Roderick Lafosse, prin.   783-5305
Other Schools – See Church Point, Iota, Midland, Rayne

Acadian Technical Institute   2-CS
PO BOX 820   70527   788-7521
Notre Dame HS   2-00011
910 N EASTERN AVE   70526   783-3519
  John Dailey, prin.

Crowville, AC 318, PC 2, Franklin
Franklin Parish SD
  Supt. — See Winnsboro
S, PO BOX 128   71230   2-11111
Shelton Kavalir, prin.   722-3244

Delcambre, AC 318, PC 4, Iberia
Iberia Parish SD
  Supt. — See New Iberia
JSHS, 601 W MAIN ST   70528   2-00111
Mary Saunier, prin.   685-2595

Delhi, AC 318, PC 5, Richland
Richland Parish SD
  Supt. — See Rayville
HS, 710 MAIN ST   71232   2-00011
  William Calvert, prin.   878-2235
JHS, 107 TOOMBS ST   71232   3-01100
  Leonard Guine, prin.   878-3748

Denham Springs, AC 504, PC 6, Livingston
Livingston Parish SD
  Supt. — See Livingston
HS, 1000 N RANGE AVE   70726   4-00011
  Joseph Wax, prin.   665-8851
JHS, 940 N RANGE AVE   70726   3-00100
  Wade Smith, prin.   665-8898
Southside JHS, PO BOX 907   70727   3-00100
  Thomas Cothern, prin.   664-4221

Community Christian Academy   2-11111
400 RIVER RD   70726   665-5696
  Joyce Wilson, prin.

Dequincy, AC 318, PC 5, Calcasieu
Calcasieu Parish SD
  Supt. — See Lake Charles
HS, 207 N OVERTON ST   70633   2-00011
  David Paine, prin.   786-5251
MS, 1603 W 4TH ST   70633   2-00100
  James Burnham, prin.   786-3000

Deridder, AC 318, PC 6, Beauregard
Beauregard Parish SD   6-11111
  PO BOX 938   70634   463-5551
  F. Brewer, supt.
HS, PO BOX 1090   70634   3-00011
  Stan Levy, prin.   463-3266
East Beauregard S   3-11111
  HC 64 BOX 61   70634   328-7511
  L. Spears, prin.
JHS, 415 N FRUSHA DR   70634   3-00100
  Hayward Steele, prin.   463-9083
Other Schools – See Fields, Longville, Merryville, Singer

Destrehan, AC 504, PC 6, St. Charles
St. Charles Parish SD
  Supt. — See Luling
HS, 1 WILDCAT LN   70047   4-00011
  John Walker, prin.   764-9946
Hurst MS, 170 ROAD RUNNER LN   70047   3-00100
  Henry Shepard, prin.   764-6367

Dodson, AC 318, PC 2, Winn
Winn Parish SD
Supt. — See Winnfield
S, PO BOX 97 71422   2-11111
Charles Fox, prin.   628-2172

Donaldsonville, AC 504, PC 6, Ascension
Ascension Parish SD   7-11111
PO BOX 189 70346   473-7981
Ralph Ricardo, supt.
HS, 100 TIGER DR 70346   3-00011
Emile Chiquet, prin.   474-2730
Lowery MS, PO BOX 311 70346   3-00100
Jesse Sanders, prin.   474-2760
Other Schools – See Geismar, Gonzales, Prairieville,
Saint Amant

Ascension Catholic S   3-11111
311 SAINT VINCENT ST 70346   473-9227
Jordan Roy, prin.

Downsville, AC 318, PC 2, Union
Union Parish SD
Supt. — See Farmerville
S, PO BOX 8 71234   2-11111
J. Lazenby, prin.   982-5318

Doyline, AC 318, PC 3, Webster
Webster Parish SD
Supt. — See Minden
JSHS, PO BOX 657 71023   2-00111
James Stewart, prin.   745-3673

Dry Prong, AC 318, PC 2, Grant
Grant Parish SD
Supt. — See Colfax
Grant HS, PO BOX 249 71423   3-00011
Dr. Joseph May, prin.   899-3331
JHS, PO BOX 147 71423   2-00100
Jerrell Paige, prin.   899-5697

Dubach, AC 318, PC 3, Lincoln
Lincoln Parish SD
Supt. — See Ruston
JSHS, PO BOX 158 71235   2-00111
Howard Brown, prin.   777-3470

Dubberly, AC 318, PC 2, Webster
Webster Parish SD
Supt. — See Minden
Central JHS, RR 1 BOX 660 71024   2-00100
Halven Carodine, prin.   377-2591

Duson, AC 318, PC 4, Lafayette
Lafayette Parish SD
Supt. — See Lafayette
Judice MS, 2645 S FIELDSPAN RD 70529   3-01100
Robert Adamson, prin.   984-1250

East Point, AC 318, PC 2, Red River

Riverdale Academy, PO BOX 4 71025   2-11111
Ernest Morgan, prin.   932-5876

Edgard, AC 504, PC 3, St. John The Baptist
St. John The Baptist Parish SD
Supt. — See Reserve
West St. John JSHS   2-00111
PO BOX 66 70049   497-3271
Leroy Keller, prin.

Elizabeth, AC 318, PC 2, Allen
Allen Parish SD
Supt. — See Oberlin
S, PO BOX 580 70638   2-11111
Larry Crawford, prin.   634-5341

Elmer, AC 318, PC 1, Rapides
Rapides Parish SD
Supt. — See Alexandria
Oak Hill HS   3-00011
7362 HIGHWAY 112 71424   793-2014
John Francis, prin.

Elm Grove, AC 318, PC 2, Bossier
Bossier Parish SD
Supt. — See Benton
MS, PO BOX 108 71051   3-00100
Robert Marlow, prin.   747-1975

Elton, AC 318, PC 4, Jefferson Davis
Jefferson Davis Parish SD
Supt. — See Jennings
JSHS, PO BOX 429 70532   2-00111
Robert Daigle, prin.   584-2991

Enterprise, AC 318, PC 2, Catahoula
Catahoula Parish SD
Supt. — See Jonesville
S, PO BOX 100 71425   2-11111
John Bartmess, prin.   744-5488

Epps, AC 318, PC 3, West Carroll
West Carroll Parish SD
Supt. — See Oak Grove
S, PO BOX 277 71237   2-11111
Donald Gwin, prin.   926-3624

Erath, AC 318, PC 4, Vermilion
Vermilion Parish SD
Supt. — See Abbeville
HS, 808 S BROADWAY ST 70533   2-00011
Garlyn Landry, prin.   937-8451
MS, 808 S BROADWAY ST 70533   3-01100
Ebrar Reaux, prin.   937-4441

Eunice, AC 318, PC 7, St. Landry
St. Landry Parish SD
Supt. — See Opelousas
HS, PO BOX 231 70535   3-00011
David Greer, prin.   457-3011
Eunice Vo Ed Ctr   Vo Tech
PO BOX 1127 70535   457-8686
Mike Corrigan, prin.
JHS, 900 W OAK AVE 70535   3-00100
Fred Alfred, prin.   457-7386

Louisiana State University at Eunice   4-CC
PO BOX 1129 70535   457-7311
St. Edmund HS   2-00111
351 W MAGNOLIA AVE 70535   457-2592
Harry Summerlin, prin.

Evans, AC 318, PC 2, Vernon
Vernon Parish SD
Supt. — See Leesville
S, PO BOX 67 70639   2-11111
William Carver, prin.   286-5289

Farmerville, AC 318, PC 5, Union
Union Parish SD, PO BOX 308 71241   5-11111
Malvin Sistrunk, supt.   368-9715
HS, 202 ANTHONY ST 71241   3-00011
Gary Walsworth, prin.   368-2661
MS, RR 3 BOX 269 71241   3-01100
Stephen Richardson, prin.   368-9542
Other Schools – See Bernice, Downsville, Lillie,
Marion, Spearsville

North Central Area Technical Institute   1-CS
PO BOX 548 71241   368-3179

Fenton, AC 318, PC 2, Jefferson Davis
Jefferson Davis Parish SD
Supt. — See Jennings
S, PO BOX 250 70640   2-11111
David Clayton, prin.   756-2326

Ferriday, AC 318, PC 5, Concordia
Concordia Parish SD
Supt. — See Vidalia
HS, 801 N EE WALLACE BLVD 71334   3-00011
Fred Butcher, prin.   757-8626
JHS, PO BOX 672 71334   2-00100
Howard Jackson, prin.   757-8695

Concordia Technical Institute   2-CS
PO BOX 152 71334   757-6501
Huntington S, 300 LYNWOOD DR 71334   2-11111
Gerald Horn, prin.   757-4515

Fields, AC 318, PC 1, Beauregard
Beauregard Parish SD
Supt. — See Deridder
Hyatt S, HC 63 BOX 221 70653   2-11111
Zack Shirley, prin.   786-6722

Florien, AC 318, PC 3, Sabine
Sabine Parish SD
Supt. — See Many
JSHS, PO BOX 70 71429   2-00111
Ivan Harless, prin.   586-3681

Folsom, AC 504, PC 2, St. Tammany
St. Tammany Parish SD
Supt. — See Covington
JHS, PO BOX F 70437   2-00110
Clemeal Harry, prin.   796-3724

Forest, AC 318, PC 2, West Carroll
West Carroll Parish SD
Supt. — See Oak Grove
S, PO BOX 368 71242   2-11111
Henry Butler, prin.   428-3672

Fort Necessity, AC 318, PC 2, Franklin
Franklin Parish SD
Supt. — See Winnsboro
S, HC 62 BOX 1 71243   2-11111
Leo Thornhill, prin.   723-4793

Franklin, AC 318, PC 6, St. Mary
St. Mary Parish SD
Supt. — See Centerville
HS, 1401 CYNTHIA ST 70538   4-00011
Charles Middleton, prin.   828-0143
JHS, 525 MORRIS ST 70538   3-00100
Michael Parrie, prin.   828-0855

Hanson Memorial HS   2-00111
903 ANDERSON ST 70538   828-3487
Wayne Coleman, prin.

Franklinton, AC 504, PC 5, Washington
Washington Parish SD   6-11111
PO BOX 587 70438   839-3436
Earle Brown, supt.
HS, 1 DEMON CIR 70438   3-00011
Michael Henley, prin.   839-6781
Pine S, 27164 HIGHWAY 62 70438   3-11011
Edward Deas, prin.   848-5243
Franklinton Vo Career Ctr   Vo Tech
616 T W BARKER DR 70438   839-6621
Robert Johnson, prin.
JHS, 617 MAIN ST 70438   3-00100
Beverly Ann Young, prin.   839-3501
Other Schools – See Angie, Mount Hermon, Varnado

Bowling Green S   2-11111
700 VARNADO ST 70438   839-5317
Lewis Murray, prin.

French Settlement, AC 504, PC 3, Livingston
Livingston Parish SD
Supt. — See Livingston
JSHS, 15875 LA HIGHWAY 16 70733   2-00111
Daniel Amond, prin.   698-3561

Galliano, AC 504, PC 5, Lafourche
Lafourche Parish SD
Supt. — See Thibodaux
South Lafourche SHS   3-00001
PO BOX 160 70354   632-5721
Lloyd Guidry, prin.

Geismar, AC 504, PC 2, Ascension
Ascension Parish SD
Supt. — See Donaldsonville
Dutchtown MS   3-01100
13078 HIGHWAY 73 70734   621-2355
Donald Songy, prin.

Georgetown, AC 318, PC 2, Grant
Grant Parish SD
Supt. — See Colfax
S, PO BOX 66 71432   2-11111
Tommy Brumley, prin.   827-5306

Gibsland, AC 318, PC 4, Bienville
Bienville Parish SD
Supt. — See Arcadia
Gibsland-Coleman S   2-11111
PO BOX 70 71028   843-6247
Arthur Smith, prin.

Gilbert, AC 318, PC 3, Franklin
Franklin Parish SD
Supt. — See Winnsboro
S, PO BOX 900 71336   2-11111
Gary Barton, prin.   435-5961

Glenmora, AC 318, PC 4, Rapides
Rapides Parish SD
Supt. — See Alexandria
JSHS, PO BOX 697 71433   2-00111
James McArthur, prin.   748-8145
Plainview S, PO BOX 1057 71433   2-11111
Calvin Johnson, prin.   634-5944

Golden Meadow, AC 504, PC 4, Lafourche
Lafourche Parish SD
Supt. — See Thibodaux
JHS, 630 S BAYOU DR 70357   2-00110
Harold Adams, prin.   475-7314

Gonzales, AC 504, PC 6, Ascension
Ascension Parish SD
Supt. — See Donaldsonville
East Ascension JSHS   4-00111
612 E WORTHY ST 70737   621-2400
Wilmon Little, prin.
MS, 1502 W ORICE ROTH RD 70737   3-01100
William Pittman, prin.   621-2505

Grambling, AC 318, PC 6, Lincoln
Lincoln Parish SD
Supt. — See Ruston
Grambling State University Lab. HS   2-00011
407 CENTRAL AVE 71245   274-2341
Clarence Kennedy, prin.
Grambling State University MS   2-00100
407 CENTRAL AVE 71245   274-2341
Vicki Brown, prin.

Grambling State University   6-UC
PO BOX 607 71245   274-2435

Grand Cane, AC 318, PC 2, De Soto

Central School, PO BOX 71 71032   2-11111
William Buck, prin.   858-3319

Grand Coteau, AC 318, PC 4, St. Landry

Academy of the Sacred Heart   2-11111
PO BOX 310 70541   662-5275
Sr. Carol Haggarty, prin.

Grand Isle, AC 504, PC 4, Jefferson
Jefferson Parish SD
Supt. — See Harvey
S, PO BOX 995 70358   2-11111
Richard Augustin, prin.   787-2577

Grant, AC 318, PC 1, Allen
Allen Parish SD
Supt. — See Oberlin
Fairview S, PO BOX 91 70644   2-11111
Richard Gallien, prin.   634-5354

Gray, AC 504, PC 4, Terrebonne
Terrebonne Parish SD
Supt. — See Houma
Bourgeois HS   4-00011
1 RESERVATION DR 70359   872-3277
Luther Fletcher, prin.
Price Vo S, PO BOX 1267 70359   Vo Tech
Glen Breerwood, prin.   868-3105

Greensburg, AC 504, PC 3, St. Helena
St. Helena Parish SD   4-11111
PO BOX 540 70441   222-6106
Myrtie Wofford, supt.

St. Helena Central HS — 2-00011
  PO BOX 490 70441 — 222-4402
  Charles Taylor, prin.
St. Helena Central MS — 3-01000
  RR 2 BOX 22 70441 — 222-6291
  Willie Johnson, prin.

Florida Parishes Technical Institute — 2-CS
  PO BOX 130 70441 — 222-4251

Gretna, AC 504, PC 7, Jefferson
Jefferson Parish SD
  Supt. — See Harvey
  JHS, 910 GRETNA BLVD 70053 — 4-00110
    Feleciano Mendoza, prin. — 366-0120
  Livaudais JHS, 925 LAMAR AVE 70056 — 3-00110
    Paul Dumas, prin. — 393-7544

Archbishop Blenk HS — 2-00011
  17 GRETNA BLVD 70053 — 367-2626
  David Pooley, prin.
Jefferson College — 2-CS
  12 WESTBANK EXPY 70053 — 362-5787
Randazzo Vocational Training Institute — 2-CS
  125 LAFAYETTE ST 70053 — 366-5409

Gueydan, AC 318, PC 4, Vermilion
Vermilion Parish SD
  Supt. — See Abbeville
  JSHS, 901 MAIN ST 70542 — 2-00111
    Robert Rizzuto, prin. — 536-6938

Hackberry, AC 318, PC 3, Cameron
Cameron Parish SD
  Supt. — See Cameron
  S, 1390 SCHOOL ST 70645 — 2-11111
    Pamela LaFleur, prin. — 762-3305

Hahnville, AC 504, PC 5, St. Charles
St. Charles Parish SD
  Supt. — See Luling
  Landry MS, RR 1 BOX 108 70057 — 2-00100
    William Picard, prin. — 783-6636

Hall Summit, AC 318, PC 2, Red River
Red River Parish SD
  Supt. — See Coushatta
  S, PO BOX 68 71034 — 2-11111
    Mary Marston, prin. — 932-4416

Hammond, AC 504, PC 7, Tangipahoa
Tangipahoa Parish SD
  Supt. — See Amite
  HS, 284 RIVER RD 70401 — 4-00011
    Al Link, prin. — 345-7235
  JHS, 111 J W DAVIS DR 70403 — 3-00100
    Edward Dillon, prin. — 345-2654

Coastal College — 2-CS
  119 YOKUM RD 70403
Hammond Area Technical Institute — 2-CS
  PO BOX 489 70404 — 549-5063
St. Thomas Aquinas HS — 2-00011
  14520 VOSS DR 70401 — 542-7662
  Philip Crawford, prin.
Seventh Ward General Hospital — HSP
  HWY 51 S 70401 — 549-6600
Southeastern Louisiana University — 6-UC
  PO BOX 784 70404 — 549-2123

Harrisonburg, AC 318, PC 2, Catahoula
Catahoula Parish SD
  Supt. — See Jonesville
  HS, 300 HIGHWAY 8 W 71340 — 2-00114
    David Mitchell, prin. — 744-5273

Harvey, AC 504, PC 7, Jefferson
Jefferson Parish SD — 8-11111
  501 MANHATTAN BLVD 70058 — 349-7802
  Barbara Turner, supt.
  West Jefferson HS, 2200 8TH ST 70058 — 4-00011
    Eldon Orgeron, prin. — 368-6055
  Cox JHS, 2200 LAPALCO BLVD 70058 — 3-00110
    John Billips, prin. — 367-6388
  Other Schools — See Avondale, Grand Isle, Gretna, Jefferson, Kenner, Lafitte, Marrero, Metairie, Westwego

West Jefferson Technical Institute — 2-CS
  475 MANHATTAN BLVD 70058 — 361-6464

Haughton, AC 318, PC 4, Bossier
Bossier Parish SD
  Supt. — See Benton
  HS, 210 E MCKINLEY AVE 71037 — 3-00011
    Jane Smith, prin. — 949-2429

Haynesville, AC 318, PC 5, Claiborne
Claiborne Parish SD
  Supt. — See Homer
  HS, 406 S 1ST ST E 71038 — 2-00011
    Keith Alexander, prin. — 624-0905
  JHS, 1000 S 1ST ST E 71038 — 2-01100
    Robert Bond, prin. — 624-0152

Claiborne Academy — 2-11111
  RR 3 BOX 174 71038 — 927-2747
  Darden Gladney, prin.

Hicks, AC 318, PC 1, Vernon
Vernon Parish SD
  Supt. — See Leesville
  S, GENERAL DELIVERY 71446 — 2-11111
    Dale Hardwick, prin. — 239-9645

Holden, AC 504, PC 2, Livingston
Livingston Parish SD
  Supt. — See Livingston
  S, GENERAL DELIVERY 70744 — 3-11111
    Paula Green, prin. — 567-9367

Homer, AC 318, PC 5, Claiborne
Claiborne Parish SD — 5-11111
  PO BOX 600 71040 — 927-3502
  James Scriber, supt.
  HS, 1008 N MAIN ST 71040 — 2-00011
    Ron Beard, prin. — 927-2985
  JHS, 1009 PEARL ST 71040 — 2-01100
    David Frye, prin. — 927-2826
  Other Schools — See Athens, Haynesville, Lisbon, Summerfield

Claiborne Technical Institute — 2-CS
  3001 MINDEN HWY 71040

Hornbeck, AC 318, PC 2, Vernon
Vernon Parish SD
  Supt. — See Leesville
  S, PO BOX 9 71439 — 2-11111
    Roger Whatley, prin. — 565-4440

Houma, AC 504, PC 8, Terrebonne
Terrebonne Parish SD — 7-11111
  PO BOX 5097 70361 — 876-7400
  Morgan Brasher, supt.
  Ellender Memorial HS — 4-00011
    3012 PATRIOT DR 70363 — 868-7903
    James Charles, prin.
  Terrebonne HS, PO BOX 2767 70361 — 3-00011
    Ulyse Louviere, prin. — 879-3377
  Terrebonne Vo-Tech HS — Vo Tech
    1 SAYRE RD 70363 — 851-1163
    Hayes Badeaux, prin.
  Terrebonne Vo Ctr, 3 SAYRE RD 70363 — Vo Tech
    Richard Bascle, prin. — 851-0558
  East Street MS, 609 EAST ST 70363 — 2-00110
    Nicholas Smith, prin. — 872-3378
  Evergreen S, 3843 W MAIN ST 70360 — 3-00110
    Rodrick Broussard, prin. — 876-2606
  Grand Caillou MS — 3-01100
    4077 GRAND CAILLOU RD 70363 — 879-3001
    Judy Gaspard, prin.
  JHS, 200 SAINT CHARLES ST 70360 — 4-00110
    Philip Martin, prin. — 872-1511
  Oaklawn JHS, 2401 ACADIAN DR 70363 — 3-00100
    Don Johnson, prin. — 872-3904
  Other Schools — See Bourg, Chauvin, Gray, Montegut

Coastal College — 2-CS
  2318 W PARK AVE 70364
Delta College — 2-CS
  3827 W MAIN ST 70360 — 362-5445
South Louisiana Technical Institute — 2-CS
  PO BOX 5033 70361 — 857-3655
Vanderbilt Catholic HS — 3-00011
  209 S HOLLYWOOD RD 70360 — 876-2551
  Alan Powers, prin.

Independence, AC 504, PC 4, Tangipahoa
Tangipahoa Parish SD
  Supt. — See Amite
  HS, PO BOX 10 70443 — 3-00011
    John Mabry, prin. — 878-9436
  MS, PO BOX 97 70443 — 2-01100
    Edward Bankston, prin. — 878-4376

Iota, AC 318, PC 4, Acadia
Acadia Parish SD
  Supt. — See Crowley
  JSHS, PO BOX 780 70543 — 3-00111
    Cal Simar, prin. — 779-2534

Iowa, AC 318, PC 5, Calcasieu
Calcasieu Parish SD
  Supt. — See Lake Charles
  HS, PO BOX 6 70647 — 2-00011
    David Buller, prin. — 582-3561

Jackson, AC 504, PC 5, East Feliciana
East Feliciana Parish SD
  Supt. — See Clinton
  HS, 3503 HIGHWAY 10 70748 — 2-00011
    C. Matthews, prin. — 634-5931
  MS, 3503 HIGHWAY 10 70748 — 2-01100
    Hattie Reed, prin. — 634-5932

Folkes Technical Institute — 2-CS
  PO BOX 808 70748 — 634-2636

Jeanerette, AC 318, PC 6, Iberia
Iberia Parish SD
  Supt. — See New Iberia
  HS, RR 1 BOX 67 70544 — 3-00011
    David Hills, prin. — 276-6038
  MS, 609 PELLERIN RD 70544 — 2-00100
    Glenn Eldridge, prin. — 276-4320

Jefferson, AC 504, PC 7, Jefferson
Jefferson Parish SD
  Supt. — See Harvey
  Riverdale JSHS — 4-00111
    240 RIVERDALE DR 70121 — 833-7288
    Diane Roussel, prin.

Jena, AC 318, PC 5, La Salle
LaSalle Parish SD, PO BOX 90 71342 — 5-11111
  Robert Coleman, supt. — 992-2161
  HS, PO BOX 89 71342 — 3-00011
    James Horton, prin. — 992-5195

JHS, PO BOX 920 71342 — 2-00100
  David Roark, prin. — 992-5815
  Other Schools — See Olla, Urania

Jennings, AC 318, PC 7, Jefferson Davis
Jefferson Davis Parish SD — 6-11111
  PO BOX 640 70546 — 824-1834
  W. Whitford, supt.
  HS, PO BOX 1090 70546 — 3-00011
    Eugene Van Hook, prin. — 824-0642
  Hathaway S — 2-11111
    4040 PINE ISLAND HWY 70546 — 824-4452
    Carl Langley, prin.
  Northside JHS — 3-00100
    208 SHANKLAND AVE 70546 — 824-0823
    Carl Benoit, prin.
  Other Schools — See Elton, Fenton, Lacassine, Lake Arthur, Roanoke, Welsh

Jefferson Davis Technical Institute — 1-CS
  1230 N MAIN ST 70546 — 824-4811

Jonesboro, AC 318, PC 5, Jackson
Jackson Parish SD — 5-11111
  PO BOX 705 71251 — 259-4456
  Clifton Milstead, supt.
  Jonesboro-Hodge HS — 2-00011
    225 PERSHING HWY 71251 — 259-4138
    Roy Barlow, prin.
  Weston S, 213 HIGHWAY 505 71251 — 2-11111
    James Staples, prin. — 259-7313
  Jonesboro-Hodge JHS — 2-00100
    401 WALKER RD 71251 — 259-6611
    Talton Barron, prin.
  Other Schools — See Chatham, Quitman

Jonesville, AC 318, PC 5, Catahoula
Catahoula Parish SD — 5-11111
  PO BOX 308 71343 — 339-7997
  L. Keith Guice, supt.
  Block JSHS, 300 DIVISION ST 71343 — 2-00111
    Carvel White, prin. — 339-7996
  Central S, HC 69 71343 — 1-11111
    Robert Smith, prin. — 339-7574
  Other Schools — See Enterprise, Harrisonburg, Sicily Island

Kaplan, AC 318, PC 5, Vermilion
Vermilion Parish SD
  Supt. — See Abbeville
  HS, 200 E PIRATE LN 70548 — 3-00011
    Randy Schexnider, prin. — 643-6385
  Pecan Island S, PO BOX 41 70548 — 2-11111
    Oran Meche, prin. — 737-2320
  Rost MS, 112 W 6TH ST 70548 — 3-01100
    Ken Broussard, prin. — 643-8545

Keithville, AC 318, PC 2, Caddo

Grawood Christian S — 2-11111
  10420 GRAWOOD SCHOOL RD 71047 — 925-9588
  Wayne Thrash, prin.

Kenner, AC 504, PC 8, Jefferson
Jefferson Parish SD
  Supt. — See Harvey
  Barbre MS, 1610 3RD ST 70062 — 3-00100
    (—), prin. — 467-6218
  Roosevelt MS, 3315 MAINE AVE 70065 — 3-00100
    Peter Breithoff, prin. — 443-1361

Kentwood, AC 504, PC 4, Tangipahoa
Tangipahoa Parish SD
  Supt. — See Amite
  JSHS, PO BOX 88 70444 — 2-00111
    Ann Smith, prin. — 229-2881
  Sumner JSHS — 2-00111
    15841 HIGHWAY 440 70444 — 229-8805
    Darrell Fairburn, prin.

Kilbourne, AC 318, PC 2, West Carroll
West Carroll Parish SD
  Supt. — See Oak Grove
  S, PO BOX 339 71253 — 2-11111
    Truman Smith, prin. — 428-3721

Kinder, AC 318, PC 4, Allen
Allen Parish SD
  Supt. — See Oberlin
  HS, RR 1 BOX 4K 70648 — 2-00011
    Charles Nevils, prin. — 738-2886

Labadieville, AC 504, PC 4, Assumption
Assumption Parish SD
  Supt. — See Napoleonville
  MS, PO BOX 127 70372 — 2-01100
    Michael Arcement, prin. — 526-4227

Labarre, AC 504, PC 2, Pointe Coupee
Point Coupee Parish SD
  Supt. — See New Roads
  Pointe Coupee JSHS — 4-00111
    GENERAL DELIVERY 70751 — 638-3085
    Glen Bowman, prin.

Lacassine, AC 318, PC 2, Jefferson Davis
Jefferson Davis Parish SD
  Supt. — See Jennings
  S, PO BOX E 70650 — 2-11111
    John Juneau, prin. — 588-4206

Lacombe, AC 504, PC 6, St. Tammany
St. Tammany Parish SD
  Supt. — See Covington
  Bayou Lacombe JHS — 2-01100
    PO BOX 787 70445 — 882-5416
    Frank Sibley, prin.

Lafayette, AC 318, PC 8, Lafayette
Lafayette Parish SD   8-11111
  PO Box 2158 70502   236-6825
  Max Skidmore, supt.
Acadiana HS, 315 RUE DE BELIER 70506   4-00011
  Judith Cox, prin.   984-2646
Carencro HS   4-00011
  721 W BUTCHER SWITCH RD 70507   896-6192
  David Lutgring, prin.
Comeaux HS   4-00011
  100 W BLUEBIRD ST 70508   984-8395
  Anatole Garret, prin.
HS, 3000 W CONGRESS ST 70506   4-00011
  Dr. Kurt Schmersahl, prin.   984-5284
Northside HS, 301 DUNAND ST 70501   4-00011
  Janet Hiatt, prin.   232-0681
Lafayette Career Ctr, 200 18TH ST 70501   Vo Tech
  Lee Ruffin, prin.   233-2026
Acadian MS, 4201 MOSS ST 70507   4-01100
  Hebert Thayer, prin.   233-2496
Alleman MS   3-01100
  600 ROSELAWN BLVD 70503   984-7210
  Sidney Roy, prin.
Breaux MS, 1400 S ORANGE ST 70501   3-01100
  Burnell Lemoine, prin.   234-2313
MS, 1301 W UNIVERSITY AVE 70506   3-00100
  Thomas Brown, prin.   234-4032
Martin MS   3-01100
  401 BROADMOOR BLVD 70503   984-9796
  Ellen Ventress, prin.
Moss MS, 801 MUDD AVE 70501   3-00100
  Preston Welcome, prin.   233-5275
Other Schools – See Broussard, Carencro, Duson,
  Scott, Youngsville

Delta Career College   1-CS
  1900 CAMERON ST 70506   235-1147
Delta Schools   3-CS
  4549 JOHNSTON ST 70503   988-2211
Lafayette General Medical Center   HSP
  PO BOX 52009 70505   261-7381
Lafayette Regional Voc.-Technical School   3-CS
  PO BOX 4909 70502   265-5766
Remington College   2-CS
  303 RUE LOUIS XIV # 8 70508   981-4010
St. Thomas Moore HS   3-00011
  450 E FARREL RD 70508   988-3700
  Raymond Simon, prin.
Teurlings Catholic JSHS   2-00111
  139 TEURLINGS DR 70501   235-5711
  Bruce Baudier, prin.
University Medical Center   HSP
  P O BOX 4016 70502   261-6004
University of Southwestern Louisiana   7-UC
  PO BOX 40400 70504   231-6457

Lafitte, AC 504, PC 4, Jefferson
Jefferson Parish SD
  Supt. — See Harvey
Fisher JSHS, HC 63 BOX 496A 70067   3-00111
  Clothilde Cobert, prin.   689-3665

Lake Arthur, AC 318, PC 5, Jefferson Davis
Jefferson Davis Parish SD
  Supt. — See Jennings
JSHS, PO BOX AP 70549   3-00111
  Tom Smith, prin.   774-5152

Lake Charles, AC 318, PC 8, Calcasieu
Calcasieu Parish SD   8-11111
  PO BOX 800 70602   491-1645
  Charles Oakley, supt.
Barbe HS, 2200 W MCNEESE ST 70605   4-00011
  Denton Henrich, prin.   478-3626
Houston HS   3-00011
  880 SAM HOUSTON JONES PKY 70611
  Kerry Durr, prin.   855-3528
LaGrange HS   4-00011
  3420 LOUISIANA AVE 70605   477-4571
  Jim Anderson, prin.
Lake Charles/Boston HS   3-00011
  1509 ENTERPRISE BLVD 70601   436-9594
  William Palmer, prin.
Washington/Marion HS   3-00011
  2802 PINEVIEW ST 70601   433-5892
  Roy Guillory, prin.
Molo Magnet MS   3-00100
  2300 MEDORA ST 70601   433-6785
  Solomon Cannon, prin.
Moss Bluff MS, RR 9 BOX 125 70611   3-00100
  Al Heimback, prin.   855-7774
Oak Park MS   2-00100
  2200 OAK PARK BLVD 70601   478-3310
  John Moore, prin.
Reynaud MS   2-00100
  745 S SHATTUCK ST 70601   436-5729
  John Moutoun, prin.
Welsh MS, 1500 W MCNEESE ST 70605   4-00100
  Cheryl Honeycutt, prin.   477-6611
White JHS, 1000 E MCNEESE ST 70605   4-00100
  William Stokes, prin.   477-1604
Other Schools – See Bell City, Dequincy, Iowa,
  Starks, Sulphur, Vinton, Westlake

Cameron Parish SD
  Supt. — See Cameron
Grand Lake S, RR 2 BOX 360B 70605   2-11111
  Pearl Leach, prin.   598-2231

Delta School of Business and Technology   2-CC
  517 BROAD ST 70601   439-5765

Hamilton Christian Academy   2-11111
  1415 8TH ST 70601   439-1178
  David Moore, prin.
Lake Charles Memorial Hospital   HSP
  1701 OAK PARK BLVD 70601   494-2481
McNeese State University   6-UC
  4100 RYAN ST 70605   475-5000
St. Louis HS, 1620 BANK ST 70601   2-00011
  Victor Bonnaffee, prin.   436-7275
St. Patrick's Hospital   HSP
  524 S RYAN ST 70601   491-7730
Sowela Regional Technical Institute   3-CS
  3820 LEGION ST 70601   491-2681

Lake Providence, AC 318, PC 6, East Carroll
East Carroll Parish SD   4-11111
  PO BOX 792 71254   559-2222
  Gerald Stanley, supt.
SHS   2-00001
  602 MRTIN LUTHER KING JR DR 71254
  Herbert Howard, prin.   559-2243
Monticello S, RR 1 BOX 314 71254   2-11111
  Phil Jackson, prin.   552-6366
JHS, 1205 GOULD BLVD 71254   2-00110
  Theodore Lane, prin.   559-1395

Briarfield Academy   2-00111
  RR 2 BOX 312 71254   559-2360
  Don Catron, prin.

La Place, AC 504, PC 7, St. John The Baptist
St. John The Baptist Parish SD
  Supt. — See Reserve
Glade JHS   3-00100
  3328 NEW HIGHWAY 51 70068   652-5935
  Roger Rankin, prin.

St. Charles Catholic HS   2-00011
  100 DOMINICAN RD 70068   652-3809
  Andrew Cupit, prin.

Larose, AC 504, PC 6, Lafourche
Lafourche Parish SD
  Supt. — See Thibodaux
Larose-Cut Off JHS   3-00110
  PO BOX 1390 70373   693-3273
  Philip Collins, prin.

Lebeau, AC 318, PC 2, St. Landry
St. Landry Parish SD
  Supt. — See Opelousas
North Central JSHS   2-00111
  PO BOX 10 71345   623-4239
  Milton Ambres, prin.

Lecompte, AC 318, PC 4, Rapides
Rapides Parish SD
  Supt. — See Alexandria
Rapides HS, PO BOX 770 71346   2-00011
  Rodney Miller, prin.   776-9371
Raymond JHS, PO BOX 429 71346   2-01100
  Causby Watson, prin.   776-5489

Leesville, AC 318, PC 6, Vernon
Vernon Parish SD   7-11111
  201 BELVIEW RD 71446   239-3401
  Sam Hinson, supt.
HS, 502 BERRY AVE 71446   4-00011
  Bill Crawford, prin.   239-3464
Pickering JSHS, 497 LEBLEU RD 71446   3-00111
  Rob Craft, prin.   537-1555
JHS, PO BOX 1570 71496   3-00100
  Jackie Self, prin.   239-3874
Other Schools – See Anacoco, Evans, Hicks,
  Hornbeck, Pitkin, Rosepine, Simpson

Salter Technical Institute   2-CS
  RR 2 BOX 25 71446   537-3135

Lena, AC 318, PC 2, Rapides
Rapides Parish SD
  Supt. — See Alexandria
Northwood S, 8830 HIGHWAY 1 N 71447   3-11111
  Sidney Cox, prin.   793-8021

Lillie, AC 318, PC 2, Union
Union Parish SD
  Supt. — See Farmerville
MS, PO BOX 3 71256   2-01100
  Vera Jackson, prin.   285-9561

Lisbon, AC 318, PC 2, Claiborne
Claiborne Parish SD
  Supt. — See Homer
Pineview HS, HC 18 BOX 1050 71048   2-11111
  Felton Evans, prin.   353-6334

Livingston, AC 504, PC 4, Livingston
Livingston Parish SD   7-11111
  PO BOX 1130 70754   686-7044
  J. Rogers Pope, supt.
Doyle JSHS, PO BOX 160 70754   2-00111
  Charles Scott, prin.   686-2318
Other Schools – See Albany, Denham Springs,
  French Settlement, Holden, Maurepas, Springfield,
  Walker, Watson

Livonia, AC 504, PC 3, Pointe Coupee
Point Coupee Parish SD
  Supt. — See New Roads
JSHS, PO BOX 549 70755   2-00111
  J. Swindler, prin.   637-2532

Lockport, AC 504, PC 5, Lafourche
Lafourche Parish SD
  Supt. — See Thibodaux

JHS, 720 MAIN ST 70374   3-00110
  Doyle Rogers, prin.   532-2597

Logansport, AC 318, PC 4, De Soto
De Soto Parish SD
  Supt. — See Mansfield
S, PO BOX 1049 71049   3-11111
  Willie Jones, prin.   697-4338
Stanley S, RR 1 BOX 371 71049   2-11111
  Debra Land, prin.   697-2664

Longville, AC 318, PC 2, Beauregard
Beauregard Parish SD
  Supt. — See Deridder
South Beauregard JSHS   3-00111
  RR 1 BOX 49A 70652   725-3536
  Bob Ensminger, prin.

Loranger, AC 504, PC 3, Tangipahoa
Tangipahoa Parish SD
  Supt. — See Amite
HS, PO BOX 560 70446   2-00011
  Stephen Boyette, prin.   878-6271
MS, PO BOX 469 70446   2-01100
  Cora Morris, prin.   878-9455

Loreauville, AC 318, PC 3, Iberia
Iberia Parish SD
  Supt. — See New Iberia
JSHS, PO BOX 446 70552   2-00111
  Russell Erikson, prin.   229-4701

Luling, AC 504, PC 5, St. Charles
St. Charles Parish SD   6-11111
  PO BOX 46 70070   785-6289
  Thomas Tocco, supt.
Other Schools – See Boutte, Destrehan, Hahnville,
  Paradis

Lutcher, AC 504, PC 5, St. James
St. James Parish SD   5-11111
  PO BOX 338 70071   869-5375
  Karen Poirrier, supt.
HS, PO BOX 489 70071   3-00011
  Terry Mullen, prin.   869-5741
JHS, 2461 N KING AVE 70071   2-00100
  George Scott, prin.   869-3305
Other Schools – See Saint James, Vacherie

Madisonville, AC 504, PC 3, St. Tammany
St. Tammany Parish SD
  Supt. — See Covington
JHS, PO BOX 850 70447   2-01100
  Hilary Tate, prin.   845-3355

Mamou, AC 318, PC 5, Evangeline
Evangeline Parish SD
  Supt. — See Ville Platte
HS, 1008 7TH ST 70554   2-00011
  James Guillory, prin.   468-5793
MS, 1205 4TH ST 70554   2-01100
  Aubrey Smith, prin.   468-3123

Mandeville, AC 504, PC 6, St. Tammany
St. Tammany Parish SD
  Supt. — See Covington
HS, 1 SKIPPER DR 70471   4-00011
  James Robertson, prin.   626-5225
JHS, 639 CARONDELET ST 70448   3-00100
  Rich Sylvest, prin.   626-4428

Mangham, AC 318, PC 3, Richland
Richland Parish SD
  Supt. — See Rayville
HS, PO BOX 348 71259   2-00011
  Althan Smith, prin.   248-2485
JHS, PO BOX 428 71259   2-00100
  Bobby Joe Chapman, prin.   248-2729

Mansfield, AC 318, PC 6, De Soto
De Soto Parish SD   6-11111
  201 CROSBY ST 71052   872-2836
  Walter Lee, supt.
HS, 401 KINGS HWY 71052   3-00011
  Gail Garcia, prin.   872-0793
De Soto JHS, PO BOX 313 71052   2-00100
  Willie Guiton, prin.   872-1309
Other Schools – See Logansport, Pelican, Stonewall

Mansura, AC 318, PC 4, Avoyelles
Avoyelles Parish SD
  Supt. — See Marksville
MS, PO BOX 188 71350   3-00100
  Albin Lemoine, prin.   964-2334

Many, AC 318, PC 5, Sabine
Sabine Parish SD   5-11111
  PO BOX 1079 71449   256-9228
  James Wood, supt.
HS, RR 2 BOX 380 71449   2-00011
  Norman Booker, prin.   256-2114
JHS, 850 HIGHLAND AVE 71449   2-01100
  James Mitchell, prin.   256-3573
Other Schools – See Converse, Florien, Negreet,
  Noble, Pleasant Hill, Zwolle

Sabine Valley Technical Institute   2-CS
  PO BOX 790 71449   256-5663

Marion, AC 318, PC 3, Union
Union Parish SD
  Supt. — See Farmerville
Linville S, RR 2 BOX 14D 71260   2-11111
  John Ellis, prin.   292-5506
S, PO BOX 67 71260   2-11111
  Lillie Davis, prin.   292-4410

Marksville, AC 318, PC 6, Avoyelles
Avoyelles Parish SD
  201 W TUNICA DR 71351   6-11111 / 253-5982
  James Bordelon, supt.
HS, 316 W BONTEMPS ST 71351   3-00011 / 253-9356
  Jerome St. Romain, prin.
MS, RR 2 BOX 283 71351   3-00100 / 253-8952
  Rufus Johnson, prin.
Other Schools – See Bunkie, Mansura, Moreauville

Marrero, AC 504, PC 8, Jefferson
Jefferson Parish SD
  Supt. — See Harvey
Ehret HS, 4300 PATRIOT ST 70072   5-00011 / 340-7651
  Arthur Majorie, prin.
Higgins HS, 7201 LAPALCO BLVD 70072   4-00011 / 341-2273
  Joseph Fennidy, prin.
Cullier Career Center   Vo Tech
  1429B AMES BLVD 70072   340-6963
  Ruth Autin, prin.
Ellender MS, 4501 E AMES BLVD 70072   4-00100 / 341-9469
  Thomas Hebert, prin.
MS, 4100 7TH ST 70072   3-00100 / 341-5842
  Etta Liccardi, prin.
Truman MS, 5417 EHRET RD 70072   4-00100 / 341-0961
  Arthur Majorie, prin.

Archbishop Shaw HS   3-00011
  1000 SALESIAN LN 70072   340-6727
  Fr. Gonder, prin.
Immaculata HS, 537 AVENUE D 70072   3-00011 / 341-6217
  Sr. Roseann Ruiz, prin.

Mathews, AC 504, PC 3, Lafourche
Lafourche Parish SD
  Supt. — See Thibodaux
Central Lafourche SHS   3-00001
  PO BOX 89 70375   532-3319
  Milton Arabie, prin.

Maurepas, AC 504, PC 2, Livingston
Livingston Parish SD
  Supt. — See Livingston
S, PO BOX 39 70449   2-11111 / 695-6111
  Gerald Bantaa, prin.

Maurice, AC 318, PC 2, Vermilion
Vermilion Parish SD
  Supt. — See Abbeville
North Vermilion JSHS   3-00011
  RR 1 BOX 55 70555   898-1491
  Michael Guilbeaux, prin.

Meraux, AC 504, PC 6, St. Bernard
St. Bernard Parish SD
  Supt. — See Chalmette
Trist MS, 3433 LIONEL DR 70075   2-00100 / 279-8578
  Tom Powell, prin.

Archbishop Hannan HS   3-00011
  2501 ARCHBISHOP HANNAN BLVD 70075   279-1921
  John Serio, prin.

Mer Rouge, AC 318, PC 3, Morehouse
Morehouse Parish SD
  Supt. — See Bastrop
Delta JSHS, PO BOX 162 71261   2-00111 / 647-3443
  Calvin Dismuke, prin.

Merryville, AC 318, PC 4, Beauregard
Beauregard Parish SD
  Supt. — See Deridder
S, RR 2 BOX 5 70653   3-11111 / 825-8046
  Earl Franks, prin.

Metairie, AC 504, PC 9, Jefferson
Jefferson Parish SD
  Supt. — See Harvey
Bonnabel HS, 8800 BRUIN DR 70003   4-00011 / 443-4564
  Julius Palone, prin.
East Jefferson HS, 400 PHLOX AVE 70001   4-00011 / 888-7171
  William Kelly, prin.
King HS, 4301 GRACE KING PL 70002   4-00011 / 888-7334
  Al Montgomery, prin.
Adams MS, 5525 HENICAN PL 70003   3-00100 / 887-5240
  Elizabeth Keller, prin.
Harris MS, 911 ELISE AVE 70003   3-00100 / 733-0867
  Paul Emenes, prin.
Haynes MS, 1416 METAIRIE RD 70005   3-00100 / 837-8300
  Jerome Helmstetter, prin.
Meisler MS, 3700 CLEARY AVE 70002   4-00100 / 888-5832
  Jay Harney, prin.

Archbishop Chappelle HS   4-00011
  8800 VETERANS BLVD 70003   467-3105
  Beth Johnson, prin.
Archbishop Rummel HS   4-00111
  1901 SEVERN AVE 70001   834-5592
  David Hardin, prin.
Crescent City Baptist S   2-11111
  4828 UTICA ST 70006   885-4700
  Helen Driscoll, prin.
Eastern College of Health Vocations   2-CS
  3540 S I 10 SERVICE RD W 70001   834-8644
Ecole Classique S   3-11111
  5236 GLENDALE ST 70006   887-3507
  Sal Federico, prin.
Heritage Academy   2-00111
  2900 WYTCHWOOD DR 70003   887-7111
  Harry Dekay, prin.
Jefferson Technical Institute   2-CS
  5200 BLAIR ST 70001   736-7072
Lutheran HS, 3864 17TH ST 70002   2-00011 / 455-4062
  Paul Buetow, prin.

Metairie Park Country S   3-11111
  300 PARK RD 70005   837-5204
  Edward Becker, prin.
RETS Training Center   3-CC
  3321 HESSMER AVE # 301 70002   888-6848
Ridgewood Prepatatory S   2-11111
  201 PASADENA AVE 70001   835-2545
  M. Montgomery, prin.
St. Martin's Episcopal S   3-11111
  5309 AIRLINE HWY 70003   733-0353
  Donald Schwartz, prin.

Midland, AC 318, PC 2, Acadia
Acadia Parish SD
  Supt. — See Crowley
JSHS, PO BOX 66 70559   2-00111 / 783-3310
  J. Clyde Briley, prin.

Minden, AC 318, PC 7, Webster
Webster Parish SD   6-11111
  PO BOX 520 71058   377-7052
  Jerry Lott, supt.
HS, PO BOX 838 71058   3-00011 / 377-2766
  Faye Newsom, prin.
Webster JHS, PO BOX 857 71058   3-00100 / 377-3847
  Len Harris, prin.
Other Schools – See Cotton Valley, Doyline, Dubberly, Sarepta, Shongaloo, Sibley, Springhill

Glenbrook S   2-11111
  COUNTRY CLUB CIRCLE 71055   377-2135
  L. Grigsby, prin.
Northwest Louisiana Technical Institute   2-CS
  PO BOX 835 71058   371-3035

Monroe, AC 318, PC 8, Ouachita
Monroe City SD, PO BOX 4180 71211   7-11111 / 325-0601
  George Cannon, supt.
Carroll HS, PO BOX 5040 71211   3-00011 / 387-8441
  Julian Gray, prin.
Neville HS, 600 FORSYTHE AVE 71201   3-00011 / 323-2237
  Charles Stewart, prin.
Wossman HS   3-00011
  1600 ARIZONA AVE 71202   387-2932
  James Johnson, prin.
Carroll JHS, 2939 RENWICK ST 71201   2-00100 / 322-1683
  Jimmy Jones, prin.
Jefferson JHS, 1009 PECAN ST 71202   3-00100 / 387-1825
  Walter Collins, prin.
Lee JHS, 1600 N 19TH ST 71201   3-00100 / 323-1143
  James Hammond, prin.

Ouachita Parish SD   7-11111
  PO BOX 1642 71212   388-2711
  Lanny Johnson, supt.
Ouachita Parish HS   4-00011
  681 HIGHWAY 594 71203   343-2769
  Tom Middleton, prin.
Ouachita MS, 5500 BLANKS ST 71203   4-00100 / 345-5100
  William Colvin, prin.
Other Schools – See Calhoun, Sterlington, West Monroe

Career Training Specialists   2-CS
  1611 LOUISVILLE AVE 71201
Delta Career College   2-CS
  1702 HUDSON LN 71201   322-8870
Northeast Louisiana University   7-UC
  700 UNIVERSITY AVE 71209   342-5252
Ouachita Christian S   3-11111
  7065 HIGHWAY 165 N 71203   325-6000
  David Watson, prin.
River Oaks S, PO BOX 4804 71211   2-11111 / 343-4185
  Robert Caiola, prin.
St. Francis Medical Center   HSP
  309 JACKSON ST 71201   362-4141
St. Frederick HS   2-00011
  3300 WESTMINISTER AVE 71201   323-9636
  Sr. Marlene Geppert, prin.

Montegut, AC 504, PC 3, Terrebonne
Terrebonne Parish SD
  Supt. — See Houma
MS, 138 DOLPHIN ST 70377   3-01100 / 594-5886
  Louise Vice Adams, prin.

Monterey, AC 318, PC 2, Concordia
Concordia Parish SD
  Supt. — See Vidalia
S, PO BOX 127 71354   2-11111 / 386-2214
  Jack Bairnsfather, prin.

Montgomery, AC 318, PC 3, Grant
Grant Parish SD
  Supt. — See Colfax
HS, PO BOX 428 71454   2-00011 / 646-2879
  Melvin Shaw, prin.
Montgomery-Gaines JHS   2-00100
  PO BOX 558 71454   646-2463
  Brian Hines, prin.

Moreauville, AC 318, PC 3, Avoyelles
Avoyelles Parish SD
  Supt. — See Marksville
Avoyelles HS, PO BOX 120 71355   3-00011 / 985-2361
  Bruce Juneau, prin.

Morgan City, AC 504, PC 7, St. Mary
St. Mary Parish SD
  Supt. — See Centerville
HS, 2400 HEMLOCK ST 70380   3-00011 / 384-1754
  Kenneth Alfred, prin.
JHS, 911 MARGUERITE ST 70380   3-00100 / 384-5922
  Jerry Cunningham, prin.

Central Catholic HS   2-00111
  2100 CEDAR ST 70380   385-5372
  Alden Foret, prin.
Young Memorial Technical Institute   2-CS
  PO BOX 2148 70381   384-6526

Mount Hermon, AC 504, PC 2, Washington
Washington Parish SD
  Supt. — See Franklinton
S, 36119 HIGHWAY 38 70450   3-11111 / 877-4642
  Gary Fowler, prin.

Napoleonville, AC 504, PC 3, Assumption
Assumption Parish SD, PO BOX B 70390   5-11111 / 369-7252
  P. Cancienne, supt.
Assumption HS, PO BOX 338 70390   4-00011 / 369-2956
  Rodney Bergeron, prin.
Assumption Magnet MS   2-01100
  PO BOX 418 70390   369-2648
  Billie Nweze, prin.
MS, PO BOX 236 70390   2-01100 / 369-6587
  Jesse Robertson, prin.
Other Schools – See Belle Rose, Labadieville, Pierre Part

Natchitoches, AC 318, PC 7, Natchitoches
Natchitoches Parish SD   6-11111
  PO BOX 16 71458   352-2358
  Mike Whitford, supt.
Natchitoches HS   4-00011
  200 HIGHWAY 3110 BYP S 71457   352-2211
  Julio Toro, prin.
JHS, 1621 WELCH ST 71457   3-00100 / 357-9410
  Don Mims, prin.
N. S. U. Lab. MS   2-00100
  NORTHWESTERN UNIV 71497   357-4509
  Jim Berry, prin.
Other Schools – See Campti

Natchitoches Technical Institute   2-CS
  PO BOX 657 71458   357-3162
Northwestern State University   6-UC
  COLLEGE AVE 71497   800-327-1903
St. Marys S, 1101 E 5TH ST 71457   2-11111 / 352-8394
  Sr. Genevieve Kamel, prin.

Negreet, AC 318, PC 2, Sabine
Sabine Parish SD
  Supt. — See Many
S, PO BOX 14 71460   2-11111 / 256-2349
  Randal Martin, prin.

Newellton, AC 318, PC 4, Tensas
Tensas Parish SD
  Supt. — See Saint Joseph
HS, PO BOX 645 71357   2-10011 / 467-5109
  Johnny Simms, prin.
Routhwood MS, PO BOX 646 71357   2-01100 / 467-5103
  James Kelly, prin.

New Iberia, AC 318, PC 8, Iberia
Iberia Parish SD, PO BOX 200 70562   7-11111 / 365-2341
  Dave Cavalier, supt.
SHS, 1301 E ADMIRAL DOYLE DR 70560   4-00001 / 369-6412
  Ernest Lancon, prin.
Iberia Parish Career Ctr   Vo Tech
  100 RECREATION DR 70560   365-7231
  Nathan Cormier, prin.
Anderson MS   3-00100
  1059 ANDERSON ST 70560   365-3932
  Stanley Small, prin.
Belle Place MS   4-00100
  2256 LOREAUVILLE RD 70560   364-2141
  Roy Johnson, prin.
New Iberia Freshman HS   3-00100
  2100 JEFFERSON ISLAND RD 70560   365-2431
  Verge Ausberry, prin.
Other Schools – See Delcambre, Jeanerette, Loreauville

Assembly Christian S   2-11111
  4219 W ADMIRAL DOYLE DR 70560   364-4340
  Rev. John Foster, prin.
Catholic HS, 1301 DELASALLE DR 70560   3-01111 / 364-5116
  Br. Kovatch, prin.
Delta Schools   2-CS
  413 W ADMIRAL DOYLE DR 70560   365-7348
Teche Area Technical Institute   2-CS
  PO BOX 11057 70562   373-0011

New Orleans, AC 504, PC 10, Orleans
Orleans Parish SD   8-11111
  4100 TOURO ST 70122   286-2868
  Morris Holmes, supt.
Abramson HS, 5552 READ BLVD 70127   4-00011 / 242-4830
  Joseph Pecarrere, prin.
Clark HS, 1301 N DERBIGNY ST 70116   3-00011 / 822-8201
  Richard Theodore, prin.
Cohen HS, 3520 DRYADES ST 70115   4-00011 / 891-8075
  Leroy Gray, prin.
Easton Fundamental HS   4-00011
  3019 CANAL ST 70119   821-0844
  Jean Demas, prin.
Fortier HS, 5624 FRERET ST 70115   4-00011 / 862-5148
  John Brown, prin.
Franklin HS   3-00011
  2001 LEON C SIMON DR 70122   286-2600
  Thomas Tews, prin.
Kennedy HS, 5700 WISNER BLVD 70124   4-00011 / 286-2680
  Anita Dumas, prin.
McDonogh HS   4-00011
  2426 ESPLANADE AVE 70119   821-6479
  Faye Johnson, prin.

McDonogh 35 HS   4-00011
 1331 KERLEREC ST 70116   942-3592
 Cynthia Caliste, prin.
Nicholls HS   4-00011
 3820 SAINT CLAUDE AVE 70117   942-3570
 Victor Gordon, prin.
Rabouin HS   3-00011
 727 CARONDELET ST 70130   592-8398
 Carol Chance, prin.
Reed HS, 5316 MICHOUD BLVD 70129   4-00011
 Clive Coleman, prin.   254-8655
Walker HS   3-00011
 2832 GENERAL MEYER AVE 70114   362-7075
 Robert Gaut, prin.
Carver JSHS, 3059 HIGGINS BLVD 70126   4-00111
 Lindsey Moore, prin.   942-1776
Karr Magnet JSHS   4-00111
 3332 HUNTLEE DR 70131   394-8161
 John Hiser, prin.
Landry JSHS, 1200 WHITNEY AVE 70114   4-00111
 Turner Thomas, prin.   366-3624
Lawless JSHS, 5300 LAW ST 70117   4-00111
 Shirley Taylor, prin.   942-3602
McMain Magnet JSHS   4-00111
 5712 S CLAIBORNE AVE 70125   862-5117
 Donalyn Hassenboehler, prin.
New Orleans Center for Creative Art S   2-00111
 6048 PERRIER ST 70118   899-0055
 John Otis, prin.
New Orleans Center for Health Careers   3-00111
 2009 PALMYRA ST 70112   592-8500
 Velma Anderson, prin.
Washington JSHS   4-00111
 1201 S ROMAN ST 70125   592-8580
 Bonnie Payton, prin.
Danneel Pre-Vo S   Vo Tech
 401 NASHVILLE AVE 70115   899-3505
 Eleanor Davis, prin.
Beauregard MS, 4621 CANAL ST 70119   3-00100
 Shelia Thomas, prin.   483-6121
Bell JHS, 1010 N GALVEZ ST 70119   4-00110
 Lucille Lloyd, prin.   821-6075
Capdau JHS, 3821 FRANKLIN AVE 70122   3-00110
 Bessye Smith, prin.   949-5700
Colton JHS   3-00110
 2300 SAINT CLAUDE AVE 70117   942-1790
 John Jones, prin.
Green MS, 2319 VALENCE ST 70115   3-00100
 Derbert Dillworth, prin.   895-8297
Gregory JHS, 1700 PRATT DR 70122   4-00110
 Stephen Boyard, prin.   286-2660
Live Oak MS   3-00100
 3128 CONSTANCE ST 70115   891-4072
 Martin Marino, prin.
Livingston MS, 7301 DWYER RD 70126   4-00100
 Denise Cates, prin.   241-4360
McDonogh 28 JHS   3-00110
 2733 ESPLANADE AVE 70119   942-3688
 Henry Elloie, prin.
Peters MS, 425 S BROAD ST 70119   3-00100
 Theresa Adams, prin.   822-4370
Phillips JHS, 1200 SENATE ST 70122   3-00110
 Walter Goodwin, prin.   286-2676
Williams MS, 11755 DWYER RD 70128   4-00100
 Clive Coleman, prin.   245-1548
Woodson MS, 2514 3RD ST 70113   3-00100
 Ron Barnett, prin.   891-7590
Wright MS, 1426 NAPOLEON AVE 70115   3-00100
 Jimmie Teague, prin.   891-6325

Bayou Technical Institute   2-CS
 PO BOX 13128 70185   866-7703
Brother Martin HS   4-00111
 4401 ELYSIAN FIELDS AVE 70122   283-1561
 John Devlin, prin.
Cabrini HS, 1400 MOSS ST 70119   2-00111
 Frances Tarantino, prin.   482-1193
Cameron College   2-CS
 2740 CANAL ST 70119   821-5881
Charity-Delgado School of Nursing   2-HSP
 450 S CLAIBORNE AVE 70112   568-6483
Charity Hospital of Louisiana   HSP
 1532 TULANE AVE 70112   568-2311
Christian Brothers Academy   1-00100
 1322 MOSS ST 70119   482-1724
 Br. Scanlon, prin.
Coastal College   4-CS
 2001 CANAL ST STE 300 70112   522-2400
De La Salle JSHS   3-00111
 5300 SAINT CHARLES AVE 70115   895-5717
 Br. Calligan, prin.
Delgado Community College   6-CC
 501 CITY PARK AVE 70119   483-4114
Dillard University   4-UC
 2601 GENTILLY BLVD 70122   283-8822
Franklin College of Court Reporting   2-CS
 1200 S CLEARVIEW PKY 70123
Ganus S, 6026 PARIS AVE 70122   2-11111
 Wayne Arnold, prin.   282-4491
Holy Cross JSHS   3-01111
 4950 DAUPHINE ST 70117   942-3100
 Br. Walsh, prin.
Isadore Newman S   4-11111
 1903 JEFFERSON AVE 70115   899-5641
 Scott McLeod, prin.
Jesuit JSHS, 4133 BANKS ST 70119   4-00111
 Paul Frederick, prin.   486-6631
Louisiana State University   4-UC
 433 BOLIVAR ST 70112   568-4829

Loyola University   5-UC
 6363 SAINT CHARLES AVE 70118   861-5990
McGehee S, 2433 PRYTANIA ST 70130   2-11111
 Margaret Wagner, prin.   561-1224
Mt. Carmel Academy   3-00111
 7027 MILNE BLVD 70124   288-7626
 Sr. Camille Campbell, prin.
NEC-Bryman Campus   2-CS
 2322 CANAL ST 70119   822-4500
Newcomb College of Tulane University   4-UC
 1229 BROADWAY ST 70118   865-5594
New Orleans Baptist Theological Seminary   3-UC
 3939 GENTILLY BLVD 70126   282-4455
New Orleans Regional Technical Institute   2-CS
 980 NAVARRE AVE 70124   483-4666
Notre Dame Seminary   2-UC
 2901 S CARROLLTON AVE 70118   866-7426
Ochsner School of Allied Health Sciences   2-CS
 880 W COMMERCE RD 70123   842-3267
Our Lady of Holy Cross College   2-UC
 4123 WOODLAND DR 70131   394-7744
Phillips Junior College   4-CC
 822 S CLEARVIEW PKY 70123   734-0123
Redeemer HS, 1453 CRESCENT DR 70122   2-00111
 Arthur Schmitt, prin.   288-1494
Sacred Heart Academy   3-11111
 4521 SAINT CHARLES AVE 70115   891-1943
 Catherine Bouzon, prin.
St. Augustine JSHS   3-00111
 2600 A P TUREAUD AVE 70119   944-2424
 Carl Blouin, prin.
St. Marys Academy   3-00111
 6905 CHEF MENTEUR HWY 70126   245-0200
 Sr. Mary Bruner, prin.
St. Marys Dominican HS   3-00111
 7701 WALMSLEY AVE 70125   865-9401
 Cynthia Thomas, prin.
Seton Academy, 3222 CANAL ST 70119   2-00011
 Joan Johnson, prin.   827-1370
Southern University in New Orleans   5-UC
 6400 PRESS DR 70126   286-5000
Touro Infirmary   HSP
 1401 FOUCHER ST 70115   897-8244
Tulane University   7-UC
 6823 SAINT CHARLES AVE 70118   865-5731
University of New Orleans 70148   7-UC
     286-6595
Ursuline Academy   2-00011
 2635 STATE ST 70118   866-2725
 Sr. Ann Barrett, prin.
William Carey College   2-UC
 2700 NAPOLEON AVE 70115   897-5906
Word of Faith Academy   2-11111
 13123 I 10 SERVICE RD 70128   242-2602
 William McInnis, prin.
Xavier University   5-UC
 7325 PALMETTO ST 70125   486-7411
Xavier University Prep HS   3-00001
 5116 MAGAZINE ST 70115   899-6061
 Sr. Eileen Sullivan, prin.

New Roads, AC 504, PC 6, Pointe Coupee
 Point Coupee Parish SD   5-11111
  PO BOX 579 70760   638-8674
  Michael Lucia, supt.
 Other Schools – See Labarre, Livonia

Catholic HS, 504 4TH ST W 70760   3-00111
 Kirk Guidry, prin.   638-3469
False River Academy   3-11111
 201 MAJOR PKY 70760   638-3783
 Bill Williams, prin.
Memorial Technical Institute   3-CS
 PO BOX 725 70760   638-8613

Noble, AC 318, PC 2, Sabine
 Sabine Parish SD
  Supt. — See Many
 Ebarb S, RR 1 BOX 774 71462   2-11111
  William Thomas, prin.   645-9402

Oakdale, AC 318, PC 6, Allen
 Allen Parish SD
  Supt. — See Oberlin
 HS, 101 S 13TH ST 71463   2-00011
  Louis Karam, prin.   335-2338
 JHS, 124 S 13TH ST 71463   3-01100
  Michael Doucet, prin.   335-1558

Oakdale Technical Institute   2-CS
 PO BOX EM 71463   335-3944

Oak Grove, AC 318, PC 4, West Carroll
 West Carroll Parish SD   5-11111
  PO BOX 1318 71263   428-2378
  John Mercer, supt.
 JSHS, PO BOX 1008 71263   2-00011
  Gene Gammill, prin.   428-2308
 Fiske Union S, PO BOX 1015 71263   2-11111
  Wayne Martin, prin.   428-2528
 Goodwill S, RR 3 BOX 120A 71263   2-11111
  Edward Bain, prin.   428-2972
 Other Schools – See Epps, Forest, Kilbourne

Oberlin, AC 318, PC 4, Allen
 Allen Parish SD, PO BOX C 70655   5-11111
  Jim Labuff, supt.   639-4311
 JSHS, PO BOX D 70655   2-00111
  Tyrus Pearce, prin.   639-4341
 Other Schools – See Elizabeth, Grant, Kinder,
  Oakdale, Reeves

Olla, AC 318, PC 4, La Salle
 LaSalle Parish SD
  Supt. — See Jena
 LaSalle HS, PO BOX 458 71465   2-00011
  Cary McGuffee, prin.   495-5165

Opelousas, AC 318, PC 7, St. Landry
 St. Landry Parish SD   7-11111
  PO BOX 310 71570   948-3657
  Raymond Fontenot, supt.
 SHS, PO BOX 906 70571   3-00001
  Raymond Cassimere, prin.   942-5634
 Northwest HS, RR 2 BOX 87 70570   2-00011
  Joe Cassimere, prin.   543-7955
 East JHS, 1000 E LEO ST 70570   2-00110
  Robert Morrison, prin.   942-4761
 JHS, PO BOX 112 70571   3-00110
  Clem Zerangue, prin.   942-4957
 Other Schools – See Arnaudville, Eunice, Lebeau,
  Port Barre, Washington

Acadiana Prep S   2-11111
 PO BOX 1505 70571   948-6551
 Gordon McGee, prin.
Amy Ware S   2-11111
 1421 GARLAND BELT RD 70570   948-1765
 Ray Bonvillain, prin.
Harris Technical Institute   2-CS
 PO BOX 713 70571   948-0239
Opelousas Catholic S   3-11111
 415 E PRUDHOMME LN 70570   942-5404
 Karen Domengeaux, prin.

Paradis, AC 504, PC 3, St. Charles
 St. Charles Parish SD
  Supt. — See Luling
 Martin MS, PO BOX 1468 70080   2-00100
  Juanita Haydel, prin.   758-7579

Patterson, AC 504, PC 5, St. Mary
 St. Mary Parish SD
  Supt. — See Centerville
 HS, 2525 MAIN ST 70392   2-00011
  Michael Brocato, prin.   395-2675
 JHS, PO BOX R 70392   3-01100
  Herman Albritton, prin.   395-6772

Pearl River, AC 504, PC 4, St. Tammany
 St. Tammany Parish SD
  Supt. — See Covington
 HS, 39110 REBEL LN 70452   3-00011
  Ron Styron, prin.   863-2591
 JHS, 39395 PINE ST 70452   2-01100
  John Downey, prin.   863-5882

Pelican, AC 318, PC 2, De Soto
 De Soto Parish SD
  Supt. — See Mansfield
 All Saints-Pelican S   2-11111
  RR 1 BOX 510 71063   755-2318
  Gary Hunt, prin.

Pierre Part, AC 504, PC 5, Assumption
 Assumption Parish SD
  Supt. — See Napoleonville
 MS, 3321 HIGHWAY 70 70339   2-01100
  Earl Martinez, prin.   252-6359

Pine Prairie, AC 318, PC 3, Evangeline
 Evangeline Parish SD
  Supt. — See Ville Platte
 S, PO BOX 200 70576   3-11111
  Terry Ardoin, prin.   599-2300

Pineville, AC 318, PC 7, Rapides
 Rapides Parish SD
  Supt. — See Alexandria
 HS, 1511 LINE ST 71360   4-00011
  Jesse Crouch, prin.   442-8990
 JHS, 501 EDGEWOOD DR 71360   3-00100
  Lemon Coleman, prin.   640-0512

Louisiana College   4-UC
 PO BOX 560 71359   487-7386

Pitkin, AC 318, PC 3, Vernon
 Vernon Parish SD
  Supt. — See Leesville
 S, PO BOX 307 70656   3-11111
  Sandra Whitlock, prin.   358-3121

Plain Dealing, AC 318, PC 4, Bossier
 Bossier Parish SD
  Supt. — See Benton
 JSHS, PO BOX 307 71064   2-00111
  Larry Towner, prin.   326-4815

Plain Dealing Academy   2-11111
 PO BOX 176 71064   326-5823
 Rebecca Walding, prin.

Plaquemine, AC 504, PC 6, Iberville
 Iberville Parish SD   6-11111
  PO BOX 151 70765   687-4341
  Charles Bujol, supt.
 HS, PO BOX 326 70765   3-00011
  David Gullatt, prin.   687-6367
 Gay MS, PO BOX 717 70765   3-01100
  William Bujol, prin.   687-3502
 Other Schools – See Rosedale, Saint Gabriel, White
  Castle

 St. John JSHS, 24250 REGINA ST 70764   2-00111
  John Fitzenberger, prin.   687-3056

Westside Technical Institute 1-CS
PO BOX 733 70765 687-6392

Plaucheville, AC 318, PC 2, Avoyelles

St. Joseph S, PO BOX 38 71362 2-11111
Br. Andre Lucia, prin. 922-3401

Pleasant Hill, AC 318, PC 3, Sabine
Sabine Parish SD
Supt. — See Many
Pleasant Hill S, PO BOX 8 71065 2-11111
Dale Skinner, prin. 796-3670

Ponchatoula, AC 504, PC 6, Tangipahoa
Tangipahoa Parish SD
Supt. — See Amite
HS, 19452 HIGHWAY 22 E 70454 4-00011
Virgil Allen, prin. 386-3514
JHS, 315 E OAK ST 70454 3-00100
Nick Vaccaro, prin. 386-3157

Port Allen, AC 504, PC 6, West Baton Rouge
West Baton Rouge Parish SD 5-11111
670 ROSEDALE RD 70767 343-8309
Beverly Triche, supt.
HS, 3553 ROSEDALE RD 70767 2-00011
Fred McKey, prin. 383-1107
West Baton Rouge Vo Skills Ctr Vo Tech
807 N 14TH ST 70767 343-3716
Alfred Johnson, prin.
DeVall MS, 11851 N RIVER RD 70767 2-01100
Arnold Chauvin, prin. 627-4268
MS, 610 ROSEDALE RD 70767 2-01100
Leroy Smith, prin. 383-5777
Other Schools – See Brusly

Port Barre, AC 318, PC 4, St. Landry
St. Landry Parish SD
Supt. — See Opelousas
JSHS, PO BOX 69 70577 3-01111
John Ryder, prin. 585-7256

Port Sulphur, AC 504, PC 5, Plaquemines
Plaquemines Parish SD 6-11111
PO BOX 70 70083 564-2743
Carroll Perlander, supt.
S, 164 SCHOOL RD 70083 3-11111
Harold Graham, prin. 564-2423
Other Schools – See Belle Chasse, Boothville,
Braithwaite, Buras

Prairieville, AC 504, PC 2, Ascension
Ascension Parish SD
Supt. — See Donaldsonville
Galvez MS 3-01100
42018 HIGHWAY 933 70769 621-2424
Lee Gaudin, prin.

Princeton, AC 318, PC 2, Bossier
Bossier Parish SD
Supt. — See Benton
MS, 1895 WINFIELD RD 71067 3-00100
Ronald Gormanous, prin. 949-2408

Quitman, AC 318, PC 2, Jackson
Jackson Parish SD
Supt. — See Jonesboro
S, PO BOX 38 71268 3-11111
Paul Walsworth, prin. 259-2698

Raceland, AC 504, PC 6, Lafourche
Lafourche Parish SD
Supt. — See Thibodaux
JHS, PO BOX C 70394 3-00110
Leonard St. Piere, prin. 537-5140

Rayne, AC 318, PC 6, Acadia
Acadia Parish SD
Supt. — See Crowley
HS, 1016 N POLK ST 70578 3-00011
James Proctor, prin. 334-3691
Armstrong MS 3-00100
700 MARTIN LUTHER KING DR 70578 334-3377
Darrell Cart, prin.

Rayville, AC 318, PC 5, Richland
Richland Parish SD 5-11111
PO BOX 599 71269 728-5964
Arlon Adams, supt.
HS, 1201 SE PEARL ST 71269 3-00011
Harry Lewis, prin. 728-3294
JHS, 1203 SE PEARL ST 71269 2-00100
Lee McDonald, prin. 728-3618
Other Schools – See Delhi, Mangham

Riverfield Academy 2-11111
RR 2 BOX 1 71269 728-3281
Charles Meador, prin.

Reeves, AC 318, PC 2, Allen
Allen Parish SD
Supt. — See Oberlin
S, PO BOX 100 70658 2-11111
Donald Bennett, prin. 666-2414

Reserve, AC 504, PC 6, St. John The Baptist
St. John The Baptist Parish SD 6-11111
PO BOX AL 70084 536-1106
Gerald Keller, supt.
East St. John HS, 1 WILDCAT DR 70084 4-00011
Michael Coburn, prin. 536-4226
Godchaux JHS, PO BOX AH 70084 3-00100
Barbara Falgoust, prin. 536-4283
Other Schools – See Edgard, La Place

River Parish Technical Institute 2-CS
PO BOX AQ 70084 536-4418
Riverside Academy 3-11111
332 RAILROAD AVE 70084 536-4246
Barry Heltz, prin.

Ringgold, AC 318, PC 4, Bienville
Bienville Parish SD
Supt. — See Arcadia
JSHS, PO BOX 608 71068 2-00111
B. Haynie, prin. 894-2271

River Ridge, AC 504, PC 7, Jefferson

Curtis Christian S 3-11111
10125 JEFFERSON HWY 70123 737-4621
John Curtis, prin.

Roanoke, AC 318, PC 3, Jefferson Davis
Jefferson Davis Parish SD
Supt. — See Jennings
Welsh-Roanoke JHS, PO BOX 9 70581 2-00100
Raymond Brown, prin. 753-2317

Rosedale, AC 504, PC 3, Iberville
Iberville Parish SD
Supt. — See Plaquemine
North Iberville S, PO BOX 198 70772 3-11111
Melvin Steele, prin. 625-2523

Rosepine, AC 318, PC 4, Vernon
Vernon Parish SD
Supt. — See Leesville
JSHS, PO BOX 369 70659 2-00111
Audrey Ashworth, prin. 463-6079

Ruston, AC 318, PC 7, Lincoln
Lincoln Parish SD 6-11111
410 S FARMERVILLE ST 71270 255-1430
Gerald Cobb, supt.
HS, 900 COOKTOWN RD 71270 4-00011
Randy Moore, prin. 255-0807
JHS, 1400 TARBUTTON RD 71270 3-00100
Sandra Henderson, prin. 251-1601
Other Schools – See Choudrant, Dubach, Grambling,
Simsboro

Cedar Creek S 3-11111
2400 CEDAR CREEK DR 71270 255-7707
Kenneth Henderson, prin.
Louisiana Technical University 6-UC
PO BOX 3168 71272 257-3036
Ruston Technical Institute 2-CS
PO BOX 1070 71273 251-4145

Saint Amant, AC 504, PC 2, Ascension
Ascension Parish SD
Supt. — See Donaldsonville
HS, 12035 HIGHWAY 431 70774 4-00011
Eva Bourgeois, prin. 621-2565
MS, 44317 HIGHWAY 429 70774 3-01100
Peggy Aime, prin. 621-2600

Saint Benedict, AC 504, PC 1, St. Tammany

St. Joseph Seminary College 1-UC
GENERAL DELIVERY 70457 892-1800

Saint Bernard, AC 504, PC 3, St. Bernard
St. Bernard Parish SD
Supt. — See Chalmette
HS, 2601 TORRES DR 70085 3-00011
Paul Granberry, prin. 682-5200
Beauregard MS, 1201 BAYOU RD 70085 2-00100
Charles Raviotta, prin. 682-5964

Saint Francisville, AC 504, PC 4, West Feliciana
West Feliciana Parish SD 4-11111
PO BOX 1910 70775 635-3891
Lloyd Lindsey, supt.
West Feliciana JSHS 3-00111
PO BOX 580 70775 635-4561
James Rougeau, prin.

Saint Gabriel, AC 504, PC 3, Iberville
Iberville Parish SD
Supt. — See Plaquemine
East Iberville S 3-11111
3285 HIGHWAY 75 70776 642-5410
Melvin Craige, prin.

Saint James, AC 504, PC 2, St. James
St. James Parish SD
Supt. — See Lutcher
HS, PO BOX 101 70086 3-00011
Abraham Williams, prin. 265-3911

Saint Joseph, AC 318, PC 4, Tensas
Tensas Parish SD, PO BOX 318 71366 4-11111
Donald Pennington, supt. 766-3269
Davidson JSHS, PO BOX 408 71366 2-00111
Ples Bell, prin. 766-3585
Other Schools – See Newellton, Waterproof

Tensas Academy, PO BOX 289 71366 2-11111
Hardy Palmer, prin. 766-4384

Saint Martinville, AC 318, PC 6, St. Martin
St. Martin Parish SD 6-11111
PO BOX 859 70582 394-6261
Roland Chevalier, supt.
HS, 762 N MAIN ST 70582 3-00011
Alvin Wiltz, prin. 394-3135

JHS 2-00100
1120 S MRTN LTHR KING JR DR 70582 394-4764
Laura Turpeau, prin.
Other Schools – See Breaux Bridge, Cecilia

Evangeline Technical Institute 2-CS
PO BOX 68 70582 394-6466

Saline, AC 318, PC 2, Bienville
Bienville Parish SD
Supt. — See Arcadia
S, PO BOX 118 71070 2-11111
Kenneth Heron, prin. 576-3215

Sarepta, AC 318, PC 3, Webster
Webster Parish SD
Supt. — See Minden
S, PO BOX 220 71071 2-11111
Ronnie Brown, prin. 847-4136

Scott, AC 318, PC 5, Lafayette
Lafayette Parish SD
Supt. — See Lafayette
MS, PO BOX 427 70583 4-01100
John Boudreaux, prin. 235-9698

Shongaloo, AC 318, PC 2, Webster
Webster Parish SD
Supt. — See Minden
S, RR 1 BOX 15 71072 2-11111
Morris Busby, prin. 846-2541

Shreveport, AC 318, PC 9, Caddo
Caddo Parish SD 8-11111
PO BOX 32000 71130 636-0210
Terry Terril, supt.
Byrd HS, 3201 LINE AVE 71104 4-00011
R. Lynne Fitzgerald, prin. 869-2567
Caddo Parish Magnet HS 4-00011
1601 VIKING DR 71101 221-2501
Ascension Smith, prin.
Captain Shreve HS 4-00011
6115 E KINGS HWY 71105 865-7137
Tommy Powell, prin.
Fair Park HS 4-00011
3222 GREENWOOD RD 71109 635-8181
John Dilworth, prin.
Green Oaks HS 3-00011
2550 PRINCE VALIANT DR 71107 425-3411
Wilmer Godfrey, prin.
Huntington HS 4-00011
6801 RASBERRY LN 71129 687-6655
Robert Hudson, prin.
Northwood HS 3-00011
5939 OLD MOORINGSPORT RD 71107 929-3513
James Festavan, prin.
Southwood HS, 9000 WALKER RD 71118 4-00011
Jewell Wagner, prin. 686-9512
Washington HS, 2104 MILAM ST 71103 3-00011
Horace Maxile, prin. 222-2186
Woodlawn HS 4-00011
7340 WYNGATE BLVD 71106 686-3161
William Robinson, prin.
Caddo Career Ctr Vo Tech
5950 UNION AVE 71108 636-5150
Gayle Flowers, prin.
Bethune MS, 4331 HENRY ST 71109 2-00100
Billie Alford, prin. 636-6336
Bickham MS 3-00100
7240 OLD MOORINGSPORT RD 71107 929-4106
Kenneth Cochran, prin.
Broadmoor MS Laboratory 4-00100
441 ATLANTIC AVE 71105 861-2403
Johanna Barker, prin.
Caddo Parish Magnet MS 4-00100
7635 CORNELIOUS LN 71106 868-6588
Judy Moncrief, prin.
Clark MS, 351 HEARNE AVE 71103 3-00100
Ecotry Fuller, prin. 425-8742
Hollywood MS, 6310 CLIFT AVE 71106 3-00100
Donald McLaurin, prin. 868-2753
Linear MS, 1845 LINEAR ST 71107 3-00100
Walter White, prin. 221-1589
Linwood MS, 401 W 70TH ST 71106 3-00100
William Lee, prin. 861-2401
Midway MS 3-00100
3840 GREENWOOD RD 71109 636-1861
Roosevelt Crosby, prin.
Ridgewood MS 3-00100
2001 RIDGEWOOD DR 71118 686-0383
Jim Lynn, prin.
Youree Drive MS 3-00100
6008 YOUREE DR 71105 868-5324
Ollie Tyler, prin.
Other Schools – See Vivian

American School of Business 2-CS
702 PROFESSIONAL DR N 71105 798-3333
Ayers Institute 2-CS
2924 KNIGHT ST STE 318 71105 868-3000
Centenary College of Louisiana 3-UC
PO BOX 41188 71134 800-234-4448
Commercial College of Shreveport 4-CS
2640 YOUREE DR 71104 865-6571
Diesel Driving Academy 1-CS
PO BOX 36949 71133 636-6300
Evangel Academy 3-11111
7425 BROADACRES RD 71129 687-0757
Lorna Skidmore, prin.
Louisiana State University 5-UC
8515 YOUREE DR 71115 797-5000

Loyola College Prep S   2-00011
  921 JORDAN ST   71101   221-2675
  Kathleen Campbell, prin.
Northwestern State University   2-UC
  1800 LINE AVE   71101
Overton Brooks VA Medical Center   HSP
  510 E STONER AVE   71101   424-6037
Schumpert Medical Center   HSP
  PO BOX 21976   71120   227-4500
Shreveport-Bossier Technical Institute   2-CS
  PO BOX 78527   71137   226-7811
Southern University   4-CC
  3050 M L KING DR   71107   674-3342
Trinity Heights Christian Academy   2-11111
  4800 OLD MOORINGSPORT RD   71107   221-2697
  Charles Anderson, prin.

Sibley, AC 318, PC 3, Webster
Webster Parish SD
  Supt. — See Minden
HS, PO BOX 8   71073   2-00011
  W. Williams, prin.   377-2133

Sicily Island, AC 318, PC 2, Catahoula
Catahoula Parish SD
  Supt. — See Jonesville
HS, PO BOX 128   71368   2-00011
  M. Nolen, prin.   389-5337
Martin JHS, PO BOX 338   71368   2-01100
  Wilbert Gardner, prin.   389-5651

Simpson, AC 318, PC 3, Vernon
Vernon Parish SD
  Supt. — See Leesville
S, PO BOX 8   71474   2-11111
  Jim Funderburk, prin.   383-7810

Simsboro, AC 318, PC 3, Lincoln
Lincoln Parish SD
  Supt. — See Ruston
S, PO BOX 118   71275   3-11111
  Harry Jones, prin.   247-6265

Singer, AC 318, PC 2, Beauregard
Beauregard Parish SD
  Supt. — See Deridder
S, PO BOX 398   70660   2-11111
  Ellis Spikes, prin.   463-5908

Slidell, AC 504, PC 7, St. Tammany
St. Tammany Parish SD
  Supt. — See Covington
Northshore HS, 100 PANTHER DR   70461   3-00011
  William Percy, prin.   649-6400
Salmen HS, 4040 BERKLEY DR   70458   3-00011
  William Heckel, prin.   643-7366
HS, 1 TIGER DR   70458   4-00011
  Joseph Buccaran, prin.   643-2992
Boyet JHS, 380 REBEL DR   70461   3-00100
  R. Magee, prin.   643-3775
Clearwood JHS   3-01100
  130 CLEARWOOD DR   70458   641-8200
  Alan Bennett, prin.
St. Tammany JHS   3-00100
  701 CLEVELAND AVE   70458   643-1592
  Willie Jeter, prin.
JHS, 333 PENNSYLVANIA AVE   70458   3-00100
  Michael Stassi, prin.   641-5914

Grantham College of Engineering   3-HMS
  34641 GRANTHAM COLLEGE DR   70460
     800-955-2527
Pope John Paul II HS   2-00111
  1901 JAGUAR DR   70461   649-0914
  Lawrence Keller, prin.
Slidell Technical Institute   2-CS
  PO BOX 827   70459   646-6430

Sorrento, AC 504, PC 4, Ascension

Ascension Technical Institute   2-CS
  PO BOX 38   70778   675-5397

Spearsville, AC 318, PC 2, Union
Union Parish SD
  Supt. — See Farmerville
S, PO BOX 18   71277   2-10011
  Cathryn Buckley, prin.   778-3752

Springfield, AC 504, PC 2, Livingston
Livingston Parish SD
  Supt. — See Livingston
JSHS, PO BOX 39   70462   2-00111
  Melvin Brown, prin.   294-3256

Springhill, AC 318, PC 6, Webster
Webster Parish SD
  Supt. — See Minden
HS, CHURCH AT ARKANSAS ST   71075   2-00011
  Wayne King, prin.   539-2563
JHS, 401 W CHURCH ST   71075   2-00100
  Ben Miller, prin.   539-5115

Starks, AC 318, PC 3, Calcasieu
Calcasieu Parish SD
  Supt. — See Lake Charles
S, PO BOX 69   70661   2-11111
  Roger Creel, prin.   743-5341

Sterlington, AC 318, PC 4, Ouachita
Ouachita Parish SD
  Supt. — See Monroe
JSHS, PO BOX 546   71280   2-00111
  Archie Evans, prin.   665-2215

Stonewall, AC 318, PC 4, De Soto
De Soto Parish SD
  Supt. — See Mansfield
North DeSoto JSHS   3-00111
  PO BOX 290   71078   925-6917
  Leon Hunt, prin.

Sulphur, AC 318, PC 7, Calcasieu
Calcasieu Parish SD
  Supt. — See Lake Charles
HS, 600 SYCAMORE ST   70663   4-00011
  John Land, prin.   527-5145
Leblanc/Drost MS   2-00100
  1100 N CROCKER ST   70663   527-5296
  E. Gerald Connor, prin.
Lewis MS, 1752 CYPRESS ST   70663   3-00100
  Charles Hansen, prin.   527-6178

Summerfield, AC 318, PC 2, Claiborne
Claiborne Parish SD
  Supt. — See Homer
S, PO BOX 158   71079   2-11111
  W. T. Bailey, prin.   927-3621

Tallulah, AC 318, PC 6, Madison
Madison Parish SD   5-11111
  PO BOX 1620   71284   574-3616
  Joe Walk, supt.
McCall HS, 800 FISH ST   71282   2-00011
  Adell Williams, prin.   574-3529
JSHS, 600 BAYOU DR   71282   3-00111
  Foe Avery, prin.   574-4747
Thomastown S, RR 2 BOX 90   71282   2-11111
  Johnny Ford, prin.   574-2405
McCall JHS, 900 W ASKEW ST   71282   2-00100
  Detra Griffin, prin.   574-0933

Tallulah Academy   2-11111
  PO BOX 911   71284   574-2606
  Robert Holstead, prin.
Tallulah Technical Institute   2-CS
  PO BOX 1740   71284   574-4820

Thibodaux, AC 504, PC 7, Lafourche
Lafourche Parish SD   7-11111
  PO BOX 879   70302   446-5631
  Ed Blanchard, supt.
SHS, 1355 TIGER DR   70301   4-00001
  Luke Ford, prin.   447-4071
East Thibodaux JHS, 802 E 7TH ST   70301   3-00110
  Edward Guillot, prin.   446-5616
West Thibodaux JHS   3-00110
  1111 E 12TH ST   70301   446-6889
  Ken Delcambre, prin.
Other Schools – See Galliano, Golden Meadow,
  Larose, Lockport, Mathews, Raceland

Nicholls State University   6-UC
  LA HWY 1   70301   448-4139
Thibodaux Area Technical Institute   2-CS
  1425 TIGER DR   70301   447-0924
White HS, 555 CARDINAL DR   70301   3-00111
  Br. Ronald Talbot, prin.   446-8486

Tickfaw, AC 504, PC 3, Tangipahoa
Tangipahoa Parish SD
  Supt. — See Amite
Nesom ES, PO BOX 280   70466   2-00100
  Alton Williams, prin.   345-2166

Tioga, AC 318, PC 4, Rapides
Rapides Parish SD
  Supt. — See Alexandria
HS, PO BOX 158   71477   3-00011
  Richard Bardwell, prin.   640-9661
JHS, PO BOX 638   71477   3-00100
  Thomas Stepp, prin.   640-9412

Urania, AC 318, PC 3, La Salle
LaSalle Parish SD
  Supt. — See Jena
LaSalle JHS, PO BOX 520   71480   2-00100
  Steve Long, prin.   495-3474

Vacherie, AC 504, PC 5, St. James
St. James Parish SD
  Supt. — See Lutcher
St. James JHS   2-00100
  3125 VALCOUR AIME ST   70090   265-4215
  John Brass, prin.
MS, 13440 HIGHWAY 644   70090   2-01100
  S. Jude Revlet, prin.   265-3674

Varnado, AC 504, PC 2, Washington
Washington Parish SD
  Supt. — See Franklinton
HS, 25543 WASHINGTON ST   70426   2-00011
  Hayward Boone, prin.   732-2025

Vidalia, AC 318, PC 5, Concordia
Concordia Parish SD   5-11111
  PO BOX 950   71373   336-4226
  James Lee, supt.
HS, PO BOX 609   71373   2-00011
  Henry Sugg, prin.   336-6231
JHS, PO BOX 429   71373   2-00100
  Willie Marsalis, prin.   336-6227
Other Schools – See Ferriday, Monterey

Ville Platte, AC 318, PC 6, Evangeline
Evangeline Parish SD   6-11111
  1101 TE MAMOU RD   70586   363-6651
  Larry Broussard, supt.
Bayou Chicot JSHS, RR 3   70586   2-01111
  Donald Smith, prin.   461-2687

JSHS, 210 W COTTON ST   70586   3-00111
  Joe Tuminaro, prin.   363-3387
Vidrine S, RR 5 BOX 200   70586   3-11111
  Roland Smith, prin.   363-4280
Ace S, RR 2 BOX 112C   70586   Vo Tech
  Paul Roy Fontenot, prin.   363-2702
Other Schools – See Basile, Chataignier, Mamou,
  Pine Prairie

Charles B Coreil Technical Institute   2-CS
  PO BOX 296   70586   363-2197
Sacred Heart HS, 114 TROJAN LN   70586   2-00011
  Larry Vidrine, prin.   363-1475

Vinton, AC 318, PC 5, Calcasieu
Calcasieu Parish SD
  Supt. — See Lake Charles
HS, 1603 GRACE AVE   70668   2-00011
  Harold Fuqua, prin.   589-7223
Vinton Northside MS   2-00100
  900 HORRIDGE ST   70668   589-7567
  M. L. Sarver, prin.

Vivian, AC 318, PC 5, Caddo
Caddo Parish SD
  Supt. — See Shreveport
North Caddo HS, 201 AIRPORT DR   71082   3-00011
  Billy Prealow, prin.   375-3258

Walker, AC 504, PC 5, Livingston
Livingston Parish SD
  Supt. — See Livingston
HS, PO BOX 249   70785   3-00011
  Charles King, prin.   664-4825
JHS, PO BOX 219   70785   3-00100
  Bobbye Impson, prin.   665-8970

Washington, AC 318, PC 4, St. Landry
St. Landry Parish SD
  Supt. — See Opelousas
Washington Vo Ed Ctr   Vo Tech
  PO BOX 438   70589   826-7360
  Andrew Leon, prin.

Waterproof, AC 318, PC 4, Tensas
Tensas Parish SD
  Supt. — See Saint Joseph
JSHS, PO BOX 307   71375   2-00111
  Caldwell Flood, prin.   749-3332

Watson, AC 504, PC 3, Livingston
Livingston Parish SD
  Supt. — See Livingston
Live Oak HS, PO BOX 190   70786   2-00011
  Lewis Norgress, prin.   665-8858
Live Oak MS, PO BOX 147   70786   3-00100
  Carl Hoover, prin.   664-3211

Welsh, AC 318, PC 5, Jefferson Davis
Jefferson Davis Parish SD
  Supt. — See Jennings
HS, 306 BOURGEOIS ST   70591   2-00011
  Harry Kyle, prin.   734-2361

Westlake, AC 318, PC 6, Calcasieu
Calcasieu Parish SD
  Supt. — See Lake Charles
HS, 1000 GARDEN DR   70669   3-00011
  Gary Anderson, prin.   433-6866
Arnett MS, 400 SULPHUR AVE   70669   3-00100
  B. Jardell, prin.   436-9657

West Monroe, AC 318, PC 7, Ouachita
Ouachita Parish SD
  Supt. — See Monroe
HS, 201 RIGGS ST   71291   4-00011
  Frank Machen, prin.   323-3771
West Ouachita HS   3-00011
  4061 CAPLES RD   71292   361-0909
  Johnny Hines, prin.
Richardson JSHS   1-00111
  910 THOMAS RD   71292   323-5991
  Louis Pargoud, prin.
Riser JHS, 100 PRICE DR   71292   2-00100
  Linda Brian, prin.   387-0567
MS, 1600 N 7TH ST   71291   3-00100
  James Brian, prin.   388-4360
Woodlawn MS   2-00100
  175 WOODLAWN SCHOOL RD   71292   325-1575
  Charles Dykes, prin.

Delta-Ouachita Technical Institute   2-CS
  609 VOCATIONAL PKY   71292   396-7431

Westwego, AC 504, PC 7, Jefferson
Jefferson Parish SD
  Supt. — See Harvey
Worley JHS   3-00110
  913 WESTBANK EXPY   70094   348-4964
  Roland Lassere, prin.

White Castle, AC 504, PC 4, Iberville
Iberville Parish SD
  Supt. — See Plaquemine
JSHS, 32695 GRAHAM ST   70788   2-00111
  Ronald Bagala, prin.   545-3621

Winnfield, AC 318, PC 6, Winn
Winn Parish SD, PO BOX 430   71483   5-11111
  Derwood Duke, supt.   628-6936
HS, PO BOX 968   71483   2-00011
  Ernest Bamburg, prin.   628-3506
MS, PO BOX 1140   71483   3-00100
  Jefferson Hobdy, prin.   628-2765
Other Schools – See Atlanta, Calvin, Dodson

Long Technical Institute	2-CS
303 S JONES ST 71483	628-4342
Winnsboro, AC 318, PC 6, Franklin	
Franklin Parish SD	5-11111
1809 PRAIRIE ST 71295	435-9046
Jacquelyn Shipp, supt.	
HS, 1600 GLOVER DR 71295	3-00011
John Sartin, prin.	435-5676
Ward III S, RR 1 71295	2-11111
John Brown, prin.	435-4749
JHS, RR 1 BOX 33 71295	3-00100
James Clark, prin.	435-5505
Other Schools — See Baskin, Crowville, Fort Necessity, Gilbert, Wisner	

Franklin Academy, 2110 LOOP RD 71295	2-11111
Carolyn Fenn, prin.	435-9520
Northeast Louisiana Technical Institute	2-CS
1710 WARREN ST 71295	435-5096
Wisner, AC 318, PC 4, Franklin	
Franklin Parish SD	
Supt. — See Winnsboro	
JSHS, PO BOX 775 71378	2-00111
Michael Caldwell, prin.	724-7599
Youngsville, AC 318, PC 4, Lafayette	
Lafayette Parish SD	
Supt. — See Lafayette	
MS, PO BOX 1049 70592	2-01100
Jesse Kebodeaux, prin.	856-5961

Zachary, AC 504, PC 6, East Baton Rouge	
East Baton Rouge Parish SD	
Supt. — See Baton Rouge	
HS, 4101 CHURCH ST 70791	4-00011
Jerry Boudreaux, prin.	654-2776
Northeast JSHS, RR 3 BOX 161 70791	3-00111
Ulysses Joseph, supt.	654-5808
Northwestern MS	3-00100
5200 E CENTRAL AVE 70791	654-9201
Ann Clark, prin.	
Zwolle, AC 318, PC 4, Sabine	
Sabine Parish SD	
Supt. — See Many	
HS, PO BOX 188 71486	2-00011
William Ruffin, prin.	645-6104
IS, PO BOX 768 71486	2-01100
Daniel Leslie, prin.	645-6369

MAINE

DEPARTMENT OF EDUCATION & CULTURAL SERVICES
Education Building
State House Station #23, Augusta 04333
(207) 287-5800

Commissioner of Education	Leo Martin
Deputy Commissioner	Polly Ward
Director Adult Learning	Paul Walker
Director Applied Technolgy	Chris Lyons
Director Certification, Placement & Teacher Education	Nancy Ibarguen
Director of Finance	Stanley Sumner
Director of Instruction	Vacant
Director Management Information	James Watkins
Director School Business Services	Walter Ruark
Director Special Services	David Stockford

STATE BOARD OF EDUCATION
State House Station #23, Augusta 04333

Chairperson	Marjorie Medd

PUBLIC, PRIVATE AND CATHOLIC SECONDARY SCHOOLS

Ashland, AC 207, PC 3, Aroostook	
SAD 32, PO BOX 289 04732	3-11111
Terrance Despres, supt.	435-3661
Ashland Community JSHS	2-00111
PO BOX N 04732	435-3481
Terrance Despres, prin.	
Auburn, AC 207, PC 7, Androscoggin	
Auburn SD, PO BOX 800 04212	5-11111
B. Eretzian, supt.	784-6431
Little SHS, 2 AUBURN HTS 04210	4-00001
James Miller, prin.	783-8528
MS, 610 COURT ST 04210	3-00100
Richard Brouillette, prin.	784-1356
Walton Freshman HS	2-00010
92 MARY CARROLL ST 04210	784-1528
Anita Campbell, prin.	
Central Maine Technical College	3-CC
1250 TURNER ST 04210	784-2385
Mid-State College	3-CC
88 E HARDSCRABBLE RD 04210	783-1478
Augusta, AC 207, PC 7, Kennebec	
Augusta SD, RR 7 BOX 2525 04330	5-11111
H. G. Nye, supt.	626-2468
Cony HS, 120 CONY ST 04330	3-00011
Maynard Young, prin.	626-2460
Buker JHS, 22 ARMORY ST 04330	2-00100
Michael Buckley, prin.	626-2450
Hodgkins JHS, 17 MALTA ST 04330	2-00100
Daniel Bigley, prin.	626-2490
Erskine Academy, PO BOX 547 04332	2-00011
James Nelson, prin.	445-2962

Mid-State College	2-CC
218 WATER ST 04330	623-3962
University of Maine	4-UC
UNIVERSITY HTS 04330	622-7131
Bangor, AC 207, PC 8, Penobscot	
Bangor SD, 73 HARLOW ST 04401	5-11111
J. Doughty, supt.	945-4400
HS, 885 BROADWAY 04401	4-00011
Norris Nickerson, prin.	941-6200
Fifth Street MS, 143 5TH ST 04401	2-00100
Robert MacDonald, prin.	941-6220
Garland Street MS	2-00100
304 GARLAND ST 04401	941-6230
Stephen Bishop, prin.	
Union SD 34, PO BOX 6360 04402	4-11111
G. MacDonald, supt.	848-3283
Hermon HS, RR 2 BOX 5460 04401	2-00011
Patricia Duran, prin.	848-3365
Bangor Theological Seminary	1-UC
300 UNION ST 04401	942-6781
Beal College	2-CC
629 MAIN ST 04401	947-4591
Eastern Maine Medical Center	HSP
489 STATE ST 04401	947-7051
Eastern Maine Technical College	3-CC
354 HOGAN RD 04401	941-4600
Husson College	4-UC
1 COLLEGE CIR 04401	947-1121
John Baptist Memorial HS	2-00011
100 BROADWAY 04401	947-0313
Joseph Sekera, prin.	
New England School of Broadcasting	1-CS
1 COLLEGE CIR 04401	947-6083

Bar Harbor, AC 207, PC 5, Hancock	
College of the Atlantic	2-UC
105 EDEN ST 04609	288-5015
Bar Mills, AC 207, PC 2, York	
SAD 6, PO BOX 38 04004	5-11111
R. Barker, supt.	929-3831
Other Schools — See Standish, West Buxton	
Bath, AC 207, PC 6, Sagadahoc	
Bath SD, 2 SHERIDAN RD 04530	4-11111
D. Wallace, supt.	443-6601
Morse SHS, 826 HIGH ST 04530	3-00001
Francis Lyons, prin.	443-8250
JHS, 6 BATH ST 04530	3-00110
Paul Timberlake, prin.	443-8270
Hyde S, 616 HIGH ST 04530	2-00111
Malcolm Gauld, prin.	443-5584
Belfast, AC 207, PC 6, Waldo	
SAD 34, PO BOX 363 04915	4-11111
F. Wills, supt.	338-1960
Belfast Area HS, 80 WALDO AVE 04915	3-00011
Ronald Gleason, prin.	338-1790
Howard MS, LINCOLNVILLE AVE 04915	2-00100
Sarah Crosby, prin.	338-3320
Berwick, AC 207, PC 4, York	
SAD 60	
Supt. — See North Berwick	
Noble HS	3-00011
46 CRANBERRY MEADOW RD 03901	698-1320
Pamela Fisher, prin.	
Noble JHS, PO BOX 693 03901	3-00100
Carol Weeks, prin.	698-1188

Bethel, AC 207, PC 4, Oxford
SAD 44, 284 WALKERS MILL RD 04217   4-11111
R. Jenkins, supt.   824-2185
Telstar HS   2-00011
  284 WALKERS MILL RD 04217   824-2136
  Theodore Davis, prin.
Telstar MS   2-00100
  284 WALKERS MILL RD 04217   824-3596
  Bruce Bell, prin.

Gould Academy, PO BOX 860 04217   2-00011
  William Clough, prin.   824-2161

Biddeford, AC 207, PC 7, York
Biddeford SD   5-11111
  2 MAPLEWOOD AVE 04005   282-8280
  Roger Spugnardi, supt.
HS, 2 MAPLEWOOD AVE 04005   3-00011
  Warren Galway, prin.   282-1596
MS, 335 HILL ST 04005   3-00100
  Suzanne Lukas, prin.   282-5957

University of New England   4-UC
  11 HILLS BEACH RD 04005   283-0171

Bingham, AC 207, PC 4, Somerset
SAD 13, PO BOX 139 04920   2-11111
  C. Barnes, supt.   672-5502
Upper Kennebec Valley JSHS   2-00111
  PO BOX 299 04920   672-3300
  Richard Morrison, prin.

Blue Hill, AC 207, PC 3, Hancock

Stevens Academy, PO BOX 816 04614   2-00011
  David Hitchings, prin.   374-2808

Boothbay Harbor, AC 207, PC 4, Lincoln
Boothbay Harbor Community SD   3-11111
  96 TOWNSEND AVE 04538   633-2874
  C. Heino, supt.
Boothbay Region HS   2-00011
  156A TOWNSEND AVE 04538   633-2421
  John Tourtillotte, prin.

Brewer, AC 207, PC 6, Penobscot
Brewer SD, 49 CAPRI ST 04412   4-11111
  P. Jordan, supt.   989-3160
HS, 79 PARKWAY S 04412   3-00011
  Jerry Goss, prin.   989-4140
MS, 5 SOMERSET ST 04412   2-00100
  William Leithiser, prin.   989-8640

Bridgton, AC 207, PC 4, Cumberland
SAD 61
  Supt. — See Naples
Lake Region HS, ROUTE 302 04009   3-00011
  Peter James, prin.   693-6221
Lake Region MS   2-00100
  RR 2 BOX 525 04009   647-8403
  Larry Thompson, prin.

Brooklin, AC 207, PC 2, Hancock
Union SD 76
  Supt. — See Deer Isle
JHS, PO BOX 120 04616   1-01100
  Michelle Jackson, prin.   359-8898

Brunswick, AC 207, PC 7, Cumberland
Brunswick SD, 35 UNION ST 04011   5-11111
  D. Douglas, supt.   729-4148
HS, 36 SPRING ST 04011   3-00011
  David Cannan, prin.   729-0107
JHS, BARROWS ST 04011   3-00100
  Truman Libby, prin.   729-1669

Bowdoin College 04011   4-UC
  725-3100

Buckfield, AC 207, PC 2, Oxford
SAD 39, PO BOX 190 04220   3-11111
  Paul Malinski, supt.   336-2666
JSHS, RR 2 BOX 255 04220   2-00111
  Carol Boyce, prin.   336-2151

Bucksport, AC 207, PC 5, Hancock
Bucksport SD, PO BOX 1519 04416   4-11111
  M. Curtis, supt.   469-7311
HS, PO BOX 400 04416   2-00011
  Thomas Comiciotto, prin.   469-6652
Gardner MS, PO BOX 910 04416   2-00100
  Carl Lusby, prin.   469-6647

Union SD 91, PO BOX V 04416   3-11100
  H. Kelley, supt.   469-2331
Other Schools – See Orrington

Calais, AC 207, PC 5, Washington
Union SD 106, CHURCH ST 04619   4-11111
  R. Marx, supt.   454-7561
HS, RR 1 BOX 22B 04619   2-00011
  Michael Chadwick, prin.   454-2591
MS, 1 WASHINGTON ST 04619   2-01100
  Ralph Shannon, prin.   454-7126

Washington County Technical College   2-CS
  RR 1 BOX 22C 04619   454-2144

Camden, AC 207, PC 5, Knox
SAD 28, PO BOX 1267 04843   4-11111
  T. Marx, supt.   236-3358
Camden-Rockport HS   3-00011
  34 KNOWLTON ST 04843   236-7800
  John Shaw, prin.

Taylor MS, 34 KNOWLTON ST 04843   2-00100
  Michael Weatherwax, prin.   236-7805

Cape Elizabeth, AC 207, PC 6, Cumberland
Cape Elizabeth SD   4-11111
  PO BOX 6267 04107   799-2217
  C. Goldman, supt.
HS, 345 OCEAN HOUSE RD 04107   2-00011
  Richard Difusco, prin.   799-3309
MS, 14 SCOTT DYER RD 04107   3-01100
  Nancy Hutton, prin.   799-8176

Caribou, AC 207, PC 6, Aroostook
Caribou SD, 348 MAIN ST 04736   4-11111
  I. Belanger, supt.   496-6311
HS, 410 SWEDEN ST 04736   3-00011
  David Ouellette, prin.   493-4260
MS, 21 GLENN ST 04736   3-01100
  John Plourde, prin.   493-4240

Carmel, AC 207, PC 2, Penobscot
SAD 23, PO BOX 208 04419   2-11100
  P. Whitney, supt.   848-5173
Caravel MS, PO BOX 142 04419   2-01100
  Harold Stewart, prin.   848-3615

Castine, AC 207, PC 3, Hancock

Maine Maritime Academy   3-UC
  BATTLE AVE 04420   326-4311

Corinna, AC 207, PC 3, Penobscot
SAD 48
  Supt. — See Newport
JHS, PO BOX 403 04928   1-00100
  Joseph Gallant, prin.   278-4201

Cornish, AC 207, PC 3, York
SAD 55 04020   4-11111
  D. Brown, supt.   625-8683
Sacopee Valley JSHS   2-00111
  RR 1 BOX 64 04020   625-3208
  Walter Ridlon, prin.

Cumberland Center, AC 207, PC 4, Cumberland
SAD 51, PO BOX 6A 04021   4-11111
  R. Hasson, supt.   829-4800
Greely HS, 303 MAIN ST 04021   3-00011
  Michael Moore, prin.   829-4805
Greely JHS, 303 MAIN ST 04021   2-00100
  Jillian Kaechele, prin.   829-4815

Danforth, AC 207, PC 3, Washington
SAD 14, RR 1 BOX 50 04424   2-11111
  D. Wells, supt.   448-2882
East Grand S, PO BOX 218 04424   2-11111
  William Grant, prin.   448-2260

Deer Isle, AC 207, PC 2, Hancock
Deer Isle-Stonington Comm. SD   3-11111
  RR 1 BOX 6 04627 – (—), supt.   348-7777
Deer Isle-Stonington JSHS   2-00111
  RR 1 BOX 81 04627   348-2303
  Howard Johnson, prin.

Union SD 76, RR 1 BOX 6 04627   2-11100
  R. Webster, supt.   348-7777
Other Schools – See Brooklin

Dexter, AC 207, PC 5, Penobscot
SAD 46, 10 SPRING ST 04930   4-11111
  P. Dahlinger, supt.   924-5262
Dexter Regional HS   2-00011
  14 ABBOTT HILL RD 04930   924-5536
  Bruce Ives, prin.

Dixfield, AC 207, PC 4, Oxford
SAD 21, 103 WELD ST 04224   3-11111
  C. Howes, supt.   562-7254
Dirigo HS, 99 WELD ST 04224   2-00011
  Patricia Conant, prin.   562-4251
Dirigo MS, SCHOOL ST 04224   2-01100
  Timothy Kelly, prin.   562-7552

Dover-Foxcroft, AC 207, PC 5, Piscataquis
SAD 68, 55 HIGH ST 04426   4-11100
  C. Bridge, supt.   564-2421
Sedomocha JHS   2-00100
  45 HARRISON AVE 04426   564-8376
  John Spruce, prin.

Foxcraft Academy   2-00011
  147 W MAIN ST 04426   564-8351
  Howard Ryder, prin.

East Corinth, AC 207, PC 2, Penobscot
SAD 64, PO BOX 279 04427   4-11111
  L. Ney, supt.   285-3334
Central HS, PO BOX 370 04427   2-00111
  Martin Gray, prin.   285-3326

East Holden, AC 207, PC 2, Penobscot
SAD 63, RR 1 BOX 22 04429   3-11100
  W. Zemer, supt.   843-7851
Holbrook MS, RR 1 BOX 22 04429   2-01100
  Ralph Russell, prin.   843-7769

East Machias, AC 207, PC 2, Washington

Washington Academy   2-00011
  PO BOX 190 04630   255-8301
  James Steenstra, prin.

East Millinocket, AC 207, PC 4, Penobscot
Union SD 113, 41 NORTH ST 04430   3-11111
  T. Jarvis, supt.   746-3500

Schenck JSHS, 41 NORTH ST 04430   2-00111
  Danny Michaud, prin.   746-3511
Other Schools – See Medway

Easton, AC 207, PC 2, Aroostook
Easton SD, PO BOX 126 04740   2-11111
  William Braun, supt.   488-7700
HS, PO BOX 66 04740   1-00011
  Thomas Jandreau, prin.   488-7702

Eastport, AC 207, PC 4, Washington
Union SD 104, HIGH ST 04631   3-11111
  Michael Belanger, supt.   853-2567
Shead HS, 89 HIGH ST 04631   2-00011
  Joseph Seeley, prin.   853-6254

Eliot, AC 207, PC 2, York
SAD 35, ROUTE 236 03903   4-11111
  Wesley Kennedy, supt.   439-2438
Marshwood HS, 204 DOW HWY 03903   3-00011
  Thomas Conrad, prin.   439-5600
Other Schools – See South Berwick

Ellsworth, AC 207, PC 6, Hancock
Ellsworth SD, 75 STATE ST 04605   4-11111
  B. Sawyer, supt.   667-8136
HS, LE JOK ST 04605   2-00011
  Leon Beal, prin.   667-4722
Moore MS, 123 STATE ST 04605   2-00100
  James Newett, prin.   667-6261

Fairfield, AC 207, PC 5, Somerset
SAD 49, 9 SCHOOL ST 04937   5-11111
  E. Fabian, supt.   453-4200
Lawrence HS, 9 SCHOOL ST 04937   3-00011
  Robert Fairbrother, prin.   453-7177
Lawrence JHS, 7 SCHOOL ST 04937   2-00100
  Stephen Cottrell, prin.   453-7175

Kennebec Valley Technical College   2-CC
  92 WESTERN AVE 04937   453-9762

Falmouth, AC 207, PC 6, Cumberland
Falmouth SD, 51 WOODVILLE RD 04105   4-11111
  G. McGiffin, supt.   781-3200
HS, 52 WOODVILLE RD 04105   2-00011
  James Veitch, prin.   781-7429
MS, 52 WOODVILLE RD 04105   2-00100
  Terrence Allen, prin.   781-3740

Farmington, AC 207, PC 5, Franklin
SAD 9, PO BOX 471 04938   5-11111
  M. Cormier, supt.   778-6571
Mt. Blue SHS, RR 2 BOX 2580 04938   3-00001
  Thomas Ward, prin.   778-3561
Mt. Blue JHS, RR 1 BOX 1441 04938   3-00110
  Paul Brown, prin.   778-3511
Other Schools – See Wilton

University of Maine   4-UC
  102 MAIN ST 04938   778-9521

Fort Fairfield, AC 207, PC 4, Aroostook
SAD 20, PO BOX 212 04742   3-11111
  R. Doody, supt.   473-4455
HS, PO BOX 112 04742   2-00011
  Gary Janosco, prin.   472-3271
MS, 20 COLUMBIA AVE 04742   2-01100
  Randall Rolfe, prin.   472-3280

Fort Kent, AC 207, PC 4, Aroostook
SAD 27, 8 W MAIN ST 04743   4-11111
  S. Bernstein, supt.   834-3189
Ft. Kent Community HS   3-00011
  51 PLEASANT ST 04743   834-5540
  James Marquis, prin.

University of Maine   3-UC
  25 PLEASANT ST 04743   834-3162

Freeport, AC 207, PC 4, Cumberland
Freeport SD, 30 MAIN ST 04032   4-11111
  R. Lyman, supt.   865-4743
HS, 30 HOLBROOK ST 04032   2-00011
  Patricia Palmer, prin.   865-4706
MS, 19 PLEASANT ST 04032   2-00100
  Christopher Toy, prin.   865-6051

Pine Tree Academy   2-11111
  16 POWNAL RD 04032   865-4747
  Ronald Kruegar, prin.

Fryeburg, AC 207, PC 4, Oxford
SAD 72, 30A PORTLAND ST 04037   3-11100
  G. Cunningham, supt.   935-2600
Ockett MS, 10 BRIDGTON RD 04037   2-00100
  Eleanor Tracy, prin.   935-2480

Fryeburg Academy, 152 MAIN ST 04037   2-00011
  Daniel Lee, prin.   935-2001

Gardiner, AC 207, PC 6, Kennebec
SAD 11, 150 HIGHLAND AVE 04345   5-11111
  Ronald Snyder, supt.   582-5346
Gardiner Area HS, 40 W HILL RD 04345   3-00011
  Mary Arno, prin.   582-3150
Gardiner Regional JHS   3-00100
  161 COBBOSSEE AVE 04345   582-1326
  Arthur Warren, prin.

Gorham, AC 207, PC 5, Cumberland
Gorham SD, 270 MAIN ST 04038   4-11111
  T. McCormack, supt.   839-5000

HS, 41 MORRILL AVE 04038 — 3-00011
  Steve Rogers, prin. — 839-5004
  Shaw JHS, 75 SOUTH ST 04038 — 2-00100
  Richard Klain, prin. — 839-5011

Gouldsboro, AC 207, PC 2, Hancock
  Flanders Bay Community SD — 2-00011
  RR 1 BOX 43 04607 — 422-3522
  D. Stewart, supt.
  Sumner Memorial HS — 2-00011
  RR 1 BOX 42 04607 — 422-3510
  David Wallin, prin.

Gray, AC 207, PC 3, Cumberland
  SAD 15, PO BOX 1080 04039 — 4-11111
  R. Woodbury, supt. — 657-3335
  Gray-New Gloucester HS — 3-00011
  10 LIBBY HILL RD 04039 — 657-3323
  Roger Lowell, prin.
  Gray-New Gloucester MS — 3-01100
  31 LIBBY HILL RD 04039 — 657-4994
  David Ross, prin.

Greenville, AC 207, PC 4, Piscataquis
  Union SD 60, PO BOX 100 04441 — 2-11111
  G. Reynolds, supt. — 695-3708
  S, PO BOX 100 04441 — 2-11111
  Gilbert Reynolds, prin. — 695-2666
  MS, PO BOX 100 04441 — 2-01100
  Gilbert Reynolds, prin. — 695-2745

Guilford, AC 207, PC 4, Piscataquis
  SAD 4, PO BOX 268 04443 — 4-11111
  R. Poulin, supt. — 876-3444
  Piscataquis Community HS — 2-00011
  PO BOX 118 04443 — 876-4625
  Norman Higgins, prin.
  MS, PO BOX 88 04443 — 2-01100
  J. Daly, prin. — 876-4301

Hallowell, AC 207, PC 5, Kennebec
  SAD 16, 11 1/2 LINCOLN ST 04347 — 3-11111
  L. Levesque, supt. — 622-6351
  Hall-Dale HS, MAPLE ST 04347 — 2-00011
  Stephen MacDougall, prin. — 622-6211
  Hall-Dale MS, MAPLE ST 04347 — 2-00100
  Suzanne Olson, prin. — 622-4162

Hampden, AC 207, PC 4, Penobscot
  SAD 22, PO BOX 279 04444 — 4-11111
  R. Lyons, supt. — 862-3255
  Hampden Academy — 3-00011
  PO BOX 279 04444 — 862-3791
  Robert Rowe, prin.
  Weatherbee MS, PO BOX 279 04444 — 3-01100
  William Cattelle, prin. — 862-3254
  Other Schools – See Winterport

Harrington, AC 207, PC 2, Washington
  SAD 37, PO BOX 79 04643 — 4-11111
  J. White, supt. — 483-2734
  Narraguagus HS — 2-00011
  RR 2 BOX 489 04643 — 483-2747
  John Sawyer, prin.

Hartland, AC 207, PC 4, Somerset
  SAD 48
  Supt. — See Newport
  JHS, ACADEMY ST 04943 — 2-00100
  Peter Campbell, prin. — 938-4770

Hebron, AC 207, PC 2, Oxford

  Hebron Academy, PO BOX 309 04238 — 2-11111
  Richard Davidson, prin. — 966-2100

Houlton, AC 207, PC 6, Aroostook
  SAD 29, PO BOX 190 04730 — 4-11111
  W. McDonnell, supt. — 532-6555
  JSHS, PO BOX 190 04730 — 3-00111
  David Wiggin, prin. — 532-6551

  SAD 70, RR 4 BOX 1870 04730 — 3-11111
  T. Comeau, supt. — 532-3015
  Hodgdon HS, RR 4 BOX 1870 04730 — 2-00011
  Woodrow Dunphy, prin. — 532-2413

Howland, AC 207, PC 4, Penobscot
  SAD 31 04448 — 3-11111
  W. Fowler, supt. — 732-3112
  Penobscot Valley HS — 2-00011
  PO BOX 328 04448 — 732-3111
  Jayne Branscombe, prin.
  Hichborn MS, CROSS ST 04448 — 2-00100
  Gary Haynes, prin. — 732-3113

Island Falls, AC 207, PC 3, Aroostook
  South Aroostook Community SD — 3-11111
  RR 1 BOX 104 04747 — 757-8223
  K. Coville, supt.
  South Aroostook Community S — 3-11111
  RR 1 BOX 104 04747 — 757-8206
  Greg Bagley, prin.

Islesboro, AC 207, PC 2, Waldo
  Islesboro SD, PO BOX 118 04848 — 1-11111
  William Dove, supt. — 734-6723
  Islesboro Central S — 1-11111
  PO BOX 118 04848 — 734-2251
  William Dove, prin.

Jackman, AC 207, PC 3, Somerset
  SAD 12, PO BOX 239 04945 — 2-11111
  Richard Curtis, supt. — 668-7749
  Forest Hills Consolidated S — 2-11111
  PO BOX 239 04945 — 668-5291
  Richard Curtis, prin.

Jay, AC 207, PC 3, Franklin
  Jay SD, 6 SCHOOL ST 04239 — 4-11111
  W. B. Parsons, supt. — 897-3936
  HS, 4 SCHOOL ST 04239 — 2-00011
  William Riley, prin. — 897-4336
  JHS, 3 SCHOOL ST 04239 — 2-00100
  Jacqueline Pelletier, prin. — 897-4319

Jonesport, AC 207, PC 4, Washington
  Moosabec Community SD — 2-00011
  PO BOX 309 04649 — 497-2154
  P. Edgecomb, supt.
  Jonesport-Beals HS — 2-00011
  PO BOX 189 04649 — 497-5454
  Nancy Melhorn, prin.

Kennebunk, AC 207, PC 5, York
  SAD 71, 1 STORER ST 04043 — 4-11111
  M. Joyce, supt. — 985-1100
  HS, 89 FLETCHER ST 04043 — 3-00011
  David McConnell, prin. — 985-1110
  MS, 87 FLETCHER ST 04043 — 2-00100
  Sandra Caldwell, prin. — 985-2912

Kennebunkport, AC 207, PC 4, York

  Heartwood School of Art — 1-CS
  PO BOX 1100 04046 — 967-8444
  Landing School of Boatbuilding & Design — 1-CS
  PO BOX 1490 04046 — 985-7976

Kents Hill, AC 207, PC 2, Kennebec

  Kents Hill S, PO BOX 257 04349 — 2-00011
  George Bonnefond, prin. — 685-4914

Kingfield, AC 207, PC 3, Franklin
  SAD 58, RR 1 BOX 1580 04947 — 4-11111
  Anthony Krapf, supt. — 265-5511
  Other Schools – See Phillips, Strong

  Carrabassett Valley Academy — 1-00111
  RR 1 BOX 2240 04947 — 237-2250
  John Ritzo, prin.

Kittery, AC 207, PC 6, York
  Kittery SD, 22 SHAPLEIGH RD 03904 — 4-11111
  B. Johnson, supt. — 439-6819
  Traip Academy — 2-00011
  12 WILLIAMS AVE 03904 — 439-1121
  Leonard Box, prin.
  Frisbee MS, 120 ROGERS RD 03904 — 2-01100
  Kevin Moran, prin. — 439-1122

Lee, AC 207, PC 2, Penobscot
  SAD 30, PO BOX 368 04455 — 2-11100
  J. Winslow, supt. — 738-2665
  Mt. Jefferson JHS, WINN ST 04455 — 2-00100
  Mary Hinse, prin. — 738-2866

  Lee Academy, PO BOX 338 04455 — 2-00011
  Edwin McLaughlin, prin. — 738-4263

Lewiston, AC 207, PC 8, Androscoggin
  Lewiston SD, 36 OAK ST 04240 — 6-11111
  R. Connors, supt. — 795-4100
  HS, 156 EAST AVE 04240 — 4-00011
  Richard Sykes, prin. — 795-4190
  JHS, 75 CENTRAL AVE 04240 — 3-00100
  Charles Douglas, prin. — 795-4180

  Bates College 04240 — 4-UC
   — 786-6000
  Central Maine Medical Center — 1-CC
  300 MAIN ST 04240 — 795-0111
  St. Dominic Regional HS — 2-00011
  179 BLAKE ST 04240 — 782-6911
  Michael Welch, prin.

Limerick, AC 207, PC 2, York

  Air Tech — 2-CS
  RR 11 BOX 170 04048 — 793-8020

Limestone, AC 207, PC 4, Aroostook
  Limestone SD, 275 MAIN ST 04750 — 4-11111
  J. Morse, supt. — 325-4888
  JSHS, 75 HIGH ST 04750 — 2-00111
  Paul Beaulieu, prin. — 325-4742

Lincoln, AC 207, PC 5, Penobscot
  SAD 67, PO BOX 250 04457 — 4-11111
  J. Turcotte, supt. — 794-6509
  Mattanawcook Academy — 2-00011
  15 REED DR 04457 — 794-6711
  Richard Greenlaw, prin.
  Mattanawcook JHS — 2-01100
  41 SCHOOL ST 04457 — 794-8935
  David Theoharides, prin.

Lisbon Falls, AC 207, PC 5, Androscoggin
  Union SD 30, 4 CAMPUS ST 04252 — 4-11111
  G. Carroll, supt. — 353-6711
  Lisbon HS, 591 LISBON ST 04252 — 2-00011
  William Schenck, prin. — 353-3030
  Sugg MS, MIDDLE SCHOOL RD 04252 — 2-00100
  Sheila McAllister, prin. — 353-3055

Litchfield, AC 207, PC 2, Kennebec
  Union SD 44
  Supt. — See Sabattus
  Libby-Tozier MS, HALLOWELL RD 04350 — 2-01100
  Thomas Soule, prin. — 268-4136

Livermore Falls, AC 207, PC 4, Androscoggin
  SAD 36, PO BOX S 04254 — 4-11111
  Emmons Pinkham, supt. — 897-6722
  HS, 25 CEDAR ST 04254 — 2-00011
  Carol Parsons, prin. — 897-3428
  MS, 1 HIGHLAND AVE 04254 — 2-00100
  Brian Oakes, prin. — 897-2121

Lubec, AC 207, PC 3, Washington
  SAD 19, 20 SOUTH ST 04652 — 2-11111
  O. Bridgham, supt. — 733-5573
  S, 20 SOUTH ST 04652 — 2-11111
  Chester Hubbard, prin. — 733-5591

Machias, AC 207, PC 4, Washington
  Union SD 102, 12 E MAIN ST 04654 — 3-11111
  W. Clark, supt. — 255-6585
  Machias Memorial HS — 2-00011
  106 COURT ST 04654 — 255-3812
  William Prescott, prin.

  University of Maine — 3-UC
  9 OBRIEN AVE 04654 — 255-3313

Madawaska, AC 207, PC 5, Aroostook
  Madawaska SD — 4-11111
  96 SAINT THOMAS ST 04756 — 728-3346
  T. Scott, supt.
  JSHS, 80 7TH AVE 04756 — 3-00111
  Kermit Pooler, prin. — 728-3371

Madison, AC 207, PC 5, Somerset
  SAD 59, 30 MAIN ST 04950 — 4-11111
  L. Ingraham, supt. — 696-3323
  Madison Area Memorial HS — 2-00011
  RR 1 BOX 229 04950 — 696-3395
  Joseph Testa, prin.
  JHS, 199 MAIN ST 04950 — 2-01100
  John Krasnavage, prin. — 696-3381

Mars Hill, AC 207, PC 4, Aroostook
  SAD 42, PO BOX 1006 04758 — 2-11111
  M. Eastman, supt. — 425-3771
  Central Aroostook JSHS — 2-00111
  PO BOX 310 04758 — 425-2811
  Roger Shaw, prin.

Medway, AC 207, PC 3, Penobscot
  Union SD 113
  Supt. — See East Millinocket
  MS, PO BOX L 04460 — 2-01100
  Robert Bouchard, prin. — 746-3470

Mexico, AC 207, PC 4, Oxford
  SAD 43, 32 PARKER ST 04257 — 3-11111
  W. Richards, supt. — 364-7896
  Mountain Valley MS — 2-00100
  HIGHLAND TERR 04257 — 364-7926
  Charles Lever, prin.
  Other Schools – See Rumford

Millinocket, AC 207, PC 6, Penobscot
  Millinocket SD — 4-11111
  AROOSTOOK AVE 04462 — 723-6400
  R. Pelletier, supt.
  Stearns HS, 199 STATE ST 04462 — 2-00011
  Terrence Baigle, prin. — 723-6430
  MS, 275 KATAHDIN AVE 04462 — 2-00100
  Arthur Greenlaw, prin. — 723-6415

Milo, AC 207, PC 4, Piscataquis
  SAD 41, 37 W MAIN ST 04463 — 4-11111
  J. K. Laux, supt. — 943-7317
  Penquis Valley HS, 35 W MAIN ST 04463 — 2-00011
  George Sincerbeaux, prin. — 943-7346
  Penquis Valley MS, 35 W MAIN ST 04463 — 2-00100
  Thomas Lechner, prin. — 943-7346

Monmouth, AC 207, PC 3, Kennebec
  Monmouth SD, PO BOX 460 04259 — 3-11111
  R. Crawford, supt. — 933-3062
  HS, RR 1 BOX 258 04259 — 2-00011
  Roy Crawford, prin. — 933-4416
  MS, PO BOX 240 04259 — 2-01100
  David Bartlett, prin. — 933-9002

Mount Desert, AC 207, PC 2, Hancock
  Mt. Desert Community SD — 2-00011
  HC 62 BOX 5 04660 — 288-5049
  H. Colter, supt.
  Mt. Desert Island HS — 2-00011
  HC 62 BOX 5 04660 — 288-5011
  Lawrence Coughlin, prin.

Naples, AC 207, PC 2, Cumberland
  SAD 61, PO BOX 989 04055 — 4-11111
  John Fontana, supt. — 693-3738
  Other Schools – See Bridgton

Newcastle, AC 207, PC 2, Lincoln

  Lincoln Academy, PO BOX 382 04553 — 2-00011
  Christopher Frost, prin. — 563-3596

Newport, AC 207, PC 4, Penobscot
  SAD 48, 65 MAIN ST 04953 — 4-11111
  R. Freve, supt. — 368-5091
  Nokomis Reg. HS — 3-00011
  RR 2 BOX 4800 04953 — 368-4354
  Lyford Beverage, prin.
  Other Schools – See Corinna, Hartland

North Anson, AC 207, PC 3, Somerset
  SAD 74, PO BOX 159 04958 — 4-11111
  R. Hatch, supt. — 635-2727
  Carrabec HS, PO BOX 220 04958 — 2-00011
  Robert Clement, prin. — 635-2296

North Berwick, AC 207, PC 4, York
SAD 60, PO BOX 819 03906 — 5-11111
P. Johnson, supt. — 676-2234
Other Schools – See Berwick

North Bridgton, AC 207, PC 3, Cumberland

Bridgton Academy — 2-00001
PO BOX 292 04057 — 647-3322
James Young, prin.

North Haven, AC 207, PC 2, Knox
SAD 7, RR 1 BOX 699 04853 — 1-11111
Pat Donahue, supt. — 867-4707
North Haven Community S — 1-11111
RR 1 BOX 699 04853 — 867-4707
Angus Hallowell, prin.

North Windham, AC 207, PC see Windham

St. Joseph's College 04062 — 5-UC
892-6766

Oakland, AC 207, PC 5, Kennebec
SAD 47, 20 HEATH ST 04963 — 4-11111
J. Albanese, supt. — 465-7384
Messalonskee HS, 62 OAK ST 04963 — 3-00011
Carroll Thompson, prin. — 465-7381
Williams JHS, 19 PLEASANT ST 04963 — 2-00100
Deborah Bobotas, prin. — 465-2167

Old Orchard Beach, AC 207, PC 6, York
Old Orchard Beach SD — 4-11111
28 JAMESON HILL RD 04064 — 934-5751
Jay Bartner, supt.
HS, 40 T FOR TURN RD 04064 — 2-00011
Grace Cantara, prin. — 934-4461
Loranger MS, 148 SACO AVE 04064 — 2-01100
Michael Pulsifer, prin. — 934-2361

Old Town, AC 207, PC 6, Penobscot
Old Town SD, 151 OAK ST 04468 — 4-11111
J. Grady, supt. — 827-7171
HS, 240 STILLWATER AVE 04468 — 3-00011
Donald Sturgeon, prin. — 827-3910
Leonard MS, 151 OAK ST 04468 — 2-00100
Frank Perry, prin. — 827-3900

Orono, AC 207, PC 7, Penobscot
Union SD 87, 18 GOODRIDGE RD 04473 — 4-11111
R. Moreau, supt. — 866-5521
JSHS, 14 GOODRICH DR 04473 — 2-00111
Thomas Perry, prin. — 866-4916

University of Maine 04469 — 6-UC
581-2600

Orrington, AC 207, PC 2, Penobscot
Union SD 91
Supt. — See Bucksport
Center Drive MS — 2-00100
RR 3 BOX 100 04474 — 825-3697
James White, prin.

Phillips, AC 207, PC 3, Franklin
SAD 58
Supt. — See Kingfield
MS, RR 4 04966 — 2-01100
(—), prin. — 639-2909

Pittsfield, AC 207, PC 5, Somerset
SAD 53, PO BOX 488 04967 — 3-11100
T. McCannell, supt. — 487-5107
Warsaw MS, 27 SCHOOL ST 04967 — 2-01100
Claton Corriveau, prin. — 487-5145

Maine Central Institute — 2-00011
125 S MAIN ST 04967 — 487-3355
Douglas Cummings, prin.

Poland Spring, AC 207, PC 2, Androscoggin

Elan HS, RR 1 BOX 370 04274 — 2-00011
Lynne Schott, prin. — 998-4666

Portland, AC 207, PC 8, Cumberland
Portland SD, 331 VERANDA ST 04103 — 6-11111
T. Edwards, supt. — 874-8100
Deering HS, 370 STEVENS AVE 04103 — 4-00011
Jan Patten, prin. — 874-8260
HS, 284 CUMBERLAND AVE 04101 — 3-00011
Dana Allen, prin. — 874-8250
King MS, 92 DEERING AVE 04102 — 2-00100
Michael McCarthy, prin. — 874-8140
Lincoln MS, 522 STEVENS AVE 04103 — 3-00100
Kathleen Rossi, prin. — 874-8145
Moore MS, 171 AUBURN ST 04103 — 3-00100
Philip McCormick, prin. — 874-8150

Andover College — 4-CC
901 WASHINGTON AVE 04103 — 774-6126
Baxter State School for the Deaf — HND
PO BOX 799 04104
Casco Bay College — 2-CC
477 CONGRESS ST 04101 — 772-0196
Catherine McAuley HS — 2-00011
631 STEVENS AVE 04103 — 797-3802
Sr. Mary Kelleher, prin.
Cheverus HS, 267 OCEAN AVE 04103 — 2-00011
John Mullen, prin. — 774-6238
Maine College of Art — 2-UC
97 SPRING ST 04101 — 775-3052
Maine Medical Center — HSP
22 BRAMHALL ST 04102 — 871-2141

Mercy Hospital — HSP
144 STATE ST 04101 — 879-3000
University of Southern Maine — 6-UC
96 FALMOUTH ST 04103 — 780-4133
W, 360 SPRING ST 04102 — 3-11111
Waynflete S, 360 SPRING ST 04102 — 772-6832
Ronald Hall, prin.
Westbrook College — 3-UC
716 STEVENS AVE 04103 — 797-7261

Presque Isle, AC 207, PC 7, Aroostook
SAD 1, PO BOX 1118 04769 — 5-11111
G. Johnson, supt. — 764-4101
HS, 16 FORT ST 04769 — 3-00011
Richard Durost, prin. — 764-0121
Cunningham MS, 5 3RD ST 04769 — 2-00100
Frank Hallett, prin. — 764-8101
Skyway MS — 2-00100
569 SKYWAY INDUSTRIAL PARK 04769
John Graves, prin. — 764-4474

Northern Maine Technical College — 3-CC
33 EDGEMONT DR 04769 — 769-2461
University of Maine — 4-UC
181 MAIN ST 04769 — 764-0311

Rangeley, AC 207, PC 3, Franklin
Union SD 37, PO BOX 97 04970 — 2-11111
R. Greenleaf, supt. — 864-3311
Rangeley Lakes Regional S — 2-11111
PO BOX 97 04970 — 864-3311
James Smith, prin.

Readfield, AC 207, PC 1, Kennebec
Maranacook Community SD — 3-00111
PO BOX 87 04355 — 685-3336
Ed LeBlanc, supt.
Maranacook Comm. JSHS — 3-00111
PO BOX 177 04355 — 685-4923
Warren Hathorne, prin.

Richmond, AC 207, PC 4, Sagadahoc
Richmond SD, PO BOX 190 04357 — 4-11111
R. Spearin, supt. — 737-2221
HS, 118 MAIN ST 04357 — 2-00011
Gregory Bartlett, prin. — 737-4348
MS, 118 MAIN ST 04357 — 2-00100
Douglas Reed, prin. — 737-8655

Rockland, AC 207, PC 6, Knox
SAD 5, 34 SCHOOL ST 04841 — 4-11111
Don Kanicki, supt. — 596-6620
Rockland District HS — 2-00011
400 BROADWAY 04841 — 596-2010
Michael Gundel, prin.
Rockland District MS — 2-00100
38 LINCOLN ST 04841 — 596-2020
G. Thomas Mellor, prin.

Rumford, AC 207, PC 6, Oxford
SAD 43
Supt. — See Mexico
Mountain Valley HS — 3-00011
799 HANCOCK ST 04276 — 364-4547
Richard Blackman, prin.

Sabattus, AC 207, PC 4, Androscoggin
Oak Hill Community SD — 2-00011
PO BOX 220 04280 — 375-4273
L. Littlefield, supt.
Oak Hill HS, PO BOX 400 04280 — 2-00011
David Wing, prin. — 375-4950

Union SD 44, PO BOX 220 04280 — 4-11100
L. Littlefield, supt. — 375-4273
Other Schools – See Litchfield

Saco, AC 207, PC 7, York
Union SD 7 — 4-11100
56 INDUSTRIAL PARK RD # 2 04072
C. Mowles, supt. — 284-4505
MS, BUXTON ROAD 04072 — 3-00100
Joseph Voci, prin. — 282-4181

Thornton Academy, 438 MAIN ST 04072 — 3-00011
Carl Stasio, prin. — 282-3361

Saint Agatha, AC 207, PC 2, Aroostook
SAD 33, PO BOX 347 04772 — 3-11111
J. White, supt. — 543-7334
Wisdom JSHS, PO BOX 137 04772 — 2-00111
P. Bouchard, prin. — 543-7717

Sanford, AC 207, PC 7, York
Sanford SD, 263 MAIN ST 04073 — 5-11111
R. Grogan, supt. — 324-2810
HS, 2R MAIN ST 04073 — 4-00011
Gary Rook, prin. — 324-4050
JHS, 8 MAIN ST 04073 — 3-00100
D. Terracin, prin. — 324-3114

Scarborough, AC 207, PC 5, Cumberland
Scarborough SD, PO BOX 370 04070 — 4-11111
S. Grover, supt. — 883-4315
HS, 30 GORHAM RD 04074 — 3-00011
Susan Gendron, prin. — 883-4354
Wentworth MS, 40 GORHAM RD 04074 — 2-00100
(—), prin. — 883-4356

Searsport, AC 207, PC 4, Waldo
SAD 56, PO BOX 467 04974 — 3-11111
R. Clukey, supt. — 548-6643
Searsport District HS, CHURCH ST 04974 — 2-00011
Darrell Gilman, prin. — 548-2313

Searsport District MS — 2-00100
MORTLAND RD 04974 — 548-2311
Susan Weaver, prin.

Sherman Station, AC 207, PC 2, Penobscot
SAD 25, PO BOX 20 04777 — 3-11111
C. Nightingale, supt. — 365-4272
Katahdin HS, ROUTE 11 04777 — 2-00011
Steven Greenlaw, prin. — 365-4218
Katahdin JHS, RR 11 04777 — 2-00100
Steven Greenlaw, prin. — 365-4285

Skowhegan, AC 207, PC 6, Somerset
SAD 54, PO BOX 69 04976 — 5-11111
Bruce McGray, supt. — 474-9508
Skowhegan Area HS — 3-00011
PO BOX 248 04976 — 474-5511
Barb Arnold, prin.
Skowhegan Area MS, WILLOW ST 04976 — 3-00100
Eileen Kohl, prin. — 474-3339

South Berwick, AC 207, PC 4, York
SAD 35
Supt. — See Eliot
Marshwood JHS, 49 ACADEMY ST 03908 — 3-00100
Thomas Parker, prin. — 384-4111

Berwick Academy — 2-11111
27 ACADEMY ST 03908 — 384-2164
Richard Ridgeway, prin.

South China, AC 207, PC 2, Kennebec
Union SD 52
Supt. — See Winslow
MS, RR 1 BOX 1162 04358 — 2-01100
Prescott Verrill, prin. — 445-2065

South Paris, AC 207, PC 4, Oxford
SAD 17, 23 MARKET SQ 04281 — 5-11111
Mary Jane McCalmon, supt. — 743-8972
Oxford Hills HS, 250 MAIN ST 04281 — 4-00011
Philip Blood, prin. — 743-8914
Oxford Hills JHS, 100 PINE ST 04281 — 3-00100
Joseph Moore, prin. — 743-5946

South Portland, AC 207, PC 7, Cumberland
South Portland SD — 5-11111
130 WESCOTT RD 04106 — 871-0555
R. MacDonald, supt.
HS, 637 HIGHLAND AVE 04106 — 3-00011
Jacqueline Soychak, prin. — 767-3266
Mahoney MS, 240 OCEAN ST 04106 — 2-00100
Kathy Germani, prin. — 799-7386
Memorial MS, 120 WESCOTT RD 04106 — 2-00100
Alan Hawkins, prin. — 773-5629

Southern Maine Technical College — 4-CC
2 FORT RD 04106 — 799-7303

Standish, AC 207, PC 2, Cumberland
SAD 6
Supt. — See Bar Mills
Bonny Eagle HS, 700 SACO RD 04084 — 4-00011
Alton Hadley, prin. — 929-3831

Strong, AC 207, PC 3, Franklin
SAD 58
Supt. — See Kingfield
Mt. Abram Reg. HS — 2-00011
RR 1 BOX 760 04983 — 678-2701
Gilbert Eaton, prin.

Thomaston, AC 207, PC 4, Knox
SAD 50, PO BOX 182 04861 — 3-11111
D. Calderwood, supt. — 354-2555
Georges Valley HS — 2-00011
PO BOX 192 04861 — 354-2502
Scott Phair, prin.
MS, WATTS LANE 04861 — 2-01100
Terry Kenniston, prin. — 354-6353

Thorndike, AC 207, PC 2, Waldo
SAD 3
Supt. — See Unity
Mt. View HS, RR 2 BOX 180 04986 — 2-00011
Wayne Suomi, prin. — 568-3255
Mt. View JHS, RR 2 BOX 180 04986 — 2-00100
Kendall Olsen, prin. — 568-7561

Topsham, AC 207, PC 6, Sagadahoc
SAD 75, PO BOX 475 04086 — 5-11111
J. Wilhelm, supt. — 729-9961
Mt. Ararat HS, ROUTE 201 04086 — 4-00011
Joseph Findlay, prin. — 729-6751
Mt. Ararat MS, ROUTE 201 04086 — 2-00100
Elizabeth Manchester, prin. — 729-6751

Turner, AC 207, PC 2, Androscoggin
SAD 52, RR 1 BOX 1220 04282 — 4-11111
S. Sawyer, supt. — 225-3795
Leavitt Area HS — 3-00011
RR 1 BOX 1251 04282 — 225-3533
Wilfred LeBlanc, prin.
Tripp MS, RR 1 BOX 1253 04282 — 2-00100
Peter Selwood, prin. — 225-3261

Unity, AC 207, PC 2, Waldo
SAD 3, PO BOX 171 04988 — 4-11111
G. Clockedile, supt. — 948-6136
Other Schools – See Thorndike

Unity College — 2-UC
HC 78 BOX 1 04988 — 948-3131

Van Buren, AC 207, PC 5, Aroostook
SAD 24, 319 MAIN ST 04785 — 3-11111 / 868-2746
W. Mowatt, supt.
Van Buren District JSHS — 2-00111
321 MAIN ST 04785 — 868-5274
Richard Cote, prin.

Vinalhaven, AC 207, PC 3, Knox
SAD 8, RR 1 BOX 112 04863 — 2-11111 / 863-4800
D. Hopkins, supt.
Lincoln S, RR 1 BOX 112 04863 — 2-11111 / 863-4800
Earl Lord, prin.

Waldoboro, AC 207, PC 4, Lincoln
SAD 40, PO BOX L 04572 — 4-11111 / 832-5358
D. Gaul, supt.
Medomack Valley HS — 3-00011
PO BOX 309 04572 — 832-5389
R. Dolloff, prin.
Gray JHS, PO BOX 329 04572 — 2-00100 / 832-2106
Barry Belyea, prin.

Washburn, AC 207, PC 4, Aroostook
SAD 45, PO BOX 507 04786 — 3-11111 / 455-8301
D. Lyon, supt.
Washburn District HS — 2-00011
PO BOX 188 04786 — 455-4501
Larry Hallowell, prin.

Waterboro, AC 207, PC 3, York
SAD 57, PO BOX 499 04087 — 5-11111 / 247-3221
Fred Bechard, supt.
Massabesic HS, PO BOX 500 04087 — 3-00011 / 247-3141
James Stephenson, prin.
Massabesic JHS, PO BOX 460 04087 — 3-00100 / 247-6121
William Fisher, prin.

Waterville, AC 207, PC 7, Kennebec
Waterville SD, 21 GILMAN ST 04901 — 4-11111 / 873-4281
A. Hall, supt.
HS, 1 BROOKLYN AVE 04901 — 3-00011 / 873-2751
Eric Haley, prin.
JHS, 120 W RIVER RD 04901 — 2-00100 / 873-2144
Peter Thiboutot, prin.

Colby College — 4-UC
150 MAYFLOWER HILL DR 04901 — 872-3168
Mid-Maine Medical Center — HSP
30 CHASE AVE 04901 — 872-4315

Thomas College — 3-UC
180 W RIVER RD 04901 — 877-0101

Wells, AC 207, PC 4, York
Wells-Ogunquit Community SD — 4-11111
PO BOX 578 04090 — 646-8331
R. Kautz, supt.
HS, PO BOX 579 04090 — 3-00011 / 646-7011
Valjeane Olenn, prin.
JHS, PO BOX 310 04090 — 2-01100 / 646-5142
Julia Phelps, prin.

Westbrook, AC 207, PC 7, Cumberland
Westbrook SD, 596 MAIN ST 04092 — 5-11111 / 854-0800
E. Connolly, supt.
HS, 125 STROUDWATER ST 04092 — 3-00011 / 854-0810
William Michaud, prin.
JHS, 426 BRIDGE ST 04092 — 3-00100 / 854-0830
Spencer Hardy, prin.

West Buxton, AC 207, PC 2, York
SAD 6
Supt. — See Bar Mills
Bonny Eagle MS — 3-00100
RR 2 BOX 250 04093 — 929-3831
Paul Vincent, prin.

Wilton, AC 207, PC 4, Franklin
SAD 9
Supt. — See Farmington
Academy Hill MS, PO BOX S 04294 — 2-01100 / 645-4488
Donald Lacharite, prin.

Windham, AC 207, PC 5, Cumberland
Windham SD — 4-11111
228 WINDHAM CENTER RD 04062 — 892-1800
J. Love, supt.
SHS, 406 GRAY RD 04062 — 2-00001 / 892-1810
Shirley Hartwell, prin.
JHS, 408 GRAY RD 04062 — 3-00110 / 892-1820
Harold Shortsleeve, prin.

Winslow, AC 207, PC 6, Kennebec
Union SD 52, 16 BENTON AVE 04901 — 4-11111 / 872-1960
L. Duff, supt.
HS, 14 DANIELSON ST 04901 — 3-00011 / 872-1990
George Davis, prin.
JHS, 10 DANIELSON ST 04901 — 2-00100 / 872-1973
Hugh Riordan, prin.
Other Schools — See South China

Winterport, AC 207, PC 4, Waldo
SAD 22
Supt. — See Hampden
Wagner MS, PO BOX 739 04496 — 2-00100 / 223-4309
Dale Williams, prin.

Winthrop, AC 207, PC 5, Kennebec
Winthrop SD, TOWN HALL LANE 04364 — 4-11111 / 377-2296
R. Pelletier, supt.
HS, 11 HIGHLAND AVE 04364 — 2-00011 / 377-2228
Philip Richardson, prin.
MS, 24 CHARLES ST 04364 — 2-00100 / 377-2240
Mark Flight, prin.

Wiscasset, AC 207, PC 4, Lincoln
Union SD 48, PO BOX 430 04578 — 4-11111 / 882-6303
J. Ashe, supt.
HS, GARDINER ROAD 04578 — 2-00011 / 882-7722
Bruce Brann, prin.
MS, PO BOX 348 04578 — 2-01100 / 882-7767
Don Siviski, prin.

Woodland, AC 207, PC 4, Washington
Union SD 107, PO BOX 580 04694 — 3-11111 / 427-6913
C. Anderson, supt.
JSHS, MAIN ST 04694 — 2-00111 / 427-3325
Earle Tourtillotte, prin.

Yarmouth, AC 207, PC 5, Cumberland
Yarmouth SD, 8 PORTLAND ST 04096 — 4-11111 / 846-5586
Ken Murphy, supt.
HS, 50 W ELM ST 04096 — 3-00011 / 846-5535
Kenneth Nye, prin.
Harrison MS, MCCARTNEY ST 04096 — 2-01100 / 846-2499
Richard Fugere, prin.

North Yarmouth Academy — 2-00111
123 MAIN ST 04096 — 846-9051
Edward Good, prin.

York, AC 207, PC 5, York
York SD, 300 YORK ST 03909 — 4-11111 / 363-3403
K. Donovan, supt.
HS, 286 LONG SANDS RD 03909 — 2-00011 / 363-3621
Robert Stevens, prin.
MS, 84 ORGANUG RD 03909 — 3-01100 / 363-4214
Elton Knowles, prin.

MARYLAND

STATE DEPARTMENT OF EDUCATION
200 W. Baltimore St., Baltimore 21201
(410) 333-2000

Superintendent of Schools	Nancy Grasmick
Deputy Superintendent	Vacant
Assistant Superintendent Certification & Accreditation	A. Sanders
Assistant Superintendent Instruction	Lorraine Costella
Assistant Superintendent Education & Support	Ellen Gonzales
Assistant Superintendent Business Services	Raymond Brown
Assistant Superintendent Special Education	Richard Steinke

STATE BOARD OF EDUCATION
200 W. Baltimore St., Baltimore 21201

President   Robert Embry

PUBLIC, PRIVATE AND CATHOLIC SECONDARY SCHOOLS

Aberdeen, AC 410, PC 7, Harford
Harford County SD
Supt. — See Bel Air
HS, 251 PARADISE RD 21001 — 4-00011 / 273-5500
Robert Magee, prin.
MS, 111 MOUNT ROYAL AVE 21001 — 4-00100 / 273-5510
Agnes Purnell, prin.

Accident, AC 301, PC 2, Garrett
Garrett County SD
Supt. — See Oakland
Northern Garrett County HS — 3-00011
RR 2 BOX 4 21520 — 746-8668
Martin Green, prin.

Northern MS, RR 2 BOX 5 21520 — 2-00100 / 746-8165
William Carlson, prin.

Accokeek, AC 301, PC 5, Prince George's
Prince Georges County SD
Supt. — See Upper Marlboro
Burroughs MS, 1400 BERRY RD 20607 — 2-00100 / 292-2500
Bruce Katz, prin.

Adelphi, AC 301, PC 7, Prince George's
Prince Georges County SD
Supt. — See Upper Marlboro
Buck Lodge MS — 3-00100
2611 BUCK LODGE 20783 — 434-0700
Gerald Kountz, prin.

Annapolis, AC 410, PC 8, Anne Arundel
Anne Arundel County SD — 8-11111
2644 RIVA RD 21401 — 222-5000
Carol Parham, supt.
Broadneck SHS — 3-00001
1265 GREEN HOLLY DR 21401 — 757-1300
Lawrence Knight, prin.
HS, 2700 RIVA RD 21401 — 4-00011 / 266-5240
Laura Webb, prin.
MS, 1399 FOREST DR 21403 — 3-00100 / 267-8658
Kevin Dennehy, prin.
Bates MS, 701 CHASE ST 21401 — 3-00100 / 263-0270
Sarah McGowan, prin.

Other Schools – See Arnold, Baltimore, Crofton,
Edgewater, Fort George G. Meade, Gambrills, Glen
Burnie, Harwood, Lothian, Millersville, Odenton,
Pasadena, Severn, Severna Park

Annapolis Christian S	2-11111
710 RIDGELY AVE 21401	266-8251
Fleet Business School	2-CS
2530 RIVA RD STE 201 21401	266-8500
Key S, 534 HILLSMERE DR 21403	3-11111
Ronald Goldblatt, prin.	263-9231
St. John's College	2-UC
PO BOX 2800 21404	800-727-9238
St. Mary HS	3-00011
113 DUKE OF GLOUCESTER ST 21401	269-1088
Sr. Phyllis McNally, prin.	
United States Naval Academy	5-UC
117 DECATUR RD 21402	267-6100

Arnold, AC 410, PC 7, Anne Arundel

Anne Arundel County SD	
Supt. — See Annapolis	
Severn River JHS	3-00110
241 PENINSULA FARM RD 21012	544-0922
Don McClenahan, prin.	

Anne Arundel Community College	7-CC
101 COLLEGE PKY 21012	647-7100

Baltimore, AC 410, PC 11, Baltimore

Anne Arundel County SD	
Supt. — See Annapolis	
Brooklyn Park JSHS	4-00111
200 HAMMONDS LN 21225	789-8500
Joel Drapalski, prin.	
Lindale MS, 200 HAMMONDS LN 21225	3-00100
Joel Drapalski, prin.	789-8500
Balitmore CSD, 200 E NORTH AVE 21202	9-11111
Walter Amprey, supt.	396-8700
Baltimore City College HS	4-00011
3220 THE ALAMEDA 21218	396-6557
Jean Johnson, prin.	
Baltimore Polytech Institute	4-00011
1400 W COLD SPRING LN 21209	396-7026
Albert Strickland, prin.	
Carver Voc. Tech. HS	4-00011
2201 PRESSTMAN ST 21216	396-0553
Michael Plitt, prin.	
Douglass HS	4-00011
2301 GWYNNS FALLS PKY 21217	396-7821
Shirley Hill, prin.	
Dunbar HS, 1400 ORLEANS ST 21231	3-00011
Charlotte Brown, prin.	396-9478
Edmondson/Westside HS	4-00011
501 N ATHOL AVE 21229	396-0685
Irby Miller, prin.	
Forest Park HS	3-00011
3701 ELDORADO AVE 21207	396-0746
Loretta Breese, prin.	
Lake Clifton/Eastern HS	4-00011
2801 SAINT LO DR 21213	396-6637
Stanley Holmes, prin.	
Mergenthaler Vo-Tech HS	4-00011
3500 HILLEN RD 21218	396-6496
Christolyne Buie, prin.	
Northern HS	4-00011
2201 PINEWOOD AVE 21214	396-6435
Douglas Norris, prin.	
Northwestern HS	4-00011
6900 PARK HEIGHTS AVE 21215	396-0646
Mary Brown, prin.	
Patterson HS, 100 KANE ST 21224	4-00011
Leon Tillet, prin.	396-9276
S for the Arts	2-00011
712 CATHEDRAL ST 21201	396-1185
David Simon, prin.	
Southern HS	4-00011
1100 COVINGTON ST 21230	396-1500
Cecelia Chesno, prin.	
Southwestern HS	4-00011
200 FONT HILL AVE 21223	396-1422
David Benson, prin.	
Walbrook HS	4-00011
2000 EDGEWOOD ST 21216	396-0721
Marilyn Rondeau, prin.	
Western HS, 4600 FALLS RD 21209	4-00011
Sandra Wighton, prin.	396-7040
Paquin JSHS, 2200 SINCLAIR LN 21213	2-00111
Rosetta Stith, prin.	396-9399
Briscoe HS, 900 DRUID HILL AVE 21201	Vo Tech
Jack Knott, prin.	396-0771
Venable HS	Vo Tech
701 E 34TH ST # 3 21218	396-6478
Wynola Cunningham, prin.	
Brown MS, 2700 SEAMON AVE 21225	3-00100
Reginald Turner, prin.	396-1525
Calverton JHS	4-00110
1100 WHITMORE AVE 21216	396-0581
Earl Lee, prin.	
Canton HS	3-00100
801 S HIGHLAND AVE 21224	396-9172
Craig Spilman, prin.	
Chinquapin MS	4-00100
900 WOODBOURNE AVE 21212	396-6424
Ian Cohen, prin.	
Diggs-Johnson JHS	3-00110
1300 HERKIMER ST 21223	396-1572
Linda Beechner, prin.	
Dunbar MS, 500 N CAROLINE ST 21205	3-00100
Raymond English, prin.	396-9296

Fallstaff MS, 3801 FALLSTAFF RD 21215	3-00100
Gloria Pegram, prin.	396-0682
Franklin MS, 1201 CAMBRIA ST 21225	2-00100
Diana Cisar, prin.	396-1373
Garrison MS	2-00100
3910 BARRINGTON RD 21207	396-0735
Andrew Harvey, prin.	
Greenspring MS	3-00100
4701 GREENSPRING AVE 21209	396-0670
Bessie Barco, prin.	
Hamilton MS, 5609 SEFTON AVE 21214	4-00100
Eugene Lawrence, prin.	396-6370
Hampstead Hill JHS	4-00100
101 S ELLWOOD AVE 21224	396-9133
Kevin Harahan, prin.	
Harlem Park MS	4-00100
1500 HARLEM AVE 21217	396-0612
Wyatt Coger, prin.	
Lemmel MS	4-00100
2801 N DUKELAND ST 21216	396-0665
Elizabeth Williams, prin.	
Lombard MS	3-00100
1601 E LOMBARD ST 21231	396-9261
Robert Hopkins, prin.	
Marshall JHS, 5001 SINCLAIR LN 21206	4-00110
Geraldine Hill, prin.	396-9102
Marshall MS	3-00100
5000 TRUESDALE AVE 21206	396-1997
Elnora Saunders, prin.	
Northeast MS, 5001 MORAVIA RD 21206	3-00100
Alease Owens, prin.	396-9221
Pimlico MS	3-00100
3500 W NORTHERN PKY 21215	396-0806
Roy Pope, prin.	
Poole MS, 1300 W 36TH ST 21211	3-00100
Doris Shaw, prin.	396-6456
Southeast MS, 6820 FAIT AVE 21224	3-00100
John Mohamed, prin.	396-9291
Washington MS	3-00100
1301 MCCULLOH ST 21217	396-7813
Ruth Bukatman, prin.	
West Baltimore MS	4-00100
201 N BEND RD 21229	396-0700
Sheila Kolman, prin.	
Winston MS, 1101 WINSTON AVE 21212	3-00100
Edith Harrison, prin.	396-6356

Baltimore County SD	
Supt. — See Towson	
Carver Center for Arts & Technology	4-00011
938 YORK RD 21204 – Mary Cary, prin.	887-2775
Catonsville High School	4-00011
421 BLOOMSBURY AVE 21228	887-0808
Donald Mohler, prin.	
Chesapeake HS	3-00011
1801 TURKEY POINT RD 21221	887-0100
George Dausch, prin.	
Dundalk HS, 1901 DELVALE AVE 21222	4-00011
Dwayne Johnson, prin.	887-7023
Eastern Vo-Tech HS	4-00011
1100 MACE AVE 21221	887-0190
Robert Kemmery, prin.	
Kenwood HS	4-00011
501 STEMMERS RUN RD 21221	887-0153
Frederick Cogswell, prin.	
Lansdowne HS	4-00011
3800 HOLLINS FERRY RD 21227	887-1415
Laurie Fogelman, prin.	
Loch Raven HS	3-00011
1212 COWPENS AVE 21286	887-3525
Joan Powell, prin.	
Milford Mill HS	3-00011
3800 WASHINGTON AVE 21244	887-0660
Deloris Mbah, prin.	
Overlea HS, 5401 KENWOOD AVE 21206	4-00011
Norman Smith, prin.	887-5241
Parkville HS	4-00011
2600 PUTTY HILL AVE 21234	887-5257
Jean Jagodzinski, prin.	
Patapsco HS, 8100 WISE AVE 21222	3-00011
Barb Russell, prin.	887-7060
Perry Hall HS, 4601 EBENEZER RD 21236	4-00011
Morton Greenberg, prin.	887-5108
Pikesville HS	3-00011
7621 LABYRINTH RD 21208	887-1217
David King, prin.	
Southeastern Vo-Tech HS	4-00011
325 SOLLERS POINT RD 21222	887-0840
Hubert Parker, prin.	
Sparrows Point HS	3-00011
7400 N POINT RD 21219	887-7517
G. Keith Harmeyer, prin.	
Western Vo-Tech HS	4-00011
100 KENWOOD AVE 21228	887-0840
Kenneth Burch, prin.	
Woodlawn HS	4-00011
1801 WOODLAWN DR 21207	887-1309
Alex Murphy, prin.	
Catonsville Comm Career Ctr	Vo Tech
106 BLOOMSBURY AVE 21228	887-0934
Rob Cullison, prin.	
Rosedale Comm Career Ctr	Vo Tech
8200 OLD PHILADELPHIA RD 21237	887-0133
Donald Hardesty, prin.	
Arbutus MS	3-00100
5525 SHELBOURNE RD 21227	887-1402
Linda Wilson, prin.	
Deep Creek MS	3-00100
1000 S MARLYN AVE 21221	887-0112
Roger Pancake, prin.	

Dumbarton MS	3-00100
300 DUMBARTON RD 21212	887-3176
Lynn Hoffman, prin.	
Dundalk MS, 7400 DUNMANWAY 21222	2-00100
John Kreiner, prin.	887-7018
Golden Ring MS	3-00100
6700 KENWOOD AVE 21237	887-0130
Bronda Mills, prin.	
Holabird MS, 1701 DELVALE AVE 21222	3-00100
Frank Passaro, prin.	887-7049
Johnnycake JHS	3-00100
6200 JOHNNYCAKE RD 21207	887-0825
Roger Proudfoot, prin.	
Lansdowne MS	3-00100
2400 LANSDOWNE RD 21227	887-1411
E. Goldian, prin.	
Loch Raven MS	3-00100
8101 LA SALLE RD 21286	887-3518
Jack Wilson, prin.	
Middle River MS	3-00100
800 MIDDLE RIVER RD 21220	887-0165
Linda Chapin, prin.	
Old Court MS	3-00100
4627 OLD COURT RD 21208	887-0742
Robert Tomback, prin.	
Parkville MS	3-00100
8711 AVONDALE RD 21234	887-5250
Sharon Norman, prin.	
Perry Hall MS	3-00100
4300 EBENEZER RD 21236	887-5100
Thomas Evans, prin.	
Pikesville MS, 7701 7 MILE LN 21208	4-00100
Ann Glazer, prin.	887-1207
Pine Grove MS	3-00100
9200 OLD HARFORD RD 21234	887-5270
Beverly Ferman, prin.	
Sparrows Point MS	2-00100
7400 N POINT RD 21219	887-7524
Jacqueline Pipkin, prin.	
Stemmers Run MS	3-00100
201 STEMMERS RUN RD 21221	887-0177
Henry Wagner, prin.	
Stricker MS, 7855 TRAPPE RD 21222	3-00100
Raymond McColgan, prin.	887-7038
Woodlawn MS	3-00100
3033 SAINT LUKES LN 21207	887-1304
D. Bergman, prin.	

Howard County SD	
Supt. — See Ellicott City	
Mayfield Woods MS	2-00100
7950 RED BARN WAY 21227	313-5022
Jesse Smith, prin.	

Actors Theatre Conservatory	1-11111
300 DUMBARTON RD 21212	337-8519
Walter Anderson, prin.	
All-State Career School	2-CS
201 S ARLINGTON AVE 21223	566-7111
Archbishop Curley HS	2-00011
3701 SINCLAIR LN 21213	485-5000
Fr. Twele, prin.	
Arlington Baptist HS	2-00011
3030 N ROLLING RD 21244	655-9300
John Stegman, prin.	
Arundel Institute of Technology	2-CS
1808 EDISON HWY 21213	327-6640
Baltimore Hebrew University	2-UC
5800 PARK HEIGHTS AVE 21215	578-6900
Baltimore International Culinary College	2-CC
17 COMMERCE ST 21202	800-624-9926
Beth Tfiloh S	3-11111
3300 OLD COURT RD 21208	486-1905
Zipora Schorr, prin.	
Boys Latin School of Maryland	2-11111
822 W LAKE AVE 21210	377-5192
Hamilton Bishop, prin.	
Broadcasting Institute of Maryland	2-CS
7200 HARFORD RD 21234	800-942-9246
Bryn Mawr S	3-11111
109 W MELROSE AVE 21210	323-8800
Barbara Chase, prin.	
Cardinal Gibbons HS	2-00111
3225 WILKENS AVE 21229	644-1770
Donald Delciello, prin.	
Catholic HS of Baltimore	2-00011
2800 EDISON HWY 21213	732-6200
Sr. Janet Thiel, prin.	
College of Notre Dame of Maryland	5-UC
4701 N CHARLES ST 21210	435-0100
Community College of Baltimore	6-CC
2901 LIBERTY HEIGHTS AVE 21215	396-0203
Community College of Baltimore	3-CC
600 E LOMBARD ST 21202	396-0203
Coppin State College	4-UC
2500 W NORTH AVE 21216	333-7427
Dundalk Community College	5-CC
7200 SOLLERS POINT RD 21222	282-6700
Essex Community College	7-CC
7201 ROSSVILLE BLVD 21237	682-6000
Father Hall MS	2-01100
2848 W LAFAYETTE AVE 21216	566-1231
Phyllis Douglas, prin.	
Friends S, 5114 N CHARLES ST 21210	3-11111
Diana McGraw, prin.	435-2800
Gilman S, 5407 ROLAND AVE 21210	3-11111
Redmond Finney, prin.	323-3800
Goucher College	3-UC
1021 DULANEY VALLEY RD 21204	337-6000
Greater Baltimore Medical Center	HSP
6701 N CHARLES ST 21204	828-2121

Harbor Hospital Center — HSP
  3001 S HANOVER ST 21225 — 347-3670
Institute of Notre Dame HS — 2-00011
  901 N AISQUITH ST 21202 — 522-7800
  Carol Goldbeck, prin.
Johns Hopkins Hospital — HSP
  600 N WOLFE ST 21205
Johns Hopkins University — 3-UC
  600 N WOLFE ST 21205
Johns Hopkins University — 7-UC
  3400 N CHARLES ST 21218 — 516-8000
Lincoln Technical Institute — 3-CS
  3200 WILKENS AVE 21229 — 646-5480
Loyola College — 6-UC
  4501 N CHARLES ST 21210 — 323-1010
Maryland General Hospital — 2-HSP
  827 LINDEN AVE 21201 — 225-8000
Maryland Institute College of Art — 4-UC
  1300 W MOUNT ROYAL AVE 21217 — 669-9200
Maryland School for the Blind — HND
  3501 TAYLOR AVE 21236
Mercy HS — 2-00011
  1300 E NORTHERN PKY 21239 — 433-8880
  Sr. Carol Wheeler, prin.
Mercy Hospital — HSP
  301 SAINT PAUL PL 21202 — 332-9202
Morgan State University — 5-UC
  1700 E COLD SPRING LN 21239 — 319-3000
Mother Seton Academy — 1-00100
  320 S REGESTER ST 21231 — 563-2833
  Sr. Ellen Smith, prin.
Mt. St. Joseph HS — 3-00011
  4403 FREDERICK AVE 21229 — 644-3300
  Charles Reiter, prin.
Ner Israel Rabbinical College — 2-UC
  400 MOUNT WILSON LN 21208 — 484-7200
New England Tractor Trailer Training — 2-CS
  1410 BUSH ST 21230 — 783-0100
Our Lady of Mt. Carmel HS — 2-00011
  1706 EASTERN AVE 21231 — 686-1023
  Kathleen Sipes, prin.
Our Lady of Pompei S — 2-11111
  201 S CONKLING ST 21224 — 276-6534
  Angela Rebbert, prin.
Park Heights Street Academy — 2-00011
  3901 PARK HEIGHTS AVE # 3903 21215
  Pamela Shaw, prin. — 367-3446
Peabody Institute Johns Hopkins Univ. — 2-UC
  1 E MOUNT VERNON PL 21202
PTC Career Institute — 2-CS
  201 E BALTIMORE ST 21202 — 837-3270
RETS Tech Training Center — 4-CC
  1520 S CATON AVE 21227 — 644-6400
Rice Aviation — 2-CS
  701 WILSON POINT RD 21220 — 682-2226
Roland Park Country S — 3-11111
  5204 ROLAND AVE 21210 — 323-5500
  Jean Brune, prin.
Rosa Parks MS — 2-00100
  3510 ELDORADO AVE 21207 — 664-9433
  Joseph Campbell, prin.
St. Frances Academy — 2-00011
  501 E CHASE ST 21202 — 539-5794
  Sr. Francis Schilling, prin.
St. Ignatius Loyola Academy — 2-00100
  740 N CALVERT ST 21202 — 539-8268
  Rev. Murray, prin.
St. Mary's Seminary & University — 2-UC
  5400 ROLAND AVE 21210 — 323-3200
Seton Keough HS — 3-00011
  1201 S CATON AVE 21227 — 646-4444
  Sr. Joan Elias, prin.
Sojourner-Douglass College — 2-UC
  500 N CAROLINE ST 21205 — 276-0306
Talmudical Academy of Baltimore — 3-11111
  4445 OLD COURT RD 21208 — 484-6600
Union Memorial Hospital — HSP
  201 E UNIVERSITY PKY 21218 — 554-2739
University of Baltimore — 6-UC
  1420 N CHARLES ST 21201 — 625-3000
University of Maryland — 5-UC
  522 W LOMBARD ST 21201 — 328-3100
Waldorf School of Baltimore — 2-01100
  4901 SPRINGGARDEN RD 21209 — 367-6808

Bel Air, AC 410, PC 6, Harford
Harford County SD — 8-11111
  45 E GORDON ST 21014 — 838-7300
  Ray Keech, supt.
Harford Technical HS — 2-00001
  200 THOMAS RUN RD 21015 — 638-3804
  David Thomas, prin.
HS, 100 HEIGHE ST 21014 — 4-00011
  William Ekey, prin. — 638-4100
Wright HS — 4-00011
  1301 N FOUNTAIN GREEN RD 21015 — 638-4110
  Ronald Webb, prin.
MS, 99 IDLEWILD ST 21014 — 3-00100
  Matthew Plevyak, prin. — 638-4140
Southampton MS — 4-00100
  1201 MOORES MILL RD 21014 — 638-4150
  Barb Canavan, prin.
Other Schools – See Aberdeen, Edgewood, Fallston,
  Havre De Grace, Joppa, Pylesville

Eastern Christian College — 3-UC
  PO BOX 629 21014 — 879-9300
Harford Community College — 5-CC
  401 THOMAS RUN RD 21015 — 836-4000

John Carroll HS — 3-00011
  703 CHURCHVILLE RD 21014 — 838-8333
  Robert Garbacik, prin.

Beltsville, AC 301, PC 7, Prince George's
Prince Georges County SD
  Supt. — See Upper Marlboro
High Point HS — 4-00011
  3601 POWDER MILL RD 20705 — 937-1000
  Ron Cunningham, prin.
King MS, 4545 AMMENDALE RD 20705 — 3-00100
  Bette Lewis, prin. — 937-6070

Berlin, AC 410, PC 5, Worcester
Worcester County SD
  Supt. — See Newark
Decatur HS, 9913 SEAHAWK RD 21811 — 3-00011
  Anthony McNabb, prin. — 641-2171
MS, 309 FRANKLIN AVE 21811 — 2-01100
  Melvin Ross, prin. — 641-3010

Worcester Country S — 2-11111
  508 S MAIN ST 21811 — 641-3575
  Barry Tull, prin.

Bethesda, AC 301, PC 8, Montgomery
Montgomery County SD
  Supt. — See Rockville
Bethesda-Chevy Chase HS — 4-00011
  4301 EAST WEST HWY 20814 — 657-4900
  Wayne Whigham, prin.
Johnson HS — 4-00011
  6400 ROCK SPRING DR 20814 — 571-6900
  Frank Masci, prin.
Whitman HS — 4-00011
  7100 WHITTIER BLVD 20817 — 320-6600
  Jerome Marco, prin.
Pyle MS, 6311 WILSON LN 20817 — 3-00100
  Harvey Strine, prin. — 320-6540
Westland MS — 2-00100
  5501 MASSACHUSETTS AVE 20816 — 320-6515
  Dan Shea, prin.

Holton Arms S, 7303 RIVER RD 20817 — 3-01111
  Diana Beebe, prin. — 365-5300
Hunter Memorial Laboratory — HSP
  8218 WISCONSIN AVE STE 202 20814
  — 656-9093
Landon S, 6101 WILSON LN 20817 — 3-01111
  Damon Bradley, prin. — 320-3200
Lycee Rochambeau — 3-11111
  9600 FOREST RD 20814 — 530-8260
National Institute of Health — 2-CS
  9000 ROCKVILLE PIKE BLDG 10 20892
  — 496-8335
St. Andrew's Episcopal S — 2-00111
  8935 BRADMOOR DR 20817 — 530-4900
  James Cantwell, prin.
Stone Ridge Country Day S — 3-11111
  9101 ROCKVILLE PIKE 20814 — 657-4322
  Sr. Anne Dyer, prin.
Washington Waldorf S — 2-11111
  4800 SANGAMORE RD 20816 — 229-6107
  Cynthia Bennett, prin.

Bladensburg, AC 301, PC 6, Prince George's
Prince Georges County SD
  Supt. — See Upper Marlboro
HS, 5610 TILDEN RD 20710 — 4-00011
  David Stofa, prin. — 779-6920

Elizabeth Seton HS — 3-00011
  5715 EMERSON ST 20710 — 864-4532
  Geraldine Buckley, prin.

Boonsboro, AC 301, PC 4, Washington
Washington County SD
  Supt. — See Hagerstown
HS, 10 CAMPUS AVE 21713 — 3-00011
  Helen Becker, prin. — 791-4360
MS, 1 JH WADE DR 21713 — 3-00100
  Deidre Shumaker, prin. — 791-4370

Bowie, AC 301, PC 8, Prince George's
Prince Georges County SD
  Supt. — See Upper Marlboro
HS, 15200 ANNAPOLIS RD 20715 — 4-00011
  John Hagan, prin. — 464-8500
Tall Oaks Vocational S — 2-00011
  2112 CHURCH RD 20721 — 249-2900
  Russell Eschbacher, prin.
Tasker MS — 3-00100
  4901 COLLINGTON RD 20715 — 464-0910
  Lee Ridgley, prin.

Bowie State University — 5-UC
  14000 JERICHO PARK RD 20715 — 464-3000

Brandywine, AC 301, PC 4, Prince George's
Prince Georges County SD
  Supt. — See Upper Marlboro
Gwynn Park HS — 4-00011
  13800 BRANDYWINE RD 20613 — 372-6186
  Mary Cunningham, prin.
Gwynn Park MS, 8000 DYSON RD 20613 — 3-00100
  John Flynn, prin. — 372-6801

Brooklandville, AC 410, PC 3, Baltimore

Maryvale Prep S, 11300 FALLS RD 21022 — 2-00111
  Sr. Shawn MaGuire, prin. — 252-3366
Park S, 2425 OLD COURT RD 21022 — 3-11111
  F. Sharpless, prin. — 825-2351

St. Paul's S, 11152 FALLS RD 21022 — 3-11111
  Robert Hallert, prin. — 825-4400
St. Paul's School for Girls — 2-01111
  11232 FALLS RD 21022 — 823-6323
  Lila Lohr, prin.

Brunswick, AC 301, PC 6, Frederick
Frederick County SD
  Supt. — See Frederick
HS, 101 CUMMINGS DR 21716 — 3-00011
  Melvin Whitfield, prin. — 834-9133
MS, 301 CUMMINGS DR 21716 — 2-00100
  Hal Mosser, prin. — 834-7723

Burtonsville, AC 301, PC 6, Montgomery
Montgomery County SD
  Supt. — See Rockville
Paint Branch HS — 4-00011
  14121 OLD COLUMBIA PIKE 20866 — 989-5600
  Rebecca Newman, prin.
Banneker MS — 4-00100
  14800 PERRYWOOD DR 20866 — 989-5747
  Fred Lowenbach, prin.

Cambridge, AC 410, PC 7, Dorchester
Dorchester County SD — 5-11111
  PO BOX 619 21613 — 228-4747
  Spicer Bell, supt.
Cambridge-South Dorchester HS — 3-00011
  2475 CAMBRIDGE BYPASS 21613 — 228-9224
  Douglas Fleetwood, prin.
Dorchester County School of Technology — 2-00011
  2485 CAMBRIDGE BYPASS 21613 — 228-3457
  Michael Asplin, prin.
Maces Lane MS, 1101 MACES LN 21613 — 3-00100
  John Hurley, prin. — 228-2111
Other Schools – See Hurlock

Capitol Heights, AC 301, PC 5, Prince George's
Prince Georges County SD
  Supt. — See Upper Marlboro
Central HS — 3-00011
  200 CABIN BRANCH RD 20743 — 336-8200
  William Watkins, prin.
Fairmont Heights HS — 3-00011
  1401 NYE ST 20743 — 773-1200
  Clarence McDonald, prin.
Walker Mill MS — 3-00100
  800 KAREN BLVD 20743 — 336-8855
  Joan Brown, prin.

Catonsville, AC 410, PC 8, Baltimore
Baltimore County SD
  Supt. — See Towson
MS, 2301 EDMONDSON AVE 21228 — 2-00100
  Penelope Booth, prin. — 887-0803

Catonsville Community College — 7-CC
  800 S ROLLING RD 21228 — 455-6050
Mt. De Sales Academy — 2-00011
  700 ACADEMY RD 21228 — 744-8498
  Sr. Ann Britton, prin.
University of Maryland — 6-UC
  5401 WILKENS AVE 21228 — 455-1000

Centreville, AC 410, PC 4, Queen Anne's
Queen Annes County SD — 6-11111
  202 CHESTERFIELD AVE 21617 — 758-2403
  Joseph Shilling, supt.
Queen Anne's County HS — 4-00011
  RR 3 BOX 16 21617 — 758-0500
  David Jones, prin.
MS, RR 3 BOX 17 21617 — 3-01100
  Thaddeus Kalmanowicz, prin. — 758-0883
Other Schools – See Stevensville, Sudlersville

Gunston S, PO BOX 200 21617 — 1-00011
  Temple Blackwood, prin. — 758-0620

Chesapeake City, AC 410, PC 3, Cecil
Cecil County SD
  Supt. — See Elkton
Bohemia Manor JSHS — 3-00011
  2755 AUGUSTINE HERMAN HWY 21915
  Delbert Jackson, prin. — 885-2075

Chestertown, AC 410, PC 5, Kent
Kent County SD — 4-11111
  215 WASHINGTON AVE 21620 — 778-1595
  James Lupis, prin.
MS, 402 E CAMPUS AVE 21620 — 2-01100
  Lloyd Taylor, prin. — 778-1771
Other Schools – See Galena, Rock Hall, Worton

Washington College — 3-UC
  WASHINGTON AVE 21620 — 778-2800

Clarksville, AC 410, PC 3, Howard
Howard County SD
  Supt. — See Ellicott City
MS, 6535 TROTTER RD 21029 — 3-00100
  Frank Scrivener, prin. — 313-7057

Clear Spring, AC 301, PC 2, Washington
Washington County SD
  Supt. — See Hagerstown
HS, 12630 BROADFORDING RD 21722 — 2-00011
  William AuMiller, prin. — 842-2125
MS, 12628 BROADFORDING RD 21722 — 2-00100
  James Conrad, prin. — 842-2118

Clinton, AC 301, PC 7, Prince George's
Prince Georges County SD
  Supt. — See Upper Marlboro

Surrattsville HS   4-00011
   6101 GARDEN DR   20735   868-0653
   Robert Dredger, prin.
Decatur MS, 8200 PINEWOOD DR   20735   3-00100
   Sandra DuVall, prin.   297-8400

Grace Brethren Christian S   4-11111
   6501 SURRATTS RD   20735   868-1600
   Daniel Grabill, prin.

Cockeysville/Hunt Valley, AC 410, PC 7, Baltimore
Baltimore County SD
   Supt. — See Towson
Cockeysville MS   3-00100
   10401 GREENSIDE DR   21030   887-7626
   Julie Syzmaszek, prin.

College Park, AC 301, PC 7, Prince George's

University of Maryland   20742   8-UC
   405-1000
University of Maryland   8-UC
   UNIV BLVD AND ADELPHI RD   20742   985-7000

Colora, AC 301, PC 1, Cecil

West Nottingham Academy   2-00011
   1079 FIRETOWER RD   21917   658-5556
   Edward Baker, prin.

Columbia, AC 410, PC 8, Howard
Howard County SD
   Supt. — See Ellicott City
Atholton HS, 6520 FREETOWN RD   21044   4-00011
   Scott Pfeifer, prin.   313-7065
Hammond HS   2-00011
   8800 GUILFORD RD   21046   313-7115
   Marshall Peterson, prin.
Oakland Mills HS   4-00011
   9410 KILIMANJARO RD   21045   313-6945
   Dave Bruzga, prin.
Wilde Lake HS   3-00011
   5460 TRUMPETER RD   21044   313-6965
   Bonnie Daniel, prin.
Brown MS   3-00100
   6700 CRADLEROCK WAY   21045   313-7107
   Michael Goins, prin.
Harper's Choice MS   3-00100
   5450 BEAVERKILL RD   21044   313-6929
   James Evans, prin.
Oakland Mills MS   3-00100
   9540 KILIMANJARO RD   21045   313-6937
   Larry Cohen, prin.
Wilde Lake MS   3-00100
   10481 CROSS FOX LN   21044   313-6957
   Ken Gill, prin.

Columbia Center   UC
   6740 ALEXANDER BELL DR   21046   290-1777
Howard Community College   5-CC
   10901 LITTLE PATUXENT PKY   21044   992-4800

Cresaptown, AC 301, PC 5, Allegany
Allegany County SD
   Supt. — See Cumberland
Center for Career & Technical Education   Vo Tech
   14211 MCMULLEN HWY   21502   729-6486
   Roger Flanagan, prin.

Crisfield, AC 410, PC 5, Somerset
Somerset County SD
   Supt. — See Princess Anne
JSHS, 210 S SOMERSET AVE   21817   2-00111
   Roger Daugherty, prin.   968-0150

Crofton, AC 410, PC 7, Anne Arundel
Anne Arundel County SD
   Supt. — See Annapolis
JHS, 2301 DAVIDSONVILLE RD   21114   3-00110
   Walter Bruso, prin.   793-0280

Cumberland, AC 301, PC 7, Allegany
Allegany County SD   7-11111
   108 WASHINGTON ST   21502   759-2000
   Robert Terrill, supt.
Allegany HS, 616 SEDGWICK ST   21502   3-00011
   Richard Stevenson, prin.   777-8110
Ft. Hill HS, 500 GREENWAY AVE   21502   3-00011
   James Thompson, prin.   777-2570
Braddock MS, 909 HOLLAND ST   21502   3-00100
   C. Sloan, prin.   777-7990
Washington MS   3-00100
   200 N MASSACHUSETTS AVE   21502   777-5360
   Joseph Sank, prin.
Other Schools – See Cresaptown, Flintstone,
   Frostburg, Lonaconing, Mount Savage, Oldtown,
   Westernport

Allegany Community College   4-CC
   12401 WILLOWBROOK RD   21502   724-7700
Bishop Walsh HS   2-00111
   700 BISHOP WALSH RD   21502   724-5360
   Patrick King, prin.

Damascus, AC 301, PC 6, Montgomery
Montgomery County SD
   Supt. — See Rockville
HS, 25921 RIDGE RD   20872   3-00011
   James Fish, prin.   253-7030
Baker MS, 25400 OAK DR   20872   3-00100
   Jerome Lynch, prin.   253-7010

Denton, AC 410, PC 5, Caroline
Caroline County SD   5-11111
   112 MARKET ST   21629   479-1460
   Allan Gorsuch, supt.
Lockerman MS   2-00100
   207 LOCKERMAN RD   21629   479-2760
   Harry Martin, prin.
Other Schools – See Federalsburg, Ridgely

District Heights, AC 301, PC 6, Prince George's
Prince Georges County SD
   Supt. — See Upper Marlboro
Suitland HS   4-00011
   5200 SILVER HILL RD   20747   568-7770
   Sterling Marshall, prin.
Key MS, 2301 SCOTT KEY DR   20747   3-00100
   Bruce Speight, prin.   735-4131

Easton, AC 410, PC 6, Talbot
Talbot County SD   5-11111
   PO BOX 1029   21601   822-0330
   J. Meek, supt.
HS, 701 MECKLENBURG AVE   21601   3-00011
   Edward Webster, prin.   822-4180
MS, OXFORD ROAD   21601   3-00100
   Kelly Griffith, prin.   822-2910
Other Schools – See Saint Michaels

MacQueen Gibbs Willis School of Nursing   HSP
   219 S WASHINGTON ST   21601   822-1000
SS. Peter & Paul S, 900 HIGH ST   21601   3-11111
   Susan Patterson, prin.   822-2251

Edgewater, AC 410, PC 4, Anne Arundel
Anne Arundel County SD
   Supt. — See Annapolis
South River HS   4-00011
   201 E CENTRAL AVE   21037   956-5600
   James Hamilton, prin.
Center of Applied Technology-South   3-00111
   211 E CENTRAL AVE   21037   956-5900
   Aretha Stubbs, prin.
Central MS, 221 E CENTRAL AVE   21037   3-00100
   Victoria Hutchins, prin.   956-5800

Edgewood, AC 410, PC 7, Harford
Harford County SD
   Supt. — See Bel Air
HS   3-00011
   2415 WILLOUGHBY BEACH RD   21040   612-1500
   Robert Williams, prin.
MS   3-00100
   2411 WILLOUGHBY BEACH RD   21040   612-1518
   Robert Depuy, prin.

Elkton, AC 410, PC 6, Cecil
Cecil County SD, 201 BOOTH ST   21921   7-11111
   Jerry Kunkle, supt.   996-5400
HS, 110 JAMES ST   21921   4-00011
   Nelsen Bolender, prin.   996-5000
Cherry Hill MS   3-00100
   2535 SINGERLY RD   21921   996-5020
   Reginald Canady, prin.
MS, 625 NORTH ST   21921   2-00100
   Stephen Asplen, prin.   996-5010
Other Schools – See Chesapeake City, North East,
   Perryville, Rising Sun

Ellicott City, AC 410, PC 6, Howard
Howard County SD   8-11111
   10910 ROUTE 108   21042   313-6600
   Michael Hickey, supt.
Centennial HS   4-00011
   4300 CENTENNIAL LN   21042   313-2856
   Edgar Markley, prin.
Howard County HS of Technology   1-00011
   10920 STATE ROUTE 108   21042   313-6982
   Mary Day, prin.
Howard HS   4-00011
   8700 OLD ANNAPOLIS RD   21043   313-2867
   Eugene Streagle, prin.
Mt. Hebron HS   4-00011
   9440 STATE ROUTE 99   21042   313-2880
   Sylvia Pattillo, prin.
Burleigh Manor MS   3-00100
   4200 CENTENNIAL LN   21042   313-2507
   James DeGeorge, prin.
Dunloggin MS   3-00100
   9129 NORTHFIELD RD   21042   313-2831
   Jesse Scharff, prin.
Ellicott Mills MS   2-00100
   4445 MONTGOMERY RD   21043   313-2839
   Sylvester Burke, prin.
Patapsco MS   3-00100
   8885 OLD FREDERICK RD   21043   313-2848
   Steve Gibson, prin.
Other Schools – See Baltimore, Clarksville,
   Columbia, Glenelg, Glenwood, Jessup, Laurel,
   Marriotsville

Emmitsburg, AC 301, PC 4, Frederick

Emergency Management Institute   1-HMS
   16825 SETON AVE   21727
Mt. St. Mary's College   4-UC
   16300 OLD EMMITSBURG RD   21727   447-6122

Fallston, AC 410, PC 6, Harford
Harford County SD
   Supt. — See Bel Air
JSHS, 2301 CARRS MILL RD   21047   4-00111
   Robert Pfau, prin.   638-4120
MS, 2301 CARRS MILL RD   21047   3-00100
   F. Pomilla, prin.   638-4129

Federalsburg, AC 410, PC 4, Caroline
Caroline County SD
   Supt. — See Denton
Richardson HS   2-00011
   25320 RICHARDSON RD   21632   754-5575
   Ralph White, prin.
Richardson MS   2-00100
   25390 RICHARDSON RD   21632   754-9922
   Greg Thornton, prin.

Flintstone, AC 301, PC 2, Allegany
Allegany County SD
   Supt. — See Cumberland
S, PO BOX O   21530   2-11111
   Robert Saville, prin.   478-2434

Forestville, AC 301, PC 7, Prince George's
Prince Georges County SD
   Supt. — See Upper Marlboro
Jackson MS, 3500 REGENCY PKY   20747   3-00100
   William Simmons, prin.   736-9700

Bishop McNamara HS   3-00011
   6800 MARLBORO PIKE   20747   735-8401
   Mathew Goyette, prin.

Fort George G. Meade, AC 410, PC see Baltimore
Anne Arundel County SD
   Supt. — See Annapolis
Meade HS, 1100 CLARK RD   20755   4-00011
   Stan Stawas, prin.   674-7710
MacArthur MS   3-00100
   3500 ROCKENBACH RD   20755   222-6550
   John Kozora, prin.

Fort Washington, AC 301, PC 7, Prince George's
Prince Georges County SD
   Supt. — See Upper Marlboro
Friendly HS   4-00011
   10000 ALLENTOWN RD   20744   248-5400
   Cheryl Riggins, prin.
Lord Baltimore MS   3-00100
   8700 ALLENTOWN RD   20744   248-3320
   Toni Menchan, prin.
Oxon Hill MS   3-00100
   9570 FORT FOOTE RD   20744   567-1555
   Maxine Bane, prin.

Frederick, AC 301, PC 8, Frederick
Frederick County SD   8-11111
   115 E CHURCH ST   21701   694-1000
   Noel Farmer, supt.
HS, 650 CARROLL PKY   21701   4-00011
   Daniel Cunningham, prin.   694-1367
Frederick Voc-Tech Center   2-00011
   7922 OPOSSUMTOWN PIKE   21702   694-1658
   Ron Neff, prin.
Johnson HS, 1501 N MARKET ST   21701   4-00011
   Joseph Heidel, prin.   694-1412
Linganore HS   4-00011
   12013 OLD ANNAPOLIS RD   21701   865-5555
   Hank Bohlander, prin.
Ballenger Creek MS   3-00100
   5525 BALLENGER CREEK PIKE   21701   293-6418
   Michael Kline, prin.
Johnson MS, 1501 N MARKET ST   21701   2-00100
   Carolyn Kimberlin, prin.   694-1433
Monocacy MS   3-00100
   8009 OPOSSUMTOWN PIKE   21702   694-1189
   Steven Arlen, prin.
West Frederick MS   4-00100
   515 W PATRICK ST   21701   694-1389
   Michael Trout, prin.
Other Schools – See Brunswick, Ijamsville,
   Middletown, New Market, Thurmont, Walkersville

Abbie Business Institute   2-CS
   5310 SPECTRUM DR BLDG A   21701   694-0211
Frederick Community College   5-CC
   7932 OPOSSUMTOWN PIKE   21702   694-5240
Hood College   4-UC
   400 ROSEMONT AVE   21701   663-3131
Maryland School for the Deaf   HND
   PO BOX 250   21705
St. Johns HS, 889 BUTTERFLY LN   21702   2-00011
   Edward Hoffman, prin.   662-4210

Frostburg, AC 301, PC 6, Allegany
Allegany County SD
   Supt. — See Cumberland
Beall JSHS, 331 E MAIN ST   21532   3-00111
   Theodore Kight, prin.   689-3377

Frostburg State University   21532   5-UC
   689-4000

Gaithersburg, AC 301, PC 8, Montgomery
Montgomery County SD
   Supt. — See Rockville
HS, 314 S FREDERICK AVE   20877   4-00011
   Frederick Evans, prin.   840-4700
Quince Orchard HS   4-00011
   15800 QUINCE ORCHARD RD   20878   840-4686
   Thomas Warren, prin.
Watkins Mill HS   3-00011
   10301 APPLE RIDGE RD   20879   840-3959
   Steve Dickoff, prin.
MS, 2 TEACHERS WAY   20877   3-00100
   David Steinberg, prin.   840-4554
Montgomery Village MS   3-00100
   19300 WATKINS MILL RD   20879   840-4660
   Darlene Simmons, prin.

Ridgeview IS | 3-00100
16600 RAVEN ROCK DR 20878 | 840-4770
Lewis Jones, prin.

Galena, AC 410, PC 2, Kent
Kent County SD
Supt. — See Chestertown
MS, PO BOX 298 21635 | 2-01100
Winton Fenner, prin. | 648-5132

Gambrills, AC 410, PC 4, Anne Arundel
Anne Arundel County SD
Supt. — See Annapolis
Arundel SHS | 4-00001
1001 ANNAPOLIS RD 21054 | 674-6500
Ken Catlin, prin.

Germantown, AC 301, PC 8, Montgomery
Montgomery County SD
Supt. — See Rockville
Seneca Valley HS | 4-00011
12700 MIDDLEBROOK RD 20874 | 353-8000
Bonnie Fox, prin.
King MS | 3-00100
11700 NEELSVILLE CHURCH RD 20876 | 353-8080
Ruth Koenigsberg, prin.

Montgomery College | 5-CC
20200 OBSERVATION DR 20876 | 353-7000

Glen Burnie, AC 410, PC 8, Anne Arundel
Anne Arundel County SD
Supt. — See Annapolis
North County SHS, 10 1ST AVE E 21061 | 4-00001
William Wentworth, prin. | 222-6970
HS | 4-00011
7550 BLTMORE ANNAPOLIS BLVD 21060
Midgie Sledge, prin. | 761-8950
Corkran MS | 3-00100
7600 QUARTERFIELD RD 21061 | 222-6493
Phyllis Cherry, prin.
Marley MS | 3-00100
7730 BLTMORE ANNAPOLIS BLVD 21060
Rob Janovsky, prin. | 761-0934

Glencoe, AC 301, PC 2, Baltimore

Oldfields S, 1500 GLENCOE RD 21152 | 2-00111
Hawley Rogers, prin. | 472-4800

Glenelg, AC 410, PC 3, Howard
Howard County SD
Supt. — See Ellicott City
HS, 14025 BURNTWOODS RD 21737 | 3-00011
James McGregor, prin. | 313-5528

Glenelg Country S | 2-11111
PO BOX 190 21737 | 531-2229
Ryland Chapman, prin.

Glenwood, AC 410, PC 2, Howard
Howard County SD
Supt. — See Ellicott City
MS, 2680 STATE ROUTE 97 21738 | 3-00100
Vincent Catania, prin. | 313-5520

Grantsville, AC 301, PC 3, Garrett

Diesel Institute of America | 1-CS
PO BOX 69 21536 | 895-5139

Great Mills, AC 301, PC 3, St. Mary's
St. Mary's County SD
Supt. — See Leonardtown
HS, HC 63 20634 | 4-00011
Patricia Martin, prin. | 863-9426

Greenbelt, AC 301, PC 7, Prince George's
Prince Georges County SD
Supt. — See Upper Marlboro
Roosevelt HS | 4-00011
7601 HANOVER PKY 20770 | 513-5400
Gerald Boarman, prin.
MS, 8950 EDMONSTON RD 20770 | 3-00100
Elizabeth Gresham, prin. | 474-2225

Hagerstown, AC 301, PC 8, Washington
Washington County SD | 7-11111
PO BOX 730 21741 | 791-4000
Wayne Gersen, supt.
Career Studies Center | 3-00001
50 W OAK RIDGE DR 21740 | 791-4276
A. Oyster, prin.
North Hagerstown HS | 4-00011
1200 PENNSYLVANIA AVE 21742 | 791-4302
Richard Gulas, prin.
South Hagerstown HS | 3-00011
1101 S POTOMAC ST 21740 | 791-4336
John Peckyno, prin.
Hicks MS, 1321 S POTOMAC ST 21740 | 3-00100
Ralph Kline, prin. | 791-4286
Northern MS | 3-00100
701 NORTHERN AVE 21742 | 791-4316
Richard Gehrman, prin.
Western Heights MS | 2-00100
1300 MARSHALL ST 21740 | 791-4351
David Reeder, prin.
Other Schools – See Boonsboro, Clear Spring,
Hancock, Smithsburg, Williamsport

Grace Academy | 2-11111
530 N LOCUST ST 21740 | 733-2033
Hagerstown Business College | 3-CC
18618 CRESTWOOD DR 21742 | 739-2670

Hagerstown Junior College | 5-CC
11400 ROBINWOOD DR 21742 | 790-2800
Heritage Academy | 2-11111
12215 WALNUT PT W 21740 | 582-2600
Highland View Academy | 2-00011
RR 1 BOX 286 21740 | 739-8480
St. Maria Goretti HS | 2-00011
1535 OAK HILL AVE 21742 | 739-4266
Sr. Susan Albert, prin.

Hampstead, AC 410, PC 5, Carroll
Carroll County SD
Supt. — See Westminster
North Carroll HS | 4-00011
3801 HAMPSTEAD MEXICO RD 21074 | 374-6105
Greg Eckles, prin.
North Carroll MS | 2-00100
2401 HANOVER PIKE 21074 | 374-6135
Richard DeLong, prin.

Hancock, AC 301, PC 4, Washington
Washington County SD
Supt. — See Hagerstown
JSHS, 289 W MAIN ST 21750 | 2-00111
Richard Martin, prin. | 678-6191

Harwood, AC 410, PC 2, Anne Arundel
Anne Arundel County SD
Supt. — See Annapolis
Southern HS | 3-00011
4400 SOLOMONS ISLAND RD 20776 | 867-7100
Don Buchanan, prin.

Havre De Grace, AC 410, PC 6, Harford
Harford County SD
Supt. — See Bel Air
HS, 700 CONGRESS AVE 21078 | 3-00011
James Bennett, prin. | 939-6600
MS, 401 LEWIS LN 21078 | 2-00100
Edwin Saunders, prin. | 939-6608

Helen, AC 301, PC 1, St. Mary's
St. Mary's County SD
Supt. — See Leonardtown
Brent MS, GENERAL DELIVERY 20635 | 3-00100
Lloyd Jenkins, prin. | 884-4635

Calverton S | 2-11111
300 CALVERTON SCHOOL RD 20639 | 855-1922
Elizabeth Bratton, prin.

Huntingtown, AC 410, PC 3, Calvert
Calvert County SD
Supt. — See Prince Frederick
Plum Point MS | 3-00100
1475 PLUM POINT RD 20639 | 535-7400
George Miller, prin.

Hurlock, AC 410, PC 4, Dorchester
Dorchester County SD
Supt. — See Cambridge
North Dorchester HS | 2-00011
5875 CLOVERDALE RD 21643 | 943-4511
James Bishop, prin.
North Dorchester MS | 2-00100
5745 CLOVERDALE RD 21643 | 943-3322
Gwen Handy, prin.

Hyattsville, AC 301, PC 7, Prince George's
Prince Georges County SD
Supt. — See Upper Marlboro
Northwestern HS | 4-00011
7000 ADELPHI RD 20782 | 779-5400
Kevin Maxwell, prin.
MS, 6001 42ND AVE 20781 | 3-00100
Joseph Lupo, prin. | 864-4655
Orem MS | 3-00100
6100 EDITORS PARK DR 20782 | 559-7181
Kevin Sawyer, prin.

De Matha Catholic HS | 3-00011
4313 MADISON ST 20781 | 864-3666
John Moylan, prin.
TESST Electronics and Computer Institute | 3-CS
5122 BALTIMORE AVE 20781 | 864-5750

Ijamsville, AC 301, PC 99, Frederick
Frederick County SD
Supt. — See Frederick
Windsor Knolls ES | 3-00100
1150 WINDSOR RD 21754 | 831-3465
Paulette Shockey, prin.

Indian Head, AC 301, PC 5, Charles
Charles County SD
Supt. — See La Plata
Lackey HS, RR 1 BOX 250 20640 | 4-00011
Richetta Acker, prin. | 743-5431
Henson MS, RR 1 BOX 6 20640 | 3-00100
Nancy Renfro, prin. | 375-8550
Smallwood MS, ROUTE 210 20640 | 3-00100
Patty Dorsey, prin. | 743-5422

Jessup, AC 410, PC 6, Anne Arundel
Howard County SD
Supt. — See Ellicott City
Patuxent Valley MS | 2-00100
9151 VOLLMERHAUSEN RD 20794 | 880-5840
David Lovewell, prin.

Joppa, AC 410, Harford
Harford County SD
Supt. — See Bel Air
Joppatowne HS | 3-00011
555 JOPPA FARM RD 21085 | 612-1510
Doris Williams, prin.

Magnolia MS | 3-00100
299 FORT HOYLE RD 21085 | 612-1525
Marilyn Owen, prin.

Kensington, AC 301, PC 4, Montgomery
Montgomery County SD
Supt. — See Rockville
Einstein HS | 4-00011
11135 NEWPORT MILL RD 20895 | 929-2200
Richard Towers, prin.

Academy of the Holy Cross | 2-00011
4920 STRATHMORE AVE 20895 | 942-2100
Sr. Katherine Kase, prin.
Newport Prep S | 2-11111
11311 NEWPORT MILL RD 20895 | 942-4550
Nina Olin, prin.

Landover, AC 301, PC 6, Prince George's
Prince Georges County SD
Supt. — See Upper Marlboro
Kenmoor MS, 2500 KENMOOR DR 20785 | 3-00100
Sylvia Markham, prin. | 322-7350

Lincoln Technical Institute | 4-CS
7800 CENTRAL AVE 20785 | 336-7250

Langley Park, AC 301, PC 7, Prince George's

Maryland Drafting Institute | 3-CS
2045 UNIVERSITY BLVD E 20783 | 439-7776

Lanham-Seabrook, AC 301, PC 7, Prince George's
Prince Georges County SD
Supt. — See Upper Marlboro
DuVal HS, 9880 GOOD LUCK RD 20706 | 4-00011
Frank Stetson, prin. | 794-7700
Goddard MS | 3-01100
9850 GOOD LUCK RD 20706 | 577-3300
Sheila Gray, prin.
Johnson MS, 5401 BARKER PL 20706 | 2-00100
John Robinson, prin. | 459-5800

Washington Bible College | 2-UC
6511 PRINCESS GARDEN PKY 20706 | 552-1400

La Plata, AC 301, PC 6, Charles
Charles County SD, PO BOX D 20646 | 7-11111
John Bloom, supt. | 932-6610
HS, PO BOX 790 20646 | 4-00011
Donald Cooke, prin. | 934-1100
Somers MS, PO BOX A 20646 | 3-00100
David Trudnak, prin. | 934-4663
Other Schools – See Indian Head, Newburg, Pomfret,
Waldorf

Charles County Community College | 6-CC
PO BOX 910 20646 | 934-2251

Largo, AC 301, PC 6, Prince George's

Prince George's Community College | 7-CC
301 LARGO RD 20772 | 336-6000

Laurel, PC 7, Prince George's
Howard County SD
Supt. — See Ellicott City
Hammond MS | 2-00100
8110 ALADDIN DR 20723 | 410-880-5830
David Oaks, prin.

Prince Georges County SD
Supt. — See Upper Marlboro
HS, 8000 CHERRY LN 20707 | 4-00011
Thomas Kirby, prin. | 301-725-8300
Eisenhower MS | 3-00100
13725 BRIARWOOD DR 20708 | 301-776-9393
Brian Giersch, prin.

Capitol College | 3-UC
11301 SPRINGFIELD RD 20708 | 800-950-1992
St. Pallotti HS, 113 8TH ST 20707 | 2-00011
Paul Leonarczyk, prin. | 301-725-3228

Leonardtown, AC 301, PC 4, St. Mary's
St. Mary's County SD | 7-11111
PO BOX 641 20650 | 475-4230
Joan Kozlovsky, supt.
HS, RR 1 BOX 49-3 20650 | 4-00011
Edward Weiland, prin. | 475-5007
St. Mary's County Technical Center | 2-00011
RR 1 BOX 49-2 20650 | 475-5501
Stephen Olczak, prin.
MS, RR 1 BOX 49-1 20650 | 3-00100
George Kirby, prin. | 475-2801
Other Schools – See Great Mills, Helen, Lexington
Park, Morganza

Leonard Hall Naval Academy | 1-01110
PO BOX 507 20650 | 475-8029
Margaret Bailey, prin.
St. Mary's Ryken HS | 2-00011
42 CAMP CALVERT RD 20650 | 475-2814
Harry Swaney, prin.

Lexington Park, AC 301, PC 6, St. Mary's
St. Mary's County SD
Supt. — See Leonardtown
Esperanza MS, 201 MAPLE RD 20653 | 3-00100
Carol Montague, prin. | 863-9451
Spring Ridge MS | 3-00100
RR 1 BOX 106 20653 | 863-9462
William Sluder, prin.

Lonaconing, AC 301, PC 4, Allegany
Allegany County SD
  Supt. — See Cumberland
Westmar HS   3-00011
  0 STATE ROUTE 36 S 21539   463-5751
  Timothy Martin, prin.

Lothian, AC 410, PC 2, Anne Arundel
Anne Arundel County SD
  Supt. — See Annapolis
Southern MS   3-00100
  5235 SOLOMONS ISLAND RD 20711   867-2170
  Deborah Montgomery, prin.

Lusby, AC 410, PC 3, Calvert
Calvert County SD
  Supt. — See Prince Frederick
Southern MS   3-00100
  9615 HG TRUEMAN RD 20657   535-7877
  Gene Bridgett, prin.

Lutherville, AC 410, PC 7, Baltimore
Baltimore County SD
  Supt. — See Towson
Ridgely MS, 121 E RIDGELY RD 21093   3-00100
  Stephen Ponzillo, prin.   887-7650

McDonogh, AC 410, PC 2, Baltimore

McDonogh S   4-11111
  8600 MCDONOGH RD 21208   363-0600
  William Mules, prin.

Mc Henry, AC 301, PC 3, Garrett

Garrett Community College   3-CC
  PO BOX 151 21541   387-6666

Mardela Springs, AC 410, PC 2, Wicomico
Wicomico County SD
  Supt. — See Salisbury
Mardela JSHS, 24940 DELMAR RD 21837   2-00111
  Richard Turner, prin.   742-5987

Marriotsville, AC 410, PC 99, Howard
Howard County SD
  Supt. — See Ellicott City
Mount View MS   3-00100
  12101 WOODFORD DR 21104   313-5545
  Marion Payne, prin.

Middletown, AC 301, PC 4, Frederick
Frederick County SD
  Supt. — See Frederick
HS, 200 HIGH ST 21769   3-00011
  George Seaton, prin.   371-5000
MS, 100 HIGH ST 21769   3-00100
  William VanHall, prin.   371-4300

Millersville, AC 410, PC 3, Anne Arundel
Anne Arundel County SD
  Supt. — See Annapolis
Old Mill HS, 600 PATRIOTS LN 21108   4-00011
  Mary Gable, prin.   969-9010
Old Mill MS-North   3-00100
  610 PATRIOTS LN 21108   969-5950
  William Callahan, prin.
Old Mill MS-South   3-00100
  620 PATRIOTS LN 21108   969-7000
  Ed Holshey, prin.

Monkton, AC 410, PC 3, Baltimore
Baltimore County SD
  Supt. — See Towson
Hereford MS, 712 CORBETT RD 21111   3-00100
  Judith Scheper, prin.   887-7902

Morganza, AC 301, PC 2, St. Mary's
St. Mary's County SD
  Supt. — See Leonardtown
Chopticon HS   4-00011
  GENERAL DELIVERY 20660   475-5655
  John Ryan, prin.

Mount Airy, PC 5, Carroll
Carroll County SD
  Supt. — See Westminster
MS, 102 WATERSVILLE RD 21771   2-00100
  Larry Barnes, prin.   410-795-1744

Mount Savage, AC 301, PC 4, Allegany
Allegany County SD
  Supt. — See Cumberland
S, RR 1 BOX 112A 21545   3-11111
  Gregory Smith, prin.   264-3220

Newark, AC 410, PC 2, Worcester
Worcester County SD   6-11111
  6270 WORCESTER HWY 21841   632-2582
  Terrance Greenwood, supt.
Wocester County Vo-Tech Ctr   2-00011
  6268 WORCESTER HWY 21841   632-2582
  Leroy Hall, prin.
  Other Schools – See Berlin, Pocomoke City, Snow Hill

Newburg, AC 301, PC 3, Charles
Charles County SD
  Supt. — See La Plata
Piccowaxen MS, RR 1 BOX 6 20664   2-00100
  Joseph Warfield, prin.   934-1977

New Carrollton, AC 301, PC 7, Prince George's
Prince Georges County SD
  Supt. — See Upper Marlboro
Carroll MS, 6130 LAMONT DR 20784   3-00100
  Herman Schiemer, prin.   577-6600

New Market, AC 301, PC 2, Frederick
Frederick County SD
  Supt. — See Frederick
MS, PO BOX 58 21774   4-00100
  Sally Smith, prin.   865-3434

New Windsor, AC 410, PC 3, Carroll
Carroll County SD
  Supt. — See Westminster
MS, 1100 GREEN VALLEY RD 21776   2-01100
  Jeffrey Kimble, prin.   635-6411

North East, AC 410, PC 4, Cecil
Cecil County SD
  Supt. — See Elkton
Cecil Vo-Tech HS, 900 N EAST RD 21901   2-00001
  Douglas Dunston, prin.   996-6250
HS, 300 IRISHTOWN RD 21901   3-00011
  Christopher Mench, prin.   996-6200
MS, 300 E CECIL AVE 21901   3-00100
  Charles Kasinec, prin.   996-6210

Cecil Community College   4-CC
  1000 N EAST RD 21901   287-6060
Tome School   2-11111
  581 MARYLAND AVE 21901   287-2050

Oakland, AC 301, PC 4, Garrett
Garrett County SD, PO BOX 59 21550   6-11111
  Jerome Ryscavage, supt.   334-8900
Southern Garrett County HS   3-00011
  1100 E OAK ST 21550   334-9447
  Arthur Refosco, prin.
Southern MS   3-00100
  903 BROADFORD RD 21550   334-8881
  John Rickman, prin.
  Other Schools – See Accident

Odenton, AC 410, PC 7, Anne Arundel
Anne Arundel County SD
  Supt. — See Annapolis
Arundel MS, 1179 HAMMOND LN 21113   3-00110
  Clifton Prince, prin.   674-6900

Oldtown, AC 301, PC 2, Allegany
Allegany County SD
  Supt. — See Cumberland
S, MAIN ST 21555   2-11111
  Jay Walbert, prin.   395-5111

Olney, AC 301, PC 7, Montgomery
Montgomery County SD
  Supt. — See Rockville
Farquhar MS   2-00100
  16915 BATCHELLORS FOREST RD 20832
  Julia Toxie, prin.   924-3100
Parks MS, 19200 OLNEY MILL RD 20832   3-00100
  Sarah Pinkney-Murkey, prin.   924-3180

Owings, AC 410, PC 2, Calvert
Calvert County SD
  Supt. — See Prince Frederick
Northern HS   4-00011
  2950 CHANEYVILLE RD 20736   257-1519
  Tommy Tucker, prin.
Northern MS   4-00100
  2954 CHANEYVILLE RD 20736   257-1622
  Earle Thorne, prin.

Owings Mills, AC 410, PC 6, Baltimore
Baltimore County SD
  Supt. — See Towson
HS, 124 S TOLLGATE RD 21117   3-00011
  Morris Hoffman, prin.   887-1700

Bais Yaakov Girls S   3-11111
  11111 PARK HEIGHTS AVE 21117   363-3300
Garrison Forest S   2-11111
  300 GARRISON FOREST RD 21117   363-1500
  Nancy Kirkland, prin.

Oxon Hill, AC 301, PC 8, Prince George's
Prince Georges County SD
  Supt. — See Upper Marlboro
Forestville HS   3-00011
  6360 OXON HILL RD 20745   567-1310
  Bruce Tyler, prin.
HS, 6701 LEYTE DR 20745   4-00011
  Cecil Short, prin.   839-1100
Potomac HS, 5211 BOYDELL AVE 20745   4-00011
  C. Anthony Thompson, prin.   894-2300

Parkton, AC 301, PC 2, Baltimore
Baltimore County SD
  Supt. — See Towson
Hereford HS, 17301 YORK RD 21120   3-00011
  Ray Gross, prin.   887-1905

Pasadena, AC 410, PC 7, Anne Arundel
Anne Arundel County SD
  Supt. — See Annapolis
Chesapeake HS   4-00011
  4798 MOUNTAIN RD 21122   255-9600
  Harry Calender, prin.
Northeast HS, 1121 DUVALL HWY 21122   3-00011
  Joseph Carducci, prin.   437-6400
Chesapeake Bay MS   4-00100
  4804 MOUNTAIN RD 21122   437-2400
  Charity McClellan, prin.
Fox MS, 7922 OUTING AVE 21122   3-00100
  John Brown, prin.   437-5512

Perry Hall, AC 410, PC 7, Baltimore

Perry Hall Christian S   2-11111
  3919 SCHROEDER AVE 21128   256-8880

Perryville, AC 410, PC 4, Cecil
Cecil County SD
  Supt. — See Elkton
HS, 1696 PERRYVILLE RD 21903   2-00011
  Maurice Tenney, prin.   996-6000
MS, 850 AIKEN AVE 21903   2-00100
  David Rudolph, prin.   996-6010

Pocomoke City, AC 410, PC 5, Worcester
Worcester County SD
  Supt. — See Newark
Pocomoke HS   2-00011
  1817 OLD VIRGINIA RD 21851   957-1484
  Fred Grant, prin.
Pocomoke MS, 800 8TH ST 21851   3-01100
  Teresa Hammerbacher, prin.   957-1567

Pomfret, AC 301, PC 2, Charles
Charles County SD
  Supt. — See La Plata
Charles County Career & Technology Ctr   2-00011
  RR 1 BOX 75 20675   934-9061
  George Harrington, prin.
McDonough HS, RR 2 BOX 74Q 20675   4-00011
  James Cornette, prin.   934-2944

Poolesville, AC 301, PC 5, Montgomery
Montgomery County SD
  Supt. — See Rockville
JSHS, 17501 W WILLARD RD 20837   3-00011
  Joan Benz, prin.   972-7900
Poolesville MS   2-00100
  17501 W WILLARD RD 20837   972-7900
  Joan Benz, prin.

Potomac, AC 301, PC 8, Montgomery
Montgomery County SD
  Supt. — See Rockville
Churchill HS   4-00011
  11300 GAINSBOROUGH RD 20854   469-1200
  Joseph Headman, prin.

Bullis S, 10601 FALLS RD 20854   2-01111
  Stephen Kurtz, prin.   299-8500
German S, 8617 CHATEAU DR 20854   2-11111
    365-4400

Prince Frederick, AC 410, PC 4, Calvert
Calvert County SD   6-11111
  1305 DARES BEACH RD 20678   535-1700
  James Hook, supt.
Calvert HS, 300 DARES BEACH RD 20678   4-00011
  James Marlett, prin.   535-7311
Calvert Career Ctr   Vo Tech
  330 DORSEY RD 20678   535-7450
  James Marlett, prin.
Calvert MS   3-00100
  435 SOLOMONS ISLAND RD N 20678   535-7355
  Patricia Young, prin.
  Other Schools – See Huntingtown, Lusby, Owings

Princess Anne, AC 410, PC 4, Somerset
Somerset County SD   5-11111
  PRINCE WILLIAM ST 21853   651-1616
  James Horn, supt.
Washington JSHS, PO BOX 189 21853   3-00111
  Herman Riggin, prin.   651-0480
  Other Schools – See Crisfield, Westover

University of Maryland Eastern Shore   4-UC
  11868 ACADEMIC OVAL 21853   651-6410

Pylesville, AC 410, PC 2, Harford
Harford County SD
  Supt. — See Bel Air
North Harford HS   3-00011
  211 PYLESVILLE RD 21132   638-3650
  Thomas Gibson, prin.
North Harford MS   3-00100
  213 PYLESVILLE RD 21132   638-3658
  Gerald Scarborough, prin.

Randallstown, AC 410, PC 8, Baltimore
Baltimore County SD
  Supt. — See Towson
HS, 4000 OFFUTT RD 21133   4-00011
  Clark Powell, prin.   887-0748
Deer Park MS, 9830 WINANDS RD 21133   3-00100
  John Jackson, prin.   887-0726

Reisterstown, AC 410, PC 7, Baltimore
Baltimore County SD
  Supt. — See Towson
Franklin HS   4-00011
  12000 REISTERSTOWN RD 21136   887-1119
  Evelyn Cogswell, prin.
Franklin MS   4-00100
  10 COCKEYSMILL RD 21136   887-1119
  Carroll Parker, prin.

Ridgely, AC 410, PC 4, Caroline
Caroline County SD
  Supt. — See Denton
North Caroline HS   3-00011
  10990 RIVER RD 21660   479-2332
  Margaret Hannah, prin.
Caroline Career & Technical Ctr   Vo Tech
  10855 CENTRAL AVE 21660   479-0100
  Brian Spiering, prin.

Rising Sun, AC 410, PC 4, Cecil
Cecil County SD
  Supt. — See Elkton
HS, 100 TIGER DR 21911   4-00111
  Terrill Stammler, prin.   658-9115

MS, 289 PEARL ST 21911   2-00100
Leonard Lundberg, prin.   658-5535

Riverdale, AC 301, PC 6, Prince George's
Prince Georges County SD
Supt. — See Upper Marlboro
Parkdale HS   4-00011
6001 GOOD LUCK RD 20737   474-4700
William LeFevre, prin.
Wirt MS   3-00100
62ND PL & TUCKERMAN ST 20782   277-7032
Ethel Engrum, prin.

Rock Hall, AC 410, PC 4, Kent
Kent County SD
Supt. — See Chestertown
MS, 21203 SHARP ST 21661   2-01100
John Sharp, prin.   639-2279

Rockville, AC 301, PC 8, Montgomery
Montgomery County SD   8-11111
850 HUNGERFORD DR 20850   279-3000
Paul Vance, supt.
Magruder HS   4-00011
5939 MUNCASTER MILL RD 20855   840-4600
John Graham, prin.
Montgomery HS   4-00011
250 RICHARD MONTGOMERY DR 20852
Thomas Quelet, prin.   279-8400
HS, 2100 BALTIMORE RD 20851   4-00011
Edward Shirley, prin.   279-8500
Wooton HS, 2100 WOOTTON PKY 20850   4-00011
Terrill Meyer, prin.   279-8550
Frost MS, 9201 SCOTT DR 20850   3-00100
Robert Domergue, prin.   279-3949
Hoover JHS, 8810 POSTOAK RD 20854   4-00110
Carole Goodman, prin.   469-1010
Parkland MS   3-00100
4610 W FRANKFORT DR 20853   460-2180
Jay Breakiron, prin.
Redland MS   3-00100
6505 MUNCASTER MILL RD 20855   840-4680
Nancy Schultze, prin.
Tilden MS   3-00100
11211 OLD GEORGETOWN RD 20852   230-5930
Arch Webster, prin.
West MS, 651 GREAT FALLS RD 20850   3-00100
John Nori, prin.   279-3979
Wood MS, 14615 BAUER DR 20853   3-00100
Sheila Dobbins, prin.   460-2150
Other Schools – See Bethesda, Burtonsville,
Damascus, Gaithersburg, Germantown,
Kensington, Olney, Poolesville, Potomac, Sandy
Spring, Silver Spring

Connelly School of the Holy Child   2-00111
9029 BRADLEY BLVD 20854   365-0955
Sr. Margaret Doyle, prin.
Georgetown Prep S   2-00011
10900 ROCKVILLE PIKE 20852   493-5000
James Power, prin.
Heights S   2-01111
10400 SEVEN LOCKS RD 20854   365-4300
Joseph McPherson, prin.
Montgomery College   7-CC
51 MANNAKEE ST 20850   279-5000
Montrose Christian S   3-11111
5100 RANDOLPH RD 20852   770-5337
Kenneth Coley, prin.
Smith Jewish Day S   3-11111
1901 E JEFFERSON ST 20852   881-1400
Geraldine Nussbaum, prin.

Saint James, AC 301, PC 2, Washington

St. James S, COLLEGE RD 21781   2-00111
Richard Baker, prin.   733-9330

Saint Mary's City, AC 301, PC 5, St. Mary's

St. Mary's College of Maryland   4-UC
GENERAL DELIVERY 20686   862-0200

Saint Michaels, AC 410, PC 4, Talbot
Talbot County SD
Supt. — See Easton
HS, SEYMOUR AVE 21663   2-00011
Roger Clark, prin.   745-2852

Salisbury, AC 410, PC 7, Wicomico
Wicomico County SD   7-11111
PO BOX 1538 21802   742-5128
Evelyn Holman, supt.
Bennett HS, 300 E COLLEGE AVE 21801   4-00011
Dan Savoy, prin.   742-5300
Parkside HS   3-00011
1015 BEAGLIN PARK DR 21801   546-2255
Timothy Bass, prin.
Wicomico HS, 201 LONG AVE 21801   3-00011
Tom Field, prin.   742-3278
Wicomico Applied Tech HS   1-00011
607 MORRIS ST 21801   546-3155
C. Andrew Buchanan, prin.
Bennett MS, 200 E COLLEGE AVE 21801   3-00100
F. Stephenson Matthes, prin.   742-9139
Wicomico MS, 635 E MAIN ST 21801   3-00100
William Evans, prin.   749-5622
Other Schools – See Mardela Springs

Salisbury State University   6-UC
1101 CAMDEN AVE 21801   543-6000
Woodridge Business Institute   2-CS
309 E MAIN ST 21801   742-6700

Wor-Wic Technical Community College   4-CC
30 WESLEY DR 21801   749-8181

Sandy Spring, AC 410, PC 4, Montgomery
Montgomery County SD
Supt. — See Rockville
Sherwood HS   4-00011
300 OLNEY SANDY SPRING RD 20860   924-3200
Elizabeth Boone, prin.

Sandy Spring Friends S   2-00111
16923 NORWOOD RD 20860   744-7455
Stephen Gessner, prin.

Severn, AC 410, PC 7, Anne Arundel
Anne Arundel County SD
Supt. — See Annapolis
Center of Applied Technology-North   4-00111
800 STEVENSON RD 21144   969-3100
John Weslow, prin.

Archbishop Spalding HS   3-00011
8080 NEW CUT RD 21144   969-9105
Barbara Schwitzer, prin.

Severna Park, AC 410, PC 8, Anne Arundel
Anne Arundel County SD
Supt. — See Annapolis
HS, 60 ROBINSON RD 21146   4-00011
Oliver Wittig, prin.   544-0900
MS, 450 JUMPERS HOLE RD 21146   3-00100
Leslie Mobray, prin.   647-7900

Severn S, 100 WATER ST 21146   2-00111
Edson Sheppard, prin.   647-7700

Silver Spring, AC 301, PC 8, Montgomery
Montgomery County SD
Supt. — See Rockville
Blair HS, 313 WAYNE AVE 20910   4-00011
Phillip Gainous, prin.   650-6600
Kennedy HS, 1901 RANDOLPH RD 20902   4-00011
Stephen Tarason, prin.   929-2100
Springbrook HS   4-00011
201 VALLEY BROOK DR 20904   649-8200
Don Kress, prin.
Wheaton HS   4-00011
12601 DALEWOOD DR 20906   929-2050
Joseph Dalton, prin.
Edison Career Center   Vo Tech
12501 DALEWOOD DR 20906   929-2175
Patricia Sweeney, prin.
Argyle MS, 2400 BEL PRE RD 20906   2-00100
Judy Docca, prin.   460-2400
Briggs-Chaney MS   3-00100
1901 RAINBOW DR 20905   989-6000
Janice Mostow, prin.
Eastern MS   3-00100
300 UNIVERSITY BLVD E 20901   650-6650
John Goodloe, prin.
Key MS, 910 SCHINDLER DR 20903   3-00100
Patricia Foster, prin.   431-7630
Lee MS, 11800 MONTICELLO AVE 20902   3-00100
Elizabeth Glowa, prin.   649-8100
Sligo MS, 1401 DENNIS AVE 20902   3-00100
Dorothy Jackson, prin.   649-8121
Takoma Park IS   3-00100
7611 PINEY BRANCH RD 20910   650-6444
Maria Montgomery, prin.
White Oak MS   3-00100
12201 NEW HAMPSHIRE AVE 20904   989-5780
Durinda Yates, prin.

Barrie Day S, 13500 LAYHILL RD 20906   2-11111
Jeffrey Moredock, prin.   871-7400
Good Counsel HS   3-00011
11601 GEORGIA AVE 20902   942-1155
Charles Dusterhoff, prin.
Hebrew Academy of Greater Washington   2-11111
2010 LINDEN LN 20910   587-4100
Holy Cross Hospital   HSP
1500 FOREST GLEN RD 20910   565-1216
Home Study International   HMS
PO BOX 4437 20914   680-6570
Maryland College of Art & Design   2-CC
10500 GEORGIA AVE 20902   649-4454
Ultrasound Diagnostic School   2-CS
1320 FENWICK LN 20910   588-0786
Washington Theological Union   2-UC
9001 NEW HAMPSHIRE AVE 20903   439-0551
Yeshiva HS of Greater Washington   2-00111
1840 UNIVERSITY BLVD W 20902   593-7273
Yeshiva HS of Greater Washington   2-00111
1216 ARCOLA AVE 20902   593-7273

Smithsburg, AC 301, PC 4, Washington
Washington County SD
Supt. — See Hagerstown
HS, 66 N MAIN ST 21783   3-00011
Michael Shockey, prin.   824-2002
MS, 68 N MAIN ST 21783   3-00100
Joseph Millward, prin.   791-4390

Snow Hill, AC 410, PC 4, Worcester
Worcester County SD
Supt. — See Newark
HS, 305 S CHURCH ST 21863   2-00011
Kelly Shumate, prin.   632-1658
MS   2-01100
5719 COULBOURNE LANE DR 21863   632-1727
Jesse Lynch, prin.

Stevenson, AC 410, PC 3, Baltimore

St. Timothy's S   2-00011
8400 GREENSPRING AVE 21153   486-7400
Galen Brewster, prin.
Villa Julie College   4-UC
1525 GREENSPRING VALLEY RD 21153
   486-7000

Stevensville, AC 410, PC 4, Queen Anne's
Queen Annes County SD
Supt. — See Centreville
MS, RT 18 21666   3-01100
Dominick Romano, prin.   643-3194

Sudlersville, AC 410, PC 2, Queen Anne's
Queen Annes County SD
Supt. — See Centreville
MS, CHURCH ST 21668   2-01100
George Henckel, prin.   438-3151

Sykesville, AC 410, PC 4, Carroll
Carroll County SD
Supt. — See Westminster
Liberty HS   4-00011
5855 BARTHOLOW RD 21784   795-8100
Robert Bastress, prin.
South Carroll HS   4-00011
1300 W OLD LIBERTY RD 21784   795-8500
David Booz, prin.
MS, 7301 SPRINGFIELD AVE 21784   2-00100
Donald Pyles, prin.   795-1313

Takoma Park, AC 301, PC 7, Montgomery

Columbia Union College   4-UC
7600 FLOWER AVE 20912   270-9200
Montgomery College   5-CC
7600 TAKOMA AVE 20912   650-1300
Takoma Academy   2-00111
8120 CARROLL AVE 20912   434-4700
Harvey Bristow, prin.
Washington Adventist Hospital   HSP
7600 CARROLL AVE 20912   891-7600

Taneytown, AC 410, PC 5, Carroll
Carroll County SD
Supt. — See Westminster
Northwest MS, 99 KINGS DR 21787   2-01100
Bronson Jones, prin.   756-6345

Temple Hills, AC 301, PC 6, Prince George's
Prince Georges County SD
Supt. — See Upper Marlboro
Crossland HS   4-00011
6901 TEMPLE HILL RD 20748   449-4100
Arthur Curry, prin.
Marshall MS, 4909 BRINKLEY RD 20748   3-00100
Regina Humaine, prin.   899-8500
Shugart MS, 2000 CALLOWAY ST 20748   3-00100
Robert Weidner, prin.   894-2425
Stoddert MS, 2501 OLSON ST 20748   3-00100
George Mitchell, prin.   423-7600

Thurmont, AC 301, PC 5, Frederick
Frederick County SD
Supt. — See Frederick
Catoctin HS   3-00011
14745 SABILLASVILLE RD 21788   271-7406
Earl Miller, prin.
MS, 408 E MAIN ST 21788   3-00100
Claire Kondig, prin.   271-7355

Timonium, AC 410, PC see Lutherville
Baltimore County SD
Supt. — See Towson
Dulaney HS, 255 E PADONIA RD 21093   4-00011
Thomas Hensley, prin.   887-7633

Towson, AC 410, PC 8, Baltimore
Baltimore County SD   8-11111
6901 N CHARLES ST 21204   887-5555
Stuart Berger, supt.
HS, 69 CEDAR AVE 21286   3-00011
Risa Schwartz, prin.   887-3608
Other Schools – See Baltimore, Catonsville,
Cockeysville/Hunt Valley, Lutherville, Monkton,
Owings Mills, Parkton, Randallstown,
Reisterstown, Timonium

Calvert Hall College HS   4-00011
8102 LA SALLE RD 21286   825-4266
Br. Johnson, prin.
Forbush S, 6501 N CHARLES ST 21204   2-11111
   938-4400
Loyola HS, 500 CHESTNUT AVE 21204   3-00111
Donald Urbancic, prin.   823-0601
Medix School   2-CS
1017 YORK RD 21204   337-5155
Notre Dame Prep S   3-00111
815 HAMPTON LN 21286   825-6202
Sr. Mary Denny, prin.
Towson Catholic HS   2-00011
114 WARE AVE 21204   823-8400
Andrew Dotterweich, prin.
Towson State University   7-UC
8000 YORK RD 21204   830-2000

Union Bridge, AC 410, PC 3, Carroll
Carroll County SD
Supt. — See Westminster
Key HS, 3825 BARK HILL RD 21791   3-00011
George Phillips, prin.   775-7888

Upper Marlboro, AC 301, PC 3, Prince George's
Prince Georges County SD   9-11111
    14201 SCHOOL LN 20772   952-6000
    Edward Felegy, supt.
Croom Vocational HS   1-00011
    15100 MOUNT CALVERT RD 20772   952-9570
    Reuben Buggs, prin.
Douglass HS, 8000 CROOM RD 20772   3-00011
                                                        952-2400
    Susan DePlatchett, prin.
Largo HS, 505 LARGO RD 20772   4-00011
    Gordon Sampson, prin.   336-8280
Kettering MS   3-00100
    65 HERRINGTON DR 20772   336-4100
    Eleanor White, prin.
Madison MS   3-00100
    7300 WOODYARD RD 20772   868-3850
    Paul Lewis, prin.
Other Schools – See Accokeek, Adelphi, Beltsville,
    Bladensburg, Bowie, Brandywine, Capitol Heights,
    Clinton, District Heights, Forestville, Fort
    Washington, Greenbelt, Hyattsville, Landover,
    Lanham-Seabrook, Laurel, New Carrollton, Oxon
    Hill, Riverdale, Temple Hills

Queen Anne S   2-00111
    14111 OAK GROVE RD 20772   249-5000
    Stanford Shutes, prin.
Riverdale Baptist S   2-00111
    1133 LARGO RD 20772   249-7000
    Rev. James Hockenberry, prin.

Waldorf, AC 301, PC 7, Charles
Charles County SD
    Supt. — See La Plata
Stone HS, PO BOX 32 20604   4-00011
    Herman Murrell, prin.   645-2601

Westlake HS   4-00011
    3300 MIDDLETOWN RD 20603   645-8857
    John Cox, prin.
Hanson MS, PO BOX 22D 20604   4-00100
    Garth Bowling, prin.   645-4520
Stoddert MS   3-00100
    2040 SAINT THOMAS DR 20602   645-1334
    William Wise, prin.

Walkersville, AC 301, PC 5, Frederick
Frederick County SD
    Supt. — See Frederick
HS, 81 FREDERICK ST 21793   3-00011
    Jay Berno, prin.   845-2711
MS, 55 FREDERICK ST 21793   3-00100
    Bruce Brown, prin.   845-2515

Westernport, AC 301, PC 4, Allegany
Allegany County SD
    Supt. — See Cumberland
Westmar MS, PHILOS AVE 21562   2-00100
    James Smith, prin.   359-3046

Westminster, AC 410, PC 7, Carroll
Carroll County SD   7-11111
    55 N COURT ST 21157   848-8280
    Edward Shilling, supt.
Carroll County Vo-Tech HS   2-00001
    1229 WASHINGTON RD 21157   848-5202
    Catherine Engel, prin.
HS, 1225 WASHINGTON RD 21157   4-00011
    Sherri-Le Bream, prin.   848-5050
Westminster East MS   2-00100
    100 LONGWELL AVE 21157   848-0191
    Don Reck, prin.
Westminster West MS   2-00100
    60 MONROE ST 21157   848-8411
    Harry Lambert, prin.

Other Schools – See Hampstead, Mount Airy, New
    Windsor, Sykesville, Taneytown, Union Bridge

Carroll Community College   4-CC
    1601 WASHINGTON RD 21157   876-9600
Western Maryland College   4-UC
    2 COLLEGE HL 21157   848-7000

Westover, AC 410, PC 3, Somerset
Somerset County SD
    Supt. — See Princess Anne
Tawes Vocational Center   Vo Tech
    PO BOX 189 21871   651-2285
    Lloyd Tyler, prin.

Williamsport, AC 301, PC 4, Washington
Washington County SD
    Supt. — See Hagerstown
HS, 5 S CLIFTON DR 21795   3-00011
    James Hardin, prin.   223-7400
Springfield MS   3-00100
    305 E SUNSET AVE 21795   223-8010
    Roger Stenersen, prin.

Worton, AC 410, PC 2, Kent
Kent County SD
    Supt. — See Chestertown
Kent County HS   3-00011
    25301 LAMBS MEADOW RD 21678   778-4540
    John Perry, prin.

Wye Mills, AC 301, PC 2, Talbot

Chesapeake College   4-CC
    PO BOX 8 21679   822-5400

MASSACHUSETTS

STATE DEPARTMENT OF EDUCATION
350 Main St., Malden 02148
(617) 388-3300

Commissioner of Education   Robert Antonucci

Deputy Commissioner Program Operations   David Driscoll

STATE BOARD OF EDUCATION
350 Main St., Malden 02148

Chairperson   Piedad Robertson

PUBLIC, PRIVATE AND CATHOLIC SECONDARY SCHOOLS

Abington, AC 617, PC 7, Plymouth
Abington SD   4-11111
    1071 WASHINGTON ST 02351   982-2150
    John Aherne, supt.
HS, 201 LINCOLN BLVD 02351   3-00011
    Paul Byron, prin.   982-2160
Frolio JHS   2-00100
    1071 WASHINGTON ST 02351   982-2170
    Joseph Rosenthal, prin.

Acton, AC 508, PC 4, Middlesex
Acton-Boxborough SD   4-00011
    16 CHARTER RD 01720   264-4700
    Isa Zimmerman, supt.
Acton-Boxborough Reg. HS   4-00011
    96 HAYWARD RD 01720   264-4700
    Stephen Donovan, prin.
Grey Regional JHS   3-00100
    16 CHARTER RD 01720   264-4700
    Clifford Card, prin.

Acushnet, AC 508, PC 6, Bristol
Acushnet SD, 130 MAIN ST 02743   4-11100
    Dawn Cameron, supt.   998-0260
Ford MS, 708 MIDDLE RD 02743   2-00100
    John Tavares, prin.   995-1877

Adams, AC 413, PC 7, Berkshire
Adams-Cheshire SD   4-11111
    5 COLUMBIA ST 01220   743-2939
    Bernard Fallon, supt.
Hoosac Valley JSHS   3-00111
    0 ROUTE 116 01220   743-5200
    Thomas Condron, prin.

Agawam, AC 413, PC 7, Hampden
Agawam SD
    Supt. — See Feeding Hills

HS, 760 COOPER ST 01001   4-00011
    John Morrissey, prin.   789-1400

Amesbury, AC 508, PC 7, Essex
Amesbury SD, 15 SCHOOL ST 01913   5-11111
    Stephen Gerber, supt.   388-0507
HS, 5 HIGHLAND ST 01913   3-00011
    Gerald Schrock, prin.   388-4800
MS, 220 MAIN ST 01913   3-00100
    Raymond Tiezzi, prin.   388-0515

Amherst, AC 413, PC 7, Hampshire
Amherst-Pelham SD   4-00111
    170 CHESTNUT ST 01002   549-3690
    Gus Sayer, supt.
Amherst Regional SHS   3-00001
    21 MATOON ST 01002   549-3710
    John Heffley, prin.
Amherst Regional JHS   3-00110
    170 CHESTNUT ST 01002   549-3975
    J. Heffley, prin.

Amherst College 01002   4-UC
                                                        542-2328
Hampshire College 01002   4-UC
                                                        582-5471
University of Massachusetts 01003   8-UC
                                                        545-0222

Andover, AC 508, PC 6, Essex
Andover SD, 26 BARTLET ST 01810   5-11111
    Mark McQuillan, supt.   470-1700
HS, 100 SHAWSHEEN RD 01810   4-00011
    Timothy Thomas, prin.   470-1700
Andover West MS   3-00100
    98 SHAWSHEEN RD 01810   470-1788
    Samuel Campbell, prin.

Doherty MS, 26 BARTLET ST 01810   3-00100
    Floyd McManus, prin.   475-1443

Greater Lawrence SD, 57 RIVER RD 01810   4-00011
    Marsha McDonough, supt.   686-0194
Greater Lawrence Regional Vo-Tech HS   4-00011
    57 RIVER RD 01810   686-0194
    Marsha McDonough, prin.

Phillips Academy, 180 MAIN ST 01810   4-00011
    Donald McNemar, prin.   475-3400

Arlington, AC 617, PC 8, Middlesex
Arlington SD, PO BOX 167 02174   5-11111
    Walter Devine, supt.   646-1000
HS, 869 MASSACHUSETTS AVE 02174   3-00011
    Charles McCarthy, prin.   646-1000
Ottoson JHS, 63 ACTON ST 02174   3-00100
    Paul Lamoureaux, prin.   646-1000

Arlington Catholic HS   3-00011
    16 MEDFORD ST 02174   646-7770
    Sr. Catherine Clifford, prin.

Ashburnham, AC 508, PC 4, Worcester
Ashburnham-Westminster SD
    Supt. — See Westminster
Oakmont Regional JSHS   3-00111
    OAKMONT DR 01430   827-5907
    William Waight, prin.

Cushing Academy   2-00011
    PO BOX 8000 01430   827-5911
    Joseph Curry, prin.

Ashland, AC 508, PC 6, Middlesex
Ashland SD, 90 CONCORD ST 01721   4-11111
    B. Ruthfield, supt.   881-0150

JSHS, 87 W UNION ST 01721 — 2-00111
James Reynolds, prin. — 881-0177

Athol, AC 508, PC 7, Worcester
Athol-Royalston SD — 4-11111
2175 MAIN ST 01331 — 249-2400
James Kelley, supt.
HS, 2363 MAIN ST 01331 — 3-00011
Thomas Casey, prin. — 249-3255
JHS, 494 SCHOOL ST 01331 — 2-00100
Robert Potter, prin. — 249-3437

Attleboro, AC 508, PC 8, Bristol
Attleboro SD — 6-11111
108 RATHBUN WILLARD DR 02703 — 222-0012
Joseph Rappa, supt.
HS, 100 RATHBUN WILLARD DR 02703 — 4-00011
Robert Bray, prin. — 222-5150
Attleboro Vo-Tech HS — Vo Tech
108 RATHBUN WILLARD DR 02703 — 222-5150
Francis Antosca, prin.
Brennan MS, 135 COUNTY ST 02703 — 3-01100
Francis Leary, prin. — 222-7750
Thatcher MS, JAMES ST 02703 — 3-01100
Edward McCarthy, prin. — 222-1922
Other Schools – See South Attleboro

Bishop Feehan HS — 3-00011
70 HOLCOTT DR 02703 — 226-6223
Br. Wickman, prin.

Auburn, AC 508, PC 7, Worcester
Auburn SD, 5 WEST ST 01501 — 4-11111
Patricia Martin, supt. — 832-7755
HS, 99 AUBURN ST 01501 — 3-00011
Paul Sturgis, prin. — 832-7711
MS, 10 SWANSON RD 01501 — 3-00100
Donald Thunberg, prin. — 832-7722

Avon, AC 508, PC 6, Norfolk
Avon SD, 265 W MAIN ST 02322 — 3-11111
Lincoln Lynch, supt. — 588-0230
JSHS, 287 W MAIN ST 02322 — 2-01111
Harry Levine, prin. — 583-4822

Ayer, AC 508, PC 6, Middlesex
Ayer SD, 141 WASHINGTON ST 01432 — 4-11111
Richard Warren, supt. — 772-3468
JSHS, 115 WASHINGTON ST 01432 — 3-00111
Don Parker, prin. — 772-3357

Babson Park, AC 617, PC see Wellesley

Babson College — 4-UC
ONE COLLEGE DR 02157 — 235-1200

Baldwinville, AC 508, PC 4, Worcester
Narragansett SD
Supt. — See Otter River
Narragansett Regional JSHS — 3-00111
133 S MAIN ST 01436 — 939-5388
Kent Dumas, prin.

Barre, AC 508, PC 4, Worcester
Quabbin SD, 40 WEST ST 01005 — 5-11111
Maureen Marshall, supt. — 355-4668
Quabbin Regional JSHS — 3-00111
SOUTH ST 01005 — 355-4651
Maureen Lacroix, prin.

Bedford, AC 617, PC 7, Middlesex
Bedford SD, 9 MUDGE WAY 01730 — 4-11111
Joseph Buckley, supt. — 275-7588
HS, 9 MUDGE WAY 01730 — 3-00011
Thomas Duggan, prin. — 275-1700
Glenn MS, 99 MCMAHON RD 01730 — 2-00100
Laurence Aronstein, prin. — 275-1700

Lincoln SD
Supt. — See Lincoln
Hanscom MS, HANSCOM A F B 01730 — 2-01100
Ronald Hadge, prin. — 274-0050

Middlesex Community College — 5-CC
210 SPRINGS RD 01730 — 280-3200

Belchertown, AC 413, PC 4, Hampshire
Belchertown SD, PO BOX 841 01007 — 4-11111
Robert Byard, supt. — 323-0423
HS, 62 N WASHINGTON ST 01007 — 2-00011
Dennis Pike, prin. — 323-6941
Chestnut Hill Community MS — 3-01100
59 STATE ST 01007 – Joe Giroux, prin. — 323-7611

Bellingham, AC 508, PC 7, Norfolk
Bellingham SD, 60 HARPIN ST 02019 — 4-11111
Malcolm Patterson, supt. — 883-1706
Bellingham Mem. JSHS — 3-00111
110 BLACKSTONE ST 02019 — 883-4220
Roger Canestrari, prin.

Belmont, AC 617, PC 7, Middlesex
Belmont SD, 644 PLEASANT ST 02178 — 5-11111
Peter Holland, supt. — 484-4180
HS, 221 CONCORD AVE 02178 — 3-00011
Foster E. Wright, prin. — 484-4700
Chenery MS — 3-00100
95 WASHINGTON ST 02178 — 484-3900
Marvin Shapiro, prin.

Belmont Hill S, 350 PROSPECT ST 02178 — 2-00111
Richard Melvoin, prin. — 484-4410

Beverly, AC 508, PC 8, Essex
Beverly SD, 4 COLON ST 01915 — 5-11111
Lawrence Chase, supt. — 921-6100
HS, 80 SOHIER RD 01915 — 4-00011
Keith Manville, prin. — 921-6132
Briscoe MS, 7 SOHIER RD 01915 — 2-00100
John Lapsley, prin. — 921-6103
Memorial MS, 502 CABOT ST 01915 — 3-00100
Ken Stowe, prin. — 921-6110

Endicott College — 3-CC
376 HALE ST 01915 — 927-0585
Montserrat College of Art — 2-UC
PO BOX 26 01915 — 800-836-0487

Billerica, AC 508, PC 6, Middlesex
Billerica SD, 365 BOSTON RD 01821 — 6-11111
Robert Calabrese, supt. — 436-9500
Billerica Mem. HS, 35 RIVER ST 01821 — 4-00011
Tom Sharkey, prin. — 436-9300
Locke MS, 132 ALLEN RD 01821 — 3-00100
Rich Loranger, prin. — 436-9420
Marshall MS, 32 FLOYD ST 01821 — 3-00100
Stan Jekanoski, prin. — 436-9440

Shawsheen Valley Vocational-Technical SD — 4-00011
100 COOK ST 01821 — 667-2111
Charles Lyons, supt.
Shawsheen Valley Vocational Technical HS — 4-00011
100 COOK ST 01821 — 667-2111
Charles Lyons, prin.

Blackstone, AC 508, PC 5, Worcester
Blackstone-Millville SD — 4-11111
LINCOLN ST 01504 — 883-6633
Aldo Cecchi, supt.
Blackstone-Millville Reg. JSHS — 3-00111
LINCOLN ST 01504 — 883-4400
Rob Powers, prin.

Bolton, AC 508, PC 3, Worcester
Nashoba SD, 12 GREEN RD 01740 — 3-00011
Roland Miller, supt. — 779-2257
Nashoba Regional HS — 3-00011
12 GREEN RD 01740 — 779-2257
Sam Pawlak, prin.

Boston, AC 617, PC 11, Suffolk
Boston SD, 26 COURT ST 02108 — 8-11111
Lois Harrison-Jones, supt. — 635-9050
HS, 152 ARLINGTON ST 02116 — 4-00011
Tom Hennessey, prin. — 451-6860
English HS, 144 MCBRIDE ST 02130 — 4-00011
Joseph Smith, prin. — 524-3373
Snowden International HS — 3-00011
150 NEWBURY ST 02116 — 635-9989
Gloria Coulter, prin.
Boston Latin Academy — 4-00111
78 AVENUE LOUIS PASTEUR 02115 — 566-2250
Michael Contompasis, prin.
O'Bryant Math/Science JSHS — 4-00111
55 NEW DUDLEY ST 02120 — 445-4381
Gustave Anglin, prin.
Other Schools – See Brighton, Charlestown, Dorchester, East Boston, Hyde Park, Jamaica Plain, Mattapan, Roslindale, Roxbury, Roxbury Crossing, South Boston, West Roxbury

---

Art Institute of Boston, The — 2-UC
700 BEACON ST 02215 — 262-1223
Bay State College — 3-CC
122 COMMONWEALTH AVE 02116 — 236-8000
Berklee College of Music — 5-UC
1140 BOYLSTON ST 02215 — 266-1400
Boston Architectural Center — 3-UC
320 NEWBURY ST 02115 — 536-3170
Boston Conservatory — 2-UC
8 FENWAY 02215 — 536-6340
Boston University — 7-UC
685 COMMONWEALTH AVE 02215 — 353-2000
Boston University Medical Center — UC
100 E NEWTON ST 02118 — 638-5300
Boston Univ. Graduate School of Mgmt. — 2-UC
685 COMMONWEALTH AVE 02215
Bunker Hill Community College — 5-CC
250 RUTHERFORD AVE 02129 — 241-8600
Burdett School — 2-CS
745 BOYLSTON ST 02116 — 859-1900
Butera School of Art — 2-CS
111 BEACON ST 02116 — 536-4623
Cathedral HS, 74 UNION PARK ST 02118 — 2-00011
Sr. Patricia Keaveney, prin. — 542-3090
Children's Hospital — HSP
300 LONGWOOD AVE 02115 — 735-6433
Commonwealth S — 2-00011
151 COMMONWEALTH AVE 02116 — 266-7525
Judith Keenan, prin.
Don Bosco Tech HS — 3-00011
300 TREMONT ST 02116 — 426-9457
John Goff, prin.
Emerson College — 4-UC
148 BEACON ST 02116 — 578-8500
Emmanuel College — 3-UC
400 FENWAY 02115 — 277-9340
Fisher College — 4-CC
118 BEACON ST 02116 — 262-3240
Forsyth School for Dental Hygienists — 2-CS
140 FENWAY 02115 — 262-5200
Franklin Institute of Boston — 2-CC
41 BERKELEY ST 02116 — 423-4630
Hickox School — 3-CC
200 TREMONT ST 02116 — 482-7655

Katharine Gibbs School — 3-CC
126 NEWBURY ST 02116 — 578-7100
Laboure College — 3-CC
2120 DORCHESTER AVE 02124 — 296-8300
Massachusetts College of Art — 4-UC
621 HUNTINGTON AVE 02115 — 232-1555
MA College of Pharmacy & Allied Health — 4-UC
179 LONGWOOD AVE 02115 — 732-2893
Massachusetts General Hospital — UC
32 FRUIT ST 02114
Massachusetts School Professional Psych. — 2-UC
221 RIVERMOOR ST 02132 — 327-6777
MGH Institute of Health Professions — 2-UC
101 MERRIMAC ST 02114 — 726-3163
New England Banking Institute — 2-CC
89 SOUTH ST 02111 — 951-2350
New England Baptist Hospital — HSP
220 FISHER AVE 02120 — 739-5266
New England College of Optometry — 2-UC
424 BEACON ST 02115 — 266-2030
New England Conservatory of Music — 3-UC
290 HUNTINGTON AVE 02115 — 262-1120
New England Deaconess Hospital — HSP
110 FRANCIS ST 02215 — 732-8001
New England Medical Center — HSP
P O BOX 451 02111 — 956-7655
New England School of Art & Design — 2-CS
28 NEWBURY ST 02116 — 536-0383
New England School of Law — 4-UC
154 STUART ST 02116 — 451-0010
New England School of Photography — 2-CS
537 COMMONWEALTH AVE 02215 — 437-1868
Newton Prepartory S — 2-00011
245 MARLBOROUGH ST 02116 — 267-4530
J Lynch, prin.
North Bennet Street School — 2-CS
39 N BENNET ST 02113 — 227-0155
Northeast Broadcasting School — 2-CS
142 BERKELEY ST 02116 — 267-7910
Northeastern University — 8-UC
360 HUNTINGTON AVE 02115 — 373-2000
Northeast Institute of Industrial Tech — 2-CS
41 PHILLIPS ST 02114 — 523-2869
RETS Electronic School — 2-CS
965 COMMONWEALTH AVE 02215 — 783-1197
School of the Museum of Fine Arts — 3-UC
230 FENWAY 02115 — 267-1218
Simmons College — 5-UC
300 FENWAY 02115 — 738-2000
Suffolk University — 5-UC
8 ASHBURTON PL 02108 — 573-8460
Tufts University — 4-UC
136 HARRISON AVE 02111
University of Massachusetts — 6-UC
100 WILLIAM T MRRISSEY BLVD 02125 — 287-5000
Veterans Administration Hospital — HSP
150 S HUNTINGTON AVE 02130 — 232-9500
Wentworth Institute of Technology — 5-UC
550 HUNTINGTON AVE 02115 — 442-9010
Wheelock College — 3-UC
200 RIVERWAY 02215 — 734-5200
Winsor S, 17 PILGRIM RD 02215 — 2-01111
Carolyn Peter, prin. — 735-9500

Bourne, AC 508, PC 4, Barnstable
Bourne SD, 36 SANDWICH RD 02532 — 4-11111
John O'Brien, supt. — 759-0660
HS, 75 WATERHOUSE RD 02532 — 3-00011
John Grondin, prin. — 759-0670
Stone MS, 5400 LINDBERGH AVE 02542 — 2-00100
William Wibel, prin. — 563-5668

Upper Cape Cod Vocational-Technical SD — 3-00011
220 SANDWICH RD 02532 — 759-7711
David Sampson, supt.
Upper Cape Cod Vo-Tech HS — 3-00011
220 SANDWICH RD 02532 — 759-7711
Barry Motta, prin.

Boylston, AC 508, PC 3, Worcester
Berlin-Boylston SD, 1001 MAIN ST 01505 — 2-00111
Donald DuPont, supt. — 869-2837
Tahanto Regional JSHS — 2-00111
1001 MAIN ST 01505 — 869-2333
John Driscoll, prin.

Bradford, AC 508, PC see Haverhill

Bradford College — 2-UC
320 S MAIN ST 01835 — 372-7161

Braintree, AC 617, PC 8, Norfolk
Braintree SD — 5-11111
482 WASHINGTON ST 02184 — 380-0130
Peter Kurzberg, supt.
HS, 128 TOWN ST 02184 — 4-00011
John Leroy, prin. — 848-4000
East MS, 305 RIVER ST 02184 — 3-00100
Michael Connelly, prin. — 380-0170
South MS, 232 PEACH ST 02184 — 2-00100
John Horstak, prin. — 380-0160

Archbishop Williams HS — 3-00011
80 INDEPENDENCE AVE 02184 — 843-3636
Mary Barnes, prin.
Thayer Academy — 3-00111
745 WASHINGTON ST 02184 — 843-3580
William Elliott, prin.

Bridgewater, AC 508, PC 6, Plymouth
Bridgewater-Raynham SD 4-00011
 166 MOUNT PROSPECT ST 02324 697-6902
 Edward O'Donoghue, supt.
Bridgewater-Raynham Regional HS 4-00011
 166 MOUNT PROSPECT ST 02324 697-6902
 Edward O'Donoghue, prin.

Bridgewater SD, 35 SOUTH ST 02324 4-11100
 Robert Blakeley, supt. 697-6914
Williams JHS, 200 SOUTH ST 02324 2-00100
 Warren Kelson, prin. 697-6968

Bridgewater State College 02325 6-UC
 697-1237

Brighton, AC 617, PC see Boston
Boston SD
 Supt. — See Boston
 HS, 25 WARREN ST 02135 4-00011
 Juliette Johnson, prin. 635-9873
 Edison JHS, 60 GLENMONT RD 02135 3-00100
 Eliot Stern, prin. 635-8436
 Taft MS, 20 WARREN ST 02135 3-00100
 Irene McCarthy, prin. 782-0080

Mt. St. Joseph Academy 2-00011
 617 CAMBRIDGE ST 02134 254-8383
 Sr. Mary Murphy, prin.
St. Elizabeth's Hospital HSP
 235 WASHINGTON ST 02135 789-2366
St. John's Seminary 2-UC
 127 LAKE ST 02135 254-2610

Brockton, AC 508, PC 8, Plymouth
Brockton SD, 43 CRESCENT ST 02401 7-11111
 Manthala George, supt. 580-7511
HS, 470 FOREST AVE 02401 5-00011
 Robert Jarvis, prin. 580-7633
East JHS, 464 CENTRE ST 02402 3-00100
 David Swift, prin. 580-7351
North JHS, 108 OAK ST 02401 2-00100
 Robert Bartlett, prin. 580-7371
South JHS, 105 KEITH AVE 02401 3-00100
 Rich Williams, prin. 580-7311
West JHS, 271 WEST ST 02401 3-00100
 Eugene Franciosi, prin. 580-7381

Brockton Hospital HSP
 680 CENTRE ST 02402 941-7044
Cardinal Spellman HS 3-00011
 738 COURT ST 02402 583-6875
 Sr. Thomasine Knowlton, prin.
Massasoit Community College 5-CC
 1 MASSASOIT BLVD 02402 588-9100
New England Tractor Trailer Training 2-CS
 1093 N MONTELLO ST 02401 587-1100

Brookline, AC 617, PC 8, Norfolk
Brookline SD 6-11111
 333 WASHINGTON ST 02146 730-2403
 James Walsh, supt.
HS, 115 GREENOUGH ST 02146 4-00011
 Mary Jennings, prin. 730-2604

Hebrew College 1-UC
 43 HAWES ST 02146 232-8710
Hellenic College 2-UC
 50 GODDARD AVE 02146 731-3500
Maimonides S, 34 PHILBRICK RD 02146 3-11111
 Rabbi Shapiro, prin. 232-4414
NEC-Bryman Campus 3-CS
 323 BOYLSTON ST 02146 232-6035
Newbury College 4-CC
 129 FISHER AVE 02146 739-0510
Northeast Hebrew Academy 2-11111
 9 PRESCOTT ST 02146 731-5330
 Judith Helman, prin.

Burlington, AC 617, PC 7, Middlesex
Burlington SD 5-11111
 123 CAMBRIDGE ST 01803 270-1800
 Robert Neely, supt.
HS, 123 CAMBRIDGE ST 01803 3-00011
 Maynard Suffredini, prin. 270-1800
Simonds MS, 144 WINN ST 01803 3-00100
 Rich Connors, prin. 270-1782

Open Bible Academy, 3 WINN ST 01803 2-11111
 Fred Irwin, prin. 272-2074

Buzzards Bay, AC 508, PC 5, Barnstable

Massachusetts Maritime Academy 4-UC
 101 ACADEMY DR 02532 800-544-3411

Byfield, AC 508, PC 4, Essex
Triton SD, PO BOX 56 01922 4-00111
 Garry Murphy, supt. 465-2476
Triton Regional JSHS, ELM ST 01922 4-00111
 J. Ward, prin. 462-8171

Governor Dummer Academy 2-00011
 1 ELM ST 01922 – Peter Bragdon, prin. 465-1763

Cambridge, AC 617, PC 8, Middlesex
Cambridge SD 6-11111
 159 THORNDIKE ST 02141 349-6400
 Mary Lou Mcgrath, supt.
Cambridge Rindge & Latin HS 4-00011
 459 BROADWAY 02138 349-6400
 Ed Sarasin, prin.

Kennedy MS, 158 SPRING ST 02141 2-01100
 Mary Mroz, prin. 349-6400

Arthur D. Little Mgmt. Education Inst. 1-UC
 35 ACORN PARK 02140 864-5770
Boston Choir S 1-01100
 29 MOUNT AUBURN ST 02138 868-8658
 John Dunn, prin.
Buckingham Browne & Nichols HS 3-11111
 9 GERRYS LANDING RD 02138 547-6100
 Mary Newmann, prin.
Cambridge College 2-UC
 1000 MSSACHUSETTS AVE # 128 02138 492-5108
Cambridge Hospital HSP
 1493 CAMBRIDGE ST 02139 498-1000
Cambridge School of Culinary Arts 2-CS
 2020 MASSACHUSETTS AVE 02140 354-3836
Computer Processing Institute 3-CS
 615 MASSACHUSETTS AVE 02139 354-6900
Episcopal Divinity School 2-UC
 99 BRATTLE ST 02138 868-3450
Harvard University 7-UC
 8 GARDEN ST 02138 495-1000
Lesley College 4-UC
 29 EVERETT ST 02138 868-9600
Longy School of Music 3-UC
 1 FOLLEN ST 02138 876-0956
Massachusetts Institute of Technology 6-UC
 77 MASSACHUSETTS AVE 02139 253-1000
Matignon HS, 1 MATIGNON RD 02140 3-00011
 Gary Lefave, prin. 876-1212
Mt. Auburn Hospital HSP
 330 MOUNT AUBURN ST 02138 499-5070
North Cambridge Catholic HS 2-00011
 40 NORRIS ST 02140 876-6068
 Sr. Ellen Powers, prin.
Weston School of Theology 2-UC
 3 PHILLIPS PL 02138 492-1960

Canton, AC 617, PC 7, Norfolk
Blue Hills Vocational SD 4-00011
 800 RANDOLPH ST 02021 828-5800
 Wilfred Savoie, supt.
Blue Hills Regional Vocational HS 4-00011
 800 RANDOLPH ST 02021 828-5800
 Wilfred Savoie, prin.

Canton SD, 960 WASHINGTON ST 02021 5-11111
 Peter Capernaros, supt. 821-5060
HS, 900 WASHINGTON ST 02021 3-00011
 Barry Parker, prin. 821-5050
Galvin MS, 55 PECUNIT ST 02021 3-00100
 Charles Howard, prin. 821-5070

Bay State School of Appliances 2-CS
 225 TURNPIKE ST 02021 828-3434

Carver, AC 508, PC 4, Plymouth
Plymouth-Carver SD
 Supt. — See Plymouth
Carver JSHS 3-00111
 SOUTH MEADOW RD 02330 830-4430
 Thomas Long, prin.

Charlemont, AC 413, PC 3, Franklin

Academy at Charlemont 1-01111
 MOHAWK TRL 01339 339-4912
 Eric Grinnell, prin.

Charlestown, AC 617, PC see Boston
Boston SD
 Supt. — See Boston
 HS, 240 MEDFORD ST 02129 4-00011
 Stacy Johnson, prin. 242-1450
 Edwards MS, 28 WALKER ST 02129 3-00100
 Charles McAfee, prin. 242-0779

Charlton, AC 508, PC 3, Worcester
South Worcester County Vocational SD 3-00011
 RR 1 BOX 277 01507 248-5971
 Charles Valera, supt.
Bay Path Vocational Technical HS 3-00011
 RR 1 BOX 277 01507 248-5971
 Steven Mondor, prin.

Chatham, AC 508, PC 4, Barnstable
Chatham SD, 147 DEPOT ST 02633 3-11111
 Vida Gavin, supt. 945-5130
JSHS, 425 CROWELL RD 02633 2-00111
 Michael Smith, prin. 945-0246

Chelmsford, AC 508, PC 8, Middlesex
Chelmsford SD
 Supt. — See North Chelmsford
McCarthy MS, 250 NORTH RD 01824 4-00100
 Robert Bennett, prin. 256-6531

Chelsea, AC 617, PC 8, Suffolk
Chelsea SD, 208 CITY HALL 02150 5-11111
 John Gawrys, supt. 889-8415
HS, 12 CLARK AVE 02150 3-00011
 Elsa Wasserman, prin. 889-0636
Williams Annex MS 2-00100
 179 CHESTNUT ST 02150 884-6501
 Stephen Soucha, prin.

TAD Technical Institute 3-CS
 45 SPRUCE ST 02150 800-370-1589

Chestnut Hill, AC 617, PC see Newton

Beaver Country Day S 2-01111
 791 HAMMOND ST 02167 734-6950
 Peter Hutton, prin.
Boston College 7-UC
 140 COMMONWEALTH AVE 02167 552-8000
Brimmer & May S 2-11111
 69 MIDDLESEX RD 02167 566-7462
 Anne Reemstierna, prin.
Pine Manor College 3-UC
 400 HEATH ST 02167 731-7000

Chicopee, AC 413, PC 8, Hampden
Chicopee SD, 180 BROADWAY ST 01020 6-11111
 Herbert Curry, supt. 594-3410
HS, 650 FRONT ST 01013 3-00011
 Frances Bigda, prin. 594-3437
Chicopee Comprehensive HS 4-00011
 209 ROLF AVE 01020 594-3534
 Mitchell Kuzdzal, prin.
Bellamy MS 3-00100
 314 PENDLETON AVE 01020 594-3527
 Julie Leonard, prin.

Allstate Institute of Technology 2-UC
 165 FRONT ST DOOR D 5TH FLR 01013
 594-8248
Elms College 3-UC
 291 SPRINGFIELD ST 01013 800-255-3567

Clinton, AC 508, PC 6, Worcester
Clinton SD, 100 CHURCH ST 01510 4-11111
 Brendon J. Bailey, supt. 365-4200
HS, 80 CHURCH ST 01510 2-00011
 Edward Philbin, prin. 365-4208
MS, 100 W BOYLSTON ST 01510 3-01100
 Gerald Gaw, prin. 365-4220

Cohasset, AC 617, PC 6, Norfolk
Cohasset SD, 143 POND ST 02025 4-11111
 Stephen Hart, supt. 383-6111
JSHS, 143 POND ST 02025 2-00111
 Mary Ellen Gallagher, prin. 383-6100

Concord, AC 508, PC 5, Middlesex
Concord-Carlisle SD 3-00011
 120 MERIAM RD 01742 371-9410
 Thomas Scott, supt.
Concord-Carlisle HS 3-00011
 500 WALDEN ST 01742 371-4610
 Elaine Dicicco, prin.

Concord SD, 120 MERIAM RD 01742 4-11100
 Thomas Scott, supt. 371-9410
Concord Peabody MS 2-00100
 1231 OLD MARLBORO RD 01742 371-8860
 Connie Pawlak, prin.
Concord Sanborn MS 2-00100
 835 OLD MARLBORO RD 01742 371-8880
 Connie Pawlak, prin.

Concord Academy, 194 MAIN ST 01742 2-00011
 Thomas Wilcox, prin. 369-6080
East Coast Aero Tech School 3-CS
 696 VIRGINIA RD 01742 371-9977
Fenn ES, 516 MONUMENT ST 01742 2-01110
 Jerry Ward, prin. 369-5800
Middlesex S, 1400 LOWELL RD 01742 2-00011
 Deirdre Ling, prin. 369-2550

Conway, AC 413, PC 3, Franklin

Conway School of Landscape Design 1-UC
 DELABARRE AVE 01341 369-4044

Dalton, AC 413, PC 6, Berkshire
Central Berkshire SD 4-11111
 PO BOX 299 01227 684-0320
 John Jangro, supt.
Wahconah Regional HS 3-00011
 150 WINDSOR RD 01226 684-1330
 Thomas Potter, prin.
Nessacus MS, 120 1ST ST 01226 3-00100
 Lee Brown, prin. 684-0780

Danvers, AC 508, PC 7, Essex
Danvers SD, 64 CABOT RD 01923 5-11111
 Richard Santeusanio, supt. 777-4539
HS, 60 CABOT RD 01923 3-00011
 Paul Coleman, prin. 777-8925
Dunn MS, 62 CABOT RD 01923 3-00100
 Betty Allen, prin. 774-8590

North Shore Community College 5-CC
 1 FERNCROFT RD 01923 762-4000
St. Johns Prep S, 72 SPRING ST 01923 3-00011
 Br. Davis, prin. 774-1050

Dedham, AC 617, PC 7, Norfolk
Dedham SD, 30 WHITING AVE 02026 5-11111
 Thomas Curran, supt. 326-5622
HS, 86 WHITING AVE 02026 3-00011
 Denise Walsh, prin. 326-4773
MS, 86 WHITING AVE 02026 3-00100
 Donald Seaber, prin. 326-6900

Noble And Greenough S 2-00111
 507 BRIDGE ST 02026 326-3700
 Richard Baker, prin.

Ursuline Academy — 2-00111
65 LOWDER ST 02026 — 326-6161
Sr. Mercedes Videira, prin.

Deerfield, AC 413, PC 3, Franklin

Deerfield Academy, MAIN ST 01342 — 3-00111
Robert Kaufmann, prin. — 772-0241
Eaglebrook ES, PO BOX 7 01342 — 2-00110
Stuart Chase, prin. — 774-7411

Dighton, AC 508, PC 4, Bristol
Bristol County Agricultural SD — 2-00011
135 CENTER ST 02715 — 669-6744
James Santos, supt.
Bristol County Agricultural HS — 2-00011
135 CENTER ST 02715 — 669-6744
Russell James, prin.

Dighton-Rehoboth SD
Supt. — See North Dighton
JHS, 1250 SOMERSET AVE 02715 — 2-00100
Paul Swett, prin. — 669-4245

Dorchester, AC 617, PC see Boston
Boston SD
Supt. — See Boston
Burke HS, 60 WASHINGTON ST 02121 — 3-00100
Albert Holland, prin. — 427-0240
HS, 9 PEACEVALE RD 02124 — 3-00011
Christopher Lane, prin. — 436-2065
Boston Latin Academy — 4-00111
205 TOWNSEND ST 02121 — 635-9957
Maria Aaronson, prin.
Cleveland MS, 11 CHARLES ST 02122 — 3-00100
Mikel Sidberry, prin. — 825-9201
King MS, 77 LAWRENCE AVE 02121 — 2-00100
Steven Leonard, prin. — 445-4120
McCormack MS — 3-00100
315 MOUNT VERNON ST 02125 — 825-7949
Robert Martin, prin.
Thompson MS, 100 MAXWELL ST 02124 — 2-00100
Ron Spratling, prin. — 282-4040
Wilson MS, 18 CROFTLAND AVE 02124 — 3-00100
Rosalyn Browne, prin. — 288-4730

Boston College HS — 4-00011
150 WILLIAM T MRRISSEY BLVD 02125 — 436-3900
William Kemeza, prin.
Msgr. Ryan Memorial HS — 2-00011
11 MAYHEW ST 02125 — 282-2818
Sr. Maureen Kane, prin.

Douglas, AC 508, PC 2, Worcester
Douglas SD, CONSTITUTION AVE 01516 — 4-11111
Concetta Verge, supt. — 476-7901
Other Schools – See East Douglas

Dover, AC 508, PC 4, Norfolk
Dover-Sherborn SD, 137 FARM ST 02030 — 3-00111
Rob Couture, supt. — 785-0036
Dover-Sherborn Regional HS — 2-00011
PO BOX 190 02030 — 785-0624
Richard Wakely, prin.
Dover-Sherborn Regional JHS — 2-00100
137 FARM ST 02030 — 785-0717
John Moore, prin.

Dracut, AC 508, PC 7, Middlesex
Dracut SD, 2063 LAKEVIEW AVE 01826 — 5-11111
Christos Daoulas, supt. — 957-2660
HS, 1540 LAKEVIEW AVE 01826 — 3-00011
Bruce Hutchins, prin. — 957-1500
Englesby JHS — 3-00100
1580 LAKEVIEW AVE 01826 — 957-3330
Roger Dumont, prin.

Dudley, AC 508, PC 5, Worcester
Dudley-Charlton Regional SD — 5-11111
68 DUDLEY OXFORD RD 01571 — 943-6888
James Walter, supt.
Shepherd Hill Regional JSHS — 4-00111
DUDLEY & OXFORD RD 01570 — 943-6700
Albert Thibadeau, prin.

Nichols College 01570 — 4-UC
943-2055

Duxbury, AC 617, PC 4, Plymouth
Duxbury SD — 5-11111
130 SAINT GEORGES ST 02332 — 934-7600
Eileen Williams, supt.
JSHS, 130 SAINT GEORGES ST 02332 — 4-00111
John Hill, prin. — 934-7650

East Boston, AC 617, PC see Boston
Boston SD
Supt. — See Boston
HS, 86 WHITE ST 02128 — 4-00011
John Poto, prin. — 567-2140
Barnes MS, 312 BORDER ST 02128 — 3-00100
George Moran, prin. — 569-1343

Savio Preparatory HS — 2-00011
145 BYRON ST 02128 — 567-2710
Rev. John Stagnaro, prin.

East Bridgewater, AC 508, PC 5, Plymouth
East Bridgewater SD — 4-11111
11 PLYMOUTH ST 02333 — 378-7241
Gordon Mitchell, supt.
HS, 11 PLYMOUTH ST 02333 — 3-00011
Judith Riordan, prin. — 378-3161
MS, 435 CENTRAL ST 02333 — 3-01100
John Collins, prin. — 378-7221

East Brookfield, AC 508, PC 4, Worcester
Spencer-East Brookfield SD
Supt. — See Spencer
Lashway JHS, SCHOOL ST 01515 — 2-00100
Eileen Prizio, prin. — 885-8537

East Douglas, AC 508, PC 4, Worcester
Douglas SD
Supt. — See Douglas
Douglas Mem. JSHS — 3-00111
CONSTITUTION AVE 01516 — 476-3332
William Mahoney, prin.

East Falmouth, AC 508, PC 6, Barnstable
Falmouth SD — 5-11111
340 TEATICKET HWY 02536 — 548-0151
Suzanne McGee, supt.
Other Schools – See Falmouth

East Freetown, AC 508, PC 3, Bristol
Freetown-Lakeville SD — 4-01111
43 BULLOCK RD 02717 — 763-5183
August Pereira, supt.
Apponequet Regional HS — 3-00011
99 E HOWLAND RD 02717 — 947-2660
James Conro, prin.
Austin MS, 99 E HOWLAND RD 02717 — 3-01100
Karl Smith, prin. — 947-7850

Easthampton, AC 413, PC 7, Hampshire
Easthampton SD, 130 MAIN ST 01027 — 4-11111
Katherine Kussy, supt. — 527-1510
HS, 70 WILLISTON AVE 01027 — 3-00011
Jeffrey Sealander, prin. — 527-3030
White Brook MS, 200 PARK ST 01027 — 3-01100
Rosemarie Bonner, prin. — 527-6000

Hampshire SD
Supt. — See Westhampton
Hampshire Regional JSHS — 3-00111
19 STAGE RD 01027 — 586-3960
Carolyn MacManus, prin.

Williston Northampton S — 2-00111
19 PAYSON AVE 01027 — 527-1520
Dennis Grubbs, prin.

East Longmeadow, AC 413, PC 7, Hampden
East Longmeadow SD — 4-11111
180 MAPLE ST 01028 — 525-5450
Michael Waring, supt.
HS, 180 MAPLE ST 01028 — 3-00011
Richard Freccero, prin. — 525-5460
Birchland Park MS — 3-00100
50 HANWARD HL 01028 — 525-5480
Ronald Lech, prin.

East Pepperell, AC 508, PC 4, Middlesex
North Middlesex SD
Supt. — See Townsend
Varnum Brook MS, HOLLIS ST 01463 — 3-01100
Mike Connolly, prin. — 433-6722

East Sandwich, AC 508, PC 3, Barnstable
Sandwich SD
Supt. — See Sandwich
Sandwich JSHS — 3-00111
365 QUAKER MEETING HOUSE RD 02537 — 888-4900
Russell Norton, prin.

East Walpole, AC 508, PC 5, Norfolk
Walpole SD
Supt. — See Walpole
Bird MS, 141 WASHINGTON ST 02032 — 2-01100
Suzanne Gillam, prin. — 660-7226

East Weymouth, AC 617, PC see Weymouth
Weymouth SD
Supt. — See Weymouth
Weymouth SHS — 4-00001
1051 COMMERCIAL ST 02189 — 337-4500
Richard Steele, prin.

Everett, AC 617, PC 8, Middlesex
Everett SD, 121 VINE ST 02149 — 5-11111
Frederick Foresteire, supt. — 389-7950
HS, 548 BROADWAY 02149 — 4-00011
Edward Leo, prin. — 387-0180
Parlin JHS, 587 BROADWAY 02149 — 3-00100
Peter Dolan, prin. — 387-1762

Pope John XXIII Central HS — 2-00011
888 BROADWAY 02149 — 389-0240
Sr. Kristin Hokanson, prin.

Fairhaven, AC 508, PC 7, Bristol
Fairhaven SD — 4-11111
128 WASHINGTON ST 02719 — 979-4000
Bernard Roderick, supt.
HS, 12 HUTTLESTON AVE 02719 — 3-00011
John Newburn, prin. — 979-4000
Hastings JHS, 30 SCHOOL ST 02719 — 3-00100
Allen Duarte, prin. — 979-4000

Fall River, AC 508, PC 8, Bristol
Fall River SD, 417 ROCK ST 02720 — 7-11111
James Gibney, supt. — 675-8420
Durfee HS, 360 ELSBREE ST 02720 — 5-00011
Albert Attar, prin. — 675-8420
Kuss MS, 289 ROCK ST 02720 — 3-00100
Angelo Stavros, prin. — 675-8420
Lord MS, 615 TUCKER ST 02721 — 3-00100
Stephen Nawrocki, prin. — 675-8420
Morton MS, 376 PRESIDENT AVE 02720 — 3-00100
George Howayeck, prin. — 675-8420

Talbot MS, 124 MELROSE ST 02723 — 3-00100
Bruce Clarke, prin. — 675-8420
Greater Fall River SD — 4-00011
STONEHAVEN RD 02723 — 678-2891
Joseph Martins, supt.
Diman Regional Vocational Technical HS — 4-00011
STONEHAVEN RD 02723 — 678-2891
John Connell, prin.

Bishop Connolly HS — 2-00011
373 ELSBREE ST 02720 — 676-1071
Fr. Murray, prin.
Bristol Community College — 5-CC
777 ELSBREE ST 02720 — 678-2811

Falmouth, AC 508, PC 5, Barnstable
Falmouth SD
Supt. — See East Falmouth
HS, 874 GIFFORD STREET EXT 02540 — 4-00011
Thomas Forcella, prin. — 540-2200
Lawrence MS — 3-00100
113 LAKEVIEW AVE 02540 — 548-0606
Howard Campbell, prin.

Falmouth Academy — 2-00111
7 HIGHFIELD DR 02540 — 457-9696
Bruce Buxton, prin.

Feeding Hills, AC 413, PC 6, Hampden
Agawam SD — 5-11111
1305 SPRINGFIELD ST 01030 — 789-1400
Bernard Ryder, supt.
Agawam JHS — 3-00100
1305 SPRINGFIELD ST 01030 — 789-1400
Kevin Littlefield, prin.
Other Schools – See Agawam

Fiskdale, AC 508, PC 4, Worcester
Tantasqua SD, PO BOX 26 01518 — 4-00111
David Roach, supt. — 347-9014
Tantasqua Regional SHS — 3-00011
319 BROOKFIELD RD 01518 — 347-9301
Francis Simanski, prin.
Tantasqua Regional Vo HS — Vo Tech
319 BROOKFIELD RD 01518 — 347-3045
George Zini, prin.
Tantasqua Regional JHS — 3-00110
320 BROOKFIELD RD 01518 — 347-7381
John Barry, prin.

Fitchburg, AC 508, PC 8, Worcester
Fitchburg SD, 376 SOUTH ST 01420 — 6-11111
Philip Fallon, supt. — 345-9300
HS, 98 ACADEMY ST 01420 — 3-00011
Bernard Welch, prin. — 345-3240
Brown JHS, 62 ACADEMY ST 01420 — 3-00100
Richard Masciarelli, prin. — 345-3278
Memorial MS — 3-00100
615 ROLLSTONE ST 01420 — 345-3295
Peter Stephens, prin.

Montachusett Vocational Technical SD — 4-00011
1050 WESTMINSTER ST 01420 — 343-2506
Stratos Dukakis, supt.
Montachusett Vocational Technical HS — 4-00011
1050 WESTMINSTER ST 01420 — 343-2506
Stratos Dukakis, prin.

Fitchburg State College — 6-UC
160 PEARL ST 01420 — 345-2151
Notre Dame HS, 171 SOUTH ST 01420 — 1-00111
Jeff Hammond, prin. — 343-7635
St. Bernards HS, 45 HARVARD ST 01420 — 2-00011
Rev. Thomas Sullivan, prin. — 342-3212

Florence, AC 413, PC see Northampton
Northampton SD
Supt. — See Northampton
Kennedy JHS, 30 BRIDGE RD 01060 — 3-00100
Richard Carnes, prin. — 586-6970

Foxboro, AC 508, PC 6, Norfolk
Foxboro SD — 4-11111
CARPENTER & SOUTH 02035 — 543-1600
Magdalene Giffune, supt.
JSHS, 120 SOUTH ST 02035 — 3-00111
William Rex, prin. — 543-1616

Framingham, AC 508, PC 8, Middlesex
Framingham SD, 454 WATER ST 01701 — 6-11111
Eugene Thayer, supt. — 626-9117
HS, 115 A ST 01701 — 4-00011
Robert Flaherty, prin. — 626-4964
Walsh MS, 301 BROOK ST 01701 — 4-00100
James Halliday, prin. — 626-9180

South Middlesex Vocational Technical SD — 3-00011
750 WINTER ST 01701 — 879-5400
Paul Bento, supt.
Keefe Technical HS — 3-00011
750 WINTER ST 01701 — 879-5400
Jack Wescott, prin.

Framingham State College — 5-UC
100 STATE ST 01701 — 620-1220
Framingham Union Hospital School/Nursing — 1-HSP
85 LINCOLN ST 01701 — 626-3514
ITT Technical Institute — 2-CS
1671 WORCESTER RD STE 100 01701 — 879-6266

Marian HS, 273 UNION AVE 01701 — 2-00011
Br. Paul Alves, prin. — 875-7646

Franklin, AC 508, PC 6, Norfolk
Franklin SD, 130 OAK ST 02038   5-11111
   Dorothy Swanbeck, supt.   528-5600
JSHS, 224 OAK ST 02038   4-00111
   Mary Moran, prin.   528-5600

Tri-County SD, 147 POND ST 02038   3-00011
   John Jones, supt.   528-5400
Tri-County Regional Vo-Tech HS   3-00011
   147 POND ST 02038   528-5400
   Peter Rickard, prin.

Dean College   4-CC
   99 MAIN ST 02038   528-9100

Gardner, AC 508, PC 7, Worcester
Gardner SD, 130 ELM ST 01440   5-11111
   Michael Pregot, supt.   632-1000
HS, 200 CATHERINE ST 01440   3-00011
   Walter Dubzinski, prin.   632-1600
JHS, 62 WATERFORD ST 01440   2-00100
   Richard Wojtukiewicz, prin.   632-1603

Mt. Wachusett Community College   4-CC
   444 GREEN ST 01440   632-6600

Georgetown, AC 508, PC 4, Essex
Georgetown SD, 1 LIBRARY ST 01833   4-11111
   Larry Borin, supt.   352-5777
JSHS, 11 WINTER ST 01833   2-00111
   Gerald Silverman, prin.   352-5790

Gloucester, AC 508, PC 8, Essex
Gloucester SD   5-11111
   99 BLACKBURN CIR 01930   281-9800
   Howard Goodrow, supt.
HS, 32 LESLIE O JOHNSON RD 01930   3-00011
   Charles Symonds, prin.   281-9870
O'Maley MS, BABSON RD 01930   3-00100
   Joan Connolly, prin.   281-9850

Grafton, AC 508, PC 4, Worcester
Grafton SD, 30 PROVIDENCE RD 01519   4-11111
   Gail Rowe, supt.   839-5421
Grafton Memorial HS   2-00011
   24 PROVIDENCE RD 01519   839-5425
   Raymond Lemay, prin.
MS, 82 NORTH ST 01519   2-01100
   John Gorman, prin.   839-5420

Granby, AC 413, PC 4, Hampshire
Granby SD, E STATE ST 01033   3-11111
   Francis Gougeon, supt.   467-7193
JSHS, 387 E STATE ST 01033   2-00111
   Albert Bessette, prin.   467-7105

St. Hyacinth College & Seminary   1-UC
   66 SCHOOL ST 01033   467-7191

Great Barrington, AC 413, PC 5, Berkshire
Berkshire Hills SD
   Supt. — See Stockbridge
Monument Mountain Regional HS   3-00011
   600 STOCKBRIDGE RD 01230   528-3346
   Linda Day, prin.
Searles MS, 79 BRIDGE ST 01230   2-00100
   Jane Forey, prin.   528-3346

Dewey Academy, 389 MAIN ST 01230   1-00001
   Thomas Bratter, prin.   528-9800
Simon's Rock of Bard College   2-UC
   80 ALFORD RD 01230   528-0771

Greenfield, AC 413, PC 7, Franklin
Greenfield SD, 141 DAVIS ST 01301   5-11111
   Ilene Turock, supt.   772-1300
HS, LENOX AVE 01301   3-00011
   William Lawson, prin.   773-3639
MS, 195 FEDERAL ST 01301   3-00100
   James Peters, prin.   773-5214

Greenfield Community College   4-CC
   1 COLLEGE DR 01301   774-3131
Stoneleigh-Burnham S   2-00011
   584 BERNARDSTON RD 01301   774-2711
   C. Wray, prin.

Groton, AC 508, PC 4, Middlesex
Groton-Dunstable SD   4-11111
   PO BOX 729 01450   448-5505
   John Barranco, supt.
Groton-Dunstable Regional HS   2-00011
   PO BOX 730 01450   448-6362
   William McGuirk, prin.
Groton/Dunstable MS   2-00100
   PO BOX 727 01450   448-2408
   Edward Roberts, prin.

Groton School, PO BOX 991 01450   2-00111
   William Polk, prin.   448-3363
Lawrence Academy   2-00011
   PO BOX 992 01450   448-6354
   Steven Hahn, prin.

Hadley, AC 413, PC 3, Hampshire
Hadley SD, 49 RUSSELL ST 01035   3-11111
   Ann Finck, supt.   586-0822
Hopkins Academy JSHS   2-00111
   127 RUSSELL ST 01035   584-1106
   Janet Selavka, prin.

Hampden, AC 413, PC 3, Hampden
Hampden SD, 85 WILBRAHAM RD 01036   3-11100
   Gwen Van Dorp, supt.   566-8814
Burgess MS, 85 WILBRAHAM RD 01036   2-01100
   Michael Rooney, prin.   566-3931

Hanover, AC 617, PC 5, Plymouth
Hanover SD, 848 MAIN ST 02339   4-11111
   Kenneth Johnson, supt.   878-0786
HS, 287 CEDAR ST 02339   3-00011
   Thomas Nee, prin.   878-5450
MS, 45 WHITING ST 02339   3-01100
   Philip O'Neil, prin.   871-1122

South Shore Regional Vocational Tech. SD   2-00011
   476 WEBSTER ST 02339   878-8822
   James Hager, supt.
South Shore Vocational Technical HS   2-00011
   476 WEBSTER ST 02339   878-8822
   James Hager, prin.

Hanson, AC 617, PC 4, Plymouth
Whitman-Hanson SD
   Supt. — See Whitman
Indian Head MS   3-01100
   750 INDIAN HEAD ST 02341   447-7065
   Patricia Johnson, prin.

Calvary Baptist S, ROUTE 58 02341   2-11111
   Rev. Ronald Secrest, prin.   293-6367

Harvard, AC 508, PC 4, Worcester
Harvard SD, 39 MASS AVE 01451   3-11111
   Lois Haslam, supt.   456-4140
Bromfield JSHS, 14 MASS AVE 01451   2-00111
   Robert Scholl, prin.   456-4152

Harwich, AC 508, PC 4, Barnstable
Cape Cod Regional Vocational-Tech SD   2-00011
   PLEASANT LAKE AVE 02645   432-4500
   F. Carroll, supt.
Cape Cod Regional Voc-Tech HS   2-00011
   PLEASANT LAKE AVE 02645   432-4500
   Richard Curcio, prin.

Harwich SD, OAK ST 02645   4-11111
   Charles Ferris, supt.   430-7200
HS, OAK ST 02645   2-00011
   Vincent Bresnahan, prin.   430-7207
MS, SISSON RD 02645   2-01100
   Robert Cronin, prin.   430-7212

Hatfield, AC 413, PC 4, Hampshire
Hatfield SD, 34 SCHOOL ST 01038   2-11111
   Linda Driscoll, supt.   247-5641
Smith Academy, 34 SCHOOL ST 01038   2-00111
   Frank Abarno, prin.   247-5641

Hathorne, AC 508, PC see Danvers
Essex Agricultural & Technical SD   3-00011
   MAPLE 01937 — Gustave Olson, supt.   774-0050
Essex Agricultural & Technical HS   3-00011
   MAPLE 01937 — Helen Hegarty, prin.   774-0050

Essex Agricultural & Technical Institute   2-CS
   GENERAL DELIVERY 01937   774-0050

Haverhill, AC 508, PC 8, Essex
Haverhill SD, 4 SUMMER ST 01830   6-11111
   Thomas Fowler-Finn, supt.   374-3400
HS, 137 MONUMENT ST 01832   4-00011
   Michael Wrenn, prin.   374-5700
Consentino MS   4-01100
   685 WASHINGTON ST 01832   374-5775
   Daniel Harrington, prin.
Hunking MS, WINCHESTER ST 01835   2-01100
   Thomas Behan, prin.   374-5787
Nettle MS, 150 BOARDMAN ST 01830   2-01100
   James Quinn, prin.   374-5792
Whittier MS, 256 CONCORD ST 01830   2-01100
   Gerald Quatrale, prin.   374-5782

Whittier Vocational SD   3-00011
   115 AMESBURY LINE RD 01830   373-4101
   Karen Prentice, supt.
Whittier Regional Vocational HS   3-00011
   115 AMESBURY LINE RD 01830   373-4101
   Karen Prentice, prin.

Northern Essex Community College   5-CC
   100 ELLIOTT ST 01830   374-3900

Hingham, AC 617, PC 6, Plymouth
Hingham SD, 14 MAIN ST 02043   5-11111
   Gary Baker, supt.   741-1500
SHS, 41 PLEASANT ST 02043   3-00001
   Richard MacLeod, prin.   749-2160
JHS, 1103 MAIN ST 02043   2-00100
   Robert Willett, prin.   749-1280

Notre Dame Academy   2-00011
   1073 MAIN ST 02043   749-5930
   Sr. Anne Ruane, prin.

Holbrook, AC 617, PC 7, Norfolk
Holbrook SD, 227 PLYMOUTH ST 02343   4-11111
   John Spillane, supt.   767-1226
JSHS, 245 S FRANKLIN ST 02343   3-00111
   David Sweeney, prin.   767-4616

Holden, AC 508, PC 5, Worcester
Holden SD, 1128 MAIN ST 01520   4-11100
   Robert Conn, supt.   829-6631

Mountview MS   3-00100
   270 SHREWSBURY ST 01520   829-5577
   Joan Barry, prin.

Wachusett SD, 1128 MAIN ST 01520   4-00011
   Robert Conn, supt.   829-6631
Wachusett Regional HS   4-00011
   1401 MAIN ST 01520 — H. Lane, prin.   829-6771

Holliston, AC 508, PC 7, Middlesex
Holliston SD, LINDEN ST 01746   5-11111
   John Drinkwater, supt.   429-0654
JSHS, 340 HOLLIS ST 01746   3-00111
   Robert Berardi, prin.   429-0678

Holyoke, AC 413, PC 8, Hampden
Holyoke SD, 57 SUFFOLK ST 01040   6-11111
   James McDonnell, supt.   534-2005
HS, 500 BEECH ST 01040   4-00011
   Edward Shevlin, prin.   534-2020
Dean Vo-Tech HS, 1045 MAIN ST 01040   Vo Tech
   Walter Welch, prin.   534-2071
Lynch JHS   2-00100
   1575 NORTHAMPTON ST 01040   534-2050
   David Dupont, prin.
Magnet MS for Arts, 325 PINE ST 01040   2-00100
   Felicita El-Ghadi, prin.   534-2007
Peck JHS   3-00100
   1916 NORTHAMPTON ST 01040   534-2040
   Alexander Borelli, prin.

Holyoke Catholic HS   2-00011
   91 CHESTNUT ST 01040   533-0347
   William Fitzgerald, prin.
Holyoke Community College   5-CC
   303 HOMESTEAD AVE 01040   538-7000

Hopedale, AC 508, PC 5, Worcester
Hopedale SD, 25 ADIN ST 01747   3-11111
   Donald Hayes, supt.   634-2220
JSHS, 25 ADIN ST 01747   2-00111
   Barry Cahill, prin.   634-2217

Hopkinton, AC 508, PC 4, Middlesex
Hopkinton SD   4-11111
   HAYDEN ROWE ST 01748   435-4511
   William Hosmer, supt.
JSHS, 83 HAYDEN ROWE ST 01748   2-00111
   Thomas Lane, prin.   435-3351

Hudson, AC 508, PC 7, Middlesex
Hudson SD, 155 APSLEY ST 01749   4-11111
   Sheldon Berman, supt.   568-8535
HS, 69 BRIGHAM ST 01749   3-00011
   John Stapelfeld, prin.   568-8361
Kennedy MS, 201 MANNING ST 01749   2-00100
   Albert Powers, prin.   562-7313

Hudson Catholic HS, 198 MAIN ST 01749   2-00011
   Mary McCarthy, prin.   562-6701

Hull, AC 617, PC 7, Plymouth
Hull SD, 81 CENTRAL AVE 02045   4-11111
   John MacLean, supt.   925-0771
JSHS, 180 MAIN ST 02045   3-00111
   Robert McIntyre, prin.   925-3000

Huntington, AC 413, PC 4, Hampshire
Gateway SD, LITTLEVILLE ROAD 01050   4-11111
   Raymond Broderick, supt.   667-8711
Gateway Regional HS   2-00011
   LITTLEVILLE ROAD 01050   667-8711
   Robert Gazda, prin.
Gateway Regional MS   3-01100
   LITTLEVILLE ROAD 01050   667-8711
   Peter Curro, prin.

Hyannis, AC 508, PC 6, Barnstable
Barnstable SD, PO BOX 955 02601   6-11111
   Edward Tynan, supt.   790-6440
Barnstable HS, 744 W MAIN ST 02601   4-00011
   Alvin Fortune, prin.   790-6445
Barnstable MS   3-00100
   895 FALMOUTH RD 02601   790-6460
   Terence Russell, prin.

Faith Christian S   2-11111
   154 BEARSES WAY 02601   775-1830
   Rev. Robedee, prin.

Hyde Park, AC 617, PC see Boston
Boston SD
   Supt. — See Boston
HS, 655 METROPOLITAN AVE 02136   4-00011
   Curtis Wells, prin.   361-8080
Rogers MS, 15 EVERETT ST 02136   3-00100
   John Daniels, prin.   361-1990

Hyde Park Academy   2-11111
   14 EVERETT ST 02136   364-5595
   Henry Lodge, prin.

Ipswich, AC 508, PC 5, Essex
Ipswich SD, 1 LORD SQ 01938   4-11111
   Richard Thompson, supt.   356-2935
HS, 130 HIGH ST 01938   2-00011
   Stephen Fortado, prin.   356-3137
MS, 23 GREEN ST 01938   2-00100
   Ronald Toleos, prin.   356-3535

Jamaica Plain, AC 617, PC see Boston
Boston SD
   Supt. — See Boston
Curley MS, 493 CENTRE ST 02130   3-00100
   Valerie Lowe, prin.   524-2020

Kingston, AC 617, PC 5, Plymouth
Silver Lake SD
  130 PEMBROKE ST 02364 — 4-00111 / 585-4313
  Paul Squarcia, supt.
Silver Lake Regional SHS
  132 PEMBROKE ST 02364 — 4-00001 / 585-3844
  John McEwan, prin.
Other Schools – See Pembroke

Sacred Heart HS
  399 BISHOPS HWY 02364 — 2-00111 / 585-7511
  Sr. Marjorie Nickel, prin.

Lancaster, AC 508, PC 3, Worcester
Lancaster SD, PO BOX 37 01523 — 3-11100 / 365-6854
  Paul Livingston, supt.
MS, PO BOX 37 01523 — 2-01100 / 365-4558
  Thomas Moore, prin.

Lawrence, AC 508, PC 8, Essex
Lawrence SD, 255 ESSEX ST 01840 — 7-11111 / 975-5900
  James Scully, supt.
HS, 58 LAWRENCE ST 01841 — 4-00011 / 975-2750
  Steven Jenkins, prin.
Kane JHS, 141 OSGOOD ST 01843 — 3-01100 / 975-5953
  Juan Rodriguez, prin.
Leonard MS, 60 ALLEN ST 01840 — 3-01100 / 975-5962
  Kathleen Borys, prin.

Central Catholic HS
  300 HAMPSHIRE ST 01841 — 3-00011 / 682-0260
  Br. Richard Carey, prin.
Lawrence General Hospital
  1 GENERAL ST 01841 — HSP / 683-4000
St. Mary HS, 301 HAVERHILL ST 01840 — 2-00011 / 682-6441
  Sr. Mary Farren, prin.

Lee, AC 413, PC 4, Berkshire
Lee SD, 0 CROSSWAY ST 01238 — 3-11111 / 243-0276
  Henry Zukauski, supt.
HS, 140 GREYLOCK ST 01238 — 2-00011 / 243-2787
  Richard Salinetti, prin.

Leicester, AC 508, PC 5, Worcester
Leicester SD, 1078 MAIN ST 01524 — 4-11111 / 892-7040
  Norman Limoges, supt.
HS, 80 WINSLOW AVE 01524 — 2-00011 / 892-7030
  James O'Donnell, prin.
Leicester Memorial MS
  400 PLEASANT ST 01524 — 2-00100 / 892-7055
  John Hartnett, prin.

Becker College
  3 PAXTON ST 01524 — 3-CC / 791-9241

Lenox, AC 413, PC 4, Berkshire
Lenox SD, 6 WALKER ST 01240 — 3-11111 / 637-5550
  Roland Miller, supt.
Lenox Memorial JSHS
  157 EAST ST 01240 — 2-00111 / 637-5560
  Bruce Walker, prin.

Leominster, AC 508, PC 8, Worcester
Leominster SD, 24 CHURCH ST 01453 — 6-11111 / 534-7700
  Louis Amadio, supt.
HS, 122 GRANITE ST 01453 — 4-00011 / 534-7715
  Kevin O'Malley, prin.
Leominster Trade SHS
  122 GRANITE ST 01453 — Vo Tech / 534-7735
  Roger Melason, prin.

Lexington, AC 617, PC 8, Middlesex
Lexington SD
  1557 MASSACHUSETTS AVE 02173 — 5-11111 / 861-2550
  Jeffrey Young, supt.
HS, 251 WALTHAM ST 02173 — 4-00011 / 861-2340
  David Wilson, prin.
Clarke JHS, 17 STEDMAN RD 02173 — 3-00100 / 861-2450
  Pamela Houlares, prin.
Diamond JHS, 99 HANCOCK ST 02173 — 2-00100 / 861-2460
  Joanne Hennessy, prin.
Minute Man Vocational Technical SD
  758 MARRETT RD 02173 — 3-00011 / 861-6500
  Ronald Fitzgerald, supt.
Minute Man Vocational Technical HS
  758 MARRETT RD 02173 — 3-00011 / 861-6500
  William Callahan, prin.

Lexington Christian Academy
  48 BARTLETT AVE 02173 — 2-00111 / 862-7850
  J. Koops, prin.
Wentworth Technical School
  191 SPRING ST 02173 — 4-CS / 674-1000

Lincoln, AC 617, PC 5, Middlesex
Lincoln SD, BALLFIELD ROAD 01773 — 4-11100 / 259-9400
  Rebecca Vanderbogert, supt.
Brooks MS, BALLFIELD RD 01773 — 2-01100 / 259-9409
  Brenda Brathwaite, prin.
Other Schools – See Bedford

Littleton, AC 508, PC 5, Middlesex
Littleton SD, SHATTUK ST 01460 — 4-11111 / 486-8951
  Vincent Franco, supt.
JSHS, RUSSELL ST 01460 — 2-00111 / 486-8938
  John Walker, prin.

Longmeadow, AC 413, PC 7, Hampden
Longmeadow SD
  811 LONGMEADOW ST 01106 — 5-11111 / 567-3351
  Thomas McGarry, supt.
HS, 95 GRASSY GUTTER RD 01106 — 3-00011 / 567-3331
  Donald Murphy, prin.

Glenbrook MS
  110 CAMBRIDGE CIR 01106 — 2-01100 / 567-1241
  James Lutat, prin.
Williams MS, 410 WILLIAMS ST 01106 — 2-01100 / 567-3391
  Mary Sedran, prin.

Bay Path College
  588 LONGMEADOW ST 01106 — 3-CC / 567-0621

Lowell, AC 508, PC 9, Middlesex
Lowell SD, 89 APPLETON ST 01852 — 7-11111 / 937-7647
  George Psapatsaris, supt.
HS, 50 FRENCH ST 01852 — 4-00011 / 937-8900
  William Samaras, prin.
Butler JHS, 1140 GORHAM ST 01852 — 3-01100 / 937-8973
  Harry Kouloheras, prin.
Daley JHS, 150 FLEMING ST 01851 — 3-01100 / 937-8981
  Joseph Hogan, prin.
Robinson MS, 110 JUNE ST 01850 — 3-01100 / 937-8974
  Donald Gagnon, prin.
Sullivan MS, 150 DRAPER ST 01852 — 3-01100 / 937-8993
  Lorraine Burgoyne, prin.
Wang MS, 365 W MEADOW RD 01854 — 3-01100 / 937-7683
  Leonard Flynn, prin.

Lowell Catholic HS
  530 STEVENS ST 01851 — 2-00011 / 452-1794
  Edward Quinn, prin.
Middlesex Community College
  33 KEARNEY SQ 01852 — 5-CC / 656-3211
St. Louis JHS, 74 BOISVERT ST 01850 — 1-00100 / 452-2332
  Sr. Irene Martineau, prin.
University of Massachusetts Lowell
  1 UNIVERSITY AVE 01854 — 7-UC / 452-5000

Ludlow, AC 413, PC 7, Hampden
Ludlow SD, 63 CHESTNUT ST 01056 — 5-11111 / 583-8372
  William Campton, supt.
HS, 500 CHAPIN ST 01056 — 3-00011 / 589-9001
  James Cavallo, prin.
Baird MS, 109 SPORTSMANS RD 01056 — 3-00100 / 589-5685
  Robert Smith, prin.

Lunenburg, AC 508, PC 4, Worcester
Lunenburg SD
  1033 MASSACHUSETTS AVE 01462 — 4-11111 / 582-4100
  Richard Carlson, supt.
HS, 1079 MASSACHUSETTS AVE 01462 — 2-00011 / 582-4115
  Frank Sambuceti, prin.
Turkey Hill MS
  129 NORTHFIELD RD 01462 — 3-01100 / 582-4110
  Mary Cringan, prin.

Twin City Christian S
  194 ELECTRIC AVE 01462 — 2-11111 / 582-4901
  Wayne Chevalier, prin.

Lynn, AC 617, PC 8, Essex
Lynn SD, 42 FRANKLIN ST 01902 — 7-11111 / 593-1680
  James Leonard, supt.
Classical HS, 33 N COMMON ST 01902 — 3-00011 / 593-3617
  Peter Arselanian, prin.
Lynn English HS
  50 GOODRIDGE ST 01902 — 4-00011 / 595-1620
  Joseph Patuleia, prin.
Lynn Vocational Technical Institute
  80 NEPTUNE BLVD 01902 — 3-00011 / 598-6020
  Albert Malagrifa, prin.
Breed JHS
  90 OCALLAGHAN WAY 01905 — 3-00100 / 581-0417
  Nicholas Kostan, prin.
Eastern JHS, 19 PORTER ST 01902 — 3-00100 / 592-3444
  Andrew Fila, prin.
Pickering JHS, 70 CONOMO AVE 01904 — 2-00100 / 593-2669
  William McGuinness, prin.

St. Mary HS, 35 TREMONT ST 01902 — 2-00111 / 595-7885
  Barbara Donovan, prin.

Lynnfield, AC 617, PC 7, Essex
Lynnfield SD, 505 MAIN ST 01940 — 4-11111 / 334-5800
  John Flores, supt.
HS, 275 ESSEX ST 01940 — 2-00011 / 334-5820
  Kristine Burke, prin.
MS, 505 MAIN ST 01940 — 3-01100 / 334-5810
  Kevin Plodzik, prin.

Malden, AC 617, PC 8, Middlesex
Malden SD, 77 SALEM ST 02148 — 6-11111 / 397-7204
  George Holland, supt.
HS, 77 SALEM ST 02148 — 4-00011 / 397-7223
  John Wright, prin.
MS, 401 PLEASANT ST 02148 — 3-00100 / 397-7218
  Camille Brandano, prin.

Malden Catholic HS
  99 CRYSTAL ST 02148 — 3-00011 / 322-3098
  Br. Puccio, prin.

Manchester, AC 508, PC 6, Essex
Manchester SD, LINCOLN ST 01944 — 3-11111 / 526-4919
  Paul Lengieza, supt.
JSHS, LINCOLN ST 01944 — 2-00111 / 526-4412
  William Foye, prin.

Mansfield, AC 508, PC 6, Bristol
Mansfield SD, PO BOX 428 02048 — 5-11111 / 261-7505
  Donald Nicoletti, supt.
HS, 250 EAST ST 02048 — 3-00011 / 339-7540
  Edward Rosa, prin.
Quarters MS, EAST ST 02048 — 3-00100 / 339-7530
  James Hunt, prin.

Marblehead, AC 617, PC 7, Essex
Marblehead SD, 2 HUMPHREY ST 01945 — 4-11111 / 631-0900
  James Kent, supt.
HS, DUNCANSLEIGH SQUARE 01945 — 3-00011 / 631-0900
  Henry Lucas, prin.
MS, 85 VILLAGE ST 01945 — 3-01100 / 631-0900
  D. Schauben-Fuerst, prin.

Marion, AC 508, PC 4, Plymouth

Tabor Academy, 226 FRONT ST 02738 — 2-00011 / 748-2000
  Jay Stroud, prin.

Marlborough, AC 508, PC 8, Middlesex
Assabet Valley SD
  109 FITCHBURG ST 01752 — 3-00011 / 485-9430
  David Tobin, supt.
Assabet Valley Vocational HS
  109 FITCHBURG ST 01752 — 3-00011 / 485-9430
  David Tobin, prin.

Marlborough SD, 255 MAIN ST 01752 — 5-11111 / 460-3509
  David Tobin, supt.
HS, 431 BOLTON ST 01752 — 3-00011 / 460-3513
  Leonard Morley, prin.
MS, 25 UNION ST 01752 — 3-00100 / 460-3502
  William Downey, prin.

Marshfield, AC 617, PC 5, Plymouth
Marshfield SD, 76 S RIVER ST 02050 — 5-11111 / 834-5010
  William Hurley, supt.
JSHS, 89 FOREST ST 02050 — 4-00111 / 834-5055
  Peter Deffos, prin.

Mattapan, AC 617, PC see Boston
Boston SD
  Supt. — See Boston
Lewenberg MS, 20 OUTLOOK RD 02126 — 3-00100 / 298-9360
  Thomas O'Neill, prin.

Mattapoisett, AC 508, PC 5, Plymouth
Old Rochester SD
  135 MARION RD 02739 — 3-00011 / 758-2772
  Joan Walsh, supt.
Old Rochester Regional HS
  135 MARION RD 02739 — 3-00011 / 758-3745
  James Egan, prin.
Old Rochester Regional JHS
  135 MARION RD 02739 — 2-00100 / 758-4928
  Robert Gardner, prin.

Maynard, AC 508, PC 7, Middlesex
Maynard SD, 1 TIGER DR 01754 — 4-11111 / 897-2222
  Donald Kennedy, supt.
HS, 197 GREAT RD 01754 — 2-00011 / 897-8891
  Donald Cranson, prin.
Fowler JHS, 67 SUMMER ST 01754 — 2-01100 / 897-6700
  Robert Brooks, prin.

Medfield, AC 508, PC 6, Norfolk
Medfield SD, 7 DALE ST 02052 — 4-11111 / 359-2302
  Thomas Reis, supt.
HS, 24 POUND ST 02052 — 2-00011 / 359-4367
  Robert Maguire, prin.
Blake MS, 88 SOUTH ST 02052 — 2-00100 / 359-2396
  Robert White, prin.

Medford, AC 617, PC 8, Middlesex
Medford SD, 489 WINTHROP ST 02155 — 6-11111 / 396-5800
  Philip Devaux, supt.
HS, 489 WINTHROP ST 02155 — 4-00011 / 396-5800
  Salvatore Todaro, prin.
Medford Vo-Tech HS
  489 WINTHROP ST 02155 — Vo Tech / 396-5800
  Lawrence Volpe, prin.
Roberts JHS, 35 COURT ST 02155 — 2-00100 / 396-5800
  M. Hickey, prin.

Lawrence Memorial Hospital
  170 GOVERNORS AVE 02155 — HSP / 396-9250
Tufts University
  520 BOSTON AVE 02155 — 6-UC / 628-5000

Medway, AC 508, PC 5, Norfolk
Medway SD, 45 HOLLISTON ST 02053 — 4-11111 / 533-3222
  Arthur Bettencourt, supt.
HS, 45 HOLLISTON ST 02053 — 2-00111 / 533-3227
  David Driscoll, prin.
MS, 45 HOLLISTON ST 02053 — 3-00100 / 533-3230
  William Lynch, prin.

Melrose, AC 617, PC 8, Middlesex
Melrose SD, 235 W FOSTER ST 02176 — 5-11111 / 662-2000
  Richard Incerto, supt.
HS, 360 LYNN FELLS PKY 02176 — 4-00011 / 662-2000
  Claude Croston, prin.
MS, 350 LYNN FELLS PKY 02176 — 3-00100 / 662-2000
  Anthony Larosa, prin.

Mendon, AC 508, PC 3, Worcester
Mendon-Upton SD
  Supt. — See Upton
Nipmuc Regional HS
  PO BOX 6 01756 — 2-00011 / 473-0994
  Irene Sherry, prin.
Miscoe Hill MS, PO BOX 7 01756 — 2-01100 / 478-2241
  Irene Sherry, prin.

Methuen, AC 508, PC 8, Essex
Methuen SD, 160 MERRIMACK ST 01844 — 6-11111 / 681-1317
  Charles Littlefield, supt.
HS, 1 RANGER RD 01844 — 4-00011 / 681-1360
  Arthur Nicholson, prin.

Timony Memorial MS
  45 PLEASANT VIEW ST 01844   3-01100
  Ruth Hasset, prin.   681-1340
Tenney MS, 75 PLEASANT ST 01844   3-01100
  James Smith, prin.   681-1352

Computer Learning Center   2-CS
  436 BROADWAY 01844   794-0233
Presentation of Mary Academy   2-00011
  209 LAWRENCE ST 01844   682-9391
  Sr. Rose Marie, prin.

Middleboro, AC 508, PC 6, Plymouth
Middleboro SD   5-11111
  1 NICKERSON AVE 02346   946-2000
  Michael Ippolito, supt.
HS, 71 E GROVE ST 02346   3-00011
  William Wassel, prin.   946-2010
Memorial JHS, 219 N MAIN ST 02346   3-00100
  Alan Lindsay, prin.   946-2020

Middleton, AC 508, PC 5, Essex
North Shore Regional Vocational SD   2-00011
  30 LOG BRIDGE RD 01949   762-0001
  Patricia Carlson, supt.
North Shore Regional Vocational HS   2-00011
  30 LOG BRIDGE RD 01949   927-6178
  John Roper, prin.

Milford, AC 508, PC 8, Worcester
Milford SD, 31 W FOUNTAIN ST 01757   5-11111
  Thomas Cullen, supt.   478-1100
HS, 31 W FOUNTAIN ST 01757   4-00011
  Robert Pagnini, prin.   478-1110
Milford MS-East, MAIN ST 01757   2-00100
  Thomas Davoren, prin.   478-1170

Millbury, AC 508, PC 5, Worcester
Millbury SD, 12 MARTIN ST 01527   4-11111
  Richard Palermo, supt.   865-9501
Millbury Memorial JSHS   3-00111
  12 MARTIN ST 01527   865-5841
  Dan Carmody, prin.

Millis, AC 508, PC 5, Norfolk
Millis SD, 247 PLAIN ST 02054   4-11111
  Daniel Kehoe, supt.   376-7000
HS, 247 PLAIN ST 02054   2-00011
  Paul Brunelle, prin.   376-7010
MS, 247 PLAIN ST 02054   2-00100
  William McIvor, prin.   376-7014

Milton, AC 617, PC 8, Norfolk
Milton SD, 391 BROOK RD 02186   5-11111
  Mary O'Neill, supt.   696-4809
HS, BROOK ROAD AT CENTRAL 02186   3-00011
  Allen Adams, prin.   696-4470
Pierce MS, 25 GILE RD 02186   3-00100
  Robert Tippo, prin.   696-4568

Aquinas College   2-CC
  303 ADAMS ST 02186   696-3100
Curry College   3-UC
  1071 BLUE HILL AVE 02186   333-0500
Fontbonne Academy   2-00011
  930 BROOK RD 02186   696-3241
  Sr. Marilyn McGoldrick, prin.
Milton Academy, 170 CENTRE ST 02186   3-11111
  Edwin Fredie, prin.   698-7800

Monson, AC 413, PC 4, Hampden
Monson SD, PO BOX 159 01057   4-11111
  V. Carbone, supt.   267-4150
JSHS, 25 THOMPSON ST 01057   2-00111
  Michael Kane, prin.   267-4155

Montague, AC 413, PC 3, Franklin
Gill-Montague SD
  Supt. — See Turners Falls
Turners Falls HS   2-00011
  TURNPIKE ROAD 01351   863-9341
  James Cokkinias, prin.
Great Falls MS, TURNPIKE ROAD 01351   2-00100
  Roma Hansis, prin.   863-9011

Nantucket, AC 508, PC 5, Nantucket
Nantucket SD, 10 SURFSIDE RD 02554   3-11111
  Alan Myers, supt.   228-7285
HS, 10 SURFSIDE RD 02554   2-00011
  Pamela Culver, prin.   228-7280
Peirce MS, 10 SURFSIDE RD 02554   2-00100
  Pamela Culver, prin.   228-7280

Natick, AC 508, PC 8, Middlesex
Natick SD, 13 E CENTRAL ST 01760   5-11111
  Joseph Keefe, supt.   651-7104
HS, 15 WEST ST 01760   3-00011
  Donald Bevelander, prin.   651-7135
Kennedy MS, 165 MILL ST 01760   3-01100
  William Donovan, prin.   651-7189
Wilson MS, 24 RUTLEDGE RD 01760   3-01100
  Harriet Safran, prin.   651-7204

Walnut Hill S, 12 HIGHLAND ST 01760   2-00011
  Stephanie Perrin, prin.   653-4312

Needham, AC 617, PC 8, Norfolk
Needham SD   5-11111
  1330 HIGHLAND AVE 02192   455-0435
  Fred Tirrell, supt.
Pollard MS, 1155 CENTRAL AVE 02192   3-00100
  Jacquelin Apsler, prin.   455-0482
Other Schools – See Needham Heights

St. Sebastians Country Day S   2-00111
  1191 GREENDALE AVE 02192   449-5200
  William Burke, prin.

Needham Heights, AC 617, PC see Needham
Needham SD
  Supt. — See Needham
Needham HS, 609 WEBSTER ST 02194   3-00011
  Paul Madden, prin.   455-0802

New Bedford, AC 508, PC 8, Bristol
Greater New Bedford SD   4-00011
  1121 ASHLEY BLVD 02745   998-3321
  Jeffrey Riley, supt.
Greater New Bedford Vocational HS   4-00011
  1121 ASHLEY BLVD 02745   998-3321
  M. Shea, prin.

New Bedford SD, 455 COUNTY ST 02740   7-11111
  C. Nanopoulos, supt.   997-4511
HS, 230 HATHAWAY BLVD 02740   5-00011
  Michael Longo, prin.   997-4511
Keith JHS, 70 HATHAWAY BLVD 02740   3-00100
  Steve Derossi, prin.   997-4511
Normandin JHS   3-00100
  240 TARKILN HILL RD 02745   997-4511
  John Viveiros, prin.
Roosevelt JHS, 120 DENNIS ST 02744   3-00100
  Leonard Rivet, prin.   997-4511

Kinyon-Campbell Business School   2-CS
  59 LINDEN ST 02740   992-5448

Newburyport, AC 508, PC 7, Essex
Newburyport SD, 70 LOW ST 01950   4-11111
  G. Dulac, supt.   465-4457
HS, 241 HIGH ST 01950   3-00011
  Mary Larnard, prin.   465-4440
Nock MS, 70 LOW ST 01950   3-01100
  Eugene Case, prin.   465-4447

Newton, AC 617, PC 8, Middlesex

Aquinas College   2-CC
  15 WALNUT PARK 02158   969-4400
Boston College Law School   3-UC
  885 CENTRE ST 02159
Lasell College   3-CC
  1844 COMMONWEALTH AVE 02166   243-2000
Mt. Alvernia Academy   2-00011
  790 CENTRE ST 02158   969-2260
  Sr. Suzanne Fondine, prin.
Newton Country Day S   2-01111
  785 CENTRE ST 02158   244-4246
  Sr. Barbara Rogers, prin.
Swedenborg School of Religion   2-UC
  48 SARGENT ST 02158   244-0504
Trinity Catholic HS   2-00011
  575 WASHINGTON ST 02158   244-1841
  Sr. Mary Gill, prin.

Newton Center, AC 617, PC see Newton
Newton SD
  Supt. — See Newtonville
Newton South HS   4-00011
  140 BRANDEIS RD 02159   552-7547
  Ernest Van Seasholes, prin.
Brown JHS   3-00100
  125 MEADOWBROOK RD 02159   552-7409
  Judith Neville, prin.

Andover Newton Theological School   2-UC
  210 HERRICK RD 02159   964-1100
Mt. Ida College   4-UC
  777 DEDHAM ST 02159   969-7000

Newton Lower Falls, AC 617, PC see Newton

Newton-Wellesley Hospital   HSP
  2014 WASHINGTON ST 02162   243-6255

Newtonville, AC 617, PC see Newton
Newton SD, 100 WALNUT ST 02160   7-11111
  Irwin Blumer, supt.   552-7591
Newton North HS   4-00011
  360 LOWELL AVE 02160   552-7422
  V. Marini, prin.
Day JHS, 21 MINOT PL 02160   3-00100
  Edward Fraktman, prin.   552-7379
Other Schools – See Newton Center

Norfolk, AC 508, PC 3, Norfolk
King Philip SD
  Supt. — See Wrentham
King Philip Regional MS North   3-00100
  18 KING ST 02056 – Ron Marino, prin.   384-8944

North Adams, AC 413, PC 7, Berkshire
North Adams SD, 191 E MAIN ST 01247   4-11111
  Robert Maroni, supt.   662-3225
Drury HS, S CHURCH ST 01247   3-00011
  Roger Cirone, prin.   662-3240
Conte MS, CHURCH ST 01247   3-00100
  Edward Lamarre, prin.   662-3200
Northern Berkshire Vocational SD   2-00011
  10 HODGES CROSS RD 01247   663-5383
  Howard Brookner, prin.
McCann Vocational Technical HS   2-00011
  10 HODGES CROSS RD 01247   663-6160
  Francis Millard, prin.

North Adams State College   4-UC
  375 CHURCH ST 01247   664-4511

Northampton, AC 413, PC 8, Hampshire
Northampton-Smith SD   2-00011
  80 LOCUST ST 01060   586-6970
  Steven Johnson, supt.
Smith Vocational & Agricultural HS   2-00011
  80 LOCUST ST 01060   586-6970
  Steven Johnson, prin.

Northampton SD, 212 MAIN ST 01060   5-11111
  Bruce Willard, supt.   586-6970
HS, 380 ELM ST 01060   3-00011
  Gordon Noseworthy, prin.   586-6970
Other Schools – See Florence

Smith College 01063   5-UC
       585-2500

North Andover, AC 508, PC 7, Essex
North Andover SD   5-11111
  675 CHICKERING RD 01845   794-1503
  George Blaisdell, supt.
HS, 675 CHICKERING RD 01845   3-00011
  J. Goggin, prin.   794-1711
MS, 495 MAIN ST 01845   3-00100
  Richard Neal, prin.   794-1870

Brooks S, 1160 GREAT POND RD 01845   2-00011
  Lawrence Becker, prin.   686-6101
Fellowship Bible S   2-11111
  525 TURNPIKE ST 01845   686-9373
  Rocco Digloria, prin.
Merrimack College   5-UC
  315 TURNPIKE ST 01845   683-7111

North Attleboro, AC 508, PC 8, Bristol
North Attleboro SD   5-11111
  570 LANDRY AVE 02760   643-2100
  Joseph McKeigue, supt.
HS, LANDRY AVE 02760   3-00011
  Wilson Whitty, prin.   643-2115
JHS, 45 S WASHINGTON ST 02760   3-00100
  Robert Stromberg, prin.   643-2130

Northborough, AC 508, PC 6, Worcester
Northborough-Southborough SD   3-00011
  75 BARTLETT ST 01532   351-7000
  Dennis Disalvo, supt.
Algonquin Regional HS   3-00011
  79 BARTLETT ST 01532   351-7010
  Carroll Paine, prin.

Northborough SD   4-11100
  75 BARTLETT ST 01532   351-7000
  Dennis Disalvo, supt.
MS, 145 LINCOLN ST 01532   3-01100
  Nadine Henderson, prin.   351-7020

Southborough SD   3-11100
  75 BARTLETT ST 01532   351-7000
  Dennis Disalvo, supt.
Other Schools – See Southborough

North Brookfield, AC 508, PC 5, Worcester
North Brookfield SD   3-11111
  10 NEW SCHOOL DR 01535   867-9821
  William Leach, supt.
JSHS, 10 NEW SCHOOL DR 01535   2-00111
  John Pipczynski, prin.   867-7131

North Chelmsford, AC 508, PC see Chelmsford
Chelmsford SD   6-11111
  75 GRANITEVILLE RD 01863   251-4981
  Richard Moser, supt.
Chelmsford SD   4-00011
  200 RICHARDSON RD 01863   251-8792
  Herbert Levine, prin.
Other Schools – See Chelmsford

North Dartmouth, AC 508, PC 6, Bristol
Dartmouth SD
  Supt. — See South Dartmouth
Dartmouth HS, 366 SLOCUM RD 02747   4-00011
  Donald King, prin.   997-9332
Dartmouth MS   3-00100
  529 HAWTHORN ST 02747   997-3178
  Douglas Pfeninger, prin.

Bishop Stang HS, 500 SLOCUM RD 02747   3-00011
  Theresa Dougall, prin.   996-5602
University of Massachusetts Dartmouth   6-UC
  285 OLD WESTPORT RD 02747   999-8000

North Dighton, AC 508, PC 4, Bristol
Dighton-Rehoboth SD   5-11111
  2700 REGIONAL RD 02764   252-5000
  Richard Kisiel, supt.
Dighton-Rehoboth Regional HS   3-00011
  2700 REGIONAL RD 02764   252-5025
  Marshall Sawyer, prin.
Other Schools – See Dighton, Rehoboth

North Eastham, AC 508, PC 4, Barnstable
Nauset SD
  Supt. — See Orleans
Nauset Regional HS, CABLE RD 02651   3-00011
  Thomas Ballerino, prin.   255-1505

North Easton, AC 508, PC 5, Bristol
Easton SD, PO BOX 359 02356   5-11111
  William Simmons, supt.   230-3202
Ames SHS, 100 LOTHROP ST 02356   3-00001
  Duncan Oliver, prin.   230-3210

Easton JHS, 98 COLUMBUS AVE 02356 3-00110
Aubrey Conrad, prin. 230-3210

Stonehill College 4-UC
320 WASHINGTON ST 02357 230-1373

Northfield, AC 413, PC 4, Franklin
Pioneer Valley SD, ROUTE 10 01360 4-11111
Kevin Courtney, supt. 498-2911
Pioneer Valley Regional JSHS 2-00111
ROUTE 10 01360 498-2931
Everett Masters, prin.

Northfield Mt. Hermon S 4-00011
206 MAIN ST 01360 498-5311
Jacqueline Smethurst, prin.

North Reading, AC 508, PC 7, Middlesex
North Reading SD 4-11111
19 SHERMAN RD 01864 664-7810
Francis O'Donoghue, supt.
HS, 191 PARK ST 01864 2-00011
William Butler, prin. 664-7800
JHS, SHERMAN RD 01864 2-00100
V. Gail Votano, prin. 664-7806

Norton, AC 508, PC 4, Bristol
Norton SD, 64 W MAIN ST 02766 4-11111
Maurice Splaine, supt. 285-0100
HS, 66 W MAIN ST 02766 3-00011
Daniel Wheeler, prin. 285-0160
MS, 64 W MAIN ST 02766 3-00100
Stanley Koss, prin. 285-0140

New Testament S 2-11111
1 NEW TAUNTON AVE 02766 285-9771
Carroll Conley, prin.
Wheaton College 4-UC
26 E MAIN ST 02766 285-7722

Norwell, AC 617, PC 4, Plymouth
Norwell SD, 322 MAIN ST 02061 4-11111
Robert Bunnell, supt. 659-8800
HS, 18 SOUTH ST 02061 2-00011
Anthony Bahros, prin. 659-8810
JHS, 334 MAIN ST 02061 2-00100
Henry Goldman, prin. 659-8814

Norwood, AC 617, PC 8, Norfolk
Norwood SD 5-11111
100 WESTOVER PKY 02062 762-6804
Ralph Toran, supt.
HS, 249 NICHOLS ST 02062 3-00011
George Usezich, prin. 769-2333
JHS South, ENDEAN PARK 02062 3-00100
Patrick Cammarata, prin. 762-7880

Ultrasound Diagnostic School 2-CS
57 PROVIDENCE HWY 02062 551-0404

Oak Bluffs, AC 508, PC 4, Dukes
Martha's Vineyard SD
Supt. — See Vineyard Haven
Martha's Vineyard Regional HS 2-00011
PO BOX 1385 02557 693-1033
Gregory Scotten, prin.

Orange, AC 508, PC 5, Franklin
Ralph C. Mahar SD, S MAIN ST 01364 3-00111
Eileen Perkins, supt. 544-2920
Mahar Regional JSHS, S MAIN ST 01364 3-00111
Francis Zak, prin. 544-2542

Orleans, AC 508, PC 4, Barnstable
Nauset SD 4-00111
78 ELDRIDGE PARK WAY 02653 255-8800
Michael Gradone, supt.
Nauset Regional MS 3-00100
64 ROUTE 28 02653 255-0016
Barbara Cooper, prin.
Other Schools — See North Eastham

Osterville, AC 508, PC 5, Barnstable

Cape Cod Academy 2-11111
PO BOX 469 02655 428-5400
Thomas Evans, prin.

Otter River, AC 508, PC 3, Worcester
Narragansett SD, 133 S MAIN ST 01436 4-11111
William Turner, supt. 939-5661
Other Schools — See Baldwinville

Oxford, AC 508, PC 6, Worcester
Oxford SD, 5 SIGOURNEY ST 01540 4-11111
Francis Driscoll, supt. 987-6050
JSHS, 351 MAIN ST 01540 3-00111
Roger Bacon, prin. 987-6081

Palmer, AC 413, PC 5, Hampden
Palmer SD, 24 CONVERSE ST 01069 4-11111
Warren Pelton, supt. 283-2650
JSHS, 105 MAIN ST 01069 3-00111
Alphonse Murray, prin. 283-6511

Pathfinder Vocational-Technical SD 3-00011
419 ROUTE 181 01069 283-9701
Gerald Paist, supt.
Pathfinder Vocational Technical HS 3-00011
419 ROUTE 181 01069 283-9701
Gerald Paist, prin.

Paxton, AC 508, PC 4, Worcester

Anna Maria College 4-UC
2 SUNSET LN 01612 757-4586

Peabody, AC 508, PC 8, Essex
Peabody SD, 70 ENDICOTT ST 01960 6-11111
James Buckley, supt. 531-1600
Veterans Memorial HS 4-00011
485 LOWELL ST 01960 531-1600
Joan Carr, prin.
Peabody Vo HS, ALLENS LANE 01960 Vo Tech
Peter Mooney, prin. 531-1600
Higgins MS, 71 KING ST 01960 4-00100
John Murtagh, prin. 531-1600

Bishop Fenwick HS 3-00011
99 MARGIN ST 01960 531-8200
Ralph Leduc, prin.

Pembroke, AC 617, PC 4, Plymouth
Silver Lake SD
Supt. — See Kingston
Silver Lake Regional JHS 4-00110
559 SCHOOL ST 02359 293-9511
William Pepper, prin.

Pittsfield, AC 413, PC 8, Berkshire
Pittsfield SD, 269 1ST ST 01201 6-11111
John Krieger, supt. 499-9512
HS, 300 EAST ST 01201 3-00011
Mark Mathews, prin. 499-9537
Taconic HS, 170 VALENTINE RD 01201 3-00011
Douglas McNally, prin. 448-9600
Pittsfield Vo HS Vo Tech
VALENTINE ROAD 01201 448-9601
Raymond Cooke, prin.
Herberg MS, 501 POMEROY AVE 01201 3-00100
Linda Porter, prin. 448-9640
Reid MS, 950 NORTH ST 01201 3-00100
Colleen Rossi, prin. 448-9620

Berkshire Community College 4-CC
1350 WEST ST 01201 499-4660
Berkshire Medical Center HSP
725 NORTH ST 01201 447-5264
Mildred Elley Business School 2-CS
400 COLUMBUS AVE 01201 499-8618
Miss Hall's S, PO BOX 1166 01202 2-00011
Trudy Hall, prin. 443-6401
Notre Dame MS, 41 MELVILLE ST 01201 2-00100
James Rivers, prin. 442-6040
St. Joseph Central HS 2-00011
22 MAPLEWOOD AVE 01201 447-9121
Rev. John Bonzagni, prin.

Plymouth, AC 508, PC 6, Plymouth
Plymouth-Carver SD, LINCOLN ST 02360 5-00111
Bernard Sidman, supt. 830-4300
Plymouth-North HS, 37 OBERY ST 02360 3-00011
Bruce Marshman, prin. 830-4400
Plymouth South HS 3-00011
490 LONG POND RD 02360 224-7512
Robert O'Day, prin.
Plymouth South Tech HS Vo Tech
490 LONG POND RD 02360 224-7512
Robert O'Day, prin.
Plymouth-Carver IS 4-00100
125 LONG POND RD 02360 830-4450
Lyman Goding, prin.
Other Schools — See Carver

Prides Crossing, AC 508, PC see Beverly

Landmark School, 412 HALE ST 01965 2-01111
Robert Broudo, prin. 927-4440

Provincetown, AC 508, PC 5, Barnstable
Provincetown SD, PRINCE ST 02657 2-11111
Vincent Yuskiewicz, supt. 487-0560
JSHS, 12 WINSLOW ST 02657 2-00111
Susan Fleming, prin. 487-1177

Quincy, AC 617, PC 8, Norfolk
Quincy SD, 70 CODDINGTON ST 02169 6-11111
Eugene Creedon, supt. 984-8700
North Quincy HS 4-00011
316 HANCOCK ST 02171 984-8744
Peter J. Chrisom, prin.
HS, 52 CODDINGTON ST 02169 4-00011
Lloyd Hill, prin. 984-8751
Atlantic MS, 86 HOLLIS AVE 02171 2-00100
Laura Bogan, prin. 984-8727
Broad Meadows MS 2-00100
50 CALVIN RD 02169 984-8723
Gerald Butler, prin.
Central MS, 1012 HANCOCK ST 02169 3-00100
Louis Dimartinis, prin. 984-8725
Sterling MS, 444 GRANITE ST 02169 2-00100
Richard Hutchison, prin. 984-8729

Eastern Nazarene College 3-UC
23 E ELM AVE 02170 773-6350
Quincy Junior College 4-CC
34 CODDINGTON ST 02169 786-8777
Woodward S, 1102 HANCOCK ST 02169 2-00111
Robert Johnson, prin. 773-5610

Randolph, AC 617, PC 8, Norfolk
Randolph SD, 40 HIGHLAND AVE 02368 5-11111
Gerard Linehan, supt. 961-6206
JSHS, 70 MEMORIAL PKY 02368 4-00111
Ellen Keane, prin. 961-6220

Raynham, AC 508, PC 4, Bristol
Raynham SD, 687 PLEASANT ST 02767 4-11100
Joseph Gilbert, supt. 824-2730
Laliberte JHS, PLEASANT ST 02767 2-00100
Alan Jaffe, prin. 824-2720

Reading, AC 617, PC 7, Middlesex
Reading SD, 82 OAKLAND RD 01867 5-11111
Robert Munnelly, supt. 944-5800
Reading Memorial HS 4-00011
62 OAKLAND RD 01867 944-8200
Rena Mirkin, prin.
Coolidge MS 2-00100
89 BIRCH MEADOW DR 01867 944-9236
Albert Lahood, prin.
Parker MS, 45 TEMPLE ST 01867 2-00100
John Delaney, prin. 944-1236

Austin Prep S, 101 WILLOW ST 01867 3-00111
Paul Moran, prin. 944-4900

Rehoboth, AC 508, PC 2, Bristol
Dighton-Rehoboth SD
Supt. — See North Dighton
Beckwith MS, 330 WINTHROP ST 02769 3-01100
Anthony Ferreira, prin. 252-5080

Revere, AC 617, PC 8, Suffolk
Revere SD, 101 SCHOOL ST 02151 5-11111
Rocco Malfitano, supt. 286-8226
HS, 101 SCHOOL ST 02151 3-00011
William McAlduff, prin. 286-8222

Rochester, AC 508, PC 3, Plymouth
Old Colony Vocational Technical SD 2-00011
476 NORTH AVE 02770 763-8011
David Ferreira, supt.
Old Colony Regional Vo-Tech HS 2-00011
476 NORTH AVE 02770 763-8011
David Ferreira, prin.

Rockland, AC 617, PC 7, Plymouth
Rockland SD, 34 GODDARD AVE 02370 5-11111
Ronald Gerhart, supt. 878-3893
JSHS, 34 GODDARD AVE 02370 3-00111
A. MacKinlay, prin. 871-0541

Rockport, AC 508, PC 6, Essex
Rockport SD, 16 JERDENS LN 01966 3-11111
Charles Martin, supt. 546-1200
JSHS, 12 JERDENS LN 01966 2-00111
Dan Fleming, prin. 546-1234

Roslindale, AC 617, PC see Boston
Boston SD
Supt. — See Boston
Irving MS, 114 CUMMINS HWY 02131 3-00100
R Maloney, prin. 323-2633

St. Clare HS, 190 CUMMINS HWY 02131 2-00011
Sr. Karen Hokanson, prin. 323-0966

Roxbury, AC 617, PC see Boston
Boston SD
Supt. — See Boston
Dearborn MS, 35 GREENVILLE ST 02119 2-00100
John Shields, prin. 427-2524
Lewis MS, 131 WALNUT AVE 02119 2-00100
Brenda Jones, prin. 427-4546
Timilty MS, 205 ROXBURY ST 02119 3-00100
Roger Harris, prin. 445-3114
Wheatley MS 2-00100
20 KEARSARGE AVE 02119 427-3340
Michael Anderson, prin.

Roxbury Crossing, AC 617, PC see Boston
Boston SD
Supt. — See Boston
Madison Park HS 4-00011
55 NEW DUDLEY ST 02120 445-2440
James Watson, prin.

Roxbury Community College 4-CC
1234 COLUMBUS AVE 02120 541-5310

Rutland, AC 508, PC 4, Worcester

Devereux Center in Massachusetts HND
60 MILES RD 01543 886-4746

Salem, AC 508, PC 8, Essex
Salem SD, 29 HIGHLAND AVE 01970 5-11111
Ed Curtin, supt. 740-1212
HS, 77 WILSON ST 01970 4-00011
Karen Baker, prin. 740-1123
Salem MS East 2-00100
211 LAFAYETTE ST 01970 740-1293
Charles Chaurette, prin.
Salem MS West 3-00100
29 HIGHLAND AVE 01970 745-1191
Mary Manning, prin.

Salem State College 6-UC
352 LAFAYETTE ST 01970 741-6000

Sandwich, AC 508, PC 5, Barnstable
Sandwich SD, 16 DEWEY AVE 02563 5-11111
Peter Cannone, prin. 888-1054
Other Schools — See East Sandwich

Saugus, AC 617, PC 8, Essex
Saugus SD, 23 MAIN ST 01906 5-11111
William Doyle, supt. 231-5000
HS, PEARCE DR 01906 3-00011
Kenneth Fabrizio, prin. 231-5027

Belmonte Saugus MS, 29 DOW ST 01906   3-00100
John Serino, prin.   231-5052

Scituate, AC 617, PC 6, Plymouth
Scituate SD   5-11111
606 CHIEF JSTCE CUSHING HWY 02066
John P. Kulevich, supt.   545-8759
HS   3-00011
606 CHIEF JSTCE CUSHING HWY 02066
Prudence Goodale, prin.   545-8750
Gates IS, 327 FIRST PARISH RD 02066   3-00100
Joan Desalvo, prin.   545-8760

Seekonk, AC 508, PC 7, Bristol
Seekonk SD, 1 SCHOOL ST 02771   4-11111
George McLaughlin, supt.   336-7711
HS, 261 ARCADE AVE 02771   3-00011
Frederick Nelson, prin.   336-7272
IS, 660 NEWMAN AVE 02771   2-00100
Gerald Kaveny, prin.   761-7570

Sharon, AC 617, PC 7, Norfolk
Sharon SD, 1 SCHOOL ST 02067   5-11111
Thomas Lagrasta, supt.   784-5937
HS, 181 POND ST 02067   3-00011
John Blanchon, prin.   784-1554
MS, 75 MOUNTAIN ST 02067   3-00100
Richard Carter, prin.   784-6717

Sheffield, AC 413, PC 4, Berkshire
Southern Berkshire SD   4-11111
PO BOX 339 01257   229-8778
Thomas Consolati, supt.
Mt. Everett Regional JSHS   3-01111
PO BOX 219 01257   229-8734
J. Wayne Eline, prin.

Berkshire S   2-00011
245 N UNDERMOUNTAIN RD 01257   229-8511
Richard Unsworth, prin.

Shelburne Falls, AC 413, PC 4, Franklin
Mohawk Trail SD   3-00111
26 ASHFIELD RD 01370   625-9811
Albert Cormier, supt.
Mohawk Trail Regional JSHS   3-00111
HC 84 BOX 30 01370   625-9811
Philip Dzialo, prin.

Shrewsbury, AC 508, PC 7, Worcester
Shrewsbury SD, 100 MAPLE AVE 01545   5-11111
John P. Collins, supt.   845-5721
JSHS, 45 OAK ST 01545   4-00111
Ray Peterson, prin.   845-4641

St. Johns HS, 378 MAIN ST 01545   3-00011
Br. Comedy, prin.   842-8934

Somerset, AC 508, PC 7, Bristol
Somerset SD   5-11111
580 WHETSTONE HILL RD 02726   674-3508
Daniel Cabral, supt.
HS, 270 GRANDVIEW AVE 02726   3-00011
Donald Rebello, prin.   678-3981
JHS, 1141 BRAYTON AVE 02726   3-00100
Walter Palmer, prin.   674-4619

Somerville, AC 617, PC 8, Middlesex
Somerville SD, 93 SCHOOL ST 02143   6-11111
Al Argenziano, supt.   625-6600
HS, 81 HIGHLAND AVE 02143   4-00011
Anthony Fedele, prin.   625-6600

Computer Learning Center   3-CS
5 MIDDLESEX AVE 02145   776-3500
St. Clement HS, 579 BOSTON AVE 02144   2-00011
Sr. Julia Fitzpatrick, prin.   776-3228
Somerville Hospital   HSP
125 LOWELL ST 02143   666-4400

South Attleboro, AC 508, PC see Attleboro
Attleboro SD
Supt. — See Attleboro
Coelho MS, 75 BROWN ST 02703   3-01100
Charles Cokonis, prin.   761-7551

Southborough, AC 508, PC 4, Worcester
Southborough SD
Supt. — See Northborough
Woodward MS, CORDAVILLE RD 01772   2-00100
P. Trottier, prin.   485-2400

St. Marks S, 25 MARLBORO RD 01772   2-00011
Christopher Mabley, prin.   485-0050

South Boston, AC 617, PC see Boston
Boston SD
Supt. — See Boston
HS, 95 G ST 02127   4-00011
Lorraine Hamilton, prin.   268-2751
Gavin MS, 215 DORCHESTER ST 02127   3-00100
Joseph Lee, prin.   269-1723

Southbridge, AC 508, PC 7, Worcester
Southbridge SD, PO BOX 665 01550   5-11111
Jo Austin, supt.   764-3285
HS, 25 COLE AVE 01550   3-00011
Joseph Baily, prin.   764-5450
Wells JHS, 82 MARCY ST 01550   3-00100
Don Cesarini, prin.   764-3514

South Dartmouth, AC 508, PC 6, Bristol
Dartmouth SD, 8 BUSH ST 02748   5-11111
Arthur Middleton, supt.   997-3391
Other Schools – See North Dartmouth

South Deerfield, AC 413, PC 4, Franklin
Frontier SD, 219 CHRISTIAN LN 01373   3-00111
John Welch, supt.   665-1155
Frontier Regional JSHS   3-00111
311 N MAIN ST 01373   665-2118
William Decker, prin.

South Dennis, AC 508, PC 5, Barnstable
Dennis-Yarmouth SD
Supt. — See South Yarmouth
Wixon MS, ROUTE 134 02660   3-01100
Richard Colby, prin.   398-7695

South Easton, AC 508, PC 4, Bristol
Southeastern SD   4-00011
250 FOUNDRY ST 02375   238-4374
Paul O'Leary, supt.
Southeastern Regional Vo-Tech HS   4-00011
250 FOUNDRY ST 02375   238-4374
John Avery, prin.

Southeastern Technical Institute   2-CS
250 FOUNDRY ST 02375   238-4374

South Hadley, AC 413, PC 6, Hampshire
South Hadley SD, 116 MAIN ST 01075   4-11111
Cynthia Seidel, supt.   538-5057
JSHS, 153 NEWTON ST 01075   3-00111
Paul Raymond, prin.   538-5063

Mt. Holyoke College   4-UC
COLLEGE ST 01075   538-2023

South Hamilton, AC 508, PC 5, Essex
Hamilton-Wenham SD   4-11111
775 BAY RD 01982   468-5310
Patricia Alger, supt.
Hamilton-Wenham Regional HS   3-00011
775 BAY RD 01982 – John Elwell, prin.   468-5300
Other Schools – See Wenham

Gordon-Conwell Theological Seminary   3-UC
130 ESSEX ST 01982   468-7111
Pingree S, 537 HIGHLAND ST 01982   2-00011
John Chandler, prin.   468-4415

South Lancaster, AC 508, PC 4, Worcester

Atlantic Union College   3-UC
PO BOX 1000 01561   800-282-2030

Southwick, AC 413, PC 4, Hampden
Southwick-Tolland SD   4-11111
86 POWDER MILL RD 01077   569-5391
Gerald Fortier, supt.
HS, 93 FEEDING HILLS RD 01077   2-00011
Paul Meagher, prin.   569-6171
Powder Mill MS   3-01100
94 POWDER MILL RD 01077   569-5951
Robert Spear, prin.

South Yarmouth, AC 508, PC 7, Barnstable
Dennis-Yarmouth SD   5-11111
296 STATION AVE 02664   398-7605
Michael McCaffray, supt.
Dennis-Yarmouth Regional HS   4-00011
210 STATION AVE 02664   398-7630
Curtis Collins, prin.
Other Schools – See South Dennis, West Yarmouth

Spencer, AC 508, PC 6, Worcester
Spencer-East Brookfield SD   4-11111
302 MAIN ST 01562   885-8500
John Begley, supt.
Prouty HS, 302 MAIN ST 01562   3-00011
John Williams, prin.   885-8505
Prouty JHS, 195 MAIN ST 01562   2-00100
J. Staiti, prin.   885-8524
Other Schools – See East Brookfield

Springfield, AC 413, PC 9, Hampden
Springfield SD, 195 STATE ST 01103   7-11111
Peter Negroni, supt.   787-7087
HS of Commerce, 415 STATE ST 01105   4-00011
Willette Johnson, prin.   787-7220
Springfield Central HS   5-00011
1840 ROOSEVELT AVE 01109   787-7085
Celeste Budd-Jackson, prin.
Putnam Vocational Technical HS   4-00011
1300 STATE ST 01109   787-7424
Clifford Flint, prin.
MA Career Development Inst   Vo Tech
140 WILBRAHAM AVE 01109   781-5640
Anthony Mole, prin.
Chestnut Street MS   3-00100
495 CHESTNUT ST 01107   787-7285
Mario Cirillo, prin.
Duggan MS   3-00100
1015 WILBRAHAM RD 01109   787-7410
Thomas Keating, prin.
Forest Park MS, 46 OAKLAND ST 01108   3-00100
Carol Fazio, prin.   787-7420
Kennedy MS   3-00100
1385 BERKSHIRE AVE 01151   787-7510
Willard Wright, prin.
Kiley JHS, 180 COOLEY ST 01128   4-00100
Edward Brennan, prin.   787-7240

American International College   4-UC
1000 STATE ST 01109   737-7000
Bay State Medical Center   HSP
759 CHESTNUT ST 01199   784-4303

Cathedral HS, 260 SURREY RD 01118   4-00011
Sr. Denise Granger, prin.   782-5285
Life Laboratories   2-CS
299 CAREW ST 01104   747-0820
MacDuffie S, 3 AMES HILL DR 01105   2-00111
Michael Cornog, prin.   734-4971
Pioneer Valley Christian S   2-11111
965 PLUMTREE RD 01119   782-8031
Timothy Duff, prin.
Salter School   2-CS
458 BRIDGE ST 01103   731-7353
Springfield College   5-UC
263 ALDEN ST 01109   788-3136
Springfield Technical Community College   5-CC
1 ARMORY SQ 01105   781-7822
Western New England College   5-UC
1215 WILBRAHAM RD 01119   800-325-1122

Stockbridge, AC 413, PC 4, Berkshire
Berkshire Hills SD   4-11111
BERKSHIRE HILLS REG 01262   298-3711
Linda Day, supt.
Other Schools – See Great Barrington

Desisto S, GENERAL DELIVERY 01262   2-00111
A. Desisto, prin.   298-3776

Stoneham, AC 617, PC 7, Middlesex
Stoneham SD, 149 FRANKLIN ST 02180   5-11111
William Hoyt, supt.   438-0600
HS, 149 FRANKLIN ST 02180   3-00011
Thomas Ryan, prin.   438-5717
MS, 101 CENTRAL ST 02180   3-00100
William Orman, prin.   438-0646

Greater Boston Academy & Edgewood ES   1-11111
20 WOODLAND RD 02180   438-4253
William Arnold, prin.

Stoughton, AC 617, PC 8, Norfolk
Stoughton SD, 232 PEARL ST 02072   5-11111
Geoffrey Fanning, supt.   344-4000
HS, 232 PEARL ST 02072   4-00011
Anthony Sarno, prin.   344-4000
JHS, 211 CUSHING ST 02072   3-00100
Deborah Levitz, prin.   344-4000

Stow, AC 508, PC 4, Middlesex
Stow SD, 403 GREAT RD 01775   3-11100
Robert Barbarisi, supt.   897-8832
Hale MS, HARTLEY RD 01775   2-01100
Gary Oakes, prin.   897-4788

Sudbury, AC 508, PC 4, Middlesex
Lincoln-Sudbury SD   3-00011
390 LINCOLN RD 01776   443-9961
Matthew King, supt.
Lincoln-Sudbury Regional HS   3-00011
390 LINCOLN RD 01776   443-9961
Matthew King, supt.

Sudbury SD, 40 FAIRBANK RD 01776   4-11100
Henry Derusha, supt.   443-1058
Curtis MS, 22 PRATTS MILL RD 01776   3-01100
Joan McKenna, prin.   443-1071

Sutton, AC 508, PC 3, Worcester
Sutton SD, BOSTON ROAD 01590   4-11111
Gordon Spence, supt.   865-9270
JSHS, BOSTON RD 01590   3-00111
Ed Grant, prin.   865-6481

Swampscott, AC 617, PC 7, Essex
Swampscott SD, 207 FOREST AVE 01907   4-11111
Richard Chrystal, supt.   596-8800
HS, 1 FOREST AVE 01907   3-00011
Peter Sack, prin.   596-8830
MS, 71 GREENWOOD AVE 01907   3-00100
Ronald Landman, prin.   596-8820

Marian Court College   2-CC
35 LITTLES POINT RD 01907   595-6768

Swansea, AC 508, PC 3, Bristol
Swansea SD   4-11111
1 GARDNERS NECK RD 02777   675-1195
Harold Devine, supt.
Case HS, 70 SCHOOL ST 02777   3-00011
David Jardin, prin.   675-7483
Case JHS, 195 MAIN ST 02777   3-00100
Ken Sheehan, prin.   675-0116

New England Christian Academy   2-11111
271 SHARPS LOT RD 02777   676-3011
Frederick Poulin, prin.

Taunton, AC 508, PC 8, Bristol
Bristol-Plymouth Vocational-Tech SD   3-00011
940 COUNTY ST 02780   823-5151
John Correia, supt.
Bristol-Plymouth Vocational Technical HS   3-00011
940 COUNTY ST 02780   823-5151
Daniel Saunders, prin.

Taunton SD, 50 WILLIAMS ST 02780   6-11111
Gerald Croteau, supt.   821-1201
HS, 50 WILLIAMS ST 02780   4-00011
Patrick Jackman, prin.   821-1101
Cohannet MS   3-01100
120A COHANNET ST 02780   821-1290
Richard Faulkner, prin.
Mulcahey MS, 28 CLIFFORD ST 02780   3-01100
Gerald Puccini, prin.   821-1255

Parker MS, 50 WILLIAMS ST 02780 — 3-01100
Richard Castro, prin. — 821-1112

Coyle & Cassidy HS — 3-00011
2 HAMILTON ST 02780 — 823-6164
Michael Donly, prin.
Taunton Catholic MS — 2-01100
61 SUMMER ST 02780 — 822-0491
Kathleen Simpson, prin.

Tewksbury, AC 508, PC 7, Middlesex
Tewksbury SD, 139 PLEASANT ST 01876 — 5-11111
Christine McGrath, supt. — 851-7347
Tewksbury Memorial HS — 3-00011
320 PLEASANT ST 01876 — 851-2022
William Degregorio, prin.
JHS, 10 VICTOR DR 01876 — 3-00100
Richard Griffin, prin. — 851-3709

Topsfield, AC 508, PC 5, Essex
Masconomet SD, 20 ENDICOTT RD 01983 — 4-00111
Richard Dussault, supt. — 887-2323
Masconomet Regional JSHS — 4-00111
20 ENDICOTT RD 01983 — 887-2323
Stephen Smith, prin.

Townsend, AC 508, PC 4, Middlesex
North Middlesex SD, 23 MAIN ST 01469 — 5-11111
James McCormick, supt. — 597-8713
North Middlesex Regional HS — 4-00111
19 MAIN ST 01469 – Ralph Olsen, prin. — 597-8721
Hawthorne Brook MS — 3-01100
BROOKLINE ROAD 01469 — 597-6914
Stephen Keating, prin.
Other Schools – See East Pepperell

Turners Falls, AC 413, PC 5, Franklin
Franklin County SD — 2-00011
200 INDUSTRIAL BLVD 01376 — 863-4239
Walter Welch, supt.
Franklin County Technical HS — 2-00011
200 INDUSTRIAL BLVD 01376 — 863-9561
Patricia Bassett, prin.

Gill-Montague SD, CROCKER AVE 01376 — 4-11111
Anthony Serio, supt. — 863-9324
Other Schools – See Montague

Hallmark Institute of Photography — 1-CS
PO BOX 308 01376 — 863-2478

Tyngsboro, AC 508, PC 2, Middlesex
Greater Lowell Vocational-Technical SD — 4-00011
107 PAWTUCKET BLVD 01879 — 454-5411
William Collins, supt.
Greater Lowell Vocational Technical HS — 4-00011
107 PAWTUCKET BLVD 01879 — 454-5411
William Collins, supt.

Tyngsboro SD, 50 NORRIS RD 01879 — 4-11111
David Hawkins, supt. — 649-7488
JSHS, 36 NORRIS RD 01879 — 3-00111
Lawrence Kelleher, prin. — 649-7571

Academy of Notre Dame — 3-11111
180 MIDDLESEX RD 01879 — 649-7611
Sr. Maureen Marr, prin.

Upton, AC 508, PC 4, Worcester
Mendon-Upton SD — 4-11111
PO BOX 176 01568 — 529-7729
Dave Crisafulli, supt.
Other Schools – See Mendon

Uxbridge, AC 508, PC 5, Worcester
Uxbridge SD, 62 CAPRON ST 01569 — 4-11111
Michael Ronan, supt. — 278-8648
HS, 62 CAPRON ST 01569 — 2-00011
John Robarts, prin. — 278-8633
Whitin IS, 120 GRANITE ST 01569 — 3-01100
Brian Lynch, prin. — 278-8640

Vineyard Haven, AC 508, PC 4, Dukes
Martha's Vineyard SD — 2-00011
RR 2 BOX 261 02568 — 693-2007
Hebert Custer, supt.
Other Schools – See Oak Bluffs

Wakefield, AC 617, PC 7, Middlesex
Northeast Metro Vocational SD — 4-00011
100 HEMLOCK RD 01880 — 246-0810
Thomas Markham, supt.
Northeast Metro Regional Vocational HS — 4-00011
100 HEMLOCK RD 01880 — 246-0810
James Pelley, prin.

Wakefield SD, 525 MAIN ST 01880 — 5-11111
Stephen F. Maio, supt. — 246-6400
Wakefield Memorial HS — 3-00011
60 FARM ST 01880 – R. Osborne, prin. — 246-6440
JHS, 525 MAIN ST 01880 — 3-00100
John Sardella, prin. — 246-6410

Our Lady of Nazareth Academy — 2-00011
14 WINSHIP DR 01880 — 245-5210
Madeline Bartlett, prin.

Walpole, AC 508, PC 6, Norfolk
Norfolk County Agricultural SD — 2-00011
400 MAIN ST 02081 — 668-0268
Richard Morse, supt.
Norfolk County Agricultural HS — 2-00011
400 MAIN ST 02081 — 668-0268
Michael Barden, prin.

Walpole SD, SCHOOL 02081 — 5-11111
Thomas Cibotti, supt. — 660-7200
HS, COMMON ST 02081 — 3-00011
Lester Burch, prin. — 660-7257
Johnson MS, ROBBINS RD 02081 — 3-01100
Stephen Driscoll, prin. — 660-7242
Other Schools – See East Walpole

Waltham, AC 617, PC 8, Middlesex
Waltham SD, 617 LEXINGTON ST 02154 — 6-11111
John Daddona, supt. — 893-8050
HS, 617 LEXINGTON ST 02154 — 4-00011
John Graceffa, prin. — 893-8050
Waltham Vo HS, 100 SUMMER ST 02154 — Vo Tech
William Nolan, prin. — 647-0309
Kennedy MS, 655 LEXINGTON ST 02154 — 2-00100
Sidney Smith, prin. — 891-9319
South MS, 510 MOODY ST 02154 — 2-00100
Paul Connolly, prin. — 899-9110

Bentley College — 6-UC
175 FOREST ST 02154 — 891-2000
Brandeis University — 5-UC
415 SOUTH ST 02154 — 736-2000
Chapel Hill-Chauncy Hall S — 2-00011
785 BEAVER ST 02154 — 894-2644
James Clements, prin.

Ware, AC 413, PC 6, Hampshire
Ware SD, PO BOX 240 01082 — 4-11111
Paul Demers, supt. — 967-4271
JSHS, 237 WEST ST 01082 — 2-00111
Charles Adams, prin. — 967-6234

Wareham, AC 508, PC 5, Plymouth
Wareham SD, 54 MARION RD 02571 — 5-11111
James Nolan, supt. — 291-3500
HS, 0 VIKING WAY 02571 — 3-00011
David MacKinnon, prin. — 291-3510
MS, 121R MARION RD 02571 — 3-00100
Barry Rabinovitch, prin. — 291-3550

Warren, AC 413, PC 4, Worcester
Quaboag Regional SD — 4-11111
OLD W BROOKFIELD RD 01083 — 436-5991
William Haggerty, supt.
Quaboag Regional JSHS — 3-00111
OLD W BROOKFIELD RD 01083 — 436-5991
Michael Diruzza, prin.

Watertown, AC 617, PC 8, Middlesex
Watertown SD, 30 COMMON ST 02172 — 5-11111
Sally Dias, supt. — 926-7700
HS, 50 COLUMBIA ST 02172 — 3-00011
Jennifer Huntington, prin. — 926-7760
MS, WAVERLEY AVE 02172 — 3-00100
John Burns, prin. — 926-7783

New England Fuel Institute — 2-CS
PO BOX 888 02272 — 924-1000
New England School of Business — 2-CS
PO BOX 888 02272 — 924-1000
Perkins School for the Blind — HND
175 N BEACON ST 02172 — 924-3434

Wayland, AC 508, PC 5, Middlesex
Wayland SD, 41 COCHITUATE RD 01778 — 4-11111
William G. Zimmerman, supt. — 358-7728
HS — 3-00011
264 OLD CONNECTICUT PATH 01778 — 358-7746
Sharon Hennessy, prin.
MS, 201 MAIN ST 01778 — 2-00100
Richard Schaye, prin. — 655-6670

Webster, AC 508, PC 7, Worcester
Webster SD, PO BOX 430 01570 — 4-11111
Anthony D'Acchioli, supt. — 943-0104
Bartlett JSHS, LAKE ST 01570 — 3-00111
Arnold Berry, prin. — 943-8552

Wellesley, AC 617, PC 8, Norfolk
Wellesley SD, 40 KINGSBURY ST 02181 — 5-11111
Carla Delitis, supt. — 446-6226
HS, 50 RICE ST 02181 — 3-00111
Mary Hayes, prin. — 446-6290
MS, 50 KINGSBURY ST 02181 — 3-00100
John D'Auria, prin. — 446-6235

Dana Hall S, 45 DANA RD 02181 — 2-00111
Elaine Betts, prin. — 235-3010
Massachusetts Bay Community College — 5-CC
50 OAKLAND ST 02181 — 237-1100
Wellesley College 02181 — 4-UC
 — 235-0320

Wendell, AC 508, PC 2, Franklin

Lake Grove School-Maple Valley — HND
PO BOX 767 01379 — 544-6913

Wenham, AC 508, PC 5, Essex
Hamilton-Wenham SD
Supt. — See South Hamilton
Buker MS, 11 SCHOOL ST 01984 — 2-00100
Kalil Boghdan, prin. — 468-5320

Gordon College — 4-UC
255 GRAPEVINE RD 01984 — 927-2300

West Barnstable, AC 508, PC 4, Barnstable

Cape Cod Community College — 5-CC
2240 ROUTE 132 02668 — 362-2131

Westborough, AC 508, PC 5, Worcester
Westborough SD, 16 PHILLIPS ST 01581 — 4-11111
John Doherty, supt. — 366-8551
HS, 90 W MAIN ST 01581 — 3-00011
Maureen Zolubos, prin. — 366-7433
Gibbons MS, 20 FISHER ST 01581 — 3-00100
William Maher, prin. — 366-8541

West Boylston, AC 508, PC 5, Worcester
West Boylston SD — 3-11111
125 CRESCENT ST 01583 — 835-2917
Leo Sullivan, supt.
JSHS, 125 CRESCENT ST 01583 — 2-00111
Francine Bullock, prin. — 835-4475

West Bridgewater, AC 508, PC 4, Plymouth
West Bridgewater SD — 4-11111
65 N MAIN ST 02379 — 586-5094
Ronald Pacy, supt.
JSHS, 155 W CENTER ST 02379 — 2-00111
S. Benson, prin. — 583-7502

New England Baptist Academy — 2-11111
560 N MAIN ST 02379 — 584-5188
Joseph Coppola, prin.

Westfield, AC 413, PC 8, Hampden
Westfield SD, 22 ASHLEY ST 01085 — 6-11111
Alton Sprague, supt. — 572-6403
HS, 177 MONTGOMERY RD 01085 — 4-00011
Carl Ostrowski, prin. — 572-6463
Westfield Vo HS, 33 SMITH AVE 01085 — Vo Tech
Steven Pippin, prin. — 572-6533
MS, 30 W SILVER ST 01085 — 3-00100
Thomas McDowell, prin. — 572-6441

St. Marys HS, 25 BARTLETT ST 01085 — 2-00011
Sr. Christine Methe, prin. — 568-5692
Westfield State College — 5-UC
577 WESTERN AVE 01085 — 568-3311

Westford, AC 508, PC 4, Middlesex
Nashoba Valley Technical SD — 2-00111
347 LITTLETON RD 01886 — 692-4711
Frederick Green, supt.
Nashoba Valley Technical HS — 2-00011
347 LITTLETON RD 01886 — 692-4711
David McLaughlin, prin.

Westford SD, 35 TOWN FARM RD 01886 — 5-11111
John Crisafulli, supt. — 692-5560
Westford Academy HS — 3-00011
PATTON ST 01886 – Joseph Lisi, prin. — 692-5571
Blanchard MS, WESTN 01886 — 3-00100
Deborah Alexander, prin. — 692-5582

Westhampton, AC 413, PC 2, Hampshire
Hampshire SD, 19 STAGE RD 01027 — 3-00111
Rich Dragon, supt. — 527-7200
Other Schools – See Easthampton

Westminster, AC 508, PC 3, Worcester
Ashburnham-Westminster SD — 4-11111
1 LEOMINSTER ST 01473 — 874-1501
William Allen, supt.
Other Schools – See Ashburnham

West Newbury, AC 508, PC 3, Essex
Pentucket SD, 22 MAIN ST 01985 — 4-00111
Henry Dembowski, supt. — 363-2280
Pentucket Reg. HS, 22 MAIN ST 01985 — 3-00011
Mike McLaughlin, prin. — 363-5507
Pentucket Reg. JHS, 24 MAIN ST 01985 — 2-00100
Steven Welford, prin. — 363-2957

Weston, AC 617, PC 7, Middlesex
Weston SD, 89 WELLESLEY ST 02193 — 4-11111
Meredith Jones, supt. — 899-0620
HS, 444 WELLESLEY ST 02193 — 2-00111
Bruce MacDonald, prin. — 899-0620
MS, 456 WELLESLEY ST 02193 — 2-00100
Ronald Harris, prin. — 899-0620

Cambridge S, 45 GEORGIAN RD 02193 — 2-00011
George Cohan, prin. — 642-8200
Pope John XXIII National Seminary — 1-UC
558 SOUTH AVE 02193 — 899-5500
Regis College — 3-UC
235 WELLESLEY ST 02193 — 800-456-1820
Rivers S, 333 WINTER ST 02193 — 2-00111
David Harman, prin. — 235-9300

Westport, AC 508, PC 3, Bristol
Westport SD, 17 MAIN RD 02790 — 4-11111
Margot Desjardins, supt. — 636-1137
HS, 19 MAIN RD 02790 — 2-00111
Charles Menard, prin. — 636-1050
MS, 400 OLD COUNTY RD 02790 — 2-01100
John Mello, prin. — 636-1090

West Roxbury, AC 617, PC see Boston
Boston SD
Supt. — See Boston
HS, 1205 VFW PKY 02132 — 4-00011
Donald Pellegrini, prin. — 323-4866
Shaw MS — 2-00100
20 MOUNT VERNON ST 02132 — 325-2727
Edward Mabardi, prin.

Catholic Memorial HS — 3-00011
235 BAKER ST 02132 — 323-7333
Anthony Polito, prin.

Roxbury Latin S   2-00111
101 SAINT THERESA AVE 02132   325-4920
Rev. Jarvis, prin.

West Springfield, AC 413, PC 8, Hampden
West Springfield SD   5-11111
26 CENTRAL ST 01089   263-3289
William O'Shea, supt.
HS, 425 PIPER RD 01089   4-00011
George Bauman, prin.   732-4147
JHS, 115 SOUTHWORTH ST 01089   2-00100
Richard Berte, prin.   732-3316

St. John's School of Business   2-CS
PO BOX 1190 01090   781-0390

West Upton, AC 508, PC 4, Worcester
Blackstone Valley Regional SD   3-00011
65 PLEASANT ST 01568   529-4593
Michael Fitzpatrick, supt.
Blackstone Valley HS   3-00011
65 PLEASANT ST 01568   529-4593
Eugene Picard, prin.

Westwood, AC 617, PC 6, Norfolk
Westwood SD, 660 HIGH ST 02090   4-11111
Robert Monson, supt.   326-7500
HS, 200 NAHATAN ST 02090   2-00011
P. Flaherty, prin.   326-7500
Thurston JHS, 850 HIGH ST 02090   2-00100
Maureen Szal, prin.   326-7500

Montrose S, 72 DEERFIELD AVE 02090   2-00111
Diane Hunter, prin.   326-0535
Xaverian Brothers HS   3-00011
800 CLAPBOARDTREE ST 02090   326-6392
Br. Daniel Skala, prin.

West Yarmouth, AC 508, PC 6, Barnstable
Dennis-Yarmouth SD
Supt. — See South Yarmouth
Mattacheese MS   3-01100
HIGGINS CROWELL RD 02673   778-7979
Charles Orloff, prin.

Weymouth, AC 617, PC 8, Norfolk
Weymouth SD, 111 MIDDLE ST 02189   6-11111
Robert West, supt.   335-1460
JHS, 360 PLEASANT ST 02190   3-00110
Paul Youngclaus, prin.   337-7500
Other Schools – See East Weymouth

Whitinsville, AC 508, PC 6, Worcester
Northbridge SD   4-11111
87 LINWOOD AVE 01588   234-8156
Joseph Ferreira, supt.
Northbridge HS   2-00011
171 LINWOOD AVE 01588   234-6221
Edward Riley, prin.
Northbridge MS, PLEASANT ST 01588   2-00100
Ronald Stead, prin.   234-8718

Whitinsville Christian S   3-11111
279 LINWOOD AVE 01588   234-8211
Jack Vandenborn, prin.

Whitman, AC 617, PC 7, Plymouth
Whitman-Hanson SD   5-11111
39 WHITMAN AVE 02382   447-7000
Raymond Avery, supt.
Whitman-Hanson Reg. HS   3-00011
600 FRANKLIN ST 02382   447-7020
Gerald Buckley, prin.
MS, 77 CORTHELL AVE 02382   3-00100
Middleton McGoodwin, prin.   447-7035
Other Schools – See Hanson

Wilbraham, AC 413, PC 5, Hampden
Hampden-Wilbraham SD   3-00011
621 MAIN ST 01095 – J. Halloran, supt.   596-3884
Minnechaug Regional HS   3-00011
621 MAIN ST 01095   596-9011
Robert Johnson, prin.

Wilbraham SD, 621 MAIN ST 01095   4-11100
J. Halloran, supt.   596-3884
MS, 269 STONY HILL RD 01095   3-00100
Richard Ullery, prin.   596-9061

Wilbraham & Monson Academy   2-00111
421 MAIN ST 01095   596-6811
Richard Malley, prin.

Williamstown, AC 413, PC 5, Berkshire
Mt. Greylock SD   3-00111
1781 COLD SPRING RD 01267   458-9582
Edward Filiault, supt.
Mt. Greylock Reg. JSHS   3-00111
1781 COLD SPRING RD 01267   458-9582
Beth Singer, prin.

Buxton S, PO BOX 646 01267   1-00011
C. William Bennett, prin.   458-3919
Highcroft S, PO BOX 548 01267   1-01111
David Milne, prin.   458-8136
Williams College 01267   4-UC
   597-2211

Wilmington, AC 508, PC 7, Middlesex
Wilmington SD, 159 CHURCH ST 01887   5-11111
Geraldine O'Donnell, supt.   694-6000
HS, 159 CHURCH ST 01887   3-00011
Paul Fleming, prin.   694-6060
North IS, SALEM ST 01887   2-00100
Michael Tikonoff, prin.   694-6040
West IS, 20 CARTER LN 01887   2-00100
James Jordan, prin.   694-6050

Winchendon, AC 508, PC 5, Worcester
Winchendon SD, 1 SUMMER DR 01475   4-11111
Coral Grout, supt.   297-0031
Murdock HS, 175 GROVE ST 01475   2-00011
Michael Mezzocchi, prin.   297-1256
MS, 28 MURDOCK AVE 01475   2-00100
David Sandmann, prin.   297-0351

Winchendon S, 172 ASH ST 01475   2-00111
J. Labelle, prin.   297-1223

Winchester, AC 617, PC 7, Middlesex
Winchester SD   5-11111
154 HORN POND BROOK RD 01890   721-7004
Robert Fitzgerald, supt.
HS, 80 SKILLINGS RD 01890   3-00011
John Ritchie, prin.   721-7020
McCall JHS, 458 MAIN ST 01890   3-00100
Evander French, prin.   721-7026

Winthrop, AC 617, PC 7, Suffolk
Winthrop SD, 45 PAULINE ST 02152   4-11111
Joseph Laino, supt.   846-5500
HS, 2 MAIN ST 02152   3-00011
Joseph Mauro, prin.   846-5500
MS, PAULINE ST 02152   2-00100
Rosemary Ditullio, prin.   846-5500

Woburn, AC 617, PC 8, Middlesex
Woburn SD, 55 LOCUST ST 01801   5-11111
Paul Andrews, supt.   935-6609
HS, 88 MONTVALE AVE 01801   4-00011
James Foley, prin.   933-8051
Joyce JHS, 75 LOCUST ST 01801   2-00100
Laurence Gilgun, prin.   935-5586
Kennedy JHS, 33 MIDDLE ST 01801   3-00100
Paul McElheney, prin.   935-7676

Associated Technical Institute   2-CS
345 W CUMMINGS PARK 01801   935-3838

Woods Hole, AC 508, PC 4, Barnstable

Woods Hole Oceanographic Institution   2-UC
02543   457-2000

Worcester, AC 508, PC 9, Worcester
Worcester SD, 20 IRVING ST 01609   7-11111
James Garvey, supt.   799-3116

Burncoat HS, 179 BURNCOAT ST 01606   4-00011
William Hynes, prin.   799-3299
Doherty Memorial HS   4-00011
299 HIGHLAND ST 01602   799-3270
Cynthia McMullen, prin.
North HS   3-00011
150 HARRINGTON WAY 01604   799-3370
Robert Boule, prin.
South Community HS   4-00011
170 APRICOT ST 01603   799-3325
James Garvey, prin.
Burncoat MS, 135 BURNCOAT ST 01606   3-00100
Dorothy Bratiotis, prin.   799-3390
Forest Grove MS, 495 GROVE ST 01605   3-00100
David O'Connor, prin.   799-3420
Sullivan MS, 14 RICHARDS ST 01603   3-00100
John Bierfeldt, prin.   799-3350
Worcester East MS   3-00100
420 GRAFTON ST 01604   799-3430
Kevin Keaney, prin.

Worcester Trade Complex SD   4-00011
26 SALISBURY ST 01609   799-1941
Joseph Lemenager, supt.
Worcester Vocational Technical HS   4-00011
2 GROVE ST 01605   799-1980
Michael Doherty, prin.

Assumption College   4-UC
500 SALISBURY ST 01609   752-5615
Bancroft S, 110 SHORE DR 01605   3-11111
Theodore Sharp, prin.   853-2640
Becker College   4-CC
61 SEVER ST 01609   791-9241
Burdett School   2-CS
100 FRONT ST 01608   849-1900
Clark University   5-UC
950 MAIN ST 01610   793-7431
College of the Holy Cross   5-UC
1 COLLEGE ST 01610   793-2443
Holy Name Central Catholic HS   3-00011
144 GRANITE ST 01604   753-6371
John Madden, prin.
New England School of Accounting   2-CS
155 ARARAT ST 01606   853-8972
Notre Dame Academy   2-00011
425 SALISBURY ST 01609   757-6200
Sr. Ann Morrison, prin.
Quinsigamond Community College   5-CC
670 W BOYLSTON ST 01606   853-2300
St. Marys Catholic S   2-11111
50 RICHLAND ST 01610   753-1170
Sr. Dorothea Jurkowski, prin.
St. Peter Marian Central HS   3-00111
781 GROVE ST 01605   852-5555
Timothy Rioux, prin.
Salter School   2-CS
155 ARARAT ST 01606   853-1074
University of Massachusetts Medical S   2-UC
55 LAKE AVE N 01655   856-6630
Worcester Academy   2-00111
81 PROVIDENCE ST 01604   754-5302
John McKenzie, prin.
Worcester City Hospital   HSP
455 MAIN ST STE 306 01608   799-8120
Worcester Polytechnic Institute   5-UC
100 INSTITUTE RD 01609   831-5286
Worcester State College   5-UC
486 CHANDLER ST 01602   793-8129
Worcester Technical Institute   2-CS
251 BELMONT ST 01605   799-1945

Wrentham, AC 508, PC 4, Norfolk
King Philip SD, PO BOX 49 02093   4-00111
Perry Davis, supt.   384-3144
King Philip Reg. HS   3-00011
PO BOX 49 02093   384-1000
Winston Fairfield, prin.
Other Schools – See Norfolk

MICHIGAN

STATE DEPARTMENT OF EDUCATION
John A. Hannah Office Building
P.O. Box 30008, Lansing 48909
(517) 373-3324

Superintendent of Public Instruction	Robert Schiller
Deputy Superintendent	Teressa Staten
Deputy Superintendent Administration	James Phelps
Deputy Superintendent Instructional Programs	Vacant
Deputy Superintendent Direct Services	Ivan Cotman

STATE BOARD OF EDUCATION
P.O. Box 30008, Lansing 48909

Co-President	Annetta Miller

INTERMEDIATE SCHOOL DISTRICTS

Allegan County ISD
James Pavelka 616-673-2161
310 THOMAS ST, Allegan 49010
Alpena/Montmorency/Alcona ISD
Thomas Lanway 517-354-3101
2118 US HIGHWAY 23 S
Alpena 49707
Barry ISD
Thomas Mohler 616-945-4192
535 W WOODLAWN AVE
Hastings 49058
Bay/Arenac ISD
Jon Whan 517-686-4410
4228 2 MILE RD, Bay City 48706
Berrien ISD
Jerry Reimann 616-471-7725
711 SAINT JOSEPH AVE
Berrien Springs 49103
Branch ISD
Robert Redmond 517-279-5730
370 MORSE ST, Coldwater 49036
Calhoun ISD
Roger LaBonte 616-781-5141
17111 G DR N, Marshall 49068
Charlevoix/Emmet ISD
Mark Eckhardt 616-547-9947
PO BOX 318, Charlevoix 49720
Cheboygan/Otsego/Presque Isle ISD
James Mick, 6065 LEARNING LN 616-238-9394
Indian River 49749
Clare/Gladwin ISD
G. Zubulake 517-386-3851
4041 E MANNSIDING RD
Clare 48617
Clinton County ISD
Larry Schwartzkopf 517-224-6831
4179 S US HIGHWAY 27
Saint Johns 48879
COOR ISD
Lyle Spalding, 11051 N CUT RD 517-275-5137
Roscommon 48653
Copper Country ISD
Paul Ollila 906-482-4250
PO BOX 27, Hancock 49930
Delta/Schoolcraft ISD
Dennis Stanek 906-786-9300
2525 3RD AVE S, Escanaba 49829
Dickinson/Iron ISD
Richard Jacobsen 906-779-2690
1074 PYLE DR, Kingsford 49801
Eastern UP ISD
Jerry Gallagher, PO BOX 883 906-632-3373
Sault Sainte Marie 49783
Eaton ISD
Jon Tomlanovich 517-543-5500
1790 PACKARD HWY
Charlotte 48813
Genesee ISD
David Spathelf 810-768-4400
2413 W MAPLE AVE, Flint 48507
Gogebic/Ontonagon ISD
Graydon Blank 906-575-3438
PO BOX 218, Bergland 49910

Gratiot/Isabella ISD
Douglas Sasse 517-875-5101
PO BOX 310, Ithaca 48847
Hillsdale ISD
David Steel 517-439-1515
3471 BECK RD, Hillsdale 49242
Huron ISD
William Mayes 517-269-6406
711 E SOPER RD, Bad Axe 48413
Ingham ISD
Donald Shebuski 517-676-1051
2630 W HOWELL RD
Mason 48854
Ionia ISD
William Schewe 616-527-4900
2191 HARWOOD RD, Ionia 48846
Iosco ISD
Jerome Allore, 686 AULERICH RD 517-362-4467
East Tawas 48730
Jackson ISD
Gerald Kratz 517-787-2800
6700 BROWNS LAKE RD
Jackson 49201
Kalamazoo Valley ISD
Larry Wile, 1819 E MILHAM RD 616-381-4620
Kalamazoo 49002
Kent ISD
George Woons, 2930 KNAPP ST NE 616-364-1333
Grand Rapids 49505
Lapeer ISD
Peter Holley, 1996 W OREGON ST 810-664-5917
Lapeer 48446
Lenawee ISD
William Ross 517-265-2119
4107 N ADRIAN HWY
Adrian 49221
Lewis Cass ISD
John Ward, 61682 DAILEY RD 616-445-3891
Cassopolis 49031
Livingston ISD
Charles Johnson 517-546-5550
1425 W GRAND RIVER AVE
Howell 48843
Macomb ISD
Joseph Nicita 810-228-3300
44001 GARFIELD RD
Clinton Township 48038
Manistee ISD
Robert Tilmann 616-723-6205
722 E PARKDALE AVE
Manistee 49660
Marquette Alger ISD
Louis Myefski 906-226-5100
427 W COLLEGE AVE
Marquette 49855
Mason/Lake ISD
Scott Russell 616-757-3716
2130 W US HIGHWAY 10
Ludington 49431
Mecosta-Osceloa ISD
Roger Dixon 616-796-3543
PO BOX 1137, Big Rapids 49307
Menominee County ISD
Ronald Peltier 906-863-5665
952 1ST ST, Menominee 49858

Midland ISD
James McKimmey 517-631-5890
3917 JEFFERSON AVE
Midland 48640
Monroe ISD
Gerald Wing 313-242-5454
1101 S RAISINVILLE RD
Monroe 48161
Montcalm Area ISD
William Seiter 517-831-5261
PO BOX 367, Stanton 48888
Muskegon Area ISD
James Perry, 630 HARVEY ST 616-777-2637
Muskegon 49442
Newaygo ISD
Roland Marmion 616-689-5906
1035 E JAMES ST
White Cloud 49349
Oakland ISD
William Keane 810-858-2121
2100 PONTIAC LAKE RD
Waterford 48328
Oceana ISD
Lawrence Stancliff 616-873-5651
844 GRISWOLD ST, Hart 49420
Ottawa Area ISD
J. Bergers 616-399-6940
13565 PORT SHELDON ST
Holland 49424
Saginaw ISD
Larry Engel, 6235 GRATIOT RD 517-799-4733
Saginaw 48603
St. Clair ISD
Joseph Caimi 810-364-8990
PO BOX 5001, Port Huron 48061
St. Joseph ISD
Larry Campbell 616-467-5400
PO BOX 219, Centreville 49032
Sanilac ISD
Frederick Cady, 46 N JACKSON ST 810-648-2200
Sandusky 48471
Shiawassee ISD
Patrick Gilbert 517-743-3471
1025 N SHIAWASSEE ST
Corunna 48817
Traverse Bay Area ISD
Michael McIntyre 616-922-6200
2325 GARFIELD RD N
Traverse City 49686
Tuscola ISD
John Moore 517-673-2144
1385 CLEAVER RD, Caro 48723
Van Buren ISD
James Mapes, 701 S PAW PAW ST 616-674-8091
Lawrence 49064
Washtenaw ISD
Michael Emlaw 313-994-8100
PO BOX 1406, Ann Arbor 48106
Wayne ISD
Michael Flanagan 313-467-1300
33500 VAN BORN RD
Wayne 48184
Wexford/Missaukee ISD
William Penny 616-775-5651
9905 E 13TH ST, Cadillac 49601

PUBLIC, PRIVATE AND CATHOLIC SECONDARY SCHOOLS

Addison, AC 517, PC 3, Lenawee
Addison Community SD
219 COMSTOCK ST 49220   4-11111
Jeffrey Kersh, supt.   547-6123
HS, 219 COMSTOCK ST 49220   2-00011
D. Britton, prin.   547-6121
MS, 240 W MAIN ST 49220   2-00100
Bradley Hamilton, prin.   547-6125

Adrian, AC 517, PC 7, Lenawee
Adrian SD, 227 N WINTER ST 49221   6-11111
Albert Meloy, supt.   263-2115
HS, 785 RIVERSIDE AVE 49221   4-00011
Gerald Burg, prin.   263-2181
Drager MS, 340 E CHURCH ST 49221   3-00100
Lindle Cochran, prin.   265-8122
Springbrook JHS   3-00100
615 SPRINGBROOK AVE 49221   263-0543
Robert Ritz, prin.

Madison SD, 3498 TREAT HWY 49221   3-11111
James Hartley, supt.   263-0741
Madison HS, 3498 TREAT HWY 49221   2-00011
Connie Ries, prin.   263-0741

Adrian College   4-UC
110 S MADISON ST 49221   265-5161
Berean Baptist Academy   2-11111
751 W MAUMEE ST 49221   263-4312
Michael Cox, prin.
Lenawee Christian S   3-11111
111 WOLF CREEK HWY 49221   263-8540
Paul Palpant, prin.
Siena Heights College   4-UC
1247 E SIENA HEIGHTS DR 49221   263-0731

Alanson, AC 616, PC 3, Emmet
Littlefield SD, PO BOX 1300 49706   3-11111
William Courliss, supt.   548-2261
Littlefield S, 7400 NORTH ST 49706   3-11111
Lawrence Krueger, prin.   548-2261

Alba, AC 616, PC 2, Antrim
Alba SD, 5935 ELM ST 49611   2-11111
Ron Militello, supt.   584-2000
S, 5935 ELM ST 49611   2-11111
Ron Militello, supt.   584-2000

Albion, AC 517, PC 7, Calhoun
Albion SD, 401 E MICHIGAN AVE 49224   4-11111
Judyth Dobbert, supt.   629-9166
Albion HS, 225 E WATSON ST 49224   3-00011
James Arnett, prin.   629-9421

Albion College   4-UC
611 E PORTER ST 49224   629-1000

Algonac, AC 810, PC 5, St. Clair
Algonac Community SD   5-11111
1216 SAINT CLAIR BLVD 48001   794-9364
Dennis Guiser, supt.
HS, 5200 TAFT RD 48001   3-00011
Tom Baldwin, prin.   794-4911
Algonquin JHS, 9185 MARSH RD 48001   3-00100
Linda Schneider-Rediske, prin.   794-9317

Allegan, AC 616, PC 5, Allegan
Allegan SD, 550 5TH ST 49010   5-11111
Douglas McCall, supt.   673-5431
SHS, 1560 LINCOLN RD 49010   3-00001
Brian McFalone, prin.   673-7002
White JHS, 3300 115TH AVE 49010   3-00110
George Mohr, prin.   673-2241

Allendale, AC 616, PC 4, Ottawa
Allendale SD   4-11111
6561 LAKE MICHIGAN DR 49401   895-4350
David Annis, supt.
JSHS, 6561 LAKE MICHIGAN DR 49401   3-00011
Steve Scholten, prin.   895-4351

Grand Valley State University   6-UC
1 CAMPUS DR 49401   895-6611

Allen Park, AC 313, PC 8, Wayne
Allen Park SD   5-11111
19001 CHAMPAIGN RD 48101   928-4667
William Kiefer, supt.
HS, 18401 CHAMPAIGN RD 48101   3-00011
G. Grundman, prin.   383-7517
MS, 8401 VINE AVE 48101   3-00100
R. Wilkinson, prin.   928-6152

Inter City Baptist S   2-11111
4700 ALLEN RD 48101   928-6900
Steven Stratford, prin.
St. Frances Cabrini HS   2-00011
15305 WICK RD 48101   388-0110
Sr. Pam Kobasic, prin.

Alma, AC 517, PC 6, Gratiot
Alma SD, 1500 PINE AVE 48801   5-11111
Wm. McKinstry, supt.   463-3111
HS, 1500 PINE AVE 48801   3-00011
Richard Chambers, prin.   463-3111
MS, 322 E DOWNIE ST 48801   3-01100
Carl Ellinger, prin.   463-3111

Alma College   4-UC
614 W SUPERIOR ST 48801   463-7111

Almont, AC 810, PC 4, Lapeer
Almont Community SD   4-11111
401 CHURCH ST 48003   798-8561
Steven Zott, supt.
JSHS, 4701 HOWLAND RD 48003   3-00011
James Jenuwine, prin.   798-8595

Alpena, AC 517, PC 7, Alpena
Alpena SD, 2373 GORDON RD 49707   6-11111
Ron LeBarre, supt.   356-4863
HS, 3303 S 3RD AVE 49707   4-00011
Brian Bronson, prin.   356-6161
Thunder Bay JHS, 375 S 2ND AVE 49707   3-00100
Lois Brinkman, prin.   354-4300

Alpena Community College   3-CC
666 JOHNSON ST 49707   356-9021

Ann Arbor, AC 313, PC 9, Washtenaw
Ann Arbor SD, 2555 S STATE ST 48104   7-11111
John Simpson, supt.   994-2230
Community HS   2-00011
401 N DIVISION ST 48104   994-2025
Robert Galardi, prin.
Huron HS, 2727 FULLER RD 48105   4-00011
Joetta Mial, prin.   994-2043
Pioneer HS   4-00011
601 W STADIUM BLVD 48103   994-2126
Donald Jones, prin.
Clague HS, 2616 NIXON ROAD 48105   3-00100
M. Thompson-Powell, prin.   994-1982
Forsyth JHS, 1655 NEWPORT RD 48103   2-00100
S. Baskerville, prin.   994-1986
Scarlett JHS, 3300 LORRAINE ST 48108   2-00100
Robin Jackson, prin.   994-2001
Slauson JHS   3-00100
1019 W WASHINGTON ST 48103   994-2005
Mark Ravlin, prin.
Tappan JHS   3-00100
2251 E STADIUM BLVD 48104   994-2012
L. Corbitt, prin.

Concordia College   3-UC
4090 GEDDES RD 48105   995-7331
Father Gabriel Richard HS   2-00011
530 ELIZABETH ST 48104   662-0496
Rev. Fride, prin.
Greenhills S   2-00011
850 GREEN HILLS DR 48105   769-4010
Anthony Paulus, prin.
Ross Technical Institute   2-CS
4703 WASHTENAW AVE 48108   434-7320
University of Michigan   8-UC
815 S UNIVERSITY AVE 48109   764-1817
University of Michigan-Ann Arbor   2-UC
109 OBSERVATORY ST 48109
Washtenaw Community College   6-CC
4800 E HURON RIVER DR 48105   973-3300

Armada, AC 810, PC 4, Macomb
Armada Area SD   4-11111
23550 ARMADA CENTER RD 48005   784-5558
Elliot Burns, supt.
HS, 23655 ARMADA CENTER RD 48005   3-00011
Dennis Kiel, prin.   784-9156
MS, 23550 ARMADA CENTER RD 48005   2-00100
Karolyn Stokley, prin.   784-9105

Ashley, AC 517, PC 3, Gratiot
Ashley Community SD   2-11111
PO BOX 6 48806   847-4000
Ken Maher, supt.
JSHS, PO BOX 6 48806   2-00111
Carl Wayer, prin.   847-2514

Athens, AC 616, PC 3, Calhoun
Athens Area SD   3-11111
300 E HOLCOMB ST 49011   729-5427
Dale Dittmer, supt.
Athens Area HS   2-00011
300 E HOLCOMB ST 49011   729-5414
David Nofz, prin.
MS, 515 E WILLIAMS ST 49011   2-01100
Joseph Chambers, prin.   729-5421

Atlanta, AC 517, PC 3, Montmorency
Atlanta Community SD   3-11111
PO BOX 407 49709   785-4877
Terry Deo, supt.
JSHS, PO BOX 407 49709   2-00111
Lester Hall, prin.   785-4842

Auburn, AC 517, PC 4, Bay
Bay City SD
Supt. — See Bay City
Western HS, 500 W MIDLAND RD 48611   4-00011
Alan Bryant, prin.   624-4481
Western HS, 500 W MIDLAND RD 48611   3-00100
Dale Dunham, prin.   662-4480

Auburn Hills, AC 810, PC 7, Oakland
Avondale SD, 260 S SQUIRREL RD 48326   5-11111
James Bird, supt.   852-4411
Avondale HS   3-00011
2800 WAUKEGAN ST 48326   852-2850
Joseph Coe, prin.
Other Schools – See Rochester Hills

Baker College of Auburn Hills   5-UC
1500 UNIVERSITY DR 48326

Oakland Christian S   3-11111
3075 SHIMMONS RD 48326   373-2700
Robert Hayes, prin.
Oakland Community College   4-CC
2900 FEATHERSTONE RD 48326   340-6500

Au Gres, AC 517, PC 3, Arenac
Au Gres-Sims SD, PO BOX 648 48703   3-11111
David Schiebel, supt.   876-7150
Au Gres-Sims JSHS   2-00111
PO BOX 648 48703   876-7157
Sue Stine, prin.

Augusta, AC 616, PC 3, Kalamazoo
Galesburg-Augusta Community SD
Supt. — See Galesburg
MS, 750 W VAN BUREN ST 49012   2-00100
Christopher Hurley, prin.   731-4136

Bad Axe, AC 517, PC 5, Huron
Bad Axe SD, 760 S VAN DYKE RD 48413   4-11111
John Males, supt.   269-9938
HS, 750 S VAN DYKE RD 48413   2-00011
Daniel Scow, prin.   269-9593
MS, 407 E WOODWORTH ST 48413   2-00100
John Rowland, prin.   269-2735

Great Lakes Junior College of Business   3-CC
150 NUGENT RD 48413   755-3444

Baldwin, AC 616, PC 3, Lake
Baldwin Community SD   3-11111
525 4TH ST 49304   745-4791
Stanley Chase, supt.
HS, 525 4TH ST 49304   2-00011
Ronald Erickson, prin.   745-4683
Yates MS, 525 4TH ST 49304   2-00100
William Boismier, prin.   745-3261

Bangor, AC 616, PC 4, Van Buren
Bangor SD, 801 W ARLINGTON ST 49013   4-11111
John Gunnell, supt.   427-7977
JSHS, 801 W ARLINGTON ST 49013   3-00111
Chris Stephens, prin.   427-6844

Baraga, AC 906, PC 4, Baraga
Baraga Area SD, 210 LYONS ST 49908   3-11111
Ken Hammerberg, supt.   353-6664
JSHS, 210 LYONS ST 49908   2-00111
Robert Maradik, prin.   353-6661

Bath, AC 517, PC 3, Clinton
Bath Community SD   4-11111
PO BOX 310 48808   641-6721
Anthony Foster, supt.
HS, PO BOX 159 48808   2-00011
Ed Sampson, prin.   641-6724
MS, PO BOX 148 48808   2-00100
Jack Brown, prin.   641-6781

Battle Creek, AC 616, PC 8, Calhoun
Battle Creek SD   6-11111
3 VAN BUREN ST W 49017   965-9500
Mike Bitar, supt.
Battle Creek Central SHS   4-00001
100 VAN BUREN ST W 49017   965-9526
Bruce Barney, prin.
Kellogg JHS, 60 VAN BUREN ST W 49017   3-00110
Carl Word, prin.   965-9655
Northwestern JHS, 176 LIMIT ST 49017   3-00110
Richard Oldham, prin.   965-9607
Southeastern JHS, 50 SPENCER ST 49017   3-00110
Michael Eubanks, prin.   965-9671
Southwestern JHS   2-00110
388 WASHINGTON AVE S 49015   965-9625
Steve Hoelscher, prin.
Springfield MS, 1023 AVENUE A 49015   2-01100
Nancy Fenton, prin.   965-9640

Harper Creek Community SD   5-11111
7290 BECKLEY RD 49017   979-1136
C. Glen Walter, supt.
Harper Creek HS   3-00011
7290 BECKLEY RD 49017   979-1121
Dan Warren, prin.
Harper Creek JHS   2-00100
7454 BECKLEY RD 49017   979-1131
Michael Ott, prin.

Lakeview SD, 15 ARBOR ST 49015   5-11111
Paul Williams, supt.   965-3080
Lakeview HS, 300 28TH ST S 49015   3-00011
Robert Ward, prin.   965-3042
Lakeview JHS   2-00100
20 WOODROW AVE S 49015   965-3074
Paul Doersam, prin.

Pennfield SD   4-11111
8587 PENNFIELD RD 49017   961-9781
Robert Grimes, supt.
Pennfield HS   2-00011
8587 PENNFIELD RD 49017   961-9770
Tom Tenney, prin.
Dunlap MS, 8587 PENNFIELD RD 49017   2-00100
Don Richards, prin.   961-9784

Battle Creek Academy   2-11111
480 PARKWAY DR 49017   965-1278
Sunimal Kulasekere, prin.
Davenport College of Business   2-UC
67 MICHIGAN AVE W 49017   968-6105

Kambly School/Developmentally Impaired HND
1003 NORTH AVE 49017
Kellogg Community College 5-CC
450 NORTH AVE 49017 965-3931
St. Philip Catholic Central S 3-11111
20 CHERRY ST 49017 963-4503
Mike Spahr, prin.

Bay City, AC 517, PC 8, Bay
Bangor Township SD 5-11111
3520 OLD KAWKAWLIN RD 48706 684-8121
Carl Hartman, supt.
Glenn HS, 3201 KIESEL RD 48706 3-00011
Richard Green, prin. 684-7510
Bangor JHS, 3281 KIESEL RD 48706 3-00100
Alan Slowinski, prin. 686-7640

Bay City SD, 910 N WALNUT ST 48706 7-11111
Joe Gonzales, supt. 686-9700
Central HS, 1624 COLUMBUS AVE 48708 4-00011
George Charles, prin. 893-9541
Handy MS, 601 BLEND ST 48706 4-00100
Patrick O'Toole, prin. 684-1723
Other Schools – See Auburn

All Saints HS, 217 S MONROE ST 48708 2-00011
Thomas Grange, prin. 892-2533
Great Lakes Junior College of Business 2-CC
3930 TRAXLER CT 686-1572
Holy Family S, 1503 22ND ST 48708 2-00100
Barbara Rakowski, prin. 892-8332
Northeastern School of Commerce 2-CS
701 N MADISON AVE 48708 893-4502

Bear Lake, AC 616, PC 2, Manistee
Bear Lake SD, PO BOX 188 49614 2-11111
James Brady, supt. 864-3133
JSHS, PO BOX 188 49614 2-00111
Harold Wingate, prin. 864-3133

Beaverton, AC 517, PC 4, Gladwin
Beaverton Rural SD, 406 ROSS ST 48612 4-11111
Thomas Randle, supt. 435-7771
HS, 440 ROSS ST 48612 3-00011
Samuel Bagnieski, prin. 435-7783
JHS, 106 TONKIN ST 48612 2-00100
W. Ashcroft, prin. 435-7774

Belding, AC 616, PC 6, Ionia
Belding Area SD, 321 WILSON ST 48809 5-11111
Bert Emerson, supt. 794-1960
JSHS, 850 HALL ST 48809 3-00111
Charles Barker, prin. 794-1976

Bellaire, AC 616, PC 4, Antrim
Bellaire SD 3-11111
204 W FORREST HOME AVE 49615 533-8141
John Hagel, supt.
JSHS 2-01111
204 W FORREST HOME AVE 49615 533-8015
Donald Vernon, prin.

Belleville, AC 313, PC 5, Wayne
Lincoln Consolidated SD
Supt. — See Ypsilanti
Lincoln JHS, 50700 WILLOW RD 48111 2-00100
David Storey, prin. 484-7033

VanBuren SD 6-11111
555 W COLUMBIA AVE 48111 697-9123
James Richendollar, supt.
HS, 501 W COLUMBIA AVE 48111 4-00011
Larry Tabor, prin. 697-9133
North MS, 47097 MCBRIDE AVE 48111 3-00100
William Sparrow, prin. 697-9171
South MS, 45201 OWEN ST 48111 3-00100
John Forsyth, prin. 697-8711

Michigan Institute of Aeronautics 2-CS
47884 D ST 48111 800-447-1310

Bellevue, AC 616, PC 4, Eaton
Bellevue Community SD 4-11111
201 WEST ST 49021 763-9432
William Kirby, supt.
HS, 575 LOVE HWY 49021 2-00011
(—), prin. 763-9413
MS, 904 W CAPITAL AVE 49021 2-01100
Bruce Johnson, prin. 763-9401

Benton Harbor, AC 616, PC 7, Berrien
Benton Harbor Area SD 6-11111
711 E BRITAIN AVE 49022 927-0600
Sherwin Allen, supt.
HS, 870 COLFAX AVE 49022 4-00011
(—), prin. 927-0616
Fair Plain JHS, 120 E NAPIER AVE 49022 2-00100
Donn Richardson, prin. 927-0658
King MS, 750 E BRITAIN AVE 49022 2-00100
Russell Tynes, prin. 927-0682
Mccord Renaissance MS 2-00100
465 S MCCORD ST 49022 927-0691
John Brown, prin.

Heathkit Educational Systems 49022 2-HMS
800-444-3284
Immanuel Christian S 2-11111
300 E NAPIER AVE 49022 925-6125
Karen Sanders, prin.
Jordan College-Berrien County Campus 2-UC
185 E MAIN ST 49022 927-3333
Lake Michigan College 4-CC
2755 E NAPIER AVE 49022 927-3571

Benzonia, AC 616, PC 2, Benzie
Benzie County Central SD 4-11111
9222 HOMESTEAD RD 49616 882-9654
David Micinski, supt.
Benzie Central JSHS 3-00111
9300 HOMESTEAD RD 49616 882-4497
Peter Olson, prin.

Berkley, AC 810, PC 7, Oakland
Berkley SD, 2211 OAKSHIRE AVE 48072 5-11111
C. Robert Maxfield, supt. 544-5800
HS, 2325 CATALPA DR 48072 4-00011
Jane Makulski, prin. 544-5850
Anderson MS, 3205 CATALPA DR 48072 3-00100
Janet Chanoine, prin. 544-5820
Other Schools – See Oak Park

Berrien Springs, AC 616, PC 4, Berrien
Berrien Springs SD 4-11111
1 SYLVESTER AVE 49103 471-2891
Tedd Morris, supt.
HS, 1 SYLVESTER AVE 49103 2-00011
David Paulson, prin. 471-1748
MS, 1 SYLVESTER AVE 49103 2-00100
Richard Bartz, prin. 471-2796

Andrews University 49104 4-UC
471-3100

Bessemer, AC 906, PC 4, Gogebic
Bessemer Area SD 3-11111
301 E SELLAR ST 49911 667-0802
Al Gaiss, supt.
Johnston HS, 100 W LEAD ST 49911 2-00011
Gary Gleason, prin. 667-0413

Beverly Hills, AC 810, PC 7, Oakland
Birmingham SD
Supt. — See Birmingham
Groves HS, 20500 W 13 MILE RD 48025 3-00011
Robert Lentz, prin. 433-8700

Big Rapids, AC 616, PC 7, Mecosta
Big Rapids SD 4-11111
500 N WARREN AVE 49307 796-2627
John Jeffery, supt.
HS, 500 N WARREN AVE 49307 3-00011
Linda Myers, prin. 796-7651
MS, 215 N STATE ST 49307 2-00100
James Van Hoven, prin. 796-9965

Ferris State University 7-UC
901 S STATE ST 49307 592-2000

Birch Run, AC 517, PC 3, Saginaw
Birch Run Area SD 4-11111
PO BOX 325 48415 624-9307
Margaret Mahaney, supt.
HS, PO BOX 325 48415 3-00011
Jerry Psotka, prin. 624-9392
Greene MS, PO BOX 325 48415 3-01100
Doug Rowley, prin. 624-5821

Birmingham, AC 810, PC 7, Oakland
Birmingham SD 6-11111
550 W MERRILL ST 48009 644-9300
John Hoeffler, supt.
Seaholm HS, 2436 W LINCOLN ST 48009 4-00011
Helene Mills, prin. 433-8400
Berkshire MS 3-00100
21707 W 14 MILE ROAD 48009 642-6606
Richard Durda, prin.
Derby MS, 1300 DERBY RD 48009 2-00100
Laura Smith, prin. 642-2440
Other Schools – See Beverly Hills, Bloomfield Hills

Detroit Country Day S 3-11111
22305 W THIRTEEN MILE RD 48025 646-7717
Brad Gilman, prin.

Blanchard, AC 517, PC 2, Isabella
Montabella Community SD
Supt. — See Edmore
Montabella HS 2-00011
1456 N COUNTY LINE RD 49310 427-5175
Lyle Thomas, prin.

Blissfield, AC 517, PC 5, Lenawee
Blissfield Community SD 4-11111
630 S LANE ST 49228 486-2205
Paul Palka, supt.
HS, 630 S LANE ST 49228 2-00011
David Thompson, prin. 486-2148
MS, 1305 BEAMER RD 49228 2-00100
Bette Kohler, prin. 486-4420

Bloomfield Hills, AC 810, PC 5, Oakland
Birmingham SD
Supt. — See Birmingham
Covington MS 2-00100
1525 COVINGTON RD 48301 642-6006
William Blackwell, prin.
West Maple MS 2-00100
6275 INKSTER RD 48301 851-8315
William Fredo, prin.

Bloomfield Hills SD 6-11111
4175 ANDOVER RD 48302 645-4500
W. Robert Docking, supt.
Andover HS, 4200 ANDOVER RD 48302 3-00011
John Toma, prin. 645-4600
Lahser HS, 3456 LAHSER RD 48302 3-00011
David Symington, prin. 339-3200

Model HS 2-00011
1661 HUNTERS RIDGE DR 48304 339-3470
Cindy Boughner, prin.
Bloomfield Hills MS 2-00100
4200 QUARTON RD 48302 932-6000
Gary Grossnickle, prin.
East Hills MS 2-00100
2800 KENSINGTON RD 48304 339-3400
Donald Hillman, prin.
Other Schools – See Orchard Lake

Academy of the Sacred Heart 2-11111
1250 KENSINGTON RD 48304 646-8900
Judy Bisignano, prin.
Brother Rice HS, 7101 LAHSER RD 48301 3-00011
Br. George Gremley, prin. 647-2526
Cranbrook Academy of Art 2-UC
PO BOX 801 48303 645-3300
Cranbrook S 2-11111
1221 N WOODWARD AVE 48304 645-3602
Daniel Behring, prin.
Marian HS, 7225 LAHSER RD 48301 2-00011
Sr. Mary Ohara, prin. 644-1750
Oakland Community College 7-CC
2480 OPDYKE RD 48304 540-1500
Roeper City & Country S 2-11111
PO BOX 329 48303 642-1500
Charles Webster, prin.

Bloomingdale, AC 616, PC 3, Van Buren
Bloomingdale SD, PO BOX 217 49026 4-11111
Thomas Hoke, supt. 521-3550
JSHS, PO BOX 217 49026 2-00111
Roger Tuinstra, prin. 521-3141

Boyne City, AC 616, PC 5, Charlevoix
Boyne City SD, PO BOX 289 49712 4-11111
Robert Nakoneczny, supt. 582-6503
HS, 1025 BOYNE AVE 49712 2-00011
Xavier Gaudard, prin. 582-6587
MS, 321 S PARK ST 49712 2-01100
Stephen Smith, prin. 582-9981

Boyne Falls, AC 616, PC 2, Charlevoix
Boyne Falls SD, PO BOX 356 49713 2-11111
Ruth Goldsmith, supt. 549-2211
S, PO BOX 356 49713 2-11111
Ruth Goldsmith, prin. 549-2212

Breckenridge, AC 517, PC 4, Gratiot
Breckenridge Community SD 4-11111
PO BOX 217 48615 842-3182
Dennis Hagey, supt.
JSHS, PO BOX 217 48615 3-00111
Rudy Godefroidt, prin. 842-3182

Brethren, AC 616, PC 2, Manistee
Kaleva-Norman-Dickson SD 3-11111
4400 N HIGH BRIDGE RD 49619 477-5353
Gregory Webster, supt.
JSHS, 4400 N HIGH BRIDGE RD 49619 2-00111
Wayne Bernier, prin. 477-5355

Bridgeport, AC 517, PC 5, Saginaw
Bridgeport-Spaulding Community SD 5-11111
PO BOX M 48722 777-1770
Marvin Hauck, supt.
HS, 6335 DIXIE HWY 48722 3-00011
Randall Danner, prin. 777-3100
Other Schools – See Saginaw

Bridgeport Baptist Academy 2-11111
2440 KING RD 48722 777-6811
William Swain, prin.

Bridgman, AC 616, PC 4, Berrien
Bridgman SD, 9964 GAST RD 49106 3-11111
Tom Smusz, supt. 465-5432
HS, 9964 GAST RD 49106 2-00011
Stewart Schofield, prin. 465-6848
Reed MS, 10254 CALIFORNIA 49106 2-01100
David Cunningham, prin. 465-5410

Brighton, AC 810, PC 6, Livingston
Brighton Area SD, 4740 BAUER RD 48116 6-11111
Dennis McMahon, supt. 229-1450
HS, 7878 BRIGHTON RD 48116 4-00011
Richard Bologna, prin. 229-1489
Maltby MS, 4740 BAUER RD 48116 3-00100
Rae McCall, prin. 229-1455
Scranton MS, 8415 MALTBY RD 48116 3-00100
Ken Hamman, prin. 229-1444

Ross Technical Institute 2-CS
5757 WHITMORE LAKE RD 48116 227-0160

Brimley, AC 906, PC 3, Chippewa
Brimley Area SD, PO BOX 156 49715 3-11111
Jacob Helms, supt. 248-3219
S, PO BOX 156 49715 3-11111
Walt Hyvarinen, prin. 248-3218

Britton, AC 517, PC 3, Lenawee
Britton-Macon Area SD 2-11111
201 COLLEGE AVE 49229 451-4581
Robert Tibo, supt.
Britton-Macon S 2-11111
201 COLLEGE AVE 49229 451-2805
Randy Salisbury, prin.

Bronson, AC 517, PC 4, Branch
Bronson Community SD 4-11111
501 E CHICAGO ST 49028 369-2015
James Thrall, supt.

JSHS, 450 E GRANT ST 49028 — 3-00111
  Norman Taylor, prin. — 369-2015

Brooklyn, AC 517, PC 4, Jackson
  Columbia SD, 11775 HEWITT RD 49230 — 4-11111
    Gary Allen, supt. — 592-6641
  Columbia HS, 11775 HEWITT RD 49230 — 3-00011
    Warren Wade, prin. — 592-6634
  Columbia MS, 321 SCHOOL ST 49230 — 2-00100
    Zachary Kanaan, prin. — 592-2181

Brown City, AC 313, PC 4, Sanilac
  Brown City Community SD — 4-11111
    4290 2ND ST 48416 — 346-2781
    Dennis Sidebottom, supt.
  JSHS, 4400 2ND ST 48416 — 2-00111
    Richard VanDrew, prin. — 346-2781

Buchanan, AC 616, PC 5, Berrien
  Buchanan Community SD — 4-11111
    401 W CHICAGO ST 49107 — 695-8401
    David Casey, supt.
  HS, 401 W CHICAGO ST 49107 — 3-00011
    William McBeth, prin. — 695-8403
  MS, 610 W 4TH ST 49107 — 2-00100
    William McBeth, prin. — 695-8406

Buckley, AC 616, PC 2, Wexford
  Buckley Community SD — 2-11111
    305 1ST ST 49620 — 269-3325
    William Howard, supt.
  S, 305 1ST ST 49620 — 2-11111
    Lawrence Davis, prin. — 269-3325

Burr Oak, AC 616, PC 3, St. Joseph
  Burr Oak Community SD — 2-11111
    PO BOX 337 49030 — 489-2213
    Terry Conklin, supt.
  S, PO BOX 337 49030 — 2-11111
    Terry Conklin, prin. — 489-5534

Burton, AC 810, PC 8, Genesee
  Atherton Community SD — 4-11111
    3354 S GENESEE RD 48519 — 742-0400
    Alvin Du Bois, supt.
  Atherton HS, 3354 S GENESEE RD 48519 — 2-00011
    Gerald Leahy, prin. — 742-0400
  Atherton MS, 3444 S GENESEE RD 48519 — 2-01100
    Bernard Romain, prin. — 742-0400

  Bendle SD — 4-11111
    2283 E SCOTTWOOD AVE 48529 — 742-2501
    John Angle, supt.
  Bendle SHS, 2294 E BRISTOL RD 48529 — 2-00001
    Robert Mills, prin. — 742-5103
  Lamb JHS, 4093 BARNES AVE 48529 — 2-00110
    William Parrish, prin. — 742-3385

  Bentley Community SD — 4-11111
    1223 S BELSAY RD 48509 — 742-4990
    Bruce Kefgen, supt.
  Bentley HS, 1150 N BELSAY RD 48509 — 2-00011
    George Gray, prin. — 742-5811
  Bentley MS, 1180 N BELSAY RD 48509 — 2-01100
    Judith Barrett, prin. — 743-9040

  Genesee Christian S — 2-11111
    1223 S BELSAY RD 48509 — 743-3108
    Dr. Shelpman, prin.
  More Academy — 2-11111
    6456 E BRISTOL RD 48519 — 742-2411
    Sr. Ellen Mullally, prin.
  Valley Christian Academy — 2-11111
    3266 S GENESEE RD 48519 — 742-4500
    Dale Farrell, prin.

Byron, AC 313, PC 3, Shiawassee
  Byron Area SD — 4-11111
    312 W MAPLE AVE 48418 — 266-4881
    Diane Scheerhorn, supt.
  HS, 312 W MAPLE AVE 48418 — 2-00011
    David Mitchell, prin. — 266-4620
  MS, 312 W MAPLE AVE 48418 — 2-00100
    Paul Fox, prin. — 266-4422

Byron Center, AC 616, PC 4, Kent
  Byron Center SD — 4-11111
    2475 84TH ST SW 49315 — 878-1541
    Philip Swainston, supt.
  HS — 2-00011
    8638 BYRON CENTER AVE SW 49315 — 878-1584
    William Skilling, prin.
  MS — 2-00100
    8542 BYRON CENTER AVE SW 49315 — 878-1543
    Tom Jeltes, prin.

Cadillac, AC 616, PC 7, Wexford
  Cadillac Area SD, 115 SOUTH ST 49601 — 5-11111
    Fred Carroll, supt. — 779-9300
  HS, 400 LINDEN ST 49601 — 3-00011
    Tom Jobson, prin. — 779-9371
  MS, 500 CHESTNUT ST 49601 — 3-00100
    Maynard Thompson, prin. — 779-9360

  Baker College of Cadillac — 2-UC
    9600 E 13TH ST 49601
  Heritage Christian S — 2-11111
    1706 WRIGHT ST 49601 — 775-4272
    Richard Roberts, prin.

Caledonia, AC 616, PC 3, Kent
  Caledonia Community SD — 5-11111
    203 E MAIN ST SE 49316 — 891-8185
    Robert Myers, supt.

  HS, 9757 DUNCAN LAKE AVE SE 49316 — 3-00011
    Tonya Porter, prin. — 891-8129
  MS, 9749 DUNCAN LAKE AVE SE 49316 — 3-00100
    Clark Volz, prin. — 891-8649

Calumet, AC 906, PC 3, Houghton
  Calumet SD, 102 CALUMET AVE 49913 — 4-11111
    Raymond Tiberg, supt. — 337-0311
  HS, 102 CALUMET AVE 49913 — 2-00011
    Bruce Grusecki, prin. — 337-0412
  Washington MS, CALUMET AVE 49913 — 2-01100
    Raymond Pomroy, prin. — 337-0211

Camden, AC 517, PC 2, Hillsdale
  Camden-Frontier SD — 3-11111
    4971 W MONTGOMERY RD 49232 — 368-5255
    Stanley DeVoir, supt.
  JSHS, 4971 W MONTGOMERY RD 49232 — 2-00111
    Bill Jedele, prin. — 368-5256

Canton, AC 313, PC 6, Wayne
  Plymouth-Canton Community SD
    Supt. — See Plymouth
  HS, 8415 N CANTON CENTER RD 48187 — 4-00011
    Thomas MacKenzie, prin. — 451-6600
  Salem HS, 46181 JOY RD 48187 — 4-00011
    Gerald Ostoin, prin. — 451-6600

  Plymouth Christian Academy — 3-11111
    43065 JOY RD 48187 — 459-3505

Capac, AC 810, PC 4, St. Clair
  Capac Community SD — 4-11111
    403 N GLASSFORD ST 48014 — 395-4321
    Mark Gaubatz, supt.
  JSHS, 541 N GLASSFORD ST 48014 — 3-00011
    Joseph Remenap, prin. — 395-4321

Carleton, AC 313, PC 5, Monroe
  Airport Community SD — 5-11111
    11270 GRAFTON RD 48117 — 654-2414
    James Orwin, supt.
  Airport HS, 11270 GRAFTON RD 48117 — 3-00011
    William Cheal, prin. — 654-6208
  Wagar MS, 11270 GRAFTON RD 48117 — 3-00100
    Gerald Bieniek, prin. — 654-6205

Carney, AC 906, PC 2, Menominee
  Carney-Nadeau SD, PO BOX 68 49812 — 2-11111
    Faye DeMarte, supt. — 639-2171
  Carney-Nadeau S, PO BOX 68 49812 — 2-11111
    Ronald Solberg, prin. — 639-2171

Caro, AC 517, PC 5, Tuscola
  Caro Community SD — 4-11111
    301 N HOOPER ST 48723 — 673-3166
    Dennis Anderson, supt.
  HS, 301 N HOOPER ST 48723 — 3-00011
    William Conway, prin. — 673-3166
  MS, 301 N HOOPER ST 48723 — 3-00100
    Robert DeBoer, prin. — 673-3166

  Great Lakes Junior College of Business — 2-CC
    1231 CLEAVER RD 48723 — 673-5857

Carrollton, AC 517, PC 6, Saginaw
  Carrollton SD, PO BOX 517 48724 — 4-11111
    Paul Novak, supt. — 754-1475
  Other Schools – See Saginaw

Carson City, AC 517, PC 4, Montcalm
  Carson City-Crystal Area SD — 4-11111
    115 E MAIN ST 48811 — 584-3138
    John Smith, supt.
  JSHS, 213 E SHERMAN ST 48811 — 3-00011
    Ron Gooding, prin. — 584-3175

Carsonville, AC 810, PC 3, Sanilac
  Carsonville-Port Sanilac SD — 3-11111
    100 N GOETZE 48419 — 657-9393
    Don Mueller, supt.
  Carsonville-Port Sanilac JSHS — 2-00111
    100 N GOETZE 48419 — 657-9394
    Gale Travis, prin.

Caseville, AC 517, PC 3, Huron
  Caseville SD, 6609 VINE ST 48725 — 2-11111
    James Stahl, supt. — 856-2940
  JSHS, 6609 VINE ST 48725 — 2-00111
    George Bednorek, prin. — 856-2311

Cass City, AC 517, PC 4, Tuscola
  Cass City SD, 4868 SEEGER ST 48726 — 4-11111
    Kenneth Micklash, supt. — 872-2200
  HS, 4868 SEEGER ST 48726 — 2-00011
    Russell Biefer, prin. — 872-2148
  MS, 4690 SEEGER ST 48726 — 3-01100
    Donald Schelke, prin. — 872-4397

  Jordan College-Thumb Area Campus — 2-UC
    6667 MAIN ST 48726 — 872-4394

Cassopolis, AC 616, PC 4, Cass
  Cassopolis SD, PO BOX 98 49031 — 4-11111
    John Ostrowski, supt. — 445-3861
  Beatty HS, PO BOX 98 49031 — 2-00011
    Bernard Abrams, prin. — 445-3861
  Adams MS, PO BOX 98 49031 — 2-01100
    Sandra Pompey, prin. — 445-3861

Cedar Lake, AC 517, PC 2, Montcalm

  Cedar Lake Academy — 2-00011
    PO BOX 68 48812 — 427-5181
    Ray Davis, prin.

Cedar Springs, AC 616, PC 5, Kent
  Cedar Springs SD — 5-11111
    204 E MUSKEGON 49319 — 696-1204
    Nyla Rypma, supt.
  HS, 204 E MUSKEGON 49319 — 3-00011
    Tom Popiel, prin. — 696-1200
  MS, 204 E MUSKEGON 49319 — 3-00100
    John Shear, prin. — 696-9100

  Jordan College — 4-UC
    360 PINE ST 49319 — 696-1180

Cedarville, AC 906, PC 4, Mackinac
  Les Cheneaux Community SD — 2-11111
    PO BOX 366 49719 — 484-2256
    Kenneth Drenth, supt.
  S, PO BOX 366 49719 — 2-11111
    John Duncan, prin. — 484-2256

Center Line, AC 810, PC 6, Macomb
  Centerline SD — 5-11111
    26400 ARSENAL ST 48015 — 757-7000
    Terry Follbaum, supt.
  HS, 26300 ARSENAL ST 48015 — 3-00011
    Lynda Bonucchi, prin. — 757-6660
  Wolfe MS, 8640 MCKINLEY ST 48015 — 3-00100
    Sue Gripton, prin. — 757-5880

  St. Clement S, 8155 RITTER ST 48015 — 3-11111
    Deborah Michon, prin. — 757-1737

Central Lake, AC 616, PC 3, Antrim
  Central Lake S, PO BOX 128 49622 — 2-11111
    C. Blamer, supt. — 544-3141
  JSHS, PO BOX 128 49622 — 2-00111
    Chet Budzynski, prin. — 544-3341

Centreville, AC 616, PC 4, St. Joseph
  Centreville SD, PO BOX 158 49032 — 3-11111
    Larry McConnell, supt. — 467-5220
  HS, 190 HOGAN ST 49032 — 2-00011
    Bill Miller, prin. — 467-5210
  MS, 190 HOGAN ST 49032 — 2-00100
    Barbara Lester, prin. — 467-5205

  Glen Oaks Community College — 3-CC
    62249 SHIMMEL RD 49032 — 467-9945

Charlevoix, AC 616, PC 5, Charlevoix
  Charlevoix SD — 4-11111
    208 W CLINTON ST 49720 — 547-3200
    Roberta Jackson, supt.
  HS, 108 E GARFIELD AVE 49720 — 2-00011
    David Smith, prin. — 547-3222
  MS, 204 GRANT ST 49720 — 2-00100
    Dennis Van Guilder, prin. — 547-3206

Charlotte, AC 517, PC 6, Eaton
  Charlotte SD, 378 STATE ST 48813 — 5-11111
    James Olin, supt. — 543-2810
  HS, 378 STATE ST 48813 — 4-00011
    Leland Wheaton, prin. — 543-4340
  MS, 301 HORATIO ST 48813 — 3-00100
    Kathy Tomlanovich, prin. — 543-6966

Chassell, AC 906, PC 3, Houghton
  Chassell Township SD — 2-11111
    PO BOX 140 49916 — 523-4691
    Daniel Bachman, supt.
  S, PO BOX 140 49916 — 2-11111
    Richard Hazzard, prin. — 523-4491

Cheboygan, AC 616, PC 6, Cheboygan
  Cheboygan Area SD — 4-11111
    PO BOX 100 49721 — 627-4436
    Gordon Van Wieren, supt.
  HS, 801 W LINCOLN AVE 49721 — 3-00011
    George Pike, prin. — 627-7191
  MS, 504 DIVISION ST 49721 — 2-00100
    Mark Dombrowski, prin. — 627-7103

Chelsea, AC 313, PC 5, Washtenaw
  Chelsea SD — 5-11111
    500 WASHINGTON ST 48118 — 475-9131
    Joseph Piasecki, supt.
  HS, 500 WASHINGTON ST 48118 — 3-00011
    Ronald Mead, prin. — 475-9131
  Beach MS, 445 MAYER DR 48118 — 3-00100
    D. Stielstra, prin. — 475-3717

Chesaning, AC 517, PC 5, Saginaw
  Chesaning UNSD, 820 S LINE ST 48616 — 4-11111
    Michael Dewey, supt. — 845-7020
  HS, 850 N 4TH ST 48616 — 3-00011
    C. Hahnenberg, prin. — 845-2040
  MS, 431 N 4TH ST 48616 — 3-01100
    Duane Ferry, prin. — 845-7040

Clare, AC 517, PC 5, Clare
  Clare SD, 201 E STATE ST 48617 — 4-11111
    John Leppanen, supt. — 386-9945
  HS, 306 SCHOOLCREST AVE 48617 — 2-00011
    Kim Kolbe, prin. — 386-7789
  MS, 209 E STATE ST 48617 — 2-01100
    Dennis Zyskowski, prin. — 386-9979

Clarkston, AC 810, PC 4, Oakland
  Clarkston Community SD — 6-11111
    PO BOX 1050 48347 — 625-4402
    Gary Haner, supt.
  SHS, 6595 MIDDLE LAKE RD 48346 — 4-00001
    Brent Cooley, prin. — 625-0900

Clarkston Vo-Tech School OTCNWC — Vo Tech
8211 BIG LAKE RD 48346 — 625-5202
Daniel Manthei, prin.
JHS, 6300 E CHURCH ST 48346 — 3-00110
Vincent Licata, prin. — 625-5361
Sashabow JHS — 3-00110
5565 PINE KNOB RD 48346 — 674-4169
Jean Lang, prin.

Clawson, AC 810, PC 7, Oakland
Clawson SD, 626 PHILLIPS AVE 48017 — 4-11111
Anthony Topoleski, supt. — 435-7500
HS, 101 JOHN M AVE 48017 — 3-00011
(—), prin. — 435-5520
MS, 150 JOHN M AVE 48017 — 2-00100
L. Ciepielowski, prin. — 435-5525

Climax, AC 616, PC 3, Kalamazoo
Climax-Scotts Community SD — 3-11111
372 S MAIN ST 49034 — 746-4211
Greg Mowen, supt.
Climax-Scotts HS, 372 S MAIN ST 49034 — 2-00011
Patrick Smith, prin. — 746-4212
Climax-Scotts MS, 372 S MAIN ST 49034 — 2-01100
James Hibbler, prin. — 746-4214

Clinton, AC 517, PC 4, Lenawee
Clinton Community SD — 4-11111
341 E MICHIGAN AVE 49236 — 456-7441
George Sargeant, supt.
HS, 340 E MICHIGAN AVE 49236 — 2-00011
James Duvall, prin. — 456-7040
MS, 120 E FRANKLIN ST 49236 — 2-01100
David Pray, prin. — 456-7267

St. Thomas More HS — 2-00111
8744 CLINTON MACON RD 49236 — 423-7451
Carl Lagore, prin.

Clinton Township, AC 810, PC 8, Macomb
Chippewa Valley SD — 6-11111
19120 CASS AVE 48038 — 228-5500
James Rivard, supt.
Chippewa Valley HS — 4-00011
18300 19 MILE RD 48038 — 228-5530
Al Diver, prin.
Algonquin MS — 3-00100
19150 BRIARWOOD LN 48036 — 954-2400
John Savel, prin.
Wyandot MS — 3-00100
39490 GARFIELD RD 48038 — 228-5600
Kathryn Dugall, prin.
Other Schools – See Macomb Township

Clintondale Community SD — 5-11111
35100 LITTLE MACK AVE 48035 — 791-6300
Raymond Contesti, supt.
Clintondale HS — 4-00011
35200 LITTLE MACK AVE 48035 — 791-6300
Mitchell Ritter, prin.
Clintondale MS — 3-00100
35300 LITTLE MACK AVE 48035 — 791-6300
Sheila Apisa, prin.

L'Anse Creuse SD
Supt. — See Harrison Township
Pankow Vo-Tech S — Vo Tech
24600 F V PANKOW 48036 — 469-4414
Chen-Lieh Chang, prin.

Baker College of Mount Clemens — 5-UC
34950 LITTLE MACK AVE 48035 — 791-6610
Macomb Community College — 4-CC
16500 HALL RD 48038
Ross Business Institute — 2-CS
37065 S GRATIOT AVE 48036 — 954-3083

Clio, AC 810, PC 5, Genesee
Clio Area SD, 430 N MILL ST 48420 — 5-11111
Albert Butler, supt. — 686-0500
HS, 1 MUSTANG DR 48420 — 4-00011
John Egloff, prin. — 686-4880
Carter MS, 300 UPLAND DR 48420 — 4-01100
Midge Dahle, prin. — 686-0503

Coldwater, AC 517, PC 6, Branch
Coldwater Community SD — 5-11111
175 S MICHIGAN AVE 49036 — 279-5910
William Chinery, supt.
HS, 275 N FREMONT ST 49036 — 3-00011
Bradford Mellor, prin. — 279-5930
Legg MS, 175 GREEN ST 49036 — 3-00100
Mitchell Zaleski, prin. — 279-5940

Coleman, AC 517, PC 4, Midland
Coleman Community SD — 4-11111
PO BOX W 48618 — 465-6060
Michael Smith, supt.
HS, PO BOX W 48618 — 2-00011
Cheryl Thomas, prin. — 465-6171
MS, PO BOX W 48618 — 2-00100
Richard Bradford, prin. — 465-6177

Coloma, AC 616, PC 4, Berrien
Coloma Community SD — 4-11111
PO BOX 550 49038 — 468-2424
Clifford Tallman, supt.
SHS, PO BOX 550 49038 — 3-00001
Harold Wheeler, prin. — 468-2400
JHS, PO BOX 550 49038 — 2-00110
John Sieber, prin. — 468-2405

Colon, AC 616, PC 4, St. Joseph
Colon Community SD — 4-11111
400 DALLAS ST 49040 — 432-3231
Roger Thelen, supt.
JSHS, 400 DALLAS ST 49040 — 2-00111
Dan Ruple, prin. — 432-3231

Commerce Township, AC 810, PC 5, Oakland
Walled Lake Consolidated SD
Supt. — See Walled Lake
Smart MS, 8500 COMMERCE RD 48382 — 3-00100
Lawrence Barlow, prin. — 363-4197

Comstock, AC 616, PC 6, Kalamazoo
Comstock SD, PO BOX 369 49041 — 5-11111
Robert Hamet, supt. — 388-9461
HS, 2107 N 26TH ST 49041 — 3-00011
Frank Stuckey, prin. — 388-9400
Northeast MS, 1424 N 28TH ST 49041 — 3-00100
Tim Fox, prin. — 388-9433

Comstock Park, AC 616, PC 6, Kent
Comstock Park SD — 4-11111
100 BETTY ST NE 49321 — 784-1740
James Van Dyk, supt.
HS, 150 6 MILE RD NE 49321 — 3-00011
Jonathan Prinz, prin. — 784-5255
Mill Creek MS, 100 BETTY ST NE 49321 — 2-00100
Byron Chitwood, prin. — 784-9847

Jordan Energy Institute — 2-UC
155 7 MILE RD NW 49321 — 784-7595

Concord, AC 517, PC 3, Jackson
Concord Community SD — 3-11111
405 S MAIN ST 49237 — 524-8850
John Sturock, supt.
HS, 219 MONROE ST 49237 — 2-00011
Gregory Huff, prin. — 524-8384
MS, 405 S MAIN ST 49237 — 2-00100
Marvelle Vannest, prin. — 524-8854

Constantine, AC 616, PC 4, St. Joseph
Constantine SD, 260 W 6TH ST 49042 — 4-11111
Ben Smith, supt. — 435-2015
HS, 260 W 6TH ST 49042 — 2-00011
Jack Deller, prin. — 435-2015
MS, 750 CANARIS ST 49042 — 2-00100
Rod Begaman, prin. — 435-2015

Cooks, AC 906, PC 2, Schoolcraft
Big Bay de Noc SD — 2-11111
HC 1 BOX 62 49817 — 644-2773
Sally Gerometta, supt.
Big Bay de Noc S — 2-11111
HC 1 BOX 62 49817 — 644-2773
Lee Potvin, prin.

Coopersville, AC 616, PC 5, Ottawa
Coopersville SD, 198 EAST ST 49404 — 4-11111
Robert Fortin, supt. — 837-8131
HS, 198 EAST ST 49404 — 3-00011
Ross Conran, prin. — 837-9753
MS, 198 EAST ST 49404 — 2-00100
Tom Fox, prin. — 837-9796

Corunna, AC 517, PC 5, Shiawassee
Corunna SD — 4-11111
106 S SHIAWASSEE ST 48817 — 743-6338
Duane Ash, supt.
HS, 417 E KING ST 48817 — 3-00011
Richard Ames, prin. — 743-3441
MS, 400 N COMSTOCK ST 48817 — 3-00100
Richard Ziegler, prin. — 743-5817

Covert, AC 616, PC 3, Van Buren
Covert SD, 35323 M 140 49043 — 3-11111
A. Hawkins, supt. — 764-0200
HS, 35323 M 140 49043 — 2-00011
Gus Calbert, prin. — 764-0230

Croswell, AC 810, PC 4, Sanilac
Croswell-Lexington SD — 4-11111
5407 PECK RD 48422 — 679-2232
Gary Davis, supt.
Croswell-Lexington HS — 3-00011
5461 PECK RD 48422 — 679-3555
Erik Bergh, prin.
Croswell-Lexington MS — 3-01100
5485 PECK RD 48422 — 679-3536
John Ferda, prin.

Crystal Falls, AC 906, PC 4, Iron
Forest Park SD, 801 FOREST PKY 49920 — 3-11111
Eugene Dziubinski, supt. — 875-6761
Forest Park JSHS — 2-00111
801 FOREST PKY 49920 — 875-6869
Therese Peterson, prin.

Custer, AC 616, PC 2, Mason
Mason County Eastern SD — 3-11111
PO BOX 111 49405 — 757-3733
Ronald Nurnberger, supt.
Mason County Eastern JSHS — 2-00111
18 S MAIN ST 49405 — 757-3734
Dana McGrew, prin.

Dansville, AC 517, PC 2, Ingham
Dansville SD, 1264 ADAMS ST 48819 — 3-11111
C. Dean Atkins, supt. — 623-6129
HS, 1264 ADAMS ST 48819 — 2-00011
Jerry Allen, prin. — 623-6141
MS, 1264 ADAMS ST 48819 — 2-00100
Roger Pollok, prin. — 623-6108

Davison, AC 810, PC 6, Genesee
Davison Community SD — 5-11111
615 E CLARK ST 48423 — 653-3531
Robert Hahn, supt.
HS, 1250 N OAK RD 48423 — 4-00011
Richard Ramsey, prin. — 653-3531
JHS, 600 S DAYTON ST 48423 — 4-00100
Carole Burley, prin. — 653-3531

Faith Baptist S — 2-11111
7306 E ATHERTON RD 48423 — 653-9661
Lawrence Nagengast, prin.

Dearborn, AC 313, PC 8, Wayne
Dearborn SD, 18700 AUDETTE ST 48124 — 7-11111
Jeremy Hughes, supt. — 730-0224
HS, 19501 OUTER DR 48124 — 4-00011
Ann Superko, prin. — 730-3074
Ford HS, 20601 ROTUNDA DR 48124 — 4-00011
Gerald Dodd, prin. — 271-8237
Fordson HS, 13800 FORD RD 48126 — 4-00011
Barbara O'Brien, prin. — 582-4359
Bryant MS, 460 N VERNON ST 48128 — 3-00100
Karl Stuef, prin. — 730-3050
Smith MS, 23851 YALE ST 48124 — 2-00100
Gary Ashcroft, prin. — 730-3185
Stout MS — 2-00100
18500 OAKWOOD BLVD 48124 — 271-8093
John Cotter, prin.

Detroit College of Business — 5-UC
4801 OAKMAN BLVD 48126 — 581-4400
Divine Child HS — 3-00011
1001 N SILVERY LN 48128 — 562-9058
Sr. Mary Sabalausky, prin.
Ford Community College — 6-CC
5101 EVERGREEN RD 48128 — 845-9650
Oakwood Hospital — HSP
PO BOX 2500 48123 — 593-7005
St. Alphonsus HS — 2-00011
7265 CALHOUN ST 48126 — 582-4266
John Rashid, prin.
University of Michigan-Dearborn — 6-UC
4901 EVERGREEN RD 48128 — 593-5000

Dearborn Heights, AC 313, PC 8, Wayne
Crestwood SD — 5-11111
1501 N BEECH DALY RD 48127 — 278-0903
Oscar Brown, supt.
Crestwood HS — 3-00011
1501 N BEECH DALY RD 48127 — 278-0900
Michael Bee, prin.
Riverside MS — 3-01100
25900 W WARREN ST 48127 — 274-0140
Gregory Pratt, prin.

Dearborn Heights SD 7 — 4-11111
20629 ANNAPOLIS ST 48125 — 278-1900
(—), supt.
Annapolis HS, 4650 CLIPPERT ST 48125 — 3-00011
Michael Vogel, prin. — 278-9870
Best JHS, 22201 POWERS AVE 48125 — 2-00100
William Nickel, prin. — 278-6200

Westwood Community SD
Supt. — See Inkster
Robichaud JSHS, 3601 JANET ST 48125 — 3-00111
Robert Yauch, prin. — 565-1900

Decatur, AC 616, PC 4, Van Buren
Decatur SD, 110 CEDAR ST 49045 — 4-11111
Ronald Chapman, supt. — 423-6111
JSHS, 110 CEDAR ST 49045 — 2-00111
Don Prediger, prin. — 423-6134

Deckerville, AC 810, PC 4, Sanilac
Deckerville Community SD — 4-11111
2633 BLACK RIVER ST 48427 — 376-3615
Tim Edwards, supt.
JSHS, 2633 BLACK RIVER ST 48427 — 2-00111
Alan Broughton, prin. — 376-3875

Deerfield, AC 517, PC 3, Lenawee
Deerfield SD — 2-11111
252 DEERFIELD ROAD 49238 — 447-3215
John McEwan, supt.
S, 252 DEERFIELD ROAD 49238 — 2-11111
Edward Osnowitz, prin. — 447-3015

Delton, AC 616, PC 2, Barry
Delton-Kellogg SD — 4-11111
327 N GROVE ST 49046 — 623-9246
M. Dean McBeth, supt.
Delton-Kellogg HS — 3-00011
327 N GROVE ST 49046 — 623-9226
Paul Blacken, prin.
Delton-Kellogg MS — 3-01100
327 N GROVE ST 49046 — 623-9251
Gary Kimble, prin.

De Tour Village, AC 906, PC 2, Chippewa
De Tour Village Area SD — 2-11111
PO BOX 68 49725 — 297-2421
Lon McCollum, supt.
JSHS, PO BOX 68 49725 — 2-00111
Richard Roan, prin. — 297-2011

Detroit, AC 313, PC 12, Wayne
Detroit SD — 9-11111
5057 WOODWARD AVE 48202 — 494-1000
David Snead, supt.
Cass Technical HS, 2421 2ND AVE 48201 — 5-00011
(—), prin. — 494-2605

Central HS, 2425 TUXEDO ST 48206 4-00011
  William Jenifer, prin. 252-3000
Chadsey HS, 5335 MARTIN ST 48210 4-00011
  Alexis Rowan, prin. 494-2381
Cody HS, 18445 CATHEDRAL ST 48228 4-00011
  Mackie Bradford, prin. 270-0529
Cooley HS, 15055 HUBBELL ST 48227 4-00011
  Posey Williams, prin. 270-0012
Denby HS, 12800 KELLY RD 48224 4-00011
  Ellword Miller, prin. 245-3200
Finney HS 4-00011
  17200 SOUTHAMPTON ST 48224 245-3325
  Carl Stone, prin.
Ford HS, 20000 EVERGREEN RD 48219 4-00011
  Elijah Porter, prin. 494-7567
Kettering HS, 6101 VAN DYKE 48213 4-00011
  Henry McKee, prin. 866-5336
King HS, 3200 E LAFAYETTE ST 48207 4-00011
  Beverly Gray, prin. 494-1802
MacKenzie HS 4-00011
  9275 WYOMING ST 48204 270-0454
  Joseph Gilbert, prin.
Mumford HS 4-00011
  17525 WYOMING ST 48221 270-0430
  Robin Oden, prin.
Murray-Wright HS 4-00011
  2001 W WARREN AVE 48208 494-2553
  Sally Polk, prin.
Northern HS 4-00011
  9026 WOODWARD AVE 48202 494-2625
  Walter Jenkins, prin.
Northwestern HS 4-00011
  2200 W GRAND BLVD 48208 895-1865
  Marian Sutton, prin.
Osborn HS, 11600 E 7 MILE RD 48205 4-00011
  Mamie Humphrey, prin. 245-3353
Pershing HS, 18875 RYAN RD 48234 4-00011
  Emeral Crosby, prin. 252-3257
Redford HS 5-00011
  21431 GRAND RIVER AVE 48219 494-7500
  Walter Mclean, prin.
Renaissance HS 3-00011
  6565 W OUTER DR 48235 270-0409
  Erma Hamilton, prin.
Southeastern HS 3-00011
  3030 FAIRVIEW ST 48214 245-3225
  Claudia Hamilton, prin.
Southwestern HS 4-00011
  6921 W FORT ST 48209 849-4521
  Betty Hines, prin.
Western HS, 1500 SCOTTEN ST 48209 4-00011
  Gloria Clark-Arnold, prin. 849-4758
Breithaupt Vo Ctr Vo Tech
  9300 HUBBELL ST 48228 270-0238
  Paula Marable, prin.
Crockett Vo-Tech S Vo Tech
  571 MACK AVE 48201 494-1805
  Rowena Ayala, prin.
Golightly Vo-Tech S Vo Tech
  900 DICKERSON ST 48215 822-4090
  L. Peoples, prin.
Randolph Vo-Tech S Vo Tech
  17101 HUBBELL ST 48235 863-6300
  Jerome Shepard, prin.
Barbour Magnet MS 4-00100
  4209 SENECA ST 48214 245-3472
  Randall Moody, prin.
Beaubien JHS 3-00110
  19701 WYOMING ST 48221 270-0314
  David Porter, prin.
Boynton MS, 12800 VISGER ST 48217 3-00100
  Vernon Nimocks, prin. 849-2776
Brooks MS, 16101 W CHICAGO ST 48228 3-00100
  Calvin McKinney, prin. 270-0287
Burbank MS 3-00100
  15600 E STATE FAIR ST 48205 245-3571
  Robert Remesz, prin.
Burroughs MS, 8950 SAINT CYRIL 48213 3-00100
  Susan Meczkowski, prin. 245-3425
Butzel MS, 2301 VAN DYKE ST 48214 2-00110
  Napoleon Jordan, prin. 245-3446
Cadillac MS 3-00100
  15125 SCHOOLCRAFT ST 48227 270-0157
  Jacqueline Miller, prin.
Cerveny JHS 3-00110
  15850 STRATHMOOR ST 48227 270-0520
  Nathanial Washington, prin.
Cleveland MS, 13322 CONANT ST 48212 3-00100
  Toni Brooks, prin. 252-3206
Coffey MS 3-00100
  17210 CAMBRIDGE AVE 48235 270-0192
  Janis Lindsay, prin.
Columbus MS, 18025 BROCK ST 48205 3-00100
  Raymond Hughes, prin. 245-3576
Drew MS, 9600 WYOMING ST 48204 3-00100
  James Lee, prin. 270-0279
Earhart MS, 1000 SCOTTEN ST 48209 3-00100
  Rosa Williams, prin. 849-3946
Farwell MS, 19955 FENELON ST 48234 3-00100
  Herbert Williams, prin. 252-3179
Guest MS, 10825 FENKELL ST 48238 3-01100
  Janet Kincannon, prin. 873-9605
Hally MS, 2585 GROVE ST 48221 3-00100
  James Bateman, prin. 270-0152
Hamilton MS 3-00100
  14223 SOUTHAMPTON ST 48213 245-3507
  Annette Temple, prin.
Hampton JHS, 3900 PICKFORD ST 48221 3-00110
  Ella Taylor, prin. 494-7070

Hutchins MS 3-00100
  8820 WOODROW WILSON ST 48206 494-2123
  Jessye Franklin, prin.
Jackson MS 3-00100
  4180 MARLBOROUGH ST 48215 245-3487
  David White, prin.
Joy MS, 4611 FAIRVIEW ST 48214 3-00100
  Rosalyn Whitehead, prin. 245-3514
Knudsen JHS, 2600 LELAND ST 48207 2-00110
  James Foster, prin. 245-3500
Lessenger MS, 8401 TRINITY ST 48228 3-00100
  Jean Nash, prin. 849-2357
Longfellow MS 2-00100
  13141 ROSA PARKS BLVD 48238 252-3249
  Shirley Lusby, prin.
Ludington MS 3-01100
  19355 EDINBOROUGH RD 48219 494-7578
  Edward Williams, prin.
McMichael MS 3-00100
  6050 LINWOOD ST 48208 494-2651
  Delma Boyce, prin.
Miller MS, 2322 DUBOIS ST 48207 3-00110
  Pierre Hendrix, prin. 494-2641
Munger MS, 5525 MARTIN ST 48210 3-00100
  Roscoe McKnight, prin. 494-2647
Murphy JHS, 23901 FENKELL ST 48223 3-00110
  Alvin Jackson, prin. 494-7585
Nolan MS, 1150 E LANTZ ST 48203 3-00100
  Carol Gray, prin. 252-3195
Parks MS, 8030 E OUTER DR 48213 3-00100
  Sadie Mahone, prin. 245-3434
Pelham MS, 2001 MYRTLE ST 48208 2-00100
  Rosa Jackson, prin. 494-2556
Post JHS, 8200 MIDLAND ST 48238 2-00110
  John Harris, prin. 270-0301
Robinson MS, 13000 ESSEX AVE 48215 3-00100
  Charles Washington, prin. 245-3461
Ruddiman MS 3-00100
  7350 SOUTHFIELD FWY 48228 849-2771
  James Stephens, prin.
Taft MS, 19501 BERG RD 48219 3-00100
  Paul Gray, prin. 494-7577
Von Steuben MS 3-00100
  12300 LINNHURST ST 48205 245-3588
  Jerry Green, prin.
Webber MS, 4700 TIREMAN ST 48204 3-01100
  William Porter, prin. 494-2437
Wilson MS, 7735 LANE ST 48209 2-00100
  Florine Calhoun, prin. 849-2419
Young MS, 2757 MACOMB ST 48207 3-00100
  Bernice Waddles, prin. 494-2416
Other Schools – See Redford

Benedictine HS 2-00011
  8001 W OUTER DR 48235 532-1274
  Sr. Jacquelyn Murray, prin.
Center for Creative Studies 3-UC
  201 E KIRBY ST 48202 872-3118
Center for Humanistic Studies 1-UC
  40 E FERRY ST 48202 875-7440
Chauffeurs Training School 1-CS
  14601 DEQUINDRE ST 48212 883-2200
Detroit Business Institute 4-CS
  115 STATE ST 48226 962-6534
Detroit College of Law 3-UC
  130 E ELIZABETH ST 48201 965-0150
Detroit Institute Ophthalmology 1-CS
  15415 E JEFFERSON AVE 48230 824-4800
Dominican Academy 2-00100
  9740 MCKINNEY ST 48224 882-9409
  Sr. Joan Weitz, prin.
Dominican HS 2-00011
  9740 MCKINNEY ST 48224 882-8500
  Sr. Joan Weitz, prin.
East Catholic HS 2-00011
  7320 SAINT ANTHONY PL 48213 921-9650
  Sr. Jeanette Salbert, prin.
Evangel Christian Academy 2-11111
  11055 GLENFIELD 48213 839-7650
  Susan Conti, prin.
Grace Hospital HSP
  18700 MEYERS RD 48235 966-3363
Harper-Grace Hospital HSP
  3990 JOHN R ST 48201 745-4330
Henry Ford Hospital HSP
  2799 W GRAND BLVD 48202 972-1928
Holy Redeemer HS 2-00011
  5668 BAKER ST 48209 841-4433
  Peter Neill, prin.
Jordan College-Detroit Campus 2-UC
  15400 GRAND RIVER AVE 48227 835-5100
Krainz Woods Academy of Medical Tech. 1-CS
  4327 E 7 MILE RD 48234 366-5204
Lewis College of Business 2-CC
  17370 MEYERS RD 48235 862-6300
Lutheran HS West 2-00111
  8181 GREENFIELD RD 48228 584-3621
  Rev. Brant Engel, prin.
Lutheran School for the Deaf HND
  6661 E NEVADA ST 48234
Marygrove College 4-UC
  8425 W MCNICHOLS RD 48221 862-8000
Michigan Career Institute 3-CS
  14520 GRATIOT AVE 48205 526-6600
NEC-Bryman Campus 2-CS
  4244 OAKMAN BLVD 48204 834-1400
Payne-Pulliam School of Trade & Commerce 2-CS
  2345 CASS AVE 48201 963-4710
Ross Medical Education Center 2-CS
  15670 E 8 MILE RD 48205 371-2131

Ross Technical Institute 2-CS
  1553 WOODWARD AVE STE 650 48226
    965-7451
Sacred Heart Major Seminary 2-UC
  2701 W CHICAGO 48206 883-8500
St. John's Hospital HSP
  22101 MOROSS RD 48236 343-3301
St. Martin DePorres HS 2-00011
  13436 GROVE ST 48235 864-3330
  Sunbeam Hughes, prin.
St. Vincent MS, 2020 14TH ST 48216 2-01100
  Kathleen McBride, prin. 961-6773
SER Business and Technical Institute 2-CS
  9301 MICHIGAN AVE 48210 846-2240
Southeast Michigan Red Cross Blood Ctr. HSP
  PO BOX 33351 48232 494-2730
Trinity Christian S 2-11111
  9540 BRAMELL 48239 255-5760
  Michael Holiday, prin.
University of Detroit Jesuit HS 3-00111
  8400 S CAMBRIDGE AVE 48221 862-5400
  John Findlater, prin.
University of Detroit-Mercy 5-UC
  PO BOX 19900 48219 993-1245
Wayne County Community College 6-CC
  801 W FORT ST 48226 496-2510
Wayne State University 7-UC
  5980 CASS AVE 48202 577-2230

DeWitt, AC 517, PC 5, Clinton

Dewitt SD, PO BOX 800 48820 4-11111
  John Cook, supt. 669-2260
HS, 2957 W HERBISON RD 48820 3-00011
  Fred Goers, prin. 669-2240
MS, 3147 W HERBISON RD 48820 2-00100
  Cynthia Sager, prin. 669-2280

Dexter, AC 313, PC 4, Washtenaw

Dexter Comm. SD 4-11111
  2615 BAKER RD 48130 426-4623
  John Hansen, supt.
HS, 2615 BAKER RD 48130 3-00011
  David Messner, prin. 426-3991
Wylie MS, 3060 KENSINGTON ST 48130 3-01100
  David Mills, prin. 426-3993

Dollar Bay, AC 906, PC 3, Houghton

Osceola Township SD 2-11111
  PO BOX 371 49922 482-5800
  Harvey Filppula, supt.
JSHS, PO BOX 371 49922 2-00111
  Mike Maino, prin. 482-5812

Dowagiac, AC 616, PC 6, Cass

Dowagiac UNSD, 206 MAIN ST 49047 5-11111
  Ronald Jones, supt. 782-4400
Union HS 3-00011
  701 W PRAIRIE RONDE ST 49047 782-4420
  Michael Swartz, prin.
Central MS, 520 MAIN ST 49047 2-00100
  Ron Walsworth, prin. 782-4440

Southwestern Michigan College 4-CC
  58900 CHERRY GROVE RD 49047 782-5113

Dryden, AC 810, PC 3, Lapeer

Dryden Community SD 3-11111
  3866 ROCHESTER RD 48428 796-2266
  Christopher Wigent, supt.
JSHS, 3866 ROCHESTER RD 48428 2-00111
  Ruth Fox, prin. 796-2266

Dundee, AC 313, PC 5, Monroe

Dundee Community SD 4-11111
  420 YPSILANTI ST 48131 529-2350
  Albert Widner, supt.
HS, 420 YPSILANTI ST 48131 2-00011
  C. Schankin, prin. 529-2350
MS, 420 YPSILANTI ST 48131 2-01100
  Sue Gaudet, prin. 529-2350

Durand, AC 517, PC 5, Schiawassee

Durand Area SD 4-11111
  310 N SAGINAW ST 48429 288-2681
  Gary Hughes, supt.
HS, 9575 MONROE RD 48429 3-00011
  Robert Doctor, prin. 288-3468
Lucas MS, 100 SYCAMORE ST 48429 2-00100
  Barbara Hoevel, prin. 288-3435

East Detroit, AC 810, PC 8, Macomb

NEC-National Institute of Technology 2-CS
  15115 DEERFIELD AVE 48021 313-779-5530

East Jordan, AC 616, PC 4, Charlevoix

East Jordan SD, PO BOX 638 49727 4-11111
  Robert Hansen, supt. 536-3131
HS, 240 S MAPLE ST 49727 2-00011
  Gus Bishop, prin. 536-2259
MS, 304 4TH ST 49727 2-00100
  Evior Swan, prin. 536-2823

East Lansing, AC 517, PC 8, Ingham

East Lansing SD 5-11111
  509 BURCHAM DR 48823 337-1781
  William Mitchell, supt.
HS, 509 BURCHAM DR 48823 4-00011
  Doris Walker, prin. 332-2545
Hannah MS, 819 ABBOTT AVE 48823 2-00100
  John Fitzpatrick, prin. 337-6462
MacDonald MS 2-00100
  1601 BURCHAM DR 48823 337-6582
  John Fitzpatrick, prin.

Educational Inst./American Hotel-Motel 2-HMS
  PO BOX 1240 48826 353-5500
Michigan State University 8-UC
  450 ADMINISTRATION BLDG 48824 355-6560

Eastpointe, AC 810, PC 8, Macomb
East Detroit SD 6-11111
  19200 STEPHENS DR 48021 445-4410
  John Gardiner, supt.
East Detroit HS 4-00011
  15501 COUZENS AVE 48021 445-4455
  James Bannan, prin.
Kelly JHS, 24701 KELLY RD 48021 3-00100
  Werner Schroeder, prin. 445-4570
Oakwood JHS, 14825 NEHLS AVE 48021 3-00100
  Gerald Lecureux, prin. 445-4600

Eaton Rapids, AC 517, PC 5, Eaton
Eaton Rapids SD, 501 KING ST 48827 5-11111
  Michael Rocca, supt. 663-8155
HS, 800 STATE ST 48827 3-00011
  Robert Lange, prin. 663-2231
MS, 301 GREYHOUND DR 48827 3-00100
  Richard Williams, prin. 663-8155

Eau Claire, AC 616, PC 2, Berrien
Eau Claire SD, PO BOX 398 49111 3-11111
  David Gray, supt. 461-6947
JSHS, 7450 HOCHBERGER RD 49111 2-00111
  Lary Schlaack, prin. 461-6997

Eben Junction, AC 906, PC 2, Alger
Superior Central SD 2-11111
  PO BOX 148 49825 439-5531
  Tony McLain, supt.
Superior Central HS 2-00111
  PO BOX 148 49825 439-5532
  Gerald Lasak, prin.

Ecorse, AC 313, PC 7, Wayne
Ecorse SD, 27385 W OUTER DR 48229 4-11111
  Emma Epps, supt. 382-6320
HS, 4165 7TH ST 48229 2-00011
  Freeman Moore, prin. 382-6320
Kennedy MS, 27225 W OUTER DR 48229 2-00100
  Paul Dallman, prin. 382-6320

Edmore, AC 517, PC 4, Montcalm
Montabella Community SD 4-11111
  302 W MAIN ST 48829 427-5148
  Dian Shaw, supt.
Montabella MS, 300 W MAIN ST 48829 2-00100
  Ronald Farrell, prin. 427-5414
Other Schools – See Blanchard

Edwardsburg, AC 616, PC 4, Cass
Edwardsburg SD 4-11111
  69410 SECTION ST 49112 663-3055
  James Bermingham, supt.
HS, 69410 SECTION ST 49112 3-00011
  S. Ostrander, prin. 663-3055
JHS, 69410 SECTION ST 49112 2-00100
  Curtis Meek, prin. 663-3055

Elk Rapids, AC 616, PC 4, Antrim
Elk Rapids SD, 707 E 3RD 49629 4-11111
  Elmer Peterman, supt. 264-8692
HS, 308 MEGUZEE PT 49629 2-00111
  S. Gallagher, prin. 264-8108
Cherryland MS, 707 E 3RD 49629 2-00100
  T. Morris, prin. 264-8991

Ellsworth, AC 616, PC 2, Antrim
Ellsworth Community SD 2-11111
  PO BOX 68 49729 588-6148
  Richard Diebold, supt.
S, PO BOX 68 49729 2-11111
  Marvin Ruis, prin. 588-2544

Elsie, AC 517, PC 3, Clinton
Ovid-Elsie Area SD 4-11111
  8989 E COLONY RD 48831 834-2271
  Wayne Petroelje, supt.
Ovid-Elsie HS 3-00011
  8989 E COLONY RD 48831 834-2271
  Kirk Baese, prin.
Ovid-Elsie MS 2-00100
  8989 E COLONY RD 48831 834-2271
  Lyle Howard, prin.

Engadine, AC 906, PC 3, Mackinac
Engadine Consolidated SD 2-11111
  RR 1 BOX 1 49827 477-6313
  R. Leveille, supt.
JSHS, RR 1 BOX 1 49827 2-00111
  John Bertucci, prin. 477-6449

Erie, AC 313, PC 3, Monroe
Mason Consolidated SD 4-11111
  2400 LAKESIDE RD 48133 848-4849
  R. W. Kackmeister, supt.
Mason HS, 2400 LAKESIDE RD 48133 2-00011
  L. Meeker, prin. 848-5755
Mason MS, 2400 LAKESIDE RD 48133 2-00100
  James Seiber, prin. 848-4944

Escanaba, AC 906, PC 7, Delta
Escanaba Area SD, 111 N 5TH ST 49829 5-11111
  Thomas Smith, supt. 786-5411
HS, 500 S LINCOLN RD 49829 4-00011
  James Hansen, prin. 786-6521
MS, 1500 LUDINGTON ST 49829 3-00100
  Robert Koski, prin. 786-7462

Bay de Noc Community College 4-CC
  2001 N LINCOLN RD 49829 786-5802

Essexville, AC 517, PC 5, Bay
Hampton SD, 303 PINE ST 48732 4-11111
  Robert Winters, supt. 894-9700
Garber HS, 213 PINE ST 48732 3-00011
  Daniel Harfst, prin. 894-9710
Cramer JHS, 313 PINE ST 48732 2-00100
  Brian Malcho, prin. 894-9740

Evart, AC 616, PC 4, Osceola
Evart SD, 139 N MAIN 49631 4-11111
  Joseph Curtin, supt. 734-5594
JSHS, 321 N HEMLOCK ST 49631 3-00111
  Steve Howell, prin. 734-5551

Ewen, AC 906, PC 3, Ontonagon
Ewen-Trout Creek SD 3-11111
  PO BOX 218 49925 988-2364
  Ray Rigoni, supt.
Ewen-Trout Creek JSHS 2-00111
  PO BOX 218 49925 988-2365
  Russell Bailey, prin.

Fairgrove, AC 517, PC 3, Tuscola
Akron-Fairgrove SD 3-11111
  1933 LIBERTY ST 48733 693-6163
  Kenneth Tahfs, supt.
Akron-Fairgrove JSHS 2-00111
  2800 N THOMAS RD 48733 693-6112
  James Ross, prin.

Fairview, AC 517, PC 3, Oscoda
Fairview Area SD 2-11111
  1879 E MILLER RD 48621 848-2480
  Genevieve Troyer, supt.
JSHS, 1879 E MILLER RD 48621 2-00111
  James Slasinski, prin. 848-2480

Farmington, AC 810, PC 7, Oakland
Farmington SD 7-11111
  32500 SHIAWASSEE ST 48336 489-3339
  Michael Flanagan, supt.
HS, 32000 SHIAWASSEE ST 48336 4-00011
  James Myers, prin. 489-3455
Harrison HS, 29995 W 12 MILE RD 48334 3-00011
  Rande Horne, prin. 489-3499
North Farmington HS 4-00011
  32900 W 13 MILE RD 48334 489-3535
  Deborah Clarke, prin.
Dunckel MS, 32800 W 12 MILE RD 48334 3-00100
  Buhl Burton, prin. 489-3577
East MS, 25000 MIDDLEBELT RD 48336 3-00100
  William Martin, prin. 489-3601
Power MS 3-00100
  34740 RHONSWOOD ST 48335 489-3622
  Laura Miner, prin.
Warner MS, 30303 W 14 MILE RD 48334 3-00100
  Darlene Russell, prin. 489-3636

Mercy HS, 29300 W 11 MILE RD 48336 3-00011
  Sr. Regina Doelker, prin. 476-8020

Farmington Hills, AC 313, PC 8, Oakland

Oakland Community College 4-CC
  27055 ORCHARD LAKE RD 48334 471-7500
William Tyndale College 2-UC
  35700 W 12 MILE RD 48331 553-7200

Farwell, AC 517, PC 3, Clare
Farwell Area SD, 395 E MAIN ST 48622 4-11111
  Thomas Pelon, supt. 588-9917
HS, 399 MICHIGAN ST 48622 2-00011
  John Maxwell, prin. 588-9913
MS, 500 E OHIO ST 48622 2-01100
  Kenneth Richardson, prin. 588-9915

Fennville, AC 616, PC 4, Allegan
Fennville SD, PO BOX 1 49408 4-11111
  Robert Hickman, supt. 561-5045
JSHS, PO BOX 2 49408 3-00111
  David Smith, prin. 561-8161

Fenton, AC 810, PC 6, Genesee
Fenton Area SD, 3100 OWEN RD 48430 5-11111
  Robert Burek, supt. 629-2268
HS, 3200 W SHIAWASSEE AVE 48430 3-00011
  Kenneth Wensel, prin. 629-4167
MS, 404 W ELLEN ST 48430 3-00100
  Neil McPhee, prin. 629-4189

Lake Fenton Community SD 4-11111
  11425 TORREY RD 48430 629-4141
  Gerald Laskey, supt.
Lake Fenton HS 2-00011
  11425 TORREY RD 48430 629-5331
  Jerry Kramer, prin.
Torrey Hills MS 2-01100
  12410 TORREY RD 48430 629-5303
  Arlene Schaefer, prin.

Ferndale, AC 810, PC 8, Oakland
Ferndale SD, 725 PINECREST DR 48220 5-11111
  W. G. Coyne, supt. 547-2202
HS, 881 PINECREST DR 48220 4-00011
  Edward Griffen, prin. 548-8600
Coolidge MS, 2521 BERMUDA ST 48220 2-00100
  Gary Sophiea, prin. 547-1700
Other Schools – See Oak Park

Hazel Park SD
  Supt. — See Hazel Park
Jardon Vo S Vo Tech
  2200 WOODWARD HTS 48220 544-5294
  William Persons, prin.
Webb JHS 2-00100
  2100 WOODWARD HTS 48220 544-5320
  Fred Nix, prin.

Fife Lake, AC 616, PC 2, Grand Traverse
Forest Area Community SD 3-11111
  7741 SHIPPY RD SW 49633 369-4191
  Fred Joles, supt.
Forest Area SD 2-00111
  7661 SHIPPY RD SW 49633 369-2884
  Paul Price, prin.

Flat Rock, AC 313, PC 6, Wayne
Flat Rock Community SD 4-11111
  PO BOX 130 48134 782-2451
  Gerald Peregord, supt.
HS, 28639 DIVISION ST 48134 2-00011
  Mary McCabe, prin. 782-2458
Simpson MS 2-00100
  24900 MEADOWS ST 48134 782-2453
  Gary Griffin, prin.

Woodhaven SD 5-11111
  24975 VAN HORN RD 48134 783-3300
  Roy Bassett, supt.
Woodhaven HS 4-00011
  24787 VAN HORN RD 48134 783-3333
  Bill Thompson, prin.
Other Schools – See Romulus

Flint, AC 810, PC 9, Genesee
Beecher Community SD 5-11111
  1020 W COLDWATER RD 48505 785-4731
  Ira Rutherford, supt.
Beecher HS 3-00011
  1020 W COLDWATER RD 48505 785-4731
  Robert Bryant, prin.
Summit MS, G5159 SUMMIT ST 48505 2-01100
  Chester Hughes, prin. 785-4731
Other Schools – See Mount Morris

Carman-Ainsworth SD 6-11111
  G3475 W COURT ST 48532 230-3200
  Thomas Svitkovich, supt.
Carmen-Ainsworth SHS 3-00001
  1300 N LINDEN RD 48532 230-3240
  Ralph Baldini, prin.
Carmen-Ainsworth JHS 4-00110
  1409 W MAPLE AVE 48507 234-2500
  Daniel Kelly, prin.

Flint SD, 923 E KEARSLEY ST 48503 8-11111
  Nathel Burtley, supt. 760-1000
Central HS, 601 CRAPO ST 48503 4-00011
  Dean Ludwig, prin. 760-1042
Northern HS, G3284 MACKIN RD 48504 4-00011
  Waldo Bronson, prin. 760-1740
Northwestern HS 4-00011
  G2138 W CARPENTER RD 48505 760-1780
  Bessie Straham, prin.
Southwest JSHS, 1420 W 12TH ST 48507 4-00111
  Richard Randels, prin. 760-1400
Schools of Choice JSHS 3-00111
  517 E 5TH AVE 48503 760-1390
  Arnett Miller, prin.
Genessee Area Skill Ctr Vo Tech
  G-5081 TORREY RD 48507 760-1444
  Doug Weir, prin.
Holmes MS, 6602 OXLEY DR 48504 3-00100
  Arthur Wright, prin. 760-1620
Longfellow MS 3-00100
  1255 N CHEVROLET AVE 48504 760-1336
  Ronald Barnett, prin.
McKinley MS, 4501 CAMDEN AVE 48507 3-00100
  Robert Twomley, prin. 760-1610
Whittier MS, 701 CRAPO ST 48503 4-00100
  Gail Ganakas, prin. 760-1175

Kearsley Community SD 5-11111
  4396 UNDERHILL DR 48506 736-8000
  Laurence MacQueen, supt.
Kearsley HS, 4302 UNDERHILL DR 48506 3-00011
  Larry Wiltse, prin. 736-8000
Armstrong MS, 6161 HOPKINS RD 48506 3-00100
  Linda Chard, prin. 736-9929

Westwood Heights SD 4-11111
  3207 FINNEY CT 48504 785-0870
  James Mitchell, supt.
Hamady HS 2-00011
  3223 W CARPENTER RD 48504 785-0890
  Steven Overweg, prin.
Hamady MS 2-01100
  3223 W CARPENTER RD 48504 785-0895
  Steven Overweg, prin.

Baker College of Flint 6-UC
  1050 W BRISTOL RD 48507 767-7600
Detroit College of Business-Flint 2-UC
  3115 LAWNDALE AVE 48504
GMI Engineering & Management Institute 5-UC
  1700 W 3RD AVE 48504 800-955-4464
Hurley Medical Center HSP
  701 W 8TH AVE 48503 257-9409
Jordan College-Flint Campus 2-UC
  3488 N JENNINGS RD 48504 789-0520
Luke Powers HS 3-00011
  G2040 W CARPENTER RD 48505 785-4741
  Joseph Forlenza, prin.

Mott Community College 6-CC
 1401 E COURT ST 48503 762-0453
Ross Medical Education Center 3-CS
 1036 GILBERT RD 48532 230-1100
St. Joseph Hospital HSP
 302 KENSINGTON AVE 48503 762-8592
University of Michigan-Flint 5-UC
 303 E KEARSLEY ST 48502 762-3000
Valley S, 3301 N VERNON AVE 48506 2-11111
 Marianne Kugler, prin. 764-4004

Flushing, AC 810, PC 6, Genesee
 Flushing Community SD 5-11111
 522 N MCKINLEY RD 48433 659-0600
 William Tunnicliff, supt.
 HS, 5039 DELAND RD 48433 4-00011
 Harvey Workman, prin. 659-0630
 MS, 409 CHAMBERLAIN ST 48433 3-00100
 Greg Jackson, prin. 659-0660

Fort Gratiot, AC 810, PC 6, St. Clair
 Port Huron Area SD
 Supt. — See Port Huron
 Port Huron Northern HS 4-00011
 1799 KRAFFT RD 48059 984-2671
 J. Goldsworthy, prin.
 MS, 3985 KEEWAHDIN RD 48059 3-00100
 James Dunn, prin. 984-6544

Fowler, AC 517, PC 3, Clinton
 Fowler SD, PO BOX 408 48835 3-11111
 Mary Ann Chartrand, supt. 593-2296
 HS, S WRIGHT ROAD 48835 2-00111
 Stephen Dembowski, prin. 593-2250

Most Holy Trinity ES 2-01100
 11144 W KENT ST 48835 593-2616
 Martha Maier, prin.

Fowlerville, AC 517, PC 5, Livingston
 Fowlerville Community SD 5-11111
 4861 N FOWLERVILLE RD 48836 223-8459
 Dave Peden, supt.
 JSHS, 7677 W SHARPE RD 48836 3-00111
 Edward Alverson, prin. 223-9171

Frankenmuth, AC 517, PC 5, Saginaw
 Frankenmuth SD 4-11111
 941 E GENESEE ST 48734 652-9958
 Erik Swanson, supt.
 HS, 525 E GENESEE ST 48734 3-00011
 Daniel Gibson, prin. 652-9955
 Rittmueller MS 2-01100
 965 E GENESEE ST 48734 652-6119
 D. Wescott, prin.

Frankfort, AC 616, PC 4, Benzie
 Frankfort-Elberta Area SD 3-11111
 613 LEELANAU AVE 49635 352-4641
 Thomas Gorang, supt.
 JSHS, 534 11TH ST 49635 2-00111
 Kevin Cowhy, prin. 352-4781

Fraser, AC 810, PC 7, Macomb
 Fraser SD, 33466 GARFIELD RD 48026 5-11111
 Gary Matsche, supt. 293-5100
 HS, 34270 GARFIELD RD 48026 4-00011
 N. Marvaso, prin. 293-5100
 Richards MS, 33500 GARFIELD RD 48026 3-00100
 R. Brunzell, prin. 294-5720

Freeland, AC 517, PC 4, Saginaw
 Freeland Community SD 4-11111
 710 POWLEY DR 48623 695-5527
 Thomas Orr, supt.
 JSHS, 8250 WEBSTER RD 48623 3-00111
 James Richardson, prin. 695-2586

Free Soil, AC 616, PC 2, Mason
 Freesoil Community SD 2-11111
 8480 N DEMOCRAT 49411 464-5651
 Stephen Lites, supt.
 Freesoil Community HS 1-00011
 8480 N DEMOCRAT 49411 464-5651
 Stephen Lites, prin.

Fremont, AC 616, PC 5, Newaygo
 Fremont SD, 220 W PINE ST 49412 4-11111
 Bradley Hansen, supt. 924-2350
 HS, 204 E MAIN ST 49412 3-00011
 John Mellema, prin. 924-5300
 MS, 500 W WOODROW ST 49412 2-00100
 James Hieftje, prin. 924-0230

Fruitport, AC 616, PC 4, Muskegon
 Fruitport Community SD 5-11111
 3255 PONTALUNA RD 49415 865-3154
 Dan Bird, supt.
 HS, 357 6TH AVE 49415 3-00011
 David Snyder, prin. 865-3101
 MS, 305 PONTALUNA RD 49415 3-00100
 Norman Heerema, prin. 865-3128

Galesburg, AC 616, PC 4, Kalamazoo
 Galesburg-Augusta Community SD 4-11111
 241 BLAKE BLVD 49053 665-7081
 Ronald Mrozinski, supt.
 Galesburg-Augusta HS 2-00100
 315 W BATTLE CREEK ST 49053 665-7081
 James Takacs, prin.
 Other Schools – See Augusta

Galien, AC 616, PC 3, Berrien
 Galien Township SD 3-11111
 PO BOX 248 49113 545-3364
 Carl Cratsenburg, supt.

JSHS 2-00111
 122 E SOUTHEASTERN AVE 49113 545-3364
 Vicky Pfauth, prin.

Garden City, AC 313, PC 8, Wayne
 Garden City SD 6-11111
 1333 RADCLIFF ST 48135 425-4900
 Michael Wilmot, supt.
 SHS, 6500 MIDDLEBELT RD 48135 4-00001
 Jerry Perttunen, prin. 421-8220
 JHS, 1851 RADCLIFF ST 48135 4-00110
 James Boogren, prin. 427-8410

Garden City Hospital HSP
 6245 INKSTER RD 48135 458-4421

Gaylord, AC 517, PC 5, Otsego
 Gaylord Community SD 5-11111
 615 S ELM AVE 49735 732-6402
 R. Mason Buckingham, supt.
 HS, 240 E 4TH ST 49735 3-00011
 Jerome Sieracki, prin. 732-6402
 MS, 600 E 5TH ST 49735 3-00100
 David Schopp, prin. 732-6402

St. Mary HS, 310 W MITCHELL ST 49735 1-00111
 James Kerfoot, prin. 732-5303

Genesee, AC 810, PC 4, Genesee
 Genesee SD, 7347 N GENESEE 48437 3-11111
 Mark Hilt, supt. 640-1650
 JSHS, 7347 N GENESEE 48437 2-00111
 Kenneth Kavula, prin. 640-1450

Gibraltar, AC 313, PC 5, Wayne
 Gibraltar SD
 Supt. — See Woodhaven
 Carlson HS 4-00011
 30550 W JEFFERSON AVE 48173 379-9617
 S. Kochanski, prin.
 Schumate MS 3-00100
 30550 W JEFFERSON AVE 48173 379-9250
 Rose Crane, prin.

Gladstone, AC 906, PC 5, Delta
 Gladstone Area SD, 400 S 10TH ST 49837 4-11111
 Ella Burton, supt. 428-2417
 HS, 300 S 10TH ST 49837 3-00011
 Thomas Warren, prin. 428-9200
 MS, 200 S 10TH ST 49837 2-00100
 Peter Brock, prin. 428-2295

Gladwin, AC 517, PC 5, Gladwin
 Gladwin Community SD 4-11111
 1206 N SPRING ST 48624 426-9255
 Michael Oakes, supt.
 HS, 1400 N SPRING ST 48624 3-00011
 B. Shellenbarger, prin. 426-7341
 MS, 401 N BOWERY AVE 48624 2-00100
 Bruce Lyon, prin. 426-3808

Skeels Northern Christian S 2-11111
 3956 N M 18 48624 426-4411
 Rev. George Coon, prin.

Gobles, AC 616, PC 3, Van Buren
 Gobles SD, 409 N STATE ST 49055 4-11111
 Tommie Saylor, supt. 628-5618
 JSHS, 409 N STATE ST 49055 3-00111
 Gary Goren, prin. 628-2113

Goodrich, AC 810, PC 3, Genesee
 Goodrich Area SD, 8029 GALE RD 48438 4-11111
 Raymond Green, supt. 636-2250
 HS, 8029 GALE RD 48438 2-00011
 K. Andrzejewski, prin. 636-2251
 MS, 8029 GALE RD 48438 2-01100
 Jerry Lawrason, prin. 636-2253

Grand Blanc, AC 810, PC 6, Genesee
 Grand Blanc Community SD 6-11111
 11920 S SAGINAW ST 48439 694-8211
 Gary Lipe, supt.
 HS, 12500 HOLLY RD 48439 4-00011
 Michael Newton, prin. 694-8211
 MS, 11920 S SAGINAW ST 48439 4-00100
 Norm Abdella, prin. 694-8211

Grand Haven, AC 616, PC 7, Ottawa
 Grand Haven SD 6-11111
 1415 S BEECHTREE ST 49417 847-4614
 William Dean, supt.
 SHS, 900 CUTLER ST 49417 4-00001
 Jay Cason, prin. 847-4600
 JHS, 1400 S GRIFFIN ST 49417 4-00110
 David Randall, prin. 847-4770

Grand Ledge, AC 517, PC 6, Eaton
 Grand Ledge SD, 1020 JENNE ST 48837 6-11111
 David Layle, supt. 627-3241
 HS, 225 W KENT ST 48837 4-00011
 Gary Kamminga, prin. 627-5194
 Beagle MS, 600 W SOUTH ST 48837 3-00100
 Charles Phillips, prin. 627-4274
 Hayes MS, 12620 NIXON RD 48837 3-00100
 Mark Christman, prin. 627-5080

Grand Marais, AC 906, PC 2, Alger
 Burt Township SD 1-11111
 PO BOX 296 49839 494-2543
 William Christensen, supt.
 Burt Township S, PO BOX 296 49839 1-11111
 Tim Murphy, prin. 494-2521

Grand Rapids, AC 616, PC 9, Kent
 East Grand Rapids SD 5-11111
 2915 HALL ST SE 49506 235-3535
 James Morse, supt.
 East Grand Rapids HS 3-00011
 2211 LAKE DR SE 49506 235-7555
 Patrick Cwayna, prin.
 East Grand Rapids MS 3-00100
 2425 LAKE DR SE 49506 235-7551
 James Ogilvie, prin.

Forest Hills SD 6-11111
 6590 CASCADE RD SE 49546 285-8800
 J. Michael Washburn, supt.
 Central HS, 5901 HALL ST SE 49546 3-00011
 Larry Curtis, prin. 285-8700
 Northern HS 3-00011
 3801 LEONARD ST NE 49546 285-8600
 Gloria Graber, prin.
 Central MS, 5810 ADA DR SE 49546 3-00100
 Bruce Vorce, prin. 285-8750
 Northern Hills MS 3-00100
 3775 LEONARD ST NE 49546 285-8650
 Carol Vorce, prin.

Grand Rapids SD, PO BOX 117 49501 8-11111
 Jeffrey Grotsky, supt. 771-2000
 Central HS, 431 FOUNTAIN ST NE 49503 3-00011
 Joe Grandy, prin. 771-2310
 Creston HS 4-00011
 1720 PLAINFIELD AVE NE 49505 771-2424
 Frank Sebastian, prin.
 Ottawa Hills HS 4-00011
 2055 ROSEWOOD AVE SE 49506 771-2900
 Sidney Bailey, prin.
 Union HS 4-00011
 1800 TREMONT BLVD NW 49504 771-3160
 K. Folkertsma, prin.
 Kent Vo Options Vo Tech
 864 CRAHEN AVE NE 49546 771-2740
 Patricia Crame, prin.
 Burton Environmental Science MS 2-00100
 2133 BUCHANAN AVE SW 49507 771-2269
 Sue Richards, prin.
 Iroquois Math/Technology MS 3-00100
 1050 IROQUOIS DR SE 49506 771-2640
 Pam Clinkscales, prin.
 Northeast MS 3-00100
 1400 FULLER AVE NE 49505 771-2818
 Mike Mabin, prin.
 Riverside Law/Govt/Intl Studies MS 3-00100
 265 ELEANOR ST NE 49505 771-2969
 Linda Scott, prin.
 Westwood Health/Science MS 3-00100
 1525 MOUNT MERCY DR NW 49504 771-3322
 Mary Beth Parker, prin.

Kelloggsville SD, 242 52ND ST SE 49548 4-11111
 William Zoller, supt. 538-7460
 Kelloggsville HS, 23 JEAN ST SW 49548 2-00111
 George Stamas, prin. 532-1570
 Kelloggsville JHS, 23 JEAN ST SW 49548 2-00100
 Rein Pukk, prin. 532-1575

Kenowa Hills SD 5-11111
 2325 4 MILE RD NW 49504 784-2511
 Terry Post, supt.
 Kenowa Hills HS 3-00011
 3950 HENDERSHOT AVE NW 49504 784-2400
 Jon McCarthy, prin.
 Kenowa Hills JHS 3-00100
 4252 3 MILE RD NW 49504 453-6351
 Eugene De Wys, prin.

Kentwood SD
 Supt. — See Kentwood
 Pinewood MS, 2100 60TH ST SE 49508 2-00100
 Michael Miles, prin. 455-1224

Northview SD 5-11111
 4365 HUNSBERGER AVE NE 49505 363-6861
 Patricia Oldt, supt.
 Northview HS 3-00011
 4451 HUNSBERGER AVE NE 49505 363-4857
 William Pappas, prin.
 Hills & Dales MS 2-00100
 4400 AMBROSE AVE NE 49505 361-3430
 Phillip Helzer, prin.

Wyoming SD
 Supt. — See Wyoming
 Kent Occupational S Vo Tech
 1800 LEFFINGWELL AVE NE 49505 361-7378
 Katherine Williams, prin.

AMR Combs Flight Training Academy 1-CS
 PO BOX 888380 49588 800-262-4953
Aquinas College 4-UC
 1607 ROBINSON RD SE 49506 800-678-9593
Blodgett Memorial Medical Center HSP
 1840 WEALTHY ST SE 49506 774-7601
Butterworth Hospital HSP
 100 MICHIGAN ST NE 49503 774-1601
Calvin College 5-UC
 3201 BURTON ST SE 49546 957-6000
Calvin Theological Seminary 2-UC
 3233 BURTON ST SE 49546 957-6036
Catholic Central HS 3-00011
 319 SHELDON BLVD SE 49503 459-4559
 James O'Donnell, prin.
Covenant Christian High S 2-00001
 1401 FERNDALE AVE SW 49504 453-5048
 Agatha Lubbers, prin.

Davenport College of Business 6-UC
415 E FULTON ST 49503 451-3511
Davenport College of Business 2-CS
3030 EASTERN AVE SE 49508 245-3030
Grace Bible College 2-UC
PO BOX 910 49509 538-2330
Grand Rapids Baptist Academy 2-00111
3101 LEONARD ST NE 49505 942-0363
Randall Ross, prin.
Grand Rapids Baptist College & Seminary 3-UC
1001 E BELTLINE AVE NE 49505 949-5300
Grand Rapids Christian HS 4-00011
2300 PLYMOUTH AVE SE 49506 241-4641
James Stapert, prin.
Grand Rapids Community College 6-CC
143 BOSTWICK AVE NE 49503 771-3900
Grand Rapids Educational Center 2-CS
1750 WOODWORTH ST NE # 100 49505
364-8464
ITT Technical Institute 2-CS
4020 SPARKS DR SE 49546 956-1060
Jordan College-Grand Rapids Campus 2-UC
1925 BRETON RD SE 49506 957-3999
Kendall College of Art & Design 3-UC
111 N DIVISION AVE 49503 800-676-2787
Plymouth Christian HS 2-00111
965 PLYMOUTH AVE NE 49505 454-9481
Richard Elshof, prin.
Reformed Bible College 4-UC
3333 E BELTLINE AVE NE 49505 363-2050
Ross Medical Education Center 2-CS
2035 28TH ST SE STE O 49508 243-3070
South Christian HS 3-00011
160 68TH ST SW 49548 455-3210
Larry Plaisier, prin.
Tri-Unity Christian S 2-00111
2104 44TH ST SW 49509 532-6766
Thomas Burkman, prin.
West Catholic HS 3-00011
1801 BRISTOL AVE NW 49504 453-4467
Frank Cody, prin.

Grandville, AC 616, PC 7, Kent
Grandville SD 5-11111
3131 BARRETT AVE SW 49418 530-1600
Brian Callaghan, supt.
HS, 3535 WILSON AVE SW 49418 4-00011
Randy Remenap, prin. 530-1659
MS, 3100 OTTAWA AVE SW 49418 3-00100
Charles Schultz, prin. 530-1623

American Education Centers 2-CS
4339 CANAL AVE SW 49418 531-1600
Calvin Christian HS 2-00011
3750 IVANREST AVE SW 49418 538-0990
Henry Zuiderveen, prin.

Grant, AC 616, PC 3, Newaygo
Grant SD, 331 W STATE RD 49327 4-11111
(—), supt. 834-5621
HS, 331 W STATE RD 49327 2-00011
L. Art Willick, prin. 834-5622
JHS, 96 E 120TH ST 49327 3-01100
Michael Ostyn, prin. 834-5910

Grass Lake, AC 517, PC 3, Jackson
Grass Lake Community SD 3-11111
899 S UNION ST 49240 522-8491
Dena Dardzinski, supt.
JSHS, 1000 GRASS LAKE RD 49240 2-00111
Barbara Bleyaert, prin. 522-8494

Grayling, AC 517, PC 4, Crawford
Crawford-AuSable SD 4-11111
403 MICHIGAN AVE 49738 348-7641
Kent Reynolds, supt.
HS 3-00011
1135 N OLD US HIGHWAY 27 49738
Joel Raddatz, prin. 348-7641
MS, 500 SPRUCE ST 49738 3-01100
Michael Branch, prin. 348-7641

Greenville, AC 616, PC 6, Montcalm
Greenville SD, 516 W CASS ST 48838 5-11111
Thomas Pridgeon, supt. 754-3686
HS, 111 N HILLCREST ST 48838 4-00011
Thomas Matchett, prin. 754-3681
MS, 1321 CHASE ST 48838 4-01100
Diane Brissette, prin. 754-9361

Grosse Ile, AC 313, PC 6, Wayne
Grosse Ile Township SD 4-11111
23270 E RIVER RD 48138 675-1550
Harrison Cass, supt.
HS, 7800 S GRAY DR 48138 3-00011
D. Yardley, prin. 675-1550
MS, 23270 E RIVER RD 48138 2-00100
Joseph Skaisgir, prin. 675-1550

Grosse Pointe, AC 313, PC 6, Wayne
Grosse Pointe SD 6-11111
389 SAINT CLAIR ST 48230 343-2000
Edward Shine, supt.
Grosse Pointe North HS 4-00011
707 VERNIER RD 48236 343-2199
Caryn Wells, prin.
Grosse Pointe South HS 4-00011
11 GROSSE POINTE BLVD 48236 343-2130
(—), prin.
Brownell MS 2-00100
260 CHALFONTE AVE 48236 343-2115
Don Messing, prin.

Parcells MS, 20600 MACK AVE 48236 3-00100
Glenn Croydon, prin. 343-2104
Pierce MS, 15430 KERCHEVAL ST 48230 3-00100
Lee Warras, prin. 343-2094

University Liggett S 3-11111
1045 COOK RD 48236 884-4444
Matthew Hanley, prin.

Gwinn, AC 906, PC 4, Marquette
Gwinn Area SD, M-35 49841 5-11111
Richard Drury, supt. 346-9283
HS, M-35 49841 3-00011
Kelvin Marjomaki, prin. 346-9247
MS, GRANITE ST 49841 2-00100
James Ghiardi, prin. 346-5914

Hale, AC 517, PC 2, Iosco
Hale Area SD, 415 MAIN ST 48739 3-11111
J. Carter, supt. 728-7661
Hale Area JSHS, 415 MAIN RD 48739 2-00111
Maxine Yetter, prin. 728-2861

Hamilton, AC 616, PC 4, Allegan
Hamilton Community SD 4-11111
PO BOX 300 49419 751-5148
James Kos, supt.
JSHS, 4845 136TH AVE 49419 3-00111
Bruce Vanderwall, prin. 751-5185

Hamtramck, AC 313, PC 7, Wayne
Hamtramck SD, PO BOX 12012 48212 5-11111
John Radwanski, supt. 892-4980
HS, 11410 CHAREST ST 48212 3-00011
Mark Decker, prin. 892-7505
Kosciuszko MS, 2333 BURGER ST 48212 3-00100
E. Malczewski, prin. 365-4625

St. Florian S, 2622 FLORIAN ST 48212 3-11111
Sr. Estelle Printz, prin. 875-6347

Hancock, AC 906, PC 5, Houghton
Hancock SD, 417 QUINCY ST 49930 4-11111
John Vaara, supt. 487-9207
Hancock Central JSHS 2-00111
417 QUINCY ST 49930 487-9202
Judy Raica, prin.

Suomi College 2-CC
601 QUINCY ST 49930 482-5300

Hanover, AC 517, PC 2, Jackson
Hanover-Horton SD 4-11111
131 FAIRVIEW 49241 563-0100
John Dardzinski, supt.
Other Schools – See Horton

Harbor Beach, AC 517, PC 4, Huron
Harbor Beach Community SD 3-11111
402 S 5TH ST 48441 479-3261
Kelly Hileman, supt.
JSHS, 402 S 5TH ST 48441 2-00111
Wayne Kadar, prin. 479-3261

Harbor Springs, AC 616, PC 4, Emmet
Harbor Springs SD 4-11111
327 E BLUFF DR 49740 526-2801
Thomas Richards, supt.
HS, 327 E BLUFF DR 49740 2-00011
Richard Bouton, prin. 526-6255
MS, 327 E BLUFF DR 49740 2-00100
Don Start, prin. 526-7352

Black Forest Hall 2-CS
PO BOX 140 49740 526-7066
Harbor Light Christian S 2-11111
8333 CLAYTON RD 49740 347-7859
Lawrence Kubovchick, prin.

Harper Woods, AC 313, PC 7, Wayne
Harper Woods SD 3-11111
20225 BEACONSFIELD ST 48225 839-1296
Arthur Toth, supt.
JSHS, 20225 BEACONSFIELD ST 48225 2-00111
James Haley, prin. 839-7400

Bishop Gallagher HS 2-00011
19360 HARPER AVE 48225 886-0855
Thomas Lutostanski, prin.
Lutheran HS East 2-00011
20100 KELLY RD 48225 371-8750
Rev. Paul Wargo, prin.
Notre Dame HS, 20254 KELLY RD 48225 2-00011
Fr. Olszamowski, prin. 371-8965
Regina HS, 20200 KELLY RD 48225 3-00011
Sr. Leanne Leszczynski, prin. 526-0220

Harris, AC 906, PC 1, Menominee
Bark River-Harris SD 49845 3-11111
William Lake, supt. 466-9981
Bark River-Harris JSHS 49845 2-00111
Gerald Sundquist, prin. 466-5321

Harrison, AC 517, PC 4, Clare
Harrison Community SD 4-11111
224 S MAIN ST 48625 539-7871
Joseph Ashcroft, supt.
HS, 700 S 5TH 48625 3-00011
Dale Barr, prin. 539-7417
MS, 224 S MAIN ST 48625 2-00100
Thomas House, prin. 539-7194

Mid-Michigan Community College 4-CC
1375 S CLARE AVE 48625 386-7792

Harrison Township, AC 810, PC 7, Macomb
L'Anse Creuse SD 6-11111
36727 JEFFERSON AVE 48045 465-1941
Francis Higgins, supt.
L'Anse Creuse HS 4-00011
38495 LANSE CREUSE ST 48045 463-5881
Richard Benedict, prin.
L'Anse Creuse Central MS 2-00100
38000 REIMOLD ST 48045 469-8818
Marna Beard, prin.
L'Anse Creuse South MS 3-00100
34641 JEFFERSON AVE 48045 791-1890
Ron Johnson, prin.
Other Schools – See Clinton Township, Macomb Township

Hart, AC 616, PC 4, Oceana
Hart SD, 300 JOHNSON ST 49420 4-11111
Patrick Gaudard, supt. 873-4080
HS, 300 JOHNSON ST W 49420 2-00111
P. Malarney, prin. 873-5691
MS, 300 JOHNSON ST W 49420 2-01100
Lawrence DeAugustine, prin. 873-2549

Hartford, AC 616, PC 4, Van Buren
Hartford SD, 115 SCHOOL ST 49057 4-11111
Robert Pobuda, supt. 621-2441
HS, 115 SCHOOL ST 49057 2-00011
D. Hellinga, prin. 621-2441
MS, 141 SCHOOL ST 49057 2-00100
James McQueen, prin. 621-2441

Hartland, AC 810, PC 3, Livingston
Hartland Consolidated SD 5-11111
PO BOX 900 48353 632-7481
Peter Caroselli, supt.
HS, PO BOX 900 48353 4-00011
James Basel, prin. 632-6363
Farms MS, PO BOX 900 48353 3-00100
James Imhoff, prin. 229-2016

Haslett, AC 517, PC 7, Ingham
Haslett SD, 5593 FRANKLIN ST 48840 4-11111
Robert Regan, supt. 339-8242
HS, 5450 MARSH RD 48840 3-00011
G. Johnson, prin. 339-8249
MS, 1535 FRANKLIN ST 48840 3-00100
Valdis Gailitis, prin. 339-8233

Hastings, AC 616, PC 6, Barry
Hastings Area SD 5-11111
232 W GRAND ST 49058 948-4400
Carl Schoessel, supt.
HS, 520 W SOUTH ST 49058 3-00011
Steve Harbison, prin. 948-4409
MS, 232 W GRAND ST 49058 3-00100
Stanley Kirkendall, prin. 948-4404

Hazel Park, AC 810, PC 7, Oakland
Hazel Park SD 6-11111
23136 HUGHES AVE 48030 542-3910
Malvin Rasmusson, supt.
HS, 23400 HUGHES AVE 48030 4-00011
James Meisinger, prin. 544-5216
Beecher JHS 2-00100
22750 HIGHLAND AVE 48030 544-5328
Leonard Sak, prin.
Other Schools – See Ferndale

Hemlock, AC 517, PC 4, Saginaw
Hemlock SD 4-11111
1095 N HEMLOCK RD 48626 642-5282
Reginald Rye, supt.
HS, 733 N HEMLOCK RD 48626 2-00011
C. Crossett, prin. 642-5287
MS, 525 S MAPLE ST 48626 2-01100
Gerald Madaleno, prin. 642-5253

Hesperia, AC 616, PC 3, Oceana
Hesperia Community SD 4-11111
PO BOX 338 49421 854-6185
Max Kessler, supt.
HS, PO BOX 338 49421 2-00011
Clifford Nordin, prin. 854-6385
MS, PO BOX 338 49421 2-00100
Karen Carter, prin. 854-6475

Hickory Corners, AC 616, PC 2, Barry
Gull Lake Community SD
Supt. — See Richland
Gull Lake MS, 9500 N 40TH ST 49060 2-00100
Jeffrey Cable, prin. 671-5135

Highland, AC 810, PC 3, Oakland
Huron Valley SD 7-11111
2390 S MILFORD RD 48357 684-8000
James Doyle, supt.
Milford HS, 2380 S MILFORD RD 48357 4-00011
Bruce Gilbert, prin. 684-8091
MS, 305 N JOHN ST 48357 3-00100
Bart Montante, prin. 684-8085
Other Schools – See Milford, White Lake

Highland Park, AC 313, PC 7, Wayne
Highland Park SD 6-11111
20 BARTLETT ST 48203 252-0440
Eugene Cain, supt.
HS, 15900 WOODWARD AVE 48203 3-00011
Gerald Golden, prin. 252-0460
Ferris MS, 60 CORTLAND ST 48203 2-01100
Eulah Peterson, prin. 252-2043

Highland Park Community College	3-CC
12541 2ND AVE 48203	252-0436

Hillman, AC 517, PC 3, Montmorency
Hillman Community SD	3-11111
PO BOX 518 49746	742-4536
Keith Moore, supt.	
Hillman Community S	3-11111
245 3RD ST 49746	742-4536
Ernest Lueder, prin.	

Hillsdale, AC 517, PC 6, Hillsdale
Hillsdale Community SD	5-11111
30 S NORWOOD AVE 49242	437-4401
Richard Lane, supt.	
HS, 30 S NORWOOD AVE 49242	3-00011
Peter Beck, prin.	439-4320
Davis MS, 30 N WEST ST 49242	3-00100
Chris Butler, prin.	439-4326

Hillsdale College	4-UC
33 E COLLEGE ST 49242	437-7341

Holland, AC 616, PC 8, Ottawa
Holland SD, 372 S RIVER AVE 49423	6-11111
Ned Curtis, supt.	393-7501
SHS, 600 VAN RAALTE AVE 49423	3-00001
Gary Sickels, prin.	393-7550
West MS, 500 W 24TH ST 49423	3-00110
Jim Zeedyk, prin.	393-7540

West Ottawa SD	6-11111
294 W LAKEWOOD BLVD 49424	395-2300
Charles Muncatchy, supt.	
West Ottawa HS, 1024 136TH AVE 49424	4-00011
Gary Lucas, prin.	786-1000
West Ottawa MS, 3700 140TH AVE 49424	4-00100
Brian Weinrich, prin.	786-2000

Calvary Baptist S	2-11111
518 PLASMAN AVE 49423	396-4494
Kim Meyering, prin.	
Holland Christian HS	3-00011
950 OTTAWA AVE 49423	396-1477
Timothy Hoeksema, prin.	
Holland Christian MS	3-00100
850 OTTAWA AVE 49423	396-5231
Kenneth Kuipers, prin.	
Hope College	5-UC
69 E 10TH ST 49423	392-5111
Western Theological Seminary	2-UC
86 E 12TH ST 49423	392-8555

Holly, AC 810, PC 6, Oakland
Holly Area SD, 111 COLLEGE ST 48442	5-11111
Wayne Peters, supt.	634-4431
HS, 920 BAIRD ST 48442	4-00011
Steven Gaynor, prin.	634-4451
Sherman MS, 14470 N HOLLY RD 48442	3-00100
John Dunlop, prin.	634-8296

Holt, AC 517, PC 7, Ingham
Holt SD, 4610 SPAHR ST 48842	5-11111
Mark Maksimowicz, supt.	694-0401
SHS, 1784 AURELIUS RD 48842	3-00001
Tom Davis, prin.	694-2162
JHS, 5780 HOLT RD 48842	3-00110
Susan York, prin.	694-7117
Washington Woods MS	2-00100
2055 S WASHINGTON RD 48842	694-8707
Valerie Smith, prin.	

St. Matthew Lutheran S	2-11111
2418 AURELIUS RD 48842	694-3182
Arthur Schroeder, prin.	

Holton, AC 616, PC 3, Muskegon
Holton SD, PO BOX 159 49425	4-11111
Mary Margaret Kusler, supt.	821-2178
JSHS, PO BOX 159 49425	3-00111
Mickey Noble, prin.	821-2123

Homer, AC 517, PC 4, Calhoun
Homer Community SD	4-11111
403 S HILLSDALE ST 49245	568-4461
Lee Robinson, supt.	
HS, 403 S HILLSDALE ST 49245	2-00011
Fred Saxton, prin.	568-4464
MS, 403 S HILLSDALE ST 49245	2-01100
Brenton Holcomb, prin.	568-4456

Hopkins, AC 616, PC 3, Allegan
Hopkins SD, 400 CLARK ST 49328	4-11111
James Cooper, supt.	793-7261
JSHS, 215 CLARK ST 49328	3-00111
(—), prin.	793-7616

Horton, AC 517, PC 2, Jackson
Hanover-Horton SD	
Supt. — See Hanover	
Hanover-Horton HS	2-00011
10000 MOSCOW RD 49246	563-8181
Donna Andrew, prin.	
Hanover-Horton MS	2-01100
10000 MOSCOW RD 49246	563-8181
Terry Catron, prin.	

Houghton, AC 906, PC 6, Houghton
Houghton-Portage Township SD	4-11111
1603 GUNDLACH RD 49931	482-0451
Dennis Harbour, supt.	

Houghton Central JSHS	3-00111
1603 GUNDLACH RD 49931	482-0450
Earl Kaurala, prin.	

Michigan Technological University	6-UC
1400 TOWNSEND DR 49931	487-1885

Houghton Lake, AC 517, PC 5, Roscommon
Houghton Lake Community SD	4-11111
6001 W HOUGHTON LAKE DR 48629	366-5376
James French, supt.	
HS, 4433 HOUGHTON LAKE DR 48629	3-00011
Ronald Szewczyk, prin.	366-5376
MS, 4441 HOUGHTON LAKE DR 48629	2-00100
Judith Gorski, prin.	366-5376

Howard City, AC 616, PC 4, Montcalm
Tri-County Area SD	4-11111
208 E EDGERTON ST 49329	937-5611
Peter Injasoulian, supt.	
Tri County HS	2-00011
21350 KENDAVILLE RD 49329	937-4338
Michael Pritchard, prin.	
Tri County MS	2-00100
21350 KENDAVILLE RD 49329	937-4318
Susan Wanner, prin.	

Howell, AC 517, PC 6, Livingston
Howell SD, 415 N BARNARD ST 48843	6-11111
Charles Manuel, supt.	548-6234
HS, 1200 W GRAND RIVER AVE 48843	4-00011
B. Campbell, prin.	548-6206
Highlander Way MS	3-01100
511 N HIGHLANDER WAY 48843	548-6252
Charles Kraegel, prin.	
McPherson MS	3-01100
1400 W GRAND RIVER AVE 48843	548-6267
G. Douglas Paige, prin.	

Cleary College - Livingston Campus	3-UC
3750 CLEARY COLLEGE DR 48843	548-3670

Hudson, AC 517, PC 5, Lenawee
Hudson Area SD	4-11111
781 N MAPLE GROVE AVE 49247	448-8912
Michael Ryan, supt.	
JSHS, 771 N MAPLE GROVE AVE 49247	3-00111
Jack Loudin, prin.	448-8912

Hudsonville, AC 616, PC 6, Ottawa
Hudsonville SD	5-11111
3866 VAN BUREN ST 49426	669-1740
Donald VanDoeselaar, supt.	
HS, 5037 32ND AVE 49426	3-00011
Joseph Beel, prin.	669-1500
MS, 5535 SCHOOL AVE 49426	2-00100
Jack VanEden, prin.	669-1510

Unity Christian HS, 3487 OAK ST 49426	3-00011
Jack Postma, prin.	669-1820

Huntington Woods, AC 810, PC 6, Oakland
American Education Centers	2-CS
26075 WOODWARD AVE 48070	399-5522

Ida, AC 313, PC 4, Monroe
Ida SD, 3145 PRAIRIE ST 48140	4-11111
H. Gabehart, supt.	269-3110
HS, 3145 PRAIRIE ST 48140	2-00011
Marvin Dick, prin.	269-3485
MS, 3143 PRAIRIE ST 48140	3-01100
Sheldon Wiens, prin.	269-2220

Imlay City, AC 810, PC 5, Lapeer
Imlay Community SD	4-11111
634 W BORLAND RD 48444	724-2765
Gary Moore, supt.	
JSHS, 495 W 1ST ST 48444	3-00111
Mark Hughes, prin.	724-2765

Indian River, AC 616, PC 2, Cheboygan
Inland Lakes SD	3-11111
5243 STRAITS HWY 49749	238-9811
Ronald Berg, supt.	
Inland Lakes HS	2-00011
5243 STRAITS HWY 49749	238-9363
Frank Holes, prin.	
Inland Lakes MS	2-00100
5243 STRAITS HWY 49749	238-6730
Pasquali Nardizzi, prin.	

Inkster, AC 313, PC 8, Wayne
Inkster SD, 29115 CARLYSLE ST 48141	5-11111
Edmond Beverly, supt.	722-5310
HS, 3250 MIDDLEBELT RD 48141	3-00011
M. Wilson, prin.	722-6700
Blanchette MS, 29193 BEECH ST 48141	2-00100
S. Mosley, prin.	722-4014

Westwood Community SD	4-11111
25912 ANNAPOLIS ST 48141	565-1900
Equilla Bradford, supt.	
Other Schools – See Dearborn Heights	

Peterson-Warren Academy	2-11111
4000 SYLVIA ST 48141	565-5808
Alvin Barnes, prin.	

Interlochen, AC 616, PC 2, Grand Traverse
Interlochen Arts Academy	2-00011
PO BOX 199 49643	276-9221
Raymond Rideout, prin.	

Ionia, AC 616, PC 6, Ionia
Ionia SD, 250 E TUTTLE RD 48846	5-11111
Terrence Conklin, supt.	527-9280
HS, 250 E TUTTLE RD 48846	3-00011
Mark Bielang, prin.	527-0600
MS, 438 UNION ST 48846	3-00100
Dan Evans, prin.	527-0040

Iron Mountain, AC 906, PC 6, Dickinson
Iron Mountain SD	4-11111
PO BOX 280 49801	779-2600
Richard Allen, supt.	
HS, 300 W B ST 49801	2-00011
Richard Debelak, prin.	779-2610
Central MS, 301 W HUGHITT ST 49801	2-00100
Marvin Harry, prin.	779-2620

North Dickinson County SD	3-11111
W6588 STATE HIGHWAY M69 49801	542-9281
Thomas Rossler, supt.	
North Dickinson S	3-11111
W6588 STATE HIGHWAY M69 49801	542-9281
Ed Davidson, prin.	

Iron River, AC 906, PC 4, Iron
West Iron County SD	
Supt. — See Stambaugh	
West Iron County JSHS	2-00111
612 W ADAMS ST 49935	265-5184
Tom Gendzwill, prin.	

Ironwood, AC 906, PC 6, Gogebic
Ironwood Area SD	4-11111
634 E AYER ST # 46 49938	932-0200
Percy Smith, supt.	
Wright JSHS	3-00111
638 E AYER ST # 46 49938	932-0932
Henry Bothwell, prin.	

Gogebic Community College	3-CC
E4946 JACKSON RD 49938	932-4231

Ishpeming, AC 906, PC 6, Marquette
Ishpeming SD, 319 E DIVISION ST 49849	4-11111
Stephen Piereson, supt.	485-5501
HS, 319 E DIVISION ST 49849	2-00011
James Thomas, prin.	485-1066
Phelps MS, 700 E NORTH ST 49849	2-01100
David Gadomski, prin.	486-4438

NICE Community SD	4-11111
300 S WESTWOOD DR 49849	485-1021
William Hyry, supt.	
Westwood HS	3-00011
300 S WESTWOOD DR 49849	485-1023
Dennis Bobula, prin.	

Ithaca, AC 517, PC 5, Gratiot
Ithaca SD, 710 UNION ST 48847	4-11111
Kenneth Federspiel, supt.	875-3700
JSHS, 710 UNION ST 48847	3-00111
F. Howes Smith, prin.	875-3373

Jackson, AC 517, PC 8, Jackson
East Jackson SD	4-11111
1404 N SUTTON RD 49202	764-2090
Bruce Van Eyck, supt.	
East Jackson HS	2-00011
1566 N SUTTON RD 49202	764-1700
Leon Hunt, prin.	
East Jackson MS, 4340 WALZ RD 49201	2-00100
Mary Ann Kessler, prin.	764-6010

Jackson SD, 1400 W MONROE ST 49202	6-11111
Darwin Johnson, supt.	789-8144
SHS, 544 WILDWOOD AVE 49201	4-00001
Thomas Stobie, prin.	784-8501
Parkside JHS, 2400 4TH ST 49203	4-00110
Donque Ellis, prin.	783-2873

Northwest SD	5-11111
4000 VAN HORN RD 49201	569-2247
Robert Halle, supt.	
Northwest HS	3-00011
4200 VAN HORN RD 49201	569-2244
David Lickfeldt, prin.	
Northwest JHS	3-00100
6700 RIVES JUNCTION RD 49201	569-2245
Bill Fitch, prin.	

Vandercook Lake SD	3-11111
1000 E GOLF AVE 49203	782-9044
Burdette Andrews, supt.	
Vandercook Lake JSHS	2-00111
1000 E GOLF AVE 49203	782-8167
Anthony Hollow, prin.	

Jackson Baptist S, 4200 LOWE RD 49203	2-11111
Ronald Hooley, prin.	783-2658
Jackson Business Institute	2-CS
234 S MECHANIC ST 49201	789-6123
Jackson Catholic ES	2-00100
915 COOPER ST 49202	784-3385
Pamela Sullivan, prin.	
Jackson Community College	5-CC
2111 EMMONS RD 49201	787-0800
Lumen Christi HS	3-00011
3483 SPRING ARBOR RD 49203	787-0630
Fr. Rieden, prin.	
Ross Medical Education Center	2-CS
1188 N WEST AVE 49202	782-7677
W. A. Foote Memorial Hospital	HSP
205 N EAST AVE 49201	788-4940

Jenison, AC 616, PC 7, Ottawa
Jenison SD, 8375 20TH AVE 49428 — 5-11111
  David Dresslar, supt. — 457-1400
HS, 2140 BAUER RD 49428 — 4-00011
  Mark Dievendorf, prin. — 457-3400
MS, 8295 20TH AVE 49428 — 3-00100
  Thomas Tenbrink, prin. — 457-1402

Johannesburg, AC 517, PC 2, Otsego
Johannesburg-Lewiston SD — 3-11111
  10854 M-32 49751 — 732-1773
  James Hilgendorf, supt.
Johannesburg-Lewiston HS — 2-00011
  10854 M-32 49751 — 732-1773
  John Bailey, prin.

Jonesville, AC 517, PC 4, Hillsdale
Jonesville Community SD — 4-11111
  417 E CHICAGO ST 49250 — 849-9075
  Dennis McComb, supt.
JSHS, 401 E CHICAGO ST 49250 — 2-00111
  Albert Roeseler, prin. — 849-9934

Kalamazoo, AC 616, PC 8, Kalamazoo
Kalamazoo SD, 1220 HOWARD ST 49008 — 7-11111
  Frank Rapley, supt. — 337-0123
Central HS, 2432 N DRAKE RD 49006 — 4-00011
  Joseph Payton, prin. — 337-0300
Norrix HS, 606 E KILGORE RD 49001 — 4-00011
  Jim O'Donnell, prin. — 337-0200
Hillside JHS, 1941 ALAMO AVE 49006 — 3-00100
  Dorothy Young, prin. — 337-0570
Milwood JHS, 2916 KONKLE ST 49001 — 3-00100
  Darrell Clay, prin. — 337-0670
South JHS, 922 W MAPLE ST 49008 — 3-00100
  John Armstrong, prin. — 337-0730

Bronson Methodist Hospital — HSP
  252 E LOVELL ST 49007 — 341-7862
Davenport College of Business — 4-UC
  4123 W MAIN ST 49006 — 382-2835
First Assembly Christian S — 2-11111
  5550 OAKLAND DR 49002 — 323-2161
  Philip McElhenny, prin.
Grand Rapids Educational Center — 2-CS
  5349 W MAIN ST 49009 — 381-9616
Heritage Baptist Academy — 2-11111
  8828 DOUGLAS AVE 49004 — 385-3344
  John Dantuma, prin.
Kalamazoo Christian HS — 3-00011
  2121 STADIUM DR 49008 — 381-2250
  Larry Baker, prin.
Kalamazoo College — 4-UC
  1200 ACADEMY ST 49006 — 383-8588
Kalamazoo Valley Community College — 6-CC
  6767 W O AVE 49009 — 372-5200
Msgr. Hackett HS — 2-00011
  1000 W KILGORE RD 49008 — 381-2646
  Samuel Accorso, prin.
Western Michigan University 49008 — 7-UC
   — 387-2000

Kalkaska, AC 616, PC 4, Kalkaska
Kalkaska SD, PO BOX 580 49646 — 4-11111
  Doyle Disbrow, supt. — 258-9109
HS, 109 N BIRCH ST 49646 — 3-00011
  Stafford Wood, prin. — 258-9167
MS, 1700 W KALKASKA ROAD 49646 — 3-00100
  Alfred DeOtte, prin. — 258-4040

Kent City, AC 616, PC 3, Kent
Kent City Community SD — 4-11111
  341 N MAIN ST 49330 — 678-7714
  Penny Klein, supt.
JSHS, 351 N MAIN ST 49330 — 3-00111
  James Hatch, prin. — 678-4210

Algoma Christian S — 2-11111
  14471 SPARTA AVE 49330 — 678-7480
  James Elenbaas, prin.

Kentwood, AC 616, PC 8, Kent
Kentwood SD — 6-11111
  5820 EASTERN AVE SE 49508 — 455-4400
  Mary Leiker, supt.
East Kentwood HS — 4-00011
  6178 CAMPUS PARK AVE SE 49508 — 698-6700
  Larry Corbett, prin.
Crestwood MS, 2674 44TH ST SE 49512 — 3-00100
  Richard Farrer, prin. — 455-1200
Valleywood MS, 1110 50TH ST SE 49508 — 3-00100
  Richard Dunn, prin. — 538-7670
Other Schools – See Grand Rapids

Kinde, AC 517, PC 2, Huron
North Huron SD, 21 MAIN ST 48445 — 3-11111
  Richard Fawcett, supt. — 874-4100
North Huron HS, 21 MAIN ST 48445 — 2-00011
  William Hogan, prin. — 874-4101
North Huron MS — 2-01100
  8321 N VAN DYKE 48445 — 738-5231
  Terrence Cupples, prin.

Kingsford, AC 906, PC 6, Dickinson
Breitung Township SD — 4-11111
  2000 W PYLE DR 49801 — 779-2650
  James Verley, supt.
HS, HAMILTON AVE 49801 — 3-00011
  Clyde Peterson, prin. — 779-2670
MS, HAMILTON AVE 49801 — 2-00100
  Mike Tomasoski, prin. — 779-2680

Kingsley, AC 616, PC 3, Grand Traverse
Kingsley Area SD, 403 BLAIR ST 49649 — 4-11111
  Joel Donaldson, supt. — 263-5262
HS, 403 BLAIR ST 49649 — 2-00011
  Dale Rieger, prin. — 263-5261
MS, 403 BLAIR ST 49649 — 2-01100
  Lugh Dixon, prin. — 263-5162

Kingston, AC 517, PC 2, Tuscola
Kingston Community SD — 3-11111
  5790 STATE ST 48741 — 683-2294
  Jerry Laycock, supt.
JSHS, 5790 STATE ST 48741 — 2-00111
  Wayne Wright, prin. — 683-2550

Laingsburg, AC 517, PC 4, Shiawassee
Lainsburg Community SD — 4-11111
  320 E GRAND RIVER RD 48848 — 651-2705
  Halsted Beatty, supt.
HS, 8008 WOODBURY RD 48848 — 2-00011
  Carl Clarke, prin. — 651-5091
MS, 320 E GRAND RIVER RD 48848 — 2-01100
  Gregory Kingdon, prin. — 651-5034

Lake City, AC 616, PC 3, Missaukee
Lake City Area SD — 4-11111
  710 E MITCHELL 49651 — 839-4333
  Lewis Burchard, supt.
HS, 251 RUSSELL ST 49651 — 2-00011
  Charles Schwedler, prin. — 839-7161
MS, 5534 W DAVIS RD 49651 — 2-00100
  Jan Thomas, prin. — 839-7163

Lake Leelanau, AC 616, PC 2, Leelanau

St. Mary S, 310 SAINT MARY ST 49653 — 2-11111
  David Eddington, prin. — 256-9636

Lake Linden, AC 906, PC 4, Houghton
Lake Linden-Hubbell SD — 3-11111
  601 CALUMET ST 49945 — 296-6211
  Dennis Christian, supt.
Lake Linden Hubbell JSHS — 2-00111
  601 CALUMET ST 49945 — 296-6271
  Dennis Christian, prin.

Lake Odessa, AC 616, PC 4, Ionia
Lakewood SD — 5-11111
  639 JORDAN LAKE ST 48849 — 374-8043
  Steven Secor, supt.
Lakewood HS, 7223 VELTE RD 48849 — 3-00011
  Timothy Wood, prin. — 374-8868
East MS, 824 3RD AVE 48849 — 2-01100
  Eric Heide, prin. — 374-8268
Other Schools – See Woodland

Lake Orion, AC 810, PC 5, Oakland
Lake Orion Community SD — 5-11111
  315 N LAPEER ST 48362 — 693-5413
  Robert Bass, supt.
SHS, 455 E SCRIPPS RD 48360 — 4-00001
  Leslie Thirjung, prin. — 693-5420
JHS, 385 E SCRIPPS RD 48360 — 3-00110
  Mortell Kinser, prin. — 693-5440

Lakeview, AC 517, PC 4, Montcalm
Lakeview Community SD — 4-11111
  123 5TH ST 48850 — 352-6226
  George Showers, supt.
HS, 9800 YOUNGMAN RD 48850 — 2-00011
  Michael Hondorp, prin. — 352-7221
MS, 516 WASHINGTON ST 48850 — 3-01100
  Robert Ivan, prin. — 352-8016

L'Anse, AC 906, PC 4, Baraga
L'Anse Area SD, 201 N 4TH ST 49946 — 3-11111
  Henry VerBerkmoes, supt. — 524-6121
JSHS, 201 N 4TH ST 49946 — 2-00111
  Sally Narhi, prin. — 524-6122

Lansing, AC 517, PC 9, Ingham
Lansing SD — 7-11111
  519 W KALAMAZOO ST 48933 — 325-6006
  Richard Halik, supt.
Eastern HS — 4-00011
  220 N PENNSYLVANIA AVE 48912 — 325-6500
  William Allen, prin.
Everett HS, 3900 STABLER ST 48910 — 4-00011
  Gary Bredahl, prin. — 325-6600
Sexton HS, 102 MCPHERSON AVE 48915 — 4-00011
  Clyde Carnegie, prin. — 325-6700
Hill Vo HS, 5815 WISE RD 48911 — Vo Tech
  Cordell Henderson, prin. — 325-6900
Gardner MS, 333 DAHLIA DR 48911 — 4-00100
  Ann Blair, prin. — 325-6540
Otto MS, 500 E THOMAS ST 48906 — 4-00100
  Walker Beverly, prin. — 325-6570
Pattengill MS, 1017 JEROME ST 48912 — 4-00100
  Saturnino Rodriguez, prin. — 325-6640
Rich MS, 2600 S HAMPDEN DR 48911 — 4-00100
  Michael Foster, prin. — 325-6670

Waverly SD, 515 SNOW RD 48917 — 5-11111
  Jon Reynolds, supt. — 321-7265
Waverly HS — 3-00011
  5027 W MICHIGAN AVE 48917 — 323-3831
  Carol Nehil, prin.
Waverly MS, 620 SNOW RD 48917 — 3-00100
  Warren Starr, prin. — 321-7240
Waverly East IS — 3-00100
  3131 W MICHIGAN AVE 48917 — 484-8830
  Dan Pappas, prin.

Davenport College of Business — 4-UC
  220 E KALAMAZOO ST 48933 — 484-2600
Great Lakes Bible College — 2-UC
  6211 W WILLOW HWY 48917 — 321-0242
Lansing Catholic Central HS — 3-00011
  501 MARSHALL ST 48912 — 484-4465
  Nora Wade, prin.
Lansing Community College — 7-CC
  521 WASHINGTON SQ N 48933 — 483-1851
Lansing Computer Institute — 2-CS
  501 MARSHALL ST # 101 48912 — 482-8896
Michigan School for the Blind — HND
  715 W WILLOW ST 48913
Ross Medical Education Center — 1-CS
  913 W HOLMES RD STE 260 48910 — 887-0180
Thomas M. Cooley Law School — 4-UC
  PO BOX 13038 48901 — 371-5140

Lapeer, AC 810, PC 6, Lapeer
Lapeer Community SD — 6-11111
  1025 W NEPESSING ST 48446 — 667-2400
  Jack McAuley, supt.
Lapeer East HS — 4-00011
  933 S SAGINAW ST 48446 — 667-2418
  Michael Linton, prin.
Lapeer West HS — 4-00011
  170 MILLVILLE RD 48446 — 667-2423
  William Slater, prin.
White MS, 201 JEFFERSON ST 48446 — 3-00100
  David Dagley, prin. — 667-2409
Zemmer MS, 1920 W OREGON ST 48446 — 3-00100
  Harold Harding, prin. — 667-2413

Lathrup Village, AC 810, PC 5, Oakland
Southfield SD
  Supt. — See Southfield
Lathrup HS, 19301 W 12 MILE RD 48076 — 4-00011
  Todd Henderson, prin. — 746-7204
Birney MS, 27225 EVERGREEN RD 48076 — 3-00100
  Ted Jennings, prin. — 746-8800

Lawrence, AC 616, PC 3, Van Buren
Lawrence SD — 3-11111
  650 W SAINT JOSEPH ST 49064 — 674-8233
  Richard Stoll, supt.
JSHS, 650 W SAINT JOSEPH ST 49064 — 2-00111
  Larry Smith, prin. — 674-8233

Lawton, AC 616, PC 4, Van Buren
Lawton Community SD — 4-11111
  880 E 2ND ST 49065 — 624-4931
  Daniel Pratley, supt.
HS, 880 E 2ND ST 49065 — 2-00011
  (—), prin. — 624-4191
MS, 880 E 2ND ST 49065 — 2-00100
  Michael McCrossin, prin. — 624-4581

Leland, AC 616, PC 3, Leelanau
Leland SD, 200 N GRAND AVE 49654 — 2-11111
  Michael Kenney, supt. — 256-9857
S, 200 N GRAND AVE 49654 — 2-11111
  Michael Hartigan, prin. — 256-9857

Le Roy, AC 616, PC 2, Oseola
Pine River Area SD — 4-11111
  6375 N PINE RIVER RD 49655 — 829-3141
  Lee Sandy, supt.
Pine River JSHS — 3-00111
  6375 N PINE RIVER RD 49655 — 829-3841
  Ted Raven, prin.

Leslie, AC 517, PC 4, Ingham
Leslie SD, 432 N MAIN ST 49251 — 4-11111
  Tom Dove, supt. — 589-8200
JSHS, 400 KIMBALL ST 49251 — 3-00111
  Barbara Knuth, prin. — 589-8294

Lincoln, AC 517, PC 2, Alcona
Alcona Community SD — 4-11111
  PO BOX 249 48742 — 736-6212
  Paul Mancine, supt.
Alcona JSHS, 51 N BARLOW RD 48742 — 3-00111
  (—), prin. — 736-8534

Lincoln Park, AC 313, PC 8, Wayne
Lincoln Park SD — 6-11111
  1545 SOUTHFIELD RD 48146 — 389-0200
  Randall Kite, supt.
JSHS, 1701 CHAMPAIGN RD 48146 — 4-00111
  Charles Kratz, prin. — 389-0234

Linden, AC 810, PC 4, Genessee
Linden Community SD — 4-11111
  202 N BRIDGE ST 48451 — 735-7821
  Thomas Riutta, supt.
HS, 7201 SILVER LAKE RD 48451 — 3-00011
  Elaine Morgan, prin. — 735-9411
MS, 325 HYATT LN 48451 — 3-01100
  Lyndon Lewis, prin. — 735-9566

Litchfield, AC 517, PC 4, Hillsdale
Litchfield Community SD — 3-11111
  210 WILLIAMS ST 49252 — 542-2388
  John Van Nieuwenhuyz, supt.
JSHS, 210 WILLIAMS ST 49252 — 2-00111
  Dwight Smith, prin. — 542-2386

Livonia, PC 9, Wayne
Clarenceville SD — 4-11111
  20210 MIDDLEBELT RD 48152 — 810-473-8900
  David Kamish, supt.
Clarenceville HS — 2-00011
  20155 MIDDLEBELT RD 48152 — 810-473-8926
  David Simowski, prin.

Clarenceville MS 2-00100
20210 MIDDLEBELT RD 48152 810-473-8915
Carl Wagner, prin.

Livonia SD 7-11111
15125 FARMINGTON RD 48154 313-523-8800
Joseph Marinelli, supt.
Churchill HS 4-00011
8900 NEWBURGH RD 48150 313-523-9200
Rodney Hosman, prin.
Franklin HS, 31000 JOY RD 48150 4-00011
Michael Fenchel, prin. 313-523-9300
Stevenson HS 4-00011
33500 6 MILE RD 48152 313-523-9400
Dale Coller, prin.
Career Education Ctr Vo Tech
8985 NEWBURGH RD 48150 313-953-3900
Stephen Smith, prin.
Emerson MS 3-00100
29100 W CHICAGO ST 48150 313-523-9456
David Butler, prin.
Frost MS, 14041 STARK RD 48154 3-00100
Carol Schnurstein, prin. 313-523-9459
Holmes MS 3-00100
16200 NEWBURGH RD 48154 313-953-3932
Richard Haertel, prin.
Riley MS 3-00100
15555 HENRY RUFF ST 48154 313-523-9463
John Kuenzel, prin.
Other Schools – See Westland

Ladywood HS 3-00011
14680 NEWBURGH RD 48154 313-591-1544
Sr. Mary Smith, prin.
Madonna University 5-UC
36600 SCHOOLCRAFT RD 48150 313-591-5000
Mo Tech Education Center 2-CS
35155 INDUSTRIAL RD 48150 313-522-9510
NEC-National Institute of Technology 4-CS
18000 NEWBURGH RD 48152 313-464-7387
Schoolcraft College 6-CC
18600 HAGGERTY RD 48152 313-462-4400

Lowell, AC 616, PC 5, Kent
Lowell Area SD 5-11111
12685 FOREMAN ST 49331 897-8415
Fritz Esch, supt.
HS, 750 FOREMAN ST 49331 3-00011
Jim DeWeerd, prin. 897-4125
MS, 12675 FOREMAN ST 49331 3-00100
Mike Matlosz, prin. 897-9222

Ludington, AC 616, PC 6, Mason
Ludington Area SD 5-11111
809 E TINKHAM AVE 49431 845-7303
James Ford, supt.
HS, 508 N WASHINGTON AVE 49431 3-00011
Mark Boon, prin. 845-7303
DeJonge MS 2-00100
706 E TINKHAM AVE 49431 845-7303
Mark Boon, prin.

Mackinac Island, AC 906, PC 2, Mackinac
Mackinac Island SD 1-11111
PO BOX 340 49757 847-3377
Gary Urman, supt.
S, PO BOX 340 49757 1-11111
Gary Urman, prin. 847-3377

Mackinaw City, AC 616, PC 3, Cheboygan
Mackinaw City SD 2-11111
609 W CENTRAL AVE 49701 436-8211
Michael Bootz, supt.
JSHS, 609 W CENTRAL AVE 49701 1-00111
William Alexander, prin. 436-8211

Macomb Township, AC 810, PC 7, Macomb
Chippewa Valley SD
Supt. — See Clinton Township
Iroquois MS 3-00100
48301 ROMEO PLANK RD 48044 228-5590
Mary Holwey, prin.

L'Anse Creuse SD
Supt. — See Harrison Township
L'Anse Creuse North HS 4-00011
23700 21 MILE RD 48042 949-4450
Tom Denewith, prin.
L'Anse Creuse North MS 3-00100
46201 FAIRCHILD RD 48042 949-4040
James Dooley, prin.

Lutheran HS North 3-00011
16825 24 MILE RD 48042 781-9151
Steven Meseke, prin.

Madison Heights, AC 810, PC 8, Oakland
Lamphere SD 4-11111
31201 DORCHESTER AVE 48071 589-1990
James McCann, supt.
Lamphere HS, 610 W 13 MILE RD 48071 3-00011
Rich Yaroch, prin. 589-3943
Page MS, 29615 TAWAS ST 48071 2-00100
John Gatz, prin. 589-3428

Madison SD, 25421 ALGER ST 48071 4-11111
Jack Myers, supt. 399-7800
Madison HS, 915 E 11 MILE RD 48071 3-00011
William Cayen, prin. 548-1800
Wilkinson MS, 26524 JOHN R RD 48071 2-00100
Dell Weitzel, prin. 399-0455

Academy of Health Careers 2-CS
27301 DEQUINDRE RD STE 200 48071
547-8400
Bishop Foley HS 3-00011
32000 CAMPBELL RD 48071 585-1210
Alex Gajewski, prin.
Dorsey Business School 2-CS
30821 BARRINGTON ST 48071 585-9200

Mancelona, AC 616, PC 4, Antrim
Mancelona SD 3-11111
112 SAINT JOHNS ST 49659 587-9764
Thomas Ross, supt.
HS, 110 CARLTON ST 49659 2-00011
Harry Ashton, prin. 587-8551
MS, 209 MICHIGAN AVE 49659 2-00100
Terry McLeod, prin. 587-9869

Manchester, AC 313, PC 4, Washtenaw
Manchester Community SD 4-11111
710 E MAIN ST 48158 428-9711
Ronald Niedzwiecki, supt.
HS, 710 E MAIN ST 48158 2-00011
Russell LeBlanc, prin. 428-7333
Ackerson SD, 410 CITY RD 48158 2-01100
Brian Shick, prin. 428-7442

Manistee, AC 616, PC 6, Manistee
Manistee Area SD, 550 MAPLE ST 49660 4-11111
John Kuenzli, supt. 723-3521
HS, 550 MAPLE ST 49660 3-00011
R. Riemersma, prin. 723-2547
MS, 550 MAPLE ST 49660 2-00100
Suzette Darbor, prin. 723-3271

Manistee Catholic ES 2-11111
1500 MANISTEE HWY 49660 723-2529
William Zamrowski, prin.

Manistique, AC 906, PC 5, Schoolcraft
Manistique Area SD 4-11111
100 N CEDAR ST 49854 341-2195
Herb Harroun, supt.
JSHS, CEDAR & MAIN STS 49854 3-00111
Michael Jarski, prin. 341-2195

Manton, AC 616, PC 4, Wexford
Manton Consolidated SD 3-11111
PO BOX 280 49663 824-6411
Robert Henthorne, supt.
JSHS, PO BOX 280 49663 2-00111
Jim Davlantes, prin. 824-6411

Maple City, AC 616, PC 2, Leelanau
Glen Lake Community SD 3-11111
3375 W BURDICKVILLE RD 49664 334-3061
William Newkirk, supt.
Glen Lake JSHS 2-00111
3375 W BURDICKVILLE RD 49664 334-3062
John Scholten, prin.

Marcellus, AC 616, PC 4, Cass
Marcellus Community SD 3-11111
PO BOX 48 49067 646-7655
Dennis McCrumb, supt.
HS, PO BOX 48 49067 2-00011
Steve Lorenz, prin. 646-5081
MS, PO BOX 48 49067 2-00100
Mark Formsma, prin. 646-3158

Howardsville Christian S 2-11111
53441 BENT RD 49067 646-9367
Kenneth Gilson, prin.

Marenisco, AC 906, PC 3, Gogebic
Marenisco SD, PO BOX 188 49947 2-11111
Henry Aapala, supt. 787-2288
Roosevelt S, PO BOX 188 49947 2-11111
Henry Aapala, supt. 787-2288

Marine City, AC 810, PC 5, St. Clair
East China SD, 1585 MEISNER RD 48054 5-11111
Thomas Shorkey, supt. 765-8817
HS, 1085 WARD ST 48039 3-00011
Gary Miller, prin. 765-8881
MS, 6373 KING RD 48039 3-00100
S. Maki, prin. 765-8891
Other Schools – See Saint Clair

Cardinal Mooney HS 2-00011
660 S WATER ST 48039 765-8825
Fr. Vandeveire, prin.

Marion, AC 616, PC 3, Osceola
Marion SD, PO BOX O 49665 3-11111
J. G. Schwartz, supt. 743-2486
JSHS, PO BOX O 49665 2-00111
Thomas Cutler, prin. 743-2836

Marlette, AC 517, PC 4, Sanilac
Marlette Community SD 4-11111
3051 MOORE ST 48453 635-7425
Tony Parker, supt.
HS, 3051 MOORE ST 48453 2-00011
John Walker, prin. 635-7425
MS, 6230 EUCLID ST 48453 2-01100
Michael Distelrath, prin. 635-7425

Marquette, AC 906, PC 7, Marquette
Marquette Area SD 6-11111
1201 W FAIR AVE 49855 225-4400
William Bergin, supt.
HS, 1203 W FAIR AVE 49855 4-00011
Lawrence Lawless, prin. 225-4254

Bothwell MS, 1200 TIERNEY ST 49855 3-01100
Robert Lantz, prin. 225-4260
Graveraet MS, 611 N FRONT ST 49855 3-00100
Bill Ostwald, prin. 225-4300

Marquette General Hospital HSP
420 W MAGNETIC ST 49855 225-3434
Northern Michigan University 6-UC
610 COHODAS ADMIN CENTER 49855 227-2920

Marshall, AC 616, PC 6, Calhoun
Marshall SD, 100 E GREEN ST 49068 4-11111
Louis Giannunzio, supt. 781-1256
HS, 701 N MARSHALL AVE 49068 3-00011
Raymond Davis, prin. 781-1252
MS, 100 E GREEN ST 49068 3-00100
Judy Shelton, prin. 781-1291

Martin, AC 616, PC 2, Allegan
Martin SD, 1619 UNIVERSITY ST 49070 3-11111
Iris Williams, supt. 672-7194
JSHS, 1556 CHALMERS 49070 2-00111
Greg Alexander, prin. 672-5554

Marysville, AC 810, PC 6, St. Clair
Marysville SD 4-11111
1111 DELAWARE AVE 48040 364-7731
Charles Andrews, supt.
HS, 1325 MICHIGAN AVE 48040 3-00011
Thomas Hadden, prin. 364-7161
MS, 400 STADIUM DR 48040 3-00100
Sandra Standel, prin. 364-6336

Mason, AC 517, PC 6, Ingham
Mason SD, 118 W OAK ST 48854 5-11111
Glenn Doran, supt. 676-2484
HS, 1001 S BARNES ST 48854 3-00011
Timothy Young, prin. 676-9055
MS, 235 TEMPLE ST 48854 3-00100
John Borgert, prin. 676-6514

Mattawan, AC 616, PC 4, Van Buren
Mattawan Consolidated SD 5-11111
56720 MURRAY ST 49071 668-3361
J. Weeldreyer, supt.
HS, 56720 MURRAY ST 49071 3-00011
Douglas Knobloch, prin. 668-3361
MS, 56720 MURRAY ST 49071 3-00100
William McNulty, prin. 668-3361

Mayville, AC 517, PC 4, Tuscola
Mayville Community SD 4-11111
6250 FULTON ST 48744 843-6115
Lawrence Geiger, supt.
HS, 6250 FULTON ST 48744 2-00011
James Wencel, prin. 843-6116
MS, 6210 FULTON ST 48744 2-01100
Douglas Foote, prin. 843-6165

Mc Bain, AC 616, PC 3, Missaukee
McBain Rural Agricultural SD 3-11111
107 E MAPLE ST 49657 825-2165
Howard Napp, supt.
JSHS, 107 E MAPLE ST 49657 2-00111
Bruce Brumels, prin. 825-2412

Northern Michigan Christian S 2-11111
128 S MARTIN ST 49657 825-2492
Peter Boonstra, prin.

Melvindale, AC 313, PC 7, Wayne
Melvindale-Northern Allen Park SD 4-11111
18530 PROSPECT ST 48122 389-3300
Gerald Wolf, supt.
HS, 18656 PROSPECT ST 48122 3-00011
Robert Wallace, prin. 389-3320
Strong MS 3-00100
3303 OAKWOOD BLVD 48122 389-3325
Mark Kavorkian, prin.

Memphis, AC 810, PC 4, St. Clair
Memphis Community SD 3-11111
34110 BORDMAN RD 48041 392-2151
Kenneth Helinski, supt.
HS, 34165 BORDMAN RD 48041 2-00011
Richard Delekta, prin. 392-2186
MS, 34165 BORDMAN RD 48041 2-01100
Kenneth Reygaert, prin. 392-2131

Mendon, AC 616, PC 3, St. Joseph
Mendon Community SD 3-11111
26393 KIRBY RD 49072 496-8491
Jay Van Hoven, supt.
JSHS, 26393 KIRBY RD 49072 2-00111
(—), prin. 496-8491

Menominee, AC 906, PC 6, Menominee
Menominee Area SD 4-11111
1230 13TH ST 49858 863-9951
Randall Neelis, supt.
HS, 2101 18TH ST 49858 3-00011
Ken Hofer, prin. 863-7814
MS, 1200 11TH AVE 49858 3-00100
Wayne Anttila, prin. 863-9929

Merrill, AC 517, PC 3, Saginaw
Merrill Community SD 4-11111
431 W ALICE ST 48637 643-7261
Ken Tesauro, supt.
HS, 555 W ALICE ST 48637 2-00011
Douglas Fillmore, prin. 643-7231
MS, 755 W ALICE ST 48637 2-01100
Keith Clark, prin. 643-7247

Mesick, AC 616, PC 2, Wexford
Mesick Consolidated SD | 3-11111
PO BOX 275 49668 | 885-1200
George Hubbard, supt.
JSHS, PO BOX 275 49668 | 2-00111
Penny Baker, prin. | 885-1200

Michigan Center, AC 517, PC 5, Jackson
Michigan Center SD | 4-11111
400 S STATE ST 49254 | 764-5779
John Jimenez, supt.
JSHS, 400 S STATE ST 49254 | 3-00111
David Sawyer, prin. | 764-1440

Middleton, AC 517, PC 3, Gratiot
Fulton SD, 8060 ELY HWY 48856 | 3-11111
Fred Cunningham, supt. | 236-7300
Fulton JSHS, 8060 ELY HWY 48856 | 2-00111
Chuck Mungall, prin. | 236-7232

Middleville, AC 616, PC 4, Barry
Thornapple-Kellogg SD | 4-11111
3885 BENDER RD 49333 | 795-3313
Stephen Garrett, supt.
Thornapple-Kellogg HS | 3-00011
3885 BENDER RD 49333 | 795-3394
Henry Dugan, prin.
Thornapple-Kellogg MS | 3-00100
509 W MAIN ST 49333 | 795-3349
Gordon Dahlgren, prin.

Midland, AC 517, PC 8, Midland
Bullock Creek SD | 4-11111
1420 S BADOUR RD 48640 | 631-9022
Michael Freeland, supt.
Bullock Creek HS | 3-00011
1420 S BADOUR RD 48640 | 631-2340
Ron Main, prin.
Bullock Creek MS | 2-00100
644 S BADOUR RD 48640 | 631-9260
Greg Climie, prin.

Midland SD | 6-11111
600 E CARPENTER ST 48640 | 839-2401
Arthur Frock, supt.
Dow SHS, 3901 N SAGINAW ST 48640 | 3-00001
Ray Roberts, prin. | 839-2482
SHS, 1301 EASTLAWN DR 48642 | 3-00001
Daniel Shepard, prin. | 839-2481
Central JHS, 305 E REARDON ST 48640 | 3-00110
Paul Warner, prin. | 839-2471
Jefferson JHS, 800 W CHAPEL LN 48640 | 3-00110
Leonard Lawry, prin. | 839-2473
Northeast JHS, 1305 E SUGNET RD 48642 | 3-00110
Carol Staples, prin. | 839-2472

Calvary Baptist Academy | 2-11111
6100 N PERRINE RD 48640 | 832-3341
Michael Reece, prin.
Great Lakes Junior College of Business | 2-CC
3555 E PATRICK RD 48642 | 835-5588
Midland Christian S | 2-11111
4417 W WACKERLY ST 48640 | 835-9881
Keith Borgstrom, prin.
Northwood University | 5-UC
3225 COOK RD 48640 | 800-457-7878

Milan, AC 313, PC 5, Washtenaw
Milan Area SD, 920 NORTH ST 48160 | 4-11111
Patricia Dignan, supt. | 439-1541
HS, 920 NORTH ST 48160 | 3-00011
William Matley, prin. | 439-2411
MS, 432 S PLATT RD 48160 | 3-01100
D. Pennington, prin. | 439-2418

Milford, AC 810, PC 6, Oakland
Huron Valley SD
Supt. — See Highland
Muir MS, 425 GEORGE ST 48381 | 3-00100
Christine Hoben, prin. | 684-8060

Millington, AC 517, PC 4, Tuscola
Millington Community SD | 4-11111
8655 GLEASON RD 48746 | 871-5227
Robert Peterson, supt.
HS, 8780 DEAN RD 48746 | 3-00011
Michael Ferguson, prin. | 871-5220
Meachum MS, 8537 GLEASON RD 48746 | 2-00100
Donald Zoller, prin. | 871-5242

Mio, AC 517, PC 4, Oscoda
Mio-AuSable SD, PO BOX 909 48647 | 3-11111
R. B. Rank, supt. | 826-3225
Mio-AuSable JSHS | 2-00111
PO BOX 909 48647 | 826-3226
Frederick Groenke, prin.

Monroe, AC 313, PC 7, Monroe
Jefferson SD, 2400 N DIXIE HWY 48161 | 5-11111
Jon Rhoades, supt. | 289-5550
Jefferson HS, 5707 WILLIAMS RD 48161 | 3-00011
Stephan Scharf, prin. | 289-5555
Jefferson MS | 3-00100
5102 N STONEY CREEK RD 48161 | 289-5565
Charles Kennon, prin.

Monroe SD, 1275 N MACOMB ST 48161 | 6-11111
David Taylor, supt. | 241-0330
SHS, 901 HERR RD 48161 | 4-00001
Marian Hellenberg, prin. | 241-1491
JHS, 503 WASHINGTON ST 48161 | 4-00110
Randall Monday, prin. | 241-0776

Monroe County Community College | 4-CC
1555 S RAISINVILLE RD 48161 | 242-7300
Ross Business Institute | 2-CS
1285 N TELEGRAPH RD 48161 | 243-5456
St. Mary Catholic HS | 2-00011
108 W ELM AVE 48161 | 241-0663
Br. Livernois, prin.

Montague, AC 616, PC 4, Muskegon
Montague Area SD | 4-11111
4900 STANTON BLVD 49437 | 893-1515
Larry Lindquist, supt.
HS, 4900 STANTON BLVD 49437 | 2-00011
Roger Finlan, prin. | 894-2661
NBC MS, 4700 STANTON BLVD 49437 | 3-01100
Gary Beaudoin, prin. | 894-5617

Montrose, AC 810, PC 4, Genesee
Montrose Community SD | 4-11111
300 NANITA ST 48457 | 639-6131
W. Cypher, supt.
Hill-McCloy HS, 301 NANITA ST 48457 | 2-00011
Douglas Kinter, prin. | 639-6131
Kuehn-Haven MS, 303 RAY ST 48457 | 3-01100
Mark Kleinhans, prin. | 639-6131

Morenci, AC 517, PC 4, Lenawee
Morenci Area SD, 500 PAGE ST 49256 | 4-11111
Dana Compton, supt. | 458-7501
HS, 700 COOMER ST 49256 | 2-00011
Raddy VanGasse, prin. | 458-7502
MS, 131 CONGRESS ST 49256 | 2-00100
Ronald Merillat, prin. | 458-7506

Morley, AC 616, PC 3, Mecosta
Morley-Stanwood Community SD | 4-11111
4808 NORTHLAND DR 49336 | 856-4392
Philip Crouse, supt.
Morley-Stanwood JSHS | 3-00111
4808 NORTHLAND DR 49336 | 856-4444
Robert Lewis, prin.

Morrice, AC 517, PC 3, Shiawassee
Morrice Area SD | 3-11111
691 PURDY LANE 48857 | 625-3141
Margo Hooper, supt.
JSHS, 691 PURDY LANE 48857 | 2-00111
David Percival, prin. | 625-3141

Mount Clemens, AC 810, PC 7, Macomb
Mount Clemens Community SD | 5-11111
167 CASS AVE 48043 | 469-7800
Blanche Fraser, supt.
HS, 155 CASS AVE 48043 | 3-00011
Wayne Ries, prin. | 469-7070
MS, 161 CASS AVE 48043 | 3-00100
Nelson Jackson, prin. | 469-7013

Mount Morris, AC 810, PC 5, Genesee
Beecher Community SD
Supt. — See Flint
Dolan MS, 6255 NEFF RD 48458 | 2-01100
James Shelley, prin. | 785-4731

Mount Morris Consolidated SD | 5-11111
12356 WALTER ST 48458 | 686-8760
Larry Allen, supt.
Johnson HS, 8041 NEFF RD 48458 | 3-00011
Dave Bickel, prin. | 686-2370
MS, 12356 WALTER ST 48458 | 3-00100
Robert Sunday, prin. | 686-7100

Mount Pleasant, AC 517, PC 7, Isabella
Beal City SD, 3117 ELIAS RD 48858 | 3-11111
Paul Ellinger, supt. | 644-3901
Beal City JSHS, 3117 ELIAS RD 48858 | 2-00111
Roger Allen, prin. | 644-3944

Mount Pleasant SD | 5-11111
201 S UNIVERSITY AVE 48858 | 773-5500
Robert Janson, supt.
HS, 1155 S ELIZABETH ST 48858 | 4-00011
David Larson, prin. | 773-5500
West MS, 440 S BRADLEY RD 48858 | 3-00100
Carol Stark, prin. | 773-5500

Central Michigan University | 7-UC
100 WARRINER HALL 48858 | 774-3131
Sacred Heart Academy | 3-11111
316 E MICHIGAN ST 48858 | 772-1457
Richard Roberts, prin.

Munising, AC 906, PC 5, Alger
Munising SD, PO BOX 70 49862 | 4-11111
Steve Cromell, supt. | 387-2251
HS, 800 W MUNISING AVE 49862 | 2-00011
Helen Peters, prin. | 387-2103
Mather MS, ELM AVE 49862 | 2-01100
Jim Landfair, prin. | 387-2448

Muskegon, AC 616, PC 8, Muskegon
Muskegon SD | 6-11111
349 W WEBSTER AVE 49440 | 722-1602
Joseph Schulze, supt.
SHS, 80 W SOUTHERN AVE 49441 | 4-00001
Arlyn Zack, prin. | 726-4811
Bunker JHS, 2312 DENMARK ST 49441 | 3-00110
Carole Kolberg, prin. | 755-2211
Steele JHS, 1150 AMITY AVE 49442 | 3-00110
Bill Scott, prin. | 773-3291

Oakridge SD | 4-11111
481 S WOLF LAKE RD 49442 | 788-2361
Stan Fortuna, supt.
Oakridge HS | 2-00011
251 N WOLF LAKE RD 49442 | 788-2324
Robert Goryl, prin.
Oakridge MS | 2-00100
481 S WOLF LAKE RD 49442 | 788-2357
Joe Coletta, prin.

Orchard View SD | 5-11111
2310 MARQUETTE AVE 49442 | 773-3334
Gary Sarut, supt.
Orchard View HS | 3-00011
2310 MARQUETTE AVE 49442 | 773-3331
Rich Brothers, prin.
Orchard View MS | 3-00100
35 S SHERIDAN RD 49442 | 773-3336
P. Engblade, prin.

Baker College of Muskegon | 4-UC
141 HARTFORD AVE 49442 | 726-4904
Calvary Baptist Church S | 2-11111
1600 CLINTON ST 49442 | 726-4946
David Holtzhouse, prin.
Catholic Central HS | 2-00111
1145 W LAKETON AVE 49441 | 755-2201
Patricia O'Toole, prin.
Muskegon Community College | 4-CC
221 S QUARTERLINE RD 49442 | 777-0311
Ross Medical Education Center | 2-CS
950 W NORTON AVE 49441 | 739-1531
Western Michigan Christian HS | 2-00111
1212 KINGSLEY ST 49442 | 773-6502
Gerald Van Woerkom, prin.

Muskegon Heights, AC 616, PC 7, Muskegon
Muskegon Heights SD | 5-11111
2603 LEAHY ST 49444 | 739-9302
Eddie West, supt.
HS, 2427 JEFFERSON ST 49444 | 3-00011
James Buress, prin. | 733-2038
MS, 55 E SHERMAN BLVD 49444 | 2-00100
Nathaniel Allen, prin. | 733-2186

Napoleon, AC 517, PC 4, Jackson
Napoleon Community SD | 4-11111
PO BOX 308 49261 | 536-8667
Robert DuBois, supt.
HS, 201-21 WEST AVE 49261 | 2-00011
Mike Snyder, prin. | 536-8613
JSHS, 204 WEST AVE 49261 | 2-00100
Dale Cutler, prin. | 536-8643

Negaunee, AC 906, PC 5, Marquette
Negaunee SD, 101 S PIONEER AVE 49866 | 4-11111
Don Mourand, supt. | 475-4157
HS, 500 W ARCH ST 49866 | 3-00011
Michael Mileski, prin. | 475-7861
MS, 102 W CASE ST 49866 | 2-00100
R. Trebilcock, prin. | 475-7866

Newaygo, AC 616, PC 4, Newaygo
Newaygo SD, PO BOX 820 49337 | 5-11111
Ralph Burde, supt. | 652-6984
HS, 200 EAST ST 49337 | 2-00011
Edward Grodus, prin. | 652-1646
MS, 25 PARK ST 49337 | 2-00100
Tom Ebels, prin. | 652-1285

New Baltimore, AC 810, PC 6, Macomb
Anchor Bay SD | 5-11111
52801 ASHLEY ST 48047 | 725-2861
Juliana Texley, supt.
Anchor Bay HS | 4-00011
48650 SUGARBUSH RD 48047 | 949-4510
Rob Slezak, prin.
Anchor Bay JHS | 3-00100
52801 ASHLEY ST 48047 | 725-7373
Steven Lutz, prin.

Newberry, AC 906, PC 4, Luce
Tahquamenon Area SD | 4-11111
700 NEWBERRY AVE 49868 | 293-3226
Margaret Goldthorpe, supt.
HS, 700 NEWBERRY AVE 49868 | 2-00011
Helen Potoczak, prin. | 293-3243
MS, 700 NEWBERRY AVE 49868 | 2-00100
William Peltier, prin. | 293-5197

New Boston, AC 313, PC 4, Wayne
Huron SD | 4-11111
32044 HURON RIVER DR 48164 | 782-2441
Gary Jackson, supt.
Huron HS | 3-00011
32044 HURON RIVER DR 48164 | 782-1436
Daniel Webster, prin.
Renton JHS | 2-00100
31578 HURON RIVER DR 48164 | 782-2483
William Balwinski, prin.

New Buffalo, AC 616, PC 4, Berrien
New Buffalo Area SD | 3-11111
222 S WHITTAKER ST 49117 | 469-2211
Michael Lindley, supt.
JSHS, 222 S WHITTAKER ST 49117 | 2-00111
Ronald Hart, prin. | 469-2770

New Haven, AC 810, PC 4, Macomb
New Haven Community SD | 4-11111
57700 GRATIOT AVE 48048 | 749-5123
James Avery, supt.
JSHS, 57700 GRATIOT AVE 48048 | 2-00111
Frances Pough, prin. | 749-5104

New Lothrop, AC 313, PC 3, Shiawassee
New Lothrop Area SD — 3-11111
  9285 EASTON RD 48460 — 638-5091
  Bruce Evans, supt.
JSHS, 9285 EASTON RD 48460 — 2-00111
  James Dohm, prin. — 638-5054

Niles, AC 616, PC 7, Berrien
Brandywine SD — 4-11111
  1620 LASALLE ST 49120 — 684-7150
  David Porrell, supt.
Brandywine JSHS, 1700 BELL RD 49120 — 3-00111
  D. Shoemake, prin. — 683-4800

Niles Community SD — 5-11111
  111 SPRUCE ST 49120 — 683-0732
  John Huffman, supt.
HS, 1441 EAGLE ST 49120 — 4-00011
  David Clark, prin. — 683-2894
Lardner MS, 801 N 17TH ST 49120 — 3-00100
  John Tanke, prin. — 683-6610

First Assembly Christian S — 2-11111
  1922 E MAIN ST 49120 — 683-3518
  Linda Fearnow, prin.

North Adams, AC 517, PC 3, Hillsdale
North Adams-Jerome SD — 3-11111
  4555 KNOWLES RD 49262 — 287-4214
  Woodrow Hall, supt.
North Adams-Jerome JSHS — 2-00111
  4555 KNOWLES RD 49262 — 287-4214
  Philip Snyder, prin.

North Branch, AC 810, PC 4, Lapeer
North Branch Area SD — 4-11111
  6600 BRUSH ST 48461 — 688-3570
  Donald Gleason, supt.
HS, PO BOX 3620 48461 — 3-00011
  Lee Schleicher, prin. — 688-3001
Fox JHS, 6570 BRUSH ST 48461 — 3-00100
  Larry Lambert, prin. — 688-3284

North Branch Wesleyan Academy — 2-11111
  3164 N BRANCH RD 48461 — 688-2575
  Larry Curell, prin.

North Muskegon, AC 616, PC 5, Muskegon
North Muskegon SD — 3-11111
  1600 MILLS AVE 49445 — 744-5257
  Barbara Gowell, supt.
HS, 1507 MILLS AVE 49445 — 2-00011
  John Borchert, prin. — 744-1681
MS, 1500 MILLS AVE 49445 — 2-00100
  John Borchert, prin. — 744-1681

Reeths-Puffer SD, 991 W GILES RD 49445 — 5-11111
  Steven Fritz, supt. — 744-4736
Reeths-Puffer SHS — 3-00001
  1500 N GETTY ST 49445 — 744-1647
  Joseph Tibaldi, prin.
Reeths-Puffer JHS — 3-00110
  1911 W GILES RD 49445 — 744-4721
  Thomas Hornik, prin.

Northport, AC 616, PC 3, Leelanau
Northport SD, PO BOX 108 49670 — 2-11111
  Shari Hogue, supt. — 386-5153
S, 104 WING ST 49670 — 2-11111
  James Bodrie, prin. — 386-5154

Northville, AC 810, PC 6, Wayne
Northville SD, 501 W MAIN ST 48167 — 5-11111
  Leonard Rezmierski, supt. — 349-3400
HS, 775 N CENTER ST 48167 — 4-00011
  Thomas Johnson, prin. — 344-8425
Cooke MS, 21200 TAFT RD 48167 — 2-00100
  Jeffrey Radwanski, prin. — 344-8491
Meads Mill MS — 2-00100
  16700 FRANKLIN RD 48167 — 344-8435
  David Longridge, prin.

Norton Shores, AC 616, PC 7, Muskegon
Mona Shores SD — 5-11111
  3374 MCCRACKEN ST 49441 — 780-4751
  Kenneth Walcott, supt.
Mona Shores HS — 4-00011
  1121 SEMINOLE RD 49441 — 780-4711
  Dave Caruso, prin.
Mona Shores MS — 3-00100
  1700 WOODSIDE RD 49441 — 759-8506
  Daniel Cwayna, prin.

Norway, AC 906, PC 5, Dickinson
Norway-Vulcan Area SD — 4-11111
  PO BOX 159 49870 — 563-9552
  Rodney Green, supt.
HS, SECTION AND 3RD AVE 49870 — 2-00011
  Donald Byczek, prin. — 563-9542
Vulcan MS — 2-01100
  SECTION AND 3RD AVE 49870 — 563-9563
  Donald Byczek, prin.

Novi, AC 810, PC 8, Oakland
Novi Community SD — 5-11111
  25345 TAFT RD 48374 — 344-8330
  Emmett Lippe, supt.
HS, 24062 TAFT RD 48375 — 4-00011
  Art Miller, prin. — 344-8300
MS, 25299 TAFT RD 48374 — 2-00100
  Milan Obrenovich, prin. — 344-8320

Oak Park, AC 810, PC 8, Oakland
Berkley SD
  Supt. — See Berkley

Norup MS — 2-00100
  14450 MANHATTAN ST 48237 — 544-5830
  Steve Frank, prin.

Ferndale SD
  Supt. — See Ferndale
Best MS, 24220 ROSEWOOD ST 48237 — 2-00100
  Michael Kownacki, prin. — 547-0880

Oak Park SD, 13900 GRANZON ST 48237 — 5-11111
  Alexander Bailey, prin. — 691-8400
HS, 13701 OAK PARK BLVD 48237 — 3-00011
  Gary Marx, prin. — 691-8412
Roosevelt MS, 23261 SCOTIA ST 48237 — 3-00100
  William Hardy, prin. — 691-8449

Lawton School — 2-CS
  21800 GREENFIELD RD 48237 — 968-2421
Ross Technical Institute — 2-CS
  20820 GREENFIELD RD 48237 — 967-3100
Saa Beth Jacob School for Girls — 2-11111
  14390 W 10 MILE RD 48237 — 544-9070
  Goldie Silverstein, prin.
Yeshiva Beth Yehuda-Yeshiva Gedolah — 2-UC
  24600 GREENFIELD RD 48237

Okemos, AC 517, PC 7, Ingham
Okemos SD, 4406 OKEMOS RD 48864 — 5-11111
  Dan Wertz, supt. — 349-9460
HS, 4000 OKEMOS RD 48864 — 4-00011
  John Lanzetta, prin. — 349-4460
Kinawa MS, 1900 KINAWA DR 48864 — 3-00100
  Thomas Tweedy, prin. — 349-9220

Olivet, AC 616, PC 4, Eaton
Olivet Community SD, 255 1ST ST 49076 — 4-11111
  Edward Richardson, supt. — 749-9129
HS, 255 1ST ST 49076 — 2-00111
  David Campbell, prin. — 749-3671
MS, 255 1ST ST 49076 — 2-01100
  Kevin Kruger, prin. — 749-9953

Olivet College — 3-UC
  300 S MAIN ST 49076 — 800-456-7189

Onaway, AC 517, PC 4, Presque Isle
Onaway Area SD — 4-11111
  4549 STATE ROUTE 33 49765 — 733-8423
  Michael Jurgensen, supt.
JSHS, 4549 STATE ROUTE 33 49765 — 2-00111
  Warren Hauer, prin. — 733-4211

Onekama, AC 616, PC 3, Manistee
Onekama Consolidated SD — 2-11111
  5016 MAIN ST 49675 — 889-4251
  Kenneth Heikkinen, supt.
Onekama Consolidated JSHS — 2-00111
  5016 MAIN ST 49675 — 889-5521
  Roy Fortin, prin.

Onsted, AC 517, PC 3, Lenawee
Onsted Community SD — 4-11111
  PO BOX 220 49265 — 467-2174
  Eugene Deuel, supt.
HS, SLEE ROAD 49265 — 2-00011
  Charles Redding, prin. — 467-2171
MS, 1008 SLEE RD 49265 — 3-01100
  Michael Horning, prin. — 467-2168

Ontonagon, AC 906, PC 4, Ontonagon
Ontonagon Area SD — 3-11111
  301 GREENLAND RD 49953 — 884-4422
  William Creger, supt.
JSHS, 701 PARKER AVE 49953 — 2-00111
  John Peterson, prin. — 884-4422

Orchard Lake, AC 810, PC 4, Oakland
Bloomfield Hills SD
  Supt. — See Bloomfield Hills
West Hills MS — 2-00100
  2601 LONE PINE RD 48323 — 932-6100
  Janette Gwinn, prin.

St. Mary's College — 2-UC
  ORCHARD LAKE & COMMERCE RDS 48324 — 683-0504
St. Marys Prep S — 2-00011
  3535 ORCHARD LAKE RD 48324 — 683-0530
  Lawrence Reeside, prin.
SS. Cyril and Methodius Seminary — 2-UC
  3535 INDIAN TRL 48324 — 683-0311

Ortonville, AC 810, PC 4, Oakland
Brandon SD — 5-11111
  1025 S ORTONVILLE RD 48462 — 627-4981
  Joy Holler, supt.
Brandon HS — 3-00011
  1025 S ORTONVILLE RD 48462 — 627-4981
  Karen Sage, prin.
Brandon-Fletcher MS — 3-00100
  300 SOUTH ST 48462 — 627-4981
  Donald Patrick, prin.

Oscoda, AC 517, PC 4, Iosco
Oscoda Area SD, 3550 E RIVER RD 48750 — 4-11111
  Craig Douglas, supt. — 739-2033
Oscoda Area HS, 3550 E RIVER RD 48750 — 3-00011
  Mary Reitler, prin. — 739-9121
Richardson JHS, 3630 E RIVER RD 48750 — 3-00100
  Kevin James, prin. — 739-9106

Otisville, AC 810, PC 3, Genesee
Lakeville Community SD — 5-11111
  11107 WASHBURN RD 48463 — 793-6211
  Howard Merriman, supt.

Lakeville HS — 3-00011
  12455 WILSON RD # G 48463 — 793-6294
  G. Doctor, prin.
Lakeville MS — 3-00100
  11107 WASHBURN RD # G 48463 — 793-6281
  Frans Luoma, prin.

Otsego, AC 616, PC 5, Allegan
Otsego SD, 313 W ALLEGAN ST 49078 — 4-11111
  John Kingsnorth, supt. — 694-5131
HS, 540 WASHINGTON ST 49078 — 3-00011
  Dennis Massingill, prin. — 692-6371
MS, 538 WASHINGTON ST 49078 — 3-01100
  John Van Bonn, prin. — 694-9426

Ottawa Lake, AC 313, PC 2, Monroe
Whiteford Agricultural SD — 3-11111
  6655 CONSEAR RD 49267 — 856-2656
  John Gasidlo, supt.
Whiteford HS, 6655 CONSEAR RD 49267 — 2-00011
  Richard Gunn, prin. — 856-1443
Whiteford MS, 6655 CONSEAR RD 49267 — 2-00100
  Richard Gunn, prin. — 856-1443

Owendale, AC 517, PC 2, Huron
Owendale-Gagetown Area SD — 2-11111
  7166 SEBEWAING RD 48754 — 678-4261
  Manuel Thies, supt.
Owen-Gage JSHS — 2-00111
  7166 SEBEWAING RD 48754 — 678-4141
  Joanne Hopper, prin.

Owosso, AC 517, PC 7, Shiawassee
Owosso SD, PO BOX 340 48867 — 5-11111
  Thomas Hicks, supt. — 723-8131
HS, 765 E NORTH ST 48867 — 4-00011
  Roger Elford, prin. — 723-8231
MS, 219 N WATER ST 48867 — 3-00100
  Dave Ross, prin. — 723-3460

Baker College of Owosso — 2-UC
  1020 S WASHINGTON ST 48867 — 723-5251

Oxford, AC 810, PC 5, Oakland
Oxford SD, 105 S PONTIAC RD 48371 — 5-11111
  Marion Ginopolis, supt. — 628-2591
HS, 1420 E LAKEVILLE RD 48371 — 3-00011
  Mike Davis, prin. — 628-2546
MS, 1400 E LAKEVILLE RD 48371 — 3-00100
  Carole Papson, prin. — 628-4831

Pontiac Business Institute — 2-CS
  PO BOX 459 48371 — 628-4847

Painesdale, AC 906, PC 3, Houghton
Adams Township SD — 3-11111
  PO BOX 37 49955 — 482-0599
  Patrick Rozich, supt.
Jeffers JSHS, PO BOX 37 49955 — 2-00111
  James Maierle, prin. — 482-0580

Paradise, AC 906, PC 2, Chippewa
Whitefish SD, PO BOX 58 49768 — 1-11111
  Anne Westlund, supt. — 492-3353
Whitefish S, PO BOX 58 49768 — 1-11111
  Anne Westlund, prin. — 492-3353

Parchment, AC 616, PC 4, Kalamazoo
Parchment SD — 4-11111
  520 N ORIENT AVE 49004 — 342-7405
  W. Misner, supt.
HS, 1916 E G AVE 49004 — 2-00011
  La Cinda Dorrance, prin. — 342-7400
MS, 307 N RIVERVIEW DR 49004 — 2-00100
  Jane Pastor, prin. — 342-7416

Parma, AC 517, PC 3, Jackson
Western SD, 1400 S DEARING RD 49269 — 4-11111
  Craig Younkman, supt. — 531-3321
Western HS, 1400 S DEARING RD 49269 — 3-00011
  Floyd Strandberg, prin. — 531-3331
Western MS, 1400 S DEARING RD 49269 — 2-00100
  Blaine Goodrich, prin. — 531-3326

Paw Paw, AC 616, PC 5, Van Buren
Paw Paw SD, 119 PAW PAW RD 49079 — 4-11111
  C. Carlson, supt. — 657-8800
HS, 313 W MICHIGAN AVE 49079 — 3-00011
  Steven Daoust, prin. — 657-8841
Michigan Avenue MS — 3-00100
  600 E MICHIGAN AVE 49079 — 657-8870
  David Aubrey, prin.

Peck, AC 810, PC 3, Sanilac
Peck Community SD — 3-11111
  222 E LAPEER ST 48466 — 378-5171
  Richard Huntington, supt.
JSHS, 222 E LAPEER ST 48466 — 2-00111
  Michael Tubbs, prin. — 378-5501

Pellston, AC 616, PC 3, Emmet
Pellston SD, PO BOX 16 49769 — 3-11111
  Thomas Litzner, supt. — 539-8682
JSHS, 127 N PARK 49769 — 2-00111
  (—), prin. — 539-8801

Pentwater, AC 616, PC 4, Oceana
Pentwater SD, 600 PARK ST 49449 — 2-11111
  Lynn Bollman, supt. — 869-4064
S, 600 PARK ST 49449 — 2-11111
  Ronald Mousel, prin. — 869-7871

Perry, AC 517, PC 4, Shiawassee
Perry SD, 2775 BRITTON RD 48872 — 4-11111
  Jacklyn Hurd, supt. — 625-3108

HS, 2775 BRITTON RD 48872   3-00011
Dr. D. Oegema, prin.   625-3104
MS, 2775 BRITTON RD 48872   2-00100
Glenn Perry, prin.   625-6196

Petersburg, AC 313, PC 4, Monroe
Summerfield SD   3-11111
   17555 IDA WEST RD 49270   279-1035
   Russell Hoogendoorn, supt.
Summerfield HS   2-00011
   17555 IDA WEST RD 49270   279-1012
   Robert Scarbrough, prin.
Summerfield MS, 232 E ELM ST 49270   2-00100
   William Ryan, prin.   279-1013

Petoskey, AC 616, PC 6, Emmet
Petoskey SD, 1130 HOWARD ST 49770   5-11111
   Franklin Ronan, supt.   348-0160
HS, 1500 HILL ST 49770   3-00011
   Leonard Trudeau, prin.   348-0101
MS, 801 NORTHMEN DR 49770   3-00100
   Carl Moser, prin.   348-0181

North Central Michigan College   3-CC
   1515 HOWARD ST 49770   348-6600

Pewamo, AC 517, PC 3, Ionia
Pewamo-Westphalia SD   3-11111
   5101 S CLINTONIA RD 48873   587-3281
   Roy Thelen, supt.
Pewamo-Westphalia JSHS   2-00111
   5101 S CLINTONIA RD 48873   587-3281
   Michael Folk, prin.

St. Joseph S, 160 E ST 48873   1-01100
   Sr. Donna Thelen, prin.   593-3400

Pickford, AC 906, PC 3, Chippewa
Pickford SD, PO BOX 278 49774   2-11111
   Keith Krahnke, supt.   647-6285
JSHS, PO BOX 278 49774   2-00111
   Keith Krahnke, prin.   647-6285

Pigeon, AC 517, PC 4, Huron
Elkton-Pigeon-Bayport SD   4-11111
   6136 PIGEON RD 48755   453-2097
   Robert Drury, supt.
Laker HS, 6136 PIGEON RD 48755   2-00011
   Lisa Dicamillo, prin.   453-2348
Laker MS, 6136 PIGEON RD 48755   2-00100
   Richard Pauly, prin.   453-3131

Pinckney, AC 313, PC 4, Livingston
Pinckney Community SD   5-11111
   PO BOX 9 48169   878-3115
   Ted Culver, supt.
HS, PO BOX 9 48169   3-00011
   Gerald Lester, prin.   878-3115
MS, PO BOX 7 48169   3-00100
   Iva Katz-Hesse, prin.   878-3115

Pinconning, AC 517, PC 4, Bay
Pinconning Area SD   4-11111
   605 W 5TH ST 48650   879-4556
   Michael Manor, supt.
HS, 605 W 5TH ST 48650   3-00011
   Kenneth Fegan, prin.   879-2311
Pinconning Area MS   2-00100
   605 W 5TH ST 48650   879-8410
   Thomas Mason, prin.

Pittsford, AC 517, PC 3, Hillsdale
Pittsford Area SD   3-11111
   3111 HAMILTON ST 49271   523-3481
   Max Baxter, supt.
JSHS, 3111 HAMILTON ST 49271   2-00111
   Eugene Shaw, prin.   523-3483

Plainwell, AC 616, PC 5, Allegan
Plainwell Community SD   5-11111
   600 SCHOOL DR 49080   685-5823
   David Jones, supt.
HS, 684 STARR RD 49080   3-00011
   Linda Iciek, prin.   685-9554
MS, 720 BRIGHAM ST 49080   3-00100
   Robert Howe, prin.   685-5813

Plymouth, AC 313, PC 6, Wayne
Plymouth-Canton Community SD   7-11111
   454 S HARVEY ST 48170   451-3120
   John M. Hoben, supt.
Central MS, 650 CHURCH ST 48170   3-00100
   Patricia Moore, prin.   451-6580
East MS, 1042 S MILL ST 48170   3-00100
   T. Workman, prin.   451-6565
Pioneer MS   3-00100
   46081 W ANN ARBOR RD 48170   451-6575
   Cheryl Johnson, prin.
West MS   3-00100
   44401 W ANN ARBOR TRL 48170   451-6570
   Judith Stone, prin.
Other Schools – See Canton, Westland

Agape Christian Academy   2-11111
   41550 E ANN ARBOR TRL 48170   459-5430
   Mark Moore, prin.

Pontiac, AC 810, PC 8, Oakland
Pontiac SD   7-11111
   350 WIDE TRACK DR E 48342   857-8123
   Darryl Lee, supt.
Central HS, 300 W HURON ST 48341   4-00011
   Ezra Sloan, prin.   857-8400

Northern HS, 1051 ARLENE AVE 48340   4-00011
   David Badger, prin.   857-8460
Jefferson/Whittier JHS   2-00100
   600 MOTOR ST 48341   857-8333
   Jimmie Randolph, prin.
Lincoln JHS, 131 HILLSIDE DR 48342   3-00100
   Larry Beamer, prin.   333-2903
Madison JHS, 1275 N PERRY ST 48340   3-00100
   Jesse Petway, prin.   857-8520
Washington JHS   3-00100
   710 MENOMINEE RD 48341   333-1555
   Leroy Williams, prin.

North Oakland Medical Center   HSP
   461 W HURON ST 48341   857-7222
Oakland Catholic SD   2-00011
   1300 GIDDINGS RD 48340   373-5300
   Frank Turk, prin.

Portage, AC 616, PC 8, Kalamazoo
Portage SD   6-11111
   8111 S WESTNEDGE AVE 49002   329-7400
   James Rikkers, supt.
Central HS   4-00011
   8135 S WESTNEDGE AVE 49002   329-7267
   Frank Gawkowski, prin.
Northern HS, 1000 IDAHO AVE 49002   4-00011
   Tim Dorgan, prin.   329-7328
Central MS   3-00100
   8035 S WESTNEDGE AVE 49002   329-7308
   Dick Tyler, prin.
North MS, 5808 OREGON AVE 49002   3-00100
   Mary Lou Wright, prin.   329-7358
West MS   3-00100
   7145 MOORS BRIDGE RD 49002   327-9104
   John Schreur, prin.

Port Hope, AC 517, PC 2, Huron
Port Hope Community SD   2-11111
   7840 PORTLAND RD 48468   428-4151
   James Hunter, supt.
S, 7840 PORTLAND RD 48468   2-11111
   Laurel Klump, prin.   428-4151

Port Huron, AC 810, PC 8, St. Clair
Port Huron Area SD   7-11111
   1925 LAPEER AVE 48060   984-3101
   Larry Moeller, supt.
HS, 2215 COURT ST 48060   4-00011
   Larry Crosby, prin.   984-2611
Central MS, 200 32ND ST 48060   3-00100
   Frank Haynes, prin.   984-6533
Chippewa MS   3-00100
   2800 CHIPPEWA TRL 48060   984-6539
   Andrew Pochodylo, prin.
Holland Woods MS   3-00100
   1617 HOLLAND AVE 48060   984-6548
   Robert Barber, prin.
Other Schools – See Fort Gratiot

Baker College of Port Huron   2-UC
   3403 LAPEER RD 48060
McCormick Consolidated Academy   2-00100
   2865 HENRY ST 48060   985-9069
   Paul Crowell, prin.
Port Huron Hospital   HSP
   1001 KEARNEY ST 48060   987-5000
St. Clair County Community College   4-CC
   323 ERIE ST 48060   984-3881

Portland, AC 517, PC 5, Ionia
Portland SD, 1100 IONIA RD 48875   4-11111
   Charles Dumas, supt.   647-4161
HS, 1100 IONIA RD 48875   3-00011
   Mannes Overweg, prin.   647-2981
MS, 745 STORZ ST 48875   2-00100
   William Adams, prin.   647-2985

St. Patricks S, 112 N WEST ST 48875   3-11111
   Elizabeth Kolarik, prin.   647-7551

Posen, AC 517, PC 2, Presque Isle
Posen Consolidated SD   2-11111
   10575 MICHIGAN AVE 49776   766-2573
   Michael Murch, supt.
JSHS, 10575 MICHIGAN AVE 49776   2-00111
   Clifford Kelly, prin.   766-2471

Potterville, AC 517, PC 4, Eaton
Potterville SD, 420 N HIGH ST 48876   4-11111
   William Heath, supt.   645-2662
JSHS, 420 N HIGH ST 48876   2-00111
   Linda Wigginton, prin.   645-7609

Powers, AC 906, PC 2, Menominee
North Central Area SD   3-11111
   PO BOX 601 49874   498-7737
   Kenneth Groh, supt.
North Central JSHS   2-00111
   PO BOX 601 49874   497-5226
   Norman McKindles, prin.

Quincy, AC 517, PC 4, Branch
Quincy Community SD   4-11111
   1 EDUCATIONAL PKY 49082   639-7141
   Rich Tait, supt.
HS, 18 COLFAX ST 49082   2-00011
   Joseph Lopez, prin.   639-9245
MS, 32 FULTON ST 49082   2-00100
   Sarah Coolman, prin.   639-4201

Rapid River, AC 906, PC 3, Delta
Rapid River SD, PO BOX 68 49878   3-11111
   John Palmer, supt.   474-6424
Tri-Twp. JSHS, PO BOX 68 49878   2-01111
   William Pistulka, prin.   474-6411

Ravenna, AC 616, PC 3, Muskegon
Ravenna SD, 12322 STAFFORD ST 49451   4-11111
   George Jacob, supt.   853-2231
HS, 2700 S RAVENNA RD 49451   2-00011
   J. Koenigsknecht, prin.   853-2218

Reading, AC 517, PC 4, Hillsdale
Reading Community SD   3-11111
   519 ELM ST 49274   283-2166
   Robert Duncan, supt.
Owens JSHS, 301 CHESTNUT ST 49274   2-00111
   Jon Burrell, prin.   283-2142

Redford, AC 313, PC 8, Wayne
Detroit SD
   Supt. — See Detroit
Ann Arbor Trail MS   3-00100
   7635 CHATHAM 48239   849-2363
   Margaret Estill, prin.

Redford Union SD   6-11111
   18499 BEECH DALY RD 48240   592-3300
   Kenneth Johnson, supt.
HS, 17711 KINLOCH 48240   3-00011
   Robert Schramke, prin.   592-3395
Hilbert MS, 26440 PURITAN 48239   3-00100
   Brian Motter, prin.   592-3380

South Redford SD   5-11111
   26141 SCHOOLCRAFT 48239   535-4000
   Jan W. Jacobs, supt.
Thurston HS   3-00011
   26255 SCHOOLCRAFT 48239   535-4000
   Stew Schauder, prin.
Pierce MS, 25605 ORANGELAWN 48239   3-00100
   Lorraine Yadach, prin.   535-4000

Bishop Borgess HS   2-00011
   11685 APPLETON 48239   255-1100
   Sr. Joan Charnley, prin.
Catholic Central HS   3-00011
   14200 BREAKFAST DR 48239   534-0660
   Fr. Moffatt, prin.
St. Agatha HS   2-00011
   25707 PEMBROKE AVE 48240   532-3317
   Roberta Clemak, prin.

Reed City, AC 616, PC 4, Osceola
Reed City SD   4-11111
   829 S CHESTNUT ST 49677   832-2201
   James Ryan, supt.
JSHS, 225 W CHURCH AVE 49677   3-00111
   Ken Kent, prin.   832-2224

Reese, AC 517, PC 4, Tuscola
Reese SD, 9535 CENTER ST 48757   4-11111
   Larry Lethorn, supt.   868-9864
HS, 1696 S VAN BUREN RD 48757   2-00011
   Larry Ostrander, prin.   868-4191
MS, 9590 SAGINAW ST 48757   2-01100
   Robert Colby, prin.   868-4157

Remus, AC 517, PC 3, Mecosta
Chippewa Hills SD   4-11111
   3226 ARTHUR RD 49340   967-3614
   Thomas Pillar, supt.
Chippewa Hills HS   3-00011
   3226 ARTHUR RD 49340   967-3614
   Joyce Shull, prin.
MS, 350 E WHEATLAND AVE 49340   2-00100
   Darryl Soper, prin.   967-3550

Republic, AC 906, PC 4, Marquette
Republic-Michigamme SD   2-11111
   RR 1 BOX 201A 49879   376-2277
   Edward Eppert, supt.
Republic-Michigamme S   2-11111
   RR 1 BOX 201A 49879   376-2277
   Edward Eppert, prin.

Richland, AC 616, PC 2, Kalamazoo
Gull Lake Community SD   5-11111
   11775 E D AVE 49083   629-5880
   Daniel Lukich, supt.
Gull Lake HS, 9550 M 89 49083   3-00011
   Rob Sickles, prin.   629-5803
Other Schools – See Hickory Corners

Richmond, AC 810, PC 5, McComb
Richmond Community SD   4-11111
   68931 S MAIN ST 48062   727-3565
   Keith Mino, supt.
Richmond Community JSHS   3-00111
   35320 DIVISION RD 48062   727-3225
   Tom Powers, prin.

River Rouge, AC 313, PC 7, Wayne
River Rouge SD   4-11111
   1411 COOLIDGE HWY 48218   297-9605
   William McCollum, supt.
JSHS, 1411 COOLIDGE HWY 48218   3-00111
   Donna Jones, prin.   297-9615

Riverview, AC 313, PC 7, Wayne
Riverview Community SD   4-11111
   13425 COLVIN ST 48192   285-9660
   Michael Krigelski, supt.
HS, 12431 LONGSDORF ST 48192   3-00011
   Charles Pike, prin.   285-7361

Seitz MS, 17800 KENNEBEC ST 48192   2-00100
Donald Lessner, prin.   285-2043

Detroit Business Institute   3-CS
19100 FORT ST 48192   479-0660

Rochester, AC 810, PC 6, Oakland
Rochester Community SD   7-11111
501 W UNIVERSITY DR 48307   651-6210
John Schultz, supt.
Adams HS, 3200 W TIENKEN RD 48306   4-00011
Caye Randolph, prin.   652-0116
HS, 180 S LIVERNOIS RD 48307   4-00011
Richard Ickes, prin.   651-5590
Hart MS, 6500 SHELDON RD 48306   3-00100
Tresa Zumsteg, prin.   651-2930
Reuther JHS, 1430 E AUBURN RD 48307   3-00100
Greg Owens, prin.   852-9221
Van Hoosen JHS   3-00100
1339 N ADAMS RD 48306   651-7370
Marv Rubin, prin.
Other Schools – See Rochester Hills

Lutheran HS Northwest   2-00011
1000 BAGLEY AVE 48309   852-6677
Timothy Ewell, prin.
Oakland University   6-UC
1 OAKLAND UNIVERSITY 48309   370-3500

Rochester Hills, AC 810, PC 8, Oakland
Avondale SD
Supt. — See Auburn Hills
Avondale MS   3-00100
1435 W AUBURN RD 48309   852-2600
Gerald Hanley, prin.

Rochester Community SD
Supt. — See Rochester
West JHS, 500 OLD PERCH RD 48309   3-00100
Pam Lesperance, prin.   375-9400

Michigan Christian College   2-UC
800 W AVON RD 48307   800-521-6010

Rock, AC 906, PC 2, Delta
Mid-Peninsula SD   2-11111
5055 SAINT NICHOLAS 31ST RD 49880
Gene DeKeyser, supt.   359-4387
Mid-Peninsula S   2-11111
5055 SAINT NICHOLAS 31ST RD 49880
Roy Vaessen, prin.   359-4387

Rockford, AC 616, PC 5, Kent
Rockford SD, 235 COURTLAND ST 49341   6-11111
Michael Shibler, supt.   866-1597
HS, 4100 KROES ST NE 49341   4-00011
Jim Haskins, prin.   866-1541
MS, 397 E DIVISION ST 49341   3-00100
Jamie Hosford, prin.   866-1534

Rogers City, AC 517, PC 5, Presque Isle
Rogers City Area SD   3-11111
251 W HURON AVE 49779   734-4013
Roger Benner, supt.
JSHS, 1033 W HURON AVE 49779   2-00111
James Connell, prin.   734-2143

Romeo, AC 810, PC 5, McComb
Romeo Community SD   5-11111
316 N MAIN ST 48065   752-0200
George Harrison, supt.
SHS, 11091 32 MILE RD 48065   3-00001
Julie Markham, prin.   752-0300
JHS, 297 PROSPECT ST 48065   3-00110
Michael LaFeve, prin.   752-0240

Romulus, AC 313, PC 7, Wayne
Romulus Community SD   5-11111
36540 GRANT ST 48174   941-1600
Wm. Bedell, supt.
HS, 9650 WAYNE RD 48174   4-00011
Thomas Dolan, prin.   941-2170
JHS, 37300 WICK RD 48174   3-00100
Andrea Williams, prin.   722-1050

Woodhaven SD
Supt. — See Flat Rock
Brownstown MS   3-00100
20135 INKSTER RD 48174   783-3400
Herbert Kehrl, prin.

Roscommon, AC 517, PC 3, Roscommon
Gerrish-Higgins SD, 814 LAKE ST 48653   4-11111
Donald Mick, supt.   275-5800
JSHS, 10600 OAKWOOD RD 48653   3-00111
Claude Rummer, prin.   275-5331

Kirtland Community College   3-CC
10775 SAINT HELEN RD # F-97 48653
   275-5121

Roseville, AC 810, PC 8, Macomb
Roseville Community SD   6-11111
18975 CHURCH ST 48066   445-5505
John Kment, supt.
HS, 17855 COMMON RD 48066   4-00011
Thomas Evans, prin.   445-5542
Eastland JHS, 18700 FRANK ST 48066   3-00110
Claudia Varblow, prin.   445-5702
JHS, 16250 MARTIN RD 48066   4-00110
Joseph Bresciami, prin.   445-5605

Calvary Christian S   2-11111
17000 EASTLAND ST 48066   776-2650
Steven Kaminski, prin.
Dorsey Business School   2-CS
31542 GRATIOT AVE 48066   296-3225

Royal Oak, AC 810, PC 8, Oakland
Royal Oak SD   6-11111
1123 LEXINGTON BLVD 48073   435-8400
Lawrence Nichols, supt.
Dondero HS   4-00011
709 N WASHINGTON AVE 48067   541-7100
Gerald Judge, prin.
Kimball HS   4-00011
1500 LEXINGTON BLVD 48073   435-8500
Thomas Neville, prin.
Addams MS   2-00100
2222 W WEBSTER RD 48073   288-3100
Joe Scheer, prin.
Churchill MS, 707 GIRARD AVE 48073   2-00100
Rita Walker, prin.   588-5050
Keller MS, 1505 N CAMPBELL RD 48067   2-00100
James Hunter, prin.   541-5225

Oakland Community College   4-CC
SOUTHEAST CAMPUS 48073   548-1252
Shrine HS, 3500 W 13 MILE RD 48073   2-00111
Thomas Kirkwood, prin.   549-2925
William Beaumont Hospital   HSP
3601 W 13 MILE RD 48073   551-0681

Rudyard, AC 906, PC 3, Chippewa
Rudyard Area SD   4-11111
2ND & WILLIAM 49780   478-3771
G. Bosshart, supt.
JSHS, 2ND & WILLIAM 49780   2-00111
Alan Kantola, prin.   478-3771

Saginaw, AC 517, PC 8, Saginaw
Bridgeport-Spaulding Community SD
Supt. — See Bridgeport
Bridgeport-Spaulding JHS   3-01100
3675 SOUTHFIELD DR 48601   777-9440
Hiram Becker, prin.

Buena Vista SD, PO BOX 4829 48601   4-11111
T. Wallace, supt.   755-2184
Buena Vista HS   2-00011
3945 E HOLLAND RD 48601   745-1493
Mildred Mason-Dennis, prin.
Ricker MS, 1925 S OUTER DR 48601   2-00100
Kenneth Waters, prin.   753-6438

Carrollton SD
Supt. — See Carrollton
Carrollton HS   2-00011
1235 MAPLERIDGE RD 48604   753-3433
Terrence Urquhart, prin.

Saginaw SD, 550 MILLARD ST 48607   7-11111
F. B. Gibbs, supt.   759-2200
Hill SHS, 3115 MACKINAW ST 48602   4-00001
Thomas Sharpe, prin.   797-4815
Saginaw SHS, 3100 WEBBER ST 48601   3-00001
Wilson Smith, prin.   759-3577
Averill Career Ctr, 2102 WEISS ST 48602   Vo Tech
Julie Walker, prin.   797-4836
Central JHS   3-00100
900 S WEADOCK AVE 48607   759-3538
John Norwood, prin.
North JHS, 1101 N BOND ST 48602   3-00110
Ostranda Lane, prin.   759-3552
South JHS, 224 N ELM ST 48602   3-00110
Thomas Barris, prin.   797-4803
Webber JHS, 2600 PRESCOTT AVE 48601   3-00110
Cliff Davis, prin.   759-3563

Saginaw Township Community SD   5-11111
PO BOX 6278 48608   797-1800
Wayne Vasher, supt.
Heritage HS, 3465 N CENTER RD 48603   4-00011
E. Sheffield, prin.   799-5790
White Pine MS, 505 N CENTER RD 48603   4-00100
David Nizinski, prin.   797-1814

Swan Valley SD, 8380 OHERN RD 48609   4-11111
Richard Syrek, supt.   781-3100
Swan Valley HS, 8400 OHERN RD 48609   3-00011
John Cuthbertson, prin.   781-2740
Swan Valley MS, 8400 OHERN RD 48609   2-00100
Richard Decker, prin.   781-2270

Community Baptist Christian S   2-11111
8331 GRATIOT RD 48609   781-2340
D. Jackson, prin.
Great Lakes Junior College of Business   3-CC
310 S WASHINGTON AVE 48607   755-3444
Michigan Lutheran Seminary   2-00011
2777 HARDIN ST 48602   793-1041
William Zeiger, prin.
Nouvel Catholic Central HS   3-00011
2555 WIENEKE RD 48603   791-4330
Marie Denome, prin.
Ross Medical Education Center   2-CS
4054 BAY RD 48603   793-9800
St. Mary's Medical Center   HSP
830 S JEFFERSON AVE 48601   776-8176
Valley Lutheran HS   2-00011
3560 MCCARTY RD 48603   790-1676
David Krause, prin.

Saint Charles, AC 517, PC 4, Saginaw
St. Charles Community SD   4-11111
891 W WALNUT ST 48655   865-9961
James Slick, supt.
HS, 881 W WALNUT ST 48655   2-00011
Michael Olson, prin.   865-9991
Thurston MS, 893 W WALNUT ST 48655   2-00100
Terry Fuller, prin.   865-9927

Saint Clair, AC 810, PC 6, St. Clair
East China SD
Supt. — See Marine City
HS, 2200 CLINTON AVE 48079   3-00011
Richard Rose, prin.   329-4757
MS, 301 N 6TH ST 48079   3-00100
Joseph Pius, prin.   329-2251

Saint Clair Shores, AC 810, PC 8, Macomb
Lake Shore SD, 30401 TAYLOR ST 48082   5-11111
John Brackett, supt.   296-8205
Lake Shore HS   3-00011
22980 E 13 MILE RD 48082   296-8242
Gloria Ehrler, prin.
Kennedy MS   3-00100
23101 MASONIC BLVD 48082   296-8315
Beatrice Ullrich, prin.

Lakeview SD, 20300 STATLER ST 48081   5-11111
David Myers, supt.   445-4015
Lakeview HS, 21100 E 11 MILE RD 48081   3-00011
William Johanns, prin.   445-4045
Jefferson MS   3-00100
27900 ROCKWOOD ST 48081   445-4130
Fred Zielke, prin.

South Lake SD   4-11111
23700 GREATER MACK AVE 48080   445-4209
Ronald Cook, supt.
South Lake HS   3-00011
21900 E 9 MILE RD 48080   445-4248
William Putney, prin.
South Lake MS   2-00100
21621 CALIFORNIA ST 48080   445-4340
Brian Campbell, prin.

Saint Ignace, AC 906, PC 5, Mackinac
St. Ignace Area SD   3-11111
840 PORTAGE ST 49781   643-8145
Fred Stearns, supt.
Lasalle HS, 840 PORTAGE ST 49781   2-00011
M. Springsteen, prin.   643-8800
St. Ignace Area MS   2-01100
860 PORTAGE ST 49781   643-7822
Mike Lehto, prin.

Saint James, AC 616, PC 2, Charlevoix
Beaver Island Community SD   1-11111
PO BOX 235 49782   448-2744
Mark Eckhardt, supt.
Beaver Island S, PO BOX 235 49782   1-11111
Kathleen McNamara, prin.   448-2744

Saint Johns, AC 517, PC 6, Clinton
St. John's SD, PO BOX 230 48879   5-11111
Stephen Bakita, supt.   224-9352
HS, 501 W SICKLES ST 48879   4-00011
William Swears, prin.   224-9341
Wilson MS, 101 W CASS ST 48879   3-00100
Robert Kudwa, prin.   224-1714

Grove Christian S   2-11111
6990 E PRICE RD 48879
Larry Kruger, prin.

Saint Joseph, AC 616, PC 6, Berrien
St. Joseph SD, 2214 S STATE ST 49085   5-11111
Fred Richardson, supt.   982-4621
HS, 2521 STADIUM DR 49085   3-00011
Thomas Miller, prin.   982-4623
Upton MS, 800 MAIDEN LN 49085   3-00100
Allen Skibbe, prin.   982-4631

Lake Michigan Catholic HS   2-00111
915 PLEASANT ST 49085   983-2511
Dale Cryan, prin.
Michigan Lutheran HS   2-00011
615 E MARQUETTE WOODS RD 49085   429-7861
Rev. Franzman, prin.

Saint Louis, AC 517, PC 5, Gratiot
St. Louis SD, 113 E SAGINAW ST 48880   4-11111
Tom Kowalski, supt.   681-2545
HS, 201 E SAGINAW ST 48880   2-00011
Keith Wing, prin.   681-2500
Nurnberger MS, 312 UNION ST 48880   2-01100
John Raab, prin.   681-5155

Saline, AC 313, PC 6, Washtenaw
Saline Area SD, 7190 N MAPLE RD 48176   5-11111
Ellen Ewing, supt.   429-5454
HS, 7190 N MAPLE RD 48176   3-00011
Paul Thibault, prin.   429-5454
MS, 7265 N ANN ARBOR ST 48176   3-00100
Joseph Schwartz, prin.   429-5454

Saline Christian S   2-11111
300 OLD CREEK DR 48176   429-7733
Ann Chatfield, prin.

Sand Creek, AC 517, PC 2, Lenawee
Sand Creek Community SD   3-11111
6850 SAND CREEK HWY 49279   436-3121
Don Barnes, supt.

JSHS, 6518 SAND CREEK HWY 49279 2-00111
Michael McAran, prin. 436-3121

Sandusky, AC 810, PC 4, Sanilac
Sandusky Community SD 4-11111
191 PINE TREE LN 48471 648-3400
James Nolan, supt.
HS, 191 PINE TREE LN 48471 2-00011
Mark Hund, prin. 648-3401
MS, 395 S SANDUSKY RD 48471 2-00100
Tim Lentz, prin. 648-3300

Sanford, AC 517, PC 3, Midland
Meridian SD, 3361 N M 30 48657 4-11111
James Gillette, supt. 687-3200
Meridian HS, 3303 N M 30 48657 2-00011
Wayne King, prin. 687-3225
Meridian MS, 3475 N M 30 48657 2-00100
Michael Rickey, prin. 687-3208

Saranac, AC 616, PC 4, Ionia
Saranac Community SD 4-11111
150 PLEASANT ST 48881 642-9102
Bruce Chadwick, supt.
HS, 150 PLEASANT ST 48881 2-00011
Nelson TerBurgh, prin. 642-9186
Harker MS, 234 WEEKS RD 48881 2-00100
David Benjamin, prin. 642-9701

Saugatuck, AC 616, PC 3, Allegan
Saugatuck SD, PO BOX 186 49453 3-11111
Terry Brooks, supt. 857-1444
JSHS, 401 ELIZABETH ST 49453 2-00111
Tom A. Nowak, prin. 857-2133

Sault Sainte Marie, AC 906, PC 7, Chippewa
Sault Sainte Marie Area SD 5-11111
460 W SPRUCE ST 49783 635-6609
David Zuhlke, supt.
HS, 904 MARQUETTE AVE 49783 3-00011
John Swart, prin. 635-6605
MS, 684 MARQUETTE AVE 49783 3-00100
(—), prin. 635-6604

Lake Superior State University 4-UC
1000 COLLEGE DR 49783 635-2202

Schoolcraft, AC 616, PC 4, Kalamazoo
Schoolcraft Community SD 4-11111
PO BOX 278 49087 679-4331
William Haug, supt.
HS, PO BOX 278 49087 2-00011
Richard Moon, prin. 679-5201
MS, PO BOX 278 49087 2-01100
Lynn Horton, prin. 679-5179

Scottville, AC 616, PC 4, Mason
Mason County Central SD 4-11111
300 W BROADWAY ST 49454 757-3713
Bruce Smith, supt.
Mason County Central HS 2-00011
300 W BROADWAY ST 49454 757-4748
Jack Murchie, prin.
Mason County Central MS 2-01100
310 W BERYL ST 49454 757-3724
Michael Robinson, prin.

West Shore Community College 2-CC
PO BOX 277 49454 845-6211

Sebewaing, AC 517, PC 4, Huron
Unionville-Sebewaing SD 3-11111
628 E MAIN ST 48759 883-2360
William D. Dodge, supt.
Unionville-Sebewaing HS 2-00011
2203 WILDNER RD 48759 883-2534
David Blossom, prin.
Unionville-Sebewaing MS 2-01100
628 E MAIN ST 48759 883-3140
Anthony Grant, prin.

Shelby, AC 616, PC 4, Oceana
Shelby SD, 155 E 6TH ST 49455 4-11111
James Peters, supt. 861-5211
HS, 525 N STATE ST 49455 2-00011
Dave Killips, prin. 861-4452
MS, FIFTH ST 49455 2-00100
Duane Shugart, prin. 861-4521

Shelby Township, AC 313, PC 8, Macomb
Utica Community SD 7-11111
51041 SHELBY RD 48316 739-0400
Joan Sergent, supt.
Shelby JHS 3-00110
51700 VAN DYKE AVE 48316 254-8325
Thomas Bodell, prin.
Other Schools – See Sterling Heights, Utica,
Washington Township

Shepherd, AC 517, PC 4, Isabella
Shepherd SD, PO BOX 219 48883 4-11111
Douglas Dodge, supt. 828-5520
HS, 100 E HALL ST 48883 3-00011
Bob Alger, prin. 828-6601
MS, 100 E HALL ST 48883 2-00100
Thomas Shepard, prin. 828-6601

Sidney, AC 517, PC 2, Montcalm

Montcalm Community College 4-CC
2800 COLLEGE DR 48885 328-2111

Southfield, AC 810, PC 8, Oakland
Southfield SD, 24661 LAHSER RD 48034 6-11111
Marlene Davis, supt. 746-8500

HS, 24675 LAHSER RD 48034 4-00011
Kenneth Wilson, prin. 746-8650
Levey MS, 25300 W 9 MILE RD 48034 3-00100
Cecil Rice, prin. 746-8740
Thompson MS 3-00100
16300 LINCOLN DR 48076 746-7400
Michael Horn, prin.
Other Schools – See Lathrup Village

Academy of Court Reporting 2-CS
26111 EVERGREEN RD STE 101 48076
353-4880
Detroit Business Institute 2-CS
21700 NORTHWESTERN HWY #515 48075
557-5744
Dorsey Business School 2-CS
24901 NRTHWSTRN HWY STE 202 48075
352-7830
Lawrence Technological University 5-UC
21000 W 10 MILE RD 48075 800-225-5588
Providence Hospital HSP
16001 W 9 MILE RD 48075 424-3293
Southfield Christian S 3-11111
28650 LAHSER RD 48034 357-3660
Phil Ackley, prin.
Specs Howard School of Broadcast Arts 3-CS
16900 W 8 MILE RD STE 115 48075
569-0101

Southgate, AC 313, PC 8, Wayne
Southgate Community SD 5-11111
13201 TRENTON RD 48195 246-4600
Thomas Withee, supt.
Allen Annex HS 2-00011
16500 MCCANN ST 48195 246-4644
Roger Dittmer, prin.
Anderson HS, 15475 LEROY ST 48195 4-00011
Michael Kell, prin. 246-4611
Gerisch MS, 12601 MCCANN ST 48195 3-00100
Marilyn Svaluto, prin. 246-4623

Aquinas HS 2-00011
15601 NORTHLINE RD 48195 283-3190
Richard Kuhn, prin.
Dorsey Business School 2-CS
15755 NORTHLINE RD 48195 285-5400

South Haven, AC 616, PC 6, Van Buren
South Haven SD, 554 GREEN ST 49090 5-11111
Larry Blackmer, supt. 637-0520
Mohr HS, 600 ELKENBURG ST 49090 3-00011
John Yelding, prin. 637-0500
Baseline MS, 7357 BASELINE RD 49090 3-01100
John Weiss, prin. 637-0530

South Lyon, AC 810, PC 6, Oakland
South Lyon Community SD 5-11111
235 W LIBERTY ST 48178 437-8127
Duane Moore, supt.
HS, 1000 N LAFAYETTE ST 48178 4-00011
Larry Jackson, prin. 437-2031
MS, 61526 9 MILE RD 48178 3-00100
Linda Martin, prin. 437-8176

Sparta, AC 616, PC 5, Kent
Sparta Area SD, 480 S STATE ST 49345 5-11111
Michael Weiler, supt. 887-8253
HS, 480 S STATE ST 49345 3-00011
Randall Morris, prin. 887-8213
JHS, 240 GLENN ST 49345 3-01100
Mary Stearns, prin. 887-8211

Spring Arbor, AC 517, PC 4, Jackson

Spring Arbor College 4-UC
106 E MAIN ST 49283 750-1200

Spring Lake, AC 616, PC 5, Ottawa
Spring Lake SD 4-11111
345 HAMMOND ST 49456 846-5500
Larry Mason, supt.
Spring Lake JSHS 3-00111
345 HAMMOND ST 49456 846-7581
Mark Westerburg, prin.

Springport, AC 517, PC 3, Jackson
Springport SD, PO BOX 100 49284 4-11111
Dale McCarty, supt. 857-3495
HS, PO BOX 100 49284 2-00111
Roland Pakonen, prin. 857-3475

Stambaugh, AC 906, PC 4, Iron
West Iron County SD 4-11111
PO BOX 580 49964 265-9218
Sharon Stockero, supt.
Other Schools – See Iron River

Standish, AC 517, PC 4, Arenac
Standish-Sterling Community SD 4-11111
3789 WYATT RD 48658 846-4526
Claude Inch, supt.
Standish-Sterling JSHS 3-00111
3789 WYATT RD 48658 846-4526
Dennis Haut, prin.

Stanton, AC 517, PC 4, Montcalm
Central Montcalm SD 4-11111
1480 SHERIDAN RD SW 48888 831-5243
Robert Spencer, supt.
Central HS, PO BOX 9 48888 3-00011
Jerry Winkler, prin. 831-5247
Central MS, PO BOX 9 48888 3-00100
Irma Baker, prin. 831-5256

Stephenson, AC 906, PC 3, Menominee
Stephenson Area SD 4-11111
526 W DIVISION ST 49887 753-2221
Charles Kalhoefer, supt.
JSHS, 526 W DIVISION ST 49887 2-00111
P. Weismantel, prin. 753-2222

Sterling Heights, AC 810, PC 9, Macomb
Utica Community SD
Supt. — See Shelby Township
Stevenson SHS 4-00001
39701 DODGE PARK RD 48313 268-4700
Susan Meyer, prin.
Ford HS 4-00011
11911 CLINTON RIVER RD 48313 254-8200
David Lathers, prin.
Bemis JHS, 12500 19 MILE RD 48313 3-00110
Joyce Spade, prin. 254-8330
Davis JHS 3-00110
11311 PLUMBROOK RD 48312 825-2200
Richard Pearson, prin.
Heritage JHS 2-00110
37400 DODGE PARK RD 48312 825-2205
F. Finkbeiner, prin.
Jeanette JHS, 40400 GULLIVER DR 48310 3-00110
Lillian Demas, prin. 825-2210

Warren Consolidated SD
Supt. — See Warren
SHS, 12901 15 MILE RD 48312 4-00001
Merle Loch, prin. 825-2700
Carleton JHS, 8900 15 MILE RD 48312 2-00110
Joyce Field, prin. 825-2590
Flynn JHS, 2899 FOX HILL DR 48310 3-00110
Charles Kluka, prin. 825-2900
Fuhrmann MS, 5155 E 14 MILE RD 48310 3-00100
Ronald Dziurda, prin. 825-2930
Grissom JHS, 35701 RYAN RD 48310 2-00110
William Hanley, prin. 825-2560

Sterling Christian S 2-11111
33380 RYAN RD 48310 268-5420
Tony Bryson, prin.

Stevensville, AC 616, PC 4, Berrien
Lakeshore SD 5-11111
5771 CLEVELAND AVE 49127 428-1400
Gary Campbell, supt.
Lakeshore HS 3-00011
5771 CLEVELAND AVE 49127 428-1400
William Scaletta, prin.
Lakeshore JHS 3-00100
1459 W JOHN BEERS RD 49127 428-1408
Dennis Kniola, prin.

Stockbridge, AC 517, PC 4, Ingham
Stockbridge Community SD 4-11111
303 W ELIZABETH ST 49285 851-7188
Andrew De Saeger, supt.
HS, 416 N CLINTON ST 49285 3-00011
Kenneth Larson, prin. 851-7770
MS, S WOOD ST 49285 3-01100
Patrick Harrington, prin. 851-8149

Sturgis, AC 616, PC 7, St. Joseph
Nottawa Community SD 2-11111
26438 M 86 49091 467-7153
Bruce Nelson, supt.
Nottawa S, 26438 M 86 49091 2-11111
Bruce Nelson, prin. 467-7153

Sturgis SD, 216 VINEWOOD AVE 49091 5-11111
Lyle Sisson, supt. 659-1500
JSHS, 216 VINEWOOD AVE 49091 4-00111
Wendell Moyer, prin. 659-1515

Suttons Bay, AC 616, PC 3, Leelanau
Suttons Bay SD, PO BOX 367 49682 3-11111
Robert MacEachran, supt. 271-3846
JSHS, PO BOX 367 49682 2-00111
William Crandell, prin. 271-3844

Swartz Creek, AC 810, PC 5, Genesee
Swartz Creek Community SD 5-11111
8354 CAPPY LN 48473 635-4441
Charles Townsend, supt.
HS, 1 DRAGON DR 48473 4-00011
Sheldon Safer, prin. 635-4441
MS, 8230 CRAPO ST 48473 4-00100
Jon Hartwig, prin. 635-4441

Tawas City, AC 517, PC 4, Iosco
Tawas Area SD, 245 M 55 W 48763 4-11111
David Conzelmann, supt. 362-4481
Tawas Area HS, 255 M 55 W 48763 2-00011
Ronald Milks, prin. 362-6127
Tawas Area MS, 255 M 55 W 48763 2-00100
Jerry Youngs, prin. 362-6129

Taylor, AC 313, PC 8, Wayne
Taylor SD, 23033 NORTHLINE RD 48180 7-11111
Barbara Van Otterloo, supt. 374-1200
Kennedy HS, 13505 PINE ST 48180 4-00011
Carl Bargamian, prin. 374-1229
Taylor Center HS, 24715 WICK RD 48180 4-00011
Robert Haarala, prin. 295-5700
Truman HS 4-00011
11211 BEECH DALY RD 48180 946-6551
Gale Mitchell, prin.
Career Center HS Vo Tech
9601 WESTLAKE ST 48180 295-5757
Paul Lammers, prin.
Brake JHS, 13500 PINE ST 48180 3-00100
A. Sebastian, prin. 374-1227

Hoover JHS, 27101 BEVERLY ST 48180   3-00100
Lee Lewis, prin.   295-5775
West JHS, 10575 WILLIAM AVE 48180   3-00100
Kenneth Nelson, prin.   295-5783

Light and Life Christian S   2-11111
8900 PARDEE RD 48180   292-1660
George Kennedy, prin.
Ross Business Institute   2-CS
22293 EUREKA RD 48180   374-2135

Tecumseh, AC 517, PC 6, Lenawee
Tecumseh SD   5-11111
304 W CHICAGO BLVD 49286   423-2167
Gerard Pound, supt.
HS, 307 N MAUMEE ST 49286   3-00011
Ben Thomas, prin.   423-6008
MS, 212 N OTTAWA ST 49286   2-00100
Ron June, prin.   423-1105

Tekonsha, AC 517, PC 3, Calhoun
Tekonsha SD, 245 S ELM ST 49092   2-11111
James Showers, supt.   767-4121
JSHS, 245 S ELM ST 49092   2-00111
Harry Hochstetler, prin.   767-4121

Temperance, AC 313, PC 6, Monroe
Bedford SD, 1623 W STERNS RD 48182   5-11111
Herbert Moyer, supt.   847-6736
Bedford HS, 8285 JACKMAN RD 48182   4-00011
Rob Flessner, prin.   847-6736
Bedford JHS, 8405 JACKMAN RD 48182   4-00100
Mary Zaums, prin.   847-6736

Three Oaks, AC 616, PC 4, Berrien
River Valley SD   4-11111
15480 S THREE OAKS RD 49128   756-9541
Charles Williams, supt.
River Valley HS   2-00011
15480 S THREE OAKS RD 49128   756-9541
Douglas Degner, prin.
River Valley MS   2-00100
15480 S THREE OAKS RD 49128   756-9541
David Zech, prin.

Three Rivers, AC 616, PC 6, St. Joseph
Three Rivers Community SD   5-11111
1008 8TH ST 49093 – Janet Allen, supt.   279-1100
HS, 207 E MICHIGAN AVE 49093   3-00011
Sherman Thurkow, prin.   279-1120
MS, 1101 JEFFERSON ST 49093   3-01100
Louis Seman, prin.   279-1130

Traverse City, AC 616, PC 7, Grand Traverse
Traverse City Area SD   7-11111
PO BOX 32 49685   922-6450
Peter Wharton, supt.
SHS, 1150 MILLIKEN DR 49686   4-00001
(—), prin.   922-6600
East JHS, 1776 3 MILE RD N 49686   4-00110
Michael Murray, prin.   922-8800
West JHS, 3950 SILVER LAKE RD 49684   4-00110
George Bourdo, prin.   922-6700

Immaculate Conception MS   2-01100
218 VINE ST 49684   947-1252
Michael Knoff, prin.
Munson Medical Center   HSP
1105 6TH ST 49684   922-9000
Northwestern Michigan College   5-CC
1701 E FRONT ST 49686   800-748-0566
St. Francis HS, 123 E 11TH ST 49684   2-00011
Wayne LaPointe, prin.   946-8038

Trenton, AC 313, PC 7, Wayne
Trenton SD, 2603 CHARLTON RD 48183   5-11111
John Doyle, supt.   676-8600
HS, 2601 CHARLTON RD 48183   3-00011
Jerome Peterson, prin.   692-4530
Monguagon MS, 4000 MARIAN DR 48183   2-00100
Bill Miller, prin.   676-8700

Troy, AC 810, PC 8, Oakland
Troy SD, 4400 LIVERNOIS RD 48098   7-11111
Janet Jopke, supt.   689-0600
Athens HS, 4333 JOHN R RD 48098   4-00011
R. Cross, prin.   524-1200
HS, 4777 NORTHFIELD PKY 48098   4-00011
Larry Boehms, prin.   952-6200
Baker MS, 1291 TORPEY DR 48083   3-00100
Larry Hahn, prin.   689-1971
Boulan Park MS   3-00100
3570 NORTHFIELD PKY 48084   643-9404
Antoinette Burke, prin.
Larson MS   3-00100
2222 E LONG LAKE RD 48098   689-8710
Leon Klein, prin.
Smith MS, 5835 DONALDSON DR 48098   3-00100
Stuart Redpath, prin.   879-0500

Bethany Christian S   2-11111
2601 JOHN R RD 48083   689-4821
Juan Moreno, prin.
Carnegie Institute   2-CS
550 STEPHENSON HWY STE 100 48083
  589-1078
ITT Technical Institute   2-CC
1225 E BIG BEAVER RD 48083   524-1800
Walsh Coll. Accountancy & Bus. Admin.   4-UC
PO BOX 7006 48007   689-8282

Twining, AC 517, PC 2, Arenac
Arenac Eastern SD   3-11111
200 SMALLEY ST 48766   867-4234
Loren Wycoff, supt.
Arenac Eastern S   3-11111
200 SMALLEY ST 48766   867-4231
John Thomas, prin.

Ubly, AC 517, PC 3, Huron
Ubly Community SD   3-11111
2020 UNION ST 48475   658-8202
David Landeryou, supt.
HS, 2020 UNION ST 48475   2-00011
Frederick Ligrow, prin.   658-8554

Union City, AC 517, PC 4, Branch
Union City Community SD   4-11111
430 SAINT JOSEPH ST 49094   741-8091
William Tebbe, supt.
HS, 430 SAINT JOSEPH ST 49094   2-00011
Mervin Miller, prin.   741-8561
MS, 435 SAINT JOSEPH ST 49094   2-01100
Eugene Pensari, prin.   741-5381

Union Lake, AC 313, PC 6, Oakland

Oakland Community College   4-CC
7350 COOLEY LAKE ROAD 48387   363-7191

University Center, AC 517, PC see Bay City

Delta College 48710   6-CC
  686-9201
Saginaw Valley State University   5-UC
2250 PIERCE RD 48710   790-4042

Utica, AC 313, PC 6, Macomb
Utica Community SD
Supt. — See Shelby Township
SHS, 47255 SHELBY RD 48317   4-00001
Richard Mann, prin.   254-8300
Eppler MS, 45461 BROWNELL ST 48317   3-00110
David Turrel, prin.   254-8320

Vanderbilt, AC 517, PC 3, Otsego
Vanderbilt Area SD   2-11111
947 DONOVAN ST 49795   983-4121
Daniel Woodward, supt.
S, 947 DONOVAN ST 49795   2-11111
Nadine O'Brien, prin.   983-2561

Vassar, AC 517, PC 5, Tuscola
Vassar SD, 220 ATHLETIC ST 48768   4-11111
Andrew Booth, supt.   823-8535
HS, 220 ATHLETIC ST 48768   3-00011
Dan Heckman, prin.   823-8534
MS, 220 ATHLETIC ST 48768   2-00100
Paul Wojno, prin.   823-8533

Vermontville, AC 517, PC 3, Eaton
Maple Valley SD   4-11111
11090 NASHVILLE HWY 49096   852-9699
Ozzie Parks, supt.
Maple Valley JSHS   3-00111
11090 NASHVILLE HWY 49096   852-9275
Larry Lenz, prin.

Vestaburg, AC 517, PC 2, Montcalm
Vestaburg Community SD   3-11111
7188 AVENUE B 48891   268-5353
Ronald Milks, supt.
JSHS, 7188 AVENUE B 48891   2-00111
Bonnie Hecker, prin.   268-5343

Vicksburg, AC 616, PC 4, Kalamazoo
Vicksburg Community SD   5-11111
301 S KALAMAZOO ST 49097   649-0550
Larry Cole, supt.
HS, 501 E HIGHWAY ST 49097   3-00011
Ronald Fuller, prin.   649-0554
MS, 348 E PRAIRIE ST 49097   3-00100
Charles Glaes, prin.   649-0552

Wakefield, AC 906, PC 4, Gogebic
Wakefield Township SD   3-11111
715 PUTNAM ST 49968   224-9421
Lawrence Kapugia, supt.
JSHS, 715 PUTNAM ST 49968   2-00111
Robert Mercure, prin.   224-7211

Waldron, AC 517, PC 3, Hillsdale
Waldron Area SD   2-11111
1338 WALDRON ROAD 49288   286-6251
Paul Kleeman, supt.
JSHS, 1338 WALDRON ROAD 49288   2-00111
David Snook, prin.   286-6251

Walkerville, AC 616, PC 2, Oceana
Walkerville Rural Community SD   2-11111
PO BOX 68 49459   873-4850
Nancy Kraska, supt.
JSHS, FRANKLIN ST 49459   2-00111
David Dewey, prin.   873-3652

Walled Lake, AC 810, PC 6, Oakland
Walled Lake Consolidated SD   7-11111
850 LADD RD BLDG D 48390   960-8300
James Geisler, supt.
Central HS   4-00011
2978 S COMMERCE RD 48390   960-8600
Richard Smith, prin.
Western HS, 600 BECK RD 48390   4-00011
D. Champnella, prin.   960-8500
MS, 46720 W PONTIAC TRL 48390   3-00100
Joan Heinz, prin.   960-8550
Other Schools – See Commerce Township

Warren, AC 810, PC 9, Macomb
Fitzgerald SD, 23200 RYAN RD 48091   5-11111
James Edoff, supt.   757-1750
Fitzgerald HS, 23200 RYAN RD 48091   3-00011
Joy Holman, prin.   757-7070
Chatterton MS, 24333 RYAN RD 48091   3-00100
Judith Ryder, prin.   757-6650

Van Dyke SD   5-11111
22100 FEDERAL AVE 48089   758-8333
Michael Dyke, supt.
Lincoln HS, 22900 FEDERAL AVE 48089   4-00011
Roger Markham, prin.   758-8305
Lincoln MS, 22500 FEDERAL AVE 48089   3-00100
Marvin Fischer, prin.   758-8320

Warren Consolidated SD   7-11111
31300 ANITA DR 48093   825-2410
Paul Stamatakis, supt.
Cousino HS, 30333 HOOVER RD 48093   3-00011
Joseph Sayers, prin.   574-3100
Warren-Mott HS   4-00011
3131 E 12 MILE RD 48092   574-3250
Philip Hutchins, prin.
Beer MS, 3200 MARTIN RD 48092   3-00100
John Mocny, prin.   574-3175
Carter MS, 12000 MASONIC BLVD 48093   3-00100
James Dolan, prin.   825-2620
Other Schools – See Sterling Heights

Warren Woods SD   5-11111
27100 SCHOENHERR RD 48093   445-6300
Thomas Dobbs, supt.
Tower HS, 27900 BUNERT RD 48093   3-00011
Robert Tyler, prin.   775-8780
Warren Woods MS   3-00100
13400 E 12 MILE RD 48093   751-1800
Alfred Cardinali, prin.

Bethesda Christian S   3-11111
12900 FRAZHO RD 48089   756-6100
John Romine, prin.
De La Salle Collegiate HS   3-00111
14600 COMMON RD 48093   778-2207
Br. Lackey, prin.
Detroit College of Business-Warren   2-UC
27500 DEQUINDRE RD 48092
Immaculate Conception HS   1-00011
29400 WESTBROOK AVE 48092   574-0510
Sr. Mary Lukiw, prin.
Macomb Christian S   2-11111
28501 LORRAINE AVE 48093   751-8980
Burton Schultz, prin.
Macomb Community College   7-CC
14500 E 12 MILE RD 48093   445-7000
Ross Medical Education Center   1-CS
26417 HOOVER RD 48089   758-7200
Sawyer School of Business   3-CS
26051 HOOVER RD 48089   758-2300

Washington Township, AC 313, PC 7, Macomb
Utica Community SD
Supt. — See Shelby Township
Eisenhower SHS, 6500 25 MILE RD 48094   4-00001
Verne Lamoreaux, prin.   781-5571
Malow JHS, 6400 25 MILE RD 48094   3-00110
Arthur Thomas, prin.   781-0400

Waterford, AC 810, PC 8, Oakland
Waterford SD   7-11111
6020 PONTIAC LAKE RD 48327   666-4000
Dale Martin, supt.
Kettering HS, 2800 BENDER AVE 48329   4-00011
Ron Kowaleswski, prin.   673-1261
Mott HS, 1151 SCOTT LAKE RD 48328   4-00011
Stuart Thorell, prin.   674-4134
NW Oakland Skill Center   Vo Tech
1415 CRESCENT LAKE RD 48327   674-4875
Keith Wunderlich, prin.
Crary JHS, 501 N CASS LAKE RD 48328   3-00100
Eugene Downie, prin.   682-9300
Mason JHS   3-00100
3835 W WALTON BLVD 48329   674-2281
Michael LeMense, prin.
Pierce JHS, 5145 HATCHERY RD 48329   3-00100
Donna Elwell, prin.   674-0331

Our Lady of the Lakes HS   2-00111
5495 DIXIE HWY 48329   623-0340
Carl Uberti, prin.
Ross Medical Education Center   2-CS
253 SUMMIT DR 48328   683-1166

Watersmeet, AC 906, PC 3, Gogebic
Watersmeet Township SD   2-11111
PO BOX 217 49969   358-4504
Don Parling, supt.
S, PO BOX 217 49969   2-11111
Parnell Basanese, prin.   358-4555

Watervliet, AC 616, PC 4, Berrien
Watervliet SD   4-11111
450 E RED ARROW HWY 49098   463-5566
Kenneth Bannen, supt.
JSHS, 450 E RED ARROW HWY 49098   3-00111
Kevin Harness, prin.   463-4221

Wayland, AC 616, PC 5, Allegan
Wayland UNSD   5-11111
835 E SUPERIOR ST 49348   792-2181
R. Brenner, supt.
HS, 870 E SUPERIOR ST 49348   3-00011
Jack Deming, prin.   792-2254

MS, 201 PINE ST 49348 — 2-00100
Jon Jensen, prin. — 792-2306

Wayne, AC 313, PC 7, Wayne
Wayne-Westland Community SD
Supt. — See Westland
Memorial SHS, 3001 4TH ST 48184 — 4-0001 / 595-2200
Ron Stratton, prin.
Franklin JHS — 3-00110
33555 ANNAPOLIS ST 48184 — 595-2400
Leo Schuster, prin.

Dorsey Business School — 2-CS
34841 VETERANS PLZ 48184 — 595-1540
United Care, Annapolis Hospital — HSP
33155 ANNAPOLIS ST 48184 — 467-4000

Webberville, AC 517, PC 4, Ingham
Webberville Community SD — 3-11111
313 GRAND RIVER RD E 48892 — 521-3422
Bruce Brown, supt.
JSHS, 309 GRAND RIVER RD E 48892 — 2-00111
Robert Gerisch, prin. — 521-3447

West Bloomfield, AC 810, PC 8, Oakland
West Bloomfield SD — 5-11111
3250 COMMERCE RD 48324 — 738-3555
Seymour Gretchko, supt.
HS, 4925 ORCHARD LAKE RD 48323 — 4-00011 / 539-2500
George Fornero, prin.
Abbott MS — 3-00100
3380 ORCHARD LAKE RD 48324 — 738-3600
Teri Giannetti, prin.
Orchard Lake MS — 2-00100
6000 ORCHARD LAKE RD 48322 — 539-2400
Esther Peterson, prin.

West Branch, AC 517, PC 4, Ogemaw
West Branch-Rose City SD — 5-11111
PO BOX 308 48661 — 345-2460
James Zubulake, supt.
Ogemaw Heights HS — 3-00011
PO BOX 308 48661 — 345-2855
Jamie Richards, prin.
Surline MS, PO BOX 308 48661 — 3-01100
Jeffrey Budge, prin. — 345-0195

Westland, AC 313, PC 8, Wayne
Livonia SD
Supt. — See Livonia
NW Wayne Skill Ctr — Vo Tech
8075 RITZ AVE 48185 — 523-9388
EARL DAWSON, prin.

Plymouth-Canton Community SD
Supt. — See Plymouth
Lowell MS, 8400 N HIX RD 48185 — 3-00100
Patricia Patton, prin. — 451-6503
Wayne-Westland Community SD — 7-11111
36745 MARQUETTE ST 48185 — 595-2000
Larry Thomas, supt.
Glenn SHS — 4-00001
36105 MARQUETTE ST 48185 — 595-2300
Dennis Connolly, prin.
Adams JHS, 33475 PALMER RD 48185 — 3-00110
Celestine Sanders, prin. — 595-2377
Marshall JHS, 35100 BAYVIEW ST 48185 — 3-00110 / 595-2444
Larry Galbraith, prin.
Stevenson JHS, 38501 PALMER RD 48185 — 3-00110
William Camp, prin. — 595-2500
Other Schools — See Wayne

Lutheran HS, 33300 COWAN RD 48185 — 2-00011
Steven Schwecke, prin. — 422-2090

White Cloud, AC 616, PC 4, Newaygo
White Cloud SD — 4-11111
553 W WILCOX AVE 49349 — 689-6820
Gary Pardike, supt.
JSHS, PO BOX 824 49349 — 3-00111
Patrick Bootz, prin. — 689-1707

Whitehall, AC 616, PC 5, Muskegon
Whitehall SD, 541 E SLOCUM ST 49461 — 4-11111
Jack Mansfield, supt. — 893-7335
HS, 541 E SLOCUM ST 49461 — 2-00011
Dennis Love, prin. — 894-5661

MS, 401 S ELIZABETH ST 49461 — 3-01100
Ilene Bosma, prin. — 894-9023

White Lake, AC 810, PC 5, Oakland
Huron Valley SD
Supt. — See Highland
Lakeland HS — 4-00011
1630 BOGIE LAKE RD 48383 — 684-8080
Sam Osborn, prin.
MS, 1450 BOGIE LAKE RD 48383 — 3-00100
Ed Jaworowicz, prin. — 684-8070

White Pigeon, AC 616, PC 4, St. Joseph
White Pigeon Community SD — 4-11111
410 E PRAIRIE AVE 49099 — 483-7676
Dale Kimball, supt.
JSHS, 410 E PRAIRIE AVE 49099 — 3-00111
Phyllis Giera, prin. — 483-7679

White Pine, AC 906, PC 4, Ontonagon
White Pine SD, PO BOX 307 49971 — 2-11111
David Koski, supt. — 885-5351
JSHS, PO BOX 307 49971 — 1-00111
John Valesano, prin. — 885-5591

Whitmore Lake, AC 313, PC 5, Washtenaw
Whitmore Lake SD, 8845 MAIN ST 48189 — 4-11111
Glenn Bachman, supt. — 449-4464
HS, 8877 MAIN ST 48189 — 2-00011
Richard Gaubatz, prin. — 449-4461
MS, 8877 MAIN ST 48189 — 2-01100
Mary Waters, prin. — 449-4715

Whittemore, AC 517, PC 2, Iosco
Whittemore-Prescott Area SD — 4-11111
PO BOX 250 48770 — 756-2061
Alan McLean, supt.
Whittemore-Prescott JSHS — 3-00111
PO BOX 250 48770 — 756-2501
Roger Spencer, prin.

Williamston, AC 517, PC 5, Ingham
Williamston Community SD — 4-11111
418 HIGHLAND ST 48895 — 655-4361
Steven Smyth, supt.
HS, 3939 VANNETER RD 48895 — 2-00011
Randy Bowles, prin. — 655-2142
MS, 3845 VANNETER RD 48895 — 2-00100
Tim Kitts, prin. — 655-4668

Wolverine, AC 616, PC 2, Cheboygan
Wolverine Community SD — 2-11111
PO BOX 219 49799 — 525-8201
Daniel Boals, supt.
JSHS, 5767 BALLARD ST 49799 — 2-00111
Daniel Boals, prin. — 525-8201

Woodhaven, AC 313, PC 7, Wayne
Gibraltar SD — 5-11111
19370 VREELAND RD 48183 — 692-4002
R. Johns, supt.
Other Schools — See Gibraltar

Woodland, AC 616, PC 2, Barry
Lakewood SD
Supt. — See Lake Odessa
MS, 233 W BROADWAY ST 48897 — 3-00100
David Doozan, prin. — 367-4475

Wyandotte, AC 313, PC 8, Wayne
Wyandotte SD, 639 OAK ST 48192 — 5-11111
Michael Williamson, supt. — 246-1070
Roosevelt HS, 540 EUREKA RD 48192 — 4-00011
Edmund Hebda, prin. — 246-1000
Wilson MS, 1275 15TH ST 48192 — 3-00100
Thomas Kell, prin. — 246-8360

Gabriel Richard HS — 2-00011
15325 PENNSYLVANIA AVE 48192 — 284-1875
John Bres, prin.
Our Lady of Mt. Carmel S — 2-11111
2609 10TH ST 48192 — 284-7311
Sr. Cordelia Szynkowski, prin.

Wyoming, AC 616, PC 8, Kent
Godfrey-Lee SD — 4-11111
1565 BURTON ST SW 49509 — 241-4722
Robert Jones, supt.

Lee HS, 1335 LEE ST SW 49509 — 2-00011
Dee Korson, prin. — 452-3295
Lee MS, 1335 LEE ST SW 49509 — 2-00100
Thomas Konow, prin. — 452-8703
Godwin Heights SD — 4-11111
15 36TH ST SW 49548 — 245-0461
Patrick Murphy, supt.
Godwin Heights HS — 3-00011
50 35TH ST SW 49548 — 245-0461
R. Noordeloos, prin.
Godwin Heights MS — 2-00100
111 36TH ST SE 49548 — 245-0461
G. Lewis, prin.

Wyoming SD — 6-11111
3575 GLADIOLA AVE SW 49509 — 530-7550
Richard Carlson, supt.
Rogers HS — 3-00011
1351 BUCKINGHAM ST SW 49509 — 530-7580
Harry Hudson, prin.
Wyoming Park HS — 3-00011
2125 WRENWOOD ST SW 49509 — 530-7560
David Glanville, prin.
Jackson Park MS — 3-00100
1331 33RD ST SW 49509 — 530-7540
Jerry Thorton, prin.
Newhall MS, 1840 38TH ST SW 49509 — 3-00100
Barbara Smith, prin. — 530-7590
Other Schools — See Grand Rapids

Calvin Christian MS — 2-00110
2500 NEWPORT ST SW 49509 — 531-7400
Raymond Vander Molen, prin.
NEC-National Institute of Technology — 3-CS
2620 REMICO ST SW 49509 — 538-3170

Yale, AC 810, PC 4, St. Clair
Yale SD, 198 SCHOOL DR 48097 — 4-11111
Ralph Darin, supt. — 387-4274
HS, 198 SCHOOL DR 48097 — 3-00011
Roger Wood, prin. — 387-3231
Yale MS, 103 W MECHANIC ST 48097 — 2-00100
James Heimbuch, prin. — 387-3231

Ypsilanti, AC 313, PC 7, Washtenaw
Lincoln Consolidated SD — 5-11111
8970 WHITTAKER RD 48197 — 484-7001
Thomas McDougall, supt.
Lincoln HS, 7425 WILLIS RD 48197 — 3-00011
Fred Boss, prin. — 484-7004
Other Schools — See Belleville

Willow Run Community SD — 5-11111
2171 E MICHIGAN AVE 48198 — 481-8200
Youssef Yomtoob, supt.
Willow Run HS, 235 SPENCER LN 48198 — 3-00011
Gayle Green, prin. — 481-8300
Edmondson MS — 3-00100
1800 E FOREST AVE 48198 — 481-8325
Melvin Anglin, prin.

Ypsilanti SD, 1885 PACKARD RD 48197 — 6-11111
Wayne Case, supt. — 482-9388
HS, 2095 PACKARD RD 48197 — 4-00011
J. Fulton, prin. — 482-8880
East MS, 510 EMERICK ST 48198 — 2-00100
William Snyder, prin. — 482-8590
West MS, 105 N MANSFIELD ST 48197 — 2-00100
Michael Galinis, prin. — 482-8076

Calvary Christian Academy — 2-11111
1007 ECORSE RD 48198 – T. Hall, prin. — 482-1990
Cleary College - Washtenaw Campus — 3-UC
2170 WASHTENAW RD 48197 — 800-686-1883
Eastern Michigan University 48197 — 7-UC
800-468-6368

Zeeland, AC 616, PC 6, Ottawa
Zeeland SD, PO BOX 110 49464 — 5-11111
Gary Feenstra, supt. — 772-7380
HS, 320 E MAIN AVE 49464 — 3-00011
Michael Jones, prin. — 772-4617
MS, 179 W ROOSEVELT AVE 49464 — 3-00100
Jae Shobbrook, prin. — 772-2149

MINNESOTA

STATE DEPARTMENT OF EDUCATION
712 Capitol Square Building
550 Cedar St., St. Paul 55101
(612) 296-6104

Commissioner of Education	Linda Powell
Deputy Commissioner	John Mercer
Assistant Commissioner Management & Support Services	Robert Wedl
Asst. Commissioner Learning & Instructional Services	Ceil Critchley

STATE BOARD OF EDUCATION
550 Cedar St., St. Paul 55101

Executive Director	Marsha Gronseth

PUBLIC, PRIVATE AND CATHOLIC SECONDARY SCHOOLS

Ada, AC 218, PC 4, Norman
Ada SD, 105 4TH AVE E 56510 — 3-11111, 784-4462
Thomas Hanson, supt.
Ada-Borup JSHS, 105 4TH AVE E 56510 — 2-00111, 784-4462
James Christianson, prin.

Adams, AC 507, PC 3, Mower
Southland SD, PO BOX 351 55909 — 3-11111, 582-3283
Larry Tompkins, supt.
Southland HS, PO BOX 351 55909 — 2-00011, 582-3568
Lawrence Croker, prin.
Other Schools – See Elkton

Adrian, AC 507, PC 4, Nobles
Adrian SD, PO BOX 40 56110 — 3-11111, 483-2266
Leroy Domagala, supt.
JSHS, PO BOX 40 56110 — 2-00111, 483-2232
Dave Edwards, prin.

Aitkin, AC 218, PC 4, Aitkin
Aitkin SD, 306 2ND ST NW 56431 — 4-11111, 927-2115
Edward Anderson, supt.
JSHS, 306 2ND ST NW 56431 — 3-00111, 927-2115
Steven Wilkowski, prin.

Albany, AC 612, PC 4, Stearns
Albany SD, PO BOX 330 56307 — 4-11111, 845-2171
John Tritabaugh, supt.
HS, PO BOX 330 56307 — 2-00011, 845-2171
Steve Dooley, prin.
JHS, PO BOX 330 56307 — 2-00100, 845-2161
Charles Griffith, prin.

Alberta, AC 612, PC 99, Stevens
Chokio-Alberta SD
Supt. – See Chokio
Chokio-Alberta JSHS — 2-00111, 324-7141
PO BOX 96 56207
Omer Durfee, prin.

Albert Lea, AC 507, PC 7, Freeborn
Albert Lea SD, 109 WEST AVE 56007 — 5-11111, 377-5800
Cy Kruse, supt.
Central HS, 504 W CLARK ST 56007 — 4-00011, 377-6500
Alan Root, prin.
Southwest JHS — 3-00100, 377-6580
901 S HIGHWAY 69 56007
Terrance Moriarty, prin.

South Central Technical College — 2-CS, 373-0656
2200 TECH DR 56007

Albertville, AC 612, PC 4, Wright
St. Michael-Albertville SD — 4-11111, 497-3180
11343 50TH ST NE 55301
Mario DeMatteis, supt.
St Michael-Albertville HS — 2-00011, 497-2192
11343 50TH ST NE 55301
Mark Minkler, prin.
Other Schools – See Saint Michael

Alden, AC 507, PC 3, Freeborn
Alden SD, PO BOX 99 56009 — 2-10011, 874-3240
Stan Ries, supt.
Alden-Conger HS, PO BOX 99 56009 — 2-00111, 874-3240
Stan Ries, prin.

Alexandria, AC 612, PC 6, Douglas
Alexandria SD, PO BOX 308 56308 — 5-11111, 762-2141
George Cassell, supt.
Jefferson SHS — 3-00001, 762-2142
1401 JEFFERSON ST 56308
Pernell Knutson, prin.
Central JHS, 715 ELM ST 56308 — 4-00110, 762-2140
Michael Ennis, prin.

Alexandria Technical College — 4-CC, 762-0221
1601 JEFFERSON ST 56308

Amboy, AC 507, PC 3, Blue Earth
Maple River SD
Supt. — See Mapleton
MS, PO BOX 70 56010 — 2-00100, 674-3046
Marcene Kluender, prin.

Annandale, AC 612, PC 4, Wright
Annandale SD, PO BOX 190 55302 — 4-11111, 274-5602
Steve Niklaus, supt.
HS, PO BOX 190 55302 — 2-00011, 274-8208
Marcia Zigler, prin.
MS, PO BOX 190 55302 — 3-00100, 274-8226
Timothy Ilse, prin.

Anoka, AC 612, PC 7, Anoka
Anoka-Hennepin SD
Supt. — See Coon Rapids
SHS, 3939 7TH AVE 55303 — 5-00001, 422-5700
Dean Soutor, prin.
Moore JHS, 1523 5TH AVE 55303 — 4-00110, 422-5100
Jerome Lerom, prin.
Sandburg MS, 1902 2ND AVE 55303 — 4-00100, 422-5170
Ronald Mitchell, prin.

Anoka Technical Institute — 2-CS, 427-1880
1355 W MAIN ST 55303
Meadow Creek Christian S — 3-11111
2937 BUNKER LAKE BLVD NW 55304

Apple Valley, AC 612, PC 8, Dakota
Rosemount-Apple Valley-Eagan SD
Supt. — See Rosemount
HS, 14450 HAYES RD 55124 — 4-00011, 431-8206
James Boesen, prin.
Scott Highlands MS — 4-00100, 423-7581
14011 PILOT KNOB RD 55124
Dennis Pregler, prin.
Valley MS, 900 GARDEN VIEW DR 55124 — 4-00100, 431-8300
Janice Jessen, prin.

Arden Hills, AC 612, PC 6, Ramsey
Mounds View SD
Supt. — See Roseville
Mounds View HS — 4-00011, 633-4031
1900 COUNTY ROAD F W 55112
Karl Brungardt, prin.

Argyle, AC 218, PC 3, Marshall
Argyle SD, PO BOX 279 56713 — 2-11111, 437-6615
James Schindele, supt.
JSHS, PO BOX 279 56713 — 2-00111, 437-6615
(—), prin.

Arlington, AC 612, PC 4, Sibley
Arlington SD, PO BOX 1000 55307 — 3-11001, 964-2292
Nordy Nelson, supt.
SHS, PO BOX 1000 55307 — 2-00001, 964-2292
James Swanson, prin.

Ashby, AC 218, PC 2, Grant
Ashby SD, PO BOX C 56309 — 2-11111, 747-2257
Raymond Dahlen, supt.
JSHS, PO BOX C 56309 — 2-00111, 747-2257
Warren Nelson, prin.

Askov, AC 612, PC 2, Pine
East Central SD
Supt. — See Sandstone
East Central MS, PO BOX 250 55704 — 2-00100, 838-3112
Leon Tuominen, prin.

Atwater, AC 612, PC 4, Kandiyohi
Atwater SD, PO BOX 760 56209 — 3-11001, 974-8841
Thomas Dickhudt, supt.
SHS, PO BOX 760 56209 — 2-00001, 974-8842
Don Grages, prin.

Aurora, AC 218, PC 4, St. Louis
Mesabi East SD, 601 N 1ST ST W 55705 — 4-11111, 229-3321
Dale Wain, supt.
Mesabi East SHS, 601 N 1ST ST W 55705 — 3-00001, 229-2571
Martin Skala, prin.
Other Schools – See Biwabik

Austin, AC 507, PC 7, Mower
Austin SD, 202 4TH AVE NE 55912 — 5-11111, 433-0966
J. Douglas Myers, supt.
HS, 301 3RD ST NW 55912 — 4-00011, 433-0401
Julia Buchanan, prin.
Ellis MS, 1700 4TH AVE SE 55912 — 4-00100, 433-7093
N. Hanson, prin.

Austin Community College — 3-CC, 433-0508
1600 8TH AVE NW 55912
Pacelli HS, 311 4TH ST NW 55912 — 2-00011, 437-3278
Terry Nelsen, prin.
Riverland Technical College — 2-CS, 433-0600
1900 8TH AVE NW 55912

Babbitt, AC 218, PC 4, St. Louis
St. Louis County SD
Supt. — See Virginia
Kennedy JSHS, 30 SOUTH DR 55706 — 2-00111, 827-3101
James Techar, prin.

Badger, AC 218, PC 2, Roseau
Badger SD, PO BOX 68 56714 — 2-11111, 528-3201
Robert Clausen, supt.
JSHS, PO BOX 68 56714 — 2-00111, 528-3201
Robert Clausen, prin.

Bagley, AC 218, PC 4, Clearwater
Bagley SD, 202 BAGLEY AVE NW 56621 — 4-11111, 694-6184
Gary Bratvold, supt.
JSHS, 202 BAGLEY AVE NW 56621 — 3-00111, 694-3120
T. Ohman, prin.

Balaton, AC 507, PC 3, Lyon
Balaton SD, PO BOX 150 56115 — 2-11111, 734-5601
Norris Oerter, supt.
JSHS, PO BOX 150 56115 — 2-00111, 734-5601
James Jones, prin.

Barnesville, AC 218, PC 4, Clay
Barnesville SD, PO BOX 189 56514 — 3-11111, 354-2217
Edward Thompson, supt.
JSHS, PO BOX 189 56514 — 2-00111, 354-2228
Gary Zirbes, prin.

Barnum, AC 218, PC 2, Carlton
Barnum SD, PO BOX 227 55707 — 3-11111, 389-6978
Ronald Luoma, supt.
JSHS, PO BOX 227 55707 — 2-00111, 389-3273
Dale Tormondsen, prin.

Battle Lake, AC 218, PC 3, Otter Tail
Battle Lake SD, PO BOX 1280 56515 — 2-11111, 864-5215
John Widvey, supt.
JSHS, PO BOX 1280 56515 — 2-00111, 864-5215
John Widvey, prin.

Baudette, AC 218, PC 4, Lake of the Woods
Lake of the Woods SD — 3-11111, 634-2735
PO BOX 310 56623
Charles Speiker, supt.

Lake of the Woods JSHS   2-00111
PO BOX 310   56623   634-2510
Gerald Turner, prin.

Baxter, PC 5, Crow Wing

Lake Region Christian S   2-11111
2110 FAIRVIEW RD N   56401

Becker, AC 612, PC 3, Sherburne
Becker SD, 12000 HANCOCK ST   55308   4-11111
Jim Mantzke, supt.   261-4502
JSHS, 12000 HANCOCK ST   55308   3-00111
Luverne Liestman, prin.   261-4501

Belgrade, AC 612, PC 3, Stearns
Belgrade-Elrosa SD   3-11110
PO BOX 339   56312   254-8212
Duane Swenson, supt.
Belgrade-Elrosa JHS   2-00110
PO BOX 339   56312   254-8211
Terry Frazee, prin.

Belle Plaine, AC 612, PC 5, Scott
Belle Plaine SD   3-11111
220 S MARKET ST   56011   873-2238
Thomas Lubovich, supt.
SHS, 220 S MARKET ST   56011   2-00001
Lowell Hoffman, prin.   873-2238
JHS, 130 S WILLOW ST   56011   2-00110
Daniel Dressen, prin.   873-2278

Belview, AC 507, PC 2, Redwood
Belview SD, PO BOX 220   56214   2-11100
Ivan Eckstrom, supt.   329-8362
MS, PO BOX 220   56214   1-00100
Janice Eilers, prin.   938-4111

Bemidji, AC 218, PC 7, Beltrami
Bemidji SD, 201 15TH ST NW   56601   6-11111
Wayne Haugen, supt.   759-3110
HS, 201 15TH ST NW   56601   4-00011
Ev Arnold, prin.   759-3135
MS   4-00100
1910 MIDDLE SCHOOL AVE NW   56601
Fred Sanford, prin.   759-3210

Bemidji State University   5-UC
1500 BIRCHMONT DR NE   56601   755-2000
Oak Hills Bible College   2-UC
1600 OAK HILLS RD SW   56601   751-8670

Benson, AC 612, PC 5, Swift
Benson SD, 1400 MONTANA AVE   56215   4-11111
Les Potas, supt.   843-2710
JSHS, 1400 MONTANA AVE   56215   3-00111
Kim Ross, prin.   843-2710

Bertha, AC 218, PC 3, Todd
Bertha-Hewitt SD, PO BOX 8   56437   3-11111
Larry Werder, supt.   924-2500
JSHS, PO BOX 8   56437   2-00111
Charles Margerum, prin.   924-2500

Bigfork, AC 218, PC 2, Itasca
Grand Rapids SD
Supt. — See Grand Rapids
JSHS, PO BOX 228   56628   2-00111
Eugene Brandt, prin.   743-3444

Big Lake, AC 612, PC 5, Sherburne
Big Lake SD, PO BOX 410   55309   4-11111
Laverne Lageson, supt.   263-2910
JSHS, PO BOX 410   55309   3-00111
Darrell Esterly, prin.   263-2912

Birchdale, AC 218, PC 1, Koochiching
South Koochiching SD
Supt. — See Northome
Indus JSHS, RR 3 BOX 301-C   56629   1-00111
Milton McCauley, prin.   634-2425

Bird Island, AC 612, PC 4, Renville
Bird Island-Olivia SD   4-11111
PO BOX 460   55310   365-4060
Virgil Green, supt.
Other Schools – See Olivia

Biwabik, AC 218, PC 4, St. Louis
Mesabi East SD
Supt. — See Aurora
Mesabi East JHS   55708   2-00110
Robert Olson, prin.   865-4111

Blackduck, AC 218, PC 3, Beltrami
Blackduck SD, 1ST ST E   56630   3-11111
Thomas Hoppe, supt.   835-4214
JSHS, 1ST ST E   56630   2-00111
Thomas Mathews, prin.   835-4214

Blaine, AC 612, PC 8, Anoka
Anoka-Hennepin SD
Supt. — See Coon Rapids
SHS, 12555 UNIVERSITY AVE NE   55434   5-00001
John Tefer, prin.   422-5800
Roosevelt JHS, 650 MAIN ST NE   55434   4-00110
Ron Olsbo, prin.   422-5450

Spring Lake Park SD
Supt. — See Spring Lake Park
Westwood JHS, 711 91ST AVE NE   55434   3-00100
Gayle Anderson, prin.   784-8625

Blooming Prairie, AC 507, PC 4, Steele
Blooming Prairie SD   4-11111
202 4TH AVE NW   55917   583-4427
Irving Peterson, supt.

JSHS, 202 4TH AVE NW   55917   2-00111
Dennis Roos, prin.   583-4428

Bloomington, AC 612, PC 8, Hennepin
Bloomington SD   7-11111
8900 PORTLAND AVE   55420   885-8452
Timothy Connors, supt.
Jefferson HS, 4001 W 102ND ST   55437   4-00011
Kent Stever, prin.   884-5000
Kennedy HS, 9701 NICOLLET AVE   55420   4-00011
Robert Schmidt, prin.   885-7800
Olson JHS, 4551 W 102ND ST   55437   4-00100
Dan Jones, prin.   884-2900

Academy of Accountancy   2-CC
3050 METRO DR STE 200   55425   851-0066
Lutheran HS, 8201 PARK AVE   55420   2-00011
Jerry Boehm, prin.   920-4311
Medical Institute of Minnesota   2-CS
5503 GREEN VALLEY DR   55437   844-0064
Normandale Community College   6-CC
9700 FRANCE AVE S   55431   832-6320
Northwestern College of Chiropractic   3-UC
2501 W 84TH ST   55431   888-4777
Trinity S, 2300 E 88TH ST   55425   2-00111

Blue Earth, AC 507, PC 5, Faribault
Blue Earth SD, 300 E 6TH ST   56013   4-11111
Donald Helmstetter, supt.   526-4168
JSHS, 300 E 6TH ST   56013   3-00111
John Huisman, prin.   526-4123

Bovey, AC 218, PC 3, Itasca
Coleraine SD
Supt. — See Coleraine
Connor-Jasper MS, PO BOX 40   55709   2-00100
Dennis Perreault, prin.   245-2661

Braham, AC 612, PC 4, Isanti
Braham SD, PO BOX 488   55006   4-11111
Pat Flanagan, supt.   396-3313
Braham Area JSHS   2-00111
PO BOX 488   55006   396-4444
Michael Shay, prin.

Brainerd, AC 218, PC 7, Crow Wing
Brainerd SD, 300 QUINCE ST   56401   6-11111
Robert Gross, supt.   828-5300
SHS, 702 S 5TH ST   56401   4-00001
James Hunt, prin.   828-5255
Franklin JHS   4-00110
1001 KINGWOOD ST   56401   828-6660
Carol Munns, prin.

Brainerd Community College   4-CC
501 W COLLEGE DR   56401   800-933-0346

Brandon, AC 612, PC 2, Douglas
Brandon SD, PO BOX 185   56315   2-11111
Mark Westby, supt.   524-2263
JSHS, PO BOX 185   56315   2-00111
Don Bakken, prin.   524-2263

Breckenridge, AC 218, PC 5, Wilkin
Breckenridge SD, 710 13TH ST N   56520   4-11111
John Klein, supt.   643-2694
HS, 710 13TH ST N   56520   2-00011
Neal Folstad, prin.   643-2694
MS, 510 8TH ST N   56520   2-00100
Jerome Mock, prin.   643-6681

Brooklyn Center, AC 612, PC 8, Hennepin
Brooklyn Center SD   4-11111
6500 HUMBOLDT AVE N   55430   561-2120
Douglas M. Rossi, supt.
JSHS, 6500 HUMBOLDT AVE N   55430   3-00111
Richard Janezich, prin.   561-2120

Minnesota School of Business   3-CS
6120 EARLE BROWN DR   55430   566-7777

Brooklyn Park, AC 612, PC 8, Hennepin
Osseo SD
Supt. — See Maple Grove
Park Center SHS   4-00001
7300 BROOKLYN BLVD   55443   566-6700
Judy Lamp, prin.
Brooklyn JHS, 7377 NOBLE AVE N   55443   3-00110
Kate McGuire, prin.   566-6893
North View JHS   4-00110
5869 69TH AVE N   55429   566-6220
Willie Johnson, prin.

North Hennepin Community College   5-CC
7411 85TH AVE N   55445   424-0811

Brooten, AC 612, PC 3, Stearns
Brooten SD, PO BOX 39   56316   2-11001
Duane Swensen, supt.   346-2244
SHS, PO BOX 39   56316   2-00001
Terry Frazee, prin.   346-2244

Browerville, AC 612, PC 3, Todd
Browerville SD, PO BOX 185   56438   3-11111
Larry Werder, supt.   594-2272
JSHS, PO BOX 185   56438   2-00111
Dahn Beaudoin, prin.   594-2272

Browns Valley, AC 612, PC 3, Traverse
Browns Valley SD, PO BOX N   56219   2-01111
Melvin Hauge, supt.   695-2103
JSHS, PO BOX N   56219   2-00111
Todd Cameron, prin.   695-2296

Brownton, AC 612, PC 3, Mcleod
Brownton SD, PO BOX 99   55312   2-11001
David Klepel, supt.   328-5216
McCleod West SHS   2-00001
PO BOX 99   55312   328-5214
Larry Corrow, prin.

Buffalo, AC 612, PC 6, Wright
Buffalo SD, 214 1ST AVE NE   55313   5-11111
M. D. Miller, supt.   682-5200
HS, 1300 HIGHWAY 25 N   55313   4-00011
Nicholas Miller, prin.   682-6800
JHS, 301 2ND AVE NE   55313   3-00100
Janet Olson, prin.   682-5200

Burnsville, AC 612, PC 8, Dakota
Burnsville SD   7-11111
100 RIVER RIDGE CT   55337   895-7200
James Rickabaugh, supt.
SHS, 600 HIGHWAY 13 E   55337   4-00001
Howard Hall, prin.   895-7333
Metcalf JHS, 2250 DIFFLEY RD   55337   4-00110
Rudolph DeLuca, prin.   895-7272
Nicollet JHS, 400 E 134TH ST   55337   4-00110
John Bednar, prin.   895-7251

Butterfield, AC 507, PC 3, Watonwan
Butterfield SD, PO BOX 189   56120   2-11111
Lloyd Fandrich, supt.   956-2771
JSHS, PO BOX 189   56120   2-00111
(—), prin.   956-2771

Byron, AC 507, PC 4, Olmsted
Byron SD, PO BOX 157   55920   4-11111
R. E. Carlson, supt.   775-2383
JSHS, PO BOX 157   55920   3-00111
Charles Skarie, prin.   775-2301

Caledonia, AC 507, PC 5, Houston
Caledonia SD, 511 W MAIN ST   55921   3-11111
M. Miller, supt.   724-3316
JSHS, 511 W MAIN ST   55921   2-00111
Brian Doty, prin.   724-3316

Cambridge, AC 612, PC 6, Isanti
Cambridge-Isanti SD   5-11111
315 7TH LN NE   55008   689-4988
Ray Hoheisel, supt.
HS, 430 8TH AVE NW   55008   4-00011
Rod Kaisler, prin.   689-2020
MS, 428 2ND AVE NW   55008   3-01100
Craig Paulson, prin.   689-3030
Other Schools – See Isanti

Anoka-Ramsey Community College   2-CC
W HIGHWAY 95   55008   422-3456

Campbell, AC 218, PC 2, Wilkin
Campbell-Tintah SD   2-11111
PO BOX 8   56522 – John Klein, supt.   630-5311
Campbell-Tintah JSHS   1-00111
PO BOX 8   56522   630-5311
Allan Jensen, prin.

Canby, AC 507, PC 4, Yellow Medicine
Canby SD, 307 1ST ST W   56220   3-11111
H. Lyle Jones, supt.   223-5965
JSHS, 307 1ST ST W   56220   2-00111
Lyle Sentz, prin.   223-7226

Southwestern Technical College   2-CS
1011 1ST ST W   56220   800-658-2535

Cannon Falls, AC 507, PC 5, Goodhue
Cannon Falls SD   4-11111
820 MINNESOTA ST E   55009   263-3562
Richard McGuire, supt.
JSHS, 820 MINNESOTA ST E   55009   3-00111
Joe Baisley, prin.   263-3331

Carlton, AC 218, PC 3, Carlton
Carlton SD, PO BOX 310   55718   3-11111
Raymond Vikander, supt.   384-4225
JSHS, PO BOX 310   55718   2-00111
(—), prin.   384-4226

Cass Lake, AC 218, PC 3, Cass
Cass Lake SD, RR 3 BOX 4   56633   3-11111
James Bottrell, supt.   335-2204
JSHS, RR 3 BOX 4   56633   2-00111
Ralph Brose, prin.   335-2203

Bug-O-Nay-Ge-Shig S   3-11111
PO BOX 100   56633   665-2282
Ted Bogda, prin.

Ceylon, AC 507, PC 2, Martin
Ceylon SD, 301 W GRANT   56121   2-11111
James Schultze, supt.   632-4291
JSHS, 301 W GRANT   56121   1-00111
James Schultze, prin.   632-4291

Champlin, AC 612, PC 7, Hennepin
Anoka-Hennepin SD
Supt. — See Coon Rapids
Champlin Park SHS   4-00001
6025 109TH AVE N   55316   493-8600
David Bonthuis, prin.
Jackson JHS, 6000 109TH AVE N   55316   4-00110
Larry Siedow, prin.   424-8586

Chaska, AC 612, PC 7, Carver
Chaska SD, 110600 VILLAGE RD   55318   5-11111
David Clough, supt.   368-3601

HS, 1700 N CHESTNUT ST 55318   4-00011
James O'Connell, prin.   448-8620
MS, 1600 PARK RIDGE DR 55318   3-00100
Leonard Takkunen, prin.   448-8700

Chatfield, AC 507, PC 4, Olmsted
Chatfield SD, 205 UNION ST NE 55923   3-10111
Jeffrey Miller, supt.   867-4210
Chosen Valley JSHS   2-00111
205 UNION ST NE 55923   867-4210
Edward Jones, prin.

Chisago City, AC 612, PC 4, Chisago

Chisago Lakes Baptist Academy   2-11111
PO BOX 350 55013

Chisholm, AC 218, PC 6, St. Louis
Chisholm SD, 300 3RD AVE SW 55719   4-11111
Robert Belluzzo, supt.   254-5726
HS, 300 3RD AVE SW 55719   2-00011
Thomas Grosland, prin.   254-5727
Chisholm MS, 301 4TH ST SW 55719   2-01100
Russell Maki, prin.   254-5715

Chokio, AC 612, PC 3, Stevens
Chokio-Alberta SD, PO BOX 68 56221   2-11111
Burton Nypen, supt.   324-7131
Other Schools – See Alberta

Circle Pines, AC 612, PC 5, Anoka
Centennial SD, 4707 NORTH RD 55014   5-11111
John McClellan, supt.   780-7610
Centennial SHS, 4707 NORTH RD 55014   3-00001
Lyle Koski, prin.   780-7646
Centennial JHS, 4707 NORTH RD 55014   4-00110
F. Neumann, prin.   780-7669

Clara City, AC 612, PC 4, Chippewa
Clara City SD, PO BOX 690 56222   2-00111
Roger Rueckert, supt.   847-2154
MacCray HS, PO BOX 690 56222   2-00011
Gary Sims, prin.   847-2478
MacCray JHS, PO BOX 690 56222   2-00100
Gary Sims, prin.   847-3525

Clarkfield, AC 612, PC 3, Yellow Medicine
Clarkfield SD, PO BOX 338 56223   2-11100
Earl Mathison, supt.   669-4423
JHS, PO BOX 338 56223   2-00100
Bruce Bergeson, prin.   669-4424

Clearbrook, AC 218, PC 3, Clearwater
Clearbrook SD, PO BOX 8 56634   2-11011
Vern Pfeifer, supt.   776-3112
HS, PO BOX 8 56634   2-00011
Daniel Hannig, prin.   776-3112

Cleveland, AC 507, PC 3, Le Sueur
Cleveland SD, PO BOX 310 56017   2-11111
Arnold Prince, supt.   931-5953
JSHS, PO BOX 310 56017   2-00111
David Machula, prin.   931-5955

Climax, AC 218, PC 2, Polk
Climax SD, PO BOX 67 56523   2-11111
Walt Aanenson, supt.   857-2385
JSHS, PO BOX 67 56523   2-00111
Tom Sedler, prin.   857-2395

Clinton, AC 612, PC 3, Big Stone
Clinton-Graceville SD   2-11111
PO BOX 361 56225   325-5282
James Torbert, supt.
Other Schools – See Graceville

Cloquet, AC 218, PC 7, Carlton
Cloquet SD, 509 CARLTON AVE 55720   4-11111
Russell Smith, supt.   879-6721
HS, 1000 18TH ST 55720   3-00011
D. Modec, prin.   879-3393
MS, 509 CARLTON AVE 55720   3-01100
John Langenbrunner, prin.   879-3328

Fond Du Lac Ojibway S   2-11111
105 UNIVERSITY RD 55720   879-4593
Thomas Peacock, prin.

Cokato, AC 612, PC 4, Wright
Dassel-Cokato SD, PO BOX 370 55321   4-11111
Ed Otto, supt.   286-5535
Dassel-Cokato HS, PO BOX 370 55321   3-00011
Paul Thomas, prin.   286-5531
Dassel-Cokato MS, PO BOX Q 55321   3-01100
Dale Johnson, prin.   286-6321

Cold Spring, AC 612, PC 4, Stearns
Cold Spring SD, 534 5TH AVE N 56320   4-11111
Tom Westerhaus, supt.   685-4901
Rocori HS, 534 5TH AVE N 56320   4-00011
James Johnson, prin.   685-8683
Rocori MS, 533 MAIN ST 56320   2-00100
Sylvan Peterson, prin.   685-3296

Coleraine, AC 218, PC 4, Itasca
Coleraine SD, PO BOX 195 55722   4-11111
Martin Duncan, supt.   245-1566
Greenway HS, PO BOX 520 55722   3-00011
Gerald Tischer, prin.   245-1287
Other Schools – See Bovey

Collegeville, AC 612, PC 2, Stearns

St. John's University   4-UC
PO BOX 7155 56321   363-2011

St. Johns Preparatory S   2-00011
PO BOX 4000 56321   363-3315
Rev. Dommer, prin.

Columbia Heights, AC 612, PC 7, Anoka
Columbia Heights SD   5-11111
1400 49TH AVE NE 55421   574-6505
Alain Holt, supt.
HS, 1400 49TH AVE NE 55421   3-00011
Jane Goodell, prin.   574-6530
Central MS, 900 49TH AVE NE 55421   3-00100
Janet Anderson, prin.   574-6550

Comfrey, AC 507, PC 2, Brown
Comfrey SD, PO BOX 68 56019   2-11111
Richard Briesath, supt.   877-3491
JSHS, PO BOX 68 56019   2-00111
Richard Briesath, prin.   877-3491

Cook, AC 218, PC 3, St. Louis
St. Louis County SD
Supt. — See Virginia
JSHS, 306 W VERMILION DR 55723   2-00111
Bonita Gurno, prin.   666-5221

Coon Rapids, AC 612, PC 8, Anoka
Anoka-Hennepin SD   8-11111
11299 HANSON BLVD NW 55433   422-5500
Douglas Otto, supt.
SHS   5-00001
2340 NORTHDALE BLVD NW 55433   422-5900
Ann Zweber, prin.
JHS, 11600 RAVEN ST NW 55433   4-00110
Dennis Psick, prin.   422-5400
Northdale JHS   4-00110
11301 DOGWOOD ST NW 55448   422-5650
Harold Boyum, prin.
Other Schools – See Anoka, Blaine, Champlin

Anoka-Ramsey Community College   5-CC
11200 MISSISSIPPI BLVD NW 55433   427-2600

Cottage Grove, AC 612, PC 7, Washington
South Washington County SD   7-11111
7362 E POINT DOUGLAS RD S 55016   458-4200
Dan Hoke, supt.
Park HS, 8040 80TH ST S 55016   4-00011
Walter Lyszak, prin.   458-4225
Other Schools – See Saint Paul Park, Woodbury

Cotton, AC 218, PC 2, St. Louis
St. Louis County SD
Supt. — See Virginia
JSHS, 9165 HIGHWAY 53 55724   2-00111
Robert Larson, prin.   482-3232

Cottonwood, AC 507, PC 3, Lyon
Cottonwood SD, PO BOX 107 56229   2-11011
Palmer Anderson, supt.   423-5164
HS, PO BOX 107 56229   2-00011
George Davis, prin.   423-5166

Cromwell, AC 218, PC 2, Carlton
Cromwell SD, PO BOX 7 55726   2-11111
Herbert Hilinski, supt.   644-3737
JSHS, PO BOX 7 55726   2-00111
Randy Thudin, prin.   644-3716

Crookston, AC 218, PC 6, Polk
Crookston SD, 415 JACKSON AVE 56716   4-11111
(—), supt.   281-5313
Central JSHS, 121 E 3RD ST 56716   3-00111
Allen Zenor, prin.   281-2144

University of Minnesota   4-UC
2900 UNIVERSITY AVE 56716   281-6510

Crosby, AC 218, PC 4, Crow Wing
Crosby-Ironton SD   4-11111
711 POPLAR ST 56441   546-5165
Bruce Grosland, supt.
Crosby-Ironton JSHS   3-00111
711 POPLAR ST 56441   546-5168
Jerald Ecklund, prin.

Danube, AC 612, PC 3, Renville
Danube SD, PO BOX 157 56230   2-01100
Ivan Eckstrom, supt.   329-8362
DRSH MS, PO BOX 157 56230   2-01100
Marshall Thorstad, prin.   826-2287

Dawson, AC 612, PC 4, Lac Qui Parle
Dawson SD, PO BOX 1018 56232   3-11111
Brad Madsen, supt.   769-2955
Dawson-Boyd JSHS   2-00111
PO BOX 1018 56232   769-2955
Brad Madsen, prin.

Deer River, AC 218, PC 3, Itasca
Deer River SD, PO BOX 307 56636   4-11111
Wallace Schoeb, supt.   246-2420
JSHS, PO BOX 307 56636   2-00111
Jack Gunderson, prin.   246-8241

Delano, AC 612, PC 5, Wright
Delano SD, 700 ELM AVE E 55328   4-11111
James Tool, supt.   479-3617
HS, 700 ELM AVE E 55328   2-00011
Ted May, prin.   479-3617
MS, 700 ELM AVE E 55328   3-01100
Richard Rominski, prin.   479-3617

Detroit Lakes, AC 218, PC 6, Becker
Detroit Lakes SD, 702 LAKE AVE 56501   5-11111
Robert Melick, supt.   847-9271

Community SHS   3-00001
1301 ROOSEVELT AVE 56501   847-4491
Robert Soukup, prin.
JHS, 510 11TH AVE 56501   3-00110
Les Perry, prin.   847-9228

Dilworth, AC 218, PC 5, Clay
Dilworth SD, PO BOX 188 56529   3-11100
Dennis Wahl, supt.   287-2371
JHS, PO BOX 188 56529   2-00100
Peggy Hanson, prin.   287-2148

Glyndon-Felton SD   3-11011
PO BOX 188 56529   287-2371
Dennis Wahl, supt.
Other Schools – See Glyndon

Dodge Center, AC 507, PC 4, Dodge
Triton SD, PO BOX 40 55927   4-11111
John Hornung, supt.   374-2192
Triton SHS, PO BOX 40 55927   2-00001
Burt Bemmels, prin.   374-2446
Other Schools – See West Concord

Duluth, AC 218, PC 8, St. Louis
Duluth SD, 215 N 1ST AVE E 55802   7-11111
Reginald Nolin, supt.   723-4150
Denfeld HS, 4405 W 4TH ST 55807   4-00011
George Holliday, prin.   624-4833
East HS, 2900 E 4TH ST 55812   4-00011
Richard Warner, prin.   724-8827
Central JSHS   4-00111
800 E CENTRAL ENTRANCE 55811   722-6343
William Westholm, prin.
Morgan Park MS   3-01100
1243 88TH AVE W 55808   626-2741
Jon Vomachka, prin.
Ordean MS, 105 S 40TH AVE E 55804   2-01100
Mary Sedin, prin.   525-1913
Woodland MS, 201 CLOVER ST 55812   3-01100
Mitchell Wiss, prin.   724-8869

College of Saint Scholastica   4-UC
1200 KENWOOD AVE 55811   800-447-5444
Duluth Business University   2-CS
412 W SUPERIOR ST 55802   722-3361
Duluth Technical College   2-CS
2101 TRINITY RD 55811   722-2801
Marshall HS   2-00111
1215 RICE LAKE RD 55811
University of Minnesota   6-UC
2400 OAKLAND AVE 55812   726-7106

Eagan, AC 612, PC 8, Dakota
Rosemount-Apple Valley-Eagan SD
Supt. — See Rosemount
HS, 4185 BRADDOCK TRL 55123   4-00011
Thomas Wilson, prin.   683-6900
Dakota Hills MS   4-00100
4183 BRADDOCK TRL 55123   683-6800
Patrick Sullivan, prin.

Rasmussen Business College   3-CS
3500 FEDERAL DR 55122   687-9000

Eagle Bend, AC 218, PC 3, Todd
Eagle Bend SD, PO BOX 299 56446   2-00111
Russell Martinson, supt.   738-6442
Eagle Valley JSHS   2-00111
PO BOX 299 56446   738-6442
Richard Lundgren, prin.

East Grand Forks, AC 218, PC 6, Polk
East Grand Forks SD   4-11111
PO BOX 151 56721   773-3494
John Roche, supt.
HS, PO BOX 151 56721   3-00011
Donald Dimond, prin.   773-2405
Central MS, PO BOX 151 56721   3-00100
Robert Simonson, prin.   773-1141

Northwest Technical College   2-CS
HWY 220 N 56721   773-3441
Sacred Heart HS, 126 3RD ST NW 56721   2-00111
Philip Meyer, prin.   773-0230

Eden Prairie, AC 612, PC 8, Hennepin
Eden Prairie SD, 8100 SCHOOL RD 55344   6-11111
Gerald McCoy, supt.   937-3686
HS, 17185 VALLEY VIEW RD 55346   4-00011
Arne Johnson, prin.   934-6900
Central MS, 8025 SCHOOL RD 55344   4-00100
John Lyngdal, prin.   937-3636

International School of Minnesota   2-11111
6385 BEACH RD 55344
Northwest Technical Institute   1-CC
11995 SINGLETREE LN 55344   944-0080
Thunderbird Aviation   1-CS
14091 PIONEER TRL 55347   941-1212

Eden Valley, AC 612, PC 3, Meeker
Eden Valley SD, PO BOX 100 55329   3-11111
Greg Vandal, supt.   453-6310
JSHS, PO BOX 100 55329   2-00111
Larry Peterson, prin.   453-2900

Edgerton, AC 507, PC 4, Pipestone
Edgerton SD, PO BOX 28 56128   2-11111
Bill Richter, supt.   442-7881
JSHS, PO BOX 28 56128   2-00111
Larry Rolsma, prin.   442-7881

Southwest Christian HS
550 ELIZABETH 56128 — 2-00011

Edina, AC 612, PC 8, Hennepin
Edina SD
5701 NORMANDALE RD 55424 — 6-11111 920-2980
Ken Dragseth, supt.
SHS, 6754 VALLEY VIEW RD 55439 — 4-00001 944-2110
Rob Lynch, prin.
South View JHS, 4725 S VIEW LN 55424 — 3-00110 927-9721
David Peterson, prin.
Valley View JHS
6750 VALLEY VIEW RD 55439 — 3-00110 944-2110
Christine Weymouth, prin.

Elbow Lake, AC 218, PC 4, Grant
Elbow Lake SD, 411 1ST ST SE 56531 — 2-10001 685-4477
Kelly Smith, supt.
West Central SHS, 411 1ST ST SE 56531 — 2-00001 685-4477
(—), prin.

Elgin, AC 507, PC 3, Wabasha
Elgin-Millville SD, PO BOX D 55932 — 3-11111 876-2212
Richard Pederson, supt.
JSHS, PO BOX D 55932 — 2-00111 876-2212
Richard Pederson, prin.

Elk River, AC 612, PC 7, Sherburne
Elk River SD, 400 SCHOOL ST 55330 — 6-11111 241-3400
David Flannery, supt.
SHS, 900 SCHOOL ST 55330 — 4-00001 241-3400
Nicholas Olsen, prin.
Salk JHS, 11970 HIGHLAND RD 55330 — 3-00110 241-3455
James Voight, prin.
Vandenberg JHS
948 PROCTOR AVE 55330 — 3-00110 241-3450
Ron Gaarder, prin.

Alliance Christian Academy
829 SCHOOL ST 55330 — 2-11111

Elkton, AC 507, PC 2, Mower
Southland SD
Supt. — See Adams
Southland MS, PO BOX 85 55933 — 2-00100 584-6641
C. Olsen, prin.

Ellsworth, AC 507, PC 3, Nobles
Ellsworth SD, PO BOX 8 56129 — 2-11111 967-2242
Leroy Domagala, supt.
JSHS, PO BOX 8 56129 — 1-00111 967-2242
George Berndt, prin.

Ely, AC 218, PC 5, St. Louis
Ely SD, 600 E HARVEY ST 55731 — 3-11111 365-6166
Terrence Merfeld, supt.
Memorial JSHS, 600 E HARVEY ST 55731 — 2-00111 365-6140
Joselyn Hennings, prin.

Vermilion Community College
1900 E CAMP ST 55731 — 4-CC 800-475-6666

Emmons, AC 507, PC 2, Freeborn
Emmons SD, PO BOX 8 56029 — 2-11100 297-5442
Stephen Malone, supt.
JHS, PO BOX 8 56029 — 1-00100 297-5441
Dave Olson, prin.

Erskine, AC 218, PC 2, Polk
Win-E-Mac SD
Supt. — See McIntosh
Win-E-Mac JHS, PO BOX 279 56535 — 2-00110 687-2237
(—), prin.

Esko, AC 218, PC 3, Carlton
Esko SD, HWY 61 55733 — 3-11111 879-2969
James Schwartz, supt.
Lincoln JSHS, HWY 61 55733 — 2-00111 879-4673
William Berglund, prin.

Evansville, AC 218, PC 3, Douglas
Evansville SD, 123 2ND AVE 56326 — 2-11111 948-2241
John Retrum, supt.
JSHS, 123 2ND AVE 56326 — 2-00111 948-2241
Tom Shea, prin.

Eveleth, AC 218, PC 5, St. Louis
Eveleth-Gilbert SD, 801 JONES ST 55734 — 4-11111 744-4380
Michael Lang, supt.
Eveleth-Gilbert SHS
801 JONES ST 55734 — 2-00001 744-4171
Robert Mohn, prin.
Other Schools – See Gilbert

Excelsior, AC 612, PC 4, Hennepin
Minnetonka SD, 261 SCHOOL AVE 55331 — 6-11111 470-3400
D. Draayer, supt.
Minnetonka West MS
6421 HAZELTINE BLVD 55331 — 4-00100 474-0907
Duane Udstuen, prin.
Other Schools – See Minnetonka

Eyota, AC 507, PC 4, Olmsted
Dover-Eyota SD, PO BOX 268 55934 — 3-11111 545-2125
Joan Wilcox, supt.
Dover-Eyota JSHS
PO BOX 268 55934 — 2-00111 545-2631
Donald Johnson, prin.

Fairfax, AC 507, PC 4, Renville
GFW SD
Supt. — See Gibbon
GFW MS, PO BOX 489 55332 — 2-01100 426-7251
Ron Johnson, prin.

Fairmont, AC 507, PC 7, Martin
Fairmont SD, 115 S PARK ST 56031 — 4-11111 238-4234
Ralph Miller, supt.
JSHS, 900 JOHNSON ST 56031 — 3-00111 238-4411
Todd McCormick, prin.

Faribault, AC 507, PC 7, Rice
Faribault SD, PO BOX 618 55021 — 5-11111 334-2291
Richard Berge, supt.
SHS, 330 9TH AVE SW 55021 — 3-00001 334-5527
Allan Johnson, prin.
JHS, 704 17TH ST SW 55021 — 3-00110 334-1864
John Currie, prin.

Bethlehem Academy
105 3RD AVE SW 55021 — 2-00111 334-3948
Sr. Kathleen Theis, prin.
Minnesota School for the Deaf
PO BOX 308 55021 — HND
Riverland Technical College
1225 3RD ST SW 55021 — 2-CS 800-422-0391
Shattuck/St. Marys S
PO BOX 218 55021 — 2-00111 332-7527
Jarek Garlinski, prin.
Wilson Center, The
PO BOX 917 55021 — HND

Farmington, AC 612, PC 6, Dakota
Farmington SD, 510 WALNUT ST 55024 — 5-11111 463-6400
Patricia Hanauer, supt.
HS, 800 DENMARK AVE 55024 — 3-00011 463-6500
Thomas Rolloff, prin.
MS, 4200 208TH ST W 55024 — 3-00100 463-6560
David Thompson, prin.

Christian Life ES
6300 212TH ST W 55024 — 2-11111

Fergus Falls, AC 218, PC 7, Otter Tail
Fergus Falls SD, 4B EAST DR 56537 — 5-11111 736-7576
Robert Block, supt.
HS, 518 FRIBERG AVE 56537 — 3-00111 736-6971
Mark Sleeper, prin.
MS, 601 RANDOLPH AVE 56537 — 4-01100 736-5601
Royal Kline, prin.

Fergus Falls Community College
1414 COLLEGE WAY 56537 — 3-CC 739-7500
Hillcrest Lutheran Academy
PO BOX 317 56538 — 2-00011

Fertile, AC 218, PC 3, Polk
Fertile-Beltrami SD
PO BOX 648 56540 — 3-11111 945-6933
Lawrence Grant, supt.
Fertile-Beltrami JSHS
PO BOX 648 56540 — 2-00111 945-6931
Richard Roragen, prin.

Fisher, AC 218, PC 2, Polk
Fisher SD, PO BOX 37 56723 — 2-11111 891-4105
Randy Bruer, supt.
JSHS, PO BOX 37 56723 — 1-00111 891-4905
Randy Bruer, prin.

Floodwood, AC 218, PC 3, St. Louis
Floodwood SD, PO BOX 287 55736 — 2-11111 476-2285
Philip Minkkinen, supt.
JSHS, PO BOX 287 55736 — 2-00111 476-2285
Philip Minkkinen, prin.

Foley, AC 612, PC 4, Benton
Foley SD, 520 DEWEY ST 56329 — 4-11111 968-7175
Noel Schroeder, supt.
HS, 621 PENN 56329 — 3-00011 968-7246
Dennis Litfin, prin.
MS, 520 DEWEY ST 56329 — 3-01100 968-6251
Paula Foley, prin.

Forest Lake, AC 612, PC 6, Washington
Forest Lake SD, 6100 210TH ST N 55025 — 6-11111 464-9100
Donald Ruble, supt.
SHS, 6101 SCANDIA TRL N 55025 — 4-00001 464-9200
Carol Kluznik, prin.
Central JHS, 200 4TH ST SW 55025 — 3-00110 464-9250
Caryn Boyd, prin.
Southwest JHS, 943 9TH AVE SW 55025 — 3-00110 464-9275
Herbert Millington, prin.

Fosston, AC 218, PC 4, Polk
Fosston SD, 301 1ST ST E 56542 — 3-11111 435-6335
Mary Ann Schmidt, supt.
JSHS, 301 1ST ST E 56542 — 2-00111 435-1909
William Leff, prin.

Frazee, AC 218, PC 4, Becker
Frazee SD, PO BOX 186 56544 — 4-11111 334-3181
Joe Merseth, supt.
JSHS, PO BOX 186 56544 — 3-00111 334-2981
R. Robinson, prin.

Freeborn, AC 507, PC 2, Freeborn
United South Central SD
Supt. — See Wells
MS, PO BOX 155 56032 — 1-01100 863-2311
Dale Brandsoy, prin.

Fridley, AC 612, PC 8, Anoka
Fridley SD
6000 MOORE LAKE DR W 55432 — 5-11111 571-6000
Dennis Rens, supt.
HS, 6000 MOORE LAKE DR W 55432 — 3-00011 571-6000
John Deir, prin.

MS, 6100 MOORE LAKE DR W 55432 — 3-00100 571-6000
Margaret Leibfried, prin.

Totino-Grace HS
1350 GARDENA AVE NE 55432 — 3-00011 571-9116
Br. Barker, prin.

Fulda, AC 507, PC 4, Murray
Fulda SD, PO BOX 247 56131 — 3-11111 425-2514
Cornelius Smit, supt.
JSHS, PO BOX 247 56131 — 2-00111 425-2516
Dale Kirsch, prin.

Garden City, AC 507, PC 2, Blue Earth
Lake Crystal-Wellcome SD
Supt. — See Lake Crystal
Lake Crystal/Welcome MS
HIGHWAY 169 56034 — 2-01100 546-3527
Bruce Melander, prin.

Gary, AC 218, PC 2, Norman
Norman County East SD
PO BOX 100 56545 — 2-11111 356-8222
Karl Schultz, supt.
Norman County East JSHS
PO BOX 100 56545 — 2-00111 356-8221
Gary Tehennepe, prin.

Gaylord, AC 612, PC 4, Sibley
Gaylord SD, PO BOX 356 55334 — 3-11110 237-5511
Nordy Nelson, supt.
Sibley East JHS, PO BOX 356 55334 — 2-00110 237-5511
Joan Anderson, prin.

Gibbon, AC 507, PC 3, Sibley
GFW SD, 323 E 11TH ST 55335 — 4-11111 834-6501
Larry Kauzlarich, supt.
Other Schools – See Fairfax, Winthrop

Gilbert, AC 218, PC 4, St. Louis
Eveleth-Gilbert SD
Supt. — See Eveleth
Eveleth-Gilbert JHS
PO BOX 698 55741 — 2-00110 741-7500
Jim Wheeler, prin.

Glencoe, AC 612, PC 5, Mcleod
Glencoe SD, 1621 16TH ST E 55336 — 4-11111 864-3165
Warren Schmidt, supt.
HS, 1825 16TH ST E 55336 — 2-00011 864-5153
Steve Wiltgen, prin.
MS, 1103 11TH ST E 55336 — 2-01100 864-3112
Mark Larson, prin.

Glenville, AC 507, PC 3, Freeborn
Glenville SD, 230 5TH ST SE 56036 — 2-11011 448-3623
Stephen Malone, supt.
HS, 230 5TH ST SE 56036 — 2-00011 448-2889
Doug Sharp, prin.

Glenwood, AC 612, PC 5, Pope
Minnewaska SD
3330 HIGHWAY 28 W 56334 — 4-11111 239-4800
Daniel Froemming, supt.
Minnewaska JSHS
3330 HIGHWAY 28 W 56334 — 3-00111 239-4800
W. Norby, prin.

Glyndon, AC 218, PC 3, Clay
Glyndon-Felton SD
Supt. — See Dilworth
Glyndon-Felton HS
513 PARKE AVE S 56547 – (—), prin. — 2-00011 498-2263

Golden Valley, AC 612, PC 7, Hennepin
Robbinsdale SD
Supt. — See New Hope
Sandburg MS
2400 SANDBURG LN 55427 — 3-00100 545-2571
Tom Henderlite, prin.

Breck School
123 OTTAWA AVE N 55422 — 4-11111

Gonvick, AC 218, PC 2, Clearwater
Gonvick SD, PO BOX 119 56644 — 2-11100 487-5262
Vern Pfeifer, supt.
JHS, PO BOX 119 56644 — 2-00100 487-5263
Richard Tronerud, prin.

Goodhue, AC 612, PC 3, Goodhue
Goodhue SD, 510 3RD AVE 55027 — 3-11111 923-4447
Mike Smith, supt.
JSHS, 510 3RD AVE 55027 — 2-00111 923-4447
Barbara Jahnke, prin.

Goodridge, AC 218, PC 2, Pennington
Goodridge SD, PO BOX 195 56725 — 2-11111 378-4133
Salvinus Hoffert, supt.
JSHS, PO BOX 195 56725 — 2-00111 378-4133
Elden Winge, prin.

Graceville, AC 612, PC 3, Big Stone
Clinton-Graceville SD
Supt. — See Clinton
Clinton-Graceville JSHS
PO BOX 398 56240 — 2-00111 748-7233
K. Tharaldson, prin.

Granada, AC 507, PC 2, Martin
Granada-Huntley-East Chain SD
PO BOX 17 56039 — 2-11111 447-2211
Jon Bathke, supt.
Granada-Huntley JSHS
PO BOX 17 56039 — 2-00111 447-2213
Jon Bathke, prin.

Grand Marais, AC 218, PC 4, Cook
Cook County SD, PO BOX 1030 55604 — 3-11111
Don Langan, supt. — 387-2271
Cook County JSHS — 2-00111
PO BOX 1030 55604 — 387-2273
Carol Aenne, prin.

Grand Meadow, AC 507, PC 3, Mower
Grand Meadow SD, PO BOX 68 55936 — 2-11111
Bob Jorstad, supt. — 754-5318
JSHS, PO BOX 68 55936 — 2-00111
Susan Roehrich, prin. — 754-5310

Grand Rapids, AC 218, PC 6, Itasca
Grand Rapids SD — 5-11111
820 N POKEGAMA AVE 55744 — 327-2261
Dan Kaler, supt.
SHS, 800 NW CONIFER DR 55744 — 3-00001
Lloyd Styrwoll, prin. — 326-9473
MS, 902 N POKEGAMA AVE 55744 — 4-00110
Henry Johnson, prin. — 327-2261
Other Schools – See Bigfork

Itasca Community College — 4-CC
1851 E HIGHWAY 169 55744 — 327-4468

Granite Falls, AC 612, PC 5, Yellow Medicine
Granite Falls SD, 450 9TH AVE 56241 — 3-11011
Earl Mathison, supt. — 564-4081
HS, 450 9TH AVE 56241 — 2-00011
Douglas McCoss, prin. — 564-4081

Southwestern Technical College — 2-CS
1593 11TH AVE 56241 — 800-657-3247

Greenbush, AC 218, PC 3, Roseau
Greenbush SD, PO BOX 70 56726 — 2-11111
Philip Dyrud, supt. — 782-2231
JSHS, PO BOX 70 56726 — 2-00111
Robert Anderson, prin. — 782-2232

Grove City, AC 612, PC 3, Meeker
Grove City SD, PO BOX 278 56243 — 2-00110
Thomas Dickhudt, supt. — 857-2271
JHS, PO BOX 278 56243 — 2-00110
Thomas Hiebert, prin. — 857-2276

Grygla, AC 218, PC 2, Marshall
Grygla SD, PO BOX 18 56727 — 2-11111
Salvinus Hoffert, supt. — 294-6155
JSHS, PO BOX 18 56727 — 2-00111
Loren Lusignan, prin. — 294-6155

Hallock, AC 218, PC 4, Kittson
Kittson Central SD — 2-11011
PO BOX 670 56728 — 843-3682
Donald Vellenga, supt.
Kittson Central HS — 2-00011
PO BOX 670 56728 — 843-3682
Edgar Warrington, prin.

Halstad, AC 218, PC 3, Norman
Halstad-Hendrum SD — 2-11111
PO BOX 328 56548 — 456-2152
Don Blaeser, supt.
Norman County West JSHS — 2-00111
PO BOX 328 56548 — 456-2151
Mary Jo Morgan, prin.

Hancock, AC 612, PC 3, Stevens
Hancock SD, PO BOX 367 56244 — 2-11111
Russell Larson, supt. — 392-5622
JSHS, PO BOX 367 56244 — 2-00111
Roger Clarke, prin. — 392-5622

Harmony, AC 507, PC 4, Fillmore
Harmony SD, 145 MAIN AVE S 55939 — 2-00011
Ken Doty, supt. — 886-6464
HS, 145 MAIN AVE S 55939 — 2-00011
Larry Jenison, prin. — 886-6464

Hastings, AC 612, PC 7, Dakota
Hastings SD — 5-11111
9TH & VERMILLION ST 55033 — 437-6111
K. LaCroix, supt.
HS, 1000 11TH ST W 55033 — 4-00011
Richard Clymer, prin. — 437-6111
MS, 9TH & VERMILLION ST 55033 — 4-00100
Garry Jensen, prin. — 437-6111

Hawley, AC 218, PC 4, Clay
Hawley SD, PO BOX 608 56549 — 3-11111
Dale Skallerud, supt. — 483-4647
JSHS, PO BOX 608 56549 — 2-00111
Mark Bezek, prin. — 483-3555

Hayfield, AC 507, PC 4, Dodge
Hayfield SD, PO BOX 6 55940 — 4-11111
Richard Guevremont, supt. — 477-3238
JSHS, PO BOX 6 55940 — 2-00111
Ronald Evjen, prin. — 477-3238

Hector, AC 612, PC 4, Renville
Buffalo Lake-Hector SD — 3-11111
PO BOX 307 55342 — 848-2232
Roy Rud, supt.
Buffalo Lake-Hector JSHS — 2-00111
PO BOX 307 55342 — 848-2233
Roy Rud, prin.

Hendricks, AC 507, PC 3, Lincoln
Hendricks SD, 200 E LINCOLN 56136 — 2-11110
Jerry Scott, supt. — 275-3116
Lincoln JHS, 200 E LINCOLN 56136 — 2-00110
Orlo Baslington, prin. — 275-3115

Henning, AC 218, PC 3, Otter Tail
Henning SD, PO BOX 15 56551 — 2-11111
Bruce Montplaiser, supt. — 583-2927
JSHS, PO BOX 15 56551 — 2-00111
Robert Koll, prin. — 583-2927

Herman, AC 612, PC 2, Grant
Herman-Norcross SD — 2-11111
PO BOX 288 56248 — 677-2291
Leroy Edlund, supt.
JSHS, PO BOX 288 56248 — 2-00111
Leroy Edlund, prin. — 677-2291

Hermantown, AC 218, PC 6, St. Louis
Hermantown SD — 4-11111
4307 UGSTAD RD 55811 — 729-9313
Michael White, supt.
HS, 4335 HAWK CIRCLE DR 55811 — 2-00111
(—), prin. — 729-8874
MS, 4289 UGSTAD RD 55811 — 2-01100
Ellen Wiss, prin. — 729-6690

Heron Lake, AC 507, PC 3, Jackson
Heron Lake-Okabena SD — 2-11110
PO BOX 378 56137 — 793-2307
John Gates, supt.
Other Schools – See Okabena

Hibbing, AC 218, PC 7, St. Louis
Hibbing SD, 800 E 21ST ST 55746 — 5-11111
Robert Sarff, supt. — 263-4850
HS, 800 E 21ST ST 55746 — 4-00011
Glenn Muster, prin. — 263-3675
Lincoln JHS — 3-00100
11TH AVE E & 23RD ST 55746 — 262-1089
Michael Richtarich, prin.

Hibbing Community College — 4-CC
1515 E 25TH ST 55746 — 262-6700
Hibbing Technical Institute — 2-CS
2900 E BELTLINE 55746 — 262-6185

Hill City, AC 218, PC 2, Aitkin
Hill City SD, 500 IONE AVE 55748 — 2-11111
Darrell Nelson, supt. — 697-2394
JSHS, 500 IONE AVE 55748 — 2-00111
(—), prin. — 697-2394

Hills, AC 507, PC 3, Rock
Hills-Beaver Creek SD — 2-11111
PO BOX 547 56138 — 962-3240
Tom Knoll, supt.
Hills-Beaver Creek JSHS — 2-00111
PO BOX 547 56138 — 962-3240
Greg Spath, prin.

Hinckley, AC 612, PC 3, Pine
Hinckley SD, PO BOX 308 55037 — 3-11111
Jack Almos, supt. — 384-6277
JSHS, PO BOX 308 55037 — 3-00111
O. Larson, prin. — 384-6132

Hoffman, AC 612, PC 3, Grant
Hoffman SD, PO BOX 306 56339 — 2-00110
Kelly Smith, supt. — 986-2032
MS, PO BOX 306 56339 — 2-00110
Gerald Ness, prin. — 986-2032

Holdingford, AC 612, PC 3, Stearns
Holdingford SD, PO BOX 250 56340 — 4-11111
Gregory Ohl, supt. — 746-2196
JSHS, PO BOX 250 56340 — 3-00111
Barbara Jahnke, prin. — 746-2221

Hopkins, AC 612, PC 7, Hennepin
Hopkins SD — 6-11111
1001 HIGHWAY 7 55305 — 933-9353
Michael Kremer, supt.
Other Schools – See Minnetonka

Alfred Adler Institute of MN — 1-UC
1001 HIGHWAY 7 # 344 55305 — 933-9363

Houston, AC 507, PC 4, Houston
Houston SD, 306 W ELM ST 55943 — 3-11111
Stephen Twitchell, supt. — 896-3161
JSHS, 306 W ELM ST 55943 — 2-00111
Mark Ruggeberg, prin. — 896-3161

Howard Lake, AC 612, PC 4, Wright
Howard Lake SD, PO BOX 708 55349 — 3-11111
Riley Hoheisel, supt. — 543-3521
Howard Lake-Waverly JSHS — 2-00111
PO BOX 708 55349 — 543-3471
David Jackson, prin.

Hutchinson, AC 612, PC 7, Mcleod
Hutchinson SD, 30 GLEN ST N 55350 — 5-11111
Gary Swenson, supt. — 587-2860
HS, 1200 ROBERTS RD 55350 — 3-00011
Scott Douglas, prin. — 587-2151
JHS, 1365 S GRADE RD 55350 — 2-00100
Michael McLoughlin, prin. — 587-2854

Hutchinson Technical College — 2-CS
2 CENTURY AVE 55350 — 587-3636
Maplewood Academy — 2-00011
700 MAIN ST N 55350

International Falls, AC 218, PC 6, Koochiching
International Falls SD, 900 5TH ST 56649 — 4-11111
David Lund, supt. — 283-8468
Falls JSHS, 900 5TH ST 56649 — 3-00111
Peggy Hanson, prin. — 283-2571

Rainy River Community College 56649 — 2-CC
— 285-7722

Inver Grove Heights, AC 612, PC 7, Dakota
Inver Grove SD, 2990 80TH ST E 55076 — 5-11111
Phillip Moye, supt. — 457-7210
Simley HS, 2920 80TH ST E 55076 — 3-00011
Richard Ehlers, prin. — 457-7230
Inver Grove Heights MS — 3-00100
8167 CAHILL AVE E 55076 — 457-7220
John Riley, prin.

Inver Hills Community College — 5-CC
8445 COLLEGE TRL 55076 — 450-8634

Iron, AC 218, PC 2, St. Louis
St. Louis County SD
Supt. — See Virginia
Cherry JSHS, 3943 TAMMINEN RD 55751 — 2-00111
Donald Hainlen, prin. — 741-1402

Isanti, AC 612, PC 4, Isanti
Cambridge-Isanti SD
Supt. — See Cambridge
MS, 201 CENTENNIAL DR 55040 — 3-01100
Fred Nolan, prin. — 444-5506

Isle, AC 612, PC 3, Mille Lacs
Isle SD, PO BOX 25 56342 — 3-01100
Dale Captain, supt. — 676-3146
JSHS, PO BOX 25 56342 — 2-00111
Gregg Allen, prin. — 676-3101

Ivanhoe, AC 507, PC 3, Lincoln
Ivanhoe SD, PO BOX 9 56142 — 2-11001
Jerry Scott, supt. — 694-1540
SHS, PO BOX 9 56142 — 2-00001
Orlo Baslington, prin. — 694-1540

Jackson, AC 507, PC 5, Jackson
Jackson SD, 1128 NORTH HWY 56143 — 4-11111
Michael Kuntz, supt. — 847-3608
HS, 1128 NORTH HWY 56143 — 2-00011
Gary Wenschlag, prin. — 847-5310
MS, 405 5TH ST 56143 — 2-00100
Steven Darkow, prin. — 847-2236

Southwestern Technical College — 2-CS
401 WEST ST 56143 — 800-658-2522

Janesville, AC 507, PC 4, Waseca
Janesville-Waldorf-Pemberton SD — 3-11111
PO BOX 389 56048 — 234-5478
Donald Wilke, supt.
Janesville-Waldorf-Pemberton HS — 2-00011
PO BOX 389 56048 — 234-5181
Jerald Kaphers, prin.
Other Schools – See Waldorf

Jeffers, AC 507, PC 2, Cottonwood
Storden-Jeffers SD
Supt. — See Storden
Storden-Jeffers JHS — 2-00100
PO BOX 68 56145 — 628-5521
Robert Meyer, prin.

Jordan, AC 612, PC 5, Scott
Jordan SD, 500 SUNSET DR 55352 — 4-11111
John Fredericksen, supt. — 492-6200
JSHS, 500 SUNSET DR 55352 — 3-00111
Donald Tillman, prin. — 492-2332

Karlstad, AC 218, PC 3, Kittson
Karlstad-Strandquist SD — 2-11111
PO BOX 178 56732 — 436-2261
Dorothy Suomala, supt.
Tri-County JSHS, PO BOX 178 56732 — 2-00111
Ron Ruud, prin. — 436-2374

Kasson, AC 507, PC 5, Dodge
Kasson-Mantorville SD — 4-11111
PO BOX 158 55944 — 634-2961
Donald Groth, supt.
Kasson-Mantorville HS — 2-00011
PO BOX 158 55944 — 634-2961
Collin Harris, prin.
Kasson-Mantorville MS — 3-01100
PO BOX 158 55944 — 634-4030
Joseph Hampl, prin.

Kelliher, AC 218, PC 2, Beltrami
Kelliher SD, PO BOX 259 56650 — 2-11111
Larry Phillips, supt. — 647-8286
JSHS, PO BOX 259 56650 — 2-00111
Darry Pink, prin. — 647-8286

Kennedy, AC 218, PC 2, Kittson
Kennedy SD, PO BOX 9 56733 — 2-11100
Donald Vellenga, supt. — 674-4136
JHS, PO BOX 9 56733 — 1-00100
Don Vellenga, prin. — 674-4136

Kenyon, AC 507, PC 4, Goodhue
Kenyon SD, 401 FOREST ST 55946 — 3-11011
Duane Stoesz, supt. — 789-6186
HS, 401 FOREST ST 55946 — 2-00011
Donald Pressnall, prin. — 789-6186

Kerkhoven, AC 612, PC 3, Swift
Kerkhoven-Murdock-Sunburg SD 56252 — 3-11111
Gary Shaw, supt. — 264-1411
JSHS 56252 — 2-00111
Harold Hagert, prin. — 264-1412

Kiester, AC 507, PC 3, Faribault
United South Central SD
  Supt. — See Wells
  MS, PO BOX 300 56051   2-01100
    Dale Brandsoy, prin.   294-3206

Kimball, AC 612, PC 3, Stearns
Kimball SD, PO BOX 368 55353   3-11111
  Kenneth Helling, supt.   398-5585
  JSHS, PO BOX 368 55353   2-00111
    Paul Wilfahrt, prin.   398-7700

La Crescent, AC 507, PC 5, Houston
La Crescent-Hokah SD   4-11111
  510 S OAK ST 55947   895-4484
  Ken Runberg, supt.
  JSHS, 1301 LANCER DR 55947   3-00111
    Don Ruud, prin.   895-4481

Lake Benton, AC 507, PC 3, Lincoln
Lake Benton SD, PO BOX 158 56149   2-11111
  Dany Castor, supt.   368-4236
  JSHS, PO BOX 158 56149   2-00111
    James Roggenbuck, prin.   368-4241

Lake City, AC 612, PC 5, Wabasha
Lake City SD, PO BOX 454 55041   4-11111
  Jerry Jensen, supt.   345-2198
  Lincoln JSHS, PO BOX 454 55041   3-00111
    Robert Svihel, prin.   345-4553

Lake Crystal, AC 507, PC 4, Blue Earth
Lake Crystal-Wellcome SD   4-11111
  PO BOX 160 56055   726-2323
  Eric Bartleson, supt.
  Lake Crystal/Wellcome Memorial HS   2-00011
  PO BOX 160 56055   726-2110
  Roger Carlson, prin.
  Other Schools – See Garden City

Lake Elmo, AC 612, PC 6, Washington
Stillwater SD
  Supt. — See Stillwater
  Oak-Land JHS   4-00110
  820 MANNING AVE N 55042   430-8313
  Thomas LeCloux, prin.

Lakefield, AC 507, PC 4, Jackson
Lakefield SD, PO BOX 338 56150   2-11001
  John Gates, supt.   662-6625
  SHS, PO BOX 338 56150   2-00001
    Gery Arndt, prin.   662-6625

Lake Park, PC 3, Becker
Lake Park SD   2-00111
  PO BOX 479 56554   218-238-5914
  Ronald Bratlie, supt.
  Lake Park-Audubon JSHS   2-00111
  PO BOX 479 56554   218-238-5916
  Ron Fleming, prin.

Lakeville, AC 612, PC 7, Dakota
Lakeville SD, 8670 210TH ST W 55044   6-11111
  Carl Wahlstrom, supt.   469-7352
  HS, 19455 KENWOOD TRL 55044   3-00011
  Harry McLenighan, prin.   469-7152
  Kenwood Trail JHS   3-00100
  19455 KENWOOD TRL 55044   469-7157
  Jerry Pederson, prin.

Lamberton, AC 507, PC 3, Redwood
Lamberton SD, PO BOX 278 56152   2-00011
  Richard Gulbranson, supt.   752-7361
  Red Rock Central HS   2-00011
  PO BOX 278 56152   752-7361
  Forrest Benz, prin.

Lancaster, AC 218, PC 2, Kittson
Lancaster SD, PO BOX 217 56735   2-11111
  Phillip Dyrud, supt.   762-5400
  JSHS, PO BOX 217 56735   1-00111
    Bradley Homstad, prin.   762-5400

Lanesboro, AC 507, PC 3, Fillmore
Lanesboro SD   2-11111
  100 KIRKWOOD ST E 55949   467-2229
  Richard Lamon, supt.
  JSHS, 100 KIRKWOOD ST E 55949   2-00111
    James Hirman, prin.   467-2229

Laporte, AC 218, PC 2, Hubbard
LaPorte SD, RR 1 BOX 1 56461   2-11111
  Dennis Kozitza, supt.   224-2288
  JSHS, RR 1 BOX 1 56461   2-00111
    Dan Brooks, prin.   224-2288

Le Center, AC 612, PC 4, Le Sueur
Le Center SD, 150 W TYRONE ST 56057   3-11111
  John Lowe, supt.   357-6802
  JSHS, 150 W TYRONE ST 56057   2-00111
    Janis Curiskis, prin.   357-6802

Le Roy, AC 507, PC 3, Mower
Le Roy SD, PO BOX 1000 55951   2-11111
  Darold Yost, supt.   324-5743
  JSHS, PO BOX 1000 55951   2-00111
    Marlene Kensrud, prin.   324-5741

Lester Prairie, AC 612, PC 4, Mcleod
Lester Prairie SD   3-11111
  131 HICKORY ST N 55354   395-2521
  R. Clifford Busch, supt.
  JSHS, 131 HICKORY ST N 55354   2-00111
    Don Hall, prin.   395-2521

Le Sueur, AC 612, PC 5, Le Sueur
Le Sueur-Henderson SD
  115 1/2 N 5TH ST 56058   4-11111
  Harold Larson, supt.   665-8828
  JSHS, 901 FERRY ST 56058   3-00111
    David Johnson, prin.   665-3305

Lewiston, AC 507, PC 4, Winona
Lewiston SD, PO BOX 741 55952   3-11111
  M. Krenz, supt.   523-2191
  JSHS, PO BOX 741 55952   2-00111
    Richard Wolter, prin.   523-2191

Lindstrom, AC 612, PC 4, Chisago
Chisago Lakes SD
  13750 LAKE BLVD 55045   5-11111
  Darrold Williams, supt.   257-5600
  Chisago Lakes HS   3-00011
  29403 OLINDA TRL N 55045   257-1130
  Rob Masche, prin.
  Chisago Lakes MS   3-00100
  13750 LAKE BLVD 55045   257-6500
  Peter Eikren, prin.

Litchfield, AC 612, PC 6, Meeker
Litchfield SD, 901 N GILMAN AVE 55355   4-11111
  Donn Hoffman, supt.   693-2444
  SHS, 901 N GILMAN AVE 55355   2-00011
  William Wold, prin.   693-2424
  JHS, 114 N HOLCOMBE AVE 55355   3-00110
    Mark Harper, prin.   693-2441

Little Falls, AC 612, PC 6, Morrison
Little Falls SD, 1001 5TH AVE SE 56345   5-11111
  Kerry Jacobson, supt.   632-5709
  HS, 1001 5TH AVE SE 56345   4-00011
  Phil Force, prin.   632-2921
  Community MS, 1000 1ST AVE NE 56345   3-00100
    William Turk, prin.   632-1976

Mary of Lourdes MS   2-01100
  205 3RD ST NW 56345   632-6742
  Debra Meyer, prin.

Littlefork, AC 218, PC 3, Koochiching
Littlefork-Big Falls SD, PO BOX D 56653   2-11111
  Terry Erholtz, supt.   278-6614
  Littlefork-Big Falls JSHS   2-00111
  PO BOX D 56653   278-6615
  Leonard Erickson, prin.

Long Lake, AC 612, PC 4, Hennepin
Orono SD, PO BOX 46 55356   4-11111
  Thomas Mich, supt.   449-8305
  Orono HS, PO BOX 26 55356   3-00011
  Carl Shutts, prin.   449-8405
  Orono MS, PO BOX 16 55356   3-01100
    Sue Kueppers, prin.   449-8450

Long Prairie, AC 612, PC 5, Todd
Long Prairie SD, 205 2ND ST S 56347   4-11111
  Donald Hansen, supt.   732-2194
  JSHS, 205 2ND ST S 56347   3-00111
    Jerry Turner, prin.   732-2194

Luverne, AC 507, PC 5, Rock
Luverne SD, PO BOX 278 56156   4-11111
  N. Miller, supt.   283-8088
  JSHS, PO BOX 278 56156   3-00111
    G. Fisher, prin.   283-4491

Lyle, AC 507, PC 3, Mower
Lyle SD, PO BOX 38 55953   2-11111
  O. Paul Trelstad, supt.   325-4146
  JSHS, PO BOX 38 55953   2-00111
    Alan Erickson, prin.   325-2201

Mabel, AC 507, PC 3, Fillmore
Mabel-Canton SD, PO BOX 337 55954   2-11111
  Marcia Love, supt.   493-5423
  Mabel-Canton JSHS   2-00111
  PO BOX 337 55954   493-5422
  Lowell Haroldson, prin.

Mc Gregor, AC 218, PC 2, Aitkin
Mc Gregor SD, PO BOX 160 55760   3-11111
  Antoinette Johns, supt.   768-2111
  JSHS, PO BOX 160 55760   2-00111
    Loren Sauter, prin.   768-2111

McIntosh, AC 218, PC 3, Polk
Win-E-Mac SD, PO BOX 280 56556   3-11111
  James Roberts, supt.   563-2900
  Win-E-Mac SHS, PO BOX 280 56556   2-00001
  (—), prin.   563-2255
  Other Schools – See Erskine

Madelia, AC 507, PC 4, Watonwan
Madelia SD, 320 BUCK AVE SE 56062   3-11111
  Will Forrey, supt.   642-3232
  JSHS, 320 BUCK AVE SE 56062   2-00111
    Neil Carpenter, prin.   642-3232

Madison, AC 612, PC 4, Lac Qui Parle
Lac Qui Parle Valley SD   3-00111
  RR 2 BOX 68A 56256   752-4200
  Marlowe Halbur, supt.
  Lac Qui Parle Valley JSHS   3-00111
  RR 2 BOX 68A 56256   752-4200
  Marlowe Halbur, prin.

Mahnomen, AC 218, PC 4, Mahnomen
Mahnomen SD, PO BOX 319 56557   3-11111
  Brent Gish, supt.   935-2211
  JSHS, PO BOX 319 56557   2-00111
    George Morrow, prin.   935-2213

Mahtomedi, AC 612, PC 6, Washington
Mahtomedi SD   4-11111
  1520 MAHTOMEDI AVE 55115   426-3224
  Don Lifto, supt.
  HS, 8000 75TH ST N 55115   3-00011
  Rick Wippler, prin.   426-3281
  MS, 8100 75TH ST N 55115   2-00100
    Russell Peterson, prin.   426-3211

Mankato, AC 507, PC 8, Blue Earth
Mankato SD, PO BOX 8741 56002   6-11111
  Paul Beilfuss, supt.   387-1868
  Mankato East HS   3-00011
  PO BOX 8726 56002   387-5671
  Donald Poplau, prin.
  Mankato West HS   4-00011
  PO BOX 8741 56002   387-3461
  John Barnett, prin.
  Mankato East JHS   3-00100
  2600 HOFFMAN RD 56001   387-5671
  Patrice Schmidt, prin.
  Other Schools – See North Mankato

Bethany Lutheran College   2-CC
  734 MARSH ST 56001   625-2977
Fitzgerald MS, 110 N 5TH ST 56001   2-00100
  Sr. Mary Miller, prin.   388-9344
Immanuel Lutheran S   2-11111
  421 N 2ND ST 56001
Loyola HS   2-00011
  145 GOOD COUNSEL DR 56001   388-2997
  James Rouse, prin.
Mankato State University   7-UC
  PO BOX 8400 56002   389-1111
Rasmussen Business College   2-CS
  GOOD COUNSEL DR 56001   625-6556

Maple Grove, AC 612, PC 8, Hennepin
Osseo SD, PO BOX 327 55369   7-11111
  Marl Ramsey, supt.   425-4131
  JHS, 7000 HEMLOCK LN N 55369   4-00110
  Wayne Melby, prin.   425-4500
  Other Schools – See Brooklyn Park, Osseo

Maple Lake, AC 612, PC 4, Wright
Maple Lake SD, PO BOX 820 55358   3-11111
  Kenneth Engel, supt.   963-3171
  JSHS, PO BOX 820 55358   2-00111
    Mary James, prin.   963-3171

Mapleton, AC 507, PC 4, Blue Earth
Maple River SD, PO BOX 515 56065   4-11111
  Don Berkland, supt.   524-3915
  Maple River HS, PO BOX 515 56065   2-00011
  David U'Ren, prin.   524-3930
  Other Schools – See Amboy, Minnesota Lake

Maplewood, AC 612, PC 8, Ramsey
North St. Paul-Maplewood SD   6-11111
  2055 LARPENTEUR AVE E 55109   770-4601
  William Gaslin, supt.
  Other Schools – See North Saint Paul, Oakdale, Saint Paul

Marshall, AC 507, PC 7, Lyon
Marshall SD   4-11111
  401 SARATOGA ST E 56258   537-0555
  Jerald Huber, supt.
  HS, 401 SARATOGA ST E 56258   3-00011
  Fred Majeski, prin.   537-0551
  MS, 207 4TH ST N 56258   2-00100
    Doug Kodet, prin.   532-2265

Southwest State University 56258   5-UC
    537-6272

Mayer, AC 612, PC 2, Carver

Lutheran HS, PO BOX 143 55360   2-00011
  John Holtmeier, prin.   657-2251

Mazeppa, AC 507, PC 3, Wabasha
Zumbrota-Mazeppa SD   4-11111
  425 CHESTNUT ST 55956   732-5107
  James Neuman, supt.
  Zumbrota/Mazeppa MS   2-01100
  425 CHESTNUT ST 55956   843-2165
  James Lehman, prin.
  Other Schools – See Zumbrota

Meadowlands, AC 218, PC 1, St. Louis
Toivola-Meadowlands SD   2-11111
  7705 WESTERN AVE 55765   427-2311
  (—), supt.
  Toivola-Meadowlands S   2-11111
  7705 WESTERN AVE 55765   427-2311
  Andrew Godnai, prin.

Medford, AC 507, PC 3, Steele
Medford SD, PO BOX 38 55049   3-11111
  William Kennedy, supt.   451-5250
  JSHS, PO BOX 38 55049   2-00111
    Byron Clemsen, prin.   451-5250

Melrose, AC 612, PC 5, Stearns
Melrose SD, 546 N 5TH AVE E 56352   4-11111
  Don Anderson, supt.   256-4224
  JSHS, 546 N 5TH AVE E 56352   3-00111
    Jim Ricklick, prin.   256-4224

Menahga, AC 218, PC 4, Wadena
Menahga SD, PO BOX 160 56464   3-11111
  Ronald Maertens, supt.   564-4141
  JSHS, PO BOX 160 56464   2-00111
    Dean Ogg, prin.   564-4141

Mendota Heights, AC 612, PC 6, Dakota
West St. Paul-Mendota Hts. SD
  Supt. — See West Saint Paul
  Sibley HS, 1897 DELAWARE AVE 55118   4-00011
    David Brom, prin.   681-2351

Middle River, AC 218, PC 2, Marshall
Middle River SD, PO BOX 130 56737   2-11111
  Philip Dyrud, supt.   222-3690
JSHS, PO BOX 130 56737   2-00111
  Eldon Sparby, prin.   222-3310

Milaca, AC 612, PC 4, Mille Lacs
Milaca SD, 500 4TH ST SW 56353   4-11111
  Darwin Bostic, supt.   983-2121
HS, 500 4TH ST SW 56353   2-00011
  Joan Bradach, prin.   983-2121
MS, 500 4TH ST SW 56353   3-00100
  Joan Bradach, prin.   983-2121

Milroy, AC 507, PC 2, Redwood
Milroy SD, PO BOX 10 56263   2-11100
  Norris Oerter, supt.   336-2563
JHS, PO BOX 10 56263   1-00100
  Scott Hammond, prin.   336-2563

Minneapolis, AC 612, PC 10, Hennepin
Minneapolis SD   8-11111
  807 BROADWAY ST NE 55413   627-2010
  Mitchell Trockman, supt.
Edison HS, 700 22ND AVE NE 55418   4-00011
  Craig Vanna, prin.   627-2982
Henry HS, 2020 43RD AVE N 55412   3-00011
  Mike Huerth, prin.   627-2897
North HS, 1500 JAMES AVE N 55411   4-00011
  Harlan Anderson, prin.   627-2778
Roosevelt HS, 4029 28TH AVE S 55406   4-00011
  Fred Meyer, prin.   627-2658
South HS, 3131 19TH AVE S 55407   4-00011
  Steve Couture, prin.   627-2508
Southwest HS, 3414 W 47TH ST 55410   4-00011
  Robert McCauley, prin.   627-2421
Washburn HS, 201 W 49TH ST 55409   4-00011
  Andre Lewis, prin.   627-2323
Anthony MS, 5757 IRVING AVE S 55419   3-00100
  Shelton Rucker, prin.   627-2471
Anwatin MS, 256 UPTON AVE S 55405   3-00100
  Cheryl Creecy, prin.   627-3150
Chiron MS, 25 N 16TH ST 55403   2-00100
  Lynn Iverson, prin.   627-3250
Folwell MS, 3611 20TH AVE S 55407   3-00100
  Joyce Lake, prin.   627-2604
Franklin MS   3-00100
  1501 ALDRICH AVE N 55411   627-2869
  Birch Jones, prin.
Northeast MS, 2955 HAYES ST NE 55418   3-00100
  Larry Lucio, prin.   627-3042
Sanford MS, 3524 42ND AVE S 55406   3-00100
  Art Indelicato, prin.   627-2720

Abbott-Northwestern Hospital   HSP
  810 E 27TH ST 55407   863-4204
Academy of Aviation   2-CC
  3050 METRO DR STE 200 55425   851-0066
Art Instruction Schools   2-HMS
  500 S 4TH ST 55415
Augsburg College   5-UC
  731 21ST AVE S 55454   330-1212
Aviation Training Academy   2-CC
  3050 METRO DR STE 200 55425   851-0066
Bethany Academy   2-11111
  2201 W 108TH ST 55431
CDI Computers - Academy   2-CC
  3050 METRO DR STE 200 55425   851-0066
ConCorde Career Institute   2-CS
  12 N 12TH ST 55403   341-3850
De La Salle HS   2-00011
  1 DE LA SALLE DR 55401   379-4671
  Barry Lieske, prin.
Dunwoody Institute   4-CC
  818 DUNWOODY BLVD 55403   374-5800
Fourth Baptist Christian S   2-11111
  2105 FREMONT AVE N 55411
Hennepin County Medical Center   HSP
  701 PARK AVE 55415   347-2338
Lakeland Medical-Dental Academy   2-CS
  1402 W LAKE ST 55408   827-5656
Lowthian College   2-CS
  825 2ND AVE S 55402   332-3361
Marantha Christian Academy   2-11111
  4021 THOMAS AVE N 55412
McConnell School   3-CS
  831 2ND AVE S 55402   332-4238
Memorial Blood Center of Minneapolis   HSP
  2304 PARK AVE 55404   871-3300
Minneapolis College of Art & Design   3-UC
  2501 STEVENS AVE 55404   874-3700
Minneapolis Community College   4-CC
  1501 HENNEPIN AVE 55403   341-7000
Minneapolis Drafting School   2-CS
  5700 W BROADWAY AVE 55428   535-8843
Minneapolis VA Medical Center   HSP
  1 VETERANS DR 55417   725-2000
Minnehaha Academy   3-11111
  3107 47TH AVE S 55406   729-8321
  Kenneth Greener, prin.
Music Tech   2-CS
  304 WASHINGTON AVE N 55401   338-0175
NEC-Brown Institute Campus   4-CC
  2225 E LAKE ST 55407   721-2481

NEI College of Technology   4-CC
  825 41ST AVE NE 55421   781-4881
North Central Bible College   4-UC
  910 ELLIOT AVE 55404   343-4779
North Memorial Medical Center   HSP
  3220 LOWRY AVE N 55422   520-5000
Queen of all Saints St. Anne MS   1-00100
  2620 RUSSELL AVE N 55411   529-8327
  Kathleen O'Hara, prin.
Risen Christ West Campus MS   2-01100
  3800 PLEASANT AVE 55409   822-5329
  James Lemmer, prin.
St. Mary's Campus Coll. of St. Catherine   3-CC
  2500 S 6TH ST 55454   332-5521
St. Mary's College of Minnesota   2-UC
  2510 PARK AVE 55404
School of Communication Arts   2-CS
  2526 27TH AVE S 55406   721-5357
University of Minnesota   8-UC
  U OF M 55455   626-1616
Walden University   2-UC
  155 5TH AVE S STE 200 55401   338-7224
Woodcrest Baptist Academy   2-11111
  6875 UNIVERSITY AVE NE 55432

Minneota, AC 507, PC 4, Lyon
Minneota SD, PO BOX 98 56264   3-11111
  H. Lyle Jones, supt.   872-6532
JSHS, PO BOX 98 56264   2-00111
  Bruce Johnson, prin.   872-6175

Minnesota Lake, AC 507, PC 3, Faribault
Maple River SD
  Supt. — See Mapleton
  MS, PO BOX 218 56068   2-00100
    James Bisel, prin.   462-3348

Minnetonka, AC 612, PC 8, Hennepin
Hopkins SD
  Supt. — See Hopkins
Hopkins SHS   4-00001
  2400 LINDBERGH DR 55305   541-7100
  Thomas Bauman, prin.
Hopkins North JHS   3-00110
  10700 CEDAR LAKE RD 55305   541-7185
  James Harders, prin.
Hopkins West JHS   3-00110
  3830 BAKER RD 55305   933-9256
  Terry Wolfson, prin.

Minnetonka SD
  Supt. — See Excelsior
HS, 18301 HIGHWAY 7 55345   4-00011
  Amy Mook, prin.   470-3500
Minnetonka East MS   3-00100
  17000 LAKE STREET EXT 55345   935-8601
  Lynn Scearcy, prin.

Rasmussen Business College   2-CS
  12450 WAYZATA BLVD STE 315 55305
     545-2000

Montevideo, AC 612, PC 6, Chippewa
Montevideo SD   4-11111
  3RD & EUREKA AVE 56265   269-8833
  Eddy Nystrom, supt.
HS, 1501 WILLIAMS AVE 56265   2-00011
  David Baukol, prin.   269-6446
MS, 302 EUREKA AVE 56265   3-01100
  Gary Radke, prin.   269-6431

Montgomery, AC 612, PC 4, Le Sueur
Montgomery SD, PO BOX 29 56069   4-11111
  Ray Farwell, supt.   364-7940
JSHS, PO BOX 29 56069   2-00111
  Karen Norell, prin.   364-5252

Monticello, AC 612, PC 5, Wright
Monticello SD, PO BOX 897 55362   5-11111
  S. Johnson, supt.   295-5184
HS, PO BOX 897 55362   3-00011
  Robert Voecks, prin.   295-2913
MS, PO BOX 897 55362   3-00100
  K. Bensen, prin.   295-5183

Moorhead, AC 218, PC 8, Clay
Moorhead SD, 810 4TH AVE S 56560   6-11111
  Bruce Anderson, supt.   299-6256
HS, 2300 4TH AVE S 56560   4-00011
  (—), prin.   299-6301
MS, 2020 11TH ST S 56560   3-00100
  Richard Jones, prin.   299-6290

Concordia College   5-UC
  901 8TH ST S 56562   299-3000
Moorhead State University   6-UC
  1104 7TH AVE S 56560   236-2243
Northwest Technical College   2-CS
  1900 28TH AVE S 56560   299-6512

Moose Lake, AC 218, PC 4, Carlton
Moose Lake SD, PO BOX 489 55767   3-11111
  Richard Buro, supt.   485-4435
JSHS, PO BOX 489 55767   2-00111
  Robert Carey, prin.   485-4622

Mora, AC 612, PC 5, Kanabec
Mora SD, 400 MAPLE AVE E 55051   4-11111
  Jon McBroom, supt.   679-3560
JSHS, 400 MAPLE AVE E 55051   3-00111
  R. Lanoue, prin.   679-2423

Morgan, AC 507, PC 3, Redwood
Morgan SD, PO BOX 188 56266   2-00111
  William Bjorklund, supt.   249-5990
Cedar Mountain JSHS   2-00111
  PO BOX 188 56266   249-5880
  Joel Whitehurst, prin.

Morris, AC 612, PC 6, Stevens
Morris SD, 201 S COLUMBIA AVE 56267   4-11111
  Dennis Rettke, supt.   589-4840
JSHS, 201 S COLUMBIA AVE 56267   3-00111
  Michael Martin, prin.   589-4400

University of Minnesota   4-UC
  600 E 4TH ST 56267   589-2211

Morristown, AC 507, PC 3, Rice
Waterville-Elysian-Morristown SD
  Supt. — See Waterville
Waterville-Elysian-Morristown JHS   2-00100
  PO BOX 278 55052   685-4222
  Harvey Anderson, prin.

Motley, AC 218, PC 2, Morrison
Motley SD, PO BOX 268 56466   2-11111
  Ray Smyth, supt.   352-6315
Motley JSHS, PO BOX 268 56466   2-00111
  (—), prin.   352-6471

Mound, AC 612, PC 6, Hennepin
Westonka SD   4-11111
  5600 LYNWOOD BLVD 55364   472-0306
  James Smith, supt.
Mound-Westonka JSHS   3-00111
  5905 SUNNYFIELD RD E 55364   472-0362
  Gene Zulk, prin.

Mounds View, AC 612, PC 7, Ramsey
Mounds View SD
  Supt. — See Roseville
Edgewood MS   3-00100
  5100 EDGEWOOD DR 55112   784-2010
  Penelope Howard, prin.

Mountain Iron, AC 218, PC 5, St. Louis
Mountain Iron-Buhl SD   3-11111
  PO BOX 537 55768   735-8271
  John Gornick, supt.
Mountain Iron-Buhl JSHS   2-00111
  PO BOX 537 55768   735-8217
  Terry Rheingans, prin.

Mountain Lake, AC 507, PC 4, Cottonwood
Mountain Lake SD   3-11111
  PO BOX 400 56159   427-2325
  Mike Novak, supt.
JSHS, PO BOX 400 56159   2-00111
  John Gates, prin.   427-2323

Nashwauk, AC 218, PC 4, Itasca
Nashwauk-Keewatin SD   3-11111
  400 2ND ST 55769 – John Klarich, supt. 885-2705
JSHS, 400 2ND ST 55769   2-00111
  Josh Robinson, prin.   885-1280

Nevis, AC 218, PC 2, Hubbard
Nevis SD, PO BOX 138 56467   2-11111
  Richard Magaard, supt.   652-3500
JSHS, PO BOX 138 56467   2-00111
  Richard Magaard, prin.   652-3500

New Brighton, AC 612, PC 7, Ramsey
Mounds View SD
  Supt. — See Roseville
Irondale HS, 2425 LONG LAKE RD 55112   4-00011
  David Groth, prin.   786-5200
Highview JHS, 2300 7TH ST NW 55112   3-00100
  Eugene Young, prin.   633-8144

United Theological Seminary/Twin Cities   2-UC
  3000 5TH ST NW 55112   633-4311

Newfolden, AC 218, PC 2, Marshall
Newfolden SD, PO BOX 277 56738   2-11111
  Ronald Paggen, supt.   874-8530
Central JSHS, PO BOX 277 56738   2-00111
  Ronald Paggen, prin.   874-7225

New Hope, AC 612, PC 7, Hennepin
Robbinsdale SD   7-11111
  4148 WINNETKA AVE N 55427   533-2781
  Jim Dahle, supt.
Cooper HS, 8230 47TH AVE N 55428   4-00011
  G. David Knutson, prin.   533-2551
Hosterman MS   3-00100
  5530 ZEALAND AVE N 55428   533-2411
  George Liliquist, prin.
Other Schools - See Golden Valley, Plymouth,
  Robbinsdale

New London, AC 612, PC 3, Kandiyohi
New London-Spicer SD   4-11111
  PO BOX 430 56273   354-2084
  Henry Lubbesmeyer, supt.
New London-Spicer HS   3-00011
  PO BOX 287 56273   354-2252
  Greg Ehresmann, prin.
New London-Spicer MS   2-01100
  PO BOX 398 56273   354-2084
  Rick Swenson, prin.

New Prague, AC 612, PC 5, Scott
New Prague SD, 101 3RD ST NW 56071   4-11111
  Robert Stepaniak, supt.   758-2506
HS, 721 CENTRAL AVE N 56071   3-00011
  Alice Woog, prin.   758-2582

MS, 405 1ST AVE NW 56071 3-01100
(—), prin. 758-2581

New Richland, AC 507, PC 4, Waseca
New Richland SD, PO BOX 427 56072 3-11011
Richard Lorenz, supt. 465-3205
HS, PO BOX 427 56072 2-00011
Anthony Boyer, prin. 465-3205

New Ulm, AC 507, PC 7, Brown
New Ulm SD, 400 S PAYNE ST 56073 5-11111
Dean Risius, supt. 359-8401
SHS, 414 S PAYNE ST 56073 3-00001
Richard Lapatka, prin. 359-8420
JHS, 15 N STATE ST 56073 3-00110
Sy Moelter, prin. 359-8480

Cathedral HS 2-00011
600 N WASHINGTON ST 56073 354-4511
David Schieffert, prin.
Dr. Martin Luther College 2-UC
1884 COLLEGE HEIGHTS DR 56073 354-8221
Holy Trinity S, 515 N STATE ST 56073 2-01100
Sr. Sharon Waldoch, prin. 354-4311
Minnesota Valley Lutheran HS 2-00011
PO BOX 52A 56073

New York Mills, AC 218, PC 3, Otter Tail
New York Mills SD 3-11111
PO BOX 218 56567 385-2553
Jerald Nesland, supt.
JSHS, PO BOX 218 56567 2-00111
James Mann, prin. 385-2553

Nicollet, AC 507, PC 3, Nicollet
Nicollet SD, PO BOX 108 56074 2-11111
Mark Hinckley, supt. 225-3411
JSHS, PO BOX 108 56074 2-00111
Richard Mayer, prin. 225-3448

North Branch, AC 612, PC 4, Chisago
North Branch SD, PO BOX 370 55056 5-11111
James Walker, supt. 674-5210
HS, PO BOX 370 55056 3-00011
Michael Trok, prin. 674-5340
MS, PO BOX 370 55056 3-00100
John Bull, prin. 674-5300

Northfield, AC 507, PC 7, Rice
Northfield SD 5-11111
1400 DIVISION ST S 55057 663-0629
Charles Kyte, supt.
HS, 1400 DIVISION ST S 55057 3-00011
William Gasho, prin. 663-0630
MS, 301 UNION ST 55057 3-00100
Don Lapp, prin. 663-0650

Carleton College 4-UC
1 N COLLEGE ST 55057 663-4000
Laura Baker School HND
PO BOX 611 55057
St. Olaf College 55057 5-UC
646-3000

North Mankato, AC 507, PC 7, Nicollet
Mankato SD
Supt. — See Mankato
Dakota Meadows MS 3-00100
1900 HOWARD DR 56003 387-1868
Jane Schuck, prin.

Northome, AC 218, PC 2, Koochiching
South Koochiching SD 2-11111
PO BOX 465 56661 897-5277
Ronald Schuster, supt.
JSHS, PO BOX 465 56661 2-00111
Ronald Schuster, prin. 897-5275
Other Schools – See Birchdale

North Saint Paul, AC 612, PC 7, Ramsey
North St. Paul-Maplewood SD
Supt. — See Maplewood
North HS, 2520 12TH AVE E 55109 4-00011
Randall Zipf, prin. 770-4703

Norwood, AC 612, PC 4, Carver
Norwood SD, 531 N MORSE ST 55368 4-11111
Patrick Desutter, supt. 467-2272
Central JSHS, 531 N MORSE ST 55368 2-00111
Charles Rick, prin. 467-2272

Oakdale, AC 612, PC 7, Washington
North St. Paul-Maplewood SD
Supt. — See Maplewood
Tartan HS 4-00011
828 GREENWAY AVE N 55128 770-4629
Lawrence Hartman, prin.

Ogilvie, AC 612, PC 3, Kanabec
Ogilvie SD, PO BOX 160 56358 3-11111
Jerald Horgen, supt. 272-4431
JSHS, PO BOX 160 56358 2-00111
Keith Lester, prin. 272-4431

Okabena, AC 507, PC 2, Jackson
Heron Lake-Okabena SD
Supt. — See Heron Lake
Heron Lake-Okabena-Lakefield JHS 2-00110
PO BOX 97 56161 853-4507
Carlton Mitchell, prin.

Oklee, AC 218, PC 2, Red Lake
Oklee SD, PO BOX 100 56742 2-11111
Dale Salberg, supt. 796-5136
JSHS, PO BOX 100 56742 2-00111
Dale Salberg, prin. 796-5136

Olivia, AC 612, PC 5, Renville
Bird Island-Olivia SD
Supt. — See Bird Island
Bold HS, 701 9TH ST S 56277 2-00011
Glenn Hegna, prin. 523-1031

Onamia, AC 612, PC 3, Mille Lacs
Onamia SD, 35465 125TH AVE 56359 3-11111
Kent Baldry, supt. 532-4174
JSHS, 35465 125TH AVE 56359 2-00111
Dennis Hitzemann, prin. 532-4174

Orr, AC 218, PC 2, St. Louis
St. Louis County SD
Supt. — See Virginia
JSHS, PO BOX 307 55771 2-00111
Judith Pearson, prin. 757-3225

Ortonville, AC 612, PC 4, Big Stone
Ortonville SD, PO BOX 247 56278 3-11111
Keith Redfield, supt. 839-6181
JSHS, PO BOX 247 56278 2-00111
Dennis Johnson, prin. 839-6183

Osakis, AC 612, PC 4, Douglas
Osakis SD, PO BOX X 56360 3-11111
Leroy Mackove, supt. 859-2191
JSHS, PO BOX X 56360 2-00111
John Peterka, prin. 859-2192

Oslo, AC 218, PC 2, Marshall
Oslo SD, PO BOX 10 56744 2-11111
James Hahn, supt. 695-2121
JSHS, PO BOX 10 56744 2-00111
Kenneth Henry, prin. 695-2121

Osseo, AC 612, PC 5, Hennepin
Osseo SD
Supt. — See Maple Grove
SHS, 317 2ND AVE NW 55369 4-00001
Richard Melvin, prin. 425-2323
JHS, 10223 93RD AVE N 55369 4-00110
Barry Drevlow, prin. 425-2422

Owatonna, AC 507, PC 7, Steele
Owatonna SD, 515 W BRIDGE ST 55060 5-11111
James Bauck, supt. 455-8612
HS, 333 E SCHOOL ST 55060 4-00011
James Herzog, prin. 451-4710
JHS, 500 15TH ST NE 55060 3-00100
Janell Salcedo, prin. 451-8410

Owatonna Christian S 2-11111
265 26TH ST NE 55060
Pillsbury Baptist Bible College 2-UC
315 S GROVE AVE 55060 451-2710

Parkers Prairie, AC 218, PC 3, Otter Tail
Parkers Prairie SD, PO BOX 46 56361 3-11111
Phillip Smith, supt. 338-6011
JSHS, PO BOX 46 56361 2-00111
Michael Bergevin, prin. 338-6011

Park Rapids, AC 218, PC 5, Hubbard
Park Rapids SD, PO BOX 591 56470 4-11111
Leslie Norman, supt. 732-3333
HS, PO BOX 591 56470 3-00011
Gary Gauldin, prin. 732-3333
MS, PO BOX 591 56470 3-01100
Bruce Gravalin, prin. 732-3333

Paynesville, AC 612, PC 4, Stearns
Paynesville SD, 217 W MILL ST 56362 4-11111
Howard Caldwell, supt. 243-3410
HS, 795 W HIGHWAY 23 56362 2-00111
John Janotta, prin. 243-3761
MS, 801 W HIGHWAY 23 56362 2-00100
(—), prin. 243-3724

Pelican Rapids, AC 218, PC 4, Otter Tail
Pelican Rapids SD, PO BOX V 56572 4-11111
Keith Klein, supt. 863-5910
JSHS, PO BOX V 56572 3-00111
Glenn Moerke, prin. 863-5910

Pequot Lakes, AC 218, PC 3, Crow Wing
Pequot Lakes SD, PO BOX 368 56472 3-11111
Martin Avelsgaard, supt. 568-4996
HS, PO BOX 368 56472 2-00111
Edward Larsen, prin. 568-9210

Perham, AC 218, PC 4, Otter Tail
Perham SD, 200 5TH ST SE 56573 4-11111
Dennis Drummond, supt. 346-4501
JSHS, 200 5TH ST SE 56573 3-00111
Kitty Krueger, prin. 346-6500

Peterson, AC 507, PC 2, Fillmore
Rushford-Peterson SD
Supt. — See Rushford
Rushford-Peterson MS 2-00100
PO BOX 8 55962 875-2238
Maynard Thompson, prin.

Pierz, AC 612, PC 4, Morrison
Pierz SD, 112 KAMNIC LN S 56364 3-11111
Reinhold Opp, supt. 468-6458
Healy JSHS, 112 KAMNIC LN S 56364 3-00111
L. Miller, prin. 468-6491

Pillager, AC 218, PC 2, Cass
Pillager SD, PO BOX 38 56473 3-11111
Douglas Hamilton, supt. 746-3772
JSHS, PO BOX 38 56473 2-00111
Robert Speed, prin. 746-3557

Pine City, AC 612, PC 5, Pine
Pine City SD, 1400 6TH ST 55063 4-11111
Candice Ames, supt. 629-7511
SHS, 1400 6TH ST 55063 2-00001
Donald Lund, prin. 629-7511
JHS, 1400 6TH ST 55063 2-00110
George Johnson, prin. 629-7511

Pine Island, AC 507, PC 4, Goodhue
Pine Island SD, PO BOX 398 55963 4-11111
Brian Grenell, supt. 356-4849
JSHS, PO BOX 398 55963 2-00111
K. DeBoer, prin. 356-8326

Pine River, AC 218, PC 3, Cass
Pine River-Backus SD 4-11111
PO BOX 610 56474 587-4720
Dudley Gerber, supt.
JSHS, PO BOX 610 56474 3-00111
William Dunshee, prin. 587-4425

Pipestone, AC 507, PC 5, Pipestone
Pipestone SD, 400 2ND AVE SW 56164 4-11111
William Burkholder, supt. 825-5861
HS, 400 2ND AVE SW 56164 2-00011
Cliff Carmody, prin. 825-5861
MS, 400 2ND AVE SW 56164 2-00100
Don Plahn, prin. 825-5861

Southwestern Technical College 2-CS
PO BOX 250 56164 825-5471

Plainview, AC 507, PC 5, Wabasha
Plainview SD, 500 W BROADWAY 55964 4-11111
James Schmitt, supt. 534-3651
JSHS, 500 W BROADWAY 55964 3-00111
Larry Fix, prin. 534-3128

Plummer, AC 218, PC 2, Red Lake
Plummer SD 2-11111
628 MINNESOTA AVE 56748 465-4222
Richard Lorenson, supt.
Pershing JSHS 2-00111
628 MINNESOTA AVE 56748 465-4222
Richard Lorenson, prin.

Plymouth, AC 612, PC 8, Hennepin
Robbinsdale SD
Supt. — See New Hope
Armstrong HS, 10635 36TH AVE N 55441 4-00011
Denis Biagini, prin. 546-3266
MS, 10011 36TH AVE N 55441 4-00100
Luverne Ahrndt, prin. 544-9147

Wayzata SD
Supt. — See Wayzata
Wayzata SHS 4-00001
305 VICKSBURG LN N 55447 476-3000
Craig Paul, prin.
Wayzata East JHS 3-00110
12000 RIDGEMOUNT AVE W 55441 476-3060
John Greupner, prin.

Preston, AC 507, PC 4, Fillmore
Preston-Fountain SD 3-11100
PO BOX 407 55965 765-3636
Ken Doty, supt.
Preston-Fountain MS 2-01100
PO BOX 407 55965 765-3843
William Bentson, prin.

Princeton, AC 612, PC 5, Mille Lacs
Princeton SD, 110 6TH AVE S 55371 5-11111
Harvey Walsh, supt. 389-4101
HS, 807 8TH AVE S 55371 3-00011
Dale Hurni, prin. 389-4101
MS, 606 3RD ST S 55371 3-00100
J. Hoff, prin. 389-9485

Prinsburg, PC 3, Kandiyohi

Central Minnesota Christian S 2-11111
PO BOX 98 56281

Prior Lake, AC 612, PC 7, Scott
Prior Lake SD, PO BOX 539 55372 5-11111
Les Sonnabend, supt. 447-2185
HS, PO BOX 539 55372 3-00011
Fred Blaisdell, prin. 447-4131
Hidden Oaks MS, PO BOX 539 55372 3-00100
Craig Olson, prin. 447-2188

Proctor, AC 218, PC 5, St. Louis
Proctor SD, 131 9TH AVE 55810 4-11111
Barbra Zakrajsek, supt. 624-4869
HS, 131 9TH AVE 55810 3-00011
Bruce Watkins, prin. 628-2273
Jedlicka MS, 201 S 1ST AVE 55810 2-00100
Sherman Carlson, prin. 628-1057

Randolph, AC 507, PC 2, Dakota
Randolph SD, PO BOX 38 55065 2-11111
Ronald James, supt. 263-2151
JSHS, PO BOX 38 55065 2-00111
Richard Whitaker, prin. 263-2151

Redlake, AC 218, PC 4, Beltrami
Redlake SD, GENERAL DELIVERY 56671 3-11111
Ed Kroenke, supt. 679-3353
JSHS, GENERAL DELIVERY 56671 2-00111
(—), prin. 679-3733

Red Lake Falls, AC 218, PC 4, Red Lake
Red Lake Falls SD 3-11111
PO BOX 399 56750 253-2139
Russel Sethre, supt.

LaFayette JSHS, PO BOX 399 56750   2-00111
Mike Verdun, prin.   253-2163

Red Wing, AC 612, PC 7, Goodhue
Red Wing SD, 444 W 6TH ST 55066   5-11111
Clayton Hovda, supt.   388-7181
Central HS, 525 EAST AVE 55066   3-00011
Larry Sonju, prin.   388-7181
Twin Bluff MS   3-00100
2120 TWIN BLUFF RD 55066   388-7144
John Quist, prin.

Redwood Falls, AC 507, PC 5, Redwood
Redwood Falls SD   4-11111
700 E COOK ST 56283   644-3531
Rick Ellingworth, supt.
Redwood Valley HS   2-00011
700 E COOK ST 56283   644-3511
Lyle Turtle, prin.
Redwood Valley MS   2-01100
700 E COOK ST 56283 – (—), prin.   644-3521

Remer, AC 218, PC 2, Cass
Remer SD, RR 1 BOX A 56672   3-11111
Linda Bauer, supt.   566-2351
JSHS, RR 1 BOX B 56672   2-00111
(—), prin.   556-2352

Renville, AC 612, PC 4, Renville
Renville SD, PO BOX 338 56284   2-00011
Ivan Eckstrom, supt.   329-8362
BDRSH HS, PO BOX 338 56284   2-00011
Robert Anderson, prin.   329-8368

Richfield, AC 612, PC 8, Hennepin
Richfield SD, 7001 HARRIET AVE 55423   5-11111
L. Larson, supt.   861-8220
HS, 7001 HARRIET AVE 55423   4-00011
Richard Maas, prin.   861-8245
JHS, 7461 OLIVER AVE S 55423   3-00100
Robin Carlson, prin.   861-8270

Holy Angels Academy   3-00111
6600 NICOLLET AVE 55423   866-8762
Sr. Mary Duval, prin.
Minnesota School of Business   4-CS
1401 W 76TH ST 55423   861-2000

Robbinsdale, AC 612, PC 7, Hennepin
Robbinsdale SD
Supt. — See New Hope
Technology Learning MS   3-01100
4139 REGENT AVE N 55422   535-1790
Susan Manikowski, prin.

Rochester, AC 507, PC 8, Olmsted
Rochester SD, 615 7TH ST SW 55902   7-11111
Vernon Johnson, supt.   285-8551
Marshall SHS, 1510 14TH ST NW 55901   4-00001
Diane Ilstrup, prin.   285-8693
Mayo SHS, 1420 11TH AVE SE 55904   4-00001
Nancy Kaldor, prin.   285-8820
Adams JHS, 1525 31ST ST NW 55901   4-00110
Malcolm McKay, prin.   285-8840
Kellogg JHS, 503 17TH ST NE 55906   3-00110
Jerry Williams, prin.   285-8701
Willow Creek JHS   4-00110
2425 11TH AVE SE 55904   285-8876
Pamela Haack, prin.

Lourdes HS, 621 W CENTER ST 55902   2-00011
Dennis Nigon, prin.   289-3991
Mayo Foundation   4-UC
200 1ST ST NW 55901   284-2511
Minnesota Bible College   1-UC
920 MAYOWOOD RD SW 55902   288-4563
Riverland Technical College   2-CS
1926 COLLEGEVIEW RD E 55904   800-247-1296
Rochester Community College   5-CC
851 30TH AVE SE 55904   285-7216
University of Minnesota Rochester Center   2-UC
855 30TH AVE SE 55904   280-2828
Victory Academy   2-11111
606 36TH AVE SE 55904

Rockford, AC 612, PC 5, Wright
Rockford SD, PO BOX 9 55373   4-11111
Allen Moen, supt.   477-5831
JSHS, PO BOX 70 55373   3-00111
John Headlee, prin.   477-5846

Roseau, AC 218, PC 4, Roseau
Roseau SD, 509 3RD ST NE 56751   4-11111
Herbert Benz, supt.   463-1471
JSHS, 509 3RD ST NE 56751   3-00111
Terry Gotziaman, prin.   463-2770

Rosemount, AC 612, PC 6, Dakota
Rosemount-Apple Valley-Eagan SD   7-11111
14445 DIAMOND PATH W 55068   423-7700
John Haro, supt.
HS, 3335 142ND ST W 55068   4-00011
J. Richard Dewey, prin.   423-7501
MS, 3135 143RD ST W 55068   3-00100
Larry Larson, prin.   423-7570
Other Schools – See Apple Valley, Eagan

Dakota Co. Technical College   4-CC
1300 145TH ST E 55068   423-8301
First Baptist S   2-11111
PO BOX 89 55068

Roseville, AC 612, PC 8, Ramsey
Mounds View SD   7-11111
2959 HAMLINE AVE N 55113   636-3650
Burton Nygren, supt.
Other Schools – See Arden Hills, Mounds View, New
Brighton, Shoreview

Roseville SD   6-11111
1251 COUNTY ROAD B2 W 55113   635-1600
Carol Ericson, supt.
Roseville SHS   4-00011
1261 HIGHWAY 36 W 55113   635-1660
Robert Rygh, prin.
Other Schools – See Saint Paul

Concordia Academy   2-00011
2400 DALE ST N 55113   484-8429
Randy Lowe, prin.
Minneapolis Business College   2-CS
1711 COUNTY ROAD B W 55113   636-7406

Rothsay, AC 218, PC 2, Wilkin
Rothsay SD, PO BOX 247 56579   2-11111
Robert Block, supt.   867-2735
JSHS, PO BOX 247 56579   2-00111
Gary Zirbes, prin.   867-2117

Round Lake, AC 507, PC 2, Nobles
Round Lake SD   2-00011
445 HARRISON ST 56167   945-8123
George Loudenslager, supt.
JSHS, 445 HARRISON ST 56167   2-00111
Louis Smith, prin.   945-8123

Royalton, AC 612, PC 3, Morrison
Royalton SD, PO BOX 5 56373   3-11111
John Franzoia, supt.   584-5531
JSHS, PO BOX 5 56373   2-00111
Philip Nelson, prin.   584-5531

Rush City, AC 612, PC 4, Chisago
Rush City SD, PO BOX 566 55069   3-11111
Tim Eklund, supt.   358-4855
JSHS, PO BOX 566 55069   2-00111
Mark Saari, prin.   358-4795

Rushford, AC 507, PC 4, Fillmore
Rushford-Peterson SD   3-11111
PO BOX 627 55971   864-7785
Ronald Breuer, supt.
Rushford-Peterson HS   2-00011
PO BOX 627 55971   864-7786
Brad Johnson, prin.
Other Schools – See Peterson

Russell, AC 507, PC 2, Lyon
Russell SD, PO BOX 310 56169   2-00100
Don Knutson, supt.   823-4371
RTR MS, PO BOX 310 56169   2-00100
Beverley Evans, prin.   823-4371

Saginaw, AC 218, PC 2, St. Louis
St. Louis County SD
Supt. — See Virginia
Albrook JSHS, PO BOX 128 55779   2-00111
Corrine Spector, prin.   729-8322

Saint Anthony, AC 612, PC 6, Hennepin
St Anthony-New Brighton SD   4-11111
3303 33RD AVE NE 55418   782-1000
Warren Rolek, supt.
HS, 3303 33RD AVE NE 55418   2-00011
Michael Sjklocha, prin.   782-1010
MS, 3303 33RD AVE NE 55418   2-00100
Eileen Beha, prin.   782-1030

Saint Bonifacius, AC 612, PC 4, Hennepin

Crown College   3-UC
6425 COUNTY ROAD 30 55375   446-4100

Saint Charles, AC 507, PC 5, Winona
St. Charles SD, 600 E 6TH ST 55972   4-11111
Thomas Ames, supt.   932-4423
JSHS, 600 E 6TH ST 55972   2-00111
Henry Welle, prin.   932-4420

Saint Clair, AC 507, PC 3, Blue Earth
St. Clair SD, PO BOX 99 56080   3-11111
Jerry Olson, supt.   245-3027
JSHS, PO BOX 99 56080   2-00111
James Buysse, prin.   245-3027

Saint Cloud, AC 612, PC 8, Stearns
St. Cloud SD, 628 ROOSEVELT RD 56301   7-11111
Ronald Jandura, supt.   253-9333
Apollo HS, 1000 44TH AVE N 56303   4-00011
Jerry Larson, prin.   253-1600
Technical HS, 233 12TH AVE S 56301   4-00011
Gayla Holmgren, prin.   252-2231
North MS, 1212 29TH AVE N 56303   3-00100
John Carlsted, prin.   251-2159
South MS, 1120 15TH AVE S 56301   3-00100
Bernice Berns, prin.   251-1322

Cathedral John XXIII S   3-00111
312 7TH AVE N 56303   251-3421
Thomas Raiche, prin.
St. Cloud Business College   3-CS
245 37TH AVE N 56303   251-5600
St. Cloud Hospital   HSP
1406 6TH AVE N 56303   255-5666
St. Cloud State University   7-UC
740 4TH AVE S 56301   800-369-4260

St. Cloud Technical College   5-CC
1540 NORTHWAY DR 56303   654-5000
Ss. Peter Paul & Michael MS   2-01100
1215 11TH AVE N 56303   251-5295
Michael Mullin, prin.

Saint Francis, AC 612, PC 5, Anoka
St. Francis SD   5-11111
3325 BRIDGE ST NW 55070   753-2241
John Noennig, supt.
HS, 3325 BRIDGE ST NW 55070   4-00011
Lila Ronn, prin.   753-2800
MS   3-00100
23026 AMBASSADOR BLVD NW 55070   753-2550
Michael Wyatt, prin.

Saint James, AC 507, PC 5, Watonwan
St. James SD, PO BOX 509 56081   4-11111
Walter Conway, supt.   375-3381
JSHS, PO BOX 509 56081   3-00111
Roger Ziemann, prin.   375-3381

Saint Joseph, AC 612, PC 5, Stearns

College of Saint Benedict   4-UC
37 COLLEGE AVE S 56374   363-5505

Saint Louis Park, AC 612, PC 8, Hennepin
St. Louis Park SD   5-11111
6425 W 33RD ST 55426   928-6001
Carl Holmstrom, supt.
HS, 6425 W 33RD ST 55426   4-00011
Francis Crisman, prin.   925-4300
JHS, 2025 TEXAS AVE S 55426   3-00100
Les Bork, prin.   541-1884

Benilde-St. Margarets HS   3-00111
2501 HIGHWAY 100 S 55416   927-4176
Robert Tift, prin.
Groves Learning Center   1-11111
3200 HIGHWAY 100 S 55416   920-6377
Sue Kirchhoff, prin.
Methodist Hospital   HSP
6500 EXCELSIOR BLVD 55426   932-5010

Saint Michael, AC 612, PC 5, Wright
St. Michael-Albertville SD
Supt. — See Albertville
St. Michael-Albertville MS   2-00100
PO BOX 10 55376   497-2655
Dennis Toskas, prin.

Saint Paul, AC 612, PC 10, Ramsey
North St. Paul-Maplewood SD
Supt. — See Maplewood
Glenn MS   3-00100
1560 COUNTY ROAD B E 55109   770-4724
Robert Meixner, prin.
Maplewood MS   4-00100
2410 HOLLOWAY AVE E 55109   770-4690
Thomas Harrold, prin.

Roseville SD
Supt. — See Roseville
Roseville JHS   4-00110
15 COUNTY ROAD B2 E 55117   482-5280
Wil Chan, prin.

St. Paul SD, 360 COLBORNE ST 55102   8-11111
Curman Gaines, supt.   293-5100
Central HS   4-00011
275 LEXINGTON PKY N 55104   293-8700
Mary Mackbee, prin.
Como Park HS, 740 ROSE AVE W 55117   4-00011
Brad Manor, prin.   293-8800
Harding HS, 1540 6TH ST E 55106   4-00011
Louis Kanavati, prin.   293-8900
Highland Park HS   4-00011
1015 SNELLING AVE S 55116   293-8940
Joanne Knuth, prin.
Humboldt HS, 30 BAKER ST E 55107   3-00011
John Ettlinger, prin.   293-8600
Johnson HS, 1349 ARCADE ST 55106   4-00011
Donald Ausemus, prin.   293-8890
Battle Creek MS, 2121 N PARK DR 55119   3-00100
Julian Stafford, prin.   293-8960
Cleveland MS, 1000 WALSH ST 55106   2-00100
Larry Gallatin, prin.   293-8880
Expo MS, 631 ALBERT ST N 55104   2-00100
Joan Sorenson, prin.   293-5970
Hazel Park MS   3-00100
1140 WHITE BEAR AVE N 55106   293-8920
Donald Sonsalla, prin.
Highland Park JHS   3-00100
975 SNELLING AVE S 55116   293-8950
Benjamin Zachary, prin.
Humboldt JHS   2-00100
640 HUMBOLDT AVE 55107   293-8630
John Ettlinger, prin.
Murray JHS, 2200 BUFORD AVE 55108   3-00100
Nancy Nielsen, prin.   293-8740
Ramsey JHS, 1700 SUMMIT AVE 55105   3-00100
Dorothy LeGault, prin.   293-8860
Washington JHS   2-00100
1041 MARION ST 55117   293-8830
Lyle Odland, prin.

Bethel College   4-UC
3900 BETHEL DR 55112   638-6400
Bethel Theological Seminary   2-UC
3949 BETHEL DR 55112   638-6182
Christ Household of Faith   2-11111
355 MARSHALL AVE 55102

College of Associated Arts ... 2-UC
344 SUMMIT AVE 55102 ... 224-3416
College of Saint Catherine ... 5-UC
2004 RANDOLPH AVE 55105 ... 690-6525
Concordia College ... 4-UC
275 SYNDICATE ST N 55104 ... 641-8278
Convent of the Visitation S ... 2-11111
2455 VISITATION DR 55120 ... 454-6474
Sr. Michelle Clarke, prin.
Cretin Hall HS, 550 ALBERT ST S 55116 ... 4-00011
Richard Engler, prin. ... 690-2443
Globe College of Business ... 2-CS
175 5TH ST E STE 201 55101 ... 224-4378
Hamline University ... 4-UC
1536 HEWITT AVE 55104 ... 641-2202
Hill-Murray HS ... 3-00111
2625 LARPENTEUR AVE E 55109 ... 777-1376
Joseph McHugh, prin.
Luther Northwestern Theological Seminary ... 3-UC
2481 COMO AVE 55108 ... 641-3211
Macalester College ... 4-UC
1600 GRAND AVE 55105 ... 696-6000
Metropolitan State University ... 5-UC
700 7TH ST E 55106 ... 373-2727
Mounds Park Academy ... 3-11111
2051 LARPENTEUR AVE E 55109 ... 777-2555
Robert Kreischer, prin.
National College ... 3-UC
1380 ENERGY LN 55108 ... 644-1265
Northwestern College ... 4-UC
3003 SNELLING AVE N 55113 ... 631-5100
St. Agnes HS, 530 LAFOND AVE 55103 ... 2-00011
William Peper, prin. ... 228-1161
St. Bernard HS, 170 ROSE AVE W 55117 ... 2-00011
John O'Neill, prin. ... 489-1338
St. Paul Academy-Summit ... 3-00111
1712 RANDOLPH AVE 55105
St. Paul-Ramsey Medical Center ... 1-HSP
640 JACKSON ST 55101 ... 221-2181
St. Paul Technical College ... 3-CC
235 MARSHALL AVE 55102 ... 221-1364
St. Thomas Academy ... 3-00111
949 MENDOTA HEIGHTS RD 55120 ... 454-4570
John Greving, prin.
Trinity S, 930 GERANIUM AVE E 55106 ... 2-00100
David Irber, prin. ... 776-5169
United Hospital ... HSP
333 SMITH AVE N 55102 ... 220-8811
University of Saint Thomas ... 6-UC
2115 SUMMIT AVE 55105 ... 647-5000
William Mitchell College of Law ... 4-UC
875 SUMMIT AVE 55105 ... 227-9171

Saint Paul Park, AC 612, PC 5, Washington
South Washington County SD
Supt. — See Cottage Grove
Oltman JHS, 1020 3RD ST 55071 ... 4-00100
Rod Thorsell, prin. ... 458-4280

Saint Peter, AC 507, PC 6, Nicollet
St. Peter SD, 803 DAVIS ST 56082 ... 4-11111
G. Carlson, supt. ... 931-5703
JSHS, 100 LINCOLN DR 56082 ... 3-00111
Jeffrey Olson, prin. ... 931-4210

Gustavus Adolphus College ... 4-UC
800 W COLLEGE AVE 56082 ... 933-8000

Sandstone, AC 612, PC 4, Pine
East Central SD, PO BOX 260 55072 ... 4-11111
Michael Hruby, supt. ... 245-2289
East Central HS, PO BOX 260 55072 ... 2-00011
R. Nentl, prin. ... 245-2216
Other Schools – See Askov

Sartell, AC 612, PC 6, Stearns
Sartell SD, PO BOX 328 56377 ... 4-11111
Duane Wrightson, supt. ... 656-0748
HS, PO BOX 328 56377 ... 3-00111
Geoffrey Saari, prin. ... 656-0748
MS, PO BOX 328 56377 ... 2-00100
Michael Spanier, prin. ... 253-2200

Sauk Centre, AC 612, PC 5, Stearns
Sauk Centre SD, 933 STATE RD 56378 ... 4-11111
Dan Brooks, supt. ... 352-2284
JSHS, 933 STATE RD 56378 ... 3-00111
Larry Sorenson, prin. ... 352-2258

Sauk Rapids, AC 612, PC 6, Benton
Sauk Rapids SD, PO BOX 520 56379 ... 5-11111
Jerry Hartley, supt. ... 253-4703
HS, PO BOX 520 56379 ... 3-00011
Thomas Blair, prin. ... 253-4700
MS, PO BOX 520 56379 ... 3-00100
John Clark, prin. ... 654-9073

Sebeka, AC 218, PC 3, Wadena
Sebeka SD, 200 1ST ST NW 56477 ... 3-11111
Russell Laposky, supt. ... 837-5101
JSHS, 200 1ST ST NW 56477 ... 2-00111
(—), prin. ... 837-5101

Shakopee, AC 612, PC 7, Scott
Shakopee SD, 505 HOLMES ST S 55379 ... 5-11111
Robert Ostlund, supt. ... 445-4884
SHS, 200 10TH AVE E 55379 ... 3-00011
James Murphy, prin. ... 445-4884
JHS, 1137 MARSCHALL RD 55379 ... 3-00110
Vicki Petzko, prin. ... 445-4884

Sherburn, AC 507, PC 4, Martin
Martin County SD
Supt. — See Welcome

Martin Co. West HS ... 2-00011
PO BOX 100 56171 ... 764-4671
Raymond Herman, prin.

Shoreview, AC 612, PC 7, Ramsey
Mounds View SD
Supt. — See Roseville
Chippewa MS ... 4-00100
5000 HODGSON RD 55126 ... 483-6635
Deloy Kramer, prin.

Silver Bay, AC 218, PC 4, Lake
Lake Superior SD
Supt. — See Two Harbors
Kelly JSHS, 137 BANKS BLVD 55614 ... 2-00111
George Starkovich, prin. ... 226-4437

Silver Lake, AC 612, PC 3, McLeod
Silver Lake SD, 229 LAKE AVE 55381 ... 2-11111
John Schoen, supt. ... 327-2118
JSHS, 229 LAKE AVE 55381 ... 2-00111
Jeffery Powers, prin. ... 327-2118

Slayton, AC 507, PC 4, Murray
Slayton SD, 2420 28TH ST 56172 ... 3-11111
Cornelius Smit, supt. ... 836-6183
JSHS, 2420 28TH ST 56172 ... 2-00111
Philip Johnson, prin. ... 836-6184

Sleepy Eye, AC 507, PC 5, Brown
Sleepy Eye SD, 400 4TH AVE SW 56085 ... 3-11111
(—), supt. ... 794-7903
JSHS, 400 4TH AVE SW 56085 ... 2-00111
(—), prin. ... 794-7904

St. Mary JSHS ... 2-00111
104 SAINT MARYS ST NW 56085 ... 794-4121
Jerry Neubauer, prin.

South Saint Paul, AC 612, PC 7, Dakota
South St. Paul SD, 700 2ND ST N 55075 ... 5-11111
David Metzen, supt. ... 457-9465
JSHS, 700 2ND ST N 55075 ... 4-00111
(—), prin. ... 457-9401

Springfield, AC 507, PC 4, Brown
Springfield SD, 12 BURNS AVE 56087 ... 3-11111
Ronald Kleven, supt. ... 723-4283
JSHS, 12 BURNS AVE 56087 ... 2-00111
John DeZeeuw, prin. ... 723-4283

Spring Grove, AC 507, PC 4, Houston
Spring Grove SD, PO BOX 626 55974 ... 2-11111
James Busta, supt. ... 498-3221
JSHS, PO BOX 626 55974 ... 2-00111
Shirley Ohl, prin. ... 498-3223

Spring Lake Park, AC 612, PC 6, Anoka
Spring Lake Park SD ... 5-11111
8000 HIGHWAY 65 NE 55432 ... 786-5570
Chris Huber, supt.
HS, 8001 ABLE ST NE 55432 ... 4-00011
Glenn Martin, prin. ... 786-5571
Other Schools – See Blaine

Spring Valley, AC 507, PC 4, Fillmore
Kingsland SD
Supt. — See Wykoff
Kingsland HS ... 2-00011
705 N SECTION AVE 55975 ... 346-7276
Sharon Kabes, prin.

Staples, AC 218, PC 5, Todd
Staples SD, 431 3RD ST NE 56479 ... 4-11111
John Nelson, supt. ... 894-2430
JSHS, 431 3RD ST NE 56479 ... 3-00111
Bruce Pederson, prin. ... 894-2431

Stephen, AC 218, PC 3, Marshall
Stephen SD, PO BOX 68 56757 ... 2-11111
J. Schindele, supt. ... 478-3315
JSHS, PO BOX 68 56757 ... 2-00111
Wayne Bauste, prin. ... 478-3314

Stewart, AC 612, PC 3, McLeod
Stewart SD, PO BOX 99 55385 ... 2-11100
David Klepel, supt. ... 562-2110
McLeod West JHS, PO BOX 99 55385 ... 2-00110
David Klepel, prin. ... 562-2414

Stewartville, AC 507, PC 5, Olmsted
Stewartville SD, 500 4TH ST SW 55976 ... 4-11111
Russell Hoeffner, supt. ... 533-8444
JSHS, 500 4TH ST SW 55976 ... 3-00111
Lyle Turtle, prin. ... 533-4261

Stillwater, AC 612, PC 7, Washington
Stillwater SD, 1875 GREELEY ST S 55082 ... 6-11111
David Wettergren, supt. ... 430-8340
SHS, 5701 STILLWATER BLVD N 55082 ... 4-00001
Jon Swenson, prin. ... 430-8262
JHS, 523 MARSH ST W 55082 ... 3-00110
Donald Hovland, prin. ... 430-8327
Other Schools – See Lake Elmo

Storden, AC 507, PC 2, Cottonwood
Storden-Jeffers SD, PO BOX 69 56174 ... 2-11100
Norman Johnson, supt. ... 445-3424
Other Schools – See Jeffers

Swanville, AC 612, PC 2, Morrison
Swanville SD, PO BOX 98 56382 ... 2-11111
James Loecken, supt. ... 547-2431
JSHS, PO BOX 98 56382 ... 2-00111
James Loecken, prin. ... 547-2431

Thief River Falls, AC 218, PC 6, Pennington
Thief River Falls SD ... 4-11111
230 S LABREE 56701 ... 681-8711
Robert Duncan, supt.
Lincoln HS, 101 KNIGHT AVE S 56701 ... 3-00011
Terry Soine, prin. ... 681-7432
Franklin MS, 300 SPRUCE AVE S 56701 ... 3-00100
Bill Hahne, prin. ... 681-8813

Northland Community College ... 3-CC
2101 HWY 1 E 56701 ... 800-628-9918

Tower, AC 218, PC 3, St. Louis
St. Louis County SD
Supt. — See Virginia
Tower-Soudan JSHS ... 2-00111
PO BOX 469 55790 – (—), prin. ... 753-4040

Tracy, AC 507, PC 4, Lyon
Tracy SD, PO BOX 30 56175 ... 3-11111
Harold Remme, supt. ... 629-4222
JSHS, PO BOX 30 56175 ... 2-00111
Ron Brand, prin. ... 629-4222

Trimont, AC 507, PC 3, Martin
Martin County SD
Supt. — See Welcome
Martin Co. West JHS, PO BOX N 56176 ... 2-00100
Dale Harbitz, prin. ... 639-2081

Truman, AC 507, PC 4, Martin
Truman, PO BOX 276 56088 ... 2-11111
Joseph Peterson, supt. ... 776-2111
JSHS, PO BOX 276 56088 ... 2-00111
Joseph Peterson, prin. ... 776-2111

Twin Valley, AC 218, PC 3, Norman
Twin Valley SD, PO BOX 420 56584 ... 2-11111
Karl Schulz, supt. ... 584-5151
JSHS, PO BOX 420 56584 ... 2-00111
Dale Svaren, prin. ... 584-5152

Two Harbors, AC 218, PC 5, Lake
Lake Superior SD, 405 4TH AVE 55616 ... 4-11111
Lyle Northey, supt. ... 834-8216
JSHS, 405 4TH AVE 55616 ... 3-00111
Dwight Moe, prin. ... 834-8201
Minnehaha MS, 421 7TH ST 55616 ... 2-01100
Robert Lackore, prin. ... 834-8221
Other Schools – See Silver Bay

Tyler, AC 507, PC 4, Lincoln
Tyler SD, PO BOX 659 56178 ... 2-00011
Don Knutson, supt. ... 247-5911
Russell-Tyler-Rothton HS ... 2-00011
PO BOX 659 56178 ... 247-5911
Gary Brosz, prin.

Ulen, AC 218, PC 3, Clay
Ulen-Hitterdal SD ... 2-11111
PO BOX 389 56585 ... 596-8853
William Durkop, supt.
Ulen-Hitterdal JSHS ... 2-00111
PO BOX 389 56585 ... 596-8853
William Durkop, prin.

Underwood, AC 218, PC 2, Otter Tail
Underwood SD, PO BOX 248 56586 ... 2-11111
Berthold Kinzler, supt. ... 826-6101
JSHS, PO BOX 248 56586 ... 2-00111
Gary Sletten, prin. ... 826-6102

Upsala, AC 612, PC 2, Morrison
Upsala SD, PO BOX 190 56384 ... 2-11111
Russell Johnson, supt. ... 573-2174
JSHS, PO BOX 190 56384 ... 2-00111
Brian Doty, prin. ... 573-2176

Verndale, AC 218, PC 3, Wadena
Verndale SD, PO BOX G 56481 ... 2-11111
James Madsen, supt. ... 445-5184
JSHS, PO BOX G 56481 ... 2-00111
Richard Rhoades, prin. ... 445-5184

Virginia, AC 218, PC 6, St. Louis
St. Louis County SD, 731 3RD ST S 55792 ... 5-11111
Daniel Mobilia, supt. ... 749-8130
Other Schools – See Babbitt, Cook, Cotton, Iron, Orr, Saginaw, Tower

Virginia SD, 411 S 5TH AVE 55792 ... 4-11111
Robert Krebsbach, supt. ... 741-5161
JSHS, 411 S 5TH AVE 55792 ... 4-00111
Bryan Kehoe, prin. ... 741-1332

Mesabi Community College ... 4-CC
210 N 9TH AVE 55792 ... 749-7700

Wabasha, AC 612, PC 4, Wabasha
Wabasha-Kellogg SD ... 3-11111
2113 HIAWATHA DR E 55981 ... 565-4603
John Mattison, supt.
Wabasha-Kellogg JSHS ... 2-00111
2113 HIAWATHA DR E 55981 ... 565-4537
Gerald Reker, prin.

Wabasso, AC 507, PC 3, Redwood
Wabasso SD, PO BOX 69 56293 ... 2-11111
George Bates, supt. ... 342-5114
JSHS, PO BOX 69 56293 ... 2-00111
Richard Pattee, prin. ... 342-5114

Waconia, AC 612, PC 5, Carver
Waconia SD, 24 S WALNUT ST 55387 ... 4-11111
Ric Dressen, supt. ... 442-6600
HS, 24 S WALNUT ST 55387 ... 2-00011
Robert Lind, prin. ... 442-6600

JHS, 24 S WALNUT ST 55387 | 2-00100
Robert Lind, prin. | 442-6600

Wadena, AC 218, PC 5, Wadena
Wadena-Deer Creek SD | 4-11111
 PO BOX 151 56482 | 631-2155
 Larry Foley, supt.
Wadena-Deer Creek JSHS | 3-00111
 PO BOX 151 56482 | 631-2155
 Lowell Roisum, prin.

Northwest Technical College | 2-CS
 PO BOX 566 56482 | 631-3530

Waldorf, AC 507, PC 2, Waseca
Janesville-Waldorf-Pemberton SD
 Supt. — See Janesville
Janesville-Waldorf-Pemberton MS | 2-00100
 PO BOX 218 56091 | 239-2176
 Shelley Schultz, prin.

Walker, AC 218, PC 3, Cass
Walker-Akeley SD | 3-11111
 PO BOX 4000 56484 | 547-1311
 Boyd McLarty, supt.
Walker-Akeley JSHS | 2-00111
 PO BOX 4000 56484 | 547-1311
 Donald Carlson, prin.

Walnut Grove, AC 507, PC 3, Redwood
Walnut Grove SD, PO BOX 278 56180 | 2-11100
 Orlyn Wiemers, supt. | 859-2141
Westbrook-Walnut Grove MS | 2-01100
 PO BOX 278 56180 | 859-2141
 Orlyn Wiemers, prin.

Wanamingo, AC 507, PC 3, Goodhue
Wanamingo SD, 225 3RD AVE S 55983 | 2-11100
 Duane Stoesz, supt. | 824-2211
JHS, 225 3RD AVE S 55983 | 2-00100
 Jeffrey Evert, prin. | 824-2211

Warren, AC 218, PC 4, Marshall
Warren-Alvarado SD | 3-11111
 224 E BRIDGE AVE 56762 | 745-5393
 Gerald Dalzell, supt.
Warren-Alvarado JSHS | 2-00111
 224 E BRIDGE AVE 56762 | 745-4636
 John Rokke, prin.

Warroad, AC 218, PC 4, Roseau
Warroad SD, 510 CEDAR AVE 56763 | 4-11111
 John Reishus, supt. | 386-1472
HS, 510 CEDAR AVE 56763 | 2-00011
 David Kragness, prin. | 386-1820
MS, 510 CEDAR AVE 56763 | 2-01100
 Charles Woolcock, prin. | 386-1877

Waseca, AC 507, PC 6, Waseca
Waseca SD, 501 E ELM AVE 56093 | 4-11111
 Francis Heinen, supt. | 835-2500
HS, 1717 2ND ST NW 56093 | 3-00011
 Richard Hansen, prin. | 835-5470
Central MS, 501 E ELM AVE 56093 | 3-01100
 James O'Regan, prin. | 835-3000

Watertown, AC 612, PC 4, Carver
Watertown-Mayer SD | 4-11111
 PO BOX 368 55388 | 955-0204
 Harvey Kraabel, supt.
HS, PO BOX 368 55388 | 2-00011
 Larry Enter, prin. | 955-0240
Watertown-Mayer MS | 2-01100
 PO BOX 368 55388 | 955-0209
 Mark Matuska, prin.

Waterville, AC 507, PC 4, Le Sueur
Waterville-Elysian-Morristown SD | 4-11111
 500 PAQUIN ST E 56096 | 362-4432
 Edward Henderson, supt.
Waterville-Elysian-Morristown HS | 2-00011
 500 PAQUIN ST E 56096 | 362-4431
 Donald McHenry, prin.
Other Schools – See Morristown

Waubun, AC 218, PC 2, Mahnomen
Waubun SD, PO BOX 98 56589 | 3-11111
 John Vorachek, supt. | 473-2171
JSHS, PO BOX 98 56589 | 2-00111
 Joan Bradach, prin. | 473-2173

Wayzata, AC 612, PC 5, Hennepin
Wayzata SD, PO BOX 660 55391 | 6-11111
 David Landswerk, supt. | 476-3100

Wayzata West JHS | 3-00110
 149 BARRY AVE N 55391 | 476-3180
 John Waight, prin.
Other Schools – See Plymouth

Blake S, 301 PEAVEY LN 55391 | 4-11111

Welcome, AC 507, PC 3, Martin
Martin County SD | 4-11111
 PO BOX 268 56181 | 728-8276
 Randy Grupe, supt.
Other Schools – See Sherburn, Trimont

Wells, AC 507, PC 4, Faribault
United South Central SD | 4-11111
 250 2ND AVE SW 56097 | 553-3134
 Robert Dell, supt.
United South Central HS | 2-00011
 250 2ND AVE SW 56097 – (—), prin. | 553-5819
Other Schools – See Freeborn, Kiester

Westbrook, AC 507, PC 3, Cottonwood
Westbrook SD, PO BOX 128 56183 | 2-10011
 Steve Kjorness, supt. | 274-5450
Westbrook-Walnut Grove HS | 2-00011
 PO BOX 129 56183 | 274-6111
 William Richards, prin.

West Concord, AC 507, PC 3, Dodge
Triton SD
 Supt. — See Dodge Center
Triton JHS, PO BOX 38 55985 | 2-00110
 Raymond Six, prin. | 527-2211

West Saint Paul, AC 612, PC 7, Dakota
West St. Paul-Mendota Hts. SD | 5-11111
 1897 DELAWARE AVE 55118 | 681-2300
 Jack Loss, supt.
Grass JHS, 181 BUTLER AVE W 55118 | 3-00100
 Ruthanne Strohn, prin. | 451-2342
Other Schools – See Mendota Heights

St. Croix Lutheran S | 2-00011
 1200 OAKDALE AVE 55118

Wheaton, AC 612, PC 4, Traverse
Wheaton SD, 1700 3RD AVE S 56296 | 3-11111
 James Torbert, supt. | 563-8283
JSHS, 1700 3RD AVE S 56296 | 2-00111
 Allan Crane, prin. | 563-8282

White Bear Lake, AC 612, PC 7, Ramsey
White Bear Lake SD | 6-11111
 3554 WHITE BEAR AVE N 55110 | 773-6000
 Theodore Blaesing, supt.
White Bear South HS | 4-00001
 3551 MCKNIGHT RD N 55110 | 653-2966
 Ronald Tesch, prin.
Central JHS, 4857 BLOOM AVE 55110 | 4-00100
 Rob Thompson, prin. | 653-2887
Sunrise Park MS | 3-00100
 2399 CEDAR AVE 55110 | 773-6300
 Kathy Baker, prin.
White Bear North JHS | 4-00010
 5040 BALD EAGLE AVE 55110 | 653-2915
 Larry Denucci, prin.

Lakewood Community College | 5-CC
 3401 CENTURY AVE N 55110 | 779-3200
Northeast Metro Technical College | 2-CS
 3300 CENTURY AVE N 55110 | 770-2351

White Earth, AC 218, PC 2, Becker

Circle of Life S | 2-11111
 PO BOX 447 56591

Willmar, AC 612, PC 7, Kandiyohi
Willmar SD, 611 5TH ST SW 56201 | 5-11111
 Orlo Almlie, supt. | 231-1100
SHS, 824 7TH ST SW 56201 | 3-00001
 Charles Briscoe, prin. | 235-4414
JHS, 201 WILLMAR AVE SE 56201 | 4-00110
 James Stoltz, prin. | 235-1252

Rice Memorial Hospital | HSP
 301 BECKER AVE SW 56201 | 231-4530
Willmar Community College | 4-CC
 PO BOX 797 56201 | 231-5116
Willmar Technical Institute | 2-CC
 PO BOX 1097 56201 | 235-5114

Willow River, AC 218, PC 2, Pine
Willow River SD, PO BOX 66 55795 | 3-11111
 D. McDonald, supt. | 372-3131
JSHS, PO BOX 66 55795 | 2-00111
 William Skarich, prin. | 372-3131

Windom, AC 507, PC 5, Cottonwood
Windom SD, PO BOX C177 56101 | 4-11111
 Richard Orcutt, supt. | 831-4885
JSHS, PO BOX C177 56101 | 3-00111
 Carl Villeneuve, prin. | 831-4881

Winona, AC 507, PC 8, Winona
Winona SD, 654 HUFF ST 55987 | 5-11111
 Ronald McIntire, supt. | 454-9461
HS, 901 GILMORE AVE 55987 | 4-00011
 John Youngstrom, prin. | 454-9507
MS, 166 W BROADWAY ST 55987 | 4-00100
 Scott Hannon, prin. | 454-9402

Cotter HS | 2-00011
 1115 W BROADWAY ST 55987 | 453-5000
 Michael Donlin, prin.
St. Mary's College of Minnesota | 4-UC
 700 TERRACE HTS STE 2 55987 | 457-1503
St. Stanislaus MS, 602 E 5TH ST 55987 | 2-01100
 Randy Althoff, prin. | 452-3766
Winona State University | 6-UC
 PO BOX 5838 55987 | 457-2017
Winona Technical College | 2-CS
 1250 HOMER RD 55987 | 454-4600

Winsted, AC 612, PC 4, McLeod

Holy Trinity HS | 2-00111
 110 WINSTED AVE W 55395 | 485-2182
 John Dokken, prin.

Winthrop, AC 507, PC 4, Sibley
GFW SD
 Supt. — See Gibbon
GFW HS, PO BOX 1001 55396 | 2-00011
 Douglas Standke, prin. | 647-5382

Woodbury, AC 612, PC 7, Washington
South Washington County SD
 Supt. — See Cottage Grove
HS, 2665 WOODLANE DR 55125 | 4-00011
 Dana Babbit, prin. | 458-4320
JHS, 1425 SCHOOL DR 55125 | 3-00100
 Mark Parr, prin. | 458-4300

New Life Christian S | 2-11111
 6758 BAILEY RD 55125 | 459-4121
 Patricia Wiens, prin.

Wood Lake, AC 507, PC 2, Yellow Medicine
Wood Lake SD, PO BOX 159 56297 | 2-00100
 Palmer Anderson, supt. | 485-3116
MS, PO BOX 159 56297 | 2-00100
 Palmer Anderson, prin. | 485-3116

Worthington, AC 507, PC 6, Nobles
Worthington SD, PO BOX 878 56187 | 4-11111
 Bruce Thomas, supt. | 372-2172
SHS, 1211 CLARY ST 56187 | 3-00001
 Bruce Blatti, prin. | 376-6121
JHS, PO BOX 459 56187 | 3-00110
 Mark Sandbo, prin. | 376-4174

Worthington Community College | 3-CC
 1450 COLLEGE WAY 56187 | 372-2107

Wrenshall, AC 218, PC 2, Carlton
Wrenshall SD, PO BOX 68 55797 | 2-11111
 E. Schulz, supt. | 384-4274
JSHS, PO BOX 68 55797 | 2-00111
 Elroy Schulz, prin. | 384-4274

Wykoff, AC 507, PC 2, Fillmore
Kingsland SD, PO BOX 96 55990 | 3-11111
 Walter Simonson, supt. | 352-4341
Kingsland MS, PO BOX 96 55990 | 2-00100
 Joanne Tierney, prin. | 352-2731
Other Schools – See Spring Valley

Zumbrota, AC 507, PC 4, Goodhue
Zumbrota-Mazeppa SD
 Supt. — See Mazeppa
Zumbrota/Mazeppa HS | 2-00011
 705 MILL ST 55992 | 732-7395
 Dennis Larson, prin.

MISSISSIPPI

STATE DEPARTMENT OF EDUCATION
Sillers State Office Building
P.O. Box 771, Jackson 39205
(601) 359-2326

Superintendent of Education	Thomas Burnham
Deputy Superintendent	R. D. Harris
Associate Superintendent Accountability	Judy Rhodes
Associate Superintendent Academic Education	Gerald Hasselman
Associate Superintendent Vocational-Technical Education	Therrell Myers
Director Management Information Systems	Nathan Slater

STATE BOARD OF EDUCATION
P.O. Box 771, Jackson 39205

Chairperson	Talmadge Portis

PUBLIC, PRIVATE AND CATHOLIC SECONDARY SCHOOLS

Aberdeen, AC 601, PC 6, Monroe
Aberdeen SSD, PO BOX 607 39730 — 4-11111
  John Curlee, supt. — 369-4682
HS, PO BOX 607 39730 — 3-00011
  Dwight McComb, prin. — 369-8933
Shivers JHS, PO BOX 607 39730 — 2-00100
  Preston Belle, prin. — 369-6241

Monroe County SD — 5-11111
PO BOX 847 39730 — 369-2022
  James Hathcock, supt.
Monroe County Vo-Tech Ctr — Vo Tech
  RR 4 BOX 16A 39730 — 369-7845
  Arlon Cox, prin.
Other Schools – See Amory, Hamilton, Smithville

Ackerman, AC 601, PC 4, Choctaw
Choctaw County SD — 4-11111
PO BOX 398 39735 — 285-6239
  Ty Cobb, supt.
JSHS, PO BOX 396 39735 — 2-00111
  Wayne McLeod, prin. — 285-3296
Choctaw County Vo-Tech Ctr — Vo Tech
  PO BOX 775 39735 — 285-3205
  MICHAEL THOMAS, prin.
Other Schools – See Weir

Amory, AC 601, PC 6, Monroe
Amory SSD, PO BOX 330 38821 — 4-11111
  Orman Bridges, supt. — 256-5991
HS, PO BOX 330 38821 — 3-00011
  L. Marett, prin. — 256-5753
Amory Vo-Tech Complex — Vo Tech
  PO BOX 330 38821 — 256-7601
  Delorise Allison, prin.
MS, 700 2ND AVE N 38821 — 2-01100
  Travis Beard, prin. — 256-5658

Monroe County SD
  Supt. — See Aberdeen
Hatley S, RR 3 BOX 69-A 38821 — 3-11111
  J. Parham, prin. — 256-4563

Anguilla, AC 601, PC 3, Sharkey
South Delta SD
  Supt. — See Rolling Fork
JSHS, PO BOX 487 38721 — 2-01111
  Lonnie McFadden, prin. — 873-6535

Arcola, AC 601, PC 3, Washington

Deer Creek S, PO BOX 376 38722 — 2-11111
  F. Allegrezza, prin. — 827-5165

Ashland, AC 601, PC 2, Benton
Benton County SD — 4-11111
PO BOX 247 38603 — 224-6252
  Ron Wilkerson, supt.
HS, 101 SCHOOL ST 38603 — 2-00111
  Jim Robinson, prin. — 224-6247
MS, PO BOX 368 38603 — 2-00100
  Bessie Tables, prin. — 224-6485
Other Schools – See Hickory Flat

Avon, AC 601, PC 2, Washington
Western Line SD, PO BOX 50 38723 — 4-11111
  Larry Green, supt. — 335-7186
Riverside S, PO BOX 80 38723 — 3-11111
  W. Cotton, prin. — 335-4527
Other Schools – See Greenville

Baldwyn, AC 601, PC 5, Prentiss
Baldwyn SSD — 4-11111
  518 HIGHWAY 45 N 38824 — 365-1000
  C. Shelton, supt.
HS, 512 HIGHWAY 45 N 38824 — 2-00011
  Sam Bryant, prin. — 365-1020
MS, 515 BENDER CIR 38824 — 2-01100
  Larry Gann, prin. — 365-1015

Bassfield, AC 601, PC 2, Jefferson Davis
Jefferson Davis County SD
  Supt. — See Prentiss
JSHS, PO BOX 128 39421 — 3-00111
  Marvin Lee, prin. — 943-5391

Batesville, AC 601, PC 6, Panola
South Panola Consolidated SD — 5-11111
PO BOX 749 38606 — 563-9361
  Tom Wren, supt.
South Panola HS, PO BOX 600 38606 — 4-00011
  Charles Barton, prin. — 563-4756
JHS, PO BOX 32 38606 — 3-00100
  Robert Chapman, prin. — 563-4503

Batesville Job Corps Center — 2-CS
  RR 3 BOX 2J 38606
North Delta S, RR 2 BOX 81 38606 — 2-11111
  Robert Foust, prin. — 563-4536

Bay Saint Louis, AC 601, PC 6, Hancock
Bay St. Louis-Waveland SD — 4-11111
  201 CARROLL AVE 39520 — 467-6621
  Paul Tisdale, supt.
Bay HS, 750 BLUE MEADOW RD 39520 — 3-00011
  Sandra Prator, prin. — 467-6611
Bay JHS, 750 BLUE MEADOW RD 39520 — 3-00100
  James Baldree, prin. — 467-4916

Hancock County SD
  Supt. — See Waveland
Hancock County Vo Ctr — Vo Tech
  7180 STENNIS AIRPORT RD 39525 — 467-3568
  Alvin Bourgeois, prin.

Our Lady Academy — 2-00111
  222 S BEACH BLVD 39520 — 467-7048
  Sr. Donella Hartman, prin.
St. Stanislaus HS — 3-00111
  304 S BEACH BLVD 39520 — 467-9057
  Michael Ryan, prin.

Bay Springs, AC 601, PC 4, Jasper
West Jasper Consolidated SD — 4-11111
PO BOX 610 39422 — 764-2280
  Charles Lyle, supt.
HS, PO BOX 389 39422 — 2-00011
  Gary Gibson, prin. — 764-4151
Jasper County Career Development Ctr — Vo Tech
  PO BOX 610 39422 — 764-2280
  Dan Williams, prin.
MS, PO BOX 587 39422 — 3-01100
  Carolyn Rhodes, prin. — 764-3378
Other Schools – See Stringer

Sylva-Bay Academy, PO BOX J 39422 — 2-11111
  Mike Tucker, prin. — 764-2157

Belmont, AC 601, PC 4, Tishomingo
Tishomingo County Special Municipal SD
  Supt. — See Iuka
Belmont S, PO BOX 250 38827 — 3-11111
  John Moore, prin. — 454-7924

Belzoni, AC 601, PC 5, Humphreys
Humphreys County SD — 5-11111
PO BOX 678 39038 — 247-3586
  Howard Austin, supt.
Humphreys County HS — 3-00011
PO BOX 658 39038 — 247-1881
  Otis Hall, prin.
Vo Complex, PO BOX 672 39038 — Vo Tech
  James Brown, prin. — 247-2764
Humphreys County JHS — 2-00100
PO BOX 678 39038 — 247-3761
  J. B. Holmes, prin.

Humphreys Academy — 2-11111
PO BOX 179 39038 — 247-1572
  Dom Bevalague, prin.

Benton, AC 601, PC 2, Yazoo
Yazoo County SD
  Supt. — See Yazoo City
Yazoo Co. HS, PO BOX 288 39039 — 2-00011
  John Smith, prin. — 673-9777

Benton Academy, PO BOX 308 39039 — 2-11111
  Bill Harbor, prin. — 673-9722

Biloxi, AC 601, PC 8, Harrison
Biloxi Public SD, PO BOX 168 39533 — 6-11111
  Virgil Strickland, supt. — 374-1810
HS, 1424 FATHER RYAN AVE 39530 — 4-00011
  Lloyd Seymour, prin. — 435-1421
Fernwood MS, 2329 PASS RD 39531 — 3-00100
  Ronnie Farris, prin. — 436-5120
Michel MS — 2-00100
  1400 FATHER RYAN AVE 39530 — 435-4540
  Murray Killebrew, prin.
Nichols MS, 340 NICHOLS DR 39530 — 2-00100
  Charles Guy, prin. — 436-4648

Jackson County SD
  Supt. — See Vancleave
St. Martin JHS — 5-00110
  16300 LEMOYNE BLVD 39532 — 392-2410
  Perry Griffis, prin.

Mercy Cross HS — 2-00111
  390 CRUSADERS DR 39530 — 374-4145
  Leo Trahan, prin.

Blue Mountain, AC 601, PC 3, Tippah
South Tippah SD
  Supt. — See Ripley
S, PO BOX 97 38610 — 2-11111
  Jerry Fowler, prin. — 685-4706

Blue Mountain College — 2-UC
PO BOX 338 38610 — 685-4771

Blue Springs, AC 601, PC 2, Union
Union County SD
  Supt. — See New Albany
East Union S, RR 3 BOX 34 38828 — 3-11111
  Leon Clark, prin. — 534-6920

Bogue Chitto, AC 601, PC 3, Lincoln
Lincoln County SD
  Supt. — See Brookhaven
S, PO BOX 128 39629 — 3-11111
  Stanton Long, prin. — 734-2723

Booneville, AC 601, PC 6, Prentiss
Booneville SD, PO BOX 358 38829 — 4-11111
  R. Griffin, supt. — 728-2171
JSHS, 100 GEORGE E ALLEN DR 38829 — 2-00111
  Robert Harmon, prin. — 728-5445

Prentiss County SD — 5-11111
  PO BOX 179 38829 — 728-4911
  Edward McCoy, supt.
Jumpertown S, RR 3 BOX 140 38829 — 2-11111
  Kenneth Chism, prin. — 728-6378
Thrasher S, RR 1 BOX 197 38829 — 3-11111
  William Buse, prin. — 728-5233
Prentiss County Vo Ctr — Vo Tech
  PO BOX 147 38829 — 728-9259
  Gary English, prin.
Other Schools – See New Site, Wheeler

Northeast Mississippi Community College — 5-CC
  101 CUNNINGHAM BLVD 38829 — 728-7751

Brandon, AC 601, PC 7, Rankin
Rankin County SD — 7-11111
  PO BOX 1359 39043 — 825-5590
  Michael Vinson, supt.
HS, 408 S COLLEGE ST 39042 — 3-00011
  Hugh Carr, prin. — 825-2261
Northwest JSHS — 4-01111
  9201 HIGHWAY 25 39042 — 992-9865
  Susan Rucker, prin.
MS, 200 SCHOOL RD 39042 — 4-01100
  John Kennedy, prin. — 825-5998
Other Schools – See Florence, Pelahatchie, Puckett,
  Richland, Sandhill

University Christian S — 2-11111
  127 PLEASANT ST 39042 — 825-1355
  Larry Mangum, prin.

Brookhaven, AC 601, PC 7, Lincoln
Brookhaven SD, PO BOX 540 39601 — 5-11111
  Charles Fulton, supt. — 833-6661
SHS, PO BOX 532 39601 — 3-00011
  Gregg Whittier, prin. — 833-4498
Brookhaven Vocational Complex — Vo Tech
  PO BOX 540 39601 — 833-8335
  Mike Warren, prin.
Alexander JHS — 3-00110
  713 BEAUREGARD ST 39601 — 833-7549
  Dan Brown, prin.

Lincoln County SD — 5-11111
  PO BOX 826 39601 — 835-3448
  Harold Smith, supt.
Enterprise S, RR 4 BOX 583 39601 — 3-11111
  Bruce Falvey, prin. — 833-7284
Star S, RR 3 BOX 486 39601 — 3-11111
  Bill Britt, prin. — 833-3473
West Lincoln S, RR 5 BOX 227 39601 — 3-11111
  Perry Miller, prin. — 833-4600
Other Schools – See Bogue Chitto

Brookhaven Academy — 2-11111
  PO BOX 946 39601 — 833-4041
  John Gray, prin.

Brooklyn, AC 601, PC 3, Forrest
Forrest County Agricultural HSD — 3-00011
  PO BOX 9 39425 — 582-4102
  Thomas Lowery, supt.
Forrest County Agricultural HS — 3-00011
  PO BOX 9 39425 — 582-4741
  Carl Shepherd, prin.

Bruce, AC 601, PC 4, Calhoun
Calhoun County SD
  Supt. — See Pittsboro
HS, PO BOX 248 38915 — 2-00011
  James Shows, prin. — 983-3350
MS, PO BOX 248 38915 — 2-01100
  Angelia Weldon, prin. — 983-3366

Byhalia, AC 601, PC 3, Marshall
Marshall County SD
  Supt. — See Holly Springs
HS, PO BOX 346 38611 — 2-00011
  Mike Hamblin, prin. — 838-2206

Caledonia, AC 601, PC 3, Lowndes
Lowndes County SD
  Supt. — See Columbus
HS, 111 CONFEDERATE DR 39740 — 2-00011
  Don Harding, prin. — 356-4988
MS, 111 CONFEDERATE DR 39740 — 2-00100
  Lee Peeples, prin. — 356-4080

Calhoun City, AC 601, PC 4, Calhoun
Calhoun County SD
  Supt. — See Pittsboro
HS, PO BOX 559 38916 — 2-00011
  Leonard Holland, prin. — 628-5112
MS, PO BOX 559 38916 — 2-01100
  Rick Vaughn, prin. — 628-6271

Calhoun Academy, PO BOX C 38916 — 2-11111
  Bill Cook, prin. — 983-4235

Camden, AC 601, PC 3, Madison
Madison County SD
  Supt. — See Canton
Jackson S, PO BOX 29 39045 — 3-11111
  George Cole, prin. — 468-2531

Canton, AC 601, PC 7, Madison
Canton SSD, 403 LINCOLN ST 39046 — 5-11111
  Joe Galloway, supt. — 859-4110

JSHS, 529 MACE ST 39046 — 4-00111
  Huey Porter, prin. — 859-5325
Canton Vo-Tech Ctr — Vo Tech
  487 N UNION STREET EXT 39046 — 859-3984
  Mike Thomas, prin.

Madison County SD — 5-11111
  1633 W PEACE ST 39046 — 355-7412
  C. Melvin Ray, supt.
Madison County Vo-Tech Ctr — Vo Tech
  1633 W PEACE ST 39046 — 859-6847
  Larry Garvin, prin.
Other Schools – See Camden, Flora, Madison

Canton Academy, PO BOX 116 39046 — 2-11111
  Mike Coggins, prin. — 859-5231

Carriere, AC 601, PC 3, Pearl River
Pearl River County SD — 4-11111
  5902 HIGHWAY 11 N 39426 — 798-7744
  Sylvia Posey, supt.
Pearl River Central HS — 3-00011
  5853 HIGHWAY 11 N 39426 — 798-1986
  Robert Lumpkin, prin.
Other Schools – See Mc Neill

Carrollton, AC 601, PC 2, Carroll
Carroll County SD — 4-11111
  PO BOX 256 38917 — 237-9276
  James Alford, supt.
Other Schools – See North Carrollton, Vaiden

Carroll Academy, PO BOX 226 38917 — 2-00011
  Robert Gordon, prin. — 237-6858

Carson, AC 601, PC 2, Jefferson Davis
Jefferson Davis County SD
  Supt. — See Prentiss
Vo-Tech Ctr, PO BOX 70 39427 — Vo Tech
  Thomas Johnson, prin. — 792-5005

Carthage, AC 601, PC 5, Leake
Leake County SD, PO BOX 478 39051 — 5-11111
  Joe Kea, supt. — 267-4579
HS, 704 N JORDAN ST 39051 — 2-00011
  Jerry Gressett, prin. — 267-7713
Edinburg S, RR 8 BOX 103 39051 — 2-11111
  John McKinney, prin. — 267-7137
Thomastown S, RR 2 BOX 345 39051 — 2-11111
  Steve Luse, prin. — 267-7896
Leake County Vo-Tech Ctr — Vo Tech
  703 N WEST ST 39051 — 267-8442
  Monte Ladner, prin.
JHS, 801 PRESLEY RD 39051 — 2-01100
  Bobby Boone, prin. — 267-8909
Other Schools – See Walnut Grove

Centreville, AC 601, PC 4, Wilkinson

Centreville Academy — 2-00011
  PO BOX 70 39631 — 645-5912
  Lea Hurst, prin.

Charleston, AC 601, PC 4, Tallahatchie
East Tallahatchie Consolidated SD — 4-11111
  411 CHESTNUT ST 38921 — 647-5524
  David Hargett, supt.
HS, COSSAR ST 38921 — 2-00011
  Jim Aven, prin. — 647-5359
East Tallahatchie Vo Ctr — Vo Tech
  COSSAR ST 38921 — 647-5524
  William Douglas, prin.
MS, INDIANA RD 38921 — 3-01100
  Levan Miller, prin. — 647-2115

Strider Academy — 2-11111
  RR 2 BOX 246 38921 — 647-5833
  Joseph Bradshaw, prin.

Clarksdale, AC 601, PC 7, Coahoma
Clarksdale SSD, PO BOX 1088 38614 — 5-11111
  Carl Weeden, supt. — 627-8500
SHS, PO BOX 1088 38614 — 3-00001
  Jeff King, prin. — 627-8530
Keen Vo Ctr, PO BOX 1088 38614 — Vo Tech
  Bernie Winkel, prin. — 627-8580
Higgins JHS, PO BOX 1088 38614 — 3-00110
  Henry Clay, prin. — 627-8550
Oakhurst JHS, PO BOX 1088 38614 — 3-00110
  Sam Kendricks, prin. — 627-8560

Coahoma Co. Agricultural SD — 2-00011
  RR 1 BOX 616 38614 — 624-8045
  Vivian Presley, supt.
Coahoma Co. Agri HS — 2-00011
  RR 1 BOX 616 38614 — 624-9814
  Olenza McBride, prin.

Coahoma County SD — 5-11111
  PO BOX 820 38614 — 624-3040
  Audrey Ball, supt.
Coahoma County HS — 2-00011
  PO BOX 820 38614 — 627-7378
  Robert Lee, prin.
Coahoma County JHS — 2-00100
  PO BOX 820 38614 — 627-7371
  Robert Willis, prin.

Coahoma Community College — 8-CC
  RR 1 BOX 616 38614 — 800-844-1222
Lee Academy, PO BOX 1027 38614 — 2-11111
  Brian Tierney, prin. — 627-7891

Cleveland, AC 601, PC 7, Bolivar
Cleveland SD, 305 MERRITT DR 38732 — 5-11111
  Peg Campbell, supt. — 843-3529
HS, 300 W SUNFLOWER RD 38732 — 3-00011
  Bill Johnson, prin. — 843-2460
East Side HS, LEE ST 38732 — 3-00011
  Leroy Byars, prin. — 843-2338
Cleveland Vo Complex, 3RD ST 38732 — Vo Tech
  John McCool, prin. — 843-8818
Eastwood JHS — 2-00100
  715 S MARTIN LUTHER KING DR 38732
  General Burton, prin. — 843-4355
Green JHS — 3-00100
  300 W SUNFLOWER RD 38732 — 843-2456
  Robert Montesi, prin.

Bayou Academy, PO BOX 417 38732 — 2-11111
  Gerald Crowe, prin. — 843-9618
Delta State University — 5-UC
  HWY 8 W 38732 — 846-4000

Clinton, AC 601, PC 7, Hinds
Clinton SD, PO BOX 300 39060 — 6-11111
  Randy McCoy, supt. — 924-7533
SHS, 711 W LAKEVIEW DR 39056 — 4-00001
  Walter Bounds, prin. — 924-5656
Clinton Vo Complex — Vo Tech
  713 W LAKEVIEW DR 39056 — 924-0247
  Billy Stack, prin.
JHS, 401 E COLLEGE ST 39056 — 3-00100
  Limmie Flowers, prin. — 924-0619
Sumner Hill JHS — 2-00010
  400 W NORTHSIDE DR 39056 — 924-5510
  Willie McInnis, prin.

Mississippi College — 5-UC
  PO BOX 4086 39058 — 925-3240

Coffeeville, AC 601, PC 3, Yalobusha
Coffeeville SD, PO BOX K 38922 — 3-11111
  Aubrey Ray, supt. — 675-8941
JSHS, PO BOX K 38922 — 2-00111
  Ethel Jenkins, prin. — 675-8904

Coldwater, AC 601, PC 4, Tate
Tate County SD
  Supt. — See Senatobia
JSHS, PO BOX CC 38618 — 3-00111
  Phernado Bearden, prin. — 622-5511
Senatobia/Tate Vo-Tech Ctr — Vo Tech
  PO BOX 440 38618 — 622-5149
  Tryce Barber, prin.

Collins, AC 601, PC 5, Covington
Covington County SD — 5-11111
  PO BOX 1269 39428 — 765-8247
  Lavahn Moss, supt.
HS, PO BOX 1479 39428 — 3-00011
  Fred Barnes, prin. — 765-3203
Covington County Vo-Tech Ctr — Vo Tech
  PO BOX 1268 39428 — 765-8253
  Cecil Easterling, prin.
MS, PO BOX 757 39428 — 3-01100
  Larry Tripp, prin. — 765-4908
Other Schools – See Mount Olive, Seminary

Collinsville, AC 601, PC 4, Lauderdale
Lauderdale County SD
  Supt. — See Meridian
West Lauderdale S — 2-11111
  RR 3 BOX 525 39325 — 737-2277
  Billy Smith, prin.

Columbia, AC 601, PC 6, Marion
Columbia SD, PO BOX 271 39429 — 4-11111
  Hugh Dickens, supt. — 736-2366
HS, 1009 BROAD ST 39429 — 3-00011
  Gary Smyly, prin. — 736-5334
Jefferson MS, 1300 WEST AVE 39429 — 2-00100
  Jerry Sharp, prin. — 736-2786

Marion County SD, 600 BROAD ST 39429 — 5-11111
  William Davis, supt. — 736-7193
East Marion S — 4-11111
  527 E MARION SCHOOL RD 39429 — 736-3006
  Bill Russell, prin.
Marion County Vo Complex — Vo Tech
  1140 HIGHWAY 13 S 39429 — 736-6095
  Ron Fortenberry, prin.
Other Schools – See Foxworth

Columbia Academy — 2-00011
  PO BOX 906 39429 — 736-6418
  Victor Blair, prin.

Columbus, AC 601, PC 7, Lowndes
Columbus Municipal SD — 6-11111
  PO BOX 1308 39703 — 328-2598
  Reuben Dilworth, supt.
SHS East, 820 N BROWDER ST 39702 — 3-00001
  Scott Murrah, prin. — 328-2082
McKellar Vo Ctr — Vo Tech
  810 N BROWDER ST 39702 — 327-0290
  William Self, prin.
Columbus Freshman HS West — 3-00010
  1815 MILITARY RD 39701 — 328-3334
  Bob Williford, prin.
Cook MS, 2217 7TH ST N 39701 — 3-00100
  Linda Guin, prin. — 329-8282

Lowndes County SD
201 AIRLINE RD   39702   5-11111 / 329-5775
Tom Smith, supt.
New Hope HS   3-00011 / 328-7999
3419 NEW HOPE RD   39702
Mike Halford, prin.
West Lowndes HS   2-00011 / 328-1369
1380 MOTLEY RD   39701
Roosevelt Bridges, prin.
Vocational Complex   Vo Tech / 327-7108
664 FRONTAGE RD   39701
Maye Youngblood, prin.
New Hope MS   3-00100 / 329-1875
3419 NEW HOPE RD   39702
Lance Eiland, prin.
West Lowndes MS   2-00100 / 327-1962
1380 MOTLEY RD   39701
Robert Smith, prin.
Other Schools – See Caledonia

Heritage Academy   3-11111 / 327-5272
625 MAGNOLIA LN   39701
Ray Wooten, prin.
Mississippi University for Women   4-UC / 329-7106
PO BOX W-1602   39701

Como, AC 601, PC 4, Panola
North Panola Consolidated SD
Supt. — See Sardis
North Panola Vocational Comp S   Vo Tech / 526-5804
PO BOX 474   38619
James Barnett, prin.

Corinth, AC 601, PC 7, Alcorn
Alcorn SD, PO BOX 1420   38834   5-11111 / 286-5591
Mike Wamsley, supt.
Biggersville JSHS   2-00111 / 286-3542
RR 4 BOX 349   38834
Victor Goolsby, prin.
Alcorn Vo Ctr, RR 5 BOX 66   38834   Vo Tech / 286-7727
MIKE McCLAMROCH, prin.
Other Schools – See Glen, Kossuth

Corinth SD, 1101 CRUISE ST   38834   4-11111 / 287-2425
O. Gann, supt.
HS, 1310 HARPER RD   38834   3-00011 / 286-1000
Harold Smith, prin.
JHS, 1000 E 5TH ST   38834   2-00100 / 286-1261
Harold Gray, prin.

Crawford, AC 601, PC 3, Lowndes
Oktibbeha County SD
Supt. — See Starkville
Moor S, PO BOX 95   39743   2-11111 / 272-5660
James Chambers, prin.

Cruger, AC 601, PC 3, Holmes

Cruger-Tchula Academy   2-11111 / 453-9149
PO BOX 130   38924
Carlton Abels, prin.

Crystal Springs, AC 601, PC 6, Copiah
Copiah County SD
Supt. — See Hazlehurst
HS, 211 NEWTON ST   39059   4-00011 / 892-4791
Charles Lewis, prin.
MS, PO BOX 520   39059   3-01100 / 892-2722
Carl Stokes, prin.

Mississippi Job Corps Center   2-CS
PO BOX 817   39059

Decatur, AC 601, PC 4, Newton
Newton County SD   4-11111 / 635-2317
PO BOX 97   39327
Charles Hand, supt.
Newton County HS   2-00011 / 635-2718
PO BOX 278   39327
Edward McGowan, prin.
Newton County Vo-Tech Center   Vo Tech / 635-4138
PO BOX 742   39327
Marcus Savell, prin.
Newton County MS   2-00100 / 635-2318
PO BOX 70   39327
Robert Strebeck, prin.

East Central Community College   4-CC / 635-2111
PO BOX 129   39327
Newton County Academy   2-11111 / 635-2756
PO BOX 25   39327
Bryan Burt, prin.

De Kalb, AC 601, PC 4, Kemper
Kemper County SD   4-11111 / 743-5657
PO BOX 219   39328
Wayne Killebrew, supt.
Kemper County JSHS   3-01111 / 743-5292
PO BOX 429   39328
Kevin Jones, prin.
Stennis Vo-Tech Complex   Vo Tech / 743-5226
PO BOX 88   39328
Howard Little, prin.

Kemper Academy   2-11111 / 743-2232
PO BOX 459   39328
Pete McCleskey, prin.

D'Iberville, AC 601, PC 6, Harrison
Harrison County SD
Supt. — See Gulfport
HS, 3320 WARRIOR DR   39532   3-00011 / 392-2678
M. Richardson, prin.
MS, 10000 GORENFLO RD   39532   3-01100 / 392-1746
Larry Evans, prin.

Drew, AC 601, PC 4, Sunflower
Drew SD, 117 W SHAW AVE   38737   4-11111 / 745-6657
James Edwards, supt.
JSHS, 288 GREEN AVE   38737   2-00111 / 745-8586
Roosevelt Ramsey, prin.

North Sunflower Academy   2-11111 / 745-2728
RR 2 BOX 821   38737
Charles Francis, prin.

Durant, AC 601, PC 5, Holmes
Durant SD, PO BOX 669   39063   3-11111 / 653-3175
Curtis Burrell, supt.
S, PO BOX 669   39063   3-11111 / 653-3429
Kermit Hutchins, prin.

Holmes County SD
Supt. — See Lexington
Sullivan S, HIGHWAY 51 S   39063   3-11111 / 653-6262
John McGee, prin.

Ecru, AC 601, PC 3, Pontotoc
Pontotoc County SD
Supt. — See Pontotoc
North Pontotoc S, RR 1 BOX 252D   38841   4-11111 / 489-5612
Steve Carr, prin.

Ellisville, AC 601, PC 5, Jones
Jones County SD, RR 4 BOX 642A   39437   6-11111 / 649-5201
William Moss, supt.
South Jones JSHS, ANDERSON ST   39437   4-00111 / 477-8451
John Bryant, prin.
Other Schools – See Laurel

Jones County Junior College   39437   5-CC / 477-4025

Enterprise, AC 601, PC 2, Clarke
Enterprise Consolidated SD   3-11111 / 659-7965
PO BOX A   39330
Michael Taylor, supt.
JSHS, PO BOX A   39330   2-00111 / 659-4435
Lavalle White, prin.

Ethel, AC 601, PC 2, Attala
Attala County SD
Supt. — See Kosciusko
JSHS, PO BOX 128   39067   2-00111 / 674-5673
David Jones, prin.

Eupora, AC 601, PC 4, Webster
Webster County SD
Supt. — See Walthall
JSHS, 212 W CLARK AVE   39744   2-00111 / 258-4041
William Reed, prin.
Webster County Vo Complex   Vo Tech / 258-8206
PO BOX 889   39744
David Faulkenbery, prin.

Falkner, AC 601, PC 2, Tippah
North Tippah SD
Supt. — See Tiplersville
JSHS, PO BOX 139   38629   2-00111 / 837-7892
Joe Horton, prin.

Fayette, AC 601, PC 4, Jefferson
Jefferson County SD   4-11111 / 786-3721
PO BOX 157   39069
Daniel Smith, supt.
Jefferson County HS   3-00011 / 786-3919
RR 1 BOX 266   39069
John Dickey, prin.
Vo-Tech Ctr, RR 2 BOX 35E   39069   Vo Tech / 786-3642
J. Heidelberg, prin.
Jefferson County JHS   3-00100 / 786-3900
RR 2 BOX 35C   39069
Inder Mitchell, prin.

Flora, AC 601, PC 4, Madison
Madison County SD
Supt. — See Canton
MS, PO BOX 159   39071   2-00100 / 879-8916
Yale Canfield, prin.

Tri-County Academy, PO BOX K   39071   2-11111 / 879-8517
Glenn Cain, prin.

Florence, AC 601, PC 4, Rankin
Rankin County SD
Supt. — See Brandon
HS, 232 HIGHWAY 469 N   39073   2-00011 / 845-2205
Sam Newman, prin.
McLaurin S, RR 1 BOX 412   39073   3-11111 / 845-2247
Terry Brister, prin.
MS, PO BOX 159   39073   3-01100 / 845-2862
Beverly Weathersby, prin.

Wesley College   1-UC / 845-2265
PO BOX 70   39073

Forest, AC 601, PC 6, Scott
Forest Municipal SD   4-11111 / 469-3250
511 CLEVELAND ST   39074
Richard Hill, supt.
HS, 511 CLEVELAND ST   39074   2-00011 / 469-3255
Bob Richardson, prin.
Hawkins MS, 803 E OAK ST   39074   3-01100 / 469-1474
James Harper, prin.

Scott County SD, 100 E FIRST ST   39074   5-11111 / 469-3861
Frank McCurdy, supt.
Scott Central S, RR 5 BOX 124   39074   4-11111 / 469-4883
Fred Yates, prin.
Forest/Scott County Vo-Tech Ctr   Vo Tech / 469-2913
521 CLEVELAND ST   39074
A. Eichelberger, prin.
Other Schools – See Lake, Morton, Sebastopol

Foxworth, AC 601, PC 3, Marion
Marion County SD
Supt. — See Columbia
West Marion JSHS   4-01111 / 736-6381
2 W MARION ST   39483
Billy Bourne, prin.

Fulton, AC 601, PC 5, Itawamba
Itawamba County SD   5-11111 / 862-2159
304 W WIYGUL ST   38843
F. Wiygul, supt.
Vo-Tech Ctr, PO BOX 548   38843   Vo Tech / 862-3137
Joel Holley, prin.
JHS, 700 W MAIN ST   38843   2-00110 / 862-4558
James Nanney, prin.
Other Schools – See Mantachie, Tremont

Itawamba Jr. College & Agricultural SD   3-00001 / 862-3104
602 W HILL ST   38843
W. Benjamin, supt.
Itawamba Agricultural SHS   3-00001 / 862-3104
602 W HILL ST   38843
Billy Loague, prin.

Itawamba Community College   5-CC / 862-3101
HWY 78   38843

Gallman, AC 601, PC 2, Copiah

Copiah Academy, PO BOX 125   39077   3-11111 / 892-3770
David Bosse, prin.

Gautier, AC 601, PC 7, Jackson
Pascagoula SSD
Supt. — See Pascagoula
JHS, 1920 GRAVELINE RD   39553   3-00110 / 938-6540
Charles Brown, prin.

Mississippi Gulf Coast Community College   2-CC / 497-9602
39553

Georgetown, AC 601, PC 2, Copiah

Union Academy, RR 1 BOX 75   39078   2-11111 / 858-2255
Richard Brown, prin.

Glen, AC 601, PC 2, Alcorn
Alcorn SD
Supt. — See Corinth
Alcorn Central HS   3-00011 / 286-8720
RR 2 BOX 280   38846
Cecil Stroup, prin.
Alcorn Central MS   2-01100 / 286-3674
RR 2 BOX 280   38846
Wayne Hindman, prin.

Gloster, AC 601, PC 4, Amite

Pine Hills Academy   2-11111 / 225-4721
PO BOX 458   39638
Bruce Penton, prin.

Goodman, AC 601, PC 4, Holmes

Holmes Community College   4-CC / 472-2312
PO BOX 369   39079

Greenville, AC 601, PC 8, Washington
Greenville SSD, PO BOX 1619   38702   6-11111 / 334-7000
William Thomas, supt.
HS, 419 E ROBERTSHAW ST   38701   4-00011 / 334-7061
Charlie Lynch, prin.
Weston HS, 901 ARCHER ST   38701   3-00011 / 334-7081
Sammy Felton, prin.
Greenville Vo Complex   Vo Tech / 334-7171
PO BOX 4620   38704
Alvin Harrington, prin.
Coleman JHS, 400 HIGHWAY 1 N   38701   3-00100 / 334-7036
Albert Calvin, prin.
Solomon JHS   3-00100 / 334-7051
556 BOWMAN BLVD   38701
Gloria Taylor, prin.

Western Line SD
Supt. — See Avon
O'Bannon S, PO BOX 1678   38702   4-11111 / 335-2637
C. Hall, prin.

Greenville Christian S   2-11111 / 332-0946
PO BOX 4398   38704
David Glasgow, prin.
St. Joseph HS, 700 GOLF ST   38701   2-00111 / 378-9711
Br. Geraghty, prin.
Washington S, 1605 E REED RD   38703   4-11111 / 334-4096
Audrey Sidney, prin.

Greenwood, AC 601, PC 7, Leflore
Greenwood SD, PO BOX 1497   38935   5-11111 / 453-4231
C. Stevenson, supt.
HS, 1209 GARRARD AVE   38930   4-00011 / 455-7450
Carey Spears, prin.
Greenwood Vo-Tech Ctr   Vo Tech / 455-7414
SYCAMORE AVE   38930
Danny Hardin, prin.
Threadgill MS, 1001 BROAD ST   38930   2-01100 / 455-7440
Margie Pulley, prin.

Leflore County SD   5-11111 / 459-7231
PO BOX 544   38935
Irvin Whittaker, supt.
Elzy JSHS, RR 4 BOX 100   38930   3-00111 / 453-3394
Tommy Spells, prin.
Leflore County Vo Ctr   Vo Tech / 453-7706
PO BOX 1158   38935
Fred Hooper, prin.

East MS, MEADOWBROOK RD 38930   3-01100
   Terry Swilley, prin.   453-9182
Other Schools – See Itta Bena

Pillow Academy   3-11111
   PO BOX 1880 38935   453-1266
   Thomas Thompson, prin.

Grenada, AC 601, PC 7, Grenada
Grenada SD, PO BOX 1940 38902   5-11111
   Buddy Pender, supt.   226-1606
HS, 1875 FAIRGROUND RD 38901   4-00011
   Larry Fry, prin.   226-8844
Grenada Vo Complex   Vo Tech
   2035 JACKSON AVE 38901   226-5969
   Don Connerley, prin.
JHS, 0 JONES RD 38901   3-00100
   Carole White, prin.   226-5135

Kirk Academy, PO BOX 1008 38902   3-11111
   A. Smithers, prin.   226-2791

Gulfport, AC 601, PC 8, Harrison
Gulfport SSD, PO BOX 220 39502   6-11111
   W. Strebeck, supt.   865-4600
SHS, 100 PERRY ST 39507   4-00001
   Leslie Steverson, prin.   896-7525
Gulfport Vocational Annex S   Vo Tech
   100 PERRY ST 39507   896-6011
   Leonard Plitt, prin.
Bayou View JHS, 212 43RD ST 39507   3-00110
   Bill Reedy, prin.   865-4633
Central JHS, 2015 15TH ST 39501   3-00110
   James Taylor, prin.   896-5711

Harrison County SD   7-11111
   1801 23RD AVE 39501   865-4052
   Henry Arledge, supt.
Harrison Central SHS   4-00001
   15600 SCHOOL RD 39503   832-2610
   Lester Denley, prin.
Harrison County Vo-Tech Ctr   Vo Tech
   15600 SCHOOL RD 39503   832-6652
   Larry Thrash, prin.
Harrison Central JHS   3-00010
   10453 KLEIN RD 39503   832-6711
   Elemuel Porter, prin.
North Gulfport MS   4-00100
   4715 ILLINOIS AVE 39501   864-8944
   C. Luckett, prin.
Other Schools – See D'Iberville

Gulfport Job Corps Center   2-CS
   3300 20TH ST 39501
Mississippi Gulf Coast Community College   2-CC
   39507   896-3355
St. John HS, 620 PASS RD 39501   2-00111
   Lanny Acosta, prin.   863-8141

Guntown, AC 601, PC 3, Lee
Lee County SD
   Supt. — See Tupelo
MS, PO BOX 8 38849   2-00100
   Harvey Brooks, prin.   348-5567

Hamilton, AC 601, PC 3, Monroe
Monroe County SD
   Supt. — See Aberdeen
Hamilton S, PO BOX 34 39746   3-11111
   Van Pearson, prin.   343-8307

Hattiesburg, AC 601, PC 8, Forrest
Forrest County SD   5-11111
   PO BOX 1977 39403   545-6055
   Walter Cartier, supt.
North Forrest JSHS   3-00111
   693 EATONVILLE RD 39401   545-9304
   Marvin Miller, prin.

Hattiesburg SD, PO BOX 1569 39403   6-11111
   Gordon Walker, supt.   584-6283
SHS, 301 N HUTCHINSON AVE 39401   4-00001
   Horace Overby, prin.   544-0811
Hawkins JHS, 526 FORREST ST 39401   3-00110
   Charles Gregg, prin.   583-4311
Rowan JHS   2-00110
   500 MARTIN LUTHER KING AVE 39401
   John Kent, prin.   583-2657

Lamar County SD
   Supt. — See Purvis
Oak Grove S   3-11111
   2543 OLD HIGHWAY 24 39402   264-7232
   Carolyn Adams, prin.

Hattiesburg Radiology Group   HSP
   116 S 25TH AVE 39401   288-4241
Moore Career College   2-CS
   1500 N 31ST AVE 39401   583-4100
University of Southern Mississippi   7-UC
   PO BOX 5165 39406   266-5000
William Carey College   4-UC
   498 TUSCAN AVE 39401   800-962-5991

Hazlehurst, AC 601, PC 5, Copiah
Copiah County SD   5-11111
   PO BOX 550 39083   894-1341
   Dale Sullivan, supt.
Other Schools – See Crystal Springs, Wesson

Hazlehurst CSD, 119 E FROST ST 39083   4-11111
   Robert McDaniel, supt.   894-1152
JSHS, 101 S HALEY ST 39083   3-00111
   James Boston, prin.   894-2489

Heidelberg, AC 601, PC 3, Jasper
East Jasper Consolidated SD   4-11111
   PO BOX E 39439   787-3281
   Audie McCormick, supt.
HS, PO BOX M 39439   2-00011
   Elijah Buckley, prin.   787-3414

Heidelberg Academy, PO BOX Q 39439   2-00011
   William Faggert, prin.   787-4589

Hernando, AC 601, PC 5, De Soto
DeSoto County SD   7-11111
   425 E COMMERCE ST 38632   429-5271
   Erlend Nichols, supt.
HS, 805 RILEY ST 38632   3-00011
   T. Long, prin.   429-4170
JHS, 2690 MAGNOLIA DR 38632   2-00010
   James Sims, prin.   429-4154
Other Schools – See Horn Lake, Olive Branch, Southaven

Hickory Flat, AC 601, PC 3, Benton
Benton County SD
   Supt. — See Ashland
S, RR 2 BOX 1C 38633   2-11111
   Ollice Massengill, prin.   333-7731

Hollandale, AC 601, PC 5, Washington
Hollandale SD, PO BOX 128 38748   4-11111
   Howard Sanders, supt.   827-2276
Simmons JSHS, PO BOX 428 38748   3-00111
   Willie Amos, prin.   827-2229

Holly Springs, AC 601, PC 6, Marshall
Holly Springs SD   4-11111
   165 N WALTHALL ST 38635   252-2183
   Earmon McSwine, supt.
HS, 165 N WALTHALL ST 38635   3-00011
   Wallace Longest, prin.   252-4371
Holly Springs Vo-Tech Ctr   Vo Tech
   165 N WALTHALL ST 38635   252-2071
   Herman Young, prin.
IS, 210 W VALLEY AVE 38635   3-01100
   Judy Smith, prin.   252-2329

Marshall County SD   5-11111
   PO BOX 38 38635   252-4271
   Donnal Ash, supt.
Byers S, RR 2 BOX 199 38635   3-11111
   John Chase, prin.   851-7826
Other Schools – See Byhalia, Potts Camp

Marshall Academy   2-11111
   100 ACADEMY DR 38635   252-3449
   Hoyte Carothers, prin.
Rust College   4-UC
   150 E RUST AVE 38635   252-4661

Horn Lake, AC 601, PC 6, De Soto
DeSoto County SD
   Supt. — See Hernando
HS, 6125 HURT RD 38637   4-00011
   M. Kuykendall, prin.   393-5273
MS, 6870 CENTER ST E 38637   3-00100
   Willie George, prin.   393-7443

Houlka, AC 601, PC 3, Chickasaw
Chickasaw County SD   3-11111
   PO BOX 480 38850   568-3333
   Raymond Paden, supt.
S, PO BOX 277 38850   3-11111
   Carol Templeton, prin.   568-2772

Houston, AC 601, PC 5, Chickasaw
Houston SSD, PO BOX 351 38851   4-11111
   Laverne Collins, supt.   456-3332
SHS, PO BOX 568 38851   2-00001
   Michael Price, prin.   456-3320
Houston Vo Ctr, PO BOX 608 38851   Vo Tech
   ALFRED BELL, prin.   456-3748
JHS, PO BOX 192 38851   3-00110
   Warren Cousin, prin.   456-5174

Hurley, AC 601, PC 3, Jackson
Jackson County SD
   Supt. — See Vancleave
East Central HS, PO BOX 13 39555   4-00011
   Tim Anderson, prin.   588-7000
East Central MS, PO BOX 13 39555   2-01100
   Mary Tanner, prin.   588-7009

Independence, AC 601, PC 3, Tate
Tate County SD
   Supt. — See Senatobia
JSHS, PO BOX 159 38638   3-00111
   Clyde Robinson, prin.   233-4691

Indianola, AC 601, PC 7, Sunflower
Indianola SD, HIGHWAY 82 E 38751   5-11111
   Robert Merritt, supt.   887-2654
Gentry HS, 801 BB KING RD 38751   3-00011
   Andrew Carter, prin.   887-2433
JHS, 701 CHAPMAN ST 38751   2-00100
   John Chance, prin.   887-1852

Sunflower County SD   5-11111
   PO BOX 70 38751   887-4919
   James Smith, supt.
Other Schools – See Moorhead, Ruleville

Indianola Academy   3-11111
   PO BOX 967 38751   887-2025
   Sam Henderson, prin.

Itta Bena, AC 601, PC 4, Leflore
Leflore County SD
   Supt. — See Greenwood

Leflore County S, PO BOX 564 38941   4-11111
   Charles Scott, prin.   254-7762

Mississippi Valley State University   4-UC
   14000 HIGHWAY 82 W 38941   254-9041

Iuka, AC 601, PC 5, Tishomingo
Tishomingo County Special Municipal SD   4-11111
   507 W QUITMAN ST 38852   423-3206
   Bob Ferguson, supt.
Tishomingo County HS   2-00011
   RR 2 BOX 748 38852   423-7300
   Robert Haggard, prin.
MS, 507 W QUITMAN ST 38852   2-01100
   Benny McClung, prin.   423-3316
Other Schools – See Belmont, Tishomingo

Jackson, AC 601, PC 9, Hinds
Hinds County SD
   Supt. — See Raymond
Byram JSHS, 5801 TERRY RD 39212   4-00111
   Phil Hannon, prin.   372-4597

Jackson SD, PO BOX 2338 39225   8-11111
   Benjamin Canada, supt.   960-8725
Callaway HS, 601 BEASLEY RD 39206   4-00011
   Aaron Jones, prin.   987-3535
Forest Hill HS   3-00011
   2607 RAYMOND RD 39212   371-4313
   Ron Sellers, prin.
Hill HS, 2185 FORTUNE ST 39204   3-00011
   Delores Hopkins, prin.   960-5354
Lanier HS, 833 MAPLE ST 39203   3-00011
   Thomas Johnson, prin.   960-5369
Murrah HS, 1400 MURRAH DR 39202   3-00011
   Linda Dick, prin.   960-5380
Provine HS, 2400 ROBINSON ST 39209   4-00011
   Emmanuel Reeves, prin.   960-5393
Wingfield HS, 1985 SCANLON DR 39204   3-00011
   Bishop Knox, prin.   371-4350
Bailey Magnet JSHS   2-00111
   1900 N STATE ST 39202   960-5343
   Marcus Burkes, prin.
Career Development Ctr   Vo Tech
   2703 FIRST AVE 39209   960-5322
   Willie Mott, prin.
Blackburn MS, 1311 W PEARL ST 39203   3-00100
   William Revies, prin.   960-5329
Brinkley MS   3-00100
   3535 ALBERMARLE RD 39213   987-3573
   Ken Acton, prin.
Chastain MS   3-00100
   4650 MANHATTAN RD 39206   987-3550
   Jack Rice, prin.
Hardy MS, 545 ELLIS AVE 39209   3-00100
   Verne Harris, prin.   355-6891
Northwest MS   3-00100
   7020 HIGHWAY 49 N 39213   987-3609
   Larry Blalock, prin.
Peeples MS, 290 TREEHAVEN DR 39212   3-00100
   Lonnie Boyd, prin.   371-4345
Powell MS, 3655 LIVINGSTON RD 39213   3-00100
   John Wicks, prin.   987-3580
Rowan MS, 136 E ASH ST 39202   2-00100
   Karl Twyner, prin.   960-5349
Siwell Road MS   3-00100
   1983 N SIWELL RD 39209   923-2550
   Beray Thigpin, prin.
Whitten MS   3-00100
   210 DANIEL LAKE BLVD 39212   371-4309
   Paul Russell, prin.

Belhaven College   3-UC
   1500 PEACHTREE ST 39202   968-5940
Hillcrest Christian S   3-11111
   4060 S SIWELL RD 39212   372-0149
   Walt Gaston, prin.
Hinds Community College   2-CC
   1750 CHADWICK DR 39204   372-6507
Jackson Academy   4-11111
   PO BOX 14978 39236   362-9676
   Keith Branning, prin.
Jackson Prep S, PO BOX 4940 39296   3-00111
   James Roberts, prin.   939-8611
Jackson State University   6-UC
   1400 LYNCH ST 39203   800-848-6817
Millsaps College   4-UC
   P O BOX 15495 39210   800-352-1050
Mississippi College   5-UC
   151 E GRIFFITH ST 39201
Mississippi Medical Center   HSP
   1225 N STATE ST 39202   968-5130
Mississippi School for the Blind   HND
   1252 EASTOVER DR 39211
Mississippi School for the Deaf   HND
   1253 EASTOVER DR 39211
Moore Career College   2-CS
   2460 TERRY RD 39204   371-2900
Phillips Junior College   3-CC
   2680 INSURANCE CENTER DR 39216   362-6341
Reformed Theological Seminary   3-UC
   5422 CLINTON BLVD 39209   922-4988
Rice College   2-CS
   2525 ROBINSON ST 39209   355-8100
St. Andrew's Episcopal S   3-11111
   4120 OLD CANTON RD 39216
   J. Bean, prin.
St. Joseph HS, 2221 BOLING ST 39213   2-00011
   Donald Flood, prin.   362-5314
St. Joseph JHS, 100 HOLLY DR 39206   2-00100
   Keith Fulcher, prin.   981-9773

The Education Center 2-11111
  4080 OLD CANTON RD 39216 982-2812
  Lynn Macon, prin.
University of Mississippi Medical Center 4-UC
  2500 N STATE ST 39216 984-1080
Wesley Biblical Seminary 1-UC
  PO BOX 9938 39286 957-1314
Woodland Hills Baptist Academy 2-11111
  5055 MANHATTAN RD 39206 366-9494
  Larry Luby, prin.

Kilmichael, AC 601, PC 3, Montgomery
Montgomery County SD
  Supt. — See Winona
Montgomery County High School 2-00011
  PO BOX 278 39747 262-5535
  Jerry Boggan, prin.

Kiln, AC 601, PC 4, Hancock
Hancock County SD
  Supt. — See Waveland
Hancock JSHS 3-00111
  7084 STENNIS AIRPORT RD 39556 467-2251
  David Kopf, prin.

Kosciusko, AC 601, PC 6, Attala
Attala County SD 4-11111
  100 COURTHOUSE 39090 289-2801
  David Spears, supt.
Kosciusko-Attala Vo Complex Vo Tech
  450 HIGHWAY 12 E 39090 289-2689
  Barry Burchfield, prin.
Other Schools – See Ethel, Mc Adams

Kosciusko SSD 4-11111
  206 S HUNTINGTON ST 39090 289-4771
  David Sistrunk, supt.
HS, 206 S HUNTINGTON ST 39090 2-00011
  Charles Hull, prin. 289-2424
JHS, 206 S HUNTINGTON ST 39090 2-00100
  Dewayne Cade, prin. 289-3737

Magnolia Bible College 1-UC
  PO BOX 1109 39090 800-748-8655

Kossuth, AC 601, PC 2, Alcorn
Alcorn SD
  Supt. — See Corinth
JSHS, RR 5 38834 3-00111
  Larry Mitchell, prin. 286-3653

Lake, AC 601, PC 2, Scott
Scott County SD
  Supt. — See Forest
Lake S, RR 1 39092 3-10011
  Huey Stone, prin. 775-3248
MS, RR 1 39092 2-01100
  Rodney Tadlock, prin. 775-3614

Laurel, AC 601, PC 7, Jones
Jones County SD
  Supt. — See Ellisville
Northeast Jones JSHS 4-00111
  RR 13 BOX 15 39440 425-2347
  Thomas Parker, prin.
West Jones JSHS 4-00111
  RR 11 BOX 324 39440 729-8144
  James Thomas, prin.
Fatherree Vo-Tech Ctr Vo Tech
  2409 MOOSE DR 39440 425-2378
  Lester Boyles, prin.

Laurel SD, PO BOX 288 39441 5-11111
  David Sheppard, supt. 649-6391
Watkins HS, 1100 W 12TH ST 39440 3-00011
  Ronnie Jones, prin. 649-4145
Watkins Vocational S Vo Tech
  1100 W 11TH ST 39440 649-4141
  Walter Strong, prin.
Gardiner JHS, 303 W 8TH ST 39440 2-00100
  William Gully, prin. 428-1880
Jones JHS, 1125 N 5TH AVE 39440 2-00100
  Kent Headrick, prin. 428-5312

South Central Regional Medical Center HSP
  PO BOX 607 39441 426-4000
Southeastern Baptist College 1-UC
  4229 HIGHWAY 15 N 39440 426-6346

Leakesville, AC 601, PC 4, Greene
Greene County SD 4-11111
  PO BOX 1329 39451 394-2364
  Jerry Smith, supt.
Greene Co. HS, RR 1 BOX 12 39451 3-00011
  David Dearman, prin. 394-5290
Green County Vo-Tech Complex Vo Tech
  RR 2 BOX 266 39451 394-2973
  Bob Walley, prin.
JHS, PO BOX 1479 39451 2-01100
  Douglas Mizell, prin. 394-2495

Learned, AC 601, PC 2, Hinds

Rebul Academy 2-11111
  5257 LEARNED RD 39154 885-6802
  Charles Mason, prin.

Leland, AC 601, PC 6, Washington
Leland SD, 408 4TH ST 38756 4-11111
  Barbara Massey, supt. 686-5000
HS, 403 E 3RD ST 38756 3-00011
  Delores Nash, prin. 686-5020
Leland Vo Complex, 408 4TH ST 38756 Vo Tech
  Walter Downs, prin. 686-5025
MS, 200 MILAM ST 38756 2-01100
  Abe Hudson, prin. 686-5017

Lexington, AC 601, PC 4, Holmes
Holmes County SD, PO BOX B 39095 5-11111
  Judge Nelson, supt. 834-2175
McClain HS, PO BOX 270 39095 2-00011
  Terry Howard, prin. 834-2172
Holmes County Vo-Tech Ctr Vo Tech
  PO BOX 390 39095 834-3052
  Jesse Lucas, prin.
McClain MS, PO BOX 270 39095 3-01100
  Larry Williams, prin. 834-2709
Other Schools – See Durant, Tchula

Central Holmes Academy 2-11111
  PO BOX J 39095 834-3011
  Phillip Chisholm, prin.

Liberty, AC 601, PC 3, Amite
Amite County SD, PO BOX 378 39645 3-11111
  Curtis Bishop, supt. 657-4361
Amite County JSHS 2-00011
  PO BOX 328 39645 657-8920
  W. L. Tobias, prin.
Amite County Vo Complex Vo Tech
  PO BOX 770 39645 657-8081
  Lloyd King, prin.

Amite HS, PO BOX 354 39645 2-11111
  Brent Caston, prin. 657-8896

Long Beach, AC 601, PC 7, Harrison
Long Beach SSD 4-11111
  111 QUARLES ST 39560 864-1146
  Bobby Jones, supt.
HS, 300 E OLD PASS RD 39560 3-00011
  Marlin Ladner, prin. 863-6945
MS, 204 N CLEVELAND AVE 39560 3-00100
  Bill Moore, prin. 864-3370

University of Southern Mississippi 2-UC
  EAST BEACH BLVD 39560

Lorman, AC 601, PC 3, Jefferson

Alcorn State University 5-UC
  PO BOX 359 39096 877-6147

Louisville, AC 601, PC 6, Winston
Louisville Municipal SD 5-11111
  PO BOX 909 39339 773-3411
  T. Fred Perkins, supt.
HS, 200 IVY AVE 39339 3-00011
  Jackie Wofford, prin. 773-3431
Waiya S, RR 7 BOX 233 39339 2-11111
  James Gregory, prin. 773-6770
Louisville Vo Complex Vo Tech
  204 IVY AVE 39339 – Jerry Webb, prin. 773-6152
Eiland MS, 508 CAMILE AVE 39339 3-01100
  Joe Wylie, prin. 773-9001
Other Schools – See Noxapater

Winston Academy 2-11111
  PO BOX 545 39339 773-3569
  Farrel Rigby, prin.

Lucedale, AC 601, PC 5, George
George County SD, 100 E MAIN ST 39452 5-11111
  Timothy Havard, supt. 947-6993
George County HS 4-00011
  500 W CHURCH ST 39452 947-3116
  Robert Walker, prin.
MS, 709 MABLE ST 39452 2-00100
  Kaye Brown, prin. 947-3106

Lumberton, AC 601, PC 4, Lamar
Lumberton SD, PO BOX 551 39455 3-11111
  Carl Hancock, supt. 796-2441
JSHS, PO BOX 551 39455 2-00111
  Allen Stevens, prin. 796-2451

Bass Memorial Academy 2-00011
  11 MARANATHA CIR 39455 794-8561
  Tui Pitman, prin.

Maben, AC 601, PC 3, Oktibbeha
Oktibbeha County SD
  Supt. — See Starkville
JSHS, PO BOX 506 39750 2-00111
  Charles Davis, prin. 263-8106

Webster County SD
  Supt. — See Walthall
East Webster JSHS 2-00111
  RR 2 BOX 468 39750 263-5321
  Eddie Woodruff, prin.

Mc Adams, AC 601, PC 2, Attala
Attala County SD
  Supt. — See Kosciusko
JSHS, PO BOX 127 39107 2-00111
  Jerry Redmond, prin. 289-3838

Mc Comb, AC 601, PC 7, Pike
McComb SD, PO BOX 868 39648 5-11111
  Leslie Daniels, supt. 684-4661
HS, 310 7TH ST 39648 3-00011
  Stephen Handley, prin. 684-5678
Mc Comb Vo Ctr Vo Tech
  1003 VIRGINIA AVE 39648 684-5288
  James Morris, prin.
Denman JHS 3-00100
  1211 LOUISIANA AVE 39648 684-2387
  S. Lucas, prin.

Parklane Academy 3-11111
  1115 PARKLANE DR 39648 684-7841
  William Swindle, prin.

Mc Neill, AC 601, PC 3, Pearl River
Pearl River County SD
  Supt. — See Carriere
Pearl River Central MS 3-01100
  PO BOX 430 39457 798-5654
  Larry Carroll, prin.

Macon, AC 601, PC 4, Noxubee
Noxubee County SD 4-11111
  PO BOX 540 39341 726-4527
  Albert Williams, supt.
Noxubee County HS 3-00011
  PO BOX 490 39341 726-4428
  Anderson Liddell, prin.
Noxubee County Vo Ctr Vo Tech
  PO BOX 387 39341 726-4225
  Felix Russ, prin.
Liddell MS, PO BOX 229 39341 3-01100
  Velma Jenkins, prin. 726-4880

Central Academy, PO BOX 231 39341 2-11111
  Travis Higginbotham, prin. 726-4817

Madden, AC 601, PC 2, Leake

Leake Academy, PO BOX 128 39109 2-11111
  Pete Lewis, prin. 267-4461

Madison, AC 601, PC 6, Madison
Madison County SD
  Supt. — See Canton
Madison Central HS 3-00011
  PO BOX 39 39130 856-7121
  Carl Lucas, prin.
Scott MS, PO BOX 339 39130 4-00100
  Mike Kent, prin. 856-6157

Madison-Ridgeland Academy 3-11111
  400 N OLD CANTON RD 39110 856-4455
  Donald Richardson, prin.

Magee, AC 601, PC 5, Simpson
Simpson County SD
  Supt. — See Mendenhall
HS, 501 E CHOCTAW ST 39111 3-00011
  John Moore, prin. 849-2263
JHS, 201 1ST ST NE 39111 3-01100
  Ernest Jaynes, prin. 849-3334

Magnolia, AC 601, PC 4, Pike
South Pike SD, 250 W BAY ST 39652 5-11111
  Lauren Lanier, supt. 783-3742
South Pike HS, 205 W MYRTLE ST 39652 3-00011
  Willie Jones, prin. 783-2312
South Pike Vo Ctr, 252 W BAY ST 39652 Vo Tech
  Bill Catchings, prin. 783-5832
South Pike MS 3-00100
  1147 N CLARK AVE 39652 783-2383
  E. Randall, prin.

Mantachie, AC 601, PC 3, Itawamba
Itawamba County SD
  Supt. — See Fulton
Mantachie S, PO BOX 38 38855 3-11111
  Ronnie Hill, prin. 282-4276

Marks, AC 601, PC 4, Quitman
Quitman County SD, PO BOX E 38646 4-11111
  S. Wright, supt. 326-5451
Quitman County HS 3-00011
  PO BOX 350 38646 326-5191
  Charles Barron, prin.
Quitman County Vo Complex Vo Tech
  PO BOX 117 38646 326-8427
  Ned Gathwright, prin.

Delta Academy, PO BOX 70 38646 2-11111
  Jim Isbell, prin. 326-8164

Mathiston, AC 601, PC 3, Webster

Wood College 2-CC
  PO BOX 289 39752 263-5352

Meadville, AC 601, PC 2, Franklin
Franklin County SD 4-11111
  PO BOX 605 39653 384-2340
  Larry Jones, supt.
Frankin HS, PO BOX 666 39653 2-00011
  James Hutto, prin. 384-2965
Franklin County Vo-Tech Ctr Vo Tech
  PO BOX 155 39653 384-5889
  MICHAEL LOFTON, prin.
Franklin JHS, PO BOX 643 39653 2-00100
  Lona Thomas, prin. 384-2441

Mendenhall, AC 601, PC 4, Simpson
Simpson County SD 5-11111
  101 COURT ST 39114 847-1562
  Troy Greer, supt.
HS, PO BOX 218 39114 3-00011
  Jack McAlpin, prin. 847-2411
Simpson County Vo-Tech Complex Vo Tech
  RR 1 BOX 1A1 39114 847-4000
  Sidney Lee, prin.
JHS, PO BOX 309 39114 3-00100
  John Hardy, prin. 847-2296
Other Schools – See Magee

Simpson County Academy — 2-11111
RR 4 BOX 334A 39114 — 847-1394
Wade Gaston, prin.

Meridian, AC 601, PC 8, Lauderdale
Lauderdale County SD — 6-11111
PO BOX 5498 39302 — 693-1683
David Everett, supt.
Northeast Lauderdale JSHS — 3-00111
RR 8 BOX 75 39305 — 679-8523
Roger Wright, prin.
Clarkdale S, RR 1 BOX 417 39301 — 3-11111
Charles Easom, prin. — 693-4463
Southeast S, RR 7 BOX 477 39301 — 2-11111
Algie Davis, prin. — 483-5501
Southeast JHS, RR 6 BOX 2B 39301 — 2-00100
Jerry Coleman, prin. — 485-5751
Northeast MS — 1-00100
7763 HIGHWAY 39 39305 — 483-3532
Richard Kelly, prin.
Other Schools – See Collinsville

Meridian SD, PO BOX 31 39302 — 6-11111
Larry Drawdy, supt. — 483-6271
SHS, 2320 32ND ST 39305 — 4-00001
Robert Turnage, prin. — 482-3191
Collins Vo Ctr, 2640 24TH AVE 39305 — Vo Tech
Archie Scarbrough, prin. — 483-3331
Griffin JHS, 2814 DAVIS ST 39301 — 2-00110
Martha Walker, prin. — 484-4073
Northwest JHS, 4400 32ND ST 39307 — 3-00110
Wade Shirley, prin. — 484-4094

Meridian Community College — 4-CC
910 HIGHWAY 19 N 39307 — 483-8241
Moore Career College — 2-CS
1500 HIGHWAY 19 N 39307 — 693-2900

Mississippi State, AC 601, PC 7, Oktibbeha

Mississippi State University — 7-UC
PO BOX J 39762 — 325-2224

Mize, AC 601, PC 2, Smith
Smith County SD
Supt. — See Raleigh
S, PO BOX 187 39116 — 3-11111
Ramon Johnston, prin. — 733-2242

Monticello, AC 601, PC 4, Lawrence
Lawrence County SD — 5-11111
PO BOX 338 39654 — 587-2506
John Bull, supt.
Lawrence County HS — 3-00011
PO BOX 488 39654 — 587-4910
Raymond Reddick, prin.
Vo-Tech Ctr, PO BOX 578 39654 — Vo Tech
John Rowley, prin. — 587-9346
JHS, PO BOX 489 39654 — 3-01100
David Collins, prin. — 587-2128

Mooreville, AC 601, PC 2, Lee
Lee County SD
Supt. — See Tupelo
S, RR 1 38857 — 4-11111
John Dye, prin. — 842-6859

Moorhead, AC 601, PC 4, Sunflower
Sunflower County SD
Supt. — See Indianola
MS, 908 WASHINGTON ST 38761 — 2-00100
Earnest Brown, prin. — 246-5680

Mississippi Delta Community College — 5-CC
PO BOX 668 38761 — 246-5631

Morton, AC 601, PC 5, Scott
Scott County SD
Supt. — See Forest
HS, 351 S FOURTH ST 39117 — 2-00011
James Caldwell, prin. — 732-6210
JHS, 121 HILLSBORO RD 39117 — 3-00100
Percy Parker, prin. — 732-6977

Moss Point, AC 601, PC 7, Jackson
Moss Point SSD, 4924 CHURCH ST 39563 — 6-11111
C. Cronin, supt. — 475-1533
SHS, 4913 WEEMS ST 39563 — 3-00001
Auwilda Polk, prin. — 475-5721
Moss Point Vo Ctr — Vo Tech
4924 CHURCH ST 39563 — 474-1455
Andrew Ellis, prin.
Magnolia JHS — 3-00110
4630 MAGNOLIA ST 39563 — 475-1429
Richard Niles, prin.
Mayo JHS — 3-00110
3416 ORANGE GROVE RD 39563 — 475-0367
Mary Holbert, prin.

Mound Bayou, AC 601, PC 4, Bolivar
Mound Bayou SD, PO BOX 901 38762 — 4-11111
William Crockett, supt. — 741-2555
Kennedy Memorial JSHS — 3-00111
PO BOX 901 38762 — 741-2510
Eltea Lambert, prin.

Mount Olive, AC 601, PC 3, Covington
Covington County SD
Supt. — See Collins
Mt. Olive S, PO BOX 309 39119 — 3-11111
Don McLeod, prin. — 797-3939

Mount Pleasant, AC 601, PC 2, Marshall

Mt. Pleasant Christian Academy — 2-11111
ACADEMY DR 38649 — 851-7271
Daniel Ray, prin.

Myrtle, AC 601, PC 2, Union
Union County SD
Supt. — See New Albany
Myrtle S, PO BOX 40 38650 — 3-11111
Paul Nolan, prin. — 988-2416
West Union S, RR 1 BOX 149 38650 — 3-11111
Ronald Scott, prin. — 534-4982

Natchez, AC 601, PC 7, Adams
Natchez-Adams SD — 6-11111
PO BOX 1188 39121 — 445-2800
William Hoskins, supt.
SHS, 319 SGT PRENTISS DR 39120 — 4-00001
Robert Barrett, prin. — 445-2863
Natchez-Adams Vo S — Vo Tech
208 LYNDA LEE DR 39120 — 445-2902
Jack Lann, prin.
Central JHS, 208 LYNDA LEE DR 39120 — 2-00110
Millicent Mayo, prin. — 445-2941
MS, 100 PINE RIDGE RD 39120 — 2-00100
H. W. Barnett, prin. — 445-2926

Adams County Christian S — 3-11111
300 CHINQUAPIN DR 39120 — 442-1422
Michael Nutt, prin.
Cathedral Unit S — 3-11111
701 MRTIN LUTHER KING JR ST 39120
Jules Michel, prin. — 442-1988
Trinity Episcopal Day S — 2-11111
RR 1 BOX 482 39120 — 442-5424
Robert Owens, prin.

Nettleton, AC 601, PC 4, Monroe
Nettleton SD, PO BOX 409 38858 — 4-11111
Larry Williams, supt. — 963-2151
HS, PO BOX 409 38858 — 2-00011
James Malone, prin. — 963-2306
JHS, PO BOX 409 38858 — 2-00100
Cornelious Armstrong, prin. — 963-2360

New Albany, AC 601, PC 6, Union
New Albany SSD, PO BOX 771 38652 — 4-11111
Kenneth Quinn, supt. — 534-1800
Daniel HS, PO BOX 771 38652 — 3-00011
Jerry Harmon, prin. — 534-1805
New Albany Vo Complex — Vo Tech
PO BOX 771 38652 — 534-1810
Jackie Ford, prin.
MS, 400 APPLE ST 38652 — 3-01100
Wade Ivy, prin. — 534-1820

Union County SD, PO BOX 939 38652 — 4-11111
Harry Adair, supt. — 534-1960
Ingomar S, RR 1 BOX 213A 38652 — 3-11111
John Weeden, prin. — 534-5463
Other Schools – See Blue Springs, Myrtle

New Augusta, AC 601, PC 3, Perry
Perry County SD, PO BOX 137 39462 — 4-11111
Joel Powell, supt. — 964-3211
Perry Central HS, PO BOX 139 39462 — 3-00011
Steve Trammell, prin. — 964-3235
Perry Co Vo Tech Center — Vo Tech
PO BOX 138 39462 — 964-8282
Rex Buckhaults, prin.

New Site, AC 601, PC 2, Prentiss
Prentiss County SD
Supt. — See Booneville
HS, RR 1 BOX 19 38859 — 2-00011
R. Thompson, prin. — 728-5205

Newton, AC 601, PC 5, Newton
Newton Municipal SD — 4-11111
PO BOX 150 39345 — 683-2451
James Nelson, supt.
HS, 201 W FIRST ST 39345 — 3-00001
Charles Beasley, prin. — 683-2232
Newton Vo Tech Ctr — Vo Tech
531 E CHURCH ST 39345 — 683-6338
Lynn Wagner, prin.
MS, 531 E CHURCH ST 39345 — 2-00100
F. Kirby, prin. — 683-3926

North Carrollton, AC 601, PC 3, Carroll
Carroll County SD
Supt. — See Carrollton
George JSHS, PO BOX 398 38947 — 2-00111
Douglas McAdams, prin. — 237-4701

Noxapater, AC 601, PC 2, Winston
Louisville Municipal SD
Supt. — See Louisville
S, 220 W ALICE ST 39346 — 3-11111
Clyde Lindley, prin. — 724-4241

Ocean Springs, AC 601, PC 7, Jackson
Jackson County SD
Supt. — See Vancleave
St. Martin SHS — 2-00001
10800 YELLOW JACKET BLVD 39564 — 875-8418
Jimmy Hodges, prin.

Ocean Springs SSD — 5-11111
PO BOX 7002 39566 — 875-7706
Dewey Herring, supt.
SHS, 406 HOLCOMB BLVD 39564 — 3-00001
Stan Partridge, prin. — 875-2872
Keys Vo Center, PO BOX 7002 39566 — Vo Tech
Dennis Illich, prin. — 872-3411

JHS, 2320 GOVERNMENT ST 39564 — 3-00110
Donald Fairley, prin. — 875-0333

Okolona, AC 601, PC 5, Chickasaw
Okolona SSD, PO BOX 510 38860 — 4-11111
Jim McCalla, supt. — 447-2353
JSHS, 404 W WINTER ST 38860 — 3-00111
Joseph Fields, prin. — 447-2362
Okolona Vo-Tech Ctr — Vo Tech
HWY 45 NORTH 38860 — 447-3331
Harold Arrington, prin.

Olive Branch, AC 601, PC 5, De Soto
DeSoto County SD
Supt. — See Hernando
HS, 6530 BLOCKER ST 38654 — 3-00011
Charles Garrett, prin. — 895-4600
MS, 8631 PIGEON ROOST RD 38654 — 3-01100
Kenneth Reid, prin. — 895-4610

Southern Baptist Education Ctr — 3-11111
7400 GETWELL RD 38654 — 349-3096
David Manley, prin.

Oxford, AC 601, PC 6, Lafayette
Lafayette County SD — 4-11111
PO BOX 110 38655 — 234-3271
J. Nelson, supt.
Lafayette JSHS, RR 5 38655 — 3-00111
W. Bigham, prin. — 234-3614

Oxford SD, 224 BRAMLETT BLVD 38655 — 5-11111
Bob McCord, supt. — 234-3541
HS, 222 BRAMLETT BLVD 38655 — 3-00011
David Sullivan, prin. — 234-1562
Oxford/Lafayette County Vo-Tech Ctr — Vo Tech
1904 HIGHWAY 7 S 38655 — 234-9469
Jim Treloar, prin.
JHS, 409 WASHINGTON AVE 38655 — 3-00100
Bob King, prin. — 234-2288

Pascagoula, AC 601, PC 8, Jackson
Pascagoula SSD, PO BOX 250 39568 — 6-11111
George Ayers, supt. — 938-6495
SHS, 2903 PASCAGOULA ST 39567 — 4-00001
James Harrison, prin. — 938-6443
Pascagoula Vo Complex — Vo Tech
2602 MARKET ST 39567 — 938-6579
Paul Johnson, prin.
HS Annex, 1520 TUCKER AVE 39567 — 3-00010
Elbert Vaughn, prin. — 938-6435
Colmer JHS, 3112 EDEN ST 39581 — 3-00110
Alan Curry, prin. — 938-6473
JHS, 2234 PASCAGOULA ST 39567 — 3-00110
James Baker, prin. — 938-6565
Other Schools – See Gautier

Resurrection Catholic HS — 2-00111
PO BOX 1267 39568 — 762-3353
Sr. Richard Burke, prin.

Pass Christian, AC 601, PC 6, Harrison
Pass Christian SD — 4-11111
701 W NORTH ST 39571 — 452-7271
Phillip Terrell, supt.
HS, 270 W 2ND ST 39571 — 2-00011
A. Swanier, prin. — 452-2008
MS, 315 CLARK AVE 39571 — 2-01100
Glen East, prin. — 452-4653

Coast Episcopal HS, PO BOX N 39571 — 2-00111
Susan Dockens, prin. — 452-9442

Pearl, AC 601, PC 7, Rankin
Pearl SD, PO BOX 5750 39288 — 5-11111
William Dodson, supt. — 932-7916
HS, PO BOX 5750 39288 — 4-00011
John MacCurlee, prin. — 932-7931
JHS, PO BOX 5750 39288 — 3-00100
Keith Crumpton, prin. — 932-7952

Pelahatchie, AC 601, PC 4, Rankin
Rankin County SD
Supt. — See Brandon
JSHS, PO BOX 569 39145 — 3-01111
Tom Henry, prin. — 854-8019

East Rankin Academy — 2-11111
PO BOX 509 39145 — 854-5691
Robert Gates, prin.

Perkinston, AC 601, PC 3, Stone

Mississippi Gulf Coast Community College — 6-CC
PO BOX 67 39573 — 928-5211

Petal, AC 601, PC 6, Forrest
Petal SSD, PO BOX 523 39465 — 5-11111
William Lewis, supt. — 545-3002
HS, 1145 HIGHWAY 42 39465 — 3-00011
Tom Clark, prin. — 583-3538
MS, CENTRAL AVE 39465 — 3-00100
Jerry Shepherd, prin. — 584-6301

Pheba, AC 601, PC 2, Clay
Clay County SD
Supt. — See West Point
West Clay County JSHS — 2-00111
RR 1 BOX 342 39755 — 494-4571
Gwendolyn Roberts, prin.

Philadelphia, AC 601, PC 6, Neshoba
Mississippi Band of Choctaw Indians — 3-11111
PO BOX 6085 39350 — 656-5251
Willa Brantley, supt.

Choctaw Central HS 2-00011
RR 7 BOX 72 39350 656-8990
James Pair, prin.
Neshoba County SD 4-11111
PO BOX 338 39350 656-3752
V. Manning, supt.
Neshoba Central JSHS 4-00111
1125 GOLF COURSE RD 39350 656-3391
Jerry Brantley, prin.

Philadelphia SD, 248 BYRD AVE 39350 4-11111
Rhonda Partridge, supt. 656-2955
JSHS, 248 BYRD AVE 39350 2-00111
Joe Wood, prin. 656-2672
Philadelphia Neshoba Vo-Tech Ctr Vo Tech
900 VALLEY VIEW DR 39350 656-8544
Harry Carter, prin.

Picayune, AC 601, PC 7, Pearl River
Picayune SD 5-11111
706 GOODYEAR BLVD 39466 798-3230
Richard McClements, supt.
Picayune Memorial HS 4-00011
800 5TH AVE 39466 798-1380
James Finley, prin.
Vo-Tech Ctr Vo Tech
600 GOODYEAR BLVD 39466 798-7601
CARL WILLIS, prin.
JHS, 702 GOODYEAR BLVD 39466 3-00100
Jack Rivers, prin. 798-5449

Piney Woods, AC 601, PC 2, Rankin

Piney Woods S 2-11111
PO BOX 99 39148
Earnest Ward, prin.

Pittsboro, AC 601, PC 2, Calhoun
Calhoun County SD 5-11111
PO BOX 58 38951 983-3152
DeWitt Spencer, supt.
Other Schools – See Bruce, Calhoun City, Vardaman

Pontotoc, AC 601, PC 5, Pontotoc
Pontotoc County SD 5-11111
285 HIGHWAY 15 S 38863 489-3932
Jerry Horton, supt.
South Pontotoc S, RR 5 38863 4-11111
Gerald Hegan, prin. 489-5925
Pontotoc Vo Complex Vo Tech
354 CENTER RIDGE DR 38863 489-1826
Phil Ryan, prin.
Other Schools – See Ecru

Pontotoc CSD, 132 N MAIN ST 38863 4-11111
Charles Harrison, supt. 489-3336
HS, 132 N MAIN ST 38863 2-00011
Sam Dowdy, prin. 489-1275
JHS, 132 N MAIN ST 38863 2-00100
Conwell Duke, prin. 489-8360

Poplarville, AC 601, PC 5, Pearl River
Poplarville SSD, 804 S JULIA ST 39470 4-11111
Larry Tynes, supt. 795-8477
JSHS, 1301 S MAIN ST 39470 3-00111
Louise Smith, prin. 795-8424
Poplarville Vo-Tech Ctr Vo Tech
1301 S MAIN ST 39470 795-8343
J. Stringfellow, prin.

Pearl River Community College 5-CC
STATION A 39470 795-6801

Port Gibson, AC 601, PC 4, Claiborne
Claiborne County SD 4-11111
PO BOX 337 39150 437-4232
F. White, supt.
HS, PO BOX 397 39150 2-00011
Shirley Reeves, prin. 437-4190
Clairborne County Vo-Tech Vo Tech
PO BOX 337 39150 437-4232
Steven Bailey, prin.
MS, 161 RAMSEY DR 39150 3-00100
Elijah Brown, prin. 437-4251

Chamberlain-Hunt Academy 2-01111
124 MCCOMB AVE 39150 437-4291
James Eidt, prin.

Potts Camp, AC 601, PC 2, Marshall
Marshall County SD
Supt. — See Holly Springs
JSHS, PO BOX 697 38659 3-01111
John Eaton, prin. 333-6354

Prentiss, AC 601, PC 4, Jefferson Davis
Jefferson Davis County SD 5-11111
PO BOX 1197 39474 792-4267
Marion Fortenberry, supt.
JSHS, PO BOX 1168 39474 3-00111
James Wiginton, prin. 792-4646
Other Schools – See Bassfield, Carson

Prentiss Christian HS 2-11111
PO BOX 1287 39474 792-8549
Jack Bailey, prin.

Puckett, AC 601, PC 2, Rankin
Rankin County SD
Supt. — See Brandon
Puckett S, PO BOX 40 39151 3-11111
Thad Haskin, prin. 825-5742

Purvis, AC 601, PC 4, Lamar
Lamar County SD, PO BOX 609 39475 6-11111
Emil Pav, supt. 794-1030

S, SCHOOL ST 39475 3-11111
Glenn Swan, prin. 794-2708
Other Schools – See Hattiesburg, Sumrall

Quitman, AC 601, PC 5, Clarke
Quitman SD, 312 E FRANKLIN ST 39355 5-11111
David Meadows, supt. 776-2186
Quitman District HS 3-00011
210 N JACKSON AVE 39355 776-3341
James Morgan, prin.
Clarke County Vo Ctr Vo Tech
HIGHWAY 45 N 39355 776-5219
CHARLES SHEPHERD JR, prin.
Quitman District JHS 3-00100
SHIRLEY DRIVE 39355 776-6243
Charles McClure, prin.

Raleigh, AC 601, PC 4, Smith
Smith County SD, PO BOX 308 39153 5-11111
C. Boyles, supt. 782-4296
JSHS, PO BOX 188 39153 2-01111
Harold Morris, prin. 782-4261
Smith County Vo Complex Vo Tech
PO BOX 37 39153 – Dan King, prin. 782-4211
Other Schools – See Mize, Taylorsville

Raymond, AC 601, PC 4, Hinds
Hinds County SD, PO BOX 100 39154 6-11111
Leslie Johnson, supt. 857-5222
HS, PO BOX E 39154 2-00011
Booker Ducksworth, prin. 857-8016
Hinds County Vo-Tech Complex Vo Tech
PO BOX 390 39154 857-5536
Eugene Brown, prin.
Other Schools – See Jackson, Utica

Central Hinds Academy 2-11111
RR 2 BOX 211 39154 857-5568
C. Bryant, prin.
Hinds Community College 39154 6-CC
857-5261

Richland, AC 601, PC 5, Rankin
Rankin County SD
Supt. — See Brandon
JSHS, 1202 HIGHWAY 49 S 39218 3-00111
Robert Luckett, prin. 939-9381

Richton, AC 601, PC 4, Perry
Richton SD, PO BOX 568 39476 4-11111
Bobby DePoyster, supt. 788-6581
JSHS, PO BOX 568 39476 2-00111
Thomas Blackledge, prin. 788-9608

Ripley, AC 601, PC 6, Tippah
South Tippah SD, PO BOX 439 38663 5-11111
Larry Robbins, supt. 837-7156
HS, 720 S CLAYTON ST 38663 2-00011
Gary King, prin. 837-7583
Pine Grove S 2-11111
3510A COUNTY ROAD 600 38663 837-7789
William Witt, prin.
N/S Tippah County Vo-Tech Ctr Vo Tech
PO BOX 533 38663 837-9798
Howard Newby, prin.
MS, 720 S CLAYTON ST 38663 3-01100
Troy Holliday, prin. 837-7959
Other Schools – See Blue Mountain

Rolling Fork, AC 601, PC 4, Sharkey
South Delta SD 4-11111
600 PARKWAY AVE 39159 873-4302
Ryan Grayson, supt.
JSHS, 600 PARKWAY AVE 39159 3-00111
Peter Jackson, prin. 873-4308
Sharkey-Issaquena Vo Complex Vo Tech
600 PARKWAY AVE 39159 873-2029
James Tankson, prin.
Other Schools – See Anguilla

Sharkey Issaquena Academy 2-11111
PO BOX 248 39159 873-4241
T. Woods, prin.

Rosedale, AC 601, PC 5, Bolivar
West Bolivar SD, PO BOX 189 38769 4-11111
Jordan Goins, supt. 759-3525
West Bolivar HS, PO BOX 398 38769 2-00011
Robert Jennings, prin. 759-3346
Barnes Vo Ctr, PO BOX 160 38769 Vo Tech
Kenneth Roberts, prin. 759-3791
West Bolivar MS, PO BOX 159 38769 2-01100
James Wilson, prin. 759-3743

Ruleville, AC 601, PC 5, Sunflower
Sunflower County SD
Supt. — See Indianola
Ruleville Central HS 4-00011
360 DIVISION AVE 38771 756-4757
Thomas Edwards, prin.
MS, PO BOX 66 38771 2-00100
Willie McDaniel, prin. 756-4698

Saltillo, AC 601, PC 4, Lee
Lee County SD
Supt. — See Tupelo
Saltillo S, PO BOX 460 38866 4-11011
Johnny Green, prin. 869-5466

Sandhill, AC 601, PC 2, Rankin
Rankin County SD
Supt. — See Brandon
Pisgah JSHS, PO BOX 70 39161 2-01111
Harlan Stanley, prin. 829-2825

Sardis, AC 601, PC 4, Panola
North Panola Consolidated SD 4-11111
PO BOX 334 38666 487-2305
James Harris, supt.
North Panola HS, PO BOX 278 38666 3-00011
Richard Palmer, prin. 487-1070
Other Schools – See Como

Scooba, AC 601, PC 3, Kemper

East Mississippi Community College 3-CC
PO BOX 158 39358 476-8442

Sebastopol, AC 601, PC 2, Scott
Scott County SD
Supt. — See Forest
Sebastopol S, PO BOX 86 39359 3-11111
J. Edwards, prin. 625-8654

Seminary, AC 601, PC 2, Covington
Covington County SD
Supt. — See Collins
S, PO BOX 34 39479 3-11111
Billy Smith, prin. 722-3220

Senatobia, AC 601, PC 5, Tate
Senatobia Municipal SD 4-11111
304 W TATE ST 38668 562-4897
Michael Waldrop, supt.
JSHS, 102 W PORTER ST 38668 3-00111
Larry Skelton, prin. 562-4230

Tate County SD, 304 W TATE ST 38668 5-11111
Greg Freeman, supt. 562-5861
Other Schools – See Coldwater, Independence

Magnolia Heights S 2-11111
1201 S PANOLA ST 38668 562-4491
Marvin Lishman, prin.
Northwest Mississippi Community College 5-CC
510 N PANOLA ST 38668 562-3200

Shannon, AC 601, PC 4, Lee
Lee County SD
Supt. — See Tupelo
JSHS, PO BOX 468 38868 3-00111
Lynn Lindsey, prin. 767-9566

Shaw, AC 601, PC 4, Bolivar
Shaw SD, PO BOX 510 38773 3-11111
Rueben Watson, supt. 754-2611
JSHS, PO BOX 510 38773 2-00111
Norman Burke, prin. 754-4181

Shelby, AC 601, PC 5, Bolivar
North Bolivar SD, PO BOX 28 38774 4-11111
Arthur Cartlidge, supt. 398-7832
Broad Street JSHS 2-00111
PO BOX 149 38774 398-7003
Maurice Smith, prin.

Smithville, AC 601, PC 3, Monroe
Monroe County SD
Supt. — See Aberdeen
S, PO BOX 149 38870 3-11111
William Stevens, prin. 651-4276

Southaven, AC 601, PC 7, De Soto
DeSoto County SD
Supt. — See Hernando
JSHS, 899 RASCO RD W 38671 4-00111
J. Baird, prin. 393-9300
DeSoto Vo-Tech Ctr Vo Tech
847 RASCO RD W 38671 393-9300
John Kelly, prin.

Northwest Mississippi Community College 2-CC
DESOTO CENTER 38671 342-1570

Star, AC 601, PC 3, Rankin

Rankin Academy, PO BOX 99 39167 2-11111
J. Neeley, prin. 845-6790

Starkville, AC 601, PC 7, Oktibbeha
Oktibbeha County SD 4-11111
105 N WASHINGTON ST 39759 323-1472
Walter Conley, supt.
Alexander S, RR 6 BOX 118 39759 2-11111
Junior Burkes, prin. 323-1462
Other Schools – See Crawford, Maben, Sturgis

Starkville SD 5-11111
401 GREENSBORO ST 39759 324-4050
Larry Box, supt.
HS, 801 HIGHWAY 25 S 39759 4-00011
Stan Miller, prin. 324-4130
Millsaps Vo Ctr, HIGHWAY 25 S 39759 Vo Tech
James Stidham, prin. 324-4170
Armstrong JHS, 303 MCKEE ST 39759 3-00100
Glenn McGee, prin. 324-4070

Starkville Academy 2-11111
505 ACADEMY RD 39759 323-7814
J. Logan, prin.

Stringer, AC 601, PC 2, Jasper
West Jasper Consolidated SD
Supt. — See Bay Springs
S, PO BOX 68 39481 3-11111
Gregory Dearman, prin. 428-5508

Sturgis, AC 601, PC 2, Oktibbeha
Oktibbeha County SD
Supt. — See Starkville
Sturgis S, RR 1 BOX 257 39769 2-11111
Ronnie Ware, prin. 465-7956

Summit, AC 601, PC 4, Pike
North Pike SD, RR 4 BOX 11AA 39666 — 4-11111 / 276-2216
  James Jones, supt.
North Pike HS, RR 4 BOX 11AA 39666 — 2-00011 / 276-2175
  Donald Magee, prin.
North Pike MS, RR 1 BOX 125 39666 — 2-00100 / 684-3283
  Lee Brewer, prin.

Southwest Mississippi Community College — 4-CC
39666 — 276-2001

Sumner, AC 601, PC 2, Tallahatchie
West Tallahatchie Consolidated SD
  Supt. — See Webb
West District MS, PO BOX 188 38957 — 3-01100 / 375-8304
  Ruth Lewis, prin.

Sumrall, AC 601, PC 3, Lamar
Lamar County SD
  Supt. — See Purvis
HS, PO BOX 187 39482 — 2-00011 / 758-4730
  Keith Waters, prin.

Taylorsville, AC 601, PC 4, Smith
Smith County SD
  Supt. — See Raleigh
S, PO BOX 8 39168 — 2-11111 / 785-6942
  Rex Keeton, prin.

Tchula, AC 601, PC 4, Holmes
Holmes County SD
  Supt. — See Lexington
Marshall JSHS, PO BOX H 39169 — 3-00011 / 235-5113
  Percy Washington, prin.

Tiplersville, AC 601, PC 2, Tippah
North Tippah SD, PO BOX 65 38674 — 4-11111 / 223-4384
  Junior Wooten, supt.
Other Schools – See Falkner, Walnut

Tishomingo, AC 601, PC 2, Tishomingo
Tishomingo County Special Municipal SD
  Supt. — See Iuka
Tishomingo County Vo Complex — Vo Tech / 438-6689
  PO BOX 60 38873
  Gary Taylor, prin.

Tougaloo, AC 601, PC see Jackson

Tougaloo College — 3-UC
500 E COUNTY LINE RD 39174 — 977-7700

Tremont, AC 601, PC 2, Itawamba
Itawamba County SD
  Supt. — See Fulton
S, PO BOX 9 38876 — 2-11111 / 652-3391
  Jerry Kuykendall, prin.

Tunica, AC 601, PC 4, Tunica
Tunica County SD — 4-11111 / 363-2811
  PO BOX 758 38676
  Jerry Gentry, supt.
Rosa Fort HS, PO BOX 997 38676 — 2-00011 / 363-1343
  James Bulloch, prin.
Tunica Vo-Tech Ctr — Vo Tech / 363-2051
  PO BOX 758 38676
  David Williams, prin.
JHS, PO BOX 967 38676 — 2-00100 / 363-1749
  Earl Dishmon, prin.

Tunica Institute of Learning S — 2-11111 / 363-1051
PO BOX 966 38676
  Edward Beach, prin.

Tupelo, AC 601, PC 8, Lee
Lee County SD, PO BOX 832 38802 — 6-11111 / 841-9144
  Cecil Weeks, supt.
Other Schools – See Guntown, Mooreville, Saltillo, Shannon

Tupelo SSD, PO BOX 557 38802 — 6-11111 / 841-8850
  Mike Walters, supt.
HS, 2500 CLIFF GOOKIN BLVD 38801 — 4-00011 / 841-8970
  Dale Dobbs, prin.
Vo-Tech Ctr, 903 FILLMORE ST 38801 — Vo Tech / 841-8990
  Jimmy Young, prin.
MS, 1009 VARSITY DR 38801 — 2-00100 / 840-9580
  Jim Hall, prin.

Mississippi University for Women-Tupelo — 1-UC
655 EASON BLVD 38801 — 329-7299
Moore Career College — 2-CS
880 CLIFF GOOKIN BLVD 38801 — 371-2900
North Mississippi Medical Center — HSP
830 S GLOSTER ST 38801 — 841-3136

Tylertown, AC 601, PC 4, Walthall
Walthall County SD — 5-11111 / 876-3401
  814A MORSE AVE 39667
  Greg Ellzey, supt.
JSHS, RR 4 BOX 257 39667 — 3-00111 / 876-3370
  Richard Willoughby, prin.
Dexter S, RR 2 BOX 234 39667 — 3-11111 / 876-3985
  Paul Graves, prin.
Salem S, RR 1 BOX 163 39667 — 3-11111 / 876-2580
  Charles Boyd, prin.

Union, AC 601, PC 4, Newton
Union SSD, 208 PEACHTREE ST 39365 — 3-11111 / 774-9579
  William Wade, supt.
Union S, 101 FOREST ST 39365 — 3-11111 / 774-8257
  Don Brantley, prin.

University, AC 601, PC see Oxford

University of Mississippi 38677 — 7-UC / 232-7226

Utica, AC 601, PC 4, Hinds
Hinds County Agricultural SD — 2-00011 / 354-2327
  PO BOX 89 39175
  Clyde Muse, supt.
Hinds County Agricultural HS — 2-00011 / 885-6062
  PO BOX 89 39175
  Charles Langston, prin.

Hinds County SD
  Supt. — See Raymond
JSHS, PO BOX H 39175 — 2-00011 / 885-8714
  George Walker, prin.

Vaiden, AC 601, PC 3, Carroll
Carroll County SD
  Supt. — See Carrollton
JSHS, PO BOX 9 39176 — 2-00111 / 464-5491
  B. Ferguson, prin.

Vancleave, AC 601, PC 5, Jackson
Jackson County SD — 6-11111 / 826-1757
  12210 COLONEL VICKERY RD 39565
  William Lee, supt.
HS, PO BOX 12424 39564 — 4-00011 / 826-4701
  Charles Brown, prin.
Jackson County Vo Ctr — Vo Tech / 826-5944
  RR 4 BOX 12425 39565
  Roger Bardwell, prin.
MS, PO BOX 12424 39564 — 2-00100 / 826-5902
  Joe Hubal, prin.
Other Schools – See Biloxi, Hurley, Ocean Springs

Vardaman, AC 601, PC 3, Calhoun
Calhoun County SD
  Supt. — See Pittsboro
JSHS, PO BOX 193 38878 — 2-00111 / 682-7574
  James Casey, prin.

Vicksburg, AC 601, PC 7, Warren
Vicksburg Warren SD — 7-11111 / 638-5122
  PO BOX 820065 39182
  Charles Craft, supt.
HS, 3701 DRUMMOND ST 39180 — 3-00011 / 636-2914
  Kermit Harness, prin.
Warren Central HS — 4-00011 / 638-3372
  1000 HIGHWAY 27 39180
  Peter Pikul, prin.
Vicksburg Central JHS — 3-00100 / 636-1966
  1533 BALDWIN FERRY RD 39180
  Charles Tolliver, prin.
Warren JHS — 4-00100 / 638-3981
  1630 BALDWIN FERRY RD 39180
  Terrance Lang, prin.

All Saints Episcopal S — 2-00111 / 636-5266
  2730 CONFEDERATE AVE 39180
  David Luckett, prin.
Hinds Community College — 3-CC / 638-0600
  755 HIGHWAY 27 39180
Porters Chapel Academy — 2-11111 / 638-3733
  3460 PORTERS CHAPEL RD 39180
  Frank Lee, prin.
Vicksburg Catholic S — 3-11111 / 636-2256
  1900 GROVE ST 39180
  George Valadie, prin.

Walnut, AC 601, PC 3, Tippah
North Tippah SD
  Supt. — See Tiplersville
Walnut S, PO BOX 230 38683 — 2-11111 / 223-4032
  Troy Shaw, prin.

Walnut Grove, AC 601, PC 2, Leake
Leake County SD
  Supt. — See Carthage
South Leake JSHS — 3-00111 / 253-2393
  PO BOX 159 39189
  Samuel Hoye, prin.

Walthall, AC 601, PC 2, Webster
Webster County SD — 4-11111 / 258-5921
  PO BOX 338 39771
  Jimmy Powell, supt.
Other Schools – See Eupora, Maben

Water Valley, AC 601, PC 5, Yalobusha
Water Valley SD, PO BOX 788 38965 — 4-11111 / 473-1203
  Keny Goodwin, supt.
JSHS, PO BOX 647 38965 — 3-00111 / 473-2468
  Jerry Holt, prin.

Waveland, AC 601, PC 6, Hancock
Hancock County SD — 5-11111 / 467-4466
  450 HIGHWAY 90 39576
  Myrna Bourgeois, supt.
Other Schools – See Bay Saint Louis, Kiln

Waynesboro, AC 601, PC 6, Wayne
Wayne County SD — 5-11111 / 735-4871
  609 AZALEA DR 39367
  Stanley Brewer, supt.
Wayne County HS — 3-00011 / 735-2851
  1325 AZALEA DR 39367
  Ben Graves, prin.
Wayne County Vo Ctr — Vo Tech / 735-5036
  800 COLLINS ST 39367
  Tullus Messemore, prin.
MS, 155 WAYNE ST 39367 — 2-01100 / 735-3159
  Taylor Mayfield, prin.

Wayne Academy, PO BOX 308 39367 — 2-11111 / 735-2921
  Gerald Nobles, prin.

Webb, AC 601, PC 3, Tallahatchie
West Tallahatchie Consolidated SD — 4-11111 / 375-9291
  PO BOX 129 38966
  Cassie Pennington, supt.

West Tallahatchie JSHS — 2-00111 / 375-8829
  PO BOX 129 38966
  Otis Anthony, prin.
Other Schools – See Sumner

Weir, AC 601, PC 3, Choctaw
Choctaw County SD
  Supt. — See Ackerman
S, PO BOX 98 39772 — 3-11111 / 547-6428
  Marion Kelley, prin.

Wesson, AC 601, PC 4, Copiah
Copiah County SD
  Supt. — See Hazlehurst
S, 1048 GROVE ST 39191 — 3-11111 / 643-2221
  Rickey Clopton, prin.

Copiah-Lincoln Community College — 4-CC
PO BOX 457 39191 — 643-5101

West, AC 601, PC 2, Holmes

East Holmes Academy — 2-11111 / 967-2226
PO BOX 247 39192
  Frank Drake, prin.

West Point, AC 601, PC 6, Clay
Clay County SD, PO BOX 759 39773 — 3-11111 / 494-2915
  Mae Brewer, supt.
Other Schools – See Pheba

West Point SD, PO BOX 656 39773 — 5-11111 / 494-4242
  Thomas Lott, supt.
SHS, PO BOX 616 39773 — 3-00001 / 494-5083
  Randy Hamblin, prin.
West Point Vo Complex — Vo Tech / 494-6176
  PO BOX 1136 39773
  Eddie Odom, prin.
JHS, PO BOX 617 39773 — 3-00110 / 494-6665
  Israel Lee, prin.

Mary Holmes College — 3-CC
PO BOX 1257 39773 — 800-634-2749
Oak Hill Academy — 3-11111 / 494-5043
PO BOX 1217 39773
  Nolan Vickers, prin.

Wheeler, AC 601, PC 3, Prentiss
Prentiss County SD
  Supt. — See Booneville
S, PO BOX 98 38880 — 3-11111 / 365-2629
  Lonnie Murphy, prin.

Wiggins, AC 601, PC 5, Stone
Stone County SD, 214 N CRITZ ST 39577 — 4-11111 / 928-7247
  Henry Rath, supt.
Stone HS, 400 E BORDER AVE 39577 — 3-00011 / 928-5492
  James Webb, prin.
Stone MS, 532 E CENTRAL AVE 39577 — 3-00100 / 928-4876
  George Hancock, prin.

Winona, AC 601, PC 6, Montgomery
Montgomery County SD — 4-11111 / 283-4533
  PO BOX 687 38967
  Joe Moore, supt.
Other Schools – See Kilmichael

Winona SSD — 4-11111 / 283-3731
  214 FAIRGROUND ST 38967
  Doris Smith, supt.
JSHS, 301 FAIRGROUND ST 38967 — 2-00111 / 283-3112
  Dwight Lollar, prin.
Winona Vo Complex — Vo Tech / 283-3601
  300 N APPLEGATE ST 38967
  Bobby Trussell, prin.

Winona Academy — 2-11111 / 283-1169
RR 3 BOX 15 38967
  Timothy Williams, prin.

Woodland, AC 601, PC 2, Chickasaw

Wilkinson County Christian Academy — 2-11111 / 888-4313
P O BOX 977 39669
  Jack Withers, prin.

Woodville, AC 601, PC 4, Wilkinson
Wilkinson County SD — 4-11111 / 888-3582
  PO BOX 785 39669
  Charles Johnson, supt.
Wilkinson County JSHS — 2-00111 / 888-4228
  PO BOX 875 39669
  Estes Taplin, prin.
Wilkinson County Vo Complex — Vo Tech / 888-4394
  PO BOX 1193 39669
  Abe Fletcher, prin.

Yazoo City, AC 601, PC 7, Yazoo
Yazoo City Municipal SD — 5-11111 / 746-2125
  PO BOX 127 39194
  Arthur Cartlidge, supt.
HS — 3-00011 / 746-2378
  1825 DR MRTN LUTHER KING DR 39194
  Lea Barrett, prin.
Yazoo City Vo Complex — Vo Tech / 746-7642
  1825 DR MRTN LUTHER KING DR 39194
  Larry Summers, prin.
JHS, 516 E CANAL ST 39194 — 3-00100 / 746-3368
  Rebecca Turner, prin.

Yazoo County SD — 4-11111 / 746-4672
  PO BOX 1088 39194
  Harold Middleton, supt.
Other Schools – See Benton

Manchester Academy — 2-11111 / 746-5913
PO BOX 155 39194
  Mike Hardwick, prin.

MISSOURI

STATE DEPARTMENT OF EDUCATION
P.O. Box 480, Jefferson City 65102
(314) 751-4212

Commissioner of Education	Robert Bartman
Deputy Commissioner	Vacant
Assistant Commisioner Administration	Terrence Stewart
Assistant Commissioner Vocational & Adult Education	Frank Drake
Assistant Commissioner Instruction	Otis Baker
Assistant Commissioner Special Education	John Allan
Assistant Commissioner Urban & Teacher Education	L. Celestine Ferguson
Assistant Commissioner Vocational Rehabilitation	Don Gann

STATE BOARD OF EDUCATION
P.O. Box 480, Jefferson City 65102

President	Susan Finke

PUBLIC, PRIVATE AND CATHOLIC SECONDARY SCHOOLS

Adrian, AC 816, PC 4, Bates
Adrian RSD 3, PO BOX 98 64720 — 3-11111
Victor Kretzschmar, supt. — 297-2158
HS, PO BOX 98 64720 — 2-00011
William Gordon, prin. — 297-2158

Advance, AC 314, PC 4, Stoddard
Advance RSD 4, PO BOX 370 63730 — 3-11111
Jerry Robison, supt. — 722-3581
JSHS, PO BOX 370 63730 — 2-00111
Michael Redman, prin. — 722-3584

Albany, AC 816, PC 4, Gentry
Albany RSD 3 — 3-11111
101 W JEFFERSON ST 64402 — 726-3911
Marilou Rogers, supt.
JSHS, 101 W JEFFERSON ST 64402 — 2-00111
Michael Adkins, prin. — 726-3911

Alma, AC 816, PC 2, Lafayette
Lafayette County RSD 10 — 2-11111
PO BOX 197 64001 — 674-2236
Greg Prather, supt.
Santa Fe HS, PO BOX 197 64001 — 2-00111
Gary Littrell, prin. — 674-2236

Alton, AC 417, PC 3, Oregon
Alton RSD 4, 2180 SCHOOL ST 65606 — 3-11111
Billy Smith, supt. — 778-7215
HS, 2180 SCHOOL ST 65606 — 2-00111
Rolla Fraley, prin. — 778-7215

Amoret, AC 816, PC 2, Bates
Miami RSD 1, RR 1 64722 — 2-11111
Lonnie Clair, supt. — 267-3480
Miami JSHS, RR 1 64722 — 2-00111
Robert McLean, prin. — 267-3484

Anderson, AC 417, PC 4, McDonald
McDonald County RSD 1 — 5-11111
PO BOX 378 64831 — 845-3321
Michael Rustman, supt.
McDonald County HS — 3-00011
RR 3 BOX 373 64831 — 845-3322
Cecil Box, prin.

Annapolis, AC 314, PC 2, Iron
South Iron RSD 1, PO BOX 218 63620 — 2-11111
Douglas Funk, supt. — 598-4241
South Iron JSHS, PO BOX 218 63620 — 2-00111
James Thomas, prin. — 598-4241

Appleton City, AC 816, PC 4, St. Clair
Appleton City RSD 2 — 2-11111
PO BOX 126 64724 — 476-2161
Mike Stevenson, supt.
JSHS,.PO BOX 126 64724 — 2-00111
Dennis McCullough, prin. — 476-2118

Archie, AC 816, PC 3, Cass
Cass County RSD 5 — 2-11111
PO BOX 106 64725 — 293-5312
William Gordon, supt.
JSHS, PO BOX 106 64725 — 2-00111
Thomas Beer, prin. — 293-5312

Arnold, AC 314, PC 7, Jefferson
Fox Consolidated SD 6 — 6-11111
745 JEFFCO BLVD 63010 — 296-8000
Charles Hudson, supt.
Fox SHS, 745 JEFFCO BLVD 63010 — 4-00001
Ron Sauer, prin. — 296-5210
Fox JHS, 745 JEFFCO BLVD 63010 — 3-00110
Michael Rudanovich, prin. — 295-5077
Ridgewood JHS — 3-00110
1401 RIDGEWOOD SCHOOL RD 63010 — 282-1459
Wesley Alkire, prin.
Other Schools – See Imperial

Ash Grove, AC 417, PC 4, Greene
Ash Grove RSD 4, PO BOX 218 65604 — 3-11111
Richard Harris, supt. — 672-2534
JSHS, PO BOX 218 65604 — 2-00111
Ralph Hill, prin. — 672-2330

Ashland, AC 314, PC 4, Boone
Southern Boone County RSD 1 — 3-11111
PO BOX 168 65010 — 657-2144
Marjorie Spaedy, supt.
Southern Boone County JSHS — 2-00111
PO BOX 168 65010 — 657-2144
Mitchell Holbrook, prin.

Atlanta, AC 816, PC 2, Macon
Atlanta Consolidated SD 3 — 2-11111
PO BOX 367 63530 — 239-4212
Gary Nuhn, supt.
JSHS, PO BOX 367 63530 — 2-01111
Rex Nelson, prin. — 239-4211

Aurora, AC 417, PC 6, Lawrence
Aurora RSD 8, 409 W LOCUST ST 65605 — 4-11111
Ronald Wilken, supt. — 678-3373
HS, 101 S ROOSEVELT AVE 65605 — 3-00011
Robert Ware, prin. — 678-3355
MS, 1044 S LINCOLN AVE 65605 — 2-00100
Larry Ewing, prin. — 678-3630

Ava, AC 417, PC 5, Douglas
Ava RSD 1, PO BOX 338 65608 — 4-11111
Tom Nichols, supt. — 683-4112
HS, PO BOX 338 65608 — 3-00011
Robert Wolhaus, prin. — 683-4112
MS, PO BOX 338 65608 — 2-01100
Jesse Blevins, prin. — 683-4112

Bakersfield, AC 417, PC 2, Ozark
Bakersfield RSD 4, PO BOX 38 65609 — 2-11111
R. Pendergrass, supt. — 284-7333
HS, PO BOX 38 65609 — 2-00011
Gary Pitchford, prin. — 284-7333

Ballwin, AC 314, PC 7, St. Louis
Parkway Consolidated SD 2
Supt. — See Chesterfield
West HS, 14653 CLAYTON RD 63011 — 4-00011
James McMillan, prin. — 391-4700

Rockwood RSD 6
Supt. — See Eureka
Lafayette HS, 17050 CLAYTON RD 63011 — 4-00011
Daniel Edwards, prin. — 458-0400

Crestview JHS — 4-00100
16025 CLAYTON RD 63011 — 227-3220
William Blackburn, prin.
Selvidge JHS — 3-00100
235 NEW BALLWIN RD 63021 — 227-1320
John Maxwell, prin.

Barnard, AC 816, PC 2, Nodaway
South Nodaway County RSD 4 — 2-11111
PO BOX 7 64423 — 652-3221
Warren Denney, supt.
South Nodaway County JSHS — 1-00111
PO BOX 7 64423 – Jeff Sumy, prin. — 652-3727

Bell City, AC 314, PC 2, Stoddard
Bell City RSD 2, PO BOX 147 63735 — 2-11111
Don Abner, supt. — 733-4444
JSHS, PO BOX 147 63735 — 1-00111
Carl Ritter, prin. — 733-4444

Belle, AC 314, PC 4, Maries
Maries County RSD 2 — 3-11111
PO BOX 819 65013 — 859-3800
Gary Boggs, supt.
HS, PO BOX 819 65013 — 2-00011
Kendall Ebersold, prin. — 859-6114
Other Schools – See Bland

Belton, AC 816, PC 7, Cass
Belton SD 124 — 5-11111
110 W WALNUT ST 64012 — 348-1000
Gordon Sunderland, supt.
HS, 107 W SUNRISE DR 64012 — 4-00011
Donald St. Louis, prin. — 348-1036
Yeokum MS, 613 MILL ST 64012 — 3-00100
Tim Coleman, prin. — 348-1042

Benton, AC 314, PC 3, Scott
Scott County RSD 4 — 3-11111
PO BOX 98 63736 — 545-3887
Mike Johnson, supt.
Kelly JSHS, PO BOX 98 63736 — 2-00111
Ernie Lawson, prin. — 545-3541

Berkeley, AC 314, PC 7, St. Louis
Ferguson-Florissant RSD 2
Supt. — See Florissant
HS, 8710 WALTER AVE 63134 — 2-00011
Vernon Mitchell, prin. — 521-4897
JHS, 8300 FROST AVE 63134 — 2-00100
Terry Proffitt, prin. — 524-3883

Bernie, AC 314, PC 4, Stoddard
Bernie RSD 13, PO BOX 470 63822 — 3-11111
Phil Dawson, supt. — 293-5333
JSHS, PO BOX 470 63822 — 2-00111
James Patmore, prin. — 293-5334

Bethany, AC 816, PC 5, Harrison
South Harrison RSD 2 — 3-11111
PO BOX 445 64424 — 425-8044
Ed Musgrove, supt.
South Harrison County JSHS — 2-00111
PO BOX 445 64424 — 425-8051
Chad Elifrits, prin.
North Central Area Vo-Tech — Vo Tech
PO BOX 445 64424 – Jim Lee, prin. — 425-2196

Bevier, AC 816, PC 3, Macon
Bevier Consolidated SD 4 — 2-11111
400 BLOOMINGTON ST 63532 — 773-6611
Joan Patrick, supt.
JSHS, 400 BLOOMINGTON ST 63532 — 2-00111
Kenneth Kelso, prin. — 773-5213

Billings, AC 417, PC 3, Christian
Billings RSD 4 — 2-11111
118 W MOUNT VERNON RD 65610 — 744-2623
Ken Spurgeon, supt.
JSHS — 2-00111
118 W MOUNT VERNON RD 65610 — 744-2551
John Lacy, prin.

Bismarck, AC 314, PC 4, St. Francois
Bismarck RSD 5, PO BOX 257 63624 — 3-11111
Jerry Milligan, supt. — 734-6111
JSHS, PO BOX 257 63624 — 2-00111
Donald Francis, prin. — 734-6111

Bland, AC 314, PC 3, Gasconade
Maries County RSD 2
Supt. — See Belle
Maries County MS, 300 S MAIN 65014 — 2-00100
Dwane Smith, prin. — 646-3912

Bloomfield, AC 314, PC 4, Stoddard
Bloomfield RSD 14, PO BOX R 63825 — 3-11111
Robert Noyes, supt. — 568-4564
HS, PO BOX R 63825 — 2-00011
Charles Myers, prin. — 568-2146

Blue Eye, AC 417, PC 2, Stone
Blue Eye RSD 5, PO BOX 38 65611 — 3-11111
William Wheeler, supt. — 779-5331
JSHS, PO BOX 38 65611 — 2-00111
Joe Kilgore, prin. — 779-5331

Blue Springs, AC 816, PC 8, Jackson
Blue Springs RSD 4 — 7-11111
1801 W VESPER ST 64015 — 224-1300
Charles McGraw, supt.
HS, 2000 ASHTON DR 64015 — 4-00011
Ted Lewman, prin. — 229-3459
Blue Springs South HS — 4-00011
1200 TAYLOR RD 64014 — 224-1315
Dennis Littrell, prin.
Georgeff-Baker JHS — 3-00100
2103 W VESPER ST 64015 — 224-1325
Don Gray, prin.
Hall-McCarter JHS — 3-00100
1609 W VALLEYVIEW RD 64015 — 224-1330
Gene Vinson, prin.

Eastern Jackson Co. Coll./Allied Health — 2-CS
808 S 15TH ST 64015 — 229-4720

Bolivar, AC 417, PC 6, Polk
Bolivar RSD 1 — 4-11111
604 W JACKSON ST 65613 — 326-5291
Richard Trout, supt.
HS, 524 W MADISON ST 65613 — 2-00011
Albert Skalicky, prin. — 326-5228
MS, 1300 N HARTFORD AVE 65613 — 2-00100
Stephen Skinner, prin. — 326-3811

Southwest Baptist University — 4-UC
1601 S SPRINGFIELD AVE 65613 — 326-5281

Bonne Terre, AC 314, PC 5, St. Francois
North St. Francois County RSD 1 — 4-11111
300 BERRY RD 63628 — 358-2247
Richard McMullin, supt.
North St. Francois County HS — 3-00011
7151 VO TEC RD 63628 — 358-8890
David Stevens, prin.
United Career Center — Vo Tech
7163 VO TEC RD 63628 — 358-2271
Don Vanherck, prin.
Other Schools – See Desloge

Boonville, AC 816, PC 6, Cooper
Boonville RSD 1, 700 MAIN ST 65233 — 4-11111
Greg Gettings, supt. — 882-7474
HS, PO BOX 74 65233 — 2-00111
Dwight Jones, prin. — 882-7426
Boonslick Area Vo S — Vo Tech
RR 4 BOX 76 65233 — 882-5306
Rodger Brewen, prin.
Elliott MS, 700 MAIN ST 65233 — 2-00100
Donald Schupp, prin. — 882-6649

Kemper Military School & College — 2-00111
701 3RD ST 65233 – Ivan Phillyis, prin. — 882-5623
Kemper Military School & College — 2-CC
701 3RD ST 65233 — 800-530-5600

Bosworth, AC 816, PC 2, Carroll
Bosworth RSD 5, RR 2 BOX 4 64623 — 2-11111
Ann Meese, supt. — 534-7702
JSHS, RR 2 BOX 4 64623 — 1-00111
Ann Meese, prin. — 534-7311

Bourbon, AC 314, PC 4, Crawford
Crawford County RSD 1 — 3-11111
PO BOX 40 65441 — 732-4426
Waymon Boast, supt.
HS, PO BOX 40 65441 — 2-00011
William Watts, prin. — 732-5615
MS, PO BOX 40 65441 — 2-00100
Donald Copeland, prin. — 732-4424

Bowling Green, AC 314, PC 5, Pike
Bowling Green RSD 1 — 4-11111
700 W ADAMS ST 63334 — 324-5441
Michael Newell, supt.
HS, 700 W ADAMS ST 63334 — 2-00011
Argil Ellison, prin. — 324-5341
JHS, 1000 W CENTENNIAL AVE 63334 — 2-00100
Kenny Youmans, prin. — 324-2181

Bradleyville, AC 417, PC 2, Taney
Bradleyville RSD 1, PO BOX 61 65614 — 2-11111
Lowell Hunt, supt. — 796-2288
JSHS, PO BOX 61 65614 — 2-00111
Chris Morrison, prin. — 796-2288

Branson, AC 417, PC 5, Taney
Branson RSD 4, 500 S 5TH ST 65616 — 4-11111
Dr. Lee J. Orth, supt. — 334-6541
HS, 1 BUCCANEER DR 65616 — 3-00011
Allen Ritchie, prin. — 334-6511
JHS, 1 BUCCANEER DR 65616 — 2-00100
Roger Newell, prin. — 334-3087

Brashear, AC 816, PC 2, Adair
Adair County RSD 2 — 2-11111
205 W DEWEY 63533 — 323-5272
Harold Means, supt.
Adair County JSHS — 2-00111
PO BOX 235 63533 — 323-5272
Terry Morrow, prin.

Braymer, AC 816, PC 3, Caldwell
Braymer Consolidated SD 4 — 2-11111
PO BOX 427 64624 — 645-2284
Lonnie Daugherty, supt.
JSHS, PO BOX 427 64624 — 2-00111
Russell Clodfelter, prin. — 645-2285

Breckenridge, AC 816, PC 2, Caldwell
Breckenridge RSD 1 — 2-11111
PO BOX 255 64625 — 644-5715
Lionel Brown, supt.
JSHS, PO BOX 255 64625 — 1-00111
Kimberly Brammer, prin. — 644-5715

Brentwood, AC 314, PC 6, St. Louis
Brentwood SD — 3-11111
1775 PARKRIDGE AVE 63144 — 962-4507
John Cleary, supt.
JSHS, 2221 HIGH SCHOOL DR 63144 — 2-00111
Christopher Corley, prin. — 962-3837

Bridgeton, AC 314, PC 7, St. Louis

Bryan Institute — 1-CS
12184 NATURAL BRIDGE RD 63044 — 291-0241

Bronaugh, AC 417, PC 2, Vernon
Bronaugh RSD 7, PO BOX 8 64728 — 2-11111
Jerry Sparks, supt. — 922-3211
JSHS, PO BOX 8 64728 — 2-00111
Douglas Hedrick, prin. — 922-3211

Brookfield, AC 816, PC 5, Linn
Brookfield RSD 3, RR 3 BOX 230D 64628 — 4-11111
Ted Davis, supt. — 258-7443
HS, RR 3 BOX 230A 64628 — 2-00011
Douglas Henry, prin. — 258-7242
Brookfield Area Career Center S — Vo Tech
RR 3 BOX 230C 64628 — 258-2682
Rick Pierson, prin.
MS, RR 3 BOX 230B 64628 — 2-00100
Paul Barger, prin. — 258-7335

Broseley, AC 314, PC 2, Butler
Twin Rivers RSD 10, HWY 51 63932 — 4-11111
Joe Knodell, supt. — 328-4321
Twin Rivers HS, PO BOX 146 63932 — 2-00011
Larry Anderson, prin. — 328-4730

Brunswick, AC 816, PC 4, Chariton
Brunswick RSD 2 — 2-11111
1008 COUNTY RD 65236 — 548-3550
William Page, supt.
JSHS, 1008 COUNTY RD 65236 — 2-00111
Roger Barnes, prin. — 548-3771

Bucklin, AC 816, PC 3, Linn
Bucklin RSD 2, PO BOX 80 64631 — 2-11111
Robert White, supt. — 695-3225
JSHS, PO BOX 80 64631 — 2-00111
Larry Crooks, prin. — 695-3225

Buffalo, AC 417, PC 4, Dallas
Dallas County RSD 1 — 4-11111
PO BOX 800 65622 — 345-2221
Paul Darnell, supt.
HS, PO BOX 800 65622 — 3-00011
William Saling, prin. — 345-2223
Buffalo Area Vo S — Vo Tech
PO BOX 800 65622 — 752-3491
Bill Stringer, prin.
JHS, PO BOX 800 65622 — 2-00100
Thomas Inman, prin. — 345-2335

Bunceton, AC 816, PC 2, Cooper
Cooper County RSD 4 — 2-11111
PO BOX 110 65237 — 427-5347
Elvin Farguhar, supt.
JSHS, PO BOX 110 65237 — 1-00111
Tim Lenz, prin. — 427-5347

Bunker, AC 314, PC 2, Reynolds
Bunker RSD 3, PO BOX 365 63629 — 2-11111
Lawrence Graves, supt. — 689-2507

JSHS, PO BOX 365 63629 — 2-00111
Ron Cook, prin. — 689-2211

Burlington Junction, AC 816, PC 3, Nodaway
West Nodaway RSD 1 — 2-11111
PO BOX 260 64428 — 725-4613
Dan Kercher, supt.
West Nodaway JSHS — 2-01111
PO BOX 260 64428 — 725-3317
Richard Morelock, prin.

Butler, AC 816, PC 5, Bates
Ballard RSD 2, RR 1 BOX 145 64730 — 2-11111
Paul Brink, supt. — 297-2656
Ballard JSHS, RR 1 BOX 145 64730 — 1-00111
Ronnie Hargrave, prin. — 297-2656

Butler RSD 5, 420 S FULTON ST 64730 — 4-11111
Gary Crabtree, supt. — 679-6121
JSHS, 420 S FULTON ST 64730 — 2-00111
Paul Joiner, prin. — 679-6121

Cabool, AC 417, PC 4, Texas
Cabool RSD 4, PO BOX N 65689 — 3-11111
Robert Fields, supt. — 962-3153
HS, PO BOX N 65689 — 2-00011
Vicki Woods, prin. — 962-3153
MS, PO BOX N 65689 — 2-01100
Larry Baker, prin. — 962-3153

Cainsville, AC 816, PC 2, Harrison
Cainsville RSD 1, PO BOX 108 64632 — 2-11111
Harvey Chauvin, supt. — 893-5213
JSHS, PO BOX 108 64632 — 1-00111
Harvey Chauvin, prin. — 893-5214

Cairo, AC 816, PC 2, Randolph
Northeast Randolph County RSD 4 — 2-11111
PO BOX 137 65239 — 263-2788
Marge Gibson, supt.
Northeast JSHS, PO BOX 137 65239 — 2-00111
Gary Wood, prin. — 263-2788

Caledonia, AC 314, PC 2, Washington
Valley RSD 6 — 3-11111
GENERAL DELIVERY 63631 — 779-3515
Harwell Lambert, supt.
Valley JSHS, GENERAL DELIVERY 63631 — 2-00111
Cliff Carver, prin. — 779-3515

Calhoun, AC 816, PC 2, Henry
Calhoun RSD 8, PO BOX 7 65323 — 2-11111
Charles Brock, supt. — 694-3422
JSHS, PO BOX 7 65323 — 1-00111
Michael Allen, prin. — 694-3422

California, AC 314, PC 5, Moniteau
Montieau County RSD 1 — 4-11111
PO BOX 168 65018 — 796-2145
Ronald Harlan, supt.
JSHS, PO BOX 168 65018 — 3-00111
Jim McDonald, prin. — 796-4911

Camdenton, AC 314, PC 5, Camden
Camdenton RSD 3 — 5-11111
PO BOX 1409 65020 — 346-5651
Ronald Hendricks, supt.
SHS, PO BOX 1409 65020 — 3-00001
R. Worthan, prin. — 346-5651
Lake Area Vo-Tech S — Vo Tech
PO BOX 1409 65020 — 346-4260
Mike Wingate, prin.
JHS, PO BOX 1409 65020 — 3-00110
Michael Bryant, prin. — 346-5651

Cameron, AC 816, PC 5, Clinton
Cameron RSD 1, 105 E 5TH ST 64429 — 4-11111
W. Anderson, supt. — 632-2170
HS, 1022 S CHESTNUT ST 64429 — 2-00011
Gerald Steele, prin. — 632-2129
MS, 116 W 4TH ST 64429 — 2-01100
Randall Relford, prin. — 632-2185

Campbell, AC 314, PC 4, Dunklin
Campbell RSD 2, HIGHWAY 53 S 63933 — 3-11111
Steve Bounds, supt. — 246-2133
JSHS, 801 S STATE ROUTE 53 63933 — 2-00111
D. Smith, prin. — 246-2576

Canton, AC 314, PC 5, Lewis
Canton RSD 5, 200 S 4TH ST 63435 — 3-11111
Richard Davis, supt. — 288-5216
JSHS, 200 S 4TH ST 63435 — 2-00111
Randy Lillard, prin. — 288-5216

Culver-Stockton College 63435 — 4-UC
— 288-5221

Cape Girardeau, AC 314, PC 8, Cape Girardeau
Cape Girardeau SD 63 — 5-11111
61 N CLARK ST 63701 — 335-6654
Neyland Clark, supt.
Central SHS, 205 CARUTHERS ST 63701 — 3-00001
Danny Milligan, prin. — 335-8228
Cape Girardeau Vo-Tech S — Vo Tech
301 N CLARK ST 63701 — 334-3358
Harold Tilley, prin.
Central JHS, 1900 THILENIUS ST 63701 — 3-00110
Lanny Barnes, prin. — 335-9473

Cape Girardeau Voc. Technical School — 2-CS
301 N CLARK ST 63701 — 334-0826
Metro Business College — 2-CS
1732 N KINGSHIGHWAY ST 63701 — 334-9181

Notre Dame Regional HS
 1912 RITTER DR 63701 2-00011
 Sr. Mary Fischer, prin.   335-6772
Southeast Missouri State University 6-UC
 1 UNIVERSITY PLZ 63701 651-2000

Cardwell, AC 314, PC 3, Dunklin
Southland Consolidated SD 9 2-11111
 PO BOX 47 63829 654-3574
 Michael Back, supt.
Southland JSHS, PO BOX 47 63829 2-00111
 Ted Wilkerson, prin. 654-3531

Carl Junction, AC 417, PC 5, Jasper
Carl Junction RSD 1, PO BOX 4 64834 4-11111
 Jerry Stark, supt. 649-7026
HS, PO BOX 4 64834 3-00011
 Raymond Dykens, prin. 649-7011
JHS, PO BOX 4 64834 2-00100
 Ron Moorehouse, prin. 649-7246

Carrollton, AC 816, PC 5, Carroll
Carrollton RSD 7, 300 E 9TH ST 64633 3-11111
 Tom Fevurly, supt. 542-2769
JSHS, 300 E 9TH ST 64633 3-00111
 Norman Grossman, prin. 542-1276
Carrollton Area Vo-Tech S Vo Tech
 305 E 10TH ST 64633 542-0000
 Joe Daniels, prin.

Carthage, AC 417, PC 7, Jasper
Carthage RSD 9, 714 S MAIN ST 64836 5-11111
 Charles Johnson, supt. 359-7000
SHS, 714 S MAIN ST 64836 3-00001
 John Ihm, prin. 359-7020
Carthage Area Vo S Vo Tech
 609 S RIVER ST 64836 359-7026
 James Honey, prin.
JHS, 827 E CENTENNIAL AVE 64836 3-00110
 Gary Reed, prin. 359-7050

Caruthersville, AC 314, PC 6, Pemiscot
Caruthersville SD 18 4-11111
 1711 WARD AVE 63830 333-4321
 Arnold Bell, supt.
HS, 1708 WARD AVE 63830 2-00011
 Cynthia Porter, prin. 333-2114
JHS, 602 E 18TH ST 63830 2-00100
 Jim Bullington, prin. 333-1210

Cassville, AC 417, PC 4, Barry
Cassville RSD 4, 14TH & MAIN 65625 4-11111
 Dan Bailey, supt. 847-2221
HS, 14TH & MAIN 65625 3-00011
 Ron Richardson, prin. 847-3137
MS, 14TH & MAIN 65625 2-01100
 Jim Orrell, prin. 847-3136

Center, AC 314, PC 3, Ralls
Ralls County RSD 2 3-11111
 PO BOX 230 63436 267-3397
 Gary Schroer, supt.
Twain JSHS, PO BOX 230 63436 2-00111
 James McCarty, prin. 267-3397

Centerview, AC 816, PC 2, Johnson
Johnson County RSD 7 3-11111
 92 NW STATE ROUTE 58 64019 656-3316
 Ray Patrick, supt.
Crest Ridge JSHS 2-00111
 92 NW STATE ROUTE 58 64019 656-3392
 Vernon Meinders, prin.

Centralia, AC 314, PC 5, Boone
Centralia RSD 6 4-11111
 635 S JEFFERSON ST 65240 682-3561
 Thomas Quinn, supt.
HS, 849 S JEFFERSON ST 65240 2-00011
 James Head, prin. 682-3508
MS, 110 N JEFFERSON ST 65240 2-01100
 Philip Gooding, prin. 682-2617

Sunnydale Academy 2-00011
 RR 2 BOX 144 65240 682-2164
 Jim Wampler, prin.

Chadwick, AC 417, PC 2, Christian
Chadwick RSD 1, HWY 125 65629 2-11111
 Ronald Wagner, supt. 278-3588
JSHS, HWY 125 65629 1-00111
 Terry Beasley, prin. 278-3588

Chaffee, AC 314, PC 5, Scott
Scott County RSD 2 3-11111
 517 W YOAKUM AVE 63740 887-3226
 Wayne Pressley, supt.
JSHS, 517 W YOAKUM AVE 63740 2-00111
 William Biggerstaff, prin. 887-3226

Chamois, AC 314, PC 2, Osage
Osage County RSD 1 2-11111
 HC 63 BOX 8A 65024 763-5666
 Vernon L. Altom, supt.
JSHS, HC 63 BOX 8A 65024 2-00111
 Harold Green, prin. 763-5666

Charleston, AC 314, PC 6, Mississippi
Charleston RSD 1, PO BOX 39 63834 4-11111
 Bill Bacchus, supt. 683-3776
HS, PO BOX 39 63834 3-00011
 Joe Forrest, prin. 683-3761
JHS, PO BOX 39 63834 2-00100
 Kevin Miller, prin. 683-3346

Chesterfield, AC 314, PC 8, St. Louis
Parkway Consolidated SD 2 7-11111
 455 N WOODS MILL RD 63017 851-8100
 Don Senti, supt.
Central HS 4-00011
 369 N WOODS MILL RD 63017 851-5220
 William Myer, prin.
Central JHS 3-00100
 471 N WOODS MILL RD 63017 851-8265
 Dan Natale, prin.
West JHS, 2312 BAXTER RD 63017 3-00100
 Salvatore Sciortino, prin. 391-4750
Other Schools – See Ballwin, Creve Coeur,
 Manchester

Rockwood RSD 6
 Supt. — See Eureka
Marquette HS 3-00011
 2351 CLARKSON RD 63017 537-5838
 Daniel Deschamp, prin.

Special SD of St. Louis County
 Supt. — See Saint Louis
West County Tech SHS Vo Tech
 13480 S OUTER 40 63017 851-2898
 Mary Giovanni, prin.

Logan College of Chiropractic 3-UC
 PO BOX 1065 63006 227-2100

Chilhowee, AC 816, PC 2, Johnson
Chilhowee RSD 4, PO BOX 98 64733 2-11111
 Jerrold Robison, supt. 678-2511
JSHS, PO BOX 98 64733 1-00111
 Dennis James, prin. 678-4511

Chillicothe, AC 816, PC 6, Livingston
Chillicothe RSD 2 4-11111
 PO BOX 530 64601 646-4566
 Orlo Shroyer, supt.
HS, 1535 CALHOUN ST 64601 3-00011
 Ron Smith, prin. 646-3414
Area Vo-Tech S, 1200 FAIR ST 64601 Vo Tech
 Ron Wolf, prin. 646-3414
JHS, 1529 CALHOUN ST 64601 2-00100
 Mark Frost, prin. 646-1916

Clarksville, AC 314, PC 2, Pike
Pike County RSD 3 2-11111
 PO BOX 218 63336 242-3546
 John Vanderford, supt.
Clopton JSHS, PO BOX 218 63336 2-00111
 Dale Miller, prin. 242-3546
Other Schools – See Eolia

Clarkton, AC 314, PC 4, Dunklin
Clarkton Consolidated SD 4 2-11111
 PO BOX 637 63837 448-3712
 Richard Reynolds, supt.
JSHS, PO BOX 637 63837 2-00111
 Linda Hodges, prin. 448-3120

Clayton, AC 314, PC 7, St. Louis
Clayton SD 4-11111
 7530 MARYLAND AVE 63105 726-5210
 Steven Adamowski, supt.
HS, 1 MARK TWAIN CIR 63105 3-00011
 Donald Hugo, prin. 726-2575
Wydown MS 3-00100
 6500 WYDOWN BLVD 63105 726-5222
 Joe Bartlett, prin.

Mid-America Paralegal Institute 2-CS
 8008 CARONDELET AVE STE 211 63105
  863-3331

Cleveland, AC 816, PC 3, Cass
Midway RSD 1, RR 1 64734 3-11111
 Bill Akers, supt. 899-2994
Midway JSHS, RR 1 64734 2-00111
 Robert Weltsch, prin. 899-2211

Clever, AC 417, PC 3, Christian
Clever RSD 5, PO BOX 128 65631 2-11111
 Larry Hale, supt. 743-2430
JSHS, PO BOX 128 65631 2-00111
 Richard Henson, prin. 743-2700

Clifton Hill, AC 816, PC 2, Randolph
Westran RSD 1
 Supt. — See Huntsville
Westran MS, RR 1 BOX 46B 65244 2-00100
 William Burns, prin. 261-4511

Climax Springs, AC 314, PC 1, Camden
Climax Springs RSD 4 2-11111
 RR 1 BOX 239 65324 347-2351
 Frances Woody, supt.
JSHS, RR 1 BOX 239 65324 2-00111
 Mickey Bowers, prin. 347-2351

Clinton, AC 816, PC 6, Henry
Clinton SD 124, 701 S 8TH ST 64735 4-11111
 Sandra Braithwait, supt. 885-2237
HS, 600 E CLINTON ST 64735 3-00011
 Gene Reid, prin. 885-2247
Clinton Area Vo S Vo Tech
 5TH AND WILSON 64735 885-6101
 James Lindsay, prin.
MS, 709 S 8TH ST 64735 2-00100
 Steven Litten, prin. 885-3353

Cole Camp, AC 816, PC 4, Benton
Cole Camp RSD 1 3-11111
 RR 2 BOX 68 65325 668-4427
 Scott Huddleston, supt.

HS, RR 2 BOX 68 65325 2-00011
 William Smart, prin. 668-3751

Columbia, AC 314, PC 8, Boone
Columbia SD 93 7-11111
 1818 W WORLEY ST 65203 886-2100
 Russell Thompson, supt.
Columbia-Hickman SHS 4-00001
 1104 N PROVIDENCE RD 65203 886-2500
 Edith Corn, prin.
Rock Bridge JSHS 3-00111
 4303 S PROVIDENCE RD 65203 886-2560
 Jim King, prin.
Columbia Area Career Ctr Vo Tech
 4043 S PROVIDENCE RD 65203 886-2610
 Don Bristow, prin.
Jefferson JHS, 713 ROGERS ST 65201 4-00110
 Dr. Roy Willard, prin. 886-2660
Oakland JHS, 3405 OAKLAND PL 65202 2-00110
 Mary Laffey, prin. 886-2710
West JHS, 401 CLINKSCALES RD 65203 4-00110
 Margaret Roberts, prin. 886-2760

Columbia College 5-UC
 1001 ROGERS ST 65216 800-231-2391
Stephens College 3-UC
 PO BOX 2121 65215 442-2211
University of Missouri 7-UC
 228 JESSE HALL 65211 882-3387

Conception, AC 816, PC 2, Nodaway

Conception Seminary College 64433 1-UC
  944-2218

Conception Junction, AC 816, PC 2, Nodaway
Jefferson Consolidated SD 123 2-11111
 PO BOX 112A 64434 944-2316
 Jerry Archer, supt.
Jefferson JSHS, PO BOX 112A 64434 1-00111
 Don Edwards, prin. 944-2316

Concordia, AC 816, PC 4, Lafayette
Concordia RSD 2, PO BOX 879 64020 2-11111
 Harold Brown, supt. 463-7235
JSHS, PO BOX 879 64020 2-00111
 Link Luttrell, prin. 463-2246

St. Paul's Lutheran HS 2-00011
 200 MAIN ST 64020 463-2238
 Richard Gove, prin.

Conway, AC 417, PC 3, Laclede
Laclede County RSD 1 3-11111
 RR 2 BOX 82B 65632 589-2951
 Larry Clinefelter, supt.
JSHS, RR 2 BOX 82B 65632 2-00111
 Hershel Nichols, prin. 589-2941

Cooter, AC 314, PC 2, Pemiscot
Cooter RSD 4, PO BOX 218 63839 2-11111
 Floyd Wilson, supt. 695-3312
JSHS, PO BOX 218 63839 2-00111
 Michael Wallace, prin. 695-4972

Craig, AC 816, PC 2, Holt
Craig RSD 3, PO BOX 7 64437 2-11111
 Hershel Ferguson, supt. 683-5351
JSHS, PO BOX 315 64437 1-00111
 Hershel Ferguson, prin. 683-5431

Crane, AC 417, PC 4, Stone
Crane RSD 3, PO BOX E 65633 3-11111
 Tyler Laney, supt. 723-5300
JSHS, PO BOX E 65633 2-00111
 Bill Redus, prin. 723-5383

Creighton, AC 816, PC 2, Cass
Sherwood-Cass RSD 8 3-11111
 PO BOX 98 64739 499-2239
 Donald Lovland, supt.
Sherwood JSHS, PO BOX 98 64739 2-00111
 Theodore Woodruff, prin. 499-2239

Creve Coeur, AC 314, PC 7, St. Louis
Parkway Consolidated SD 2
 Supt. — See Chesterfield
North HS, 12860 FEE FEE RD 63146 4-00011
 Gretchen Fleming, prin. 851-8300
Fern Ridge HS 1-00011
 13157 N OLIVE SPUR RD 63141 542-0042
 Mary Plunkett, prin.
East JHS 3-00100
 181 COEUR DE VILLE DR 63141 542-0001
 Michael Shipman, prin.

De Smet Jesuit HS 3-00011
 233 N NEW BALLAS RD 63141 567-3500
 Gregory Densberger, prin.
St. Louis Priory S 2-00111
 500 S MASON RD 63141 434-3690
 Fr. Frerking, prin.

Crocker, AC 314, PC 4, Pulaski
Crocker RSD 2, PO BOX 488 65452 3-11111
 Roger Nash, supt. 736-2215
HS, PO BOX 488 65452 2-00111
 James Tillman, prin. 736-2214
MS, PO BOX 488 65452 2-01100
 Doyle Swiney, prin. 736-2214

Crystal City, AC 314, PC 5, Jefferson
Crystal City SD 47 3-11111
 1100 MISSISSIPPI AVE 63019 937-4411
 James Maze, supt.

HS, 1100 MISSISSIPPI AVE 63019   2-00011
David Stader, prin.   937-2005

Cuba, AC 314, PC 5, Crawford
Crawford County RSD 2   4-11111
208 ELM AVE 65453   885-2534
Ronald Kettler, supt.
HS, 208 ELM AVE 65453   2-00011
Robert Heigele, prin.   885-2534
MS, 208 ELM AVE 65453   2-00100
Greg Lentz, prin.   885-2534

Dadeville, AC 417, PC 2, Dade
Dadeville RSD 2, PO BOX 188 65635   2-11111
Henry McBride, supt.   995-2201
JSHS, PO BOX 188 65635   1-00111
Roger Hall, prin.   995-2231

Dearborn, AC 816, PC 2, Platte
North Platte County RSD 1   3-11111
PO BOX 68 64439   992-3511
Francis Moran, supt.
North Platte HS, PO BOX 68 64439   2-00011
John Green, prin.   992-3344
Other Schools – See Edgerton

Deepwater, AC 417, PC 2, Henry
Lakeland RSD 3   2-11111
RR 1 BOX 230-1 64740   644-2223
James Lewis, supt.
Lakeland JSHS   2-00111
RR 1 BOX 230-1 64740   644-2223
Jeff Osner, prin.

Deering, AC 314, PC 2, Pemiscot
Pemiscot County Consolidated SD 7   2-11111
PO BOX 297 63840   757-6648
Russell Gilmore, supt.
Delta JSHS, PO BOX 297 63840   2-00111
Kenneth Emerson, prin.   757-6611

De Kalb, AC 816, PC 2, Buchanan
Buchanan County RSD 4   2-11111
PO BOX 48 64440   685-3160
Robert Couldry, supt.
JSHS, PO BOX 48 64440   2-00111
Eric Sorensen, prin.   685-3211

Delta, AC 314, PC 2, Cape Girardeau
Delta RSD 5, PO BOX 787 63744   2-11111
Larry Beshears, supt.   794-2500
JSHS, PO BOX 787 63744   2-00111
William Price, prin.   794-2511

Desloge, AC 314, PC 5, St. Francois
North St. Francois County RSD 1
Supt. — See Bonne Terre
North County JHS   2-00100
406 E CHESTNUT ST 63601   431-6700
Harold Huff, prin.

De Soto, AC 314, PC 6, Jefferson
Desoto SD 73, PO BOX 579 63020   5-11111
E. Dean Burns, supt.   586-8811
HS, 731 AMVETS DR 63020   4-00011
Sharon Waite, prin.   586-3347
JHS, 815 AMVETS DR 63020   3-00100
Gwen Lewis, prin.   586-2267

Dexter, AC 314, PC 6, Stoddard
Dexter RSD 11, 915 W GRANT ST 63841   4-11111
Jerry Waddle, supt.   624-4078
HS, 1101 W GRANT ST 63841   3-00011
James Hall, prin.   624-2622
Hill MS, 1107 BROWN PILOT LN 63841   3-00100
Ken Jackson, prin.   624-5965

Diamond, AC 417, PC 3, Newton
Diamond RSD 4, PO BOX 68 64840   3-11111
Dan Chapman, supt.   325-5186
HS, PO BOX 68 64840   2-00011
Richard Giles, prin.   325-5188

Dixon, AC 314, PC 4, Pulaski
Dixon RSD 1, PO BOX A 65459   4-11111
Norman Herren, supt.   759-7163
HS, PO BOX A 65459   2-00011
Martin White, prin.   759-7119
MS, PO BOX A 65459   2-00100
Randy Hoffman, prin.   759-7139

Doniphan, AC 314, PC 4, Ripley
Doniphan RSD 1, 309 PINE ST 63935   4-11111
Eugene Croarkin, supt.   996-3819
HS, 5 BALL PARK RD 63935   3-00011
C. Bonnell, prin.   996-3312
Current River Vo S   Vo Tech
301 SPRING ST 63935   996-2915
John Braschler, prin.
MS, 605 E SUMMIT ST 63935   2-00100
Tom Bridges, prin.   996-3614

Dora, AC 417, PC 2, Ozark
Dora RSD 3, PO BOX 14 65637   2-11111
Donald Collins, supt.   261-2346
JSHS, PO BOX 14 65637   2-01111
John Hood, prin.   261-2263

Drexel, AC 816, PC 3, Cass
Drexel RSD 4, PO BOX 860 64742   2-11111
Richard Larson, supt.   657-4715
HS, PO BOX 860 64742   1-00011
Phillip Denney, prin.   657-4504

Eagleville, AC 816, PC 2, Harrison
North Harrison County RSD 3   2-11111
PO BOX 98 64442   867-5222
David Cross, supt.
North Harrison County JSHS   2-00111
PO BOX 98 64442   867-5221
Keith Nowland, prin.

Earth City, AC 314, PC 99, St. Louis

ITT Technical Institute   4-UC
13505 LAKEFRONT DR 63045   298-7800

Easton, AC 816, PC 2, Buchanan
East Buchanan County Consolidated SD 1
Supt. — See Gower
East Buchanan MS   2-00100
301 COUNTY PARK RD N 64443   473-2451
Gary Summers, prin.

East Prairie, AC 314, PC 5, Mississippi
East Prairie RSD 2   4-11111
304 E WALNUT ST 63845   649-3562
Jared Williams, supt.
HS, 304 E WALNUT ST 63845   2-00011
Michael Miller, prin.   649-3564
JHS, 304 E WALNUT ST 63845   2-00100
Michael Miller, prin.   649-3564

Edgerton, AC 816, PC 3, Platte
North Platte County RSD 1
Supt. — See Dearborn
MS, 900 LEWIS ST 64444   2-01100
Ron Ressler, prin.   227-3622

Edina, AC 816, PC 4, Knox
Knox County RSD 1   3-11111
RR 3 BOX 59 63537   397-2228
Mark Yehle, supt.
Knox County JSHS   2-00111
RR 3 BOX 59 63537   397-2231
Gary Gordy, prin.

Eldon, AC 314, PC 5, Miller
Eldon RSD 1, 110 S OAK ST 65026   4-11111
Howard Neeley, supt.   392-8000
HS, NORTH & PINE STS 65026   3-00011
Larry Leech, prin.   392-8010
Tri-County Tech S   Vo Tech
2ND AND PINE ST 65026   392-8060
Sterling Green, prin.
MS, 110 S OAK ST 65026   2-00100
Jim Wilson, prin.   392-8020

El Dorado Springs, AC 417, PC 5, Cedar
El Dorado Springs RSD 2   4-11111
PO BOX 191 64744   876-3112
George Bates, supt.
HS, PO BOX 191 64744   2-00011
Lonnie Leatherman, prin.   876-3112
MS, PO BOX 191 64744   2-00100
Marsha Gilbert, prin.   876-3112

Ellington, AC 314, PC 3, Reynolds
Southern Reynolds County RSD 2   3-11111
PO BOX 430 63638   663-2291
Philip Hall, supt.
Southern Reynolds County JSHS   2-00111
PO BOX 430 63638   663-2291
Robert Hill, prin.

Ellsinore, AC 314, PC 2, Carter
East Carter County RSD 2   3-11111
PO BOX D 63937   322-5625
Ronald Yarbro, supt.
East Carter JSHS, PO BOX D 63937   2-00111
Douglas Daugherty, prin.   322-5653

Elsberry, AC 314, PC 4, Lincoln
Elsberry RSD 2, PO BOX 106 63343   3-11111
Winston Bailey, supt.   898-5554
HS, PO BOX 106 63343   2-00011
Clinton Waters, prin.   898-5553

Eminence, AC 314, PC 3, Shannon
Eminence RSD 1, PO BOX F 65466   2-11111
Eric Mansfield, supt.   226-3251
JSHS, PO BOX F 65466   2-00111
James Keeling, prin.   226-3252

Eolia, AC 314, PC 2, Pike
Pike County RSD 3
Supt. — See Clarksville
Pike/Lincoln Tech Ctr   Vo Tech
PO BOX 38 63344   485-2900
Terry Eivins, prin.

Essex, AC 314, PC 3, Stoddard
Richland RSD 1, PO BOX 8 63846   2-11111
Carrell Odom, supt.   283-5332
Richland JSHS, PO BOX 8 63846   2-00111
Carrell Odom, prin.   283-5332

Eugene, AC 314, PC 2, Cole
Cole County RSD 5   3-11111
PO BOX 78 65032   498-3888
Gregory Wilson, supt.
Cole County JSHS, PO BOX 78 65032   2-00111
Mark Blythe, prin.   498-3311

Eureka, AC 314, PC 5, St. Louis
Rockwood RSD 6   7-11111
111 E NORTH ST 63025   938-5225
Dennis Peterson, supt.
HS, PO BOX 37 63025   4-00011
Kenneth Johnson, prin.   938-5350

Other Schools – See Ballwin, Chesterfield, Fenton, Glencoe

Everton, AC 417, PC 2, Dade
Everton RSD 3, PO BOX 107 65646   2-11111
Hershel Bledsoe, supt.   535-2221
JSHS, PO BOX 107 65646   1-00111
Leon Haden, prin.   535-2221

Ewing, AC 314, PC 2, Lewis
Lewis County Consolidated SD 1   4-11111
PO BOX 366 63440   494-3217
William Cornett, supt.
Highland JSHS, PO BOX 366 63440   3-00111
Aldace Naughton, prin.   494-3215

Excelsior Springs, AC 816, PC 7, Clay
Excelsior Springs SD 40   5-11111
PO BOX 248 64024   637-3165
James Botts, supt.
HS, PO BOX 248 64024   3-00011
Neill Wheeler, prin.   637-2187
Excelsior Springs Career Ctr   Vo Tech
PO BOX 248 64024   637-6096
Marvin Wright, prin.
Excelsior Springs Technical HS   Vo Tech
PO BOX 248 64024   637-5501
Tom Mayfield, prin.
Lewis MS, PO BOX 248 64024   3-00100
Margret Anderson, prin.   637-5516

Exeter, AC 417, PC 3, Barry
Exeter RSD 6, RR 1 BOX 509 65647   2-11111
Marvin Spragg, supt.   835-2922
HS, RR 1 BOX 509 65647   2-00011
Don Reynolds, prin.   835-3745

Fairfax, AC 816, PC 3, Atchison
Fairfax RSD 3, PO BOX 79 64446   2-11111
Martin Sweatman, supt.   686-2421
JSHS, PO BOX 79 64446   2-00111
Jodee Drake, prin.   686-2851

Fair Grove, AC 417, PC 3, Greene
Fairgrove RSD 10   3-11111
RR 3 BOX 75 65648   759-2554
Gary Yarber, supt.
HS, RR 3 BOX 75 65648   2-00011
David Hunter, prin.   759-2554
MS, RR 3 BOX 75 65648   2-01100
Dean Crayton, prin.   759-2554

Fair Play, AC 417, PC 2, Polk
Fair Play RSD 2   2-11111
RR 1 BOX 1020 65649   654-2231
Jim Rich, supt.
JSHS, RR 1 BOX 1020 65649   2-00111
Randal Breshears, prin.   654-2232

Farmington, AC 314, PC 7, St. Francois
Farmington RSD 7   5-11111
1022 SAINTE GENEVIEVE AVE 63640   756-4569
Robert Webb, supt.
HS, 1 BLACK KNIGHT DR 63640   4-00011
David Cramp, prin.   756-6631
JHS, 506 S FLEMING ST 63640   3-00100
Howard Hoehn, prin.   756-6638

Mineral Area Regional Medical Center   HSP
1212 WEBER RD 63640   756-4581

Faucett, AC 816, PC 2, Buchanan
Mid-Buchanan County RSD 5   3-11111
RR 1 64448 – Gary Bell, supt.   238-1646
Mid-Buchanan JSHS, RR 1 64448   2-00111
Steve Johnson, prin.   238-0372

Fayette, AC 816, PC 5, Howard
Fayette RSD 3, 704 LUCKY ST 65248   3-11111
Gary Schurz, supt.   248-2153
HS, 509 HERNDON ST 65248   2-00011
Ron Anderson, prin.   248-2124
Clark MS, 704 LUCKY ST 65248   2-00100
Donna Telle, prin.   248-3800

Central Methodist College   3-UC
411 CENTRAL METHODIST SQ 65248   248-3391

Fenton, AC 314, PC 5, St. Louis
Rockwood RSD 6
Supt. — See Eureka
Rockwood Summit HS   3-00011
1780 HAWKINS RD 63026   861-3424
Thomas Hensley, prin.
Rockwood South JHS   3-00100
1628 HAWKINS RD 63026   225-6161
Charles Yates, prin.

Ferguson, AC 314, PC 7, St. Louis
Ferguson-Florissant RSD 2
Supt. — See Florissant
MS, 701 JANUARY AVE 63135   4-00100
Daryl Hall, prin.   521-5792

Festus, AC 314, PC 6, Jefferson
Festus RSD 6   4-11111
1515 MIDMEADOW LN 63028   937-4920
Robert Taylor, supt.
HS, 501 WESTWIND DR 63028   3-00011
Rob Selinger, prin.   937-5410
MS, 1717 W MAIN ST 63028   3-00100
John Richeson, prin.   937-5417

Jefferson County RSD 7 — 3-11100
1250 DOOLING HOLLOW RD 63028 — 937-9188
Wayne Brower, supt.
Jefferson MS — 2-01100
1250 DOOLING HOLLOW RD 63028 — 937-9188
Diana Vittetoe, prin.

St. Pius X HS — 2-00011
1030 SAINT PIUS DR 63028 — 937-3695
Adele Greaving, prin.

Fillmore, AC 816, PC 2, Andrew
North Andrew County RSD 6
Supt. — See Rosendale
North Andrew MS, PO BOX 99 64449 — 2-00100 — 487-2135
Tim Roush, prin.

Flat River, AC 314, PC 5, St. Francois
Central RSD 3 — 4-11111
200 DARREL S COLE DR 63601 — 431-2616
Orville Adams, supt.
Other Schools – See Park Hills

Mineral Area College 63601 — 4-CC — 431-4593

Florissant, AC 314, PC 8, St. Louis
Ferguson-Florissant RSD 2 — 7-11111
1005 WATERFORD DR 63033 — 831-4411
G. Robert Fritz, supt.
McCluer HS — 4-00011
1896 S FLORISSANT RD 63031 — 521-7432
Wayne Fields, prin.
McCluer North HS — 4-00011
705 WATERFORD DR 63033 — 831-6600
Larry Kreyling, prin.
Cross Keys JHS — 3-00100
14205 COUGAR DR 63033 — 831-2700
Dolores Graham, prin.
Other Schools – See Berkeley, Ferguson

Hazelwood SD — 7-11111
15955 NEW HALLS FERRY RD 63031 — 839-9400
Larry Humphries, supt.
Hazelwood Central HS — 4-00011
15875 NEW HALLS FERRY RD 63031 — 839-9500
Graham Weir, prin.
Hazelwood JHS — 4-00100
1605 SHACKELFORD RD 63031 — 839-9600
John Dougherty, prin.
Other Schools – See Hazelwood, Saint Louis

Special SD of St. Louis County
Supt. — See Saint Louis
North County Tech S — Vo Tech
1700 DERHAKE RD 63033 — 839-6104
Charles Harris, prin.

St. Louis Christian College — 2-UC
1360 GRANDVIEW DR 63033 — 837-6777
St. Thomas Aquinas-Mercy HS — 3-00011
845 DUNN RD 63031 — 837-1144
Paul Frein, prin.

Fordland, AC 417, PC 3, Webster
Fordland RSD 3, PO BOX 118 65652 — 2-11111 — 738-2296
John Garton, supt.
JSHS, PO BOX 118 65652 — 2-00111 — 738-2296
William Marcus, prin.

Forsyth, AC 417, PC 4, Taney
Forsyth RSD 3, PO BOX 187 65653 — 3-11111 — 546-2501
Maynard Wallace, supt.
HS, PO BOX 187 65653 — 2-00011 — 546-4561
Richard Forcum, prin.
MS, PO BOX 187 65653 — 2-01100 — 546-4561
Galen Chambers, prin.

Fort Leonard Wood, AC 314, PC 7, Pulaski
Waynesville RSD 6
Supt. — See Waynesville
Wood MS, 7076 PULASKI AVE 65473 — 3-00100 — 329-2311
Leroy Fulmer, prin.

Fredericktown, AC 314, PC 5, Madison
Fredericktown RSD 1, HWY 72 E 63645 — 4-11111 — 783-2570
Jerry Kinder, supt.
HS, HWY 72 E 63645 — 3-00011 — 783-3628
Harry Lane, prin.
MS, HWY 72 E 63645 — 2-00100 — 783-6555
Kevin Dunn, prin.

Fulton, AC 314, PC 7, Callaway
Fulton SD 58, 2320 N BLUFF ST 65251 — 4-11111 — 642-2206
Robert Fessler, supt.
HS, 2250 BLUFF ST 65251 — 3-00011 — 642-2023
James Barton, prin.
MS, 403 E 10TH ST 65251 — 3-00100 — 642-7221
Mark Enderle, prin.

Missouri School for the Deaf 65251 — HND
Westminister College — 3-UC
501 WESTMINSTER AVE 65251 — 642-3361
William Woods College — 3-UC
200 W 12TH ST 65251 — 642-2251

Gainesville, AC 417, PC 3, Ozark
Gainesville RSD 5 — 3-11111
HC 3 BOX 170 65655 — 679-4200
Jerry Merrell, supt.
JSHS, HC 3 BOX 170 65655 — 2-00111 — 679-4200
Bill Looney, prin.

Galena, AC 417, PC 2, Stone
Galena RSD 2, PO BOX 286 65656 — 2-11111 — 357-6027
David Burns, supt.
JSHS, PO BOX 286 65656 — 2-00111 — 357-6618
Jerry Parrett, prin.

Gallatin, AC 816, PC 4, Daviess
Gallatin RSD 5, 602 S OLIVE ST 64640 — 3-11111 — 663-2171
James Ruse, supt.
JSHS, 602 S OLIVE ST 64640 — 2-00111 — 663-2171
Charles Burrell, prin.

Galt, AC 816, PC 2, Grundy
Grundy County RSD 5 — 2-11111
PO BOX 6 64641 — 673-6511
Harry Wheeler, supt.
Grundy County JSHS — 2-00111
PO BOX 6 64641 — 673-6511
Stanley Ingraham, prin.

Gideon, AC 314, PC 4, New Madrid
Gideon SD 37, PO BOX 227 63848 — 2-11111 — 448-3911
James Evans, supt.
JSHS, PO BOX 227 63848 — 2-00111 — 448-3471
Ron Buchanan, prin.

Gilman City, AC 816, PC 2, Harrison
Gilman City RSD 4, PO BOX 45 64642 — 2-11111 — 876-5221
Lyle Oliver, supt.
JSHS, PO BOX 45 64642 — 1-00111 — 876-5221
John Williams, prin.

Glasgow, AC 816, PC 4, Howard
Howard County RSD 2 — 2-11111
860 RANDOLPH ST 65254 — 338-2014
Larry Flanagan, supt.
JSHS, 860 RANDOLPH ST 65254 — 2-00111 — 338-2012
Richard Baldwin, prin.

Glencoe, AC 314, PC 3, St. Louis
Rockwood RSD 6
Supt. — See Eureka
LaSalle Springs MS — 3-00100
3300 HIGHWAY 109 63038 — 938-5513
Scott Francin, prin.
Rockwood Valley MS — 3-00100
1220 HIGHWAY 109 63038 — 458-3632
Mary Riedel, prin.

Golden City, AC 417, PC 3, Barton
Golden City RSD 3 — 2-11111
PO BOX 248 64748 — 537-4900
Gary Kaufman, supt.
JSHS, PO BOX 248 64748 — 2-00111 — 537-8311
Henry Taffner, prin.

Gower, AC 816, PC 4, Buchanan
East Buchanan County Consolidated SD 1 — 3-11111
100 SMITH ST 64454 — 424-6466
Donald Quick, supt.
East Buchanan HS, 100 SMITH ST 64454 — 2-00011 — 424-6460
Scott Antle, prin.
Other Schools – See Easton

Graham, AC 816, PC 2, Nodaway
Nodaway-Holt RSD 7
Supt. — See Maitland
Nodaway-Holt HS — 2-00011
318 S TAYLOR ST 64455 — 939-2135
Tyran Sumy, prin.

Grain Valley, AC 816, PC 4, Jackson
Grain Valley RSD 5 — 4-11111
714 S MAIN ST 64029 — 229-4685
David Hackett, supt.
JSHS, 714 S MAIN ST 64029 — 2-00111 — 229-4663
Dan Jones, prin.

Granby, AC 417, PC 4, Newton
East Newton County RSD 6 — 4-11111
RR 1 64844 – Doyle Price, supt. — 472-6231
East Newton County HS, RR 1 64844 — 2-00011 — 472-6238
Max Newell, prin.

Grandview, AC 816, PC 7, Jackson
Grandview Consolidated SD 4 — 5-11111
724 MAIN ST 64030 — 761-7486
Jerry Thornsberry, supt.
HS, 2300 HIGH GROVE RD 64030 — 4-00011 — 761-1812
Jim Jenkins, prin.
MS, 12650 MANCHESTER AVE 64030 — 3-00100 — 763-6066
Tim Donovan, prin.

Grant City, AC 816, PC 3, Worth
Worth County RSD 3 — 2-11111
PO BOX 40 64456 — 564-3389
Richard Nagel, supt.
Worth County JSHS — 2-00111
PO BOX 40 64456 — 564-2218
Dale Healy, prin.

Green City, AC 816, PC 3, Sullivan
Green City RSD 1 — 2-11111
RR 1 BOX 1133 63545 — 874-4127
Dick Phillips, supt.
JSHS, RR 1 BOX 1133 63545 — 2-00111 — 874-4127
John Williams, prin.

Greenfield, AC 417, PC 4, Dade
Greenfield RSD 4 — 2-11111
410 W COLLEGE ST 65661 — 637-5321
Lowell Keltner, supt.
JSHS, 410 W COLLEGE ST 65661 — 2-00111 — 637-5328
Greg Sewell, prin.

Green Ridge, AC 816, PC 2, Pettis
Green Ridge RSD 8, PO BOX 38 65332 — 2-11111 — 527-3315
Judith Brown, supt.
JSHS, PO BOX 38 65332 — 2-00111 — 527-3315
Andy Henley, prin.

Greenville, AC 314, PC 2, Wayne
Greenville RSD 2, PO BOX 277A 63944 — 3-11111 — 224-3844
Eugene Oakley, supt.
JSHS, PO BOX 277 63944 — 2-00111 — 224-3618
Charles Barker, prin.

Hale, AC 816, PC 2, Carroll
Hale RSD 1, PO BOX 248 64643 — 2-11111 — 565-2417
Stephen Andes, supt.
HS, PO BOX 248 64643 — 1-00011 — 565-2417
Garry Becker, prin.

Half Way, AC 417, PC 2, Polk
Halfway RSD 3, PO BOX 98 65663 — 2-11111 — 445-2351
Larry King, supt.
JSHS, PO BOX 98 65663 — 2-00111 — 445-2211
A. Roweton, prin.

Hallsville, AC 314, PC 3, Boone
Boone County RSD 4 — 3-11111
421 E HIGHWAY 124 65255 — 696-5512
Ralph Powell, supt.
JSHS, 421 E HIGHWAY 124 65255 — 2-00111 — 696-2281
James Stinson, prin.

Hamilton, AC 816, PC 4, Caldwell
Hamilton RSD 2, PO BOX 128 64644 — 3-11111 — 583-2171
Dr. Thomas Trail, supt.
Penney HS, PO BOX 128 64644 — 2-00011 — 583-2136
Darell Hawley, prin.
MS, PO BOX 128 64644 — 2-01100 — 583-2173
Darell Hawley, prin.

Hannibal, AC 314, PC 7, Marion
Hannibal SD 60 — 5-11111
4650 MCMASTERS AVE 63401 — 221-1258
W. Taveau, supt.
HS, 4500 MCMASTERS AVE 63401 — 4-00011 — 221-2733
Michael Lewton, prin.
Hannibal Area Vo S — Vo Tech
4500 MCMASTERS AVE 63401 — 221-4430
Harold Ward, prin.
MS, 4700 MCMASTERS AVE 63401 — 3-00100 — 221-5840
Jerry Rash, prin.

Hannibal Area Voc. Technical School — 2-CS
4550 MCMASTERS AVE 63401 — 221-4430
Hannibal-LaGrange College — 3-UC
2800 PALMYRA RD 63401 — 221-3675
St. Thomas Aquinas HS — 1-00011
245 N LEVERING AVE 63401 — 221-4330
Fr. Daly, prin.

Hardin, AC 816, PC 3, Ray
Hardin-Central Consolidated SD 2 — 2-11111
PO BOX 548 64035 — 398-4394
Rick Edwards, supt.
Hardin-Central JSHS — 2-00111
PO BOX 548 64035 — 398-4394
Gary O'Neal, prin.

Harrisburg, AC 314, PC 2, Boone
Harrisburg RSD 8 — 2-11111
180 W SEXTON ST 65256 — 875-5604
Gene Garrison, supt.
JSHS, 221 S HARRIS ST 65256 — 2-00111 — 875-5602
G. Lowrey, prin.

Harrisonville, AC 816, PC 6, Cass
Harrisonville RSD 9 — 4-11111
402 EASTWOOD RD 64701 — 884-2727
David Smith, supt.
HS, 1504 E ELM ST 64701 — 3-00011 — 884-3273
Rob Barrett, prin.
Cass County Area Vo S — Vo Tech
1600 E ELM ST 64701 — 884-3253
Patricia Matthews, prin.
MS, 601 S HIGHLAND DR 64701 — 2-00100 — 885-3295
Todd White, prin.

Hartville, AC 417, PC 2, Wright
Hartville RSD 2, PO BOX F 65667 — 3-11111 — 741-7676
Bob Dryer, supt.
JSHS, PO BOX F 65667 — 2-00111 — 741-6223
Larry Mays, prin.

Hayti, AC 314, PC 5, Pemiscot
Hayti RSD 2, PO BOX 469 63851 — 3-11111 — 359-0180
George Byers, supt.
HS, PO BOX 469 63851 — 2-00111 — 359-1188
Wilburn Simmons, prin.
MS, PO BOX 469 63851 — 2-00100 — 359-1681
Coy Wilson, prin.

Pemiscot County Special SD — 3-00001
RR 2 BOX 886K 63851 — 359-0021
Keith Smith, supt.
Pemiscot County Vo HS — Vo Tech
RR 2 BOX 886K 63851 — 359-2601
Nicholas Thiele, prin.

Hazelwood, AC 314, PC 7, St. Louis
Hazelwood SD
Supt. — See Florissant
Hazelwood West JSHS — 4-00111
1 WILDCAT LN 63042 — 731-9100
George Gerdeman, prin.

Sanford-Brown Business College 4-CS
355 BROOKES DR 63042 731-5200

Herculaneum, AC 314, PC 4, Jefferson
Dunklin RSD 5, PO BOX 306 63048 4-11111
James Whitmer, supt. 479-5604
HS, PO BOX 306 63048 3-00011
Richard Borman, prin. 479-5602
Senn-Thomas MS, 204 MAIN ST 63048 2-00100
James Chandler, prin. 479-4055

Hermann, AC 314, PC 5, Gasconade
Gasconade County RSD 1 4-11111
RR 2 BOX 154 65041 486-2116
Dan Doerhoff, supt.
HS, RR 2 BOX 154 65041 2-00011
Gordon Laboube, prin. 486-5425
MS, 800 WASHINGTON ST 65041 2-00100
Ronald Combs, prin. 486-3121

Hermitage, AC 417, PC 3, Hickory
Hermitage RSD 4, PO BOX 327 65668 2-11111
Harold McCoy, supt. 745-6418
JSHS, PO BOX 327 65668 2-00111
Barbara McCaslin, prin. 745-6417

Higbee, AC 816, PC 3, Randolph
Higbee RSD 8, PO BOX 128 65257 2-11111
Phillip Palmer, supt. 456-7277
JSHS, PO BOX 128 65257 2-00111
Archie Derboven, prin. 456-7206

Higginsville, AC 816, PC 5, Lafayette
Lafayette County Consolidated SD 1 4-11111
2818 HIGHWAY BLVD 64037 584-3631
Gary Evans, supt.
Lafayette County HS 2-00011
803 W 31ST ST 64037 584-3661
James Tompkins, prin.
Lafayette County JHS 2-00100
805 W 31ST ST 64037 584-7161
Ray Sutherland, prin.

Hillsboro, AC 314, PC 4, Jefferson
Grandview RSD 2 3-11111
11470 HIGHWAY C 63050 944-3941
Gerald Moenster, supt.
Grandview JSHS 2-00111
11470 HIGHWAY C 63050 944-3390
Maurice Creason, prin.

Hillsboro RSD 3, 20 HAWK DR 63050 5-11111
James Sucharski, supt. 789-3378
HS, 12 HAWK DR 63050 3-00011
Larry Wells, prin. 789-3554
JHS, 10478 HIGHWAY 21 63050 3-00100
James Knuckles, prin. 789-3567

Jefferson College 5-CC
1000 VIKING DR 63050 789-3951

Holcomb, AC 314, PC 3, Dunklin
Holcomb RSD 3, PO BOX 187 63852 2-11111
Joe Morrow, supt. 792-3631
JSHS, PO BOX 187 63852 2-00111
Darrell Wilburn, prin. 792-3362

Holden, AC 816, PC 4, Johnson
Holden RSD 3, 900 MARKET ST 64040 4-11111
Robert V. Hoffman, supt. 732-5568
HS, 1901 S MAIN ST 64040 2-00011
James Moore, prin. 732-5523
MS, 902 MARKET ST 64040 2-00100
Greg Montgomery, prin. 732-4125

Hollister, AC 417, PC 5, Taney
Hollister RSD 5 3-11111
1798 STATE HIGHWAY BB 65672 334-6119
Gordon Logsdon, supt.
JSHS, 1798 STATE HIGHWAY BB 65672 2-00111
Gordon Logsdon, prin. 334-6119

Hopkins, AC 816, PC 3, Nodaway
North Nodaway County RSD 6 2-11111
PO BOX 256 64461 778-3411
William Couldry, supt.
North Nodaway County JSHS 2-00111
PO BOX 256 64461 778-3315
George Carroll, prin.

Hornersville, AC 314, PC 3, Dunklin
Senath-Hornersville Cons. SD 8
Supt. — See Senath
MS, PO BOX 258 63855 2-01100
Barth Larsen, prin. 737-2455

House Springs, AC 314, PC 3, Jefferson
Northwest RSD 1, PO BOX 500 63051 6-11111
John Gibson, supt. 677-3473
Northwest HS, PO BOX 500 63051 4-00011
Richard Boyle, prin. 375-3243
Cedar Hill MS, PO BOX 500 63051 2-00100
Gerald Glidewell, prin. 285-2301
MS, PO BOX 500 63051 3-00100
James Cashion, prin. 375-3288
North Jefferson MS 3-00100
PO BOX 500 63051 376-5844
James Pickett, prin.

Houston, AC 417, PC 4, Texas
Houston RSD 1, 423 W PINE ST 65483 4-11111
Terry Reid, supt. 967-3024
HS, 423 W PINE ST 65483 2-00011
Dennis Powell, prin. 967-4883
MS, 423 W PINE ST 65483 2-00100
Duane Widhalm, prin. 967-4886

Hughesville, AC 816, PC 2, Pettis
Pettis County RSD 5 2-11111
PO BOX 36 65334 827-0772
Eldon Kreisel, supt.
Northwest JSHS, PO BOX 36 65334 2-00111
Warren Ripley, prin. 827-0774

Humansville, AC 417, PC 4, Polk
Humansville RSD 4 2-11111
PO BOX 307 65674 754-2535
Douglas Wright, supt.
JSHS, PO BOX 307 65674 2-00111
Janice Hogan, prin. 754-2219

Hume, AC 816, PC 2, Bates
Hume RSD 8, PO BOX 402 64752 2-11111
Elaine Brame, supt. 643-7411
JSHS, PO BOX 402 64752 1-00111
Larry Berry, prin. 643-7411

Huntsville, AC 816, PC 4, Randolph
Westran RSD 1, 210 W DEPOT ST 65259 3-11111
Stephen Pharr, supt. 277-4429
Westran HS, RR 2 BOX 26A 65259 2-00011
James Otten, prin. 277-4415
Other Schools – See Clifton Hill

Hurley, AC 417, PC 1, Stone
Hurley RSD 1, PO BOX 248 65675 2-11111
Dennis Williams, supt. 748-3271
JSHS, PO BOX 248 65675 1-00111
Dennis Williams, prin. 748-3271

Iberia, AC 314, PC 3, Miller
Iberia RSD 5, PO BOX 156 65486 3-11111
Stan Johnson, supt. 793-6818
JSHS, PO BOX 156 65486 2-00111
Keith Jerome, prin. 793-6818

Imperial, AC 314, PC 3, Jefferson
Fox Consolidated SD 6
Supt. — See Arnold
Seckman JHS, 2810 SECKMAN RD 63052 3-00110
Lindell Stacy, prin. 296-5707

Windsor Consolidated SD 1 5-11111
6208 US HIGHWAY 61/67 63052 464-1123
Randall Boyer, supt.
Windsor HS 3-00011
6208 US HIGHWAY 61/67 63052 464-4430
Richard Riggs, prin.
Windsor MS 3-00100
6208 US HIGHWAY 61/67 63052 464-4417
Neil Penberthy, prin.

Independence, AC 816, PC 9, Jackson
Fort Osage RSD 1 6-11111
2101 N TWYMAN RD 64058 249-6131
Paul James, supt.
Ft. Osage SHS 4-00001
2101 N TWYMAN RD 64058 249-6106
Kim Schaberg, prin.
Area Vo-Tech S Vo Tech
2101 N TWYMAN RD 64058 249-6377
WALTER KENNON, prin.
Ft. Osage JHS 4-00110
2101 N TWYMAN RD 64058 249-6104
Jerry Soendker, prin.

Independence SD 30 7-11111
1231 WINDSOR ST 64055 833-3433
Robert Watkins, supt.
Chrisman HS 4-00011
1223 N NOLAND RD 64050 252-1200
Thomas Herrick, prin.
Truman HS, 3301 S NOLAND RD 64055 4-00011
Jeff White, prin. 833-1313
Bridger JHS 4-00100
18200 E STATE ROUTE 78 64057 796-4200
G. Gelven, prin.
Palmer JHS, 218 N PLEASANT ST 64050 3-00100
Jerry Moore, prin. 254-7474

Kansas City SD 33
Supt. — See Kansas City
Van Horn HS 3-00011
1109 S ARLINGTON AVE 64053 871-8200
William Smith, prin.
Nowlin MS, 2800 S HARDY AVE 64052 3-00100
Evelyn Belser, prin. 871-8300

National Career Institute 2-CS
17601 E US HIGHWAY 40 64055 373-6292
St. Mary Bundschu Memorial HS 2-00011
622 N MAIN ST 64050 252-8733
David Woolwine, prin.
Vatterott College 2-CS
210 S MAIN ST 64050 252-3997

Ironton, AC 314, PC 4, Iron
Arcadia Valley RSD 2 4-11111
750 W PARK DR 63650 546-7313
Terry Adams, supt.
Arcadia Valley HS 2-00011
520 W PARK DR 63650 546-3933
James Erpenbach, prin.
Arcadia Valley Area Vo S Vo Tech
520 W PARK DR 63650 546-3907
Bill Sheehy, prin.
Arcadia Valley MS 2-00100
550 W PARK DR 63650 546-3302
Patricia Mertens, prin.

Jackson, AC 314, PC 6, Cape Girardeau
Jackson RSD 2 5-11111
221 S OKLAHOMA ST 63755 243-3579
Wayne Maupin, supt.
SHS, 221 S OKLAHOMA ST 63755 3-00001
Vernon Huck, prin. 243-3234
Hawkins JHS 3-00110
221 S OKLAHOMA ST 63755 243-3584
Dennis Parham, prin.

Jameson, AC 816, PC 2, Daviess
North Daviess RSD 3 2-11111
RR 1 BOX 34 64647 828-4123
E. Schoppenhorst, supt.
North Daviess JSHS 1-00111
RR 1 BOX 34 64647 828-4123
Julie Kirby, prin.

Jamesport, AC 816, PC 3, Daviess
Tri-County RSD 7 2-11111
PO BOX 224 64648 684-6118
Art Heriford, supt.
Tri-County JSHS, PO BOX 227 64648 1-00111
Stan Coulson, prin. 684-6116

Jamestown, AC 816, PC 2, Moniteau
Moniteau County Consolidated SD 1 2-11111
200 SCHOOL ST 65046 849-2141
Don Lawrence, supt.
Moniteau County JSHS 2-00111
200 SCHOOL ST 65046 849-2141
Stanley Mantle, prin.

Jasper, AC 417, PC 3, Jasper
Jasper County RSD 5 3-11111
RR 3 BOX 20 64755 394-2416
Greg Koetting, supt.
Jasper County HS 2-00011
RR 3 BOX 20 64755 394-2511
Gerald Portman, prin.

Jefferson City, AC 314, PC 8, Cole
Cole County RSD 2 3-11111
6124 FALCON LN 65101 636-2020
Larry Reed, supt.
Blair Oaks JSHS 2-00111
6124 FALCON LN 65101 635-8514
Chuck Schmidt, prin.

Jefferson City SD 6-11111
315 E DUNKLIN ST 65101 659-3000
Chris Straub, supt.
JSHS, 609 UNION ST 65101 4-00001
Richard Pemberton, prin. 659-3200
Nichols Career Ctr, 609 UNION ST 65101 Vo Tech
Harold Lynch, prin. 659-3100
Jefferson MS 3-00100
1201 FAIRGROUNDS RD 65109 659-3140
Fern Ward, prin.
Simonsen JHS, 501 E MILLER ST 65101 3-00010
Charles Dorch, prin. 659-3125

Helias HS, 1305 SWIFTS HWY 65109 3-00011
Joseph Gulino, prin. 635-6139
Lincoln University 4-UC
820 CHESTNUT ST 65101 681-5042
Linn Technical College 2-CS
308 E HIGH ST 65101 634-7897
Metro Business College 2-CS
1407 SOUTHWEST BLVD 65109 635-6600

Jennings, AC 314, PC 7, St. Louis
Jennings SD, 8888 CLIFTON AVE 63136 5-11111
W. Bell, supt. 867-8900
HS, 8850 COZENS AVE 63136 3-00011
Robert Bax, prin. 867-4600
JHS, 8831 COZENS AVE 63136 2-00100
Clarence Holman, prin. 867-6445

Joplin, AC 417, PC 8, Jasper
Joplin RSD 8, PO BOX 128 64802 6-11111
William Brill, supt. 625-5200
SHS, 2104 INDIANA AVE 64804 4-00001
Frank Zeka, prin. 625-5230
Franklin Tech S, 2020 IOWA AVE 64804 Vo Tech
Fred Green, prin. 625-5260
JHS, 310 W 8TH ST 64801 4-00110
Darrel Warren, prin. 625-5250

College Heights Christian S 2-00011
RR 7 BOX 947 64801 782-4114
Lee Pelham, prin.
McAuley Regional HS 2-00011
930 S PEARL AVE 64801 624-9320
Martin Bambick, prin.
Missouri Southern State College 5-UC
3950 NEWMAN RD 64801 624-8181
Ozark Christian College 3-UC
1111 N MAIN ST 64801 800-299-4662
St. John's Regional Medical Center HSP
2727 MC CLELLAND BLVD 64804 781-2727
St. Peters MS, 802 BYERS AVE 64801 1-00100
Steven Johnson, prin. 624-5605
Vatterott College 2-CS
N MAIN ST 64801 781-5633

Kahoka, AC 816, PC 4, Clark
Clark County RSD 1 4-11111
427 W CHESTNUT ST 63445 727-2377
Randy Sheriff, supt.
Clark County JSHS 3-00111
384 N JEFFERSON ST 63445 727-3316
Howard Berlin, prin.

Kansas City, AC 816, PC 10, Jackson
Center SD 58, 8701 HOLMES ST 64131   5-11111
  Raymond Feltner, supt.   363-6060
Center HS, 8715 HOLMES ST 64131   3-00011
  Darlene Jones, prin.   363-2260
Center MS, 326 E 103RD ST 64114   2-00100
  James Kenworthy, prin.   942-0326

Hickman Mills Consolidated SD 1   6-11111
  9000 OLD SANTA FE RD 64138   761-6111
  Coy Goodwin, supt.
Hickman Mills HS   3-00011
  9010 OLD SANTA FE RD 64138   763-8374
  Charles Greene, prin.
Ruskin HS   3-00011
  7000 E 111TH ST # 46 64134   761-5514
  William Elliott, prin.
Ervin JHS   3-00100
  10530 GREENWOOD RD 64134   763-1525
  Linda Roberts, prin.
Smith-Hale JHS   3-00100
  8925 LONGVIEW RD 64134   761-4544
  Debra Nelson, prin.

Kansas City SD 33   8-11111
  1211 MCGEE ST 64106   871-7000
  Walter Marks, supt.
Central HS, 3221 INDIANA AVE 64128   4-00011
  Emmerson Payme, prin.   871-8900
East HS, 1924 VAN BRUNT BLVD 64127   3-00011
  Gary Maricle, prin.   871-1800
NE Law/Public Service HS   4-00011
  415 VAN BRUNT BLVD 64124   871-1900
  Stephen Brown, prin.
Paseo Academy HS   3-00011
  4747 FLORA AVE 64110   871-7900
  Dorothy Shepherd, prin.
Southeast HS   3-00011
  3500 E MEYER BLVD 64132   871-0800
  Manuel Isquierdo, prin.
Southwest HS   4-00011
  6512 WORNALL RD 64113   871-0900
  Thomas Reefer, prin.
Westport HS, 315 E 39TH ST 64111   3-00011
  Vonnelle Middleton, prin.   871-6500
Lincoln College Prep. JSHS   3-00111
  2111 WOODLAND AVE 64108   871-1500
  Barbara Lusk, prin.
Metro Tech HS   Vo Tech
  1215 E TRUMAN RD 64106   871-8150
  R. M. Turvey, prin.
Arts & Science MS, 6903 OAK ST 64113   2-00100
  Linda Kondris, prin.   871-4770
Bingham Magnet MS   3-00100
  7618 WYANDOTTE ST 64114   871-1877
  Mark Lewis, prin.
Central Magnet MS   3-00100
  3611 E LINWOOD BLVD 64128   871-0100
  Mark Harrison, prin.
MS of the Arts-Magnet   3-00100
  8201 HOLMES ST 64131   871-4900
  Roger Williams, prin.
High School Prep   2-00010
  6330 SWOPE PKY 64132   871-2780
  Diane Stevenson, prin.
King MS, 4201 INDIANA AVE 64130   3-00100
  Juanita Hempstead, prin.   871-0150
Lincoln Magnet MS   3-00100
  2012 E 23RD ST 64127   871-1700
  John Anderson, prin.
Northeast MS   3-00100
  4904 INDEPENDENCE AVE 64124   871-6830
  Lloyd Seals, prin.
Robeson MS, 4610 E 24TH ST 64127   3-00100
  Cleo Washington, prin.   871-6950
Southeast Magnet MS   3-00100
  6410 SWOPE PKY 64132   926-2800
  Martin Gill, prin.
Westport MS, 3845 MCGEE ST 64111   3-00100
  Charles Green, prin.   871-6050
Other Schools – See Independence

Park Hill RSD 5   6-11111
  7703 NW BARRY RD 64153   741-1521
  Harold Gaarde, supt.
Park Hill HS, 7701 NW BARRY RD 64153   4-00011
  L. Papenfuhs, prin.   741-4070
Lakeview MS, 6720 NW 64TH ST 64151   3-00100
  Raymond Smither, prin.   741-8665
Plaza MS, 6501 NW 72ND ST 64151   3-00100
  Georgina Chambers, prin.   741-1511

Raytown Consolidated SD 2
Supt. — See Raytown
Raytown MS, 4900 PITTMAN RD 64133   4-00100
  Chris Richardson, prin.   737-6305

Archbishop O'Hara HS   3-00011
  9001 JAMES A REED RD 64138   763-4800
  Stuart Bintner, prin.
Avila College   3-UC
  11901 WORNALL RD 64145   942-8400
Barstow S, 11511 STATE LINE RD 64114   2-11111
  James Achterberg, prin.   942-3255
Bishop Hogan HS   2-00011
  1221 E MEYER BLVD 64131   444-3464
  Charles Wurth, prin.
Calvary Bible College   3-UC
  15800 CALVARY RD 64147   322-0110
Cleveland Chiropractic College   2-UC
  6401 ROCKHILL RD 64131   800-467-2252

ConCorde Career Institute   3-CS
  3239 BROADWAY ST 64111   531-5223
DeVry Institute of Technology   4-UC
  11224 HOLMES ST 64131   941-2810
Diamond Council of America   1-HMS
  9140 WARD PKY 64114
Electronic Institutes   3-CS
  15329 KENSINGTON AVE 64147   331-5700
Farmland Industries   1-HMS
  PO BOX 7305 64116
Kansas City Art Institute   3-UC
  4415 WARWICK BLVD 64111   800-522-5224
Lutheran HS, 414 WALLACE AVE 64125   1-00011
  Richard Klatt, prin.   241-5478
Maple Woods Community College   5-CC
  2601 NE BARRY RD 64156   436-6500
Menorah Medical Center   HSP
  4949 ROCKHILL RD 64110   276-8101
Midwestern Baptist Theological Seminary   2-UC
  5001 N OAK TRFY 64118   453-4600
Missouri Auction School   1-CS
  1600 GENESSEE ST 64102   421-7117
Nazarene Theological Seminary   2-UC
  1700 E MEYER BLVD 64131   333-6254
Notre Dame De Sion S   2-00011
  10631 WORNALL RD 64114   942-3282
  Alice Munninghoff, prin.
Pembroke Hill S, 400 W 51ST ST 64112   4-11111
  Thomas Harvey, prin.   753-1300
Penn Valley Community College   5-CC
  3201 SW TRAFFIC WAY 64111   932-7610
Research College of Nursing   2-UC
  2316 E MEYER BLVD 64132   926-4100
Research Medical Center   2-HSP
  2316 E MEYER BLVD 64132   276-4000
Rockhurst College   4-UC
  1100 ROCKHURST RD 64110   926-4250
Rockhurst HS   3-00011
  9301 STATE LINE RD 64114   363-2036
  Fred Campisano, prin.
St. Luke's Hospital   HSP
  4400 WORNALL RD 64111   932-2233
St. Monica S, 1524 PASEO BLVD 64108   2-01100
  Sr. Michael Allegri, prin.   421-0305
St. Paul School of Theology   2-UC
  5123 E TRUMAN RD 64127   483-9600
St. Teresas Academy   2-00011
  5600 MAIN ST 64113   523-3522
  Faith Wilson, prin.
Sanford-Brown Business College   2-CS
  3901 BLUE RIDGE CUT OFF 64133   737-5858
TAD Technical Institute   3-CS
  7910 TROOST AVE 64131   361-5140
Trans World Technical Academy   2-CS
  533 MEXICO CITY AVE 64153   800-892-8324
Trinity Lutheran Hospital   HSP
  31ST & WYANDOTTE STS 64108   751-2000
United Health Careers Institute   2-CS
  1100 MAIN ST STE 10 64105   474-4750
University of Health Sciences   3-UC
  2105 INDEPENDENCE AVE 64124   283-2000
University of Missouri   6-UC
  5100 ROCKHILL RD 64110   235-1101
Wright Business School   2-CC
  5528 NE ANTIOCH RD 64119   452-4411

Kearney, AC 816, PC 4, Clay
Kearney RSD 1   4-11111
  1002 S JEFFERSON ST 64060   635-4116
  Richard Logerwell, supt.
SHS, 715 E 19TH ST 64060   2-00001
  Randall Smith, prin.   635-4585
JHS, PO BOX 78 64060   3-00110
  Karl Morrow, prin.   635-4115

Kennett, AC 314, PC 7, Dunklin
Kennett SD 39, 510 COLLEGE AVE 63857   4-11111
  Larry Ewing, supt.   888-2861
HS, 1400 W WASHINGTON ST 63857   3-00011
  Terry Turlington, prin.   888-4578
Kennett Area Vo S   Vo Tech
  1400 W WASHINGTON ST 63857   888-9067
  Ralph Hemann, prin.
MS, 510 COLLEGE AVE 63857   2-00100
  Ward Billings, prin.   888-4787

Keytesville, AC 816, PC 3, Chariton
Keytesville RSD 3   2-11111
  RR 2 BOX 55 65261   288-3767
  Kyle Stephenson, supt.
JSHS, RR 2 BOX 55 65261   1-00111
  Lonnie Jackson, prin.   288-3767

King City, AC 816, PC 3, Gentry
King City RSD 1, PO BOX 188 64463   2-11111
  Terry Karr, supt.   535-4319
JSHS, PO BOX 188 64463   2-00111
  Noel Fischer, prin.   535-4319

Kingdom City, AC 314, PC 2, Callaway
North Callaway County RSD 1   4-11111
  PO BOX 33 65262   386-2214
  R. Howard, supt.
North Callaway HS   2-00011
  PO BOX 33 65262   386-2211
  Trevis Brown, prin.

Kingsville, AC 816, PC 2, Johnson
Kingsville RSD 1, PO BOX 7 64061   2-11111
  Dean Schnakenberg, supt.   597-3422
JSHS, PO BOX 7 64061   2-00111
  Larry Potthast, prin.   597-3422

Kirksville, AC 816, PC 7, Adair
Kirksville RSD 3, 1209 S 1ST ST 63501   4-11111
  Kenneth Southard, supt.   665-7774
HS   3-00011
  1300 S COTTAGE GROVE AVE 63501   665-4631
  Patrick Williams, prin.
Kirksville Area Vo S   Vo Tech
  1300 S COTTAGE GROVE AVE 63501   665-2865
  Paul Wootten, prin.
MS   3-00100
  1515 S COTTAGE GROVE AVE 63501   665-3793
  Gary Drummond, prin.

Kirksville Coll. of Osteopathic Medicine   3-UC
  800 W JEFFERSON ST 63501   800-626-5266
Northeast Missouri State University   6-UC
  63501   785-4000

Kirkwood, AC 314, PC 8, St. Louis
Kirkwood RSD 7   6-11111
  11289 MANCHESTER RD 63122   965-9570
  Deborah Holmes, supt.
HS, 801 W ESSEX AVE 63122   4-00011
  Franklin McCallie, prin.   966-5700
Nipher MS, 700 S KIRKWOOD RD 63122   3-00100
  Carol Migneron, prin.   965-9580
North Kirkwood MS   3-00100
  11287 MANCHESTER RD 63122   965-9530
  Kathleen Keusenkothen, prin.

Midwest Institute for Medical Assistants   2-CS
  112 W JEFFERSON AVE 63122   965-8363
St. Louis Community College   6-CC
  11333 BIG BEND RD 63122   984-7608
Ursuline Academy   3-00011
  341 S SAPPINGTON RD 63122   966-4556
  Sr. Mary Agnew, prin.
Vianney HS   3-00011
  1311 S KIRKWOOD RD 63122   965-4853
  Lawrence Furrer, prin.

Knob Noster, AC 816, PC 4, Johnson
Knob Noster RSD 8   4-11111
  401 E WIMER ST 65336   563-3186
  Larry Ficken, supt.
HS, 504 S WASHINGTON AVE 65336   2-00011
  Gerald Jenkins, prin.   563-2283
MS, 211 E WIMER ST 65336   2-00100
  Minter Ringen, prin.   563-2260

Koshkonong, AC 417, PC 2, Oregon
Oregon-Howell RSD 3   2-11111
  PO BOX 398 65692   867-3321
  Ronald Taylor, supt.
JSHS, PO BOX 398 65692   2-00111
  Robert Gillham, prin.   867-3251

Laddonia, AC 314, PC 3, Audrain
Community RSD 6   2-11111
  RR 1 BOX 196 63352   492-6222
  Ted Spessard, supt.
Community HS, RR 1 BOX 196 63352   2-00011
  Charlotte Baker, prin.   492-6222

Lake Ozark, AC 314, PC 3, Miller
School of the Osage RSD 2   4-11111
  PO BOX 1960 65049   365-4091
  Dalton Ham, supt.
Osage HS, PO BOX 1960 65049   2-00011
  Gary Carrender, prin.   348-0115
Osage MS, PO BOX 1960 65049   2-01100
  Jeffrey Fishburn, prin.   365-5343

Lamar, AC 417, PC 5, Barton
Lamar RSD 1, 202 W 7TH ST 64759   4-11111
  Barb Burns, supt.   682-3527
HS, 503 MAPLE ST 64759   2-00011
  Charles Blaney, prin.   682-5571
Lamar Area Vo S, 202 W 7TH ST 64759   Vo Tech
  Karl Morey, prin.   682-3384
MS, 7TH & GULF 64759   2-01100
  Herbert Gailey, prin.   682-3548

La Monte, AC 816, PC 3, Pettis
La Monte RSD 4   2-11111
  301 S WASHINGTON ST 65337   347-5439
  Douglas Domer, supt.
JSHS, 301 S WASHINGTON ST 65337   2-00111
  Gary Littrell, prin.   347-5439

Lancaster, AC 816, PC 3, Schuyler
Schuyler County RSD 1
  Supt. — See Queen City
Schuyler County HS   2-00011
  PO BOX 220 63548   457-3701
  Daniel Day, prin.

La Plata, AC 816, PC 4, Macon
La Plata RSD 2, 201 W MOORE ST 63549   2-11111
  Richard Ray, supt.   332-7001
JSHS, 201 W MOORE ST 63549   2-00111
  Richard Burns, prin.   332-7001

Laquey, AC 314, PC 2, Pulaski
Laquey RSD 5, PO BOX 130 65534   3-11111
  Dale Passmore, supt.   765-3716
JSHS, PO BOX 130 65534   2-00111
  Paul Miller, prin.   765-4051

Lathrop, AC 816, PC 4, Clinton
Lathrop RSD 2, 700 EAST ST 64465   3-11111
  Olin Parks, supt.   528-4225
JSHS, 612 CENTER ST 64465   2-00111
  Charles Nance, prin.   528-4224

Lawson, AC 816, PC 4, Ray
Lawson RSD 14, PO BOX 157 64062 — 4-11111 296-3214
  Steve Sellers, supt.
HS, PO BOX 157 64062 — 2-00011 296-3296
  Standlea Petty, prin.
Central MS, PO BOX 157 64062 — 2-01100 296-3513
  Edward Duncan, prin.

Leadwood, AC 314, PC 4, St. Francois
West St. Francis County RSD 4 — 3-11111 562-7535
  1124 MAIN ST 63653
  Claude Lynch, supt.
West County JSHS, 1124 MAIN ST 63653 — 2-00111 562-7521
  Terrence Scandrett, prin.

Lebanon, AC 417, PC 6, Laclede
Lebanon RSD 3 — 5-11111 532-9141
  321 S JEFFERSON AVE 65536
  Jack Howard, supt.
SHS, 777 BRICE ST 65536 — 3-00001 532-9144
  Richard Tiller, prin.
Laclede Area Vo S — Vo Tech 532-5494
  HWY 64 BYPASS 65536
  Jon Presley, prin.
JHS, 500 S ADAMS AVE 65536 — 3-00110 532-9121
  Clark Mershon, prin.

Lee's Summit, AC 816, PC 8, Jackson
Lee's Summit RSD 7 — 7-11111 524-3368
  600 SE MILLER ST 64063
  Gail Williams, supt.
HS, 400 SE BLUE PKY 64063 — 5-00011 524-3369
  Jim Lemery, prin.
Campbell JHS — 3-00100 524-3050
  1201 NE COLBERN RD 64086
  Dennis Smith, prin.
Pleasant Lea JHS — 3-00100 524-4730
  630 SW PERSELS RD 64081
  Carl Grigsby, prin.

Longview Community College — 5-CC 672-2000
  500 SW LONGVIEW RD 64081

Leeton, AC 816, PC 3, Johnson
Leeton RSD 10, 500 N MAIN ST 64761 — 2-11111 653-4314
  Tom McGuire, supt.
HS, 500 N MAIN ST 64761 — 1-00011 653-4314
  Brian Gaub, prin.

Leopold, AC 314, PC 2, Bollinger
Leopold RSD 3, 100 W MAIN ST 63760 — 2-11111 238-2211
  Robert Turner, supt.
JSHS, 100 W MAIN ST 63760 — 1-00111 238-2211
  Greg Nenninger, prin.

Lesterville, AC 314, PC 2, Reynolds
Lesterville RSD 4, PO BOX 120 63654 — 2-11111 637-2201
  Daniel Cashion, supt.
JSHS, PO BOX 120 63654 — 2-00111 637-2201
  Robert Declue, prin.

Lexington, AC 816, PC 5, Lafayette
Lexington RSD 5, 100 S 13TH ST 64067 — 4-11111 259-4369
  Joe Aull, supt.
HS, 2307 AULL LN 64067 — 2-00011 259-4391
  Marvin Misemer, prin.
Lex La-Ray Tech Ctr — Vo Tech 259-2264
  2323 HIGH SCHOOL DR 64067
  Charles Houseworth, prin.
MS, 101 N 16TH ST 64067 — 2-00100 259-4611
  Tom Hayes, prin.

Wentworth Military Academy — 2-00011 259-2221
  1880 WASHINGTON AVE 64067
  Terence Davis, prin.
Wentworth Military Academy — 2-CC 259-2221
  1800 WASHINGTON AVE 64067

Liberal, AC 417, PC 3, Barton
Liberal RSD 2, PO BOX 38 64762 — 2-11111 843-5115
  Derrall Beasley, supt.
HS, PO BOX 38 64762 — 2-00011 843-2125
  Robert Hays, prin.
JHS, PO BOX 38 64762 — 1-00100 843-6033
  Yolanda Hermsen, prin.

Liberty, AC 816, PC 7, Clay
Liberty SD 53, 14 S MAIN ST 64068 — 5-11111 781-4541
  Ron Anderson, supt.
SHS, 200 BLUE JAY DR 64068 — 3-00001 781-3432
  Martin Jacobs, prin.
JHS, 600 W KANSAS AVE 64068 — 3-00110 781-4540
  Joanie Hartnett, prin.

William Jewell College 64068 — 4-UC 781-7700

Licking, AC 314, PC 4, Texas
Licking RSD 8, PO BOX 179 65542 — 3-11111 674-2911
  Dewayne Collins, supt.
JSHS, PO BOX 149 65542 — 2-00111 674-2711
  Stephen Denbow, prin.

Lincoln, AC 816, PC 3, Benton
Lincoln RSD 2, PO BOX 39 65338 — 2-11111 547-3514
  David Decker, supt.
JSHS, PO BOX 39 65338 — 2-00111 547-3514
  David Wright, prin.

Linn, AC 314, PC 4, Osage
Osage County RSD 2 — 3-11111 897-4200
  1212 E MAIN ST 65051
  Brian Kirk, prin.

HS, 1212 E MAIN ST 65051 — 2-00011 897-4216
  Lonnie Thompson, prin.
Linn Tech S, 1 TECHNOLOGY DR 65051 — Vo Tech 897-3603
  Don Claycomb, prin.
Osage County MS — 2-00100 897-2228
  1212 E MAIN ST 65051
  Veronica Smith, prin.

Linn Technical College — 2-CS 897-3603
  1 TECHNOLOGY DR 65051

Lockwood, AC 417, PC 4, Dade
Lockwood RSD 1, PO BOX W 65682 — 2-11111 232-4513
  Joann Berlekamp, supt.
HS, PO BOX W 65682 — 2-00011 232-4513
  Mackie Diefenderfer, prin.

Lone Jack, AC 816, PC 2, Jackson
Lone Jack Consolidated SD 6 — 2-11111 566-2215
  201 W LNE JACK LEES SMMT RD 64070
  David Cooper, supt.
JSHS — 2-00111 566-2215
  201 W LNE JACK LEES SMMT RD 64070
  Ron Inman, prin.

Louisiana, AC 314, PC 5, Pike
Louisiana RSD 2 — 3-11111 754-4261
  515 JACKSON ST 63353
  Onofrio Monachino, supt.
HS, 3321 GEORGIA ST 63353 — 2-00011 754-6181
  Dan Johnson, prin.
MS, 515 JACKSON ST 63353 — 2-01100 754-5340
  Betty Dolbeare, prin.

Ludlow, AC 816, PC 2, Livingston
Southwest Livingston County RSD 1 — 2-11111 738-4433
  RR 1 BOX 68 64656
  Franklin E. Schottel, supt.
Southwest Livingston County JSHS — 2-00111 738-4433
  RR 1 BOX 68 64656
  Larry Chapman, prin.

Macks Creek, AC 314, PC 2, Camden
Macks Creek RSD 5 — 2-11111 363-5911
  PO BOX 38 65786
  William Jones, supt.
JSHS, PO BOX 38 65786 — 2-00111 363-5911
  Gail Aubuchon, prin.

Macon, AC 816, PC 6, Macon
Macon County RSD 1 — 4-11111 385-5719
  700 N MISSOURI ST 63552
  J. King, supt.
Macon County HS — 3-00011 385-5748
  700 N MISSOURI ST 63552
  John Wallace, prin.
Macon Area Vo S — Vo Tech 385-2158
  700 N MISSOURI ST 63552
  Larry Theerman, prin.
Macon County MS — 2-00100 385-2189
  700 N MISSOURI ST 63552
  James Cerva, prin.

Madison, AC 816, PC 3, Monroe
Madison Consolidated SD 3 — 2-11111 291-5115
  PO BOX 123 65263
  Paul Franklin, supt.
JSHS, PO BOX 123 65263 — 2-00111 291-5115
  Raymond Clem, prin.

Maitland, AC 816, PC 2, Holt
Nodaway-Holt RSD 7 — 2-11111 935-2515
  PO BOX 29NH 64466
  John Zeliff, supt.
Nodaway-Holt MS, PO BOX 29NH 64466 — 2-01100 935-2514
  Jill Wolken, prin.
Other Schools – See Graham

Malden, AC 314, PC 6, Dunklin
Malden RSD 1, PO BOX 296 63863 — 4-11111 276-5794
  James Whitledge, supt.
JSHS, 407 STATE ROUTE J 63863 — 3-00111 276-4546
  Dewain Ward, prin.

Malta Bend, AC 816, PC 2, Saline
Malta Bend RSD 5, PO BOX 10 65339 — 2-11111 595-2371
  Joyce Briggs, supt.
JSHS, PO BOX 10 65339 — 1-00111 595-2371
  Phil Nelson, prin.

Manchester, AC 314, PC 6, St. Louis
Parkway Consolidated SD 2
  Supt. — See Chesterfield
South HS, 801 HANNA RD 63021 — 4-00011 394-8300
  Craig Larson, prin.
South JHS, 760 WOODS MILL RD 63011 — 4-00100 256-1300
  James Cockrell, prin.

John F. Kennedy HS — 2-00011 227-5900
  500 WOODS MILL RD 63011
  Donald Burkhart, prin.

Mansfield, AC 417, PC 4, Wright
Mansfield RSD 4, PO BOX 418 65704 — 3-11111 924-8458
  Robert Perry, supt.
HS, PO BOX 107 65704 — 2-00011 924-3236
  Jerry Armstrong, prin.
JHS, PO BOX 419 65704 — 2-00100 924-8625
  Fred Doherty, prin.

Maplewood, AC 314, PC 6, St. Louis
Maplewood-Richmond Heights SD — 4-11111 644-4400
  7539 MANCHESTER RD 63143
  Jerry Elliott, supt.

Maplewood-Richmond Heights HS — 2-00011 644-4400
  7539 MANCHESTER RD 63143
  Carol McCormack, prin.
Other Schools – See Richmond Heights

Marble Hill, AC 314, PC 4, Bollinger
Woodland RSD 4 — 3-11111 238-3343
  RR 3 BOX 3210 63764
  Ron Wene, supt.
Woodland JSHS — 2-00111 238-2663
  RR 3 BOX 3210 63764
  Mark Engelhardt, prin.

Marceline, AC 816, PC 5, Linn
Marceline RSD 5 — 3-11111 376-3371
  314 E SANTA FE AVE 64658
  Jay Reese, supt.
HS, 314 E SANTA FE AVE 64658 — 2-00011 376-2411
  Tom Hauser, prin.
MS, 314 E SANTA FE AVE 64658 — 2-00100 376-2411
  Tom Hauser, prin.

Marionville, AC 417, PC 4, Lawrence
Marionville RSD 9, PO BOX J 65705 — 3-11111 463-2514
  Ron Bilyeu, supt.
HS, PO BOX J 65705 — 2-00111 463-2521
  Jamey Parks, prin.

Marquand, AC 314, PC 2, Madison
Marquand-Zion RSD 6, PO BOX A 63655 — 2-11111 783-3388
  Gerald Deardorff, supt.
Marquand-Zion JSHS, PO BOX A 63655 — 2-00111 783-3388
  Nicholas Elfrink, prin.

Marshall, AC 816, PC 7, Saline
Marshall SD — 4-11111 886-7414
  468 S JEFFERSON AVE 65340
  Bruce Brock, supt.
HS, 805 S MIAMI AVE 65340 — 3-00011 886-2244
  James Tobin, prin.
Saline County Career Ctr — Vo Tech 886-6958
  900 W VEST ST 65340
  Don Ward, prin.
Bueker MS, 565 S ODELL AVE 65340 — 3-01100 886-6833
  Spencer Fricke, prin.

Missouri Valley College — 4-UC 886-6924
  500 E COLLEGE ST 65340

Marshfield, AC 417, PC 5, Webster
Marshfield RSD 1, PO BOX B 65706 — 4-11111 468-2120
  Joyce Dana, supt.
HS, PO BOX B 65706 — 3-00011 468-2165
  Tom Hibbs, prin.
JHS, PO BOX B 65706 — 2-00100 468-4050
  Michael Arnold, prin.

Maryland Heights, AC 314, PC 8, St. Louis
Pattonville RSD 3 — 6-11111 298-4502
  115 HARDING AVE 63043
  Roger Clough, supt.
Pattonville HS — 4-00011 739-0776
  2497 CREVE COEUR MILL RD 63043
  John Glore, prin.
Pattonville Hts. MS — 3-00100 298-4440
  195 FEE FEE RD 63043
  Bernard Epstein, prin.
Other Schools – See Saint Ann

Maryville, AC 816, PC 7, Nodaway
Maryville RSD 2 — 4-11111 562-3255
  109 E SUMMIT DR 64468
  Roland Tullberg, supt.
HS, 1503 S MUNN AVE 64468 — 3-00011 562-3511
  Ronald Landherr, prin.
NW Tech S, 1515 S MUNN AVE 64468 — Vo Tech 562-3022
  Paul Coffman, prin.
Washington MS, 301 E 1ST ST 64468 — 2-01100 562-3244
  Glen Jonagan, prin.

Northwest Missouri State University — 6-UC 562-1110
  800 UNIVERSITY DR 64468

Maysville, AC 816, PC 4, DeKalb
Maysville RSD 1, 601 W MAIN 64469 — 3-11111 449-2308
  Kenneth Tipton, supt.
JSHS, PO BOX 68 64469 — 2-00111 449-2154
  Paul Neice, prin.

Meadville, AC 816, PC 2, Linn
Meadville RSD 4 — 2-11111 938-4111
  101 E CRANDALL ST 64659
  Kenneth Dudley, supt.
JSHS, 101 E CRANDALL ST 64659 — 2-00111 938-4112
  Velma Trentham, prin.

Memphis, AC 816, PC 4, Scotland
Scotland County RSD 1 — 3-11111 465-8531
  PO BOX 337 63555
  Daniel O'Donnell, supt.
JSHS, PO BOX 337 63555 — 2-00111 465-8907
  Arthur Huff, prin.

Mendon, AC 816, PC 2, Chariton
Northwestern RSD 1 — 2-11111 272-3201
  PO BOX 43 64660
  Frank Darling, supt.
Northwestern JSHS — 2-00111 272-3201
  PO BOX 43 64660
  Michael Spears, prin.

Mercer, AC 816, PC 2, Mercer
North Mercer County RSD 3 — 2-11111 382-4214
  PO BOX 648 64661
  William Casey, supt.

JSHS, PO BOX 648 64661 1-00111
Douglas Reed, prin. 382-4214

Mexico, AC 314, PC 7, Audrain
Mexico SD 59 5-11111
920 S JEFFERSON ST 65265 581-3773
Gary Hieronymus, supt.
HS, 639 N WADE ST 65265 3-00011
Darriel Douglas, prin. 581-4296
Mexico Area Vo S Vo Tech
905 N WADE ST 65265 581-5684
Donald Walker, prin.
JHS, 1200 W BOULEVARD ST 65265 3-00100
Glenn Wheeler, prin. 581-4664

Missouri Military Academy 2-01111
204 N GRAND ST 65265 581-1776
Frank Meredith, prin.

Milan, AC 816, PC 4, Sullivan
Milan Consolidated SD 2 3-11111
373 S MARKET ST 63556 265-4414
Wallace Stiles, supt.
JSHS, 373 S MARKET ST 63556 2-00111
Daniel Van Ingen, prin. 265-4415

Miller, AC 417, PC 3, Lawrence
Miller RSD 2, 500 SCHOOL ST 65707 3-11111
James Young, supt. 452-3515
JSHS, 500 SCHOOL ST 65707 2-00111
Michael Ferraro, prin. 452-3271

Moberly, AC 816, PC 7, Randolph
Moberly SD, 101 JOHNSON ST 65270 5-11111
Lance Hutton, supt. 263-5712
HS, 1625 GRATZ BROWN ST 65270 3-00011
Robert Gordon, prin. 269-2660
Moberly Area Vo S Vo Tech
1625 GRATZ BROWN ST 65270 269-2690
William Goodrick, prin.
JHS, 920 KWIX RD 65270 3-00100
Arthur Yocum, prin. 269-2680

Central Christian College of the Bible 1-UC
911 E URBANDALE DR 65270 263-3900
Moberly Area Community College 4-CC
COLLEGE & ROLLINS ST 65270 263-4110

Mokane, AC 314, PC 2, Callaway
South Callaway County RSD 2 3-11111
PO BOX 37 65059 676-5211
Paul Skeans, supt.
South Callaway HS 2-00011
PO BOX 37 65059 676-5211
Terry Cain, prin.
South Callaway MS 2-01100
PO BOX 37 65059 676-5216
Stephen Walkenbach, prin.

Monett, AC 417, PC 6, Barry
Monett RSD 1, 800 E SCOTT ST 65708 4-11111
Charles Cudney, supt. 235-7422
HS, 700 9TH ST 65708 3-00011
Ken Brumley, prin. 235-5445
Monett Area Vo S, 700 9TH ST 65708 Vo Tech
Ken Rhuems, prin. 235-7022
MS, 1010 7TH ST 65708 3-00100
Roy Knight, prin. 235-8270

Monroe City, AC 314, PC 5, Monroe
Monroe City RSD 1 3-11111
401 US HIGHWAY 24 AND 36 E 63456 735-4631
William Miles, supt.
HS 2-00011
401 US HIGHWAY 24 AND 36 E 63456 735-4626
Walter Hazelrigg, prin.
JHS, 420 N WASHINGTON ST 63456 2-00100
Fred Cochrane, prin. 735-4742

Montgomery City, AC 314, PC 4, Montgomery
Montgomery County RSD 2 4-11111
RR 1 BOX 16B 63361 564-2278
William Lord, supt.
Montgomery County HS 2-00011
RR 1 BOX 16A 63361 564-2213
James Luetjen, supt.
Montgomery County MS 2-00100
RR 1 BOX 16B 63361 564-2253
Bryan Knowles, prin.

Montrose, AC 816, PC 2, Henry
Montrose RSD 14, PO BOX 175 64770 1-11111
John Warmbrodt, supt. 693-4812
HS, PO BOX 175 64770 1-00011
Charles Campbell, prin. 693-4812

Morrisville, AC 417, PC 2, Polk
Marion C. Early RSD 5 3-11111
PO BOX 96 65710 756-2255
James Horton, supt.
Early JSHS, PO BOX 96 65710 2-00111
Thomas Keller, prin. 756-2216

Mound City, AC 816, PC 4, Holt
Holt County RSD 2 2-11111
PO BOX 147 64470 442-3737
Bill View, supt.
Holt County JSHS 2-00111
PO BOX 147 64470 442-5429
Richard Vest, prin.

Mountain Grove, AC 417, PC 5, Wright
Mountain Grove RSD 3 4-11111
PO BOX 806 65711 926-3177
Dan Lawson, supt.

HS, 420 N MAIN ST 65711 2-00011
Alan Benson, prin. 926-3116
Mountain Grove Area Vo-Tech S Vo Tech
PO BOX 806 65711 926-3119
EVERETT MITCHELL, prin.
MS, 400 E 17TH ST 65711 3-01100
Bob Cossin, prin. 926-3168

Mountain View, AC 417, PC 4, Howell
Mountain View-Birch Tree RSD 3 4-11111
PO BOX 464 65548 934-2021
Charles Snider, supt.
Liberty JSHS, PO BOX 464 65548 3-00111
Stan Whitson, prin. 934-2029

Mount Vernon, AC 417, PC 5, Lawrence
Mt. Vernon RSD 5 4-11111
731 S LANDRUM ST 65712 466-7573
Dennis Cooper, supt.
JSHS, 731 S LANDRUM ST 65712 3-00111
Dan Breeden, prin. 466-7526

Myrtle, AC 417, PC 2, Oregon
Couch RSD 1, RR 1 BOX 1187 65778 2-11111
Doyle Wood, supt. 938-4211
Couch JSHS, RR 1 65778 2-00111
William Garrison, prin. 938-4212

Naylor, AC 314, PC 3, Ripley
Naylor RSD 2, RR 1 BOX 512 63953 2-11111
David Templemire, supt. 399-2505
JSHS, RR 1 BOX 512 63953 2-00111
Bernard Allen, prin. 399-2506

Neelyville, AC 314, PC 2, Butler
Neelyville RSD 4, PO BOX 8 63954 3-11111
John Green, supt. 989-3813
JSHS, PO BOX 8 63954 2-00111
Gerald Rich, prin. 989-3815

Neosho, AC 417, PC 6, Newton
Neosho RSD 5 5-11111
511 S NEOSHO BLVD 64850 451-8600
Roy Shaver, supt.
SHS, 511 S NEOSHO BLVD 64850 3-00011
Howard Spencer, prin. 451-8670
JHS, 511 S NEOSHO BLVD 64850 3-00110
William Rogers, prin. 451-8660

Crowder College 4-CC
601 LACLEDE AVE 64850 451-3226

Nevada, AC 417, PC 6, Vernon
Nevada RSD 5 5-11111
800 W HICKORY ST 64772 448-2000
Kenneth Bowman, supt.
HS, 810 W HICKORY ST 64772 3-00011
Henry Gretlein, prin. 448-2020
Nevada Area Vo S Vo Tech
900 W ASHLAND ST 64772 448-2090
Barbara Parsons, prin.
MS, 900 N OLIVE ST 64772 3-01100
Manley Jackson, prin. 448-2040

Cottey College 2-CC
1000 W AUSTIN BLVD 64772 667-8181

New Bloomfield, AC 314, PC 2, Callaway
Callaway County RSD 3 3-11111
PO BOX 188 65063 491-3700
W. Wilcox, supt.
Callaway County JSHS 2-00111
PO BOX 188 65063 491-3315
Rodney Haley, prin.

Newburg, AC 314, PC 3, Phelps
Newburg RSD 2, PO BOX C 65550 3-11111
Larry Ament, supt. 762-2211
JSHS, PO BOX C 65550 2-00111
Michael Brooks, prin. 762-2331

New Cambria, AC 816, PC 2, Macon
Macon County RSD 4 2-11111
PO BOX 70 63558 226-5615
George Carter, supt.
Macon County JSHS 2-00111
PO BOX 70 63558 226-5615
George Carter, prin.

New Franklin, AC 816, PC 4, Howard
New Franklin RSD 1 2-11111
412 E BROADWAY 65274 848-2141
Jeanie Pierce, supt.
JSHS, 412 E BROADWAY 65274 2-00111
Kelvin McMillin, prin. 848-2314

New Haven, AC 314, PC 4, Franklin
New Haven SD, 100 PARK DR 63068 2-11111
Colin Moran, supt. 237-3231
HS, 100 PARK DR 63068 2-00011
Timothy Strobel, prin. 237-2629
MS, 100 PARK DR 63068 1-00100
David Menke, prin. 237-2900

New Madrid, AC 314, PC 5, New Madrid
New Madrid County RSD 1 4-11111
310 US HIGHWAY 61 63869 688-2161
Mike Barnes, supt.
Central HS 3-00011
310 US HIGHWAY 61 63869 688-2165
Jerry Noble, prin.
Vo-Tech Skills Ctr Vo Tech
310 US HIGHWAY 61 63869 688-2161
William Glaus, prin.

Newtown, AC 816, PC 2, Sullivan
Newtown-Harris RSD 3, PO BOX D 64667 1-11111
H. K. Myers, supt. 794-2245
Newtown-Harris JSHS, PO BOX D 64667 1-00111
H. K. Myers, prin. 794-2245

Niangua, AC 417, PC 2, Webster
Niangua RSD 5, PO BOX 77 65713 2-11111
Roy Manion, supt. 473-6101
JSHS, PO BOX 77 65713 2-00111
Ronald Shawgo, prin. 473-6101

Nixa, AC 417, PC 5, Christian
Nixa RSD 2, 205 NORTH ST 65714 4-11111
Kenneth Holloway, supt. 725-7400
HS, 205 NORTH ST 65714 3-00011
Jordan Needham, prin. 725-7450
MS, 301 S MAIN ST 65714 3-00100
Mark Sellenriek, prin. 725-7430

Norborne, AC 816, PC 3, Carroll
Norborne RSD 8, PO BOX 192 64668 2-11111
Dennis Williams, supt. 594-3319
HS, PO BOX 192 64668 1-00011
Nancy Gillespie, prin. 594-3319

Normandy, AC 314, PC 5, St. Louis
Normandy SD 6-11111
7837 NATURAL BRIDGE RD 63121 389-8005
Bruce Smith, supt.
JHS, 7855 NATURAL BRIDGE RD 63121 3-00100
Steven Huber, prin. 389-8005
Other Schools – See Saint Louis

Incarnate Word Academy 2-00011
2788 NORMANDY DR 63121 725-5850
Randy Berzon, prin.

North Kansas City, AC 816, PC 5, Clay
North Kansas City SD 74 7-11111
2000 NE 46TH ST 64116 453-5050
Eugene Denisar, supt.
HS, 620 E 23RD AVE 64116 4-00011
Vicki Baker, prin. 221-0185
Oak Park HS, 825 NE 79TH TER 64118 4-00011
Robert West, prin. 436-1400
Winnetonka HS, 5815 NE 48TH ST 64119 4-00011
Harold Condra, prin. 452-7900
Antioch MS, 2100 NE 65TH ST 64118 3-00100
Robert Russell, prin. 452-2587
Eastgate MS, 4700 NE PARVIN RD 64117 3-00100
Phyllis Budesheim, prin. 453-2900
Maple Park MS 3-00100
5300 N BENNINGTON AVE 64119 452-7005
Max Horton, prin.
New Mark MS, 515 NE 106TH ST 64155 4-00100
John Hagan, prin. 734-8900

North Kansas City Hospital HSP
2800 HOSPITAL DR 64116 346-7000
St. Pius X HS, 1500 NE 42ND TER 64116 2-00011
Edward Carlin, prin. 453-3450

Norwood, AC 417, PC 2, Wright
Norwood RSD 1 2-11111
GENERAL DELIVERY 65717 746-4343
Leon Pendergrass, supt.
JSHS, GENERAL DELIVERY 65717 2-00111
Don Johnson, prin. 746-4343

Novinger, AC 816, PC 3, Adair
Adair County RSD 1, PO BOX B 63559 2-11111
Robert Wallace, supt. 488-6411
Adair County JSHS, PO BOX B 63559 2-00111
John Ahern, prin. 488-6411

Oak Grove, AC 816, PC 2, Jackson
Oak Grove RSD 6, PO BOX N 64075 4-11111
Roger Adamson, supt. 625-4156
HS, PO BOX N 64075 2-00011
Roger Nelson, prin. 625-4152
MS, PO BOX N 64075 2-00100
Katherine Barton, prin. 625-4154

Oak Ridge, AC 314, PC 2, Cape Girardeau
Oak Ridge RSD 6, PO BOX 10 63769 2-11111
Roger Tatum, supt. 266-3232
JSHS, PO BOX 10 63769 2-00111
Duane Schindler, prin. 266-3630

Odessa, AC 816, PC 5, Lafayette
Odessa RSD 7, 701 S 3RD ST 64076 4-11111
Bert Kimble, supt. 633-5316
HS, 713 S 3RD ST 64076 3-00011
Dahlman Davis, prin. 633-5533
JHS, 310 S 1ST ST 64076 2-00100
John Brantley, prin. 633-5396

O'Fallon, AC 314, PC 7, St. Charles
Ft. Zumwalt RSD 2, 110 VIRGIL ST 63366 7-11111
Bernard Dubray, supt. 272-6620
Fort Zumwalt North HS 4-00011
1230 TOM GINNEVER AVE 63366 272-6620
David Hoekel, prin.
Fort Zumwalt North MS 4-00100
210 VIRGIL ST 63366 272-6620
Larry Lusch, prin.
Other Schools – See Saint Peters

St. Dominic HS 3-00011
31 SAINT DOMINIC DR 63366 272-8303
Sr. Carolyn Wolfbauer, prin.

Oran, AC 314, PC 4, Scott
Oran RSD 3, PO BOX 250 63771   2-11111   262-2330
  Jack McIntosh, supt.
HS, PO BOX 250 63771   2-00011   262-3345
  Don Moore, prin.

Oregon, AC 816, PC 3, Holt
South Holt County RSD 1   2-11111   446-2282
PO BOX 257 64473
  George Munro, supt.
South Holt County JSHS   2-00111   446-3454
PO BOX 257 64473
  Jerry Golden, prin.

Orrick, AC 816, PC 3, Ray
Orrick RSD 11, PO BOX 37 64077   2-11111   496-2336
  Stephen Meyer, supt.
JSHS, PO BOX 37 64077   2-00111   496-3327
  Kendall Simcox, prin.

Osborn, AC 816, PC 2, DeKalb
Osborn RSD 0, RR 1 BOX 1 64474   2-11111   675-2217
  Bruce Johnson, supt.
JSHS, RR 1 BOX 1 64474   1-00111   675-2217
  David Gilliland, prin.

Osceola, AC 417, PC 3, St. Clair
Osceola SD, HIGHWAY WW S 64776   2-11111   646-8143
  Don Neidt, supt.
JSHS, HIGHWAY WW S 64776   2-00111   646-8144
  Val Bennett, prin.

Otterville, AC 816, PC 3, Cooper
Otterville RSD 6, PO BOX 177 65348   2-11111   366-4391
  Lloyd Best, supt.
JSHS, PO BOX 177 65348   2-00111   366-4391
  Linda Fry, prin.

Overland, AC 314, PC 7, St. Louis
Ritenour SD
  Supt. — See Saint Louis
Ritenour HS   4-00011   426-9531
9100 SAINT CHARLES ROCK RD 63114
  Ned Richardson, prin.
Ritenour MS East   3-00100   426-9544
2500 MARSHALL AVE 63114
  John Breen, prin.

Owensville, AC 314, PC 4, Gasconade
Gasconade RSD 2, PO BOX 536 65066   4-11111   437-2177
  Randall Kristofferson, supt.
HS, PO BOX 536 65066   3-00011   437-2174
  Mark Leach, prin.
MS, PO BOX 536 65066   2-00100   437-2172
  Catherine Lahmeyer, prin.

Ozark, AC 417, PC 5, Christian
Ozark RSD 6, PO BOX 166 65721   5-11111   485-7694
  Johnny Fite, supt.
HS, PO BOX 166 65721   3-00011   485-7521
  Dennis Miller, prin.
JHS, PO BOX 166 65721   2-00100   485-7624
  Jerry Bough, prin.

Pacific, AC 314, PC 5, Franklin
Meramec Valley RSD 3   5-11111   257-2438
126 N PAYNE ST 63069
  Ed Hillhouse, supt.
HS, 425 UDE DR 63069   3-00011   257-2449
  Kirk Eidson, prin.
JHS, 913 W UNION ST 63069   3-00100   257-2413
  Jon Heisel, prin.

Palmyra, AC 314, PC 5, Marion
Palmyra RSD 1, PO BOX 151 63461   4-11111   769-2069
  Ray Church, supt.
HS, PO BOX 151 63461   2-00011   769-2067
  James Lowe, prin.
MS, PO BOX 151 63461   2-01100   769-2174
  Christine Crawford, prin.

Paris, AC 816, PC 4, Monroe
Paris RSD 2, RR 2 BOX 7 65275   3-11111   327-4112
  John Gibbs, supt.
HS, RR 2 BOX 7 65275   2-00011   327-4111
  Bill Lewis, prin.
JHS, 112 S MAIN ST 65275   2-01100   327-4563
  Joe Branham, prin.

Park Hills, AC 314, PC 99, St. Francois
Central RSD 3
  Supt. — See Flat River
Central HS, 116 REBEL DR 63601   3-00011   431-1211
  Terry Brashers, prin.
Central JHS, 801 COLUMBIA ST 63601   2-00100   431-1322
  Terry Noble, prin.

Parkville, AC 816, PC 4, Platte

Park College 64152   4-UC   741-2000

Patton, AC 314, PC 2, Bollinger
Meadow Heights RSD 2   3-11111   866-0060
RR 1 BOX 210D 63662
  Thomas Waller, supt.
Meadow Heights JSHS   2-00111   866-2924
RR 1 BOX 210D 63662
  Rick Chastain, prin.

Pattonsburg, AC 816, PC 2, Daviess
Pattonsburg RSD 2, 504 W 4TH ST 64670   2-11111   367-2111
  William Walker, supt.
JSHS, 504 W 4TH ST 64670   1-00111   367-2111
  Jeffrey McNeely, prin.

Peculiar, AC 816, PC 4, Cass
Raymore-Peculiar RSD 2   5-11111   758-5191
PO BOX 366 64078
  Martha Nicholson, supt.
Raymore-Peculiar HS   3-00011   758-6656
PO BOX 366 64078
  Robert Bach, prin.
Raymore-Peculiar MS   3-00100   758-6865
PO BOX 366 64078
  G. Sagaser, prin.

Perryville, AC 314, PC 6, Perry
Perry County SD 32   4-11111   547-6588
326 COLLEGE ST 63775
  Ron Fitch, supt.
HS, 326 COLLEGE ST 63775   3-00011   547-6527
  Daniel Steska, prin.
Perryville Area Career Center   Vo Tech   547-2542
326 COLLEGE ST 63775
  Marvin Ruehling, prin.
JHS, 326 COLLEGE ST 63775   3-01100   547-4572
  Rick Francis, prin.

St. Vincent HS, 210 S WATERS ST 63775   2-00111   547-2560
  John Eck, prin.

Philadelphia, AC 314, PC 2, Marion
Marion County RSD 2   2-11111   439-5913
PO BOX 100 63463
  Randy Spratt, supt.
Marion County JSHS   2-00111   439-5913
PO BOX 100 63463
  Randy Spratt, prin.

Piedmont, AC 314, PC 4, Wayne
Clearwater RSD 1, RR 1 BOX 1A 63957   4-11111   223-7426
  Wayne Cook, supt.
Clearwater JSHS, RR 1 BOX 1A 63957   2-00111   223-4524
  Blane Keel, prin.

Pierce City, AC 417, PC 4, Lawrence
Pierce City RSD 6, PO BOX E 65723   3-11111   476-2555
  Gene Rice, supt.
JSHS, PO BOX E 65723   2-00111   476-2515
  Randy Anderson, prin.

Pilot Grove, AC 816, PC 3, Cooper
Cooper County Consolidated SD 4   2-11111   834-6915
107 SCHOOL ST 65276
  Ralph Damon, supt.
Cooper County JSHS   2-00111   834-4415
107 SCHOOL ST 65276
  Curtis Twenter, prin.

Plato, AC 417, PC 2, Texas
Plato RSD 5, PO BOX A 65552   3-11111   458-4706
  James Carlton, supt.
JSHS, PO BOX A 65552   2-00111   458-4687
  Jerry Hobbs, prin.

Platte City, AC 816, PC 5, Platte
Platte County RSD 3   4-11111   464-3995
PO BOX 1400 64079
  Donald Siegrist, supt.
HS, PO BOX 1400 64079   2-00011   464-3996
  Benita Pearce, prin.
Northland Career Center   Vo Tech   464-2442
PO BOX 1700 64079
  John Hall, prin.
MS, PO BOX 1400 64079   2-01100   464-3982
  Terry Hart, prin.

Plattsburg, AC 816, PC 4, Clinton
Clinton County RSD 3   3-11111   539-2183
800 W FROST ST 64477
  Richard Mandell, supt.
JSHS, 800 W FROST ST 64477   2-00111   539-2184
  Frank Cox, prin.

Pleasant Hill, AC 816, PC 5, Cass
Pleasant Hill RSD 3   4-11111   987-3161
301 N MCKISSOCK ST 64080
  Mitchel Hanna, supt.
HS, 1301 E MYRTLE ST 64080   2-00011   987-3111
  Cliff Borgstadt, prin.
MS, 327 N MCKISSOCK ST 64080   2-01100   987-2149
  Robert Baldwin, prin.

Pleasant Hope, AC 417, PC 2, Polk
Pleasant Hope RSD 6   3-11111   467-2850
PO BOX 387 65725
  Donald Dittman, supt.
JSHS, PO BOX 387 65725   2-00111   467-2271
  Harriet Blackburn, prin.

Point Lookout, AC 417, PC 3, Taney

College of the Ozarks   4-UC   334-6411
GENERAL DELIVERY 65726

Polo, AC 816, PC 3, Caldwell
Polo RSD 7, RR 1 BOX 38A 64671   2-11111   354-2326
  Kenneth Schaeffer, supt.
JSHS, RR 1 BOX 38A 64671   2-00111   354-2524
  Bryan Prewitt, prin.

Poplar Bluff, AC 314, PC 7, Butler
Poplar Bluff RSD 1, PO BOX 47 63902   6-11111   785-7751
  Thomas Hoover, supt.
HS, 1300 VICTORY LN 63901   4-00011   785-6471
  James Daniels, prin.
Poplar Bluff Area Vo S   Vo Tech   785-2248
RR 10 BOX 452 63901
  James Ellis, prin.
JHS, 550 N WESTWOOD BLVD 63901   3-00100   785-7751
  Thomas Schlimpert, prin.

Three Rivers Community College   4-CC   686-4101
THREE RIVERS BLVD 63901

Portageville, AC 314, PC 5, New Madrid
Portageville SD, 904 KING AVE 63873   3-11111   379-3855
  John Thomas, supt.
HS, 904 KING AVE 63873   2-00011   379-3819
  John Smith, prin.
MS, 902 KING AVE 63873   2-01100   379-3853
  Jim McKay, prin.

Potosi, AC 314, PC 5, Washington
Potosi RSD 3, 400 N MINE ST 63664   5-11111   438-5485
  Jesse Jarvis, supt.
HS, 200 TROJAN DR 63664   3-00011   438-2156
  Ray Ballard, prin.
Evans MS, 303 S LEAD ST 63664   3-00100   438-2101
  Don Young, prin.

Prairie Home, AC 816, PC 2, Cooper
Prairie Home RSD 5   2-11111   841-5296
PO BOX 105 65068
  E. Gene Adkison, supt.
JSHS, PO BOX 105 65068   1-00111   841-5296
  David Dicke, prin.

Princeton, AC 816, PC 4, Mercer
Princeton RSD 5   2-11111   748-3211
1008 E COLEMAN ST 64673
  Neita Collins, supt.
JSHS, 1008 E COLEMAN ST 64673   2-00111   748-3490
  Michael Parnell, prin.

Purdin, AC 816, PC 2, Linn
Linn County RSD 1   2-11111   244-5035
PO BOX 130 64674
  Glenn Brown, supt.
Linn County JSHS   2-00111   244-5035
PO BOX 130 64674
  Ken Kennedy, prin.

Purdy, AC 417, PC 3, Barry
Purdy RSD 2, PO BOX 248 65734   3-11111   442-3216
  Roger Blakely, supt.
JSHS, PO BOX 248 65734   2-00111   442-3215
  Robert Abeln, prin.

Puxico, AC 314, PC 3, Stoddard
Puxico RSD 8, PO BOX 37 63960   3-11111   222-3762
  William Pogue, supt.
JSHS, PO BOX 37 63960   2-00111   222-3175
  Naemon Townsend, prin.

Queen City, AC 816, PC 3, Schuyler
Schuyler County RSD 1   3-11111   766-2204
PO BOX 338 63561
  David Grubb, supt.
Schuyler County MS   2-00100   766-2296
PO BOX 248 63561
  Linda Berry, prin.
Other Schools – See Lancaster

Ravenwood, AC 816, PC 2, Nodaway
Northeast Nodaway County RSD 5   2-11111   937-3125
PO BOX 206 64479
  Tim Gutzmer, supt.
Northeast Nodaway County JSHS   2-00111   937-3125
PO BOX 206 64479
  Marlin Kinman, prin.

Raytown, AC 816, PC 8, Jackson
Raytown Consolidated SD 2   6-11111   737-6200
10500 E 60TH TER 64133
  Grenvell Foraker, supt.
HS, 6019 BLUE RIDGE BLVD 64133   4-00011   737-6325
  Richard Atha, prin.
Raytown South HS   4-00011   737-6340
8211 STERLING AVE 64138
  Robert Blaine, prin.
Herndon Area Vo-Tech S   Vo Tech   737-6315
11501 E HIGHWAY 350 64138
  JAMES GAINES, prin.
South MS, 8401 E 83RD ST 64138   3-00100   737-6310
  Larry Taylor, prin.
Other Schools – See Kansas City

Reeds Spring, AC 417, PC 2, Stone
Reeds Spring RSD 4   3-11111   272-8173
PO BOX 169 65737
  John Williams, supt.
HS, PO BOX 169 65737   2-00011   272-8171
  Christopher Dean, prin.
Gibson Technical Center   Vo Tech   272-3271
PO BOX 169 65737
  Larry Carnes, prin.
MS, PO BOX 209 65737   2-01100   272-8245
  Jack Frisbie, prin.

Republic, AC 417, PC 6, Greene
Republic RSD 3   5-11111   732-1812
518 N HAMPTON AVE 65738
  Allan Crader, supt.
HS, 688 E HINES ST 65738   3-00011   732-2616
  Donald Farwell, prin.
MS, 518 N HAMPTON AVE 65738   3-00100   732-1814
  Larry Carter, prin.

Revere, AC 816, PC 2, Clark
Revere Consolidated SD 3   2-11111   948-2621
PO BOX 300 63465
  Erwin Neighbors, supt.
JSHS, PO BOX 300 63465   1-00111   948-2621
  Erwin Neighbors, prin.

Rich Hill, AC 417, PC 4, Bates
Rich Hill RSD 4, 110 W OLIVE ST 64779 2-11111
Michael Mendon, supt. 395-2418
Bryant JSHS, FIRST & OLIVE ST 64779 2-00111
Roy Glynn, prin. 395-4191

Richland, AC 314, PC 4, Pulaski
Pulaski County RSD 4 3-11111
HC 75 BOX 45 65556 765-3241
Mark Mitchell, supt.
JSHS, HC 75 BOX 45 65556 2-00111
Terry Evans, prin. 765-3711

Richmond, AC 816, PC 6, Ray
Richmond RSD 16 4-11111
849 E SOUTH ST 64085 776-6912
Roy Cozad, supt.
HS, 451 E SOUTH ST 64085 2-00111
Dick Michael, prin. 776-2226
MS, 200 SUMMIT ST 64085 3-01100
Gary Hancock, prin. 776-5841

Richmond Heights, AC 314, PC 7, St. Louis
Maplewood-Richmond Heights SD
Supt. — See Maplewood
Green JHS, 1313 BOLAND PL 63117 2-00100
Arline Kalishman, prin. 644-4400

Ridgeway, AC 816, PC 2, Harrison
Ridgeway RSD 5, PO BOX 179A 64481 2-11111
Bob Newman, supt. 872-6813
JSHS, PO BOX 179A 64481 1-00111
Nancy Parman, prin. 872-6813

Risco, AC 314, PC 2, New Madrid
Risco RSD 2, PO BOX 17 63874 2-11111
Charles Smith, supt. 396-5568
JSHS, PO BOX 17 63874 2-00111
Michael Walker, prin. 396-5568

Riverside, AC 816, PC 5, Platte

Aero Mechanics School 2-CS
200 NORTHWEST PKY 64150 741-7700

Rock Port, AC 816, PC 4, Atchison
Rock Port RSD 2 2-11111
600 S NEBRASKA ST 64482 744-6294
Gary Arthaud, supt.
JSHS, 600 S NEBRASKA ST 64482 2-00111
Rodney Bastow, prin. 744-6296

Rogersville, AC 417, PC 3, Greene
Greene County RSD 8 4-11111
PO BOX 587 65742 753-2891
Albert Erb, supt.
Logan-Rogersville HS 2-00011
RR 4 BOX 75 65742 753-2813
John Hetherington, prin.
Logan-Rogersville MS 2-00100
304 S MILL ST 65742 753-2896
William Hurst, prin.

Rolla, AC 314, PC 7, Phelps
Rolla SD 31, 6TH & MAIN STS 65401 5-11111
Kent King, supt. 364-1329
SHS, 900 BULLDOG RUN 65401 3-00001
Roger Berkbuegler, prin. 364-4746
Rolla Area Vo-Tech S Vo Tech
1304 E 10TH ST 65401 364-3726
Bob Chapman, prin.
JHS, 1360 SOEST RD 65401 3-00110
Geraldine Johnson, prin. 364-3014

Metro Business College 2-CS
2305 N BISHOP AVE 65401 364-8464
Rolla Area Vocational-Technical School 2-CS
1304 E 10TH ST 65401 364-3726
University of Missouri 5-UC
102 PARKER HALL 65401 341-4114

Rosendale, AC 816, PC 2, Andrew
North Andrew County RSD 6 2-11111
RR 1 BOX 29 64483 567-2965
Michael Newman, supt.
North Andrew HS 2-00011
RR 1 BOX 29 64483 567-2525
Jane Snyder, prin.
Other Schools – See Fillmore

Russellville, AC 314, PC 3, Cole
Cole County RSD 1, 100 PARK ST 65074 3-11111
Ronald Griffin, supt. 782-3313
JSHS, 100 PARK ST 65074 2-00111
Kevin Kohler, prin. 782-4915

Saint Ann, AC 314, PC 7, St. Louis
Pattonville RSD 3
Supt. — See Maryland Heights
Holman MS 3-00100
11055 SAINT CHARLES ROCK RD 63074
John Pohl, prin. 298-4438

Ritenour SD
Supt. — See Saint Louis
Hoech MS West, 3312 ASHBY RD 63074 3-00100
Jack Williams, prin. 426-9561

AL-MED Academy 2-CS
10963 SAINT CHARLES ROCK RD 63074
739-4450
Vatterott College 5-CC
3925 INDUSTRIAL DR 63074 428-5900

Saint Charles, AC 314, PC 8, St. Charles
Francis Howell RSD 3 7-11111
4545 CENTRAL SCHOOL RD 63304 441-0088
John Oldani, supt.
Howell HS 4-00011
7001 S HIGHWAY 94 63304 441-0050
Robert Schoewe, prin.
Howell North HS 4-00011
2549 HACKMANN RD 63303 441-2707
Kyle Thrasher, prin.
Barnwell JHS 4-00100
1035 JUNGS STATION RD 63303 441-6363
Constance McCallum, prin.
Hollenbeck JHS 3-00100
4555 CENTRAL SCHOOL RD 63304 441-1501
James Lange, prin.
Howell JHS, 825 OFALLON RD 63304 2-00100
Bernard Schreck, prin. 926-8882

St. Charles County RSD 5 4-11111
2165 HIGHWAY V 63301 258-4466
Gary VanMeter, supt.
Orchard Farm HS 2-00011
2165 HIGHWAY V 63301 258-4466
Lanny Hradek, prin.
Orchard Farm MS 2-00100
2165 HIGHWAY V 63301 258-4466
Allen Hollrah, prin.

St. Charles RSD 6, 1916 ELM ST 63301 6-11111
M. Keen, supt. 724-5840
HS, 725 N KINGSHIGHWAY ST 63301 3-00011
Jerry Cook, prin. 724-3940
St. Charles West HS 4-00011
3601 DROSTE RD 63301 723-7900
Clark Cilek, prin.
Lewis & Clark Vo S Vo Tech
2400 ZUMBEHL RD 63301 723-4829
Kenneth Cobb, prin.
Hardin MS, 1950 ELM ST 63301 3-00100
Michael Ebert, prin. 724-7217
Jefferson MS, 2660 ZUMBEHL RD 63301 3-00100
Virginia Beaver, prin. 723-4934

Duchesne HS, 2550 ELM ST 63301 3-00011
Charles Nolan, prin. 946-6767
Lewis & Clark Technical School 2-CS
2400 ZUMBEHL RD 63301 723-4829
Lindenwood College 4-UC
209 S KINGSHIGHWAY ST 63301 949-2000
Sanford-Brown Business College 2-CS
3555 FRANKS DR 63301 724-7100

Saint Clair, AC 314, PC 5, Franklin
St. Clair RSD 13, 905 BARDOT ST 63077 4-11111
Russell Ford, supt. 629-3500
HS, 900 E GRAVOIS AVE 63077 3-00111
William Morgan, prin. 629-3103
JHS, 900 E GRAVOIS AVE 63077 2-00100
Fredrick Marshaus, prin. 629-0588

Saint Elizabeth, AC 314, PC 2, Miller
St. Elizabeth RSD 4 2-11111
PO BOX 68 65075 493-2414
Jim Christal, supt.
JSHS, PO BOX 68 65075 2-00111
Ron Weiskopf, prin. 493-2414

Sainte Genevieve, AC 314, PC 5, Ste. Genevieve
St. Genevieve County RSD 2 4-11111
375 N 5TH ST 63670 883-5720
Mikel Stewart, supt.
HS, 715 WASHINGTON ST 63670 3-00011
Dannie Clark, prin. 883-3583
MS, 211 N 5TH ST 63670 2-00100
Joe Shirey, prin. 883-2744

Valle HS, 40 N 4TH ST 63670 2-00011
Sr. Mary Bauman, prin. 883-7496

Saint James, AC 314, PC 5, Phelps
St. James RSD 1, 101 E SCIOTO ST 65559 4-11111
Jim Porter, supt. 265-3261
Hodge JSHS, 101 E SCIOTO ST 65559 3-00111
Dennis Wilson, prin. 265-3263

Saint Joseph, AC 816, PC 8, Buchanan
St. Joseph SD, 925 FELIX ST 64501 7-11111
Dan Colgan, supt. 233-1301
Benton HS, 5655 S 4TH ST 64504 3-00011
Lamar Hicks, prin. 238-4531
Central HS, 2602 EDMOND ST 64501 4-00011
Sam Carmeal, prin. 279-6303
Lafayette HS 3-00011
412 N HIGHLAND AVE 64505 279-6373
Wallace Prawl, prin.
Hillyard Vo S, 3434 FARAON ST 64506 Vo Tech
Jim Cornett, prin. 232-5459
Bode MS, 720 N NOYES BLVD 64506 3-00100
Donald Lentz, prin. 233-3116
Robidoux MS 2-00100
4212 SAINT JOSEPH AVE 64505 364-2780
Rex Geary, prin.
Spring Garden MS 2-00100
5802 S 22ND ST 64503 238-0032
Robert Clemens, prin.
Truman MS 3-00100
3227 OLIVE ST # 45 64507 232-6590
Kenneth Quick, prin.

Bishop Le Blond HS 2-00011
3529 FREDERICK AVE 64506 279-1629
Sr. Corrine Connelly, prin.
Missouri Western State College 5-UC
4525 DOWNS DR 64507 800-662-7041
Northwest Missouri Community College 3-CC
4315 PICKETT RD 64503 364-5700

Saint Louis, AC 314, PC 10, St. Louis
Affton SD 101 5-11111
8701 MACKENZIE RD 63123 638-8770
Gary Benedict, supt.
Affton HS, 8309 MACKENZIE RD 63123 3-00011
David Wilde, prin. 638-6330
Rogers MS, 7550 MACKENZIE RD 63123 3-00100
John Kosash, prin. 351-9679

Bayless SD, 4530 WEBER RD 63123 4-11111
Allan Ellis, supt. 631-2244
Bayless HS, 4532 WEBER RD 63123 2-00011
Dr. Douglas Morris, prin. 544-6342
Bayless MS, 4529 WEBER RD 63123 2-00100
James Knackstedt, prin. 544-6306

Hancock Place SD 4-11111
9101 S BROADWAY 63125 544-6403
Al Bourisaw, supt.
Hancock JSHS, 229 W RIPA AVE 63125 3-00111
Jerry Schloss, prin. 544-1200

Hazelwood SD
Supt. — See Florissant
Hazelwood East HS 4-00011
11300 DUNN RD 63138 653-2300
Jerry Ellersieck, prin.
Kirby JHS, 1865 DUNN RD 63138 3-00100
Ray Taylor, prin. 653-3200

Ladue SD, 9703 CONWAY RD 63124 5-11111
Charles Mckenna, supt. 994-7080
Watkins HS, 1201 S WARSON RD 63124 3-00111
William Raisch, prin. 993-6447
Ladue JHS, 9701 CONWAY RD 63124 3-00100
Frank Fischel, prin. 993-3900

Lindbergh RSD 8 6-11111
4900 S LINDBERGH BLVD 63126 842-3800
James Sandfort, supt.
Lindbergh HS 4-00011
4900 S LINDBERGH BLVD 63126 849-2000
David Skillman, prin.
Sperreng MS 4-00100
12111 TESSON FERRY RD 63128 849-0123
Robert Ayres, prin.

Mehlville RSD 9 7-11111
3120 LEMAY FERRY RD 63125 892-5000
Robert Rogers, supt.
Mehlville HS 4-00011
3200 LEMAY FERRY RD 63125 892-5000
Ron Jones, prin.
Oakville HS, 5557 MILBURN RD 63129 4-00011
Edgar Chard, prin. 892-8800
Buerkle JHS, 623 BUCKLEY RD 63125 3-00100
Jack Jordan, prin. 892-8100
Oakville JHS 3-00100
5950 TELEGRAPH RD 63129 846-8338
Harry Hadd, prin.
Washington JHS, 5165 AMBS RD 63128 2-00100
Michael Mc Gough, prin. 892-7100

Normandy SD
Supt. — See Normandy
Normandy HS 4-00011
6701 SAINT CHARLES ROCK RD 63133
John Young, prin. 389-8006

Ritenour SD, 2420 WOODSON RD 63114 6-11111
John DeArman, supt. 429-3500
Other Schools – See Overland, Saint Ann

Riverview Gardens SD 6-11111
1370 NORTHUMBERLAND DR 63137 869-2505
Edwin Benton, supt.
Riverview Gardens HS 4-00011
1218 SHEPLEY DR 63137 869-4700
Bruce Beaver, prin.
Riverview Gardens MS 3-00100
9800 PATRICIA BARKALOW DR 63137 869-2505
Terry Laux, prin.

Special SD of St. Louis County 6-00001
12110 CLAYTON RD 63131 569-8100
Ronald Rebore, supt.
South County Tech HS Vo Tech
12721 W WATSON RD 63127 822-6604
Jerome Berni, prin.
Other Schools – See Chesterfield, Florissant

St. Louis City SD, 911 LOCUST ST 63101 8-11111
David Mahan, supt. 231-3720
Beaumont HS 4-00011
3836 NATURAL BRIDGE AVE 63107 533-2410
Charles Brasfield, prin.
Central Visual and Performing Arts HS 3-00011
3616 N GARRISON AVE 63107 371-1045
Carl Landis, prin.
Cleveland NJROTC Academy 3-00011
4352 LOUISIANA AVE 63111 832-0933
Richard Stumpe, prin.
Metro HS, 5017 WASHINGTON PL 63108 2-00011
Betty Wheeler, prin. 367-5210
Roosevelt HS 4-00011
3125 S KINGSHIGHWAY BLVD 63139 776-6040
Thomas Daly, prin.

Soldan International Studies HS   2-00011
918 UNION BLVD 63108   367-9222
Harold Greer, prin.
Sumner HS, 4248 COTTAGE AVE 63113   4-00011
Joseph Dubose, prin.   371-1048
Vashon HS, 3405 BELL AVE 63106   4-00011
Ivory Lofton, prin.   533-9487
Gateway HS, 5101 MCREE AVE 63110   Vo Tech
Antoinette Tieber, prin.   776-3300
Blewett MS, 1927 CASS AVE 63106   2-00100
Odell Johnson, prin.   231-7738
Blow MS   3-00100
516 LOUGHBOROUGH AVE 63111   353-1349
Richard Sirna, prin.
Busch Academic Athletic Academy   2-00100
5910 CLIFTON AVE 63109   772-1038
William Bullerdick, prin.
Enright Classical Jr Academy   2-00100
5351 ENRIGHT AVE 63112   367-0555
Mary Purdy, prin.
Fanning MS, 3417 GRACE AVE 63116   3-00100
Joann Perkins, prin.   772-1038
International Studies MS   2-00100
4265 CLARENCE AVE 63115   382-7186
Doris Johnson, prin.
Langston MS, 5511 WABADA AVE 63112   2-00100
Robert Hudson, prin.   383-2908
Long MS, 5028 MORGANFORD RD 63116   2-00100
David Eaton, prin.   481-3440
L'Ouverture MS   2-00100
3021 HICKORY ST 63104   664-3579
William Boyd, prin.
Mason MS   2-00100
6031 SOUTHWEST AVE 63139   645-1201
Doris Reece, prin.
Northwest MS   2-00100
5140 RIVERVIEW BLVD 63120   385-4774
Terell Wayne, prin.
Nottingham MS   2-00100
4915 DONOVAN AVE 63109   352-6085
Albert Reinsch, prin.
Pruitt Military Academy   2-00100
1212 N 22ND ST 63106   231-1443
Maurice Grant, prin.
Simmons MS   2-00100
4318 SAINT LOUIS AVE 63115   535-5844
Barbara Harvey, prin.
Stevens MS, 1033 WHITTIER ST 63113   2-00100
Arthur Sharpe, prin.   533-8550
Stowe MS, 5750 LOTUS AVE 63112   2-00100
Jim Billups, prin.   382-7310
Turner MS   3-00100
2615 PENDLETON AVE 63113   535-8482
Clarence Ward, prin.
Webster MS, 2127 N 11TH ST 63106   2-00100
Charles Shelton, prin.   231-9196
Williams MS   2-00100
3955 SAINT FERDINAND AVE 63113   652-4545
Walter Glenn, prin.
Yeatman MS   2-00100
4265 ATHLONE AVE 63115   261-8132
James Strughold, prin.

Wellston SD   3-11111
6574 SAINT LOUIS AVE 63121   382-8111
Ronald Stodghill, supt.
Eskridge HS, 1200 SUTTER AVE 63133   2-00011
Henry Anderson, prin.   727-8850

Academy of the Visitation   3-11111
3020 N BALLAS RD 63131   432-5353
Patricia Hurst, prin.
Aquinas Institute of Theology   1-UC
3642 LINDELL BLVD 63108   658-3882
Barnes College   1-HSP
416 S KINGSHIGHWAY BLVD 63110   362-5225
Barnes Hospital   2-HSP
4949 BARNES HOSPITAL PLZ 63110   362-5190
Basic Institute of Technology   2-CC
4455 CHIPPEWA ST 63116   771-1200
Bishop DuBourg HS   3-00011
5850 EICHELBERGER ST 63109   832-3030
Tom Jokerst, prin.
Block Yeshiva HS   1-00011
9723 GRANDVIEW DR 63132   997-3940
Rabbi Gary Menschel, prin.
Cardinal Ritter College Prep HS   2-00011
5421 THEKLA AVE 63120   381-7979
Carmele Hall, prin.
Central Institute for the Deaf   1-UC
818 S EUCLID AVE 63110   652-3200
Chaminade College Preparatory S   3-00111
425 N LINDBERGH BLVD 63131   993-4400
James Gerker, prin.
Christian Brothers College HS   3-00011
6501 CLAYTON RD 63117   721-1200
James Gerdes, prin.
Concordia Seminary   2-UC
801 DE MUN AVE 63105   721-5934
Cor Jesu Academy   3-00011
10320 GRAVOIS RD 63123   842-1546
Sr. Sheila Oneil, prin.
Covenant Theological Seminary   2-UC
12330 CONWAY RD 63141   800-264-8064
Crossroads S   2-00111
500 DE BALIVIERE AVE 63112   367-8085
Anne Spencer, prin.
Deaconess College of Nursing   2-UC
6150 OAKLAND AVE 63139   768-3040
Florissant Upholstery School   1-CS
1420 N VANDEVENTER AVE 63113   534-1886

Fontbonne College   3-UC
6800 WYDOWN BLVD 63105   889-1419
Harris-Stowe State College   3-UC
3026 LACLEDE AVE 63103   340-3300
Hickey School   3-CS
940 WESTPORT PLZ STE 101 63146

   434-2212
Jewish Hospital of St. Louis   HSP
216 S KINGSHIGHWAY BLVD 63110   454-8686
John Burroughs S, 755 S PRICE RD 63124   3-00111
Keith Shahan, prin.   993-4040
Kenrick School of Theology   1-UC
5200 GLENNON DR 63119   644-0266
Lutheran HS North   2-00011
5401 LUCAS AND HUNT RD 63121   389-3100
Edward Reitz, prin.
Lutheran HS South   3-00011
9515 TESSON FERRY RD 63123   631-1400
David Waterman, prin.
Lutheran Medical Center   HSP
3547 S JEFFERSON AVE 63118   577-5853
Mallinckrodt Institute of Radiology   1-CS
510 S KINGSHIGHWAY BLVD 63110   362-7100
Mary Institute   4-11111
101 N WARSON RD 63124   993-5100
John Johnson, prin.
Maryville University of St. Louis   4-UC
13550 CONWAY RD 63141   576-9300
Missouri Baptist College   3-UC
12542 CONWAY RD 63141   434-1115
Missouri Baptist Medical Center   2-HSP
3015 N BALLAS RD 63131   569-5193
Missouri School for Doctors' Assistants   2-CC
10121 MANCHESTER RD 63122   821-7700
Missouri School for the Blind   HND
3815 MAGNOLIA AVE 63110
Missouri Technical School   2-UC
1167 CORPORATE LAKE DR 63132   569-3600
Notre Dame HS, 320 E RIPA AVE 63125   2-00011
Sr. Shelley Hogan, prin.   544-1015
Patricia Stevens Career College   2-CS
1000 SAINT LOUIS UNION STA 63103   421-0949
Principia S, 13201 CLAYTON RD 63131   3-11111
William Truitt, prin.   434-2100
Ranken Technical College   3-CC
4431 FINNEY AVE 63113   371-0236
Rosary HS, 1720 REDMAN RD 63138   3-00011
Sr. Mary Winkelmann, prin.   741-1333
Rosati-Kain HS   2-00011
4389 LINDELL BLVD 63108   533-8513
Sr. Joan Andert, prin.
St. Elizabeth Academy   2-00011
3401 ARSENAL ST 63118   771-5134
Sr. Linda Zechmeister, prin.
St. John Baptist HS   2-00011
5021 ADKINS AVE 63116   351-5604
George Wingbermuehle, prin.
St. John's Mercy Medical Center   HSP
615 S NEW BALLAS RD 63141   569-6182
St. Joseph Academy   3-00011
2307 S LINDBERGH BLVD 63131   965-7205
Sr. Nancy Folkl, prin.
St. Josephs Institute for the Deaf   HND
1483 82ND BLVD 63132
St. Louis College of Health Careers   1-CS
4484 W PINE BLVD 63108   652-0300
St. Louis College of Pharmacy   3-UC
4588 PARKVIEW PL 63110   367-8700
St. Louis Community College   6-CC
3400 PERSHALL RD 63135   595-4244
St. Louis Community College   5-CC
5600 OAKLAND AVE 63110   644-9127
St. Louis Conservatory of Music   2-UC
560 TRINITY AVE 63130   863-3033
St. Louis Tech   2-CS
9741 SAINT CHARLES ROCK RD 63114
   427-3600
St. Louis University   6-UC
221 N GRAND BLVD 63103   658-2474
St. Louis University HS   4-00011
4970 OAKLAND AVE 63110   531-0330
Paul Owens, prin.
St. Mary's HS   2-00011
4701 S GRAND BLVD 63111   481-8400
Daniel Mosley, prin.
Sanford-Brown Business College   2-CS
1655 DES PERES RD STE 150 63131
   965-6606
   2-HMS
Trans World Travel Academy
11495 NATURAL BRDGE RD #214 63044
   895-6754
University of Missouri   6-UC
8001 NATURAL BRIDGE RD 63121   553-5254
Vanderschmidt School   1-CS
4625 LINDELL BLVD 63108   361-6000
Vatterott Education Center   4-CS
3854 WASHINGTON BLVD 63108   534-2586
Villa Duchesne HS   2-00111
801 S SPOEDE RD 63131   432-2021
Renee Allen, prin.
Washington University   6-UC
1 BROOKINGS DR 63130   889-5000
Washington University   3-UC
4559 SCOTT AVE 63110
Webster University   6-UC
470 E LOCKWOOD AVE 63119   968-6900
Westminster Christian Academy   2-00111
10900 LADUE RD 63141   997-2900
Jim Marsh, prin.

Whitfield S, 175 S MASON RD 63141   2-00111
Mary Burke, prin.   434-5141

Saint Peters, AC 314, PC 8, St. Charles
Ft. Zumwalt RSD 2
Supt. — See O'Fallon
Fort Zumwalt South HS   4-00011
8050 MEXICO RD 63376   281-1212
Tom Byrnes, prin.
Fort Zumwalt South MS   4-00100
300 KNAUST RD 63376   272-6620
Michael Clemens, prin.

Lutheran HS, 5100 MEXICO RD 63376   2-00011
Larry Marty, prin.   928-5100
St. Charles County Community College   4-CC
PO BOX 76975 63376   723-1220

Salem, AC 314, PC 5, Dent
Salem RSD 80, 1400 W 3RD ST 65560   4-11111
Keith Robertson, supt.   729-6642
SHS, 1400 W 3RD ST 65560   3-00000
James Simpson, prin.   729-6641
JHS, 1400 W 3RD ST 65560   2-00110
Jack Hays, prin.   729-4261

Salisbury, AC 816, PC 4, Chariton
Salisbury RSD 4, PO BOX B 65281   3-11111
Roger Dorson, supt.   388-6442
JSHS, PO BOX B 65281   2-00111
Bob Fuka, prin.   388-6442

Sarcoxie, AC 417, PC 4, Jasper
Sarcoxie RSD 2, PO BOX 310 64862   3-11111
Ellis Sneed, supt.   548-3134
JSHS, PO BOX 310 64862   2-00111
Sam Knight, prin.   548-2153

Savannah, AC 816, PC 5, Andrew
Savannah RSD 3, PO BOX 151 64485   4-11111
William Ray, supt.   324-3144
HS, 701 E WILLIAM ST 64485   3-00011
Steve Kellepouris, prin.   324-3128
JHS, 701 W CHESTNUT ST 64485   2-00100
Neil Anderson, prin.   324-3126

Schell City, AC 417, PC 2, Vernon
Schell City RSD 1, PO BOX 68 64783   2-11111
William Belt, supt.   432-3511
JSHS, PO BOX 68 64783   1-00111
Nancy Fagan, prin.   432-3511

Scott City, AC 314, PC 5, Scott
Scott City RSD 1, 3000 MAIN ST 63780   3-11111
Douglas Berry, supt.   264-2381
JSHS, 3000 MAIN ST 63780   2-00111
Fred Graham, prin.   264-2138

Sedalia, AC 816, PC 7, Pettis
Sedalia SD 200, PO BOX 109 65302   5-11111
Bob Griffey, supt.   826-1054
Smith-Cotton HS   4-00011
312 E BROADWAY BLVD 65301   826-1115
Lynn Snow, prin.
MS, 2205 S INGRAM AVE 65301   3-00100
Marvin Ebersold, prin.   827-3100

Sacred Heart S, 416 W 3RD ST 65301   2-11111
Mark Register, prin.   827-3800
State Fair Community College   4-CC
3201 W 16TH ST 65301   826-7100

Senath, AC 314, PC 4, Dunklin
Senath-Hornersville Cons. SD 8   3-11111
PO BOX G 63876 – Lawayne Law, supt.   738-2669
Senath-Hornersville HS, PO BOX G 63876   2-00011
Benny McAtee, prin.   738-2661
Other Schools – See Hornersville

Seneca, AC 417, PC 4, Newton
Seneca RSD 7, PO BOX 469 64865   4-11111
Arch Gordanier, supt.   776-3426
HS, PO BOX 469 64865   2-00011
William McEntire, prin.   776-3926
Wells MS, PO BOX 469 64865   2-00100
Thomas Marrs, prin.   776-3911

Seymour, AC 417, PC 4, Webster
Seymour RSD 2, PO BOX 397 65746   3-11111
(—), supt.   935-2287
JSHS, PO BOX 397 65746   2-00111
Dan Ray, prin.   935-4508

Shelbina, AC 314, PC 4, Shelby
Shelby County RSD 4, HWY 36 W 63468   3-11111
Timothy Dunaway, supt.   588-4961
South Shelby HS, HIGHWAY 36 W 63468   2-00011
Andrew Crist, prin.   588-4163
JHS, 400 S CENTER ST 63468   2-00100
Ronald Smoot, prin.   588-2208

Shelbyville, AC 314, PC 3, Shelby
Shelby County Consolidated SD 1   2-11111
PO BOX 150 63469   633-2410
Dale Wallace, supt.
North Shelby JSHS   2-00111
PO BOX 150 63469   633-2410
Larry Smoot, prin.

Sheldon, AC 417, PC 2, Vernon
Sheldon RSD 8, PO BOX 68 64784   2-11111
Wayne Rumans, supt.   884-5113
JSHS, PO BOX 68 64784   1-00111
Donald Hendrix, prin.   884-5111

Sikeston, AC 314, PC 7, Scott
Scott County Central SD, RR 1 63801 — 2-11111 / 471-2686
  Ray Shoaf, supt.
Scott Central JSHS, RR 1 63801 — 2-00111 / 471-2001
  Jerry Crites, prin.

Sikeston RSD 6 — 5-11111
  1002 VIRGINIA ST 63801 — 472-2581
  Robert Buchanan, supt.
  SHS, 200 PINE ST 63801 — 3-00001 / 471-5440
  Randall Fidler, prin.
  Sikeston Area Vo S, 200 PINE ST 63801 — Vo Tech / 471-5440
  Gerald Jackson, prin.
  JHS, 100 TWITTY DR 63801 — 3-00110 / 471-0792
  Harley Barnes, prin.

Silex, AC 314, PC 2, Lincoln
Silex RSD 1, PO BOX 46 63377 — 2-11111 / 384-5227
  James Farmer, supt.
JSHS, PO BOX 46 63377 — 2-00111 / 384-5227
  Millard Kinkead, prin.

Slater, AC 816, PC 4, Saline
Slater SD, 515 ELM ST 65349 — 3-11111 / 529-2278
  Darrel Lee, supt.
HS, 515 ELM ST 65349 — 2-00011 / 529-3133
  Paul Vaillancourt, prin.

Smithton, AC 816, PC 3, Pettis
Smithton RSD 6, PO BOX 97 65350 — 3-11111 / 343-5316
  Gerald Fillinger, supt.
JSHS, PO BOX 97 65350 — 2-00111 / 343-5318
  Ralph Spurrier, prin.

Smithville, AC 816, PC 5, Clay
Smithville RSD 2, PO BOX 290 64089 — 4-11111 / 532-0406
  David Leggard, supt.
HS, 645 S COMMERCIAL AVE 64089 — 2-00011 / 532-0405
  Robert Leachman, prin.
MS, 675 S COMMERCIAL AVE 64089 — 2-00100 / 532-0415
  William Maus, prin.

Sparta, AC 417, PC 3, Christian
Sparta RSD 3, PO BOX 160 65753 — 3-11111 / 278-4284
  Don Call, supt.
JSHS, PO BOX 160 65753 — 2-00111 / 278-3224
  Douglas Hayter, prin.

Spokane, AC 417, PC 1, Christian
Spokane RSD 7, PO BOX 218 65754 — 3-11111 / 587-3841
  Floyd Jarvis, supt.
JSHS, PO BOX 218 65754 — 2-01111 / 587-3841
  Larry Woolf, prin.

Springfield, AC 417, PC 9, Greene
Springfield RSD 12 — 7-11111
  940 N JEFFERSON AVE 65802 — 864-3800
  Gerald Moseman, supt.
  Central HS, 423 E CENTRAL ST 65802 — 4-00011 / 864-3822
  Bob Maggi, prin.
  Glendale HS — 4-00011
  2727 S INGRAM MILL RD 65804 — 887-0438
  Emmett Sawyer, prin.
  Hillcrest HS, 3319 N GRANT AVE 65803 — 4-00011 / 833-9780
  John Laurie, prin.
  Kickapoo HS — 4-00011
  3710 S JEFFERSON AVE 65807 — 887-0496
  Pamela McGinnis, prin.
  Parkview HS — 4-00011
  516 W MEADOWMERE ST 65807 — 831-4584
  Michael Kohr, prin.
  Cherokee JHS — 3-00100
  420 E PLAINVIEW RD 65810 — 887-0293
  Charles Hawkins, prin.
  Hickory Hills JHS — 2-00100
  3429 E TRAFFICWAY ST 65802 — 831-0871
  Thomas Wyrick, prin.
  Jarrett JHS, 840 S JEFFERSON AVE 65806 — 3-00100 / 895-2165
  Allen Grymes, prin.
  Pershing JHS — 3-00100
  2120 S VENTURA AVE 65804 — 888-2590
  Frank Wann, prin.
  Pipkin JHS — 2-00100
  1215 N BOONVILLE AVE 65802 — 895-2170
  Robert Isreal, prin.
  Pleasant View JHS — 2-00100
  RR 1 BOX 401 65803 — 833-0432
  Charles Brown, prin.
  Reed JHS, 2000 N LYON AVE 65803 — 2-00100 / 895-2175
  Judy Brunner, prin.
  Study JHS, 2343 W OLIVE ST 65802 — 2-00110 / 895-2180
  Stephen Seal, prin.

Assemblies of God Theological Seminary — 2-UC
  1445 N BOONVILLE AVE 65802 — 862-3344
Baptist Bible College — 3-UC
  628 E KEARNEY ST 65803 — 869-9811
Berean College — 1-HMS
  1445 N BOONVILLE AVE 65802
Bryan Travel College — 2-CS
  520 W UNIVERSITY ST # B 65807 — 862-5700
Central Bible College — 3-UC
  3000 N GRANT AVE 65803 — 833-2551
Dick Hill International Flight — 1-CS
  PO BOX 10603 65808 — 485-3474
Drury College — 4-UC
  900 N BENTON AVE 65802 — 865-8731
Evangel College — 4-UC
  1111 N GLENSTONE AVE 65802 — 865-2811
Forest Inst./Professional Psychology — 2-UC
  1322 S CAMPBELL AVE 65807 — 831-7902
Lester E. Cox Medical Center — HSP
  1423 N JEFFERSON AVE 65802 — 836-3424

Phillips Junior College — 2-CC
  1010 W SUNSHINE ST 65807 — 864-7220
St. John's Regional Health Center — HSP
  1235 E CHEROKEE ST 65804 — 885-2848
St. John's School of Nursing — HSP
  4431 S FREMONT AVE 65804 — 885-2098
Southwest Missouri State University — 7-UC
  901 S NATIONAL AVE 65804 — 800-492-7900
Southwest School of Broadcasting — 2-CS
  1031 E BATTLEFIELD ST #212B 65807 — 883-4060
Springfield Catholic HS — 2-00011
  2340 S EASTGATE AVE 65809 — 887-8817
  James Skahan, prin.
Vatterott College — 2-CS
  1258 E TRAFFICWAY ST 65802 — 831-8116

Stanberry, AC 816, PC 4, Gentry
Gentry County RSD 2 — 2-11111
  610 N PARK ST 64489 — 783-2136
  Gerald Shineman, supt.
JSHS, 610 N PARK ST 64489 — 2-00111 / 783-2163
  Larry Heaps, prin.

Steele, AC 314, PC 4, Pemiscot
South Pemiscot County RSD 5 — 3-11111
  611 BEASLEY RD 63877 — 695-4426
  Mitchell Fisher, supt.
South Pemiscot County JSHS — 2-00111
  611 BEASLEY RD 63877 — 695-3342
  Randy McDaniel, prin.

Steelville, AC 314, PC 4, Crawford
Steelville RSD 3, PO BOX 339 65565 — 3-11111 / 775-2175
  Dale Houck, supt.
HS, PO BOX 339 65565 — 2-00011 / 775-2144
  Bruce Forrest, prin.
MS, PO BOX 339 65565 — 2-00100 / 775-2176
  Vicki Sandberg, prin.

Stet, AC 816, PC 1, Ray
Stet RSD 15, 1 CARDINAL LN 64680 — 2-11111 / 484-3122
  Paula Sprouse, supt.
JSHS, 1 CARDINAL LN 64680 — 1-00111 / 484-3122
  Steven Street, prin.

Stewartsville, AC 816, PC 3, DeKalb
Stewartsville Consolidated SD 2 — 2-11111
  RR 2 BOX 23 64490 — 669-3792
  Gaylon Whitmer, supt.
JSHS, RR 2 BOX 23 64490 — 2-00111 / 669-3258
  Michael Morgan, prin.

Stockton, AC 417, PC 4, Cedar
Stockton RSD 1, PO BOX 190 65785 — 3-11111 / 276-5141
  Raymond Scott, supt.
HS, PO BOX 190 65785 — 2-00011 / 276-3315
  Larry Sommerer, prin.
MS, PO BOX 190 65785 — 2-00100 / 276-5141
  Fredrick Erickson, prin.

Stoutland, AC 417, PC 2, Camden
Camden County RSD 2 — 3-11111
  HWYS T & H 65567 — 286-3711
  Rex Dameron, supt.
JSHS, HWYS T & H 65567 — 2-00111 / 286-3711
  Bobby Burns, prin.

Stover, AC 314, PC 3, Morgan
Morgan County RSD 1 — 3-11111
  PO BOX 337 65078 — 377-2217
  Joe Dyke, supt.
Morgan County JSHS — 2-00111
  PO BOX 337 65078 — 377-2218
  James Bellis, prin.

Strafford, AC 417, PC 4, Greene
Strafford RSD 6, PO BOX 97 65757 — 3-11111 / 736-3600
  James Tice, supt.
JSHS, PO BOX 97 65757 — 2-00111 / 736-2111
  R. Evans, prin.

Sturgeon, AC 314, PC 3, Boone
Sturgeon RSD 5, PO BOX 248 65284 — 2-11111 / 687-3515
  Franklin Curtis, supt.
JSHS, PO BOX 248 65284 — 2-00111 / 687-3512
  Lloyd Carr, prin.

Sullivan, AC 314, PC 6, Franklin
Spring Bluff RSD 15 — 2-11111
  RR 2 BOX 286 63080 — 457-8302
  Robert Sinclair, supt.
Spring Bluff S, RR 2 BOX 286 63080 — 2-11111 / 457-8302
Sullivan Consolidated SD 2 — 4-11111
  138 TAYLOR ST 63080 — 468-5171
  Gary Keltner, supt.
  HS, 1073 E VINE ST 63080 — 3-00011 / 468-5181
  Dan McWhorter, prin.
  MS, 1156 ELMONT RD 63080 — 3-00100 / 468-5191
  James Thornsberry, prin.

Summersville, AC 417, PC 3, Texas
Summersville RSD 2 — 3-11111
  PO BOX 198 65571 — 932-4045
  Mike McAdams, supt.
JSHS, PO BOX 198 65571 — 2-00111 / 932-4929
  Dan Shockley, prin.

Sweet Springs, AC 816, PC 4, Saline
Sweet Springs RSD 7 — 2-11111
  105 MAIN ST 65351 — 335-4860
  Lindell Harrison, supt.
JSHS, 105 MAIN ST 65351 — 2-00111 / 335-6341
  James Collins, prin.

Tarkio, AC 816, PC 4, Atchison
Tarkio RSD 1, 312 S 11TH ST 64491 — 2-11111 / 736-4161
  Robert Bruner, supt.
JSHS, 312 S 11TH ST 64491 — 2-00111 / 736-4118
  Eddie Defenbaugh, prin.

Thayer, AC 417, PC 4, Oregon
Thayer RSD 2, PO BOX 195 65791 — 3-11111 / 264-7261
  Merle Williams, supt.
JSHS, PO BOX 195 65791 — 2-00111 / 264-7261
  Mark House, prin.

Theodosia, AC 417, PC 2, Ozark
Lutie RSD 6, HC 4 BOX 4177 65761 — 2-11111 / 273-4274
  Robert Campbell, supt.
Lutie HS, PO BOX 380 65761 — 1-00011 / 273-4274
  Gerald Portman, prin.

Tina, AC 816, PC 2, Carroll
Tina-Avalon RSD 2 — 2-11111
  HIGHWAY 65 64682 — 622-4211
  Merle O'Neal, supt.
Tina-Avalon JSHS, HWY 65 64682 — 1-00111 / 622-4212
  David Garber, prin.

Tipton, AC 816, PC 4, Moniteau
Moniteau County RSD 6 — 3-11111
  PO BOX P 65081 – Sam Bayne, supt. — 433-5520
JSHS, PO BOX P 65081 — 2-00111 / 433-5529
  Nelson Kohler, prin.

Trenton, AC 816, PC 6, Grundy
Grundy County RSD 9 — 4-11111
  PO BOX 279 64683 — 359-3994
  Gary Howren, supt.
  HS, 1415 OKLAHOMA AVE 64683 — 2-00011 / 359-2291
  Larry Odom, prin.
  Adams MS, 1312 E 9TH ST 64683 — 2-00100 / 359-4328
  Brian Blankenship, prin.

North Central Missouri College — 3-CC
  1301 MAIN ST 64683 — 359-3948

Troy, AC 314, PC 5, Lincoln
Troy RSD 3, 711 W COLLEGE ST 63379 — 5-11111 / 528-6098
  Dr. John Lawrence, supt.
Buchanan HS, 711 W COLLEGE ST 63379 — 3-00011 / 528-4618
  Donnie Gaddis, prin.
JHS, 711 W COLLEGE ST 63379 — 2-00100 / 528-7464
  Darrell Harvey, prin.

Tuscumbia, AC 314, PC 2, Miller
Miller County RSD 3 — 2-11111
  PO BOX 1 65082 — 369-2375
  Roy W. True, supt.
JSHS, PO BOX 1 65082 — 1-00111 / 369-2375
  Michael Haines, prin.

Union, AC 314, PC 6, Franklin
Union RSD 11, PO BOX 440 63084 — 5-11111 / 583-8626
  Terry Holder, supt.
HS, PO BOX 440 63084 — 3-00011 / 583-2513
  Wayne Dreier, prin.
MS, PO BOX 440 63084 — 3-00100 / 583-5855
  Charles Penberthy, prin.

East Central College — 4-CC
  PO BOX 529 63084 — 583-5193

Union Star, AC 816, PC 2, DeKalb
Union Star RSD 2, PO BOX 98 64494 — 2-11111 / 593-2294
  Thomas Foraker, supt.
JSHS, PO BOX 98 64494 — 1-00111 / 593-2294
  Bruce Skoglund, prin.

Unionville, AC 816, PC 4, Putnam
Putnam County RSD 1 — 3-11111
  RR 3 BOX 15 63565 — 947-3361
  Darl Davis, supt.
Putnam County JSHS — 2-00111
  RR 3 BOX 15 63565 — 947-3361
  Wayne Hines, prin.

University City, AC 314, PC 8, St. Louis
University City SD — 5-11111
  8346 DELCREST DR 63124 — 872-1932
  Lynn Beckwith, supt.
  HS, 7401 BALSON AVE 63130 — 4-00011 / 863-1710
  Michael Thacker, prin.
  Brittany Woods MS — 3-00100
  8125 GROBY RD 63130 — 997-6570
  Verona Bowers, prin.

Urbana, AC 417, PC 2, Dallas
Hickory County RSD 1 — 3-11111
  RR 1 BOX 838 65767 — 993-4241
  David Edge, supt.
Skyline JSHS, RR 1 BOX 838 65767 — 2-00111 / 993-4226
  Rex Barclay, prin.

Valley Park, AC 314, PC 5, St. Louis
Valley Park SD — 3-11111
  356 MERAMEC STATION RD 63088 — 225-4151
  Dennis Lea, supt.
JSHS — 2-00111
  356 MERAMEC STATION RD 63088 — 225-4151
  Michael Cowen, prin.

Van Buren, AC 314, PC 3, Carter
Van Buren RSD 1, PO BOX 550 63965 — 3-11111 / 323-4281
  Lewis Hux, supt.
JSHS, PO BOX 550 63965 — 2-00111 / 323-4295
  Jeff Lindsey, prin.

Vandalia, AC 314, PC 5, Audrain
Van-Far RSD 1 — 3-11111
  2200 W US HIGHWAY 54 63382 — 594-6111
  Ronald McSorley, supt.
Vandalia JSHS — 2-00111
  2200 W US HIGHWAY 54 63382 — 594-6111
  Rick Swisher, prin.

Verona, AC 417, PC 3, Lawrence
Verona RSD 7, PO BOX 98 65769 — 2-11111
  Leon Cunningham, supt. — 498-6418
JSHS, PO BOX 98 65769 — 2-00111
  William Sorrells, prin. — 498-6775

Versailles, AC 314, PC 4, Morgan
Morgan County RSD 2 — 4-11111
  309 S MONROE ST 65084 — 378-4231
  Gary Dixon, supt.
Morgan County HS — 2-00011
  309 S MONROE ST 65084 — 378-4697
  George Arnold, prin.
Morgan County MS — 2-00100
  309 S MONROE ST 65084 — 378-5432
  Terry Wolfe, prin.

Viburnum, AC 314, PC 3, Iron
Iron County Consolidated SD 4 — 3-11111
  PO BOX 368 65566 — 244-5422
  Tom Nathe, supt.
Iron County HS, PO BOX 368 65566 — 2-00011
  Carol Chitwood, prin. — 244-5521
Iron County JHS, PO BOX 368 65566 — 2-00100
  Steve McIntosh, prin. — 244-5521

Vienna, AC 314, PC 3, Maries
Maries County RSD 1 — 3-11111
  PO BOX 218 65582 — 422-3304
  Jim Dean, supt.
JSHS, PO BOX 218 65582 — 2-00111
  Andrew Parker, prin. — 422-3363

Walker, AC 417, PC 2, Vernon
Walker RSD 4, 216 E LESLIE AVE 64790 — 2-11111
  William Malone, supt. — 465-2222
JSHS, 216 E LESLIE AVE 64790 — 1-00111
  Linda Ott, prin. — 465-2222

Walnut Grove, AC 417, PC 3, Greene
Walnut Grove RSD 5 — 2-11111
  PO BOX 187 65770 — 994-2543
  Lee Creemer, supt.
JSHS, PO BOX 187 65770 — 2-00111
  Glenn Hoover, prin. — 994-2544

Wardell, AC 314, PC 2, Pemiscot
North Pemiscot County RSD 1 — 3-11111
  PO BOX 38 63879 — 628-3471
  Keith Henke, supt.
North Pemiscot County JSHS — 2-00111
  PO BOX 38 63879 — 628-3465
  James Gore, prin.

Warrensburg, AC 816, PC 7, Johnson
Warrensburg RSD 6 — 5-11111
  PO BOX 638 64093 — 747-7823
  Michael Jinks, supt.
HS, 1411 S RIDGEVIEW DR 64093 — 3-00011
  Kenneth Walker, prin. — 747-2262
Warrensburg Vo-Tech S — Vo Tech
  205 S RIDGEVIEW DR 64093 — 747-2283
  Larry Reiter, prin.
MS, 522 E GAY ST 64093 — 3-00100
  James Davis, prin. — 747-5612

Central Missouri State University 64093 — 6-UC
                                             543-4111

Warrenton, AC 314, PC 5, Warren
Warren County RSD 3 — 4-11111
  302 KUHL ST 63383 — 456-4311
  James Dishman, supt.
Warren County HS, 302 KUHL ST 63383 — 3-00011
  John Deutch, prin. — 456-4311
Warren JHS, 302 KUHL ST 63383 — 2-00100
  Michael Bain, prin. — 456-4311

Warsaw, AC 816, PC 4, Benton
Warsaw RSD 9, PO BOX 248 65355 — 4-11111
  John Boise, supt. — 438-7351
HS, PO BOX 248 65355 — 2-00011
  Frank Rowles, prin. — 438-7351
MS, PO BOX 1750 65355 — 2-00100
  Randy Morrow, prin. — 438-9079

Washburn, AC 417, PC 2, Barry
Southwest RSD 5, PO BOX 297 65772 — 3-11111
  Jim Roe, supt. — 826-5411

Southwest JSHS, PO BOX 297 65772 — 2-00111
  Robert Borman, prin. — 826-5413

Washington, AC 314, PC 7, Franklin
Washington SD, PO BOX 357 63090 — 5-11111
  Jerry Chambers, supt. — 239-2727
HS, 600 E 11TH ST 63090 — 4-00011
  Ed Stockwell, prin. — 239-4717
Washington Area Vo S — Vo Tech
  550 E 11TH ST 63090 — 239-7777
  Paul MacKay, prin.
JHS, 401 E 14TH ST 63090 — 2-00100
  Robert Wessels, prin. — 239-4783

St. Francis Borgia Regional HS — 3-00011
  1000 BORGIA DR 63090 — 239-7871
  Sr. Mary Owens, prin.

Waynesville, AC 314, PC 5, Pulaski
Waynesville R6 — 6-11111
  399 SCHOOL ST 65583 — 774-6497
  Ervin Morriss, supt.
HS, 1001 BUSINESS I44 W 65583 — 4-00011
  Dwight Hensley, prin. — 774-6401
Waynesville Area Vo-Tech — Vo Tech
  810 ROOSEVELT ST 65583 — 774-6106
  William Fullbright, prin.
MS, 403 SCHOOL ST 65583 — 3-00100
  Jack King, prin. — 774-6198
Other Schools – See Fort Leonard Wood

Weaubleau, AC 417, PC 2, Hickory
Weaubleau RSD 3 — 2-11111
  PO BOX 198 65774 — 428-3668
  Leland Foster, supt.
JSHS, PO BOX 198 65774 — 2-00111
  James Rogers, prin. — 428-3368

Webb City, AC 417, PC 6, Jasper
Webb City RSD 7 — 5-11111
  411 N MADISON ST 64870 — 673-6000
  Ronald Barton, supt.
HS, 621 N MADISON ST 64870 — 3-00011
  Mark Porter, prin. — 673-6010
JHS, 807 W 1ST ST 64870 — 2-00100
  Tom Gosch, prin. — 673-6030

Webster Groves, AC 314, PC 7, St. Louis
Webster Groves SD — 5-11111
  400 E LOCKWOOD AVE 63119 — 961-1233
  William Gussner, supt.
HS, 100 SELMA AVE 63119 — 4-00011
  Yvonne Kauffman, prin. — 961-1240
Hixson JHS, 630 S ELM AVE 63119 — 3-00100
  Donald Morrison, prin. — 963-6450

Eden Theological Seminary — 2-UC
  475 E LOCKWOOD AVE 63119 — 961-3627
Nerinx HS — 3-00011
  530 E LOCKWOOD AVE 63119 — 968-1505
  Mary Schenkenberg, prin.

Wellington, AC 816, PC 3, Lafayette
Wellington-Napoleon RSD 9 — 2-11111
  PO BOX J 64097 – Al Gilliam, supt. — 934-2531
Wellington-Napoleon JSHS — 2-00111
  PO BOX J 64097 – Steve Smith, prin. — 934-2621

Wellsville, AC 314, PC 4, Montgomery
Wellsville-Middletown RSD 1 — 2-11111
  BURLINGTON ROAD 63384 — 684-2428
  Jeff Carter, supt.
JSHS, 900 BURLINGTON ST 63384 — 2-00111
  Michael Stolle, prin. — 684-2017

Wentzville, AC 314, PC 6, St. Charles
Wentzville RSD 4, 1 CAMPUS DR 63385 — 5-11111
  Ronald Berrey, supt. — 327-3800
Holt HS, 600 CAMPUS DR 63385 — 4-00011
  G. Mosher, prin. — 327-3876
MS, 405 CAMPUS DR 63385 — 4-00100
  William Solomon, prin. — 327-3815

Weston, AC 816, PC 4, Platte
West Platte County RSD 2 — 3-11111
  1103 WASHINGTON ST 64098 — 386-2236
  Ken Harpst, supt.
West Platte County JSHS — 2-00111
  935 WASHINGTON ST 64098 — 386-2292
  Robert Foster, prin.

Westphalia, AC 314, PC 2, Osage
Osage County RSD 3 — 3-11111
  PO BOX 37 65085 — 455-2375
  Rex Miller, supt.

JSHS, PO BOX 37 65085 — 2-00111
  Larry Hutchcraft, prin. — 455-2550

West Plains, AC 417, PC 6, Howell
West Plains RSD 7, 613 W 1ST ST 65775 — 5-11111
  Wayne Lovan, supt. — 256-6150
HS, 602 E OLDEN ST 65775 — 4-00011
  James Minner, prin. — 256-6150
South Central Area Vo S — Vo Tech
  610 E OLDEN ST 65775 — 256-6150
  Stephen Bryant, prin.
MS, 730 E OLDEN ST 65775 — 3-01100
  Davis Roush, prin. — 256-6150

Southwest Missouri State University — 2-UC
  905 W MAIN ST 65775 — 256-5533

Wheatland, AC 417, PC 2, Hickory
Wheatland RSD 2, PO BOX 68 65779 — 2-11111
  Ray Aubuchon, supt. — 282-6433
JSHS, PO BOX 68 65779 — 2-00111
  Roger Schmiedeskamp, prin. — 282-5833

Wheaton, AC 417, PC 3, Barry
Wheaton RSD 3, PO BOX 249 64874 — 2-11111
  Robert Murray, supt. — 652-3914
JSHS, PO BOX 249 64874 — 2-00111
  Lowell McInturff, prin. — 652-7249

Willard, AC 417, PC 4, Greene
Willard RSD 2, PO BOX 98 65781 — 4-11111
  Jerry Bouse, supt. — 742-2584
HS, PO BOX 98 65781 — 3-00011
  John Brummel, prin. — 742-3524
JHS, PO BOX 98 65781 — 2-00100
  Jan Cole, prin. — 742-2588

Willow Springs, AC 417, PC 4, Howell
Willow Springs RSD 4 — 4-11111
  215 W 4TH ST 65793 — 469-3260
  John Enloe, supt.
HS, 215 W 4TH ST 65793 — 2-00111
  Don Hamby, prin. — 469-2114
MS, 215 W 4TH ST 65793 — 2-00100
  Malcolm Gum, prin. — 469-3211

Windsor, AC 816, PC 5, Henry
Henry County RSD 1 — 3-11111
  210 NORTH ST 65360 — 647-3533
  Albert Winkle, supt.
JSHS, 210 NORTH ST 65360 — 2-00111
  Keith Willis, prin. — 647-3106

Winfield, AC 314, PC 3, Lincoln
Winfield RSD 4, 701 ELM ST 63389 — 4-11111
  Lyle Laughman, supt. — 668-8188
HS, 701 ELM ST 63389 — 2-00111
  David Gorski, prin. — 668-8130
JHS, 701 ELM ST 63389 — 2-00100
  Paul Behle, prin. — 668-8001

Winona, AC 314, PC 4, Shannon
Winona RSD 3, PO BOX 248 65588 — 2-11111
  Michael Greene, supt. — 325-4221
HS, PO BOX 248 65588 — 2-00011
  Winston Reed, prin. — 325-8101

Winston, AC 816, PC 2, Daviess
Winston RSD 6, PO BOX 38 64689 — 2-11111
  Nylen Lewis, supt. — 749-5456
JSHS, PO BOX 38 64689 — 1-00111
  Steve Yost, prin. — 749-5456

Wright City, AC 314, PC 4, Warren
Wright City RSD 2 — 4-11111
  PO BOX 198 63390 — 745-3290
  Maurice Overlander, supt.
HS, PO BOX 198 63390 — 2-00011
  Dale Ridder, prin. — 745-3341
MS, PO BOX 198 63390 — 2-00100
  Richard Lagemann, prin. — 745-3347

Wyaconda, AC 816, PC 2, Clark
Wyaconda Consolidated SD 1 — 2-11111
  PO BOX 168 63474 — 479-5431
  Terry Sherer, supt.
HS, PO BOX 168 63474 — 1-00011
  Terry Sherer, prin. — 479-5431

Zalma, AC 314, PC 1, Bollinger
Zalma RSD 5, HC 2 BOX 184 63787 — 2-11111
  Carol Blanton, supt. — 722-3320
JSHS, HC 2 BOX 184 63787 — 2-00111
  Daniel Sitze, prin. — 722-3320

MONTANA

OFFICE OF PUBLIC INSTRUCTION
106 State Capitol, Helena 59620
(405) 444-3095

State Superintendent of Public Instruction	Nancy Keenan
Deputy Superintendent	Jack Copps
Assistant Superintendent Operations	Gregg Groepper
Assistant Superintendent Accreditation & Curriculum Services	Gail Gray
Assistant Superintendent Educational Technology	Scott Buswell

STATE BOARD OF EDUCATION
106 State Capitol, Helena 59620

Chairperson   John Kinna

COUNTY SUPERINTENDENTS OF SCHOOLS

Beaverhead County
Dorothy Donoban
2 S PACIFIC ST, Dillon 59725   406-683-5632
Big Horn County
Robert Harlin
PO BOX H, Hardin 59034   406-665-1507
Blaine County
Carrol Elliot
PO BOX 819, Chinook 59523   406-357-3270
Broadwater County
Fleda Brammer
PO BOX 489, Townsend 59644   406-266-3445
Carbon County
Jerry Scott
PO BOX 116, Red Lodge 59068   406-446-1301
Carter County
Darlene Carter, Ekalaka 59324   406-775-8721
Cascade County
Helen Hagen, 415 2ND AVE N
Great Falls 59401   406-761-6700
Chouteau County
L. Stollfuss
PO BOX 459, Fort Benton 59442   406-622-3242
Custer County
Ellen Zook
1010 MAIN ST, Miles City 59301   406-232-7800
Daniels County
Patricia McDonnell
PO BOX 67, Scobey 59263   406-487-2651
Dawson County
Jean Grow
207 W BELL ST, Glendive 59330   406-365-3963
Deer Lodge County
Carl Stetzner
COURTHOUSE, Anaconda 59711   406-563-8421
Fallon County
Marlene Ferrell
PO BOX 1117, Baker 59313   406-778-2883
Fergus County
Shirley Barrick
COURTHOUSE, Lewistown 59457   406-538-3136
Flathead County
Dorothy Laird
723 5TH AVE E, Kalispell 59901   406-758-5720
Gallatin County
M. Brown, 311 W MAIN ST # 101
Bozeman 59715   406-585-1375
Garfield County
Joann Stanton
PO BOX 28, Jordan 59337   406-557-6115
Glacier County
Daryl Omsberg
1210 E MAIN ST, Cut Bank 59427   406-873-2295
Golden Valley County
S. Carpenter, Ryegate 59074   406-568-2342

Granite County
Jo Ann Husbyn
PO BOX 520, Philipsburg 59858   406-859-3831
Hill County
Shirley Isbell
315 4TH ST, Havre 59501   406-265-5481
Jefferson County
Sandra Streib
PO BOX H, Boulder 59632   406-225-4251
Judith Basin County
Cynthia Denton, Stanford 59479   406-566-2272
Lake County
Joyce Wegner
106 4TH AVE E, Polson 59860   406-883-6211
Lewis & Clark County
Warren Morehouse
316 N PARK AVE, Helena 59623   406-447-8344
Liberty County
Krystyna Cole
PO BOX 684, Chester 59522   406-759-5216
Lincoln County
Mary Hudspeth
418 MINERAL AVE, Libby 59923   406-293-7781
Madison County
Pat Miller
PO BOX 247, Virginia City 59755   406-843-5392
McCone County
Janet McCabe
PO BOX 180, Circle 59215   406-485-3590
Meagher County
Joseph Phillips, PO BOX 354
White Sulphur Springs 59645   406-547-3612
Mineral County
Billye Ann Bricker
Superior 59872   406-822-4542
Missoula County
Rachel Vielleux, 301 W ALDER ST
Missoula 59802   406-721-5700
Musselshell County
Kathryn Pfister
506 MAIN ST, Roundup 59072   406-323-1104
Park County
Mary Sarver
414 E CALLENDER ST
Livingston 59047   406-222-6120
Petroleum County
Stephanie Downs, Winnett 59087   406-429-5551
Phillips County
Gary Baden
PO BOX DD, Malta 59538   406-654-2010
Pondera County
Linda Bruner, Conrad 59425   406-278-7681
Powder River County
Charlotte Miller
PO BOX L, Broadus 59317   406-436-2488

Powell County
Karl Roosa, 409 MISSOURI AVE
Deer Lodge 59722   406-846-3680
Prairie County
Edna Irion
PO BOX 566, Terry 59349   406-637-5575
Ravalli County
Greg Danelz
PO BOX 5021, Hamilton 59840   406-363-2322
Richland County
Joan Ritter
210 W MAIN ST, Sidney 59270   406-482-1608
Roosevelt County
Traci Harada
COURTHOUSE, Wolf Point 59201   406-653-1590
Rosebud County
Sharyn Thomas
PO BOX 407, Forsyth 59327   406-356-2537
Sanders County
Joyce Decker-Wegner
106 4TH AVE E, Polson 59860   406-827-4397
Sheridan County
Robert Smith, COURTHOUSE
Plentywood 59254   406-765-2310
Silver Bow County
Bob Kelly
155 W GRANITE ST, Butte 59701   406-723-8262
Stillwater County
Teresa Miller
PO BOX 1098, Columbus 59019   406-322-5333
Sweet Grass County
Linda DeCock
PO BOX 220, Big Timber 59011   406-932-5147
Teton County
Gwyn Anderson
PO BOX 610, Choteau 59422   406-466-2907
Toole County
Maria Harrison, Shelby 59474   406-434-2112
Treasure County
Kathleen Thomas
PO BOX 429, Hysham 59038   406-342-5545
Valley County
Jan Allie, 501 COURT SQ # 114
Glasgow 59230   406-228-8221
Wheatland County
Effie Winsky
PO BOX 637, Harlowton 59036   406-632-4893
Wibaux County
Patricia Zinda
PO BOX 291, Wibaux 59353   406-795-2485
Yellowstone County
Buzz Christianson
PO BOX 35022, Billings 59107   406-256-6850

PUBLIC, PRIVATE AND CATHOLIC SECONDARY SCHOOLS

Absarokee, AC 406, PC 4, Stillwater
Absarokee SD, RR 1 BOX 2020 59001   2-11111
Michael Reynolds, supt.   328-4583
JSHS, RR 1 BOX 2020 59001   2-00111
Michael Reynolds, prin.   328-4583

Alberton, AC 406, PC 2, Mineral
Alberton SD 2, PO BOX 118 59820   2-11111
Gary Weber, supt.   722-4413
HS, PO BOX 118 59820   1-00011
Carl Dehne, prin.   722-4413

Anaconda, AC 406, PC 7, Deer Lodge
Anaconda SD 10   4-11111
PO BOX 1281 59711   563-6361
Mary Jo Oreskovich, supt.
HS, 5TH & MAIN 59711   3-00011
Earl Sager, prin.   563-5269
JHS, 3RD & CHERRY 59711   2-00100
Mike Thompson, prin.   563-6242

Arlee, AC 406, PC 2, Lake
Arlee SD JT & 8, PO BOX 37 59821   2-11111
Gayle Crane, supt.   726-3216
HS, PO BOX 37 59821   2-00011
Deanna Brady-Leader, prin.   726-3216
JHS, PO BOX 37 59821   1-00100
(—), prin.   726-3216

Ashland, AC 406, PC 2, Rosebud

St. Labre Catholic S   2-11111
1 MISSION RD 59004   784-2278
Anne Amsden, prin.

Augusta, AC 406, PC 2, Lewis and Clark
Augusta SD 45, PO BOX 307 59410   2-11111
Tom Lockyer, supt.   562-3384
HS, PO BOX 307 59410   1-00011
Tom Lockyer, prin.   562-3384

Bainville, AC 406, PC 2, Roosevelt
Bainville SD, PO BOX 177 59212   2-11111
Frank Loehding, supt.   769-2321
HS, PO BOX 177 59212   1-00011
Frank Loehding, prin.   769-2321

Baker, AC 406, PC 4, Fallon
Baker SD 12, PO BOX 659 59313   3-11111
James Stanton, supt.   778-3329
HS, 1015 S 3RD W 59313   2-00011
Don Schillinger, supt.   778-3329
JHS, PO BOX 659 59313   1-00100
J. Dobyns, prin.   778-3614

Belfry, AC 406, PC 2, Carbon
Belfry SD, PO BOX 28 59008   2-11111
Don Bidwell, supt.   664-3323
HS, PO BOX 28 59008   1-00011
Don Bidwell, prin.   664-3319

Belgrade, AC 406, PC 5, Gallatin
Belgrade SD 44, PO BOX 166 59714   3-11111
Harry Erickson, supt.   388-6951
HS, PO BOX 166 59714   2-00011
Pat Kramarich, prin.   388-4224
JHS, PO BOX 166 59714   2-00100
Kevin McNelis, prin.   388-1309

Belt, AC 406, PC 3, Cascade
Belt SD, PO BOX 197 59412   2-11111
Daryl Bertelsen, supt.   277-3351
HS, PO BOX 197 59412   1-00011
Daryl Bertelsen, prin.   277-3351

Bigfork, AC 406, PC 4, Flathead
Bigfork SD 38, PO BOX 188 59911   3-11111
Joseph Malletta, supt.   837-4240
HS, PO BOX 188 59911   2-00011
Steve Racki, prin.   837-5271
MS, PO BOX 188 59911   2-00100
Jackie Boshka, prin.   837-5221

Big Sandy, AC 406, PC 3, Chouteau
Big Sandy SD, PO BOX 570 59520   2-11111
Richard Shaffer, supt.   378-2501
HS, PO BOX 570 59520   1-00011
James Barsotti, prin.   378-2502
JHS, PO BOX 570 59520   1-00100
James Barsotti, prin.   378-2502

Big Timber, AC 406, PC 4, Sweet Grass
Sweet Grass County HSD   2-00011
PO BOX 886 59011   932-5993
Richard Webb, supt.
Sweet Grass County HS   2-00011
PO BOX 886 59011   932-5993
Alvin Buerkle, prin.

Billings, AC 406, PC 8, Yellowstone
Billings SD 2, 415 N 30TH ST 59101   7-11111
Peter Carparelli, supt.   255-3500
HS, 425 GRAND AVE 59101   4-00011
Joseph Cross, prin.   255-3630
Billings West HS   4-00011
2201 SAINT JOHNS AVE 59102   255-3670
David Irion, prin.
Skyview HS   4-00011
1775 HIGH SIERRA BLVD 59105   255-3650
Leo Wohler, prin.

Billings Career Center   Vo Tech
3723 CENTRAL AVE 59102   655-3111
Robert Whalen, prin.
Castle Rock JHS, 415 N 30TH ST 59101   3-00100
Peggy Parker, prin.   255-3710
James JHS, 1200 30TH ST W 59102   3-00100
Don Dundas, prin.   655-3124
Lewis & Clark JHS   3-00100
1315 LEWIS AVE 59102   255-3720
William Twilling, prin.
Riverside JHS   3-00100
3700 MADISON AVE 59101   255-3740
Harold Olson, prin.

Lockwood ESD 26   4-11100
1932 US HIGHWAY 87 E 59101   252-6022
Joe McCracken, supt.
Lockwood JHS   2-00100
1932 US HIGHWAY 87 E 59101   259-0154
Cameron Cronk, prin.

Billings Business College   2-CS
2520 5TH AVE S 59101   256-1000
Billings Vocational Technical Center   2-CS
3803 CENTRAL AVE 59102   255-3801
Central Catholic HS   2-00011
3 BROADWATER AVE 59101   245-6651
Ronald Nistler, prin.
May Technical Colleges   2-CS
1306 CENTRAL AVE 59102   259-7000
Montana State University - Billings   5-UC
1500 N 30TH ST 59101   657-2158
Rocky Mountain College   3-UC
1511 POLY DR 59102   800-877-6259
St. Francis MS, 205 N 32ND ST 59101   2-00100
Sidney Sulser, prin.   259-5037
St. Vincent's Hospital   HSP
2915 12TH AVE N 59101   657-7102

Bonner, AC 406, PC 2, Missoula
Bonner ESD 14, PO BOX 1004 59823   2-11100
Christopher Hagar, supt.   258-6151
MS, PO BOX 4 59836   2-00100
Christopher Hagar, prin.   258-6151

Boulder, AC 406, PC 4, Jefferson
Boulder SD, PO BOX 176 59632   2-11111
Richard Moe, supt.   225-3740
Jefferson HS, PO BOX 176 59632   2-00011
Roger Brewer, prin.   225-3317

Box Elder, AC 406, PC 2, Hill
Box Elder SD, PO BOX 205 59521   2-11111
Carroll Lindsey, supt.   352-4955
HS, PO BOX 205 59521   1-00011
Carroll Lindsey, prin.   352-4195

Rocky Boy ESD 87J   2-11111
PO BOX 620 59521   395-4291
Sandra Murie, supt.
Rocky Boy HS, PO BOX 620 59521   1-00011
Voyd St. Pierre, prin.   395-4270
Rocky Boy MS, PO BOX 620 59521   1-00100
Voyd St. Pierre, prin.   395-4474

Stone Child College 59521   2-CC
  395-4313

Bozeman, AC 406, PC 7, Gallatin
Bozeman SD 7, PO BOX 520 59771   5-11111
Paula Butterfield, supt.   585-1500
HS, 205 N 11TH AVE 59715   4-00011
Louis Gappmayer, prin.   585-1650
Chief Joseph MS, 309 N 11TH AVE 59715   4-00100
Anne Olson, prin.   585-1613

Monforton ESD 27   2-11100
6001 MONFORTON SCHOOL RD 59715
Katherine Pattee, supt.   586-1557
Monforton MS   2-01100
6001 MONFORTON SCHOOL RD 59715
Katherine Pattee, prin.   586-1557

Montana State University   7-UC
103 CULBERTSON HALL 59717   994-2452
Mt. Ellis Academy   1-11111
3641 BOZEMAN TRAIL RD 59715   587-5178
Douglas Ammon, prin.

Brady, AC 406, PC 2, Pondera
Brady SD 19, PO BOX 166 59416   1-11111
James Palmer, supt.   753-2522
HS, PO BOX 166 59416   1-00011
James Palmer, prin.   753-2522

Bridger, AC 406, PC 3, Carbon
Bridger SD, PO BOX 467 59014   2-11111
Duane Synoground, supt.   662-3588
HS, 429 W PARK AVE 59014   1-00011
Duane Synoground, prin.   662-3533

Broadus, AC 406, PC 3, Powder River
Broadus SD 79J, PO BOX 500 59317   2-11111
Brian Patrick, supt.   436-2658
Powder River County District JSHS   2-00111
PO BOX 500 59317   436-2658
Allen Burgad, prin.

Broadview, AC 406, PC 2, Yellowstone
Broadview SD 21-J   2-11111
PO BOX 106 59015   667-2337
Dan Nelsen, supt.
HS, PO BOX 106 59015   1-00011
Daniel Nelson, prin.   667-2337

Brockton, AC 406, PC 2, Roosevelt
Brockton SD, PO BOX 198 59213   2-11111
James Hall, supt.   786-3311
HS, PO BOX 198 59213   1-00011
James Hall, prin.   786-3311

Browning, AC 406, PC 4, Glacier
Browning SD 9, PO BOX 610 59417   4-11111
Lee Clark, supt.   338-2715
HS, PO BOX 610 59417   2-00011
Larry McDonald, prin.   338-2745
MS, PO BOX 610 59417   2-00100
Robert Parsons, prin.   338-2725

Blackfeet Community College   2-CC
PO BOX 819 59417   338-5421

Butte, AC 406, PC 8, Silver Bow
Butte SD 1, 111 N MONTANA ST 59701   6-11111
William Nachatilo, supt.   496-2000
HS, 401 S WYOMING ST 59701   4-00011
Dan Peters, prin.   496-2030
East MS, 2600 GRAND AVE 59701   3-00100
William Bartholomew, prin.   496-2060

Butte Central HS, 9 S IDAHO ST 59701   2-00011
Patrick Prendergast, prin.   782-9500
Butte Vocational-Technical Center 59701   2-CS
  494-2894
Central JHS, 400 W PARK ST 59701   2-00100
Sr. Roberta O'Leary, prin.   782-1233
Montana Tech   4-UC
1300 W PARK ST 59701   800-445-8324
St. James Community Hospital   HSP
400 S CLARK ST 59701   782-8361

Cascade, AC 406, PC 3, Cascade
Cascade SD   2-11111
W END CENTRAL AVE 59421   468-2212
Kirk Miller, supt.
JSHS, W END CENTRAL AVE 59421   2-00111
James Donovan, prin.   468-2212

Charlo, AC 406, PC 2, Lake
Charlo SD 7-J, PO BOX 10 59824   2-11111
Steven Gaub, supt.   644-2207
HS, PO BOX 10 59824   1-00011
Dave Herries, prin.   644-2206
MS, PO BOX 10 59824   1-00100
Dave Herries, prin.   644-2206

Chester, AC 406, PC 3, Liberty
Chester SD 33, PO BOX 550 59522   2-11111
Joel Voytoski, supt.   759-5108
JSHS, PO BOX 550 59522   2-00111
William Schlepp, prin.   759-5108

Chinook, AC 406, PC 4, Blaine
Chinook SD 10, PO BOX 1059 59523   3-11111
Dan Haugen, supt.   357-2628
HS, PO BOX 1059 59523   2-00011
Walt Acra, prin.   357-2236
MS, PO BOX 1059 59523   1-00100
Walt Acra, prin.   357-2237

Choteau, AC 406, PC 4, Teton
Choteau SD 1, PO BOX 857 59422   2-11111
Rick Ripley, supt.   466-5303
HS, PO BOX 857 59422   2-00011
John Maloney, prin.   466-5303

Circle, AC 406, PC 3, McCone
Circle SD 1, PO BOX 99 59215   2-11111
Gene Markuson, supt.   485-2332
HS, PO BOX 99 59215   2-00011
Richard Bailey, prin.   485-3600
Redwater MS, PO BOX 99 59215   2-01100
Peggy Nerud, prin.   485-2140

Clancy, AC 406, PC 2, Jefferson
Montana City ESD 27   2-11100
HC BOX 127 59634   442-6779
Penny Koke, supt.
Montana City MS, HC BOX 127 59634   1-00100
Penny Koke, prin.   442-6779

Colstrip, AC 406, PC 5, Rosebud
Colstrip SD 19, PO BOX 159 59323   4-11111
James Anderson, supt.   748-2271
HS, 5000 PINE BUTTE DR 59323   2-00011
Carol Wicker, prin.   748-2920
Brattin MS, 216 OLIVE DRIVE 59323   2-00100
Eileen Johnson, prin.   748-4150

Columbia Falls, AC 406, PC 5, Flathead
Columbia Falls SD 6   4-11111
PO BOX 1259 59912   892-6550
Ryan Taylor, supt.
HS, 610 13TH ST W 59912   3-00011
William Anderson, prin.   892-6500
Eagle HS, PO BOX 1259 59912   1-00011
JoEllen Estenson, prin.   387-5319
JHS, 540 4TH AVE W 59912   2-00100
John Giacomino, prin.   892-6530

Columbus, AC 406, PC 4, Stillwater
Columbus SD 6, PO BOX 899 59019   3-11111
   Duane Denny, supt.   322-5373
JSHS, PO BOX 899 59019   2-00111
   George McKay, prin.   322-5373

Conrad, AC 406, PC 5, Pondera
Conrad SD 10   3-11111
   215 S MARYLAND ST 59425   278-5521
   Dennis Williams, supt.
HS, 308 S ILLINOIS ST 59425   2-00011
   Paul Stenerson, prin.   278-3285
Utterback MS, 24 2ND AVE SW 59425   2-00100
   Fred Zaino, prin.   278-3227

Corvallis, AC 406, PC 3, Ravalli
Corvallis SD 1, PO BOX 700 59828   4-11111
   K. Maki, supt.   961-4211
HS, PO BOX 700 59828   2-00011
   Sarah Schumacher, prin.   961-3201
JHS, PO BOX 700 59828   2-00100
   Allyson Hoiland, prin.   961-3007

Crow Agency, AC 406, PC 4, Big Horn

Little Big Horn College 59022   2-CC
  638-2228

Culbertson, AC 406, PC 3, Roosevelt
Culbertson SD, PO BOX 516 59218   2-11111
   Patrick Stuber, supt.   787-6246
HS, PO BOX 516 59218   1-00011
   Gerald Jennex, prin.   787-6243

Custer, AC 406, PC 2, Yellowstone
Custer SD 15, PO BOX 69 59024   1-11111
   Louise Jenkins, supt.   856-4117
HS, PO BOX 69 59024   1-00011
   Louise Jenkins, prin.   856-4117

Cut Bank, AC 406, PC 5, Glacier
Cut Bank SD 15, 101 3RD AVE SE 59427   4-11111
   Barbara Parker, supt.   873-2229
HS, 300 1ST ST SE 59427   2-00011
   Dennis Roseleip, prin.   873-5629
JHS, 101 3RD AVE SE 59427   2-00100
   Sharon Dale, prin.   873-4421

Darby, AC 406, PC 3, Ravalli
Darby SD 9, 209 SCHOOL DR 59829   3-11111
   Jack Eggensperger, supt.   821-3841
HS, 209 SCHOOL DR 59829   2-00011
   John Hughes, prin.   821-3252

Deer Lodge, AC 406, PC 5, Powell
Deer Lodge ESD 1   3-11100
   444 MONTANA AVE 59722   846-1553
   Tom Cotton, supt.
Duvall MS, 444 MONTANA AVE 59722   2-00100
   Pat Rogers, prin.   846-1684

Powell County HSD   2-00011
   709 MISSOURI AVE 59722   846-2757
   Jerry Claussen, supt.
Powell County HS   2-00011
   709 MISSOURI AVE 59722   846-2757
   Mike Doyle, prin.

Denton, AC 406, PC 2, Fergus
Denton SD 84, PO BOX 1048 59430   2-11111
   Les Cabot, supt.   567-2370
JSHS, PO BOX 1048 59430   2-00111
   Les Cabot, supt.   567-2370

Dillon, AC 406, PC 5, Beaverhead
Beaverhead County HSD   2-00011
   104 N PACIFIC ST 59725   683-2361
   Dennis Kimzey, supt.
Beaverhead County HS   2-00011
   104 N PACIFIC ST 59725   683-2361
   John Wilkerson, prin.

Dillon ESD 10, 225 E REEDER ST 59725   4-11100
   Larry Blades, supt.   683-4311
MS, 14 COTTOM DR 59725   2-00100
   Janelle Beers, prin.   683-2368

Western Montana College   3-UC
   710 S ATLANTIC ST 59725   683-7331

Dodson, AC 406, PC 2, Phillips
Dodson SD, PO BOX 278 59524   2-11111
   Nellie Sherman, supt.   383-4362
HS, PO BOX 278 59524   1-00011
   Nellie Sherman, prin.   383-4362

Drummond, AC 406, PC 2, Granite
Drummond SD, PO BOX 349 59832   2-11111
   Walter Piippo, supt.   288-3281
HS, PO BOX 349 59832   1-00011
   Walter Piippo, prin.   288-3281

Dutton, AC 406, PC 2, Teton
Dutton SD 28, PO BOX 50 59433   2-11111
   Kathleen Lockyer, supt.   476-3424
HS, PO BOX 50 59433   1-00011
   Robert Mutch, prin.   476-3424

East Helena, AC 406, PC 4, Lewis and Clark
East Helena ESD 9   4-11100
   PO BOX 1280 59635   227-6631
   Ronald Stegmann, supt.
Radley MS, PO BOX 1280 59635   2-00100
   Ron Whitmoyer, prin.   227-5851

Ekalaka, AC 406, PC 2, Carter
Carter County HSD   1-00011
   PO BOX 458 59324   775-8767
   Glenn Hageman, supt.
Carter County HS, PO BOX 458 59324   1-00011
   Glenn Hageman, prin.   775-8767

Ennis, AC 406, PC 3, Madison
Madison Valley Cons Public SD   2-11111
   PO BOX 517 59729   682-4258
   John Overstreet, supt.
Madison Valley Consolidated HS   1-00011
   PO BOX 517 59729   682-4258
   Jay Willet, prin.

Eureka, AC 406, PC 4, Lincoln
Eureka SD, PO BOX 2000 59917   3-11111
   Ron Blake, supt.   296-2502
Lincoln County JSHS   2-00111
   PO BOX 2000 59917   296-2525
   Richard Stavenow, prin.

Fairfield, AC 406, PC 3, Teton
Fairfield SD 21, PO BOX 99 59436   2-11111
   Ward Fifield, supt.   467-2103
HS, PO BOX 99 59436   2-00011
   Wayne Stiffler, prin.   467-2528

Fairview, AC 406, PC 3, Richland
Fairview SD, PO BOX 467 59221   2-11111
   Ken Avison, supt.   747-5265
HS, PO BOX 467 59221   2-00011
   Rusty Martin, prin.   747-5265

Flaxville, AC 406, PC 1, Daniels
Flaxville SD, PO BOX 89 59222   1-11111
   Marvin Rich, supt.   474-2211
HS, PO BOX 89 59222   1-00011
   Marvin Rich, prin.   474-2211

Florence, AC 406, PC 2, Ravalli
Florence-Carlton SD 15-6   3-11111
   5602 OLD US HIGHWAY 93 59833   273-6751
   Ernest Jean, supt.
Florence-Carlton JSHS   2-00111
   5602 OLD US HIGHWAY 93 59833   273-6301
   Brady Selle, prin.

Forsyth, AC 406, PC 4, Rosebud
Forsyth SD 4, PO BOX 319 59327   3-11111
   Fred Seybert, supt.   356-2796
HS, PO BOX 319 59327   2-00011
   Ed Peterson, prin.   356-2705
MS, PO BOX 319 59327   2-00100
   Kathleen Byron, prin.   356-2791

Fort Benton, AC 406, PC 4, Chouteau
Ft. Benton SD 1, PO BOX 399 59442   3-11111
   Kurt Hilyard, supt.   622-5691
HS, 1820 WASHINGTON 59442   2-00011
   Randy Durr, prin.   622-3213
JHS, 1820 WASHINGTON 59442   1-00100
   Randy Durr, prin.   622-5112

Frazer, AC 406, PC 2, Valley
Frazer SD, PO BOX 488 59225   2-11111
   Dennis Maasjo, supt.   695-2241
HS, PO BOX 488 59225   1-00011
   Dennis Maasjo, prin.   695-2241

Frenchtown, AC 406, PC 2, Missoula
Frenchtown SD 40   3-11111
   PO BOX 117 59834   626-5762
   Michael Nicosia, supt.
HS, PO BOX 117 59834   2-00011
   Thomas Kallay, prin.   626-5222

Froid, AC 406, PC 2, Roosevelt
Froid SD, PO BOX 218 59226   2-11111
   Bill Parker, supt.   766-2343
HS, PO BOX 218 59226   1-00011
   Steve Sammons, prin.   766-2342

Fromberg, AC 406, PC 2, Carbon
Fromberg SD, PO BOX 188 59029   2-11111
   Jay Eslick, supt.   668-7611
JSHS, PO BOX 188 59029   1-00111
   Jay Eslick, prin.   668-7611

Gardiner, AC 406, PC 3, Park
Gardiner SD, PO BOX 26 59030   2-11111
   Lynn Mavencamp, supt.   848-7261
HS, PO BOX 26 59030   1-00011
   Lynn Mavencamp, prin.   848-7261

Geraldine, AC 406, PC 2, Chouteau
Geraldine SD, PO BOX 347 59446   2-11111
   Ed Zabrocki, supt.   737-4311
HS, PO BOX 347 59446   1-00011
   Ed Zabrocki, prin.   737-4371

Geyser, AC 406, PC 2, Judith Basin
Geyser SD 58, PO BOX 70 59447   2-11111
   Ben Beaudry, supt.   735-4368
HS, PO BOX 70 59447   1-00011
   Ben Beaudry, prin.   735-4368

Gildford, AC 406, PC 2, Hill
Kremlin-Gildford SD   2-11111
   PO BOX 166 59525   376-3183
   Paul Preeshl, supt.
Kremlin-Gilford JSHS   1-00111
   PO BOX 166 59525   376-3183
   Paul Preeshl, prin.

Glasgow, AC 406, PC 5, Valley
Glasgow SD, PO BOX 28 59230   4-11111
   Gary Martin, supt.   228-2406
HS, PO BOX 28 59230   2-00011
   Robert Farrell, prin.   228-2485
MS, PO BOX 28 59230   2-00100
   Glen Monson, prin.   228-8268

Glendive, AC 406, PC 5, Dawson
Dawson County HSD   3-00011
   PO BOX 701 59330   365-5293
   Dan Martin, supt.
Dawson County HS   3-00011
   900 N MERRILL AVE 59330   365-5265
   Hilary Hopfauf, prin.

Dawson Community College   3-CC
   PO BOX 421 59330   365-3396

Grass Range, AC 406, PC 2, Fergus
Grass Range SD 27, PO BOX 58 59032   2-11111
   Claire Garrick, supt.   428-2122
HS, PO BOX 58 59032   1-00011
   Claire Garrick, prin.   428-2341

Great Falls, AC 406, PC 8, Cascade
Great Falls SD, PO BOX 2429 59403   7-11111
   Larry Williams, supt.   791-2350
HS, 1900 2ND AVE S 59405   4-00011
   Gary Davis, prin.   791-2167
Russell HS, 228 17TH AVE NW 59404   4-00011
   Herman Plass, prin.   791-2387
East MS, 4040 CENTRAL AVE 59405   3-00100
   Gordon Dahl, prin.   791-2312
Gibson MS, 2400 CENTRAL AVE 59401   4-00100
   Dick Kuntz, prin.   791-2145
North MS, 2601 8TH ST NE 59404   3-00100
   Ted Snow, prin.   791-2330

College of Great Falls   4-UC
   1301 20TH ST S 59405   761-8210
Columbus Hospital   HSP
   500 15TH AVE S 59405   727-3333
Great Falls Vocational Technical Center   3-CC
   2100 16TH AVE S 59405   771-1240
May Technical College   2-CS
   1807 3RD ST NW 59404   761-4000
Montana Deaconess Medical Center   HSP
   1101 26TH ST S 59405   761-1200
Montana School for the Deaf and Blind   HND
   3800 2ND AVE N 59405

Hamilton, AC 406, PC 5, Ravalli
Hamilton SD 3, 217 DALY AVE 59840   4-11111
   Jean Hagen, supt.   363-2280
HS, 209 S 5TH ST 59840   2-00011
   Hyrum Tatton, prin.   363-2021
Westview JHS, 103 S 9TH ST 59840   2-00100
   Robert Smith, prin.   363-2121

Hardin, AC 406, PC 5, Big Horn
Hardin SD, RR 1 BOX 1001 59034   4-11111
   Rodney Svee, supt.   665-1304
HS, 702 N TERRY AVE 59034   2-00011
   Jerry Slyker, prin.   665-1908
MS, 611 5TH ST W 59034   2-00100
   Don Gilbertson, prin.   665-1408

Harlem, AC 406, PC 3, Blaine
Harlem SD 12, PO BOX 339 59526   3-11111
   Donald Wetzel, supt.   353-2674
HS, PO BOX 339 59526   2-00011
   James Owens, prin.   353-2887
MS, PO BOX 339 59526   1-00100
   James Owens, prin.   353-2287

Fort Belknap College 59526   2-CC
  353-2205

Harlowton, AC 406, PC 4, Wheatland
Harlowton SD 16, PO BOX 288 59036   2-11111
   JoAnne Ackermann, supt.   632-4822
HS, PO BOX 288 59036   2-00011
   Dale Kari, prin.   632-4822

Harrison, AC 406, PC 2, Madison
Harrison SD 23, PO BOX 7 59735   2-11111
   Dan Rask, supt.   685-3471
HS, PO BOX 7 59735   1-00011
   Dan Rask, prin.   685-3471

Havre, AC 406, PC 7, Hill
Havre SD, PO BOX 7791 59501   5-11111
   Robert Windel, supt.   265-4356
HS, PO BOX 7791 59501   3-00011
   Jan Ophus, prin.   265-6731
MS, 1441 11TH ST W 59501   3-00100
   Jeff Pratt, prin.   265-9613

Northern Montana College   4-UC
   PO BOX 7751 59501   265-3700

Hays, AC 406, PC 2, Blaine
Hays-Lodge Pole SD 50   2-11111
   PO BOX 110 59527   673-3120
   Dale Shupe, supt.
Hays-Lodge Pole HS   1-00011
   PO BOX 110 59527   673-3120
   Bernard Lambert, prin.

Hays-Lodge Pole MS — 1-00100
PO BOX 110 59527 — 673-3120
Tim Peterson, prin.

Heart Butte, AC 406, PC 2, Pondera
Heart Butte SD 1, PO BOX 259 59448 — 2-11111
Edward Parisian, supt. — 338-2200
HS, PO BOX 259 59448 — 1-00011
Robert Small, prin. — 338-2200

Helena, AC 406, PC 7, Lewis and Clark
Helena SD 1, PO BOX 5417 59604 — 6-11111
Gary Toothaker, supt. — 447-8595
Capital HS, 100 VALLEY DR 59601 — 4-00011
Dwight Moose, prin. — 442-8600
HS, 1300 BILLINGS AVE 59601 — 4-00011
Gregory Moo, prin. — 442-8090
Anderson MS, 1200 KNIGHT ST 59601 — 3-00100
Ken Stuker, prin. — 442-4101
MS, 1025 N RODNEY ST 59601 — 3-00100
Pep Jewell, prin. — 442-5720

Carroll College — 4-UC
1610 N BENTON AVE 59625 — 442-3450
Helena College of Tech of the Univ of MT — 3-CC
1115 N ROBERTS ST 59601 — 444-6800

Highwood, AC 406, PC 2, Chouteau
Highwood SD, RR 1 BOX 100 59450 — 2-11111
Jeff Blessum, supt. — 733-2081
HS, RR 1 BOX 100 59450 — 1-00011
Jeff Blessum, prin. — 733-2671

Hinsdale, AC 406, PC 2, Valley
Hinsdale SD, PO BOX 398 59241 — 1-11111
Michael Button, supt. — 364-2314
HS, PO BOX 398 59241 — 1-00011
Michael Button, prin. — 364-2314

Hobson, AC 406, PC 2, Judith Basin
Hobson SD 25 59452 — 2-11111
Dennis Fry, supt. — 423-5483
HS 59452 — 1-00011
Dennis Fry, prin. — 423-5483

Hot Springs, AC 406, PC 2, Sanders
Hot Springs SD 14J, PO BOX T 59845 — 2-11111
Merle Farrier, supt. — 741-3285
JSHS, PO BOX T 59845 — 1-00111
Lloyd Redmond, prin. — 741-3285

Hysham, AC 406, PC 2, Treasure
Hysham SD, PO BOX 272 59038 — 2-11111
William Colter, supt. — 342-5237
JSHS, PO BOX 272 59038 — 1-00111
William Colter, prin. — 342-5237

Joliet, AC 406, PC 3, Carbon
Joliet SD 7, PO BOX G 59041 — 2-11111
Leo Lorenz, supt. — 962-3541
HS, PO BOX G 59041 — 2-00011
Vance Blatter, prin. — 962-3541
MS, PO BOX G 59041 — 1-00100
Vance Blatter, prin. — 962-3541

Joplin, AC 406, PC 2, Liberty
J-I SD, PO BOX 89 59531 — 2-11111
Ronald Blomquist, supt. — 292-3832
Joplin-Inverness HS — 1-00011
PO BOX 89 59531 — 292-3832
Ronald Blomquist, prin.
Joplin-Inverness MS — 1-00100
PO BOX 89 59531 — 292-3832
Ronald Blomquist, prin.

Jordan, AC 406, PC 2, Garfield
Garfield County HSD — 1-00011
PO BOX 409 59337 — 557-2259
Elbert Hatcher, supt.
Garfield County HS — 1-00011
PO BOX 409 59337 — 557-2259
Elbert Hatcher, prin.

Judith Gap, AC 406, PC 2, Wheatland
Judith Gap SD 21J, PO BOX 64 59453 — 2-11111
Robert Korthuis, supt. — 473-2211
HS, PO BOX 64 59453 — 1-00011
Robert Korthuis, prin. — 473-2211

Kalispell, AC 406, PC 7, Flathead
Cayuse Prairie ESD 10 — 2-11100
897 LAKE BLAINE RD 59901 — 756-4562
John Babcock, supt.
Cayuse Prairie MS — 2-01100
897 LAKE BLAINE RD 59901 — 756-4560
John Babcock, prin.

Evergreen ESD 50 — 3-11100
18 W EVERGREEN DR 59901 — 752-0101
Robert Aumaugher, supt.
Evergreen MS — 2-01100
18 W EVERGREEN DR 59901 — 752-1189
Robert Aumaugher, prin.

Kalispell SD 5, 233 1ST AVE E 59901 — 5-11111
William Cooper, supt. — 756-5015
Flathead SHS, 644 4TH AVE W 59901 — 4-00001
Cathryn McDevitt, prin. — 756-5075
JHS, 205 NORTHWEST LN 59901 — 2-00110
Patrick Feeley, prin. — 756-5030

Smith Valley ESD 89 — 2-11100
600 BATAVIA LN 59901 – (—), supt. — 756-4536
Smith Valley MS — 1-00100
600 BATAVIA LN 59901 — 756-4536
Harold Welling, prin.

Flathead Valley Community College — 4-CC
777 GRANDVIEW DR 59901 — 756-3846

Lambert, AC 406, PC 2, Richland
Lambert SD, PO BOX 236 59243 — 2-11111
Richard Hughes, supt. — 774-3333
HS, PO BOX 236 59243 — 1-00011
Richard Hughes, prin. — 774-3333

Lame Deer, AC 406, PC 3, Rosebud

Dull Knife Memorial College — 2-CC
GENERAL DELIVERY 59043 — 477-6215

Laurel, AC 406, PC 6, Yellowstone
Laurel SD, 410 COLORADO AVE 59044 — 4-11111
Wayne Severtson, supt. — 628-8623
HS, 203 E 8TH ST 59044 — 3-00011
Mike Michunovich, prin. — 628-7911
MS, 410 COLORADO AVE 59044 — 2-00100
Richard Trerise, prin. — 628-6919

Lavina, AC 406, PC 2, Golden Valley
Lavina SD, PO BOX 146 59046 — 1-11111
Richard Cameron, supt. — 636-2761
HS, PO BOX 146 59046 — 1-00011
Richard Cameron, prin. — 636-2761

Lewistown, AC 406, PC 6, Fergus
Lewistown SD 1, 215 7TH AVE S 59457 — 4-11111
Conrad Robertson, supt. — 538-8777
Fergus HS — 2-00011
201 CASINO CREEK DR 59457 — 538-2321
Richard Wilson, prin.
MS, 914 W MAIN ST 59457 — 2-00100
Pat Hould, prin. — 538-5168

Libby, AC 406, PC 5, Lincoln
Libby SD 4, 724 LOUISIANA AVE 59923 — 4-11111
William Donahue, supt. — 293-8811
HS, 150 EDUCATION WAY 59923 — 3-00011
Stanley Evans, prin. — 293-6398
MS, 101 SKI RD 59923 — 3-00100
Dave Stephenson, prin. — 293-5803

Lima, AC 406, PC 2, Beaverhead
Lima SD 12, PO BOX AA 59739 — 2-11111
Dale Huhtanen, supt. — 276-3571
HS, PO BOX AA 59739 — 1-00011
Jerry Allen, prin. — 276-3571

Lincoln, AC 406, PC 3, Lewis and Clark
Lincoln SD 38, PO BOX 39 59639 — 2-11111
John Loucks, supt. — 362-4201
JSHS, PO BOX 39 59639 — 1-00111
Kathy Heisler, prin. — 362-4201

Livingston, AC 406, PC 6, Park
Livingston SD, 132 S B ST 59047 — 4-11111
Verne Beffert, supt. — 222-0861
Park HS, 6 VIEW VISTA DR 59047 — 3-00011
Timothy Dunn, prin. — 222-0448
Sleeping Giant MS — 2-00100
301 VIEW VISTA DR 59047 — 222-3292
Tena Versland, prin.

Lodge Grass, AC 406, PC 3, Big Horn
Lodge Grass SD, PO BOX AF 59050 — 3-11111
Ray Phipps, supt. — 639-2304
HS, PO BOX AF 59050 — 2-00011
Elaine Forrest, prin. — 639-2385
MS, PO BOX AF 59050 — 2-00100
Elaine Forrest, prin. — 639-2385

Lolo, AC 406, PC 5, Missoula
Lolo ESD 7 — 3-11100
11395 US HIGHWAY 93 S 59847 — 273-6141
Elmer Myers, supt.
MS, 11395 US HIGHWAY 93 S 59847 — 2-01100
Alice Kupilik, prin. — 273-6141

Malta, AC 406, PC 4, Phillips
Malta SD, PO BOX 670 59538 — 3-11111
Robert Rust, supt. — 654-2225
HS, 219 S 5TH ST E 59538 — 2-00011
Kelly Taylor, prin. — 654-2002
JHS, 219 S 5TH ST E 59538 — 2-00100
Kelly Taylor, prin. — 654-2002

Manhattan, AC 406, PC 4, Gallatin
Manhattan SD 3, PO BOX 425 59741 — 3-11111
Ronald Zier, supt. — 284-6460
HS, PO BOX 425 59741 — 2-00011
Bob Moore, prin. — 284-3341

Manhattan Christian S — 2-11111
8000 CHURCHILL RD 59741

Medicine Lake, AC 406, PC 2, Sheridan
Medicine Lake SD 7 — 2-11111
PO BOX 265 59247 — 789-2211
Calvin Moore, supt.
JSHS, PO BOX 265 59247 — 2-00111
Lynn Utterback, prin. — 789-2211

Melstone, AC 406, PC 2, Musselshell
Melstone SD, PO BOX 97 59054 — 2-11111
Terry Quintus, supt. — 358-2346

HS, 5 6TH AVE E 59054 — 1-00011
Terry Quintus, prin. — 358-2352

Miles City, AC 406, PC 6, Custer
Miles City SD 1, 1604 MAIN ST 59301 — 4-11111
Robert Richards, supt. — 232-3840
Custer County District HS — 3-00011
20 S CENTER AVE 59301 — 232-4920
Fred Anderson, prin.
Washington MS, 210 N 9TH ST 59301 — 2-00100
Rick Powell, prin. — 232-2084

Miles Community College — 3-CC
2715 DICKINSON ST 59301 — 232-3031

Missoula, AC 406, PC 8, Missoula
Hellgate ESD 4, 2385 FLYNN LN 59802 — 4-11100
Craig Brewington, supt. — 728-5626
Hellgate MS, 2385 FLYNN LN 59802 — 2-00100
Terry Vanderpan, prin. — 549-6109

Missoula County HSD — 5-00011
915 SOUTH AVE W 59801 — 728-2400
Mary Vagner, supt.
Big Sky HS, 3100 SOUTH AVE W 59801 — 4-00011
Darlene Smith, prin. — 728-2401
Hellgate HS, 900 S HIGGINS AVE 59801 — 4-00011
Jon Fimmel, prin. — 728-2402
Sentinel HS, 901 SOUTH AVE W 59801 — 4-00011
Bruce Zinne, prin. — 728-2403
Other Schools – See Seeley Lake

Missoula ESD 1, 215 S 6TH ST W 59801 — 6-11100
Jacob Block, supt. — 728-4000
Meadow Hill MS — 3-00100
4210 S RESERVE ST 59803 — 542-4045
Mike Maxwell, prin.
Porter MS, 2510 W CENTRAL AVE 59801 — 2-00100
Mark Thane, prin. — 542-4060
Rattlesnake MS — 2-00100
120 PINEVIEW DRIVE 59802 — 542-4070
David Dorn, prin.
Washington MS — 3-00100
645 W CENTRAL AVE 59801 — 542-4085
Joe Stauduhar, prin.

Loyola-Sacred Heart HS — 2-00011
320 EDITH ST 59801 — 549-6101
Joe Caciari, prin.
Missoula Vocational Technical Center — 3-CC
909 SOUTH AVE W 59801 — 542-6882
St. Patrick Hospital — HSP
PO BOX 4587 59806 — 543-7271
University of Montana 59812 — 6-UC
800-462-8636

Moore, AC 406, PC 2, Fergus
Moore SD 44, PO BOX 1 59464 — 2-11111
Kathleen Eaton, supt. — 374-2231
HS, PO BOX 1 59464 — 1-00011
Kathleen Eaton, prin. — 374-2231

Nashua, AC 406, PC 2, Valley
Nashua SD, PO BOX 170 59248 — 2-11111
David Kloker, supt. — 746-3411
HS, PO BOX 170 59248 — 1-00011
David Kloker, prin. — 746-3411

Noxon, AC 406, PC 2, Sanders
Noxon SD 10, PO BOX 1506 59853 — 2-11111
John Baule, supt. — 847-2443
JSHS, PO BOX 1506 59853 — 2-00111
Jim Watts, prin. — 847-2442

Opheim, AC 406, PC 2, Valley
Opheim SD, PO BOX 108 59250 — 2-11111
Ken Halverson, supt. — 762-3214
HS, PO BOX 108 59250 — 1-00011
Ken Halverson, prin. — 762-3214

Outlook, AC 406, PC 2, Sheridan
Outlook SD 29, PO BOX 296 59252 — 1-11111
Michael Smith, supt. — 895-2466
HS, PO BOX 296 59252 — 1-00011
Michael Smith, prin. — 895-2466

Pablo, AC 406, PC 2, Lake

Salish Kootenai College — 3-CC
PO BOX 117 59855 — 675-4800

Park City, AC 406, PC 2, Stillwater
Park City SD 5, PO BOX 278 59063 — 2-11111
Bob Barnes, supt. — 633-2406
JSHS, PO BOX 278 59063 — 2-00111
Terry Laughery, prin. — 633-2350

Peerless, AC 406, PC 2, Daniels
Peerless SD 2, PO BOX 475 59253 — 1-11111
Roger Britton, supt. — 893-4377
HS, PO BOX 475 59253 — 1-00011
Roger Britton, prin. — 893-4377

Philipsburg, AC 406, PC 3, Granite
Philipsburg SD 1, PO BOX 400 59858 — 3-11111
Jim Kelly, supt. — 859-3232
Granite HS, PO BOX 400 59858 — 1-00011
Jim Kelly, prin. — 859-3232

Plains, AC 406, PC 3, Sanders
Plains SD 1, PO BOX 549 59859 — 3-11111
Ron Rude, supt. — 826-3666

HS, PO BOX 549   59859 | 2-00011
James French, prin. | 826-3666
MS, PO BOX 549   59859 | 1-00100
James French, prin. | 826-3666

Plentywood, AC 406, PC 4, Sheridan
Plentywood SD 20 | 3-11111
100 E LAUREL AVE   59254 | 765-1803
Lowell Young, supt.
JSHS, 100 E LAUREL AVE   59254 | 2-00111
James Germann, prin. | 765-1803

Plevna, AC 406, PC 2, Fallon
Plevna SD 55, PO BOX 158   59344 | 2-11111
Carter Christiansen, supt. | 772-5666
HS, PO BOX 158   59344 | 1-00011
Carter Christiansen, prin. | 772-5666

Polson, AC 406, PC 5, Lake
Polson SD 23, 111 4TH AVE E   59860 | 4-11111
Andrew Veis, supt. | 883-6355
HS, 111 4TH AVE E   59860 | 2-00011
Ed Longin, prin. | 883-6350
MS, 111 4TH AVE E   59860 | 3-01100
Darryl Dupuis, prin. | 883-6335

Poplar, AC 406, PC 3, Roosevelt
Poplar SD, PO BOX 458   59255 | 3-11111
Douglas Sullivan, supt. | 768-3637
HS, 400 4TH AVE W   59255 | 2-00011
Daniel Farr, prin. | 768-3410
JHS, PO BOX 458   59255 | 2-01100
Calvin Johnson, prin. | 768-3409

Fort Peck Community College   59255 | 2-CC
| 768-5551

Power, AC 406, PC 2, Teton
Power SD 30, PO BOX 155   59468 | 2-11111
Kathleen Lockyer, supt. | 463-2251
HS, PO BOX 155   59468 | 1-00011
Kathleen Lockyer, prin. | 463-2251

Pryor, AC 406, PC 3, Big Horn
Pryor SD, PO BOX 229   59066 | 1-11111
Daniel Sybrant, supt. | 259-7329
Plenty Coups JSHS | 1-00111
PO BOX 229   59066 | 259-7329
Daniel Sybrant, prin.

Rapelje, AC 406, PC 2, Stillwater
Rapelje SD 32, PO BOX 89   59067 | 1-11111
Gary Scott, supt. | 663-2216
HS, PO BOX 89   59067 | 1-00011
Gary Scott, prin. | 663-2216

Red Lodge, AC 406, PC 4, Carbon
Red Lodge SD 1, PO BOX 1090   59068 | 3-11111
Ken Miller, supt. | 446-1428
HS, PO BOX 1090   59068 | 2-00011
Steve Bradshaw, prin. | 446-1903
MS, PO BOX 1090   59068 | 1-00100
Steve York, prin. | 446-2110

Reedpoint, AC 406, PC 2, Stillwater
Reedpoint SD 9-9, PO BOX 338   59069 | 1-11111
Rod Olson, supt. | 326-2245
HS, PO BOX 338   59069 | 1-00011
Rod Olson, prin. | 326-2245

Richey, AC 406, PC 2, Dawson
Richey SD, PO BOX 60   59259 | 2-11111
Carol Ruf, supt. | 773-5680
HS, PO BOX 60   59259 | 1-00011
Carol Ruf, prin. | 773-5523
MS, PO BOX 60   59259 | 1-00100
Carol Ruf, prin. | 773-5680

Roberts, AC 406, PC 2, Carbon
Roberts SD, PO BOX 78   59070 | 2-11111
Ron Marshall, supt. | 445-2421
HS, 106 MAPLE   59070 | 1-00011
Ron Marshall, prin. | 445-2421

Ronan, AC 406, PC 4, Lake
Ronan SD 30, PO BOX R   59864 | 4-11111
Bob Voth, supt. | 676-3390
HS, PO BOX R   59864 | 2-00011
Richard Gallagher, prin. | 676-8410
JHS, PO BOX R   59864 | 2-01100
Jim Gillhouse, prin. | 676-5831

Rosebud, AC 406, PC 2, Rosebud
Rosebud SD 12, PO BOX 38   59347 | 2-11111
Norm Hagen, supt. | 347-5353
HS, PO BOX 38   59347 | 1-00011
Norm Hagen, prin. | 347-5353

Roundup, AC 406, PC 4, Musselshell
Roundup SD, PO BOX 717   59072 | 3-11111
J. Jay Erdie, supt. | 323-1507
HS, 6TH AVE & 5TH ST W   59072 | 2-00011
Allen Cherry, prin. | 323-2402
MS, 6TH AVE & 5TH ST W   59072 | 2-00100
Allen Cherry, prin. | 323-2402

Roy, AC 406, PC 2, Fergus
Roy SD 74, PO BOX 9   59471 | 1-11111
George Bewick, supt. | 464-2511
HS, PO BOX 9   59471 | 1-00011
George Bewick, prin. | 464-2511

Rudyard, AC 406, PC 3, Hill
Blue Sky SD, PO BOX 129   59540 | 2-11111
James Smith, supt. | 355-4481
Blue Sky HS, PO BOX 129   59540 | 1-00011
Joe Jurenka, prin. | 355-4460
Blue Sky MS, PO BOX 129   59540 | 1-00100
Joe Jurenka, prin. | 355-4481

Ryegate, AC 406, PC 2, Golden Valley
Ryegate SD, PO BOX 129   59074 | 1-11111
Robert Heppner, supt. | 568-2211
HS, PO BOX 129   59074 | 1-00011
Robert Heppner, prin. | 568-2211

Saco, AC 406, PC 2, Phillips
Saco SD, PO BOX 298   59261 | 2-11111
Carl Knudsen, supt. | 527-3531
HS, PO BOX 298   59261 | 1-00011
Larry Crowder, prin. | 527-3531

Saint Ignatius, AC 406, PC 3, Lake
St. Ignatius SD 28 | 3-11111
PO BOX 400   59865 | 745-4420
Richard Mutterer, supt.
JSHS, PO BOX 400   59865 | 2-00111
Timothy Skinner, prin. | 745-3811

Saint Regis, AC 406, PC 3, Mineral
St. Regis SD, PO BOX K   59866 | 2-11111
Linda Carlsen, supt. | 649-2427
HS, PO BOX K   59866 | 1-00011
Linda Carlsen, prin. | 649-2311

Sand Coulee, AC 406, PC 2, Cascade
Centerville SD | 2-11111
693 HIGHWAY 227   59472 | 736-5123
Stan Perkins, supt.
Centerville JSHS | 2-00111
693 HIGHWAY 227   59472 | 736-5167
Mark Brajcich, prin.

Savage, AC 406, PC 2, Richland
Savage SD, PO BOX 110   59262 | 2-11111
John McNeil, supt. | 776-2317
HS, PO BOX 110   59262 | 1-00011
John Pehrson, prin. | 776-2317

Scobey, AC 406, PC 4, Daniels
Scobey SD 1, PO BOX 10   59263 | 2-11111
Dustin Hill, supt. | 487-2202
JSHS, PO BOX 10   59263 | 2-00111
George Rider, prin. | 487-2202

Seeley Lake, AC 406, PC 3, Missoula
Missoula County HSD
Supt. — See Missoula
Seeley-Swan HS   59868 | 2-00011
Kim Haines, prin. | 677-2224

Shelby, AC 406, PC 5, Toole
Shelby SD 14 | 3-11111
622 N GRANITE AVE   59474 | 434-2622
Dennis Parman, supt.
HS, 1001 6TH ST N   59474 | 2-00011
Douglas Helgeson, prin. | 434-5523
MS, 133 6TH AVE S   59474 | 2-00100
Charles Topley, prin. | 434-5236

Shepherd, AC 406, PC 2, Yellowstone
Shepherd SD 37, PO BOX 8   59079 | 3-11111
Calvin Spangler, supt. | 373-5461
HS, 7842 SHEPHERD RD   59079 | 2-00011
Gary DeGooyer, prin. | 373-5284
MS, PO BOX 8   59079 | 2-00100
Larry Leikam, prin. | 373-5873

Sheridan, AC 406, PC 3, Madison
Sheridan SD 5, PO BOX 586   59749 | 2-11111
William Walker, supt. | 842-5401
HS, PO BOX 586   59749 | 1-00011
William Walker, prin. | 842-5401

Sidney, AC 406, PC 6, Richland
Sidney SD, 121 5TH ST SW   59270 | 4-11111
Phil Waber, supt. | 482-4081
HS, 1012 4TH ST SW   59270 | 3-00011
James Wood, prin. | 482-2330
JSHS, 415 S CENTRAL AVE   59270 | 2-00100
Bill Nankivel, prin. | 482-4050

Simms, AC 406, PC 2, Cascade
Sun River Valley SD | 2-11111
PO BOX 38   59477 | 264-5111
Penny Bertelsen, supt.
HS, PO BOX 38   59477 | 2-00011
Richard Walker, prin. | 264-5110
Other Schools – See Sun River

Stanford, AC 406, PC 3, Judith Basin
Stanford SD 12, 104 4TH AVE S   59479 | 2-11111
Larry Biere, supt. | 566-2265
JSHS, 104 4TH AVE S   59479 | 1-00011
Larry Biere, prin. | 566-2265

Stevensville, AC 406, PC 4, Ravalli
Stevensville SD 2, 300 PARK ST   59870 | 4-11111
Anthony Tognetti, supt. | 777-5481
HS, 300 PARK ST   59870 | 2-00011
Ron Nicholas, prin. | 777-5481
JHS, 300 PARK ST   59870 | 2-00100
Jim Notaro, prin. | 777-5533

Sunburst, AC 406, PC 2, Toole
Sunburst SD 2, PO BOX 710   59482 | 2-11111
Alan Ryan, supt. | 937-7366

HS, PO BOX 710   59482 | 1-00011
Thomas Nau, prin. | 937-2811

Sun River, AC 406, PC 2, Cascade
Sun River Valley SD
Supt. — See Simms
MS, PO BOX 1   59483 | 1-00100
Carl Roy, prin. | 264-5330

Superior, AC 406, PC 3, Mineral
Superior SD 3, PO BOX 400   59872 | 2-11111
Fred Maker, supt. | 822-4851
HS, 410 ARIZONA AVE   59872 | 2-00011
Allan Labbe, prin. | 822-4851
MS, PO BOX 400   59872 | 1-00100
Allan Labbe, prin. | 822-4851

Terry, AC 406, PC 3, Prairie
Terry SD 5, PO BOX 187   59349 | 2-11111
Bruce Clausen, supt. | 637-5533
HS, PO BOX 187   59349 | 2-00011
Bruce Clausen, prin. | 637-5533

Thompson Falls, AC 406, PC 4, Sanders
Thompson Falls SD 2 | 3-11111
PO BOX 129   59873 | 827-3541
Jerry Pauli, supt.
JSHS, PO BOX 129   59873 | 2-00111
Don Jensen, prin. | 827-3561

Three Forks, AC 406, PC 4, Gallatin
Three Forks SD, 212 E NEAL ST   59752 | 2-11111
Charles Ansley, supt. | 285-6830
JSHS, 210 E NEAL ST   59752 | 2-00111
Jack Heebner, prin. | 285-3503

Townsend, AC 406, PC 4, Broadwater
Townsend ESD 7, PO BOX N   59644 | 3-11111
Al McMilin, supt. | 266-3455
Broadwater County HS, PO BOX N   59644 | 2-00011
Rick Rafter, prin. | 266-3455
MS, PO BOX N   59644 | 2-00100
Gerald Rodacker, prin. | 266-3942

Troy, AC 406, PC 3, Lincoln
Troy SD 1, PO BOX O   59935 | 3-11111
Doug Reisig, supt. | 295-4606
JSHS, PO BOX O   59935 | 2-00111
John Konzen, prin. | 295-4520

Turner, AC 406, PC 2, Blaine
Turner SD 43, PO BOX 40   59542 | 2-11111
Earl McKinley, supt. | 379-2315
HS, PO BOX 40   59542 | 1-00011
Earl McKinley, prin. | 379-2219

Twin Bridges, AC 406, PC 2, Madison
Twin Bridges SD 7, PO BOX AC   59754 | 2-11111
Rand Bradley, supt. | 684-5656
HS, PO BOX AC   59754 | 1-00011
Rand Bradley, prin. | 684-5656

Valier, AC 406, PC 3, Pondera
Valier SD 18, PO BOX 528   59486 | 2-11111
Joe Brott, supt. | 279-3311
HS, PO BOX 528   59486 | 1-00011
Joe Brott, prin. | 279-3311

Victor, AC 406, PC 3, Ravalli
Victor SD 7, 425 4TH AVE   59875 | 2-11111
Lucy Braach, supt. | 642-3551
HS, 425 4TH AVE   59875 | 1-00011
Michael Williams, prin. | 642-3551

Westby, AC 406, PC 2, Sheridan
Westby SD 3, PO BOX 108   59275 | 2-11111
Robert Otheim, supt. | 385-2258
HS, PO BOX 108   59275 | 1-00011
Robert Otheim, prin. | 385-2258

West Yellowstone, AC 406, PC 3, Gallatin
West Yellowstone SD 69 | 2-11111
PO BOX 460   59758 | 646-7617
John Hargrove, supt.
HS, PO BOX 460   59758 | 1-00011
Doug Woods, prin. | 646-7617

Whitefish, AC 406, PC 5, Flathead
Whitefish SD 44, 600 2ND ST E   59937 | 4-11111
David Peters, supt. | 862-8640
HS, 600 2ND ST E   59937 | 3-00011
Dorothy Chatlain, prin. | 862-8600
Whitefish-Central JHS | 2-00100
600 2ND ST E   59937 | 862-8650
Terry Nelson, prin.

Whitehall, AC 406, PC 4, Jefferson
Whitehall SD, PO BOX 400   59759 | 3-11111
Lyle Barringer, supt. | 287-3455
HS, 1 SCHOOL WAY   59759 | 2-00011
Jim McCrossin, prin. | 287-3862
JHS, 1 SCHOOL WAY   59759 | 1-00100
Dan Reum, prin. | 287-3862

White Sulphur Springs, AC 406, PC 3, Meagher
White Sulphur Springs SD 8 | 2-11111
PO BOX C   59645 – Sandra Scott, supt. | 547-3351
HS, 405 CENTRAL AVE S   59645 | 1-00011
Dennis Davis, prin. | 547-3351
MS, 405 CENTRAL AVE S   59645 | 1-00100
Sandra Scott, prin. | 547-3351

Whitewater, AC 406, PC 2, Phillips
Whitewater SD, PO BOX 46   59544 | 1-11111
Steve Cascaden, supt. | 674-5418

HS, PO BOX 46 59544   1-00011
  Steve Cascaden, prin.   674-5417

Wibaux, AC 406, PC 3, Wibaux
  Wibaux SD 6, PO BOX 220 59353   2-11111
    Glen Mader, supt.   795-2474
  HS, PO BOX 220 59353   1-00011
    Larry Helvik, prin.   795-2474

Willow Creek, AC 406, PC 2, Gallatin
  Willow Creek SD, PO BOX 198 59760   1-11111
    Dale Sailer, supt.   285-6991
  HS, PO BOX 198 59760   1-00011
    Dale Sailer, prin.   285-6991

Wilsall, AC 406, PC 2, Park
  Shields Valley SD   2-11111
    PO BOX 131 59086   578-2176
    Fred Bull, supt.

Shields Valley HS   1-00011
  PO BOX 131 59086   578-2176
    Ed Barich, prin.

Winifred, AC 406, PC 2, Fergus
  Winifred SD 115 59489   2-11111
    Dennis Coulter, supt.   462-5349
  HS 59489   1-00011
    Dennis Coulter, prin.   462-5420

Winnett, AC 406, PC 2, Petroleum
  Winnett SD, PO BOX 167 59087   2-11111
    Marvin Koch, supt.   429-2251
  HS, PO BOX 167 59087   1-00011
    Marvin Koch, prin.   429-2251

Wolf Point, AC 406, PC 5, Roosevelt
  Wolf Point SD, 220 4TH AVE S 59201   4-11111
    Robert Joscelyn, supt.   653-2361

HS, 220 4TH AVE S 59201   2-00011
  Michael Preyer, prin.   653-1200
JHS, 213 6TH AVE S 59201   2-00100
  Dave Madsen, prin.   653-1200

Worden, AC 406, PC 2, Yellowstone
  Huntley Project SD 24   3-11111
    1477 ASH ST 59088   967-2540
    Romona Stout, supt.
  Huntley Project HS, 1477 ASH ST 59088 2-00011
    Leonard Sargent, prin.   967-2540
  Huntley Project MS, 1477 ASH ST 59088 2-00100
    Nickolas Schuering, prin.   967-2540

NEBRASKA

STATE DEPARTMENT OF EDUCATION
301 Centennial Mall South
P.O. Box 94987, Lincoln 68509
(402) 471-2295

Commissioner of Education	Joe Lutjeharms
Deputy Commissioner	Douglas Christensen
Interim Director Rehabilitation Services	Margaret Hoffman
Assistant Commissioner Internal Administrative Services	Polly Feis
Assistant Commissioner Education Services	Marge Harouff
Assistant Commissioner Special Programs	Robert Kellogg

STATE BOARD OF EDUCATION
P.O. Box 94987, Lincoln 68509

President   Russell Worthman

PUBLIC, PRIVATE AND CATHOLIC SECONDARY SCHOOLS

Adams, AC 402, PC 2, Gage
  Adams SD, PO BOX 259 68301   2-11111
    K. Nelson, supt.   988-2525
  JSHS, PO BOX 259 68301   1-00111
    Larry Coorts, prin.   988-2525

Ainsworth, AC 402, PC 4, Brown
  Ainsworth SD, PO BOX 65 69210   3-11111
    Gerald Ehlers, supt.   387-2333
  JSHS, PO BOX 65 69210   2-00111
    Davin Clayton, prin.   387-2082

Albion, AC 402, PC 4, Boone
  Albion SD, PO BOX 391 68620   3-11111
    Richard Stephens, supt.   395-2134
  JSHS, PO BOX 391 68620   2-00111
    Duane Backstrom, prin.   395-2134

Allen, AC 402, PC 2, Dixon
  Allen SD, PO BOX 190 68710   2-11111
    John Werner, supt.   635-2484
  JSHS, PO BOX 190 68710   2-00111
    (—), prin.   635-2484

Alliance, AC 308, PC 6, Box Butte
  Alliance SD   4-11111
    1604 SWEETWATER AVE 69301   762-5475
    Martin Peterson, supt.
  HS, 100 W 14TH ST 69301   3-00011
    Richard Boness, prin.   762-3359
  MS, 1112 LARAMIE AVE 69301   2-00100
    Derald Morgan, prin.   762-3079

Alma, AC 308, PC 4, Harlan
  Alma SD, PO BOX 170 68920   3-11111
    Eugene McCue, supt.   928-2131
  JSHS, PO BOX 170 68920   2-00111
    Paul Joseph, prin.   928-2131

Amherst, AC 308, PC 2, Buffalo
  Amherst SD, PO BOX 8 68812   2-11111
    Elton Teter, supt.   826-3131
  JSHS, PO BOX 8 68812   1-00111
    Jerry Beekman, prin.   826-3131

Ansley, AC 308, PC 3, Custer
  Ansley SD, PO BOX 370 68814   2-11111
    Gary Myers, supt.   935-1121
  JSHS, PO BOX 370 68814   1-00111
    Larry Ferguson, prin.   935-1121

Arapahoe, AC 308, PC 4, Furnas
  Arapahoe SD, PO BOX 466 68922   2-11111
    Eldean Stewart, supt.   962-5458
  HS, PO BOX 466 68922   1-00011
    Jack Moles, prin.   962-5458

Arcadia, AC 308, PC 2, Valley
  Arcadia SD, PO BOX 248 68815   2-11111
    Charles Finley, supt.   789-6523
  JSHS, PO BOX 248 68815   1-00111
    Milton Carter, prin.   789-6522

Arlington, AC 402, PC 4, Washington
  Arlington SD, PO BOX 580 68002   3-11111
    Kristine Wolzen, supt.   478-4172
  JSHS, PO BOX 580 68002   2-00111
    Lloyd Kilmer, prin.   478-4171

Arnold, AC 308, PC 3, Custer
  Arnold SD, PO BOX 66 69120   2-11111
    Robert Reed, supt.   848-2226
  JSHS, PO BOX 66 69120   2-00111
    Michael Harvey, prin.   848-2226

Arthur, AC 308, PC 2, Arthur
  Arthur County HSD   1-00011
    PO BOX 145 69121   764-2253
    Leo Turner, supt.
  Arthur County JSHS   1-00011
    PO BOX 145 69121   764-2253
    Leo Turner, prin.

Ashland, AC 402, PC 4, Saunders
  Ashland-Greenwood SD   2-11111
    1200 BOYD ST 68003   944-2128
    Craig Pease, supt.
  Ashland-Greenwood HS   2-00011
    1200 BOYD ST 68003   944-2114
    Ray Bentzen, prin.

Ashland-Greenwood MS   2-00100
  1200 BOYD ST 68003   944-7083
    Ray Bentzen, prin.

Atkinson, AC 402, PC 4, Holt
  West Holt RHSD, PO BOX 457 68713   2-00011
    George Shinker, supt.   925-2890
  West Holt HS   2-00011
    PO BOX 457 68713   925-2890
    Gerald Burns, prin.

Auburn, AC 402, PC 5, Nemaha
  Auburn SD, 1406 22ND ST 68305   3-11111
    Myron Ballain, supt.   274-4830
  HS, 1829 CENTRAL AVE 68305   2-00011
    Gerald Beach, prin.   274-4328
  MS, 1713 J ST 68305   2-00100
    Leo Dietrich, prin.   274-4220

Aurora, AC 402, PC 5, Hamilton
  Aurora SD, 300 L ST 68818   4-11111
    Donald Burling, supt.   694-6923
  SHS, 300 L ST 68818   2-00001
    Roland Carter, prin.   694-6968
  JHS, 300 L ST 68818   2-00110
    Kenneth Thiele, prin.   694-6915

Axtell, AC 308, PC 3, Kearney
  Axtell Community SD   2-11111
    PO BOX 97 68924   743-2414
    Thomas Sandberg, supt.
  JSHS, PO BOX 97 68924   2-00111
    James Doyle, prin.   743-2415

Bancroft, AC 402, PC 2, Cuming
  Bancroft-Rosalie SD   2-11111
    PO BOX 128 68004   648-3337
    Jon Cerny, supt.
  Bancroft JSHS, PO BOX 128 68004   2-00111
    Mike Sjuts, prin.   648-3336

Bartlett, AC 308, PC 2, Wheeler
  Wheeler Central SD   2-11111
    PO BOX 68 68622   654-3273
    Ronald Gilham, supt.

Wheeler Central JSHS 1-00111
PO BOX 68 68622 – (—), prin. 654-3273

Bartley, AC 308, PC 2, Red Willow
Bartley SD, PO BOX 187 69020 2-11111
Donald Hafer, supt. 692-3223
HS, PO BOX 187 69020 1-00011
Myron Deterding, prin. 692-3223

Bassett, AC 402, PC 3, Rock
Rock County HSD 2-00011
PO BOX 448 68714 684-3411
Dennis Spence, supt.
Rock County HS, PO BOX 448 68714 2-00011
Matthew Fisher, prin. 684-3411

Battle Creek, AC 402, PC 3, Madison
Battle Creek SD, PO BOX 190 68715 2-11111
Delno Fuelberth, supt. 675-6905
JSHS, PO BOX 190 68715 2-00111
Richard Cleveland, prin. 675-3705

Bayard, AC 308, PC 4, Morrill
Bayard SD, PO BOX 607 69334 3-11111
Clayton Cundall, supt. 586-1700
JSHS, PO BOX 607 69334 2-00111
Robert Armstrong, prin. 586-1700

Beatrice, AC 402, PC 7, Gage
Beatrice SD, 213 N 5TH ST 68310 4-11111
Stephen Joel, supt. 223-1500
SHS, 213 N 5TH ST 68310 2-00001
Richard Kunde, prin. 223-1515
JHS, 510 ELK ST 68310 3-00110
Dennis Hynek, prin. 223-1545

Southeast Community College 2-CC
RR 2 BOX 35A 68310 228-3468

Beaver City, AC 308, PC 3, Furnas
Furnas County SD
Supt. — See Oxford
JSHS, PO BOX 130 68926 1-00111
Bernard Phillips, prin. 268-4085

Beemer, AC 402, PC 3, Cuming
Beemer SD, PO BOX 10 68716 2-11111
David Watters, supt. 528-3380
JSHS, PO BOX 10 68716 1-00111
Larry Bausch, prin. 528-3232

Bellevue, AC 402, PC 8, Sarpy
Bellevue SD, 2009 FRANKLIN ST 68005 6-11111
Richard Triplett, supt. 293-4000
Bellevue East SHS 3-00001
1401 HIGH SCHOOL DR 68005 293-4150
Herbert Barelman, prin.
Bellevue West SHS 3-00001
PO BOX 1596 68005 293-4040
Randolph Boardman, prin.
Bellevue Mission JHS 3-00110
2202 WASHINGTON ST 68005 293-4260
Judith Porter, prin.
Fontenelle JHS, 701 KAYLEEN DR 68005 3-00110
John Ott, prin. 293-4360

Bellevue College 4-UC
1000 GALVIN RD S 68005 291-8100

Benedict, AC 402, PC 2, York
Benedict SD, PO BOX 135 68316 2-11111
Stanley Kravig, supt. 732-6677
HS, PO BOX 135 68316 1-00011
Ron Nickel, prin. 732-6677
MS, PO BOX 135 68316 1-00100
Ron Nickel, prin. 732-6677

Benkelman, AC 308, PC 4, Dundy
Dundy County, PO BOX 586 69021 2-11111
Dallas Watkins, supt. 423-2773
Dundy County HS 2-00011
PO BOX 586 69021 423-2738
Douglas Stutzman, prin.

Bennington, AC 402, PC 3, Douglas
Bennington SD, PO BOX 265 68007 3-11111
Douglas Townsend, supt. 238-2447
JSHS, PO BOX 265 68007 2-00111
Ron Boner, prin. 238-2447

Bertrand, AC 308, PC 3, Phelps
Bertrand SD, 503 SCHOOL ST 68927 2-11111
Kendell Moseley, supt. 472-3427
JSHS, 503 SCHOOL ST 68927 2-00111
Carl Wells, prin. 472-3427

Big Springs, AC 308, PC 2, Deuel
Big Springs SD, PO BOX 457 69122 2-11111
Max Kroger, supt. 889-3622
JSHS, PO BOX 457 69122 1-00111
Max Kroger, prin. 889-3622

Blair, AC 402, PC 6, Washington
Blair Community SD 4-11111
140 S 16TH ST 68008 426-2610
Lawrence Bock, supt.
JSHS, 9TH & PARK 68008 3-00110
Steven Shanahan, prin. 426-4941

Dana College 2-UC
2848 COLLEGE DR 68008 426-7200

Bloomfield, AC 402, PC 4, Knox
Bloomfield SD, 311 E BENTON 68718 2-11111
John Post, supt. 373-4800

JSHS, 203 E BENTON 68718 2-00111
David Fricke, prin. 373-4800

Blue Hill, AC 402, PC 3, Webster
Blue Hill SD, PO BOX 217 68930 2-11111
Vaden Lane, supt. 756-2085
JSHS, PO BOX 217 68930 2-00111
James Duval, prin. 756-3043

Boys Town, AC 402, PC 3, Douglas

Boys Town HS 2-00011
125 HEROES BLVD 68010 498-1800
Patrick McGinnis, prin.

Bradshaw, AC 402, PC 2, York
Bradshaw SD, PO BOX 98 68319 2-11111
Richard Berthold, supt. 736-4353
JSHS, PO BOX 98 68319 1-00111
Richard Berthold, supt. 736-4351

Brady, AC 308, PC 2, Lincoln
Brady SD, PO BOX 68 69123 2-11111
Lewis Shoff, supt. 584-3317
JSHS, PO BOX 68 69123 1-00111
Douglas Pearson, prin. 584-3317

Brainard, AC 402, PC 2, Butler
East Butler SD, PO BOX 36 68626 2-11111
Paul Limas, supt. 545-2081
JSHS, PO BOX 36 68626 2-00111
Gerald Reinsch, prin. 545-2081

Bridgeport, AC 308, PC 4, Morrill
Bridgeport SD, PO BOX 430 69336 2-11111
John Bond, supt. 262-1470
JSHS, PO BOX 430 69336 2-00111
William Jacobsen, prin. 262-0346

Broken Bow, AC 308, PC 5, Custer
Broken Bow SD, 323 N 7TH AVE 68822 3-11111
Donald Vanderheiden, supt. 872-6821
HS, 322 N 9TH AVE 68822 2-00111
Robert Brown, prin. 872-2475
MS, 322 N 9TH AVE 68822 2-00100
Louis Stithem, prin. 872-6441

Brule, AC 308, PC 2, Keith
Brule SD, 714 STATE ST 69127 2-11111
John Frates, supt. 287-2354
JSHS, 714 STATE ST 69127 1-00111
Stanley Krajewski, prin. 287-2354

Bruning, AC 402, PC 2, Thayer
Bruning SD, PO BOX 70 68322 2-11111
Wayne Koehler, supt. 353-4445
JSHS, PO BOX 70 68322 1-00111
Dale Buller, prin. 353-4685

Burwell, AC 308, PC 4, Garfield
Burwell HSD, PO BOX 670 68823 2-00111
Ken O'Mara, supt. 346-4189
JSHS, PO BOX 670 68823 2-00111
Larry Pfeiffer, prin. 346-4150

Butte, AC 402, PC 2, Boyd
Butte SD, PO BOX 139 68722 2-11111
William Minchow, supt. 775-2201
JSHS, PO BOX 139 68722 1-00111
Kevin Kirwan, prin. 775-2201

Cairo, AC 308, PC 3, Hall
Centura SD, PO BOX 430 68824 3-11111
Robert Norvell, supt. 485-4258
JSHS, PO BOX 430 68824 2-00111
David Karr, prin. 485-4258

Callaway, AC 308, PC 3, Custer
Callaway SD, PO BOX 188 68825 2-11111
James Grove, supt. 836-2272
JSHS, PO BOX 188 68825 1-00111
David Weber, prin. 836-2272

Cambridge, AC 308, PC 4, Furnas
Cambridge SD, PO BOX 100 69022 2-11111
James Tenopir, supt. 697-3323
HS, PO BOX 100 69022 2-00111
Ronald Streit, prin. 697-3322

Cedar Bluffs, AC 402, PC 3, Saunders
Cedar Bluffs SD, PO BOX 66 68015 2-11111
Lawrence McMann, supt. 628-2060
JSHS, PO BOX 66 68015 2-00111
Scott Buchanan, prin. 628-2080

Cedar Rapids, AC 402, PC 2, Boone
Cedar Rapids SD, PO BOX 218 68627 2-11111
Donald Pieper, supt. 358-0640
JSHS, PO BOX 218 68627 1-00111
Leonard Homan, prin. 358-0640

Central City, AC 308, PC 5, Merrick
Central City SD, 1804 14TH AVE 68826 3-11111
Ronald Wall, supt. 946-3055
HS, 1804 14TH AVE 68826 2-00111
Raymond Huggett, prin. 946-3086
MS, 1804 14TH AVE 68826 2-00100
Gregg Wibbels, prin. 946-3056

Nebraska Christian HS 2-00111
RR 2 BOX 124 68826 946-3836
Richard Musgrave, prin.

Chadron, AC 308, PC 6, Dawes
Chadron SD, 7TH & ANN 69337 4-11111
Stephen Sexton, supt. 432-3000

HS, 901 CEDAR ST 69337 2-00011
Wayne Jones, prin. 432-5548
MS, 551 E 6TH ST 69337 2-01100
Henry Reitz, prin. 432-3090

Chadron State College 4-UC
1000 MAIN ST 69337 432-4451

Chambers, AC 402, PC 2, Holt
Chambers SD, PO BOX 218 68725 2-11111
Larry Tangeman, supt. 482-5233
JSHS, PO BOX 218 68725 1-00111
Gregory Barnes, prin. 482-5233

Chappell, AC 308, PC 3, Deuel
Chappell SD 2-11111
3RD & WASHINGTON 69129 874-2911
Gene Panning, supt.
JSHS, 3RD & WASHINGTON 69129 2-00111
Harold Hardy, prin. 874-2911

Chester, AC 402, PC 2, Thayer
Chester-Hubbell-Byron SD 2-11111
PO BOX 337 68327 324-5555
Daniel Jantzen, supt.
Chester-Hubbell-Byron JSHS 1-00111
PO BOX 337 68327 324-5555
Roger Hill, prin.

Clarks, AC 308, PC 2, Merrick
Clarks SD, PO BOX 205 68628 2-11111
Richard Ziegler, supt. 548-2216
JSHS, PO BOX 205 68628 1-00111
Douglas Gilson, prin. 548-2216

Clarkson, AC 402, PC 3, Colfax
Clarkson SD, PO BOX G 68629 2-11111
Charles Tonnies, supt. 892-3454
JSHS, PO BOX G 68629 1-00111
Gene Finke, prin. 892-3454

Clay Center, AC 402, PC 3, Clay
Clay Center SD, PO BOX 125 68933 2-11111
Sam Townsend, supt. 762-3561
JSHS, PO BOX 125 68933 1-00111
Steven Senff, prin. 762-3561

Clearwater, AC 402, PC 2, Antelope
Clearwater SD, PO BOX 38 68726 2-11111
Robert Rabe, supt. 485-2505
JSHS, PO BOX 38 68726 1-00111
Mike Sieh, prin. 485-2505

Cody, AC 402, PC 2, Cherry
Cody-Kilgore SD, PO BOX 216 69211 2-11111
Franklin Rempp, supt. 823-4190
JSHS, PO BOX 216 69211 1-00111
Franklin Rempp, prin. 823-4190

Coleridge, AC 402, PC 3, Cedar
Coleridge Community SD 2-11111
PO BOX 37 68727 283-4844
W. Schnoor, supt.
JSHS, PO BOX 37 68727 1-00111
Daniel Hoesing, prin. 283-4844

Columbus, AC 402, PC 7, Platte
Columbus SD, PO BOX 947 68602 5-11111
Fred Bellum, supt. 563-4912
HS, 2200 26TH ST 68601 3-00011
Robert Dierman, prin. 564-3224
MS, 2410 16TH ST 68601 2-00100
Richard Meyer, prin. 564-7284

Lakeview HSD, PO BOX 170 68602 2-00011
Richard Kamm, supt. 563-2345
Lakeview HS, RR 3 68601 2-00011
Robert Arp, prin. 563-2345

Central Community College 2-CC
PO BOX 1027 68602 564-7132
Scotus Central Catholic HS 2-00111
1554 18TH AVE 68601 564-7165
Robert Kobza, prin.

Cook, AC 402, PC 2, Johnson
Nemaha Valley SD 2-11111
PO BOX 255 68329 864-4171
Chris Effken, supt.
JSHS, 401 1ST ST 68329 2-00111
Gary Anderson, prin. 864-4171

Cozad, AC 308, PC 5, Dawson
Cozad CSD, PO BOX 268 69130 3-11111
Rodney Koch, supt. 784-2744
HS, PO BOX 268 69130 2-00011
William Gettman, prin. 784-2744
MS, 815 AVENUE C 69130 2-00100
John Grinde, prin. 784-2746

Crawford, AC 308, PC 4, Dawes
Crawford SD, PO BOX 543 69339 2-11111
Wayne Ferguson, supt. 665-1531
JSHS, PO BOX 543 69339 2-00111
Merrell Nelsen, prin. 665-1531

Creighton, AC 402, PC 4, Knox
Creighton SD, PO BOX 10 68729 2-11111
Fred Boelter, supt. 358-3663
Creighton Community JSHS 2-00111
PO BOX 10 68729 358-3663
Bradley Best, prin.

Crete, AC 402, PC 5, Saline
Crete SD, 920 LINDEN AVE 68333 4-11111
Jody Isernhagen, supt. 471-3464

JSHS, 1500 E 15TH ST 68333   3-00111
Linda Wyatt, prin.   471-3463

Doane College   4-UC
1014 BOSWELL AVE 68333   826-2161

Crofton, AC 402, PC 3, Knox
Crofton Community SD   2-11111
PO BOX 229 68730   388-2440
Randall Anderson, supt.
JSHS, PO BOX 229 68730   2-00111
Richard Allen, prin.   388-2440

Culbertson, AC 308, PC 3, Hitchcock
Culbertson SD, PO BOX 128 69024   2-11111
Marvin Schleeman, supt.   278-2131
JSHS, PO BOX 128 69024   2-00111
Larry Casper, prin.   278-2131

Curtis, AC 308, PC 3, Frontier
Medicine Valley SD, PO BOX 9 69025   2-11111
Dennis Chipman, supt.   367-4106
JSHS, PO BOX 9 69025   2-00111
Steven Vanderbeek, prin.   367-4106

University of Nebraska   5-UC
PO BOX 69 69025   367-4124

Dalton, AC 308, PC 2, Cheyenne
Leyton SD, PO BOX 97 69131   2-11111
William Pile, supt.   377-2303
Leyton HS, PO BOX 97 69131   1-00011
Harlin Dormann, prin.   377-2303

Davenport, AC 402, PC 2, Thayer
Davenport Community SD   2-11111
PO BOX 190 68335   364-2225
Wayne Koehler, supt.
JSHS, PO BOX 190 68335   1-00111
Jeffrey Walburn, prin.   364-2225

David City, AC 402, PC 5, Butler
David City SD, 750 D ST 68632   2-11111
Larry Jess, supt.   367-4590
JSHS, 750 D ST 68632   2-00111
Timothy Hoffman, prin.   367-3187

Aquinas HS, PO BOX 149 68632   2-00111
David McMahon, prin.   367-3175

Dawson, AC 402, PC 2, Richardson
Dawson-Verdon SD   2-11111
PO BOX 128 68337   855-2645
Ray Blackburn, supt.
JSHS, PO BOX 128 68337   1-00111
Ray Blackburn, prin.   855-2645

Daykin, AC 402, PC 2, Jefferson
Meridian SD, PO BOX 190 68338   2-11111
Stephen Deger, supt.   446-7265
Meridian JSHS, PO BOX 190 68338   1-00111
Kenneth Stauss, prin.   446-7265

Deshler, AC 402, PC 3, Thayer
Deshler SD, PO BOX 547 68340   2-11111
Larry Wilbeck, supt.   365-7272
JSHS, PO BOX 547 68340   2-00111
Bradley Cabrera, prin.   365-7272

De Witt, AC 402, PC 3, Saline
Tri County SD, RR 1 BOX 164A 68341   3-11111
Gary Oxley, supt.   683-2015
Tri County JSHS, RR 1 BOX 164A 68341   2-00111
Russell Hicks, prin.   683-2015

Diller, AC 402, PC 2, Jefferson
Diller Community SD   2-11111
PO BOX 8 68342   793-5570
Rolland Fenster, supt.
JSHS, PO BOX 8 68342   1-00111
Rolland Fenster, prin.   793-5570

Dix, AC 308, PC 2, Kimball
Potter-Dix SD
Supt. — See Potter
Potter-Dix MS, PO BOX 149 69133   1-01100
Dan Hoesly, prin.   682-5231

Dodge, AC 402, PC 3, Dodge
Dodge SD, PO BOX 337 68633   2-11111
James Havelka, supt.   693-2207
JSHS, PO BOX 337 68633   2-00111
William Johnson, prin.   693-2207

Doniphan, AC 402, PC 3, Hall
Doniphan SD, PO BOX D 68832   2-11111
Gerald Carnes, supt.   845-2282
JSHS, PO BOX D 68832   2-00111
Robert Fish, prin.   845-6531

Dorchester, AC 402, PC 3, Saline
Dorchester SD, PO BOX 7 68343   2-11111
Galen Johnson, supt.   946-2781
JSHS, PO BOX 7 68343   2-00111
Terrence Gautreaux, prin.   946-2781

Dunning, AC 308, PC 2, Blaine
Sandhills SD, PO BOX 460 68833   2-11111
Patrick Osmond, supt.   538-2224
JSHS, PO BOX 460 68833   1-00111
Michael Cullen, prin.   538-2224

Elba, AC 308, PC 2, Howard
Elba SD, PO BOX 100 68835   2-11111
William Lewis, supt.   863-2228

JSHS, PO BOX 100 68835   1-00111
William Lewis, prin.   863-2228

Elgin, AC 402, PC 3, Antelope
Elgin SD, PO BOX 399 68636   2-11111
Dwaine Uttecht, supt.   843-2455
HS, PO BOX 399 68636   1-00011
Daniel Schiefelbein, prin.   843-2457

Pope John XXIII Central Catholic HS   2-00111
PO BOX 179 68636   843-5325
Joe Stureck, prin.

Elkhorn, AC 402, PC 4, Douglas
Elkhorn SD, 502 GLENN ST 68022   4-11111
Roger Breed, supt.   289-2579
HS, 711 VETERANS DR 68022   3-00011
Terry Haack, prin.   289-4239
MS, 500 HILLCREST ST 68022   2-00100
Kevin Riggert, prin.   289-2428

Mt. Michael HS   2-00011
22520 MOUNT MICHAEL RD 68022   289-2541
Brian Osborne, prin.

Elm Creek, AC 308, PC 3, Buffalo
Elm Creek SD, PO BOX 490 68836   2-11111
S. Sterling Troxel, supt.   856-4300
JSHS, PO BOX 490 68836   2-00111
Fred Hansen, prin.   856-4300

Elmwood, AC 402, PC 3, Cass
Elmwood-Murdock SD
Supt. — See Murdock
MS, PO BOX 100 68349   1-00100
Dale Hall, prin.   994-2125

Elwood, AC 308, PC 3, Gosper
Elwood SD, PO BOX 107 68937   2-11111
David Wade, supt.   785-2491
JSHS, PO BOX 107 68937   2-00111
Richard Einspahr, prin.   785-2491

Emerson, AC 402, PC 3, Dakota
Emerson-Hubbard SD   2-11111
PO BOX 8733   695-2621
Bradley Manard, supt.
Emerson-Hubbard JSHS   2-00111
PO BOX 9 68733   695-2636
Gary Klahn, prin.

Eustis, AC 308, PC 2, Frontier
Eustis SD, PO BOX 9 69028   2-11111
Steven Wallick, supt.   486-3991
JSHS, PO BOX 9 69028   1-00111
Timothy De Waard, prin.   486-3211

Ewing, AC 402, PC 2, Holt
Ewing SD, PO BOX 98 68735   2-11111
Donald Clark, supt.   626-7235
JSHS, PO BOX 98 68735   1-00111
Ed Lowe, prin.   626-7235

Exeter, AC 402, PC 3, Fillmore
Exeter SD, PO BOX 139 68351   2-11111
Joseph Reinert, supt.   266-5911
JSHS, PO BOX 139 68351   1-00111
Charles Evans, prin.   266-5911

Fairbury, AC 402, PC 5, Jefferson
Fairbury SD, 1121 8TH ST 68352   4-11111
Mark Alderman, supt.   729-6104
JSHS, 1501 9TH ST 68352   2-00111
Terrence Kenealy, prin.   729-6116

Fairfield, AC 402, PC 2, Clay
Sandy Creek SD   2-11111
RR 1 BOX 127 68938   726-2151
Lawrence Ramaekers, supt.
JSHS, RR 1 BOX 127 68938   2-00111
Robert Siemsen, prin.   726-2151

Fairmont, AC 402, PC 3, Fillmore
Fairmont SD, PO BOX 157 68354   2-11111
(—), supt.   268-3491
JSHS, PO BOX 157 68354   1-00111
David Bottrell, prin.   268-3411

Falls City, AC 402, PC 5, Richardson
Falls City SD, 1415 MORTON ST 68355   3-11111
Duane Stehlik, supt.   245-2825
HS, 1400 FULTON ST 68355   2-00111
John Brooke, prin.   245-2116
MS, 1415 MORTON ST 68355   2-00100
Rick Johnson, prin.   245-3455

Sacred Heart S, 807 E 19TH ST 68355   2-11111
Fr. Morin, prin.   245-4151

Farnam, AC 308, PC 2, Dawson
Farnam SD, PO BOX 126 69029   1-11111
Larry Hermsmeyer, supt.   569-2552
JSHS, PO BOX 126 69029   1-00111
Larry Hermsmeyer, prin.   569-2552

Filley, AC 402, PC 2, Gage
Filley SD, PO BOX 87 68357   2-11111
Larry Smith, supt.   662-3595
JSHS, PO BOX 87 68357   1-00111
Larry Smith, prin.   662-3595

Firth, AC 402, PC 2, Lancaster
Norris SD, RR 1 68358   4-11111
Dennis Nosal, supt.   791-5381
Norris HS, RR 1 68358   2-00011
Galen Boldt, prin.   791-5301

MS 68358   2-00100
D. Larry Grosshans, prin.   791-5302

Fort Calhoun, AC 402, PC 3, Washington
Ft. Calhoun SD, 1506 LINCOLN ST 68023   3-11111
Jerry Barabas, supt.   468-5592
JSHS, 1506 LINCOLN ST 68023   2-00111
Donald Johnson, prin.   468-5591

Franklin, AC 308, PC 4, Franklin
Franklin SD, 1001 M ST 68939   2-11111
Richard Kennedy, supt.   425-6283
JSHS, 1001 M ST 68939   2-00111
Larry Weaver, prin.   425-6283

Fremont, AC 402, PC 7, Dodge
Fremont SD, 957 N PIERCE ST 68025   5-11111
James Merritt, supt.   727-3000
SHS, 1750 N LINCOLN AVE 68025   3-00001
Kenneth Thomson, prin.   727-3050
JHS, 130 E 9TH ST 68025   3-00110
Gary Bolton, prin.   727-3100

Archbishop Bergan HS   2-00111
PO BOX 259 68025   721-9683
Joseph Vojtech, prin.
Midland Lutheran College   3-UC
900 N CLARKSON ST 68025   721-5480

Friend, AC 402, PC 4, Saline
Friend SD, PO BOX 67 68359   2-11111
Leo Stokes, supt.   947-2781
JSHS, PO BOX 67 68359   2-00111
Leroy Garrels, prin.   947-2781

Fullerton, AC 308, PC 4, Nance
Fullerton SD, PO BOX 520 68638   2-11111
Gene Burton, supt.   536-2431
JSHS, PO BOX 520 68638   2-00111
Max Irvin, prin.   536-2431

Geneva, AC 402, PC 4, Fillmore
Geneva North SD, RR 1 BOX 23A 68361   1-00111
(—), supt.   759-3164
Geneva North HS, RR 1 BOX 23A 68361   1-00111
(—), prin.   759-3164
Geneva North MS, RR 1 BOX 23A 68361   1-00100
(—), prin.   759-3164

Geneva SD, 1410 L ST 68361   3-11111
William Anderson, supt.   759-4955
JSHS, 1410 L ST 68361   2-00111
Larry Molacek, prin.   759-3141

Genoa, AC 402, PC 4, Nance
Genoa SD, PO BOX 640 68640   2-11111
Don Day, supt.   993-2274
JSHS, PO BOX 640 68640   2-00111
Kenneth Heinz, prin.   993-2274

Gering, AC 308, PC 6, Scotts Bluff
Gering SD, 1800 8TH ST 69341   4-11111
Mary Kamerzell, supt.   436-3125
SHS, 1500 U ST 69341   3-00001
Bruce Epstein, prin.   436-3121
JHS, 800 Q ST 69341   3-00110
Thomas Wlaschin, prin.   436-3123

Gibbon, AC 308, PC 4, Buffalo
Gibbon SD, PO BOX 790 68840   3-11111
Dan Ernst, supt.   468-5721
JSHS, PO BOX 790 68840   2-00111
Kevin Madsen, prin.   468-5721

Giltner, AC 402, PC 2, Hamilton
Giltner SD, PO BOX 157 68841   2-11111
Donald Ferguson, supt.   849-2238
JSHS, PO BOX 157 68841   1-00111
Douglas Bandemer, prin.   849-2238

Gordon, PC 4, Sheridan
Gordon SD, PO BOX 530 69343   2-00011
Rodney Borders, supt.   308-282-1322
HS, PO BOX 530 69343   2-00111
Raymond Stone, prin.   308-282-1322

Sheridan County SD
Supt. — See Rushville
JHS, PO BOX 530 69343   2-00100
Raymond Stone, prin.   308-282-1322

Gothenburg, AC 308, PC 5, Dawson
Gothenburg SD, 1415 AVENUE G 69138   3-11111
Wayne Bell, supt.   537-3653
JSHS, 1415 AVENUE G 69138   2-00111
Fred Helmink, prin.   537-3651

Grand Island, AC 308, PC 8, Hall
Grand Island SD, 615 N ELM ST 68801   6-11111
Lane Plugge, supt.   385-5900
SHS, 2124 N LAFAYETTE AVE 68803   4-00001
Kenton Mann, prin.   385-5950
Barr JHS   2-00110
602 W STOLLEY PARK RD 68801   385-5875
Allan Satterly, prin.
Walnut JHS, 1600 N CUSTER AVE 68803   2-00110
Vikki Deuel, prin.   385-5990
Westridge MS   2-00100
1812 MANSFIELD RD 68803   385-5886
Daniel Woods, prin.

Northwest HSD   3-00011
2710 N NORTH RD 68803   385-6398
Joseph Toczek, supt.
Northwest HS, 2710 N NORTH RD 68803   3-00011
Michael Zulkowski, prin.   385-6398

Central Catholic HS | 2-00111
1200 RUBY AVE 68803 | 384-2440
Robert Ripp, prin. |
Central Community College | 4-CC
PO BOX 4903 68802 | 384-5220
Spencer School of Business | 2-CS
410 W 2ND ST 68801 | 382-8044

Grant, AC 308, PC 4, Perkins
Grant Public SD, PO BOX 829 69140 | 2-11111
Jonathan Burkey, supt. | 352-4735
HS, PO BOX 829 69140 | 2-00111
George Yerger, prin. | 352-4735

Greeley, AC 308, PC 3, Greeley
Greeley SD, PO BOX 160 68842 | 2-11111
Tom Jochum, supt. | 428-5435
JSHS, PO BOX 160 68842 | 1-00111
James Beck, prin. | 428-3145

Gretna, AC 402, PC 4, Sarpy
Gretna SD, 801 SOUTH ST 68028 | 3-11111
Gail Kopplin, supt. | 332-3265
JSHS, 805 S COUNTY RD 68028 | 2-00111
Kevin Riley, prin. | 332-3936

Guide Rock, AC 402, PC 2, Webster
Guide Rock SD, PO BOX 128 68942 | 1-11111
Donald Osborn, supt. | 257-3105
JSHS, PO BOX 128 68942 | 1-00111
Donald Osborn, prin. | 257-3105

Hampton, AC 402, PC 2, Hamilton
Hampton SD, 458 5TH ST 68843 | 2-11111
R. W. Hoppner, supt. | 725-3116
JSHS, 458 5TH ST 68843 | 1-00111
Gerald Eickhoff, prin. | 725-3116

Harrisburg, AC 308, PC 1, Banner
Banner County SD, PO BOX 5 69345 | 2-11111
Dennis O'Connor, supt. | 436-5263
Banner County JSHS | 2-00111
PO BOX 5 69345 | 436-5263
Eldon Hubbard, prin. |

Harrison, AC 308, PC 2, Sioux
Sioux County HSD, PO BOX 38 69346 | 1-00111
Wesley Moench, supt. | 668-2415
Sioux County HS, PO BOX 38 69346 | 1-00011
Wesley Moench, prin. | 668-2415

Hartington, AC 402, PC 4, Cedar
Hartington SD | 2-11111
BROADWAY & PARK 68739 | 254-3947
Don Flakus, supt. |
JSHS, BROADWAY & PARK 68739 | 2-00111
Myron Riddle, prin. | 254-3947

Cedar Catholic HS | 2-00011
401 S BROADWAY 68739 | 254-3906
Gerald Dunn, prin. |
Holy Trinity ES | 2-01100
502 S BROADWAY 68739 | 254-6496
Gordon Beavers, prin. |

Harvard, AC 402, PC 3, Clay
Harvard SD, PO BOX 100 68944 | 2-11111
Larry Turnquist, supt. | 772-2171
JSHS, PO BOX 100 68944 | 2-00111
Brent Williamson, prin. | 772-2171

Hastings, AC 402, PC 7, Adams
Adams Central RHSD | 2-00111
PO BOX 1088 68902 | 463-3285
Glen Larsen, supt. |
Adams Central JSHS | 2-00111
PO BOX 1088 68902 | 463-3285
James A. Karloff, prin. |

Hastings SD, 714 W 5TH ST 68901 | 5-11111
Kenneth Anderson, supt. | 461-7500
HS, 1100 W 14TH ST 68901 | 3-00011
Michael Marymee, prin. | 461-7550
JHS, 505 N HASTINGS AVE 68901 | 2-00100
Larry Bornschlegl, prin. | 461-7520

Central Community College | 2-CC
PO BOX 1024 68902 | 463-9811
Hastings College | 3-UC
PO BOX 269 68902 | 463-2402
Mary Lanning Memorial Hospital | HSP
715 N SAINT JOSEPH AVE 68901 | 463-4521
St. Cecilia HS | 2-00111
521 N KANSAS AVE 68901 | 462-2105
Marie Butler, prin. |

Hayes Center, AC 308, PC 2, Hayes
Hayes Center SD, PO BOX 8 69032 | 2-11111
Johnnie Simmons, supt. | 286-3341
JSHS, PO BOX 8 69032 | 1-00111
Harry Grimminger, prin. | 286-3341

Hay Springs, AC 308, PC 3, Sheridan
Hay Springs SD, PO BOX 280 69347 | 2-11111
Ronald G. Hiles, supt. | 638-4434
JSHS, PO BOX 280 69347 | 1-00111
Michael Montgomery, prin. | 638-4434

Hebron, AC 402, PC 4, Thayer
Hebron SD, PO BOX 9 68370 | 2-11111
Donald Crowder, supt. | 768-6117
JSHS, PO BOX 9 68370 | 2-00111
Dennis Shipp, prin. | 768-6117

Hemingford, AC 308, PC 3, Box Butte
Hemingford SD, PO BOX 217 69348 | 3-11111
Donald Hanks, supt. | 487-3328
JSHS, PO BOX 217 69348 | 2-00111
Lyle Fodnes, prin. | 487-3328

Henderson, AC 402, PC 3, York
Henderson SD, PO BOX 626 68371 | 2-11111
Norman Yoder, supt. | 723-4434
JSHS, PO BOX 626 68371 | 2-00111
Blaine Friesen, prin. | 723-4434

Hershey, AC 308, PC 3, Lincoln
Hershey SD, PO BOX 369 69143 | 2-11111
George Rogers, supt. | 368-5574
JSHS, PO BOX 369 69143 | 2-00111
Patrick Moore, prin. | 368-5572

Hildreth, AC 402, PC 2, Franklin
Hildreth SD, PO BOX 157 68947 | 2-11111
Gary Fisher, supt. | 938-3825
JSHS, PO BOX 157 68947 | 1-00111
Richard Alt, prin. | 938-3825

Holdrege, AC 308, PC 6, Phelps
Holdrege SD, 505 14TH AVE 68949 | 4-11111
D. Deriese, supt. | 995-8663
HS, 600 12TH AVE 68949 | 2-00011
Dan Twarling, prin. | 995-6558
MS, 600 14TH AVE 68949 | 3-01100
Charles Featherston, prin. | 995-5421

Homer, AC 402, PC 3, Dakota
Homer Community SD | 2-11111
PO BOX 340 68030 | 698-2377
Mel Waldner, supt. |
JSHS, PO BOX 340 68030 | 2-00111
Phillip Wineland, prin. | 698-2377

Hooper, AC 402, PC 3, Dodge
Logan View HSD | 2-00111
RR 1 BOX 104 68031 | 654-3317
Harlan Schrieber, supt. |
Logan View JSHS | 2-00111
RR 1 BOX 104 68031 | 654-3317
Jerald Ribbe, prin. |

Hordville, AC 402, PC 2, Hamilton
Polk-Hordville SD
Supt. — See Polk
Polk-Hordville MS, PO BOX 45 68846 | 1-00100
Dennis Gray, prin. | 757-3351

Howells, AC 308, PC 3, Colfax
Howells SD, PO BOX 159 68641 | 1-11111
James Havelka, supt. | 986-1621
HS, PO BOX 159 68641 | 1-00111
Richard Hoelscher, prin. | 986-1621
JHS, PO BOX 159 68641 | 1-00100
Richard Hoelscher, prin. | 986-1621

Humboldt, AC 402, PC 4, Richardson
Humboldt SD, PO BOX 278 68376 | 2-11111
Robert Eastman, supt. | 862-2151
JSHS, PO BOX 278 68376 | 2-00111
John James, prin. | 862-2151

Humphrey, AC 402, PC 3, Platte
Humphrey SD, PO BOX 278 68642 | 2-11111
Robert Heckathorn, supt. | 923-1230
JSHS, PO BOX 278 68642 | 2-00111
Steven Robb, prin. | 923-1230

St. Francis Central HS | 2-00111
PO BOX 277 68642 | 923-0818
Thomas Ridder, prin. |

Hyannis, AC 308, PC 2, Grant
Hyannis HSD, PO BOX 286 69350 | 1-00111
Tom Carlstrom, supt. | 458-2202
Hyannis JSHS, PO BOX 286 69350 | 1-00111
Walter Dyer, prin. | 458-2202

Imperial, AC 308, PC 4, Chase
Chase County HSD | 2-00111
PO BOX 577 69033 | 882-4304
Glen Beran, supt. |
Chase County HS, PO BOX 577 69033 | 2-00011
Raymond Martin, prin. | 882-4304

Indianola, AC 308, PC 3, Red Willow
Republican Valley SD, RR 1 69034 | 2-11111
John W. Symington, supt. | 364-2202
Red Willow JSHS, RR 1 69034 | 2-00111
Don Farley, prin. | 364-2202

Johnson, AC 402, PC 2, Nemaha
Johnson-Brock SD | 2-11111
PO BOX 186 68378 | 868-5235
Joe Anderson, supt. |
JSHS, PO BOX 186 68378 | 2-00111
Jacquelyn Kelsay, prin. | 868-5235

Kearney, AC 308, PC 7, Buffalo
Kearney SD, 310 W 24TH ST 68847 | 5-11111
Gary Hammack, supt. | 237-2278
HS, 3610 6TH AVE 68847 | 4-00011
William Kenagy, prin. | 234-1720
Horizon MS, 915 W 35TH ST 68847 | 3-00100
Gerald Menke, prin. | 234-1911

Kearney West HSD | 2-00111
YOUTH DEVELOPMENT CENTER 68847
(—), supt. | 237-3181
Kearney West JSHS | 2-00111
YOUTH DEVELOPMENT CENTER 68847
Timothy O'Dea, prin. | 237-3181

Catholic HS, PO BOX 1866 68848 | 2-00111
Terrence Torson, prin. | 234-2610
University of Nebraska | 6-UC
905 W 25TH ST 68849 | 234-8208

Kenesaw, AC 402, PC 3, Adams
Kenesaw SD, PO BOX 129 68956 | 2-11111
Mark Schweer, supt. | 752-3215
JSHS, PO BOX 129 68956 | 2-00111
Donald Eberle, prin. | 752-3215

Kimball, AC 308, PC 5, Kimball
Kimball SD, 301 S HOWARD ST 69145 | 3-11111
Deloy Bremer, supt. | 235-2188
HS, 901 S NADINE ST 69145 | 2-00011
Jerry Williams, prin. | 235-4861
Kimball MS, 301 S HOWARD ST 69145 | 2-00100
Steven Pattison, prin. | 235-3005

Laurel, AC 402, PC 3, Cedar
Laurel-Concord SD, PO BOX 8 68745 | 2-11111
William Gannon, supt. | 256-3133
Laurel-Concord JSHS | 2-00111
PO BOX 8 68745 | 256-3133
Leslie Owen, prin. |

La Vista, AC 402, PC 6, Sarpy
Papillion-La Vista SD | 6-11111
7552 S 84TH ST 68128 | 339-3411
Harlan Metschke, supt. |
JHS, 7900 EDGEWOOD BLVD 68128 | 3-00110
Henry Alfrey, prin. | 592-5510
Other Schools – See Papillion

Lawrence, AC 402, PC 2, Nuckolls
Lawrence SD, PO BOX 128 68957 | 2-11111
Kent Miller, supt. | 756-7013
JSHS, PO BOX 128 68957 | 1-00111
Kent Miller, prin. | 756-7013

Lebanon, AC 308, PC 1, Red Willow
Beaver Valley SD, PO BOX 157 69036 | 2-11111
Dwight Parrish, supt. | 375-4215
JSHS, PO BOX 157 69036 | 1-00111
(—), prin. | 375-4215

Leigh, AC 402, PC 2, Colfax
Leigh SD, PO BOX 98 68643 | 2-11111
Cecil Fields, supt. | 487-2228
JSHS, PO BOX 98 68643 | 2-00111
Roland Hoppes, prin. | 487-2228

Lewellen, AC 308, PC 2, Garden
Lewellen RHSD, PO BOX F 69147 | 1-00011
Donald Newth, supt. | 778-5571
Lewellen Rural HS, PO BOX F 69147 | 1-00011
Donald Newth, prin. | 778-5571

Lewiston, AC 402, PC 1, Pawnee
Lewiston SD, PO BOX 74 68380 | 2-11111
Charles Griffith, supt. | 865-4675
JSHS, PO BOX 74 68380 | 2-00111
Linda Rempe, prin. | 865-4675

Lexington, AC 308, PC 6, Dawson
Lexington SD | 4-11111
1610 N WASHINGTON ST 68850 | 324-4681
Gary Druckemiller, supt. |
SHS, 13TH & ADAMS 68850 | 2-00001
Doyle Denney, prin. | 324-4691
JHS, 1100 N WASHINGTON ST 68850 | 2-00110
Roger Boyer, prin. | 324-2349

Lincoln, AC 402, PC 9, Lancaster
Lincoln SD, PO BOX 82889 68501 | 8-11111
Philip Schoo, supt. | 436-1000
Lincoln Northeast SHS | 4-00001
2635 N 63RD ST 68507 | 436-1303
Jerry Wilks, prin. |
Lincoln Southeast SHS | 4-00001
2930 S 37TH ST 68506 | 436-1304
Nancy Becker, prin. |
SHS, 2229 J ST 68510 | 4-00001
Kathryn Piller, prin. | 436-1301
Lincoln East JSHS | 4-00111
1000 S 70TH ST 68510 | 436-1302
Eugene Armstrong, prin. |
Culler JHS, 5201 VINE ST 68504 | 3-00110
William Bucher, prin. | 436-1210
Dawes JHS, 5130 COLFAX AVE 68504 | 2-00110
Darlene Rischling, prin. | 466-1211
Goodrich JHS, 4600 LEWIS AVE 68521 | 3-00110
Thomas Furby, prin. | 436-1213
Irving JHS, 2745 S 22ND ST 68502 | 3-00110
David Vanhorn, prin. | 436-1214
Lefler JHS, 1100 S 48TH ST 68510 | 3-00110
Hugh McDermott, prin. | 436-1215
Mickle JHS, 2500 N 67TH ST 68507 | 3-00110
Curtis Crandall, prin. | 436-1216
Park JHS, 714 F ST 68508 | 3-00110
Kevin Wibbels, prin. | 436-1212
Pound JHS, 4740 S 45TH ST 68516 | 3-00110
Royce Holtgrewe, prin. | 436-1217

Bryan Memorial Hospital | HSP
5000 SUMNER ST 68506 | 483-3801
College View Academy | 2-11111
5240 CALVERT ST 68506 | 486-2899
Michael Schwartz, prin. |
Gateway Electronics Institute | 2-CC
1033 O ST STE 130 68508 | 434-6060
Lincoln Christian S | 2-11111
6410 S 70TH ST 68516 | 488-2363
James Peters, prin. |

Lincoln Lutheran JHS — 2-00110
1100 N 56TH ST 68504 — 467-5404
Daniel Heibel, prin.
Lincoln School of Commerce — 3-CC
PO BOX 82826 68501 — 474-5315
Nebraska Wesleyan University — 4-UC
5000 SAINT PAUL AVE 68504 — 466-2371
Pius X HS, 6000 A ST 68510 — 3-00011
Gregory Logsdon, prin. — 488-0931
Southeast Community College — 5-CC
8800 O ST 68520 — 471-3413
Union College — 3-UC
3800 S 48TH ST 68506 — 488-2331
University of Nebraska — 7-UC
14TH & R STS 68588 — 472-7211

Lindsay, AC 402, PC 2, Platte

Holy Family S, PO BOX 158 68644 — 2-11111
Michael McCabe, prin. — 428-3215

Litchfield, AC 308, PC 2, Sherman
Litchfield SD, PO BOX 167 68852 — 2-11111
Eldon Epley, supt. — 446-2244
JSHS, PO BOX 167 68852 — 1-00111
Russell Flamig, prin. — 446-2244

Lodgepole, AC 308, PC 2, Cheyenne
Lodgepole SD, PO BOX 158 69149 — 2-11111
James Stansbury, supt. — 483-5252
HS, PO BOX 158 69149 — 1-00011
Robert Davis, prin. — 483-5252

Loomis, AC 308, PC 2, Phelps
Loomis SD, PO BOX 250 68958 — 2-11111
Keith Fagot, supt. — 876-2111
JSHS, PO BOX 250 68958 — 2-00111
Steven Smith, prin. — 876-2111

Louisville, AC 402, PC 3, Cass
Louisville SD, PO BOX 489 68037 — 2-11111
Edward Kasl, supt. — 234-3585
JSHS, PO BOX 489 68037 — 2-00111
Michael Minnihan, prin. — 234-3585

Loup City, AC 308, PC 4, Sherman
Loup City SD, 140 N 6TH ST 68853 — 3-11111
David Rokusek, supt. — 745-0120
HS, PO BOX 628 68853 — 2-00011
Donald Penner, prin. — 745-0548
MS, 800 N 8TH ST 68853 — 2-01100
Larry Hiatt, prin. — 745-0603

Lynch, AC 402, PC 2, Boyd
Lynch SD, PO BOX 98 68746 — 2-11111
Nelson Dahl, supt. — 569-2081
JSHS, PO BOX 98 68746 — 1-00111
Nelson Dahl, prin. — 569-2081

Lyons, AC 402, PC 4, Burt
Lyons-Decatur Northeast SD — 2-11111
PO BOX 526 68038 — 687-2472
F. Forsberg, supt.
Northeast JSHS, 5TH & CRYSTAL 68038 — 2-00111
Alan Wiese, prin. — 687-2349

Mc Cook, AC 308, PC 6, Red Willow
McCook SD, 700 W 7TH ST 69001 — 4-11111
Ron Karr, supt. — 345-2510
SHS, 600 W 7TH ST 69001 — 2-00001
Leroy Hoehner, prin. — 345-5422
JHS, 800 W 7TH ST 69001 — 2-00110
Leroy Hoehner, prin. — 345-6940

McCook Community College — 2-CC
1205 E 3RD ST 69001 — 800-348-5343

Mc Cool Junction, AC 402, PC 2, York
McCool Junction SD — 2-11111
PO BOX 278 68401 — 724-2231
George Bauer, supt.
JSHS, PO BOX 278 68401 — 1-00111
Daniel Ohlrich, prin. — 724-2231

Macy, AC 402, PC 3, Thurston
Macy SD, PO BOX 280 68039 — 2-11111
Lee Rottman, supt. — 837-5622
JSHS, PO BOX 280 68039 — 2-00111
Henry Eggert, prin. — 837-5260

Madison, AC 402, PC 4, Madison
Madison SD, PO BOX 450 68748 — 3-11111
Eugene Cerny, supt. — 454-3336
JSHS, PO BOX 450 68748 — 2-00111
Stanley Turner, prin. — 454-3336

Madrid, AC 308, PC 2, Perkins
Wheatland SD, PO BOX 38 69150 — 2-11111
Daniel Navrkal, supt. — 326-4201
Wheatland JSHS, PO BOX 38 69150 — 1-00111
Ken Beeman, prin. — 326-4201

Malcolm, AC 402, PC 2, Lancaster
Malcolm SD, PO BOX 198 68402 — 2-11111
Leland Knobel, supt. — 796-2152
JSHS, PO BOX 198 68402 — 2-00111
Earl Nannen, prin. — 796-2152

Marquette, AC 402, PC 2, Hamilton
Marquette SD, PO BOX 100 68854 — 2-11111
Charles Holt, supt. — 854-2241
JSHS, PO BOX 100 68854 — 1-00111
Charles Holt, prin. — 854-2241

Maxwell, AC 308, PC 2, Lincoln
Maxwell SD, PO BOX 188 69151 — 2-11111
John Brown, supt. — 582-4585
JSHS, PO BOX 188 69151 — 2-00111
Randy Pierce, prin. — 582-4585

Maywood, AC 308, PC 2, Frontier
Maywood SD, PO BOX 46 69038 — 2-11111
Dennis Krominga, supt. — 362-4223
JSHS, PO BOX 46 69038 — 1-00111
Stephen Morford, prin. — 362-4223

Mead, AC 402, PC 3, Saunders
Mead SD, PO BOX 158 68041 — 2-11111
George Robertson, supt. — 624-2745
JSHS, PO BOX 158 68041 — 2-00111
Roy Ingram, prin. — 624-3435

Merna, AC 308, PC 2, Custer
Anselmo-Merna SD — 2-11111
PO BOX 68 68856 — 643-2224
James Lofquist, supt.
JSHS, PO BOX 68 68856 — 2-00111
Larry Caudle, prin. — 643-2224

Milford, AC 402, PC 4, Seward
Milford SD, PO BOX C 68405 — 3-11111
Alan Katzberg, supt. — 761-3321
JSHS, PO BOX C 68405 — 2-00111
Gerald Bond, prin. — 761-2525

Southeast Community College — 3-CC
RR 2 BOX D 68405 — 761-2131

Milligan, AC 402, PC 2, Fillmore
Milligan SD, PO BOX 40 68406 — 1-11111
Thomas Sharp, supt. — 629-4265
JSHS, PO BOX 40 68406 — 1-00111
Lenoris Girmus, prin. — 629-4265

Minatare, AC 308, PC 3, Scotts Bluff
Minatare SD, PO BOX 425 69356 — 2-11111
Gerald Van Buskirk, supt. — 783-1232
JSHS, PO BOX 425 69356 — 1-00111
Gerald Van Buskirk, prin. — 783-1232

Minden, AC 308, PC 5, Kearney
Minden, 520 W 3RD ST 68959 — 3-11111
Scott Maline, supt. — 832-2440
HS, 325 YATES AVE 68959 — 2-00011
Gerald Gilder, prin. — 832-2254
Jones MS, 520 W 3RD ST 68959 — 2-01100
John Osgood, prin. — 832-2338

Mitchell, AC 308, PC 4, Scotts Bluff
Mitchell SD, 1819 19TH AVE 69357 — 3-11111
Donald Wagner, supt. — 623-1707
JSHS, 1819 19TH AVE 69357 — 2-00111
Kent Halley, prin. — 623-1707

Monroe, AC 402, PC 2, Platte
Monroe SD, PO BOX 156 68647 — 2-11111
Dale Heth, supt. — 495-2125
JSHS, PO BOX 156 68647 — 1-00111
(—), prin. — 495-2125

Morrill, AC 308, PC 3, Scotts Bluff
Morrill SD, PO BOX 486 69358 — 2-11111
Dennis Schmitz, supt. — 247-2149
JSHS, PO BOX 486 69358 — 2-00111
Kenton McLellan, prin. — 247-2149

Mullen, AC 308, PC 3, Hooker
Mullen SD, PO BOX 127 69152 — 2-11111
Robert Mandeville, supt. — 546-2223
JSHS, PO BOX 127 69152 — 2-00111
Randall Marymee, prin. — 546-2223

Murdock, AC 402, PC 2, Cass
Elmwood-Murdock SD — 2-11111
PO BOX 407 68407 — 867-2341
James Putnam, supt.
Elmwood-Murdock HS — 1-00011
PO BOX 407 68407 — 867-2341
Daniel Novak, prin.
Other Schools – See Elmwood

Murray, AC 402, PC 2, Cass
Conestoga SD, PO BOX 40 68409 — 3-11111
Rick Black, supt. — 235-2271
Conestoga JSHS, PO BOX 40 68409 — 2-00111
Vincent McAndrew, prin. — 235-2271

Nebraska City, AC 402, PC 6, Otoe
Nebraska City SD, 215 N 12TH ST 68410 — 4-11111
Keith Rohwer, supt. — 873-6033
SHS, STEINHART PARK ROAD 68410 — 2-00001
Erwin Friesen, prin. — 873-3360
JHS, 217 S 9TH ST 68410 — 2-00110
Charles Stoner, prin. — 873-5591

Lourdes Central S, 412 2ND AVE 68410 — 2-11111
Valerie Able, prin. — 873-6154
Nebraska School for Visually Handicapped — HND
10TH ST & 10TH AVE 68410

Neligh, AC 402, PC 4, Antelope
Neligh-Oakdale SD — 3-11111
PO BOX 149 68756 — 887-4166
Roger Macklem, supt.
HS, PO BOX 149 68756 — 2-00011
Terry Weber, prin. — 887-4166
MS, PO BOX 149 68756 — 2-00100
Terry Weber, prin. — 887-4166

Nelson, AC 402, PC 3, Nuckolls
Nelson SD, PO BOX 368 68961 — 2-11111
Kenneth Brown, supt. — 225-5421
JSHS, PO BOX 368 68961 — 2-00111
Susan Smidt, prin. — 225-3371

Newcastle, AC 402, PC 2, Dixon
Newcastle SD, PO BOX 187 68757 — 2-11111
Nelson Hinkle, supt. — 355-2231
JSHS, PO BOX 187 68757 — 2-00111
Stanford Hendricks, prin. — 355-2231

Newman Grove, AC 402, PC 3, Madison
Newman Grove SD — 2-11111
PO BOX 370 68758 — 447-2721
Luther Heller, supt.
JSHS, PO BOX 370 68758 — 2-00111
David Rich, prin. — 447-6294

Niobrara, AC 402, PC 2, Knox
Niobrara SD, PO BOX 310 68760 — 2-11111
Ronald Wright, supt. — 857-3322
JSHS, PO BOX 310 68760 — 1-00111
James Tinglehoff, prin. — 857-3322

Santee SD, RR 2 BOX 207 68760 — 2-11111
James Berryman, supt. — 857-3741
Santee JSHS, RR 2 BOX 207 68760 — 1-00111
James Berryman, prin. — 857-3741

Norfolk, AC 402, PC 7, Madison
Norfolk SD, PO BOX 139 68702 — 5-11111
Randy Nelson, supt. — 371-9370
SHS, 801 RIVERSIDE BLVD 68701 — 3-00001
Jeff Burkink, prin. — 371-0952
JHS, 510 PASEWALK AVE 68701 — 3-00110
Dee Zanders, prin. — 371-2241

Nebraska Christian College — 2-UC
1800 SYRACUSE AVE 68701 — 371-5960
Norfolk Catholic HS — 2-00011
2300 MADISON AVE 68701 — 371-2784
Jeff Bellar, prin.
Northeast Community College — 4-CC
PO BOX 469 68702 — 371-2020

North Bend, AC 402, PC 4, Dodge
North Bend Central HSD — 2-00111
PO BOX 160 68649 — 652-3268
Michael Ough, supt.
North Bend Central JSHS — 2-00111
PO BOX 160 68649 — 652-3268
Randall McIntyre, prin.

North Platte, AC 308, PC 7, Lincoln
North Platte SD, PO BOX 1557 69103 — 5-11111
Lynn Richardson, supt. — 535-7100
HS, 1000 W 2ND ST 69101 — 4-00011
Richard Zarkowski, prin. — 535-7105
Adams MS, 1200 MCDONALD RD 69101 — 3-00100
Jo Ann Stevens, prin. — 532-7112
Madison MS — 2-00100
1400 N MADISON AVE 69101 — 535-7126
Thomas Best, prin.

Mid-Plains Community College — 2-CC
INTERSTATE 80 & HIGHWAY 83 69101 — 800-658-4308
Mid-Plains Community College — 2-CC
1101 HALLIGAN DR 69101 — 800-658-4308
St. Patrick JSHS — 2-00111
500 S SILBER AVE 69101 — 532-1874
John Hannagan, prin.

Oakland, AC 402, PC 4, Burt
Oakland Craig SD — 2-11111
309 N DAVIS AVE 68045 — 685-5661
David Jones, supt.
Oakland Craig HS — 2-00011
309 N DAVIS AVE 68045 — 685-5661
Harold Hawkins, prin.
Oakland Craig JHS — 1-00100
309 N DAVIS AVE 68045 — 685-5661
Harold Hawkins, prin.

Odell, AC 402, PC 2, Gage
Odell SD — 2-11111
188 EDUCATIONAL AVE 68415 — 766-4171
Milford Smith, supt.
JSHS, 188 EDUCATIONAL AVE 68415 — 1-00111
Gerald Rupprecht, prin. — 766-4171

Ogallala, AC 308, PC 6, Keith
Ogallala SD, 602 E G ST 69153 — 4-11111
John Windhusen, supt. — 284-4060
HS, 602 E G ST 69153 — 2-00111
Dale Kruse, prin. — 284-4029
MS, 205 E 6TH ST 69153 — 2-00100
Marlin Spellmeyer, prin. — 284-4478

Omaha, AC 402, PC 10, Douglas
Millard SD, 5606 S 147TH ST 68137 — 7-11111
Ronald Witt, supt. — 895-8200
Millard North HS — 4-00011
1010 S 144TH ST 68154 — 691-1365
Ike Pane, prin.
Millard South HS, 14905 Q ST 68137 — 4-00011
Dick Wollman, prin. — 895-8268
West HS, 180TH & Q 68135 — 4-00011
Richard Kolowski, prin. — 895-8200
Andersen MS, 15405 ADAMS ST 68137 — 3-00100
Robert Lykke, prin. — 895-8440
Kiewit MS, 15650 HOWARD ST 68118 — 3-00100
Philip Koch, prin. — 691-1470

Millard Central MS, 12801 L ST 68137   3-00100
  Michael Fjell, prin.   895-8225
Millard North MS   3-00100
  2828 S 139TH ST 68144   691-1280
  Gary Barta, prin.
Russell MS, 5304 S 172ND ST 68135   3-00100
  Larry Roth, prin.   895-8200

Omaha SD, 3215 CUMING ST 68131   8-11111
  Norbert Schuerman, supt.   557-2300
Benson HS, 5120 MAPLE ST 68104   4-00011
  Frank Hoy, prin.   557-3000
Bryan HS, 4700 GILES RD 68157   4-00011
  Robert Whitehouse, prin.   557-3100
Burke HS, 12200 BURKE ST 68154   4-00011
  Karen Burmood, prin.   557-3200
Central HS, 124 N 20TH ST 68102   4-00011
  Gaylord Moller, prin.   557-3300
Omaha North HS, 4410 N 36TH ST 68111   4-00011
  Thomas Harvey, prin.   557-3400
Omaha Northwest HS   4-00011
  8204 CROWN POINT AVE 68134   557-3500
  Frank Bell, prin.
Omaha South HS, 4519 S 24TH ST 68107   4-00011
  Jerry Bartee, prin.   557-3600
Magnet Career Ctr, 3230 BURT ST 68131   Vo Tech
  Marvin Decker, prin.   557-3700
Beveridge JHS, 1616 S 120TH ST 68144   2-00100
  James Wilson, prin.   557-4000
Bryan JHS, 8210 S 42ND ST 68147   2-00100
  Raymond Ramsey, prin.   557-4100
Hale JHS, 6143 WHITMORE ST 68152   3-00100
  H. James Anding, prin.   557-4200
Lewis & Clark JHS, 6901 BURT ST 68132   2-00110
  Gary Thompson, prin.   557-4300
Marrs JHS, 5619 S 19TH ST 68107   2-00100
  James Hubschman, prin.   557-4400
McMillan JHS, 3802 REDICK AVE 68112   2-00100
  Norma Deeb, prin.   557-4500
Monroe JHS, 5105 BEDFORD AVE 68104   2-00100
  James Vincent, prin.   557-4600
Morton JHS, 4606 TERRACE DR 68134   2-00100
  Douglas Kyles, prin.   557-4700
Norris JHS, 2235 S 46TH ST 68106   2-00110
  Douglas Bahle, prin.   557-4800

Westside Community SD   5-11111
  909 S 76TH ST 68114   390-2100
  Kenneth Bird, supt.
Westside HS, 8701 PACIFIC ST 68114   4-00011
  James Findley, prin.   390-3300
Westside MS, 8601 MARTHA ST 68124   3-00100
  Bill Krueger, prin.   390-6464

Archbishop Bergan Mercy Hospital   HSP
  7500 MERCY RD 68124   398-6193
Bellevue Christian S   2-11111
  1722 S 16TH ST 68108   342-6506
  Paulette Bangert, prin.
Bishop Clarkson Memorial Hospital   HSP
  4350 DEWEY AVE 68105   559-3203
Brownell Talbot S   3-11111
  400 N HAPPY HOLLOW BLVD 68132   556-3772
  Ann Nordin, prin.
Cathedral HS, 3900 WEBSTER ST 68131   2-00011
  Denise Hoge, prin.   556-1255
Clarkson College   2-UC
  101 S 42ND ST 68131   559-2288
College of Saint Mary   3-UC
  1901 S 72ND ST 68124   399-2400
Creighton Prepatory S   3-00011
  7400 WESTERN AVE 68114   393-1190
  John Naatz, prin.
Creighton University   6-UC
  2500 CALIFORNIA ST 68178   280-2700
Daniel Gross HS, 7700 S 43RD ST 68147   3-00011
  William Ford, prin.   734-2000
Duchesne Academy   2-00011
  3601 BURT ST 68131   558-3800
  Sr. Marie Flick, prin.
Father Flanagan HS   2-00011
  2606 HAMILTON ST 68131   498-3000
  Norman Ridder, prin.
Gateway Electronics Institute   2-CC
  4862 S 96TH ST 68127   593-9000
Grace College of the Bible   2-UC
  1515 S 10TH ST 68108   449-2800
Immanuel Medical Center   HSP
  6901 N 72ND ST 68122   572-2270
Institute of Computer Science   2-CS
  808 S 74TH PLZ STE 200 68114   393-7064
ITT Technical Institute   2-CC
  9814 M ST 68127   331-2900
Marian HS, 7400 MILITARY AVE 68134   3-00011
  Elizabeth Kish, prin.   571-2618
Mercy HS, 1501 S 48TH ST 68106   2-00011
  Carolyn Jaworski, prin.   553-9424
Methodist College of Nursing & Health   2-UC
  8501 W DODGE RD 68114   390-4915
Metropolitan Community College   5-CC
  PO BOX 3777 68103   449-8415
Metropolitan Community College   3-CC
  30TH & FORT STS 68111   449-8300
Metropolitan Community College   3-CC
  204TH & DODGE ST 68022
Nebraska College of Business   3-CC
  3636 CALIFORNIA ST 68131   553-8600
Nebraska Custom Diesel Drivers Training   2-CS
  14243 C CIR 68144   393-7773

Nebraska School for the Deaf   HND
  3223 N 45TH ST 68104
Omaha Christian S   2-11111
  225 N 80TH ST 68114   399-9565
  Charles Ramsey, prin.
Omaha College of Business   2-CS
  1052 PARK AVE 68105   342-1818
Omaha College of Health Careers   1-CC
  10845 HARNEY ST 68154   333-1400
Omaha Opportunities Industrial Center   2-CS
  2724 N 24TH ST 68110   457-4222
Roncalli HS, 6401 REDICK AVE 68152   2-00011
  Kevin Nolan, prin.   571-7670
St. Joseph Hospital   HSP
  601 N 30TH ST 68131   449-4812
Skutt HS, 3131 S 156TH ST 68130   2-00011
  W. Durow, prin.   333-0818
Universal Technical Institute   2-CS
  902 CAPITOL AVE 68102   345-2422
University of Nebraska at Omaha   7-UC
  60TH AND DODGE ST 68182   554-2311
University of Nebraska Medical Center   4-UC
  600 S 42ND AND DEWEY 68198   559-4200

O'Neill, AC 402, PC 5, Holt
O'Neil SD, PO BOX 230 68763   3-11111
  Paul Nollette, supt.   336-3775
JSHS, PO BOX 230 68763   2-00111
  Boyd Blomenkamp, prin.   336-1544

St. Marys HS, 300 N 4TH ST 68763   2-00111
  Casper Ningen, prin.   336-4455

Orchard, AC 402, PC 2, Antelope
Orchard SD, PO BOX 269 68764   2-11111
  J. Allen Schlueter, supt.   893-4155
JSHS, PO BOX 269 68764   2-00111
  Dan Hadden, prin.   893-3215

Ord, AC 308, PC 4, Valley
Ord SD, 320 N 19TH ST 68862   3-11111
  Tucker Lillis, supt.   728-5013
JSHS, 1800 K ST 68862   2-00111
  Gerain Spatz, prin.   728-3241

Orleans, AC 308, PC 2, Harlan
Furnas County SD
  Supt. — See Oxford
JSHS, PO BOX 477 68966   2-00111
  David Brady, prin.   473-3185

Osceola, AC 402, PC 3, Polk
Osceola SD, PO BOX 198 68651   2-11111
  Kenneth Mahlin, supt.   747-3121
JSHS, PO BOX 198 68651   2-00111
  Larry Miller, prin.   747-3121

Oshkosh, AC 308, PC 3, Garden
Garden County HSD   1-00011
  PO BOX 230 69154   772-3242
  Richard Finley, supt.
Garden County HS   1-00011
  PO BOX 230 69154   772-3242
  Roger Gray, prin.

Osmond, AC 402, PC 3, Pierce
Osmond SD, PO BOX 458 68765   2-11111
  Bill Mowinkel, supt.   748-3777
JSHS, PO BOX 458 68765   2-00111
  Marlyn Washburn, prin.   748-3777

Overton, AC 308, PC 3, Dawson
Overton SD, PO BOX 310 68863   2-11111
  David Hendricks, supt.   987-2424
JSHS, PO BOX 310 68863   2-00111
  William Patterson, prin.   987-2424

Oxford, AC 308, PC 3, Furnas
Furnas County SD, PO BOX 7 68967   2-11111
  Nathan Stineman, supt.   824-3209
JSHS, PO BOX 7 68967   2-00111
  Gary Brouillette, prin.   824-3209
  Other Schools – See Beaver City, Orleans

Palisade, AC 308, PC 2, Hitchcock
Wauneta-Palisade SD
  Supt. — See Wauneta
Wauneta Palisade JHS, PO BOX O 69040   1-00100
  Charles Hervert, prin.   285-3219

Palmer, AC 308, PC 3, Merrick
Palmer SD, PO BOX 248 68864   2-11111
  Richard Chochon, supt.   894-3065
JSHS, PO BOX 248 68864   1-00111
  David Tickner, prin.   894-3065

Palmyra, AC 402, PC 3, Otoe
Palmyra SD, PO BOX 130 68418   2-11111
  Gary Fritch, supt.   780-5328
JSHS, PO BOX 130 68418   2-00111
  Wayne Johnson, prin.   780-5327

Papillion, AC 402, PC 7, Sarpy
Papillion-La Vista SD
  Supt. — See La Vista
Papillion-Lavista SHS   4-00001
  402 CENTENNIAL RD 68046   339-0405
  Dennis Smith, prin.
JHS, 423 S WASHINGTON ST 68046   3-00110
  Robert Hahn, prin.   339-3262

Pawnee City, AC 402, PC 4, Pawnee
Pawnee City SD, PO BOX 393 68420   2-11111
  Gary Amen, supt.   852-2988
JSHS, PO BOX 393 68420   2-00111
  Robert West, prin.   852-2988

Paxton, AC 308, PC 3, Keith
Paxton Consolidated SD   2-11111
  PO BOX 368 69155   239-4283
  Robert Conn, supt.
JSHS, PO BOX 368 69155   1-00111
  Robert Conn, prin.   239-4283

Pender, AC 402, PC 4, Thurston
Pender SD, 609 WHITNEY 68047   2-11111
  Terry Hazard, supt.   385-3044
JSHS, 609 WHITNEY 68047   2-00111
  Ernest McIntyre, prin.   385-3044

Peru, AC 402, PC 4, Nemaha

Peru State College 68421   4-UC
   872-3815

Petersburg, AC 402, PC 2, Boone
Petersburg SD, PO BOX 240 68652   2-11111
  Earl Fickenscher, supt.   386-5302
JSHS, PO BOX 240 68652   1-00111
  Mary Thieman, prin.   386-5302

Pierce, AC 402, PC 4, Pierce
Pierce SD, 300 S 1ST ST 68767   2-11111
  Donald Jones, supt.   329-4677
JSHS, 300 S 1ST ST 68767   2-00111
  Lynn Moeller, prin.   329-4677

Plainview, AC 402, PC 4, Pierce
Plainview SD, PO BOX 638 68769   2-11111
  Donovan Betterman, supt.   582-4993
JSHS, PO BOX 638 68769   2-00111
  Gale Retzlaff, prin.   582-4993

Plattsmouth, AC 402, PC 6, Cass
Plattsmouth SD, 1724 8TH AVE 68048   4-11111
  Virgil Likness, supt.   296-3361
HS, 1724 8TH AVE 68048   2-00011
  Stanton Kroon, prin.   296-3322
MS, 1724 8TH AVE 68048   2-00100
  Cheryl Blue, prin.   296-3174

Pleasanton, AC 308, PC 2, Buffalo
Pleasanton SD, PO BOX 190 68866   2-11111
  Larry Johnson, supt.   388-2041
JSHS, PO BOX 190 68866   2-00111
  Ron Wymore, prin.   388-2041

Polk, AC 402, PC 2, Polk
Polk-Hordville SD, PO BOX 29 68654   2-11111
  Dennis Gray, supt.   765-2271
Polk-Hordville HS, PO BOX 29 68654   1-00111
  Keith Leckron, prin.   765-3331
  Other Schools – See Hordville

Ponca, AC 402, PC 3, Dixon
Ponca SD, PO BOX 568 68770   2-11111
  Kevin Johnson, supt.   755-2241
JSHS, PO BOX 568 68770   2-00111
  Michelle Rinas, prin.   755-2241

Potter, AC 308, PC 2, Cheyenne
Potter-Dix SD, PO BOX P 69156   2-11111
  Virgil Combs, supt.   879-4434
Potter-Dix HS, PO BOX P 69156   1-00111
  Kevin Thomas, prin.   879-4434
  Other Schools – See Dix

Prague, AC 402, PC 2, Saunders
Prague SD, PO BOX 98 68050   2-11111
  Dale Meritt, supt.   663-4388
JSHS, PO BOX 98 68050   1-00111
  Dale Meritt, prin.   663-4388

Ralston, AC 402, PC 6, Douglas
Ralston SD, 8545 PARK DR 68127   5-11111
  Kenneth Rippe, supt.   331-4700
HS, 8969 PARK DR 68127   4-00011
  Martha Bruckner, prin.   331-7373
MS, 8202 LAKEVIEW ST 68127   3-00100
  Lonnie Bernth, prin.   331-4701

Randolph, AC 402, PC 3, Cedar
Randolph SD, PO BOX 440 68771   2-11111
  W. Troshynski, supt.   337-0385
JSHS, PO BOX 440 68771   2-00111
  Ron Iles, prin.   337-0385

Ravenna, AC 308, PC 4, Buffalo
Ravenna SD
  740 W CARTHAGE ST 68869   452-3249
  Edwin Hollinger, supt.
JSHS, 740 W CARTHAGE ST 68869   2-00111
  Gary Larsen, prin.   452-3249

Raymond, AC 402, PC 2, Lancaster
Raymond Central SD   3-11111
  PO BOX 180A 68428   785-2615
  Robert Broomfield, supt.
JSHS, PO BOX 180A 68428   2-00111
  Gladys Helm, prin.   785-2685

Red Cloud, AC 402, PC 4, Webster
Red Cloud SD, 334 N CHERRY ST 68970   2-11111
  Donald Osborn, supt.   746-3413
JSHS, 121 W 7TH AVE 68970   2-00111
  Wendel Cass, prin.   746-2818

Rising City, AC 402, PC 2, Butler
Rising City SD, PO BOX 160 68658   2-11111
  Jonathan Habben, supt.   542-2216
JSHS, PO BOX 160 68658   1-00111
  Virgil Hartsock, prin.   542-2216

Roseland, AC 402, PC 2, Adams
Silver Lake SD, PO BOX 8 68973 — 2-11111, 756-6611
  Gale McDonald, supt.
Silver Lake JSHS, PO BOX 8 68973 — 2-00111, 756-6611
  Kenneth Mahoney, prin.

Rushville, AC 308, PC 4, Sheridan
Rushville HSD, PO BOX 590 69360 — 2-00111, 327-2682
  Lewis Gellett, supt.
HS, PO BOX 590 69360 — 2-00111, 327-2682
  Glen Mitchell, prin.

Sheridan County SD — 3-11100, 327-2272
  PO BOX 409 69360
  Charles Smith, supt.
JHS, PO BOX 590 69360 — 2-00100, 327-2682
  Glen Mitchell, prin.
Other Schools – See Gordon

Saint Edward, AC 402, PC 3, Boone
St. Edward SD, PO BOX C 68660 — 2-11111, 678-2282
  Benard Straatmeyer, supt.
JSHS, PO BOX C 68660 — 2-00111, 678-2282
  Wayne Morfield, prin.

Saint Paul, AC 308, PC 4, Howard
St. Paul SD, 1305 HOWARD AVE 68873 — 3-11111, 754-4433
  Douglas Ackles, supt.
JSHS, 1305 HOWARD AVE 68873 — 2-00111, 754-4433
  John Weitzel, prin.

Sargent, AC 308, PC 3, Custer
Sargent SD, PO BOX 366 68874 — 2-11111, 527-4119
  Lyn Johnson, supt.
JSHS, PO BOX 366 68874 — 2-00111, 527-4119
  Donald Seifried, prin.

Schuyler, AC 402, PC 5, Colfax
Colfax County SD, 411 E 11TH ST 68661 — 3-11100, 352-3233
  Larry Jensen, supt.
Schuyler West Ward MS — 2-01100, 352-5514
  200 W 10TH ST 68661
  James Deblauw, prin.

Schuyler Central HSD — 2-00011, 352-2421
  401 ADAM ST 68661
  Robert Brandt, supt.
Schuyler Central HS — 2-00011, 352-2421
  401 ADAM ST 68661
  David Melick, prin.

Scotia, AC 308, PC 2, Greeley
North Loup Scotia SD — 2-11111, 245-3201
  PO BOX 307 68875
  David Kroger, supt.
JSHS, PO BOX 307 68875 — 2-00111, 245-3571
  Glen Hawley, prin.

Scottsbluff, AC 308, PC 7, Scotts Bluff
Scottsbluff SD, 2601 BROADWAY 69361 — 5-11111, 635-6200
  David Reichert, supt.
HS, 313 E 27TH ST 69361 — 3-00011, 635-6230
  Joie Baker, prin.
Bluffs MS, 23RD & BROADWAY 69361 — 3-00100, 635-6270
  Nicholas Marick, prin.

Regional West Medical Center — HSP, 635-3711
  4021 AVENUE B 69361
Western Nebraska Community College — 3-CC, 635-3606
  1601 E 27TH ST 69361

Scribner, AC 402, PC 3, Dodge
Scribner-Snyder SD, PO BOX L 68057 — 2-11111, 664-2567
  Loyal Vincent, supt.
Scribner-Snyder JSHS, PO BOX L 68057 — 2-00111, 664-2567
  Donald Bartek, prin.

Seward, AC 402, PC 6, Seward
Seward SD, 410 SOUTH ST 68434 — 4-11111, 643-2941
  Marshall Adams, supt.
SHS — 2-00001, 643-2988
  532 NORTHERN HEIGHTS DR 68434
  Doug Radtke, prin.
JHS, 2375 3RD ST 68434 — 2-00110, 643-2986
  Eldon Lindquist, prin.

Concordia College — 3-UC, 643-3651
  800 N COLUMBIA AVE 68434

Shelby, AC 402, PC 3, Polk
Shelby SD, PO BOX 218 68662 — 2-11111, 527-5946
  Kenneth Bowe, supt.
JSHS, PO BOX 218 68662 — 2-00111, 527-5946
  Keith Jurrens, prin.

Shelton, AC 308, PC 3, Buffalo
Shelton SD, PO BOX 610 68876 — 2-11111, 647-6742
  David Schley, supt.
JSHS, PO BOX 610 68876 — 2-00111, 647-6742
  Ronald Hudson, prin.

Platte Valley SDA Academy — 2-00011, 647-5151
  19338 W CAMPUS DR 68876
  Kenneth Turpen, prin.

Shickley, AC 402, PC 2, Fillmore
Shickley SD, PO BOX 407 68436 — 2-11111, 627-3375
  Edward Briscoe, supt.
JSHS, PO BOX 407 68436 — 1-00111, 627-3375
  Paul Hull, prin.

Sidney, AC 308, PC 6, Cheyenne
Sidney SD, 21ST & KING ST 69162 — 4-11111, 254-5855
  Charles Bunner, supt.
HS, 1128 20TH AVE 69162 — 2-00011, 254-5893
  John McLane, prin.

JHS, 1122 19TH AVE 69162 — 2-00100, 254-5853
  Jeffrey West, prin.

Western Nebraska Community College — 2-CC, 800-221-9682
  69162

Silver Creek, AC 308, PC 3, Merrick
Silver Creek SD, PO BOX 247 68663 — 2-11111, 773-2233
  Larry Meyer, supt.
JSHS, PO BOX 247 68663 — 1-00111, 773-2233
  Theodore Cremers, prin.

South Sioux City, AC 402, PC 6, Dakota
South Sioux City SD — 4-11101, 494-2425
  PO BOX 158 68776
  Vandle Phillips, supt.
SHS, 3301 G ST 68776 — 2-00001, 494-2433
  Steve Rector, prin.
JHS, PO BOX 158 68776 — 3-00100, 494-3061
  John Laughhunn, prin.

Spalding, AC 308, PC 3, Greeley
Spalding SD, PO BOX 220 68665 — 2-11111, 497-2431
  Benje Hookstra, supt.
JSHS, PO BOX 220 68665 — 1-00111, 497-2431
  Benje Hookstra, prin.

Spalding Academy — 1-11111, 497-2103
  PO BOX 310 68665
  Dennis Hellman, prin.

Spencer, AC 402, PC 3, Boyd
Spencer-Naper SD — 2-11111, 589-1333
  PO BOX 109 68777
  Dale Reber, supt.
Spencer-Naper JSHS — 2-00111, 589-1333
  PO BOX 109 68777
  Charles Kadlecek, prin.

Springfield, AC 402, PC 4, Sarpy
South Sarpy SD 46 — 4-11111, 592-1300
  PO BOX 365 68059
  Robert Diekmann, supt.
Platteview HS, PO BOX 365 68059 — 2-00011, 339-3606
  Robert Olander, prin.
Platteview Central JHS — 2-00100, 339-5052
  PO BOX 365 68059
  Ralph Glock, prin.

Springview, AC 402, PC 2, Keya Paha
Keya Paha County HSD — 1-00011, 497-3501
  PO BOX 219 68778
  Joe Matrisciano, supt.
Keya Paha County HS — 1-00011, 497-3501
  PO BOX 219 68778 – (—), prin.

Stanton, AC 402, PC 4, Stanton
Stanton Community SD — 2-11111, 439-2233
  PO BOX 749 68779
  Don Schmidt, supt.
JSHS, PO BOX 749 68779 — 2-00111, 439-2250
  Dennis Dolliver, prin.

Stapleton, AC 308, PC 2, Logan
Stapleton SD, PO BOX 128 69163 — 2-11111, 636-2252
  Jon Broadbent, supt.
JSHS, PO BOX 128 69163 — 2-00111, 636-2252
  Jay Muma, prin.

Stella, AC 402, PC 2, Richardson
Southeast Consolidated SD — 2-11111, 883-2600
  PO BOX 73 68442
  Larry Marcusson, supt.
JSHS, PO BOX 73 68442 — 2-00111, 883-2400
  Michael Apple, prin.

Sterling, AC 402, PC 2, Johnson
Sterling SD, PO BOX 39 68443 — 2-11111, 866-4761
  Robert Norton, supt.
JSHS, PO BOX 39 68443 — 1-00111, 866-4761
  Brad Buller, prin.

Stratton, AC 308, PC 2, Hitchcock
Stratton SD, PO BOX 324 69043 — 2-11111, 276-2281
  Larry Schall, supt.
JSHS, PO BOX 324 69043 — 1-00111, 276-2281
  Larry Schall, prin.

Stromsburg, AC 402, PC 4, Polk
Stromsburg SD, PO BOX 525 68666 — 2-11111, 764-2156
  Donald Holmberg, supt.
JSHS, PO BOX 525 68666 — 2-00111, 764-5521
  Ronald Cornwell, prin.

Stuart, AC 402, PC 3, Holt
Stuart SD, PO BOX G 68780 — 2-11111, 924-3302
  Rodger Lenhard, supt.
JSHS, PO BOX G 68780 — 1-00111, 924-3302
  Gary Addison, prin.

Sumner, AC 402, PC 2, Dawson
Sumner-Eddyville-Miller SD — 2-11111, 752-2925
  PO BOX 126 68878
  Richard Hodge, supt.
JSHS, PO BOX 126 68878 — 1-00111, 752-2925
  Randy Lee Evans, prin.

Superior, AC 402, PC 4, Nuckolls
Superior SD, PO BOX 288 68978 — 3-11111, 879-3258
  Dennis Mehlhaff, supt.
JSHS, PO BOX 288 68978 — 2-00111, 879-3257
  Melvin Crowe, prin.

Sutherland, AC 308, PC 4, Lincoln
Sutherland SD, PO BOX 217 69165 — 2-11111, 386-4656
  Michael Cunning, supt.

JSHS, PO BOX 217 69165 — 2-00111, 386-4656
  Michael Troxel, prin.

Sutton, AC 402, PC 4, Clay
Sutton SD, PO BOX 590 68979 — 2-11111, 773-5569
  Dennis Wittman, supt.
JSHS, PO BOX 590 68979 — 2-00111, 773-4303
  Susan Miller, prin.

Syracuse, AC 402, PC 4, Otoe
Syracuse-Dunbar-Avoca SD — 3-11111, 269-2381
  PO BOX P 68446
  Edwin Johnson, supt.
JSHS, 1500 EDUCATION DR 68446 — 2-00111, 269-2381
  Gene Neddenriep, prin.

Table Rock, AC 402, PC 2, Pawnee
Table Rock SD, PO BOX F 68447 — 2-11111, 839-4755
  (—), supt.
JSHS, PO BOX F 68447 — 1-00111, 839-4755
  Howard Hanson, prin.

Taylor, AC 308, PC 2, Loup
Loup County SD, PO BOX 170 68879 — 2-11111, 942-6115
  William Smith, supt.
Loup County JSHS — 1-00111, 942-6115
  PO BOX 170 68879
  William Smith, prin.

Tecumseh, AC 402, PC 4, Johnson
Tecumseh SD, PO BOX 338 68450 — 2-11111, 335-3320
  Thomas Rother, supt.
JSHS, PO BOX 338 68450 — 2-00111, 335-3328
  Richard Lester, prin.

Tekamah, AC 402, PC 4, Burt
Tekamah-Herman SD — 3-11111, 374-2157
  112 N 13TH ST 68061
  Raymond Chase, supt.
JSHS, 112 N 13TH ST 68061 — 2-00111, 374-2156
  Billy Anderson, prin.

Thedford, PC 2, Thomas
Thedford RHSD — 1-00111, 308-645-2230
  PO BOX 248 69166
  Percy Morgan, supt.
Thedford Rural JSHS — 1-00111, 308-645-2230
  PO BOX 248 69166
  (—), prin.

Tilden, AC 402, PC 3, Madison
Elkhorn Valley SD — 2-11111, 368-5301
  PO BOX 430 68781
  Randall Peck, supt.
Elkhorn Valley JSHS — 2-00111, 368-5338
  PO BOX 430 68781
  Carl Johnson, prin.

Trenton, AC 308, PC 3, Hitchcock
Trenton SD, PO BOX 368 69044 — 2-11111, 334-5575
  Kurt Harrison, supt.
JSHS, PO BOX 368 69044 — 1-00111, 334-5575
  Lewis Evert, prin.

Trumbull, AC 402, PC 2, Clay
Trumbull SD, PO BOX 94 68980 — 2-11111, 743-2307
  Francis Shaughnessy, supt.
JSHS, PO BOX 94 68980 — 1-00111, 743-2306
  Dave Scribner, prin.

Tryon, AC 308, PC 2, McPherson
McPherson County HSD — 1-00011, 587-2262
  PO BOX 38 69167
  Clyde Robertson, supt.
McPherson County HS — 1-00011, 587-2262
  PO BOX 38 69167 – (—), prin.

Utica, AC 402, PC 3, Seward
Centennial SD, PO BOX 187 68456 — 3-11111, 534-2291
  Ronald Oswald, supt.
JSHS, PO BOX 187 68456 — 2-00111, 534-2321
  Leroy Ernst, prin.

Valentine, AC 402, PC 5, Cherry
Cherry County SD, 365 N MAIN ST 69201 — 3-11100, 376-1680
  Jean Stolzenburg, supt.
MS, 239 N WOOD ST 69201 — 2-00100, 376-3367
  Stephen Saum, prin.
Valentine Rural HSD — 2-00011, 376-2730
  PO BOX 90 69201
  Calvin Loughran, supt.
Valentine Rural HS — 2-00011, 376-2730
  PO BOX 90 69201
  Dale Naprstek, prin.

Valley, AC 402, PC 4, Douglas
Valley SD, 401 S PINE ST 68064 — 3-11111, 359-2583
  Gil Kettelhut, supt.
JSHS, 401 S PINE ST 68064 — 2-00111, 359-2121
  Donovan Ginger, prin.

Verdigre, AC 402, PC 3, Knox
Verdigre SD, PO BOX 220 68783 — 2-11111, 668-2275
  John Erickson, supt.
JSHS, PO BOX 220 68783 — 2-00111, 668-2275
  Ronald Wecker, prin.

Waco, AC 402, PC 2, York

Nebraska Evangelist Lutheran HS — 2-00011, 728-5236
  RR 2 BOX 103B 68460
  James Pasbrig, prin.

Wahoo, AC 402, PC 5, Saunders
Wahoo SD, 2201 LOCUST ST 68066 — 3-11111, 443-3051
  John Brennan, supt.

HS, 2201 LOCUST ST 68066 — 2-00011 / 443-4332
Richard Williams, prin.
MS, 2201 LOCUST ST 68066 — 2-00100 / 443-3101
Mark Wilson, prin.

Bishop Neumann Central HS — 2-00111 / 443-4151
202 S LINDEN AVE 68066
Sr Michelle Hayek, prin.

Wakefield, AC 402, PC 4, Dixon
Wakefield SD, PO BOX 575 68784 — 2-11111 / 287-2012
Derwin Hartman, supt.
JSHS, PO BOX 575 68784 — 2-00111 / 287-2012
Joseph Coble, prin.

Wallace, AC 308, PC 2, Lincoln
Wallace SD, PO BOX 127 69169 — 2-11111 / 387-4323
Gene Haddix, supt.
JSHS, PO BOX 127 69169 — 1-00111 / 387-4323
Larry Seger, prin.

Walthill, AC 402, PC 3, Thurston
Walthill SD, PO BOX 3C 68067 — 2-11111 / 846-5432
Rich Schlesselman, supt.
JSHS, PO BOX 3C 68067 — 2-00111 / 846-5432
Jack White, prin.

Waterloo, AC 402, PC 2, Douglas
Waterloo SD — 2-11111 / 779-2646
7TH & WASHINGTON 68069
Thomas McMahon, supt.
JSHS, 7TH & WASHINGTON 68069 — 2-00111 / 779-2646
Michael Lynch, prin.

Wauneta, AC 308, PC 3, Chase
Wauneta-Palisade SD — 2-11111 / 394-5700
PO BOX 368 69045
Dennis Wentz, supt.
Wauneta-Palisade HS — 2-00011 / 394-5650
PO BOX 368 69045
James Manker, prin.
Other Schools – See Palisade

Wausa, AC 402, PC 3, Knox
Wausa SD, PO BOX 159 68786 — 2-11111 / 586-2255
Robert Rogers, supt.
JSHS, PO BOX 159 68786 — 1-00111 / 586-2255
Dale Wamberg, prin.

Waverly, AC 402, PC 4, Lancaster
Waverly SD, PO BOX 426 68462 — 4-11111 / 786-2321
James Ossian, supt.
HS, PO BOX 426 68462 — 2-00011 / 786-2765
Robert Meyers, prin.

JHS, PO BOX 426 68462 — 2-00100 / 786-2348
Dennis Bellinger, prin.

Wayne, AC 402, PC 6, Wayne
Wayne SD, 611 W 7TH ST 68787 — 3-11111 / 375-3150
Dennis Jensen, supt.
HS, 611 W 7TH ST 68787 — 2-00011 / 375-3150
Donald Zeiss, prin.
MS, 312 DOUGLAS ST 68787 — 2-01100 / 375-2230
Richard Metteer, prin.

Wayne State College — 5-UC / 800-228-9972
200 E 10TH ST 68787

Weeping Water, AC 402, PC 4, Cass
Weeping Water SD — 2-11111 / 267-2435
PO BOX 206 68463
Louis Eberhart, supt.
JSHS, PO BOX 206 68463 — 2-00111 / 267-2435
Charles Haag, prin.

West Point, AC 402, PC 5, Cuming
West Point SD — 3-11111 / 372-5546
1200 E WASHINGTON ST 68788
Darryl Kile, supt.
JSHS, 1200 E WASHINGTON ST 68788 — 2-00111 / 372-5546
Richard Lemmerman, prin.

Central Catholic HS — 2-00011 / 372-5326
419 E DECATUR ST 68788
Sr. Carol Diederich, prin.

Wilber, AC 402, PC 4, Saline
Wilber-Clatonia SD — 3-11111 / 821-2266
9TH & FRANKLIN 68465
Richard Becker, supt.
Wilber Clatonia JSHS — 2-00111 / 821-2508
9TH & FRANKLIN 68465
Ernie Talarico, prin.

Wilcox, AC 308, PC 2, Kearney
Wilcox SD, PO BOX 190 68982 — 2-11111 / 478-5265
Glen Lewis, supt.
JSHS, PO BOX 190 68982 — 1-00111 / 478-5265
Victor Young, prin.

Winnebago, AC 402, PC 3, Thurston
Winnebago SD, PO BOX KK 68071 — 2-11111 / 878-2224
William McCoy, supt.
JSHS, PO BOX KK 68071 — 2-00111 / 878-2224
Bruce Haag, prin.

Nebraska Indian Community College — 2-CC / 878-2414
PO BOX 752 68071

Winside, AC 402, PC 2, Wayne
Winside SD, PO BOX 158 68790 — 2-11111 / 286-4466
Donavon Leighton, supt.
JSHS, PO BOX 158 68790 — 2-00111 / 286-4465
Ronald Leapley, prin.

Wisner, AC 402, PC 4, Cuming
Wisner-Pilger SD, PO BOX 580 68791 — 2-11111 / 529-3249
William Hakonson, supt.
JSHS, PO BOX 580 68791 — 2-00111 / 529-3249
Alan Harms, prin.

Wolbach, AC 308, PC 2, Greeley
Wolbach SD, PO BOX 67 68882 — 2-11111 / 246-5232
Clyde Childers, supt.
JSHS, PO BOX 67 68882 — 1-00111 / 246-5232
Greg Peterson, prin.

Wood River, AC 308, PC 4, Hall
Wood River RHSD — 2-00111 / 583-2249
PO BOX 518 68883
Larry Harnisch, supt.
Wood River Rural JSHS — 2-00111 / 583-2249
PO BOX 518 68883
Kenneth Navratil, prin.

Wymore, AC 402, PC 4, Gage
Southern SD 1, 115 S 11TH ST 68466 — 2-11111 / 645-3326
Larry Humphrey, supt.
Southern JSHS, 115 S 11TH ST 68466 — 2-00111 / 645-3326
Steven Whitwer, prin.

Wynot, AC 402, PC 2, Cedar
Wynot SD, PO BOX 157 68792 — 2-11111 / 357-2121
Tedsen Hillman, supt.
JSHS, PO BOX 157 68792 — 1-00111 / 357-2121
Tedsen Hillman, prin.

York, AC 402, PC 6, York
York SD, 611 PLATTE AVE 68467 — 4-11111 / 362-6655
Paul Toms, supt.
HS, 1005 DUKE DR 68467 — 2-00011 / 362-6655
Scott Koch, prin.
MS, 1200 EAST AVE 68467 — 2-00100 / 362-6655
Richard Moses, prin.

York College — 2-UC / 362-4441
912 KIPLINGER AVE 68467

Yutan, AC 402, PC 3, Saunders
Yutan SD, PO BOX 220 68073 — 2-11111 / 625-2243
Dewey Harouff, supt.
JSHS, PO BOX 220 68073 — 2-00111 / 625-2243
James Moore, prin.

NEVADA

STATE DEPARTMENT OF EDUCATION
Capitol Complex
400 W. King St., Carson City 89710
(702) 687-3100

Interim Superintendent of Instruction	Mary Peterson
Deputy Superintendent Administrative & Fiscal Services	Vacant
Deputy Superintendent Instructional, Research, Evaluative Services	Vacant

STATE BOARD OF EDUCATION
400 W. King St., Carson City 89710

President	Yvonne Shaw

PUBLIC, PRIVATE AND CATHOLIC SECONDARY SCHOOLS

Alamo, AC 702, PC 2, Lincoln
Lincoln County SD
Supt. — See Panaca
Pahrangat Valley JSHS — 2-00111 / 725-3321
PO BOX 198 89001
Larry Lytle, prin.

Austin, AC 702, PC 2, Lander
Lander County SD
Supt. — See Battle Mountain
JSHS, PO BOX 160 89310 — 1-00111 / 964-2467
Tom Brannan, prin.

Baker, AC 702, PC 1, White Pine
White Pine County SD
Supt. — See East Ely

MS, PO BOX 120 89311 — 1-00100 / 234-7333
(—), prin.

Battle Mountain, AC 702, PC 5, Lander
Lander County SD — 4-11111 / 635-2886
PO BOX 1300 89820
Dr. Leon Hensley, supt.
HS, PO BOX 1330 89820 — 2-00011 / 635-5436
James Huckaby, prin.
JHS, PO BOX 1360 89820 — 2-00100 / 635-2415
Steve Larsgaard, prin.
Other Schools – See Austin

Beatty, AC 702, PC 4, Nye
Nye County SD
Supt. — See Tonopah

HS, PO BOX 806 89003 — 2-00011 / 553-2595
Keith Koerner, prin.

Boulder City, AC 702, PC 7, Clark
Clark County SD
Supt. — See Las Vegas
HS, 1101 5TH ST 89005 — 3-00011 / 799-8200
Bill Garis, prin.
Garrett JHS, 1200 AVENUE G 89005 — 3-00100 / 799-8290
Pamela Hawkins, prin.

Carlin, AC 702, PC 4, Elko
Elko County SD
Supt. — See Elko
JSHS, PO BOX 729 89822 — 2-00111 / 754-6317
Gwen Thacker, prin.

Carson City, AC 702, PC 8, (Indep. City)
Carson City SD, PO BOX 603 89702 — 6-11111 / 885-6310
  Robert Scott, supt.
Carson HS, 1111 N SALIMAN RD 89701 — 4-00011 / 885-6500
  Glen Adair, prin.
Carson MS — 3-00100
  W KING ST & RICHMOND 89701 — 885-6400
  Tom Badillo, prin.
Eagle Valley MS, 4151 E 5TH ST 89701 — 3-00100 / 885-6570
  Judith Elges, prin.

Western Nevada Community College — 6-CC
2201 W NYE LN 89703 — 887-3000

Dayton, AC 702, PC 3, Lyon
Lyon County SD
  Supt. — See Yerington
HS, PO BOX 729 89403 — 2-00011 / 246-0123
  Patricia Haller, prin.
IS, 315 DAYTON VALLEY RD 89403 — 2-01100 / 246-7777
  Dave Regalado, prin.

East Ely, AC 702, PC see Ely
White Pine County SD — 4-11111 / 289-4851
  PO BOX 150400 89315
  Jan Cahill, supt.
Other Schools — See Baker, Ely, Lund

Elko, AC 702, PC 7, Elko
Elko County SD, PO BOX 1012 89803 — 6-11111 / 738-5196
  Paul Billings, supt.
HS, 987 COLLEGE AVE 89801 — 4-00011 / 738-7281
  Moyal Kump, prin.
Spring Creek HS — 3-00111 / 753-5575
  14550 LAMOILLE HWY 89803
  Joe DeBraga, prin.
JHS, 777 COUNTRY CLUB DR 89801 — 3-00100 / 738-7236
  Glade Oberhansli, prin.
Other Schools — See Carlin, Jackpot, Owyhee, Wells

Northern Nevada Community College — 4-CC
901 ELM ST 89801 — 800-343-2724

Ely, AC 702, PC 5, White Pine
White Pine County SD
  Supt. — See East Ely
White Pine County HS — 2-00011 / 289-4811
  844 AULTMAN ST 89301
  Robert Dolezal, prin.
White Pine County MS — 2-00100 / 289-4841
  616 HIGH ST 89301
  Virginia Goddard, prin.

Eureka, AC 702, PC 3, Eureka
Eureka County SD — 2-11111 / 237-5373
  PO BOX 249 89316
  David Lannigan, supt.
JSHS, PO BOX 237 89316 — 2-00111 / 237-5361
  Neil Stevens, prin.

Fallon, AC 702, PC 6, Churchill
Churchill County SD — 5-11111 / 423-5184
  545 E RICHARDS ST 89406
  Robert Quisenberry, supt.
Churchill County HS — 4-00011 / 423-2181
  1222 S TAYLOR ST 89406
  Dan Corcoran, prin.
Churchill County JHS — 3-00100 / 423-7701
  650 S MAINE ST 89406
  Thomas Brennan, prin.

Fernley, AC 702, PC 4, Lyon
Lyon County SD
  Supt. — See Yerington
HS, PO BOX 837 89408 — 2-00011 / 575-4439
  Carl Schaff, prin.
IS, PO BOX 835 89408 — 3-01100 / 789-1170
  Cheryl Sample, prin.

Gabbs, AC 702, PC 3, Nye
Nye County SD
  Supt. — See Tonopah
S, PO BOX 147 89409 — 2-11111 / 285-2692
  Gene Berg, prin.

Gardnerville, AC 702, PC 4, Douglas
Douglas County SD
  Supt. — See Minden
Carson Valley MS — 3-00100 / 782-2265
  PO BOX 157 89410
  Roger Gerson, prin.

Gerlach, AC 702, PC 2, Washoe
Washoe County SD
  Supt. — See Reno
JSHS, 555 E SUNSET BLVD 89412 — 1-00111 / 557-2326
  David Green, prin.

Hawthorne, AC 702, PC 5, Mineral
Mineral County SD — 4-11111 / 945-2403
  PO BOX 1540 89415
  Granville Gage, supt.
Mineral County HS — 2-00011 / 945-3332
  PO BOX 938 89415
  Joe Blaney, prin.

Henderson, AC 702, PC 8, Clark
Clark County SD
  Supt. — See Las Vegas
Basic HS, 400 PALO VERDE DR 89015 — 4-00011 / 799-8000
  Stephen Augspurger, prin.
Green Valley HS — 5-00011 / 799-0950
  460 ARROYO GRANDE BLVD 89014
  Carroll Johnston, prin.
Brown JHS, 307 CANNES ST 89015 — 3-00100 / 799-8900
  Emilio Fernandez, prin.

Burkholder JHS — 4-00100 / 799-8080
  355 W VAN WAGENEN ST 89015
  Janice Swartz, prin.
Greenspun JHS — 4-00100 / 799-0920
  140 VALLE VERDE DR 89014
  LeRoy Hurd, prin.
White JHS, 1661 GALLERIA DR 89014 — 4-00100 / 799-0777
  Frank Lamping, prin.

Incline Village, AC 702, PC 5, Washoe
Washoe County SD
  Supt. — See Reno
Incline HS, PO BOX 6860 89450 — 2-00011 / 832-4200
  Andrew Jezycki, prin.
Incline MS, PO BOX 7816 89452 — 2-00100 / 832-4220
  Burke Stancill, prin.

Sierra Nevada College-Lake Tahoe — 2-UC
PO BOX 4269 89450 — 800-332-8666

Indian Springs, AC 702, PC 4, Clark
Clark County SD
  Supt. — See Las Vegas
JSHS, PO BOX 539 89018 — 2-00111 / 382-8011
  Bob Chesto, prin.

Jackpot, AC 702, PC 3, Elko
Elko County SD
  Supt. — See Elko
JSHS, PO BOX 463 89825 — 2-00111 / 755-2374
  John Barrus, prin.

Jean, AC 702, PC 2, Clark
Clark County SD
  Supt. — See Las Vegas
Sandy Valley JHS — 1-00100 / 799-5344
  HC 70 BOX 111 89019
  Norman Parker, prin.

Las Vegas, AC 702, PC 10, Clark
Clark County SD — 9-11111 / 799-5310
  2832 E FLAMINGO RD 89121
  Dr. Brian Cram, supt.
Southern Nevada Vo-Tech HS — 4-00011 / 799-7500
  5710 MOUNTAIN VISTA ST 89120
  Daniel Berg, prin.
Bonanza HS, 6665 DEL REY AVE 89102 — 4-00011 / 799-4000
  Judy Cameron, prin.
Chaparral HS — 5-00011 / 799-7580
  3850 ANNIE OAKLEY DR 89121
  Mike West, prin.
Cimarron Memorial HS — 5-00011 / 799-4400
  2301 N TENAYA WAY 89128
  Ken Bedrosian, prin.
Clark HS, 4291 PENNWOOD AVE 89102 — 4-00011 / 799-5800
  Wayne Tanaka, prin.
Durango HS, 7100 W DEWEY DR 89113 — 4-00011 / 799-5850
  Allen Coles, prin.
Eldorado HS, 1139 LINN LN 89110 — 4-00011 / 799-7200
  Gail Dixon, prin.
Las Vegas Academy HS — 3-00011 / 799-7800
  315 S 7TH ST 89101 — Bob Gerye, prin.
Las Vegas HS — 4-00011 / 799-1080
  6500 E SAHARA AVE 89122
  Frank Brusa, prin.
Silverado HS — 3-00011 / 799-5790
  2832 E FLAMINGO RD 89121
  (—), prin.
Valley HS, 2839 BURNHAM AVE 89109 — 5-00011 / 799-5450
  Aldeane Ries, prin.
Western HS — 4-00011 / 799-4080
  4601 W BONANZA RD 89107
  Lanny Lund, prin.
Becker MS — 3-00100 / 799-4460
  9151 PINEWOOD HILLS DR 89134
  Cathy Andrews, prin.
Brinley JHS, 2480 MAVERICK ST 89108 — 4-00100 / 799-4550
  Alan McNulty, prin.
Cannon JHS, 5850 EUCLID ST 89120 — 4-00100 / 799-5600
  Chris Erbe, prin.
Cashman JHS — 4-00100 / 799-5880
  4622 W DESERT INN RD 89102
  Evans Rutledge, prin.
Fremont JHS — 4-00100 / 799-5558
  1100 E SAINT LOUIS AVE 89104
  Matti Smith, prin.
Garside JHS — 4-00100 / 799-4245
  300 S TORREY PINES DR 89107
  Marlin Nielsen, prin.
Gibson JHS — 4-00100 / 799-4700
  3900 W WASHINGTON AVE 89107
  Lois Venger, prin.
Guinn JHS — 3-00100 / 799-5900
  4150 S TORREY PINES DR 89103
  Shauna Zobel, prin.
Hyde Park JHS, 900 HINSON ST 89107 — 3-00100 / 799-4260
  Patricia LaMonica, prin.
Johnson JHS — 4-00100 / 799-4480
  7701 DUCHARME AVE 89128
  Paul Oisboid, prin.
Knudson JHS, 2400 ATLANTIC ST 89104 — 3-00100 / 799-7470
  S. Weiner, prin.
Martin JHS, 2800 STEWART AVE 89101 — 3-00100 / 799-7922
  John Kelley, prin.
O'Callaghan JHS — 4-00100 / 799-7340
  1450 RADWICK DR 89110
  Kay Samolovitch, prin.
Orr JHS, 1562 E KATIE AVE 89119 — 4-00100 / 799-5573
  Joe Pursell, prin.
Robison JHS, 825 MARION DR 89110 — 4-00100 / 799-7300
  Mary Ramirez, prin.
Sawyer MS, 5450 REDWOOD ST 89118 — 3-00100 / 799-5980
  Theresa Smith, prin.

Swainston MS — 4-00100 / 799-4860
  3500 W GILMORE AVE 89031
  Susan Overmoen, prin.
Woodbury JHS — 4-00100 / 799-7660
  3875 E HARMON AVE 89121
  Donald Cheneyworth, prin.
Other Schools — See Boulder City, Henderson, Indian Springs, Jean, Laughlin, Mesquite, North Las Vegas, Overton

American Academy for Career Education — 2-CS / 732-7748
  3120 E DESERT INN RD 89121
Bishop Gorman HS — 3-00011 / 732-1945
  1801 S MARYLAND PKY 89104
  David Erbach, prin.
Century Schools — 2-CS / 451-6666
  3075 E FLAMINGO RD STE 114 89121
Clark County Christian S — 2-11111 / 382-5998
  3005 CEDAR AVE 89101
  Elma Chenevert, prin.
Columbia School of Broadcasting — 2-HMS
  2840 E FLAMINGO RD STE F 89121
Education Dynamics Institute — 3-CC / 648-1522
  2635 N DECATUR BLVD 89108
Education Dynamics Institute — 2-CS / 731-6421
  953 E SAHARA AVE # 102 89104
Faith Lutheran HS — 2-00111 / 648-7047
  1251 ROBIN ST 89106
  Steven Glandorf, prin.
Interior Design Institute — 2-CS / 369-9944
  4225 S EASTERN AVE STE 4 89119
International Dealers School — 2-CS / 385-7665
  503 FREMONT ST 89101
Las Vegas Gaming & Technical School — 2-CS / 800-847-5484
  3030 S HIGHLAND DR 89109
Meadows S, 8601 SCHOLAR LN 89128 — 3-11111 / 254-1610
  William Richardson, prin.
Mountain View Christian S — 2-11111 / 452-1300
  3901 E BONANZA RD 89110
  Jeanne Truesdale, prin.
National Academy for Casino Dealers — 2-CS / 735-4884
  557 E SAHARA AVE STE 108 89104
PCI Dealers School — 2-CS / 877-4724
  920 S VALLEY VIEW BLVD 89107
Phillips Junior College — 2-CC / 434-0486
  3320 E FLAMINGO RD STE 30 89121
Professional Careers — 2-CS / 368-2338
  3305 SPRING MOUNTAIN RD 89102
Trinity Christian S — 2-11111 / 734-0562
  950 E SAINT LOUIS AVE 89104
  Walter Smith, prin.
University of Nevada Las Vegas — 7-UC / 800-334-8658
  4505 S MARYLAND PKY 89154
Vegas Career School — 2-CS / 362-8488
  1110 E CHARLESTON BLVD 89104

Laughlin, AC 702, PC 2, Clark
Clark County SD
  Supt. — See Las Vegas
JSHS, PO BOX 29190 89028 — 2-00111 / 298-1996
  Estella Hodgkin, prin.

Lovelock, AC 702, PC 4, Pershing
Pershing County SD — 3-11111 / 273-7819
  PO BOX 389 89419
  Daniel Fox, supt.
Pershing County HS — 2-00011 / 273-2625
  PO BOX 389 89419
  Ronald Beck, prin.
Pershing County MS — 2-00100 / 273-1200
  PO BOX 389 89419
  Anita Fisk, prin.

Lund, AC 702, PC 2, White Pine
White Pine County SD
  Supt. — See East Ely
JSHS, PO BOX 29 89317 — 1-00111 / 238-5273
  Jolynn Maynard, prin.

Mc Dermitt, AC 702, PC 2, Humboldt
Humboldt County SD
  Supt. — See Winnemucca
HS, PO BOX 98 89421 — 1-00011 / 532-8761
  Gerald Lugert, prin.

Mesquite, AC 702, PC 4, Clark
Clark County SD
  Supt. — See Las Vegas
Virgin Valley JSHS — 3-00111 / 346-2780
  GENERAL DELIVERY 89024
  John McLaren, prin.

Minden, AC 702, PC 4, Douglas
Douglas County SD — 6-11111 / 782-5134
  PO BOX 1888 89423
  Pendery Clark, supt.
Douglas HS, PO BOX 429 89423 — 4-00011 / 782-5136
  William Butler, prin.
Other Schools — See Gardnerville, Zephyr Cove

North Las Vegas, AC 702, PC 8, Clark
Clark County SD
  Supt. — See Las Vegas
Cheyenne HS — 4-00011 / 799-4830
  3200 W ALEXANDER RD 89030
  Richard Brown, prin.
Rancho HS, 1900 E OWENS AVE 89030 — 5-00011 / 799-7000
  Barry Gunderson, prin.

Area Tech Trade Ctr	Vo Tech	HS, 395 BOOTH ST 89509	4-00011
444 W BROOKS AVE 89030	799-8300	Patrick Rogan, prin.	333-5050
Michael Kinnaird, prin.		Wooster HS, 1331 E PLUMB LN 89502	4-00011
Bridger JHS, 2505 N BRUCE ST 89030	4-00100	Bernard Zunino, prin.	333-5100
Douglas Gougar, prin.	799-7185	Washoe JSHS, 777 W 2ND ST 89503	3-00111
Smith JHS, 1301 E TONOPAH AVE 89030	3-00100	Robert Floyd, prin.	333-5150
Sue DeFrancesco, prin.	799-7080	Hare Occupational Ctr	Vo Tech
Von Tobel JHS, 2436 N PECOS DR 89115	4-00100	350 HUNTER LAKE DR 89509	333-5380
Charles Jaurequi, prin.	799-7280	CAROL CHAPIN, prin.	

HS, 820 15TH ST 89431 — 4-00011 / Jan Shoemaker, prin. — 353-5550 / Dilworth MS, 255 PRATER WAY 89431 — 3-00100 / Gary Longson, prin. — 353-5740 / MS, 2275 18TH ST 89431 — 3-00100 / John Genasci, prin. — 353-5770

Community College of Southern Nevada	7-CC	Billinghurst MS	3-00100
3200 E CHEYENNE AVE 89030	643-6060	6685 CHESTERFIELD LN 89523	746-5870

Western Truck School — 2-CS / 39 GLEN CARRAN CIR 89431 — 331-4441

Overton, AC 702, PC 4, Clark
Clark County SD
Supt. — See Las Vegas
Moapa Valley HS 89040 — 2-00011 / Larry Moses, prin. — 397-2611
Lyon MS, 179 S ANDERSON 89040 — 2-00100 / Kate Christensen, prin. — 799-2611

Ken Vaughn, prin. — 746-5860
Clayton MS, 1295 WYOMING AVE 89503 — 3-00100 / Hank Vanderbeek, prin. — 746-5860
O'Brien MS, 10500 STEAD BLVD 89506 — 3-00100 / Gil Folk, prin. — 677-5420
Pine MS, 4800 NEIL RD 89502 — 3-00100 / Dan Garfinkle, prin. — 689-2500

Tonopah, AC 702, PC 5, Nye
Nye County SD, PO BOX 113 89049 — 5-11111 / Robert Ragar, supt. — 482-6258
HS, PO BOX 2001 89049 — 2-00011 / Ray DePalma, prin. — 482-3698
Other Schools – See Beatty, Gabbs, Pahrump, Round Mountain

Owyhee, AC 702, PC 3, Elko
Elko County SD
Supt. — See Elko
JSHS, PO BOX 100 89832 — 2-00111 / Gloria Jim, prin. — 757-3400

Swope MS, 901 KEELE DR 89509 — 3-00100 / William Campbell, prin. — 333-5330
Traner MS, 1700 CARVILLE DR 89512 — 3-00100 / Raul Hernandez, prin. — 333-5130
Vaughn MS, 1200 BRESSON AVE 89502 — 3-00100 / Deborah Cylke, prin. — 333-5160
Other Schools – See Gerlach, Incline Village, Sparks

Virginia City, AC 702, PC 3, Storey
Storey County SD, PO BOX C 89440 — 2-11111 / William Kolton, supt. — 847-0983
HS, GENERAL DELIVERY 89440 — 2-00011 / Daniel Piel, prin. — 847-0992
MS, 127 S D ST 89440 — 1-00100 / Melinda Johnson, prin. — 847-0980

Pahrump, AC 702, PC 4, Nye
Nye County SD
Supt. — See Tonopah
HS, PO BOX 610 89041 — 3-00011 / Ron Eason, prin. — 727-7737
JHS, PO BOX 3380 89041 — 2-00100 / Selway Mulkey, prin. — 727-5546

Bishop Manogue HS — 2-00011 / 400 BARTLETT ST 89512 — 329-0011 / Robert Sullivan, prin.
Career College of Northern Nevada — 2-CC / 1195A CORPORATE BLVD 89502 — 856-2266
International Dealers School — 2-CS / 1055 S VIRGINIA ST 89502 — 322-8330

Wells, AC 702, PC 4, Elko
Elko County SD
Supt. — See Elko
JSHS, PO BOX 338 89835 — 2-00111 / Theodore Paulson, prin. — 752-3477

Panaca, AC 702, PC 3, Lincoln
Lincoln County SD — 4-11111
PO BOX 118 89042 — 728-4471 / D. Francom, supt.
Lincoln County HS — 2-00011
PO BOX 268 89042 — 728-4481 / N. Lorell Bleak, prin.
Meadow Valley MS — 2-00100
PO BOX 567 89042 — 728-4655 / Willard Phillips, prin.
Other Schools – See Alamo

Morrison College — 3-UC / 140 WASHINGTON ST 89503 — 323-4145
Truckee Meadows Community College — 6-CC / 7000 DANDINI BLVD 89512 — 673-7040
University of Nevada 89557 — 7-UC / 784-6865

Winnemucca, AC 702, PC 6, Humboldt
Humboldt County SD — 5-11111
PO BOX 1070 89446 — 623-8100 / Kenneth Lords, supt.
Lowry HS, PO BOX 831 89446 — 3-00011 / Ronald Mullanix, prin. — 623-8130
JHS, 451 REINHART ST 89445 — 3-00100 / Peter Stein, prin. — 623-8120
Other Schools – See Mc Dermitt

Round Mountain, AC 702, PC 2, Nye
Nye County SD
Supt. — See Tonopah
JSHS, PO BOX 777 89045 — 2-00111 / Clarence Price, prin. — 377-2690

Reno, AC 702, PC 9, Washoe
Washoe County SD, 425 E 9TH ST 89512 — 8-11111 / Mary Nebgen, supt. — 348-0200
Galena HS — 4-00011 / 3600 BUTCH CASSIDY WAY 89511 — 851-5630 / Jaculine Jones, prin.
Hug HS, 2880 SUTRO ST 89512 — 4-00011 / Steven Hull, prin. — 333-5300
McQueen HS, 6055 LANCER ST 89523 — 4-00011 / Mike Whellams, prin. — 746-5880

Smith, AC 702, PC 2, Lyon
Lyon County SD
Supt. — See Yerington
Smith Valley JSHS, PO BOX 30 89430 — 2-00111 / Arnold Locklear, prin. — 465-2332

Yerington, AC 702, PC 4, Lyon
Lyon County SD — 6-11111
25 JOE PARR WAY 89447 — 463-2205 / Nat Lommori, supt.
HS, 114 PEARL ST 89447 — 2-00011 / Daryl Hart, prin. — 463-2203
IS, 215 PEARL ST 89447 — 2-01100 / John Prida, prin. — 463-3506
Other Schools – See Dayton, Fernley, Smith

Sparks, AC 702, PC 8, Washoe
Washoe County SD
Supt. — See Reno
Reed HS, 1350 BARING BLVD 89434 — 4-00011 / Thomas Griffin, prin. — 353-5700

Zephyr Cove, AC 702, PC 4, Douglas
Douglas County SD
Supt. — See Minden
Whittell HS, PO BOX 677 89448 — 2-00011 / David Sheets, prin. — 588-2446
Kingsbury MS, PO BOX 648 89448 — 2-01100 / Beverle Pine, prin. — 588-6281

NEW HAMPSHIRE

STATE DEPARTMENT OF EDUCATION
State Office Park South
101 Pleasant St., Concord 03301
(603) 271-3494

Commissioner of Education	Charles Marston
Deputy Commissioner	Elizabeth Twomey
Director Division of Instructional Services	Paul Fillion
Director Division of Standards & Certification	Judith Fillion
Director Division of Vocational Rehabilitation	Bruce Archambault

STATE BOARD OF EDUCATION
101 Pleasant St., Concord 03301

Chairperson	Judith Thayer

PUBLIC, PRIVATE AND CATHOLIC SECONDARY SCHOOLS

Allenstown, AC 603, PC 2, Merrimack
School Administrative Unit 53
Supt. — See Pembroke
Dupont MS, 10 SCHOOL ST 03275   2-01100
Frederick Dunlop, prin.   485-4474

Alstead, AC 603, PC 3, Cheshire
School Administrative Unit 60
Supt. — See Charlestown
Fall Mountain Regional HS   2-00011
RR 1 BOX 89 03602   835-6318
Jeff Taylor, prin.
Vilas MS, PO BOX 98 03602   2-00100
Douglas Hubbell, prin.   835-6351

Alton, AC 603, PC 3, Belknap
School Administrative Unit 51
Supt. — See Center Barnstead
Alton Central S, PO BOX 910 03809   3-11111
George Rogers, prin.   875-7500

Amherst, AC 603, PC 3, Hillsborough
School Administrative Unit 39   4-11111
PO BOX 849 03031   673-2690
Richard Lalley, supt.
Souhegan Corp. HS   3-00011
412 BOSTON POST RD 03031   673-9940
Mackin Robert, prin.
MS, PO BOX 966 03031   3-01100
Paul Collins, prin.   673-8944

Andover, AC 603, PC 2, Merrimack

Proctor Academy, PO BOX 500 03216   2-00011
David Fowler, prin.   735-5126

Antrim, AC 603, PC 4, Hillsborough
School Administrative Unit 1
Supt. — See Peterborough
Great Brook MS, SUMMER ST 03440   2-01100
Richard Nannicelli, prin.   588-6630

Barrington, AC 603, PC 3, Strafford
School Administrative Unit 44
Supt. — See Strafford
MS, HCR 03825   2-01100
John Freeman, prin.   664-2127

Bedford, AC 603, PC 4, Hillsborough
School Administrative Unit 25   4-11100
103 COUNTY RD UNIT 25 03110   472-3755
Dennis Pope, supt.
McKelvie MS   3-01100
108 LIBERTY HILL RD 03110   472-3951
Arnold MacDonald, prin.

Belmont, AC 603, PC 3, Belknap
School Administrative Unit 46
Supt. — See Penacook
Belmont Memorial JSHS   3-00111
SCHOOL ST 03220   267-6525
Robert Norton, prin.

Berlin, AC 603, PC 7, Coos
School Administrative Unit 3   4-11111
183 HILLSIDE AVE 03570   752-6500
Richard Steudle, supt.
HS, 550 WILLARD ST 03570   3-00011
R. Bruce MacKay, prin.   752-4122
MS, 200 STATE ST 03570   3-01100
Anthony Urban, prin.   752-5311

New Hampshire Technical College   2-CC
2020 RIVERSIDE DR 03570   752-1113

Bethlehem, AC 603, PC 3, Grafton
School Administrative Unit 35
Supt. — See Littleton
Profile JSHS, RR 1 BOX 418 03574   2-00111
Stephen North, prin.   823-7411

Bow, AC 603, PC 3, Merrimack
School Administrative Unit 19
Supt. — See Goffstown
Bow Memorial JHS   2-01110
20 BOW CENTER RD 03304   225-3212
Kirk Spofford, prin.

Bristol, AC 603, PC 4, Grafton
School Administrative Unit 4   4-11111
5 N MAIN ST UNIT 4 03222   744-5555
John Davis, supt.
Newfound Regional HS   2-00011
NEWFOUND RD 03222   744-6006
Gail Sullivan, prin.
Newfound Memorial MS, LAKE ST 03222   3-01100
Archie Auger, prin.   744-8162

Canaan, AC 603, PC 3, Grafton
School Administrative Unit 62
Supt. — See Enfield
Mascoma Valley Regional HS   2-00011
RR 1 BOX 168A 03741   632-4308
Deborah Scheer, prin.
Indian River MS   2-01100
RR 1 BOX 169 03741   632-4357
Andrew Mellow, prin.

Cardigan Mountain S   2-00110
PO BOX 58 03741   523-4321
Cameron Dewar, prin.

Center Barnstead, AC 603, PC 2, Belknap
School Administrative Unit 51   4-11111
PO BOX 220 03225   269-8200
Elaine Brigman, supt.
Other Schools — See Alton, Pittsfield

Charlestown, AC 603, PC 4, Sullivan
School Administrative Unit 60   4-11111
PO BOX 600 03603   826-7756
Leo Corriveau, supt.
MS, S MAIN ST 03603   2-00100
Wayne Evans, prin.   826-7711
Other Schools — See Alstead, Walpole

Chester, AC 603, PC 3, Rockingham

White Pines College   1-CC
40 CHESTER ST 03036   887-4401

Claremont, AC 603, PC 7, Sullivan
School Administrative Unit 6   5-11111
165 BROAD ST 03743   543-4200
Barbara Krysiak, supt.
Stevens HS, 175 BROAD ST 03743   3-00011
Carol Curtis, prin.   542-4931
MS, 107 SOUTH ST 03743   2-00100
Mark Elgart, prin.   543-3392

New Hampshire Technical College   2-CC
1 COLLEGE DR 03743   542-7744

Colebrook, AC 603, PC 4, Coos
School Administrative Unit 7   3-11111
3 ACADEMY ST 03576   237-5571
Paul Allen, supt.
Colebrook Academy   2-00011
1 ACADEMY ST 03576   237-4280
Robert Mills, prin.
MS, 166 MAIN ST 03576   2-00100
Patricia Callioras, prin.   237-4801
Other Schools — See Pittsburg, West Stewartstown

Concord, AC 603, PC 8, Merrimack
School Administrative Unit 8   6-11111
16 RUMFORD ST 03301   225-0811
Curtis Sokness, supt.
SHS, 170 WARREN ST 03301   4-00001
Christine Rath, prin.   225-0800
Rundlett JHS, 152 SOUTH ST 03301   4-00110
Pam Melanson, prin.   225-0862

Bishop Brady HS   2-00011
25 COLUMBUS AVE 03301   224-7418
Jean Barker, prin.
Concord Christian S   2-11111
20 N STATE ST 03301   224-7428
Bernard Cornell, prin.
Franklin Pierce College   2-UC
130 PEMBROKE RD 03301
Franklin Pierce Law Center   2-UC
2 WHITE ST 03301   228-1541
New Hampshire Technical Institute   4-CC
PO BOX 2039 03302   225-1800
St. Paul's S, 325 PLEASANT ST 03301   2-00011
David Hicks, prin.   225-3341

Contoocook, AC 603, PC 4, Merrimack
School Administrative Unit 66
Supt. — See Hopkinton
Hopkinton JSHS, 27A PARK AVE 03229   2-00111
James Gorman, prin.   746-4167

Conway, AC 603, PC 4, Carroll
School Administrative Unit 9
Supt. — See North Conway
Kennett JSHS, 176 MAIN ST 03818   3-00111
Lawrence Urda, prin.   447-6364

Derry, AC 603, PC 7, Rockingham
Approved Public Academies   5-00011
PINKERTON ST 03038   432-2588
Bradford Ek, supt.
Pinkerton Academy   5-00011
PINKERTON ST 03038   432-2588
Bradford Ek, prin.

School Administrative Unit 10   5-11100
18 S MAIN ST 03038   432-1210
David Brown, supt.
Hood Memorial JHS, 15 HOOD RD 03038   3-00100
Kathleen Murphy, prin.   432-1224

Calvary Christian S   2-11111
PO BOX 303 03038   434-1501
Donald Batchelder, prin.

Dover, AC 603, PC 8, Strafford
School Administrative Unit 11   5-11111
288 CENTRAL AVE 03820   742-6400
Gerald Daley, supt.
HS, 25 ALUMNI DR 03820   4-00011
Gregory Kageleiry, prin.   742-3176
JHS, 61 LOCUST ST 03820   3-00100
Paul Mauceri, prin.   742-3172

McIntosh College   3-CC
23 CATARACT AVE 03820   742-3518
St. Thomas Aquinas HS   3-00011
197 DOVER POINT RD 03820   742-3206
Brian Newhall, prin.

Dublin, AC 603, PC 3, Cheshire

Dublin Christian Academy   2-11111
PO BOX 521 03444   563-8505
Melvin Moody, prin.
Dublin S, PO BOX 77 03444   2-00011
Samuel Eliot, prin.   563-8584

Durham, AC 603, PC 6, Strafford
School Administrative Unit 5   4-11111
36 COE DR 03824 – John Powers, supt.   868-5100
Oyster River HS, 99 COE DR 03824   2-00011
Ann Brown, prin.   868-2838
Oyster River MS   2-00100
47 GARRISON AVE 03824   868-2820
Donald Wilson, prin.

School for Lifelong Learning 03824   4-UC
   862-1692
University of New Hampshire 03824   7-UC
   862-2263

East Swanzey, AC 603, PC 99, Cheshire
School Administrative Unit 38   5-11111
600 OLD HOMESTEAD HWY UNIT 03446
William Wheeler, supt.   352-6955
Monadnock Regional JSHS   4-00111
580 OLD HOMESTEAD HWY 03446   352-6575
Daniel Stockwell, prin.
Other Schools — See Hinsdale, Winchester

Enfield, AC 603, PC 4, Grafton
School Administrative Unit 62   4-11111
PO BOX 789 03748   632-5563
Keith Pfeifer, supt.
Other Schools — See Canaan

Epping, AC 603, PC 4, Rockingham
School Administrative Unit 14   4-11111
213 MAIN ST 03042   679-5402
Robert Retchless, supt.
JSHS, ACADEMY ST 03042   2-00111
Victor Petzy, prin.   679-5472

Exeter, AC 603, PC 6, Rockingham
School Administrative Unit 16   5-11111
24 FRONT ST 03833   772-4040
William Clancy, supt.
Exeter Area HS, 30 LINDEN ST 03833   3-00011
Walter Borkowski, prin.   778-7772
Exeter Area JHS, 30 LINDEN ST 03833   3-00100
Thomas Meehan, prin.   778-7772

Phillips Exeter Academy   4-00011
20 MAIN ST 03833   772-4311
Kendra O'Donnell, prin.

Farmington, AC 603, PC 5, Strafford
School Administrative Unit 61   4-11111
MEMORIAL DR 03835   755-2627
Robin Leveille, supt.
Farmington HS, MEMORIAL DR 03835   2-00011
John Graziano, prin.   755-2811
Main Street MS, 41 S MAIN ST 03835   2-00100
William Patison, prin.   755-2181

Franklin, AC 603, PC 6, Merrimack
School Administrative Unit 18   4-11111
119 CENTRAL ST 03235   934-3108
Edgar Melanson, supt.
HS, 115 CENTRAL ST 03235   2-00111
Jonathan Freeman, prin.   934-5441
MS, 200 SANBORN ST 03235   2-01100
Barry Albert, prin.   934-5829

Sant Bani S, RR 1 03235   2-11111
Kent Bicknell, prin.   934-4240

Gilford, AC 603, PC 2, Belknap
School Administrative Unit 30
Supt. — See Laconia
JSHS, 88 ALVAH WILSON RD 03246   3-00111
Don Engelbert, prin.   524-7135

Goffstown, AC 603, PC 7, Hillsboro
School Administrative Unit 19   5-11111
11 SCHOOL ST UNIT 19 03045   497-4818
Owen Conway, supt.
HS, 27 WALLACE RD 03045   3-00011
William Marston, prin.   497-4841
Mountain View MS   4-01100
41 LAUREN LN 03045   487-8288
Stephen O'Neil, prin.
Other Schools — See Bow

Gorham, AC 603, PC 4, Coos
School Administrative Unit 20   3-11111
115 MAIN ST UNIT 20 03581   466-3632
Daniel Whitaker, supt.
JSHS, 120 MAIN ST 03581   2-00111
James Hunt, prin.   466-2776

Groveton, AC 603, PC 4, Coos
School Administrative Unit 58   3-11111
8 PREBLE ST 03582   636-1437
Alfred St. Cyr, supt.
JSHS, 38 STATE ST 03582   2-00111
Frederick Bailey, prin.   636-1619
Other Schools — See North Stratford

Hampstead, AC 603, PC 3, Rockingham
School Administrative Unit 55
Supt. — See Plaistow

MS, 28 HEATH RD   03841   2-01100
  Robert Little, prin.   329-6743

Hampton, AC 603, PC 6, Rockingham
School Administrative Unit 21   5-11111
  ALUMNI DRIVE   03842   926-8992
  James Weiss, supt.
Winnacunnet HS, 1 ALUMNI DR   03842   3-00011
  Roberta Neuman, prin.   926-3395
Hampton Academy JHS   2-01100
  29 ACADEMY AVE   03842   926-2000
  Patricia Goyette, prin.

Hanover, AC 603, PC 6, Grafton
School Administrative Unit 22   4-11111
  41 LEBANON ST UNIT 22   03755   643-6050
  Joseph Della Badia, supt.
HS, 41 LEBANON ST   03755   3-00011
  Uwe Bagnato, prin.   643-3431
Richmond MS, 35 LEBANON ST   03755   2-00100
  Susan Finer, prin.   643-6040
Other Schools – See Orford

Dartmouth College   03755   6-UC
  228-1541

Henniker, AC 603, PC 4, Merrimack
School Administrative Unit 24   4-11111
  PO BOX 516   03242   428-3269
  Donald Jones, supt.
Cogswell Memorial MS   2-01100
  PO BOX 585   03242   428-3476
  Fred Roberts, prin.
Other Schools – See Weare

New England College   4-UC
  26 BRIDGE ST   03242   428-2211

Hillsborough, AC 603, PC 4, Hillsboro
School Administrative Unit 34   4-11111
  PO BOX 893   03244   464-4466
  Arthur Tate, supt.
Hillsboro-Deering HS   2-00011
  12 HILLCAT DR   03244   464-4555
  Patrick O'Shea, prin.
Hillsboro-Deering MS   2-01100
  SCHOOL STREET   03244   464-5904
  Barry Ring, prin.

Hinsdale, AC 603, PC 4, Cheshire
School Administrative Unit 38
  Supt. – See East Swanzey
JSHS, PO BOX 46   03451   2-00111
  Michael Abbott, prin.   336-5984

Hollis, AC 603, PC 3, Hillsboro
School Administrative Unit 41   4-11111
  PO BOX 1588   03049   465-7118
  Damon Russell, supt.
Hollis/Brookline HS, 25 MAIN ST   03049   2-00011
  Denis Joy, prin.   465-2269
Hollis/Brookline JHS   2-00100
  12 DRURY LN   03049   465-2233
  Robert McGittigan, prin.

Hooksett, AC 603, PC 5, Merrimack
School Administrative Unit 15   4-11100
  90 FARMER RD   03106   622-3731
  Paul Fillion, supt.
Hooksett-Memorial JHS   2-00100
  1550 HOOKSETT RD   03106   485-9959
  Robert Suprenant, prin.

Hopkinton, AC 603, PC 2, Merrimack
School Administrative Unit 66   3-11111
  271 MAIN ST STE 1   03229   746-5186
  Ed McHale, supt.
Other Schools – See Contoocook

Hudson, AC 603, PC 6, Hillsborough
School Administrative Unit 27   5-11111
  20 LIBRARY ST   03051   883-7765
  Peter Dolloff, supt.
Alvirne HS, 200 DERRY ST   03051   4-00011
  G. Leonard Nase, prin.   886-1260
Hudson Memorial MS   4-01100
  1 MEMORIAL DR   03051   886-1240
  Barbara Stone, prin.
Litchfield MS, MCELWAIN DR   03051   2-00100
  Francis Flood, prin.   886-1267

Jaffrey, AC 603, PC 5, Cheshire
School Administrative Unit 47   4-11111
  41 MAIN ST UNIT 47   03452   532-8100
  John Wheeler, supt.
Conant HS, 109 STRATTON RD   03452   2-00011
  Thomas Brennan, prin.   532-8131
Jaffrey-Rindge MS   2-00100
  109 STRATTON RD   03452   532-8122
  Timothy Woodward, prin.

Keene, AC 603, PC 7, Cheshire
School Administrative Unit 29   5-11111
  34 WEST ST   03431   357-9002
  Phillip McCormack, supt.
HS, 43 ARCH ST   03431   4-00011
  Richard Larcom, prin.   352-0640
JHS, 17 WASHINGTON ST   03431   3-00100
  Jonathan Proctor, prin.   352-5830

Antioch New England   2-UC
  40 AVON ST   03431   357-3122
Franklin Pierce College   2-UC
  43 ARCH ST   03431

Keene State College   5-UC
  229 MAIN ST   03435   358-2276

Kingston, AC 603, PC 2, Rockingham
School Administrative Unit 17   4-11111
  178 MAIN ST UNIT 17   03848   642-3688
  John Handfield, supt.
Sanborn Regional HS   3-00011
  13 CHURCH ST   03848   642-3341
  Victor Daly, prin.
Other Schools – See Newton Junction

Laconia, AC 603, PC 7, Belknap
School Administrative Unit 30   5-11111
  PO BOX 309   03247   524-5710
  Richard Ayers, supt.
HS, 345 UNION AVE   03246   3-00011
  Robert St. Lawrence, prin.   524-3350
Memorial MS, 150 MCGRATH ST   03246   3-00100
  Douglas Whittum, prin.   524-4632
Other Schools – See Gilford

Laconia Christian S   2-11111
  RR 3 BOX 50   03246   524-3250
  David Borchers, prin.
New Hampshire Technical College   3-CC
  PRESCOTT HILL   03246   524-3207

Lebanon, AC 603, PC 7, Grafton
School Administrative Unit 32   5-11111
  PO BOX 488   03766   448-1634
  John Fontana, supt.
Other Schools – See West Lebanon

Lebanon College   2-CC
  1 COURT ST   03766   448-2445

Lincoln, AC 603, PC 3, Grafton
School Administrative Unit 23
  Supt. — See Woodsville
Lin-Wood S, PO BOX 97   03251   2-11111
  Michael Morgan, prin.   745-2214

Lisbon, AC 603, PC 4, Grafton
School Administrative Unit 35
  Supt. — See Littleton
Lisbon Regional S   2-11111
  24 HIGHLAND AVE   03585   838-5506
  Glenn Stillings, prin.

Littleton, AC 603, PC 5, Grafton
School Administrative Unit 35   4-11111
  30 MAPLE ST   03561   444-3925
  Robert Horan, supt.
HS, SCHOOL ST   03561   2-00011
  Robert Morrill, prin.   444-5601
Bronson JHS, HIGH ST   03561   2-00100
  Robert Morrill, prin.   444-3361
Other Schools – See Bethlehem, Lisbon

White Mountain S   1-00011
  W FARM ROAD   03561   444-2928
  Chris Landry, prin.

Londonderry, AC 603, PC 3, Rockingham
School Administrative Unit 12   5-11111
  268 MAMMOTH RD   03053   432-6920
  Arthur Ouillette, supt.
HS, 295 MAMMOTH RD   03053   4-00011
  Edmond Thibodeau, prin.   432-6941
JHS, 313 MAMMOTH RD   03053   3-00100
  Nancy Meyers, prin.   432-6925

Victory Christian S   2-11111
  42 MAMMOTH RD   03053   434-2237
  Bruce Richards, prin.

Manchester, AC 603, PC 8, Hillsborough
School Administrative Unit 37   7-11111
  196 BRIDGE ST   03104   624-6300
  Leonard Bernard, supt.
Manchester Central HS   4-00011
  207 LOWELL ST   03104   624-6363
  William Burns, prin.
Manchester Memorial HS   4-00011
  403 S PORTER ST   03103   624-6378
  Ray Downton, prin.
Manchester West HS   4-00011
  9 NOTRE DAME AVE   03102   624-6384
  Robert Baines, prin.
Hillside JHS, 112 RESERVOIR AVE   03104   3-00100
  Wendy Jack, prin.   624-6352
Parkside JHS, 75 PARKSIDE AVE   03102   3-00100
  Edward Wade, prin.   624-6356
Southside JHS, 140 S JEWETT ST   03103   3-00100
  David Messier, prin.   624-6359

Derryfield S, 2108 RIVER RD   03104   2-00111
  Nancy Boettiger, prin.   669-4524
Hesser College   4-CC
  3 SUNDIAL AVE   03103   668-6660
New Hampshire College   5-UC
  2500 RIVER RD   03106   645-9611
New Hampshire Technical College   4-CC
  1066 FRONT ST   03102   668-6706
Northeast Career Schools   2-CS
  749 E INDUSTRIAL PARK DR   03109   669-1151
Notre Dame College   3-UC
  2321 ELM ST   03104   669-4298
St. Anselm College   4-UC
  87 SAINT ANSELMS DR   03102   641-7084
St. Joseph JHS, 460 PINE ST   03104   2-00100
  Sr. Barbara McLean, prin.   624-4811

Trinity HS, 581 BRIDGE ST   03104   2-00011
  Br. Lunny, prin.   668-2910
University of New Hampshire   2-UC
  220 HACKETT HILL RD   03102   668-0700

Meredith, AC 603, PC 4, Belknap
School Administrative Unit 2   4-11111
  103 MAIN ST STE 2   03253   279-7947
  Gary Burton, supt.
Inter-Lakes JSHS, 1 LAKER LN   03253   2-00111
  Robert Braman, prin.   279-6162

Meriden, AC 603, PC 3, Sullivan

Kimball Union Academy   2-00011
  PO BOX 188   03770   469-3211
  Timothy Knox, prin.

Merrimack, AC 603, PC 4, Hillsborough
School Administrative Unit 26   5-11111
  36 MCELWAIN ST   03054   424-6200
  James O'Neil, supt.
HS, 38 MCELWAIN ST   03054   4-00011
  Timothy Mayes, prin.   424-6204
Mastricola MS   4-00100
  26 BABOOSIC LAKE RD   03054   424-6221
  Kenneth Taylor, prin.

Milford, AC 603, PC 6, Hillsborough
School Administrative Unit 40   5-11111
  100 WEST ST UNIT 40   03055   673-2202
  Elizabeth McCoy, supt.
Milford Area HS, 100 WEST ST   03055   3-00011
  James Hayes, prin.   673-4201
Milford Area MS, OSGOOD ROAD   03055   3-01100
  James Stetson, prin.   673-5221

Milton, AC 603, PC 4, Strafford
School Administrative Unit 64
  Supt. — See Union
Nute JSHS, FARMINGTON ROAD   03851   2-00111
  Donald Desmarais, prin.   652-4591

Moultonborough, AC 603, PC 2, Carroll
School Administrative Unit 45   3-11111
  PO BOX 419   03254   476-5247
  Kenneth Greenbaum, supt.
Moultonborough Academy   2-00111
  PO BOX 228   03254   476-5517
  Thomas Tunny, prin.

Nashua, AC 603, PC 8, Hillsborough
School Administrative Unit 42   7-11111
  PO BOX 687   03061   594-4300
  Berard Masse, supt.
SHS, 25 RIVERSIDE DR   03062   4-00001
  Ronald Jean, prin.   594-4311
Elm Street JHS, 105 ELM ST   03060   4-00110
  Pauline Caron, prin.   594-4322
Fairground JHS   3-00110
  27 CLEVELAND ST   03060   594-4393
  John Daniels, prin.
Pennichuck JHS   3-00110
  207 MANCHESTER ST   03060   594-4308
  Ernest Mercier, prin.

Bishop Guertin HS, 194 LUND RD   03060   3-00011
  Br. Labbe, prin.   889-4107
Daniel Webster College   3-UC
  20 UNIVERSITY DR   03063   883-3556
Franklin Pierce College   2-UC
  20 COTTON RD   03063
Nashua Catholic JHS   2-00110
  6 BARTLETT AVE   03060   882-7011
  George Lavoice, prin.
New Hampshire Technical College   3-CC
  505 AMHERST ST   03063   882-6923
Rivier College   4-UC
  420 S MAIN ST   03060   888-1311

New Hampton, AC 603, PC 2, Belknap

New Hampton S, PO BOX 579   03256   2-00011
  Jeffrey Beedy, prin.   744-5401

New Ipswich, AC 603, PC 3, Hillsborough
School Administrative Unit 63
  Supt. — See Wilton
Mascenic Regional HS   2-00011
  TURNPIKE ROAD   03071   878-1113
  Robin Pierce, prin.
Boynton MS, ROUTE 124   03071   2-01100
  David Dube, prin.   878-4800

New London, AC 603, PC 4, Merrimack
School Administrative Unit 65   4-11111
  190 MAIN ST UNIT 65   03257   526-2051
  Jean Richards, supt.
Kearsarge Regional MS   2-00100
  PO BOX 2330   03257   526-6415
  Thomas Poliseno, prin.
Other Schools – See North Sutton

Colby-Sawyer College   2-UC
  100 MAIN ST   03257   526-2010

Newmarket, AC 603, PC 5, Rockingham
School Administrative Unit 31   3-11111
  211 S MAIN ST   03857   659-5020
  Chadwick Chase, supt.
Newmarket Central JSHS   2-00111
  213 S MAIN ST   03857   659-3271
  Ann Papagiotas, prin.

Newport, AC 603, PC 5, Sullivan
School Administrative Unit 43   4-11111
  15 SUNAPEE ST UNIT 43   03773   863-3540
  Elizabeth Durocher, supt.
JSHS, 245 S MAIN ST   03773   3-00111
  Edward Gallagher, prin.   863-2414
Other Schools – See Sunapee

Newton Junction, AC 603, PC 2, Rockingham
School Administrative Unit 17
  Supt. — See Kingston
Sanborn Regional MS   2-00100
  31A W MAIN ST   03859   382-6226
  Gardner Hurlburt, prin.

North Conway, AC 603, PC 4, Carroll
School Administrative Unit 9   4-11111
  19 PINE ST UNIT 9   03860   356-5534
  Harry Benson, supt.
Other Schools – See Conway

North Haverhill, AC 603, PC 2, Grafton
School Administrative Unit 23
  Supt. — See Woodsville
Haverhill Cooperative MS   2-01100
  PO BOX 207A   03774   787-2100
  Donald Weisburger, prin.

North Stratford, AC 603, PC 3, Coos
School Administrative Unit 58
  Supt. — See Groveton
Stratford S   03590   2-11111
  David Ross, prin.   922-3387

North Sutton, AC 603, PC 2, Merrimack
School Administrative Unit 65
  Supt. — See New London
Kearsage Regional HS   2-00011
  NORTH ROAD   03260 – Paul Ezen, prin.   927-4261

Northwood, AC 603, PC 2, Rockingham
Approved Public Academies   2-00011
  RR 4   03261 – David Smith, supt.   942-5531
Coe Brown Academy, RR 4   03261   2-00011
  David Smith, prin.   942-5531

Orford, AC 603, PC 2, Grafton
School Administrative Unit 22
  Supt. — See Hanover
S, RR 1 BOX 82B   03777   2-11111
  Patricia Davenport, prin.   353-4321

Pelham, AC 603, PC 3, Hillsborough
School Administrative Unit 28
  Supt. — See Windham
HS, 85 MARSH RD   03076   2-00011
  Robert Pedersen, prin.   635-2115
Pelham Memorial MS   3-01100
  59 MARSH RD   03076   635-2321
  Dennis Goyette, prin.

Pembroke, AC 603, PC 99, Suncook
School Administrative Unit 53   5-11111
  267 PEMBROKE ST UNIT 53   03275   485-5188
  Paul Deminico, supt.
Pembroke Academy   3-00011
  209 ACADEMY RD   03275   485-7881
  George Edwards, prin.
Three Rivers MS, ACADEMY ST   03275   2-01100
  Allen Zipke, prin.   485-9539
Other Schools – See Allenstown

Penacook, AC 603, PC see Concord
School Administrative Unit 46   5-11111
  105 CENTER ST   03303   753-6561
  Phillip Bell, supt.
Merrimack Valley HS   3-00011
  163 S MAIN ST   03303   753-4311
  Pamela Burke, prin.
Merrimack Valley MS   3-00100
  14 ALLEN ST   03303   753-6336
  Harvey Burke, prin.
Other Schools – See Belmont

Peterborough, AC 603, PC 5, Hillsborough
School Administrative Unit 1   4-11111
  ROUTE 202 N   03458   924-3336
  Larry Bramblett, supt.
Conval Regional HS   3-00011
  184 ROUTE 202 N   03458   924-3869
  William Breiner, prin.
Other Schools – See Antrim, Pittsburg

Pittsburg, AC 603, PC 2, Coos
School Administrative Unit 7
  Supt. — See Colebrook
S, RR 1 BOX 1   03592   2-11111
  Norma Chenevert, prin.   538-6996

School Administrative Unit 1
  Supt. — See Peterborough
South Meadow MS, ROUTE 202 N   03458   3-01100
  Howard Gilmore, prin.   924-7105

Pittsfield, AC 603, PC 4, Merrimack
School Administrative Unit 51
  Supt. — See Center Barnstead
HS, 5 ONEIDA ST   03263   2-00011
  Robert Simpson, prin.   435-6701
Pittsfield MS, ONEIDA ST   03263   2-00100
  Robert Simpson, prin.   435-6701

Plaistow, AC 603, PC 4, Rockingham
School Administrative Unit 55   5-11111
  30 GREENOUGH RD   03865   382-6119
  Terrance Holmes, supt.

Timberlane Regional HS   3-00011
  36 GREENOUGH RD   03865   382-6541
  William Mealey, prin.
Timberlane Regional MS   3-00100
  44 GREENOUGH RD   03865   382-7131
  Judith DeShaies, prin.
Other Schools – See Hampstead

Plymouth, AC 603, PC 5, Grafton
School Administrative Unit 48   4-11111
  3 OLD WARDBRIDGE RD UNIT 48   03264   536-1254
  John True, supt.
Plymouth Regional HS   3-00011
  1 OLD WARDBRIDGE RD   03264   536-1444
  Mary Cronin, prin.

Calvary Christian S   2-11111
  RR 4 BOX 740   03264   536-4022
  Norman Fuller, prin.
Holderness S, RR 3   03264   2-00011
  Rev. Brinton Woodward, prin.   536-1257
Plymouth State College   03264   5-UC
   535-2237

Portsmouth, AC 603, PC 8, Rockingham
School Administrative Unit 52   5-11111
  50 CLOUGH DR   03801   436-7100
  Nathan Greenberg, supt.
HS, 50 ALUMNI DR   03801   3-00011
  David Matthews, prin.   436-7100
MS, 155 PARROTT AVE   03801   3-00100
  John Stokel, prin.   436-7100

Franklin Pierce College   2-UC
  PO BOX 3060   03802

Raymond, AC 603, PC 5, Rockingham
School Administrative Unit 33   4-11111
  43 HARRIMAN HILL RD UNIT 33   03077
  Cheryl Stratchko, supt.   895-4299
HS, 45 HARRIMAN HILL RD   03077   2-00011
  Christopher George, prin.   895-6616
Gove MS, 10 SCHOOL ST   03077   3-01100
  Edward Donovan, prin.   895-3394

Rindge, AC 603, PC 2, Cheshire

Franklin Pierce College   03461   5-UC
   899-5111
Hampshire Country S   03461   1-01111
  Peter Ray, prin.   899-3325
The Meeting S, 116 THOMAS RD   03461   1-00011
  Jacqueline Stilwell, prin.   899-3366

Rochester, AC 603, PC 8, Strafford
School Administrative Unit 54   5-11111
  62 S MAIN ST   03867   332-3678
  Raymond Yeagley, supt.
Spaulding HS   4-00011
  130 WAKEFIELD ST   03867   332-0757
  Robert Bouchard, prin.
MS, 46 BROCK ST   03867   4-00100
  Paul Asbell, prin.   332-4090

Rye, AC 603, PC 3, Rockingham
School Administrative Unit 50   3-11100
  PO BOX 560   03870   964-5153
  Daniel Durgin, supt.
JHS, 501 WASHINGTON RD   03870   2-00100
  George Cushing, prin.   964-5591

Salem, AC 603, PC 7, Rockingham
School Administrative Unit 57   5-11111
  38 GEREMONTY DR UNIT 57   03079
  Henry LaBranche, supt.   893-7040
HS, 44 GEREMONTY DR   03079   4-00011
  Richard Desimone, prin.   893-7069
Woodbury MS, 206 MAIN ST   03079   3-00100
  Michael Delahanty, prin.   893-7055

Franklin Pierce College   2-UC
  12 INDUSTRIAL WAY   03079

Somersworth, AC 603, PC 7, Strafford
School Administrative Unit 56   4-11111
  414 HIGH ST   03878   692-4450
  Brian Beeler, supt.
HS, 10 MEMORIAL DR   03878   2-00011
  Robert Langelier, prin.   692-2431
MS, 20 MEMORIAL DR   03878   2-00100
  Paul Maskwa, prin.   692-2126

S.E. New Hampshire Christian Academy   2-11111
  ROCKY HILL ROAD   03878   692-3043
  Donald Ainsworth, prin.
Tri-City Christian Academy   2-11111
  150 W HIGH ST   03878   692-2093
  Paul Edgar, prin.

Strafford, AC 603, PC 4, Strafford
School Administrative Unit 44   4-11100
  PO BOX 317   03884   664-5422
  George Reid, supt.
Other Schools – See Barrington

Stratham, AC 603, PC 3, Rockingham

New Hampshire Technical College   3-CC
  277 R PORTSMOUTH AVE   03885   772-1194

Sunapee, AC 603, PC 3, Sullivan
School Administrative Unit 43
  Supt. — See Newport
JSHS, NORTH ROAD   03782   2-00111
  Richard Leone, prin.   763-5615

Tilton, AC 603, PC 5, Belknap
School Administrative Unit 59   4-11111
  PO BOX 709   03276   286-4116
  Mark Beauvais, supt.
Winnisquam Regional HS   2-00011
  PO BOX 209   03276   286-4531
  Norman Couture, prin.
Winnisquam Regional MS   2-01100
  PO BOX 318   03276   286-7143
  Larry Dicenzo, prin.

Tilton S, 30 SCHOOL ST   03276   2-00011
  Michael Baker, prin.   286-4342

Union, AC 603, PC 3, Strafford
School Administrative Unit 64   3-11111
  RR 2 BOX 1018   03887   473-2326
  Sheldon Damon, supt.
Other Schools – See Milton

Walpole, AC 603, PC 3, Cheshire
School Administrative Unit 60
  Supt. — See Charlestown
MS, TURNPIKE ROAD   03608   2-01100
  Grant Harris, prin.   756-4728

Weare, AC 603, PC 2, Hillsboro
School Administrative Unit 24
  Supt. — See Henniker
Stark Regional HS   2-00011
  618 N STARK HWY   03281   428-3546
  Mark Roth, prin.

West Lebanon, AC 603, PC see Lebanon
School Administrative Unit 32
  Supt. — See Lebanon
Lebanon HS, 195 HANOVER ST   03766   3-00011
  Michael Healey, prin.   448-2055
Lebanon JHS, 75 BANK ST   03766   2-00100
  Jacqueline Guillette, prin.   448-3056

West Stewartstown, AC 603, PC 2, Coos
School Administrative Unit 7
  Supt. — See Colebrook
West Side MS, PO BOX 120   03597   1-01100
  Paula Noll, prin.   246-8630

Whitefield, AC 603, PC 4, Coos
School Administrative Unit 36   4-11111
  21 HIGHLAND ST   03598   837-9363
  James Gaylord, supt.
White Mountains Regional HS   03598   2-00011
  Patrick Kelly, prin.   837-2528

Wilton, AC 603, PC 4, Hillsboro
School Administrative Unit 63   4-11111
  PO BOX 479   03086   654-2171
  Richard Lates, supt.
Wilton-Lyndeborough JSHS   2-00111
  PO BOX 255   03086   654-6123
  Ernest Belanger, prin.
Other Schools – See New Ipswich

High Mowing S, RR 2 BOX 133   03086   1-00011
  Louis Rossi, prin.   654-2391

Winchester, AC 603, PC 4, Cheshire
School Administrative Unit 38
  Supt. — See East Swanzey
Thayer JSHS, PO BOX 7   03470   2-00111
  Dennis Littky, prin.   239-4381

Windham, AC 603, PC 2, Rockingham
School Administrative Unit 28   5-11111
  PO BOX 510   03087   890-3760
  Raymond Raudonis, supt.
MS, 112 LOWELL RD   03087   2-00100
  Stephen Plocharczyk, prin.   893-2636
Other Schools – See Pelham

Castle College   2-CC
  21 SEARLES RD   03087   893-6111

Wolfeboro, AC 603, PC 5, Carroll
School Administrative Unit 49   4-11111
  PO BOX 190   03894   569-1658
  Sherwood Fleury, supt.
Kingswood Regional HS   3-00011
  RR 1 BOX 610   03894   569-2055
  Deborah Brooks, prin.
Kingswood Regional MS   2-00100
  RR 1 BOX 1268   03894   569-3689
  Robert Stimson, prin.

Brewster Academy, S MAIN ST   03894   2-00011
  David Smith, prin.   569-1600

Woodsville, AC 603, PC 4, Grafton
School Administrative Unit 23   4-11111
  35 S COURT ST UNIT 23   03785   747-2701
  Douglas McDonald, supt.
HS, 10 HIGH ST   03785   2-00011
  Bruce Labs, prin.   747-2781
Other Schools – See Lincoln, North Haverhill

NEW JERSEY

STATE DEPARTMENT OF EDUCATION
225 W. State St., CN 500, Trenton 08625
(609) 292-4469

Commissioner of Education	Leo Klagholz
Assistant Commissioner Academic Programs & Standards	Vacant
Assistant Commissioner Administration & Finance	Robert Davis
Assistant Commissioner Policy & Planning	Winifred Tillery
Assistant Commissioner Professional Development & Licensing	Vacant
Assistant Commissioner Urban & Field Services	Vacant

STATE BOARD OF EDUCATION
225 W. State St., CN 500, Trenton 08625

President   Anne Dillman

COUNTY SUPERINTENDENTS OF SCHOOLS

Atlantic County
Sandra Loewe   609-625-0004
1200 HARDING HWY W
Mays Landing 08330
Bergen County
Alfred Marbaise   201-599-6256
327 E RIDGEWOOD AVE
Paramus 07652
Burlington County
Arthur Merz, UNION & HIGHS STS   609-265-5060
Mount Holly 08060
Camden County
William Kile, 6981 N PARK DR   609-756-5700
Pennsauken 08109
Cape May County
Patricia Horton   609-465-1283
CREST HAVEN ROAD
Cape May Court House 08210
Cumberland County
Glenn Earl   609-451-0211
19 LANDIS AVE, Bridgeton 08302
Essex County
Peter Carter, 155 FAIRVIEW AVE   201-857-5700
Cedar Grove 07009

Gloucester County
Peter Contini   609-468-6500
RR 4 BOX 184D, Sewell 08080
Hudson County
Louis Acocella, 595 NEWARK AVE   201-915-1250
Jersey City 07306
Hunterdon County
Bruce Quinn   908-788-1414
1 E MAIN ST, Flemington 08822
Mercer County
Barbara Anderson   609-588-5884
PO BOX 8068, Trenton 08650
Middlesex County
Mary Guidette   908-390-6000
200 OLD MATAWAN RD
Old Bridge 08857
Monmouth County
Milton Hughes   908-431-7816
PO BOX 1264, Freehold 07728
Morris County
Sharon Clover   201-285-8320
CN 900, Morristown 07960

Ocean County
Joseph Zack   908-929-2078
212 WASHINGTON ST
Toms River 08753
Passaic County
Melindo Persi, 31 MCBRIDE AVE   201-881-7123
Paterson 07501
Salem County
Willetta Mulhorn   609-769-2700
RR 2 BOX 344, Woodstown 08098
Somerset County
John Nemeth   908-231-7171
PO BOX 3000, Somerville 08876
Sussex County
Bernard Andrews   201-579-6996
18 CHURCH ST, Newton 07860
Union County
Michael Maddaluna   908-654-9860
300 NORTH AVE E
Westfield 07090
Warren County
Jane Keehn   908-475-6326
413 2ND ST, Belvidere 07823

PUBLIC, PRIVATE AND CATHOLIC SECONDARY SCHOOLS

Absecon, AC 609, PC 6, Atlantic
Absecon CSD   3-11100
IRELAN AVE & WEBB RD 08201   641-5375
Walter Krug, supt.
Attales MS, 800 IRELAND AVE 08201   2-01100
(—), prin.   641-3329

Galloway Township SD   5-11100
PO BOX 728 08201   748-1250
Gary Bowen, supt.
Rann MS, 515 S 8TH AVE 08201   3-00100
Amos Kraybill, prin.   652-8200

Greater Egg Harbor Regional HSD
Supt. — See Mays Landing
Absegami HS   4-00011
201 S WRANGLEBORO RD 08201   625-1372
Lynn Basner, prin.

Holy Spirit HS, 500 S NEW RD 08201   3-00011
Fr. Joseph Perreault, prin.   646-3000

Adelphia, AC 908, PC 3, Monmouth

Talmudical Academy of New Jersey   1-UC
ROUTE 524 07710   431-1600
Talmudical HS, PO BOX 7 07710   1-00011
                                                431-1600

Allendale, AC 201, PC 6, Bergen
Allendale SD, BROOKSIDE AVE 07401   3-11100
J. Morton, supt.   327-2020
Brookside MS   2-01100
100 BROOKSIDE AVE 07401   327-2021
Noreen Hajinlian, prin.

Northern Highlands Regional SD   3-00011
298 HILLSIDE AVE 07401   327-8700
David Garrahan, supt.
Northern Highlands Regional HS   3-00011
298 HILLSIDE AVE 07401   327-8700
Vincent Herold, prin.

Allentown, AC 609, PC 4, Monmouth
Upper Freehold Regional SD   4-11111
27 HIGH ST 08501   259-7292
Stephen Sokolow, supt.
HS, HIGH ST 08501   3-00011
Thomas Vona, prin.   259-2160

Allenwood, AC 908, PC 99, Monmouth

Baxter Christian Academy   2-11111
PO BOX 515 08720   938-3565

Annandale, AC 908, PC 4, Hunterdon
Clinton Township SD   4-11100
PO BOX 6 08801   735-8320
Richard Byrnes, supt.
Other Schools – See Lebanon

North Hunterdon/Vorhees Regional HSD   4-00011
1445 STATE ROUTE 31 08801   735-5191
Joseph Appel, supt.
North Hunterdon HS   4-00011
1445 STATE ROUTE 31 08801   735-5191
Thomas Finnegan, prin.
Other Schools – See Glen Gardner

Asbury, AC 908, PC 2, Hunterdon
Bethlehem Township SD   2-11100
160 W PORTAL RD 08802   537-4044
Bernard O'Brien, supt.
Hoppock MS, 160 W PORTAL RD 08802   2-01100
Emil Suarez, prin.   479-6336

Central Jersey Christian S   2-11111
PO BOX 470 07712   775-5898

Asbury Park, AC 908, PC 7, Monmouth
Asbury Park SD, 1506 PARK AVE 07712   5-11111
James Mundy, supt.   776-2606
HS, 1003 SUNSET AVE 07712   3-00011
Daniel Murphy, prin.   776-2638

MS, 1200 BANGS AVE 07712   3-01100
Antonio Lewis, prin.   776-2559

Atco, AC 609, PC 4, Camden
Lower Camden County Regional HSD 1   5-00111
200 COOPER FOLLY RD 08004   767-2850
Michael Schreiner, supt.
Edgewood Regional HS   4-00011
250 COOPER FOLLY RD 08004   767-1850
Michele Spence, prin.
Edgewood Regional JHS   4-00110
200 COOPER FOLLY RD 08004   767-7222
Clifton Matthew, prin.
Other Schools – See Lindenwold, Pine Hill

Atlantic City, AC 609, PC 8, Atlantic
Atlantic City SD   6-11111
1809 PACIFIC AVE 08401   343-7200
R. Harris, supt.
HS, 3701 ATLANTIC AVE 08401   4-00011
Ernest Harper, prin.   343-7300
Chelsea MS, 2523 ARCTIC AVE 08401   2-00100
Herbert Milan, prin.   343-7350

Atlantic City Medical Center   HSP
1925 PACIFIC AVE 08401   344-4081
Boardwalk & Marina Casino Dealers School   2-CS
2709 ATLANTIC AVE 08401   344-1986

Audubon, AC 609, PC 6, Camden
Audubon SD   4-11111
350 EDGEWOOD AVE 08106   547-7695
John Palomano, supt.
JSHS, 350 EDGEWOOD AVE 08106   3-00111
William Westphal, prin.   547-7695

Avenel, AC 908, PC see Woodbridge
Woodbridge Township SD
Supt. — See Woodbridge
MS, 85 WOODBINE AVE 07001   3-00100
Dennis Kozar, prin.   396-7020

Barnegat, AC 609, PC 4, Ocean
Barnegat Township SD — 4-11100
  25 BIRDSALL ST   08005 — 698-5800
  Robert Horbelt, supt.
Brackman MS, 25 BIRDSALL ST   08005 — 3-00100
  William Carson, prin. — 698-5880

Barrington, AC 609, PC 6, Camden
Barrington Borough SD — 3-11100
  208 WHITE HORSE PIKE   08007 — 547-8467
  Nelson Malony, supt.
Woodland MS, 1 SCHOOL LN   08007 — 2-01100
  Michael Klaszky, prin. — 547-8402

Basking Ridge, AC 908, PC 5, Somerset
Bernards Township SD — 4-11111
  200 PEACHTREE RD   07920 — 204-2601
  Adrienne O'Neill, supt.
Ridge HS, 268 S FINLEY AVE   07920 — 3-00011
  Ron Stevens, prin. — 204-2585
Annin MS, 70 QUINCY RD   07920 — 3-00100
  Joan Tonnarelli, prin. — 204-2610

Bayonne, AC 201, PC 8, Hudson
Bayonne SD — 6-11111
  AVENUE A AND 29TH ST   07002 — 858-5814
  Richard Malanowski, supt.
HS, 667 AVENUE A   07002 — 4-00011
  Michael Wanko, prin. — 858-5900

Bayonne Hospital — HSP
  12 W 30TH ST   07002 — 339-9656
Holy Family Academy — 2-00011
  239 AVENUE A   07002 — 339-7341
  Sr. Joan O'Donnell, prin.
Hudson Area School of Radiologic Tech. — HSP
  29 E 29TH ST   07002 — 858-5000
Marist HS, 1241 KENNEDY BLVD   07002 — 2-00011
  Br. Handibode, prin. — 437-4544

Bayville, AC 908, PC 3, Ocean
Central Regional HSD — 4-00111
  FORREST HILLS PKWY   08721 — 269-1100
  Ronald DeConde, supt.
Central Regional HS — 4-00011
  509 FOREST HILLS PKY   08721 — 269-1100
  Norman Brown, prin.
Central Regional MS — 3-00100
  FORREST HILLS PKWY   08721 — 269-1100
  James McConnell, prin.

Belle Mead, AC 908, PC 3, Somerset
Hillsborough Township SD
  Supt. — See Neshanic Station
Hillsborough HS — 4-00011
  466 RAIDER BLVD   08502 — 874-4200
  Anthony Radano, prin.

Belleville, AC 201, PC 8, Essex
Belleville SD — 5-11111
  190 CORTLANDT ST   07109 — 450-3507
  Michael Lally, supt.
HS, 100 PASSAIC AVE   07109 — 4-00011
  Joseph Ciccone, prin. — 450-3542
MS, 279 WASHINGTON AVE   07109 — 3-00100
  Mario DiMaggio, prin. — 450-3532

Bellmawr, AC 609, PC 7, Camden
Bellmawr Borough SD — 3-11100
  256 ANDERSON AVE   08031 — 931-3620
  Timothy Bell, supt.
Bell Oaks MS — 2-01100
  256 ANDERSON AVE   08031 — 931-6273
  Robert Scharlach, prin.

Belmar, AC 908, PC 6, Monmouth

St. Rose HS, 607 7TH AVE   07719 — 3-00011
  Sr. Kathleen Letts, prin. — 681-2858

Belvidere, AC 908, PC 5, Warren
Belvidere SD, 537 OXFORD ST   07823 — 3-11111
  Robert Gratz, supt. — 475-6601
HS, 809 OXFORD ST   07823 — 2-00011
  John Pappas, prin. — 475-4025
Oxford Street MS — 2-01100
  801 OXFORD ST   07823 — 475-6616
  Deborah Grefe, prin.

Bergenfield, AC 201, PC 7, Bergen
Bergenfield SD — 5-11111
  100 S PROSPECT AVE   07621 — 385-8202
  John Galish, supt.
HS, 80 S PROSPECT AVE   07621 — 3-00011
  Ross Medlar, prin. — 385-8600
Brown MS — 3-00100
  130 S WASHINGTON AVE   07621 — 385-8847
  Rita Eberhard, prin.

Berkeley Heights, AC 908, PC 7, Union
Berkeley Heights SD — 4-11100
  PO BOX 147   07922 — 464-1718
  Robert Stowell, supt.
Columbia MS — 2-00100
  345 PLAINFIELD AVE   07922 — 464-1600
  Ralph Ferrie, prin.

Union County Regional HSD
  Supt. — See Springfield
Livingston Regional HS — 3-00011
  175 WATCHUNG BLVD   07922 — 464-3100
  Rosalie Lamonte, prin.

Bernardsville, AC 908, PC 6, Somerset
Bernardsville Borough SD — 3-11111
  25 OLCOTT AVE   07924 — 953-2149
  Melvin Klein, supt.
Bernards HS, 25 OLCOTT AVE   07924 — 2-00011
  Lynn Caravello, prin. — 766-8220
MS, SENEY DR   07924 — 2-01100
  Robert Pollack, prin. — 953-2168

Beverly, AC 609, PC 5, Burlington

Star Technical Institute — 2-CS
  2224 ROUTE 130   08010 — 877-2727

Blackwood, AC 609, PC 6, Camden
Black Horse Pike Regional SD — 5-00011
  580 ERIAL RD   08012 — 227-4106
  Gerald Kileen, supt.
Highland HS, 450 ERIAL RD   08012 — 4-00011
  Frank Palatucci, prin. — 227-4100
Other Schools — See Runnemede

Gloucester Township SD — 6-11100
  17 ERIAL RD   08012 — 227-1400
  Robert Suessmuth, supt.
Glen Landing MS — 4-00100
  85 LITTLE GLOUCESTER RD   08012 — 227-3534
  Arthur Brown, prin.
Lewis MS, 1200 ERIAL RD   08012 — 4-00100
  Kevin Kitchenmann, prin. — 227-8400

Camden County College — 7-CC
  PO BOX 200   08012 — 227-7200
Pennco Tech — 3-CS
  PO BOX 1427   08012 — 232-0310

Blairstown, AC 908, PC 3, Warren
North Warren Regional SD — 3-00111
  PO BOX 410   07825 — 362-8211
  Edward Herbert, supt.
North Warren Regional JSHS — 3-00111
  PO BOX 410   07825 — 362-8211
  Edward Herbert, prin.

Blair Academy   07825 — 2-00011
  Chandler Hardwick, prin. — 362-6121

Bloomfield, AC 201, PC 8, Essex
Bloomfield Township SD — 5-11111
  155 BROAD ST   07003 — 680-8555
  Ed Glickman, supt.
HS, 160 BROAD ST   07003 — 4-00011
  John Szabo, prin. — 680-8600
MS, 60 HUCK RD   07003 — 3-00100
  Charles Nankivell, prin. — 680-8620

Essex County Vocational SD
  Supt. — See East Orange
Essex County Vocational HS-Bloomfield — 2-00011
  209 FRANKLIN ST   07003 — 429-8893
  Robert Fiorini, prin.

Bloomfield College — 4-UC
  1 PARK PL   07003 — 748-9000

Bloomingdale, AC 201, PC 6, Passaic
Bloomingdale SD — 3-11100
  31 CAPTOLENE AVE   07403 — 838-3282
  Roger Tesi, supt.
Bergen MS, 225 GLENWILD AVE   07403 — 2-00100
  Michael Mintz, prin. — 838-4835

Bloomsbury, AC 908, PC 3, Hunterdon
Pohatcong Township SD — 2-11100
  45 ROUTE 519   08804 — 995-7715
  Jerry Clymer, supt.
Glen MS, RR 1 BOX 167   08804 — 2-01100
  Jerry Clymer, prin. — 995-7715

Bogota, AC 201, PC 6, Bergen
Bogota SD, 1 HENRY C LUTHIN PL   07603 — 4-11111
  Salvatore Montagna, supt. — 441-4800
JSHS, 111 KOVAR ST   07603 — 3-00111
  Roy Corso, prin. — 441-4809

Boonton, AC 201, PC 6, Morris
Boonton SD, 434 LATHROP AVE   07005 — 4-11111
  Harry Powers, supt. — 335-3994
HS, 306 LATHROP AVE   07005 — 3-00011
  Robert Kane, prin. — 335-9700
Hill MS, 435 LATHROP AVE   07005 — 2-01100
  Daniel Davis, prin. — 316-9235

Bordentown, AC 609, PC 5, Burlington
Bordentown Regional SD — 4-11111
  78 CROSSWICKS ST   08505 — 298-3041
  James Black, supt.
Bordentown Regional HS — 2-00011
  DUNNS MILL RD   08505 — 298-0025
  Dennis Sabo, prin.
McFarland JHS — 2-00100
  87 CROSSWICKS ST   08505 — 298-0674
  Norine Gerepka, prin.

Bound Brook, AC 908, PC 6, Somerset
Bound Brook Borough SD — 4-11111
  133 W MAPLE AVE   08805 — 271-2830
  Osborne Abbey, supt.
JSHS, 111 W UNION AVE   08805 — 3-00111
  Edgar Alster, prin. — 271-2851

Brick, AC 908, PC 8, Ocean
Brick Township SD — 6-11111
  101 HENDRICKSON AVE   08724 — 477-2800
  Louis Aragona, supt.

Brick Twp. HS — 4-00011
  346 CHAMBERSBRIDGE RD   08723 — 477-2800
  Joseph Tomaselli, prin.
Brick Twp. Memorial HS — 4-00011
  2001 LANES MILL RD   08724 — 477-2800
  M. Daniel Regan, prin.
Lake Riviera MS — 3-00100
  171 BEAVERSON BLVD   08723 — 477-2800
  Richard Handschuch, prin.
Veterans Memorial MS — 4-00100
  41 HARRISON AVE   08724 — 477-2800
  Raymond Messemer, prin.

Ocean County Vocational SD
  Supt. — See Toms River
Brick Center Vo S — Vo Tech
  350 CHAMBERSBRIDGE RD   08723 — 920-0050
  Craig Coleman, prin.

Brick Computer Science Institute — 2-CS
  515 ROUTE 70   08723 — 477-0975

Bridgeton, AC 609, PC 7, Cumberland
Bridgeton SD, PO BOX 657   08302 — 5-11111
  Donald D'Amico, supt. — 453-3200
JSHS, WEST AVE   08302 — 4-00111
  Robert Sharp, prin. — 453-3300

Cumberland County Vocational Ed SD — 2-00000
  601 BRIDGETON AVE   08302 — 451-9000
  Don Schreiber, supt.
Cumberland County Vo-Tech Ctr — Vo Tech
  601 BRIDGETON AVE   08302 — 451-9000
  Lorne Davidson, prin.

Fairfield Township SD — 3-11100
  RR 4 BOX 337   08302 — 451-1128
  Dan Mastrobuono, supt.
Fairfield Twp. IS — 2-01100
  RR 7 BOX 387   08302 — 451-2164
  Ed Gibson, prin.

South Jersey Hospital System — HSP
  MAGNOLIA & IRVING AVES   08302 — 451-6600

Bridgewater, AC 908, PC 6, Somerset
Bridgewater-Raritan Regional SD — 6-11111
  PO BOX 6030   08807 — 563-1888
  Joseph McGarry, supt.
Bridgewater-Raritan HS — 4-00011
  PO BOX 6569   08807 — 231-8660
  Charles Crosby, prin.
Eisenhower MS — 3-00100
  791 EISENHOWER AVE   08807 — 231-0230
  Dorothy Baldwin, prin.
Hillside MS, 844 BROWN RD   08807 — 3-00100
  Wilson Bethard, prin. — 231-1905

Somerset County Vocational SD — 2-00011
  PO BOX 6350   08807 — 526-8900
  Richard Messner, supt.
Somerset County Vo-Tech HS — Vo Tech
  PO BOX 6350   08807 — 526-8900
  Edmund Jones, prin.
Somerset County Tech Inst   08807 — Vo Tech
  Joseph Malone, prin. — 526-8900

Brigantine, AC 609, PC 7, Atlantic
Brigantine CSD, PO BOX 947   08203 — 4-11100
  Daniel Loggi, supt. — 266-7671
Brigantine North MS — 2-01100
  PO BOX 947   08203 — 266-3603
  Myron Plotkin, prin.

Brookside, AC 201, PC 3, Morris
Mendham Township SD — 2-11100
  W MAIN ST   07926 — 543-9334
  Joseph Cornell, supt.
Mendham Twp. MS — 2-00100
  16 WASHINGTON VALLEY RD   07926 — 543-2505
  Elizabeth Shrader, prin.

Browns Mills, AC 609, PC 7, Burlington
Pemberton Township SD — 6-11111
  PO BOX 98   08015 — 893-8141
  Robert Elder, supt.
Other Schools — See Pemberton

Budd Lake, AC 201, PC 6, Morris
Mount Olive Township SD — 5-11111
  89 US HIGHWAY 46   07828 — 691-4005
  Dennis Daggett, supt.
Mt. Olive MS, 99 SUNSET DR   07828 — 3-00100
  Joseph Morris, prin. — 691-4065
Other Schools — See Flanders

Buena, AC 609, PC 5, Atlantic
Buena Regional SD — 4-11111
  HARDING HWY   08310 — 697-0800
  Stuart Schnur, supt.
Buena Regional HS — 3-00011
  WEYMOUTH RD   08310 — 697-2400
  Ken Soboloski, prin.
Other Schools — See Minotola

Burlington, AC 609, PC 6, Burlington
Burlington CSD, 518 LOCUST AVE   08016 — 4-11111
  Patricia Abernethy, supt. — 387-5874
Burlington City JSHS — 3-00111
  100 DEWEY ST   08016 — 387-5800
  Robert Williams, prin.

Burlington Township SD 4-11111
PO BOX 428 08016 387-3955
Joseph Fritz, supt.
Burlington Twp. HS 2-00011
610 FOUNTAIN AVE 08016 387-1713
Patrick Ragosta, prin.
Hopkins MS 2-01100
700 JACKSONVILLE RD 08016 387-3774
Gerald Gares, prin.

Life Center Academy 2-11111
2045 BURLINGTON-COLUMBUS RD 08016
499-2100
St. Mary's Hall-Doane Academy 2-11111
RIVERBANK ST 08016 386-3500
Charles Toll, prin.

Butler, AC 201, PC 6, Morris
Butler SD, 38 BARTHOLDI AVE 07405 4-11111
Frank Stranzl, supt. 492-2032
HS, 38 BARTHOLDI AVE 07405 3-00011
Manuel Ferriera, prin. 492-2000
MS, 34 PEARL PL 07405 2-01100
James Smith, prin. 492-2079

Caldwell, AC 201, PC 6, Essex
Caldwell-West Caldwell SD 4-11111
30 PROSPECT ST 07006 228-6979
Daniel Gerardi, supt.
HS, 265 WESTVILLE AVE 07006 3-00011
Joe Jacangelo, prin. 228-6981
Cleveland MS, 36 ACADEMY RD 07006 2-00100
Richard Schenk, prin. 228-9115

Caldwell College 4-UC
9 RYERSON AVE 07006 228-4424
Mt. St. Dominic Academy 2-00011
3 RYERSON AVE 07006 226-0660
Sr. Doris Bowles, prin.

Califon, AC 908, PC 4, Hunterdon
Lebanon Township SD 3-11100
70 BUNNVALE RD 07830 638-4111
John Deibert, supt.
Woodglen MS, RR 2 BOX 295 07830 2-01100
William Jarvis, prin. 638-4111

Tewksbury Township SD 2-11100
173 COUNTY ROAD 517 07830 439-3101
Kenneth Gross, supt.
Old Turnpike MS 2-01100
171 COUNTY ROAD 517 07830 439-2010
Richard Ireland, prin.

Camden, AC 609, PC 8, Camden
Camden CSD, 201 N FRONT ST 08102 7-11111
Preston Gunning, supt. 966-2000
HS, 1700 PARK BLVD 08103 4-00011
Ruthie Green-Brown, prin. 966-5100
Wilson HS, 3100 FEDERAL ST 08105 4-00011
Herbert Factor, prin. 966-5300
East Camden MS 3-01100
3067 STEVENS ST 08105 966-5111
Marilyn Allen, prin.
Hatch MS, 1875 PARK BLVD 08103 3-00100
Jan Gillespie, prin. 966-5122
Morgan Village MS 3-01100
3107 FAIRVIEW ST 08104 966-5330
Patricia Cook, prin.
Pyne Poynt MS, 920 N 7TH ST 08102 3-01100
Vernon Dover, prin. 966-5360
Veterans Memorial MS 3-00100
26TH & HAYES 08105 966-5360
Yvonne deDaniels, prin.

Cooper Medical Center HSP
6TH & STEVENS STS 08103 342-2010
Divers Academy of the Eastern Seaboard 2-CS
2500 S BROADWAY 08104 800-238-3483
Our Lady of Lourdes School of Nursing HSP
1565 VESPER BLVD 08103 757-3729
Rowan College of New Jersey 3-UC
200 N BROADWAY 08102 757-2857
Rutgers-The State U of NJ/Camden Coll. 4-UC
08102 757-1766
Rutgers-The State U of NJ/Univ. Coll. 3-UC
08102 757-1766
West Jersey Hospital HSP
1000 ATLANTIC AVE 08104 342-4008

Cape May, AC 609, PC 5, Cape May
Cape May County Vocational Technical SD
Supt. — See Cape May Court House
Cape May County Tech Institute Vo Tech
CREST HAVEN RD 08210 465-2161
Louise Karwowski, prin.

Lower Cap May Regional SD 4-00111
687 ROUTE 9 08204 884-3475
Richard Strauss, supt.
Lower Cape May Regional HS 3-00011
687 ROUTE 9 08204 884-3475
Harvey Allen, prin.
Teitelman MS, 687 ROUTE 9 08204 3-00100
Christopher Kobik, prin. 884-3475

Cape May Court House, AC 609, PC 5, Cape May
Cape May County Vocational Technical SD 2-00000
CREST HAVEN ROAD 08210 465-2161
Wilbur Kistler, supt.
Cape May County Vo-Tech Ctr Vo Tech
CREST HAVEN RD 08210 465-3064
Norman Zimmerman, prin.
Other Schools – See Cape May

Middle Township SD 5-11111
216 S MAIN ST 08210 465-1800
Victor Rossetti, supt.
Middle Twp. HS 3-00011
212 BAYBERRY DR 08210 465-1852
Charles Eck, prin.
Middle Twp. MS 4 3-00100
300 E PACIFIC AVE 08210 – (—), prin. 465-1834

Burdette Tomlin Memorial Hospital HSP
2 STONE HARBOR BLVD 08210 463-2180
Cape Christian Academy 2-10111
1159 S ROUTE 9 08210 465-4132

Carney's Point, AC 609, PC 5, Salem
Penns Grove-Carneys Point SD
Supt. — See Penns Grove
Penns Grove HS 3-00011
334 HARDING HWY 08069 299-6300
Paul Rufino, prin.

Salem Community College 4-CC
460 HOLLYWOOD AVE 08069 299-2100

Carteret, AC 908, PC 7, Middlesex
Carteret Borough SD 5-11111
300 CARTERET AVE 07008 541-8961
Robert Hausner, supt.
HS, 199 WASHINGTON AVE 07008 3-00011
Joseph Torre, prin. 541-8963
Hale MS, 674 ROOSEVELT AVE 07008 2-01100
J. Terebetsky, prin. 541-8968

Cedar Grove, AC 201, PC 7, Essex
Cedar Grove Township SD 4-11111
520 POMPTON AVE 07009 239-1550
John DeCesare, supt.
HS, 90 RUGBY RD 07009 2-00011
Robert Reis, prin. 239-6400
Memorial MS, 90 RUGBY RD 07009 2-00100
Dennis Murphy, prin. 239-5233

Chatham, AC 201, PC 6, Morris
Chatham SD 4-11111
54 FAIRMOUNT AVE 07928 635-5656
Carol Conger, supt.
HS, 255 LAFAYETTE AVE 07928 3-00011
Arthur Ebeling, prin. 635-9075
MS, 480 MAIN ST 07928 3-01100
Michael Conte, prin. 635-7200

Cherry Hill, AC 609, PC 8, Camden
Cherry Hill Township SD 6-11111
PO BOX 5015 08034 429-5600
Phillip Esbrandt, supt.
Cherry Hill HS-East 4-00011
1750 KRESSON RD 08003 424-2222
James Gallagher, prin.
Cherry Hill HS-West 4-00011
2101 CHAPEL AVE W 08002 663-8006
Richard Simon, prin.
Beck JHS, 936 CROPWELL RD 08003 3-00100
Giacamo Rosa, prin. 424-4505
Carusi JHS, 315 ROOSEVELT DR 08002 3-00100
Maxwell Wald, prin. 667-1220

Camden Catholic HS 3-00011
300 CUTHBERT RD 08002 663-2247
Fr. Martin, prin.
Harris School of Business 2-CS
654 LONGWOOD AVE 08002 662-5300
Kane Business Institute 2-CS
206 HADDONFIELD RD 08002 488-1166
Kings Christian HS 2-00111
WINSTON WAY 08034 428-8866

Chester, AC 908, PC 4, Morris
Chester Township SD 3-11100
415 STATE ROUTE 24 07930 879-7383
Thomas Butler, supt.
Black River MS, 133 NORTH RD 07930 2-00100
Andrew Lindstedt, prin. 879-6363

West Morris Regional HSD 4-00011
FOUR BRIDGES RD 07930 879-6404
Judith Ferguson, supt.
West Morris Central HS 4-00011
BARTLEY NAUGHTRIGHT RD 07930 879-5212
Michael Reilly, prin.
Other Schools – See Mendham

Devereux Center in New Jersey HND
PO BOX 520 07930 879-4500

Cinnaminson, AC 609, PC 7, Burlington
Cinnaminson Township SD 4-11111
PO BOX 224 08077 829-7600
Timothy Wade, supt.
HS, RIVERTON ROAD 08077 3-00011
Robert Wisor, prin. 829-7770
MS, 312 N FORK LANDING RD 08077 3-01100
Judith Hamm, prin. 786-8012

Omega Institute 3-CS
ROUTE 130 S 08077 786-2200

Clark, AC 908, PC 7, Union
Clark Township SD 4-11100
10 SCHINDLER RD 07066 574-9600
Paul Ortenzio, supt.
Kumpf MS, 65 MILDRED TER 07066 2-00100
James Carovillano, prin. 381-0400

Union County Regional HSD
Supt. — See Springfield
Johnson Regional HS 3-00011
365 WESTFIELD AVE 07066 382-0910
David Carl, prin.

Mother Seton Regional HS 2-00011
50 BRANT AVE 07066 382-1952
Sr. Regina Martin, prin.

Clarksburg, AC 908, PC 3, Monmouth
Millstone Township SD 3-11100
18 SCHOOLHOUSE RD 08510 446-0890
Ernest Donnelly, supt.
Millstone Twp. MS 3-01100
308 MILLSTONE RD 08510 446-6802
Jerue Irons, prin.

Clayton, AC 609, PC 6, Gloucester
Clayton SD, 300 W CHESTNUT ST 08312 4-11111
Michael Greene, supt. 881-8700
HS, 350 E CLINTON ST 08312 2-00011
Gary Goldberg, prin. 881-8701
MS, CLINTON ST E 08312 2-00100
Gary Goldberg, prin. 881-8702

Cliffside Park, AC 201, PC 7, Bergen
Cliffside Park SD 4-11111
525 PALISADE AVE 07010 313-2310
James Colagreco, supt.
HS, 64 RIVERVIEW AVE 07010 3-00011
George Gundersen, prin. 313-2370

Cliffwood, AC 908, PC 5, Monmouth
Matawan-Aberdeen Regional SD
Supt. — See Matawan
Matawan Avenue MS 3-00100
447 MATAWAN AVE 07721 290-2850
Kathleen Sidoti, prin.

Clifton, AC 201, PC 8, Passaic
Clifton SD, PO BOX 2209 07015 6-11111
William Liess, supt. 470-2260
HS, 333 COLFAX AVE 07013 4-00011
Robert Mooney, prin. 470-2312
Columbus MS, 350 PIAGET AVE 07011 3-00100
Severin Palydowycz, prin. 470-2360
Wilson MS 3-00100
1400 VAN HOUTEN AVE 07013 470-2350
William Hahn, prin.

Closter, AC 201, PC 6, Bergen
Closter SD, 340 HOMANS AVE 07624 3-11100
Jeff Feifer, supt. 768-3001
Village MS, 511 DURIE AVE 07624 2-00100
Allan Deroian, prin. 768-7633

Collingswood, AC 609, PC 7, Camden
Collingswood Borough SD 4-11111
200 LEES AVE 08108 962-5732
Adam Pfeffer, supt.
HS, 416 W COLLINGS AVE 08108 3-00011
John Bach, prin. 962-5701
MS, 414 W COLLINGS AVE 08108 2-00100
Edward Kurkian, prin. 962-5702

Colonia, AC 908, PC see Woodbridge
Woodbridge Township SD
Supt. — See Woodbridge
Colonia HS, 180 EAST ST 07067 4-00011
John Belz, prin. 499-6500
MS, 100 DELAWARE AVE 07067 3-00100
Modesta Clausen, prin. 396-7000

Colts Neck, AC 908, PC 3, Monmouth
Colts Neck Township SD 3-11100
70 CONOVER RD 07722 946-0055
Gregg Hauser, supt.
Cedar Drive MS, 73 CEDAR DR 07722 2-01100
Joan Kilcommons, prin. 462-1156

Monmouth County Vocational SD 4-00011
41 STATE ROUTE 34 S 07722 431-7942
Brian McAndrew, supt.
Monmouth County Vo-Tech HS Vo Tech
41 STATE ROUTE 34 S 07722 431-7942
Brian McAndrew, prin.
Other Schools – See Freehold, Highlands, Lincroft

Columbus, AC 609, PC 3, Burlington
Northern Burlington County Regional SD 4-00111
160 MANSFIELD RD E 08022 267-7878
James Sarruda, supt.
Northern Burlington County Regional HS 3-00011
160 MANSFIELD RD E 08022 267-7878
Joseph Jones, prin.
Northern Burlington County Regional JHS 3-00100
160 MANSFIELD RD E 08022 267-7878
Richard Bryfogle, prin.

Convent Station, AC 201, PC 4, Morris

Academy of St. Elizabeth 2-00011
PO BOX 297 07961 292-6414
College of Saint Elizabeth 07961 4-UC
292-6300

Cranbury, AC 609, PC 4, Middlesex
Monroe Township SD
Supt. — See Jamesburg
Applegarth MS, APPLEGARTH RD 08512 2-00100
John Dorney, prin. 655-0604

Cranford, AC 908, PC 7, Union
Cranford Township SD 5-11111
PO BOX 646 07016 272-9100
Emalene Renna, supt.

HS, 201 W END PL 07016   3-00011
Robert Seyfarth, prin.   272-9100

Union County College   6-CC
1033 SPRINGFIELD AVE 07016   709-7000

Cresskill, AC 201, PC 6, Bergen
Cresskill SD, 50 LINCOLN DR 07626   4-11111
Alfred DiDonato, supt.   567-5919
JSHS, 1 LINCOLN DR 07626   2-00111
Henry McNally, prin.   567-5479

Delanco, AC 609, PC 5, Burlington
Delanco Township SD   2-11100
411 WALNUT ST 08075   461-0859
Joseph Miller, supt.
Walnut Street MS   2-00100
411 WALNUT ST 08075   461-0874
Paul Winkie, prin.

Delran, AC 609, PC 7, Burlington
Delran Township SD, CREEK RD 08075   4-11111
Carl Johnson, supt.   461-1778
HS, HARTFORD & CONROW RDS 08075   3-00011
Michael Gallucci, prin.   461-6100
MS, 411 S CHESTER AVE 08075   3-00100
Stephen Falcone, prin.   461-8822

Holy Cross HS   4-00011
5035 ROUTE 130 08075   461-5400
Sr. Mary Persico, prin.

Demarest, AC 201, PC 5, Bergen
Demarest SD, 568 PIERMONT RD 07627   3-11100
Paul Saxton, supt.   768-6060
MS, 568 PIERMONT RD 07627   2-00100
Dennis McDonald, prin.   768-6060

Northern Valley Regional SD   4-00011
162 KNICKERBOCKER RD 07627   768-3200
Eugene Westlake, supt.
Northern Valley Regional HS   3-00011
150 KNICKERBOCKER RD 07627   768-3200
Herbert Annerman, prin.
Other Schools – See Old Tappan

Academy of the Holy Angels S   3-00011
315 HILLSIDE AVE 07627   768-7822
Sr. Marie Danielle, prin.

Denville, AC 201, PC 7, Morris
Denville Township SD   4-11100
501 OPENAKI RD 07834   366-1001
Sandra Dohrenwend, supt.
Valleyview MS   2-00100
320 DIAMOND SPRING RD 07834   627-7050
George Deamer, prin.

Morris County Vocational Technical SD   2-00000
400 E MAIN ST 07834   627-4600
James Deworken, supt.
Morris County Area Vo-Tech S   Vo Tech
400 E MAIN ST 07834   627-4600
Stephen O'Malley, prin.

Morris Catholic HS   2-00011
200 MORRIS AVE 07834   627-6660
Br. Hugh McGrath, prin.

Deptford, AC 609, PC 3, Gloucester
Deptford Township SD   5-11111
2022 GOOD INTENT RD 08096   232-2707
David Moyer, supt.
Deptford Twp. HS   3-00011
575 FOX RUN RD 08096   232-2713
Harry Gallagher, prin.
Other Schools – See Sewell

Dover, AC 201, PC 7, Morris
Dover Town SD, 100 GRACE ST 07801   4-11111
Margaret Fischer, supt.   989-2000
HS, 100 GRACE ST 07801   3-00011
Don Alperti, prin.   989-2010
East Dover MS   3-00100
302 E MCFARLAN ST 07801   989-2040
Charles DeLorenzo, prin.

Dover Business College   2-CS
15 E BLACKWELL ST 07801   366-6700
Kubert School of Cartoon & Graphic Arts   2-CS
37 MYRTLE AVE 07801   361-1327

Dumont, AC 201, PC 7, Bergen
Dumont SD, 25 DEPEW ST 07628   4-11111
Thomas Roberts, supt.   387-3082
HS, 101 NEW MILFORD AVE 07628   3-00011
Jeff Scheetz, prin.   387-3060

Dunellen, AC 908, PC 6, Middlesex
Dunellen SD, 434 DUNELLEN AVE 08812   3-11111
Gerald Stefanski, supt.   968-3226
JSHS, 434 DUNELLEN AVE 08812   2-00111
John Feldman, prin.   968-0884

East Brunswick, AC 908, PC 8, Middlesex
East Brunswick Township SD   6-11111
22 MILLTOWN RD 08816   613-6705
Jon Kopko, supt.
SHS, 380 CRANBURY RD 08816   4-00001
Charles King, prin.   613-6904
Churchill JHS, 18 NORTON RD 08816   4-00110
Robert Janderval, prin.   613-6800

Middlesex Co. Vocational-Technical HSD   4-00011
PO BOX 220 08816   257-3300
J. Zanzalari, supt.
East Brunswick Vocational HS   4-00011
112 RUES LN 08816   254-8700
Bernard Siegel, prin.
Other Schools – See New Brunswick, Perth Amboy,
Piscataway, Woodbridge

Eastampton, AC 609, PC 99, Burlington
Eastampton Township SD   3-11100
1 STUDENT DR 08060   267-9172
John Holcroft, supt.
Other Schools – See Mount Holly

East Hanover, AC 201, PC 6, Morris
East Hanover Township SD   3-11100
20 SCHOOL AVE 07936   887-2112
Joan Lukowiak, supt.
MS, 477 RIDGEDALE AVE 07936   2-00100
Preston Pratola, prin.   887-8810

Hanover Park Regional HSD   4-00011
75 MOUNT PLEASANT AVE 07936   887-0320
John Adamus, supt.
Hanover Park HS   3-00011
63 MOUNT PLEASANT AVE 07936   887-0300
Carmen Buono, prin.
Other Schools – See Whippany

East Orange, AC 201, PC 8, Essex
East Orange SD, 715 PARK AVE 07017   7-11111
John Howard, supt.   266-5760
HS, 34 N WALNUT ST 07017   4-00011
Stephen Cowan, prin.   266-5800
Scott HS, 129 RENSHAW AVE 07017   4-00011
Irene Nichols, prin.   266-5900
Costley MS, 116 HAMILTON ST 07017   2-01100
R. Leonard Moore, prin.   266-5660
Davey MS, 161 ELMWOOD AVE 07018   3-00100
Laura Trimmings, prin.   266-5970
Healy MS, 116 HAMILTON ST 07017   2-00100
Loretta Onyeani, prin.   266-5670
Truth MS, 116 HAMILTON ST 07017   2-00100
Vivette Peacock, prin.   266-5665

Essex County Vocational SD   4-00011
68 S HARRISON ST 07018   676-4979
Robert Noonan, supt.
Other Schools – See Bloomfield, Newark

Drake College of Business   2-CS
60 EVERGREEN PL 07018   673-6009
Empire Technical School/New Jersey   3-CS
576 CENTRAL AVE 07018   675-0565
Essex Catholic HS   2-00011
135 GLENWOOD AVE 07017   674-4200
Br. Thomas Leto, prin.
SCS Business & Technical Institute   2-CS
516 MAIN ST 07018   675-4300
Upsala College   4-UC
345 PROSPECT ST 07017   266-7000

East Rutherford, AC 201, PC 6, Bergen
Carlstadt-East Rutherford Regional HSD   2-00011
280 PATERSON AVE 07073   935-4155
Sam Feldman, supt.
Becton Regional HS   2-00011
120 PATERSON AVE 07073   935-3007
Donald Wernes, prin.

East Rutherford SD   3-11100
GROVE & UHLAND STS 07073   804-3103
James Opiekun, supt.
Faust MS, GROVE & UHLAND STS 07073   2-01100
Louis Ravettine, prin.   804-3110

Eatontown, AC 908, PC 7, Monmouth
Eatontown SD, 215 BROAD ST 07724   4-11100
Richard Kaplan, supt.   542-1055
Memorial MS, 7 GRANT AVE 07724   2-00100
Ron Danielson, prin.   542-1055

Monmouth Regional HSD
Supt. — See Tinton Falls
Monmouth Regional HS   4-00011
535 TINTON AVE 07724   542-1170
William Kupersmith, prin.

Ranney S, 235 HOPE RD 07724   3-11111
Margaret Mahon, prin.   542-4777

Edgewater Park, AC 609, PC 6, Burlington
Edgewater Park Township SD   3-11100
25 WASHINGTON AVE 08010   877-2124
Walt Dold, supt.
Ridgeway MS, 300 DELANCO RD 08010   2-01100
Dennis Corbett, prin.   871-3434

Edison, AC 908, PC 8, Middlesex
Edison Township SD   7-11111
100 MUNICIPAL BLVD 08817   287-4400
Joseph Kreskey, supt.
HS, 1 BOULEVARD OF EAGLES 08817   4-00011
Frank Cangelosi, prin.   985-2900
Stevens HS, 930 GROVE AVE 08820   4-00011
Cedric Richardson, prin.   549-5543
Adams MS, NEW DOVER ROAD 08820   3-00100
Harry Olsen, prin.   548-9257
Hoover MS, 180 JACKSON AVE 08837   3-00100
Arlene Illes, prin.   225-9390
Jefferson MS, 450 DIVISION ST 08817   3-00100
Ross Capaccio, prin.   985-2500

Wilson MS   3-00100
WOODROW WILSON DRIVE 08820   548-2550
Rose Traficante, prin.

Academy of Professional Development   2-CS
98 MAYFIELD AVE 08837   417-9100
Bishop Ahr-St. Thomas HS   4-00011
1 TINGLEY LN 08820   549-1108
Sr. Donna Trukowski, prin.
Cittone Institute   4-CS
1697 OAK TREE RD 08820   548-8798
John F. Kennedy Medical Center   HSP
65 JAMES ST 08820   321-7515
Middlesex County College   7-CC
PO BOX 3050 08818   548-6000
Rabbi Jacob Joseph School   2-UC
1 PLAINFIELD AVE 08817
Wardlaw Hartridge S   2-00111
1295 INMAN AVE 08820   754-1882
Burgess Ayres, prin.

Egg Harbor City, AC 609, PC 5, Atlantic
Egg Harbor City SD   3-11100
527 PHILADELPHIA AVE 08215   965-7722
L. Rhine, supt.
Rittenberg MS   2-01100
528 PHILADELPHIA AVE 08215   965-0138
Irving Marshall, prin.

Pilgrim Academy, PO BOX 322 08215   2-11111
   965-2866

Elizabeth, AC 908, PC 9, Union
Elizabeth SD, 500 N BROAD ST 07208   7-11111
Thomas Dunn, supt.   558-3025
HS, 600 PEARL ST 07202   5-00011
Frank Cicarell, prin.   558-3105
Cleveland MS, 436 1ST AVE 07206   2-00100
Deborah Dixon, prin.   558-3361
Hamilton MS, 310 CHERRY ST 07208   3-00100
Paul Macciachera, prin.   558-3274
Holmes MS, 436 ELIZABETH AVE 07206   2-00100
Mark Jackson, prin.   558-4621
Lafayette MS, 1071 JULIA ST 07201   2-00100
Miguel Guilarte, prin.   558-3281
Roosevelt MS, 650 BAYWAY AVE 07202   2-00100
Jean Cina, prin.   558-3346

Benedictine Academy   2-00011
840 N BROAD ST 07208   352-0670
Sr. Marcia Lammerding, prin.
Drake College of Business   2-CS
9 CALDWELL PL 07201   352-5509
Elizabeth General Medical Center School   HSP
925 E JERSEY ST 07201   558-8082
Jewish Education Center   3-11111
330 ELMORA AVE 07208   353-4446
St. Mary Assumption HS   2-00011
237 S BROAD ST 07202   352-4350
Janet Malko, prin.
St. Patrick HS, 221 COURT ST 07206   2-00011
Joseph Picaro, prin.   353-5220
Trinity Christian Academy   2-11111
417 PENNINGTON ST 07202   352-9725
Union County College 07206   3-CC
   965-6000

Elmer, AC 609, PC 4, Salem
Pittsgrove Township SD   4-11111
RR 1 BOX 341C 08318   358-3094
John Daspro, supt.
Schalick JSHS, RR 1 BOX 312 08318   3-00111
William Jolley, prin.   358-2054

Elmwood Park, AC 201, PC 7, Bergen
Elmwood Park SD, 375 RIVER DR 07407   4-11111
Melindo Persi, supt.   794-2979
Memorial JSHS, 375 RIVER DR 07407   3-00111
Thomas Fedor, prin.   794-2933

Elwood, AC 609, PC 4, Atlantic
Mullica Township SD   3-11100
PO BOX 318 08217   561-3868
Gerald Toscano, supt.
Mullica Twp. MS, PO BOX 318 08217   2-01100
Mary Lou DeFrancisco, prin.   561-3735

Emerson, AC 201, PC 6, Bergen
Emerson SD, 182 MAIN ST 07630   3-11111
Charles Montesano, supt.   262-2828
JSHS, 182 MAIN ST 07630   2-00111
Ann Wilks, prin.   262-4447

Englewood, AC 201, PC 7, Bergen
Englewood Cliffs SD
Supt. — See Englewood Cliffs
Upper MS, 143 CHARLOTTE PL 07632   2-01100
Nicholas Mamola, prin.   567-6151

Englewood CSD, 12 TENAFLY RD 07631   4-11111
Henry Oliver, supt.   833-6060
Morrow JSHS   3-00111
274 KNICKERBOCKER RD 07631   833-6142
Edward Henderson, prin.

Dwight Englewood S   3-11111
315 E PALISADE AVE 07631   569-9500
James Van Amberg, prin.
Englewood Hospital   HSP
350 ENGLE ST 07631   894-3243

Englewood Cliffs, AC 201, PC 6, Bergen
Englewood Cliffs SD 2-11100
143 CHARLOTTE PL 07632 567-7292
Greg Hauser, supt.
Other Schools – See Englewood

St. Peter's College 07632 3-UC
568-7730

Englishtown, AC 908, PC 4, Monmouth
Freehold Regional HSD 6-00011
11 PINE ST 07726 – Dan McGuire, supt. 431-8538
Manalapan HS, 30 CHURCH LN 07726 4-00011
R. McChesney, prin. 431-8324
Other Schools – See Farmingdale, Freehold, Marlboro

Manalapan-Englishtown Regional SD 5-11100
54 MAIN ST 07726 446-5506
Joseph Scozzari, supt.
Manalapan-Englishtown MS 3-00100
155 MILLHURST RD 07726 446-8108
Gail Petricek, prin.

Ewing, AC 609, PC 8, Mercer

Academy of Professional Development 2-CS
934 PARKWAY AVE 08618 538-0400

Fairfield, AC 201, PC 6, Essex

Metropolitan Technical Institute 2-CS
11 DANIEL RD 07004 227-8191

Fair Haven, AC 908, PC 6, Monmouth
Fair Haven Borough SD 3-11100
224 HANCE RD 07704 747-2294
Robert Chartier, supt.
Knollwood ES, 224 HANCE RD 07704 2-10100
Wallace Wolff, prin. 747-0320

Fair Lawn, AC 201, PC 8, Bergen
Fair Lawn SD 5-11111
35-01 MORLOT AVE 07410 794-5511
Robert Byrne, supt.
HS, 14-00 BERDAN AVE 07410 4-00011
Elizabeth Panella, prin. 794-5454
Memorial MS 3-00100
1ST & LAMBERT ROAD 07410 794-5473
John Kane, prin.

Farmingdale, AC 908, PC 4, Monmouth
Freehold Regional HSD
Supt. — See Englishtown
Howell HS 4-00011
405 SQUANKUM YELLOWBROOK RD 07727
Harvey Casey, prin. 431-8490

Flanders, AC 201, PC 5, Morris
Mount Olive Township SD
Supt. — See Budd Lake
Mount Olive HS, 18 COREY RD 07836 3-00011
Joan Tucker, prin. 927-2200

Flemington, AC 908, PC 5, Hunterdon
Flemington-Raritan Regional SD 5-11100
50 COURT ST 08822 782-8074
James Swalm, supt.
Reading-Fleming MS 3-00100
50 COURT ST 08822 782-8070
Paul Metzger, prin.

Hunterdon Central Regional HSD 4-00011
84 STATE ROUTE 31 08822 782-5727
Raymond Farley, supt.
Hunterdon Central HS 4-00011
84 STATE ROUTE 31 08822 782-5727
David Myers, prin.

Hunterdon Co Vocational SD 2-00000
1 E MAIN ST 08822 806-4394
Richard Van Gulik, supt.
Hunterdon County Vocational S Vo Tech
1 E MAIN ST 08822 – (—), prin. 284-7155
North Hunterdon Vocational S Vo Tech
1 E MAIN ST 08822 735-5191
Thomas Finnegan, prin.
Voorhees Vocational S Vo Tech
1 E MAIN ST 08822 638-6116
Edward Barry, prin.

Florence, AC 609, PC 5, Burlington
Florence Township SD 4-11111
201 CEDAR ST 08518 499-4600
Michael Zapicchi, supt.
Florence Twp. Memorial HS 2-00011
500 E FRONT ST 08518 499-4620
Gerard Steffe, prin.
Florence Township MS 2-00100
500 E FRONT ST 08518 499-4647
Bernard D'Emidio, prin.

Florham Park, AC 201, PC 6, Morris
Florham Park SD 3-11100
BRIARWOOD ROAD 07932 822-3880
Fred Ferrone, supt.
Ridgedale MS 2-00100
75 RIDGEDALE AVE 07932 822-3855
Elsa Hill, prin.

Fords, AC 908, PC see Woodbridge
Woodbridge Township SD
Supt. — See Woodbridge
MS, 100 FANNING ST 08863 3-00100
Carl Anthony, prin. 417-5400

Fort Lee, AC 201, PC 8, Bergen
Ft. Lee SD, 255 WHITEMAN ST 07024 5-11111
A. Sugarman, supt. 585-4612
HS, 3000 LEMOINE AVE 07024 3-00011
John Richardson, prin. 585-4675
Cole MS, 467 STILLWELL AVE 07024 2-00100
Chris Onorato, prin. 585-4660

Franklin Lakes, AC 201, PC 6, Bergen
Franklin Lakes SD, 490 PULIS AVE 07417 4-11100
Ed Sullivan, supt. 891-1856
Franklin Avenue MS 2-00100
755 FRANKLIN AVE 07417 891-0202
Joseph Klingler, prin.

Ramapo Indian Hills Regional HSD 4-00011
331 GEORGE ST 07417 891-1505
John Pennoyer, supt.
Ramapo HS, 331 GEORGE ST 07417 3-00011
Richard Van Hoff, prin. 891-1500
Other Schools – See Oakland

Franklinville, AC 609, PC 4, Gloucester
Southern Gloucester County Regional HSD 4-00111
PO BOX 405 08322 694-0100
Boyd Sands, supt.
Delsea Regional HS 3-00011
BLACKWOODTOWN ROAD 08322 694-0100
Frank Borelli, prin.
Delsea Regional MS 3-00100
BLACKWOODTOWN ROAD 08322 694-0100
Michael Kopakowski, prin.

Freehold, AC 908, PC 7, Monmouth
Freehold Borough SD 4-11100
280 PARK AVE 07728 462-0450
Janet Kalafat, supt.
IS, 280 PARK AVE 07728 2-00100
Mark Chitwood, prin. 462-0453

Freehold Regional HSD
Supt. — See Englishtown
Freehold Borough HS 3-00011
65 BROADWAY 07728 431-8364
Carol Mulhare, prin.
Freehold Twp. HS 4-00011
281 ELTON ADELPHIA RD 07728 431-8464
James Hayden, prin.

Freehold Township SD 5-11100
237 STONEHURST BLVD 07728 462-8400
David Cole, supt.
Barkalow MS 2-00100
498 STILLWELLS CORNER RD 07728 431-4403
Rob MacMillan, prin.
Eisenhower MS 2-00100
279 BURLINGTON RD 07728 431-3910
Joe Quirk, prin.

Monmouth County Vocational SD
Supt. — See Colts Neck
Monmouth County Career Ctr Vo Tech
KOZLOSKI RD 07728 431-3773
Joseph Scelfo, prin.

Frenchtown, AC 908, PC 4, Hunterdon
Delaware Valley Regional HSD 3-00011
RR 1 BOX 188 08825 996-2131
Martin Matula, supt.
Delaware Valley Reg. HS 3-00011
RR 1 BOX 188 08825 996-2131
Joe Mammana, prin.

Garfield, AC 201, PC 8, Bergen
Garfield SD, 125 OUTWATER LN 07026 5-11111
Thomas Cangialosi, supt. 340-5000
HS, 125 OUTWATER LN 07026 3-00011
James Tantillo, prin. 340-5010
Jefferson MS, 62 ALPINE ST 07026 2-00100
Nicholas Perrapato, prin. 340-5039

Garwood, AC 908, PC 5, Union
Garwood SD, 500 EAST ST 07027 2-11100
Renee Howard, supt. 789-0165
Lincoln/Franklin ES 2-01100
WALNUT ST & SECOND AVE 07027 789-0331
Randy Pratt, prin.

Gibbstown, AC 609, PC 5, Gloucester
Greenwich Township SD 3-11100
225 W BROAD ST 08027 224-4913
William Carpenter, supt.
Nehaunsey MS 2-00100
415 SWEDESBORO RD 08027 224-4920
T. Porreca, prin.

Gladstone, AC 201, PC 4, Somerset

Gill/St. Bernard's S 2-11111
PO BOX 604 07934 234-1611
Christine Gorham, prin.
Mount Saint John Academy 1-00111
MOSLE RD 07934 234-1074
Sr. Mary Gilmore, prin.

Glassboro, AC 609, PC 7, Gloucester
Glassboro SD 4-11111
506 J BOWE MEMORIAL BLVD 08028 881-0123
Nicholas Mitcho, supt.
HS 3-00011
500 J BOWE MEMORIAL BLVD 08028 881-2200
Harry Alexandrowicz, prin.
IS, 250 DELSEA DR N 08028 2-00100
Carmen Mitcho, prin. 881-2313

Rowan College of New Jersey 08028 6-UC
863-5000

Glen Gardner, AC 908, PC 4, Hunterdon
North Hunterdon/Vorhees Regional HSD
Supt. — See Annandale
Voorhees HS 3-00011
256 COUNTY ROAD 513 08826 638-6116
Edward Barry, prin.

Glen Ridge, AC 201, PC 6, Essex
Glen Ridge SD 4-11111
235 RIDGEWOOD AVE 07028 429-8300
Marcia Bossart, supt.
JSHS, 200 RIDGEWOOD AVE 07028 2-00111
Michael Buonomo, prin. 429-8300

Glen Rock, AC 201, PC 7, Bergen
Glen Rock SD 4-11111
620 HARRISTOWN RD 07452 251-8948
Dario Valcarcel, supt.
JSHS, 600 HARRISTOWN RD 07452 3-00111
David Schein, prin. 251-8958

Gloucester City, AC 609, PC 7, Camden
Gloucester City SD 4-11111
520 CUMBERLAND ST 08030 456-9394
James Hetherington, supt.
JSHS, 1313 ROUTE 130 08030 3-00111
Ron Pritchett, prin. 456-7000

Gloucester Catholic HS 3-00011
333 RIDGEWAY ST 08030 456-4400
Fr. Kenneth Johnston, prin.

Green Brook, AC 908, PC 4, Somerset
Green Brook Township SD 2-11100
132 JEFFERSON AVE 08812 968-1171
Jeffrey Klein, supt.
MS, 132 JEFFERSON AVE 08812 2-00100
Jeffrey Klein, prin. 968-1051

Hackensack, AC 201, PC 8, Bergen
Bergen County Vocational SD 4-00011
200 HACKENSACK AVE 07601 343-5691
John Grieco, supt.
Hackensack Vo-Tech HS Vo Tech
200 HACKENSACK AVE 07601 343-6000
Evan Dopf, prin.
Other Schools – See Paramus, Teterboro

Hackensack SD, 355 STATE ST 07601 5-11111
Anthony Marseglia, supt. 646-7830
HS, 135 1ST ST 07601 4-00011
Mark Bauman, prin. 646-7910
MS, 360 UNION ST 07601 3-00100
Michael Burke, prin. 646-7842

American Business Academy 2-CS
66 MOORE ST 07601 488-9400
Fairleigh Dickinson University 3-CC
150 KOTTE PL 07601 692-2675
Hackensack Christian S 2-11111
15 CONKLIN PL 07601 487-7212
Hackensack Medical Center HSP
30 PROSPECT AVE 07601 441-2000

Hackettstown, AC 908, PC 6, Warren
Hackettstown SD, PO BOX 465 07840 4-11111
James Sheerin, supt. 852-2800
HS, 701 WARREN ST 07840 3-00011
William Cashill, prin. 852-8150
MS, 500 WASHINGTON ST 07840 2-01100
David Osmun, prin. 852-8554

Centenary College 3-UC
400 JEFFERSON ST 07840 852-1400

Haddonfield, AC 609, PC 7, Camden
Haddonfield Borough SD 4-11111
1 LINCOLN AVE 08033 429-4130
Barry Ersek, supt.
Haddonfield Memorial HS 3-00011
401 KINGS HWY E 08033 429-3960
Joseph Serico, prin.
MS, 1 LINCOLN AVE 08033 2-00100
John Caggiano, prin. 429-5851

Pope Paul VI HS 4-00011
901 HOPKINS RD 08033 858-4900
Fr. Rock, prin.

Haddon Heights, AC 609, PC 6, Camden
Haddon Heights SD, 300 2ND AVE 08035 4-11111
Edward Snyder, supt. 547-1412
JSHS, 301 2ND AVE 08035 3-00111
David Sandowich, prin. 547-1920

Baptist HS 2-00111
THIRD & STATION AVE 08035 547-2996
Graham Gilbert, prin.
Kings Christian S, 18 8TH AVE 08035 2-00111
Ernest Rebstock, prin. 546-7921

Haledon, AC 201, PC 6, Passaic
Passaic County Manchester Regional HSD 3-00011
70 CHURCH ST 07508 956-2584
Char Stanko, supt.
Manchester Regional HS 3-00011
70 CHURCH ST 07508 956-2560
Cheryl Metrey, prin.

Hamburg, AC 201, PC 5, Sussex
Wallkill Valley Regional SD — 3-00011
RR 2 BOX 247 07419 — 827-4100
Joseph DiPasquale, supt.
Wallkill Valley Regional HS — 3-00011
RR 2 BOX 247 07419 — 827-4100
Joseph DiPasquale, prin.

Hammonton, AC 609, PC 7, Atlantic
Hammonton Town SD — 4-11111
PO BOX 631 08037 — 567-7004
Warren Benedetto, supt.
HS, 169 LIBERTY ST 08037 — 3-00011 — 567-7000
Ron Lukas, prin.
MS, CENTRAL AVE 08037 — 2-00100 — 567-7007
Nicholas DeRosa, prin.

St. Joseph S, 133 N 3RD ST 08037 — 3-11111 — 561-0689
James Cavalieri, prin.

Harrison, AC 201, PC 7, Hudson
Harrison SD, 430 WILLIAM ST 07029 — 4-11111 — 483-4627
O. DiSalvo, supt.
HS, 1 N 5TH ST 07029 — 3-00011 — 482-5050
Robert Censullo, prin.
Washington MS — 2-00100
223 HAMILTON ST 07029 — 483-2285
Richard Lyons, prin.

Hasbrouck Heights, AC 201, PC 7, Bergen
Hasbrouck Heights SD — 4-11111
379 BOULEVARD 07604 — 393-8145
Howard Herbert, supt.
JSHS, 365 BOULEVARD 07604 — 3-00111 — 288-3971
Paul Palek, prin.

Hawthorne, AC 201, PC 7, Passaic
Hawthorne SD, PO BOX 2 07507 — 4-11111 — 423-6401
Frank Chiofalo, supt.
HS, 118 PARMELEE AVE 07506 — 2-00111 — 423-6417
Joan Hall, prin.
Lincoln MS — 2-00100
230 HAWTHORNE AVE 07506 — 423-6459
Joseph Vitale, prin.

Hawthorne Christian Academy — 2-11111
2000 ROUTE 208 07506 — 423-3331

Hazlet, AC 908, PC 7, Monmouth
Hazlet Township SD — 5-11111
305 MIDDLE RD 07730 — 264-8402
Michael Cleffi, supt.
Raritan HS, 419 MIDDLE RD 07730 — 3-00011 — 264-8411
Ralph Guadagno, prin.
Beers Street MS, 610 BEERS ST 07730 — 2-00100 — 264-1107
Susan Sposato, prin.
Union Avenue MS — 2-00100
1639 UNION AVE 07730 — 264-0940
J. Richard Sherman, prin.

Hibernia, AC 201, PC 99, Morris
Rockaway Township SD — 4-11100
PO BOX 500 07842 — 627-8200
Thomas Parciak, supt.
Other Schools – See Rockaway

High Bridge, AC 908, PC 5, Hunterdon
High Bridge Borough SD — 3-11100
40 FAIRVIEW AVE 08829 — 638-4105
Joseph Stuby, supt.
MS, 50 THOMAS ST 08829 — 2-01100 — 638-4101
James Moriarty, prin.

Highland Park, AC 908, PC 7, Middlesex
Highland Park SD — 4-11111
435 MANSFIELD ST 08904 — 572-6990
Peter Bastardo, supt.
JSHS, 102 N 5TH AVE 08904 — 3-00111 — 572-2400
Robert Terrano, prin.

Highlands, AC 908, PC 5, Monmouth
Henry Hudson Regional SD — 2-00111
1 GRAND TOUR 07732 — 872-0900
R. Dziadosz, supt.
Hudson Regional JSHS — 2-00111
1 GRAND TOUR 07732 — 872-0900
R. Dziadosz, prin.

Monmouth County Vocational SD
Supt. — See Colts Neck
Marine Academy of Science & Tech — Vo Tech
BUILDING 25 07732 — 291-0995
Paul Christopher, prin.

Hightstown, AC 609, PC 6, Mercer
East Windsor Regional SD — 5-11111
384 STOCKTON ST 08520 — 443-7704
David Witmer, supt.
HS, 25 LESHIN LN 08520 — 4-00011 — 443-7738
Martin Barlow, prin.
Kreps MS, 5 KENT LN 08520 — 3-01100 — 443-7767
Katherine Goerss, prin.

Peddie S, SOUTH MAIN ST 08520 — 2-00111 — 490-7514
Thomas DeGray, prin.

Hillsdale, AC 201, PC 6, Bergen
Hillsdale SD, 32 RUCKMAN RD 07642 — 4-11100 — 664-0282
Anthony DeNorchia, supt.
White MS, 120 MAGNOLIA AVE 07642 — 2-01100 — 664-0286
Ronald Sands, prin.

Pascack Valley Regional HSD
Supt. — See Montvale
Pascack Valley HS — 3-00011
200 PIERMONT AVE 07642 — 358-7056
Barbara Sapienza, prin.

Hillside, PC 7, Union
Hillside Township SD — 5-11111
195 VIRGINIA ST 07205 — 908-352-2433
Rose Stahnten, supt.
HS, 1085 LIBERTY AVE 07205 — 3-00011 — 908-352-7662
Milton James, prin.
Krumbiegel MS — 2-00100
145 HILLSIDE AVE 07205 — 201-923-2601
John Kaszak, prin.

Hoboken, AC 201, PC 8, Hudson
Hoboken SD, 1115 CLINTON ST 07030 — 5-11111 — 420-2151
Edwin Duroy, supt.
HS, NINTH ST & CLINTON ST 07030 — 3-00011 — 420-2301
Charles Tortorella, prin.
Brandt MS, 215 9TH ST 07030 — 2-01100 — 420-2336
Frank Spano, prin.
DeMarest MS, 158 4TH ST 07030 — 2-01100 — 420-2291
Peter Hetzel, prin.

Academy of the Sacred Heart HS — 2-00011
713 WASHINGTON ST 07030 — 659-7139
Sr. Diane Collesano, prin.
Hudson S, 506 PARK AVE 07030 — 2-01110 — 659-8335

Stevens Institute of Technology — 5-UC
6TH & HUDSON STS 07030 — 420-5100

Holmdel, AC 908, PC 3, Monmouth
Holmdel Township SD — 4-11111
PO BOX 407 07733 — 946-1800
Susan LaGlise, supt.
HS, 36 CRAWFORDS CORNER RD 07733 — 3-00011 — 946-1832
Richard White, prin.
Satz IS — 3-00100
24 CRAWFORDS CORNER RD 07733 — 946-1808
Paul Hart, prin.

St. John Vianney Regional HS — 3-00011
301 LINE RD 07733 — 739-0800
Joseph Deroba, prin.

Hopatcong, AC 201, PC 7, Sussex
Hopatcong Borough SD — 5-11111
PO BOX 1029 07843 — 398-8801
Wayne Threlkeld, supt.
HS, PO BOX 1029 07843 — 3-00011 — 398-8803
Roy DeFranci, prin.
MS, PO BOX 1029 07843 — 3-00100 — 398-8804
Theresa Guiliano, prin.

Howell, AC 908

Lakewood Preparatory S — 2-11111
152 LANES MILL RD 07731 — 364-2812
Lois Hirshkowitz, prin.

Irvington, AC 201, PC 8, Essex
Irvington Township SD — 6-11111
1150 SPRINGFIELD AVE 07111 — 399-6801
Rodgers Lewis, supt.
Morrell HS — 5-00011
1253 CLINTON AVE # 1273 07111 — 399-6897
Priscilla Butts, prin.
Myrtle Avenue MS — 3-00100
255 MYRTLE AVE 07111 — 399-6877
Anthony Pilone, prin.

Iselin, AC 908, PC see Woodbridge
Woodbridge Township SD
Supt. — See Woodbridge
Kennedy Memorial HS — 3-00011
200 WASHINGTON AVE 08830 — 602-8650
Robert Kasko, prin.
MS, 900 WOODRUFF ST 08830 — 3-00100 — 602-8450
Regis Sloan, prin.

Ultrasound Diagnostic School — 2-CS
PLAZA 1 AT GILL LN #6B 08830 — 634-1131

Jackson, AC 908, PC 3, Ocean
Jackson Township SD — 6-11111
DON CONNOR BLVD 08527 — 928-1400
Dominic Cotugno, supt.
Jackson Memorial HS — 4-00011
0 DON CONNOR BLVD 08527 — 928-1400
Francis Bygott, prin.
Goetz MS, 0 PATTERSON RD 08527 — 4-01100 — 928-5112
Faith Lessig, prin.
McAuliffe MS — 3-01100
35 HOPE CHAPEL RD 08527 — 928-1400
Margaret Hengel, prin.

Ocean County Vocational SD
Supt. — See Toms River
Jackson Vo S, RR 12 BOX 401 08527 — Vo Tech — 928-3830
Frank Adam, prin.

Jamesburg, AC 908, PC 6, Middlesex
Jamesburg SD, 17 AUGUSTA ST 08831 — 2-11100 — 521-0303
Adam Drapczuk, supt.
Breckwedel MS, 13 AUGUSTA ST 08831 — 2-01100 — 521-0640
Adam Drapckuk, prin.

Monroe Township SD — 5-11111
RR 2 BOX 300 08831 — 521-2111
Richard Marasco, supt.
Monroe Township HS — 3-00011
PERRINEVILLE RD 08831 — 521-2882
Charles Stein, prin.
Other Schools – See Cranbury

Jersey City, AC 201, PC 9, Hudson
Hudson County Board of Trustees
Supt. — See North Bergen
Hudson Co. AVTS Jersey City Vo-Tech Ctr — Vo Tech
525 MONTGOMERY ST 07302 — 413-5954
Barbara Mendolla, prin.

Jersey CSD — 8-11111
346 CLAREMONT AVE 07305 — 915-6202
Victor Demming, supt.
Academic HS, 16 BENTLEY AVE 07304 — 2-00011 — 915-6400
Roberts Roggenstein, prin.
Dickinson HS, 2 PALISADE AVE 07306 — 4-00011 — 714-4400
Frank Dooley, prin.
Ferris HS, 35 COLGATE ST 07302 — 4-00011 — 915-6660
Terrence Matthews, prin.
Lincoln HS, 60 CRESCENT AVE 07304 — 4-00011 — 915-6700
Charles Cooper, prin.
Snyder HS, 239 BERGEN AVE 07305 — 4-00011 — 915-6600
Michael Mintz, prin.
Jersey City MS 31 — 2-00100
3055 JOHN F KENNEDY BLVD 07306 — 714-4370
Mary Louf, prin.

Academy of St. Aloysius — 2-00111
2495 JOHN F KENNEDY BLVD 07304 — 433-8877
Tara Brunt, prin.
Al-Ghazaly School, 17 PARK ST 07304 — 2-11111 — 433-5002
Bergen S, 36 EMORY ST 07304 — 2-11111 — 433-3138
Denise Davis, prin.
Christ Hospital — HSP
176 PALISADE AVE 07306 — 795-8360
Chubb Institute — 2-CS
40 JOURNAL SQ 07306 — 656-0330
Hudson Catholic HS — 3-00011
790 BERGEN AVE 07306 — 332-5970
Br. Gerrow, prin.
Hudson County Community College — 5-CC
168 SIP AVE 07306 — 714-2127
Jersey City State College — 6-UC
2039 JOHN F KENNEDY BLVD 07305 — 200-3234
St. Aloysius HS, 721 W SIDE AVE 07306 — 2-00011 — 435-9240
Sr. Gloria O'Brien, prin.
St. Anthony HS, 175 8TH ST 07302 — 2-00011 — 653-5143
Sr. Mary Felicia, prin.
St. Dominic Academy — 3-00011
2572 JOHN F KENNEDY BLVD 07304 — 434-5938
Sr. Betty Schultz, prin.
St. Francis Hospital — HSP
1 MCWILLIAMS PL 07302 — 795-7001
St. Mary HS, 209 3RD ST 07302 — 2-00011 — 656-8008
Sr. Jacqueline Carey, prin.
St. Peter Prep S, 144 GRAND ST 07302 — 3-00011 — 434-4400
John Raslowsky, prin.
St. Peter's College — 5-UC
2641 JOHN F KENNEDY BLVD 07306 — 915-9000

Keansburg, AC 908, PC 7, Monmouth
Keansburg Borough SD — 4-11111
69 CHURCH ST 07734 – J. Caruso, supt. — 787-7578
HS, 140 PORT MONMOUTH RD 07734 — 2-00011 — 787-7575
Olga Kupczak, prin.
Bolger MS, 100 PALMER PL 07734 — 3-01100 — 495-7900
Robert Seidel, prin.

Kearny, AC 201, PC 8, Hudson
Kearny SD, 336 DEVON ST 07032 — 5-11111 — 955-5021
John McGeehan, supt.
HS, 336 DEVON ST 07032 — 4-00011 — 995-5048
Salvatore Valanzola, prin.

Keyport, AC 908, PC 6, Monmouth
Keyport SD, 335 BROAD ST 07735 — 4-11111 — 264-2840
John Dumford, supt.
HS, 351 BROAD ST 07735 — 2-00011 — 264-0902
Anthony Gaita, prin.

Kinnelon, AC 201, PC 6, Morris
Kinnelon Borough SD — 4-11111
170 KINNELON RD RM 35 07405 — 838-1921
Lois McGuire, supt.
HS, 121 KINNELON RD 07405 — 2-00011 — 838-5500
Charles Khuory, prin.
Miller MS, 117 KIEL AVE 07405 — 2-01100 — 838-5250
Joseph Palladino, prin.

Lake Hopatcong, AC 201, PC 4, Morris
Jefferson Township SD — 5-11111
28 BOWLING GREEN PKY 07849 — 663-5780
Sheldon Rubin, supt.
Other Schools – See Oak Ridge

Lakehurst, AC 908, PC 5, Ocean
Manchester Township SD
Supt. — See Whiting
Manchester Twp. HS — 3-00011
101 S COLONIAL DR 08733 — 657-2121
Richard Fosko, prin.
Manchester Twp. MS — 3-00100
2759 RIDGEWAY RD 08733 — 657-1717
Kevin Burger, prin.

Lakewood, AC 908, PC 8, Ocean
Lakewood Township SD 6-11111
655 PRINCETON AVE 08701 905-3633
Ernest Cannava, supt.
HS, 855 SOMERSET AVE 08701 4-00011
Arthur Turner, prin. 905-3502
MS, 755 SOMERSET AVE 08701 3-00100
Robert Ostrove, prin. 905-3600

Ocean County Vocational SD
Supt. — See Toms River
Career & Tech Inst Vo Tech
1515 ROUTE 70 08701 364-5300
Patricia Dacey, prin.

Bais Kaila Torah Prep HS 2-00011
PO BOX 952 08701 370-4300
Beth Medrash Govoha 3-UC
617 6TH ST 08701 367-1060
Calvary Academy 2-11111
1133 COUNTY LINE RD E 08701 363-3633
Georgian Court College 4-UC
900 LAKEWOOD AVE 08701 364-2200
Star Technical Institute 2-CS
1255 HIGHWAY 70 STE 12N 08701 901-0001

Lambertville, AC 609, PC 5, Hunterdon
South Hunterdon Regional HSD 2-00111
301 MOUNT AIRY HRBOURTON RD 08530
Thomas Davidson, supt. 397-2060
South Hunterdon Regional JSHS 2-00111
301 MOUNT AIRY HRBOURTON RD 08530
Louis Piccolo, prin. 397-2060

Lanoka Harbor, AC 609, PC 3, Ocean
Lacey Township SD 5-11111
PO BOX 216 08734 971-2001
Richard Starodub, supt.
Lacey Twp. HS, PO BOX 206 08734 4-00011
Michael Adamski, prin. 971-2021
Lacey Twp. MS, PO BOX 197 08734 3-00100
Paul Berkowicz, prin. 971-2070

Lawrenceville, AC 609, PC 4, Mercer
Lawrence Township SD 5-11111
2565 PRINCETON PIKE 08648 530-8609
Claire Kohn, supt.
Lawrence HS 3-00011
2525 PRINCETON AVE 08648 530-8369
Anthony Watson, prin.
Lawrence MS 2-00100
2455 PRINCETON AVE 08648 530-8429
Walter Woolley, prin.

Lawrenceville S, PO BOX 6008 08648 2-00111
Josiah Bunting, prin. 896-0400
Rider University 6-UC
2083 LAWRENCEVILLE RD 08648 896-5000

Lebanon, AC 908, PC 4, Hunterdon
Clinton Township SD
Supt. — See Annandale
Round Valley MS, RR 4 08833 2-00100
John Scott, prin. 236-6341

Leonardo, AC 908, PC 5, Monmouth
Middletown Township SD
Supt. — See Middletown
Bayshore MS 3-00100
36 LEONARDVILLE RD 07737 291-1380
Robert Murphy, prin.

Leonia, AC 201, PC 6, Bergen
Leonia SD, 500 BROAD AVE 07605 4-11111
Frank Marlow, supt. 461-9100
HS, 100 CHRISTIE HEIGHTS ST 07605 3-00011
Donald Yates, prin. 461-9100
MS, 500 BROAD AVE 07605 3-01100
Don Kouba, prin. 461-9100

Lincoln Park, AC 201, PC 7, Morris
Lincoln Park Borough SD 3-11100
19 STATION RD 07035 696-5500
Frank Sinatra, supt.
Chapel Hill MS 2-00100
31 CHAPEL HILL RD 07035 696-5510
Joseph DiBrigida, prin.

Lincroft, AC 908, PC 6, Monmouth
Monmouth County Vocational SD
Supt. — See Colts Neck
High Tech HS, PO BOX 119 07738 Vo Tech
William Pollock, prin. 842-8444

Brookdale Community College 6-CC
765 NEWMAN SPRINGS RD 07738 842-1900
Christian Brothers Academy 3-00011
850 NEWMAN SPRINGS RD 07738 747-1959
Br. Montedoro, prin.

Linden, AC 908, PC 8, Union
Linden SD, 728 N WOOD AVE 07036 5-11111
James Clarke, supt. 486-5818
HS, 121 W SAINT GEORGES AVE 07036 4-00011
Seymour Kaplowitz, prin. 486-5432
McManus MS 2-00100
300 EDGEWOOD RD 07036 486-7751
Joseph Placa, prin.
Soehl MS, 300 E HENRY ST 07036 3-00100
Gregory Martucci, prin. 486-0550

General Technical Institute 2-CS
1118 BALTIMORE AVE 07036 486-9353

Lindenwold, AC 609, PC 7, Camden
Lower Camden County Regional HSD 1
Supt. — See Atco
Overbrook Regional JHS 4-00100
0 WHITE HORSE AVE 08021 346-3330
Nicholas Guerere, prin.

Linwood, AC 609, PC 6, Atlantic
Linwood CSD, 51 BELHAVEN AVE 08221 3-11100
Ralph Schiavo, supt. 927-6355
Belhaven Avenue MS 2-01100
51 BELHAVEN AVE 08221 927-3552
Walter Dull, prin.

Mainland Regional HSD 4-00011
1301 OAK AVE 08221 927-2461
Alfred Arena, supt.
Mainland Regional HS 4-00011
1301 OAK AVE 08221 - (—), prin. 927-4151

Little Falls, AC 201, PC 7, Passaic
Little Falls Township SD 3-11100
36 STEVENS AVE 07424 256-1034
James Nash, supt.
MS 1, STEVENS AVE 07424 2-01100
Raymond Mead, prin. 256-1033

Passaic County Regional HSD 1 4-00011
160 E MAIN ST 07424 890-2560
Louis Centolanza, supt.
Passaic County Regional HS 4-00011
160 E MAIN ST 07424 890-2500
Louis Centolanza, prin.

Little Ferry, AC 201, PC 6, Bergen
Little Ferry SD, 130 LIBERTY ST 07643 3-11100
Stacy Holmes, supt. 641-6186
Memorial MS, 130 LIBERTY ST 07643 2-01100
Carmen Holster, prin. 641-6186

Little Silver, AC 908, PC 6, Monmouth
Little Silver Borough SD 3-11100
124 WILLOW DR 07739 741-2188
Thomas Gallagher, supt.
Markham Place MS 2-01100
99 MARKHAM PL 07739 741-7112
Donald Merce, prin.

Red Bank Regional HSD 4-00011
101 RIDGE RD 07739 842-7884
Donald Warner, supt.
Red Bank Regional HS 4-00011
101 RIDGE RD 07739 842-8000
Robert Nogueria, prin.

Livingston, AC 201, PC 8, Essex
Livingston Township SD 5-11111
11 FOXCROFT DR 07039 535-8010
Robert Kish, supt.
HS, 30 ROBERT H HARP DR 07039 4-00011
Rob Grady, prin. 535-8100
Heritage MS, 20 FOXCROFT DR 07039 3-00100
Anita Codey, prin. 535-8090
Mt. Pleasant MS 2-00100
11 BROADLAWN DR 07039 535-8070
Arthur Saliceti, prin.

Newark Academy 3-00111
91 S ORANGE AVE 07039 992-7000
Allan Strand, prin.
St. Barnabas Medical Center HSP
94 OLD SHORT HILLS RD 07039 533-5628

Lodi, AC 201, PC 7, Bergen
Lodi SD, PO BOX 815 07644 4-11111
Paula Feduccia, supt. 778-4620
HS, 71 PUTNAM ST 07644 3-00011
Rob Bentsen, prin. 478-6100
Jefferson MS, 75 1ST ST 07644 2-00100
Gary Carabin, prin. 478-8662

Felician College 3-UC
262 S MAIN ST 07644 778-1190
Immaculate Conception HS 2-00011
258 S MAIN ST 07644 773-2400
Sr. Mary Tomasiak, prin.

Long Branch, AC 908, PC 8, Monmouth
Long Branch SD, 6 W END CT 07740 5-11111
Herbert Korey, supt. 571-2868
HS, 391 WESTWOOD AVE 07740 3-00011
John Crotty, prin. 229-7300
MS, 364 INDIANA AVE 07740 3-00100
Robert Celli, prin. 229-5533

Monmouth Medical Center HSP
3RD & PAVILION AVE 07740 222-5200

Long Valley, AC 908, PC 4, Morris
Washington Township SD 4-11100
53 W MILL RD 07853 876-4172
George Wilhelm, supt.
MS, 51 E MILL RD 07853 4-01100
Kevin Walsh, prin. 876-3434

Lumberton, AC 609, PC 3, Burlington
Lumberton Township SD 3-11100
30 FALMOUTH RD 08048 - (—), supt. 265-0123
MS, 30 FALMOUTH RD 08048 2-01100
Leonard Kelpsh, prin. 265-0123

Lyndhurst, AC 201, PC 7, Bergen
Lyndhurst Township SD 4-11111
281 RIDGE RD 07071 438-5683
Joseph Abate, supt.
HS, 400 WEART AVE 07071 3-00011
James Corino, prin. 896-2100
Lincoln MS, 281 RIDGE RD 07071 1-00100
Thomas Grillo, prin. 438-5683

Madison, AC 201, PC 7, Morris
Madison SD, 359 WOODLAND RD 07940 4-11111
Lawrence Feinsod, supt. 593-3100
HS, 170 RIDGEDALE AVE 07940 3-00011
R. Padian, prin. 593-3117
JHS, 285 MAIN ST 07940 2-00100
Florence Senyk, prin. 593-3149

Bayley Ellard HS 2-00011
205 MADISON AVE 07940 377-2486
Jeanne Gradone, prin.
Drew University 4-UC
36 MADISON AVE 07940 408-3000
Fairleigh Dickinson University 4-UC
07940 800-338-8803

Mahwah, AC 201, PC 6, Bergen
Mahwah Township SD 4-11111
60 RIDGE RD 07430 529-5000
H. Blueglass, supt.
HS, 50 RIDGE RD 07430 3-00011
Bruce Segall, prin. 529-5000
Ramapo Ridge MS, 150 RIDGE RD 07430 2-00100
Les Weintraub, prin. 529-5000

Lincoln Technical Institute 3-CS
70 MCKEE DR 07430 529-1414
Ramapo College of New Jersey 5-UC
505 RAMAPO VALLEY RD 07430 529-7600

Manahawkin, AC 609, PC 4, Ocean
Southern Regional HSD 5-00111
75 CEDAR BRIDGE RD 08050 597-9481
Robert Daria, supt.
Southern Regional HS 4-00011
600 N MAIN ST 08050 597-9481
Peter Righi, prin.
Southern Regional MS 4-00110
75 CEDAR BRIDGE RD 08050 597-9481
Stephen Klemens, prin.

Manasquan, AC 908, PC 6, Monmouth
Manasquan SD, 169 BROAD ST 08736 4-11111
Carole Morris, supt. 528-8800
HS, 169 BROAD ST 08736 3-00011
Jeff Osborn, prin. 528-8820

Manville, AC 908, PC 7, Somerset
Manville Borough SD 4-11111
410 BROOKS BLVD 08835 231-8545
Francis Heelan, supt.
JSHS, 1100 BROOKS BLVD 08835 2-00111
Barbara Feldman, prin. 231-8504

Maple Shade, AC 609, PC 7, Burlington
Maple Shade Township SD 4-11111
FREDERICK & CLINTON AVE 08052 779-1750
James Kerfoot, supt.
JSHS, 180 FREDERICK AVE 08052 3-00111
Martin Harmon, prin. 779-2880

Maplewood, AC 201, PC 7, Essex
South Orange-Maplewood SD 5-11111
525 ACADEMY ST 07040 378-9630
Ralph Lieber, supt.
Columbia HS, 17 PARKER AVE 07040 4-00011
Judith Weiss, prin. 378-5266
MS, 7 BURNETT ST 07040 3-01100
Bernard Ryan, prin. 378-2849
Other Schools – See South Orange

Margate City, AC 609, PC 6, Atlantic
Margate City SD 3-11100
GRANVILLE & WINCHESTER AVES 08402
Dominick Potena, supt. 822-1686
Tighe MS 2-01100
ESSEX & AMHERST AVE 08402 822-2353
Philip Munafo, prin.

Marlboro, AC 908, PC 3, Monmouth
Freehold Regional HSD
Supt. — See Englishtown
HS, 95 N MAIN ST 07746 4-00011
Matthew Herman, prin. 431-8424

Marlboro Township SD 5-11100
1980 TOWNSHIP DR 07746 972-2000
William Foley, supt.
MS, 355 COUNTY ROAD 520 07746 3-00100
Harvey Abramson, prin. 972-2100

Marlton, AC 609, PC 7, Burlington
Evesham Township SD 5-11100
26 S MAPLE AVE 08053 983-1800
Douglas Groff, supt.
Demasi MS 3-00100
199 EVESBORO MEDFORD RD 08053 988-0777
Frank Sama, prin.
MS, 4 TOMLINSON LN 08053 3-00100
Norman Allison, prin. 983-0684

Lenape Regional HSD
Supt. — See Medford
Cherokee HS 4-00011
WILLOW BEND ROAD 08053 983-5140
Don Stecher, prin.

Martinsville, AC 908, PC 4, Somerset

The Pingry S, PO BOX 366 08836 3-11111
John Hanly, prin. 647-5555

Matawan, AC 908, PC 6, Monmouth
Matawan-Aberdeen Regional SD   5-11111
  1 CREST WAY   07747   290-2705
  Kenneth Hall, supt.
Matawan Regional HS   3-00011
  450 ATLANTIC AVE   07747   290-2800
  Roger Tuccillo, prin.
Other Schools – See Cliffwood

Old Bridge Township SD   6-11111
  519 COUNTY ROAD 516   07747   290-3976
  Andrew Korshalla, supt.
Other Schools – See Old Bridge

Mays Landing, AC 609, PC 4, Atlantic
Atlantic County Vocational SD   2-00000
  5080 ATLANTIC AVE   08330   625-2249
  William Flynn, supt.
Atlantic County Vo-Tech S   Vo Tech
  5080 ATLANTIC AVE   08330   625-2249
  Charles Mossbrucker, prin.

Greater Egg Harbor Regional HSD   4-00011
  1824 VIENNA AVE   08330   625-1456
  John Dugan, supt.
Oakcrest HS, 1824 VIENNA AVE   08330   4-00011
  Dennis Foreman, prin.   625-2242
Other Schools – See Absecon

Hamilton Township SD   4-11100
  202 FARRAGUT AVE   08330   625-6595
  Claude McAllister, supt.
Davies MS, 1876 VIENNA AVE   08330   2-00100
  Philip Zuba, prin.   625-6616

Atlantic Community College   5-CC
  5100 BLACK HORSE PIKE   08330   625-1111

Maywood, AC 201, PC 6, Bergen
Maywood SD   3-11100
  452 MAYWOOD AVE   07607   845-9114
  (—), supt.
Maywood Avenue MS   2-01100
  452 MAYWOOD AVE   07607   845-9110
  Raymond Bauer, prin.

Medford, AC 609, PC 4, Burlington
Burlington County Vocational SD
  Supt. — See Mount Holly
Institute of Technology   3-00011
  10 HAWKIN RD   08055   654-0200
  Ronald Ruilova, prin.

Lenape Regional HSD   6-00011
  235 HARTFORD RD   08055   654-5111
  Daniel Hicks, supt.
Lenape HS, 235 HARTFORD RD   08055   4-00011
  John Furgione, prin.   654-5111
Shawnee HS   4-00011
  600 TABERNACLE RD   08055   654-7544
  John Johnsen, prin.
Other Schools – See Marlton

Medford Township SD   5-11100
  320 STOKES RD   08055   654-6416
  Patrick Johnson, supt.
Medford Township Memorial MS   3-00100
  55 MILL ST   08055   654-7707
  Joseph Del Rossi, prin.

Aviation Career Academy   2-CS
  FOSTERTOWN RD   08055   267-1200

Medford Lakes, AC 609, PC 5, Burlington
Medford Lakes Borough SD   3-11100
  135 MUDJEKEEWIS TRL   08055   654-0991
  Donald Gross, supt.
Neeta MS, NEETA TRL   08055   2-01100
  Anita Homola, prin.   654-5155

Mendham, AC 201, PC 5, Morris
Mendham Borough SD   3-11100
  12 HILLTOP RD   07945   543-2295
  William Frank, supt.
Mountain View MS, 100 DEAN RD   07945   2-01100
  Robert Marold, prin.   543-7075

West Morris Regional HSD
  Supt. — See Chester
West Morris Mendham HS   3-00011
  65 E MAIN ST   07945   543-2501
  Angela DeMartino, prin.

Assumption College for Sisters   1-CC
  MALLINCKRODT CONVENT   07945   543-6528

Metuchen, AC 908, PC 7, Middlesex
Metuchen SD   4-11111
  596 MIDDLESEX AVE   08840   321-8710
  Gennaro Lepre, supt.
JSHS, 400 GROVE AVE   08840   3-00111
  John Novak, prin.   321-8743

St. Josephs HS   3-00011
  145 PLAINFIELD RD   08840   549-7600
  Br. Cairns, prin.

Middlesex, AC 908, PC 7, Middlesex
Middlesex Borough SD   4-11111
  300 JOHN F KENNEDY DR   08846   968-2666
  Ron Campbell, supt.
HS, 300 JOHN F KENNEDY DR   08846   3-00011
  Peter Diskin, prin.   968-0202
Mauger MS, FISHER AVE   08846   3-01100
  Thomas Grifa, prin.   356-6108

Middletown, AC 908, PC 8, Monmouth
Middletown Township SD   7-11111
  59 TINDALL RD   07748   706-6002
  Peter Merluzzi, supt.
Middletown-North HS   4-00011
  63 TINDALL RD   07748 – (—), prin.   706-6061
Middletown-South HS   4-00011
  501 NUTSWAMP RD   07748   706-6111
  Ronald Pietkewicz, prin.
Thompson MS   3-00100
  1001 MIDDLETOWN LINCROFT RD   07748
  Patrick Houston, prin.   671-2212
Other Schools – See Leonardo, Port Monmouth

Midland Park, AC 201, PC 6, Bergen
Midland Park Borough SD   4-11111
  31 HIGHLAND AVE   07432   444-1400
  August DePreker, supt.
JSHS, 250 PROSPECT ST   07432   3-00111
  William Freeman, prin.   444-7400

Millburn, AC 201, PC 7, Essex
Millburn Township SD   5-11111
  434 MILLBURN AVE   07041   376-3600
  Gerald Kohn, supt.
HS, 462 MILLBURN AVE   07041   3-00011
  Keith Neigel, prin.   376-3600
MS, 25 OLD SHORT HILLS RD   07041   3-00100
  Nicholas Navarino, prin.   379-2600

Milburn School for Hearing Handicapped   HND
  SPRING & WILLOW STS   07041

Milltown, AC 908, PC 6, Middlesex
Milltown SD, VIOLET TER   08850   3-11100
  Walter Boright, supt.   828-8620
Kilmer MS, W CHURCH ST   08850   2-01100
  Bertram Nussbaum, prin.   828-0500

Millville, AC 609, PC 8, Cumberland
Millville SD, PO BOX 1278   08332   6-11111
  Gene Stanley, supt.   327-6001
SHS, 200 N WADE BLVD   08332   4-00001
  Warren Elliot, prin.   327-6040
Memorial Freshman HS   3-00110
  500 E BROAD ST   08332   327-6042
  Stephen Burke, prin.

Titan Helicopter Academy   2-CS
  BLDG 90 EASTERWOOD ST   08332   327-5203

Minotola, AC 609, PC see Buena
Buena Regional SD
  Supt. — See Buena
Cleary MS, 1309 CENTRAL AVE   08341   3-00100
  Joseph Capizola, prin.   697-0100

Monmouth Junction, AC 908, PC 4, Middlesex
South Brunswick Township SD   4-11111
  PO BOX 181   08852   297-7800
  Samuel Stewart, supt.
South Brunswick HS   3-00011
  PO BOX 183   08852   329-4044
  Richard Kaye, prin.
Crossroads MS, GEORGES ROAD   08852   3-00100
  Gary Abbamont, prin.   329-4633

Monroeville, AC 609, PC 2, Salem
Upper Pittsgrove Township SD   2-11100
  RR 2 BOX 63   08343   358-8163
  Lillian Chambers, supt.
Upper Pittsgrove MS   2-01100
  RR 2 BOX 63   08343   358-8163
  Lillian Chambers, prin.

Montclair, AC 201, PC 8, Essex
Montclair SD, 22 VALLEY RD   07042   6-11111
  William Librera, supt.   509-4010
HS, 100 CHESTNUT ST   07042   4-00011
  Elaine Davis, prin.   509-4100
Glenfield MS, 25 MAPLE AVE   07042   3-00100
  David Gidich, prin.   509-4171
Mt. Hebron MS   3-01100
  173 BELLEVUE AVE   07043   509-4207
  Frank Alvarez, prin.

Immaculate Conception HS   2-00011
  33 COTTAGE PL   07042   744-7445
  Sr. Maureen Crowley, prin.
Katharine Gibbs School   3-CC
  33 PLYMOUTH ST   07042   744-6967
Lacordaire Academy   1-00011
  155 LORRAINE AVE   07043   744-1156
  Sr. Suzanne McCaffrey, prin.
Montclair-Kimberley Academy   3-11111
  201 VALLEY RD   07042   746-9800
  Francis O'Connor, prin.
Mountainside Hospital   HSP
  1 BAY AVE   07042   429-6061

Montvale, AC 201, PC 6, Bergen
Montvale SD   3-11100
  47 SPRING VALLEY RD   07645   391-1662
  Richard Rice, supt.
Fieldstone MS   2-01100
  47 SPRING VALLEY RD   07645   391-9000
  Roy Montesano, prin.

Pascack Valley Regional HSD   4-00011
  46 AKERS AVE   07645   358-7006
  Richard Willett, supt.
Pascack Hills HS   3-00011
  225 W GRAND AVE   07645   358-7020
  Bart DiPaola, prin.
Other Schools – See Hillsdale

St. Joseph Regional HS   2-00011
  40 CHESTNUT RIDGE RD   07645   391-3300
  Br. Cushing, prin.

Montville, AC 201, PC 5, Morris
Montville Township SD
  Supt. — See Pine Brook
HS, 100 HORSENECK RD   07045   3-00011
  Mario Cardinale, prin.   331-7100
Lazar MS   3-00100
  123 CHANGEBRIDGE RD   07045   331-4140
  Edward Michaelson, prin.

Moorestown, AC 609, PC 7, Burlington
Moorestown Township SD   5-11111
  803 N STANWICK RD   08057   235-4000
  Vito Germinario, supt.
HS, 350 BRIDGEBORO RD   08057   3-00011
  Lawrence Ludd, prin.   235-4000
Allen MS, 801 N STANWICK RD   08057   3-01100
  Cheryl Simone, prin.   235-4000

Moorestown Friends S   3-11111
  110 E MAIN ST   08057   235-2900
  Allan Craig, prin.

Morris Plains, AC 201, PC 6, Morris
Morris Plains SD   2-11100
  500 SPEEDWELL AVE   07950   539-8818
  Thomas Jones, supt.
Borough MS   2-01100
  500 SPEEDWELL AVE   07950   538-1650
  Ed Paone, prin.

Parsippany-Troy Hills Township SD
  Supt. — See Parsippany
Parsippany Hills HS, 20 RITA DR   07950   4-00011
  Anthony Sciaino, prin.   682-2826

Morristown, AC 201, PC 7, Morris
Morris SD, 27 NORMANDY PKY   07960   5-11111
  William McIvor, supt.   292-2010
HS, 50 EARLY ST   07960   4-00011
  James Galbraith, prin.   292-2100
Frelinghuysen MS   3-00100
  200 W HANOVER AVE   07960   292-2200
  Dan Skelton, prin.

Delbarton JSHS   3-00111
  270 MENDHAM RD   07960   538-3231
  Fr. Beatus Lucey, prin.
Morristown-Beard S   2-00111
  PO BOX 1999   07962   539-3032
  Phillip Anderson, prin.
Morristown Memorial Hospital   HSP
  100 MADISON AVE   07960   540-5177
Rabbinical College of America   2-UC
  226 SUSSEX AVE   07960   267-9404
Villa Walsh Academy   2-00111
  455 WESTERN AVE   07960   538-3680
  Sr. Patricia Pompa, prin.

Mountain Lakes, AC 201, PC 5, Morris
Mountain Lakes SD   4-11111
  400 BOULEVARD   07046   334-8280
  John Sakala, supt.
JSHS, 96 POWERVILLE RD   07046   2-00111
  Douglas Wilkins, prin.   334-8400

Mount Arlington, AC 201, PC 5, Morris
Mt. Arlington SD   2-11100
  235 HOWARD BLVD   07856   398-4400
  William Desmond, supt.
MS, 235 HOWARD BLVD   07856   2-01100
  JoAnn Cowing, prin.   398-4400

Mount Ephraim, AC 609, PC 5, Camden
Mt. Ephraim Borough SD   2-11100
  121 S BLACK HORSE PIKE   08059   931-1634
  Richard Serfling, supt.
Kershaw MS   2-01100
  125 S BLACK HORSE PIKE   08059   931-1634
  Richard Serfling, prin.

Mount Holly, AC 609, PC 7, Burlington
Burlington County Vocational SD   4-00011
  695 WOODLANE RD   08060   267-4226
  Walter Rudder, supt.
Institute of Technology   3-00011
  695 WOODLANE RD   08060   267-4226
  Daniel Money, prin.
Other Schools – See Medford

Eastampton Township SD
  Supt. — See Eastampton
Eastampton MS, 1 STUDENT DR   08060   2-01100
  John Holcroft, prin.   267-9172

Mt. Holly Township SD   4-11100
  301 LEVIS DR   08060   267-7108
  Donald Lucas, supt.
Holbein MS, 301 LEVIS DR   08060   2-01100
  Lawrence Donahue, prin.   267-7200

Rancocas Valley Regional HSD   4-00011
  520 JACKSONVILLE RD   08060   267-0830
  Henry Cram, supt.
Rancocas Valley Regional HS   4-00011
  520 JACKSONVILLE RD   08060   267-0830
  Henry Cram, prin.

Westampton Township SD   3-11100
  710 RANCOCAS RD   08060   261-1969
  Dan Martin, supt.
Westampton MS   2-01100
  700 RANCOCAS RD   08060   267-2722
  D. Harris, prin.

Burlington Co. Memorial Hospital   HSP
  175 MADISON AVE   08060   267-0700

Mount Laurel, AC 609, PC 2, Burlington
Mt. Laurel Township SD   5-11100
  330 MRESTOWN MOUNT LAURE RD   08054   235-3387
  James Anzide, supt.
Harrington MS   4-00100
  514 MRESTOWN MOUNT LAURE RD   08054   234-1610
  James Waskovich, prin.

Cittone Institute   2-CS
  523 FELLOWSHIP RD   08054   722-9333
Heritage Christian Academy   2-11111
  530 UNION MILL RD   08054   234-1145

Mullica Hill, AC 609, PC 4, Gloucester
Clearview Regional SD   4-00111
  PO BOX 429   08062   478-0044
  Michael Toscano, supt.
Clearview Regional SHS   3-00001
  PO BOX 429   08062   478-4400
  Greg Amiriantz, prin.
Clearview Regional JHS   3-00110
  PO BOX 429   08062   478-4400
  Charles Bishop, prin.

Neptune, AC 908, PC 8, Monmouth
Neptune Township SD   5-11111
  2106 W BANGS AVE   07753   776-2001
  Michael Lake, supt.
HS, 55 NEPTUNE BLVD   07753   4-00100
  Robert Morgan, prin.   776-2200
MS, 2100 HECK AVE   07753   3-00100
  Sylvia Thomas, prin.   776-2100

Jersey Shore Medical Center   HSP
  1945 STATE ROUTE 33   07753   680-4400

Neshanic Station, AC 908, PC 2, Somerset
Hillsborough Township SD   6-11111
  555 AMWELL RD   08853   369-0030
  Robert Gulick, supt.
Other Schools – See Belle Mead, Somerville

Newark, AC 201, PC 10, Essex
Essex County Vocational SD
  Supt. — See East Orange
Essex County Vocational HS-Market Street   3-00011
  91 W MARKET ST   07103   622-1100
  Robert Fiorini, prin.
Essex County Vocational HS-13th Street   3-00011
  300 N 13TH ST   07107   483-5466
  James Southers, prin.
Essex County Tech Career Ctr   07107   Vo Tech
  Samuel Carollo, prin.   622-1100
Newark SD, 2 CEDAR ST   07102   8-11111
  Eugene Campbell, supt.   733-7333
Arts HS   2-00011
  556 MRTN LTHER KING JR BLVD   07102
  Eleta Caldwell, prin.   733-6757
Barringer HS, 90 PARKER ST   07104   4-00011
  Ben O'Neal, prin.   268-5125
Central HS, 100 SUMMIT ST   07103   3-00011
  Norma Brown, prin.   733-6897
East Side HS, 238 VAN BUREN ST   07105   4-00011
  Rob Wujciak, prin.   465-4900
Science HS, 40 RECTOR ST   07102   2-00011
  Christine Taylor, prin.   733-8689
Shabazz HS, 80 JOHNSON AVE   07108   4-00011
  Mary Bennett, prin.   733-6760
Weequahic HS   4-00011
  279 CHANCELLOR AVE   07112   705-3900
  Richard Williams, prin.
West Side HS   4-00011
  403 S ORANGE AVE   07103   733-6977
  Fernard Williams, prin.
University JSHS, 55 CLINTON PL   07108   2-00111
  Doris Culver, prin.   374-3190
Barringer Prep. School   3-00010
  163 WEBSTER ST   07111   268-5100
  John Petrozzino, prin.
Brown Academy MS   3-01100
  695 BERGEN ST   07108   733-6844
  Frank Walters, prin.
Camden MS, 321 BERGEN ST   07103   3-01100
  Dorothea Brownlee, prin.   733-8350
Chancellor Avenue MS   2-01100
  321 CHANCELLOR AVE   07112   705-3870
  Geneva Wardell, prin.
Maple Avenue MS   2-01100
  33 MAPLE AVE   07112   705-3850
  Esther Wright, prin.
Marin MS, 663 BROADWAY   07104   3-00100
  Lius Lopez, prin.   268-5330
Vailsburg MS, 107 IVY ST   07106   3-00100
  August Alamo, prin.   374-3295

Bilingual Institute   2-CS
  685 BROAD ST   07102   624-3883
Chad Science Academy   2-00011
  370 S 7TH ST   07103   623-4806
Essex County College   5-CC
  303 UNIVERSITY AVE   07102   877-3100

Link Community S   2-00100
  139 LIVINGSTON ST   07103   642-0529
  Sr. Patricia McKearney, prin.
Newark Beth Israel Medical Center   HSP
  201 LYONS AVE   07112   926-7000
New Jersey Institute of Technology   6-UC
  323 MRTN LTHER KING JR BLVD   07102   596-3000
Our Lady of Good Counsel HS   2-00011
  243 WOODSIDE AVE   07104   482-6493
  Sr. Ann Fagan, prin.
PTC Career Institute   2-CS
  200 WASHINGTON ST   07102   623-1100
Rutgers-The State U of NJ/Newark Coll.   5-UC
  249 UNIVERSITY AVE   07102   648-5205
Rutgers-The State U of NJ/Nursing   2-UC
  249 UNIVERSITY AVE   07102   648-5205
Rutgers-The State U of NJ/Univ. Coll.   3-UC
  249 UNIVERSITY AVE   07102   648-5205
St. Benedict Prep S   3-00111
  520 MRTN LTHER KING JR BLVD   07102
  Fr. Leahy, prin.   643-4800
St. Michael's Medical Center   HSP
  268 MRTN LTHER KING JR BLVD   07102   877-5411
St. Vincent Academy   2-00010
  228 W MARKET ST   07103   622-1613
  Sr. June Favata, prin.
SCS Business & Technical Institute   2-CS
  756 BROAD ST   07102   623-3939
Seton Hall University   4-UC
  1095 RAYMOND BLVD   07102   642-8750
University of Medicine & Dentistry   5-UC
  30 BERGEN ST   07107   456-4300

New Brunswick, AC 908, PC 8, Middlesex
Middlesex Co. Vocational-Technical HSD
  Supt. — See East Brunswick
New Brunswick Vocational HS   3-00011
  256 EASTON AVE   08901   247-3832
  Gerald Bohrer, prin.

New Brunswick SD   5-11111
  24 BAYARD ST   08901   745-5414
  Ron Larkin, supt.
JSHS, 1125 LIVINGSTON AVE   08901   3-00111
  Fred Brown, prin.   745-5334

New Brunswick Theological Seminary   2-UC
  17 SEMINARY PL   08901   247-5241
Rutgers-The State U of NJ   08903   3-UC   932-1766
Rutgers-The State U of NJ/Cook   5-UC
  GEORGE ST   08901   932-1766
Rutgers-The State U of NJ/Douglass   08903   5-UC   932-1766
Rutgers-The State U of NJ/Livingston   5-UC
  08903   932-1766
Rutgers-The State U of NJ/Mason Gross   2-UC
  08903   932-1766
Rutgers-The State U of NJ/Pharmacy   3-UC
  08903   932-1766
Rutgers-The State U of NJ/Rutgers Coll.   6-UC
  08903   932-1766
Rutgers-The State U of NJ/Univ. Coll.   4-UC
  GEORGE ST   08901   932-1766
St. Peter HS, 175 SOMERSET ST   08901   2-00011
  Sr. Maureen Cawley, prin.   846-8046
St. Peter's Medical Center   HSP
  254 EASTON AVE   08901   745-8600
Shoreless Lake HS, 75 MORRIS ST   08901   1-01111
  Fr. Pascual, prin.   725-4879

Newfield, AC 609, PC 4, Gloucester

Our Lady of Mercy Academy HS   2-00011
  RR 1 BOX 159   08344   697-2008
  Sr. Grace Scandale, prin.

New Milford, AC 201, PC 7, Bergen
New Milford SD   4-11111
  145 MADISON AVE   07646   261-2952
  Mario Volpe, supt.
JSHS, 330 RIVER RD   07646   3-00111
  John Moncrief, prin.   262-0172

New Monmouth, AC 908, PC see Middletown

Mater Dei HS, 538 CHURCH ST   07748   2-00011
  Frank Poleski, prin.   671-9100

Newport, AC 609, PC 2, Cumberland
Downe Township SD   2-11100
  ROUTE 553   08345   447-3878
  Joseph Webb, supt.
Downe Twp. MS, ROUTE 553   08345   2-01100
  Mary Ann Russell, prin.   447-4673

New Providence, AC 908, PC 7, Union
New Providence SD   4-11111
  340 CENTRAL AVE   07974   464-9050
  David Sousa, supt.
HS, 35 PIONEER DR   07974   2-00011
  Geoffrey Gorden, prin.   464-4700
MS, 35 PIONEER DR   07974   2-00100
  Frank Delasandro, prin.   464-4700

Newton, AC 201, PC 6, Sussex
Andover Regional SD   3-11100
  707 LIMECREST RD   07860   383-3746
  Dennis Pallozzi, supt.
Burd MS   2-01100
  219 NEWTON SPARTA RD   07860   383-3721
  Frank Mobilio, prin.

Kittatinny Regional SD   3-00111
  RR 10 BOX 10255   07860   383-1800
  Rob Walker, supt.
Kittatinny Regional JSHS   3-00111
  RR 10 BOX 10255   07860   383-1800
  Benjamin Miller, prin.

Newton SD, 57 TRINITY ST   07860   4-11111
  Roberta Watson, supt.   383-1900
HS, 44 RYERSON AVE   07860   3-00111
  John Frank, prin.   383-7993
Halsted Street MS, HALSTED ST   07860   2-01100
  John Hannum, prin.   383-7440

Sussex County Community College   4-CC
  COLLEGE HILL   07860   300-2100

North Arlington, AC 201, PC 7, Bergen
North Arlington SD, 222 RIDGE RD   07031   4-11111
  William Mancuso, supt.   955-5200
JSHS, 222 RIDGE RD   07031   3-00111
  Robert Kinloch, prin.   955-5216

Queen of Peace HS   3-00011
  191 RUTHERFORD PL   07031   998-8227
  Br. Olert, prin.

North Bergen, AC 201, PC 8, Hudson
Hudson County Board of Trustees   3-00000
  8511 TONNELLE AVE   07047   854-6800
  Frank Gargiulo, supt.
Hudson County AVTS North Hudson Ctr   Vo Tech
  2000 85TH ST   07047   854-4797
  Russel Pascale, prin.
Hudson County AVTS at Bayonne   Vo Tech
  8511 TONNELLE AVE   07047   858-5861
  Yvonne Hatchett, prin.
Other Schools – See Jersey City

North Bergen SD   6-11111
  7317 KENNEDY BLVD   07047   868-1000
  Leo Gattoni, supt.
HS, 7417 KENNEDY BLVD   07047   4-00011
  Paschal Tennaro, prin.   868-1000

North Brunswick, AC 908, PC 8, Middlesex
North Brunswick Twp. SD   5-11111
  PO BOX 1807   08903   297-9000
  Ed Leppert, supt.
North Brunswick Twp. HS   4-00011
  1 RAIDER RD   08902   821-8200
  Leonard Simkin, prin.
Linwood MS, 25 LINWOOD PL   08902   3-00100
  Vito D'Eufemia, prin.   247-5712

North Caldwell, AC 201, PC 5, Essex
West Essex Regional SD   4-00111
  65 W GREENBROOK RD   07006   228-1200
  Gary Vitta, supt.
West Essex SHS   3-00001
  65 W GREENBROOK RD   07006   228-1200
  Joseph Garvey, prin.
West Essex JHS   3-00110
  65 W GREENBROOK RD   07006   228-1200
  August Belotti, prin.

Northfield, AC 609, PC 6, Atlantic
Northfield CSD, 547 TILTON RD   08225   3-11100
  Don Adams, supt.   641-5181
Mill Road MS, 400 W MILL RD   08225   2-00100
  Cliff Nusbaum, prin.   641-1731

North Haledon, AC 201, PC 6, Passaic
North Haledon SD   3-11100
  515 HIGH MOUNTAIN RD   07508   427-1220
  Charles Ferraro, supt.
High Mountain MS   2-01100
  515 HIGH MOUNTAIN RD   07508   427-1220
  Donna Cardiello, prin.

Eastern Christian S   2-00011
  50 OAKWOOD AVE   07508   427-0900
  Jan Lucas, prin.
Mary Help Christians Academy   2-00011
  659 BELMONT AVE   07508   790-6200
  Sr. Karen Dunn, prin.

North Plainfield, AC 908, PC 7, Somerset
North Plainfield SD   5-11111
  33 MOUNTAIN AVE   07060   769-6060
  Dwight Pfennig, supt.
JSHS, 34 WILSON AVE   07060   4-00111
  Roger Weber, prin.   769-6003

Northvale, AC 201, PC 5, Bergen
Northvale SD, 441 TAPPAN RD   07647   2-11100
  Robert McGuire, supt.   768-8485
Hale MS, PARIS AVE   07647   2-01100
  Janice Krasilovsky, prin.   768-0635

Nutley, AC 201, PC 8, Essex
Nutley SD, 375 BLOOMFIELD AVE   07110   5-11111
  James Fadule, supt.   661-8798
HS, 300 FRANKLIN AVE   07110   4-00011
  John Jacone, prin.   661-8832
Franklin MS, 325 FRANKLIN AVE   07110   3-00100
  James Vivinetto, prin.   661-8871

NEC-RETS Campus   3-CS
  103 PARK AVE   07110   661-0600

Oakhurst, AC 908, PC 5, Monmouth
Ocean Township SD   5-11111
  163 MONMOUTH RD   07755   531-5600
  Robert Mahon, supt.

Ocean Twp. HS, 550 W PARK AVE 07755   4-00011
  John Tighe, prin.   531-5650
  Other Schools – See Ocean

Oakland, AC 201, PC 7, Bergen
  Oakland SD   4-11100
    315 RAMAPO VALLEY RD 07436   337-3133
    Lawrence Ksanznak, supt.
  Valley MS, 71 OAK ST 07436   2-00100
    Richard Heflich, prin.   337-8185

Ramapo Indian Hills Regional HSD
  Supt. — See Franklin Lakes
  Indian Hills HS, 97 YAWPO AVE 07436   3-00011
    Ronald Frederick, prin.   337-0100

Oaklyn, AC 609, PC 5, Camden
  Oaklyn Borough SD   2-11110
    136 KENDALL BLVD 08107   858-0335
    Barry MacGibeny, supt.
  JHS, 136 KENDALL BLVD 08107   2-00110
    Patricia Moore, prin.   858-0335

Oak Ridge, AC 201, PC 3, Morris
  Jefferson Township SD
    Supt. — See Lake Hopatcong
  Jefferson Twp. HS   3-00011
    RR 2 BOX 142 07438   697-3535
    Robert Ross, prin.
  Jefferson Twp. MS   3-00100
    RR 2 BOX 141 07438   697-1980
    Leonard Goduto, prin.

Ocean, AC 908, PC 7, Monmouth
  Ocean Township SD
    Supt. — See Oakhurst
  Ocean Twp. IS, 1200 W PARK AVE 07712   4-01100
    Donald Vineburg, prin.   532-5631

Hillel Yeshiva ES, 1025 DEAL RD 07712   3-1111
     493-9300
Star Technical Institute   2-CS
  2105 HIGHWAY 35 07712   493-1660

Ocean City, AC 609, PC 7, Cape May
  Ocean City SD, 801 ASBURY AVE 08226   4-11111
    Donald Dearborn, supt.   399-5150
  HS, 701 E 6TH ST 08226   4-00011
    Michael Cipriano, prin.   399-1290
  IS, 1801 BAY AVE 08226   3-01100
    Lyle Alverson, prin.   399-5611

Oceanport, AC 908, PC 6, Monmouth
  Oceanport Borough SD   3-11100
    55 WOLFHILL AVE 07757   544-8588
    Glenn Morgan, supt.
  Maple Place MS, 2 MAPLE PL 07757   2-01100
    Susan Sposato, prin.   229-0267

Old Bridge, AC 908, PC 6, Middlesex
  Old Bridge Township SD
    Supt. — See Matawan
  Cedar Ridge HS, RR 1 08857   4-00011
    Patrick Burns, prin.   290-3901
  Madison Central HS   4-00011
    3439 COUNTY ROAD 516 08857   360-4401
    Joseph Sweeney, prin.
  Salk MS, RR 2 08857   3-00100
    Joseph Alvarez, prin.   360-4519
  Sandburg MS, ROUTE 516 08857   3-00100
    Joseph Wydra, prin.   290-3886

Old Tappan, AC 201, PC 5, Bergen
  Northern Valley Regional SD
    Supt. — See Demarest
  Northern Valley Regional HS   4-00011
    150 CENTRAL AVE 07675   768-3200
    Anthony Panico, prin.

Old Tappan SD, 1 SCHOOL ST 07675   3-11100
    Raymond Albano, supt.   664-7231
DeWolf MS, 275 OLD TAPPAN RD 07675   2-01100
    Robert Lynch, prin.   664-1475

Oradell, AC 201, PC 6, Bergen
  River-Dell Regional HSD   4-00111
    55 PYLE ST 07649   599-7206
    Robert Van Zanten, supt.
  River Dell SHS, 55 PYLE ST 07649   3-00001
    Lorraine Brooks, prin.   599-7240
  River Dell JHS, 55 PYLE ST 07649   3-00110
    Richard Lukesh, prin.   599-7246

Bergen Catholic HS   3-00011
  1040 ORADELL AVE 07649   261-1816
  Br. Sullo, prin.

Orange, AC 201, PC 8, Essex
  Orange CSD, 369 MAIN ST 07050   5-11111
    Bernice Davis, supt.   677-4040
  HS, 400 LINCOLN AVE 07050   3-00011
    Richard Gardner, prin.   677-4050
  MS, 400 CENTRAL AVE 07050   3-00100
    Gloria Taylor, prin.   677-4135

Hospital Center at Orange   HSP
  188 S ESSEX AVE 07050   266-2060
Islamic Day S, 261 WILLIAM ST 07050   2-11111
     672-4124

Palisades Park, AC 201, PC 7, Bergen
  Palisades Park SD, 270 1ST ST 07650   4-11111
    James Nichols, supt.   947-3560
  JSHS, 1 TRAFALGAR RD 07650   3-00111
    Anthony Caruso, prin.   941-1100

Notre Dame S, 312 1ST ST 07650   2-01100
  Sr. Ellen McMahon, prin.   947-5262

Palmyra, AC 609, PC 6, Burlington
  Palmyra Borough SD   4-11111
    301 DELAWARE AVE 08065   786-9300
    Dennis Hurley, supt.
  JSHS, 5TH & WEART BLVD 08065   3-00111
    Matthew Busillo, prin.   786-9400

Paramus, AC 201, PC 8, Bergen
  Bergen County Vocational SD
    Supt. — See Hackensack
  Paramus Vo S, 265 PASCACK RD 07652   Vo Tech
    Phillip Allocca, prin.   986-0008

Paramus SD   5-11111
  145 SPRING VALLEY RD 07652   261-7800
  Harry Galinsky, supt.
HS, 99 E CENTURY RD 07652   4-00011
  Richard Zanella, prin.   261-7800
East Brook MS   2-01100
  190 SPRING VALLEY RD 07652   261-1566
  Charles Brown, prin.
West Brook MS   3-01100
  550 ROOSEVELT BLVD 07652   652-3907
  Barbara Hyde, prin.

Bergen Community College   7-CC
  400 PARAMUS RD 07652   447-7100
Business Training Institute   2-CS
  4 FOREST AVE 07652   845-9300
Computer Learning Center   3-CS
  160 E ROUTE 4 07652   845-6868
Dover Business College   2-CS
  E-81 ROUTE 4 W 07652   843-8500
Frisch School, 243 FRISCH CT 07652   2-00011
  Rabbi Meier, prin.   845-0555
Paramus Catholic HS   2-00011
  425 PARAMUS RD 07652   445-6465
  Br. Stolz, prin.
Plaza School of Technology   2-CS
  BERGEN MALL 07652   843-0344

Park Ridge, AC 201, PC 6, Bergen
  Park Ridge SD, 2 PARK AVE 07656   4-11111
    Catherine Mozak, supt.   930-4856
  JSHS, 2 PARK AVE 07656   2-00111
    Emil Binotto, prin.   930-4867

Parlin, AC 908, PC see Sayreville
  Sayreville SD, 1 TAFT PL 08859   5-11111
    Marie Parnell, supt.   525-5224
  War Memorial HS   4-00011
    820 WASHINGTON RD 08859   525-5252
    Dennis Fyffe, prin.
  Sayreville MS   4-01100
    800 WASHINGTON RD 08859   525-5290
    Soren Thomsen, prin.

Parsippany, AC 201, PC 8, Morris
  Parsippany-Troy Hills Township SD   6-11111
    PO BOX 52 07054   263-7250
    Timothy Brennan, supt.
  HS, 309 BALDWIN RD 07054   3-00011
    Melvin Zerkes, prin.   263-7022
  Brooklawn MS   3-00100
    250 BEECHWOOD RD 07054   428-7551
    Kenneth Graham, prin.
  Central MS, 1602 ROUTE 46 07054   3-00100
    Angelo Guiliana, prin.   263-7125
  Other Schools – See Morris Plains

Chubb Institute   4-CS
  PO BOX 342 07054   682-4900
Parsippany Christian S   2-11111
  PO BOX 5365 07054   539-7012

Passaic, AC 201, PC 8, Passaic
  Passaic CSD, 101 PASSAIC ST 07055   6-11111
    Robert Holster, supt.   470-5201
  HS, 186 PAULISON AVE 07055   4-00011
    Marjorie Bunnell, prin.   470-5600
  Lincoln MS   4-00100
    300 LAFAYETTE AVE 07055   470-5504
    Lawrence Everett, prin.

Collegiate S, 7 PASSAIC AVE 07055   1-11111
  Angela Gibson, prin.   777-1714

Paterson, AC 201, PC 9, Passaic
  Paterson SD, 33 CHURCH ST 07505   7-11111
    Laval Wilson, supt.   881-6213
  Eastside HS, MARKET ST 07501   4-00011
    Charles Lighty, prin.   881-6301
  Kennedy HS   4-00011
    127 PREAKNESS AVE 07522   881-6263
    Judith Sampson, prin.
  Parks Arts HS   2-00011
    12TH AVE AND 28TH ST 07514   881-6365
    Tony Wells, prin.
  MS 4, 55 CLINTON ST 07522   2-01100
    Richard Garibel, prin.   881-6012
  Paterson City ES 7   2-01100
    106 RAMSEY ST 07501   881-6038
    Henry Focacci, prin.

Barnett Memorial Hospital   HSP
  680 BROADWAY 07514   977-6730
Bilingual Institute   2-CS
  2 W BROADWAY 07505   279-8988

Don Bosco Technical HS   2-00011
  202 UNION AVE 07502   595-8800
  Fr. Alejunas, prin.
Passaic Co. Community College   5-CC
  170 COLLEGE BLVD 07505   684-6800
Paterson Catholic HS   2-00011
  764 11TH AVE 07514   278-1024
  Sr. Gloria Perez, prin.
St. Joseph's Medical Center   HSP
  703 MAIN ST 07503   977-2001

Paulsboro, AC 609, PC 6, Gloucester
  Paulsboro SD   4-11111
    700 N DELAWARE ST 08066   423-5515
    Walter Quint, supt.
  JSHS, 700 N DELAWARE ST 08066   3-00111
    Joseph Manzione, prin.   423-2222

Pedricktown, AC 609, PC 4, Salem
  Oldmans Township SD   2-11100
    RR 1 BOX 336B 08067   299-4240
    Maurice Madden, supt.
  Oldmans MS, RR 1 BOX 336B 08067   2-01100
    Maurice Madden, prin.   299-4240

Pemberton, AC 609, PC 4, Burlington
  Pemberton Township SD
    Supt. — See Browns Mills
  Pemberton Township HS   4-00011
    0 ARNEYS MOUNT PEMBERTON RD 08068   894-4833
    Robert Holmes, prin.
  Fort MS   3-00100
    FORT DIX PEMBERTON RD 08068   894-8223
    Wendy Schadt, prin.

Burlington County College   6-CC
  COUNTY ROUTE 530 08068   894-9311

Pennington, AC 609, PC 5, Mercer
  Hopewell Valley Regional SD   5-11111
    425 S MAIN ST 08534   737-0105
    David Thomas, supt.
  Central HS   3-00011
    259 PNNINGTON TITUSVILLE RD 08534   737-1411
    David Oliver, prin.
  Timberlane MS   2-00100
    50 TIMBERLANE DR 08534   737-0200
    Michael Fitzpatrick, prin.

Pennington S   2-00111
  112 W DELAWARE AVE 08534   737-1838
  Deborah Cook, prin.

Pennsauken, AC 609, PC 8, Camden
  Camden County Vocational SD
    Supt. — See Sicklerville
  Camden County Vocational-Technical HS   3-00011
    6008 BROWNING RD 08109   663-1040
    Robert Morelli, prin.

Pennsauken Township SD   6-11111
  800 HYLTON RD 08110   662-8500
  Harold Kurtz, supt.
HS, 800 HYLTON RD 08110   4-00011
  John Ritchie, prin.   662-8500
Phifer MS, 8201 PARK AVE 08109   4-00100
  James Chapman, prin.   662-8500

Bishop Eustace Prep S   3-00011
  ROUTE 70 08109   662-2160
  Fr. Firneno, prin.
Lincoln Technical Institute   4-CS
  2100 HADDONFIELD RD STE F 08110   665-3010

Penns Grove, AC 609, PC 6, Salem
  Penns Grove-Carneys Point SD   4-11111
    113 W HARMONY ST 08069   299-4250
    Robert Bender, supt.
  MS, 351 E MAPLE AVE 08069   3-00100
    (—), prin.   299-0576
  Other Schools – See Carney's Point

St. James HS   2-00011
  350 GEORGETOWN RD 08069   299-0400
  Fr. Osinski, prin.

Pennsville, AC 609, PC 7, Salem
  Pennsville Township SD   4-11111
    30 CHURCH ST 08070   540-6210
    Ron Capasso, supt.
  Pennsville Memorial HS   3-00011
    110 S BROADWAY 08070   540-6220
    Michael Gorman, prin.
  MS, 4 WILLIAM PENN AVE 08070   3-00100
    Anthony Iatarola, prin.   540-6240

Park Bible Academy   2-11111
  104 SPARKS AVE 08070   678-9464

Perth Amboy, AC 908, PC 8, Middlesex
  Middlesex Co. Vocational-Technical HSD
    Supt. — See East Brunswick
  Perth Amboy Vocational HS   2-00011
    618 NEW BRUNSWICK AVE 08861   442-9595
    Carl Klumb, prin.

Perth Amboy SD   6-11111
  178 BARRACKS ST 08861   826-3360
  Jack De Talvo, supt.
HS, 300 EAGLE AVE 08861   4-00011
  Ben Rotella, prin.   826-3360
McGinnis MS, 271 STATE ST 08861   4-01100
  Alvin Mattes, prin.   826-3360

Shull MS, 380 HALL AVE 08861　　3-01100
　Robert Mantz, prin.　　826-3360

Raritan Bay Medical Center　　HSP
530 NEW BRUNSWICK AVE 08861　　324-5232

Phillipsburg, AC 908, PC 7, Warren
Phillipsburg SD　　5-11111
675 CORLISS AVE 08865　　454-3400
　Thomas Seidenberger, supt.
HS, 200 HILLCREST BLVD 08865　　4-00011
　Kenneth Lutz, prin.　　454-6551
MS, 525 WARREN ST 08865　　3-00100
　H. Pethick, prin.　　454-5577

All Saints HS, 137 ROSEBERRY ST 08865　　2-00111
James Duris, prin.　　859-1244

Pine Beach, AC 908, PC 4, Ocean

Admiral Farragut Academy　　2-01111
601 RIVERSIDE DR 08741　　349-1253
Col. Harrington, prin.

Pine Brook, AC 201, PC 3, Morris
Montville Township SD　　5-11111
39 WOODMONT RD 07058　　808-2020
　Richard Bozza, supt.
Other Schools – See Montville

Pine Hill, AC 609, PC 6, Camden
Lower Camden County Regional HSD 1
　Supt. — See Atco
Overbrook Regional HS　　4-00011
1200 TURNERVILLE RD 08021　　767-8000
Paul Harmelin, prin.

Piscataway, AC 908, PC 8, Middlesex
Middlesex Co. Vocational-Technical HSD
　Supt. — See East Brunswick
Piscataway Vocational HS　　3-00011
21 SUTTONS LN 08854　　985-0717
Richard Stone, prin.
Piscataway Township SD　　6-11111
1515 STELTON RD 08854　　572-2289
　Philip Geiger, supt.
Piscataway Twp. HS　　4-00011
325 HOES LN 08854 – (—), prin.　　981-0700
Conackamack MS　　2-00100
5001 WITHERSPOON ST 08854　　981-0700
　John Gardner, prin.
Quibbletown MS　　2-00100
WASHINGTON AVE 08854　　981-0700
　James Koch, prin.
Schor MS　　2-00100
289 N RANDOLPHVILLE RD 08854　　981-0700
　Carol Rigney, prin.

Johnson Medical School　　2-UC
PO BOX 101 08855
Katharine Gibbs School　　2-CS
80 KINGSBRIDGE RD 08854　　885-1580
Timothy Christian S　　3-11111
2008 ETHEL RD 08854　　985-0116

Pitman, AC 609, PC 6, Gloucester
Pitman SD, PO BOX 88 08071　　4-11111
　Michael DiPaola, supt.　　589-2145
HS, 225 LINDEN AVE 08071　　2-00011
　Leonard Stevens, prin.　　589-0635

Gloucester Co. Christian S　　2-11111
PO BOX 89 08071　　589-1665

Pittstown, AC 908, PC 3, Hunterdon
Alexandria Township SD　　2-11100
RR 2 BOX 80 08867　　996-6811
　John Ammon, supt.
Alexandria MS, RR 2 BOX 80 08867　　2-01100
　John Ammon, prin.　　996-6811

Plainfield, AC 908, PC 8, Union
Plainfield SD, 504 MADISON AVE 07060　　6-11111
　Annette Kearney, supt.　　753-3155
JSHS, 950 PARK AVE 07060　　4-00111
　Lance Rosza, prin.　　753-3182
Hubbard MS, 661 W 8TH ST 07060　　2-00100
　(—), prin.　　753-3298
Maxson MS, 920 E 7TH ST 07062　　3-00100
　Edward Michaelson, prin.　　753-3330

Du Cret School of the Arts　　2-CS
1030 CENTRAL AVE 07060　　757-7171
Mt. St. Mary Academy　　2-00011
1645 US HIGHWAY 22 07060　　757-1750
　Sr. Eloise Kays, prin.
Muhlenberg Regional Medical Center　　HSP
1200 RANDOLPH RD 07060　　668-2418

Plainsboro, AC 609, PC 4, Middlesex
West Windsor-Plainsboro Regional SD
　Supt. — See Princeton Junction
West Windsor-Plainsboro MS　　4-00100
GROVERS MILL RD 08536　　799-9600
　Arthur Downs, prin.

Pleasantville, AC 609, PC 7, Atlantic
Egg Harbor Township SD　　5-11111
202 NAPLES AVE 08232　　646-7911
　Fred Nickles, supt.
Egg Harbor Twp. HS　　4-00011
24 HIGH SCHOOL DR 08232　　653-0100
　Ed Betts, prin.

Egg Harbor Twp MS　　3-00100
4034 FERNWOOD AVE 08232　　383-3355
　Donald Robertson, prin.

Pleasantville CSD　　5-11111
115 W DECATUR AVE 08232　　383-6810
　Judith Wilcox, supt.
HS, 350 S FRANKLIN AVE 08232　　3-00011
　Norman King, prin.　　383-6900

Point Pleasant, AC 908, PC 7, Ocean
Point Pleasant Beach SD　　3-11111
309 COOKS LN 08742　　899-8840
　F. Crawley, supt.
HS, 700 TRENTON AVE 08742　　2-00011
　Raymond Ellis, prin.　　899-1817

Point Pleasant Borough SD　　5-11111
2100 PANTHER PATH 08742　　892-0265
　George Kane, supt.
HS, 808 LAURA HERBERT DR 08742　　3-00011
　Richard Blake, prin.　　892-7500
Memorial MS　　3-00100
808 LAURA HERBERT DR 08742　　892-4050
　Roy Feldman, prin.

Pomona, AC 609, PC 5, Atlantic

Stockton State College　　6-UC
GENERAL DELIVERY 08240　　652-1776

Pompton Lakes, AC 201, PC 7, Passaic
Pompton Lakes SD, 237 VAN AVE 07442　　4-11111
　Joel McKenzie, supt.　　835-4334
HS, 44 LAKESIDE AVE 07442　　3-00011
　Ernest Fisher, prin.　　835-7100
Lakeside MS, 316 LAKESIDE AVE 07442　　2-00100
　Vincent Iraggi, prin.　　835-2221

Pompton Plains, AC 201, PC see Pequannock
Pequannock Township SD　　4-11111
85 SUNSET RD 07444　　616-6040
　Glenn Grube, supt.
Pequannock Twp. HS　　3-00011
85 SUNSET RD 07444　　616-6000
　Ralph Rizzolo, prin.
Pequannock Valley MS　　3-01100
493 TURNPIKE 07444　　616-6050
　Leslie Conlon, prin.

Chancellor Academy　　2-00011
PO BOX 218 07444　　835-4989
　Richard Sheridan, prin.

Port Elizabeth, AC 609, PC 3, Cumberland
Maurice River Township SD　　2-11100
PO BOX 464 08348　　825-7411
　Albert Monillas, supt.
Maurice River Twp. MS　　2-01100
PO BOX 464 08348　　825-7411
　Albert Monillas, prin.

Port Monmouth, AC 908, PC 5, Monmouth
Middletown Township SD
　Supt. — See Middletown
Thorne MS, 70 MURPHY RD 07758　　3-00100
　Marshall Culver, prin.　　787-1220

Port Norris, AC 609, PC 4, Cumberland
Commercial Township SD　　3-11100
RR 1 BOX 193 08349　　785-0222
　Barry Ballard, supt.
MS, RR 1 BOX 10A 08349　　2-01100
　Michael Killeen, prin.　　785-1611

Pottersville, AC 908, PC 3, Somerset

Purnell School for Girls　　1-00011
GENERAL DELIVERY 07979　　439-2154
　William Moran, prin.

Princeton, AC 609, PC 7, Mercer
Princeton Regional SD　　5-11111
PO BOX 711 08542　　924-9322
　Richard Willever, supt.
HS, 151 MOORE ST 08540　　3-00011
　Owen Snyder, prin.　　683-4480
Witherspoon MS　　3-00100
217 WALNUT LN 08540　　921-3135
　William Johnson, prin.

American Boy Choir S　　1-01100
19 LAMBERT DR 08540　　924-5858
　Thomas Thompson, prin.
Cittone Institute　　2-CS
100 CANAL POINTE BLVD 08540　　520-8798
Hun School of Princeton　　2-00111
176 EDGERSTOUNE RD 08540　　921-7600
　Gerald Donaldson, prin.
Princeton Day S, PO BOX 75 08544　　3-11111
　Duncan Alling, prin.　　924-6700
Princeton Theological Seminary　　3-UC
CN821 64 MERCER ST 08542　　921-8300
Princeton University 08544　　6-UC
　　258-3000
Raritan Valley Flying School　　1-CS
ROUTE 206 08540　　921-3100
Stuart Country Day S　　2-11111
1200 STUART RD 08540　　921-2330
　Margaret Schorr, prin.
Waldorf S, 1062 CHERRY HILL RD 08540　　2-01100
　　466-1970
Westminster Choir College of Rider Univ.　　2-UC
101 WALNUT LN 08540　　921-7100

Princeton Junction, AC 609, PC 4, Mercer
West Windsor-Plainsboro Regional SD　　6-11111
PO BOX 248 08550　　799-0200
　Ray Bandlow, supt.
West Windsor-Plainsboro HS　　4-00011
346 CLARKSVILLE RD 08550　　799-3200
　Michael Carr, prin.
Other Schools – See Plainsboro

Rahway, AC 908, PC 8, Union
Rahway SD, 1200 KLINE PL 07065　　5-11111
　Anthony Cavanna, supt.　　396-1020
HS, 1012 MADISON AVE 07065　　3-00011
　Antonio Garay, prin.　　396-1090
IS, 1200 KLINE PL 07065　　3-00100
　Ralph Manfredi, prin.　　396-1025

Ramsey, AC 201, PC 7, Bergen
Ramsey SD, 266 E MAIN ST 07446　　4-11111
　Bruce DeYoung, supt.　　327-6800
HS, 230 E MAIN ST 07446　　3-00011
　George Rizzo, prin.　　327-6800
Smith MS, 2 MONROE ST 07446　　2-00100
　Richard Weiner, prin.　　327-3022

Don Bosco Prep HS　　3-00011
492 N FRANKLIN TPKE 07446　　327-8003
　Fr. Connolly, prin.
Ho-Ho-Kus School　　2-CS
27 S FRANKLIN TPKE 07446　　327-8877

Randolph, AC 201
Randolph Township SD　　5-11111
SCHOOLHOUSE ROAD 07869　　328-2775
　Robert Gordon, supt.
HS, 507 MILLBROOK AVE 07869　　4-00011
　Cecil Beavers, prin.　　361-2400
IS, 507 MILLBROOK AVE 07869　　3-00100
　Milton Ortiz, prin.　　366-8700

County College of Morris　　7-CC
200 CENTER GROVE RD 07869　　361-5000

Readington, AC 908, PC 3, Hunterdon
Readington Township SD　　4-11100
PO BOX 2 08870　　534-2195
　Thomas Gannon, supt.
MS, PO BOX 2 08870　　3-01100
　Michael Billis, prin.　　534-2113

Red Bank, AC 908, PC 7, Monmouth
Red Bank SD, 76 BRANCH AVE 07701　　3-11100
　Christine Kane, supt.　　758-1506
MS, 101 HARDING RD 07701　　2-01100
　John Dorsey, prin.　　758-1515

Red Bank Catholic HS　　3-00011
10 PETERS PL 07701　　747-1774
　Sr. Mary Ronan, prin.
Riverview Medical Center　　HSP
35 UNION ST 07701　　530-2232

Richland, AC 609, PC 3, Atlantic

St. Augustine Prep S　　2-00011
PO BOX 279 08350　　697-2600
　Jerome McGowan, prin.

Ridgefield, AC 201, PC 6, Bergen
Ridgefield SD, 555 CHESTNUT ST 07657　　4-11111
　Richard Sabella, supt.　　945-9236
Ridgefield Memorial JSHS　　3-00111
555 WALNUT ST 07657　　945-4455
　Harvey Weiss, prin.

Ridgefield Park, AC 201, PC 7, Bergen
Ridgefield Park SD　　4-11111
98 CENTRAL AVE 07660　　641-0806
　David Rightmeyer, supt.
JSHS, 250 E GRAND AVE 07660　　3-00111
　Joe Celauro, prin.　　440-1440

Ridgewood, AC 201, PC 7, Bergen
Ridgewood Village SD　　5-11111
49 COTTAGE PL 07450　　670-2700
　Fred Stokley, supt.
HS, 627 E RIDGEWOOD AVE 07450　　4-00011
　John Crews, prin.　　670-2800
Franklin MS, 15 N VAN DIEN AVE 07450　　3-00100
　Paul Folkemer, prin.　　670-2780
Washington MS　　3-00100
155 WASHINGTON PL 07450　　670-2790
　George Neville, prin.

Valley Hospital　　HSP
301 LINWOOD AVE 07450　　447-8002

Ringwood, AC 201, PC 7, Passaic
Ringwood SD　　4-11100
121 CARLETONDALE RD 07456　　962-7028
　R. Sellitti, supt.
Ryerson MS, 130 VALLEY RD 07456　　2-00100
　David Paulus, prin.　　962-7063

Riverside, AC 609, PC 6, Burlington
Riverside Township SD　　4-11111
112 E WASHINGTON ST 08075　　461-1255
　J. Ferner, supt.
JSHS, 112 E WASHINGTON ST 08075　　3-00111
　Orvyl Wilson, prin.　　461-1255

River Vale, AC 201, PC 6, Bergen
River Vale SD   4-11100
  613 WESTWOOD AVE 07675   358-4020
  Carmine Ceresa, supt.
  Holdrum MS, 385 RIVERVALE RD 07675   2-00100
  Jack Dennis, prin.   358-4016

Rockaway, AC 201, PC 6, Morris
Morris Hills Regional SD   4-00011
  48 KNOLL DR 07866   989-2707
  James McNasby, supt.
  Morris Hills HS, 520 W MAIN ST 07866   3-00011
  Barry Spetter, prin.   989-2800
  Morris Knolls HS, 50 KNOLL DR 07866   4-00011
  Kurt Weinheimer, prin.   989-2750

Rockaway Borough SD   3-11100
  103 E MAIN ST 07866   625-8601
  John Phillips, supt.
  Jefferson MS, 95 E MAIN ST 07866   2-01100
  James Esposito, prin.   625-8603

Rockaway Township SD
  Supt. — See Hibernia
Copeland MS   3-00100
  100 LAKESHORE DR 07866   627-2465
  Stephen Gottlieb, prin.

Roselle, AC 908, PC 7, Union
Roselle Borough SD   4-11111
  710 LOCUST ST 07203   298-2000
  George Sliwiak, supt.
  Clark JSHS, 122 E 6TH AVE 07203   3-00111
  Andrew Brown, prin.   298-2000

Roselle Catholic HS   3-00011
  1 RARITAN RD 07203   245-2350
  Br. Mullin, prin.

Roselle Park, AC 908, PC 7, Union
Roselle Park SD, 500 LARCH ST 07204   4-11111
  William Clarke, supt.   245-1197
  JSHS, 185 W WEBSTER AVE 07204   3-00111
  John Hutchinson, prin.   241-4550

Rumson, AC 908, PC 6, Monmouth
Rumson-Fair Haven Regional HSD   3-00011
  74 RIDGE RD 07760   842-1597
  James Mullevey, supt.
  Rumson-Fair Haven HS   3-00011
  74 RIDGE RD 07760   842-1597
  James Mullevey, prin.

Rumson Borough SD   3-11100
  60 FORREST AVE 07760   842-4747
  John Woodbury, supt.
  Forrestdale MS, 60 FORREST AVE 07760   2-01100
  Nancy Guthrie, prin.   842-0383

Runnemede, AC 609, PC 6, Camden
Black Horse Pike Regional SD
  Supt. — See Blackwood
  Triton HS, 250 SCHUBERT AVE 08078   4-00011
  Louis Cappelli, prin.   939-4500

Runnemede Borough SD   3-11100
  505 W 3RD AVE 08078   931-5365
  Joseph Sweeney, supt.
  Volz MS, 505 W 3RD AVE 08078   2-00100
  Joe Koch, prin.   931-5353

Rutherford, AC 201, PC 7, Bergen
Rutherford SD, 176 PARK AVE 07070   4-11111
  Luke Sarsfield, supt.   939-1717
  HS, 54 ELLIOTT PL 07070   3-00011
  William Bauman, prin.   438-7675

St. Mary HS, 64 CHESTNUT ST 07070   2-00011
  Mary Lanni, prin.   933-5220

Saddle Brook, AC 201, PC 7, Bergen
Saddle Brook Township SD   4-11111
  355 MAYHILL ST 07663   843-2133
  Mel Klein, supt.
  JSHS, 355 MAYHILL ST 07663   3-00111
  Jane Moffet, prin.   843-2880

Saddle River, AC 201, PC 5, Bergen

Saddle River Country Day S   2-11111
  147 CHESTNUT RIDGE RD 07458   327-4050
  Robert Kuhlman, prin.

Salem, AC 609, PC 6, Salem
Salem CSD, 51 NEW MARKET ST 08079   4-11111
  Richard Rhau, supt.   935-3800
  HS, 219 WALNUT ST 08079   3-00011
  Norman Wilson, prin.   935-3900
  MS, 51 NEW MARKET ST 08079   2-01100
  Gwyndolyn Alston, prin.   935-2700

Scotch Plains, AC 908, PC 7, Union
Scotch Plains-Fanwood Regional SD   5-11111
  EVERGREEN AVE & CEDAR ST 07076   232-6161
  Carol Choye, supt.
  Scotch Plains-Fanwood HS   4-00011
  667 WESTFIELD RD 07076   889-8600
  Terry Riegel, prin.
  Park MS, PARK AVE 07076   2-00100
  Chester Janusz, prin.   322-4445
  Terrill MS, 1301 TERRILL RD 07076   2-00100
  John Foulks, prin.   322-5215

Union County Vocational SD   2-00000
  1776 RARITAN RD 07076   889-8828
  Vito Gagliardi, supt.
Union County Vo-Tech Inst   Vo Tech
  1776 RARITAN RD 07076   889-8828
  Vito Gagliardi, prin.

Union Catholic Regional HS   3-00011
  1600 MARTINE AVE 07076   889-1600
  Sr. Percylee Hart, prin.
Union County College 07076   3-CC
     889-8000

Seabrook, AC 609, PC 4, Cumberland
Cumberland Regional SD   4-00011
  PO BOX 5115 08302   451-9400
  William Caldwell, supt.
  Cumberland Regional HS   4-00011
  PO BOX 5115 08302   451-9400
  Robert Bumpus, prin.

Upper Deerfield Township SD   4-11100
  0 HIGHWAY 77 08302   455-2267
  Barbara Shellenberger, supt.
  Woodruff MS, 0 HIGHWAY 77 08302   2-00100
  James Turner, prin.   451-4610

Secaucus, AC 201, PC 7, Hudson
Secaucus SD, 685 5TH ST 07094   4-11111
  Constantino Scerbo, supt.   974-2004
  HS, MILLRIDGE ROAD 07094   2-00011
  William Koenig, prin.   974-2033
  MS, MILLRIDGE ROAD 07094   2-00100
  Edward Rittberg, prin.   974-2022

Sewell, AC 609, PC 4, Gloucester
Deptford Township SD
  Supt. — See Deptford
  Monongahela MS   3-00100
  RR 4 BOX 204 08080   232-2732
  Calantha Davis, prin.

Gloucester County Vo-Tech SD   2-00000
  PO BOX 800 08080   468-1445
  Victor Morella, supt.
Gloucester County Vo-Tech S   Vo Tech
  PO BOX 186 08080   468-1445
  Jay Tregellas, prin.

Washington Township SD   6-11111
  206 E HOLLY AVE 08080 – (—), supt.   589-6644
  Washington Twp. SHS   4-00001
  529 HURFFVILLE CROSSKEYS RD 08080
  Joseph Vandenburg, prin.   589-8500
  Washington Twp. Mid HS   4-00010
  509 HURFFVILLE CROSSKEYS RD 08080
  Craig Daniels, prin.   589-8500
  Chestnut Ridge MS   4-00100
  641 HURFFVILLE CROSSKEYS RD 08080
  Maria Carpenter, prin.   582-3535
  Orchard Valley MS   4-00100
  238 PITMAN DOWNER RD 08080   582-5353
  Joanne Robertson, prin.

Gloucester County College   5-CC
  RR 4 BOX 203 08080   468-5000
Lambs Road Academy   2-11111
  190 LAMBS RD 08080   589-3655

Sicklerville, AC 609, PC 4, Camden
Camden County Vocational SD   4-00011
  PO BOX 566 08081   767-7000
  R. Haldemann, supt.
  Camden County Vocational-Technical HS   4-00011
  343 BERLIN CROSS KEYS RD 08081   767-7000
  Charles Buchheim, prin.
  Other Schools – See Pennsauken

Camden Co. Vocational/Technical Schools   2-CS
  PO BOX 556 08081   767-7000

Skillman, AC 908, PC 3, Somerset
Montgomery Township SD   4-11111
  405 BURNT HILL RD 08558   874-5200
  Jamie Savedoff, supt.
  Montgomery HS   2-00011
  375 BURNT HILL RD 08558   874-4600
  Anne Marie Current, prin.
  Montgomery MS   2-00100
  375 BURNT HILL RD 08558   874-3248
  Arthur Firestone, prin.

Somerdale, AC 609, PC 6, Camden
Sterling HSD, 501 S WARWICK RD 08083   3-00011
  Gary Kasprack, supt.   784-1287
  Sterling HS, 501 S WARWICK RD 08083   3-00011
  Winfred Powell, prin.   784-1333

Star Technical Institute   2-CS
  2 WHITE HORSE RD 08083   435-7827

Somerset, AC 908, PC 7, Somerset
Franklin Township SD   5-11111
  1755 AMWELL RD 08873   873-2400
  Dennis Clancy, supt.
  Franklin HS, 415 FRANCIS ST 08873   4-00011
  William Westfield, prin.   249-6410
  Smith MS, 1645 AMWELL RD 08873   4-00100
  Carl Wade, prin.   873-2800

Rutgers Prep S   3-11111
  1345 EASTON AVE 08873   545-5600
  Edward Lingenheld, prin.

Somerville, AC 908, PC 7, Somerset
Branchburg Township SD   4-11100
  140 CEDAR GROVE RD 08876   722-3265
  John Pastre, supt.
  Central MS, 220 BAIRD RD 08876   2-00100
  George Resavy, prin.   526-1415

Hillsborough Township SD
  Supt. — See Neshanic Station
  Hillsborough MS   4-00100
  260 TRIANGLE RD 08876   874-3420
  Jane Benner, prin.

Somerville Borough SD   4-11111
  51 W CLIFF ST 08876   218-4101
  Carolyn Leary, supt.
  HS, 222 DAVENPORT ST 08876   3-00011
  Steven Kramer, prin.   218-4108
  MS, 53 W CLIFF ST 08876   2-00100
  Theodore Stanik, prin.   218-4107

Immaculata HS   3-00011
  240 MOUNTAIN AVE 08876   722-0200
  Sr. Mary Birster, prin.
Raritan Valley Community College   6-CC
  PO BOX 3300 08876   526-1200
Somerset Medical Center   HSP
  100 REHILL AVE 08876   685-2200

South Amboy, AC 908, PC 6, Middlesex
South Amboy SD, 240 JOHN ST 08879   4-11111
  Anthony Novembre, supt.   525-2102
  Hoffman HS, 249 JOHN ST 08879   2-00011
  William Beattie, prin.   525-2108
  MS, LINCOLN ST 08879   2-01100
  Carol Galley, prin.   525-2121

St. Mary Regional HS   2-00011
  310 AUGUSTA ST 08879   721-0748
  John Gloss, prin.

South Bound Brook, AC 908, PC 5, Somerset
South Bound Brook SD   2-11100
  125 MADISON ST 08880   356-0018
  Fred Cooley, supt.
  Brampton MS, 125 MADISON ST 08880   2-01100
  Barney Fabbo, prin.   356-1936

South Orange, AC 201, PC 7, Essex
South Orange-Maplewood SD
  Supt. — See Maplewood
  MS, 444 S ORANGE AVE 07079   3-01100
  Nancy Murray, prin.   378-5216

Immaculate Conception Seminary   2-UC
  400 S ORANGE AVE 07079   761-9575
Marylawn of the Oranges S   2-00011
  445 SCOTLAND RD 07079   762-9222
  Sr. Virginia Thomas, prin.
Seton Hall University   6-UC
  457 CENTRE ST 07079   761-9000

South Plainfield, AC 908, PC 7, Middlesex
South Plainfield SD   5-11111
  CROMWELL PL 07080   754-4620
  Steven Cole, supt.
  HS, 200 LAKE ST 07080   3-00011
  Leroy Seitz, prin.   754-4620
  MS, 2201 PLAINFIELD AVE 07080   3-00100
  Anthony Massaro, prin.   754-4620

South River, AC 908, PC 7, Middlesex
South River SD   4-11111
  MONTGOMERY ST 08882   613-4006
  John Ambrogi, supt.
  HS, 20 MONTGOMERY ST 08882   2-00011
  James Pope, prin.   613-4016
  MS, 20 THOMAS ST 08882   2-00100
  Ron Grygo, prin.   613-4048

Sparta, AC 201, PC 6, Sussex
Sparta Township SD   5-11111
  328 SPARTA AVE 07871   729-7886
  Carolyn Hartley, supt.
  HS, 70 W MOUNTAIN RD 07871   3-00011
  Frank Calabria, prin.   729-6191
  JHS, 18 MOHAWK AVE 07871   2-00100
  William Calvani, prin.   729-3151

Sussex County Vo-Tech SD   3-00011
  105 N CHURCH RD 07871   383-6700
  William Rooney, supt.
Sussex County Vo-Tech HS   Vo Tech
  105 N CHURCH RD 07871   383-6700
  Dennis Nick, prin.

Pope John XXIII HS   3-00011
  28 ANDOVER RD 07871   729-6125
  Fr. McHugh, prin.

Spotswood, AC 908, PC 6, Middlesex
Spotswood SD, SUMMERHILL RD 08884   4-11111
  Ronald Chiste, supt.   251-6800
  Spotswood Memorial HS   3-00011
  65 SUMMERHILL RD 08884   251-6800
  Peter Karycki, prin.
  Spotswood Memorial MS   2-00100
  MEMORIAL DR 08884   251-6800
  Kathleen Mulligan, prin.

Springfield, AC 201, PC 7, Union
Springfield Township SD   4-11100
  PO BOX 210 07081   376-0060
  Gary Friedland, supt.

Gaudineer MS | 2-01100
1 SPRINGFIELD AVE 07081 | 376-5080
Kenneth Bernabe, prin.

Union County Regional HSD | 4-00011
101 MOUNTAIN AVE 07081 | 376-6300
Donald Merachnik, supt.
Dayton Regional HS | 3-00011
101 MOUNTAIN AVE 07081 | 376-6300
Judith Wickline, prin.
Other Schools – See Berkeley Heights, Clark

Stanhope, AC 201, PC 5, Sussex
Byram Township SD | 4-11100
12 MANSFIELD DR 07874 | 347-1019
James DiRenzo, supt.
Byram Twp. IS | 3-01100
12 MANSFIELD DR 07874 | 347-1019
James Direnzo, prin.
Lenape Valley Regional HSD | 3-00011
PO BOX 578 07874 | 347-7600
J. M. Stracco, supt.
Lenape Valley Regional HS | 3-00011
PO BOX 578 07874 | 347-7600
Marylu Coviello, prin.

Stanhope Borough SD | 2-11100
VALLEY RD 07874 | 347-0008
Louis Ripatrazone, supt.
Valley Road MS, VALLEY RD 07874 | 2-01100
Patricia Supplee, prin. | 347-0008

Stewartsville, AC 908, PC 3, Warren
Greenwich Township SD | 2-11100
269 S MAIN ST 08886 | 859-2022
James Alercia, supt.
MS, 269 S MAIN ST 08886 | 2-01100
James Alercia, prin. | 859-2022

Stirling, AC 908, PC 4, Morris
Long Hill Township SD | 3-11100
331 ELM ST 07980 | 647-1200
Mary Louise Malyska, supt.
Central MS, 90 CENTRAL AVE 07980 | 2-01100
Ronald Hoffman, prin. | 647-2311

Stratford, AC 609, PC 6, Camden
Stratford Borough SD | 3-11100
317 PRINCETON AVE 08084 | 783-2555
Gene Iannette, supt.
Yellin MS, 111 WARWICK RD 08084 | 2-01100
James Dailey, prin. | 783-1094

School of Osteopathic Medicine | 2-UC
40 LAUREL RD E 08084 | 346-6990

Succasunna, AC 201, PC 6, Morris
Roxbury Township SD | 5-11111
25 MEEKER ST 07876 | 584-6867
Leonard Elovitz, supt.
Roxbury HS, 1 BRYANT DR 07876 | 4-00011
Lewis Ludwig, prin. | 584-1200
Eisenhower MS, 47 EYLAND AVE 07876 | 3-00100
Owen Toale, prin. | 584-2973

Summit, AC 908, PC 7, Union
Summit CSD, 90 MAPLE ST 07901 | 5-11111
Paul Rossey, supt. | 273-3023
HS, 125 KENT PLACE BLVD 07901 | 3-00011
Don Geddis, prin. | 273-1494
MS, 272 MORRIS AVE 07901 | 3-00100
Gerard Murphy, prin. | 273-1190

Kent Place S, 42 NORWOOD AVE 07901 | 2-11111
Arlene Gibson, prin. | 273-0900
Oak Knoll S, 44 BLACKBURN RD 07901 | 2-11111
Joanne Ainsworth, prin. | 522-8100
Oratory Prep S, 1 BEVERLY RD 07901 | 2-00111
Fr. Rotunno, prin. | 273-1084
Overlook Hospital | HSP
193 MORRIS AVE 07901 | 522-2020

Sussex, AC 201, PC 4, Sussex
High Point Regional HSD | 3-00011
299 PIDGEON HILL RD 07461 | 875-7204
Bernard Andrews, supt.
High Point HS | 3-00011
299 PIDGEON HILL RD 07461 | 875-3101
John Killoy, prin.
Sussex-Wantage Regional SD | 4-11100
31 RYAN RD 07461 | 875-3175
Arthur DiBenedetto, supt.
MS, 10 LOOMIS AVE 07461 | 3-00100
Alfred Annunziata, prin. | 875-4138

Upsala College | 2-UC
RR 3 BOX 138-A 07461 | 875-7187

Swedesboro, AC 609, PC 4, Gloucester
Kingsway Regional HSD | 4-00111
RR 1 BOX 277 08085 | 467-3300
Terrence Crowley, supt.
Kingsway Regional JSHS | 4-00111
RR 1 BOX 278A 08085 | 467-3300
James Granato, prin.

Teaneck, AC 201, PC 8, Bergen
Teaneck SD, 1 MERRISON ST 07666 | 5-11111
Harold Morris, supt. | 833-5510
HS, 100 ELIZABETH AVE 07666 | 4-00011
James Delaney, prin. | 833-5400
Franklin MS, 1315 TAFT RD 07666 | 3-01100
Frank Allen, prin. | 833-5450

Jefferson MS, 655 TEANECK RD 07666 | 3-01100
Victor Klein, prin. | 833-5470

Fairleigh Dickinson University | 6-UC
1000 RIVER RD 07666 | 692-2000
Holy Name Hospital | HSP
690 TEANECK RD 07666 | 833-3007

Tenafly, AC 201, PC 7, Bergen
Tenafly SD, 500 TENAFLY RD 07670 | 4-11111
John Fitzsimons, supt. | 569-4400
HS, 19 COLUMBUS DR 07670 | 3-00011
Louis Visco, prin. | 569-4400
MS, 36 SUNSET LN 07670 | 3-00100
Robert Weldon, prin. | 569-4400

Teterboro, AC 201, PC 1, Bergen
Bergen County Vocational SD
Supt. — See Hackensack
Teterboro Vo S | Vo Tech
RT 46 & CENTRAL AVE 07608 | 288-6632
Salvatore Mastroeni, prin.

Teterboro School of Aeronautics | 3-CS
80 MOONACHIE AVE 07608 | 288-6300

Tinton Falls, AC 908, PC 7, Monmouth
Monmouth Regional HSD | 4-00011
1 NORMAN J FIELD WAY 07724 | 542-1170
Patrick Collum, supt.
Other Schools – See Eatontown

Tinton Falls SD, 620 TINTON AVE 07724 | 4-11100
Edward Miklus, supt. | 542-0444
MS, 674 TINTON AVE 07724 | 2-00100
Larry Kostula, prin. | 542-0775

Toms River, AC 908, PC 6, Ocean
Ocean County Vocational SD | 3-00000
137 BEY LEA RD 08753 | 240-6414
Frederick Felice, supt.
Toms River Vo S | Vo Tech
1299 OLD FREEHOLD RD 08753 | 349-8425
Jeanne Andrews, prin.
Other Schools – See Brick, Jackson, Lakewood, Waretown

Toms River Regional SD | 7-11111
1144 HOOPER AVE 08753 | 505-5506
Michael Ritacco, supt.
Toms River HS-North | 4-00011
1201 OLD FREEHOLD RD 08753 | 505-5702
Raymond Ryan, prin.
Toms River HS-South | 4-00011
101 HYERS ST 08753 | 505-5738
John Holloway, prin.
Toms River HS-East, DUNDEIN ST 08753 | 4-00011
Peter Kohl, prin. | 505-5668
Toms River IS-East, HOOPER AVE 08753 | 4-00100
John Fitzgerald, prin. | 505-5777
Toms River IS-West | 4-00100
INDIAN HEAD RD 08753 | 505-5800
Mark Regan, prin.

Monsignor Donovan HS | 3-00011
711 HOOPER AVE 08753 | 349-8801
Edward Gere, prin.
Ocean County College | 6-CC
0 COLLEGE DR 08753 | 255-4000

Totowa, AC 201, PC 7, Passaic
Totowa SD, 294 TOTOWA RD 07512 | 3-11100
Viktor Joganow, supt. | 956-2125
Memorial MS, 294 TOTOWA RD 07512 | 2-01100
Eugene Ridgeway, prin. | 942-2562

Berdan Institute | 2-CS
265 STATE RT 46 07512 | 256-3444

Tranquility, AC 908, PC 2, Sussex

Garden State Academy | 2-00011
PO BOX 10 07879 | 852-0300

Trenton, AC 609, PC 8, Mercer
Ewing Township SD | 5-11111
1331 LOWER FERRY RD 08618 | 883-3388
Leonard Kelpsh, supt.
Ewing SHS, 900 PARKWAY AVE 08618 | 3-00011
Wayne Fuller, prin. | 771-1300
Fisher JHS | 3-00110
1325 LOWER FERRY RD 08618 | 883-2882
Warren Schuster, prin.

Hamilton Township SD | 7-11111
90 PARK AVE 08690 | 890-3723
James Donovan, supt.
Hamilton East-Steinert HS | 4-00011
2900 KLOCKNER RD 08690 | 890-3743
Frank Lugossy, prin.
Hamilton North-Nottingham HS | 4-00011
1055 KLOCKNER RD 08619 | 890-3758
Carol Chiacchio, prin.
Hamilton West-Watson HS | 4-00011
2720 S CLINTON AVE 08610 | 890-3605
Neil Bencivengo, prin.
Crockett MS, 2631 KUSER RD 08691 | 3-00100
Joan Sigafoos, prin. | 890-3800
Grice MS | 3-00100
901 WHITE HORSE HAMILTON RD 08610
James Gilroy, prin. | 890-3602
Reynolds MS | 3-00100
2145 YRDVLL HAMILTON SQU RD 08690
Anthony Armenti, prin. | 890-3761

Mercer County Vocational SD | 2-00000
1085 OLD TRENTON RD 08690 | 586-2129
Elric Cicchetti, supt.
MCVS Assunpink Vo S | Vo Tech
1085 OLD TRENTON RD 08690 | 586-5144
BRUCE WHITE, prin.
MCVS Health Occupations Ctr 08690 | Vo Tech
Virginia Clevenger, prin. | 587-7640
MCVS Sypek Center Vo S | Vo Tech
129 BULL RUN RD 08638 | 737-9785
Martha Koblish, prin.

Trenton SD, 108 N CLINTON AVE 08609 | 7-11111
Bernice Venable, supt. | 989-2408
Trenton Central HS | 5-00011
400 CHAMBERS ST 08609 | 989-2496
Charlie Ramsey, prin.
Dunn MS, 401 DAYTON ST 08610 | 3-00100
Paul Gmitter, prin. | 989-2582
Hedgepeth-Williams MS | 3-00100
301 GLADSTONE AVE 08629 | 989-2781
Michael Rothstein, prin.
King MS | 3-00100
800 MRTN LTHER KING JR BLVD 08638
Albert Williams, prin. | 989-2690
Holland MS, 1001 W STATE ST 08618 | 3-00100
Morris Kimble, prin. | 989-2730

Helene Fuld Medical Center | HSP
750 BRUNSWICK AVE 08638 | 394-3174
McCorristin HS | 3-00011
175 LEONARD AVE 08610 | 586-3705
Sr. Marguerite O'Beirne, prin.
Mercer Christian Academy | 2-11111
PO BOX 7299 08628 | 882-7300
Mercer County Community College | 6-CC
1200 OLD TRENTON RD 08690 | 586-0505
Mercer County Community College | 2-CC
N BROAD & ACADEMY STS 08608 | 586-0505
Mercer Medical Center | HSP
PO BOX 1658 08607 | 394-4050
Notre Dame HS | 4-00011
601 LAWRENCEVILLE RD 08648 | 882-7900
Barry Breen, prin.
St. Francis Medical Center | HSP
601 HAMILTON AVE 08629 | 599-5190
Thomas Edison State College | 6-UC
101 W STATE ST 08608 | 984-1100
Trenton State College | 6-UC
HILLWOOD LAKES CN 4700 08650 | 771-1855
Villa Victoria Academy | 2-11111
376 W UPPER FERRY RD 08628 | 883-1700
Sr. Helen Sanchez, prin.

Tuckahoe, AC 609, PC 3, Cape May
Upper Township SD | 4-11100
PO BOX 158 08250 | 390-8448
John Tredinnick, supt.
Upper Twp. MS, PO BOX 158 08250 | 3-00100
Raymond Cavanaugh, prin. | 628-2633

Tuckerton, AC 609, PC 5, Ocean
Pinelands Regional SD | 4-00111
PO BOX 248 08087 | 296-3106
Clement Crea, supt.
Pinelands Regional HS | 3-00011
PO BOX 248 08087 | 296-3106
John Graig, prin.
Pinelands Regional MS | 3-00100
PO BOX 248 08087 | 296-3106
Lawrence Mesarick, prin.

Union, AC 908, PC 8, Union
Union Township SD | 6-11111
2369 MORRIS AVE 07083 | 851-6420
James Caulfield, supt.
HS, 2350 N 3RD ST 07083 | 4-00011
Samuel Fortunato, prin. | 851-6500
Burnet MS, 1000 CALDWELL AVE 07083 | 3-00100
Gary Malles, prin. | 851-6490
Kawameeh MS | 3-00100
DAVID & GOLF TERRACE 07083 | 851-6570
Gloria Hines, prin.

Engine City Technical Institute | 2-CS
2365 ROUTE 22 W 07083 | 964-1450
Kean College of New Jersey | 7-UC
1000 MORRIS AVE 07083 | 527-2000
Lincoln Technical Institute | 4-CS
2299 VAUXHALL RD 07083 | 964-7800

Union City, AC 201, PC 8, Hudson
Union City SD | 6-11111
3912 BERGENLINE AVE 07087 | 348-5851
Thomas Highton, supt.
Union Hill HS | 4-00011
3808 HUDSON AVE 07087 | 348-5936
Frank Acinapura, prin.
Columbus MS | 2-00100
1500 NEW YORK AVE 07087 | 271-2085
Robert Fazio, prin.

Holy Rosary Secondary Academy | 2-00011
1509 BERGENLINE AVE 07087 | 864-5236
Sr. Alice Donofrio, prin.
Mesivta Sanz Hudson City S | 2-11111
3400 NEW YORK AVE 07087 | 867-8690
SCS Business & Technical Institute | 2-CS
2200 BERGENLINE AVE 07087 | 867-3500

Upper Montclair, AC 201, PC see Montclair

Montclair State College 7-UC
1 NORMAL AVE 07043 893-4000

Upper Saddle River, AC 201, PC 6, Bergen
Upper Saddle River SD 3-11100
395 W SADDLE RIVER RD 07458 327-4401
Nathan Parker, supt.
Cavallini MS 2-01100
395 W SADDLE RIVER RD 07458 327-4028
James Meisterich, prin.

Ventnor City, AC 609, PC 7, Atlantic
Ventnor CSD, LAFAYETTE AVE N 08406 3-11100
William Gussie, supt. 822-9295
MS, LAFAYETTE AVE N 08406 2-01100
Anthony DiCosola, prin. 822-2151

Vernon, AC 201, PC 4, Sussex
Vernon Township SD 5-11111
PO BOX 99 07462 764-4486
Anthony Macerino, supt.
Vernon Twp. HS, PO BOX 800 07462 4-00011
Kenneth Hart, prin. 875-7111
Glen Meadow MS 3-01100
PO BOX 516 07462 764-1700
Linda Heady, prin.
Lounsberry Hollow MS 3-01100
PO BOX 219 07462 764-4041
John Paskey, prin.

Verona, AC 201, PC 7, Essex
Verona SD, 30 GOULD ST 07044 4-11111
Robert Rosado, supt. 239-2100
HS, 151 FAIRVIEW AVE 07044 2-00011
Benedict Tantillo, prin. 239-3300
Whitehorne MS 2-00100
600 BLOOMFIELD AVE 07044 239-1300
Edward Berk, prin.

Vincentown, AC 609, PC 3, Burlington
Shamong Township SD 3-11100
256 MEDFORD INDIAN MILLS RD 08088
(—), supt. 268-0440
Indian Mills Memorial MS 2-01100
99 MEDFORD INDIAN MILLS RD 08088
Roger Wagner, prin. 268-0440

Southampton Township SD 3-11100
177 MAIN ST 08088 859-2256
William Martin, supt.
Southampton Twp. MS 2-01100
26 PLEASANT ST 08088 859-2256
Susan Peternich, prin.

Tabernacle Township SD 4-11100
132 NEW RD 08088 268-0153
Diane DeGiacomo, supt.
Tabernacle MS, 132 NEW RD 08088 3-01100
Roger Hladky, prin. 268-0153

Vineland, AC 609, PC 8, Cumberland
Vineland CSD, 625 PLUM ST 08360 6-11111
Charles Valentine, supt. 794-6700
Vineland HS-South 4-00011
2880 E CHESTNUT AVE 08360 794-6800
Gerald Luongo, prin.
D'Ippolito IS 3-01100
1578 N VALLEY AVE 08360 794-6934
Belinda Hall, prin.
Landis IS, 61 W LANDIS AVE 08360 3-01100
Thomas McCann, prin. 794-6925
Memorial IS, 424 S MAIN RD 08360 3-01100
Jaqueline Harvard, prin. 794-6918
Rossi IS, 2572 PALERMO AVE 08360 3-01100
Eugene Lera, prin. 794-6961
Vineland Freshman HS North 4-00010
3010 E CHESTNUT AVE 08360 794-6800
Theodore Peters, prin.

Cumberland Christian S 3-11111
1100 W SHERMAN AVE 08360 696-1600
Cumberland County College 4-CC
PO BOX 517 08360 691-8600
Sacred Heart HS, 21 N EAST AVE 08360 2-00011
Sr. Evarista Farley, prin. 691-4491
Star Technical Institute 1-CS
1386 S DELSEA DR 08360 696-0500

Voorhees, AC 609, PC 7, Camden
Eastern Camden County Regional HSD 4-00011
PO BOX 2500 08043 346-6740
Barry Galasso, supt.
Eastern SHS, PO BOX 2500 08043 3-00001
Suzanne Gongol, prin. 346-6720
Eastern Freshman HS 3-00010
PO BOX 2500 08043 782-4225
Fred Rapp, prin.
Voorhees Township SD 5-11100
329 ROUTE 73 08043 751-2435
Raymond Brosel, supt.
Voorhees MS, HOLLY OAK DRIVE 08043 3-00100
Samuel Citron, prin. 795-2025

Waldwick, AC 201, PC 6, Bergen
Waldwick SD, 155 SUMMIT AVE 07463 4-11111
Patrick Piegari, supt. 445-3340
JSHS, 155 WYCKOFF AVE 07463 3-01100
Delores Torralbas, prin. 652-9000

Berkeley College of Business 2-CC
100 W PROSPECT ST 07463 652-0388

Wall, AC 908, PC see Glendora
Wall Township SD 5-11111
PO BOX 1199 07719 681-7900
Eileen Smith-Stevens, supt.
HS, PO BOX 1199 07719 3-00011
Ronald Grigoletto, prin. 681-4300
IS, PO BOX 1199 07719 3-00100
Douglas Bohrer, prin. 449-3131

Stuart School of Business Administration 2-CS
2400 BELMAR BLVD 07719 681-7200

Wallington, AC 201, PC 7, Bergen
Wallington SD, 30 PINE ST 07057 4-11111
Frank Cocchiola, supt. 777-4421
JSHS, 234 MAIN AVE 07057 3-00011
Joseph Pompeo, prin. 777-0808

Wanaque, AC 201, PC 6, Passaic
Lakeland Regional SD 4-00011
205 CONKLINTOWN RD 07465 835-1900
Gerald Lysik, supt.
Lakeland Regional HS 4-00011
205 CONKLINTOWN RD 07465 835-1900
Alan Niamoli, prin.

Waretown, AC 609, PC 4, Ocean
Ocean County Vocational SD
Supt. — See Toms River
Ocean Center Vo School Vo Tech
RR 2 BOX 81V 08758 693-3434
Peter Flipse, prin.

Warren, AC 908, PC 4, Somerset
Warren Township SD 4-11100
114 STIRLING RD 07060 647-0535
Pamela Fiander, supt.
MS, 100 OLD STIRLING RD 07059 2-00100
Michael Hoffman, prin. 753-5300

Watchung Hills Regional SD 4-00011
108 STIRLING RD 07060 647-4890
Robert Baly, supt.
Watchung Hills Regional HS 4-00011
108 STIRLING RD 07060 647-4800
Robert Baly, prin.

Koinonia Academy 2-11111
114 STIRLING RD 07059 647-1770

Washington, AC 908, PC 6, Warren
Warren County Vocational SD 2-00011
RR 1 BOX 168A 07882 689-7650
Frank Mancuso, supt.
Warren County Vo-Tech Institute Vo Tech
RR 1 BOX 168A 07882 689-7650
Steven Kramer, prin.

Warren Hills Regional HSD 4-00111
89 BOWERSTOWN RD 07882 689-3143
John Mulhern, supt.
Warren Hills Regional HS 3-00011
150 JACKSON VALLEY RD 07882 689-3050
Richard Cunningham, prin.
Warren Hills JHS 3-00100
64 CARLTON AVE 07882 689-0750
Carl Weber, prin.

Good Shepherd Christian S 2-11111
PO BOX 65 07882 689-6804
Warren County Community College 3-CC
ROUTE 57 W BOX 55A 07882 689-1090

Watchung, AC 908, PC 6, Somerset
Watchung Borough SD 2-11100
50 VALLEYVIEW RD 07060 755-8121
Patrick Parenty, supt.
Valley View MS 2-01100
50 VALLEYVIEW RD 07060 755-4422
Thomas DaGanci, prin.

Wayne, AC 201, PC 8, Passaic
Passaic County Technical-Vocational HSD 4-00011
45 REINHARDT RD 07470 790-6000
William Galese, supt.
Passaic County Tech-Vo HS 4-00011
45 REINHARDT RD 07470 790-6000
Diana Lobosco, prin.

Wayne Township SD 6-11111
50 NELLIS DR 07470 633-3032
Rob Winter, supt.
Wayne Hills HS 4-00011
272 BERDAN AVE 07470 633-3090
Eugene Sudol, prin.
Wayne Valley HS, 551 VALLEY RD 07470 4-00011
Russell De Vries, prin. 633-3066
Schuyler-Colfax JHS 3-00100
1500 HAMBURG TPKE 07470 633-3130
Frank Markowick, prin.
Washington MS, 68 LENOX RD 07470 3-00100
Americo Romeo, prin. 633-3140

De Paul Diocesan HS 3-00011
1512 ALPS RD 07470 694-3702
Sr. Patricia Flarity, prin.
William Paterson College 6-UC
300 POMPTON RD 07470 595-2000

Weehawken, AC 201, PC 7, Hudson
Weehawken Township SD 4-11111
53 LIBERTY PL 07087 867-2243
Joseph Wisniewski, supt.

JSHS, 53 LIBERTY PL 07087 2-00111
Peter Olivieri, prin. 867-1774

West Caldwell, AC 201, PC 7, Essex

Essex County College 3-CC
730 BLOOMFIELD AVE 07006 228-3968

West Deptford, AC 609, PC 7, Gloucester
West Deptford Township SD 5-11111
675 GROVE RD 08066 848-4300
Lawrence Hobdell, supt.
MS, 675 GROVE RD 08066 3-01100
Fred Gilfillin, prin. 848-1200
Other Schools – See Westville

Westfield, AC 908, PC 8, Union
Westfield SD, 302 ELM ST 07090 5-11111
Mark Smith, supt. 789-4420
HS, 550 DORIAN RD 07090 4-00011
Robert Petix, prin. 789-4500
Edison IS, 800 RAHWAY AVE 07090 3-00100
Samuel Hazell, prin. 789-4470
Roosevelt IS, 301 CLARK ST 07090 3-00100
Kenneth Shulack, prin. 789-4560

West Long Branch, AC 908, PC 6, Monmouth
Shore Regional HSD 3-00011
132 STATE ROUTE 36 07764 222-9300
Leonard Schnappauf, supt.
Shore Regional HS 3-00011
132 STATE ROUTE 36 07764 222-9300
Leonard Schnappauf, prin.

West Long Branch SD 3-11100
135 LOCUST AVE 07764 222-5900
Betty McElmon, supt.
Antonides MS, 135 LOCUST AVE 07764 2-01100
Kenneth Knops, prin. 222-5080

Monmouth College 5-UC
400 CEDAR AVE 07764 571-3400

West Milford, AC 201, PC 4, Passaic
West Milford Township SD 5-11111
46 HIGHLANDER DR 07480 697-1700
Thomas Kraft, supt.
HS, 67 HIGHLANDER DR 07480 4-00011
Richard Linkh, prin. 697-1700
Macopin MS, 70 HIGHLANDER DR 07480 3-00100
Charles Romain, prin. 697-1700

Westmont, AC 609, PC 6, Camden
Haddon Township SD 4-11111
500 RHOADS AVE 08108 854-2900
John McGovern, supt.
Haddon Twp. JSHS 3-00111
406 MEMORIAL AVE 08108 854-6525
Victor Mignogna, prin.

West New York, AC 201, PC 8, Hudson
West New York SD, 100 51ST ST 07093 6-11111
Rose DeFino, supt. 902-1120
Memorial HS, 5501 PARK AVE 07093 4-00011
Frank Grosso, prin. 902-1130

St. Joseph Palisades HS 2-00011
5400 BROADWAY 07093 864-9700
Fr. Petrillo, prin.

West Orange, AC 201, PC 8, Essex
West Orange SD 5-11111
179 EAGLE ROCK AVE 07052 669-5430
Richard Suprina, supt.
HS, 51 CONFORTI AVE 07052 4-00011
Jerry Tarnoff, prin. 669-5301
Edison MS, 75 WILLIAM ST 07052 2-00100
Errol Scales, prin. 669-5360
Roosevelt MS, 36 GILBERT PL 07052 3-00100
Joseph Del Guercio, prin. 669-5373

Seton Hall Preparatory HS 3-00011
120 NORTHFIELD AVE 07052 325-6624
Fr. Kelly, prin.
Solomon Schecter HS 2-00111
1418 PLEASANT VALLEY WAY 07052 669-8000
Ruth Ritterbrand, prin.

West Paterson, AC 201, PC 7, Passaic
West Paterson SD 3-11100
853 MCBRIDE AVE 07424 278-5535
Anthony De Pasquale, supt.
Memorial MS, 15 MEMORIAL DR 07424 2-01100
Alfred Baumann, prin. 256-5800

Berkeley College of Business 4-CC
44 RIFLE CAMP RD 07424 278-5400

West Trenton, AC 609, PC see Ewing

Marie Katzenbach School for the Deaf HND
320 SULLIVAN WAY # CN535 08628

Westville, AC 609, PC 5, Gloucester
West Deptford Township SD
Supt. — See West Deptford
West Deptford HS 3-00011
1600 CROWN POINT RD 08093 848-6110
William Stubbs, prin.

St. John of God Community Services HND
532 DELSEA DR 08093 848-4700

Westwood, AC 201, PC 7, Bergen
Westwood Regional SD   4-11111
  701 RIDGEWOOD RD 07675   664-0880
  Joseph Fisler, supt.
JSHS, 701 RIDGEWOOD RD 07675   3-00111
  Donald Korneski, prin.   664-0880

Immaculate Heart Academy   3-00011
  PO BOX 300 07675   445-6800
  Sr. Ellen Cronan, prin.
Pascak Valley Hospital   HSP
  250 OLD HOOK RD 07675   358-3010

Wharton, AC 201, PC 6, Morris
Wharton Borough SD   3-11100
  137 E CENTRAL AVE 07885   361-2592
  Michael Chirichello, supt.
MacKinnon MS   2-00100
  137 E CENTRAL AVE 07885   361-2506
  Richard Bitondo, prin.

Whippany, AC 201, PC 6, Morris
Hanover Park Regional HSD
  Supt. — See East Hanover
Whippany Park HS   3-00011
  165 WHIPPANY RD 07981   887-3004
  John Kirchberger, prin.

Hanover Township SD   4-11100
  61 HIGHLAND AVE 07981   515-2404
  Salvatore Sansone, supt.
Memorial JHS, 61 HIGHLAND AVE 07981   2-00100
  Harvey Altman, prin.   515-2427

Whiting, AC 908, PC 3, Ocean
Manchester Township SD   5-11111
  121 ROUTE 539 08759   350-5901
  Joel Oppenheim, supt.
Other Schools – See Lakehurst

Wildwood, AC 609, PC 5, Cape May
Wildwood CSD   3-11111
  4300 PACIFIC AVE 08260   522-4157
  Arthur Motz, supt.
JSHS, 4300 PACIFIC AVE 08260   2-00111
  Bruce Myers, prin.   522-7922

Wildwood Catholic HS   2-00011
  1500 CENTRAL AVE 08260   522-7257
  Sr. Maryellen Ford, prin.

Williamstown, AC 609, PC 7, Gloucester
Monroe Township SD   5-11111
  75 E ACADEMY ST 08094   629-6400
  Robert La Porta, supt.
HS, CLAYTON ROAD 08094   4-00011
  James Greczek, prin.   629-7444
Oak Knoll MS, 23 BODINE AVE 08094   3-00100
  Max Bienstock, prin.   728-3944

Victory Christian S   2-11111
  PO BOX 806 08094   629-4300

Willingboro, AC 609, PC 8, Burlington
Willingboro Township SD   6-11111
  50 SALEM RD 08046   871-9000
  Geraldyn Foster, supt.
SHS   4-00001
  20 S JOHN F KENNEDY WAY 08046   871-9000
  John Wasinda, prin.
Willingboro Memorial JHS   4-00110
  451 VAN SCIVER PKY 08046   871-9000
  Charles Boden, prin.

Woodbridge, AC 908, PC 7, Middlesex
Middlesex Co. Vocational-Technical HSD
  Supt. — See East Brunswick
Woodbridge Vocational HS   2-00011
  1 CONVERY BLVD 07095 – (—), prin.   634-5858

Woodbridge Township SD   7-11111
  PO BOX 428 07095   602-8549
  Fred Buonocore, supt.
HS, 25 KELLY ST 07095   4-00011
  David Peterson, prin.   602-8600
MS, 525 BARRON AVE 07095   2-00100
  James Sullivan, prin.   602-8690
Other Schools – See Avenel, Colonia, Fords, Iselin

Berkeley College of Business   2-CC
  430 RAHWAY AVE 07095   800-446-5400
DeVry Technical Institute   5-CS
  479 GREEN ST 07095   634-9510

Woodbury, AC 609, PC 7, Gloucester
Woodbury SD, 25 N BROAD ST 08096   4-11111
  R. Craig Barry, supt.   853-0123
JSHS, 25 N BROAD ST 08096   3-00111
  John Gamble IV, prin.   853-0123

Woodbury Heights, AC 609, PC 5, Gloucester
Gateway Regional SD   3-00111
  801 EGG HARBOR RD 08096   848-8172
  Malcolm Dawson, supt.

Gateway Regional JSHS   3-00111
  801 EGG HARBOR RD 08096   848-8200
  Michael Pilacik, prin.

Woodcliff Lake, AC 201, PC 6, Bergen
Woodcliff Lake SD   3-11100
  134 WOODCLIFF AVE 07675   391-6570
  Elliot Soloman, supt.
Woodcliff Lake MS   2-00100
  134 WOODCLIFF AVE 07675   930-4840
  Joan Lipkowitz, prin.

Wood-Ridge, AC 201, PC 6, Bergen
Wood-Ridge SD   3-11111
  89 HACKENSACK ST 07075   933-6777
  Robert Smith, supt.
JSHS, 258 HACKENSACK ST 07075   2-00111
  Regina White, prin.   939-0810

Woodstown, AC 609, PC 5, Salem
Salem County Board Vocational SD   2-00000
  PO BOX 350 08098   769-0101
  William Adams, supt.
Employment Prep Center   Vo Tech
  172 SALEM - WOODSTOWN RD 08098   769-0101
  Robert Lawson, prin.
Vo-Tech Career Ctr   Vo Tech
  PO BOX 350 08098   769-0101
  Jack McCulley, prin.

Woodstown-Pilesgrove Regional SD   4-11111
  135 EAST AVE 08098   769-0144
  Kristine Stanwood, supt.
HS, 140 EAST AVE 08098   3-00011
  Steven Merkel, prin.   769-0144
MS, 15 LINCOLN AVE 08098   2-01100
  William Stanwood, prin.   769-0144

Wrightstown, AC 609, PC 5, Burlington

Kings Academy, 131 E MAIN ST 08562   2-11111
                                            723-8216

Wyckoff, AC 201, PC 7, Bergen
Wyckoff Township SD   4-11100
  241 MORSE AVE 07481   848-5700
  George Wolthoff, supt.
Eisenhower MS, 344 CALVIN CT 07481   3-00100
  Joseph Desiderio, prin.   848-5750

Eastern Christian MS   2-01100
  518 SICOMAC AVE 07481   891-3663

NEW MEXICO

STATE DEPARTMENT OF EDUCATION
Education Building
300 Don Gaspar, Santa Fe 87501
(505) 827-6696

Superintendent of Public Instruction   Alan Morgan

Deputy Superintendent   Henry Gonzales

Associate Superintendent Learning Services   Jeanne Knight

Associate Superintendent School Management & Accountability   Michael Davis

Director Agency Support   Tres Giron

Assistant Superintendent Vocational Education   Albert Zamora

STATE BOARD OF EDUCATION
300 Don Gaspar, Santa Fe 87501

President   Virginia Trujillo

PUBLIC, PRIVATE AND CATHOLIC SECONDARY SCHOOLS

Alamogordo, AC 505, PC 8, Otero
Alamogordo SD, PO BOX 617 88311 — 6-11111
  Stan Rounds, supt. — 439-3200
HS, 103 CUBA AVE 88310 — 4-00011
  Larry DeWees, prin. — 439-3300
Chaparral JHS — 3-00100
  1401 COLLEGE AVE 88310 — 439-3350
  Charles Wride, prin.
Other Schools – See Holloman AFB

Community Christian S — 2-11111
  2907 THUNDER RD 88310 — 434-0352
  Philip Brown, prin.
International Business College — 2-CS
  3200 N WHITE SANDS BLVD 88310 — 437-1854
New Mexico School Visually Handicapped — HND
  1900 N WHITE SANDS BLVD 88310
New Mexico State University — 3-CC
  PO BOX 477 88311 — 437-6860

Albuquerque, AC 505, PC 10, Bernalillo
Albuquerque SD — 8-11111
  PO BOX 25704 87125 — 842-8211
  Jack Bobroff, supt.
HS, 800 ODELIA RD NE 87102 — 4-00011
  Tom Savage, prin. — 843-6400
Cibola HS, 1510 ELLISON DR NW 87114 — 4-00011
  Don Duran, prin. — 897-0110
Del Norte HS — 4-00011
  5323 MONTGOMERY BLVD NE 87109 — 883-7222
  Martha Bass, prin.
Eldorado HS — 4-00011
  11300 MONTGOMERY BLVD NE 87111
  H. Russell Goff, prin. — 296-4871
Highland HS, 4700 COAL AVE SE 87108 — 4-00011
  Evalynne Hunemuller, prin. — 265-3711
La Cueva HS — 4-00011
  7801 WILSHIRE AVE NE 87122 — 823-2327
  Sue Griffith, prin.
Manzano HS — 4-00011
  12200 LOMAS BLVD NE 87112 — 292-0090
  Tim Whalen, prin.
Rio Grande HS — 4-00011
  2300 ARENAL RD SW 87105 — 873-0220
  Veronica Garcia, prin.
Sandia HS — 4-00011
  7801 CANDELARIA RD NE 87110 — 294-1511
  Jim Juarez, prin.
Valley HS — 4-00011
  1505 CANDELARIA RD NW 87107 — 345-9021
  Charles Stoughton, prin.
West Mesa HS — 4-00011
  6701 FORTUNA RD NW 87121 — 831-6993
  Bob Hennig, prin.
Career Enrichment Ctr — Vo Tech
  807 MOUNTAIN RD NE 87102 — 247-3658
  Jim Simpson, prin.
Adams MS — 4-00100
  5401 GLENRIO RD NW 87105 — 831-0400
  Joann Coffee, prin.
Cleveland MS — 3-00100
  6910 NATALIE AVE NE 87110 — 881-9227
  Mary Lou Anderson, prin.
Eisenhower MS — 4-00100
  11001 CAMERO AVE NE 87111 — 292-2530
  Susie Peck, prin.
Garfield MS, 3501 6TH ST NW 87107 — 3-00100
  Rommie Compher, prin. — 344-1647
Grant MS — 3-00100
  1111 EASTERDAY DR NE 87112 — 299-2113
  Helen Johnson, prin.
Harrison MS — 3-00100
  3912 ISLETA BLVD SW 87105 — 877-1279
  Mary Jane Detson, prin.
Hayes MS, 1100 TEXAS ST NE 87110 — 3-00100
  Jimmie Lueder, prin. — 265-7741
Hoover MS, 12015 TIVOLI AVE NE 87111 — 4-00100
  Don Wolfley, prin. — 298-6896
Jackson MS — 3-00100
  10600 INDIAN SCHOOL RD NE 87112 — 299-7377
  Milton Baca, prin.
Jefferson MS — 3-00100
  712 GIRARD BLVD NE 87106 — 255-8691
  Julie Ambrogi, prin.
Johnson MS — 3-00100
  6811 TAYLOR RD NW 87120 — 898-1492
  Ruth Owens, prin.
Kennedy MS — 3-00100
  721 TOMASITA ST NE 87123 — 298-6701
  Terrence Hannon, prin.
Madison MS, 3501 MOON ST NE 87111 — 4-00100
  Barbara Blackwell, prin. — 299-4735
McKinley MS — 3-00100
  4500 COMANCHE RD NE 87110 — 881-9390
  Julieta Contreras, prin.
Polk MS, 2220 RAYMAC RD SW 87105 — 3-00100
  Doug Johnson, prin. — 877-6444
Pyle MS, 1820 VALDORA RD SW 87105 — 3-00100
  Louis Martinez, prin. — 877-3770
Taft MS, 620 SCHULTE RD NW 87107 — 3-00100
  Larry Adkins, prin. — 344-7670
Taylor MS — 3-00100
  8200 GUADALUPE TRL NW 87114 — 898-3666
  Eugene Johnson, prin.
Truman MS — 3-00100
  400 BENAVIDES RD SW 87105 — 836-3030
  Edgar Briggs, prin.

Van Buren MS — 3-00100
  700 LOUISIANA BLVD SE 87108 — 268-3833
  Gary Hocevar, prin.
Washington MS — 3-00100
  1101 PARK AVE SW 87102 — 764-2000
  Mary Mercado, prin.
Wilson MS — 3-00100
  1138 CARDENAS DR SE 87108 — 268-3961
  Tim Thomassen, prin.
Other Schools – See Rio Rancho, Tijeras

Albuquerque Academy — 3-00111
  6400 WYOMING BLVD NE 87109 — 828-3201
  Robert Bovinette, prin.
Albuquerque Technical-Vocational Inst — 6-CC
  525 BUENA VISTA DR SE 87106 — 224-3000
Amritsar Academy — 2-11111
  1650 GABALDON DR NW 87104 — 247-8939
  Avtar Greeley, prin.
Art Center — 2-CC
  2268 WYOMING AVE NE 87112 — 298-1828
AzTech College — 2-CS
  2201 SAN PEDRO DR NE BLDG 3 87110 — 888-5800
Hope Christian HS — 3-00011
  6800 PALOMAS AVE NE 87109 — 828-1114
  Wayne Ehlert, prin.
ITT Technical Institute — 2-CC
  5100 MASTHEAD ST NE 87109 — 828-1114
Menaul HS — 2-00111
  301 MENAUL BLVD NE 87107 — 345-7727
  Ron Hodges, prin.
Metropolitan College of Court Reporting — 2-CS
  2201 SN PDR DR N BLDG 1-300 87110 — 888-3400
National College — 2-UC
  1202 PENNSYLVANIA ST NE 87110 — 265-7518
Northern Arizona Institute of Technology — 2-CS
  11300 LOMAS BLVD NE 87112 — 291-1700
Parks College — 2-CC
  1023 TIJERAS AVE NW 87102 — 843-7500
Pima Medical Institute — 2-CS
  2201 SAN PEDRO DR NE 87110 — 881-2893
St. Pius X HS — 3-00011
  5301 SAINT JOSEPHS DR NW 87120 — 831-8400
  Fr. Schwenzer, prin.
Sandia Prep S, 532 OSUNA RD NE 87113 — 2-00111
  Richard Heath, prin. — 344-1671
Southwestern Indian Polytechnic Inst. — 2-CS
  PO BOX 10146 87184 — 766-3197
Temple Baptist Academy — 2-11111
  1620 SAN PEDRO DR NE 87110 — 262-0969
  S. Hlad, prin.
University of New Mexico 87131 — 7-UC
  277-2626
University of Phoenix-NM Division — 2-UC
  7471 PAN AMERICAN FWY NE 87109 — 821-4800
Victory Christian S — 2-11111
  220 EL PUEBLO RD NW 87114 — 898-3060
  Glenn Frey, prin.

Animas, AC 505, PC 2, Hidalgo
Animas SD, PO BOX 85 88020 — 3-11111
  George York, supt. — 548-2299
HS 88020 — 2-00011
  Haskell Sinclair, prin. — 548-2296
MS 88020 — 2-00100
  Ted Hopkins, prin. — 548-2333

Anthony, AC 505, PC 6, Dona Ana
Gadsden SD, PO BOX 70 88021 — 7-11111
  Richard Anderson, supt. — 882-3525
Gadsden HS, RR 1 BOX 268 88021 — 4-00001
  Charles Pogue, prin. — 882-4551
Gadsden JHS, RR 1 BOX 196 88021 — 4-00110
  Thomas Miller, prin. — 882-2372
Other Schools – See Chaparral, Santa Teresa

Artesia, AC 505, PC 7, Eddy
Artesia SD, 1106 W QUAY AVE 88210 — 5-11111
  James Phipps, prin. — 746-3585
SHS, 1006 W RICHARDSON AVE 88210 — 3-00001
  Steve Starkey, prin. — 746-9816
Park JHS, 15TH & CANNON 88210 — 3-00110
  John Spradling, prin. — 746-9892

Aztec, AC 505, PC 6, San Juan
Aztec SD, 1117 W AZTEC BLVD 87410 — 5-11111
  Ron Helland, supt. — 334-9474
SHS, 500 E CHACO ST 87410 — 3-00001
  Andrew Sweet, prin. — 334-9414
Koogler JHS — 3-00110
  455 N LIGHT PLANT RD 87410 — 334-6102
  Connie Sanders, prin.

Bayard, AC 505, PC 5, Grant
Cobre SD, PO BOX R 88023 — 4-11111
  Harrell Holder, supt. — 537-3371
Cobre HS, 1111 W CENTRAL AVE 88023 — 3-00001
  David Jacquez, prin. — 537-3321
Snell MS, HIGHWAY 180 88023 — 3-00100
  Marc Space, prin. — 537-3359

Belen, AC 505, PC 6, Valencia
Belen SD, 520 N MAIN ST 87002 — 5-11111
  Barbara Armbruster, supt. — 864-4466
HS, 1619 W DELGADO AVE 87002 — 4-00011
  James Danner, prin. — 864-7468
JHS, 400 S 4TH ST 87002 — 3-00100
  Jerry Martinez, prin. — 864-7453

Bernalillo, AC 505, PC 6, Sandoval
Bernalillo SD, PO BOX 640 87004 — 5-11111
  Gilbert Sena, supt. — 867-2317
HS, PO BOX 640 87004 — 3-00011
  Tom Crespin, prin. — 867-2361
MS, PO BOX 640 87004 — 3-00100
  Patrick Lopez, prin. — 867-3300
Other Schools – See Santo Domingo Pueblo

Bloomfield, AC 505, PC 6, San Juan
Bloomfield SD, 325 N BERGIN LN 87413 — 5-11111
  Clifford Weber, supt. — 632-3316
HS, 520 N 1ST ST 87413 — 3-00011
  Jim Cromartie, prin. — 632-3373
Mesa Alta JHS, 329 N BERGIN LN 87413 — 3-00100
  Wally Feldman, prin. — 632-8021

Capitan, AC 505, PC 3, Lincoln
Capitan SD, PO BOX 278 88316 — 3-11111
  Diana Sonnamaker, supt. — 354-2239
JSHS 88316 — 2-00111
  Darrel Stierwalt, prin. — 354-2567

Carlsbad, AC 505, PC 7, Eddy
Carlsbad SD, 408 N CANYON ST 88220 — 6-11111
  Anna Perez, supt. — 887-2821
SHS, 3000 W CHURCH ST 88220 — 4-00001
  Tom Hansen, prin. — 887-3511
Leyva JHS, 800 W CHURCH ST 88220 — 4-00110
  Benny Willmon, prin. — 887-3586

New Mexico State University — 3-CC
  1500 UNIVERSITY DR 88220 — 885-8831

Carrizozo, AC 505, PC 4, Lincoln
Carrizozo SD, PO BOX 99 88301 — 2-11111
  James Bayless, supt. — 648-2347
HS 88301 — 1-00011
  Gabriel Papponi, prin. — 648-2346
MS 88301 — 1-01100
  Kay Patterson, prin. — 648-2346

Chama, AC 505, PC 4, Rio Arriba
Chama Valley SD
Supt. — See Tierra Amarilla
MS, PO BOX 337 87520 — 1-00100
  Benjamin Leyba, prin. — 756-2161

Chaparral, AC 505, PC 5, Dona Ana
Gadsden SD
Supt. — See Anthony
MS, PO BOX 129 88021 — 2-00100
  David Garcia, prin. — 824-4847

Cimarron, AC 505, PC 3, Colfax
Cimarron SD, PO BOX 605 87714 — 3-11111
  Thelma Coker, supt. — 376-2445
HS, N COLLISON AV 87714 — 2-00011
  Mark Feddersen, prin. — 376-2241
MS, 320 W 9TH ST 87714 — 1-01100
  Marjorie Haynie, prin. — 376-2519
Other Schools – See Eagle Nest

Clayton, AC 505, PC 4, Union
Clayton SD, 323 S 5TH ST 88415 — 3-11111
  Claude Austin, supt. — 374-9611
HS, 323 S 5TH ST 88415 — 2-00011
  John Burgess, prin. — 374-2596
JHS, 3RD & SPRUCE 88415 — 2-00100
  Jack Wiley, prin. — 374-9543

Cliff, AC 505, PC 2, Grant
Silver SD
Supt. — See Silver City
JSHS, GENERAL DELIVERY 88028 — 2-00111
  Lyman Bayles, prin. — 535-2051

Cloudcroft, AC 505, PC 3, Otero
Cloudcroft SD, PO BOX 198 88317 — 3-11111
  Vernon Asbill, supt. — 682-2361
HS 88317 — 2-00011
  Eddy Coleman, prin. — 682-2524
MS 88317 — 2-01100
  Donna McGee, prin. — 682-3336

Clovis, AC 505, PC 8, Curry
Clovis SD, PO BOX 19000 88102 — 6-11111
  Mack Mitchell, supt. — 769-4300
SHS, 1900 N THORNTON ST 88101 — 4-00001
  Jim McDaniel, prin. — 769-4350
Gattis JHS, 1400 CAMEO ST 88101 — 3-00110
  Tony Adrian, prin. — 769-4400
Marshall JHS — 3-00110
  100 COMMERCE WAY 88101 — 769-4410
  Dale Fullerton, prin.
Yucca JHS, 1500 SYCAMORE ST 88101 — 3-00110
  George Boal, prin. — 769-4420

Clovis Community College — 3-CC
  417 SCHEPPS BLVD 88101 — 769-2811

Corona, AC 505, PC 2, Lincoln
Corona SD, PO BOX 258 88318 — 1-11111
  Linda Coy, supt. — 849-1911
JSHS 88318 — 1-00111
  Linda Coy, prin. — 849-1711

Crownpoint, AC 505, PC 4, McKinley
Gallup-McKinley SD
Supt. — See Gallup
JSHS, PO BOX D 87313 — 3-00111
  Jodie Wallace, prin. — 786-5664

Cuba, AC 505, PC 3, Sandoval
Cuba SD, PO BOX 70 87013 — 3-11111
Joe Lopez, supt. — 289-3211
HS 87013 — 2-00011
Greg Spradling, prin. — 289-3211
MS 87013 — 2-00100
Edumenio Gurule, prin. — 289-3211

Deming, AC 505, PC 7, Luna
Deming SD, 501 W FLORIDA ST 88030 — 5-11111
Carlos Viramontes, supt. — 546-8841
SHS, 1100 S NICKEL ST 88030 — 3-00001
Hector Madrid, prin. — 546-2678
JHS, 1400 S IRON ST 88030 — 3-00110
Armando Reyes, prin. — 546-4863

Des Moines, AC 505, PC 2, Union
Des Moines SD, PO BOX 38 88418 — 2-11111
Michael Hall, supt. — 278-2611
JSHS 88418 — 1-00111
Michael Hall, prin. — 278-2611

Dexter, AC 505, PC 3, Chaves
Dexter SD, PO BOX 159 88230 — 3-11111
Jimmy Derrick, supt. — 734-5420
HS, PO BOX 159 88230 — 2-00011
Don Warren, prin. — 734-6814
JHS, PO BOX 159 88230 — 2-00100
Sam Witt, prin. — 734-5414

Dora, AC 505, PC 2, Roosevelt
Dora SD, PO BOX 327 88115 — 2-11111
Terrill Mitchell, supt. — 477-2216
JSHS, GENERAL DELIVERY 88115 — 1-00111
Kenneth Shaw, prin. — 477-2211

Dulce, AC 505, PC 4, Rio Arriba
Dulce SD, PO BOX 547 87528 — 3-11111
Levi Pesata, supt. — 759-3353
HS, GENERAL DELIVERY 87528 — 2-00011
Peter Gallagher, prin. — 759-3282
MS, GENERAL DELIVERY 87528 — 2-00100
Peter Gallagher, prin. — 759-3282

Eagle Nest, AC 505, PC 2, Colfax
Cimarron SD
Supt. — See Cimarron
MS 87718 — 1-01100
Lee Mills, prin. — 377-6991

Elida, AC 505, PC 2, Roosevelt
Elida SD, PO BOX 8 88116 — 2-11111
T. Goodwin, supt. — 274-6211
JSHS 88116 — 1-00111
T. D. Goodwin, prin. — 274-6211

El Pueblo, AC 505, PC 1, San Miguel
Las Vegas West SD
Supt. — See Las Vegas
Valley MS 87560 — 1-00100
Eddie Atencio, prin. — 421-5069

El Rito, AC 505, PC 2, Rio Arriba
Mesa Vista SD, PO BOX 6 87530 — 3-11111
Vernon Jaramillo, supt. — 581-4504
Other Schools – See Ojo Caliente

Espanola, AC 505, PC 6, Rio Arriba
Espanola SD, 714 DON DIEGO RD 87532 — 6-11111
Jose Chavez, supt. — 753-2254
Espanola Valley HS 87532 — 4-00011
George Gonzales, prin. — 753-7357
JHS 87532 — 3-00100
Jake Henderson, prin. — 753-2294

McCurdy S, PO BOX 127 87532 — 2-11111
Joyce Sass, prin. — 753-7221
Northern New Mexico Community College — 4-CC
1002 N ONATE ST 87532 — 753-7141

Estancia, AC 505, PC 3, Torrance
Estancia SD, PO BOX 68 87016 — 3-11111
Carolyn Renteria, supt. — 384-2243
HS 87016 — 2-00011
Danielle Johnston, prin. — 384-2761
MS 87016 — 2-00100
Paul Benoit, prin. — 384-2363

Eunice, AC 505, PC 5, Lea
Eunice SD, PO BOX 129 88231 — 3-11111
John Turner, supt. — 394-2524
HS, PO BOX 129 88231 — 2-00011
Joey Morin, prin. — 394-2332
Caton MS, PO BOX 129 88231 — 2-00100
Joe Rasor, prin. — 394-3338

Farmington, AC 505, PC 8, San Juan
Farmington SD, PO BOX 5850 87499 — 6-11111
Michael Hogan, supt. — 599-8615
SHS, 2200 N SUNSET AVE 87401 — 4-00001
Barry Sigmon, prin. — 599-8614
Rocinante Tech HS — Vo Tech
406 AIRPORT DR 87401 — 599-8627
Robert Rank, prin.
Heights JHS, 3700 COLLEGE BLVD 87402 — 3-00110
Roberta Brummett, prin. — 599-8611
Hermosa JHS, 1500 E 25TH ST 87401 — 3-00110
Floyd Causey, prin. — 599-8612
Mesa View JHS — 3-00110
4451 WILDFLOWER DR 87401 — 599-8622
Hugh Easterday, prin.
Tibbetts JHS, 312 E APACHE ST 87401 — 3-00110
Joanie Burris, prin. — 599-8613

Catholic Academy — 1-00110
2100 E 20TH ST 87401 — 326-3012
Vasco Seavy, prin.
Navajo Prep S — 2-00011
1200 W APACHE ST 87401 — 326-6571
Betty Ojaye, prin.
San Juan College — 4-CC
4601 COLLEGE BLVD 87402 — 326-3311

Floyd, AC 505, PC 2, Roosevelt
Floyd SD, PO BOX 75 88118 — 2-11111
George Langan, supt. — 478-2211
JSHS 88118 — 1-00111
Craig Terry, prin. — 478-2211

Fort Sumner, AC 505, PC 4, De Baca
Ft. Sumner SD, PO BOX 387 88119 — 2-11111
T. Richards, supt. — 355-7734
HS 88119 — 1-00011
Dick Haynes, prin. — 355-2231
MS 88119 — 2-00100
Dick Haynes, prin. — 355-7633

Gallina, AC 505, PC 2, Rio Arriba
Jemez Mountain SD — 2-11111
PO BOX 230 87017 — 638-5419
Mary Robinson, supt.
Coronado JSHS 87017 — 2-00111
Henry Andazola, prin. — 638-5549
MS, PO BOX 230 87017 — 1-00100
Henry Andazola, prin. — 638-5549

Gallup, AC 505, PC 7, McKinley
Gallup-McKinley SD — 7-11111
PO BOX 1318 87305 — 722-7711
Ramon Vigil, supt.
HS, PO BOX 39 87305 — 4-00011
Joe Gill, prin. — 863-3821
MS, 1001 S GRANDVIEW DR 87301 — 4-00100
Craig Pirlot, prin. — 863-3824
Kennedy MS — 3-00100
600 S BOARDMAN AVE 87301 — 722-7721
Peter Belletto, prin.
Other Schools – See Crownpoint, Navajo, Ramah, Thoreau, Tohatchi

University of New Mexico — 4-CC
PO BOX 1756 87305 — 863-7608

Grady, AC 505, PC 2, Curry
Grady SD, PO BOX 71 88120 — 2-11111
Carolyn Luck, supt. — 357-2192
JSHS, PO BOX 71 88120 — 1-00111
Carolyn Luck, prin. — 357-2192

Grants, AC 505, PC 6, Cibola
Grants/Cibola County SD — 5-11111
PO BOX 8 87020 — 287-2961
Thomas Jackson, supt.
HS, 500 MOUNTAIN RD 87020 — 3-00011
Ron Marquez, prin. — 285-4677
Los Alamitos MS — 3-00100
ELM DRIVE & MOUNT TAYLOR 87020 — 287-4414
David Jiron, prin.
Other Schools – See New Laguna

New Mexico State University — 2-CC
PO BOX 906 87020 — 287-7981

Hagerman, AC 505, PC 3, Chaves
Hagerman SD, PO BOX B 88232 — 2-11111
Bob Posey, supt. — 752-3254
HS 88232 — 2-00011
Richard Acosta, prin. — 752-3283
JHS 88232 — 1-00100
Richard Acosta, prin. — 752-3283

Hatch, AC 505, PC 4, Dona Ana
Hatch Valley SD, PO BOX 790 87937 — 4-11111
Cecil Davis, supt. — 267-3076
Hatch Valley HS, PO BOX 790 87937 — 2-00011
Jose Griego, prin. — 267-3051
Hatch Valley JHS, PO BOX 790 87937 — 2-00100
Judd Nordyke, prin. — 267-9238

Hobbs, AC 505, PC 8, Lea
Hobbs SD, PO BOX 1040 88241 — 6-11111
Rusty Heskett, supt. — 393-9183
SHS, 800 N JEFFERSON ST 88240 — 4-00001
Cliff Burch, prin. — 397-3241
Heizer JHS, 100 E STANOLIND RD 88240 — 2-00110
Tony Baker, prin. — 393-4614
Highland JHS — 3-00110
2500 N JEFFERSON ST 88240 — 392-5511
Jim Gardner, prin.
Houston JHS, 300 N HOUSTON ST 88240 — 3-00110
John Notaro, prin. — 393-7129

College of the Southwest — 2-UC
6610 N LOVINGTON HWY 88240 — 392-6561
New Mexico Junior College — 4-CC
5317 N LOVINGTON HWY 88240 — 392-4510

Holloman AFB, AC 505, PC 6, Otero
Alamogordo SD
Supt. — See Alamogordo
Holloman MS, PO BOX 1149 88330 — 2-00100
Susan Jim, prin. — 479-2282

Hondo, AC 505, PC 2, Lincoln
Hondo Valley SD, PO BOX 55 88336 — 2-11111
Gilbert Candelaria, supt. — 653-4412
JSHS 88336 — 1-00111
Cheryl Bowman, prin. — 653-4411

House, AC 505, PC 1, Quay
House SD, PO BOX 673 88121 — 1-11111
Wayne Anderson, supt. — 279-7353
JSHS, PO BOX 673 88121 — 1-00111
Wayne Anderson, prin. — 279-7353

Jal, AC 505, PC 4, Lea
Jal SD, PO BOX 1386 88252 — 3-11111
Guan Miller, supt. — 395-2101
JSHS, 105 E UTAH AVE 88252 — 2-00111
Rick Ferguson, prin. — 395-2277

Jemez Pueblo, AC 505, PC 4, Sandoval
Jemez Valley SD — 4-11111
8501 HIGHWAY 4 87024 — 834-7391
Gary Dwyer, supt.
Jemez Valley HS 87024 — 2-00011
Louise Garcia-Sanchez, prin. — 834-7392
Jemez Valley MS 87024 — 2-00100
Michael Garcia, prin. — 834-7593
Other Schools – See Rio Rancho

Kirtland, AC 505, PC 5, San Juan
Central Consolidated SD
Supt. — See Shiprock
Central HS, 550 ROAD 6100 87417 — 3-00011
Jane Owens, prin. — 598-5881
MS, 538 ROAD 6100 87417 — 3-00100
Charles Trujillo, prin. — 598-6114

Lake Arthur, AC 505, PC 2, Chaves
Lake Arthur SD, PO BOX 98 88253 — 2-11111
Mason Costin, supt. — 365-2001
HS 88253 — 1-00011
Gynn Langford, prin. — 365-2001
MS 88253 — 1-00100
Gynn Langford, prin. — 365-2001

Las Cruces, AC 505, PC 8, Dona Ana
Las Cruces SD — 7-11111
505 S MAIN ST # 249 88001 — 527-5800
Jesse Gonzales, supt.
Mayfield SHS, 1955 N VALLEY DR 88005 — 4-00001
Robert Ogas, prin. — 527-9415
HS, 1755 EL PASEO ST 88001 — 4-00011
Manuel Rodriguez, prin. — 527-9400
Onate SHS, 6800 N MAIN ST 88012 — 4-00001
Carl Montoya, prin. — 527-9430
Excel the Career Program — Vo Tech
410 W COURT AVE 88005 — 527-6050
John Krause, prin.
Lynn MS, 950 S WALNUT ST 88001 — 3-00100
Dorris Hamilton, prin. — 527-9445
Picacho MS — 3-00100
2700 W PICACHO AVE 88005 — 527-9445
Erlinda Martinez, prin.
Sierra MS, 1700 SPRUCE AVE 88001 — 4-00100
Jean De La Pena, prin. — 527-9640
Vista MS, 4465 ELKS RD 88005 — 4-00100
Olivia Ogas, prin. — 527-9465
Zia MS, 1300 W UNIVERSITY AVE 88005 — 4-00100
Tom Hayes, prin. — 527-9475
Other Schools – See Mesilla, White Sands Missile Range

Dona Ana Branch Community College — 3-CC
PO BOX 3001 88003 — 527-7510
International Business College — 3-CS
650 MONTANA AVE # F 88001 — 526-5579
Memorial Medical Center — HSP
2801 E UNIVERSITY AVE 88001 — 522-8641
Mesilla Valley Christian S — 2-11111
3850 STERN DR 88001 — 525-8515
Karl Kanning, prin.
New Mexico State University — 7-UC
PO BOX 30001 88003 — 646-2035

Las Vegas, AC 505, PC 7, San Miguel
Las Vegas City SD — 5-11111
901 DOUGLAS AVE 87701 — 425-5277
Joseph Padilla, supt.
Robertson HS, 1240 5TH ST 87701 — 3-00011
Phil Leger, prin. — 425-9385
Memorial MS — 3-00100
OLD NATIONAL RD 87701 — 425-6729
Carmen Holquin, prin.

Las Vegas West SD — 4-11111
179 BRIDGE ST 87701 — 425-9316
David Salazar, supt.
West Las Vegas HS — 3-00011
157 MORENO ST 87701 — 425-3531
Ray Collins, prin.
West Las Vegas MS — 2-00100
1310 S GONZALES ST 87701 — 425-9301
Frank Montenegro, prin.
Other Schools – See El Pueblo

Luna Vocational Technical Institute — 3-CC
PO BOX K 87701 — 454-2500
New Mexico Highlands University 87701 — 4-UC
425-7511

Logan, AC 505, PC 3, Quay
Logan SD, PO BOX 67 88426 — 2-11111
Doug Hulce, supt. — 487-2252
JSHS 88426 — 1-00111
W Carter, prin. — 487-2252

Lordsburg, AC 505, PC 5, Hidalgo
Lordsburg SD, PO BOX 430 88045 — 3-11111
Phillip DeFoor, supt. — 542-9361
HS, 501 W 4TH ST 88045 — 2-00011
J. Lee, prin. — 542-3782

Dugan-Tarango MS | 2-00100
1352 HARDIN DR 88045 | 542-9806
Fred La Marca, prin.

Los Alamos, AC 505, PC 7, Los Alamos
Los Alamos SD, PO BOX 90 87544 | 5-11111
Denny Holder, supt. | 662-4141
HS, 1300 DIAMOND DR 87544 | 4-00011
Cheryl Pongratz, prin. | 662-4136
MS, 2101 CUMBRES DR 87544 | 3-00100
Andy Trottier, prin. | 662-5251

Los Lunas, AC 505, PC 6, Valencia
Los Lunas SD, PO BOX 1300 87031 | 6-11111
Charles Tafoya, supt. | 865-9636
HS, 1776 MAIN ST SW 87031 | 4-00011
Patricia Parkinson, prin. | 865-4646
MS, 220 LUNA ST 87031 | 3-00100
Jesus Sedillos, prin. | 865-7273

Loving, AC 505, PC 4, Eddy
Loving SD, PO BOX 98 88256 | 3-11111
David Chavez, supt. | 745-2339
HS, 602 S 6TH ST 88256 | 2-00011
Tom Quintela, prin. | 745-3349
MS, 312 S 6TH ST 88256 | 2-00100
Dennis Atherton, prin. | 745-3612

Lovington, AC 505, PC 6, Lea
Lovington SD, PO BOX 1537 88260 | 5-11111
John Wilbanks, supt. | 396-3020
SHS, 701 W AVENUE K 88260 | 3-00011
Art Karger, prin. | 396-2425
JHS, 500 W JEFFERSON AVE 88260 | 3-00110
Hal Roueche, prin. | 396-3233

Magdalena, AC 505, PC 3, Socorro
Magdalena SD, PO BOX 24 87825 | 2-11111
Tim McCoy, supt. | 854-2241
HS 87825 | 1-00011
Tim McCoy, prin. | 854-2477
MS 87825 | 1-00100
Robert Jiron, prin. | 854-2424

Maxwell, AC 505, PC 2, Colfax
Maxwell SD, PO BOX 275 87728 | 2-11111
David Lock, supt. | 375-2371
JSHS 87728 | 1-00111
Linda Caspar, prin. | 375-2371

Melrose, AC 505, PC 3, Curry
Melrose SD, PO BOX 275 88124 | 2-11111
Bruce Hegwer, supt. | 253-4269
JSHS, 100 E MISSOURI 88124 | 2-00111
Patricia Scott, prin. | 253-4267

Mesilla, AC 505, PC 4, Dona Ana
Las Cruces SD
Supt. — See Las Cruces
San Andres HS, HIGHWAY 28 88046 | 2-00011
Eric Cress, prin. | 527-6058

Montezuma, AC 505, PC 2, San Miguel

Hammer United World College | 2-00001
PO BOX 248 87731 | 454-4200
Theodore Lockwood, prin.

Mora, AC 505, PC 4, Mora
Mora SD, PO BOX 179 87732 | 3-11111
Leroy Sanchez, supt. | 387-2224
HS, PO BOX 180 87732 | 2-00111
Douglas Velarde, prin. | 387-2121

Moriarty, AC 505, PC 4, Torrance
Moriarty SD, PO BOX 2000 87035 | 5-11111
James Murlless, supt. | 832-4471
HS, PO BOX 2000 87035 | 3-00011
Freddie Cardenas, prin. | 832-4254
MS, PO BOX 2000 87035 | 3-00100
Buck Glenn, prin. | 832-6200

Mosquero, AC 505, PC 2, Harding
Mosquero SD, PO BOX 258 87733 | 1-11111
Sam Sandoval, supt. | 673-2271
JSHS, PO BOX 258 87733 | 1-00111
Sam Sandoval, prin. | 673-2271

Mountainair, AC 505, PC 3, Torrance
Mountainair SD, PO BOX 456 87036 | 2-11111
Jack Snyder, supt. | 847-2333
HS, PO BOX 456 87036 | 2-00111
Ernest Renteria, prin. | 847-2211

Navajo, AC 505, PC 4, McKinley
Gallup-McKinley SD
Supt. — See Gallup
Navajo Pine JSHS | 2-00111
PO BOX 1286 87305 | 777-2288
Gilbert Sage, prin.

Newcomb, AC 505, PC 2, San Juan
Central Consolidated SD
Supt. — See Shiprock
HS, PO BOX 7973 87455 | 2-00011
Sam Alonzo, prin. | 696-3417
JHS, PO BOX 7973 87455 | 2-00100
Sam Alonzo, prin. | 696-3417

New Laguna, AC 505, PC 3, Cibola
Grants/Cibola County SD
Supt. — See Grants
Laguna-Acoma JSHS | 2-00111
PO BOX 76 87038 | 287-3796
Kilino Marquez, prin.

Ojo Caliente, AC 505, PC 2, Taos
Mesa Vista SD
Supt. — See El Rito
Mesa Vista JSHS | 2-00111
PO BOX 1037 87549 | 583-2275
Raul Guerrero, prin.

Pecos, AC 505, PC 4, San Miguel
Pecos SD, PO BOX 368 87552 | 3-11111
Hank Dominguez, supt. | 757-6120
JSHS, PO BOX 368 87552 | 2-00111
Christino Griego, prin. | 757-6126

Penasco, AC 505, PC 3, Taos
Penasco SD, PO BOX 520 87553 | 3-11111
Nelson Lopez, supt. | 587-2230
JSHS, PO BOX 520 87553 | 2-00111
Mike Chavez, prin. | 587-2503

Portales, AC 505, PC 7, Roosevelt
Portales SD, 501 S ABILENE AVE 88130 | 5-11111
Dr. Howard Overby, supt. | 356-6641
HS, 201 S KNOXVILLE ST 88130 | 3-00011
David Jenkins, prin. | 356-5831
JHS, 300 E 5TH ST 88130 | 2-00100
Forrest Wellman, prin. | 356-8578

Eastern New Mexico University 88130 | 5-UC
| 562-2121

Quemado, AC 505, PC 2, Catron
Quemado SD, PO BOX 128 87829 | 2-11111
Wilfred Lackey, supt. | 773-4700
JSHS, PO BOX 128 87829 | 1-00111
Carm Chavez, prin. | 773-4645

Questa, AC 505, PC 4, Taos
Questa SD, PO BOX 440 87556 | 3-11111
Levi Duran, supt. | 586-0421
HS, PO BOX 440 87556 | 2-00011
Ruben Lucero, prin. | 586-1604
MS 87556 | 2-00100
Reuben Lucero, prin. | 586-0510

Ramah, AC 505, PC 3, McKinley
Gallup-McKinley SD
Supt. — See Gallup
JSHS, PO BOX 849 87321 | 2-00111
Tim Bond, prin. | 783-4211

Raton, AC 505, PC 6, Colfax
Raton SD, PO BOX 940 87740 | 4-11111
Butch McGowen, supt. | 445-9111
HS, 1535 TIGER CIR 87740 | 3-00011
Bill Naccarato, prin. | 445-3541
MS, 500 S 3RD ST 87740 | 2-00100
Joe Gagliardi, prin. | 445-9881

Rehoboth, AC 505, PC 2, McKinley

Rehoboth Christian HS | 2-11111
PO BOX 41 87322 | 863-4412
Mike DeYoung, prin.

Reserve, AC 505, PC 2, Catron
Reserve SD, PO BOX 350 87830 | 2-11111
Mary Sanchez, supt. | 533-6241
JSHS, PO BOX 350 87830 | 2-00111
Everett Banister, prin. | 533-6242

Rio Rancho, AC 505, PC 8, Sandoval
Albuquerque SD
Supt. — See Albuquerque
Lincoln MS, 2287 LEMA RD SE 87124 | 4-00100
Catherine Harvey-Baca, prin. | 892-1100

Jemez Valley SD
Supt. — See Jemez Pueblo
Mountain View MS | 2-00100
7100 IDALIA RD 87124 | 867-1021
George Jackson, prin.

Roswell, AC 505, PC 8, Chaves
Roswell SD, PO BOX 1437 88202 | 7-11111
Fred Pomeroy, supt. | 625-8100
Goddard HS | 4-00011
701 E COUNTRY CLUB RD 88201 | 625-8115
David Biringer, prin.
HS, 500 W HOBBS ST 88201 | 4-00011
Lee Kyser, prin. | 625-8130
University HS, 25 MARTIN 88201 | 2-00011
Amarante Fresquez, prin. | 625-8245
Berrendo MS | 2-00100
800 MARION RICHARDS RD 88201 | 625-8175
Edward Phillips, prin.
Mesa MS, 1601 E BLAND ST 88201 | 3-00100
Robert Cobos, prin. | 625-8179
Mt. View MS | 2-00100
312 E MOUNTAIN VIEW RD 88201 | 625-8173
Dan Gomez, prin.
Sierra MS, 605 S SYCAMORE AVE 88201 | 2-00100
John Allensworth, prin. | 625-8183

Eastern New Mexico Medical Center | HSP
405 W COUNTRY CLUB RD 88201 | 622-8170
Eastern New Mexico University | 4-CC
PO BOX 6000 88202 | 624-7000
New Mexico Military Institute | 2-00011
101 W COLLEGE BLVD 88201 | 622-6250
Charles Featherstone, prin.
New Mexico Military Institute | 3-CC
101 W COLLEGE BLVD 88201 | 800-421-5376

Roy, AC 505, PC 2, Harding
Roy SD, PO BOX C 87743 | 2-11111
William Maes, supt. | 485-2242
JSHS 87743 | 1-00111
William Maes, prin. | 485-2242

Ruidoso, AC 505, PC 5, Lincoln
Ruidoso SD, 200 HORTON CIR 88345 | 4-11111
Mike Gladden, supt. | 257-4051
HS, 200 WARRIOR DR 88345 | 3-00011
Don Weems, prin. | 258-4910
MS, 100 REESE DR 88345 | 2-00100
Paula Papponi, prin. | 257-7324

San Jon, AC 505, PC 2, Quay
San Jon SD, PO BOX 5 88434 | 2-11111
Mike Chambers, supt. | 576-2466
JSHS, PO BOX 5 88434 | 2-00111
Mike Chambers, prin. | 576-2466

Santa Fe, AC 505, PC 8, Santa Fe
Pojoaque Valley SD | 4-11111
PO BOX 3468 87501 | 455-2284
Art Blea, supt.
Pojoaque SHS 87504 | 3-00001
Dulces Guardiola, prin. | 455-2234
Pojoaque JHS 87504 | 2-00110
Carlos Alarid, prin. | 455-2238

Santa Fe SD, 610 ALTA VISTA ST 87505 | 7-11111
Amos Melendez, supt. | 982-2631
Capital HS, 4851 PASEO DEL SOL 87505 | 3-00011
Andrew Rendon, prin. | 989-5555
HS, 2100 YUCCA ST 87505 | 4-00011
Pete Aguilar, prin. | 989-5507
Alameda JHS, 400 MADERA ST 87501 | 3-00100
Wilfred Quintana, prin. | 989-5464
Capshaw JHS, ZIA ROAD 87505 | 3-00100
Tom Sweitzer, prin. | 989-5438
DeVargas JHS, 1750 LLANO ST 87505 | 3-00100
Rexie Baca, prin. | 989-5453

Brush Ranch School | HND
PO BOX 2450 87504 | 757-6114
College of Santa Fe | 3-UC
1600 SAINT MICHAELS DR 87505 | 473-6234
Institute of American Indian Arts | 2-CC
PO BOX 20007 87504 | 988-6463
New Mexico School for the Deaf | HND
1060 CERRILLOS RD 87501
St. Catherines Indian HS | 2-00111
801A GRIFFIN ST 87501 | 982-1889
Joe Atencio, prin.
St. John's College | 2-UC
1160 CAMINO DE CRUZ BLANCA 87501
| 982-3691
St. Michaels HS, 100 SIRINGO RD 87505 | 3-00111
Br. Walsh, prin. | 983-7353
Santa Fe Community College | 3-CC
PO BOX 4187 87502 | 471-8200
Santa Fe Prep S | 2-00111
1101 CAMINO DE CRUZ BLANCA 87501
Stephen Machen, prin. | 982-1829
Sante Fe Community S | 2-11111
PO BOX 2241 87504 | 471-6928
Ed Nagel, prin.

Santa Rosa, AC 505, PC 4, Guadalupe
Santa Rosa SD, 344 S 4TH ST 88435 | 3-11111
Dan Flores, supt. | 472-3171
HS, 717 S 3RD ST 88435 | 2-00011
Amos Estrada, prin. | 472-3422
MS, 244 S 4TH ST 88435 | 2-00100
Cathy Garcia-Vega, prin. | 472-3633

Santa Teresa, AC 505, PC 3, Dona Ana
Gadsden SD
Supt. — See Anthony
Mt Cristo Rey HS, PO BOX 899 88008 | 2-00011
Russell Phipps, prin. | 589-5477
JHS, 4800 MCNUTT 88008 | 3-00110
Rafael Gallegos, prin. | 589-1922

Santo Domingo Pueblo, AC 505, PC 5, Sandoval
Bernalillo SD
Supt. — See Bernalillo
Santo Domingo MS | 2-00100
PO BOX 100 87052 | 867-4441
Gilbert Duran, prin.

Shiprock, AC 505, PC 6, San Juan
Central Consolidated SD | 6-11111
PO BOX 1179 87420 | 368-4984
William Horton, supt.
HS, PO BOX 6003 87420 | 3-00011
Elmer Hall, prin. | 368-5161
Tse' Bit'ai MS, PO BOX 1873 87420 | 3-00100
Tom Bryant, prin. | 368-4741
Other Schools – See Kirtland, Newcomb

Silver City, AC 505, PC 7, Grant
Silver SD, 2810 N SWAN ST 88061 | 5-11111
Herb Torrez, supt. | 388-1527
Silver HS, 32ND & SILVER ST 88061 | 4-00011
Frank Quarrell, prin. | 388-1563
La Plata MS, N SILVER ST 88061 | 3-00100
Don Aycock, prin. | 538-3774
Other Schools – See Cliff

Western New Mexico University | 4-UC
PO BOX 680 88062 | 800-222-9668

Socorro, AC 505, PC 6, Socorro
Socorro SD, PO BOX 1157 87801 | 4-11111
Delbert Fraissinet, supt. | 835-0300

HS, PO BOX 1367 87801 3-00011
  Bernard Saiz, prin. 835-0700
Sarracino MS 2-00100
  1425 EL CAMINO REAL ST 87801 835-0283
  Frank Jaramillo, prin.

New Mexico Institute Mining & Technology 3-UC
801 LEROY PL 87801 835-5600

Springer, AC 505, PC 4, Colfax
Springer SD, PO BOX 308 87747 2-11111
  Michael Dickson, supt. 483-2482
JSHS, PO BOX 308 87747 2-00111
  Art Romero, prin. 483-2436

Taos, AC 505, PC 5, Taos
Taos SD, 213 PASEO DEL CANON 87571 5-11111
  Juan Aragon, supt. 758-5201
SHS, 134 CERVANTES ST 87571 3-00001
  Gilbert Archuleta, prin. 758-5233
JHS, 235 PASEO DEL CANON 87571 3-00110
  Reynaldo Quintana, prin. 758-5242

Tatum, AC 505, PC 3, Lea
Tatum SD, PO BOX 685 88267 3-11111
  John Ingle, supt. 398-4455
JSHS, PO BOX 685 88267 2-00111
  T J Parks, prin. 398-4555

Texico, AC 505, PC 3, Curry
Texico SD, PO BOX 237 88135 3-11111
  R. L. Richards, supt. 482-3801
HS, PO BOX 237 88135 2-00011
  Carolyn Abell, prin. 482-3305
JHS, PO BOX 237 88135 2-00100
  Anna Southard, prin. 482-9520

Thoreau, AC 505, PC 4, McKinley
Gallup-McKinley SD
  Supt. — See Gallup
HS, PO BOX 96 87323 2-00011
  James Pina, prin. 862-7488
MS, PO BOX A 87323 2-00100
  David Oakes, prin. 862-7463

Blessed Kateri Tekakwitha S 2-11111
  200 CENTRAL AVE 87323 862-7465
  Sr. Natalie Bussiere, prin.

Tierra Amarilla, AC 505, PC 3, Rio Arriba
Chama Valley SD, PO BOX 10 87575 3-11111
  Manuel Valdez, supt. 588-7285
Escalante HS, PO BOX 157 87575 2-00011
  Gumercindo Salazar, prin. 588-7201
MS, PO BOX 159 87575 1-00100
  Gumercindo Salazar, prin. 588-7297
Other Schools – See Chama

Tijeras, AC 505, PC 2, Bernalillo
Albuquerque SD
  Supt. — See Albuquerque
Roosevelt MS, PO BOX 310 87059 2-00100
  Ruth Johnson, prin. 281-3316

Toadlena, AC 505, PC 2, San Juan

Toadlena Boarding S 2-11111
  PO BOX 857 87324

Tohatchi, AC 505, PC 3, McKinley
Gallup-McKinley SD
  Supt. — See Gallup
HS, PO BOX 248 87325 2-00011
  Benny Roanhorse, prin. 733-2216
MS, PO BOX 322 87325 2-00100
  Joe Cotner, prin. 733-2555

Truth or Consequences, AC 505, PC 6, Sierra
Truth or Consequences SD 4-11111
  PO BOX 952 87901 894-7141
  Janel Ryan, supt.
Hot Springs HS 2-00011
  1200 N PERSHING ST 87901 894-2839
  Vernel Trujillo, prin.
MS 2-00100
  NEW MIDDLE SCHOOL ROAD 87901 894-2257
  Claudie Thompson, prin.

Tucumcari, AC 505, PC 6, Quay
Tucumcari SD, PO BOX 1046 88401 4-11111
  William Coker, supt. 461-3910
HS, 1100 S 7TH ST 88401 2-00011
  Don Sparks, prin. 461-3830
JHS, 914 S 5TH ST 88401 2-00100
  Pilar Gonzalez de Killough, prin. 461-2310

Tularosa, AC 505, PC 5, Otero
Tularosa SD, 504 1ST ST 88352 4-11111
  Susanna Murphy, supt. 585-2782
HS, 998 TULAROSA AVE 88352 2-00011
  Ron Geisheimer, prin. 585-2282
MS, 504 1ST ST 88352 2-00100
  Max Salcido, prin. 585-4561

Vaughn, AC 505, PC 3, Guadalupe
Vaughn SD, PO BOX 158 88353 2-11111
  Roman Garcia, supt. 584-2283
JSHS, PO BOX 158 88353 1-00111
  Roman Garcia, prin. 584-2283

Wagon Mound, AC 505, PC 2, Mora
Wagon Mound SD 2-11111
  PO BOX 158 87752 666-2206
  Tony Garcia, supt.
JSHS, PO BOX 158 87752 1-00111
  Mary Schutz, prin. 666-2206

White Sands Missile Range, AC 505, PC 5, Dona Ana
Las Cruces SD
  Supt. — See Las Cruces
White Sands MS 88002 2-00100
  Phil Allen, prin. 678-1064

Zuni, AC 505, PC 6, McKinley
Zuni SD, PO BOX A 87327 4-11111
  James West, supt. 782-5511
HS, PO BOX 550 87327 2-00011
  Christopher Carson, prin. 782-4451
Twin Buttes JSHS 1-00111
  PO BOX 680 87327 782-4446
  Linda Belarde, prin.
MS, PO BOX 447 87327 2-00100
  Marilyn Feathers, prin. 782-5561

NEW YORK

STATE EDUCATION DEPARTMENT
111 Education Building
Washington Ave., Albany 12234
(518) 474-5844

Commissioner of Education	Thomas Sobol
Executive Deputy Commissioner	Thomas Sheldon
Acting Deputy Commissioner Education	Lawrence Gloeckler
Associate Commissioner Regional Field Services	Terry Ann Schwartz
Associate Commissioner Central Services	James Kadamus

BOARD OF REGENTS, UNIVERSITY OF THE STATE OF NEW YORK
Washington Ave., Albany 12234

Chancellor	Martin Barell

BOARDS OF COOPERATIVE EDUCATIONAL SERVICES

Albany/Schoharie/Schenectady BOCES
  Custer Quick 518-456-9215
  1015 WATERVLIET SHAKER RD
  Albany 12205
Broome/Delaware/Tioga BOCES
  Lawrence Kiley 607-729-9301
  421 UPPER GLENWOOD RD
  Binghamton 13905
Cattargus/Allegany/Erie/Wyoming BOCES
  James Cross 716-372-8293
  PO BOX 424B, Olean 14760
Cayuga/Onondaga BOCES
  Frank Ambrosie 315-253-0361
  234 S STREET RD, Auburn 13021
Clinton/Essex/Warren/Washington BOCES
  William Fritz 518-561-0100
  PO BOX 455, Plattsburgh 12901
Delaware/Chenango/Madison/Otsego BOCES
  F. Van Wickler 607-334-2771
  RR 3, Norwich 13815

Dutchess BOCES
  Duane Hutton 914-471-9200
  SALT POINT TURNPIKE
  Poughkeepsie 12601
Erie 1 BOCES
  Robert Loretan 716-686-2000
  2 PLEASANT AVE W
  Lancaster 14086
Erie 2/Chautauqua/Cattaraugus BOCES
  Gary Barr, 3340 BAKER RD 716-662-0135
  Orchard Park 14127
Franklin/Essex/Hamilton BOCES
  David DeSantis 518-483-6420
  PO BOX 28, Malone 12953
Genesee/Wyoming BOCES
  Edwin Dunmire 716-343-1400
  8250 STATE STREET RD
  Batavia 14020
Hamilton/Fulton/Montgomery BOCES
  Joseph Iraci 518-762-4633
  PO BOX 665, Johnstown 12095

Herkimer/Fulton/Hamilton/Otsego BOCES
  William Whitehill 315-867-2023
  301 GROS BLVD, Herkimer 13350
Jeffrsn/Lewis/Hamltn/Herkmr/Oneida BOCES
  Charles Bohlen 315-788-0400
  OUTER ARSENAL ST ROAD
  Watertown 13601
Livingston/Steuben/Wyoming BOCES
  Charles Moore 716-658-2291
  LACKAWANNA AVE
  Mount Morris 14510
Madison/Oneida BOCES
  Edward Shafer 315-363-8000
  SPRING ROAD, Verona 13478
Monroe 2/Orleans BOCES
  Richard Haken 716-352-2410
  3599 BIG RIDGE RD
  Spencerport 14559
Monroe 1 BOCES
  Joseph Farinola 716-383-2200
  41 OCONNOR RD, Fairport 14450

Nassau BOCES
Ira Singer   516-997-8700
VALENTINE RD & THE PLAIN RD
Westbury 11590
Oneida/Herkimer/Madison BOCES
Robert Sekowski   315-768-4560
PO BOX 70, New Hartford 13413
Onondaga/Cortland/Madison BOCES
Lee Peters   315-433-2602
PO BOX 4754, Syracuse 13221
Ontario/Seneca/Yates/Cayuga/Wayne BOCES
Harold Bowman   716-526-6400
3501 COUNTY ROAD 20
Stanley 14561
Orange/Ulster BOCES
Emanuel Axelrod   914-294-5431
GIBSON ROAD, Goshen 10924
Orleans/Niagara BOCES
Peter Kachris   716-798-4800
4232 SHELBY BASIN RD
Medina 14103
Oswego BOCES
Burton Ramer   315-963-7251
PO BOX 488, Mexico 13114
Otsego/Delaware/Schoharie/Greene BOCES
Austin Leahy   607-652-7531
REXMERE PARK, Stamford 12167

Putnam/Westchester BOCES
John Battles   914-245-2700
Yorktown Heights 10598
Rensselaer/Columbia/Greene BOCES
John Sackett   518-477-8771
1550 SCHUURMAN RD
Castleton 12033
Rockland BOCES
Anthony Campo, 61 PARROT RD   914-623-3828
West Nyack 10994
Saratoga/Warren BOCES
B. Evans, 112 SPRING ST   518-584-3411
Saratoga Springs 12866
Schuyler/Chemung/Tioga BOCES
Ronald Poletto   607-739-3581
431 PHILO RD, Elmira 14903
St. Lawrence/Lewis BOCES
Richard Callan   315-386-4504
PO BOX 231, Canton 13617
Steuben/Allegany BOCES
Rene Bouchard, RR 1, Bath 14810   607-776-7631
Suffolk 1 BOCES
Raymond DeFeo   516-288-6400
215 RIVERHEAD RD
Westhampton Beach 11978

Suffolk 2 BOCES
Edward Milliken   516-289-2200
201 E SUNRISE HWY
Patchogue 11772
Suffolk 3 BOCES
Edward Murphy   516-549-4900
507 DEER PARK AVE
Dix Hills 11746
Sullivan BOCES
Gary Moore   914-292-0082
RR 1 BOX 522, Liberty 12754
Tompkins/Seneca/Tioga BOCES
Roy Dexheimer   607-257-1551
555 WARREN RD, Ithaca 14850
Ulster BOCES
Laura Fleigner   914-255-1400
RR 32 BOX 175, New Paltz 12561
Washington/Warren/Hamilton/Essex BOCES
Gerald Carozza   518-793-7721
WASHINGTON CO BLDG ANNEX
Hudson Falls 12839
Westchester BOCES
R. Lerer, 17 BERKLEY DR   914-937-3820
Port Chester 10573

PUBLIC, PRIVATE AND CATHOLIC SECONDARY SCHOOLS

Accord, AC 914, PC 3, Ulster
Rondout Valley Central SD   5-11111
PO BOX 9   12404   626-7383
H. Ross O'Sullivan, supt.
Rondout Valley HS, PO BOX 9 12404   3-00011
William Cafiero, prin.   687-7631
Rondout Valley JHS, PO BOX 9 12404   2-00100
Peter Beckwith, prin.   687-7632

Adams, AC 315, PC 4, Jefferson
South Jefferson Central SD   4-11111
6 INSTITUTE ST 13605   583-6104
David Paciencia, supt.
South Jefferson JSHS   3-00111
ROUTE 11 13605   232-4531
Ronald Sloan, prin.

Addison, AC 607, PC 4, Steuben
Addison Central SD   4-11111
1 COLWELL ST 14801   359-2243
Harold Hall, supt.
JSHS, 1 COLWELL ST 14801   3-00111
Betsy Stiker, prin.   359-2241

Afton, AC 607, PC 3, Chenango
Afton Central SD, 18 SAND ST 13730   3-11111
Vernice Church, supt.   639-1111
JSHS, 18 SAND ST 13730   2-00111
Joseph Collea, prin.   639-1111

Akron, AC 716, PC 5, Erie
Akron Central SD   4-11111
47 BLOOMINGDALE AVE 14001   542-5532
William Bolton, supt.
JSHS, 47 BLOOMINGDALE AVE 14001   3-00111
R. Black, prin.   542-5416

Albany, AC 518, PC 9, Albany
Albany CSD, 1 ACADEMY PARK 12207   6-11111
John Bach, supt.   462-7200
Albany HS   4-00011
700 WASHINGTON AVE 12203   454-3987
David McGuire, prin.
Hackett MS, 45 DELAWARE AVE 12202   3-00100
Kevin Justice, prin.   462-7144
Livingston MS   2-00100
315 NORTHERN BLVD 12210   462-7154
Gerald Guzik, prin.

South Colonie Central SD   6-11111
102 LORALEE DR 12205   869-3576
Thomas Brown, supt.
Colonie Central HS   4-00011
100 HACKETT AVE 12205   459-1220
Albert Aldi, prin.
Lisha Kill MS   3-01100
100 WATERMAN AVE 12205   456-2306
Joseph Sheperd, prin.
Sand Creek MS   3-01100
329 SAND CREEK RD 12205   459-1333
Henry Kaiser, prin.

Academy of the Holy Names   2-00011
1075 NEW SCOTLAND AVE 12208   489-2559
Mary Vigliante, prin.
Albany Academy for Boys   2-11111
135 ACADEMY RD 12208   465-1461
Carmen Marnell, prin.
Albany Academy for Girls   2-11111
140 ACADEMY RD 12208   463-2201
Ronald Fay, prin.
Albany College of Pharmacy   3-UC
106 NEW SCOTLAND AVE 12208   445-7221
Albany Law School of Union University   3-UC
80 NEW SCOTLAND AVE 12208   445-2321
Albany Medical Center   3-HSP
43 NEW SCOTLAND AVE 12208   445-3830
Albany Medical College   3-UC
47 NEW SCOTLAND AVE 12208   445-4970
Albany Memorial Hospital   HSP
600 NORTHERN BLVD 12204   471-3262

Albany School of Cytotechnology   1-CS
432 WESTERN AVE 12203   445-5298
Bishop Maginn HS   2-00011
99 SLINGERLAND ST 12202   463-2247
Joseph Grasso, prin.
Bryant & Stratton Business Institute   3-CC
1259 CENTRAL AVE 12205   437-1802
Chauffeurs Training School   3-CS
12 RAILROAD AVE 12205   482-8601
Christian Brothers Academy   2-00111
1 DE LA SALLE RD 12208   462-5447
Br. Wilder, prin.
College of Saint Rose   5-UC
432 WESTERN AVE 12203   454-5111
Doane Stuart S, 799 S PEARL ST 12202   2-11111
Edward Dougherty, prin.   465-5222
LaSalle JSHS, 391 WESTERN AVE 12203   2-00111
Anne Moscinski, prin.   489-4731
Maria College of Albany   3-CC
700 NEW SCOTLAND AVE 12208   438-7170
Mildred Elley Business School   2-CS
2 COMPUTER DR S 12205   446-0590
New School of Contemporary Radio   1-CS
50 COLVIN AVE 12206   438-7682
Regents Coll of the Univ of State of NY   7-UC
7 COLUMBIA CIR 12203   464-8500
Russell Sage Junior College of Albany   4-CC
140 NEW SCOTLAND AVE 12208   445-1711
St. Anne Institute   2-00111
160 N MAIN AVE 12206   489-7411
Richard Riccio, prin.
SUNY at Albany   7-UC
1400 WASHINGTON AVE 12222   442-5431
SUNY Center for the Capital District   2-UC
845 CENTRAL AVE 12206   485-5964

Albertson, AC 516, PC 6, Nassau
Herricks UFD
Supt. — See New Hyde Park
Herricks MS, 7 HILLDALE DR 11507   3-00100
Seth Weitzman, prin.   625-6463

Viscardi S, 201 I U WILLETS RD 11507   2-11111
Robert Falvo, prin.   747-5400

Albion, AC 716, PC 6, Orleans
Albion Central SD, 324 EAST AVE 14411   5-11111
Ronald Sodoma, supt.   589-6656
HS, 302 EAST AVE 14411   3-00011
John Greene, prin.   589-5644
MS, 254 EAST AVE 14411   3-01100
Kim Houserman, prin.   589-7033

Alden, AC 716, PC 4, Erie
Alden Central SD, 13190 PARK ST 14004   4-11111
Thomas Boedicker, supt.   937-9116
HS, 13190 PARK ST 14004   3-00011
William Tupay, prin.   937-9116
MS, CRITTENDEN RD 14004   2-00100
Francine Fritz, prin.   937-9116

Alexander, AC 716, PC 2, Genesee
Alexander Central SD   4-11111
3314 BUFFALO ST 14005   591-1551
John Lutz, supt.
JSHS, 3314 BUFFALO ST 14005   2-00111
R. Parkman, prin.   591-1551

Alexandria Bay, AC 315, PC 4, Jefferson
Alexandria Central SD   3-11111
34 BOLTON AVE 13607   482-9971
Myrjean Koster, supt.
Alexandria Central JSHS   2-00111
34 BOLTON AVE 13607   482-9971
Terry Fralick, prin.

Alfred, AC 607, PC 5, Allegany

Alfred University   4-UC
26 N MAIN ST 14802   871-2111

NY State College Ceramics at Alfred   2-UC
14802   800-541-9229
SUNY College of Technology 14802   5-CC
   587-4215

Allegany, AC 716, PC 4, Cattaraugus
Allegany Central SD, 80 N 4TH ST 14706   4-11111
Charles Chester, supt.   373-0060
JSHS, 80 N 4TH ST 14706   3-00111
Frank Petruzzi, prin.   373-0060

Almond, AC 607, PC 2, Allegany
Alfred-Almond Central SD   3-11111
6795 ROUTE 21 14804   276-2981
Diana Luellen, supt.
Alfred-Almond JSHS   2-00111
6795 ROUTE 21 14804   276-2961
Richard Nicol, prin.

Amenia, AC 914, PC 4, Dutchess
Northeast Central SD, HAIGHT RD 12501   4-11111
Brenda Luck, supt.   373-8146
Webutuck JSHS, HAIGHT RD 12501   2-00111
Janice Volpe, prin.   373-8104

Amherst, AC 716, PC 8, Erie
Amherst Central SD   5-11111
55 KINGS HWY 14226   836-3000
R O'Neill, supt.
Amherst Central HS   3-00011
4301 MAIN ST 14226   836-3000
Joseph Podgorski, prin.
MS, 55 KINGS HWY 14226   3-00100
Anton Schwarzmueller, prin.   836-3000

Sweet Home Central SD   5-11111
1901 SWEET HOME RD 14228   689-5201
Gary Cooper, supt.
Sweet Home HS   4-00011
1901 SWEET HOME RD 14228   689-5301
Paul Hendel, prin.
Sweet Home MS, 4150 MAPLE RD 14226   3-00100
Craig Allwes, prin.   837-3500

Buffalo Academy of the Sacred Heart   2-00011
3860 MAIN ST 14226   834-2101
Sr. Edith Wyss, prin.
Daemen College   4-UC
4380 MAIN ST 14226   839-8225
Park School of Buffalo   2-11111
4625 HARLEM RD 14226   839-1242
Donald Graff, prin.
SUNY at Buffalo 14260   8-UC
   636-2901

Amityville, AC 516, PC 6, Suffolk
Amityville UFD, 150 PARK AVE 11701   5-11111
Edward Mavragis, supt.   691-7900
Amityville Memorial HS   3-00011
250 MERRICK RD 11701   598-6550
Richard Cohen, prin.
Miles MS, 501 ROUTE 110 11701   3-00100
James Jackson, prin.   789-6200

Island Drafting & Technical Institute   3-CS
128 BROADWAY 11701   691-8733

Amsterdam, AC 518, PC 7, Montgomery
Amsterdam CSD, 11 LIBERTY ST 12010   5-11111
Arthur Cotungo, supt.   843-5217
HS, SARATOGA AVE 12010   4-00011
Umberto DeRose, prin.   843-4932
Lynch MS, COOLIDGE ROAD 12010   3-00100
Harry Kilfoile, prin.   843-3716

Broadalbin-Perth Central SD
Supt. — See Broadalbin
Broadalbin-Perth MS, RR 4 12010   2-00100
Paul Williamsen, prin.   842-3919

Perth Bible Christian Academy   2-11111
  1863 COUNTY HIGHWAY 107   12010
  Frederick Spier, prin.   843-0734

Andes, AC 914, PC 2, Delaware
Andes Central SD   2-11111
  DELAWARE AVE   13731   676-3167
  Jean-Pierre Dumortier, supt.
Andes Central S, DELAWARE AVE   13731   2-11111
  Joseph Grieco, prin.   676-3167

Andover, AC 607, PC 4, Allegany
Andover Central SD, 35 ELM ST   14806   2-11111
  Jacqueline Bellamy, supt.   478-8491
S, 35 ELM ST   14806   2-11111
  Louis McIntosh, prin.   478-8491

Angelica, AC 716, PC 3, Allegany
Angelica Central SD   2-11111
  21 E MAIN ST   14709   466-7601
  Joe Backer, supt.
Angelica Central S, 21 E MAIN ST   14709   2-11111
  Ronald Pierce, prin.   466-7601

Angola, AC 716, PC 4, Erie
Evans-Brant Central SD   5-11111
  8855 ERIE RD   14006   549-2300
  W. Houston, supt.
Lake Shore SHS, 959 BEACH RD   14006   3-00001
  Kenneth Keipper, prin.   549-2300
Lake Shore Central MS   3-00110
  8855 ERIE RD   14006   549-2300
  Gifford Swyers, prin.

Annandale-on-Hudson, AC 914, PC 2, Dutchess

Bard College   12504   4-UC
   758-6822

Ardsley, AC 914, PC 5, Westchester
Ardsley UFD, 500 FARM RD   10502   4-11111
  Stanley Toll, supt.   693-6300
HS, 300 FARM RD   10502   2-00011
  Lawrence Mayer, prin.   693-6300
MS, 700 ASHFORD AVE   10502   3-01100
  Rose Willner, prin.   693-7564

Argyle, AC 518, PC 2, Washington
Argyle Central SD, SHERIDAN ST   12809   3-11111
  Lawrence Patzwald, supt.   638-8243
Argyle Central S, SHERIDAN ST   12809   3-11111
  Richard Broome, prin.   638-8243

Arkport, AC 607, PC 3, Steuben
Arkport Central SD, 35 EAST AVE   14807   3-11111
  Ralph Kerr, supt.   295-7471
Arkport Central S, 35 EAST AVE   14807   3-11111
  William Locke, prin.   295-7471

Armonk, AC 914, PC 5, Westchester
Byram Hills Central SD   4-11111
  10 TRIPP LN   10504   273-4082
  Thomas Maguire, supt.
Byram Hills HS, 12 TRIPP LN   10504   2-00011
  Rennie Schwartz, prin.   273-9200
Crittenden MS   3-01100
  10 MACDONALD AVE   10504   273-4250
  Evan Powderly, prin.

Arverne, AC 718, PC see New York
Queens Borough SD 27
  Supt. — See Ozone Park
Cardozo JHS, 365 BEACH 56TH ST   11692   3-00110
  Elizabeth Baxter, prin.   945-3300

Astoria, AC 718, Queens

St. Demetrios S, 3003 30TH DR   11102   3-11111
  Andreas Zachariow, prin.   728-1754

Athol Springs, AC 716, PC 3, Erie

St. Francis HS   3-00011
  4129 LAKE SHORE ROAD   14010   627-2386
  Fr. Hartmayer, prin.

Attica, AC 716, PC 5, Wyoming
Attica Central SD   4-11111
  3338 E MAIN STREET RD   14011   591-0400
  Ed Stores, supt.
HS, 3338 E MAIN STREET RD   14011   3-00011
  Barbara Jones, prin.   591-0400
JHS, 3338 E MAIN STREET RD   14011   3-01100
  Ernest Lusky, prin.   591-0400

Auburn, AC 315, PC 8, Cayuga
Auburn CSD, 76 THORNTON AVE   13021   6-11111
  Hollis Palmer, supt.   255-5835
HS, 200 LAKE AVE   13021   4-00011
  Olivia Borncamp, prin.   255-5858
East MS, 157 FRANKLIN ST   13021   3-00100
  Paul Delpiano, prin.   255-5820
West MS, 217 GENESEE ST   13021   3-00100
  Michael Orofino, prin.   255-5824

SUNY Cayuga County Community College   5-CC
  197 FRANKLIN ST   13021   255-1743

Aurora, AC 315, PC 3, Cayuga
Southern Cayuga Central SD   4-11111
  2384 STATE ROUTE 34B   13026   364-7211
  A. Edward Dimiceli, supt.
Other Schools – See Poplar Ridge

Wells College   13026   2-UC
   364-3264

Averill Park, AC 518, PC 5, Rensselaer
Averill Park Central SD   5-11111
  20 GETTLE RD   12018   674-3816
  John Thero, supt.
HS, 16 GETTLE RD   12018   3-00011
  Kathryn Oppedisano, prin.   674-3826
Algonquin MS, RR 4 BOX 92   12018   3-00100
  Michael Purdy, prin.   674-3848

Avoca, AC 607, PC 4, Steuben
Avoca Central SD, OLIVER ST   14809   3-11111
  Sharon Muth, supt.   566-2221
Avoca Central S, OLIVER ST   14809   3-11111
  Robert Cleeves, prin.   566-2221

Avon, AC 716, PC 5, Livingston
Avon Central SD   4-11111
  161 CLINTON ST   14414   226-2455
  Albert Plouffe, supt.
JSHS, 161 CLINTON ST   14414   3-00111
  Richard Letvin, prin.   226-2457

Babylon, AC 516, PC 7, Suffolk
Babylon UFD, 171 RALPH AVE   11702   4-11111
  James Hunderfund, supt.   661-5810
JSHS, 50 RAILROAD AVE   11702   3-00111
  Michael Lobasso, prin.   661-5810

Bainbridge, AC 607, PC 4, Chenango
Bainbridge-Guilford Central SD   4-11111
  18 JULIAND ST   13733   967-2421
  W. Ermlich, supt.
Bainbridge-Guilford JSHS   3-00111
  18 JULIAND ST   13733   967-6323
  Ellen O'Donnell, prin.

Baldwin, AC 516, PC 7, Nassau
Baldwin Central SD, 960 HASTINGS ST   11510   5-11111
  Gene Lanzaro, supt.   377-9271
HS, 841 HIGH SCHOOL DR   11510   4-00011
  Ranier Melucci, prin.   377-9203
JHS, 3211 SCHREIBER PL   11510   3-00100
  Raymond White, prin.   377-9321

Baldwinsville, AC 315, PC 6, Onondaga
Baldwinsville Central SD   6-11111
  29 E ONEIDA ST   13027   638-6043
  Thomas McGowan, supt.
Baker SHS, OSWEGO ST   13027   4-00001
  Jerry Hill, prin.   638-6000
Durgee JHS, 29 E ONEIDA ST   13027   3-00110
  Irving Gray, prin.   638-6086

Ballston Spa, AC 518, PC 5, Saratoga
Ballston Spa Central SD   5-11111
  70 MALTA AVE   12020   884-7110
  Roger Gorham, supt.
HS, 480 GARRETT RD   12020   3-00011
  Michael Palma, prin.   884-7150
MS, 100 WOOD RD   12020   3-00100
  Stephen Toussaint, prin.   884-7201

Barker, AC 716, PC 3, Niagara
Barker Central SD   4-11111
  1628 QUAKER RD   14012   795-3832
  Robert Bouldin, supt.
JSHS, 1628 QUAKER RD   14012   2-00111
  Norman Kahler, prin.   795-3201

Barrytown, AC 914, PC 2, Dutchess

Unification Theological Seminary   2-UC
  10 DOCK RD   12507   758-6881

Batavia, AC 716, PC 7, Genesee
Batavia CSD   5-11111
  39 WASHINGTON AVE   14020   344-8217
  David Van Scoy, supt.
HS, 260 STATE ST   14020   3-00011
  Glenn Young, prin.   344-8280
MS, 96 ROSS ST   14020   3-01100
  John Jakubowski, prin.   344-8260

New York State School for the Blind   HND
  RICHMOND AVE   14020
Notre Dame HS, 73 UNION ST   14020   2-00011
  Nicholas Borrelli, prin.   343-2783
SUNY Genesee Community College   5-CC
  1 COLLEGE RD   14020   343-0055

Bath, AC 607, PC 6, Steuben
Bath Central SD, 25 ELLIS AVE   14810   4-11111
  Charlotte Gregory, supt.   776-3301
Haverling JSHS, 25 ELLIS AVE   14810   3-00111
  Peter Robbins, prin.   776-4107

Bayport, AC 516, PC 6, Suffolk
Bayport-Blue Point UFD   4-11111
  189 ACADEMY ST   11705   472-4040
  Richard Curtis, supt.
Bayport-Blue Point HS   3-00011
  200 SNEDECOR AVE   11705   472-1800
  Peter Sellitto, prin.
Young MS, 602 SYLVAN AVE   11705   2-00100
  John Emery, prin.   472-0800

Bay Shore, AC 516, PC 8, Suffolk
Bay Shore UFD, 75 PERKAL ST   11706   5-11111
  Crescent Bellamore, supt.   968-1117
HS, 155 3RD AVE   11706   4-00011
  Robert Consigli, prin.   968-1156

MS, 393 BROOK AVE   11706   4-00100
  Selven Powell, prin.   968-1208

Bayside, AC 718, PC see New York
Queens Borough HSD
  Supt. — See Corona
HS, 32ND AVE & 208TH ST   11361   4-00011
  Andrea Kanner, prin.   229-7600
Cardozo HS, 5720 223RD ST   11364   5-00011
  Bertram Linder, prin.   631-4880

Queens Borough SD 26   7-11110
  6115 OCEANIA ST   11364   423-0902
  Irwin Altman, supt.
Curie JHS, 4635 OCEANIA ST   11361   4-00110
  Michael Roth, prin.   423-8100
Hawthorne IS, 6115 OCEANIA ST   11364   3-00100
  Michael Shyman, prin.   631-6800
Other Schools – See Floral Park, Flushing, Little Neck

CUNY Queensborough Community College   7-CC
  22205 56TH AVE   11364   631-6262

Beacon, AC 914, PC 7, Dutchess
Beacon CSD, 88 SARGENT AVE   12508   5-11111
  Richard Sagar, supt.   838-2105
HS, 72 FISHKILL AVE   12508   3-00011
  George Billups, prin.   831-3050
Rombout MS   3-00100
  MATTEAWAN ROAD   12508   831-2300
  Edward Mancari, prin.

St. Joachim MS, 60 LIBERTY ST   12508   2-01100
  Stephanie Giammatteo, prin.   831-6550

Beaver Falls, AC 315, PC 3, Lewis
Beaver River Central SD, ARTZ RD   13305   4-11111
  Richard Green, supt.   346-1211
Beaver River JSHS, ARTZ RD   13305   3-00111
  D. Terry Williams, prin.   346-1211

Bedford, AC 914, PC 4, Westchester
Bedford Central SD
  Supt. — See Mount Kisco
Fox Lane HS, S BEDFORD ROAD   10506   3-00011
  Richard Kraemer, prin.   241-6065
Fox Lane MS, S BEDFORD ROAD   10506   3-00100
  James Alloy, prin.   241-6144

Belfast, AC 716, PC 4, Allegany
Belfast Central SD   3-11111
  PO BOX 336   14711   365-2646
  Donald Klem, supt.
S, KING ST   14711   3-11111
  Dennis Doell, prin.   365-2646

Belleville, AC 315, PC 2, Jefferson
Belleville-Henderson Central SD   3-11111
  2500 ACADEMY ST   13611   846-5411
  Gerald Hale, supt.
Bellville-Henderson Central S   3-11111
  2500 ACADEMY ST   13611   846-5411
  Shawn Baker, prin.

Bellmore, AC 516, PC 7, Nassau
Bellmore-Merrick Central SD
  Supt. — See North Merrick
Kennedy HS   3-00011
  3000 BELLMORE AVE   11710   623-8900
  Fred Cohen, prin.
Mepham HS, 2401 CAMP AVE   11710   4-00011
  John Didden, prin.   623-8900
Grand Avenue JHS   3-00100
  2301 GRAND AVE   11710   623-8900
  Frederick Gimpel, prin.

Bellport, AC 516, PC 5, Suffolk
South Country Central SD
  Supt. — See East Patchogue
MS, 35 KREAMER ST   11713   4-00100
  Denis Desesa, prin.   286-4352

Belmont, AC 716, PC 4, Allegany
Belmont Central SD, 24 SOUTH ST   14813   2-11111
  Charles Smith, supt.   268-7629
Belmont Central S, 24 SOUTH ST   14813   2-11111
  James Arthur, prin.   268-7627

Bemus Point, AC 716, PC 2, Chautauqua
Bemus Point Central SD   3-11111
  DUTCH HOLLOW ROAD   14712   386-2375
  Albert D'Attilio, supt.
Maple Grove JSHS   2-00111
  DUTCH HOLLOW ROAD   14712   386-2855
  Kenneth Gaiser, prin.

Bergen, AC 716, PC 4, Genesee
Byron-Bergen Central SD   4-11111
  6917 TOWNLINE RD   14416   494-1220
  William Hayes, supt.
Byron-Bergen HS   2-00111
  6917 W BERGEN RD   14416   494-1220
  Edward Bishop, prin.
Byron-Bergen MS   2-01100
  6917 W BERGEN RD   14416   494-1220
  Susan Hustlbey, prin.

Berlin, AC 518, PC 4, Rensselaer
Berlin Central SD, PO BOX 259   12022   4-11111
  Wayne Jones, supt.   658-2690
Berlin Central JSHS   3-00111
  PO BOX 259   12022   658-2515
  David Seaver, prin.

Berne, AC 518, PC 3, Albany
Berne-Knox-Westerlo Central SD   4-11111
   2021 HELDERBERG TRL 12023   872-1117
   Robert Drake, supt.
Berne-Knox-Westerlo JSHS   3-00111
   2021 HELDERBERG TRL 12023   872-1117
   Steven Schrade, prin.

Bethpage, AC 516, PC 7, Nassau
Bethpage UFD, 10 CHERRY AVE 11714   4-11111
   David Nydick, supt.   733-3700
HS, 10 CHERRY AVE 11714   3-00011
   Antoinette MacLeod, prin.   733-3700
Kennedy MS, 500 BROADWAY 11714   3-00100
   Clifford Jaeger, prin.   733-3791

Bible School Park, AC 607, PC see Johnson City

Practical Bible Training School   2-UC
   PO BOX 601 13737   729-1581

Binghamton, AC 607, PC 8, Broome
Binghamton CSD, 98 OAK ST 13905   6-11111
   James Lee, supt.   762-8131
HS, 31 MAIN ST 13905   4-00011
   Joseph Holly, prin.   762-8200
East MS, 167 E FREDERICK ST 13904   3-00100
   Gary Worden, prin.   762-8300
West MS, W JUNIOR AVE 13905   3-00100
   Thomas Corgel, prin.   763-8400

Chenango Forks Central SD   4-11111
   PO BOX 204A 13903   648-8511
   R. David Andrus, supt.
Chenango Forks HS   3-00011
   1 GORDON DR 13901   648-8511
   Joseph Stoner, prin.
Chenango Forks MS   3-00100
   1 GORDON DR 13901   648-8511
   Edward Petras, prin.

Chenango Valley Central SD   4-11111
   1222 E ARTERIAL HWY 13901   779-4710
   Michael Grenis, supt.
Chenango Valley JSHS   3-00111
   1160 CHENANGO ST 13901   779-4742
   Rodney Eldridge, prin.

Central Baptist Christian Academy   2-11111
   1606 STATE ROUTE 12 13901   648-6210
   Rev. Hanel, prin.
Ridley-Lowell Business & Technical Inst   2-CS
   116 FRONT ST 13905   724-2941
St. Patrick's MS, 58 OAK ST 13905   2-01100
   Charles McGlynn, prin.   723-4601
Seton Catholic Central HS   3-00011
   70 SEMINARY AVE 13905   723-5307
   Kathleen Dwyer, prin.
SUNY at Binghamton   7-UC
   PO BOX 6001 13902   777-2000
SUNY Broome Community College   6-CC
   907 UPPER FRONT ST 13905   771-5000

Blauvelt, AC 914, PC 5, Rockland
South Orangetown Central SD   4-11111
   160 VAN WYCK RD 10913   365-4200
   Morton Sherman, supt.
South Orangetown MS   3-00100
   160 VAN WYCK RD 10913   365-4251
   Emanuel Kostakis, prin.
Other Schools – See Orangeburg

Bohemia, AC 516, PC 6, Suffolk
Connetquot Central SD   6-11111
   780 OCEAN AVE 11716   244-2211
   John Maloney, supt.
Connetquot SHS, 190 7TH ST 11716   4-00001
   Joseph O'Brien, prin.   244-2226
Other Schools – See Oakdale, Ronkonkoma

Boiceville, AC 914, PC 3, Ulster
Onteora Central SD, ROUTE 28 12412   4-11111
   Gary Loewenberg, supt.   657-6383
Onteora JSHS 12412   3-00111
   F. Galluccio-Steele, prin.   657-2373

Bolivar, AC 716, PC 4, Allegany
Bolivar Central SD   3-11111
   100 SCHOOL ST 14715   928-2561
   Robert Mountain, supt.
JSHS, 100 SCHOOL ST 14715   2-00111
   Vincent Di Tanna, prin.   928-2561

Bolton Landing, AC 518, PC 4, Warren
Bolton Central SD, HORICON AVE 12814   2-11111
   Richard Grimm, supt.   644-3531
Bolton Central S, HORICON AVE 12814   2-11111
   Franklin McKinney, prin.   644-3531

Boonville, AC 315, PC 4, Oneida
Adirondack Central SD   4-11111
   110 FORD ST 13309   942-4411
   Harry Fensom, supt.
Adirondack HS, 110 FORD ST 13309   2-00111
   Richard Wheeler, prin.   942-4411

Bradford, AC 607, PC 2, Steuben
Bradford Central SD   2-11111
   2820 STATE ROUTE 226 14815   583-4616
   Wendell Binley, supt.
Bradford Central S   2-11111
   2820 STATE ROUTE 226 14815   583-4616
   Marilyn Sokira, prin.

Brasher Falls, AC 315, PC 3, St. Lawrence
Brasher Falls Central SD   4-11111
   ROUTE 11 13613   389-5131
   Kathleen Farrell, supt.
St. Lawrence JSHS   3-00111
   PO BOX 307 13613   389-5131
   Anthony Francello, prin.

Breesport, AC 607, PC 3, Chemung

Twin Tiers Baptist S, PO BOX K 14816   2-00111
   Harold Wolcott, prin.   739-3619

Brentwood, AC 516, PC 8, Suffolk
Brentwood UFD, 1 3RD AVE 11717   7-11111
   Frank Mauro, supt.   434-2325
SHS, 2 6TH AVE 11717   5-00001
   Gary Mintz, prin.   434-2391
JHS, 33 LEAHY AVE 11717   3-00010
   John Galaris, prin.   434-2541
East MS, 70 HILLTOP DR 11717   3-00100
   Ross Herzog, prin.   434-2473
North MS, 350 WICKS RD 11717   3-00100
   Mark Nizewitz, prin.   434-2356
South MS, 785 CANDLEWOOD RD 11717   3-00100
   Ann Quinn, prin.   434-2341
West MS, UDALL ROAD 11717   3-00100
   Kevin McNicholas, prin.   434-2371

Academy of St. Joseph   3-11111
   1725 BRENTWOOD RD 11717   273-2406
   Sr. Valerie Scholl, prin.
Long Island University   4-UC
   2ND AVE 11717   273-5112
SUNY Suffolk County Community College   5-CC
   1001 CROOKED HILL RD 11717   434-6750

Brewster, AC 914, PC 4, Putnam
Brewster Central SD   5-11111
   RR 2 BOX 400 10509   279-8001
   Gregory Vogt, supt.
HS, FOGGINTOWN ROAD 10509   3-00011
   George Coan, prin.   279-8001
Wells MS, ROUTE 312 10509   3-01100
   William Shannon, prin.   279-8001

Briarcliff Manor, AC 914, PC 6, Westchester
Briarcliff Manor UFD   4-11111
   45 INGHAM RD 10510   941-8880
   Michael Mackin, supt.
JSHS, 444 PLEASANTVILLE RD 10510   2-00111
   Joseph Troy, prin.   769-9400

King's College, The 10510   3-UC
   941-7200

Bridgehampton, AC 516, PC 4, Suffolk
Bridgehampton UFD   2-11111
   MONTAUK HWY 11932   537-0271
   John Edwards, supt.
S, MONTAUK HWY 11932   2-11111
   John Edwards, supt.   537-0271

Broadalbin, AC 518, PC 4, Fulton
Broadalbin-Perth Central SD   4-11111
   14 SCHOOL ST 12025   883-3442
   Harry Brooks, supt.
Broadalbin-Perth HS   3-00011
   BRIDGE ST EXT 12025   883-3442
   Nancy Allegretto, prin.
Other Schools – See Amsterdam

Brockport, AC 716, PC 6, Monroe
Brockport Central SD   5-11111
   40 ALLEN ST 14420   637-5303
   Patricia Horkan, supt.
HS, 40 ALLEN ST 14420   4-00011
   Jeffrey Brown, prin.   637-5303
Oliver MS, 40 ALLEN ST 14420   4-00100
   Jack Milner, prin.   637-5303

SUNY College at Brockport 14420   6-UC
   395-2211

Brocton, AC 716, PC 4, Chautauqua
Brocton Central SD   3-11111
   138 W MAIN ST 14716   792-9121
   Richard Gloss, supt.
JSHS, 138 W MAIN ST 14716   2-00111
   Richard Thom, prin.   792-9121

Bronx, AC 718, PC see New York
Bronx Borough HSD   8-00011
   3000 E TREMONT AVE 10461   892-9926
   Carmen Russo, supt.
Addams Vocational HS   4-00011
   900 TINTON AVE 10456   292-4513
   Cynthia List, prin.
Bronx HS of Science   5-00011
   75 W 205TH ST 10468   295-0200
   Vincent Galasso, prin.
Childs HS, 800 E GUN HILL RD 10467   5-00011
   Richard Urovsky, prin.   519-7700
Clinton HS   5-00011
   100 W MOSHOLU PKY S 10468   543-1000
   Norman Wechsler, prin.
Columbus HS, 925 ASTOR AVE 10469   5-00011
   Frank Melia, prin.   231-5000
Dodge Vocational HS   4-00011
   2474 CROTONA AVE 10458   584-2700
   Irma Nesci, prin.
Gompers HS   4-00011
   455 SOUTHERN BLVD 10455   665-0950
   Maryann Hawthorne, prin.

Kennedy HS   5-00011
   99 TERRACE VIEW AVE 10463   562-5500
   Charles Saltzman, prin.
Lehman HS   5-00011
   3000 E TREMONT AVE 10461   824-0500
   Robert Leder, prin.
Monroe HS, 1300 BOYNTON AVE 10472   5-00011
   Roberta Goldman, prin.   893-5800
Morris HS, 1110 BOSTON RD 10456   4-00011
   Lourdes Garcia, prin.   542-3700
Roosevelt HS   5-00011
   500 E FORDHAM RD 10458   733-8100
   Thelma Baxter, prin.
Smith HS, 333 E 151ST ST 10451   4-00011
   Stephen Applebaum, prin.   993-5000
South Bronx HS   3-00011
   701 SAINT ANNS AVE 10455   993-6354
   Sonia Rivera, prin.
Stevenson HS   5-00011
   1980 LAFAYETTE AVE 10473   918-2700
   Caesar Previdi, prin.
Taft HS, 240 E 172ND ST 10457   5-00011
   Mary Ann Macon, prin.   293-7200
Truman HS   5-00011
   750 BAYCHESTER AVE 10475   904-5400
   Mark Orfinger, prin.
Walton HS, 2780 RESERVOIR AVE 10468   5-00011
   Nicola Genco, prin.   364-7400
University Heights JHS   2-00010
   UNIVERSITY AVE & W 181ST ST 10453
   Nancy Mohr, prin.   220-6397

Bronx Borough SD 10   8-11100
   1 FORDHAM PLZ 10458   220-8300
   F. Goldberg, supt.
Browning IS, 120 E 184TH ST 10468   3-00100
   Ira Goldberg, prin.   584-0350
Giordano JHS   4-00100
   2502 LORILLARD PL 10458   584-1660
   Joseph Solanto, prin.
Mosholu Parkway JHS   4-00100
   149 E MOSHOLU PKY N 10467   405-6300
   Lawrence Gluck, prin.
Niles JHS, 577 E 179TH ST 10457   4-00100
   Gerald Friedlander, prin.   584-2330
Patri IS, 2225 WEBSTER AVE 10457   3-00100
   Michael Spivak, prin.   584-0980
Riverdale JHS, 660 W 237TH ST 10463   4-00100
   Melvin Katz, prin.   796-8516
Tetard JHS, 120 W 231ST ST 10463   4-00100
   Henry Yurek, prin.   796-8170

Bronx Borough SD 11   7-11100
   1250 ARNOW AVE 10469   519-8000
   Frank Arricale, supt.
Casals IS, 800 BAYCHESTER AVE 10475   3-01100
   Steven Bennett, prin.   904-5600
Castle Hill JHS, 1560 PURDY ST 10462   4-01100
   Frank Paliotta, prin.   892-8600
Green JHS, 3710 BARNES AVE 10467   4-00100
   Frank Uzzo, prin.   653-2130
Michelangelo IS   4-00100
   2545 GUNTHER AVE 10469   379-7400
   Ernst Gisolfi, prin.
Northeast Education Park IS   3-01100
   700 BAYCHESTER AVE 10475   904-5650
   James Duffy, prin.
Sousa JHS   4-00100
   3750 BAYCHESTER AVE 10466   231-0100
   Al Thomas, prin.
Whalen JHS, 2441 WALLACE AVE 10467   4-00100
   Frank Perfito, prin.   653-1237

Bronx Borough SD 12   7-11100
   1000 JENNINGS ST 10460   328-2310
   Welfredo Abreu, supt.
Gathings IS, 800 HOME ST 10456   3-00100
   Jean Keizs, prin.   542-1155
Hansberry IS, 1970 W FARMS RD 10460   3-00100
   Franklyn Sanchez, prin.   542-5362
Hernandez IS, 977 FOX ST 10459   4-00100
   Louis Corominas, prin.   589-4844
Ridder JHS, 1619 BOSTON RD 10460   2-00100
   Roy Rivera, prin.   589-3200
Young IS, 1919 PROSPECT AVE 10457   3-00100
   Allan Brandt, prin.   294-8503

Bronx Borough SD 7   7-11110
   501 COURTLANDT AVE 10451   292-0481
   Carmen Rodriguez, supt.
Bilingual IS, 778 FOREST AVE 10456   3-00100
   Juan Fonseca, prin.   292-1684
Burger IS, 345 BROOK AVE 10454   3-00100
   Adolph Rotter, prin.   292-0269
Clark JHS, 360 E 145TH ST 10454   3-00110
   Dennis Pradier, prin.   292-2211
De Tio IS, 600 SAINT ANNS AVE 10455   3-00100
   Joel Sklar, prin.   292-0880
Gehrig IS   3-00100
   250 THURMAN MUNSON WAY 10451   292-0260
   (—), prin.
Robeson IS, 339 MORRIS AVE 10451   3-00100
   John Crawford, prin.   292-1052

Bronx Borough SD 8   7-11110
   650 WHITE PLAINS RD 10473   822-5140
   Max Messer, supt.
Dunbar JHS   2-00110
   890 CAULDWELL AVE 10456   822-5398
   Arnold Nager, prin.
Einstein IS, 885 BOLTON AVE 10473   4-01100
   Jonathan Worth, prin.   822-5067

Hudson JHS, 1111 PUGSLEY AVE 10472   3-00100
  Mathew Cowit, prin.   822-5186
Kiernan JHS   3-00110
  1025 MORRISON AVE 10472   822-5021
  Ken Orefice, prin.
Knowlton IS, 681 KELLY ST 10455   3-00100
  Iraida Fuentes, prin.   822-5082
Maleska IS   3-01100
  456 WHITE PLAINS RD 10473   822-5035
  Chester Cohen, prin.
Peninsula IS, 730 BRYANT AVE 10474   3-01100
  Donald Fulton, prin.   822-5124
Piagentini-Jones IS   4-00100
  650 HOLLYWOOD AVE 10465   822-5317
  Robert Barrett, prin.

Bronx Borough SD 9   8-11100
  1377 JEROME AVE 10452   681-5000
  Anne Wolinsky, supt.
Clemente IS, 250 E 164TH ST 10456   4-01100
  Nelson Abreu, prin.   681-6334
Drew IS, 3630 3RD AVE 10456   3-00100
  Steven Issman, prin.   681-7105
Macombs JHS   4-01100
  1700 MACOMBS RD 10453   583-7007
  Verdi Avila, prin.
Mott JHS   4-01100
  E 167TH ST & COLLEGE AVE 10456   681-6847
  Victor Lozano, prin.
Patterson IS   3-01100
  275 ROBERTO CLMNT STATE BRG 10453
  Willie Moore, prin.   583-6266
Sands IS, 1600 WEBSTER AVE 10457   4-00100
  William Green, prin.   583-6766
Tosacanini JHS, 1000 TELLER AVE 10456   4-01100
  Glenn Bader, prin.   681-7219
Wade JHS, 1865 MORRIS AVE 10453   3-00100
  Saul Brodsky, prin.   681-6220

New York City Special Schools
  Supt. — See Brooklyn
Bronx Occupation Training Ctr   Vo Tech
  2697 WESTCHESTER AVE 10461   597-6404
  ANNE PONTECORVO, prin.
School for Career Development   Vo Tech
  470 JACKSON AVE 10455   993-5581
  JEFFREY RAPPORT, prin.

Academy of Mt. St. Ursula   3-00011
  330 BEDFORD PARK BLVD 10458   364-5353
  Sr. Mary Read, prin.
All Hallows Institute   2-00011
  111 E 164TH ST 10452   293-4545
  Gerald Grimmeyer, prin.
Aquinas HS, 685 E 182ND ST 10457   3-00011
  Sr. Margaret Ryan, prin.   367-2113
Cardinal Hayes HS   4-00011
  650 GRAND CONCOURSE 10451   292-6100
  Fr. Graham, prin.
Cardinal Spellman HS   4-00011
  1 NEEDHAM AVE 10466   881-8000
  Msgr. Monahan, prin.
College of New Rochelle   3-UC
  950 BAYCHESTER AVE 10475   320-0300
College of New Rochelle   3-UC
  332 E 149TH ST 10451   665-1310
CUNY Bronx Community College   6-CC
  W 181ST & UNIVERSITY AVE 10453   220-6920
CUNY Hostos Community College   5-CC
  475 GRAND CONCOURSE 10451   518-6622
CUNY Lehman College   6-UC
  250 BEDFORD PARK BLVD W 10468   960-8881
Drake Business School   3-CS
  2488 GRAND CONCOURSE 10458   295-6200
Fieldston S, 3901 FIELDSTON RD 10471   3-00111
  David Shapiro, prin.   543-5000
Fordham Prep S   3-00011
  441 E FORDHAM RD 10458   367-7500
  Cornelius McCarthy, prin.
Fordham University   7-UC
  441 E FORDHAM RD 10458   817-1000
Horace Mann-Barnard S   3-00111
  231 W 246TH ST 10471   548-4000
  Norman Fountain, prin.
Lavelle School/Blind-Visually Impaired   HND
  E 221 ST & PAULDING AVE 10469
Mercy College   3-UC
  50 ANTIN PL 10462   798-8952
Monroe College   2-CS
  2501 JEROME AVE 10468   933-6700
Monsignor Scanlan HS   3-00011
  915 HUTCHINSON RIVER PKY 10465   430-0100
  Sr. Marie O'Donnell, prin.
Montefiore Medical Center   HSP
  111 E 210TH ST 10467   920-4001
Mt. St. Michael Academy   4-00011
  4300 MURDOCK AVE 10466   515-6400
  Br. Kearney, prin.
Mt. St. Michael Academy   2-00100
  4300 MURDOCK AVE 10466   515-6400
  Br. Grogan, prin.
New York Institute for Special Education   HND
  999 PELHAM PKY N 10469   519-7000
Our Savior Lutheran S   3-11111
  1734 WILLIAMSBRIDGE RD 10461   792-5665
  Lewis Williams, prin.
Pace Business School   2-CS
  210 E 188TH ST 10458   933-7400
Preston HS, 2780 SCHURZ AVE 10465   2-00011
  Sr. Lucille Coldrick, prin.   863-9134

Riverdale Country S   3-11111
  5250 FIELDSTON RD 10471   549-8810
  Roger Boocock, prin.
Sacred Heart MS   2-01100
  1248 NELSON AVE 10452   293-6040
  Br. Lamagna, prin.
St. Barnabas HS, 425 E 240TH ST 10470   2-00011
  Sr. Margaret McEntee, prin.   325-8800
St. Catherine Academy   3-00011
  2350 WILLIAMSBRIDGE RD 10469   882-2882
  Ralph Napolitano, prin.
St. Helena Commercial HS   2-00011
  925 HUTCHINSON RIVER PKY 10465   792-1395
  Sr. Jean McHenry, prin.
St. Pius V HS   2-00011
  500 COURTLANDT AVE 10451   292-3636
  Sr. Mary Lynch, prin.
St. Raymond Academy   2-00011
  2380 E TREMONT AVE 10462   824-4220
  Sr. Marian Byrne, prin.
St. Raymond's HS   3-00011
  2151 SAINT RAYMONDS AVE 10462   824-5050
  Br. Meagher, prin.
SCS Business & Technical Institute   4-CS
  2467 JEROME AVE 10468   733-5200
SUNY Maritime College   3-UC
  6 PENNYFIELD AVE 10465   409-7200

Bronxville, AC 914, PC 6, Westchester
Bronxville UFD   4-11111
  81 PONDFIELD RD 10708   337-5600
  John Chambers, supt.
HS, 177 PONDFIELD RD 10708   2-00011
  Maureen Grolnick, prin.   337-5600
MS, PONDFIELD ROAD 10708   2-00100
  John Kehoe, prin.   337-5600

Concordia College   3-UC
  171 WHITE PLAINS RD 10708   337-9300
Sarah Lawrence College 10708   4-UC
      337-0700

Brookfield, AC 315, PC 3, Madison
Brookfield Central SD   2-11111
  FAIRGROUND RD 13314   899-3324
  Patricia Archambault, supt.
Brookfield Central S   2-11111
  FAIRGROUND RD 13314   899-3324
  Patricia Archambault, prin.

Brookhaven, AC 516, PC 5, Suffolk
South Country Central SD
  Supt. — See East Patchogue
Bellport HS   4-00011
  205 BEAVER DAM RD 11719   286-4331
  Howard Dodd, prin.

Brooklyn, AC 718, PC see New York
Brooklyn Borough HSD   8-00011
  1600 AVENUE L 11230   258-4826
  Joyce Coppin, supt.
Automotive HS, 50 BEDFORD AVE 11222   4-00011
  Steven Gilbert, prin.   388-6318
Barton HS, 901 CLASSON AVE 11225   5-00011
  Jerry Resnick, prin.   636-4901
Brooklyn College Academy   2-00011
  BEDFORD AVE 11210   951-5941
  Madaline Lumachi, prin.
Bushwick HS, 400 IRVING AVE 11237   4-00011
  Jose Fraga, prin.   381-7100
Canarsie HS   5-00011
  1600 ROCKAWAY PKY 11236   649-4820
  Jacqueline Muse, prin.
Dewey HS, 50 AVENUE X 11223   5-00011
  William Sigelakis, prin.   373-6400
East New York Vocational HS   4-00011
  1 WELLS ST 11208   647-5204
  Jesse Lazarus, prin.
Erasmus Hall HS   5-00011
  911 FLATBUSH AVE 11226   282-7803
  Norman Green, prin.
Grady HS, 25 BRIGHTON 4TH RD 11235   4-00011
  Anthony Valenti, prin.   332-5000
Jefferson HS   4-00011
  400 PENNSYLVANIA AVE 11207   345-1801
  Lena Medley, prin.
Madison HS, 3787 BEDFORD AVE 11229   5-00011
  Connie Ranieri, prin.   377-0400
Maxwell Vocational HS   4-00011
  145 PENNSYLVANIA AVE 11207   345-9100
  Barb Elk, prin.
Midwood HS   5-00011
  2839 BEDFORD AVE 11210   859-9200
  Lewis Forhlich, prin.
Murrow HS, 1600 AVENUE L 11230   5-00011
  Saul Bruckner, prin.   258-9283
New Utrecht HS, 1601 80TH ST 11214   5-00011
  Al Leibowitz, prin.   232-2500
Prospect Heights HS   4-00011
  883 CLASSON AVE 11225   636-5800
  Jerry Cioffi, prin.
Robeson HS of Business/Tech   4-00011
  150 ALBANY AVE 11213   774-0300
  Marcia Lyles, prin.
Roosevelt HS, 5800 20TH AVE 11204   5-00011
  Adele Vocel, prin.   256-1346
Sheepshead Bay HS   5-00011
  3000 AVENUE X 11235   332-2003
  Richard Tardalo, prin.
South Shore HS   5-00011
  6565 FLATLANDS AVE 11236   531-4454
  Rena Stempel, prin.

Tilden HS, 5800 TILDEN AVE 11203   4-00011
  Welton Sawyer, prin.   629-4523
Van Arsdale HS, 257 N 6TH ST 11211   4-00011
  John Woodman, prin.   387-7658
Westinghouse Vo & Tech HS   4-00011
  105 JOHNSON ST 11201   625-6130
  Lewis Rappaport, prin.
Wingate HS, 600 KINGSTON AVE 11203   5-00011
  Richard Organisciak, prin.   467-7400
NYC Vocational Training Center   Vo Tech
  1171 65TH ST 11219   258-4826
  Frank Quiroga, prin.
Other Schools – See Jamaica

Brooklyn Borough SD 13   7-11100
  355 PARK PL 11238   636-3204
  Argie Johnson, supt.
Edmonds JHS, 300 ADELPHI ST 11205   3-00100
  Katherine Corbett, prin.   834-6778
Key IS, 300 WILLOUGHBY AVE 11205   3-00100
  Frances Horne, prin.   834-6904
McKinney JHS, 101 PARK AVE 11205   3-00100
  Henry Pankey, prin.   834-6760
Ruggles JHS, 141 MACON ST 11216   3-00100
  Noreen Hosier, prin.   834-6916

Brooklyn Borough SD 14   7-11110
  215 HEYWARD ST 11206   963-4800
  William Rogers, supt.
Campos IS, 215 HEYWARD ST 11206   3-00100
  Ken Mittler, prin.   963-0713
DeHostos IS, 101 WALTON ST 11206   3-00100
  Alan Fierstein, prin.   782-0589
Ericsson JHS, 424 LEONARD ST 11222   4-00110
  Sheldon Toback, prin.   782-2527
Gaynor IS, 223 GRAHAM AVE 11206   3-00100
  Henry Whitney, prin.   387-7697
Hopkins IS, 70 TOMPKINS AVE 11206   3-00100
  Linon Pretty, prin.   782-9500
Wells JHS, 183 S 3RD ST 11211   4-00110
  Joseph Gryzlo, prin.   387-4184

Brooklyn Borough SD 15   7-11110
  360 SMITH ST 11231   330-9300
  William Casey, supt.
Alexander JHS, 350 5TH AVE 11215   4-00100
  Michael Schlar, prin.   330-9315
Dewey JHS, 4004 4TH AVE 11232   3-00100
  Hector Rivera, prin.   330-9360
Hale IS, 285 BALTIC ST 11201   3-00110
  Charles Dluzniewski, prin.   330-9390
Rouget JHS, 544 7TH AVE 11215   3-00100
  Eugene Weiss, prin.   330-9325
Stranahan JHS, 610 HENRY ST 11231   3-00110
  Walter Sadowski, prin.   330-9365

Brooklyn Borough SD 16   7-11110
  1010 LAFAYETTE AVE 11221   574-2323
  Minta Spain, supt.
Garnett JHS, 800 GATES AVE 11221   3-00110
  Zephrine Cummings, prin.   574-2424
Reid JHS, 125 STUYVESANT AVE 11221   3-00100
  Robert Norris, prin.   574-2357

Brooklyn Borough SD 17   8-11100
  402 EASTERN PKY 11225   462-4900
  Thelma Harper, supt.
Atwell IS, 400 EMPIRE BLVD 11225   4-00100
  Marvin Barksdale, prin.   774-1002
Bethune IS, 188 ROCHESTER AVE 11213   3-00100
  Letha Terry, prin.   774-7900
Jackson IS, 790 E NEW YORK AVE 11203   4-00100
  Albert Wiley, prin.   493-8920
Public MS 248, 15 SNYDER AVE 11226   3-00100
  Claudette Murray, prin.   469-9478
Robinson IS, 46 MCKEEVER PL 11225   4-00100
  Vergie Muhammed, prin.   693-6655
Walker IS, 1224 PARK PL 11213   4-00100
  Mark Oberst, prin.   493-5446
Whitman IS, 72 VERONICA PL 11226   4-00100
  Claude Winfield, prin.   282-5230

Brooklyn Borough SD 18   7-11100
  755 E 100TH ST 11236   257-7500
  H. Garner, supt.
Bildersee JHS, 956 E 82ND ST 11236   4-00100
  Fred Dubinsky, prin.   241-4800
Levin JHS, 5909 BEVERLEY RD 11203   4-00100
  Anthony Raziano, prin.   451-2200
Somers JHS, 1084 LENOX RD 11212   3-00100
  Bernard Taab, prin.   342-1144
Wilson JHS, 1001 E 100TH ST 11236   4-00100
  Marion Kendall, prin.   251-4411
Winthrop JHS, 905 WINTHROP ST 11203   4-00100
  Roslyn Schley, prin.   773-2662

Brooklyn Borough SD 19   7-11100
  2057 LINDEN BLVD 11207   257-6900
  Levander Lily, supt.
Cordero IS, 350 LINWOOD ST 11208   4-00100
  Ronald Jones, prin.   647-9500
Douglas IS, 300 WYONA ST 11207   3-00100
  Levi Brisbane, prin.   498-6560
Gateway IS   2-00100
  1426 FREEPORT LOOP 11239   642-3007
  Richard Ferri, prin.
Gershwin JHS   3-00100
  800 VAN SICLEN AVE 11207   649-0765
  Milton Strong, prin.
Lincoln IS, 528 RIDGEWOOD AVE 11208   3-00100
  Victor Rodriguez, prin.   647-0111
Sinnott IS, 370 FOUNTAIN AVE 11208   3-00100
  Ronald Attivissimo, prin.   647-9050

Brooklyn Borough SD 20 7-11100
  1031 59TH ST 11219 851-3200
  Ralph Fabrizio, supt.
Ditmas JHS, 700 CORTELYOU RD 11218 4-00100
  Nancy Brogan, prin. 941-5450
Dyker Heights JHS 4-00100
  8010 12TH AVE 11228 833-9363
  Madeleine Brennan, prin.
McKinley JHS 4-00100
  7305 FORT HAMILTON PKY 11228 833-1000
  Carl Sanfilippo, prin.
Montauk JHS, 4200 16TH AVE 11204 3-00100
  James Hayden, prin. 438-0155
Pershing JHS, 4812 9TH AVE 11220 4-00100
  Beverly McCormick, prin. 633-8200
Shallow JHS, 6500 16TH AVE 11204 4-00100
  Donald Delseni, prin. 256-8218

Brooklyn Borough SD 21 7-11110
  345 VAN SICKLEN ST 11223 266-1714
  Donald Weber, supt.
Boody JHS, 228 AVENUE S 11223 4-00100
  Steve Ganzell, prin. 375-7635
Cavallaro JHS, 8787 24TH AVE 11214 4-00100
  Rose Molinelli, prin. 996-6706
Low IS, 99 AVENUE P 11204 4-00110
  John Mancini, prin. 236-1344
Reynolds IS, 1401 EMMONS AVE 11235 4-00100
  Richard Pearl, prin. 891-9005
Tilyou JHS, 501 WEST AVE 11224 3-00100
  Marian Nagler, prin. 999-0100
Twain IS, 2401 NEPTUNE AVE 11224 4-00100
  Gary Goldstein, prin. 266-0814

Brooklyn Borough SD 22 8-11100
  2525 HARING ST 11235 648-5550
  John Comer, supt.
Cunningham IS, 1875 E 17TH ST 11229 4-00100
  Jeffrey Latto, prin. 645-1334
Hudde IS, 2500 NOSTRAND AVE 11210 4-00100
  Mel Brand, prin. 253-3700
Mann IS, 1420 E 68TH ST 11234 4-00100
  Patrick Timpone, prin. 763-4700
Marine Park IS, 1925 STUART ST 11229 4-00100
  Robert Sheedy, prin. 375-3523
Shell Bank IS 4-00100
  2424 BATCHELDER ST 11235 743-0220
  Ilene Agranoff, prin.

Brooklyn Borough SD 23 7-11110
  2240 DEAN ST 11233 495-7711
  Michael Vega, supt.
Coleman JHS, 1137 HERKIMER ST 11233 3-00100
  Judith West, prin. 495-7787
Hamilton JHS 3-00110
  985 ROCKAWAY AVE 11212 495-7833
  Priscilla Williams, prin.
Hunter JHS, 210 CHESTER ST 11212 3-00100
  Margo Spielberg, prin. 495-7781
Ocean Hill IS, 2021 BERGEN ST 11233 3-00100
  Ernest Logan, prin. 495-7736

Brooklyn Borough SD 32 7-11100
  797 BUSHWICK AVE 11221 574-0212
  Marco Hernandez, supt.
Fermi IS, 35 STARR ST 11221 4-00100
  Maria Diaz, prin. 821-4277
Halsey JHS, 125 COVERT ST 11207 4-00100
  Norman Letow, prin. 574-0288
Hayes IS, 231 PALMETTO ST 11221 3-00100
  Alberto Bryan, prin. 574-0361
Schuyler IS, 1300 GREENE AVE 11237 4-01100
  Mildred Boyce, prin. 574-0390
Willoughby JHS 3-00100
  1390 WILLOUGHBY AVE 11237 821-4860
  Aida Rivera, prin.

New York City Special Schools 7-00000
  110 LIVINGSTON ST 11201
  Ed Bayardelle, supt.
Brooklyn Occupational Training Ctr Vo Tech
  8310 21ST AVE 11214 266-0509
  NEIL WASSERMAN, prin.
Other Schools – See Bronx, Corona, Jamaica, New
  York, Staten Island

Richmond Borough HSD 7-00011
  1171 65TH ST 11219 236-5455
  Charles Schonhaut, supt.
Boys & Girls HS, 1700 FULTON ST 11213 5-00011
  Frank Micken, prin. 467-1700
Brooklyn Tech HS 5-00011
  29 FORT GREEN PL 11217 858-5150
  Lee McCaskill, prin.
Eastern District HS 5-00011
  850 GRAND ST 11211 387-2800
  Louis La Bosco, prin.
Ft. Hamilton HS, 8301 SHORE RD 11209 5-00011
  Alice Farkouh, prin. 748-1537
Hale HS, 345 DEAN ST 11217 4-00011
  Raymond Martinez, prin. 855-2412
Jay HS, 237 7TH AVE 11215 5-00011
  Henry Brun, prin. 788-1514
Lafayette HS, 2630 BENSON AVE 11214 5-00011
  Rosemary Ferrara, prin. 372-3480
Lincoln HS 5-00011
  OCEAN PKY & WEST AVE 11235 372-5474
  Martin Kopelowitz, prin.
HS of Telecommunications 4-00100
  350 67TH ST 11220 745-4800
  Charles Amundsen, prin.
Other Schools – See Staten Island

Adelphi Academy 2-11111
  8515 RIDGE BLVD 11209 238-3308
  Roy Blash, prin.
Advanced Software Analysis 2-CS
  151 LAWRENCE ST FL 2 11201 522-9073
Allen School for Physicians Aides 2-CS
  188 MONTAGUE ST 11201 243-1700
Bais Esther, 1353 50TH ST 11219 3-11111
  Rabbi Abraham Green, prin. 436-1234
Bais Rachel S of Boro Park 4-11111
  5301 14TH AVE 11219 436-9279
  Mindi Margulies, prin.
Bais Yaakov Academy 3-11111
  1213 ELM AVE 11230 339-4747
  Rabbi Greenberg, prin.
Bais Yaakov D'Gur HS 2-00011
  1975 51ST ST 11204 338-5600
  Leah Lederman, prin.
Beer Hagolah Inst HS 2-00111
  293 NEPTUNE AVE 11235 332-7000
  Lillian German, prin.
Berkeley Carroll Street S 3-11111
  181 LINCOLN PL 11217 789-6060
  Bongsoon Zubay, prin.
Beth Chana School for Girls 2-11111
  620 BEDFORD AVE 11211 522-7422
  Rabbi Scheiner, prin.
Beth HaMedrash Shaarei Yosher 1-UC
  4102 16TH AVE # 10 11204 854-2290
Beth HaTalmud Rabbinical College 2-UC
  2127 82ND ST 11214 259-2525
Beth Jacob HS, 4421 15TH AVE 11219 3-00011
  P. Handelsman, prin. 851-2255
Beth Medrash Emek Halacha Rabbncl. Coll. 1-UC
  1763 63RD ST 11204 232-1600
Beth Rachel Girls S 5-11111
  227 MARCY AVE 11211 963-9595
  Rabbi Frankel, prin.
Beth Rivkah S, 310 CROWN ST 11225 4-11111
  Chaya Laine, prin. 735-0400
Bishop Ford Central Catholic HS 4-00011
  500 19TH ST 11215 965-6400
  Br. Nawrocki, prin.
Bishop Kearney HS, 2202 60TH AVE 11204 4-00011
  Sr. Joan Mcavoy, prin. 236-6363
Bishop Loughlin Memorial HS 3-00011
  357 CLERMONT AVE 11238 857-2700
  Br. Bonilla, prin.
Bnei Shimon Yisroel of Sopron 2-11111
  215 HEWES ST 11211 387-5588
  Rosa Friedman, prin.
Bnos Yaakov S for Girls 3-11111
  206 WILSON ST 11211 963-3940
  Rabbi Samet, prin.
Bnos Yakov, 1581 52ND ST 11219 3-11111
  David Oberlander, prin. 963-1212
Bnos Yerushalayim S 3-11111
  600 MCDONALD AVE 11218 871-0500
  Rabbi Klein, prin.
Bnos Zion of Bobov 4-11111
  5000 14TH AVE 11219 438-3080
  Jacob Zucker, prin.
Boricua College 2-UC
  186 N 6TH ST 11211 782-2200
Brooklyn Friends S, 375 PEARL ST 11201 2-11111
  James Handlin, prin. 852-1029
Brooklyn Hospital HSP
  121 DEKALB AVE 11201 403-8005
Brooklyn Law School 4-UC
  250 JORALEMON ST 11201 625-2200
Catherine McAuley HS 2-00011
  710 E 37TH ST 11203 462-7282
  Sr. Peggy Lake, prin.
Central Yeshiva Tomchei Tmimim Lubavitz 2-UC
  841 OCEAN PKY 11230 434-0784
College of New Rochelle 2-UC
  1368 FULTON ST 11216 638-2500
CUNY Brooklyn College 7-UC
  2900 BEDFORD AVE 11210 780-5485
CUNY Kingsborough Community College 7-CC
  2001 ORIENTAL BLVD 11235 934-5000
CUNY Medgar Evan College 4-UC
  1150 CARROLL ST 11225 270-4900
CUNY New York City Technical College 7-UC
  300 JAY ST 11201 643-4900
Darkei Noam Rabbinical College 2-UC
  2822 AVENUE J 11210
FEGS Trades & Business School 2-CS
  199 JAY ST 11201 488-0120
Fontbonne Hall Academy 3-00011
  9901 SHORE RD 11209 748-2244
  Sr. Anne Clancy, prin.
Free S, 1383 PRESIDENT ST 11213 2-01110
  Rabbi Okunov, prin. 467-0860
Genesis S, 1201 66TH ST 11219 1-00100
  Gerald Cattaro, prin. 259-5317
Interfaith Medical Center HSP
  567 PROSPECT PL 11238 935-7902
Kehilath Yakov Rabbinical Seminary 1-UC
  206 WILSON ST 11211 963-3940
Kennedy MS, 284 WARWICK ST 11207 1-00100
  Br. Fannon, prin. 235-0744
Long Island College Hospital HSP
  340 HENRY ST 11201 780-1952
Long Island University-Brooklyn Campus 6-UC
  1 UNIVERSITY PLZ 11201 403-1001
Machon Bais Yaakov 2-00011
  1681 42ND ST 11204 972-7900
  Moishe Yanofsky, prin.

Machzikei Hadath Rabbinical College 2-UC
  PO BOX 190799 11219 331-6613
Magen David Yeshivah HS 2-00011
  7801 BAY PKY 11214 331-4002
  Norman Fisher, prin.
Merkaz Bnos HS, 1400 W 6TH ST 11204 2-00011
  Rabbi Waldman, prin. 259-5600
Mesifta Vyoel Moshei 3-00011
  1010 45TH ST 11219 438-7109
  Seemee Rozenberg, prin.
Mesivia Eitz Chaim, 1577 48TH ST 11219 2-00011
  Rabbi Grumfeld, prin. 438-2018
Mesivta Eastern Parkway Rabbinical Sem. 1-UC
  510 DAHILL RD 11218 438-1002
Mesivta Haichel Hatorah 2-11111
  2449 OCEAN AVE 11229 646-8900
  M. London, prin.
Mesivta HS 2-00011
  1585 CONEY ISLAND AVE 11230 377-0777
  Jack Shonek, prin.
Mesivta Tiferes Yisroel S 2-11011
  1271 E 35TH ST 11210 258-9006
  Philip Kipust, prin.
Mesivta Torah Vodaath Seminary 2-UC
  425 E 9TH ST 11218 941-8000
Methodist Hospital of Brooklyn HSP
  506 6TH ST 11215 780-3000
Mirrer Yeshiva 2-UC
  1795 OCEAN PKY 11223 645-0536
Mirrer Yeshiva HS 2-00011
  1795 OCEAN PKY 11223 375-0771
  Rabbi Engelberg, prin.
Mount Carmel Academy 1-00100
  10 WITHERS ST 11211 782-1110
  Sr. Helen Gulczynski, prin.
MSFTA Chsan Sofer & Rabbi Kluger 3-11111
  1876 50TH ST 11204 236-1171
  David Schonbrun, prin.
Nazareth Regional HS 3-00011
  475 E 57TH ST 11203 763-1100
  Robert Muccigrosso, prin.
Nefesh Academy 2-11111
  1226 OCEAN PKY 11230 951-0600
  Rabbi London, prin.
Our Lady of Perpetual Help HS 3-00011
  550 59TH ST 11220 492-5800
  Sr. Mary Febronia, prin.
Packer Collegiate Institute 3-11111
  170 JORALEMON ST 11201 875-6644
  Frank Bookhout, prin.
Polytechnic University 5-UC
  333 JAY ST 11201 260-3600
Polytech Prep S, 9216 7TH AVE 11228 3-01111
  William Williams, prin. 836-9800
Pratt Institute 5-UC
  200 WILLOUGHBY AVE 11205 636-3600
Prospect Park Bnos Leah 2-00011
  1601 AVENUE R 11229 376-3337
  Rabbi Kramer, prin.
Rabbinical Academy Mesivta Rabbi Chaim 2-UC
  1593 CONEY ISLAND AVE 11230 377-0777
Rabbinical Coll. Bobovr Yeshiva Bnei Zn. 2-UC
  1577 48TH ST 11219 438-2018
Rabbinical Coll. Ch' San Sofer of NY 1-UC
  1876 50TH ST 11204 236-1171
Rabbinical Seminary Adas Yereim 2-UC
  185 WILSON ST 11211 388-1751
Rabbinical Seminary M'Kor Chaim 2-UC
  1571 55TH ST 11219 851-0183
St. Ann's S, 129 PIERREPONT ST 11201 3-11111
  Stanley Bosworth, prin. 522-1660
St. Edmund HS, 2474 OCEAN AVE 11229 2-00011
  Sr. Muriel Smithwick, prin. 743-6100
St. Francis College 4-UC
  180 REMSEN ST 11201 522-2300
St. Joseph HS 2-00011
  80 WILLOUGHBY ST 11201 624-3618
  Sr. Eugenia Calabrese, prin.
St. Joseph's College 2-UC
  245 CLINTON AVE 11205 636-6800
St. Saviour HS, 588 6TH ST 11215 2-00011
  Sr. Mary Monica, prin. 768-4406
SCS Business & Technical Institute 4-CS
  884 FLATBUSH AVE 11226 856-6100
SCS Business & Technical Institute 3-CS
  394 BRIDGE ST 11201 802-9500
Shaare Torah S 2-00011
  1680 CONEY ISLAND AVE 11230 645-8145
  Rabbi Cohen, prin.
Shulamith Girls HS 2-00011
  1277 E 14TH ST 11230 338-7154
  Susan Katz, prin.
Sinai Academy Center 2-00111
  2025 79TH ST 11214 256-7400
  Fred Hochbaum, prin.
Stuart School of Diamond Cutting 2-CS
  1420 KINGS HWY 11229 339-2640
SUNY Health Science Center 4-UC
  450 CLARKSON AVE 11203 270-1000
SYRIT Computer School Systems 1-CS
  1760 53RD ST 11204 853-1212
Talmudical Seminary Oholei Torah 2-UC
  667 EASTERN PKY 11213 774-5500
Talmud Torah D'Rabinu Yoel S 4-11111
  5411 FORT HAMILTON PKY 11219 438-7109
  Sally Browne, prin.
Talmud Torah Tolds Yosef 2-11111
  105 HEYWARD ST 11206 852-0502
  Imse Tambor, prin.

Tiferes Bais Yaakov HS 2-00011
    4508 16TH AVE 11204 436-7009
    Judi Greenwald, prin.
Tomer Dvora Girls Mesivta 2-00011
    1413 45TH ST 11219 851-0024
    H. Mosesoh, prin.
Torah Temimah Talmudical Seminary 1-UC
    555 OCEAN PKY 11218
Torah Vodaath S, 425 E 9TH ST 11218 2-00011
    Chaim Schilit, prin. 941-8000
United Talmudical Academy 2-UC
    82 LEE AVE 11211 963-9260
Xaverian HS, 7100 SHORE RD 11209 4-00011
    Br. Abel, prin. 836-7100
Yeshiva and Kollel Harbotzas Torah 2-UC
    1049 E 15TH ST 11230
Yeshiva and Mesivta Kol Torah 2-UC
    4823B 48TH ST 11224
Yeshiva Bnos Ahavas 3-11111
    12 FRANKLIN AVE 11211 330-0222
    Eva Rozman, prin.
Yeshiva Congregation Toras Yufa S 2-10001
    1056 54TH ST 11219 436-5683
    Chaya Lieberman, prin.
Yeshiva Derech Chaim 2-UC
    1573 39TH ST 11218
Yeshiva Gedolah Academy 2-11111
    2261 BRAGG ST 11229 646-8646
    Rabbi Mayerfeld, prin.
Yeshiva Gedolah Bais Yisroel 2-UC
    2002 AVENUE J 11210
Yeshiva Gedolah Imrei Yosef D'Spinka 2-UC
    1460 56TH ST 11219
Yeshiva Harma for Girls 2-00011
    2600 OCEAN AVE 11229 743-3141
    Hanania Elbaz, prin.
Yeshivah of Flatbush Braverman 3-00011
    1609 AVENUE J 11230 377-1100
    Rabbi Eliach, prin.
Yeshiva Imrei Yosef Spinka 2-11111
    5801 15TH AVE 11219 851-1600
    Rabbi Rubin, prin.
Yeshiva Karlin Stolin 2-11111
    1818 54TH ST 11204 232-7800
    Azriel Hoshander, prin.
Yeshiva Karlin Stolin 1-UC
    1818 54TH ST 11204 232-7800
Yeshiva Kehilath Yakov 3-11111
    206 WILSON ST 11211 963-1212
    David Oberlander, prin.
Yeshiva Machzikei Hadas 2-11111
    1601 42ND ST 11204 436-4445
    Rabbi Scheinert, prin.
Yeshiva of Brooklyn 4-11111
    1470 OCEAN PKY 11230 376-3775
    Harriet Schechter, prin.
Yeshiva of Nitra 2-UC
    194 DIVISION AVE 11211 384-5460
Yeshivas Novominsk-Kol Yehuda 2-00011
    1569 47TH ST 11219 438-2727
    Rabbi Spira, prin.
Yeshivat Ateret Torah 3-11111
    901 QUENTIN RD 11223 375-7100
    Rabbi Weinberg, prin.
Yeshiva Tifereth Elimelech 2-11111
    5801 16TH AVE 11204 438-1177
    Rabbi Goldberg, prin.
Yeshivat Mikdash Melech 1-UC
    1326 OCEAN PKY 11230 339-1090
Yeshiva Torah Temimah 3-11111
    555 OCEAN PKY 11218 853-8500
    Israel Hisiger, prin.
Yeshiva Toras Chesed S 2-00011
    5506 16TH AVE 11204 972-3077
    Rabbi Leifer, prin.
Yeshiva T'Tiferes Bunim 3-11111
    5202 13TH AVE 11219 436-6870
    Isaac Perl, prin.
Yesh Mesivta Arugath Habrsm 2-11111
    171 HOOPER ST 11211 388-7534
    Gedalya Cohen, prin.

Brookville, AC 516, PC 5, Nassau

Long Island University-C. W. Post Campus 7-UC
    RT 25A 11548 299-2501

Brushton, AC 518, PC 3, Franklin
Brushton-Moira Central SD 3-11111
    GALE ROAD 12916 – Paul Fiacco, supt. 529-8948
Brushton-Moira Central JSHS 2-00111
    GALE ROAD 12916 529-7342
    Holly Daniels, prin.

Buffalo, AC 716, PC 10, Erie
Buffalo CSD, 712 CITY HALL 14202 8-11111
    Albert Thompson, supt. 851-3575
Bennett HS, 2885 MAIN ST 14214 3-00011
    Marilyn Wittman, prin. 838-7500
Burgard Vocational HS 2-00011
    400 KENSINGTON AVE 14214 838-7544
    Thomas Kopera, prin.
Cleveland HS, 110 14TH ST 14213 4-00011
    Ben Randle, prin. 888-7150
Emerson Vocational HS 2-00011
    1405 SYCAMORE ST 14211 897-8158
    Salvatore Sedita, prin.
Hutchinson Central Tech HS 4-00011
    256 S ELMWOOD AVE 14201 851-3888
    Joseph Gentile, prin.
Kensington HS, 319 SUFFOLK ST 14215 3-00011
    Robert Barton, prin. 838-7528

Lafayette HS 3-00011
    370 LAFAYETTE AVE 14213 888-7177
    F. Ganter, prin.
McKinley Vocational HS 4-00011
    1500 ELMWOOD AVE 14207 871-6060
    Crystal Barton, prin.
Riverside HS, 51 ONTARIO ST 14207 3-00011
    John Vella, prin. 871-6050
Seneca Vocational HS 3-00011
    666 E DELAVAN AVE 14215 897-8170
    Mark Balen, prin.
South Park HS 4-00011
    150 SOUTHSIDE PKY 14220 828-4828
    Paul Lafornara, prin.
Buffalo Acad Visual-Perf. Arts 3-01111
    CLINTON AND CEDAR ST 14204 851-3868
    Ronald Meer, prin.
Buffalo Traditional JSHS 4-01111
    450 MASTEN AVE 14209 888-7130
    David Greco, prin.
City Honors JSHS 3-01111
    186 E NORTH ST 14204 888-7141
    Michael Anneli, prin.
Occupational Training Ctr Vo Tech
    1695 ELMWOOD AVE 14207 871-6000
    LAUREN WATSON, prin.
Badillo Community MS 3-01100
    300 S ELMWOOD AVE 14201 851-3848
    David Caban, prin.
Black Rock MS, 101 HERTEL AVE 14207 3-01100
    John Bargnesi, prin. 871-6006
Hillery Park MS, 73 PAWNEE PKY 14210 2-01100
    Anthony Muscarella, prin. 828-4770
Houghton MS, 1725 CLINTON ST 14206 2-01100
    Jacqueline Morana, prin. 828-4794
Indian Park MS, 76 BUFFUM ST 14210 2-01100
    Phyllis Robinson, prin. 828-4800
Lincoln MS, 1369 BROADWAY ST 14212 3-01100
    Gilbert Hargrave, prin. 897-8028
Lorraine MS, 71 LORRAINE AVE 14220 2-00100
    Joel Weiss, prin. 828-4809
North Park MS 2-01100
    780 PARKSIDE AVE 14216 838-7447
    Robert Curtin, prin.
Public MS 56 2-01100
    716 W DELAVAN AVE 14222 888-7100
    Judith Ricca, prin.
Riverside MS, 238 ONTARIO ST 14207 3-01100
    Arlene Shappee, prin. 871-6016
Roosevelt MS, 249 SKILLEN ST 14207 2-01100
    Carol Allen, prin. 871-6030
Triangle MS, 1515 S PARK AVE 14220 2-01100
    Jean Polino, prin. 828-4777
West Hertel MS, 489 HERTEL AVE 14207 3-01100
    Gregg Hejmanowski, prin. 871-6072

Cheektowago-Sloan UFD 4-11111
    166 HALSTEAD AVE 14212 891-6402
    James Mazgajewski, supt.
Other Schools – See Cheektowaga

West Seneca Central SD
    Supt. — See West Seneca
West Seneca East HS 4-00011
    4760 SENECA ST 14224 674-2020
    Rene Goshin, prin.

Bishop Timon St. Jude HS 2-00011
    601 MCKINLEY PKY 14220 826-3610
    Timothy Lynch, prin.
Bryant & Stratton Business Institute 5-CC
    1028 MAIN ST 14202 884-9120
Buffalo Seminary 2-00011
    205 BIDWELL PKY 14222 885-6780
    Sarah Briggs, prin.
Canisius College 5-UC
    2001 MAIN ST 14208 883-7000
Canisius HS 2-00011
    1180 DELAWARE AVE 14209 882-0466
    Fr. Ciancimino, prin.
D'Youville College 4-UC
    320 PORTER AVE 14201 800-777-3921
Medaille College 4-UC
    18 AGASSIZ CIR 14214 884-3281
Millard Fillmore Hospital HSP
    3 GATES CIR 14209 887-4860
Mt. Mercy Academy 3-00011
    88 RED JACKET PKY 14220 825-8796
    Barbara Ochterski, prin.
Nardin Academy 3-11111
    135 CLEVELAND AVE 14222 881-6262
    Rebecca Reeder, prin.
National Tractor Trailer School 2-CS
    175 KATHERINE ST 14210 849-6887
Nichols School 3-01111
    1250 AMHERST ST 14216 875-8212
    Peter Cobb, prin.
Northeast Institute 2-CS
    2643 MAIN ST 14214 838-6984
St. Joseph Collegiate Institute 3-00011
    845 KENMORE AVE 14223 874-4024
    Br. Corry, prin.
St. Mary's School for the Deaf HND
    2253 MAIN ST 14214
Sisters School of Nursing HSP
    2157 MAIN ST 14214 862-2774
SUNY at Buffalo 7-UC
    17 CAPEN HALL BOX 601660 14260
     645-6900
SUNY College at Buffalo 7-UC
    1300 ELMWOOD AVE 14222 878-4000

SUNY Erie Community College City 5-CC
    121 ELLICOTT ST 14203 842-2770
SUNY Niagara Frontier Regional Center 2-UC
    564 FRANKLIN ST 14202 886-8020
Trocaire College 3-CC
    110 RED JACKET PKY 14220 826-1200
Turner Carroll HS, 185 LANG AVE 14215 2-00011
    Judith Talbot, prin. 896-4911
Villa Maria Academy 2-00011
    600 DOAT ST 14211 894-0398
    Sr. Maria Bielski, prin.
Villa Maria College of Buffalo 3-CC
    240 PINE RIDGE RD 14225 896-0700

Burnt Hills, AC 518, PC 4, Saratoga
Burnt Hills-Ballston Lake CSD
    Supt. — See Scotia
Burnt Hills-Ballston Lake HS 4-00011
    LAKEHILL RD 12027 399-9141
    Jennie Pennington, prin.
Burnt Hills-Ballston Lake MS 3-00100
    LAKEHILL RD 12027 399-1625
    David Guilmette, prin.

Cairo, AC 518, PC 4, Greene
Cairo-Durham Central SD 4-11111
    PO BOX 780 12413 622-8534
    Donald Gibson, supt.
Cairo-Durham JSHS 3-00111
    PO BOX 598 12413 622-8543
    David Arnone, prin.

Caledonia, AC 716, PC 4, Livingston
Caledonia-Mumford Central SD 4-11111
    99 NORTH ST 14423 538-6811
    William Donlon, supt.
Caledonia-Mumford JSHS 3-00111
    99 NORTH ST 14423 538-6811
    Tom Moran, prin.

Callicoon, AC 914, PC 3, Sullivan
Delaware Valley Central SD 3-11111
    ROUTE 97 12723 887-5301
    Charles Grottenthaler, supt.
Delaware Valley Central S 3-11111
    ROUTE 97 12723 887-5301
    Edwin Chellis, prin.

Cambria Heights, AC 718, PC see New York
Queens Borough HSD
    Supt. — See Corona
Jackson HS, 20701 116TH AVE 11411 5-00011
    Leslie Embriano, prin. 528-4220

Cambridge, AC 518, PC 4, Washington
Cambridge Central SD 4-11111
    23 W MAIN ST 12816 677-2653
    Thomas Markle, supt.
JSHS, 24 S PARK ST 12816 3-00111
    Charles Noe, prin. 677-8527

Camden, AC 315, PC 5, Oneida
Camden Central SD, 51 3RD ST 13316 5-11111
    Martin Handler, supt. 245-2500
HS, 1 OSWEGO ST 13316 3-00011
    Susan Whitney, prin. 245-3168
MS, 32 UNION ST 13316 3-00100
    Terry Schaal, prin. 245-0080

Camillus, AC 315, PC 4, Onondaga
West Genesee Central SD 5-11111
    5525 IKE DIXON RD 13031 672-3120
    Rudolph Rubeis, supt.
West Genesee HS 4-00011
    5201 W GENESEE ST 13031 487-4592
    Helen White, prin.
MS, 5525 IKE DIXON RD 13031 2-00100
    Dean Desantis, prin. 672-3159
West Genesee MS 3-00100
    500 SANDERSON DR 13031 487-4615
    Joseph Pecori, prin.

Campbell, AC 607, PC 2, Steuben
Campbell Central SD 4-11111
    8455 COUNTY ROAD 125 14821 527-4548
    Stephen Morley, supt.
JSHS 3-00111
    8455 COUNTY ROAD 125 14821 527-4551
    Benjamin Gustafson, prin.

Canaan, AC 518, PC 2, Columbia
Berkshire Farm UFD 2-00111
    ROUTE 22 12029 781-4567
    John Richman, supt.
Berkshire Farm JSHS 2-00111
    ROUTE 22 12029 781-3500
    Peter Mulvaney, prin.

Canajoharie, AC 518, PC 4, Montgomery
Canajoharie Central SD 4-11111
    10 ERIE BLVD 13317 – Rich Rose, supt. 673-8008
HS, 10 ERIE BLVD 13317 3-00011
    Donald Bowden, prin. 673-2611
JHS, 51 BURCH ST 13317 2-00100
    Joseph Thomas, prin. 673-3274

Canandaigua, AC 716, PC 7, Ontario
Canandaigua Central SD 5-11111
    143 N PEARL ST 14424 396-3700
    Stephen Uebbing, supt.
Canandaigua Academy HS 4-00011
    1 ACADEMY CIR 14424 396-3800
    Chester Starowitz, prin.
Canandaigua MS 3-00100
    215 GRANGER ST 14424 396-3850
    Charles Carlson, prin.

SUNY Community College Finger Lakes 5-CC
LINCOLN HILL ROAD 14424 394-3500

Canaseraga, AC 607, PC 3, Allegany
Canaseraga Central SD 2-11111
4 W MAIN ST 14822 545-6421
Donald Raw, supt.
S, 4 W MAIN ST 14822 2-11111
Kathy Dimitrievski, prin. 545-6421

Canastota, AC 315, PC 5, Madison
Canastota Central SD 4-11111
120 ROBERTS ST 13032 697-2025
Craig King, supt.
JSHS, 102 ROBERTS ST 13032 3-00111
Garad Williams, prin. 697-2003

Candor, AC 607, PC 3, Tioga
Candor Central SD 4-11111
PO BOX 145 13743 659-5010
Rich Kelly, supt.
JSHS, PO BOX 145 13743 2-00111
Fred Farah, prin. 659-5020

Canisteo, AC 607, PC 4, Steuben
Canisteo Central SD 4-11111
84 GREENWOOD ST 14823 698-4225
Charles Carlton, supt.
JSHS, 84 GREENWOOD ST 14823 3-01111
Josephine Barnard, prin. 698-4225

Canton, AC 315, PC 6, St. Lawrence
Canton Central SD, 99 STATE ST 13617 4-11111
Howard Smith, supt. 386-8561
Williams HS, 99 STATE ST 13617 3-00011
David Crosby, prin. 386-8561
McKenney MS, 99 STATE ST 13617 3-01100
Arthur Quackenbush, prin. 386-8561

St. Lawrence University 4-UC
2501 SAINT LAWRENCE UNIV 13617 379-5011
SUNY College of Technology 4-CC
34 CORNELL DR 13617 386-7011

Carle Place, AC 516, PC 6, Nassau
Carle Place UFD, CHERRY LANE 11514 4-11111
Albert Inserra, supt. 334-1900
JSHS, 168 CHERRY LN 11514 3-00111
Richard Piva, prin. 334-1900

Ultrasound Diagnostic School 2-CS
1 OLD COUNTRY RD 11514 794-2383

Carmel, AC 914, PC 5, Putnam
Carmel Central SD
Supt. — See Patterson
HS, 30 FAIR ST 10512 4-00011
J. MacDonald, prin. 225-8441
Fischer MS, 275 FAIRWAY DR 10512 4-01100
Stephen Helman, prin. 225-0035

Carthage, AC 315, PC 5, Jefferson
Carthage Central SD 5-11111
RR 2 BOX 57B 13619 493-0510
Kenn Rishel, supt.
HS, MARTIN STREET RD 13619 3-00011
Robert Melia, prin. 493-1690
MS, COLE RD 13619 3-00100
James Newell, prin. 493-1400

Castleton, AC 518, PC 4, Rensselaer
Schodack Central SD 4-11111
1216 MAPLE HILL RD 12033 732-2297
James Butterworth, supt.
Maple Hill HS 2-00011
1216 MAPLE HILL RD 12033 732-7701
Ralph Dimarino, prin.
Maple Hill MS 2-01100
1477 S SCHODACK RD 12033 732-7736
Thomas Rabone, prin.

Cato, AC 315, PC 3, Cayuga
Cato-Meridian Central SD 4-11111
PO BOX 100 13033 626-2121
Henry Safnauer, supt.
Cato-Meridian JSHS 2-00111
PO BOX 100 13033 626-2121
James Obernesser, prin.

Catskill, AC 518, PC 5, Greene
Catskill Central SD 4-11111
347 W MAIN ST 12414 943-4696
Raymond O'Connell, supt.
HS, 347 W MAIN ST 12414 3-00011
John Turek, prin. 943-2300
MS, 347 W MAIN ST 12414 2-00100
Buddy Lee Appel, prin. 943-5665

Cattaraugus, AC 716, PC 4, Cattaraugus
Cattaraugus Central SD 3-11111
1 CARTER ST 14719 257-3483
John Mormile, supt.
JSHS, 1 CARTER ST 14719 2-00111
John Mormile, prin. 257-3483

Cazenovia, AC 315, PC 5, Madison
Cazenovia Central SD 4-11111
31 EMORY AVE 13035 655-1317
Charles Read, supt.
JSHS, 31 EMORY AVE 13035 3-00111
Thomas Long, prin. 655-1314

Cazenovia College 13035 4-UC
655-8283

Cedarhurst, AC 516, PC 6, Nassau
Lawrence UFD
Supt. — See Lawrence
Lawrence HS, REILLY ROAD 11516 4-00011
Jayson Stoller, prin. 295-8000

Hebrew Academy of Five Towns 2-00011
635 CENTRAL AVE 11516 569-3807
Daniel Vitow, prin.

Centereach, AC 516, PC 8, Suffolk
Middle Country Central SD 7-11111
8 43RD ST 11720 – Frank Flood, supt. 468-5514
HS, 14 43RD ST 11720 4-00011
Joseph Durrigo, prin. 468-5600
Dawnwood MS, 10 43RD ST 11720 4-00100
John Reid, prin. 468-5550
Selden MS, 22 JEFFERSON AVE 11720 4-00100
Elizabeth McCarville, prin. 468-5760
Other Schools – See Selden

Center Moriches, AC 516, PC 6, Suffolk
Center Moriches UFD 4-11111
511 MAIN ST 11934 878-0052
Joe Donovan, supt.
JSHS, 311 FROWEIN RD 11934 3-00111
Francis Mazura, prin. 878-0092

Central Islip, AC 516, PC 8, Suffolk
Central Islip UFD 5-11111
50 WHEELER RD 11722 348-5001
Howard Koenig, supt.
HS, 50 WHEELER RD 11722 4-00011
D. Meehan, prin. 348-5078
Reed MS, HALF MILE ROAD 11722 3-00100
John Cassidy, prin. 348-5065

New York Institute of Technology 11722 5-UC
348-7516

Central Square, AC 315, PC 4, Oswego
Central Square Central SD 5-11111
MAIN ST 13036 – Dale Hesser, supt. 668-2611
Moore HS, CAUGHDENOY ROAD 13036 4-00011
Robert Sherman, prin. 668-4231
MS, ROUTE 11 13036 4-00100
William McKee, prin. 668-4216

Central Valley, AC 914, PC 4, Orange
Monroe-Woodbury Central SD 6-11111
ROUTE 32 10917 928-2321
Terrence Olivo, supt.
Monroe-Woodbury HS 4-00011
265 DUNDERBERG RD 10917 928-2321
Gary Heller, prin.
Monroe-Woodbury MS 3-00100
ROUTE 32 10917 928-2321
Charles Kreutz, prin.

Champlain, AC 518, PC 4, Clinton
Northeastern Clinton Central SD 4-11111
ROUTE 276 12919 298-8242
Christopher Degrandpre, supt.
HS, ROUTE 276 12919 2-00011
Robert Mooso, prin. 298-8638
JHS, ROUTE 276 12919 2-00100
John Mahoney, prin. 298-8681

Chappaqua, AC 914, PC 6, Westchester
Chappaqua Central SD 5-11111
PO BOX 21 10514 238-7200
Donald Parker, supt.
Greeley HS 3-00011
70 ROARING BROOK RD 10514 238-3911
Edward Hart, prin.
Bell MS, 50 SENTER ST 10514 3-00100
Thomas Cardellichio, prin. 238-6170

Chateaugay, AC 518, PC 3, Franklin
Chateaugay Central SD, RIVER ST 12920 3-11111
Patrick Calnon, supt. 497-6420
JSHS, RIVER ST 12920 2-00111
Paul Harrica, prin. 497-6611

Chatham, AC 518, PC 4, Columbia
Chatham Central SD 4-11111
48 WOODBRIDGE AVE 12037 392-2400
Lee Wilson, supt.
HS, 48 WOODBRIDGE AVE 12037 2-00011
Brian Howard, prin. 392-4181
MS, WOODBRIDGE AVE 12037 2-01100
Gordan Fitting, prin. 392-2409

Chaumont, AC 315, PC 3, Jefferson
Lyme Central SD, ACADEMY ST 13622 2-11111
Pasquale Caramanna, supt. 649-2417
Lyme Central S, ACADEMY ST 13622 2-11111
E. Mazura, prin. 649-2417

Chautauqua, AC 716, PC 3, Chautauqua
Chautauqua Central SD 2-11111
PO BOX 1097 14722 789-3506
Edward Fisk, supt.
JSHS, PO BOX 1097 14722 2-00111
James Scarnati, prin. 357-2235

Chazy, AC 518, PC 4, Clinton
Chazy UFD, MAIN ST 12921 3-11111
Charles O'Connor, supt. 846-7135
Chazy Central Rural JSHS 2-00111
MAIN ST 12921 846-7135
Charles O'Connor, prin.

Cheektowaga, AC 716, PC 8, Erie
Cheektowaga-Maryvale UFD 4-11111
1050 MARYVALE DR 14225 631-7407
Gary Brader, supt.

Maryvale HS 3-00011
1050 MARYVALE DR 14225 631-7481
Robert Moscato, prin.
Maryvale MS 3-00100
1050 MARYVALE DR 14225 631-7425
Burt Sellers, prin.

Cheektowaga Central SD 4-11111
3600 UNION RD 14225 686-3606
Leslie Lewis, supt.
JSHS, 3600 UNION RD 14225 3-00111
George Radka, prin. 686-3602

Cheektowago-Sloan UFD
Supt. — See Buffalo
Kennedy JSHS 3-00111
305 CAYUGA CREEK RD 14227 891-6406
Daniel Mahoney, prin.

Cleveland Hill UFD 4-11111
105 MAPLEVIEW RD 14225 836-7200
Kenneth Dyl, supt.
Cleveland Hill HS 2-00011
105 MAPLEVIEW RD 14225 836-7200
Martin Heavey, prin.
Cleveland Hill MS 2-00100
105 MAPLEVIEW RD 14225 836-7200
Edward Knab, prin.

Cherry Valley, AC 607, PC 3, Otsego
Cherry Valley-Springfield Central SD 3-11111
COUNTY ROUTE 54 13320 264-9332
Michael Marcelle, prin.
Cherry Valley-Springfield JSHS 2-00111
COUNTY ROUTE 54 13320 264-3265
Charles Strange, prin.

Chester, AC 914, PC 5, Orange
Chester UFD, 3 MAPLE AVE 10918 3-11111
Edward Stoddard, supt. 469-2231
JSHS, 3 MAPLE AVE 10918 2-00111
Paul Reh, prin. 469-2231

Sugarloaf UFD, GIBSON HILL RD 10918 2-00111
Arnold Jaeger, supt. 469-2157
Sugarloaf JSHS, GIBSON HILL RD 10918 2-00111
Angelo Gandolfini, prin. 469-2136

Chestertown, AC 518, PC 3, Warren
North Warren Central SD
Supt. — See Pottersville
North Warren HS, MAIN ST 12817 2-00011
Michael Prescott, prin. 494-2323

Chestnut Ridge, AC 914, PC 6, Rockland
East Ramapo Central SD
Supt. — See Spring Valley
Spring Valley JHS, 892 S MAIN ST 10977 3-00110
Albert Gyuricza, prin. 577-6304

Chittenango, AC 315, PC 5, Madison
Chittenango Central SD, RR 2 13037 5-11111
William Moth, supt. 687-7271
HS, 222 GENESEE ST 13037 3-00011
Harold Talbot, prin. 687-7271
MS, 1732 FYLER RD 13037 3-00100
Linda Frye, prin. 687-7271

Churchville, AC 716, PC 4, Monroe
Churchville-Chili Central SD 5-11111
139 FAIRBANKS RD 14428 293-1800
David Ryan, supt.
Churchville-Chili HS 4-00011
5786 BUFFALO RD 14428 293-1800
Kathleen Fromel, prin.
Churchville-Chili MS 4-00100
139 FAIRBANKS RD 14428 293-1800
Joe Hoff, prin.

Cicero, AC 315, PC 4, Onondaga
North Syracuse Central SD
Supt. — See North Syracuse
Cicero-North Syracuse SHS 4-00001
6002 STATE ROUTE 31 13039 699-2611
Lee Aldrich, prin.

Bryant & Stratton Business Institute 4-CC
5775 S BAY RD 13039 452-1105

Cincinnatus, AC 607, PC 2, Cortland
Cincinnatus Central SD 3-11111
2809 CINCINNATUS RD 13040 863-3335
Donald Hickman, supt.
JSHS, 2809 CINCINNATUS RD 13040 2-00111
Anthony Dilucci, prin. 863-4101

Circleville, AC 914, PC 4, Orange
Pine Bush Central SD
Supt. — See Pine Bush
MS, ROUTE 302 10919 3-00100
Maureen Connaughton, prin. 361-2167

Clarence, AC 716, PC 4, Erie
Clarence Central SD 5-11111
9625 MAIN ST 14031 759-8311
Thomas Coseo, supt.
HS, 9625 MAIN ST 14031 4-00011
Terry Piper, prin. 759-8311
JHS, 10150 GREINER RD 14031 3-00100
James Ballard, prin. 759-2030

Clayton, AC 315, PC 4, Jefferson
Thousand Islands Central SD 4-11111
HIGH ST 13624 686-5521
William Montonna, supt.

Thousand Islands HS   2-00011
    SAND BAY ROAD   13624   686-5594
    Don Brennan, prin.
Thousand Islands MS   13624   2-00100
    James Waterson, prin.   686-5199

Clifton Park, AC 518, PC 3, Saratoga
Shenendehowa Central SD   6-11111
    PO BOX 57   12065   877-6251
    John Yagielski, supt.
Shenendehowa SHS   4-00001
    970 ROUTE 146   12065   371-4763
    Gary Adelson, prin.
Gowana JHS, 970 ROUTE 146   12065   3-00110
    Ronald Coleman, prin.   371-6363
Koda JHS, 970 ROUTE 146   12065   3-00110
    Joseph Nicolella, prin.   371-7392

Clifton Springs, AC 315, PC 4, Ontario
Phelps-Clifton Springs Central SD   4-11111
    1500 STATE ROUTE 488   14432   548-9511
    A. Warner, supt.
Midlakes HS   3-00110
    1500 STATE ROUTE 488   14432   548-9481
    Hugh Kane, prin.
Other Schools – See Phelps

Clinton, AC 315, PC 4, Oneida
Clinton Central SD   4-11111
    75 CHENANGO AVE   13323   853-5574
    James Torrance, supt.
HS, 75 CHENANGO AVE   13323   3-00110
    Frank Perretta, prin.   853-5574
MS, 75 CHENANGO AVE   13323   2-00100
    Ruthann Fuller, prin.   853-5574

Hamilton College   4-UC
    198 COLLEGE HILL RD   13323   859-4011

Clintonville, AC 518, PC 2, Clinton
Ausable Valley Central SD   4-11111
    1273 ROUTE 9N   12944   834-2845
    John Gratto, supt.
Ausable Valley JSHS   3-00111
    1490 ROUTE 9N   12944   834-2800
    Donald Hollingsworth, prin.

Clyde, AC 315, PC 4, Wayne
Clyde-Savannah Central SD   4-11111
    215 GLASGOW ST   14433   923-7747
    William Gilbert, supt.
JSHS, 215 GLASGOW ST   14433   2-00111
    Anthony Patanzo, prin.   923-2411

Clymer, AC 716, PC 3, Chautauqua
Clymer Central SD   3-11111
    8672 E MAIN ST   14724   355-4447
    Robert Reagle, supt.
JSHS, 8672 E MAIN ST   14724   2-00111
    Robert Reagle, prin.   355-4444

Cobleskill, AC 518, PC 6, Schoharie
Cobleskill Richmondville Central SD   4-11111
    WASHINGTON HTS   12043   234-4032
    Samuel Shevat, supt.
Golding HS, ELM ST   12043   3-00011
    William Downs, prin.   234-3565
Golding MS, ELM ST   12043   3-00100
    William Walling, prin.   234-8368

SUNY College of Agriculture & Technology   5-UC
    12043   234-5011

Cohoes, AC 518, PC 7, Albany
Cohoes CSD, 21 PAGE AVE   12047   4-11111
    Gerald Thompson, supt.   237-0100
HS, 73 ELM ST   12047   3-00011
    Craig Brown, prin.   237-9100
MS, 7 BEVAN ST   12047   2-00100
    Ronald Gabriel, prin.   237-4131

St. Agnes Catholic S   2-01100
    45 JOHNSTON AVE   12047   237-8876
    Bede McGuinness, prin.

Cold Spring, AC 914, PC 4, Putnam
Haldane Central SD   3-11111
    10 CRAIGSIDE DR   10516   265-9254
    Joanne Marien, supt.
Haldane JSHS, 10 CRAIGSIDE DR   10516   2-00111
    Geraldine Page, prin.   265-3593

Cold Spring Harbor, AC 516, PC 5, Suffolk
Cold Spring Harbor Central SD   4-11111
    75 GOOSE HILL RD   11724   692-8036
    Francis Roberts, supt.
JSHS, 82 TURKEY LN   11724   3-00111
    Thomas Hall, prin.   692-8600

College Point, AC 718, PC see New York

St. Agnes Academic HS   3-00011
    1320 124TH ST   11356   353-6276
    Sr. Marguerite Warren, prin.

Colton, AC 315, PC 3, St. Lawrence
Colton-Pierrepont Central SD   2-11111
    5 MAPLE ST   13625   262-2100
    Joyce Monroe, supt.
Colton-Pierrepont JSHS   2-00111
    5 MAPLE ST   13625 – Joe Zelinski, prin.   262-2100

Commack, AC 516, PC 8, Suffolk
Commack UFD, PO BOX 150   11725   6-11111
    Joseph Del Russo, supt.   754-7210

Commack HS, 1 SCHOLAR LN   11725   4-00011
    Ronald Vale, prin.   754-7256
MS, VANDERBILT PKWY   11725   4-00100
    Pamela Travis-Moore, prin.   493-3752

Long Island Business Institute   2-CS
    6500 JERICHO TPKE   11725   499-7100

Congers, AC 914, PC 6, Rockland

Rockland Country Day S   2-11111
    32 PITKIN LN E   10920   268-6802
    Nicholas Ohan, prin.

Conklin, AC 607, PC 4, Broome
Susquehanna Valley Central SD   4-11111
    1040 CONKLIN RD   13748   775-0170
    Richard Stank, supt.
Susquehanna Valley SHS   2-00001
    1040 CONKLIN RD   13748   775-0304
    John Paske, prin.
Susquehanna Valley JHS   3-00110
    1040 CONKLIN RD   13748   775-0303
    Gerardo Tagliaferri, prin.

Cooperstown, AC 607, PC 4, Otsego
Cooperstown Central SD   4-11111
    38 LINDEN AVE   13326   547-5364
    Douglas Bradshaw, supt.
Cooperstown Central HS   2-00011
    38 LINDEN AVE   13326   547-8181
    Barry Gould, prin.
MS, 38 LINDEN AVE   13326   2-00100
    David Pearlman, prin.   547-5512

Copenhagen, AC 315, PC 3, Lewis
Copenhagen Central SD   3-11111
    MECHANIC ST   13626   688-4411
    Thomas Kirkwood, supt.
JSHS, MECHANIC ST   13626   2-00111
    Thomas Kirkwood, supt.   688-4411

Copiague, AC 516, PC 7, Suffolk
Copiague UFD   5-11111
    2650 GREAT NECK RD   11726   842-4000
    George Apuzzi, supt.
HS, 1100 DIXON AVE   11726   4-00011
    G. Dachs, prin.   842-4000
JHS, 2650 GREAT NECK RD   11726   3-00100
    Albert Voorneveld, prin.   842-4000

Corfu, AC 716, PC 3, Genesee
Pembroke Central SD   4-11111
    ROUTES 5 & 77   14036   599-4525
    William Cala, supt.
Pembroke JSHS   3-00111
    ROUTES 5 & 77   14036   599-4525
    Robert D'Angelo, prin.

Corinth, AC 518, PC 5, Saratoga
Corinth Central SD, 105 OAK ST   12822   4-11111
    Thomas Gould, supt.   654-2601
JSHS, 105 OAK ST   12822   3-00111
    Fredda Berger, prin.   654-9005

Corning, AC 607, PC 7, Steuben
Corning CSD
    Supt. — See Painted Post
Corning-Painted Post East HS   3-00011
    201 CANTIGNY ST   14830   936-3746
    Ed Robinson, prin.
Corning Free Academy MS   3-00100
    11 W 3RD ST   14830   936-3788
    Roger Grigsby, prin.
Northside Blodgett MS   3-00100
    143 PRINCETON AVE   14830   936-3791
    Sheldon Guss, prin.

Christian Learning Center   2-11111
    109 ELLICOTT ST   14830   962-4220
    Rev. Tietje, prin.
SUNY Corning Community College   5-CC
    SPENCER HILL ROAD   14830   962-9011

Cornwall, AC 914, PC 5, Orange
Cornwall Central SD   4-11111
    130 MAIN ST   12518   534-8009
    Richard Brodow, supt.
Cornwall Central JSHS   3-00111
    122 MAIN ST   12518   534-8908
    Robert Maher, prin.

Cornwall on Hudson, AC 914, PC 5, Orange

New York Military Academy   2-01111
    70 ACADEMY AVE   12520   534-3710
    Dennis Costello, prin.
Storm King S, 314 MOUNTAIN RD   12520   2-00011
    John Suitor, prin.   534-7892

Corona, AC 718, PC see New York
New York City Special Schools
    Supt. — See Brooklyn
Queens Occupational Training Ctr   Vo Tech
    4115 104TH ST   11368   424-8584
    BLANCHE FIERSTEIN, prin.

Queens Borough HSD   8-00011
    10525 HORACE HARDING EXPY   11368
    Samuel Kostman, supt.   592-4496
Other Schools – See Bayside, Cambria Heights,
    Elmhurst-A, Far Rockaway, Flushing, Forest Hills,
    Jamaica, Long Island City, Ozone Park, Queens
    Village, Richmond Hill, Ridgewood, Rockaway
    Park, Springfield Gardens

Queens Borough SD 24
    Supt. — See Middle Village
Da Vinci IS, 9850 50TH AVE   11368   4-00100
    Phyllis Laperchia, prin.   760-3233

Sister Clara Muhammed S   2-11111
    10501 NORTHERN BLVD   11368   779-1060
    Sr. Shirley Dye, prin.

Cortland, AC 607, PC 7, Cortland
Cortland CSD, 1 VALLEY VIEW DR   13045   5-11111
    Per Omland, supt.   753-6061
JSHS, 8 VALLEY VIEW DR   13045   4-00111
    Christopher Tanski, prin.   753-6061

Cortland Christian Academy   2-11111
    15 STATE ROUTE 281   13045   756-5838
    Craig Miller, prin.
SUNY College at Cortland   6-UC
    PO BOX 2000   13045   753-2201

Coxsackie, AC 518, PC 5, Greene
Coxsackie-Athens Central SD   4-11111
    90 SUNSET BLVD   12051   731-1710
    L. Jeffery Baltes, supt.
Coxsackie-Athens HS   2-00011
    24 SUNSET BLVD   12051   731-1800
    James Maxwell, prin.
Coxsackie-Athens MS   2-00100
    24 SUNSET BLVD   12051   731-1850
    Terrance Nash, prin.

Crestwood, AC 914, PC see Yonkers

St. Vladimir's Orthodox Theological Sem.   2-UC
    575 SCARSDALE RD   10707   961-8313

Croton, AC 914, PC 6, Westchester
Croton-Harmon UFD   4-11111
    10 GERSTEIN ST   10520   271-4793
    Sherry King, supt.
Croton-Harmon HS   2-00011
    36 OLD POST RD S   10520   271-2147
    Robert Kuklis, prin.
Van Cortlandt MS, 3 GLEN PL   10520   2-00100
    Susan McMahon, prin.   271-2191

Crown Point, AC 518, PC 3, Essex
Crown Point Central SD, MAIN ST   12928   2-11111
    Marilyn Terranova, supt.   597-3285
Crown Point Central S, MAIN ST   12928   2-11111
    Michael Redzich, prin.   597-3285

Cuba, AC 716, PC 4, Allegany
Cuba-Rushford Central SD   4-11111
    15 ELM ST   14727   968-1556
    Michael O'Brien, supt.
JSHS, 15 ELM ST   14727   3-00111
    Donald McClarin, prin.   968-2650

Dansville, AC 716, PC 6, Livingston
Dansville Central SD   4-11111
    285 MAIN ST   14437   335-4000
    Donald Bartalo, supt.
HS, 282 MAIN ST   14437   3-00011
    Michael Depew, prin.   335-4010
MS, 31 CLARA BARTON ST   14437   3-00100
    Cynthia Hinman, prin.   335-4020

Davenport, AC 607, PC 2, Delaware
Charlotte Valley Central SD   2-11111
    ROUTE 23   13750   278-5511
    David Whipple, supt.
Charlotte Valley S, ROUTE 23   13750   2-11111
    John Tucci, prin.   278-5511

Deer Park, AC 516, PC 8, Suffolk
Deer Park UFD   5-11111
    1881 DEER PARK AVE   11729   242-6505
    Ronald Paras, supt.
HS, 30 ROCKAWAY AVE   11729   4-00011
    Joseph Delucia, prin.   242-6548
Frost MS, 450 HALF HOLLOW RD   11729   3-00100
    Julia Bingham, prin.   242-6596

De Kalb Junction, AC 315, PC 2, St. Lawrence
Hermon-DeKalb Central SD   3-11111
    RR 1 BOX 13   13630   347-3442
    Richard Nelson, supt.
Hermon-DeKalb JSHS   2-00111
    RR 1 BOX 13   13630   347-3442
    John Davis, prin.

Delanson, AC 518, PC 2, Schenectady
Duanesburg Central SD   12053   3-11111
    John Markell, supt.   895-2957
Duanesburg JSHS   12053   2-00111
    Ralph Lyons, prin.   895-2355

Delhi, AC 607, PC 5, Delaware
Delhi Central SD, 2 SHELDON DR   13753   4-11111
    R. Zajack, supt.   746-2101
Delaware Academy JSHS   3-00111
    2 SHELDON DR   13753   746-2103
    Charles Stratton, prin.

SUNY College of Technology   4-CC
    2 MAIN ST   13753   746-4111

Delmar, AC 518, PC 6, Albany
Bethlehem Central SD   5-11111
    90 ADAMS PL   12054   439-7098
    Leslie Loomis, supt.

Bethlehem Central HS | 4-00011
700 DELAWARE AVE 12054 | 439-4921
Jon Hunter, prin.
Bethlehem Central MS | 4-00100
332 KENWOOD AVE 12054 | 439-7460
F. Burdick, prin.

Depew, AC 716, PC 7, Erie
Depew UFD, 591 TERRACE BLVD 14043 | 5-11111
Eugene Hale, supt. | 686-2251
HS, 5201 TRANSIT RD 14043 | 3-00011
George Morse, prin. | 686-2421
MS, 5201 TRANSIT RD 14043 | 3-01100
Edward Mooradian, prin. | 686-2440

Deposit, AC 607, PC 4, Broome
Deposit Central SD, 121 2ND ST 13754 | 3-11111
John Oakes, supt. | 467-2197
JSHS, 171 2ND ST 13754 | 2-00111
Robert MacFarland, prin. | 467-2197

De Ruyter, AC 315, PC 3, Madison
De Ruyter Central SD | 3-11111
711 RAILROAD ST 13052 | 852-3321
Tiffany Phillips, supt.
JSHS, 711 RAILROAD ST 13052 | 2-00111
Donald Hickman, prin. | 852-3321

De Witt, AC 315, PC 6, Onondaga
Jamesville-DeWitt Central SD | 4-11111
PO BOX 606 13214 | 445-8300
Gene Spanneut, supt.
Jamesville-DeWitt HS | 3-00011
PO BOX 606 13214 | 445-8340
Barbara Goessling, prin.
Other Schools – See Jamesville

Manlius Pebble Hill S | 2-11111
5300 JAMESVILLE RD 13214 | 446-2452
Baxter Ball, prin.

Dexter, AC 315, PC 4, Jefferson
General Brown Central SD | 4-11111
415 E GROVE ST 13634 | 639-4711
Don Grant, supt.
Brown JSHS, 1017 CEMETERY RD 13634 | 3-00111
C. Hoard, prin. | 639-6234

Dix Hills, AC 516, PC 8, Suffolk
Half Hollow Hills Central SD | 6-11111
525 HALF HOLLOW RD 11746 | 351-6632
Kevin McGuire, supt.
Half Hollow Hills HS East | 4-00011
50 VANDERBILT PKY 11746 | 421-6540
James McCaffrey, prin.
Half Hollow Hills HS West | 3-00011
375 WOLF HILL RD 11746 | 421-6480
James Lofrese, prin.
Candlewood MS | 3-00100
1200 CARLLS STRAIGHT PATH 11746 | 595-2784
Linda Bruno, prin.
Other Schools – See Melville

Five Towns College | 2-CC
305 N SERVICE RD 11746 | 783-8800
Upper Room Christian S | 2-11111
722 DEER PARK AVE 11746 | 242-5359
Gregory Eck, prin.

Dobbs Ferry, AC 914, PC 6, Westchester
Dobbs Ferry UFD | 4-11111
505 BROADWAY 10522 | 693-1506
R. Gerson, supt.
HS, 505 BROADWAY 10522 | 2-00011
Karen Benedict, prin. | 693-7645
MS, 505 BROADWAY 10522 | 2-01100
Frank Zappone, prin. | 693-7640

Long Island University | 3-UC
555 BROADWAY 10522 | 693-4500
Masters School for Girls | 2-00111
49 CLINTON AVE 10522 | 693-1400
Pamela Clarke, prin.
Mercy College | 5-UC
555 BROADWAY 10522 | 693-4500
Our Lady of Victory Academy | 2-00011
565 BROADWAY 10522 | 693-1633
Sr. Patricia Vetrano, prin.

Dolgeville, AC 315, PC 4, Herkimer
Dolgeville Central SD | 4-11111
SLAWSON ST 13329 | 429-3155
Robert Smith, supt.
Green JSHS, 38 SLAWSON ST 13329 | 3-00111
James Donnelly, prin. | 429-3156

Douglaston, AC 718, PC see New York

Cathedral College Immaculate Conception | 1-UC
7200 DOUGLASTON PKY 11362

Dover Plains, AC 914, PC 4, Dutchess
Dover UFD, PO BOX 6311 12522 | 4-11111
J. Bruce McKenna, supt. | 832-6501
Dover JSHS, PO BOX 6311 12522 | 3-00111
Jan Furman, prin. | 832-6631

Downsville, AC 607, PC 4, Delaware
Downsville Central SD, PO BOX J 13755 | 2-11111
Ted Grocki, supt. | 363-2100
Downsville Central S, PO BOX J 13755 | 2-11111
Joseph Fulgieri, prin. | 363-2100

Dryden, AC 607, PC 4, Tompkins
Dryden Central SD, PO BOX 88 13053 | 4-11111
Don Trombley, supt. | 844-8694
JSHS, PO BOX 88 13053 | 3-00111
Robert Barraco, prin. | 844-8694

SUNY Tompkins Cortland Community College | 5-CC
PO BOX 139 13053 | 844-8211

Dundee, AC 607, PC 4, Yates
Dundee Central SD, 55 WATER ST 14837 | 4-11111
Nancy Zimar, supt. | 243-5533
JSHS, 55 WATER ST 14837 | 2-00111
Charles Tyo, prin. | 243-5533

Dunkirk, AC 716, PC 7, Chautauqua
Dunkirk CSD | 4-11111
201 LAKE SHORE DR E 14048 | 366-6700
Terry Wolfenden, supt.
HS, 75 W 6TH ST 14048 | 3-00011
Richard Peterson, prin. | 366-9390
MS, 525 EAGLE ST 14048 | 3-00100
Thomas Boris, prin. | 366-9380

East Amherst, AC 716, PC 3, Erie
Williamsville Central SD
Supt. — See Williamsville
Williamsville East HS | 3-00011
151 PARADISE RD 14051 | 626-8400
John Olsen, prin.
Casey MS, 105 CASEY RD 14051 | 3-01100
Robert Miller, prin. | 626-8585
Transit MS, 8730 TRANSIT RD 14051 | 3-01100
Jill Bartkowski, prin. | 626-8700

East Aurora, AC 716, PC 6, Erie
East Aurora UFD, 430 MAIN ST 14052 | 4-11111
Robert Fort, supt. | 652-1000
HS, 1003 CENTER ST 14052 | 3-00011
James Hoagland, prin. | 655-0700
MS, 430 MAIN ST 14052 | 2-00100
Dennis Leach, prin. | 652-1004

Christ the King Seminary | 1-UC
PO BOX 607 14052 | 652-8900

East Bloomfield, AC 716, PC 3, Ontario
East Bloomfield Central SD | 4-11111
OAKMOUNT AVE 14443 | 657-6121
R. Jack Siring, supt.
Bloomfield JSHS | 3-00111
OAKMOUNT AVE 14443 | 657-6190
Stephen Beaulieu, prin.

Eastchester, AC 914, PC see New York
Eastchester UFD | 4-11111
580 WHITE PLAINS RD 10707 | 793-6130
Robert Pellicone, supt.
HS, 65 STEWART PL 10707 | 2-00011
John Sullivan, prin. | 793-6130
MS, 550 WHITE PLAINS RD 10707 | 2-00100
Richard Dellinger, prin. | 793-6130

Tuckahoe UFD | 3-11111
65 SIWANOY BLVD 10707 | 337-5376
Charles Eible, supt.
Tuckahoe JSHS | 2-00111
65 SIWANOY BLVD 10707 | 337-5376
Lawrence Glickman, prin.

East Elmhurst, AC 718, PC see New York
Queens Borough SD 33 | 4-01100
3202 JUNCTION BLVD 11369 | 335-7500
Charles Schonhout, supt.
Armstrong IS | 4-01100
3202 JUNCTION BLVD 11369 | 335-7500
Laverne Flowers, prin.

East Greenbush, AC 518, PC 5, Rensselaer
East Greenbush Central SD | 5-11111
11 TROY RD 12061 | 477-2755
Terrance Brewer, supt.
Columbia HS 12061 | 4-00011
James MacArevey, prin. | 477-8711
Goff MS, GILLIGAN ROAD 12061 | 3-00100
Matthew Sanzone, prin. | 477-2731

East Hampton, AC 516, PC 4, Suffolk
East Hampton UFD | 4-11111
76 NEWTOWN LN 11937 | 324-4104
Cornelius O'Connell, supt.
HS, 2 LONG LN 11937 | 3-00011
Leigh Byron, prin. | 329-4132
MS, 76 NEWTOWN LN 11937 | 2-01100
Jay Niles, prin. | 329-4116

East Islip, AC 516, PC 7, Suffolk

Suburban Technical School | 2-CS
2650 SUNRISE HWY 11730 | 224-5001

East Meadow, AC 516, PC 8, Nassau
East Meadow UFD | 6-11111
101 CARMAN AVE 11554 | 228-5200
Frank Saracino, supt.
HS, 101 CARMAN AVE 11554 | 4-00011
Richard Barry, prin. | 228-5331
Woodland MS | 4-00100
690 WENWOOD DR 11554 | 564-6523
Diana Todaro, prin.
Other Schools – See Westbury

East Northport, AC 516, PC 7, Suffolk
Elwood UFD
Supt. — See Greenlawn

Elwood/Glenn HS | 3-00011
478 ELWOOD RD 11731 | 266-5410
Kathleen Semergieff, prin.
Elwood MS, 478 ELWOOD RD 11731 | 2-00100
Arthur Strassle, prin. | 266-5420

Northport-East Northport UFD
Supt. — See Northport
MS, 1075 5TH AVE 11731 | 3-00100
William Muller, prin. | 261-9000

East Norwich, AC 516, PC 5, Nassau
Oyster Bay-East Norwich Central SD
Supt. — See Oyster Bay
Vernon MS, 880 OYSTER BAY RD 11732 | 2-01100
Martin Malone, prin. | 624-6560

East Patchogue, AC 516, PC 7, Suffolk
South Country Central SD | 5-11111
189 N DUNTON AVE 11772 | 286-4304
Joe Laria, supt.
Other Schools – See Bellport, Brookhaven

Eastport, AC 516, PC 4, Suffolk
Eastport UFD | 3-11111
390 MONTAUK HWY 11941 | 325-0800
Robert Dillon, supt.
JSHS, 390 MONTAUK HWY 11941 | 2-00111
J. Gagliano, prin. | 325-0800

East Rochester, AC 716, PC 6, Monroe
East Rochester UFD | 4-11111
222 WOODBINE AVE 14445 | 248-6302
Lorenzo Benati, supt.
Obourn HS, 200 WOODBINE AVE 14445 | 2-00011
H Maffucci, prin. | 248-6350
Morgan MS, 108 EAST AVE 14445 | 2-01100
Joseph Bascom, prin. | 248-6330

East Rockaway, AC 516, PC 7, Nassau
East Rockaway UFD | 4-11111
443 OCEAN AVE 11518 | 887-8300
Rob Parry, supt.
JSHS, 443 OCEAN AVE 11518 | 3-00111
William Fortgang, prin. | 887-8310

East Setauket, AC 516, PC 4, Suffolk
Three Village Central SD | 6-11111
200 NICOLLS RD 11733 | 474-7514
Mary Barter, supt.
Melville SHS, 380 OLD TOWN RD 11733 | 4-00001
Robert McKean, prin. | 474-5704
Murphy JHS, OXHEAD ROAD 11733 | 3-00110
Arnold Dodge, prin. | 474-7621
Other Schools – See Setauket

East Syracuse, AC 315, PC 5, Onondaga
East Syracuse-Minoa Central SD | 5-11111
407 FREMONT RD 13057 | 656-7201
Gary Minns, supt.
East Syracuse-Minoa Central SHS | 3-00001
6400 KIRKVILLE RD 13057 | 656-7242
Henry Santulli, prin.
Pine Grove JHS | 3-00110
6320 FREMONT RD 13057 | 656-7201
Edgar Ames, prin.

Bishop Grimes HS | 2-00111
6653 KIRKVILLE RD 13057 | 437-0356
Fr. Heizman, prin.

Eden, AC 716, PC 5, Erie
Eden Central SD, PO BOX 267 14057 | 4-11111
Thomas Christopher, supt. | 992-3629
JSHS, PO BOX 267 14057 | 3-00111
Paul Ludwig, prin. | 992-3641

Edmeston, AC 607, PC 3, Otsego
Edmeston Central SD | 3-11111
11 NORTH ST 13335 | 965-8931
John Holdorf, supt.
Edmeston Central S, 11 NORTH ST 13335 | 3-11111
Casey Barduhn, prin. | 965-8931

Elba, AC 716, PC 3, Genesee
Elba Central SD, 57 S MAIN ST 14058 | 3-11111
Rob Smith, supt. | 757-9967
JSHS, 57 S MAIN ST 14058 | 2-00111
Paul Ballard, prin. | 757-9967

Eldred, AC 914, PC 3, Sullivan
Eldred Central SD | 3-11111
600 STATE ROUTE 55 12732 | 557-6141
Anthony Lanni, supt.
Eldred Central S | 3-11111
600 STATE ROUTE 55 12732 | 557-6014
Albert Wojtaszek, prin.

Elizabethtown, AC 518, PC 3, Essex
Elizabethtown-Lewis Central SD | 2-11111
COURT ST 12932 – Paul Bona, supt. | 873-6371
Elizabethtown-Lewis Central S | 2-11111
COURT ST 12932 | 873-6371
James Tromblee, supt.

Ellenburg Depot, AC 518, PC 3, Clinton
Northern Adirondack Central SD | 4-11111
PO BOX 164 12935 | 594-7060
William Scott, supt.
Northern Adirondack JSHS | 3-00111
PO BOX 164 12935 | 594-3962
Norman Kavanaugh, prin.

Ellenville, AC 914, PC 5, Ulster
Ellenville Central SD | 4-11111
28 MAPLE AVE 12428 | 647-7100
Ed Rhine, supt.

JSHS, 28 MAPLE AVE 12428   3-00111
  Mark Ellison, prin.   647-7100

Ellicottville, AC 716, PC 3, Cattaraugus
Ellicottville Central SD   3-11111
  5873 ROUTE 219 S 14731   699-2368
  Ed Ahrens, supt.
JSHS, 5873 ROUTE 219 S 14731   2-00111
  Mark Ward, prin.   699-2316

Elma, AC 716, PC 4, Erie
Iroquois Central SD, GIRDLE RD 14059   5-11111
  Lawrence Pereira, supt.   652-9300
Iroquois HS, PO BOX 32 14059   3-00111
  Richard Marotto, prin.   652-3000
Iroquois MS, GIRDLE RD 14059   3-00100
  Charles Funke, prin.   652-3000

Elmhurst-A, AC 718, PC see New York
Queens Borough HSD
  Supt. — See Corona
Newtown HS, 4801 90TH ST 11373   5-00011
  John Ficalora, prin.   592-4300

Cathedral Prep Seminary   2-00111
  5625 92ND ST 11373   592-6800
  Msgr. Catanello, prin.

Elmira, AC 607, PC 8, Chemung
Elmira CSD, 951 HOFFMAN ST 14905   6-11111
  Ann Fuqua, supt.   737-7400
Elmira Free Academy   4-00011
  933 HOFFMAN ST 14905   735-3100
  Joseph Nikiel, prin.
Southside HS, 777 S MAIN ST 14904   4-00011
  Kenneth Thomas, prin.   735-3200
Broadway MS   3-00100
  1000 BROADWAY ST 14904   735-3300
  Patricia McKinney, prin.
Davis MS   3-00100
  E CLINTON AND LAKE ST 14901   735-3400
  Daile Rose, prin.

Arnot-Ogden Medical Center   HSP
  600 ROE AVE 14905   737-4289
Arnot-Ogden Memorial Hospital   HSP
  600 ROE AVE 14905
Elmira Business Institute   2-CS
  180 CLEMENS CENTER PKY 14901   733-7177
Elmira Christian Academy   2-11111
  235 E MILLER ST 14904   734-7195
  Katherine Mattoon, prin.
Elmira College   4-UC
  PARK PLACE 14901   735-1800
Holy Family JHS, 1010 DAVIS ST 14901   2-00100
  Elizabeth Berliner, prin.   734-0336
Notre Dame HS, 1400 MAPLE AVE 14904   2-00011
  Sr. Mary Hickey, prin.   734-2267

Elmira Heights, AC 607, PC 5, Chemung
Elmira Heights Central SD   4-11111
  ROBINWOOD AVE 14903   734-7114
  Charles Clemens, supt.
Edison JSHS, 135 COLLEGE AVE 14903   2-00111
  Theodore Bowen, prin.   733-5604

Elmont, AC 516, PC 8, Nassau
Sewanhaka Central HSD   6-00111
  555 RIDGE RD 11003   488-9800
  George Goldstein, supt.
Elmont Memorial JSHS   4-00111
  555 RIDGE RD 11003   488-9200
  Diane Scricca, prin.
Other Schools – See Floral Park, Franklin Square,
  New Hyde Park

Elmsford, AC 914, PC 5, Westchester
Elmsford UFD, S GOODWIN AVE 10523   3-11111
  Rob Pauline, supt.   592-8440
Hamilton JSHS   2-00111
  50 S GOODWIN AVE 10523   592-8440
  Leonard Mecca, prin.

Ultrasound Diagnostic School   2-CS
  2269 S SAW MILL RIVER RD 10523   347-6817

Endicott, AC 607, PC 7, Broome
Union-Endicott Central SD   5-11111
  1401 BROAD ST 13760   757-2112
  Dennis Sweeney, supt.
Union-Endicott HS   4-00011
  1200 E MAIN ST 13760   757-2181
  James Bossong, prin.
Snapp MS, 101 S LODER AVE 13760   3-00100
  David Zandy, prin.   757-2156

Seton Catholic MS   2-01100
  1112 BROAD ST 13760   748-7423
  Anne Cowling, prin.

Endwell, AC 607, PC 7, Broome
Maine-Endwell Central SD   5-11111
  712 FARM TO MARKET RD 13760   754-1400
  Dennis Ford, supt.
Maine-Endwell HS   3-00011
  720 FARM TO MARKET RD 13760   754-1400
  Keith Mathews, prin.
Maine-Endwell MS   3-00100
  1119 FARM TO MARKET RD 13760   786-8271
  John Touhey, prin.

Fabius, AC 315, PC 2, Onondaga
Fabius-Pompey Central SD   3-11111
  7811 MAIN ST 13063   683-5301
  Fred Thomsen, supt.
JSHS, 1211 MILL ST 13063   2-00111
  Steven Hubbard, prin.   683-5811

Fairport, AC 716, PC 6, Monroe
Fairport Central SD   6-11111
  38 W CHURCH ST 14450   223-7600
  Paul Doyle, supt.
SHS, 1358 AYRAULT RD 14450   4-00001
  Robert Reiter, prin.   421-2100
Brown MS, 665 AYRAULT RD 14450   3-00100
  Michael Hagerman, prin.   421-2065
Minerva-Deland JHS   3-00010
  140 HULBURT RD 14450   421-2030
  Robert Reiter, prin.
Perrin MS, 85 POTTER PL 14450   3-00100
  James Valentine, prin.   421-2080

Falconer, AC 716, PC 5, Chautauqua
Falconer Central SD   4-11111
  2 EAST AVE N 14733   665-6624
  Robert Niver, supt.
JSHS, 2 EAST AVE N 14733   3-00111
  Donald Conway, prin.   665-6624

Levant Christian S   2-11111
  PO BOX 236 14733   665-2422
  Charles Hill, prin.

Fallsburg, AC 914, PC 3, Sullivan
Fallsburg Central SD   4-11111
  BRICKMAN RD 12733   434-5884
  Marilyn Wranek, supt.
JSHS, BRICKMAN RD 12733   3-00111
  Barry Foster, prin.   434-6800

Farmingdale, AC 516, PC 6, Nassau
Farmingdale UFD   6-11111
  50 VAN COTT AVE 11735   752-6510
  Gerald Dempsey, supt.
HS, 150 LINCOLN ST 11735   4-00011
  Arthur Sumbler, prin.   752-6600
Howitt MS, 70 VAN COTT AVE 11735   3-00100
  Robert Schultz, prin.   752-6525

Polytechnic University   3-UC
  901 ROUTE 110 11735   454-5101
SUNY College of Technology   7-UC
  ROUTE 110 11735   420-2000

Farmingville, AC 516, PC 7, Suffolk

Faith Academy   2-11111
  1070 PORTION RD 11738   732-7088
  Rev. Cotrone, prin.

Far Rockaway, AC 718, PC see New York
Queens Borough HSD
  Supt. — See Corona
HS, 821 BEACH 25TH ST 11691   4-00011
  Robert Kane, prin.   327-6000

Queens Borough SD 27
  Supt. — See Ozone Park
Piccolo IS, 1045 NAMEOKE ST 11691   4-00100
  Vito Martino, prin.   471-6900

Global Business Institute   2-CS
  1931 MOTT AVE 11691   327-2220
Peninsula Hospital Center   HSP
  5115 BEACH CHANNEL DR 11691   945-7100
Shor Yoshuv Rabbinical College   1-UC
  1526 CENTRAL AVE 11691   327-2048
Torah Academy for Girls   2-00111
  444 BEACH 6TH ST 11691   471-8444
  Abraham Aufrichtig, prin.

Fayetteville, AC 315, PC 5, Onondaga
Fayetteville-Manlius Central SD
  Supt. — See Manlius
Wellwood MS   3-01100
  700 S MANLIUS ST 13066   682-1300
  David Wheeler, prin.

Fillmore, AC 716, PC 2, Allegany
Fillmore Central SD, 104 MAIN ST 14735   3-11111
  Eddie Husted, supt.   567-2251
Fillmore Central S, 104 MAIN ST 14735   3-11111
  David Hanks, prin.   567-2251

Fishers Island, AC 516, PC 3, Suffolk
Fishers Island UFD, PO BOX A 06390   1-11111
  Carmine Antonelli, supt.   788-7444
Fishers Island Central S   1-11111
  PO BOX A 06390   788-7444
  Carmine Antonelli, prin.

Floral Park, AC 718, PC 7, Nassau
Queens Borough SD 26
  Supt. — See Bayside
Hillside JHS, 8114 257TH ST 11004   4-00110
  Marcel Kshensky, prin.   831-4000

Sewanhaka Central HSD
  Supt. — See Elmont
Floral Park Memorial JSHS   4-00111
  210 LOCUST ST 11001   488-9300
  Diane Kelly, prin.
Sewanhaka JSHS, 500 TULIP AVE 11001   4-00111
  David Kreutz, prin.   488-9600

Florida, AC 914, PC 4, Orange
Florida UFD, 51 N MAIN ST 10921   3-11111
  Michael Lesick, supt.   651-3095
Seward Institute JSHS   2-00111
  53 N MAIN ST 10921   651-4038
  Brian Hunt, prin.

Flushing, AC 718, PC see New York
Queens Borough HSD
  Supt. — See Corona
Bowne HS, 6325 MAIN ST 11367   5-00011
  Patricia Kobbetts, prin.   263-1919
HS, 3501 UNION ST 11354   4-00011
  Jay Cohen, prin.   762-8360
Harris HS, 7540 PARSONS BLVD 11366   3-00011
  Malcolm Largman, prin.   969-1433
Lewis HS, 5820 UTOPIA PKY 11365   5-00011
  Robert Burns, prin.   357-7740
Island Academy Alternative HS   2-00010
  1800 HAZEN ST 11370   728-6774
  Timothy Lisante, prin.

Queens Borough SD 25   7-11110
  7030 164TH ST 11365   591-2100
  Jacqueline Browne, supt.
Beard JHS, 14480 BARCLAY AVE 11355   4-00110
  Emily Tom, prin.   359-6676
Bleeker JHS, 14726 25TH DR 11354   4-00110
  Theodore Solow, prin.   445-3232
Block IS, 3465 192ND ST 11358   4-00110
  Manfred Korman, prin.   961-3480
Carson IS, 4621 COLDEN ST 11355   4-00110
  Oscar Cohen, prin.   353-6464
Parson JHS, 15840 76TH RD 11366   3-00110
  Nathan Blaivas, prin.   591-9000
Other Schools – See Whitestone

Queens Borough SD 26
  Supt. — See Bayside
Ryan JHS, 6420 175TH ST 11365   4-00110
  Frank Schimmel, prin.   358-2005

College of Aeronautics   4-UC
  LAGUARDIA AIRPORT 11371   429-6600
CUNY Queens College   7-UC
  6530 KISSENA BLVD 11367   520-7000
Drake Business School   3-CS
  3609 MAIN ST APT 6 11354   353-3535
Ezra Academy of Queens   2-00111
  11945 UNION TPKE 11375   263-5500
  Francine Hirschman, prin.
Garden S, 3316 79TH ST 11372   2-11111
  Richard Marotta, prin.   335-6263
Greater New York Academy   2-00011
  4132 58TH ST 11377   639-1752
  Del Metellus, prin.
Holy Cross HS   3-00011
  2620 FRANCIS LEWIS BLVD 11358   886-7250
  Br. Branigan, prin.
Monsignor McClancy HS   3-00011
  7106 31ST AVE 11370   898-3800
  Br. Rocco, prin.
St. Francis Prep S   5-00011
  6100 FRANCIS LEWIS BLVD 11365   423-8810
  Br. Conway, prin.
Shevach HS, 7509 MAIN ST 11367   2-00111
  Rivkah Blau, prin.   263-0525
Windsor S, 4160 KISSENA BLVD 11355   2-00111
  Philip Stewart, prin.   359-8300

Fonda, AC 518, PC 4, Montgomery
Fonda-Fultonville Central SD   4-11111
  EDUCATIONAL PLAZA 12068   853-4415
  William Higgins, supt.
Fonda-Fultonville HS   3-00011
  CEMETERY ST 12068   853-3182
  Michael Mongin, prin.
Fonda-Fultonville MS   3-01100
  CEMETERY ST 12068   853-4747
  John West, prin.

Forest Hills, AC 718, PC see New York
Queens Borough HSD
  Supt. — See Corona
HS, 6701 110TH ST 11375   5-00011
  Rowena O'Shaughnessy, prin.   268-3137

Queens Borough SD 28   7-11110
  10855 69TH AVE 11375   830-3230
  Joe Petrella, supt.
Sage HS, 6817 AUSTIN ST 11375   4-00110
  Richard Anastasio, prin.   830-4970
Other Schools – See Jamaica, Rego Park

Kew Forest S, 11917 UNION TPKE 11375   2-11111
  Philip Rogers, prin.   268-4667
Mestiva Ohr Torah   2-00111
  6635 108TH ST 11375   268-3444
  Bernard Wolinez, prin.
New York School for Medical Dental Asst.   2-CS
  11616 QUEENS BLVD 11375   793-2330
Rabbinical Seminary of America   2-UC
  9215 69TH AVE 11375   268-4700
Torah Academy HS   2-00111
  11945 UNION TPKE 11375   575-3077
  Rabbi Bryks, prin.
Yeshiva Rabi Dov Revel   2-10110
  7102 113TH ST 11375   261-9624
  Rachel Goldman, prin.

Forestville, AC 716, PC 3, Chautauqua
Forestville Central SD   3-11111
  12 WATER ST 14062   965-2785
  J Rodriguez, supt.

Forestville Central JSHS 2-00111
4 ACADEMY ST 14062 965-2711
Charles Nebral, prin.

Fort Ann, AC 518, PC 2, Washington
Ft. Ann Central SD 3-11111
CATHERINE ST 12827 639-5594
Robert Meldrum, supt.
S, CATHERINE ST 12827 3-11111
John Whelan, prin. 639-5594

Fort Covington, AC 518, PC 4, Franklin
Salmon River Central SD 4-11111
BOMBAY RD 12937 358-2215
Robert Jaeger, supt.
Salmon River JSHS, BOMBAY RD 12937 3-00111
W. Perkins, prin. 358-9510

Fort Edward, AC 518, PC 5, Washington
Ft. Edward UFD, 220 BROADWAY 12828 3-11111
Joe Murphy, supt. 747-6880
JSHS, 220 BROADWAY 12828 2-00111
Peter Livshin, prin. 747-4529

Fort Plain, AC 518, PC 4, Montgomery
Ft. Plain Central SD, 1 WEST ST 13339 4-11111
John Metallo, supt. 993-2123
HS, 1 WEST ST 13339 2-00011
John Metallo, prin. 993-4463

Frankfort, AC 315, PC 5, Herkimer
Frankfort-Schuyler Central SD 4-11111
PALMER ST 13340 894-5083
Francis Saraceno, supt.
Frankfort-Schuyler Central JSHS 3-00111
PALMER ST 13340 – Gary Tutty, prin. 895-7461

Franklin, AC 607, PC 2, Delaware
Franklin Central SD 2-11111
PO BOX 888 13775 829-3551
Douglas Ido, supt.
Franklin Central S 2-11111
15 INSTITUTE ST 13775 829-3551
Douglas Ido, prin.

Franklin Square, AC 516, PC 8, Nassau
Sewanhaka Central HSD
Supt. — See Elmont
Carey JSHS, 230 POPPY AVE 11010 4-00111
Thomas Dolan, prin. 560-8600

Valley Stream Central HSD
Supt. — See Valley Stream
Valley Stream North JSHS 3-00111
750 HERMAN AVE 11010 564-5510
Robert Alden, prin.

Franklinville, AC 716, PC 4, Cattaraugus
Franklinville Central SD 3-11111
32 N MAIN ST 14737 676-3723
Richard Wachter, supt.
JSHS, 31 N MAIN ST 14737 2-00111
Daniel McCarthy, prin. 676-3222

Fredonia, AC 716, PC 7, Chautauqua
Fredonia Central SD 4-11111
425 E MAIN ST 14063 679-1581
James Merrins, supt.
HS, 425 E MAIN ST 14063 3-00011
R. Redman, prin. 679-1581
MS, 425 E MAIN ST 14063 2-00100
R. Redman, prin. 679-1581

SUNY College at Fredonia 14063 5-UC
673-3111

Freeport, AC 516, PC 8, Nassau
Freeport UFD, 235 N OCEAN AVE 11520 6-11111
Richard Bonen, supt. 867-5205
HS, PO BOX 50 11520 4-00011
Michael Campbell, prin. 867-5305
Dodd JHS, PO BOX 50 11520 3-00100
James Brown, prin. 867-5286

Frewsburg, AC 716, PC 4, Chautauqua
Frewsburg Central SD 4-11111
26 INSTITUTE ST 14738 569-9250
Paul Grekalski, supt.
JSHS, 26 INSTITUTE ST 14738 2-00111
Steve Vanstrom, prin. 569-3255

Friendship, AC 716, PC 4, Allegany
Friendship Central SD 2-11111
46 W MAIN ST 14739 973-3534
Whitney Vantine, supt.
Friendship Central S 3-11111
46 W MAIN ST 14739 – D. Mazur, prin. 973-3311

Fulton, AC 315, PC 7, Oswego
Fulton CSD, 167 S 4TH ST 13069 5-11111
Harvey Kaufman, supt. 593-5510
Bodley HS, 6 GILLARD DR 13069 4-00011
James Granozio, prin. 593-5400
JHS, 129 CURTIS ST 13069 3-00100
Mark Slosek, prin. 593-5440

Gainesville, AC 716, PC 2, Wyoming
Letchworth Central SD 4-11111
5550 SCHOOL RD 14066 493-5450
Charles Pegan, supt.
Letchworth JSHS, SCHOOL ROAD 14066 3-00111
Thomas Kelleher, prin. 493-2571

Galway, AC 518, PC 2, Saratoga
Galway Central SD 4-11111
5317 SACANDAGA RD 12074 882-1221
Ronald Gillespie, supt.

JSHS, 5317 SACANDAGA RD 12074 3-00111
Wallace Vanderwerker, prin. 882-1221

Garden City, AC 516, PC 7, Nassau
Garden City UFD 5-11111
56 CATHEDRAL AVE 11530 294-3004
Robert Dema, supt.
HS, 170 ROCKAWAY AVE 11530 3-00011
John Okulski, prin. 294-3030
MS, 98 CHERRY VALLEY AVE 11530 3-00100
John Glancy, prin. 294-3065

Adelphi University 6-UC
1 SOUTH AVE 11530 294-8700
Cathedral School of St. Mary 4-11111
37 CATHEDRAL AVE 11530 747-3377
Kimberton Barton, prin.
SUNY Nassau Community College 7-CC
1 EDUCATION DR 11530 222-7501
Waldorf S, 225 CAMBRIDGE AVE 11530 2-11111
Marilyn Ruppart, prin. 742-3434

Garden City Park, AC 516, PC 6, Nassau
Mineola UFD
Supt. — See Mineola
Mineola HS, 10 ARMSTRONG RD 11040 3-00011
John Lewis, prin. 741-1206

Garnerville, AC 914, PC see West Haverstraw
Haverstraw-Stony Point Central SD 6-11111
65 CHAPEL ST 10923 942-3000
A. Everhart, supt.
Other Schools – See Haverstraw, Stony Point, Thiells

Geneseo, AC 716, PC 6, Livingston
Geneseo Central SD 4-11111
4050 AVON RD 14454 243-3450
Jerome Ochs, supt.
JSHS, 4050 AVON RD 14454 3-00111
Barb Francis, prin. 243-3450

SUNY College at Geneseo 6-UC
1 COLLEGE CIR 14454 245-5211

Geneva, AC 315, PC 7, Ontario
Geneva CSD, 400 W NORTH ST 14456 4-11111
Vincent Scalise, supt. 781-0276
HS, 101 CARTER RD 14456 3-00011
Brian Mazza, prin. 781-0402
MS, 63 PULTENEY ST 14456 3-00100
Ann Goldfarb, prin. 781-0404

De Sales HS, 90 PULTENEY ST 14456 2-00011
Edward Tracey, prin. 789-5111
Hobart & William Smith College 4-UC
PULTENEY ST 14456 789-5500

Germantown, AC 518, PC 4, Columbia
Germantown Central SD 3-11111
123 MAIN ST 12526 537-6280
Peter Hughes, supt.
Germantown Central S 3-11111
123 MAIN ST 12526 537-6281
John Smith, prin.

Ghent, AC 518, PC 3, Columbia

Hawthorne Valley S 2-11111
ROAD 2 BOX 225 12075 672-7092
Candace Christiansen, prin.

Gilbertsville, AC 607, PC 2, Otsego
Gilbertsville-Mt. Upton Central SD
Supt. — See Mount Upton
Gilbertsville-Mount Upton JSHS 2-00111
GROVE ST 13776 – Patricia Scott, prin. 783-2246

Gilboa, AC 607, PC 2, Schoharie
Gilboa-Conesville Central SD 2-11111
WYCKOFF RD 12076 588-7541
John Barnes, supt.
Gilboa-Conesville Central S 2-11111
RR 1 BOX 6 12076 588-7555
Matthew Murray, prin.

Glen Cove, AC 516, PC 7, Nassau
Glen Cove CSD, 150 DOSORIS LN 11542 5-11111
Charles Murphy, supt. 759-7217
HS, 150 DOSORIS LN 11542 3-00011
Stan Saretsky, prin. 759-7261
MS, 189 FOREST AVE 11542 3-01100
Carl LaPointe, prin. 759-7241

All Saints MS, 12 PEARSALL AVE 11542 2-01100
Sr. Mary Dolan, prin. 676-0762
North Shore University Hospital HSP
ST ANDREWS LN 11542 676-5000
Webb Institute of Naval Architecture 1-UC
200 CRESCENT BEACH RD 11542 671-2213

Glendale, AC 718, PC see New York
Queens Borough SD 24
Supt. — See Middle Village
JHS, 7401 78TH AVE 11385 3-00100
Bernadette Boyle, prin. 326-8261

Glen Head, AC 516, PC 5, Nassau
North Shore Central SD
Supt. — See Sea Cliff
North Shore HS 3-00011
450 GLEN COVE AVE 11545 671-5500
Elaine Boyrer, prin.
North Shore MS 2-00100
505 GLEN COVE AVE 11545 671-5500
James Curran, prin.

Long Island Lutheran HS 2-00111
131 BROOKVILLE RD 11545 626-1700
David Hahn, prin.

Glens Falls, AC 518, PC 7, Warren
Glens Falls CSD, 15 QUADE ST 12801 5-11111
Dalen Showalter, supt. 792-1212
HS, 10 QUADE ST 12801 3-00011
William Kennedy, prin. 792-6564
MS, 20 QUADE ST 12801 3-00100
Harriet Finch, prin. 793-3418

Glens Falls Hospital HSP
100 PARK ST 12801 792-3151

Gloversville, AC 518, PC 7, Fulton
Gloversville CSD, 90 N MAIN ST 12078 5-11111
Don Lomanto, supt. 725-2612
HS, 199 LINCOLN ST 12078 3-00011
Randall Gilbert, prin. 725-0671
Estee MS, 90 N MAIN ST 12078 3-00100
Richard Santelli, prin. 773-7351

Goshen, AC 914, PC 6, Orange
Goshen Central SD, MAIN ST 10924 4-11111
Joseph Colistra, supt. 294-2410
Goshen Central HS 3-00011
SCOTCHTOWN AVE 10924 294-2430
Roy Reese, prin.
Hooker MS, 41 LINCOLN AVE 10924 3-00100
K. Hubley, prin. 294-2470

Burke Catholic HS, FLETCHER ST 10924 2-00011
Sr. Josephine Ortner, prin. 294-5481

Gouverneur, AC 315, PC 5, St. Lawrence
Gouverneur Central SD 4-11111
133 E BARNEY ST 13642 287-4870
Gary Buehler, supt.
JSHS, 113 E BARNEY ST 13642 3-00111
James Hawley, prin. 287-1900

Gowanda, AC 716, PC 5, Cattaraugus
Gowanda Central SD 4-11111
24 PROSPECT ST 14070 532-3325
William Berg, supt.
JSHS, 24 PROSPECT ST 14070 3-00111
Scott Smith, prin. 532-3325

Grahamsville, AC 914, PC 3, Sullivan
Tri Valley Central SD 4-11111
STATE ROUTE 55 12740 985-2296
George Vanderzell, supt.
Tri Valley HS 2-00011
STATE ROUTE 55 12740 985-2296
John Jordan, prin.
Tri Valley MS 2-01100
STATE ROUTE 55 12740 985-2296
Boris Oleksiuk, prin.

Grand Island, AC 716, PC 3, Erie
Grand Island Central SD 5-11111
1100 RANSOM RD 14072 773-9100
Paul Fields, supt.
HS, 1100 RANSOM RD 14072 3-00011
Gus Young, prin. 773-9100
MS, 1100 RANSOM RD 14072 3-00100
Agnes Becker, prin. 773-9100

Granville, AC 518, PC 5, Washington
Granville Central SD 4-11111
60 QUAKER ST 12832 642-1051
Robert Urzillo, supt.
JSHS, 61 QUAKER ST 12832 3-00111
Daryl Hammond, prin. 642-1051

Great Neck, AC 516, PC 6, Nassau
Great Neck UFD 6-11111
345 LAKEVILLE RD 11020 773-1405
William Shine, supt.
Great Neck North HS, 35 POLO RD 11023 3-00011
Bernard Kaplan, prin. 773-1513
Great Neck South HS 3-00011
341 LAKEVILLE RD 11020 773-1600
Thomas Heinegg, prin.
Great Neck North MS, 77 POLO RD 11023 3-00100
Patrick Sullivan, prin. 773-1570
Great Neck South MS 3-00100
349 LAKEVILLE RD 11020 773-1660
Salvatore Lipari, prin.

Greene, AC 607, PC 4, Chenango
Greene Central SD 4-11111
40 S CANAL ST 13778 656-4161
Fred Tarolli, supt.
HS, 40 S CANAL ST 13778 2-00011
Herbert Dickson, prin. 656-4161
MS, 40 S CANAL ST 13778 2-00100
D. Gordon Daniels, prin. 656-4161

Green Island, AC 518, PC 4, Albany
Green Island UFD 2-11111
171 HUDSON AVE 12183 273-1422
Matthew Breitenbach, supt.
Heatley S, 171 HUDSON AVE 12183 2-11111
Charles Dedrick, prin. 273-1422

Greenlawn, AC 516, PC 7, Suffolk
Elwood UFD, 100 KENNETH AVE 11740 4-11111
Michael Maina, supt. 266-5402
Other Schools – See East Northport

Harborfields Central SD | 5-11111
2 OLDFIELD RD 11740 | 754-5320
  Raymond Walters, supt.
Harborfields HS, 98 TAYLOR AVE 11740 | 3-00011
  David Hanna, prin. | 754-5360
Oldfield MS, 2 OLDFIELD RD 11740 | 3-01100
  Neil Lederer, prin. | 754-5310

Greenport, AC 516, PC 4, Suffolk
Greenport UFD, 720 FRONT ST 11944 | 3-11111
  Charles Kozora, supt. | 477-1950
JSHS, 800 FRONT ST 11944 | 2-00111
  William Ellwood, prin. | 477-1950

Greenville, AC 518, PC 3, Greene
Greenville Central SD | 4-11111
  ROUTE 81 12083 | 966-5065
  Linda Gush, supt.
JSHS, ROUTE 81 12083 | 3-00111
  John Andrie, prin. | 966-5190

Greenwich, AC 518, PC 4, Washington
Greenwich Central SD | 4-11111
  10 GRAY AVE 12834 | 692-9542
  James Lagoy, supt.
JSHS, WOODLAWN AVE 12834 | 3-00111
  J. Fitzgerald, prin. | 692-9542

Greenwood, AC 607, PC 3, Steuben
Greenwood Central SD, MAIN ST 14839 | 2-11111
  Grover Weller, supt. | 225-4292
Greenwood Central S, MAIN ST 14839 | 2-11111
  William Tammaro, prin. | 225-4292

Greenwood Lake, AC 914, PC 5, Orange
Greenwood Lake UFD, LAKES RD 10925 | 3-11100
  John Canzoneri, supt. | 782-8678
MS, LAKES RD 10925 | 2-01100
  Ronald De Pace, prin. | 986-8624

Groton, AC 607, PC 4, Tompkins
Groton Central SD, 400 PERU RD 13073 | 4-11111
  Gordon Klumpp, supt. | 898-5801
JSHS, 400 PERU RD 13073 | 2-00111
  J. Pabis, prin. | 898-5801

Guilderland, AC 518, PC 4, Albany
Guilderland Central SD | 5-11111
  6094 STATE FARM RD 12084 | 456-6200
  Harold McCarthy, supt.
Farnsworth MS | 4-00100
  6094 STATE FARM RD 12084 | 456-6010
  Penelope Heath, prin.
Other Schools – See Guilderland Center

Guilderland Center, AC 518, PC 3, Albany
Guilderland Central SD
  Supt. — See Guilderland
HS 12085 | 4-00011
  John Whipple, prin. | 861-8591

Hamburg, AC 716, PC 7, Erie
Frontier Central SD | 5-11111
  4432 BAY VIEW RD 14075 | 649-6001
  Charles Little, supt.
Frontier HS, 4432 BAY VIEW RD 14075 | 4-00011
  M. Courtney, prin. | 646-2151
Frontier MS, 2751 AMSDELL RD 14075 | 4-00100
  Rodney Will, prin. | 646-2249

Hamburg Central SD | 5-11111
  5305 ABBOTT RD 14075 | 649-6850
  Don Ogilvie, supt.
SHS, 4111 LEGION DR 14075 | 3-00001
  Lawrence Hood, prin. | 649-6850
JHS, 360 DIVISION ST 14075 | 3-00110
  Arthur Robinson, prin. | 649-6850

Hopevale UFD, 3780 HOWARD RD 14075 | 2-00111
  Joseph Caligiuri, supt. | 648-2062
Hopevale JSHS | 2-00111
  3780 HOWARD RD 14075 | 648-1930
  James McGowan, prin.

Hilbert College | 3-CC
  5200 S PARK AVE 14075 | 649-7900
Immaculata Academy | 2-00011
  5138 S PARK AVE 14075 | 649-6161
  Thomas Sullivan, prin.

Hamilton, AC 315, PC 5, Madison
Hamilton Central SD | 3-11111
  47 W KENDRICK AVE 13346 | 824-3300
  Edmund Backus, supt.
JSHS, 47 W KENDRICK AVE 13346 | 2-00111
  Vincent Condro, prin. | 824-3300

Colgate University | 5-UC
  13 OAK DR 13346 | 824-1000

Hamlin, AC 716, PC 3, Monroe

St. John's Lutheran ES | 2-10100
  1107 LAKE ROAD EAST FRK 14464 | 964-2550
  Karl Meyer, prin.

Hammond, AC 315, PC 2, St. Lawrence
Hammond Central SD | 2-11111
  PO BOX 185 13646 | 324-5931
  Robert Scofield, supt.
Hammond Central S | 2-11111
  PO BOX 185 13646 | 324-5931
  Robert Scofield, prin.

Hammondsport, AC 607, PC 3, Steuben
Hammondsport Central SD | 3-11111
  MAIN STREET EXT 14840 | 569-5200
  Bruce Inglis, supt.
JSHS, MAIN STREET EXT 14840 | 2-00111
  Daniel Perrine, prin. | 569-5300

Hampton Bays, AC 516, PC 6, Suffolk
Hampton Bays UFD | 4-11111
  86 ARGONNE RD 11946 | 723-2100
  Carl Nelson, supt.
JSHS, 88 ARGONNE RD 11946 | 3-00111
  Robert Feger, prin. | 723-2110

Hancock, AC 607, PC 4, Delaware
Hancock Central SD, 16 READ ST 13783 | 3-11111
  Richard Dillon, supt. | 637-2511
JSHS, 16 READ ST 13783 | 2-01111
  George Wacker, prin. | 637-2511

Hannibal, AC 315, PC 3, Oswego
Hannibal Central SD, AUBURN ST 13074 | 4-11111
  Frank Ferrando, supt. | 564-5212
JSHS, CAYUGA ST 13074 | 3-00111
  Roger Thompson, prin. | 564-5188

Harpursville, AC 607, PC 3, Broome
Harpursville Central SD | 4-11111
  PO BOX 147 13787 | 693-2500
  Albert Oatman, supt.
JSHS, PO BOX 147 13787 | 3-00111
  Rexford Hurlburt, prin. | 693-2500

Harrison, AC 914, PC 7, Westchester
Harrison Central SD | 4-11111
  50 UNION AVE 10528 | 835-3300
  Ron Valenti, supt.
HS, 251 UNION AVE 10528 | 3-00011
  David Goodhart, prin. | 835-3300
Klein MS, UNION & NELSON AVE 10528 | 3-00100
  Rosemary Brooke, prin. | 835-3300

Harrisville, AC 315, PC 3, Lewis
Harrisville Central SD | 3-11111
  PO BOX 189 13648 | 543-2707
  Bonnie Sanderson, supt.
JSHS, PO BOX 189 13648 | 2-00111
  Lloyd Dashnaw, prin. | 543-2920

Hartford, AC 518, PC 2, Washington
Hartford Central SD | 3-11111
  PO BOX 79 12838 | 632-5931
  Rob Hanna, supt.
Hartford Central S, PO BOX 79 12838 | 3-11111
  Douglas Burton, prin. | 632-5923

Hartsdale, AC 914, PC 6, Westchester
Greenburgh Central SD | 4-11111
  475 W HARTSDALE AVE 10530 | 761-6000
  Anthony Mazzullo, supt.
Woodlands HS | 3-00011
  475 W HARTSDALE AVE 10530 | 761-6052
  Kathy Mason, prin.
Woodland JHS | 2-00100
  475 W HARTSDALE AVE 10530 | 761-6052
  Barbara Harris, prin.

Daytop Village HS | 2-00111
  246 CENTRAL AVE 10530 | 949-6674
  Kenneth Silver, prin.
Maria Regina HS | 2-00011
  500 W HARTSDALE AVE 10530 | 761-3300
  Sr. Danielle Baran, prin.
SUNY Hudson Valley Regional Center | 2-UC
  200 N CENTRAL AVE 10530 | 948-6208

Hastings on Hudson, AC 914, PC 6, Westchester
Greenburgh-Graham UFD | 2-11111
  1 BROADWAY 10706 | 478-1106
  Vincent Ziccolella, supt.
Greenburgh-Graham HS | 2-00011
  1 BROADWAY 10706 | 478-1161
  Charles Earle, prin.

Hastings on Hudson UFD | 4-11111
  27 FARRAGUT AVE 10706 | 478-2011
  Vincent Beni, supt.
Hastings HS, MOUNT HOPE BLVD 10706 | 2-00011
  Thomas Fazio, prin. | 478-2902
Farragut MS, 282 FARRAGUT AVE 10706 | 2-00100
  Jennifer Dolan, prin. | 478-4454

Hauppauge, AC 516, PC 7, Suffolk
Hauppauge UFD | 5-11111
  600 TOWNLINE RD 11788 | 265-3630
  Robert Dallow, supt.
HS, 500 LINCOLN BLVD 11788 | 4-00011
  Patrick Perpignano, prin. | 265-3630
MS, 600 TOWNLINE RD 11788 | 3-00100
  Jerome Giaimo, prin. | 265-3630

Haverstraw, AC 914, PC 6, Rockland
Haverstraw-Stony Point Central SD
  Supt. — See Garnerville
Haverstraw MS, 16 GRANT ST 10927 | 3-00100
  Raymond Hagadorn, prin. | 942-3400

SUNY Rockland Community College | 3-CC
  36 MAIN ST 10927 | 942-0624

Hawthorne, AC 914, PC 5, Westchester

Polytechnic University | 2-UC
  36 SAW MILL RIVER RD 10532 | 347-6940

Hempstead, AC 516, PC 8, Nassau
Hempstead UFD | 6-11111
  185 PENINSULA BLVD 11550 | 292-7001
  Eddy Bayardelle, supt.
HS, 185 PENINSULA BLVD 11550 | 4-00011
  Barbara Williams, prin. | 292-7014
Schultz MS, 70 GREENWICH ST 11550 | 3-00100
  Tyree Curry, prin. | 292-7124

Uniondale UFD
  Supt. — See Uniondale
Lawrence Road JHS | 3-00110
  50 LAWRENCE RD 11550 | 565-5730
  Robert Tucker, prin.

Computer Career Center | 2-CS
  474 FULTON AVE 11550 | 486-2526
Hofstra University | 7-UC
  1000 FULTON AVE 11550 | 463-6600
Sacred Heart Academy | 3-00011
  47 CATHEDRAL AVE 11550 | 483-7383
  Sr. Edyth Fitzsimmons, prin.
Suburban Technical School | 4-CS
  175 FULTON AVE 11550 | 481-6660

Henrietta, AC 716, PC 4, Monroe
Rush-Henrietta Central SD | 6-11111
  2034 LEHIGH STATION RD 14467 | 359-5010
  Robert McKanna, supt.
Rush-Henrietta HS | 4-00011
  1799 LEHIGH STATION RD 14467 | 359-5208
  Morris Mallory, prin.
Roth MS, 4000 E HENRIETTA RD 14467 | 3-00100
  Donna Kleinhans, prin. | 359-5108
Other Schools – See West Henrietta

Herkimer, AC 315, PC 6, Herkimer
Herkimer Central SD | 4-11111
  801 W GERMAN ST 13350 | 866-2230
  Robert Moorhead, supt.
JSHS, 801 W GERMAN ST 13350 | 3-00111
  Harold Stoffolano, prin. | 866-1770

SUNY Herkimer County Community College | 4-CC
  100 RESERVOIR RD 13350 | 866-0300

Heuvelton, AC 315, PC 3, St. Lawrence
Heuvelton Central SD | 3-11111
  100 WASHINGTON ST 13654 | 344-2414
  Clive Chambers, supt.
Heuvelton Central S | 3-11111
  100 WASHINGTON ST 13654 | 344-2414
  C. David Lansford, prin.

Hewlett, AC 516, PC 6, Nassau
Hewlett-Woodmere UFD | 5-11111
  1180 HENRIETTA PL 11557 | 374-8100
  Bert Nelson, supt.
HS, 60 EVERIT AVE 11557 | 3-00011
  Don Robbins, prin. | 374-8005
Woodmere MS | 3-00100
  1170 PENINSULA BLVD 11557 | 374-8068
  Charles Terry, prin.

Hicksville, AC 516, PC 8, Nassau
Hicksville UFD | 5-11111
  200 DIVISION AVE 11801 | 733-6600
  Salvatore Mugavero, supt.
HS, 200 DIVISION AVE 11801 | 4-00011
  Richard Hogan, prin. | 733-6623
MS, 215 JERUSALEM AVE 11801 | 4-00100
  Marie Marshall, prin. | 733-6523

Holy Trinity Diocesan HS | 4-00011
  98 CHERRY LN 11801 | 433-2900
  James Boglioli, prin.

Highland, AC 914, PC 5, Ulster
Highland Central SD | 4-11111
  320 PANCAKE HOLLOW RD 12528 | 691-7241
  Ron Revelle, supt.
HS, 320 PANCAKE HOLLOW RD 12528 | 2-00011
  Robert Rua, prin. | 691-2933
MS, 71 MAIN ST 12528 | 2-00100
  Michael Hinchey, prin. | 691-2968

Highland Falls, AC 914, PC 5, Orange
Highland Falls Central SD | 4-11111
  PO BOX 287 10928 | 446-9575
  Herbert Donlan, supt.
O'Neill HS, ROUTE 9W 10928 | 2-00011
  John Guarracino, prin. | 446-4914
MS, PO BOX 287 10928 | 2-01100
  Carolyn McNally, prin. | 446-4761

Hillburn, AC 914, PC 3, Rockland
Ramapo Central SD | 5-11111
  MOUNTAIN AVE 10931 | 357-7783
  Ticknor Litchfield, supt.
Other Schools – See Suffern

Hillsdale, AC 518, PC 2, Columbia
Copake-Taconic Hills Central SD | 4-11111
  ADMINISTRATIVE CENTER 12529 | 851-3301
  John Oates, supt.
Roeliff-Jansen MS | 2-00100
  9065 STATE ROUTE 22 12529 | 325-4471
  Gerald Sadoski, prin.
Other Schools – See Philmont

Hilton, AC 716, PC 6, Monroe
Hilton Central SD, 225 WEST AVE 14468 | 5-11111
  Christopher Bogden, supt. | 392-3450
HS, 400 EAST AVE 14468 | 4-00011
  George Goodwin, prin. | 392-4940

Williams MS, 200 SCHOOL LN 14468   3-00100
   M. Brooke, prin.   392-3450

Hinsdale, AC 716, PC 3, Cattaraugus
Hinsdale Central SD   3-11111
   3701 MAIN ST 14743 – Kurt Pfaff, supt. 557-2228
Hinsdale Central S, 3701 MAIN ST 14743   3-11111
   Kurt Pfaff, prin.   557-2227

Holbrook, AC 516, PC 8, Suffolk
Sachem Central SD   7-11111
   245 UNION AVE 11741   467-8202
   James Ruck, supt.
Seneca JHS, 850 MAIN ST 11741   4-00100
   Thomas McLaughlin, prin.   467-8448
Other Schools – See Holtsville, Lake Ronkonkoma

Holland, AC 716, PC 4, Erie
Holland Central SD, CANADA ST 14080   4-11111
   Peter Roswell, supt.   537-2231
HS, 114 PEARL ST 14080   2-00011
   Ronald Roma, prin.   537-2231
MS, PARTRIDGE RD 14080   2-01100
   David Walling, prin.   537-2231

Holland Patent, AC 315, PC 2, Oneida
Holland Patent Central SD   4-11111
   MAIN ST 13354   865-4101
   Anthony Barretta, supt.
Holland Patent Central HS 13354   3-00011
   William Blynt, prin.   865-8154
MS 13354   3-00100
   Johnnie Jones, prin.   865-8152

Holley, AC 716, PC 4, Orleans
Holley Central SD   4-11111
   3800 N MAIN STREET RD 14470   638-6316
   Russell Rees, supt.
HS, LYNCH ROAD 14470   2-00011
   John Heise, prin.   638-6335
MS, LYNCH RD 14470   2-00100
   William Pileggi, prin.   638-6337

Hollis, AC 718, PC see New York
Queens Borough SD 29
   Supt. — See Rosedale
Anthony IS, 8815 182ND ST 11423   4-00100
   Robert Anastasio, prin.   297-9821

Holtsville, AC 516, PC 7, Suffolk
Sachem Central SD
   Supt. — See Holbrook
Sagamore JHS, 57 DIVISION ST 11742   4-00100
   Thomas Toscano, prin.   736-5050

Homer, AC 607, PC 5, Cortland
Homer Central SD, 80 S WEST ST 13077   5-11111
   John Grant, supt.   749-7241
HS, 80 S WEST ST 13077   3-00011
   Margaret Perfetti, prin.   749-7246
IS, 58 CLINTON ST 13077   4-01100
   Lawrence King, prin.   749-2693

Honeoye, AC 716, PC 3, Ontario
Honeoye Central SD   3-11111
   78 E MAIN ST 14471   229-4125
   Ray Spadafora, supt.
JSHS, 78 E MAIN ST 14471   3-00111
   Mark Mondanaro, prin.   229-4127

Honeoye Falls, AC 716, PC 4, Monroe
Honeoye Falls-Lima Central SD   4-11111
   20 CHURCH ST 14472   624-7010
   Diane Reed, supt.
Honeoye Falls-Lima HS   3-00011
   83 EAST ST 14472   624-7050
   Jack Eckdahl, prin.
Honeoye Falls-Lima MS   3-00100
   619 QUAKER MEETING HOUSE RD 14472
   Garcia Reed, prin.   624-7100

Hoosick, AC 518, PC 2, Rensselaer

Hoosac School, PO BOX 9 12089   1-00111
   Richard Lomuscio, prin.   686-7331

Hoosick Falls, AC 518, PC 5, Rensselaer
Hoosick Falls Central SD   4-11111
   RIVER RD 12090 – Tim Clay, supt. 686-7012
JSHS, RIVER RD 12090   3-00111
   William Auty, prin.   686-7321

Hopewell Junction, AC 914, PC 4, Dutchess
Wappingers Central SD
   Supt. — See Wappingers Falls
Jay HS, ROUTE 52 12533   4-00011
   Joseph Corrigan, prin.   897-9600

Hornell, AC 607, PC 6, Steuben
Hornell CSD, 14 ALLEN ST 14843   4-11111
   G. Gray, supt.   324-1301
JSHS, MAPLE CITY PARK 14843   4-00111
   R. Christopher Roser, prin.   324-1303

St. James Mercy Hospital   HSP
   411 CANISTEO ST 14843   324-0841

Horseheads, AC 607, PC 6, Chemung
Horseheads Central SD   5-11111
   1 RAIDER LN 14845   739-5601
   Robert Reidy, supt.
HS, 401 FLETCHER ST 14845   4-00011
   Jack Kent, prin.   739-5601
MS, 341 SING SING RD 14845   3-00100
   Harry Hillman, prin.   739-6356

Houghton, AC 716, PC 4, Allegany

Houghton Academy, THAYER ST 14744   2-00111
   Philip Stockin, prin.   567-8115
Houghton College   4-UC
   PO BOX 128 14744   567-9200

Hudson, AC 518, PC 6, Columbia
Hudson CSD, 401 STATE ST 12534   5-11111
   N. Howard, supt.   828-4815
JSHS, 215 HARRY HOWARD AVE 12534   3-00111
   George Baseheart, prin.   828-4132

SUNY Columbia Greene Community College   4-CC
   PO BOX 1000 12534   828-4181

Hudson Falls, AC 518, PC 6, Washington
Hudson Falls Central SD   5-11111
   85 NOTRE DAME ST 12839   747-2121
   John Zeis, supt.
HS, 80 E LA BARGE ST 12839   3-00011
   Don Bernhoft, prin.   747-2121
JHS, 83 NOTRE DAME ST 12839   2-00100
   Nicholas Resetar, prin.   747-2121

Huntington, AC 516, PC 7, Suffolk
Huntington UFD   5-11111
   PO BOX 1500 11743   673-2038
   Richard Stock, supt.
HS, 188 OAKWOOD RD 11743   4-00011
   Mary Griffin, prin.   673-2003
Finley JHS, 20 GREENLAWN RD 11743   3-00100
   Craig Springer, prin.   673-2020

Seminary of the Immaculate Conception   2-UC
   440 W NECK RD 11743   423-0483
Touro College   2-UC
   300 NASSAU RD 11743   421-2244

Huntington Station, AC 516, PC 8, Suffolk
South Huntington UFD   6-11111
   60 WESTON ST 11746   673-1610
   Daniel Domenech, supt.
Whitman HS, 301 W HILLS RD 11746   4-00011
   John O'Farrell, prin.   673-1714
Stimson MS, 401 OAKWOOD RD 11746   4-00100
   Marie Connelly, prin.   673-1694

St. Anthonys HS   4-00011
   275 WOLF HILL RD 11747   271-2020
   Br. Dawson, prin.

Hurley, AC 914, PC 5, Ulster

Coleman HS, 430 HURLEY AVE 12443   2-00011
   Joseph Fusco, prin.   338-2750

Hyde Park, AC 914, PC 5, Dutchess
Hyde Park Central SD   5-11111
   HAVILAND ROAD 12538   229-8873
   Lloyd Jaeger, supt.
Roosevelt HS   4-00011
   SOUTH CROSS ROAD 12538   229-7101
   John Hoctor, prin.
Haviland MS, 20 HAVILAND RD 12538   3-00100
   R. Kuralt, prin.   229-2181

Culinary Institute of America   4-CC
   651 ALBANY POST RD 12538   452-9600

Ilion, AC 315, PC 6, Herkimer
Ilion Central SD, PO BOX 480 13357   4-11111
   J. Fusco, supt.   894-9934
JSHS, 99 WEBER AVE 13357   3-00111
   George Deluco, prin.   895-7471

Indian Lake, AC 518, PC 3, Hamilton
Indian Lake Central SD   2-11111
   28 W MAIN ST 12842   648-5024
   Carmine Giangreco, supt.
Indian Lake Central S   2-11111
   28 W MAIN ST 12842   648-5024
   Carmine Giangreco, prin.

Industry, AC 716, PC see Rochester

State Agriculture & Industrial S   2-00111
   GENERAL DELIVERY 14474   533-1700
   Carl Jutzin, prin.

Interlaken, AC 607, PC 3, Seneca
South Seneca Central SD   4-11111
   8236 MAIN ST 14847   532-8395
   John Plume, supt.
Other Schools – See Ovid

Irvington, AC 914, PC 6, Westchester
Irvington UFD, 40 N BROADWAY 10533   4-11111
   Stephen Fisher, supt.   591-8500
HS, 40 N BROADWAY 10533   2-00011
   Rich Hajek, prin.   591-8500
MS, 101 MAIN ST 10533   2-00100
   Andrew Kerfut, prin.   591-9494

Island Park, AC 516, PC 5, Nassau
Island Park UFD   3-11100
   150 TRAFALGAR BLVD 11558   431-7268
   G. Marr, supt.
Lincoln Orens MS   2-01100
   TRAFALGAR BLVD 11558   431-7194
   Sy Rosen, prin.

Islip, AC 516, PC 7, Suffolk
Islip UFD, 215 MAIN ST 11751   5-11111
   Mel Rubinstein, supt.   581-2560
HS, 2508 UNION BLVD 11751   3-00011
   C. Fenton, prin.   581-2560
MS, 211 MAIN ST 11751   3-00100
   Alan Van Cott, prin.   581-2560

Islip Terrace, AC 516, PC 6, Suffolk
East Islip UFD   5-11111
   1 CRAIG B GARIEPY ST 11752   581-1600
   Michael Griffin, supt.
East Islip HS, 1 REDMEN ST 11752   4-00011
   Clyde Payne, prin.   581-1600
Islip Terrace JHS, 100 REDMEN ST 11752   3-00100
   Robert Stelling, prin.   581-1600

Ithaca, AC 607, PC 8, Tompkins
Ithaca CSD, 400 LAKE ST 14850   6-11111
   James Lorthridge, supt.   274-2101
HS, 1401 N CAYUGA ST 14850   4-00011
   Mark Piechota, prin.   274-2145
Boynton MS, 1601 N CAYUGA ST 14850   3-00100
   Joseph Stone, prin.   274-2241
De Witt MS, 560 WARREN RD 14850   3-00100
   Ronald Acerra, prin.   257-3222

Cascadilla Prep S, PO BOX 878 14851   1-00011
   John Kendall, prin.   272-3110
Cornell University   7-UC
   410 THURSTON AVE 14850   255-2000
Ithaca College   6-UC
   953 DANBY RD 14850   274-3013
Tompkins Community Hospital   HSP
   101 DATES DR 14850   274-4443

Jackson Heights, AC 718, PC see New York
Queens Borough SD 30
   Supt. — See Long Island City
Pulitzer IS, 3334 80TH ST 11372   4-00100
   Perry Sandler, prin.   457-1242

Plaza Business Institute   3-CC
   7409 37TH AVE 11372   779-1430

Jamaica, AC 718, PC see New York
Brooklyn Borough HSD
   Supt. — See Brooklyn
Lane HS, 8600 DEXTER CT 11421   5-00011
   Morton Damasek, prin.   647-2100

New York City Special Schools
   Supt. — See Brooklyn
School for Career Development   Vo Tech
   14210 LINDEN BLVD 11436   322-3500
   Suzanne Merkel, prin.

Queens Borough HSD
   Supt. — See Corona
Edison Vo-Tech HS   4-00011
   16565 84TH AVE 11432   297-6580
   Lawrence Block, prin.
Hillcrest HS   5-00011
   16005 HIGHLAND AVE 11432   658-5407
   Nicholas Coletto, prin.
HS, 16701 GOTHIC DR 11432   5-00011
   Barbara Pleener, prin.   739-5942
Martin HS, 15610 BAISLEY BLVD 11434   4-00011
   Leslie Gurka, prin.   528-2920

Queens Borough SD 28
   Supt. — See Forest Hills
Grossley JHS, 10835 167TH ST 11433   3-00110
   Ken Berson, prin.   739-6883
Schlesinger JHS   3-00110
   133-25 GUY BREWER BLVD 11434   723-6200
   Beverly Simpson, prin.
Van Wyck JHS, 8505 144TH ST 11435   4-00110
   Hermann Fischer, prin.   657-1120

Archbishop Molloy HS   4-00011
   8353 MANTON ST 11435   441-2100
   Br. Palmieri, prin.
Catholic Medical Center   HSP
   88-25 153RD ST 11408   849-1200
Christopher Robin S   2-11111
   22216 MERRICK BLVD 11413   525-1330
   Robert Donus, prin.
CUNY York College   5-UC
   9420 GUY R BREWER BLVD 11451   262-2000
Dominican Commercial HS   2-00011
   16106 89TH AVE 11432   739-2060
   Sr. Bernadette Assant, prin.
Mary Louis Academy   4-00011
   17621 WEXFORD TER 11432   297-2120
   Sr. Joan Petito, prin.
St. John's University   7-UC
   GRAND CENTRAL AND UTOP PKY 11439
    990-6161
SCS Business & Technical Institute   4-CS
   16302 JAMAICA AVE 11432   658-8855
Yeshiva HS, 8686 PALO ALTO ST 11423   2-00011
   Rabbi Witty, prin.   479-8550

Jamestown, AC 716, PC 8, Chautauqua
Jamestown CSD, 200 E 4TH ST 14701   6-11111
   C. Tod Eagle, supt.   483-4420
HS, 350 E 2ND ST 14701   4-00011
   J. McElrath, prin.   483-4376
Jefferson MS, 195 MARTIN RD 14701   3-01100
   Katherine Burch, prin.   483-4411
Persell MS, 375 BAKER ST 14701   3-01100
   Joann DeMarco, prin.   483-4406

Washington MS, 159 BUFFALO ST 14701   3-01100
  Samuel Pellerito, prin.   483-4413

Southwestern Central SD   4-11111
  600 HUNT RD 14701   484-1136
  Ed Harvey, supt.
Southwestern HS, 600 HUNT RD 14701   3-00011
  James De Rusha, prin.   664-6273
Southwestern MS, 600 HUNT RD 14701   2-00100
  Gregory Paterniti, prin.   664-6270

Bethel Baptist Christian Academy   2-11111
  200 HUNT RD 14701   484-7420
  Dale Fillmore, prin.
Jamestown Business College   2-CC
  PO BOX 429 14702   664-5100
SUNY Jamestown Community College   5-CC
  525 FALCONER ST 14701   665-5220
Woman's Christian Assoc. Hospital   HSP
  207 FOOTE AVE 14701   487-0141

Jamesville, AC 315, PC 3, Onondaga
Jamesville-DeWitt Central SD
  Supt. — See De Witt
Jamesville-DeWitt MS   3-01100
  RANDALL ROAD 13078   445-8360
  Ronald Ramsden, prin.

Jasper, AC 607, PC 3, Steuben
Jasper-Troupsburg Central SD   3-11111
  PO BOX 81 14855   792-3675
  John Ditondo, supt.
Jasper-Troupsburg JSHS   2-00111
  PO BOX 81 14855   792-3675
  Sylvia Root, prin.

Jefferson, AC 607, PC 3, Schoharie
Jefferson Central SD, MAIN ST 12093   2-11111
  Edward Roche, supt.   652-7821
Jefferson Central S, MAIN ST 12093   2-11111
  John Righi, prin.   652-7821

Jeffersonville, AC 914, PC 2, Sullivan
Jeffersonville-Youngsville Central SD   3-11111
  PO BOX 308 12748   482-5110
  Albert Larson, supt.
S, PO BOX 308 12748   3-11111
  Judith Highhouse, prin.   482-4610

Jericho, AC 516, PC 7, Nassau
Jericho UFD   4-11111
  CEDAR SWAMP ROAD 11753   681-4100
  Rob Manheimer, supt.
HS, CEDAR SWAMP ROAD 11753   3-00011
  Mathew Mandery, prin.   681-5820
MS, CEDAR SWAMP ROAD 11753   2-00100
  Edward Corallo, prin.   681-5820

Johnson City, AC 607, PC 7, Broome
Johnson City Central SD   5-11111
  666 REYNOLDS RD 13790   729-1722
  Albert Mamary, supt.
JSHS, 666 REYNOLDS RD 13790   4-00111
  Richard Gulbin, prin.   763-1256

St. James MS, 143 MAIN ST 13790   2-01100
  Maria Carucci, prin.   797-5444

Johnstown, AC 518, PC 6, Fulton
Johnstown CSD, 501 GLEBE ST 12095   4-11111
  Tim Morell, supt.   762-4611
HS, 12 PEARL ST 12095   3-00011
  Curt Woodcock, prin.   762-4661
Knox JHS, 400 S PERRY ST 12095   2-00100
  Anthony Eppolito, prin.   762-3711

SUNY Fulton-Montgomery Community College 6-CC
  ALUMNI BUILDING 67 12095   762-4651
Tryon S   2-00111
  PERTH JOHNSTOWN ROAD 12095   762-4681
  Dennis Sherman, prin.

Jordan, AC 315, PC 4, Onondaga
Jordan-Elbridge Central SD   4-11111
  CHAPPELL ST 13080   689-3978
  Dwayne Adsitt, supt.
Jordan-Elbridge JSHS   3-00111
  5721 HAMILTON RD 13080   689-9553
  Noel Hotchkiss, prin.

Katonah, AC 914, PC 4, Westchester
Katonah Lewisboro UFD 10536   5-11111
  Karen McCarthy, supt.   763-5000
Jay HS, ROUTE 121 10536   3-00011
  Laura Frenck, prin.   763-3126
Jay MS, ROUTE 121 10536   3-00100
  Doug Dwyer, prin.   763-3194

Harvey S, 260 JAY ST 10536   2-00111
  Barry Fenstermacher, prin.   232-3161

Keene Valley, AC 518, PC 2, Essex
Keene Central SD, MARKET ST 12943   2-11111
  Martin Ruglis, supt.   576-4555
Keene Central S, MARKET ST 12943   2-11111
  Diana Greene, prin.   576-4555

Kendall, AC 716, PC 3, Orleans
Kendall Central SD   4-11111
  KENDALL ROAD 14476   659-2741
  Harlow Fisher, supt.
JSHS, ROOSEVELT HWY 14476   3-00111
  Michael O'Laughlin, prin.   659-2706

Kenmore, AC 716, PC 7, Erie
Kenmore UFD   6-11111
  1500 COLVIN BLVD 14223   874-8400
  John Helfrich, supt.
Kenmore West HS   4-00011
  33 HIGHLAND PKY 14223   874-8401
  Charles Kristich, prin.
Franklin MS   3-00100
  540 PARKHURST BLVD 14223   874-8404
  Mary Kermis, prin.
Hoover MS, 249 THORNCLIFF RD 14223   3-00100
  William Jack, prin.   874-8405
Kenmore MS, 155 DELAWARE RD 14217   3-00100
  Florence Kern, prin.   874-8403
Other Schools – See Tonawanda

Mt. St. Mary Academy   2-00011
  3756 DELAWARE AVE 14217   877-1358
  Sr. Eileen Quinn, prin.

Keuka Park, AC 315, PC 4, Yates

Keuka College   3-UC
  PO BOX 98 14478   536-4411

Kew Gardens, AC 718, PC see New York

Yeshiva Shaar HaTorah Talmudic Research   1-UC
  8396 117TH ST 11418   846-1940

Kings Park, AC 516, PC 7, Suffolk
Kings Park Central SD   5-11111
  101 CHURCH ST 11754   269-3210
  Mary Derose, supt.
HS, 200 ROUTE 25A 11754   3-00011
  John Merone, prin.   269-3245
Rogers MS, 97 OLD DOCK RD 11754   3-00100
  George Duffy, prin.   269-3269

Kings Point, AC 516, PC 5, Nassau

United States Merchant Marine Academy   3-UC
  11024   773-5000

Kingston, AC 914, PC 7, Ulster
Kingston CSD, 61 CROWN ST 12401   6-11111
  William Ledoux, supt.   339-3000
HS, 403 BROADWAY 12401   4-00011
  Douglas Goodemote, prin.   331-1970
Bailey MS, MERILINA AVE 12401   3-00100
  Daniel Bigelow, prin.   338-6390
Other Schools – See Lake Katrine

Lackawanna, AC 716, PC 7, Erie
Lackawanna CSD, 30 JOHNSON ST 14218   5-11111
  Nellie King, supt.   827-6767
JSHS, 550 MARTIN RD 14218   4-00111
  William Bilowus, prin.   827-6727

Bryant & Stratton Business Institute   2-CC
  1214 ABBOTT RD 14218   821-9331

La Fargeville, AC 315, PC 3, Jefferson
La Fargeville Central SD, MAIN ST 13656   2-11111
  Richard Sauer, supt.   658-2241
La Fargeville Central S, MAIN ST 13656   3-11111
  Ula Alton, prin.   658-2241

La Fayette, AC 315, PC 3, Onondaga
La Fayette Central SD   4-11111
  5955 ROUTE 20 W 13084   677-9728
  Joseph Coleman, supt.
JSHS, ROUTE 11 N 13084   2-00111
  Robert Ramsden, prin.   677-3131

Lagrangeville, AC 914, PC 3, Dutchess
Arlington Central SD
  Supt. — See Poughkeepsie
Arlington HS, 263 ROUTE 55 12540   4-00011
  Linda Horisk, prin.   471-7301

Lake George, AC 518, PC 3, Warren
Lake George Central SD   4-11111
  425 CANADA ST 12845   668-5456
  Sherman Parker, supt.
JSHS, 425 CANADA ST 12845   3-00111
  Ann Jaeger, prin.   668-5452

Lake Grove, AC 516, PC 6, Suffolk

Lake Grove School   HND
  PO BOX 712 11755   585-8776

Lake Katrine, AC 914, PC 4, Ulster
Kingston CSD
  Supt. — See Kingston
Miller JHS, FORDING PL ROAD 12449   3-00100
  Bythema Bagley, prin.   382-2960

Lake Luzerne, AC 518, PC 4, Warren
Hadley-Luzerne Central SD   4-11111
  2213 LAKE AVE 12846   696-2461
  Douglas Huntley, supt.
Hadley-Luzerne HS   2-00111
  2213 LAKE AVE 12846   696-2461
  Irwin Sussman, prin.
Townsend MS, HYLAND DRIVE 12846   2-01100
  Clinton Freeman, prin.   696-2461

King's S, PO BOX 300 12846   2-11111
  Gayle Frase, prin.   654-6230

Lakemont, AC 607, PC 2, Yates

Freedom Academy   2-11111
  FREEDOM VILLAGE 14857   243-8126
  Allen Greeno, prin.

Lake Placid, AC 518, PC 4, Essex
Lake Placid Central SD   3-11111
  250 MAIN ST 12946   523-2474
  Gerald Blair, supt.
JSHS, 250 MAIN ST 12946   2-00111
  Robert Schiller, prin.   523-2474

National Sports Academy   1-00111
  12 LAKE PLACID CLUB DR 12946   523-3460
  James Manning, prin.
Northwood S, PO BOX 1070 12946   2-00011
  John Friedlander, prin.   523-3357

Lake Ronkonkoma, AC 516, PC 7, Suffolk
Sachem Central SD
  Supt. — See Holbrook
Sachem HS, 212 SMITH RD 11779   5-00011
  Dennis James, prin.   467-0417

Lancaster, AC 716, PC 7, Erie
Lancaster Central SD   5-11111
  177 CENTRAL AVE 14086   686-3200
  Joseph Girardi, supt.
HS, 1 FORTON DR 14086   4-00011
  Dan Paveljack, prin.   686-3250
Aurora MS, 148 AURORA ST 14086   4-00100
  Terrence Smerka, prin.   686-3220

St. Mary's HS   2-00011
  142 LAVERACK AVE 14086   683-4824
  Mary Sciandra, prin.

Lansing, AC 607, PC 5, Tompkins
Lansing Central SD, 264 RIDGE RD 14882   4-11111
  R. Buckley, supt.   533-4294
HS, 300 RIDGE RD 14882   2-00111
  W. Rankin, prin.   533-4868
MS, 6 LUDLOWVILLE RD 14882   2-01100
  Mary Bente, prin.   533-4271

South Lansing Center for Girls   2-00111
  270 AUBURN RD 14882   533-4262
  Linda Albrecht, prin.

Larchmont, AC 914, PC 6, Westchester
Mamaroneck UFD
  Supt. — See Mamaroneck
Hommocks MS   3-00100
  10 HOMMOCKS RD 10538   834-6550
  Richard North, prin.

Latham, AC 518, PC 7, Albany
North Colonie Central SD
  Supt. — See Newtonville
Shaker HS   4-00011
  445 WATERVLIET SHAKER RD 12110   785-5511
  James Jackson, prin.
Shaker JHS   3-00100
  475 WATERVLIET SHAKER RD 12110   785-1341
  Russell Moore, prin.

Latham Christian Academy   2-11111
  495 WATERVLIET SHAKER RD 12110   785-5916
  Neil Shupp, prin.

Laurens, AC 607, PC 2, Otsego
Laurens Central SD, 64 MAIN ST 13796   2-11111
  Jeffrey Hahn, supt.   432-2050
Laurens Central S, 64 MAIN ST 13796   2-11111
  Pat Grasso, prin.   432-2050

Lawrence, AC 516, PC 6, Nassau
Lawrence UFD, 195 BROADWAY 11559   5-11111
  Stewart Weinberg, supt.   295-7031
MS, 195 BROADWAY 11559   3-00100
  Ed Sallie, prin.   295-7000
Other Schools – See Cedarhurst

Le Roy, AC 716, PC 5, Genesee
Le Roy Central SD   4-11111
  26 TRIGON PARK 14482   768-8133
  Mark Lewis, supt.
JSHS, 2 TRIGON PARK 14482   3-00111
  Charles Herring, prin.   768-8134

Levittown, AC 516, PC 8, Nassau
Island Trees UFD, 100 OWL PL 11756   4-11111
  Rich Segerdahl, supt.   520-2100
Island Trees HS, 59 STRAIGHT LN 11756   3-00011
  Victor Longaro, prin.   520-2135
Island Trees MS   3-00100
  45 WANTAGH AVE 11756   520-2157
  Jon Segerdahl, prin.

Levittown UFD, 150 ABBEY LN 11756   6-11111
  Herman Sirois, supt.   520-5674
Division Avenue HS   3-00011
  120 DIVISION AVE 11756   520-5705
  John Allen, prin.
MacArthur HS   4-00011
  3369 N JERUSALEM RD 11756   520-5802
  Alfonse Celentano, prin.
Salk MS, 3359 N JERUSALEM RD 11756   3-00100
  Regina Lamarca, prin.   731-9076
Wisdom Lane MS   3-00100
  120 CENTER LN 11756   731-9360
  Tim Chambers, prin.

Hunter Business School | 2-CS
3601 HEMPSTEAD TPKE 11756 | 796-1000
South Shore Christian S | 2-11111
40 FARMEDGE RD 11756 | 796-9301
Rev. Cole, prin.

Liberty, AC 914, PC 5, Sullivan
Liberty Central SD | 4-11111
115 BUCKLEY ST 12754 | 292-6990
Richard Beruk, supt.
JSHS, 115 BUCKLEY ST 12754 | 3-00111
Glenn Spielmann, prin. | 292-5400

Lima, AC 716, PC 4, Livingston

Lima Christian S | 2-11111
1575 ROCHESTER ST 14485 | 624-3841
Kirk House, prin.

Limestone, AC 716, PC 2, Cattaraugus
Limestone UFD, 640 N MAIN ST 14753 | 2-11111
John Pionzio, supt. | 925-8873
Limestone Union Free S | 2-11111
640 N MAIN ST 14753 | 925-8873
John Pionzio, prin.

Lincolndale, AC 914, PC 3, Westchester
Somers Central SD | 4-11111
PO BOX 620 10540 | 248-7872
Joe Ennis, supt.
Somers HS, PO BOX 640 10540 | 3-00011
Rip Economou, prin. | 248-8585
Other Schools – See Somers

Ives S, GENERAL DELIVERY 10540 | 2-00111
Alan Hilliard, prin. | 248-7474

Lindenhurst, AC 516, PC 8, Suffolk
Lindenhurst UFD, 350 DANIEL ST 11757 | 6-11111
Anthony Pecorale, supt. | 226-6511
HS, 300 CHARLES ST 11757 | 4-00011
Paul Fried, prin. | 226-6445
JHS, 350 S WELLWOOD AVE 11757 | 4-00100
Joe Pezzullo, prin. | 226-6521

Lisbon, AC 315, PC 2, St. Lawrence
Lisbon Central SD, MAIN ST 13658 | 3-11111
Wayne Chesbrough, supt. | 393-4951
Lisbon Central S, MAIN ST 13658 | 3-11111
Philip Snyder, prin. | 393-4951

Little Falls, AC 315, PC 6, Herkimer
Little Falls CSD, 770 E MAIN ST 13365 | 4-11111
Geoffrey Davis, supt. | 823-1470
JSHS, 1 HIGH SCHOOL RD 13365 | 3-00111
Craig Fox, prin. | 823-4300

Little Neck, AC 718, PC see New York
Queens Borough SD 26
Supt. — See Bayside
Pasteur JHS | 4-00110
5160 MARATHON PKY 11362 | 423-8138
Mae Fong, prin.

Little Valley, AC 716, PC 4, Cattaraugus
Little Valley Central SD | 2-11111
207 ROCK CITY ST 14755 | 938-9155
Stephen Bocciolatt, supt.
Little Valley Central S | 2-11111
207 ROCK CITY ST 14755 | 938-9155
Paul Stetz, prin.

Liverpool, AC 315, PC 5, Onondaga
Liverpool Central SD, 800 4TH ST 13088 | 6-11111
Jerome Melvin, supt. | 453-0225
HS, 4338 WETZEL RD 13090 | 5-00011
Raymond Savarese, prin. | 453-1112
Chestnut Hill MS | 2-00100
204 SASLON PARK DR 13088 | 453-0245
Carl Beck, prin.
MS, 700 7TH ST 13088 | 2-00100
John Dixon, prin. | 453-0258
Soule Road MS, 8340 SOULE RD 13090 | 3-00100
Joanne Wetter, prin. | 453-1283

National Tractor Trailer School | 2-CS
PO BOX 208 13088 | 451-2430

Livingston Manor, AC 914, PC 4, Sullivan
Livingston Manor Central SD | 3-11111
SCHOOL ST 12758 – Ken Gray, supt. | 439-4400
JSHS, SCHOOL ST 12758 | 2-00111
John Healy, prin. | 439-5621

Livonia, AC 716, PC 4, Livingston
Livonia Central SD, PO BOX E 14487 | 4-11111
James Franklin, supt. | 346-4000
JSHS, PO BOX E 14487 | 3-00111
Michael Haugh, prin. | 346-4042

Loch Sheldrake, AC 914, PC 3, Sullivan

SUNY Sullivan County Community College | 4-CC
PO BOX 4002 12759 | 434-5750

Lockport, AC 716, PC 7, Niagara
Lockport CSD, 130 BEATTIE AVE 14094 | 6-11111
Russell Dever, supt. | 439-6411
HS, 250 LINCOLN AVE 14094 | 4-00011
John Essler, prin. | 439-6422
Belknap MS, 491 HIGH ST 14094 | 3-00100
Paul Pignataro, prin. | 439-6431
North Park JHS, 160 PASSAIC AVE 14094 | 3-00100
Nicholas Cedrone, prin. | 439-6464

Star Point Central SD | 4-11111
4363 MAPLETON RD 14094 | 625-7269
Lowell Brinnen, supt.
Starpoint JSHS | 4-00111
4363 MAPLETON RD 14094 | 625-7280
James Allen, prin.

Locust Valley, AC 516, PC 5, Nassau
Locust Valley Central SD | 4-11111
99 HORSE HOLLOW RD 11560 | 674-6350
Matt Dirisio, supt.
JSHS, 99 HORSE HOLLOW RD 11560 | 3-00111
Edward Tronolone, prin. | 674-6305

Friends Academy | 3-11111
355 DUCK POND RD 11560 | 676-0393
Marcus Hurlbut, prin.
Portledge S, 355 DUCK POND RD 11560 | 2-11111
Huson Gregory, prin. | 671-1475

Long Beach, AC 516, PC 8, Nassau
Long Beach SD, 235 LIDO BLVD 11561 | 5-11111
Elliot Landon, supt. | 897-2104
HS, 322 LAGOON DR W 11561 | 4-00011
Helen Cheliotes, prin. | 897-2012
MS, 239 LIDO BLVD 11561 | 3-00100
Frederick Brand, prin. | 897-2166

Rabbinical College of Long Island | 1-UC
201 MAGNOLIA BLVD 11561 | 431-7414
Torah HS, 205 W BEECH ST 11561 | 2-00011
Rabbi Eckstein, prin. | 431-7144

Long Island City, AC 718, PC see New York
Queens Borough HSD
Supt. — See Corona
Aviation HS, 3500 QUEENS BLVD 11101 | 4-00011
Eileen Taylor, prin. | 361-2032
Bryant HS, 4810 31ST AVE 11103 | 5-00011
Rose DePinto, prin. | 721-5404
International HS | 2-00011
3110 THOMSON AVE 11101 | 482-5455
Eric Nadelstern, prin.
HS, 2801 41ST AVE 11101 | 4-00011
Frank Nappi, prin. | 937-1610
Queens Vocational HS | 4-00011
3702 47TH AVE 11101 | 937-3010
Steven Serber, prin.

Queens Borough SD 30 | 7-11110
3625 CRESCENT ST 11106 | 729-6380
Angelo Gimondo, supt.
Astoria IS, 3151 21ST ST 11106 | 3-00100
Dorothy Hively, prin. | 274-8316
Greeley JHS, 4501 31ST AVE 11103 | 4-00110
Ira Rudin, prin. | 278-7054
Holmes JHS, 3641 28TH ST 11106 | 4-00110
Philip Composto, prin. | 937-1463
Steinway JHS, 3711 21ST AVE 11105 | 4-00110
Carl Thomaselli, prin. | 278-6403
Other Schools – See Jackson Heights

CUNY LaGuardia Community College | 6-CC
31-10 THOMPSON AVE 11101 | 482-5000
St. John's Prep S | 4-00011
2121 CRESCENT ST 11105 | 721-7200
William Higgins, prin.

Long Lake, AC 518, PC 3, Hamilton
Long Lake Central SD, SCHOOL ST 12847 | 2-11111
Jacqueline Backus, supt. | 624-2221
Long Lake Central S, SCHOOL ST 12847 | 2-11111
Jacqueline Backus, prin. | 624-2221

Loudonville, AC 518, PC 7, Albany

Siena College 12211 | 5-UC
783-2300

Lowville, AC 315, PC 5, Lewis
Lowville Central SD | 4-11111
7668 N STATE ST 13367 | 376-3544
William Wormuth, supt.
JSHS, 7668 N STATE ST 13367 | 3-00111
Kenneth McAuliffe, prin. | 376-3544

Lynbrook, AC 516, PC 7, Nassau
Lynbrook UFD | 5-11111
111 ATLANTIC AVE 11563 | 887-0253
William Metkiff, supt.
HS, 9 UNION AVE 11563 | 3-00011
Santo Barbarino, prin. | 887-0200
Lynbrook North MS | 2-00100
529 MERRICK RD 11563 | 887-0282
Thomas McDonald, prin.
Lynbrook South MS | 2-00100
333 UNION AVE 11563 | 887-0267
Gary Rugg, prin.

Briarcliffe School | 2-CC
10 PENINSULA BLVD 11563 | 596-1313

Lyndonville, AC 716, PC 3, Orleans
Lyndonville Central SD | 3-11111
HOUSEL AVE 14098 | 765-2282
Richard Pucher, supt.
Webber JSHS, HOUSEL AVE 14098 | 2-00111
Charles Bostwick, prin. | 765-2251

Lyons, AC 315, PC 5, Wayne
Lyons Central SD | 4-11111
9 LAWRENCE ST 14489 | 946-4214
Noel Mcstay, supt.

JSHS, 10 CLYDE RD 14489 | 3-00111
Fred Goodrich, prin. | 946-9010

Macedon, AC 315, PC 4, Wayne
Gananda Central SD | 3-11111
PO BOX 609 14502 | 986-3506
Larry Pedersen, supt.
Gananda JSHS, PO BOX 609 14502 | 2-00111
Ken Dehn, prin. | 986-3521

Mc Graw, AC 607, PC 4, Cortland
Mc Graw Central SD | 3-11111
W ACADEMY ST 13101 | 836-3636
Donato Leopardi, supt.
JSHS, W ACADEMY ST 13101 | 2-00111
Richard During, prin. | 836-3600

Madison, AC 315, PC 2, Madison
Madison Central SD | 3-11111
ROUTE 20 13402 | 893-1878
Arthur Wilson, supt.
Madison Central S, ROUTE 20 13402 | 3-11111
Cliff Moses, prin. | 893-1878

Madrid, AC 315, PC 3, St. Lawrence
Madrid-Waddington Central SD | 3-11111
ROUTE 345 13660 | 322-5746
James Boyle, supt.
Madrid-Waddington JSHS | 2-00111
ROUTE 345 13660 | 322-5746
John Dineen, prin.

Mahopac, AC 914, PC 6, Putnam
Mahopac Central SD | 5-11111
112 LAKEVIEW DR 10541 | 628-3415
Jerry Cicchelli, supt.
HS, 421 BALDWIN PLACE RD 10541 | 4-00011
Thomas Readyoff, prin. | 628-3256
MS, 421 BALDWIN PLACE RD 10541 | 3-00100
John Reilly, prin. | 621-1330

Malone, AC 518, PC 6, Franklin
Malone Central SD, WEST ST 12953 | 5-11111
Thomas Helmer, supt. | 483-7370
Franklin Academy HS | 3-00111
54 STATE ST 12953 | 483-7807
Richard Spataro, prin.
MS, WEBSTER ST 12953 | 3-00100
Wayne Walbridge, prin. | 483-7801

SUNY North Country Community College | 3-CC
12953 | 483-4550

Malverne, AC 516, PC 6, Nassau
Malverne UFD, 301 WICKS LN 11565 | 4-11111
Barry Schoenholz, supt. | 596-2005
HS, 75 OCEAN AVE 11565 | 3-00111
James Lennon, prin. | 596-2020
Herber MS, 75 OCEAN AVE 11565 | 3-01100
Raymond Rodecker, prin. | 596-2044

Mamaroneck, AC 914, PC 7, Westchester
Mamaroneck UFD | 5-11111
1000 W BOSTON POST RD 10543 | 698-9000
Norman Colb, supt.
HS, 1000 W BOSTON POST RD 10543 | 4-00011
James Coffey, prin. | 698-9000
Other Schools – See Larchmont

Rye Neck UFD, 310 HORNIDGE RD 10543 | 4-11111
Peter Mustich, supt. | 698-6171
Rye Neck HS, 300 HORNIDGE RD 10543 | 2-00011
Barbara Ferraro, prin. | 698-6171
Rye Neck MS, 300 HORNIDGE RD 10543 | 2-01100
Paul Siragusa, prin. | 698-6171

Westchester Hebrew HS | 2-00011
856 ORIENTA AVE 10543 | 698-0806
Rabbi Majerowicz, prin.

Manhasset, AC 516, PC 6, Nassau
Manhasset UFD | 4-11111
200 MEMORIAL PL 11030 | 627-4400
Maria Petraglia, supt.
HS, 200 MEMORIAL PL 11030 | 3-00011
Michael Keany, prin. | 627-4400
MS, 200 MEMORIAL PL 11030 | 2-00100
Thomas Gilroy, prin. | 627-4400

St. Marys HS, 51 CLAPHAM AVE 11030 | 3-00011
Br. George, prin. | 627-2711

Manlius, AC 315, PC 5, Onondaga
Fayetteville-Manlius Central SD | 5-11111
8199 E SENECA TPKE 13104 | 682-1200
Philip Martin, supt.
Fayetteville-Manlius HS | 4-00011
8201 E SENECA TPKE 13104 | 682-1240
James Chupaila, prin.
Eagle Hill MS, 4645 ENDERS RD 13104 | 3-01100
Anita Pisano, prin. | 682-1280
Other Schools – See Fayetteville

Manorville, AC 516, PC 3, Suffolk
South Manor UFD | 4-11110
151 DAYTON AVE 11949 | 878-4441
Gary Schneider, supt.
Dayton Avenue MS | 3-01110
151 DAYTON AVE 11949 | 878-4441
William Burger, prin.

Marathon, AC 607, PC 4, Cortland
Marathon Central SD, MAIN ST 13803 | 3-11111
Larry Hayes, supt. | 849-3251
JSHS, PO BOX 339 13803 | 2-00111
David Rosetti, prin. | 849-3251

Marcellus, AC 315, PC 4, Onondaga
Marcellus Central SD, 2 REED PKY 13108   4-11111
Paul Bristol, supt.   673-0201
HS, 2 REED PKY 13108   3-00011
Salvatore Vitale, prin.   673-0296
Driver MS, REED PKY 13108   3-01100
Joanne Downes, prin.   673-0219

Marcy, AC 315, PC 6, Oneida
Whitesboro Central SD
Supt. — See Yorkville
Whitesboro HS, ROUTE 291 13403   4-00011
Martin Sweeney, prin.   768-9800

Margaretville, AC 914, PC 3, Delaware
Margaretville Central SD, MAIN ST 12455   3-11111
Gary Wank, supt.   586-2647
Margaretville Central S, MAIN ST 12455   3-11111
Reed Schultz, prin.   586-2647

Marion, AC 315, PC 4, Wayne
Marion Central SD   4-11111
4034 WARNER RD 14505   926-4228
B. Fleegel, supt.
JSHS, 4034 WARNER RD 14505   3-00111
Warren Crouse, prin.   926-4228

Marlboro, AC 914, PC 4, Ulster
Marlboro Central SD   4-11111
50 CROSS RD 12542   236-5802
Edward Sagarese, supt.
Marlboro Central HS   3-00011
50 CROSS RD 12542   236-5810
John O'Donnell, prin.
MS, 1375 ROUTE 9W 12542   2-00100
Kenneth Mitchell, prin.   236-5842

Maspeth, AC 718, PC see New York
Queens Borough SD 24
Supt. — See Middle Village
Cowper IS, 7002 54TH AVE 11378   5-01100
Patricia Ruddy, prin.   639-3817

Martin Luther HS   2-00011
6002 MASPETH AVE # 17 11378   894-4000
Ben Herbrich, prin.

Massapequa, AC 516, PC 7, Nassau
Massapequa UFD   6-11111
4925 MERRICK RD 11758   797-6160
James Brucia, supt.
SHS, 4925 MERRICK RD 11758   4-00011
James Maloney, prin.   797-6110
Berner JHS, 50 CARMAN MILL RD 11758   4-00110
Robert Hackett, prin.   797-6080

Plainedge UFD
Supt. — See North Massapequa
Plainedge HS, 299 WYNGATE DR 11758   3-00011
Jeffrey Hollman, prin.   797-4465

Massena, AC 315, PC 7, St. Lawrence
Massena Central SD   5-11111
290 S MAIN ST 13662   769-2471
V. Sue Davis, supt.
HS, HIGHLAND AVE 13662   4-00011
Kendall Straight, prin.   764-0533
Leary JHS   3-00100
RANSOM AVE & SCHOOL ST 13662   764-0562
Sandra Long, prin.

Mastic Beach, AC 516, PC 7, Suffolk
William Floyd UFD   6-11111
240 MASTIC BEACH RD 11951   281-3020
Wayne Williams, supt.
Floyd HS, 240 MASTIC BEACH RD 11951   5-00011
Robert Feeney, prin.   281-3020
Paca JHS, 240 BLANCO DR 11951   4-00100
Philip Marconi, prin.   281-3020

Mattituck, AC 516, PC 5, Suffolk
Mattituck-Cutchogue UFD   4-11111
PO BOX 1438 11952   298-8460
Lee Ellwood, supt.
Mattituck-Cutchogue JSHS   3-00111
ROUTE 25 11952   298-8471
James McKenna, prin.

Mayfield, AC 518, PC 3, Fulton
Mayfield Central SD, SCHOOL ST 12117   4-11111
William Gokey, supt.   661-5431
JSHS, 27 SCHOOL ST 12117   3-00111
Kathleen Koehnen, prin.   661-7820

Mayville, AC 716, PC 4, Chautauqua
Mayville Central SD   3-11111
2 ACADEMY ST 14757   753-7138
Lawrence Zacher, supt.
JSHS, 2 ACADEMY ST 14757   2-00111
Samuel De Angelo, prin.   753-7138

Mechanicville, AC 518, PC 6, Saratoga
Mechanicville CSD, 10 N MAIN ST 12118   4-11111
Frank Greenhall, supt.   664-5727
HS, KNISKERN AVE 12118   2-00011
Michael McCarthy, prin.   664-9888
MS, 25 KNISKERN AVE 12118   2-00100
Kevin Duffy, prin.   664-6303

Medford, AC 516, PC 7, Suffolk
Patchogue-Medford UFD
Supt. — See Patchogue
Patchogue-Medford SHS   4-00001
181 BUFFALO AVE 11763   758-1010
Frances Candia, prin.

Oregon Avenue MS   3-00110
109 OREGON AVE 11763   758-1100
Anthony Diclemente, prin.

Medina, AC 716, PC 6, Orleans
Medina Central SD   4-11111
1016 GWINN ST 14103   798-2700
David Gee, supt.
HS, 11235 MAPLE RIDGE RD 14103   3-00011
F. Snyder, prin.   798-2710
Wise MS, 1016 GWINN ST 14103   3-00100
Nunzio Maiorana, prin.   798-2100

Melville, AC 516, PC 7, Suffolk
Half Hollow Hills Central SD
Supt. — See Dix Hills
West Hollow MS   3-00100
250 OLD EAST NECK RD 11747   755-8660
Vincent Deland, prin.

Katharine Gibbs School   2-CC
535 BROADHOLLOW RD 11747   293-2460

Merrick, AC 516, PC 7, Nassau
Bellmore-Merrick Central SD
Supt. — See North Merrick
Calhoun HS, 1786 STATE ST 11566   4-00011
Ben Ciuffo, prin.   623-8900
Merrick Avenue JHS   3-00100
1870 MERRICK AVE N 11566   623-8900
Mary Levin, prin.

Mexico, AC 315, PC 4, Oswego
Mexico Central SD   5-11111
5390 ACADEMY ST 13114   963-7831
Robert McGruder, supt.
HS, MAIN ST 13114   3-00011
John Proud, prin.   963-3812
MS, FRAVOR RD 13114   3-01100
John Ruf, prin.   963-3775

Middleburgh, AC 518, PC 4, Schoharie
Middleburgh Central SD   4-11111
181 MAIN ST 12122   827-5155
Walter Doherty, supt.
HS, 181 MAIN ST 12122   2-00011
R. Herodes, prin.   827-5155
MS, 181 MAIN ST 12122   2-00100
Scott Hubble, prin.   827-5186

Middle Island, AC 516, PC 6, Suffolk
Longwood Central SD   6-11111
35 YAPHANK MIDDLE ISLAND RD 11953
Jeffrey Smith, supt.   345-2172
Longwood SHS   4-00001
100 LONGWOOD RD 11953   345-9200
R. Viera, prin.
Longwood JHS   4-00110
198 LONGWOOD RD 11953   345-2701
Levi McIntyre, prin.

Middleport, AC 716, PC 4, Niagara
Royalton-Hartland Central SD   4-11111
50 PARK AVE 14105   735-3654
Lawrence Shanley, supt.
Royalton-Hartland JSHS   3-00111
56 STATE ST 14105   735-3800
Robert Farkas, prin.

Middletown, AC 914, PC 7, Orange
Middletown CSD   6-11111
223 WISNER AVE 10940   343-2233
Charles Skiptunas, supt.
HS, GARDNER AVE EXTENSION 10940   4-00011
Dennis Hand, prin.   341-5900
JHS, 112 GRAND AVE 10940   3-00100
Thomas Buckheit, prin.   341-5400

Harmony Christian S   2-11111
RR 2 BOX 730 10940   692-5353
Richard Clift, prin.
SUNY Orange County Community College   6-CC
115 SOUTH ST 10940   341-4030

Middle Village, AC 718, PC see New York
Queens Borough SD 24   8-11100
6754 80TH ST 11379 – John Iorio, supt. 326-8241
Other Schools – See Corona, Glendale, Maspeth,
Ridgewood, Woodside

Christ the King HS   4-00011
6802 METROPOLITAN AVE 11379   366-7400
Hugh Kirwan, prin.

Milford, AC 607, PC 2, Otsego
Milford Central SD, W MAIN ST 13807   2-11111
Bruce Burritt, supt.   286-7721
Milford Central S, W MAIN ST 13807   2-11111
Gary Turtis, prin.   286-7721

Millbrook, AC 914, PC 4, Dutchess
Millbrook Central SD, ALDEN PL 12545   3-11111
Robert Knapp, supt.   677-8214
JSHS, ALDEN PL 12545   2-00111
Ann St. Germain, prin.   677-8212

Millbrook S, RR 1 BOX 1000 12545   2-00100
Drew Casertano, prin.   677-8261

Miller Place, AC 516, PC 6, Suffolk
Miller Place UFD   5-11111
191 N COUNTRY RD 11764   474-2700
Raymond Sommerstad, supt.
HS, 15 MEMORIAL DR 11764   3-00011
Daniel Nolan, prin.   474-2723

North Country Road MS   2-00100
191 N COUNTRY RD 11764   474-2710
Harry Faulknor, prin.

Mill Neck, PC 3, Nassau

Mill Neck Lutheran School   HND
FROST MILL ROAD B12 11765

Mineola, AC 516, PC 7, Nassau
Mineola UFD, 200 EMORY RD 11501   5-11111
Harry Jaroslaw, supt.   741-5036
MS, 200 EMORY RD 11501   3-00100
Ken Handler, prin.   741-4943
Other Schools – See Garden City Park

Chaminade HS, 240 EMORY RD 11501   4-00011
Br. McAward, prin.   742-5555
Winthrop University Hospital   HSP
259 1ST ST 11501   663-2201

Mohawk, AC 315, PC 5, Herkimer
Mohawk Central SD, 28 GROVE ST 13407   4-11111
Rob Service, supt.   866-7717
JSHS, 28 GROVE ST 13407   2-00111
Daniel Nolan, prin.   866-2623

Monroe, AC 914, PC 6, Orange
Kiryas Joel Village UFSD   2-11111
500 FOREST RD 10950   782-2300
Steven Benardo, supt.
Kiryas Joel Village S, KAHAN DR 10950   2-11111
Steven Benardo, prin.   782-2300

Monsey, AC 914, PC 7, Rockland

Bais Yaakov HS of Spring Valley   2-00011
11 SMOLLEY DR 10952   356-3113
R. Soloveitchik, prin.
Beth Rochel School for Girls   3-11111
145 SADDLE RIVER RD 10952   352-5000
Herschel Leiner, prin.
Kol Yaakov Torah Center   2-UC
29 W MAPLE 10952
National Tax Training School   2-HMS
PO BOX 382 10952
Ohr Somayach Tanenbaum Educational Ctr.   1-UC
PO BOX 334 10952   425-1370
Rabbinical College Beth Shraga   1-UC
PO BOX 412 10952   356-1980
United Talmudical Academy   3-11111
PO BOX 188 10952   425-0392
Rabbi Wagschal, prin.
Yesh Ahavath Israel-Bnos Visnitz S   4-11111
PO BOX 446 10952   356-1010
Rabbi Luria, prin.
Yeshiva and Kolel Bais Medrash Elyon   2-UC
73 MAIN ST 10952
Yeshivath Viznitz   1-UC
PO BOX 446 10952   356-1010

Montgomery, AC 914, PC 5, Orange
Valley Central SD, 944 ROUTE 17K 12549   5-11111
Beverly Ouderkirk, supt.   457-3030
Valley Central HS   4-00011
1175 STATE ROUTE 17K 12549   457-3122
Joseph Dibello, prin.
Valley Central MS   3-00100
1189 STATE ROUTE 17K 12549   457-3124
John Hunter, prin.

Monticello, AC 914, PC 6, Sullivan
Monticello Central SD   5-11111
99 PORT JERVIS ROAD 12701   794-7700
John Lawler, supt.
HS, 99 PORT JERVIS ROAD 12701   3-00011
Robert Harding, prin.   794-8840
MS, 25 SAINT JOHN ST 12701   3-00100
Robert Falcone, prin.   794-6020

Montrose, AC 914, PC 4, Westchester
Hendrick Hudson Central SD   4-11111
61 TROLLEY RD 10548   736-5200
Virginia Rederer, supt.
Hendrick Hudson HS   3-00011
2 ALBANY POST RD 10548   736-5250
Joseph Minadeo, prin.
Blue Mountain MS, PO BOX 14 10548   2-00100
Oscar Scherer, prin.   736-5351

Moravia, AC 315, PC 4, Cayuga
Moravia Central SD   4-11111
50 N MAIN ST 13118   497-2670
A. Beaudry, supt.
JSHS, 50 N MAIN ST 13118   3-00111
Judith Shearer, prin.   497-2670

Morris, AC 607, PC 3, Otsego
Morris Central SD, W MAIN ST 13808   2-11111
Wayne Hess, supt.   263-5110
Morris Central S, W MAIN ST 13808   2-11111
Joseph Brillinger, prin.   263-5110

Morristown, AC 315, PC 2, St. Lawrence
Morristown Central SD   2-11111
GOUVERNEUR ST 13664   375-8814
Garry Billington, supt.
Morristown Central S   2-11111
GOUVERNEUR ST 13664   375-8814
Raymond Kondrat, prin.

Morrisville, AC 315, PC 5, Madison
Morrisville-Eaton Central SD   3-11111
CAMBRIDGE AVE 13408   684-9300
John Stoothoff, supt.

JSHS, FEARON RD 13408 — 2-00111 / 684-9121
Arthur Thormahlen, prin.

SUNY College of Agriculture & Technology — 5-CC / 684-6000
13408

Mount Kisco, AC 914, PC 6, Westchester
Bedford Central SD — 5-11111
PO BOX 180 10549 — 241-6000
Bruce Dennis, supt.
Other Schools – See Bedford

Northern Westchester Hospital Center — HSP
400 E MAIN ST 10549 — 666-1301

Mount Morris, AC 716, PC 5, Livingston
Mt. Morris Central SD — 3-11111
30 BONADONNA AVE 14510 — 658-2568
Ron Service, supt.
JSHS, BONADONNA AVE 14510 — 2-00111 / 658-3331
Gary Mix, prin.

Mount Sinai, AC 516, PC 6, Suffolk
Mt. Sinai UFD, N COUNTRY RD 11766 — 4-11111 / 473-1991
Peter Paciolla, supt.
HS, GERTRUDE GOODMAN DR 11766 — 3-00011 / 473-1991
Edward Walters, prin.
MS, N COUNTRY RD 11766 — 3-01100 / 473-1991
Bernard Creedon, prin.

Mount Upton, AC 607, PC 3, Chenango
Gilbertsville-Mt. Upton Central SD — 3-11111
MAIN ST 13809 – Fred Loveland, supt. — 764-8202
Other Schools – See Gilbertsville

Mount Vernon, AC 914, PC 8, Westchester
Mt. Vernon CSD — 6-11111
165 N COLUMBUS AVE 10553 — 665-5201
W. Prattella, supt.
HS, 100 CALIFORNIA RD 10552 — 5-00011 / 665-5302
Andrew Jones, prin.
Davis MS, 350 GRAMATAN AVE 10552 — 3-00011 / 665-5120
Mario Sclafani, prin.
Franco MS, 455 N HIGH ST 10552 — 3-00011 / 665-5150
Alfonzo Grimes, prin.

Mt. Vernon Hospital — HSP
VALENTINE ST 10550 — 664-8000

Munnsville, AC 315, PC 2, Madison
Stockbridge Valley Central SD — 3-11111
MAIN ST 13409 – Ed Reid, supt. — 495-6512
Stockbridge Valley Central JSHS — 2-00111
MAIN ST 13409 – Ed Reid, supt. — 495-6512

Nanuet, AC 914, PC 7, Rockland
Nanuet UFD, 101 CHURCH ST 10954 — 4-11111 / 623-1430
Dr. David Rightmyer, supt.
HS, 103 CHURCH ST 10954 — 3-00011 / 623-1665
John Burke, prin.
Barr MS, 143 CHURCH ST 10954 — 3-01100 / 623-1263
Peter Bydlik, prin.

Albertus Magnus HS — 2-00011
798 ROUTE 304 10954 — 623-8842
Sr. Helen Boyd, prin.

Naples, AC 716, PC 4, Ontario
Naples Central SD, MAIN ST 14512 — 4-11111 / 374-6381
Walter Zerrahn, supt.
JSHS, MAIN ST 14512 — 2-00111 / 374-6381
Richard Arnold, prin.

Narrowsburg, AC 914, PC 3, Sullivan
Narrowsburg Central SD — 2-11111
BRIDGE ST & ERIE AVE 12764 — 252-3922
Joseph Kilker, supt.
Narrowsburg Central S, 7 ERIE ST 12764 — 2-11111 / 252-3922
Robert Kennedy, prin.

Nedrow, AC 315, PC 5, Onondaga
Onondaga Central SD — 4-11111
4543 S ONONDAGA RD 13120 — 492-1701
Daniel Connor, supt.
Onondaga JSHS — 2-00111
4479 S ONONDAGA RD 13120 — 492-1705
William Rasbeck, prin.

Newark, AC 315, PC 6, Wayne
Newark Central SD — 5-11111
132 HARRISON ST 14513 — 331-2260
Robert Christmann, supt.
HS, 625 PEIRSON AVE 14513 — 3-00011 / 331-5150
David Paddock, prin.
JHS, 316 W MILLER ST 14513 — 3-00100 / 331-5150
Robert Palmateer, prin.

Newark Valley, AC 607, PC 4, Tioga
Newark Valley Central SD — 4-11111
77 WHIG ST 13811 — 642-3221
William Starkweather, supt.
JSHS, WILSON CREEK ROAD 13811 — 3-00111 / 642-8351
I. McGraw, prin.

New Berlin, AC 607, PC 4, Chenango
New Berlin Central SD — 3-11111
SCHOOL ST 13411 — 847-6551
David Burroughs, supt.
JSHS, 17 MAIN ST 13411 — 2-01111 / 847-6184
Michael Virgil, prin.

Newburgh, AC 914, PC 8, Orange
Newburgh CSD, 124 GRAND ST 12550 — 7-11111 / 563-7221
Phillip Leahy, supt.
Newburgh Free Academy — 4-00011
201 FULLERTON AVE 12550 — 563-7500
Thomas Fogarty, prin.

Newburgh Magnet MS — 2-00100
191 WASHINGTON ST 12550 — 563-7744
Louis Tullo, prin.
North JHS, 301 ROBINSON AVE 12550 — 4-00110 / 563-7300
John Mee, prin.
South JHS, 33 MONUMENT ST 12550 — 4-00110 / 563-7400
Vincent Hufford, prin.

Mt. St. Mary College — 4-UC
330 POWELL AVE 12550 — 561-0800

New City, AC 914, PC 8, Rockland
Clarkstown Central SD
Supt. — See West Nyack
Clarkstown North HS — 4-00011
151 CONGERS RD 10956 — 639-6504
Daniel Nicholson, prin.

Newcomb, AC 518, PC 3, Essex
Newcomb Central SD, ROUTE 28N 12852 — 1-11111 / 582-3341
Barbara Kearns, supt.
Newcomb Central S, ROUTE 28 N 12852 — 1-11111 / 582-3341
Barbara Kearns, prin.

Newfane, AC 716, PC 5, Niagara
Newfane Central SD — 4-11111
6273 CHARLOTTEVILLE RD 14108 — 778-7101
Charlotte Sawyer, supt.
HS, 2649 TRANSIT RD 14108 — 3-00011 / 778-0130
N. Kopeck, prin.
MS, 2700 TRANSIT RD 14108 — 2-00100 / 778-0101
Barbara Bradley, prin.

Newfield, AC 607, PC 3, Tompkins
Newfield Central SD — 4-11111
247 MAIN ST 14867 – Ed Sakal, supt. — 564-9955
HS, 247 MAIN ST 14867 — 2-00011 / 564-9955
Suzanne France, prin.
MS, 247 MAIN ST 14867 — 2-01100 / 564-9955
John Boronkay, prin.

New Hartford, AC 315, PC 4, Oneida
New Hartford Central SD — 5-11111
33 OXFORD RD 13413 — 738-9218
Robert Bradley, supt.
SHS, 33 OXFORD RD 13413 — 3-00001 / 738-9214
Edward Martin, prin.
Perry JHS, WESTON ROAD 13413 — 3-00110 / 733-9300
Michael Hargreaves, prin.

Marantha Christian Academy — 2-11111
MIDDLE SETTLEMENT RD 13413 — 733-8837
James Wessing, prin.

New Hyde Park, AC 516, PC 6, Nassau
Herricks UFD — 5-11111
99 SHELTER ROCK RD 11040 — 248-3105
Sidney Freund, supt.
Herricks HS — 4-00011
100 SHELTER ROCK RD 11040 — 248-3142
Patricia Randall, prin.
Other Schools – See Albertson

Sewanhaka Central HSD
Supt. — See Elmont
New Hyde Park Memorial JSHS — 4-00111
500 LEONARD BLVD 11040 — 488-9500
Gerard Conners, prin.

New Lebanon, AC 518, PC 3, Columbia
New Lebanon Central SD — 3-11111
PO BOX 850 12125 — 794-9016
Thaddeus Obloy, supt.
New Lebanon JSHS — 2-00111
PO BOX 850 12125 — 794-7600
Timothy Price, prin.

Darrow S, SHAKER RD 12125 — 2-00011 / 794-7700
Michael Clarke, prin.

New Paltz, AC 914, PC 6, Ulster
New Paltz Central SD — 4-11111
196 MAIN ST 12561 – Ira Glick, supt. — 255-1300
HS, S PUTT CORNERS ROAD 12561 — 3-00011 / 255-1306
Gunnar Hagstrom, prin.
MS, 75 S MANHEIM BLVD 12561 — 3-00100 / 255-1304
Richard Wiesenthal, prin.

SUNY College at New Paltz — 6-UC
75 MANHEIM BLVD 12561 — 257-2121

Newport, AC 315, PC 3, Herkimer
West Canada Valley Central SD — 4-11111
PO BOX 360 13416 — 845-8802
Richard Steet, supt.
West Canada Valley JSHS — 2-00111
PO BOX 360 13416 — 845-8802
Frank Sutliff, prin.

New Rochelle, AC 914, PC 8, Westchester
New Rochelle CSD — 6-11111
515 NORTH AVE 10801 — 576-4200
Linda Kelly, supt.
HS, 265 CLOVE RD 10801 — 4-00011 / 576-4502
Don Baughman, prin.
Leonard MS, 25 GERADA LN 10804 — 3-00100 / 576-4339
Don Zaccagnino, prin.
Young MS, 270 CENTRE AVE 10805 — 3-00100 / 576-4360
Thelma Esteves, prin.

Blessed Sacrament-St. Gabriel HS — 2-00011
24 SHEA PL 10801 – Br. Ramos, prin. — 632-2595
College of New Rochelle — 6-UC
29 CASTLE PL 10805 — 632-5300

Iona College — 6-UC
715 NORTH AVE 10801 — 633-2000
Iona Prep S, 255 WILMOT RD 10804 — 3-00011 / 632-0714
Br. Stoldt, prin.
Monroe College — 2-CS
434 MAIN ST 10801 — 632-5400
Salesian HS, 148 E MAIN ST 10801 — 2-00011 / 632-0248
John Flaherty, prin.
Thornton-Donovan S — 2-1111
100 OVERLOOK CIR 10804 — 632-8836
Douglas Fleming, prin.
Ursuline JSHS, 1354 NORTH AVE 10804 — 2-00111 / 636-3950
Sr. Jean Nicholson, prin.

Newtonville, AC 518, PC 4, Albany
North Colonie Central SD — 5-11111
543 NEW LOUDON RD 12110 — 785-8591
Marya Levenson, supt.
Other Schools – See Latham

New York, AC 212, PC 12, New York
Manhattan Borough HSD — 8-00111
525 W 50TH ST 10019 — 496-2690
Pat Black, supt.
Art & Design HS, 1075 2ND AVE 10022 — 4-00011 / 752-4340
Diana Cagle, prin.
Bacon Vocational HS — 2-00011
345 E 15TH ST 10003 — 475-6875
Claudette Cutlar-Day, prin.
Bergtraum HS, 411 PEARL ST 10038 — 5-00011 / 964-9610
Elise Chan, prin.
Brandeis HS, 145 W 84TH ST 10024 — 5-00011 / 799-0300
Marlene Lazar, prin.
Central Park East HS — 2-00011
1573 MADISON AVE 10029 — 860-8935
Debra Meier, prin.
Chelsea Vocational HS — 4-00011
131 AVENUE OF THE AMERICAS 10013 — 925-1080
Janice Medina, prin.
Fashion Industries HS — 4-00011
225 W 24TH ST 10011 — 255-1235
Charles Bonnici, prin.
HS for the Humanities — 4-00011
351 W 18TH ST 10011 — 675-5350
Ron Bing, prin.
HS of Communication/Graphic Arts — 4-00011
439 W 49TH ST 10019 — 245-5925
Stanley Turetsky, prin.
Irving HS, 40 IRVING PL 10003 — 5-00011 / 674-5000
Robert Durkin, prin.
King HS, 122 AMSTERDAM AVE 10023 — 5-00011 / 874-1202
Stephanie Ferrandino, prin.
La Guardia HS — 5-00011
108 AMSTERDAM AVE 10023 — 496-0700
Paul Saronson, prin.
Manhattan HS for Science/Math — 4-00011
E 116TH ST & FDR DR 10029 — 876-4639
Patricia Cook, prin.
Park West HS, 525 W 50TH ST 10019 — 4-00011 / 262-5861
Stephen Budikas, prin.
Randolph HS — 4-00011
CONVENT AVE & 135TH ST 10031 — 926-0113
Nathalie McFarlane, prin.
Richman HS, 317 E 67TH ST 10021 — 4-00011 / 879-6866
Gino Silvestri, prin.
Seward Park HS, 350 GRAND ST 10002 — 5-00011 / 674-7000
Jules Levine, prin.
Stuyvesant HS — 5-00011
345 CHAMBERS ST 10282 — 312-4800
Abraham Baumel, prin.
Thomas HS, 111 E 33RD ST 10016 — 4-00011 / 532-8910
John Rogers, prin.
Washington HS — 5-00011
549 AUDUBON AVE 10040 — 927-1841
Barbara Hauptman, prin.
Career Employment Ctr HS — Vo Tech
351 W 18TH ST 10011 — 206-0570
SHERRY ZEKOWSKI, prin.
Liberty Mid HS, 250 W 18TH ST 10011 — 3-00010 / 691-0934
Bruce Schnur, prin.
Wadleigh JHS, 215 W 114TH ST 10026 — 2-00110 / 749-5800
Bruce Moody, prin.

Manhattan Borough SD 1 — 7-11110
80 MONTGOMERY ST 10002 — 577-0200
Fran Goldstein, supt.
Beha JHS, 420 E 12TH ST 10009 — 2-00110 / 673-7010
Henry Staiman, prin.
Corlears JHS, 220 HENRY ST 10002 — 4-00110 / 962-7205
Bonnie Long, prin.
Straubenmuller JHS — 3-00110
111 COLUMBIA ST 10002 — 677-5190
Kenneth Baron, prin.
Valle JHS, 145 STANTON ST 10002 — 2-00110 / 473-8152
Pat Fascina, prin.

Manhattan Borough SD 2 — 7-11110
210 E 33RD ST 10016 — 481-1651
Anthony Alvarado, supt.
Baruch JHS, 330 E 21ST ST 10010 — 3-00110 / 674-4545
Marge Struk, prin.
Henry JHS, 333 W 17TH ST 10011 — 2-00110 / 255-6770
Irma Straughn, prin.
Pro Perf Arts JHS, 328 W 48TH ST 10036 — 4-00100 / 247-8652
Claudia DiSalvo, prin.
Sen JHS, 100 HESTER ST 10002 — 4-00110 / 219-1204
Archer Wah Dong, prin.
Wagner JHS, 220 E 76TH ST 10021 — 4-00110 / 535-8610
John Wittekind, prin.

Manhattan Borough SD 3   7-11110
  300 W 96TH ST   10025   678-2800
  Anton Klein, supt.
Joan of Arc JHS, 154 W 93RD ST   10025   4-00100
  Clara Garrett, prin.   678-2902
O'Shea IS, 100 W 77TH ST   10024   4-00100
  William Colavito, prin.   678-2817
Washington JHS, 103 W 107TH ST   10025   4-00110
  Jules Linden, prin.   678-2861

Manhattan Borough SD 4   7-11110
  319 E 117TH ST   10035   860-5893
  Carlos Medina, supt.
DeBurgos JHS, 410 E 100TH ST   10029   4-00110
  Leslie Moore, prin.   860-5854
Jefferson Park JHS   4-00110
  240 E 109TH ST   10029   860-5872
  Joyce Duncan, prin.
Roberts JHS, 2351 1ST AVE   10035   3-00110
  David Vazquez, prin.   860-5838
Robinson JHS   2-00110
  1573 MADISON AVE   10029   860-5822
  Deborah Meier, prin.

Manhattan Borough SD 5   7-11110
  433 W 123RD ST   10027   690-5858
  Bertrand Brown, supt.
Clemente IS, 625 W 133RD ST   10027   4-00100
  Aura Rivera, prin.   690-5848
Douglas MS   2-00100
  2581 ADM CLYTN PWLL JR BLVD   10039
  Lorraine Monroe, prin.   690-5968
Powell JHS, 509 W 129TH ST   10027   4-00110
  Charlotte Graham, prin.   690-5977

Manhattan Borough SD 6   7-11100
  665 W 182ND ST   10033   795-4111
  Anthony Amato, supt.
Hall IS   2-01100
  131ST ST & CONVENT AVE   10027   927-9466
  Miriam Sing, prin.
Inwood JHS, 650 ACADEMY ST   10034   4-01100
  Leonard Latronica, prin.   927-9652
Roosevelt JHS, 511 W 182ND ST   10033   4-00100
  Phyllis Williams, prin.   927-7739
Stitt IS, 401 W 164TH ST   10032   4-00100
  Donald Tippitt, prin.   927-8380
Stowe IS, 6 EDGECOMBE AVE   10030   4-00100
  Elizabeth Pruger, prin.   491-7676
Urena MS, 4600 BROADWAY   10040   4-00100
  Mark Kavarsky, prin.   567-2322

New York City Special Schools
  Supt. — See Brooklyn
Manhattan Occupational Trng Cntr   Vo Tech
  250 W HOUSTON ST   10014   675-7926
  Kevin McCormack, prin.
School for Career Development   Vo Tech
  113 E 4TH ST   10003   477-2090
  Richard Blum, prin.

Advanced Software Analysis   2-CS
  5 BEEKMAN ST RM 700   10038   349-9768
AFS Intercultural Programs   2-UC
  313 E 43RD ST   10017   949-4242
American Academy McAllister Institute   1-CC
  450 W 56TH ST FL 2   10019   757-1190
American Academy of Dramatic Arts   2-CC
  120 MADISON AVE   10016   686-9244
American Business Institute   4-CS
  1657 BROADWAY   10019   315-2400
American University of Paris   4-UC
  80 E 11TH ST # 434   10003   677-4870
Apex Technical School   3-CS
  635 AVENUE OF THE AMERICAS   10011
     645-3300
Bank Street College of Education   3-UC
  610 W 112TH ST   10025   222-6700
Barnard College   4-UC
  3009 BROADWAY   10027   854-5262
Barnard S   1-11111
  554 FORT WASHINGTON AVE   10033   795-1050
  Thomas Tinker, prin.
Bellevue Hospital Center   HSP
  462 1ST AVE   10016   481-7557
Berkeley School   3-CC
  3 E 43RD ST   10017   986-4343
Berk Trade School   4-CS
  311 W 35TH ST   10001   629-3736
Birch Wathen Lenox S   2-11111
  210 E 77TH ST   10021   861-0404
  Frank Carnibuci, prin.
Blake Business School   4-CS
  20 COOPER SQ   10003   254-1233
Boricua College   4-UC
  3755 BROADWAY   10032   694-1000
Brearley S, 610 E 83RD ST   10028   3-11111
  Evelyn Halpert, prin.   744-8582
Browning S, 52 E 62ND ST   10021   2-11111
  Stephen Clement, prin.   838-6280
Calhoun S, 433 WEST END AVE   10024   2-11111
  Mariana Leighton, prin.   724-1980
Career Institute   2-CS
  500 8TH AVE FL 4   10018   564-0589
Cashier Training Institute   4-CS
  500 8TH AVE   10018   564-0500
Cathedral HS, 350 E 56TH ST   10022   3-00011
  Sr. Mary Kilmartin, prin.   688-1545
Chapin S, 100 E END AVE   10028   3-11111
  Sandra Theunick, prin.   744-2335
Churchill S, 22 E 95TH ST   10128   2-00100
  Kristine Baxter, prin.   722-0610

College for Human Services   3-UC
  345 HUDSON ST   10014   989-2002
College of Insurance   3-UC
  101 MURRAY ST   10007   962-4111
College of New Rochelle   2-UC
  125 BARCLAY ST   10007   815-1710
College of New Rochelle   2-UC
  144 DR MRTN L KING JR BLVD   10027   662-7500
College of New Rochelle   2-UC
  5 W 29TH ST   10001   689-6208
Collegiate S, 370 WEST END AVE   10024   3-11111
  Jacob Dresden, prin.   769-6520
Columbia Grammar & Prep S   3-11111
  5 W 93RD ST   10025   749-6200
  Richard Soghoian, prin.
Columbia University   2-UC
  617 W 168TH ST   10032   305-5756
Columbia University General Studies   7-UC
  612 W 115TH ST   10025   854-1754
Convent of Sacred Heart   2-11111
  1 E 91ST ST   10128   722-4745
  Sr. Nancy Salisbury, prin.
Cooper Union   4-UC
  41 COOPER SQ   10003   254-6300
Cope Institute   2-CS
  84 WILLIAM ST FL 4   10038   809-5935
Cornell University Medical College   3-UC
  525 E 68TH ST   10021   746-5144
CUNY Baruch College   7-UC
  17 LEXINGTON AVE   10010   447-3000
CUNY Borough/Manhattan Community College   7-CC
  199 CHAMBERS ST   10007   618-1000
CUNY City College   7-UC
  CONVENT & 138TH ST   10031   690-6741
CUNY Graduate School University Center   5-UC
  33 W 42ND ST   10036   642-1600
CUNY Hunter College   7-UC
  695 PARK AVE   10021   772-4000
CUNY John Jay College Criminal Justice   6-UC
  445 W 59TH ST   10019   237-8000
CUNY Mt. Sinai School of Medicine   2-UC
  1 LEVY PLACE   10029
Dalton S, 108 E 89TH ST   10128   4-11111
  Gardner Dunnan, prin.   722-5160
Day S, 11 E 89TH ST   10128   3-11111
  John Dexter, prin.   369-8040
De La Salle Academy   2-00100
  202 W 97TH ST   10025 – Br. Carty, prin.   316-5840
Dominican Academy   2-00011
  44 E 68TH ST   10021   744-0195
  Sr. Martha Kunesh, prin.
Drake Business School   3-CS
  225 BROADWAY # 2   10007   349-7900
Dwight S, 18 W 89TH ST   10024   2-11111
  William Goodin, prin.   724-6360
FEGS Trades & Business School   2-CS
  17 BATTERY PL   10004   440-8130
Folk Art Institute   1-CS
  61 W 62ND ST   10023   977-7170
Fordham University   4-UC
  113 W 60TH ST   10023   636-6300
French Culinary Institute   1-CS
  462 BROADWAY   10013   219-8890
Friends Seminary S   3-11111
  222 E 16TH ST   10003   979-5030
  Richard Eldridge, prin.
Fuld School of Nursing Joint Diseases   2-CC
  1919 MADISON AVE   10035   650-4460
General Hospital   HSP
  1919 MADISON AVE   10035   650-4455
General Theological Seminary   2-UC
  175 9TH AVE   10011   243-5150
Global Business Institute   2-CS
  209 DR MRTN L KING JR BLVD   10027   663-1500
Hebrew Union College   1-UC
  1 W 4TH ST   10012   674-5300
Hewitt S, 45 E 75TH ST   10021   2-11111
  Mary Yurchak, prin.   288-1919
Hunter College & Campus S   4-11111
  71 E 94TH ST   10128   860-1291
  Anthony Miserandino, prin.
Institute of Allied Medical Professions   2-CS
  106 CENTRAL PARK S APT 23D   10019   757-0520
Institute of Audio Research   3-CS
  64 UNIVERSITY PL   10003   677-7580
Interboro Institute   3-CC
  450 W 56TH ST   10019   399-0091
Jewish Theological Seminary of America   2-UC
  3080 BROADWAY   10027   678-8000
Juilliard School   3-UC
  60 LINCOLN CENTER PLZ   10023   799-5000
Katharine Gibbs School   4-CC
  200 PARK AVE   10166   867-9307
Laboratory Institute of Merchandising   2-UC
  12 E 53RD ST   10022   752-1530
LaSalle Academy, 44 E 2ND ST   10003   3-00011
  Br. Bradley, prin.   475-8940
La Scuola New York G. Marconi S   2-11111
  12 E 96TH ST   10128   369-3290
  Lavina Lorch, prin.
Loyola HS, 980 PARK AVE   10028   2-00011
  Fr. Fox, prin.   288-3522
Lycee Francais De New York   3-11111
  3 E 95TH ST   10128   369-1400
  Gerard Roubichou, prin.
Mandl School   3-CS
  254 W 54TH ST   10019   247-3434
Manhattan Christian S   2-11111
  401 W 205TH ST   10034   567-2276
  Richard Bonifas, prin.

Manhattan School of Music   3-UC
  120 CLAREMONT AVE   10027   749-3025
Mannes College of Music   2-UC
  150 W 85TH ST   10024   580-0210
Marymount Manhattan College   4-UC
  221 E 71ST ST   10021   517-0400
Marymount School of New York   2-11111
  1026 5TH AVE   10028   744-4486
  Kathleen Fagan, prin.
Memorial Sloan Kettering Cancer Center   2-CS
  1275 YORK AVE   10021   639-6561
Mesivta Tifereth Jerusalem of America   1-UC
  145 E BROADWAY   10002   964-2830
Mesivta Tifereth Jerusalem S   2-11111
  141 E BROADWAY   10002   964-2830
  Stanley Bronfeld, prin.
Mother Cabrini HS   2-00111
  701 FORT WASHINGTON AVE   10040   923-3540
  Joan Demarco, prin.
Nativity Mission MS   1-00100
  204 FORSYTH ST   10002   477-2472
  Fr. Podsiadlo, prin.
New School for Social Research   6-UC
  66 W 12TH ST   10011   741-5600
New York Business School   3-CS
  269 W 40TH ST   10018   944-9200
New York City Health & Hospitals   HSP
  346 BROADWAY   10013   391-7407
New York College of Podiatric Medicine   3-UC
  53 E 124TH ST   10035   410-8000
New York Eye & Ear Infirmary   HSP
  310 E 14TH ST   10003   979-4375
New York Food & Hotel Management School   3-CS
  154 W 14TH ST   10011   675-6655
New York Hospital Cornell Medical Center   HSP
  525 E 68TH ST   10021   746-4000
New York Institute of Technology   5-UC
  1855 BROADWAY   10023   399-8300
New York Inst. of Business Technology   4-CS
  401 PARK AVE S FRNT 2   10016   725-9400
New York Law School   4-UC
  57 WORTH ST   10013   431-2100
New York School of Interior Design   3-UC
  170 E 70TH ST   10021   800-336-9743
New York Theological Seminary   2-UC
  5 W 29TH ST   10001   532-4012
New York University   7-UC
  70 WASHINGTON SQ S   10012   998-1212
New York University Medical Center   3-UC
  550 1ST AVE   10016   340-5111
Nightingale Bamford S   2-11111
  20 E 92ND ST   10128   289-5020
  Dorothy Hutcheson, prin.
Northeastern Academy   2-00011
  532 W 215TH ST   10034   569-4800
  Melcher Monk, prin.
Notre Dame HS   2-00011
  104 SAINT MARKS PL   10009   982-0740
  John Joven, prin.
Pace University   6-UC
  1 PACE PLZ   10038   346-1200
Parsons School of Design   2-UC
  66 5TH AVE   10011   229-8953
Phillips Beth Israel School of Nursing   HSP
  310 E 22ND ST   10010   614-6110
Printing Trades School   3-CS
  233 PARK AVE S   10003   677-0505
Professional Business Institute   1-CS
  125 CANAL ST   10002   226-7300
Professional Children's S   2-01111
  132 W 60TH ST   10023   582-3116
  Jeffrey Lawrence, prin.
Ramaz S, 60 E 78TH ST   10021   3-00111
  Rabbi Bakst, prin.   427-1000
Regis HS, 55 E 84TH ST   10028   3-00011
  Fr. Kuntz, prin.   288-1100
Rice HS, 74 W 124TH ST   10027   2-00011
  Br. Casey, prin.   369-4100
St. Agnes HS, 555 WEST END AVE   10024   2-00011
  Br. Potenza, prin.   873-9100
St. George Academy, 215 E 6TH ST   10003   2-00011
  Sr. Monica Lesnick, prin.   473-3323
St. Hilda's & St. Hugh's S   2-11111
  619 W 114TH ST   10025   932-1980
  Lynne Allen, prin.
St. Jean Baptiste HS   2-00011
  173 E 75TH ST   10021   288-1645
  Sr. Patricia Ells, prin.
St. Michael's HS, 425 W 33RD ST   10001   2-00011
  Sr. Kathleen Cusack, prin.   563-2547
St. Vincent Ferrer HS   2-00011
  151 E 65TH ST   10021   535-4680
  Sr. Gilmary McCabe, prin.
St. Vincent's Hospital   2-HSP
  27 CHRISTOPHER ST   10014   790-8492
School for the Deaf   HND
  225 E 23RD ST   10010
School of Visual Arts   6-UC
  209 E 23RD ST   10010   679-7350
SCS Business & Technical Institute   4-CS
  25 W 17TH ST   10011   366-1666
Sotheby's Educational Studies   2-CS
  1334 YORK AVE   10021   606-7822
Spanish-American Institute   2-CS
  215 W 43RD ST   10036   840-7111
Spence S, 22 E 91ST ST   10128   3-11111
  Edes Gilbert, prin.   289-5940
Steiner S, 15 E 79TH ST   10021   2-11111
  Lucy Schneider, prin.   535-2130

Stenotype Academy 3-CS
  15 PARK ROW 10038 962-0002
SUNY College of Optometry 2-UC
  100 E 24TH ST 10010 420-5100
SUNY Fashion Institute of Technology 7-UC
  227 W 27TH ST 10001 760-7700
SUNY Metropolitan Regional Center 2-UC
  666 BROADWAY 10012 598-0640
Superior Career Institute 4-CS
  116 W 14TH ST 10011 675-2140
Swedish Institute 3-CS
  226 W 26TH ST FL 5 10001 924-5900
Taylor Business Institute 4-CC
  1 PENN PLZ 10119 279-0510
Teachers College of Columbia University 5-UC
  525 W 120TH ST 10027 678-3000
Technical Careers Institutes 4-CC
  320 W 3LST ST 10001 594-4000
Techno-Dental Training Center 2-CS
  101 W 31ST ST FL 4 10001 695-1818
Tobe-Coburn School for Fashion Careers 2-CC
  8 E 40TH ST 10016 686-9040
Touro College 5-UC
  844 AVENUE OF THE AMERICAS 10001
    447-0700
Touro College 2-UC
  240 E 123RD ST 10035 722-1575
Travel Institute 2-CS
  15 PARK ROW RM 617 10038 349-3331
Trinity S, 139 W 91ST ST 10024 3-1111
  Henry Moses, prin. 873-1650
Ultrasound Diagnostic School 2-CS
  121 W 27TH ST 10001 645-9116
U.N. International S, 2450 FDR DR 10010 4-11111
  Joseph Blaney, prin. 684-7400
Union Settlement Assoc. Training School 2-CS
  174 E 104TH ST 10029 348-1822
Union Theological Seminary 2-UC
  3041 BROADWAY 10027 662-7100
Universal Business and Media School 2-CS
  220 E 106TH ST 10029 360-1210
Wood School 2-CC
  8 E 40TH ST 10016 686-9040
Xavier HS, 30 W 16TH ST 10011 3-00011
  Fr. Baum, prin. 924-7900
Yeshiva University HS 3-00011
  2540 AMSTERDAM AVE 10033 960-5345
  Rabbi Finkelstein, prin.
Yeshiva Rabbi S.R. Hirsch 3-11111
  91 BENNETT AVE 10033 568-6200
  M. Hyman, prin.
Yeshiva University 5-UC
  500 W 185TH ST 10033 960-5400
Yeshiva University 3-UC
  55 5TH AVE 10003
York Prep S, 116 E 85TH ST 10028 2-00111
  Ronald Stewart, prin. 628-1220

New York Mills, AC 315, PC 5, Oneida
New York Mills UFD 3-11111
  1 MARAUDER BLVD 13417 768-8124
  Debbie Smith, supt.
S, 1 MARAUDER BLVD 13417 3-11111
  Dave Langone, prin. 768-8124

Niagara Falls, AC 716, PC 8, Niagara
Niagara Falls CSD 6-11111
  607 WALNUT AVE 14301 286-4203
  Carmen Granto, supt.
La Salle HS, 1500 MILITARY RD 14304 4-00011
  Russell Murgia, prin. 286-1000
HS, 1201 PINE AVE 14301 4-00011
  Robert DiFrancesco, prin. 284-3355
Gaskill MS 4-00100
  910 HYDE PARK BLVD 14301 284-3311
  Gary Myers, prin.
La Salle JHS, 7436 BUFFALO AVE 14304 3-00100
  Thomas Franklin, prin. 283-1151

American Institute of Music 1-HMS
  PO BOX 1706 14302
Fell's School of Business 1-CS
  2541 MILITARY RD 14304 297-2750
Niagara Catholic HS, 520 66TH ST 14304 2-00011
  Ronald Buggs, prin. 283-8771

Niagara University, AC 716, PC 4, Niagara

Niagara University 5-UC
  GENERAL DELIVERY 14109 285-1212

North Babylon, AC 516, PC 7, Suffolk
North Babylon UFD, 5 JARDINE PL 11703 5-11111
  Margaret Doyle, supt. 321-3226
HS, 1 PHELPS LN 11703 4-00011
  Eugene Cuneo, prin. 321-3233
Moses MS, 250 PHELPS LN 11703 3-00100
  Alice Gordon, prin. 321-3251

North Collins, AC 716, PC 4, Erie
North Collins Central SD 3-11111
  2045 SCHOOL ST 14111 337-0101
  John McDonough, supt.
JSHS, 2045 SCHOOL ST 14111 2-00111
  Gary Nicholson, prin. 337-0101

North Creek, AC 518, PC 3, Warren
Johnsburg Central SD, MAIN ST 12853 2-11111
  Ann Adams, supt. 251-2814
Johnsburg Central S, MAIN ST 12853 2-11111
  Nicholas Savin, prin. 251-3504

North Greece, AC 716, PC 3, Monroe
Greece Central SD 7-11111
  PO BOX 300 14515 621-1000
  Raymond Page, supt.
  Other Schools – See Rochester

North Massapequa, AC 516, PC 7, Nassau
Plainedge UFD 5-11111
  241 WYNGATE DR 11758 797-4410
  Clinton Barter, supt.
Packard JHS 3-00100
  IDAHO AVE & CENTRAL 11758 755-5700
  Andrew Greene, prin.
  Other Schools – See Massapequa

North Merrick, AC 516, PC 7, Nassau
Bellmore-Merrick Central SD 5-00111
  1260 MEADOWBROOK RD 11566 623-8900
  Marc Bernstein, supt.
  Other Schools – See Bellmore, Merrick

Northport, AC 516, PC 6, Suffolk
Northport-East Northport UFD 6-11111
  110 ELWOOD RD 11768 261-9000
  William Brosnan, supt.
HS, 152 LAUREL HILL RD 11768 4-00011
  Theresa Oropallo, prin. 261-9000
MS, 158 LAUREL AVE 11768 3-00100
  Martin Nadler, prin. 261-9000
  Other Schools – See East Northport

Northport Veterans Administration Hosp. HSP
  79 MIDDLEVILLE RD 11768 261-4400

North Salem, AC 914, PC 3, Westchester
North Salem Central SD 4-11111
  RT 124 10560 669-5414
  Charles Wilson, supt.
JSHS, RT 124 10560 3-00111
  Patricia Cyganovich, prin. 669-5414

North Syracuse, AC 315, PC 6, Onondaga
North Syracuse Central SD 6-11111
  5355 W TAFT RD 13212 452-3128
  Albert Furici, supt.
JHS, 5353 W TAFT RD 13212 4-00110
  Vito Testone, prin. 452-3151
  Other Schools – See Cicero

North Tarrytown, AC 914, PC 6, Westchester
Tarrytown UFD 4-11111
  200 N BROADWAY 10591 631-9404
  Donald Kusel, supt.
Sleepy Hollow JSHS 3-00111
  210 N BROADWAY 10591 631-8838
  Gregg Doonan, prin.

North Tonawanda, AC 716, PC 8, Niagara
North Tonawanda CSD 6-11111
  175 HUMPHREY ST 14120 694-3206
  John George, supt.
HS, 405 MEADOW DR 14120 4-00011
  Frank Ruggiero, prin. 694-8022
Lowry JHS, 621 PAYNE AVE 14120 3-00100
  Ralph Hilliard, prin. 694-8030
Reszel MS 3-00100
  1500 VANDERBILT AVE 14120 694-8040
  Gloria Mierzwa, prin.

Northville, AC 518, PC 4, Fulton
Northville Central SD, 3RD ST 12134 3-11111
  Gerald Fitzgerald, supt. 863-2663
JSHS, 3RD ST 12134 2-00111
  Janet Meuwissen, prin. 863-4332

Norwich, AC 607, PC 6, Chenango
Norwich CSD, 112 S BROAD ST 13815 5-11111
  Robert Cleveland, supt. 334-3211
HS, MIDLAND DRIVE 13815 3-00011
  James Walters, prin. 334-3211
MS, MIDLAND DRIVE 13815 2-00100
  Michael McCollough, prin. 334-3211

Valley Heights Christian Academy 2-11111
  75 CALVARY DR 13815 336-8422
  Kenneth Lont, prin.

Norwood, AC 315, PC 4, St. Lawrence
Norwood-Norfolk Central SD 4-11111
  PO BOX 194 13668 353-6631
  Yvonne Watkins, supt.
JSHS, PO BOX 194 13668 3-00111
  James Kramer, prin. 353-6631

Nunda, AC 716, PC 4, Livingston
Dalton-Nunda Central SD, MILL ST 14517 4-11111
  M. Zoller, supt. 468-2541
Keshequa JSHS, MILL ST 14517 2-00111
  Mike Baker, prin. 468-2513

Nyack, AC 914, PC 6, Rockland
Nyack UFD, 41 DICKINSON AVE 10960 5-11111
  Perry Berkowitz, supt. 353-7010
MS, 98 S HIGHLAND AVE 10960 3-00100
  Martin Fiedler, prin. 353-7200
  Other Schools – See Upper Nyack

Nyack College 10960 3-UC
  358-1710
SUNY Rockland Community College 3-CC
  21 N BROADWAY 10960 358-9392

Oakdale, AC 516, PC 6, Suffolk
Connetquot Central SD
  Supt. — See Bohemia

Oakdale-Bohemia Road JHS 3-00110
  60 OAKDALE BOHEMIA RD 11769 244-2279
  Richard Cantin, prin.

Dowling College 5-UC
  150 IDLE HOUR BLVD 11769 244-3000
La Salle Center 2-10111
  500 MONTAUK HWY 11769 589-0900
  Br. Blixt, prin.

Oakfield, AC 716, PC 4, Genesee
Oakfield-Alabama Central SD 4-11111
  7001 LEWISTON RD 14125 948-5211
  Michael Hall, supt.
Oakfield-Alabama JSHS 3-00111
  7001 LEWISTON RD 14125 948-5211
  W. Burns, prin.

Oceanside, AC 516, PC 8, Nassau
Oceanside UFD, 145 MERLE AVE 11572 6-11111
  Elliot Garfinkle, supt. 678-1215
HS, 3160 SKILLMAN AVE 11572 4-00011
  Jess Resnick, prin. 678-7526
MS, 186 ALICE AVE 11572 3-00100
  Enid D'Arrigo, prin. 678-8518

South Nassau Communities Hospital HSP
  2445 OCEANSIDE RD 11572 763-2030

Odessa, AC 607, PC 3, Schuyler
Odessa-Montour Central SD 4-11111
  COLLEGE AVE 14869 594-3341
  Donald Gooley, supt.
Odessa-Montour JSHS 2-00111
  COLLEGE AVE 14869 594-3341
  Michael Johnston, prin.

Ogdensburg, AC 315, PC 7, St. Lawrence
Ogdensburg CSD, 1100 STATE ST 13669 4-11111
  James Kelly, supt. 393-0900
Ogdensburg Free Academy HS 3-00011
  1100 STATE ST 13669 393-0900
  Steven Barlow, prin.
MS, 1100 STATE ST 13669 3-00100
  Rich Lockwood, prin. 393-0900

Mater Dei College 3-CC
  RIVERSIDE DR 13669 393-5930
Wadhams Hall Seminary College 1-UC
  RR 4 BOX 80 13669 393-4231

Old Forge, AC 315, PC 4, Herkimer
Town of Webb UFD, MAIN ST 13420 2-11111
  Joseph Phelan, supt. 369-3222
Town of Webb S, MAIN ST 13420 2-11111
  Carl Klossner, prin. 369-3222

Old Westbury, AC 516, PC 5, Nassau
East Williston UFD, 11 BACON RD 11568 4-11111
  David Helme, supt. 876-4740
Wheatley JSHS, 11 BACON RD 11568 3-00111
  Steven Kussin, prin. 876-4701

New York Institute of Technology 6-UC
  OLD WESTBURY CAMPUS 11568 686-7516
On-Line Campus NY Inst of Technology 7-HMS
  PO BOX 8000 11568 800-222-6948
School of the Holy Child 2-00111
  25 STORE HILL RD 11568 626-3433
  Elizabeth McCann, prin.
SUNY College at Old Westbury 5-UC
  PO BOX 210 11568 876-3000
SUNY Long Island Regional Center 2-UC
  PO BOX 130 11568 997-4700

Olean, AC 716, PC 7, Cattaraugus
Olean CSD, 410 W SULLIVAN ST 14760 5-11111
  John Edwards, supt. 375-4417
HS, 410 W SULLIVAN ST 14760 3-00011
  Louis Chistolini, prin. 375-4419
MS, 420 N 7TH ST 14760 3-00100
  Fred Nichols, prin. 375-4461

Archbishop Walsh HS 2-00011
  204 N 24TH ST 14760 372-8122
  Edward Butler, prin.
Olean Business Institute 2-CC
  301 N UNION ST 14760 372-7978
SUNY Jamestown Community College 3-CC
  14760 372-1661

Olmstedville, AC 518, PC 2, Essex
Minerva Central SD 2-11111
  PO BOX 39 12857 251-2000
  Raymond Ciccarelli, supt.
Minerva Central S, PO BOX 39 12857 2-11111
  Raymond Ciccarelli, prin. 251-2000

Oneida, AC 315, PC 7, Madison
Oneida CSD, 565 SAYLES ST 13421 5-11111
  Frederick Volp, supt. 363-2550
HS, 560 SENECA ST 13421 3-00011
  James Vitale, prin. 363-6901
  Other Schools – See Wampsville

Oneonta, AC 607, PC 7, Otsego
Oneonta CSD, 290 CHESTNUT ST 13820 4-11111
  Hans Dellith, supt. 433-8232
HS, 130 EAST ST 13820 3-00011
  William Pirone, prin. 433-8241
JHS, 130 EAST ST 13820 2-00100
  Thomas Duffy, prin. 433-8262

Hartwick College　13820　4-UC
431-4200

SUNY College at Oneonta　13820　6-UC
431-3730

Ontario Center, AC 315, PC 3, Wayne
Wayne Central SD　5-11111
　PO BOX 155　14520　524-2811
　R. Spring, supt.
Wayne HS　3-00011
　6200 ONTARIO CENTER RD　14520　524-2811
　Ronald Miller, prin.
Armstrong MS　3-00100
　6076 ONTARIO CENTER RD　14520　524-2811
　Thomas Cox, prin.

Orangeburg, AC 914, PC 5, Rockland
South Orangetown Central SD
　Supt. — See Blauvelt
Tappan Zee HS　3-00011
　15 DUTCH HILL RD　10962　365-5504
　Lynn Trager, prin.

Dominican College of Blauvelt　4-UC
　470 WESTERN HWY　10962　359-7800
Iona College　3-UC
　1 DUTCH HILL RD　10962　359-2252
Long Island University　2-UC
　ROUTE 340　10962　359-7200
New York University　4-UC
　10 WESTERN HWY　10962　990-1212

Orchard Park, AC 716, PC 5, Erie
Orchard Park Central SD　5-11111
　3330 BAKER RD　14127　662-6280
　Charles Stoddart, supt.
HS, 4040 BAKER RD　14127　4-00011
　J. Ables, prin.　662-6243
MS, 60 S LINCOLN AVE　14127　4-00100
　Lurly Hunsberger, prin.　662-6227

SUNY Erie Community College South　5-CC
　4140 SOUTHWESTERN BLVD　14127　648-5400

Oriskany, AC 315, PC 4, Oneida
Oriskany Central SD　3-11111
　1313 UTICA ST　13424　768-7824
　Richard Timbs, supt.
JSHS, UTICA ST　13424　2-00111
　Richard Alito, prin.　768-7821

Ossining, AC 914, PC 7, Westchester
Ossining UFD, 190 CROTON AVE　10562　5-11111
　Robert Roelle, supt.　941-7700
HS, 29 S HIGHLAND AVE　10562　3-00011
　Kathleen Zazza, prin.　762-5760
Dorner MS　3-00100
　90 VAN CORTLANDT AVE　10562　762-5740
　Richard Maurer, prin.

Oswego, AC 315, PC 7, Oswego
Oswego CSD, 120 E 1ST ST　13126　6-11111
　Lee Cravotta, supt.　341-5885
HS, 2 BUCCANEER BLVD　13126　4-00011
　David Cowell, prin.　341-5869
MS, FITZGIBBONS DR　13126　3-00100
　Edward Matott, prin.　341-5856

SUNY at Oswego　13126　6-UC
341-2500

Otego, AC 607, PC 4, Otsego
Otego-Unadilla Central SD　4-11111
　RR 1 BOX 451A　13825　988-2516
　Richard Molatch, supt.
Unatego JSHS, RR 1 BOX 451A　13825　3-00111
　Douglas Parker, prin.　988-7065

Ovid, AC 607, PC 3, Seneca
South Seneca Central SD
　Supt. — See Interlaken
South Seneca JSHS, 7263 MAIN ST　14521　3-00111
　Paul Davie, prin.　869-9636

Owego, AC 607, PC 5, Tioga
Owego-Apalachin Central SD　5-11111
　36 TALCOTT ST　13827　687-6224
　Francis Murphy, supt.
Owego Free Academy, GEORGE ST　13827　3-00011
　Bernard Dolan, prin.　687-6230
Owego Apalachin MS, 100 ELM ST　13827　3-00100
　Robert Snyder, prin.　687-6248

Oxford, AC 607, PC 4, Chenango
Oxford Academy & Central SD　4-11111
　S WASHINGTON AVE　13830　843-2025
　Anthony Micha, supt.
Oxford Academy HS　2-00011
　S WASHINGTON AVE　13830　843-2025
　Alford Orcutt, prin.
Oxford Academy MS, FORT HILL　13830　2-01100
　H. Grayson Stevens, prin.　843-2025

Oyster Bay, AC 516, PC 6, Nassau
Oyster Bay-East Norwich Central SD　4-11111
　1 MCCOUNS LN　11771　624-6504
　Francis Banta, supt.
HS, 150 E MAIN ST　11771　2-00011
　Elizabeth Scott, prin.　624-6523
Other Schools — See East Norwich

St. Dominic's HS　2-00011
　110 ANSTICE ST　11771　922-4888
　Frank Brancato, prin.

Ozone Park, AC 718, PC see New York
Queens Borough HSD
　Supt. — See Corona
Adams HS　5-00011
　10101 ROCKAWAY BLVD　11417　843-8180
　Gerard Beirne, prin.

Queens Borough SD 27　8-11110
　8201 ROCKAWAY BLVD　11416　642-5701
　Colman Genn, supt.
Blackwell JHS, 9311 101ST AVE　11416　4-00100
　Matthew Bromme, prin.　845-5942
Goddard JHS　4-00100
　13830 LAFAYETTE ST　11417　848-0001
　Raymond Gregory, prin.
Other Schools — See Arverne, Far Rockaway,
　Rockaway Park, South Ozone Park

Painted Post, AC 607, PC 4, Steuben
Corning CSD, 165 CHARLES ST　14870　6-11111
　George Hamaty, supt.　936-3704
Corning-Painted Post West HS　3-00011
　35 VICTORY HWY　14870　936-3794
　Andrea Schmookler, prin.
Other Schools — See Corning

Palisades, AC 914, PC 4, Rockland

Lamont-Doherty Earth Observatory　10964　1-UC
365-8546

Palmyra, AC 315, PC 5, Wayne
Palmyra-Macedon Central SD　4-11111
　151 HYDE PKY　14522　597-3401
　James Tobin, supt.
Palmyra-Macedon HS　3-00011
　151 HYDE PKY　14522　597-3420
　David Borland, prin.
Palmyra-Macedon MS　3-00100
　163 HYDE PKY　14522　597-3450
　Susan Allen, prin.

Panama, AC 716, PC 2, Chautauqua
Panama Central SD, SCHOOL ST　14767　3-11111
　Raymond Fashano, supt.　782-3245
JSHS, SCHOOL ST　14767　2-00111
　Merle Elkin, prin.　782-2455

Parish, AC 315, PC 2, Oswego
Altmar-Parish-Williamstown Central SD　4-11111
　COUNTY ROUTE 22　13131　625-7298
　Marcia Schwarz, supt.
Altmar-Parish-Williamstown HS　3-00011
　COUNTY RT 22　13131　625-7255
　Bruce Amey, prin.
Altmar-Parish-Williamstown MS　2-00100
　COUNTY RT 22　13131　625-4711
　Stanley Finkle, prin.

Parishville, AC 315, PC 3, St. Lawrence
Parishville-Hopkinton Central SD　3-11111
　SCHOOL ST　13672 – A Kilcoyne, supt.　265-4642
JSHS, SCHOOL ST　13672　2-00111
　Christine Greenwood, prin.　265-4642

Patchogue, AC 516, PC 7, Suffolk
Patchogue-Medford UFD　6-11111
　241 S OCEAN AVE　11772　758-1017
　Raymond Fell, supt.
Saxton Street MS　4-00100
　121 SAXTON ST　11772　758-1011
　Karl Haerr, prin.
South Ocean Avenue MS　3-00110
　225 S OCEAN AVE　11772　758-1030
　Susan Kahl, prin.
Other Schools — See Medford

Briarcliffe School　2-CC
　10 LAKE ST　11772　654-5300
St. Joseph's College　4-UC
　25 AUDUBON AVE　11772　654-3200

Patterson, AC 914, PC 4, Putnam
Carmel Central SD, SOUTH ST　12563　5-11111
　Ralph Bilbao, supt.　878-2094
Other Schools — See Carmel

Paul Smiths, AC 518, PC 3, Franklin

Paul Smith's College　12970　3-CC
327-6211

Pavilion, AC 716, PC 3, Genesee
Pavilion Central SD　4-11111
　7014 BIG TREE RD　14525　584-3115
　R. Westacott, supt.
JSHS, 7014 BIG TREE RD　14525　2-00111
　L. Graham, prin.　584-3070

Pawling, AC 914, PC 4, Dutchess
Pawling Central SD, 7 HAIGHT ST　12564　4-11111
　Thomas Wolf, supt.　855-1320
JSHS, RESERVOIR ROAD　12564　2-00111
　Frank Tolan, prin.　855-1620

Trinity Pawling S　2-00011
　300 STATE ROUTE 22　12564　855-3100
　Archibald Smith, prin.

Pearl River, AC 914, PC 7, Rockland
Pearl River UFD　4-11111
　275 E CENTRAL AVE　10965　620-3900
　Michael Osnato, supt.
JSHS, 275 E CENTRAL AVE　10965　3-00111
　Robert Nardella, prin.　620-3800

Peekskill, AC 914, PC 7, Westchester
Lakeland CSD
　Supt. — See Shrub Oak
Panas HS, 300 CROTON AVE　10566　3-00011
　Arthur Maloney, prin.　739-2823

Peekskill CSD, 1031 ELM ST　10566　4-11111
　Salvatore Corda, supt.　737-3300
HS, 1072 ELM ST　10566　3-00011
　Sheldon Levine, prin.　737-0201
MS, 212 RINGGOLD ST　10566　2-00100
　Anthony Ciaglia, prin.　737-4542

Ohr HaMeir Theological Seminary　1-UC
　PO BOX 2130　10566　736-1500

Pelham, AC 914, PC 6, Westchester
Pelham UFD, 17 FRANKLIN PL　10803　4-11111
　Dudley Hare, supt.　738-3434
Pelham Memorial HS　2-00011
　640 COLONIAL AVE　10803　738-8110
　John Conroy, prin.
MS, FRANKLIN PL　10803　2-00100
　Joseph Longobardi, prin.　738-8190

Penfield, AC 716, PC 6, Monroe
Penfield Central SD　5-11111
　PO BOX 900　14526　248-3220
　Richard Mace, supt.
HS, HIGHSCHOOL DR　14526　4-00011
　Donald Burt, prin.　248-3000
Bay Trail MS, 1760 SCRIBNER RD　14526　4-00100
　Ron Bailey, prin.　248-3610

Penn Yan, AC 315, PC 6, Yates
Penn Yan Central SD　4-11111
　1 SCHOOL ST　14527　536-3371
　Gloria Carroll, supt.
Penn Yan Academy HS　3-00011
　305 COURT ST　14527　536-4408
　Thomas Rakovan, prin.
MS, 515 LIBERTY ST　14527　2-00100
　Edward Bronson, prin.　536-3366

Perry, AC 716, PC 5, Wyoming
Perry Central SD　4-11111
　59 LEICESTER ST　14530　237-6156
　Charles Chester, supt.
JSHS, 33 WATKINS AVE　14530　3-00111
　Carol McMullin, prin.　237-2121

Peru, AC 518, PC 4, Clinton
Peru Central SD, PO BOX 68　12972　5-11111
　Warren Grund, supt.　643-9494
JSHS, 17 SCHOOL ST　12972　4-00111
　Ronald Wilson, prin.　643-2396

Phelps, AC 315, PC 4, Ontario
Phelps-Clifton Springs Central SD
　Supt. — See Clifton Springs
Midlakes HS, 144 MAIN ST　14532　2-00100
　David Dinolfo, prin.　548-5641

Philadelphia, AC 315, PC 4, Jefferson
Indian River Central SD　5-11111
　COUNTY ROUTE 29　13673　642-3441
　Henry Zygadlo, supt.
Indian River HS, US ROUTE 11　13673　3-00011
　Wayne Walbridge, prin.　642-3427
Indian River MS　4-01100
　COUNTY ROUTE 29　13673　642-0125
　Richard Deforest, prin.

Philmont, AC 518, PC 4, Columbia
Copake-Taconic Hills Central SD
　Supt. — See Hillsdale
Taconic Hills HS　2-00011
　GENERAL DELIVERY　12565　851-7261
　Muriel Lanciault, prin.

Phoenix, AC 315, PC 4, Oswego
Phoenix Central SD　5-11111
　400 VOLNEY ST　13135　695-1511
　J. Robert Johnson, supt.
Birdlebough HS, 470 MAIN ST　13135　3-00011
　James McLaughlin, prin.　695-1631
Dillon MS, 400 VOLNEY ST　13135　3-01100
　Mark Montoney, prin.　695-1521

Pine Bush, AC 914, PC 4, Orange
Pine Bush Central SD　6-11111
　ROUTE 302　12566　744-2031
　William Bassett, supt.
HS, ROUTE 302　12566　4-00011
　Kenneth Sherman, prin.　744-2031
Crispell MS, MAPLE AVE　12566　3-00100
　Patrick Mataraza, prin.　744-2031
Other Schools — See Circleville

Pine Plains, AC 518, PC 4, Dutchess
Pine Plains Central SD　4-11111
　RR 1 BOX 86　12567　398-7181
　William Wilson, supt.
Stissing Mt. JSHS　3-00111
　3731 STATE ROUTE 199　12567　398-7181
　Frank Dougherty, prin.

Pittsford, AC 716, PC 4, Monroe
Pittsford Central SD　6-11111
　42 W JEFFERSON RD　14534　381-9940
　John O'Rourke, supt.
Pittsford-Sutherland HS　3-00011
　SUTHERLAND ST　14534　381-9940
　Jerry Sollenne, prin.
Pittsford-Mendon HS　3-00011
　472 PITTSFORD MENDON RD　14534　385-6750
　Kathleen Quigley, prin.

MS, BARKER ROAD 14534   3-00100
   Sherman Craig, prin.   385-6750

Plainview, AC 516, PC 8, Nassau
Plainview-Old Bethpage Central SD   5-11111
   85 JAMAICA AVE 11803   937-6301
   Henry Grishman, supt.
Plainview-Old Bethpage/JFK HS   4-00011
   50 KENNEDY DR 11803   937-6370
   Randolph Ross, prin.
Mattlin MS   3-01100
   50 WASHINGTON AVE 11803   937-6393
   Lawrence Napolitano, prin.
Plainview-Old Bethpage MS   3-01100
   121 CENTRAL PARK RD 11803   349-4750
   Edward Metzendorf, prin.

Stenotopia The World of Court Reporting   2-CS
   45 S SERVICE RD 11803   777-1117

Plattsburgh, AC 518, PC 7, Clinton
Beekmantown Central SD   4-11111
   PO BOX 829 12901   563-8250
   David Walter, supt.
Beekmantown JSHS   4-00111
   PO BOX 829 12901   563-8787
   Michael Retherford, prin.

Plattsburgh CSD, 1 CLIFFORD DR 12901   4-11111
   Arthur Momot, supt.   561-6670
HS, RUGAR ST 12901   3-00011
   John Gallagher, prin.   561-7500
MS, 17 BROAD ST 12901   3-00100
   Paul Dingman, prin.   563-6800

Champlain Valley Physicians Hospital   HSP
   100 BEEKMAN ST 12901   561-2000
Seton Catholic HS   2-00011
   5035 S CATHERINE ST 12901   561-4031
   Sr. Gwenda Cote, prin.
SUNY Clinton Community College   4-CC
   BLUFF POINT 12901   561-6650
SUNY College at Plattsburgh 12901   6-UC
      564-2000

Pleasantville, AC 914, PC 6, Westchester
Pleasantville UFD, 40 ROMER AVE 10570   4-11111
   Frank Gray, supt.   741-1440
HS, 40 ROMER AVE 10570   2-00011
   Don Antonecchia, prin.   741-1420
Pleasantville North MS   2-01100
   63 ROMER AVE 10570   741-1450
   George Cancro, prin.

Pace University   5-UC
   BEDFORD ROAD 10570   769-3200

Poland, AC 315, PC 2, Herkimer
Poland Central SD, ROUTE 8 13431   3-11111
   John Stewart, supt.   826-7481
JSHS, ROUTE 8 13431   2-00111
   Jon Speich, prin.   826-7500

Poplar Ridge, AC 315, PC 2, Cayuga
Southern Cayuga Central SD
   Supt. — See Aurora
Southern Cayuga HS   2-00011
   GENERAL DELIVERY 13139   364-7111
   Maria Fragnoli-Ryan, prin.
Southern Cayuga MS   2-01100
   GENERAL DELIVERY 13139   364-7098
   Robert Honcharski, prin.

Port Byron, AC 315, PC 4, Cayuga
Port Byron Central SD   4-11111
   40 MAPLE AVE 13140   776-5728
   Robert Harris, supt.
HS, 40 MAPLE AVE 13140   2-00011
   Thomas Shannon, prin.   776-4598
MS, 40 MAPLE AVE 13140   2-01100
   Scott Miller, prin.   776-8939

Port Chester, AC 914, PC 7, Westchester
Port Chester-Rye UFD   5-11111
   PO BOX 246 10573   934-7901
   Anthony Napoli, supt.
HS, 1 TAMARACK RD 10573   3-00011
   Albert Vazquez, prin.   934-7950
MS, 113 BOWMAN AVE 10573   3-01100
   Carmen Macchia, prin.   934-7930

United Hospital Medical Center   HSP
   406 BOSTON POST RD 10573   939-7000

Port Henry, AC 518, PC 4, Essex
Moriah Central SD, HC 1 BOX 7A 12974   3-11111
   Harold Bressett, supt.   546-3301
Moriah JSHS, HC 1 BOX 7A 12974   2-00111
   Jack Deweese, prin.   546-3301

Port Jefferson Station, AC 516, PC 6, Suffolk
Brookhaven-Comsewogue UFD   5-11111
   290 NORWOOD AVE 11776   474-8105
   Alan Austen, supt.
Comsewogue HS   3-00011
   568 BICYCLE PATH 11776   474-8182
   Leon Beckerman, prin.
Kennedy MS, 200 JAYNE BLVD 11776   3-00100
   Jack Zamek, prin.   474-8160

Port Jefferson UFD   4-11111
   500 SCRAGGY HILL RD 11777   473-3210
   Leonard Adler, supt.
Vandermeulen JSHS   3-00111
   350 OLD POST RD 11777   473-3333
   Lynn Schwartz, prin.

Port Jervis, AC 914, PC 6, Orange
Port Jervis CSD, 9 THOMPSON ST 12771   5-11111
   Patrick Hamill, supt.   858-3175
HS, ROUTE 209 12771   3-00011
   John Latini, prin.   858-3100
MS, 118 E MAIN ST 12771   3-00100
   Robert Witherow, prin.   858-3148

Portville, AC 716, PC 4, Cattaraugus
Portville Central SD, ELM ST 14770   4-11111
   James Piscitelli, supt.   933-8701
JSHS, ELM ST 14770   3-00111
   George Nuffer, prin.   933-8701

Port Washington, AC 516, PC 7, Nassau
Port Washington UFD   5-11111
   100 CAMPUS DR 11050   767-4326
   William Heebink, supt.
Schreiber HS, 101 CAMPUS DR 11050   4-00011
   Sidney Barish, prin.   767-4351
Weber JHS   3-00100
   PORT WASHINGTON BLVD 11050   767-4484
   Faith Cleary, prin.

Potsdam, AC 315, PC 7, St. Lawrence
Potsdam Central SD, 29 LEROY ST 13676   4-11111
   Gary Snell, supt.   265-2000
HS, 29 LEROY ST 13676   3-00011
   Michael Valley, prin.   265-2000
Kingston MS, 29 LEROY ST 13676   3-01100
   Edward Hanlon, prin.   265-2000

Clarkson University   5-UC
   PO BOX 5725 13699   268-6400
SUNY College at Potsdam 13676   5-UC
      267-2000

Pottersville, AC 518, PC 3, Warren
North Warren Central SD   3-11111
   OLMSTEDVILLE RD 12860   494-3015
   Gerald Kusler, supt.
North Warren HS   2-00100
   OLMSTEDVILLE RD 12860   494-3015
   Michael McSweeney, prin.
Other Schools – See Chestertown

Poughkeepsie, AC 914, PC 8, Dutchess
Arlington Central SD   6-11111
   8 NOXON RD 12603   471-0089
   Donald Rothman, supt.
Arlington MS, 5 DUTCHESS TPKE 12603   4-00100
   E. Fox, prin.   471-0090
Titusville MS   3-00100
   GREEN MEADOW PK 12603   454-5220
   Anthony Celenza, prin.
Other Schools – See Lagrangeville

Poughkeepsie CSD   5-11111
   11 COLLEGE AVE 12603   451-4950
   Matthew Clarke, supt.
HS, 70 FORBUS ST 12603   3-00011
   Theodore Petersen, prin.   451-4850
MS, 55 COLLEGE AVE 12603   3-00100
   William Evans, prin.   471-4800

Spackenkill UFD, 42 HAGAN DR 12603   4-11111
   Michael Muffs, supt.   462-3636
Spackenkill HS   2-00011
   112 SPACKENKILL RD 12603   462-6140
   Scott Sanford, prin.
Todd JHS, 11 CROFT RD 12603   2-00100
   John Pinna, prin.   462-4755

Krissler Business Institute   2-CS
   166 MANSION ST 12601   471-0330
Marist College   6-UC
   290 NORTH RD 12601   575-3226
Our Lady of Lourdes HS   2-00011
   29 N HAMILTON ST 12601   471-4000
   Br. Lavallee, prin.
Poughkeepsie Day S   2-11111
   39 NEW HACKENSACK RD 12603   452-7600
   Anthony Buccelli, prin.
SUNY Dutchess Community College   6-CC
   53 PENDELL RD 12601   471-4500
Tabernacle Christian Acad   2-11111
   153 ACADEMY ST 12601   454-2792
   Edwin Hostetter, prin.
Union College Poughkeepsie Center   3-UC
   249 HOOKER AVE 12603   454-4490
Vassar College   4-UC
   125 RAYMOND AVE 12601   437-7000

Prattsburg, AC 607, PC 3, Steuben
Prattsburg Central SD   3-11111
   ACADEMY ST 14873   522-3795
   James McCormick, supt.
Prattsburg Central S 14873   3-11111
   David Jones, prin.   522-3795

Pulaski, AC 315, PC 5, Oswego
Pulaski Central SD, 7319 LAKE ST 13142   4-11111
   W. Leib, supt.   298-5188
JSHS, 7250 SALINA ST 13142   3-00111
   Frank House, prin.   298-5103

Purchase, AC 914, PC see Harrison

Keio Academy of New York   2-00011
   3 COLLEGE RD 10577   694-2703
   Nancy Russo, prin.
Manhattanville College   4-UC
   2900 PURCHASE ST 10577   694-2200
New York University   4-UC
   PURCHASE ST 10577
SUNY College at Purchase   5-UC
   735 ANDERSON HILL RD 10577   251-6000

Putnam Valley, AC 914, PC 4, Putnam
Putnam Valley Central SD   4-11110
   142 PEEKSKILL HOLLOW RD 10579   528-8143
   Donald McKenzie, supt.
JHS, 142 PEEKSKILL HOLLOW RD 10579   2-00110
   Charles Hill, prin.   528-8101

Queensbury, AC 518, PC 3, Warren
Queensbury UFD   5-11111
   83 AVIATION RD 12804 – J. Irion, supt.   793-8811
HS, 99 AVIATION RD 12804   3-00011
   Roger Marcy, prin.   793-8811
MS, 75 AVIATION RD 12804   4-01100
   Arthur Gottleib, prin.   793-8811

SUNY Adirondack Community College   5-CC
   439 BAY RD 12804   793-4491

Queens Village, AC 718, PC see New York
Queens Borough HSD
   Supt. — See Corona
Van Buren HS   5-00011
   23017 HILLSIDE AVE 11427   776-4728
   Burt Zuckerman, prin.

Queens Borough SD 29
   Supt. — See Rosedale
Nuzzi IS, 21310 92ND AVE 11428   4-00100
   Lewis Trager, prin.   465-0651

Randolph, AC 716, PC 4, Cattaraugus
Randolph Central SD, 18 MAIN ST 14772   4-11111
   Richard Chubon, supt.   358-6161
JSHS, 18 MAIN ST 14772   3-00111
   Terry Dangle, prin.   358-6161

Ravena, AC 518, PC 5, Albany
Ravena-Coeymans-Selkirk CSD
   Supt. — See Selkirk
HS, ROUTE 9W 12143   3-00011
   Andrew Defeo, prin.   756-2155
MS, ROUTE 9W 12143   3-01100
   Robert DeSarbo, prin.   756-2155

Red Creek, AC 315, PC 3, Wayne
Red Creek Central SD   4-11111
   PO BOX 190 13143   754-6304
   Sylvio Albert, supt.
JSHS, PO BOX 190 13143   2-00111
   Charles Paice, prin.   754-6277

Red Hook, AC 914, PC 4, Dutchess
Red Hook Central SD, MILL ROAD 12571   4-11111
   Willard Rock, supt.   758-2241
HS, 52 W MARKET ST 12571   3-00011
   Peter Lawson, prin.   758-2261
MS, 63 W MARKET ST 12571   2-00100
   Donald Germain, prin.   758-8825

Devereux Center in New York   HND
   PO BOX 40 12571   758-1899

Rego Park, AC 718, PC see New York
Queens Borough SD 28
   Supt. — See Forest Hills
Halsey JHS, 6400 102ND ST 11374   4-00110
   Martin Mayerson, prin.   830-4910

Remsen, AC 315, PC 3, Oneida
Remsen Central SD, DAVIS DR 13438   3-11111
   James Rizzo, supt.   831-3797
JSHS, MAIN ST 13438   2-00111
   Anthony Nicotera, prin.   831-3851

Rensselaer, AC 518, PC 6, Rensselaer
Rensselaer CSD, 555 BROADWAY 12144   4-11111
   Stephen Urgenson, supt.   465-7509
JSHS, 555 BROADWAY 12144   2-00111
   Michael Dawkins, prin.   436-8561

Retsof, AC 716, PC 2, Livingston
York Central SD, ROUTE 63 14539   4-11111
   Maurice Dalton, supt.   243-1730
York JSHS, ROUTE 63 14539   2-00111
   Joseph Scanlan, prin.   243-2990

Rhinebeck, AC 914, PC 5, Dutchess
Rhinebeck Central SD   4-11111
   NORTH PARK RD 12572   871-5522
   Joe Bickford, supt.
JSHS, NORTH PARK RD 12572   2-00111
   Thomas Mawhinney, prin.   871-5500

Rhinecliff, AC 914, PC 3, Dutchess
Rhinecliff UFD, MORTON RD 12574   2-00111
   Michael Frazier, supt.   876-6414
JSHS, MORTON RD 12574   2-00111
   Don Bartlett, prin.   876-6414

Richburg, AC 716, PC 2, Allegany
Richburg Central SD, MAIN ST 14774   2-11111
   Robert Klucik, supt.   928-1380
S, MAIN ST 14774   2-11111
   Joseph Decerbo, prin.   928-1380

Richfield Springs, AC 315, PC 4, Otsego
Richfield Springs Central SD   3-11111
  PO BOX 631 13439   858-0610
  Steven Szatko, supt.
Richfield Springs Central S   3-11111
  PO BOX 631 13439   858-0610
  R. Erwin, prin.

Richmond Hill, AC 718, PC see New York
Queens Borough HSD
  Supt. — See Corona
  HS, 8930 114TH ST 11418   5-00011
  Susan Feldman, prin.   846-3335

Shaar Hatorah HS   2-00011
  11706 84TH AVE 11418   846-1940
  Rabbi Spitz, prin.

Ridgewood, AC 718, PC see New York
Queens Borough HSD
  Supt. — See Corona
  Cleveland HS, 2127 HIMROD ST 11385   5-00011
  Myron Liebrader, prin.   381-9600

Queens Borough SD 24
  Supt. — See Middle Village
  IS 77, 976 SENECA AVE 11385   4-00100
  Anthony Lettieri, prin.   366-7120
  JHS, 6656 FOREST AVE 11385   4-00100
  Catherine Powis, prin.   821-4882

Academy for Career Education   2-CS
  5505 MYRTLE AVE 11385   497-4900

Ripley, AC 716, PC 4, Chautauqua
Ripley Central SD, 12 N STATE ST 14775   3-11111
  James Coon, supt.   736-6201
Ripley Central S, 12 N STATE ST 14775   3-11111
  Janeil Rey, prin.   736-2631

Riverdale, AC 718, PC see New York

College of Mount Saint Vincent   4-UC
  6301 RIVERDALE AVE 10471   549-8000
Manhattan College   5-UC
  4513 MANHATTAN COLLEGE PKY 10471   920-0100

Riverhead, AC 516, PC 6, Suffolk
Riverhead Central SD   5-11111
  700 OSBORNE AVE 11901   369-6716
  Dorothy Lipsky, supt.
  HS, 700 HARRISON AVE 11901   4-00011
  James Butler, prin.   369-6723
  MS, 600 HARRISON AVE 11901   3-00100
  Willie Patterson, prin.   369-6759

Central Suffolk Hospital   HSP
  1300 ROANOKE AVE 11901   548-6000
Mercy HS, 1225 OSTRANDER AVE 11901   2-00011
  Sr. Mary Hanson, prin.   727-5900
SUNY Suffolk County Community College   4-CC
  2 SPEONK RIVERHEAD RD 11901   548-2500

Rochester, AC 716, PC 9, Monroe
Brighton Central SD   5-11111
  2035 MONROE AVE 14618   461-9670
  John Eckhardt, supt.
Brighton HS, 1150 WINTON RD S 14618   3-00011
  Thomas Jones, prin.   242-5000
Twelve Corners MS   3-00100
  2643 ELMWOOD AVE 14618   242-5100
  Leroy Welkley, prin.

East Irondequoit Central SD   5-11111
  600 PARDEE RD 14609   336-7000
  Josephine Kehoe, supt.
Eastridge HS, 2350 RIDGE RD E 14622   3-00011
  Alfred Masino, prin.   336-7050
Eastridge JHS, 2350 RIDGE RD E 14622   2-00100
  George Batterson, prin.   336-7100

Gates-Chili Central SD   5-11111
  910 WEGMAN RD 14624   247-5050
  William Dadey, supt.
Gates-Chili HS, 910 WEGMAN RD 14624   4-00011
  Stephen Tisa, prin.   247-5050
Gates-Chili MS, 910 WEGMAN RD 14624   4-00100
  Roger Klimek, prin.   247-5050

Greece Central SD
  Supt. — See North Greece
Greece Arcadia HS   4-00011
  120 ISLAND COTTAGE RD 14612   621-3860
  Donald Ramsey, prin.
Greece-Athena HS   4-00011
  800 LONG POND RD 14612   225-9600
  Robert Lewis, prin.
Olympia HS, 1139 MAIDEN LN 14615   4-00011
  David Fischer, prin.   621-1500
Apollo MS, 740 MAIDEN LN 14615   3-00100
  Paul Schiffman, prin.   865-1000
Arcadia MS, 130 IS COTTAGE RD 14612   4-00100
  Douglas Skeet, prin.   663-3200
Greece Athena MS   4-00100
  800 LONG POND RD 14612   225-4080
  Richard Snyder, prin.
Hoover Drive MS   2-00100
  133 HOOVER DR 14615   865-4880
  Ronald Nigro, prin.

Rochester CSD, 131 W BROAD ST 14614   8-11111
  Manuel Rivera, supt.   262-8378
East HS, 1801 MAIN ST E 14609   4-00011
  Edward Cavalier, prin.   288-3130
Edison Tech HS, 655 COLFAX ST 14606   4-00011
  James Wedderburn, prin.   647-2200
Franklin HS, 950 NORTON ST 14621   4-00011
  Gloria Nowlin, prin.   467-3131
HS of the Arts, 494 AVERILL AVE 14607   2-00011
  David Silver, prin.   325-7594
Marshall HS, 180 RIDGEWAY AVE 14615   4-00011
  C. Robinson, prin.   458-2110
Wilson Magnet HS   3-00011
  501 GENESEE ST 14611   328-3440
  Mary Johnston, prin.
Charlotte MS, 4115 LAKE AVE 14612   4-00100
  G. Alexander, prin.   663-7070
Douglass MS   4-00100
  940 FERNWOOD PARK 14609   482-2000
  Bert Alexander, prin.
Jefferson MS, 1 EDGERTON PARK 14608   4-00100
  Joseph Accongio, prin.   458-2280
Monroe MS, 164 ALEXANDER ST 14607   4-00100
  Rob Pedzick, prin.   232-1530
Rochester MS, 85 ADAMS ST 14608   3-00100
  Wilhelmina Glover, prin.   454-3525

West Irondequoit Central SD   5-11111
  370 COOPER RD 14617   342-5500
  Joseph Sproule, supt.
Irondequoit HS, 260 COOPER RD 14617   4-00011
  Stewart Agor, prin.   266-7351
Dake MS, 350 COOPER RD 14617   3-00100
  Deborah Springpeace, prin.   342-2140

Allendale Columbia S   2-11111
  519 ALLENS CREEK RD 14618   381-4560
  Charles Hertrick, prin.
All Saints Catholic JHS   2-00100
  170 SPENCERPORT RD 14606   429-6010
  Mary Caffrey, prin.
Aquinas Institute   3-00011
  1127 DEWEY AVE 14613   254-2020
  Fr. Noelke, prin.
Bexley Hall School   2-UC
  1100 GOODMAN ST S 14620   271-1320
Bishop Kearney HS   3-00011
  125 KINGS HWY S 14617   342-4000
  Sr. Elaine Englert, prin.
Bryant & Stratton Business Institute   3-CC
  82 SAINT PAUL ST 14604   325-6010
Bryant & Stratton Business Institute   2-CC
  1225 JEFFERSON RD 14623   292-5627
Colgate Rochestr-Bexly-Crozer Seminaries   2-UC
  1100 GOODMAN ST S 14620   271-1320
Continental Dental Assistant School   2-CS
  633 JEFFERSON RD 14623   272-8060
David Hochstein Memorial Music School   2-CS
  50 PLYMOUTH AVE N 14614   454-4596
Eastman School of Music   3-UC
  26 GIBBS ST 14604   274-1060
Genesee Hospital   HSP
  224 ALEXANDER ST 14607   263-5947
Harley S, 1981 CLOVER ST 14618   2-11111
  Richard Blumenthal, prin.   442-1770
McQuaid Jesuit HS   3-00011
  1800 CLINTON AVE S 14618   473-1130
  Franklin Kamp, prin.
Nazareth Academy   2-00011
  1001 LAKE AVE 14613   458-8583
  Olena Lylak, prin.
Nazareth College of Rochester   5-UC
  4245 EAST AVE 14618   586-2525
Northeastern Catholic JHS   2-00100
  125 KINGS HWY S 14617   544-0560
  Sr. Kathryn Wahl, prin.
North Star Christian Academy   2-11111
  332 SPENCERPORT RD 14606   429-5530
  Frederick Fabry, prin.
Our Lady of Mercy HS   3-00111
  1437 BLOSSOM RD 14610   288-7120
  Sr. Barbara Hamm, prin.
Roberts Wesleyan College   3-UC
  2301 WESTSIDE DR 14624   594-9471
Rochester Business Institute   3-CC
  1850 RIDGE RD E 14622   266-0430
Rochester General Hospital   HSP
  1425 PORTLAND AVE 14621   338-4430
Rochester Institute of Technology   7-UC
  1 LOMB MEMORIAL DR 14623   475-2400
Rochester Institute of Technology (NTID)   2-CC
  1 LOMB MEMORIAL DR 14623   475-6376
Rochester School for the Deaf   HND
  1545 SAINT PAUL ST 14621   544-1240
St. Bernard's Institute   1-UC
  1100 GOODMAN ST S 14620   271-1320
St. John Fisher College   4-UC
  3690 EAST AVE 14618   385-8000
St. Mary's Hospital   HSP
  89 GENESEE ST 14611   464-3033
Siena Catholic Academy   2-00100
  2617 EAST AVE 14610   381-1220
  Steve Schockow, prin.
SUNY Genessee Valley Regional Center   2-UC
  8 PRINCE ST 14607   244-3641
SUNY Monroe Community College   7-CC
  1000 E HENRIETTA RD 14623   292-2000
Talmudical Institute of Upstate New York   1-UC
  796 PARK AVE 14607   473-2810

University of Rochester   6-UC
  500 JOSEPH C WILSON BLVD 14627   275-2121
University of Rochester Medical Center   3-UC
  14642   275-8831

Rockaway Park, AC 718, PC see New York
Queens Borough HSD
  Supt. — See Corona
Beach Channel HSD   4-00011
  10000 BEACH CHANNEL DR 11694   945-6900
  Sandra Hassan, prin.

Queens Borough SD 27
  Supt. — See Ozone Park
Rockaway Beach JHS   3-00110
  320 BEACH 104TH ST 11694   945-4200
  Robert Spata, prin.

Stella Maris HS   3-00011
  111 BEACH 112TH ST 11694   634-4994
  Sr. Jane Bannon, prin.

Rockville Centre, AC 516, PC 7, Nassau
Rockville Centre UFD   5-11111
  128 SHEPHERD ST 11570   255-8920
  William Johnson, supt.
South Side HS, 140 SHEPHERD ST 11570   3-00011
  Robin Calitri, prin.   255-8944
South Side MS, 67 HILLSIDE AVE 11570   3-00100
  Lawrence Vanderwater, prin.   255-8976

Mercy Hospital   HSP
  1000 N VILLAGE AVE 11570   255-2201
Molloy College   6-UC
  1000 HEMPSTEAD AVE 11570   678-5000

Rocky Point, AC 516, PC 6, Suffolk
Rocky Point UFD   5-11111
  82 ROCKY POINT YAPHANK RD 11778
  Ray Kwak, supt.   744-1600
JSHS   4-00111
  82 ROCKY POINT YAPHANK RD 11778
  Daniel Galvin, prin.   744-1600

Rome, AC 315, PC 8, Oneida
Rome CSD, 112 E THOMAS ST 13440   6-11111
  Dan Farsaci, supt.   336-0383
Rome Free Academy SHS   4-00001
  500 TURIN ST 13440   338-9200
  Fred Lampman, prin.
Staley JHS   3-00110
  620 E BLOOMFIELD ST 13440   338-9300
  Guy Giamporcaro, prin.
Strough JHS, 801 LAUREL ST 13440   4-00110
  John Vero, prin.   338-9325

New York State School for the Deaf   HND
  401 TURIN ST 13440
Rome Catholic JSHS   2-00111
  800 CYPRESS ST 13440   336-6190
  Sr. Depaul Juliano, prin.

Romulus, AC 607, PC 2, Seneca
Romulus Central SD   3-11111
  5705 MAIN ST 14541   869-5391
  Nelson Wellspeak, supt.
Romulus Central S, 5705 MAIN ST 14541   3-11111
  Barbara Quinn, prin.   869-5391

Ronkonkoma, AC 516, PC 7, Suffolk
Connetquot Central SD
  Supt. — See Bohemia
  JHS, 501 PECONIC ST 11779   3-00110
  Arthur Coccaro, prin.   467-6000

Roosevelt, AC 516, PC 7, Nassau
Roosevelt UFD, 240 DENTON PL 11575   5-11111
  Susan Savitt, supt.   867-8616
JSHS, 1 WAGNER AVE 11575   4-00111
  David Bluford, prin.   867-8666

Roscoe, AC 607, PC 3, Sullivan
Roscoe Central SD, ACADEMY ST 12776   2-11111
  Frederic Philley, supt.   498-4126
Roscoe Central S, ACADEMY ST 12776   2-11111
  George Glantzis, prin.   498-4126

Rosedale, AC 718, PC see New York
Queens Borough SD 29   7-11110
  1 CROSS ISLAND PLZ 11422   740-1000
  Reginald Landeau, supt.
Other Schools – See Hollis, Queens Village, Saint
  Albans, Springfield Gardens

Roslyn, AC 516, PC 4, Nassau
Roslyn UFD, HARBOR HILL ROAD 11576   4-11111
  Frank Tassone, supt.   625-6303
Other Schools – See Roslyn Heights

Roslyn Heights, AC 516, PC 6, Nassau
Roslyn UFD
  Supt. — See Roslyn
Roslyn HS, 145 ROSLYN RD 11577   3-00011
  Mark Weyne, prin.   625-6340
Roslyn MS, 315 LOCUST LN 11577   3-00100
  Richard Holahan, prin.   625-6408

Roxbury, AC 607, PC 3, Delaware
Roxbury Central SD, MAIN ST 12474   2-11111
  Lee Quackenbush, supt.   326-4151
Roxbury Central S, MAIN ST 12474   2-11111
  Leone Schermerhorn, prin.   326-4151

Rushville, AC 716, PC 3, Ontario
Gorham-Middlesex Central SD   4-11111
  BALDWIN RD 14544   554-4848
  Michael Singleton, supt.

Whitman JSHS   3-00111
   4100 BALDWIN RD   14544   554-6441
   Dean Duffy, prin.

Russell, AC 315, PC 2, St. Lawrence
Edwards-Knox Central SD   3-11111
   PO BOX 630   13684   562-8326
   William Cartwright, supt.
Edwards-Knox JSHS   2-00111
   PO BOX 630   13684   562-3227
   Alan Eggleston, prin.

Rye, AC 914, PC 7, Westchester
Rye CSD, 324 MIDLAND AVE   10580   4-11111
   Barry Farnham, supt.   967-6108
HS, 1 PARSONS ST   10580   3-00011
   James Rooney, prin.   967-6100
MS, 1 PARSONS ST   10580   2-00100
   Willis Bott, prin.   967-6100

Cathedral Prep Seminary   1-00011
   946 POST RD   10580 – Fr. Lasala, prin.   921-3994
Rye Country Day S   3-11111
   1271 BOSTON POST RD   10580   867-1417
   Scott Nelson, prin.
School of the Holy Child   2-00111
   2205 WESTCHESTER AVE   10580   967-5622
   Sr. Jean O'Meara, prin.

Rye Brook, AC 914, PC 6, Westchester
Blind Brook-Rye SD   3-11111
   NORTH RIDGE ST   10573   937-3600
   Bruno Ponterio, supt.
Blind Brook JSHS, 840 KING ST   10573   2-00111
   Ron Wilson, prin.   937-3600

Sackets Harbor, AC 315, PC 4, Jefferson
Sackets Harbor Central SD   3-11111
   BROAD ST   13685   646-3575
   Howard Lapidus, supt.
Sackets Harbor Central S   3-11111
   BROAD ST   13685   646-3575
   Robert Wagoner, prin.

Sag Harbor, AC 516, PC 4, Suffolk
Sag Harbor UFD, RR 2 BOX 11   11963   3-11111
   Thomas Roy, supt.   725-5020
Pierson JSHS, JERMAIN AVE   11963   2-00111
   John Luciano, prin.   725-5302

Saint Albans, AC 718, PC see New York
Queens Borough SD 29
   Supt. — See Rosedale
Linden JHS, 10989 204TH ST   11412   4-00110
   Martin Drew, prin.   479-5540

Saint Bonaventure, AC 716, PC 4, Cattaraugus

St. Bonaventure University   5-UC
   GENERAL DELIVERY   14778   375-2000

Saint James, AC 516, PC 7, Suffolk
Smithtown Central SD
   Supt. — See Smithtown
Smithtown MS, 10 SCHOOL ST   11780   4-00100
   Harry Ortgies, prin.   361-2500

Knox School   2-00111
   100 LONG BEACH RD   11780   584-5500
   Clifford Eriksen, prin.
Suffolk Lutheran S   2-11111
   248 MORICHES RD   11780   862-7740
   Rev. Thernanger, prin.

Saint Johnsville, AC 518, PC 4, Montgomery
Oppenheim-Ephratah Central SD   3-11111
   RR 2   13452   568-2014
   Richard Casadonte, supt.
Oppenheim-Ephratah Central S   3-11111
   RR 2   13452 – Paul Carroll, prin.   568-2014

St. Johnsville Central SD   3-11111
   50 CENTER ST   13452   568-2011
   David Lapone, supt.
JSHS, 44 CENTER ST   13452   2-00111
   David Lapone, prin.   568-2011

Saint Regis Falls, AC 518, PC 3, Franklin
St. Regis Falls Central SD   2-11111
   PO BOX 309   12980   856-9421
   Edwin Zacunski, supt.
S, MAIN ST   12980   2-11111
   Ernest Witkowski, prin.   856-9421

Salamanca, AC 716, PC 6, Cattaraugus
Salamanca CSD, 50 IROQUOIS DR   14779   4-11111
   John Hogle, supt.   945-2403
HS, 50 IROQUOIS DR   14779   2-00111
   Ronald DeCarli, prin.   945-2404
MS, 50 IROQUOIS DR   14779   2-00100
   Robert Bell, prin.   945-2405

Salem, AC 518, PC 3, Washington
Salem Central SD, E BROADWAY   12865   3-11111
   Greg Aidala, supt.   854-7855
JSHS, E BROADWAY   12865   2-00111
   Donnalee Francis, prin.   854-7600

Sanborn, AC 716, PC 3, Niagara
Niagara-Wheatfield Central SD   5-11111
   2794 SAUNDERS SETTLEMENT RD   14132
   Joel Radin, supt.   731-7341
Niagara-Wheatfield HS   4-00011
   2292 SAUNDERS SETTLEMENT RD   14132
   C. Pelcin, prin.   731-7356

Town MS   3-00100
   2292 SAUNDERS SETTLEMENT RD   14132
   F. Pierce, prin.   731-7413

SUNY Niagara County Community College   6-CC
   3111 SAUNDERS SETTLEMENT RD   14132
       731-3271

Sandy Creek, AC 315, PC 3, Oswego
Sandy Creek Central SD   4-11111
   PO BOX 248   13145   387-3445
   Jerald Quimby, supt.
JSHS, PO BOX 248   13145   3-00111
   James Beardsley, prin.   387-3465

Saranac, AC 518, PC 2, Clinton
Saranac Central SD   12981   4-11111
   Donald Parks, supt.   492-7451
HS   12981   2-00011
   James Votraw, prin.   293-8200
JHS   12981   2-00100
   Kenneth Kringle, prin.   293-6602

Saranac Lake, AC 518, PC 6, Franklin
Saranac Lake Central SD   4-11111
   99 GEORGE LAPAN HWY   12983   891-5460
   Nancy Will, supt.
HS, 99 GEORGE LAPAN HWY   12983   3-00011
   Gerald Goldman, prin.   891-4450
Petrova MS, PETROVA AVE   12983   2-00100
   John Raymond, prin.   891-4221

SUNY North Country Community College   4-CC
   PO BOX 89   12983   891-2915

Saratoga Springs, AC 518, PC 8, Saratoga
Saratoga Springs CSD, 7 WELLS ST   12866   6-11111
   John MacFadden, supt.   583-4710
SHS, 238 W CIRCULAR ST   12866   4-00001
   Frank Crowley, prin.   587-6690
JHS, 238 W CIRCULAR ST   12866   4-00110
   J. Michael Gonroff, prin.   584-7443

Saratoga Central Catholic HS   2-00111
   247 BROADWAY   12866   587-7070
   Edwin Hammond, prin.
Skidmore College   12866   5-UC
       584-5000

SUNY Empire State College   6-UC
   1 UNION AVE   12866   587-2100

Saugerties, AC 914, PC 5, Ulster
Saugerties Central SD   5-11111
   WASHINGTON AVE EXT   12477   246-4934
   Daniel Lee, supt.
JSHS, WASHINGTON AVE EXT   12477   4-00111
   Robert Potter, prin.   246-4988

Sauquoit, AC 315, PC 3, Oneida
Sauquoit Valley Central SD   4-11111
   2601 ONEIDA ST   13456   839-6311
   Don MacLane, supt.
Sauquoit Valley HS   2-00011
   2601 ONEIDA ST   13456   839-6316
   Kenneth Ford, prin.
MS, SULPHUR SPRING RD   13456   2-00100
   Marianne DeGraaf, prin.   839-6371

Sayville, AC 516, PC 7, Suffolk
Sayville UFD, 99 GREELEY AVE   11782   5-11111
   Joseph Verdone, supt.   244-6510
MS, JOHNSON AVE   11782   3-00100
   Maureen Dowling, prin.   244-6650
Other Schools — See West Sayville

Scarsdale, AC 914, PC 7, Westchester
Edgemont UFSD   4-11111
   GLENDALE ROAD   10583   472-7768
   Nancy Taddiken, supt.
Edgemont JSHS   3-00111
   199 WHITE OAK LN   10583   725-1500
   William Smith, prin.

Scarsdale UFD, 2 BREWSTER RD   10583   5-11111
   Rich Hibschman, supt.   721-2410
HS, 1057 POST RD   10583   4-00011
   Judith Fox, prin.   721-2450
MS, 134 MAMARONECK RD   10583   3-00100
   Peter Telfer, prin.   721-2600

Schaghticoke, AC 518, PC 3, Rensselaer
Hoosic Valley Central SD   4-11111
   ROUTE 40   12154   753-4450
   Jayne Miller, supt.
Hoosic Valley JSHS, RR 1 BOX 8B   12154   3-00111
   Allan Rydinsky, prin.   753-4432

Schenectady, AC 518, PC 8, Schenectady
Niskayuna Central SD   5-11111
   1239 VAN ANTWERP RD   12309   377-4666
   J. McAndrews, supt.
Niskayuna HS   4-00011
   1626 BALLTOWN RD   12309   382-2521
   Ed Carangelo, prin.
Iroquois MS   2-00100
   2495 ROSENDALE RD   12309   377-2233
   Naomi Woolsey, prin.
Van Antwerp MS   2-00100
   2253 STORY AVE   12309   370-1243
   Anthony Brandone, prin.

Rotterdam-Mohanasen SD   5-11111
   2072 CURRY RD   12303   356-5063
   Frederick Betschen, supt.
Mohonasen HS, 2072 CURRY RD   12303   3-00011
   Niel Tebbano, prin.   356-5010

Draper MS, 2070 CURRY RD   12303   3-00100
   Dan Lucca, prin.   356-5015

Schalmont Central SD   4-11111
   401 DUANESBURG RD   12306   355-9200
   Alan Longshore, supt.
Schalmont HS, 1 SABRE DR   12306   3-00011
   Ludwig Wallner, prin.   355-6110
Schalmont MS, 2 SABRE DR   12306   3-00100
   Michael Kondratowicz, prin.   355-6110

Schenectady CSD   6-11111
   108 N BRANDYWINE AVE   12307   370-8101
   Michael Coury, supt.
HS, 1401 THE PLAZA   12308   4-00011
   Eileen Camasso, prin.   370-8190
Central Park MS, 425 ELM ST   12304   3-00100
   Eric Neils, prin.   370-8250
Mont Pleasant MS, FOREST RD   12303   3-00100
   Edmond Stevens, prin.   370-8160
Oneida MS, 1501 ONEIDA ST   12308   2-00100
   Gail Smith, prin.   370-8260

Ellis Hospital   HSP
   1101 NOTT ST   12308   382-4471
Modern Welding School   2-CS
   1740 BROADWAY   12306   374-1216
New Life Academy   2-11111
   150 CORLAER AVE   12304   370-4392
   Michael Kochan, prin.
Notre Dame-Bishop Gibbons HS   2-00111
   2600 ALBANY ST   12304   393-3131
   Br. Staniecki, prin.
Spencer Business Institute   2-CS
   200 STATE ST   12305   374-7619
SUNY Schenectady County Community Coll.   4-CC
   78 WASHINGTON AVE   12305   346-6211
Union College   12308   5-UC
       370-6000

Schenevus, AC 607, PC 3, Otsego
Schenevus Central SD   2-11111
   100 MAIN ST   12155   638-5530
   Peter Bowers, supt.
Schenevus Central S   2-11111
   100 MAIN ST   12155   638-5881
   Marjorie Kelly, prin.

Schoharie, AC 518, PC 4, Schoharie
Schoharie Central SD, MAIN ST   12157   4-11111
   Peter Bassett, supt.   295-8188
JSHS, MAIN ST   12157   3-00111
   Lawrence Clarke, prin.   295-8188

Schroon Lake, AC 518, PC 4, Essex
Schroon Lake Central SD   2-11111
   MAIN ST   12870   532-7164
   Daniel MacGregor, supt.
Schroon Lake Central S, MAIN ST   12870   2-11111
   Richard Kahn, prin.   532-7164

Mountainside Christian Academy   12870   2-11111
   William Bowman, prin.   532-7128

Schuylerville, AC 518, PC 4, Saratoga
Schuylerville Central SD   4-11111
   14 SPRING ST   12871   695-3255
   Leon Reed, supt.
JSHS, 14 SPRING ST   12871   3-00111
   Thomas Martin, prin.   695-3255

Scio, AC 716, PC 3, Allegany
Scio Central SD   3-11111
   WASHINGTON ST   14880   593-5510
   John Dubots, supt.
Scio Central S, WASHINGTON ST   14880   3-11111
   James Watkins, prin.   593-5510

Scotia, AC 518, PC 6, Schenectady
Burnt Hills-Ballston Lake CSD   5-11111
   50 CYPRESS DR   12302   399-6407
   Richard O'Rourke, supt.
Other Schools – See Burnt Hills

Scotia-Glenville Central SD   5-11111
   BUSINESS BLVD   12302   382-1215
   Patrick Dicaprio, supt.
Scotia-Glenville HS   3-00011
   1 TARTAN WAY   12302   382-1231
   James Proper, prin.
Scotia-Glenville JHS   2-00100
   900 PRESTIGE PKY   12302   382-1263
   Anne Sterman, prin.

Schenectady Christian S   2-11111
   SACANDAGA ROAD   12302   370-4272
   Noleen Hathaway, prin.

Scottsville, AC 716, PC 4, Monroe
Wheatland-Chili Central SD   4-11111
   940 NORTH RD   14546   889-4500
   Ronald Mathews, supt.
Wheatland-Chili JSHS   2-00111
   940 NORTH RD   14546   889-4500
   Doreen Decamp, prin.

Sea Cliff, AC 516, PC 6, Nassau
North Shore Central SD   4-11111
   112 FRANKLIN AVE   11579   671-5500
   Michael McGill, supt.
Other Schools – See Glen Head

Seaford, AC 516, PC 7, Nassau
Seaford UFD   4-11111
   1600 WASHINGTON AVE   11783   783-0711
   Dwayne Poll, supt.

HS, 1575 SEAMANS NECK RD 11783   3-00011
  Raymond Buckley, prin.   783-0750
MS, 3940 SUNSET AVE 11783   3-00100
  John Dirr, prin.   783-0730

Selden, AC 516, PC 7, Suffolk
Middle Country Central SD
  Supt. — See Centereach
Newfield HS, 145 MARSHALL DR 11784   4-00011
  Cecil Ramsey, prin.   468-5700

SUNY Suffolk County Community College   7-CC
  533 COLLEGE RD 11784   451-4110

Selkirk, AC 518, PC 3, Albany
Ravena-Coeymans-Selkirk CSD   4-11111
  26 THATCHER ST 12158   767-2513
  William Schwartz, supt.
Other Schools – See Ravena

Seneca Falls, AC 315, PC 6, Seneca
Seneca Falls Central SD   4-11111
  10 FALL ST 13148 – David Giles, supt.   568-5818
Mynderse Academy HS   2-00011
  105 TROY ST 13148   568-9824
  Anthony Ferrara, prin.
MS, 95 TROY ST 13148   2-01100
  Irene Angell, prin.   568-9828

New York Chiropractic College   3-UC
  PO BOX 800 13148   626-2700

Setauket, AC 516, PC 5, Suffolk
Three Village Central SD
  Supt. — See East Setauket
Gelinas JHS, 25 MUD RD 11733   3-00110
  Marion Gaigal, prin.   474-7562

Sharon Springs, AC 518, PC 3, Schoharie
Sharon Springs Central SD   2-11111
  ROUTE 20 13459   284-2266
  Terrance Wissick, supt.
Sharon Springs Central S   2-11111
  ROUTE 20 13459 – Jane Roth, prin.   284-2267

Shelter Island, AC 516, PC 4, Suffolk
Shelter Island UFD   2-11111
  33 N FERRY RD 11964   749-0302
  Marlene Berman, supt.
Shelter Island Central S   2-11111
  33 N FERRY RD 11964   749-0302
  Lydia Axelrod, prin.

Sherburne, AC 607, PC 4, Chenango
Sherburne-Earlville Central SD   4-11111
  15 UTICA RD 13460   674-7300
  Mary Cannie, supt.
Sherburne-Earlville HS   2-00011
  ROUTE 12 13460   674-7380
  Michael Sandore, prin.
Sherburne-Earlville MS   3-01100
  ROUTE 12 13460   674-7350
  Douglas Exley, prin.

Sherman, AC 716, PC 3, Chautauqua
Sherman Central SD, PARK ST 14781   3-11111
  Raymond Cenni, supt.   761-6121
JSHS, PARK ST 14781   2-00111
  Raymond Cenni, prin.   761-6121

Shoreham, AC 516, PC 3, Suffolk
Shoreham-Wading River Central SD   4-11111
  250 ROUTE 25A 11786   821-8104
  David Jackson, supt.
Shoreham-Wading River HS   3-00011
  250 ROUTE 25A 11786   821-8264
  Joseph Hayward, prin.
Shoreham-Wading River MS   2-00100
  RANDALL ROAD 11786   821-8268
  Cary Bell, prin.

Shortsville, AC 716, PC 4, Ontario
Manchester-Shortsville SD   4-11111
  RT 21 14548 – Philip Grajko, supt.   289-3964
Red Jacket JSHS 14548   2-00111
  Scott MacDonnell, prin.   289-3966

Shrub Oak, AC 914, PC 4, Westchester
Lakeland CSD, 1086 E MAIN ST 10588   6-11111
  Patrick Bernardo, supt.   245-1700
Lakeland HS, 1086 E MAIN ST 10588   3-00011
  Brian Gould, prin.   528-0600
Lakeland-Copper Beech MS   3-00100
  ROUTE 132 10588   245-1885
  Susan Rosengrant, prin.
Other Schools – See Peekskill

Sidney, AC 607, PC 5, Delaware
Sidney Central SD, 95 W MAIN ST 13838   4-11111
  Kevin Mack, supt.   563-4277
HS, 95 W MAIN ST 13838   2-00011
  Gary Scavo, prin.   563-4250
MS, 11 PEARL ST E 13838   2-00100
  John Cappello, prin.   563-4225

Silver Creek, AC 716, PC 5, Chautauqua
Silver Creek Central SD   4-11111
  DICKINSON ST 14136   934-2603
  James Mills, supt.
JSHS, DICKINSON ST 14136   3-00111
  Alvin Crowe, prin.   934-2603

Sinclairville, AC 716, PC 3, Chautauqua
Cassadaga Valley Central SD   4-11111
  ROUTE 60 14782   962-5155
  Kenneth Connolly, supt.

Cassadaga Valley JSHS   3-00111
  ROUTE 60 14782   962-8581
  David Abram, prin.

Skaneateles, AC 315, PC 5, Onondaga
Skaneateles Central SD   4-11111
  49 E ELIZABETH ST 13152   685-8361
  Walter Sullivan, supt.
HS, 49 E ELIZABETH ST 13152   2-00011
  Georgette Hoskins, prin.   685-8361
MS, 35 EAST ST 13152   2-00100
  William Palombella, prin.   685-8361

Slate Hill, AC 914, PC 3, Orange
Minisink Valley Central SD   5-11111
  RR 6 10973   355-5100
  Harvey Hilburgh, supt.
Minisink Valley HS, RR 6 10973   3-00011
  Brian Burke, prin.   355-5150
Minisink Valley MS, RR 6 10973   3-00100
  Frank Dimarco, prin.   355-5200

Smithtown, AC 516, PC 8, Suffolk
Smithtown Central SD   6-11111
  26 NEW YORK AVE 11787   361-2206
  Michael Walsh, supt.
SHS, 100 CENTRAL RD 11787   4-00001
  Roger Sullivan, prin.   361-2400
Smithtown Ninth Grade Annex   3-00010
  660 MEADOW RD 11787   366-4709
  Fred Stellhorn, prin.
Other Schools – See Saint James

Smithtown Christian ES   2-11111
  2 HIGBIE DR 11787 – Sal Greco, prin.   265-3334

Sodus, AC 315, PC 4, Wayne
Sodus Central SD, PO BOX 220 14551   4-11111
  Thomas Miller, supt.   483-2331
JSHS, PO BOX 220 14551   3-00111
  Weston Somerville, prin.   483-2331

Solvay, AC 315, PC 6, Onondaga
Solvay UFD, 95 HAZARD ST 13209   4-11111
  Carmen D'Eredita, supt.   468-1111
HS, 600 GERTRUDE AVE 13209   3-00011
  Robert O'Donnell, prin.   468-2551
Hazard Street JHS, 95 HAZARD ST 13209   2-00100
  Terry MacNabb, prin.   468-1421

Somers, AC 914, PC 3, Westchester
Somers Central SD
  Supt. — See Lincolndale
MS, ROUTE 202 10589   2-00100
  Ettore Manfredi, prin.   277-3399

John F. Kennedy HS   3-00011
  54 ROUTE 138 10589   232-5061
  Sr. Christopher O'Toole, prin.

Southampton, AC 516, PC 5, Suffolk
Southampton UFD, 70 LELAND LN 11968   4-11111
  Richard Malone, supt.   283-6800
HS, 141 NARROW LN 11968   3-00011
  Josephine Devincenzi, prin.   283-6800
IS, 70 LELAND LN 11968   2-01100
  John O'Mahoney, prin.   283-6800

Friends World Program   2-UC
  MONTAUK HWY 11968
Long Island University-Southampton   4-UC
  11968   283-4000

South Dayton, AC 716, PC 3, Chautauqua
Pine Valley-South Dayton Central SD   3-11111
  7827 ROUTE 83 14138   988-3276
  Lucinda Miner, supt.
Pine Valley Central JSHS   2-00111
  7827 ROUTE 83 14138   988-3276
  Lucinda Miner, prin.

South Fallsburg, AC 914, PC 4, Sullivan

Yeshivah Zichron Moshe   2-11111
  LAUREL PARK ROAD 12779   434-5240
  James Brennan, prin.
Yeshivah Zichron Moshe   2-UC
  LAUREL PARK ROAD 12779   434-5240

South Glens Falls, AC 518, PC 5, Saratoga
South Glens Falls Central SD   5-11111
  6 BLUEBIRD RD 12803   793-9617
  James McCarthy, supt.
SHS, 42 MERRITT RD 12803   3-00001
  C. Pelkie, prin.   792-9987
Winch JHS, 99 HUDSON ST 12803   3-00110
  Michael Kuzdzal, prin.   792-5891

Community Christian S 12803   2-11111
  William Bidwell, prin.   793-6443

South Kortright, AC 607, PC 2, Delaware
South Kortright Central SD   2-11111
  ROUTE 10 13842   538-9111
  W. Keating, supt.
South Kortright Central S   2-11111
  ROUTE 110 13842   538-9111
  Lynda Race, prin.

South New Berlin, AC 607, PC 3, Chenango
South New Berlin Central SD   2-11111
  N MAIN ST 13843 – Joe Busch, supt.   859-2221
South New Berlin Central S   2-11111
  N MAIN ST 13843   859-2555
  Fredric Johnson, prin.

Southold, AC 516, PC 6, Suffolk
Southold UFD   3-11111
  420 OAKLAWN AVE 11971   765-5400
  Patricia Hennessey, supt.
JSHS, 420 OAKLAWN AVE 11971   2-00111
  Mary Fitzpatrick, prin.   765-5400

South Otselic, AC 315, PC 3, Chenango
Georgetown-South Otselic Central SD   3-11111
  MAPLE ST 13155   653-7591
  Robert Reardon, supt.
Otselic Valley JSHS, MAPLE ST 13155   2-00111
  Anna Deglee, prin.   653-7218

South Ozone Park, AC 718, PC see New York
Queens Borough SD 27
  Supt. — See Ozone Park
Grissom JHS   4-00110
  12110 ROCKAWAY BLVD 11420   843-2260
  John Baxter, prin.

South Wales, AC 716, PC 2, Erie

Gow S, EMERY RD 14139   2-00111
  J. William Adams, prin.   652-3450

Sparkill, AC 914, PC 4, Rockland

St. Thomas Aquinas College   4-UC
  RT 340 10976   359-9500

Spencer, AC 607, PC 3, Tioga
Spencer-Van Etten Central SD
  Supt. — See Van Etten
Spencer-Van Etten JSHS   3-00111
  DARTT CROSSROAD 14883   589-4451
  Paul Zoltowski, prin.

Spencerport, AC 716, PC 5, Monroe
Spencerport Central SD   5-11111
  71 LYELL AVE 14559   352-3421
  Henry Peris, supt.
HS, 2707 SPENCERPORT RD 14559   4-00011
  Edward Groszewski, prin.   352-3421
Cosgrove JHS   3-00100
  2749 SPENCERPORT RD 14559   352-3421
  Edward Przybycien, prin.

Springfield Gardens, AC 718, PC see New York
Queens Borough HSD
  Supt. — See Corona
Springfield Gardens HS   5-00011
  14310 SPRINGFIELD BLVD 11413   341-3033
  Pamela Lemelle, prin.

Queens Borough SD 29
  Supt. — See Rosedale
Springfield Gardens IS   4-00100
  13255 RIDGEDALE ST 11413   527-3501
  Kenwin Lewis, prin.
Tri-Community JHS   4-00110
  14500 SPRINGFIELD BLVD 11413   276-5140
  James Stanton, prin.

Spring Valley, AC 914, PC 7, Rockland
East Ramapo Central SD   6-11111
  105 S MADISON AVE 10977   577-6011
  Jack Anderson, supt.
Ramapo SHS, 400 VIOLA RD 10977   4-00001
  Martin Goldmeer, prin.   577-6402
SHS, ROUTE 59 10977   3-00001
  Sydney Farber, prin.   577-6505
Kakiat JHS, 465 VIOLA RD 10977   2-00110
  Gerald Pollack, prin.   577-6104
Other Schools – See Chestnut Ridge, Suffern

Bais Medrash L'Torah Rabbinical College   2-UC
  118 W CENTRAL AVE 10977
Green Meadow Waldorf S   2-11111
  303 HUNGRY HOLLOW RD 10977   356-2556
  David Sloan, prin.
Gruss School for Girls   3-11111
  15 ROOSEVELT AVE 10977   354-7555
  Zlata Hoffman, prin.
SUNY Rockland Community College   3-CC
  766 N MAIN ST 10977   352-5535
SUNY Rockland Community College   3-CC
  185 N MAIN ST 10977   352-5535
Yeshiva of New Square S   3-11111
  766 N MAIN ST 10977   354-7555
  M. Neustadt, prin.

Springville, AC 716, PC 5, Erie
Springville-Griff Institute SD   4-11111
  307 NEWMAN ST 14141   592-3236
  William Nennstiel, supt.
Griffith Institute HS   3-00011
  290 N BUFFALO ST 14141   592-3237
  Charles Vredenburg, prin.
Griffith Institute MS   3-01100
  267 NEWMAN ST 14141   592-3270
  Stephen Bell, prin.

Staatsburg-on-Hudson, AC 914, PC 4, Dutchess

Anderson S, 875 ROUTE 9 12580   2-00111
  Frank Mulhern, prin.   889-4046

Stamford, AC 607, PC 4, Delaware
Stamford Central SD, 1 RIVER ST 12167   2-11111
  William Lister, supt.   652-7301
Stamford Central S, 1 RIVER ST 12167   3-11111
  Joe Beck, prin.   652-7301

Star Lake, AC 315, PC 4, St. Lawrence
Clifton-Fine Central SD   3-11111
  PO BOX 75   13690   848-3335
  Donald Belcer, supt.
Clifton-Fine JSHS, MAIN ST   13690   2-00111
  Lonnie Avery, prin.   848-3333

Staten Island, AC 718, PC see New York
New York City Special Schools
  Supt. — See Brooklyn
Richmond Career & Vo Ctr   Vo Tech
  MOUNT LORETTO   10309   984-1526
  STEPHEN DICARLO, prin.
Richmond Occupational Training Ctr   Vo Tech
  155 TOMPKINS   10304   273-8622
  MARY MCINERNEY, prin.

Richmond Borough HSD
  Supt. — See Brooklyn
Curtis HS, 105 HAMILTON AVE   10301   4-00011
  Edward Seto, prin.   273-7380
McKee Voc. Tech. HS   3-00011
  290 SAINT MARKS PL   10301   273-4000
  Jonathan Greene, prin.
New Dorp HS, 465 NEW DORP LN   10306   4-00011
  Elizabeth Sciabarra, prin.   667-8686
Port Richmond HS, 45 INNIS ST   10302   4-00011
  Suzanne Weber, prin.   273-3600
Staten Island Tech HS   3-00011
  485 CLAWSON ST   10306   667-5725
  Nicholas Bilotti, prin.
Tottenville HS, 100 LUTEN AVE   10312   5-00011
  Michael Marotta, prin.   356-2220
Wagner HS, 1200 MANOR RD   10314   4-00011
  Ralph Musco, prin.   698-4200

Richmond Borough SD 31   8-11100
  211 DANIEL LOW TER   10301   447-3300
  Louis DeSario, supt.
Barnes IS, 225 CLEVELAND AVE   10308   4-00100
  Maureen O'Brien, prin.   356-4200
Bernstein IS   3-00100
  1270 HUGUENOT AVE   10312   356-2314
  Joseph Corriero, prin.
Dreyfus IS, 101 WARREN ST   10304   3-00100
  Bertram Levinson, prin.   727-6040
Egbert IS, 333 MIDLAND AVE   10306   3-00100
  Allan Newman, prin.   987-5336
Laurie IS, 33 FERNDALE AVE   10314   4-00100
  Barb Glassman, prin.   698-5757
Markham IS, 20 HOUSTON ST   10302   4-00100
  Ed Barbini, prin.   981-0521
Morris IS, 445 CASTLETON AVE   10301   4-00100
  Andrew Monahan, prin.   727-8481
Paulo IS, 455 HUGUENOT AVE   10312   4-00100
  Anthony Polomene, prin.   356-0130
Prall IS, 11 CLOVE LAKE PL   10310   3-00100
  Greg Gallo, prin.   981-8800
Totten IS, 34 ACADEMY AVE   10307   3-00100
  Frank Moschella, prin.   984-0772

Bayley Seton Hospital   HSP
  75 VANDERBILT AVE   10304   390-6007
CUNY College of Staten Island   7-UC
  130 STUYVESANT PL   10301   390-7733
CUNY College of Staten Island   3-UC
  715 OCEAN TER   10301   390-7664
Drake Business School   3-CS
  25 VICTORY BLVD   10301   447-1515
Francis HS, 4240 AMBOY RD   10308   2-00111
  Barbara Gil, prin.   967-0400
Monsignor Farrell HS   4-00011
  2900 AMBOY RD   10306   987-2900
  Fr. Bergin, prin.
Moore Catholic HS   3-00011
  100 MERRILL AVE   10314   761-9200
  Fr. Kelly, prin.
Notre Dame Academy   2-00011
  134 HOWARD AVE   10301   447-8878
  Sr. Maria Cassano, prin.
St. John's University   4-UC
  300 HOWARD AVE   10301   447-4343
St. John's Villa Academy   2-00111
  26 LANDIS AVE   10305   442-6240
  Sr. Rita Carey, prin.
St. Joseph HS, 5150 HYLAN BLVD   10312   4-00011
  Fr. Ansaldi, prin.   984-6500
St. Joseph Hill Academy   2-00111
  850 HYLAN BLVD   10305   447-1374
  Sr. Mary Charlotte, prin.
St. Peter's Boys HS   3-00011
  200 CLINTON AVE   10301   447-1676
  John Fodera, prin.
St. Peter's Girls HS   2-00011
  300 RICHMOND TER   10301   447-0304
  Sr. Bernardine Denning, prin.
St. Vincent's Medical Center   HSP
  2 GRIDLEY AVE   10303   876-1300
Staten Island Academy   2-11111
  715 TODT HILL RD   10304   987-8100
  Graham Brown, prin.
Wagner College   4-UC
  631 HOWARD AVE   10301   390-3100
Yeshiva & Mesivta Tiferes Torah S   2-00011
  641 DELAFIELD AVE   10310   447-1151
  Er Friedman, prin.

Stillwater, AC 518, PC 4, Saratoga
Stillwater Central SD   4-11111
  N HUDSON AVE   12170   664-8656
  John Clark, supt.

HS, N HUDSON AVE   12170   2-00011
  Douglas Leavens, prin.   664-6141
MS, N HUDSON AVE   12170   2-00100
  Jacqueline Going, prin.   664-2416

Stone Ridge, AC 914, PC 3, Ulster

SUNY Ulster County Community College   5-CC
  12484   687-7621

Stony Brook, AC 516, PC 7, Suffolk

Stony Brook S, 11 CEDAR ST   11790   2-00111
  Judith Oulund, prin.   751-1800
SUNY at Stony Brook   11794   7-UC
  689-6000
SUNY Health Science Center   11790   4-UC
  632-6265

Stony Point, AC 914, PC 7, Rockland
Haverstraw-Stony Point Central SD
  Supt. — See Garnerville
Farley MS, 140 CENTRAL DR   10980   3-00100
  Eugene White, prin.   942-3200

Suffern, AC 914, PC 7, Rockland
East Ramapo Central SD
  Supt. — See Spring Valley
Pomona JHS, 101 POMONA RD   10901   3-00110
  David Brown, prin.   577-6204

Ramapo Central SD
  Supt. — See Hillburn
HS, 45 VIOLA RD   10901   4-00011
  Patrick Faherty, prin.   357-3800
JHS, 60 HEMION RD   10901   3-00100
  Richard Kaufman, prin.   357-7400

SUNY Rockland Community College   6-CC
  145 COLLEGE RD   10901   356-4650
Yeshiva Chofetz Chaim S   2-11111
  24 HIGHVIEW RD   10901   357-9821
  Y. Ginsberg, prin.

Syosset, AC 516, PC 7, Nassau
Syosset Central SD, 99 PELL LN   11791   6-11111
  Carole Hankin, supt.   364-5605
HS, 70 SOUTHWOODS RD   11791   4-00011
  Jorge Schneider, prin.   364-5675
South Woods MS, 99 PELL LN   11791   3-00100
  James Dougherty, prin.   364-5663
Thompson MS, 98 ANN DR   11791   3-00100
  James Collins, prin.   364-5760

Our Lady of Mercy Academy   2-00011
  999 CONVENT RD   11791   921-1047
  Sr. Madelaine Moore, prin.

Syracuse, AC 315, PC 9, Onondaga
Syracuse CSD, 725 HARRISON ST   13210   7-11111
  Henry Williams, supt.   435-4161
Corcoran HS   4-00011
  919 GLENWOOD AVE   13207   435-4321
  Yvonne Young, prin.
Fowler HS, 227 MAGNOLIA ST   13204   4-00011
  Ronald Spadafora, prin.   435-4376
Henninger HS, 600 ROBINSON ST   13206   4-00011
  Anthony Dibello, prin.   435-4343
Nottingham HS   4-00011
  3100 E GENESEE ST   13224   435-4380
  Granger Ward, prin.
Clary MS, AMIDON DR   13205   3-00100
  Thomas Kenah, prin.   435-4411
Grant MS, 2400 GRANT BLVD   13208   3-00100
  Jean Phillips, prin.   435-4433
Levy MS, 100 FELLOWS AVE   13210   3-00100
  Donnell Hicks, prin.   435-4444
Lincoln MS, 1613 JAMES ST   13203   3-00100
  F. Beyer, prin.   435-4450
Shea MS, 1607 S GEDDES ST   13207   3-00100
  Josephine Crisafulli, prin.   435-4480

Westhill Central SD   4-11111
  4501 ONONDAGA BLVD   13219   476-5329
  Mark De Sanctis, supt.
Westhill HS   3-00011
  4501 ONONDAGA BLVD   13219   475-1621
  Richard Cavallaro, prin.
Onondaga Hill MS   2-00100
  4860 ONONDAGA RD   13215   492-1736
  Douglas Hutson, prin.

All Saints JHS, 301 VALLEY DR   13207   1-00100
  Joan Smith, prin.   472-7488
Bishop Ludden HS, 815 FAY RD   13219   2-00011
  Dennis Meehan, prin.   468-2591
Bishop Ludden JHS, 815 FAY RD   13219   2-00100
  Dennis Meehan, prin.   468-2591
Bryant & Stratton Business Institute   4-CC
  953 JAMES ST   13203   472-6603
Central City Business Institute   4-CC
  224 HARRISON ST   13202   800-945-2224
Christian Brothers Academy   3-00111
  6245 RANDALL RD   13214   446-5960
  Br. McCabe, prin.
Crouse-Irving Memorial Hospital   HSP
  736 IRVING AVE   13210   470-7481
Faith Heritage S   3-11111
  3740 MIDLAND AVE   13205   469-7777
  Paul Foster, prin.
Le Moyne College   4-UC
  1419 SALT SPRINGS RD   13214   800-333-4733

Living Word Academy   2-11111
  6101 COURT STREET RD   13206   437-6744
  Louis Levanti, prin.
St. Josephs Hospital & Health Center   2-HSP
  206 PROSPECT AVE   13203   448-5046
Simmons Institute of Funeral Service   2-CS
  1828 SOUTH AVE   13207   475-5142
SUNY College Environ. Science - Forestry   4-UC
  1 FORESTRY DR   13210   800-777-7373
SUNY Health Science Center   4-UC
  155 ELIZABETH BLACKWELL ST   13210
  464-5540
SUNY Onondaga Community College   6-CC
  4941 ONONDAGA RD   13215   469-7741
Syracuse University   13244   7-UC
  443-1870

Tannersville, AC 518, PC 2, Greene
Hunter-Tannersville Central SD   2-11111
  MAIN ST   12485 – Joe Pezak, supt.   589-5400
Hunter-Tannersville JSHS   12485   2-00111
  Jon Van Eyk, prin.   589-5880

Tarrytown, AC 914, PC 7, Westchester

Hackley School   3-11111
  293 BENEDICT AVE   10591   631-0128
  Peter Gibbon, prin.
Marymount College   4-UC
  100 MARYMOUNT AVE   10591   631-3200

Thiells, AC 914, PC 6, Rockland
Haverstraw-Stony Point Central SD
  Supt. — See Garnerville
North Rockland HS   4-00011
  106 HAMMOND RD   10984   942-3300
  Israel Bordainick, prin.

Thornwood, AC 914, PC 6, Westchester
Mt. Pleasant Central SD   4-11111
  825 WESTLAKE DR   10594   769-5500
  J. Whearty, supt.
Westlake HS, 825 WESTLAKE DR   10594   2-00011
  James Mullin, prin.   769-8311
Westlake MS, 825 WESTLAKE DR   10594   2-00100
  N. Castrataro, prin.   769-8541

Ticonderoga, AC 518, PC 5, Essex
Ticonderoga Central SD   4-11111
  351 AMHERST AVE   12883   585-6674
  Rob Collins, supt.
HS, CALKINS PL   12883   2-00011
  Ralph Corbo, prin.   585-6661
MS, ALEXANDRIA AVE   12883   2-00100
  Michael Vigliotti, prin.   585-7442

SUNY North Country Community College   3-CC
  PO BOX 311   12883   585-4454

Tioga Center, AC 607, PC 3, Tioga
Tioga Central SD, 5TH AVE   13845   4-11111
  Beverly Ouderkirk, supt.   687-9233
Tioga HS, 27 5TH AVE   13845   2-00011
  Patrick Dougherty, prin.   687-8001
Tioga MS, 27 5TH AVE   13845   2-01100
  Robert James, prin.   687-8004

Tonawanda, AC 716, PC 8, Erie
Kenmore UFD
  Supt. — See Kenmore
Kenmore East HS, 350 FRIES RD   14150   4-00011
  Barbara Field, prin.   874-8402

Tonawanda CSD, 202 BROAD ST   14150   5-11111
  Carl Mangee, supt.   694-7784
HS, 150 HINDS ST   14150   3-00011
  Patrick Slavin, prin.   694-7670
JHS, HINDS & FLETCHER ST   14150   2-00100
  Richard Catlin, prin.   694-7660

Cardinal O'Hara HS   2-00011
  39 OHARA RD   14150   695-2600
  James Walline, prin.

Troy, AC 518, PC 8, Rensselaer
Brunswick Central SD   4-11111
  RR 3 BOX 200A   12180   279-4602
  Barbara Nagler, supt.
Tamarac HS, RR 3 BOX 200A   12180   2-00011
  Donald Newell, prin.   279-4620
Tamarac MS, RR 3 BOX 200A   12180   2-00100
  William Gilbert, prin.   279-4630

Lansingburgh CSD, 576 5TH AVE   12182   4-11111
  Lee Bordick, supt.   235-4404
Lansingburgh HS, 320 7TH AVE   12182   3-00011
  Warren Gemmill, prin.   235-1910
Knickerbacker MS, 320 7TH AVE   12182   3-00100
  Howard Lustig, prin.   235-1910

Troy CSD, 1728 TIBBITS AVE   12180   6-11111
  Mario Scalzi, supt.   271-5210
HS, 1950 BURDETT AVE   12180   4-00011
  Armand Reo, prin.   271-5300
Doyle MS, 1976 BURDETT AVE   12180   4-00100
  James Gorman, prin.   271-5350

Catholic Central HS, 625 7TH AVE   12182   3-00111
  Sr. Carolyn Schanz, prin.   235-7100
Emma Willard School   2-00011
  285 PAWLING AVE   12180   274-4440
  Robin Robertson, prin.

La Salle Institute
 174 WILLIAMS RD 12180 3-00111
 Br. Romond, prin. 283-2500
Rensselaer Polytechnic Institute 12180 6-UC
  276-6000
Russell Sage College 4-UC
 51 1ST ST 12180 270-2000
Samaritan Hospital HSP
 2215 BURDETT AVE 12180 271-3285
SUNY Hudson Valley Community College 6-CC
 80 VANDENBURGH AVE 12180 283-1100

Trumansburg, AC 607, PC 4, Tompkins
Trumansburg Central SD 4-11111
 100 WHIG ST 14886 387-7551
 John Delaney, supt.
Dickerson HS, 100 WHIG ST 14886 2-00011
 John Furey, prin. 387-7551
Doig MS, 100 WHIG ST 14886 2-01100
 Gary Astles, prin. 387-7551

Tully, AC 315, PC 3, Onondaga
Tully Central SD, 20 STATE ST 13159 4-11111
 Daniel Porter, supt. 696-6200
JSHS, 6 ELM ST 13159 3-00111
 Gary Heymann, prin. 696-6235

Tupper Lake, AC 518, PC 5, Franklin
Tupper Lake Central SD 4-11111
 25 CHENEY AVE 12986 359-3371
 Charles Button, supt.
JSHS, 25 CHENEY AVE 12986 3-00111
 James Ellis, prin. 359-3322

Turin, AC 315, PC 2, Lewis
South Lewis Central SD 4-11111
 JR-SR HS BLDG 13473 348-8471
 Jack Mylan, supt.
South Lewis JSHS, EAST ROAD 13473 3-00111
 David Daniels, prin. 348-8421

Tuxedo Park, AC 914, PC 3, Orange
Tuxedo UFD, ROUTE 17 10987 2-11111
 Herbert Fliegner, supt. 351-4786
Tuxedo JSHS, ROUTE 17 10987 2-00111
 Carmine Antonelli, prin. 351-4786

Uniondale, AC 516, PC 7, Nassau
Uniondale UFD 5-11111
 933 GOODRICH ST 11553 560-8824
 Alan Hernandez, supt.
SHS, 933 GOODRICH ST 11553 4-00001
 Edward Beyrer, prin. 560-8957
Turtle Hook JHS 3-00110
 975 JERUSALEM AVE 11553 489-8046
 Eustace Thompson, prin.
Other Schools – See Hempstead

Hebrew Academy of Nassau 2-00111
 215 OAK ST 11553 538-8161
 Rabbi Schonbrun, prin.
Kellenberg Memorial HS 4-00111
 1400 GLENN CURTISS BLVD 11553 292-0200
 Br. Ormond, prin.

Union Springs, AC 315, PC 4, Cayuga
Union Springs Central SD 4-11111
 27 N CAYUGA ST 13160 889-4101
 Randolph Coon, supt.
Union Springs Central SHS 2-00001
 27 N CAYUGA ST 13160 889-4110
 Bruce Sharpe, prin.
MS, 27 N CAYUGA ST 13160 2-00110
 Mary Ann Dobmeier, prin. 889-4112

Upper Nyack, AC 914, PC 4, Rockland
Nyack UFD
 Supt. — See Nyack
HS, 360 CHRISTIAN HERALD RD 10960 3-00011
 Ira Oustatcher, prin. 353-7100

Utica, AC 315, PC 8, Oneida
Utica CSD, 13 ELIZABETH ST 13501 6-11111
 Taras Herbowy, supt. 792-2222
Proctor SHS, 1203 HILTON AVE 13501 4-00001
 Irving Jones, prin. 792-2111
Donovan JHS, EUCLID RD 13502 3-00110
 Carol Fox, prin. 792-2157
Kennedy JHS 3-00110
 500 DEERFIELD DR E 13502 792-2086
 Ronald Mancuso, prin.

Munson-Williams-Proctor Institute 2-CS
 310 GENESEE ST 13502 797-8260
Notre Dame HS 2-00011
 2 NOTRE DAME LN 13502 724-5118
 Brian McNamara, prin.
Notre Dame JHS North 1-00100
 309 GENESEE ST 13501 735-4631
 Sr. Melissa Scholl, prin.
Notre Dame JHS-South 2-00100
 13 BARTON AVE 13502 732-7130
 Lorraine Ciaccia, prin.
St. Elizabeth Hospital HSP
 2209 GENESEE ST 13501 798-8125
St. Lukes Memorial Hospital Center HSP
 PO BOX 479 13503 798-6136
SUNY Institute of Technology Utica/Rome 5-UC
 PO BOX 3050 13504 792-7208
SUNY Mohawk Valley Community College 6-CC
 1101 SHERMAN DR 13501 792-5400
Utica College of Syracuse University 5-UC
 1600 BURRSTONE RD 13502 792-3111

Utica School of Commerce 3-CC
 201 BLEECKER ST 13501 733-2307

Valatie, AC 518, PC 4, Columbia
Kinderhook Central SD 4-11111
 CENT ADMIN OFFICE 12184 758-7575
 Jerome Callahan, supt.
Crane HS, US ROUTE 09 12184 3-00011
 David Golden, prin. 758-7577
Crane MS, US ROUTE 09 12184 3-00100
 Gerard Gretzinger, prin. 758-7676

Valhalla, AC 914, PC 6, Westchester
Mt. Pleasant-Blythedale UFD 1-11111
 BRADHURST AVE 10595 592-7555
 Corinne Bloomer, supt.
Blythedale S, BRADHURST AVE 10595 2-11111
 Carol Squires, prin. 592-2155
Valhalla UFD 3-11111
 300 COLUMBUS AVE 10595 683-5040
 Mike Knowlton, supt.
JSHS, 300 COLUMBUS AVE 10595 3-00111
 Frank Ehrhart, prin. 683-5000

New York Medical College 10595 4-UC
  347-5000
SUNY Westchester Community College 6-CC
 75 GRASSLANDS RD 10595 285-6600

Valley Stream, AC 516, PC 8, Nassau
Valley Stream Central HSD 5-00111
 1 KENT RD 11580 872-5601
 Donald Howard, supt.
Valley Stream Central SHS 3-00001
 135 FLETCHER AVE 11580 561-4410
 J. Glynn, prin.
Valley Stream South JSHS 3-00111
 150 JEDWOOD PL 11581 791-0310
 Christine Cutting, prin.
Valley Stream Memorial JHS 3-00110
 398 FLETCHER AVE 11580 872-7710
 Timothy Melchior, prin.
Other Schools – See Franklin Square

Business Informatics Center 2-CS
 134 S CENTRAL AVE 11580 561-0050

Van Etten, AC 607, PC 3, Chemung
Spencer-Van Etten Central SD 4-11111
 LANGFORD ST 14889 – C. Bailey, supt. 589-4458
Other Schools – See Spencer

Van Hornesville, AC 315, PC 2, Herkimer
Hornesville-Young Central SD 2-11111
 ROUTE 80 13475 858-0729
 Martin Swenson, supt.
Young Central S, ROUTE 80 13475 2-11111
 Martin Swenson, prin. 858-0729

Verona, AC 315, PC 4, Oneida
Sherrill CSD, ROUTE 31 13478 5-11111
 Patrick Curtain, supt. 363-4200
Vernon-Verona-Sherrill HS 3-00011
 ROUTE 31 13478 363-4200
 Pam Fuller, prin.
Vernon-Verona-Sherrill Ms 2-00100
 ROUTE 31 13478 363-4200
 Norman Reed, prin.

Vestal, AC 607, PC 6, Broome
Vestal Central SD, 201 MAIN ST 13850 5-11111
 Michael Pavlovich, supt. 757-2241
HS, 200 WOODLAWN DR 13850 4-00011
 Albert Guzzi, prin. 757-2281
African Road JHS 4-00100
 620 S BENITA BLVD 13850 757-2331
 Marlyn Geres, prin.

Ross Corners Christian Academy 2-11111
 2101 OWEGO RD 13850 748-3301
 Richard Roberts, prin.

Victor, AC 716, PC 4, Ontario
Victor Central SD, 953 HIGH ST 14564 5-11111
 Tim Wisniewski, supt. 924-3252
HS, 953 HIGH ST 14564 3-00011
 Douglas Hamlin, prin. 924-3252
JHS, HIGH ST 14564 2-00100
 Jeffrey Crane, prin. 924-3252

Voorheesville, AC 518, PC 5, Albany
Voorheesville Central SD 4-11111
 ROUTE 85A 12186 765-3313
 Alan McCartney, supt.
Bouton JSHS, ROUTE 85A 12186 3-00111
 Terence Barlow, prin. 765-3314

Wallkill, AC 914, PC 4, Ulster
Wallkill Central SD, 13 MAIN ST 12589 5-11111
 Don Andrews, supt. 895-3301
HS, ROBINSON DR 12589 3-00011
 Victor Liviccori, prin. 895-2048
MS, ROUTE 208 12589 2-00100
 Lorna Thompson, prin. 895-2001

Walton, AC 607, PC 5, Delaware
Walton Central SD 4-11111
 47 STOCKTON AVE 13856 865-4116
 George Mack, supt.
JSHS, 47 STOCKTON AVE 13856 2-00011
 Roger Hutchinson, prin. 865-4116
MS, 47 STOCKTON AVE 13856 2-00100
 James Hoover, prin. 865-4116

Wampsville, AC 315, PC 3, Madison
Oneida CSD
 Supt. — See Oneida
Shortell MS, PO BOX 716 13163 2-00100
 Frank Del Favero, prin. 363-1051

Wantagh, AC 516, PC 7, Nassau
Wantagh UFD 5-11111
 3303 BELTAGH AVE 11793 781-8000
 George Besculides, supt.
HS, 3303 BELTAGH AVE 11793 3-00011
 John Pisani, prin. 781-8000
MS, 3301 BELTAGH AVE 11793 3-00100
 Anthony DeNapoli, prin. 781-8000

Wappingers Falls, AC 914, PC 5, Dutchess
Wappingers Central SD 7-11111
 15 MYERS CORNERS RD 12590 298-3600
 John Marmillo, supt.
Ketcham HS 4-00011
 99 MYERS CORNERS RD 12590 297-3727
 John Biasotti, prin.
Van Wyck JHS 4-00100
 10 HILLSIDE LAKE RD 12590 221-9135
 Gretchen Carpenter, prin.
JHS, 90 S REMSEN AVE 12590 4-00100
 Michael DeFillipo, prin. 297-5741
Other Schools – See Hopewell Junction

Warrensburg, AC 518, PC 5, Warren
Warrensburg Central SD 4-11111
 1 JAMES ST 12885 623-2861
 Roger Mcquain, supt.
JSHS, HORICON AVE 12885 2-00111
 Daniel Roberts, prin. 623-2862

Warsaw, AC 716, PC 5, Wyoming
Warsaw Central SD 4-11111
 153 W BUFFALO ST 14569 786-8000
 Edmund Kulakowski, supt.
JSHS, 153 W BUFFALO ST 14569 3-00111
 William Schofield, prin. 786-8010

Warwick, AC 914, PC 6, Orange
Warwick Valley Central SD 5-11111
 WEST ST 10990 – Joe Natale, supt. 987-3010
Warwick Valley HS, WEST ST 10990 3-00011
 David Trizano, prin. 987-3050
Warwick Valley MS, WEST ST 10990 4-01100
 Ann Paduch, prin. 987-3100

Washingtonville, AC 914, PC 5, Orange
Washingtonville Central SD 5-11111
 52 W MAIN ST 10992 496-2221
 Peter Brenner, supt.
HS, 54 W MAIN ST 10992 4-00011
 Samuel Black, prin. 496-2231
MS, 38 W MAIN ST 10992 4-00100
 Richard Denton, prin. 496-2261

Waterford, AC 518, PC 4, Saratoga
Waterford-Halfmoon UFD 3-11111
 125 MIDDLETOWN RD 12188 237-3466
 Ward Patton, supt.
JSHS, 125 MIDDLETOWN RD 12188 2-00111
 Carl Heiner, prin. 237-0800

Waterloo, AC 315, PC 6, Seneca
Waterloo Central SD 4-11111
 202 W MAIN ST 13165 539-1500
 Michael Hunsinger, supt.
HS, 65 CENTER ST 13165 3-00011
 Vincent Hemmer, prin. 539-1550
MS, 202 W MAIN ST 13165 2-00100
 Richard Byndas, prin. 539-1540

Watertown, AC 315, PC 8, Jefferson
Watertown CSD 5-11111
 376 BUTTERFIELD AVE 13601 785-3700
 Warren Fargo, supt.
HS, 1335 WASHINGTON ST 13601 4-00011
 Stephen Williamson, prin. 785-3800
Case JHS, 1237 WASHINGTON ST 13601 3-00100
 Philip Pratt, prin. 785-3870

Immaculate Heart Central HS 2-00011
 1316 IVES ST 13601 788-4670
 Pat Fontana, prin.
SUNY Jefferson Community College 4-CC
 1220 COFFEEN ST 13601 782-5250

Waterville, AC 315, PC 4, Oneida
Waterville Central SD 4-11111
 381 MADISON ST 13480 841-4161
 Michael Glover, supt.
JSHS, MADISON ST 13480 3-00111
 James VanWormer, prin. 841-4161

Watervliet, AC 518, PC 7, Albany
Watervliet CSD, 2557 10TH AVE 12189 4-11111
 Richard Hogan, supt. 273-4661
JSHS, WISWALL AVE 12189 3-00111
 John Weaver, prin. 273-4240

Watkins Glen, AC 607, PC 4, Schuyler
Watkins Glen Central SD 4-11111
 301 12TH ST 14891 535-9718
 Donald Dryden, supt.
Watkins Glen Central HS 2-00011
 301 12TH ST 14891 535-2761
 Brian O'Donnell, prin.
MS, 200 10TH ST 14891 2-01100
 Richard Warters, prin. 535-2725

Waverly, AC 607, PC 5, Tioga
Waverly Central SD 4-11111
15 FREDERICK ST 14892 565-2841
Walter Cain, supt.
JSHS, 1 FREDERICK ST 14892 3-00111
Michael McMahon, prin. 565-8101

Wayland, AC 716, PC 4, Steuben
Wayland-Cohocton Central SD 4-11111
2350 STATE ROUTE 63 14572 728-2211
J. Burroughs, supt.
Wayland-Cohocton HS 3-00011
2350 STATE ROUTE 63 14572 728-2211
Thomas Dutchess, prin.
Wayland MS 3-01100
2350 STATE ROUTE 63 14572 728-2551
Peter Cosola, prin.

Webster, AC 716, PC 6, Monroe
Webster Central SD 6-11111
119 SOUTH AVE 14580 265-3600
Philip Chirico, supt.
SHS, 800 FIVE MILE LINE RD 14580 4-00001
Douglas Smith, prin. 671-1880
JHS, 875 RIDGE RD 14580 4-00110
Loren Penman, prin. 671-7520

Webster Christian S, 675 HOLT RD 14580 2-11111
C. Ormsby, prin. 872-5150

Weedsport, AC 315, PC 4, Cayuga
Weedsport Central SD 4-11111
2821 E BRUTUS ST 13166 834-6637
Gary Gilchrist, supt.
JSHS, 2821 E BRUTUS ST 13166 3-00111
Nelson Bauersfeld, prin. 834-6652

Wells, AC 518, PC 3, Hamilton
Wells Central SD, ROUTE 30 12190 2-11111
Glenn Goodale, supt. 924-2272
S, ROUTE 30 12190 2-11111
Glenn Goodale, prin. 924-2272

Wellsville, AC 716, PC 6, Allegany
Wellsville Central SD 4-11111
126 W STATE ST 14895 593-5761
Keith Reester, supt.
HS, 126 W STATE ST 14895 3-00011
Michael McArdle, prin. 593-2291
MS, 30 N BROOKLYN AVE 14895 2-00100
Joseph Backhaus, prin. 593-1317

SUNY College of Technology 14895 3-CC
587-3105

West Babylon, AC 516, PC 8, Suffolk
West Babylon UFD 5-11111
10 FARMINGDALE RD 11704 321-3142
Robert Manley, supt.
HS, 500 GREAT EAST NECK RD 11704 4-00011
P. O'Brien, prin. 321-3003
JHS, 200 OLD FARMINGDALE RD 11704 3-00100
Melvin Noble, prin. 321-3084

Commercial Driver Training School 3-CS
600 PATTON AVE 11704 249-1330

Westbury, AC 516, PC 7, Nassau
East Meadow UFD
Supt. — See East Meadow
Clarke HS, 740 EDGEWOOD DR 11590 3-00011
Vincent Cirello, prin. 876-7451
Clarke MS, 740 EDGEWOOD DR 11590 3-00100
Robert Feirsen, prin. 876-7401

Westbury UFD, 2 HITCHCOCK LN 11568 5-11111
Charles Swensen, supt. 876-5016
HS, 151 POST RD 11568 3-00011
Pless Dickerson, prin. 876-5047
MS, 455 ROCKLAND ST 11590 3-00100
Mary Haynes, prin. 876-5082

Westfield, AC 716, PC 5, Chautauqua
Westfield Central SD 4-11111
189 E MAIN ST 14787 326-2151
Robert Olczak, supt.
JSHS, 201 E MAIN ST 14787 3-00111
Jeffrey Greabell, prin. 326-2151

Westhampton Beach, AC 516, PC 4, Suffolk
Westhampton Beach UFD 4-11111
340 MILL RD 11978 288-3800
Ed Broderick, supt.
HS, LILAC ROAD 11978 3-00011
Anthony Salvi, prin. 288-3800
MS, 340 MILL RD 11978 2-00100
Phillip Debrita, prin. 288-3800

West Hempstead, AC 516, PC 7, Nassau
West Hempstead UFD 4-11111
252 CHESTNUT ST 11552 489-8511
Richard Varriale, supt.
HS, 400 NASSAU BLVD 11552 3-00011
Anthony Dibettetto, prin. 489-7738
West Hempstead MS 2-00100
450 NASSAU BLVD 11552 489-7738
Joseph Cirnigliaro, prin.

West Henrietta, AC 716, PC 3, Monroe
Rush-Henrietta Central SD
Supt. — See Henrietta
Burger MS, 639 ERIE STATION RD 14586 2-00100
Michael Sturgeon, prin. 359-5308

West Islip, AC 516, PC 8, Suffolk
West Islip UFD 5-11111
100 SHERMAN AVE 11795 422-1560
Paul Lochner, supt.
HS, 3 HIGBIE LN 11795 4-00011
Kenneth Hartill, prin. 422-1500
Beach Street MS, 1765 BEACH ST 11795 3-01100
James Lanzarotta, prin. 422-1580
Udall Road MS, 900 UDALL RD 11795 3-01100
Harold Anderson, prin. 422-1590

St. John Baptist Diocesan HS 3-00011
1170 MONTAUK HWY 11795 587-8000
Allan Degnan, prin.

Westmoreland, AC 315, PC 3, Oneida
Westmoreland Central SD 4-11111
ROUTE 233 13490 853-6199
Marilyn Pirkle, supt.
JSHS, ROUTE 233 13490 3-00111
Rich Stanley, prin. 853-5571

West Nyack, AC 914, PC 5, Rockland
Clarkstown Central SD 6-11111
30 PARROT RD 10994 634-4941
John Krause, supt.
Clarkstown South HS 4-00011
31 DEMAREST MILL RD 10994 624-3400
Gerold Bierker, prin.
Festa East JHS, 30 PARROT RD 10994 2-00100
(—), prin. 639-6410
Festa South JHS, 30 PARROT RD 10994 3-00100
Carol Conklin, prin. 639-6400
Festa West JHS, 30 PARROT RD 10994 2-00100
Gloria Robertson, prin. 639-6420
Other Schools – See New City

West Park, AC 914, PC 3, Ulster
West Park UFSD, ROUTE 9W 12493 1-00111
Jeffrey Hanna, supt. 384-6412
WEST PARK JSHS, ROUTE 9W 12493 1-00111
JOHN FARRELL, prin. 384-6710

West Point, AC 914, PC 6, Orange

United States Military Academy 5-UC
606 THAYER RD 10996 938-3122

Westport, AC 518, PC 3, Essex
Westport Central SD, SISCO ST 12993 2-11111
Norman Koslofsky, supt. 962-8244
S, SISCO ST 12993 2-11111
Norman Koslofsky, prin. 962-8244

West Sayville, AC 516, PC 5, Suffolk
Sayville UFD
Supt. — See Sayville
Sayville HS, 20 BROOK ST 11796 4-00011
Joseph Buderman, prin. 244-6600

West Seneca, AC 716, PC 8, Erie
West Seneca Central SD 6-11111
1397 ORCHARD PARK RD 14224 674-5300
Vincent Coppola, supt.
West Seneca West HS 4-00011
3330 SENECA ST 14224 674-9964
James Brotz, prin.
East MS, 1445 CENTER RD 14224 3-00100
William Kennedy, prin. 674-1215
West JHS, 395 CENTER RD 14224 3-00100
Richard Caputi, prin. 674-9367
Other Schools – See Buffalo

Houghton College 2-UC
910 UNION RD 14224 674-6363
West Seneca Christian S 2-11111
511 UNION RD 14224 674-1820
John Fenton, prin.

West Valley, AC 716, PC 2, Cattaraugus
West Valley Central SD 2-11111
5359 SCHOOL ST 14171 942-3293
Theron Hotaling, supt.
West Valley Central S, SCHOOL ST 14171 2-11111
Virginia Williams, prin. 942-3293

West Winfield, AC 315, PC 3, Herkimer
Bridgewater-West Winfield Central SD 4-11111
FAIRGROUND RD 13491 822-6161
Donald Covell, supt.
Mount Markham HS 13491 2-00100
John Skahill, prin. 822-6343
Mount Markham MS 13491 3-01100
Renee Rudd, prin. 822-6361

Whitehall, AC 518, PC 5, Washington
Whitehall Central SD 3-11111
BUCKLEY RD 12887 499-1772
James Watson, supt.
JSHS, BUCKLEY RD 12887 2-00111
James Allegretto, prin. 499-1770

White Plains, AC 914, PC 8, Westchester
White Plains CSD 6-11111
5 HOMESIDE LN 10605 422-2019
Saul Yanofsky, supt.
HS, 550 NORTH ST 10605 4-00011
Jack Tate, prin. 422-2182
MS, 128 GRANDVIEW AVE 10605 4-00100
Bernard Cropsey, prin. 422-2092

Academy of Our Lady of Good Counsel HS 2-00011
52 N BROADWAY 10603 949-0178
Sr. Ellen Curry, prin.

Archbishop Stepinac HS 3-00011
950 MAMARONECK AVE 10605 946-4800
Ronald Tedesco, prin.
Berkeley College 3-CC
40 W RED OAK LN 10604 694-1122
German S, 50 PARTRIDGE RD 10605 2-11111
Johannes Kettlack, prin. 948-6514
Mercy College 3-UC
MARTINE AVE & S BROADWAY 10601
948-3666
New York School for the Deaf HND
555 KNOLLWOOD RD 10603
Pace University 5-UC
78 N BROADWAY 10603 773-3200
Simmons School 1-CS
190 E POST RD 10601 761-2701
Westchester Business Institute 3-CC
325 CENTRAL AVE 10606 948-4442
Westchester Conservatory of Music 3-CS
20 SOUNDVIEW AVE 10606 761-3715
Windward S, 7 WINDWARD AVE 10605 2-11111
Judith Hochman, prin. 949-6968

Whitesboro, AC 315, PC 5, Oneida
Whitesboro Central SD
Supt. — See Yorkville
MS, 75 ORISKANY BLVD 13492 3-00100
John Pickett, prin. 768-9750

Whitestone, AC 718, PC see New York
Queens Borough SD 25
Supt. — See Flushing
Carr JHS, 15460 17TH AVE 11357 3-00110
Michelle Fratti, prin. 746-0818

Whitesville, AC 607, PC 3, Allegany
Whitesville Central SD 2-11111
692 MAIN ST 14897 356-3301
J. Dennis Kirst, supt.
Whitesville Central S 2-11111
692 MAIN ST 14897 356-3301
J. Dennis Kirst, prin.

Whitney Point, AC 607, PC 4, Broome
Whitney Point Central SD 4-11111
PO BOX 249 13862 692-3222
Dale Schumacher, supt.
HS, KEIBEL RD 13862 3-00011
John Storer, prin. 692-8201
JHS, ROUTE 11 13862 3-00100
Michael Heller, prin. 692-8232

Williamson, AC 315, PC 4, Wayne
Williamson Central SD 4-11111
MILLER ST 14589 - H. Spink, supt. 589-9661
HS, 5891 STATE ROUTE 21 14589 2-00011
Charles Monsees, prin. 589-9621
MS, MILLER ST 14589 2-01100
Patrick Wright, prin. 589-9661

Williamsville, AC 716, PC 6, Erie
Williamsville Central SD 6-11111
415 LAWRENCE BELL DR 14221 626-7220
Howard Welker, supt.
Williamsville North HS 4-00011
1595 HOPKINS RD 14221 626-8503
S. Gang, prin.
Williamsville South HS 3-00011
5950 MAIN ST 14221 626-8200
Nicholas Deangelo, prin.
Heim MS, 175 HEIM RD 14221 3-01100
Charles Osborne, prin. 626-8600
Mill MS, 505 MILL ST 14221 3-01100
William Grobe, prin. 626-8300
Other Schools – See East Amherst

Bryant & Stratton Business Institute 3-CC
200 BRYANT AND STRATTON WAY 14221
631-0260
Christian Central Academy 2-11111
PO BOX 436 14231 634-4821
Ruth Adams, prin.
SUNY Erie Community College North 6-CC
6205 MAIN ST 14221 634-0800

Williston Park, AC 516, PC 6, Nassau

St. Aidan Upper Division ES 2-01100
510 WILLIS AVE 11596 747-6150
Joan Siecke, prin.

Willsboro, AC 518, PC 3, Essex
Willsboro Central SD, SCHOOL ST 12996 2-11111
Dodge Watkins, supt. 963-4456
Willsboro Central S, SCHOOL ST 12996 2-11111
Dodge Watkins, prin. 963-4456

Wilson, AC 716, PC 4, Niagara
Wilson Central SD, 412 LAKE ST 14172 4-11111
R. Zipp, supt. 751-9341
JSHS, 374 LAKE ST 14172 3-00111
Bruce Fraser, prin. 751-9341

Windham, AC 518, PC 2, Greene
Windham-Ashland-Jewett Central SD 3-11111
MAIN ST 12496 - A. Peterson, supt. 734-3400
Windham-Ashland Central S 3-11111
MAIN ST 12496 734-3400
Deborah Elmendorf, prin.

Windsor, AC 607, PC 4, Broome
Windsor Central SD, 215 MAIN ST 13865 4-11111
Oliver Blaise, supt. 655-8216
Windsor Central HS 3-00011
1191 NY ROUTE 79 13865 655-8250
Lawrence Chizak, prin.

Wolcott, AC 315, PC 4, Wayne
North Rose-Wolcott Central SD   4-11111
  11631 SALTER COLVIN RD   14590   594-8051
  Norman Fagnan, supt.
North Rose-Wolcott HS   3-00011
  11631 SALTER COLVIN RD   14590   594-3100
  Robert Ceccarelli, prin.
North Rose-Wolcott MS   2-00100
  30 NEW HARTFORD ST   14590   594-3115
  John Boogaard, prin.

Woodbury, AC 516, PC 6, Nassau

Briarcliffe School   4-CC
  250 CROSSWAYS PARK DR   11797   364-2055

Woodmere, AC 516, PC 7, Nassau

Woodmere Academy   2-11111
  336 WOODMERE BLVD   11598   374-9000
  Richard Hanson, prin.

Woodside, AC 718, PC see New York
Queens Borough SD 24
  Supt. — See Middle Village
JHS, 4602 47TH AVE   11377   4-01100
  John Jangl, prin.   937-0320

Joseph Bulova School   1-CS
  4024 62ND ST   11377   424-2929

Worcester, AC 607, PC 3, Otsego
Worcester Central SD   2-11111
  RR 1 BOX 1C   12197   397-8785
  Lawrence Bobnick, supt.
S, RR 1 BOX 1C   12197   2-11111
  Marilyn Lubell, prin.   397-8785

Wyandanch, AC 516, PC 6, Suffolk
Wyandanch UFD   4-11111
  STRAIGHT PATH   11798   491-1013
  Calvin Wilson, supt.
Wyandanch Memorial JSHS   3-00111
  54 S 32ND ST   11798   491-1022
  William Wheeler, prin.

Yonkers, AC 914, PC 9, Westchester
Yonkers CSD, 145 PALMER RD   10701   7-11111
  Don Batista, supt.   376-8000
Gorton HS, 100 SHONNARD PL   10703   4-00011
  Robert Santa Morena, prin.   376-8350
Lincoln HS, 375 KNEELAND AVE   10704   4-00011
  Bedelia Fries, prin.   376-8400
Roosevelt HS, 631 TUCKAHOE RD   10710   4-00011
  Michael Yazurlo, prin.   376-8500
Saunders Trades & Tech HS   4-00011
  183 PALMER RD   10701   376-8150
  Bernard Pierorazio, prin.
Burroughs JHS   3-00100
  150 ROCKLAND AVE   10705   376-8200
  Marylou MacDonald, prin.
Emerson JHS, 160 BOLMER AVE   10703   3-00100
  Charles Whelan, prin.   376-8300
Museum JHS   3-00110
  565 WARBURTON AVE   10701   376-8000
  Andrea Groepler, prin.
Twain JHS, WAKEFIELD AVE   10704   3-00100
  Ivan Toper, prin.   376-8540

Pace Business School   2-CS
  164 ASHBURTON AVE   10701   963-7945
Sacred Heart HS   3-00011
  34 CONVENT AVE   10703   965-3114
  Br. Hoatson, prin.
St. John's Riverside Hospital   HSP
  967 N BROADWAY   10701   964-4283
St. Joseph's Seminary   1-UC
  201 SEMINARY AVE   10704   968-6200

Yorkshire, AC 716, PC 4, Cattaraugus
Yorkshire-Pioneer Central SD   5-11111
  PO BOX 579   14173   492-1051
  David Kurzawa, supt.
Pioneer HS, PO BOX 619   14173   3-00011
  Christopher Tracey, prin.   492-4066
Pioneer MS, PO BOX 619   14173   4-01100
  Karen MacGamwell, prin.   492-3154

Yorktown Heights, AC 914, PC 6, Westchester
Yorktown Central SD   5-11111
  2723 CROMPOND RD   10598   243-8000
  Steven Dimuzio, supt.
Yorktown HS   4-00011
  2727 CROMPOND RD   10598   243-8050
  Michael Frischman, prin.
Strang MS, 2701 CROMPOND RD   10598   3-00100
  John Sieverding, prin.   243-8100

Mercy College   3-UC
  2651 STRANG BLVD   10598   245-6100

Yorkville, AC 315, PC 5, Oneida
Whitesboro Central SD   5-11111
  67 WHITESBORO ST   13495   768-9700
  Richard Robinson, supt.
Other Schools – See Marcy, Whitesboro

Youngstown, AC 716, PC 4, Niagara
Lewiston-Porter Central SD   5-11111
  4061 CREEK RD   14174   754-8281
  Walter Polka, supt.
Lewiston-Porter HS   3-00011
  4061 CREEK RD   14174   754-8281
  Roberta Love, prin.
Lewiston-Porter MS   3-00100
  4061 CREEK RD   14174   754-8281
  Dennis Tosetto, prin.

NORTH CAROLINA

STATE DEPARTMENT OF PUBLIC INSTRUCTION
Education Building
301 N. Wilmington St., Raleigh 27601
(919) 715-1000

Superintendent of Public Instruction	Bob Etheridge
Deputy Superintendent	Roger Jackson
Assistant Superintendent Instructional Services	Henry Johnson
Assistant Superintendent Auxiliary Services	Charles Weaver
Assistant Superintendent Financial & Personnel Services	James Barber
Assistant Superintendent Accountability Services	Suzanne Triplett

STATE BOARD OF EDUCATION
301 N. Wilmington St., Raleigh 27601

Chairperson	Kenneth Harris

PUBLIC, PRIVATE AND CATHOLIC SECONDARY SCHOOLS

Aberdeen, AC 919, PC 5, Moore
Moore County SD
  Supt. — See Carthage
MS, 503 SANDHILLS BLVD N   28315   3-01100
  William Moore, prin.   944-1124

Ahoskie, AC 919, PC 5, Hertford
Hertford County SD
  Supt. — See Winton
Hertford County HS   4-00011
  PO BOX 1326   27910   332-4096
  Terence Taylor, prin.

Ridgecroft S, RR 3 BOX 35   27910   2-11111
  Carolyn Jackson, prin.   332-2964
Roanoke-Chowan Community College   3-CC
  RR 2 BOX 46A   27910   332-5921

Albemarle, AC 704, PC 7, Stanly
Albemarle CSD, 1503 W MAIN ST   28001   4-11111
  William Church, supt.   982-1148
HS, 311 PARK RIDGE RD   28001   3-00011
  Thomas Taylor, prin.   982-3711

MS, 266 N 3RD ST   28001   2-00100
  Joe Sinclair, prin.   982-5480

Stanly County SD, 223 S 2ND ST   28001   6-11111
  Jim Martin, supt.   983-5151
Other Schools – See New London, Norwood, Oakboro

Stanly Community College   4-CC
  RR 4 BOX 55   28001   982-0121

Andrews, AC 704, PC 5, Cherokee
Cherokee County SD
  Supt. — See Murphy
JSHS   28901   2-00111
  Stephen Coffey, prin.   321-5415

Angier, AC 919, PC 4, Harnett
Harnett County SD
  Supt. — See Lillington
Harnett Central HS, RR 4   27501   3-00011
  Don Wilson, prin.   639-6161
Harnett Central MS, RR 4   27501   3-00100
  James Futrell, prin.   639-6000

Apex, AC 919, PC 5, Wake
Wake County SD
  Supt. — See Raleigh
HS, 1501 LAURA DUNCAN RD   27502   4-00011
  Thomas Dixon, prin.   387-2208
MS, 400 E MOORE ST   27502   3-00100
  Darrell Helm, prin.   387-2181
West Lake MS, 4600 W LAKE RD   27502   3-00100
  Ramey Beavers, prin.   662-2900

Arden, AC 704, PC 2, Buncombe
Buncombe County SD
  Supt. — See Asheville
Valley Springs MS   3-00100
  RR 1 BOX 16   28704   684-0886
  Arbie Rhodes, prin.

Alliance Tractor Trailer Training Center   1-CS
  PO BOX 883   28704   684-4454
Christ S, 500 CHRIST SCHOOL RD   28704   2-00111
  Peter Conway, prin.   684-6232

Asheboro, AC 919, PC 7, Randolph
Asheboro CSD, 1126 S PARK ST 27203   5-11111
Dr. Bob Gordon, supt.   625-5104
HS, 1221 S PARK ST 27203   3-00011
Michael Warren, prin.   625-6185
North Asheboro MS   2-00100
1861 N ASHEBORO JR HIGH RD 27203 672-1900
Daryl Barnes, prin.
South Asheboro MS   2-00100
523 W WALKER AVE 27203   629-4141
Curt Lorimer, prin.

Randolph County SD   7-11111
2222 S FAYETTEVILLE ST 27203   318-6100
Worth Hatley, supt.
Southwestern HS   3-00011
1641 HOPEWELL FRIENDS RD 27203   629-4390
Donnie Baxter, prin.
South West Randolph MS   3-00100
1509 HOPEWELL FRIENDS RD 27203   381-3900
Deborah Williams, prin.
Other Schools – See Ramseur, Randleman, Trinity

Fayetteville St. Christian S   2-11111
151 W PRITCHARD ST 27203   869-2128
James Deal, prin.
Randolph Community College   4-CC
PO BOX 1009 27204   629-1471

Asheville, AC 704, PC 8, Buncombe
Asheville CSD, 16 BILTMORE AVE 28801   5-11111
E. Trogdon, supt.   255-5304
HS, 419 MCDOWELL ST 28803   3-00011
L. Liggett, prin.   255-5352
MS, 197 S FRENCH BROAD AVE 28801   3-00100
Gerald Gault, prin.   255-5306

Buncombe County SD   7-11111
175 BINGHAM RD 28806   255-5921
J. Frank Yeager, supt.
Erwin HS, 60 LEES CREEK RD 28806   4-00011
Malcolm Brown, prin.   258-1086
Reynolds HS, 1 ROCKET DR 28803   4-00011
Ronald Dalton, prin.   298-2500
Roberson HS, 250 OVERLOOK RD 28803   4-00011
Richard Greene, prin.   684-8548
Career Education Center   Vo Tech
175 BINGHAM RD 28806   251-0499
Larry McCallum, prin.
Erwin MS, 20 ERWIN HILLS RD 28806   3-00100
Allen Credle, prin.   253-4866
Reynolds MS, 2 ROCKET DR 28803   3-00100
Kaye Lamb, prin.   298-7484
Other Schools – See Arden, Black Mountain,
Candler, Enka, Swannanoa, Weaverville

Asheville Buncombe Technical Comm. Coll.   5-CC
340 VICTORIA RD 28801   254-1921
Asheville Christian Academy   2-11111
PO BOX 9038 28815   298-1600
William George, prin.
Asheville S   2-00011
360 ASHEVILLE SCHOOL RD 28806   254-6345
William Peebles, prin.
Carolina S   2-11111
1345 HENDERSONVILLE RD 28803   274-0757
Gilbert Webb, prin.
Cecil's College   2-CC
PO BOX 6407 28816   252-2486
Temple Baptist S   2-11111
985 1/2 PATTON AVE 28806   252-3712
Raymond Bailey, prin.
University of North Carolina   5-UC
1 UNIVERSITY HTS 28804   251-6481
Warren Wilson College   3-UC
PO BOX 9000 28802   800-727-1894

Aurora, AC 919, PC 3, Beaufort
Beaufort County SD
Supt. — See Washington
HS, RR 2 BOX 249 27806   2-00011
Tony Harrison, prin.   322-4524

Ayden, AC 919, PC 5, Pitt
Pitt County SD
Supt. — See Greenville
Ayden-Grifton HS   3-00011
RR 3 BOX 172 28513   746-4183
James Gray, prin.
MS, 1207 W 3RD ST 28513   2-01100
Denise Streeter, prin.   746-3672

Bailey, AC 919, PC 3, Nash
Nash-Rocky Mount County SD
Supt. — See Nashville
Southern Nash SHS   3-00001
RR 1 BOX 318 27807   478-5450
Jerry Congleton, prin.

Bakersville, AC 704, PC 2, Mitchell
Mitchell County SD   4-11111
115 SCHOOL RD 28705   688-4432
Roger Duncan, supt.
Mitchell HS, 217 SCHOOL RD 28705   3-00011
Don Baucom, prin.   688-2101
Bowman MS 28705   2-01100
Larry Fortner, prin.   688-2752
Other Schools – See Spruce Pine

Banner Elk, AC 704, PC 3, Avery

Lees-McRae College   3-UC
PO BOX 128 28604   898-6698

Barco, AC 919, PC 2, Currituck
Currituck County SD
Supt. — See Currituck
Currituck County HS   3-00011
HCR BOX 825 27917   453-2171
Richard Wardle, prin.

Battleboro, AC 919, PC 2, Edgecombe
Edgecombe County SD
Supt. — See Tarboro
Phillips MS, RR 2 BOX 1 27809   3-01100
Leonard Thompson, prin.   446-8824

Bayboro, AC 919, PC 3, Pamlico
Pamlico County SD   4-11111
507 ANDERSON DR 28515   745-4171
S. Russell Cotton, supt.
Pamlico HS, PO BOX 699 28515   3-00011
Joshua Potter, prin.   745-3151
Pamlico JHS, RR 1 BOX JH1 28515   3-01100
James Lanier, prin.   745-4062

Bear Creek, AC 919, PC 2, Chatham
Chatham County SD
Supt. — See Pittsboro
Chatham Central HS   2-00011
NC HIGHWAY 902 27207   837-2251
John Glover, prin.

Beaufort, AC 919, PC 5, Carteret
Carteret County SD   6-11111
107 SAFRIT DR 28516   728-4583
Tom Davis, supt.
East Carteret HS, RR 1 28516   3-00011
James Walker, prin.   728-3514
MS, 100 CARRAWAY DR 28516   2-00100
Renne Newman, prin.   728-4520
Other Schools – See Morehead City, Newport

Beaufort Christian Academy   2-11111
PO BOX 568 28516   728-3465
Mary Rice, prin.

Belhaven, AC 919, PC 4, Beaufort
Beaufort County SD
Supt. — See Washington
JHS, 321 S MAIN RD 27810   2-00100
Mary Barnes, prin.   943-2208

Belmont, AC 704, PC 6, Gaston
Gaston County SD
Supt. — See Gastonia
South Point SHS   3-00001
906 SOUTHPOINT RD 28012   825-3351
Robert Hager, prin.
JHS, 110 N CENTRAL AVE 28012   3-00110
Marcia Hunter, prin.   825-9619

Belmont Abbey College   3-UC
1 ABBEY PL 28012   800-523-2355

Benson, AC 919, PC 5, Johnston
Johnston County SD
Supt. — See Smithfield
Benson MS, 401 S ELM ST 27504   2-01100
Almond Barefoot, prin.   894-4233

Alliance Tractor Trailer Training Center   2-CS
PO BOX 579 27504   892-8370

Bessemer City, AC 704, PC 5, Gaston
Gaston County SD
Supt. — See Gastonia
SHS, 119 YELLOW JACKET LN 28016   3-00001
Robert Carpenter, prin.   629-2258
JHS, PO BOX 624 28016   3-00110
William Helms, prin.   629-3281

Bethel, AC 919, PC 4, Pitt
Pitt County SD
Supt. — See Greenville
North Pitt HS, RR 1 BOX 313 27812   3-00011
Lenwood Simpson, prin.   825-0054

Beulaville, AC 919, PC 3, Duplin
Duplin County SD
Supt. — See Kenansville
East Duplin HS, PO BOX 188 28518   3-00011
Kenneth Kennedy, prin.   298-4535

Biscoe, AC 919, PC 4, Montgomery
Montgomery County SD
Supt. — See Troy
East Montgomery HS   3-00011
RR 1 BOX 194 27209   428-9641
F. Crisco, prin.
East MS, RR 1 BOX 196 27209   2-00100
Eddie Henderson, prin.   428-3278

Black Mountain, AC 704, PC 6, Buncombe
Buncombe County SD
Supt. — See Asheville
Owen HS, 99 LAKE EDEN RD 28711   3-00011
Fred Ivey, prin.   686-3852

Bladenboro, AC 919, PC 4, Bladen
Bladen County SD
Supt. — See Elizabethtown
HS, PO BOX 459 28320   3-00011
Donald Kelly, prin.   863-4821
Spaulding-Monroe MS   2-00100
PO BOX 579 28320   863-3232
Lillian Graham, prin.

Boiling Springs, AC 704, PC 4, Cleveland

Gardner-Webb University   4-UC
GENERAL DELIVERY 28017   434-2361

Boone, AC 704, PC 7, Watauga
Watauga County SD, HWY 194 28607   5-11111
C. David Greene, supt.   264-7190
Watauga HS, RR 6 BOX 30 28607   4-00011
Sherell Carreker, prin.   264-2407

Appalachian State University   7-UC
ASU STATION 28608   262-2120

Boonville, AC 919, PC 4, Yadkin
Yadkin County SD
Supt. — See Yadkinville
Starmount HS, RR 2 BOX 206 27011   3-00011
Eddie Campbell, prin.   468-4949

Brevard, AC 704, PC 6, Transylvania
Transylvania County SD   5-11111
400 ROSENWALD LN 28712   884-6173
A. Mickey Church, supt.
HS, COUNTRY CLUB ROAD 28712   3-00011
James Williams, prin.   884-4103
MS, 198 FISHER RD 28712   3-00100
John Tinsley, prin.   884-2091
Other Schools – See Rosman

Brevard College   3-CC
N BROAD ST 28712   883-8292

Bryson City, AC 919, PC 4, Swain
Swain County SD   4-11111
280 SCHOOL DR 28713   488-3129
Joseph Johnson, supt.
Swain County HS   3-00011
1415 NEW FONTANA RD 28713   488-2152
Gerald McKinney, prin.
Swain County MS   2-00100
10 ALMOND SCHOOL RD 28713   488-3480
Robert White, prin.

Buies Creek, AC 919, PC 4, Harnett

Campbell University   5-UC
PO BOX 127 27506   800-334-4111

Bunn, AC 919, PC 2, Franklin
Franklin County SD
Supt. — See Louisburg
HS, PO BOX 146 27508   3-00011
D. Wayne Wilbourne, prin.   496-3975

Burgaw, AC 919, PC 4, Pender
Pender County SD   6-11111
925 PENDERLEA HWY 28425   259-2187
Wendell Murray, supt.
Pender HS, RR 2 BOX 2335 28425   4-00011
Larry Baysden, prin.   259-5761
MS, PO BOX 757 28425   3-00100
Franklin Rivenbark, prin.   259-2344
West Pender MS   2-00100
10750 NC HIGHWAY 53 W 28425   283-5626
H. Blake, prin.
Other Schools – See Hampstead

Burlington, AC 910, PC 8, Alamance
Burlington CSD   6-11111
1712 VAUGHN RD 27217   570-6060
Joseph Sinclair, supt.
Cummings HS   3-00011
2200 N MEBANE ST 27217 – (—), prin. 570-6100
Williams HS, 1307 S CHURCH ST 27215   4-00011
James Daye, prin.   570-6161
Sellers-Gunn Vo Ctr   Vo Tech
612 APPLE ST 27217   570-6130
Sheldon Southerland, prin.
Broadview MS   3-00100
2229 BROADVIEW DR 27217   570-6195
Randall Bryan, prin.
Turrentine MS   3-00100
1710 EDGEWOOD AVE 27215   570-6150
Patricia Bason, prin.

Burnsville, AC 704, PC 4, Yancey
Yancey County SD   5-11111
100 SCHOOL CIR 28714   682-6101
Vernon Chapman, supt.
Mountain Heritage HS   3-00011
PO BOX 70 28714   682-6103
Larry Howell, prin.
Cane River MS, RR 3 28714   2-00100
Ivan Whitson, prin.   682-2202
East Yancey MS, RR 6 BOX 87 28714   2-00100
Kenny Sparks, prin.   682-2281

Buxton, AC 919, PC 4, Dare
Dare County SD
Supt. — See Manteo
Cape Hatteras S, PO BOX 948 27920   3-11111
Joyce Bornfriend, prin.   995-5730

Calypso, AC 919, PC 2, Duplin
Duplin County SD
Supt. — See Kenansville
North Duplin JSHS   2-00111
PO BOX 306 28325   658-3051
Larry Cooper, prin.

Camden, AC 919, PC 2, Camden
Camden County SD   4-11111
174 NC HIGHWAY 343 N 27921   335-0831
Frederick Denning, supt.

Camden County HS   2-00011
  103 US HIGHWAY 158 W 27921   338-0114
  Vann Pennell, prin.
  MS, 248 SCOTLAND RD 27921   2-01100
  Ron Melchiorre, prin.   338-3349

Cameron, AC 919, PC 2, Moore
Moore County SD
  Supt. — See Carthage
Union Pines HS   3-00011
  1981 UNION CHURCH RD 28326   947-5511
  Larry Riggan, prin.

Camp Lejeune, AC 919, PC 8, Onslow
Camp Lejeune SD, BLDG 855 28542   5-11111
  James Pirkle, supt.   451-2461
Lejeune HS 28542   3-00011
  Rick Scroggs, prin.   451-2451
Brewster JHS 28542   3-00100
  Tom King, prin.   451-2561

Candler, AC 704, PC 3, Buncombe
Buncombe County SD
  Supt. — See Asheville
Enka MS, 390 ASBURY RD 28715   3-00100
  Ivan Randolph, prin.   667-1388

Mt. Pisgah Academy   2-00011
  75 ACADEMY DR 28715   667-2535
  Arne Nielsen, prin.

Canton, AC 704, PC 5, Haywood
Haywood County SD
  Supt. — See Waynesville
Pisgah HS, SUBSTATION RD 28716   3-00011
  Mike Mathews, prin.   646-3440
JHS, 60 PENLAND ST 28716   2-00100
  Mary Fowler, prin.   646-3467

Carthage, AC 919, PC 3, Moore
Moore County SD   6-11111
  PO BOX 1180 28327   947-2976
  Gene Riddle, supt.
  Other Schools – See Aberdeen, Cameron, Pinehurst,
  Robbins, Southern Pines

Cary, AC 919, PC 8, Wake
Wake County SD
  Supt. — See Raleigh
HS, 638 WALNUT ST 27511   4-00011
  Donna Hargens, prin.   460-3549
East Cary MS   3-00100
  1111 SE MAYNARD RD 27511   460-3504
  Luther Cherry, prin.
West Cary MS, 1000 EVANS RD 27513   3-00100
  Elvia Walker, prin.   460-3528

Catawba, AC 704, PC 2, Catawba
Catawba County SD
  Supt. — See Newton
Bandys HS, RR 1 BOX 98 28609   3-00011
  W. Sipe, prin.   241-3171
MS, PO BOX 448 28609   2-00100
  Richard Johnson, prin.   241-3131

Cerro Gordo, AC 919, PC 2, Columbus
Columbus County SD
  Supt. — See Whiteville
West Columbus HS 28430   3-00011
  Dan McPherson, prin.   654-4111

Chadbourn, AC 919, PC 4, Columbus
Columbus County SD
  Supt. — See Whiteville
MS, 801 W SMITH ST 28431   3-01100
  Eugene Sturdivant, prin.   654-4300

Chapel Hill, AC 919, PC 8, Orange
Chapel Hill-Carrboro CSD   6-11111
  750 S MERRITT MILL RD 27516   967-8211
  Neil Pedersen, supt.
HS, 1709 HIGH SCHOOL RD 27516   4-00011
  Charles Patterson, prin.   929-2106
Culbreth MS, 225 CULBRETH RD 27516   3-00100
  Charles Stewart, prin.   929-7161
Phillips MS, 606 N ESTES DR 27514   3-00100
  Alton Cheek, prin.   929-2188

North Carolina Memorial Hospital   HSP
  101 MANNING DR 27514   966-5111
University of North Carolina 27599   7-UC
      966-3621

Charlotte, AC 704, PC 10, Mecklenburg
Charlotte/Mecklenburg Co SD   8-11111
  701 E 2ND ST 28202   379-7000
  John Murphy, supt.
East Mecklenburg SHS   4-00001
  6800 MONROE RD 28212   343-6430
  Eugene Hawley, prin.
Garinger SHS, 1100 EASTWAY DR 28205   4-00001
  Buddy Coleman, prin.   343-6450
Independence SHS   4-00001
  1967 PATRIOT DR 28227   343-6900
  James Murchison, prin.
Myers Park SHS   4-00001
  2400 COLONY RD 28209   343-5800
  James Amendum, prin.
Providence SHS, 1800 PINEVILLE 28226   3-00001
  Gregory Clemmer, prin.   343-5800
West Charlotte SHS   4-00001
  2219 SENIOR DR 28216   343-6060
  Barbara Ledford, prin.
Harding University HS   4-00011
  2001 ALLEGHANY ST 28208   343-6007
  Venton Bell, prin.

Olympic HS   4-00011
  4301 SANDY PORTER RD 28273   343-3800
  Jerald Moore, prin.
South Mecklenburg HS   4-00011
  8900 PARK RD 28210   343-3600
  Ken Wells, prin.
West Mecklenburg HS   4-00011
  7400 TUCKASEEGEE RD 28214   343-6080
  Dennis Williams, prin.
Albemarle Road JHS   3-00110
  6900 DEMOCRACY DR 28212   343-6420
  Russell Sgro, prin.
Carmel JHS, 5001 CAMILLA DR 28226   4-00110
  Ernest Thompson, prin.   343-6705
Cochrane JHS   3-00110
  6200 STARHAVEN DR 28215   343-6460
  Ken Simmons, prin.
Coulwood MS   2-00100
  1901 KENTBERRY DR 28214   343-6090
  Judy Phillips, prin.
Davis MS, 3343 GRIFFITH ST 28203   2-00100
  Christine Waggoner, prin.   343-5832
Eastway JHS, 3333 BISCAYNE DR 28205   3-00110
  Larry Lewis, prin.   343-6410
Graham JHS   3-00110
  1800 RUNNYMEDE LN 28211   343-5810
  Ann Clark, prin.
Hawthorne JHS, 1400 PEGRAM ST 28205   3-00110
  Calvin Lewers, prin.   343-5490
Kennedy JHS, 4000 GALLANT RD 28273   3-00110
  Zandra Johnson, prin.   343-5540
McClintock JHS, 2101 RAMA RD 28212   4-00110
  Joel Ritchie, prin.   343-6425
Northeast JHS   4-00110
  5960 BRICKSTONE DR 28227   343-6920
  Marian Yates, prin.
Northwest JHS   2-00100
  1415 BEATTIES FORD RD 28216   343-5500
  Rosalind Anderson, prin.
Piedmont Open MS   3-00110
  1241 E 10TH ST 28204   343-5435
  Tom Spivey, prin.
Quail Hollow JHS   4-00100
  2901 SMITHFIELD CHURCH RD 28210   343-3620
  Sandra Niedzialek, prin.
Randolph JHS   4-00110
  4400 WATER OAK RD 28211   343-6700
  Diana Bagwell, prin.
Ranson JHS   3-00110
  5850 STATESVILLE RD 28269   343-6800
  Laird Lewis, prin.
Sedgefield JHS   3-00110
  2700 DORCHESTER PL 28209   343-5840
  Jackie Menser, prin.
Smith JHS, 1600 TYVOLA RD 28210   3-00100
  Catherine Munn, prin.   343-5815
South Charlotte MS   4-00110
  8040 STRAWBERRY LN 28277   343-3670
  Maureen Cockerline, prin.
Spaugh MS   2-00100
  1901 HERBERT SPAUGH LN 28208   343-6025
  William Crawford, prin.
Williams JHS, 2400 CARMINE ST 28206   3-00110
  Rick Hinson, prin.   343-5544
Wilson MS   3-00100
  7020 TUCKASEEGEE RD 28214   343-6070
  Gayle Aughtry, prin.
Other Schools – See Huntersville

American Business and Fashion Institute   2-CS
  1515 MOCKINGBIRD LN STE 600 28209
      523-3738
Brookstone College of Business   2-CS
  8307 UNVERSITY EXEC PARK DR 28262
      547-8600
Calvary Christian S   2-11111
  8101 FALLSDALE DR 28214   394-5566
  Richard Hardee, prin.
Carolinas Medical Center   2-HSP
  PO BOX 32861 28232   355-2145
Catholic HS, 3100 PARK RD 28209   3-00011
  Sr. Paulette Williams, prin.   523-5671
Central Piedmont Community College   7-CC
  PO BOX 35009 28235   342-6687
Charlotte Christian S   3-11111
  7301 SARDIS RD 28270   366-5657
  Jerald Hubbard, prin.
Charlotte Country Day S   4-11111
  1440 CARMEL RD 28226   366-1241
  Margaret Gragg, prin.
Charlotte Diesel Driving School   2-CS
  6000 N TRYON ST 28213   597-9550
Charlotte Latin S   4-11111
  PO BOX 6143 28207   846-1100
  Edward Fox, prin.
Charlotte Memorial Hospital   HSP
  1000 BLYTHE BLVD 28203   355-5043
Crown Christian Academy   2-11111
  5901 NATIONS FORD RD 28217   521-6030
  Anthony Shiflett, prin.
East Coast Bible College   2-CC
  6900 WILKINSON BLVD 28214   394-2307
ECPI Computer Institute   2-CS
  1121 WOODRIDGE CENTER DR 28217   357-0077
Johnson C. Smith University   4-UC
  100 BEATTIES FORD RD 28216   378-1000
King's College   2-CC
  322 LAMAR AVE 28204   372-0266
Mercy School of Nursing   HSP
  1921 VAIL AVE 28207   379-5841

Northside Christian Academy   3-11111
  333 JEREMIAH BLVD 28262   596-4856
  Barry Shearer, prin.
Paw Creek Christian Academy   2-11111
  1209 LITTLE ROCK RD 28214   394-7191
  Daniel Woods, prin.
Presbyterian Hospital   2-HSP
  PO BOX 33549 28233   384-4141
Providence Day S   4-11111
  5800 SARDIS RD 28270   364-6848
  Eugene Bratek, prin.
Queens College   4-UC
  1900 SELWYN AVE 28274   337-2212
Trinity Christian Academy   3-11111
  5815 NATIONS FORD RD 28217
  Jerald Hubbard, prin.
University of North Carolina 28223   7-UC
      547-2213
Victory Christian S   2-11111
  PO BOX 240433 28224   522-8566
  Michael Pratt, prin.

Cherokee, AC 704, PC 3, Swain

Oconaluftee Job Corps Center   2-CS
  200 PARK CIRCLE 28719

Cherryville, AC 704, PC 5, Gaston
Gaston County SD
  Supt. — See Gastonia
JSHS, 313 RIDGE AVE 28021   3-00111
  Lee Dedmon, prin.   435-4506

China Grove, AC 704, PC 5, Rowan
Rowan-Salisbury County SD
  Supt. — See Salisbury
South Rowan HS   4-00011
  1655 PATTERSON ST 28023   857-1161
  Alan King, prin.
MS, 1013 N MAIN ST 28023   3-00100
  Theodore Bowen, prin.   857-7038

Chinquapin, AC 919, PC 2, Duplin
Duplin County SD
  Supt. — See Kenansville
MS, PO BOX 8 28521   2-01100
  Denny Rutledge, prin.   285-3476

Chocowinity, AC 919, PC 3, Beaufort
Beaufort County SD
  Supt. — See Washington
JSHS, PO BOX 100 27817   3-00111
  James Henderson, prin.   946-6191

Claremont, AC 704, PC 3, Catawba
Catawba County SD
  Supt. — See Newton
Bunker Hill HS   3-00011
  4675 OXFORD SCHOOL RD 28610   241-3355
  John Stiver, prin.

Clarkton, AC 919, PC 3, Bladen
Bladen County SD
  Supt. — See Elizabethtown
MS, PO BOX 127 28433   2-00100
  James Coleman, prin.   647-6531

Clayton, AC 919, PC 5, Johnston
Johnston County SD
  Supt. — See Smithfield
HS, PO BOX 39 27520   3-00011
  William Parrish, prin.   553-4064
MS, PO BOX 687 27520   3-00100
  Gerald Toler, prin.   553-5811

Clemmons, AC 919, PC 6, Forsyth
Winston-Salem/Forsyth SD
  Supt. — See Winston-Salem
West Forsyth HS   4-00011
  1735 LEWISVILLE CLEMMONS RD 27012
  Jerry Peoples, prin.   766-6467

Cleveland, AC 704, PC 3, Rowan
Rowan-Salisbury County SD
  Supt. — See Salisbury
West Rowan MS, PO BOX 106 27013   2-00100
  Rick Hampton, prin.   633-9667

Clinton, AC 919, PC 6, Sampson
Clinton CSD, 303 LISBON ST 28328   5-11111
  Charles Gainey, supt.   592-3132
HS, 1201 W ELIZABETH ST 28328   3-00011
  Larry Price, prin.   592-2067
Sampson MS, 211 FINCH ST 28328   3-00100
  Frederick Bogue, prin.   592-3327

Sampson County SD   6-11111
  313 ROWAN RD 28328   592-1401
  Larry Bell, supt.
Union HS, RR 4 BOX 338 28328   2-00011
  Freddie Williamson, prin.   592-4026
Union MS, RR 4 BOX 346 28328   3-00100
  Garry Smith, prin.   592-4547
Other Schools – See Dunn, Newton Grove, Roseboro

Sampson Community College   4-CC
  PO BOX 318 28328   592-8084

Clyde, AC 704, PC 4, Haywood

Haywood Community College   3-CC
  FREEDLANDER DRIVE 28721   627-2821

Columbia, AC 919, PC 3, Tyrrell
Tyrrell County SD — 3-11111
PO BOX 328 27925 — 796-1121
Betsey Stallings, supt.
JSHS, PO BOX 419 27925 — 2-00111
James Cahoon, prin. — 796-0191

Columbus, AC 704, PC 3, Polk
Polk County SD, 202 E MILLS ST 28722 — 4-11111
James Causby, supt. — 894-3051
Polk County HS, RR 1 BOX 812 28722 — 3-00011
David Jones, prin. — 894-2525
Other Schools – See Tryon

Concord, AC 704, PC 8, Cabarrus
Cabarrus County SD — 7-11111
PO BOX 388 28026 — 786-6191
Daniel Freeman, supt.
Central Cabarrus HS — 4-00011
505 HIGHWAY 49 S 28025 — 786-0125
John Lentz, prin.
HS, 481 BURRAGE RD NE 28025 — 3-00011
Bert Thomas, prin. — 786-4161
Northwest Cabarrus HS — 3-00011
5130 NW CABARRUS DR 28027 — 788-4111
Larry Woods, prin.
MS, 120 MARSH AVE NW 28025 — 3-00100
Barry Little, prin. — 786-4121
Fries MS, 133 CIRCLE DR 28027 — 3-00100
Terrence Ford, prin. — 788-4140
Northwest Cabarrus MS — 3-00100
5140 NW CABARRUS DR 28027 — 788-4135
(—), prin.
Other Schools – See Mount Pleasant

Barber-Scotia College — 2-UC
145 CABARRUS AVE W 28025 — 786-5171
Cabarrus Memorial Hospital — HSP
920 CHURCH ST N 28025 — 783-1556
First Assembly Christian S — 2-11111
154 HIGHWAY 601 BYP N 28027 — 786-5199
Thomas Snipes, prin.

Conover, AC 704, PC 6, Catawba

Catawba Valley Lutheran HS — 2-00011
PO BOX 1012 28613 — 327-8490
Nancy Pingel, prin.

Conway, AC 919, PC 3, Northampton
Northampton County SD
Supt. — See Jackson
Northampton HS East — 3-00011
RR 2 BOX 270 27820 – (—), prin. — 585-0627
MS, RR 2 BOX 152 27820 — 2-00100
Charles Tyner, prin. — 585-0312

Cramerton, AC 704, PC 4, Gaston
Gaston County SD
Supt. — See Gastonia
JHS, 236 8TH AVE 28032 — 2-00110
Gary Short, prin. — 824-2285

Cramerton Christian Academy — 2-11111
426 WOODLAWN AVE 28032 — 824-2840
Rev. King, prin.

Creedmoor, AC 919, PC 4, Granville
Granville County SD
Supt. — See Oxford
South Granville HS — 3-00011
PO BOX 398 27522 — 528-1507
Michael Fedewa, prin.
Hawley MS, PO BOX 67 27522 — 3-00100
Abram Liles, prin. — 528-0091

Creswell, AC 919, PC 2, Washington
Washington County SD
Supt. — See Plymouth
Creswell S, PO BOX 188 27928 — 2-11111
David Cahoon, prin. — 797-4766

Cullowhee, AC 704, PC 5, Jackson

Western Carolina University 28723 — 6-UC
227-7317

Currituck, AC 919, PC 3, Currituck
Currituck County SD — 5-11111
PO BOX 40 27929 — 232-2223
William Capps, supt.
Knapp JHS 27929 — 2-00100
Maurice Green, prin. — 232-3107
Other Schools – See Barco

Dallas, AC 704, PC 5, Gaston
Gaston County SD
Supt. — See Gastonia
North Gaston SHS, RR 3 28034 — 4-00001
William Adams, prin. — 922-5285
Church Street JSHS — 3-00111
300 CHURCH ST 28034 — 922-5061
James Watson, prin.
Friday JHS, RR 3 28034 — 3-00110
Sheri Little, prin. — 922-5297

Gaston College — 5-CC
201 HIGHWAY 321 S 28034 — 922-6200

Danbury, AC 919, PC 2, Stokes
Stokes County SD, PO BOX 50 27016 — 6-11111
G. Sells, supt. — 593-8146

North Stokes JSHS — 3-00111
RR 1 BOX 346 27016 — 593-8134
Larry Cooke, prin.
Other Schools – See King, Walnut Cove

Davidson, AC 704, PC 5, Mecklenburg

Davidson College — 4-UC
PO BOX 1737 28036 — 892-2230

Deep Run, AC 919, PC 2, Lenoir
Lenoir County SD
Supt. — See Kinston
South Lenoir HS 28525 — 3-00011
Thomas Salter, prin. — 568-6161

Delco, AC 919, PC 3, Columbus
Columbus County SD
Supt. — See Whiteville
Acme-Delco MS, PO BOX 40 28436 — 3-00100
Edward Thompson, prin. — 655-3200

Denton, AC 704, PC 4, Davidson
Davidson County SD
Supt. — See Lexington
South Davidson JSHS — 3-00111
RR 2 BOX 2000 27239 — 869-3533
Ronnie Robbins, prin.

Denver, AC 704, PC 2, Lincoln
Lincoln County SD
Supt. — See Lincolnton
East Lincoln HS — 3-00011
1800 HIGHWAY 73 W 28037 — 483-5681
Joy Schrum, prin.

Dobson, AC 919, PC 4, Surry
Surry County SD, PO BOX 364 27017 — 6-11111
Glenn Cook, supt. — 386-8211
Surry Central HS, PO BOX 8 27017 — 3-00011
Larry Couch, prin. — 386-8842
Central MS, 1990 ZEPHYR RD 27017 — 3-00100
Rickey Dobbins, prin. — 386-4018
Other Schools – See Mount Airy, Pilot Mountain

Surry Community College — 5-CC
PO BOX 304 27017 — 386-8121

Dublin, AC 919, PC 2, Bladen

Bladen Community College — 3-CC
PO BOX 266 28332 — 862-2164

Dudley, AC 919, PC 2, Wayne
Wayne County SD
Supt. — See Goldsboro
Southern Wayne HS — 4-00011
RR 4 BOX 55 28333 — 705-6060
George Seagraves, prin.
Brogden MS — 3-01100
3761 US HWY 117 SOUTH ALT 28333 — 705-6010
R. Jones, prin.

Dunn, AC 919, PC 6, Harnett
Harnett County SD
Supt. — See Lillington
MS, N ORANGE AVE 28334 — 3-00100
Newanda Colvin, prin. — 892-1016

Sampson County SD
Supt. — See Clinton
Midway HS, RR 5 BOX 525 28334 — 3-00011
Richard Walters, prin. — 567-6664

Durham, AC 919, PC 9, Durham
Durham County SD — 8-11111
511 CLEVELAND ST 27701 — 560-2000
C. Phillips, supt.
HS, 401 N DUKE ST 27701 — 4-00011
Howard Johnson, prin. — 560-3926
Hillside HS, 1900 CONCORD ST 27707 — 4-00011
Richard Hicks, prin. — 560-3925
Jordan HS, 6806 GARRETT RD 27707 — 4-00011
Harold Rogers, prin. — 560-3912
Northern HS, 117 MASSEY RD 27712 — 4-00011
Isaac Thomas, prin. — 560-3956
Riverside HS — 3-00011
3218 ROSE OF SHARON RD 27712 — 560-3965
William Batchelor, prin.
Southern HS, 800 CLAYTON RD 27703 — 4-00011
Joseph Gilliard, prin. — 560-3968
Brogden MS, 1001 LEON ST 27704 — 3-00100
John Hunter, prin. — 560-3906
Carrington MS, 227 MILTON RD 27712 — 4-00100
Fred Putney, prin. — 560-3916
Chewning MS, 6819 RED MILL RD 27704 — 3-00100
Raymond Paris, prin. — 560-3914
Githens MS — 3-00100
4800 CHAPEL HILL RD 27707 — 560-3966
Brandon Smith, prin.
Holton MS, 401 N DRIVER ST 27703 — 2-00100
William Payne, prin. — 560-3931
Lowes Grove MS — 3-00100
4418 S ALSTON AVE 27713 — 560-3946
John Elledge, prin.
Neal MS, 201 BAPTIST RD 27704 — 3-00100
Edward Forsythe, prin. — 560-3955
Rogers-Herr MS — 2-00100
911 W CORNWALLIS RD 27707 — 560-3970
John Howard, prin.
Shepard MS, 2401 DAKOTA ST 27707 — 2-00100
Queen Bass, prin. — 560-3938

Carolina Friends S — 2-11111
RR 1 BOX 183 27705 — 383-6602
John Baird, prin.
Cresset Christian Academy — 2-11111
3707 GARRETT RD 27707 — 489-7258
Robert Cooke, prin.
Duke University 27706 — 7-UC
684-3214
Durham Academy, 3601 RIDGE RD 27705 — 3-11111
Donald North, prin. — 489-6569
Durham County General Hospital — HSP
3643 N ROXBORO RD 27704 — 470-7347
Durham Technical Community College — 5-CC
1637 E LAWSON ST 27703 — 598-9224
Hill Learning Center — 2-11111
3130 PICKETT RD 27705 — 489-7464
Sharon Maskel, prin.
Liberty Christian S — 2-11111
1606 LIBERTY ST 27703 — 683-5522
Loren Kurtz, prin.
Mount Zion Christian Academy — 2-11111
3519 FAYETTEVILLE ST 27707 — 682-4605
Marcheta Riley, prin.
North Carolina Central University — 6-UC
PO BOX 19617 27707 — 560-6298

East Bend, AC 919, PC 3, Yadkin
Yadkin County SD
Supt. — See Yadkinville
Forbush HS, RR 2 BOX 944 27018 — 3-00011
Patricia Craver-Beck, prin. — 961-4644

East Flat Rock, AC 704, PC 5, Henderson
Henderson County SD
Supt. — See Hendersonville
East Henderson HS — 3-00011
110 UPWARD RD 28726 — 697-4768
Carroll Mullins, prin.
Flat Rock JHS — 3-00100
1028 W BLUE RIDGE RD 28726 — 697-4775
David Jones, prin.

East Spencer, AC 704, PC 4, Rowan
Rowan-Salisbury County SD
Supt. — See Salisbury
North Rowan MS, PO BOX 429 28039 — 3-00100
Harold Thomas, prin. — 639-3018

Eden, AC 919, PC 7, Rockingham
Rockingham County SD — 5-11111
511 HARRINGTON HWY 27288 — 627-2600
Ira Trollinger, supt.
Morehead HS, 134 N PIERCE ST 27288 — 3-00011
Robert Harger, prin. — 627-7731
Holmes MS, 211 N PIERCE ST 27288 — 3-00100
George Reynolds, prin. — 623-9791
Other Schools – See Madison, Mayodan, Reidsville,
Ruffin, Wentworth

Edenton, AC 919, PC 6, Chowan
Edenton/Chowan County SD — 5-11111
PO BOX 206 27932 — 482-4436
John Dunn, supt.
Holmes HS, 600 WOODARD ST 27932 — 3-00011
James Boyce, prin. — 482-8426
Other Schools – See Tyner

Elizabeth City, AC 919, PC 7, Pasquotank
Elizabeth City/Pasquotank County SD — 6-11111
1200 HALSTEAD BLVD 27909 — 335-2981
Joseph Peel, supt.
Northeastern HS — 4-00011
963 OAK STUMP RD 27909 — 335-2932
Gene Yarbrough, prin.
MS, 306 N ROAD ST 27909 — 3-00100
Diane Bradford, prin. — 335-2974

College of the Albemarle — 4-CC
PO BOX 2327 27906 — 335-0821
Elizabeth City State University — 4-UC
1704 WEEKSVILLE RD 27909 — 335-3305
Roanoke Bible College — 2-UC
714 1ST ST 27909 — 338-5191
Victory Christian S — 2-11111
684 OLD HERTFORD HWY 27909 — 264-2011
Rev. R. Parker, prin.

Elizabethtown, AC 919, PC 5, Bladen
Bladen County SD, PO BOX 37 28337 — 6-11111
Ray Brayboy, supt. — 862-4136
East Bladen HS, PO BOX 578 28337 — 3-00011
John Foye, prin. — 862-3033
Bladen MS, PO BOX 638 28337 — 3-00100
John Kirk, prin. — 862-4071
Other Schools – See Bladenboro, Clarkton, Tar Heel

Elkin, AC 919, PC 5, Surry
Elkin CSD, 241 CHURCH ST 28621 — 3-11111
Donald Lassiter, supt. — 835-3135
JSHS, 334 ELK SPUR ST 28621 — 2-00111
Charles Parsons, prin. — 835-3858

Elm City, AC 919, PC 4, Wilson
Wilson County SD
Supt. — See Wilson
MS, 215 CHURCH ST E 27822 — 2-00100
Dan Williams, prin. — 236-4148

Elon College, AC 919, PC 5, Alamance
Alamance County SD
Supt. — See Graham
Western HS — 3-00011
1731 N NC HIGHWAY 87 27244 — 538-6020
Sam Fowler, prin.

Western MS, 2100 ELDON DR 27244   3-00100
Sondra Aheron, prin.   538-6010

Elon College   5-UC
PO BOX 2700 27244   800-334-8448

Enfield, AC 919, PC 5, Halifax
Halifax County SD
   Supt. — See Halifax
Eastman MS, RR 2 BOX 143A 27823   2-00100
   Alfred Riddick, prin.   445-3720
MS, PO BOX 128 27823   2-00100
   Claude Cooper, prin.   445-5502

Enka, AC 704, PC 6, Buncombe
Buncombe County SD
   Supt. — See Asheville
HS, 475 ENKA LAKE RD 28728   4-00011
   Bruce Peterson, prin.   667-5421

Erwin, AC 919, PC 5, Harnett
Harnett County SD
   Supt. — See Lillington
Triton HS, RR 1 BOX 210 28339   4-00011
   Daniel Honeycutt, prin.   897-8121
MS, 301 S 10TH ST 28339   2-01100
   Willard McCaskill, prin.   897-7178

Cape Fear Christian Academy   2-11111
   RR 1 BOX 139A 28339   897-5423
   William Autry, prin.

Fairmont, AC 919, PC 4, Robeson
Robeson County SD
   Supt. — See Lumberton
HS, RR 4 BOX 190A 28340   3-00011
   Dallas Freeman, prin.   628-6727
Fairgrove MS, RR 1 BOX 40 28340   2-01100
   Donald Frye, prin.   628-8290
MS, 402 IONA ST 28340   3-01100
   Janet Owen, prin.   628-9728

Farmville, AC 919, PC 5, Pitt
Pitt County SD
   Supt. — See Greenville
Farmville Central HS   3-00011
   PO BOX 209 27828   753-5138
   Charles Long, prin.
MS, PO BOX 50 27828   3-00100
   Richard Cutler, prin.   753-2116

Fayetteville, AC 910, PC 8, Cumberland
Cumberland County SD   8-11111
   PO BOX 2357 28302   678-2300
   John Griffin, supt.
Byrd SHS, 1624 IRELAND DR 28304   4-00001
   E. Jackson, prin.   484-8121
Cape Fear SHS, 4000 CLINTON RD 28301   3-00001
   Rufus Hales, prin.   483-0191
Pine Forest SHS   4-00001
   525 ANDREWS RD 28311   488-2384
   Wayne Byrd, prin.
Sanford SHS   4-00001
   2301 FORT BRAGG RD 28303   484-1151
   David Pugh, prin.
Seventy-First SHS   4-00001
   6764 RAEFORD RD 28304   867-3116
   Gerald Patterson, prin.
Smith SHS, 1800 SEABROOK RD 28301   4-00001
   Lonnie McAllister, prin.   483-0153
Westover SHS, 277 BONANZA DR 28303   4-00001
   William Shipp, prin.   864-0190
Armstrong JHS, RR 1 BOX 121C 28301   2-00110
   Gwen Edwards, prin.   483-2425
Byrd JHS, 1616 IRELAND DR 28304   4-00110
   Larry Lancaster, prin.   483-3101
Chapel JHS, 2150 SKIBO RD 28314   3-00110
   Paris Jones, prin.   864-1407
Chesnutt JHS, 2121 SKIBO RD 28314   3-00110
   E. Freeman, prin.   867-9147
Hillcrest JHS   3-00110
   590 WINDING CREEK RD 28305   323-2201
   Mary McDoffie, prin.
Pine Forest JHS, 6737 RAMSEY ST 28311   3-00110
   Marvin Lucas, prin.   488-2711
Ross JHS, 3200 RAMSEY ST 28301   3-00110
   Robert Lucas, prin.   488-8415
Westover JHS, 275 BONANZA DR 28303   3-00110
   J. Williams, prin.   864-0813
Other Schools – See Hope Mills, Spring Lake,
   Stedman

Berean Baptist Academy   2-11111
   518 GLENSFORD DR 28314   868-2511
   Mark French, prin.
Cornerstone Christian Academy   2-11111
   3000 SCOTTY HILL RD 28303   867-1166
   Rick Williamson, prin.
Fayetteville Academy   2-11111
   3200 CLIFFDALE RD 28303   868-5131
   Benjamine Crabtree, prin.
Fayetteville Christian S   2-11111
   1428 IRELAND DR 28304   483-3905
   Tammi Peters, prin.
Fayetteville State University   5-UC
   1200 MURCHISON RD 28301   486-1157
Fayetteville Technical Community College   5-CC
   PO BOX 35236 28303   678-8437
Methodist College   4-UC
   5400 RAMSEY ST 28311   488-7110

Flat Rock, AC 704, PC 4, Henderson

Blue Ridge Community College   4-CC
   RR 2 BOX 133A 28731   692-3572

Fletcher, AC 704, PC 5, Henderson

Fletcher Academy   2-00011
   PO BOX 5440 28732   687-8738
   Spencer Hannah, prin.

Forest City, AC 704, PC 6, Rutherford
Rutherford County SD
   Supt. — See Spindale
Chase HS, RR 5 28043   3-00011
   Patricia Keeter, prin.   245-7668
East Rutherford HS   4-00011
   PO BOX 635 28043   245-6424
   Connie Hamrick, prin.
Cool Springs MS, 428 W MAIN ST 28043   2-00100
   Phillip Cook, prin.   245-2411

Fort Bragg, AC 919, PC 8, Cumberland
Fort Bragg SD, PO BOX 70089 28307   5-11110
   Frank Cleary, supt.   436-5410
Albritton MS, PO BOX 70089 28307   2-00110
   Richard Ensley, prin.   436-0025

Four Oaks, AC 919, PC 4, Johnston
Johnston County SD
   Supt. — See Smithfield
South Johnston HS   4-00011
   10381 US HIGHWAY 301 S 27524   894-3146
   Ann Williams, prin.
Four Oaks MS, HATCHER ST 27524   2-00100
   Robert Deaton, prin.   963-4022

Franklin, AC 704, PC 5, Macon
Macon County SD   5-11111
   PO BOX 1029 28734   524-3314
   Lonnie Crawford, supt.
HS, 23 SCHOOL DR 28734   3-00011
   Gary Sheilds, prin.   524-6467
Macon MS   2-00100
   121 WELLS GROVE RD 28734   524-3766
   C. Sanders, prin.
Other Schools – See Highlands, Topton

Lyndon B Johnson Conservation Center   2-CS
   466 JOB CORP DR 28734

Franklinton, AC 919, PC 4, Franklin
Franklinton CSD, 1 N MAIN ST 27525   4-11111
   Peggy McGhee, supt.   494-2185
JSHS, 1 N MAIN ST 27525   3-00111
   John Daniels, prin.   494-2332

Fremont, AC 919, PC 4, Wayne
Wayne County SD
   Supt. — See Goldsboro
Norwayne MS, RR 2 27830   3-00100
   Rich Sauls, prin.   242-3414

Fuquay-Varina, AC 919, PC 5, Wake
Wake County SD
   Supt. — See Raleigh
HS, 201 BROAD ST 27526   3-00011
   Charles Rose, prin.   557-2511
MS, 104 N WOODROW ST 27526   3-00100
   Carroll Reed, prin.   557-2727

Garner, AC 919, PC 7, Wake
Wake County SD
   Supt. — See Raleigh
HS, 2101 SPRING DR 27529   4-00011
   James Knox, prin.   662-2379
East Garner MS   3-00100
   900 E GARNER RD 27529   662-2339
   R. Cobb, prin.
North Garner MS, 720 POWELL DR 27529   3-00100
   Gregory Norris, prin.   662-2434

Gaston, AC 919, PC 4, Northampton
Northampton County SD
   Supt. — See Jackson
Northampton HS West   2-00011
   100 BROUGHTON ST 27832   537-1910
   Willie Gilchrist, prin.
JHS, PO BOX 258 27832   2-00100
   Phil Matthews, prin.   535-2511

Gastonia, AC 704, PC 8, Gaston
Gaston County SD   8-11111
   943 OSCEOLA ST 28054   866-6100
   Edwin West, supt.
Ashbrook SHS   4-00001
   2222 S NEW HOPE RD 28054   866-6600
   Elaine Jenkins, prin.
Huss SHS, 1518 EDGEFIELD AVE 28052   4-00001
   Gary Henry, prin.   866-6610
Grier JHS   3-00110
   1622 E GARRISON BLVD 28054   866-6086
   Steve Huffstetler, prin.
Highland JHS, 1600 N MORRIS ST 28052   2-00110
   Bob Wilkerson, prin.   866-6091
Southwest JHS   3-00110
   1 ROADRUNNER DR 28052   866-6290
   Stephen Brittain, prin.
York-Chester JHS, 601 S CLAY ST 28052   3-00110
   Robert Guthrie, prin.   866-6105
Other Schools – See Belmont, Bessemer City,
   Cherryville, Cramerton, Dallas, Lowell, Mount
   Holly, Stanley

Gaston Day S   2-11111
   2001 GASTON DAY SCHOOL RD 28056
   Phillip Brady, prin.   864-7744
Gaston Memorial Hospital   HSP
   2525 COURT DR 28054   866-2121
Victory Christian Academy   2-11111
   310 CAROLINA AVE 28052   867-1731
   Kenneth Peek, prin.

Gatesville, AC 919, PC 2, Gates
Gates County SD, PO BOX 125 27938   4-11111
   Cleveland Hawkins, supt.   357-1113
Gates County HS, RR 1 BOX 93A 27938   2-00011
   William Lawrence, prin.   357-0720
Central JHS, RR 1 BOX 81 27938   2-00100
   James Norfleet, prin.   357-0470

Gibsonville, AC 919, PC 5, Guilford
Guilford County SD
   Supt. — See Greensboro
Eastern Guilford HS   3-00011
   415 PEEDEN DR 27249   274-8461
   Linda Teague, prin.

Glenville, AC 704, PC 3, Jackson
Jackson County SD
   Supt. — See Sylva
Blue Ridge S, PO BOX 429 28736   2-11111
   Fred Harris, prin.   743-2646

Goldsboro, AC 919, PC 8, Wayne
Wayne County SD   7-11111
   301 N HERMAN ST 27530   736-1104
   W. Flowers, supt.
Eastern Wayne HS   4-00011
   1135 NEW HOPE RD 27534   751-7120
   Freddie Carroll, prin.
HS, 901 BEECH ST 27530   4-00011
   Gerald Whitley, prin.   731-5930
Rosewood JSHS   2-00111
   900 ROSEWOOD RD 27530   705-6050
   Wayne Williams, prin.
Eastern Wayne MS   3-00100
   3518 CENTRAL HEIGHTS RD 27534   751-7110
   William Turner, prin.
MS, 801 LIONEL ST 27530   3-00100
   (—), prin.   731-5940
Greenwood MS, 3209 E ASH ST 27534   3-01100
   Sandra McCullen, prin.   751-7100
Other Schools – See Dudley, Fremont, Mount Olive,
   Pikeville

Faith Christian Academy   2-11111
   1200 W GRANTHAM ST 27530   734-8700
   Walter Sloan, prin.
Wayne Christian S   2-11111
   1704 BEECH ST 27530   734-5684
   Fred Clifford, prin.
Wayne Community College   4-CC
   PO BOX 8002 27533   735-5151
Wayne Country Day S   2-11111
   PO BOX 10279 27532   736-1045
   David Wachter, prin.

Graham, AC 919, PC 7, Alamance
Alamance County SD, 609 RAY ST 27253   7-11111
   Mary Jo Utley, supt.   226-8465
HS, 903 TROLLINGER RD 27253   3-00011
   Bradford Evans, prin.   570-6440
Southern HS   3-00011
   631 SOUTHERN HIGH SCHOOL RD 27253
   Mark Rumley, prin.   570-6400
MS, 311 E PINE ST 27253   3-00100
   Dorothy Humble, prin.   570-6460
Southern MS   3-00100
   771 SOUTHERN HIGH SCHOOL RD 27253
   J. Barrett, prin.   570-6500
Other Schools – See Elon College, Mebane

Alamance Christian S   2-11111
   PO BOX 838 27253   578-3340
   Robert La Tour, prin.

Granite Falls, AC 704, PC 5, Caldwell
Caldwell County SD
   Supt. — See Lenoir
MS, 90 N MAIN ST 28630   3-00100
   C. Burns, prin.   396-2341

Grantsboro, AC 919, PC 3, Pamlico

Pamlico Community College   2-CC
   PO BOX 185 28529   249-1851

Greensboro, AC 919, PC 9, Guilford
Guilford County SD   8-11111
   712 N EUGENE ST 27401   370-8100
   Jerry West, supt.
Dudley HS, 1200 LINCOLN ST 27401   4-00011
   (—), prin.   370-8130
Grimsley HS, 801 WESTOVER TER 27408   4-00011
   (—), prin.   370-8180
Northwest Guilford HS   4-00011
   5240 NW SCHOOL RD 27409   605-3300
   Roger Nelson, prin.
Page HS, 201 ALMA PINNIX DR 27405   4-00011
   Paul Puryear, prin.   370-8200
Smith HS, 2407 S HOLDEN RD 27407   4-00011
   Barry Williams, prin.   294-7300
Southeast Guilford HS   4-00011
   4530 SE SCHOOL RD 27406   674-4300
   Barb Murr, prin.

Southern Guilford HS 3-00011
5700 DRAKE RD 27406 674-0526
James Foster, prin.
Western Guilford HS 3-00011
409 FRIENDWAY RD 27410 292-2088
Debra Barham, prin.
Allen MS, 1108 GLENDALE DR 27406 3-00100
Joseph Johnson, prin. 819-2890
Aycock MS, 811 CYPRESS ST 27405 3-00100
James Long, prin. 370-8110
Guilford MS, 401 COLLEGE RD 27410 4-01100
Oakley Mabe, prin. 316-5833
Jackson MS, 2200 ONTARIO ST 27403 3-00100
Jerry Hairston, prin. 294-7350
Kiser MS, 716 BENJAMIN PKY 27408 3-00100
Margaret Bray, prin. 370-8240
Lincoln MS, 1016 LINCOLN ST 27401 3-00100
(—), prin. 370-8250
Mendenhall MS 3-00100
205 WILLOUGHBY BLVD 27408 545-2000
Charles Benton, prin.
Northwest Guilford MS 3-00100
5300 NW SCHOOL RD 27409 605-3333
Robert Boles, prin.
Southeast MS 3-00100
4825 WOODY MILL RD 27406 674-4280
Mary Jones, prin.
Other Schools – See Gibsonville, High Point,
Jamestown, Mc Leansville

Bennett College 3-UC
900 E WASHINGTON ST 27401 800-338-2366
Brookstone College of Business 2-CS
7815 NATIONAL SERVICE RD 27409 668-2627
Central North Carolina Sch. for the Deaf HND
PO BOX 14670 27415
ECPI Computer Institute 2-CS
7015G ALBERT PICK RD 27409 665-1400
Greensboro College 3-UC
815 W MARKET ST 27401 800-346-8226
Greensboro Day S 3-11111
PO BOX 26805 27429 288-8590
Ralph Davidson, prin.
Guilford College 4-UC
5800 W FRIENDLY AVE 27410 800-992-7759
Moses H. Cone Memorial Hospital HSP
1200 N ELM ST 27401 379-3881
North Carolina A&T State University 6-UC
1601 E MARKET ST 27411 334-7946
University of North Carolina 7-UC
1000 SPRING GARDEN ST 27412 334-5243
Vandalia Christian S 2-11111
3919 PLEASANT GARDEN RD 27406 379-8380
Donald Oates, prin.

Greenville, AC 919, PC 8, Pitt
Pitt County SD, 1717 W 5TH ST 27834 7-11111
Howard Sosne, supt. 830-4200
Conley HS, RR 13 BOX 230 27858 4-00011
N. Baldree, prin. 756-3440
Rose HS 4-00011
600 W ARLINGTON BLVD 27834 752-3169
(—), prin.
Aycock MS 3-00100
1325 RED BRICKS ROAD 27834 756-4181
Carl Tadlock, prin.
Eppes MS, 1100 S ELM ST 27858 3-00100
Carolyn Ferebee, prin. 757-2160
Wellcome MS, RR 6 BOX 76 27834 3-00100
Bruce Gray, prin. 752-5938
Other Schools – See Ayden, Bethel, Farmville,
Winterville

East Carolina University 7-UC
1000 E 5TH ST 27858 757-6640
Greenville Christian Academy 2-11111
2001 GREENVILLE BLVD SW 27834 756-0939
Westley Smith, prin.
Pitt Community College 5-CC
PO BOX 7007 27835 355-4245
Trinity Christian S 2-11111
3111 GOLDEN RD 27858 758-0037
Larry Bryan, prin.

Grifton, AC 919, PC 4, Lenoir
Lenoir County SD
Supt. — See Kinston
Savannah MS, RR 2 BOX 275 28530 2-00100
Linwood Grant, prin. 527-8897

Halifax, AC 919, PC 2, Halifax
Halifax County SD 6-11111
PO BOX 468 27839 583-5111
Steven Wrenn, supt.
Southeast Halifax HS 3-00011
RR 1 BOX 206 27839 445-2027
Wayne Miller, prin.
Other Schools – See Enfield, Littleton, Roanoke
Rapids, Scotland Neck

Hallsboro, AC 919, PC 3, Columbus
Columbus County SD
Supt. — See Whiteville
MS 28442 3-01100
Bill Shipman, prin. 646-4192

Hamlet, AC 919, PC 6, Richmond
Richmond County SD 6-11111
522 W HAMLET AVE 28345 582-5860
M. James, supt.
JHS, 1406 MCDONALD AVE 28345 3-00110
Robert Beck, prin. 582-7903
Other Schools – See Rockingham

Richmond Community College 3-CC
PO BOX 1189 28345 582-7052

Hampstead, AC 919, PC 3, Pender
Pender County SD
Supt. — See Burgaw
Topsail HS 3-00011
17445 US HIGHWAY 17 N 28443 270-2755
Larry Poore, prin.
Topsail MS 2-00100
17447 US HIGHWAY 17 N 28443 270-2612
E. Highsmith, prin.

Harrells, AC 919, PC 2, Sampson

Harrells Christian Academy 2-11111
PO BOX 88 28444 532-4575
Robert Vanderslice, prin.

Havelock, AC 919, PC 7, Craven
Craven County SD
Supt. — See New Bern
HS, 101 WEBB BLVD 28532 4-00011
O. Gainey, prin. 444-5112
MS, 102 HIGH SCHOOL DR 28532 4-00100
Alvin West, prin. 444-5125

Haw River, AC 919, PC 4, Alamance

Alamance Community College 5-CC
PO BOX 623 27258 578-2002

Hayesville, AC 704, PC 2, Clay
Clay County SD 4-11111
178 YELLOW JACKET DR 28904 389-8513
Douglas Penland, supt.
HS, 177 YELLOW JACKET DR 28904 2-00011
Gail Criss, prin. 389-6532
MS, 300 YELLOW JACKET DR 28904 2-01100
Connie Bristol, prin. 389-9924

Hays, AC 919, PC 4, Wilkes
Wilkes County SD
Supt. — See Wilkesboro
North Wilkes HS 28635 3-00011
Peggy Martin, prin. 957-8601

Henderson, AC 919, PC 7, Vance
Vance County SD 6-11111
128 CHURCH ST 27536 – (—), supt. 492-2127
Northern Vance HS 4-00011
RR 6 BOX 285 27536 492-6041
J. Adcock, prin.
Southern Vance HS 3-00011
RR 1 BOX 937 27536 430-6000
Celeste Brown, prin.
Eaton-Johnson MS 3-00100
500 W ROCK SPRING ST 27536 438-5017
Beverly Smith, prin.
MS, 219 CHARLES ST 27536 3-00100
Anna Hager, prin. 492-0054

Kerr Vance Academy 2-11111
RR 4 BOX 213 27536 492-0018
Sarah Sponenberg, prin.
Vance-Granville Community College 5-CC
PO BOX 917 27536 492-2061

Hendersonville, AC 704, PC 6, Henderson
Henderson County SD 6-11111
125 E ALLEN ST 28792 697-4733
Dan Lunsford, supt.
HS, 311 8TH AVE W 28739 3-00011
William Dalbec, prin. 693-3381
North Henderson HS 3-00011
35 FRUITLAND RD 28792 697-4500
Charles Thomas, prin.
West Henderson HS 3-00011
3600 HAYWOOD RD 28739 891-6571
Kathy Revis, prin.
Apple Valley MS 3-00100
43 FRUITLAND RD 28792 697-4545
William Sink, prin.
JHS, 930 9TH AVE W 28739 2-00100
W. Wilkins, prin. 697-4800
Rugby MS, 3555 HAYWOOD RD 28739 3-00100
Catherine Credle, prin. 891-6566
Other Schools – See East Flat Rock

Faith Christian S 2-11111
708 OLD SPARTANBURG RD 28792 692-0556
Donald Schearer, prin.

Henrietta, AC 704, PC 4, Rutherford
Rutherford County SD
Supt. — See Spindale
Tri-Community MS 2-01100
PO BOX 649 28076 657-6373
Douglas Clark, prin.

Hertford, AC 919, PC 4, Perquimans
Perquimans County SD 4-11111
411 S EDENTON ROAD ST 27944 426-5741
Randall Henion, supt.
Perquimans HS, PO BOX 398 27944 2-00011
W. Byrum, prin. 426-5778
Other Schools – See Winfall

Hickory, AC 704, PC 8, Catawba
Catawba County SD
Supt. — See Newton
St. Stephen's HS 4-00011
3205 34TH STREET DR NE 28601 256-9841
J. Carraway, prin.

Arndt MS, RR 2 BOX 145 28601 3-00100
Kenneth Throneburg, prin. 256-9545

Hickory CSD, 432 4TH AVE SW 28602 5-11111
Stuart Thompson, supt. 322-2855
HS, 1234 3RD ST NE 28601 4-00011
Dan Massey, prin. 322-5860
College Park MS, 409 8TH AVE NE 28601 2-00100
Martha Hill, prin. 322-4660
Grandview MS, 737 12TH ST SW 28602 2-00100
Tanya Honeycutt, prin. 328-2289

Catawba Valley Community College 5-CC
RR 3 BOX 283 28602 327-9124
Lenoir-Rhyne College 4-UC
PO BOX 292 28603 800-277-5721
Tabernacle Christian Academy 2-11111
1225 29TH AVENUE DR NE 28601 324-9936
David Hicks, prin.

Hiddenite, AC 704, PC 3, Alexander
Alexander County SD
Supt. — See Taylorsville
East JHS, RR 2 BOX 358-C 28636 3-00110
Charles Sherrill, prin. 632-7670

Highlands, AC 704, PC 3, Macon
Macon County SD
Supt. — See Franklin
S, PO BOX 940 28741 2-11111
W. Brooks, prin. 526-2147

High Point, AC 919, PC 8, Guilford
Guilford County SD
Supt. — See Greensboro
Andrews HS, 1920 MCGUINN DR 27265 4-00011
E Thomas, prin. 819-2810
High Point Central HS 3-00011
801 FERNDALE BLVD 27262 882-6839
R. Krall, prin.
Southwest HS, 4364 BARROW RD 27265 3-00011
Earl Crotts, prin. 819-2882
Ferndale MS 3-00100
701 FERNDALE BLVD 27262 819-2900
Jules Crowell, prin.
Griffin MS, E WASHINGTON DR 27260 2-00100
Michael Seamon, prin. 819-2910
Jay MS, 1201 E FAIRFIELD RD 27263 3-00100
Charles Williard, prin. 431-1968
Welborn MS, 1710 MCGUINN DR 27265 3-00100
John Schroeder, prin. 819-2929
Southwest MS, 4368 BARROW RD 27265 3-00100
Helen Langford, prin. 819-2933

High Point College 4-UC
933 MONTLIEU AVE 27262 841-9000
John Wesley College 1-UC
2314 N CENTENNIAL ST 27265 889-2262
Mount Calvary Christian S 2-11111
RR 4 BOX 1057 27263 434-6800
Richard Callahan, prin.
Wesleyan Academy 3-11111
1917 N CENTENNIAL ST 27262 884-3333
Joel Farlow, prin.
Westchester Academy 2-11111
204 PINE TREE LN 27265 869-2128
Peter Cowen, prin.

Hillsborough, AC 919, PC 5, Orange
Orange County SD, 200 E KING ST 27278 6-11111
N. Andrew Overstreet, supt. 732-8126
Orange HS 4-00011
500 ORANGE HIGH RD 27278 732-6133
Steve Halkiotis, prin.
Stanford MS 3-00100
308 ORANGE HIGH SCHOOL RD 27278
Gary Hodgson, prin. 732-6121

Abundant Life Christian Academy 2-11111
512 US HIGHWAY 70 E 27278 732-0888
Daniel Peters, prin.
St. Mary S, 7500 SCHLEY RD 27278 2-11111
Milton Little, prin. 732-7200

Hobgood, AC 919, PC 2, Halifax

Hobgood Academy 2-11111
PO BOX 307 27843 826-4116
John Hardison, prin.

Holly Ridge, AC 919, PC 3, Onslow
Onslow County SD
Supt. — See Jacksonville
Dixon HS 3-00011
160 DIXON SCHOOL RD 28445 347-2958
James Rochelle, prin.
Dixon MS 2-01100
200 DIXON SCHOOL RD 28445 347-2738
Albert James, prin.

Hookerton, AC 919, PC 2, Greene

Mount Calvary Christian Academy 2-11111
PO BOX 250 28538 747-8111
Gary Crawford, prin.

Hope Mills, AC 919, PC 6, Cumberland
Cumberland County SD
Supt. — See Fayetteville
South View SHS 4-00001
4800 ELK MILL RD 28348 425-8181
J. Buffaloe, prin.

JHS, 220 CAMERON RD 28348 — 3-00110
Mary Johnson, prin. — 425-5106
South View JHS — 3-00110
4800 ELK MILL RD 28348 — 424-3131
Peter Stallings, prin.

Hudson, AC 704, PC 5, Caldwell
Caldwell County SD
Supt. — See Lenoir
South Caldwell HS — 4-00011
RR 3 BOX 600 28638 — 396-2188
W. Anderson, prin.
MS, 291 PINE MOUNTAIN RD 28638 — 3-00100
Bryon Tolbert, prin. — 728-4281

Harris Chapel Christian Academy — 2-11111
RR 2 BOX 393 28638 — 728-2370
Allen Norrod, prin.

Huntersville, AC 704, PC 5, Mecklenburg
Charlotte/Mecklenburg Co SD
Supt. — See Charlotte
North Mecklenburg SHS — 4-00001
11201 OLD STATESVILLE RD 28078 — 343-3840
M. Turner, prin.
Alexander JHS — 3-00110
12201 HAMBRIGHT RD 28078 — 343-3830
Jim Poole, prin.

Icard, AC 704, PC 5, Burke
Burke County SD
Supt. — See Morganton
East Burke HS, PO BOX 515 28666 — 4-00011
Charles Williams, prin. — 397-5541
East Burke MS, PO BOX 1150 28666 — 3-00100
Robert Patton, prin. — 397-7446

Iron Station, AC 704, PC 2, Lincoln
Lincoln County SD
Supt. — See Lincolnton
East Lincoln MS — 3-00100
4137 HIGHWAY 73 28080 — 732-0761
Henry Barkley, prin.

Jackson, AC 919, PC 3, Northampton
Northampton County SD — 5-11111
PO BOX 158 27845 — 534-1371
Charles Slemenda, supt.
Other Schools – See Conway, Gaston

Jacksonville, AC 910, PC 8, Onslow
Onslow County SD — 7-11111
200 BROADHURST RD 28540 — 455-2211
Ronald Singletary, supt.
HS, 1021 HENDERSON DR 28540 — 4-00011
Jay Randall, prin. — 346-9706
Southwest HS — 3-00011
500 BURGAW HWY 28540 — 455-4888
James Collins, prin.
White Oak HS — 3-00011
1950 PINEY GREEN RD 28546 — 455-1541
Paul Wiggins, prin.
Hunters Creek MS — 3-00100
85 HUNTERS TRL 28546 — 353-2147
R. Whaley, prin.
MS, 401 NEW BRIDGE ST 28540 — 3-00100
Edward Herring, prin. — 346-9504
Northwoods Park MS — 3-00100
904 SIOUX DR 28540 — 347-1202
Alex Boyle, prin.
Southwest MS, 1013 FURIA DR 28540 — 3-00100
Donald Parker, prin. — 455-1105
Other Schools – See Holly Ridge, Richlands, Swansboro

Coastal Carolina Community College — 5-CC
444 WESTERN BLVD 28546 — 455-1221

Jamestown, AC 919, PC 5, Guilford
Guilford County SD
Supt. — See Greensboro
Ragsdale HS, 602 E MAIN ST 27282 — 3-00011
Kathryn Rogers, prin. — 819-2855
MS, 4401 VICKREY CHAPEL RD 27282 — 4-00011
David Kemp, prin. — 819-2920

Guilford Technical Community College — 6-CC
PO BOX 309 27282 — 334-4822

Jamesville, AC 919, PC 3, Martin
Martin County SD
Supt. — See Williamston
S, PO BOX 189 27846 — 3-11111
Phillip Griffin, prin. — 792-4428

Jefferson, AC 919, PC 4, Ashe
Ashe County SD, PO BOX 604 28640 — 5-11111
Morris Walker, supt. — 246-7175
Ashe Central JSHS — 3-00111
626 ASHE CENTRAL SCHOOL RD 28640
Nancy Reeves, prin. — 982-2126
Other Schools – See Warrensville, West Jefferson

Kannapolis, AC 704, PC 8, Cabarrus
Kannapolis CSD, 100 DENVER ST 28083 — 5-11111
Edward Tyson, supt. — 938-1131
Brown HS, 415 E 1ST ST 28083 — 4-00011
John Maye, prin. — 932-6125
MS, 525 E C ST 28083 — 3-00100
Ronald Honbarrier, prin. — 932-4102

Kenansville, AC 919, PC 3, Duplin
Duplin County SD — 6-11111
PO BOX 128 28349 — 296-1521
Leonard Guy, supt.

Smith MS, PO BOX 368 28349 — 2-00100
Pat Matthis, prin. — 296-0309
Other Schools – See Beulaville, Calypso, Chinquapin, Rose Hill, Teachey, Warsaw

James Sprunt Community College — 3-CC
PO BOX 398 28349 — 296-2500

Kenly, AC 919, PC 4, Johnston
Johnston County SD
Supt. — See Smithfield
North Johnston HS — 3-00011
PO BOX 338 27542 — 284-2031
Gary Carter, prin.
North Johnston MS — 2-00100
RR 4 BOX 139 27542 — 284-3374
Hilda White, prin.

Kernersville, AC 919, PC 7, Forsyth
Winston-Salem/Forsyth SD
Supt. — See Winston-Salem
East Forsyth HS — 4-00011
2500 W MOUNTAIN ST 27284 — 727-2265
Deborah Brooks, prin.
Glenn HS, 1600 UNION CROSS RD 27284 — 4-00011
Adolpus Coplin, prin. — 788-2932

Kerwin Baptist Christian S — 2-11111
4520 OLD HOLLOW RD 27284 — 993-3791
Ted Aschenbrand, prin.

Kill Devil Hills, AC 919, PC 5, Dare
Dare County SD
Supt. — See Manteo
First Flight MS, 109 RUN HILL RD 27948 — 2-00100
Sandy Brooks, prin. — 441-8888

King, AC 919, PC 5, Stokes
Stokes County SD
Supt. — See Danbury
Chestnut Grove JHS — 3-00110
RR 4 BOX 185 27021 — 983-2106
William Collins, prin.

Calvary Christian S — 2-11111
PO BOX 136 27021 — 983-3728
Anthony Keel, prin.

Kings Mountain, AC 704, PC 6, Cleveland
King's Mountain CSD — 5-11111
500 W PARKER ST 28086 — 734-5637
Robert McRae, supt.
HS, 500 PHIFER RD 28086 — 3-00011
J. Lavender, prin. — 734-5647
MS, 1000 PHIFER RD 28086 — 3-00100
John Goforth, prin. — 734-5667

Kinston, AC 919, PC 8, Lenoir
Lenoir County SD, 201 E KING ST 28501 — 7-11111
James Wilson, supt. — 527-1109
HS, 2601 N QUEEN ST 28501 — 4-00011
Brenda Canup, prin. — 527-8067
Rochelle MS — 4-00100
300 N ROCHELLE BLVD 28501 — 527-4290
William Heath, prin.
Woodington MS — 3-00100
RR 5 BOX 274 28501 — 527-9570
Vaughn Fowler, prin.
Other Schools – See Deep Run, Grifton, La Grange

Arendell Parrott Academy — 2-11111
PO BOX 1314 28503 — 522-4222
Ike Southerland, prin.
Bethel Christian Academy — 2-11111
RR 2 BOX 385 28501 — 522-4636
Richard Barnard, prin.
Lenoir Community College — 5-CC
PO BOX 188 28502 — 527-6223
Lenoir Memorial Hospital — HSP
PO BOX 1678 28503 — 522-7797

La Grange, AC 919, PC 5, Lenoir
Lenoir County SD
Supt. — See Kinston
North Lenoir HS — 4-00011
RR 1 BOX 194 28551 — 527-9184
Hermon Carraway, prin.
Frink MS, 102 WALTERS ST 28551 — 3-00100
Gerald Roberson, prin. — 566-3326

Lake Waccamaw, AC 919, PC 3, Columbus
Columbus County SD
Supt. — See Whiteville
East Columbus HS — 3-00011
RR 1 BOX 825 28450 — 646-4094
Reginald Lewis, prin.

Landis, AC 704, PC 4, Rowan
Rowan-Salisbury County SD
Supt. — See Salisbury
Corriher Lipe MS, 214 W RICE ST 28088 — 3-00100
Betty Yates, prin. — 857-7946

Lasker, AC 919, PC 99, Northampton

Northeast Academy — 2-11111
PO BOX 126 27848 — 539-2461
Carl Britt, prin.

Laurel Hill, AC 919, PC 4, Scotland
Scotland County SD
Supt. — See Laurinburg
Carver MS, RR 2 BOX 7 28351 — 2-00100
James Tapp, prin. — 462-3601

Laurinburg, AC 919, PC 7, Scotland
Scotland County SD — 6-11111
233 E CHURCH ST 28352 — 276-1138
David Martin, supt.
Scotland HS, 1000 W CHURCH ST 28352 — 4-00011
Raymond Oxendine, prin. — 276-7370
Johnson MS — 2-00100
815 MCGIRTS BRIDGE RD 28352 — 277-4324
Norwood Randolph, prin.
Shaw MS, RR 2 BOX 293 28352 — 2-00100
S. Burgin, prin. — 276-0611
Sycamore Lane MS — 3-00100
2100 SYCAMORE LN 28352 — 277-4350
L. Thomas Clark, prin.
Other Schools – See Laurel Hill

St. Andrews Presbyterian College — 3-UC
1700 DOGWOOD MILE ST 28352 — 277-5555

Lawndale, AC 704, PC 3, Cleveland
Cleveland County SD
Supt. — See Shelby
Burns HS — 3-00011
307 E STAGECOACH TRL 28090 — 538-7403
Ronald Wilson, prin.
Burns JHS, 215 SHADY GROVE RD 28090 — 3-00100
Richard Cornwell, prin. — 538-3126

Leland, AC 919, PC 4, Brunswick
Brunswick County SD
Supt. — See Southport
North Brunswick HS — 3-00011
PO BOX 340 28451 — 371-2261
Robert Harris, prin.
MS, PO BOX 40 28451 — 3-01100
Diana Mintz, prin. — 371-3030

Lenoir, AC 704, PC 7, Caldwell
Caldwell County SD — 7-11111
1914 HICKORY BLVD SE 28645 — 728-8407
Kenneth Roberts, supt.
Hibriten HS, 550 EAST BLVD 28645 — 3-00011
H. Stevens, prin. — 758-7376
West Caldwell HS — 4-00011
300 W CALDWELL DR 28645 — 758-5583
(—), prin.
Gamewell MS, RR 6 BOX 272 28645 — 3-00100
Donnie Bassinger, prin. — 754-6204
MS, 332 GREENHAVEN DR NW 28645 — 2-00100
Helen Hall, prin. — 758-1570
Other Schools – See Granite Falls, Hudson

Caldwell Community College — 5-CC
PO BOX 600 28645 — 726-2200
Morgan School/Patterson Preserve — 1-00111
RR 5 BOX 170 28645
Michael Bradshaw, prin.

Lewisville, AC 919, PC 5, Forsyth

Forsyth Country Day S — 3-11111
PO BOX 549 27023 — 945-3151
Gordon Bingham, prin.

Lexington, PC 7, Davidson
Davidson County SD — 7-11111
PO BOX 2057 27293 — 704-249-8182
W. Max Walser, supt.
Central HS — 3-00011
RR 6 BOX 2265 27292 — 704-352-2920
D. Burt Wagner, prin.
North Davidson HS — 3-00011
RR 10 BOX 1685 27292 — 704-731-8431
Phillip Rapp, prin.
West Davidson HS — 3-00011
RR 5 BOX 334 27292 — 704-956-5580
Kevin Firquin, prin.
Central MS — 3-00100
RR 6 BOX 2275 27292 — 704-352-2310
Kenneth Severt, prin.
North Davidson MS — 3-00100
RR 10 BOX 1660 27292 — 704-731-2331
Stephen Teague, prin.
Other Schools – See Denton, Linwood, Thomasville

Lexington CSD, 1010 FAIR ST 27292 — 5-11111
James Simeon, supt. — 704-242-1527
HS, 26 PENRY ST 27292 — 3-00111
Ashley Hinson, prin. — 704-242-1574
MS, HEMSTEAD ST 27292 — 3-00100
Johnnie Van Roekel, prin. — 704-242-1557

Davidson County Community College — 5-CC
PO BOX 1287 27293 — 704-249-8186
Sheets Memorial Christian S — 2-11111
307 HOLT ST 27292
Dan Hightower, prin.

Lillington, AC 919, PC 4, Harnett
Harnett County SD, 700 MAIN ST 27546 — 7-11111
Ivo Wortman, supt. — 893-1201
Western Harnett HS — 3-00011
RR 2 BOX 175 27546 — 892-1400
Henry Holt, prin.
Western Harnett MS — 2-00100
RR 2 BOX 175A 27546 — 892-4826
Ned White, prin.
Other Schools – See Angier, Dunn, Erwin

Lincolnton, AC 704, PC 6, Lincoln
Lincoln County SD — 6-11111
2682 N HIGHWAY 321 28092 — 732-2261
Martin Eaddy, supt.

HS, 803 N ASPEN ST 28092   3-00011
  Max Houser, prin.   735-3089
West Lincoln HS, 172 SHOAL RD 28092   3-00011
  Kelly Childers, prin.   276-1402
Lincoln S of Tech, 1 TIMKEN DR 28092   Vo Tech
  Mildred Costner, prin.   732-4084
MS, 301 JEB SEAGLE DR 28092   3-00100
  Burlene Eaker, prin.   735-1120
West Lincoln MS, 260 SHOAL RD 28092   3-00100
  Larry Wise, prin.   276-1760
Other Schools – See Denver, Iron Station

Linwood, AC 704, PC 2, Davidson
Davidson County SD
  Supt. — See Lexington
Tyro MS, RR 1 27299   2-00100
  Michael Scott, prin.   956-7795

Littleton, AC 919, PC 3, Halifax
Halifax County SD
  Supt. — See Halifax
Northwest HS, RR 2 BOX 274 27850   4-00011
  Gary Moss, prin.   586-4125

Louisburg, AC 919, PC 5, Franklin
Franklin County SD   5-11111
  105 S BICKETT BLVD 27549   496-4159
  Russell Allen, supt.
HS, 201 ALLEN LN 27549   3-00011
  Robert Barnes, prin.   496-3725
Terrell Lane MS, 101 TERRELL LN 27549   3-00100
  Carl Harris, prin.   496-1855
Other Schools – See Bunn

Louisburg College   3-CC
  501 N MAIN ST 27549   496-2521

Lowell, AC 704, PC 5, Gaston
Gaston County SD
  Supt. — See Gastonia
Holbrook JHS, 418 S CHURCH ST 28098   3-00110
  Anna Cooke, prin.   824-2381

Lucama, AC 919, PC 3, Wilson
Wilson County SD
  Supt. — See Wilson
Springfield MS   2-00100
  7037 SPRINGFIELD SCHOOL RD 27851   239-1347
  Robert Pope, prin.

Lumberton, AC 919, PC 7, Robeson
Robeson County SD   7-11111
  PO BOX 2909 28359   738-4841
  Purnell Swett, supt.
SHS, 3901 FAYETTEVILLE RD 28358   3-00001
  Anthony Parker, prin.   738-5271
Robeson County Career Ctr   Vo Tech
  PO BOX 1328 28359   671-6095
  STACY LOCKLEAR, prin.
Littlefield MS, RR 7 BOX 174 28358   3-01100
  Allen Faircloth, prin.   671-6065
JHS, 82 MARION RD 28358   3-00110
  Dale Maynor, prin.   738-9611
Other Schools – See Fairmont, Maxton, Orrum,
  Pembroke, Red Springs, Rowland, Saint Pauls

Robeson Community College   4-CC
  PO BOX 1420 28359   738-7101

Mc Leansville, AC 919, PC 4, Guilford
Guilford County SD
  Supt. — See Greensboro
Northeast Guilford HS   3-00011
  6700 MCLEANSVILLE RD 27301   375-2500
  Henry Alston, prin.
MS, 5315 FRIEDEN CHURCH RD 27301   3-00100
  David Turner, prin.   697-3199
Northeast Guilford MS   3-00100
  6720 MCLEANSVILLE RD 27301   375-2525
  Kenneth Wheat, prin.

Madison, AC 919, PC 4, Rockingham
Rockingham County SD
  Supt. — See Eden
Western Rockingham MS   3-00100
  915 AYERSVILLE RD 27025   548-2168
  Judy Fowler, prin.

Maiden, AC 704, PC 5, Catawba
Catawba County SD
  Supt. — See Newton
HS, W MAIN ST 28650   2-00011
  William Gatewood, prin.   428-8197
Tuttle MS, RR 1 BOX 38 28650   2-00100
  Kermit Whisnant, prin.   465-7014

Manteo, AC 919, PC 3, Dare
Dare County SD, PO BOX 640 27954   5-11111
  H. Leon Holleman, supt.   473-1151
HS 27954   3-00011
  Linda Holmes, prin.   473-5841
MS 27954   3-00100
  Bobby Hudspeth, prin.   473-5549
Other Schools – See Buxton, Kill Devil Hills

Marion, AC 704, PC 5, McDowell
McDowell County SD   6-11111
  320 S MAIN ST 28752   652-4535
  Dr. David Ricketts, supt.
McDowell HS, HWY 70-W 28752   4-00011
  Gary Laney, prin.   652-7920
East McDowell JHS, 700 STATE ST 28752   3-00110
  Larry Wilkerson, prin.   652-7711
West McDowell JHS, HWY 70-W 28752   3-00110
  Larry Ramsey, prin.   652-3390

McDowell Technical Community College   4-CC
  RR 1 BOX 170 28752   652-6021

Marshall, AC 704, PC 3, Madison
Madison County SD   5-11111
  2 BLANNHASSETT IS 28753   649-9276
  David Wyatt, supt.
Madison HS, 102 MARSHALL BYP 28753   3-00011
  Theresa Banks, prin.   649-2876
Madison MS   3-00100
  1 TURNING POINT PL 28753   649-2269
  Nancy Allen, prin.

Mars Hill, AC 704, PC 4, Madison

Mars Hill College   4-UC
  MAIN ST 28754   800-543-1514

Marshville, AC 704, PC 4, Union
Union County SD
  Supt. — See Monroe
Forest Hills MS   3-00011
  100 FREST HILLS SCHOOL RD S 28103   233-4001
  Barry Aycock, prin.
East Union MS, PO BOX 666 28103   3-00100
  J. McAfee, prin.   624-2114

Matthews, AC 704, PC 7, Mecklenburg
Union County SD
  Supt. — See Monroe
Sun Valley MS   3-00100
  1409 WESLEY CHAPEL RD 28105   283-2161
  G. Faris, prin.

Bible Baptist Christian S   2-11111
  2724 MARGARET WALLACE RD 28105
  Robert Brinkley, prin.   535-1694

Maxton, AC 919, PC 4, Robeson
Robeson County SD
  Supt. — See Lumberton
Townsend MS   2-01100
  134 W CAROLINA ST 28364   844-5086
  Lindsey Quick, prin.

Mayodan, AC 919, PC 4, Rockingham
Rockingham County SD
  Supt. — See Eden
McMichael HS   3-00011
  6845 NC HIGHWAY 135 27027   427-5165
  Pam Riley, prin.

Mebane, AC 919, PC 5, Alamance
Alamance County SD
  Supt. — See Graham
Eastern Alamance HS   3-00011
  4040 MEBANE ROGERS RD 27302   563-5991
  James Pickens, prin.
Woodlawn MS   3-00100
  3970 MEBANE ROGERS RD 27302   563-3222
  Lynn Briggs, prin.

Merry Hill, AC 919, PC 1, Bertie

Lawrence Academy   2-11111
  PO BOX 36 27957   482-4748
  Thomas Gregory, prin.

Millers Creek, AC 919, PC 4, Wilkes
Wilkes County SD
  Supt. — See Wilkesboro
West Wilkes HS 28651   3-00011
  Jerry McGuire, prin.   973-4503
IS, RR 1 BOX 113 28651   3-01100
  Mike Dancy, prin.   838-4065

Misenheimer, AC 704, PC 4, Stanly

Pfeiffer College   3-UC
  GENERAL DELIVERY 28109   463-1360

Mocksville, PC 5, Davie
Davie County SD   5-11111
  220 CHERRY ST 27028   704-634-5921
  William Steed, supt.
Davie County SHS   4-00001
  1200 SALISBURY RD 27028   704-634-5905
  W. Potts, prin.
North Davie JHS   3-00110
  RR 2 BOX 44 27028   919-998-5555
  Larry Bridgewater, prin.
South Davie JHS   3-00110
  135 HARDISON ST 27028   704-634-5941
  Robert Landry, prin.

Monroe, AC 704, PC 7, Union
Union County SD   7-11111
  500 N MAIN ST STE 600 28112   283-2733
  Clifton Dodson, supt.
HS, 1 HIGH SCHOOL DR 28112   3-00011
  Jamie Collins, prin.   289-1556
Parkwood HS   3-00011
  3220 PARKWOOD SCHOOL RD 28112   764-7418
  Joe Caldwell, prin.
Piedmont HS   3-00011
  1619 PIEDMONT SCHOOL RD 28110   753-4713
  Archie Price, prin.
Sun Valley HS   4-00011
  5211 OLD CHARLOTTE HWY 28110   289-8571
  Robert Smith, prin.
Union County Career Center   Vo Tech
  600 BREWER DR 28112   289-5505
  C. Bill Tyson, prin.
MS, 601 E SUNSET DR 28112   3-00100
  Raymond Holman, prin.   289-5471

Parkwood MS   3-00100
  3219 PARKWOOD SCHOOL RD 28112   764-7339
  Larry Stinson, prin.
Piedmont MS   3-00100
  2816 SIKES MILL RD 28110   753-4716
  Gwyn Griffin, prin.
Other Schools – See Marshville, Matthews

Tabernacle Christian S   2-11111
  2900 WALKUP AVE 28110   289-2490
  Robert Sumner, prin.

Montreat, PC 3, Buncombe

Montreat-Anderson College   2-UC
  PO BOX 1267 28757   800-622-6968

Mooresville, AC 704, PC 6, Iredell
Iredell-Statesville SD
  Supt. — See Statesville
Brawley MS, RR 7 BOX 259 28115   2-00100
  Roberta Ellis, prin.   664-4430

Mooresville CSD, 305 N MAIN ST 28115   5-11111
  Jane Carrigan, supt.   664-5553
HS, 659 E CENTER AVE 28115   2-00011
  Joyce Sloop, prin.   664-5545
Woods Tech/Arts HS   Vo Tech
  574 W MCLELLAND AVE 28115   663-3274
  J. Young, prin.
MS, 160 S MAGNOLIA AVE 28115   3-00100
  Randy Bolton, prin.   663-3841

Morehead City, AC 919, PC 6, Carteret
Carteret County SD
  Supt. — See Beaufort
West Carteret HS   4-00011
  RR 2 BOX 390 28557   726-1176
  Dale Patrick, prin.
MS 28557   3-00100
  Harry Stanfield, prin.   726-1126

Carteret Community College   3-CC
  3505 ARENDELL ST 28557   247-4142

Morganton, AC 704, PC 7, Burke
Burke County SD   7-11111
  700 E PARKER RD 28655   433-4300
  Carlos Hicks, supt.
Freedom HS   4-00011
  511 INDEPENDENCE BLVD 28655   433-1310
  David Burleson, prin.
Liberty MS, 529 ENOLA RD 28655   3-00100
  Betty Terrell, prin.   437-1330
Table Rock MS, 1585 NC 126 28655   3-00100
  Susan Fetner, prin.   437-5212
Other Schools – See Icard, Valdese

North Carolina School for the Deaf   HND
  517 W FLEMING DR 28655
Tabernacle Christian S   2-11111
  201 TABERNACLE RD 28655   437-1897
  Robert Key, prin.
Western Piedmont Community College   5-CC
  1001 BURKEMONT AVE 28655   438-6051

Mount Airy, AC 919, PC 6, Surry
Mt. Airy CSD, 119 CHURCH ST 27030   4-11111
  Charles Morris, supt.   786-8355
HS, 1011 N SOUTH ST 27030   2-00011
  Donnie Johnson, prin.   789-5147
JHS, 1019 N SOUTH ST 27030   2-00100
  David Long, prin.   789-9021

Surry County SD
  Supt. — See Dobson
North Surry HS, 2102 W PINE ST 27030   4-00011
  C. Edwards, prin.   789-5055
Gentry MS, 1811 W PINE ST 27030   3-00100
  Bill Sawyers, prin.   786-4155

Northern Hospital of Surry County   2-HSP
  PO BOX 1101 27030   789-9541

Mount Gilead, AC 919, PC 4, Montgomery
Montgomery County SD
  Supt. — See Troy
West Montgomery HS   3-00011
  RR 3 BOX 228 27306   439-6191
  Fred Davis, prin.
West MS, RR 2 BOX 600 27306   2-00100
  Frances Reaves, prin.   572-9378

Mount Holly, AC 704, PC 6, Gaston
Gaston County SD
  Supt. — See Gastonia
East Gaston SHS, 710 S LANE RD 28120   4-00001
  Jim Costner, prin.   827-7251
JHS, 124 S HAWTHORNE ST 28120   3-00110
  Mark Hollar, prin.   827-4811

Mount Olive, AC 919, PC 5, Wayne
Wayne County SD
  Supt. — See Goldsboro
MS, 309 WOOTEN ST 28365   2-01100
  James Williams, prin.   658-7329

Mt. Olive College   3-UC
  209 N BREAZEALE AVE 28365   658-2502

Mount Pleasant, AC 704, PC 4, Cabarrus
Cabarrus County SD
  Supt. — See Concord

HS, 700 WALKER RD 28124 3-00011
Judy Misenheimer, prin. 436-9321
MS, 8325 HIGHWAY 49 N 28124 2-00100
Paul Shouse, prin. 436-9302

Mount Ulla, AC 704, PC 2, Rowan
Rowan-Salisbury County SD
Supt. — See Salisbury
West Rowan HS 3-00011
8050 NC 801 HWY 28125 278-9233
Henry Kluttz, prin.

Murfreesboro, AC 919, PC 5, Hertford
Hertford County SD
Supt. — See Winton
Hertford County MS 3-00100
RR 1 BOX 422B 27855 398-4091
Ronald Hignite, prin.

Chowan College 3-CC
PO BOX 1848 27855 800-488-4101

Murphy, AC 704, PC 4, Cherokee
Cherokee County SD 5-11111
104 HIGH SCHOOL CIR 28906 837-2722
Donald Bentley, supt.
JSHS, 104 HIGH SCHOOL CIR 28906 3-00111
Robert Hendrix, prin. 837-2426
Hiwasee Dam S, RR 4 BOX 207B 28906 2-11111
Ernest Jones, prin. 644-5115
Other Schools – See Andrews

Tri-County Community College 3-CC
PO BOX 40 28906 837-6810

Nashville, AC 919, PC 5, Nash
Nash-Rocky Mount County SD 7-11111
930 EASTERN AVE 27856 459-5220
Travis Twiford, supt.
Nash Central JHS, RR 5 BOX 10 27856 4-00110
Robert Spencer, prin. 459-5292
Other Schools – See Bailey, Rocky Mount, Spring
Hope

New Bern, AC 919, PC 7, Craven
Craven County SD 7-11111
3600 TRENT RD 28562 514-6300
Brad Sneeden, supt.
HS, 4200 ACADEMIC DR 28562 4-00011
William Dill, prin. 514-6400
Fields MS 3-00100
2000 CLARENDON BLVD 28560 514-6438
Terrence Hicks, prin.
MacDonald MS 4-00100
3127 ELIZABETH AVE 28562 514-6450
Glenn Haworth, prin.
West Craven MS 3-00100
515 NW CRVN MDDLE SCHOOL RD 28562
W. Perry, prin. 514-6488
Other Schools – See Havelock, Vanceboro

Craven Community College 4-CC
PO BOX 885 28563 638-4131
Ruths Chapel Christian S 2-11111
2709 OAKS RD 28560 638-1297
David Thompson, prin.

Newland, AC 704, PC 3, Avery
Avery County SD 4-11111
PO BOX 1360 28657 733-6006
Michael Manis, supt.
Avery County HS 3-00011
PO BOX 1300 28657 733-0151
Stephen Sneed, prin.
Avery County MS 2-00100
PO BOX 697 28657 733-0145
Keith Tutterow, prin.

New London, AC 704, PC 2, Stanly
Stanly County SD
Supt. — See Albemarle
North Stanly HS, RR 3 BOX 8 28127 3-00011
George White, prin. 463-7358

Newport, AC 919, PC 5, Carteret
Carteret County SD
Supt. — See Beaufort
Broad Creek MS, RR 1 BOX 13M 28570 3-00100
William Blair, prin. 247-3135

Newton, AC 704, PC 6, Catawba
Catawba County SD 7-11111
PO BOX 1000 28658 464-8333
Glenn Barger, supt.
Foard HS, RR 1 BOX 295 28658 3-00011
J. Biggerstaff, prin. 462-1496
Blackburn MS, RR 1 BOX 231 28658 3-00100
James Christenbury, prin. 462-1827
Other Schools – See Catawba, Claremont, Hickory,
Maiden

Newton-Conover City SD 5-11111
PO BOX 149 28658 464-3191
Everette Simmons, supt.
Newton-Conover HS 3-00011
338 W 15TH ST 28658 465-0920
Gerald Bowman, prin.
Newton-Conover MS 3-00100
221 W 26TH ST 28658 464-4221
Larry Harris, prin.

Newton Grove, AC 919, PC 3, Sampson
Sampson County SD
Supt. — See Clinton

Hobbton HS, RR 2 BOX 153 28366 2-00011
Kenny Bass, prin. 594-0242
Hobbton MS, RR 2 28366 2-00100
Donald Boykin, prin. 592-1401

North Wilkesboro, AC 919, PC 5, Wilkes

Wilkes Regional Medical Center HSP
PO BOX 609 28659 651-8100

Norwood, AC 704, PC 4, Stanly
Stanly County SD
Supt. — See Albemarle
South Stanly JSHS 3-00111
RR 1 BOX 107 28128 474-3155
William Anderson, prin.

Oakboro, AC 704, PC 3, Stanly
Stanly County SD
Supt. — See Albemarle
West Stanly HS 3-00011
16686 NC 24 27 HWY 28129 485-3012
Thomas Rogers, prin.

Oak Ridge, AC 910, PC 3, Guilford

Oak Ridge Military Academy 2-00111
PO BOX 498 27310 643-4131
Robert Rossi, prin.

Ocracoke, AC 919, PC 3, Hyde
Hyde County SD
Supt. — See Swanquarter
S, PO BOX 189 27960 1-11111
E. Thompson, prin. 928-3251

Olin, AC 704, PC 2, Iredell
Iredell-Statesville SD
Supt. — See Statesville
North Iredell HS, RR 1 BOX 15 28660 4-00011
James Edmiston, prin. 876-4191
North Iredell MS, RR 1 28660 2-00100
Wayne Hall, prin. 876-4802

Orrum, AC 919, PC 2, Robeson
Robeson County SD
Supt. — See Lumberton
MS, PO BOX 129 28369 3-01100
Ardeen Hunt, prin. 628-8408

Oxford, AC 919, PC 6, Granville
Granville County SD 6-11111
101 DELACROIX ST 27565 693-4613
Michael Ward, supt.
Webb HS 3-00011
3200 WEBB SCHOOL RD 27565 693-2521
Neill McDonald, prin.
Northern Granville MS 2-00100
3144 WEBB SCHOOL RD 27565 693-1483
Andre Henry, prin.
Other Schools – See Creedmoor

Pantego, AC 919, PC 2, Beaufort

Terra Ceia Christian S 2-11111
RR 2 BOX 159 27860 943-2485
Ken Leys, prin.

Pembroke, AC 919, PC 4, Robeson
Robeson County SD
Supt. — See Lumberton
Swett HS, PO BOX 1210 28372 4-00011
Bill Brewington, prin. 521-3253
MS, RR 2 BOX 52A 28372 3-00100
Kelly Sanderson, prin. 521-9464

Pembroke State University 5-UC
PO BOX 1510 28372 521-6262

Pikeville, AC 919, PC 3, Wayne
Wayne County SD
Supt. — See Goldsboro
Aycock HS, PO BOX 159 27863 3-00011
Dexter Simms, prin. 242-3400

Pilot Mountain, AC 919, PC 4, Surry
Surry County SD
Supt. — See Dobson
East Surry HS, 705 W MAIN ST 27041 3-00011
Bob Ward, prin. 368-2251
ES, PO BOX 97 27041 3-00100
F. Van Dearmin, prin. 368-2641

Pinehurst, AC 910, PC 6, Moore
Moore County SD
Supt. — See Carthage
MS, PO BOX 729 28374 2-01100
Betty Martin, prin. 295-6969

Sandhills Community College 5-CC
2200 AIRPORT RD 28374 692-6185

Pinetops, AC 919, PC 4, Edgecombe
Edgecombe County SD
Supt. — See Tarboro
Southwest Edgecombe HS 3-00011
RR 1 BOX 25 27864 827-5016
Lowell Thomas, prin.
South Edgecomb MS 3-01100
RR 1 BOX 255 27864 827-5083
James Lamm, prin.

Pinetown, AC 919, PC 2, Beaufort
Beaufort County SD
Supt. — See Washington

Northside HS, RR 1 BOX 177 27865 3-00011
John Phillips, prin. 943-6341

Pisgah Forest, AC 704, PC 4, Transylvania

Schenck Civilian Conservation Center 2-CS
98 SCHENCK DR 28768

Pittsboro, AC 919, PC 4, Chatham
Chatham County SD 6-11111
PO BOX 128 27312 542-3626
Perry Harrison, supt.
Northwood HS, RR 4 BOX 61 27312 3-00011
Wade Lehman, prin. 542-4934
Horton MS, PO BOX 636 27312 3-00100
Ernest Alston, prin. 542-2303
Other Schools – See Bear Creek, Siler City

Plymouth, AC 919, PC 5, Washington
Washington County SD 5-11111
802 WASHINGTON ST 27962 793-5171
R. Alligood, supt.
HS, E MAIN ST 27962 3-00011
Julius Walker, prin. 793-3031
Other Schools – See Creswell, Roper

Polkton, AC 704, PC 3, Anson

Anson Community College 3-CC
PO BOX 126 28135 800-766-0319

Powellsville, AC 919, PC 2, Bertie
Bertie County SD
Supt. — See Windsor
White MS, PO BOX 9 27967 2-00100
William Peele, prin. 332-2491

Princeton, AC 919, PC 4, Johnston
Johnston County SD
Supt. — See Smithfield
S, PO BOX 38 27569 3-11111
Fred Bartholomew, prin. 936-5011

Raeford, AC 919, PC 5, Hoke
Hoke County SD, 310 WOOLEY ST 28376 6-11111
William Harrison, supt. 875-4106
Hoke County HS 4-00011
600 S BETHEL RD 28376 875-2156
Randy Bridges, prin.
East Hoke MS, 200 US 401 N 28376 3-00100
Ron Alexander, prin. 875-5048
West Hoke MS, 200 NC 211 W 28376 3-00100
C. Langdon, prin. 875-3411

Raleigh, AC 919, PC 9, Wake
Wake County SD 8-11111
3600 WAKE FOREST RD 27609 850-1600
Robert Wentz, supt.
Athens Drive HS 4-00011
1420 ATHENS DR 27606 233-4050
Walter Sherlin, prin.
Broughton HS 4-00011
723 SAINT MARYS ST 27605 856-7810
Diane Payne, prin.
Enloe HS, 128 CLARENDON CRES 27610 4-00011
Bob Allen, prin. 856-7860
Millbrook HS 4-00011
2201 SPRING FOREST RD 27615 850-8787
Joann Patton, prin.
Sanderson HS, 5500 DIXON DR 27609 3-00011
Jane Currin, prin. 881-4800
Carnage MS, 1425 CARNAGE DR 27610 3-00100
William Crockett, prin. 856-7600
Carroll MS, 4520 SIX FORKS RD 27609 4-00100
Leon Herndon, prin. 881-1370
Daniels MS, 2816 OBERLIN RD 27608 4-00100
John Modest, prin. 881-4860
East Millbrook MS 3-00100
3801 SPRING FOREST RD 27604 850-8755
Patricia Gole, prin.
East Wake MS 3-00100
2700 OLD MILBURNIE RD 27604 266-8500
Gene Yeargin, prin.
Leesville Road MS 4-00100
8405 LEESVILLE RD 27613 870-4141
Jeanette Beckwith, prin.
Leesville Road HS 3-00010
8409 LEESVILLE RD 27613 870-4250
Richard Murphy, prin.
Ligon MS, 706 E LENOIR ST 27601 4-00100
Crystal Helm, prin. 856-7929
Martin MS, 1701 RIDGE RD 27607 4-00100
David Coley, prin. 881-4970
West Millbrook MS 4-00100
8115 STRICKLAND RD 27615 870-4050
Daniel Bowers, prin.
Other Schools – See Apex, Cary, Fuquay-Varina,
Garner, Wake Forest, Wendell, Zebulon

Cardinal Gibbons HS 2-00011
2401 WESTERN BLVD 27606 834-1625
Duane Kockx, prin.
ECPI Computer Institute 2-CS
4509 CREEDMOOR RD 27612 571-0057
Friendship Christian S 2-11111
5510 FALLS OF NEUSE RD 27609 872-2133
Rev. Peterson, prin.
Hale HS, 3400 WHITE OAK RD 27609 2-00111
Margaret Evans, prin. 782-3331
Meredith College 4-UC
3800 HILLSBOROUGH ST 27607 829-8581

Neuse Baptist Christian S | 2-11111
PO BOX 61146 27661 | 876-0990
  Charles Bright, prin.
North Carolina State University | 7-UC
PO BOX 7001 27695 | 737-2434
Peace College | 2-CC
15 E PEACE ST 27604 | 832-2881
Raleigh Christian Academy | 3-11111
2110 TRAWICK RD 27604 | 872-2215
  Richard Tippett, prin.
Raleigh Christian Community S | 2-11111
7000 DESTINY DR 27604 | 266-7227
  Kathie Thompson, prin.
Ravenscroft S | 3-11111
7409 FALLS OF NEUSE RD 27615 | 847-0900
  James Ledyard, prin.
St. Augustine's College | 4-UC
1315 OAKWOOD AVE 27610 | 824-1415
St. Mary's College | 2-CC
900 HILLSBOROUGH ST 27603 | 839-4100
St. Mary's College Prep S | 2-00001
900 HILLSBOROUGH ST 27603 | 828-2521
  Clauston Jenkins, prin.
Shaw University | 4-UC
118 E SOUTH ST 27601 | 546-8222
Wake Christian Academy | 3-11111
5500 ACADEMY DR 27603 | 772-6264
  Philip Crane, prin.
Wake Technical Community College | 5-CC
9101 FAYETTEVILLE RD 27603 | 772-7500

Ramseur, AC 919, PC 4, Randolph
Randolph County SD
  Supt. — See Asheboro
Eastern Randolph HS | 4-00011
RR 2 BOX 180 27316 | 824-2351
  Pat Chappell, prin.
Randolph MS, 5302 FOUSHEE RD 27316 | 3-00100
  Barry Cole, prin. | 824-6700

Faith Christian S | 2-11111
5449 BROOKHAVEN RD 27316 | 824-4156
  William Hohneisen, prin.

Randleman, AC 919, PC 5, Randolph
Randolph County SD
  Supt. — See Asheboro
HS, 4396 TIGERS DEN RD 27317 | 3-00011
  Mike Steed, prin. | 498-2682
MS, 800 HIGH POINT ST 27317 | 3-00100
  Gary Davis, prin. | 498-2606

Red Springs, AC 919, PC 5, Robeson
Robeson County SD
  Supt. — See Lumberton
HS, N VANCE ST 28377 | 3-00011
  Harold Livingston, prin. | 843-4211

MacDonald Academy | 2-11111
200 N COLLEGE ST 28377 | 843-4995
  George Erickson, prin.

Reidsville, AC 919, PC 7, Rockingham
Rockingham County SD
  Supt. — See Eden
HS, 1901 S PARK DR 27320 | 3-00011
  Eddie Daniel, prin. | 349-6361
MS, 1903 S PARK DR 27320 | 3-00100
  Jeff Paris, prin. | 342-4726

Richlands, AC 919, PC 3, Onslow
Onslow County SD
  Supt. — See Jacksonville
HS, PO BOX 218 28574 | 3-00011
  Nace Ridge, prin. | 324-4191
Trexler MS, PO BOX 188 28574 | 2-00100
  James Rivenbark, prin. | 324-4414

Roanoke Rapids, AC 919, PC 7, Halifax
Halifax County SD
  Supt. — See Halifax
Davie MS, RR 1 BOX 191 27870 | 3-00100
  Michael Hedgepeth, prin. | 537-5243

Roanoke Rapids CSD | 5-11111
536 HAMILTON ST 27870 | 535-3111
  Michael Williams, supt.
HS, 800 HAMILTON ST 27870 | 3-00011
  Chester Rogerson, prin. | 537-8563
Chaloner MS, 2100 VIRGINIA AVE 27870 | 3-00100
  Kathryn Landen, prin. | 537-8540

Halifax Academy | 2-11111
RR 2 BOX 355 27870 | 537-8527
  William Mayo, prin.

Robbins, AC 919, PC 3, Moore
Moore County SD
  Supt. — See Carthage
North Moore HS, PO BOX 9 27325 | 3-00100
  Charles Todd, prin. | 948-2228
Elise MS, PO BOX 850 27325 | 2-01100
  Charles Lambert, prin. | 948-2421

Robbinsville, AC 704, PC 3, Graham
Graham County SD | 4-11111
PO BOX 605 28771 | 479-3413
  Lowell Crisp, supt.
HS, PO BOX 625 28771 | 2-00011
  Ginger Cody, prin. | 479-3330
MS, 301 SWEETWATER RD 28771 | 2-00100
  (—), prin. | 479-8488

Robersonville, AC 919, PC 4, Martin
Martin County SD
  Supt. — See Williamston
Roanoke HS, RR 2 BOX 19 27871 | 3-00011
  Barbara Mallory, prin. | 795-4081
MS, PO BOX 118 27871 | 2-00100
  Ernest Brooks, prin. | 795-3910

Rockingham, AC 919, PC 6, Richmond
Richmond County SD
  Supt. — See Hamlet
Richmond SHS, PO BOX 1748 28379 | 4-00001
  Ralph Robertson, prin. | 997-9812
JHS, 415 WALL ST 28379 | 3-00110
  John Langley, prin. | 997-9827
Rohanen JHS, 100 SCHOOL ST 28379 | 2-00110
  Joe Richardson, prin. | 997-9839

Temple Christian S | 2-11111
413 AIRPORT RD 28379 | 997-3179
  Rev. Joseph Byrd, prin.

Rocky Mount, AC 919, PC 8, Edgecombe
Edgecombe County SD
  Supt. — See Tarboro
West Edgecombe MS | 3-01100
RR 2 BOX 223 27801 | 446-9434
  Josie Davis, prin.

Nash-Rocky Mount County SD
  Supt. — See Nashville
Northern Nash SHS, RR 5 27804 | 4-00001
  Robert Hurley, prin. | 937-5600
SHS, 308 S TILLERY ST 27804 | 4-00001
  Jerry Carter, prin. | 977-3085
Edwards JHS, 720 EDWARDS ST 27803 | 3-00110
  Wayne Doll, prin. | 977-3328

Falls Road Baptist S | 2-11111
113 TREVATHAN ST 27804 | 977-2401
  Kris Bjorgen, prin.
Grace Christian S | 2-11111
509 KINGSTON AVE 27803 | 442-1857
  Stephen Ellis, prin.
Nash Community College | 4-CC
PO BOX 7488 27804 | 443-4011
North Carolina Wesleyan College | 4-UC
3400 N WESLEYAN BLVD 27804 | 977-7171
Rocky Mount Academy | 2-11111
1313 AVONDALE AVE 27803 | 443-4126
  Michael Bailey, prin.

Ronda, AC 919, PC 2, Wilkes
Wilkes County SD
  Supt. — See Wilkesboro
East Wilkes HS, PO BOX 368 28670 | 3-00011
  Phillip Couch, prin. | 957-2979

Roper, AC 919, PC 3, Washington
Washington County SD
  Supt. — See Plymouth
Washington Union MS | 3-01100
PO BOX 188 27970 | 793-2835
  Clifford Phifer, prin.

Roseboro, AC 919, PC 4, Sampson
Sampson County SD
  Supt. — See Clinton
Lakewood HS, PO BOX 859 28382 | 3-00011
  John Blanton, prin. | 525-5171
Roseboro-Salemburg MS | 2-00100
PO BOX 976 28382 | 525-4764
  Carolyn Royal, prin.

Rose Hill, AC 919, PC 4, Duplin
Duplin County SD
  Supt. — See Kenansville
Charity MS, PO BOX 70 28458 | 2-00100
  (—), prin. | 289-3323

Rosman, AC 704, PC 2, Transylvania
Transylvania County SD
  Supt. — See Brevard
JSHS 28772 | 2-00111
  William Cathey, prin. | 862-4284

Rowland, AC 919, PC 4, Robeson
Robeson County SD
  Supt. — See Lumberton
South Robeson HS | 3-00011
PO BOX 309 28383 | 422-3987
  Josephine Locklear, prin.
MS, 408 W CHAPEL ST 28383 | 2-00100
  Larry Brooks, prin. | 422-3983

Roxboro, AC 919, PC 6, Person
Person County SD | 6-11111
304 S MORGAN ST 27573 | 599-2191
  Ronnie Bugnar, supt.
Person HS, 1010 RIDGE RD 27573 | 4-00011
  Larry Oakley, prin. | 599-8321
Northern MS, PO BOX 3130 27573 | 3-00100
  Jean Rogers, prin. | 599-6344
Southern MS, PO BOX 642 27573 | 3-00100
  Dennis Walker, prin. | 599-6995

Piedmont Community College | 4-CC
PO BOX 1197 27573 | 599-1181
Roxboro Christian Academy | 2-11111
360 WESLEYAN HTS 27573 | 599-0208
  David Bess, prin.

Ruffin, AC 919, PC 2, Rockingham
Rockingham County SD
  Supt. — See Eden

Lincoln MS | 2-01100
2610 OREGON HILL RD 27326 | 939-2435
  Ralph Clayton, prin.

Rutherfordton, AC 704, PC 5, Rutherford
Rutherford County SD
  Supt. — See Spindale
Rutherfordton Central HS | 4-00011
PO BOX 1119 28139 | 287-3304
  Hampton Casebolt, prin.
R. S. MS, 605 E CHARLOTTE RD 28139 | 2-00100
  Don Hastings, prin. | 286-4461

Saint Pauls, AC 919, PC 4, Robeson
Robeson County SD
  Supt. — See Lumberton
HS, 302 N OLD STAGE RD 28384 | 2-00011
  Colon Lane, prin. | 865-4177
MS, 510 W SHAW ST 28384 | 2-00100
  Harriet Jackson, prin. | 865-4070

Salisbury, AC 704, PC 7, Rowan
Rowan-Salisbury County SD | 7-11111
314 N ELLIS ST 28144 | 636-7500
  Donald Martin, supt.
East Rowan HS | 3-00011
175 SAINT LUKES CHURCH RD 28146 | 279-5232
  Harry Starr, prin.
HS, 500 LINCOLNTON RD 28144 | 3-00011
  N. Eagle, prin. | 636-1221
Erwin MS | 3-00100
170 SAINT LUKES CHURCH RD 28146 | 279-7265
  Everette Corriher, prin.
Knox MS, 1625 PARK RD W 28144 | 3-00100
  Larry Britt, prin. | 633-2922
Other Schools – See China Grove, Cleveland, East
  Spencer, Landis, Mount Ulla, Spencer

Catawba College | 3-UC
2300 W INNES ST 28144 | 800-228-2922
Gospel Light Baptist S | 2-11111
1010 AIRPORT RD 28147 | 633-7250
  Roscoe Morgan, prin.
Hood Theological Seminary | 1-UC
800 W THOMAS ST 28144 | 638-5644
Livingstone College | 3-UC
701 W MONROE ST 28144 | 638-5500
Rowan-Cabarrus Community College | 5-CC
PO BOX 1595 28145 | 637-0760
Salisbury Business College | 2-CS
1400 JAKE ALEXANDER BLVD W 28147 | 636-4071

Sanford, AC 919, PC 7, Lee
Lee County SD, 200 WICKER ST 27330 | 6-11111
  James Harrell, supt. | 774-6226
Lee HS, 1708 NASH ST 27330 | 4-00011
  (—), prin. | 776-7541
East MS, 1337 BROADWAY RD 27330 | 3-00100
  Eric Pittard, prin. | 776-8441
West MS | 3-00100
3301 WICKER STREET EXT 27330 | 775-7351
  Dr. Jon Burwell, prin.

Central Carolina Community College | 5-CC
1105 KELLY DR 27330 | 775-5401
Grace Christian S | 2-11111
2601 S JEFFERSON DAVIS HWY 27330 | 774-4415
  Stephen Coble, prin.

Scotland Neck, AC 919, PC 5, Halifax
Halifax County SD
  Supt. — See Halifax
Brawley MS, PO BOX 449 27874 | 2-00100
  Steve Thornton, prin. | 826-4513

Selma, AC 919, PC 5, Johnston
Johnston County SD
  Supt. — See Smithfield
Selma MS | 2-01100
1533 US HIGHWAY 301 N 27576 | 965-2555
  Renee Sanders, prin.

Shallotte, AC 919, PC 3, Brunswick
Brunswick County SD
  Supt. — See Southport
West Brunswick HS | 3-00011
RR 3 BOX 999 28459 | 754-4338
  Harry Lemon, prin.
MS, RR 2 BOX 5 28469 | 4-01100
  Sandra Robinson, prin. | 754-6882

Sharpsburg., AC 919, PC 4, Nash

N.E.W. Academy, PO BOX 129 27878 | 2-11111
  Ronald Bourgoin, prin. | 446-1239

Shelby, AC 704, PC 7, Cleveland
Cleveland County SD | 6-11111
130 S POST RD 28152 | 487-8581
  W. Watson, supt.
Crest HS | 3-00011
800 OLD BOILING SPRINGS RD 28152 | 482-5354
  Leonard Litton, prin.
Crest JHS | 4-00100
315 BEAVER DAM CHURCH RD 28152 | 482-0343
  Brenda Sharts, prin.
Other Schools – See Lawndale

Shelby SD, 315 PATTON DR 28150 | 5-11111
  Steve Curtis, supt. | 487-6367
HS, 230 E DIXON BLVD 28152 | 1-00011
  Clifford Wilson, prin. | 482-3409

MS, 400 W MARION ST 28150   3-00100
Dina Braddy, prin.   482-6331

Cleveland Community College   4-CC
137 S POST RD 28152   484-4000

Siler City, AC 919, PC 5, Chatham
Chatham County SD
Supt. — See Pittsboro
Matthews HS   3-00011
910 E CARDINAL ST 27344   742-2916
William Hamilton, prin.
Chatham MS, 439 E 5TH ST 27344   2-00100
Brenda Griffin, prin.   663-2414

Smithfield, AC 919, PC 6, Johnston
Johnston County SD   7-11111
PO BOX 1336 27577   934-6031
G. Thomas Houlihan, supt.
Smithfield-Selma HS   4-00011
PO BOX 1497 27577   934-5191
Ava Thompson, prin.
MS, PO BOX 2270 27577   3-00100
Linda Stevens, prin.   934-4696
Other Schools — See Benson, Clayton, Four Oaks,
Kenly, Princeton, Selma

Johnston Community College   4-CC
PO BOX 2350 27577   934-3051

Snow Hill, AC 919, PC 4, Greene
Greene County SD   5-11111
301 KINGOLD BLVD 28580   747-3425
Paul Browning, supt.
Greene Central HS   3-00011
RR 1 BOX 11 28580   747-3814
William Smith, prin.
Greene County MS   2-00100
RR 1 BOX 12 28580   747-8191
George Farrow, prin.

Southern Pines, AC 919, PC 6, Moore
Moore County SD
Supt. — See Carthage
Pinecrest HS, PO BOX 1259 28388   4-00011
Ben Greene, prin.   692-6554
MS, 255 S MAY ST 28387   3-01100
Ed Jackson, prin.   692-2357

Calvary Christian S   2-11111
400 S BENNETT ST 28387   692-8311
Rev. Kent Kelly, prin.
Wallace O'Neal Day S   2-11111
PO BOX 290 28388   692-6920
Gardiner Dodd, prin.

Southport, AC 919, PC 4, Brunswick
Brunswick County SD   6-11111
NC HIGHWAY 133 28461   457-5241
Ralph Johnston, supt.
South Brunswick HS, COUGAR DR 28461   3-00011
Sue Sellers, prin.   457-5765
South Brunswick MS   3-00100
COUGAR DR 28461   845-2771
Richard Lawson, prin.
Other Schools — See Leland, Shallotte

Sparta, AC 919, PC 4, Alleghany
Alleghany County SD   4-11111
1 PEACHTREE ST 28675   372-4345
Suzanne Mellow, supt.
Alleghany HS, PO BOX 909 28675   2-00100
James Halsey, prin.   372-4554

Spencer, AC 704, PC 5, Rowan
Rowan-Salisbury County SD
Supt. — See Salisbury
North Rowan HS   3-00011
300 N WHITEHEAD AVE 28159   636-4420
Allen Eury, prin.

Spindale, AC 704, PC 5, Rutherford
Rutherford County SD   6-11111
219 FAIRGROUND RD 28160   286-2757
Roger Petty, supt.
Other Schools — See Forest City, Henrietta,
Rutherfordton, Union Mills

Isothermal Community College   4-CC
PO BOX 804 28160   286-3636

Spring Hope, AC 919, PC 4, Nash
Nash-Rocky Mount County SD
Supt. — See Nashville
Southern Nash JHS   3-00110
RR 3 BOX 54 27882   478-4807
R. McMahon, prin.

Spring Lake, AC 919, PC 6, Cumberland
Cumberland County SD
Supt. — See Fayetteville
JHS, 612 SPRING AVE 28390   3-00110
Nina Corders, prin.   497-1175

Spruce Pine, AC 704, PC 4, Mitchell
Mitchell County SD
Supt. — See Bakersville
Harris MS, 231 HARRIS ST 28777   3-01100
William Buchanan, prin.   765-2321

Mayland Community College   3-CC
PO BOX 547 28777   765-7356

Stanley, AC 704, PC 5, Gaston
Gaston County SD
Supt. — See Gastonia
JHS, 317 HOVIS RD 28164   3-00110
Byron Rickman, prin.   263-2941

Statesville, AC 704, PC 7, Iredell
Iredell-Statesville SD   7-11111
PO BOX 911 28687   872-8931
Jesse Register, supt.
South Iredell HS, RR 10 BOX 90A 28677   4-00011
Glen Weddington, prin.   528-4536
HS, 474 N CENTER ST 28677   3-00011
Penny Howard, prin.   873-3491
West Iredell HS, RR 6 BOX 13 28677   3-00011
Miriam Evans, prin.   873-2181
East MS, RIVER HILL RD 28677   2-00100
Rose Dorton, prin.   878-0070
MS, 321 CLEGG ST 28677   2-00100
James Millsaps, prin.   872-2135
West Iredell MS, RR 6 28677   2-00100
Lucy Martin, prin.   873-2887
Other Schools — See Mooresville, Olin, Troutman

Mitchell Community College   4-CC
500 W BROAD ST 28677   878-3200
Southview Christian S   2-11111
RR 16 BOX 57 28677   872-9554
James Peterson, prin.

Stedman, AC 919, PC 3, Cumberland
Cumberland County SD
Supt. — See Fayetteville
JHS, RR 2 BOX 2 28391   3-00110
James Surles, prin.   483-3326

Supply, AC 919, PC 2, Brunswick

Brunswick Community College   4-CC
PO BOX 30 28462   754-6900

Swannanoa, AC 704, PC 5, Buncombe
Buncombe County SD
Supt. — See Asheville
Owen MS   3-00100
730 OLD US HIGHWAY 70 28778   686-7739
Roger Capps, prin.

Swanquarter, AC 919, PC 3, Hyde
Hyde County SD, PO BOX 217 27885   3-11111
Morgan Harris, supt.   926-3281
Mattamuskeet JSHS   2-00111
RR 1 BOX 155A 27885   926-4701
Alfred Lockamy, prin.
Other Schools — See Ocracoke

Swansboro, AC 919, PC 4, Onslow
Onslow County SD
Supt. — See Jacksonville
HS, PO BOX 827 28584   3-00011
J. Beasley, prin.   326-4300
MS, 1240 W CORBETT AVE 28584   2-00100
Frances Corbett, prin.   326-3601

Sylva, AC 704, PC 4, Jackson
Jackson County SD   5-11111
43 HOSPITAL RD 28779   586-2311
Charles McConnell, supt.
Smoky Mountain HS   3-00011
505 E MAIN ST 28779   586-2177
Judy Wolfe, prin.
Other Schools — See Glenville

Southwestern Community College   4-CC
275 WEBSTER RD 28779   586-4091

Tabor City, AC 919, PC 4, Columbus
Columbus County SD
Supt. — See Whiteville
South Columbus HS   3-00011
RR 1 BOX 28A 28463   653-4073
William Sugg, prin.
Tabor City MS, 505 W 6TH ST 28463   3-00100
John Williams, prin.   653-3637

Tarboro, AC 919, PC 7, Edgecombe
Edgecombe County SD   5-11111
412 PEARL ST 27886   823-6151
David Bryant, supt.
North Edgecombe HS   3-00011
RR 2 BOX 195 27886   823-3562
William Ellis, prin.
HS, 1400 W HOWARD AVE 27886   3-00011
(—), prin.   823-4284
Martin MS, 300 E JOHNSTON ST 27886   3-00100
Shelvia Whitehurst, prin.   823-8167
Other Schools — See Battleboro, Pinetops, Rocky
Mount

Edgecombe Community College   4-CC
2009 W WILSON ST 27886   446-0436

Tar Heel, AC 919, PC 2, Bladen
Bladen County SD
Supt. — See Elizabethtown
JSHS, PO BOX 128 28392   2-00111
Charles Tedder, prin.   862-2475

Taylorsville, AC 704, PC 4, Alexander
Alexander County SD   5-11111
250 LILEDOUN RD SW 28681   632-7001
W. Austin, supt.
Alexander Central SHS   4-00001
241 SCHOOL AVE SW 28681   632-7063
Robert Young, prin.

West JHS, RR 8 BOX 220 28681   3-00110
Tony Harper, prin.   495-4611
Other Schools — See Hiddenite

Teachey, AC 919, PC 2, Duplin
Duplin County SD
Supt. — See Kenansville
Wallace-Rose Hill HS   3-00011
RR 1 BOX 200 28464   285-7501
Charles Blanchard, prin.

Thomasville, AC 919, PC 7, Davidson
Davidson County SD
Supt. — See Lexington
East Davidson HS, 501 LAKE RD 27360   3-00011
Benjamin Terrell, prin.   476-4814
Ledford HS, RR 4 BOX 773 27360   3-00011
Max Cole, prin.   769-9671
Brown MS   3-00100
1140 KENDALL MILL RD 27360   475-8845
James Kiger, prin.
Ledford MS, RR 4 BOX 786 27360   3-00100
Gilbert Buck, prin.   476-4816

Thomasville CSD, 400 TURNER ST 27360   4-11111
Daniel Cockman, supt.   475-1386
HS, 410 UNITY ST 27360   3-00011
Wayne Thrift, prin.   476-4811
MS, 400 UNITY ST 27360   2-00100
Mike Allred, prin.   472-7977

Topton, AC 704, PC 2, Cherokee
Macon County SD
Supt. — See Franklin
Nantahala S, HC 307 28781   2-11111
Richard Baldwin, prin.   321-4388

Trenton, AC 919, PC 2, Jones
Jones County SD, 320 JONES RD 28585   4-11111
Norma Sermon-Boyd, supt.
Jones HS, 2500 NC HIGHWAY 58 S 28585   2-00011
Clarence Willie, prin.   448-2451
Jones MS, 150 OLD NEW BERN RD 28585   2-00100
Amos Taylor, prin.   448-3956

Trinity, AC 919, PC 6, Randolph
Randolph County SD
Supt. — See Asheboro
HS   4-00011
5746 TRINITY HIGH SCHOOL DR 27370
Darrell Saunders, prin.   861-6870
Archdale Trinity MS   4-00100
PO BOX 232 27370   431-2589
Robert Upchurch, prin.

Troutman, AC 704, PC 4, Iredell
Iredell-Statesville SD
Supt. — See Statesville
MS 28166   2-00100
Marlin Tate, prin.   528-5137

Troy, AC 919, PC 5, Montgomery
Montgomery County SD   5-11111
441 PAGE ST 27371 - R. Jackson, supt.   576-6511
Other Schools — See Biscoe, Mount Gilead

Montgomery Community College   3-CC
PO BOX 787 27371   572-3691

Tryon, AC 704, PC 4, Polk
Polk County SD
Supt. — See Columbus
MS, 147 HARMON FIELD RD 28782   2-00100
Andy Millard, prin.   859-6636

Tyner, AC 919, PC 2, Chowan
Edenton/Chowan County SD
Supt. — See Edenton
Chowan MS, RR 1 BOX 66 27980   2-00100
Maxter Allen, prin.   221-4131

Union Mills, AC 704, PC 2, Rutherford
Rutherford County SD
Supt. — See Spindale
MS 28167   2-01100
Loretta Bailey, prin.   287-7561

Valdese, AC 704, PC 5, Burke
Burke County SD
Supt. — See Morganton
Heritage MS, 1951 ENON RD 28690   2-00100
Dan Hoyle, prin.   874-0731

Vanceboro, AC 919, PC 3, Craven
Craven County SD
Supt. — See New Bern
West Craven HS   4-00011
2600 STREETS FERRY RD 28586   244-3200
Robert Jolly, prin.

Wadesboro, AC 704, PC 5, Anson
Anson County SD   5-11111
400 N GREEN ST 28170   694-4417
John Batchelor, supt.
Anson SHS, PO BOX 513 28170   4-00001
Frank Richardson, prin.   694-9301
Anson JHS, PO BOX 678 28170   4-00110
Franklin Cooper, prin.   694-3945

Wake Forest, AC 919, PC 6, Wake
Wake County SD
Supt. — See Raleigh
Wake Forest-Rolesville HS   3-00011
420 STADIUM DR 27587   554-8611
Robert Winston, prin.
Wake Forest-Rolesville MS   3-00100
1800 S MAIN ST 27587   554-8440
Dan Barnes, prin.

Southeastrn Baptist Theological Seminary 3-UC
PO BOX 1889 27588 556-3101

Walkertown, AC 919, PC 4, Forsyth
Winston-Salem/Forsyth SD
Supt. — See Winston-Salem
MS, 3175 RUXTON DR 27051 3-00100
Bonnie Welsh, prin. 595-2161

Gospel Light Christian S 3-11111
PO BOX 70 27051 595-4311
Robert Roberson, prin.

Walnut Cove, AC 919, PC 4, Stokes
Stokes County SD
Supt. — See Danbury
South Stokes SHS 4-00011
RR 1 BOX 307 27052 994-2995
John Booth, prin.
Southeastern Stokes JHS 2-00110
PO BOX 68 27052 591-4371
Edward Hairston, prin.

Warrensville, AC 919, PC 2, Ashe
Ashe County SD
Supt. — See Jefferson
Northwest JSHS, PO BOX 259 28693 3-00111
Larry Lewis, prin. 384-3591

Warrenton, AC 919, PC 3, Warren
Warren County SD 5-11111
109 COUSIN LUCYS LN 27589 257-3184
James Wilkerson, supt.
Warren County HS 3-00011
RR 1 BOX 149 27589 257-4413
Costel Evans, prin.
Warren County MS 3-00100
US 158 BYPASS 27589 257-3751
W. Ramey, prin.

Warsaw, AC 919, PC 5, Duplin
Duplin County SD
Supt. — See Kenansville
Kenan HS, RR 2 BOX 160 28398 3-00011
Willie Gillespie, prin. 293-4218
MS, 718 W COLLEGE ST 28398 2-00100
H. Bowden, prin. 293-7997

Washington, AC 919, PC 6, Beaufort
Beaufort County SD 5-11111
321 SMAW RD 27889 946-8131
George Thigpen, supt.
Other Schools — See Aurora, Belhaven, Chocowinity,
Pinetown

Washington CSD, 321 SMAW RD 27889 5-11111
George Thigpen, supt. 946-8131
HS, 400 SLATESTONE RD 27889 3-00011
James Boyette, prin. 946-0858
Jones MS, 230 E 8TH ST 27889 3-00100
Michael Baker, prin. 946-0874

Beaufort County Community College 4-CC
PO BOX 1069 27889 946-6194

Waynesville, AC 704, PC 6, Haywood
Haywood County SD 6-11111
1615 N MAIN ST 28786 456-2400
Karen Campbell, supt.
Tuscola HS 3-00100
350 TUSCOLA SCHOOL RD 28786 456-2408
Charles Starnes, prin.
Bethel MS, RR 3 BOX 256 28786 2-00100
Tom Daily, prin. 646-3443
MS, 507 BROWN AVE 28786 3-00100
Fred Chandler, prin. 456-2403
Other Schools — See Canton

Weaverville, AC 704, PC 4, Buncombe
Buncombe County SD
Supt. — See Asheville
North Buncombe HS 4-00011
890 CLARKS CHAPEL RD 28787 645-4221
R. Mangum, prin.
North Buncombe MS 3-00100
51 N BUNCOMBE SCHOOL RD 28787 645-7944
A. Taylor, prin.

Weldon, AC 919, PC 4, Halifax
Weldon CSD, 120 COWARD ST 27890 4-11111
George Hood, supt. 536-4821
JSHS, PO BOX 31 27890 2-00111
Clemon Williamson, prin. 536-4829

Halifax Community College 3-CC
PO BOX 809 27890 536-2551

Wendell, AC 919, PC 5, Wake
Wake County SD
Supt. — See Raleigh
East Wake HS 4-00011
5101 ROLESVILLE RD 27591 365-2625
Del Burns, prin.

Wentworth, AC 919, PC 2, Rockingham
Rockingham County SD
Supt. — See Eden
Rockingham County HS 4-00011
PO BOX 41 27375 634-3220
Raymond Cooke, prin.

Rockingham Community College 4-CC
PO BOX 38 27375 342-4261

West Jefferson, AC 919, PC 4, Ashe
Ashe County SD
Supt. — See Jefferson
Beaver Creek JSHS, PO BOX 48 28694 3-00111
James Blackburn, prin. 246-5311
Ashe County Career Center Vo Tech
MT JEFFERSON RD 28694 246-2112
Duane Pennington, prin.

Whitakers, AC 919, PC 3, Nash

Enfield Academy, PO BOX 700 27891 2-11111
Peter Lawrence, prin. 437-7711

White Plains, AC 919, PC 2, Surry

White Plains Christian S 2-11111
PO BOX 84 27031 786-6310
C. Fred Tolbert, prin.

Whiteville, AC 919, PC 6, Columbus
Columbus County SD 6-11111
PO BOX 729 28472 642-5168
Thomas Nance, supt.
Other Schools — See Cerro Gordo, Chadbourn, Delco,
Hallsboro, Lake Waccamaw, Tabor City

Whiteville CSD 5-11111
107 W WALTER ST 28472 642-4116
Otis McNeil, supt.
HS, 413 N LEE ST 28472 3-00011
Coleman Barbour, prin. 642-8054
Central MS, 300 S MEMORY ST 28472 3-00100
Milton Frink, prin. 642-3546

Columbus Christian Academy 2-11111
115 W CALHOUN ST 28472 642-6196
Rev. Keith Bartholomew, prin.
Southeastern Community College 4-CC
PO BOX 151 28472 642-7141
Waccamaw Academy 2-11111
PO BOX 507 28472 642-7530
Frank Walters, prin.

Wilkesboro, AC 919, PC 5, Wilkes
Wilkes County SD 7-11111
201 W MAIN ST 28697 667-1121
Marsh Lyall, supt.
Wilkes Central HS 3-00011
RR 3 BOX 525 28697 667-5277
Ned Pierce, prin.
Wilkes County Career Ctr HS Vo Tech
RR 2 BOX 232 28697 667-3653
James Davis, prin.
Woodward MS, 400 WINSTON ST 28697 3-00100
Coleen Bush, prin. 838-2618
Other Schools — See Hays, Millers Creek, Ronda

Wilkes Community College 5-CC
PO BOX 120 28697 651-8600

Williamston, AC 919, PC 6, Martin
Martin County SD 5-11111
300 N WATTS ST 27892 792-1575
Willie Peele, supt.
HS, 200 GODWIN AVE 27892 3-00011
Dennis Mills, prin. 792-7881
Bear Grass JSHS 2-00110
RR 4 BOX 336 27892 792-3721
Hallet Davis, prin.
MS, PO BOX 427 27892 2-00100
William Matthews, prin. 792-1111
Other Schools — See Jamesville, Robersonville

Martin Community College 3-CC
KEHUKEE PARK ROAD 27892 792-1521

Wilmington, AC 910, PC 8, New Hanover
New Hanover County SD 7-11111
1802 S 15TH ST 28401 763-5431
W. McNeel, supt.
Hoggard HS 4-00011
4305 SHIPYARD BLVD 28403 791-0230
Hugh McManus, prin.
Laney HS, 2700 N COLLEGE RD 28405 4-00011
Maryann Nunnally, prin. 799-8400
New Hanover HS 4-00011
1307 MARKET ST 28401 251-6100
Robert Bayzle, prin.
Lakeside JSHS, 1805 S 13TH ST 28401 2-00111
Bonnie Page, prin. 251-6161
Myrtle Grove MS, 901 PINER RD 28409 3-00100
Robert Moore, prin. 791-2223
Noble MS, 6520 MARKET ST 28405 3-00100
William Moore, prin. 791-8724
Roland-Grise MS, 4412 LAKE AVE 28403 3-00100
Dennis Brandon, prin. 791-2363
Trask JHS, 2900 N COLLEGE RD 28405 3-00100
Dewey Furr, prin. 799-2826
Virgo JHS, 813 NIXON ST 28401 3-00100
Russell Simmons, prin. 251-6146
Williston MS, 401 S 10TH ST 28401 3-00100
Kenneth McLaurin, prin. 763-7684

Cape Fear Academy 2-11111
4002 S COLLEGE RD 28412 791-0287
Eric Cluxton, prin.
Cape Fear Community College 5-CC
411 N FRONT ST 28401 343-0481
Miller-Motte Business College 3-CS
606 S COLLEGE RD 28403 392-4660

New Hanover Memorial Hospital HSP
2131 S 17TH ST 28401 343-7074
University of North Carolina 6-UC
601 S COLLEGE RD 28403 395-3243
Wilmington Christian Academy 3-11111
1401 N COLLEGE RD 28405 791-4248
Barren Nobles, prin.

Wilson, AC 919, PC 8, Wilson
Wilson County SD 7-11111
117 TARBORO ST SW 27893 399-7700
Ann Denlinger, supt.
Beddingfield HS 4-00011
4510 OLD STANTONSBURG RD 27893 399-7880
Luther Bryant, prin.
Fike HS, 500 HARRISON DR N 27893 4-00011
Shirley Pierce, prin. 399-7905
Hunt HS, 4559 LAMM RD 27893 4-00011
Philip Deadmon, prin. 399-7930
Darden-Vick MS 2-00100
504 CARROLL ST E 27893 399-7886
Russell Landen, prin.
Forest Hills MS 3-00100
1210 FOREST HILLS RD NW 27896 399-7913
Herman Dollar, prin.
Speight MS 2-00100
6640 SPEIGHT SCHOOL RD 27893 238-3983
(—), prin.
Toisnot MS 3-00100
1301 CORBETT AVE N 27893 399-7973
Allen Johnson, prin.
Other Schools — See Elm City, Lucama

Barton College 4-UC
COLLEGE STATION 27893 399-6318
Eastern North Carolina Sch. for the Deaf HND
PO BOX 2768 27894
Greenfield S, PO BOX 3525 27895 2-11111
Janet Beaman, prin. 237-8046
Wilson Christian Academy 2-11111
PO BOX 3818 27895 237-8064
Roland Pittman, prin.
Wilson Technical Community College 4-CC
PO BOX 4305 27893 291-1195

Windsor, AC 919, PC 4, Bertie
Bertie County SD 5-11111
222 COUNTY FARM RD 27983 794-3173
Joseph Nelson, supt.
Bertie HS, 715 US HIGHWAY 13 N 27983 4-00011
Glen Mitchell, prin. 794-3034
Southwestern MS 3-00100
819 GOVERNORS RD 27983 794-2358
Norman Cherry, prin.
Other Schools — See Powellsville

Winfall, AC 919, PC 3, Perquimans
Perquimans County SD
Supt. — See Hertford
Perquimans MS, PO BOX 117 27985 3-00100
Henry Felton, prin. 426-7355

Wingate, AC 704, PC 5, Union

Wingate College 28174 4-UC
800-755-5550

Winston-Salem, AC 910, PC 9, Forsyth
Winston-Salem/Forsyth SD 8-11111
1065 MILLER ST 27103 727-2816
Larry Coble, supt.
Carver HS 4-00011
3545 CARVER SCHOOL RD 27105 727-2987
Daniel Piggott, prin.
Mt. Tabor HS, 342 PETREE RD 27106 4-00011
Martha Land, prin. 765-6831
North Forsyth HS 4-00011
5705 SHATTALON DR 27105 767-6611
W. Kaye Shutt, prin.
Parkland HS, 1600 BREWER RD 27127 4-00011
James Brandon, prin. 727-2828
Reynolds HS 4-00011
301 N HAWTHORNE RD 27104 727-2061
Stan Elrod, prin.
Career Ctr HS, 1615 MILLER ST 27103 Vo Tech
Loretta Elliot, prin. 727-8181
Ashley MS, 1647 E 21ST ST 27105 3-00100
John Beaty, prin. 727-2085
Atkins MS 3-00100
1215 N CAMERON AVE 27101 727-2781
Donald Golding, prin.
Cook MS, 920 W 11TH ST 27105 3-00100
Ed Armstrong, prin. 727-2784
Hanes MS, 28TH & IVY AVE 27105 3-00100
Ron Montaquila, prin. 727-2252
Hill MS, 2200 TRYON ST 27107 3-00100
Patricia Holiday, prin. 788-7422
Kennedy MS 3-00100
100 N HIGHLAND AVE 27101 727-2343
Norma Harbin, prin.
Mineral Springs MS 3-00100
4559 OGBURN AVE 27105 767-2331
Jim Wheeler, prin.
Northwest MS, 5501 MURRAY RD 27106 3-00100
W. Kurt Telford, prin. 924-5126
Paisley MS, 1400 GRANT AVE 27105 3-00100
Tom Bohlinger, prin. 727-2775
Philo MS, 410 HAVERHILL ST 27127 3-00100
William Peay, prin. 784-0420
Wiley MS 3-00100
1400 W NORTHWEST BLVD 27104 727-2378
Dawn Wooten, prin.

Other Schools – See Clemmons, Kernersville, Walkertown

Bishop McGuiness HS   2-00011
   1730 LINK RD   27103   725-4247
   George Repass, prin.
Forsyth Memorial Hospital   HSP
   3333 SILAS CREEK PKY   27103   760-5111
Forsyth Technical Community College   5-CC
   2100 SILAS CREEK PKY   27103   723-0371
North Carolina School of the Arts   2-UC
   200 WAUGHTOWN ST   27127   770-3291
Piedmont Bible College   2-UC
   716 FRANKLIN ST   27101   725-8344
Salem Academy   2-00011
   PO BOX 10548   27108   721-2646
   David Black, prin.
Salem College   3-UC
   PO BOX 10548   27108   800-327-2536
Union Grove Christian S   2-11111
   RR 8 BOX 1228   27106   764-3105
   Rev. Ken Harris, prin.

Wake Forest University   5-UC
   2240 REYNOLDA RD   27106   759-6074
Wake Forest University   3-UC
   MEDICAL CENTER BLVD   27157   748-4424
Winston-Salem State University   5-UC
   601 S MRTN LTHER KING JR DR   27110
Woodland Baptist Christian HS   2-11111
   3665 PATTERSON AVE   27105   767-6176
   Joel Groce, prin.

Winterville, AC 919, PC 5, Pitt
Pitt County SD
   Supt. — See Greenville
   Cox MS, PO BOX 550   28590   3-00100
   John Pinner, prin.   756-3105

Winton, AC 919, PC 3, Hertford
Hertford County SD   5-11111
   PO BOX 158   27986   358-1761
   Jane Burke, supt.
Other Schools – See Ahoskie, Murfreesboro

Yadkinville, AC 919, PC 5, Yadkin
Yadkin County SD   5-11111
   RR 6 BOX 105   27055   679-2051
   Cleve Hollar, supt.
Other Schools – See Boonville, East Bend

Yanceyville, AC 919, PC 4, Caswell
Caswell County SD   5-11111
   PO BOX 160   27379   694-4116
   Carl McGee, supt.
Yancey HS, PO BOX 190   27379   4-00011
   Steven Williamson, prin.   694-4212
Dillard JHS, PO BOX 310   27379   2-00100
   Larry Briggs, prin.   694-4941

Zebulon, AC 919, PC 5, Wake
Wake County SD
   Supt. — See Raleigh
   MS, 1000 OLD US 64 E   27597   3-00100
   Thomas Benton, prin.   269-3630

Baptist Temple Christian S   2-11111
   615 US HIGHWAY 64 BUS W   27597   269-6504
   Rev. Dupree, prin.

NORTH DAKOTA

DEPARTMENT OF PUBLIC INSTRUCTION
600 Boulevard Ave., E., Bismarck 58505
(701) 224-4920

Superintendent of Public Instruction	Wayne Sanstead
Assistant Superintendent	Ronald Stastney
Director Support Services & Instructional Technology	Joseph Linnertz

STATE BOARD OF PUBLIC SCHOOL EDUCATION
600 Boulevard Ave., E., Bismark 58505

Chairperson	Melvin Olson

COUNTY SUPERINTENDENTS OF SCHOOLS

Adams County
   Reva Frieze   701-567-2805
   PO BOX 150, Hettinger   58639
Barnes County
   Pat Beil, Valley City   58072   701-845-8514
Benson County
   Jean Olson, PO BOX 347   701-473-5370
   Minnewaukan   58351
Billings County
   Lana O'Brien, Medora   58645   701-623-4366
Bottineau County
   Dwane Getzlaff, Bottineau   58318   701-228-2815
Bowman County
   Lois Anderson, Bowman   58623   701-523-3478
Burke County
   Joan Sorum, Bowbells   58721   701-377-2918
Burleigh County
   Eileen Mack, Bismarck   58504   701-222-6679
Cass County
   Bruce Hoefs   701-241-5740
   PO BOX 2806, Fargo   58108
Cavalier County
   Shirley Peterson   701-256-2285
   901 3RD ST, Langdon   58249
Dickey County
   Helen Sprouse, Ellendale   58436   701-349-3049
Divide County
   Wilma Anderson, Crosby   58730   701-965-6622
Dunn County
   Candice Benz, Manning   58642   701-573-4442
Eddy County
   Alice Allmaras   701-947-5615
   524 CENTRAL AVE
   New Rockford   58356
Emmons County
   Del Svalen, Linton   58552   701-254-4486
Foster County
   Diantha Nilles, Carrington   58421   701-652-2641
Golden Valley County
   Virginia Bares   701-872-4543
   PO BOX 35, Beach   58621
Grand Forks County
   Kathryn Haltli   701-780-8291
   PO BOX 1435, Grand Forks   58206

Grant County
   Karen Witkowski   701-622-3238
   PO BOX 279, Carson   58529
Griggs County
   Ardis Oettle   701-797-2433
   PO BOX 566, Cooperstown   58425
Hettinger County
   Diane Senn, Mott   58646   701-824-2500
Kidder County
   Clarilyn Riedinger, Steele   58482   701-475-2311
Lamoure County
   Margaret Witt   701-883-5301
   PO BOX 235, La Moure   58458
Logan County
   Gary Schumacker   701-754-2756
   Napoleon   58561
McHenry County
   Maxine Rognlien, Towner   58788   701-537-5642
McIntosh County
   Bruce Speidel, Ashley   58413   701-288-3346
McKenzie County
   Jessie Goddard   701-842-3616
   PO BOX 503, Watford City   58854
McLean County
   Melford Samuelson   701-462-8541
   PO BOX 10, Washburn   58577
Mercer County
   Clyde Boyko, Stanton   58571   701-745-3392
Morton County
   Karen Kautzmann   701-667-3315
   210 2ND AVE NW
   Mandan   58554
Mountrail County
   W. Ray Stewart   701-628-2955
   PO BOX 490, Stanley   58784
Nelson County
   Grace Carlson   701-247-2472
   PO BOX 566, Lakota   58344
Oliver County
   Alice Husfloen, Center   58530   701-794-8782
Pembina County
   Lois Olson, Cavalier   58220   701-265-4336
Pierce County
   Ioane Schmidt, Rugby   58368   701-776-5227

Ramsey County
   Beverly Schmidt   701-662-7062
   Devils Lake   58301
Ransom County
   Sheryl Dagman, Lisbon   58054   701-683-5823
Renville County
   Shanette Haarsager, Mohall   58761   701-756-6370
Richland County
   Peggy Carlson   701-642-7713
   PO BOX 126, Wahpeton   58074
Rolette County
   Dwane Getzlaff, Rolla   58367   701-477-5265
Sargent County
   Elaine Marquette   701-724-6241
   PO BOX 249, Forman   58032
Sheridan County
   Anton Klein   701-363-2207
   PO BOX 667, Mc Clusky   58463
Sioux County
   Virginia Luger   701-854-3481
   PO BOX L, Fort Yates   58538
Slope County
   Lois Anderson   701-879-6277
   PO BOX MM, Amidon   58620
Stark County
   Patricia Hardy   701-264-7656
   PO BOX 130, Dickinson   58602
Steele County
   Barbara Dekker, Finley   58230   701-524-2830
Stutsman County
   Joan Nayes, Jamestown   58401   701-252-9033
Towner County
   Patrick Delmore, Cando   58324   701-968-3523
Traill County
   Barbara Dekker, Hillsboro   58045   701-436-4459
Walsh County
   Lois Olson, Grafton   58237   701-352-1060
Ward County
   Joan Holum, Minot   58701   701-857-6495
Wells County
   Alice Allmaras, Fessenden   58438   701-547-3221
Williams County
   Grant Archer, Williston   58801   701-572-1712

PUBLIC, PRIVATE AND CATHOLIC SECONDARY SCHOOLS

Adams, AC 701, PC 2, Walsh
Adams SD 128, PO BOX 76 58210 — 2-11111 944-2745
  Douglas Grove, supt.
S, PO BOX 76 58210 — 2-11111 944-2745
  Dennis Hammer, prin.

Alexander, AC 701, PC 2, McKenzie
Alexander SD 2, PO BOX 66 58831 — 2-11111 828-3335
  William Maxwell, supt.
S, PO BOX 66 58831 — 2-11111 828-3334
  Murray Kline, prin.

Anamoose, AC 701, PC 2, McHenry
Anamoose SD 14, RR 1 BOX 18 58710 — 2-11111 465-3258
  David Zwingel, supt.
S, RR 1 BOX 18 58710 — 2-11111 465-3258
  David Zwingel, prin.

Argusville, AC 701, PC 2, Cass
Cass Valley North SD 76 — 2-11111 484-5331
  PO BOX 38 58005
  Mark Weston, supt.
Cass Valley North JSHS — 2-00111 484-5331
  PO BOX 38 58005
  Mark Weston, prin.

Arthur, AC 701, PC 2, Cass
Dakota SD 3, PO BOX 68 58006 — 2-11111 967-8344
  Helmuth Haberman, supt.
Dakota JSHS, PO BOX 68 58006 — 1-00111 967-8344
  Ronald Hensler, prin.

Ashley, AC 701, PC 4, McIntosh
Ashley SD 9, PO BOX H 58413 — 2-11111 288-3456
  B. McShane, supt.
S, PO BOX H 58413 — 2-11111 288-3457
  Donald Kosel, prin.

Beach, AC 701, PC 4, Golden Valley
Beach SD 3, PO BOX 368 58621 — 2-11111 872-4161
  Vern Brenner, supt.
JSHS, PO BOX 368 58621 — 2-00111 872-4161
  Victor Demaniow, prin.

Belcourt, AC 701, PC 4, Rolette
Belcourt SD 7, PO BOX 440 58316 — 4-11111 477-6471
  Wayne Keplin, supt.
Turtle Mtn. Community HS — 3-00011 477-6471
  PO BOX 440 58316
  Rosemary Jaros, prin.
Turtle Mtn. Community MS — 2-00100 477-6471
  PO BOX 440 58316
  Louis Dauphinais, prin.

Turtle Mountain Community College — 2-CC 477-5605
  PO BOX 340 58316

Belfield, AC 701, PC 3, Stark
Belfield SD 13, PO BOX 97 58622 — 2-11111 575-4275
  Arno Jorgenson, supt.
S, PO BOX 97 58622 — 2-11111 575-4275
  Perry Braunagel, prin.

Berthold, AC 701, PC 2, Ward
Berthold SD 54, PO BOX 185 58718 — 2-11111 453-3484
  Marcia Hall, supt.
S, PO BOX 185 58718 — 2-11111 453-3484
  Clyde T. Huber, prin.

Beulah, AC 701, PC 5, Mercer
Beulah SD 27, 205 5TH ST NW 58523 — 4-11111 873-2263
  Dale Gilje, supt.
JSHS, 205 5TH ST NW 58523 — 2-00111 873-2261
  Kelly Rasch, prin.

Binford, AC 701, PC 2, Griggs
Glenfield-Sutton-McHenry SD — 2-00111 676-2511
  PO BOX 38 58416
  Kerwin Borgen, supt.
Other Schools – See Glenfield

Bisbee, AC 701, PC 2, Towner
West Central SD 2 — 1-00111 656-3536
  PO BOX 217 58317
  Wayne Lingen, supt.
Bisbee-Egeland JSHS — 1-00111 656-3536
  PO BOX 217 58317
  Glen Weinmann, prin.

Bismarck, AC 701, PC 8, Burleigh
Bismarck SD 1, 400 E AVENUE E 58501 — 7-11111 221-3705
  Lowell Jensen, supt.
HS, 800 N 8TH ST 58501 — 4-00001 221-3521
  Thomas Hesford, prin.
Century SHS — 3-00001 221-3545
  1000 E CENTURY AVE 58501
  Jeffrey Geiger, prin.
Bismarck Vo Ctr — Vo Tech 221-3790
  1500 EDWARDS AVE 58501
  Serenus Hoffner, prin.
Hughes JHS — 3-00110 221-3555
  806 N WASHINGTON ST 58501
  Al Ault, prin.
Simle JHS, 1215 N 19TH ST 58501 — 3-00110 221-3570
  Douglas Johnson, prin.
Wachter JHS, 1107 S 7TH ST 58504 — 3-00110 221-3585
  James Potter, prin.

Naughton SD 25 — 1-00100
  9101 123RD AVE NE 58501 – (—), supt. 673-3324
Naughton MS — 1-00100
  9101 123RD AVE NE 58501 673-3119
  Lisa Martel, prin.

Bismarck State College — 4-CC 224-5400
  1500 EDWARDS AVE 58501
Interstate Business College — 2-CS 255-0779
  520 E MAIN AVE 58501
Medcenter One College of Nursing — 1-UC 224-6271
  512 N 7TH ST 58501
Quain & Ramstad Clinic — HSP 222-5413
  221 N 5TH ST 58501
St. Alexius Medical Center — HSP 224-7070
  PO BOX 5510 58502
St. Marys Central HS — 2-00011 223-4113
  1025 N 2ND ST 58501
  Scott Halvorson, prin.
Shiloh Christian S — 2-11111 221-2104
  6117 E MAIN AVE 58501
  Donna Kennedy, prin.
United Tribes Technical College — 2-CC 255-3285
  3315 UNIVERSITY DR 58504
University of Mary — 4-UC 255-7500
  7500 UNIVERSITY DR 58504

Bottineau, AC 701, PC 5, Bottineau
Bottineau County SD 1, 301 BRANDER ST 58318 — 3-11111 228-2266
  Dean Koppelman, supt.
JSHS, 301 BRANDER ST 58318 — 3-01111 228-2266
  Ross Roemmich, prin.

North Dakota State University-Bottineau — 2-CC 228-2277
  1ST & SIMRALL BLVD 58318
Turtle Mt. School/Paramedical Technique — 1-CS 228-3390
  58318

Bowbells, AC 701, PC 2, Burke
Bowbells SD 14, PO BOX 279 58721 — 2-11111 377-2396
  Lloyd Gjovik, supt.
S, PO BOX 279 58721 — 2-11111 377-2396
  Lloyd Gjovik, prin.

Bowdon, AC 701, PC 2, Wells
Bowdon SD 23, PO BOX 429 58418 — 1-11111 962-3477
  Dale Hogie, supt.
S, PO BOX 429 58418 — 1-11111 962-3477
  Norbert J. Schlegel, prin.

Bowman, AC 701, PC 4, Bowman
Bowman SD 1, PO BOX H 58623 — 2-11111 523-3283
  Wilfred Volesky, supt.
S, PO BOX H 58623 — 2-11111 523-3283
  Glenn Moser, prin.

Sheets SD 14, RR 1 BOX 21 58623 — 1-01100 523-5727
  (—), supt.
Cottage MS, RR 1 BOX 21 58623 — 1-01100 523-5553
  Sheryl Craig, prin.

Butte, AC 701, PC 2, McLean
Butte SD 62, PO BOX 287 58723 — 1-11111 626-7118
  Leonard Bubach, supt.
S, PO BOX 287 58723 — 1-11111 626-7118
  Stanley Paschke, prin.

Buxton, AC 701, PC 2, Traill
Central Valley SD 3 — 2-11111 847-2220
  RR 1 BOX 152B 58218
  Dale Duggan, supt.
Central Valley S, RR 1 BOX 152B 58218 — 2-11111 847-2220
  Robert Schneck, prin.

Calvin, AC 701, PC 1, Cavalier
Border Central SD, PO BOX 98 58323 — 1-11111 697-5111
  Russell Fletschock, supt.
Border Central S, PO BOX 98 58323 — 1-11111 697-5111
  Daniel Darling, prin.

Cando, AC 701, PC 4, Towner
Southern SD 8, PO BOX 489 58324 — 2-11111 968-4416
  Lewis Getz, supt.
S, PO BOX 489 58324 — 2-11111 968-4416
  Walter Beseler, prin.

Carrington, AC 701, PC 4, Foster
Carrington SD 10, 100 3RD AVE S 58421 — 3-11111 652-3136
  Charles Brickner, supt.
JSHS, 100 3RD AVE S 58421 — 2-00111 652-3136
  Allen Larson, prin.

Carson, AC 701, PC 2, Grant
Roosevelt SD 18, PO BOX 197 58529 — 2-11111 622-3263
  Samuel Tollefson, supt.
Roosevelt S, PO BOX 197 58529 — 2-11111 622-3263
  Jerome Sondag, prin.

Cartwright, AC 701, PC 1, McKenzie
Horse Creek SD 32 — 1-01100 828-3482
  HC 2 BOX 9 58838 – (—), supt.
Horse Creek MS, HC 2 BOX 9 58838 — 1-01100 481-1373
  Linda Schieffer, prin.

Casselton, AC 701, PC 4, Cass
Central Cass SD 17 — 3-11111 347-5352
  PO BOX 250 58012
  Larry Nybladh, supt.
Central Cass S, PO BOX 250 58012 — 2-11111 347-5352
  Steve Lorentzen, prin.

Cavalier, AC 701, PC 4, Pembina
Cavalier SD 6, PO BOX N 58220 — 3-11111 265-8417
  Melvin Olson, supt.
S, PO BOX N 58220 — 3-11111 265-8417
  Loren Scheer, prin.

Center, AC 701, PC 3, Oliver
Center SD 18, PO BOX 248 58530 — 2-11111 794-8776
  Michael Ness, supt.

S, PO BOX 248 58530 — 2-11111 794-8778
  Edwin Boger, prin.

Chaffee, AC 701, PC 1, Cass
Chaffee SD 26, PO BOX 110 58014 — 1-11111 347-4016
  Larry Davis, supt.
S, PO BOX 110 58014 — 1-11111 347-4016
  Merry Kellerman, prin.

Colfax, AC 701, PC 1, Richland
Richland SD 44, PO BOX 26 58018 — 2-11111 372-3713
  Ron Julson, supt.
Richland JSHS, PO BOX 26 58018 — 2-00111 372-3714
  Bruce Hackey, prin.

Cooperstown, AC 701, PC 4, Griggs
Cooperstown SD 18 — 2-11111 797-3114
  PO BOX 487 58425
  Wade Faul, supt.
Griggs County Central JSHS — 2-00111 797-3114
  PO BOX 487 58425
  Kirk Ham, prin.

Crosby, AC 701, PC 4, Divide
Divide County SD 1, PO BOX G 58730 — 2-11111 965-6313
  Donald Nielsen, supt.
Divide County JSHS, PO BOX G 58730 — 2-00111 965-6392
  Norman Sortland, prin.

Des Lacs, AC 701, PC 2, Ward
United SD 7, PO BOX 117 58733 — 3-11111 725-4334
  Donald Strang, supt.
Des Lacs Burlington JSHS — 2-00111 725-4334
  PO BOX 117 58733
  Alton M. Nygaard, prin.

Devils Lake, AC 701, PC 6, Ramsey
Devils Lake SD 1 — 4-11111 662-7640
  1601 COLLEGE DR 58301
  Ronald Bommersbach, supt.
HS, 1601 COLLEGE DR 58301 — 3-00011 662-1200
  Steven Swiontek, prin.
Lake Area Vo-Tech Ctr, HWY 20 N 58301 — Vo Tech 662-7650
  Elroy Burkle, prin.
Central MS, 325 7TH ST 58301 — 3-01100 662-7664
  Robert Gibson, prin.

North Dakota School for the Deaf — HND
  58301
University of North Dakota-Lake Region — 3-CC 662-8683
  58301

Dickinson, AC 701, PC 7, Stark
Dickinson SD 1, PO BOX 1057 58602 — 5-11111 225-1550
  Rollie Morud, supt.
HS, PO BOX 1057 58602 — 3-00011 225-6736
  Eugene Boyle, prin.
Hagen JHS, PO BOX 1057 58602 — 2-00100 225-5117
  Ronald Steiner, prin.

Dickinson State University 58601 — 4-UC 227-2507
Trinity HS, 815 EMPIRE RD 58601 — 2-00111 225-6081
  Rod Torgerson, prin.

Drake, AC 701, PC 2, McHenry
Drake SD 57, PO BOX 256 58736 — 2-11111 465-3634
  George Wieland, supt.
S, PO BOX 256 58736 — 2-11111 465-3735
  Marvin Goplen, prin.

Drayton, AC 701, PC 3, Pembina
Drayton SD 19, PO BOX 399 58225 — 2-11111 454-3324
  Kurt Eddy, supt.
S, PO BOX 399 58225 — 2-11111 454-3324
  Robert Klein, prin.

Driscoll, AC 701, PC 2, Burleigh
Driscoll SD 36, PO BOX 46 58532 — 1-11111 387-4312
  Elmer Reiner, supt.
S, PO BOX 46 58532 — 1-11111 387-4312
  Elmer Reiner, prin.

Dunseith, AC 701, PC 3, Rolette
Dunseith SD 1, PO BOX 789 58329 — 3-11111 244-5434
  Myron Haugse, supt.
Dunseith JSHS, PO BOX 789 58329 — 2-00111 244-5249
  Leslie Jensen, prin.

Edgeley, AC 701, PC 3, La Moure
Edgeley SD 3, PO BOX 37 58433 — 2-11111 493-2772
  Arlyn Irion, supt.
JSHS, PO BOX 37 58433 — 2-00111 493-2292
  Myron Luttschwager, prin.

Edinburg, AC 701, PC 2, Walsh
Edinburg SD 106, PO BOX 6 58227 — 2-11111 993-8312
  Mike Klabo, supt.
S, PO BOX 6 58227 — 2-11111 993-8312
  John M. Evenson, prin.

Edmore, AC 701, PC 2, Ramsey
Edmore SD 2, PO BOX 188 58330 — 2-11111 644-2282
  David Schneider, supt.
S, PO BOX 188 58330 — 2-11111 644-2282
  Rick Jacobson, prin.

Elgin, AC 701, PC 3, Grant
Elgin SD 16, PO BOX 70 58533 — 2-11111 584-2374
  Martin Schock, supt.
S, PO BOX 70 58533 — 2-11111 584-2374
  John Lynch, prin.

Ellendale, AC 701, PC 4, Dickey
Ellendale SD 40, PO BOX 400 58436   2-11111
  Kirk A Hansen, supt.   349-3232
Ellendale JSHS, PO BOX 400 58436   2-00111
  Tim Graf, prin.   349-4148

Trinity Bible College   2-UC
  50 6TH AVE S 58436   349-3621

Enderlin, AC 701, PC 3, Ransom
Enderlin SD 22, 410 BLUFF ST 58027   2-11111
  Kenneth Scarbrough, supt.   437-2240
S, 410 BLUFF ST 58027   2-11111
  Timothy Michaelson, prin.   437-2240

Fairmount, AC 701, PC 2, Richland
Fairmount SD 18, PO BOX 228 58030   2-11111
  Kenneth Rusten, supt.   474-5469
S, PO BOX 228 58030   2-11111
  Douglas Bertsch, prin.   474-5987

Fargo, AC 701, PC 8, Cass
Fargo SD 1, 1104 2ND AVE S 58103   7-11111
  Vern Bennett, supt.   241-4801
North SHS, 801 17TH AVE N 58102   3-00001
  Edward Raymond, prin.   241-4785
South HS, 1840 15TH AVE S 58103   4-00011
  Richard Warner, prin.   241-4711
Wilson HS   2-00011
  315 N UNIVERSITY DR 58102   241-4889
  Jerry Hasche, prin.
Agassiz JHS, 1305 9TH AVE S 58103   4-00100
  Charles Krumwiede, prin.   241-4881
Franklin JHS, 1420 8TH ST N 58102   3-00110
  Warren Gullickson, prin.   241-4792

Dakota Aero Technical   1-CS
  1801 23RD AVE N RM 111 58102   237-5305
Interstate Business College   3-CS
  2720 32ND AVE S 58103   232-2477
North Dakota State University 58105   6-UC
      237-7211
Oak Grove Lutheran HS   2-00111
  124 N TERRACE 58102   237-0210
  Clarke Tufte, prin.
St. Anthony JHS, 719 9TH ST S 58103   2-00100
  Robert Dignan, prin.   293-3780
St. Luke's Hospital   HSP
  5TH ST & MILLS AVE 58105   280-5102
Shanley HS, 705 13TH AVE N 58102   2-00011
  Kim Colwell, prin.   235-5581
Tri-College University 58105   2-UC
      237-8170

Fessenden, AC 701, PC 3, Wells
Fessenden SD 40, PO BOX 67 58438   2-11111
  Dale Hogie, supt.   547-3296
S, PO BOX 67 58438   2-11111
  Curtis Pierce, prin.   547-3296

Finley, AC 701, PC 3, Steele
Finley Sharon SD 19   2-11111
  PO BOX 447 58230 – (—), supt.   524-2588
Finley Sharon S, PO BOX 447 58230   2-11111
  Virgil Babinski, prin.   524-2420

Flasher, AC 701, PC 2, Morton
Flasher SD 39, PO BOX 267 58535   2-11111
  Leon Johnson, supt.   597-3355
S, PO BOX 267 58535   2-11111
  R. Honrath, prin.   597-3355

Fordville, AC 701, PC 2, Walsh
Fordville SD 79, PO BOX 127 58231   1-11111
  Morgan J. Huset, supt.   229-3297
S, PO BOX 127 58231   1-11111
  Dennis Dryburgh, prin.   229-3297

Forman, AC 701, PC 3, Sargent
Sargent Central SD   2-11111
  PO BOX 289 58032   724-3205
  Rodney Jones, supt.
Sargent Central S, PO BOX 289 58032   2-11111
  B. Schumacher, prin.   724-3205

Fort Totten, AC 701, PC 3, Benson
Fort Totten SD 30   2-00011
  PO BOX 239 58335   766-4282
  Charles Guthrie, supt.
Four Winds Community HS   2-00011
  PO BOX 239 58335   766-4282
  Charles Guthrie, prin.

Little Hoop Community College   2-CC
  PO BOX 269 58335   766-4415

Fort Yates, AC 701, PC 2, Sioux
Fort Yates SD 4, PO BOX 428 58538   2-11111
  (—), supt.   854-3887
Fort Yates S, PO BOX 428 58538   2-11111
  Bruce Benz, prin.   854-3819

Standing Rock College   2-CC
  HC 1 BOX 4 58538   854-3861

Gackle, AC 701, PC 2, Logan
Gackle SD 14, PO BOX 375 58442   2-11111
  Duane Zwinger, supt.   485-3692
S, PO BOX 375 58442   2-11111
  Ron Groth, prin.   485-3693

Garrison, AC 701, PC 4, McLean
Garrison SD 51, PO BOX 249 58540   2-11111
  Alan Taylor, supt.   463-2818

JSHS, PO BOX 249 58540   2-00111
  Michael Heilman, prin.   463-2218

Glenburn, AC 701, PC 2, Renville
Glenburn SD 26, PO BOX 138 58740   2-11111
  Charles Dunlop, supt.   362-7426
S, PO BOX 138 58740   2-11111
  Bruce Henderson, prin.   362-7426

Glenfield, AC 701, PC 2, Foster
Glenfield-Sutton-McHenry SD
  Supt. — See Binford
Midkota HS, PO BOX 98 58443   2-00111
  Gilbert Black, prin.   785-2126

Glen Ullin, AC 701, PC 3, Morton
Glen Ullin SD 48, PO BOX 548 58631   2-11111
  Patrick Feist, supt.   348-3590
S, PO BOX 548 58631   2-11111
  R. Johnson, prin.   348-3365

Golden Valley, AC 701, PC 2, Mercer
Golden Valley SD 20   1-00111
  PO BOX 158 58541   983-4256
  John Hvidsten, supt.
JSHS, PO BOX 158 58541   1-00111
  M. Beckwith, prin.   983-4256

Goodrich, AC 701, PC 2, Sheridan
Goodrich SD 16, PO BOX 159 58444   1-11111
  Rodney Scherbenske, supt.   884-2469
S, PO BOX 159 58444   1-11111
  Rodney Scherbenske, prin.   884-2469

Grafton, AC 701, PC 5, Walsh
Grafton SD 3, 1548 SCHOOL RD 58237   4-11111
  Julian Bjornson, supt.   352-1930
SHS, 1548 SCHOOL RD 58237   2-00001
  Lynn F. Flanagan, prin.   352-1930
North Valley Vo Ctr   Vo Tech
  RR 1 BOX 4 58237   352-3705
  Elizabeth Daby, prin.
Grafton Central JHS   3-01110
  725 GRIGGS AVE 58237   352-1469
  Norman Dutot, prin.

Grand Forks, AC 701, PC 8, Grand Forks
Grand Forks SD 1   6-11111
  PO BOX 6000 58206   746-2200
  Mark Sanford, supt.
Central SHS, 115 N 4TH ST 58203   3-00001
  Gordon Opstad, prin.   746-2375
Red River SHS, 2211 17TH AVE S 58201   3-00001
  Everett Knudsvig, prin.   746-2400
Community HS   1-00011
  911 COTTONWOOD ST 58201   746-2425
  David Godfread, prin.
Schroeder JHS, 800 32ND AVE S 58201   3-00110
  Owen Graupe, prin.   746-2330
South JHS, 1224 WALNUT ST 58201   3-00110
  Nancy Dutot, prin.   746-2345
Valley JHS, 2100 5TH AVE N 58203   3-00110
  James Stenehjem, prin.   746-2360

Aaker's Business College   2-CS
  PO BOX 876 58206   772-6646
North Dakota School for the Blind   HND
  500 STANFORD RD 58203
University of North Dakota   7-UC
  BOX 8193 UNIVERSITY STATION 58203
      777-2121

Granville, AC 701, PC 2, McHenry
Granville SD 25, PO BOX 158 58741   2-11111
  Larry Gegelman, supt.   728-6694
S, PO BOX 158 58741   2-11111
  Gary Volk, prin.   728-6641

Grenora, AC 701, PC 2, Williams
Grenora SD 99, PO BOX 38 58845   2-11111
  Clifton Lee, supt.   694-2711
S, PO BOX 38 58845   2-11111
  Carlyle Norby, prin.   694-2711

Gwinner, AC 701, PC 3, Sargent
North Sargent SD 3   2-11111
  PO BOX 158 58040   678-2492
  Walter Robinson, supt.
North Sargent S, PO BOX 158 58040   2-11111
  Bradley Rinas, prin.   678-2492

Halliday, AC 701, PC 2, Dunn
Halliday SD 19, PO BOX 188 58636   2-11111
  Keith Laite, supt.   938-4391
S, PO BOX 188 58636   2-11111
  Keith Laite, prin.   938-4391

Hankinson, AC 701, PC 4, Richland
Hankinson SD 8, PO BOX 220 58041   2-11111
  Robert Scrivner, supt.   242-7516
S, PO BOX 220 58041   2-11111
  Gary Engberg, prin.   242-7138

Harvey, AC 701, PC 4, Wells
Harvey SD 38, 811 BURKE AVE 58341   3-11111
  George Brackin, supt.   324-2265
HS, 200 NORTH ST E 58341   2-00011
  Robert Marthaller, prin.   324-2267

Hatton, AC 701, PC 3, Traill
Hatton SD 7, PO BOX 200 58240   2-11111
  Jack Maus, supt.   543-3455
S, PO BOX 200 58240   2-11111
  Kevin Rogers, prin.   543-3455

Hazelton, AC 701, PC 2, Emmons
Hazelton-Moffit SD   2-11111
  PO BOX 528 58544   782-6232
  Edo Johnston, supt.
JSHS, PO BOX 528 58544   1-00111
  Anthony Storey, prin.   782-6232

Hazen, AC 701, PC 5, Mercer
Hazen SD 3, PO BOX 487 58545   3-11111
  Jerome Enget, supt.   748-2345
HS, PO BOX 487 58545   2-00011
  Bryan Dinkins, prin.   748-2345
MS, PO BOX 487 58545   2-00100
  Gary Zimmerman, prin.   748-6649

Hebron, AC 701, PC 3, Morton
Hebron SD 13, PO BOX Q 58638   2-11111
  George Ding, supt.   878-4442
S, PO BOX Q 58638   2-11111
  George Ding, prin.   878-4442

Hettinger, AC 701, PC 4, Adams
Hettinger SD 13, PO BOX 1188 58639   2-11111
  Steven Rassier, supt.   567-4501
S, PO BOX 1188 58639   2-11111
  Leonard Bjerklie, prin.   567-4501

Hillsboro, AC 701, PC 4, Traill
Hillsboro SD 9, PO BOX 579 58045   2-11111
  Gerald Bartholomay, supt.   436-4360
JSHS, PO BOX 579 58045   2-00111
  Rick Alfson, prin.   436-4360

Hoople, AC 701, PC 2, Walsh
Valley SD 12, PO BOX 150 58243   2-11111
  James McGurran, supt.   894-6226
Valley HS, PO BOX 150 58243   1-00111
  John Oistad, prin.   894-6226

Hope, AC 701, PC 2, Steele
Hope SD 10, PO BOX 100 58046   2-11111
  Douglas Burlingame, supt.   945-2511
S, PO BOX 100 58046   2-11111
  Dale Krueger, prin.   945-2473

Inkster, AC 701, PC 1, Grand Forks
Midway SD 128, RR 2 BOX 31 58244   2-11111
  Robert White, supt.   869-2432
Midway S, RR 2 BOX 31 58244   2-11111
  Ordean Hosna, prin.   869-2432

Jamestown, AC 701, PC 7, Stutsman
Jamestown SD 1, PO BOX 269 58402   5-11111
  David Haney, supt.   252-1950
HS, PO BOX 269 58402   3-00011
  Larry Ukestad, prin.   252-0559
James Valley Multidistrict Vo S   Vo Tech
  910 12TH AVE NE 58401   252-8841
  Arlo Stevick, prin.
JHS, PO BOX 269 58402   3-00100
  Nace Haugen, prin.   252-0317

Jamestown College 58405   3-UC
      252-3467

Jud, AC 701, PC 1, La Moure
Jud SD 5, PO BOX 487 58454   1-11111
  Neil Trottier, supt.   685-2217
S, PO BOX 487 58454   1-11111
  Neil Trottier, prin.   685-2217

Karlsruhe, AC 701, PC 2, McHenry
Karlsruhe SD 54, PO BOX 365 58744   1-11111
  Donald Ost, supt.   525-6371
S, PO BOX 365 58744   1-11111
  Donald Ost, prin.   525-6371

Kenmare, AC 701, PC 4, Ward
Kenmare SD 28, PO BOX 667 58746   2-11111
  Greg Haugland, supt.   385-4996
JSHS, PO BOX 667 58746   2-01111
  Arnold Jordan, prin.   385-4996

Kensal, AC 701, PC 2, Stutsman
Kensal SD 19, PO BOX 8 58455   2-11111
  Tom Tracy, supt.   435-2857
S, PO BOX 8 58455   2-11111
  Allen Zerr, prin.   435-2857

Killdeer, AC 701, PC 3, Dunn
Killdeer SD 16, PO BOX 579 58640   2-11111
  Gary Engebretson, supt.   764-5877
S, PO BOX 579 58640   2-11111
  Roger Gunderson, prin.   764-5877

Kindred, AC 701, PC 3, Cass
Kindred SD 2, 55 1ST AVE S 58051   3-11111
  Adam Boschee, supt.   428-3149
S, 55 1ST AVE S 58051   2-11111
  Steven Hall, prin.   428-3646

Kulm, AC 701, PC 3, La Moure
Kulm SD 7, PO BOX G 58456   2-11111
  Daniel Bauer, supt.   647-2303
JSHS, PO BOX G 58456   1-00111
  Dennis Hehr, prin.   647-2485

Lakota, AC 701, PC 3, Nelson
Lakota SD 66, PO BOX 388 58344   2-11111
  Harold Bergquist, supt.   247-2992
JSHS, PO BOX 388 58344   2-00111
  Dennis Winkler, prin.   247-2992

La Moure, AC 701, PC 3, La Moure
La Moure SD 8, PO BOX 656 58458   2-11111
  Robert Kummeth, supt.   883-5396

S, PO BOX 656 58458   1-11111
Caline Olson, prin.   883-5397

Langdon, AC 701, PC 4, Cavalier
Langdon SD 23, 715 14TH AVE 58249   3-11111
Bernard Lipp, supt.   256-5291
JSHS, 715 14TH AVE 58249   2-00111
Kevin Coles, prin.   256-5291

Larimore, AC 701, PC 4, Grand Forks
Larimore SD 44, PO BOX 769 58251   3-11111
Terry Bartness, supt.   343-2366
JSHS, PO BOX 769 58251   2-00111
Sherryl Houdek, prin.   343-2366

Leeds, AC 701, PC 3, Benson
Leeds SD 6, PO BOX K 58346   2-11111
James Isaak, supt.   466-2422
S, PO BOX K 58346   2-11111
Jeff Carpenter, prin.   466-2461

Lehr, AC 701, PC 2, Logan
Lehr SD 10, PO BOX 68 58460   1-11111
Paul Wagner, supt.   378-2283
S, PO BOX 68 58460   1-11111
Paul Wagner, prin.   378-2283

Leonard, AC 701, PC 2, Cass
Leonard SD 54, PO BOX 369 58052   1-11111
Clay Dunlap, supt.   645-2478
S, PO BOX 369 58052   1-11111
Oliveann Dunlap, prin.   645-2478

Lidgerwood, AC 701, PC 3, Richland
Lidgerwood SD 28   2-11111
PO BOX 468 58053   538-7341
Kenneth Reed, supt.
S, PO BOX 468 58053   2-11111
Rudy Hanson, prin.   538-7341

Lignite, AC 701, PC 2, Burke
Burke Central SD 36   2-11111
PO BOX 91 58752   933-2821
C. Dvorak, supt.
Burke Central S, PO BOX 91 58752   2-11111
C. Dvorak, prin.   933-2821

Linton, AC 701, PC 4, Emmons
Linton SD 36, PO BOX 970 58552   2-11111
Steven Nelson, supt.   254-4138
S, PO BOX 970 58552   2-11111
Corbley Ogren, prin.   254-4717

Lisbon, AC 701, PC 4, Ransom
Lisbon SD 19, PO BOX 593 58054   3-11111
Steven Johnson, supt.   683-4106
HS, PO BOX 593 58054   2-00011
Wayne Levang, prin.   683-4106
MS, PO BOX 593 58054   2-01100
(—), prin.   683-4106

Mc Clusky, AC 701, PC 2, Sheridan
Mc Clusky SD 19, PO BOX 426 58463   2-11111
Steven Stevenson, supt.   363-2470
JSHS, PO BOX 426 58463   1-00111
James Legg, prin.   363-2470

McVille, AC 701, PC 3, Nelson
Dakota Prairie SD 1
Supt. — See Petersburg
S, PO BOX E 58254   2-11111
Maynard Loibl, prin.   322-4771

Maddock, AC 701, PC 3, Benson
Maddock SD 9, PO BOX G 58348   2-11111
Richard Cheatley, supt.   438-2531
S, PO BOX G 58348   2-11111
Timothy Cross, prin.   438-2531

Makoti, AC 701, PC 2, Ward
North Shore SD 158   2-11111
PO BOX 127 58756   726-5591
Roland Loney, supt.
North Shore JSHS   1-00111
PO BOX 127 58756   726-5591
Robert Holte, prin.

Mandan, AC 701, PC 7, Morton
Mandan SD 1, 309 COLLINS AVE 58554   5-11111
Wallace Schmeling, supt.   663-9531
HS, 905 8TH AVE NW 58554   4-00011
Dale Ekstrom, prin.   663-9532
JHS, 406 4TH ST NW 58554   3-00100
Harlan Haak, prin.   663-7491

Mandaree, AC 701, PC 2, McKenzie
Mandaree SD 36, PO BOX 488 58757   2-11111
Frank Taylor, supt.   759-3274
S, PO BOX 488 58757   2-11111
Tex Hall, prin.   759-3311

Marion, AC 701, PC 2, La Moure
Marion SD 9, PO BOX 159 58466   2-00111
James Gross, supt.   669-2261
Litchville-Marion JSHS   2-00111
PO BOX 159 58466   669-2261
Mark Woodbury, prin.

Max, AC 701, PC 2, McLean
Max SD 50, PO BOX 297 58759   2-11111
Norman Batterberry, supt.   679-2685
S, PO BOX 297 58759   2-11111
S. M. Hannegrefs, prin.   679-2685

Mayville, AC 701, PC 4, Traill
Mayville-Portland SD   3-11111
900 MAIN ST W 58257   786-2281
William Julson, supt.

Mayville-Portland JSHS   2-00111
900 MAIN ST W 58257   786-2281
Douglas Jacobson, prin.

Mayville State University   3-UC
330 3RD ST NE 58257   786-2301

Medina, AC 701, PC 2, Stutsman
Medina SD 3, PO BOX 547 58467   2-11111
Jerry Fischer, supt.   486-3121
S, PO BOX 547 58467   2-11111
Jerry Fischer, prin.   486-3121

Milnor, AC 701, PC 3, Sargent
Milnor SD 2, PO BOX 9 58060   2-11111
Dale Fuhrman, supt.   427-9361
S, PO BOX 9 58060   2-11111
Glenn Dorr, prin.   427-5237

Milton, AC 701, PC 2, Cavalier
Milton SD 30, PO BOX 2020 58260   1-00111
Kent Hart, supt.   496-3425
Milton-Osnabrock JSHS   1-00111
PO BOX 2020 58260   496-3425
Kent Hart, prin.

Minnewaukan, AC 701, PC 2, Benson
Minnewaukan SD 5   2-11111
PO BOX 348 58351   473-5306
Myron Jury, supt.
S, PO BOX 348 58351   2-11111
Ronald Carlson, prin.   473-5306

Minot, AC 701, PC 8, Ward
Minot SD 1, 215 2ND ST SE 58701   6-11111
Richard Larson, supt.   857-4443
Magic City Campus SHS   4-00001
1100 11TH AVE SW 58701   857-4500
Richard Olthoff, prin.
Central Campus JHS   4-00010
215 1ST ST SE 58701   857-4660
Thomas McDonald, prin.
Hill JHS, 1000 6TH ST SW 58701   3-00100
Leslie Anderson, prin.   857-4477
Memorial JHS, 1 ROCKET RD 58704   2-00100
Larry Grindy, prin.   727-6125
Ramstad JHS, 501 LINCOLN AVE 58701   3-00100
Larry Wahlund, prin.   857-4465

Bishop Ryan JSHS   2-00111
316 11TH AVE NW 58701   852-4004
Patrick Nally, prin.
Meyer Voc-Tech School   2-CS
PO BOX 2126 58702   852-0427
Minot School for Allied Health   2-CS
20 BURDICK EXPY W STE 603 58701
  857-5620
Minot State University   5-UC
500 UNIVERSITY AVE W 58701   857-3300
St. Joseph's Hospital   HSP
3RD ST & 4TH AVE SE 58701   857-2300
Trinity Medical Center   HSP
3 BURDICK EXPY 58701   857-5000

Minto, AC 701, PC 3, Walsh
Minto SD 20, PO BOX 377 58261   2-11111
Harold A. Mach, supt.   248-3479
S, PO BOX 377 58261   2-11111
Frank M. Mitzell, prin.   248-3400

Mohall, AC 701, PC 3, Renville
Mohall SD 9, PO BOX 187 58761   2-11111
Milton Hoyt, supt.   756-6660
S, PO BOX 187 58761   2-11111
Roger Gendreau, prin.   756-6660

Montpelier, AC 701, PC 1, Stutsman
Montpelier SD 14, PO BOX 10 58472   2-11111
Rick Maddock, supt.   489-3348
S, PO BOX 10 58472   2-11111
Bruce Haarsager, prin.   489-3348

Mott, AC 701, PC 4, Hettinger
Mott SD 6, 205 DAKOTA AVE 58646   2-11111
Darrel Remington, supt.   824-2249
S, RR 1 BOX 227 58646   2-11111
Norman Fries, prin.   824-2795

Munich, AC 701, PC 2, Cavalier
Munich SD 19, PO BOX 39 58352   2-11111
R. R. Fletschock, supt.   682-5321
S, PO BOX 39 58352   2-11111
Jack DeMaine, prin.   682-5321

Napoleon, AC 701, PC 3, Logan
Napoleon SD 2, PO BOX 69 58561   2-11111
Timothy Ketterling, supt.   754-2244
S, PO BOX 69 58561   2-11111
Wayne Lucht, prin.   754-2787

Neche, AC 701, PC 2, Pembina
Neche SD 55, PO BOX 50 58265   2-11111
Larry Durand, supt.   886-7777
S, PO BOX 50 58265   2-11111
Larry Durand, prin.   886-7604

Newburg, AC 701, PC 2, Bottineau
Newburg United SD   2-11111
PO BOX 427 58762   272-6151
John Rintala, supt.
JSHS, PO BOX 427 58762   1-00111
Joseph Harder, prin.   272-6151

New England, AC 701, PC 3, Hettinger
New England SD 9   2-11111
PO BOX 307 58647   579-4462
Roger Pommerer, supt.
S, PO BOX 307 58647   2-11111
Lawrence Lechler, prin.   579-4160

New Leipzig, AC 701, PC 2, Grant
New Leipzig SD 15   2-11111
PO BOX 50 58562   584-2518
Martin Schock, supt.
S, PO BOX 50 58562   2-11111
Terry Bentz, prin.   584-2518

New Rockford, AC 701, PC 4, Eddy
New Rockford SD 1   2-11111
430 1ST AVE N 58356   947-5036
Dean Vorland, supt.
S, 430 1ST AVE N 58356   2-11111
Tim Guler, prin.   947-5036

New Salem, AC 701, PC 3, Morton
New Salem SD 7, PO BOX 378 58563   2-11111
Dale Hurt, supt.   843-7846
JSHS, PO BOX 378 58563   2-00111
Gordon Davis, prin.   843-7610

New Town, AC 701, PC 4, Mountrail
New Town SD 1, PO BOX 700 58763   3-11111
Edward Slocum, supt.   627-3658
JSHS, PO BOX 700 58763   2-00111
Doris McGrady, prin.   627-3658

Fort Bethold Community College   2-CC
PO BOX 490 58763   627-4738

Northwood, AC 701, PC 4, Grand Forks
Northwood SD 129   2-11111
PO BOX 250 58267   587-5221
Kevin Keenaghan, supt.
S, PO BOX 250 58267   2-11111
John Holien, prin.   587-6201

Oakes, AC 701, PC 4, Dickey
Oakes SD 41, 804 MAIN AVE 58474   3-11111
Arthur Conklin, supt.   742-3234
JSHS, 804 MAIN AVE 58474   2-00111
Donald Warren, prin.   742-3234
Southeast Vo Ctr, PO BOX 372 58474   Vo Tech
Wayne Kutzer, prin.   742-3248

Oriska, AC 701, PC 2, Barnes
Oriska SD 13, PO BOX 337 58063   1-11111
Roger Mulvaney, supt.   845-2846
S, PO BOX 337 58063   1-11111
Greg Jenkins, prin.   845-2846

Page, AC 701, PC 2, Cass
Page SD 80, PO BOX 26 58064   2-11111
Arthur Mitzel, supt.   668-2292
S, PO BOX 26 58064   2-11111
Bernard Hummel, prin.   668-2520

Park River, AC 701, PC 4, Walsh
Park River SD 78, PO BOX 240 58270   3-11111
Claude Sheldon, supt.   284-7164
JSHS, PO BOX 240 58270   2-00111
David Beckman, prin.   284-7164

Parshall, AC 701, PC 3, Mountrail
Parshall SD 3, PO BOX 158 58770   2-11111
Michael Severson, supt.   862-3129
JSHS, PO BOX 158 58770   2-00111
Mark Grueneich, prin.   862-3129

Pembina, AC 701, PC 3, Pembina
Pembina SD 1, PO BOX 409 58271   2-11111
Wade Defoe, supt.   825-6261
S, PO BOX 409 58271   2-11111
Wade Defoe, prin.   825-6261

Petersburg, AC 701, PC 2, Nelson
Dakota Prairie SD 1   3-11111
PO BOX 37 58272   345-8455
Jack Adkins, supt.
Unity JSHS, PO BOX 37 58272   2-00111
Janet Edlund, prin.   345-8233
Other Schools – See McVille, Tolna

Pettibone, AC 701, PC 1, Kidder
Pettibone SD 11, PO BOX 63 58475   1-11111
Tony Grubb, supt.   273-6695
S, PO BOX 63 58475   1-11111
Tony Grubb, prin.   273-6695

Pingree, AC 701, PC 1, Stutsman
Pingree Buchanan SD   2-11111
111 LINCOLN AVE 58476   252-5563
Dennis Adair, supt.
Pingree Buchanan JSHS   1-00111
111 LINCOLN AVE 58476   252-5563
Dennis Adair, prin.

Plaza, AC 701, PC 2, Mountrail
Plaza SD 137, PO BOX 38 58771   2-11111
Roland Loney, supt.   497-3734
S, PO BOX 38 58771   2-11111
Janene Lee, prin.   497-3734

Powers Lake, AC 701, PC 2, Burke
Powers Lake SD 27   2-11111
PO BOX 346 58773   464-5432
Stanley Miller, supt.
JSHS, PO BOX 346 58773   2-00111
John Albertson, prin.   464-5432

Ray, AC 701, PC 3, Williams
Nesson SD 2, PO BOX 564 58849 — 2-11111
David Huwe, supt. — 568-3301
S, PO BOX 564 58849 — 2-11111
Arley Larson, prin. — 568-3301

Reeder, AC 701, PC 2, Adams
Reeder SD 3, PO BOX 248 58649 — 1-11111
(—), supt. — 853-2311
S, PO BOX 248 58649 — 1-11111
Sharon Soehren, prin. — 853-2311

Regent, AC 701, PC 2, Hettinger
Regent SD 14, PO BOX 219 58650 — 2-11111
Duane Martin, supt. — 563-4315
S, PO BOX 219 58650 — 2-11111
Duane Martin, prin. — 563-4314

Rhame, AC 701, PC 2, Bowman
Mud Butte SD 30 — 1-01100
HC 2 BOX 26 58651 – (—), supt. — 279-6653
Mud Butte MS, HC 2 BOX 26 58651 — 1-01100
Roberta Bleth, prin. — 279-6659

Rhame SD 17, PO BOX 39 58651 — 2-11111
Wilfred Volesky, supt. — 279-5527
S, PO BOX 39 58651 — 2-11111
Pam Nagel, prin. — 279-5753

Richardton, AC 701, PC 3, Stark
Richardton SD 4, PO BOX 289 58652 — 2-00111
John Jankowski, supt. — 974-2111
JSHS, PO BOX 289 58652 — 2-00111
J. Gengler, prin. — 974-2111

Robinson, AC 701, PC 1, Kidder
Robinson SD 14, PO BOX 38 58478 — 1-11111
Mark Bernier, supt. — 392-8542
S, PO BOX 38 58478 — 1-11111
Mark Bernier, prin. — 392-8542

Rocklake, AC 701, PC 2, Towner
North Central SD 28 — 2-11111
PO BOX 188 58365 — 266-5539
Wayne Lingen, supt.
North Central S, PO BOX 188 58365 — 2-11111
Duane Paulsrud, prin. — 266-5539

Rogers, AC 701, PC 1, Barnes
North Central SD 65 — 2-11111
RR 1 BOX 37A 58479 – Lee Kelm, supt. — 646-6202
North Central S, RR 1 BOX 37A 58479 — 2-11111
Clyde Eriksen, prin. — 646-6202

Rolette, AC 701, PC 3, Rolette
Rolette SD 29, PO BOX 97 58366 — 2-11111
Merrill Krueger, supt. — 246-3595
S, PO BOX 97 58366 — 2-11111
Wayne Johnson, prin. — 246-3596

Rolla, AC 701, PC 4, Rolette
Mt. Pleasant SD 4 — 2-11111
RR 1 BOX 93 58367 — 477-3151
Norman Baumgarn, supt.
JSHS, RR 1 BOX 93 58367 — 2-00111
Scott Mitchell, prin. — 477-3151

Roseglen, AC 701, PC 1, McLean
White Shield SD 85 — 2-11111
HC 1 BOX 45 58775 — 743-4350
Gene Lafromboise, supt.
S, HC 1 BOX 45 58775 — 2-11111
Thomas Parsley, prin. — 743-4350

Rugby, AC 701, PC 5, Pierce
Rugby SD 5, 1123 S MAIN AVE 58368 — 3-11111
H. Lavik, supt. — 776-5201
JSHS, 1123 S MAIN AVE 58368 — 2-00111
George Dendinger, prin. — 776-5201

Saint John, AC 701, PC 2, Rolette
St. John SD 3, PO BOX 200 58369 — 2-11111
Donald Davis, supt. — 477-5651
S, PO BOX 200 58369 — 2-11111
Carey Kakela, prin. — 477-5651

Saint Thomas, AC 701, PC 2, Pembina
St. Thomas SD 43 — 2-11111
PO BOX 150 58276 — 257-6424
Steven Dick, supt.
S, PO BOX 150 58276 — 2-11111
David Hanson, prin. — 257-6424

Sawyer, AC 701, PC 2, Ward
Sawyer SD 16, PO BOX 167 58781 — 2-11111
James McQueen, supt. — 624-5167
S, PO BOX 167 58781 — 2-11111
James McQueen, prin. — 624-5167

Scranton, AC 701, PC 2, Bowman
Scranton SD 33, PO BOX 126 58653 — 2-11111
Clarke Ranum, supt. — 275-8897
S, PO BOX 126 58653 — 2-11111
Dennis Schaff, prin. — 275-8266

Selfridge, AC 701, PC 2, Sioux
Selfridge SD 8, PO BOX 45 58568 — 1-11111
Robert Braun, supt. — 422-3353
S, PO BOX 45 58568 — 1-11111
Russell Kronberg, prin. — 422-3353

Sheldon, AC 701, PC 2, Ransom
Sheldon SD 2, RR 1 BOX 1 58068 — 1-11111
Larry Davis, supt. — 882-3434
S, RR 1 BOX 1 58068 — 1-11111
Patricia Schroeder, prin. — 882-3221

Sherwood, AC 701, PC 2, Renville
Sherwood SD 2, PO BOX 9 58782 — 2-11111
P. Pearson, supt. — 459-2214
S, PO BOX 9 58782 — 2-11111
Terry L. Miller, prin. — 459-2214

Sheyenne, AC 701, PC 2, Eddy
Sheyenne SD 12, PO BOX 67 58374 — 2-11111
Myron Jury, supt. — 996-3461
S, PO BOX 67 58374 — 2-11111
Lorell Jungling, prin. — 996-3461

Solen, AC 701, PC 1, Sioux
Solen SD 3, PO BOX 128 58570 — 2-11111
Robert Schubert, supt. — 544-3332
JSHS, PO BOX 128 58570 — 2-00111
Robert Abrahamson, prin. — 544-3331

South Heart, AC 701, PC 2, Stark
South Heart SD 9, PO BOX 159 58655 — 2-11111
Duane Darling, supt. — 677-5671
S, PO BOX 159 58655 — 2-11111
D. Jablonsky, prin. — 677-5671

Stanley, AC 701, PC 4, Mountrail
Stanley SD 2, PO BOX 10 58784 — 3-11111
Elroy Hagen, supt. — 628-3811
JSHS, PO BOX 10 58784 — 2-00111
Joseph Lukach, prin. — 628-2342

Stanton, AC 701, PC 3, Mercer
Stanton SD 22, PO BOX 40 58571 — 2-11111
Gerald Quintus, supt. — 745-3319
S, PO BOX 40 58571 — 2-11111
Gerald Quintus, prin. — 745-3319

Starkweather, AC 701, PC 2, Ramsey
Starkweather SD 44 — 2-11111
PO BOX 45 58377 — 292-4381
Thomas Birchem, supt.
S, PO BOX 45 58377 — 2-11111
Dennis Dockter, prin. — 292-4381

Steele, AC 701, PC 3, Kidder
Steele-Dawson SD 26 — 2-11111
PO BOX 380 58482 — 475-2243
V. Erdelt, supt.
Steele-Dawson S, PO BOX 380 58482 — 2-11111
Raymond Jund, prin. — 475-2243

Strasburg, AC 701, PC 3, Emmons
Strasburg SD 15, PO BOX 308 58573 — 2-11111
James Eiseman, supt. — 336-2667
S, PO BOX 308 58573 — 2-11111
Frances Kuhn, prin. — 336-2667

Surrey, AC 701, PC 3, Ward
Surrey SD 41, PO BOX 40 58785 — 2-11111
Terry Mcleod, supt. — 838-8822
S, PO BOX 40 58785 — 2-11111
Robert Briggs, prin. — 838-3282

Sykeston, AC 701, PC 2, Wells
Sykes SD 39, PO BOX 367 58486 — 1-11111
Robert Stringer, supt. — 984-2392
Sykes S, PO BOX 367 58486 — 1-11111
Cheryl Hogie, prin. — 984-2392

Tappen, AC 701, PC 2, Kidder
Tappen SD 28, PO BOX 127 58487 — 2-11111
Leland Ham, supt. — 327-4256
S, PO BOX 127 58487 — 2-11111
Leland Ham, prin. — 327-4256

Thompson, AC 701, PC 3, Grand Forks
Thompson SD 61, PO BOX 265 58278 — 3-11111
Albert Peterson, supt. — 599-2765
S, PO BOX 265 58278 — 3-11111
Allan Boedeker, prin. — 599-2765

Tioga, AC 701, PC 4, Williams
Tioga SD 15, PO BOX 279 58852 — 2-11111
David S. Rust, supt. — 664-2333
JSHS, PO BOX 279 58852 — 2-00111
Ron Dockter, prin. — 664-2333

Tolna, AC 701, PC 2, Nelson
Dakota Prairie SD 1
Supt. — See Petersburg
S, PO BOX 404 58380 — 2-11111
Eddie Poehls, prin. — 262-4713

Tower City, AC 701, PC 2, Cass
Maple Valley SD 4 — 2-11111
PO BOX 168 58071 — 749-2570
Ronald Wendel, supt.
Maple Valley JSHS — 2-00111
PO BOX 168 58071 — 749-2570
Gary Milbrandt, prin.

Towner, AC 701, PC 3, McHenry
Newport SD 4, PO BOX 270 58788 — 2-11111
Larry Gegelman, supt. — 537-5414
S, PO BOX 270 58788 — 2-11111
Harry Renke, prin. — 537-5414

Trenton, AC 701, PC 2, Williams
Eight Mile SD 6, PO BOX 239 58853 — 2-11111
Lincoln Napton, supt. — 774-8040
Eight Mile S, PO BOX 239 58853 — 2-11111
Matthew Herman, prin. — 774-8221

Turtle Lake, AC 701, PC 3, McLean
Turtle Lake Mercer SD — 2-11111
PO BOX 160 58575 — 448-2365
Darryl Frederick, supt.
Turtle Lake Mercer S — 2-11111
PO BOX 160 58575 — 448-2365
Lui Ravnaas, prin.

Tuttle, AC 701, PC 2, Kidder
Tuttle SD 20, PO BOX 8 58488 — 2-11111
Leon Ableidinger, supt. — 867-2564
S, PO BOX 8 58488 — 2-11111
Jess Smith, prin. — 867-2564

Underwood, AC 701, PC 3, McLean
Underwood SD 8, PO BOX 100 58576 — 2-11111
Dean Koppelman, supt. — 442-3201
S, PO BOX 100 58576 — 2-11111
James Dunnigan, prin. — 442-3201

Upham, AC 701, PC 2, McHenry
Upham SD 29, PO BOX 26 58789 — 2-11111
Harlan Heinrich, supt. — 768-2531
S, PO BOX 26 58789 — 2-11111
Harlan Heinrich, prin. — 768-2531

Valley City, AC 701, PC 6, Barnes
Valley City SD 2 — 4-11111
460 CENTRAL AVE N 58072 — 845-0483
Paul Johnson, supt.
SHS, 460 CENTRAL AVE N 58072 — 2-00001
Robert Toso, prin. — 845-1498
Valley City Area Vo-Tech S — Vo Tech
PO BOX 30 58072 — 845-0256
Anneus Meester, prin.
JHS, 460 CENTRAL AVE N 58072 — 2-00110
Donald Bauer, prin. — 845-4181

Valley City State University — 3-UC
101 COLLEGE ST SW 58072 — 845-7100

Velva, AC 701, PC 3, McHenry
Velva SD 1, PO BOX 179 58790 — 2-11111
Ron Stahlecker, supt. — 338-2022
S, PO BOX 179 58790 — 2-11111
Ken Henderson, prin. — 338-2022

Verona, AC 701, PC 2, La Moure
Verona SD 11, PO BOX 76 58490 — 1-11111
Richard Berg, supt. — 432-5544
S, PO BOX 76 58490 — 1-11111
Richard Berg, prin. — 432-5544

Wahpeton, AC 701, PC 6, Richland
Wahpeton SD 37, 1505 11TH ST N 58075 — 4-11111
Michael Connell, supt. — 642-6741
HS, 1021 11TH ST N 58075 — 3-00011
Clark Williams, prin. — 642-2604
Richland County Vo Ctr — Vo Tech
2101 9TH ST N 58075 — 642-8701
Dan Rood, prin.
MS, 1209 LOY AVE 58075 — 2-00100
Lynn Sabbe, prin. — 642-6688

North Dakota State College of Science — 4-CC
800 6TH ST N 58075 — 671-2221

Walhalla, AC 701, PC 4, Pembina
Walhalla SD 27, PO BOX 558 58282 — 2-11111
Merlin Dahl, supt. — 549-3751
S, PO BOX 558 58282 — 2-11111
Mark Lindahl, prin. — 549-3751

Warwick, AC 701, PC 1, Benson
Warwick SD 29, PO BOX 7 58381 — 2-11111
Rocklyn Cofer, supt. — 294-2561
S, PO BOX 7 58381 — 2-11111
Donald Tennancour, prin. — 294-2561

Washburn, AC 701, PC 4, McLean
Washburn SD 4, PO BOX 280 58577 — 3-11111
Robert Tollefson, supt. — 462-3228
S, PO BOX 280 58577 — 3-11111
Keith Altendorf, prin. — 462-3221

Watford City, AC 701, PC 4, McKenzie
McKenzie County SD 1 — 3-11111
PO BOX 589 58854 — 842-3626
Sherman Sylling, supt.
JSHS, PO BOX 589 58854 — 2-00111
Jay Diede, prin. — 842-3625

West Fargo, AC 701, PC 7, Cass
West Fargo SD 6 — 5-11111
207 MAIN AVE W 58078 — 282-3387
M. Leidal, supt.
HS, 801 9TH ST E 58078 — 4-00011
M. P. Drew, prin. — 282-3357
MS, 109 3RD ST E 58078 — 3-00100
Steven Kent, prin. — 282-0530

Westhope, AC 701, PC 3, Bottineau
Westhope SD 17, PO BOX 406 58793 — 2-11111
John Rintala, supt. — 245-6444
S, PO BOX 406 58793 — 2-11111
L. L. Legg, prin. — 245-6444

Wildrose, AC 701, PC 2, Williams
Wildrose/Alamo SD — 1-11111
PO BOX 697 58795 — 539-2269
Kenneth Kaylor, supt.
Wildrose/Alamo S — 1-11111
PO BOX 697 58795 — 539-2261
Marlyn Vatne, prin.

Williston, AC 701, PC 7, Williams
Williston SD 1, PO BOX 1407 58802 — 5-11111
Norman Zielinski, supt. — 572-1580
HS, PO BOX 1407 58802 — 3-00011
John Salwei, prin. — 572-0967

JHS, PO BOX 1407 58802	2-00100	**Wimbledon, AC 701, PC 2, Barnes**		**Wolford, AC 701, PC 1, Pierce**
Mike Norland, prin.	572-5618	Wimbledon Court SD 82	2-11111	Wolford SD 1, PO BOX 478 58385

JHS, PO BOX 1407 58802 — 2-00100
Mike Norland, prin. — 572-5618

University of North Dakota — 3-CC
PO BOX 1326 58802 — 774-4200

Willow City, AC 701, PC 2, Bottineau
Willow City SD 13, PO BOX 37 58384 — 2-11111
Dean Koppelman, supt. — 366-4595
S, PO BOX 37 58384 — 2-11111
Brett Gibbs, prin. — 366-4595

Wilton, AC 701, PC 3, McLean
Montefiore SD 1, PO BOX 157 58579 — 2-11111
Clement Boechler, supt. — 734-6559
S, PO BOX 157 58579 — 2-11111
R. Norris, prin. — 734-6944

Wimbledon, AC 701, PC 2, Barnes
Wimbledon Court SD 82 — 2-11111
PO BOX 255 58492 — 435-2494
G. Gauderman, supt.
Wimbledon Court S — 2-11111
PO BOX 255 58492 — 435-2494
Brian Ramberg, prin.

Wing, AC 701, PC 2, Burleigh
Wing SD 28, PO BOX 130 58494 — 2-11111
Gene Kotaska, supt. — 943-2319
S, PO BOX 130 58494 — 2-11111
Gary Simmons, prin. — 943-2319

Wishek, AC 701, PC 4, McIntosh
Wishek SD 19, PO BOX 247 58495 — 2-11111
D. Zimmerman, supt. — 452-2892
S, PO BOX 247 58495 — 2-11111
Cleo Boschee, prin. — 452-2995

Wolford, AC 701, PC 1, Pierce
Wolford SD 1, PO BOX 478 58385 — 1-11111
Merrill Krueger, supt. — 583-2387
S, PO BOX 478 58385 — 1-11111
Gary Arlien, prin. — 583-2387

Wyndmere, AC 701, PC 3, Richland
Wyndmere SD 42, PO BOX 190 58081 — 2-11111
Dennis Nathan, supt. — 439-2287
S, PO BOX 190 58081 — 2-11111
John Hamann, prin. — 439-2287

Zeeland, AC 701, PC 2, McIntosh
Zeeland SD 4, PO BOX 2 58581 — 1-11111
Edward Wickre, supt. — 423-5429
S, PO BOX 2 58581 — 1-11111
Edward Wickre, prin. — 423-5429

OHIO

STATE DEPARTMENT OF EDUCATION
Ohio Departments Building
65 S. Front St. #808, Columbus 43266
(614) 466-3641

Superintendent of Public Instruction	Ted Sanders
Deputy Superintendent	John Goff
Assistant Superintendent Finance & Administration	James Van Keuren
Assistant Superintendent Internal Operations	Raymond Horn
Assistant Superintendent School Improvement	Irene Bandy-Hedden
Assistant Superintendent School Results & Accountability	Robert Moore

STATE BOARD OF EDUCATION
65 S. Front St. #808, Columbus 43266

President   Oliver Ocasek

COUNTY SUPERINTENDENTS OF SCHOOLS

Adams County
Philip Satterfield — 513-544-5586
3359 STATE ROUTE 125
West Union 45693

Allen County
Dale Kistler — 419-222-1836
204 N MAIN ST STE 303
Lima 45801

Ashland County
Douglas Staggs — 419-289-0000
COUNTY OFFICE BUILDING
Ashland 44805

Ashtabula County
Jerome Brockway — 216-576-9023
PO BOX 186, Jefferson 44047

Athens County
Gerald Stotts, 26 W STIMSON AVE — 614-593-8001
Athens 45701

Auglaize County
Larry Goodes — 419-738-3422
211 S BLACKHOOF ST
Wapakoneta 45895

Belmont County
Steven Grimm — 614-695-9773
410 FOX SHANNON PL
Saint Clairsville 43950

Brown County
Homer Castle, 325 W STATE ST — 513-378-6118
Georgetown 45121

Butler County
James Boyd — 513-887-3710
301 S 3RD ST, Hamilton 45011

Carroll County
James Betts — 216-863-1170
401 W MAIN ST, Malvern 44644

Champaign County
Carroll Meadows — 513-653-5296
PO BOX 269, Urbana 43078

Clark County
Larry Zerkle — 513-325-7671
1115 N LIMESTONE ST
Springfield 45503

Clermont County
Robert Whitman — 513-753-3114
809 EASTGATE SOUTH DR STE G
Cincinnati 45245

Clinton County
Rod Lane, 62 LAUREL DR — 513-382-6921
Wilmington 45177

Columbiana County
Paul Hood, 38720 SALTWELL RD — 216-424-9591
Lisbon 44432

Coshocton County
Roger Ames — 614-622-2924
23640 COUNTY ROAD 202
Coshocton 43812

Crawford County
Judy Howard — 419-562-8741
112 E MANSFIELD ST
Bucyrus 44820

Cuyahoga County
William Gesinsky — 216-524-3000
5700 W CANAL RD
Valley View 44125

Darke County
Robert Lantz — 513-548-4915
5279 EDUCATION DR
Greenville 45331

Defiance County
Robert Breisinger — 419-782-2921
506 COURT ST, Defiance 43512

Delaware-Union County SD
Ronald Smith — 614-548-7880
22 COURT ST, Delaware 43015

Erie County
Richard Acierto — 419-625-6274
2902 COLUMBUS AVE
Sandusky 44870

Fairfield County
H. Klein — 614-653-3193
126 W MAIN ST, Lancaster 43130

Fayette County
Douglas Male, PO BOX 624 — 614-335-3010
Washington Court House 43160

Franklin County
David Cottrell — 614-445-3750
1717 ALUM CREEK DR
Columbus 43207

Fulton County
Roy Vivian — 419-335-1070
PO BOX 338, Wauseon 43567

Gallia County
Robert Lanning, 230 SHAWNEE LN — 614-446-7883
Gallipolis 45631

Geauga County
Mathew Galemmo — 216-285-2222
470 CENTER ST, Chardon 44024

Greene County
William Wright, 360 E ENON RD — 513-372-0091
Yellow Springs 45387

Guernsey County
Carol Austin, 749 WHEELING AVE — 614-439-3558
Cambridge 43725

Hamilton County
James Hyre — 513-742-2200
11083 HAMILTON AVE
Cincinnati 45231

Hancock County
Bradley Cox — 419-422-7525
604 LIMA AVE, Findlay 45840

Hardin County
Charles Renner — 419-674-2288
1 COURT HOUSE SQ RM 50
Kenton 43326

Harrison County
Roy Cherry — 614-269-2000
7205 CUMBERLAND RD SW
Bowerston 44695

Henry County
John Wilhelm, 660 N PERRY ST — 419-592-1861
Napoleon 43545

Highland County
James Gibson, 106 1/2 N HIGH ST — 513-393-1331
Hillsboro 45133

Hocking County
Joseph Murtha — 614-385-8517
57 S WALNUT ST, Logan 43138

Holmes County
Joel Roscoe   216-674-1941
10 S CLAY ST, Millersburg 44654
Huron County
Don Schick   419-668-1658
180 MILAN AVE, Norwalk 44857
Jackson County
Howard Smith   614-682-7595
265 W CROSS ST, Oak Hill 45656
Jefferson County
Craig Closser, 2023 SUNSET BLVD   614-283-3347
Steubenville 43952
Knox County
Bruce Hawkins, 106 E HIGH ST   614-393-6767
Mount Vernon 43050
Lake County
James Porter   216-357-2563
PO BOX 490, Painesville 44077
Lawrence County
Oakley Collins   614-532-4223
COURT HOUSE, Ironton 45638
Licking County
Donald Boehm   614-349-6084
675 PRICE RD NE, Newark 43055
Logan County
Max McGowan, 125 S OPERA ST   513-599-5195
Bellefontaine 43311
Lorain County
Wayne Ross   216-323-7518
1885 LAKE AVE, Elyria 44035
Lucas County
Thomas Baker   419-245-4150
1 GOVERNMENT CTR
Toledo 43604
Madison County
Robert Groff   614-852-2174
59 N MAIN ST, London 43140
Mahoning County
Ronald Kendall, 2801 MARKET ST   216-788-2481
Youngstown 44507
Marion County
James Traveline   614-387-6625
134 E CENTER ST, Marion 43302
Medina County
James Boyes   216-723-6393
144 N BROADWAY ST
Medina 44256
Meigs County
John Reibel   614-992-5592
PO BOX 684, Pomeroy 45769
Mercer County
Ken Taylor   419-586-6628
311 S MAIN ST, Celina 45822

Miami County
John Decker   513-332-6987
215 W MAIN ST, Troy 45373
Monroe County
Richard Edge   614-472-5801
304 MILL ST, Woodsfield 43793
Montgomery County
Raymond Hopper   513-225-4598
451 W 3RD ST, Dayton 45422
Morgan County
Jerry Russell, PO BOX 509   614-962-2377
Mc Connelsville 43756
Morrow County
Douglas Whitaker, 27 W HIGH ST   419-946-7070
Mount Gilead 43338
Muskingum County
Larry Miller   614-452-4518
205 N 7TH ST, Zanesville 43701
Noble County
Donald Donatelli   614-732-2084
20977 STATE ROUTE 146
Sarahsville 43779
Ottawa County
(—), 314 W WATER ST   419-898-1318
Oak Harbor 43449
Paulding County
Paul Clark   419-399-4711
PO BOX 176, Paulding 45879
Perry County
Richard Fisher, PO BOX 307   614-342-3502
New Lexington 43764
Pickaway County
Donald Dowdy   614-474-7529
139 W FRANKLIN ST
Circleville 43113
Pike County
Larry Meredith   614-289-4171
PO BOX 578, Piketon 45661
Portage County
Donald Szostak   216-297-1436
224 W RIDDLE AVE
Ravenna 44266
Preble County
Ralph Shell   513-456-1187
COURT HOUSE, Eaton 45320
Putnam County
Jan Osborn   419-523-5951
PO BOX 190, Ottawa 45875
Richland County
David Cardwell   419-755-5520
50 PARK AVE E, Mansfield 44902
Ross County
Edwin Schiller   614-775-7229
PO BOX 326, Chillicothe 45601

Sandusky County
Gary Keller   419-332-8214
602 W STATE ST, Fremont 43420
Scioto County
George Lawson   614-354-7761
602 7TH ST RM 405
Portsmouth 45662
Seneca County
R. Lichtle   419-447-2927
244 S WASHINGTON ST
Tiffin 44883
Shelby County
Mary Lou Holly   513-498-1354
129 E COURT ST, Sidney 45365
Stark County
Curtis Hinds   216-492-8136
2100 38TH ST NW, Canton 44709
Summit County
R. Louis Daugherty   216-945-5600
420 WASHINGTON AVE # 200
Cuyahoga Falls 44221
Trumbull County
Herbert Thomas   216-392-4400
347 N PARK AVE, Warren 44481
Tuscarawas County
Richard Ronald   216-364-1242
172 N BROADWAY ST
New Philadelphia 44663
Van Wert County
David Rhoades   419-238-4746
216 E CENTRAL AVE
Van Wert 45891
Vinton County
James Pack, 112 N MARKET ST   614-596-5218
Mc Arthur 45651
Warren County
Gerald Powell   513-932-3851
416 S EAST ST, Lebanon 45036
Washington County
Patricia Foor   614-373-6669
RR 2 BOX 1A, Marietta 45750
Wayne County
Douglas Staggs   216-345-6771
2534 BURBANK RD
Wooster 44691
Williams County
John Granger   419-636-5078
COURT HOUSE, Bryan 43506
Wood County
Delbert Brown   419-354-9010
1 COURT HOUSE SQ
Bowling Green 43402
Wyandot County
Richard Verhoff   419-927-2414
295 STATE HIGHWAY 231
Sycamore 44882

PUBLIC, PRIVATE AND CATHOLIC SECONDARY SCHOOLS

Ada, AC 419, PC 6, Hardin
Ada EVD, 500 GRAND AVE 45810   3-11111
James Reiter, supt.   634-6421
JSHS, 500 GRAND AVE 45810   2-00111
Sam Beckley, prin.   634-2746

Ohio Northern University   5-UC
525 S MAIN ST 45810   772-2000

Akron, AC 216, PC 9, Summit
Akron CSD, 70 N BROADWAY ST 44308   8-11111
Terry Grier, supt.   434-1661
Buchtel HS, 1040 COPLEY RD 44320   3-00011
Sylvester Small, prin.   836-7905
Central Hower HS   4-00011
123 S FORGE ST 44308   434-3444
Greg Kavinsky, prin.
East HS, 80 BRITTAIN RD 44305   3-00011
Terry Wheeler, prin.   784-5433
Ellet HS, 309 WOOLF AVE 44312   4-00011
Alex Rachita, prin.   784-0451
Firestone HS, 333 RAMPART AVE 44313   4-00011
Cynthia Wheeler, prin.   836-2294
Garfield HS   4-00011
435 N FIRESTONE BLVD 44301   773-6831
Fredric Schuett, prin.
Kenmore HS, 2140 13TH ST SW 44314   4-00011
Harold Jordan, prin.   848-4141
North HS, 985 GORGE BLVD 44310   3-00011
Donna Loomis, prin.   434-7106
Goodrich MS   3-00100
700 LAFOLLETTE ST 44306   773-6689
James McCoy, prin.
Goodyear MS, 49 N MARTHA AVE 44305   3-00100
Elora Dees, prin.   784-0454
Hyre JHS, 2443 WEDGEWOOD DR 44312   3-00100
Sam Orlando, prin.   733-6286
Innes MS, 1999 EAST AVE 44314   3-00100
Paul Green, prin.   745-1138
Jennings MS   3-00100
225 E TALLMADGE AVE 44310   434-0243
Anthony Marano, prin.
Kent MS, 1445 HAMMEL ST 44306   2-00100
Lawrence Weigle, prin.   773-7631
Litchfield MS, 1540 FAIRFAX RD 44313   3-00100
Brenda Eich, prin.   836-7951
Miller-South Education Center MS   2-01100
1055 EAST AVE 44307   434-7531
Betty Chatman, prin.
Perkins MS, 630 MULL AVE 44313   3-00100
James Bell, prin.   864-2126

Riedinger MS   2-00100
77 W THORNTON ST 44311   376-3912
Joanne Smith, prin.

Coventry Local SD   4-11111
3257 CORMANY RD 44319   644-8489
Gerald Wargo, supt.
Coventry HS, 3257 CORMANY RD 44319   3-00011
Bruce Morris, prin.   644-2232
Erwine MS   3-01100
1135 PORTAGE LAKES DR 44319   644-2281
David Redd, prin.

Manchester Local SD   4-11111
6075 MANCHESTER RD 44319   882-6926
Marco Burnette, supt.
Manchester HS   2-00011
437 W NIMISILA RD 44319   882-3291
James France, prin.
Manchester MS   3-01100
760 W NIMISILA RD 44319   882-3812
Richard Brokow, prin.

Springfield Local SD   5-11111
2960 SANITARIUM RD 44312   784-0421
Tucker Self, supt.
Springfield HS   4-00011
2966 SANITARIUM RD 44312   794-0200
Larry Roberson, prin.
Spring Hill MS, 660 LESSIG AVE 44312   3-00100
Roger Plaster, prin.   628-9922

Academy of Court Reporting   2-CS
2930 W MARKET ST 44333   867-4030
Akron General Medical Center   HSP
400 WABASH AVE 44307   384-6548
Archbishop Hoban HS   3-00011
400 ELBON AVE 44306   773-6658
Mary Beiting, prin.
Children's Hospital & Medical Center   HSP
281 LOCUST ST 44302   379-8293
Cooperative Medical Technology Program   HSP
1 PERKINS SQ 44308   379-8720
Hammel College   3-CS
885 E BUCHTEL AVE 44305   762-7491
McKim Technical Institute   2-CS
1791 JACOBY RD 44321   666-4014
Our Lady of the Elms HS   2-00011
1375 W EXCHANGE ST 44313   867-0880
Edna Dierker, prin.

St. Thomas Medical Center   HSP
41 ARCH ST 44304   375-7560
St. Vincent-St. Mary HS   3-00011
15 N MAPLE ST 44303   253-9113
Margaret Lynch, prin.
Southern Ohio College   4-CC
2791 MOGADORE RD 44312   733-8766
Summa Health System/Akron City Hospital   2-HSP
525 E MARKET ST 44304   375-3101
University of Akron   7-UC
381 BUCHTEL COMMON 44325   972-7117

Albany, AC 614, PC 3, Athens
Alexander Local SD   4-11111
6091 AYERS RD 45710   698-8831
Rick Rolston, supt.
Alexander HS, 6125 SCHOOL RD 45710   2-00011
David Angles, prin.   698-8951
Other Schools – See Shade

Alexandria, AC 614, PC 2, Licking
Northridge Local SD
Supt. — See Johnstown
Northridge JHS, PO BOX 68 43001   2-00100
William Yeager, prin.   924-5281

Alliance, AC 216, PC 7, Stark
Alliance CSD   5-11111
200 GLAMORGAN ST 44601   821-2100
John Thomas, supt.
HS, 400 GLAMORGAN ST 44601   4-00011
Gregory Backus, prin.   821-2100
Stanton MS, 311 S UNION AVE 44601   2-00100
Nadine McIlwain, prin.   821-2100
State Street MS, 150 E STATE ST 44601   2-00100
James Sabin, prin.   821-2100

Marlington Local SD   5-11111
10320 MOULIN AVE NE 44601   823-7458
Alan Andreani, supt.
Marlington HS   3-00011
10450 MOULIN AVE NE 44601   823-1300
Rick Engle, prin.
Marlington MS   3-00100
10325 MOULIN AVE NE 44601   823-7566
J. Turner, prin.

Mt. Union College   4-UC
1972 CLARK AVE 44601   821-5320

Amanda, AC 614, PC 3, Fairfield
Amanda-Clearcreek Local SD 4-11111
414 N SCHOOL ST 43102 969-4112
Virginia Isele, supt.
Amanda-Clearcreek HS 2-00011
414 N SCHOOL ST 43102 969-4435
Willard Kobel, prin.

Amherst, AC 216, PC 7, Lorain
Amherst EVD, 185 FOREST ST 44001 5-11111
Howard Dulmage, supt. 988-4406
Steele HS, 450 WASHINGTON ST 44001 4-00011
Robert Boynton, prin. 988-4433
Nord JHS, 501 LINCOLN ST 44001 3-00100
William Marley, prin. 988-4441

Amsden, AC 419, PC 2, Seneca
Lakota Local SD
Supt. — See Risingsun
Lakota JHS, 8351 W SENECA 44803 2-00100
William Fries, prin. 435-2497

Andover, AC 216, PC 4, Ashtabula
Pymatuning Valley Local SD 4-11111
ROUTE 6 W 44003 293-6488
Keith Thimons, supt.
Pymatuning Valley HS 2-00011
5571 US HIGHWAY 6 44003 293-6263
Paul Freeman, prin.
Pymatuning Valley MS 3-01100
5571 US HIGHWAY 6 44003 293-6981
Patricia French, prin.

Anna, AC 513, PC 4, Shelby
Anna Local SD, PO BOX 169 45302 3-11111
Charles Rhyan, supt. 394-4251
JSHS, PO BOX 169 45302 2-00111
Clifford Clements, prin. 394-4251

Ansonia, AC 513, PC 4, Darke
Ansonia Local SD 3-11111
PO BOX 279 45303 337-4000
Edwin Leas, supt.
HS, PO BOX 279 45303 2-00011
Anne Cox, prin. 337-5591
MS, PO BOX 279 45303 2-00100
Stephen Garman, prin. 337-1801

Antwerp, AC 419, PC 4, Paulding
Antwerp Local SD, ARCHER DR 45813 3-11111
David Bagley, supt. 258-5421
JSHS, ARCHER DR 45813 2-00111
James Miller, prin. 258-5421

Apple Creek, AC 216, PC 3, Wayne
Southeast Local SD 4-11111
9048 DOVER RD 44606 698-3001
Lynn Dildine, supt.
Waynedale HS, 9050 DOVER RD 44606 2-00011
Patrick Peterman, prin. 698-3071
Lea MS, 9130 DOVER RD 44606 2-00100
Willis Kaderly, prin. 698-3151

Arcadia, AC 419, PC 3, Hancock
Arcadia Local SD 3-11111
19033 STATE ROUTE 12 44804 894-6431
Duane Seiling, supt.
JSHS, 19033 STATE ROUTE 12 44804 2-00111
Gary Lathrop, prin. 894-6431

Arcanum, AC 513, PC 4, Darke
Arcanum Butler Local SD 4-11111
2 WEISENBARGER CT 45304 692-5174
James Lambert, supt.
HS, 310 N MAIN ST 45304 2-00011
Gregory Place, prin. 692-5175
Butler MS 2-00100
1481 STATE ROUTE 127 45304 678-6571
Stephen Gruber, prin.

Archbold, AC 419, PC 5, Fulton
Archbold Area Local SD 4-11111
600 LAFAYETTE ST 43502 445-5579
Kenneth Cline, supt.
HS, 600 LAFAYETTE ST 43502 2-00011
Mark Fruth, prin. 445-5579
MS, 306 STRYKER ST 43502 2-00100
David Rex, prin. 446-2726

Four County JVSD 4-00011
RR 1 BOX 245A 43502 267-3331
Otto Meyer, supt.
Four County Joint Vocational SHS 4-00011
RR 1 BOX 245A 43502 267-3331
Linda Watkins, prin.

Northwest State Community College 3-CC
22600 STATE ROUTE 34 43502 267-5511

Arlington, AC 419, PC 3, Hancock
Arlington Local SD, S MAIN ST 45814 3-11111
David Ingram, supt. 365-5121
JSHS, S MAIN ST 45814 2-00111
Rodney Russell, prin. 365-5121

Ashland, AC 419, PC 7, Ashland
Ashland County-West Holmes JVSD 2-00001
1783 STATE ROUTE 60 44805 289-3313
David Kovach, supt.
Ashland County-West Holmes JVSHS 2-00001
1783 STATE ROUTE 60 44805 289-3313
Donald Dilgard, prin.

Ashland CSD, 416 ARTHUR ST 44805 5-11111
Michael Richardson, supt. 289-1117
HS, 1440 KING RD 44805 4-00011
Carl Roloff, prin. 289-7968

MS, 345 COTTAGE ST 44805 3-00100
Jeffrey Patterson, prin. 289-7966

Crestview Local SD 4-11111
1575 STATE ROUTE 96 44805 895-1198
Roger Harraman, supt.
Crestview HS 2-00011
1575 STATE ROUTE 96 44805 895-1700
Delwin Herz, prin.
Crestview MS 2-01100
1575 STATE ROUTE 96 44805 895-1700
Leroy Russell, prin.

Mapleton Local SD 4-11111
635 COUNTY ROAD 801 44805 945-2123
Steven Willeke, supt.
Mapleton HS 2-00011
635 COUNTY ROAD 801 44805 945-2188
William Snyder, prin.
Other Schools – See Nova

Ashland University 5-UC
401 COLLEGE AVE 44805 289-4142

Ashtabula, AC 216, PC 7, Ashtabula
Ashtabula Area CSD 6-11111
PO BOX 290 44004 993-2500
John Rose, supt.
HS, 401 W 44TH ST 44004 3-00011
Joseph Petros, prin. 993-2522
Ashtabula Harbor HS 3-00011
221 LAKE AVE 44004 993-2553
William Licate, prin.
Columbus JHS 2-00100
1326 COLUMBUS AVE 44004 993-2618
Theresa DiCesare, prin.
West JHS, 1231 W 47TH ST 44004 2-00100
Steve Candela, prin. 993-2577

Buckeye Local SD 4-11111
3436 EDGEWOOD DR 44004 998-4411
Joseph Donatone, supt.
Edgewood HS, 2428 BLAKE RD 44004 3-00011
Thomas Diringer, prin. 997-5301
Braden JHS, 3436 EDGEWOOD DR 44004 2-00100
Sam Kent, prin. 998-0550

Kent State University-Ashtabula Campus 3-CC
3431 W 13TH ST 44004 964-2237
St. John HS, 3320 STATION AVE 44004 2-00011
Elinor Scricca, prin. 997-5531

Ashville, AC 614, PC 4, Pickaway
Teays Valley Local SD 5-11111
385 CIRCLEVILLE AVE 43103 983-4111
Ronald Thornton, supt.
Teays Valley HS 3-00011
3887 STATE ROUTE 752 43103 983-3121
Ronald Claibourne, prin.
Teays Valley MS 3-00100
383 CIRCLEVILLE AVE 43103 983-4074
Robert Thompson, prin.

Athens, AC 614, PC 7, Athens
Athens CSD
Supt. — See The Plains
MS, 51 W STATE ST 45701 2-00100
Paul Grippa, prin. 593-7107

Ohio University 7-UC
PO BOX 640 45701 593-2571

Attica, AC 419, PC 3, Seneca
Seneca East Local SD 4-11111
PO BOX 462 44807 426-7041
David Getter, supt.
Seneca East HS, PO BOX 462 44807 2-00011
Judy Watson, prin. 426-3312
Other Schools – See Republic

Atwater, AC 216, PC 3, Portage
Waterloo Local SD 4-11111
1464 INDUSTRY RD 44201 947-2664
Fred Crewse, supt.
Waterloo HS, 1464 INDUSTRY RD 44201 2-00011
Robert Wolf, prin. 947-2124
Other Schools – See Randolph

Aurora, AC 216, PC 6, Portage
Aurora CSD, 102 E GARFIELD RD 44202 4-11111
James Costanza, supt. 562-6106
HS, 100 W PIONEER TRL 44202 3-00011
Linda Robertson, prin. 562-3501
Harmon MS 3-01100
130 AURORA HUDSON RD 44202 562-3375
Jerry Brodsky, prin.

Austinburg, AC 216, PC 3, Ashtabula

Grand River Academy 2-00011
PO BOX 222 44010 275-2811
Randy Blum, prin.

Avon, AC 216, PC 6, Lorain
Avon Local SD 4-11111
36600 DETROIT RD 44011 934-6191
John Bianchi, supt.
JSHS, 3075 STONEY RIDGE RD 44011 3-00111
Rick Buckosh, prin. 934-6171

Avon Lake, AC 216, PC 7, Lorain
Avon Lake CSD 5-11111
175 AVON BELDEN RD 44012 933-6210
Clayton Dusek, supt.
HS, 175 AVON BELDEN RD 44012 3-00011
Richard Lund, prin. 933-6290

Learwood MS, 340 LEAR RD 44012 3-00100
William Hamilton, prin. 933-8142

Bainbridge, AC 614, PC 3, Ross
Paint Valley Local SD 4-11111
7454 US HIGHWAY 50 W 45612 634-2826
T. Williamson, supt.
Paint Valley JSHS 3-00111
7454 US HIGHWAY 50 W 45612 634-3582
Donald Anderson, prin.

Baltimore, AC 614, PC 5, Fairfield
Liberty Union-Thurston Local SD 4-11111
621 W WASHINGTON ST 43105 862-4171
John Schiller, supt.
Liberty Union HS 2-00011
500 W WASHINGTON ST 43105 862-4107
Rodney Moorman, prin.
Liberty Union MS 2-00100
600 W WASHINGTON ST 43105 862-4406
Paul Mathews, prin.

Barberton, AC 216, PC 8, Summit
Barberton CSD, 479 NORTON AVE 44203 5-11111
Ronald Clemmer, supt. 753-1025
HS, 489 W HOPOCAN AVE 44203 4-00011
Gail Blunt, prin. 753-1084
Highland MS 3-00100
1152 BELLEVIEW AVE 44203 825-0806
Donald Smith, prin.
Light MS, 292 ROBINSON AVE 44203 3-00100
John Vargo, prin. 848-4236

Akron Machining Institute 2-CS
2959 BARBER RD 44203 745-1111

Barnesville, AC 614, PC 5, Belmont
Barnesville EVD 4-11111
210 W CHURCH ST 43713 425-3615
David Wilson, supt.
HS, 910 SHAMROCK DR 43713 2-00011
Gary Norris, prin. 425-3617

Bartlett, AC 614, PC 2, Washington
Warren Local SD
Supt. — See Vincent
MS, PO BOX 26 45713 2-01100
Patrick Levine, prin. 551-2461

Bascom, AC 419, PC 3, Seneca
Hopewell-Loudon Local SD 3-11111
PO BOX 400 44809 937-2216
James Getz, supt.
Hopewell-Loudon JSHS 2-00111
PO BOX 400 44809 937-2216
Dean Kirian, prin.

Batavia, AC 513, PC 4, Clermont
Batavia Local SD, 800 BAUER AVE 45103 4-11111
Michael Wells, supt. 732-2343
JSHS, 800 BAUER AVE 45103 3-00111
Terry Sheehan, prin. 732-2341

Clermont-Northeastern Local SD 4-11111
5347 HUTCHINSON RD 45103 625-5478
Thomas Rice, supt.
Clermont-Northeastern HS 3-00011
5327 HUTCHINSON RD 45103 732-2551
Thomas Bill, prin.
Northeastern MS 2-00100
2792 US HIGHWAY 50 45103 625-7075
James Sallee, prin.

West Clermont Local SD
Supt. — See Cincinnati
Amelia HS, 1351 CLOUGH PIKE 45103 4-00011
Richard Hamilton, prin. 753-5120
Amelia MS, 1341 CLOUGH PIKE 45103 4-00100
Larry Lucas, prin. 753-5010

University of Cincinnati 3-CC
725 COLLEGE DR 45103 732-2990

Bath, AC 216, PC 3, Summit
Revere Local SD, PO BOX 340 44210 4-11111
Patrick Corbett, supt. 762-9491
Revere MS 2-00100
3195 SPRING VALLEY RD 44210 762-9491
Ed Wolski, prin.
Other Schools – See Richfield

Bay Village, AC 216, PC 7, Cuyahoga
Bay Village CSD 4-11111
377 DOVER CENTER RD 44140 871-2322
Randy Stortz, supt.
Bay HS, 29230 WOLF RD 44140 3-00011
Joseph Loomis, prin. 835-6486
Bay MS, 27725 WOLF RD 44140 3-01100
David Wilson, prin. 835-6481

Beachwood, AC 216, PC 7, Cuyahoga
Beachwood CSD 4-11111
24601 FAIRMOUNT BLVD 44122 464-2600
Lee McMurrin, supt.
HS, 25100 FAIRMOUNT BLVD 44122 2-00011
Randy Boroff, prin. 831-2080
MS, 2860 RICHMOND RD 44122 2-00100
Edward Bernetich, prin. 831-0355

Cleveland College of Jewish Studies 2-UC
26500 SHAKER BLVD 44122 464-4050

Beallsville, AC 614, PC 2, Monroe
Switzerland of Ohio Local SD
Supt. — See Woodsfield
JSHS, PO BOX 262 43716 2-00111
Ken Phillips, prin. 926-1302

Beaver, AC 614, PC 2, Pike
Eastern Local SD 4-11111
1170 TILE MILL RD 45613 226-4851
Harold Sayre, supt.
Eastern HS, 1170 TILE MILL RD 45613 2-00011
Gary Jenkins, prin. 226-2231

Beavercreek, AC 513, PC 8, Greene
Beavercreek Local SD 6-11111
2940 DAYTON XENIA RD 45434 426-1522
R. Ferguson, supt.
SHS, 2940 DAYTON XENIA RD 45434 4-00011
Eugene Bennington, prin. 429-7547
Ankeney JHS 3-00110
2940 DAYTON XENIA RD 45434 429-7567
David Elliott, prin.
Ferguson JHS 3-00110
2940 DAYTON XENIA RD 45434 429-7577
Barry Corson, prin.

Bedford, AC 216, PC 7, Cuyahoga
Bedford CSD 5-11111
475 NORTHFIELD RD 44146 439-1500
George Bowdouris, supt.
HS, 481 NORTHFIELD RD 44146 4-00011
Dennis Blackburn, prin. 439-4848
Heskett MS, 5771 PERKINS RD 44146 3-00100
Miles Carter, prin. 439-4452

Chanel HS, 480 NORTHFIELD RD 44146 2-00011
Roger Abood, prin. 232-5900

Bellaire, AC 614, PC 6, Belmont
Bellaire CSD, 3517 GUERNSEY ST 43906 4-11111
Gilbert Dunn, supt. 676-1826
HS, 349 35TH ST 43906 3-00011
Frank Danadic, prin. 676-3652
Gravel Hill MS, 46TH ST 43906 2-00100
Robert Fialkowski, prin. 676-3014

St. John Central HS 2-00011
3625 GUERNSEY ST 43906 676-4932
David Vitlip, prin.

Bellbrook, AC 513, PC 6, Greene
Sugarcreek Local SD 4-11111
60 E SOUTH ST 45305 848-6251
Albert Mikula, supt.
HS, 3491 UPPER BELLBROOK RD 45305 3-00011
Steve Rhoades, prin. 848-6361
JHS, 3545 UPPER BELLBROOK RD 45305 2-00100
Larry Will, prin. 848-6131

Bellefontaine, AC 513, PC 7, Logan
Bellefontaine CSD 5-11111
820 LUDLOW RD 43311 593-9060
R. Carter, supt.
HS, 555 E LAKE AVE 43311 3-00011
George Harris, prin. 593-0545
MS, 511 N PARK ST 43311 3-00100
Randall Myers, prin. 593-9010

Benjamin Logan Local SD 4-11111
2091 STATE ROUTE 47 E 43311 593-9211
Dwight Spencer, supt.
Logan HS 3-00011
6609 STATE ROUTE 47 E 43311 468-7333
Robert Ohler, prin.
Other Schools – See Zanesfield

Ohio Hi-Point JVSD 3-00001
2280 STATE ROUTE 540 43311 599-3010
Marilyn Boyd, supt.
Ohio Hi-Point Joint Vocational SHS 3-00001
2280 STATE ROUTE 540 43311 599-3010
(—), prin.

Bellevue, AC 419, PC 6, Huron
Bellevue CSD, 125 NORTH ST 44811 4-11111
Jon Kiger, supt. 483-5171
HS, 200 OAKLAND AVE 44811 3-00011
Charles Palsa, prin. 483-3775
JHS, 215 NORTH ST 44811 2-00100
John Redd, prin. 483-7710

Bellville, AC 419, PC 4, Richland
Clear Fork Valley Local SD 4-11111
107 MAIN ST 44813 886-3855
David Southward, supt.
Clear Fork HS 3-00011
987 STATE ROUTE 97 E 44813 886-2601
Edward Platzer, prin.

Belmont, AC 614, PC 2, Belmont
Union Local SD 4-11111
66859 BELMONT MORRISTOWN RD 43718
Robert Butts, supt. 695-5776
Union Local HS 3-00011
66859 BELMONT MORRISTOWN RD 43718
Steven Mumma, prin. 782-1181

Beloit, AC 216, PC 4, Mahoning
West Branch Local SD 5-11111
14277 S MAIN ST 44609 938-9324
Paul D'Eramo, supt.
West Branch HS 3-00011
14277 S MAIN ST 44609 938-2183
Michael Bosick, prin.
Other Schools – See Damascus

Belpre, AC 614, PC 6, Washington
Belpre CSD 4-11111
2014 WASHINGTON BLVD 45714 423-9511
G. Bickert, supt.
JSHS, 300 STONE RD 45714 3-00111
R. Wallace, prin. 423-3000

Berea, AC 216, PC 7, Cuyahoga
Berea CSD, 390 FAIR ST 44017 6-11111
R. Krivak, supt. 243-6000
HS, 165 E BAGLEY RD 44017 4-00011
Paul Winkel, prin. 234-5418
Roehm MS, 7220 PLEASANT AVE 44017 3-00100
Barry Garguilo, prin. 234-1326
Other Schools – See Brook Park, Middleburg Heights

Baldwin-Wallace College 5-UC
275 EASTLAND RD 44017 826-2222

Bergholz, AC 614, PC 3, Jefferson
Edison Local SD
Supt. — See Hammondsville
Springfield JHS, RR 1 43908 2-00110
Robert Burdge, prin. 768-2420

Berlin, AC 216, PC 3, Holmes
East Holmes Local SD 4-11111
PO BOX 182 44610 893-2610
Lewis Bevington, supt.
Hiland JSHS, PO BOX 275 44610 2-00111
Gary Sterrett, prin. 893-2626
Other Schools – See Charm

Berlin Center, AC 216, PC 2, Mahoning
Western Reserve Local SD 3-11111
13850 W AKRON CANFIELD RD 44401 547-4100
Charles Swindler, supt.
Western Reserve HS 2-00011
13850 W AKRON CANFIELD RD 44401 547-3911
Jeanne Vild, prin.
Western Reserve MS 2-01100
15904 W AKRON CANFIELD RD 44401 547-3941
Dale Reese, prin.

Berlin Heights, AC 419, PC 3, Erie
Berlin-Milan Local SD
Supt. — See Milan
Berlin-Milan MS, 20 CENTER ST 44814 2-00100
Gary Bankert, prin. 588-2078

Bethel, AC 513, PC 4, Clermont
Bethel-Tate Local SD 4-11111
200 W PLANE ST 45106 734-2238
William Shula, supt.
Bethel-Tate HS 3-00011
3101 STATE ROUTE 125 45106 734-2271
Lester Tacy, prin.
Hill East MS, 150 FOSSYL DR 45106 3-01100
Steven Gill, prin. 734-2261

U.S. Grant JVSD 2-00001
3046 STATE ROUTE 125 45106 734-6222
Ken Morrison, supt.
Grant Joint Vocational SHS 2-00001
3046 STATE ROUTE 125 45106 734-6222
William Shepherd, prin.

Bettsville, AC 419, PC 3, Seneca
Bettsville Local SD, PO BOX 6 44815 2-11111
Richard Van Mooy, supt. 986-5166
JSHS, PO BOX 6 44815 2-00111
James Metcalf, prin. 986-5166

Beverly, AC 614, PC 4, Washington
Fort Frye Local SD, PO BOX 98 45715 4-11111
Ronald Curry, supt. 984-2497
Ft. Frye JSHS, PO BOX 68 45715 3-00111
Samuel Sells, prin. 984-2376

Bexley, AC 614, PC 7, Franklin
Bexley CSD 4-11111
348 S CASSINGHAM RD 43209 231-7611
Philip Tieman, supt.
HS, 326 S CASSINGHAM RD 43209 3-00011
Kip Greenhill, prin. 231-4591
MS, 300 S CASSINGHAM RD 43209 2-00100
Thomas Fletcher, prin. 237-4277

Blanchester, AC 513, PC 5, Clinton
Blanchester Local SD 4-11111
410 E JOHN ST 45107 783-3523
Raymond Bauer, supt.
HS, 3482 STATE ROUTE 28 45107 3-00011
James Brockman, prin. 783-2461
MS, 3482 STATE ROUTE 28 45107 2-00100
James Brockman, prin. 783-3642

Bloomdale, AC 419, PC 3, Wood
Elmwood Local SD 4-11111
7650 JERRY CITY RD 44817 655-2681
Kenneth Hawley, supt.
Elmwood HS 2-00111
7650 JERRY CITY RD 44817 655-3420
Harold Bower, prin.
Other Schools – See Cygnet

Bloomingburg, AC 614, PC 3, Fayette
Miami Trace Local SD
Supt. — See Washington Court House
Miami Trace JHS 3-00100
103 MAIN STREET 43106 437-7344
Daniel Roberts, prin.

Bloomingdale, AC 614, PC 2, Jefferson
Jefferson County JVSD, RR 1 43910 2-00011
Burchard Sheehy, supt. 264-5545
Jefferson County Joint Vocational SHS 2-00011
RR 1 43910 264-5545
Burchard Sheehy, prin.

Bluffton, AC 419, PC 3, Allen
Bluffton EVD, 102 S JACKSON ST 45817 4-11111
Larry Brunswick, supt. 358-5901
JSHS, 106 W COLLEGE AVE 45817 2-00111
Dan Rumer, prin. 358-7941

Bluffton College 3-UC
COLLEGE AVE 45817 358-8015

Botkins, AC 513, PC 4, Shelby
Botkins Local SD, PO BOX 550 45306 3-11111
James Degen, supt. 693-4241
JSHS, PO BOX 550 45306 2-00111
Connie Schneider, prin. 693-4241

Bowerston, AC 614, PC 2, Harrison
Conotton Valley Union Local SD 3-11111
7205 CUMBERLAND RD SW 44695 269-2000
Roy Cherry, supt.
Conotton Valley JSHS 2-00111
7205 CUMBERLAND RD SW 44695 269-2711
Patrick Peterman, prin.

Bowling Green, AC 419, PC 8, Wood
Bowling Green CSD 5-11111
140 S GROVE ST 43402 352-3576
Richard Cummings, supt.
HS, 530 W POE RD 43402 4-00011
Eric Myers, prin. 354-0100
JHS, 215 W WOOSTER ST 43402 3-00100
Donald Morrison, prin. 354-0200

Bowling Green State University 43403 7-UC
372-2211

Bradford, AC 513, PC 4, Miami
Bradford EVD, 712 N MIAMI AVE 45308 3-11111
Robert Crafton, supt. 448-2770
JSHS, 712 N MIAMI AVE 45308 2-00111
Kent Shafer, prin. 448-2719

Brecksville, AC 216, PC 7, Cuyahoga
Brecksville-Broadview Heights CSD 5-11111
6638 MILL RD 44141 526-4370
L. Neil Johnson, supt.
Brecksville-Broadview Heights MS 3-00100
27 PUBLIC SQ 44141 546-5401
Mark Robinson, prin.
Other Schools – See Broadview Heights

Cuyahoga Valley JVSD 3-00001
8001 BRECKSVILLE RD 44141 526-5200
Jerry Shuck, supt.
Cuyahoga Valley Joint Vocational SHS 3-00001
8001 BRECKSVILLE RD 44141 526-5200
Gary Romes, prin.

Bridgeport, AC 614, PC 4, Belmont
Bridgeport EVD, 501 BENNETT ST 43912 4-11111
Sam Lucas, supt. 635-1713
HS, 501 BENNETT ST 43912 2-00011
Mark Matz, prin. 635-0853
Kirkwood MS, 501 BENNETT ST 43912 2-00110
Mark Matz, prin. 635-0613

Brilliant, AC 614, PC 4, Jefferson
Buckeye Local SD
Supt. — See Rayland
Buckeye North MS, 1004 3RD ST 43913 2-00100
Alan Zerla, prin. 598-4540

Bristolville, AC 216, PC 3, Trumbull
Bristol Local SD, PO BOX 260 44402 4-11111
Marty Santillo, supt. 889-2700
Bristol HS, PO BOX 260 44402 2-00011
Richard Thomas, prin. 889-2621
Bristol MS, PO BOX 260 44402 2-01100
James Hungerford, prin. 889-2700

Broadview Heights, AC 216, PC 7, Cuyahoga
Brecksville-Broadview Heights CSD
Supt. — See Brecksville
Brecksville-Broadview Heights HS 3-00011
6376 MILL RD 44147 546-5301
James Harbuck, prin.

Brookfield, AC 216, PC 4, Trumbull
Brookfield Local SD 4-11111
PO BOX 209 44403 448-4930
Joseph White, supt.
HS, PO BOX 209 44403 3-00011
John Yensick, prin. 448-3001
JHS, PO BOX 209 44403 2-00100
John Young, prin. 448-3003

Brooklyn, AC 216, PC 7, Cuyahoga
Brooklyn CSD 4-11111
9200 BIDDULPH RD 44144 351-8477
Carol Witherow, supt.
JSHS, 9200 BIDDULPH RD 44144 3-00111
Louis Syroney, prin. 351-8477

Brook Park, AC 216, PC 7, Cuyahoga
Berea CSD
Supt. — See Berea
Ford MS, 17001 HOLLAND RD 44142 3-00100
Barbara Webb, prin. 433-1133

Brookville, AC 513, PC 5, Montgomery
Brookville Local SD 4-11111
325 SIMMONS AVE 45309 833-2181
Larry Henry, supt.
HS, 106 S HILL ST 45309 2-00011
Dale Creamer, prin. 833-6761
MS, 128 S HILL ST 45309 3-01100
Michael Gray, prin. 833-6731

Brunswick, AC 216, PC 8, Medina
Brunswick CSD, PO BOX 310 44212 6-11111
Edward Myracle, supt. 225-7731
HS, 3581 CENTER RD 44212 4-00011
James Hayas, prin. 225-7731
Willetts MS, 1045 HADCOCK RD 44212 3-00100
Ronald Bishop, prin. 225-7731

Bryan, AC 419, PC 6, Williams
Bryan CSD, 120 S BEECH ST   43506   4-11111
James Garber, supt.   636-6973
HS, 150 S PORTLAND ST   43506   3-00011
Cameron Vanarsdalen, prin.   636-4536
MS, 1301 CENTER ST   43506   3-01100
Tom Dominque, prin.   636-6766

Bucyrus, AC 419, PC 7, Crawford
Bucyrus CSD, 630 JUMP ST   44820   4-11111
William Hall, supt.   562-4045
HS, 900 W PERRY ST   44820   3-00011
Robert Hamm, prin.   562-7721
MS, 245 WOODLAWN AVE   44820   3-01100
Daniel Freund, prin.   562-0003

Wynford Local SD   4-11111
3288 HOLMES CENTER RD   44820   562-7828
Charles Barr, supt.
Wynford JSHS   3-00011
3288 HOLMES CENTER RD   44820   562-7828
Scott Langenderfer, prin.

Burton, AC 216, PC 4, Geauga
Berkshire Local SD   4-11111
PO BOX 364   44021 – (—), supt.   834-4123
Berkshire JSHS, PO BOX 365   44021   3-00111
David Beten, prin.   834-4110

Kent State University-Geauga Campus   3-CC
14111 CLARIDON TROY RD   44021   834-4187

Byesville, AC 614, PC 4, Guernsey
Rolling Hills Local SD   4-11111
PO BOX 38   43723   432-6952
Norman Blanchard, supt.
Meadowbrook HS   3-00011
58615 MARIETTA RD   43723   685-5561
Charles Chippi, prin.
Meadowbrook MS   3-00100
58607 MARIETTA RD   43723   685-2561
Larry Touvell, prin.

Cadiz, AC 614, PC 5, Harrison
Belmont-Harrison Area JVSD
Supt. — See Saint Clairsville
Harrison Career Ctr Joint Vo HS   1-00011
82500 CADIZ JEWETT RD   43907   942-2148
James Mowery, prin.

Harrison Hills CSD
Supt. — See Hopedale
JSHS, 440 E MARKET ST   43907   3-00111
Donald Hyde, prin.   942-2184

Caldwell, AC 614, PC 4, Noble
Caldwell EVD   4-11111
516 FAIRGROUND ST   43724   732-5634
Dennis Demcho, supt.
HS, 516 FAIRGROUND ST   43724   2-00011
Granville Flesher, prin.   732-5635

Cambridge, AC 614, PC 7, Guernsey
Cambridge CSD   5-11111
152 HIGHLAND AVE   43725   439-5021
Regis Woods, supt.
HS, 1201 CLAIRMONT AVE   43725   3-00011
William Lee, prin.   439-3692
MS, 701 STEUBENVILLE AVE   43725   2-00100
Deborah Kapp, prin.   439-3506

Camden, AC 513, PC 4, Preble
Preble-Shawnee Local SD   4-11111
124 BLOOMFIELD ST   45311   452-3323
Larry Russell, supt.
Shawnee HS   3-00011
5495 SOMERS GRATIS RD   45311   787-3541
Rod Schockey, prin.
Shawnee MS   2-00100
5495 SOMERS GRATIS RD   45311   787-3519
Richard Collier, prin.

Campbell, AC 216, PC 7, Mahoning
Campbell CSD, 280 6TH ST   44405   4-11111
Charles Shreve, supt.   755-9841
Memorial JSHS, 280 6TH ST   44405   3-00111
James Ciccolelli, prin.   755-1491

Canal Fulton, AC 216, PC 5, Stark
Northwest Local SD   4-11111
8590 ERIE AVE N   44614   854-2291
Dennis Lambes, supt.
Northwest HS, 8590 ERIE AVE N   44614   3-00011
John Hexamer, prin.   854-2205
Northwest MS, 8540 ERIE AVE N   44614   2-00100
Larry Minamyer, prin.   854-3303

Canal Winchester, AC 614, PC 5, Franklin
Canal Winchester Local SD   3-11111
300 WASHINGTON ST   43110   837-4533
Vernon Noggle, supt.
HS, 300 WASHINGTON ST   43110   2-00011
Stephen Donahue, prin.   833-2151
MS, 100 WASHINGTON ST   43110   2-00100
Rick Weininger, prin.   833-2159

World Harvest Christian Academy   3-11111
4595 GENDER RD   43110   837-1990
Edward Reck, prin.

Canfield, AC 216, PC 6, Mahoning
Canfield Local SD   4-11111
100 WADSWORTH ST   44406   533-3303
James Watkins, supt.
HS, 100 CARDINAL DR   44406   3-00011
William Kay, prin.   533-5507

MS, 42 WADSWORTH ST   44406   3-00100
Dante Zambrini, prin.   533-5544

Mahoning County JVSD   3-00001
7300 N PALMYRA RD   44406   533-6871
Robert Lantz, supt.
Mahoning County Joint Vocational SHS   3-00001
7300 N PALMYRA RD   44406   533-6871
Barbara Ciccotelli, prin.

Canton, AC 216, PC 8, Stark
Canton CSD   7-11111
617 MCKINLEY AVE SW   44707   438-2500
Fred Blosser, supt.
McKinley HS, 2323 17TH ST NW   44708   4-00011
Verner Russell, prin.   438-2712
Timken HS   4-00011
521 TUSCARAWAS ST W   44702   438-2602
Xenophon Griveas, prin.
Crenshaw MS, 2525 19TH ST NE   44705   3-00100
George Burwell, prin.   454-7717
Hartford MS, 1824 3RD ST SE   44707   3-00100
Richard Brown, prin.   453-6012
Lehman MS, 1120 15TH ST NW   44703   3-00100
Robert Neading, prin.   456-1963
Souers MS, 2800 13TH ST SW   44710   3-00100
Joseph Andalora, prin.   456-8779

Canton Local SD   5-11111
4526 RIDGE AVE SE   44707   484-8010
David Bowman, supt.
Canton South HS   3-00011
600 FAIRCREST ST SE   44707   484-8000
Lorenda Tiscornia, prin.
Faircrest Memorial MS   3-01100
616 FAIRCREST ST SW   44706   484-8015
Timothy Welker, prin.

Plain Local SD, 901 44TH ST NW   44709   6-11111
Larry Morgan, supt.   492-3500
Pleasant View MS   2-01100
3000 COLUMBUS RD NE   44705   452-7453
Carmela Lioi, prin.
Taft MS   3-00100
3829 GUILFORD AVE NW   44718   493-5505
Dennis Miller, prin.
Other Schools – See North Canton

Aultman Hospital   HSP
2600 6TH ST SW   44710   452-9911
Central Catholic HS   3-00011
4824 TUSCARAWAS ST W   44708   478-2131
Fr. Robert Kaylor, prin.
Heritage Christian Academy   2-11111
2107 6TH ST SW   44706   452-8271
Bruce Barkhurst, prin.
Kent State University-Stark Campus   4-CC
6000 FRANK AVE NW   44720   499-9600
Malone College   4-UC
515 25TH ST NW   44709   489-0800
Raedel College & Industrial Welding Sch.   2-CS
137 6TH ST NE   44702   454-9006
Stark Technical College   5-CC
6200 FRANK AVE NW   44720   494-6170
Timken Mercy Medical Center   HSP
1320 TIMKEN MERCY DR NW   44708   489-1001
Walsh College   4-UC
2020 EASTON ST NW   44720   499-7090

Cardington, AC 419, PC 4, Morrow
Cardington-Lincoln Local SD   4-11111
121 NICHOLS ST   43315   864-3691
Patrick Drouhard, supt.
Cardington-Lincoln JSHS   3-00111
349 CHESTERVILLE AVE   43315   864-2691
William Clauss, prin.

Carey, AC 419, PC 5, Wyandot
Carey EVD, 357 E SOUTH ST   43316   3-11111
Raymond Funk, supt.   396-7922
JSHS, 357 E SOUTH ST   43316   2-00111
Mark Miller, prin.   396-7638

Carlisle, AC 513, PC 5, Warren
Carlisle Local SD   4-11111
724 FAIRVIEW DR   45005   746-0710
Bobby Grigsby, supt.
HS, 250 JAMAICA RD   45005   3-00011
Ernest Dalton, prin.   746-4481
MS, 720 FAIRVIEW DR   45005   2-00100
Mark Upton, prin.   746-3227

Carroll, AC 614, PC 3, Fairfield
Bloom-Carroll Local SD   4-11111
69 N BEAVER ST   43112   837-6560
Richard Snelling, supt.
Bloom-Carroll HS   2-00011
69 N BEAVER ST   43112 – (—), prin.   756-4311
Bloom-Carroll MS   2-00100
69 N BEAVER ST   43112   756-9231
Thomas Petty, prin.

Eastland JVSD
Supt. — See Groveport
Fairfield Career Ctr Joint Vo SHS   2-00011
4000 COLUMBUS LNCSTER RD NW   43112
Patricia McGee, prin.   756-9243

Carrollton, AC 216, PC 5, Carroll
Carrollton EVD, 252 3RD ST NE   44615   5-11111
L. Pontuti, supt.   627-2181
HS, 252 3RD ST NE   44615   3-00011
Kathleen Chain, prin.   627-2134
Bell-Herron MS, 252 3RD ST NE   44615   3-00100
Fred Boggs, prin.   627-7188

Casstown, AC 513, PC 2, Miami
Miami East Local SD   4-11111
3825 N STATE ROUTE 589   45312   335-7505
Keith St. Pierre, supt.
Miami East HS   2-00011
3825 N STATE ROUTE 589   45312   335-7070
Jeffrey Lewis, prin.
Other Schools – See Troy

Castalia, AC 419, PC 3, Erie
Margaretta Local SD   4-11111
305 S WASHINGTON ST   44824   684-5322
Don Ruck, supt.
Margaretta JSHS, 209 LOWELL ST   44824   3-00111
Keith Bonnigson, prin.   684-5351

Cedarville, AC 513, PC 5, Greene
Cedar Cliff Local SD   3-11111
PO BOX 45   45314   766-6000
David Baits, supt.
JSHS, PO BOX 45   45314   2-00111
John Taylor, prin.   766-1871

Cedarville College   4-UC
PO BOX 601   45314   766-2211

Celina, AC 419, PC 6, Mercer
Celina CSD   5-11111
585 E LIVINGSTON ST   45822   586-8300
Ralph Stelzer, supt.
HS, 715 E WAYNE ST   45822   4-00011
Fred Wiswell, prin.   586-8300
MS, 615 HOLLY ST   45822   3-00100
Glenn Hux, prin.   586-8300

Wright State University   3-CC
7600 STATE ROUTE 703   45822   586-2365

Centerburg, AC 614, PC 4, Knox
Centerburg Local SD   3-11111
PO BOX 728   43011   625-6346
Barbara Lambert, supt.
JSHS, PO BOX 728   43011   2-00111
Todd Nauman, prin.   625-6634

Centerville, AC 513, PC 7, Montgomery
Centerville CSD   6-11111
111 VIRGINIA AVE   45458   433-8841
Frank DePalma, supt.
HS, 500 E FRANKLIN ST   45459   4-00011
Dave McDaniel, prin.   439-3500
Magsig MS, 192 W FRANKLIN ST   45459   3-00100
Margaret Barclay, prin.   433-0965
Tower Heights MS   3-00100
195 N JOHANNA DR   45459   434-0383
Thomas Henderson, prin.
Other Schools – See Dayton

RETS Technical Center   3-CC
PO BOX 130   45459   433-3410
Spring Valley Academy   2-11111
1461 E SPRING VALLEY PIKE   45458   433-0790
John Wheaton, prin.

Chagrin Falls, AC 216, PC 5, Cuyahoga
Chagrin Falls EVD   4-11111
77 E WASHINGTON ST   44022   247-5500
Jake Hudson, supt.
HS, 400 E WASHINGTON ST   44022   2-00011
James Trusso, prin.   247-5500
MS, 77 E WASHINGTON ST   44022   2-00100
David Axner, prin.   247-5500

Kenston Local SD   4-11111
17419 SNYDER RD   44023   543-9677
Robert Lee, supt.
Kenston HS, 17425 SNYDER RD   44023   3-00011
David Rathz, prin.   543-9821
Kenston MS, 17419 SNYDER RD   44023   3-00100
Donald Menefee, prin.   543-8241

English Nanny and Governess School   1-CS
30 S FRANKLIN ST   44022   800-733-1984
University HS   2-00011
2785 SOM CENTER RD   44022   831-2200
Richard Hawley, prin.

Chardon, AC 216, PC 5, Geauga
Chardon Local SD, 428 NORTH ST   44024   5-11111
Bruce Armstrong, supt.   285-4052
HS, 151 CHARDON AVE   44024   3-00011
Richard Bonde, prin.   285-4057
MS, 424 NORTH ST   44024   3-00100
Roberta Rowley, prin.   285-4062

Notre Dame-Catholic Latin S   3-00011
13000 AUBURN RD   44024   946-3314
Sr. Donna Paluf, prin.

Charm, AC 216, PC 2, Holmes
East Holmes Local SD
Supt. — See Berlin
Flat Ridge MS, PO BOX 159   44617   1-01100
Joe Wengerd, prin.   893-3156

Chesapeake, AC 614, PC 4, Lawrence
Chesapeake Union EVD   4-11111
PO BOX 458   45619   867-3135
Fred Wood, supt.
HS, PO BOX 458   45619   2-00011
G. L. Smith, prin.   867-5906
MS, PO BOX 10   45619   2-01100
Benjamin Coleman, prin.   867-3972

Lawrence County JVSD 2-00011
RR 2 BOX 262 45619 867-6641
Perry Walls, supt.
Lawrence County Joint Vocational SHS 2-00011
RR 2 BOX 262 45619 867-6641
Ronnie Blair, prin.

Cheshire, AC 614, PC 2, Gallia
Gallia County Local SD
Supt. — See Gallipolis
River Valley HS 3-00011
1428 LITTLE KYGER RD 45620 367-7377
Patrick Stout, prin.
Cheshire Kyger MS 2-01100
350 WATSON GROVE RD 45620 367-7721
Ronald Paxton, prin.

Chesterland, AC 216, PC 4, Geauga
West Geauga Local SD 4-11111
13445 CHILLICOTHE RD 44026 729-7212
Robert Szakovits, supt.
West Geauga HS 3-00011
13401 CHILLICOTHE RD 44026 729-9543
William Pierce, prin.
West Geauga MS, 8611 CEDAR RD 44026 2-00100
Glenn Bitner, prin. 729-9561

Chillicothe, AC 614, PC 7, Ross
Chillicothe CSD, 235 CHERRY ST 45601 5-11111
Richard Cline, supt. 775-4250
HS, 381 YOCTANGEE PKY 45601 4-00011
Rodney Jenkins, prin. 773-5200
Mt. Logan MS, 841 E MAIN ST 45601 2-00100
Robert Crabtree, prin. 773-2638
Smith MS, 345 ARCH ST 45601 3-00100
Michael MacCarter, prin. 773-2241

Huntington Local SD 4-11111
188 HUNTSMAN RD 45601 663-5892
James McGuire, supt.
Huntington JSHS 3-00111
188 HUNTSMAN RD 45601 663-2230
John Barr, prin.

Pickaway-Ross County JVSD
Supt. — See Lucasville
Pickaway-Ross County Joint Vo SHS 4-00011
895 CROUSE CHAPEL RD 45601 642-2550
Ronald Vetter, prin.

Union-Scioto Local SD 4-11111
1432 EGYPT PIKE 45601 773-4102
Ronald Vaughan, supt.
Union-Scioto JSHS 3-00111
1432 EGYPT PIKE 45601 773-4105
Stephen Stirn, prin.

Zane Trace Local SD 4-11111
946 STATE ROUTE 180 45601 775-1809
James Dunkle, supt.
Zane Trace HS 2-00011
946 STATE ROUTE 180 45601 775-1809
Darren Jenkins, prin.
Other Schools – See Kingston

Ohio University 45601 4-UC
774-7200
Southeastern Business College 2-CS
1855 WESTERN AVE 45601 774-6300

Cincinnati, AC 513, PC 10, Hamilton
Cincinnati CSD, 230 E 9TH ST 45202 8-11111
J. Michael Brandt, supt. 369-4000
Aiken HS, 5641 BELMONT AVE 45224 4-00011
John Schroder, prin. 853-2500
Hughes Alternative HS 4-00011
2515 CLIFTON AVE 45219 559-3000
Mary Gladden, prin.
Taft HS 3-00011
420 EZZARD CHARLES DR 45214 977-8000
Orlando Henderson, prin.
Western Hills HS 4-00011
2144 FERGUSON RD 45238 244-8700
Thomas Shaver, prin.
Withrow HS, 2488 MADISON RD 45208 4-00011
Patricia Rice, prin. 533-5700
Cincinnati Academy of Physical Education 3-00111
5425 WINTON RIDGE LN 45232 681-1445
Doris Frye, prin.
Creative & Performing Arts School 4-01111
1310 SYCAMORE ST 45210 632-5900
Rosalyn England, prin.
Walnut Hills JSHS 4-00111
3250 VICTORY PKY 45207 569-5500
Marvin Koenig, prin.
Woodward JSHS 4-00111
7001 READING RD 45237 758-1200
Michael Hicks, prin.
Bloom JHS, 1941 BAYMILLER ST 45214 3-00100
Dorothy Battle, prin. 357-4340
Crest Hills MS 3-00100
1908 SEYMOUR AVE 45237 458-2000
Jeffrey Brokamp, prin.
Dater JHS, 2840 BOUDINOT AVE 45238 3-00110
Kenneth Smith, prin. 244-3020
Gamble MS 3-00100
2601 WESTWOOD NORTHERN BLVD 45211
Charles Staley, prin. 389-7410
Peoples MS, 3030 ERIE AVE 45208 3-00100
Dorothy Wells, prin. 533-6360
Porter JHS, 1030 CUTTER ST 45203 3-00100
Edward Jung, prin. 763-4440
Schwab MS 3-00100
4370 BEECH HILL AVE 45223 681-2945
Dennis Matthews, prin.

Shroder JHS, 3500 LUMFORD PL 45213 3-00100
Robert Suess, prin. 731-2012

Deer Park Community CSD 4-11111
8688 DONNA LN 45236 891-0222
Robert Flury, supt.
Deer Park JSHS 3-00111
8351 PLAINFIELD RD 45236 891-0010
Timothy Feeley, prin.

Finneytown Local SD 4-11111
8916 FONTAINEBLEAU TER 45231 728-3700
Donald Schmidt, supt.
Finneytown JSHS 3-00111
8916 FONTAINEBLEAU TER 45231 931-0712
Joseph Speaks, prin.

Forest Hills Local SD 6-11111
7550 FOREST RD 45255 231-3600
John Patzwald, supt.
Anderson JSHS, 7560 FOREST RD 45255 4-00111
Michael Hall, prin. 232-2772
Turpin JSHS, 2650 BARTELS RD 45244 4-00111
Robert Shahan, prin. 232-7770

Great Oaks JVSD 5-00111
3254 E KEMPER RD 45241 771-8840
Harold Carr, supt.
Diamond Oaks CDC Vocational S 3-00011
6375 HARRISON AVE 45247 574-1300
B. Jackson, prin.
Scarlet Oaks CDC SHS 3-00111
3254 E KEMPER RD 45241 771-8810
W. Hunter, prin.
Other Schools – See Milford, Wilmington

Indian Hill EVD, 6855 DRAKE RD 45243 4-11111
David Quattrone, supt. 561-5211
Indian Hill HS, 6845 DRAKE RD 45243 2-00011
Karl Feltman, prin. 561-4225
Indian Hill MS, 6845 DRAKE RD 45243 2-00100
Robert Baas, prin. 561-4670

Madeira CSD, 7465 LOANNES DR 45243 4-11111
Dennis Hockney, supt. 791-0016
Madeira JSHS, 7465 LOANNES DR 45243 2-00111
Martin Strifler, prin. 891-8222

Mariemont CSD 4-11111
6743 CHESTNUT ST 45227 272-2722
Donald Thompson, supt.
Mariemont JSHS 3-00111
3812 POCAHONTAS AVE 45227 271-8310
Gerald Harris, prin.

Mt. Healthy CSD 5-11111
7615 HARRISON AVE 45231 729-0077
Joseph Epplen, supt.
Mt. Healthy HS, 2046 ADAMS RD 45231 4-00011
Carey Owens, prin. 729-0130
North MS, 2170 STRUBLE RD 45231 2-00100
Carole Miller, prin. 825-4581
South MS, 1917 MILES RD 45231 2-00100
Lawrence Westerfield, prin. 742-0666

North College Hill CSD 4-11111
1498 W GALBRAITH RD 45231 931-8181
Stanley Wernz, supt.
North College Hill HS 2-00011
1620 W GALBRAITH RD 45239 521-4311
Gary Gellert, prin.
North College Hill MS 2-00100
1620 W GALBRAITH RD 45239 521-4311
C. Hoock, prin.

Northwest Local SD 7-11111
3240 BANNING RD 45239 923-1000
Russell Sammons, supt.
Colerain HS, 8801 CHEVIOT RD 45251 4-00011
Albert Early, prin. 385-6424
Northwest HS, 10761 PIPPIN RD 45231 3-00011
Frank Margello, prin. 851-7300
Colerain MS, 4700 POOLE RD 45251 3-00100
James Sullivan, prin. 385-8490
Pleasant Run MS 4-00100
11770 PIPPIN RD 45231 851-2400
Harry Meyer, prin.
White Oak MS, 3130 JESSUP RD 45239 3-00100
Terrence Byrne, prin. 741-4300

Oak Hills Local SD 6-11111
6479 BRIDGETOWN RD 45248 574-3200
Lawrence Borcherding, supt.
Oak Hills SHS 4-00001
3200 EBENEZER RD 45248 922-2300
James Williamson, prin.
Bridgetown JHS, 3900 RACE RD 45211 4-00110
Paul Sallada, prin. 574-3511
Delhi JHS, 5280 FOLEY RD 45238 3-00110
Franklyn Shaut, prin. 922-8400

Princeton CSD, 25 W SHARON RD 45246 6-11111
Richard Denoyer, supt. 771-8560
Princeton HS, 11080 CHESTER RD 45246 4-00011
Richard Bell, prin. 771-8470
Princeton JHS 4-00100
11157 CHESTER RD 45246 771-0780
Aaron Mackey, prin.

Sycamore CSD, 4881 COOPER RD 45242 6-11111
Garth Errington, supt. 791-4848
Sycamore HS, 7400 CORNELL RD 45242 4-00011
Douglas Gorham, prin. 489-0405
Sycamore JHS, 5757 COOPER RD 45242 3-00100
James Sears, prin. 791-8013

West Clermont Local SD 6-11111
550 BATAVIA PIKE 45244 528-0664
Dennis Devine, supt.
Glen Este HS 4-00011
4342 GLEN ESTE WTHMSVLLE RD 45245
Robert Hoover, prin. 943-8211
West Clermont Career Ctr Vo Tech
4342 GLEN ESTE WTHMSVLLE RD 45245
Mary Ossman, prin. 943-8200
Glen Este MS 4-00100
4342 GLEN ESTE WTHMSVLLE RD 45245
Mark Peters, prin. 943-8250
Other Schools – See Batavia

Winton Woods CSD 5-11111
1215 W KEMPER RD 45240 825-5700
Thomas Richey, supt.
Winton Woods HS 4-00011
1231 W KEMPER RD 45240 825-7840
Annie Wade, prin.
Winton Woods MS 3-00100
147 FARRAGUT RD 45218 825-7140
James Anthony, prin.

Wyoming CSD 4-11111
100 PENDERY AVE 45215 761-7857
Robert Yearout, supt.
Wyoming HS, 106 PENDERY AVE 45215 2-00011
Brandon Cordes, prin. 761-7722
Wyoming MS, 17 WYOMING AVE 45215 3-01100
Angela Davis, prin. 761-7248

ACA College of Design 1-CC
2528 KEMPER LN 45206 751-1206
Antonelli Institute of Art & Photography 2-CC
124 E 7TH ST 45202 241-4338
Art Academy of Cincinnati 2-UC
1125 SAINT GREGORY ST 45202 721-5202
Art Advertising Academy 1-CC
4343 BRIDGETOWN RD 45211 574-1010
Athenaeum of Ohio 2-UC
6616 BEECHMONT AVE 45230 231-2223
Christ Hospital HSP
2139 AUBURN AVE 45219 369-2498
Cincinnati Bible College 3-UC
PO BOX 04320 45204 244-8100
Cincinnati College of Mortuary Science 2-UC
3860 PACIFIC AVE/COHEN CTR 45207 745-3631
Cincinnati Country Day S 3-11111
6905 GIVEN RD 45243 561-7298
John Raushenbush, prin.
Cincinnati School of Court Reporting 2-CS
35 E 7TH ST STE 600 45202 241-1011
Cincinnati Technical College 5-CC
3520 CENTRAL PKY 45223 569-1500
College of Mount Saint Joseph 4-UC
5701 DELHI RD 45233 800-654-9314
Connecticut School of Broadcasting 2-CS
4790 RED BANK RD STE 102 45227
271-6060
Elder HS, 3900 VINCENT AVE 45205 3-00011
Fr. Schaeper, prin. 921-3744
God's Bible School and College 2-UC
1810 YOUNG ST 45210 721-7944
Good Samaritan Hospital HSP
3217 CLIFTON AVE 45220 872-2494
Hebrew Union College 2-UC
3101 CLIFTON AVE 45220 221-1875
Institute of Medical & Dental Technology 2-CS
375 GLENSPRINGS DR STE 201 45246
851-8500
Institute of Medical & Dental Technology 2-CS
4452 EASTGATE BLVD STE 209 45245
383-3187
Landmark Christian S 2-11111
500 OAK DR 45246 771-7050
Richard Schrenker, prin.
La Salle HS, 3091 N BEND RD 45239 3-00011
Donald Ehrhart, prin. 741-3000
McAuley HS 3-00011
6000 OAKWOOD AVE 45224 681-1800
Cheryl Sucher, prin.
McNicholas HS 3-00011
6536 BEECHMONT AVE 45230 231-3500
John Laudeman, prin.
Moeller HS 3-00011
9001 MONTGOMERY RD 45242 791-1680
Daniel Ledford, prin.
Mother of Mercy HS 3-00011
3036 WERK RD 45211 661-2740
Sr. Nancy Merkle, prin.
Providence Hospital HSP
2446 KIPLING AVE 45239 853-5000
Purcell Marian HS 3-00011
2935 HACKBERRY ST 45206 751-1230
Janice Rich, prin.
Roger Bacon HS, 4320 VINE ST 45217 3-00011
Fr. Bosse, prin. 641-1300
St. Rita School for the Deaf HND
1720 GLENDALE MILFORD RD 45215 771-7600
St. Ursula Academy 2-00011
1339 E MCMILLAN ST 45206 961-3410
Sr. Katherine Beimesche, prin.
St. Xavier HS 4-00011
600 W NORTH BEND RD 45224 761-7600
David Mueller, prin.
Seton HS, 3901 GLENWAY AVE 45205 3-00011
Sr. Brenda Busch, prin. 471-2600
Seven Hills S, 5400 RED BANK RD 45227 3-11111
Henry Briggs, prin. 271-9027

Southern Ohio College 5-CC
1055 LAIDLAW AVE 45237 242-3791
Patricia Oster, prin.
Southwestern College of Business 2-CC
9910 PRINCETON GLENDALE RD 45246
874-0432
Southwestern College of Business 4-CC
717 RACE ST 45202 421-3212
Summit Country Day S 3-11111
2161 GRANDIN RD 45208 871-4700
Edward Tyrrell, prin.
Union Institute 4-UC
440 E MCMILLAN ST 45206 861-6400
University of Cincinnati 8-UC
2700 CLIFTON AVE 45221 556-6000
University of Cincinnati 4-CC
9555 PLAINFIELD RD 45236 745-5661
University of Cincinnati/OMI College 3-UC
2220 VICTORY PKY 45206 556-6564
Ursuline Academy 3-00011
5535 PFEIFFER RD 45242 791-5791
Shirley Speaks, prin.
Xavier University 5-UC
3800 VICTORY PKY 45207 745-3501

Circleville, AC 614, PC 7, Pickaway
Circleville CSD, 388 CLARK DR 43113 4-11111
Dinzle Brown, supt. 474-4340
HS, 380 CLARK DR 43113 3-00011
Ronald Malone, prin. 474-4846
Everts MS, 520 S COURT ST 43113 3-00100
Harold Cullum, prin. 474-2345

Logan Elm Local SD 4-11111
9579 TARLTON RD 43113 474-7501
John Edgar, supt.
Logan Elm HS, 9575 TARLTON RD 43113 3-00011
James Liddle, prin. 474-7503
McDowell-Exchange JHS 2-00100
9579 TARLTON RD 43113 474-7538
Michael Kneece, prin.

Circleville Bible College 2-UC
PO BOX 458 43113 477-7701

Clarksville, AC 513, PC 2, Clinton
Clinton-Massie Local SD 4-11111
2556 LEBANON RD 45113 289-2471
Thomas Hubler, supt.
Clinton-Massie HS 2-00011
2556 LEBANON RD 45113 289-2109
Danny Nier, prin.
Clinton-Massie MS 2-00100
2556 LEBANON RD 45113 289-2932
Ronald Rudduck, prin.

Clay Center, AC 419, PC 2, Ottawa
Genoa Area Local SD 4-11111
PO BOX 148 43408 855-7741
Nelson McCray, supt.
Other Schools – See Genoa

Clayton, AC 513, PC 3, Montgomery
Montgomery County JVSD 4-00111
6800 HOKE RD 45315 837-7781
C. Baughman, supt.
Montgomery County Joint Vocational SHS 4-00111
6800 HOKE RD 45315 837-7781
Ralph Craft, prin.

Northmont CSD
Supt. — See Englewood
Northmont HS 4-00011
4916 NATIONAL RD 45315 836-8605
P. Eugene Klaus, prin.
Northmont JHS 3-00100
4810 NATIONAL RD 45315 836-5151
James Krueckeberg, prin.

Cleveland, AC 216, PC 11, Cuyahoga
Cleveland CSD, 1380 E 6TH ST 44114 8-11111
Sammie Parrish, supt. 574-8000
Adams HS, 3817 E 116TH ST 44105 4-00011
Darryl Smith, prin. 561-2200
Collinwood HS 4-00011
15210 SAINT CLAIR AVE 44110 451-8782
William Martin, prin.
East HS, 1349 E 79TH ST 44103 4-00011
Mary Stokes, prin. 431-5361
East Tech HS, 2439 E 55TH ST 44104 3-00011
Terry Butler, prin. 431-2626
Glenville HS, 650 E 113TH ST 44108 4-00011
Elbert Cobbs, prin. 851-9400
Hay HS, 2075 E 107TH ST 44106 4-00011
Leroy Melton, prin. 421-7700
Kennedy HS 4-00011
17100 HARVARD AVE 44128 921-1450
Livesteen Carter, prin.
King Law HS, 1651 E 71ST ST 44103 2-00011
Melvin Jones, prin. 391-1208
Lincoln-West HS, 3202 W 30TH ST 44109 4-00011
Hozie Crittenden, prin. 631-1505
Marshall HS, 3952 W 140TH ST 44111 3-00011
Gilbert Freolino, prin. 251-5740
Rhodes HS, 5100 BIDDULPH RD 44144 4-00011
Alean Stewart, prin. 351-6285
South HS, 7415 BROADWAY AVE 44105 4-00011
Jerry Mitchell, prin. 641-0410
West Technical HS 4-00011
2201 W 93RD ST 44102 281-9100
Bobby McDowell, prin.
Cleveland HS, 2064 STEARNS RD 44106 3-01111
Anthony Vitanza, prin. 791-2496

Cleveland S of Science 3-00111
4016 WOODBINE AVE 44113 281-6188
Patricia Oster, prin.
Davis Aviation HS Vo Tech
4101 N MARGINAL RD 44114 621-1357
Joseph Takacs, prin.
Hayes HS, 4600 DETROIT AVE 44102 Vo Tech
Theodis Fipps, prin. 631-1528
Health Career Ctr, 1740 E 32ND ST 44114 Vo Tech
Robert Black, prin. 579-9984
Audubon JHS, 3055 EAST BLVD 44104 3-00100
Arthur Lawson, prin. 421-3132
Central JHS, 2225 E 40TH ST 44103 3-00100
David Petschauer, prin. 431-4410
Davis JHS 2-00100
10700 CHURCHILL AVE 44106 791-6272
Delphya Gagliardi, prin.
Eliot JHS, 15700 LOTUS DR 44128 3-00100
Clarine Boles, prin. 752-0100
Gallagher JHS 3-00100
6601 FRANKLIN BLVD 44102 961-0057
Alvin Bradley, prin.
Hale HS, 3588 EAST BLVD 44105 2-00100
Rose Davis, prin. 641-4485
Hamilton JHS, 3465 E 130TH ST 44120 2-00100
Edward Dietsche, prin. 561-3880
Hart JHS, 3901 E 74TH ST 44105 3-00100
C. Dean Fleenor, prin. 341-0874
Henry JHS, 11901 DURANT AVE 44108 3-00100
Charlene Hobbs, prin. 851-6600
Jefferson JHS, 3145 W 46TH ST 44102 3-00100
Joseph Mueller, prin. 631-5962
Lincoln JHS, 1701 CASTLE AVE 44113 3-00100
James Joyner, prin. 241-7440
Mooney JHS 3-00100
3213 MONTCLAIR AVE 44109 741-1183
Micheline Jackson, prin.
Roosevelt JHS, 800 LINN DR 44108 3-00100
David Volosin, prin. 541-0587
Shuler JHS 3-00100
13501 TERMINAL AVE 44135 671-0272
Marilyn Cargile, prin.
Spellacy JHS, 655 E 162ND ST 44110 3-00100
Marcella Boozer, prin. 531-2872
Willson JHS, 1625 E 55TH ST 44103 3-00100
Sandra Cohen, prin. 432-4593
Wright JHS 4-00100
11005 PARKHURST DR 44111 671-6430
Cynthia Metzger, prin.
Young JHS, 17900 HARVARD AVE 44128 2-00100
Betty English, prin. 283-5220

Cleveland Heights-University Heights CSD
Supt. — See University Heights
Roxboro MS, 2400 ROXBORO RD 44106 3-00100
Annamaria Tabernik, prin. 371-7440

Cuyahoga Heights Local SD 3-11111
4820 E 71ST ST 44125 341-1313
John Ramicone, supt.
Cuyahoga Heights JSHS 2-00111
4820 E 71ST ST 44125 341-1313
James Jackson, prin.

Orange CSD 4-11111
32000 CHAGRIN BLVD 44124 831-8600
Albert Roberts, supt.
Orange JSHS 3-00111
32000 CHAGRIN BLVD 44124 831-8600
John Branham, prin.

Academy of Court Reporting 2-CS
614 W SUPERIOR AVE 44113 861-3222
American Red Cross Blood Services HSP
3747 EUCLID AVE 44115 431-3053
Benedictine HS 2-00011
2900 MRTN LUTHER KING JR DR 44104
Fr. Mondzelewski, prin. 421-2080
Bryant & Stratton Business Institute 3-CS
12955 SNOW RD 44130 265-3151
Case Western Reserve University 6-UC
2040 ADELBERT RD 44106 368-4344
Cleveland Central Catholic HS 3-00011
6550 BAXTER AVE 44105 441-4700
Sr. Patricia Finn, prin.
Cleveland Clinic Foundation 2-CS
9500 EUCLID AVE 44195 444-2300
Cleveland Institute Dental Medical Asst. 2-CS
1836 EUCLID AVE STE 401 44115 241-2930
Cleveland Institute of Art 2-UC
11141 EAST BLVD 44106 421-7000
Cleveland Institute of Electronics 4-CC
1776 E 17TH ST 44114 800-243-6446
Cleveland Institute of Music 2-UC
11021 EAST BLVD 44106 795-3107
Cleveland Machining Institute 2-CS
2500 BROOKPARK RD 44134 741-1100
Cleveland State University 7-UC
1983 E 24TH ST 44115 687-2000
Cuyahoga Community College 6-CC
2900 COMMUNITY COLLEGE AVE 44115
987-6000
Dyke College 3-UC
112 PROSPECT AVE E 44115 696-9000
ETI Technical College 4-UC
4300 EUCLID AVE 44103 431-4300
Fairview General Hospital HSP
18101 LORAIN AVE 44111 467-7135
John Carroll University 5-UC
20700 N PARK BLVD 44118 397-1886

Marti College of Fashion 2-CC
PO BOX 580 44107 221-8584
Meridia Hillcrest Hospital HSP
6780 MAYFIELD RD 44124 445-4500
MetroHealth Medical Center HSP
3395 SCRANTON RD 44109 459-5701
MetroHealth Medical Ctr. School/Nursing 2-HSP
1803 VALENTINE AVE 44109 459-3546
MTI Business College 2-CS
1901 E 13TH ST STE 310 44114 621-8228
NEC-National Education Center 2-CS
14445 BROADWAY AVE 44125 475-7520
Northshore Technical Institute 2-CS
8815 BROADWAY AVE 44105 883-2800
Notre Dame College 3-UC
4545 COLLEGE RD 44121 381-1680
Ohio Auto/Diesel Technical Institute 3-CS
1421 E 49TH ST 44103 881-1700
Ohio College of Podiatric Medicine 2-UC
10515 CARNEGIE AVE 44106 800-238-7903
Parmadale S, 6753 STATE RD 44134 2-01100
Audrey Price, prin. 845-7700
PTC Career Institute 2-CS
1140 EUCLID AVE 44115 575-1100
St. Ignatius HS, 1911 W 30TH ST 44113 2-00011
Richard Clark, prin. 651-0222
St. Joseph Academy 2-00011
3430 ROCKY RIVER DR 44111 251-6788
Jacqualine Kasprowiski, prin.
St. Luke's Hospital 2-HSP
11311 SHAKER BLVD 44104 368-7000
Sawyer College of Business 2-CC
13027 LORAIN AVE 44111 941-7666
University Hospital of Cleveland HSP
2065 ADELBERT RD 44106 844-3815
Ursuline College 4-UC
2550 LANDER RD 44124 449-4200
Villa Angela/St. Joseph HS 3-00011
18491 LAKE SHORE BLVD 44119 481-8414
Sr. Maria Berlec, prin.
West Side Institute of Technology 3-CC
9801 WALFORD AVE 44102 651-1656

Cleveland Heights, AC 216, PC 8, Cuyahoga
Cleveland Heights-University Heights CSD
Supt. — See University Heights
HS, 13263 CEDAR RD 44118 4-00011
Charles Shaddow, prin. 371-7100
Monticello MS 3-00100
3665 MONTICELLO BLVD 44121 371-6520
William Byrd, prin.

Beaumont School for Girls 2-00011
3301 N PARK BLVD 44118 321-2954
Sr. Susan Rathburn, prin.
Hebrew Academy 3-11111
1860 S TAYLOR RD 44118 321-5838
David Bernstein, prin.
Lutheran East HS 2-00011
3565 MAYFIELD RD 44118 382-6100
Timothy Ewell, prin.
Sawyer College of Business 3-CS
3150 MAYFIELD RD 44118 932-0911

Cleves, AC 513, PC 4, Hamilton
Three Rivers Local SD 4-11111
92 CLEVES AVE 45002 941-6400
Richard Scherer, supt.
Three Rivers MS 2-00100
8575 BRIDGETOWN RD 45002 941-5784
Gary Smith, prin.
Other Schools – See North Bend

Clyde, AC 419, PC 6, Sandusky
Clyde-Green Springs EVD 4-11111
106 S MAIN ST 43410 547-0588
Stanley Mounts, supt.
HS, 1015 RACE ST 43410 3-00011
Larry Schultz, prin. 547-9511
JHS, 201 SPRING ST 43410 2-00100
Gregory Elchert, prin. 547-9150

Coal Grove, AC 614, PC 4, Lawrence
Dawson-Bryant Local SD 4-11111
423 MARION PIKE 45638 532-6451
Donald Washburn, supt.
Dawson-Bryant HS 2-00011
427 MARION PIKE 45638 532-6345
William Morgan, prin.
Dawson-Bryant IS, 222 LANE ST 45638 2-01100
Steven Easterling, prin. 532-1664

Coldwater, AC 419, PC 5, Mercer
Coldwater EVD, 310 N 2ND ST 45828 4-11111
Clete Biersack, supt. 678-2611
JSHS, 310 N 2ND ST 45828 3-00111
Larry Fair, prin. 678-4821

College Hill, AC 513, PC see Cincinnati

Central Baptist S 2-11111
7645 WINTON RD 45224 521-5481
James Voiles, prin.

Collins, AC 216, PC 2, Huron
Western Reserve Local SD
Supt. — See Wakeman
Western Reserve HS 2-00011
3841 STATE ROUTE 20 44826 668-8470
(—), prin.
Western Reserve MS 2-01100
9941 US ROUTE 20 E 44826 668-1924
Andrew Valachek, prin.

Columbiana, AC 216, PC 5, Columbiana
Columbiana EVD | 4-11111
  720 NEW WATERFORD ROAD 44408 | 482-5352
  Roger Stiller, supt.
  HS, 28 PITTSBURGH ST 44408 | 2-00011
  Richard Wagner, prin. | 482-3818
  South Side MS | 2-01100
  720 COLUMBIANA WATERFORD RD 44408
  Ronald Burger, prin. | 482-5354

Crestview Local SD | 4-11111
  3062 FAIRFIELD SCHOOL RD 44408 | 482-5526
  Phillip Roudebush, supt.
  Crestview HS | 2-00011
  44100 CRESTVIEW RD 44408 | 482-4744
  John Gecina, prin.
  Crestview MS | 2-01100
  3062 FAIRFIELD SCHOOL RD 44408 | 482-4648
  Daniel Meta, prin.

Columbia Station, AC 216, PC 3, Lorain
Columbia Local SD | 4-11111
  25796 ROYALTON RD 44028 | 236-5008
  Joseph Aguiar, supt.
  Columbia HS, 14168 W RIVER RD 44028 | 2-00011
  John Dickerson, prin. | 236-5001
  Columbia MS, 13646 W RIVER RD 44028 | 2-01100
  Robert Hope, prin. | 236-5741

Columbus, AC 614, PC 11, Franklin
Columbus CSD, 270 E STATE ST 43215 | 8-11111
  Lawrence Mixon, supt. | 365-5000
  Beechcroft HS | 3-00011
  6100 BEECHCROFT RD 43229 | 365-5364
  Norman Kushen, prin.
  Briggs HS, 2555 BRIGGS RD 43223 | 3-00011
  Katherine Ricketts, prin. | 365-5915
  Brookhaven HS, 4077 KARL RD 43224 | 4-00011
  Thomas Schleub, prin. | 365-5985
  Centennial HS, 1441 BETHEL RD 43220 | 3-00011
  Stephen Oldham, prin. | 365-5491
  Columbus Alternative HS | 3-00011
  2632 MCGUFFEY RD 43211 | 365-6006
  Jacqueline Ralls, prin.
  East HS, 1500 E BROAD ST 43205 | 4-00011
  Henry Scott, prin. | 365-6096
  Eastmoor HS, 417 S WEYANT AVE 43213 | 3-00011
  Phillip Hobbs, prin. | 365-6158
  Independence HS | 3-00011
  5175 REFUGEE RD 43232 | 365-5372
  James Osborn, prin.
  Linden-McKinley HS | 3-00011
  1320 DUXBERRY AVE 43211 | 365-5583
  Mary Thomas, prin.
  Marion-Franklin HS | 3-00011
  1265 KOEBEL RD 43207 | 365-5432
  Barbara Horcher, prin.
  Mifflin HS, 3245 OAK SPRING DR 43219 | 3-00011
  Donald Taylor, prin. | 365-5466
  Northland HS | 4-00011
  1919 NORTHCLIFF DR 43229 | 365-5342
  Brian Terrell, prin.
  South HS, 1160 ANN ST 43206 | 4-00011
  Emma Henderson, prin. | 365-5541
  Walnut Ridge HS | 4-00011
  4841 E LIVINGSTON AVE 43227 | 365-5400
  Robert Cochrun, prin.
  West HS, 179 S POWELL AVE 43204 | 4-00011
  Shirley Hamilton, prin. | 365-5956
  Whetstone HS, 4405 SCENIC DR 43214 | 3-00011
  Jewelyn Dicello, prin. | 365-6060
  Northeast Career Ctr | Vo Tech
  3871 STELZER RD 43219 | 365-5478
  Ernest Landis, prin.
  Southeast Career Ctr | Vo Tech
  3500 ALUM CREEK DR 43207 | 365-5442
  Delores Webster, prin.
  Barrett MS, 345 E DESHLER AVE 43206 | 3-00100
  Jock Harris, prin. | 365-5514
  Beery MS, 2740 LOCKBOURNE RD 43207 | 2-00100
  Phillip Ikehorn, prin. | 365-5414
  Buckeye MS, 2950 PARSONS AVE 43207 | 3-00100
  James Hamer, prin. | 365-5417
  Champion Alternative MS | 2-00100
  1270 HAWTHORNE AVE 43203 | 365-6082
  Andrew Melton, prin.
  Clearbrook MS, 31 N 17TH ST 43203 | 2-00100
  Erline Sager, prin. | 365-6085
  Clinton MS, 3940 KARL RD 43224 | 3-00100
  James Thomas, prin. | 365-5996
  Crestview MS, 251 E WEBER RD 43202 | 3-00100
  Daniel Jerman, prin. | 365-6014
  Dominion MS | 2-00100
  330 E DOMINION BLVD 43214 | 365-6020
  Dolores Blankenship, prin.
  Eastmoor MS | 3-00100
  3450 MEDWAY AVE 43213 | 365-6166
  Elouise Knight, prin.
  Everett MS, 100 W 4TH AVE 43201 | 3-00100
  Clarence Reavling, prin. | 365-5558
  Franklin Alternative MS | 3-00100
  1390 BRYDEN RD 43205 | 365-6113
  Pam VanHorn, prin.
  Hilltonia Alternative MS | 3-00100
  2345 W MOUND ST 43204 | 365-5937
  Robert Jones, prin.
  Indianola MS, 420 E 19TH AVE 43201 | 3-00100
  Walter Richardson, prin. | 365-5575
  Johnson Park MS | 3-00100
  1130 S WAVERLY ST 43227 | 365-6501
  Marvena Bosley, prin.

Linmoor Alternative MS | 2-00100
  2001 HAMILTON AVE 43211 | 365-5595
  George Rich, prin.
Medina MS, 1425 HUY RD 43224 | 3-00100
  Jack Culp, prin. | 365-6050
Mifflin Alternative MS | 3-00100
  3000 AGLER RD 43219 | 365-5474
  Stephen Tankovich, prin.
Mohawk Alternative MS | 3-00100
  300 E LIVINGSTON AVE 43215 | 365-6517
  Dennis Dorsey, prin.
Monroe Alternative MS | 3-00100
  474 N MONROE AVE 43203 | 365-6124
  Ralph Taylor, prin.
Ridgeview MS, 4241 RUDY RD 43214 | 2-00100
  Lorenzo Hunt, prin. | 365-5506
Sherwood Alternative MS | 3-00100
  1400 SHADY LANE RD 43227 | 365-5393
  Charmaine Tinker, prin.
Southmoor MS, 1201 MOLER RD 43207 | 3-00100
  Henderson Days, prin. | 365-5550
Starling MS, 120 S CENTRAL AVE 43222 | 3-00100
  Michael Ochab, prin. | 365-5945
Wedgewood MS, 3771 EAKIN RD 43228 | 3-00100
  Terence Schreiber, prin. | 365-5947
Westmoor MS | 3-00100
  3001 VALLEYVIEW DR 43204 | 365-5974
  Lynn Boetcher, prin.
Woodward Park MS | 3-00100
  5151 KARL RD 43229 | 365-5354
  Jeffery Forster, prin.
Yorktown MS | 2-00100
  5600 E LIVINGSTON AVE 43232 | 365-5408
  William Lude, prin.
Other Schools – See Dublin

Groveport Madison Local SD
  Supt. — See Groveport
  Groveport Madison MS North | 3-00100
  5474 SEDALIA DR 43232 | 837-5508
  Arthur Soroka, prin.

Hamilton Local SD | 4-11111
  4999 LOCKBOURNE RD 43207 | 491-8044
  Elmo Kallner, supt.
  Hamilton HS | 3-00011
  4999 LOCKBOURNE RD 43207 | 491-3330
  Robert Crable, prin.
  Hamilton MS, 775 RATHMELL RD 43207 | 3-00100
  John Cornette, prin. | 491-3468

South-Western CSD
  Supt. — See Grove City
Franklin Heights HS | 4-00011
  1001 DEMOREST RD 43204 | 272-7100
  Edward Palmer, prin.
Finland MS, 1825 FINLAND AVE 43223 | 3-00100
  James Voyles, prin. | 276-5324
Norton MS, 215 NORTON RD 43228 | 3-00100
  Billy Mullins, prin. | 878-7278

Academy of Court Reporting | 1-CS
  630 E BROAD ST 43215 | 221-7770
American School of Technology | 2-CS
  2100 MORSE RD # 4599 43229 | 436-4820
Bishop Hartley HS | 3-00011
  1285 ZETTLER RD 43227 | 237-5421
  James Silcott, prin.
Bishop Ready HS | 2-00011
  707 SALISBURY RD 43204 | 276-5263
  Celene Seamen, prin.
Bishop Waterson HS | 3-00011
  99 E COOKE RD 43214 | 268-8671
  John Durant, prin.
Bradford School | 2-CC
  6170 BUSCH BLVD 43229 | 846-9410
Capital University | 5-UC
  2199 E MAIN ST 43209 | 236-6908
Capital University Law School | 2-UC
  665 S HIGH ST 43215
Columbus College of Art & Design | 4-UC
  107 N 9TH ST 43215 | 224-9101
Columbus Para-Professional Institute | 2-CS
  1077 LEXINGTON AVE 43201 | 299-0200
Columbus School for Girls | 3-11111
  56 S COLUMBIA AVE 43209 | 252-0781
  Patricia Hayot, prin.
Columbus State Community College | 6-CC
  550 E SPRING ST 43215 | 227-2400
De Sales HS, 4212 KARL RD 43224 | 3-00011
  Patrick Rossetti, prin. | 267-7808
DeVry Institute of Technology | 5-UC
  1350 ALUM CREEK DR 43209 | 253-1525
Franklin University | 5-UC
  201 S GRANT AVE 43215 | 224-6237
Liberty Christian Academy | 3-11111
  4938 BEATRICE DR 43227 | 864-5332
  David McIlrath, prin.
Mt. Carmel Medical Center | HSP
  793 W STATE ST 43222 | 225-5032
NHAW Home Study Institute | 2-HMS
  PO BOX 16790 43216
Ohio Dominican College | 4-UC
  1216 SUNBURY RD 43219 | 800-955-6446
Ohio School for the Deaf | HND
  500 MORSE RD 43214
Ohio State School for the Blind | HND
  5220 N HIGH ST 43214
Ohio State University | 8-UC
  190 N OVAL MALL 43210 | 292-2424
Ohio State University Hospitals | HSP
  410 W 10TH AVE 43210 | 292-8900

Pontifical College Josephinum | 2-UC
  7625 N HIGH ST 43235 | 885-5585
Riverside Methodist Hospital | HSP
  3535 OLENTANGY RIVER RD 43214 | 261-5424
St. Charles Prep S | 2-00011
  2010 E BROAD ST 43209 | 252-6714
  Dominic Cavello, prin.
Technology Education College | 2-CC
  288 S HAMILTON RD 43213 | 759-7700
Tree of Life HS | 2-00111
  935 NORTHRIDGE RD 43224 | 263-2688
  Jayne Marrah, prin.
Trinity Lutheran Seminary | 2-UC
  2199 E MAIN ST 43209 | 235-4136
Wellington S, 3650 REED RD 43220 | 3-11111
  David Blanchard, prin. | 457-7883

Columbus Grove, AC 419, PC 4, Putnam
Columbus Grove Local SD | 3-11111
  201 W CROSS ST 45830 | 659-2639
  Gary Jones, supt.
  HS, 201 W CROSS ST 45830 | 2-00011
  Scott Hummel, prin. | 659-2157
  MS, 201 W CROSS ST 45830 | 2-01100
  James Kincaid, prin. | 659-2631

Conneaut, AC 216, PC 7, Ashtabula
Conneaut Area CSD | 5-11111
  263 LIBERTY ST 44030 | 599-8135
  James Crawford, supt.
  HS, 381 MILL ST 44030 | 3-00011
  Richard Fill, prin. | 599-8135
  Rowe MS, 360 ROWE ST 44030 | 3-00100
  Richard Belconis, prin. | 599-8135

Continental, AC 419, PC 4, Putnam
Continental Local SD | 3-11111
  PO BOX 479 45831 | 596-3671
  Eugene Linton, supt.
  JSHS, PO BOX 479 45831 | 2-00111
  Jim Martin, prin. | 596-3871

Convoy, AC 419, PC 4, Van Wert
Crestview Local SD | 3-11111
  531 N TULLY ST 45832 | 749-2893
  Denny Howell, supt.
  Crestview JSHS, 531 E TULLY ST 45832 | 3-00111
  Dan Norris, prin. | 749-2719

Copley, AC 216, PC 5, Summit
Copley-Fairlawn CSD | 4-11111
  3797 RIDGEWOOD RD 44321 | 668-3200
  John Litzel, supt.
  HS, 3807 RIDGEWOOD RD 44321 | 3-00011
  James Cowgill, prin. | 668-3222
  Copley-Fairlawn JHS | 2-00100
  1531 S CLVLAND MASSILLON RD 44321
  Janet Monroe, prin. | 668-3275

Cortland, AC 216, PC 6, Trumbull
Lakeview Local SD | 4-11111
  300 HILLMAN DR 44410 | 637-8741
  Richard Raidel, supt.
  Lakeview JSHS, 300 HILLMAN DR 44410 | 3-00111
  Robert Wilson, prin. | 637-4921

Maplewood Local SD | 4-11111
  2414 GREENVILLE RD 44410 | 637-7506
  D. McClain, supt.
  Maplewood JSHS | 3-00111
  2414 GREENVILLE RD 44410 | 637-8466
  Michael Conrath, prin.

Coshocton, AC 614, PC 7, Coshocton
Coshocton County JVSD | 2-00001
  23640 COUNTY ROAD 202 43812 | 622-0211
  Roger Ames, supt.
  Coshocton County Joint Vocational SHS | 2-00001
  23640 COUNTY ROAD 202 43812 | 622-0211
  Roger Bartunek, prin.

Coshocton CSD | 4-11111
  1207 CAMBRIDGE RD 43812 | 622-1901
  Dennis Demcho, supt.
  JSHS, 1205 CAMBRIDGE RD 43812 | 3-00111
  Jeffrey Watson, prin. | 622-9433

Covington, AC 513, PC 5, Miami
Covington EVD, 25 N GRANT ST 45318 | 3-11111
  David Jones, supt. | 473-2249
  HS, 807 CHESTNUT ST 45318 | 2-00011
  Robert Huelsman, prin. | 473-3746
  MS, 25 N GRANT ST 45318 | 2-00100
  David Jones, prin. | 473-2833

Crestline, AC 419, PC 5, Crawford
Crestline EVD, 401 HEISER CT 44827 | 4-11111
  Mike Cline, supt. | 683-1834
  HS, 7854 OLDFIELD RD 44827 | 2-00011
  Tom Wolff, prin. | 683-1964
  MS, 215 N COLUMBUS ST 44827 | 2-01100
  Timothy Hamman, prin. | 683-1966

Creston, AC 216, PC 4, Wayne
North Central Local SD | 4-11111
  350 S MAIN ST 44217 | 435-6382
  Larry Acker, supt.
  Norwayne HS, 350 S MAIN ST 44217 | 2-00011
  William Hanna, prin. | 435-4276
  MS, PO BOX 4443 44217 | 2-01100
  Paul Stellar, prin. | 435-4255

Cridersville, AC 419, PC 4, Auglaize
Perry Local SD, 2770 E BREESE RD 45806 | 3-11111
  Michael Lamb, supt. | 221-2770
  Perry HS, 2770 E BREESE RD 45806 | 2-00011
  Michael Richards, prin. | 221-2773

Crooksville, AC 614, PC 5, Perry
Crooksville EVD 4-11111
91 S BUCKEYE ST 43731 982-7040
Timm Mackley, supt.
HS, 4075 CERAMIC WAY 43731 2-00011
Steven Pompey, prin. 982-7015

Cuyahoga Falls, AC 216, PC 8, Summit
Cuyahoga Falls CSD 6-11111
PO BOX 396 44222 929-0581
Ronald Overfield, supt.
HS, 2300 4TH ST 44221 4-00011
H. James Schulz, prin. 929-0581
Bolich MS, 2630 13TH ST 44223 3-00100
Barbara Greene, prin. 920-3623
Roberts MS, 3333 CHARLES ST 44221 2-00100
Thomas Ratcliff, prin. 920-3607
Sill MS, 1910 SEARL ST 44221 2-00100
Joseph Iacano, prin. 920-3604

Woodridge Local SD 3-11111
3097 NORTHAMPTON RD 44223 928-9074
Richard Clapp, supt.
Other Schools – See Peninsula

Akron Medical-Dental Institute 2-CS
1625 PORTAGE TRL W 44223 762-9788
Cuyahoga Valley Christian Academy 3-00111
4687 WYOGA LAKE RD 44224 929-0575
Roger Taylor, prin.
NEC-National Institute of Technology 4-CS
1225 ORLEN AVE 44221 923-9959

Cygnet, AC 419, PC 3, Wood
Elmwood Local SD
Supt. — See Bloomdale
Elmwood MS, WASHINGTON ST 43413 2-00100
Larry Coffelt, prin. 655-3651

Dalton, AC 216, PC 4, Wayne
Dalton Local SD, 177 MILL ST N 44618 3-11111
Duane Miller, supt. 828-2267
HS, 177 MILL ST N 44618 2-00011
Judith Kenny, prin. 828-2261
IS, 151 E MAIN ST 44618 2-00100
Milton Troyer, prin. 828-2405

Damascus, AC 216, PC 3, Columbiana
West Branch Local SD
Supt. — See Beloit
West Branch MS, PO BOX 308 44619 2-00100
Louis Ramunno, prin. 537-3511

Danville, AC 614, PC 4, Knox
Danville Local SD, PO BOX 30 43014 3-11111
John Jurkowitz, supt. 599-6116
JSHS, PO BOX 30 43014 2-00111
Juris Klavins, prin. 599-6116

Dayton, AC 513, PC 9, Montgomery
Centerville CSD
Supt. — See Centerville
Watts MS, 7056 MCEWEN RD 45459 2-00100
Fred Lindley, prin. 434-0370

Dayton CSD, 348 W 1ST ST 45402 8-11111
James Williams, supt. 461-3000
Belmont HS 4-00011
2323 MAPLEVIEW AVE 45420 253-8881
William Martin, prin.
Dunbar HS, 2222 RICHLEY DR 45408 3-00011
Leon Love, prin. 268-6893
Meadowdale HS 4-00011
4417 WILLIAMSON DR 45416 278-9605
Marlea Jordan, prin.
Patterson Career Center HS 4-00011
118 E 1ST ST 45402 222-6301
Timothy Nealon, prin.
White HS, 501 NIAGARA AVE 45405 4-00011
Craig Williams, prin. 276-2107
Greene Vocational Ctr Vo Tech
503 EDISON ST 45407 223-3058
Learwinson Jackson, prin.
Fairport MS, 1952 FAIRPORT AVE 45406 2-00100
Vondia Jackson, prin. 276-2101
Fairview MS 3-00100
2408 PHILADELPHIA DR 45406 278-9625
Cheryl Johnson, prin.
Kiser MS, 1401 LEO ST 45404 3-00100
James Brytus, prin. 224-1753
MacFarlane MS 3-00100
215 S SUMMIT ST 45407 224-7486
James Dorsey, prin.
Roth MS, 4535 HOOVER AVE 45417 3-00100
Melvin Crafter, prin. 268-6754
Stivers MS, 1313 E 5TH ST 45402 3-00100
Richard Penry, prin. 223-3175
Wright MS, 1361 HUFFMAN AVE 45403 3-00100
Byron Day, prin. 253-3175

Jefferson Township Local SD 4-11111
2989 S UNION RD 45418 835-5682
Herbert Franklin, supt.
Jefferson HS, 2701 S UNION RD 45418 2-00011
Richard Bullard, prin. 835-5691
Radcliff Heights MS 2-01100
120 KNOX AVE 45427 835-5126
William Schooler, prin.

Mad River Local SD 5-11111
801 HARSHMAN RD 45431 259-6606
L. Draffen, supt.
Stebbins HS 3-00011
1900 HARSHMAN RD 45424 237-4250
Donald Kuntz, prin.
Spinning Hills MS 3-00100
5001 EASTMAN AVE 45432 259-6635
Phyllis Clingner, prin.

Northridge Local SD 4-11111
2011 TIMBER LN 45414 278-5885
C. W. Jarboe, supt.
Northridge HS, 2251 TIMBER LN 45414 3-00011
B. Johnston, prin. 275-7469
Dennis MS, 5120 N DIXIE DR 45414 3-00100
Stanley Kuck, prin. 274-2135

Oakwood City SD 4-11111
20 RUBICON RD 45409 297-5332
Timothy Ilg, supt.
Oakwood HS 2-00011
1200 FAR HILLS AVE 45419 297-5325
Ed Bowman, prin.
Oakwood JHS 2-00100
1200 FAR HILLS AVE 45419 297-5328
John Hagan, prin.

Trotwood-Madison CSD
Supt. — See Trotwood
Trotwood-Madison JHS 3-00100
3594 N SNYDER RD 45426 854-0017
Willie Brown, prin.

Vandalia-Butler CSD
Supt. — See Vandalia
Smith MS, 3625 LITTLE YORK RD 45414 3-01100
Samuel Lickiter, prin. 454-6115

Carroll HS, 4524 LINDEN AVE 45432 3-00011
Joseph Sens, prin. 253-8188
Chaminade Julienne HS 3-00011
505 S LUDLOW ST 45402 461-3740
Theodore Wallace, prin.
Dayton Christian ES 3-01100
501 HICKORY ST 45410 461-2868
James Rakestraw, prin.
Dayton Christian HS 3-00011
325 HOMEWOOD AVE 45405 278-9645
David Rough, prin.
Hillel Academy of Dayton 2-11111
100 E WOODBURY DR 45415 277-8966
David Lamm, prin.
International College of Broadcasting 2-CS
6 S SMITHVILLE RD 45431 258-8251
ITT Technical Institute 3-CC
3325 STOP 8 RD 45414 454-2267
Miami-Jacobs Junior College of Business 3-CC
PO BOX 1433 45401 461-5174
Miami Valley S, 5151 DENISE DR 45429 2-11111
Thomas Elmer, prin. 434-4444
Ohio Institute of Photography & Tech 2-CC
2029 EDGEFIELD RD 45439 294-6155
St. Elizabeth Medical Center HSP
601 S EDWIN C MOSES BLVD 45408 229-6600
Sinclair Community College 6-CC
444 W 3RD ST 45402 226-2525
Southwestern College of Business 3-CC
225 W 1ST ST 45402 224-0061
United Theological Seminary 2-UC
1810 HARVARD BLVD 45406 278-5817
University of Dayton 6-UC
300 COLLEGE PARK AVE 45469 800-837-7433
Wright State University 7-UC
3640 COLONEL GLENN HWY 45435 873-2312

Defiance, AC 419, PC 7, Defiance
Ayersville Local SD 3-11111
28046 WATSON RD 43512 395-1111
Ken Jones, supt.
Ayersville JSHS 2-00111
28046 WATSON RD 43512 395-1112
Thomas Duck, prin.

Defiance CSD, 629 ARABELLA ST 43512 5-11111
Gary Dowler, supt. 782-0070
HS, 1755 PALMER DR 43512 4-00011
Cary Frisinger, prin. 784-2777
JHS, 629 ARABELLA ST 43512 3-00100
Charles Beard, prin. 782-0050

Northeastern Local SD 4-11111
5921 DOMERSVILLE RD 43512 497-3461
Roger Whitacre, supt.
Tinora HS 2-00011
5921 DOMERSVILLE RD 43512 497-2621
Wayne Johnson, prin.
Tinora MS 2-00100
5921 DOMERSVILLE RD 43512 497-2361
Larry Acocks, prin.

Defiance College 3-UC
701 N CLINTON ST 43512 783-2330

De Graff, AC 513, PC 4, Logan
Riverside Local SD 3-11111
PO BOX 190 43318 585-5981
Phillip Trout, supt.
Riverside JSHS, PO BOX 190 43318 2-00111
James A. Grove, prin. 585-5981

Delaware, AC 614, PC 7, Delaware
Buckeye Valley Local SD 4-11111
901 COOVER RD 43015 369-8735
Samuel Martin, supt.
Buckeye Valley HS 3-00011
901 COOVER RD 43015 363-1349
Larry Oehler, prin.
Other Schools – See Radnor

Delaware CSD 5-11111
248 N WASHINGTON ST 43015 363-1188
Don Dyck, supt.
Hayes HS, 289 EUCLID AVE 43015 4-00011
Robert Bixler, prin. 369-7656
Willis IS, 74 W WILLIAM ST 43015 3-00100
Santha Stall-Friedman, prin. 369-8728

Delaware JVSD 2-00001
1610 STATE ROUTE 521 43015 363-1993
William Stalets, supt.
Delaware Joint Vocational SHS 2-00001
1610 STATE ROUTE 521 43015 363-1993
Carlene Thompson, prin.

Olentangy Local SD 4-11111
814 SHANAHAN RD 43015 548-6111
Keith Richards, supt.
Olentangy HS 3-00011
675 LEWIS CENTER RD 43015 548-5800
Robert Thompson, prin.
Olentangy MS 3-00100
814 SHANAHAN RD 43015 – (—), prin. 548-4141

Methodist Theological School in Ohio 2-UC
3081 COLUMBUS PIKE 43015 363-1146
Ohio Wesleyan University 4-UC
61 S SANDUSKY ST 43015 369-3000

Delphos, AC 419, PC 6, Allen
Delphos CSD 4-11111
227 N JEFFERSON ST 45833 692-6466
Bruce Sommers, supt.
Jefferson HS, 925 N STATE ST 45833 2-00011
George Ervin, prin. 695-1786
Jefferson MS 2-00100
227 N JEFFERSON ST 45833 695-2523
Mark Downey, prin.

St. John HS, 515 E 2ND ST 45833 2-00011
George Adams, prin. 692-5371

Delta, AC 419, PC 5, Fulton
Pike-Delta-York Local SD 4-11111
419 FERNWOOD ST 43515 822-3391
Charles Atkins, supt.
Pike-Delta-York HS 2-00011
605 TAYLOR ST 43515 822-3391
Robin Rayfield, prin.
MS, 419 FERNWOOD ST 43515 2-00100
David Ibarra, prin. 822-3391

Dennison, AC 614, PC 5, Tuscarawas
Claymont CSD, PO BOX 111 44621 4-11111
William Wenger, supt. 922-5478
Claymont JHS, 220 N 3RD ST 44621 3-00100
Ronnie Vinci, prin. 922-1901
Other Schools – See Uhrichsville

Diamond, AC 216, PC 2, Portage

Truck Driver Development Service 2-CS
1688 N PRICETOWN RD 44412 538-2216

Dola, AC 419, PC 2, Hardin
Hardin Northern Local SD 3-11111
11589 STATE ROUTE 81 45835 759-2331
Daniel Marshman, supt.
Hardin Northern JSHS 2-00111
11589 STATE ROUTE 81 45835 759-3515
Raymond Frazier, prin.

Dover, AC 216, PC 7, Tuscarawas
Dover CSD, 219 W 6TH ST 44622 5-11111
F. William Zanders, supt. 364-1906
HS, 520 N WALNUT ST 44622 3-00011
Frederick Delphia, prin. 364-7148
MS, 220 W 6TH ST 44622 2-00100
Ronald Bond, prin. 364-7128

Doylestown, AC 216, PC 5, Wayne
Chippewa Local SD, 257 HIGH ST 44230 4-11111
Steve Caples, supt. 658-6368
Chippewa HS 2-00011
100 VALLEY VIEW RD 44230 658-2011
William Adams, prin.
Chippewa MS, 257 HIGH ST 44230 2-01100
Howard Morris, prin. 658-2214

Dresden, AC 614, PC 4, Muskingum
Tri-Valley Local SD 5-11111
PO BOX 125 43821 754-1572
Dean Sarbaugh, supt.
Tri-Valley HS, PO BOX 125 43821 3-00011
John Larson, prin. 754-2921
Tri-Valley JHS, PO BOX 125 43821 2-00100
Terry Kopchak, prin. 754-3531

Dublin, AC 614, PC 7, Franklin
Columbus CSD
Supt. — See Columbus
Northwest Career Ctr Vo Tech
2960 CRANSTON DR 43017 365-5325
Pete Maneff, prin.

Dublin CSD, 7030 COFFMAN RD 43017 6-11111
John Fink, supt. 764-5913
Dublin Coffman HS 4-00011
6780 COFFMAN RD 43017 764-5900
Robert Rich, prin.
Davis MS, 2400 SUTTER PKY 43017 4-00100
Gary Wetherill, prin. 761-5820
Sells MS, 150 W BRIDGE ST 43017 4-00100
Carol King, prin. 764-5919

Duncan Falls, AC 614, PC 4, Muskingum
Franklin Local SD — 5-11111
PO BOX 428 43734 — 674-5203
William Parrett, supt.
JHS, MILL ST 43734 — 2-00100
Robert Walden, prin. — 674-5208
Other Schools – See Philo, Roseville

East Canton, AC 216, PC 4, Stark
Osnaburg Local SD — 4-11111
BROWNING ST 44730 — 488-1609
Phillip Warner, supt.
JSHS, 310 BROWNING CT N 44730 — 2-00111
John McIntosh, prin. — 488-0316

East Cleveland, AC 216, PC 8, Cuyahoga
East Cleveland CSD — 6-11111
15305 TERRACE RD 44112 — 268-6570
Hayward Sims, supt.
Shaw HS, 15320 EUCLID AVE 44112 — 4-00011
Stephen Lloyd, prin. — 268-6500
Kirk MS, 14410 TERRACE RD 44112 — 4-00100
Iris Fields, prin. — 268-6610

Huron Road Hospital — HSP
13951 TERRACE RD 44112 — 761-7996

Eastlake, AC 216, PC 7, Lake
Willoughby-Eastlake CSD
Supt. — See Willoughby
North HS, 34041 STEVENS BLVD 44095 — 4-00011
George Spinner, prin. — 975-3667
Industrial Training Ctr — Vo Tech
34041 STEVENS BLVD 44095 — 975-3687
Timothy Code, prin.
MS, 36000 LAKE SHORE BLVD 44095 — 3-01100
Rolanda Schonauer, prin. — 942-5696

East Liverpool, AC 216, PC 7, Columbiana
East Liverpool CSD — 5-11111
202 MAPLEWOOD AVE 43920 — 385-7132
Thomas Ash, supt.
HS, 100 MAINE BLVD 43920 — 4-00011
John Weaver, prin. — 386-8750
MS, 810 W 8TH ST 43920 — 3-00100
Glenn Dickinson, prin. — 386-8765

Kent State University-East Liverpool — 2-CC
400 E 4TH ST 43920 — 385-3805
Ohio Valley Business College — 2-CS
500 MARYLAND ST 43920 — 385-1070

East Palestine, AC 216, PC 6, Columbiana
East Palestine CSD — 4-11111
166 E NORTH AVE 44413 — 426-4191
Jeffrey Richardson, supt.
HS, 360 W GRANT ST 44413 — 2-00111
David Guy, prin. — 426-9401
MS, 200 W NORTH AVE 44413 — 3-01100
Joseph Shivers, prin. — 426-9451

Eaton, AC 513, PC 6, Preble
Eaton CSD, 307 N CHERRY ST 45320 — 4-11111
David Dolph, supt. — 456-1107
HS, 307 N CHERRY ST 45320 — 3-00011
James Brinckerhoff, prin. — 456-1141
Dixon-Isreal MS — 2-00100
7183 CALIFORNIA SCHOOL RD 45320 — 456-2286
Harry McCabe, prin.

Edgerton, AC 419, PC 4, Williams
Edgerton Local SD — 3-11111
217 E RIVER ST 43517 — 298-2112
Gregg Reink, supt.
HS, 324 S MICHIGAN AVE 43517 — 2-00011
Randy Earl, prin. — 298-2331
MS, 217 E RIVER ST 43517 — 2-00100
Lu Ann Hulbert, prin. — 298-2166

Edon, AC 419, PC 3, Williams
Edon-Northwest Local SD — 2-11111
309 W INDIANA ST 43518 — 272-3213
G. Kent Adams, supt.
HS, 309 W INDIANA ST 43518 — 2-00011
Michael Struble, prin. — 272-3113
MS, 309 W INDIANA ST 43518 — 2-01100
Michael Struble, prin. — 272-3213

Elida, AC 419, PC 4, Allen
Elida Local SD, 101 E NORTH ST 45807 — 5-11111
John Olds, supt. — 331-4155
HS, 101 E NORTH ST 45807 — 3-00011
Stephen Dackin, prin. — 331-4115
MS, 4500 SUNNYDALE ST 45807 — 3-00100
Mike Estes, prin. — 331-2505

Elmore, AC 419, PC 4, Ottawa
Woodmore Local SD
Supt. — See Woodville
Woodmore JSHS — 3-00111
633 FREMONT ST 43416 — 862-2721
Dennis Mock, prin.

Elyria, AC 216, PC 8, Lorain
Elyria CSD, 355 GRISWOLD RD 44035 — 7-11111
Lester Schultz, supt. — 284-8000
HS, 311 6TH ST 44035 — 4-00011
Bela Molnar, supt. — 324-7500
Elyria West HS — 3-00011
42101 GRISWOLD RD 44035 — 324-7500
Paul Rigda, prin.
Eastern Heights JHS — 3-00100
528 GARFORD AVE 44035 — 324-7500
Michael Jackson, prin.
Northwood MS, 700 GULF RD 44035 — 3-00100
Richard Ackerman, prin. — 324-7500

Westwood MS — 2-00100
42350 ADELBERT ST 44035 — 324-7500
(—), prin.

Elyria Catholic HS, 725 GULF RD 44035 — 2-00011
Sr. Barbara Piscopo, prin. — 365-1821
Kings Academy, 300 ABBE ROAD 44035 — 2-01100
Leslie Cornett, prin. — 365-2215
Lorain County Community College — 5-CC
1005 ABBE RD N 44035 — 365-4191
Open Door Christian HS — 2-00111
8287 W RIDGE RD 44035 — 322-6386
Craig Koehler, prin.

Englewood, AC 513, PC 7, Montgomery
Northmont CSD — 6-11111
4001 OLD SALEM RD 45322 — 836-2601
Robert Mengerink, supt.
Other Schools – See Clayton

Enon, AC 513, PC 5, Clark
Mad River-Green Local SD
Supt. — See Springfield
Indian Valley MS — 3-01100
510 S ENON XENIA PIKE 45323 — 864-7348
Eugene Evilsizor, prin.

Euclid, AC 216, PC 8, Cuyahoga
Euclid CSD, 651 E 222ND ST 44123 — 6-11111
Kurt Stanic, supt. — 261-2900
HS, 711 E 222ND ST 44123 — 4-00011
William Scoggan, prin. — 261-2900
Euclid Central MS — 3-00100
20701 EUCLID AVE 44117 — 261-2900
Ronald Seymour, prin.

ESI Career Center — 1-CS
25301 EUCLID AVE 44117 — 289-1299
Meridia Euclid Hospital — HSP
18901 LAKE SHORE BLVD 44119 — 531-9000

Fairborn, AC 513, PC 8, Greene
Fairborn CSD — 6-11111
306 E WHITTIER AVE 45324 — 878-3961
Stephen Scovic, supt.
HS — 4-00011
900 E DYTN YELLOW SPRNGS RD 45324
Richard Murphy, prin. — 879-3611
Baker JHS, 200 LINCOLN DR 45324 — 4-00100
John Jahoda, prin. — 878-4681

Fairfield, AC 513, PC 8, Butler
Fairfield CSD, 211 DONALD DR 45014 — 6-11111
Charles Wiedenmann, supt. — 829-6300
SHS, 1111 NILLES RD 45014 — 4-00011
Erick Cook, prin. — 829-3838
Fairfield Freshman HS — 3-00010
5050 DIXIE HWY 45014 — 829-8300
Robert Polson, prin.
MS, 255 DONALD DR 45014 — 4-00100
Elizabeth Griffel, prin. — 829-4433

Southern Ohio College — 4-CC
4641 BACH LN 45014 — 829-7100

Fairport Harbor, AC 216, PC 5, Lake
Fairport Harbor EVD, 329 VINE ST 44077 — 3-11111
Michael Whitacre, supt. — 354-5400
Fairport Harding JSHS — 2-00111
329 VINE ST 44077 — 354-3592
Gary Doberstyn, prin.

Fairview Park, AC 216, PC 7, Cuyahoga
Fairview Park CSD — 4-11111
20770 LORAIN RD 44126 — 331-5500
Gregg Morris, supt.
Fairview HS, 4507 W 213TH ST 44126 — 3-00011
Michael Loewy, prin. — 356-3500
Mayer JHS, 21200 CAMPUS DR 44126 — 2-00100
Charles Kullik, prin. — 356-3510

Fayette, AC 419, PC 4, Fulton
Gorham-Fayette Local SD — 3-11111
GAMBER ST 43521 — 237-2573
Joseph Long, supt.
Gorham-Fayette JSHS — 2-00111
N EAGLE ST 43521 – Mark North, prin. — 237-2114

Fayetteville, AC 513, PC 2, Brown
Fayetteville-Perry Local SD — 3-11111
PO BOX 281 45118 — 875-2423
James Frazier, supt.
HS, PO BOX 281 45118 — 2-00011
William Garrett, prin. — 875-3520
MS, PO BOX 281 45118 — 2-01100
Alan Simmons, prin. — 875-2829

Felicity, AC 513, PC 3, Clermont
Felicity-Franklin Local SD — 4-11111
415 WASHINGTON 45120 — 876-2111
Roger Hornsby, supt.
Felicity-Franklin JSHS — 3-00111
WASHINGTON ST 45120 — 876-2113
Phillip Carter, prin.

Findlay, AC 419, PC 8, Hancock
Findlay CSD, 227 S WEST ST 45840 — 6-11111
Steven Farnsworth, supt. — 425-8213
HS, 1200 BROAD AVE 45840 — 4-00011
Robert Shamp, prin. — 425-8289
Millstream South Campus — Vo Tech
1100 BROAD AVE 45840 — 425-8293
Ramon Myers, prin.
Central MS — 2-00100
200 W MAIN CROSS ST 45840 — 425-8257
Robert Fox, prin.

Donnell MS, 301 BALDWIN AVE 45840 — 2-00100
Kathleen Crates, prin. — 425-8370
Glenwood MS, 1715 N MAIN ST 45840 — 2-00100
John Celebrezze, prin. — 425-8373

Liberty-Benton Local SD — 3-11111
9050 W STATE ROUTE 12 45840 — 422-8526
Dennis Recker, supt.
Liberty-Benton JSHS — 2-00111
9050 W STATE ROUTE 12 45840 — 422-9166
Joseph Mihalik, prin.

Owens Community College — 3-CC
300 DAVIS ST 45840 — 423-6827
Stautzenberger College — 3-CS
1637 TIFFIN AVE 45840 — 423-2211
University of Findlay — 4-UC
1000 N MAIN ST 45840 — 422-8313
Winebrenner Theological Seminary — 1-UC
PO BOX 478 45839 — 422-4824

Fort Jennings, AC 419, PC 2, Putnam
Jennings Local SD, PO BOX 98 45844 — 2-11111
Frank Sukup, supt. — 286-2238
JSHS, PO BOX 98 45844 — 2-00111
Thomas Sakemiller, prin. — 286-2238

Fort Loramie, AC 513, PC 4, Shelby
Fort Loramie Local SD — 3-11111
PO BOX 26 45845 — 295-3931
Larry Ludlow, supt.
HS, PO BOX 26 45845 — 2-00111
Michael Roche, prin. — 295-3342

Fort Recovery, AC 419, PC 4, Mercer
Fort Recovery Local SD — 3-11111
PO BOX 612 45846 — 375-4139
Patrick Niekamp, supt.
HS, PO BOX 604 45846 — 2-00011
Edward Snyder, prin. — 375-4111
MS, PO BOX 604 45846 — 2-00100
Edward Snyder, prin. — 375-4111

Fostoria, AC 419, PC 7, Seneca
Fostoria CSD, 114 W HIGH ST 44830 — 5-11111
Jerry Argabrite, supt. — 435-8163
HS, 1001 PARK AVE 44830 — 3-00011
Joseph Johnson, prin. — 436-4110
Emerson MS, 140 W HIGH ST 44830 — 2-00100
James Williamson, prin. — 436-4120

St. Wendelin HS — 2-00011
533 N COUNTYLINE ST 44830 — 435-8144
Fr. Hite, prin.

Fowler, AC 216, PC 2, Trumbull
Mathews Local SD
Supt. — See Vienna
Neal MS, PO BOX 37 44418 — 2-00100
John Sofikitis, prin. — 637-3066

Frankfort, AC 614, PC 4, Ross
Adena Local SD, 119 W HIGH ST 45628 — 4-11111
Ken Putnam, supt. — 998-4633
Adena HS, 167 W HIGH ST 45628 — 2-00111
Jake Grooms, prin. — 998-2313

Franklin, AC 513, PC 7, Warren
Franklin CSD, 150 E 6TH ST 45005 — 5-11111
Albert Porter, supt. — 746-1699
HS, 750 E 4TH ST 45005 — 3-00011
Clarence Wilkinson, prin. — 743-8610
JHS, 136 E 6TH ST 45005 — 2-00100
Thomas Wurzelbacher, prin. — 743-8630

Franklin Furnace, AC 614, PC 4, Scioto
Green Local SD, RR 2 BOX 13A 45629 — 3-11111
Frank Barnett, supt. — 354-9221
Green JSHS, RR 2 BOX 18AA 45629 — 2-00111
Michael Hughes, prin. — 354-9150

Fredericktown, AC 614, PC 4, Knox
Fredericktown Local SD — 4-11111
134 W 2ND ST 43019 — 694-2956
Morris James, supt.
HS, 117 COLUMBUS RD 43019 — 2-00011
Anthony Deiuliis, prin. — 694-2726
IS, 39 TAYLOR ST 43019 — 3-01100
Edward Erick, prin. — 694-2966

Freeport, AC 614, PC 2, Harrison
Harrison Hills CSD
Supt. — See Hopedale
Lakeland JSHS, RR 3 43973 — 2-00111
Gerald Hickman, prin. — 658-3600

Fremont, AC 419, PC 7, Sandusky
Fremont CSD, 211 S PARK AVE 43420 — 6-11111
Kent Watkins, supt. — 332-6454
Fremont-Ross SHS — 3-00001
1100 NORTH ST 43420 — 332-8221
Earnie Jones, prin.
JHS, 501 CROGHAN ST 43420 — 4-00110
Lois Livingston, prin. — 332-5569

Vanguard/Sentinel JVSD — 4-00001
1306 CEDAR ST 43420 — 332-2626
Larry Graser, supt.
Vanguard Joint Vocational SHS — 3-00001
1306 CEDAR ST 43420 — 332-2626
Terri Clark, prin.
Other Schools – See Tiffin

St. Joseph Central HS — 2-00011
702 CROGHAN ST 43420 — 332-9947
Fr. Hartigan, prin.

Terra Technical College 4-CC
2830 NAPOLEON RD 43420 334-8400

Gahanna, AC 614, PC 8, Franklin
Gahanna-Jefferson CSD 6-11111
160 HAMILTON ROAD 43230 471-7065
John Sonedecker, supt.
Lincoln HS, 140 S HAMILTON RD 43230 4-00011
Jill Martin, prin. 478-5500
Gahanna East MS, 730 CLOTTS RD 43230 3-00100
Phillip Koppel, prin. 478-5550
Gahanna West MS 3-00100
350 N STYGLER RD 43230 478-5570
John Allen, prin.
Gahanna South MS 3-00100
349 SHADY SPRING DR 43230 337-3730
Dennis Souder, prin.

Columbus Academy 3-11111
4300 CHERRY BOTTOM RD 43230 475-2311
Douglas Mackelcan, prin.

Galion, AC 419, PC 7, Crawford
Galion CSD, 200 W CHURCH ST 44833 5-11111
Michael Traugh, supt. 468-3432
HS, 200 N UNION ST 44833 3-00011
Fritz Caudle, prin. 468-6500
MS, 200 W WALNUT ST 44833 2-00100
Robert Casey, prin. 468-3134

Northmor Local SD 4-11111
5189 COUNTY ROAD 57 44833 946-8861
Glenn Sprague, supt.
Northmor JSHS 3-00111
5353 COUNTY ROAD 29 44833 946-3946
Larry Cawley, prin.

Gallipolis, AC 614, PC 5, Gallia
Gallia County Local SD 5-11111
230 SHAWNEE LN 45631 446-7917
Robert Lanning, supt.
Other Schools – See Cheshire

Gallipolis CSD, 61 STATE ST 45631 5-11111
Patricia Brenneman, supt. 446-3211
Gallia Academy JSHS 4-00111
340 4TH AVE 45631 446-3212
John Ellingson, prin.

Gallipolis State Institute 45631 HND
Southeastern Business College 2-CS
1176 JACKSON PIKE # 312 45631 446-4367

Galloway, AC 614, PC 2, Fayette
South-Western CSD
Supt. — See Grove City
Westland HS, 146 GALLOWAY RD 43119 4-00011
Richard Caster, prin. 878-7217

Gambier, AC 614, PC 4, Knox

Kenyon College 4-UC
1 KENYON COLLEGE 43022 427-5000

Garfield Heights, AC 216, PC 8, Cuyahoga
Garfield Heights CSD 5-11111
5640 BRIARCLIFF DR 44125 475-8100
Ronald Victor, supt.
HS, 12000 MAPLE LEAF DR 44125 3-00011
Marlene Remesch, prin. 475-8105
MS, 4900 TURNEY RD 44125 3-01100
Frank Surace, prin. 641-1489

Trinity HS, 12425 GRANGER RD 44125 3-00011
Sr. Catherine Britton, prin. 581-1644

Garrettsville, AC 216, PC 4, Portage
James A. Garfield Local SD 4-11111
8235 PARK AVE 44231 527-4336
Charles Klamer, supt.
Garfield HS 2-00011
10233 STATE ROUTE 88 44231 527-4341
Thomas Rayburn, prin.
Garfield MS, 8233 PARK AVE 44231 2-00100
Daryl Bateman, prin. 527-2151

Gates Mills, AC 216, PC 5, Cuyahoga

Gilmour Academy 3-11111
34001 CEDAR RD 44040 442-1104
Robert Lavelle, prin.
Hawken S, PO BOX 8002 44040 2-00011
Richard Barter, prin. 423-4446

Geneva, AC 216, PC 6, Ashtabula
Geneva Area CSD 5-11111
135 S EAGLE ST 44041 466-4831
R. Taylor, supt.
Geneva Area HS 3-00011
839 SHERMAN ST 44041 466-4831
Ronald Donatone, prin.
JHS, 819 SHERMAN ST 44041 3-00100
Joanna Daniels, prin. 466-4831

Genoa, AC 419, PC 4, Ottawa
Genoa Area Local SD
Supt. — See Clay Center
Genoa Area HS 3-00011
2980 N GENOA CLAY CENTER RD 43430
William McFarland, prin. 855-7735
Genoa Area JHS, 303 W 4TH ST 43430 2-00100
Paul Orshoski, prin. 855-7781

Georgetown, AC 513, PC 5, Brown
Georgetown EVD, PO BOX 299 45121 4-11111
Larry Grooms, supt. 378-3730

JSHS, PO BOX 299 45121 2-00111
David Winks, prin. 378-6730

Southern Hills JVSD 2-00001
PO BOX 179 45121 378-4577
Rodney Glover, supt.
Southern Hills Joint Vocational SHS 2-00001
PO BOX 179 45121 378-6131
Eric Scott, prin.

Germantown, AC 513, PC 5, Montgomery
Valley View Local SD 4-11111
64 COMSTOCK ST 45327 855-6581
Herschel Cornn, supt.
Valley View HS 3-00011
6027 FRMRSVLL GERMANTN PIKE 45327
(—), prin. 855-4116
Valley View MS 2-01100
64 COMSTOCK ST 45327 855-4203
Michael Eckert, prin.

Gibsonburg, AC 419, PC 5, Sandusky
Gibsonburg EVD 4-11111
300 S HARRISON ST 43431 637-2479
Bruce Smith, supt.
JSHS, 300 S HARRISON ST 43431 3-00111
Kathleen Reed, prin. 637-2873

Gilboa, AC 419, PC 2, Putnam
Pandora-Gilboa Local SD
Supt. — See Pandora
MS, FRANKLIN ST 45847 2-01100
Hugh Terrell, prin. 456-3301

Girard, AC 216, PC 7, Trumbull
Girard CSD, 31 N WARD AVE 44420 4-11111
Anthony D'Ambrosio, supt. 545-2596
JSHS, 31 N WARD AVE 44420 3-00111
Joseph Cochran, prin. 545-5437

Glouster, AC 614, PC 4, Athens
Trimble Local SD, 1 TOMCAT DR 45732 4-11111
Virginia Mace, supt. 767-4444
Trimble HS, 1 TOMCAT DR 45732 2-00011
Thomas Vitchner, prin. 767-4444
Trimble MS 2-01100
18500 JACKSONVILLE RD 45732 767-2810
Darrell Dugan, prin.

Gnadenhutten, AC 614, PC 4, Tuscarawas
Indian Valley Local SD 4-11111
PO BOX 171 44629 254-4334
Robert Fogler, supt.
Indian Valley HS, PO BOX 130 44629 3-00011
John Coutts, prin. 254-4262
Other Schools – See Tuscarawas

Goshen, AC 513, PC 4, Clermont
Goshen Local SD 5-11111
6785 GOSHEN RD 45122 722-2222
B. Dennison, supt.
HS, 6692 GOSHEN RD 45122 3-00011
George Rise, prin. 722-2227
Spaulding MS, 6755 LINTON RD 45122 2-00100
Paul Varney, prin. 722-2226

Grafton, AC 216, PC 5, Lorain
Midview Local SD, 1097 ELM ST 44044 5-11111
Linda Gesinsky, supt. 926-3737
Midview HS, 38199 CAPEL RD 44044 3-00011
Alan Pavelschak, prin. 748-2121
Midview MS, 37999 CAPEL RD 44044 3-00100
Richard Schibely, prin. 748-2121

Grand Rapids, AC 419, PC 3, Wood
Otsego Local SD
Supt. — See Tontogany
Otsego MS, E 2ND ST 43522 2-00100
William Hale, prin. 832-2261

Grandview Heights, AC 614, PC 6, Franklin
Grandview Heights CSD 4-11111
1587 W 3RD AVE 43212 481-3600
Ted Knapke, supt.
JSHS, 1587 W 3RD AVE 43212 2-00111
Joseph Boyle, prin. 481-3620

Granville, AC 614, PC 5, Licking
Granville EVD, PO BOX 417 43023 4-11111
James McCord, supt. 587-0332
HS, 248 NEW BURG ST 43023 2-00111
Charles Dilbone, prin. 587-0395
MS, 210 NEW BURG ST 43023 2-00100
Richard Daly, prin. 587-1484

Denison University 4-UC
PO BOX B 43023 587-0810

Graysville, AC 614, PC 1, Monroe
Switzerland of Ohio Local SD
Supt. — See Woodsfield
Skyvue JSHS 2-00111
33329 HARTSHORN RIDGE RD 45734 567-3313
Gary Davis, prin.

Green Camp, AC 614, PC 2, Marion
Elgin Local SD
Supt. — See Marion
Elgin JHS, PO BOX 214 43322 2-00100
Brian Napper, prin. 528-2320

Greenfield, AC 513, PC 6, Highland
Greenfield EVD, 200 N 5TH ST 45123 4-11111
Phillip Cornett, supt. 981-2152
McClain HS, 200 N 5TH ST 45123 3-00011
Dan Strain, prin. 981-7731
MS, 200 N 5TH ST 45123 3-00100
Michael Shumate, prin. 981-2197

Greenford, AC 216, PC 3, Mahoning
South Range Local SD
Supt. — See North Lima
South Range West IS 2-01100
PO BOX 86 44422 533-3335
Stephen Krivan, prin.

Greensburg, AC 216, PC 5, Summit
Green Local SD, PO BOX 218 44232 5-11111
John Haschak, supt. 896-3903
Green HS, PO BOX 218 44232 3-00011
John Goldsberry, prin. 896-1907
Green MS, PO BOX 218 44232 3-00100
Larry Brown, prin. 896-1994

Portage Lakes JVSD 3-00001
PO BOX 248 44232 896-3757
David Kleinschmidt, supt.
Portage Lakes Career Center 3-00001
PO BOX 248 44232 896-3757
Brett Smith, prin.

Greenville, AC 513, PC 7, Darke
Greenville CSD, MEMORIAL HALL 45331 5-11111
Kenneth Peters, supt. 548-3185
HS, 100 GREENWAVE WAY 45331 4-00011
Kenneth Baker, prin. 548-4188
JHS, 100 CENTRAL AVE 45331 3-00100
Michael Calland, prin. 548-3202

Greenwich, AC 419, PC 4, Huron
South Central Local SD 3-11111
3305 ANGLING RD 44837 752-3815
Robert Shaffer, supt.
South Central JSHS 2-00111
3305 ANGLING RD 44837 752-3354
Edwin Holland, prin.

Grove City, AC 614, PC 7, Franklin
South-Western CSD 7-11111
2975 KINGSTON AVE 43123 875-2318
Bob Bowers, supt.
HS, 4665 HOOVER RD 43123 4-00011
Tom Rutan, prin. 875-9550
Hayes Tech HS Vo Tech
4436 HAUGHN RD 43123 875-2318
Donald Wohrle, prin.
Brookpark MS 3-00100
2803 SOUTHWEST BLVD 43123 875-2341
Elaine Wank-Burton, prin.
Park Street MS, 3191 PARK ST 43123 3-00100
Gregory Grinch, prin. 875-2318
Pleasant View MS 3-00100
7255 KROPP RD 43123 878-5324
Robert Skinner, prin.
Other Schools – See Columbus, Galloway

Groveport, AC 614, PC 5, Franklin
Eastland JVSD 4-00011
4300 AMALGAMATED PL 43125 836-5725
Claude Graves, supt.
Eastland Career Ctr Joint Vo SHS 3-00011
4465 S HAMILTON RD 43125 836-5725
Walter Armes, prin.
Other Schools – See Carroll

Groveport Madison Local SD 6-11111
5055 S HAMILTON RD 43125 836-5371
Charles Barr, supt.
Groveport Madison SHS 4-00001
4475 S HAMILTON RD 43125 836-4964
Mary Pierce, prin.
Groveport Madison Freshman HS 2-00010
751 MAIN ST 43125 836-4957
Thomas Tussing, prin.
Groveport Madison MS South 3-00100
4400 GLENDENNING DR 43125 836-4953
Steven Friece, prin.
Other Schools – See Columbus

Hamilton, AC 513, PC 8, Butler
Butler County JVSD 4-00011
3603 HAMILTON MIDDLETOWN RD 45011
James Boyd, supt. 868-6300
Lee Joint Vocational HS 4-00011
3603 HAMILTON MIDDLETOWN RD 45011
Joseph Pyfrin, prin. 868-6300

Edgewood CSD
Supt. — See Trenton
Edgewood MS 3-01100
3440 BUSENBARK RD 45011 863-4692
Steven Moeckel, prin.

Hamilton CSD, PO BOX 627 45012 7-11111
Janet Baker, supt. 887-5000
SHS, 1165 EATON AVE 45013 4-00001
Robert Bierly, prin. 868-7700
Garfield JHS, 250 N FAIR AVE 45011 4-00110
Thomas Alf, prin. 887-5035
Washington JHS 3-00110
5000 MADISON AVE 45015 887-5090
Dennis Malone, prin.
Wilson JHS, 714 EATON AVE 45013 3-00110
Paul Burkhardt, prin. 887-5170

New Miami Local SD 4-11111
600 SEVEN MILE AVE 45011 863-0833
Gene Troy, supt.
New Miami JSHS 2-00111
600 SEVEN MILE AVE 45011 863-4917
Gene Troy, prin.

Ross Local SD
3371 HAMILTON CLEVES RD 45013   5-11111
Kenneth Rupe, supt.   863-1253
Ross HS
3425 HAMILTON CLEVES RD 45013   3-00011
Gregory Young, prin.   863-1252
Ross MS
3371 HAMILTON CLEVES RD 45013   3-01100
Steve Kidd, prin.   863-1251

Mercy Hospital   HSP
116 DAYTON ST 45011   867-6464
Miami University-Hamilton Campus   4-CC
1601 PECK BLVD 45011   863-8833
Stephen Badin HS   3-00011
571 HAMILTON NEW LONDON RD 45013
M. Winkeljohn, prin.   863-3993

Hamler, AC 419, PC 3, Henry
Patrick Henry Local SD   4-11111
6900 STATE ROUTE 18 43524   274-5451
James Gooding, supt.
Henry HS   2-00011
6900 STATE ROUTE 18 43524   274-3015
Linda Krauskopf, prin.
MS, PO BOX 328 43524   2-01100
Keith Ruhe, prin.   274-3431

Hammondsville, AC 216, PC 3, Jefferson
Edison Local SD, PO BOX 158 43930   5-11111
R. Roquemore, supt.   532-1594
Stanton JHS, PO BOX 158 43930   2-00110
Dixie Leedy, prin.   532-1594
Other Schools – See Bergholz, Richmond

Hannibal, AC 614, PC 3, Monroe
Switzerland of Ohio Local SD
Supt. — See Woodsfield
River HS   2-00011
52560 RIVER HIGH SCHOOL RD 43931   483-1358
Gary Hunter, prin.

Hanoverton, AC 216, PC 2, Columbiana
United Local SD   4-11111
8143 STATE ROUTE 9 44423   223-1521
Glenn Willis, supt.
United JSHS   3-00111
8143 STATE ROUTE 9 44423   223-1521
Wayne McDevitt, prin.

Harrison, AC 513, PC 6, Hamilton
Southwest Local SD   5-11111
230 S ELM ST 45030   367-4139
Kay Bowling, supt.
HS, 9860 WEST RD 45030   4-00011
Carroll Roberts, prin.   367-4169
MS, 9830 WEST RD 45030   3-00100
Don Jostworth, prin.   367-4831

Harrod, AC 419, PC 3, Allen
Allen East Local SD   4-11111
9520 HARROD RD 45850   648-3333
Joel Scott, supt.
Allen East MS, 9520 HARROD RD 45850   2-01100
Charles Wolf, prin.   648-3571
Other Schools – See Lafayette

Hartville, AC 216, PC 4, Stark
Lake Local SD, 12077 LISA ST NW 44632   5-11111
Robert Dunnerstick, supt.   877-9383
Lake MS, 12001 MARKET AVE N 44632   3-00110
Mark Filicky, prin.   877-4290
Other Schools – See Uniontown

Haviland, AC 419, PC 2, Paulding
Wayne Trace Local SD
Supt. — See Payne
Wayne Trace JSHS   3-00111
4915 US HIGHWAY 127 45851   399-4100
Larry Pressler, prin.

Heath, AC 614, PC 6, Licking
Heath CSD, 107 LANCASTER DR 43056   4-11111
Dan Dupps, supt.   522-2816
JSHS, 300 LICKING VIEW DR 43056   2-00111
Jeff Thompson, prin.   522-1348

Hebron, AC 614, PC 4, Licking
Lakewood Local SD   4-11111
525 E MAIN ST 43025   928-5878
Robert Heigle, supt.
Lakewood HS   3-00011
5222 NATIONAL RD SE 43025   928-4526
Frederick Eickelberger, prin.
Lakewood JHS, 9370 LANCER RD 43025   3-00100
James Mitchen, prin.   928-8330

Hemlock, AC 614, PC 2, Perry
Southern Local SD   4-11111
10390 STATE ROUTE 155 SE 43730   394-2402
Carol Spangler, supt.
Miller HS   2-00011
10397 STATE ROUTE 155 SE 43730   394-2426
David Lanning, prin.
Miller MS   2-01100
10397 STATE ROUTE 155 SE 43730   394-1173
Robert Towner, prin.

Hicksville, AC 419, PC 5, Defiance
Hicksville EVD, 101 E SMITH ST 43526   4-11111
Robert Smith, supt.   542-7665
JSHS, 101 E SMITH ST 43526   2-00111
Dale Nienberg, prin.   542-7636

Hilliard, AC 614, PC 7, Franklin
Hilliard CSD, 5323 CEMETERY RD 43026   6-11111
Roger Nehls, supt.   771-4273

HS, 5100 DAVIDSON RD 43026   4-00011
T. Webb, prin.   771-2299
MS, 5600 SCIOTO DARBY RD 43026   4-00100
Jeffrey Reinhard, prin.   771-2800

Hillsboro, AC 513, PC 6, Highland
Hillsboro CSD, 410 E MAIN ST 45133   5-11111
Patrick Hagan, supt.   393-3475
JSHS, 358 W MAIN ST 45133   4-00111
Monti Mallow, prin.   393-3485

Southern State Community College   4-CC
200 HOBART RD 45133   393-3431

Hiram, AC 216, PC 4, Portage

Hiram College   4-UC
PO BOX 96 44234   569-3211

Holgate, AC 419, PC 4, Henry
Holgate Local SD   3-11111
103 FRAZIER AVE 43527   264-5141
John Mohler, supt.
JSHS, 103 FRAZIER AVE 43527   2-00111
Robert Vennekotter, prin.   264-2521

Holland, AC 419, PC 4, Lucas
Springfield Local SD   5-11111
6900 HALL ST 43528   867-5600
George Tombaugh, supt.
Springfield HS   4-00011
1470 S MCCORD RD 43528   867-5633
William Dais, prin.
Springfield MS   3-00100
7001 MADISON AVE 43528   867-5644
James Wightman, prin.

Hopedale, AC 614, PC 3, Harrison
Harrison Hills CSD   5-11111
PO BOX 356 43976   937-2728
Lynn King, supt.
Other Schools – See Cadiz, Freeport, Scio

Houston, AC 513, PC 2, Shelby
Hardin-Houston Local SD   3-11111
5300 HOUSTON RD 45333   295-3010
Anthony Frierott, supt.
JSHS, 5300 HOUSTON RD 45333   2-00111
Fred Nuss, prin.   295-3010
Hardin-Houston MS   2-00100
5300 HOUSTON RD 45333   295-3010
Fred Nuss, prin.

Howard, AC 614, PC 2, Knox
East Knox Local SD   3-11111
PO BOX 68 43028   599-7493
John Loudermelt, supt.
East Knox JSHS, PO BOX 128 43028   2-00111
Dorothy Holden, prin.   599-7007

Hoytville, AC 419, PC 2, Wood
McComb Local SD
Supt. — See Mc Comb
McComb MS, PO BOX 157 43529   2-01100
Diane Tache, prin.   278-0907

Hubbard, AC 216, PC 6, Trumbull
Hubbard EVD, 150 HALL AVE 44425   4-11111
Kevin Turner, supt.   534-1921
HS, 350 HALL AVE 44425   3-00011
Richard Buchenic, prin.   534-1113
Reed MS, 150 HALL AVE 44425   3-01100
Geno Buonamici, prin.   534-1129

Huber Heights, AC 513, PC 8, Montgomery
Huber Heights CSD   6-11111
5954 LONGFORD RD 45424   237-6300
Richard Burke, supt.
Wayne SHS   4-00001
5400 CHAMBERSBURG RD 45424   233-6431
Barbara Townsend, prin.
Studebaker JHS   4-00110
5950 LONGFORD RD 45424   237-6345
Tom Heid, prin.

Hudson, AC 216, PC 6, Summit
Hudson Local SD   5-11111
77 N OVIATT ST 44236   653-1200
Dennis Allen, supt.
HS, 2500 HUDSON AURORA RD 44236   4-00011
Robert Hardesty, prin.   653-1416
MS, 77 N OVIATT ST 44236   4-00100
David Root, prin.   653-1316

Hospitality Training Center   1-CS
220 N MAIN ST 44236   653-9151
Western Reserve Academy   2-00011
115 COLLEGE ST 44236   650-4400
Henry Flanagan, prin.

Huron, AC 419, PC 6, Erie
Huron CSD   4-11111
712 CLEVELAND RD E 44839   433-3911
David Ritter, supt.
HS, 710 CLEVELAND RD W 44839   3-00011
Andrew Garrick, prin.   433-3171
McCormick MS, 325 OHIO ST 44839   2-01100
Will Folger, prin.   433-5658

Bowling Green State University   3-CC
901 RYE BEACH RD 44839   433-5560

Independence, AC 216, PC 6, Cuyahoga
Independence Local SD   3-11111
7733 STONE RD 44131   642-5850
Stanley Skoczen, supt.

HS, 6111 ARCHWOOD RD 44131   2-00011
David Laurenzi, prin.   642-5860
MS, 6565 BRECKSVILLE RD 44131   2-01100
Robert Sykora, prin.   642-5865

Connecticut School of Broadcasting   2-CS
6701 ROCKSIDE RD STE 204 44131   447-9117
Ironton, AC 614, PC 7, Lawrence
Ironton CSD, 105 S 5TH ST 45638   4-11111
James Payne, supt.   532-4133
JSHS, 1701 S 7TH ST 45638   3-00111
Michael Whitehead, prin.   532-3911

Rock Hill Local SD, RR 3 45638   4-11111
Lloyd Evans, supt.   533-6046
Rock Hill HS, RR 3 45638   3-00011
Steve Lambert, prin.   533-6048
Rock Hill MS, RR 3 45638   2-00100
James Wipert, prin.   533-6066

Ohio University   4-UC
1804 LIBERTY AVE 45638   533-4600
St. Joseph Central HS   1-00111
912 S 6TH ST 45638 – Fr. Nau, prin.   532-0485
Jackson, AC 614, PC 6, Jackson
Jackson CSD, 379 E SOUTH ST 45640   5-11111
Jack Coyan, supt.   286-6442
JSHS, 21 TROPIC ST 45640   4-00111
Thomas Slater, prin.   286-7575

Southeastern Business College   2-CS
420 E MAIN ST 45640   286-1554
Jackson Center, AC 513, PC 4, Shelby
Jackson Center Local SD   3-11111
204 S LINDEN ST 45334   596-6053
Donald Knight, supt.
JSHS, 204 S LINDEN ST 45334   2-00111
Charlyne Perrine, prin.   596-6149

Jamestown, AC 513, PC 4, Greene
Greeneview Local SD   4-11111
4 S CHARLESTON RD 45335   675-2728
Arthur Reiber, supt.
Greeneview HS   2-00011
53 N LIMESTONE ST 45335   675-9711
Timothy McLinden, prin.
Greeneview Central MS   2-00100
51 N LIMESTONE ST 45335   675-9391
Steven Black, prin.

Jefferson, AC 216, PC 5, Ashtabula
Ashtabula County JVSD   3-00001
1565 STATE ROUTE 167 44047   576-6015
Jerome Brockway, supt.
Ashtabula County Joint Vocational SHS   3-00001
1565 STATE ROUTE 167 44047   576-6015
Nancy Settles, prin.
Jefferson Area Local SD   4-11111
45 E SATIN ST 44047   576-9180
Charles Jeffords, supt.
Jefferson Area JSHS   3-00111
125 S POPLAR ST 44047   576-4731
Laurence Bragga, prin.

Jeromesville, AC 419, PC 3, Ashland
Hillsdale Local SD   4-11111
485 TOWNSHIP ROAD 1902 44840   368-8231
Joel Roscoe, supt.
Hillsdale HS   2-00111
485 TOWNSHIP ROAD 1902 44840   368-6841
Sam Cook, prin.
Hillsdale MS, PO BOX 57 44840   2-01100
Robert Blanchard, prin.   368-4911

Johnstown, AC 614, PC 5, Licking
Johnstown-Monroe Local SD   4-11111
441 S MAIN ST 43031   967-6846
James Tarantine, supt.
Johnstown-Monroe HS   2-00011
401 S OREGON ST 43031   967-2721
Gary Hunter, prin.
Adams MS, 80 W MAPLE ST 43031   2-00100
Larry Furniss, prin.   967-8766

Northridge Local SD   4-11111
6097 JOHNSTOWN UTICA RD 43031   967-6631
John Hollingsworth, supt.
Northridge HS   2-00011
6066 JOHNSTOWN UTICA RD 43031   967-6651
Donald Sullivan, prin.
Other Schools – See Alexandria

Kalida, AC 419, PC 3, Putnam
Kalida Local SD, PO BOX 269 45853   3-11111
Ronald Heitmeyer, supt.   532-3534
JSHS, PO BOX 269 45853   2-00111
Richard Kortokrax, prin.   532-3529

Kansas, AC 419, PC 2, Seneca
Lakota Local SD
Supt. — See Risingsun
Lakota HS   2-00011
5186 COUNTY ROAD 13 44841   986-5161
Dwight Schmiesing, prin.

Kent, AC 216, PC 8, Portage
Kent CSD, 321 N DEPEYSTER ST 44240   5-11111
Marc Crail, supt.   673-6515
Roosevelt HS   4-00011
1400 N MANTUA ST 44240   673-9595
Judith Kirman, prin.
Davey MS, 701 PARK AVE 44240   3-00100
John Fender, prin.   673-6693

Kent State University 7-UC
PO BOX 5190 44242 672-3000

Kenton, AC 419, PC 6, Hardin
Kenton CSD, 222 W CARROL ST 43326 4-11111
Sandra Vasu-Sarver, supt. 673-0775
HS, 200 HARDING AVE 43326 3-00011
David Sturgeon, prin. 673-1286
MS, 300 ORIENTAL ST 43326 2-00100
Douglas Roberts, prin. 673-1237

Kettering, AC 513, PC 8, Montgomery
Kettering CSD 6-11111
3750 FAR HILLS AVE 45429 296-7600
Joseph Madak, supt.
Kettering-Fairmont SHS 4-00001
3301 SHROYER RD 45429 296-7700
William Stager, prin.
JHS, 3000 GLENGARRY DR 45420 4-00110
Ronald Sinclair, prin. 297-1900
Van Buren JHS 3-00110
3775 SHROYER RD 45429 297-1985
Robert McCoy, prin.

Alter HS, 940 E DAVID RD 45429 3-00011
Walt Klimaski, prin. 434-4434
Kettering College of Medical Arts 3-CC
3737 SOUTHERN BLVD 45429 296-7218
School of Advertising Art 2-CS
2900 ACOSTA ST 45420 294-0592

Kidron, AC 216, PC 3, Wayne

Central Christian HS 2-00111
PO BOX 9 44636 857-7311
Frederic Miller, prin.

Kings Mills, AC 513, PC 3, Warren
Kings Local SD 5-11111
5620 COLUMBIA RD 45034 398-3776
John Lazares, supt.
Kings HS, 5500 COLUMBIA RD 45034 3-00011
John Faulkner, prin. 398-8050
Kings JHS, 5620 COLUMBIA RD 45034 2-00100
Charles Willis, prin. 398-1777

Kingston, AC 614, PC 4, Ross
Zane Trace Local SD
Supt. — See Chillicothe
Zane Trace MS, PO BOX 615 45644 2-01100
Richard Stevens, prin. 642-2271

Kinsman, AC 216, PC 3, Trumbull
Joseph Badger Local SD 4-11111
7000 STATE ROUTE 88 44428 772-2020
Richard Packuk, supt.
Badger HS, 8319 MAIN ST 44428 2-00011
Alan Harris, prin. 876-8011
Badger MS 2-00100
6144 STATE ROUTE 7 44428 772-4731
Robert Moon, prin.

Victory Christian S 2-11111
6759 STATE ROUTE 5 44428 924-2044
Frank Jara, prin.

Kirkersville, AC 614, PC 3, Licking
Southwest Licking Local SD 5-11111
PO BOX 400 43033 927-3941
Thomas Gay, supt.
Other Schools – See Pataskala

Kirtland, AC 216, PC 6, Lake
Kirtland Local SD 3-11111
9152 CHILLICOTHE RD 44094 256-3311
Jack Porter, supt.
HS, 9150 CHILLICOTHE RD 44094 2-00011
Vernon Fawcett, prin. 256-3366
MS, 9152 CHILLICOTHE RD 44094 2-00100
Stan Lipinski, prin. 256-3358

Lakeland Community College 5-CC
7700 CLOCKTOWER DR 44094 953-7100

Kunkle, AC 419, PC 2, Williams
North Central Local SD
Supt. — See Pioneer
North Central MS, PO BOX 92 43531 2-00100
Thomas Balser, prin. 737-2293

Lafayette, AC 419, PC 2, Allen
Allen East Local SD
Supt. — See Harrod
Allen East HS 2-00011
105 N WASHINGTON ST 45854 649-6311
Ronald Goodwin, prin.

LaGrange, AC 216, PC 4, Lorain
Keystone Local SD 4-11111
301 LIBERTY ST 44050 355-5131
David Ring, supt.
Keystone HS, 301 LIBERTY ST 44050 3-00011
Thomas Hlavsa, prin. 355-5132
Keystone MS, 301 LIBERTY ST 44050 3-01100
Timothy Jenkins, prin. 355-5133

Lakeside, AC 419, PC 3, Ottawa
Danbury Local SD 3-11111
9451 E HARBOR RD 43440 798-5185
Joyce Plummer, supt.
Danbury JSHS 2-00111
9451 E HARBOR RD 43440 798-4037
Randal Harner, prin.

Lakewood, AC 216, PC 8, Cuyahoga
Lakewood CSD, 1470 WARREN RD 44107 6-11111
Daniel Kalish, supt. 529-4092
HS, 14100 FRANKLIN BLVD 44107 4-00011
Charlane Bowden, prin. 529-4021
Emerson MS 3-00100
13439 CLIFTON BLVD 44107 529-4241
Robert Hayden, prin.
Harding MS, 16600 HILLIARD RD 44107 3-00100
Allen Senkovich, prin. 529-4261
Mann MS, 1215 W CLIFTON BLVD 44107 2-00100
Gilbert Fritzsche, prin. 529-4287

St. Augustine Academy 2-00011
14808 LAKE AVE 44107 221-4227
Sr. Patricia Lenard, prin.
St. Edward HS 3-00011
13500 DETROIT AVE 44107 221-3776
Br. Spooner, prin.

Lancaster, AC 614, PC 8, Fairfield
Fairfield Union Local SD
Supt. — See West Rushville
Fairfield Union HS 3-00011
6401 CNCNNT ZNESVILLE RD NE 43130
Dale Ferbrache, prin. 536-7306
Fairfield Union JHS 2-00100
6401 CNCNNT ZNESVILLE RD NE 43130
Dale Ferbrache, prin. 536-7846

Lancaster CSD 6-11111
345 E MULBERRY ST 43130 687-7300
John Baughman, supt.
SHS, 1312 GRANVILLE PIKE 43130 4-00001
William Hughes, prin. 687-7370
Ewing JHS, 825 E FAIR AVE 43130 3-00100
Carl Spencer, prin. 687-7347
Sherman JHS, 701 UNION ST 43130 3-00100
Michael Binion, prin. 687-7344
Stanbery Freshman HS 3-00010
315 E MULBERRY ST 43130 687-7324
Jerry White, prin.

Ohio University 4-UC
1570 GRANVILLE PIKE 43130 654-6711
Southeastern Business College 2-CS
1522 SHERIDAN DR 43130 687-6126
William Fisher Catholic HS 2-00011
1803 GRANVILLE PIKE 43130 654-1231
Sr. Gail Morgan, prin.

Latham, AC 614, PC 2, Pike
Western Local SD
Supt. — See Piketon
Western JSHS 2-00111
8640 STATE ROUTE 124 45646 493-2514
John Payne, prin.

Leavittsburg, AC 216, PC 4, Trumbull
Labrae Local SD 4-11111
1015 N LEAVITT RD 44430 898-1393
George Geordan, supt.
Labrae JSHS, 4650 W MARKET ST 44430 3-00111
David Bowser, prin. 898-0800

Lebanon, AC 513, PC 7, Warren
Lebanon CSD, 25 OAKWOOD AVE 45036 5-11111
Stephen Yambor, supt. 932-0999
HS, 160 MILLER RD 45036 3-00011
Dwight Goins, prin. 932-6798
Berry JHS, 23 OAKWOOD AVE 45036 3-00100
Gail Rose, prin. 932-2993

Warren County JVSD 3-00001
3525 N STATE ROUTE 48 45036 932-5677
Edward Perkins, supt.
Warren County Career Ctr Joint Vo SHS 3-00001
3525 N STATE ROUTE 48 45036 932-5677
Vincent Roessner, prin.

Leesburg, AC 513, PC 4, Highland
Fairfield Local SD 3-11111
PO BOX 347 45135 780-2221
Scott Wilson, supt.
Fairfield JSHS, PO BOX 347 45135 2-00111
Robert Kratzer, prin. 780-2966

Lees Creek, AC 513, PC 2, Clinton
East Clinton Local SD 4-11111
97 COLLEGE ST 45138 584-2461
J. Richard Gieringer, supt.
East Clinton HS, 174 LARRICK RD 45138 2-00011
Terrence Fouch, prin. 584-2474

Leetonia, AC 216, PC 4, Columbiana
Leetonia EVD, 450 WALNUT ST 44431 3-11111
Joseph Bertolini, supt. 427-6594
JSHS, 181 WALNUT ST 44431 2-00111
Daniel Simcox, prin. 427-2115

Leipsic, AC 419, PC 4, Putnam
Leipsic Local SD, 232 OAK ST 45856 3-11111
Kenneth Boyer, supt. 943-2165
JSHS, 232 OAK ST 45856 2-00111
John Hall, prin. 943-2164

Lewisburg, AC 513, PC 4, Preble
Tri-County North Local SD 4-11111
436 N COMMERCE ST 45338 962-2671
Timothy Hopkins, supt.
Tri-County North HS 2-00011
500 PANTHER WAY 45338 962-2675
Russell Mielbrecht, prin.
Tri-County North MS 2-01100
530 PANTHER WAY 45338 962-2631
James Scherman, prin.

Lewistown, AC 513, PC 2, Logan
Indian Lake Local SD 4-11111
6210 STATE ROUTE 235 N 43333 686-8601
Robert Van Osdol, supt.
Indian Lake HS 3-00011
6210 STATE ROUTE 235 N 43333 686-8851
Charles Blair, prin.
Indian Lake MS 3-00100
8144 COUNTY ROAD 54 43333 686-8833
James Jenkins, prin.

Lexington, AC 419, PC 5, Richland
Lexington Local SD 5-11111
103 CLEVER LN 44904 884-2132
Robert Earnest, supt.
HS, 103 CLEVER LN 44904 3-00011
James Ziegelhofer, prin. 884-1111
JHS, 90 FREDERICK ST 44904 2-00100
William Ferguson, prin. 884-2112

Liberty Center, AC 419, PC 4, Henry
Liberty Center Local SD 3-11111
PO BOX 434 43532 533-5011
Myrna Ritterling, supt.
JSHS, PO BOX 434 43532 2-00111
Rick Utz, prin. 533-6641

Lima, AC 419, PC 8, Allen
Apollo JVSD, 3325 SHAWNEE RD 45806 3-00001
Jon Rockhold, supt. 999-3015
Apollo Career Ctr Joint Vocational SHS 3-00001
3325 SHAWNEE RD 45806 999-3015
Carol Blass, prin.

Bath Local SD, 2650 BIBLE RD 45801 4-11111
Charles Montgomery, supt. 221-0807
Bath HS, 2850 BIBLE RD 45801 3-00011
Paul Kugler, prin. 221-0176
Bath MS, 2700 BIBLE RD 45801 3-01100
Paul Whittington, prin. 221-0176

Lima CSD, 515 CALUMET AVE 45804 6-11111
Charles Buroker, supt. 998-2400
HS, 600 S PIERCE ST 45804 4-00011
Mitchell Black, prin. 998-2000
North MS, 1135 N WEST ST 45801 2-00100
Oscar Marshall, prin. 998-2100
South MS, 560 S PINE ST 45804 3-00100
John Brown, prin. 998-2120
West MS, 816 COLLEGE AVE 45805 2-00100
Jonathan Cox, prin. 998-2150

Shawnee Local SD 5-11111
3255 ZURMEHLY RD 45806 991-6085
Bill Lodermeier, supt.
Shawnee HS 3-00011
3333 ZURMEHLY RD 45806 991-4153
Don Wade, prin.
Shawnee MS 3-01100
3235 ZURMEHLY RD 45806 991-6095
Michael Archer, prin.

Lima Central Catholic HS 2-00011
720 S CABLE RD 45805 222-4276
Daniel Rupert, prin.
Lima Technical College 4-CC
4240 CAMPUS DR 45804 222-8324
Northwestern College 4-CC
1441 N CABLE RD 45805 227-3141
Ohio State University-Lima Campus 3-UC
4240 CAMPUS DR 45804 221-1641

Lisbon, AC 216, PC 5, Columbiana
Beaver Local SD 5-11111
13052 STATE ROUTE 7 44432 385-6831
Frank Blankenship, supt.
Beaver HS 3-00011
13187 STATE ROUTE 7 44432 386-8700
James Patsey, prin.
Beaver MS 3-01100
13052 STATE ROUTE 7 44432 386-8707
William Baker, prin.

Columbiana County JVSD 2-00001
9364 STATE ROUTE 45 44432 424-9561
John Dilling, supt.
Columbiana County Joint Vocational SHS 2-00001
9364 STATE ROUTE 45 44432 424-9561
John Gecina, prin.

Lisbon EVD, 431 E CHESTNUT ST 44432 4-11111
Anthony Krukowski, supt. 424-7714
Anderson JSHS 3-00111
260 W LINCOLN WAY 44432 424-3215
John Krotky, prin.

Lockland, AC 513, PC 5, Hamilton
Lockland CSD 3-11111
210 N COOPER AVE 45215 563-5000
Nita Clayton, supt.
JSHS, 249 W FORRER ST 45215 2-00111
Carl Parks, prin. 733-4991

Lodi, AC 216, PC 5, Medina
Cloverleaf Local SD 5-11111
8525 FRIENDSVILLE RD 44254 948-2500
Charles Spade, supt.
Cloverleaf SHS 3-00001
8525 FRIENDSVILLE RD 44254 948-2500
William Thombs, prin.
Other Schools – See Seville

Logan, AC 614, PC 6, Hocking
Logan-Hocking Local SD 5-11111
57 S WALNUT ST 43138 385-8517
Joseph Murtha, supt.

HS, 50 NORTH ST 43138   4-00011
  David McAllister, prin.   385-2069
Logan-Hocking MS   3-00100
  13579 MAYSVILLE WILLIAMS RD 43138
  David Snipes, prin.   385-8764

London, AC 614, PC 6, Madison
London CSD, 60 S WALNUT ST 43140   4-11111
  Jacob Froning, supt.   852-5700
HS, 336 ELM ST 43140   3-00011
  Steven Allen, prin.   852-5700
MS, 60 S WALNUT ST 43140   2-00100
  James Jones, prin.   852-5700

Madison-Plains Local SD   4-11111
  55 LINSON RD 43140   852-3712
  James Stauffer, supt.
Madison-Plains HS   3-00011
  800 LINSON RD 43140   852-0364
  John Varnell, prin.
Madison-Plains MS   2-00100
  9940 STATE ROUTE 38 SW 43140   852-1707
  James James, prin.

Lorain, AC 216, PC 8, Lorain
Clearview Local SD   4-11111
  4700 BROADWAY 44052   233-5412
  Richard Sulewski, supt.
Clearview JSHS   2-00111
  4700 BROADWAY 44052   233-6313
  Ed Kershaw, prin.

Lorain CSD, 2350 POLE AVE 44052   7-11111
  Thomas Bollin, supt.   233-2232
King HS, 2600 ASHLAND AVE 44052   4-00011
  David Coleman, prin.   282-9191
HS, 602 WASHINGTON AVE 44052   4-00011
  Paul Sink, prin.   244-0200
Southview HS, 2270 E 42ND ST 44055   4-00011
  Ramon Pagan, prin.   277-7271
Irving MS   3-01100
  4TH & HAMILTON AVE 44052   244-3171
  David Karolak, prin.
Whittier MS, 3201 SENECA AVE 44055   3-00100
  Henry Harsar, prin.   277-7261
Longfellow/Emerson ES   2-10100
  MAINE AVE & D ST 44052   288-4146
  Barbara Evans, prin.

Sheffield-Sheffield Lake CSD   4-11111
  1824 HARRIS RD 44054   949-6181
  Charles Krepop, supt.
Brookside HS, 1812 HARRIS RD 44054   3-00011
  Burton Daugherty, prin.   949-4220
Sheffield MS, 1919 HARRIS RD 44054   3-00100
  Pam Purses, prin.   949-4228

ESI Career Center   2-CS
  1985 N RIDGE RD E 44055   277-8832
Lorain Catholic HS   2-00111
  760 TOWER BLVD 44052   282-8216
  Sr. Joanne Miller, prin.
Southeastern Business College   5-CS
  1907 N RIDGE RD E 44055   277-0021

Loudonville, AC 419, PC 5, Ashland
Loudonville-Perrysville EVD   4-11111
  210 E MAIN ST 44842   994-3912
  Tom Lavinder, supt.
HS, 421 CAMPUS AVE 44842   2-00011
  Ben Blubaugh, prin.   994-4101
Other Schools — See Perrysville

Louisville, AC 216, PC 6, Stark
Louisville CSD, 418 E MAIN ST 44641   5-11111
  Clyde Lepley, supt.   875-1666
HS, 1201 S NICKELPLATE ST 44641   3-00011
  William Stetler, prin.   875-1438
MS, 300 E GORGAS ST 44641   3-00100
  David Varner, prin.   875-5597

St. Thomas Aquinas HS   2-00011
  2121 RENO DR 44641 – Fr. Hazel, prin.   875-1631

Loveland, AC 513, PC 6, Hamilton
Loveland CSD   5-11111
  757 S LEBANON RD 45140   683-5600
  Ronald DeWitt, supt.
Loveland Hurst HS, 1 TIGER TRL 45140   3-00011
  Thomas Hausterman, prin.   683-1920
Loveland Hutst MS   3-00100
  801 S LEBANON RD 45140   683-3100
  Edward Lenney, prin.

Lowellville, AC 216, PC 4, Mahoning
Lowellville Local SD   2-11111
  2 E GRANT ST 44436   536-6318
  Robert Kwiat, supt.
S, 2 E GRANT ST 44436   2-11111
  Michael Katula, prin.   536-8426

Lucas, AC 419, PC 3, Richland
Lucas Local SD, PO BOX 307 44843   3-11111
  Robert Delane, supt.   892-2338
HS, PO BOX 327 44843   2-00011
  Jacque Daup, prin.   892-2291
Lucas Heritage MS   2-00100
  PO BOX 327 44843   892-2291
  Jacque Daup, prin.

Lucasville, AC 614, PC 4, Scioto
Pickaway-Ross County JVSD   4-00011
  VERN RIFFE DR 45648   642-2550
  Jack Derr, supt.
Other Schools — See Chillicothe

Scioto County JVSD   3-00001
  PO BOX 766 45648   259-5522
  Tom Reiser, supt.
Scioto County Joint Vocational SHS   3-00001
  PO BOX 766 45648   259-5522
  David Bowling, prin.

Valley Local SD, PO BOX 888 45648   4-11111
  Douglas Booth, supt.   259-5551
Valley HS, PO BOX 888 45648   2-00111
  Lawrence Comer, prin.   259-5551
Valley MS, PO BOX 490 45648   2-00100
  Paul Miller, prin.   259-2651

Lynchburg, AC 513, PC 4, Highland
Lynchburg-Clay Local SD   4-11111
  263 N MAIN ST 45142   364-2338
  Gregory Hawk, supt.
Lynchburg-Clay JSHS   2-00111
  8250 STATE ROUTE 134 45142   364-2250
  C. Davidson, prin.

Lyndhurst, AC 216, PC 7, Cuyahoga
South Euclid-Lyndhurst CSD   5-11111
  5044 MAYFIELD RD 44124   691-2000
  Lawrence Marazza, supt.
Brush HS, 4875 GLENLYN RD 44124   4-00011
  Walt Conte, prin.   691-2065
Memorial JHS   3-00100
  1250 PROFESSOR RD 44124   691-2140
  Larry Cirillo, prin.

Cleveland Institute Dental Medical Asst.   2-CS
  5564 MAYFIELD RD 44124   473-6273

Mc Arthur, AC 614, PC 4, Vinton
Vinton County Local SD   5-11111
  112 N MARKET ST 45651   596-5218
  James Pack, supt.
Vinton County Cons. HS   3-00011
  307 W HIGH ST 45651   596-5258
  John Simmons, prin.
Vinton County JHS, RR 1 45651   2-00100
  Daniel Murray, prin.   596-5243

Mc Comb, AC 419, PC 4, Hancock
McComb Local SD   3-11111
  328 S TODD ST 45858   293-3979
  Rahman Dyer, supt.
HS, 328 S TODD ST 45858   2-00011
  T. Heidlebaugh, prin.   293-3853
Other Schools — See Hoytville

Mc Connelsville, AC 614, PC 4, Morgan
Morgan Local SD, PO BOX 509 43756   5-11111
  Jerry Russell, supt.   962-2782
Morgan HS, 800 RAIDER DR 43756   3-00011
  John Mental, prin.   962-2944

Mc Dermott, AC 614, PC 3, Scioto
Northwest Local SD, RR 1 45652   4-11111
  A. McCoy, supt.   259-5558
Northwest HS, RR 1 45652   3-00011
  D. Diehlmann, prin.   259-2366

Mc Donald, AC 216, PC 5, Trumbull
McDonald Local SD   3-11111
  600 IOWA AVE 44437   530-8051
  Matt Chojnacki, supt.
JSHS, 600 IOWA AVE 44437   2-00111
  Robert Blonairz, prin.   530-2528

Macedonia, AC 216, PC 6, Summit
Nordonia Hills CSD
  Supt. — See Northfield
Nordonia HS   3-00011
  8006 S BEDFORD RD 44056   467-0580
  J. Blankenship, prin.

Mc Guffey, AC 419, PC 3, Hardin
Upper Scioto Valley Local SD   3-11111
  S COURTRIGHT 45859   757-4451
  John Reno, supt.
Upper Scioto Valley JSHS   2-00111
  S COURTRIGHT 45859   757-3231
  John Merriman, prin.

Madison, AC 216, PC 4, Lake
Madison Local SD   5-11111
  6741 N RIDGE RD 44057   428-2166
  Stan Heffner, supt.
HS, 3100 BURNS RD 44057   3-00011
  Clinton Keener, prin.   428-2161
MS, 1941 RED BIRD RD 44057   3-00100
  Robert Nobles, prin.   428-1196

Magnolia, AC 216, PC 5, Stark
Sandy Valley Local SD   4-11111
  RR 2 BOX 100 44643   866-3339
  Dennis Woods, supt.
Sandy Valley JSHS   3-00111
  RR 2 BOX 100 44643   866-9371
  Warren Van Fossen, prin.

Malvern, AC 216, PC 4, Carroll
Brown Local SD, 401 W MAiN ST 44644   4-11111
  James Betts, supt.   863-1170
JSHS, 401 W MAIN ST 44644   2-00111
  Edwin Bode, prin.   863-1355

Manchester, AC 513, PC 4, Adams
Adams County/Ohio Valley SD
  Supt. — See West Union
JSHS, 309 E 9TH ST 45144   2-00111
  Charles Kimble, prin.   549-3971

Mansfield, AC 419, PC 8, Richland
Madison Local SD   5-11111
  1379 GRACE ST 44905   589-2600
  Frederick Slater, supt.
Madison HS, 600 ESLEY LN 44905   4-00011
  Allen Pease, prin.   589-2112
Beer MS, 103 BAHL AVE 44905   1-00110
  (—), prin.   589-9549
Madison JHS, 690 ASHLAND RD 44905   4-00110
  Michael Shambre, prin.   522-0471

Mansfield CSD, PO BOX 1448 44901   6-11111
  Mel Coleman, supt.   525-6400
SHS, 145 W PARK BLVD 44906   4-00001
  James White, prin.   525-6369
Mansfield Freshman HS   2-00010
  314 CLINE AVE 44907   525-6347
  Michael Dick, prin.
Malabar MS, 205 W COOK RD 44907   3-00100
  Steve Miller, prin.   525-6374
Simpson MS, 218 W 4TH ST 44903   3-00100
  William Castle, prin.   525-6348

Ontario Local SD   4-11111
  2200 BEDFORD BLVD 44906   747-4311
  Gene Hancock, supt.
Ontario HS   3-00011
  467 SHELBY ONTARIO RD 44906   529-3969
  Bryan Neff, prin.
Ontario MS, 3560 PARK AVE W 44906   3-01100
  Andrew Johnson, prin.   529-5507

Mansfield Christian HS   2-00111
  500 LOGAN RD 44907   756-5651
  Paul Rohrer, prin.
Mansfield General Hospital   HSP
  335 GLESSNER AVE 44903   526-8595
North Central Technical College   4-CC
  PO BOX 698 44901   755-4800
Ohio State University-Mansfield Campus   3-UC
  1680 UNIVERSITY DR 44906   755-4226
St. Peters HS, 104 W 1ST ST 44902   2-00011
  Fr. Richard Kennedy, prin.   524-0979

Mantua, AC 216, PC 4, Portage
Crestwood Local SD   4-11111
  4565 W PROSPECT ST 44255   274-8511
  David Singleton, supt.
Crestwood HS, 10919 MAIN ST 44255   3-00011
  David Broman, prin.   274-2214
Crestwood MS   3-01100
  10880 JOHN EDWARD DR 44255   274-2249
  Robert Jurca, prin.

Maple Heights, AC 216, PC 8, Cuyahoga
Maple Heights CSD   5-11111
  5500 CLEMENT AVE 44137   587-3200
  Jack Neal, supt.
HS, 5500 CLEMENT AVE 44137   4-00011
  Kim Meyer, prin.   587-3200
MS, 5460 WEST BLVD 44137   3-00100
  Josephine Dodge, prin.   587-3200

Maria Stein, AC 419, PC 2, Mercer
Marion Local SD   3-11111
  1901 STATE ROUTE 716 45860   925-4597
  R. Huelsman, supt.
Marion HS   2-00011
  1901 STATE ROUTE 716 45860   925-4597
  Kenneth Doseck, prin.

Marietta, AC 614, PC 7, Washington
Marietta CSD, 701 3RD ST 45750   5-11111
  Dora Jean Bumgarner, supt.   374-6500
HS, 208 DAVIS AVE 45750   4-00011
  Paul Remke, prin.   374-6540
MS, 242 7TH ST 45750   3-00100
  Mark Doebrich, prin.   374-6530

Washington County JVSD, RR 2 45750   2-00111
  Patricia Foor, supt.   373-2766
Washington County Career Center SHS   2-00001
  RR 2 45750   373-2766
  Charles Milhoan, prin.

Marietta College   4-UC
  210 5TH ST 45750   373-4643
Memorial Hospital   HSP
  401 MATTHEW ST 45750   374-1412
Washington Community College   4-CC
  710 COLEGATE DR 45750   374-8716

Marion, AC 614, PC 8, Marion
Elgin Local SD   4-11111
  4616 LARUE PROSPECT RD W 43302   382-1101
  John Fernbaugh, supt.
Elgin HS, 1239 KEENER RD S 43302   2-00011
  John Millisor, prin.   383-5118
Other Schools — See Green Camp

Marion CSD, 910 E CHURCH ST 43302   6-11111
  Robert Thiede, supt.   387-3300
Harding HS, 420 SEMINOLE AVE 43302   4-00011
  Vaughan Williams, prin.   387-3300
Baker MS   2-00100
  400 PENNSYLVANIA AVE 43302   389-6362
  Joseph Parish, prin.
Edison MS, 871 CHATFIELD RD 43302   2-00100
  Edwin Schoonmaker, prin.   387-5716
Taft MS, 474 N STATE ST 43302   3-00100
  Thomas Clary, prin.   387-5890

Pleasant Local SD 4-11111
3541 SMELTZER RD 43302 389-4476
C. Richard Arndt, supt.
Pleasant HS, 1101 OWENS RD W 43302 2-00011
Robert Dendinger, prin. 389-2389
Pleasant MS, 3507 SMELTZER RD 43302 2-01100
Michael Terry, prin. 389-5167

River Valley Local SD 4-11111
1239 COLUMBUS SANDUSKY RD N 43302
David Kirkton, supt. 387-4261
River Valley HS 3-00011
1267 COLUMBUS SANDUSKY RD N 43302
Joseph Catera, prin. 387-1281
River Valley JHS 2-00100
1199 COLUMBUS SANDUSKY RD N 43302
Glenn Crawford, prin. 387-1283

Tri-Rivers JVSD 3-00001
2222 MARION MOUNT GILEAD RD 43302
James Craycraft, supt. 389-4681
Tri-Rivers Career Center Joint Vo SHS 3-00001
2222 MARION MOUNT GILEAD RD 43302
Dennis Swartz, prin. 389-4681
_____

Marion Catholic HS 2-00111
1001 MOUNT VERNON AVE 43302 389-2381
David Roesch, prin.
Marion General Hospital HSP
96 MCKINLEY PARK DR 43302 383-8700
Marion Technical College 3-CC
1467 MOUNT VERNON AVE 43302 389-4636
Ohio State University-Marion 4-UC
1465 MOUNT VERNON AVE 43302 389-2361

Martins Ferry, AC 614, PC 6, Belmont
Martins Ferry CSD 4-11111
631 HANOVER ST 43935 633-1732
Steve Kish, supt.
HS, 832 HANOVER ST 43935 3-00011
Robert McNabb, prin. 633-0684
MS, 56731 COLERAIN PIKE 43935 2-00100
Anthony Collette, prin. 633-3341

Marysville, AC 513, PC 6, Union
Marysville EVD 5-11111
1000 EDGEWOOD DR 43040 644-8105
Jerry Stackhouse, supt.
HS, 800 AMRINE MILL RD 43040 3-00011
Gregory Hanson, prin. 642-0010
MS, 833 N MAPLE ST 43040 3-00100
M. Sweeney, prin. 642-1721

Mason, AC 513, PC 7, Warren
Mason CSD 5-11111
200 NORTHCREST DR 45040 398-0474
David Lewis, supt.
HS 3-00011
770 S MASON MONTGOMERY RD 45040
Charles Birkholtz, prin. 398-5025
MS, 211 N EAST ST 45040 2-00100
Mark Henderson, prin. 398-9035

Massillon, AC 216, PC 8, Stark
Jackson Local SD 5-11111
7984 FULTON DR NW 44646 830-8000
Joe Larson, supt.
Jackson HS, 7600 FULTON DR NW 44646 4-00011
Thomas Chain, prin. 837-3501
Jackson Memorial MS 4-01100
7355 MUDBROOK RD NW 44646 830-8034
Robert Glassburn, prin.

Massillon CSD, 207 OAK AVE SE 44646 5-11111
Alexander Paris, supt. 830-1810
Washington HS 4-00011
1 PAUL E BROWN DR SE 44646 830-1800
Alfred Hennon, prin.
Andrews MS 3-00100
661 TREMONT AVE SW 44647 830-1831
Donald Green, prin.
Longfellow MS 3-00100
514 NORTH AVE NE 44646 830-1841
David Limbach, prin.

Perry Local SD 6-11111
4201 HARSH AVE SE 44646 477-8121
David Mancini, supt.
Perry SHS, 3737 HARSH AVE SE 44646 4-00011
Ray Fortner, prin. 477-3486
Edison JHS, 4201 HARSH AVE SE 44646 3-00110
Paul Carver, prin. 478-6167

Starke County Area JVSD 2-00001
6805 RICHVILLE DR SW 44646 832-1591
Dan Risaliti, supt.
Drage Career Education Center 2-00001
6805 RICHVILLE DR SW 44646 832-9856
Richard Faiello, prin.

Tuslaw Local SD 4-11111
1723 MANCHESTER AVE NW 44647 837-7813
Alan Osler, supt.
Tuslaw JSHS 3-00111
1723 MANCHESTER AVE NW 44647 837-3511
Robert Horner, prin.
_____

Massillon Christian S 2-11111
965 OVERLOOK AVE SW 44647 833-1039
Robert Sampsel, prin.

Maumee, AC 419, PC 7, Lucas
Maumee CSD, 2345 DETROIT AVE 43537 5-11111
Paul Murphy, supt. 893-3200

HS, 1147 SACO ST 43537 3-00011
Lee Black, prin. 893-8778
Gateway MS 3-00100
GIBBS AND SACKETT STS 43537 893-3386
Paul Raczkowski, prin.

Mayfield, AC 216, PC 5, Cuyahoga
Mayfield CSD 5-11111
784 SOM CENTER RD 44143 442-2200
David Abbott, supt.
JSHS, 6116 WILSON MILLS RD 44143 4-00111
Robert Lombardo, prin. 442-2200

Mechanicsburg, AC 513, PC 4, Champaign
Mechanicsburg EVD, 60 HIGH ST 43044 3-11111
Kevin Turner, supt. 834-2453
JSHS, 60 HIGH ST 43044 2-00111
Mark Weedy, prin. 834-2494

Medina, AC 216, PC 7, Medina
Buckeye Local SD 4-11111
3044 COLUMBIA RD 44256 725-3735
Darryl Graves, supt.
Buckeye HS, 3084 COLUMBIA RD 44256 3-00011
David Kuhn, prin. 722-3604
Buckeye MS, 3024 COLUMBIA RD 44256 2-00100
Karl Duerr, prin. 725-0118

Highland Local SD 4-11111
3880 RIDGE RD 44256 239-1903
Michael Carlson, supt.
Highland HS, 3880 RIDGE RD 44256 3-00011
Bruce Hulme, prin. 239-1901
Highland MS, 3940 RIDGE RD 44256 2-00100
Craig Bailey, prin. 239-2487

Medina County JVSD 3-00001
1101 W LIBERTY ST 44256 725-8461
Thomas Horwedel, supt.
Medina County Joint Vocational SHS 3-00001
1101 W LIBERTY ST 44256 725-8461
John Youngblood, prin.
Medina CSD 6-11111
120 W WASHINGTON ST 44256 725-8831
Charles Irish, supt.
HS, 777 E UNION ST 44256 4-00011
Charles Pfeiffer, prin. 725-9210
Medina Claggett JHS 3-00100
420 E UNION ST 44256 725-9250
Thomas McKenna, prin.
_____

First Baptist Christian S 2-11111
3646 MEDINA RD 44256 725-3227
Jerry Kramer, prin.
Hamrick Truck Driving School 2-CS
1156 MEDINA RD 44256 239-2229

Mentor, AC 216, PC 8, Lake
Mentor EVD, 6451 CENTER ST 44060 7-11111
William Hiller, supt. 255-4444
Mentor SHS, 6477 CENTER ST 44060 4-00001
Joe Webb, prin. 255-4444
Memorial JHS 3-00110
8979 MENTOR AVE 44060 255-4444
Larry Disbro, prin.
Mentor Shore JHS 3-00110
5670 HOPKINS RD 44060 255-4444
Neil Sharp, prin.
Ridge JHS 3-00110
7860 JOHNNYCAKE RIDGE RD 44060 255-4444
Joffrey Jones, prin.
_____

Cleveland Institute Dental Medical Asst. 2-CS
5733 HOPKINS RD 44060 257-5524
Lake Catholic HS 3-00011
6733 REYNOLDS RD 44060 951-0077
Sr. St. Ann Waldron, prin.

Metamora, AC 419, PC 3, Fulton
Evergreen Local SD 4-11111
14544 COUNTY ROAD 6 # 6 43540 644-3521
Russell Griggs, supt.
Evergreen HS 2-00011
14544 COUNTY ROAD 6 43540 644-2951
Mark Basilius, prin.
Evergreen MS, 310 SWANTON ST 43540 2-00100
Duane Elliott, prin. 644-2331

Miamisburg, AC 513, PC 7, Montgomery
Miamisburg CSD, 540 PARK AVE 45342 5-11111
Carl Berg, supt. 866-3381
HS, 1860 BELVO RD 45342 4-00011
Gregory Whitehead, prin. 866-0771
Wantz MS, 115 S 7TH ST 45342 3-00100
Thomas Klingel, prin. 866-3431

Middleburg Heights, AC 216, PC 7, Cuyahoga
Berea CSD
Supt. — See Berea
Midpark MS, 7000 PAULA DR 44130 4-00011
Jay Gradisher, prin. 676-8400

Polaris JVSD 3-00011
7285 OLD OAK BLVD 44130 243-8600
John Church, supt.
Polaris Career Ctr Joint Vocational SHS 3-00011
7285 OLD OAK BLVD 44130 243-8600
Ernest Mason, prin.
_____

Southwest General Hospital HSP
18697 BAGLEY RD 44130 826-8051

Middlefield, AC 216, PC 4, Geauga
Cardinal Local SD 4-11111
PO BOX 188 44062 632-0261
Leslie Harris, supt.
Cardinal HS, PO BOX 7 44062 2-00011
Robert Longfellow, prin. 632-0264
Cardinal MS, 16000 E HIGH ST 44062 2-00100
Thomas Moss, prin. 632-0263

Middleport, AC 614, PC 5, Meigs
Meigs Local SD
Supt. — See Pomeroy
Meigs MS, 621 S 3RD AVE 45760 2-00100
David Gaul, prin. 992-3058

Middletown, AC 513, PC 8, Butler
Lakota Local SD
Supt. — See West Chester
Liberty MS 4-00100
7055 DUTCHLAND BLVD 45044 777-4420
Ronald Brooks, prin.
Madison Local SD, 601 HILL ST 45042 4-11111
Daniel Hare, supt. 420-4750
Madison HS 2-00011
1368 MIDDLETOWN EATON RD 45042 420-4760
Robert Leahy, prin.
Madison MS 3-01100
1380 MIDDLETOWN EATON RD 45042 420-4766
Edward Dulle, prin.
Middletown CSD 6-11111
1515 GIRARD AVE 45044 423-0781
Harry Eastridge, supt.
HS, 601 N BREIEL BLVD 45042 4-00011
James Brown, prin. 420-4500
Manchester Technical Center Vo Tech
4420 MANCHESTER RD 45042 420-4522
(—), prin.
Vail MS, 1415 GIRARD AVE 45044 3-00100
Peggy McClusky, prin. 420-4528
Verity MS, 1900 JOHNS RD 45044 3-00100
Larry Knapp, prin. 420-4538
Other Schools – See Monroe
_____

Fenwick HS 2-00011
3800 MANCHESTER RD 45042 423-0723
John Rossi, prin.
Miami University-Middletown Campus 4-CC
4200 N UNIVERSITY BLVD 45042 424-4444
Middletown Christian S 2-11111
PO BOX 100 45044 423-4542
Jerry Smith, prin.
Middletown Regional Hospital HSP
105 MCKNIGHT DR 45044 420-5100
Southwestern College of Business 3-CC
631 S BREIEL BLVD 45044 423-3346

Milan, AC 419, PC 4, Erie
Berlin-Milan Local SD 4-11111
140 MAIN ST S 44846 499-4272
Don Gfell, supt.
Edison HS 3-00011
2603 STATE ROUTE 113 E 44846 499-4652
Daniel McCarthy, prin.
Other Schools – See Berlin Heights

Ehove JVSD, 316 MASON RD W 44846 3-00011
Joseph DeRose, supt. 499-4663
Ehove Career Center Vocational S 3-00011
316 MASON RD W 44846 499-4663
Larry Hodge, prin.

Milford, AC 513, PC 6, Clermont
Great Oaks JVSD
Supt. — See Cincinnati
Live Oaks CDC SHS 3-00011
5956 BUCKWHEAT RD 45150 575-1900
James Dixon, prin.

Milford EVD, 525 LILA AVE 45150 6-11111
Loren Wilson, supt. 831-5100
HS, 1 EAGLES WAY 45150 4-00011
Michael Chandler, prin. 831-2990
JHS, 5733 PLEASANT HILL RD 45150 3-00100
David Gomon, prin. 831-1900
_____

St. Andrew ES, 555 MAIN ST 45150 2-01100
James Renner, prin. 831-5277

Milford Center, AC 513, PC 3, Union
Fairbanks Local SD 3-11111
11158 STATE ROUTE 38 43045 349-3731
Stephen Weller, supt.
Fairbanks HS 2-00011
11158 STATE ROUTE 38 43045 349-3721
Edward Pleasant, prin.
Fairbanks MS 2-01100
11158 STATE ROUTE 38 43045 349-6841
Debora Binkley, prin.

Millbury, AC 419, PC 4, Wood
Lake Local SD, PO BOX 151 43447 4-11111
Robert Walter, supt. 836-2552
Lake HS, 28080 LEMOYNE RD 43447 3-00011
James Ingham, prin. 838-6645
Lake JHS, 28100 LEMOYNE RD 43447 2-00100
Carl Brubaker, prin. 838-6395

Miller City, AC 419, PC 2, Putnam
Miller City-New Cleveland Local SD 3-11111
PO BOX 38 45864 876-3172
William Kreinbrink, supt.
JSHS, PO BOX 38 45864 2-00111
Kevin McGlaughlin, prin. 876-3173

Millersburg, AC 216, PC 5, Holmes
West Holmes Local SD — 5-11111
10901 STATE ROUTE 39 44654 — 674-3546
Dean Werstler, supt.
West Holmes HS — 3-00011
10901 STATE ROUTE 39 44654 — 674-6085
Gary Gehm, prin.
West Holmes MS — 2-00100
430 E JACKSON ST 44654 — 674-4761
Roger Saurer, prin.

Millersport, AC 614, PC 4, Fairfield
Walnut Township Local SD — 3-11111
PO BOX 278 43046 — 467-2802
Howard Martin, supt.
JSHS, PO BOX 278 43046 — 2-00111
(—), prin. — 467-2929

Mineral Ridge, AC 216, PC 4, Trumbull
Weathersfield Local SD — 4-11111
3750 MAIN ST 44440 — 652-0287
Richard Murray, supt.
HS, 1334 SEABORN ST 44440 — 2-00011
Thomas Laskovac, prin. — 652-1451
MS, 3750 MAIN ST 44440 — 2-01100
Richard Dell, prin. — 652-2120

Minerva, AC 216, PC 5, Stark
Minerva Local SD — 5-11111
303 LATZER AVE 44657 – (—), supt. — 868-4332
HS, 501 ALMEDA AVE 44657 — 3-00011
John Bair, prin. — 868-4134
Hazen MS, 401 N MARKET ST 44657 — 3-00100
Richard Mikes, prin. — 868-4497

Minford, AC 614, PC 3, Scioto
Minford Local SD, PO BOX 204 45653 — 4-11111
Dennis Meade, supt. — 820-3896
HS, PO BOX 204 45653 — 2-00011
Robert Shaffer, prin. — 820-3445
MS, PO BOX 204 45653 — 3-01100
Jerry Ruark, prin. — 820-2181

Mingo Junction, AC 614, PC 5, Jefferson
Indian Creek Local SD — 5-11111
707 WILSON AVE 43938 — 282-3671
Victor Cardenzana, supt.
Indian Creek MS — 2-01100
110 STEUBEN ST 43938 — 535-0043
Stanley Harasick, prin.
Other Schools – See Wintersville

Minster, AC 419, PC 5, Auglaize
Minster Local SD, 100 E 7TH ST 45865 — 3-11111
Halver Belcher, supt. — 628-3397
HS, 100 E 7TH ST 45865 — 2-00011
Larry Smith, prin. — 628-2324

Mogadore, AC 216, PC 5, Summit
Field Local SD, 1473 SAXE RD 44260 — 4-11111
Thomas Shoup, supt. — 673-2659
Field SHS — 3-00001
2900 STATE ROUTE 43 44260 — 673-9591
John Evans, prin.
Field JHS, 1379 SAXE RD 44260 — 3-00110
Gino Calcie, prin. — 673-4176

Mogadore Local SD — 3-11111
144 S CLEVELAND AVE 44260 — 628-9946
Clement Yaskowitz, supt.
JSHS, 130 S CLEVELAND AVE 44260 — 2-00111
James Montaquila, prin. — 628-9943

Monroe, AC 513, PC 5, Warren
Middletown CSD
Supt. — See Middletown
Lemon-Monroe HS, 101 W ELM ST 45050 — 3-00011
William Heflin, prin. — 539-8471

Monroeville, AC 419, PC 4, Huron
Monroeville Local SD — 3-11111
101 WEST ST 44847 — 465-2610
William Pahl, supt.
JSHS, 101 WEST ST 44847 — 2-00111
Harry Lombard, prin. — 465-2531

Montpelier, AC 419, PC 5, Williams
Montpelier EVD, 110 N EAST AVE 43543 — 4-11111
John Kaylor, supt. — 485-3676
HS, 309 E MAIN ST 43543 — 2-00011
David Ruhe, prin. — 485-3186
Superior MS, RR 3 43543 — 3-01100
Aloysius Marcinek, prin. — 485-5546

Morral, AC 614, PC 2, Marion
Ridgedale Local SD — 4-11111
3105 HILLMAN FORD RD 43337 — 382-6065
Gary Troll, supt.
Ridgedale JSHS — 2-00111
3165 HILLMAN FORD RD 43337 — 383-2168
Thomas Crowe, prin.

Morrow, AC 513, PC 4, Warren
Little Miami Local SD — 4-11111
5819 MORROW ROSSBURG RD 45152 — 899-2264
Fred Williams, supt.
Little Miami HS, 605 WELCH RD 45152 — 2-00011
David Janson, prin. — 899-3781
Little Miami JHS, 605 WELCH RD 45152 — 2-00100
Barry Schaad, prin. — 899-3408

Mount Blanchard, AC 419, PC 2, Hancock
Riverdale Local SD — 4-11111
20613 STATE ROUTE 37 45867 — 694-4994
John Roettger, supt.

Riverdale JSHS — 2-00111
20613 STATE ROUTE 37 45867 — 694-2211
John Dunn, prin.
Other Schools – See Wharton

Mount Gilead, AC 419, PC 5, Morrow
Mt. Gilead EVD, PO BOX 239 43338 — 4-11111
Hartsell Dodrill, supt. — 946-1646
HS, 338 W PARK AVE 43338 — 2-00011
Steven Selvey, prin. — 947-6065
JHS, 145 N CHERRY ST 43338 — 2-00100
R. Steven Selvey, prin. — 946-6511

Mount Orab, AC 513, PC 4, Brown
Western Brown Local SD — 5-11111
211 S HIGH ST 45154 — 444-2044
James Rosendahl, supt.
Western Brown HS — 3-00011
PO BOX 386 45154 — 444-2544
Denver Jackson, prin.

Mount Vernon, AC 614, PC 7, Knox
Knox County JVSD — 3-00001
306 MARTINSBURG RD 43050 — 397-5820
Ray Richardson, supt.
Knox County Joint Vocational SHS — 3-00001
306 MARTINSBURG RD 43050 — 397-5820
Rick Hornick, prin.

Mt. Vernon CSD — 5-11111
302 MARTINSBURG RD 43050 — 397-7422
Jeffrey Sittason, supt.
HS, 304 MARTINSBURG RD 43050 — 4-00011
John Crecelius, prin. — 397-7422
MS, 301 N MULBERRY ST 43050 — 3-00100
Jeffrey Kuntz, prin. — 397-7422

Mt. Vernon Academy — 2-00011
PO BOX 311 43050 — 397-5411
Steve Davis, prin.
Mt. Vernon Nazarene College — 4-UC
800 MARTINSBURG RD 43050 — 397-1244

Mount Victory, AC 513, PC 3, Hardin
Ridgemont Local SD — 3-11111
PO BOX 8 43340 — 354-2441
Cheryl Grimm, supt.
Other Schools – See Ridgeway

Mowrystown, AC 513, PC 2, Highland
Bright Local SD, PO BOX 9 45155 — 3-11111
James Evilsizer, supt. — 442-3114
Whiteoak JSHS, PO BOX 297 45155 — 2-00111
John Butler, prin. — 442-2241

Munroe Falls, AC 216, PC 6, Summit
Stow CSD
Supt. — See Stow
Kimpton MS, 380 N RIVER RD 44262 — 3-00100
John Schwartzhoff, prin. — 688-6461

Napoleon, AC 419, PC 6, Henry
Napoleon CSD — 5-11111
701 BRIARHEATH DR 43545 — 599-7015
Michael Russell, supt.
HS, 701 BRIARHEATH DR 43545 — 3-00011
Larry Long, prin. — 599-1050
Central MS, 303 W MAIN ST 43545 — 3-00100
Thomas Condit, prin. — 592-6991

Navarre, AC 216, PC 4, Stark
Fairless Local SD — 4-11111
11885 NAVARRE RD SW 44662 — 767-3444
Gary Stamm, supt.
Fairless JSHS — 3-00111
11885 NAVARRE RD SW 44662 — 767-3444
Howard Scheetz, prin.

Nelsonville, AC 614, PC 5, Athens
Nelsonville-York CSD — 4-11111
1 BUCKEYE DR 45764 — 753-1964
Jack Hillyer, supt.
Nelsonville-York HS — 2-00011
1 BUCKEYE DR 45764 — 753-1964
Richard Rogers, prin.
Nelsonville-York MS — 2-00100
189 FAYETTE ST 45764 — 753-1254
John Anderson, prin.

Tri County JVSD — 3-00011
15676 STATE ROUTE 691 45764 — 753-3511
Ronald Smith, supt.
Tri County Joint Vocational HS — 3-00011
15676 STATE ROUTE 691 45764 — 753-3511
Carmen Lorubbio, prin.

Hocking College — 5-CC
3301 HOCKING PKY 45764 — 753-3591

New Albany, AC 614, PC 4, Franklin
Plain Local SD — 3-11111
6425 NEW ALBANY CONDIT RD 43054 — 855-2040
Ralph Johnson, supt.
HS — 2-00011
6425 NEW ALBANY CONDIT RD 43054 — 855-7331
Paul King, prin.
MS — 2-00100
6425 NEW ALBANY CONDIT RD 43054 — 855-2030
Linda Martin, prin.

Newark, AC 614, PC 8, Licking
Licking County JVSD — 3-00001
150 PRICE RD 43055 — 366-3351
William Mann, supt.

Licking County Joint Vocational SHS — 3-00001
150 PRICE RD 43055 — 366-3351
David Cisler, prin.

Licking Valley Local SD — 4-11111
1379 LICKING VALLEY RD NE 43055 — 763-3525
Donald Urban, supt.
Licking Valley HS — 3-00011
1379 LICKING VALLEY RD NE 43055 — 763-3721
Daniel Montgomery, prin.
Licking Valley MS — 2-00100
1379 LICKING VALLEY RD NE 43055 — 763-3396
Robert Tharp, prin.

Newark CSD, 85 E MAIN ST 43055 — 6-11111
Leslie Johnson, supt. — 345-9891
HS, 314 GRANVILLE ST 43055 — 4-00011
Ronald Wheeler, prin. — 345-9831
Lincoln MS, 471 E MAIN ST 43055 — 3-00100
Judy Mullins, prin. — 345-4440
Roosevelt MS — 3-00100
621 MOUNT VERNON RD 43055 — 349-2320
Stanley Kaiser, prin.
Wilson MS, 805 W CHURCH ST 43055 — 3-00100
Raymond Kress, prin. — 349-2315

Central Ohio Technical College — 4-CC
UNIVERSITY DR 43055 — 366-1351
Newark Catholic HS — 2-00111
1 GREEN WAVE DR 43055 — 344-3594
Carol Hatem, prin.
Ohio State University-Newark — 3-UC
1179 UNIVERSITY DR 43055 — 366-3321

New Boston, AC 614, PC 5, Scioto
New Boston Local SD — 3-11111
522 GLENWOOD AVE 45662 — 456-4626
Lowell Howard, supt.
Glenwood JSHS — 2-00111
522 GLENWOOD AVE 45662 — 456-4559
Jerry Bentley, prin.

Southeastern Business College — 2-CS
3879 RHODES AVE 45662 — 456-4124

New Bremen, AC 419, PC 5, Auglaize
New Bremen Local SD — 3-11111
202 S WALNUT ST 45869 — 629-2373
James Roeth, supt.
JSHS, 202 S WALNUT ST 45869 — 2-00111
Frank Borchers, prin. — 629-2373

Newbury, AC 216, PC 2, Geauga
Newbury Local SD — 3-11111
14775 AUBURN RD 44065 — 564-5501
Edward Armon, supt.
JSHS, 14775 AUBURN RD 44065 — 2-00111
Marilyn Foote, prin. — 564-2281

New Carlisle, AC 513, PC 6, Clark
Tecumseh Local SD — 5-11111
9760 W NATIONAL RD 45344 — 845-3576
Boyd Marcum, supt.
Tecumseh HS — 4-00011
9830 W NATIONAL RD 45344 — 845-4500
Jack Poore, prin.
MS, 1203 KENNISON AVE 45344 — 2-00100
Margaret McAtee, prin. — 845-4460
Olive Branch MS — 2-00100
9712 W NATIONAL RD 45344 — 845-4465
David Campbell, prin.

Newcomerstown, AC 614, PC 5, Tuscarawas
Newcomerstown EVD — 4-11111
702 S RIVER ST 43832 — 498-8373
David Branch, supt.
HS, 659 BEAVER ST 43832 — 2-00011
Robert Glazier, prin. — 498-5111
MS, 325 W STATE ST 43832 — 2-00100
Cathy McCrea, prin. — 498-8151

New Concord, AC 614, PC 4, Muskingum
East Muskingum Local SD — 4-11111
13505 JOHN GLENN SCHOOL RD 43762 — 826-7655
James Mahoney, supt.
Glenn HS — 3-00011
13115 JOHN GLENN SCHOOL RD 43762 — 826-7641
Gary Lucas, prin.
East Muskingum MS — 3-01100
13125 JOHN GLENN SCHOOL RD 43762 — 826-7631
John Hazard, prin.

Muskingum College — 4-UC
147 CENTER ST 43762 — 826-8115

New Knoxville, AC 419, PC 3, Auglaize
New Knoxville Local SD — 2-11111
345 S MAIN ST 45871 — 753-2431
Martin Fanning, supt.
HS, 345 S MAIN ST 45871 — 2-00011
Steve Castle, prin. — 753-2431

New Lebanon, AC 513, PC 5, Montgomery
New Lebanon Local SD — 4-11111
1105 W MAIN ST 45345 — 687-1301
Michael Virelli, supt.
Dixie HS, 200 S FULS RD 45345 — 2-00011
Tim Barrett, prin. — 687-1366
MS, 1100 W MAIN ST 45345 — 2-01100
Thomas Geglein, prin. — 687-3508

New Lexington, AC 614, PC 6, Perry
New Lexington CSD, 310 1ST ST 43764 — 4-11111
Clyde Metz, supt. — 342-4133

HS, 2549 PANTHER DR NE 43764   3-00011
James Leckrone, prin.   342-3528
MS, 2550 PANTHER DR NE 43764   3-00100
Dennis Love, prin.   342-4128

New London, AC 419, PC 5, Huron
New London Local SD   4-11111
100 E MAIN ST 44851   929-8433
Stephen Schumm, supt.
JSHS, 17 PARK AVE 44851   3-00011
James Vansickle, prin.   929-1586

New Madison, AC 513, PC 3, Darke
Tri-Village Local SD   3-11111
PO BOX 31 45346   996-6261
John Montgomery, supt.
Tri-Village JSHS, PO BOX 31 45346   2-00011
Bonnie Coe, prin.   996-1511

New Matamoras, AC 614, PC 4, Washington
Frontier Local SD, PO BOX 134 45767   4-11111
John Hoff, supt.   865-3473
Frontier HS, PO BOX 134 45767   2-00011
Mike Romick, prin.   865-3441

New Middletown, AC 216, PC 4, Mahoning
Springfield Local SD, PO BOX AK 44442   4-11111
Gerald Kotchmar, supt.   542-2929
Springfield HS   2-00011
11335 YNGSTWN PITTSBURGH RD 44442
Thomas Davis, prin.   542-3626
Springfield IS   2-01100
11333 YNGSTWN PITTSBURGH RD 44442
Nick Visingardi, prin.   542-3624

New Paris, AC 513, PC 4, Preble
C. R. Coblentz Local SD   4-11111
115 N SPRING ST 45347   437-0331
James Williams, supt.
National Trail HS   2-00011
6940 OXFORD GETTYSBURG RD 45347
Kern Carpenter, prin.   437-2061
Other Schools – See West Manchester

New Philadelphia, AC 216, PC 7, Tuscarawas
Buckeye JVSD   3-00001
545 UNIVERSITY DR NE 44663   339-2288
C. Fries, supt.
Buckeye Joint Vocational SHS   3-00001
545 UNIVERSITY DR NE 44663   339-2288
Linda Earley, prin.

New Philadelphia CSD   5-11111
303 4TH ST NW 44663   364-0600
Hank Smith, supt.
HS, 343 RAY AVE NW 44663   4-00011
Michael Herchik, prin.   364-0644
Welty MS, 315 4TH ST NW 44663   3-00100
Joseph Williams, prin.   364-0645

Central Catholic HS   2-00011
777 3RD ST NE 44663   343-3302
Paul Sullivan, prin.
Kent State University   2-CC
UNIVERSITY DR NE 44663   339-3391

New Richmond, AC 513, PC 4, Clermont
New Richmond EVD   5-11111
1139 BETHEL NEW RICHMOND RD 45157
Larry Graves, supt.   553-2616
HS   3-00011
1131 BETHEL NEW RICHMOND RD 45157
R. Kirk Hamilton, prin.   553-3191
MS   2-00100
1135 BETHEL NEW RICHMOND RD 45157
Michael Kelly, prin.   553-3161

New Riegel, AC 419, PC 2, Seneca
New Riegel Local SD   2-11111
PO BOX 157 44853   595-2265
Robert Brickner, supt.
JSHS, PO BOX 157 44853   2-00111
Richard Gross, prin.   595-2256

Newton Falls, AC 216, PC 5, Trumbull
Newton Falls EVD   4-11111
909 1/2 MILTON BLVD 44444   872-5445
Gary Kriston, supt.
HS, 907 MILTON BLVD 44444   3-00011
Phillip Clacko, prin.   872-5121
JHS, 907 1/2 MILTON BLVD 44444   2-00100
Richard Hura, prin.   872-0905

New Washington, AC 419, PC 4, Crawford
Buckeye Central Local SD   3-11111
PO BOX 368 44854   492-2864
Chris Boyd, supt.
Buckeye Central JSHS   2-00111
PO BOX 368 44854   492-2266
Chris Boyd, prin.

Niles, AC 216, PC 7, Trumbull
Niles CSD, 345 WARREN AVE 44446   5-11111
John Bruno, supt.   652-2509
McKinley HS, 616 DRAGON DR 44446   3-00011
Michael Lastic, prin.   652-9968
Edison JHS, 36 W CHURCH ST 44446   2-00100
Barbara Weaver, prin.   652-5656

ETI Technical College   3-CC
2076 YOUNGSTOWN WARREN RD 44446
   652-9919

North Baltimore, AC 419, PC 5, Wood
North Baltimore Local SD   3-11111
110 S 2ND ST 45872   257-3531
Donald King, supt.
HS, 124 S 2ND ST 45872   2-00011
Robert Reublin, prin.   257-3464
MS, 124 S 2ND ST 45872   2-00100
Robert Reublin, prin.   257-3464

North Bend, AC 513, PC 3, Hamilton
Three Rivers Local SD
Supt. — See Cleves
Taylor HS, 36 HARRISON AVE 45052   3-00011
Marshall Brumback, prin.   941-2510

North Bloomfield, AC 216, PC 3, Trumbull
Bloomfield-Mespo Local SD   2-11111
2077 PARK WEST RD 44450   685-4711
Manlius Fults, supt.
Bloomfield HS   2-00011
2077 PARK WEST RD 44450   685-4711
Robert Rostan, prin.
Bloomfield MS   2-00100
2077 PARK WEST RD 44450   685-4711
Robert Rostan, prin.

North Canton, AC 216, PC 7, Stark
North Canton CSD, 525 7TH ST NE 44720   5-11111
Robert Roden, supt.   497-5600
Hoover HS   4-00011
605 FAIR OAKS AVE SW 44720   497-5620
T. Isue, prin.
MS, 200 CHARLOTTE ST NW 44720   3-00100
Mario Mattachione, prin.   497-5635

Plain Local SD
Supt. — See Canton
Glenoak HS   4-00011
2300 SCHNEIDER ST NE 44721   492-7455
Jacqueline Riegner, prin.
Middlebranch MS   3-00100
7500 MIDDLEBRANCH AVE NE 44721   493-5525
Thomas Kauth, prin.

ETI Technical College   2-CC
1320 W MAPLE ST 44720   494-1214

Northfield, AC 216, PC 5, Summit
Nordonia Hills CSD   5-11111
9370 OLDE 8 RD 44067   467-0580
Paul Pendleton, supt.
Nordonia MS, 73 LEONARD AVE 44067   3-00100
Wayne Greene, prin.   467-0580
Other Schools – See Macedonia

North Jackson, AC 216, PC 3, Mahoning
Jackson-Milton Local SD   4-11111
14110 MAHONING AVE 44451   538-3232
James Infante, supt.
Jackson-Milton JSHS   3-00111
10748 MAHONING AVE 44451   538-3308
J. Smik, prin.

North Lewisburg, AC 513, PC 4, Champaign
Triad Local SD   3-11111
7920 BRUSH LAKE RD 43060   826-4961
Albert Shelton, supt.
Triad JSHS   2-00111
7941 BRUSH LAKE RD 43060   826-3771
Daniel Kaffenbarger, prin.

North Lima, AC 216, PC 3, Mahoning
South Range Local SD   4-01111
11836 SOUTH AVE 44452   549-5226
James Hall, supt.
South Range HS   2-00011
11836 SOUTH AVE 44452   549-2163
Donald Bobovnik, prin.
Other Schools – See Greenford

North Olmsted, AC 216, PC 8, Cuyahoga
North Olmsted CSD   6-11111
24100 PALM DR 44070   779-3548
Rick Fenton, supt.
HS, 5755 BURNS RD 44070   4-00011
Douglas Fagan, prin.   777-7700
MS   4-00100
27351 BUTTERNUT RIDGE RD 44070   777-7700
William Burkhardt, prin.

North Ridgeville, AC 216, PC 7, Lorain
North Ridgeville CSD   5-11111
5490 MILLS CREEK LN 44039   327-4444
James Levero, supt.
SHS, 7000 PITTS BLVD 44039   3-00001
David Livingston, prin.   327-4444
JHS, 35895 CENTER RIDGE RD 44039   3-00110
Philip Binkley, prin.   327-4444

Lake Ridge Academy   2-11111
37501 CENTER RIDGE RD 44039   327-1175
Joseph Ferber, prin.

North Robinson, AC 419, PC 2, Crawford
Colonel Crawford Local SD   4-11111
STATE ROUTE 602 44856   562-4666
William Ferrell, supt.
Crawford HS   2-00011
STATE ROUTE 602 44856   562-4666
James Hudson, prin.
Crawford IS   2-00100
STATE ROUTE 602 44856   562-3503
Ted Bruner, prin.

North Royalton, AC 216, PC 7, Cuyahoga
North Royalton CSD   5-11111
6579 ROYALTON RD 44133   237-8800
Albert Vasek, supt.
HS, 14713 RIDGE RD 44133   4-00011
Charles Gibson, prin.   237-8800
MS, 14725 RIDGE RD 44133   3-00100
Diane Kee, prin.   237-8800

Northwood, AC 419, PC 6, Wood
Northwood Local SD   4-11111
600 LEMOYNE RD 43619   691-3888
Michael Carmean, supt.
HS, 700 LEMOYNE RD 43619   2-00011
Jeff Szabo, prin.   691-4651
MS, 500 LEMOYNE RD 43619   2-00100
Phil Eaton, prin.   691-4621

Norton, AC 216, PC 7, Summit
Norton CSD   4-11111
4128 CLEVELAND MASSILLON RD 44203
James Gides, supt.   825-0863
HS   3-00011
4108 CLEVELAND MASSILLON RD 44203
Thomas Smicklas, prin.   825-7300
MS   3-00100
3390 CLEVELAND MASSILLON RD 44203
Bruce Kumer, prin.   825-5607

Norwalk, AC 419, PC 7, Huron
Norwalk CSD, 134 BENEDICT AVE 44857   5-11111
Virginia Poling, supt.   668-2779
HS, 80 E MAIN ST 44857   3-00011
Charles Bertschman, prin.   668-2079
MS, 64 CHRISTIE AVE 44857   3-00100
Stephen Cillo, prin.   668-8370

St. Paul HS, 93 E MAIN ST 44857   2-00011
Dennis Doughty, prin.   668-3005

Norwood, AC 513, PC 7, Hamilton
Norwood CSD   5-11111
2132 WILLIAMS AVE 45212   396-5521
James Ballinger, supt.
HS, 2020 SHERMAN AVE 45212   3-00011
David Griffel, prin.   396-5560
MS, 2060 SHERMAN AVE 45212   3-00100
Douglas King, prin.   396-5538

Nova, AC 419, PC 2, Ashland
Mapleton Local SD
Supt. — See Ashland
Mapleton HS, PO BOX 37 44859   2-01100
John Neighbor, prin.   652-3540

Oak Harbor, AC 419, PC 5, Ottawa
Benton Carroll Salem Local SD   4-11111
11685 W STATE ROUTE 163 43449   898-6210
Terry Clark, supt.
HS   3-00011
11661 W STATE ROUTE 163 43449   898-6216
Richard Thorbahn, prin.
MS, 315 N CHURCH ST 43449   3-00100
Daniel Kaylo, prin.   898-6217

Oak Hill, AC 614, PC 4, Jackson
Oak Hill Union Local SD   4-11111
265 W CROSS ST 45656   682-7595
Howard Smith, supt.
JSHS, 205 WESTERN AVE 45656   3-00111
William Haines, prin.   682-7055

Oberlin, AC 216, PC 6, Lorain
Firelands Local SD   4-11111
11970 VERMILION RD 44074   965-5821
Finn Laursen, supt.
Firelands HS   3-00011
10643 VERMILION RD 44074   965-5351
Paul Haeuptle, prin.
Other Schools – See South Amherst

Lorain County JVSD   4-00001
15181 STATE ROUTE 58 44074   774-1051
William Ruth, supt.
Burton Vocational Center HS   4-00001
15181 STATE ROUTE 58 44074   774-1051
Diane Checkelhoff, prin.

Oberlin CSD   4-11111
218 N PLEASANT ST 44074   774-1458
(—), supt.
HS, 281 N PLEASANT ST 44074   2-00011
Fredrick Holland, prin.   774-1295
Langston MS   2-00100
150 N PLEASANT ST 44074   775-7961
Larry Thomas, prin.

Oberlin College   5-UC
135 W LORAIN ST 44074   775-8400

Old Fort, AC 419, PC 2, Seneca
Old Fort Local SD   3-11111
7635 N COUNTY ROAD 51 44861   992-4291
James Meeker, supt.
JSHS   2-00111
7635 N COUNTY ROAD 51 44861   992-4291
Daniel Colvin, prin.

Old Washington, AC 614, PC 2, Guernsey
East Guernsey Local SD   4-11111
PO BOX 128 43768   489-5190
Clint Born, supt.
Buckeye Trail HS, PO BOX 128 43768   2-00011
John Alleman, prin.   489-5005

Olmsted Falls, AC 216, PC 6, Cuyahoga
Olmsted Falls CSD 5-11111
PO BOX 38010 44138 243-4050
Robert Kreiner, supt.
HS, 26939 BAGLEY RD 44138 3-00011
Gregory Ludwig, prin. 235-1200
MS, 26184 BAGLEY RD 44138 3-00100
Charles Murphy, prin. 235-8400

Oregon, AC 419, PC 7, Lucas
Oregon CSD, 5721 SEAMAN ST 43616 5-11111
Robert Pfefferle, supt. 693-0661
Clay HS, 5665 SEAMAN ST 43616 4-00011
William Lindeman, prin. 693-0665
Eisenhower MS 3-00100
331 N CURTICE RD N 43618 836-8498
Arthur Prince, prin.
Fassett MS, 3025 STARR AVE 43616 2-00100
Dean Ensey, prin. 693-0455

Cardinal Stritch HS 2-00011
3225 PICKLE RD 43616 693-0466
Fr. Yeager, prin.
St. Charles Hospital HSP
2600 NAVARRE AVE 43616 698-7341

Orrville, AC 216, PC 6, Wayne
Orrville CSD, 815 N ELLA ST 44667 5-11111
Richard Thomas, supt. 682-4651
HS, 841 N ELLA ST 44667 3-00011
Robert Sickman, prin. 682-4661
JHS, 217 E CHURCH ST 44667 2-00100
James Curtis, prin. 682-1791

University of Akron-Wayne College 3-CC
1901 SMUCKER RD 44667 683-2010

Orwell, AC 216, PC 4, Ashtabula
Grand Valley Local SD 4-11111
7527 STATE ROUTE 45 44076 437-6570
Hiram Lynch, supt.
Grand Valley HS 2-00011
44 N SCHOOL ST 44076 437-6260
Richard Cooper, prin.

Ottawa, AC 419, PC 5, Putnam
Ottawa-Glandorf Local SD 4-11111
360 N LOCUST ST 45875 523-5261
Michael Ruhe, supt.
Ottawa-Glandorf HS 3-00011
630 GLENDALE AVE 45875 523-5702
John Cunningham, prin.

Ottoville, AC 419, PC 3, Putnam
Ottoville Local SD 3-11111
PO BOX 248 45876 453-3356
Rusty MacDonald, supt.
JSHS, PO BOX 248 45876 2-00111
Wilbur Altenburger, prin. 453-3358

Oxford, AC 513, PC 7, Butler
Talawanda CSD 5-11111
131 W CHESTNUT ST 45056 523-4716
Dennis Leone, supt.
Talawanda HS 4-00011
101 W CHESTNUT ST 45056 523-4137
Rob Walker, prin.
Talawanda MS 3-00100
4030 OXFORD REILY RD 45056 523-1989
Philip Cagwin, prin.

Miami University 7-UC
E HIGH ST 45056 529-2345

Painesville, AC 216, PC 7, Lake
Auburn JVSD, 8140 AUBURN RD 44077 2-00001
Peter Oberson, supt. 357-7542
Auburn Career Ctr Joint Vocational SHS 2-00001
8140 AUBURN RD 44077 357-7542
Peter Oberson, prin.

Painesville City Local SD 5-11111
58 JEFFERSON ST 44077 639-7000
Fritz Overs, supt.
Harvey HS 3-00011
167 W WASHINGTON ST 44077 639-7020
Donald Ehas, prin.
Hobart JSHS, 200 W WALNUT ST 44077 3-00111
Brent McGarvey, prin. 639-7040

Painesville Township Local SD 5-11111
585 RIVERSIDE DR 44077 352-0668
Barry Morrison, supt.
Riverside SHS, 585 RIVERSIDE DR 44077 3-00001
John Weiss, prin. 352-3341
Williams JHS, 625 RIVERSIDE DR 44077 3-00110
Richard Hronek, prin. 352-3345

Lake Erie College 3-UC
391 W WASHINGTON ST 44077 352-3361

Pandora, AC 419, PC 4, Putnam
Pandora-Gilboa Local SD 3-11111
N JEFFERSON ST 45877 384-3227
Ray Graves, supt.
Pandora-Gilboa HS 2-00011
N JEFFERSON ST 45877 384-3225
Mark Stall, prin.
Other Schools – See Gilboa

Parma, AC 216, PC 8, Cuyahoga
Parma CSD, 6726 RIDGE RD 44129 7-11111
Carl Hilling, supt. 842-5300
Normandy HS 4-00011
2500 W PLEASANT VALLEY RD 44134 885-2400
James Kubinski, prin.
HS, 6285 W 54TH ST 44129 4-00011
Patricia Raiff, prin. 885-2300
Greenbriar JHS 3-00100
11810 HUFFMAN RD 44130 885-2370
Ronald Sterle, prin.
Shiloh MS 3-00100
2303 GRANTWOOD DR 44134 351-2376
Joseph Kornick, prin.
Other Schools – See Parma Heights, Seven Hills

Padua Franciscan HS 3-00011
6740 STATE RD 44134 845-2444
Timothy Guilivo, prin.
Southwest Christian S 2-11111
5983 W 54TH ST 44129 845-8840
Carol Bost, prin.

Parma Heights, AC 216, PC 7, Cuyahoga
Parma CSD
Supt. — See Parma
Valley Forge HS 4-00011
9999 INDEPENDENCE BLVD 44130 885-2330
John Roberts, prin.

Cuyahoga Community College 5-CC
11000 W PLEASANT VALLEY RD 44130
842-7773
Holy Name HS 4-00011
6000 QUEENS HWY 44130 886-0300
Eugene Krakowiak, prin.
Total Technical Institute 3-CS
6500 PEARL RD STE 45 44130 843-2323

Pataskala, AC 614, PC 5, Licking
Southwest Licking Local SD
Supt. — See Kirkersville
Watkins Memorial HS 3-00011
8868 WATKINS RD SW 43062 927-3846
W. McKinley, prin.
Watkins MS 3-00100
8808 WATKINS RD SW 43062 927-5767
Harry Gardner, prin.

Paulding, AC 419, PC 5, Paulding
Paulding EVD, 405 N WATER ST 45879 4-11111
Stanley Searing, supt. 399-4656
HS, 405 N WATER ST 45879 3-00011
Don DeWitt, prin. 399-4656
MS, 405 N WATER ST 45879 2-00100
Jack Griner, prin. 399-4656

Payne, AC 419, PC 4, Paulding
Wayne Trace Local SD 4-11111
501 W TOWNLINE ST 45880 263-2415
Steven Keller, supt.
Other Schools – See Haviland

Peebles, AC 513, PC 4, Adams
Adams County/Ohio Valley SD
Supt. — See West Union
JSHS, PO BOX 307 45660 3-00111
Michael McFarland, prin. 587-2681

Pemberville, AC 419, PC 4, Wood
Eastwood Local SD 4-11111
4800 SUGAR RIDGE RD 43450 833-6411
Frederick Schnoor, supt.
Eastwood HS 3-00011
4900 SUGAR RIDGE RD 43450 833-3611
James Jerdonek, prin.
Eastwood MS 2-00100
4800 SUGAR RIDGE RD 43450 833-6011
Susan Wynn, prin.

Peninsula, AC 216, PC 3, Summit
Woodridge Local SD
Supt. — See Cuyahoga Falls
Woodridge HS, 4440 QUICK RD 44264 2-00011
David MacRaild, prin. 929-3191
Woodridge MS 2-01100
1930 BRONSON AVE 44264 657-2351
David Harris, prin.

Perry, AC 216, PC 4, Lake
Perry Local SD, 3961 MAIN ST 44081 4-11111
Charles Howard, supt. 259-3881
HS, 4261 MANCHESTER AVE 44081 3-00011
Robert Geisler, prin. 259-3511
MS, 4261 MANCHESTER AVE 44081 2-00100
Douglas Jenkins, prin. 259-3026

Perrysburg, AC 419, PC 7, Wood
Penta County JVSD 5-00011
30095 OREGON RD 43551 666-1120
Louise Fought, supt.
Penta County Joint Vocational SHS 4-00001
30095 OREGON RD 43551 666-1120
James Pease, prin.
Penta Skill Center Joint Vocational SHS 4-00011
30095 OREGON RD 43551 666-1120
Charles Gibbons, prin.

Perrysburg EVD 5-11111
140 E INDIANA AVE 43551 874-9131
Ronald Eaton, supt.
HS, 550 E SOUTH BOUNDARY ST 43551 4-00011
Robert Phillips, prin. 874-3181
JHS, 140 E INDIANA AVE 43551 3-00100
T. Waltzer, prin. 874-9193

Perrysville, AC 419, PC 3, Ashland
Loudonville-Perrysville EVD
Supt. — See Loudonville
JHS, 155 W 3RD ST 44864 2-00100
Steve Brown, prin. 938-7193

Pettisville, AC 419, PC 3, Fulton
Pettisville Local SD, PO BOX 1 43553 2-11111
Stephen Switzer, supt. 446-2705
JSHS, PO BOX 1 43553 2-00111
Stephen Brannan, prin. 446-2705

Philo, AC 614, PC 3, Muskingum
Franklin Local SD
Supt. — See Duncan Falls
HS, 200 BROAD ST 43771 3-00011
Kenneth Budd, prin. 674-4355

Pickerington, AC 614, PC 6, Fairfield
Pickerington Local SD 5-11111
777 LONG RD 43147 833-2110
Daniel Ross, supt.
HS, 300 OPPORTUNITY WAY 43147 4-00011
James Reed, prin. 833-3025
JHS, 130 HILL RD S 43147 3-00100
Jim Barry, prin. 833-2100

Piketon, AC 614, PC 4, Pike
Pike County Area JVSD 2-00011
PO BOX 577 45661 289-2721
Larry Meredith, supt.
Riffe Joint Vocational SHS 2-00011
PO BOX 577 45661 289-2721
David Buckwalter, prin.

Scioto Valley Local SD 4-11111
PO BOX 600 45661 289-4456
Ernest Hamilton, supt.
HS, PO BOX 488 45661 3-00011
Keith Willson, prin. 289-2254
JHS, 2379 SCHUSTER RD 45661 2-00100
Steve McCann, prin. 289-2871

Western Local SD 3-11111
12599 STATE ROUTE 124 45661 493-3113
Joseph Morrison, supt.
Other Schools – See Latham

Pioneer, AC 419, PC 4, Williams
North Central Local SD 3-11111
201 WYANDOT ST 43554 737-2392
Charles Tank, supt.
North Central HS 2-00011
400 BAUBICE ST 43554 737-2366
Brion Deitsch, prin.
Other Schools – See Kunkle

Piqua, AC 513, PC 7, Miami
Piqua CSD, 316 N COLLEGE ST 45356 5-11111
Jerry Clark, supt. 773-4321
HS, 1 INDIAN TRL 45356 4-00011
Glenn Honeycutt, prin. 773-6314
Bennett JHS, 625 S MAIN ST 45356 2-00100
Robert Luby, prin. 773-0386
Wilder MS, 1120 NICKLIN AVE 45356 2-00100
Ted Bayat, prin. 773-2017

Upper Valley JVSD 3-00001
8811 CAREER DR 45356 778-1980
James Stickley, supt.
Upper Valley Joint Vocational SHS 3-00001
8811 CAREER DR 45356 778-1980
Larry Householder, prin.

Edison State Community College 4-CC
1973 EDISON DR 45356 778-8600

Pitsburg, AC 513, PC 2, Darke
Franklin-Monroe Local SD 3-11111
PO BOX 78 45358 692-8637
David Gray, supt.
Franklin-Monroe JSHS 2-00111
PO BOX 78 45358 692-8761
Neal Hans, prin.

Plain City, AC 614, PC 4, Madison
Central Ohio JVSD 2-00001
7877 US HIGHWAY 42 NE 43064 873-4666
Brian O'Mara, supt.
Tolles Technical Center Joint Voc. SHS 2-00001
7877 US HIGHWAY 42 S 43064 873-4666
Tony Sherry, prin.

Jonathan Alder Local SD 4-11111
6440 KILBURY HUBER RD 43064 873-5621
Douglas Carpenter, supt.
Alder HS 2-00011
6440 KILBURY HUBER RD 43064 873-4642
Phillip Harris, prin.
ES, 340 W MAIN ST 43064 2-10100
Victoria Kilbury, prin. 873-4609

Pleasant Hill, AC 513, PC 4, Miami
Newton Local SD, PO BOX 68 45359 3-11111
Shelby Warren, supt. 676-3271
Newton JSHS, PO BOX 68 45359 2-00111
Steven Brandeberry, prin. 676-3081

Plymouth, AC 419, PC 4, Richland
Plymouth Local SD 4-11111
365 SANDUSKY ST 44865 687-4733
Jeffrey Slauson, supt.
HS, 184 SANDUSKY ST 44865 2-00011
Kevin Reidy, prin. 687-4051
Other Schools – See Shiloh

Poland, AC 216, PC 5, Mahoning
Poland Local SD
30 RIVERSIDE DR 44514 — 5-11111 / 757-7000
Robert Zorn, supt.
Poland Seminary HS — 3-00011 / 757-7018
3199 DOBBINS RD 44514
Brian Wolf, prin.
MS, 47 COLLEGE ST 44514 — 3-00100 / 757-7003
Thomas Shook, prin.

Pomeroy, AC 614, PC 4, Meigs
Meigs Local SD, PO BOX 272 45769 — 4-11111 / 992-2153
William Buckley, supt.
Meigs HS, 42091 POMEROY PIKE 45769 — 3-00011 / 992-2158
Fenton Taylor, prin.
Other Schools – See Middleport

Port Clinton, AC 419, PC 6, Ottawa
Port Clinton CSD — 4-11111 / 732-2103
431 PORTAGE DR 43452
Dennis Rectenwald, supt.
HS, 821 JEFFERSON ST 43452 — 3-00011 / 734-2147
Jack Nitz, prin.
MS, E 4TH ST 43452 — 2-00100 / 734-4448
Dale Van Lerberghe, prin.

Portsmouth, AC 614, PC 7, Scioto
Clay Local SD, 44 CLAY HIGH ST 45662 — 3-11111 / 354-6645
Ted Adams, supt.
Clay JSHS, 44 CLAY HIGH ST 45662 — 2-00111 / 354-6644
Rodney Walker, prin.

Portsmouth CSD, 411 COURT ST 45662 — 5-11111 / 354-5663
H. Osborn, supt.
Portsmouth East HS — 2-00011 / 776-6777
MARSHALL & FARNEY AVE 45662
Joseph Knapp, prin.
HS, 1149 GALLIA ST 45662 — 3-00011 / 353-2398
Thomas Walker, prin.
Grant MS, 1225 4TH ST 45662 — 2-00100 / 353-6129
Jerry Skiver, prin.
McKinley MS, 1729 KINNEYS LN 45662 — 2-00100 / 353-6719
Michael Welton, prin.
Portsmouth East MS — 2-00100 / 776-6777
MARSHALL & FARNEY AVE 45662
L. Knapp, prin.

Notre Dame HS — 3-00111 / 353-0719
2220 SUNRISE AVE 45662
Fred Ellsesser, prin.
Shawnee State University — 4-UC / 355-2202
940 2ND ST 45662

Proctorville, AC 614, PC 3, Lawrence
Fairland Local SD — 4-11111 / 886-8606
PO BOX 201 45669
Jerry McConnell, supt.
Fairland HS, PO BOX 805 45669 — 3-00011 / 886-6430
David Judd, prin.
Fairland West MS, PO BOX 90 45669 — 2-00100 / 886-6242
John Lewis, prin.

Put-in-Bay, AC 419, PC 2, Ottawa
Put-in-Bay Local SD — 1-11111 / 285-3614
PO BOX 659 43456
Kelly Faris, supt.
JSHS, PO BOX 659 43456 — 1-00111 / 285-3614
Kelly Faris, prin.

Racine, AC 614, PC 3, Meigs
Southern Local SD — 3-11111 / 949-2669
PO BOX 176 45771
Bobby Ord, supt.
Southern HS, PO BOX 98 45771 — 2-00011 / 949-2611
Gordon Fisher, prin.
Southern JHS, PO BOX 326 45771 — 2-00100 / 949-2233
Michaela Kucsma, prin.

Radnor, AC 614, PC 2, Delaware
Buckeye Valley Local SD
Supt. – See Delaware
Buckeye Valley MS — 3-00100 / 363-6626
4230 STATE ROUTE 203 43066
Steven Jackson, prin.

Randolph, AC 216, PC 3, Portage
Waterloo Local SD
Supt. – See Atwater
Waterloo MS, PO BOX 216 44265 — 2-01100 / 325-7272
Thomas Giovangnoli, prin.

Ravenna, AC 216, PC 7, Portage
Maplewood Area JVSD — 3-00001 / 296-2892
7075 STATE ROUTE 88 44266
John Kilchenman, prin.
Maplewood Area Joint Vocational SHS — 3-00001 / 296-2892
7075 STATE ROUTE 88 44266
Jerry Smith, prin.

Ravenna CSD, 507 E MAIN ST 44266 — 5-11111 / 296-9679
Philip Warner, supt.
HS, 345 E MAIN ST 44266 — 3-00011 / 296-9679
R. Green, prin.
Brown MS, 228 S SCRANTON ST 44266 — 3-00100 / 296-3849
Frank Seman, prin.

Southeast Local SD — 4-11111 / 654-5841
8423 TALLMADGE RD 44266
Terry Byers, supt.
Southeast HS — 3-00011 / 654-5841
8423 TALLMADGE RD 44266
Charles Vrabel, prin.
Southeast MS — 3-01100 / 654-5842
8301 TALLMADGE RD 44266
Frank Little, prin.

Bohecker's Business College — 2-CS / 297-7319
326 E MAIN ST 44266

Rawson, AC 419, PC 2, Hancock
Cory-Rawson Local SD — 3-11111 / 963-3415
3930 COUNTY ROAD 26 45881
Walter Baney, supt.
Cory-Rawson HS — 2-00011 / 963-2611
3930 COUNTY ROAD 26 45881
Richard Steiner, prin.
Cory-Rawson MS — 2-01100 / 963-3161
3930 COUNTY ROAD 26 45881
Lawrence Grove, prin.

Rayland, AC 614, PC 2, Jefferson
Buckeye Local SD — 5-11111 / 859-2114
PO BOX 300 43943
Anne Stephens, supt.
Buckeye HS, RR 2 BOX 275 43943 — 3-00011 / 859-2196
Daniel Stephens, prin.
Other Schools – See Brilliant, Tiltonsville

Reading, AC 513, PC 7, Hamilton
Reading Community CSD — 4-11111 / 554-1800
1301 BONNELL ST 45215
John Varis, supt.
Reading Community JSHS — 3-00011 / 733-4422
810 E COLUMBIA AVE 45215
Robert Dalton, prin.

Mt. Notre Dame HS — 3-00011 / 821-3044
711 E COLUMBIA AVE 45215
Maureen Baldock, prin.

Reedsville, AC 614, PC 2, Meigs
Eastern Local SD — 3-11111 / 985-4292
38900 STATE ROUTE 7 45772
Ronald Minard, supt.
Eastern JSHS — 2-00111 / 985-3329
38900 STATE ROUTE 7 45772
Charles Moore, prin.

Republic, AC 419, PC 3, Seneca
Seneca East Local SD
Supt. — See Attica
Seneca East MS, PO BOX 39 44867 — 2-00100 / 585-4291
Theodore George, prin.

Reynoldsburg, AC 614, PC 8, Franklin
Reynoldsburg CSD — 5-11111 / 866-2815
6549 E LIVINGSTON AVE 43068
Richard Ross, supt.
SHS, 6699 E LIVINGSTON AVE 43068 — 4-00001 / 866-6397
Dan Hoffman, prin.
JHS, 2300 BALDWIN PL 43068 — 3-00110 / 868-0500
Michael Cox, prin.

Richfield, AC 216, PC 5, Summit
Revere Local SD
Supt. — See Bath
Revere HS, 3420 EVERETT RD 44286 — 3-00011 / 659-6111
William Holko, prin.

Richmond, AC 614, PC 2, Jefferson
Edison Local SD
Supt. — See Hammondsville
Edison SHS, PO BOX 308 43944 — 3-00001 / 765-4313
Richard Wilinski, prin.

Richmond Dale, AC 614, PC 3, Ross
Scioto Valley Local SD — 4-11111 / 884-4553
PO BOX 108 45673
Tom Shoemaker, supt.
Southeastern JSHS — 3-00111 / 884-4654
PO BOX 108 45673
John Skaggs, prin.

Richmond Heights, AC 216, PC 6, Cuyahoga
Richmond Heights Local SD — 3-11111 / 692-0086
447 RICHMOND RD 44143
Stephen Franko, supt.
HS, 447 RICHMOND RD 44143 — 2-00011 / 692-0094
Hans Pesch, prin.
MS, 447 RICHMOND RD 44143 — 2-00100 / 692-0094
Hans Pesch, prin.

Bryant & Stratton Business Institute — 2-CS / 461-3151
691 RICHMOND RD 44143
Richmond Heights General Hospital — HSP / 585-6500
27100 CHARDON RD 44143

Richwood, AC 614, PC 4, Union
North Union Local SD — 4-11111 / 943-2509
401 N FRANKLIN ST 43344
John Roller, supt.
North Union HS — 2-00011 / 943-3012
401 N FRANKLIN ST 43344
Thomas Forman, prin.
North Union MS, 16 NORRIS ST 43344 — 2-00100 / 943-2369
Duane Tron, prin.

Ridgeway, AC 513, PC 2, Hardin
Ridgemont Local SD
Supt. — See Mount Victory
Ridgemont JSHS, PO BOX 87 43345 — 2-00111 / 363-3611
Dale Diddle, prin.

Rio Grande, AC 614, PC 3, Gallia
Gallia-Jackson-Vinton JVSD — 3-00011 / 245-5334
PO BOX 157 45674
John Shump, supt.
Buckeye Hills Career Ctr Joint Vo SHS — 3-00011 / 245-5334
PO BOX 157 45674
Ponney Cisco, prin.

University of Rio Grande — 4-UC / 245-5353
GENERAL DELIVERY 45674

Ripley, AC 513, PC 4, Brown
Ripley-Union-Lewis Local SD — 3-11111 / 392-4396
PO BOX 6 45167
Charles Osborn, supt.
Ripley-Union-Lewis JSHS — 3-00111 / 392-4384
1317 S 2ND ST 45167 – J. Walters, prin.

Risingsun, AC 419, PC 3, Wood
Lakota Local SD, PO BOX 5 43457 — 4-11111 / 457-2911
Robert Ludwig, supt.
Other Schools – See Amsden, Kansas

Rittman, AC 216, PC 6, Wayne
Rittman EVD, 220 N 1ST ST 44270 — 4-11111 / 927-3155
Larry Stucky, supt.
HS, 100 SAURER ST 44270 — 2-00011 / 927-3115
Orville Ullman, prin.
MS, 75 N MAIN ST 44270 — 2-00100 / 927-3145
Frank Holloway, prin.

Rockford, AC 419, PC 4, Mercer
Parkway Local SD — 4-11111 / 363-3045
401 S FRANKLIN ST 45882
Gary Graham, supt.
Parkway HS, 401 S FRANKLIN ST 45882 — 2-00011 / 363-2894
Norman Vantilburg, prin.
Other Schools – See Willshire

Rocky River, AC 216, PC 7, Cuyahoga
Rocky River CSD — 4-11111 / 333-6000
21600 CENTER RIDGE RD 44116
Victor Smole, supt.
HS, 20951 DETROIT RD 44116 — 3-00011 / 333-6000
George Steyer, prin.
MS, 1631 LAKEVIEW AVE 44116 — 2-00100 / 333-6000
Kathleen Komnenovich, prin.

Lutheran West HS — 2-00011 / 333-1660
3850 LINDEN RD 44116
Dwayne Jobst, prin.
Magnificat HS — 3-00011 / 331-1572
20770 HILLIARD BLVD 44116
Sr. Carolyn Marshall, prin.

Rootstown, AC 216, PC 3, Portage
Rootstown Local SD — 4-11111 / 325-9911
4190 STATE ROUTE 44 44272
Donald Crewse, supt.
HS, 4190 STATE ROUTE 44 44272 — 2-00011 / 325-7911
Roger Sidoti, prin.
Schnee MS — 2-00100 / 325-9956
4190 STATE ROUTE 44 44272
Gary Savage, prin.

Northeastern Ohio Univ Coll of Medicine — 2-UC / 325-2511
PO BOX 95 44272

Roseville, AC 614, PC 4, Muskingum
Franklin Local SD
Supt. — See Duncan Falls
MS, 76 W ATHENS RD 43777 — 2-01100 / 697-7317
Karen Miller, prin.

Rossford, AC 419, PC 6, Wood
Rossford EVD — 4-11111 / 666-2010
229 EAGLE POINT RD 43460
Bill Spargur, supt.
HS, 701 SUPERIOR ST 43460 — 3-00011 / 666-5262
Joseph Gagel, prin.
JHS, 651 SUPERIOR ST 43460 — 2-00100 / 666-5254
Timothy Lenahan, prin.

Russellville, AC 513, PC 2, Brown
Eastern Local SD
Supt. — See Sardinia
MS, 203 E MAIN ST 45168 — 2-01100 / 377-4771
Gregory Stephenson, prin.

Russia, AC 513, PC 2, Shelby
Russia Local SD, PO BOX 8 45363 — 2-11111 / 295-3454
Steven Miller, supt.
JSHS, PO BOX 8 45363 — 2-00111 / 295-3454
Vernon Rosenbeck, prin.

Saint Bernard, AC 513, PC 6, Hamilton
St. Bernard-Elmwood Place CSD — 4-11111 / 641-2020
105 WASHINGTON AVE 45217
Robert Carroll, supt.
St. Bernard-Elmwood Place JSHS — 3-00111 / 641-2020
4615 TOWER AVE 45217
Guy Popplewell, prin.

Saint Clairsville, AC 614, PC 6, Belmont
Belmont-Harrison Area JVSD — 3-00011 / 695-9130
110 FOX SHANNON PL 43950
Charles Grimes, supt.
Belmont Career Ctr Joint Vocational SHS — 2-00001 / 695-9130
110 FOX SHANNON PL 43950
Gwen Morgenstern, prin.
Other Schools – See Cadiz

St. Clairsville-Richland CSD — 4-11111 / 695-1624
108 WOODROW AVE 43950
Lorrinda Saxby, supt.
HS, 102 WOODROW AVE 43950 — 3-00011 / 695-1584
Richard Polinsky, prin.
MS, 104 WOODROW AVE 43950 — 3-01100 / 695-1591
Wayne Ogilbee, prin.

Belmont Technical College — 4-CC / 695-9500
120 FOX SHANNON PL 43950

Ohio University
45425 NATIONAL RD W   43950
4-UC
695-1720

Saint Henry, AC 419, PC 4, Mercer
St. Henry Consolidated Local SD
371 E COLUMBUS ST   45883
James Dippold, supt.
4-11111
678-4834
HS, 181 S WALNUT ST   45883
Rob Condon, prin.
2-00011
678-2373
MS, 381 E COLUMBUS ST   45883
Marvin Wourms, prin.
2-00100
678-2302

Saint Martin, AC 513, PC 2, Brown

Chatfield College
20918 STATE ROUTE 251   45118
1-CC
875-3344

Saint Marys, AC 419, PC 6, Auglaize
St. Mary's CSD, 101 W SOUTH ST   45885
Paul Blaine, supt.
5-11111
394-4312
Memorial HS, 101 W SOUTH ST   45885
Dan Griffin, prin.
3-00011
394-4011
McBroom MS, 210 S FRONT ST   45885
Newton Triplett, prin.
2-00100
394-2112

Saint Paris, AC 513, PC 4, Champaign
Graham Local SD, PO BOX 910   43072
Dennis Curtin, supt.
4-11111
663-4123
Graham HS, PO BOX 710   43072
Edwin Hauk, prin.
3-00011
663-4127
Graham MS, PO BOX 830   43072
Ron Coder, prin.
2-00100
663-5339

Salem, AC 216, PC 7, Columbiana
Salem CSD, 1226 E STATE ST   44460
Burton Schoffman, supt.
5-11111
332-0316
HS, 1200 E 6TH ST   44460
Charles McShane, prin.
3-00011
332-8905
JHS, 230 N LINCOLN AVE   44460
James Irvin, prin.
2-00100
332-8914

Kent State University-Salem Campus
SALEM CAMPUS   44460
2-CC
332-0361

Salineville, AC 216, PC 4, Columbiana
Southern Local SD
38095 STATE ROUTE 39   43945
John Fieldhouse, supt.
4-11111
679-2343
Southern JSHS
38095 STATE ROUTE 39   43945
William Bucey, prin.
2-00011
679-2305

Sandusky, AC 419, PC 8, Erie
Perkins Local SD
1210 E BOGART RD   44870
Maxwell Shoff, supt.
4-11111
625-0484
Perkins HS, 3714 CAMPBELL ST   44870
George Scheckelhoff, prin.
3-00011
625-1252
Perkins MS, 3700 SOUTH AVE   44870
Larry Pitts, prin.
3-00100
625-0132

Sandusky CSD, 407 DECATUR ST   44870
Gene Kleindienst, supt.
5-11111
626-6940
HS, 2130 HAYES AVE   44870
C. Kidwell, prin.
4-00011
626-6940
Jackson MS, 314 W MADISON ST   44870
John Kaszonyi, prin.
2-00100
626-6940
Barker IS, 1925 BARKER ST   44870
Robert Beck, prin.
1-01100
626-6940

Providence Hospital
1912 HAYES AVE   44870
HSP
625-8450
St. Mary HS
410 W JEFFERSON ST   44870
Fr. Quinn, prin.
2-00011
626-1892
Southeastern Business College
4020 MILAN RD   44870
2-CS
627-8345

Sarahsville, AC 614, PC 2, Noble
Noble Local SD
20977 STATE ROUTE 146   43779
Donald Donatelli, supt.
4-11111
732-2084
Shenandoah HS
49346 STATE ROUTE 147   43779
Don Ullmann, prin.
2-00011
732-2361

Sardinia, AC 513, PC 3, Brown
Eastern Local SD, PO BOX 500   45171
Thomas Miller, supt.
4-11111
378-3981
Eastern Local HS, PO BOX 500   45171
Ted Downing, prin.
2-00011
378-6016
Other Schools – See Russellville

Southern State Community College
12681 US ROUTE 62   45171
3-CC

Scio, AC 614, PC 3, Harrison
Harrison Hills CSD
Supt. — See Hopedale
Jewett-Scio JSHS, 322 W MAIN ST   43988
James Drexler, prin.
2-00111
945-2501

Seaman, AC 513, PC 4, Adams
Adams County/Ohio Valley SD
Supt. — See West Union
North Adams JSHS
355 BROADWAY ST   45679
James Rose, prin.
2-00111
386-2528

Sebring, AC 216, PC 5, Mahoning
Sebring Local SD
225 E INDIANA AVE   44672
Richard Archer, supt.
3-11111
938-6165

McKinley JSHS
225 E INDIANA AVE   44672
Edward Kapusinski, prin.
2-00111
938-2963

Senecaville, AC 614, PC 2, Guernsey
Mid-East Ohio JVSD
Supt. — See Zanesville
Guernsey-Noble Career Ctr
57090 VOCATIONAL RD   43780
Deborah Kapp, prin.
2-00001
685-2516

Seven Hills, AC 216, PC 7, Cuyahoga
Parma CSD
Supt. — See Parma
Hillside JHS, 1320 HILLSIDE RD   44131
John Spinner, prin.
2-00100
885-2373

Seville, AC 216, PC 4, Medina
Cloverleaf Local SD
Supt. — See Lodi
Cloverleaf JHS
7500 BUFFHAM RD   44273
Ronald Tisher, prin.
3-00110
948-2500

Shade, AC 614, PC 1, Athens
Alexander Local SD
Supt. — See Albany
Alexander JHS
2380 US ROUTE 33   45776
Frank Doudna, prin.
2-00100
696-1155

Shadyside, AC 614, PC 5, Belmont
Shadyside Local SD
3890 LINCOLN AVE   43947
Jerry Narcisi, supt.
3-11111
676-3121
JSHS, 3890 LINCOLN AVE   43947
David Sommers, prin.
2-00011
676-3235

Shaker Heights, AC 216, PC 8, Cuyahoga
Shaker Heights CSD
15600 PARKLAND DR   44120
Mark Freeman, supt.
5-11111
295-1400
HS, 15911 ALDERSYDE DR   44120
A. Jack Rumbaugh, prin.
4-00011
295-4200
MS, 20600 SHAKER BLVD   44122
Brent Wendling, prin.
3-00100
295-4100

Hathaway Brown S
19600 N PARK BLVD   44122
William Christ, prin.
3-11111
932-4214
Laurel S, 1 LYMAN CIR   44122
Helen Marter, prin.
3-11111
464-1441

Shelby, AC 419, PC 6, Richland
Pioneer JVSD, PO BOX 309   44875
Richard Jones, supt.
3-00001
347-7926
Pioneer Joint Vocational SHS
PO BOX 309   44875
Donald Plotts, prin.
3-00001
347-7744

Shelby CSD
25 HIGH SCHOOL AVE   44875
E. Frost, supt.
4-11111
342-3520
HS, 109 W SMILEY AVE   44875
E. Steven Rhodes, prin.
3-00011
342-5065
JHS, 16 PARK AVE   44875
Mark Stock, prin.
2-00100
347-5451

Sherwood, AC 419, PC 3, Defiance
Central Local SD
6289 US HIGHWAY 127   43556
Douglas Johnson, supt.
4-11111
658-2808
Fairview HS
6829 US HIGHWAY 127   43556
Stephen Young, prin.
2-00011
658-2186
Fairview MS
6289 US HIGHWAY 127   43556
Gary Rettig, prin.
2-00100
658-2331

Shiloh, AC 419, PC 3, Richland
Plymouth Local SD
Supt. — See Plymouth
MS, MECHANIC ST   44878
John Hart, prin.
2-00100
896-3721

Sidney, AC 513, PC 7, Shelby
Fairlawn Local SD
18800 JOHNSTON RD   45365
Tom Coyne, supt.
3-11111
492-1974
Fairlawn JSHS
18800 JOHNSTON RD   45365
Joseph Fargo, prin.
2-00111
492-5930

Sidney CSD, 232 N MIAMI AVE   45365
Lewis Blackford, supt.
5-11111
497-2200
HS, 1215 CAMPBELL RD   45365
Gregory Johnson, prin.
4-00011
497-2238
Bridgeview MS, 320 E NORTH ST   45365
Thomas Roll, prin.
3-00100
497-2225

Lehman HS
2400 SAINT MARYS RD   45365
Michael Barhorst, prin.
2-00011
498-1161

Smithville, AC 216, PC 4, Wayne
Green Local SD, PO BOX 438   44677
Thomas Rolf, supt.
4-11111
669-3921
HS, PO BOX 156   44677
Michael Larson, prin.
2-00011
669-3165
Greene MS, PO BOX 367   44677
Richard Zimmerly, prin.
2-01100
669-2751

Wayne County JVSD
518 W PROSPECT ST   44677
Kenneth Packard, supt.
3-00001
669-2134
Wayne County Career Ctr Joint Vo SHS
518 W PROSPECT ST   44677
Steve Miller, prin.
3-00001
669-2134

Solon, AC 216, PC 7, Cuyahoga
Solon CSD, 33425 ARTHUR RD   44139
Joseph Regano, supt.
5-11111
248-1600
HS, 33600 INWOOD DR   44139
E. James Kotora, prin.
4-00011
349-6230
MS, 6835 SOM CENTER RD   44139
Michael Doney, prin.
3-00100
349-3848

South Amherst, AC 216, PC 4, Lorain
Firelands Local SD
Supt. — See Oberlin
MS, 152 W MAIN ST   44001
Robert Telloni, prin.
2-00100
986-7021

South Charleston, AC 513, PC 4, Clark
Southeastern Local SD
195 E JAMESTOWN ST   45368
Bruce Stewart, supt.
3-11111
462-8388
Southeastern HS
195 E JAMESTOWN ST   45368
Susan Cline, prin.
2-00011
462-8308

South Euclid, AC 216, PC 7, Cuyahoga

Regina HS, 1857 S GREEN RD   44121
Sr. Maureen Burke, prin.
2-00011
382-2110

Southington, AC 216, PC 3, Trumbull
Southington Local SD
4432 STATE ROUTE 305   44470
James Allen, supt.
3-11111
898-7480
Chalker HS
4432 STATE ROUTE 305   44470
William Pfahler, prin.
2-00011
898-1781
MS, 4432 STATE ROUTE 305   44470
William Pfahler, prin.
2-01100
898-1781

South Point, AC 614, PC 5, Lawrence
South Point Local SD
203 PARK AVE   45680
Andrew Nameth, supt.
5-11111
377-4315
HS, 302 HIGH ST   45680
John Sherman, prin.
3-00011
377-4323
MS, 201 PARK AVE   45680
Ken Cook, prin.
3-00100
377-4343

South Webster, AC 614, PC 3, Scioto
Bloom-Vernon Local SD
PO BOX 237   45682
Paul White, supt.
4-11111
778-2281
HS, PO BOX 100   45682
Rick Carrington, prin.
2-00011
778-2320
Bloom MS, PO BOX 237   45682
John Eaton, prin.
2-01100
778-2974

Sparta, AC 419, PC 2, Morrow
Highland Local SD, PO BOX 98   43350
Gary Burggraf, supt.
4-11111
768-2206
Highland HS, PO BOX 98   43350
Randy Miller, prin.
3-00011
253-7670
Highland JHS, PO BOX 68   43350
Anthony Deiuliis, prin.
2-00100
768-2781

Spencer, AC 216, PC 3, Medina
Black River Local SD
PO BOX 26   44275
Herbert Young, supt.
4-11111
648-2025
Black River MS, PO BOX 128   44275
Curtis Kennedy, prin.
2-01100
648-2310
Other Schools – See Sullivan

Spencerville, AC 419, PC 4, Allen
Spencerville Local SD
600 SCHOOL ST   45887
Donald Smith, supt.
4-11111
647-4111
HS, 600 SCHOOL ST   45887
Joel Hatfield, prin.
2-00011
647-4111
MS, 436 E 4TH ST   45887
Charles Violet, prin.
2-00100
647-4111

Springboro, AC 513, PC 6, Warren
Springboro Community SD
270 W CENTRAL AVE   45066
Gary Meier, supt.
4-11111
748-3960
HS, 1605 S MAIN ST   45066
Keith Harring, prin.
3-00011
748-3950
JHS, 705 S MAIN ST   45066
Joseph Deluca, prin.
3-00100
748-3953

Springfield, AC 513, PC 8, Clark
Mad River-Green Local SD
1215 OLD MILL RD   45506
Alvin Pridemore, supt.
4-11111
328-5351
Greenon HS
3950 S TECUMSEH RD   45502
William Hill, prin.
3-00011
325-7343
Other Schools – See Enon

Northeastern Local SD
1414 BOWMAN RD   45502
Roger Compton, supt.
5-11111
325-7615
Kenton Ridge HS
4444 MIDDLE URBANA RD   45503
Douglas Mowrey, prin.
3-00011
390-1274
Northeastern HS
1480 BOWMAN RD   45502
Roger Woodworth, prin.
2-00011
328-6575

Northwestern Local SD 4-11111
5610 TROY RD 45502 964-1318
Charles Cornett, supt.
Northwestern HS, 5650 TROY RD 45502 3-00011
Richard Littell, prin. 964-1324
Northwestern MS, 5610 TROY RD 45502 3-01100
Milton Palmer, prin. 964-1391

Springfield-Clark County JVSD 3-00001
1901 SELMA RD 45505 325-7368
Ralph Alexander, supt.
Springfield-Clark County Joint Vo SHS 3-00001
1901 SELMA RD 45505 325-7368
Kathryn Limes, prin.

Springfield CSD 7-11111
49 E COLLEGE AVE 45504 328-2000
James Frantz, supt.
Springfield North HS 4-00011
701 E HOME RD 45503 328-2017
Gerald Gochenour, prin.
Springfield South HS 4-00011
700 S LIMESTONE ST 45505 328-2027
Homer Evans, prin.
Clark MS, 1315 W HIGH ST 45506 2-00100
Richard Broderick, prin. 328-2001
Franklin MS 2-00100
1525 KENWOOD AVE 45505 328-2004
Rita Phipps, prin.
Hayward MS, 1700 CLIFTON AVE 45505 2-00100
Joetta Cooper, prin. 328-2007
Roosevelt MS 3-00100
1600 N LIMESTONE ST 45503 328-2011
R. Bash, prin.
Schaefer MS, 130 S BURNETT RD 45505 3-00100
David Calhoun, prin. 328-2014

Springfield Local SD 4-11111
1561 E POSSUM RD 45502 328-5378
Myron Smith, supt.
Shawnee HS, 1675 E POSSUM RD 45502 3-00011
Herbert Swiger, prin. 325-9296

Catholic Central HS 2-00011
1200 E HIGH ST 45505 325-9204
Fr. Kreidler, prin.
Clark State Community College 4-CC
570 E LEFFEL LN 45505 325-0691
Community Hospital HSP
PO BOX 1228 45501 328-8900
Wittenberg University 4-UC
PO BOX 720 45501 327-7916

Steubenville, AC 614, PC 7, Jefferson
Steubenville CSD, PO BOX 189 43952 5-11111
Charles Joyce, supt. 283-3767
HS, 420 N 4TH ST 43952 3-00011
Richard Ranallo, prin. 282-9741
Harding MS, 1928 SUNSET BLVD 43952 3-00100
Peter Basil, prin. 282-3481

Catholic Central HS 2-00011
320 WESTVIEW AVE 43952 264-5538
Kenneth Voss, prin.
Franciscan University of Steubenville 4-UC
100 FRANCISCAN WAY 43952 800-783-6220
Jefferson Technical College 4-CC
4000 SUNSET BLVD 43952 264-5591
Ohio Valley Hospital HSP
1 ROSS PARK BLVD 43952 283-7273

Stewart, AC 614, PC 2, Athens
Federal Hocking Local SD 4-11111
PO BOX 117 45778 662-6691
Tim Lairson, supt.
Federal Hocking HS 2-00011
STATE ROUTE 144 45778 662-3211
George Wood, prin.
Federal Hocking MS 2-00100
PO BOX 117 45778 662-4321
Martha Singleton, prin.

Stow, AC 216, PC 8, Summit
Stow CSD, 1819 GRAHAM RD 44224 6-11111
Dean Mizer, supt. 688-8266
HS, 3227 GRAHAM RD 44224 4-00011
Jay Morgan, prin. 678-0700
Other Schools – See Munroe Falls

Walsh Jesuit HS 3-00011
4550 WYOGA LAKE RD 44224 929-4205
William Ricco, prin.

Strasburg, AC 216, PC 4, Tuscarawas
Strasburg-Franklin Local SD 3-11111
140 N BODMER AVE 44680 878-5571
Terry Miller, supt.
Strasburg-Franklin JSHS 2-00111
140 N BODMER AVE 44680 878-5571
Robert Sattler, prin.

Streetsboro, AC 216, PC 6, Portage
Streetsboro CSD, 9000 KIRBY LN 44241 4-11111
Robert Love, supt. 626-4900
HS, 1900 ANNALANE DR 44241 3-00011
Thomas Jesse, prin. 626-4902
MS, 1951 ANNALANE DR 44241 2-00100
(—), prin. 626-4905

Strongsville, AC 216, PC 8, Cuyahoga
Strongsville CSD 6-11111
13200 PEARL RD 44136 238-2650
Kathleen Ferrone Neal, supt.

SHS, 20025 LUNN RD 44136 4-00001
Theodore Barto, prin. 238-2650
Albion JHS, 11109 WEBSTER RD 44136 3-00110
Gary Novak, prin. 238-2650
Center JHS, 13200 PEARL RD 44136 3-00110
Walter Hoffman, prin. 238-2650

Struthers, AC 216, PC 7, Mahoning
Struthers CSD, 99 EUCLID AVE 44471 4-11111
Samuel Crow, supt. 750-1061
HS, 111 EUCLID AVE 44471 3-00011
Pete Pirone, prin. 750-1062
MS, 800 5TH ST 44471 3-01100
Albert Toth, prin. 750-1064

Stryker, AC 419, PC 4, Williams
Stryker Local SD, PO BOX 624 43557 3-11111
David Nicholls, supt. 682-4591
JSHS, PO BOX 624 43557 2-00111
(—), prin. 682-4591

Sugarcreek, AC 216, PC 4, Tuscarawas
Garaway Local SD 4-11111
PO BOX 339 44681 852-2421
W. Russell McGlothlin, supt.
Garaway JSHS, PO BOX 339 44681 2-00111
Onley Heath, prin. 852-2422

Sugar Grove, AC 614, PC 2, Fairfield
Berne Union Local SD 3-11111
506 N MAIN ST 43155 746-8341
Donna Boylan, supt.
Berne Union HS, 506 N MAIN ST 43155 2-00011
William Chesser, prin. 746-9956
Berne Union MS, 506 N MAIN ST 43155 2-00100
Charles Byers, prin. 746-9738

Sullivan, AC 419, PC 2, Ashland
Black River Local SD
Supt. — See Spencer
Black River HS 2-00011
233 COUNTY ROAD 40 44880 625-3211
Martha Brand, prin.

Summit Station, AC 614, PC 4, Licking
Licking Heights Local SD 4-11111
6539 SUMMIT RD SW 43073 927-6926
Charles Crist, supt.
Licking Heights HS 2-00011
6539 SUMMIT RD SW 43073 927-6926
John Martino, prin.
Licking Heights MS 2-00100
6539 SUMMIT RD SW 43073 927-9046
Karl VanDeest, prin.

Sunbury, AC 614, PC 4, Delaware
Big Walnut Local SD 4-11111
PO BOX 5001 43074 965-2706
Carl Martin, supt.
Big Walnut HS, PO BOX 5001 43074 3-00011
Charles Workman, prin. 965-3766
Big Walnut IS, PO BOX 5002 43074 3-00100
Steven Butler, prin. 965-3006

Swanton, AC 419, PC 5, Fulton
Swanton Local SD 4-11111
108 N MAIN ST 43558 826-7085
Roger Barnes, supt.
HS, 206 CHERRY ST 43558 3-00011
Ray Orben, prin. 826-3045
JHS, 206 CHERRY ST 43558 2-00100
Ken Baumgartner, prin. 826-4016

Sycamore, AC 419, PC 3, Wyandot
Mohawk Local SD 4-11111
295 STATE HIGHWAY 231 44882 927-2414
David Danhoff, supt.
Mohawk HS 2-00011
295 STATE HIGHWAY 231 44882 927-6292
John Bowen, prin.

Sylvania, AC 419, PC 7, Lucas
Sylvania CSD, 6850 MONROE ST 43560 6-11111
Patrick Bernardo, supt. 885-7900
Sylvania Northview HS 3-00011
5403 SILICA DR 43560 885-7932
Richard Roberts, prin.
Sylvania Southview HS 4-00011
7225 SYLVANIA AVE 43560 885-7943
Gail Mirrow, prin.
Sylvania Arbor Hills JHS 3-00100
5334 WHITEFORD RD 43560 885-7919
Thomas Hauman, prin.
Sylvania McCord MS 3-00100
4304 N MCCORD RD 43560 885-7921
Jack Smith, prin.

Lourdes College 3-UC
6832 CONVENT BLVD 43560 885-5291

Tallmadge, AC 216, PC 7, Summit
Tallmadge CSD, 486 EAST AVE 44278 3-11111
Dennis Buzzelli, supt. 633-3291
HS, 484 EAST AVE 44278 3-00011
John McKee, prin. 633-5505
MS, 76 NORTH AVE 44278 3-00100
Richard Banig, prin. 633-4994

Akron Christian S 2-11111
508 NEWTON ST 44278 784-1284
Lawrence Inks, prin.

The Plains, AC 614, PC 5, Athens
Athens CSD, PO BOX 68 45780 5-11111
Richard Bongiorno, supt. 797-4544

Athens HS, 1 HIGH SCHOOL RD 45780 3-00011
David Liggitt, prin. 797-4521
Other Schools – See Athens

Thompson, AC 216, PC 2, Geauga
Ledgemont Local SD 3-11111
16200 BURROWS RD 44086 298-3341
Robert Fenn, supt.
Ledgemont HS 2-00011
16700 THOMPSON RD 44086 298-3343
Kathleen Malobenski, prin.

Thornville, AC 614, PC 3, Perry
Northern Local SD 4-11111
8700 SHERIDAN DR 43076 743-1303
Steve Johnson, supt.
Sheridan HS, 8660 SHERIDAN DR 43076 3-00011
Steve Holekamp, prin. 743-1335
Sheridan MS, 8700 SHERIDAN DR 43076 3-00100
John Simmons, prin. 743-1315

Tiffin, AC 419, PC 7, Seneca
Tiffin CSD, 244 S MONROE ST 44883 5-11101
Forest Yocum, supt. 447-2515
Columbian SHS 3-00001
300 S MONROE ST 44883 447-6331
John Frye, prin.
JHS, 138 E MARKET ST 44883 2-00100
Joseph Silardi, prin. 447-4149

Vanguard/Sentinel JVSD
Supt. — See Fremont
Sentinel Joint Vocational SHS 3-00001
793 E TOWNSHIP ROAD 201 44883
Ronald Seman, prin. 448-1212

Calvert HS, PO BOX 836 44883 2-00011
Joseph Noonan, prin. 447-3844
Heidelberg College 4-UC
310 E MARKET ST 44883 448-2202
Tiffin University 3-UC
155 MIAMI ST 44883 800-968-6446

Tiltonsville, AC 614, PC 4, Jefferson
Buckeye Local SD
Supt. — See Rayland
Buckeye Southwest MS 2-00100
100 WALDEN AVE 43963 859-2357
Jerome Vinci, prin.

Tipp City, AC 513, PC 6, Miami
Bethel Local SD 4-11111
7490 STATE ROUTE 201 45371 845-9414
Judith Campbell, supt.
Bethel HS 2-00011
7490 STATE ROUTE 201 45371 845-9487
J. Graham, prin.
Bethel JHS 2-00100
7490 STATE ROUTE 201 45371 845-9430
(—), prin.

Tipp City EVD 4-11111
90 S TIPPECANOE DR 45371 667-8444
W. Dean Pond, supt.
Tippecanoe HS, 555 N HYATT ST 45371 3-00011
Anthony Armocida, prin. 667-8448
Ball JHS, 575 N HYATT ST 45371 2-00100
John Zigler, prin. 667-8454

Toledo, AC 419, PC 10, Lucas
Ottawa Hills Local SD 3-11111
2532 EVERGREEN RD 43606 536-6371
William Reimer, supt.
Ottawa Hills JSHS 2-00111
2532 EVERGREEN RD 43606 536-4647
Jo Ann Burkhardt, prin.

Toledo CSD 8-11111
420 E MANHATTAN BLVD 43608 729-8200
Crystal Ellis, supt.
Bowsher HS 4-00011
3548 S DETROIT AVE 43614 385-5776
Louis Woods, prin.
Libbey HS, 1250 WESTERN AVE 43609 4-00011
Patricia Scharf, prin. 385-5341
Rogers HS, 5539 NEBRASKA AVE 43615 4-00011
Bunk Adams, prin. 531-1648
Scott HS 4-00011
2400 COLLINGWOOD BLVD 43620 244-8303
Stanley Woody, prin.
Start HS 4-00011
2100 TREMAINSVILLE RD 43613 473-1446
John Patroulis, prin.
Waite HS, 301 MORRISON DR 43605 4-00011
Ricardo Cervantes, prin. 691-4687
Woodward HS 4-00011
600 E STREICHER ST 43608 729-7131
Kay Ladd, prin.
Byrnedale JHS 3-00100
3645 GLENDALE AVE 43614 382-3427
Rebecca Johnson, prin.
DeVeaux JHS 3-00100
2626 W SYLVANIA AVE 43613 475-4213
Earl Apgar, prin.
East Toledo JHS 3-00100
355 DEARBORN AVE 43605 691-4692
(—), prin.
Jones JHS, 550 WALBRIDGE AVE 43609 3-00100
Alexander Davis, prin. 244-8391
Leverette JHS 3-00100
1111 E MANHATTAN BLVD 43608 726-3449
(—), prin.
McTigue JHS, 5700 HILL AVE 43615 3-00100
Richard St. John, prin. 531-4264

Old West End JHS
3131 CAMBRIDGE ST 43610
Pariss Coleman, prin.
2-00100
244-5581

Robinson JHS, 1007 GRAND AVE 43606
Richard Jackson, prin.
2-00100
244-3753

Washington Local SD
3505 W LINCOLNSHIRE BLVD 43606
Kenneth Bishop, supt.
6-11111
531-9066

Whitmer HS, 5601 CLEGG DR 43613
Thomas Jennings, prin.
4-00011
473-8402

Jefferson JHS, 5530 WHITMER DR 43613
Kenneth Aerni, prin.
3-00100
473-8452

Washington JHS
5700 WHITMER DR 43613
Thomas Gschwind, prin.
3-00100
473-8487

Central Catholic HS
2550 CHERRY ST 43608
Jack Altenburger, prin.
4-00011
255-2280

Davis Junior College
4747 MONROE ST 43623
3-CC
473-2700

Maumee Valley Country Day S
1715 S REYNOLDS RD 43614
Richard Cadigan, prin.
3-11111
381-1313

Medical College of Ohio
PO BOX 10008 43699
3-UC
381-4260

Mercy Hospital
2200 JEFFERSON AVE 43624
HSP
259-1279

Notre Dame Academy
3535 W SYLVANIA AVE 43623
Sr. Carol Gregory, prin.
3-00011
475-9359

Owens Community College
PO BOX 10000 43699
5-CC
661-7225

Professional Skills Institute
1232 FLAIRE DR 43615
1-CS
531-9610

RETS Institute of Technology
1606 W LASKEY RD 43612
2-CC
478-7387

Riverside Hospital
1600 N SUPERIOR ST 43604
HSP
729-6059

St. Francis De Sales HS
2323 W BANCROFT ST 43607
M. Lukas, prin.
3-00011
531-1618

St. John's HS
5901 AIRPORT HWY 43615
Carl Wagner, prin.
3-00011
865-5743

St. Ursula Academy
4025 INDIAN RD 43606
Jane Charette, prin.
3-00011
531-1693

St. Vincent Medical Center
2201 CHERRY ST 43608
HSP
321-4319

Stautzenberger College
5355 SOUTHWYCK BLVD 43614
5-CS
866-0261

Stautzenberger College
4404 SECOR RD 43623
4-CS
474-2220

Stautzenberger College
5405 SOUTHWYCK BLVD 43614
2-CS
866-4882

Toledo Christian Academy
2303 BROOKFORD DR 43614
Randy Taylor, prin.
3-11111
389-8700

University of Toledo
2801 W BANCROFT ST 43606
7-UC
537-2211

Tontogany, AC 419, PC 2, Wood
Otsego Local SD, PO BOX 290 43565
Larry Busdeker, supt.
4-11111
823-4381

Otsego HS, PO BOX 290 43565
Robert Nicholson, prin.
2-00011
823-4911

Other Schools – See Grand Rapids

Toronto, AC 614, PC 6, Jefferson
Toronto CSD, 300 MYERS ST 43964
George Allan, supt.
4-11111
537-2456

HS, 300 MYERS ST 43964
Gary Fisher, prin.
2-00011
537-2442

Karaffa MS, 1307 DENNIS WAY 43964
James Ray, prin.
2-01100
537-2471

Trenton, AC 513, PC 6, Butler
Edgewood CSD
5005 OXFORD STATE RD 45067
Ron Kash, supt.
4-11111
863-4692

Edgewood HS
5005 OXFORD STATE RD 45067
Frederick Breyer, prin.
3-00011
867-0089

Other Schools – See Hamilton

Trotwood, AC 513, PC 6, Montgomery
Trotwood-Madison CSD
444 S BROADWAY ST 45426
William Smith, supt.
5-11111
854-3050

Trotwood-Madison HS
221 E TROTWOOD BLVD 45426
Dale Stearner, prin.
4-00011
854-0878

Other Schools – See Dayton

Troy, AC 513, PC 7, Miami
Miami East Local SD
Supt. — See Casstown
Miami East JHS
2901 N STRINGTOWN RD 45373
Mike Mullen, prin.
2-00100
339-2101

Troy CSD, 500 N MARKET ST 45373
Glenn Kiefer, supt.
5-11111
332-6700

HS, 151 W STAUNTON RD 45373
Robert Fletcher, prin.
4-00011
332-6710

JHS, 556 ADAMS ST 45373
Marcia Rarick, prin.
3-00100
332-6720

Hobart Institute of Welding Technology
400 TRADE SQ E 45373
2-CS
800-332-9448

Tuscarawas, AC 614, PC 3, Tuscarawas
Indian Valley Local SD
Supt. — See Gnadenhutten
MS, PO BOX 356 44682
Roger Bond, prin.
2-00100
922-4226

Twinsburg, AC 216, PC 6, Summit
Twinsburg CSD
11136 RAVENNA RD 44087
Jeffrey Miller, supt.
4-11111
963-8300

Chamberlin HS
10270 RAVENNA RD 44087
Derran Wimer, prin.
3-00011
963-8305

Dodge MS, 10225 RAVENNA RD 44087
Edward Vittardi, prin.
3-00100
963-8310

Uhrichsville, AC 614, PC 6, Tuscarawas
Claymont CSD
Supt. — See Dennison
Claymont HS, 215 E 6TH ST 44683
Jeffrey Gyurko, prin.
3-00011
922-3471

Union City, AC 513, PC 4, Darke
Mississinawa Valley Local SD
419 E ELM ST 45390
Michael Gray, supt.
3-11111
968-5656

Mississinawa Valley JSHS
1469 STATE ROAD 47 E 45390
Warren Scholler, prin.
2-00111
968-4464

Uniontown, AC 216, PC 5, Stark
Lake Local SD
Supt. — See Hartville
Lake SHS
1025 LAKE CENTER ST NW 44685
David DeHaven, prin.
3-00001
877-4282

University Heights, AC 216, PC 7, Cuyahoga
Cleveland Heights-University Heights CSD
2155 MIRAMAR BLVD 44118
Roger Vince, supt.
6-11111
371-7171

Wiley MS, 2181 MIRAMAR BLVD 44118
James Cipolletti, prin.
3-00100
371-7270

Other Schools – See Cleveland, Cleveland Heights

Upper Arlington, AC 614, PC 8, Franklin
Upper Arlington CSD
1950 N MALLWAY DR 43221
William Schaefer, supt.
5-11111
487-5000

HS, 1650 RIDGEVIEW RD 43221
Paul Martin, prin.
4-00011
487-5200

Hastings MS, 1850 HASTINGS LN 43220
Edward Orazen, prin.
3-00100
487-5100

Jones MS
2100 NW ARLINGTON AVE 43221
Timothy Reno, prin.
3-00100
487-5080

Upper Sandusky, AC 419, PC 6, Wyandot
Upper Sandusky EVD
390 W WALKER ST 43351
James McGlamery, supt.
4-11111
294-2306

HS, 800 N SANDUSKY AVE 43351
Thomas Baker, prin.
3-00011
294-2308

Union MS, 390 W WALKER ST 43351
Thomas Patton, prin.
2-00100
294-5721

Urbana, AC 513, PC 7, Champaign
Urbana CSD, 711 WOOD ST 43078
Stanley Imhulse, supt.
4-11111
652-2141

HS, 500 WASHINGTON AVE 43078
Mitchell Smith, prin.
3-00011
653-3517

JHS, 500 WASHINGTON AVE 43078
Nick Mescher, prin.
2-00100
653-4102

Urbana University
100 COLLEGE ST 43078
3-UC
652-1301

Utica, AC 614, PC 4, Licking
North Fork Local SD
PO BOX 497 43080
Linda Booth, supt.
4-11111
892-3666

HS, PO BOX 666 43080
Douglas Burdette, prin.
3-00011
892-2855

MS, PO BOX 647 43080
(—), prin.
2-00100
892-2691

Van Buren, AC 419, PC 2, Hancock
Van Buren Local SD
PO BOX 229 45889
Larry Cook, supt.
3-11111
299-3578

JSHS, PO BOX 229 45889
Michael Brand, prin.
2-00111
299-3384

Vandalia, AC 513, PC 7, Montgomery
Vandalia-Butler CSD
306 S DIXIE DR 45377
Norman Burkhardt, supt.
5-11111
898-4618

Butler HS, 600 S DIXIE DR 45377
John Beckley, prin.
4-00011
454-6100

Morton MS, 231 W NATIONAL RD 45377
George Kenworthy, prin.
2-01100
454-6110

Other Schools – See Dayton

Vanlue, AC 419, PC 2, Hancock
Vanlue Local SD, PO BOX 250 45890
Donald Coletta, supt.
2-11111
387-7724

JSHS, PO BOX 250 45890
Gregg Lang, prin.
2-00111
387-7724

Van Wert, AC 419, PC 7, Van Wert
Lincolnview Local SD
15945 MIDDLE POINT RD 45891
James Grant, supt.
3-11111
238-6493

Lincolnview JSHS
15945 MIDDLE POINT RD 45891
Ralph Snyder, prin.
2-00111
238-1289

Lincolnview Marsh MS
PO BOX 150 45891
James Grant, prin.
1-01100
238-1695

Vantage JVSD
818 N FRANKLIN ST 45891
Robert Brandt, supt.
3-00001
238-5411

Vantage Joint Vocational SHS
818 N FRANKLIN ST 45891
Robert Brinkman, prin.
3-00001
238-5411

Van Wert CSD
205 W CRAWFORD ST 45891
Milton Levy, supt.
5-11111
238-0648

HS, 205 W CRAWFORD ST 45891
Wallace Grimm, prin.
3-00011
238-3350

Lincoln JHS
305 W CRAWFORD ST 45891
William Swank, prin.
2-00100
238-0727

Vermilion, AC 216, PC 7, Erie
Vermilion Local SD
1230 BEECHVIEW DR 44089
Mark Gagyi, supt.
5-11111
967-5210

HS, 1250 SANFORD ST 44089
Marcia Hershey, prin.
3-00011
967-3183

Sailorway MS
5355 SAILORWAY DR 44089
Phillip Machcinski, prin.
3-00100
967-6196

Versailles, AC 513, PC 4, Darke
Versailles EVD, PO BOX 72 45380
Gregory Taylor, supt.
4-11111
526-4773

JSHS, PO BOX 72 45380
C. Knore, prin.
3-00111
526-4427

Vienna, AC 216, PC 3, Trumbull
Mathews Local SD
4429 WARREN SHARON RD 44473
John Leeper, supt.
4-11111
394-1800

Mathews HS
4429 WARREN SHARON RD 44473
Louis Demarco, prin.
2-00011
394-1138

Other Schools – See Fowler

Vincent, AC 614, PC 2, Washington
Warren Local SD, PO BOX 1 45784
Robert Caldwell, supt.
5-11111
678-2366

Warren HS, RR 1 45784
Dennis Blatt, prin.
3-00011
678-2393

Other Schools – See Bartlett

Wadsworth, AC 216, PC 7, Medina
Wadsworth CSD, 360 COLLEGE ST 44281
Charles Parsons, supt.
5-11111
336-3571

HS, 625 BROAD ST 44281
Anthony Pallija, prin.
4-00011
336-3571

Central MS, 151 MAIN ST 44281
Stephen Dishauzi, prin.
3-00100
336-3571

Wakeman, AC 216, PC 3, Huron
Western Reserve Local SD
28 RIVER ST 44889
Gary Zoldesky, supt.
4-11111
839-2066

Other Schools – See Collins

Wapakoneta, AC 419, PC 6, Auglaize
Wapakoneta CSD, 3 N PINE ST 45895
Dean Wittwer, supt.
5-11111
738-2315

HS, 1 REDSKIN TRL 45895
Douglas Graham, prin.
3-00011
738-3111

MS, W HARRISON ST 45895
Gregory Douglass, prin.
3-00100
738-3420

Warren, AC 216, PC 8, Trumbull
Champion Local SD
5759 MAHONING AVE NW 44483
Lewis Strohm, supt.
4-11111
847-2330

Champion HS
5976 MAHONING AVE NW 44483
Dick Wagner, prin.
3-00011
847-2300

Champion MS
5435 KUSZMAUL AVE NW 44483
J. Thomas Manning, prin.
2-00100
847-2340

Howland Local SD
8200 SOUTH ST SE 44484
Richard Baringer, supt.
5-11111
856-8200

Howland HS
200 SHAFFER DR NE 44484
William Paczak, prin.
4-00011
856-8200

Howland MS, 8100 SOUTH ST SE 44484
Robert Gribling, prin.
3-00100
856-8200

Lordstown Local SD
1824 SALT SPRINGS RD 44481
Ronald Schuster, supt.
4-11111
824-2534

Lordstown JSHS
1824 SALT SPRINGS RD W 44481
Lawrence Crawford, prin.
2-00111
824-2581

James Career Ctr
1776 SALT SPRINGS RD 44481
Felix Carmello, prin.
Vo Tech
824-2588

Trumbull County JVSD
528 EDUCATIONAL HWY NW 44483
Robert Williams, supt.
3-00001
847-0503

Trumbull County Joint Vocational SHS
528 EDUCATIONAL HWY NW 44483
Bartley DuBois, prin.
3-00001
847-0503

Warren CSD
261 MONROE ST NW 44483
Louis Cardameno, supt.
6-11111
841-2321

Harding SHS, 860 ELM RD NE 44483
Rozen Lymor, prin.
4-00001
841-2316

Warren Western Reserve JHS — 4-00110
200 LOVELESS AVE SW 44485 — 841-2345
Gordon Hazen, prin.

Howland Christian S — 2-11111
8957 E MARKET ST 44484 — 856-5612
Douglas Hounshell, prin.
John F. Kennedy HS — 2-00011
2550 CENTRAL PARKWAY AVE SE 44484 — 369-1804
Ann Salva, prin.
Kent State University-Trumbull Campus — 4-CC
4314 MAHONING AVE NW 44483 — 847-0571
St. Mary ES, 261 ELM RD NE 44483 — 2-01100
James Ruffing, prin. — 399-5154
Trumbull Business College — 2-CS
3200 RIDGE AVE SE 44484 — 369-3200
Trumbull Memorial Hospital — HSP
1350 E MARKET ST 44483 — 841-9117

Warrensville Heights, AC 216, PC 7, Cuyahoga
Warrensville Heights CSD — 5-11111
4500 WARRENSVILLE CENTER RD 44128 — 663-2770
Jack Hearnes, supt.
SHS, 4270 NORTHFIELD RD 44128 — 3-00001
Jennifer Morrison, prin. — 752-8585
JHS — 3-00110
4285 WARRENSVILLE CENTER RD 44128
Lu Wims, prin. — 752-4050

Cuyahoga Community College — 5-CC
25444 HARVARD RD 44122

Warsaw, AC 614, PC 3, Coshocton
River View Local SD — 5-11111
26496 STATE ROUTE 60 43844 — 824-3521
Don Rushing, supt.
River View HS — 3-00011
26496 STATE ROUTE 60 43844 — 824-3521
David Mast, prin.
River View MS — 2-00100
26546 STATE ROUTE 60 43844 — 824-3521
Tom Gable, prin.

Washington Court House, AC 614, PC 7, Fayette
Miami Trace Local SD — 5-11111
PO BOX 624 43160 — 335-3010
Douglas Male, supt.
Miami Trace HS — 3-00011
3722 STATE ROUTE 41 NW 43160 — 335-5891
Don Trainer, prin.
Other Schools — See Bloomingburg

Washington Courthouse CSD — 4-11111
306 HIGHLAND AVE 43160 — 335-6620
Terrance Feick, supt.
Washington HS — 3-00011
1200 WILLARD ST 43160 — 335-0820
Jon Creamer, prin.
Washington MS, 318 N NORTH ST 43160 — 3-00100
Thomas Gauldin, prin. — 335-0291

Waterford, AC 614, PC 3, Washington
Wolf Creek Local SD — 3-11111
PO BOX 67 45786 — 984-2373
Clyde Crewey, supt.
HS, PO BOX 67 45786 — 2-00011
Albert Martin, prin. — 984-2373

Wauseon, AC 419, PC 6, Fulton
Wauseon EVD — 4-11111
120 E CHESTNUT ST 43567 — 335-6616
Neil Weber, supt.
HS, 840 PARKVIEW ST 43567 — 3-00011
Joseph Sevenich, prin. — 335-5756
Burr Road MS, 717 BURR RD 43567 — 3-01100
Richard Darcy, prin. — 335-2701

Waverly, AC 614, PC 5, Pike
Waverly CSD, 500 E 2ND ST 45690 — 4-11111
Dwight Hampton, supt. — 947-4770
HS, 500 E 2ND ST 45690 — 3-00011
David Surrey, prin. — 947-7701
North MS, 610 E 3RD ST 45690 — 3-00100
Roger Ramsey, prin. — 947-4527

Waynesfield, AC 419, PC 3, Auglaize
Waynesfield-Goshen Local SD — 3-11111
PO BOX 370 45896 — 568-2391
Joseph Allen, supt.
Waynesfield-Goshen Local JSHS — 2-00111
PO BOX 370 45896 — 568-5261
Amy Anderson, prin.

Waynesville, AC 513, PC 4, Warren
Wayne Local SD, 659 DAYTON RD 45068 — 4-11111
Charles Williams, supt. — 897-6971
HS, 735 DAYTON RD 45068 — 2-00011
James Barton, prin. — 897-2776
MS, 659 DAYTON RD 45068 — 2-00100
Dennis Bunnell, prin. — 897-4706

Wellington, AC 216, PC 5, Lorain
Wellington EVD, 201 S MAIN ST 44090 — 4-11111
James Hayes, supt. — 647-4286
HS, 629 N MAIN ST 44090 — 3-00011
Bradley Felkey, prin. — 647-3734
McCormick MS, 201 S MAIN ST 44090 — 3-01100
Richard Forney, prin. — 647-2342

Wellston, AC 614, PC 6, Jackson
Wellston CSD — 4-11111
416 N PENNSYLVANIA AVE 45692 — 384-2152
Franklin Vostatek, supt.
HS, 600 S PENNSYLVANIA AVE 45692 — 2-00011
Thomas Baker, prin. — 384-2162

JHS, 118 S NEW YORK AVE 45692 — 2-00100
Dan Brisker, prin. — 384-2251

Wellsville, AC 216, PC 5, Columbiana
Wellsville Local SD — 4-11111
931 CENTER ST 43968 — 532-2643
Raymond Rolley, supt.
HS, 929 CENTER ST 43968 — 2-00011
James Brown, prin. — 532-1188
Daw MS, 929 CENTER ST 43968 — 2-00100
Richard Bereschik, prin. — 532-1372

West Alexandria, AC 513, PC 4, Preble
Twin Valley Community Local SD — 4-11111
1 S MAIN ST 45381 – Paul Erslan, supt. — 839-4688
Twin Valley South HS — 2-00011
45 N MAIN ST 45381 — 839-4693
Kent McIntire, prin.
Lanier MS — 2-01100
3225 STATE ROUTE 503 S 45381 — 839-4165
Thomas Isaacs, prin.

West Carrollton, AC 513, PC 7, Montgomery
West Carrollton CSD — 5-11111
430 E PEASE AVE 45449 — 859-5121
Vance Ramage, supt.
SHS, 5833 STUDENT ST 45449 — 3-00001
James Van Tine, prin. — 435-2211
JHS, 424 E MAIN ST 45449 — 3-00110
Algott Herman, prin. — 859-8296

West Chester, AC 513, PC 3, Butler
Lakota Local SD — 6-11111
5030 TYLERSVILLE RD 45069 — 874-5505
Thomas Hayden, supt.
Lakota SHS — 4-00011
5050 TYLERSVILLE RD 45069 — 874-8390
Craig Ullery, prin.
Hopewell MS, 8200 COX RD 45069 — 3-00100
Michael Taylor, prin. — 777-2258
Lakota Freshman HS — 3-00010
6199 BECKETT RIDGE BLVD 45069 — 777-0552
Ed Rudder, prin.
Other Schools — See Middletown

Westerville, AC 614, PC 8, Franklin
Westerville CSD — 7-11111
336 S OTTERBEIN AVE 43081 — 895-6080
Ernest Husarik, supt.
Westerville North HS — 4-00011
950 COUNTY LINE RD 43081 — 895-6060
James McCann, prin.
Westerville South HS — 4-00011
303 S OTTERBEIN AVE 43081 — 895-6040
Jim Dalrymple, prin.
Blendon MS — 3-00100
223 S OTTERBEIN AVE 43081 — 895-6000
Sam Dorff, prin.
Heritage MS, 390 S SPRING RD 43081 — 4-00100
Robert Schultz, prin. — 895-5928
Walnut Springs MS — 4-00100
888 E WALNUT ST 43081 — 895-6030
Ralph Collins, prin.

Aristotle Institute Medical Dental Tech. — 2-CS
5900 WESTERVILLE RD 43081 — 891-1800
Grace Brethren Christian S — 2-00100
8225 WORTHINGTON GALENA RD 43081
Robert Baeslack, prin. — 431-8230
Otterbein College 43081 — 4-UC
898-1656

West Jefferson, AC 614, PC 5, Madison
Jefferson Local SD, PO BOX 47 43162 — 4-11111
James York, supt. — 879-7654
HS — 2-00011
561 W JEFFERSON KSVLL RD SE 43162
Gregory Place, prin. — 879-7681
Jefferson Memorial MS — 2-00100
177 S FREY AVE 43162 — 879-8345
Gary Bell, prin.

West Lafayette, AC 614, PC 4, Coshocton
Ridgewood Local SD — 4-11111
225 W UNION AVE 43845 — 545-6354
Grant Sheppard, supt.
Ridgewood HS, 517 S OAK ST 43845 — 2-00011
Daniel Groff, prin. — 545-6345

Westlake, AC 216, PC 7, Cuyahoga
Westlake CSD — 5-11111
2260 DOVER CENTER RD 44145 — 871-7300
Beverly Reep, supt.
HS, 27830 HILLIARD BLVD 44145 — 4-00011
David Minich, prin. — 835-6351
Burneson MS — 3-00100
2240 DOVER CENTER RD 44145 — 835-6340
G. Newman, prin.
Parkside MS — 2-00100
24525 HILLIARD BLVD 44145 — 835-6325
Laura Watson, prin.

West Liberty, AC 513, PC 4, Logan
West Liberty-Salem Local SD — 4-11111
7208 US HIGHWAY 68 N 43357 — 465-1075
George McGuire, supt.
West Liberty-Salem JSHS — 2-00111
7208 US HIGHWAY 68 N 43357 — 465-1060
James Hare, prin.

West Manchester, AC 513, PC 2, Preble
C. R. Coblentz Local SD
Supt. — See New Paris

Coblentz MS — 2-01100
9088 MONROE CENTRAL RD 45382 — 678-7111
Dale Thompson, prin.

West Milton, AC 513, PC 5, Miami
Milton-Union EVD — 4-11111
112 S SPRING ST 45383 — 698-4136
Darlene Duchene, supt.
Milton-Union HS — 3-00011
221 S JEFFERSON ST 45383 — 698-4138
Allen Smith, prin.
Milton-Union MS — 2-00100
146 S SPRING ST 45383 — 698-6645
Samuel Ison, prin.

West Portsmouth, AC 614, PC 5, Scioto
Washington Local SD — 4-11111
1420 13TH ST W 45663 — 858-6100
Patricia Cirasco, supt.
Portsmouth West HS — 3-00011
1420 13TH ST W 45663 — 858-6668
John Distel, prin.
Nauvoo MS, 401 CALVERTS LN 45663 — 3-01100
Robert Eichenlaub, prin. — 858-4558

West Rushville, AC 614, PC 2, Fairfield
Fairfield Union Local SD — 4-11111
PO BOX 67 43163 — 536-7384
Clark Davis, supt.
Other Schools — See Lancaster

West Salem, AC 419, PC 4, Wayne
Northwestern Local SD — 4-11111
7569 N ELYRIA RD 44287 — 846-3151
Robert Grueser, supt.
Northwestern HS — 2-00011
7569 N ELYRIA RD 44287 — 846-3833
James Jones, prin.
Congress MS, RR 2 44287 — 2-00100
Phillip Genis, prin. — 846-3974

West Union, AC 513, PC 5, Adams
Adams County/Ohio Valley SD — 6-11111
3359 STATE ROUTE 125 45693 — 544-5586
Philip Satterfield, supt.
JSHS, 201 W SOUTH ST 45693 — 3-00111
Dale Grooms, prin. — 544-5553
Ohio Valley Vo HS — Vo Tech
175 LLOYD RD 45693 — 544-2336
Thomas Potts, prin.
Other Schools — See Manchester, Peebles, Seaman

Adams County Christian S — 2-11111
212 E SPARKS ST 45693 — 544-5502
Shirley Lewis, prin.

West Unity, AC 419, PC 4, Williams
Millcreek-West Unity Local SD — 3-11111
113 S DEFIANCE ST 43570 — 924-2365
J. Hutchinson, supt.
Hilltop JSHS, 113 S DEFIANCE ST 43570 — 2-00111
Mick Belcher, prin. — 924-2365

West Worthington, AC 614, PC see Bristolville
Worthington CSD
Supt. — See Worthington
Worthington Kilbourne HS — 4-00011
1499 HARD RD 43235 — 431-6220
Ronald Porta, prin.

Wharton, AC 419, PC 2, Wyandot
Riverdale Local SD
Supt. — See Mount Blanchard
MS 43359 — 2-00100
J. Hohn, prin. — 458-2343

Wheelersburg, AC 614, PC 6, Scioto
Wheelersburg Local SD — 4-11111
PO BOX 340 45694 — 574-8484
Frank Miller, supt.
HS, 701 PIRATE DR 45694 — 2-00011
Randall Parker, prin. — 574-2527

Whitehall, AC 614, PC 7, Franklin
Whitehall CSD — 5-11111
625 S YEARLING RD 43213 — 235-2385
John Conrath, supt.
Whitehall-Yearling HS — 3-00011
675 S YEARLING RD 43213 — 235-1632
Stephen House, prin.
Rosemore JHS, 4735 KAE AVE 43213 — 2-00100
Carole Jarrell, prin. — 866-1701

Whitehouse, AC 419, PC 5, Lucas
Anthony Wayne Local SD — 5-11111
PO BOX 2487 43571 — 877-5377
Randy Hardy, supt.
Wayne JSHS, 5967 FINZEL RD 43571 — 4-00111
Robert Slykhuis, prin. — 877-0466

Wickliffe, AC 216, PC 7, Lake
Wickliffe CSD, PO BOX 195 44092 — 4-11111
David Tanski, supt. — 943-6900
HS, 2255 ROCKEFELLER RD 44092 — 3-00011
Robert Smith, prin. — 944-0800
MS, 29240 EUCLID AVE 44092 — 2-01100
Gordon Gerber, prin. — 943-3220

Rabbinical College of Telshe — 2-UC
28400 EUCLID AVE 44092 — 943-5300
St. Mary Seminary — 1-UC
28700 EUCLID AVE 44092 — 943-7600
Telshe HS, 28400 EUCLID AVE 44092 — 2-00011
David Klems, prin. — 944-0299

Wilberforce, AC 513, PC 5, Greene

Central State University	5-UC
1400 BRUSH ROW RD 45384	376-6332
Payne Theological Seminary	1-UC
PO BOX 474 45384	376-2946
Wilberforce University	3-UC
GENERAL DELIVERY 45384	376-2911

Willard, AC 419, PC 6, Huron

Willard CSD, PO BOX 150 44890	4-11111
David Hirschy, supt.	935-1541
HS, PO BOX 410 44890	3-00011
Douglas Garling, prin.	935-0181
MS, 949 S MAIN ST 44890	3-01100
Dan Major, prin.	933-8312

Williamsburg, AC 513, PC 4, Clermont

Williamsburg Local SD	4-11111
549 W MAIN ST 45176	724-3077
Glenn Alexander, supt.	
JSHS, 549 W MAIN ST 45176	2-00111
Sam Snyder, prin.	724-2211

Williamsport, AC 614, PC 3, Pickaway

Westfall Local SD	4-11111
19463 PHERSON PIKE 43164	986-3671
Roger Crago, supt.	
Westfall HS	3-00011
19463 PHERSON PIKE 43164	986-2911
Dennis Karshner, prin.	
Westfall MS	2-00100
19545 PHERSON PIKE 43164	986-2941
Michael Johnsen, prin.	

Willoughby, AC 216, PC 7, Lake

Willoughby-Eastlake CSD	6-11111
37047 RIDGE RD 44094	946-5000
Roger Lulow, supt.	
South HS, 5000 SHANKLAND RD 44094	4-00011
Glenn Caroff, prin.	975-3647
Willoughby-Eastlake Tech Ctr	Vo Tech
25 PUBLIC SQ 44094	946-7085
Ronald Haworth, prin.	
MS, 36901 RIDGE RD 44094	3-01100
Gary Barta, prin.	975-3601
Other Schools – See Eastlake, Willowick	

Andrews S, 38588 MENTOR AVE 44094	2-00111
Charles Marsee, prin.	942-3600

Willowick, AC 216, PC 7, Lake

Willoughby-Eastlake CSD	
Supt. — See Willoughby	
MS, 31500 ROYALVIEW DR 44095	3-01100
Thomas Mobily, prin.	943-2950

Willow Wood, AC 614, PC 1, Lawrence

Symmes Valley Local SD	3-11111
14778 STATE ROUTE 141 45696	643-2451
Thomas Ben, supt.	
Symmes Valley HS	2-00011
14778 STATE ROUTE 141 45696	643-2371
(—), prin.	

Willshire, AC 419, PC 3, Van Wert

Parkway Local SD	
Supt. — See Rockford	
Parkway MS, GREEN ST 45898	2-00100
David Williamson, prin.	495-2000

Wilmington, AC 513, PC 7, Clinton

Great Oaks JVSD	
Supt. — See Cincinnati	
Laurel Oaks CDC SHS	3-00111
300 OAK DR 45177	382-1411
Guy Hopkins, prin.	
Wilmington CSD	5-11111
341 S NELSON AVE 45177	382-1641
Charles Dowler, supt.	
HS, 300 RICHARDSON PL 45177	3-00011
Michael Wells, prin.	382-7716
MS, 365 W LOCUST ST 45177	3-00100
Bennie Trail, prin.	382-7556

Southern State Community College	2-CC
2698 OLD ST ROUTE 73 45177	
Wilmington College	4-UC
PO BOX 1185 45177	382-6661

Windham, AC 216, PC 5, Portage

Windham EVD, 9530 BAUER AVE 44288	4-11111
Jack Raymond, supt.	326-2711
HS, 9530 BAUER AVE 44288	2-00011
Vincent Frammartino, prin.	326-3916
MS, 9530 BAUER AVE 44288	2-00100
Douglas Kilbreath, prin.	326-3490

Wintersville, AC 614, PC 5, Jefferson

Indian Creek Local SD	
Supt. — See Mingo Junction	
Indian Creek HS, 200 PARK DR 43952	3-00001
William Huber, prin.	264-1163
Indian Creek JHS, 100 PARK DR 43952	3-00110
Courtland Stewart, prin.	264-5521

Woodsfield, AC 614, PC 5, Monroe

Switzerland of Ohio Local SD	5-11111
304 MILL ST 43793	472-5801
Richard Edge, supt.	
HS, 204 S PAUL ST 43793	2-00011
Tim Haught, prin.	472-0954

Swiss Hills Vo HS	Vo Tech
46601 E STATE ROUTE 78 43793	472-0722
Joseph Smith, prin.	
Other Schools – See Beallsville, Graysville, Hannibal	

Woodville, AC 419, PC 4, Sandusky

Woodmore Local SD	4-11111
708 W MAIN ST 43469	849-2381
Thomas Robey, supt.	
Other Schools – See Elmore	

Wooster, AC 216, PC 7, Wayne

Triway Local SD	4-11111
3205 SHREVE RD 44691	264-9491
Kevin DiDonato, supt.	
Triway HS, 3205 SHREVE RD 44691	3-00011
Larry Foltz, prin.	264-8685
Triway JHS, 3145 SHREVE RD 44691	2-00100
James Butler, prin.	264-2114
Wooster CSD, 144 N MARKET ST 44691	5-11111
H. Davidson, supt.	264-0869
HS, 101 W BOWMAN ST 44691	4-00011
David Burnison, prin.	264-9948
Edgewood MS	3-00100
2695 GRAUSTARK PATH 44691	345-6475
Davis Baker, prin.	

College of Wooster	4-UC
1189 BEALL AVE 44691	263-2311
Ohio State University-A & T Institute	3-CC
1328 DOVER RD 44691	264-3911

Worthington, AC 614, PC 7, Franklin

Worthington CSD, 752 HIGH ST 43085	6-11111
Damon Asbury, supt.	431-6500
HS, 300 W GRANVILLE RD 43085	4-00011
William Northrup, prin.	431-6565
McCord MS, 1500 HARD RD 43235	3-00100
Jeanne Paliotto, prin.	431-6550
Perry MS, 2341 SNOUFFER RD 43085	2-00100
Bill Billinghurs, prin.	431-6555
Worthingway MS, 6625 GUYER ST 43085	2-00100
Paul Cynkar, prin.	431-6560
Other Schools – See West Worthington	

Worthington Christian HS	2-00011
6670 WORTHINGTON GALENA RD 43085	
Taylor Smith, prin.	431-8210

Xenia, AC 513, PC 7, Greene

Greene County JVSD	3-00001
2960 W ENON RD 45385	372-6941
James Clendening, supt.	
Greene County Career Ctr Joint Vo SHS	3-00001
2960 W ENON RD 45385	372-6941
Terry Bissett, prin.	
Xenia CSD, 578 E MARKET ST 45385	6-11111
Robert Williams, supt.	376-2961
SHS, 303 KINSEY RD 45385	4-00001
Steve Clifton, prin.	372-6983
Central JHS, 425 EDISON BLVD 45385	3-00110
Edward Stidham, prin.	372-7635
Warner JHS, 600 BUCKSKIN TRL 45385	3-00110
Gale Adkins, prin.	376-9488

Woodrow Wilson School	HND
690 HOME AVE 45385	

Yellow Springs, AC 513, PC 5, Greene

Yellow Springs EVD	3-11111
201 S WALNUT ST 45387	767-7381
Kenneth Yonkee, supt.	
JSHS, 420 E ENON RD 45387	2-00111
Cynthia Holt, prin.	767-7224

Antioch University	5-UC
795 LIVERMORE ST 45387	767-7331

Youngstown, AC 216, PC 8, Mahoning

Austintown Local SD	6-11111
225 IDAHO RD 44515	797-3911
Richard Denamen, supt.	
Fitch HS, 4560 FALCON DR 44515	4-00011
Thomas Inchak, prin.	797-3900
Austintown MS	3-01100
5800 MAHONING AVE 44515	797-3923
Daniel Bokesch, prin.	
Ohl MS, 255 IDAHO RD 44515	3-01100
Anthony Zoccali, prin.	797-3915

Boardman Local SD	6-11111
7410 MARKET ST 44512	726-3404
Richard Selby, supt.	
Boardman HS	4-00011
7777 GLENWOOD AVE 44512	758-7511
Louis Rucci, prin.	
Center MS, 7410 MARKET ST 44512	3-01100
Terry Samuels, prin.	726-3400
Glenwood MS	3-01100
7635 GLENWOOD AVE 44512	726-3414
Anthony Alvino, prin.	

Liberty Local SD, 4115 SHADY RD 44505	4-11111
Bruce Jones, supt.	759-0807
Liberty HS	3-00011
317 CHURCHILL HUBBARD RD 44505	759-2301
Larry Prince, prin.	
Guy MS, 4115 SHADY RD 44505	2-01100
Mark Lucas, prin.	759-1733

Youngstown CSD, PO BOX 550 44501	7-11111
Alfred Tutela, supt.	744-6900
Chaney HS	4-00011
731 S HAZELWOOD AVE 44509	744-8822
William Terlesky, prin.	
East HS, 1544 E HIGH AVE 44505	3-00011
George Ritz, prin.	744-8845
Rayen HS, 250 BENITA AVE 44504	4-00011
Anthony Cassano, prin.	744-8550
Wilson HS, 2725 GIBSON ST 44502	4-00011
Vincent Procopio, prin.	744-8525
Choffin Career Ctr	Vo Tech
200 E WOOD ST 44503 – (—), prin.	744-8700
Adams MS, 2537 COOPER ST 44502	2-00100
Richard DeVincentis, prin.	744-8955
Hayes MS, 1616 FORD AVE 44504	3-01100
Laurence Lushinsky, prin.	744-7602
Hillman MS, 164 W MYRTLE AVE 44507	2-01100
(—), prin.	744-7535
North MS, 2724 MARINER AVE 44505	2-00100
Fred Canning, prin.	744-7823
Princeton MS, 2546 HILLMAN ST 44507	2-00100
Larry Spires, prin.	744-7847
Rogers JHS	2-00100
2400 S SCHENLEY AVE 44511	744-7996
Richard Saul, prin.	

Calvary Christian Academy	2-11111
1812 OAK HILL AVE 44507	747-4445
Arnold Wagner, prin.	
Cardinal Mooney HS	3-00011
2545 ERIE ST 44507	788-5007
Sr. Jane Kudlacz, prin.	
Choffin Career Center	2-CS
PO BOX 550 44501	744-6915
ITT Technical Institute	3-CC
PO BOX 779 44501	747-5555
Penn-Ohio College	2-CS
3517 MARKET ST 44507	788-5084
St. Elizabeth Hospital	HSP
PO BOX 1790 44501	746-7211
Ursuline HS, 750 WICK AVE 44505	3-00011
Fr. Venglarik, prin.	744-4563
Western Reserve Care System	HSP
345 OAK HILL AVE 44502	747-0777
Youngstown Christian S	2-11111
125 WYCHWOOD LN 44512	788-8088
John Stone, prin.	
Youngstown State University	7-UC
410 WICK AVE 44555	742-3101

Zanesfield, AC 513, PC 2, Logan

Benjamin Logan Local SD	
Supt. — See Bellefontaine	
Logan MS, PO BOX 98 43360	2-00100
Michael Moore, prin.	599-2386

Zanesville, AC 614, PC 8, Muskingum

Maysville Local SD	4-11111
PO BOX 1818 43702	453-0754
Gary Reed, supt.	
Maysville SHS	2-00001
2805 PINKERTON LN 43701	453-0726
Paul Frederick, prin.	
Maysville JHS	2-00110
2725 PINKERTON LN 43701	454-9738
Steve German, prin.	
Mid-East Ohio JVSD	4-00011
1965 CHANDLERSVILLE RD 43701	454-0105
Joseph Lupo, supt.	
Muskingum-Perry Career Center SHS	3-00011
400 RICHARDS RD 43701	454-0101
Joseph Smith, prin.	
Other Schools – See Senecaville	
West Muskingum Local SD	4-11111
4880 WEST PIKE 43701	455-4052
J. Steinbrecher, supt.	
West Muskingum HS	3-00011
200 KIMES RD 43701	452-6312
Gary Ankrum, prin.	
West Muskingum MS	2-01100
100 KIMES RD 43701	455-4055
Kenton Stillwell, prin.	
Zanesville CSD, 160 N 4TH ST 43701	5-11111
James Robinson, supt.	454-9751
HS, 1701 BLUE AVE 43701	4-00011
Paul Langland, prin.	453-0335
Cleveland JHS, 714 PERSHING RD 43701	2-00100
James Lear, prin.	453-0636
Roosevelt JHS	2-00100
1275 ROOSEVELT AVE 43701	453-0711
H. Henderson, prin.	

Bishop Rosecrans HS	2-00011
1040 E MAIN ST 43701	452-7504
Mike Ross, prin.	
Muskingum Area Technical College	4-CC
1555 NEWARK RD 43701	454-2501
Ohio University	4-UC
1425 NEWARK RD 43701	453-0762

Zoarville, AC 216, PC 2, Tuscarawas

Tuscarawas Valley Local SD	4-11111
2637 TUSCARAWAS VALLEY NE 44656	
Robert Bowden, supt.	859-2213
Tuscarawas Valley JSHS	3-00111
2637 TUSCARAWAS VALLEY NE 44656	
James Brown, prin.	859-2421

OKLAHOMA

STATE DEPARTMENT OF EDUCATION
2500 N. Lincoln Blvd., Oklahoma City 73105
(405) 521-3301

Superintendent of Public Instruction	Sandy Garrett
Deputy Superintendent Accreditation/Standards	Hugh McCrabb
Assistant Superintendent Financial Services	Don Shive
Assistant Superintendent Federal/Special Services	Sid Hudson
Assistant Superintendent Professional Services	Ramona Paul

STATE BOARD OF EDUCATION
2500 N. Lincoln Blvd., Oklahoma City 73105

Chairperson   Sandy Garrett

PUBLIC, PRIVATE AND CATHOLIC SECONDARY SCHOOLS

Achille, AC 405, PC 2, Bryan
Achille ISD, PO BOX 280 74720 — 2-11111 283-3775
  Roy Davis, supt.
HS, PO BOX 280 74720 — 2-00011 283-3775
  Linda Scribner, prin.

Ada, AC 405, PC 7, Pontotoc
Ada ISD, PO BOX 1359 74821 — 4-11111 332-0255
  Zane Bowman, supt.
SHS, 1400 STADIUM DR 74820 — 3-00001 332-6711
  Bill Nelson, prin.
JHS, 223 W 18TH ST 74820 — 2-00110 332-6900
  David Smith, prin.

Byng ISD, RR 3 BOX 215 74820 — 4-11111 436-3020
  Marvin Stokes, supt.
Byng SHS, RR 3 BOX 215 74820 — 2-00001 332-4282
  Phil Parks, prin.
Byng JHS, PO BOX 2509 74821 — 2-00110 332-4282
  Tim Green, prin.

Latta ISD, RR 8 BOX 811 74820 — 3-11111 332-2092
  Donald Hoover, supt.
Latta SHS, RR 8 BOX 811 74820 — 2-00001 332-3300
  Bill Johnson, prin.
Latta JHS, RR 8 BOX 811 74820 — 2-00110 332-8180
  Shelby Morgan, prin.

Vanoss ISD, RR 5 BOX 119 74820 — 2-11111 759-2251
  Kenneth Smith, supt.
Vanoss HS, RR 5 BOX 119 74820 — 2-00011 759-2503
  Gary Self, prin.

East Central University 74820 — 5-UC 332-8000
Valley View Regional Hospital — HSP
  430 N MONTE VISTA ST 74820 — 332-2323

Adair, AC 918, PC 3, Mayes
Adair ISD, PO BOX 197 74330 — 3-11111 785-2424
  Jack Dryden, supt.
HS, PO BOX 197 74330 — 2-00011 785-2424
  Lonnie Midgley, prin.
MS, PO BOX 197 74330 — 2-00100 785-2425
  Clifton Collins, prin.

Afton, AC 918, PC 3, Ottawa
Afton ISD, PO BOX 100 74331 — 2-11111 257-8303
  Randy Gardner, supt.
HS, PO BOX 100 74331 — 2-00011 257-8305
  Tom Linihan, prin.

Agra, AC 918, PC 2, Lincoln
Agra ISD, PO BOX 279 74824 — 2-11111 375-2262
  Wesley McFarland, supt.
HS, PO BOX 279 74824 — 2-00011 375-2261
  Rick Storey, prin.

Alex, AC 405, PC 3, Grady
Alex ISD, PO BOX 188 73002 — 2-11111 785-2605
  Vernon Florence, supt.
JSHS, PO BOX 188 73002 — 2-00111 785-2264
  Jim Coale, prin.

Aline, AC 405, PC 2, Alfalfa
Aline-Cleo ISD, PO BOX 49 73716 — 2-11111 463-2255
  Gene Velharticky, supt.
Aline-Cleo JSHS, PO BOX 49 73716 — 1-00111 463-2256
  Melvin Ricke, prin.

Allen, AC 405, PC 3, Pontotoc
Allen ISD, PO BOX 430 74825 — 2-11111 857-2416
  Doyle Wilson, supt.
HS, PO BOX 430 74825 — 2-00011 857-2481
  Gregory Caldwell, prin.

Altus, AC 405, PC 7, Jackson
Altus ISD, PO BOX 558 73522 — 5-11111 481-2100
  Mike Copeland, supt.
SHS, PO BOX 558 73522 — 3-00001 481-2167
  Jerry Winkle, prin.
JHS, PO BOX 558 73522 — 3-00110 481-2173
  Bruce May, prin.

Navajo ISD, RR 2 BOX 84A 73521 — 2-11111 482-7742
  Gary Montgomery, supt.
Navajo JSHS, RR 2 BOX 84A 73521 — 1-00111 482-7742
  Robert Bowers, prin.

Western Oklahoma State College — 4-CC 477-2000
  2801 N MAIN ST 73521

Alva, AC 405, PC 6, Woods
Alva ISD, 501 14TH ST 73717 — 4-11111 327-4823
  Lynn Hoskins, supt.
HS, 501 14TH ST 73717 — 2-00011 327-3682
  Steve Parkhurst, prin.
MS, 800 FLYNN ST 73717 — 2-00100 327-0608
  John Edelmann, prin.
Other Schools — See Carmen

Northwestern State University — 4-UC 327-1700
  705 OKLAHOMA BLVD 73717

Amber, AC 405, PC 2, Grady
Amber-Pocasset ISD — 2-11111 224-5768
  PO BOX 38 73004
  W. Jackson, supt.
Amber-Pocasset JSHS — 2-00111 224-4017
  PO BOX 38 73004
  Jack Jerman, prin.

Ames, AC 405, PC 2, Major
Cimarron ISD
  Supt. — See Lahoma
MS, PO BOX 508 73718 — 2-01100 753-4605
  Chris Sparks, prin.

Anadarko, AC 405, PC 6, Caddo
Anadarko ISD — 4-11111 247-6605
  1400 S MISSION ST 73005
  Roy Swan, supt.
SHS, 1400 S MISSION ST 73005 — 3-00001 247-2486
  Sherrill Neal, prin.
JHS, 1400 S MISSION ST 73005 — 2-00110 247-6671
  Don Coble, prin.

Antlers, AC 405, PC 5, Pushmataha
Antlers ISD, 306 NE A ST 74523 — 3-11111 298-5504
  James Begin, supt.
HS, 306 NE A ST 74523 — 2-00011 298-2141
  Bob Barnes, prin.
Obuch MS, 306 NE A ST 74523 — 2-00100 298-3308
  Jerry Brown, prin.

Apache, AC 405, PC 4, Caddo
Boone-Apache ISD — 3-11111 588-3369
  PO BOX 354 73006
  Marvin Rehl, supt.
HS, PO BOX 354 73006 — 2-00011 588-3358
  Joe Stick, prin.
MS, PO BOX 354 73006 — 2-00100 588-2122
  Linda Myers, prin.

Arapaho, AC 405, PC 3, Custer
Arapaho ISD, PO BOX 160 73620 — 2-11111 323-3261
  Palmer Mosely, supt.

JSHS, PO BOX 160 73620 — 2-00111 323-3261
  Bob Haggard, prin.

Ardmore, AC 405, PC 7, Carter
Ardmore ISD, PO BOX 1709 73402 — 5-11111 223-2483
  Richard Ohara, supt.
HS, PO BOX 1709 73402 — 3-00011 226-7680
  James Meece, prin.
MS, PO BOX 1709 73402 — 3-00100 223-2475
  J. Thompson, prin.

Dickson ISD, RR 4 BOX 122 73401 — 4-11111 223-9557
  Bill Russell, supt.
Dickson HS, RR 4 BOX 122 73401 — 2-00011 226-0633
  Bob Parkhill, prin.
Dickson MS, RR 4 BOX 122 73401 — 2-00100 223-2700
  Brad Jones, prin.

Plainview ISD — 4-11111 223-6319
  1140 N PLAINVIEW RD 73401
  John Merlyn, supt.
Plainview HS — 2-00011 223-5877
  1140 N PLAINVIEW RD 73401
  Stephen Matthews, prin.
Plainview MS — 2-00100 223-6502
  1140 N PLAINVIEW RD 73401
  Glenn Smith, prin.

Oklahoma State Horseshoeing School — 2-CS 223-0064
  RR 1 BOX 28B 73401

Arkoma, AC 918, PC 4, Leflore
Arkoma ISD, PO BOX 349 74901 — 3-11111 875-3351
  Neil Brannon, supt.
JSHS, PO BOX 349 74901 — 2-00111 875-3353
  Paul Rainwater, prin.

Arnett, AC 405, PC 3, Ellis
Arnett ISD, PO BOX 317 73832 — 2-11111 885-7811
  Darrell Gunsaulis, supt.
HS, PO BOX 317 73832 — 1-00111 885-7285
  Darrell Gunsaulis, prin.

Asher, AC 405, PC 2, Pottawatomie
Asher ISD, PO BOX 168 74826 — 2-11111 784-2332
  John Hamilton, supt.
HS, PO BOX 168 74826 — 1-00011 784-2331
  Tom Larmen, prin.

Atoka, AC 405, PC 5, Atoka
Atoka ISD, PO BOX 720 74525 — 4-11111 889-6611
  Bill Crow, supt.
SHS, PO BOX 720 74525 — 3-00001 889-3361
  Curtis Inge, prin.
JHS, PO BOX 720 74525 — 2-00110 889-3553
  Gary McDonald, prin.

Tushka ISD, RR 4 BOX 2630 74525 — 2-11111 889-7355
  Dan Cooper, supt.
Tushka HS, RR 4 BOX 2630 74525 — 2-00011 889-7355
  Bill Pingleton, prin.

Balko, AC 405, PC 2, Beaver
Balko ISD, RR 1 BOX 37 73931 — 2-11111 646-3385
  Ed Thomas, supt.
HS, RR 1 BOX 37 73931 — 1-00011 646-3385
  Ed Thomas, prin.

Barnsdall, AC 918, PC 4, Osage
Barnsdall ISD, PO BOX 629 74002 — 3-11111 847-2271
  James Caldwell, supt.
JSHS, PO BOX 629 74002 — 2-00111 847-2721
  J. P. Hukill, prin.

Bartlesville, AC 918, PC 8, Washington
Bartlesville ISD, PO BOX 1357 74005 — 6-11111
John Scroggins, supt. — 336-8600
SHS, 1700 HILLCREST DR 74004 — 4-00001
Bill Denton, prin. — 336-3311
Mid. HS, 5900 BAYLOR DR 74006 — 3-00010
Ron Jared, prin. — 333-4444
Central MS, PO BOX 1357 74005 — 3-00100
Earl Sears, prin. — 336-9302
Madison MS — 3-00100
500 S MADISON BLVD 74006 — 333-3176
John Ward, prin.

Bartlesville Wesleyan College — 2-UC
2201 SILVERLAKE RD 74006 — 335-6234

Battiest, AC 405, PC 2, McCurtain
Battiest ISD, PO BOX 199 74722 — 2-11111
Ken Keeling, supt. — 241-7810
JSHS, PO BOX 199 74722 — 2-00111
Joanna Walden, prin. — 241-5550

Beaver, AC 405, PC 4, Beaver
Beaver ISD, PO BOX 580 73932 — 3-11111
Glen Love, supt. — 625-3444
HS, PO BOX 580 73932 — 2-00011
Rodger Hilton, prin. — 625-3444

Beggs, AC 918, PC 4, Okmulgee
Beggs ISD, PO BOX 690 74421 — 3-11111
Leslie Johnston, supt. — 267-3625
HS, PO BOX 690 74421 — 2-00011
Doyle Patterson, prin. — 267-3625
MS, PO BOX 690 74421 — 2-00100
David Haynes, prin. — 267-4916

Bennington, AC 405, PC 2, Bryan
Bennington ISD, PO BOX 10 74723 — 2-11111
A. McDonald, supt. — 847-2737
HS, PO BOX 10 74723 — 2-00011
Mary Knight, prin. — 847-2310

Bethany, AC 405, PC 7, Oklahoma
Bethany ISD, 6721 NW 42ND ST 73008 — 2-11111
G. Dickerson, supt. — 789-3801
HS, 6721 NW 42ND ST 73008 — 2-00011
Jay Griffis, prin. — 789-6370
MS, 6721 NW 42ND ST 73008 — 2-00100
Jim Eason, prin. — 787-3240

Putnam City ISD
Supt. — See Oklahoma City
Western Oaks MS — 3-00100
7200 NW 23RD ST 73008 — 789-4434
Ken O'Hagan, prin.

Southern Nazarene University — 4-UC
6729 NW 39TH EXPY 73008 — 491-6304
Southwestern Coll. Christian Ministries — 1-UC
PO BOX 340 73008 — 789-7661

Billings, AC 405, PC 3, Noble
Billings ISD, PO BOX 39 74630 — 2-11111
(—), supt. — 725-3271
HS, PO BOX 39 74630 — 1-00011
William Thomas, prin. — 725-3271

Binger, AC 405, PC 3, Caddo
Binger-Oney ISD, PO BOX 280 73009 — 2-11111
Wayne Britton, supt. — 656-2304
Binger-Oney HS, PO BOX 280 73009 — 1-00011
Ted George, prin. — 656-2304

Bixby, AC 918, PC 6, Tulsa
Bixby ISD, PO BOX 160 74008 — 4-11111
George Hayes, supt. — 366-4421
SHS, PO BOX 160 74008 — 3-00001
Tom Outhier, prin. — 366-4421
JHS, PO BOX 160 74008 — 3-00110
G Michael Cox, prin. — 366-4421

Blackwell, AC 405, PC 6, Kay
Blackwell ISD, 934 S 1ST ST 74631 — 4-11111
Dr. Richard Strahorn, supt. — 363-2570
HS, 303 E COOLIDGE AVE 74631 — 2-00011
Kendall Evans, prin. — 363-3553
MS, 934 S 1ST ST 74631 — 2-00100
Dan Bringham, prin. — 363-2100

Blair, AC 405, PC 3, Jackson
Blair ISD, PO BOX 428 73526 — 2-11111
Gary McLaughlin, supt. — 563-2632
HS, PO BOX 428 73526 — 2-00011
Jim Dollar, prin. — 563-2486

Blanchard, AC 405, PC 4, McClain
Blanchard ISD, PO BOX 2620 73010 — 4-11111
Ray Woodson, supt. — 485-3391
JSHS, PO BOX 2620 73010 — 2-00111
Glen Castle, prin. — 485-3392

Bridge Creek ISD — 3-11111
RR 1 BOX 407 73010 — 387-4880
Jim Pothorst, supt.
Bridge Creek SHS — 2-00001
RR 1 BOX 407 73010 — 387-3981
Terry Brown, prin.
Bridge Creek JHS — 2-00110
RR 1 BOX 407 73010 — 387-9681
Dan Beck, prin.

Bluejacket, AC 918, PC 2, Craig
Bluejacket ISD, PO BOX 29 74333 — 2-11111
Duane Thomas, supt. — 784-2365

JSHS, PO BOX 29 74333 — 1-00111
Duane Thomas, prin. — 784-2365

Boise City, AC 405, PC 4, Cimarron
Boise City ISD, PO BOX 1116 73933 — 2-11111
Bill Terry, supt. — 544-3110
HS, PO BOX 1116 73933 — 2-00011
Bill Ramsey, prin. — 544-3111

Bokchito, AC 405, PC 3, Bryan
Rock Creek SD, PO BOX 208 74726 — 2-11111
David Dailey, supt. — 295-3761
Rock Creek HS, PO BOX 208 74726 — 1-00011
Clyde Smith, prin. — 295-3761

Bokoshe, AC 918, PC 2, Leflore
Bokoshe ISD, PO BOX 158 74930 — 2-11111
Bill Reece, supt. — 969-2491
JSHS, PO BOX 158 74930 — 2-00111
J. Norman Hoffman, prin. — 969-2341

Boley, AC 918, PC 3, Okfuskee
Boley ISD, PO BOX 248 74829 — 2-11111
Frank Parrino, supt. — 667-3324
JSHS, PO BOX 248 74829 — 1-00111
Frank Parrino, prin. — 667-3324

Boswell, AC 405, PC 3, Choctaw
Boswell ISD, PO BOX 839 74727 — 2-11111
Jerry Combrink, supt. — 566-2735
JSHS, PO BOX 839 74727 — 2-00111
Curtis Cockrell, prin. — 566-2735

Bowlegs, AC 405, PC 2, Seminole
Bowlegs ISD, PO BOX 88 74830 — 2-11111
Charles Bundy, supt. — 398-4322
HS, PO BOX 88 74830 — 2-00011
Glen Bryan, prin. — 398-4376

Boynton, AC 918, PC 2, Muskogee
Boynton ISD, PO BOX 97 74422 — 2-11111
Donald Arney, supt. — 472-7330
HS, PO BOX 97 74422 — 1-00011
Jerry Belton, prin. — 472-7310

Braggs, AC 918, PC 2, Muskogee
Braggs ISD, PO BOX 59 74423 — 2-11111
Jerry Allen, supt. — 487-5265
HS, PO BOX 59 74423 — 1-00011
Dudley Hume, prin. — 487-5265

Braman, AC 405, PC 2, Kay
Braman ISD, PO BOX 130 74632 — 2-11111
Duncan Coons, supt. — 385-2191
HS, PO BOX 130 74632 — 1-00011
Jerry Frieouf, prin. — 385-2191

Bray, AC 405, PC 3, Stephens
Bray-Doyle ISD, PO BOX 711 73055 — 2-11111
R Kevin Mckinley, supt. — 658-5076
HS, PO BOX 711 73055 — 2-00011
Jack Williams, prin. — 658-5071

Bristow, AC 918, PC 5, Creek
Bristow ISD, 134 W 9TH AVE 74010 — 4-11111
Bill Stephens, supt. — 367-5555
SHS, 134 W 9TH AVE 74010 — 2-00001
Bob Steward, prin. — 367-2241
JHS, 134 W 9TH AVE 74010 — 2-00110
Jerry Lomenick, prin. — 367-3551

Broken Arrow, AC 918, PC 8, Tulsa
Broken Arrow ISD, 601 S MAIN ST 74012 — 7-11111
Jerry Hill, supt. — 251-8541
SHS, 1901 E ALBANY ST 74012 — 4-00001
Max Smith, prin. — 355-2696
Central MS, 210 N MAIN ST 74012 — 2-00100
Steve Smith, prin. — 251-8551
Childers MS, 301 E TUCSON ST 74011 — 2-00100
Barbara Evans, prin. — 451-3022
Haskell MS, 412 S 9TH ST 74012 — 3-00100
Sally Parker, prin. — 251-1563
North IS, 808 E COLLEGE ST 74012 — 4-00010
Paul Collins, prin. — 258-8696
Sequoyah MS, 2701 S ELM PL 74012 — 4-00100
John Stockstill, prin. — 455-5030
South IS — 4-00010
301 W NEW ORLEANS ST 74011 — 455-3600
Randy Pierce, prin.

Union ISD
Supt. — See Tulsa
Union JHS, 7616 S GARNETT RD 74012 — 4-00010
Art Naylor, prin. — 254-8644

Broken Bow, AC 405, PC 5, McCurtain
Broken Bow ISD, 108 W 5TH ST 74728 — 4-11111
Gwyn Slaton, supt. — 584-3306
HS, 108 W 5TH ST 74728 — 3-00011
Mike Vadnais, prin. — 584-3365
MS, 108 W 5TH ST 74728 — 2-00100
Howard Minor, prin. — 584-9603

Buffalo, AC 405, PC 4, Harper
Buffalo ISD, PO BOX 130 73834 — 2-11111
Michael Parkhurst, supt. — 735-2419
JSHS, PO BOX 130 73834 — 2-00111
Gene Baird, prin. — 735-2448

Burlington, AC 405, PC 2, Alfalfa
Burlington ISD, PO BOX 17 73722 — 2-11111
Glen Elliott, supt. — 431-2501
HS, PO BOX 17 73722 — 1-00011
Terry Carris, prin. — 431-2222

Burneyville, AC 405, PC 1, Love
Turner ISD, PO BOX 159 73430 — 2-11111
Lanny Sliger, supt. — 276-3873
Turner HS, PO BOX 159 73430 — 2-00011
John Cartwright, prin. — 276-4365

Burns Flat, AC 405, PC 4, Washita
Burns Flat-Dill City ISD — 2-11111
PO BOX 129 73624 — 562-4844
Donald Lemke, supt.
Burns Flat HS, PO BOX 129 73624 — 1-00011
Robert Birdwell, prin. — 562-4846

Butler, AC 405, PC 2, Custer
Butler ISD, PO BOX 127 73625 — 2-11111
Larry Mills, supt. — 664-3295
HS, PO BOX 127 73625 — 1-00011
Larry Mills, prin. — 664-3295

Cache, AC 405, PC 4, Comanche
Cache ISD, PO BOX 418 73527 — 3-11111
Don Colwell, supt. — 429-3266
HS, PO BOX 418 73527 — 2-00011
Dale Munyon, prin. — 429-3214
MS, PO BOX 418 73527 — 2-00100
Terry Stricker, prin. — 429-8489

Caddo, AC 405, PC 3, Bryan
Caddo ISD, PO BOX 128 74729 — 2-11111
Terry Ragan, supt. — 367-2210
HS, PO BOX 128 74729 — 2-00011
Tom Frederick, prin. — 367-2210

Calera, AC 405, PC 5, Bryan
Calera ISD, PO BOX 386 74730 — 2-11111
Hall Alexander, supt. — 434-5700
HS, PO BOX 386 74730 — 2-00011
Charles Hawthorne, prin. — 434-5158

Calumet, AC 405, PC 3, Canadian
Calumet ISD, PO BOX 10 73014 — 2-11111
Larry Davison, supt. — 893-2222
HS, PO BOX 10 73014 — 2-00011
Dennis Hix, prin. — 893-2222

Calvin, AC 405, PC 2, Hughes
Calvin ISD, PO BOX 127 74531 — 2-11111
Leroy Orr, supt. — 645-2411
JSHS, PO BOX 127 74531 — 2-00011
Shelly Turpin, prin. — 645-2411

Cameron, AC 918, PC 2, Leflore
Cameron ISD, PO BOX 190 74932 — 2-11111
Charles Caughern, supt. — 654-3412
HS, PO BOX 190 74932 — 2-00011
Marvin Stewart, prin. — 654-3412

Canadian, AC 918, PC 2, Pittsburg
Canadian ISD, PO BOX 168 74425 — 2-11111
Charles Caughern, supt. — 339-2705
HS, PO BOX 168 74425 — 1-00011
Gary Rind, prin. — 339-2705

Caney, AC 405, PC 2, Atoka
Caney ISD, PO BOX 60 74533 — 2-11111
S. Maxwell, supt. — 889-6607
JSHS, PO BOX 60 74533 — 2-00111
Nick Brister, prin. — 889-6607

Canton, AC 405, PC 3, Blaine
Canton ISD, PO BOX 639 73724 — 2-11111
Gayle Hajny, supt. — 886-3516
HS, PO BOX 639 73724 — 2-00011
DeWayne Sinclair, prin. — 886-2256

Canute, AC 405, PC 3, Washita
Canute ISD, PO BOX 490 73626 — 2-11111
Ken Leddy, supt. — 472-3295
HS, PO BOX 490 73626 — 1-00011
Mike Maddox, prin. — 472-3782

Carmen, AC 405, PC 2, Alfalfa
Alva ISD
Supt. — See Alva
Carmen-Dacoma JSHS — 2-00111
PO BOX 129 73726 — 987-2348
Raymond Moss, prin.

Carnegie, AC 405, PC 4, Caddo
Carnegie ISD, RR 2 BOX 44C 73015 — 3-11111
Harold Butler, supt. — 654-1470
SHS, RR 2 BOX 44C 73015 — 2-00001
Lonnie Bliss, prin. — 654-1266
JHS, RR 2 BOX 44C 73015 — 2-00110
Dan Faulkner, prin. — 654-1766

Carney, AC 405, PC 3, Lincoln
Carney ISD, PO BOX 240 74832 — 2-11111
Charles O'Donnell, supt. — 865-2344
HS, PO BOX 240 74832 — 1-00011
Charles O'Donnell, prin. — 865-2345

Carter, AC 405, PC 2, Beckham
Carter ISD, PO BOX 520 73627 — 2-11111
Hal Scott, supt. — 486-3241
HS, PO BOX 520 73627 — 1-00011
Hal Scott, prin. — 486-3241

Cashion, AC 405, PC 2, Kingfisher
Cashion ISD, PO BOX 100 73016 — 2-11111
Larry Mays, supt. — 433-2741
HS, PO BOX 100 73016 — 2-00011
Dwain Jindra, prin. — 433-2575

Catoosa, AC 918, PC 5, Rogers
Catoosa ISD — 4-11111
2000 S CHEROKEE ST 74015 — 266-1631
Darrell Gwartney, supt.

HS, 2000 S CHEROKEE ST 74015 | 3-00011 266-2224
Everitt Putman, prin.
Wells MS, 2000 S CHEROKEE ST 74015 | 2-00100 266-1170
Raymond Dunbar, prin.

Cement, AC 405, PC 3, Caddo
Cement ISD, PO BOX 60 73017 | 2-11111 489-3216
Jessee Middick, supt.
HS, PO BOX 60 73017 | 2-00011 489-3218
Dale Osborn, prin.

Chandler, AC 405, PC 5, Lincoln
Chandler ISD, 515 STEELE AVE 74834 | 3-11111 258-1450
Carl Moore, supt.
SHS, 515 STEELE AVE 74834 | 2-00001 258-1269
Charles Miller, prin.
JHS, 515 STEELE AVE 74834 | 2-00110 258-0183
Joe Telford, prin.

Chattanooga, AC 405, PC 2, Comanche
Chattanooga ISD, PO BOX 129 73528 | 2-11111 597-3347
Bob Piguet, supt.
HS, PO BOX 129 73528 | 2-00011 597-3347
Alvie Claborn, prin.

Checotah, AC 918, PC 5, McIntosh
Checotah ISD, PO BOX 289 74426 | 4-11111 473-5610
Patricia Sholar, supt.
HS, PO BOX 289 74426 | 2-00011 473-2239
Jack Pugh, prin.
MS, PO BOX 289 74426 | 2-00100 473-2384
Dennis Holland, prin.

Chelsea, AC 918, PC 4, Rogers
Chelsea ISD, 306 W 6TH ST 74016 | 3-11111 789-2528
Joe Gill, supt.
HS, 306 W 6TH ST 74016 | 2-00011 789-2533
Gary Berry, prin.
MS, 306 W 6TH ST 74016 | 2-00100 789-2521
Randy Wassam, prin.

Cherokee, AC 405, PC 4, Alfalfa
Cherokee ISD, PO BOX 325 73728 | 2-11111 596-3391
Merlin Overton, supt.
JSHS, PO BOX 325 73728 | 2-00111 596-3391
Rick Brown, prin.

Cheyenne, AC 405, PC 3, Roger Mills
Cheyenne ISD, PO BOX 650 73628 | 2-11111 497-2666
Galeard Roper, supt.
JSHS, PO BOX 650 73628 | 2-00011 497-3371
Jim Burns, prin.

Chickasha, AC 405, PC 7, Grady
Chickasha ISD
900 W CHOCTAW AVE 73018 | 5-11111 222-6500
Merrill Smith, supt.
SHS, 900 W CHOCTAW AVE 73018 | 3-00001 222-6550
Sharon Elkouri, prin.
JHS, 900 W CHOCTAW AVE 73018 | 2-00110 222-6530
Richard Weidenmaier, prin.

University of Sciences & Arts of OK | 4-UC 224-3140
PO BOX 82345 73018

Choctaw, AC 405, PC 6, Oklahoma
Choctaw/Nicoma Park ISD
12880 NE 10TH ST 73020 | 8-11111 769-4859
Roger Damerow, supt.
SHS, 14300 NE 10TH ST 73020 | 4-00001 390-8899
Stephen Beall, prin.
JHS, 14667 NE 3RD ST 73020 | 3-00110 390-2208
Roy Howell, prin.
Other Schools – See Nicoma Park

Chouteau, AC 918, PC 4, Mayes
Chouteau-Mazie ISD
PO BOX 969 74337 | 3-11111 476-8336
Harvey Dooley, supt.
Chouteau-Mazie HS
PO BOX 969 74337 | 2-00011 476-8334
Glinna Fleming, prin.
Chouteau-Mazie MS
PO BOX 969 74337 | 2-00100 476-5912
Joe Straw, prin.

Claremore, AC 918, PC 7, Rogers
Claremore ISD, PO BOX 907 74018 | 5-11111 341-2213
Keith Ballard, supt.
SHS, 1910 N FLORENCE AVE 74017 | 3-00001 341-0724
Cleve Kinnear, prin.
Rogers JHS, 100 W 4TH ST 74017 | 3-00110 341-7411
James Griggs, prin.

Sequoyah ISD, RR 3 BOX 200 74017 | 3-11111 341-5472
Tom Cameron, supt.
Sequoyah HS, RR 3 BOX 200 74017 | 2-00011 341-0642
Reggie Baughman, prin.
Sequoyah MS, RR 3 BOX 200 74017 | 2-00100 341-5537
John Rhine, prin.

Verdigris ISD | 2-11110 266-2336
6101 SW VERDIGRIS RD 74017
Richard Holmes, supt.
Verdigris JHS | 2-00110 266-2336
6101 SW VERDIGRIS RD 74017
Richard Holmes, prin.

Rogers State College | 4-CC 341-7510
1701 W WILL ROGERS BLVD 74017

Clarita, AC 405, PC 2, Coal
Olney ISD, PO BOX 129 74535 | 2-11111 428-3293
Charles Lewis, supt.

Olney HS, PO BOX 129 74535 | 1-00011 428-3293
Charles Lewis, prin.

Clayton, AC 918, PC 3, Pushmataha
Clayton ISD, PO BOX 190 74536 | 2-11111 569-4492
Gary Newberry, supt.
HS, PO BOX 190 74536 | 2-00011 569-4156
Raymond Richards, prin.

Cleveland, AC 918, PC 5, Pawnee
Cleveland ISD, 600 N GILBERT ST 74020 | 4-11111 358-2210
Dan Poindexter, supt.
HS, 600 N GILBERT ST 74020 | 3-00011 358-2529
Ronald Ward, prin.
MS, 600 N GILBERT ST 74020 | 1-00100 358-2533
Doug Thomas, prin.

Clinton, AC 405, PC 6, Custer
Clinton ISD, PO BOX 729 73601 | 4-11111 323-1800
Don Scales, supt.
HS, PO BOX 729 73601 | 3-00011 323-1230
Robert Roshell, prin.
MS, PO BOX 729 73601 | 2-00100 323-4228
Fred Friedrich, prin.

Coalgate, AC 405, PC 4, Coal
Coalgate ISD, PO BOX 368 74538 | 3-11111 927-2351
John Linton, supt.
HS, PO BOX 368 74538 | 2-00011 927-2592
Jim Faubion, prin.
Byrd MS, PO BOX 368 74538 | 2-00100 927-3560
Allen Hicks, prin.

Colbert, AC 405, PC 4, Bryan
Colbert ISD, PO BOX 310 74733 | 2-11111 296-2624
James Lowrance, supt.
JSHS, PO BOX 310 74733 | 2-00111 296-2590
David Hughes, prin.

Colcord, AC 918, PC 3, Delaware
Colcord ISD, PO BOX 188 74338 | 3-11111 326-4116
Kelly Hampton, supt.
JSHS, PO BOX 188 74338 | 2-00111 326-4107
Dell Heavener, prin.

Coleman, AC 405, PC 2, Johnston
Coleman ISD, PO BOX 218 73432 | 2-11111 937-4418
Randel Johnson, supt.
HS, PO BOX 218 73432 | 1-00011 937-4418
Ronald Germany, prin.

Collinsville, AC 918, PC 5, Tulsa
Collinsville ISD
2400 W BROADWAY ST 74021 | 4-11111 371-2326
Pat Herald, supt.
HS, 2400 W BROADWAY ST 74021 | 3-00011 371-3382
Denny Prince, prin.
MS, 2400 W BROADWAY ST 74021 | 2-00100 371-2541
Nancy Travers, prin.

Comanche, AC 405, PC 4, Stephens
Comanche ISD, PO BOX 310 73529 | 4-11111 439-8826
Dewayne Baxter, supt.
HS, PO BOX 310 73529 | 2-00011 439-8824
Dan Mitchell, prin.
JHS, PO BOX 310 73529 | 2-00100 439-6635
Clarese Barnett, prin.

Commerce, AC 918, PC 4, Ottawa
Commerce ISD, 420 D ST 74339 | 3-11111 675-4343
Jim Haynes, supt.
HS, 420 D ST 74339 | 2-00011 675-4343
John Greenfield, prin.
MS, 420 D ST 74339 | 2-00100 675-4101
Jerry Miller, prin.

Copan, AC 918, PC 3, Washington
Copan ISD, PO BOX 429 74022 | 2-11111 532-4344
Delbert Moreland, supt.
HS, PO BOX 429 74022 | 1-00011 532-4344
Val Coleman, prin.

Cordell, AC 405, PC 5, Washita
Cordell ISD, PO BOX 290 73632 | 3-11111 832-3420
Jerry Burrows, supt.
SHS, PO BOX 290 73632 | 2-00001 832-3432
Gary Maynard, prin.
JHS, PO BOX 290 73632 | 2-00110 832-2233
Joe Crabb, prin.

Corn, AC 405, PC 3, Washita
Washita Heights ISD
PO BOX 8 73024 | 2-11111 343-2228
Mike Southall, supt.
Washita Heights JSHS
PO BOX 8 73024 | 1-00111 343-2298
Larry Wichert, prin.

Council Hill, AC 918, PC 2, Muskogee
Midway ISD, PO BOX 127 74428 | 2-11111 474-3434
Harley Whitman, supt.
Midway HS, PO BOX 127 74428 | 1-00011 474-3434
Harley Whitman, prin.

Covington, AC 405, PC 3, Garfield
Covington-Douglas ISD
PO BOX 9 73730 | 2-11111 864-7644
Don Boynton, supt.
HS, PO BOX 9 73730 | 1-00011 864-7482
Charles Metscher, prin.

Coweta, AC 918, PC 6, Wagoner
Coweta ISD, PO BOX 550 74429 | 4-11111 486-6506
Sam Farmer, supt.
SHS, PO BOX 550 74429 | 3-00001 486-4474
Henry Bias, prin.

JHS, PO BOX 550 74429 | 3-00110 486-2127
Lloyd Keaton, prin.

Coyle, AC 405, PC 2, Logan
Coyle ISD, PO BOX 287 73027 | 2-11111 466-2242
Larry Northcutt, supt.
HS, PO BOX 287 73027 | 2-00011 466-2242
Cliff Johnson, prin.

Crescent, AC 405, PC 4, Logan
Crescent ISD, PO BOX 719 73028 | 3-11111 969-3738
Robert Howard, supt.
HS, PO BOX 719 73028 | 2-00011 969-2545
Richard McCombs, prin.
JHS, PO BOX 719 73028 | 2-00100 969-2545
Richard McCombs, prin.

Cromwell, AC 405, PC 2, Seminole
Butner ISD, PO BOX 157 74837 | 2-11111 944-5530
Donald Davenport, supt.
Butner HS, PO BOX 157 74837 | 1-00011 944-5526
(—), prin.

Crowder, AC 918, PC 2, Pittsburg
Crowder ISD, PO BOX B 74430 | 2-11111 334-3203
David Jones, supt.
HS, PO BOX B 74430 | 2-00011 334-3204
Jim Colclasure, prin.

Cushing, AC 918, PC 6, Payne
Cushing ISD, PO BOX 1609 74023 | 4-11111 225-3425
Billy Childress, supt.
HS, 1700 E WALNUT ST 74023 | 3-00011 225-6622
James Lauerman, prin.
MS, 316 N STEELE AVE 74023 | 2-00100 225-1311
Ray Brumley, prin.

Custer City, AC 405, PC 2, Custer
Custer ISD, PO BOX 200 73639 | 2-11111 593-2259
James Sweeney, supt.
Custer JSHS, PO BOX 200 73639 | 1-00111 593-2257
Andy Goodson, prin.

Cyril, AC 405, PC 4, Caddo
Cyril ISD, PO BOX 449 73029 | 2-11111 464-2419
Jim Conger, supt.
HS, PO BOX 449 73029 | 2-00011 464-2272
Don Meason, prin.

Dale, AC 405, PC 2, Pottawatomie
Dale ISD, PO BOX 748 74851 | 3-11111 964-5558
Russell Whitehead, supt.
JSHS, PO BOX 748 74851 | 2-00111 964-5555
Harold Jones, prin.

Davenport, AC 918, PC 3, Lincoln
Davenport ISD, PO BOX 849 74026 | 2-11111 377-2277
Lowell Wallace, supt.
JSHS, PO BOX 849 74026 | 2-00111 377-2277
Mike Mays, prin.

Davidson, AC 405, PC 2, Tillman
Davidson ISD, PO BOX 338 73530 | 2-11111 568-2423
Phillip Ratcliff, supt.
HS, PO BOX 338 73530 | 1-00011 568-2261
Gene Gable, prin.

Davis, AC 405, PC 5, Murray
Davis ISD, 400 E ATLANTA AVE 73030 | 3-11111 369-2386
Linda Bessett, supt.
HS, 400 E ATLANTA AVE 73030 | 2-00011 369-2482
Jack Kapella, prin.
MS, 400 E ATLANTA AVE 73030 | 2-00100 369-2415
Sheri Knight, prin.

Delaware, AC 918, PC 2, Nowata
Delaware ISD, PO BOX 69 74027 | 2-11111 467-3225
Ray Pebsworth, supt.
HS, PO BOX 69 74027 | 1-00011 467-3216
Mary Carmichael, prin.

Del City, AC 405, PC 7, Oklahoma
Midwest City-Del City ISD
Supt. — See Midwest City
SHS, 1900 S SUNNYLANE RD 73115 | 4-00001 677-5777
Judd Porter, prin.

Mid-Del College | 2-CS 677-8311
3420 S SUNNYLANE RD 73115

Depew, AC 918, PC 3, Creek
Depew ISD, PO BOX 257 74028 | 2-11111 324-5466
Bruce Terronez, supt.
HS, PO BOX 257 74028 | 2-00011 324-5466
Charles Pyle, prin.

Dewar, AC 918, PC 3, Okmulgee
Dewar ISD, PO BOX 790 74431 | 2-11111 652-9625
Harry Atkins, supt.
JSHS, PO BOX 790 74431 | 2-00111 652-9625
Roger Smith, prin.

Dewey, AC 918, PC 5, Washington
Dewey ISD, 1 BULLDOGGER RD 74029 | 4-11111 534-2241
Paul Smith, supt.
HS, 1 BULLDOGGER RD 74029 | 2-00011 534-0933
Bob White, prin.
JHS, 1 BULLDOGGER RD 74029 | 2-00100 534-0111
Wendell Stacy, prin.

Dibble, AC 405, PC 2, McClain
Dibble ISD, PO BOX 9 73031 | 3-11111 344-6380
Jesse Wilburn, supt.
JSHS, PO BOX 9 73031 | 2-00111 344-6375
Marion Claborn, prin.

Dover, AC 405, PC 2, Kingfisher
Dover ISD, PO BOX 195 73734 — 2-11111
  Gene Benson, supt. — 828-4204
HS, PO BOX 195 73734 — 1-00011
  Larry Long, prin. — 828-4204

Drummond, AC 405, PC 2, Garfield
Drummond ISD, PO BOX 220 73735 — 2-11111
  Jerry Ott, supt. — 493-2216
HS, PO BOX 220 73735 — 1-00011
  Jerry Ott, prin. — 493-2271

Drumright, AC 918, PC 5, Creek
Drumright ISD, PO BOX 191 74030 — 3-11111
  Arthur Johnson, supt. — 352-2492
HS, PO BOX 191 74030 — 2-00011
  Larry Erwin, prin. — 352-2152
Edison MS, PO BOX 191 74030 — 2-00100
  Tom Hollis, prin. — 352-2318

Olive ISD, RR 1 BOX 337 74030 — 3-11111
  Leroy Corbett, supt. — 352-9567
Olive HS, RR 1 BOX 337 74030 — 2-00011
  Delbo Leach, prin. — 352-9568

Duke, AC 405, PC 2, Jackson
Duke ISD, PO BOX 160 73532 — 2-11111
  Don Harris, supt. — 679-3311
HS, PO BOX 160 73532 — 1-00011
  Darrel Humphries, prin. — 679-3311

Duncan, AC 405, PC 7, Stephens
Duncan ISD, PO BOX 1548 73534 — 5-11111
  Jack Herron, supt. — 255-0686
HS, PO BOX 1548 73534 — 4-00011
  John Hopper, prin. — 255-0700
MS, PO BOX 1548 73534 — 3-00100
  Mike Reding, prin. — 255-1020

Empire ISD, RR 1 BOX 155 73533 — 3-11111
  Paul Griggs, supt. — 252-5392
Empire HS, RR 1 BOX 155 73533 — 2-00011
  Sam Downs, prin. — 255-7515

Durant, AC 405, PC 7, Bryan
Durant ISD, 118 N 7TH AVE 74701 — 5-11111
  Ken English, supt. — 924-1276
HS, 802 W WALNUT ST 74701 — 3-00011
  Pat Morgan, prin. — 924-4424
MS, 410 N 6TH AVE 74701 — 3-00100
  Delbert Birdsong, prin. — 924-1321

Silo ISD, HC 62 BOX 227 74701 — 3-11111
  Larry Snider, supt. — 924-7000
Silo JSHS, HC 62 BOX 227 74701 — 2-00111
  Bobby Hicks, prin. — 924-7000

Southeastern Oklahoma State University — 5-UC
STATION A 74701 — 924-0121

Dustin, AC 918, PC 2, Hughes
Dustin ISD, PO BOX 390660 74839 — 2-11111
  Rod McDonald, supt. — 656-3211
HS, PO BOX 390660 74839 — 1-00011
  Paula Oliver, prin. — 656-3230

Eagletown, AC 405, PC 3, McCurtain
Eagletown ISD, PO BOX 38 74734 — 2-11111
  J. D. Smith, supt. — 835-7220
HS, PO BOX 38 74734 — 1-00011
  John Meredith, prin. — 835-2242

Eakly, AC 405, PC 2, Caddo
Eakly ISD, PO BOX 308 73033 — 2-11111
  Jimmy Buie, supt. — 797-3231
HS, PO BOX 308 73033 — 1-00011
  Ernest Copus, prin. — 797-3231

Earlsboro, AC 405, PC 3, Pottawatomie
Earlsboro ISD, PO BOX 95 74840 — 2-11111
  Paul McGee, supt. — 997-5616
HS, PO BOX 95 74840 — 1-00011
  Jim Motes, prin. — 997-5252

Edmond, AC 405, PC 8, Oklahoma
Deer Creek ISD, RR 1 BOX 137 73003 — 3-11111
  William White, supt. — 348-6100
Deer Creek HS, RR 1 BOX 137 73003 — 2-00011
  Steve Davis, prin. — 348-5720
Deer Creek MS, RR 1 BOX 137 73003 — 2-00100
  Jan Seely, prin. — 348-4830

Edmond ISD, 1216 S RANKIN ST 73034 — 7-11111
  Randall Raburn, supt. — 340-2800
SHS, 1000 SE 15TH ST 73013 — 4-00001
  Larry Maxwell, prin. — 340-2850
Central Mid. HS, 500 E 9TH ST 73034 — 4-00110
  Linda Everett, prin. — 340-2890
Cimarron MS
  3701 S BRYANT AVE 73013 — 4-00100
  Mona Warren, prin. — 340-2935
North Mid HS
  215 W DANFORTH RD 73003 — 1-00010
  Charles Woodham, prin. — 340-2875
Santa Fe JHS, 1216 S RANKIN ST 73034 — 3-00010
  Roberta Gaston, prin. — 340-2230
Sequoyah MS
  1125 E DANFORTH RD 73034 — 4-00100
  Jeff Edwards, prin. — 340-2900
Summit MS, 1705 NW 150TH ST 73013 — 3-00100
  Joanne McCarthy, prin. — 340-2920

University of Central Oklahoma — 6-UC
100 N UNIVERSITY DR 73034 — 341-2980

Eldorado, AC 405, PC 3, Jackson
Eldorado ISD, PO BOX J 73537 — 2-11111
  Carl Baker, supt. — 633-2219
HS, PO BOX J 73537 — 1-00011
  Marvin Gamble, prin. — 633-2219

Elgin, AC 405, PC 3, Comanche
Elgin ISD, PO BOX 369 73538 — 3-11111
  Tom Crimmins, supt. — 492-3663
HS, PO BOX 369 73538 — 2-00011
  Gene Jarvis, prin. — 492-3670
MS, PO BOX 369 73538 — 2-00100
  Phil Harred, prin. — 492-3655

Elk City, AC 405, PC 7, Beckham
Elk City ISD — 4-11111
  222 W BROADWAY AVE 73644 — 225-0175
  Bruce Miller, supt.
SHS, 222 W BROADWAY AVE 73644 — 2-00001
  Rick McNeil, prin. — 225-0105
JHS, 222 W BROADWAY AVE 73644 — 3-00110
  Terry Armstrong, prin. — 225-0476

Merritt ISD, RR 4 BOX 393 73644 — 3-11111
  Elwood Simmons, supt. — 225-5460
Merritt HS, RR 4 BOX 393 73644 — 2-00011
  Steven Wilburn, prin. — 225-5460
Merritt JHS, RR 4 BOX 393 73644 — 2-00100
  Steven Wilburn, prin. — 225-5460

Elmore City, AC 405, PC 2, Garvin
Elmore City-Pernell ISD — 2-11111
  PO BOX 97 73035 — 788-2566
  Gary Johnson, supt.
JSHS, PO BOX 97 73035 — 2-00111
  David Divine, prin. — 788-2565

El Reno, AC 405, PC 7, Canadian
El Reno ISD, PO BOX 580 73036 — 4-11111
  Sandy Wisley, supt. — 262-1703
SHS, PO BOX 580 73036 — 3-00001
  Charles Leipart, prin. — 262-3254
Dale JHS, PO BOX 580 73036 — 3-00110
  Mark Woolard, prin. — 262-3253

El Reno Junior College — 3-CC
PO BOX 370 73036 — 262-2552

Enid, AC 405, PC 8, Garfield
Chisholm ISD — 4-11111
  300 COLORADO AVE 73701 — 237-5512
  Kenneth New, supt.
Chisholm HS — 2-00011
  300 COLORADO AVE 73701 — 233-2852
  Joe Haskit, prin.

Enid ISD — 6-11111
  500 S INDEPENDENCE ST 73701 — 234-5270
  Garland Keithly, supt.
SHS, 611 W WABASH AVE 73701 — 4-00001
  Ron Garrison, prin. — 234-2404
Emerson JHS, 700 W ELM AVE 73701 — 3-00110
  Alan Corr, prin. — 237-3017
Longfellow JHS — 2-00110
  900 E BROADWAY AVE 73701 — 234-7023
  John Wright, prin.
Waller JHS — 3-00110
  2604 W RANDOLPH AVE 73703 — 234-5931
  Tom Worley, prin.

Phillips University — 3-UC
100 S UNIVERSITY AVE 73701 — 800-238-1185
St. Mary's Hospital — HSP
305 S 5TH ST 73701 — 233-6100

Erick, AC 405, PC 4, Beckham
Erick ISD, PO BOX 9 73645 — 2-11111
  Clifford Macklin, supt. — 526-3476
HS, PO BOX 9 73645 — 2-00011
  Jim Reynolds, prin. — 526-3351

Eufaula, AC 918, PC 5, McIntosh
Eufaula ISD, PO BOX 609 74432 — 4-11111
  James Howard, supt. — 689-2152
SHS, PO BOX 609 74432 — 2-00001
  Ray Cooper, prin. — 689-2556
Homan JHS, PO BOX 609 74432 — 2-00110
  Ronald Curtis, prin. — 689-2711

Fairfax, AC 918, PC 4, Osage
Woodland SD, 100 N 6TH ST 74637 — 2-11111
  Phyllis Rottmann, supt. — 642-3297
Woodland HS, 100 N 6TH ST 74637 — 2-00011
  Marvin Sparks, prin. — 642-3295
Woodland MS, 100 N 6TH ST 74637 — 2-01100
  Karen Rodenberg, prin. — 738-4287

Fairland, AC 918, PC 3, Ottawa
Fairland ISD, PO BOX 689 74343 — 2-11111
  Steve Wilmouth, supt. — 676-3811
HS, PO BOX 689 74343 — 1-00011
  Joe Clapp, prin. — 676-3246

Fairview, AC 405, PC 5, Major
Fairview ISD — 3-11111
  408 E BROADWAY ST 73737 — 227-2531
  Bob Van Meter, supt.
HS, 316 N 8TH ST 73737 — 2-00011
  Jim Slater, prin. — 227-4446
Chamberlain MS, 1000 E ELM ST 73737 — 2-00100
  Richard Beck, prin. — 227-2555

Fargo, AC 405, PC 2, Ellis
Fargo ISD, PO BOX 200 73840 — 2-11111
  Larry Hixon, supt. — 698-2298

HS, PO BOX 200 73840 — 1-00011
  Steve Peretto, prin. — 698-2298

Felt, AC 405, PC 2, Cimarron
Felt ISD, PO BOX 47 73937 — 1-11111
  Wyley Mauldin, supt. — 426-2220
HS, PO BOX 47 73937 — 1-00011
  Wyley Mauldin, prin. — 426-2220

Fittstown, AC 405, PC 3, Pontotoc
McLish ISD, PO BOX 29 74842 — 2-11111
  Kenneth Rhoten, supt. — 777-2221
McLish HS, PO BOX 29 74842 — 1-00011
  Kenneth Rhoten, prin. — 777-2240

Fletcher, AC 405, PC 4, Comanche
Fletcher ISD, PO BOX 489 73541 — 2-11111
  Gary Nightingale, supt. — 549-6015
JSHS, PO BOX 489 73541 — 2-00111
  Stan Looper, prin. — 549-6015

Forgan, AC 405, PC 2, Beaver
Forgan ISD, PO BOX 406 73938 — 2-11111
  Lanny Sells, supt. — 487-3366
HS, PO BOX 406 73938 — 1-00011
  Bill Nichols, prin. — 487-3366

Fort Cobb, AC 405, PC 3, Caddo
Ft. Cobb-Broxton ISD — 2-11111
  PO BOX 130 73038 — 643-2336
  Dennis Klugh, supt.
Ft. Cobb-Broxton JSHS — 2-00111
  PO BOX 130 73038 — 643-2335
  William Morgan, prin.

Fort Gibson, AC 918, PC 5, Muskogee
Ft. Gibson ISD, PO BOX 280 74434 — 4-11111
  Earl Garrison, supt. — 478-2474
HS, PO BOX 280 74434 — 2-00011
  Curtis Johnson, prin. — 478-2452
MS, PO BOX 280 74434 — 2-00100
  Larry Corley, prin. — 478-2471

Fort Supply, AC 405, PC 2, Woodward
Ft. Supply ISD, PO BOX 160 73841 — 2-11111
  Merle Hosler, supt. — 766-2611
HS, PO BOX 160 73841 — 1-00011
  Floyd Kirk, prin. — 766-2071

Fort Towson, AC 405, PC 3, Choctaw
Ft. Towson ISD, PO BOX 39 74735 — 2-11111
  James Gibbs, supt. — 873-2712
HS, PO BOX 39 74735 — 2-00011
  Ira Banta, prin. — 873-2325

Fox, AC 405, PC 2, Carter
Fox ISD, PO BOX 248 73435 — 2-11111
  Harold McCreary, supt. — 673-2081
HS, PO BOX 248 73435 — 1-00011
  Mike Hopper, prin. — 673-2082

Foyil, AC 918, PC 1, Rogers
Foyil ISD, PO BOX 49 74031 — 2-11113
  Michael Mcgregor, supt. — 341-1113
JSHS, PO BOX 49 74031 — 2-00111
  Douglas Dodd, prin. — 342-1782

Frederick, AC 405, PC 6, Tillman
Frederick ISD, PO BOX 370 73542 — 4-11111
  Mike Hagy, supt. — 335-5516
HS, PO BOX 610 73542 — 2-00011
  Harold McDaniel, prin. — 335-5521
MS, PO BOX 490 73542 — 2-00100
  Donald Mitchell, prin. — 335-2014

Freedom, AC 405, PC 2, Woods
Freedom ISD, PO BOX 5 73842 — 1-11111
  Gene Sullivan, supt. — 621-3271
HS, PO BOX 5 73842 — 1-00011
  Gene Sullivan, prin. — 621-3271

Gage, AC 405, PC 2, Ellis
Gage ISD, PO BOX 19 73843 — 2-11111
  Jim Langston, supt. — 923-7666
JSHS, PO BOX 19 73843 — 1-00111
  Jim Beierschmitt, prin. — 923-7909

Gans, AC 918, PC 2, Sequoyah
Gans ISD, PO BOX 70 74936 — 2-11111
  Charles Bullard, supt. — 775-2236
HS, PO BOX 70 74936 — 2-00011
  Charles Bullard, prin. — 775-2236

Garber, AC 405, PC 3, Garfield
Garber ISD, PO BOX 539 73738 — 2-11111
  Jim Lamer, supt. — 863-2220
HS, PO BOX 539 73738 — 2-00011
  Rod Reese, prin. — 863-2231

Geary, AC 405, PC 4, Blaine
Geary ISD, PO BOX 188 73040 — 3-11111
  Billy Cox, supt. — 884-2989
JSHS, PO BOX 188 73040 — 2-00111
  Yvonne Christensen, prin. — 884-2362

Geronimo, AC 405, PC 3, Comanche
Geronimo ISD, PO BOX 98 73543 — 2-11111
  Vol Woods, supt. — 355-3801
HS, PO BOX 98 73543 — 2-00011
  Ron Baughman, prin. — 355-3160

Glencoe, AC 405, PC 2, Payne
Glencoe ISD, PO BOX 218 74032 — 2-11111
  Bill Collins, supt. — 669-2261
JSHS, PO BOX 218 74032 — 1-00111
  Rick McDaniel, prin. — 669-2261

Glenpool, AC 918, PC 6, Tulsa
Glenpool ISD, PO BOX 1149 74033 — 4-11111
Dennis Chaffin, supt. — 322-9500
HS, PO BOX 1149 74033 — 3-00011
Jim Bridges, prin. — 322-3285
MS, PO BOX 1149 74033 — 2-00100
Ed Robison, prin. — 322-3823

Goodwell, AC 405, PC 4, Texas
Goodwell ISD, PO BOX 580 73939 — 2-11111
Jim Holmes, supt. — 349-2271
HS, PO BOX 580 73939 — 2-00001
Jim Holmes, prin. — 349-2271

Yarbrough ISD, RR 1 BOX 31 73939 — 2-11111
Jim Archer, supt. — 545-3329
Yarbrough JSHS, RR 1 BOX 31 73939 — 1-00111
Dorothy Williams, prin. — 545-3328

Oklahoma Panhandle State University — 4-UC
PO BOX 430 73939 — 349-2610

Gore, AC 918, PC 3, Sequoyah
Gore ISD, PO BOX 580 74435 — 2-11111
W J Pete Bennett, supt. — 489-5587
HS, PO BOX 580 74435 — 2-00011
Steven Barrick, prin. — 489-5587

Gracemont, AC 405, PC 2, Caddo
Gracemont ISD, PO BOX 5 73042 — 2-11111
Darrell Thompson, supt. — 966-2233
HS, PO BOX 5 73042 — 1-00011
Wayne Taggart, prin. — 966-2233

Grandfield, AC 405, PC 4, Tillman
Grandfield ISD, PO BOX 639 73546 — 2-11111
Darrell Brite, supt. — 479-5237
HS, PO BOX 639 73546 — 2-00011
Donney Dorton, prin. — 479-3140

Granite, AC 405, PC 4, Greer
Granite ISD, PO BOX 98 73547 — 2-11111
Don Blankenship, supt. — 535-2104
JSHS, PO BOX 98 73547 — 2-00111
Roy Jaye, prin. — 535-2104

Grant, AC 405, PC 2, Choctaw
Grant ISD, PO BOX 149 74738 — 2-11111
Eldon Moffitt, supt. — 326-8315
HS, PO BOX 149 74738 — 2-00011
Thomas Moffitt, prin. — 326-8316

Grove, AC 918, PC 5, Delaware
Grove ISD, PO BOX 789 74344 — 4-11111
Herbert Bacon, supt. — 786-3003
HS, PO BOX 789 74344 — 3-00011
Rodney Dillinger, prin. — 786-2208
MS, PO BOX 789 74344 — 2-00100
Fred Clouse, prin. — 786-2209

Guthrie, AC 405, PC 7, Logan
Guthrie ISD, 802 E VILAS AVE 73044 — 5-11111
Jeff Maddox, supt. — 282-8900
HS, 200 CROOKS DR 73044 — 4-00011
Earl Sykes, prin. — 282-5906
JHS, 705 E OKLAHOMA AVE 73044 — 3-00100
John Haney, prin. — 282-5936

Guymon, AC 405, PC 6, Texas
Guymon ISD, PO BOX 1307 73942 — 4-11111
Don Bowman, supt. — 338-3371
SHS, PO BOX 1307 73942 — 3-00001
Rae Annis, prin. — 338-3371
Central JHS, PO BOX 1307 73942 — 3-00110
Monte Walgamott, prin. — 338-3371

Haileyville, AC 918, PC 3, Pittsburg
Haileyville ISD, PO BOX 29 74546 — 2-11111
John Cope, supt. — 297-2626
HS, PO BOX 29 74546 — 2-00011
Gary Fullerton, prin. — 297-2627

Hammon, AC 405, PC 3, Roger Mills
Hammon ISD, PO BOX 279 73650 — 2-11111
Albert Motsenbocker, supt. — 473-2221
JSHS, PO BOX 279 73650 — 1-00111
Kenneth Walker, prin. — 473-2737

Hanna, AC 918, PC 1, McIntosh
Hanna ISD, PO BOX H 74845 — 2-11111
Robert Miller, supt. — 657-2523
HS, PO BOX H 74845 — 1-00011
James Reed, prin. — 657-2527

Hardesty, AC 405, PC 2, Texas
Hardesty ISD, PO BOX 129 73944 — 1-11111
Tim Puett, supt. — 888-4258
HS, PO BOX 129 73944 — 1-00011
Greg Caldwell, prin. — 888-4258

Harrah, AC 405, PC 5, Oklahoma
Harrah ISD, 20670 WALKER ST 73045 — 4-11111
William Wilson, supt. — 454-6244
HS, 20458 ELM ST 73045 — 3-00011
David Rutledge, prin. — 454-2416
MS, 303 WALKER ST 73045 — 3-00100
Lloyd Walker, prin. — 454-2406

Hartshorne, AC 918, PC 4, Pittsburg
Hartshorne ISD, 520 S 5TH ST 74547 — 3-11111
James Barnes, supt. — 297-2534
SHS, 520 S 5TH ST 74547 — 2-00001
Mark Ichord, prin. — 297-2536
JHS, 520 S 5TH ST 74547 — 2-00110
John Bernardi, prin. — 297-2433

Haskell, AC 918, PC 4, Muskogee
Haskell ISD, PO BOX 278 74436 — 3-11111
J. Dixon, supt. — 482-5555
HS, PO BOX 278 74436 — 2-00011
Foye Cash, prin. — 482-5223
MS, PO BOX 278 74436 — 2-00100
Carlos Knight, prin. — 482-5223

Haworth, AC 405, PC 2, McCurtain
Haworth ISD, PO BOX 99 74740 — 3-11111
Donald Ray, supt. — 245-1406
SHS, PO BOX 99 74740 — 2-00001
Edward Alford, prin. — 245-1440
JHS, PO BOX 99 74740 — 2-00110
John Crabtree, prin. — 245-1461

Healdton, AC 405, PC 5, Carter
Healdton ISD, PO BOX 490 73438 — 3-11111
William Nixon, supt. — 229-0540
HS, PO BOX 490 73438 — 2-00011
Bill Brown, prin. — 229-0541
MS, PO BOX 490 73438 — 2-00100
Dennis Idleman, prin. — 229-0303

Heavener, AC 918, PC 5, Leflore
Heavener ISD, PO BOX 698 74937 — 3-11111
Roger Stacy, supt. — 653-7223
HS, PO BOX 698 74937 — 2-00011
Gary Conway, prin. — 653-4436

Helena, AC 405, PC 4, Alfalfa
Timberlake ISD, PO BOX 287 73741 — 2-11111
Ron Frech, supt. — 852-3307
Timberlake High School — 1-00011
PO BOX 287 73741 — 852-3281
Terry Chapman, prin.
Other Schools – See Jet

Hennessey, AC 405, PC 4, Kingfisher
Hennessey ISD — 3-11111
604 E OKLAHOMA ST 73742 — 853-4321
Jerry Pippin, supt.
HS, 707 E OKLAHOMA ST 73742 — 2-00011
Cavin Boettger, prin. — 853-4394
Binkley MS — 2-01100
604 E OKLAHOMA ST 73742 — 853-4303
Betty Kinney, prin.

Henryetta, AC 918, PC 6, Okmulgee
Henryetta ISD, 618 W MAIN ST 74437 — 4-11111
Jim Wills, supt. — 652-6523
HS, 1800 TROY AIKMAN DR 74437 — 2-00011
Rick Enis, prin. — 652-2571
JHS, 618 W MAIN ST 74437 — 2-00100
Morris Warden, prin. — 652-6578

Wilson ISD, RR 1 BOX 274 74437 — 2-11111
Fred Adams, supt. — 652-3374
Wilson HS, RR 1 BOX 274 74437 — 1-00011
James Warden, prin. — 652-3374

Hinton, AC 405, PC 4, Caddo
Hinton ISD, PO BOX 1036 73047 — 3-11111
Max Townsend, supt. — 542-3257
HS, PO BOX 1036 73047 — 2-00011
Ron Schnee, prin. — 542-3235
MS, PO BOX 1036 73047 — 1-00100
Ron Schnee, prin. — 542-3235

Hobart, AC 405, PC 5, Kiowa
Hobart ISD, PO BOX 899 73651 — 3-11111
June Knight, supt. — 726-5691
HS, PO BOX 899 73651 — 2-00011
Mike York, prin. — 726-5611
MS, PO BOX 899 73651 — 2-00100
Kenneth O'Neal, prin. — 726-5615

Holdenville, AC 405, PC 5, Hughes
Holdenville ISD, PO BOX 977 74848 — 4-11111
W. Andrew Young, supt. — 379-5483
SHS, PO BOX 977 74848 — 2-00001
Gary LaValley, prin. — 379-6893
JHS, PO BOX 977 74848 — 2-00110
Bill Brown, prin. — 379-3387

Moss ISD, RR 2 BOX 57 74848 — 2-11111
Bennie Taylor, supt. — 379-2273
Moss HS, RR 2 BOX 57 74848 — 1-00011
Bob Sifers, prin. — 379-2882

Hollis, AC 405, PC 5, Harmon
Hollis ISD, 415 N MAIN ST 73550 — 3-11111
Ed Robinson, supt. — 688-3450
HS, 415 N MAIN ST 73550 — 2-00011
Larry Palmore, prin. — 688-2707
Hollis MS, 415 N MAIN ST 73550 — 2-00100
Deanna Davidson, prin. — 688-2706

Hominy, AC 918, PC 4, Osage
Hominy ISD, PO BOX 400 74035 — 3-11111
Gerald Christy, supt. — 885-6511
HS, PO BOX 400 74035 — 2-00011
Ron Wolf, prin. — 885-2141
MS, PO BOX 400 74035 — 2-00100
Ron Harmon, prin. — 885-6253

Hooker, AC 405, PC 4, Texas
Hooker ISD, PO BOX 247 73945 — 2-11111
Fred Weibling, supt. — 652-2162
HS, PO BOX 247 73945 — 2-00011
James Hogg, prin. — 652-2516

Howe, AC 918, PC 3, Leflore
Howe ISD, PO BOX 259 74940 — 2-11111
Dennis Hemphill, supt. — 658-3666

HS, PO BOX 259 74940 — 2-00011
Joe Hemphill, prin. — 658-3368

Hugo, AC 405, PC 6, Choctaw
Hugo ISD, 208 N 2ND ST 74743 — 4-11111
Shelby Koonce, supt. — 326-6483
HS, 201 E BROWN ST 74743 — 3-00011
Mike Armes, prin. — 326-9648
MS, 208 N 2ND ST 74743 — 2-00100
Ray Young, prin. — 326-3365

Hulbert, AC 918, PC 2, Cherokee
Hulbert ISD, PO BOX 188 74441 — 2-11111
Jake Crutchfield, supt. — 772-2501
JSHS, PO BOX 188 74441 — 2-00111
Don Lucas, prin. — 772-2565

Hydro, AC 405, PC 3, Caddo
Hydro ISD, PO BOX 5 73048 — 2-11111
Doyle Greteman, supt. — 663-2774
HS, PO BOX 5 73048 — 2-00011
Jerald Hamar, prin. — 663-2246

Idabel, AC 405, PC 6, McCurtain
Idabel ISD, PO BOX 29 74745 — 4-11111
Cecil Ford, supt. — 286-7639
Gray HS, PO BOX 29 74745 — 3-00011
Hubert Langley, prin. — 286-7693
MS, PO BOX 29 74745 — 2-00100
Richard Miller, prin. — 286-6558

Indiahoma, AC 405, PC 2, Comanche
Indiahoma ISD, PO BOX 8 73552 — 2-11111
Denver Rowley, supt. — 246-3448
HS, PO BOX 8 73552 — 1-00011
Lawrence Overcast, prin. — 246-3333

Indianola, AC 918, PC 2, Pittsburg
Indianola ISD, PO BOX 119 74442 — 2-11111
Dan Edwards, supt. — 823-4231
HS, PO BOX 119 74442 — 2-00011
Ron Rippy, prin. — 823-4231

Inola, AC 918, PC 4, Rogers
Inola ISD, PO BOX 1149 74036 — 3-11111
Perry Adams, supt. — 543-2255
HS, PO BOX 789 74036 — 2-00011
Jim Peters, prin. — 543-2404
MS, PO BOX 819 74036 — 2-00100
Dale Runyan, prin. — 543-2434

Jay, AC 918, PC 4, Delaware
Jay ISD, PO BOX 2000 74346 — 4-11111
Roy Drake, supt. — 253-4293
HS, PO BOX 2000 74346 — 2-00011
Jim Heard, prin. — 253-4466
MS, PO BOX 2000 74346 — 2-00100
Glen Hamby, prin. — 253-8510

Jenks, AC 918, PC 6, Tulsa
Jenks ISD, 205 E B ST 74037 — 6-11111
Kirby Lehman, supt. — 299-4411
HS, 205 E B ST 74037 — 4-00011
Michael Means, prin. — 299-4411
Central MS, 205 E B ST 74037 — 2-00100
Diana Sample, prin. — 299-4411
East MS, 205 E B ST 74037 — 2-00100
Susan Dare, prin. — 299-4411

Jet, AC 405, PC 2, Alfalfa
Timberlake ISD
Supt. — See Helena
Timberlake MS, PO BOX 188 73749 — 1-00100
Rick Kibbe, prin. — 626-4411

Jones, AC 405, PC 4, Oklahoma
Jones ISD, PO BOX 790 73049 — 3-11111
John Wilson, supt. — 399-9215
HS, PO BOX 790 73049 — 2-00011
Mike Hill, prin. — 399-9122
MS, PO BOX 790 73049 — 2-00100
Jack Moery, prin. — 399-9114

Kansas, AC 918, PC 3, Delaware
Kansas ISD, PO BOX 196 74347 — 3-11111
Jim Burgess, supt. — 868-2562
JSHS, PO BOX 196 74347 — 2-00111
John Odle, prin. — 868-3308

Kellyville, AC 918, PC 3, Creek
Kellyville ISD, PO BOX 99 74039 — 3-11111
Dwight Davidson, supt. — 247-6133
HS, PO BOX 99 74039 — 2-00011
Bill Harlow, prin. — 247-6333
JHS, PO BOX 99 74039 — 2-00100
Jon Sissom, prin. — 247-6134

Keota, AC 918, PC 3, Haskell
Keota ISD, PO BOX 160 74941 — 2-11111
John Shaw, supt. — 966-3950
HS, PO BOX 160 74941 — 2-00011
Royce Rainwater, prin. — 966-3950

Ketchum, AC 918, PC 2, Craig
Ketchum ISD, PO BOX 720 74349 — 2-11111
Thomas Jones, supt. — 782-3241
HS, PO BOX 720 74349 — 1-00011
Clayton Edwards, prin. — 782-3242

Keyes, AC 405, PC 2, Cimarron
Keyes ISD, PO BOX 47 73947 — 2-11111
Richard Dally, supt. — 546-7231
HS, PO BOX 47 73947 — 1-00011
Bob Miller, prin. — 546-7641

Kiefer, AC 918, PC 3, Creek
Kiefer ISD, PO BOX 850 74041 — 2-11111
John Coker, supt. — 321-3421
HS, PO BOX 850 74041 — 2-00011
John Phillips, prin. — 321-3533

Kingfisher, AC 405, PC 5, Kingfisher
Kingfisher ISD, PO BOX 29 73750 — 4-11111
C Jack Harrel, supt. — 375-4194
HS, 600 S 9TH ST 73750 — 2-00011
Robert Barnett, prin. — 375-4191
MS, PO BOX 29 73750 — 2-01100
Pam Deering, prin. — 375-6607

Kingston, AC 405, PC 4, Marshall
Kingston ISD, PO BOX 370 73439 — 2-11111
Ronald Craig, supt. — 564-9033
HS, PO BOX 370 73439 — 2-00011
Wendell Peoples, prin. — 564-2384
MS, PO BOX 370 73439 — 2-00100
Randall Monroe, prin. — 564-2996

Kinta, AC 918, PC 2, Haskell
Kinta ISD, PO BOX 219 74552 — 2-11111
Mark Roye, supt. — 768-3338
HS, PO BOX 219 74552 — 1-00011
Mark Roye, supt. — 768-3339

Kiowa, AC 918, PC 3, Pittsburg
Kiowa ISD, PO BOX 6 74553 — 2-11111
Dennis Trammell, supt. — 432-5631
JSHS, PO BOX 6 74553 — 2-00111
Michael Kellog, prin. — 432-5641

Konawa, AC 405, PC 4, Seminole
Konawa ISD, RR 1 BOX 3 74849 — 3-11111
Charles McFarland, supt. — 925-3244
SHS, RR 1 BOX 3 74849 — 2-00011
Wayne Smith, prin. — 925-3221
JHS, RR 1 BOX 3 74849 — 2-00110
Ted Oliphant, prin. — 925-3222

Kremlin, AC 405, PC 2, Garfield
Kremlin-Hillsdale ISD — 2-11111
PO BOX 198 73753 — 874-2284
Mary Light, supt.
Kremlin-Hillsdale HS — 2-00011
PO BOX 198 73753 — 874-2281
Carl Barnes, prin.

Lahoma, AC 405, PC 3, Garfield
Cimarron ISD, PO BOX 8 73754 — 2-11111
W. Hassler, supt. — 796-2204
Cimarron HS, PO BOX 8 73754 — 1-00011
James Lewis, prin. — 796-2204
Other Schools – See Ames

Lamont, AC 405, PC 2, Grant
Deer Creek-Lamont ISD — 2-11111
PO BOX 10 74643 — 388-4335
Preston Brown, supt.
Deer Creek-Lamont JSHS — 1-00011
PO BOX 10 74643 — 388-4333
Preston Brown, prin.

Langston, AC 405, PC 4, Logan

Langston University — 4-UC
PO BOX 907 73050 — 466-2231

Laverne, AC 405, PC 4, Harper
Laverne ISD, PO BOX 40 73848 — 2-11111
David Harriman, supt. — 921-3361
JSHS, PO BOX 40 73848 — 2-00111
Mac Branscum, prin. — 921-3361

Lawton, AC 405, PC 8, Comanche
Lawton ISD, PO BOX 1009 73502 — 7-11111
Dick Neptune, supt. — 357-6900
Eisenhower SHS — 4-00001
5201 W GORE BLVD 73505 — 355-9144
Jerry Moon, prin.
SHS, 601 NW FORT SILL BLVD 73507 — 4-00001
Henry Ray, prin. — 355-5170
MacArthur SHS — 3-00001
4402 E GORE BLVD 73501 — 355-5230
Ann Coody, prin.
Central JHS, 801 SW C AVE 73501 — 4-00110
Butch Edwards, prin. — 355-8544
Eisenhower JHS — 4-00110
5225 W GORE BLVD 73505 — 353-1040
Dan McClure, prin.
MacArthur JHS, 510 NE 45TH ST 73507 — 3-00110
Linda Dzialo, prin. — 353-5111
Tomlinson JHS — 3-00110
702 NW HOMESTEAD DR 73505 — 353-8553
Jerry Boucher, prin.

Cameron University — 5-UC
2800 W GORE BLVD 73505 — 581-2201
Comanche Co. Memorial Hospital — HSP
3401 W GORE BLVD 73505 — 355-8620
Great Plains Area Voc. Tech. School — 2-CS
4500·SW LEE BLVD 73505 — 355-6371

Leedey, AC 405, PC 2, Dewey
Leedey ISD, PO BOX 67 73654 — 2-11111
Roy Baker, supt. — 488-3424
SHS, PO BOX 67 73654 — 1-00001
Sherman Lauder, prin. — 488-3377
JHS, PO BOX 67 73654 — 1-00110
Sherman Lauder, prin. — 488-3377

Leflore, AC 918, PC 2, Leflore
Leflore ISD, PO BOX 147 74942 — 2-11111
Louis Maggia, supt. — 753-2345
HS, PO BOX 147 74942 — 1-00011
Jimmie Peters, prin. — 753-2253

Lenapah, AC 918, PC 2, Nowata
Oklahoma Union SD — 2-11111
PO BOX 159 74042 — 255-6550
Jim Woody, supt.
Oklahoma Union JSHS — 2-00111
PO BOX 159 74042 — 255-6551
Sherman Jones, prin.

Lexington, AC 405, PC 4, Cleveland
Lexington ISD, 420 NE 4TH ST 73051 — 3-11111
Rick Moss, supt. — 527-7236
HS, 420 NE 4TH ST 73051 — 2-00011
Floyd West, prin. — 527-6586
MS, 420 NE 4TH ST 73051 — 2-00100
Randall Fuller, prin. — 527-6588

Lindsay, AC 405, PC 5, Garvin
Lindsay ISD, 800 W CREEK ST 73052 — 4-11111
Bill Patton, supt. — 756-3131
HS, 800 W CREEK ST 73052 — 3-00011
Bill Owens, prin. — 756-3132
Lindsay MS, 800 W CREEK ST 73052 — 2-00100
Bob Ashley, prin. — 756-3133

Locust Grove, AC 918, PC 4, Mayes
Locust Grove ISD, PO BOX 399 74352 — 3-11111
Bob Neel, supt. — 479-5243
HS, PO BOX 399 74352 — 2-00011
Clarence Austin, prin. — 479-5247
MS, PO BOX 399 74352 — 2-00100
Janice Tramel, prin. — 479-5244

Lone Grove, AC 405, PC 5, Carter
Lone Grove ISD, PO BOX 1330 73443 — 4-11111
Gary Scott, supt. — 657-3131
HS, PO BOX 1330 73443 — 2-00011
Lynn Henderson, prin. — 657-3133
MS, PO BOX 1330 73443 — 2-00100
Ted Clardy, prin. — 657-3132

Lone Wolf, AC 405, PC 3, Kiowa
Lone Wolf ISD, PO BOX 158 73655 — 2-11111
James Sutherland, supt. — 846-9091
HS, PO BOX 158 73655 — 1-00011
Lloyd Buckley, prin. — 846-9092

Lookeba, AC 405, PC 2, Caddo
Lookeba-Sickles ISD — 2-11111
RR 1 BOX 34 73053 — 457-6623
Dennis Byrd, supt.
Lookeba-Sickles JSHS — 2-00111
RR 1 BOX 34 73053 — 457-6621
Jack Whitman, prin.

Luther, AC 405, PC 4, Oklahoma
Luther ISD, PO BOX 430 73054 — 3-11111
Joe Ballard, supt. — 277-3233
HS, PO BOX 430 73054 — 2-00011
Walter Wilson, prin. — 277-3263
MS, PO BOX 430 73054 — 2-00100
Dennis Delano, prin. — 277-3270

McAlester, AC 918, PC 7, Pittsburg
McAlester ISD, PO BOX 1027 74502 — 5-11111
Lucy Smith, supt. — 423-4771
SHS, PO BOX 1027 74502 — 3-00001
Charles Randall, prin. — 423-4776
Parker Mid HS, PO BOX 1027 74502 — 3-00100
Allen Wadsworth, prin. — 423-4647
Puterbaugh MS, PO BOX 1027 74502 — 2-00100
Randall Peters, prin. — 423-5445

McCurtain, AC 918, PC 2, Haskell
McCurtain SD, PO BOX 189 74944 — 2-11111
Dwight Henry, supt. — 945-7237
HS, PO BOX 189 74944 — 1-00011
Perry Arnwine, prin. — 945-7236

Mc Loud, AC 405, PC 4, Pottawatomie
Mc Loud ISD, PO BOX 40 74851 — 4-11111
Mike Steele, supt. — 964-3314
SHS, PO BOX 40 74851 — 2-00001
Martin Mangieri, prin. — 964-3352
JHS, PO BOX 40 74851 — 2-00110
Bill Caruthers, prin. — 964-3312

Macomb, AC 405, PC 1, Pottawatomie
Macomb ISD, PO BOX 10 74852 — 2-11111
J E Pryor, supt. — 598-3892
HS, PO BOX 10 74852 — 2-00011
Mike Rutherford, prin. — 598-5420

Madill, AC 405, PC 5, Marshall
Madill ISD, 601 W MCARTHUR ST 73446 — 4-11111
John Carter, supt. — 795-3303
HS, 601 W MCARTHUR ST 73446 — 1-00011
Bill Weldon, prin. — 795-3339
MS, 601 W MCARTHUR ST 73446 — 2-00100
Jim Green, prin. — 795-7373

Mangum, AC 405, PC 5, Greer
Mangum ISD — 3-11111
400 N PENNSYLVANIA AVE 73554 — 782-3371
Gary Tyler, supt.
SHS, 300 N OKLAHOMA AVE 73554 — 2-00001
Bob Travis, prin. — 782-3343
JHS, 400 N PENNSYLVANIA AVE 73554 — 2-00110
Jim Bull, prin. — 782-2702

Mannford, AC 918, PC 4, Creek
Mannford ISD, PO BOX 100 74044 — 4-11111
Thomas Stiles, supt. — 865-4062
HS, PO BOX 100 74044 — 3-00011
Robert Owsley, prin. — 865-3841
MS, PO BOX 100 74044 — 2-00100
Molly Gregory, prin. — 865-4680

Marietta, AC 405, PC 4, Love
Marietta ISD, PO BOX 289 73448 — 3-11111
James Marshall, supt. — 276-9444
HS, PO BOX 289 73448 — 2-00011
Steve Henderson, prin. — 276-3204
MS, PO BOX 289 73448 — 2-00100
Jeff Dooley, prin. — 276-3886

Marlow, AC 405, PC 5, Stephens
Central High ISD — 2-11111
RR 3 BOX 249 73055 — 658-6858
Leonard Garrison, supt.
Central HS, RR 3 BOX 249 73055 — 2-00011
Ross Ridge, prin. — 658-2929

Marlow ISD, PO BOX 73 73055 — 4-11111
Ray McCarter, supt. — 658-2719
HS, PO BOX 73 73055 — 2-00011
Mickey Hoy, prin. — 658-2718
MS, PO BOX 73 73055 — 2-00100
Tommy Williams, prin. — 658-6625

Mason, AC 918, PC 1, Okfuskee
Mason ISD, RR 1 BOX 143B 74859 — 2-11111
H Dale Smart, supt. — 623-0231
HS, RR 1 BOX 143B 74859 — 1-00011
Eddie Weaver, prin. — 623-2218

Maud, AC 405, PC 4, Pottawatomie
Maud ISD, PO BOX 130 74854 — 2-11111
Larry Stogner, supt. — 374-2416
HS, PO BOX 130 74854 — 2-00011
Donna Alloway, prin. — 374-2425
MS, PO BOX 130 74854 — 2-00100
Karen Pearcy, prin. — 374-2404

Maysville, AC 405, PC 4, Garvin
Maysville ISD, PO BOX 780 73057 — 3-11111
Larry Garner, supt. — 867-5595
JSHS, PO BOX 780 73057 — 1-00111
Rick Worden, prin. — 867-4410

Medford, AC 405, PC 4, Grant
Medford ISD, 301 N MAIN ST 73759 — 2-11111
Ron Gordon, supt. — 395-2392
HS, 300 N MAIN ST 73759 — 2-00011
David Bailey, prin. — 395-2392

Meeker, AC 405, PC 4, Lincoln
Meeker SD, PO BOX 68 74855 — 3-11111
Robert Hightower, supt. — 279-3511
HS, PO BOX 68 74855 — 2-00011
Brent Walden, prin. — 279-2113
MS, PO BOX 68 74855 — 2-00100
Darrell Roe, prin. — 279-2414

Miami, AC 918, PC 7, Ottawa
Miami ISD, 418 G ST SE 74354 — 4-11111
Dean Hughes, supt. — 542-8455
HS, 2000 E CENTRAL AVE 74354 — 3-00011
Ray Judkins, prin. — 542-4421
Rogers MS, 504 GOODRICH BLVD 74354 — 3-00100
Robert Blizzard, prin. — 542-5588

Northeastern Oklahoma A&M College — 4-CC
200 I ST NE 74354 — 542-8441

Midwest City, AC 405, PC 8, Oklahoma
Midwest City-Del City ISD — 7-11111
PO BOX 10630 73140 — 737-4461
John Folks, supt.
Albert SHS, 2009 S POST RD 73130 — 3-00001
Rick Bachman, prin. — 739-1726
Midwest City SHS, 213 E ELM ST 73110 — 4-00001
Jim Miller, prin. — 739-1741
Albert JHS, 2515 S POST RD 73130 — 3-00110
Don Colston, prin. — 739-1761
Del Crest JHS, 4731 JUDY DR 73115 — 3-00110
Roger Epperly, prin. — 671-8615
Jarman JHS, 5 W MACARTHUR DR 73110 — 3-00110
Clinton Groves, prin. — 739-1771
Kerr JHS, 2300 LINDA LN 73115 — 3-00110
Marie Davis, prin. — 671-8625
Monroney JHS, 7400 E RENO AVE 73110 — 3-00110
Marty Corder, prin. — 739-1786
Other Schools – See Del City

Rose State College — 6-CC
6420 SE 15TH ST 73110 — 733-7300

Milburn, AC 405, PC 2, Johnston
Milburn ISD, PO BOX 276 73450 — 2-11111
Richard McKee, supt. — 443-5522
HS, PO BOX 276 73450 — 2-00011
Rick Meadows, prin. — 443-5522

Mill Creek, AC 405, PC 2, Johnston
Mill Creek ISD, PO BOX 118 74856 — 2-11111
Ray Dodd, supt. — 384-5514
HS, PO BOX 118 74856 — 1-00011
Leon Sorrels, prin. — 384-5447

Minco, AC 405, PC 4, Grady
Minco ISD, PO BOX 428 73059 — 2-11111
Gary Smith, supt. — 352-4867
JSHS, PO BOX 428 73059 — 2-00111
Tom Cobble, prin. — 352-4377

Moore, AC 405, PC 8, Cleveland
Moore ISD, 400 N BROADWAY ST 73160   7-11111
  Dan Foreman, supt.   793-3000
SHS, 300 N EASTERN AVE 73160   4-00001
  Gene Burr, prin.   793-3100
Brink JHS   3-00110
  11420 S WESTERN AVE 73170   692-5620
  Theresa Mitchell, prin.
Highland East JHS   3-00110
  1200 SE 4TH ST 73160   793-3200
  Donna Abraham, prin.
Highland West JHS   3-00110
  901 N SANTA FE AVE 73160   793-3210
  Glen Moore, prin.
Other Schools – See Oklahoma City

Hillsdale Free Will Baptist College   2-UC
  PO BOX 7208 73153   800-735-4455

Mooreland, AC 405, PC 4, Woodward
Mooreland ISD, PO BOX 75 73852   2-11111
  Terry Kellner, supt.   994-5388
JSHS, PO BOX 75 73852   2-00111
  John Major, prin.   994-5426

Morris, AC 918, PC 4, Okmulgee
Morris ISD, PO BOX 80 74445   3-11111
  Don Shoemake, supt.   733-4213
HS, PO BOX 80 74445   2-00011
  Jim Ledford, prin.   733-2223
MS, PO BOX 80 74445   2-00100
  Derril Etchison, prin.   733-4539

Morrison, AC 405, PC 3, Noble
Morrison ISD, PO BOX 176 73061   2-11111
  Orin Harrington, supt.   724-3341
JSHS, PO BOX 176 73061   2-00111
  Bill Seitter, prin.   724-3307

Mounds, AC 918, PC 3, Creek
Liberty ISD, RR 1 BOX 354 74047   2-11111
  David Martin, supt.   366-8496
Liberty HS, RR 1 BOX 354 74047   2-00011
  Michael Calvert, prin.   366-8784
Liberty MS, RR 1 BOX 354 74047   2-00100
  Jerry Hale, prin.   366-8494
Mounds ISD, PO BOX 189 74047   3-11111
  Dennis Campbell, supt.   827-6100
HS, PO BOX 189 74047   2-00011
  Stanley White, prin.   827-6200
JHS, PO BOX 189 74047   2-00100
  Frank Paullus, prin.   827-6300

Mountain View, AC 405, PC 4, Kiowa
Mountain View-Gotebo ISD   2-11111
  PO BOX B 73062 – Rick Webb, supt.   347-2211
HS, PO BOX B 73062   2-00011
  Steven Black, prin.   347-2211

Muldrow, AC 918, PC 5, Sequoyah
Muldrow ISD, PO BOX 660 74948   4-11111
  Roger Sharp, supt.   427-7406
HS, PO BOX 660 74948   3-00011
  Ron Etheridge, prin.   427-3274
MS, PO BOX 660 74948   2-00100
  Monty Wight, prin.   427-5421

Muskogee, AC 918, PC 8, Muskogee
Hilldale ISD   4-11111
  500 E SMITH FERRY RD 74403   683-0273
  D. B. Merrill, supt.
Hilldale HS   2-00011
  500 E SMITH FERRY RD 74403   683-3253
  Dwayne Pemberton, prin.
Hilldale MS   2-00100
  500 E SMITH FERRY RD 74403   683-0763
  Ron Fast, prin.
Muskogee ISD, 570 N 6TH ST 74401   6-11111
  Barbara Staggs, supt.   684-3700
HS, 3200 E SHAWNEE RD 74403   4-00011
  James Wilson, prin.   684-3750
Robertson MS, 570 N 6TH ST 74401   3-00100
  Ted Clements, prin.   684-3775
West MS, 570 N 6TH ST 74401   3-00100
  Louis Gregorio, prin.   684-3725

Bacone College   3-CC
  99 BACONE RD 74403   683-4581
Muskogee General Hospital   HSP
  300 ROCKEFELLER DR 74401   682-5501
Parkview School OK School for the Blind   HND
  74401

Mustang, AC 405, PC 7, Canadian
Mustang ISD, 906 S HEIGHTS DR 73064   6-11111
  Theron Croisant, supt.   376-2461
HS, 906 S HEIGHTS DR 73064   4-00011
  Jim Burkey, prin.   376-2404
MS, 906 S HEIGHTS DR 73064   3-00100
  Roger Hill, prin.   376-2448
North MS, 906 S HEIGHTS DR 73064   2-00100
  Ralph Smith, prin.   324-2236

Mutual, AC 405, PC 1, Woodward
Sharon-Mutual ISD, PO BOX 1 73853   2-11111
  John Froage, supt.   989-3120
Sharon-Mutual HS, PO BOX 1 73853   2-00011
  Kenneth Krause, prin.   989-3231

Newcastle, AC 405, PC 5, McClain
Newcastle ISD, 101 N MAIN ST 73065   4-11111
  Earl Myers, supt.   387-2890

HS, 101 N MAIN ST 73065   2-00011
  Joe Cox, prin.   387-4304
MS, 101 N MAIN ST 73065   2-00100
  Roy Giles, prin.   387-3139

Newkirk, AC 405, PC 4, Kay
Newkirk ISD, PO BOX 91 74647   3-11111
  Ray Sinor, supt.   362-6241
HS, PO BOX 91 74647   2-00011
  Emet Callaway, prin.   362-2515
MS, PO BOX 91 74647   2-00100
  Jim Wiersig, prin.   362-2516

Nicoma Park, AC 405, PC 4, Oklahoma
Choctaw/Nicoma Park ISD
  Supt. — See Choctaw
JHS, PO BOX 917 73066   2-00110
  Larry Worden, prin.   769-3106

Ninnekah, AC 405, PC 4, Grady
Ninnekah ISD, PO BOX 275 73067   3-11111
  Rocky Stone, supt.   224-4092
HS, PO BOX 275 73067   2-00011
  Chris Stickney, prin.   224-4299
JHS, PO BOX 275 73067   2-00100
  John Nations, prin.   222-1046

Noble, AC 405, PC 5, Cleveland
Noble ISD, PO BOX 499 73068   5-11111
  Troy Compston, supt.   872-3452
SHS, PO BOX 519 73068   3-00001
  Jim Middaugh, prin.   872-3441
JHS, PO BOX 539 73068   3-00110
  Susan Moreu, prin.   872-3495

Norman, AC 405, PC 8, Cleveland
Little Axe ISD   4-11111
  2000 168TH AVE NE 73071   329-7691
  Joe Work, supt.
Little Axe HS   2-00011
  2000 168TH AVE NE 73071   329-1612
  Larry Birden, prin.
Little Axe MS   2-00100
  2000 168TH AVE NE 73071   329-2156
  Barbara Webster, prin.
Norman ISD, 131 S FLOOD AVE 73069   6-11111
  James Gray, supt.   321-5014
SHS, 911 W MAIN ST 73069   4-00001
  Ed Costa, prin.   366-5812
Central Mid-HS   3-00010
  215 N PONCA AVE 73071   366-5936
  Johnelle Jones, prin.
Irving MS, 1920 E ALAMEDA ST 73071   3-00100
  David Goin, prin.   366-5941
Longfellow MS   3-00100
  1809 STUBBEMAN AVE 73069   366-5948
  Jim Conatser, prin.
West Mid-HS, 1919 W BOYD ST 73069   3-00010
  Teena Nations, prin.   366-5918
Whittier MS, 2000 W BROOKS ST 73069   3-00100
  Lynne Miller, prin.   366-5956

City College   2-CS
  1370 N INTERSTATE DR 73072   329-5627
University of Oklahoma at Norman   7-UC
  660 PARRINGTON OVAL 73019   325-3916

Nowata, AC 918, PC 5, Nowata
Nowata ISD, 707 W OSAGE AVE 74048   4-11111
  Betsy Graham, supt.   273-3425
HS, 700 W OSAGE AVE 74048   2-00011
  Robert Jobe, prin.   273-2221
MS, 700 W OSAGE AVE 74048   2-00100
  Ken Hewitt, prin.   273-1346

Oaks, AC 918, PC 2, Delaware
Oaks-Mission ISD   2-11111
  PO BOX 160 74359   868-2183
  Ed Turlington, supt.
Oaks-Mission HS, PO BOX 160 74359   2-00011
  Wyman Thompson, prin.   868-2499

Oilton, AC 918, PC 4, Creek
Oilton ISD, PO BOX 130 74052   2-11111
  Terry Powell, supt.   862-3747
HS, PO BOX 130 74052   2-00011
  Lanny Davidson, prin.   862-3272

Okarche, AC 405, PC 4, Kingfisher
Okarche ISD, PO BOX 276 73762   2-11111
  Richard Buswell, supt.   263-7300
JSHS, PO BOX 276 73762   2-00111
  Phil Wallace, prin.   263-7212

Okay, AC 918, PC 3, Wagoner
Okay ISD, PO BOX 830 74446   2-11111
  Gene Slaton, supt.   682-2548
HS, PO BOX 830 74446   2-00011
  John Adams, prin.   682-0371

Okeene, AC 405, PC 4, Blaine
Okeene ISD, PO BOX 409 73763   2-11111
  Robert Holladay, supt.   822-3268
JSHS, PO BOX 409 73763   2-00111
  Wynona Knopp, prin.   822-3219

Okemah, AC 918, PC 5, Okfuskee
Okemah ISD, 204 W DATE ST 74859   3-11111
  O Mac Smith, supt.   623-1874
HS, 204 W DATE ST 74859   2-00011
  Frank Thompson, prin.   623-1274
MS, 204 W DATE ST 74859   2-00100
  Bill Green, prin.   623-0212

Oklahoma City, AC 405, PC 10, Oklahoma
Crooked Oak ISD   3-11111
  1901 SE 15TH ST 73129   677-5252
  Kathy Roberts, supt.
Crooked Oak HS, 1901 SE 15TH ST 73129   2-00011
  Alford Nichols, prin.   677-3452
Crooked Oak MS   2-00100
  1901 SE 15TH ST 73129   677-5133
  Violet Greene, prin.
Millwood ISD   4-11111
  6724 N MRTN LUTHER KING AVE 73111   478-1336
  Leon Edd, supt.
Millwood HS   2-00011
  6724 N MRTN LUTHER KING AVE 73111   478-0504
  Johnnie Roseburr, prin.
Millwood MS   1-01100
  6724 N MRTN LUTHER KING AVE 73111   478-0360
  Edgar Scott, prin.
Moore ISD
  Supt. — See Moore
Westmoore SHS   4-00001
  12613 S WESTERN AVE 73170   691-8000
  Wayne Canaday, prin.
West JHS   4-00110
  9400 S PENNSYLVANIA AVE 73159   692-5600
  JoEd Savage, prin.
Oklahoma City ISD   8-11111
  900 N KLEIN AVE 73106   297-6522
  Betty Mason, supt.
Capitol Hill HS, 500 SW 36TH ST 73109   3-00011
  Sally Cole, prin.   634-1461
Douglas HS, 900 N EASTERN AVE 73117   4-00011
  Walter Mason, prin.   424-4391
Grant HS   4-00011
  5016 S PENNSYLVANIA AVE 73119   685-6621
  Dick Vrooman, prin.
Marshall HS   4-00011
  9017 N UNIVERSITY AVE 73114   848-6871
  Vallene Cooks, prin.
Northeast HS   4-00011
  3100 N KELLEY AVE 73111   424-1491
  James Robinson, prin.
Northwest Classen HS   4-00011
  2801 NW 27TH ST 73107   942-5551
  Rita Bilbe, prin.
Harding MS   3-00100
  3333 N SHARTEL AVE 73118   528-0562
  James Senter, prin.
Hoover MS, 2401 NW 115TH ST 73120   3-00100
  Joe Hodges, prin.   751-1210
Jackson MS, 2601 S VILLA AVE 73108   3-00100
  Larry Fry, prin.   634-6357
Jefferson MS   3-00100
  6800 S BLACKWELDER AVE 73159   632-2341
  Troy Vincent, prin.
Moon MS, 1901 NE 13TH ST 73117   3-00100
  Warren Baugher, prin.   427-8391
Roosevelt MS, 3200 SW 44TH ST 73119   3-00100
  Ron Maxfield, prin.   685-7795
Taft MS, 2901 NW 23RD ST 73107   3-00100
  Rafael White, prin.   946-1431
Webster MS   4-00100
  6708 S SANTA FE AVE 73139   632-6653
  Jan Borelli, prin.
Other Schools – See Spencer

Putnam City ISD   7-11111
  5401 NW 40TH ST 73122   495-5200
  Randy Dewar, supt.
Putnam City HS   4-00011
  5300 NW 50TH ST 73122   789-4350
  Robert Butler, prin.
Putnam City North HS   4-00011
  11800 N ROCKWELL AVE 73162   722-4220
  Kent Mathers, prin.
Putnam City West HS   4-00011
  8500 NW 23RD ST 73127   787-1140
  Jerry Rickerts, prin.
Central JHS, 4020 N GROVE AVE 73122   4-00100
  Mike Fry, prin.   787-3660
Cooper MS, 5401 NW 40TH ST 73122   3-00100
  Jan Miller, prin.   720-9887
Hefner MS   4-00100
  8400 N MACARTHUR BLVD 73132   721-2411
  Elbert Meek, prin.
Mayfield MS   3-00100
  1600 N PURDUE AVE 73127   947-8693
  Jerry Cramer, prin.
Other Schools – See Bethany

Western Heights ISD   4-11111
  8401 SW 44TH ST 73179   745-6300
  Sharon Lease, supt.
Western Heights HS   3-00011
  8401 SW 44TH ST 73179   745-4623
  Frank Hughes, prin.
Western Heights JHS   3-00100
  8005 SW 44TH ST 73179   745-2743
  Ron Larchick, prin.

Bishop McGuinness HS   3-00011
  801 NW 50TH ST 73118   842-6639
  Stephen Parsons, prin.
Casady S   4-11111
  9500 N PENNSYLVANIA AVE 73120   755-0550
Heritage Hall S   3-11111
  1400 NW 115TH ST 73114
Mercy Health Center   HSP
  4300 W MEMORIAL RD 73120   755-1515

Metropolitan College of Court Reporting 2-CS
2525 NW EXPRESSWAY ST 73112 840-2181
Mid-America Bible College 2-UC
3500 SW 119TH ST 73170 691-3800
Mt. St. Mary's HS 2-00011
2801 S SHARTEL AVE 73109 631-8865
Benno Schluterman, prin.
Oklahoma Christian University 4-UC
PO BOX 11000 73136 425-5000
Oklahoma City Community College 5-CC
7777 S MAY AVE 73159 682-7503
Oklahoma City University 5-UC
2501 N BLACKWELDER AVE 73106 521-5032
Oklahoma Horseshoeing School 1-CS
3000 N I 35 SERVICE RD 73111 424-3842
Oklahoma Junior College 2-CC
3232 NW 65TH ST 73116 848-3400
Oklahoma State University 4-CC
900 N PORTLAND AVE 73107 947-4421
Platt College 3-CS
3737 N PORTLAND AVE 73112 942-8683
Presbyterian Hospital HSP
700 NE 13TH ST 73104 271-5194
St. Anthony Hospital HSP
1000 N LEE AVE 73102 272-7273
Southwestern College of Meat Cutters 1-CS
1301 S MAY AVE 73108 681-2633
Tuttle Vocational Technical Center 2-CS
12777 N ROCKWELL AVE 73142 722-7799
University of Oklahoma Health Sciences 4-UC
PO BOX 26901 73126 271-2125
Westminister Upper Day S 2-01100
540 NW 44TH ST 73118
Wright Business School 2-CS
2219 SW 74TH ST STE 122 73159 681-2300

Okmulgee, AC 918, PC 7, Okmulgee
Okmulgee ISD, PO BOX 1346 74447 5-11111
Kerry Roberts, supt. 758-2000
HS, PO BOX 1346 74447 3-00011
Tom Turner, prin. 758-2075
MS, PO BOX 1346 74447 3-00100
John Whitfield, prin. 758-2050

Oklahoma State University 4-CC
1801 E 4TH ST 74447 800-722-4471

Oktaha, AC 918, PC 2, Muskogee
Oktaha ISD, PO BOX 9 74450 2-11111
Jerry Needham, supt. 687-3672
HS, PO BOX 9 74450 2-00011
Bill Hoots, prin. 687-3672

Olustee, AC 405, PC 3, Jackson
Olustee ISD, PO BOX 70 73560 2-11111
Roger Allen, supt. 648-2243
HS, PO BOX 70 73560 1-00011
Darinda Welch, prin. 648-2243

Omega, AC 405, PC 2, Kingfisher
Lomega ISD, RR 1 BOX 46 73764 2-11111
Reith Claflin, supt. 729-4215
Lomega HS, RR 1 BOX 46 73764 1-00011
Reith Claflin, prin. 729-4281

Oologah, AC 918, PC 3, Rogers
Oologah-Talala ISD 4-11111
PO BOX 189 74053 443-2422
Terry Tillery, supt.
HS, PO BOX 189 74053 2-00011
Jim Clemmens, prin. 443-2410
MS, PO BOX 189 74053 2-00100
Derald Buckley, prin. 443-2446

Orlando, AC 405, PC 2, Logan
Mulhall-Orlando ISD 2-11111
PO BOX 8 73073 455-2211
Carla Lewis, supt.
Mulhall-Orlando HS 1-00011
PO BOX 8 73073 455-2212
Stacey Harris, prin.

Owasso, AC 918, PC 7, Tulsa
Owasso ISD, 1501 N ASH ST 74055 5-11111
Dale Johnson, supt. 272-5367
SHS, 1501 N ASH ST 74055 4-00001
Rick Dossett, prin. 272-5334
JHS, 1501 N ASH ST 74055 3-00110
Ted Vancuren, prin. 272-6274

Paden, AC 405, PC 2, Okfuskee
Paden ISD, PO BOX 370 74860 2-11111
Gary Pollard, supt. 932-5053
HS, PO BOX 370 74860 2-00011
Kelly Bowen, prin. 932-4465

Panama, AC 918, PC 4, Leflore
Panama ISD, PO BOX 550 74951 3-11111
Nelson Davis, supt. 963-2217
HS, PO BOX 550 74951 2-00011
Harold Arter, prin. 963-2215
MS, PO BOX 550 74951 2-00100
Larry Greenwood, prin. 963-2213

Panola, AC 918, PC 2, Latimer
Panola ISD, PO BOX 6 74559 2-11111
Chester Jordan, supt. 465-3298
HS, PO BOX 6 74559 1-00011
Rowland Glenn, prin. 465-3813

Paoli, AC 405, PC 3, Garvin
Paoli ISD, PO BOX 278 73074 2-11111
Thomas King, supt. 484-7336

HS, PO BOX 278 73074 1-00011
Greg Benson, prin. 484-7336

Pauls Valley, AC 405, PC 6, Garvin
Pauls Valley ISD, PO BOX 780 73075 4-11111
Terry Simpson, supt. 238-6453
HS, PO BOX 780 73075 2-00011
David Jackson, prin. 238-6497
Lee MS, PO BOX 780 73075 2-00100
Russell Payton, prin. 238-7336

Pawhuska, AC 918, PC 5, Osage
Pawhuska ISD, 1505 LYNN AVE 74056 4-11111
Nancy Woodyard, supt. 287-1281
HS, 1505 LYNN AVE 74056 2-00011
Patsy Simmons, prin. 287-1262
JHS, 1505 LYNN AVE 74056 2-00100
Rick Peters, prin. 287-1264

Pawnee, AC 918, PC 4, Pawnee
Pawnee ISD, 615 DENVER ST 74058 3-11111
Ned Williams, supt. 762-3676
HS, 615 DENVER ST 74058 2-00011
Alan Hughes, prin. 762-3676
JHS, 615 DENVER ST 74058 2-00100
David Tanner, prin. 762-3676

Perkins, AC 405, PC 4, Payne
Perkins-Tryon ISD 4-11111
PO BOX 549 74059 547-2172
Jim Hyder, supt.
Perkins-Tryon HS 2-00011
PO BOX 549 74059 547-2425
Margaret Hrencher, prin.
Perkins-Tryon MS 2-00100
PO BOX 549 74059 547-2475
Milton Davis, prin.

Perry, AC 405, PC 5, Noble
Perry ISD, 900 FIR ST 73077 4-11111
Larry Fry, supt. 336-4511
JSHS, 900 FIR ST 73077 2-00111
Bill Rotter, prin. 336-4415

Picher, AC 918, PC 4, Ottawa
Picher-Cardin ISD 3-11111
PO BOX 280 74360 673-1714
Joe Layton, supt.
Picher-Cardin JSHS 2-00111
PO BOX 280 74360 673-1713
Robert Walker, prin.

Piedmont, AC 405, PC 5, Canadian
Piedmont ISD 3-11111
713 PIEDMONT RD N 73078 373-2311
Ronald Roblyer, supt.
HS, 713 PIEDMONT RD N 73078 2-00011
John Hyatt, prin. 373-2865
JHS, 713 PIEDMONT RD N 73078 2-00100
Joyce Anderson, prin. 373-1315

Pittsburg, AC 918, PC 2, Pittsburg
Pittsburg ISD, PO BOX 200 74560 2-11111
John Wood, supt. 432-5351
HS, PO BOX 200 74560 1-00011
Ronald Slawson, prin. 432-5513

Pocola, AC 918, PC 5, Leflore
Pocola ISD, PO BOX 640 74902 3-11111
Larry Sockey, supt. 436-2424
HS, PO BOX 640 74902 2-00011
Warner Baxter, prin. 436-2042
MS, PO BOX 640 74902 2-00100
John Currens, prin. 436-2091

Ponca City, AC 405, PC 8, Kay
Ponca City ISD, PO BOX 271 74602 6-11111
Wynona Winn, supt. 767-8000
SHS, 1022 N 7TH ST 74601 4-00001
Don Sjoberg, prin. 767-9500
East JHS, 612 E GRAND AVE 74601 3-00110
Steve Nida, prin. 767-8010
West JHS, 1401 W GRAND AVE 74601 3-00110
Michael Mitchell, prin. 767-8020

Pond Creek, AC 405, PC 3, Grant
Pond Creek-Hunter ISD 2-11111
PO BOX 56 73766 532-4242
James White, supt.
JSHS, PO BOX 56 73766 1-00011
Tom Sorrels, prin. 532-4241

Porter, AC 918, PC 3, Wagoner
Porter ISD, PO BOX 120 74454 2-11111
Lee Cobb, supt. 483-2401
HS, PO BOX 120 74454 2-00011
Calvin Moore, prin. 483-7011

Porum, AC 918, PC 3, Muskogee
Porum ISD, PO BOX 189 74455 2-11111
Pete Vanzant, supt. 484-5121
HS, PO BOX 189 74455 2-00011
Bill Belger, prin. 484-5122

Poteau, AC 918, PC 6, Leflore
Poteau ISD 4-11111
100 MOCKINGBIRD LN 74953 647-2251
Bert Corr, supt.
HS, 100 MOCKINGBIRD LN 74953 3-00011
George Reaves, prin. 647-4102
Kidd JHS, 100 MOCKINGBIRD LN 74953 2-00100
Alice Smith, prin. 647-9156

Carl Albert State College 4-CC
PO BOX 606 74953 647-8600

Prague, AC 405, PC 4, Lincoln
Prague ISD, NBU 3504 74864 3-11111
David Cox, supt. 567-4455
HS, NBU 3504 74864 2-00011
Ted Gillispie, prin. 567-2281
MS, NBU 3504 74864 2-00100
Jackie Hargrove, prin. 567-2281

Preston, AC 918, PC 3, Okmulgee
Preston ISD, PO BOX 418 74456 2-11111
Jim Waller, supt. 756-3388
HS, PO BOX 418 74456 2-00011
Terry Jones, prin. 756-8636

Prue, AC 918, PC 2, Osage
Prue ISD, PO BOX 130 74060 2-11111
Ronald Meadows, supt. 242-3351
HS, PO BOX 130 74060 2-00011
Charles Biggs, prin. 242-3384

Pryor, AC 918, PC 6, Mayes
Pryor ISD, PO BOX 548 74362 4-11111
Larry Burdick, supt. 825-1255
SHS, 521 SE 1ST ST 74361 3-00001
Gary Sharp, prin. 825-2340
JHS, 521 SE 1ST ST 74361 3-00110
Stephen Elliott, prin. 825-2371

Purcell, AC 405, PC 5, McClain
Purcell ISD, 919 N 9TH AVE 73080 3-11111
George Hatfield, supt. 527-2146
HS, 201 S 4TH AVE 73080 2-00011
Tom Pannell, prin. 527-6591
MS, 919 N 9TH AVE 73080 2-00100
Danny Jacobs, prin. 527-5561

Quapaw, AC 918, PC 3, Ottawa
Quapaw ISD, PO BOX 767 74363 3-11111
David Hardage, supt. 674-2501
HS, PO BOX 767 74363 2-00011
Tom Merritt, prin. 674-2474
MS, PO BOX 767 74363 2-00100
Larry Radford, prin. 674-2496

Quinton, AC 918, PC 4, Pittsburg
Quinton ISD, PO BOX 670 74561 3-11111
Arthur Schofield, supt. 469-3100
HS, PO BOX 670 74561 2-00011
Darrell Adcock, prin. 469-3309

Ramona, AC 918, PC 3, Washington
Caney Valley ISD, PO BOX B 74061 2-11101
Bob Smith, supt. 536-2500
Caney Valley SHS, PO BOX B 74061 2-00001
Holly Ward, prin. 536-3425
Caney Valley MS, PO BOX B 74061 2-00100
Brian Beagles, prin. 536-2705

Randlett, AC 405, PC 2, Cotton
Big Pasture ISD, PO BOX 167 73562 2-11111
Aubrey Ritter, supt. 281-3831
Big Pasture HS, PO BOX 167 73562 1-00011
James Mise, prin. 281-3276

Rattan, AC 405, PC 2, Pushmataha
Rattan ISD, PO BOX 44 74562 2-11111
Loyd Deaton, supt. 587-2546
SHS, PO BOX 44 74562 2-00001
Pete Smith, prin. 587-2715
JHS, PO BOX 44 74562 1-00110
Steve Crawford, prin. 587-2715

Red Oak, AC 918, PC 3, Latimer
Red Oak ISD, PO BOX 310 74563 2-11111
Wes Watson, supt. 754-2426
HS, PO BOX 310 74563 2-00011
James Gilmartin, prin. 754-2283

Red Rock, AC 405, PC 2, Noble
Frontier SD, PO BOX 130 74651 2-11111
Stephen Shiever, supt. 723-4361
HS, PO BOX 130 74651 1-00011
Randy Robinson, prin. 723-4360
MS, PO BOX 130 74651 2-01100
Greg Jackson, prin. 723-4223

Reydon, AC 405, PC 2, Rogers Mills
Reydon ISD, PO BOX 37 73660 2-11111
Tom McKinney, supt. 655-4375
HS, PO BOX 37 73660 1-00011
Melvin Cardwell, prin. 655-4375

Ringling, AC 405, PC 4, Jefferson
Ringling ISD, PO BOX 1010 73456 2-11111
Rick Gandy, supt. 662-2385
HS, PO BOX 1010 73456 2-00011
Grey Shivers, prin. 662-2386
JHS, PO BOX 1010 73456 2-00100
Grey Shivers, prin. 662-2387

Ringwood, AC 405, PC 2, Major
Ringwood ISD, PO BOX 239 73768 2-11111
Jim Knox, supt. 883-2202
HS, PO BOX 239 73768 2-00011
Larry Nance, prin. 883-2201

Ripley, AC 918, PC 2, Payne
Ripley ISD, PO BOX 97 74062 2-11111
Roger Shaw, supt. 372-4242
HS, PO BOX 97 74062 2-00011
Joe Powell, prin. 372-4245

Roff, AC 405, PC 3, Pontotoc
Roff ISD, PO BOX 157 74865 2-11111
Steven Crawford, supt. 456-7663
HS, PO BOX 157 74865 1-00011
Wayne Cope, prin. 456-7252

Roland, AC 918, PC 4, Sequoyah
Roland ISD, RR 1 BOX 1 74954 — 4-11111
  Howard Harrell, supt. — 427-4601
SHS, RR 1 BOX 1 74954 — 2-00001
  Gary Lattimore, prin. — 427-7419
JHS, RR 1 BOX 1 74954 — 2-00110
  Vickie Earnhart, prin. — 427-4631

Rush Springs, AC 405, PC 4, Grady
Rush Springs ISD, PO BOX 308 73082 — 3-11111
  Roy Larmar, supt. — 476-3929
HS, PO BOX 308 73082 — 2-00011
  Darrel Haynes, prin. — 476-3596
MS, PO BOX 308 73082 — 2-00100
  Bill Chambers, prin. — 476-3447

Ryan, AC 405, PC 3, Jefferson
Ryan ISD, PO BOX 369 73565 — 2-11111
  Roy Goldston, supt. — 757-2308
HS, PO BOX 369 73565 — 1-00011
  Larry Ninman, prin. — 757-2296

Salina, AC 918, PC 4, Mayes
Salina ISD, PO BOX 98 74365 — 3-11111
  Don Woodson, supt. — 434-5091
HS, PO BOX 98 74365 — 2-00011
  William Gage, prin. — 434-5347
MS, PO BOX 98 74365 — 2-00100
  Sally Cox, prin. — 434-5311

Sallisaw, AC 918, PC 6, Sequoyah
Central ISD, RR 1 BOX 36 74955 — 2-11111
  Bob Barbee, supt. — 775-5525
Central HS, RR 1 BOX 36 74955 — 2-00011
  Clyde Parsons, prin. — 775-5525
Sallisaw ISD, 604 E CHEROKEE ST 74955 — 5-11111
  Ronald Wyrick, supt. — 775-5544
HS, 200 W CREEK ST 74955 — 3-00011
  Larry Lewis, prin. — 775-7761
MS, 1206 E CREEK ST 74955 — 2-00100
  Dwight Phillips, prin. — 775-3015

Sand Springs, AC 918, PC 7, Tulsa
Sand Springs ISD, PO BOX 970 74063 — 6-11111
  George Paden, supt. — 245-3206
Page SHS, PO BOX 970 74063 — 4-00001
  Don Moore, prin. — 245-1201
Boyd JHS, PO BOX 970 74063 — 3-00110
  Larry Cale, prin. — 245-6363
Central JHS, PO BOX 970 74063 — 3-00110
  Gary Coots, prin. — 245-3211

Sapulpa, AC 918, PC 7, Creek
Sapulpa ISD, 1 S MISSION ST 74066 — 5-11111
  Charles Dodson, supt. — 224-3400
SHS, 1 S MISSION ST 74066 — 4-00001
  Joe Ligon, prin. — 224-6560
JHS, 1 S MISSION ST 74066 — 3-00110
  Michael Shanahan, prin. — 224-6710

Sasakwa, AC 405, PC 2, Seminole
Sasakwa ISD, PO BOX 323 74867 — 2-11111
  Wade Glover, supt. — 941-3213
HS, PO BOX 323 74867 — 2-00011
  Wade Glover, prin. — 941-3250

Savanna, AC 918, PC 3, Pittsburg
Savanna ISD, PO BOX 266 74565 — 2-11111
  Joe Brown, supt. — 548-3777
HS, PO BOX 266 74565 — 2-00011
  Mitch Tidwell, prin. — 548-3887

Sayre, AC 405, PC 5, Beckham
Sayre ISD — 3-10111
  716 NE HIGHWAY 66 73662 — 928-5531
  Paul Conner, supt.
SHS, 716 NE HIGHWAY 66 73662 — 2-00001
  John Wilson, prin. — 928-5576
JHS, 716 NE HIGHWAY 66 73662 — 2-00110
  Ronald Largent, prin. — 928-5578

Southwestern Oklahoma State University — 2-CC
  409 E MISSISSIPPI AVE 73662 — 928-5533

Schulter, AC 918, PC 3, Okmulgee
Schulter ISD, PO BOX 203 74460 — 2-11111
  Charles Thompson, supt. — 652-8219
HS, PO BOX 203 74460 — 1-00011
  Carroll Brooksher, prin. — 652-8200

Seiling, AC 405, PC 4, Dewey
Seiling ISD, PO BOX 780 73663 — 3-11111
  Bobby Russell, supt. — 922-7383
JSHS, PO BOX 780 73663 — 2-00111
  C. Oakes, prin. — 922-7382

Seminole, AC 405, PC 6, Seminole
Pleasant Grove ISD — 2-11111
  RR 1 BOX 247 74868 — 382-0454
  Paul Pettigrew, supt.
Pleasant Grove HS — 1-00011
  RR 1 BOX 247 74868 — 382-5865
  Charlotte Hickman, prin.
Seminole ISD, PO BOX 1031 74818 — 4-11111
  Randy Allison, supt. — 382-5085
HS, PO BOX 1031 74818 — 3-00011
  Larry Walters, prin. — 382-1415
MS, PO BOX 1031 74818 — 2-00100
  Roger Little, prin. — 382-1415
Strother ISD, RR 3 BOX 265 74868 — 2-11111
  Kenneth Speer, supt. — 382-4014
Strother JSHS, RR 3 BOX 265 74868 — 2-00111
  Ann Morris, prin. — 382-0982

Varnum ISD, RR 4 BOX 148 74868 — 2-11111
  James Scantlen, supt. — 382-1448
Varnum JSHS, RR 4 BOX 148 74868 — 1-00111
  Charles Lee, prin. — 382-1408

Seminole Junior College — 4-CC
  PO BOX 351 74818 — 382-9950

Sentinel, AC 405, PC 3, Washita
Sentinel ISD, PO BOX 640 73664 — 2-11111
  Gary Higgins, supt. — 393-2101
Thomas JSHS, PO BOX 640 73664 — 1-00111
  Tom O'Hara, prin. — 393-2112

Shattuck, AC 405, PC 4, Ellis
Shattuck ISD, PO BOX 159 73858 — 2-11111
  Donny Darrow, supt. — 938-2586
JSHS, PO BOX 159 73858 — 2-00111
  Kenny Wiley, prin. — 938-2586

Shawnee, AC 405, PC 8, Pottawatomie
Bethel ISD — 4-11111
  36000 CLEARPOND RD 74801 — 273-0385
  Charles Shields, supt.
Bethel HS, 3600 CLEAR POND RD 74801 — 2-00011
  Steve Carpenter, prin. — 273-3633
Bethel MS, 3600 CLEAR POND RD 74801 — 2-00100
  Gary Cartwright, prin. — 273-5944
Shawnee ISD, 326 N UNION ST 74801 — 5-11111
  John Broberg, supt. — 273-0653
HS, 1001 N KENNEDY ST 74801 — 3-00011
  Brenda Hodges, prin. — 273-3084
MS, 501 N UNION ST 74801 — 3-00100
  Rocky Arrington, prin. — 273-0403

Oklahoma Baptist University — 4-UC
  500 W UNIVERSITY ST 74801 — 275-2850
St. Gregory's College — 2-CC
  1900 W MACARTHUR ST 74801 — 878-5444

Shidler, AC 918, PC 2, Osage
Shidler ISD, PO BOX 85 74652 — 2-11111
  Lewis Mann, supt. — 793-2021
JSHS, PO BOX 85 74652 — 2-00111
  Lewis Mann, prin. — 793-2461

Skiatook, AC 918, PC 5, Osage
Skiatook ISD, 355 S OSAGE ST 74070 — 4-11111
  Jim Newman, supt. — 396-1792
HS, 355 S OSAGE ST 74070 — 2-00011
  Curtis Risner, prin. — 396-1790
MS, 355 S OSAGE ST 74070 — 2-00100
  Carma Burd, prin. — 396-2307

Smithville, AC 405, PC 2, McCurtain
Smithville ISD, PO BOX 8 74957 — 2-11111
  Claude Eberle, supt. — 244-3333
HS, PO BOX 8 74957 — 1-00011
  Larry Cheek, prin. — 244-3281

Snyder, AC 405, PC 4, Kiowa
Snyder ISD, PO BOX 368 73566 — 3-11111
  DeDe Graham, supt. — 569-2773
HS, PO BOX 368 73566 — 2-00011
  Mike Atchley, prin. — 569-2730
MS, PO BOX 368 73566 — 2-01100
  Carol McPhail, prin. — 569-2691

Soper, AC 405, PC 2, Choctaw
Soper ISD, PO BOX 149 74759 — 2-11111
  Olen Jestis, supt. — 345-2211
HS, PO BOX 149 74759 — 1-00011
  Scott Thompson, prin. — 345-2212

South Coffeyville, AC 918, PC 3, Nowata
South Coffeyville ISD — 2-11110
  PO BOX 190 74072 — 255-6202
  Dick Todd, supt.
JHS, PO BOX 190 74072 — 1-00110
  Terry Downing, prin. — 255-6202

Spencer, AC 405, PC 5, Oklahoma
Oklahoma City ISD
  Supt. — See Oklahoma City
Star Spencer HS — 3-00011
  3001 SPENCER RD 73084 — 771-4700
  Joyce Henderson, prin.
Rogers MS, 4000 SPENCER RD 73084 — 3-00100
  Joe Hornbeak, prin. — 771-3205

Sperry, AC 918, PC 3, Tulsa
Sperry ISD, PO BOX 610 74073 — 3-11111
  Harry Red Eagle, supt. — 288-6258
HS, PO BOX 610 74073 — 2-00011
  Guynn Hammack, prin. — 288-7213
MS, PO BOX 610 74073 — 2-00100
  David Jobe, prin. — 288-7213

Oklahoma Farriers College — 1-CS
  RR 2 BOX 88 74073 — 288-7221

Spiro, AC 918, PC 4, Leflore
Spiro ISD, 600 W BROADWAY ST 74959 — 4-11111
  J. L. Williams, supt. — 962-2463
HS, 600 W BROADWAY ST 74959 — 2-00011
  Kenneth Perrin, prin. — 962-2493
MS, 600 W BROADWAY ST 74959 — 2-00100
  Ronnie Parent, prin. — 962-2488

Springer, AC 405, PC 2, Carter
Springer ISD, PO BOX 249 73458 — 2-11111
  Charles King, supt. — 653-2471
HS, PO BOX 249 73458 — 1-00011
  Charles King, prin. — 653-2471

Sterling, AC 405, PC 3, Comanche
Sterling ISD, PO BOX 158 73567 — 2-11111
  Joe Stafford, supt. — 365-4307
JSHS, PO BOX 158 73567 — 2-00111
  Roy Cross, prin. — 365-4303

Stigler, AC 918, PC 5, Haskell
Stigler ISD, 302 NW E ST 74462 — 4-11111
  Greg Kashbaum, supt. — 967-2805
HS, 302 NW E ST 74462 — 2-00011
  Bill Self, prin. — 967-8834
MS, 302 NW E ST 74462 — 2-00100
  Rick Prentice, prin. — 967-2521

Stillwater, AC 405, PC 8, Payne
Stillwater ISD, PO BOX 879 74076 — 5-11111
  Howard Jones, supt. — 743-6300
SHS, PO BOX 879 74076 — 4-00001
  Mike Turk, prin. — 743-6450
JHS, PO BOX 879 74076 — 3-00110
  Joe Payne, prin. — 743-6420

Indian Meridian Vocational Tech School — 2-CS
  1312 S SANGRE RD 74074 — 377-3333
Oklahoma State University 74078 — 7-UC
  — 744-6384

Stilwell, AC 918, PC 5, Adair
Cave Springs ISD — 2-11111
  RR 1 BOX 1555 74960 — 775-2364
  Joe Lindsey, supt.
Cave Springs HS — 2-00011
  RR 1 BOX 1555 74960 — 696-4322
  John Mays, prin.
Stilwell ISD, 1801 W LOCUST ST 74960 — 4-11111
  Pat Martin, supt. — 696-7001
HS, 1801 W LOCUST ST 74960 — 3-00011
  Barb Martens, prin. — 696-7276
MS, 1801 W LOCUST ST 74960 — 2-00100
  Jim McGee, prin. — 696-2685

Stonewall, AC 405, PC 3, Pontotoc
Stonewall ISD, RR 2 BOX 1A 74871 — 2-11111
  Floyd Gibson, supt. — 265-4241
HS, RR 2 BOX 1A 74871 — 1-00011
  Terry Scott, prin. — 265-4242

Stratford, AC 405, PC 4, Garvin
Stratford ISD, PO BOX 589 74872 — 3-11111
  William Stokes, supt. — 759-3615
JSHS, PO BOX 589 74872 — 2-00111
  Larry Marlow, prin. — 759-2381

Stringtown, AC 405, PC 2, Atoka
Stringtown ISD, PO BOX 130 74569 — 2-11111
  Richard Quaid, supt. — 346-7423
HS, PO BOX 130 74569 — 1-00011
  Tony Potts, prin. — 346-7741

Stroud, AC 918, PC 5, Lincoln
Stroud ISD, PO BOX 410 74079 — 3-11111
  Dean Morrison, supt. — 968-2541
HS, PO BOX 410 74079 — 2-00011
  Ernest Wayland, prin. — 968-2542
MS, PO BOX 410 74079 — 2-00100
  Ed Wilkinson, prin. — 968-2200

Stuart, AC 918, PC 2, Hughes
Stuart ISD, RR 1 BOX 7 74570 — 2-11111
  Harold Lasiter, supt. — 546-2474
HS, RR 1 BOX 7 74570 — 1-00011
  Ken Hokit, prin. — 546-2627

Sulphur, AC 405, PC 5, Murray
Sulphur ISD, 1021 W 9TH ST 73086 — 4-11111
  Lloyd Snow, supt. — 622-2061
HS, 1021 W 9TH ST 73086 — 2-00011
  Rendell Cole, prin. — 622-3174
MS, 1021 W 9TH ST 73086 — 2-00100
  Keith Foreman, prin. — 622-4010

Oklahoma School for the Deaf 73086 — HND

Sweetwater, AC 405, PC 2, Roger Mills
Sweetwater ISD, RR 1 BOX 6 73666 — 2-11111
  Don Riley, supt. — 534-2272
HS, RR 1 BOX 6 73666 — 1-00011
  Don Riley, prin. — 534-2272

Tahlequah, AC 918, PC 7, Cherokee
Tahlequah ISD, PO BOX 517 74465 — 5-11111
  Janice Sheets, supt. — 458-4100
SHS, 625 N JONES AVE 74464 — 3-00011
  Gary Gore, prin. — 458-4150
JHS, 400 W MORGAN ST 74464 — 3-00110
  Edwin Dukes, prin. — 458-4140

Northeastern State University — 6-UC
  600 N GRAND AVE 74464 — 456-5511

Talihina, AC 918, PC 4, Leflore
Buffalo Valley ISD — 2-11111
  RR 2 BOX 3505 74571 — 522-4426
  Jerry Mason, supt.
Buffalo Valley HS — 1-00011
  RR 2 BOX 3505 74571 — 522-4803
  Chester Knight, prin.
Talihina ISD, PO BOX 38 74571 — 3-11111
  Ray Henson, supt. — 567-2259
SHS, PO BOX 38 74571 — 2-00001
  Jim Hibdon, prin. — 567-2266
JHS, PO BOX 38 74571 — 2-00110
  Robert Perryman, prin. — 567-2138

Taloga, AC 405, PC 2, Dewey
Taloga ISD, PO BOX 158 73667 — 2-11111
Jeff Gray, supt. — 328-5577
HS, PO BOX 158 73667 — 1-00011
Ron Brown, prin. — 328-5586

Tecumseh, AC 405, PC 6, Pottawatomie
Tecumseh ISD, 302 S 9TH ST 74873 — 4-11111
Jim Myers, supt. — 598-3739
HS, 302 S 9TH ST 74873 — 3-00011
James Blue, prin. — 598-2113
MS, 315 W PARK ST 74873 — 2-00100
Marty Lewis, prin. — 598-3744

Temple, AC 405, PC 4, Cotton
Temple ISD, PO BOX 400 73568 — 2-11111
Lane Garner, supt. — 342-6230
JSHS, PO BOX 400 73568 — 2-00111
Loren Tackett, prin. — 342-6221

Texhoma, AC 405, PC 3, Texas
Texhoma ISD, PO BOX 648 73949 — 2-11111
Mel Yates, supt. — 423-7433
HS, PO BOX 648 73949 — 2-00011
Ron Murphy, prin. — 423-7371

Thackerville, AC 405, PC 2, Love
Thackerville ISD, PO BOX 377 73459 — 2-11111
Clifford Boatright, supt. — 276-2630
HS, PO BOX 377 73459 — 2-00011
Novella Wilson, prin. — 276-3610

Thomas, AC 405, PC 4, Custer
Thomas ISD, PO BOX 190 73669 — 2-11111
David Self, supt. — 661-3521
JSHS, PO BOX 190 73669 — 2-00111
Terry Green, prin. — 661-3522

Tipton, AC 405, PC 4, Tillman
Tipton ISD, PO BOX 340 73570 — 2-11111
Larry Osborne, supt. — 667-5268
HS, PO BOX 340 73570 — 2-00011
Clay Shannon, prin. — 667-5268

Tishomingo, AC 405, PC 5, Johnston
Tishomingo ISD, RR 1 BOX 47 73460 — 3-11111
Ronald Hutchings, supt. — 371-9190
HS, RR 1 BOX 47 73460 — 2-00011
Larry Woods, prin. — 371-2322
MS, RR 1 BOX 47 73460 — 2-00100
Rex Lokey, prin. — 371-3602

Murray State College 73460 — 4-CC
371-2371

Tonkawa, AC 405, PC 5, Kay
Tonkawa ISD, PO BOX 10 74653 — 3-11111
Ron Hodges, supt. — 628-3597
JSHS, PO BOX 10 74653 — 2-00111
Robert Smith, prin. — 628-2566

Northern Oklahoma College — 4-CC
1220 E GRAND AVE 74653 — 628-2581

Tulsa, AC 918, PC 10, Tulsa
Berryhill ISD — 3-11111
3128 S 63RD WEST AVE 74107 — 446-1966
Leonard Wood, supt.
Berryhill SHS — 2-00001
3128 S 63RD WEST AVE 74107 — 446-1636
Charles Prater, prin.
Berryhill JHS — 2-00110
3128 S 63RD WEST AVE 74107 — 446-8765
Jo Etta Terrell, prin.

Tulsa ISD, PO BOX 470208 74147 — 8-11111
Robert Burton, supt. — 745-6800
Central HS, 3101 W EDISON ST 74127 — 4-00011
Betty Sprankle, prin. — 599-6200
East Central HS, 12150 E 11TH ST 74128 — 4-00011
Tim Cameron, prin. — 234-2200
Edison HS, 2906 E 41ST ST 74105 — 4-00011
Betty Rector, prin. — 748-1200
Hale HS, 6960 E 21ST ST 74129 — 4-00011
Stanley Fields, prin. — 831-7300
McClain HS, 4929 N PEORIA AVE 74126 — 4-00011
Frederick Wright, prin. — 428-0200
Memorial HS — 4-00011
5840 S HUDSON AVE 74135 — 491-2200
Bill Bond, prin.
Rogers HS, 3909 E 5TH PL 74112 — 4-00011
James Sharp, prin. — 831-3300
Washington HS — 4-00011
1631 E WOODROW PL 74106 — 428-6000
James Furch, prin.
Webster HS, 1919 W 40TH ST 74107 — 3-00011
Jerry Billings, prin. — 445-3600
Byrd MS, 7502 E 57TH ST 74145 — 3-00100
Steve Mayfield, prin. — 627-2616
Carver MS, 624 E OKLAHOMA PL 74106 — 3-00100
Bobbie Johnson, prin. — 587-5583
Cleveland MS — 2-00100
724 N BIRMINGHAM AVE 74110 — 834-3451
Nilda Reyes, prin.
Clinton MS, 2224 W 41ST ST 74107 — 3-00100
Cleta Driver, prin. — 446-5556
Edison MS, 2800 E 41ST ST 74105 — 2-00100
Ernie Thompson, prin. — 748-1250
Foster MS, 12121 E 21ST ST 74129 — 3-00100
Manuel Domingos, prin. — 437-4124
Gilcrease MS — 3-00100
5550 N CINCINNATI AVE 74126 — 425-5505
Fred Latimer, prin.

Hamilton MS — 3-00100
2316 N NORWOOD PL 74115 — 835-9537
Irvin Brown, prin.
Lewis and Clark MS — 2-00100
737 S 113 E AVE 74128 — 437-2220
Kenneth Yates, prin.
Madison MS — 2-00100
4132 W CAMERON ST 74127 — 587-9414
Michael Hacker, prin.
Monroe MS, 2010 E 48TH ST N 74130 — 3-00100
Travis Henderson, prin. — 425-7517
Nimitz MS, 3111 E 56TH ST 74105 — 3-00100
Jill Blackwelder, prin. — 743-6696
Whitney MS — 3-00100
2177 S 67TH EAST AVE 74129 — 835-9431
Derrick Schmidt, prin.
Wilson MS — 3-00100
1127 S COLUMBIA AVE 74104 — 592-3242
Garry Nichols, prin.

Union ISD — 4-11111
5656 S 129TH EAST AVE 74134 — 252-3561
Timothy Jenney, supt.
Union SHS, 6636 S MINGO RD 74133 — 4-00001
Mike O'Hara, prin. — 252-2581
Eighth Grade Center — 2-00100
5656 S 129TH EAST AVE 74134 — 250-9541
Jamie Lindsey, prin.
Other Schools – See Broken Arrow

Bishop Kelley HS — 3-00011
3905 S HUDSON AVE 74135 — 627-3390
Br. Poos, prin.
Bryan Institute — 2-CS
2843 E 51ST ST 74105 — 749-6891
Career Point Business School — 3-CS
3138 S GARNETT RD 74146 — 622-4100
Cascia Hall Prep S — 3-00011
PO BOX 52247 74152 — 742-7373
Fr. Tack, prin.
Climate Control Institute — 2-CS
708 S SHERIDAN RD 74112 — 836-6656
College of Osteopathic Medicine of OSU — 2-UC
1111 W 17TH ST 74107 — 582-1972
Holland Hall S — 3-11111
5666 E 81ST ST 74137
Metro Christian Academy — 3-11111
6363 S TRENTON AVE 74136 — 745-9868
Wanda Hartman, prin.
Metropolitan College of Legal Studies — 2-CS
2865 E SKELLY DR 74105 — 745-9946
NEC-Spartan School of Aeronautics — 5-CC
8820 E PINE ST # 51133 74115
800-331-1204
Oral Roberts University — 5-UC
7777 S LEWIS AVE 74171 — 495-7349
Platt College — 3-CS
4821 S 72ND EAST AVE 74145 — 663-9000
St. Francis Hospital — HSP
6161 S YALE AVE 74136 — 494-1370
Tulsa Co. Area Voc Tech District 18 — 2-CS
3420 S MEMORIAL DR 74145 — 627-7200
Tulsa Junior College — 6-CC
6111 E SKELLY DR STE 200 74135 — 622-5100
Tulsa Welding School — 2-CS
3038 SOUTHWEST BLVD 74107 — 800-331-2934
United States Truck Driving School — 2-CS
7500 NEW SAPULPA RD 74131 — 227-4100
University of Tulsa — 5-UC
600 S COLLEGE AVE 74104 — 631-2000

Tupelo, AC 405, PC 2, Coal
Tupelo ISD, PO BOX 310 74572 — 2-11111
Robert Pickens, supt. — 845-2460
HS, PO BOX 310 74572 — 1-00011
Frank Brewer, prin. — 845-2381

Turpin, AC 405, PC 2, Beaver
Turpin SD, PO BOX 187 73950 — 3-11111
Mike Scott, supt. — 778-3333
Turpin HS, PO BOX 187 73950 — 2-00111
Ed Chatham, prin. — 778-3333

Tuttle, AC 405, PC 5, Grady
Tuttle ISD, PO BOX 780 73089 — 4-11111
Hershel Busby, supt. — 381-2605
HS, PO BOX 780 73089 — 2-00011
Rick Banta, prin. — 381-2396
MS, PO BOX 780 73089 — 2-00100
James Stewart, prin. — 381-2062

Tyrone, AC 405, PC 3, Texas
Tyrone ISD, PO BOX 168 73951 — 2-11111
Gerald Miller, supt. — 854-6298
HS, PO BOX 168 73951 — 1-00011
Vernon Newman, prin. — 854-6298

Union City, AC 405, PC 4, Canadian
Union City ISD, PO BOX 279 73090 — 2-11111
Gary Swart, supt. — 483-3531
HS, PO BOX 279 73090 — 1-00011
Roy Tate, prin. — 483-5326

Valliant, AC 405, PC 3, McCurtain
Valliant ISD, PO BOX 777 74764 — 4-11111
Earl Wright, supt. — 933-7231
HS, PO BOX 777 74764 — 2-00011
Arnold Gregory, prin. — 933-7292
MS, PO BOX 777 74764 — 2-00100
Cynthia Ellis, prin. — 933-4253

Velma, AC 405, PC 3, Stephens
Velma-Alma ISD, PO BOX 8 73091 — 3-11111
Barbara Wood, supt. — 444-3355
Velma-Alma JSHS, PO BOX 8 73091 — 2-00111
James Miller, prin. — 444-3356

Verden, AC 405, PC 3, Grady
Verden ISD, PO BOX 99 73092 — 2-11111
S. Cook, supt. — 453-7247
HS, PO BOX 99 73092 — 1-00011
Steve James, prin. — 453-7836

Vian, AC 918, PC 4, Sequoyah
Vian ISD, PO BOX 434 74962 — 3-11111
Rick Watson, supt. — 773-5798
HS, PO BOX 434 74962 — 2-00011
Joe Smith, prin. — 773-5475
MS, PO BOX 434 74962 — 2-00100
Bill Reynolds, prin. — 773-8631

Vici, AC 405, PC 3, Dewey
Vici ISD, PO BOX 60 73859 — 2-11111
Don Rader, supt. — 995-4744
JSHS, PO BOX 60 73859 — 2-00111
Gene Van Campen, prin. — 995-4251

Vinita, AC 918, PC 6, Craig
Vinita ISD, PO BOX 408 74301 — 3-11111
Jerry Greenwood, supt. — 256-6778
HS, PO BOX 408 74301 — 2-00011
Henry Haynes, prin. — 256-6777
MS, PO BOX 408 74301 — 2-00100
Jeff Williams, prin. — 256-2402

White Oak ISD, RR 4 BOX 274 74301 — 2-11111
George Wickliffe, supt. — 256-7673
White Oak HS, RR 4 BOX 274 74301 — 1-00011
John Seifried, prin. — 256-7673

Wagoner, AC 918, PC 6, Wagoner
Wagoner ISD, PO BOX 707 74477 — 4-11111
Dennis Shoemaker, supt. — 485-9539
SHS, 300 N WARD AVE 74467 — 2-00001
Bill Benham, prin. — 485-5553
JHS, 204 N CASAVER AVE 74467 — 2-00110
Darrell Morgan, prin. — 485-9541

Wakita, AC 405, PC 2, Grant
Wakita ISD, PO BOX 45 73771 — 2-11111
Fred Ferguson, supt. — 594-2261
HS, PO BOX 45 73771 — 1-00011
Nancy Oldham, prin. — 594-2262

Walters, AC 405, PC 5, Cotton
Walters ISD — 3-11111
418 S BROADWAY ST 73572 — 875-2568
Roy Masoner, supt.
HS, 418 S BROADWAY ST 73572 — 2-00011
Tim Merchant, prin. — 875-3257
MS, 418 S BROADWAY ST 73572 — 2-00100
Gary Ledford, prin. — 875-3214

Wanette, AC 405, PC 2, Pottawatomie
Wanette ISD, PO BOX 161 74878 — 2-11111
Glenn Haswell, supt. — 383-2656
HS, PO BOX 161 74878 — 2-00011
Eugene Blue, prin. — 383-2254

Wapanucka, AC 405, PC 2, Johnston
Wapanucka ISD, PO BOX 188 73461 — 2-11111
Clint Dildeck, supt. — 937-4288
HS, PO BOX 188 73461 — 1-00011
Julie Renfro, prin. — 937-4288

Warner, AC 918, PC 4, Muskogee
Warner ISD, RR 1 BOX 1240 74469 — 3-11111
Eddie Ogden, supt. — 463-5171
HS, RR 1 BOX 1240 74469 — 2-00011
John Englebrecht, prin. — 463-5172

Connors State College — 4-CC
RR 1 BOX 1000 74469 — 463-2931

Washington, AC 405, PC 2, McClain
Washington ISD, PO BOX 98 73093 — 3-11111
L. McAlister, supt. — 288-6190
SHS, PO BOX 98 73093 — 2-00001
Dale Pope, prin. — 288-2354
JHS, PO BOX 98 73093 — 2-00110
A. J. Brewer, prin. — 288-2354

Watonga, AC 405, PC 5, Blaine
Watonga ISD, PO BOX 310 73772 — 3-11111
Michael May, supt. — 623-7364
HS, PO BOX 310 73772 — 2-00011
Lynn Wilt, prin. — 623-4961
MS, PO BOX 310 73772 — 2-00100
Lanna Chaloupek, prin. — 623-7361

Watts, AC 918, PC 2, Adair
Watts ISD, PO BOX 10 74964 — 2-11111
Jim Newby, supt. — 422-5311
HS, PO BOX 10 74964 — 2-00011
Joe Gunter, prin. — 422-5132

Waukomis, AC 405, PC 4, Garfield
Pioneer-Pleasant Vale ISD — 3-11111
RR 1 BOX 219 73773 — 758-3282
Bob Bush, supt.
Pioneer-Pleasant Vale JSHS — 2-00111
RR 1 BOX 219 73773 — 758-3282
Bill Noak, prin.

Waukomis ISD, PO BOX 729 73773 — 3-11111
  Gerald Hoeltzel, supt. — 758-3247
HS, PO BOX 729 73773 — 2-00011
  Gary Lundy, prin. — 758-3245
MS, PO BOX 729 73773 — 2-00100
  Ralph Jones, prin. — 758-3247

Waurika, AC 405, PC 4, Jefferson
Waurika ISD, PO BOX 330 73573 — 2-11111
  William Martin, supt. — 228-3373
SHS, PO BOX 330 73573 — 2-00001
  Larry Snider, prin. — 228-2341
JHS, PO BOX 330 73573 — 2-00110
  Larry Snider, prin. — 228-2341

Wayne, AC 405, PC 3, McClain
Wayne ISD, PO BOX 40 73095 — 3-11111
  Terry Selman, supt. — 449-3646
HS, PO BOX 40 73095 — 2-00011
  Earl Shephard, prin. — 449-3317
MS, PO BOX 40 73095 — 2-00100
  David Powell, prin. — 449-7047

Waynoka, AC 405, PC 3, Woods
Waynoka ISD, RR 1 BOX 1 73860 — 2-11111
  Rocky Burchfield, supt. — 824-6561
HS, RR 1 BOX 1 73860 — 1-00011
  Bob Yadon, prin. — 824-4341

Weatherford, AC 405, PC 7, Custer
Weatherford ISD — 4-11111
  516 N BROADWAY ST 73096 — 772-3327
  Greg Moss, supt.
HS, 1500 N WASHINGTON ST 73096 — 3-00011
  Floyd Lamke, prin. — 772-3385
MS, 516 N BROADWAY ST 73096 — 2-00100
  Ed Bennett, prin. — 772-2270

Southwestern Oklahoma State University — 5-UC
  100 CAMPUS DR 73096 — 772-6611

Webbers Falls, AC 918, PC 3, Muskogee
Webbers Falls ISD — 2-11111
  PO BOX 300 74470 — 464-2580
  Robert Perkins, supt.
JSHS, PO BOX 300 74470 — 2-00111
  Charles Coleman, prin. — 464-2334

Welch, AC 918, PC 2, Craig
Welch ISD, PO BOX 189 74369 — 2-11111
  Gregory Holleyman, supt. — 788-3319
JSHS, PO BOX 189 74369 — 2-00111
  Frank Hecksher, prin. — 788-3222

Weleetka, PC 4, Okfuskee
Graham ISD, RR 1 BOX 91 74880 — 2-11111
  Dusty Chancey, supt. — 918-652-8935
Graham HS, RR 1 BOX 91 74880 — 1-00011
  Dusty Chancey, prin. — 918-652-8935

Weleetka ISD — 2-11111
  PO BOX 278 74880 — 405-786-2442
  Dan Parrish, supt.
HS, PO BOX 278 74880 — 1-00011
  James Lyons, prin. — 405-786-2203

Wellston, AC 405, PC 3, Lincoln
Wellston ISD, PO BOX 60 74881 — 2-11111
  Thomas Crawley, supt. — 356-2534
HS, PO BOX 60 74881 — 2-00011
  Mike Telford, prin. — 356-2533
MS, PO BOX 60 74881 — 1-00100
  Jerald Price, prin. — 356-2533

Westville, AC 918, PC 4, Adair
Westville ISD, PO BOX 410 74965 — 3-11111
  Philip Williams, supt. — 723-3181
SHS, PO BOX 410 74965 — 2-00001
  Dan Collins, prin. — 723-5644
JHS, PO BOX 410 74965 — 2-00110
  Darrell Stephens, prin. — 723-3432

Wetumka, AC 405, PC 4, Hughes
Wetumka ISD, PO BOX 8 74883 — 3-11111
  Ron Renfrow, supt. — 452-5150
HS, PO BOX 8 74883 — 2-00011
  Vernon Stout, prin. — 452-3291
MS, PO BOX 8 74883 — 1-00100
  James Rayburn, prin. — 452-3292

Wewoka, AC 405, PC 5, Seminole
New Lima ISD, RR 1 BOX 96 74884 — 2-11111
  Bryce Hill, supt. — 257-5771
New Lima HS, RR 1 BOX 96 74884 — 1-00011
  E. Stafford, prin. — 257-5771

Wewoka ISD, PO BOX 870 74884 — 4-11111
  Bill Bentley, supt. — 257-5475
HS, PO BOX 870 74884 — 2-00011
  John Herzig, prin. — 257-5473
MS, PO BOX 870 74884 — 2-00100
  Jim Mathews, prin. — 257-2340

Whitesboro, AC 918, PC 2, Leflore
Whitesboro ISD, PO BOX 150 74577 — 2-11111
  Jim Olive, supt. — 567-2556
HS, PO BOX 150 74577 — 1-00011
  John Elrod, prin. — 567-2624

Wilburton, AC 918, PC 5, Latimer
Wilburton ISD — 4-11111
  1201 W BLAIR AVE 74578 — 465-2100
  Charles Enis, supt.
SHS, 1201 W BLAIR AVE 74578 — 2-00001
  Nancy Taylor, prin. — 465-3125
JHS, 1201 W BLAIR AVE 74578 — 2-00110
  John Garofoli, prin. — 465-2281

Eastern Oklahoma State College — 4-CC
  1301 W MAIN ST 74578 — 465-2361

Wilson, AC 405, PC 4, Carter
Wilson ISD, PO BOX 730 73463 — 3-11111
  Bill Farnham, supt. — 668-2306
HS, PO BOX 730 73463 — 2-00011
  Rick Ruckman, prin. — 668-2317

Wister, AC 918, PC 3, Leflore
Wister ISD, PO BOX 489 74966 — 2-11111
  Larry Culwell, supt. — 655-3132

HS, PO BOX 489 74966 — 2-00011
  Dart Drummonds, prin. — 655-7276

Woodward, AC 405, PC 7, Woodward
Woodward ISD, PO BOX 668 73802 — 7-11111
  Michael McClaren, supt. — 256-6063
HS, PO BOX 668 73802 — 3-00011
  Ed Story, prin. — 256-5329
JHS, PO BOX 668 73802 — 2-00100
  Mike King, prin. — 256-7901

Wright City, AC 405, PC 3, McCurtain
Wright City ISD, PO BOX 329 74766 — 3-11111
  Terry Davidson, supt. — 981-2824
JSHS, PO BOX 329 74766 — 2-00111
  Bob Finley, prin. — 981-2558

Wyandotte, AC 918, PC 2, Ottawa
Wyandotte ISD, PO BOX 360 74370 — 3-11111
  Bob Martin, supt. — 678-2255
SHS, PO BOX 360 74370 — 2-00001
  Joe Lippe, prin. — 678-2222
JHS, PO BOX 360 74370 — 2-00110
  Don Barr, prin. — 678-2222

Wynnewood, AC 405, PC 4, Garvin
Wynnewood ISD — 2-11111
  702 E KERR BLVD 73098 — 665-2004
  Jim Stark, supt.
HS, 702 E KERR BLVD 73098 — 2-00011
  Gaylon Jackson, prin. — 665-2045
MS, 702 E KERR BLVD 73098 — 2-00100
  Tom McKay, prin. — 665-4105

Wynona, AC 918, PC 3, Osage
Wynona ISD, PO BOX 700 74084 — 2-11111
  H. M. Garrett, supt. — 846-2467
HS, PO BOX 700 74084 — 1-00011
  Don Jennings, prin. — 846-2467

Yale, AC 918, PC 4, Payne
Yale ISD, 315 E CHICAGO AVE 74085 — 3-11111
  Jeannette Williams, supt. — 387-2434
HS, 315 E CHICAGO AVE 74085 — 2-00011
  Judy Sims, prin. — 387-2118
JHS, 315 E CHICAGO AVE 74085 — 2-00100
  Kirk Warnick, prin. — 387-2282

Yukon, AC 405, PC 7, Canadian
Yukon ISD, 950 POPLAR AVE 73099 — 6-11111
  Darrell Hill, supt. — 354-2587
SHS, 1000 YUKON AVE 73099 — 3-00001
  John Riley, prin. — 354-6661
Independence MS — 3-00100
  500 E VANDAMENT AVE 73099 — 354-5274
  Janice McComas, prin.
Mid HS — 3-00010
  1029 GARTH BROOKS BLVD 73099 — 354-6692
  Betty Novak, prin.

OREGON

STATE DEPARTMENT OF EDUCATION
Public Service Building
255 Capitol St. N.E., Salem 97310
(503) 378-3569

Superintendent of Public Instruction	Norma Paulus
Deputy Superintendent	Bob Burns
Director Management Services	Chris Durham
Associate Superintendent Professional/Technical Education	J. D. Hoye
Associate Superintendent Special Education	Karen Brazeau
Associate Superintendent Curriculum & Instruction	Roberta Hutton
Deputy Superintendent Educational Support Services	Greg McMurdo

STATE BOARD OF EDUCATION
700 Pringle Parkway, S.E., Salem 97310

Chairperson	Jeana Woolley

EDUCATION SERVICE DISTRICTS

Baker ESD
Ruth Whitnah   503-523-5801
2100 MAIN ST, Baker City   97814
Clackamas ESD
David Campbell   503-635-0500
PO BOX 216, Marylhurst   97036
Clatsop ESD
Richard Laughlin   503-325-2862
3194 MARINE DR, Astoria   97103
Columbia ESD
Verle Bechtel   503-397-0028
PO BOX 900, Saint Helens   97051
Coos ESD
Rolland Lippold   503-269-1611
1350 TEAKWOOD AVE
Coos Bay   97420
Curry ESD
Sam Wilson   503-247-6681
PO BOX 786, Gold Beach   97444
Deschutes ESD
Dennis Douglass   503-382-3171
1340 NW WALL ST, Bend   97701
Douglas ESD
Vernon Bittner   503-440-4777
1871 NE STEPHENS ST
Roseburg   97470
Gilliam ESD
Dale Coles   503-384-2732
PO BOX 637, Condon   97823
Grant ESD
Robert Batty   503-575-1349
835 S CANYON BLVD
John Day   97845

Harney ESD
Dennis Mills   503-573-2426
450 N BUENA VISTA AVE
Burns   97720
Jackson ESD
Shelby Price   503-776-8590
101 N GRAPE ST, Medford   97501
Jefferson ESD
Phil Riley   503-475-6192
445 SE BUFF ST, Madras   97741
Lake ESD
Johnathan Hill   503-947-3371
357 N L ST, Lakeview   97630
Lane ESD
James Maxwell   503-689-6500
1200 HIGHWAY 99 N
Eugene   97402
Linn-Benton ESD
Gerald Bennett   503-967-8822
905 4TH AVE SE, Albany   97321
Malheur ESD
Edwin Morgan   503-473-3138
363 A ST W, Vale   97918
Marion ESD
Ron Wilkerson   503-588-5330
3400 PORTLAND RD NE
Salem   97303
Multnomah ESD
James Jacobson   503-255-1841
PO BOX 301039, Portland   97230
Polk ESD
Peyton Lieuallen   503-623-6691
322 MAIN ST, Dallas   97338

Sherman ESD
Dale Coles   503-565-3509
65912 HIGH SCHOOL LOOP
Moro   97039
Tillamook ESD
William Molendyke   503-842-8423
PO BOX 416, Tillamook   97141
Umatilla ESD
Boyd Swent, 2001 SW NYE AVE   503-276-6616
Pendleton   97801
Union ESD
Ken Kramer   503-963-4106
10100 N MCALISTER RD
Island City   97850
Wallowa ESD
Dave Smyth, 301 W NORTH ST   503-426-4997
Enterprise   97828
Wasco ESD
Fred Krauss   503-298-5155
422 E 3RD ST, The Dalles   97058
Washington ESD
John Young   503-690-5400
17705 NW SPRINGVILLE RD
Portland   97229
Wheeler ESD
Dale Coles   503-763-2131
PO BOX 268, Fossil   97830
Yamhill ESD
James Redmond, 800 E 2ND ST   503-472-1431
McMinnville   97128

PUBLIC, PRIVATE AND CATHOLIC SECONDARY SCHOOLS

Adrian, AC 503, PC 2, Malheur
Adrian SD 61, PO BOX 108   97901   2-11111
Irvin Easom, supt.   372-3744
JSHS, PO BOX 108   97901   2-00111
Henry Mahler, prin.   372-2335

Albany, AC 503, PC 8, Linn
Greater Albany SD 8J   6-11111
718 7TH AVE SW   97321   967-4501
Robert Stalick, supt.
South Albany HS   4-00011
3705 COLUMBUS ST SE   97321   967-4522
John DeBoie, prin.
West Albany HS   4-00011
1130 QUEEN AVE SW   97321   967-4545
Ronald Brown, prin.
Calapooia MS, 830 24TH AVE SE   97321   3-00100
Paul Nys, prin.   967-4555
Memorial MS   3-00100
1050 QUEEN AVE SW   97321   967-4537
Ric Blasquez, prin.
North Albany MS   3-00100
1205 NW NORTH ALBANY RD   97321   967-4541
Jerry Bennett, prin.

Fairview Christian HS   2-00011
35100 GOLTRA RD SE   97321
Linn-Benton Community College   7-CC
6500 PACIFIC BLVD SW   97321   967-6105

Aloha, AC 503, PC 7, Washington

Faith Bible Christian S   2-11111
PO BOX 5335   97006   642-4112

Alsea, AC 503, PC 2, Benton
Alsea SD 7J, PO BOX B   97324   2-11111
Art Anderson, supt.   487-5555
JSHS, PO BOX B   97324   2-00111
Art Anderson, prin.   487-4305

Amity, AC 503, PC 4, Yamhill
Amity SD 4J, PO BOX 138   97101   3-11111
George Lanning, supt.   835-2171
HS, PO BOX 138   97101   2-00011
Herb Romey, prin.   835-2181
MS, PO BOX 138   97101   2-00100
Alan Riddell, prin.   835-0518

Perrydale SD 21   2-11111
7445 PERRYDALE RD   97101   835-3184
Tim Adsit, supt.
Perrydale HS   1-00011
7445 PERRYDALE RD   97101   835-3184
Tim Adsit, prin.

Arlington, AC 503, PC 2, Gilliam
Arlington SD 3, PO BOX 10   97812   2-11111
Laurence Jones, supt.   454-2632
HS, PO BOX 10   97812   1-00011
Laurence Jones, prin.   454-2632

Ashland, AC 503, PC 7, Jackson
Ashland SD 5   5-11111
885 SISKIYOU BLVD   97520   482-2811
John Daggett, supt.
HS, 201 S MOUNTAIN AVE   97520   4-00011
Mary Cornish, prin.   482-8771
MS, 100 WALKER AVE   97520   3-00100
Dale Rooklyn, prin.   482-1611

Southern Oregon State College   6-UC
1250 SISKIYOU BLVD   97520   552-6411

Astoria, AC 503, PC 7, Clatsop
Astoria SD 1, 3196 MARINE DR   97103   4-11111
Len Carpenter, supt.   325-6441
HS, 1001 W MARINE DR   97103   3-00011
Bill Parrish, prin.   325-3911
MS, 1100 KLASKANINE AVE   97103   3-01100
John Jenson, prin.   325-4331

Columbia SD 5J
Supt. — See Westport
Knappa HS, RR 6 BOX 226   97103   2-00011
Bernie Reinbold, prin.   458-6166

Clatsop Community College   6-CC
1653 JEROME AVE   97103   325-0910

Athena, AC 503, PC 3, Umatilla
Athena-Weston SD 29J   3-11111
PO BOX 240   97813   566-3551
Lynn Harris, supt.
Weston-McEwen HS   2-00011
PO BOX 707   97813   566-3555
Wayne Kostur, prin.
Other Schools – See Weston

Aurora, AC 503, PC 3, Marion
North Marion SD 15   4-11111
20256 GRIM RD NE   97002   678-5835
Gary Holmberg, supt.
North Marion HS   2-00011
20167 GRIM RD NE   97002   982-9887
Roger DeVille, prin.
North Marion MS   2-01100
20246 GRIM RD NE   97002   678-5835
Marvin Binegar, prin.

Baker City, AC 503, PC 6, Baker
Baker SD 5J, 2090 4TH ST   97814   4-11111
Arnold Coe, supt.   523-5814
Baker HS, 2500 E ST   97814   3-00011
Jerry Peacock, prin.   523-6336
Baker MS, 2025 4TH ST   97814   2-00100
Frank Bishop, prin.   523-6301

Bandon, AC 503, PC 4, Coos
Bandon SD 54, 455 9TH ST SW   97411   3-11111
Bob Sisk, supt.   347-4411
HS, 550 9TH ST SW   97411   2-00011
Rick Howell, prin.   347-4413
Harbor Lights MS, 390 9TH ST SW   97411   2-01100
Gerald Prickett, prin.   347-4415

Banks, AC 503, PC 3, Washington
Banks SD 13, 450 S MAIN ST   97106   3-11111
Will Duke, supt.   324-8591
HS, 450 S MAIN ST   97106   2-00011
Gene Harp, prin.   324-2281
JHS, 450 S MAIN ST   97106   2-00100
Ted Faro, prin.   324-3111

Beaverton, AC 503, PC 8, Washington
Beaverton SD 48J, PO BOX 200   97075   8-11111
Yvonne Katz, supt.   591-8000
Aloha SHS, PO BOX 200   97075   4-00001
Sue Tarrant, prin.   591-8000
SHS, PO BOX 200   97075   4-00001
Bruce Weitzel, prin.   591-8000
Five Oaks IS, PO BOX 200   97075   3-00110
Mark Carlton, prin.   591-8000

Highland Park IS, PO BOX 200   97075   4-00110
Pat Everett, prin.   591-8000
Meadow Park IS, PO BOX 200   97075   3-00110
Fred Sutherland, prin.   591-8000
Mountain View IS   4-00110
PO BOX 200   97075   591-8000
Mike Smith, prin.
Whitford IS, PO BOX 200   97075   3-00110
Toni Painter, prin.   591-8000
Other Schools – See Portland

Oregon Graduate Institute/Science & Tech   2-UC
19600 NW VON NEUMANN DR   97006   690-1020
Paramedic Training Institute   1-CS
PO BOX 1878   97075   226-1455
Valley Catholic HS   2-00111
4275 SW 148TH AVE   97007   644-3745
Charles Lee, prin.

Bend, AC 503, PC 7, Deschutes
Bend Administrative SD 1   7-11111
520 NW WALL ST   97701   383-6000
Scott Mutchie, supt.
HS, 230 NE 6TH ST   97701   4-00011
Peter Miller, prin.   383-6290
Mt. View HS, 2755 NE 27TH   97701   4-00011
Ed Tillinghast, prin.   383-6360
Cascade JHS   4-00100
19619 SW MOUNTAINEER WAY   97702
Tom Achterman, prin.   383-6230
High Desert MS, 61111 27TH ST   97702   3-00100
Vic Marchek, prin.   383-6480
Pilot Butte JHS   4-00100
1500 NE PENN AVE   97701 – (—), prin.   383-6260
Other Schools – See La Pine

Central Oregon Academy in Bend   2-11111
22580 MARTEE LN   97701
Central Oregon Christian HS   2-00011
PO BOX 144   97709
Central Oregon Community College   5-CC
2600 NW COLLEGE WAY   97701   383-7500

Blachly, AC 503, PC 1, Lane
Blachly SD 90   2-11111
20264 BLACHLY GRANGE RD   97412   925-3262
John Sackman, supt.
Triangle Lake JSHS   1-00111
20264 BLACHLY GRANGE RD   97412   925-3262
John Sackman, prin.

Boardman, AC 503, PC 4, Morrow
Morrow SD 1
Supt. — See Lexington
Riverside HS, PO BOX 140   97818   2-00011
Dave Youngbluth, prin.   481-2525

Bonanza, AC 503, PC 2, Klamath
Klamath County SD
Supt. — See Klamath Falls
JSHS, PO BOX 128   97623   3-00111
Paul Poetsch, prin.   545-6581

Klamath-Lake Co. Youth Ranch HS   2-00011
RR 1 BOX 751   97623   545-6742

Boring, AC 503, PC 3, Clackamas
Boring SD 44   2-11100
12240 SE SCHOOL AVE   97009   663-5909
William Jordan, supt.

MS, 27801 SE DEE ST 97009   2-01100
Robert Backstrom, prin.   663-3531

Damascus UNSD 26   3-11100
14151 SE 242ND AVE 97009   658-4416
Joseph Bucher, supt.
Damascus MS   2-01100
14151 SE 242ND AVE 97009   658-3171
Caren Reese, prin.

Damascus Christian HS   2-00011
14251 SE RUST WAY 97009

Brookings, AC 503, PC 5, Curry
Brookings-Harbor SD 17   4-11111
564 FERN ST 97415   469-7443
Bob Strickland, supt.
Brookings-Harbor HS   3-00011
564 FERN ST 97415   469-2108
Donald Bryant, prin.
Azalea MS, 564 FERN ST 97415   3-01100
Chuck Weller, prin.   469-7427

Burns, AC 503, PC 5, Harney
Harney County SD 3   4-11111
458 E WASHINGTON ST 97720   573-6811
Richard Adair, supt.
Burns Union HS   2-00011
1100 OREGON AVE 97720   573-2044
Tom Puskarich, prin.
Lincoln JHS, 550 N COURT AVE 97720   2-00100
Roy Reed, prin.   573-2058

Butte Falls, AC 503, PC 2, Jackson
Butte Falls SD 91, PO BOX 197 97522   2-11111
Harvey Boyle, supt.   865-3563
HS, PO BOX 167 97522   1-00011
Fred Lucas, prin.   865-3563

Camas Valley, AC 503, PC 2, Douglas
Camas Valley SD 21J   2-11111
PO BOX 57 97416   445-2131
Robert Kloss, supt.
JSHS, PO BOX 57 97416   1-00111
Robert Kloss, prin.   445-2131

Canby, AC 503, PC 6, Clackamas
Canby SD 86, 117 NE 3RD AVE 97013   4-11100
Boyd Applegarth, supt.   266-5871
Ackerman JHS, 350 SE 13TH AVE 97013   3-00100
Michael Zagyva, prin.   266-2751
Canby UNHSD 1   4-00011
811 SW 5TH AVE 97013   266-7861
Stephen Miller, supt.
Canby Union HS   4-00011
721 SW 4TH AVE 97013   266-5811
James Gadberry, prin.

Canyonville, AC 503, PC 4, Douglas

Canyonville Bible Academy   2-00011
PO BOX 1100 97417

Cascade Locks, AC 503, PC 3, Hood River
Hood River County SD
Supt. — See Hood River
HS, PO BOX 279 97014   1-00100
Lyle Harpe, prin.   374-8467

Cave Junction, AC 503, PC 4, Josephine
Josephine County Unit SD
Supt. — See Murphy
Illinois Valley HS   2-00011
RIVER ST & LAUREL RD 97523   592-2116
Linda Hoback, prin.
Byrne MS, 101 S JUNCTION AVE 97523   2-00100
Jann Taylor, prin.   592-2163

Community Christian Academy   2-00011
207 E LISTER ST 97523

Central Point, AC 503, PC 6, Jackson
Central Point SD 6, 451 N 2ND ST 97502   5-11111
Mike McClain, supt.   664-6611
Crater HS   4-00011
4410 ROGUE VALLEY HWY 97502   664-6611
David Gardner, prin.
Scenic JHS, 1955 SCENIC AVE 97502   3-00100
Harvey Tonn, prin.   664-6611
Other Schools – See Gold Hill

Central Assembly Christian S   2-11111
310 N 10TH ST 97502

Chiloquin, AC 503, PC 3, Klamath
Klamath County SD
Supt. — See Klamath Falls
JSHS, PO BOX 397 97624   2-00111
William McCadden, prin.   783-2321

Clackamas, AC 503, PC 5, Clackamas
North Clackamas SD 12
Supt. — See Milwaukie
Sunrise JHS, 14331 SE 132ND AVE 97015   3-00100
Rose Perkin, prin.   698-2040

Laurelwood Adventist Academy   2-00011
13400 SE 97TH AVE 97015

Clatskanie, AC 503, PC 4, Columbia
Columbia SD 5J
Supt. — See Westport

HS, PO BOX 68 97016   2-00011
Earl Fisher, prin.   728-2146
MS, PO BOX 188 97016   2-00100
W. Reinhart, prin.   728-2179

Cloverdale, AC 503, PC 2, Tillamook
Cloverdale SD 22   2-11100
36925 HIGHWAY 101 S 97112   392-3435
Gary Anderson, supt.
Cloverdale MS   1-00100
36925 HIGHWAY 101 S 97112   392-3435
Gary Anderson, prin.

Nestucca UNHSD 3   2-00011
PO BOX 38 97112   392-3194
Walter Wilson, supt.
Nestucca HS, PO BOX 38 97112   2-00100
Walter Wilson, prin.   392-3194

Colton, AC 503, PC 2, Clackamas
Colton SD 53, 30138 S WALL ST 97017   3-11100
Gerald Rust, supt.   824-3535
HS, 30205 S WALL ST 97017   2-00011
Gary Zosel, prin.   824-2311
MS, 30205 S WALL ST 97017   2-00100
Mark Rediske, prin.   824-2319

Condon, AC 503, PC 3, Gilliam
Condon SD 25J, PO BOX 615 97823   2-11111
June Ringheimer, supt.   384-2581
HS, PO BOX 575 97823   1-00011
Rita Rattray, prin.   384-2441

Coos Bay, AC 503, PC 7, Coos
Coos Bay SD 9, PO BOX 509 97420   5-11111
Giles Parker, supt.   267-3104
Marshfield HS, PO BOX 509 97420   4-00011
Arnold Roblan, prin.   267-3104
Sunset MS, PO BOX 509 97420   3-00100
Charles Sharps, prin.   267-3104
Other Schools – See Eastside

Southwestern Oregon Community College   5-CC
1988 NEWMARK AVE 97420   888-7423

Coquille, AC 503, PC 5, Coos
Coquille SD 8, 140 E 10TH ST 97423   4-11111
Jim Harris, supt.   396-2181
HS, 499 W CENTRAL ST 97423   2-00011
Tim Pflaum, prin.   396-2163
Coquille Valley MS   2-00100
1115 N BAXTER ST 97423   396-2914
Carl Wilson, prin.

Corbett, AC 503, PC 2, Multnomah
Corbett SD 39   3-11111
35800 E CROWN POINT HWY 97019   695-3612
Lawrence McClellan, supt.
HS, 35800 E CROWN POINT HWY 97019   2-00011
Jim Kuhlmann, prin.   695-3626
MS, 35800 E CROWN POINT HWY 97019   2-00100
Jim Kuhlmann, prin.   695-3626

Corvallis, AC 503, PC 8, Benton
Corvallis SD 509J   6-11111
1555 SW 35TH ST 97333   757-5811
Bruce Harter, supt.
HS, 836 NW 11TH ST 97330   4-00011
Steve Kunke, prin.   757-5871
Crescent Valley HS   4-00011
4444 NW HIGHLAND DR 97330   757-5801
Richard Behn, prin.
Cheldelin MS   3-00100
987 NE CONIFER BLVD 97330   757-5971
William Starnes, prin.
Highland View MS   3-00100
1920 NW HIGHLAND DR 97330   757-5975
Sharon Thornagle, prin.
Western View MS   3-00100
1435 SW 35TH ST 97333   757-5961
Margo Garton, prin.

Oregon State University 97333   7-UC
   737-4411

Santiam Christian S   2-11111
237 NE ARNOLD AVE 97330   745-5524

Cottage Grove, AC 503, PC 6, Lane
South Lane SD 45J3   5-11111
PO BOX 218 97424   942-3381
Steve Swisher, supt.
HS, 1000 TAYLOR AVE 97424   3-00011
Ed Otton, prin.   942-3391
Lincoln JHS, 1565 S 4TH ST 97424   3-00100
Judd VanGorder, prin.   942-3316

Cove, AC 503, PC 3, Union
Cove SD 15, PO BOX 68 97824   2-11111
Gene Mills, supt.   568-4424
JSHS, PO BOX 68 97824   2-00111
Gene Mills, prin.   568-4424

Crane, AC 503, PC 2, Harney
Harney County UNHSD 1J   2-00011
PO BOX 828 97732   493-2642
Robert Sari, supt.
Crane Union HS, PO BOX 828 97732   2-00011
Robert Sari, prin.   493-2642

Creswell, AC 503, PC 4, Lane
Creswell SD 40, 182 S 2ND ST 97426   4-11111
Duane Lyons, supt.   895-2108

HS, 33390 NIEBLOCK LN 97426   2-00011
Mike Hood, prin.   895-2137
MS, 655 W OREGON AVE 97426   2-00100
Doug Orton, prin.   895-2135

Culver, AC 503, PC 3, Jefferson
Culver SD 4, PO BOX 228 97734   2-11111
Brian Say, supt.   546-2541
HS, PO BOX 228 97734   1-00011
Brian Say, prin.   546-2251

Dallas, AC 503, PC 6, Polk
Dallas SD 2, 111 SW ASH ST 97338   5-11111
David Voves, supt.   623-5594
HS, 901 SE ASH ST 97338   3-00011
Dennis Newton, prin.   623-8336
LaCreole JHS   3-00100
701 SE LACREOLE DR 97338   623-6662
Don Wildfang, prin.

Days Creek, AC 503, PC 2, Douglas
Days Creek SD 15, PO BOX 10 97429   2-11111
Al Wells, supt.   825-3296
HS, PO BOX 10 97429   1-00011
Al Wells, prin.   825-3296

Milo Adventist Academy   2-00011
PO BOX 278 97429   825-3291
Edward Starkebaum, prin.

Dayton, AC 503, PC 4, Yamhill
Dayton SD 8, 526 FERRY ST 97114   3-11111
Steve Johnson, supt.   864-2215
HS, 801 FERRY ST 97114   2-00011
Joanne Flint, prin.   864-2273
JHS, 801 FERRY ST 97114   2-00100
Roger Lorenzen, prin.   864-2246

Dayville, AC 503, PC 2, Grant
Dayville SD 16J, PO BOX C 97825   1-11111
Maurice Thorne, supt.   987-2412
JSHS, PO BOX C 97825   1-00111
Maurice Thorne, prin.   987-2412

Detroit, AC 503, PC 2, Marion
Detroit SD 123J, PO BOX 500 97342   2-11111
(—), supt.   854-3363
JSHS 97342   1-00111
(—), prin.   854-3363

Dillard, AC 503, PC 2, Douglas
Winston-Dillard SD 116   4-11111
PO BOX 288 97432   679-3121
Jim Burton, supt.
Douglas HS, PO BOX 288 97432   3-00011
Donald Fisher, prin.   679-3121
Other Schools – See Winston

Drain, AC 503, PC 4, Douglas
North Douglas SD 22   3-11111
PO BOX 428 97435   836-2223
Otis Falls, supt.
North Douglas JSHS   2-00111
PO BOX 488 97435   836-2222
Art Johns, prin.

Dufur, AC 503, PC 3, Wasco
Dufur SD 29, PO BOX 98 97021   2-11111
Gary Delvin, supt.   467-2509
HS, PO BOX 98 97021   1-00011
Jeff Morris, prin.   467-2509

Eagle Creek, AC 503, PC 2, Clackamas

Eagle Creek Christian Academy   2-00011
PO BOX 429 97022

Eagle Point, AC 503, PC 5, Jackson
Eagle Point SD 9, PO BOX 548 97524   5-11111
Ted Adams, supt.   830-1200
HS, PO BOX 198 97524   4-00011
Richard Cloud, prin.   830-1300
JHS, PO BOX 218 97524   3-00100
Dennis Quiring, prin.   830-1250

Eastside, AC 503, PC see Coos Bay
Coos Bay SD 9
Supt. — See Coos Bay
Millicoma MS, 2ND AVE E 97420   3-00100
Gary Gehlert, prin.   267-3104

Echo, AC 503, PC 2, Umatilla
Echo SD 5, 600 GEROME 97826   2-11111
Earl Miller, supt.   376-8436
JSHS, 600 GEROME 97826   1-00111
Dave Pomeroy, prin.   376-8436

Eddyville, AC 503, PC 2, Lincoln
Lincoln County SD
Supt. — See Newport
JSHS, PO BOX 43 97343   2-00111
Robert Folkers, prin.   875-2942

Elgin, AC 503, PC 4, Union
Elgin SD 23, PO BOX 68 97827   3-11111
Ed Schumacher, supt.   437-1211
HS, PO BOX 68 97827   2-00011
Monty Nash, prin.   437-2021
JHS, PO BOX 638 97827   1-00100
Richard Mack, prin.   437-2321

Elkton, AC 503, PC 2, Douglas
Elkton SD 34, PO BOX 390 97436   2-11111
Charles Farrell, supt.   584-2228

HS, PO BOX 390 97436   1-00011
Charles Farrell, prin.   584-2228

Elmira, AC 503, PC 3, Lane
Fern Ridge SD 28J   4-11111
   88834 TERRITORIAL RD 97437   935-2253
   Patrick Burke, supt.
   HS, 24936 FIR GROVE LN 97437   3-00011
   Darrell Seely, prin.   935-8200
   Fern Ridge MS   2-00100
   88831 TERRITORIAL RD 97437   935-8230
   Greg Tippett, prin.

Fern Ridge Christian Academy   2-00011
   24918 WARTHEN RD 97437

Enterprise, AC 503, PC 4, Wallowa
Enterprise SD 21, PO BOX 520 97828   3-11111
   Larry Christman, supt.   426-3193
   HS, PO BOX 520 97828   2-00011
   Ron Brown, prin.   426-3193

Estacada, AC 503, PC 4, Clackamas
Estacada SD 108, PO BOX 519 97023   4-11111
   Scott Clark, supt.   630-6871
   HS, PO BOX 519 97023   3-00011
   Steve Woods, prin.   630-8515
   JHS, PO BOX 519 97023   2-00100
   Charles Juenemann, prin.   630-8516

Eugene, AC 503, PC 9, Lane
Bethel SD 52, 4640 BARGER DR 97402   5-11111
   Kent Hunsaker, supt.   689-3280
   Willamette HS   4-00011
   1801 ECHO HOLLOW RD 97402   689-0731
   Jim Jamieson, prin.
   Cascade MS   2-00100
   1525 ECHO HOLLOW RD 97402   689-0641
   Steve Waddell, prin.
   Shasta MS, 4656 BARGER DR 97402   3-00100
   Randy Harvey, prin.   688-9611

Crow-Applegate-Lorane SD 66   2-11111
   85955 TERRITORIAL RD 97402   935-2100
   Daniel Barker, supt.
   Crow HS, 25863 CROW RD 97402   2-00011
   Ed Davidson, prin.   935-2227
   Crolane MS   2-00100
   85955 TERRITORIAL RD 97402   935-2896
   Claude Offenbacher, prin.

Eugene SD 4J, 200 N MONROE ST 97402   7-11111
   Margaret Nichols, supt.   687-3123
   Churchill HS   4-00011
   1850 BAILEY HILL RD 97405   687-3421
   Elton Sorensen, prin.
   North Eugene HS, 200 SILVER LN 97404   4-00011
   Robert Anderson, prin.   687-3261
   Sheldon HS   4-00011
   2455 WILLAKENZIE RD 97401   687-3381
   Jim Ford, prin.
   South Eugene HS   4-00011
   400 E 19TH AVE 97401   687-3201
   Lynne George, prin.
   Jefferson MS, 1650 W 22ND AVE 97405   2-00100
   Bob Bolden, prin.   687-3221
   Kelly MS, 850 HOWARD AVE 97404   2-00100
   Jane Harrison, prin.   687-3224
   Kennedy MS   3-00100
   2200 BAILEY HILL RD 97405   687-3241
   Doug Smith, prin.
   Madison MS, 875 WILKES DR 97404   3-00100
   Cecil Kribs, prin.   687-3278
   Monroe MS, 2800 BAILEY LN 97401   3-00100
   Teresa Smith, prin.   687-3254
   Roosevelt MS, 680 E 24TH AVE 97405   3-00100
   Dan Barnum, prin.   687-3227
   Spencer Butte MS   2-00100
   500 E 43RD AVE 97405   687-3237
   Evelyn Matthews, prin.
   Young MS, 2555 GILHAM RD 97401   3-00100
   Tom Tomlinson, prin.   687-3234

Diesel Truck Driver Training School   2-CS
   90801 HIGHWAY 99 N 97402   800-888-7075
Eugene Bible College   2-UC
   2155 BAILEY HILL RD 97405   485-1780
Lane Community College   6-CC
   4000 E 30TH AVE 97405   726-2207
Marist HS, 1900 KINGSLEY RD 97401   2-00011
   Fr. Lopez, prin.   686-2234
Northwest Christian College   2-UC
   828 E 11TH AVE 97401   800-888-1641
Santa Clara Christian HS   2-00011
   815 IRVING RD 97404
Trend College   2-CS
   1050 GREEN ACRES RD 97401   342-5377
University of Oregon   7-UC
   1 UNIVERSITY OF OREGON 97403   346-3216

Falls City, AC 503, PC 3, Polk
Falls City SD 57   2-11111
   81 E NORTH MAIN ST 97344   787-3521
   Dennis Hickey, supt.
   JSHS, 81 E NORTH MAIN ST 97344   1-00111
   Dennis Hickey, prin.   787-3521

Finn Rock, AC 503, PC 1, Lane
McKenzie SD 68   2-11111
   51187 BLUE RIVER DR 97488   822-3338
   Edward Curtis, supt.

McKenzie JSHS   2-00111
   51187 BLUE RIVER DR 97488   822-3313
   Russ Conklin, prin.

Florence, AC 503, PC 6, Lane
Siuslaw SD 97J, 750 QUINCE ST 97439   4-11111
   Glenn Butler, supt.   997-2651
   Siuslaw HS, 750 QUINCE ST 97439   2-00111
   John Weeks, prin.   997-3448
   Siuslaw MS, 750 QUINCE ST 97439   2-00100
   Duane Wright, prin.   997-8241

Siuslaw Christian HS   2-00011
   PO BOX 2020 97439

Forest Grove, AC 503, PC 7, Washington
Forest Grove SD 15   5-11111
   1343 PACIFIC AVE 97116   357-6171
   Irv Nikholai, supt.
   HS, 1401 NICHOLS LN 97116   4-00011
   Bob Schlegel, prin.   359-2432
   Armstrong MS   2-00100
   1777 MOUNTAIN VIEW LN 97116   359-2465
   Mike Totman, prin.
   McCall MS, 1341 PACIFIC AVE 97116   3-00100
   Robert Thomason, prin.   359-2506

Pacific University   4-UC
   2043 COLLEGE WAY 97116   800-635-0561

Fossil, AC 503, PC 2, Wheeler
Fossil SD 21J, PO BOX 206 97830   2-11111
   Robert Smith, supt.   763-4384
   Wheeler HS, PO BOX 266 97830   1-00011
   Robert Smith, prin.   763-4146

Gaston, AC 503, PC 3, Washington
Gaston SD 511J, PO BOX 68 97119   3-11111
   Fred Loomis, supt.   985-7112
   HS, PO BOX 68 97119   2-00011
   Fred Loomis, prin.   985-7516
   JHS, PO BOX 68 97119   1-00100
   Fred Loomis, prin.   985-7516

Gervais, AC 503, PC 3, Marion
Gervais SD 1, PO BOX 100 97026   3-11111
   David Nuss, supt.   792-3801
   HS, PO BOX 195 97026   2-00011
   Tony Ramos, prin.   792-3656

Gilchrist, AC 503, PC 3, Klamath
Klamath County SD
   Supt. — See Klamath Falls
   JSHS, PO BOX 668 97737   3-00111
   Duane Barstad, prin.   433-2295

Gladstone, AC 503, PC 7, Clackamas
Gladstone SD 115   4-11111
   17789 WEBSTER RD 97027   655-2777
   Mike Vermillion, supt.
   HS, 18800 PORTLAND AVE 97027   3-00011
   Daniel Zenor, prin.   655-2544
   Kraxberger MS   3-01100
   17789 WEBSTER RD 97027   655-3636
   Richard Thompson, prin.

Serendipity Center   2-11111
   PO BOX 156 97027   761-7139
   Susan Schriver, prin.

Glendale, AC 503, PC 3, Douglas
Glendale SD 77, PO BOX E 97442   3-11111
   Gerald Stinnett, supt.   832-2133
   JSHS, PO BOX E 97442   2-00111
   Richard Johnstone, prin.   832-2171
   Glendale Azalea Skills Center   Vo Tech
   PO BOX E 97442 – Shaun Brink, prin.   832-2133

Glide, AC 503, PC 3, Douglas
Glide SD 12, 301 GLIDE LOOP DR 97443   4-11111
   P. Romney, supt.   496-3521
   HS, 18990 N UMPQUA HWY 97443   2-00011
   Darrell Koeppen, prin.   496-3554
   JHS, 301 GLIDE LOOP DR 97443   2-00100
   Dean Pindell, prin.   496-3516

Gold Beach, AC 503, PC 4, Curry
Gold Beach UNHSD 1   2-00011
   757 S ELLENSBURG AVE 97444   247-6647
   Jay Johnson, supt.
Gold Beach Union HS   2-00011
   757 S ELLENSBURG AVE 97444   247-6647
   Bill Stuart, prin.

Gold Hill, AC 503, PC 3, Jackson
Central Point SD 6
   Supt. — See Central Point
   Hanby JHS, 806 6TH AVE 97525   2-00100
   Mary Barker, prin.   664-6611

Grants Pass, AC 503, PC 7, Josephine
Grants Pass SD 7, 610 NE A ST 97526   5-11111
   Dale Smith, supt.   474-5700
   HS, 522 NE OLIVE ST 97526   4-00011
   Gregg Ross, prin.   474-5710
   North MS   3-00100
   1725 NW HIGHLAND AVE 97526   474-5740
   Jack Woodhead, prin.
   South MS, 350 W HARBECK RD 97527   2-00100
   Bill Bigelow, prin.   474-5750

Josephine County Unit SD
   Supt. — See Murphy
   Hidden Valley HS   3-00011
   651 MURPHY CREEK RD 97527   862-2124
   Janet Figoni, prin.
   North Valley HS   3-00011
   6741 MONUMENT DR 97526   479-3388
   James Peters, prin.
   Fleming MS   3-00100
   6001 MONUMENT DR 97526   476-8284
   John Codington, prin.
   Lincoln Savage MS   3-00100
   8551 NEW HOPE RD 97527   862-2171
   Craig Binkley, prin.

Downtown Learning HS   2-00011
   290 NE C ST 97526
New Hope Christian S   2-11111
   5961 NEW HOPE RD 97527   476-4588
Pine Valley HS   2-01111
   4523 AVERILL DR 97526
Rogue Community College   6-CC
   3345 REDWOOD HWY 97527   479-5541

Gresham, AC 503, PC 8, Multnomah
Barlow-Gresham UNHSD U2-20J   5-00011
   1331 NW EASTMAN PKY 97030   669-2450
   Zeno Katterle, supt.
   Barlow HS, 5105 SE 302ND AVE 97080   4-00011
   Linda Jessell, prin.   663-4112
   HS, 1200 N MAIN AVE 97030   4-00011
   Rich Correa, prin.   666-8033

Centennial SD 28J
   Supt. — See Portland
   Centennial HS   4-00011
   3505 SE 182ND AVE 97030   661-7612
   Clark Brody, prin.

Gresham Grade SD 4   6-11100
   1331 NW EASTMAN PKY 97030   669-2450
   Zeno Katterle, supt.
   Clear Creek MS   3-00100
   219 NE 219TH AVE 97030   666-2199
   Wally Scherler, prin.
   McCarty MS, 1400 SE 5TH ST 97080   3-00100
   Carol Beatty, prin.   665-0148
   Russell MS   4-00100
   3625 E POWELL VALLEY RD 97080   667-6900
   Jodie Hajduk, prin.

Orient SD 6J   3-11100
   29805 SE ORIENT DR 97080   663-3323
   Thomas Greene, supt.
   West Orient MS   2-01100
   29805 SE ORIENT DR 97080   663-3323
   Mike Plass, prin.

Mt. Hood Community College   6-CC
   26000 SE STARK ST 97030   667-7391
New Country S   2-11111
   2229 E BURNSIDE ST #70 97030

Halfway, AC 503, PC 2, Baker
Pine Eagle SD 61, PO BOX 677 97834   2-11111
   Steve Peterson, supt.   742-2811
   Pine Eagle HS, PO BOX 737 97834   2-00011
   Rus Steinebach, prin.   742-2421

Halsey, AC 503, PC 3, Linn
Central Linn SD 552   3-11111
   32433 HIGHWAY 228 97348   369-2720
   John Dallum, supt.
   Central Linn HS   2-00011
   32433 HIGHWAY 228 97348   369-2811
   (—), prin.
   Central Linn MS   2-00100
   32433 HIGHWAY 228 97348   369-2811
   Maria Delapoer, prin.

Lake Creek Mennonite HS   2-00011
   26585 PEORIA RD 97348

Harper, AC 503, PC 2, Malheur
Harper SD 66, PO BOX 800 97906   1-11111
   Jim Payne, supt.   358-2473
   HS, PO BOX 800 97906   1-00011
   Jim Payne, prin.   358-2473

Harrisburg, AC 503, PC 4, Linn
Harrisburg UNHSD 5J   2-00011
   400 S 9TH ST 97446   995-6680
   James Nerdin, supt.
   HS, 400 S 9TH ST 97446   2-00011
   James Nerdin, prin.   995-6626

Helix, AC 503, PC 2, Umatilla
Helix SD 1, PO BOX 398 97835   2-11111
   Don Parkin, supt.   457-2175
   Griswold HS, PO BOX 398 97835   1-00011
   Don Parkin, prin.   457-2175

Heppner, AC 503, PC 4, Morrow
Morrow SD 1
   Supt. — See Lexington
   HS, PO BOX 67 97836   2-00011
   Steve Dickenson, prin.   676-9138

Hermiston, AC 503, PC 7, Umatilla
Hermiston SD 8, 341 NE 3RD ST 97838   5-11111
   Jer Pratton, supt.   567-5574
   HS, 600 SW 1ST PL 97838   4-00011
   Diana Cutsforth, prin.   567-8311

Larive JHS, 199 E RIDGEWAY AVE 97838 3-00100
Shannon Gorham, prin. 567-6427

Interfaith Christian Center HS 2-00011
PO BOX 779 97838

Hillsboro, AC 503, PC 8, Washington
Hillsboro UNHSD 3J 6-00111
759 SE WASHINGTON ST 97123 640-4604
Nikki Squire, supt.
Glencoe SHS 4-00001
2700 NW GLENCOE RD 97124 640-8971
Joe Rodriguez, prin.
SHS, 3285 SE ROOD BRIDGE RD 97123 4-00001
Phil Barnekoff, prin. 648-8561
Brown JHS, 1505 SW 219TH AVE 97123 3-00110
Don Kilgras, prin. 642-5656
Evergreen JHS 3-00110
550 NE EVERGREEN ST 97124 640-8900
Mary Barnekoff, prin.
Poynter JHS, 1535 NE GRANT ST 97124 3-00110
Ken Wellman, prin. 640-3691
Thomas JHS, 645 NE LINCOLN ST 97124 3-00110
Carlos Perez, prin. 640-8939

Airman Proficiency Center 2-CS
3565 NE CORNELL RD 97124 648-2831

Hood River, AC 503, PC 5, Hood River
Hood River County SD 5-11111
PO BOX 920 97031 386-2511
Charles Bugge, supt.
Hood River Valley HS 3-00011
1220 INDIAN CREEK RD 97031 386-4500
Jan Donnelly, prin.
MS, 1602 MAY ST 97031 2-00100
Robert Dias, prin. 386-2114
Wy'East MS, 3000 WYEAST RD 97031 2-00100
Dennis Price, prin. 354-1548
Other Schools – See Cascade Locks

Baptist Christian HS 2-00011
1889 BELMONT DR 97031
Christian Mission Alliance Academy 2-00011
2650 MONTELLO AVE 97031
Concordia Lutheran HS 2-00011
1107 PINE ST 97031
Hood River Bible Fellowshp HS 2-00011
508 9TH ST 97031

Huntington, AC 503, PC 3, Baker
Huntington SD 16J, PO BOX 69 97907 2-11111
Peter Bolz, supt. 869-2204
JSHS, PO BOX 69 97907 1-00111
Peter Bolz, prin. 869-2204

Imbler, AC 503, PC 2, Union
Imbler SD 11, PO BOX 164 97841 2-11111
Newell Cleaver, supt. 534-5331
JSHS, PO BOX 164 97841 2-00111
Gus Forster, prin. 534-5331

Independence, AC 503, PC 5, Polk
Central SD 13J 5-11111
1610 MONMOUTH ST 97351 838-0030
John Dracon, supt.
Central HS, 1530 MONMOUTH ST 97351 3-00011
Robert Prichard, prin. 838-0480
Talmadge MS, 510 16TH ST 97351 3-00100
Jannice Link-Jobe, prin. 838-1424

Ione, AC 503, PC 2, Morrow
Morrow SD 1
Supt. — See Lexington
JSHS, PO BOX 167 97843 2-00111
Dick Allen, prin. 422-7131

Irrigon, AC 503, PC 3, Morrow
Morrow SD 1
Supt. — See Lexington
Columbia JHS, PO BOX K 97844 2-00100
Don Holes, prin. 922-5551

Jefferson, AC 503, PC 4, Marion
Jefferson SD 14J, 1328 N 2ND ST 97352 4-11111
Jim Moskal, supt. 327-3337
HS, 336 TALBOT RD SE 97352 2-00011
Robert Tower, prin. 327-1122
MS, 1334 N 2ND ST 97352 2-00100
J. Garza, prin. 327-2208

John Day, AC 503, PC 4, Grant
Grant Administrative SD 3 4-11111
PO BOX 729 97845 575-1280
Cliff Walters, supt.
Grant Union HS, PO BOX 129 97845 2-00011
C. Lino, prin. 575-1799
JHS, 116 NW BRIDGE ST 97845 2-00100
Jeff Kleck, prin. 575-1969

Jordan Valley, AC 503, PC 2, Malheur
Jordan Valley SD 3, PO BOX 99 97910 2-11111
Jack Crippen, supt. 586-2213
JSHS, PO BOX 99 97910 1-00111
Jack Crippen, prin. 586-2213

Joseph, AC 503, PC 4, Wallowa
Joseph SD 6, PO BOX W 97846 2-11111
Clark Bray, supt. 432-7311
HS, PO BOX W 97846 2-00111
Randall Sanders, prin. 432-7311
JHS, PO BOX W 97846 2-01100
Randall Sanders, prin. 432-7311

Junction City, AC 503, PC 5, Lane
Junction City SD 69 4-11111
325 MAPLE ST 97448 998-6311
Don Anderson, supt.
HS, 1135 W 6TH AVE 97448 3-00011
Keith Gillis, prin. 998-2343
Oaklea MS, 1515 ROSE ST 97448 3-01100
Tom Endersby, prin. 998-3381

Christ's Center, 530 W 7TH AVE 97448 2-11111
998-3015

Klamath Falls, AC 503, PC 7, Klamath
Klamath County SD 6-11111
10501 WASHBURN WAY 97603 883-5000
Frank Ellis, supt.
Henley HS 3-00011
8245 HIGHWAY 39 97603 883-5040
Chris Yaeger, prin.
Brixner JHS, 4272 HOMEDALE RD 97603 2-00100
Gregory Thede, prin. 883-5025
Henley JHS 2-00100
7925 HIGHWAY 39 97603 883-5050
Leonard Harrington, prin.
Other Schools – See Bonanza, Chiloquin, Gilchrist, Merrill

Klamath Falls Elementary SD 1 4-11100
475 S ALAMEDA AVE 97603 883-4700
Ray Crawford, supt.
Ponderosa JHS, 2554 MAIN ST 97601 3-00100
Kenneth Womer, prin. 883-4740

Klamath Union and Mazama HSD 2 4-00011
475 S ALAMEDA AVE 97603 883-4700
Ray Crawford, supt.
Klamath Union HS 3-00011
MONCLAIRE ST 97601 883-4710
Theodore Marr, prin.
Mazama HS, 3009 SUMMERS LN 97603 3-00011
Bob Simonson, prin. 883-4730

Oregon Institute of Technology 5-UC
3201 CAMPUS DR 97601 800-343-6653

La Grande, AC 503, PC 7, Union
La Grande SD 1 5-11111
2802 ADAMS AVE 97850 963-1902
Richard Prather, supt.
HS, 708 K AVE 97850 3-00011
Roland Bevell, prin. 963-1969
MS, 1108 4TH ST 97850 2-00100
James Thompson, prin. 963-1954

Eastern Oregon State College 5-UC
1410 L AVE 97850 962-3393
La Grande College of Business 1-CS
703 WASHINGTON AVE 97850 963-6485

Lake Oswego, AC 503, PC 8, Clackamas
Lake Oswego SD 7J 6-11111
PO BOX 70 97034 636-7691
William Korach, supt.
HS, PO BOX 310 97034 4-00011
Earl Ingle, prin. 635-0313
Lakeridge HS, PO BOX 739 97034 3-00011
Sandra Nelson, prin. 635-0319
JHS, 2500 COUNTRY CLUB RD 97034 3-00100
Faith Chapel, prin. 635-0335
Waluga JHS, 4700 JEAN RD 97035 3-00100
Rudolph Mundy, prin. 635-0343

Lakeview, AC 503, PC 5, Lake
Lake County SD 7, 1341 S 1ST ST 97630 4-11111
Howard Ottman, supt. 947-3347
HS, 906 S 3RD ST 97630 3-00011
Duane Yecha, prin. 947-2287
Daly MS, 220 S H ST 97630 2-00100
Duane Yecha, prin. 947-2257

La Pine, AC 503, PC 3, Deschutes
Bend Administrative SD 1
Supt. — See Bend
HS, PO BOX 306 97739 2-00011
Rick Barber, prin. 536-1783
MS, PO BOX 305 97739 2-00100
Dan Korber, prin. 536-5967

Lebanon, AC 503, PC 7, Linn
Crowfoot SD 89, PO BOX 127 97355 3-11100
Bob Nelson, supt. 451-1371
Seven Oak MS, 550 CASCADE DR 97355 2-00100
Gary Sehorn, prin. 451-8416

Lebanon SD 16, PO BOX 518 97355 4-11100
Ivan Launstein, supt. 451-1250
MS, PO BOX 518 97355 3-00100
Rod Leland, prin. 451-7300

Lebanon UNHSD 1 4-00011
PO BOX 518 97355 451-1250
Ivan Launstein, supt.
Lebanon Union HS 4-00011
PO BOX 518 97355 451-1250
Richard Reiling, prin.

Crowfoot Christian Academy 2-00011
699 CASCADE DR 97355
East Linn Christian Academy 2-11111
30337 FAIRVIEW RD 97355 451-1076

Lexington, AC 503, PC 2, Morrow
Morrow SD 1, PO BOX 368 97839 4-11111
Chuck Starr, supt. 989-8202
Other Schools – See Boardman, Heppner, Ione, Irrigon

Lincoln City, AC 503, PC 6, Lincoln
Lincoln County SD
Supt. — See Newport
Taft HS 3-00011
4040 SE HIGH SCHOOL DR 97367 996-2115
Tom Correia, prin.

Long Creek, AC 503, PC 2, Grant
Long Creek SD 17 2-11111
PO BOX 429 97856 421-3896
Larry Chamberlain, supt.
HS, PO BOX 546 97856 1-00011
Larry Chamberlain, prin. 421-3976

Lowell, AC 503, PC 3, Lane
Lowell SD 71, PO BOX 460 97452 2-11111
Ronald Johnson, supt. 937-2105
JSHS, PO BOX 460 97452 2-00111
Glenn Syron, prin. 937-2124

McMinnville, AC 503, PC 7, Yamhill
McMinnville SD 40 5-11111
1500 N BAKER ST 97128 434-6551
Michael Brott, supt.
HS, 615 E 15TH ST 97128 4-00011
Tom Chapman, prin. 472-6108
Duniway MS 3-00100
575 MICHELBOOK LN 97128 434-6551
Mark Hyder, prin.
Patton MS, 1175 E 19TH ST 97128 3-00100
Leon Mayer, prin. 472-6148

Linfield College 4-UC
900 S BAKER ST 97128 472-4121

Madras, AC 503, PC 5, Jefferson
Jefferson County SD 509J 5-11111
445 SE BUFF ST 97741 475-6192
Phil Riley, supt.
HS, 390 SE 10TH ST 97741 3-00011
Ken Cantrell, prin. 475-7265
JHS, 410 SW 4TH ST 97741 2-00100
Dick Junge, prin. 475-7253

Mapleton, AC 503, PC 3, Lane
Mapleton SD 32, PO BOX 388 97453 2-11111
Leroy Edwards, supt. 268-4312
HS, PO BOX 98 97453 2-00011
Merry Holland, prin. 268-4322
MS, PO BOX 98 97453 2-00100
Merry Holland, prin. 268-4322

Marcola, AC 503, PC 3, Lane
Marcola SD 79J 2-11111
38300 WENDING RD 97454 933-2817
Doss Bradford, supt.
Mohawk HS 97454 2-00011
Doss Bradford, prin. 933-2512

Marylhurst, AC 503, PC 2, Clackamas

Marylhurst College for Lifelong Learning 4-UC
PO BOX 261 97036 800-634-9982

Maupin, AC 503, PC 2, Wasco
Wasco County UNHSD 1 1-00011
PO BOX 347 97037 395-2225
Ray Hanson, supt.
Wasco County HS 1-00011
PO BOX 347 97037 395-2225
Ray Hanson, prin.

Medford, AC 503, PC 8, Jackson
Medford SD 549, 500 MONROE ST 97501 7-11111
Steve Wisely, supt. 776-8600
North Medford HS 4-00011
1900 N KEENEWAY DR 97504 776-8726
Don Lacey, prin.
South Medford HS 4-00011
815 S OAKDALE AVE 97501 776-8661
Floyd Pawlowski, prin.
Hedrick JHS, 1501 E JACKSON ST 97504 3-00100
Ron Williams, prin. 776-8778
McLoughlin JHS, 320 W 2ND ST 97501 3-00100
Cliff Gibson, prin. 776-8811

Cascade Christian HS 2-00111
2715 TABLE ROCK RD 97501 772-1519
St. Marys HS, 816 BLACK OAK DR 97504 2-00111
Barbara Callaway, prin. 773-7877
Trend College 2-CS
400 EARHART ST 97501 779-5581

Merrill, AC 503, PC 3, Klamath
Klamath County SD
Supt. — See Klamath Falls
Lost River JSHS 2-00111
2330 HIGHWAY 50 97633 798-5666
Jim Fletcher, prin.

Mill City, AC 503, PC 4, Linn
Mill City-Gates SD 129J 3-11111
PO BOX 197 97360 897-2321
John Campbell, prin.
Santiam HS, PO BOX 199 97360 2-00011
Larry Reeser, prin. 897-2311

MS, PO BOX 198 97360 — 2-01100
James Beck, prin. — 897-2368

Milton-Freewater, AC 503, PC 6, Umatilla
Ferndale SD 10, RR 3 BOX 179 97862 — 2-11100
William Keyser, supt. — 938-5412
Pleasant View MS — 1-00011
RR 2 BOX 314 97862 — 938-7086
Marilyn McBride, prin.

McLoughlin UNHSD 3 — 2-00011
138 S MAIN ST 97862 — 938-3551
Ronald Hackbarth, supt.
McLoughlin HS, 120 S MAIN ST 97862 — 2-00011
Robert Wimberly, prin. — 938-5591

Milton-Freewater Elementary SD 31 — 4-11100
PO BOX 707 97862 — 938-6614
A. Jorgenson, supt.
Central MS, 306 SW 2ND AVE 97862 — 2-00100
Bryan Traylor, prin. — 938-5504

Milwaukie, AC 503, PC 7, Clackamas
North Clackamas SD 12 — 7-11111
4444 SE LAKE RD 97222 — 653-3600
B. Schellenberg, supt.
Clackamas HS — 4-00011
13801 SE WEBSTER RD 97267 — 653-3722
Elaine Drakulich, prin.
HS, 11300 SE 23RD AVE 97222 — 4-00011
Dean Winder, prin. — 653-3750
Putnam HS, 4950 SE ROETHE RD 97267 — 4-00011
Deno Edward, prin. — 653-3800
Sabin Occupational Skills Ctr HS — Vo Tech
14211 SE JOHNSON RD 97267 — 653-3812
Ron Dexter, prin.
McLoughlin JHS — 2-00100
14450 SE JOHNSON RD 97267 — 653-3704
Brian Kleiner, prin.
JHS, 2300 SE HARRISON ST 97222 — 2-00100
Cindy Phillips, prin. — 653-3709
Rowe JHS, 3606 SE LAKE RD 97222 — 3-00100
Kelly Hood, prin. — 653-3718
Other Schools — See Clackamas

LaSalle HS, 11999 SE FULLER RD 97222 — 2-00011
Timothy Edwards, prin. — 659-4155
Oregon Denturist College — 2-CC
19001 SE MCLOUGHLIN BLVD 97267 — 655-7561
West Coast Training — 2-CS
2525 SE STUBB ST 97222 — 659-5181

Mitchell, AC 503, PC 2, Wheeler
Mitchell SD 55, PO BOX 247 97750 — 1-11111
Michael Carroll, supt. — 462-3311
HS, PO BOX 247 97750 — 1-00011
Michael Carroll, prin. — 462-3311

Molalla, AC 503, PC 5, Clackamas
Molalla River SD 35 — 4-11111
PO BOX 188 97038 — 829-2350
John Rogers, supt.
HS, 357 E FRANCIS ST 97038 — 2-00011
Pia Leonard, prin. — 829-2355
MS, PO BOX 225 97038 — 3-01100
Julie Clark, prin. — 829-6133

Country Christian HS — 2-00011
16975 S HIGHWAY 211 97038

Monmouth, AC 503, PC 6, Polk

Western Oregon State College — 5-UC
345 MONMOUTH AVE N 97361 — 838-8211

Monroe, AC 503, PC 2, Benton
Monroe UNHSD 1 — 2-00011
PO BOX 280 97456 — 847-5161
Del Coursey, supt.
Monroe Union HS — 2-00011
PO BOX 280 97456 — 847-5161
Del Coursey, prin.

Monument, AC 503, PC 2, Grant
Monument SD 8, PO BOX 127 97864 — 1-11111
Ron Barin, supt. — 934-2646
JSHS, PO BOX 127 97864 — 1-00111
Ron Baron, prin. — 934-2646

Moro, AC 503, PC 2, Sherman
Sherman UNHSD 1 — 2-00011
65912 HIGH SCHOOL LOOP 97039 — 565-3500
Rick Eggers, supt.
Sherman HS — 2-00011
65912 HIGH SCHOOL LOOP 97039 — 565-3500
Rick Eggers, prin.

Mount Angel, AC 503, PC 5, Marion
Mt. Angel SD 91, PO BOX 1129 97362 — 3-11111
Toni Hardman, supt. — 845-2345
Kennedy HS — 2-00011
890 E MARQUAM ST 97362 — 845-6128
Jay Kosik, prin.
MS, 460 E MARQUAM ST 97362 — 2-01100
Dave Kohler, prin. — 845-6137

Murphy, AC 503, PC 2, Josephine
Josephine County Unit SD — 6-11111
PO BOX 160 97533 — 862-3111
Carole Ricotta, supt.
Other Schools — See Cave Junction, Grants Pass

Myrtle Creek, AC 503, PC 5, Douglas
South Umpqua SD 19 — 4-11111
558 CHADWICK LN 97457 — 863-3115
Richard Risener, supt.
South Umpqua HS — 3-00011
501 CHADWICK LN 97457 — 863-3118
Ron Green, prin.
Coffenberry JHS, 591 RICE ST 97457 — 2-00100
Bill Burnett, prin. — 863-3104

Myrtle Point, AC 503, PC 5, Coos
Myrtle Point SD 41 — 4-11111
212 SPRUCE ST 97458 — 572-2811
Tom Roe, supt.
JSHS, 717 4TH ST 97458 — 2-00111
Scott MacCluer, prin. — 572-2811

Newberg, AC 503, PC 7, Yamhill
Newberg SD 29J, 714 E 6TH ST 97132 — 5-11111
H. Smith, supt. — 538-8361
HS, 1300 ELLIOTT RD 97132 — 4-00011
Debbie Rickey, prin. — 538-8364
Renne MS, 620 E 6TH ST 97132 — 2-00100
Paul Jellum, prin. — 538-8369
Springbrook MS, 2015 EMORY DR 97132 — 3-00100
Judy Wayland, prin. — 538-8371

Christian Life Center HS — 2-00011
502 S ST PAUL HWY 97132
George Fox College — 3-UC
414 N MERIDIAN ST 97132 — 538-8383

Newport, AC 503, PC 6, Lincoln
Lincoln County SD — 6-11111
PO BOX 1110 97365 — 265-9211
William Liebertz, supt.
HS, 322 NE EADS ST 97365 — 3-00011
Elaine Wells, prin. — 265-9281
MS, 311 NE EADS ST 97365 — 2-00100
Terry Gillies, prin. — 265-6601
Other Schools — See Eddyville, Lincoln City, Toledo, Waldport

North Bend, AC 503, PC 6, Coos
North Bend SD 13 — 5-11111
1313 AIRPORT LN 97459 — 756-2521
Marshall Herron, supt.
HS, 1600 14TH ST 97459 — 3-00011
Monita Johnson, prin. — 756-2521
JHS, 1500 16TH ST 97459 — 3-00100
Ronald Handke, prin. — 756-2521

North Powder, AC 503, PC 2, Union
North Powder SD 8J — 2-11111
PO BOX 10 97867 — 898-2244
Rich Cason, supt.
Powder Valley HS, PO BOX 10 97867 — 1-00011
Rich Cason, prin. — 898-2244

Nyssa, AC 503, PC 5, Malheur
Nyssa SD 26, 810 ADRIAN BLVD 97913 — 4-11111
Dennis Savage, supt. — 372-2275
HS, 820 ADRIAN BLVD 97913 — 2-00011
Glenn Walker, prin. — 372-2287
JHS, 804 ADRIAN BLVD 97913 — 2-00100
Ronald Manley, prin. — 372-3891

Oakland, AC 503, PC 3, Douglas
Oakland SD 1, PO BOX 390 97462 — 3-11111
Linda Burton, supt. — 459-4341
HS, PO BOX 390 97462 — 2-00011
Roger Stewart, prin. — 459-2597
Lincoln MS, PO BOX 390 97462 — 2-01100
Rod Kalmbach, prin. — 459-3407

Oakridge, AC 503, PC 5, Lane
Oakridge SD 76, 76499 ROSE ST 97463 — 3-11111
Michael Keown, supt. — 782-2813
JSHS, 47997 1ST ST 97463 — 2-00111
Gary Peterson, prin. — 782-2231

Oakridge Christian HS — 2-00011
PO BOX 928 97463

Ontario, AC 503, PC 6, Malheur
Ontario SD 8, 195 SW 3RD AVE 97914 — 5-11111
Dave Cloud, supt. — 889-5374
HS, 1115 W IDAHO AVE 97914 — 3-00011
Mike Taylor, prin. — 889-5309
JHS, 521 SW 2ND AVE 97914 — 3-00100
Eugene Bates, prin. — 889-5377

Treasure Valley Community College — 5-CC
650 COLLEGE BLVD 97914 — 889-6493

Oregon City, AC 503, PC 7, Clackamas
Oregon City SD 62 — 6-11111
PO BOX 591 97045 — 656-4283
Donald Tank, supt.
SHS, 1306 12TH ST 97045 — 4-00001
Sharon Rodgers, prin. — 657-2411
Gardiner MS, 180 ETHEL ST 97045 — 2-00100
Warren Burley, prin. — 657-2415
Ogden MS — 3-00100
14133 S DONOVAN RD 97045 — 657-2425
Dennis Paldi, prin.
JHS, 19761 S BEAVERCREEK RD 97045 — 2-00010
(—), prin. — 657-2437

Associated Education Services HS — 2-11111
20499 S MOLALLA AVE 97045

Clackamas Community College — 7-CC
19600 S MOLALLA AVE 97045 — 655-5153
North Clackamas Christian S — 2-11111
19651 S MOLALLA AVE 97045 — 655-5961

Paisley, AC 503, PC 2, Lake
Paisley SD 11, PO BOX 97 97636 — 2-11111
Dan Thomas, supt. — 943-3111
JSHS, PO BOX 97 97636 — 1-00111
Dan Thomas, prin. — 943-3111

Pendleton, AC 503, PC 7, Umatilla
Pendleton SD 16 — 5-11111
1207 SW FRAZER AVE 97801 — 276-6711
Al Meunier, supt.
SHS, 1800 NW CARDEN AVE 97801 — 3-00001
R. Krout, prin. — 276-3621
JHS, 700 SW RUNNION AVE 97801 — 3-00110
Mike Moore, prin. — 276-4560

Blue Mountain Community College — 5-CC
2411 NW CARDEN AVE 97801 — 276-1260
Pendleton Christian HS — 2-00011
4450 SW QUINNEY AVE 97801

Philomath, AC 503, PC 5, Benton
Philomath SD 17J, PO BOX 591 97370 — 4-11111
Chuck Jackson, supt. — 929-3169
HS, PO BOX 391 97370 — 2-00011
Nels Thompson, prin. — 929-3211
MS, PO BOX 271 97370 — 3-01100
Larry Sleeman, prin. — 929-3167

Nazarene Christian HS — 2-00011
132 S 15TH ST 97370

Phoenix, AC 503, PC 5, Jackson
Phoenix-Talent SD 4 — 4-11111
PO BOX 698 97535 — 535-1517
David Willard, supt.
HS, PO BOX 697 97535 — 3-00011
Jeff Schlecht, prin. — 535-1526
Other Schools — See Talent

Pilot Rock, AC 503, PC 4, Umatilla
Pilot Rock SD 2, PO BOX BB 97868 — 3-11111
Darce Driskel, supt. — 443-8291
JSHS, PO BOX BB 97868 — 2-00111
Ed Sherman, prin. — 443-2671

Pilot Rock Christian Academy 97868 — 2-00011

Pleasant Hill, AC 503, PC 2, Lane
Pleasant Hill SD 1 — 4-11111
36386 HIGHWAY 58 97455 — 746-9646
J. Howard, supt.
HS, 36386 HIGHWAY 58 97455 — 2-00011
Marv Brenneman, prin. — 747-4541
JHS, 36386 HIGHWAY 58 97455 — 2-00100
Dennis Biggerstaff, prin. — 746-8311

Portland, AC 503, PC 10, Multnomah
Beaverton SD 48J
Supt. — See Beaverton
Sunset SHS — 4-00001
13840 NW CORNELL RD 97229 — 591-8000
Mick Finn, prin.
Cedar Park IS — 3-00110
11100 SW PARKWAY ST 97225 — 591-8000
Verna Bailey, prin.
Centennial SD 28J — 6-11111
18135 SE BROOKLYN ST 97236 — 760-7990
George Benson, supt.
Centennial HS — 3-00100
17650 SE BROOKLYN ST 97236 — 251-2206
Ron Hoppes, prin.
Other Schools — See Gresham

David Douglas SD 40 — 6-11111
1500 SE 130TH AVE 97233 — 252-2900
Anthony Palermini, supt.
Douglas HS, 1001 SE 135TH AVE 97233 — 4-00011
John Harrington, prin. — 252-2900
Light MS — 3-00100
10800 SE WASHINGTON ST 97216 — 252-2900
Daryl Girod, prin.
Ott MS, 12500 SE RAMONA ST 97236 — 2-00100
Dick St Claire, prin. — 252-2900
Parkrose SD 3 — 5-11111
10636 NE PRESCOTT ST 97220 — 257-5200
Jackie Cottingim, supt.
Parkrose HS — 3-00011
11717 NE SHAVER ST 97220 — 257-5270
William McGovern, prin.
Parkrose MS — 3-00100
11800 NE SHAVER ST 97220 — 257-5260
Peter Nordbye, prin.

Portland SD 1J, PO BOX 3107 97208 — 8-11111
John Bierwirth, supt. — 249-2000
Benson Polytechnic HS — 4-00011
546 NE 12TH AVE 97232 — 280-5100
Tom Parr, prin.
Cleveland HS, 3400 SE 26TH AVE 97202 — 4-00011
Robert O'Neill, prin. — 280-5120
Franklin HS — 4-00011
5405 SE WOODWARD ST 97206 — 280-5140
Nate Jones, prin.
Grant HS, 2245 NE 36TH AVE 97212 — 4-00011
Myra Rose, prin. — 280-5160

Jefferson HS, 5210 N KERBY AVE 97217 — 4-00011
Alcena Boozer, prin. — 280-5180
Lincoln HS, 1600 SW SALMON ST 97205 — 4-00011
Velma Johnson, prin. — 280-5200
Madison HS, 2735 NE 82ND AVE 97220 — 4-00011
Luke Fiorante, prin. — 280-5220
Marshall HS, 3905 SE 91ST AVE 97266 — 4-00011
Colin Morse, prin. — 280-5240
Roosevelt HS — 4-00011
6941 N CENTRAL ST 97203 — 280-5260
George Galati, prin.
Wilson HS — 4-00011
1151 SW VERMONT ST 97219 — 280-5280
Eugene Valjean, prin.
Vocational Village HS — Vo Tech
8020 NE TILLAMOOK ST 97213 — 280-5747
Paul Erickson, prin.
Beaumont MS — 3-00100
4043 NE FREMONT ST 97212 — 280-5610
Lynne Smith, prin.
Binnsmead MS — 3-00100
2225 SE 87TH AVE 97216 — 280-5700
Don Starr, prin.
Fernwood MS, 1915 NE 33RD AVE 97212 — 3-00100
John Ubik, prin. — 280-6480
George MS, 10000 N BURR AVE 97203 — 3-00100
Jane Arkes, prin. — 280-6262
Gray MS, 5505 SW 23RD AVE 97201 — 3-00100
Joe Williams, prin. — 280-5676
Green MS — 3-00100
6031 N MONTANA AVE 97217 — 280-5660
Willie Poinsette, prin.
Gregory Heights MS — 3-00100
7334 NE SISKIYOU ST 97213 — 280-5600
John Alkire, prin.
Hosford MS, 2303 SE 28TH PL 97214 — 3-00100
Ronald Hanlon, prin. — 280-5640
Jackson MS, 10625 SW 35TH AVE 97219 — 3-00100
Delores Crawford, prin. — 280-5680
Kellogg MS, 3330 SE 69TH AVE 97206 — 3-00100
Sue Parker, prin. — 280-5707
Lane MS, 7200 SE 60TH AVE 97206 — 3-00100
Mike Harris, prin. — 280-6355
Mt. Tabor MS, 5800 SE ASH ST 97215 — 3-00100
Greg Wolleck, prin. — 280-5646
Portsmouth MS — 3-00100
5103 N WILLIS BLVD 97203 — 280-5666
Tom Pickett, prin.
Sellwood MS, 8300 SE 15TH AVE 97202 — 3-00100
Allan Luethe, prin. — 280-5656
Tubman MS, 2231 N FLINT AVE 97227 — 3-00100
Paul Coakley, prin. — 280-5630
West Sylvan MS — 3-00100
8111 SW WEST SLOPE DR 97225 — 280-5690
Peter Hamilton, prin.
Whitaker MS, 5700 NE 39TH AVE 97211 — 3-00100
Harriet Adair, prin. — 280-5620

Reynolds SD 7
Supt. — See Troutdale
Lee MS, 1121 NE 172ND AVE 97230 — 3-00100
Terry Brown, prin. — 255-5686

Apollo Coll. of Medical & Dental Careers — 2-CS
2600 SE 98TH AVE 97266 — 288-4400
Bassist College — 2-UC
2000 SW 5TH AVE 97201 — 800-547-0937
Cascade College — 2-UC
9101 E BURNSIDE ST 97216 — 800-550-7678
Catlin-Gabel S — 2-11111
8825 SW BARNES RD 97225 — 297-1894
James Scott, prin.
Central Catholic HS — 3-00011
2401 SE STARK ST 97214 — 235-3138
Fr. Murphy, prin.
CollegeAmerica — 2-CS
921 SW WSHINGTON ST STE 200 97205
— 242-9000
College of Legal Arts — 2-CS
527 SW HALL ST STE 308 97201 — 223-5100
Columbia Christian S — 2-11111
413 NE 91ST AVE 97220 — 257-1362
Commercial Training Services — 2-CS
2416 N MARINE DR 97217 — 285-7542
ConCorde Career Institute — 2-CS
1827 NE 44TH AVE 97213 — 281-4181
Concordia College — 3-UC
2811 NE HOLMAN ST 97211 — 800-321-9371
Franciscan Montessori Earth School — 2-11111
14030 NE SACRAMENTO ST 97230 — 257-7707
Good Samaritan Hospital — HSP
2255 NW NORTHRUP ST 97210
ITT Technical Institute — 2-UC
6035 NE 78TH CT 97218 — 255-6500
Jesuit HS — 3-00011
9000 SW BVRTN HILLSDALE HWY 97225
Richard Gedrose, prin. — 292-2663
Lents Education Center — 2-00111
447 NE 47TH AVE 97213 — 774-6358
Lewis & Clark College — 5-UC
0615 SW PALATINE HILL RD 97219
— 800-444-4111
Linfield College — 2-UC
2215 NW NORTHRUP ST 97210
Lutheran S, 740 SE 182ND AVE 97233 — 2-11111
Thomas Wolbrecht, prin. — 677-3199
Multnomah Biblical Seminary — 3-UC
8435 NE GLISAN ST 97220 — 255-0332
Open Meadow Learning Center — 2-00111
7602 N CRAWFORD ST 97203 — 285-0508

Oregon Episcopal S — 2-00111
6300 SW NICOL RD 97223 — 246-7771
Peter Stevens, prin.
Oregon Health Sciences University — 4-UC
3181 SW SAM JACKSON PARK RD 97201
— 494-7800
Oregon Polytechnic Institute — 2-CC
900 SE SANDY BLVD 97214 — 234-9333
Oregon School of Arts & Crafts — 2-UC
8245 SW BARNES RD 97225 — 297-5544
Pacific Northwest College of Art — 2-UC
1219 SW PARK AVE 97205 — 226-0462
Pacific NW Red Cross Blood Services — HSP
3131 N VANCOUVER AVE 97227 — 284-1234
Portland Adventist Academy — 2-00111
1500 SE 96TH AVE 97216 — 255-8372
Michael Conner, prin.
Portland Christian S — 2-00111
12456 NE BRAZEE ST 97230 — 256-3540
Michael Demkowicz, prin.
Portland Community College — 8-CC
PO BOX 19000 97280 — 800-634-7999
Portland State University — 7-UC
PO BOX 751 97207 — 800-547-8887
Reed College — 4-UC
3202 SE WOODSTOCK BLVD 97202
— 800-547-4750
St. Mary's Academy — 2-00011
1615 SW 5TH AVE 97201 — 228-8306
Patricia Thompson, prin.
St. Vincent Hospital & Medical Center — 2-HSP
9205 SW BARNES RD 97225 — 297-4411
Sylvan Learning Centers HS — 2-00011
4300 NE FREMONT ST STE 150 97213
Tree of Learning HS — 1-00011
9000 SW BVRTN HILLSDALE HWY 97225
Jocelyn Tuthill, prin. — 297-2336
Trend College — 3-CS
1950 SW 6TH AVE 97201 — 224-6410
Tucker-Maxon Oral S — 2-11111
2860 SE HOLGATE BLVD 97202 — 235-6551
University of Portland — 5-UC
5000 N WILLAMETTE BLVD 97203
— 800-227-4568
Veterans Administration Medical Center — HSP
PO BOX 1034 97207 — 220-8262
Walla Walla School of Nursing — 1-UC
10345 SE MARKET ST 97216 — 251-6115
Warner Pacific College — 2-UC
2219 SE 68TH AVE 97215 — 775-4366
West Coast Training — 2-CS
11919 N JENSEN AVE #292 97217 — 289-8661
Western Business College — 4-CS
425 SW WASHINGTON ST 97204 — 222-3225
Western Conservative Baptist Seminary — 3-UC
5511 SE HAWTHORNE BLVD 97215 — 233-8561
Western Culinary Institute — 1-CS
1316 SW 13TH AVE 97201 — 223-2245
Western Evangelical Seminary — 2-UC
12753 SW 68TH AVE 97223 — 639-0559
Western States Chiropractic College — 2-UC
2900 NE 132ND AVE 97230 — 800-641-5641
Westside Christian HS — 2-00011
9806 SW BOONES FERRY RD 97219 — 246-9536

Port Orford, AC 503, PC 4, Curry
Port Orford-Langlois SD 2J — 3-11111
PO BOX 8 97465 — 332-5241
Richard Wold, supt.
Pacific HS, PO BOX 8 97465 — 2-00011
Jon Bates, prin. — 332-3131
Blanco JHS, PO BOX 8 97465 — 2-00100
Piney Van Riper, prin. — 348-2326

Powers, AC 503, PC 3, Coos
Powers SD 31, PO BOX 479 97466 — 2-11111
Lester Fettig, supt. — 439-2291
JSHS, PO BOX 479 97466 — 1-00111
Lester Fettig, prin. — 439-2291

Prairie City, AC 503, PC 4, Grant
Prairie City SD 4, PO BOX 345 97869 — 2-11111
Bradley Raphel, supt. — 820-3314
JSHS, PO BOX 345 97869 — 2-00111
Bradley Raphel, prin. — 820-3314

Prineville, AC 503, PC 6, Crook
Crook County Unit SD — 5-11111
1390 SE 2ND ST 97754 — 447-5664
Bruce Anderson, supt.
Crook County HS — 3-00011
100 N KNOWLEDGE ST 97754 — 447-5661
Richard Darst, prin.
Crook County MS — 3-00100
1400 SE 2ND ST 97754 – (—), prin. — 447-6283

Prospect, AC 503, PC 4, Jackson
Prospect SD 59, PO BOX 40 97536 — 2-11111
Rodney Hascall, supt. — 560-3653
HS 97536 — 1-00111
Don Alexander, prin. — 560-3653

Rainier, AC 503, PC 4, Columbia
Ranier SD 13, PO BOX 160 97048 — 4-11111
Gene Carlson, supt. — 556-3777
HS, PO BOX 280 97048 — 2-00011
Hugh Fulton, prin. — 556-4215
MS, PO BOX 190 97048 — 2-00100
John Lewis, prin. — 556-4218

Redmond, AC 503, PC 6, Deschutes
Redmond SD 2J — 5-11111
716 SW EVERGREEN AVE 97756 — 923-5437
Elton Gregory, supt.
HS, 675 SW RIMROCK DR 97756 — 4-00011
Dan Purple, prin. — 923-4800
Obsidian JHS — 3-00100
1335 SW OBSIDIAN AVE 97756 — 923-4900
Tim Gleeson, prin.

Reedsport, AC 503, PC 5, Douglas
Reedsport SD 105, 100 RANCH RD 97467 — 4-11111
James Robinson, supt. — 271-3656
JSHS, 2260 LONGWOOD DR 97467 — 2-00111
William Gieber, prin. — 271-2141

Riddle, AC 503, PC 4, Douglas
Riddle SD 70, PO BOX 45 97469 — 3-11111
Margaret Dutton, supt. — 874-3131
JSHS, PO BOX 45 97469 — 2-00111
Jim Thomas, prin. — 874-2251

Rockaway, AC 503, PC 3, Tillamook
Neah-Kah-Nie SD 56 — 3-11111
PO BOX 28 97136 — 355-2222
Joseph Curelo, supt.
Neah-Kah-Nie JSHS, PO BOX 8 97136 — 2-00111
James Cornoyer, prin. — 355-2272

Rogue River, AC 503, PC 4, Jackson
Rogue River SD 35 — 4-11111
PO BOX 1045 97537 — 582-3235
Charles Hellman, supt.
HS, PO BOX 1045 97537 — 2-00011
John Bond, prin. — 582-3297
MS, PO BOX 1045 97537 — 2-00100
Nancy Lockwood, prin. — 582-3233

Roseburg, AC 503, PC 7, Douglas
Douglas County SD 4 — 6-11111
1419 NW VALLEY VIEW DR 97470 — 440-4015
Ronald Zook, supt.
SHS, 547 W CHAPMAN AVE 97470 — 4-00001
Karen Goirigolzarri, prin. — 440-4142
Fremont JHS, 850 W KEADY CT 97470 — 3-00110
Daniel Faught, prin. — 440-4055
Lane JHS, 2153 NE VINE ST 97470 — 3-00110
Diana Peterson, prin. — 440-4104

Douglas County Christian S — 2-11111
2079 NW WITHERSPOON AVE 97470 — 672-2199
Phoenix S, PO BOX 2404 97470 — 1-00111
Ron Breyne, prin. — 673-3036
Umpqua Comunity College — 4-CC
PO BOX 967 97470 — 440-4604

Saint Benedict, AC 503, PC 1, Marion

Mt. Angel Seminary — 1-UC
GENERAL DELIVERY 97373 — 845-3951

Saint Helens, AC 503, PC 6, Columbia
St. Helens SD 502, 474 N 16TH ST 97051 — 5-11111
Zan Freeburn, supt. — 397-3085
HS, 2375 GABLE RD 97051 — 3-00011
Robert Kunders, prin. — 397-1900
JHS, 354 N 15TH ST 97051 — 2-00100
Donald Hogan, prin. — 397-1094

Saint Paul, AC 503, PC 2, Marion
St. Paul SD 45, 20449 MAIN ST NE 97137 — 2-11111
Charles Geis, supt. — 633-2541
HS, 20449 MAIN ST NE 97137 — 1-00011
Charles Geis, prin. — 633-2541

Salem, AC 503, PC 9, Marion
Salem/Keizer SD 24J — 8-11111
PO BOX 12024 97309 — 399-3000
Homer Kearns, supt.
McKay HS — 4-00011
2440 LANCASTER DR NE 97305 — 399-3080
Guido Caldarazzo, prin.
McNary HS, 505 SANDY DR N 97303 — 4-00011
David Annala, prin. — 399-3233
North HS, 765 14TH ST NE 97301 — 4-00011
Judy Patterson, prin. — 399-3241
South HS, 1910 CHURCH ST SE 97302 — 4-00011
George Dyer, prin. — 399-3252
Sprague HS, 2373 KUEBLER RD S 97302 — 4-00011
Gil James, prin. — 399-3261
Judson MS, 4512 JONES RD SE 97302 — 3-00100
Robert Keller, prin. — 399-3201
Leslie MS, 710 HOWARD ST SE 97302 — 3-00100
Richard Hanson, prin. — 399-3206
Parrish MS, 802 CAPITOL ST NE 97301 — 3-00100
Richard Krepel, prin. — 399-3210
Waldo MS — 3-00100
2805 LANSING AVE NE 97303 — 399-3215
Mike Kolb, prin.
Walker MS, 1075 8TH ST NW 97304 — 2-00100
Patricia Mack, prin. — 399-3220
Whiteaker MS — 3-00100
1605 LOCKHAVEN DR NE 97303 — 399-3224
David Cook, prin.

Center Street S — 2-00111
3030 CENTER ST NE 97301 — 588-5331
Chemeketa Community College — 7-CC
PO BOX 14007 97309 — 399-5038
Oregon State School for the Blind — HND
700 CHURCH ST SE 97301

Oregon State School for the Deaf HND
999 LOCUST ST NE 97303
Salem Academy 2-00111
942 LANCASTER DR NE 97301 378-1221
Cynthia Daniels, prin.
Trend College 3-CS
210 LIBERTY ST SE 97301 581-1476
Western Baptist College 97301 2-UC
800-845-3005
Western Medical College of Allied Health 2-CS
3000 MARKET ST NE STE 541 97301
363-4473
Western Mennonite HS 2-00011
9045 WALLACE RD NW 97304 363-2000
Eric Martin, prin.
Willamette University 4-UC
900 STATE ST 97301 370-6148

Sandy, AC 503, PC 5, Clackamas
Sandy ESD 46, PO BOX 547 97055 4-11100
Darrell Shepherd, supt. 668-5541
Cedar Ridge MS, PO BOX 547 97055 2-00100
Gary Wilson, prin. 668-8067

Sandy UNHSD 2 4-00011
17100 SE BLUFF RD 97055 668-5266
Dennis Crow, supt.
Sandy Union HS 4-00011
17100 SE BLUFF RD 97055 668-8011
Michael Funderburg, prin.

Scappoose, AC 503, PC 5, Columbia
Scappoose SD 1J, PO BOX V 97056 4-11111
Ed Danielson, supt. 543-6374
HS, 33700 HIGH SCHOOL WAY 97056 3-00011
Ted Moon, prin. 543-6376
MS, PO BOX 490 97056 2-00100
Delburt Powell, prin. 543-7163

Scio, AC 503, PC 3, Linn
Scio SD 95, 38875 NW 1ST AVE 97374 3-11111
John Rollofson, supt. 394-3261
HS, 38875 NW 1ST AVE 97374 2-00011
Dick Horyna, prin. 394-3276
MS, 38875 NW 1ST AVE 97374 2-00100
Judy Wells, prin. 394-3271

Seaside, AC 503, PC 6, Clatsop
Jewell SD 8 2-11111
ELSIE RT BOX 1280 97138 755-2451
Kenneth Lehman, supt.
Jewell JSHS, PO BOX 1280 97138 1-00111
Kenneth Lehman, prin. 755-2451

Seaside SD 10 4-11111
1801 S FRANKLIN ST 97138 738-5591
Harold Riggan, supt.
HS, 1901 N HOLLADAY DR 97138 3-00011
Don Wickersham, prin. 738-5586
Broadway MS 2-00100
1120 BROADWAY ST 97138 738-6892
Jim White, prin.

Sheridan, AC 503, PC 5, Yamhill
Sheridan SD 48J 3-11111
339 NW SHERMAN ST 97378 843-2433
Leroy Key, supt.
HS, 433 S BRIDGE ST 97378 2-00011
Graig Prough, prin. 843-2162
Chapman MS 2-01100
332 SW CORNWALL ST 97378 843-3732
Rosalie Ayora, prin.

Delphian S 2-11111
20950 ROCK CREEK RD 97378 843-3521
West Valley Academy 2-11111
PO BOX 127 97378 843-4123

Sherwood, AC 503, PC 5, Washington
Sherwood SD 88J 4-11111
400 N SHERWOOD BLVD 97140 625-8100
Bill Hill, supt.
HS, 1155 NW MEINECKE RD 97140 2-00011
Mary Simeone, prin. 625-8110
IS, 400 N SHERWOOD BLVD 97140 2-00100
John Kelly, prin. 625-8120

Silver Lake, AC 503, PC 2, Lake
North Lake SD 14 2-11111
HC 61 BOX 96 97638 576-2121
Mike Costello, supt.
North Lake HS, HC 61 BOX 96 97638 1-00011
Art Tassie, prin. 576-2121
North Lake JHS, HC 61 BOX 96 97638 1-00100
Art Tassie, prin. 576-2121

Silverton, AC 503, PC 6, Marion
Silverton SD 4, 210 E C ST 97381 4-11100
Craig Roessler, supt. 873-5303
Twain MS, 425 N CHURCH ST 97381 2-00100
Dale Koger, prin. 873-5317

Silverton UNHSD 7J, 210 E C ST 97381 3-00011
Craig Roessler, supt. 873-5303
HS, 802 SCHLADOR ST 97381 3-00011
Dick Kromminga, prin. 873-6331

World Outreach HS 2-00011
502 OAK ST 97381

Sisters, AC 503, PC 3, Deschutes
Sisters SD 6, PO BOX 3099 97759 3-11111
Judith May, supt. 549-8521
JSHS, PO BOX 3099 97759 3-00111
Dennis Dempsey, prin. 549-4045

Spray, AC 503, PC 2, Wheeler
Spray SD 1, PO BOX 230 97874 1-11111
Gerald Slind, supt. 468-2226
JSHS, PO BOX 230 97874 1-00111
Gerald Slind, prin. 468-2226

Springfield, AC 503, PC 8, Lane
Springfield SD 19, 525 MILL ST 97477 7-11111
Paul Plath, supt. 747-3331
HS, 875 N 7TH ST 97477 4-00011
Ronald Schiessl, prin. 726-3280
Thurston HS, 333 N 58TH ST 97478 4-00011
Wayne Hill, prin. 726-3320
Briggs MS, 2355 YOLANDA AVE 97477 3-00100
Larry Bentz, prin. 726-3350
Hamlin MS 3-00100
326 CENTENNIAL BLVD 97477 726-3356
Len Arney, prin.
MS, 1084 G ST 97477 2-00100
Mary Pilgreen, prin. 726-3362
Thurston MS 3-00100
6300 THURSTON RD 97478 726-3368
Lynda Fredrickson, prin.

Stanfield, AC 503, PC 4, Umatilla
Stanfield SD 61, 1100 N MAIN ST 97875 3-11111
Harvey Hazen, supt. 449-8766
HS, 1100 N MAIN ST 97875 2-00011
Ivan Ritchie, prin. 449-3851
MS, PO BOX 189 97875 2-00100
Ivan Ritchie, prin. 449-3881

Stayton, AC 503, PC 6, Marion
Stayton SD 77J, 757 W LOCUST ST 97383 4-11100
Gary Moore, supt. 769-6924
MS, 1021 SHAFF RD 97383 2-01100
Christopher Brantley, prin. 769-2198

Stayton UNHSD 4J 3-00011
757 W LOCUST ST 97383 769-2171
Gary Moore, supt.
HS, 757 W LOCUST ST 97383 3-00011
John Lehmann, prin. 769-2171

Regis HS, 550 W REGIS ST 97383 2-00011
Douglas Wasko, prin. 769-2159

Sunriver, AC 503, PC 3, Deschutes

Sunriver Preparatory S 2-11111
PO BOX 4425 97707 593-1244
Frederick Boyle, prin.

Sutherlin, AC 503, PC 6, Douglas
Sutherlin SD 130, PO BOX 500 97479 4-11111
Richard Smith, supt. 459-2228
HS, PO BOX 1068 97479 2-00011
John Lahley, prin. 459-9551
JHS, PO BOX 1164 97479 2-00100
Gerry Galbraith, prin. 459-2668

Sweet Home, AC 503, PC 6, Linn
Sweet Home SD 55, 1920 LONG ST 97386 4-11111
William Hampton, supt. 367-6111
HS, 1641 LONG ST 97386 3-00011
William Westphal, prin. 367-7145
JHS, 880 22ND AVE 97386 2-00100
Victor Zgorzelski, prin. 367-7187

Talent, AC 503, PC 5, Jackson
Phoenix-Talent SD 4
Supt. — See Phoenix
JHS, PO BOX 359 97540 3-00100
Stephen Trout, prin. 535-1552

The Dalles, AC 503, PC 7, Wasco
Chenowith SD 9, 3632 W 10TH ST 97058 4-11111
James Kiefert, supt. 296-6149
Wahtonka HS, 3601 W 10TH ST 97058 2-00011
Jack Norton, prin. 296-4633
Chenowith MS, 3718 W 13TH ST 97058 2-01100
Dick Kessler, prin. 296-5446

The Dalles SD 12, 2525 E 14TH ST 97058 4-11111
Ivan Hernandez, supt. 296-2139
HS, 220 E 10TH ST 97058 3-00011
Dave Beasley, prin. 296-4601
JHS, 1401 I ST 97058 3-00100
Phil Fox, prin. 296-4616

Tigard, AC 503, PC 8, Washington
Tigard-Tualatin SD 23J 6-11111
13137 SW PACIFIC HWY 97223 620-1620
Russell Joki, supt.
HS, PO BOX 23059 97281 4-00011
Mark Kubiaczyk, prin. 620-1620
Fowler MS 3-00100
10865 SW WALNUT ST 97223 620-1620
Susan Carlile, prin.
Twality MS, 14650 SW 97TH AVE 97224 3-00100
Jim Wassom, prin. 620-1620
Other Schools – See Tualatin

Broadcast Professionals 2-CS
11507 SW PACIFIC HWY # D 97223 244-5113

Tillamook, AC 503, PC 5, Tillamook
Tillamook SD 9 4-11111
6825 OFFICER ROW 97141 842-4414
Elaine Hopson, supt.
HS, 2605 12TH ST 97141 3-00011
Rick Knode, prin. 842-2566
JHS, 3906 ALDER LN 97141 2-00100
James Wickman, prin. 842-7531

Tillamook Christian HS 2-00011
701 MAROLF LOOP RD 97141

Toledo, AC 503, PC 5, Lincoln
Lincoln County SD
Supt. — See Newport
HS, 1800 NE STURDEVANT RD 97391 2-00011
Ron Williams, prin. 336-5104
MS, 620 NE STURDEVANT RD 97391 2-00100
Hal Janneck, prin. 336-2299

Troutdale, AC 503, PC 6, Multnomah
Reynolds SD 7 6-11111
1204 NE 201ST AVE 97060 661-7200
Hudson Lasher, supt.
Reynolds HS 4-00011
1698 SW CHERRY PARK RD 97060 667-3186
Ed Smith, prin.
Reynolds MS, 1200 NE 201ST AVE 97060 3-00100
LaDyle Simpson, prin. 665-8166
Other Schools – See Portland

Tualatin, AC 503, PC 7, Washington
Tigard-Tualatin SD 23J
Supt. — See Tigard
HS 3-00011
22300 SW BOONES FERRY RD 97062 620-1620
Larry Pettersen, prin.
Hazelbrook MS 3-00100
11300 SW HAZELBROOK RD 97062 620-1620
Maryalice Russell, prin.

Western Truck School 2-CS
PO BOX 826 97062 691-0113

Turner, AC 503, PC 4, Marion
Cascade UNHSD 5 3-00111
10226 MARION RD SE 97392 743-2137
F James McBride, supt.
Cascade HS 3-00011
10226 MARION RD SE 97392 743-2139
Harry Walker, prin.
Cascade JHS 2-00100
10226 MARION RD SE 97392 743-2138
Milt Biddington, prin.

Ukiah, AC 503, PC 2, Umatilla
Ukiah SD 80, PO BOX 218 97880 1-11111
Frank Odegard, supt. 427-3431
HS, PO BOX 218 97880 1-00011
Frank Odegard, prin. 427-3431

Umatilla, AC 503, PC 5, Umatilla
Umatilla SD 6, PO BOX 131 97882 3-11111
George Fenton, supt. 922-4882
HS, PO BOX 131 97882 2-00011
Curt Wheeler, prin. 922-3261
Brownell MS, PO BOX 131 97882 2-00100
William Delong, prin. 922-4841

Union, AC 503, PC 4, Union
Union SD 5, PO BOX K 97883 3-11111
Russell Snodgrass, supt. 562-6115
JSHS, PO BOX 908 97883 2-00111
Bruce Mulvany, prin. 562-5166

Unity, AC 503, PC 1, Baker
Burnt River SD 30J, PO BOX 8 97884 1-11111
Ted Knivila, supt. 446-3466
Burnt River JSHS, PO BOX 8 97884 1-00111
Ted Knivila, prin. 446-3336

Vale, AC 503, PC 4, Malheur
Vale SD 84, 403 E ST W 97918 4-11111
Robert Crawford, supt. 473-3291
HS, 505 NACHEZ ST S 97918 2-00011
Bob Bates, prin. 473-3181

Vernonia, AC 503, PC 4, Columbia
Vernonia SD 47J, 475 BRIDGE ST 97064 3-11111
Ellis Mason, supt. 429-5891
HS, 299 BRIDGE ST 97064 2-00011
Steve Giere, prin. 429-3521
Washington MS, 199 BRIDGE ST 97064 2-01100
R Randall Aultman, prin. 429-7941

Waldport, AC 503, PC 4, Lincoln
Lincoln County SD
Supt. — See Newport
HS, PO BOX 370 97394 2-00011
Ron LaBreche, prin. 563-3243
MS, 380 NW SPRING ST 97394 2-00100
Beau Horn, prin. 563-3235

Wallowa, AC 503, PC 3, Wallowa
Wallowa SD 12, PO BOX 425 97885 2-11111
Edward Jensen, supt. 886-2951
JSHS, PO BOX 425 97885 2-00111
John Nesemann, prin. 886-2951

Warrenton, AC 503, PC 5, Clatsop
Warrenton-Hammond SD 30 3-11111
820 SW CEDAR AVE 97146 861-2281
Bernard LaCasse, supt.
HS, 1700 S MAIN AVE 97146 2-00011
Vince Zanobelli, prin. 861-3317

Welches, AC 503, PC 3, Clackamas
Welches SD 13 — 3-11100
  24903 E SALMON RIVER RD 97067 — 622-3165
  Judith Warren, supt.
MS, SALMON RIVER PARK ROAD 97067 — 2-01100
  Jerry McGuire, prin. — 622-3166

West Linn, AC 503, PC 7, Clackamas
West Linn-Wilsonville SD 3J — 6-11111
  STAFFORD RD 97068 — 638-9869
  Roger Woehl, supt.
HS, 5464 W A ST 97068 — 4-00011
  Clark Irwin, prin. — 656-2618
Athey Creek MS — 3-00100
  2900 SW BORLAND RD 97068 — 638-6005
  Glenn Gwynn, prin.
Bolton MS, 5933 HOLMES ST 97068 — 2-00100
  Paul Boly, prin. — 656-3842
Other Schools – See Wilsonville

Weston, AC 503, PC 3, Umatilla
Athena-Weston SD 29J
  Supt. — See Athena
Athena-Weston JHS — 2-00100
  PO BOX 158 97886 — 566-3548
  John McDonough, prin.

Westport, AC 503, PC 2, Columbia
Columbia SD 5J — 4-11111
  RR 2 BOX 2178 97016 — 455-2275
  Duane Scott, supt.
Other Schools – See Astoria, Clatskanie

Willamina, AC 503, PC 4, Yamhill
Willamina SD 30J — 4-11111
  324 SE ADAMS ST 97396 — 876-4525
  Larry Audet, supt.
HS, PO BOX 67 97396 — 2-00011
  Donald Yates, prin. — 876-9122
MS, 1100 NE OAKEN HILLS DR 97396 — 2-00100
  Buz Tautfest, prin. — 876-2545

Tri-City Christian S — 2-11111
  PO BOX 957 97396

Wilsonville, AC 503, PC 6, Clackamas
West Linn-Wilsonville SD 3J
  Supt. — See West Linn
Wood MS — 2-00100
  11055 SW WILSONVILLE RD 97070 — 682-0101
  Cherryl Brounstein, prin.

Winston, AC 503, PC 5, Douglas
Winston-Dillard SD 116
  Supt. — See Dillard
MS, 330 THOMPSON RD 97496 — 2-00100
  Joe Harris, prin. — 679-3121

Foursquare Gospel Center HS — 2-00011
  PO BOX 760 97496
Winston Mennonite HS — 2-00011
  PO BOX 392 97496

Woodburn, AC 503, PC 7, Marion
Woodburn SD 103 — 5-11111
  965 N BOONES FERRY RD 97071 — 981-9555
  Keith Robinson, supt.
HS, 1785 N FRONT ST 97071 — 3-00011
  Jack Bimrose, prin. — 981-2600
French Prairie MS — 3-00100
  1025 N BOONES FERRY RD 97071 — 981-2650
  Gary Haugen, prin.

Elliott Prairie Christian HS — 2-00011
  5383 S SCHNEIDER RD 97071
Faith Christian HS — 2-00011
  602 YOUNG ST 97071

Yamhill, AC 503, PC 3, Yamhill
Yamhill-Carlton SD 1 — 4-11111
  PO BOX 68 97148 — 662-4911
  Nolan Ferguson, supt.
Yamhill-Carlton HS — 2-00011
  275 N MAPLE ST 97148 – (—), prin. — 662-3228
MS, 310 E MAIN ST 97148 — 3-01100
  T. Bessonette, prin. — 662-3263

Yoncalla, AC 503, PC 3, Douglas
Yoncalla SD 32, PO BOX 568 97499 — 2-11111
  Ken Sprute, supt. — 849-2782
HS, PO BOX 568 97499 — 2-00011
  Terry Duncan, prin. — 849-2175

Yoncalla Christian HS — 2-00011
  PO BOX 8 97499

PENNSYLVANIA

STATE DEPARTMENT OF EDUCATION
333 Market St., Harrisburg 17126
(717) 783-6788

Secretary of Education	Donald Carroll
Office of Administration	Terry Dellmuth
Office of Elementary/Secondary Education	Joseph Bard

STATE BOARD OF EDUCATION
333 Market St., Harrisburg 17126

Chairperson	Sr. M. Antoun

INTERMEDIATE UNITS

Intermediate Unit 1
  Samuel Craighead — 412-938-3241
  RR 2 BOX 700, Coal Center 15423
Pittsburgh/Mt. Oliver IU 2
  Louise Brennen — 412-488-4482
  2100 WHARTON ST STE 600
  Pittsburgh 15203
Allegheny IU 3
  Joseph Lagana — 412-394-5700
  4 STATION SQ STE 2
  Pittsburgh 15219
Midwestern IU 4
  Angelo Pezzuolo — 412-458-6700
  453 MAPLE ST, Grove City 16127
Northwest Tri-County IU 5
  John Leuenberger — 814-734-5610
  252 WATERFORD ST # 5
  Edinboro 16412
Riverview IU 6
  R. Don Means — 814-226-7103
  880 GREENCREST DR
  Shippenville 16254
Westmoreland IU 7
  Bruce Paul, RR 12 BOX 205 — 412-836-2460
  Greensburg 15601
Appalachia IU 8
  Michael Dillon — 814-472-7690
  119 PARK ST, Ebensburg 15931
Seneca Highlands IU 9
  M. Wetzel — 814-887-5512
  PO BOX 1566, Smethport 16749
Central IU 10
  Nancy Robbins, RR 1 BOX 374 — 814-342-0884
  West Decatur 16878

Tuscarora IU 11
  Anthony Labriola, RR 1 BOX 70A — 717-899-7143
  Mc Veytown 17051
Lincoln IU 12
  Robert Piatt — 717-624-4616
  PO BOX 70, New Oxford 17350
Lancaster/Lebanon IU 13
  Richard Sherr — 717-569-7331
  1110 ENTERPRISE RD
  East Petersburg 17520
Berks County IU 14
  K. Robert Hohl — 610-987-2248
  PO BOX 16050, Reading 19612
Capital Area IU 15
  Edward Frye — 717-732-8400
  PO BOX 489, Summerdale 17093
Central Susquehanna IU 16
  Patrick Toole — 717-523-1155
  PO BOX 213, Lewisburg 17837
Blast IU 17
  Clair Goodman, 469 HEPBURN ST — 717-323-8561
  Williamsport 17701
Luzerne IU 18
  Kevin O'Connor — 717-287-9681
  PO BOX 1649, Kingston 18704
Northeastern Educational IU 19
  David Petrosky — 717-282-9200
  OLD PLANK RD, Mayfield 18433
Colonial Northampton IU 20
  Joseph Mickley — 610-252-5550
  6 DANFORTH DR, Easton 18042
Carbon-Lehigh IU 21
  Jerry Stout, 4750 ORCHARD RD — 610-799-4111
  Schnecksville 18078

Bucks County IU 22
  A. William Vantine — 215-348-2940
  705 SHADY RETREAT RD
  Doylestown 18901
Montgomery County IU 23
  Dennis Harken — 610-539-8550
  1605 W MAIN ST UNIT 23
  Norristown 19403
Chester County IU 24
  John Baillie — 610-524-5000
  150 JAMES HANCE COURT
  Exton 19341
Delaware County IU 25
  James Shields — 610-565-4880
  6TH & OLIVE STS, Media 19063
Philadelphia IU 26
  Theresa Lemme — 215-299-7000
  2120 WINTER ST UNIT 26
  Philadelphia 19103
Beaver Valley IU 27
  S. Marziano — 412-774-7800
  225 CENTER GRANGE RD
  Aliquippa 15001
Arin IU 28
  Thomas Carey — 412-463-5300
  PO BOX 175, Shelocta 15774
Schuylkill IU 29
  R. Alspach — 717-544-9131
  PO BOX 130, Mar Lin 17951

PUBLIC, PRIVATE AND CATHOLIC SECONDARY SCHOOLS

Abington, AC 215, PC 7, Montgomery
Abington SD, 970 HIGHLAND AVE 19001　6-11111
James McCaffery, supt.　884-4700
SHS, 900 HIGHLAND AVE 19001　4-00001
Norman Schmid, prin.　884-4700
JHS, 2056 SUSQUEHANNA RD 19001　4-00110
Sheldon Erwine, prin.　884-4700

Abington Memorial Hospital　2-HSP
1200 OLD YORK RD 19001　576-2650
Pennsylvania State University　4-CC
1600 WOODLAND RD 19001　886-9400

Albion, AC 814, PC 4, Erie
Northwestern SD　4-11111
1 HARTHAN WAY 16401　756-4116
Lynn Corder, supt.
Northwestern HS　3-00011
200 HARTHAN WAY 16401　756-4117
Joseph Meako, prin.
Northwestern MS　2-00100
150 HARTHAN WAY 16401　756-4118
James Henderson, prin.

Alexandria, AC 814, PC 2, Huntingdon
Juniata Valley SD, PO BOX 318 16611　4-11111
Ellis Griffith, supt.　669-9150
Juniata Valley JSHS　2-00111
PO BOX 318 16611　669-4401
Peter Ludwig, prin.

Aliquippa, AC 412, PC 7, Beaver
Aliquippa SD, 100 HARDING AVE 15001　4-11111
Paul Dinello, supt.　857-7500
HS, 100 HARDING AVE 15001　3-00011
John Thomas, prin.　857-7515
MS, 100 HARDING AVE 15001　2-00100
James George, prin.　857-7565

Hopewell Area SD　5-11111
2121 BRODHEAD RD 15001　375-6691
Francis Barnes, supt.
Hopewell HS　3-00011
1215 LONGVUE AVE 15001　378-8565
Robert Frioni, prin.
Hopewell JHS　3-01100
2121 BRODHEAD RD 15001　375-7765
Stanley Yukica, prin.

Aliquippa Hospital　HSP
2500 HOSPITAL DR 15001　857-1246

Allentown, AC 610, PC 9, Lehigh
Allentown CSD, PO BOX 328 18105　7-11111
Diane Scott, supt.　821-2621
Allen HS, 126 N 17TH ST 18104　4-00011
Louis Delorenzo, prin.　820-2223
Dieruff HS, 815 N IRVING ST 18103　4-00011
Michael Meilinger, prin.　820-2200
Harrison-Morton MS　3-00100
137 N 2ND ST 18101　820-2175
Robert McCrea, prin.
Raub MS, 102 S SAINT CLOUD ST 18104　3-00100
Robert Doran, prin.　820-2156
South Mountain MS　3-00100
709 W EMMAUS AVE 18103　820-2149
Bruce Hutchinson, prin.
Trexler MS, 851 N 15TH ST 18102　3-00100
Raymond O'Connell, prin.　820-2171

Parkland SD　6-11111
1210 SPRINGHOUSE RD 18104　366-1910
Gary McCartney, supt.
Springhouse JHS　3-00110
1200 SPRINGHOUSE RD 18104　398-0303
(—), prin.
Troxell JHS　3-00110
2219 N CEDAR CREST BLVD 18104　437-4631
Frank Reed, prin.
Other Schools – See Orefield

Salisbury Twp. SD　4-11111
1140 SALISBURY RD 18103　797-2062
F. Laird Evans, supt.
Salisbury SHS　2-00001
500 E MONTGOMERY ST 18103　791-3641
Michael Platt, prin.
Salisbury MS　3-00110
3301 DEVONSHIRE RD 18103　791-0830
Allen Fields, prin.

Allentown-Lehigh Valley Hospital Center　2-HSP
PO BOX 1110 18105　778-2204
Cedar Crest College　4-UC
100 COLLEGE DR 18104　437-4471
Central Catholic HS, 301 N 4TH ST 18102　3-00011
James Hodrick, prin.　437-4601
Information Computer Systems Institute　2-CC
2201 HANGAR PL 18103　264-8029
Lincoln Technical Institute　4-CC
5151 W TILGHMAN ST 18104　398-5301
Muhlenberg College　4-UC
2400 W CHEW ST 18104　821-3100
NEC-Allentown Campus　3-CC
1501 LEHIGH ST 18103　791-5100
Sacred Heart Hospital　HSP
421 W CHEW ST 18102　776-4745
Welder Training Institute　2-CC
729 E HIGHLAND ST 18103　437-9720

Allison Park, AC 412, PC 6, Allegheny
Area Vocational Technical SD
Supt. — See Harrisburg
Beattie AVTS　Vo Tech
9600 BABCOCK BLVD 15101　366-2800
Daniel Jacobs, prin.

Hampton Township SD　5-11111
4482 MOUNT ROYAL BLVD 15101　486-6000
Kenneth Scholtz, supt.
Hampton HS, 2929 MCCULLY RD 15101　3-00011
Charles Erdeljac, prin.　486-6000
Hampton MS, 4589 SCHOOL RD 15101　3-00100
Harold Sarver, prin.　486-6000

Altoona, AC 814, PC 8, Blair
Altoona Area SD, 1415 6TH AVE 16602　6-11111
George Cardone, supt.　946-8211
SHS, 1415 6TH AVE 16602　4-00001
Walter Betar, prin.　946-8274
Keith JHS, 1318 19TH AVE 16601　4-00110
Thomas Foose, prin.　946-8355
Roosevelt JHS, 1501 7TH AVE 16602　4-00110
William Pfeffer, prin.　946-8340

Area Vocational Technical SD
Supt. — See Harrisburg
Altoona AVTS, 1500 4TH AVE 16602　Vo Tech
Walter Kearney, prin.　946-8450

Altoona Hospital　HSP
620 HOWARD AVE 16601　946-2126
Altoona School of Commerce　2-CS
508 58TH ST 16602　944-6134
Bishop Guilfoyle HS　2-00011
2400 PLEASANT VALLEY BLVD 16602　944-4014
William Neugebauer, prin.
Calvary Baptist Academy　2-11111
810 RUSKIN DR 16602　942-9710
Computer Learning Network　2-CS
2900 FAIRWAY DR 16602　944-5643
Mercy Hospital　HSP
2601 8TH AVE 16602　944-4101
Pennsylvania State University　4-CC
3000 IVYSIDE PARK 16601　949-5000

Alverton, AC 412, PC 2, Westmoreland
Southmoreland SD
Supt. — See Scottdale
Southmoreland HS, PO BOX A 15612　3-00011
John Beck, prin.　887-2019
Southmoreland JHS, PO BOX B 15612　2-00100
A. Scott Logan, prin.　887-2031

Ambler, AC 215, PC 6, Montgomery
Wissahickon SD, 601 KNIGHT RD 19002　5-11111
Bruce Kowalski, supt.　628-1600
Wissahickon HS　3-00011
521 HOUSTON RD 19002　628-1692
Dale Stauffer, prin.
Wissahickon MS　3-00100
500 HOUSTON RD 19002　628-1668
Austin Snyder, prin.

Temple University 19002　4-UC
283-1292

Ambridge, AC 412, PC 6, Beaver
Ambridge Area SD, 740 PARK RD 15003　5-11111
Samuel DePaul, supt.　266-8800
Ambridge Area HS, 909 DUSS AVE 15003　4-00011
David Parry, prin.　266-5112
Other Schools – See Freedom

Trinity Episcopal School for Ministry　2-UC
311 11TH ST 15003　978-2133

Annville, AC 717, PC 5, Lebanon
Annville-Cleona SD　4-11111
520 S WHITE OAK ST 17003　867-4131
Carole Spahr, supt.
Annville-Cleona JSHS　3-00111
500 S WHITE OAK ST 17003　867-4661
Glenn Worcester, prin.

Lebanon Valley College　4-UC
101 N COLLEGE AVE 17003　867-6100

Archbald, AC 717, PC 6, Lackawanna
Valley View SD, 1 COLUMBUS DR 18403　4-11111
Daniel Corazzi, supt.　876-5080
Valley View HS, 1 COLUMBUS DR 18403　3-00011
Anthony DeCarli, prin.　876-4110
Valley View MS, 1 COLUMBUS DR 18403　3-01100
Louis Pilch, prin.　876-6461

Ardmore, AC 215, PC 7, Montgomery
Lower Merion SD　6-11111
301 E MONTGOMERY AVE 19003　645-1930
David Magill, supt.
Lower Merion HS　4-00011
245 E MONTGOMERY AVE 19003　645-1810
Robert Ruoff, prin.
Other Schools – See Bala-Cynwyd, Narberth,
Rosemont

Torah Academy　2-11111
ARGYLE & WYNNEWD ROADS 19003　642-7870

Armagh, AC 804, PC 2, Indiana
United SD, PO BOX 168 15920　4-11111
Raymond Aucker, supt.　446-5618

United JSHS, PO BOX 168 15920　3-00111
Harvey Long, prin.　446-5618

Arnold, AC 412, PC 6, Westmoreland
New Kensington-Arnold SD
Supt. — See New Kensington
Valley MS, 1701 ALCOA DR 15068　2-00100
James Haser, prin.　335-2511

Ashland, AC 717, PC 5, Schuylkill
North Schuylkill SD　4-11111
STATE ROUTE 61 17921　874-0466
Charles Greco, supt.
North Schuylkill JSHS, RR 2 17921　4-00111
Barton Philipps, prin.　874-0495

Ashland State General Hospital　HSP
RURAL ROUTE 61 17921　875-2000
Cardinal Brennan HS, RR 2 17921　2-00011
Sr. Mary Bednar, prin.　874-3921

Aston, AC 610, PC see Village Green
Area Vocational Technical SD
Supt. — See Harrisburg
Delaware County AVTS-Aston　Vo Tech
BIRNEY HWY & CROZERVILLE RD 19014　459-3050
Patsy Griffith, prin.

Penn-Delco SD, 95 CONCORD RD 19014　5-11111
Timothy Kirby, supt.　497-6310
Sun Valley HS　3-00011
2881 PANCOAST AVE 19014　497-6350
William Snyder, prin.
Northley MS, CONCORD ROAD 19014　3-00100
Bruce Williams, prin.　497-6330

American Christian ES　2-11111
2140 BRIDGEWATER RD 19014　558-1430
Neumann College　4-UC
CONCORD ROAD 19014　459-0905

Atglen, AC 215, PC 3, Chester
Octorara Area SD, PO BOX 500 19310　4-11111
Timothy Daniels, supt.　593-8211
Octorara Area HS, PO BOX 501 19310　3-00011
Patrick Hallock, prin.　593-8254
Octorara Area IS, PO BOX 500 19310　3-01100
Margaret Thomas, prin.　593-8223

Athens, AC 717, PC 5, Bradford
Athens Area SD, 204 WILLOW ST 18810　5-11111
Wayne Boyer, supt.　888-7766
Athens Area HS　3-00011
401 W FREDERICK ST 18810　888-7766
T. Salapino, prin.
Rowe MS, 0 PENNSYLVANIA AVE 18810　2-00100
Eugene Cerutti, prin.　888-7766
Other Schools – See East Smithfield

Austin, AC 814, PC 3, Potter
Austin Area SD, PO BOX 7 16720　2-11111
Charlene Philp, supt.　647-8603
Austin Area JSHS, PO BOX 7 16720　2-00111
Charlene Philp, prin.　647-8603

Avella, AC 412, PC 4, Washington
Avella Area SD, RR 2 BOX 194A 15312　3-11111
Thomas Zellars, supt.　356-2218
Avella Area JSHS, RR 2 BOX 194A 15312　2-00111
Daniel Cecchini, prin.　356-2216

Baden, AC 412, PC 6, Beaver

Quigley HS, 1065 FRANKLIN AVE 15005　2-00011
Fr. Menegay, prin.　869-2188

Bala-Cynwyd, AC 610, PC 6, Montgomery
Lower Merion SD
Supt. — See Ardmore
MS, 510 BRYN MAWR AVE 19004　3-00100
Patricia Haupt, prin.　664-4500

Bangor, AC 215, PC 6, Northampton
Bangor Area SD, 44 S 3RD ST 18013　5-11111
Wilford Ottey, supt.　588-2163
Bangor Area SHS　3-00001
RR 2 BOX 2069 18013 – (—), prin.　588-2105
Bangor Area JHS　3-00110
RR 2 BOX 2071 18013　588-2112
John Gower, prin.

Barnesboro, AC 814, PC 5, Cambria
Northern Cambria SD　4-11111
600 JOSEPH ST 15714　948-5481
H. Robert Mencer, supt.
Northern Cambria HS　3-00011
807 N 11TH ST 15714　948-6800
John Bernard, prin.
Northern Cambria MS　3-01100
600 JOSEPH ST 15714　948-5880
Robert Williams, prin.

Bartonsville, AC 717, PC 2, Monroe
Area Vocational Technical SD
Supt. — See Harrisburg
Monroe County AVTS　Vo Tech
PO BOX 66 18321　629-2001
David Lapinsky, prin.

Northeast Institute of Education　2-CS
PO BOX 574 18321　629-5555

Beaver, AC 412, PC 6, Beaver
Beaver Area SD, 855 2ND ST 15009   4-11111   774-4010
  Betty Schaughency, supt.
Beaver Area HS
  0 GYPSY GLEN RD 15009   4-00011   774-0251
  John Plesha, prin.
Beaver Area IS, 0 GYPSY GLEN RD 15009   2-00100   774-0251
  Lawrence Horchnak, prin.

Medical Center of Beaver County   HSP
  1000 DUTCH RIDGE RD 15009   728-7000

Beaver Falls, AC 412, PC 7, Beaver
Big Beaver Falls Area SD   4-11111
  820 16TH ST 15010   843-3470
  Jean Higgins, supt.
Beaver Falls Area HS   3-00011
  1701 8TH AVE 15010   843-7470
  Frank Jute, prin.
MS, 1601 8TH AVE 15010   3-01100   846-5470
  George Potter, prin.

Blackhawk SD   5-11111
  500 BLACKHAWK RD 15010   846-6600
  John Duff, supt.
Blackhawk JSHS   4-00111
  500 BLACKHAWK RD 15010   846-9600
  Edward Giannini, prin.

Geneva College   4-UC
  3200 COLLEGE AVE 15010   846-5100

Beaver Springs, AC 717, PC 3, Snyder
Midd-West SD
  Supt. — See Middleburg
West Snyder JSHS   2-00111
  RR 1 BOX 292 17812   658-8144
  Warren Dutrow, prin.

Bedford, AC 814, PC 5, Bedford
Bedford Area SD, 330 E JOHN ST 15522   5-11111   623-1168
  Clyde Colwell, supt.
HS, 330 E JOHN ST 15522   3-00011   623-2171
  (—), prin.
MS, E WATSON ST 15522   2-00100   623-4200
  Robert Gervinski, prin.
  Other Schools — See Hyndman

Bellefonte, AC 814, PC 6, Centre
Bellefonte Area SD   5-11111
  301 N ALLEGHENY ST 16823   355-4814
  Douglas Bleggi, supt.
Bellefonte Area HS   3-00011
  830 E BISHOP ST 16823 – (—), prin.   355-4833
Bellefonte Area MS   3-00100
  100 N SCHOOL ST 16823   355-5466
  Joseph Goodnack, prin.

Centre County Christian Academy   2-11111
  PO BOX 47 16823   355-7805

Belle Vernon, AC 412, PC 4, Fayette
Belle Vernon Area SD, RR 2 15012   5-11111   929-5262
  G. Caruso, supt.
HS, RR 2 15012   3-00011   929-9800
  W. Kubin, prin.
Bellmar JHS, 500 PERRY AVE 15012   2-00100   929-9030
  Stephen Russell, prin.
Rostraver JHS, RR 2 15012   2-00100   929-9800
  J. Bush, prin.

Belleville, AC 717, PC 4, Mifflin

Belleville Mennonite S   2-11111
  PO BOX 847 17004   935-2184

Bellwood, AC 814, PC 4, Blair
Bellwood-Antis SD   4-11111
  PO BOX 69 16617   742-2275
  Rodney Kuhns, supt.
Bellwood-Antis HS   2-00011
  220 MARTIN ST 16617   742-2274
  Michael Sakash, prin.
Bellwood-Antis MS   2-01100
  400 MARTIN ST 16617   742-2273
  Robert Fisher, prin.

Bensalem, AC 215, PC 6, Bucks
Bensalem Township SD   6-11111
  3000 DONALLEN DR 19020   750-2810
  Robert Dampman, supt.
Bensalem Twp. HS   4-00011
  4319 HULMEVILLE RD 19020   244-2881
  Stephen Smith, prin.
Armstrong MS, 2201 STREET RD 19020   3-00100   244-2817
  William Nichols, prin.
Shafer MS, 3333 HULMEVILLE RD 19020   3-00100   244-2857
  William Aiken, prin.
Snyder MS   3-00100
  3333 HULMEVILLE RD 19020   244-2837
  Gary Rowe, prin.

De La Salle Vocational HS   2-00011
  STREET RD & BRISTOL 19020   464-0344
  Francis Piperno, prin.
Holy Ghost Prep S   2-00011
  2429 BRISTOL PIKE 19020   639-2102
  Fr. McCloskey, prin.

Bentleyville, AC 412, PC 5, Washington
Bentworth SD
  Supt. — See Ellsworth
Bentworth HS, 500 LINCOLN AVE 15314   2-00011   239-5911
  Frank Watson, prin.

Benton, AC 717, PC 3, Columbia
Benton Area SD, RR 2 BOX 8 17814   3-11111   925-6651
  Edwin Hartman, supt.
JSHS, RR 2 BOX 8 17814   2-00111   925-2651
  Edwin Hartman, prin.

Berlin, AC 814, PC 4, Somerset
Berlin-Brothersvalley SD   4-11111
  1025 MAIN ST 15530   267-4621
  John Cornish, supt.
Berlin-Brothersvalley JSHS   3-00111
  1025 MAIN ST 15530   267-4622
  John Prendergast, prin.

Bernville, AC 215, PC 3, Berks
Tulpehocken Area SD   4-11111
  430 NEW SCHAEFFERSTOWN RD 19506
  Charles Snyder, supt.   488-6286
Tulpehocken HS   2-00011
  430 NEW SCHAEFFERSTOWN RD 19506
  Linda Misterkiewicz, prin.   488-6286
  Other Schools — See Bethel

Berwick, AC 717, PC 7, Columbia
Berwick Area SD   5-11111
  500 N MARKET ST 18603   759-6400
  David Force, supt.
Berwick Area HS   3-00011
  1100 FOWLER AVE 18603   759-6407
  Richard Walton, prin.
Berwick Area MS   3-00100
  1100 EVERGREEN DR 18603   759-6416
  Walter Lutz, prin.

Berwyn, AC 610, PC 6, Chester
Tredyffrin-Easttown SD   5-11111
  738 1ST AVE 19312   644-6600
  Theodore Foot, supt.
Conestoga SHS, 200 IRISH RD 19312   3-00001   644-1440
  Daniel Waters, prin.
Tredyffrin-Easttown JHS   3-00110
  840 OLD LANCASTER RD 19312   644-1460
  Harry Riggs, prin.
  Other Schools — See Wayne

Bessemer, AC 412, PC 4, Lawrence
Mohawk Area SD   4-11111
  MOHAWK SCHOOL RD 16112   667-7723
  Edmund Retort, supt.
Mohawk JSHS   3-00111
  MOHAWK SCHOOL RD 16112   667-7782
  Donald Matchett, prin.

Bethel, AC 717, PC 3, Berks
Tulpehocken Area SD
  Supt. — See Bernville
MS, 8390 LANCASTER AVE 19507   2-01100   933-4131
  L. Messersmith, prin.

Bethel Park, AC 412, PC 8, Allegheny
Bethel Park SD, 301 CHURCH RD 15102   5-11111   833-5000
  Victor Morrone, supt.
HS, 309 CHURCH RD 15102   4-00011   854-8581
  Lawrence Bukowski, prin.
Independence MS   3-00100
  2807 BETHEL CHURCH RD 15102   854-8677
  Robert David, prin.

Bethlehem, AC 610, PC 8, Northampton
Area Vocational Technical SD
  Supt. — See Harrisburg
Bethlehem AVTS   Vo Tech
  3300 CHESTER AVE 18017   866-8013
  Donald Foellner, prin.

Bethlehem Area SD   7-11111
  1516 SYCAMORE ST 18017   861-0500
  Thomas Doluisio, supt.
Freedom HS, 3149 CHESTER AVE 18017   4-00011   867-5843
  Richard Jay, prin.
Liberty HS, 1115 LINDEN ST 18018   4-00011   691-7200
  William Burkhardt, prin.
Broughal MS, 125 W PACKER AVE 18015   3-00100   866-5041
  Joe Petraglia, prin.
East Hills MS, 2005 CHESTER AVE 18017   3-00100   867-0541
  Monty Perfetti, prin.
Nitschmann MS   3-00100
  909 W UNION BLVD 18018   866-5781
  A. Thomas Kartsotis, prin.
Northeast MS   3-00100
  1110 FERNWOOD ST 18018   868-8581
  David Shelly, prin.

Bethlehem Catholic HS   3-00011
  2133 MADISON AVE 18017   866-0791
  Richard Culver, prin.
Lehigh University   6-UC
  27 MEMORIAL DR W 18015   758-3000
Moravian Academy   2-00011
  4313 GREEN POND RD 18017   691-1600
  Peter Sipple, prin.
Moravian Academy   2-00100
  11 W MARKET ST 18018   866-6677
Moravian College   4-UC
  1200 MAIN ST 18018   861-1577
Moravian Theological Seminary   3-UC
  60 W LOCUST ST 18018   861-1516
Northampton Co. Area Community College   6-CC
  3835 GREEN POND RD 18017   861-5300
St. Luke's Hospital   HSP
  801 OSTRUM ST 18015   954-3400

Biglerville, AC 717, PC 3, Adams
Upper Adams SD, N MAIN ST 17307   4-11111   677-7191
  Robert Witten, supt.

JSHS, N MAIN ST 17307   3-00111   677-7191
  Robert Klokis, prin.

Birdsboro, AC 215, PC 5, Berks
Daniel Boone Area SD
  Supt. — See Douglassville
Boone JSHS, PO BOX 450 19508   3-00111   582-2261
  Stephen Brotschul, prin.

Berks Christian S   2-11111
  926 PHILADELPHIA TER 19508   582-4191

Blairsville, AC 412, PC 5, Indiana
Blairsville-Saltsburg SD   4-11111
  195 N WALNUT ST 15717   459-5500
  Thomas Meloy, supt.
HS, 100 SCHOOL LN 15717   2-00011   459-8882
  Stephen Sarokan, prin.
JHS, 195 N WALNUT ST 15717   2-00100   459-8880
  Louis Oliver, prin.
  Other Schools — See Saltsburg

NEC-Vale Technical Institute   3-CC
  135 W MARKET ST 15717   459-9500

Bloomsburg, AC 717, PC 7, Columbia
Area Vocational Technical SD
  Supt. — See Harrisburg
Columbia-Montour AVTS   Vo Tech
  5050 SWEPPENHEISER DR 17815   784-8040
  James Lupini, prin.

Bloomsburg Area SD   4-11111
  1200 RAILROAD ST 17815   784-5000
  Alex Dubil, supt.
Bloomsburg Area HS   2-00011
  1200 RAILROAD ST 17815   784-6100
  John Klusman, prin.
Bloomsburg Area MS   2-00100
  1100 RAILROAD ST 17815   784-9100
  Robert Rupp, prin.

Central Columbia SD   4-11111
  4777 OLD BERWICK RD 17815   784-2850
  Ivan Shibley, supt.
Central Columbia HS   3-00011
  4777 OLD BERWICK RD 17815   784-2833
  John Grabert, prin.
Central Columbia MS   3-01100
  4777 OLD BERWICK RD 17815   784-6103
  Joe Kelly, prin.

Bloomsburg Christian S   2-11111
  728 E 5TH ST 17815   784-7661
Bloomsburg University 17815   6-UC   389-4000

Learning and Evaluation Center   HMS
  PO BOX 616 17815

Blossburg, AC 717, PC 4, Tioga
Southern Tioga SD, 241 MAIN ST 16912   4-11111   638-2183
  Ronald Boyanowski, supt.
North Penn JSHS, 300 MORRIS ST 16912   2-00111   638-2158
  Albert Lindner, prin.
  Other Schools — See Liberty, Mansfield

Blue Bell, AC 610, PC 6, Montgomery

Montgomery County Community College   6-CC
  340 DEKALB PIKE 19422   641-6560

Boiling Springs, AC 717, PC 4, Cumberland
South Middleton SD, 4 FORGE RD 17007   4-11111   258-6484
  Robert Miller, supt.
JSHS, 4 FORGE RD 17007   3-00111   258-6484
  Stephen Andrejack, prin.

Boothwyn, AC 215, PC 6, Delaware
Chichester SD, PO BOX 2100 19061   5-11111   485-6881
  Salvatore Illuzzi, supt.
Chichester HS   4-00011
  3333 CHICHESTER AVE 19061   485-6881
  Robert Di Nicola, prin.
Chichester MS   3-00100
  925 MEETINGHOUSE RD 19061   485-6881
  Barbara Kenney, prin.

Boswell, AC 814, PC 4, Somerset
North Star SD, 1200 MORRIS AVE 15531   4-11111   629-5631
  Wallace Berkebile, supt.
North Star HS, 400 OHIO ST 15531   2-00111   629-6651
  J. Pat Terlingo, prin.

Boyertown, AC 215, PC 5, Berks
Boyertown Area SD   6-11111
  911 MONTGOMERY AVE 19512   367-6031
  Alan Fager, supt.
Boyertown Area SHS   4-00001
  4TH AND MONROE ST 19512   369-7435
  Richard Gross, prin.
Boyertown Area JHS West   3-00110
  200 S MADISON ST 19512   369-7471
  Thomas Blocher, prin.
  Other Schools — See Gilbertsville

Bradford, AC 814, PC 5, McKean
Bradford Area SD, PO BOX 375 16701   5-11111   362-3841
  Maureen O'Mara, supt.
Bradford Area HS   3-00011
  81 INTERSTATE PKY 16701   362-3845
  David Sapala, prin.
Fretz JHS, 140 LORANA AVE 16701   2-00100   362-3500
  Terrance Hoover, prin.

Bradford Central Christian HS   2-00111
   450 W WASHINGTON ST 16701   362-3815
   Fr. McGee, prin.
Bradford Regional Medical Center   HSP
   116 INTERSTATE PKY 16701   362-8292
University of Pittsburgh at Bradford   3-UC
   300 CAMPUS DR 16701   362-7555

Bridgeville, AC 412, PC 6, Allegheny
Chartiers Valley SD
   Supt. — See Pittsburgh
Chartiers Valley HS   3-00011
   50 THOMS RUN RD 15017   429-2241
   Michael Bonacci, prin.

Bristol, AC 215, PC 7, Bucks
Bristol Borough SD   4-11111
   420 BUCKLEY ST 19007   781-1010
   Michael McCool, supt.
Bristol JSHS, 1801 WILSON AVE 19007   3-00111
   (—), prin.   781-1030

Bristol Township SD   6-11111
   800 COATES AVE 19007   943-3200
   Richard Reilly, supt.
Roosevelt JHS   3-00110
   1001 NEW RODGERS RD 19007   788-0436
   George Shissler, prin.
Other Schools – See Fairless Hills, Levittown

Pennco Tech   3-CC
   3815 OTTER ST 19007   824-3200

Brockway, AC 814, PC 4, Jefferson
Brockway Area SD, 95 NORTH ST 15824   4-11111
   Stephen Zarlinski, supt.   265-8411
Brockway Area JSHS   3-00111
   100 ALEXANDER ST 15824   265-8414
   H. Shaffer, prin.

Brodheadsville, AC 717, PC 4, Monroe
Pleasant Valley SD, RTE 115 18322   5-11111
   Kenneth Reid, supt.   992-5711
Pleasant Valley HS   3-00011
   ROUTE 209 18322   992-7178
   Angelo Senese, prin.
Pleasant Valley MS   3-00100
   ROUTE 115 18322   992-7688
   Donald Rinker, prin.

Brookville, AC 814, PC 5, Jefferson
Brookville Area SD   4-11111
   PO BOX 479 15825   849-8372
   John Grottenthaler, supt.
Brookville Area JSHS, JENKS ST 15825   3-00111
   Herbert McConnell, prin.   849-8372

Broomall, AC 610, PC 7, Delaware
Marple-Newtown SD
   Supt. — See Newtown Square
Paxon Hollow MS   3-00100
   815 PAXON HOLLOW RD 19008   359-4320
   Robert Pittman, prin.

RETS Education Center   4-CC
   2641 W CHESTER PIKE 19008   353-7630

Brownstown, AC 717, PC 3, Cambria
Area Vocational Technical SD
   Supt. — See Harrisburg
Lancaster County AVTS-Brownstown   Vo Tech
   PO BOX 519 17508   859-1111
   Robert Burchfield, prin.

Brownsville, AC 412, PC 5, Fayette
Brownsville Area SD
   Supt. — See Grindstone
Brownsville Area HS   3-00011
   1300 BRASHEAR AVE 15417   785-8200
   John Mazzocco, prin.

Bryn Athyn, AC 215, PC 4, Montgomery

Academy of the New Church-Boys   2-00011
   PO BOX 278 19009   947-4200
   Dudley Davis, prin.
Academy of the New Church College   1-UC
   PO BOX 278 19009   947-4200
Academy of the New Church-Girls   1-00011
   PO BOX 278 19009   947-4200
   Gloria Wetzel, prin.

Bryn Mawr, AC 610, PC 5, Montgomery

American College   8-UC
   270 S BRYN MAWR AVE 19010   526-1000
Baldwin S   2-11111
   701 MONTGOMERY AVE 19010   525-2700
   Blair Stambaugh, prin.
Bryn Mawr College   4-UC
   101 N MERION AVE 19010   526-5000
Bryn Mawr Hospital   HSP
   130 S BRYN MAWR AVE 19010   526-3010
Country Day School of the Sacred Heart   2-11111
   480 S BRYN MAWR AVE 19010   527-3915
   Sr. Anita MacDonald, prin.
Harcum Junior College 19010   3-CC
      525-4100
Shipley S, 814 YARROW ST 19010   3-11111
      525-4300

Buckingham, AC 215, PC 4, Bucks
Central Bucks SD
   Supt. — See Doylestown

Central Bucks SHS-East   4-00001
   HOLICONG & ANDERSON RDS 18912   794-7481
   A. Joseph Jennelle, prin.
Holicong MS, PO BOX 426 18912   3-00110
   Louis White, prin.   794-7434

Burgettstown, AC 412, PC 4, Washington
Burgettstown Area SD   4-11111
   99 MAIN ST 15021   947-3324
   William Price, supt.
JSHS, 99 MAIN ST 15021   3-00111
   Constance Gottardi, prin.   947-3324

Butler, AC 412, PC 7, Butler
Area Vocational Technical SD
   Supt. — See Harrisburg
Butler County AVTS   Vo Tech
   161 NEW CASTLE RD 16001   282-0735
   Donald Drake, prin.

Butler Area SD   6-11111
   167 NEW CASTLE RD 16001   287-8721
   Robert Paserba, supt.
Butler Area SHS   4-00001
   165 NEW CASTLE RD 16001   287-8721
   Richard Adams, prin.
Butler Area Inter. HS   4-00010
   551 FAIRGROUND HILL RD 16001   287-8721
   Michael Strutt, prin.
Butler Area JHS, 225 E NORTH ST 16001   4-00100
   Vincent Burke, prin.   287-8721

Butler County Community College   5-CC
   PO BOX 1203 16003   287-8711

Cairnbrook, AC 814, PC 4, Somerset
Shade-Central CSD, PO BOX 7 15924   3-11111
   Hubert Donahue, supt.   754-4648
Shade JSHS, PO BOX 7 15924   2-00111
   Joseph Renzi, prin.   754-4648

California, AC 412, PC 6, Washington
California Area SD   4-11111
   750 ORCHARD ST 15419   938-2511
   Frank Ameruoso, supt.
Other Schools – See Coal Center

California University of Pennsylvania   6-UC
   3RD STREET 15419   938-4000

Cambridge Springs, AC 814, PC 4, Crawford
Penncrest SD
   Supt. — See Saegertown
JSHS, 698 VENANGO AVE 16403   3-00111
   Rob Englebert, prin.   398-4631

Camp Hill, AC 717, PC 6, Cumberland
Camp Hill SD   3-11111
   2627 CHESTNUT ST 17011   763-5120
   William Freed, supt.
JSHS, 100 S 24TH ST 17011   2-00111
   C. Richard Brandt, prin.   763-5103

West Shore SD
   Supt. — See New Cumberland
Cedar Cliff HS, 1301 CARLISLE RD 17011   3-00011
   Michael Murphy, prin.   737-8654
Allen MS, 4225 GETTYSBURG RD 17011   3-00100
   James Carter, prin.   761-1500

Computer Learning Network   2-CS
   1110 FERNWOOD AVE 17011   761-1481
Holy Spirit Hospital   HSP
   505 N 21ST ST 17011   763-2106
Trinity HS   2-00111
   3601 SIMPSON FERRY RD 17011   761-1116
   Sr. Francine Gagne, prin.

Canonsburg, AC 412, PC 6, Washington
Area Vocational Technical SD
   Supt. — See Harrisburg
Western AVTS, RR 1 BOX 178A 15317   Vo Tech
   Dean Karns, prin.   746-2890

Canon-McMillan SD   5-11111
   1 N JEFFERSON AVE 15317   746-2940
   Bruce Bovard, supt.
Canon-McMillan HS   4-00011
   0 ELM STREET EXT 15317   745-1400
   Eugene Buchleitner, prin.
MS, 25 E COLLEGE ST 15317   3-00100
   Denise Sedlacek, prin.   745-9030
Other Schools – See Mc Donald

Canton, AC 717, PC 4, Bradford
Canton Area SD, 139 E MAIN ST 17724   4-11111
   Richard Neff, supt.   673-3191
JSHS, 139 E MAIN ST 17724   3-00111
   William Krause, prin.   673-5134

Carbondale, AC 717, PC 7, Lackawanna
Carbondale Area SD   4-11111
   101 BROOKLYN ST 18407   876-1740
   Martin Lawler, supt.
Carbondale Area JSHS   3-00111
   100 BROOKLYN ST 18407   282-4500
   Paul Kaczmarcik, prin.

Sacred Heart HS, 44 S CHURCH ST 18407   2-00111
   Sr. Theresa Dougherty, prin.   282-2790

Carlisle, AC 717, PC 7, Cumberland
Carlisle Area SD, 623 W PENN ST 17013   6-11111
   Gerald Fowler, supt.   240-6800

Carlisle Area HS, 723 W PENN ST 17013   3-00011
   Randall Drake, prin.   240-6855
Lamberton MS   3-00100
   777 S HANOVER ST 17013   240-6760
   Edward Plocki, prin.
Wilson MS   3-00100
   900 WAGGONERS GAP RD 17013   240-6740
   Wilfred Brousse, prin.

Carlisle Hospital   HSP
   PO BOX 310 17013   245-5440
Dickinson College   4-UC
   PO BOX 1773 17013   243-5121
Dickinson School of Law   3-UC
   150 S COLLEGE ST 17013   243-4611
Gleim Technical Institute   2-CS
   200 S SPRING GARDEN ST 17013   800-922-8399

Carmichaels, AC 412, PC 3, Greene
Carmichaels Area SD   4-11111
   225 N VINE ST 15320 – Jim Zalar, supt.   966-5045
Carmichaels Area SHS   2-00001
   300 W GREENE ST 15320   966-5046
   Patrick Sherlock, prin.
Carmichaels Area JHS   2-00110
   300 W GREENE ST 15320   966-5047
   Patrick Sherlock, prin.

Carnegie, AC 412, PC 6, Allegheny
Carlynton SD, 435 KINGS HWY 15106   4-11111
   James Johnston, supt.   429-2500
Carlynton JSHS, 435 KINGS HWY 15106   3-00111
   Fred Usher, prin.   429-2511

Catasauqua, AC 215, PC 6, Lehigh
Catasauqua Area SD   4-11111
   201 N 14TH ST 18032   264-5571
   Charles D'Amuso, supt.
HS, 850 PINE ST 18032   3-00111
   Frederick Hackett, prin.   264-0506
Lincoln MS   3-01100
   330 HOWERTOWN RD 18032   264-4341
   Frank Snyder, prin.

Catawissa, AC 717, PC 4, Columbia
Southern Columbia Area SD   4-11111
   RR 2 BOX 372B 17820   356-2331
   Bryan Balavage, supt.
Southern Columbia Area JSHS   3-00111
   RR 2 BOX 372A 17820   356-2331
   Morris Terizzi, prin.

Center Valley, AC 215, PC 3, Lehigh
Southern Lehigh SD   4-11111
   5775 MAIN ST 18034   282-3121
   Paula Fantaski, supt.
Southern Lehigh HS   3-00011
   5800 MAIN ST 18034   282-1421
   John Squarcia, prin.
Southern Lehigh MS   2-00100
   3715 PRESTON LN 18034   282-3700
   John Yeager, prin.

Allentown College of St. Frances de Sale   4-UC
   2755 STATION AVE 18034   282-1100

Chalfont, AC 215, PC 5, Bucks
Central Bucks SD
   Supt. — See Doylestown
Unami MS, 160 MOYER RD 18914   3-00110
   David Spahr, prin.   822-3317

Chambersburg, AC 717, PC 7, Franklin
Area Vocational Technical SD
   Supt. — See Harrisburg
Franklin County AVTS   Vo Tech
   2463 LOOP RD 17201   263-9033
   Dalton Paul, prin.

Chambersburg Area SD   6-11111
   511 S 6TH ST 17201   263-9281
   Edwin Sponseller, supt.
Chambersburg Area SHS   4-00001
   511 S 6TH ST 17201 – P. Rearick, prin.   261-3328
Chambersburg Area MS   4-00100
   1151 E MCKINLEY ST 17201   261-3385
   Dana Baker, prin.
Faust JHS, 1957 SCOTLAND AVE 17201   3-00110
   Rick Keller, prin.   261-3369

Chambersburg Hospital   HSP
   112 N 7TH ST 17201   267-7138
Cumberland Valley Christian S   2-11111
   600 MILLER ST 17201   264-4869
Shalom Christian Academy   2-11111
   126 SOCIAL ISLAND RD 17201   375-2223
Wilson College   3-UC
   1015 PHILADELPHIA AVE 17201   264-4141

Charleroi, AC 412, PC 6, Washington
Area Vocational Technical SD
   Supt. — See Harrisburg
Mon Valley AVTS   Vo Tech
   GUTTMAN AVE 15022   489-9581
   Bradley Deicas, prin.

Charleroi SD, 100 FECSEN DR 15022   4-11111
   Donald Celaschi, supt.   483-3509
Charlerio Area HS   3-00011
   100 FECSEN DR 15022   483-3573
   Thomas Hisiro, prin.
Charleroi Area MS   2-00100
   100 FECSEN DR 15022   483-3600
   Joseph Ritacco, prin.

Chester, AC 610, PC 8, Delaware
Chester-Upland SD — 6-11111
1720 MELROSE AVE 19013 — 447-3600
JoAnn Manning, supt.
HS, 20 W 9TH ST 19013 — 4-00011
Robert Morgan, prin. — 447-3772
Pulaski MS, 2820 W 7TH ST 19013 — 3-00100
Howard Grider, prin. — 447-3777
Showalter MS, 1000 W 10TH ST 19013 — 3-00100
John Brown, prin. — 447-3650
Smedley MS, 1701 UPLAND ST 19013 — 3-00100
Dexter Davis, prin. — 447-3660

Crozer-Chester Medical Center — HSP
401 W 15TH ST 19013 — 447-2000
Delaware County Institute of Training — 2-CS
615 AVENUE OF THE STATES 19013 — 874-1888
Sacred Heart Medical Center — HSP
9TH & WILSON ST 19013 — 494-0700
Widener University — 6-UC
700 E 14TH ST 19013 — 499-4000

Cheswick, AC 412, PC 4, Allegheny
Allegheny Valley SD, PEARL AVE 15024 — 4-11111
Ronald Wasilak, supt. — 274-5300
Other Schools – See Springdale

Cheswick Christian Academy — 2-11111
1407 PITTSBURGH ST 15024 — 274-4846

Cheyney, AC 215, PC 3, Delaware

Cheyney University of Pennsylvania — 4-UC
PO BOX 200 19319 — 399-2000

Clairton, AC 412, PC 6, Allegheny
Area Vocational Technical SD
Supt. — See Harrisburg
Steel Center AVTS — Vo Tech
565 N LEWIS RUN RD 15025 — 469-3200
Andrew D'Alesandro, prin.

Clairton CSD, 501 WADDELL AVE 15025 — 4-11111
Carmen Sarnicola, supt. — 233-3717
JSHS, 501 WADDELL AVE 15025 — 4-00111
Patrick Risha, prin. — 233-9200

West Jefferson Hills SD
Supt. — See Pittsburgh
Jefferson HS — 3-00011
310 OLD CLAIRTON RD 15025 — 655-8610
James Collins, prin.

Claridge, AC 412, PC 4, Westmoreland
Penn-Trafford SD
Supt. — See Harrison City
Penn MS, PO BOX 368 15623 — 2-00100
Ronald Darragh, prin. — 744-4431

Clarion, AC 814, PC 6, Clarion
Clarion Area SD — 4-11111
800 BOUNDARY ST 16214 — 226-6110
William Kaufman, supt.
Clarion Area JSHS — 2-00111
219 LIBERTY ST 16214 — 226-8112
Thomas Shirey, prin.

Clarion University of Pennsylvania — 6-UC
840 WOOD ST 16214 — 226-2000

Clarks Summit, AC 717, PC 6, Lackawanna
Abington Heights SD — 5-11111
218 E GROVE ST 18411 — 586-2511
Elvin LaCoe, supt.
Abington Heights HS — 4-00011
222 NOBLE RD 18411 — 586-2511
Peter Smith, prin.
Abington Heights MS, RR 4 18411 — 4-01100
Edward Kairis, prin. — 586-1281

Baptist Bible College of Pennsylvania — 3-UC
538 VENARD RD 18411 — 587-1172
Baptist HS, 660 GRIFFIN POND RD 18411 — 2-00111
— 587-1545

Claysburg, AC 814, PC 4, Blair
Claysburg-Kimmel SD — 4-11111
BEDFORD ST 16625 — 239-5141
James O'Harrow, supt.
Claysburg-Kimmel JSHS — 2-00111
BEDFORD ST 16625 — 239-5141
Robert Cunningham, prin.

Claysville, AC 412, PC 3, Washington
McGuffey SD, PO BOX 431 15323 — 5-11111
Frank Zito, supt. — 663-7745
McGuffey HS, RR 1 BOX 219 15323 — 3-00011
James Tershel, prin. — 948-3328
McGuffey MS, RR 1 BOX 219 15323 — 3-00100
Kevin Kucherawy, prin. — 948-3323

Clearfield, AC 814, PC 6, Clearfield
Area Vocational Technical SD
Supt. — See Harrisburg
Clearfield County AVTS — Vo Tech
RR 1 BOX 5 16830 — 765-5308
Terry Horton, prin.

Clearfield Area SD — 5-11111
PO BOX 710 16830 — 765-5511
Patricia Smith, supt.
Clearfield Area JSHS — 4-00111
PO BOX 910 16830 — 765-2401
Timothy Meckey, prin.

Clearfield Alli Christian S — 2-11111
RR 2 BOX 257 16830 — 765-0216
Clearfield Hospital — 2-HSP
PO BOX 992 16830 — 765-5341
Lock Haven University-Clearfield Campus — 2-CC
119 BYERS ST 16830 — 765-0616

Clymer, AC 412, PC 4, Indiana
Penns Manor Area SD, RR 2 15728 — 4-11111
Edward Meshanko, supt. — 254-4332
Penns Manor Area JSHS, RR 2 15728 — 3-00111
Edward Federinko, prin. — 254-4332

Calvary Baptist Academy — 2-11111
RR 1 BOX 636 15728 — 254-2140

Coal Center, AC 412, PC 2, Washington
California Area SD
Supt. — See California
California Area HS, RR 1 15423 — 2-00011
Charles Geyer, prin. — 785-4202

Coal Township, AC 717, PC 99, Northumberland

Our Lady of Lourdes Regional HS — 2-00011
2001 CLINTON AVE 17866 — 644-0375
Sr. Rita O'Leary, prin.

Coatesville, AC 610, PC 7, Chester
Area Vocational Technical SD
Supt. — See Harrisburg
Center For Arts & Technology-Brandywine — Vo Tech
1635 E LINCOLN HWY 19320 — 384-1585
Ronald Dutton, prin.

Coatesville Area SD — 6-11111
1515 E LINCOLN HWY 19320 — 383-7900
Louis Laurento, supt.
Coatesville Area SHS — 3-00001
1445 E LINCOLN HWY 19320 — 383-3730
Paul Chenger, prin.
IS, 351 KERSEY ST 19320 — 2-00100
Albert Bullock, prin. — 383-3740
North Brandywine MS — 3-00100
200 REECEVILLE RD 19320 — 383-3745
Jerome Smith, prin.
Coatesville Intermediate HS — 4-00010
1425 E LINCOLN HWY 19320 — 383-3735
William Brunson, prin.
South Brandywine MS — 3-00100
RR 3 BOX 121 19320 — 383-3750
Howard Simon, prin.

Brandywine Hospital — HSP
201 REECEVILLE RD 19320 — 383-9000
Lan-Chester Christian S — 2-11111
200 AIRPORT RD 19320 — 383-5784

Cochranton, AC 814, PC 4, Crawford
Crawford Central SD
Supt. — See Meadville
JSHS, PO BOX 127 16314 — 2-00111
Don Wigton, prin. — 425-7421

Cocolamus, AC 717, PC 1, Juniata
Juniata County SD
Supt. — See Mifflintown
East Juniata JSHS, PO BOX 60 17014 — 3-00111
Ray R. Baker, prin. — 463-2111

Collegeville, AC 610, PC 5, Montgomery
Perkiomen Valley SD — 4-11111
3 IRON BRIDGE DR 19426 — 489-8506
Richard Devaney, supt.
Other Schools – See Graterford

Spring-Ford Area SD — 5-11111
199 BECHTEL RD 19426 — 489-1666
Edwin Coyle, supt.
Other Schools – See Royersford

Ursinus College — 4-UC
601 E MAIN ST 19426 — 489-4111

Columbia, AC 717, PC 7, Lancaster
Columbia Borough SD — 4-11111
45 N 9TH ST 17512 – Jon Rednak, supt. — 684-2283
JSHS, 901 IRONVILLE PIKE 17512 — 3-00111
Charles Coombs, prin. — 684-7500

Commodore, AC 412, PC 2, Indiana
Purchase Line SD — 4-11111
RR 1 BOX 374 15729 — 254-4311
Dwight Brocious, supt.
Purchase Line JSHS — 3-00111
RR 1 BOX 374 15729 — 254-4312
Stanley Bem, prin.

Concordville, AC 215, PC 3, Delaware
Garnet Valley SD, PO BOX 233 19331 — 4-11111
Anthony Costello, supt. — 459-7733
Garnet Valley HS, PO BOX 233 19331 — 3-00011
Kathie Estock, prin. — 459-7745
Garnet Valley MS, PO BOX 233 19331 — 2-00100
Joseph Bruton, prin. — 459-7732

Confluence, AC 814, PC 3, Somerset
Turkeyfoot Valley Area SD — 3-11111
RR 1 BOX 78 15424 — 395-3621
Ronald Keefer, supt.
Turkeyfoot Valley Area JSHS — 2-00111
RR 1 BOX 78 15424 — 395-3621
Gary Greeley, prin.

Conneaut Lake, AC 814, PC 3, Crawford
Conneaut SD
Supt. — See Linesville
JSHS, RR 4 BOX 1144 16316 — 3-00111
C. Deemer, prin. — 382-5315

Conneautville, AC 814, PC 3, Crawford
Conneaut SD
Supt. — See Linesville
Conneaut Valley JSHS — 2-00111
RR 3 BOX 330A 16406 — 587-2091
Sandra McArdle, prin.

Connellsville, AC 412, PC 6, Fayette
Area Vocational Technical SD
Supt. — See Harrisburg
North Fayette County AVTS — Vo Tech
720 LOCUST ST 15425 — 626-0236
Kenneth Parker, prin.

Connellsville Area SD — 6-11111
125 N 7TH ST 15425 — 628-3300
Gerald Browell, supt.
Connellsville Area SHS — 4-00001
201 FALCON DR 15425 — 628-1350
Stephen Zavatsky, prin.
Connellsville JHS East — 4-00110
710 LOCUST ST 15425 — 628-8910
Robert McLuckey, prin.
Connellsville JHS West — 2-00110
215 FALLS AVE 15425 — 628-4497
John Shavel, prin.

Geibel HS, 611 E CRAWFORD AVE 15425 — 2-00011
Reynold Peduzzi, prin. — 628-5600

Conshohocken, AC 610, PC 6, Montgomery

Archbishop Kennedy HS — 2-00011
1 SAINT MATTHEWS AVE 19428 — 828-8606
William McCusker, prin.

Coraopolis, AC 412, PC 6, Allegheny
Cornell SD — 3-11111
1099 MAPLE STREET EXT 15108 — 264-5010
Orlando Falcione, supt.
Cornell JSHS — 2-00111
1099 MAPLE STREET EXT 15108 — 264-5012
Dennis Johnson, prin.
Montour SD, 90 GRANT ST 15108 — 5-11111
Joseph Karlik, supt. — 778-1060
Williams JHS — 2-00100
PORTERS HOLLOW ROAD 15108 — 778-1060
Ronald Oliver, prin.
Other Schools – See Mc Kees Rocks

Moon Area SD — 5-11111
1407 BEERS SCHOOL RD 15108 — 264-9440
Donald Deep, supt.
Moon HS — 3-00011
904 BEAVER GRADE RD 15108 — 262-9040
David Hays, prin.
Moon MS — 3-00100
1407 BEERS SCHOOL RD 15108 — 262-4140
Ruth Walsh, prin.

Our Lady of Sacred Heart HS — 2-00011
1500 WOODCREST AVE 15108 — 264-5140
Sr. Christopher Moore, prin.
Robert Morris College — 6-UC
NARROWS RUN RD 15108 — 262-8200

Corry, AC 814, PC 6, Erie
Corry Area SD, 800 E SOUTH ST 16407 — 5-11111
John McCracken, supt. — 664-4677
JSHS, 534 E PLEASANT ST 16407 — 4-00111
Harry Beil, prin. — 665-8297

Coudersport, AC 814, PC 5, Potter
Coudersport Area SD — 3-11111
698 DWIGHT ST 16915 — 274-9480
Edward Goulding, supt.
Coudersport Area JSHS — 2-00111
698 DWIGHT ST 16915 — 274-8500
Russell Cutshall, prin.

Cresson, AC 814, PC 4, Cambria
Penn-Cambria SD, 201 6TH ST 16630 — 4-11111
Russell Strange, supt. — 886-8121
Penn-Cambria SHS — 3-00001
401 LINDEN AVE 16630 — 886-8188
Milan Gjurich, prin.
Other Schools – See Gallitzin

Mt. Aloysius College — 4-UC
1 COLLEGE DR 16630 — 886-4131

Curwensville, AC 814, PC 5, Clearfield
Curwensville Area SD — 4-11111
650 BEACH ST 16833 — 236-1101
Robert Dreibelbis, supt.
Curwensville Area JSHS — 3-00111
650 BEACH ST 16833 — 236-1100
Timothy Glunt, prin.

Dallas, AC 717, PC 5, Luzerne
Dallas SD, PO BOX 2000 18612 — 4-11111
Gerald Wycallis, supt. — 675-5201
HS, CONYNGHAM AVE 18612 — 3-00011
Frank Galicki, prin. — 675-5201
MS, CONYNGHAM AVE 18612 — 3-00100
Anthony Martinelli, prin. — 675-5201

College Misericordia   4-UC
301 LAKE ST 18612   674-6400

Dallastown, AC 717, PC 5, York
Dallastown Area SD   5-11111
700 NEW SCHOOL LN 17313   244-4021
A. Neil Harvey, supt.
Dallastown Area HS   4-00011
700 NEW SCHOOL LN 17313   244-4021
G. Jones, supt.
Dallastown Area MS   4-00100
700 NEW SCHOOL LN 17313   244-4021
Robert Krantz, prin.

Danville, AC 717, PC 6, Montour
Danville Area SD   5-11111
600 WALNUT ST 17821   275-7575
Richard Martz, supt.
Danville Area HS   3-00011
600 WALNUT ST 17821   275-4111
David Price, prin.
Danville Area MS   3-00100
120 NORTHUMBERLAND ST 17821   275-0114
Thomas Farr, prin.

Geisinger Medical Center   HSP
N ACADEMY AVE 17822   271-6276
St. Cyril Academy   1-00011
580 RAILROAD ST 17821   275-1505
Sr. Donna Marie, prin.

Darby, AC 610, PC 7, Delaware
William Penn SD
Supt. — See Yeadon
Penn Wood West JHS   2-00110
121 SUMMIT ST 19023   586-1804
Salvatore Salamone, prin.

Davidsville, AC 814, PC 4, Somerset
Conemaugh Township Area SD   4-11111
PO BOX 407 15928   479-7575
Richard Watson, supt.
Conemaugh Twp. Area JSHS   3-00111
PO BOX 407 15928   479-4014
Jerry Davitch, prin.

Dayton, AC 814, PC 3, Armstrong
Armstrong SD
Supt. — See Ford City
Dayton JSHS, COLLEGE AVE 16222   2-00111
Herbert Crawford, prin.   257-8222

Denver, AC 215, PC 5, Lancaster
Cocalico SD, 800 S 4TH ST 17517   4-11111
William Worley, supt.   267-1413
Cocalico HS, 800 S 4TH ST 17517   3-00011
Sylvan Hershey, prin.   267-1421
Cocalico MS, S 6TH ST 17517   3-00100
David Davies, prin.   267-1471

Derry, AC 412, PC 5, Westmoreland
Derry Area SD, RR 1 BOX 169 15627   5-11111
Robert Critchfield, supt.   694-8383
Derry Area SHS, RR 1 BOX 169 15627   3-00001
C. Shirley, prin.   694-2780
Derry Area JHS, RR 1 BOX 169 15627   3-00110
Richard Burchill, prin.   694-8231

Devault, AC 215, PC 2, Chester
Great Valley SD, PO BOX 617 19432   5-11111
Rita Jones, supt.   889-2100
Other Schools – See Malvern

Devon, AC 610, PC 6, Chester

Devereux-Edward L French Center in PA   2-HND
119 OLD LANCASTER RD 19333   964-3269
Devereux Foundation in Pennsylvania   HND
PO BOX 400 19333   964-3000
Devon Preparatory HS   2-00111
363 N VALLEY FORGE RD 19333   688-7337
Fr. Callen, prin.

Dillsburg, AC 717, PC 4, York
Northern York County SD   5-11111
149 S BALTIMORE ST 17019   432-8691
John Allison, supt.
Northern HS   3-00011
655 S BALTIMORE ST 17019   432-8691
R. Dietrich, prin.
Northern MS   3-00100
650 S BALTIMORE ST 17019   432-8691
Ashley Steffy, prin.

Dimock, AC 717, PC 2, Susquehanna
Area Vocational Technical SD
Supt. — See Harrisburg
Susquehanna County AVTS   Vo Tech
PO BOX 100 18816   278-9229
Charles Rushefski, prin.

Elk Lake SD, PO BOX 100 18816   4-11111
Richard Serfass, supt.   278-1106
Elk Lake JSHS, PO BOX 100 18816   3-00111
C. Rushefski, prin.   278-1106

Douglassville, AC 215, PC 4, Berks
Daniel Boone Area SD   4-11111
1445 E MAIN ST 19518   582-6140
Lewis Cuthbert, supt.
Other Schools – See Birdsboro

Dover, AC 717, PC 4, York
Dover Area SD, 0 SCHOOL LN 17315   5-11111
George Severns, supt.   292-3671

Dover Area HS, 0 W CANAL ST 17315   3-00011
John Brill, prin.   292-3671
Dover Area MS   3-00100
4500 INTERMEDIATE AVE 17315   292-3671
Kenneth Walter, prin.

Downingtown, AC 610, PC 6, Chester
Downingtown Area SD   6-11111
122 WALLACE AVE 19335   269-8460
Dan Jones, supt.
SHS, 445 MANOR AVE 19335   4-00001
Edward Spang, prin.   269-4400
JHS, 335 MANOR AVE 19335   3-00110
Joseph Hamelton, prin.   269-8181
Lionville JHS, 50 DEVON DR 19335   4-00110
Walter Kottmeyer, prin.   363-6400

Doylestown, AC 215, PC 6, Bucks
Central Bucks SD   7-11111
315 W STATE ST 18901   345-1400
N. Robert Laws, supt.
Central Bucks SHS-West   4-00001
375 W COURT ST 18901   345-1661
W. Stone, prin.
Lenape MS, 313 W STATE ST 18901   3-00110
Thomas Roberts, prin.   345-0660
Other Schools – See Buckingham, Chalfont

Delaware Valley College   3-UC
ROUTE 202 & NEW BRITAIN RD 18901   345-1500
Doylestown Hospital   HSP
595 W STATE ST 18901   345-2224

Dresher, AC 215, PC 4, Montgomery
Upper Dublin SD   5-11111
530 TWINING RD 19025   576-3293
Clair Brown, supt.
Sandy Run MS, 520 TWINING RD 19025   3-00100
Robert Bortz, prin.   576-3251
Other Schools – See Fort Washington

Drexel Hill, AC 610, PC 8, Delaware
Upper Darby SD, 4611 BOND AVE 19026   6-11111
Joseph Batory, supt.   789-7200
MS, 3001 STATE RD 19026   3-00100
Joseph Galli, prin.   853-4580
Other Schools – See Upper Darby

Archbishop Prendergast HS   4-00011
401 N LANSDOWNE AVE 19026   259-0265
Carol Blair, prin.
Monsignor Bonner HS   3-00011
401 N LANSDOWNE AVE 19026   259-0280
Fr. Denny, prin.

Du Bois, AC 814, PC 6, Clearfield
Du Bois Area SD   5-11111
500 LIBERTY BLVD 15801   371-2700
Michael Ferko, supt.
Du Bois Area HS   4-00011
400 ORIENT AVE 15801   371-8111
David Distler, prin.
Du Bois Area JHS   3-00100
404 LIBERTY BLVD 15801   371-0121
A. Sebring, prin.

Central Christian HS   2-00111
200 HOSPITAL AVE 15801   371-3060
Fr. Walk, prin.
Du Bois Business College   3-CC
1 BEAVER DR 15801   371-6920
First Baptist Church Academy   2-11111
MAPLE AVE EXT 15801   371-7395
Pennsylvania State University   3-CC
COLLEGE PLACE 15801   371-2800
Triangle Tech   2-CC
PO BOX 551 15801   371-2090

Duke Center, AC 814, PC 3, McKean
Otto-Eldred SD   3-11111
143 SWEITZER DR 16729   966-3214
Robert Falk, supt.
Otto-Eldred JSHS   2-00111
143 SWEITZER DR 16729   966-3212
John Zinzi, prin.

Duncannon, AC 717, PC 4, Perry
Susquenita SD   4-11111
1725 SCHOOLHOUSE RD 17020   957-2303
Steven Messner, supt.
Susquenita HS   3-00110
1725 SCHOOLHOUSE RD 17020   957-2552
Ray Barner, prin.
Susquenita MS   2-00100
1725 SCHOOLHOUSE RD 17020   957-2303
Ken Viani, prin.

Duncansville, AC 814, PC 4, Blair

Blair County Christian S   2-11111
PO BOX 840 16635   696-3702

Dunmore, AC 717, PC 7, Lackawanna
Dunmore SD   4-11111
QUINCY AVE & WARREN ST 18509   346-2652
Joseph Haggerty, supt.
HS, 300 W WARREN ST 18512   2-00011
Charles Mecca, prin.   346-2043

Bishop O'Hara HS   2-00011
501 E DRINKER ST 18512   346-7541
Sr. Claudette Naylor, prin.

Pennsylvania State University   4-CC
120 RIDGEVIEW DR 18512   963-4757

Duquesne, AC 412, PC 6, Allegheny
Duquesne CSD, 28 S 3RD ST 15110   3-11111
Ronald Mento, supt.   466-5300
JSHS, 28 S 3RD ST 15110   2-00111
Archie Perrin, prin.   466-8130

Dushore, AC 717, PC 3, Sullivan
Sullivan County SD   3-11111
PO BOX 346 18614   928-8194
Jack Shaw, supt.
Other Schools – See Laporte

East Greenville, AC 215, PC 5, Montgomery
Upper Perkiomen SD   5-11111
201 W 5TH ST 18041   679-7961
Nelson Weber, supt.
Upper Perkiomen MS   3-01100
0 JEFFERSON ST 18041   679-6288
Celine Matz, prin.
Other Schools – See Pennsburg

Easton, AC 610, PC 8, Northampton
Area Vocational Technical SD
Supt. — See Harrisburg
Eastern Northampton County AVTS   Vo Tech
5335 KESSLERVILLE RD 18042   258-2857
Joseph Cammarata, prin.

Easton Area SD   6-11111
811 NORTHAMPTON ST 18042   250-2400
William Moloney, supt.
Easton Area SHS   4-00001
2601 WILLIAM PENN HWY 18045   250-2481
Thomas Evans, prin.
Shawnee IS, 1010 ECHO TRL 18040   3-00110
Constance Mazza, prin.   250-2460

Wilson Area SD   4-11111
2040 WASHINGTON BLVD 18042   258-0841
Albert Zarbatany, supt.
Wilson Area HS   3-00011
2200 WASHINGTON BLVD 18042   258-2732
Fred Bartosh, prin.
Lauer MS, 2400 FIRMSTONE ST 18042   3-01100
Dennis Harper, prin.   258-3041

Churchman Business School   2-CC
355 SPRING GARDEN ST 18042   258-5345
Lafayette College   4-UC
0 LAFAYETTE COLLEGE 18042   250-5000
Notre Dame HS, 3417 CHURCH RD 18045   2-00011
Joseph Kramer, prin.   868-1431

East Smithfield, AC 717, PC 3, Bradford
Athens Area SD
Supt. — See Athens
S.R.U. MS, FOURTH & MONROE 18817   2-00100
Paul Hewitt, prin.   596-3171

East Stroudsburg, AC 717, PC 6, Monroe
East Stroudsburg Area SD   5-11111
PO BOX 298 18301   424-8500
John Grogan, supt.
HS, PO BOX 298 18301   3-00011
James Bonner, prin.   424-8471
Lambert IS, 2000 MILFORD RD 18301   3-00100
Patricia Baughman, prin.   424-8430

East Stroudsburg University of PA 18301   6-UC
   424-3545
Notre Dame HS   2-00111
60 SPANGENBURG AVE 18301   421-0466
Jeffrey Lyons, prin.

Ebensburg, AC 814, PC 5, Cambria
Area Vocational Technical SD
Supt. — See Harrisburg
Admiral Peary AVTS   Vo Tech
RR 4 BOX 900 15931   472-6490
Joseph Berdomas, prin.

Central Cambria SD   4-11111
RR 4 BOX 800 15931   472-8870
Joseph Derubis, supt.
Central Cambria HS   3-00011
RR 4 BOX 800 15931   472-8860
Jules Dill, prin.
Central Cambria MS   3-00100
205 W HIGHLAND AVE 15931   472-6505
Thomas Estep, prin.

Bishop Carroll HS, PO BOX 57 15931   2-00011
Charles Koren, prin.   472-7500

Edinboro, AC 814, PC 6, Erie
General McLane SD   5-11111
11771 EDINBORO RD 16412   734-1033
Therese Walter, supt.
McLane HS, 11761 EDINBORO RD 16412   3-00011
Thomas Glover, prin.   734-1602
Parker MS, 11781 EDINBORO RD 16412   3-01100
Patricia Crist, prin.   734-1151

Edinboro University of Pennsylvania   6-UC
16444   732-2000

Elderton, AC 412, PC 2, Armstrong
Armstrong SD
Supt. — See Ford City
JSHS, LYTLE ST 15736   3-00111
Paul Hopkins, prin.   354-2153

Elizabeth, AC 412, PC 4, Allegheny
Elizabeth Forward SD — 5-11111
401 ROCK RUN RD 15037 — 751-9413
Herbert Morgan, supt.
Elizabeth Forward SHS — 3-00001
1000 WEIGLES HILL ST 15037 — 384-5600
Tim Petty, prin.
Elizabeth Forward JHS — 3-00110
401 ROCK RUN RD 15037 — 751-5903
Jay McElravy, prin.

Elizabethtown, AC 717, PC 6, Lancaster
Elizabethtown Area SD — 5-11111
600 E HIGH ST 17022 — 367-1521
Dale Williams, supt.
Elizabethtown Area HS — 3-00011
600 E HIGH ST 17022 — 367-1521
Lawrence Mayes, prin.
Elizabethtown Area MS — 3-00100
600 E HIGH ST 17022 — 367-1521
Gerald Lorson, prin.

Elizabethtown College — 4-UC
1 ALPHA DR 17022 — 367-1151
Mt. Calvary Christian S — 2-11111
629 HOLLY ST 17022 — 367-1649

Elizabethville, AC 717, PC 4, Dauphin
Upper Dauphin Area SD
Supt. — See Lykens
Upper Dauphin Area HS — 2-00011
RR 1 BOX 24 17023 — 362-8181
Dermot Garrett, prin.

Elkins Park, AC 215, PC 5, Montgomery
Cheltenham Township SD — 5-11111
1000 ASHBOURNE RD 19117 — 886-9500
Charles Stefanski, supt.
Other Schools – See Wyncote

Rolling Hill Hospital Diagnostic Center — HSP
60 TOWNSHIP LINE RD 19117 — 663-6365

Elkland, AC 814, PC 4, Tioga
Northern Tioga SD — 5-11111
117 COATES AVE 16920 — 258-5642
James Davis, supt.
JSHS, 110 ELLISON RD 16920 — 2-00111
Gary Miller, prin. — 258-5115
Other Schools – See Tioga, Westfield

Elliottsburg, AC 717, PC 2, Perry
West Perry SD, RR 1 BOX 7A 17024 — 5-11111
Winston Cleland, supt. — 789-3934
West Perry HS, RR 1 17024 — 3-00011
James Zimmerman, prin. — 789-3931
Other Schools – See New Bloomfield

Ellsworth, AC 412, PC 4, Washington
Bentworth SD, PO BOX 610 15331 — 4-11111
Thomas Turnbaugh, supt. — 239-2861
Bentworth MS, S PINE ST 15331 — 2-00100
Edward Palla, prin. — 239-4431
Other Schools – See Bentleyville

Ellwood City, AC 412, PC 6, Lawrence
Ellwood City Area SD — 4-11111
501 CRESCENT AVE 16117 — 752-1591
Francis Keller, supt.
Lincoln JSHS — 4-00111
501 CRESCENT AVE 16117 — 752-1591
Frank Aloi, prin.

Riverside Beaver County SD — 4-11111
RR 2 BOX 4010 16117 — 758-7512
Jennifer Pasuit, supt.
Riverside HS, RR 2 BOX 4010 16117 — 3-00011
D. Barto, prin. — 758-7512
Riverside MS, RR 2 BOX 4010 16117 — 3-01100
J. Meehan, prin. — 758-7512

Elverson, AC 215, PC 2, Chester
Twin Valley SD, RR 3 BOX 52 19520 — 5-11111
Creeden Coulson, supt. — 286-8600
Twin Valley HS, RR 3 BOX 51 19520 — 4-00011
Gary Otto, prin. — 286-8600
Twin Valley MS, RR 3 BOX 53 19520 — 2-00100
Lyle Bliss, prin. — 286-8660

Emmaus, AC 610, PC 7, Lehigh
East Penn SD — 6-11111
640 MACUNGIE AVE 18049 — 967-3101
Alrita Morgan, supt.
SHS, 851 NORTH ST 18049 — 4-00001
Herman Corradetti, prin. — 967-3101
JHS, 660 MACUNGIE AVE 18049 — 3-00110
Robert Misko, prin. — 965-1508
Other Schools – See Macungie

Emporium, AC 814, PC 5, Cameron
Cameron County SD — 4-11111
601 WOODLAND AVE 15834 — 486-3825
Michael Grimone, supt.
Cameron County JSHS — 2-00111
601 WOODLAND AVE 15834 — 486-3774
J. Timothy Kinsler, prin.

Enola, AC 717, PC 6, Cumberland
East Pennsboro Area SD — 4-11111
890 VALLEY ST 17025 — 732-3601
Glenn Zehner, supt.
East Pennsboro Area HS — 3-00011
425 W SHADY LN 17025 — 732-0723
Richard Zerbe, prin.

East Pennsboro Area MS — 3-00100
529 N ENOLA DR 17025 — 732-0771
Keith Voelker, prin.

Ephrata, AC 717, PC 7, Lancaster
Ephrata Area SD, 803 OAK BLVD 17522 — 5-11111
Theodore Soistmann, supt. — 733-1513
HS, 803 OAK BLVD 17522 — 4-00011
Gary Oberly, prin. — 733-1478
MS, 1000 HAMMON AVE 17522 — 3-00100
David Jones, prin. — 733-1468

Erdenheim, AC 215, PC see Flourtown
Springfield Township SD
Supt. — See Oreland
Springfield Twp. HS — 2-00011
1801 PAPER MILL RD 19118 — 233-6035
Joseph Schwartz, prin.

Erie, AC 814, PC 9, Erie
Area Vocational Technical SD
Supt. — See Harrisburg
Erie County AVTS — Vo Tech
8500 OLIVER RD 16509 — 864-0641
Richard Deluca, prin.

Erie CSD, 1511 PEACH ST 16501 — 7-11111
James Barker, supt. — 871-6200
Central HS, 3325 CHERRY ST 16508 — 4-00011
Gerald Mifsud, prin. — 871-6661
East HS, 1151 ATKINS ST 16503 — 3-00011
Helen Jackson, prin. — 871-6567
Strong Vincent HS — 3-00011
1330 W 8TH ST 16502 — 871-6433
Marilyn Whalen, prin.
Roosevelt MS — 3-00100
2300 CRANBERRY ST 16502 — 871-6416
Paul Perowicz, prin.
Wayne MS, 650 EAST AVE 16503 — 3-00100
Donald Feeney, prin. — 871-6657
Wilson MS, 718 E 28TH ST 16504 — 3-00100
Robert Polito, prin. — 871-6501

Iroquois SD, 4231 MORSE ST 16511 — 4-11111
William Konzal, supt. — 899-7641
Iroquois JSHS, 4301 MAIN ST 16511 — 3-00111
Joseph Buzanowski, prin. — 899-7641

Millcreek Township SD — 6-11111
3740 W 26TH ST 16506 — 835-5300
Robert Agnew, supt.
McDowell SHS, 3580 W 38TH ST 16506 — 4-00001
Edward Grzelak, prin. — 835-5403
McDowell Freshman HS — 4-00010
3320 CAUGHEY RD 16506 — 835-5487
Alan Karns, prin.
Westlake MS, 4330 W LAKE RD 16505 — 3-00100
Joseph Cuzzola, prin. — 835-5382
Wilson MS, 900 W 54TH ST 16509 — 3-00100
Donald Douglass, prin. — 835-5569
Other Schools – See Fairview

Wattsburg Area SD
Supt. — See Wattsburg
Seneca HS — 3-00011
10770 WATTSBURG RD 16509 — 825-4250
Albert Leonzi, prin.

Bethel Christian School of Erie — 2-11111
1781 W 38TH ST 16508 — 868-2365
Charles Bllomfield, prin.
Cathedral Prep HS, 225 W 9TH ST 16501 — 3-00011
Joann Mullen, prin. — 453-7737
Erie Business Center — 2-CC
246 W 9TH ST 16501 — 456-7504
Erie Institute of Technology — 2-CC
2221 PENINSULA DR 16506 — 838-2711
Gannon University — 5-UC
109 UNIVERSITY SQ 16541 — 871-7000
Hamot Medical Center — HSP
201 STATE ST 16507 — 870-6000
Mercyhurst College — 4-UC
501 E 38TH ST 16546 — 825-0200
Mercyhurst Prep S — 3-00011
538 E GRANDVIEW BLVD 16504 — 824-2210
Anita Squeglia, prin.
Pennsylvania State University — 4-UC
5091 STATION RD 16563 — 898-6100
St. Vincent Health Center — HSP
232 W 25TH ST 16544 — 452-5675
Thompson's Academies — 3-CS
2908 STATE ST 16508 — 456-6217
Triangle Tech — 2-CC
2000 LIBERTY ST 16502 — 453-6016
Tri-State Business Institute — 2-CS
5757 W 26TH ST 16506 — 838-7673
Villa Maria Academy — 2-00011
2403 W 8TH ST 16505 — 838-2061
Sr. Ann Joint, prin.

Everett, AC 814, PC 4, Bedford
Area Vocational Technical SD
Supt. — See Harrisburg
Bedford-Everett AVTS — Vo Tech
RR 1 BOX 460 15537 — 623-2760
Thomas Wildauer, prin.

Everett Area SD — 4-11111
15 E SOUTH STREET EXT 15537 — 652-9114
Edward Vollbrecht, supt.
JSHS, 12 N RIVER LN 15537 — 3-00111
Joseph Summerville, prin. — 652-9114

Exeter, AC 717, PC 6, Luzerne
Wyoming Area SD, MEMORIAL ST 18643 — 4-11111
Robert Fumanti, supt. — 655-3733
Wyoming Area JSHS — 3-00111
20 MEMORIAL ST 18643 — 655-2836
Paul Melvin, prin.

Exton, AC 610, PC 5, Chester
Area Vocational Technical SD
Supt. — See Harrisburg
Center for Arts and Technology — Vo Tech
150 JAMES HANCE CT 19341 — 524-5000
Alan Slobojan, prin.

Automotive Training Center — 2-CS
114 PICKERING WAY 19341 — 363-6716

Factoryville, AC 717, PC 4, Wyoming
Lackawanna Trail SD — 4-11111
PO BOX 85 18419 — 945-5185
John Micco, supt.
Lackawanna Trail JSHS — 3-00111
PO BOX 85 18419 — 945-5181
Donald Golden, prin.

Fairfield, AC 717, PC 3, Adams
Fairfield Area SD, PO BOX 245 17320 — 3-11111
Carol Saylor, supt. — 642-8525
Fairfield Area HS, PO BOX 245 17320 — 2-00011
Ronald Straley, prin. — 642-8228
Fairfield Area MS — 2-00100
4840 FAIRFIELD RD 17320 — 642-6600
Clifton Vanartsdalen, prin.

Fairless Hills, AC 215, PC 6, Bucks
Area Vocational Technical SD
Supt. — See Harrisburg
Bucks County AVTS — Vo Tech
610 WISTAR RD 19030 — 949-1700
Lamar Snyder, prin.

Bristol Township SD
Supt. — See Bristol
Armstrong JHS, 475 WISTAR RD 19030 — 4-00110
James Mannion, prin. — 945-4940

Pennsbury SD
Supt. — See Fallsington
Pennsbury SHS, 705 HOOD BLVD 19030 — 4-00001
William Katz, prin. — 949-6700
Bair Freshman HS — 4-00010
608 S OLDS BLVD 19030 — 949-6780
Charles Long, prin.

Conwell-Egan HS, 611 WISTAR RD 19030 — 4-00011
Helen Chaykowsky, prin. — 945-6200

Fairview, AC 814, PC 4, Erie
Fairview SD, 7460 MCCRAY RD 16415 — 4-11111
William Stockebrand, supt. — 474-1311
HS, 7460 MCCRAY RD 16415 — 3-00011
Douglas Allen, prin. — 474-1362
Garwood MS, 4967 GARWOOD ST 16415 — 3-01100
Greg Baran, prin. — 474-1342

Millcreek Township SD
Supt. — See Erie
Walnut Creek MS — 3-00100
5901 STERRETTANIA RD 16415 — 835-5700
Kenneth Borland, prin.

Fallsington, AC 215, PC 4, Bucks
Pennsbury SD, 134 YARDLEY AVE 19054 — 6-11111
Matthew Constanzo, supt. — 428-4100
Other Schools – See Fairless Hills, Yardley

Farrell, AC 412, PC 6, Mercer
Farrell Area SD — 4-11111
1600 ROEMER BLVD 16121 — 346-6585
John Sava, supt.
Farrell Area HS — 2-00011
1700 ROEMER BLVD 16121 — 346-6585
Frank Sincek, prin.
Farrell Area MS — 2-00100
1700 ROEMER BLVD 16121 — 346-6585
Thomas Nevant, prin.

Fawn Grove, AC 717, PC 2, York
South Eastern SD, PO BOX 217 17321 — 4-11111
Nicholas Corbo, supt. — 382-4843
Kennard-Dale HS — 3-00011
RR 1 BOX 26 17321 — 382-4871
Marianne Zimmerman, prin.
South Eastern MS, RR 1 BOX 27A 17321 — 3-01100
Bernard Loman, prin. — 382-4851

Feasterville, AC 215, PC 6, Bucks
Neshaminy SD
Supt. — See Langhorne
Poquessing JHS, 300 HEIGHTS LN 19053 — 3-00110
Michael Stanford, prin. — 322-0350

Finleyville, AC 412, PC 2, Washington
Ringgold SD
Supt. — See Monongahela
Finley MS, 6023 ROUTE 88 15332 — 3-00100
Richard Borchilo, prin. — 348-7154

South Hills Christian S — 2-11111
ROUTE 88 15332 — 833-4440

Fishertown, AC 814, PC 3, Bedford
Chestnut Ridge SD, PO BOX 80 15539 — 4-11111
Larry Giovacchini, supt. — 839-4195

Chestnut Ridge MS | 3-01100
PO BOX 80 15539 | 839-4195
James Dull, prin.
Other Schools – See New Paris

Fleetwood, AC 215, PC 5, Berks
Fleetwood Area SD | 4-11111
407 N RICHMOND ST 19522 | 944-9598
George Cooke, supt.
HS, 409 N RICHMOND ST 19522 | 2-00011
Bruce Piker, prin. | 944-7656
MS, 407 N RICHMOND ST 19522 | 2-00100
Ronald Rill, prin. | 944-7634

Flinton, AC 814, PC 2, Cambria
Glendale SD, RR 1 BOX 41D 16640 | 4-11111
Carol Blundell, supt. | 687-4261
Glendale JSHS, RR 1 BOX 41D 16640 | 2-00111
(—), prin. | 687-4261

Flourtown, AC 215, PC 5, Montgomery

Mt. St. Joseph Academy | 3-00011
120 W WISSAHICKON AVE 19031 | 233-3177
Sr. Mary Dacey, prin.

Fogelsville, AC 215, PC 3, Lehigh

Pennsylvania State University | 3-CC
ALLENTOWN CAMPUS 18051 | 285-4811

Folcroft, AC 215, PC 6, Delaware
Area Vocational Technical SD
Supt. — See Harrisburg
Delaware County AVTS-Folcroft | Vo Tech
DELMAR DR & HENDERSON BLVD 19032
Thomas Jakubczyk, prin. | 583-7620

Southeast Delco SD | 5-11111
PO BOX 328 19032 | 522-4300
Stephen Wesley, supt.
Other Schools – See Glenolden, Sharon Hill

Folsom, AC 215, PC 6, Delaware
Ridley SD, 1001 MORTON AVE 19033 | 5-11111
John Cochran, supt. | 534-1900
Ridley HS, 1001 MORTON AVE 19033 | 4-00011
William Del Vescovo, prin. | 237-8034
Other Schools – See Ridley Park

Ford City, AC 412, PC 5, Armstrong
Area Vocational Technical SD
Supt. — See Harrisburg
Lenape AVTS | Vo Tech
2215 CHAPLIN AVE 16226 | 763-7116
Raymond Rogalski, prin.

Armstrong SD, 410 MAIN ST 16226 | 6-11111
John Invernizzi, supt. | 763-7161
JSHS, 4TH AVE 16226 | 4-00011
Joseph Mauro, prin. | 763-3171
Other Schools – See Dayton, Elderton, Kittanning,
Rural Valley

Forest City, AC 717, PC 4, Susquehanna
Forest City Regional SD | 3-11111
100 SUSQUEHANNA ST 18421 | 785-3121
Michael De Stefano, supt.
Forest City Regional JSHS | 2-00111
100 SUSQUEHANNA ST 18421 | 785-3121
Michael Lisowski, prin.

Fort Washington, AC 215, PC 5, Montgomery
Upper Dublin SD
Supt. — See Dresher
Upper Dublin HS | 4-00011
800 LOCH ALSH AVE 19034 | 643-8880
Robert Field, prin.

Germantown Academy | 3-11111
340 MORRIS RD 19034 | 646-3300

Foxburg, AC 412, PC 2, Clarion
Allegheny-Clarion Valley SD | 4-11111
PO BOX 345 16036 | 659-5820
Patrick Lukasavich, supt.
Allegheny-Clarion Valley JSHS | 2-00111
PO BOX 345 16036 | 659-4661
Richard Varrati, prin.

Frackville, AC 717, PC 5, Schuylkill
Area Vocational Technical SD
Supt. — See Harrisburg
Schuylkill County AVTS-North | Vo Tech
101 TECHNOLOGY DR 17931 | 874-1034
(—), prin.

Franklin, AC 814, PC 6, Venango
Franklin Area SD, 417 13TH ST 16323 | 5-11111
Gene Rexford, supt. | 432-8917
Franklin Area HS | 3-00011
RR 4 BOX 325 16323 | 432-2121
Ronald Paranick, prin.
Franklin Area MS | 2-00100
RR 4 BOX 325 16323 | 432-2224
James Ruby, prin.

Valley Grove SD, 429 WILEY AVE 16323 | 4-11111
Charles Cagno, supt. | 432-4919
Rocky Grove JSHS | 3-00111
403 ROCKY GROVE AVE 16323 | 437-3759
Raymond Brown, prin.

Franklin Hospital | HSP
1 SPRUCE ST 16323 | 437-7000

Fredericksburg, AC 717, PC 4, Lebanon
Northern Lebanon SD | 4-11111
PO BOX 100 17026 | 865-2117
Wayne Martin, supt.
Northern Lebanon HS | 4-00011
PO BOX 100 17026 | 865-2117
Daniel Sidelnick, prin.
Northern Lebanon JHS | 3-00100
PO BOX 100 17026 | 865-2117
Kenneth Weaver, prin.

Fredericktown, AC 412, PC 4, Washington
Bethlehem-Center SD | 4-11111
RR 1 BOX 28C 15333 | 377-2328
Thomas Knight, supt.
Bethlehem-Center SHS | 2-00001
RR 1 BOX 28A 15333 | 377-2180
Thomas Katruska, prin.
Bethlehem-Center JHS | 2-00110
RR 1 BOX 28B 15333 – E. Renko, prin. | 377-0136

Freedom, AC 412, PC 4, Beaver
Ambridge Area SD
Supt. — See Ambridge
Ambridge Area JHS, 1ST ST 15042 | 3-00100
Richard Wellendorf, prin. | 869-2146

Freedom Area SD, 1701 8TH AVE 15042 | 4-11111
Robert Cercone, supt. | 775-7644
Freedom Area HS, 1701 8TH AVE 15042 | 3-00011
William Hewko, prin. | 775-7400
Freedom Area MS, 1701 8TH AVE 15042 | 3-01100
Anthony Mullen, prin. | 775-7641

Freeland, AC 717, PC 5, Luzerne
Hazleton Area SD
Supt. — See Hazleton
JHS, ROUTE 940 & HAZLE ST 18224 | 2-00110
Betty Corcoran, prin. | 636-1270

MMI Prep S, PO BOX 89 18224 | 2-00111
Joseph Rudawski, prin. | 636-1108

Freeport, AC 412, PC 4, Armstrong
Freeport Area SD, PO BOX C 16229 | 4-11111
Donald Tylinski, supt. | 295-5141
Freeport Area HS, PO BOX H 16229 | 3-00011
(—), prin. | 295-5143
Freeport Area JHS, 325 4TH ST 16229 | 2-00100
Joseph Malak, prin. | 295-9020

Galeton, AC 814, PC 4, Potter
Galeton Area SD, 3 BRIDGE ST 16922 | 3-11111
Frank Flamish, supt. | 435-6571
Galeton Area S, 3 BRIDGE ST 16922 | 3-11111
G. Grant, prin. | 435-6571

Gallitzin, AC 814, PC 4, Cambria
Penn-Cambria SD
Supt. — See Cresson
Penn-Cambria IS | 2-00110
401 MAXWELL ST 16641 | 886-4181
Linda Miller, prin.

Gap, AC 717, PC 4, Lancaster

Fairhaven Christian S | 2-11111
1031 SIMMONTOWN RD 17527 | 442-9840

Geigertown, AC 215, PC 3, Berks

High Point Baptist Academy | 2-11111
GENERAL DELIVERY 19523 | 286-5942

Gettysburg, AC 717, PC 6, Adams
Gettysburg SD | 5-11111
900 BIGLERVILLE RD 17325 | 334-6254
David Mowery, supt.
SHS, 0 LEFEVER ST 17325 | 3-00001
Forrest Adams, prin. | 334-6254
JHS, 0 LEFEVER ST 17325 | 3-00110
Carolyn Nunamaker, prin. | 334-6254

Gettysburg College | 4-UC
300 N WASHINGTON ST 17325 | 337-6000
Lutheran Theological Seminary | 2-UC
61 N WEST CONFEDERATE AVE 17325 | 334-6286

Gibsonia, AC 412, PC 5, Allegheny
Pine-Richland SD | 4-11111
4046 EWALT RD 15044 | 443-7276
George Szymanski, supt.
Pine-Richland HS | 3-00011
4300 WARRENDALE RD 15044 | 443-7851
Robert Johnson, prin.
Pine-Richland MS, RR 1 15044 | 2-00100
Sherry Burnett, prin. | 625-3111

Gilbertsville, AC 215, PC 5, Montgomery
Boyertown Area SD
Supt. — See Boyertown
Boyertown Area JHS East | 3-00110
2020 BIG RD 19525 – Leslie King, prin. | 754-9550

Girard, AC 814, PC 5, Erie
Girard SD, 1100 RICE AVE 16417 | 4-11111
Walter Blucas, supt. | 774-5666
JSHS, 1135 LAKE ST 16417 | 3-00111
Randy Newson, prin. | 774-5607

Girard Alliance Christian Academy | 2-11111
229 RICE AVE 16417 | 774-9537

Glenmoore, AC 215, PC 3, Chester

Devereux-Brandywine Center in PA | 2-HND
DEVEREUX RD 19343 | 942-5968

Glenolden, AC 610, PC 6, Delaware
Southeast Delco SD
Supt. — See Folcroft
Ashland MS | 3-00100
801 W ASHLAND AVE 19036 | 522-4375
David Tannenbaum, prin.

Glen Rock, AC 717, PC 4, York
Southern York County SD | 5-11111
PO BOX 128 17327 | 235-4811
Richard Hupper, supt.
Susquehannock HS | 3-00011
PO BOX 128 17327 | 235-4811
William Linnane, prin.
Southern MS, PO BOX 128 17327 | 3-00100
John Wright, prin. | 235-4811

Glenshaw, AC 412, PC 8, Allegheny
Shaler Area SD | 5-11111
1800 MOUNT ROYAL BLVD 15116 | 492-1200
Susan Taylor, supt.
Shaler Area MS, 700 SCOTT AVE 15116 | 4-00110
Paul Surloff, prin. | 492-1300
Other Schools – See Pittsburgh

Glenside, AC 215, PC 6, Montgomery

Beaver College | 4-UC
450 S EASTON RD 19038 | 800-767-2328

Grantham, AC 717, PC 3, Cumberland

Messiah College | 4-UC
GENERAL DELIVERY 17027 | 766-2511

Graterford, AC 215, PC 3, Montgomery
Perkiomen Valley SD
Supt. — See Collegeville
Perkiomen Valley JSHS | 3-00111
ROUTE 29 & TRAPPE ROAD 19426 | 489-1230
Franklin Manley, prin.

Greencastle, AC 717, PC 5, Franklin
Greencastle-Antrim SD | 4-11111
500 LEITERSBURG ST 17225 | 597-2187
Robert Pascale, supt.
Greencastle-Antrim HS | 3-00011
300 S RIDGE AVE 17225 | 597-2186
Jack Appleby, prin.
Greencastle-Antrim MS | 2-00100
370 S RIDGE AVE 17225 | 597-2185
C. Hoover, prin.

Greensboro, AC 412, PC 2, Greene
Southeastern Green SD, RR 1 15338 | 3-11111
Ken Ganocy, supt. | 943-3630
Mapletown HS, RR 1 15338 | 2-00011
William Guappone, prin. | 943-3401
Mapletown JHS, RR 1 15338 | 2-00100
Bernard Kubitza, prin. | 943-3401

Greensburg, AC 412, PC 7, Westmoreland
Greensburg-Salem SD, 11 PARK ST 15601 | 5-11111
Robert Nevin, supt. | 832-2901
Greensburg-Salem HS | 3-00011
65 MENNEL DR 15601 | 832-2960
William Albaugh, prin.
Greensburg-Salem JHS | 3-00100
301 N MAIN ST 15601 | 832-2930
Thomas Marshall, prin.

Hempfield Area SD | 6-11111
RR 6 BOX 76 15601 | 834-2590
C. Nichols, supt.
Hempfield Area HS | 4-00011
RR 6 BOX 78 15601 | 834-9000
George Vollrath, prin.
Harrold MS, RR 6 BOX 75 15601 | 3-00100
Richard Mori, prin. | 834-5870
Wendover MS, 425 ARTHUR PL 15601 | 3-00100
Dennis Leshock, prin. | 836-1334
Other Schools – See Irwin

Business Careers Institute | 2-CC
33 W OTTERMAN ST 15601 | 834-1258
Greensburg Central Catholic HS | 2-00011
901 ARMORY DR 15601 | 834-0310
Br. Monroe, prin.
Greensburg Institute of Technology | 2-CS
302 W OTTERMAN ST 15601 | 837-3330
Seton Hill College | 3-UC
SETON HILL DR 15601 | 800-826-6234
Triangle Tech | 1-CC
222 E PITTSBURGH ST 15601 | 832-1050
University of Pittsburgh | 4-UC
1150 MOUNT PLEASANT RD 15601 | 837-7040
Westmoreland Hospital Assoc. | HSP
532 W PITTSBURGH ST 15601 | 832-4000

Greenville, AC 412, PC 6, Mercer
Greenville Area SD | 4-11111
9 DONATION RD 16125 | 588-2500
Patricia Homer, supt.
JSHS, 9 DONATION RD 16125 | 3-00111
Stephen Ross, prin. | 588-2500

Reynolds SD, 531 REYNOLDS RD 16125	4-11111	
Maddox Stokes, supt.	646-3240	
Reynolds JSHS	3-00111	
531 REYNOLDS RD 16125	646-3221	
William Taylor, prin.		
Thiel College	3-UC	
75 COLLEGE AVE 16125	589-2000	

Grindstone, AC 412, PC 3, Fayette
Brownsville Area SD, RR 1 15442	5-11111
Dexston Reed, supt.	785-2021
Other Schools – See Brownsville, Republic	

Grove City, AC 412, PC 6, Mercer
Grove City Area SD	5-11111
511 HIGHLAND AVE 16127	458-6733
Robert Post, supt.	
Grove City Area HS	3-00011
511 HIGHLAND AVE 16127	458-5456
Ralph Packard, prin.	
Republic JSHS, P O BOX 471 16127	2-00111
George Tucci, prin.	458-9330
Grove City Area MS	2-00100
130 E MAIN ST 16127	458-8040
Francis Staph, prin.	
Grove City College	4-UC
100 CAMPUS DR 16127	458-2000

Guys Mills, AC 814, PC 2, Crawford
Penncrest SD	
Supt. – See Saegertown	
Maplewood JSHS	3-00111
RR 1 BOX 44 16327	789-3666
Robert Rusek, prin.	

Gwynedd Valley, AC 215, PC 3, Montgomery
Gwynedd-Mercy Academy	2-00011
SUMNEYTOWN PIKE & EVANS 19437	646-8815
Sr. Mary Alice, prin.	
Gwynedd-Mercy College	4-UC
SUMNEYTOWN PIKE 19437	800-342-5462

Hadley, AC 412, PC 2, Mercer
Commodore Perry SD	3-11111
RR 1 BOX 1059 16130	253-3255
Oliver Rodax, supt.	
Commodore Perry S	3-11111
RR 1 BOX 1059 16130	253-2232
Leslie Cattron, prin.	

Halifax, AC 717, PC 3, Dauphin
Halifax Area SD	4-11111
3940 PETERS MOUNTAIN RD 17032	896-3416
Ken Koberlein, supt.	
Halifax Area HS	2-00011
3940 PETERS MOUNTAIN RD 17032	896-3416
Richard Miller, prin.	
Halifax Area MS	2-00100
3940 PETERS MOUNTAIN RD 17032	896-8853
Hannah Leigey, prin.	

Hamburg, AC 215, PC 5, Berks
Hamburg Area SD, WINDSOR ST 19526	4-11111
Charles Miller, supt.	562-2241
Hamburg Area JSHS, WINDSOR ST 19526	4-00111
Leo Lenick, prin.	562-3861
Blue Mountain Academy	2-11111
RR 3 BOX 3642 19526	562-2291
Stanley Rouse, prin.	

Hanover, AC 717, PC 7, York
Hanover Public SD	4-11111
403 MOUL AVE 17331	637-9000
Solomon Lausch, supt.	
HS, 401 MOUL AVE 17331	2-00011
John Cokefair, prin.	637-9000
MS, 300 KEAGY AVE 17331	2-00100
Michael Shirey, prin.	637-9000
South Western SD	5-11111
225 BOWMAN RD 17331	632-2500
Michael Clemens, supt.	
South Western HS	3-00011
200 BOWMAN RD 17331	632-2500
John Quashnoc, prin.	
Markle IS, 225 BOWMAN RD 17331	4-01100
Bradley Arnold, prin.	632-2500

Harborcreek, AC 814, PC 4, Erie
Harbor Creek SD	5-11111
6375 BUFFALO RD 16421	898-5700
Paul Hartmann, supt.	
JSHS, 6375 BUFFALO RD 16421	4-00111
Donald Papesch, prin.	898-5726

Harleysville, AC 215, PC 6, Montgomery
Souderton Area SD	
Supt. – See Souderton	
Indian Valley MS	2-00100
130 MAPLE AVE 19438	256-8896
Nicholas Chubb, prin.	

Harmony, AC 412, PC 4, Butler
Seneca Valley SD	6-11111
124 SENECA SCHOOL RD 16037	452-6040
Gerald Malecki, supt.	
Seneca Valley SHS	4-00001
124 SENECA SCHOOL RD 16037	452-6040
Thomas Norris, prin.	

Seneca Valley JHS	4-00110
122 SENECA SCHOOL RD 16037	452-6040
(—), prin.	

Harrisburg, AC 717, PC 8, Dauphin
Area Vocational Technical SD 17126	5-00011
(—), supt.	783-6788
Dauphin County AVTS	Vo Tech
6001 LOCUST LN 17109	652-3170
Ronald Stammel, prin.	
Harrisburg-Steelton-Highspire AVTS	Vo Tech
PO BOX 5100 17110	234-2611
Juanita Moore, prin.	
Other Schools – See Allison Park, Altoona, Aston, Bartonsville, Bethlehem, Bloomsburg, Brownstown, Butler, Canonsburg, Chambersburg, Charleroi, Clairton, Clearfield, Coatesville, Connellsville, Dimock, Easton, Ebensburg, Erie, Everett, Exton, Fairless Hills, Folcroft, Ford City, Frackville, Hazleton, Hughesville, Indiana, Jamison, Jim Thorpe, Johnstown, Kingston, Lansdale, Latrobe, Lebanon, Leesport, Lewistown, Limerick, Mc Connellsburg, Mc Keesport, Mar Lin, Meadville, Mechanicsburg, Media, Mercer, Mil l Creek, Monaca, Monroeville, Mount Joy, New Berlin, New Castle, New Kensington, New Stanton, Norristown, Oakdale, Oil City, Oley, Perkasie, Philadelphia, Phoenixville, Pittsburgh, Pleasant Gap, Port Allegany, Reading, Reynoldsville, Schnecksville, Scranton, Shamokin, Shippenville, Somerset, Towanda, Uniontown, Warren, Waynesburg, Wilkes-Barre, Willow Grove, Willow Street, York	
Central Dauphin SD	6-11111
600 RUTHERFORD RD 17109	545-4703
Carolyn Dumaresq, supt.	
Central Dauphin East SHS	3-00001
626 RUTHERFORD RD 17109	545-4703
Lucinda Radich, prin.	
Central Dauphin SHS	4-00001
4600 LOCUST LN 17109	540-4606
Lawrence Mussoline, prin.	
Central Dauphin East JHS	3-00110
628 RUTHERFORD RD 17109	545-4703
Robert Holbrook, prin.	
Linglestown JHS	3-00110
1200 N MOUNTAIN RD 17112	657-3060
John Zemba, prin.	
Other Schools – See Steelton	
Harrisburg CSD, PO BOX 2645 17105	6-11111
Randolph Outen, supt.	255-2511
HS, 2451 MARKET ST 17103	4-00011
Joseph Brown, prin.	255-2617
Rowland IS, 1901 WAYNE AVE 17109	3-00100
Frank Gantz, prin.	255-2480
Scott IS, 1901 WAYNE AVE 17109	3-00100
John Grove, prin.	257-8760
Susquehanna Township SD	4-11111
3550 ELMERTON AVE 17109	657-5100
Thomas Holtzman, supt.	
Susquehanna Twp. HS	3-00011
3500 ELMERTON AVE 17109	657-5117
Mark Galowitz, prin.	
Susquehanna Twp. MS	2-00100
801 WOOD ST 17109	657-5125
Kermit Leitner, prin.	
Academy of Medical Arts and Business	2-CS
279 BOAS ST 17102	233-2172
Bishop McDevitt HS	3-00011
2200 MARKET ST 17103	236-7973
Fr. Quinlan, prin.	
Christian S	2-11111
2000 BLUE MOUNTAIN PKY 17112	545-3728
Harrisburg Area Community College	6-CC
3300 N CAMERON STREET RD 17110	780-2300
NEC-Thompson Institute	4-CC
5650 DERRY ST 17111	564-8710
Polyclinic Medical Center	HSP
2601 N 3RD ST 17110	782-2136

Harrison City, AC 412, PC 3, Westmoreland
Penn-Trafford SD, ADMIN BLDG 15636	5-11111
Joseph Marasti, supt.	744-4496
Penn-Trafford HS, PO BOX 366 15636	4-00011
Patrick Ratesic, prin.	744-4471
Other Schools – See Claridge, Trafford	

Hastings, AC 814, PC 4, Cambria
Cambria Heights SD	
Supt. – See Patton	
Cambria Heights MS, BEAVER ST 16646	2-00100
John Seymour, prin.	247-6271

Hatboro, AC 215, PC 6, Montgomery
Upper Moreland Township SD	
Supt. – See Willow Grove	
Upper Moreland MS	3-00100
4000 ORANGEMANS RD 19040	674-4185
William Lessa, prin.	

Hatfield, AC 215, PC 5, Montgomery
Biblical Theological Seminary	2-UC
200 N MAIN ST 19440	368-5000

Haverford, AC 610, PC 6, Montgomery
Haverford College	4-UC
370 LANCASTER AVE 19041	896-1000

Haverford S	3-11111
450 LANCASTER AVE 19041	642-3020
Joseph Healey, prin.	

Havertown, AC 610, PC 8, Delaware
Haverford Township SD	5-11111
1801 DARBY RD 19083	853-5900
Ewald Kalmbach, supt.	
Haverford HS, 200 MILL RD 19083	4-00011
John Meehan, prin.	853-5955
Haverford MS, 1701 DARBY RD 19083	4-00100
Michael Bianco, prin.	853-5927

Hawley, AC 717, PC 4, Wayne
Wallenpaupack Area SD	4-11111
HC 6 BOX 6075 18428	226-4557
Thomas Peifer, supt.	
Wallenpaupack Area HS	3-00011
HC 6 BOX 6075 18428	226-4511
Louis Zefran, prin.	
Wallenpaupack Area MS	3-01100
HC 6 BOX 6071 18428	226-2183
William Walker, prin.	

Hazleton, AC 717, PC 7, Luzerne
Area Vocational Technical SD	
Supt. — See Harrisburg	
Hazleton AVTS, 1451 W 23RD ST 18201	Vo Tech
Dale Long, prin.	459-3170
Hazleton Area SD	6-11111
101 S CHURCH ST 18201	459-3111
Geraldine Shepperson, supt.	
Hazleton Area SHS	4-00001
1601 W 23RD ST 18201	459-3221
Rocco Mussoline, prin.	
JHS, 700 N WYOMING ST 18201	3-00110
Edward Ecker, prin.	459-3140
Other Schools – See Freeland, West Hazleton	
Bishop Hafey HS	2-00011
1700 W 22ND ST 18201	455-9431
Fr. Tressler, prin.	
Hazelton-St. Joseph Medical Center	HSP
687 N CHURCH ST 18201	459-4444
Hazleton Prep S, 762 N VINE ST 18201	2-00100
Fr. Tressler, prin.	455-9160
Pennsylvania State University	4-CC
HAZELTON CAMPUS 18201	450-3000

Hegins, AC 717, PC 4, Schuylkill
Tri-Valley SD	
Supt. — See Valley View	
Tri-Valley JSHS, 155 E MAIN ST 17938	3-00111
William Gallagher, prin.	682-3125

Hellertown, AC 610, PC 6, Northampton
Saucon Valley SD, 1050 MAIN ST 18055	4-11111
Carl Manone, supt.	838-7026
Saucon Valley HS	3-00011
701 POLK VALLEY RD 18055	838-7001
Francis Kawtoski, prin.	
Saucon Valley MS, 1050 MAIN ST 18055	2-00100
(—), prin.	838-7071

Herminie, AC 412, PC 4, Westmoreland
Yough SD, 99 LOWBER RD 15637	5-11111
Earl Lutz, supt.	446-7272
Yough SHS, 99 LOWBER RD 15637	3-00001
Joseph Makar, prin.	446-5520
Other Schools – See Ruffs Dale	

Hermitage, AC 412, PC 7, Mercer
Hermitage SD, PO BOX 1227 16148	4-11111
Louis Mastrian, supt.	981-1673
Hickory HS, PO BOX 1227 16148	3-00011
Kathleen Nogay, prin.	981-8750
MS, PO BOX 1227 16148	2-00100
Sandra Dunham, prin.	981-8750
Kennedy Christian HS	2-00011
2120 SHENANGO VALLEY FWY 16148	346-5531
Peter Iacino, prin.	

Herndon, AC 717, PC 2, Northumberland
Line Mountain SD	4-11111
RR 2 BOX 320 17830	758-6511
David Monsour, supt.	
Line Mountain HS	2-00011
RR 1 BOX 1660 17830	758-2011
Alexander Menio, prin.	
Other Schools – See Trevorton	

Hershey, AC 717, PC 7, Dauphin
Derry Township SD	4-11111
PO BOX 898 17033	534-2501
Barbara Hasson, supt.	
HS, PO BOX 898 17033	3-00011
John Scola, prin.	531-2244
MS, PO BOX 898 17033	3-00100
Thomas Davis, prin.	531-2222
Milton Hershey S, PO BOX 830 17033	4-11111
Frances O'Connor, prin.	534-3537
Milton S. Hershey Medical Center Hosp.	HSP
PO BOX 850 17033	531-8803
Penn. State Univ. Medical College	3-UC
500 UNIVERSITY DR 17033	534-8521

Holland, AC 215, PC 6, Bucks
Council Rock SD	
Supt. — See Richboro	
Council Rock JHS, E HOLLAND RD 18966	3-00110
Lois Wilson, prin.	968-0845

Villa Joseph Marie HS — 2-00011
1180 HOLLAND RD 18966 — 357-8810
Sr. Mary Elaine, prin.

Hollidaysburg, AC 814, PC 6, Blair
Hollidaysburg Area SD — 5-11111
201 JACKSON ST 16648 — 695-5584
Leo Gensante, supt.
Hollidaysburg Area SHS — 3-00001
1500 N MONTGOMERY ST 16648 — 695-5585
Gary Robinson, prin.
Hollidaysburg Area JHS — 3-00110
1000 HEWIT ST 16648 — 695-4416
Richard Wylie, prin.

Hollsopple, AC 814, PC 3, Somerset

Johnstown Christian S, RR 2 15935 — 2-11111 / 288-2588

Homer City, AC 412, PC 4, Indiana
Homer-Center SD — 4-11111
15 WILDCAT LN 15748 — 479-8080
Joseph Marcoline, supt.
Homer-Center JSHS — 3-00111
20 WILDCAT LN 15748 — 479-8026
B. Liscik, prin.

Honesdale, AC 717, PC 5, Wayne
Wayne Highlands SD — 5-11111
474 GROVE ST 18431 — 253-4661
Daniel O'Neill, supt.
HS, 459 TERRACE ST 18431 — 3-00011
Thomas Jenkins, prin. — 253-2046
Wayne Highlands MS — 3-01100
482 GROVE ST 18431 — 253-5900
James Rodda, prin.

Hookstown, AC 412, PC 2, Beaver
South Side Area SD — 4-11111
4949 STATE ROUTE 151 15050 — 573-9540
Susan Goodwin, supt.
South Side HS — 2-00011
4949 STATE RTE 151 15050 — 573-9582
William Suit, prin.
South Side MS — 2-00100
4949 STATE ROUTE 151 15050 — 573-9582
(—), prin.

Horsham, AC 215, PC 7, Montgomery
Hatboro-Horsham SD — 5-11111
229 MEETINGHOUSE RD 19044 — 672-5660
Gerald Strock, supt.
Hatboro-Horsham HS — 3-00011
899 HORSHAM RD 19044 — 441-7900
David Hottenstein, prin.
Keith Valley MS — 3-00100
227 MEETINGHOUSE RD 19044 — 956-2910
Harrison Woodruff, prin.

Pennsylvania Coll. Straight Chiropractic — 2-UC
200 TOURNAMENT DR STE 100 19044 — 800-833-6080

Houston, AC 412, PC 4, Washington
Chartiers-Houston SD — 4-11111
2080 W PIKE ST 15342 — 746-1400
Richard Bishop, supt.
Chartiers-Houston JSHS — 3-00111
2050 W PIKE ST 15342 — 745-3350
Robert Dell, prin.

Houtzdale, AC 814, PC 4, Clearfield
Moshannon Valley SD — 4-11111
RR 1 BOX 314 16651 — 378-7616
James Lebda, supt.
Moshannon Valley JSHS — 3-00111
RR 1 BOX 314 16651 — 378-7616
Marshall Wagner, prin.

Hughesville, AC 717, PC 4, Lycoming
Area Vocational Technical SD
Supt. — See Harrisburg
Lycoming County AVTS — Vo Tech
349 CEMETARY ST 17737 — 584-5030
Richard Holodick, prin.

East Lycoming SD — 4-11111
349 CEMETARY ST 17737 — 584-2131
Edward Harrington, supt.
JSHS, 349 CEMETARY ST 17737 — 3-00111
David Reese, prin. — 584-5111

Hummelstown, AC 717, PC 5, Dauphin
Lower Dauphin SD — 5-11111
291 E MAIN ST 17036 — 566-3721
Jeffrey Miller, supt.
Lower Dauphin JSHS — 4-00011
201 S HANOVER ST 17036 — 566-3721
Landry Appleby, prin.

Mountain View Christian S — 2-11111
34 SIPE AVE 17036 — 534-2929

Huntingdon, AC 814, PC 6, Huntingdon
Huntingdon Area SD — 5-11111
2400 CASSADY AVE 16652 — 643-4140
Derry Stufft, supt.
Huntingdon Area HS — 3-00011
2400 CASSADY AVE 16652 — 643-1080
C. Williams, prin.
Huntingdon Area MS — 3-00100
2500 CASSADY AVE 16652 — 643-2900
Jill Adams, prin.

Juniata College — 4-UC
1700 MOORE ST 16652 — 643-4310

Huntingdon Valley, AC 215, PC 7, Montgomery
Lower Moreland Township SD — 4-11111
2551 MURRAY AVE 19006 — 938-0270
David Archibald, supt.
Lower Moreland JSHS — 3-00111
555 RED LION RD 19006 — 938-0220
Gregory Doviak, prin.

Hyndman, AC 814, PC 4, Bedford
Bedford Area SD
Supt. — See Bedford
JSHS, PO BOX 695 15545 — 2-00111
(—), prin. — 842-3918

Immaculata, AC 610, PC 4, Chester

Immaculata College 19345 — 4-UC / 647-4400

Imperial, AC 412, PC 5, Allegheny
West Allegheny SD — 4-11111
PO BOX 55 15126 — 695-3422
Reggie Bonfield, supt.
West Allegheny HS — 3-00011
205 W ALLEGHENY RD 15126 — 695-7368
Richard Moran, prin.
West Allegheny MS — 3-00100
207 W ALLEGHENY RD 15126 — 695-3422
J. Kevin Lordon, prin.

Indiana, AC 412, PC 7, Indiana
Area Vocational Technical SD
Supt. — See Harrisburg
Indiana County AVTS — Vo Tech
441 HAMILL RD 15701 — 349-6700
John Jahoda, prin.

Indiana Area SD, 501 E PIKE 15701 — 5-11111 / 463-8713
David Laird, supt.
Indiana Area SHS, 450 N 5TH ST 15701 — 3-00001 / 463-8562
Daniel Cilo, prin.
Indiana Area JHS, 245 N 5TH ST 15701 — 3-00110 / 463-8568
Rodney Ruddock, prin.

Cambria-Rowe Business College — 2-CS
422 S 13TH ST 15701 — 463-0222
Indiana University of Pennsylvania 15705 — 7-UC / 357-2100

Industry, AC 412, PC 4, Beaver
Western Beaver County SD
Supt. — See Midland
Western Beaver County JSHS — 3-00111
216 ENGLE RD 15052 — 643-8500
Ronald Young, prin.

Irwin, AC 412, PC 5, Westmoreland
Hempfield Area SD
Supt. — See Greensburg
West Hempfield MS, RR 3 15642 — 3-00100 / 863-1944
Timothy Welty, prin.

Norwin SD
Supt. — See North Huntingdon
Norwin SHS, 251 MCMAHON DR 15642 — 4-00001 / 863-6500
Ronald Peduzzi, prin.
Norwin JHS-East, 1 MAIN ST 15642 — 3-00110 / 863-5707
Robert Randolph, prin.
Norwin JHS-West — 3-00110
10870 MOCKINGBIRD DR 15642 — 863-1250
King Weber, prin.

Jamestown, AC 412, PC 3, Mercer
Jamestown Area SD — 3-11111
PO BOX 217 16134 — 932-5557
David Shaffer, supt.
Jamestown Area JSHS — 2-00111
PO BOX 217 16134 — 932-3186
Michael Krepps, prin.

Jamison, AC 215, PC 3, Bucks
Area Vocational Technical SD
Supt. — See Harrisburg
Middle Bucks County AVTS — Vo Tech
2740 YORK RD 18929 — 343-2480
Robert Lees, prin.

Jeannette, AC 412, PC 7, Westmoreland
Jeannette CSD, 320 S 4TH ST 15644 — 4-11111 / 523-5497
Vincent Aiello, supt.
HS, 200 FLORIDA AVE 15644 — 3-00011 / 523-5591
Paul Noonan, prin.
MS, 320 S 4TH ST 15644 — 2-00100 / 527-1592
Paul Noonan, prin.

Monsour Medical Center — HSP
70 LINCOLN HWY E 15644 — 527-1511

Jefferson, AC 412, PC 2, Greene
Jefferson-Morgan SD — 4-11111
PO BOX 158 15344 — 883-2310
K. Macek, supt.
Jefferson-Morgan JSHS — 3-00111
PO BOX 158 15344 — 883-2310
John Ballentyne, prin.

Jeffersonville, AC 215

Pathway School — HND
162 EGYPT RD 19403 — 277-0660

Jenkintown, AC 215, PC 5, Montgomery
Jenkintown SD — 2-11111
325 HIGHLAND AVE 19046 — 885-3722
David Barrett, supt.
JSHS, 325 HIGHLAND AVE 19046 — 2-00111 / 884-1801
Alastair Nisbet, prin.

Abington Friends S — 3-11111
575 WASHINGTON LN 19046 — 886-4350
Bruce Stewart, prin.
Manor Junior College — 2-CC
710 FOX CHASE RD 19046 — 885-2360

Jermyn, AC 717, PC 4, Lackawanna
Lakeland SD, RR 1 BOX 313 18433 — 4-11111 / 254-9485
Robert Ghigiarelli, supt.
Lakeland JSHS, RR 1 18433 — 3-00111 / 254-9485
Alexander Chelik, prin.

Jersey Shore, AC 717, PC 5, Lycoming
Jersey Shore Area SD — 5-11111
201 S BROAD ST 17740 — 398-1561
Gary Mowery, supt.
Jersey Shore Area SHS — 3-00001
701 CEMETERY ST 17740 — 398-7170
David Gunther, prin.
Jersey Shore Area JHS — 3-00110
601 THOMPSON ST 17740 – (—), prin. — 398-7400

Jim Thorpe, AC 717, PC 6, Carbon
Area Vocational Technical SD
Supt. — See Harrisburg
Carbon County AVTS — Vo Tech
150 W 13TH ST 18229 — 325-3682
George Seiler, prin.

Jim Thorpe Area SD — 4-11111
140 W 10TH ST 18229 — 325-3691
Thomas Sangiuliano, supt.
Jim Thorpe Area HS — 2-00011
1100 CENTER ST 18229 — 325-3663
James Pfingstler, prin.
Jim Thorpe Area JHS — 2-00100
410 CENTER AVE 18229 — 325-2771
Jeffery James, prin.

Johnsonburg, AC 814, PC 5, Elk
Johnsonburg Area SD, ELK AVE 15845 — 3-11111 / 965-2536
William Printz, supt.
Johnsonburg Area JSHS, ELK AVE 15845 — 2-00111 / 965-2556
Barbara Lias, prin.

Johnstown, AC 814, PC 8, Cambria
Area Vocational Technical SD
Supt. — See Harrisburg
Greater Johnstown AVTS — Vo Tech
445 SCHOOLHOUSE RD 15904 — 269-4545
Barry Dallara, prin.

Conemaugh Valley SD — 4-11111
1451 FRANKSTOWN RD 15902 — 535-3957
Edwin Hasson, supt.
Conemaugh Valley JSHS — 3-00111
RR 1 BOX 132 15906 — 535-5523
Joseph Macharola, prin.

Ferndale Area SD — 3-11111
100 DARTMOUTH AVE 15905 — 535-1507
Anthony Labriola, supt.
Ferndale JSHS, 600 HARLAN AVE 15905 — 2-00111 / 288-5757
James Devorick, prin.

Greater Johnstown SD — 5-11111
220 MESSENGER ST 15902 — 533-5651
June Merryman, supt.
Greater Johnstown HS — 4-00011
222 CENTRAL AVE 15902 — 533-5603
David Singer, prin.
Greater Johnstown MS — 3-00100
280 DECKER AVE 15906 — 533-5573
Paul Neatrour, prin.

Richland SD, 340 THEATRE DR 15904 — 4-11111 / 266-6063
Elizabeth Gensante, supt.
Richland HS, 1740 HIGHFIELD ST 15904 — 3-00011 / 266-6081
Steven Rakoczy, prin.
Richland MS, 280 THEATRE DR 15904 — 3-01100 / 266-1435
Robert Wertz, prin.

Westmont Hilltop SD — 4-11111
827 DIAMOND BLVD 15905 — 255-6751
Gary Estadt, supt.
Westmont Hilltop HS — 3-00011
200 FAIR OAKS DR 15905 — 255-6751
Patrick Duffy, prin.
Westmont Hilltop MS — 2-01100
827 DIAMOND BLVD 15905 — 255-6751
Austin Greenland, prin.

Bishop McCort HS — 3-00011
25 OSBORNE ST 15905 — 536-8991
William Rushin, prin.
Cambria-Rowe Business College — 2-CC
221 CENTRAL AVE 15902 — 536-5168
Conemaugh Valley Memorial Hospital — HSP
1086 FRANKLIN ST 15905 — 533-9118
Hiram G. Andrews Center — 2-CC
727 GOUCHER ST 15905 — 255-8200
Lee Hospital — HSP
320 MAIN ST 15901 — 533-0821
University of Pittsburgh at Johnstown — 5-UC
450 SCHOOLHOUSE RD 15904 — 269-7050

Kane, AC 814, PC 5, McKean
Kane Area SD, W HEMLOCK AVE 16735   4-11111
    Laverne Johnson, supt.   837-9570
Kane Area HS   2-00011
    ROUTE 321 & HEMLOCK AVE 16735   837-6821
    Jack Hedlund, prin.
Kane Area MS   3-00100
    400 W HEMLOCK AVE 16735   837-6030
    Richard Buckley, prin.

Karns City, AC 412, PC 2, Butler
Karns City Area SD   4-11111
    RR 2 BOX 135 16041   756-2030
    David Pisani, supt.
JSHS, RR 2 BOX 135 16041   3-00111
    Kenneth Fair, prin.   756-2030

Kennett Square, AC 610, PC 6, Chester
Kennett Cons. SD   4-11111
    300 E SOUTH ST 19348   444-6600
    Larry Bosley, supt.
Kennett HS, S UNION ST 19348   3-00011
    Kathleen Thorton, prin.   444-6620
Kennett MS, S UNION ST 19348   2-00100
    John Carr, prin.   444-6640

Unionville-Chadds Ford SD   5-11111
    740 UNIONVILLE RD 19348   347-0970
    Charles Garris, supt.
Unionville HS   3-00011
    750 UNIONVILLE RD 19348   347-1600
    John Maher, prin.
Patton MS, 760 UNIONVILLE RD 19348   3-00100
    Bruce Vosburgh, prin.   347-2000

Kimberton, AC 610, PC 2, Chester

Kimberton Waldorf S   2-11111
    GENERAL DELIVERY 19442   933-3635
    Mary Echlin, prin.

King of Prussia, AC 610, PC 7, Montgomery
Upper Merion Area SD   5-11111
    435 CROSSFIELD RD 19406   337-6006
    Laura Michener, supt.
Upper Merion HS   3-00011
    435 CROSSFIELD RD 19406   337-6032
    Kevin Hart, prin.
Upper Merion MS   3-01100
    CROSSFIELD ROAD 19406   337-6053
    Jacqueline Hollrah, prin.

Kingsley, AC 717, PC 2, Susquehanna
Mountain View SD   4-11111
    RR 1 BOX 339 18826   434-2180
    Andrew Chichura, supt.
Mountain View JSHS   3-00111
    RR 1 BOX 339 18826   434-2501
    David Sapala, prin.

Kingston, AC 717, PC 7, Luzerne
Area Vocational Technical SD
    Supt. — See Harrisburg
West Side AVTS, 75 EVANS ST 18704   Vo Tech
    Stephen Stahl, prin.   288-8493

Wyoming Valley West SD   6-11111
    450 N MAPLE AVE 18704   288-6551
    Norman Namey, supt.
Wyoming Valley West MS   4-00100
    201 CHESTER ST 18704   287-2131
    Charles Suppon, prin.
Other Schools – See Plymouth

Allied Medical Careers   2-CS
    PO BOX 1648 18704   288-8400
Bishop O'Reilly HS   2-00011
    PO BOX 1346 18704   288-1404
    Anita Sirak, prin.
Star Technical Institute   2-CS
    212 WYOMING AVE 18704   287-9777

Kintnersville, AC 215, PC 2, Bucks
Palisades SD, 39 SHORT DR 18930   4-11111
    Tom Free, supt.   847-5131
Palisades HS   3-00011
    35 CHURCH HILL RD 18930   847-2051
    Ken Nickischer, prin.
Palisades MS, 4710 DURHAM RD 18930   2-00100
    Frank Kuebler, prin.   847-5131

Kinzers, AC 717, PC 2, Lancaster
Pequea Valley SD   4-11111
    166 S NEW HOLLAND RD 17535   768-5530
    Ann Keim, supt.
Pequea Valley HS   3-00011
    4033 E NEWPORT RD 17535   768-5500
    J. King, prin.
Pequea Valley IS   2-00100
    166 S NEW HOLLAND RD 17535   768-5535
    Victoria Danehower, prin.

Faith Mennonite HS   2-00011
    5085 WOODLAND DR 17535   442-8818

Kittanning, AC 412, PC 6, Armstrong
Armstrong SD
    Supt. — See Ford City
SHS, 1200 ORR AVE 16201   3-00001
    D. Ralph Bouch, prin.   543-1591

Armstrong County Memorial Hospital   HSP
    1 NOLTE DR 16201   543-8404

Knox, AC 814, PC 4, Clarion
Keystone SD, RR 2 BOX 3D 16232   4-11111
    Horace Darlington, supt.   797-5921
Keystone JSHS, RR 2 BOX 3D 16232   3-00111
    John Colantonio, prin.   797-1261

Kutztown, AC 215, PC 5, Berks
Kutztown Area SD   4-11111
    50 TREXLER AVE 19530   683-7361
    Richard Karr, supt.
HS, 50 TREXLER AVE 19530   2-00011
    A. Machamer, prin.   683-7346
JHS, 10 DEISHER LN 19530   2-00100
    Albert Cunningham, prin.   683-3575

Kutztown University of Pennsylvania   6-UC
    19530   683-4000

Lake Ariel, AC 717, PC 3, Wayne
Western Wayne SD
    Supt. — See South Canaan
Western Wayne HS, RR 2 18436   3-00011
    Donald Shaffer, prin.   937-4113
Western Wayne MS, RR 2 18436   2-00100
    Patrick Torquati, prin.   937-3010

Canaan Christian Academy   2-11111
    RR 2 BOX 378 18436   937-4848

Lampeter, AC 717, PC 3, Lancaster
Lampeter-Strasburg SD   4-11111
    PO BOX 428 17537   464-3311
    Melvin Rosier, supt.
Lampeter-Strasburg HS   3-00011
    PO BOX 428 17537   464-3311
    H. Spaulding, prin.
Meylin MS, PO BOX 428 17537   2-00100
    Michael Burcin, prin.   464-3311

Lancaster, AC 717, PC 8, Lancaster
Conestoga Valley SD   5-11111
    2110 HORSESHOE RD 17601   397-2421
    Harry Wirth, supt.
Conestoga Valley HS   3-00011
    2110 HORSESHOE RD 17601   397-5231
    Joseph Crawshaw, prin.
Other Schools – See Leola

Hempfield SD
    Supt. — See Landisville
Centerville JHS   3-00100
    865 CENTERVILLE RD 17601   898-5580
    William Reinking, prin.

Lancaster SD, PO BOX 150 17608   7-11111
    Robert Shekletski, supt.   291-6121
McCaskey SHS   4-00001
    445 N RESERVOIR ST 17602   291-6211
    (—), prin.
Hand JHS, PO BOX 150 17608   3-00110
    Henry Longenberger, prin.   291-6161
Lincoln JHS, 1001 LEHIGH AVE 17602   3-00110
    (—), prin.   291-6187
Reynolds JHS, 650 W WALNUT ST 17603   3-00110
    Kathy Kuzmiak, prin.   291-6257
Wheatland JHS   3-00110
    919 HAMILTON PARK DR 17603   291-6285
    Monet Daniels, prin.

Manheim Township SD   5-11111
    PO BOX 5134 17606   569-8231
    Sharron Nelson, supt.
Manheim Twp. HS   4-00011
    PO BOX 5134 17606   569-8231
    C. Wendell Hower, prin.
Manheim Twp. MS   3-00100
    PO BOX 5134 17606   569-8231
    Robert Ruder, prin.

Catholic HS, 650 JULIETTE AVE 17601   3-00011
    Fr. Pallard, prin.   393-0454
Consolidated School of Business   2-CS
    1817 OLDE HOMESTEAD LN # J 17601   394-6211
Franklin & Marshall College   4-UC
    PO BOX 3003 17604   291-3993
Lancaster Bible College   2-UC
    901 EDEN RD 17601   800-544-7335
Lancaster Christian S   2-11111
    651 LAMPETER RD 17602   392-8092
    Jeffrey Martin, prin.
Lancaster Country Day S   2-11111
    725 HAMILTON RD 17603   392-2916
    Richard Johnson, prin.
Lancaster General Hospital   HSP
    PO BOX 3555 17604   295-8312
Lancaster Mennonite HS   3-00011
    2176 LINCOLN HWY E 17602   299-0436
    Richard Thomas, prin.
Lancaster Theological Seminary   2-UC
    555 W JAMES ST 17603   393-0654
Pennsylvania School of Art and Design   2-CS
    204 N PRINCE ST 17603   396-7833
St. Joseph's Hospital   HSP
    250 COLLEGE AVE 17603   291-6042
Thaddeus Stevens State School of Tech   2-CC
    17602   299-7730
The Living Word Academy   2-11111
    2384 NEW HOLLAND PIKE 17601   656-4271
    Kenneth Godshall, prin.

Landisville, AC 717, PC 4, Lancaster
Hempfield SD, 200 CHURCH ST 17538   6-11111
    J. Collins, supt.   898-5560

Hempfield HS, STANLEY AVE 17538   4-00011
    Douglas Minnich, prin.   898-5510
Other Schools – See Lancaster

Langhorne, AC 215, PC 4, Bucks
Neshaminy SD   6-11111
    2001 OLD LINCOLN HWY 19047   752-6300
    Gary Bowman, supt.
Neshaminy SHS   4-00001
    2001 OLD LINCOLN HWY 19047   752-6451
    Bruce Wyatt, prin.
Maple Point MS   3-00110
    2250 LANGEHORNE YARDLEY RD 19047   752-6900
    Raymond Kelly, prin.
Neshaminy JHS   3-00110
    1200 LANGHORNE NEWTOWN RD 19047   752-3600
    W. McMasters, prin.
Other Schools – See Feasterville, Levittown

Philadelphia College of Bible   3-UC
    200 MANOR AVE 19047   800-366-0049
Woods Schools 19047   HND

Lansdale, AC 610, PC 7, Montgomery
Area Vocational Technical SD
    Supt. — See Harrisburg
North Montco AVTS   Vo Tech
    1297 SUMNEYTOWN PIKE 19446   368-1177
    Michael Erwin, prin.

North Penn SD   7-11111
    401 E HANCOCK ST 19446   368-0400
    Alan Elko, supt.
North Penn SHS   4-00001
    1340 S VALLEY FORGE RD 19446   368-9800
    Juan Baughn, prin.
North Penn JHS, 400 PENN ST 19446   4-00110
    Stephen Frederick, prin.   368-2700

Calvary Baptist Christian S   2-11111
    1450 S VALLEY FORGE RD 19446   368-1100
Christopher Dock Mennonite HS   2-00011
    1000 FORTY FOOT RD 19446   362-2675
    Elaine Moyer, prin.
Lansdale Catholic HS   3-00011
    700 LANSDALE AVE 19446   262-6160
    Salvatore Dinenna, prin.

Lansdowne, AC 610, PC 7, Delaware
William Penn SD
    Supt. — See Yeadon
Penn Wood SHS   3-00011
    ESSEX & GREEN AVES 19050   284-8080
    James O'Toole, prin.

Lansford, AC 717, PC 5, Carbon
Panther Valley SD, PO BOX 40 18232   4-11111
    Joseph Dispenziere, supt.   645-3176
Panther Valley HS, PO BOX 40 18232   2-00011
    Philip Rader, prin.   645-2171
Panther Valley MS, PO BOX 7 18232   3-01100
    Mary Desei, prin.   645-2175

La Plume, AC 717, PC 2, Lackawanna

Keystone Junior College   3-CC
    PO BOX 50 18440   945-5141

Laporte, AC 717, PC 2, Sullivan
Sullivan County SD
    Supt. — See Dushore
Sullivan County JSHS   2-00111
    PO BOX 98 18626   946-7001
    Mark DiRocco, prin.

Latrobe, AC 412, PC 6, Westmoreland
Area Vocational Technical SD
    Supt. — See Harrisburg
Eastern Westmoreland County AVTS   Vo Tech
    849 HILLVIEW AVE 15650   539-9788
    Enoch Wootton, prin.

Greater Latrobe SD, 410 MAIN ST 15650   5-11111
    William Stavisky, supt.   539-4200
Greater Latrobe SHS   4-00001
    131 COUNTRY CLUB RD 15650   539-4225
    John Andrighetti, prin.
Greater Latrobe JHS   3-00110
    131 COUNTRY CLUB RD 15650   539-4265
    John Kozusko, prin.

Latrobe Area Hospital   HSP
    101 W 2ND AVE 15650   537-1001
St. Vincent College   4-UC
    300 FRASER PURCHASE RD 15650   539-9761

Lebanon, AC 717, PC 8, Lebanon
Area Vocational Technical SD
    Supt. — See Harrisburg
Lebanon County AVTS   Vo Tech
    833 METRO DR 17042   273-8551
    Stephen Kachniasz, prin.

Cornwall-Lebanon SD   5-11111
    105 E EVERGREEN RD 17042   272-2031
    John Menser, supt.
Cedar Crest HS   4-00011
    115 E EVERGREEN RD 17042   272-2031
    Joseph Hartman, prin.
Cedar Crest MS   3-00100
    101 E EVERGREEN RD 17042   272-2031
    Thomas Sherk, prin.

Lebanon SD, 1000 S 8TH ST 17042   5-11111
  William Starr, supt.   273-9391
HS, 1000 S 8TH ST 17042   4-00011
  Kenneth Mawritz, prin.   273-9391
JHS, 350 N 8TH ST 17046   3-00100
  E. Grier, prin.   273-9391

Lebanon Catholic HS   2-00111
  1400 CHESTNUT ST 17042   273-3731
  Fr. Dechico, prin.
Lebanon Christian Academy   2-11111
  875 ACADEMY DR 17046   273-8114

Leechburg, AC 412, PC 5, Armstrong
Leechburg Area SD   4-11111
  200 SIBERIAN AVE 15656   845-7701
  Edward Warnick, supt.
Leechburg Area JSHS, 215 1ST ST 15656   3-00111
  W. Carroll, prin.   842-0571

Leesport, AC 215, PC 4, Berks
Area Vocational Technical SD
  Supt. — See Harrisburg
Berks County AVTS   Vo Tech
  RR 1 BOX 1370 19533   378-4884
  Robert Runkle, prin.
Berks County AVTS-West   Vo Tech
  RR 1 BOX 1370 19533   374-4073
  Clyde Hornberger, prin.

Schuylkill Valley SD   4-11111
  RR 2 BOX 2165 19533   926-1706
  Joseph Yarworth, supt.
Schuylkill Valley JSHS   3-00111
  RR 2 BOX 2165 19533   926-1706
  John Rio, prin.

Leetsdale, AC 412, PC 4, Allegheny
Quaker Valley SD
  Supt. — See Sewickley
Quaker Valley SHS   2-00001
  625 BEAVER ST 15056   741-3600
  Jeanne Johnson, prin.

Lehighton, AC 610, PC 6, Carbon
Lehighton Area SD   5-11111
  200 BEAVER RUN RD 18235   377-4490
  Shirley Ball, supt.
Lehighton Area HS   3-00011
  301 BEAVER RUN RD 18235   377-6180
  G. Ripkey, prin.
Lehighton Area JHS   2-00100
  301 BEAVER RUN RD 18235   377-6535
  Dennis Serfass, prin.

Lehman, AC 717, PC 2, Luzerne
Lake-Lehman SD, MARKET ST 18627   4-11111
  Nancy Davis, supt.   675-2165
Lake-Lehman HS   3-00011
  OLD ROUTE 115 18627   675-2165
  John Oliver, prin.
Lake-Lehman JHS, OUTLET RD 18627   2-00100
  Robert Roberts, prin.   675-2165

Pennsylvania State University   3-CC
  PO BOX PSU 18627   675-2171

Lemont Furnace, AC 412, PC 3, Fayette

West Virginia Career College   2-CS
  200 COLLEGE DR 15456   437-4600

Lemoyne, AC 717, PC 5, Cumberland
West Shore SD
  Supt. — See New Cumberland
MS, 701 MARKET ST 17043   3-00100
  Barry Houser, prin.   761-6345

Leola, AC 717, PC 4, Lancaster
Conestoga Valley SD
  Supt. — See Lancaster
Conestoga Valley JHS   2-00100
  11 SCHOOL DR 17540   656-2627
  Wayne Heim, prin.

Lester, AC 215, PC 4, Philadelphia

All-State Career School   4-CS
  501 SEMINOLE ST 19029   521-1818

Levittown, AC 215, PC 8, Bucks
Bristol Township SD
  Supt. — See Bristol
Truman SHS, 3001 GREEN LN 19057   4-00001
  Joseph Boles, prin.   547-3000

Neshaminy SD
  Supt. — See Langhorne
Sandburg JHS, 30 HARMONY RD 19056   3-00110
  Elwood Stetler, prin.   943-0360

Bishop Conwell HS   3-00011
  200 LEVITTOWN PKY 19054   943-4300
  Helen Chaykowsky, prin.

Lewisberry, AC 717, PC 2, York
West Shore SD
  Supt. — See New Cumberland
Red Land HS   4-00011
  560 FISHING CREEK RD 17339   938-6561
  Jeffery Breighner, prin.

Lewisburg, AC 717, PC 6, Union
Lewisburg Area SD   4-11111
  PO BOX 351 17837   523-3220
  William Torok, supt.

HS, 815 MARKET ST 17837   2-00011
  Lawrence Potash, prin.   523-3220
MS, 2051 WASHINGTON AVE 17837   3-01100
  Joseph Galanti, prin.   523-3220

West Shore SD
  Supt. — See New Cumberland
Crossroads MS   3-00100
  535 FISHING CREEK RD 17339   932-1295
  Joseph Gargiulo, prin.

Bucknell University 17837   5-UC
  523-1271

Lewistown, AC 717, PC 6, Mifflin
Area Vocational Technical SD
  Supt. — See Harrisburg
Juniata-Mifflin County AVTS   Vo Tech
  1010 BELLE VERNON AVE 17044   248-3933
  Carolyn Foust, prin.

Mifflin County SD, 201 8TH ST 17044   6-11111
  Robert Bohn, supt.   248-0148
Indian Valley HS   3-00011
  HIGHLAND PARK 17044   248-5441
  Andrew Pollock, prin.
Lewistown Area HS, 2 MANOR DR 17044   3-00011
  Donald Willis, prin.   242-1401
MS, 212 GREEN AVE 17044   2-00100
  Edward Curry, prin.   248-0145
Other Schools – See Mc Veytown, Reedsville

Liberty, AC 717, PC 2, Tioga
Southern Tioga SD
  Supt. — See Blossburg
JSHS, PO BOX 135 16930   2-00111
  Robert Wirth, prin.   324-2071

Library, AC 412, PC 5, Allegheny
South Park SD, 2178 RIDGE RD 15129   4-11111
  Lawrence Muir, supt.   655-3111
South Park HS, 2178 RIDGE RD 15129   3-00011
  Edwin Moyer, prin.   655-4900
South Park MS   3-01100
  2500 STEWART RD 15129   831-7200
  Douglas Broglie, prin.

Ligonier, AC 412, PC 4, Westmoreland
Ligonier Valley SD   5-11111
  120 E MAIN ST 15658   238-5696
  James Dick, supt.
Ligonier Valley SHS   2-00001
  40 SPRINGER RD 15658   238-9531
  Vanessa Roddy, prin.
Ligonier Valley JHS, BELL ST EXT 15658   2-00110
  Barbara McEvoy, prin.   238-6407
Other Schools – See New Florence

Limerick, AC 215, PC 3, Montgomery
Area Vocational Technical SD
  Supt. — See Harrisburg
Western Montgomery County AVTS   Vo Tech
  77 GRATERSFORD RD 19468   489-7272
  Richard Frank, prin.

Lincoln University, AC 215, PC 4, Chester

Lincoln University 19352   4-UC
  932-8300

Linesville, AC 814, PC 4, Crawford
Conneaut SD, 302 E ERIE ST 16424   5-11111
  Andrew Pollus, supt.   683-5900
Linesville-Conneaut-Summit JSHS   2-00111
  RR 3 BOX 135C 16424   683-5551
  William Minick, prin.
Other Schools – See Conneaut Lake, Conneautville

Lititz, AC 717, PC 6, Lancaster
Warwick SD, 301 W ORANGE ST 17543   5-11111
  John Bonfield, supt.   626-3734
Warwick HS, 301 W ORANGE ST 17543   4-00011
  Frederick Cummins, prin.   626-3700
Warwick MS, 401 MAPLE ST 17543   3-00100
  Michael O'Hara, prin.   626-3701

Linden Hall, 212 E MAIN ST 17543   1-00011
  Douglas Peterson, prin.   626-8512

Littlestown, AC 717, PC 5, Adams
Littlestown Area SD, MAPLE AVE 17340   4-11111
  Patricia Dovey, supt.   359-4146
HS, 200 E MYRTLE ST 17340   2-00011
  Bryant Meckley, prin.   359-4146
Maple Avenue MS   3-01100
  75 MAPLE AVE 17340   359-4146
  Donna Leese, prin.

Lock Haven, AC 717, PC 6, Clinton
Keystone Central SD, 95 W 4TH ST 17745   6-11111
  Thomas O'Rourke, supt.   893-4900
JSHS, 301 W CHURCH ST 17745   4-00111
  John Glantz, prin.   748-5626
Other Schools – See Loganton, Mill Hall, Renovo

Lock Haven University 17745   5-UC
  893-2011

Loganton, AC 717, PC 2, Clinton
Keystone Central SD
  Supt. — See Lock Haven
Sugar Valley Area S   2-11111
  RR 2 BOX 10 17747   725-3521
  Stephen Caruso, prin.

Loretto, AC 814, PC 4, Cambria

St. Francis College   4-UC
  PO BOX 600 15940   472-3000

Lower Burrell, AC 412, PC 7, Westmoreland
Burrell SD   4-11111
  1021 PUCKETY CHURCH RD 15068   339-1026
  John George, supt.
Burrell HS   3-00011
  1021 PUCKETY CHURCH RD 15068   337-7621
  Frank Prazenica, prin.
Huston MS   3-01100
  1020 PUCKETY CHURCH RD 15068   339-6621
  Donald Balla, prin.

Loysburg, AC 814, PC 2, Bedford
Northern Bedford County SD   4-11111
  HC 1 BOX 200 16659   766-2221
  Lanny Ross, supt.
Northern Bedford County JSHS   3-00111
  HC 1 BOX 200 16659   766-2221
  David Smith, prin.

Lykens, AC 717, PC 4, Dauphin
Upper Dauphin Area SD, RR 1 17048   4-11111
  Andrew Hills, supt.   362-8134
Upper Dauphin Area MS, RR 1 17048   2-01100
  Keith Boyer, prin.   362-8177
Other Schools – See Elizabethville

Mc Clellandtown, AC 412, PC 3, Fayette
Albert Galltn Area SD
  Supt. — See Masontown
Gallatin North JHS   2-00110
  PO BOX 308 15458   737-6325
  Denise Martin, prin.

Mc Connellsburg, AC 717, PC 4, Fulton
Area Vocational Technical SD
  Supt. — See Harrisburg
Fulton County AVTS   Vo Tech
  151 E CHERRY ST 17233   485-5813
  Julia Cigola, prin.

Central Fulton SD   4-11111
  151 E CHERRY ST 17233   485-3195
  Robert Swadley, supt.
JSHS, 151 E CHERRY ST 17233   3-00111
  Hervey Hann, prin.   485-3195

Mc Donald, AC 412, PC 4, Washington
Canon-McMillan SD
  Supt. — See Canonsburg
Cecil MS, RR 3 15057   2-00100
  Frank Brettschneider, prin.   745-2623
Fort Cherry SD   4-11111
  110 FORT CHERRY RD 15057   796-1581
  Jesse King, supt.
Fort Cherry JSHS   3-00111
  110 FORT CHERRY RD 15057   796-1551
  Linda Nichols, prin.
South Fayette Township SD   4-11111
  2250 OLD OAKDALE RD 15057   221-4542
  Joel Carr, supt.
South Fayette Twp. JSHS   3-00111
  2254 OLD OAKDALE RD 15057   221-4542
  Linda Hippert, prin.

Mc Keesport, AC 412, PC 8, Allegheny
Area Vocational Technical SD
  Supt. — See Harrisburg
McKeesport AVTS   Vo Tech
  3600 ONEIL BLVD 15132   664-3690
  Nelda Renner, prin.

McKeesport Area SD   5-11111
  2225 5TH AVE 15132   664-3610
  Robert Weinfurtner, supt.
McKeesport Area HS   4-00011
  1960 EDEN PARK BLVD 15132   664-3650
  Robert Meredith, prin.
Cornell MS, 1600 CORNELL ST 15132   3-01100
  Frank McLaughlin, prin.   664-3720
McClure MS, 500 LONGVUE DR 15131   3-01100
  Adolph Vay, prin.   664-3740
South Allegheny SD   4-11111
  2743 WASHINGTON BLVD 15133   675-5460
  Donald Lee, supt.
South Allegheny JSHS   3-00111
  2743 WASHINGTON BLVD 15133   675-5460
  R. Zukaukas, prin.

Pennsylvania State University   4-CC
  0 UNIVERSITY DR 15132   675-9000
Serra District HS   2-00011
  200 HERSHEY DR 15132   751-2020
  Fr. Sysol, prin.

Mc Kees Rocks, AC 412, PC 6, Allegheny
Montour SD
  Supt. — See Coraopolis
Montour HS, 225 CLEVER RD 15136   3-00011
  Robert Pantuso, prin.   778-1060

Sto-Rox SD   4-11111
  600 RUSSELLWOOD AVE 15136   771-3213
  Robert Perry, supt.
Sto-Rox JSHS, 1105 VALLEY ST 15136   3-00111
  Steve Wargo, prin.   771-3213

Ohio Valley General Hospital   HSP
  25 HECKEL RD 15136   777-6207

Mc Murray, AC 412, PC 5, Washington
Peters Township SD 5-11111
631 E MCMURRAY RD 15317 941-6251
Dennis Urso, supt.
Peters Twp. HS 3-00011
264 E MCMURRAY RD 15317 941-6250
Thomas Hajzus, prin.
Peters Twp. MS 3-00100
625 E MCMURRAY RD 15317 941-2688
Anthony Merante, prin.

Mc Sherrystown, AC 717, PC 5, Adams

Delone Catholic HS 2-00011
140 S OXFORD AVE 17344 637-5969
Maureen Thiec, prin.

Macungie, AC 610, PC 5, Lehigh
East Penn SD
Supt. — See Emmaus
Eyer JHS, 5616 BUCKEYE RD 18062 3-00110
Michael Waddell, prin. 965-1604

Salem Christian S, RR 1 BOX 486B 18062 2-11111
966-5823

Mc Veytown, AC 717, PC 2, Mifflin
Mifflin County SD
Supt. — See Lewistown
Strodes Mills MS, RR 2 17051 2-01100
Teresa Hughes, prin. 248-5488

Mahanoy City, AC 717, PC 6, Schuylkill
Mahanoy Area SD, PO BOX 54 17948 4-11111
John Murtin, supt. 773-3443
Mahanoy Area HS 2-00011
800 E SOUTH ST 17948 773-4011
Richard Boyle, prin.
Mahanoy Area MS 2-01100
400 E SOUTH ST 17948 773-2522
John Murtin, prin.

McCann School of Business 2-CS
47 S MAIN ST 17948 773-1820

Malvern, AC 610, PC 5, Chester
Great Valley SD
Supt. — See Devault
Great Valley HS 3-00011
225 PHOENIXVILLE PIKE 19355 644-6610
Levi Wingard, prin.
Wayne MS, 20 DEVON RD 19355 3-00100
Stephen Swymer, prin. 644-6440

Devereux-Mapleton Center in PA 2-HND
655 SUGARTOWN RD 19355 296-6975
King of Prussia Graduate Center 2-UC
30 SWEDESFORD RD 19355
Malvern Prep S 2-00111
418 S WARREN AVE 19355 644-5454
James Stewart, prin.
Phelps S, 583 SUGARTOWN RD 19355 2-00111
Norman Phelps, prin. 644-1754
Villa Maria HS 2-00011
370 OLD LINCOLN HWY 19355 644-2551
Sr. Mary Kelly, prin.

Manchester, AC 717, PC 4, York
Northeastern York SD 4-11111
41 HARDING ST 17345 266-3667
David Krauser, supt.
Northeastern HS, 260 HIGH ST 17345 3-00011
(—), prin. 266-3644
Northeastern MS, HARTMAN ST 17345 3-00100
Fred Hainley, prin. 266-3676

Manheim, AC 717, PC 6, Lancaster
Manheim Central SD 5-11111
71 N HAZEL ST 17545 665-3422
Joseph McSparran, supt.
Manheim Central HS 3-00011
0 ADELE AVE 17545 665-2451
Jere Murphy, prin.
Manheim Central JHS 2-00100
E GRAMBY ST 17545 – L. Stitzel, prin. 665-2246

Mansfield, AC 717, PC 5, Tioga
Southern Tioga SD
Supt. — See Blossburg
JSHS, 73 W WELLSBORO ST 16933 2-00111
(—), prin. 662-2674

Mansfield University of Pennsylvania 5-UC
16933 662-4000
New Covenant Academy 2-11111
310 EXTENSION ST 16933 662-2996

Marienville, AC 814, PC 4, Forest
Forest Area SD
Supt. — See Tionesta
East Forest JSHS, BIRCH ST 16239 2-00111
Arthur Van Nort, prin. 927-6688

Marietta, AC 717, PC 5, Lancaster
Donegal SD
Supt. — See Mount Joy
Donegal MS, 1175 RIVER RD 17547 3-00100
James Lawrence, prin. 426-4915

Marion Center, AC 412, PC 2, Indiana
Marion Center Area SD 5-11111
PO BOX 156 15759 397-4911
Michael Vetere, supt.
Marion Center Area JSHS 3-00111
PO BOX 156 15759 397-5551
A. Martz, prin.

Markleysburg, AC 412, PC 2, Fayette
Uniontown Area SD
Supt. — See Uniontown
McMullen MS, RR 1 BOX 110B 15459 2-00100
Charles Machesky, prin. 329-8811

Mar Lin, AC 717, PC 3, Schuylkill
Area Vocational Technical SD
Supt. — See Harrisburg
Schuylkill County AVTS Vo Tech
PO BOX 130 17951 544-9131
Ralph Morgan, prin.
Schuylkill County AVTS-South Vo Tech
PTTSVLLE/MNRSVLL HWY 17951 544-4748
George Harris, prin.

Mars, AC 412, PC 4, Butler
Mars Area SD, RR 2 BOX 150 16046 4-11111
William Pettigrew, supt. 625-1518
Mars Area HS 3-00011
1775 THREE DEGREE RD 16046 625-1581
John Coury, prin.
Mars Area MS 2-00100
520 STATE ROUTE 228 16046 625-3145
Mark Feris, prin.

Martinsburg, AC 814, PC 4, Blair
Spring Cove SD
Supt. — See Roaring Spring
Central SHS, RR 1 BOX 420 16662 3-00001
David Thompson, prin. 793-2111

Masontown, AC 412, PC 5, Fayette
Albert Galltn Area SD 5-11111
10 W CHURCH AVE 15461 583-1654
Denise Martin, supt.
Other Schools – See Mc Clellandtown, Point Marion, Uniontown

Meadville, AC 814, PC 7, Crawford
Area Vocational Technical SD
Supt. — See Harrisburg
Crawford County AVTS Vo Tech
860 THURSTON RD 16335 724-6024
Broderic Fisher, prin.

Crawford Central SD 5-11111
RR 9 BOX 462 16335 724-3960
James Lascola, supt.
Meadville Area SHS 3-00001
930 NORTH ST 16335 336-1121
George Deshner, prin.
Meadville Area JHS 3-00110
847 N MAIN ST 16335 333-1188
Armendia Dixon, prin.
Other Schools – See Cochranton

Allegheny College 4-UC
520 N MAIN ST 16335 332-3100

Mechanicsburg, AC 717, PC 6, Cumberland
Area Vocational Technical SD
Supt. — See Harrisburg
Cumberland-Perry AVTS Vo Tech
110 OLD WILLOW MILL RD 17055 697-0354
Anthony Vicic, prin.

Cumberland Valley SD 6-11111
6746 CARLISLE PIKE 17055 697-8261
Orr Brenneman, supt.
Cumberland Valley HS 4-00011
6746 CARLISLE PIKE 17055 766-0217
Harold Bricker, prin.
Good Hope MS, 451 SKYPORT RD 17055 3-00100
Kaye Wishard, prin. 761-1865
Cumberland Valley MS West 3-00100
6746 CARLISLE PIKE 17055 766-0217
Eugene Baldwin, prin.

Mechanicsburg Area SD 5-11111
500 S BROAD ST 17055 691-4500
Robert Curtis, supt.
Mechanicsburg Area HS 4-00011
500 S BROAD ST 17055 691-4530
Richard Bollinger, prin.
Mechanicsburg Area IS 3-00100
100 E ELMWOOD AVE 17055 691-4560
Leonard Ference, prin.

Faith Tabernacle S 2-11111
1410 GOODHOPE RD 17055 975-0641

Media, AC 610, PC 6, Delaware
Area Vocational Technical SD
Supt. — See Harrisburg
Delaware County AVTS Vo Tech
SIXTH & OLIVE STS 19063 565-4880
Thomas Pivnichny, prin.

Rose Tree Media SD 5-11111
901 N PROVIDENCE RD 19063 565-1200
Henry Nacrelli, supt.
Penncrest HS, 134 BARREN RD 19063 3-00011
Anthony Hicks, prin. 566-6010
Springton Lake MS 3-00100
1900 N PROVIDENCE RD 19063 566-2900
Robert Towson, prin.

Delaware County Community College 6-CC
901 MEDIA LINE RD 19063 359-5000
Pennsylvania Institute of Technology 2-CC
800 MANCHESTER AVE 19063 565-7900
Pennsylvania State University 4-CC
25 YEARSLEY MILL RD 19063 565-3300
The Christian Academy 3-11111
704 S OLD MIDDLETOWN RD 19063 872-7600
Timothy Sierer, prin.
Williamson Free School/Trades and Tech 2-CS
106 S NEW MIDDLETOWN RD 19063 566-1776

Mercer, AC 412, PC 4, Mercer
Area Vocational Technical SD
Supt. — See Harrisburg
Mercer County AVTS Vo Tech
PO BOX 152 16137 662-3000
Rachel Martin, prin.

Mercer Area SD, PO BOX 32 16137 4-11111
Lawrence Connelly, supt. 662-5100
Mercer Area JSHS 3-00111
WEST BUTLER ST 16137 662-5104
Lawrence Connelly, prin.

Mercersburg, AC 717, PC 4, Franklin
Tuscarora SD 5-11111
118 E SEMINARY ST 17236 328-3127
Ted Rabold, supt.
Buchanan HS 3-00011
4773 FORT LOUDON RD 17236 328-2146
Ronald Maslanik, prin.
Buchanan MS 3-00100
5191 FORT LOUDON RD 17236 328-5221
Charles Rahauser, prin.

Mercersburg Academy 2-00011
300 E SEMINARY ST 17236 328-2151
Walter Burgin, prin.

Merion Station, AC 610, PC 6, Montgomery

Akiba Hebrew Academy 2-00111
223 N HIGHLAND AVE 19066 839-3540
Rabbi Field, prin.
Episcopal Academy 4-11111
376 N LATCHES LN 19066 667-9612
James Crawford, prin.
Merion Mercy HS 2-00011
515 MONTGOMERY AVE 19066 664-6655
Sr. Teresa Mary, prin.

Mertztown, AC 215, PC 2, Berks

Gateway Christian S 2-11111
245 FREDERICKSVILLE RD 19539 682-2748

Meyersdale, AC 814, PC 5, Somerset
Meyersdale Area SD 4-11111
RR 3 BOX 60 15552 634-5123
Curtis Kerns, supt.
Meyersdale Area JSHS, RR 3 15552 3-00111
W. Bowman, prin. 634-8311

Middleburg, AC 717, PC 4, Snyder
Midd-West SD, 568 E MAIN ST 17842 5-11111
William Sheaffer, supt. 837-0046
JSHS, 540 E MAIN ST 17842 3-00111
Robert Apple, prin. 837-0046
Other Schools – See Beaver Springs

Middletown, AC 717, PC 6, Dauphin
Middletown Area SD 5-11111
55 W WATER ST 17057 948-3300
Gary Shank, supt.
Middletown Area HS 3-00011
1155 N UNION ST 17057 948-3333
Casper Voithofer, prin.
Feaser MS, 214 N RACE ST 17057 3-00100
Russ Eppinger, prin. 948-3390

Electronic Institutes 2-CC
19 JAMESWAY PLZ 17057 944-2731
Pennsylvania State University 4-UC
RT 230 17057 948-6250

Midland, AC 412, PC 5, Beaver
Western Beaver County SD 4-11111
343 RIDGEMONT DR 15059 643-9310
Victor George, supt.
Other Schools – See Industry

Mifflinburg, AC 717, PC 5, Union
Mifflinburg Area SD 4-11111
PO BOX 285 17844 966-1553
Ben Van Horn, supt.
Mifflinburg Area HS 3-00011
75 MARKET ST 17844 966-1063
Dan Martin, prin.
Mifflinburg Area MS 3-01100
EAST MARKET ST 17844 966-1086
David Long, prin.

Mifflintown, AC 717, PC 3, Juniata
Juniata County SD 5-11111
PO BOX 227 17059 436-2111
Kenneth Stuck, supt.
Juniata SHS, RR 4 BOX 99 17059 3-00011
Harry Fulton, prin. 436-2193
Tuscarora JHS, RR 4 BOX 99 17059 2-00110
Fred Harris, prin. 436-2165
Other Schools – See Cocolamus

Milford, AC 717, PC 4, Pike
Delaware Valley SD 5-11111
HC 77 BOX 379A 18337 296-6431
H. James Melody, supt.

Delaware Valley HS | 3-00011
HC 77 BOX 379C 18337 | 296-6496
Thomas Finan, prin.
Delaware Valley MS | 3-01100
HC 77 BOX 379B 18337 | 296-6488
Paul Blaum, prin.

Mill Creek, AC 814, PC 2, Huntingdon
Area Vocational Technical SD
Supt. — See Harrisburg
Huntingdon County AVTS | Vo Tech
PO BOX E 17060 | 643-0951
Kenneth Erisman, prin.

Millersburg, AC 717, PC 5, Dauphin
Millersburg Area SD | 4-11111
799 CENTER ST 17061 | 692-2108
Edwin Schlegel, supt.
Millersburg Area HS | 2-00011
799 CENTER ST 17061 | 692-2108
S. Kirk Miller, prin.
Millersburg Area MS | 2-00100
799 CENTER ST 17061 | 692-2108
Sara Berchock, prin.

Millerstown, AC 717, PC 3, Perry
Greenwood SD | 3-11111
405 E SUNBURY ST 17062 | 589-3115
Norman Shea, supt.
Greenwood JSHS, RR 2 17062 | 2-00111
Ed Burns, prin. | 589-3115

Millersville, AC 717, PC 6, Lancaster
Penn Manor SD, PO BOX 1001 17551 | 5-11111
Noel Taylor, supt. | 872-9500
Penn Manor HS, PO BOX 1001 17551 | 4-00011
Valerie Breneisen, prin. | 872-9520
Other Schools – See Pequea

Millersville University of Pennsylvania | 6-UC
17551 | 872-3011

Mill Hall, AC 717, PC 4, Clinton
Keystone Central SD
Supt. — See Lock Haven
Bald Eagle-Nittany JSHS | 3-00111
200 BEN AVE 17751 | 726-3141
Norman Palovcsik, prin.

Millville, AC 717, PC 3, Columbia
Millville Area SD, PO BOX 260 17846 | 3-11111
Roy Antolick, supt. | 458-5538
JSHS, PO BOX 260 17846 | 2-00111
George Jones, prin. | 458-5547

Milton, AC 717, PC 6, Northumberland
Milton Area SD | 5-11111
700 MAHONING ST 17847 | 742-7614
James Baugher, supt.
SHS, 700 MAHONING ST 17847 | 3-00001
Philip Hoff, prin. | 742-7611
Milton Area JHS | 3-00110
700 MAHONING ST 17847 | 742-7685
Stephen Bish, prin.

Meadowbrook Christian S | 2-11111
RR 2 BOX 2000 17847 | 742-2638

Minersville, AC 717, PC 5, Schuylkill
Minersville Area SD | 4-11111
PO BOX 787 17954 | 544-4764
M. Brady, supt.
Minersville Area JSHS | 3-00111
PO BOX 787 17954 | 544-4761
Ercole Lacianca, prin.

Monaca, AC 412, PC 6, Beaver
Area Vocational Technical SD
Supt. — See Harrisburg
Beaver County AVTS, POPLAR DR 15061 | Vo Tech
Rody Polojac, prin. | 728-5800

Center Area SD, BAKER RD EXT 15061 | 4-11111
Edward Elder, supt. | 775-5600
Center Area HS | 3-00011
0 BAKER ROAD EXT 15061 | 775-4300
Philip Kanfush, prin.
Center Area JHS | 2-00100
BAKER ROAD EXT 15061 | 775-8200
Samuel Gagliardi, prin.

Monaca SD, 1500 ALLEN AVE 15061 | 3-11111
Alan Guandolo, supt. | 775-3252
JSHS, 1500 ALLEN AVE 15061 | 2-00111
Edward Drake, prin. | 775-4320

Community College of Beaver County | 5-CC
COLLEGE DR 15061 | 775-8561
Pennsylvania State University | 5-UC
BROADHEAD RD 15061 | 773-3800

Monessen, AC 412, PC 6, Westmoreland
Monessen CSD, 600 REED AVE 15062 | 4-11111
R. Malarbi, supt. | 684-3600
HS, 600 REED AVE 15062 | 2-00011
Fred Usher, prin. | 684-7100
MS, 600 REED AVE 15062 | 2-00100
Cynthia Chelen, prin. | 684-6282

Douglas School of Business | 2-CS
130 7TH ST 15062 | 684-7644

Monongahela, AC 412, PC 5, Washington
Ringgold SD, 1200 CHESS ST 15063 | 5-11111
Byron Phillips, supt. | 258-9329

Ringgold HS, RR 4 BOX 604 15063 | 4-00011
L. Weinrich, prin. | 258-2200
Carroll MS, 120 ALEXANDER AVE 15063 | 2-00100
Edward Repka, prin. | 258-8454
Other Schools – See Finleyville

Monroeville, AC 412, PC 8, Allegheny
Area Vocational Technical SD
Supt. — See Harrisburg
Forbes Road East AVTS | Vo Tech
607 BEATTY RD 15146 | 373-8100
Linda Karns, prin.

Gateway SD, 2609 MOSSIDE BLVD 15146 | 5-11111
Wayne Doyle, supt. | 372-5300
Gateway HS, 2629 MOSSIDE BLVD 15146 | 4-00011
George Vurgich, prin. | 373-5744
Gateway JHS | 3-00100
OLD WM PENN HWY 15146 | 373-5780
Victor Maccarelli, prin.

Career Training Academy | 2-CS
244 CENTER RD STE 101 15146 | 372-3900
Community College of Allegheny County | 5-CC
595 BEATTY RD 15146 | 371-8651
Greater Works Academy | 3-11111
301 COLLEGE PARK DR 15146 | 327-6500
Monroeville School of Business | 2-CC
105 MALL BLVD FL 3 15146 | 856-8040
Western School of Health & Bus. Careers | 2-CS
3824 NORTHERN PIKE 15146 | 373-6400

Mont Alto, AC 717, PC 4, Franklin

Pennsylvania State University | 3-CC
MONT ALTO CAMPUS 17237 | 749-3111

Montgomery, AC 717, PC 4, Lycoming
Montgomery Area SD | 4-11111
120 PENN ST 17752 | 547-1608
David Robbins, supt.
Montgomery Area JSHS | 2-00111
120 PENN ST 17752 | 547-1608
David Becker, prin.

Montoursville, AC 717, PC 5, Lycoming
Montoursville Area SD | 4-11111
1304 WEAVER ST 17754 | 368-2491
John Zimmerman, supt.
Montoursville Area HS | 3-00011
100 N ARCH ST 17754 | 368-2611
Daniel Chandler, prin.
McCall MS, 600 WILLOW ST 17754 | 3-01100
J. Kustanbauter, prin. | 368-2441

Montrose, AC 717, PC 4, Susquehanna
Montrose Area SD | 4-11111
RR 3 BOX 28 18801 | 278-3731
Augustine Grant, supt.
JSHS, RR 3 BOX 28 18801 | 3-00111
Michael Ognosky, prin. | 278-3731

Morgantown, AC 215, PC 3, Berks

Conestoga Christian S | 2-11111
2760 MAIN ST 19543 | 286-0353
Glenna Hershberger, prin.

Morrisdale, AC 814, PC 3, Clearfield
West Branch Area SD | 4-11111
RR 2 BOX 194 16858 | 345-6832
John McDannel, supt.
West Branch Area JSHS | 3-00111
RR 2 BOX 194 16858 | 345-5615
Andrew Pollock, prin.

Morrisville, AC 215, PC 6, Bucks
Morrisville Boro SD | 4-11111
550 W PALMER ST 19067 | 736-2681
Elizabeth Fineburg, supt.
Morrisville Borough JSHS | 3-00111
550 W PALMER ST 19067 | 736-2681
Stephen Young, prin.

Moscow, AC 717, PC 4, Lackawanna
North Pocono SD, CHURCH ST 18444 | 5-11111
John Buscarini, supt. | 842-7659
North Pocono HS | 3-00011
701 CHURCH ST 18444 | 842-7606
Joseph Castrogiovanni, prin.
North Pocono MS | 3-01100
701 CHURCH ST 18444 | 842-4588
William Wright, prin.

Mountain Top, AC 717, PC 3, Luzerne
Crestwood SD | 4-11111
281 S MOUNTAIN BLVD 18707 | 474-6888
Gordon Snow, supt.
Crestwood HS | 3-00111
281 S MOUNTAIN BLVD 18707 | 474-6782
Anthony Fadule, prin.

Mount Carmel, AC 717, PC 6, Northumberland
Mt. Carmel Area SD | 4-11111
600 W 5TH ST 17851 | 339-3473
Dennis Namey, supt.
Mt. Carmel Area JSHS | 3-00111
600 W 5TH ST 17851 | 339-1500
Richard Beierschmitt, prin.

Mount Joy, AC 717, PC 6, Lancaster
Area Vocational Technical SD
Supt. — See Harrisburg
Lancaster County AVTS-Mt. Joy | Vo Tech
PO BOX 537 17552 | 653-2061
John Bowers, prin.

Donegal SD, PO BOX 304 17552 | 4-11111
Woodrow Sites, supt. | 653-1447
Donegal HS, PO BOX 304 17552 | 3-00011
(—), prin. | 653-1871
Other Schools – See Marietta

Mount Pleasant, AC 412, PC 5, Westmoreland
Mt. Pleasant Area SD | 5-11111
RR 4 BOX 2222 15666 | 547-5706
Edward Hoffman, supt.
Mt. Pleasant Area JSHS | 4-00111
RR 4 BOX 2222 15666 | 547-5763
Michael Picarsic, prin.

Mount Union, AC 814, PC 5, Huntingdon
Mt. Union Area SD | 4-11111
28 W MARKET ST 17066 | 542-8631
Jerry Dunkle, supt.
Mt. Union Area JSHS | 3-00111
706 N SHAVER ST 17066 | 542-8631
Russell Quay, prin.

Muncy, AC 717, PC 5, Lycoming
Muncy SD, W PENN ST 17756 | 4-11111
Thomas Scholvin, supt. | 546-3125
JSHS, 200 W PENN ST 17756 | 3-00111
William Ramsey, prin. | 546-3127

Munhall, AC 412, PC 7, Allegheny
Steel Valley SD, 220 E OLIVER RD 15120 | 4-11111
Ronald Grimm, supt. | 464-3650
Steel Valley HS, 3113 MAIN ST 15120 | 3-00011
Aldine Coleman, prin. | 464-3690
Woodlawn MS | 3-00100
300 WOODLAWN AVE 15120 | 464-3645
Raymond Supak, prin.

Murrysville, AC 412, PC 7, Westmoreland
Franklin Regional SD | 5-11111
3210 SCHOOL RD 15668 | 327-5456
Paul Johnson, supt.
Franklin Regional SHS | 3-00001
3200 SCHOOL RD 15668 | 327-5298
Jane Tachoir, prin.
Franklin Regional JHS | 3-00110
4660 OLD WILLIAM PENN HWY 15668 | 327-5250
Daniel Stoner, prin.

Myerstown, AC 717, PC 5, Lebanon
Eastern Lebanon County SD | 4-11111
60 EVERGREEN DR 17067 | 866-7117
Harry Zechman, supt.
Eastern Lebanon County HS | 3-00011
180 ELCO DR 17067 | 866-7447
Stephen George, prin.
Eastern Lebanon County MS | 3-00100
180 ELCO DR 17067 | 866-6591
Keith DuBois, prin.

Evangelical School of Theology | 2-UC
121 S COLLEGE ST 17067 | 866-5775
Myerstown Mennonite S | 2-11111
739 E LINCOLN AVE 17067 | 866-5667

Nanticoke, AC 717, PC 7, Luzerne
Greater Nanticoke Area SD | 4-11111
PO BOX 126 18634 | 735-1270
Anthony Trosan, supt.
Fine HS, 425 KOSCIUSZKO ST 18634 | 3-00011
John Gregorowicz, prin. | 735-7781
Greater Nanticoke Area MS | 3-00100
555 E MAIN ST 18634 | 735-2770
Dennis Matzoni, prin.

Luzerne Co. Community College | 6-CC
1333 S PROSPECT ST 18634 | 829-7300

Nanty Glo, AC 814, PC 5, Cambria
Blacklick Valley SD, 555 BIRCH ST 15943 | 4-11111
Donald Thomas, supt. | 749-9211
Blacklick Valley JSHS | 2-00111
555 BIRCH ST 15943 | 749-9213
Thomas Kupchella, prin.

Narberth, AC 610, PC 5, Montgomery
Lower Merion SD
Supt. — See Ardmore
Welsh Valley MS | 2-00100
1320 HAGYS FORD RD 19072 | 664-3112
Alan Rosenau, prin.

Natrona, AC 412, PC see Natrona Heights

Allegheny Valley Hospital | HSP
1301 CARLISLE ST 15065 | 226-7000

Natrona Heights, AC 412, PC 7, Allegheny
Highlands SD, PO BOX 288 15065 | 5-11111
Louis Baldassare, supt. | 226-2400
Highlands HS | 4-00011
IDAHO AT PACIFIC AVE 15065 | 226-1000
Robert Susini, prin.
Highlands MS | 3-00100
1350 BROADVIEW BLVD 15065 | 226-0600
Allan Reyer, prin.

St. Joseph HS | 2-00011
800 MONTANA AVE 15065 | 224-5552
Beverly Kaniecki, prin.

Nazareth, AC 610, PC 6, Northampton
Nazareth Area SD, 8 CENTER SQ 18064 | 5-11111
John Jenkins, supt. | 759-1170

Nazareth Area SHS 3-00001
  501 E CENTER ST 18064 759-1730
  Victor Lesky, prin.
Nazareth Area MS 3-00110
  1 EDUCATION PLAZA 18064 759-3350
  Robert Jones, prin.

Nesquehoning, AC 717, PC 5, Carbon

Pennsylvania Business Institute 2-CS
  1 ANGELINI AVE 18240 669-9894

New Berlin, AC 717, PC 3, Union
Area Vocational Technical SD
  Supt. — See Harrisburg
  Sun AVTS, 815 E MARKET ST 17855 Vo Tech
  John Bohn, prin. 966-1034

New Bethlehem, AC 814, PC 4, Clarion
Redbank Valley SD 4-11111
  920 BROAD ST 16242 275-2426
  R. David Farley, supt.
Redbank Valley JSHS 3-00111
  910 BROAD ST 16242 275-2424
  Edward Bula, prin.

New Bloomfield, AC 717, PC 4, Perry
West Perry SD
  Supt. — See Elliottsburg
West Perry MS, RR 2 17068 2-00100
  Wilfred Brousse, prin. 582-4328

Carson Long Military Institute 2-00011
  PO BOX 98 17068 582-2121
  Col. Holman, prin.

New Brighton, AC 412, PC 6, Beaver
New Brighton Area SD 4-11111
  3225 43RD ST 15066 – J. Ross, supt. 843-1795
New Brighton Area HS 3-00011
  3200 43RD ST 15066 846-1050
  Enrico Antonini, prin.
New Brighton Area MS 2-00100
  901 PENN AVE 15066 846-8100
  Bonita McShane, prin.

Beaver County Christian S 2-00111
  601 PENN AVE 15066 843-3002
Garfield Business Institute 2-CS
  709 3RD AVE 15066 847-4510

New Castle, AC 412, PC 8, Lawrence
Area Vocational Technical SD
  Supt. — See Harrisburg
Lawrence County AVTS Vo Tech
  750 PHELPS WAY 16101 658-3583
  Robert Hooven, prin.

Laurel SD, RR 4 BOX 30 16101 4-11111
  Phillip Bollenbacher, supt. 658-8940
Laurel JSHS, RR 4 BOX 30 16101 3-00111
  Leonard Rich, prin. 658-9056

Neshannock Township SD 4-11111
  301 MITCHELL RD 16105 658-4793
  J. Scungio, supt.
Neshannock JSHS 3-00111
  301 MITCHELL RD 16105 658-5513
  Karen Humphrey, prin.

New Castle Area SD, 420 FERN ST 16101 5-11111
  J. Martin, supt. 656-4756
HS, 300 E LINCOLN AVE 16101 3-00011
  F. Dattilo, prin. 656-4700
Franklin JHS 3-00100
  815 CUNNINGHAM AVE 16101 656-4720
  Amen Hassen, prin.

Shenango Area SD 4-11111
  2501 OLD PITTSBURGH RD 16101 658-7287
  William Foster, supt.
Shenango Area JSHS 3-00111
  2550 ELLWOOD RD 16101 658-5537
  Conrad Palumbo, prin.

Union Area SD 3-11111
  500 S SCOTLAND LN 16101 658-4775
  Domenic Ionta, supt.
Union Area HS 2-00011
  2106 CAMDEN AVE 16101 658-4501
  Richard Rossi, prin.
Union Area MS 2-01100
  2106 CAMDEN AVE 16101 658-4501
  John Leitera, prin.

Erie Business Center South 1-CS
  700 MORAVIA ST 16101 658-9066
Jameson Memorial Hospital HSP
  1211 WILMINGTON AVE 16105 656-4052
St. Francis Hospital of New Castle HSP
  1000 S MERCER ST 16101 656-6000
Shenango Valley School of Business 2-CS
  500 S MILL ST 16101 654-1976

New Cumberland, AC 717, PC 6, Cumberland
West Shore SD, PO BOX 803 17070 6-11111
  Larry Sayre, supt. 938-9577
MS, 331 8TH ST 17070 3-00100
  Gerard Rosolie, prin. 774-0162
  Other Schools – See Camp Hill, Lemoyne,
  Lewisberry, Lewisburg

New Florence, AC 412, PC 3, Westmoreland
Ligonier Valley SD
  Supt. — See Ligonier

Laurel Valley JSHS, RR 1 15944 3-00111
  Stephen Whisdosh, prin. 238-4034

New Freedom, AC 717, PC 5, York

New Freedom Christian S 2-11111
  PO BOX 519 17349 235-6877

New Holland, AC 717, PC 5, Lancaster
Eastern Lancaster County SD 5-11111
  PO BOX 609 17557 354-1500
  William Rohrer, supt.
Garden Spot HS, 669 E MAIN ST 17557 3-00011
  Donald Reed, prin. 354-4031
Garden Spot MS, PO BOX 609 17557 2-00100
  Joyce Syphard, prin. 354-4031

New Hope, AC 215, PC 4, Bucks
New Hope-Solebury SD 3-11111
  180 W BRIDGE ST 18938 862-2552
  Robert Jannone, supt.
New Hope-Solebury JSHS 2-00111
  180 W BRIDGE ST 18938 862-2028
  Robert Anderson, prin.

Solebury S, PO BOX 429 18938 2-00111
  John Brown, prin. 862-5261

New Kensington, AC 412, PC 7, Westmoreland
Area Vocational Technical SD
  Supt. — See Harrisburg
Northern Westmoreland County AVTS Vo Tech
  705 STEVENSON BLVD 15068 335-9389
  Albert Kanaan, prin.

New Kensington-Arnold SD 5-11111
  701 STEVENSON BLVD 15068 335-8581
  Cy Yusten, supt.
Valley HS, 703 STEVENSON BLVD 15068 3-00011
  Charles Marchetti, prin. 337-4536
Other Schools – See Arnold

Career Training Academy 2-CS
  703 5TH AVE 15068 337-1000
Citizens General Hospital HSP
  651 4TH AVE 15068 337-5090
New Kensington Commercial School 2-CC
  945 GREENSBURG RD 15068 339-7542
Oakbridge Academy of Arts 1-CS
  401 9TH ST 15068 335-5336
Pennsylvania State University 4-CC
  3550 7TH STREET RD 15068 339-7561

New Milford, AC 717, PC 3, Susquehanna
Blue Ridge SD, RR 2 BOX 220 18834 4-11111
  Edward Harris, supt. 465-3141
Blue Ridge JSHS, RR 2 18834 3-00111
  James Close, prin. 465-3144

New Oxford, AC 717, PC 4, Adams
Conewago Valley SD 5-11111
  130 BERLIN RD 17350 624-2157
  William Landauer, supt.
SHS, 130 BERLIN RD 17350 3-00001
  Michael Wilson, prin. 624-2157
JHS, 130 BERLIN RD 17350 3-00110
  David Teets, prin. 624-2157

New Paris, AC 814, PC 2, Bedford
Chestnut Ridge SD
  Supt. — See Fishertown
Chestnut Ridge HS, RR 1 BOX 79A 15554 3-00011
  Wayne Henderson, prin. 839-4195

Newport, AC 717, PC 4, Perry
Newport SD, PO BOX 9 17074 4-11111
  Suzanne McGill, supt. 567-3806
JSHS, 300 N 6TH ST 17074 3-00111
  Jeffery Zimmerman, prin. 567-3105

New Stanton, AC 412, PC 4, Westmoreland
Area Vocational Technical SD
  Supt. — See Harrisburg
Central Westmoreland County AVTS Vo Tech
  240 ARONA RD 15672 925-3532
  Clentin Martin, prin.

Newtown, AC 215, PC 5, Bucks
Council Rock SD
  Supt. — See Richboro
Council Rock SHS, 62 SWAMP RD 18940 4-00001
  Jane Wilson, prin. 968-7000
Council Rock JHS 3-00110
  GREEN LN & RICHBORO RD 18940 968-7200
  F. Yates, prin.

Bucks County Community College 7-CC
  SWAMP ROAD 18940 968-8000
George S 3-00011
  1690 LANGHORNE NEWTOWN RD 18940
  David Bourns, prin. 968-3811

Newtown Square, AC 610, PC 7, Delaware
Marple-Newtown SD 5-11111
  120 MEDIA LINE RD 19073 359-4200
  Stephen Frederick, supt.
Marple-Newtown HS 3-00011
  120 MEDIA LINE RD 19073 359-4218
  John Wingerter, prin.
  Other Schools – See Broomall

Delaware County Christian S 3-11111
  464 MALIN RD 19073 353-6522
  Kenneth Tanis, prin.

New Tripoli, AC 215, PC 2, Lehigh
Northwestern Lehigh SD 4-11111
  6493 ROUTE 309 18066 298-8661
  David Fallinger, supt.
Northwestern Lehigh HS 3-00011
  RR 2 BOX 67 18066 298-8931
  Dennis Nemes, prin.
Northwestern Lehigh MS 2-00100
  RR 2 BOX 67 18066 298-2121
  James Warfel, prin.

Newville, AC 717, PC 4, Cumberland
Big Spring SD 5-11111
  45 MOUNT ROCK RD 17241 776-2000
  William Cowden, supt.
Big Spring HS 3-00011
  45 MOUNT ROCK RD 17241 776-2000
  Lindley Black, prin.
Big Spring MS 3-00100
  47 MOUNT ROCK RD 17241 776-2000
  Glenn Gow, prin.

New Wilmington, AC 412, PC 5, Lawrence
Wilmington Area SD 4-11111
  300 WOOD ST 16142 946-8726
  C. Leon Ahlum, supt.
Wilmington Area HS 3-00011
  350 WOOD ST 16142 – (—), prin. 946-3591
Wilmington Area MS 2-00100
  400 WOOD ST 16142 946-8105
  Benjamin Fenwick, prin.

Westminster College 16172 4-UC
946-7100

Norristown, AC 610, PC 8, Montgomery
Area Vocational Technical SD
  Supt. — See Harrisburg
Central Montgomery County AVTS Vo Tech
  NEW HOPE ST & PLYMOUTH RD 19401 277-2301
  John Williams, prin.

Colonial SD
  Supt. — See Plymouth Meeting
Colonial MS, 716 BELVOIR RD 19401 3-00100
  Patricia Iannelli, prin. 275-5100

Methacton SD 5-11111
  1001 KRIEBEL MILL RD 19403 489-5000
  Laird Warner, supt.
Methacton HS 4-00011
  1001 KRIEBEL MILL RD 19403 489-5026
  Franklin Congdon, prin.
Arcola MS, EAGLEVILLE ROAD 19403 3-00100
  Andrew Case, prin. 631-9403

Norristown Area SD 6-11111
  401 N WHITEHALL RD 19403 630-5000
  John Gould, supt.
Norristown Area HS 4-00011
  1900 EAGLE DR 19403 630-5090
  Barry Spencer, prin.
East Norriston MS 2-00100
  330 ROLAND DR 19401 275-6520
  Patricia Hopkins, prin.
Eisenhower MS 2-00100
  1601 MARKLEY ST 19401 277-8720
  John Haines, prin.
Stewart MS 2-00100
  1315 W MARSHALL ST 19401 275-6870
  Joseph Howell, prin.

Bishop Kenrick HS 3-00011
  250 E JOHNSON HWY 19401 275-2846
  Sr. Veronica Brooks, prin.

Northampton, AC 610, PC 6, Northampton
Northampton Area SD 6-11111
  PO BOX 118 18067 262-7811
  Ralph Tarola, supt.
Northampton Area SHS 4-00001
  1619 LAUBACH AVE 18067 262-7811
  Frank Kovacs, prin.
Northampton Area JHS 4-00110
  1617 LAUBACH AVE 18067 262-7811
  Roger Washburn, prin.

North East, AC 814, PC 5, Erie
North East SD, 50 E DIVISION ST 16428 4-11111
  Robert Towsey, supt. 725-8671
HS, 1901 FREEPORT RD 16428 2-00011
  Robert Rhodes, prin. 725-8672
MS, 1903 FREEPORT RD 16428 2-00100
  Tim Welsh, prin. 725-8672

North Huntingdon, AC 412, Westmoreland
Norwin SD, 281 MCMAHON DR 15642 6-11111
  Gary Russell, supt. 863-5052
  Other Schools – See Irwin

Northumberland, AC 717, PC 5, Northumberland

Northumberland Christian S 2-11111
  205 QUEEN ST 17857 473-9786

North Versailles, AC 412, PC 7, Allegheny
East Allegheny SD 4-11111
  1150 JACKS RUN RD 15137 824-8012
  John Dunlap, supt.
East Allegheny JSHS 3-00111
  1150 JACKS RUN RD 15137 824-9700
  Joseph Carroll, prin.

North Wales, AC 215, PC 5, Montgomery

Lansdale School of Business	2-CS
201 CHURCH RD 19454	699-5700

Oakdale, AC 412, PC 4, Allegheny
Area Vocational Technical SD
Supt. — See Harrisburg

Parkway West AVTS	Vo Tech
7101 STEUBENVILLE PIKE 15071	923-1772
Mary Ravita, prin.	

Oakmont, AC 412, PC 6, Allegheny

Riverview SD, 701 10TH ST 15139	4-11111
R. Knapp, supt.	828-6010
Riverview JSHS, 100 HULTON RD 15139	2-00111
Brad Ferko, prin.	828-1800

Oil City, AC 814, PC 7, Venango
Area Vocational Technical SD
Supt. — See Harrisburg

Venango County AVTS	Vo Tech
1 VO TECH DR 16301	677-3097
William Clark, prin.	
Oil City Area SD, PO BOX 929 16301	5-11111
Stephen Pikna, supt.	676-1867
HS, 10 LYNCH BLVD 16301	3-00011
D. Snyder, prin.	676-2771
Oil City Area MS, 69 SPRING ST 16301	3-00100
John Downing, prin.	676-5702

Clarion University of Pennsylvania	2-UC
VENANGO CAMPUS 16301	676-6591
Venango Christian HS	1-00011
1505 W 1ST ST 16301	677-3098
Fr. Schultz, prin.	

Old Forge, AC 717, PC 6, Lackawanna

Old Forge SD, 300 MARION ST 18518	3-11111
Richard Prisuta, supt.	457-6721
JSHS, 300 MARION ST 18518	2-00111
Walter Ermolovich, prin.	457-6721

Oley, AC 215, PC 3, Berks
Area Vocational Technical SD
Supt. — See Harrisburg

Berks County AVTS-East	Vo Tech
RR 3 BOX 2G 19547	987-6201
Robert Harrison, prin.	
Oley Valley SD, JEFFERSON ST 19547	4-11111
Robert Lesko, supt.	987-4134
Oley Valley HS, RR 4 19547	3-00011
Jeffery Zacon, prin.	987-4101
Oley Valley MS, RR 4 19547	2-00100
Robert Dziedzic, prin.	987-4142

Orefield, AC 215, PC 3, Lehigh
Parkland SD
Supt. — See Allentown

Parkland SHS	4-00001
2675 PA ROUTE 309 18069	395-2021
Carl Tershak, prin.	

Oreland, AC 215, PC 6, Montgomery

Springfield Township SD	4-11111
1901 PAPER MILL RD 19075	233-6000
William Leary, supt.	
Enfield MS, 1901 PAPER MILL RD 19075	2-00100
Rosemarie Retacco, prin.	233-6072
Other Schools – See Erdenheim	

Orwigsburg, AC 717, PC 5, Schuylkill

Blue Mountain SD	5-11111
PO BOX 279 17961	366-0515
Raymond Froling, supt.	
Blue Mountain MS	3-00100
675 REDDALE RD 17961	366-0546
William Toomey, prin.	
Other Schools – See Schuylkill Haven	

Oxford, AC 215, PC 5, Chester

Oxford Area SD, 119 S 5TH ST 19363	4-11111
Robert Meckes, supt.	932-6600
Oxford Area HS, 301 S 5TH ST 19363	3-00011
Kenneth Woodward, prin.	932-6640
Penn's Grove MS	3-00100
602 GARFIELD ST 19363	932-6615
Robert Farr, prin.	

Palmerton, AC 610, PC 6, Carbon

Palmerton Area SD	4-11111
PO BOX 350 18071	826-2364
Ronald Mihalko, supt.	
Palmerton Area HS	3-00011
RR 3 BOX 3681 18071	826-3155
James Davis, prin.	
Palmerton Area JHS	2-00100
RR 3 BOX 3682 18071	826-2492
Thaddeus Kosciolek, prin.	

Palmyra, AC 717, PC 6, Lebanon

Palmyra Area SD, 1125 PARK DR 17078	5-11111
Clarence Fox, supt.	838-1331
Palmyra Area SHS, 1125 PARK DR 17078	3-00011
Connie Armstrong, prin.	838-1331
Palmyra Area JHS	3-00110
10 W CHERRY ST 17078	838-2119
David Appleby, prin.	

Paoli, AC 610, PC 6, Chester

Church Farm S, PO BOX S 19301	2-00111
Charles Schreiner, prin.	363-7500

Royer-Greaves School for Blind	HND
118 S VALLEY RD 19301	

Patton, AC 814, PC 4, Cambria

Cambria Heights SD	4-11111
510 BEECH AVE 16668	674-3626
Stephen Trovato, supt.	
Cambria Heights HS	3-00011
RR 1 BOX 6 16668	674-3601
Trudy Peterman, prin.	
Other Schools – See Hastings	

Pen Argyl, AC 610, PC 5, Northampton

Pen Argyl Area SD	4-11111
1620 TEELS RD 18072	863-9093
William Haberl, supt.	
Pen Argyl Area JSHS	2-00111
501 W LAUREL AVE 18072	863-9093
Anthony Renaldo, prin.	

Penn Hills, AC 412, PC 8, Allegheny
Penn Hills SD
Supt. — See Pittsburgh

SHS, 12200 GARLAND DR 15235	4-00001
Ray Devito, prin.	793-6400
Linton JHS, 250 ASTER ST 15235	4-00110
David Wilson, prin.	795-3000

Pennsburg, AC 215, PC 4, Montgomery
Upper Perkiomen SD
Supt. — See East Greenville

Upper Perkiomen HS, 2 WALT RD 18073	3-00011
John Semet, prin.	679-5935

Perkiomen S, PO BOX 130 18073	2-01111
George Allison, prin.	679-9511

Penns Creek, AC 717, PC 3, Snyder

Penn View Bible Institute	1-UC
PO BOX 970 17862	
Penn View Christian Academy	2-11111
MOUNTAIN RD 17862	837-1855

Pequea, AC 717, PC 2, Lancaster
Penn Manor SD
Supt. — See Millersville

Marticville MS	3-00100
356 FROGTOWN RD 17565	291-9854
William Ziegler, prin.	

Perkasie, AC 215, PC 6, Bucks
Area Vocational Technical SD
Supt. — See Harrisburg

Upper Bucks County AVTS	Vo Tech
RR 2 BOX 207 18944	795-2911
Joseph Harosky, prin.	

Pennridge SD, 1506 N 5TH ST 18944	6-11111
John Slattery, supt.	257-5016
Pennridge HS, 1228 N 5TH ST 18944	4-00011
James Schultz, prin.	257-5011
Pennridge Central JHS	2-00100
1500 N 5TH ST 18944	257-5011
K. Svanson, prin.	
Pennridge South JHS	2-00100
5TH & CEDAR STS 18944	257-0467
Thomas Rutter, prin.	

Perryopolis, AC 412, PC 4, Fayette

Frazier SD	4-11111
403 W CONSTITUTION ST 15473	736-4432
Fred Smeigh, supt.	
Frazier HS	2-00011
403 W CONSTITUTION ST 15473	736-4426
Richard Martin, prin.	
Frazier MS	2-00100
403 CONSTITUTION ST 15473	736-4426
Linda Nelson, prin.	

Philadelphia, AC 215, PC 12, Philadelphia
Area Vocational Technical SD
Supt. — See Harrisburg

Bok AVTS	Vo Tech
8TH AND MIFFLIN STS 19148	952-6200
Joseph Sweeney, prin.	
Dobbins AVTS	Vo Tech
22ND ST AND LEHIGH AVE 19132	227-4421
Edward Magliocco, prin.	
Mastbaum AVTS	Vo Tech
FRANKFORD & CLEMENTINE 19134	291-4703
Charles Clark, prin.	
Randolph Skills Center	Vo Tech
HENRY & ROBERTS AVE 19129	227-4421
Edward Magliocco, prin.	
Saul Agriculture S	Vo Tech
7100 HENRY AVE 19128	487-4467
James Kerr, prin.	
Swenson Skills Center	Vo Tech
RED LION RD & ROOSEVELT BLV 19114	
Barbara Braman, prin.	961-2009
Aviation Sply Off Adult AVTS	Vo Tech
700 ROBBINS ST 19111	697-2603
Lynn Kalsh, prin.	
Defense Supply Adult AVTS	Vo Tech
2800 S 20TH ST 19145	737-2383
Sylvia Gay, prin.	
Martin Adult AVTS	Vo Tech
RED LION RD & ROOSEVELT BLV 19114	
Richard Brown, prin.	739-5788
JFK Adult AVTS	Vo Tech
734 SCHUYLKILL AVE 19146	875-3737
George Cifelli, prin.	

Philadelphia CSD	8-11111
2120 WINTER ST 19103	299-7000
Theresa Lemme, supt.	
Audenried HS, 3301 TASKER ST 19145	2-00011
Ernestine Smith, prin.	952-6204
Bartram HS, 2429 S 67TH ST 19142	5-00011
Joel Bartolomeo, prin.	492-6450
Bodine HS, 4TH & GEORGE STS 19133	2-00011
P. Hill, prin.	351-7332
Carver HS, 17TH & NORRIS STS 19116	3-00011
Ella Travis, prin.	684-5079
Central HS, 1700 W OLNEY AVE 19141	4-00011
Sheldon Pavel, prin.	276-5262
Creative & Performing Arts HS	3-00011
1122 CATHARINE ST 19147	351-7140
(—), prin.	
Edison HS, 151 W LUZERNE ST 19140	4-00011
Raul Torres, prin.	324-9440
Frankford HS, 5000 OXFORD AVE 19124	4-00011
Carolyn Perry, prin.	537-2519
Franklin HS, 550 N BROAD ST 19130	4-00011
Tilghman Moore, prin.	299-4662
Furness HS, 1900 S 3RD ST 19148	3-00011
Joseph Bergin, prin.	952-6226
Germantown HS, 50 E HIGH ST 19144	4-00011
Jesse Gardner, prin.	951-4004
Gratz HS	4-00011
1798 W HUNTING PARK AVE 19140	227-4408
Deidre Farmbry, prin.	
Kensington HS	4-00011
2059 E CUMBERLAND ST 19125	291-4700
Ana Kender, prin.	
King HS, 6100 STENTON AVE 19138	5-00011
Patricia Harris, prin.	927-7200
Lincoln HS, 3201 RYAN AVE 19136	4-00011
Barbara Braman, prin.	335-5653
Northeast HS	4-00011
1601 COTTMAN AVE 19111	728-5018
Thomas Sebastian, prin.	
Olney HS	5-00011
100 E DUNCANNON AVE 19120	456-3014
Patrick Taggert, prin.	
Overbrook HS	4-00011
5898 LANCASTER AVE 19131	581-5507
Yvonne Jones, prin.	
Penn HS, 1333 N BROAD ST 19122	4-00011
Ellen Linky, prin.	978-7200
Philadelphia HS for Girls	4-00011
1400 W OLNEY AVE 19141	276-5258
Chris Peacock, prin.	
Philadelphia Regional HS	4-00011
62ND & LEBANON AVE 19151	581-5668
Keith Rose, prin.	
Roxborough HS, 6498 RIDGE AVE 19128	4-00011
Liston Knowles, prin.	487-4464
South Philadelphia HS	5-00011
2101 S BROAD ST 19148	952-6220
George Di Pilato, prin.	
University City HS	4-00011
3601 FILBERT ST 19104	387-5100
J. Logan, prin.	
Washington HS	5-00011
11000 BUSTLETON AVE 19116	961-2001
Harry Gutelius, prin.	
West Philadelphia HS	4-00011
4700 WALNUT ST 19139	471-2902
George Roesser, prin.	
Fels JSHS	4-00111
DEVEREAUX & LANGDON STS 19111	537-2516
William Williams, prin.	
Masterman JSHS	3-01111
1699 SPRING GARDEN ST 19130	299-4661
Barbara Bravo, prin.	
Strawberry Mansion JSHS	4-00111
RIDGE AND SUSQUEHANNA AVES 19132	
Karen Del Guercio, prin.	684-5089
Girard S, 1800 SNYDER AVE 19145	4-11111
Emilio Matticoli, prin.	952-8554
Lamberton S	4-11111
7501 WOODBINE AVE 19151	581-5650
Warren Pross, prin.	
Baldi MS, 8801 VERREE RD 19115	4-00100
Max Ehrlich, prin.	961-2003
Barratt JHS, 1599 WHARTON ST 19146	4-01100
Dolores Coleman-Kirby, prin.	952-6217
Beeber JHS, 5901 MALVERN AVE 19131	4-00100
Armita Sims, prin.	581-5513
Central East MS	3-00100
B ST & WYOMING AVE 19120	456-3012
Renee Yampolsky, prin.	
Clemente MS, 3999 N 5TH ST 19140	4-01100
Anibal Soler, prin.	227-4403
Conwell MS	3-01100
1849 E CLEARFIELD ST 19134	291-4722
Bruce Rachild, prin.	
Cooke JHS, 1300 W LOUDEN ST 19141	4-01100
Craig Browne, prin.	456-3002
Deburgos Bilingual Magnet MS	4-00100
801 W LEHIGH AVE 19133	227-4405
Jose Lebron, prin.	
Fitzsimons MS	4-00100
2601 W CUMBERLAND ST 19132	227-4431
Steven Bailey, prin.	
Gillespie JHS, 1751 W PIKE ST 19140	3-00100
Thomas Lynch, prin.	227-4409
Harding JHS, 2000 WAKELING ST 19124	4-00100
Harry Gaffney, prin.	537-2528
Jones JHS, 2300 E ANN ST 19134	3-01100
Ruben Flores, prin.	291-4709

Labrum MS 2-00100
  HAWLEY & BROOKVIEW ROADS 19154
  Catherine Casselberry, prin. 281-2607
Leeds MS 3-00100
  1100 E MOUNT PLEASANT AVE 19150
  Adrienne Carpenter, prin. 248-6602
Lewis MS, 6199 ARDLEIGH ST 19138 4-00100
  Dahlia Johnson, prin. 224-5484
Meehan MS, 3001 RYAN AVE 19152 3-00100
  Chris McGinley, prin. 335-5654
Penn Treaty JHS 3-01100
  201 MONTGOMERY AVE 19118 291-4715
  Deanna Burney, prin.
Pepper MS, 2901 S 84TH ST 19153 3-01100
  Nancy McGinley, prin. 492-6457
Pickett MS, 5700 WAYNE AVE 19144 4-01100
  Samuel Gottlieb, prin. 951-4002
Peirce MS, 2400 CHRISTIAN ST 19146 3-01100
  Mary Randall, prin. 875-5743
Rhodes MS 4-01100
  2900 W CLEARFIELD ST 19132 227-4402
  Dora Campbell, prin.
Roosevelt JHS 3-00100
  WASHINGTON LN & MUSGRAVE ST 19144
  Gary McManimen, prin. 951-4170
Rush MS 3-00100
  KNIGHTS AND FAIRDALE ROAD 19154
  Elaine Chernicoff, prin. 281-2603
Sayre MS, 5820 WALNUT ST 19139 4-00100
  Janis Butler, prin. 471-2904
Shaw MS 3-00100
  5400 WARRINGTON AVE 19143 727-2161
  Albert Bichner, prin.
Shoemaker MS, 5301 MEDIA ST 19131 3-00100
  Richard Phipps, prin. 581-5501
Stetson MS, 3200 B ST 19134 4-00100
  John Bravo, prin. 291-4720
Stoddart-Fleisher MS 2-00100
  528 N 13TH ST 19123 351-7375
  Florence Campbell, prin.
Sulzberger MS 3-00100
  4725 FAIRMOUNT AVE 19139 581-5510
  Brenda Artwell, prin.
Thomas MS, 927 JOHNSTON ST 19148 3-01100
  Fred Donatucci, prin. 952-6225
Tilden MS, 6601 ELMWOOD AVE 19142 3-01100
  William Shumake, prin. 492-6454
Turner MS 3-01100
  5900 BALTIMORE AVE 19143 471-2906
  Charles D'Alphonso, prin.
Vare MS 3-01100
  MORRIS AND MOYAMENSIN 19148 952-8620
  Barbara Lepore, prin.
Vaux MS, 24TH & MASTER STS 19121 3-00100
  Harold Adams, prin. 684-5068
Wagner MS, 1701 CHELTEN AVE 19126 3-00100
  Rosemarie McNeil-Sampson, prin. 276-5252
Wanamaker MS 3-00100
  1111 CECIL B MOORE AVE 19122 684-5069
  James Clements, prin.
Wilson MS 4-00100
  LORETTO & COTTMAN AVE 19111 728-5015
  Arlene Holtz, prin.
Childs ES, 15415 S 17TH ST 19148 3-10110
  Frances Williams, prin. 952-6213

Albert Einstein Medical Center HSP
  5501 OLD YORK RD 19141 456-6090
American Institute of Design 2-CS
  1616 ORTHODOX ST 19124 288-8200
Archbishop Ryan HS 5-00011
  11201 ACADEMY RD 19154 637-1800
  Fr. Newman, prin.
Art Institute of Philadelphia 4-CC
  1622 CHESTNUT ST 19103 567-7080
Berean Institute 2-CC
  1901 W GIRARD AVE 19130 763-4833
Blairs Christian S 2-11111
  220 W UPSAL ST 19119 438-6557
Cardinal Dougherty HS 4-00011
  6301 N 2ND ST 19120 276-2300
  Eileen Poroszok, prin.
Career Institute 2-CS
  1825 KENNEDY BLVD 19103 561-7600
Cedar Grove Christian Academy 3-11111
  TABOR RD & RISING SUN 19120 455-9334
Chestnut Hill Academy 3-11111
  50 W WILLOW GROVE AVE 19118 247-4700
  Richard Parker, prin.
Chestnut Hill College 4-UC
  9601 GERMANTOWN AVE 19118 248-7000
Community College of Philadelphia 7-CC
  1700 SPRING GARDEN ST 19130 751-8000
Computer Learning Center 3-CS
  3600 MARKET ST 19104 222-6450
Court Reporting Institute, The 2-CS
  1845 WALNUT ST STE 7 19103 854-1853
Craft Institute 2-CC
  9 S 12TH ST 19107 665-8546
Curtis Institute of Music 2-UC
  1726 LOCUST ST 19103 893-5252
Delaware Valley Academy-Medical & Dental 2-CS
  3330 GRANT AVE 19114 676-1200
Drexel University 7-UC
  3141 CHESTNUT ST 19104 895-2000
Episcopal Hospital HSP
  100 E LEHIGH AVE 19125 427-7468
Evelyn Graves Christian Academy 2-11111
  5447 CHESTER AVE 19143 727-7782
Faith Tabernacle S 2-11111
  3611 N RANDOLPH ST 19140 221-0909

Father Judge HS, 3301 SOLLY AVE 19136 4-00011
  Fr. Dimauro, prin. 338-9494
Frankford Hospital HSP
  4918 PENN ST 19124 831-2362
Friends Select S 3-11111
  1651 BENJAMIN FRANKLIN PKY 19103
    561-5900
Germantown Friends S 3-11111
  31 W COULTER ST 19144 951-2300
  Richard Wade, prin.
Germantown Hospital & Medical Center HSP
  1 PENN BLVD 19144 951-8850
Girard College S 3-11111
  2101 S COLLEGE AVE 19121 787-2600
  Joseph Devlin, prin.
Gratz College 3-UC
  7611 OLD YORK RD 19126 635-7300
Hahnemann University 4-UC
  230 N BROAD ST 19102 448-7000
Holy Family College 4-UC
  9701 FRANKFORD AVE 19114 637-3050
Hussian School of Art 2-CC
  1118 MARKET ST 19107 238-9000
James Martin School 2-CS
  2600 RED LION RD 19114 961-2131
John Hallahan HS, 311 N 19TH ST 19103 3-00011
  Sr. Mary Jean, prin. 563-8930
LaSalle College HS 3-00011
  8605 CHELTENHAM AVE 19118 233-2911
  David Diehl, prin.
La Salle University 6-UC
  1900 W OLNEY AVE 19141 951-1000
La Salle University 4-UC
  11101 ACADEMY RD 19154 632-3449
Liberty Academy of Business 2-CS
  511 N BROAD ST STE 2000 19123 925-8670
Lincoln Technical Institute 3-CC
  9191 TORRESDALE AVE 19136 335-0800
Little Flower Catholic HS 3-00011
  10TH & LYCOMING ST 19140 455-6900
  Marie Gallagher, prin.
Lutheran HS, 6101 W OXFORD ST 19151 2-01111
  Donna Coursey, prin. 878-8480
Lutheran Theological Seminary 2-UC
  7301 GERMANTOWN AVE 19119 248-4616
Manna Bible Institute 1-UC
  700 E CHURCH LN 19144
McCarrie School Health Sciences & Tech. 3-CC
  512 S BROAD ST 19146 545-7772
Medical College of Pennsylvania 2-UC
  3300 HENRY AVE 19129 842-6000
Mercy Vocational HS 2-00011
  2900 W HUNTINGTON PARK AVE 19129
  Sr. Patricia Flynn, prin. 226-1225
Messiah College 3-UC
  2026 N BROAD ST 19121 769-2526
Methodist Hospital HSP
  2301 S BROAD ST 19148 952-9402
Moore College of Art and Design 3-UC
  1920 RACE ST 19103 568-4515
Nazareth Academy 2-00011
  4001 GRANT AVE 19114 637-0237
  Sr. Rosemarie Griffin, prin.
Nazareth Hospital HSP
  2601 HOLME AVE 19152 335-6000
NEC-Thompson Institute 4-CC
  3440 MARKET ST 19104 387-1530
New England Tractor Trailer Training 2-CS
  3715 E THOMPSON ST 19137 288-7800
Northeast Catholic HS 3-00011
  1840 TORRESDALE AVE 19124 831-1234
  Fr. Murray, prin.
Northeastern Hospital HSP
  2301 E ALLEGHENY AVE 19134 291-3135
Northeast Prep S 2-00011
  1309 COTTMAN AVE 19111 342-5500
Orleans Technical Institute 2-CS
  1330 RHAWN ST 19111 728-4700
Overbrook School for the Blind HND
  64TH ST & MALVERN AVE 19151
Peirce Junior College 4-CC
  1420 PINE ST 19102 545-6400
Pennsylvania Academy of the Fine Arts 2-CS
  118 N BROAD ST 19102 972-7625
Pennsylvania College of Optometry 3-UC
  1200 W GODFREY AVE 19141 276-6200
Pennsylvania College Podiatric Medicine 2-UC
  148 N 8TH ST 19107 629-0300
Pennsylvania Hospital HSP
  800 SPRUCE ST 19107 829-3312
Pennsylvania School for the Deaf HND
  100 W SCHOOL HOUSE LN 19144
Philadelphia Coll. of Pharmacy & Science 4-UC
  600 S 43RD ST 19104 596-8800
Philadelphia Coll. of Textiles & Science 5-UC
  4201 HENRY AVE 19144 951-2700
Philadelphia Coll. Osteopathic Medicine 3-UC
  4170 CITY AVE 19131 871-1000
Philadelphia Theological Seminary 2-UC
  7372 HENRY AVE 19128 483-2480
Phila. Montgomery Christian Academy 2-00111
  35 HILLCREST RD 19118 233-0782
  Samuel Pennington, prin.
PTC Career Institute 2-CS
  40 N 2ND ST 19106 922-4400
Restaurant School 2-CC
  4207 WALNUT ST 19104 222-4200
Rittenhouse Academy 2-00011
  1516 SPRUCE ST 19102 545-2800
  Harvey Levitan, prin.

Roman Catholic HS 3-00011
  301 N BROAD ST 19107 627-1270
  Gerard Hoffman, prin.
Roxborough Memorial Hospital HSP
  5800 RIDGE AVE 19128 487-4458
St. Basil Academy 2-00011
  711 FOX CHASE RD 19111 885-3771
  Sr. Carla Hernandez, prin.
St. Edwards Center Delaware Valley HS BU 2-00011
  13550 BUSTLETON AVE 19116 677-6107
St. Hubert's Catholic HS 4-00011
  7320 TORRESDALE AVE 19136 624-6840
  Joanne Walls, prin.
St. John Neumann HS 3-00011
  2600 MOORE ST 19145 389-4900
  Fr. Rossi, prin.
St. Joseph's Prep S 3-00011
  1733 W GIRARD AVE 19130 978-1950
  Fr. Keller, prin.
St. Joseph's University 6-UC
  5600 CITY AVE 19131 660-1000
St. Maria Goretti HS 3-00011
  1736 S 10TH ST 19148 465-8437
  Candida Antonelli, prin.
St. Monica Catholic S 1-00011
  1720 W RITNER ST 19145 467-4696
  Sr. Ellen Francis, prin.
SCS Business & Technical Institute 2-CS
  714 MARKET ST 19106 592-8600
Settlement Music School 2-CS
  416 QUEEN ST 19147 336-0400
Sister Clara Muhammad S 2-11111
  4700 WYALUSING AVE 19131 877-8600
Springside S, 8000 CHEROKEE ST 19118 2-11111
    247-7200
Talmudical Yeshiva of Philadelphia 2-00011
  6063 DREXEL RD 19131 477-1000
Talmudical Yeshiva of Philadelphia 1-UC
  6063 DREXEL RD 19131 477-1000
Temple University 8-UC
  BROAD ST & MONTGOMERY AVE 19122
    787-7000
Temple University 4-UC
  3307 N BROAD ST 19140 787-7000
Temple University City Center 4-UC
  1616 WALNUT ST 19103
The Community HS 2-00111
  2820 N 4TH ST 19133 425-1213
Thomas Jefferson University 4-UC
  111 S 11TH ST 19107 955-6000
Ultrasound Diagnostic School 2-CS
  3511 COTTMAN AVE 19149 624-8245
University of Pennsylvania 7-UC
  0 LEVY PARK 19104 898-5000
University of the Arts 4-UC
  320 S BROAD ST 19102 875-4800
Westminster Theological Seminary 3-UC
  PO BOX 27009 19118 887-5511
West Philadephia Catholic HS 3-00011
  4501 CHESTNUT ST 19139 386-2244
  Sr. Mary Bur, prin.
William Penn Charter S 3-11111
  3000 W SCHOOL HOUSE LN 19144 844-3460
  Earl Ball, prin.
Wireless Technical Institute 2-CS
  1533 PINE ST 19102 546-0745

Philipsburg, AC 814, PC 5, Centre
Philipsburg-Osceola Area SD 5-11111
  200 SHORT ST 16866 342-1050
  John Bender, supt.
Philipsburg-Osceola Area SHS 3-00001
  502 PHILIPS ST 16866 342-1521
  Ronald Koble, prin.
Philipsburg-Osceola JHS 2-00110
  100 6TH ST 16866 – Leon Muir, prin. 342-4860

Johnson Technical Institute 2-CS
  200 SHADYLANE DR 16866 342-5680

Phoenixville, AC 610, PC 7, Chester
Area Vocational Technical SD
  Supt. — See Harrisburg
Center for Arts & Tech-Pickering Vo Tech
  CHARLESTOWN RD 19460 933-8877
  Richard Saylor, prin.

Phoenixville Area SD 5-11111
  1120 GAY ST 19460 933-8861
  Dennis Blanton, supt.
SHS, GAY ST & CITY LINE AVE 19460 3-00001
  James Calhoun, prin. 933-6694
JHS, 1330 S MAIN ST 19460 3-00110
  Victoria Danehower, prin. 933-1912

Valley Forge Christian College 3-UC
  1401 CHARLESTOWN RD 19460 935-0450

Pine Forge, AC 215, PC 2, Berks

Pine Forge Academy 2-00011
  PO BOX 338 19548 326-5800
  Richard Mills, prin.

Pine Grove, AC 717, PC 4, Schuylkill
Pine Grove Area SD, 0 SCHOOL ST 17963 4-11111
  Edward Brewer, supt. 345-2731
Pine Grove Area HS, 0 SCHOOL ST 17963 3-00011
  Ralph Ascione, prin. 345-2731
Pine Grove Area MS 3-01100
  0 SCHOOL ST 17963 345-2731
  Edward Kimmel, prin.

Pittsburgh, AC 412, PC 10, Allegheny
Area Vocational Technical SD
  Supt. — See Harrisburg
Connelly Skill Center   Vo Tech
  1501 BEDFORD AVE 15219   338-3700
  Alfred Fascetti, prin.

Avonworth SD   3-11111
  1324 ROOSEVELT RD 15237   369-8738
  (—), supt.
Avonworth JSHS   2-00111
  250 JOSEPHS LN 15237   366-6360
  Thomas Hisiro, prin.

Baldwin-Whitehall SD   5-11111
  4900 CURRY RD 15236   885-7810
  Charles Faust, supt.
Baldwin HS   4-00011
  4653 CLAIRTON BLVD 15236   885-7500
  Jan Richard Garda, prin.
Harrison JHS, 129 WINDVALE DR 15236   3-00100
  Donna Milanovich, prin.   885-7530

Brentwood Borough SD   4-11111
  3601 BROWNSVILLE RD 15227   881-2227
  Eugene Bolt, supt.
Brentwood JSHS   3-00111
  3601 BROWNSVILLE RD 15227   881-4940
  Anthony Chiappetta, prin.

Chartiers Valley SD   5-11111
  2030 SWALLOW HILL RD 15220   429-2201
  Bernard Sulkowski, supt.
Chartiers Valley MS   3-00100
  2030 SWALLOW HILL RD 15220   429-2220
  Edward Dlugos, prin.
Other Schools – See Bridgeville

Fox Chapel Area SD   5-11111
  611 FIELD CLUB RD 15238   963-9600
  Robert Myers, supt.
Fox Chapel Area HS   4-00011
  611 FIELD CLUB RD 15238   963-9600
  Charles Territo, prin.
Dorseyville MS   3-00100
  550 SAXONBURG RD 15238   767-5343
  Robert Chiappetta, prin.

Keystone Oaks SD   5-11111
  1000 KELTON AVE 15216   571-6000
  Chester Kent, supt.
Keystone Oaks HS   3-00011
  1000 KELTON AVE 15216   571-6037
  Felix Yerace, prin.
Neff MS, 3200 ANNAPOLIS AVE 15216   3-00100
  (—), prin.   571-6146

Mt. Lebanon SD, 7 HORSMAN DR 15228   5-11111
  Glenn Smartschan, supt.   344-2077
Mt. Lebanon HS   4-00011
  155 COCHRAN RD 15228   344-2002
  Otto Graf, prin.
Mt. Lebanon JHS   3-00100
  601 LEBANON AVE 15228   344-2121
  J. Lordon, prin.

North Allegheny SD   6-11111
  200 HILLVUE LN 15237   366-2100
  Lawrence Bozzomo, supt.
Carson MS, 200 HILLVUE LN 15237   3-00100
  Marcia Martin, prin.   369-5520
Ingomar MS   3-00100
  INGOMAR HEIGHTS ROAD 15237   369-5470
  Steve Duchi, prin.
North Allegheny Inter. HS   4-00010
  350 CUMBERLAND RD 15237   369-5530
  John Schwoebel, prin.
Other Schools – See Wexford

Northgate SD, 90 GRANT AVE 15202   4-11111
  James Manley, supt.   734-8001
Northgate JSHS, 589 UNION AVE 15202   3-00111
  William Caldwell, prin.   734-8002

North Hills SD, 135 6TH AVE 15229   5-11111
  John Esaias, supt.   367-6000
North Hills SHS   4-00011
  53 ROCHESTER RD 15229   367-1073
  Jack McCurry, prin.
North Hills JHS   3-00110
  55 ROCHESTER RD 15229   367-1064
  Frank Sylvester, prin.

Penn Hills SD, 309 COLLINS DR 15235   6-11111
  Joseph Saeli, supt.   793-7000
Other Schools – See Penn Hills

Pittsburgh CSD   8-11111
  341 S BELLEFIELD AVE 15213   622-3500
  Louise Brennen, supt.
Allderdice HS, 2409 SHADY AVE 15217   4-00011
  John Brill, prin.   422-4800
Brashear HS, 590 CRANE AVE 15216   4-00011
  Robert Nicklos, prin.   571-7300
Carrick HS, 125 PARKFIELD ST 15210   4-00011
  Brian White, prin.   885-7700
Langley HS   4-00011
  2940 SHERADEN BLVD 15204   778-2100
  Daniel Belisario, prin.
Oliver HS, 2323 BRIGHTON RD 15212   4-00011
  Andrew King, prin.   323-3250
Peabody HS   4-00011
  515 N HIGHLAND AVE 15206   665-2050
  Vincent Carr, prin.

Perry Traditional Academy   3-00011
  3875 PERRYSVILLE AVE 15214   323-3400
Pittsburgh HS/Creative & Perform. Arts   2-00011
  925 BRUSHTON AVE 15208   247-7860
  Harry Clark, prin.
Schenley HS   4-00011
  4101 BIGELOW BLVD 15213   622-8200
  Normandie Fulson, prin.
South Vo-Tech HS   3-00011
  930 E CARSON ST 15203   488-5160
  Edward Schuerle, prin.
Westinghouse HS   3-00011
  1101 N MURTLAND AVE 15208   665-3940
  Lester Young, prin.
Washington Polytechnic Academy   Vo Tech
  169 40TH ST 15201   622-3480
  Richard Smith, prin.
Allegheny MS, 810 ARCH ST 15212   3-00100
  Henry Stephens, prin.   323-4100
Arsenal MS, 3900 BUTLER ST 15201   3-00100
  Ruthane Reginella, prin.   622-5740
Columbus Traditional Academy   2-00100
  1805 BUENA VISTA ST 15212   323-4171
  Carl Jurkiewicz, prin.
Frick International Studies Academy   2-00100
  107 THACKERAY ST 15213   622-5980
  Ernestine Reed, prin.
Gladstone MS   3-00100
  327 HAZELWOOD AVE 15207   422-3500
  Theodore Vasser, prin.
Greenway MS, 1400 CRUCIBLE ST 15205   3-00100
  William Brim, prin.   928-2800
Knoxville MS, 324 CHARLES ST 15210   3-00100
  Jerry Minsinger, prin.   488-2910
Milliones MS, 3117 CENTRE AVE 15219   3-00100
  Delphina Briscoe, prin.   622-5900
Prospect MS, 3 COWAN ST 15211   3-00100
  Robert Pipkin, prin.   488-3391
Reizenstein MS   4-00100
  129 DENNISTON AVE 15206   665-2260
  Roberta Feldman, prin.
Rogers Center for Performing Arts   2-00100
  5525 COLUMBO ST 15206   665-2000
  Neal Huguley, prin.
Shiller Classical Academy   2-00100
  1018 PERALTA ST 15212   323-4190
  Gussie Johnson, prin.
Sterrett Classical Academy   2-00100
  7100 REYNOLDS ST 15208   247-7870
  Carl Berdnik, prin.

Plum Borough SD   5-11111
  200 SCHOOL RD 15239   793-1352
  John Cummings, supt.
Plum HS, 900 ELICKER RD 15239   4-00011
  Frank Prazenica, prin.   795-4880
O'Block MS   3-00100
  440 PRESQUE ISLE DR 15239   733-2400
  Robert Shearer, prin.

Shaler Area SD   5-11111
  Supt. — See Glenshaw
Shaler Area SHS   4-00001
  381 WIBLE RUN RD 15209   492-1254
  William Hewko, prin.

West Jefferson Hills SD   5-11111
  PO BOX 18019 15236   655-8450
  Myles Stepanovich, supt.
Pleasant Hills MS   3-00100
  NTNL DR & OLD CLAIRTON ROAD 15236
  John Pavesi, prin.   655-8680
Other Schools – See Clairton

Woodland Hills SD   6-11111
  2430 GREENSBURG PIKE 15221   731-1300
  Stanley Herman, supt.
Woodland Hills SHS   4-00011
  2550 GREENSBURG PIKE 15221   244-1100
  Frank Sockman, prin.
Woodland Hills JHS-West   3-00110
  7600 EVANS ST 15218   351-0698
  John Rocco, prin.
Other Schools – See Turtle Creek

Allegheny Business Institute   2-CS
  339 BLVD OF THE ALLIES 15222   456-7100
Allegheny General Hospital   HSP
  320 E NORTH AVE 15212   359-3005
Art Institute of Pittsburgh   4-CS
  526 PENN AVE 15222   800-275-2470
Bidwell Training Center   2-CC
  1815 METROPOLITAN ST 15233   323-4000
Boyd Career School   4-CS
  1 CHATHAM CTR 15219   456-1800
Bradford School   3-CS
  355 5TH AVE 15222   391-6710
Canevin Catholic HS   3-00011
  2700 MORANGE RD 15205   922-7400
  John Maurer, prin.
Carlow College   4-UC
  3333 5TH AVE 15213   578-6000
Carnegie Mellon University   6-UC
  5000 FORBES AVE 15213   268-2000
Central District Catholic HS   3-00011
  4720 5TH AVE 15213 – Br. Zewe, prin.   621-8189
Chatham College   3-UC
  WOODLAND ROAD 15232   365-1100
Clarissa School of Fashion Design   2-CC
  322 5TH AVE 15222   471-4414

Community College of Allegheny County   6-CC
  808 RIDGE AVE 15212   237-2525
Community College of Allegheny County   5-CC
  111 PINE RD 15237   366-7000
Community College of Allegheny County   4-CC
  701 N HOMEWOOD AVE 15208   323-2323
Computer Systems Institute   2-CC
  900 PENN AVE 15222   261-6110
Computer Tech   3-CS
  107 6TH ST FL 8 15222   391-4197
Dean Institute of Technology   2-CC
  1501 W LIBERTY AVE 15226   531-4433
Duffs Business Institute   4-CC
  110 9TH ST 15222   261-4520
Duquesne University   6-UC
  600 FORBES AVE 15282   396-6000
Electronic Institutes   2-CC
  4634 BROWNS HILL RD 15217   521-8686
Ellis S, 6425 5TH AVE 15206   2-11111
  Helen Chinitz, prin.   661-5992
Gateway Technical Institute   3-CS
  100 7TH ST 15222   281-4111
Home for Crippled Children   HND
  1426 DENNISTON AVE 15217
ICM School of Business   4-CC
  10 WOOD ST 15222   261-2647
ITT Technical Institute   2-CS
  8 PARKWAY CTR 15220   937-9150
La Roche College   4-UC
  9000 BABCOCK BLVD 15237   367-9300
Louise S. McClintic School of Nursing   1-HSP
  4631 DAVISON ST 15201   622-7075
Median School of Allied Health Careers   3-CC
  125 7TH ST 15222   391-7021
Mercy Hospital   HSP
  1401 BLVD OF THE ALLIES 15219   232-7940
Mt. Alvernia HS   2-00011
  146 HAWTHORNE RD 15209   821-3858
  Sr. Charlene Mader, prin.
North Catholic HS   3-00011
  1400 TROY HILL RD 15212   321-4823
  James Detrude, prin.
North Hills Christian S   2-11111
  PO BOX 11161 15237   741-3233
North Hills School of Health Occupations   2-CS
  1500 NORTHWAY MALL 15237   367-8003
Oakland Catholic HS   3-00011
  144 N CRAIG ST 15213   682-6633
  Madeline Vincunas, prin.
Oakland S, 5915 BEACON ST 15217   1-11111
  June Himelstein, prin.   422-0090
Pennsylvania Gunsmith School   1-CS
  812 OHIO RIVER BLVD 15202   766-1812
Pennsylvania Institute of Culinary Arts   2-CC
  717 LIBERTY AVE 15222   566-2433
Penn Technical Institute   2-CC
  110 9TH ST 15222   355-0455
Pittsburgh Institute of Aeronautics   3-CC
  PO BOX 10897 15236   800-444-1440
Pittsburgh Institute of Mortuary Science   1-CS
  5808 BAUM BLVD 15206   362-8500
Pittsburgh Technical Institute   2-CC
  635 SMITHFIELD ST 15222   471-1011
Pittsburgh Theological Seminary   2-UC
  616 N HIGHLAND AVE 15206   362-5610
Point Park College   5-UC
  201 WOOD ST 15222   391-4100
Point Park College-St. Francis Med. Ctr.   HSP
  400 45TH ST 15201   622-4749
Presbyterian-University Hospital   HSP
  230 LOTHROP ST 15213   647-3010
Pressley Ridge School   HND
  530 MARSHALL AVE 15214
Reformed Presbyterian Theological Sem.   2-UC
  7418 PENN AVE 15208   731-8690
Robert Morris College   3-UC
  600 5TH AVE 15219   227-6800
Rosedale Technical Institute   3-CS
  4634 BROWNS HILL RD 15217   521-6200
Sawyer School   4-CS
  717 LIBERTY AVE 15222   261-5700
Seton-LaSalle HS   3-00011
  1000 MCNEILLY RD 15226   561-3583
  Br. Crawford, prin.
Shady Side Academy   3-11111
  423 FOX CHAPEL RD 15238   963-8800
  Ellis Wasson, prin.
Shadyside Hospital   HSP
  5230 CENTRE AVE 15232   622-2353
Swanson's Driving Schools   2-CS
  9915 FRANKSTOWN RD 15235   241-6963
Triangle Tech   2-CC
  1940 PERRYSVILLE AVE 15214   359-1000
Trinity Christian S   2-11111
  299 RIDGE AVE 15221   242-8886
University Health Center   HSP
  FORBES AVE & HALKET ST 15213   647-4664
University of Pittsburgh   8-UC
  4200 5TH AVE 15260   624-4141
Vincentian HS   2-00011
  PEEBLES & MCKNIGHT ROAD 15237   364-1616
  Sr. Camille Panich, prin.
Western Pennsylvania Hospital   HSP
  4800 FRIENDSHIP AVE 15224   578-5539
Western Pennsylvania School for Blind   HND
  BAYARD AT BELLEFIELD 15213
Western Pennsylvania School for the Deaf   HND
  300 E SWISSVALE AVE 15218
Western Pennsylvania School of Health & Bus. Careers   1-CS
  411 7TH AVE # 2 15219   281-2600

Winchester Thurston S   2-11111
  555 MOREWOOD AVE 15213   578-7500
  Judith Chamberlain, prin.
Yeshiva Achei Tmimim S   2-11111
  2100 WIGHTMAN ST 15217   422-7300
  Rabbi Rosenfeld, prin.

Pittston, AC 717, PC 6, Luzerne
Pittston Area SD, 5 STOUT ST 18640   5-11111
  Gerard Musto, supt.   654-2271
Pittston Area HS, 5 STOUT ST 18640   4-00011
  John Donovan, prin.   654-3541
Pittston Area MS, 0 NEW ST 18640   3-00100
  Constantin Turco, prin.   655-2927

Seton Catholic HS   2-00011
  37 WILLIAM ST 18640   654-4831
  James Redington, prin.

Plains, AC 717, PC 5, Luzerne
Wilkes-Barre Area SD
  Supt. — See Wilkes-Barre
JHS, 33 W CAREY ST 18705   2-00110
  Frank Nockley, prin.   826-7224

Pleasant Gap, AC 814, PC 4, Centre
Area Vocational Technical SD
  Supt. — See Harrisburg
Centre County AVTS 16823   Vo Tech
  Edward Geer, prin.   359-2793

Plumsteadville, AC 215, PC 4, Bucks

Plumstead Christian S   2-11111
  PO BOX 216 18949   766-8073
  Larry Green, prin.

Plymouth, AC 717, PC 6, Luzerne
Wyoming Valley West SD
  Supt. — See Kingston
Wyoming Valley West HS   4-00011
  150 WADHAM ST 18651   779-5361
  J. Ferris, prin.

Plymouth Meeting, AC 215, PC 6, Montgomery
Colonial SD   5-11111
  230 FLOURTOWN RD 19462   834-1670
  Stanley Durtan, supt.
Plymouth-Whitemarsh HS   4-00011
  100 E GERMANTOWN PIKE 19462   825-1500
  Patricia Campbell, prin.
Other Schools – See Norristown

Antonelli Institute of Art & Photography   2-CC
  PO BOX 570 19462   275-3040

Point Marion, AC 412, PC 4, Fayette
Albert Galltn Area SD
  Supt. — See Masontown
Gallatin South JHS   3-00110
  RR 1 BOX 150 15474   725-5241
  Edward Colebank, prin.

Portage, AC 814, PC 5, Cambria
Portage Area SD, 750 MEADE ST 15946   4-11111
  Jerome Yetsko, supt.   736-9637
Portage Area JSHS, 800 HIGH ST 15946   3-00111
  Christine Kelly, prin.   736-9635

Port Allegany, AC 814, PC 4, McKean
Area Vocational Technical SD
  Supt. — See Harrisburg
Seneca Highlands AVTS   Vo Tech
  PO BOX 219 16743   642-2573
  Donald Raydo, prin.

Port Allegany SD, 200 OAK ST 16743   4-11111
  R. Marks, supt.   642-2596
JSHS, 200 OAK ST 16743   3-00111
  E. Babcock, prin.   642-2544

Portersville, AC 412, PC 2, Butler

Portersville Christian S   2-11111
  RR 1 BOX 44 16051   368-8787
  Joseph Detzner, prin.

Pottstown, AC 610, PC 7, Montgomery
Owen J. Roberts SD, RR 1 19465   5-11111
  Terrance Furin, supt.   469-6261
Roberts HS, RR 1 19465   3-00111
  W. Faulkner, prin.   469-6261
Roberts MS, RR 1 19465   3-00100
  Frank Scalise, prin.   469-6261

Pottsgrove SD   5-11111
  1301 KAUFFMAN RD 19464   327-2277
  Sharon Richardson, supt.
Pottsgrove HS   3-00011
  1345 KAUFFMAN RD 19464   326-5105
  Gary Reed, prin.
Pottsgrove MS, 1329 BUCHERT RD 19464   3-00100
  J. Benton McCue, prin.   326-8243

Pottstown SD   5-11111
  BEACH & PENN STS 19464   323-8200
  Frank Heifer, supt.
HS, 749 N WASHINGTON ST 19464   3-00011
  Barry Flicker, prin.   970-6700
JHS, FRANKLIN & EAST STS 19464   3-00100
  George Giovanis, prin.   970-6665

Antonelli Medical & Professional Inst   2-CS
  1700 INDUSTRIAL HWY 19464   323-7270

Hill School   2-00111
  717 E HIGH SCHOOL ST 19464   326-1000
  Charles Watson, prin.
Pennsylvania Business Institute   3-CS
  81 ROBINSON ST 19464   326-6150
St. Pius X HS, 844 N KEIM ST 19464   2-00011
  Fr. Lowe, prin.   326-8990
West-Mont Christian Academy   2-11111
  2675 E HIGH ST 19464   326-7690

Pottsville, AC 717, PC 7, Schuylkill
Pottsville Area SD   5-11111
  1501 LAUREL BLVD 17901   621-2900
  James Gallagher, supt.
Pottsville Area HS   3-00011
  16TH AND ELK AVE 17901   621-2960
  James Gallagher, prin.
Lengel MS, 1541 LAUREL BLVD 17901   3-01100
  John Keating, prin.   621-2923

Franklin Academy   2-CS
  324 N CENTRE ST 17901   622-8370
Nativity BVM HS, 1 LAWTONS HL 17901   2-00011
  Fr. Bocian, prin.   622-8110
Pottsville Hospital School of Nursing   2-HSP
  420 S JACKSON ST 17901   621-5028
Schuylkill Business Institute   2-CS
  2400 W END AVE 17901   622-4835

Prospect Park, AC 215, PC 6, Delaware
Interboro SD   5-11111
  900 WASHINGTON AVE 19076   461-6700
  Edmond Sacchetti, supt.
Interboro HS, 500 16TH AVE 19076   3-00011
  Nicholas Cianci, prin.   237-6410

Pulaski, AC 412, PC 2, Lawrence

New Castle School of Trades   3-CC
  RR 1 16143   964-8811

Punxsutawney, AC 814, PC 6, Jefferson
Punxsutawney Area SD   5-11111
  PO BOX 478 15767   938-5110
  John Ivey, supt.
Punxsutawney Area HS   3-00011
  450 N FINDLEY ST 15767   938-5123
  Anthony Parise, prin.
Punxsutawney Area JHS   3-00100
  200 N JEFFERSON ST 15767   938-5113
  Kenneth Denne, prin.

Quakertown, AC 215, PC 6, Bucks
Quakertown Community SD   5-11111
  600 PARK AVE 18951   538-5010
  George Taylor, supt.
Quakertown Community SHS   4-00001
  600 PARK AVE 18951   538-5050
  James Beerer, prin.
Milford JHS   2-00110
  2255 ALLENTOWN RD 18951   538-5090
  John Skari, prin.
Strayer JHS, 349 S 9TH ST 18951   3-00110
  Richard Zinck, prin.   538-5080

Quarryville, AC 717, PC 4, Lancaster
Solanco SD, 121 S HESS ST 17566   5-11111
  Elizabeth Logan, supt.   786-8401
Solanco HS, 585 SOLANCO RD 17566   4-00011
  Daniel Deninnon, prin.   786-2151
Smith MS, 645 KIRKWOOD PIKE 17566   2-00100
  Leon Trager, prin.   786-2244
Swift MS   2-00100
  1866 ROBERT FULTON HWY 17566   548-2187
  Gary Harold, prin.

Radnor, AC 610, PC 8, Delaware
Radnor Township SD
  Supt. — See Wayne
HS, 130 KING OF PRUSSIA RD 19087   3-00011
  Anne Janson, prin.   293-0855

Archbishop Carroll HS   3-00011
  211 MATSONFORD RD 19087   688-7610
  Fr. Kestler, prin.
Cabrini College   4-UC
  610 KING OF PRUSSIA RD 19087   971-8100

Reading, AC 610, PC 8, Berks
Antietam SD, 100 ANTIETAM RD 19606   3-11111
  John DiNunzio, supt.   779-0554
Antietam JSHS   2-00111
  100 ANTIETAM RD 19606   779-3545
  Francis Leskowicz, prin.

Area Vocational Technical SD
  Supt. — See Harrisburg
Reading-Muhlenberg AVTS   Vo Tech
  PO BOX 13068 19612   921-7305
  Gerald Cunningham, prin.

Exeter Township SD   5-11111
  3650 PERKIOMEN AVE 19606   779-0700
  William Harst, supt.
Exeter Twp. SHS, 201 E 37TH ST 19606   3-00001
  Jeffery Keller, prin.   779-3060
Exeter Twp. JHS, 151 E 39TH ST 19606   3-00110
  James Smith, prin.   779-3320

Muhlenberg SD   4-11111
  801 E BELLEVUE AVE 19605   921-8000
  Lynn Phillips, supt.
Muhlenberg JSHS   3-00111
  SHARP AVE & FRANCES ST 19605   921-8078
  Robert Wolfe, prin.

Reading SD   7-11111
  800 WASHINGTON ST 19601   371-5611
  James Goodhart, supt.
SHS, 801 N 13TH ST 19604   4-00011
  Ronald Lubas, prin.   371-5710
Northeast JHS, 1216 N 13TH ST 19604   3-00110
  Samuel Frankhouser, prin.   371-5772
Northwest JHS, 1000 N FRONT ST 19601   3-00110
  Inez Brooks, prin.   371-5881
Southern JHS, 931 CHESTNUT ST 19602   3-00110
  (—), prin.   371-5802
Southwest JHS   3-00110
  300 CHESTNUT ST 19602   371-5934
  Thaddeus Jamula, prin.

Albright College   4-UC
  PO BOX 15234 19612   921-2381
Alvernia College   4-UC
  400 BERNARDINE ST 19607   777-5411
Central Catholic HS, 1400 HILL RD 19602   2-00011
  Vincent Shemanski, prin.   373-4178
Community General Hospital   HSP
  145 N 6TH ST 19601   378-8355
Holy Name HS   2-00011
  955 E WYOMISSING BLVD 19611   374-8361
  Fr. Davis, prin.
Pace Institute   2-CS
  606 COURT ST 19601   375-1212
Pennsylvania State University   4-CC
  PO BOX 7009 19610   320-4800
Reading Area Community College   4-CC
  PO BOX 1706 19603   372-4721
Reading Hospital & Medical Center   HSP
  300 S 6TH ST 19602   378-6331
St. Joseph's Hospital   HSP
  215 N 12TH ST 19604   378-2000

Red Lion, AC 717, PC 6, York
Red Lion Area SD, 700 DELTA RD 17356   5-11111
  Larry Macaluso, supt.   244-4518
Red Lion Area HS   4-00011
  200 HORACE MANN AVE 17356   246-1611
  C. Rhine, prin.
Red Lion Area JHS   3-00100
  412 COUNTRY CLUB RD 17356   244-1448
  Paul DiPangrazio, prin.

Red Lion Christian S, RR 3 17356   2-11111
  244-3905

Reedsville, AC 717, PC 4, Mifflin
Mifflin County SD
  Supt. — See Lewistown
Indian Valley MS   3-00100
  GARDENVIEW RD 17084   667-2123
  Mary Sigler, prin.

Renovo, AC 717, PC 4, Clinton
Keystone Central SD
  Supt. — See Lock Haven
Bucktail Area JSHS   2-00111
  1300 BUCKTAIL AVE 17764   923-1166
  Mark Delany, prin.

Republic, AC 412, PC 4, Fayette
Brownsville Area SD
  Supt. — See Grindstone
Redstone MS, PO BOX 752 15475   2-00100
  Herman Jackson, prin.   246-9682

Reynoldsville, AC 814, PC 5, Jefferson
Area Vocational Technical SD
  Supt. — See Harrisburg
Jefferson County-Dubois AVTS   Vo Tech
  100 JEFF TECH DR 15851   653-8265
  Roger Keith, prin.

Richboro, AC 215, PC 6, Bucks
Council Rock SD   6-11111
  251 TWINING FORD RD 18954   355-9901
  David Blatt, supt.
Council Rock JHS   3-00110
  150 UPPER HOLLAND RD 18954   355-0500
  Joseph Zaleski, prin.
Other Schools – See Holland, Newtown

Ridgway, AC 814, PC 5, Elk
Ridgway Area SD   4-11111
  213 FILLMORE AVE 15853   773-3146
  Francis Grandinetti, supt.
Ridgway Area JSHS, 1403 HILL ST 15853   3-00111
  Gerald Zawacki, prin.   773-3164

Ridley Park, AC 610, PC 6, Delaware
Ridley SD
  Supt. — See Folsom
Ridley MS, 400 FREE ST 19078   3-00100
  Gail Heinemeyer, prin.   237-8028

Rimersburg, AC 814, PC 4, Clarion
Union SD, RR 2 BOX 12A 16248   3-11111
  Robert McWilliams, supt.   473-6311
Union JSHS, RR 2 BOX 43A 16248   2-00111
  Robert McWilliams, prin.   473-3121

Roaring Spring, AC 814, PC 5, Blair
Spring Cove SD, 230 POPLAR ST 16673   4-11111
  James Scott, supt.   224-5124

Spring Cove JHS, 1150 E MAIN ST   16673   3-00110
  Charles Kensinger, prin.   224-2106
Other Schools – See Martinsburg

Robesonia, AC 215, PC 4, Berks
Conrad Weiser Area SD   4-11111
  RR 1 BOX 7   19551   693-8545
  Larry Schmidt, supt.
Weiser JSHS, RR 1 BOX 7   19551   4-00111
  Betsy Adams, prin.   693-8528

Rochester, AC 412, PC 5, Beaver
Rochester Area SD, 540 RENO ST   15074   4-11111
  Stephen Whisdosh, supt.   775-7504
Rochester Area JSHS   3-00111
  540 RENO ST   15074   775-7500
  John Barnes, prin.

Beaver Valley Christian Academy   2-11111
  350 ADAMS ST   15074   728-2860

Rockwood, AC 814, PC 4, Somerset
Rockwood Area SD   4-11111
  515 SOMERSET AVE   15557   926-4913
  Mary Ann Nobers, supt.
Rockwood Area JSHS   2-00111
  437 SOMERSET AVE   15557   926-4631
  Donna Johnson, prin.

Rome, AC 717, PC 2, Bradford
Northeast Bradford SD   4-11111
  RR 1 BOX 211B   18837   744-2521
  Thomas Neilson, supt.
Northeast Bradford JSHS   3-00111
  RR 1 BOX 211B   18837   744-2521
  Ray Fleming, prin.

Rosemont, AC 215, PC 3, Montgomery
Lower Merion SD
  Supt. — See Ardmore
Harriton HS, 600 N ITHAN AVE   19010   3-00011
  Norton Seaman, prin.   525-1270

Agnes Irwin S   3-11111
  S ITHAN AVE & CONESTOGA AVE   19010
  Margaret Moss, prin.   525-8400
Rosemont College   3-UC
  1400 MONTGOMERY AVE   19010   525-6420

Roseto, AC 610, PC 4, Northampton

Faith Christian S, 122 DANTE ST   18013   2-11111
   588-3414
Pius X HS, 580 3RD AVE   18013   2-00111
  Leonard Litzi, prin.   588-3291

Royersford, AC 610, PC 5, Montgomery
Spring-Ford Area SD
  Supt. — See Collegeville
Spring-Ford HS, 413 S LEWIS RD   19468   3-00011
  Michael Fabel, prin.   948-7500
Spring-Ford MS   3-00100
  700 WASHINGTON ST   19468   948-7800
  William Marion, prin.

Ruffs Dale, AC 412, PC 3, Westmoreland
Yough SD
  Supt. — See Herminie
Yough JHS, RR 1 BOX 574   15679   3-00110
  Lawrence Nemec, prin.   872-5164

Rural Valley, AC 412, PC 3, Armstrong
Armstrong SD
  Supt. — See Ford City
Shannock Valley JSHS   2-00111
  PO BOX 325   16249   783-7142
  Walter Poleski, prin.

Russell, AC 814, PC 4, Warren
Warren County SD
  Supt. — See Warren
Eisenhower JSHS   3-00111
  RR 2 BOX 2276   16345   757-8878
  Gary Breese, prin.

Russellton, AC 412, PC 1, Allegheny
Deer Lakes SD, PO BOX 10   15076   4-11111
  John Disanti, supt.   265-1511
Deer Lakes JSHS, PO BOX 10   15076   3-00111
  Raymond Buchko, prin.   265-1511

Saegertown, AC 814, PC 4, Crawford
Penncrest SD, PO BOX 808   16433   5-11111
  Paul Harakal, supt.   763-2323
JSHS, RR 1   16433   3-00111
  Ronald Reyer, prin.   763-2615
Other Schools – See Cambridge Springs, Guys Mills

Saint Davids, AC 215, PC 4, Delaware

Eastern College   4-UC
  10 FAIRVIEW DR   19087   341-5800

Saint Marys, AC 814, PC 6, Elk
St. Mary's Area SD   4-11111
  977 S SAINT MARYS RD   15857   834-7831
  William Williams, supt.
St. Mary's Area HS   3-00011
  977 S SAINT MARYS RD   15857   834-7831
  Richard Danielson, prin.
Saint Marys Area MS   3-00100
  979 S SAINT MARYS RD   15857   834-7831
  Clythera Hornung, prin.

Elk County Christian HS   2-00011
  600 MAURUS ST   15857   834-7800
  John Kowach, prin.

Salisbury, AC 814, PC 3, Somerset
Salisbury-Elk Lick SD   2-11111
  PO BOX 68   15558   662-2733
  Peter Miller, supt.
Salisbury-Elk Lick JSHS   2-00111
  PO BOX 68   15558   662-2741
  S. Thomas, prin.

Saltsburg, AC 412, PC 3, Indiana
Blairsville-Saltsburg SD
  Supt. — See Blairsville
JSHS, 84 TROJAN LN   15681   2-00111
  Thomas Sgriccia, prin.   639-3547

The Kiski S, 1888 BRETT LN   15681   2-00011
  John Pidgeon, prin.   639-3586

Saxonburg, AC 412, PC 4, Butler
South Butler County SD   5-11111
  PO BOX 657   16056   352-9451
  Merrill Arnold, supt.
Knoch JSHS, PO BOX 628   16056   4-00111
  James Ola, prin.   352-9451

Saxton, AC 814, PC 3, Bedford
Tussey Mountain SD   4-11111
  RR 1 BOX 178A   16678   635-3670
  Walter Curfman, supt.
Tussey Mountain JSHS, RR 1   16678   3-00111
  Jacob Snyder, prin.   635-2975

Sayre, AC 717, PC 6, Bradford
Sayre Area SD   4-11111
  333 W LOCKHART ST   18840   888-7615
  Donald Houck, supt.
Sayre Area JSHS   3-00111
  331 W LOCKHART ST   18840   888-6622
  Samuel Signorino, prin.

Robert Packer Hospital   HSP
  1 GUTHRIE SQ   18840   888-6666

Schnecksville, AC 610, PC 4, Lehigh
Area Vocational Technical SD
  Supt. — See Harrisburg
Lehigh County AVTS   Vo Tech
  4500 EDUCATION PARK DR   18078   799-1322
  Joseph Rothdeutsch, prin.

Lehigh County Community College   5-CC
  2370 MAIN ST   18078   799-2121

Schuylkill Haven, AC 717, PC 6, Schuylkill
Blue Mountain SD
  Supt. — See Orwigsburg
Blue Mountain HS, RR 1   17972   3-00011
  John Wabby, prin.   366-0511
Schuylkill Haven Area SD   4-11111
  120 HAVEN ST   17972   385-6705
  Richard Rada, supt.
Schuylkill Haven Area HS   2-00111
  E MAIN ST   17972   385-6717
  Frank Radzievich, prin.
Schuylkill Haven MS   2-01100
  120 HAVEN ST   17972   385-6709
  Kim LeVan, prin.

Pennsylvania State University   3-CC
  200 UNIVERSITY DR   17972   385-6000

Scottdale, AC 412, PC 6, Westmoreland
Southmoreland SD   5-11111
  609 PARKER AVE   15683   887-2000
  John Kenney, supt.
Other Schools – See Alverton

Scranton, AC 717, PC 8, Lackawanna
Area Vocational Technical SD
  Supt. — See Harrisburg
Lackawanna County AVTS   Vo Tech
  3201 ROCKWELL AVE   18508   346-8471
  Arthur Lucarelli, prin.
Scranton CSD   6-11111
  425 N WASHINGTON AVE   18503   348-3400
  John Williams, supt.
HS, 723 ADAMS AVE   18510   3-00011
  Albert Karam, prin.   348-3481
West Scranton HS   3-00011
  1201 LUZERNE ST   18504   348-3616
  Joseph Triano, prin.
East Scranton IS   2-00100
  528 QUINCY AVE   18510   348-3651
  Karen Sandis, prin.
South Scranton IS, 355 MAPLE ST   18505   3-00100
  Vincent Montoro, prin.   348-3631
West Scranton IS   3-00100
  0 FELLOWS AND PARROTT AVE   18504
  Michael Langan, prin.   348-3475

Allied Medical Careers   2-CS
  2901 PITTSTON AVE   18505   342-8000
Bishop Hannan HS   2-00111
  330 WYOMING AVE   18503   346-4643
  William Lademan, prin.
Community Medical Center   HSP
  1822 MULBERRY ST   18510   969-8952
ICS Center for Degree Studies   6-HMS
  925 OAK ST   18508   342-7701

Johnson Technical Institute   3-CC
  3427 N MAIN AVE   18508   342-6404
Lackawanna Junior College   3-CC
  901 PROSPECT AVE   18505   961-7810
Marywood College   5-UC
  2300 ADAMS AVE   18509   348-6231
NEC-International Correspondence Schools   4-HMS
  925 OAK ST   18508   342-7701
Northeast Institute of Education   2-CS
  PO BOX 470   18501   346-6666
St. Pauls MS, 1527 PENN AVE   18509   2-01100
  James McDermott, prin.   343-7880
Scranton Medical Technology Consortium   2-CS
  700 QUINCY AVE   18510   963-2100
Scranton Prep S   3-00011
  1000 WYOMING AVE   18509   941-7737
  Rev. Herbert Keller, prin.
Scranton State School for the Deaf   HND
  1800 N WASHINGTON AVE   18509
Star Technical Institute   2-CS
  1600 NAY AUG AVE   18509   963-0144
University of Scranton   6-UC
  800 LINDEN ST   18510   961-7500
Yeshiva Beth Moshe   1-UC
  930 HICKORY ST   18505   346-1747

Selinsgrove, AC 717, PC 6, Snyder
Selinsgrove Area SD, 401 18TH ST   17870   5-11111
  William Register, supt.   374-1144
Selinsgrove Area HS   3-00111
  600 BROAD ST   17870   374-1144
  James Crawford, prin.
Selinsgrove Area MS, 401 18TH ST   17870   3-01100
  Gregory Benshoff, prin.   374-1144

Susquehanna University   4-UC
  514 UNIVERSITY AVE   17870   374-0101
Welder Training & Testing Institute   2-CC
  100 PENNSYLVANIA AVE   17870   800-326-9306

Sellersville, AC 215, PC 5, Bucks

Faith Christian Academy   2-11111
  700 N MAIN ST   18960   257-5031
Upper Bucks Christian S   2-11111
  754 E ROCKHILL RD   18960   536-9200

Seneca, AC 814, PC 4, Venango
Cranberry Area SD   4-11111
  3 EDUCATION DR   16346   676-5628
  A. Myers, supt.
Cranberry Area JSHS   3-00111
  1 EDUCATION DR   16346   676-8504
  Elden Walthour, prin.

Christian Life Academy, MAIN ST   16346   2-11111
   676-9360

Sewickley, AC 412, PC 5, Allegheny
Quaker Valley SD   4-11111
  400 CHESTNUT RD   15143   741-3600
  R. Longo, supt.
Quaker Valley JHS   2-00110
  618 HARBAUGH ST   15143   741-3600
  Paul Gallagher, prin.
Other Schools – See Leetsdale

D. T. Watson Home for Crippled Children   HND
  95 CAMPMEETING RD   15143
Sewickley Academy   3-11111
  315 ACADEMY AVE   15143   741-2230
  Hamilton Clark, prin.
Sewickley Valley Hospital   HSP
  700 BLACKBURN RD   15143   741-7300

Shamokin, AC 717, PC 6, Northumberland
Area Vocational Technical SD
  Supt. — See Harrisburg
Northumberland County AVTS   Vo Tech
  1700 W MONTGOMERY ST   17866   644-0304
  Roland Holvey, prin.

Shamokin Area SD   5-11111
  2000 W STATE ST   17866   648-5752
  Ned Sodrick, supt.
Shamokin Area HS   3-00011
  2000 W STATE ST   17866   648-5731
  Eugene Boughner, prin.
Shamokin Area MS   3-00100
  8TH & ARCH ST   17872   644-0301
  Michael Leshock, prin.

Shanksville, AC 814, PC 2, Somerset
Shanksville-Stonycreek SD   2-11111
  PO BOX 128   15560   267-4649
  Gary Singel, supt.
Shanksville-Stonycreek S   2-11111
  PO BOX 128   15560   267-4649
  Constance Hummel, prin.

Sharon, AC 412, PC 7, Mercer
Sharon CSD, 215 FORKER BLVD   16146   5-11111
  Donald Thomas, supt.   983-4000
JSHS, 1129 E STATE ST   16146   4-00111
  Russell George, prin.   983-4030

Pennsylvania State University   3-CC
  147 SHENANGO AVE   16146   983-5800
Sharon Regional Health System   HSP
  740 E STATE ST   16146   983-3911
Shenango Valley School of Business   2-CS
  335 BOYD DR   16146   983-0700

Sharon Hill, AC 610, PC 6, Delaware
Southeast Delco SD
Supt. — See Folcroft
Academy Park HS 3-00011
300 CALCON HOOK RD 19079 522-4330
James Wigo, prin.

Sharpsville, AC 412, PC 5, Mercer
Sharpsville Area SD 4-11111
100 HITTLE AVE 16150 962-7874
Kenneth Vuletic, supt.
Sharpsville Area HS 2-00011
301 QUARRY WAY 16150 962-7861
Christ Hodges, prin.
Sharpsville Area MS 2-00100
303 QUARRY WAY 16150 962-7863
Douglas Hazlett, prin.
Snyder MS, 100 W RIDGE AVE 16150 2-00100
Douglas Hazlett, prin. 962-7863

Sheffield, AC 814, PC 4, Warren
Warren County SD
Supt. — See Warren
JSHS, HC BOX 600 16347 2-00111
Darrell Jaskolka, prin. 968-3720

Shenandoah, AC 717, PC 6, Schuylkill
Shenandoah Valley SD 3-11111
W CENTER ST 17976 462-1936
Gerald Nesvold, supt.
Shenandoah Valley JSHS 2-00111
W CENTER ST 17976 462-1957
Thomas Dando, prin.

Shickshinny, AC 717, PC 4, Luzerne
Northwest Area SD 4-11111
RR 2 BOX 2271 18655 542-4126
Karl Martin, supt.
Northwest Area JSHS, RR 2 18655 3-00111
J. Moss, prin. 542-4126

Shillington, AC 610, PC 6, Berks
Governor Mifflin SD 5-11111
10 S WAVERLY ST 19607 775-1461
Jack Harf, supt.
Mifflin SHS, 101 S WAVERLY ST 19607 3-00001
Chris Sherk, prin. 775-5089
Mifflin JHS 3-00110
130 E LANCASTER AVE 19607 775-1465
James Howland, prin.

Shinglehouse, AC 814, PC 4, Potter
Oswayo Valley SD 3-11111
PO BOX 610 16748 697-7175
Larry Henry, supt.
Oswayo Valley JSHS 2-00111
PO BOX 610 16748 697-6132
Dale Ishman, prin.

Shippensburg, AC 717, PC 6, Cumberland
Shippensburg Area SD 5-11111
317 N MORRIS ST 17257 530-2700
David Landis, supt.
Shippensburg Area SHS 3-00001
201 EBERLY DR 17257 530-2730
H. Frederick Shilling, prin.
Shippensburg Area SHS 3-00110
101 PARK PL 17257 530-2750
Rodney Young, prin.

Shippensburg University 17257 6-UC
532-9121

Shippenville, AC 814, PC 2, Clarion
Area Vocational Technical SD
Supt. — See Harrisburg
Clarion County AVTS Vo Tech
1976 CAREER WAY 16254 226-4391
W. Knorr, prin.

Shiremanstown, AC 717, PC 4, Cumberland

Bible Baptist S, 201 W MAIN ST 17011 2-11111
737-3550

Sidman, AC 814, PC 3, Cambria
Forest Hills SD, PO BOX 158 15955 5-11111
Paul Robinson, supt. 487-5924
Forest Hills HS, PO BOX 158 15955 3-00011
Donald Bailey, prin. 487-7613
Forest Hills MS, PO BOX 216 15955 3-00100
Raymond Wotkowski, prin. 495-4611

Sinking Spring, AC 215, PC 4, Berks
Wilson SD
Supt. — See West Lawn
Wilson Southern JHS 2-00110
3100 IROQUOIS AVE 19608 670-0544
S. Henry, prin.

Slatington, AC 215, PC 5, Lehigh
Northern Lehigh SD 4-11111
1201 SHADOW OAKS LN 18080 767-9800
Michael Clark, supt.
Northern Lehigh SHS 2-00001
1 BULLDOG LN 18080 767-9837
Nicholas Sham, prin.
Northern Lehigh JHS 3-00110
600 DIAMOND ST 18080 767-9812
Lynn Solt, prin.

Slippery Rock, AC 412, PC 5, Butler
Slippery Rock Area SD 4-11111
201 KEISTER RD 16057 794-2960
Gerald Heller, supt.
Slippery Rock Area HS 3-00011
201 KEISTER RD 16057 794-2960
David Vodila, prin.
Slippery Rock Area MS 3-00100
201 KEISTER RD 16057 794-2960
Paul Makarevich, prin.

Slippery Rock University 16057 6-UC
738-0512

Smethport, AC 814, PC 4, McKean
Smethport Area SD 4-11111
414 S MECHANIC ST 16749 887-5543
Paul Hite, supt.
JSHS, 412 S MECHANIC ST 16749 3-00111
Frank Kartesz, prin. 887-5545

Somerset, AC 814, PC 6, Somerset
Area Vocational Technical SD
Supt. — See Harrisburg
Somerset County AVTS, RR 5 15501 Vo Tech
Leroy Derstine, prin. 443-3651

Somerset Area SD 5-11111
821 S COLUMBIA AVE 15501 445-9714
Dennis Afton, supt.
Somerset Area SHS 3-00001
835 S COLUMBIA AVE 15501 443-2831
William Kuhlman, prin.
Somerset Area JHS 3-00110
827 S COLUMBIA AVE 15501 443-2831
Richard Shockey, prin.

Somerset Community Hospital HSP
225 S CENTER AVE 15501 443-5028

Souderton, AC 215, PC 6, Montgomery
Souderton Area SD 5-11111
139 HARLEYSVILLE PIKE 18964 723-6061
Alexander Grande, supt.
Souderton Area HS 4-00011
41 N SCHOOL LN 18964 723-6061
Andreas Demidont, prin.
Indian Crest MS 3-00100
139 HARLEYSVILLE PIKE 18964 723-6061
Frank D'Aiuto, prin.
Other Schools – See Harleysville

Southampton, AC 215, PC 7, Bucks
Centennial SD
Supt. — See Warminster
Klinger MS 3-00100
1415 2ND STREET PIKE 18966 364-5953
Janice Spirk, prin.

CHI Institute 2-CC
520 STREET RD 18966 357-5100

South Canaan, AC 717, PC 2, Wayne
Western Wayne SD 4-11111
GENERAL DELIVERY 18459 937-4270
Patricia Leamy, supt.
Other Schools – See Lake Ariel

South Williamsport, AC 717, PC 6, Lycoming
South Williamsport Area SD 4-11111
515 W CENTRAL AVE 17701 327-1581
James Street, supt.
S Williamsport Area JSHS 3-00111
700 PERCY ST 17701 326-2684
Paul Anderson, prin.

Spring Church, AC 412, PC 2, Armstrong
Apollo-Ridge SD, PO BOX 219 15686 4-11111
David Leckvarcik, supt. 478-1141
Apollo-Ridge HS, HC BOX 46A 15686 3-00011
Harry Notto, prin. 478-1131
Apollo-Ridge MS, HC BOX 46B 15686 2-00100
Guy De Toma, prin. 478-3721

Springdale, AC 412, PC 5, Allegheny
Allegheny Valley SD
Supt. — See Cheswick
JSHS, 501 BUTLER RD 15144 3-00111
Michael Panza, prin. 274-8100

Springfield, AC 610, PC 7, Delaware
Springfield SD 5-11111
111 W LEAMY AVE 19064 690-1781
Roger Place, supt.
HS, 49 W LEAMY AVE 19064 3-00011
Joseph O'Brien, prin. 690-1734
Richardson MS 3-01100
20 W WOODLAND AVE 19064 690-1734
Thomas Grubb, prin.

Cardinal O'Hara HS 4-00011
1701 S SPROUL RD 19064 544-3800
William McCusker, prin.
Chubb Institute-Keystone School 2-CC
965 BALTIMORE PIKE 19064 543-1747

Spring Grove, AC 717, PC 4, York
Spring Grove Area SD 5-11111
220 W JACKSON ST 17362 225-4731
Alan Lindquist, supt.
Spring Grove Area SHS, RR 4 17362 3-00001
Jeffrey Giano, prin. 225-5711
Spring Grove Area JHS 3-00110
RR 4 BOX 4621 17362 225-4758
Donna Hake, prin.

Spring Mills, AC 814, PC 3, Centre
Penns Valley Area SD 4-11111
RR 2 BOX 116 16875 422-8814
Parker Martin, supt.
Penns Valley Area JSHS 3-00111
RR 2 BOX 116 16875 422-8854
Albert D'Ambrosia, prin.

State College, AC 814, PC 8, Centre
State College Area SD 6-11111
131 W NITTANY AVE 16801 231-1016
William Opdenhoff, supt.
State College Area HS 4-00011
653 WESTERLY PKY 16801 231-1111
Michael Griffin, prin.
State College Area JHS 3-00100
2180 SCHOOL DR 16803 237-5301
John Casey, prin.

South Hills Business School 2-CS
480 WAUPELANI DR 16801 234-7755

Steelton, AC 717, PC 6, Dauphin
Central Dauphin SD
Supt. — See Harrisburg
Swatara JHS, 1101 HIGHLAND ST 17113 3-00110
Ronald Clemson, prin. 939-9363

Steelton-Highspire SD 4-11111
PO BOX 7645 17113 939-9823
Timothy Lafferty, supt.
Steelton-Highspire JSHS 3-00111
250 REYNDERS ST 17113 939-9895
James Deibler, prin.

Stoneboro, AC 412, PC 4, Mercer
Lakeview SD, RR 1 BOX 173 16153 4-11111
Alton Fell, supt. 376-7911
Lakeview HS, RR 1 16153 2-00011
William Carlson, prin. 376-7911
Lakeview MS, RR 1 16153 2-01100
Fred McConnell, prin. 376-7911

Strattanville, AC 814, PC 2, Clarion
Clarion-Limestone Area SD 4-11111
RR 1 BOX 205 16258 764-5111
J. Richard Slack, supt.
Clarion-Limestone JSHS 2-00111
RR 1 BOX 205 16258 764-5111
Lawrence Bornak, prin.

Stroudsburg, AC 717, PC 6, Monroe
Stroudsburg Area SD 5-11111
123 LINDEN ST 18360 421-1990
Russell Treible, supt.
HS, 1100 W MAIN ST 18360 4-00011
William Stoudt, prin. 421-1990
MS, CHIPPERFIELD DR 18360 4-01100
Judith Landry, prin. 421-4834

Summerdale, AC 717, PC 3, Cumberland

Central Pennsylvania Business School 3-CC
COLLEGE HILL ROAD 17093 732-0702

Sunbury, AC 717, PC 7, Northumberland
Shikellamy SD, 350 ISLAND BLVD 17801 5-11111
James Hartman, supt. 286-3720
Shikellamy HS, 600 WALNUT ST 17801 4-00011
Richard Smith, prin. 286-3713
Rice MS, 4TH & HANOVER STS 17801 2-00100
David Doran, prin. 473-3547
MS, 115 FAIRMOUNT AVE 17801 3-00100
John Gotaskie, prin. 286-3736

Susquehanna, AC 717, PC 4, Susquehanna
Susquehanna Community SD 4-11111
RR 3 BOX 5A 18847 853-4921
William Stracka, supt.
Susquehanna Community JSHS 2-00111
RR 3 BOX 5A 18847 853-4921
Robert McNamara, prin.

Swarthmore, AC 610, PC 6, Delaware

Swarthmore College 4-UC
500 COLLEGE AVE 19081 328-8000

Swiftwater, AC 717, PC 3, Monroe
Pocono Mountain SD 6-11111
PO BOX 200 18370 839-7121
David Krauser, supt.
Pocono Mountain SHS 4-00001
PO BOX 200 18370 839-7121
Joseph Yannuzzi, prin.
Pocono Mountain JHS 4-00110
PO BOX 200 18370 839-7121
William Forte, prin.

Tamaqua, AC 717, PC 6, Schuylkill
Tamaqua Area SD 4-11111
PO BOX 112 18252 668-2570
Raymond Kinder, supt.
Tamaqua Area HS, STADIUM RD 18252 3-00011
Bruce Krasley, prin. 668-1901
Tamaqua Area JHS, STADIUM RD 18252 2-00100
Robert Lombardo, prin. 668-1210

Marian HS, RR 4 BOX 446 18252 2-00011
John Malarkey, prin. 668-2225

Taylor, AC 717, PC 6, Lackawanna
Riverside SD 4-11111
DAVIS & STORRS STS 18517 562-2651
John Rooney, supt.

Riverside JSHS, 300 DAVIS ST 18517   3-00111
Dennis Kryzanowski, prin.   562-2880

Terre Hill, AC 215, PC 4, Lancaster

Terre Hill Mennonite S   2-00011
1416 UNION GROVE RD 17581   445-4618

Three Springs, AC 814, PC 2, Huntingdon
Southern Huntingdon County SD   4-11111
RR 1 BOX 1124 17264   447-5529
Harry King, supt.
Southern Huntingdon County JSHS   3-00111
RR 1 BOX 1124 17264   447-5529
Edwin Hasson, prin.

Throop, AC 717, PC 5, Lackawanna
Mid Valley SD   4-11111
52 UNDERWOOD RD 18512   489-0932
Joseph Crotti, supt.
Mid Valley JSHS   3-00111
52 UNDERWOOD RD 18512   489-1691
Robert Warzecha, prin.

Tidioute, AC 814, PC 3, Warren
Warren County SD
Supt. — See Warren
JSHS, 241 MAIN ST 16351   2-00111
Kenneth Fitzsimmons, prin.   484-3888

Tioga, AC 717, PC 3, Tioga
Northern Tioga SD
Supt. — See Elkland
Williamson JSHS, RR 2 16946   3-00111
L. Jones, prin.   827-2191

Tionesta, AC 814, PC 3, Forest
Forest Area SD, 210 VINE ST 16353   3-1111
Howard Ferguson, supt.   755-4491
West Forest JSHS, VINE ST 16353   2-00111
Ronald Paranick, prin.   755-3611
Other Schools — See Marienville

North Clarion County SD   3-1111
RR 1 BOX 194 16353   744-8536
Richard Priester, supt.
North Clarion County JSHS   2-00111
RR 1 BOX 194 16353   744-8544
Rodney Hartle, prin.

Titusville, AC 814, PC 6, Crawford
Titusville Area SD   5-11111
221 N WASHINGTON ST 16354   827-2715
Richard Carr, supt.
SHS, 302 E WALNUT ST 16354   3-00001
Walter Funk, prin.   827-9687
JHS, 302 E WALNUT ST 16354   3-00110
Terry Kerr, prin.   827-2717

Shenango Valley School of Business   2-CS
124 W SPRING ST 16354   827-9567
University of Pittsburgh at Titusville   2-UC
504 E MAIN ST # 287 16354   827-2702

Topton, AC 215, PC 4, Berks
Brandywine Heights Area SD   4-11111
200 W WEIS ST 19562   682-5100
Terry Mancini, supt.
Brandywine Heights HS   2-00011
200 W WEIS ST 19562   682-5102
Roger Hendrickson, prin.
Brandywine Heights MS   2-00100
200 W WEIS ST 19562   682-5131
William Hayes, prin.

Towanda, AC 717, PC 5, Bradford
Area Vocational Technical SD
Supt. — See Harrisburg
Bradford County AVTS   Vo Tech
RR 1 BOX 157A 18848   265-8111
Walter Becker, prin.

Towanda Area SD, 101 N 4TH ST 18848   4-11111
Daniel Paul, supt.   265-9894
Towanda Area HS   3-00011
0 STATE AND WESTERN AVE 18848   265-3690
Donald Butler, prin.
Towanda Area MS, STATE ST 18848   3-01100
Charles Rundell, prin.   265-2288

Tower City, AC 717, PC 4, Schuylkill
Williams Valley SD, RR 1 17980   4-11111
Gerald Bau, supt.   647-2167
Williams Valley JSHS, RTE 209 17980   3-00111
Robert Nestlerode, prin.   647-2167

Trafford, AC 412, PC 5, Westmoreland
Penn-Trafford SD
Supt. — See Harrison City
MS, 100 BRINTON AVE 15085   2-00100
David Spudy, prin.   372-6600

Trevorton, AC 717, PC 4, Northumberland
Line Mountain SD
Supt. — See Herndon
Line Mountain MS   2-00100
500 W SHAMOKIN ST 17881   797-2189
Mary Mikulka, prin.

Troy, AC 717, PC 4, Bradford
Troy Area SD, PO BOX 67 16947   4-11111
B. Schoonover, supt.   673-3081
Troy Area HS, 250 HIGH ST 16947   3-00011
Paul Ulrich, prin.   297-2176
Troy Area MS, 350 HIGH ST 16947   2-00100
Clyde Moate, prin.   297-2176

Martha Lloyd School   HND
W MAIN ST 16947

Tunkhannock, AC 717, PC 4, Wyoming
Tunkhannock Area SD   5-11111
200 FRANKLIN AVE 18657   836-3111
Kent Kresge, supt.
HS, 120 W TIOGA ST 18657   4-00011
C. Ellsworth, prin.   836-3111
MS, 41 PHILADELPHIA AVE 18657   4-01100
Russell Hons, prin.   836-3111

St. Michael's S, PO BOX 370 18657   2-01111
William Evans, prin.   388-6155

Turbotville, AC 717, PC 3, Northumberland
Warrior Run SD, RR 2 BOX 151A 17772   4-11111
Samuel Cooper, supt.   649-5138
Warrior Run HS, RR 2 BOX 151A 17772   3-00011
Sarah Kowalski, prin.   649-5166
Warrior Run MS, RR 2 BOX 151A 17772   3-01100
John Zeigler, prin.   649-5135

Turtle Creek, AC 412, PC 6, Allegheny
Woodland Hills SD
Supt. — See Pittsburgh
Woodland Hills JHS-East   2-00110
126 MONROEVILLE AVE 15145   824-2450
William Biesecker, prin.

Tyrone, AC 814, PC 6, Blair
Tyrone Area SD   4-11111
1317 LINCOLN AVE 16686   684-4830
William Miller, supt.
Tyrone Area JSHS   3-00111
1001 CLAY AVE 16686   684-4240
N. Smith, prin.

Grier School for Girls, RR 1 16686   2-00111
Mime Wertz, prin.   684-3000

Ulysses, AC 814, PC 3, Potter
Northern Potter SD   3-1111
RR 1 BOX 401 16948   848-7506
Robert Smith, supt.
Northern Potter JSHS   2-00111
RR 1 BOX 401 16948   848-7534
David White, prin.

Union City, AC 814, PC 5, Erie
Union City Area SD, 91 MILES ST 16438   4-11111
Thomas Ford, supt.   438-3804
HS, 105 CONCORD ST 16438   2-00111
Charles Thompson, prin.   438-7673
MS, 105 CONCORD ST 16438   2-00100
Thomas Fortin, prin.   438-2111

Uniontown, AC 412, PC 7, Fayette
Albert Galltn Area SD
Supt. — See Masontown
Gallatin SHS, RR 5 BOX 175A 15401   3-00001
Mario Tiberi, prin.   564-2024

Area Vocational Technical SD
Supt. — See Harrisburg
Fayette County AVTS   Vo Tech
RR 2 BOX 122A 15401   437-2721
John Trees, prin.

Laurel Highlands SD   5-11111
304 BAILEY AVE 15401   437-2821
Ronald Sheba, supt.
Laurel Highlands HS   4-00011
300 BAILEY AVE 15401   437-4741
Michael Carbonara, prin.
Laurel Highlands MS   3-00100
18 HOOKTON AVE 15401   437-2865
Melvin Sepic, prin.

Uniontown Area SD   5-11111
23 E CHURCH ST 15401   438-4501
James Burns, supt.
HS, 146 E FAYETTE ST 15401   4-00011
Richard Constantine, prin.   439-5000
Other Schools — See Markleysburg

Laurel Business Institute   2-CS
11 E PENN ST 15401   439-4900
Pennsylvania State University   3-CC
PO BOX 519 15401   237-2525
Uniontown Hospital   HSP
500 W BERKELEY ST 15401   430-5340

University Park, AC 814, PC see State College

Pennsylvania State University   8-UC
201 SHIELDS BLDG 16802   865-4700

Upper Darby, AC 610, PC 8, Delaware
Upper Darby SD
Supt. — See Drexel Hill
HS, 601 N LANSDOWNE AVE 19082   4-00011
Gilbert Minacci, prin.   622-7000
Beverly Hills MS   4-00100
1400 GARRETT RD 19082   626-9317
Melvyn Brodsky, prin.

PJA School   1-CS
7900 W CHESTER PIKE 19082   789-6700

Upper Saint Clair, AC 412, PC 7, Allegheny
Upper St. Clair SD   5-11111
1820 MCLAUGHLIN RUN RD 15241   833-1604
William Pope, prin.

HS, 1825 MCLAUGHLIN RUN RD 15241   4-00011
Parnell Hoffman, prin.   833-1600
Ft. Couch MS   3-00100
515 FORT COUCH RD 15241   854-3046
Thomas Harshman, prin.

Valley View, AC 717, PC 4, Schuylkill
Tri-Valley SD, 1801 W MAIN ST 17983   4-11111
Robert Franklin, supt.   682-9013
Other Schools — See Hegins

Vandergrift, AC 412, PC 6, Westmoreland
Kiski Area SD, 200 POPLAR ST 15690   5-11111
Stephen Vak, supt.   845-2022
Kiski Area HS, 200 POPLAR ST 15690   4-00011
John Shaner, prin.   845-8181
Kiski Area IS, 200 POPLAR ST 15690   3-00100
David Aiello, prin.   845-2219

Villanova, AC 610, PC 7, Delaware

Academy of Notre Dame De Namur   2-00111
560 SPROUL RD 19085   687-0650
Sr. Regina Finnegan, prin.
Northeastern Christian Junior College   2-CC
1860 MONTGOMERY AVE 19085   525-6780
Villanova University   7-UC
845 E LANCASTER AVE 19085   645-4500

Wallingford, AC 610, PC 5, Delaware
Wallingford-Swarthmore SD   5-11111
200 S PROVIDENCE RD 19086   892-3404
George Slick, supt.
Strath Haven HS   3-00011
205 S PROVIDENCE RD 19086   892-3428
Valdimar Sandberg, prin.
Strath Haven MS   3-00100
200 S PROVIDENCE RD 19086   982-3462
Sharon Parker, prin.

Warfordsburg, AC 717, PC 2, Fulton
Southern Fulton SD   3-1111
RR 2 BOX 45 17267   294-2203
Mary Coleman, supt.
Southern Fulton JSHS, RR 2 17267   2-00111
Larry Palmer, prin.   294-3251

Warminster, AC 215, PC 8, Bucks
Centennial SD   6-11111
433 CENTENNIAL RD 18974   441-6000
Thomas Sexton, supt.
Tennent HS, 333 CENTENNIAL RD 18974   4-00011
Kenneth Kastle, prin.   441-6166
Log College MS   3-00100
730 NORRISTOWN RD 18974   441-6072
Harry Clark, prin.
Other Schools — See Southampton

Archbishop Wood HS   4-00011
655 YORK RD 18974 – Fr. Close, prin.   672-5050
La Salle University   4-UC
675 YORK RD 18974   672-7293

Warren, AC 814, PC 7, Warren
Area Vocational Technical SD
Supt. — See Harrisburg
Warren County AVTS   Vo Tech
347 E 5TH AVE 16365   726-1260
Michael Hampsey, prin.

Warren County SD   6-11111
185 HOSPITAL DR 16365   723-6900
Leroy Rieck, supt.
Warren Area HS, 345 E 5TH AVE 16365   4-00011
Larry Frank, prin.   723-3370
Beaty-Warren MS, 2 E 3RD AVE 16365   4-01100
Sandra Hernan, prin.   723-5200
Other Schools — See Russell, Sheffield, Tidioute,
Youngsville

Washington, AC 412, PC 7, Washington
Trinity Area SD, 231 PARK AVE 15301   5-11111
James Husk, supt.   225-9880
Trinity HS, 231 PARK AVE 15301   4-00011
Rick Logue, prin.   225-5380
Trinity MS, 50 SCENIC DR 15301   3-00100
Angel Rodriguez, prin.   228-2112

Washington SD   4-11111
201 ALLISON AVE 15301   223-5000
Thomas Conner, supt.
HS, 201 ALLISON AVE 15301   3-00011
William Watson, prin.   223-5080

Penn Commercial College   2-CC
82 S MAIN ST 15301   222-5330
Washington & Jefferson College   4-UC
60 S LINCOLN ST 15301   222-4400
Washington Hospital   HSP
155 WILSON AVE 15301   223-3172
Washington Institute of Technology   2-CS
82 S MAIN ST 15301   222-1942

Waterfall, AC 814, PC 2, Fulton
Forbes Road SD   3-1111
HC 1 BOX 222 16689   685-3866
Charles Dunn, supt.
Forbes Road JSHS   2-00111
HC 1 BOX 222 16689   685-3866
J. Heroux, prin.

Waterford, AC 814, PC 4, Erie
Ft. LeBoeuf SD, PO BOX 367 16441   4-11111
J. Wolf, supt.   796-2638

Ft. LeBoeuf HS, 931 HIGH ST 16441   3-00011
  Clarence Schrimper, prin.   796-2616
Ft. LeBoeuf MS, 865 CHERRY ST 16441   3-01100
  Cindy Hargest, prin.   796-2681

Watsontown, AC 717, PC 4, Northumberland

Marantha Christian S, RR 2 17777   2-11111
    649-5250
Watsontown Christian Academy   2-11111
  RR 3 BOX 453 17777   538-9276

Wattsburg, AC 814, PC 2, Erie
Wattsburg Area SD   4-11111
  PO BOX 219 16442   739-2291
  L. Hurlburt, supt.
Wattsburg Area MS   3-01100
  PO BOX 199 16442   739-2217
  Gerald Malarik, prin.
  Other Schools – See Erie

Wayne, AC 610, PC 6, Delaware
Radnor Township SD   4-11111
  135 S WAYNE AVE 19087   688-8100
  John DeFlaminis, supt.
Radnor MS, 131 S WAYNE AVE 19087   3-01100
  E. Dodd, prin.   688-8100
  Other Schools – See Radnor

Tredyffrin-Easttown SD
  Supt. — See Berwyn
Valley Forge JHS   3-00110
  105 W WALKER RD 19087   688-8980
  Thomas Hughes, prin.

Valley Forge Military Academy   2-00111
  1001 EAGLE RD 19087   688-1800
  Col. Donn Miller, prin.
Valley Forge Military Academy & College   2-CC
  1001 EAGLE RD 19087   800-234-8362

Waynesboro, AC 717, PC 6, Franklin
Waynesboro Area SD   5-11111
  PO BOX 72 17268   762-1191
  Michael Moskalski, supt.
Waynesboro Area HS   4-00011
  550 E 2ND ST 17268   762-1191
  George Atherholt, prin.
Waynesboro Area MS   3-00100
  702 E 2ND ST 17268   762-1191
  John Krebs, prin.

Waynesburg, AC 412, PC 5, Greene
Area Vocational Technical SD
  Supt. — See Harrisburg
Greene County AVTS   Vo Tech
  RR 2 BOX 40 15370   627-3106
  Richard Ohler, prin.

Central Green SD, PO BOX 472 15370   5-11111
  Donald Painter, supt.   627-8151
Waynesburg Central HS, RR 2 15370   3-00011
  John Barbero, prin.   852-1050
Miller MS, 126 E LINCOLN ST 15370   3-01100
  (—), prin.   852-2722

West Greene SD, RR 5 BOX 36-B 15370   4-11111
  Charles Rembold, supt.   499-5183
West Greene JSHS, RR 5 BOX 36A 15370   3-00111
  Ken Ganocy, prin.   499-5107

Waynesburg College   4-UC
  51 W COLLEGE ST 15370   800-225-7393

Weatherly, AC 717, PC 5, Carbon
Weatherly Area SD, 602 6TH ST 18255   3-11111
  Peter McMonigle, supt.   427-8681
Weatherly Area HS, 601 6TH ST 18255   2-00011
  Peter McMonigle, prin.   427-8521
Weatherly Area MS, 602 6TH ST 18255   2-00100
  John Kudlick, prin.   427-8689

Wellsboro, AC 717, PC 5, Tioga
Wellsboro Area SD   4-11111
  2 CHARLES ST 16901   724-4424
  David Spearly, supt.
Wellsboro Area HS   3-00011
  67 NICHOLS ST 16901   724-3547
  William Wade, prin.
Wellsboro Area MS   3-01100
  9 NICHOLS ST 16901   724-2306
  Terry Erway, prin.

Pennsylvania College of Technology   4-CC
  MANSFIELD RD 16901

West Chester, AC 610, PC 7, Chester
West Chester Area SD   6-11111
  829 PAOLI PIKE 19380   436-7000
  Thomas Kent, supt.
East HS, 450 ELLIS LN 19380   4-00011
  Lee McFadden, prin.   436-7204
Henderson HS   4-00011
  400 MONTGOMERY AVE 19380   436-7221
  Michael Dibartolomeo, prin.
Fugett MS, 500 ELLIS LN 19380   3-00100
  Eliot Larson, prin.   436-7242
Pierce MS, 1314 BURKE RD 19380   3-00100
  Joseph Jackson, prin.   436-7252
Stetson MS   3-00100
  1060 WILMINGTON PIKE 19382   436-7262
  Clarence Grasty, prin.

Bishop Shanahan HS   3-00011
  101 N EVERHART AVE 19380   696-7604
  Sr. Helen Rapine, prin.
Chester County Hospital   HSP
  701 E MARSHALL ST 19380   431-5165
Devereux-Leo Kanner Center in PA   2-HND
  390 E BOOT RD 19380   431-8174
West Chester Christian S   2-11111
  1237 PAOLI PIKE 19380   692-3700
West Chester University of Pennsylvania   7-UC
  S HIGH ST 19383   436-1000

Westfield, AC 814, PC 4, Tioga
Northern Tioga SD
  Supt. — See Elkland
Cowanesque Valley JSHS, RR 16950   2-00111
  Michael Schwartz, prin.   367-2233

West Grove, AC 610, PC 4, Chester
Avon-Grove SD   5-11111
  375 KELTON JENNERSVILLE RD 19390
  Ronald Ferrari, supt.   869-2441
Avon-Grove HS, 327 STATE RD 19390   3-00011
  John Sengia, prin.   869-2446
Engle MS   3-01100
  207 SCHOOLHOUSE RD 19390   869-3022
  Augustus Massaro, prin.

West Hazleton, AC 717, PC 5, Luzerne
Hazleton Area SD
  Supt. — See Hazleton
JHS, 325 NORTH ST 18201   3-00110
  Frank Victor, prin.   459-3160

West Lawn, AC 215, PC 4, Berks
Wilson SD   5-11111
  2601 GRANDVIEW BLVD 19609   670-0180
  Lee Fredericks, supt.
Wilson SHS, GRANDVIEW BLVD 19609   3-00001
  Frank Herron, prin.   670-0185
Wilson Central JHS   2-00110
  GRANDVIEW BLVD 19609   670-1454
  Mark Hazara, prin.
  Other Schools – See Sinking Spring

West Middlesex, AC 412, PC 3, Mercer
West Middlesex Area SD   4-11111
  SHARON-NEW CASTLE RD 16159   528-2002
  Albert Jones, supt.
JSHS   3-00111
  SHARON & NEWCASTLE RD 16159   528-9951
  Russell Ridenbaugh, prin.

West Mifflin, AC 412, PC 7, Allegheny
West Mifflin Area SD   5-11111
  515 CAMP HOLLOW RD 15122   466-9131
  Joseph Dimperio, supt.
West Mifflin Area HS   3-00011
  91 COMMONWEALTH AVE 15122   466-7220
  Donald Teti, prin.
West Mifflin Area MS   3-00100
  371 CAMP HOLLOW RD 15122   466-3200
  Fred Botti, prin.

Community College of Allegheny County   6-CC
  1750 CLAIRTON RD 15122   469-1100

Westover, AC 814, PC 2, Clearfield
Harmony SD, RR 1 BOX 71 16692   3-11111
  James Kiscaden, supt.   845-2300
Harmony Area HS, RR 1 16692   2-00011
  James Sybert, prin.   845-7655
Harmony Area MS, RR 1 16692   2-00100
  Linda Brown, prin.   845-2300

West Sunbury, AC 412, PC 2, Butler
Moniteau SD, RR 2 BOX 2035 16061   4-11111
  William Marburger, supt.   637-2117
Moniteau JSHS, RR 1 16061   3-00111
  John Fecich, prin.   637-2091

Westtown, AC 215, PC 3, Chester

Westtown School 19395   3-11111
  Thomas Farquhar, prin.   399-0123

Wexford, AC 412, PC 4, Allegheny
North Allegheny SD
  Supt. — See Pittsburgh
North Allegheny SHS   4-00011
  10375 PERRY HWY 15090   935-5767
  Lawrence Butterini, prin.
Marshall MS   3-00100
  5145 WEXFORD RUN RD 15090   366-2100
  John Schwoebel, prin.

Whitehall, AC 610, PC 7, Lehigh
Whitehall-Coplay SD   5-11111
  2940 MACARTHUR RD 18052   439-1431
  Loren Keim, supt.
HS, 3800 MECHANICSVILLE RD 18052   3-00011
  Rosalee Sabo, prin.   437-5081
Whitehall-Coplay MS   3-01100
  2930 MACARTHUR RD 18052   439-1439
  Robert Rothenberger, prin.

Star Technical Institute   2-CS
  1541 ALTA DR STE 1 18052   434-9963

Wilkes-Barre, AC 717, PC 8, Luzerne
Area Vocational Technical SD
  Supt. — See Harrisburg
Wilkes-Barre AVTS   Vo Tech
  PO BOX 1699 18705   822-4131
  Thomas O'Donnell, prin.

Hanover Area SD   4-11111
  1600 SANS SOUCI PKY 18702   823-5159
  John Kmetz, supt.
Hanover Area JSHS   3-00111
  1600 SANS SOUCI PKY 18702   823-2184
  J. Sabatini, prin.

Wilkes-Barre Area SD   6-11111
  730 S MAIN ST 18702   826-7111
  Leo Solomon, supt.
Coughlin SHS   3-00001
  80 N WASHINGTON ST 18701   826-7201
  William Schwab, prin.
G.A.R. Memorial JSHS   3-00111
  2505 GRANT ST 18702   826-7165
  Phillip Latinski, prin.
Meyers JSHS, 341 CAREY AVE 18702   4-00111
  F. Wempa, prin.   826-7145
  Other Schools – See Plains

Bishop Hoban HS   3-00011
  159 S PENNSYLVANIA AVE 18701   829-2424
  Frank Majikes, prin.
King's College   4-UC
  133 N RIVER ST 18711   826-5900
Regis Academy   2-00100
  316 N MAPLE AVE 18704   287-3133
  Colleen Hogan, prin.
Wilkes Barre General Hospital   HSP
  575 N RIVER ST 18702   829-8111
Wilkes University   5-UC
  184 S RIVER ST 18766   824-4651

Wilkinsburg, AC 412, PC 7, Allegheny
Wilkinsburg Borough SD   4-11111
  718 WALLACE AVE 15221   371-9667
  Walter Watson, supt.
JSHS, 747 WALLACE AVE 15221   3-00111
  (—), prin.   371-9500

Williamsburg, AC 814, PC 4, Blair
Williamsburg Community SD   3-11111
  515 W 3RD ST 16693   832-2125
  Lee Swinsburg, supt.
Williamsburg Community JSHS   2-00111
  515 W 3RD ST 16693   832-2125
  Steven De Lisle, prin.

Williamsport, AC 717, PC 8, Lycoming
Loyalsock Township SD   4-11111
  1225 CLAYTON AVE 17701   326-6508
  Nelson Wruble, supt.
Loyalsock Twp. HS   2-00011
  1801 LOYALSOCK DR 17701   326-3581
  C. Thomas Little, prin.
Loyalsock Twp. JHS   2-00100
  2101 LOYALSOCK DR 17701   323-9439
  Wayne Rose, prin.

Williamsport Area SD   6-11111
  201 W 3RD ST 17701   327-5500
  Martha Johnston, supt.
Williamsport Area HS   4-00011
  2990 W 4TH ST 17701   323-8411
  Philip Thomas, prin.
Curtin MS, 85 ELDRED ST 17701   3-00100
  James Dougherty, prin.   323-4785
Lycoming Valley MS   2-00100
  1825 HAYS LN 17701   494-1700
  Robert Eichensehr, prin.
Roosevelt MS, 2800 W 4TH ST 17701   3-00100
  Geralyn Fausnaught, prin.   323-6177

Bishop Neumann HS   2-00111
  901 PENN ST 17701   323-9953
  Fr. Kurovsky, prin.
Divine Providence Hospital   HSP
  1100 GRAMPIAN BLVD 17701   326-8101
Lycoming College 17701   4-UC
    321-4000
Pennsylvania College of Technology   5-CC
  1 COLLEGE AVE 17701   800-367-9222
Williamsport Hospital   HSP
  777 RURAL AVE 17701   321-2101
Williamsport School of Commerce   2-CC
  941 W 3RD ST 17701   326-2869

Willow Grove, AC 215, PC 7, Montgomery
Area Vocational Technical SD
  Supt. — See Harrisburg
Eastern Montgomery County AVTS   Vo Tech
  3075 TERWOOD RD 19090   657-7080
  Joseph Colaneri, prin.

Upper Moreland Township SD   5-11111
  2900 TERWOOD RD 19090   659-6800
  Paul Beck, supt.
Upper Moreland HS   3-00011
  3000 TERWOOD RD 19090   659-6800
  John DeLaurentis, prin.
  Other Schools – See Hatboro

Willow Hill, AC 717, PC 2, Franklin
Fannett-Metal SD, PO BOX 91 17271   3-11111
  Patrick Crawford, supt.   349-7172
Fannett-Metal JSHS   2-00111
  PO BOX 91 17271   349-2363
  James Peterson, prin.

Willow Street, AC 717, PC 6, Lancaster
Area Vocational Technical SD
  Supt. — See Harrisburg

Lancaster County AVTS-Willow St | Vo Tech
PO BOX 527 17584 | 464-2771
Richard Burley, prin.
Lancaster County AVTS | Vo Tech
1730 HANS HERR DR 17584 | 464-2771
Richard Burley, prin.

Windber, AC 814, PC 5, Somerset
Windber Area SD | 4-11111
2301 GRAHAM AVE 15963 | 467-5551
Salvatore Marro, supt.
Windber Area HS | 2-00011
2301 GRAHAM AVE 15963 | 467-4567
Virgil Palumbo, prin.
Windber Area MS | 2-00100
2301 GRAHAM AVE 15963 | 467-4620
Glenn Gaye, prin.

Wingate, AC 814, PC 2, Centre
Bald Eagle Area SD, PO BOX 4 16823 | 4-11111
Daniel Fisher, supt. | 355-4860
Bald Eagle JSHS, PO BOX 4 16823 | 4-00111
Robert Vadella, prin. | 355-4868

Wormleysburg, AC 717, PC 5, Cumberland

Harrisburg Academy | 2-11111
10 ERFORD RD 17043 | 763-7811
Gregory Morgan, prin.

Wrightsville, AC 717, PC 4, York
Eastern York SD, PO BOX 150 17368 | 4-11111
Robert McGraw, supt. | 252-1555
Eastern JSHS, PO BOX 2002 17368 | 4-00111
Frederick Hackett, prin. | 252-1551

Wyalusing, AC 717, PC 3, Bradford
Wyalusing Area SD | 4-11111
PO BOX 157 18853 | 746-1605
Warner Stark, supt.
Wyalusing Valley JSHS, RR 2 18853 | 3-00111
Martin Weisgold, prin. | 746-1218

Wyncote, AC 215, PC 5, Montgomery
Cheltenham Township SD
Supt. — See Elkins Park
Cheltenham Twp. HS | 4-00011
500 RICES MILL RD 19095 | 881-6400
Joseph Rodgers, prin.
Cedarbrook MS | 3-00100
300 LONGFELLOW RD 19095 | 881-6421
Joseph Cifelli, prin.

Bishop McDevitt HS | 3-00011
101 ROYAL AVE 19095 | 887-5575
Fr. Brugger, prin.
Reconstructionist Rabbinical College | 1-UC
GREENWOOD AVE & CHURCH RD 19095 | 576-0800

Wynnewood, AC 610, PC 6, Montgomery

Eastern Baptist Theological Seminary | 2-UC
6 E LANCASTER AVE 19096 | 896-5000
Friends Central S, 1101 CITY AVE 19096 | 2-01111
| 649-7440
Lankenau Hospital | 2-HSP
120 E LANCASTER AVE 19096 | 645-2025

St. Charles Borromeo Seminary | 2-UC
1000 E WYNNEWOOD RD 19096 | 667-3394

Wyoming, AC 717, PC 5, Luzerne

McCann School of Business | 2-CC
2004 WYOMING AVE 18644 | 287-4400

Wyomissing, AC 215, PC 6, Berks
Wyomissing Area SD | 4-11111
30 EVANS AVE 19610 | 374-4031
Charles Walker, supt.
Wyomissing Area JSHS | 3-00111
630 EVANS AVE 19610 | 374-4035
Peter Cellucci, prin.

Berks Technical Institute | 1-CS
4 PARK PLZ 19610 | 372-1722

Yardley, AC 215, PC 4, Bucks
Pennsbury SD
Supt. — See Fallsington
Boehm MS, 866 BIG OAK RD 19067 | 3-00100
Thomas Hoy, prin. | 428-4220
Penn MS, 1524 DERBYSHIRE RD 19067 | 3-00100
Karen Casto, prin. | 428-4280
Pennwood MS | 3-00100
1523 MAKEFIELD RD 19067 | 428-4237
Roger Hedeman, prin.

Yeadon, AC 215, PC 7, Delaware
William Penn SD, PO BOX 405 19050 | 5-11111
Thomas Jenkins, supt. | 284-8052
Penn Wood East JHS | 3-00110
600 CYPRESS ST 19050 | 626-3223
Richard Bell, prin.
Other Schools – See Darby, Lansdowne

York, AC 717, PC 8, York
Area Vocational Technical SD
Supt. — See Harrisburg
York County AVTS | Vo Tech
2179 S QUEEN ST 17402 | 741-0820
Roger Apple, prin.

Central York SD, 775 MARION RD 17402 | 5-11111
W. Snyder, supt. | 846-6789
Central York HS, 300 E 7TH AVE 17404 | 3-00011
Glenn Caufman, prin. | 846-6789
Central York MS | 3-00100
1950 N HILLS RD 17402 | 846-6789
Richard Burd, prin.

West York Area SD | 4-11111
2605 W MARKET ST 17404 | 792-3067
Albert Glennon, supt.
West York Area HS | 3-00011
1800 BANNISTER ST 17404 | 845-6634
Barbara Rupp, prin.
West York Area JHS | 2-00100
1700 BANNISTER ST 17404 | 845-1671
Kathy Carbaugh, prin.

York CSD, PO BOX 1927 17405 | 6-11111
Jack Van Newkirk, supt. | 845-3571
Penn HS, 101 W COLLEGE AVE 17403 | 4-00011
Richard Grieg, prin. | 845-3571
Penn MS, 415 E BOUNDARY AVE 17403 | 3-00100
Ronald Trimmer, prin. | 845-3571

Smith MS, 701 TEXAS AVE 17404 | 3-00100
Eugene Radel, prin. | 845-3571

York Suburban SD | 4-11111
HOLLYWOOD AND SOUTHERN RD 17403
Robert Dovey, supt. | 848-2814
York Suburban HS | 3-00011
HOLLYWOOD AND SOUTHERN RD 17403
Paul Englert, prin. | 843-3881
York Suburban MS | 2-00100
SUNDALE DRIVE 17402 | 755-2841
Jere Eckenroth, prin.

Bradley Academy for the Visual Arts | 1-CC
625 E PHILADELPHIA ST 17403 | 848-1447
Christian S of York | 3-11111
907 GREENBRIAR RD 17404 | 767-6842
Charles Bloomfield, prin.
Consolidated School of Business | 2-CS
1605 CLUGSTON RD 17404 | 764-9550
Pennsylvania State University | 4-CC
1031 EDGECOMBE AVE 17403 | 771-4000
York Catholic HS | 3-00111
601 E SPRINGETTSBURY AVE 17403 | 846-8871
Fr. Grab, prin.
York College of Pennsylvania | 5-UC
PO BOX 15199 17405 | 846-7788
York Country Day S | 2-11111
1071 COUNTRY CLUB RD 17403 | 843-9805
Taylor Smith, prin.
York Hospital | HSP
1001 S GEORGE ST 17403 | 771-2121
York Technical Institute | 2-CS
3351 WHITEFORD RD 17402 | 757-1100
Yorktowne Business Institute | 3-CS
0 W 7TH AVE 17404 | 846-5000

York Springs, AC 717, PC 3, Adams
Bermudian Springs SD | 4-11111
PO BOX 501 17372 | 528-4113
Herbert Phelps, supt.
Bermudian Springs HS | 2-00011
PO BOX 501 17372 | 528-4113
Dale Heineman, prin.
Bermudian Springs MS | 3-01100
PO BOX 501 17372 | 528-4113
Clifton Vanartsdalen, prin.

Youngsville, AC 814, PC 4, Warren
Warren County SD
Supt. — See Warren
JSHS, 227 COLLEGE ST 16371 | 3-00111
Duane Vicini, prin. | 563-7573

Warren County Christian S | 2-11111
ROUTE 6W 16371 | 563-4457

Youngwood, AC 412, PC 5, Westmoreland

Westmoreland County Community College | 6-CC
400 ARMBRUST RD 15697 | 925-4000

RHODE ISLAND

STATE DEPARTMENT OF EDUCATION
22 Hayes St., Providence 02908
(401) 277-2031

Commissioner of Education	Peter McWalters
Deputy Commissioner	Janice Baker
Director Administration & Finance	Frank Pontarelli
Director Career & Technical Education	Frank Santoro
Director Human Resource Development	Paula Rossi
Director of Instruction	Marie DiBiasio
Director Outcomes & Assessment	Pasquale DeVito
Director Social Services	Phil Zarlengo
Director Special Needs	Robert Pryhoda
Director Teacher Education & Certification	Louis DelPapa

BOARD OF REGENTS FOR ELEMENTARY & SECONDARY EDUCATION
22 Hayes St., Providence 02908

Chairperson	Frederick Lippitt

PUBLIC, PRIVATE AND CATHOLIC SECONDARY SCHOOLS

Barrington, AC 401, PC 7, Bristol
Barrington SD, 283 COUNTY RD 02806   4-11111
  Ralph Malafronte, supt.   245-5000
HS, 220 LINCOLN AVE 02806   3-00011
  John Gray, prin.   247-3150
MS, MIDDLE HWY 02806   3-00100
  Robert Miller, prin.   247-3160

St. Andrew's S, 63 FEDERAL RD 02806   2-01111
  Everett Wilson, prin.   246-1230

Block Island, AC 401, PC 3, Washington
New Shoreham SD, HIGH ST 02807   2-11111
  M. Scherza, supt.   466-5600
Block Island Consolidated S   2-11111
  PO BOX 249 02807   466-5600
  M. Scherza, prin.

Bristol, AC 401, PC 7, Bristol
Bristol-Warren SD, 151 STATE ST 02809   4-11111
  Guy DiBiasio, supt.   253-4000
Mount Hope HS   3-00011
  199 CHESTNUT ST 02809   253-4000
  Edward Jawor, prin.
Other Schools – See Warren

Roger Williams College   5-UC
1 OLD FERRY RD 02809   253-1967

Central Falls, AC 401, PC 7, Providence
Central Falls SD, 21 HEDLEY AVE 02863   5-11111
  Maureen Chevrette, supt.   727-7700
JSHS, 24 SUMMER ST 02863   3-00111
  Charles Van Gordon, prin.   727-7710

Chepachet, AC 401, PC 3, Providence
Foster-Glocester SD, PO BOX D 02814   4-00111
  Raymond Reilly, supt.   568-4175
Other Schools – See North Scituate

Coventry, AC 401, PC 6, Kent
Coventry SD, 60 WOOD ST 02816   6-11111
  Raymond Spear, supt.   822-9400
HS, 40 RESERVOIR RD 02816   4-00011
  John Deasy, prin.   822-9499
West Bay Area Vo-Tech Center   Vo Tech
15 FOSTER DR 02816   822-9467
  Alfred Berard, prin.
MS, 19 FOSTER DR 02816   3-00100
  Donna Vigneau, prin.   822-9466

St. Xavier Academy   1-00011
2 SAINT VINCENT DE PAUL ST 02816   826-2130
  Kathleen Siok, prin.

Cranston, AC 401, PC 8, Providence
Cranston SD, 845 PARK AVE 02910   6-11111
  Edward Myers, supt.   785-8170
East SHS, 899 PARK AVE 02910   4-00001
  William Paolino, prin.   785-8126

West SHS   3-00001
80 METROPOLITAN AVE 02920   785-8049
  Lyle Perra, prin.
Cranston Area Vo-Tech Ctr   Vo Tech
100 METROPOLITAN AVE 02920   785-8070
  Edward Lemoi, prin.
Bain JHS, 135 GANSETT AVE 02910   3-00110
  Gary Spremuilo, prin.   785-8010
Park View JHS   3-00110
25 PARKVIEW BLVD 02910   785-8090
  Jon Choiniere, prin.
Western Hills JHS   3-00110
400 PHENIX AVE 02920   785-8030
  Joseph DiLorenzo, prin.

Rhode Island Medical Center   HSP
PO BOX 8269 02920   464-3666

Cumberland, AC 401, PC see Valley Falls
Cumberland SD   5-11111
2602 MENDON RD 02864   658-1600
  Robert Wallace, supt.
HS, 2600 MENDON RD 02864   4-00011
  Rose Marie Cipriano, prin.   658-2600
MS, 280 HIGHLAND AVE 02864   2-00100
  Joyce Hindle-Koutsogiane, prin.   725-2092
North Cumberland MS   2-00100
30 NATE WHIPPLE HWY 02864   333-6306
  Joseph Nasif, prin.

East Greenwich, AC 401, PC 7, Kent
East Greenwich SD, 5 DIVISION ST 02818   4-11111
  David Connolly, supt.   885-3300
HS, 300 AVENGER DR 02818   3-00011
  Stephen Coppinger, prin.   886-3292
Cole JHS, 100 CEDAR AVE 02818   2-00100
  Joseph Militello, prin.   886-3260

Rocky Hill S, IVES ROAD 02818   2-11111
  R Herrmann, prin.   884-9070

East Providence, AC 401, PC 8, Providence
East Providence SD   6-11111
80 BURNSIDE AVE 02915   437-0750
  John Degoes, supt.
SHS, 2000 PAWTUCKET AVE 02914   4-00001
  Arthur Elmasian, prin.   437-0750
East Providence Area Vo-Tech Ctr   Vo Tech
2000 PAWTUCKET AVE 02914   437-0750
  Stephen Propatier, prin.
Martin JHS, 111 BROWN ST 02914   3-00110
  John Rezendes, prin.   437-0750
Other Schools – See Riverside

Providence Country Day S   2-01111
2117 PAWTUCKET AVE 02914   438-5170
  Christopher Corkery, prin.

Esmond, AC 401, PC 5, Providence
Smithfield SD, 49 FARNUM PIKE 02917   4-11111
  Richard Lynch, supt.   231-6606
Smithfield HS   3-00011
90 PLEASANT VIEW AVE 02917   949-2050
  Robert Salisbury, prin.
Gallagher JHS   2-00100
INDIAN RUN TRAIL 02917   949-2056
  Roger Depot, prin.

Harrisville, AC 401, PC 4, Providence
Burrillville SD, 425 EAST AVE 02830   5-11111
  Dennis Flynn, supt.   568-1301
Burrillville HS, 425 EAST AVE 02830   4-00011
  Stephen Mitchell, prin.   568-1310
Burrillville MS   3-00100
2220 BRONCOS HWY 02830   568-1320
  Robert Morissette, prin.

Jamestown, AC 401, PC 5, Newport
Jamestown SD, 76 MELROSE AVE 02835   2-11100
  Phyllis Schmidt, supt.   423-7020
MS, PO BOX 318 02835   2-01100
  Phyllis Schmidt, prin.   423-7010

Johnston, AC 401, PC 8, Providence
Johnston SD, 10 MEMORIAL AVE 02919   5-11111
  Mary Carroll, supt.   233-1900
HS, 345 CHERRY HILL RD 02919   3-00011
  (—), prin.   233-1920
Ferri MS, 10 MEMORIAL AVE 02919   3-00100
  Frederick Pasquariello, prin.   233-1930

Kingston, AC 401, PC 6, Washington

University of Rhode Island 02881   7-UC
  792-2766

Lincoln, AC 401, PC 5, Providence
Lincoln SD, 1624 LONSDALE AVE 02865   5-11111
  Colette Trailor, supt.   726-2150
JSHS, 135 OLD RIVER RD 02865   4-00111
  Howard Boyaj, prin.   333-1850

Community College of Rhode Island   4-CC
1762 LOUISQUISSET PIKE 02865   333-7265

Middletown, AC 401, PC 5, Newport
Middletown SD, 350 E MAIN RD 02842   5-11111
  D. William Wheetley, supt.   849-2122
HS, 128 VALLEY RD 02842   3-00011
  John Regan, prin.   846-7250
Gaudet MS   3-01100
1017 AQUIDNECK AVE 02842   846-6395
  Vincent Guillano, prin.

Sawyer School   3-CS
PO BOX 4288 02842   849-1580

Narragansett, AC 401, PC 5, Washington
Narragansett SD, 25 5TH AVE 02882   4-11111
  John Wedlock, supt.   792-9450
JSHS, 245 S PIER RD 02882   3-00111
  James DiPrete, prin.   792-9400

Ocean State Business Institute   2-CS
  140 POINT JUDITH RD STE 3A 02882   789-0287

Newport, AC 401, PC 8, Newport
Newport SD, 437 BROADWAY 02840   5-11111
  Donald Beaudette, supt.   847-2100
Rogers HS, 1 WICKHAM RD 02840   4-00011
  Mihran Keoseian, prin.   847-6235
Newport County Vo-Tech Ctr   Vo Tech
  RUGGLES AVE 02840   849-3608
  Mary Canole, prin.
Thompson JHS, 39 BROADWAY 02840   3-00100
  Brian Abdallah, prin.   847-1493

St. George's S, PURGATORY RD 02840   2-00011
  Charles Hamblet, prin.   847-7565
Salve Regina University   4-UC
  1 OCHRE POINT AVE 02840   847-6650

North Kingstown, AC 401, PC 5, Washington
North Kingstown SD   5-11111
  100 FAIRWAY DR 02852   294-4581
  Paul Rennick, supt.
HS, 150 FAIRWAY DR 02852   4-00011
  Gerald Foley, prin.   294-4581
Davisville MS, 200 SCHOOL ST 02852   3-00100
  E. Jane Kondon, prin.   294-4581
Wickford MS   2-00100
  250 TOWER HILL RD 02852   294-4581
  Martin Hellewell, prin.

West Bay Christian Academy   1-01100
  6356 POST RD 02852   884-3600
  Michael Marrapodi, prin.

North Providence, AC 401, PC 8, Providence
North Providence SD   5-11111
  9 GEORGE ST 02911   233-1100
  David Heimbecker, supt.
HS, 1828 MINERAL SPRING AVE 02904   3-00011
  Louis Lanni, prin.   233-1150
Birchwood MS   2-00100
  10 BIRCHWOOD DR 02904   233-1120
  Kenneth Ferrara, prin.

St. Joseph's Hospital   HSP
  200 HIGH SERVICE AVE 02904   456-3050

North Scituate, AC 401, PC 2, Providence
Foster-Glocester SD
  Supt. — See Chepachet
Ponaganset HS   3-00011
  137 ANAN WADE RD 02857   647-3377
  Richard Oswald, prin.
Ponaganset MS   2-00100
  91 ANAN WADE RD 02857   647-3361
  Patrick Hannigan, prin.

Scituate SD   4-11111
  197 DANIELSON PIKE 02857   647-4100
  Allen Brown, supt.
Scituate JSHS, 94 TRIMTOWN RD 02857   3-00111
  David Light, prin.   647-4120

Hall Institute of Tech   2-CS
  PO BOX 773 02857   722-2003

North Smithfield, AC 401, PC 6, Providence
North Smithfield SD   4-11111
  450 GREENVILLE RD 02896   769-5492
  John Moretti, supt.
JSHS, 412 GREENVILLE RD 02896   3-00111
  Richard Smith, prin.   766-2500

Pawtucket, AC 401, PC 8, Providence
Pawtucket SD, PO BOX 388 02862   6-11111
  Emile Chevrette, supt.   729-6315
Shea HS, 485 EAST AVE 02860   3-00011
  James McNaught, prin.   729-6445
Tolman HS, 150 EXCHANGE ST 02860   4-00011
  Francis Moran, prin.   729-6400
Goff JHS, 974 NEWPORT AVE 02861   2-00100
  Clifford Wallace, prin.   729-6500
Jenks JHS, 350 DIVISION ST 02860   3-00100
  Joseph Cunha, prin.   729-6520
Slater JHS   2-00100
  281 MINERAL SPRING AVE 02860   729-6480
  Walter Guest, prin.

Bishop Keough Regional HS   1-00011
  145 POWER RD 02860   726-0335
  Jeanne LeClerc, prin.
Memorial Hospital of Rhode Island   HSP
  111 BREWSTER ST 02860   722-6000
Nasson Institute   2-CS
  1080 NEWPORT AVE 02861   728-1570
New England Tractor Trailer Training   3-CS
  10 DUNNELL LN 02860   725-1220
St. Raphael Academy   3-00011
  123 WALCOTT ST 02860   723-8100
  Thomas Casey, prin.
Sawyer School   3-CS
  101 MAIN ST 02860   272-8400

Peace Dale, AC 401, PC 5, Washington
South Kingstown SD
  Supt. — See Wakefield
South Kingstown JHS   2-00100
  301 CURTIS CORNER RD 02879   792-9682
  Robert Smith, prin.

Portsmouth, AC 401, PC 5, Newport
Portsmouth SD, 29 MIDDLE RD 02871   5-11111
  Mario Mancieri, supt.   683-1039
HS, 126 EDUCATION LN 02871   3-00011
  John Lucas, prin.   683-2124
MS, 125 JEPSON LN 02871   3-01100
  Timothy Ryan, prin.   849-3700

Portsmouth Abbey S   2-00011
  285 CORYS LN 02871   683-2000
  John Wilkinson, prin.

Providence, AC 401, PC 9, Providence
Providence SD   7-11111
  797 WESTMINSTER ST 02903   456-9211
  Arthur Zarrella, supt.
Central HS, 70 FRICKER ST 02903   4-00011
  Rickie Wilson, prin.   456-9111
Classical HS   4-00011
  770 WESTMINSTER ST 02903   456-9145
  Thomas Mezzanotte, prin.
Hope HS, 324 HOPE ST 02906   3-00011
  Gordon Hill, prin.   456-9161
Mt. Pleasant HS   4-00011
  434 MOUNT PLEASANT AVE 02908   456-9183
  Maria Wilk, prin.
Birch Vo Ctr   Vo Tech
  434 MOUNT PLEASANT AVE 02908   456-9198
  Larry Roberti, prin.
Hanley Vo-Tech Ctr   Vo Tech
  91 FRICKER ST 02903   456-9136
  Yusuf Munir, prin.
Occupational Ed Program   Vo Tech
  550 BRANCH AVE 02904   456-9217
  Lawrence Roberti, prin.
Bishop MS, 101 SESSIONS ST 02906   3-00100
  Albin Moser, prin.   456-9344
Bridgham MS   3-00100
  1655 WESTMINSTER ST 02909   456-9360
  Robert Lee, prin.
Greene MS   3-00100
  721 CHALKSTONE AVE 02908   456-9347
  Katia Paris, prin.
Hopkins MS, 480 CHARLES ST 02904   2-00100
  Nancy Mullen, prin.   456-9203
Perry MS, 370 HARTFORD AVE 02909   3-01100
  John Hernandez, prin.   456-9352
Williams MS   3-00100
  278 THURBERS AVE 02905   456-9355
  Joe Maguire, prin.

Bishop McVinney ES   2-01100
  155 HARRISON ST 02907   331-5714
  Theresina Scully, prin.
Brown University 02906   6-UC
     863-2378
Community College of Rhode Island   4-CC
  1 HILTON ST 02905
Johnson & Wales University   6-UC
  111 DORRANCE ST 02903   456-1000
Katharine Gibbs School   2-CS
  178 BUTLER AVE 02906   861-1420
LaSalle Academy   3-00011
  612 ACADEMY AVE 02908   351-7750
  Br. Mueller, prin.
Lincoln S, 301 BUTLER AVE 02906   2-11111
  Joan Countryman, prin.   331-9696
Moses Brown S, 250 LLOYD AVE 02906   3-11111
  David Burnham, prin.   831-7350
Providence College   6-UC
  RIVER AVE 02918   865-2535
Providence Hebrew Day S   2-11111
  450 ELMGROVE AVE 02906   331-5327
  Daniel Goodman, prin.
Rhode Island College   6-UC
  600 MOUNT PLEASANT AVE 02908   456-8014
Rhode Island Hospital   HSP
  593 EDDY ST 02903   277-5123
Rhode Island School of Design   4-UC
  2 COLLEGE ST 02903   331-3511
Rhode Island School of Photography   2-CS
  241 WEBSTER AVE 02909   943-7722
Roger Williams College   5-UC
  612 ACADEMY AVE 02908
St. Dunstan's Day S   2-01111
  220 UNIVERSITY AVE 02906
Sawyer School   3-CS
  550 HARTFORD AVE 02909   272-3280
School/Medical-Legal Secretarial Science   1-CS
  60 S ANGELL ST 02906   331-1171
School One   1-00011
  220 UNIVERSITY AVE 02906   331-2497
  Denise Jenkins, prin.
Wheeler S, 216 HOPE ST 02906   3-11111
  William Prescott, prin.   421-8100

Riverside, AC 401, PC see East Providence
East Providence SD
  Supt. — See East Providence
JHS, 179 FORBES ST 02915   2-00110
  Howard Levine, prin.   437-0750

St. Mary's Academy Bay View   3-00111
  3070 PAWTUCKET AVE 02915   438-9071
  Sr. Maureen McElroy, prin.

Smithfield, AC 401, PC 7, Providence

Bryant College   5-UC
  1150 DOUGLAS PIKE 02917   232-6100

Tiverton, AC 401, PC 6, Newport
Tiverton SD, 100 N BRAYTON RD 02878   4-11111
  Esther Campbell, supt.   624-8475
HS, 100 N BRAYTON RD 02878   3-00011
  Stephen Chrabaszcz, prin.   624-8494
MS, 10 QUINTAL DR 02878   3-01100
  George Costa, prin.   624-6668

Wakefield, AC 401, PC 5, Washington
South Kingstown SD   5-11111
  307 CURTIS CORNER RD 02879   792-9681
  Arthur Campbell, supt.
South Kingston HS   3-00011
  215 COLUMBIA ST 02879   792-9611
  Eric Wertheimer, prin.
Other Schools – See Peace Dale

Prout Memorial HS   2-00111
  4640 TOWER HILL RD 02879   789-9262
  Peter Davis, prin.

Warren, AC 401, PC 7, Bristol
Bristol-Warren SD
  Supt. — See Bristol
MS, CHILD ST 02885   2-00100
  Michael Carbone, prin.   245-2010

Our Lady of Fatima HS   2-00111
  360 MARKET ST 02885   245-4449
  Sr. Margaret Souza, prin.

Warwick, AC 401, PC 8, Kent
Warwick SD   7-11111
  34 WARWICK LAKE AVE 02889   737-3300
  Henry Tarlian, supt.
Tollgate SHS   3-00001
  575 CENTERVILLE RD 02886   737-3300
  Julius Breit, prin.
Pilgrim HS, 111 PILGRIM PKY 02888   4-00011
  Edmund Miley, prin.   737-3300
Warwick Veterans Memorial HS   4-00011
  2401 W SHORE RD 02886   737-3300
  Richard Rouleau, prin.
Warwick Area Vo-Tech Ctr   Vo Tech
  575 CENTERVILLE RD 02886   737-3300
  Richard Greene, prin.
Aldrich JHS, 789 POST RD 02888   3-00100
  Anthony Carcieri, prin.   737-3300
Gorton JHS, 69 DRAPER AVE 02889   3-00100
  Dan Sheehan, prin.   737-3300
Winman JHS   3-00110
  575 CENTERVILLE RD 02886   737-3300
  David Johnson, prin.

Bishop Hendricken HS   3-00111
  2615 WARWICK AVE 02889   739-3450
  Br. Walsh, prin.
Community College of Rhode Island   6-CC
  400 EAST AVE 02886   825-1000
Nasson Institute   2-CS
  1276 BALD HILL RD 02886   823-3773
NEC-Rhode Island Trades Shop School   3-CS
  106 ACCESS RD 02886   331-3008
New England Institute of Technology   4-CC
  2500 POST RD 02886   739-5000
New England Technical College   2-UC
  2500 POST RD 02886   739-5000
Sawyer School   2-CS
  1109 WARWICK AVE 02888   781-2887

Westerly, AC 401, PC 7, Washington
Westerly SD, 44 PARK AVE 02891   5-11111
  Andrew Carrano, supt.   596-0315
JSHS, 43 TERRACE AVE 02891   4-00111
  Walter Gibson, prin.   596-2109

Sawyer School   3-CS
  PO BOX 733 02891   348-8383

West Greenwich, AC 401, PC 5, Kent
Exeter-West Greenwich SD   4-11111
  859 NOOSENECK HILL RD 02817   397-5125
  Robert Hicks, supt.
Exeter-West Greenwich Regional HS   2-00011
  930 NOOSENECK HILL RD 02817   397-6893
  Claremary Pratt, prin.
Exeter-West Greenwich Regional JHS   2-00100
  930 NOOSENECK HILL RD 02817   397-6897
  Lewis Klaiman, prin.

West Warwick, AC 401, PC 8, Kent
West Warwick SD   5-11111
  10 HARRIS AVE 02893   821-1180
  William Jutras, supt.
SHS, 4 WEBSTER KNIGHT DR 02893   3-00001
  Donald Gainey, prin.   821-6596
Deering JHS   3-00110
  2 WEBSTER KNIGHT DR 02893   822-8445
  Trent Danella, prin.

Wood River Junction, AC 401, PC 2, Washington
Chariho SD, 455 SWITCH RD 02894 — 4-11111
John Pini, supt. — 364-7575
Chariho Regional HS — 3-00011
445 SWITCH RD 02894 — 364-7778
Edward Morgan, prin.
Chariho Area Vo-Tech Ctr — Vo Tech
SWITCH RD 02894 — 364-6869
James DeLuca, prin.
Chariho Regional MS — 3-01100
455 SWITCH RD 02894 — 364-0651
Robert Miller, prin.

Woonsocket, AC 401, PC 8, Providence
Woonsocket SD, 108 HIGH ST 02895 — 6-11111
Josephine Kelleher, supt. — 767-4600
HS, 777 CASS AVE 02895 — 4-00011
Ed Chmiel, prin. — 767-4600
Woonsocket Area Vo-Tech Ctr — Vo Tech
400 AYLSWORTH AVE 02895 — 767-4662
Doreen Bellucci, prin.
JHS, 357 PARK PL 02895 — 4-00110
(—), prin. — 767-4600

Good Shepherd JHS — 2-00110
1210 MENDON RD 02895 — 767-5906
Louise Kane, prin.
Mt. St. Charles Academy — 3-00111
800 LOGEE ST 02895 — 769-0310
Br. Croteau, prin.
Nasson Institute — 2-CS
191 SOCIAL ST 02895 — 769-2066
Sawyer School — 2-CS
1 CUMBERLAND ST 02895 — 762-0502

SOUTH CAROLINA

STATE DEPARTMENT OF EDUCATION
Rutledge Building
1429 Senate St., Columbia 29201
(803) 734-8500

Superintendent of Education	Barbara Nielsen
Senior Executive Assistant Communications	Jerry Adams
Senior Executive Assistant Business	Bob Davis
Senior Executive Assistant Collaboration	Nancy Dunlap
Senior Executive Assistant Curriculum	Luther Seabrook
Senior Executive Assistant Budgets	Jean McDaniel
Senior Executive Assistant Internal Administration	Jackie Rosswurm
Senior Executive Assistant Policy	Valerie Truesdale
Senior Executive Assistant Support Services	Donald Tudor
Senior Executive Assistant Development	W. Ben Nesbit

STATE BOARD OF EDUCATION
1429 Senate St., Columbia 29201

Chairperson   Samuel Greer

PUBLIC, PRIVATE AND CATHOLIC SECONDARY SCHOOLS

Abbeville, AC 803, PC 6, Abbeville
Abbeville County SD — 5-11111
500 CHESTNUT ST 29620 — 459-5427
W. Richard Garrett, supt.
HS, PO BOX 927 29620 — 3-00011
Carl Campbell, prin. — 459-5916
Abbeville Career Vo Ctr — Vo Tech
PO BOX 280 29620 — 459-9069
Bob Crosby, prin.
Wright MS, PO BOX 848 29620 — 2-00100
Henry Madden, prin. — 459-5998
Other Schools – See Calhoun Falls, Due West

Aiken, AC 803, PC 7, Aiken
Aiken County SD — 7-11111
PO BOX 1137 29802 — 641-2462
Joseph Brooks, supt.
HS, 211 RUTLAND DR 29801 — 4-00011
William Gassman, prin. — 641-2500
Silver Bluff HS, 300 DESOTO DR 29803 — 3-00011
H. Andrew Reeves, prin. — 652-8100
South Aiken HS — 4-00011
701 E PINE LOG RD 29803 — 641-2600
James Dawsey, prin.
Kennedy MS, 659 E PINE LOG RD 29803 — 4-00100
George Rogers, prin. — 641-2470
Schofield MS, 220 SUMTER ST NE 29801 — 4-00100
Rosie Berry, prin. — 641-2770
Other Schools – See Graniteville, Jackson, Langley, Monetta, New Ellenton, North Augusta, Wagener, Warrenville

Aiken Technical College — 4-CC
PO BOX 696 29802 — 593-9231
University of South Carolina — 4-UC
171 UNIVERSITY PKY 29801 — 648-6851

Allendale, AC 803, PC 5, Allendale
Allendale County SD — 4-11111
PO BOX 458 29810 — 584-4603
Dill Gamble, supt.

Other Schools – See Fairfax

University of South Carolina — 3-CC
PO BOX 617 29810 — 584-3446

Anderson, AC 803, PC 8, Anderson
Anderson SD 5, PO BOX 439 29622 — 7-11111
Karen Woodward, supt. — 260-5000
Hanna HS, 2600 HIGHWAY 81 N 29621 — 4-00011
Michael Sams, prin. — 260-5110
McDuffie HS — 3-00011
1225 S MCDUFFIE ST 29624 — 260-5160
Jacky Stamps, prin.
Westside HS — 4-00011
806 PEARMAN DAIRY RD 29625 — 260-5230
Henry Adair, prin.
Lakeside MS — 3-00100
315 PEARMAN DAIRY RD 29625 — 260-5135
Donnie Saxon, prin.
McCants MS — 4-00100
2123 MARCHBANKS AVE 29621 — 260-5145
Melvin Poore, prin.
Southwood MS — 3-00100
1110 SOUTHWOOD ST 29624 — 260-5205
Patricia Seawright, prin.

Anderson College — 4-UC
316 BOULEVARD 29621 — 800-542-3594
Anderson Memorial Hospital — HSP
800 N FANT ST 29621 — 261-1109
Forrest Junior College — 2-CS
601 E RIVER ST 29624 — 225-7653
Oakwood Christian S — 2-11111
304 PEARMAN DAIRY RD 29625 — 225-6262
Ronald Wilkins, prin.

Andrews, AC 803, PC 5, Georgetown
Georgetown County SD
Supt. — See Georgetown
HS, 201 S MAPLE AVE 29510 — 3-00011
R. King, prin. — 264-3414

Rosemary MS, PO BOX 4 29510 — 3-01100
Joseph Bryant, prin. — 264-3404

Andrews Academy — 2-11111
PO BOX 468 29510 — 264-8413
Mary Sowell, prin.

Aynor, AC 803, PC 2, Horry
Horry County SD
Supt. — See Conway
JSHS, PO BOX 128 29511 — 3-00111
Edward Curlee, prin. — 358-6262

Ballentine, AC 803, PC 3, Richland
Lexington SD 5 — 7-11111
1020 DUTCH FORK RD 29002 — 732-8000
Edith Jensen, supt.
Other Schools – See Chapin, Columbia, Irmo

Bamberg, AC 803, PC 5, Bamberg
Bamberg SD 1, PO BOX 526 29003 — 4-11111
Betty Bagley, supt. — 245-3053
Bamberg-Ehrhardt HS — 2-00011
PO BOX 89 29003 – (—), prin. — 245-3030
Bamberg-Ehrhardt MS — 2-00100
PO BOX 548 29003 — 245-3058
Charles Richardson, prin.

Barnwell, AC 803, PC 6, Barnwell
Barnwell SD 45 — 5-11111
2008 HAGOOD AVE 29812 — 541-1300
James Benson, supt.
HS, JACKSON ST 29812 — 3-00011
Phil Flynn, prin. — 541-1390
Guinyard-Butler MS — 3-00100
2211 ALLEN ST 29812 – Jeff Still, prin. — 541-1370

Batesburg, AC 803, PC 5, Lexington
Lexington SD 3 — 4-11111
121 W COLUMBIA AVE 29006 — 532-4423
F. Raymond Geddings, supt.

Batesburg-Leesville HS 3-00011
600 SUMMERLAND AVE 29006 532-9251
Thomas Bartone, prin.
Batesburg-Leesville MS 3-00100
101 W COLUMBIA AVE 29006 532-3831
Robert Williams, prin.

Beaufort, AC 803, PC 6, Beaufort
Beaufort County SD 7-11111
PO BOX 309 29901 525-4200
Richard Flynn, supt.
HS, 2501 MOSSY OAKS RD 29902 4-00011
Jonathan Francis, prin. 525-4241
Ladys Island MS, 1 COUGAR DR 29902 4-00100
Randall Wall, prin. 525-4264
Other Schools – See Burton, Hilton Head Island

Beaufort Academy, HC 5 29902 2-11111
E. Hubbard, prin. 524-3393
Technical College of the Lowcountry 3-CC
100 S RIBAUT RD 29902 525-8324
University of South Carolina 3-CC
801 CARTERET ST 29902 524-7112

Belton, AC 803, PC 5, Anderson
Anderson SD 2
Supt. — See Honea Path
MS, 102 CHEROKEE RD 29627 2-00100
Dan Hawkins, prin. 338-6595

Calvary Baptist Christian S 2-11111
PO BOX 863 29627 338-9623
Earl Green, prin.

Bennettsville, AC 803, PC 6, Marlboro
Marlboro County SD 6-11111
PO BOX 947 29512 479-4016
Joseph Delaney, supt.
Marlboro County HS 4-00011
951 FAYETTEVILLE AVENUE EXT 29512
Herbert Gould, prin. 479-5900
MS, 701 CHERAW ST 29512 3-00100
Henry Byrd, prin. 479-5941
Other Schools – See Clio

Marlboro Academy 2-11111
1035 BENNETTSVILLE TOWER RD 29512
John Jones, prin. 479-6501

Bethune, AC 803, PC 2, Kershaw
Kershaw County SD
Supt. — See Camden
HS, PO BOX 217 29009 2-00011
(—), prin. 334-6262
MS, PO BOX 217 29009 2-00100
(—), prin. 334-6262

Bishopville, AC 803, PC 5, Lee
Lee County SD, PO BOX 507 29010 5-11111
John Wall, supt. 484-5327
HS, 600 N MAIN ST 29010 3-00011
G. Kennington, prin. 484-5366
Lee County Vo Ctr Vo Tech
310 ROLAND ST 29010 484-5337
Bernice Wright, prin.
JHS, 321 ROLAND ST 29010 3-01100
James Gary, prin. 484-5386
Other Schools – See Elliott

Lee Academy, PO BOX 488 29010 3-11111
James Dozier, prin. 484-5532

Blacksburg, AC 803, PC 4, Cherokee
Cherokee SD
Supt. — See Gaffney
JSHS, 201 W RAMSEUR ST 29702 3-00111
James Leigh, prin. 839-6371

Blackville, AC 803, PC 5, Barnwell
Barnwell SD 19, PO BOX 185 29817 4-11111
Richard Huggins, supt. 284-2234
HS, PO BOX 245 29817 2-00011
D. Atkins, prin. 284-2280
MS, PO BOX 186 29817 2-00100
William Scott, prin. 284-3160

Davis Academy, PO BOX 338 29817 2-11111
William Kight, prin. 284-2017

Bonneau, AC 803, PC 2, Berkeley
Berkeley County SD
Supt. — See Moncks Corner
Bonneau Vo Ctr, 1917 MAIN ST 29431 Vo Tech
Bertha Washington, prin. 825-3397

Bowman, AC 803, PC 4, Orangeburg
Orangeburg SD 2, PO BOX 36 29018 3-11111
Joseph Rice, supt. 829-2541
JSHS, PO BOX 186 29018 2-00111
B. Brown, prin. 829-2873

Bowman Academy, PO BOX 98 29018 2-11111
Debbie Bair, prin. 829-2770

Branchville, AC 803, PC 4, Orangeburg
Orangeburg SD 8, PO BOX 248 29432 3-11111
Nelson Perry, supt. 274-8900
JSHS, PO BOX 188 29432 2-00111
Sidney Zemp, prin. 274-8875

Burton, AC 803, PC 6, Beaufort
Beaufort County SD
Supt. — See Beaufort

Battery Creek HS 4-00011
1 BLUE DOLPHIN DR 29902 525-4220
John McVey, prin.
Smalls MS, RR 4 BOX 210 29902 4-00100
William Gabrielson, prin. 525-4250

Calhoun Falls, AC 803, PC 4, Abbeville
Abbeville County SD
Supt. — See Abbeville
JSHS, PO BOX 336 29628 2-00111
James Tisdale, prin. 447-8014

Camden, AC 803, PC 6, Kershaw
Kershaw County SD 6-11111
1301 DUBOSE CT 29020 432-8416
H. Corley, supt.
HS, 1022 EHRENCLOU DR 29020 4-00011
Edward Dean, prin. 425-8930
Applied Technical Education Campus Vo Tech
874 VOCATIONAL LN 29020 425-8980
Betty Sue Webber, prin.
MS, 416 LAURENS ST 29020 3-00100
(—), prin. 432-4124
Other Schools – See Bethune, Kershaw, Lugoff

Camden Military Academy 2-00111
520 HIGHWAY 1 N 29020 432-6001
Lanning Richer, prin.

Campobello, AC 803, PC 2, Spartanburg
Spartanburg SD 1, PO BOX 218 29322 5-11111
James Littlefield, supt. 468-4542
Other Schools – See Inman, Landrum

Cayce, AC 803, PC 7, Lexington
Lexington SD 2
Supt. — See West Columbia
Brookland-Cayce HS 4-00011
1300 STATE ST 29033 791-5000
Barry Bolen, prin.
Busbee MS, 1407 DUNBAR RD 29033 2-00100
Joseph English, prin. 739-4070

Centenary, AC 803, PC 3, Marion
Marion SD 3
Supt. — See Rains
Terrells Bay JSHS, PO BOX 335 29519 2-00111
Charles McFadden, prin. 362-0011

Central, AC 803, PC 4, Pickens
Pickens SD
Supt. — See Easley
Daniel SHS, 1819 6 MILE HWY 29630 3-00001
Earl Gilstrap, prin. 654-2362
Edwards JHS 3-00110
1157 MADDEN BRIDGE RD 29630 654-1400
Randy Gilstrap, prin.

Central Wesleyan College 3-UC
PO BOX 1020 29630 639-2453

Chapin, AC 803, PC 2, Lexington
Lexington SD 5
Supt. — See Ballentine
HS, 300 COLUMBIA AVE 29036 3-00011
John Anderson, prin. 345-2246
MS, 1130 OLD LEXINGTON HWY 29036 2-00100
Lee Bollman, prin. 345-1466

Charleston, AC 803, PC 8, Charleston
City of Charleston Constituent SD 6-11111
220 NASSAU ST 29403 724-7761
James Gray, supt.
Burke HS, 244 PRESIDENT ST 29403 4-00011
L. Gaillard, prin. 724-7785
Courtenay Mid School 2-00100
382 MEETING ST 29403 724-7768
Charles Holmes, prin.
Rivers MS, 1002 KING ST 29403 3-00100
Walter Burke, prin. 724-7789

Cooper River Constituent SD
Supt. — See North Charleston
Stall HS, 7749 PINEHURST ST 29420 4-00011
William Turner, prin. 764-2200
Birney MS, 7750 PINEHURST ST 29420 4-00100
Michael Casey, prin. 764-2212
Toole MS, 2950 CARNER AVE 29405 3-00100
Andrea Heyer, prin. 745-7102

James Island Constituent SD 5-11111
1825 CAMP RD # B 29412 762-2780
Gary Awkerman, supt.
James Island HS 4-00011
1000 FORT JOHNSON RD 29412 762-2754
Floyd Hiott, prin.
Ft. Johnson MS, 1825 CAMP RD 29412 3-00100
John Rhodes, prin. 762-2740
James Island MS, 1484 CAMP RD 29412 3-00100
Franklin McCrea, prin. 762-2784

St. Andrews Constituent 6-11111
725 WAPPOO RD 29407 763-1500
Michael Sullivan, supt.
Middleton HS 4-00011
1776 WILLIAM KENNERTY DR 29407 763-1546
Joan Mandeville, prin.
St. Andrews HS, 721 WAPPOO RD 29407 3-00011
Robert Olson, prin. 763-1533
Hall MS, 3181 ASHLEY RIVER RD 29414 3-00100
Melanie Reynolds, prin. 763-1541
Williams MS, 640 BUTTE ST 29414 3-00100
James Mobley, prin. 763-1529

St. Johns Constituent SD 4-11111
1825 CAMP RD # B 29412 762-2780
Gary Awkerman, supt.
Other Schools – See Johns Island

Ashley Hall S 2-11111
172 RUTLEDGE AVE 29403 772-4088
Margaret MacDonald, prin.
Bishop England HS 3-00011
203 CALHOUN ST 29401 723-3637
Nicholas Theos, prin.
Charleston Southern University 4-UC
PO BOX 10087 29411 800-947-7474
Citadel, The 5-UC
171 MOULTRIE ST 29409 792-5230
College of Charleston 6-UC
66 GEORGE ST 29424 792-5670
First Baptist Church S 3-11111
48 MEETING ST 29401 722-6646
Arthur Earp, prin.
Johnson & Wales University 2-CC
701 E BAY ST 29403 727-3008
Medical University of South Carolina 4-UC
171 ASHLEY AVE 29425 792-2109
Neilsen Electronics Institute 2-CC
1600 MEETING STREET RD 29405 722-2344
Northside Christian S 3-11111
7800 NORTHSIDE DR 29420 797-2690
Cecil Beach, prin.
Porter-Gaud S 3-11111
300 ALBEMARLE RD 29407 556-3620
Gordon Bondurant, prin.
Trident Technical College 6-CC
PO BOX 10367 29411 572-6123

Cheraw, AC 803, PC 6, Chesterfield
Chesterfield SD
Supt. — See Chesterfield
HS, 649 HIGHWAY 9 29520 3-00011
Edward Shuford, prin. 537-7851
Long JHS, 1010 W GREENE ST 29520 2-00100
Melvin Wilkerson, prin. 537-5488

Chesterfield-Marlboro Technical College 3-CC
PO BOX 1007 29520 537-5286

Chesnee, AC 803, PC 4, Spartanburg
Spartanburg SD 2
Supt. — See Spartanburg
HS, 795 S ALABAMA AVE 29323 3-00011
Joseph Bullington, prin. 461-7318
MS, 715 S ALABAMA AVE 29323 2-00100
Thomas Ezell, prin. 461-3900

Chester, AC 803, PC 6, Chester
Chester SD, 121 COLUMBIA ST 29706 6-11111
Thomas Smith, supt. 385-6122
HS, PO BOX 810 29706 4-00011
Keith McAlister, prin. 377-3161
Chester Career Center Vo Tech
HWY 72 BYPASS 29706 377-1991
Jake Strickland, prin.
MS, 112 CALDWELL ST 29706 3-00100
Gaither Bumgardner, prin. 377-8192
Other Schools – See Great Falls, Richburg

Chesterfield, AC 803, PC 4, Chesterfield
Chesterfield SD 6-11111
401 BOULEVARD ST W 29709 623-2175
Joe Bradham, supt.
HS, RR 1 BOX 2 29709 2-00011
R. Allen Teal, prin. 623-2161
MS, 344 BOULEVARD ST E 29709 2-01100
Jessie Gaskins, prin. 623-2465
Other Schools – See Cheraw, Mc Bee, Pageland

Clemson, AC 803, PC 7, Pickens

Clemson University 7-UC
201 SIKES HALL 29634 656-3311

Clinton, AC 803, PC 6, Laurens
Laurens SD 56, PO BOX 484 29325 5-11111
Charles Cummins, supt. 833-0800
HS, 800 N ADAIR ST 29325 3-00011
A. Keith Bridges, prin. 833-0817
Bell Street MS, LYDIA MILL RD 29325 3-00100
Ralphine Patterson, prin. 833-0807
Dendy MS, PO BOX 668 29325 2-00100
Henry Simmons, prin. 833-0831

Presbyterian College 4-UC
503 S BROAD ST 29325 833-8230
Thornwell S, PO BOX 1157 29325 2-11111
William Alexander, prin. 833-2316

Clio, AC 803, PC 3, Marlboro
Marlboro County SD
Supt. — See Bennettsville
MS, PO BOX 68 29525 2-01100
Richard Dixon, prin. 586-9391

Clover, AC 803, PC 5, York
York SD 2, PO BOX 99 29710 5-11111
Bill Floyd, supt. 222-7191
HS, 1625 HIGHWAY 55 E 29710 3-00011
Melvin Bouknight, prin. 222-4591
JHS, 1555 HIGHWAY 55 E 29710 2-00100
Ronald Wright, prin. 222-4521

Columbia, AC 803, PC 8, Richland
Lexington SD 5
Supt. — See Ballentine

Irmo HS 4-00011
6671 SAINT ANDREWS RD 29212 732-8100
Anna Hicks, prin.
Lake Murray Technology Center Vo Tech
6745 SAINT ANDREWS RD 29212 732-8400
Jim Bull, prin.
Irmo MS Campus I 4-00100
6949 SAINT ANDREWS RD 29212 732-8300
Judy Starnes, prin.
Irmo MS Campus R 4-00100
6051 WESCOTT RD 29212 732-8200
Phyllis Pendarvis, prin.

Richland SD 1 8-11111
1616 RICHLAND ST 29201 733-6000
John Stevenson, supt.
HS, 1701 WESTCHESTER DR 29210 3-00011
Gary Geddens, prin. 731-8950
Dreher HS, 701 ADGER RD 29205 4-00011
Rae McPherson, prin. 256-1695
Eau Claire HS 4-00011
4800 MONTICELLO RD 29203 735-7600
Ellen Mosely, prin.
Flora HS, 100 FALCON DR 29204 3-00011
Bernadette Scott, prin. 738-7300
Johnson HS 3-00011
2219 BARHAMVILLE RD 29204 253-7092
Henry Young, prin.
Keenan HS, 3455 PINE BELT RD 29204 3-00011
James Wright, prin. 738-7232
Heyward Career Ctr Vo Tech
3560 LYNHAVEN DR 29204 735-3325
Wayman Stover, prin.
Alcorn MS, 5125 FAIRFIELD RD 29203 3-00100
Jeannetta Scott, prin. 735-3439
Crayton MS, 5000 CLEMSON AVE 29206 3-00100
Ellen Cooper, prin. 738-7224
Gibbes MS, 500 SUMMERLEA DR 29203 3-00100
Kenneth Richardson, prin. 343-2942
Hand MS, 2600 WHEAT ST 29205 3-00100
Dorothy Turbeville, prin. 343-2947
Perry MS 3-00100
2600 BARHAMVILLE RD 29204 256-6347
(—), prin.
St. Andrews MS 3-00100
1231 BLUE FIELD DR 29210 731-8910
Carlos Smith, prin.
Sanders MS, 6000 ALIDA ST 29203 3-00100
Gladys Cureton, prin. 735-3445
Other Schools – See Hopkins

Richland SD 2 7-11111
6831 BROOKFIELD RD 29206 787-1910
John Hudgens, supt.
Richland Northeast HS 4-00011
7500 BROOKFIELD RD 29223 699-2800
Ronald Hill, prin.
Spring Valley HS 4-00011
120 SPARKLEBERRY LN 29223 699-3500
Ronald Cowden, prin.
Richland Northeast Vo Annex Vo Tech
7500 BROOKFIELD RD 29223 788-6911
Robert West, prin.
Wilson Vo Annex Vo Tech
120 SPARKLEBERRY LN 29223 699-3600
Genevieve White, prin.
Dent MS, 2719 DECKER BLVD 29206 4-00100
J. Earl Rankin, prin. 699-2750
Summit Parkway MS 4-00100
200 SUMMIT PKY 29223 699-3580
Jo Hecker, prin.
Wright MS, 2740 ALPINE RD 29223 4-00100
Roosevelt Garrick, prin. 736-8740

State Supported Schools 4-11111
RUTLEDGE BLDG 29201 734-8500
Charlie Williams, supt.
Other Schools – See Hartsville

Allen University 2-UC
1530 HARDEN ST 29204 254-4165
Baptist Medical Centers HSP
1519 MARION ST 29201 771-5043
Benedict College 4-UC
1600 HARDEN ST 29204 800-868-6598
Ben Lippen S, PO BOX 3999 29230 2-00111
Les Lehman, prin. 786-7200
Cardinal Newman HS 2-00111
4701 FOREST DR 29206 782-2814
Harold Bayerl, prin.
Central Carolina Christian S 2-11111
2739 COVENANT RD 29204 252-3457
Theodore Myers, prin.
Columbia Biblical Seminary 2-UC
PO BOX 3122 29230 800-845-2721
Columbia College 4-UC
1301 COLUMBIA COLLEGE DR 29203 786-3871
Columbia International University 3-UC
PO BOX 3122 29230 800-777-2227
Columbia Junior College of Business 3-CC
PO BOX 1196 29202 799-9082
Hammond Academy 3-11111
845 GALWAY LN 29209 776-0295
Herbert Barks, prin.
Heathwood Hall Episcopal S 3-11111
3000 S BELTLINE BLVD 29201 765-2309
Robert Shirley, prin.
Lutheran Theological Southern Seminary 2-UC
4201 MAIN ST 29203 786-5150
Midlands Technical College 6-CC
PO BOX 2408 29202 738-7764

Sloans S, 171 STARLIGHT DR 29210 2-11111
J. Sloan, prin. 772-1677
University of South Carolina 29208 7-UC
777-7700

Conway, AC 803, PC 6, Horry
Horry County SD, 1600 9TH AVE 29526 7-11111
Gary Smith, supt. 248-2206
HS, 2201 CHURCH ST 29526 4-00011
Thomas Lewis, prin. 248-6321
Aynor-Conway Career Ctr Vo Tech
335 FOUR MILE RD 29526 365-5534
Winston Barr, prin.
MS, 1104 ELM ST 29526 3-00100
Gilbert Stefanides, prin. 248-2279
Whittemore Park MS 3-00100
1808 RHUE ST 29527 248-2233
Marjorie McIver, prin.
Other Schools – See Aynor, Green Sea, Little River, Loris, Myrtle Beach

---

Horry-Georgetown Technical College 4-CC
PO BOX 1966 29526 347-3186
North American Institute of Aviation 2-CS
PO BOX 680 29526 397-9111

Cope, AC 803, PC 2, Orangeburg
Orangeburg SD 4
Supt. — See Cordova
Cope Area Vo Ctr, PO BOX 128 29038 Vo Tech
E. Neumeister, prin. 534-7661

Cordova, AC 803, PC 2, Orangeburg
Orangeburg SD 4, PO BOX 69 29039 4-11111
David Coleman, supt. 534-7420
Edisto HS, PO BOX 101 29039 3-00011
George Benton, prin. 534-0098
Carver-Edisto MS, PO BOX 65 29039 3-01100
Rosa Kennerly, prin. 536-0231
Other Schools – See Cope

Cowpens, AC 803, PC 4, Spartanburg
Spartanburg SD 3
Supt. — See Glendale
MS, PO BOX 70 29330 3-00100
Harvey Dailey, prin. 463-3310

Cross, AC 803, PC 2, Berkeley
Berkeley County SD
Supt. — See Moncks Corner
JSHS, RR 2 BOX 365 29436 3-00111
Sylvester Madison, prin. 753-2121

Dalzell, AC 803, PC 2, Sumter
Sumter SD 2
Supt. — See Sumter
Hillcrest SHS, PO BOX 151 29040 3-00001
Frederick Maples, prin. 499-3341

Sumter Academy, PO BOX 869 29040 2-11111
Charles Owens, prin. 499-3378

Darlington, AC 803, PC 6, Darlington
Darlington SD, PO BOX 493 29532 7-11111
Betty Cox, supt. 398-5200
Mayo HS, 405 CHESTNUT ST 29532 3-00011
Roosevelt Davis, prin. 398-5050
Saint Johns High School 4-00011
525 SPRING ST 29532 398-5140
Edward Jones, prin.
Brunson Dargan JHS 3-00100
400 WELLS ST 29532 398-5080
Jack Dearhart, prin.
Gary MS, 100 MAGNOLIA ST 29532 2-00100
Otto Wingate, prin. 398-5088
Other Schools – See Hartsville, Lamar

Denmark, AC 803, PC 5, Bamberg
Bamberg SD 2, PO BOX 345 29042 4-11111
Gerald Wright, supt. 793-3346
Denmark-Olar HS, PO BOX 98 29042 2-00011
Charles Gallagher, prin. 793-3307
Denmark-Olar MS 2-00100
PO BOX 343 29042 793-3383
Rodney Anderson, prin.

Denmark Technical College 3-CC
PO BOX 327 29042 793-3301
Voorhees College 3-UC
VOORHEES ROAD 29042 793-3351

Dillon, AC 803, PC 6, Dillon
Dillon SD 2 5-11111
401 W WASHINGTON ST 29536 774-1200
D. Ray Rogers, supt.
SHS, 1332 N 2ND AVE 29536 3-00001
A. Steele, prin. 774-1230
Martin JHS, 301 N 3RD AVE 29536 4-00110
Thomas Byron, prin. 774-1212

Avalon Academy 2-11111
PO BOX 1246 29536 774-4491
Henry Meares, prin.

Dorchester, AC 803, PC 2, Dorchester
Dorchester SD 4
Supt. — See Saint George
Harleyville-Ridgeville JSHS 2-00111
1650 E MAIN ST 29437 462-7671
Willie Frazier, prin.

Due West, AC 803, PC 4, Abbeville
Abbeville County SD
Supt. — See Abbeville

Dixie JSHS, PO BOX 158 29639 2-00111
Tracy Carter, prin. 379-2186

Erskine College & Seminary 3-UC
WASHINGTON ST 29639 800-542-8838

Duncan, AC 803, PC 4, Spartanburg
Spartanburg SD 5, PO BOX 307 29334 5-11111
Marvin Woodson, supt. 949-2350
Byrnes HS, PO BOX 187 29334 4-00011
Clifton Edwards, prin. 949-2355
Hill MS, PO BOX 277 29334 4-00100
Gary Burgess, prin. 949-2370

Easley, AC 803, PC 7, Pickens
Pickens SD 7-11111
1348 GRIFFIN MILL RD 29640 855-8150
Richard Gettys, supt.
SHS, PO BOX 192 29641 4-00001
Bill Houston, prin. 855-8180
Skelton Career Ctr Vo Tech
1400 GRIFFIN MILL RD 29640 859-4064
Annette Craig, prin.
Dacusville JHS 2-00110
2671 EARLS BRIDGE RD 29640 859-7429
Ronny Hall, prin.
JHS, PO BOX 447 29641 4-00110
J. Barbary, prin. 855-8170
Other Schools – See Central, Liberty, Pickens

Landmark Christian S 2-11111
116 LANDMARK CT 29640 859-0793
John Larrabee, prin.

Edgefield, AC 803, PC 5, Edgefield
Edgefield County SD 5-11111
PO BOX 608 29824 275-4601
Clarence Dickert, supt.
Other Schools – See Johnston, North Augusta

Elliott, AC 803, PC 3, Lee
Lee County SD
Supt. — See Bishopville
Mt. Pleasant JSHS 2-00111
PO BOX 177 29046 428-3610
John Haynesworth, prin.

Elloree, AC 803, PC 3, Orangeburg
Orangeburg SD 7 29047 3-11111
James Wright, supt. 897-2211
JSHS, 200 WARRIOR ST 29047 2-00111
(—), prin. 897-2232

Estill, AC 803, PC 4, Hampton
Hampton SD 2, PO BOX 1028 29918 4-11111
Albert Eads, supt. 625-2875
HS, PO BOX 757 29918 2-00011
Anderson Taylor, prin. 625-3291
MS, PO BOX 817 29918 2-01100
Jacqueline Hopkins, prin. 625-2658

Henry Academy, PO BOX 788 29918 2-11111
Philip Spotts, prin. 625-2440

Fairfax, AC 803, PC 4, Allendale
Allendale County SD
Supt. — See Allendale
Allendale-Fairfax HS 3-00011
RR 2 BOX 222 29827 584-2311
Ronald Perry, prin.
Allendale-Fairfax MS 2-00100
RR 2 BOX 221A 29827 584-3489
Henry Smalls, prin.

Fairforest, AC 803, PC 3, Spartanburg
Spartanburg SD 6
Supt. — See Spartanburg
MS, PO BOX A 29336 3-00100
Joseph Cox, prin. 576-1270

Florence, AC 803, PC 8, Florence
Florence SD 1, 319 S DARGAN ST 29506 7-11111
Thomas Truitt, supt. 669-4141
South Florence HS 4-00011
3200 S IRBY ST 29505 664-8190
Curtis Boswell, prin.
West Florence HS 4-00011
221 BELTLINE DR 29501 664-8472
Alan Harrison, prin.
Wilson HS 4-00011
1411 OLD MARION HWY 29506 664-8440
A. Brooks, prin.
Florence Career Ctr Vo Tech
126 HOWE SPRINGS RD 29505 664-8465
Larry Hughes, prin.
Moore MS, 1101 CHERAW DR 29501 3-00100
Patricia Hanna, prin. 664-8171
Southside MS 4-00100
200 HOWE SPRINGS RD 29505 664-8467
Patsy Slice, prin.
Williams MS, 1119 N IRBY ST 29501 3-00100
Larry Jackson, prin. 664-8162

Byrnes Academy, RR 6 29506 2-11111
Gayle Robertson, prin. 662-0131
Florence Christian S 3-11111
2308 S IRBY ST 29505 662-0453
Raymond Miles, prin.
Florence Darlington Technical College 4-CC
P O BOX 8000 29501 661-8151
Francis Marion College 5-UC
PO BOX 100547 29501 661-1231

Marantha Christian S   2-11111
  2624 W PALMETTO ST   29501   669-7657
  Dale Edwards, prin.
McLeod Regional Medical Center   HSP
  555 E CHEVES ST   29506   667-2297

Fort Mill, AC 803, PC 5, York
Lancaster SD
  Supt. — See Lancaster
Indian Land HS, RR 2   29715   2-00011
  Sam Cook, prin.   547-7571

York SD 4, PO BOX 669   29716   5-11111
  Joseph Bonds, supt.   548-2527
HS, 118 MUNN RD E   29715   3-00011
  Terry Holliday, prin.   548-1900
MS, 513 BANKS ST   29715   3-00100
  Julia Gregory, prin.   547-5553

Gaffney, AC 803, PC 7, Cherokee
Cherokee SD, PO BOX 460   29342   6-11111
  V. Sue Cleveland, supt.   489-0261
SHS, 805 E FREDERICK ST   29340   4-00001
  Thomas White, prin.   489-2544
Cherokee Technology Center   Vo Tech
  3206 CHEROKEE AVE   29340   489-3191
  Fred Wilkins, prin.
Ewing JHS   3-00110
  171 E JUNIOR HIGH RD   29340   489-3176
  Marcia Duncan, prin.
Granard JHS   3-00110
  815 W RUTLEDGE AVE   29341   489-6833
  (—), prin.
Other Schools – See Blacksburg

Heritage Christian S   2-11111
  4279 CHEROKEE AVE   29340   489-0788
  William Covington, prin.
Limestone College   3-UC
  1115 COLLEGE DR   29340   800-345-3792

Georgetown, AC 803, PC 6, Georgetown
Georgetown County SD   7-11111
  624 FRONT ST   29440   546-2561
  Johnathan Moultrie, supt.
Choppee HS, RR 3 BOX 423   29440   2-00011
  Mary Rice, prin.   546-2461
HS, PO BOX 1778   29442   4-00011
  Richard Summey, prin.   546-8516
Beck MS, PO BOX 1747   29442   4-00100
  Celestine Pringle, prin.   527-4495
Choppee MS, RR 3 BOX 422A   29440   2-01100
  Mary Rice, prin.   546-9424
Other Schools – See Andrews, Hemingway, Pawleys
  Island

Gilbert, AC 803, PC 2, Lexington
Lexington SD 1
  Supt. — See Lexington
JSHS, 146 MAIN ST   29054   3-00111
  Bob Whitehead, prin.   892-2166
MS, 120 RICARD CIR   29054   2-01100
  Louis Ellis, prin.   892-6210

Glendale, AC 803, PC 4, Spartanburg
Spartanburg SD 3, PO BOX 267   29346   5-11111
  Evalyn Jerkins, supt.   579-8000
Other Schools – See Cowpens, Pacolet, Spartanburg

Goose Creek, AC 803, PC 7, Berkeley
Berkeley County SD
  Supt. — See Moncks Corner
HS, 1137 REDBANK RD   29445   4-00011
  John Fulmer, prin.   553-5300
Stratford HS   4-00011
  951 CROWFIELD BLVD   29445   820-4000
  George McCracken, prin.
Marrington MS, 109 GEARING ST   29445   3-01100
  Leonard Turner, prin.   572-0313
Sedgefield MS   3-00100
  131 CHARLES B GIBSON BLVD   29445   797-2620
  Willis Sanders, prin.
Westview MS, 101 WESTVIEW DR   29445   3-01100
  Lavinia Turner, prin.   572-1700

Graniteville, AC 803, PC 4, Aiken
Aiken County SD
  Supt. — See Aiken
Leavelle-McCampbell MS   3-00100
  82 CANAL ST   29829   663-4300
  Alfonso Lamback, prin.

Gray Court, AC 803, PC 3, Laurens
Laurens SD 55
  Supt. — See Laurens
Gray Court-Owings MS   2-01100
  PO BOX 187   29645   876-2171
  Eugene Marlar, prin.

Great Falls, AC 803, PC 4, Chester
Chester SD
  Supt. — See Chester
HS, 411 SUNSET AVE   29055   2-00011
  H. Starnes, prin.   482-2210
MS, 850 CHESTER AVE   29055   2-01100
  Debra Short, prin.   482-2220

Greeleyville, AC 803, PC 2, Williamsburg
Williamsburg County SD
  Supt. — See Kingstree
Murray JSHS, PO BOX 188   29056   3-00111
  Wallace Bartelle, prin.   426-2121

Green Sea, AC 803, PC 2, Horry
Horry County SD
  Supt. — See Conway

Green Sea-Floyds JSHS   3-00111
  5625 HIGHWAY 9   29545   392-3131
  Rodney McPherson, prin.

Greenville, AC 803, PC 8, Greenville
Anderson SD 1
  Supt. — See Williamston
Powdersville MS, 135 HOOD RD   29611   2-01100
  Monty Oxendine, prin.   269-1821

Greenville County SD   8-11111
  PO BOX 2848   29602   241-3100
  Thomas Kerns, supt.
Fine Arts SHS   2-00001
  1613 W WASHINGTON ST   29601   241-3327
  Roy Fluhrer, prin.
Berea HS, 515 BEREA DR   29611   3-00011
  Harold Batson, prin.   294-4200
Carolina HS, 2725 ANDERSON RD   29611   3-00011
  Charles Poole, prin.   295-5185
HS, 1 VARDRY ST   29601   4-00011
  Marilyn Hendrix, prin.   241-3220
Hampton HS, 100 PINE KNOLL DR   29609   4-00011
  Gaston Holland, prin.   292-7587
Mann HS, 61 ISBELL LN   29607   3-00011
  Fred Crawford, prin.   281-1150
Southside HS   3-00011
  100 BLASSINGAME RD   29605   299-8393
  David Samore, prin.
Donaldson Vo Ctr   Vo Tech
  VOCATIONAL DR   29605   299-8414
  Ed Jones, prin.
Enoree AVC, 108 SCALYBARK RD   29609   Vo Tech
  Thomas Moore, prin.   294-4343
Golden Strip Career Ctr, RR 10   29607   Vo Tech
  Don Skelton, prin.   288-1244
Berea MS   3-00100
  151 BEREA MIDDLE SCHOOL RD   29611
  David Russell, prin.   294-4323
Beck MS, 302 MCALISTER RD   29607   3-00100
  Dennis Varner, prin.   241-3268
MS, 339 LOWNDES AVE   29607   3-00100
  William Stubbs, prin.   241-3360
Hughes MS, 122 DEOYLEY AVE   29605   3-00100
  Karen Kapp, prin.   299-8363
Lakeview MS   3-00100
  3801 OLD BUNCOMBE RD   29609   294-4353
  Brenda Humbert, prin.
League MS, 125 TWIN LAKE RD   29609   3-00100
  Sandra Watkins, prin.   292-7688
Parker MS, 900 WOODSIDE AVE   29611   2-00100
  Jessie Bowens, prin.   241-3285
Sevier MS, 101 SUNNYDALE DR   29609   3-00100
  Brenda Moody, prin.   292-7578
Tanglewood MS   3-00100
  44 MERRIWOODS DR   29611   295-5165
  James Gardner, prin.
Other Schools – See Greer, Mauldin, Piedmont,
  Simpsonville, Taylors, Travelers Rest

Bob Jones Academy   2-00011
  1700 WADE HAMPTON BLVD   29614   242-5100
  Sid Cates, prin.
Bob Jones University   3-UC
  1700 WADE HAMPTON BLVD   29614   242-5100
Christ Church Episcopal S   3-11111
  100 CAVALIER DR   29607   299-1522
  James Rumrill, prin.
Furman University   5-UC
  3300 POINSETT HWY   29613   294-2034
Greenville Technical College   6-CC
  PO BOX 5616   29606   250-8000
Hampton Park Christian S   3-11111
  875 STATE PARK RD   29609   233-0556
  Bruce Mizell, prin.
ITT Technical Institute   2-CS
  1 MARCUS DR STE 402   29615   288-0773
Shannon Forest Christian S   2-11111
  829 GARLINGTON RD   29615   288-0436
  Charles Crane, prin.

Greenwood, AC 803, PC 7, Greenwood
Greenwood SD 50   6-11111
  PO BOX 248   29648   223-4348
  Michael McKenzie, supt.
SHS, 1710 COKESBURY RD   29649   4-00001
  Drew Geoly, prin.   229-2528
Greenwood County Area Vo Ctr   Vo Tech
  601 E NORTHSIDE DR   29649   229-5402
  George Russell, prin.
Emerald JHS, 150 BYPASS 225   29646   3-00110
  Gary Gredlein, prin.   223-1566
Northside JHS   3-00110
  400 GLENWOOD ST   29649   229-3519
  Furman Mauldin, prin.
Southside JHS   3-00110
  705 MARSHALL RD   29646   227-6711
  Charles Graves, prin.

Cambridge Academy   2-11111
  PO BOX 249   29648   229-2875
  Steven Landry, prin.
Lander College   4-UC
  320 STANLEY AVE   29649   800-768-3600
Piedmont Technical College   4-CC
  PO BOX 1467   29648   223-8357

Greer, AC 803, PC 7, Greenville
Greenville County SD
  Supt. — See Greenville
HS, 505 N MAIN ST   29650   3-00011
  Alex Martin, prin.   848-2363

Riverside HS, 1300 S SUBER RD   29650   4-00011
  D. Wayne Rhodes, prin.   848-2323
Blue Ridge JSHS   3-00111
  2151 FEWS CHAPEL RD   29651   895-0130
  Kenneth Southerlin, prin.
Blue Ridge MS   3-00100
  2423 E TYGER BRIDGE RD   29651   895-0123
  Charles Bright, prin.
MS, 301 CHANDLER RD   29651   3-00100
  Marion Waters, prin.   848-2350

Gresham, AC 803, PC 2, Marion
Marion SD 4, RR 1 BOX 499   29546   3-11111
  Thomas Chapman, supt.   362-0331
Brittons Neck JSHS   2-00111
  RR 1 BOX 499   29546   362-3500
  Burnie Bell, prin.

Hampton, AC 803, PC 5, Hampton
Hampton SD 1, PO BOX 177   29924   5-11111
  C. Phillips, supt.   943-4576
Hampton HS, PO BOX 338   29924   3-00011
  James Berry, prin.   943-3568
Other Schools – See Varnville

Hanahan, AC 803, PC 7, Berkeley
Berkeley County SD
  Supt. — See Moncks Corner
HS, 6015 N MURRAY AVE   29406   3-00011
  D. Gross, prin.   747-4767
MS, 5815 N MURRAY AVE   29406   3-01100
  John Harper, prin.   744-3434

Hardeeville, AC 803, PC 4, Jasper

Abundant Life Academy   2-11111
  PO BOX 310   29927   784-3171
  Charles Bowman, prin.

Hartsville, AC 803, PC 6, Darlington
Darlington SD
  Supt. — See Darlington
SHS, 701 LEWELLYN DR   29550   4-00001
  Ken Dinkins, prin.   383-3130
JHS, 437 W CAROLINA AVE   29550   3-00110
  Kaye McElveen, prin.   383-3121

State Supported Schools
  Supt. — See Columbia
Governers School Science/Math   2-00001
  306 E HOME AVE   29550   383-3900
  Leland Cox, prin.

Coker College   3-UC
  300 E COLLEGE AVE   29550   383-8050
Emmanuel Baptist S   2-11111
  1001 N MARQUIS HWY   29550   332-0164
  Ben Radin, prin.

Hemingway, AC 803, PC 3, Williamsburg
Georgetown County SD
  Supt. — See Georgetown
Pleasant Hill HS   2-00011
  RR 3 BOX 181   29554   558-9441
  E. Little, prin.
Pleasant Hill MS   2-01100
  RR 3 BOX 178   29554   558-2387
  Denise Applewhite, prin.

Williamsburg County SD
  Supt. — See Kingstree
HS, PO BOX 1430   29554   3-00011
  W. Ronald Williamson, prin.   558-9413
Hemingway Vo Ctr   Vo Tech
  RR 2 BOX 12   29554   558-5813
  Regina McKnight, prin.
Chavis MS, PO BOX 977   29554   2-01100
  David Thompson, prin.   558-5605

Hilton Head Island, AC 803, PC 7, Beaufort
Beaufort County SD
  Supt. — See Beaufort
HS, 70 WILBORN RD   29926   4-00011
  William Evans, prin.   689-7550
McCracken MS, 55 WILBORN RD   29926   3-00100
  Richard Hitch, prin.   689-7600

Hilton Head Christian Academy   2-11111
  55 GARDNER RD   29926   681-2878
  Mike Lindsay, prin.
Hilton Head Prep S   2-11111
  8 FOXGRAPE RD   29928   671-2286
  Lucy Crowley, prin.

Holly Hill, AC 803, PC 4, Orangeburg
Orangeburg SD 3, PO BOX 98   29059   5-11111
  David Longshore, supt.   496-3288
Holly Hills-Roberts JSHS   3-00111
  PO BOX 338   29059   496-3818
  Gerald Wright, prin.
MS, PO BOX 878   29059   3-00100
  Ida Bailey, prin.   496-5525

Holly Hill Academy   2-11111
  PO BOX 757   29059   496-3243
  John Gasque, prin.

Hollywood, AC 803, PC 4, Charleston

St. Paul Country Day S   2-11111
  PO BOX 580   29449   889-2702
  Brett Maddox, prin.

Honea Path, AC 803, PC 5, Anderson
Anderson SD 2, PO BOX 266 29654 — 5-11111
  Roger Burnett, supt. — 369-7364
Belton-Honea Path HS
  11000 BELTON HONEA PATH HWY 29654 — 4-00011
  Judy Davis, prin. — 369-7382
MS, 107 BROCK AVE 29654 — 2-01100
  Michael Hall, prin. — 369-7641
Other Schools – See Belton

Hopkins, AC 803, PC 4, Richland
Richland SD 1
  Supt. — See Columbia
Lower Richland HS
  2615 LOWER RICHLAND BLVD 29061 — 4-00011
  Titus Duren, prin. — 695-3000
MS, CLARKSON RD 29061 — 4-00100
  Marvin Byers, prin. — 776-5770

Huger, AC 803, PC 1, Berkeley
Berkeley County SD
  Supt. — See Moncks Corner
Cainhoy JSHS, HC 65 BOX 239 29450 — 2-00111
  Frank Legree, prin. — 336-3226

Inman, AC 803, PC 4, Spartanburg
Spartanburg SD 1
  Supt. — See Campobello
Chapman HS, 35 OAKLAND AVE 29349 — 3-00011
  Harry McMillan, prin. — 472-2836
Mabry JHS, 10 W MILLER ST 29349 — 2-00100
  Rebecca Miller, prin. — 472-8402

Irmo, AC 803, PC 7, Richland
Lexington SD 5
  Supt. — See Ballentine
Dutch Fork HS — 3-00011
  1400 OLD TAMAH RD 29063 — 732-8050
  Keith Callicutt, prin.

Iva, AC 803, PC 4, Anderson
Anderson SD 3, PO BOX 118 29655 — 4-11111
  Jeffrey Radnor, supt. — 348-6196
Crescent HS, 9104 HIGHWAY 81 S 29655 — 3-00011
  Richard Gaines, prin. — 352-6175
Other Schools – See Starr

Jackson, AC 803, PC 4, Aiken
Aiken County SD
  Supt. — See Aiken
MS, 8217 ATOMIC RD 29831 — 2-00100
  David Caver, prin. — 279-3525

Johns Island, AC 803, PC 2, Charleston
St. Johns Constituent SD
  Supt. — See Charleston
St. Johns HS, 1518 MAIN RD 29455 — 2-00011
  Harrison Washington, prin. — 559-6400
Haut Gap MS, 1861 BOHICKET RD 29455 — 2-00100
  Roberta Frasier, prin. — 559-6418

Sea Island Academy — 2-11111
  2024 ACADEMY RD 29455 — 559-5506
  Larry Shurlds, prin.

Johnsonville, AC 803, PC 4, Florence
Florence SD 5, PO BOX 98 29555 — 4-11111
  Paul Shaw, supt. — 386-2358
HS, RR 1 BOX A 29555 — 2-00011
  Sam Harrelson, prin. — 386-2707
MS, PO BOX 67 29555 — 2-01100
  Kenneth Watson, prin. — 386-2066

Johnston, AC 803, PC 5, Edgefield
Edgefield County SD
  Supt. — See Edgefield
Thurmond HS, RR 1 BOX 82 29832 — 3-00011
  Philip Musgrave, prin. — 275-1768
Thurmond Vo HS, RR 1 BOX 81A 29832 — Vo Tech
  J. Wates, prin. — 275-1767
Jet MS, RR 1 BOX 85 29832 — 2-00100
  Robert Heflin, prin. — 275-1997

Wardlaw Academy — 2-11111
  RR 1 BOX 92 29832 — 275-4794
  Tom Fedricci, prin.

Jonesville, AC 803, PC 4, Union
Union County SD
  Supt. — See Union
JSHS, PO BOX 835 29353 — 2-00111
  Bill James, prin. — 674-5272

Kershaw, AC 803, PC 4, Lancaster
Kershaw County SD
  Supt. — See Camden
North Central JSHS — 3-00111
  3000 LOCKHART RD 29067 — 432-9858
  Henry Baggett, prin.

Lancaster SD
  Supt. — See Lancaster
Jackson HS, RR 2 BOX 139A 29067 — 3-00011
  James Neal, prin. — 475-2381
Jackson MS, RR 2 29067 — 2-00100
  Mitch Lucas, prin. — 475-6021

Kingstree, AC 803, PC 5, Williamsburg
Williamsburg County SD — 6-11111
  PO BOX 1067 29556 — 354-5571
  James Franklin, supt.
HS, 615 LANE RD 29556 — 4-00011
  (—), prin. — 354-6525
JHS, 710 3RD AVE 29556 — 2-00100
  Guy Godwin, prin. — 354-6823
Other Schools – See Greeleyville, Hemingway

Williamsburg Academy — 2-11111
  PO BOX 770 29556 — 354-6539
  Larry Berry, prin.
Williamsburg Technical College — 3-CC
  601 LANE RD 29556 — 354-7423

Ladson, AC 803, PC 7, Berkeley
Berkeley County SD
  Supt. — See Moncks Corner
College Park MS, UNIVERSITY DR 29456 — 4-00100
  Richard Van Brunt, prin. — 553-8300

Dorchester SD 2
  Supt. — See Summerville
Oakbrook MS, 4704 OLD FORT RD 29456 — 4-00100
  Garland Crump, prin. — 873-9750

Lake City, AC 803, PC 6, Florence
Florence SD 3, PO BOX 128 29560 — 5-11111
  Lane Floyd, supt. — 394-8652
HS, PO BOX 1157 29560 — 4-00011
  Michael Gaskin, prin. — 394-3321
McNair JHS, PO BOX 1019 29560 — 3-00100
  Gloria Boyd, prin. — 394-8651

Carolina Academy — 2-11111
  351 S COUNTRY CLUB RD 29560 — 394-3317
  Anthony Atkinson, prin.

Lake View, AC 803, PC 3, Dillon
Dillon SD 1, PO BOX 644 29563 — 4-11111
  Stephen Laird, supt. — 759-3001
JSHS, PO BOX 624 29563 — 2-00111
  Edison Arnette, prin. — 759-3009

Lamar, AC 803, PC 4, Darlington
Darlington SD
  Supt. — See Darlington
HS, RR 2 BOX 3 29069 — 2-00011
  Andrea Kelly, prin. — 326-5543
Spaulding JHS, RR 2 BOX 65 29069 — 2-00100
  Eddie Pauley, prin. — 326-5335

Lancaster, AC 803, PC 6, Lancaster
Lancaster SD, 300 S CATAWBA ST 29720 — 6-11111
  Thomas Paquin, supt. — 286-6972
Buford HS, RR 9 29720 — 3-00011
  James Jordan, prin. — 286-7068
HS, 655 N CATAWBA ST 29720 — 4-00011
  Richard Lifsey, prin. — 283-2001
Barr Street MS, 610 W BARR ST 29720 — 3-00100
  L. Roland Freeman, prin. — 285-1531
Buford MS, RR 9 29720 — 2-01100
  Charles Clyburn, prin. — 283-3967
South MS, 602 BILLINGS DR 29720 — 3-00100
  H. Boucher, prin. — 283-8416
Other Schools – See Fort Mill, Kershaw

University of South Carolina — 3-CC
  PO BOX 889 29721 — 285-7471

Landrum, AC 803, PC 4, Spartanburg
Spartanburg SD 1
  Supt. — See Campobello
JSHS, 102 REDLAND RD 29356 — 3-00111
  James Debruhl, prin. — 457-2606

Langley, AC 803, PC 4, Aiken
Aiken County SD
  Supt. — See Aiken
Midland Valley HS — 4-00011
  PO BOX 500 29834 — 593-7100
  Warren Whitson, prin.
Langley-Bath-Clearwater MS — 3-00100
  PO BOX 327 29834 — 593-7260
  Joseph Padget, prin.

Latta, AC 803, PC 4, Dillon
Dillon SD 3, PO BOX 458 29565 — 4-11111
  John Kirby, supt. — 752-7101
HS, 606 N RICHARDSON ST 29565 — 2-00011
  Randy Fitzpatrick, prin. — 752-5751
MS, 502 WILLIS ST 29565 — 2-00100
  Willie Sneed, prin. — 752-7117

Laurens, AC 803, PC 6, Laurens
Laurens SD 55, 1029 W MAIN ST 29360 — 6-11111
  W. Hucks, supt. — 984-3568
Laurens District 55 HS — 4-00011
  PO BOX 309 29360 — 682-3151
  James Moncrief, prin.
JHS, PO BOX 288 29360 — 3-00100
  Rick Charles, prin. — 984-2400
Other Schools – See Gray Court

Lexington, AC 803, PC 5, Lexington
Lexington SD 1, PO BOX 1869 29071 — 7-11111
  J. Floyd, supt. — 359-4178
SHS, 2463 AUGUSTA HWY 29072 — 4-00011
  Joe Bedenbaugh, prin. — 359-5565
Lexington Applied Tech Ctr — Vo Tech
  2421 AUGUSTA HWY 29072 — 359-4151
  Kenneth Lake, prin.
MS, 702 N LAKE DR 29072 — 4-00110
  (—), prin. — 359-6169
Other Schools – See Gilbert, Pelion, West Columbia

Liberty, AC 803, PC 5, Pickens
Pickens SD
  Supt. — See Easley
HS, 319 SUMMIT DR 29657 — 3-00011
  Oscar Thorsland, prin. — 843-9224
MS, 310 W MAIN ST 29657 — 3-01100
  Dennis Somerville, prin. — 843-1238

Little River, AC 803, PC 5, Horry
Horry County SD
  Supt. — See Conway
North Myrtle Beach HS — 3-00011
  3750 SEA MOUNTAIN HWY 29566 — 399-6171
  Harriet Blanton, prin.
North Myrtle Beach MS — 3-00100
  655 HIGHWAY 90 29566 — 399-6136
  Michael Blanton, prin.

Lockhart, AC 803, PC 1, Union
Union County SD
  Supt. — See Union
JSHS, PO BOX 220 29364 — 2-00111
  Henry Sparrow, prin. — 545-6501

Loris, AC 803, PC 4, Horry
Horry County SD
  Supt. — See Conway
HS, 301 HERITAGE RD 29569 — 3-00011
  Bob Nalley, prin. — 756-4041
Finklea Career Ctr — Vo Tech
  3501 HIGHWAY 917 29569 — 756-0061
  Sarah Elliott, prin.
MS, 3410 CHURCH ST 29569 — 3-00100
  James McCall, prin. — 756-2181

Lugoff, AC 803, PC 5, Kershaw
Kershaw County SD
  Supt. — See Camden
Lugoff-Elgin HS, PO BOX 278 29078 — 3-00011
  Creig Tyler, prin. — 438-3481
Lugoff-Elgin MS, PO BOX 68 29078 — 3-00100
  Larry Patrick, prin. — 438-3591

Lynchburg, AC 803, PC 2, Lee

Hudgens Academy — 2-11111
  RR 2 BOX 427 29080 — 453-5464
  Robert Griggs, prin.

Manning, AC 803, PC 5, Clarendon
Clarendon SD 2, PO BOX 1252 29102 — 5-11111
  Sylvia Weinberg, supt. — 435-4435
HS, HIGHWAY 261 WEST 29102 — 3-00011
  John Bassard, prin. — 435-4417
MS, 311 W BOYCE ST 29102 — 3-00100
  Michael Shorter, prin. — 435-8195

Manning Academy — 3-11111
  PO BOX 278 29102 — 435-2114
  Eugene Nalley, prin.

Marion, AC 803, PC 6, Marion
Marion SD 1 — 5-11111
  616 E NORTHSIDE AVE 29571 — 423-1811
  Charles Bethea, supt.
HS, 1205 S MAIN ST 29571 — 4-00011
  Ed McDowell, prin. — 423-2571
Johnakin MS, GURLEY ST 29571 — 3-00100
  Lannie Edwards, prin. — 423-8360

Mauldin, AC 803, PC 7, Greenville
Greenville County SD
  Supt. — See Greenville
HS, 701 E BUTLER AVE 29662 — 4-00011
  Joseph Broadus, prin. — 281-1200

Mc Bee, AC 803, PC 3, Chesterfield
Chesterfield SD
  Supt. — See Chesterfield
JSHS, PO BOX 218 29101 — 2-00111
  Walter Baker, prin. — 335-8251

Mc Clellanville, AC 803, PC 2, Charleston
St. James-Santee Constituent
  Supt. — See Mount Pleasant
Lincoln HS, PO BOX 348 29458 — 2-00011
  Jennings Austin, prin. — 577-0970
MS, 711 PINCKNEY ST 29458 — 2-00100
  Diane Ricciardi, prin. — 887-3231

Mc Cormick, AC 803, PC 4, Mc Cormick
McCormick SD, PO BOX 548 29835 — 4-11111
  Charles Parnell, supt. — 465-2435
HS, 516 MIMS ST 29835 — 2-00011
  G. W. Yeldell, prin. — 465-2253
MS, 801 CAROLINA ST 29835 — 2-01100
  Jim Nolan, prin. — 465-2243

Moncks Corner, AC 803, PC 6, Berkeley
Berkeley County SD — 8-11111
  PO BOX 608 29461 — 761-8600
  James Hyman, supt.
Berkeley HS, 406 W MAIN ST 29461 — 4-00011
  Ben Hodges, prin. — 761-8123
Macedonia HS — 3-00011
  HC 69 BOX 437 29461 — 565-3226
  Dan Parler, prin.
Berkeley MS — 4-00100
  320 HIGHWAY 17A 29461 — 761-8152
  Joe Espinosa, prin.
Macedonia MS — 3-00100
  HC 69 BOX 436 29461 — 565-3217
  Janie Langley, prin.
Other Schools – See Bonneau, Cross, Goose Creek,
  Hanahan, Huger, Ladson, Oakley, Saint Stephen

Monetta, AC 803, PC 2, Aiken
Aiken County SD
  Supt. — See Aiken
Ridge Spring-Monetta HS — 2-00011
  10 J P KNEECE DR 29105 — 685-7077
  Mack Gantt, prin.

Mount Pleasant, AC 803, PC 8, Charleston
Charleston Moultrie Constituent SD — 6-11111
  665 COLEMAN BLVD 29464 — 849-2878
  Lynda Davis, supt.
Wando HS — 4-00011
  1560 MATHIS FERRY RD 29464 — 849-2830
  Robert Strous, prin.
Laing MS, 2213 HIGHWAY 17 N 29464 — 3-00100
  Walter Pusey, prin. — 849-2809
Moultrie MS — 3-00100
  645 COLEMAN BLVD 29464 — 849-2819
  Michael Cox, prin.

St. James-Santee Constituent — 3-11111
  665 COLEMAN BLVD 29464 — 849-2878
  Lynda Davis, supt.
Other Schools – See Mc Clellanville

Trident Academy, PO BOX 804 29465 — 1-11111
  Myron Harrington, prin. — 884-7046

Mullins, AC 803, PC 6, Marion
Marion SD 2, PO BOX 689 29574 — 5-11111
  William Foil, supt. — 464-3700
HS, RR 3 BOX 451 29574 — 3-00011
  John Drummond, prin. — 464-3710
Palmetto MS, 305 ONEAL ST 29574 — 3-00100
  Ronald Taylor, prin. — 464-3730

Pee Dee Academy — 2-11111
  PO BOX 449 29574 — 423-1771
  Jerry Wolff, prin.

Myrtle Beach, AC 803, PC 8, Horry
Horry County SD
  Supt. — See Conway
HS, 3300 CENTRAL PKY 29577 — 4-00011
  Donald Carlisle, prin. — 448-7140
Socastee HS — 4-00011
  4900 SOCASTEE BLVD 29575 — 293-2513
  Myra Bryan, prin.
Grand Strand Career Ctr — Vo Tech
  900 79TH AVE N 29572 — 449-3349
  James Powell, prin.
MS, 3301 OAK ST 29577 — 3-00100
  Thomas Currie, prin. — 448-3932
St. James MS — 3-00100
  9775 SAINT JAMES RD 29575 — 650-5543
  Wendell Shealy, prin.
Socastee MS — 3-00100
  4950 SOCASTEE BLVD 29575 — 293-4553
  Zebedee Pack, prin.

Calvary Christian S — 2-11111
  4511 DICK POND RD 29575 — 650-2829
  Robert Weeks, prin.
Chris Logan Career College — 4-CS
  505 7TH AVE N 29577 — 448-6302
Coastal Carolina College — 5-UC
  PO BOX 1954 29578 — 347-3161

Newberry, AC 803, PC 7, Newberry
Newberry County SD — 6-11111
  PO BOX 718 29108 — 321-2600
  Thomas Dowling, supt.
HS, PO BOX 458 29108 — 4-00011
  Steve Wilson, prin. — 321-2621
Newberry Career Ctr — Vo Tech
  PO BOX 799 29108 — 321-2674
  Mitchell Strickland, prin.
MS, 1829 NANCE ST 29108 — 3-00100
  Robert Heath, prin. — 321-2640
Other Schools – See Prosperity, Whitmire

Newberry College — 3-UC
  2100 COLLEGE ST 29108 — 321-5127

New Ellenton, AC 803, PC 5, Aiken
Aiken County SD
  Supt. — See Aiken
MS, 814 MAIN ST S 29809 — 2-00100
  Gayle Galick, prin. — 652-8200

Ninety Six, AC 803, PC 4, Greenwood
Greenwood SD 52 — 4-11111
  605 JOHNSTON RD 29666 — 543-3100
  Gerald Robinson, supt.
HS, 651 JOHNSTON RD 29666 — 2-00011
  Willis Burroughs, prin. — 543-2911
Edgewood MS, 120 KINARD AVE 29666 — 2-00100
  Byron Bowers, prin. — 543-3511

North, AC 803, PC 3, Orangeburg
Orangeburg SD 6, PO BOX 640 29112 — 3-11111
  William Lynn, supt. — 247-2163
JSHS, PO BOX 370 29112 — 2-00111
  Ceasar Leysath, prin. — 247-2541

North Augusta, AC 803, PC 7, Aiken
Aiken County SD
  Supt. — See Aiken
HS, 2000 KNOBCONE AVE 29841 — 4-00011
  Clarence Jackson, prin. — 442-6100
Knox MS, 1804 WELLS RD 29841 — 3-00100
  Sara Twiggs, prin. — 442-6300
MS, 725 OLD EDGEFIELD RD 29841 — 3-00100
  Franklin Hyers, prin. — 442-6200

Edgefield County SD
  Supt. — See Edgefield
Merriwether MS, PO BOX 7010 29841 — 2-00100
  Herman Thompson, prin. — 279-2511

Victory Christian S — 2-11111
  620 MARTINTOWN ROAD 29841 — 278-2138
  E. Martin, prin.

North Charleston, AC 803, PC 8, Charleston
Cooper River Constituent SD — 7-11111
  4720 JENKINS AVE 29405 — 745-7150
  Jean Murray, supt.
HS, 1087 E MONTAGUE AVE 29405 — 4-00011
  Thomas Mullins, prin. — 745-7140
Cooper River Ed Ctr — Vo Tech
  1600 SARANAC ST 29405 — 745-7087
  Mary Wilson, prin.
Brentwood MS, 2685 LEEDS AVE 29405 — 3-00100
  Annette Goodwin, prin. — 745-7094
Morningside MS — 3-00100
  1999 SINGLEY ST 29405 – (—), prin. — 745-7122
Other Schools – See Charleston

Dorchester SD 2
  Supt. — See Summerville
Fort Dorchester JHS — 3-00010
  8500 LINCOLN BLVD 29420 — 760-4450
  James Atkinson, prin.

Ferndale Baptist S — 2-11111
  4870 PIEDMONT AVE 29406 — 544-0535
  Gladys Besancon, prin.

Norway, AC 803, PC 2, Orangeburg
Orangeburg SD 1
  Supt. — See Springfield
Hunter-Kinard-Tyler JSHS — 2-00111
  PO BOX 158 29113 — 263-4832
  Sinclair Abraham, prin.

Oakley, AC 803, PC 2, Berkeley
Berkeley County SD
  Supt. — See Moncks Corner
Oakley Vo Ctr, RR 2 BOX 891 29461 — Vo Tech
  Harvey Owens, prin. — 761-3110

Orangeburg, AC 803, PC 7, Orangeburg
Orangeburg SD 5 — 6-11111
  578 ELLIS AVE NE 29115 — 534-5454
  Walter Tobin, supt.
Orangeburg-Wilkinson HS — 4-00011
  601 BRUIN PKY 29115 — 534-6180
  Lemeul Stephens, prin.
COVEC S, HIGHWAY 601 N 29115 — Vo Tech
  Mildred Rice, prin. — 536-4473
Brookdale MS — 2-01100
  394 BROOKDALE DR NE 29115 — 534-9652
  Charles Spell, prin.
Clark MS, 919 BENNETT ST NE 29115 — 3-01100
  Thomasenia Benson, prin. — 531-2200
Howard MS — 3-01100
  1255 BELLEVILLE RD NE 29115 — 534-5470
  Charles Gadsden, prin.

Claflin College — 3-UC
  700 COLLEGE ST NE 29115 — 534-2710
Garden City Christian S — 2-11111
  630 BROUGHTON ST SW 29115 — 534-7353
  Cynthia Poor, prin.
Orangeburg-Calhoun Technical College — 4-CC
  3250 SAINT MATTHEWS RD NE 29115
  — 536-0311
Orangeburg Prep S — 3-11111
  2651 NORTH RD NW 29115 — 536-1698
  Ann Glover, prin.
South Carolina State University — 5-UC
  PO BOX 7127 29117 — 536-7185
Southern Methodist College — 3-UC
  PO BOX 1027 29116 — 534-7826
Wesley Christian S — 2-11111
  PO BOX 628 29116 — 536-6167
  Robert Morgan, prin.

Pacolet, AC 803, PC 4, Spartanburg
Spartanburg SD 3
  Supt. — See Glendale
MS, PO BOX 159 29372 — 2-00100
  Gary Barnard, prin. — 474-4080

Pageland, AC 803, PC 5, Chesterfield
Chesterfield SD
  Supt. — See Chesterfield
Central HS, PO BOX 37 29728 — 3-00011
  (—), prin. — 672-6115
MS, PO BOX 187 29728 — 3-01100
  Daisy Wiley, prin. — 672-2400

New Covenent Christian S — 2-11111
  RR 1 BOX 24-5 29728 — 672-2760
  Gaye Hill, prin.

Pamplico, AC 803, PC 4, Florence
Florence SD 2, RR 1 BOX 36B 29583 — 4-11111
  Steve Quick, supt. — 493-2502
Hannah-Pamplico HS — 2-00011
  RR 1 BOX 36A 29583 — 493-5781
  Robert Sullivan, prin.
Hannah-Pamplico MS — 2-00100
  PO BOX 158 29583 — 493-5588
  Bernard McDaniel, prin.

New Prospect Christian S — 2-11111
  RR 2 BOX 84D 29583 — 493-2189
  Rev. Cagle, prin.

Pawleys Island, AC 803, PC 2, Georgetown
Georgetown County SD
  Supt. — See Georgetown
Waccamaw JSHS, 2688 RIVER RD 29585 — 3-00111
  William Royster, prin. — 237-9899

Pelion, AC 803, PC 2, Lexington
Lexington SD 1
  Supt. — See Lexington
JSHS, PO BOX 68 29123 — 3-00111
  Jean Haggard, prin. — 894-3377

Pendleton, AC 803, PC 5, Anderson
Anderson SD 4, PO BOX 545 29670 — 4-11111
  Wray Smith, supt. — 646-8000
HS, PO BOX 218 29670 — 3-00011
  Irvin Cunningham, prin. — 646-8040
JHS, 902 E QUEEN ST 29670 — 2-00100
  Joyce Beckett, prin. — 646-8030

Tri-County Tech College — 5-CC
  PO BOX 587 29670 — 646-8361

Pickens, AC 803, PC 5, Pickens
Pickens SD
  Supt. — See Easley
SHS, 111 BLUE FLAME DR 29671 — 3-00001
  Phil Greer, prin. — 878-6354
JHS, 467 SPARKS LN 29671 — 3-00110
  Floyd Jones, prin. — 878-4726

Piedmont, AC 803, PC 5, Greenville
Anderson SD 1
  Supt. — See Williamston
Wren HS, 905 WREN SCHOOL RD 29673 — 4-00011
  James Johnson, prin. — 232-4842
Wren MS — 3-01100
  1010 WREN SCHOOL RD 29673 — 232-4838
  Gregory Cantrell, prin.

Greenville County SD
  Supt. — See Greenville
Woodmont HS, RR 4 BOX 402 29673 — 3-00011
  Susan Hoover, prin. — 299-8300
Woodmont MS, RR 2 BOX 289 29673 — 3-00100
  David Ledbetter, prin. — 299-8373

Pinewood, AC 803, PC 3, Sumter
Sumter SD 2
  Supt. — See Sumter
Manchester MS, PO BOX 188 29125 — 3-01100
  Deborah Hill, prin. — 452-5454

Prosperity, AC 803, PC 4, Newberry
Newberry County SD
  Supt. — See Newberry
Mid-Carolina HS, RR 3 29127 — 3-00011
  George Kinard, prin. — 364-2134
Mid-Carolina MS, RR 3 29127 — 2-00100
  Clarence Chick, prin. — 364-3634

Rains, AC 803, PC 3, Marion
Marion SD 3, PO BOX 439 29589 — 3-11111
  Frank Hart, supt. — 423-2891
Other Schools – See Centenary

Richburg, AC 803, PC 2, Chester
Chester SD
  Supt. — See Chester
Lewisville HS, RR 1 BOX 3 29729 — 2-00011
  Ray Anderson, prin. — 789-5131
Lewisville MS, PO BOX 56 29729 — 2-00100
  Eugene Neely, prin. — 789-5858

Ridgeland, AC 803, PC 4, Jasper
Jasper County SD, PO BOX 848 29936 — 5-11111
  A. Dale Strickland, supt. — 726-7200
Jasper County HS, PO BOX 760 29936 — 3-00011
  Hugie Peterson, prin. — 726-7230
Ridgeland MS, PO BOX 250 29936 — 2-00100
  Mike Duncan, prin. — 726-7250

Heyward Academy — 3-11111
  RR 2 BOX 333 29936 — 726-3673
  John Rogers, prin.

Rock Hill, AC 803, PC 8, York
York SD 3, PO BOX 10072 29731 — 7-11111
  Phillip McDaniel, supt. — 324-5360
Northwestern HS — 4-00011
  2503 W MAIN ST 29732 — 328-6118
  W. Lovelace, prin.
HS, 320 S SPRINGDALE RD 29730 — 4-00011
  Eric Lessmeister, prin. — 324-3100
Rock Hill Career Development Ctr — Vo Tech
  2399 W MAIN ST 29732 — 327-2003
  Decosta Muckenfuss, prin.
Castle Heights MS — 3-00100
  1234 FLINT STREET EXT 29730 — 324-3165
  Edward Buddin, prin.
Rawlinson Road MS — 4-00100
  2631 W MAIN ST 29732 — 328-2451
  Tena Neely, prin.
Sullivan MS, 1825 EDEN TER 29730 — 4-00100
  Ruth Greer, prin. — 366-8181

Trinity Christian S — 2-11111
  505 UNIVERSITY DR 29730 — 366-3121
  Steve Norris, prin.
Westminster Catawba Christian S — 2-11111
  2650 INDIA HOOK RD 29732 — 366-4119
  John Hunter, prin.
Winthrop University — 6-UC
  701 W OAKLAND AVE 29733 — 323-2191

York Technical College 5-CC
452 S ANDERSON RD   29730   327-8000

Roebuck, AC 803, PC 4, Spartanburg
Spartanburg SD 6
Supt. — See Spartanburg
Gable MS, 198 OTTS SHOALS RD   29376   3-00100
Gwendolyn Smith, prin.   576-3500

Ruffin, AC 803, PC 2, Colleton
Colleton County SD
Supt. — See Walterboro
HS, RR 1 BOX 105   29475   2-00011
Quenie Crawford, prin.   562-2291

Saint George, AC 803, PC 4, Dorchester
Dorchester SD 4, 500 RIDGE ST   29477   5-11111
Ed Laughinghouse, supt.   563-4535
HS, 600 MINUS ST   29477   2-00011
Peter Weathers, prin.   563-3171
Williams Memorial MS
290 S METTS ST   29477   3-01100
Kenneth Jenkins, prin.   563-3231
Other Schools – See Dorchester

Dorchester Academy   2-11111
PO BOX 901   29477   563-9511
Carolyn Baker, prin.

Saint Matthews, AC 803, PC 4, Calhoun
Calhoun SD, 101 RICHLAND AVE   29135   4-11111
Roy Holloway, supt.   655-7310
Calhoun County HS   3-00011
RR 4 BOX 30   29135   874-3071
James Franklin, prin.
Ford MS, PO BOX 287   29135   2-00100
Ken Westbury, prin.   655-7222

Calhoun Academy   2-11111
PO BOX 526   29135   874-2734
Milly McLauchlin, prin.

Saint Stephen, AC 803, PC 4, Berkeley
Berkeley County SD
Supt. — See Moncks Corner
HS, RR 1 BOX 11A   29479   2-00011
Cleve Hawkins, prin.   567-3214
MS, PO BOX 248   29479   2-00100
Wyman Boyd, prin.   567-3128

Salem, AC 803, PC 2, Oconee
Oconee County SD
Supt. — See Walhalla
Tamassee-Salem JSHS   2-00111
PO BOX 96   29676   944-0444
Richard Alexander, prin.

Saluda, AC 803, PC 5, Saluda
Saluda SD, 404 N WISE RD   29138   4-11111
Moody Oswald, supt.   445-8441
HS, 400 W BUTLER AVE   29138   3-00011
William Whitfield, prin.   445-2564
Riverside MS   3-01100
404 N BOUKNIGHT FERRY RD   29138   445-7012
N. Burton, prin.

Seneca, AC 803, PC 6, Oconee
Oconee County SD
Supt. — See Walhalla
HS, PO BOX 917   29679   4-00011
H. Hamilton, prin.   885-5000
Hamilton Career Ctr   Vo Tech
100 VOCATIONAL DR   29678   885-5011
Frank Lanford, prin.
MS, PO BOX 607   29679   3-00100
Alphonzo Gaines, prin.   885-5016

Simpsonville, AC 803, PC 7, Greenville
Greenville County SD
Supt. — See Greenville
Hillcrest HS, PO BOX 188   29681   4-00011
Leroy Hamilton, prin.   967-1811
Bryson MS   4-00100
3657 S INDUSTRIAL DR   29681   967-1836
Judy James, prin.
Hillcrest MS, 510 GARRISON RD   29681   4-00100
Keith Russell, prin.   967-1826

Smoaks, AC 803, PC 2, Colleton
Colleton County SD
Supt. — See Walterboro
MS, RR 1 BOX 216-A   29481   2-00100
Harry Jenkins, prin.   562-2221

Spartanburg, AC 803, PC 8, Spartanburg
Spartanburg SD 2   6-11111
3655 BOILING SPRINGS RD   29303   578-0128
James Jennings, supt.
Boiling Springs HS   4-00011
2251 OLD FURNACE RD   29303   578-8465
Charles Moore, prin.
Boiling Springs JHS   3-00100
3655 BOILING SPRINGS RD   29303   578-5954
Donald Barnette, prin.
Other Schools – See Chesnee

Spartanburg SD 3
Supt. — See Glendale
Broome HS, 381 CHERRY HILL RD   29307   3-00011
Russel Wright, prin.   579-8040

Spartanburg SD 6   6-11111
1493 W O EZELL BLVD   29301   576-4212
Dr. David Eubanks, supt.
Dorman HS   4-00011
1491 W O EZELL BLVD   29301   576-4202
Wofford O'Sullivan, prin.
Dawkins MS   3-00100
150 LINCOLN SCHOOL RD   29301   576-8088
Charles Bagwell, prin.
Other Schools – See Fairforest, Roebuck

Spartanburg SD 7, PO BOX 970   29304   7-11111
Karen Angello, supt.   594-4400
SHS, 500 DUPRE DR   29307   4-00011
Joseph Clarke, prin.   594-4410
Carver JHS, 449 S CHURCH ST   29306   3-00110
Tyrone Gilmore, prin.   594-4435
McCracken JHS, 300 WEBBER RD   29307   3-00110
(—), prin.   594-4457
Whitlock JHS, 580 SUNSET DR   29303   3-00110
Joan Narron, prin.   594-4482

Converse College   4-UC
580 E MAIN ST   29302   596-9000
Sherman College of Straight Chiropractic   2-UC
PO BOX 1452   29304   578-8770
South Carolina School for Deaf and Blind   HND
29302
Spartanburg Day S   3-11111
1701 SKYLYN DR   29307   582-7539
Gary Clark, prin.
Spartanburg Methodist College   3-CC
1200 TEXTILE RD   29301   800-772-7286
Spartanburg Technical College   4-CC
PO BOX 4386   29305   591-3800
University of South Carolina   5-UC
800 UNIVERSITY WAY   29303   599-2246
Wofford College   4-UC
429 N CHURCH ST   29303   585-4821

Springfield, AC 803, PC 3, Orangeburg
Orangeburg SD 1, PO BOX 337   29146   4-11111
John Tindal, supt.   258-3418
Other Schools – See Norway

Starr, AC 803, PC 2, Anderson
Anderson SD 3
Supt. — See Iva
Starr-Iva MS, PO BOX 68   29684   3-00100
Bill Daniel, prin.   352-6146

Summerton, AC 803, PC 3, Clarendon
Clarendon SD 1, PO BOX 38   29148   4-11111
Milton Marley, supt.   485-2325
Scotts Branch JSHS   3-00111
PO BOX 67   29148   485-8184
Kenneth Mance, prin.

Clarendon Hall S, PO BOX 609   29148   2-11111
Miles Elliott, prin.   485-3550

Summerville, AC 803, PC 7, Dorchester
Dorchester SD 2   7-11111
102 GREENWAVE BLVD   29483   873-2901
William Reeves, supt.
SHS, 1101 BOONE HILL RD   29483   4-00011
Stan Yarborough, prin.   873-6460
Alston MS, 500 BRYAN ST   29483   4-00100
Robert Polk, prin.   873-3890
DuBose MS   4-00100
1000 DUBOSE SCHOOL RD   29483   875-7012
Archie Franchini, prin.
Summerville HS-Gregg Campus   4-00010
500 GREENWAVE BLVD   29483   871-3150
Nick Gaspars, prin.
Other Schools – See Ladson, North Charleston

Sumter, AC 803, PC 8, Sumter
Sumter SD 17, PO BOX 1180   29151   6-11111
Andrena Ray, supt.   469-8536
HS, 2580 MCCRAYS MILL RD   29154   5-00011
Harold Starr, prin.   481-4480
Alice Drive MS, 40 MILLER RD   29150   4-00100
Ellison Lawson, prin.   775-0821
Bates MS, 700 BAILEY ST   29150   4-00100
Lloyd Hunter, prin.   775-0711

Sumter SD 2   6-11111
1345 WILSON HALL RD   29150   469-6900
Frank Baker, supt.
Furman HS, 3400 BETHEL RD   29154   3-00011
Harold Chandler, prin.   481-8510
Mayewood HS, RR 10 BOX 310   29153   2-00011
William Hamilton, prin.   495-8014
Ebenezer JHS, 3440 EBENEZER RD   29153   3-00110
Rudy Wheeler, prin.   469-8571
Other Schools – See Dalzell, Pinewood

Central Carolina Technical College   4-CC
506 N GUIGNARD DR   29150   778-6640
Morris College   3-UC
100 W COLLEGE ST   29150   775-9371
Sumter Catholic S   2-00111
PO BOX 1090   29151   775-0119
John Monnig, prin.
Sumter Christian S   2-11111
PO BOX 1855   29151   773-1902
Ronald Davis, prin.
University of South Carolina   3-CC
200 MILLER RD   29150   775-6341
Wilson Hall S, PO BOX 246   29151   2-11111
Frederick Moulton, prin.   469-3475

Swansea, AC 803, PC 3, Lexington
Lexington SD 4, PO BOX 569   29160   4-11111
Franklin Vail, supt.   568-3886
HS, 500 E 1ST ST   29160   3-00011
Larry Rabon, prin.   568-3881
Pickney MS, 607 E 5TH ST   29160   3-00100
Cecil McClary, prin.   568-3351

Taylors, AC 803, PC 7, Greenville
Greenville County SD
Supt. — See Greenville
Eastside HS   4-00011
1300 BRUSHY CREEK RD   29687   292-7715
Kenneth Peake, prin.
Foothills Career Ctr   Vo Tech
100 HARNITHA LN   29687   292-7675
Amos Hykes, prin.
Northwood MS, 710 IKES RD   29687   4-00100
Rosia Gardner, prin.   292-7640

Tigerville, AC 803, PC 2, Greenville

North Greenville College   2-CC
PO BOX 1892   29688   895-1410

Timmonsville, AC 803, PC 4, Florence
Florence SD 4   4-11111
112 S KERSHAW ST   29161   346-5391
Paul Vivian, supt.
HS, 605 W MARKET ST   29161   2-00011
Marion Newman, prin.   346-4046
Timmonsville Vo Ctr   Vo Tech
104 N KERSHAW ST   29161   346-4035
Shirley Martin, prin.
Johnson MS   2-01100
620 N BROCKINGTON ST   29161   346-4041
Earline McClary, prin.

Travelers Rest, AC 803, PC 5, Greenville
Greenville County SD
Supt. — See Greenville
HS, 115 WILHELM WINTER ST   29690   4-00011
Randall Dozier, prin.   834-6464
Northwest MS, 1606 GEER HWY   29690   3-00100
Lacy Wilkins, prin.   834-6434

Turbeville, AC 803, PC 3, Clarendon
Clarendon SD 3, PO BOX 270   29162   4-11111
Ed Taylor, supt.   659-2188
East Clarendon JSHS   2-00111
PO BOX 67   29162   659-2185
Dwayne Howell, prin.
East Clarendon MS   2-00100
PO BOX 65   29162   659-2187
Linda Boston, prin.

Union, AC 803, PC 6, Union
Union County SD, PO BOX 907   29379   6-11111
Harold Broome, supt.   429-1740
HS, PO BOX 907   29379   4-00011
(—), prin.   429-1750
Sims JHS, PO BOX F   29379   3-00100
Thomas Sinclair, prin.   429-1755
Other Schools – See Jonesville, Lockhart

University of South Carolina   2-CC
PO BOX 729   29379   429-8728

Varnville, AC 803, PC 4, Hampton
Hampton SD 1
Supt. — See Hampton
North District MS, PO BOX 368   29944   2-00100
Willie Coker, prin.   943-3507

Wagener, AC 803, PC 3, Aiken
Aiken County SD
Supt. — See Aiken
Wagener-Salley HS   2-00011
272 MAIN ST S   29164   564-5277
Robert Taylor, prin.
Corbett MS, PO BOX 188   29164   2-01100
Joy Shealy, prin.   564-5586

Walhalla, AC 803, PC 5, Oconee
Oconee County SD   7-11111
PO BOX 649   29691   638-4000
James Brown, supt.
HS, 151 RAZORBACK LN   29691   3-00011
John Hostetler, prin.   638-4582
MS, 177 RAZORBACK LN   29691   3-00100
Troy Hawkins, prin.   638-4575
Other Schools – See Salem, Seneca, Westminster

Walterboro, AC 803, PC 6, Colleton
Colleton County SD   6-11111
PO BOX 290   29488   549-5715
Bill Cason, supt.
HS, PO BOX 1215   29488   4-00011
Bob Pence, prin.   538-2904
Colleton Area Vo Ctr   Vo Tech
525 RECOLD RD   29488   538-5538
Gordon Chipukites, prin.
Colleton A MS   4-00100
603 COLLETON LOOP   29488   549-2690
Ken Pickney, prin.
Other Schools – See Ruffin, Smoaks

Colleton Prep Academy   2-11111
PO BOX 1426   29488   538-8959
Raymond Quarles, prin.

Ware Shoals, AC 803, PC 4, Greenwood
Greenwood SD 51   4-11111
42 SPARKS AVE   29692   456-7496
J. McAbee, supt.

JSHS, 56 S GREENWOOD AVE 29692   3-00111
Charles Stone, prin.   456-7923

Warrenville, AC 803, PC 4, Aiken
Aiken County SD
Supt. — See Aiken
Aiken County Vo S   Vo Tech
2455 JEFFERSON DAVIS HWY 29851   593-7300
Joe Dowling, prin.

West Columbia, AC 803, PC 7, Lexington
Lexington SD 1
Supt. — See Lexington
White Knoll MS   3-00110
116 WHITE KNOLL WAY 29170   957-4400
Allan Whitacre, prin.

Lexington SD 2, 715 9TH ST 29169   6-11111
Michael Woodall, supt.   796-4708
Airport HS, 1315 BOSTON AVE 29170   4-00011
Jimmy Taylor, prin.   822-5600
Fulmer MS   3-00100
1614 WALTERBORO ST 29170   822-5660
Kay Gossett, prin.
Northside MS   3-00100
1218 BATCHELOR ST 29169   739-4190
Marion Thompkins, prin.
Pine Ridge MS   2-01100
735 PINE RIDGE DR 29172   755-7400
Marilyn Ward, prin.
Other Schools – See Cayce

Grace Christian S   2-11111
416 DENHAM AVE 29169   794-8996
James Stephens, prin.

Westminster, AC 803, PC 5, Oconee
Oconee County SD
Supt. — See Walhalla
West-Oak HS, 130 WARRIOR LN 29693   3-00011
Samuel Bass, prin.   647-3065

Oakway MS   2-00100
150B SCHOOL HOUSE RD 29693   972-9531
Larry Lawhorne, prin.
MS, 501 WESTMINSTER HWY 29693   3-01100
Bryan Jenkins, prin.   647-3050

Whitmire, AC 803, PC 4, Newberry
Newberry County SD
Supt. — See Newberry
JSHS, 1402 COLEMAN AVE 29178   2-00111
Gary Manuse, prin.   694-3400

Williamston, AC 803, PC 5, Anderson
Anderson SD 1, PO BOX 99 29697   6-11111
Reginald Christopher, supt.   847-7344
Palmetto HS, PO BOX 429 29697   3-00011
Doug Atkins, prin.   847-7311
Palmetto MS, PO BOX 489 29697   3-01100
Roger Wolfe, prin.   847-4333
Other Schools – See Greenville, Piedmont

Williston, AC 803, PC 5, Barnwell
Barnwell SD 29, 410 E MAIN ST 29853   4-11111
Christopher Guerrieri, supt.   266-7031
Williston-Elko HS, 408 E MAIN ST 29853   2-00011
Steven Carter, prin.   266-3110
Williston-Elko MS, 404 E MAIN ST 29853   2-00100
Lee Davis, prin.   266-3476

Winnsboro, AC 803, PC 5, Fairfield
Fairfield County SD   5-11111
PO BOX 622 29180   635-4607
Joseph Watson, supt.
Fairfield Central HS   4-00011
RR 5 BOX 60 29180   635-1441
Ned Middleton, prin.
Fairfield Co Career Ctr   Vo Tech
RR 2 BOX 5T 29180   635-5506
Robert Sharpe, prin.
Fairfield MS, RR 5 BOX 50 29180   3-00100
William Prows, prin.   635-4270

Winn Academy   2-11111
311 OLD CHESTER RD 29180   635-5494
Carroll Taylor, prin.

Woodruff, AC 803, PC 5, Spartanburg
Spartanburg SD 4, PO BOX 669 29388   4-11111
William Howell, supt.   476-3186
SHS, PO BOX 759 29388   2-00011
Rallie Liston, prin.   476-7045
JHS, PO BOX 309 29388   3-00110
John Stankus, prin.   476-3150

Yonges Island, AC 803, PC 2, Charleston
Charleston St. Paul Constituent District   4-11111
7226 HIGHWAY 162 29449   889-2291
Carlretta Wright, supt.
Baptist Hill HS   3-00011
5117 BAPTIST HILL RD 29449   889-2276
A. Pinckney, prin.
Schroder MS   3-00100
7224 HIGHWAY 162 29449   889-2391
Theodore Coker, prin.

York, AC 803, PC 6, York
York SD 1, PO BOX 770 29745   5-11111
Ellison Smith, supt.   684-9916
York Comprehensive HS   4-00011
HWY 321 S 29745   684-2336
Robert Harrison, prin.
Johnson Vo Ctr, HWY 321 S 29745   Vo Tech
John Morrison, prin.   684-1910
JHS, 1280 JOHNSON RD 29745   3-00100
Wilbert Holmes, prin.   684-5008

Blessed Hope Baptist S   2-11111
PO BOX 609 29745   684-9819
Joyce Cook, prin.

SOUTH DAKOTA

STATE DEPARTMENT OF EDUCATION
Kneip Building
700 Governors Dr., Pierre 57501
(605) 733-3243

Secretary of Education	John Bonaiuto
Deputy Secretary	Karon Schaack
Director Educational Services	Donlynn Rice
Director Finance & Management	Dale Hegg
Director Vocational & Technical Education	Larry Zikmund

STATE BOARD OF EDUCATION
700 Governors Dr., Pierre 57501

President	Dick Turner

PUBLIC, PRIVATE AND CATHOLIC SECONDARY SCHOOLS

Aberdeen, AC 605, PC 8, Brown
Aberdeen SD 6-1, 203 3RD AVE SE 57401   5-11111
Paul Kinder, supt.   622-7188
Central SHS, 205 3RD AVE SE 57401   3-00001
Cynthia Heupel, prin.   622-7900
Holgate JHS, 2200 N DAKOTA ST 57401   2-00110
Greg Aas, prin.   622-7940
Simmons JHS, 1300 S 3RD ST 57401   3-00110
Curt Asleson, prin.   622-7944

Northern State University   4-UC
1200 S JAY ST 57401   622-2521
Presentation College   2-UC
1500 N MAIN ST 57401   225-0420
Roncalli HS, 1400 N DAKOTA ST 57401   2-00111
William O'Keefe, prin.   226-2100
St. Luke's Midland Regional Medical Ctr.   HSP
305 S STATE ST 57401   622-5230
South Dakota School Visually Handicapped   HND
423 17TH AVE SE 57401

Agar, AC 605, PC 1, Sully
Agar SD 58-1, PO BOX 40 57520   1-11111
George Levin, supt.   258-2180

HS, PO BOX 40 57520   1-00011
George Levin, prin.   258-2180

Alcester, AC 605, PC 3, Union
Alcester-Hudson SD 61-1   3-11111
PO BOX 248 57001   934-1890
Don Zingler, supt.
Alcester-Hudson HS   2-00011
PO BOX 248 57001   934-1890
Jerry Joachim, prin.
Alcester-Hudson JHS   2-01100
PO BOX 248 57001   934-1890
Jerry Joachim, prin.

Alexandria, AC 605, PC 3, Hanson
Hanson SD 30-1, PO BOX 490 57311   2-11111
Darwin Peterson, supt.   239-4387
Hanson HS, PO BOX 490 57311   2-00011
Jim Goodall, prin.   239-4387
Hanson JHS, PO BOX 490 57311   1-00100
Jim Goodall, prin.   239-4387

Alpena, AC 605, PC 2, Jerauld
Alpena SD 36-1, PO BOX 38 57312   2-11111
Wallace Weatherford, supt.   849-3258

JSHS, PO BOX 38 57312   1-00111
Wallace Weatherford, prin.   849-3258

Arlington, AC 605, PC 3, Kingsbury
Arlington SD 38-1   2-11111
PO BOX 359 57212   983-5597
Alwyn Thoreson, supt.
HS, PO BOX 359 57212   2-00011
Lowell Gilbertson, prin.   983-5598
JHS, PO BOX 359 57212   1-00100
Lowell Gilbertson, prin.   983-5598

Armour, AC 605, PC 3, Douglas
Armour SD 21-1, PO BOX 640 57313   2-11111
Richard Fuller, supt.   724-2153
HS, PO BOX 640 57313   1-00011
Brad Preheim, prin.   724-2153
MS, PO BOX 640 57313   1-01100
Crystal McGuire, prin.   724-2698

Artesian, AC 605, PC 2, Sanborn
Artesian-Letcher SD 55-1   2-11111
RR 2 BOX 88A 57314   527-2239
Dean Cook, supt.

Artesian-Letcher HS
PO BOX 7 57314 — 1-00011 527-2239
Pamela Greene, prin.
Artesian-Letcher MS — 1-00100
PO BOX 7 57314 248-2210
Connie Ebersdorfer, prin.

Avon, AC 605, PC 3, Bon Homme
Avon SD 4-1, PO BOX 407 57315 — 2-11111 286-3291
John Fathke, supt.
HS, PO BOX 407 57315 — 1-00011 286-3291
Thomas Oster, prin.
JHS, PO BOX 407 57315 — 1-00100 286-3291
Thomas Oster, prin.

Baltic, AC 605, PC 3, Minnehaha
Baltic SD 49-1, PO BOX 309 57003 — 2-11111 529-5461
John Biegler, supt.
HS, PO BOX 309 57003 — 2-00011 529-5461
Bob Sittig, prin.
JHS, PO BOX 309 57003 — 1-00100 529-5461
Bob Sittig, prin.

Barnard, AC 605, PC 1, Brown
Elm Valley SD 6-2, PO BOX 6 57426 — 2-11111 329-2355
Leighton Getty, supt.
Elm Valley HS, PO BOX 6 57426 — 1-00011 329-2145
Randy Barondeau, prin.
Elm Valley JHS, PO BOX 6 57426 — 1-00100 329-2145
Randy Barondeau, prin.

Belle Fourche, AC 605, PC 5, Butte
Belle Fourche SD 9-1 — 4-11111
1113 NATIONAL ST 57717 892-3355
Robert Luce, supt.
HS, 1301 12TH AVE 57717 — 2-00011 892-2035
Bevin Brown, prin.
Roosevelt MS — 2-00100
1113 NATIONAL ST 57717 892-2708
Jean Dahlinger, prin.

Beresford, AC 605, PC 4, Union
Beresford SD 61-2 — 3-11111
301 W MAPLE ST 57004 763-5012
C. Carnes, supt.
HS, 301 W MAPLE ST 57004 — 2-00011 763-2145
Bruce Wendling, prin.
MS, 301 W MAPLE ST 57004 — 2-00100 763-2139
Charles VonEschen, prin.

Bison, AC 605, PC 2, Perkins
Bison SD 52-1, PO BOX 9 57620 — 2-11111 244-5271
Roger Slotsve, supt.
HS, PO BOX 9 57620 — 1-00011 244-5961
Jerold Grayot, prin.
JHS, PO BOX 9 57620 — 1-00100 244-5961
Jerold Grayot, prin.

Bonesteel, AC 605, PC 2, Gregory
Bonesteel-Fairfax SD 26-5 — 2-11111
PO BOX 410 57317 654-2623
Bruce Houck, supt.
Bonesteel-Fairfax HS — 1-00011
PO BOX 97 57317 654-2314
Dennis Leonard, prin.
Bonesteel-Fairfax JHS — 1-00100
PO BOX 97 57317 654-2314
Dennis Leonard, prin.

Bowdle, AC 605, PC 3, Edmunds
Bowdle SD 22-1, PO BOX 563 57428 — 2-11111 285-6272
Richard Ulrich, supt.
HS, PO BOX 563 57428 — 1-00011 285-6590
Paul Swenson, prin.
JHS, PO BOX 563 57428 — 1-00100 285-6590
Paul Swenson, prin.

Brandon, AC 605, PC 5, Minnehaha
Brandon Valley SD 49-2 — 4-11111
301 S SPLITROCK BLVD 57005 582-6375
Carleton Holt, supt.
Brandon Valley HS — 3-00011
301 S SPLITROCK BLVD 57005 582-3211
Donald Kuchel, prin.
Brandon Valley JHS — 2-00100
301 S SPLITROCK BLVD 57005 582-3214
G. Gulson, prin.

Bridgewater, AC 605, PC 3, McCook
Bridgewater SD 43-6 — 2-11111
PO BOX 350 57319 729-2541
Steve McCormick, supt.
HS, PO BOX 350 57319 — 1-00011 729-2541
Steve Quintas, prin.
JHS, PO BOX 350 57319 — 1-00100 729-2541
Steve Quintas, prin.

Bristol, AC 605, PC 2, Day
Bristol SD 18-1, PO BOX 107 57219 — 2-11111 492-3149
Darrell Hildebrandt, supt.
HS, PO BOX 107 57219 — 1-00011 492-3661
Gerold Beck, prin.
JHS, PO BOX 107 57219 — 1-00100 492-3661
Gerold Beck, prin.

Britton, AC 605, PC 4, Marshall
Britton SD 45-1, PO BOX 190 57430 — 2-11111 448-2234
Thomas Butler, supt.
HS, PO BOX 190 57430 — 2-00011 448-2234
Donald Kirkegaard, prin.
JHS, PO BOX 190 57430 — 1-00100 448-2234
Donald Kirkegaard, prin.

Brookings, AC 605, PC 7, Brookings
Brookings SD 5-1 — 5-11111
700 22ND AVE S 57006 692-6371
Bruce Crosswait, supt.
HS, 530 ELM AVE 57006 — 3-00011 692-6181
Douglas Beste, prin.
MS, 601 4TH ST 57006 — 3-00100 692-6261
Dan Neiles, prin.

South Dakota State University — 6-UC
PO BOX 2201 57007 688-4173

Buffalo, AC 605, PC 2, Harding
Harding County SD 31-1 — 2-11111
PO BOX 367 57720 375-3241
Charles Maxon, supt.
Harding County HS — 1-00011
PO BOX 367 57720 375-3241
Donald Kraemer, prin.
Harding County JHS — 1-00100
PO BOX 367 57720 375-3241
Donald Kraemer, prin.

Burke, AC 605, PC 3, Gregory
Burke SD 26-2, PO BOX 382 57523 — 2-11111 775-2644
Jack Broome, supt.
JSHS, PO BOX 382 57523 — 2-00111 775-2645
Randy DeWolf, prin.

Canistota, AC 605, PC 3, McCook
Canistota SD 43-1, PO BOX 8 57012 — 2-11111 296-3158
Robert Wilson, supt.
HS, PO BOX 8 57012 — 1-00011 296-3458
Keith Ligtenberg, prin.
MS 57012 — 1-01100 296-3458
Donald Kom, prin.

Canton, AC 605, PC 5, Lincoln
Canton SD 41-1, 112 E ELDER ST 57013 — 3-11111 987-2706
Michael Morgan, supt.
HS, 200 E ELDER ST 57013 — 2-00011 987-2706
David Beckman, prin.
MS, 112 E ELDER ST 57013 — 2-00100 987-2706
Jerry Moen, prin.

Castlewood, AC 605, PC 3, Hamlin
Castlewood SD 28-1 — 2-11111
PO BOX 98 57223 793-2497
Jeff Taylor, supt.
HS, PO BOX 98 57223 — 1-00011 793-2351
Rodger Gross, prin.
JHS, PO BOX 98 57223 — 1-00100 793-2351
Rodger Gross, prin.

Centerville, AC 605, PC 3, Turner
Centerville SD 60-1 — 2-11111
PO BOX 100 57014 563-2291
Rick Pedersen, supt.
HS, PO BOX 100 57014 — 2-00011 563-2291
Rick Pedersen, prin.
JHS 57014 — 1-00100 563-2291
Norma Thomson, prin.

Chamberlain, AC 605, PC 4, Brule
Chamberlain SD 7-1 — 4-11111
PO BOX 119 57325 734-6867
James Kenton, supt.
HS, PO BOX 119 57325 — 2-00011 734-5404
Bruce Hart, prin.
MS, PO BOX 119 57325 — 2-00100 734-5404
Bruce Hart, prin.

Chester, AC 605, PC 2, Lake
Chester Area SD 39-1 — 2-11111
PO BOX 159 57016 489-2416
John Pederson, supt.
HS, PO BOX 159 57016 — 1-00011 489-2411
Mark Greguson, prin.
JHS, PO BOX 159 57016 — 1-00100 489-2411
Mark Greguson, prin.

Clark, AC 605, PC 4, Clark
Clark SD 12-2, PO BOX 278 57225 — 3-11111 532-3603
Roland Smit, supt.
HS, 220 N CLINTON ST 57225 — 2-00011 532-3605
Kim Janisch, prin.
JHS, 220 N CLINTON ST 57225 — 1-00100 532-3605
Kim Janisch, prin.

Clear Lake, AC 605, PC 4, Deuel
Deuel SD 19-4, PO BOX 770 57226 — 3-11111 874-2161
Roger Hansen, supt.
Deuel HS, PO BOX 770 57226 — 2-00011 874-2163
Jean Haar, prin.
JHS, PO BOX 770 57226 — 1-00100 874-2163
Jean Haar, prin.

Colman, AC 605, PC 2, Moody
Colman-Egan SD 50-5, PO BOX I 57017 — 2-11111 534-3534
Roger Fritz, supt.
Colman-Egan HS, PO BOX I 57017 — 1-00011 534-3534
Terrance Stulken, prin.
Colman-Egan JHS, PO BOX I 57017 — 1-00100 534-3534
Terrance Stulken, prin.

Colome, AC 605, PC 2, Tripp
Colome SD 59-1, PO BOX 367 57528 — 2-11111 842-0583
Faye Fossum, supt.
HS, PO BOX 367 57528 — 1-00011 842-1624
Alan Armstrong, prin.
JHS, PO BOX 367 57528 — 1-00100 842-1624
Alan Armstrong, prin.

Colton, AC 605, PC 3, Minnehaha
Tri-Valley SD 49-6 — 3-11111
PO BOX 300 57018 543-5500
Dwane Pecks, supt.
Other Schools – See Lyons

Conde, AC 605, PC 2, Spink
Conde SD 56-1, PO BOX 328 57434 — 2-11111 382-5231
Craig Kono, supt.
JSHS, PO BOX 328 57434 — 1-00111 382-5231
Craig Kono, prin.

Corsica, AC 605, PC 3, Douglas
Corsica SD 21-2, PO BOX 299 57328 — 2-11111 946-5475
Vern DeGeest, supt.
HS, PO BOX 299 57328 — 1-00011 946-5475
Scott Muckey, prin.
MS, PO BOX 299 57328 — 1-00100 946-5475
Vern Degeest, prin.

Cresbard, AC 605, PC 2, Faulk
Cresbard SD 24-1, PO BOX 168 57435 — 2-11111 324-3241
Clifford Nygaard, supt.
HS, PO BOX 128 57435 — 1-00011 324-3382
Frank Larson, prin.
JHS, PO BOX 128 57435 — 1-00100 324-3382
Frank Larson, prin.

Custer, AC 605, PC 4, Custer
Custer SD 16-1, 215 N 3RD ST 57730 — 4-11111 673-3154
Tom Martin, supt.
HS, 527 MONTGOMERY ST 57730 — 2-00011 673-4473
Dean Keith, prin.
JHS, 527 MONTGOMERY ST 57730 — 2-00100 673-4473
Larry Luitjens, prin.

Dell Rapids, AC 605, PC 4, Minnehaha
Dell Rapids SD 49-3 — 3-11111
1216 GARFIELD AVE 57022 428-5473
John Jewett, supt.
HS, 1216 GARFIELD AVE 57022 — 2-00011 428-5473
Douglas Druse, prin.
JHS, 1216 GARFIELD AVE 57022 — 2-00100 428-5473
Douglas Druse, prin.

St. Mary HS, 812 STATE AVE 57022 — 1-00011 428-5591
Richard Krenke, prin.

De Smet, AC 605, PC 4, Kingsbury
De Smet SD 38-2, PO BOX K 57231 — 2-11111 854-3070
Donovan Twite, supt.
HS, PO BOX K 57231 — 2-00011 854-3423
Larry Janish, prin.
MS, PO BOX K 57231 — 2-00100 854-3423
Larry Janish, prin.

Doland, AC 605, PC 2, Spink
Doland SD 56-2, PO BOX 385 57436 — 2-11111 635-6302
Joel Druley, supt.
HS, PO BOX 385 57436 — 1-00011 635-6302
Chris Lund, prin.
JHS, PO BOX 385 57436 — 1-00100 635-6302
Chris Lund, prin.

Dupree, AC 605, PC 2, Ziebach
Dupree SD 64-2, PO BOX 10 57623 — 2-11111 365-5138
Bruce Carrier, supt.
HS, PO BOX 10 57623 — 1-00011 365-5138
Bruce Carrier, prin.
JHS, PO BOX 10 57623 — 1-00100 365-5138
Bruce Carrier, prin.

Eagle Butte, AC 605, PC 2, Dewey
Eagle Butte SD 20-1 — 3-11111
PO BOX 260 57625 964-4911
Gerald Stapert, supt.
HS, PO BOX 260 57625 — 2-00011 964-8744
Gloria Wilkinson, prin.
JHS, PO BOX 260 57625 — 1-00100 964-7841
Jessie Mendoza, prin.

Edgemont, PC 3, Fall River
Edgemont SD 23-1 — 2-11111
PO BOX 29 57735 605-662-7254
Donald Sondergard, supt.
HS, PO BOX 29 57735 — 1-00011 605-662-7294
Douglas Roberts, prin.
MS, PO BOX 29 57735 — 1-00100 605-662-7294
Douglas Roberts, prin.

Elk Point, AC 605, PC 4, Union
Elk Point SD 61-3, PO BOX 578 57025 — 2-11111 356-2606
Veryl Conner, supt.
HS, PO BOX 578 57025 — 2-00011 356-2606
Robert Slaba, prin.
MS, PO BOX 578 57025 — 2-01100 356-2606
Don Long, prin.

Elkton, AC 605, PC 3, Brookings
Elkton SD 5-3, PO BOX 190 57026 — 2-11111 542-5361
Gordon Fuhr, supt.
HS, PO BOX 190 57026 — 2-00011 542-2541
Donald Magnus, prin.
JHS, PO BOX 190 57026 — 1-00100 542-2541
Donald Magnus, prin.

Ellsworth A F B, AC 605, PC 6, Meade
Douglas SD 51-1, 1 PATRIOT DR 57706 — 5-11111 923-1431
Joseph Schmitz, supt.
Douglas HS, 1 PATRIOT DR 57706 — 3-00011 923-1464
Michael Garnos, prin.
Douglas MS, 1 PATRIOT DR 57706 — 3-00100 923-5724
Milton Kramer, prin.

Emery, AC 605, PC 2, Hanson
Emery SD 30-2, PO BOX 265 57332   2-11111
  Dean Christensen, supt.   449-4271
HS, PO BOX 265 57332   1-00011
  Chris Schultz, prin.   449-4271
JHS, PO BOX 265 57332   1-00100
  Chris Schultz, prin.   449-4271

Estelline, AC 605, PC 3, Hamlin
Estelline SD 28-2, PO BOX F 57234   2-11111
  Errol Johnson, supt.   873-2201
HS, PO BOX F 57234   1-00011
  Dennis Riekman, prin.   873-2201

Ethan, AC 605, PC 2, Davison
Ethan SD 17-1, PO BOX 169 57334   2-11111
  Glenn Turner, supt.   227-4211
HS, PO BOX 169 57334   1-00011
  Larry Wiegandt, prin.   227-4211
MS, PO BOX 169 57334   1-00100
  Glenn Turner, supt.   227-4211

Eureka, AC 605, PC 4, McPherson
Eureka SD 44-1, PO BOX 10 57437   2-11111
  Sherlock Hirning, supt.   284-2875
HS, PO BOX 10 57437   1-00011
  David Fjeldheim, prin.   284-2521
JHS, PO BOX 10 57437   1-00100
  David Fjeldheim, prin.   284-2521

Faith, AC 605, PC 3, Meade
Faith SD 46-2, PO BOX 619 57626   2-11111
  Dennis Fernau, supt.   967-2125
HS, PO BOX 619 57626   1-00011
  Dennis Fernau, prin.   967-2125
JHS, PO BOX 619 57626   1-00100
  Wanda Petz, prin.   967-2152

Faulkton, AC 605, PC 3, Faulk
Faulkton SD 24-2, PO BOX 308 57438   2-11111
  Iro Mogen, supt.   598-6266
HS, PO BOX 308 57438   1-00011
  Brenda Kwasniewski, prin.   598-6266
JHS, PO BOX 308 57438   1-00100
  Brenda Kwasniewski, prin.   598-6266

Flandreau, AC 605, PC 4, Moody
Flandreau SD 50-3   3-11111
  600 W 1ST AVE 57028   997-3263
  Mark Froke, supt.
HS, 600 W 1ST AVE 57028   2-00011
  Gary Markuson, prin.   997-2455
MS, 600 W 1ST AVE 57028   2-01100
  Dawn Olson, prin.   997-2705

Florence, AC 605, PC 2, Codington
Florence SD 14-1, PO BOX 66 57235   2-11111
  Gary Leighton, supt.   758-2412
HS, PO BOX 66 57235   1-00011
  Gary Leighton, prin.   758-2412

Fort Pierre, AC 605, PC 4, Stanley
Stanley County SD 57-1   3-11111
  PO BOX 370 57532   223-2929
  Jerry Kleinsasser, supt.
Stanley County HS   2-00011
  PO BOX 370 57532   223-2161
  Rodney Link, prin.
Stanley County JHS   2-00100
  PO BOX 370 57532   223-2161
  Rodney Link, prin.

Freeman, AC 605, PC 4, Hutchinson
Freeman SD 33-1, PO BOX 220 57029   2-11111
  Alvin Mudder, supt.   925-4214
HS, PO BOX 220 57029   1-00011
  Donald Hotchkiss, prin.   925-4214
JHS, PO BOX 220 57029   1-00100
  Donald Hotchkiss, prin.   925-4214

Garretson, AC 605, PC 3, Minnehaha
Garretson SD 49-4, PO BOX C 57030   2-11111
  Robert Arend, supt.   594-3451
HS, PO BOX C 57030   2-00011
  James Jones, prin.   594-3452
JHS, PO BOX C 57030   1-00100
  James Jones, prin.   594-3452

Gayville, AC 605, PC 2, Yankton
Gayville-Volin SD 63-1   2-11111
  PO BOX 158 57031   267-4476
  Dale Waysman, supt.
Gayville-Volin HS   1-00011
  PO BOX 158 57031   267-4476
  Dale Waysman, prin.
Gayville-Volin JHS   1-00100
  PO BOX 158 57031   267-4476
  Dale Waysman, prin.

Geddes, AC 605, PC 2, Charles Mix
Geddes Community SD 11-2   2-11111
  PO BOX 197 57342   337-3382
  Richard Rockafellow, supt.
HS, PO BOX 197 57342   1-00011
  Richard Rockafellow, prin.   337-3382
JHS, PO BOX 197 57342   1-00100
  Richard Rockafellow, prin.   337-3382

Gettysburg, AC 605, PC 4, Potter
Gettysburg SD 53-1   2-11111
  100 E KING AVE 57442   765-2436
  Larry Nudell, supt.
HS, 100 E KING AVE 57442   2-00011
  Thomas Fairbanks, prin.   765-2436
JHS, 100 E KING AVE 57442   1-00100
  Thomas Fairbanks, prin.   765-2436

Gregory, AC 605, PC 4, Gregory
Gregory SD 26-4, PO BOX 438 57533   3-11111
  David Gellerman, supt.   835-9651
HS, PO BOX 438 57533   2-00011
  Michael Dacy, prin.   835-9672
MS, PO BOX 438 57533   2-00100
  Sharon Pederson, prin.   835-9672

Groton, AC 605, PC 4, Brown
Groton SD 6-3, PO BOX 410 57445   3-11111
  Larry Klapperich, supt.   397-2351
HS, PO BOX 410 57445   2-00011
  Larry Ball, prin.   397-8381
JHS, PO BOX 410 57445   1-00100
  Larry Ball, prin.   397-8381

Harrisburg, AC 605, PC 3, Lincoln
Harrisburg SD 41-2   3-11111
  PO BOX 187 57032   743-2567
  James Hargens, supt.
HS, PO BOX 187 57032   2-00011
  Keith Huber, prin.   743-2567
JHS, PO BOX 187 57032   2-00100
  Keith Huber, prin.   743-2567

Harrold, AC 605, PC 2, Hughes
Harrold SD 32-1, PO BOX 160 57536   2-11111
  Roland Stekl, supt.   875-3298
JSHS, PO BOX 160 57536   1-00011
  Keith Grunert, prin.   875-3298

Hartford, AC 605, PC 4, Minnehaha
West Central SD 49-7   4-11111
  PO BOX 259 57033   528-3217
  David Fischer, supt.
West Central HS, PO BOX 259 57033   2-00011
  John Schmidt, prin.   528-6237
West Central JHS, PO BOX 259 57033   2-00100
  Julie Mentele, prin.   528-3215

Hayti, AC 605, PC 2, Hamlin
Hamlin SD 28-3, PO BOX 298 57241   3-11111
  Gene Carr, supt.   783-3631
Hamlin HS, PO BOX 298 57241   2-00011
  John Campbell, prin.   783-3644
Hamlin MS, PO BOX 298 57241   2-00100
  Douglas Brusseau, prin.   628-2642

Hecla, AC 605, PC 2, Brown
Hecla-Houghton SD 6-4   2-11111
  PO BOX 185 57446   994-2280
  Dale Larson, supt.
HS, PO BOX 185 57446   1-00011
  Robert Trapp, prin.   994-2280
MS, PO BOX 185 57446   1-00100
  Dale Larson, prin.   994-2280

Henry, AC 605, PC 2, Codington
Henry SD 14-2, PO BOX 8 57243   2-11111
  Bruce Carson, supt.   532-5364
JSHS, PO BOX 8 57243   1-00111
  Leslie Dale, prin.   532-5364

Herreid, AC 605, PC 2, Campbell
Herreid SD 10-1, PO BOX 276 57632   2-11111
  Gordon Baumgartner, supt.   437-2263
HS, PO BOX 276 57632   1-00011
  Ray Wikenheiser, prin.   437-2263
JHS, PO BOX 276 57632   1-00100
  Ray Wikenheiser, prin.   437-2263

Highmore, AC 605, PC 3, Hyde
Hyde SD 34-1, PO BOX 416 57345   2-11111
  Maurice Peterson, supt.   852-2389
HS, PO BOX 416 57345   1-00011
  Brian Shanks, prin.   852-2275

Hill City, AC 605, PC 3, Pennington
Hill City SD 51-2, PO BOX 659 57745   3-11111
  Donald Emch, supt.   574-3030
HS, PO BOX 659 57745   2-00011
  Bruce Jordan, prin.   574-3030
MS, PO BOX 659 57745   2-00100
  Detlev Prautzsch, prin.   574-3020

Hitchcock, AC 605, PC 1, Beadle
Hitchcock SD 2-1, PO BOX 8 57348   2-11111
  Steven Selchert, supt.   266-2151
HS, PO BOX 8 57348   1-00011
  Frank Podraza, prin.   266-2151

Hot Springs, AC 605, PC 5, Fall River
Hot Springs SD 23-2   4-11111
  1609 UNIVERSITY AVE 57747   745-4145
  Orville Creighton, supt.
HS, 1609 UNIVERSITY AVE 57747   2-00011
  Gary Peters, prin.   745-4147
MS, 1609 UNIVERSITY AVE 57747   2-00100
  Vern Hagedorn, prin.   745-4146

Hoven, AC 605, PC 3, Potter
Hoven SD 53-2, PO BOX 128 57450   2-11111
  Sharyl Hofer, supt.   948-2252
HS, PO BOX 128 57450   1-00011
  Larry Birchem, prin.   948-2252
JHS, PO BOX 128 57450   1-00100
  Larry Birchem, prin.   948-2252

Howard, AC 605, PC 4, Miner
Howard SD 48-3, PO BOX E 57349   3-11111
  Loren Scott, supt.   772-5515
HS, PO BOX E 57349   2-00011
  Earl Nebelsick, prin.   772-5515
JHS, PO BOX E 57349   2-00100
  Earl Nebelsick, prin.   772-5515

Hurley, AC 605, PC 2, Turner
Hurley SD 60-2, PO BOX 278 57036   2-11111
  Ronald Erickson, supt.   238-5221
HS, PO BOX 278 57036   1-00011
  Ronald Erickson, prin.   238-5221
JHS, PO BOX 278 57036   1-00100
  Ronald Erickson, prin.   238-5221

Huron, AC 605, PC 7, Beadle
Huron SD 2-2, PO BOX 949 57350   5-11111
  Randall Zitterkopf, supt.   352-8461
HS, 18TH & NEVADA SW 57350   3-00011
  Frank Ochsner, prin.   352-8495
MS, 535 ILLINOIS AVE SW 57350   3-00100
  Jon Campbell, prin.   352-6742

Huron University   3-UC
  333 9TH ST SW 57350   352-8721
James Valley Christian S   2-11111
  RR 2 BOX 230 57350   352-7737
  Jim Friesen, prin.

Ipswich, AC 605, PC 3, Edmunds
Ipswich SD 22-3, PO BOX 306 57451   2-11111
  Russ Monroe, supt.   426-6561
HS, PO BOX 306 57451   2-00011
  Edwin Miller, prin.   426-6571
JHS, PO BOX 306 57451   1-00100
  Edwin Miller, prin.   426-6571

Irene, AC 605, PC 2, Turner
Irene SD 63-2, PO BOX 5 57037   2-11111
  Larry Johnke, supt.   263-3311
HS, PO BOX 5 57037   2-00011
  Alvin Wiebenga, prin.   263-3313
JHS, PO BOX 5 57037   1-00100
  Alvin Wiebenga, prin.   263-3313

Iroquois, AC 605, PC 2, Beadle
Iroquois SD 2-3, PO BOX 98 57353   2-11111
  Donald Olson, supt.   546-2210
HS, PO BOX 98 57353   1-00011
  Donald Olson, prin.   546-2426
JHS, PO BOX 98 57353   1-00100
  Donald Olson, prin.   546-2426

Isabel, AC 605, PC 2, Dewey
Isabel SD 20-2, PO BOX 134 57633   2-11111
  Charles Begeman, supt.   466-2125
JSHS, PO BOX 134 57633   1-00011
  Charles Begeman, prin.   466-2125

Jefferson, AC 605, PC 3, Union
Jefferson SD 61-6, PO BOX 309 57038   3-11111
  Robert Olson, supt.   966-5731
HS, PO BOX 309 57038   2-00011
  Chris Bernard, prin.   966-5642
McCook MS, PO BOX 309 57038   2-01100
  Harlan Halverson, prin.   232-4653

Kadoka, AC 605, PC 3, Jackson
Kadoka SD 35-1, PO BOX 99 57543   2-11111
  Joe Blando, supt.   837-2175
HS, PO BOX 99 57543   1-00011
  Gene Stone, prin.   837-2172

Kimball, AC 605, PC 3, Brule
Kimball SD 7-2, PO BOX 479 57355   2-11111
  Gene Horn, supt.   778-6232
JSHS, PO BOX 479 57355   2-00111
  Arlen Nordhagen, prin.   778-6651

Kyle, AC 605, PC 3, Shannon

Oglala Lakota Community College   3-UC
  PO BOX 490 57752   455-2321

Lake Andes, AC 605, PC 3, Charles Mix
Andes Central SD 11-1   2-11111
  PO BOX 40 57356   487-7671
  Janet Varejcka, supt.
Andes Central HS, PO BOX 40 57356   1-00011
  George McGrath, prin.   487-7671
Andes Central MS, PO BOX 40 57356   1-00100
  George McGrath, prin.   487-7671

Lake Preston, AC 605, PC 3, Kingsbury
Lake Preston SD 38-3   2-11111
  PO BOX 38 57249   847-4455
  Calvin Higgins, supt.
HS, PO BOX 38 57249   1-00011
  Paul Nelson, prin.   847-4455
JHS, PO BOX 38 57249   1-00100
  Paul Nelson, prin.   847-4455

Langford, AC 605, PC 2, Marshall
Langford SD 45-2, PO BOX 127 57454   2-11111
  L. Wattier, supt.   493-6454
HS, PO BOX 127 57454   1-00011
  Trevor Osborne, prin.   493-6454
JHS, PO BOX 127 57454   1-00100
  Trevor Osborne, prin.   493-6454

Lead, AC 605, PC 5, Lawrence
Lead-Deadwood SD 40-1   4-11111
  320 S MAIN ST 57754   584-1301
  Robert Stuerman, supt.
HS, 320 S MAIN ST 57754   2-00011
  Terry Nebelsick, prin.   584-3013
Deadwood MS, 320 S MAIN ST 57754   2-00100
  Mary Ticknor, prin.   578-3698

Lemmon, AC 605, PC 4, Perkins
Lemmon SD 52-2, 209 3RD ST W 57638   3-11111
  Rick Herbel, supt.   374-3762

HS, 209 3RD ST W 57638 — 2-00011 374-3762
Mel Maxon, prin.
JHS, 209 3RD ST W 57638 — 1-00100 374-3762
Mel Maxon, prin.

Lennox, AC 605, PC 4, Lincoln
Lennox SD 41-4, PO BOX 38 57039 — 4-11111 647-2202
Robert Mayer, supt.
HS, 208 E 5TH ST 57039 — 2-00011 647-2203
Alan Rops, prin.
Chancellor MS, 305 W 5TH AVE 57039 — 1-00100 647-2204
Verlyn Schmidt, prin.
MS, 305 W 5TH AVE 57039 — 2-00100 647-2204
Verlyn Schmidt, prin.
Tea MS, 131 POPLAR AVE N 57039 — 2-00100 368-2593
Roger DeGroot, prin.
Worthing MS, 305 W 5TH AVE 57039 — 1-00100 368-2593
Roger Degroot, prin.

Leola, AC 605, PC 3, McPherson
Leola SD 44-2, PO BOX 350 57456 — 2-11111 439-3477
Richard Ellefson, supt.
HS, PO BOX 350 57456 — 1-00011 439-3142
Marvin Maule, prin.
JHS, PO BOX 350 57456 — 1-00100 439-3142
Marvin Maule, prin.

Lyons, AC 605, PC 2, Minnehaha
Tri-Valley SD 49-6
Supt. — See Colton
Tri-Valley HS, PO BOX 8 57041 — 2-00011 446-3207
Allan Beyer, prin.
Tri-Valley MS, PO BOX 8 57041 — 2-01100 543-5500
Allan Beyer, prin.

Mc Intosh, AC 605, PC 2, Corson
McIntosh SD 15-1, PO BOX 80 57641 — 2-11111 273-4298
Terry Kraft, supt.
HS, PO BOX 80 57641 — 1-00011 273-4227
Terry Kraft, prin.
JHS, PO BOX 80 57641 — 1-00100 273-4227
Terry Kraft, prin.

Mc Laughlin, AC 605, PC 3, Corson
Mc Laughlin SD 15-2 — 2-11111 823-4484
PO BOX 880 57642
Harlan Krein, supt.
HS, PO BOX 880 57642 — 2-00011 823-4482
Tom Frankenhoff, prin.
MS, PO BOX 880 57642 — 1-00100 823-4482
Tom Frankenhoff, prin.

Madison, AC 605, PC 6, Lake
Lake Central SD 39-2 — 4-11111 256-2021
800 NE 9TH ST 57042
John Sweet, supt.
HS, 800 NE 9TH ST 57042 — 2-00011 256-3501
Dennis Germann, prin.
JHS, 210 W CENTER ST 57042 — 2-00100 256-3023
Dale Waba, prin.

Dakota State University — 3-UC 256-5112
820 N WASHINGTON AVE 57042

Marion, AC 605, PC 3, Turner
Marion SD 60-3, PO BOX 207 57043 — 2-11111 648-3615
Earl Boyum, supt.
HS, PO BOX 207 57043 — 2-00111 648-3615
John Landgaard, prin.

Martin, AC 605, PC 4, Bennett
Bennett County SD 3-1 — 3-11111 685-6697
PO BOX 580 57551
Gordon Diedtrich, supt.
Bennet County HS — 2-00011 685-6330
PO BOX 580 57551
Greg Vander Lugt, prin.
Bennett County MS — 1-00100 685-6300
PO BOX 580 57551
Greg Vander Lugt, prin.

Mellette, AC 605, PC 2, Spink
Northwestern SD 56-3 — 2-11111 887-3467
PO BOX 45 57461
Michael Steinhoff, supt.
Northwestern HS, PO BOX 45 57461 — 1-00011 887-3467
Ray Sauerwein, prin.
Northwestern MS, PO BOX 45 57461 — 1-00100 887-3467
Merle Bomesberger, prin.

Menno, AC 605, PC 3, Hutchinson
Menno SD 33-2, PO BOX 346 57045 — 2-11111 387-5161
Roger Schumacher, supt.
HS, PO BOX 346 57045 — 1-00011 387-5161
Ervin Ptak, prin.
JHS, PO BOX 346 57045 — 1-00100 387-5161
Ervin Ptak, prin.

Midland, AC 605, PC 2, Haakon
Midland SD 27-2, PO BOX 226 57552 — 2-11111 843-2561
Richard Christensen, supt.
HS, PO BOX 226 57552 — 1-00011 843-2561
Lee Ochsner, prin.
JHS, PO BOX 226 57552 — 1-00100 843-2561
Lee Ochsner, prin.

Milbank, AC 605, PC 5, Grant
Milbank SD 25-4 — 4-11111 432-5579
PO BOX 1190 57252
George Smith, supt.
HS, PO BOX 1190 57252 — 2-00011 432-5546
David Bergan, prin.
MS, PO BOX 1190 57252 — 2-00100 432-5510
Marlin Smart, prin.

Miller, AC 605, PC 4, Hand
Miller SD 29-1, PO BOX 257 57362 — 3-11111 853-2711
Tom Marso, supt.
JSHS, PO BOX 257 57362 — 2-00111 853-2385
Gerry Hunter, prin.

Sunshine Bible Academy — 2-11111 853-3071
HC 63 BOX 29 57362
Jack Jones, prin.

Mission, AC 605, PC 3, Todd
Todd County SD 66-1 — 4-11111 856-4457
PO BOX 87 57555
Richard Bordeaux, supt.
Todd County HS, PO BOX 87 57555 — 2-00011 856-2324
Wayne Johnson, prin.
Todd County MS, PO BOX 87 57555 — 1-00100 856-2341
Craig Freed, prin.

Mitchell, AC 605, PC 7, Davison
Mitchell SD 17-2 — 5-11111 995-3010
PO BOX 7760 57301
John Christiansen, supt.
HS, 900 N CAPITAL ST 57301 — 3-00011 995-3034
Robert Brooks, prin.
MS, 800 W 10TH AVE 57301 — 3-00100 995-3051
Deborah Dusseau, prin.

Dakota Wesleyan University — 3-UC 995-2600
1300 W UNIVERSITY AVE 57301
Mitchell Christian S — 2-11111 996-8861
723 E ASH AVE 57301
Marv Retzer, prin.
Mitchell Vocational-Technical School — 3-CS 996-3024
821 N CAPITAL ST 57301
St. Joseph Hospital — HSP 995-2250
5TH & FOSTER 57301

Mobridge, AC 605, PC 5, Walworth
Mobridge SD 62-3, 114 10TH ST E 57601 — 3-11111 845-7227
Clifford Moser, supt.
HS, 114 10TH ST E 57601 — 2-00011 845-3460
Michael Bezenek, prin.
MS, 114 10TH ST E 57601 — 2-00100 845-2768
Brian Liedtke, prin.

Central Indian Bible College — 2-UC 845-7801
PO BOX 550 57601

Montrose, AC 605, PC 2, McCook
Montrose SD 43-2, PO BOX 8 57048 — 2-11111 363-5025
Stephen Giedosh, supt.
HS, PO BOX 8 57048 — 1-00011 363-5025
Kenneth Greeno, prin.
JHS, PO BOX 8 57048 — 1-00100 363-5025
Kenneth Greeno, prin.

Mount Vernon, AC 605, PC 2, Davison
Mt. Vernon SD 17-3 — 2-11111 236-5237
PO BOX 46 57363
Francis Determan, supt.
HS, PO BOX 46 57363 — 1-00011 236-5237
Albert Schulz, prin.
MS, PO BOX 46 57363 — 1-01100 236-5237
Francis Determan, prin.

Murdo, AC 605, PC 3, Jones
Jones County SD 37-3 — 2-11111 669-2258
PO BOX 109 57559
Jack Cranston, supt.
Jones County HS, PO BOX 109 57559 — 1-00011 669-2258
Jerald Applebee, prin.
Jones County MS, PO BOX 109 57559 — 1-00100 669-2258
Jerald Applebee, prin.

Nemo, AC 605, PC 1, Lawrence
Bureau of Indian Affairs
Supt. — See Pierre
Black Hills Forest School — 1-11111 733-2222
PO BOX 110 57759 – (—), prin.

Newell, AC 605, PC 3, Butte
Newell SD 9-2, PO BOX 99 57760 — 3-11111 456-2393
Carl Remmers, supt.
HS, PO BOX 99 57760 — 2-00011 456-2393
Edward Wegner, prin.
Preston MS, PO BOX 99 57760 — 2-00100 456-2982
Kay Smeenk, prin.

New Underwood, AC 605, PC 3, Pennington
New Underwood SD 51-3 — 2-11111 754-6485
PO BOX 128 57761
Tim Creal, supt.
JSHS, PO BOX 128 57761 — 1-00111 754-6485
Bradley Tucker, prin.

Oelrichs, AC 605, PC 2, Fall River
Oelrichs SD 23-3, PO BOX 65 57763 — 1-11111 535-2631
Morris Bates, supt.
HS, PO BOX 65 57763 — 1-00011 535-2631
Galen Arbogast, prin.

Onida, AC 605, PC 3, Sully
Sully Buttes SD 58-2 — 2-11111 258-2619
PO BOX 2000 57564
Donald Rykhus, supt.
Sully Buttes HS, PO BOX 2000 57564 — 2-00011 258-2618
Doug Froke, prin.
Sully Buttes MS, PO BOX 2000 57564 — 1-01100 258-2617
Alvin Birkholz, prin.

Parker, AC 605, PC 3, Turner
Parker SD 60-4, PO BOX 517 57053 — 2-11111 297-3456
Darrell Salter, supt.

HS, PO BOX 517 57053 — 2-00011 297-4474
Wallace Hortness, prin.
JHS, PO BOX 517 57053 — 1-00100 297-4474
Wallace Hortness, prin.

Parkston, AC 605, PC 4, Hutchinson
Parkston SD 33-3, PO BOX D 57366 — 3-11111 928-3368
Donald Quimby, supt.
HS, PO BOX D 57366 — 2-00011 928-3368
Joseph Kollman, prin.
JHS, PO BOX D 57366 — 2-00100 928-3368
Joseph Kollman, prin.

Philip, AC 605, PC 4, Haakon
Haakon SD 27-1, PO BOX 730 57567 — 3-11111 859-2679
Ted Kunz, supt.
HS, PO BOX 730 57567 — 2-00011 859-2680
Dominic Calvetti, prin.
MS, PO BOX 730 57567 — 1-00100 859-2680
Dominic Calvetti, prin.

Pierre, AC 605, PC 7, Hughes
Bureau of Indian Affairs — 4-11111 733-3243
700 GOVERNORS DR 57501
(—), supt.
Other Schools – See Nemo

Pierre SD 32-2 — 5-11111 224-8896
302 E DAKOTA AVE 57501
Kenneth Rasmussen, supt.
Riggs SHS — 3-00001 224-5931
1010 E BROADWAY AVE 57501
Michael Stroup, prin.
JHS, 309 E CAPITOL AVE 57501 — 3-00110 224-8891
John Lakner, prin.

Pine Ridge, AC 605, PC 5, Shannon

Oglala Lakota Community College — 1-CC 867-5857
PO BOX 861 57770
Red Cloud Indian S, MISSION DR 57770 — 3-11111 867-1289
Robert Heart, prin.

Plankinton, AC 605, PC 3, Aurora
Plankinton SD 1-1 — 2-11111 942-7743
PO BOX 190 57368
Joe Schlimgen, supt.
HS, PO BOX 190 57368 — 1-00011 942-7743
Joe Schlimgen, prin.
JHS, PO BOX 190 57368 — 1-00100 942-7743
Joe Schlimgen, prin.

Platte, AC 605, PC 4, Charles Mix
Platte Community SD 11-3 — 3-11111 337-3391
PO BOX 140 57369
Tom Ludens, supt.
HS, PO BOX 140 57369 — 2-00011 337-3391
Steve Randall, prin.
MS, PO BOX 140 57369 — 1-00100 337-3391
Steve Randall, prin.

Pollock, AC 605, PC 2, Campbell
Pollock SD 10-2, PO BOX 207 57648 — 2-11111 889-2831
John Lafave, supt.
JSHS, PO BOX 207 57648 — 1-00111 889-2831
Gordan Gray, prin.

Presho, AC 605, PC 3, Lyman
Lyman SD 42-1, PO BOX 1000 57568 — 2-11111 895-2579
Chris Anderson, supt.
Lyman HS, PO BOX 1000 57568 — 2-00111 895-2662
Ivan Dixon, prin.
Lyman MS, PO BOX 1000 57568 — 2-00100 869-2213
Richard Willard, prin.

Ramona, AC 605, PC 2, Lake
Oldham-Ramona SD 39-5 — 2-11111 482-8244
PO BOX 8 57054
Dal Williams, supt.
HS, PO BOX 8 57054 — 1-00011 482-8244
Mike Cullen, prin.
JHS, PO BOX 8 57054 — 1-00100 482-8244
Mike Cullen, prin.

Rapid City, AC 605, PC 8, Pennington
Rapid City Area SD 51-4 — 7-11111 394-4031
300 6TH ST 57701
Maurice Haugland, supt.
Central HS — 4-00011 394-4023
433 MOUNT RUSHMORE RD 57701
Keith Coates, prin.
Stevens HS, 1200 44TH ST 57702 — 4-00011 394-4051
Ken Burnham, prin.
Dakota MS, 600 COLUMBUS ST 57701 — 3-00100 394-4092
Harold Brenden, prin.
North MS, 1501 N MAPLE AVE 57701 — 3-00100 394-4042
Jerry Peterson, prin.
South MS, 2 INDIANA ST 57701 — 3-00100 394-4024
Curt Voight, prin.
Southwest MS, 300 6TH ST 57701 — 3-00100 394-6792
Bill Hines, prin.
West JHS, 1003 SOO SAN DR 57702 — 3-00100 394-4033
Wesley Storm, prin.

National College — 4-UC 394-4800
321 KANSAS CITY ST 57701
Rapid City Christian S — 2-00111 341-3377
PO BOX 5657 57709
David Blackhurst, prin.
Rapid City Regional Hospital — HSP 341-7111
353 FAIRMONT BLVD 57701
St. Thomas Moore HS — 2-00011 394-5003
321 KANSAS CITY ST 57701
Shirley Boyd, prin.

South Dakota School Mines and Technology 4-UC
501 E SAINT JOSEPH ST 57701 394-2256
Western Dakota Technical Institute 3-CS
1600 SEDIVY LN 57701 394-4034

Redfield, AC 605, PC 5, Spink
Redfield SD 56-4, PO BOX 560 57469 3-11111
Bob Graham, supt. 472-2315
HS, PO BOX 560 57469 2-00011
Dave Wolf, prin. 472-0561
JHS, PO BOX 560 57469 2-00100
Tom Cameron, prin. 472-0561

Revillo, AC 605, PC 2, Grant
Grant-Deuel SD 25-3 2-11111
RR 1 BOX 9 57259 623-4241
Arlo Levisen, supt.
Grant-Deuel HS, RR 1 BOX 9 57259 1-00011
Barry Pickner, prin. 623-4246
Grant-Deuel JHS, RR 1 BOX 9 57259 1-00100
Barry Pickner, prin. 623-4246

Roscoe, AC 605, PC 2, Edmunds
Edmunds Central SD 22-5 2-11111
PO BOX 317 57471 287-4251
Lew Paulson, supt.
Edmunds Central HS 1-00011
PO BOX 8 57471 287-4251
Lew Paulson, prin.
Edmunds Central JHS 1-00100
PO BOX 8 57471 287-4251
Lew Paulson, prin.

Rosebud, AC 605, PC 4, Todd

Sinte Gleska College 2-UC
PO BOX 490 57570 747-2263

Rosholt, AC 605, PC 2, Roberts
Rosholt SD 54-4, PO BOX 106 57260 2-11111
Gene Harstad, supt. 537-4283
JSHS, PO BOX 106 57260 1-00111
Gene Harstad, prin. 537-4278

Roslyn, AC 605, PC 2, Day
Roslyn SD 18-2, PO BOX 196 57261 2-11111
Darold Rounds, supt. 486-4561
HS, PO BOX 196 57261 1-00011
Marc Frankenstein, prin. 486-4311
JHS, PO BOX 196 57261 1-00100
Marc Frankenstein, prin. 486-4311

Rutland, AC 605, PC 1, Lake
Rutland SD 39-4, PO BOX 89 57057 2-11111
Dal Williams, supt. 586-4352
HS, PO BOX 89 57057 1-00011
Allen Dvorak, prin. 586-4352
JHS, PO BOX 89 57057 1-00100
Allen Dvorak, prin. 586-4352

Salem, AC 605, PC 4, McCook
McCook Central SD 43-7 2-11111
PO BOX 310 57058 425-2264
Dallas Preheim, supt.
McCook Central HS 2-00011
PO BOX 310 57058 425-2264
Tom Ludens, prin.
McCook Central MS 1-00100
PO BOX 310 57058 425-2264
Trudie Myers, prin.

Scotland, AC 605, PC 3, Bon Homme
Scotland SD 4-3, PO BOX 327 57059 2-11111
Eugene Schneider, supt. 583-2239
HS, PO BOX 327 57059 2-00011
Mike Taplett, prin. 583-2237
JHS, PO BOX 327 57059 1-00100
Mike Taplett, prin. 583-2237

Selby, AC 605, PC 3, Walworth
Selby SD 62-5, PO BOX 324 57472 2-11111
Donald Akre, supt. 649-7818
HS, PO BOX 324 57472 1-00011
Ron Jacobson, prin. 649-7818
JHS, PO BOX 324 57472 1-00100
Ron Jacobson, prin. 649-7818

Sioux Falls, AC 605, PC 9, Minnehaha
Sioux Falls SD 49-5 7-11111
PO BOX 5051 57117 331-7920
Robert Kiner, supt.
Lincoln HS, 2900 S CLIFF AVE 57105 4-00011
Fred Stephens, prin. 331-7990
Roosevelt HS, 201 E 38TH ST 57105 4-00011
Bob Perdaems, prin. 338-8400
Washington HS 4-00011
501 N SYCAMORE AVE 57103 331-7970
Janice Nicolay, prin.
Axtell Park MS, 201 N WEST AVE 57104 3-00100
Brad Meeks, prin. 331-7647
Edison MS, 2101 S WEST AVE 57105 4-00100
Joanne Smith, prin. 331-7643
Henry MS, 2200 S 5TH AVE 57105 4-00100
Dan Griffith, prin. 331-7639
Whittier MS, 930 E 6TH ST 57103 4-00100
Diana Messick, prin. 331-7630

Augustana College 4-UC
29TH AND S SMT 57197 336-4111
Kilian Community College 2-CC
224 N PHILLIPS AVE 57102 336-1711
McKennan Hospital HSP
800 E 21ST ST 57105 339-8113

National College 3-UC
3201 S KIWANIS AVE 57105 334-5430
Nettleton Academy of Hair Design 2-CS
400 W 9TH ST 57104 336-1837
Nettleton Junior College 3-CC
100 S SPRING AVE 57104 336-1837
North American Baptist Seminary 2-UC
1525 S GRANGE AVE 57105 336-6588
O'Gorman HS 3-00011
3201 S KIWANIS AVE 57105 336-3644
Brett Bradfield, prin.
Sioux Falls Christian HS 2-00111
1000 S SYCAMORE AVE 57103 334-1422
Vernon Napel, prin.
Sioux Falls College 3-UC
1501 S PRAIRIE AVE 57105 331-6710
Sioux Valley Hospital HSP
1123 S EUCLID AVE 57105 333-6424
South Dakota School for the Deaf HND
1800 E 10TH ST 57103
Southeast Vocational-Technical Institute 3-CS
2301 N CAREER PL 57107 331-7624
Stenotype Institute 2-CS
705 W AVENUE N 57104 336-1442

Sisseton, AC 605, PC 4, Roberts
Sisseton SD 54-8, 302 MAPLE ST E 57262 4-11111
Verlin Hosmer, supt. 698-7613
HS, 302 MAPLE ST E 57262 2-00011
Murdean Olson, prin. 698-7613
Thollehauge MS, 302 MAPLE ST E 57262 2-00100
Craig Ebert, prin. 698-7613

Sisseton Wahpeton Community College 2-CC
PO BOX 689 57262 698-3966

South Shore, AC 605, PC 2, Codington
South Shore SD 14-3 2-11111
PO BOX 638 57263 756-4120
Max Nawroth, supt.
HS, PO BOX 638 57263 1-00011
Dorman Hansen, prin. 756-4120
JHS, PO BOX 638 57263 1-00100
Dorman Hansen, prin. 756-4120

Spearfish, AC 605, PC 6, Lawrence
Spearfish SD 40-2 4-11111
400 E HUDSON ST 57783 642-5711
James Anderson, supt.
HS, 1700 N 5TH ST 57783 3-00011
Joe Termes, prin. 642-2612
JHS, 400 E ILLINOIS ST 57783 3-00100
Tom Riedel, prin. 642-2748

Black Hills State University 4-UC
1200 UNIVERSITY ST 57799 642-6111

Stickney, AC 605, PC 2, Aurora
Stickney SD 1-2, PO BOX 67 57375 2-11111
Frank Odens, supt. 732-4221
HS, PO BOX 67 57375 1-00011
Robert Krietlow, prin. 732-4221

Sturgis, AC 605, PC 6, Meade
Meade SD 46-1 5-11111
1230 DOUGLAS ST 57785 347-2523
Dr. Barry Furze, supt.
Brown HS, 1230 DOUGLAS ST 57785 3-00011
Richard Deaver, prin. 347-2686
Williams MS, 1425 CEDAR ST 57785 3-01100
Lonny Harter, prin. 347-5232

Summit, AC 605, PC 2, Roberts
Summit SD 54-6, PO BOX 791 57266 2-11111
Patrick Mullen, supt. 398-6211
HS, PO BOX 791 57266 1-00011
Patrick Mullen, prin. 398-6211
JHS, PO BOX 791 57266 1-00100
Patrick Mullen, prin. 398-6211

Timber Lake, AC 605, PC 3, Dewey
Timber Lake SD 20-3 2-11111
PO BOX 1000 57656 865-3654
Frank Seiler, supt.
HS, PO BOX 1000 57656 1-00011
Loris Lindskov, prin. 865-3646
JHS, PO BOX 1000 57656 1-00100
Loris Lindskov, prin. 865-3646

Toronto, AC 605, PC 2, Deuel
Deubrook Area SD 5-6
Supt. — See White
Deubrook HS, PO BOX 399 57268 1-00011
Don Ray, prin. 629-3201

Tripp, AC 605, PC 3, Hutchinson
Tripp-Delmont SD 33-5 2-11111
PO BOX 430 57376 935-6766
G. Schnieder, supt.
Tripp-Delmont HS 1-00011
PO BOX 430 57376 935-6766
Brian Jones, prin.
Tripp-Delmont MS 1-01100
PO BOX 430 57376 935-6766
Marilyn Kepplinger, prin.

Tulare, AC 605, PC 2, Spink
Tulare SD 56-5, PO BOX 108 57476 2-11111
Barry Erickson, supt. 596-4171
JSHS, PO BOX 108 57476 1-00111
Dennis Smith, prin. 596-4172

Tyndall, AC 605, PC 4, Bon Homme
Bon Homme SD 4-2 3-11111
PO BOX 28 57066 589-3388
Larry Lickfelt, supt.
Bon Homme HS, PO BOX 28 57066 2-00011
Constance Larson, prin. 589-3387
Springfield JHS 57066 1-00100
Constance Miller, prin. 369-2282
Tabor JHS 57066 1-00100
Delight Paulson, prin. 463-2271
JHS, PO BOX 28 57066 1-00100
Constance Larsen, prin. 589-3387

Veblen, AC 605, PC 2, Marshall
Veblen SD 45-3, PO BOX 169 57270 2-11111
Herbert Samson, supt. 738-2391
HS, PO BOX 169 57270 1-00011
Charles Fredrickson, prin. 738-2391
JHS, PO BOX 169 57270 1-00100
Charles Fredrickson, prin. 738-2391

Vermillion, AC 605, PC 7, Clay
Vermillion SD 13-1 4-11111
17 PROSPECT ST 57069 624-8051
Leon Swier, supt.
HS, 1001 E MAIN ST 57069 2-00011
Al Leber, prin. 624-2627
MS, 422 PRINCETON ST 57069 3-01100
Pat Anderson, prin. 624-2093

University of South Dakota 6-UC
414 E CLARK ST 57069 677-5434

Viborg, AC 605, PC 3, Turner
Viborg SD 60-5, PO BOX 397 57070 2-11111
James Holbeck, supt. 326-5418
HS, PO BOX 397 57070 1-00011
Ray Schulte, prin. 326-5418
JHS, PO BOX 397 57070 1-00100
Ray Schulte, prin. 326-5418

Volga, AC 605, PC 4, Brookings
Sioux Valley SD 5-5 3-11111
PO BOX 278 57071 627-5657
Ronald Bennett, supt.
Sioux Valley HS, PO BOX 278 57071 2-00011
Sam Holderby, prin. 627-5657
Sioux Valley MS, PO BOX 278 57071 2-01100
Virgil Newman, prin. 627-5657

Wagner, AC 605, PC 4, Charles Mix
Wagner Community SD 11-4 3-11111
PO BOX 310 57380 384-3677
Vernal Anderson, supt.
HS, PO BOX 310 57380 2-00011
Roger Wiltz, prin. 384-5426
JHS, PO BOX 310 57380 2-00100
Roger Wiltz, prin. 384-5426

Wakonda, AC 605, PC 2, Clay
Wakonda SD 13-2 2-11111
PO BOX 268 57073 267-2644
Larry Wynia, supt.
HS, PO BOX 268 57073 1-00011
Ronald Flynn, prin. 267-2645
JHS, PO BOX 268 57073 1-00100
Ronald Flynn, prin. 267-2645

Wakpala, AC 605, PC 2, Corson
Smee SD 15-3, PO BOX B 57658 2-11111
Jerry Hills, supt. 845-3040
JSHS, PO BOX B 57658 1-00111
Jerry Hills, prin. 845-3040

Wall, AC 605, PC 3, Pennington
Wall SD 51-5, PO BOX 414 57790 2-11111
K. Poppe, supt. 279-2156
HS, PO BOX 414 57790 2-00011
Gale Patterson, prin. 279-2156

Warner, AC 605, PC 2, Brown
Warner SD 6-5, PO BOX 20 57479 2-11111
Terrance Eckstaine, supt. 225-6397
HS, PO BOX 20 57479 1-00011
Lewis Borge, prin. 225-6194
MS, PO BOX 20 57479 1-00100
Lewis Borge, prin. 225-6194

Watertown, AC 605, PC 7, Codington
Watertown SD 14-4 5-11111
PO BOX 730 57201 886-7212
Ernest Edwards, supt.
HS, PO BOX 730 57201 4-00011
Randall McCune, prin. 886-5851
JHS, PO BOX 730 57201 3-00100
Daniel Albertsen, prin. 882-1406

Lake Area Vocational-Technical Institute 3-CS
PO BOX 730 57201 886-5872

Waubay, AC 605, PC 3, Day
Waubay SD 18-3, RR 1 BOX 11 57273 2-11111
Dennis Nelson, supt. 947-4529
HS, RR 1 BOX 11 57273 1-00011
Gene Furness, prin. 947-4529
JHS, RR 1 BOX 11 57273 1-00100
Gene Furness, prin. 947-4529

Waverly, AC 605, PC 1, Codington
Waverly SD 14-5, PO BOX 81 57202 2-11111
Leroy Bergan, supt. 886-9174
HS, PO BOX 81 57202 1-00011
Leroy Bergan, prin. 886-9174
JHS, PO BOX 81 57202 1-00100
Leroy Bergan, prin. 886-9174

Webster, AC 605, PC 4, Day
Webster SD 18-4, 102 E 9TH AVE 57274 — 3-11111
  Arnold Anderson, supt. — 345-3548
HS, 102 E 9TH AVE 57274 — 2-00011
  Bruce Olson, prin. — 345-4651
MS, 102 E 9TH AVE 57274 — 2-00100
  Laura Schuster, prin. — 345-4651

Wessington, AC 605, PC 2, Beadle
Wessington SD 2-4 — 2-11111
  PO BOX 167 57381 — 458-2248
  Chris Christensen, supt.
HS, PO BOX 167 57381 — 1-00011
  Chris Christensen, prin. — 458-2248
JHS, PO BOX 167 57381 — 1-00100
  Chris Christensen, prin. — 458-2248

Wessington Springs, AC 605, PC 4, Jerauld
Wessington Springs SD 36-2 — 2-11111
  PO BOX 449 57382 — 539-9311
  James Heinert, supt.
HS, PO BOX 449 57382 — 2-00011
  Tom Long, prin. — 539-9391

White, AC 605, PC 3, Brookings
Deubrook Area SD 5-6 — 2-11111
  PO BOX 346 57276 — 629-3211
  Douglas Nelson, supt.
Deubrook JHS, PO BOX 399 57268 — 1-00100
  Don Ray, prin. — 629-3201
Other Schools – See Toronto

White Lake, AC 605, PC 2, Aurora
White Lake SD 1-3 — 2-11111
  PO BOX 246 57383 — 249-2251
  Terry Mayer, supt.

HS, PO BOX 246 57383 — 1-00011 / 249-2251
  Terry Mayer, prin.
JHS, PO BOX 246 57383 — 1-00100 / 249-2251
  Terry Mayer, prin.

White River, AC 605, PC 3, Mellette
White River SD 47-1 — 2-11111
  PO BOX 273 57579 — 259-3311
  Don Barnhart, supt.
HS, PO BOX 273 57579 — 2-00011 / 259-3311
  Michael Campbell, prin.
MS, PO BOX 273 57579 — 1-00100 / 259-3311
  Jim Calhoon, prin.

Willow Lake, AC 605, PC 2, Clark
Willow Lake SD 12-3 — 2-11111
  PO BOX 170 57278 — 625-5945
  Leland Poppen, supt.
HS, PO BOX 170 57278 — 1-00011 / 625-5924
  Darrell McFarland, prin.
JHS, PO BOX 170 57278 — 1-00100 / 625-5924
  Darrell McFarland, prin.

Wilmot, AC 605, PC 3, Roberts
Wilmot SD 54-7, PO BOX 100 57279 — 2-11111 / 938-4272
  Jerry Martinson, supt.
HS, PO BOX 100 57279 — 1-00011 / 938-4647
  Robert Tennis, prin.
JHS, PO BOX 100 57279 — 1-00100 / 938-4647
  Robert Tennis, prin.

Winner, AC 605, PC 5, Tripp
Winner SD 59-2, PO BOX 231 57580 — 4-11111 / 842-0626
  Michael Elsberry, supt.
HS, PO BOX 231 57580 — 2-00011 / 842-2427
  Donald Claeys, prin.

MS, PO BOX 231 57580 — 2-00100 / 842-0880
  David Nicholas, prin.

Wolsey, AC 605, PC 2, Beadle
Wolsey SD 2-5, PO BOX 187 57384 — 2-11111 / 883-4221
  Douglas Voss, supt.
HS, PO BOX 187 57384 — 1-00011 / 883-4221
  Duwane Decker, prin.

Woonsocket, AC 605, PC 3, Sanborn
Woonsocket SD 55-4 — 2-11111
  PO BOX 428 57385 — 796-4431
  Dan Moran, supt.
HS, PO BOX 428 57385 — 2-00011 / 796-4432
  Jens Andree, prin.
JHS, PO BOX 428 57385 — 1-00100 / 796-4432
  Jens Andree, prin.

Yankton, AC 605, PC 7, Yankton
Yankton SD 63-3, 1900 FERDIG ST 57078 — 5-11111 / 665-3998
  Joseph Gertsema, supt.
HS, 1900 FERDIG ST 57078 — 3-00011 / 665-2073
  David Bitter, prin.
JHS, 710 WALNUT ST 57078 — 3-00100 / 665-2419
  Randy Mead, prin.

Mt. Marty College — 3-UC
  1105 W 8TH ST 57078 — 668-1514
Sacred Heart Hospital — HSP
  501 SUMMIT ST 57078 — 655-9371

TENNESSEE

STATE DEPARTMENT OF EDUCATION
Gateway Plaza
710 James Robertson Parkway, Nashville 37219
(615) 741-2731

Commissioner of Education	Wayne Qualls
Deputy Commissioner	Kip Reel
Acting Assistant Commissioner Accountability	James Abernathy
Assistant Commissioner Finance & Administration	Patrick Lynnisse
Assistant Commissioner Vocational-Technical Education	Marvin Flatt
Assistant Commissioner Curriculum and Instruction	Tom Cannon
Assistant Commissioner Special Education	Joseph Fisher

STATE BOARD OF EDUCATION
710 James Robertson Parkway, Nashville 37219

Executive Director	Dr. Brent Poulton

PUBLIC, PRIVATE AND CATHOLIC SECONDARY SCHOOLS

Adamsville, AC 901, PC 4, McNairy
McNairy County SD
  Supt. — See Selmer
JSHS, PO BOX 407 38310 — 3-00111 / 632-3273
  Mark Massey, prin.

Afton, AC 615, PC 2, Greene
Greene County SD
  Supt. — See Greeneville
Chuckey-Doak HS — 3-00011
  120 CHUCKEY DOAK RD 37616 — 639-9300
  Jack Kilday, prin.

Alamo, AC 901, PC 4, Crockett
Crockett County SD — 4-11111
  RR 2 BOX 132 38001 — 696-2604
  Bill Emerson, supt.
Crockett County HS — 3-00011
  RR 2 BOX 121B 38001 — 696-4525
  Jim Wards, prin.
Crockett County MS — 3-00100
  RR 1 BOX 102 38001 — 696-5583
  Pauline Wade, prin.

Alcoa, AC 615, PC 6, Blount
Alcoa CSD, 524 FARADAY ST 37701 — 4-11111 / 984-0531
  William Symons, supt.

HS, 532 FARADAY ST 37701 — 2-00011 / 982-4631
  Odis Abbott, prin.
MS, 229 E WATT ST 37701 — 2-00100 / 982-5211
  Vaughn Belcher, prin.

Altamont, AC 615, PC 3, Grundy
Grundy County SD, PO BOX 97 37301 — 4-11111 / 692-3467
  Ronald Fults, supt.
Other Schools – See Tracy City

Antioch, AC 615, PC see Nashville
Davidson County SD
  Supt. — See Nashville
HS, 5050 BLUE HOLE RD 37013 — 4-00011 / 333-5001
  Sharon Anthony, prin.
Apollo MS, 631 RICHARDS RD 37013 — 3-00100 / 333-5025
  Charles Garrett, prin.

Ezell Harding Christian S — 4-11111
  574 BELL RD 37013
  Luther Hays, prin.

Arlington, AC 901, PC 4, Shelby
Shelby County SD
  Supt. — See Memphis

Bolton HS, 7323 BRUNSWICK RD 38002 — 4-00011 / 873-8150
  Snowden Carrothers, prin.
Shadowlawn MS — 4-00100
  4734 SHADOWLAWN RD 38002 — 373-2654
  Rob Hatton, prin.

Ashland City, AC 615, PC 5, Cheatham
Cheatham County SD — 6-11111
  102 ELIZABETH ST 37015 — 792-5664
  James Stack, supt.
Cheatham County HS, 1 CUB CIR 37015 — 4-00011 / 792-5641
  Tom Pardue, prin.
Other Schools – See Kingston Springs, Pleasant View

Athens, AC 615, PC 7, McMinn
Athens CSD, 943 CRESTWAY DR 37303 — 4-11110 / 745-2863
  Robin Pierce, supt.
JHS, 200 KEITH LN 37303 — 2-00110 / 745-1177
  Jerry Howell, prin.

McMinn County SD — 6-11111
  COURTHOUSE 37303 — 745-1612
  John Forgety, supt.
McMinn HS — 4-00011
  2215 CONGRESS PKY NW 37303 — 745-4142
  J. Burris, prin.
Other Schools – See Englewood

State Area Vocational-Technical School — 2-CS
PO BOX 848 37371 — 745-6940
Tennessee Wesleyan College — 3-UC
PO BOX 40 37371 — 745-7504

Atwood, AC 901, PC 4, Carroll
West Carroll SD
Supt. — See Trezevant
West Carroll HS — 2-00011
RR 1 BOX 179 38220 — 662-7116
Judy McGregor, prin.

Bartlett, AC 901, PC 8, Shelby
Shelby County SD
Supt. — See Memphis
HS, 5688 WOODLAWN ST 38134 — 4-00011
Tate Thomas, prin. — 373-2620
Elmore Park MS — 4-00100
6330 ALTHORNE RD 38134 — 373-2642
Marjorie Lowe, prin.

Baxter, AC 615, PC 4, Putnam
Putnam County SD
Supt. — See Cookeville
Upperman JSHS, 371 1ST AVE S 38544 — 3-00111
Frank Medley, prin. — 858-3112

Bell Buckle, AC 615, PC 2, Bedford

Webb S, PO BOX 488 37020 — 2-00111
Jon Frere, prin. — 389-9322

Benton, AC 615, PC 3, Polk
Polk County SD, PO BOX A 37307 — 5-11111
Deborah Williams, supt. — 338-4506
Polk County HS, PO BOX 188 37307 — 2-00011
Larry Cross, prin. — 338-4514
Other Schools – See Copperhill

Big Sandy, AC 901, PC 3, Benton
Benton County SD
Supt. — See Camden
S, MAIN ST 38221 — 2-11111
Jim Rushing, prin. — 593-3221

Blountville, AC 615, PC 5, Sullivan
Sullivan County SD — 7-11111
PO BOX 306 37617 — 279-2300
John O'Dell, supt.
Sullivan Central HS — 4-00011
131 SHIPLEY FERRY RD 37617 — 279-2400
David Ward, prin.
MS, 1651 STATE ROUTE 37 37617 — 2-00100
Phillip Herron, prin. — 279-2301
Holston MS — 2-00100
2348 HIGHWAY 75 37617 — 279-2311
David Burrell, prin.
Other Schools – See Bluff City, Bristol, Kingsport

Northeast State Tech Community College — 4-CC
PO BOX 246 37617 — 323-3191

Bluff City, AC 615, PC 4, Sullivan
Sullivan County SD
Supt. — See Blountville
Sullivan East HS — 4-00011
4180 WEAVER PIKE 37618 — 878-1900
Wendall Gates, prin.
MS, 715 CARTER ST 37618 — 2-00100
Keith Glover, prin. — 538-1800

Bolivar, AC 901, PC 6, Hardeman
Hardeman County SD — 5-11111
PO BOX 112 38008 — 658-5181
Billy Joe Sanders, supt.
Central SHS, JEFFERSON ST 38008 — 3-00001
Charles Brown, prin. — 658-3151
JHS, 915 PRUITT ST 38008 — 3-00110
Stephen Young, prin. — 658-3656
Other Schools – See Middleton

Bradford, AC 901, PC 4, Gibson
Bradford CSD, PO BOX 220 38316 — 3-11111
Bobby McCartney, supt. — 742-3180
S, PO BOX 70 38316 — 3-11111
Joe Denning, prin. — 742-3152

Brentwood, AC 615, PC 7, Williamson
Williamson County SD
Supt. — See Franklin
HS, 5312 MURRAY LN 37027 — 4-00011
James Parker, prin. — 373-8237
MS, 5324 MURRAY LN 37027 — 4-00100
Patricia Bissell, prin. — 373-3232

Brentwood Academy — 2-00111
219 GRANNY WHITE PIKE 37027 — 373-0611
William Brown, prin.

Bristol, AC 615, PC 7, Sullivan
Bristol CSD, 615 EDGEMONT AVE 37620 — 5-11111
James Street, supt. — 652-9451
Tennessee HS — 4-00011
1112 EDGEMONT AVE 37620 — 652-9494
Randall Jones, prin.
Vance JHS, 815 EDGEMONT AVE 37620 — 3-00100
Jim Arnold, prin. — 652-9449

Sullivan County SD
Supt. — See Blountville
Holston Valley MS — 2-00100
1717 BRISTOL CAVERNS HWY 37620 — 878-1940
Robert Seaton, prin.

Bristol University — 3-UC
PO BOX 4366 37625 — 968-1442
King College — 3-UC
1350 KING COLLEGE RD 37620 — 968-1187

Brownsville, AC 901, PC 7, Haywood
Haywood County SD — 5-11111
900 E MAIN ST 38012 — 772-9613
Tom Morris, prin.
Haywood HS, 1175 E COLLEGE ST 38012 — 4-00011
Gordon Perry, prin. — 772-1845
Haywood JHS — 3-00100
1201 HARALSON ST 38012 — 772-3265
Elvin Wells, prin.

Bruceton, AC 901, PC 4, Carroll
Hollow Rock-Bruceton SD — 3-11111
PO BOX 135 38317 — 586-7657
John Sturdivant, supt.
Central JSHS, PO BOX 135 38317 — 2-00111
Jack McGee, prin. — 586-2161

Brunswick, AC 901, PC 2, Shelby

American Technical Institute — 1-UC
8760 BAYLOR RD 38014 — 382-5857

Byrdstown, AC 615, PC 3, Pickett
Pickett County SD — 3-11111
420 WOODLAWN DR 38549 — 864-3123
Charles Mitchell, supt.
Pickett County JSHS — 2-00111
200 SKYLINE DR 38549 — 864-3422
James Dillon, prin.

Camden, AC 901, PC 5, Benton
Benton County SD — 4-11111
197 BRIARWOOD ST 38320 — 584-6111
Jerry Dinwiddie, supt.
Central HS, 75 SCHOOLS DR 38320 — 3-00011
Bill Kee, prin. — 584-7254
Benton County Vo Ctr — Vo Tech
155 SCHOOLS DR 38320 — 584-4492
Luther Wiseman, prin.
Briarwood MS, BRIARWOOD ST 38320 — 3-01100
Randall Robertson, prin. — 584-4257
Other Schools – See Big Sandy

Carthage, AC 615, PC 4, Smith
Smith County SD, PO BOX 155 37030 — 5-11111
Robert Richardson, supt. — 735-9625
Smith County JSHS — 3-00011
235 COLLEGE AVE E 37030 — 735-9219
Roger Lewis, prin.
Smith County Vo Ctr — Vo Tech
PO BOX 155 37030 — 735-1264
Wilma McDonald, prin.
Other Schools – See Gordonsville

Caryville, AC 615, PC 4, Campbell
Campbell County SD
Supt. — See Jacksboro
Stony Fork S, RR 2 BOX 238 37714 — 1-11111
Hugh Perry, prin. — 324-5500

Cedar Hill, AC 615, PC 2, Robertson
Robertson County SD
Supt. — See Springfield
Byrns S, 7025 HIGHWAY 41 N 37032 — 3-11111
John Mantooth, prin. — 696-2251

Celina, AC 615, PC 4, Clay
Clay County SD, PO BOX 469 38551 — 4-11111
Alan West, supt. — 243-3310
HS 38551 — 2-00011
Dennis Smith, prin. — 243-2340
Other Schools – See Red Boiling Springs

Centerville, AC 615, PC 5, Hickman
Hickman County SD — 5-11111
108 COLLEGE AVE 37033 — 729-3391
Dale Dunn, supt.
Hickman County HS — 3-00011
1645 HIGH SCHOOL DR 37033 — 729-2616
Bert Mathis, prin.
Hickman County MS — 3-01100
1639 BULLDOG BLVD 37033 — 729-4234
Douglas True, prin.
Other Schools – See Lyles

Chapel Hill, AC 615, PC 3, Marshall
Marshall County SD
Supt. — See Lewisburg
Forrest S, PO BOX 97 37034 — 3-11111
Dean Delk, prin. — 364-7260

Charleston, AC 615, PC 3, Bradley
Bradley County SD
Supt. — See Cleveland
S, PO BOX 435 37310 — 2-11111
Gary Davis, prin. — 336-2232

Charlotte, AC 615, PC 3, Dickson
Dickson County SD
Supt. — See Dickson
JHS, 250 HUMPHRIES ST 37036 — 2-00110
William Caldwell, prin. — 789-4138

Chattanooga, AC 615, PC 9, Hamilton
Chattanooga CSD — 7-11111
1161 W 40TH ST 37409 — 825-7200
Harry Reynolds, supt.
Brainerd HS, 1020 N MOORE RD 37411 — 3-00011
Otto Taylor, prin. — 855-2615

Howard Tech HS — 4-00011
2500 S MARKET ST 37408 — 757-4970
Lurone Jennings, prin.
Phoenix 3 HS, 1301 DALLAS RD 37405 — 3-00011
Edward Greene, prin. — 757-5000
Tyner HS, 6836 TYNER RD 37421 — 3-00011
Fred Wunderlich, prin. — 855-2635
Lookout Valley JSHS — 3-00111
350 LOOKOUT HIGH ST 37419 — 825-0111
Angelo Naplatano, prin.
Chattanooga Arts & Sciences S — 4-11111
865 E 3RD ST 37403 — 757-5495
William Kennedy, prin.
Alton Park MS, 200 E 37TH ST 37410 — 2-00100
William Kelly, prin. — 757-5138
Brainerd MS — 2-00100
4201 CHERRYTON DR 37411 — 697-1206
Ervin Mitchell, prin.
Dalewood MS — 2-00100
1300 SHALLOWFORD RD 37411 — 697-1209
Morris Chapman, prin.
East Lake MS, 3600 13TH AVE 37407 — 2-00100
Hardin Satterfield, prin. — 697-1213
Orchard Knob MS — 2-00100
500 N HIGHLAND PARK AVE 37404 — 697-1216
Amelia Allen, prin.
Phoenix 2 MS — 2-01100
1219 W MISSISSIPPI AVE 37405 — 757-5206
Edna Varner, prin.
Tyner MS, 6837 TYNER RD 37421 — 3-00100
Luther Shockley, prin. — 855-2648
Other Schools – See Hixson

Hamilton County SD — 7-11111
201 BROAD ST 37402 — 757-1781
Don Loftis, supt.
East Ridge HS, 4320 BENNETT RD 37412 — 4-00011
Edward Foster, prin. — 867-6200
Red Bank HS — 4-00011
640 MORRISON SPRINGS RD 37415 — 874-1900
Don Bishop, prin.
East Ridge MS, 4400 BENNETT RD 37412 — 3-00100
Rick Smith, prin. — 867-6214
Red Bank MS — 3-00100
3715 DAYTON BLVD 37415 — 874-1908
Thomas Sterchi, prin.
Other Schools – See Harrison, Ooltewah, Sale Creek, Signal Mountain, Soddy-Daisy

Baylor S, PO BOX 1337 37401 — 3-00111
Lawrence Davies, prin. — 267-8505
Boyd-Buchanan S — 3-11111
4626 BONNIE WAY DR 37411 — 624-9063
Mary Wood, prin.
Branell Institute — 2-CS
182 EASTGATE CENTER 37411 — 899-3060
Chattanooga Christian S — 3-11111
3354 BROAD ST 37409 — 265-6411
Don Holwerda, prin.
Chattanooga State Tech. Comm. College — 6-CC
4501 AMNICOLA HWY 37406 — 697-4401
Electronic Computer Programming Inst. — 2-CC
3805 BRAINERD RD 37411 — 624-0077
Girls Preparatory S — 3-00111
200 BARTON AVE 37405 — 634-7600
Stanley Tucker, prin.
McCallie S, 2850 MCCALLIE AVE 37404 — 3-00111
Spencer McCallie, prin. — 622-2163
Notre Dame HS — 2-00011
2701 VERMONT AVE 37404 — 624-4618
Gilbert Saenz, prin.
Tennessee Temple University — 4-UC
1815 UNION AVE 37404 — 493-4100
University of Tennessee — 6-UC
615 MCCALLIE AVE 37403 — 800-882-6627

Church Hill, AC 615, PC 5, Hawkins
Hawkins County SD
Supt. — See Rogersville
Volunteer HS, PO BOX 247 37642 — 3-00011
James Hughes, prin. — 357-3641
MS, PO BOX 38 37642 — 3-00100
William Christian, prin. — 357-3051

Clarkrange, AC 615, PC 2, Fentress
Fentress County SD
Supt. — See Jamestown
Clarkrange JSHS — 2-00111
RR 1 BOX 257 38553 — 863-3401
Joe Pennycuff, prin.

Clarksburg, AC 901, PC 2, Carroll
South Carroll SD, PO BOX 15 38324 — 2-11111
Charlotte Tucker, supt. — 986-4534
JSHS, PO BOX 15 38324 — 2-00111
Joe Wooten, prin. — 986-3165

Clarksville, AC 615, PC 8, Montgomery
Montgomery County SD — 7-11111
PO BOX 867 37041 — 648-5600
Charles Lindsey, supt.
HS, 151 RICHVIEW RD 37043 — 4-00011
(—), prin. — 648-5690
Northeast HS, 3701 TRENTON RD 37040 — 4-00011
John Hill, prin. — 648-5640
Northwest HS — 4-00011
800 LAFAYETTE RD 37042 — 648-5675
Jim Huggins, prin.
Montgomery Vo-Tech Ctr — Vo Tech
435 APPLETON DR 37042 — 648-5638
Bob Petties, prin.

Greenwood MS   3-00100
430 GREENWOOD AVE 37040   648-5650
Lynn Workman, prin.
New Providence MS   4-00100
146 CUNNINGHAM LN 37042   648-5655
Tom Barnard, prin.
Northeast MS, 3703 TRENTON RD 37040   4-00100
George Giles, prin.   648-5665
Richview MS   3-00100
2350 MEMORIAL DR 37043   648-5620
Chris Winters, prin.
Other Schools – See Cunningham

Austin Peay State University   5-UC
601 COLLEGE ST 37044   648-7011
Clarksville Academy   2-11111
710 N 2ND ST 37040   647-6311
John Miller, prin.
Draughons Junior College   2-CC
1860 WILMA RUDOLPH BLVD 37040   552-7600
Miller-Motte Business College   2-CS
1820 BUSINESS PARK DR 37040   553-0071

Cleveland, AC 615, PC 8, Bradley
Bradley County SD   6-11111
PO BOX 399 37364   476-0620
Jerry Frazier, supt.
Bradley SHS, 1000 S LEE HWY 37311   4-00001
Dale Hughes, prin.   476-0650
Bradley JHS, 2200 N OCOEE ST 37311   4-00110
Jim Barger, prin.   476-0630
Trewhitt JHS   3-00110
610 KILE LAKE RD SE 37323   478-8821
James Howard, prin.
Other Schools – See Charleston

Cleveland CSD   5-11111
4300 MOUSE CREEK RD NW 37312   472-9571
Frederick Denning, supt.
HS, 850 RAIDER DR NW 37312   4-00011
Doug Greene, prin.   478-1113
JHS, 880 RAIDER DR NW 37312   3-00100
Ashley Smith, prin.   479-9641

Church of God School of Theology   2-UC
900 WALKER ST NE 37311   478-1131
Cleveland State Community College   4-CC
PO BOX 3570 37320   472-7141
Lee College   4-UC
PO BOX 3450 37320   800-533-9930

Clifton, AC 615, PC 3, Wayne
Wayne County SD
Supt. — See Waynesboro
Hughes S, PO BOX A 38425   2-11111
Terry Hampton, prin.   676-3325

Clinton, AC 615, PC 6, Anderson
Anderson County SD   6-11111
101 S MAIN ST 37716 – J. Sailors, supt.   457-5400
Anderson County HS   3-00011
2131 ANDERSONVILLE HWY 37716   457-4716
Tom Heffern, prin.
HS, DRAGON DRIVE 37716   4-00011
Tony Hale, prin.   457-2611
Anderson County Vo Center   Vo Tech
2085 ANDERSONVILLE HWY 37716   457-4205
Larry Foster, prin.
MS, 311 W BROAD ST 37716   3-00100
Debbie Warrington, prin.   457-3451
Other Schools – See Lake City, Norris, Oliver Springs

Coalfield, AC 615, PC 2, Morgan
Morgan County SD
Supt. — See Wartburg
S, PO BOX 98 37719   3-11111
Ron Wilson, prin.   435-7332

Collegedale, AC 615, PC 6, Hamilton

Collegedale Academy   2-00011
PO BOX 628 37315   396-2124
Kermise Rowe, prin.
Southern Missionary College   4-UC
PO BOX 370 37315

Collierville, AC 901, PC 7, Shelby
Shelby County SD
Supt. — See Memphis
HS, 146 COLLEGE ST 38017   4-00011
Timothy Setterlund, prin.   853-3310
MS, 1101 N BYHALIA RD 38017   4-01100
Sherry Phillips, prin.   853-3320

Collinwood, AC 615, PC 4, Wayne
Wayne County SD
Supt. — See Waynesboro
HS, RR 1 BOX 301 38450   2-00011
Herbert Luker, prin.   724-4316
MS, RR 1 BOX 300 38450   2-01100
Bob Montgomery, prin.   724-9510

Columbia, AC 615, PC 8, Maury
Maury County SD, 501 W 8TH ST 38401   7-11111
Jerry Battles, supt.   388-8403
Columbia Central HS   4-00011
921 LION PKY 38401   381-2222
Tom Hudson, prin.
Spring Hill JSHS, 1 RAIDER LN 38401   4-00111
Roy Vick, prin.   486-2207
Whitthorne MS   4-00100
1325 HAMPSHIRE PIKE 38401   388-2558
Bernard Childress, prin.

Other Schools – See Culleoka, Hampshire, Mount Pleasant, Santa Fe

Columbia Academy   3-11111
1101 W 7TH ST 38401   388-5363
Douglas Dodge, prin.
Columbia State Community College   5-CC
PO BOX 1315 38402   388-0120

Cookeville, AC 615, PC 7, Putnam
Putnam County SD   6-11111
1400 E SPRING ST 38501   526-9777
Mark Gentry, supt.
SHS, 230 CAVALIER DR 38501   4-00001
Thomas Parker, prin.   526-9721
Putnam County Vo Ctr 38501   Vo Tech
Joe Bertram, prin.   528-5457
JHS, 242 E 10TH ST 38501   4-00110
Robert Hargis, prin.   526-4531
Other Schools – See Baxter, Monterey

Cumberland School of Technology   1-CC
1065 E 10TH ST 38501   526-3660
Tennessee Technological University   8-UC
PO BOX 5006 38505   372-3888

Copperhill, AC 615, PC 2, Polk
Polk County SD
Supt. — See Benton
Copper Basin JSHS   3-00111
RR 1 BOX 250 37317   496-3291
Dave Bigham, prin.

Cordova, AC 901, PC 2, Shelby
Shelby County SD
Supt. — See Memphis
Mt. Pisgah MS, 1444 PISGAH RD 38018   4-01100
Barbara Marshall, prin.   756-2386

Evangelical Christian S   3-00111
7600 MACON RD 38018   754-7774
William Doss, prin.
St. Benedict S   3-11111
2100 N GERMANTOWN PKY 38018   388-7320
Fr. Mickey, prin.

Cornersville, AC 615, PC 3, Marshall
Marshall County SD
Supt. — See Lewisburg
S, 323 S MAIN ST 37047   3-11111
Danny Hanson, prin.   293-2341

Corryton, AC 615, Knox
Knox County SD
Supt. — See Knoxville
Gibbs HS, 7628 TAZEWELL PIKE 37721   3-00011
Jerry Sharp, prin.   687-5221

Cosby, AC 615, PC 2, Cocke
Cocke County SD
Supt. — See Newport
S, 3320 COSBY HWY 37722   3-11111
Ron McGaha, prin.   487-5602

Covington, AC 901, PC 6, Tipton
Covington SD   4-11100
764 BERT JOHNSTON AVE 38019   476-8626
Ray Newbill, supt.
MS, 800 BERT JOHNSTON AVE 38019   2-00100
Marshall Hadley, prin.   476-4620

Tipton County SD   6-11111
PO BOX 486 38019   476-7148
Tim Fite, supt.
HS, 803 S COLLEGE ST 38019   4-00011
John Jones, prin.   476-9847
Crestview MS   3-00100
201 MARK WALKER DR 38019   476-7148
Dornetha Taylor, prin.
Other Schools – See Munford

State Area Vocational-Technical School   2-CS
PO BOX 249 38019   476-8634

Cowan, AC 615, PC 4, Franklin
Franklin County SD
Supt. — See Winchester
South JHS   3-00110
601 CUMBERLAND ST W 37318   967-7355
Dan Wilkinson, prin.

Cross Plains, AC 615, PC 4, Robertson
Robertson County SD
Supt. — See Springfield
East Robertson JSHS   3-00111
158 KILGORE TRCE 37049   654-2191
Rick Ballard, prin.

Crossville, AC 615, PC 6, Cumberland
Cumberland County SD   6-11111
W STANLEY ST 38557 – Jim Hall, supt.   484-6135
Cumberland County SHS   4-00001
918 STANLEY ST 38555   484-6194
Gary Nixon, prin.
Martin JHS, 314 S MILLER AVE 38555   3-00110
Larry McDuffee, prin.   484-7547

State Area Vocational-Technical School   2-CS
PO BOX 2959 38557   484-7502

Crump, AC 901, PC 4, Hardin

State Area Vocational-Technical School   2-CS
PO BOX 89 38327   632-3393

Culleoka, AC 615, PC 2, Maury
Maury County SD
Supt. — See Columbia
S, RR 1 BOX 128 38451   3-11111
Harry Underwood, prin.   987-2511

Cunningham, AC 615, PC 1, Montgomery
Montgomery County SD
Supt. — See Clarksville
Montgomery Central HS   3-00011
3955 HIGHWAY 48 37052   387-3201
Barbara Smith, prin.
Montgomery Central MS   3-00100
3941 HIGHWAY 48 37052   387-2575
B. Worthington, prin.

Dandridge, AC 615, PC 4, Jefferson
Jefferson County SD   6-11111
PO BOX 190 37725   397-3194
Kenneth Scott, supt.
Jefferson County HS   4-00011
115 W DUMPLIN VALLEY RD 37725   397-3182
William Taylor, prin.
Maury MS, PO BOX 336 37725   2-00100
Tom Bettis, prin.   397-3424
Other Schools – See Jefferson City

Dayton, AC 615, PC 6, Rhea
Rhea County SD   5-11111
250 W CALIFORNIA AVE 37321   775-7813
Jerry Young, supt.
Other Schools – See Evensville

Bryan College   2-UC
PO BOX 7000 37321

Decatur, AC 615, PC 4, Meigs
Meigs County SD, PO BOX 68 37322   4-11111
Robert Greene, supt.   334-5793
Meigs County HS, PO BOX 128 37322   3-00011
Donald Roberts, prin.   334-5797

Decaturville, AC 901, PC 3, Decatur
Decatur County SD   4-11111
PO BOX 369 38329   852-3781
J. Wayne Stanfill, supt.
Other Schools – See Parsons, Scotts Hill

Denmark, AC 901, PC 1, Madison
Jackson-Madison County SD
Supt. — See Jackson
West MS, RR 1 BOX 132 38391   3-00100
Larry Lewis, prin.   427-8581

Dickson, AC 615, PC 6, Dickson
Dickson County SD   6-11111
817 N CHARLOTTE ST 37055   446-7571
David Peeler, supt.
Dickson County SHS   4-00001
509 HENSLEE DR 37055   446-9003
Ralph Overton, prin.
JHS, 401 E COLLEGE ST 37055   4-00110
Reed Evans, prin.   446-2273
Other Schools – See Charlotte, White Bluff

State Area Vocational-Technical School   2-CS
740 HIGHWAY 46 S 37055   446-4710

Donelson, PC see Nashville

Tennessee School for the Blind   HND
115 STEWARTS FERRY PIKE 37214

Dover, AC 615, PC 4, Stewart
Stewart County SD   4-11111
PO BOX 433 37058   232-5176
Phillip Wallace, supt.
Stewart County HS   2-00011
PO BOX 422 37058   232-5179
Francis Carson, prin.

Dresden, AC 901, PC 4, Weakley
Weakley County SD   6-11111
ROOM 309 COURTHOUSE 38225   364-2247
Richard Barber, supt.
HS, HIGHWAY 22 38225   2-00011
Charles West, prin.   364-2949
Weakley County Vo Ctr   Vo Tech
HIGHWAY 22 38225   364-2110
Jeff Kelley, prin.
JHS, 250 S WILSON ST 38225   2-00100
Jim Dunn, prin.   364-2407
Other Schools – See Gleason, Greenfield, Martin, Palmersville, Sharon

Dunlap, AC 615, PC 5, Sequatchie
Bledsoe County SD
Supt. — See Pikeville
Sequatchie/Bledsoe Vo Tech   Vo Tech
RR 1 BOX 1976 37327   554-3293
Robert Taylor, prin.

Sequatchie County SD   4-11111
PO BOX 488 37327   949-3617
John Brown, supt.
Sequatchie County HS   2-00011
PO BOX 759 37327   949-2154
Harry Rowland, prin.
Sequatchie County MS   3-01100
PO BOX 789 37327   949-4149
Jimmy Worley, prin.

Dyer, AC 901, PC 4, Gibson
Gibson County SD, PO BOX D 38330   4-11111
Bill Carey, supt.   692-3803

Gibson County HS 3-00011
PO BOX 190 38330 692-3616
B. Booth, prin.

Dyersburg, AC 901, PC 7, Dyer
Dyer County SD 5-11111
159 EVERETT AVE 38024 285-6712
Dwight Hedge, supt.
Other Schools – See Newbern

Dyersburg CSD, PO BOX 1507 38025 5-11111
George Nerren, supt. 286-3600
HS, N HIGHWAY 51 BYPASS 38024 4-00011
Billy Taylor, prin. 286-3630
MS, 305 COLLEGE ST 38024 2-00100
Ed Eller, prin. 286-3625

Dyersburg State Community College 4-CC
PO BOX 648 38025 286-3200

Eagleville, AC 615, PC 2, Rutherford
Rutherford County SD
Supt. — See Murfreesboro
S, 500 HIGHWAY 99 37060 2-11111
James Russ, prin. 274-6336

Eidson, AC 615, PC 1, Hawkins
Hawkins County SD
Supt. — See Rogersville
Clinch S, RR 1 BOX 171 37731 2-11111
Melville Bailey, prin. 272-3110

Elizabethton, AC 615, PC 7, Carter
Carter County SD, ACADEMY ST 37643 6-11111
Ernest Rasar, supt. 543-3591
Happy Valley HS 3-00011
RR 11 BOX 3500 37643 547-4094
Bob Kerley, prin.
Unaka HS, RR 10 BOX 3075 37643 2-00011
John Fine, prin. 474-4100
Happy Valley MS 2-00100
RR 11 BOX 3400 37643 547-4070
Richard Brewster, prin.
Siam MS, RR 1 BOX 2965 37643 2-00100
Robert Linberg, prin. 547-4036
Other Schools – See Hampton, Roan Mountain

Elizabethton CSD 4-11111
804 S WATAUGA AVE 37643 542-4631
David Wetzel, supt.
HS, 907 W E ST 37643 3-00011
Ed Alexander, prin. 543-1133
Dugger JHS, 306 W E ST 37643 3-00100
Larry White, prin. 542-2312

State Area Vocational-Technical School 2-CS
PO BOX 789 37644 542-4174

Englewood, AC 615, PC 4, McMinn
McMinn County SD
Supt. — See Athens
Central HS 3-00011
145 COUNTY ROAD 46 37329 263-5541
William Quirk, prin.

Erin, AC 615, PC 4, Houston
Houston County SD 4-11111
PO BOX 209 37061 289-4148
Mark Beal, supt.
Houston County HS 2-00011
RR 2 BOX 280 37061 289-4447
Bruce Glaze, prin.

Erwin, AC 615, PC 6, Unicoi
Unicoi County SD 5-11111
600 N ELM AVE 37650 743-1600
Ronald Wilcox, supt.
Unicoi County HS 3-00011
500 UNAKA WAY ST 37650 743-1632
Ellis Murphy, prin.
Unicoi Co. MS 3-00100
600 S MOHAWK DR 37650 743-1653
Allen Rogers, prin.

Evensville, AC 615, PC 2, Rhea
Rhea County SD
Supt. — See Dayton
Rhea County HS, 405 PIERCE RD 37332 4-00011
Pat Conner, prin. 775-7812

Fairview, AC 615, PC 5, Williamson
Williamson County SD
Supt. — See Franklin
HS, 1601 FAIRVIEW BLVD E 37062 3-00011
Paul Bullard, prin. 799-2614
MS, 7200 CROW CUT RD SW 37062 3-01100
Ollie Keller, prin. 799-9720

Fayetteville, AC 615, PC 6, Lincoln
Fayetteville CSD, 110 ELK AVE S 37334 3-11110
Bill Evans, supt. 433-5542
JHS, 1800 WILSON PKY 37334 2-00110
Thomas Young, prin. 433-3158

Lincoln County SD 5-11111
208 DAVIDSON DR E 37334 433-3565
James Golden, supt.
Lincoln County SHS 4-00001
1233 HUNTSVILLE HWY 37334 433-6505
Paulette McCown, prin.
Central JHS, 900 MAIN AVE S 37334 2-00110
Sam Ezell, prin. 433-6156
Other Schools – See Flintville

Flintville, AC 615, PC 2, Lincoln
Lincoln County SD
Supt. — See Fayetteville
JHS, RR 1 BOX 273 37335 2-00110
Terrell Bain, prin. 937-8271

Franklin, AC 615, PC 7, Williamson
Franklin CSD 5-11100
507 NEW HIGHWAY 96 W 37064 794-6624
Cecil Stroud, supt.
Freedom MS 4-00100
750 NEW HIGHWAY 96 W 37064 794-0987
Gary Peevely, prin.

Williamson County SD 7-11111
1320 W MAIN ST STE 202 37064 790-5850
Rebecca Schwab, supt.
HS, 810 HILLSBORO RD 37064 4-00011
Doug Crosier, prin. 794-3736
Page HS, 6281 ARNO RD 37064 3-00011
Joe Yeager, prin. 794-6385
Grassland MS 3-00100
2390 HILLSBORO RD 37064 373-8669
Barry Watkins, prin.
Page MS, 6262 ARNO RD 37064 3-00100
Mayes Waters, prin. 791-0152
Other Schools – See Brentwood, Fairview

Battleground Academy 2-00111
1314 COLUMBIA AVE 37064 794-3501
Ronald Griffeth, prin.
O'More College of Design 2-UC
PO BOX 908 37065 794-4254

Gainesboro, AC 615, PC 4, Jackson
Jackson County SD 4-11111
205 W GIBSON AVE 38562 268-0268
John Fox, supt.
Jackson County HS 2-00011
190 BLUE DEVIL LN 38562 268-9771
Jack Meadows, prin.
Fox MS, 707 SCHOOL DR 38562 2-01100
Angelia Smith, prin. 268-9779

Gallatin, AC 615, PC 7, Sumner
Sumner County SD 7-11111
PO BOX 1199 37066 451-5200
Levonn Hubbard, supt.
HS, 700 DAN P HERRON DR 37066 4-00011
Bentley Rawdon, prin. 452-2621
MS, 695 E MAIN ST 37066 3-00100
Merrol Hyde, prin. 452-9100
Other Schools – See Hendersonville, Portland, Westmoreland, White House

Volunteer State Community College 5-CC
1360 NASHVILLE PIKE 37066 452-8600

Gatlinburg, AC 615, PC 5, McMinn
Sevier County SD
Supt. — See Sevierville
Gatlinburg-Pittman HS 3-00011
150 PROFFITT RD 37738 436-5637
Joe Zavona, prin.

Germantown, AC 901, PC 8, Shelby
Shelby County SD
Supt. — See Memphis
HS, 7653 OLD POPLAR PIKE 38138 4-00011
Ernst Chism, prin. 756-2350
Houston HS, 9755 DOGWOOD RD 38139 4-00011
John Clayton, prin. 756-2370
MS, 7925 CD SMITH RD 38138 4-01100
Russell Joy, prin. 756-2338
Houston MS, 9400 DOGWOOD RD 38139 4-00100
Mike Morrison, prin. 756-2366

Bodine S 1-11111
2432 YESTER OAKS DR 38139
Rene Lee, prin.

Gleason, AC 901, PC 4, Weakley
Weakley County SD
Supt. — See Dresden
S 3-11111
1992 STATE CHAMPIONSHIP DR 38229
Jerry Simmons, prin. 648-5351

Goodlettsville, AC 615, PC 7, Davidson
Davidson County SD
Supt. — See Nashville
MS, 300 S MAIN ST 37072 2-00100
Dennis Crowder, prin. 859-8956

Branell Institute 2-CS
786 TWO MILE PKY 37072 851-1881
Nossi College of Art 2-CC
907 TWO MILE PKY STE E6 37072 851-1088

Gordonsville, AC 615, PC 3, Smith
Smith County SD
Supt. — See Carthage
S, MAIN ST 38563 3-11111
Steve Armistead, prin. 683-8245

Gray, AC 615, PC 4, Washington
Washington County SD
Supt. — See Jonesborough
Boone HS, 1440 SUNCREST DR 37615 4-00011
Herman Tester, prin. 477-7195

Greenback, AC 615, PC 3, Loudon
Loudon County SD
Supt. — See Loudon
S, 400 CHILHOWEE AVE 37742 2-11111
Helen Cole, prin. 856-3028

Greenbrier, AC 615, PC 5, Robertson
Robertson County SD
Supt. — See Springfield
HS, PO BOX 250 37073 3-00011
P. Kavanagh, prin. 643-4526
MS, 2450 HIGHWAY 41 S 37073 3-00100
Weldon Gibbs, prin. 643-7835

Greeneville, AC 615, PC 7, Greene
Greene County SD 6-11111
910 W SUMMER ST 37743 639-4194
Alford Taylor, supt.
North Greene HS 2-00011
4675 OLD BAILEYTON RD 37743 234-1752
Rich Morrison, prin.
South Greene HS 3-00011
7469 ASHEVILLE HWY 37743 639-2700
Andrew Renner, prin.
Other Schools – See Afton, Mosheim

Greeneville CSD, PO BOX 1420 37744 5-11111
Jerry Ward, supt. 638-8138
HS, 210 TUSCULUM BLVD 37743 3-00011
Hilton Seay, prin. 638-6221
Greenville Ctr for Tech Vo Tech
RR 3 BOX 48 37743 639-0171
Jerry Renner, prin.
MS, 930 VANN RD 37743 3-00100
R. Jordon, prin. 639-7841

Tusculum College 3-UC
PO BOX 5035 37743 800-251-0256

Greenfield, AC 901, PC 4, Weakley
Weakley County SD
Supt. — See Dresden
S, 319 W MAIN ST 38230 3-11111
John Vaughan, prin. 235-3424

Halls, AC 901, PC 4, Lauderdale
Lauderdale County SD
Supt. — See Ripley
HS, 800 W TIGRETT ST 38040 2-00011
Larry Winegarden, prin. 836-9642
JHS, 800 W TIGRETT ST 38040 2-00100
Pam Sirmans, prin. 836-5579

Hampshire, AC 615, PC 2, Maury
Maury County SD
Supt. — See Columbia
S, 4235 OLD STATE RD 38461 2-11111
Ronald Hines, prin. 285-2300

Hampton, AC 615, PC 4, Carter
Carter County SD
Supt. — See Elizabethton
HS, RR 2 BOX 76 37658 2-00011
Shirley Ellis, prin. 725-5200

Harriman, AC 615, PC 6, Roane
Harriman CSD, 1001 ROANE ST 37748 4-11111
Gene Thurman, supt. 882-9242
HS, 600 GEORGIA ST 37748 2-00011
Mariam Bowman, prin. 882-1821
MS, CUMBERLAND ST 37748 2-00100
James Reeves, prin. 882-1727

Roane County SD
Supt. — See Kingston
Roane County Vo Ctr Vo Tech
RR 8 BOX 200 37748 882-0242
Thomas Smith, prin.

Roane State Community College 5-CC
276 PATTON LN 37748 354-3000
State Area Vocational-Technical School 2-CS
PO BOX 1109 37748 882-6703

Harrison, AC 615, PC 6, Hamilton
Hamilton County SD
Supt. — See Chattanooga
Central HS 4-00011
5728 HIGHWAY 58 37341 344-1447
Charles Preston, prin.
Brown MS, 5716 HIGHWAY 58 37341 3-00100
Warren Hill, prin. 344-1439

Harrogate, AC 615, PC 4, Claiborne
Claiborne County SD
Supt. — See Tazewell
Forge Ridge S, RR 2 BOX 164 37752 2-11111
Dan Redmond, prin. 869-2768
Livesay MS, PO BOX 460 37752 2-01100
Don Wilder, prin. 869-4663

Lincoln Memorial University 4-UC
PO BOX 2012 37752 869-3611
White Academy 2-00111
CUMBERLAND GAP PKY 37752 869-6295
Judith Beal, prin.

Hartsville, AC 615, PC 4, Trousdale
Trousdale County SD 4-11111
214 BROADWAY 37074 374-2193
Jim Satterfield, supt.
Trousdale County JSHS 3-00111
100 CATO ST 37074 374-2201
Toby Woodmore, prin.

State Area Vocational-Technical School 1-CS
716 MCMURRY BLVD 37074 374-2147

Henderson, AC 901, PC 5, Chester
Chester County SD — 4-11111
PO BOX 327 38340 — 989-5134
Kathy Coatney Mays, supt.
Chester County HS — 3-00011
930 E MAIN ST 38340 — 989-2261
Jim Poteete, prin.
Chester County JHS — 2-00100
HIGHWAY 100 E 38340 — 989-2447
Joann Jones, prin.

Freed-Hardeman University — 4-UC
158 E MAIN ST 38340 — 800-342-7837

Hendersonville, AC 615, PC 8, Sumner
Sumner County SD
Supt. — See Gallatin
Beech HS — 4-00011
3126 LONG HOLLOW PIKE 37075 — 824-6200
Mary Clouse, prin.
HS, 123 CHEROKEE RD 37075 — 4-00011
Paul Decker, prin. — 824-6162
Doss MS, 128 TOWNSHIP DR 37075 — 2-00100
Lonnie Newton, prin. — 824-5693
Hawkins MS — 3-00100
487 WALTON FERRY RD 37075 — 824-3456
Bernard Matta, prin.
Hunter MS — 3-00100
3140 LONG HOLLOW PIKE 37075 — 822-4720
Olivia Isenberg, prin.

Hermitage, AC 615, PC see Nashville
Davidson County SD
Supt. — See Nashville
Dupont MS, 431 TYLER DR 37076 — 3-00100
Nelda Watts, prin. — 885-8827

Hixson, AC 615, PC see Chattanooga
Chattanooga CSD
Supt. — See Chattanooga
HS, 5705 MIDDLE VALLEY RD 37343 — 4-00011
Gerald Bailey, prin. — 842-4141
MS, 5401 SCHOOL DR 37343 — 3-00100
Larry DeWeese, prin. — 870-0600

Hohenwald, AC 615, PC 5, Lewis
Lewis County SD — 4-11111
206 S COURT ST 38462 — 796-3264
Dennis Whittenburg, supt.
Lewis County HS, 818 W MAIN ST 38462 — 3-00011
William Lynch, prin. — 796-4085
Lewis County MS — 3-01100
207 S COURT ST 38462 — 796-4586
Dean Heady, prin.

State Area Vocational-Technical School — 2-CS
813 W MAIN ST 38462 — 796-5822

Humboldt, AC 901, PC 6, Gibson
Humboldt CSD — 4-11111
1421 OSBORNE ST 38343 — 784-2652
Larry Sanders, supt.
HS, 2600 VIKING DR 38343 — 3-00011
Tom Colvin, prin. — 784-2781
JHS, 1811 FERRELL ST 38343 — 2-00100
Betty Denton, prin. — 784-9514

Huntingdon, AC 901, PC 5, Carroll
Carroll County SD — 1-00001
PO BOX 510 38344 — 986-4482
Billy Crum, supt.
Carroll County Vo Ctr — Vo Tech
BUENA VISTA ROAD 38344 — 986-8908
Hershel Wilkes, prin.

Huntingdon CSD, PO BOX 648 38344 — 4-11111
Dan Truett, supt. — 986-2222
HS, 75 FAIRGROUNDS 38344 — 2-00011
Farris Lowery, prin. — 986-8223
MS, 199 BROWNING AVE 38344 — 3-01100
Lynn Twyman, prin. — 986-4544

Huntland, AC 615, PC 3, Franklin
Franklin County SD
Supt. — See Winchester
S, GORE ST 37345 — 3-11111
Morris Rogers, prin. — 469-7506

Huntsville, AC 615, PC 3, Scott
Scott County SD, PO BOX 37 37756 — 5-11111
Amon Lay, supt. — 663-2159
Scott HS, PO BOX 390 37756 — 4-00011
Gary Cross, prin. — 663-2801
MS, 220 MAIN ST 37756 — 2-01100
Frank Blakeley, prin. — 663-2192

Jacksboro, AC 615, PC 4, Campbell
Campbell County SD — 6-11111
PO BOX 445 37757 — 562-8377
Arliss Chapman, supt.
Campbell County Comprehensive HS — 4-00011
RR 3 BOX 61 37757 — 562-8308
Glen Morton, prin.
MS, PO BOX 438 37757 — 2-00100
Linda Agee, prin. — 562-3773
Other Schools – See Caryville, Jellico, La Follette

State Area Vocational-Technical School — 2-CS
PO BOX 419 37757 — 562-8648

Jackson, AC 901, PC 8, Madison
Jackson-Madison County SD — 7-11111
310 N PARKWAY 38305 — 664-2500
Buddy McMillin, supt.

Jackson Central-Merry HS — 4-00011
200 ALLEN AVE 38301 — 424-2200
O'Neal Henley, prin.
North Side HS — 4-00011
3070 N HIGHLAND AVE 38305 — 668-7866
Clarence Boone, prin.
South Side HS — 3-00011
44 HARTS BRIDGE RD 38301 — 427-4416
Raybon Moore, prin.
MS, 666 LEXINGTON ST 38301 — 3-00100
Willie Jones, prin. — 427-1236
Northeast MS — 3-00100
2665 CHRISTMASVILLE RD 38305 — 988-5413
John Werthing, prin.
North Parkway MS — 3-00100
1341 N PARKWAY 38305 — 427-3384
George Freeman, prin.
Tigrett MS, 716 WESTWOOD AVE 38301 — 3-00100
Maxine Stewart, prin. — 422-2342
Other Schools – See Denmark

Jackson Christian S — 3-1111
832 COUNTRY CLUB LN 38305
Ronnie Sewell, prin.
Jackson State Community College — 5-CC
PO BOX 2467 38302 — 424-3520
Lambuth College — 3-UC
705 LAMBUTH BLVD 38301 — 800-526-2884
Lane College — 3-UC
545 LANE AVE 38301 — 426-7500
State Area Vocational-Technical School — 2-CS
MCKELLER-SIPES FIELD 38301 — 424-0691
Union University — 4-UC
2447 US HIGHWAY 45 BYP 38305 — 668-1818
University S — 3-1111
1981 HOLLYWOOD DR 38305 — 664-0812
James Vaught, prin.
West Tennessee Business College — 3-CS
PO BOX 1668 38302 — 668-7240

Jamestown, AC 615, PC 4, Fentress
Fentress County SD — 4-11111
PO BOX 963 38556 — 879-9218
Martha Wiley, supt.
Other Schools – See Clarkrange

Jasper, AC 615, PC 5, Marion
Marion County SD — 5-11111
908 RIDLEY AVE 37347 — 942-3434
Paul Turney, supt.
Marion County HS — 3-00011
814 RIDLEY AVE 37347 — 942-5161
Bill Baxter, prin.
MS, 601 ELM AVE 37347 — 3-01100
Jerry McNabb, prin. — 942-6251
Other Schools – See South Pittsburg, Whitwell

Jefferson City, AC 615, PC 6, Jefferson
Jefferson County SD
Supt. — See Dandridge
Jefferson HS — 3-00100
361 W BROADWAY BLVD 37760 — 475-6133
Mike McClane, prin.

Carson-Newman College — 4-UC
PO BOX 70552 37760 — 471-3223

Jellico, AC 615, PC 4, Campbell
Campbell County SD
Supt. — See Jacksboro
HS, RR 1 BOX 134 37762 — 2-00011
John Clifton, prin. — 784-9455

Joelton, AC 615, PC see Nashville
Davidson County SD
Supt. — See Nashville
MS — 2-00100
3500 OLD CLARKSVILLE PIKE 37080 — 876-5100
Ronald Harris, prin.

Johnson City, AC 615, PC 8, Washington
Johnson City CSD — 6-11111
PO BOX 1517 37605 — 434-5200
R. Mike Simmons, supt.
Science Hill HS — 4-00011
1509 JOHN EXUM PKY 37604 — 461-1684
Jim Heaton, prin.
Liberty Bell MS — 4-00100
LIBERTY BELL BLVD 37601 — 461-1620
Beverly Campbell, prin.

Washington County SD
Supt. — See Jonesborough
University S, PO BOX 70632 37614 — 3-11111
Sam Humphreys, prin. — 929-4333
Boones Creek MS — 2-01100
4352 KINGSPORT HWY 37615 — 282-6421
Virginia Clark, prin.

East Tennessee State University — 7-UC
PO BOX 70731 37614 — 800-462-3878
Emmanuel School of Religion — 2-UC
1 WALKER DR 37601 — 926-1186

Jonesborough, AC 615, PC 5, Washington
Washington County SD — 6-11111
405 W COLLEGE ST 37659 — 753-2131
Grant Rowland, supt.
Crockett HS — 4-00011
684 OLD STATE ROUTE 34 37659 — 753-4683
Max Williams, prin.
MS, 308 FOREST DR 37659 — 3-01100
Henry Marable, prin. — 753-4681
Other Schools – See Gray, Johnson City

Kingsport, AC 615, PC 8, Sullivan
Kingsport CSD, 1701 E CENTER ST 37664 — 6-11111
George Norris, supt. — 378-2100
Dobyns-Bennett HS — 4-00011
1800 LEGION DR 37664 — 378-8400
Toni Eubank, prin.
Robinson MS, 1515 JESSEE ST 37664 — 3-00100
Richard Everroad, prin. — 378-8515
Sevier MS, 1200 WATEREE ST 37660 — 3-00100
Carolyn McPherson, prin. — 378-8550

Sullivan County SD
Supt. — See Blountville
Sullivan North HS — 3-00011
2533 N JOHN B DENNIS HWY 37660 — 288-1400
Walter Vanhuss, prin.
Sullivan South HS — 4-00011
1236 MORELAND DR 37664 — 239-1300
John Dixon, prin.
Colonial Heights MS — 3-00100
415 LEBANON RD 37663 — 239-1362
Norman Tunnell, prin.
Ketron MS — 2-00100
3301 BLOOMINGDALE PIKE 37660 — 288-1450
Clyde Groseclose, prin.
Lynn View MS, 257 WALKER ST 37665 — 2-00100
Dennis Houser, prin. — 224-1210
Sullivan MS, 4154 S WILCOX DR 37660 — 2-00100
Tom Kerney, prin. — 349-2600

Holston Valley Hospital & Medical Center — HSP
W RAVINE ROAD 37660 — 246-3322

Kingston, AC 615, PC 5, Roane
Roane County SD, 105 BLUFF ST 37763 — 6-11111
Jess Plemons, supt. — 376-5592
Midway HS, RR 1 BOX 302 37763 — 2-00011
Houston Raby, prin. — 376-5645
Roane County HS — 3-00011
540 W CUMBERLAND ST 37763 — 376-6534
Jody McLoud, prin.
Cherokee MS — 3-00100
200 PAINT ROCK FERRY RD 37763 — 376-9281
Roger Eichelberger, prin.
Other Schools – See Harriman, Oliver Springs, Rockwood

Kingston Springs, AC 615, PC 4, Cheatham
Cheatham County SD
Supt. — See Ashland City
Harpeth JSHS — 3-00111
170 HARPETH VIEW TRL 37082 — 952-2811
Gary Hines, prin.

Knoxville, AC 615, PC 9, Knox
Knox County SD — 8-11111
PO BOX 2188 37901 — 594-1800
Allen Morgan, supt.
Austin-East HS — 3-00011
2800 MRTN LTHER KING JR AVE 37914 — 594-3792
Henrietta Grant, prin.
Bearden HS — 4-00011
8352 KINGSTON PIKE 37919 — 539-7800
Alvin Scott, prin.
Central HS — 4-00011
5321 JACKSBORO PIKE 37918 — 689-1400
Patricia Mashburn, prin.
Farragut HS — 4-00011
11237 KINGSTON PIKE 37922 — 966-9775
Edwin Hedgepeth, prin.
Fulton HS — 3-00011
2509 N BROADWAY ST 37917 — 594-1240
Ed Cloud, prin.
Halls HS, 4321 EMORY RD NE 37938 — 4-00011
David Sexton, prin. — 922-7757
Karns HS — 4-00011
2710 BYINGTON SOLWAY RD 37931 — 690-0821
Tom Everette, prin.
Doyle HS — 4-00011
2020 TIPTON STATION RD 37920 — 577-4475
Sandra Quillin, prin.
West HS — 4-00011
3326 SUTHERLAND AVE 37919 — 594-4477
Jim McClain, prin.
Byington-Solway Vo Ctr — Vo Tech
2700 BYINGTON SOLWAY RD 37931 — 693-3511
H. Jenkins, prin.
North Knox Vo Ctr — Vo Tech
7411 LEDGERWOOD RD 37938 — 922-7576
David Sexton, prin.
Bearden MS, 1000 FRANCIS RD 37909 — 4-00100
Mary Kanipe, prin. — 539-7839
Cedar Bluff MS — 3-00100
707 N CEDAR BLUFF RD 37923 — 539-7891
George Perry, prin.
Farragut MS, 200 W END AVE 37922 — 4-00100
Don Rhodes, prin. — 966-9756
Gresham MS, 500 GRESHAM RD 37918 — 3-00100
Paul Williams, prin. — 689-1430
Halls MS, 4317 EMORY RD NE 37938 — 4-00100
James Ivey, prin. — 922-7494
Holston MS — 3-00100
600 CHILHOWEE DR NE 37924 — 594-1300
Bob Gratz, prin.
Karns MS — 3-00100
2925 GRAY HENDRIX RD 37931 — 539-7732
Ron Thomas, prin.
Northwest MS — 3-00100
5301 PLEASANT RIDGE RD 37912 — 594-1345
Howard Rash, prin.
Doyle MS, 3900 DECATUR RD 37920 — 4-00100
Gary Mahoney, prin. — 579-2133

Vine MS, 1401 E VINE AVE 37915 2-00100
William Anderson, prin. 594-4461
Whittle Springs MS 3-00100
2700 WHITE OAK LN 37917 594-4474
Charles Branam, prin.
Other Schools – See Corryton, Powell, Strawberry Plains

Christian Academy Knoxville 3-11111
9426 DUTCHTOWN RD 37923
Steven Degeorge, prin.
Cooper Institute 2-CC
724 N 5TH AVE 37917 637-3573
Fort Sanders School of Nursing 1-HSP
1915 WHITE AVE 37916
ITT Technical Institute 2-CC
1637 DWNTWN WST BLVD STE 22 37919 691-8111
Johnson Bible College 3-UC
7900 JOHNSON DR 37998 573-4517
Knoxville Business College 2-CC
720 N 5TH AVE 37917 524-3043
Knoxville Catholic HS 2-00011
1610 E MAGNOLIA AVE 37917 525-0262
Fr. Garrity, prin.
Knoxville College 4-UC
901 COLLEGE ST 37921 800-627-3491
Knoxville Job Corps Center 2-CS
621 DALE AVE 37921
Pellissippi State Technical Comm. Coll. 6-CC
PO BOX 22990 37933 800-548-6925
Rice College 2-CS
1515 E MAGNOLIA AVE 37917 637-9899
State Area Vocational-Technical School 2-CS
1100 LIBERTY ST 37919 546-5567
Tennessee Institute of Electronics 2-CC
3203 TAZEWELL PIKE 37918 688-9422
Tennessee School for the Deaf HND
2725 ISLAND HOME BLVD 37920
University of Tennessee 7-UC
527 ANDY HOLT TOWER 37996 974-1000
University of Tennessee Medical Center 2-CS
600 HENLEY ST STE 100 37902 544-6404
Webb School of Knoxville 3-01111
RR 21 37923 693-0011
William Pfeifer, prin.

Lafayette, AC 615, PC 5, Macon
Macon County SD 5-11111
501 COLLEGE ST 37083 666-2125
Jimmy Wheeley, supt.
Macon County HS 3-00011
PO BOX 338 37083 666-4320
Carolyn O'Neal, prin.
Macon Co. JHS, 401 MEADOR DR 37083 2-00100
Harry Matthews, prin. 666-7545
Other Schools – See Red Boiling Springs

La Follette, AC 615, PC 6, Campbell
Campbell County SD
Supt. — See Jacksboro
MS, 1116 MIDDLESBORO HWY 37766 3-00100
Clayton Ray, prin. 562-8448

Lake City, AC 615, PC 4, Anderson
Anderson County SD
Supt. — See Clinton
MS, RR 1 BOX 208 37769 2-00100
Jim Stewart, prin. 426-2609

La Vergne, AC 615, PC 6, Rutherford
Rutherford County SD
Supt. — See Murfreesboro
HS, PO BOX 766 37086 4-00011
Carl Buckner, prin. 793-3515
Waldron MS, PO BOX 400 37086 3-01100
Mike Swanson, prin. 793-7738

Lawrenceburg, AC 615, PC 7, Lawrence
Lawrence County SD 6-11111
410 W GAINES ST 38464 762-3581
Larry Morrow, supt.
Lawrence County HS 4-00011
1800 SPRINGER RD 38464 762-9412
Mickey Dunn, prin.
Lawrence County Vo Ctr Vo Tech
1906 SPRINGER RD 38464 762-6472
Mickey Dunn, prin.
Coffman MS 2-00100
111 LAFAYETTE AVE 38464 762-6395
Sid James, prin.
Other Schools – See Loretto, Summertown

Lebanon, AC 615, PC 7, Wilson
Lebanon CSD 4-11100
701 COLES FERRY PIKE 37087 449-6060
Andy Brummet, supt.
Baird MS, 509 COLES FERRY PIKE 37087 3-00100
Mark Willoughby, prin. 444-2190

Wilson County SD 7-11111
415 E MARKET ST 37087 444-3282
Karl Puryear, supt.
HS, 415 HARDING DR 37087 4-00011
Steve Maloan, prin. 444-9610
Wilson County Vo Ctr Vo Tech
418 HARDING DR 37087 444-1104
Clifton Tribble, prin.
Other Schools – See Mount Juliet, Watertown

Alliance Tractor Trailer Training Center CS
PO BOX 950 37088 449-6363
Cumberland University 3-UC
220 S GREENWOOD ST 37087 444-2562
Friendship Christian S 2-11111
PO BOX 727 37088 449-1573
Pat Hackney, prin.

Lenoir City, AC 615, PC 6, Loudon
Lenoir City CSD 4-11111
2145 HARRISON AVE 37771 986-8058
Patricia Smith, supt.
HS, 1485 OLD HIGHWAY 95 37771 3-00011
Jack Henderson, prin. 986-2072
MS, 2141 HARRISON AVE 37771 2-00100
Jerry Burnett, prin. 986-2038

Loudon County SD
Supt. — See Loudon
Chestnut Ridge Learning Center Vo Tech
4386 HARRISON RD 37771 986-2036
Sam Davis, prin.
North MS 2-00100
421 HICKORY CREEK RD 37771 986-9944
Charles Kinstiver, prin.

Lewisburg, AC 615, PC 6, Marshall
Marshall County SD 5-11111
700 JONES CIR 37091 359-1581
Fred Shelton, supt.
Marshall County HS 3-00011
500 TIGER BLVD 37091 359-1549
Bob Cagle, prin.
Connelly MS, 330 5TH AVE N 37091 3-00100
Hugh Adams, prin. 359-1265
Other Schools – See Chapel Hill, Cornersville

Lexington, AC 901, PC 6, Henderson
Henderson County SD 5-11111
PO BOX 190 38351 968-3661
Jerry Graves, supt.
HS, 284 WHITE ST 38351 4-00011
Steve Wilkerson, prin. 968-2961
Henderson County Vo HS Vo Tech
S BROAD 38351 – Celia Barrow, prin. 968-5233
Other Schools – See Scotts Hill

Linden, AC 615, PC 4, Perry
Perry County SD, RR 10 BOX 3B 37096 4-11111
David Rhodes, supt. 589-2102
Perry County HS, RR 10 BOX 4 37096 2-00011
R. Morris, prin. 589-2831

Livingston, AC 615, PC 5, Overton
Overton County SD 5-11111
112 BUSSELL ST 38570 823-1287
Edwin Garrett, supt.
Livingston Academy HS 38570 3-00011
Thomas Brown, prin. 823-5911
MS, 312 BILBREY ST 38570 2-01100
Michael Garrett, prin. 823-5917

State Area Vocational-Technical School 2-CS
PO BOX 219 38570 823-5525

Loretto, AC 615, PC 4, Lawrence
Lawrence County SD
Supt. — See Lawrenceburg
HS, 525 2ND AVE S 38469 2-00011
David Daniel, prin. 853-4324

Loudon, AC 615, PC 5, Loudon
Loudon County SD, 100 RIVER RD 37774 5-11111
A. Edward Headlee, supt. 458-5411
HS, 1039 MULBERRY ST 37774 3-00011
William Hauhee, prin. 458-4326
Ft. Loudon MS, 1703 ROBERTS RD 37774 2-00100
Phillip Bettis, prin. 458-2026
Other Schools – See Greenback, Lenoir City

Lyles, AC 615, PC 2, Hickman
Hickman County SD
Supt. — See Centerville
East MS, RR 1 37098 2-01100
Michael Wright, prin. 670-4183

Lynchburg, AC 615, PC 5, Moore
Moore County SD, PO BOX 219 37352 3-11111
Wayne Stewart, supt. 759-7303
Moore County JSHS 2-00111
HIGHWAY 55 37352 759-4231
Phillip Farrar, prin.

Lynnville, AC 615, PC 2, Giles
Giles County SD
Supt. — See Pulaski
Richland HS, RR 1 BOX 215 38472 2-00011
Wayne Hobbs, prin. 527-3577

Madison, AC 615, PC see Nashville
Davidson County SD
Supt. — See Nashville
Neelys Bend MS 2-00100
1251 NEELYS BEND RD 37115 860-1477
Marshall Foster, prin.

Goodpasture S 4-11111
619 W DUE WEST AVE 37115 868-3700
John McCarley, prin.
Madison Academy 2-00011
PO BOX 6257 37116 865-4055
Jack Stiles, prin.
Nashville College 2-CS
1160 GALLATIN RD S 37115 868-2963

Madisonville, AC 615, PC 5, Monroe
Monroe County SD 6-11111
103 COLLEGE ST 37354 442-2373
Bob Lovingood, supt.
HS, RR 3 37354 3-00011
Don Jenkins, prin. 442-2383
Monroe County Vo Ctr, RR 3 37354 Vo Tech
Joe Helms, prin. 442-3297
MS, 538 MONROE ST 37354 3-01100
Gus Davis, prin. 442-4137
Other Schools – See Sweetwater, Tellico Plains, Vonore

Hiwassee College 3-CC
HIWASSEE RD 37354 442-3283

Manchester, AC 615, PC 6, Coffee
Coffee County SD 5-11111
300 HILLSBORO BLVD 37355 723-5150
Bobby Cummins, supt.
Coffee County Central HS 4-00011
2001 MCARTHUR ST 37355 723-5159
Nelson Johnson, prin.
Coffee County MS 3-00100
MCMINNVILLE HIGHWAY 37355 723-5177
Melvin Duke, prin.

Manchester CSD, 215 E FORT ST 37355 4-11110
Keith Brewer, supt. 728-2316
Westwood JHS 2-00110
505 W TAYLOR ST 37355 728-2071
Pat Barton, prin.

Martin, AC 901, PC 6, Weakley
Weakley County SD
Supt. — See Dresden
Westview HS, RR 1 BOX 151 38237 3-00011
David Heath, prin. 587-4202
JHS, 670 N MCCOMB ST 38237 2-00100
Nate Holmes, prin. 587-2346

University of Tennessee 38238 5-UC
587-7020

Maryville, AC 615, PC 7, Blount
Blount County SD 6-11111
831 E GRANDVIEW DR 37801 984-1212
John Davis, supt.
Blount HS 4-00011
229 COUNTY FARM RD 37801 984-5500
James French, prin.
Heritage HS 4-00011
3741 E LAMAR ALEXANDER PKY 37801
Ben Dalton, prin. 984-8110
Other Schools – See Walland

Maryville CSD 5-11111
833 LAWRENCE AVE 37801 982-7122
Mike Dalton, supt.
HS, 825 LAWRENCE AVE 37801 4-00011
David Messer, prin. 982-1132
MS 3-00100
805 MONTVALE STATION RD 37801 983-2070
Joel Giffin, prin.

Maryville College 3-UC
800 COURT ST 37801 800-456-8150

Maynardville, AC 615, PC 4, Union
Union County SD 5-11111
OLD HIGHWAY 33 BOX 10 37807 992-5466
David Coppock, supt.
Maynard JSHS 3-00111
OLD HIGHWAY 33 BOX C 37807 992-5232
Robert Lloyds, prin.

Mc Ewen, AC 615, PC 4, Humphreys
Humphreys County SD
Supt. — See Waverly
S 37101 3-11111
Glen Shivers, prin. 582-6913

Mc Kenzie, AC 901, PC 6, Carroll
Mc Kenzie CSD, 203 W BELL AVE 38201 4-11111
Joe Williams, supt. 352-2246
HS, 120 W WOODROW AVE 38201 2-00011
Dewey Chism, prin. 352-2133
JHS, 106 W WOODROW AVE 38201 2-00100
James Jackson, prin. 352-2792

Bethel College 2-UC
CHERRY ST 38201 352-5321
State Area Vocational-Technical School 2-CS
PO BOX 427 38201 352-5364

Mc Minnville, AC 615, PC 7, Warren
Warren County SD, 109 LYON ST 37110 6-11111
Pedro Paz, supt. 473-2331
Warren County SHS 4-00001
200 CALDWELL ST 37110 473-5577
Edd Cantrell, prin.
Warren County JHS 4-00110
504 N CHANCERY ST 37110 473-6557
Donna Trevathan, prin.

State Area Vocational-Technical School 2-CS
1507 VO TECH DR 37110 473-5587

Memphis, AC 901, PC 11, Shelby
Memphis CSD, 2597 AVERY AVE 38112 9-11111
E. Gerry House, supt. 325-5300
Central SHS 4-00001
306 S BELLEVUE BLVD 38104 722-4500
Barry Owens, prin.

Fairley SHS, 4950 FAIRLEY RD 38109 4-00001
  Harry Durham, prin. 789-8060
Kingsbury SHS 3-00001
  1270 N GRAHAM ST 38122 320-6060
  Wayne Finch, prin.
Middle College SHS 2-00001
  737 UNION AVE 38103 544-5360
  Joyce Mitchell, prin.
Northside SHS 3-00001
  1212 VOLLINTINE AVE 38107 722-4582
  Odell Nathaniel, prin.
Overton SHS, 1770 LANIER LN 38117 3-00001
  Clark White, prin. 684-2136
Whitehaven SHS 4-00001
  4851 ELVIS PRESLEY BLVD 38116 348-3000
  Tracy Norville, prin.
Hamilton HS 3-00011
  1363 E PERSON AVE 38106 775-7838
  Oliver Johnson, prin.
Raleigh Egypt HS 4-00011
  3970 VOLTAIRE AVE 38128 385-4108
  Bill McClain, prin.
South Side HS 4-00011
  1880 PROSPECT ST 38106 775-7380
  Willie Johnson, prin.
Washington HS 2-00011
  715 S LAUDERDALE ST 38126 775-7240
  Elsie Bailey, prin.
White Station HS 4-00011
  514 S PERKINS RD 38117 761-8880
  Steve Simpson, prin.
Woodale HS 3-00011
  5151 SCOTTSDALE AVE 38118 366-2440
  George Williams, prin.
Carver JSHS 3-00111
  1591 PENNSYLVANIA ST 38109 775-7594
  Reynolds McDonald, prin.
Craigmont JSHS 4-00111
  3333 COVINGTON PIKE 38128 385-4312
  Ada Walters, prin.
East JSHS, 3206 POPLAR AVE 38111 4-00111
  Ron Bynum, prin. 320-6160
Frayser JSHS 4-00111
  1530 DELLWOOD AVE 38127 357-3880
  Rebecca Howard, prin.
Hillcrest JSHS 4-00111
  4184 GRACELAND DR 38116 348-3104
  Elmer Ray, prin.
Manassas JSHS 3-00111
  781 FIRESTONE AVE 38107 579-3244
  Rob White, prin.
Melrose JSHS 3-00111
  2870 DEADRICK AVE 38114 325-5974
  Lavaugn Bridges, prin.
Mitchell Road JSHS 3-00111
  658 W MITCHELL RD 38109 789-8174
  Alfred Motlow, prin.
Oakhaven JSHS 3-00111
  3125 LADBROOK RD 38118 366-2300
  Claude Bowers, prin.
Ridgeway JSHS 4-00111
  2009 RIDGEWAY RD 38119 761-8820
  William Wyatt, prin.
Sheffield JSHS 4-00111
  4315 SHEFFIELD AVE 38118 366-2370
  Margaret Kiihnl, prin.
Treadwell JSHS 3-00111
  920 N HIGHLAND ST 38122 320-6100
  John Malone, prin.
Trezevant JSHS 4-00111
  3350 N TREZEVANT ST 38127 357-3760
  Ann Herron, prin.
Westside JSHS, 3389 DAWN DR 38127 3-00111
  William Hudson, prin. 357-3700
Westwood JSHS 4-00111
  4480 WESTMONT RD 38109 789-8000
  Harold McRae, prin.
Kansas Vo HS, 80 W OLIVE AVE 38106 Vo Tech
  Ethel Harrison, prin. 775-7300
Kingsbury Vo HS Vo Tech
  1328 N GRAHAM ST 38122 320-6000
  Milton Burchfield, prin.
Messick Vo S, 703 S GREER ST 38111 Vo Tech
  Jim Lovelace, prin. 325-4841
Southwest Vo-Tech HS Vo Tech
  3747 HORN LAKE RD 38109 789-8186
  Theresa Franklin, prin.
Trezevant Vo HS Vo Tech
  3224 RANGE LINE RD 38127 357-3800
  Joanne Gateley, prin.
Airway JHS, 2601 KETCHUM RD 38114 2-00110
  Clifton Lashley, prin. 744-5006
Bellvue JHS 3-00110
  575 S BELLEVUE BLVD 38104 722-4488
  Joan Miles, prin.
Chickasaw JHS 3-00110
  4060 WESTMONT RD 38109 789-8134
  Osceola Hicks, prin.
Colonial JHS, 4778 SEA ISLE RD 38117 4-00110
  Donna Essary, prin. 761-8980
Corry JHS, 2230 CORRY RD 38106 2-00110
  Joyce Kelly, prin. 775-7804
Cypress JHS, 2109 HOWELL AVE 38108 2-00110
  Tony Wall, prin. 722-4524
Fairview JHS, 750 E PARKWAY S 38104 2-00110
  B. Burrus, prin. 722-4536
Geeter JHS, 4649 HORN LAKE RD 38109 3-00110
  Joe Emmons, prin. 789-8157
Georgian Hills JHS 3-00110
  3925 DENVER ST 38127 357-3740
  Louis Holmes, prin.

Hamilton MS, 1478 WILSON ST 38106 3-00100
  Raybon Hawkins, prin. 775-7832
Havenview JHS, 1481 HESTER RD 38116 3-00110
  Cynthia Gentry, prin. 348-3093
Humes JHS, 659 N MANASSAS ST 38107 3-00110
  Marion Brewer, prin. 579-3226
Kingsbury JHS 3-00110
  1276 N GRAHAM ST 38122 320-6040
  Janet Henson, prin.
Lanier JHS, 817 BROWNLEE RD 38116 3-00110
  James Catchings, prin. 348-3128
Longview MS 3-01100
  1895 S ORLEANS ST 38106 775-7420
  Betty Mason, prin.
Raleigh Egypt MS 3-00100
  4215 ALICE ANN DR 38128 385-4141
  Leslie Fortner, prin.
Riverview MS, 241 MAJUBA AVE 38109 2-00100
  Freeman Robinson, prin. 775-7340
Sherwood JHS, 3480 RHODES AVE 38111 3-00110
  Lemuel Osborne, prin. 325-4870
Vance MS, 673 VANCE AVE 38126 3-00100
  Ben Greene, prin. 579-3256
White Station JHS 3-00100
  5456 MASON RD 38120 684-2184
  Harold Russell, prin.
Wooddale JHS 3-00100
  3467 CASTLEMAN ST 38118 366-2420
  Wayne Mangum, prin.

Shelby County SD 8-11111
  160 S HOLLYWOOD ST 38112 325-7900
  James Anderson, supt.
Kirby HS, 4080 KIRBY PKY 38115 4-00011
  James Boyd, prin. 369-1960
Kirby MS, 6670 E RAINES RD 38115 4-00100
  John Sadowski, prin. 369-1980
Other Schools – See Arlington, Bartlett, Collierville, Cordova, Germantown, Millington

Baptist Memorial Hospital HSP
  899 MADISON AVE 38146 522-4301
Bishop Byrne HS 2-00111
  1475 E SHELBY DR 38116 346-3060
  Sr. Jean Warner, prin.
Briarcrest HS 3-00111
  6000 BRIARCREST AVE 38120 765-4628
  Dan Childs, prin.
CCI Travel Careers Division 2-CS
  568 COLONIAL RD # 102 38117 761-5730
Christian Brothers College 4-UC
  650 E PARKWAY S 38104 800-278-7576
Christian Brothers HS 3-00111
  5900 WALNUT GROVE RD 38120 682-7801
  Br. Englert, prin.
ConCorde Career Institute 2-CS
  5100 POPLAR AVE STE 132 38137 761-9494
Crichton College 2-UC
  6655 WINCHESTER RD 38115 367-9800
De Neuville Hts HS 1-00111
  3060 BASKIN ST 38127 357-7316
  Jackie Mahr, prin.
Draughons Junior College 3-CC
  3200 ELVIS PRESLEY BLVD 38116 332-7800
Elliston Baptist Academy 2-00011
  4179 ELLISTON RD 38111 743-4250
  Floyd Simmons, prin.
First Assembly Christian S 3-11111
  PO BOX 11487 38111 357-0461
  Howard Freeman, prin.
Harding Academy 3-00111
  1100 CHERRY RD 38117 767-4949
  Chris Dahlberg, prin.
Harding Univ Graduate School of Religion 2-UC
  1000 CHERRY RD 38117 800-680-0809
Health Care Training Institute 2-CS
  430 N CLEVELAND ST 38104 722-2288
Hutchison S, 1740 RIDGEWAY RD 38119 3-11111
  Jack Stanford, prin. 761-2220
Immaculate Conception JSHS 2-00111
  1725 CENTRAL AVE 38104 276-6341
  Cheri Kamler, prin.
Lausanne Collegiate S 3-11111
  1381 W MASSEY RD 38120 683-5233
  George Elder, prin.
Le Moyne-Owen College 4-UC
  807 WALKER AVE 38126 942-7302
Memphis Area Voc.-Tech. School 3-CS
  620 MOSBY AVE 38105 527-8455
Memphis Catholic JSHS 2-00111
  61 N MCLEAN BLVD 38104 725-8277
  Fr. Moore, prin.
Memphis College of Art 2-UC
  1930 POPLAR AVE 38104 800-727-1088
Memphis Theological Seminary 2-UC
  168 E PARKWAY S 38104 458-8232
Memphis University S 3-00111
  6191 PARK AVE 38119 761-5271
  William Campbell, prin.
Methodist Hospital HSP
  1265 UNION AVE 38104 726-8525
Mid-America Baptist Theological Seminary 2-UC
  1255 POPLAR AVE 38104 726-9171
Miller Hawkins Business College 2-CS
  1399 MADISON AVE 38104 725-6614
Moore School of Technology 1-CS
  1200 POPLAR AVE 38104 726-1977
Rhodes College 4-UC
  2000 N PARKWAY 38112 800-238-6788
Rice College 2-CS
  2485 UNION AVE 38112 324-7423

St. Agnes Academy 2-00011
  4830 WALNUT GROVE RD 38117 767-1377
  Marian Swicker, prin.
St. Francis Hospital HSP
  5959 PARK AVE 38119 765-1800
St. Joseph Hospital HSP
  220 OVERTON AVE 38105 577-2955
St. Mary's Episcopal S 3-11111
  60 PERKINS EXT 38117 682-4626
  Virginia Pretti, prin.
Shelby State Community College 5-CC
  PO BOX 40568 38174 528-6707
Southeast College of Technology 2-CC
  2731 NONCONNAH BLVD 38132 345-1000
Southern College of Optometry 2-UC
  1245 MADISON AVE 38104 800-238-0180
State Area Vocational-Technical School 2-CS
  620 MOSBY AVE 38105 527-8455
State Technical Institute 6-CC
  5983 MACON CV 38134 377-4111
University of Memphis 38152 7-UC
  678-2000
University of Tennessee 4-UC
  800 MADISON AVE 38163 800-821-6682

Middleton, AC 901, PC 3, Hardeman
  Hardeman County SD
    Supt. — See Bolivar
  JSHS, 138 FLORIDA 38052 3-00111
    William Beibers, prin. 376-8391

Milan, AC 901, PC 6, Gibson
  Milan CSD, PO BOX 528 38358 4-11111
    Janice Nowell, supt. 686-0844
  HS, 7060 E VAN HOOK ST 38358 3-00011
    Ron Parks, prin. 686-0841
  Milan MS, 2014 SMITH ST 38358 2-00100
    Glenda Zarecor, prin. 686-7232

Milligan College, AC 615, PC 3, Carter
  Milligan College 3-UC
    PO BOX 210 37682 800-262-8337

Millington, AC 901, PC 7, Shelby
  Shelby County SD
    Supt. — See Memphis
  HS, 8057 WILKINSVILLE RD 38053 4-00011
    William Person, prin. 873-8100
  MS, 4964 CUBA MILLINGTON RD 38053 3-00100
    Roger Deans, prin. 873-8130

Monterey, AC 615, PC 5, Putnam
  Putnam County SD
    Supt. — See Cookeville
  JSHS, 710 E COMMERCIAL AVE 38574 2-00111
    Robert Weatherholt, prin. 839-2970

Morristown, AC 615, PC 7, Hamblen
  Hamblen County SD 6-11111
    210 E MORRIS BLVD 37813 586-7700
    Earnest Walker, supt.
  Morristown-Hamblen HS East 4-00011
    1 HURRICANE LN 37813 586-2543
    Jerry Williams, prin.
  Morristown-Hamblen HS West 4-00011
    1025 SULPHUR SPRINGS RD 37813 581-1600
    Mike Reed, prin.
  Lincoln Heights MS 2-00100
    219 LINCOLN AVE 37813 581-3200
    Ed Goan, prin.
  Meadowview MS 2-00100
    1623 MEADOWVIEW LN 37814 581-6360
    Ron Wright, prin.
  West View MS 3-00100
    555 W ECONOMY RD 37814 581-2407
    Sanford Harville, prin.
  Other Schools – See Russellville

Morristown College 2-CC
  417 N JAMES ST 37814
State Area Vocational-Technical School 2-CS
  PO BOX 130 37815 586-5771
Walters State Community College 5-CC
  500 S DAVY CROCKETT PKY 37813 587-9722

Mosheim, AC 615, PC 4, Greene
  Greene County SD
    Supt. — See Greeneville
  West Greene HS 3-00011
    275 W GREENE DR N 37818 422-4061
    Hal Pruitt, prin.

Mountain City, AC 615, PC 4, Johnson
  Johnson County SD 4-11111
    211 N CHURCH ST 37683 727-2640
    Gerald Buckles, supt.
  Johnson County HS 3-00011
    500 FAIRGROUND LN 37683 727-9231
    Paul Wellborn, prin.
  Johnson County MS 2-00100
    500A FAIRGROUND LN 37683 727-2600
    Morris Woodring, prin.

Mount Juliet, AC 615, PC 6, Wilson
  Wilson County SD
    Supt. — See Lebanon
  SHS, 3565 N MOUNT JULIET RD 37122 4-00001
    Phil Barnes, prin. 758-5606
  JHS, 935 N MOUNT JULIET RD 37122 4-00110
    James Farley, prin. 758-5152

Mount Pleasant, AC 615, PC 5, Maury
  Maury County SD
    Supt. — See Columbia

JSHS, 600 GREENWOOD ST 38474 — 3-00111
W. Johnson, prin. — 379-5583

Munford, AC 901, PC 4, Tipton
Tipton County SD
Supt. — See Covington
HS, PO BOX L 38058 — 4-00011
Daryl Walker, prin. — 837-0173
MS, 1147 EDUCATION AVE 38058 — 4-00100
Isaiah Davidson, prin. — 476-7148

Murfreesboro, AC 615, PC 8, Rutherford
Rutherford County SD — 7-11111
502 MEMORIAL BLVD 37129 — 893-5812
Elam Carlton, supt.
Holloway HS — 2-00011
619 S HIGHLAND AVE 37130 — 890-6004
Cliff Brothers, prin.
Oakland HS, 865 PATRIOT DR 37130 — 4-00011
Gayle Blair, prin. — 890-5920
Riverdale HS, 802 WARRIOR DR 37129 — 4-00011
James Watson, prin. — 890-6450
Central MS, 701 E MAIN ST 37130 — 4-00100
William Vaughn, prin. — 893-8262
Other Schools — See Eagleville, La Vergne, Smyrna

Middle Tennessee Christian S — 3-11111
1720 MEMORIAL BLVD 37129
Susan Cantrell, prin.
Middle Tennessee State University 37132 — 7-UC
— 898-2111
State Area Vocational-Technical School — 2-CS
1303 OLD FORT PKY 37129 — 893-4095

Nashville, AC 615, PC 10, Davidson
Davidson County SD — 8-11111
2601 BRANSFORD AVE 37204 — 259-8419
Richard Benjamin, supt.
Glencliff HS, 160 ANTIOCH PIKE 37211 — 4-00011
Sam Snow, prin. — 333-5070
Hillsboro HS — 4-00011
3812 HILLSBORO RD 37215 — 298-8400
Jean Litterer, prin.
Hillwood HS — 4-00011
6215 HICKORY VALLEY RD 37205 — 353-2025
Robert Myers, prin.
Hume-Fogg Magnet HS — 3-00011
700 BROADWAY 37203 — 742-6300
Anne Whitefield, prin.
Hunters Lane Comprehensive HS — 4-00011
1150 HUNTERS LN 37207 — 860-1401
Julie Williams, prin.
Maplewood HS — 4-00011
401 MAPLEWOOD LN 37216 — 262-6770
James Armstrong, prin.
McGavock HS — 5-00011
3150 MCGAVOCK PIKE 37214 — 885-8850
Howard Baltimore, prin.
Overton HS, 4820 FRANKLIN RD 37220 — 4-00011
Michael Hammond, prin. — 333-5135
Pearl-Cohn HS, 904 26TH AVE N 37208 — 3-00011
James Currie, prin. — 329-8150
Stratford HS — 4-00011
1800 STRATFORD AVE 37216 — 262-6730
Jim Neely, prin.
King JSHS, 613 17TH AVE N 37203 — 3-00111
Samella Junior-Spence, prin. — 329-8400
Bass MS, 5200 DELAWARE AVE 37209 — 2-00100
James Turbeyville, prin. — 298-8065
Bellevue MS — 3-00100
656 COLICE JEANNE RD 37221 — 662-3000
Robert Wilson, prin.
Cameron MS, 1034 1ST AVE S 37210 — 3-01100
Gerald Martin, prin. — 291-6365
East MS, 110 GALLATIN RD 37206 — 3-00100
Elbert Ross, prin. — 262-6650
Ewing Park MS, 3410 KNIGHT RD 37207 — 3-00110
William Terrell, prin. — 876-5115
Highland Heights MS — 2-00100
123 DOUGLAS AVE 37207 — 262-6690
Henry Flenory, prin.
Litton MS, 4601 HEDGEWOOD DR 37216 — 3-00100
Donald Wynn, prin. — 262-6700
McMurray MS — 3-00100
520 MCMURRAY DR 37211 — 333-5126
Ron Webb, prin.
Meigs Magnet MS — 3-01100
713 RAMSEY ST 37206 — 291-6390
Thomas Ward, prin.
Moore MS — 3-00100
4425 GRANNY WHITE PIKE 37204 — 298-8095
L. Batson, prin.
Two Rivers MS — 3-00100
2991 MCGAVOCK PIKE 37214 — 885-8931
Mildred Smith, prin.
West End MS, 3529 W END AVE 37205 — 2-00100
Paul Mays, prin. — 298-8425
Wharton MS — 3-01100
1625 DR DB TODD JR BLVD 37208 — 329-8180
Barbara Crawford, prin.
Wright MS, 180 MCCALL ST 37211 — 3-00100
Nancy Dill, prin. — 333-5189
Other Schools — See Antioch, Goodlettsville,
Hermitage, Joelton, Madison, Old Hickory, Whites
Creek

American Baptist College — 2-UC
1800 WORLD BPTIST CENTER DR 37207
— 262-1369
Aquinas Junior College — 2-CC
4210 HARDING RD 37205 — 297-7545

Belmont College — 5-UC
1900 BELMONT BLVD 37212 — 385-6785
Blair School of Music of Vanderbilt U. — 2-UC
2400 BLAKEMORE AVE 37212 — 322-7651
Court Reporting Institute of Tennessee — 2-CS
51 CENTURY BLVD STE 350 37214 — 855-9770
David Lipscomb S — 4-11111
3901 GRANNY WHITE PIKE 37204 — 269-1000
Richard Jones, prin.
David Lipscomb University — 4-UC
3901 GRANNY WHITE PIKE 37204
— 800-333-4358
Davidson Academy — 4-11111
1414 OLD HICKORY BLVD 37207
Art Mayernick, prin.
Davidson Technical College — 2-CS
212 PAVILION BLVD 37217
Devereux Genesis Learning Centers — 2-HND
430 B ALLIED DR 37211 — 832-4222
Donelson Christian Academy — 3-11111
3151 STAFFORD DR 37214
Daniel Kellum, prin.
Draughons Junior College — 4-CC
PLUS PARK AT PAVILION BLVD 37217
— 361-7555
Father Ryan HS — 3-00011
700 NORWOOD DR 37204 — 383-4200
Edward Krenson, prin.
Fisk University — 3-UC
1000 17TH AVE N 37208 — 329-8665
Franklin Road Academy — 3-11111
4800 FRANKLIN RD 37220 — 832-8845
Robert Welch, prin.
Free Will Baptist Bible College — 2-UC
PO BOX 50117 37205 — 383-1340
Fugazzi College — 2-CS
5042 LINBAR DR 37211 — 333-3344
Harpeth Hall, 3801 HOBBS RD 37215 — 2-01111
Leah Rhys, prin. — 297-9543
ITT Technical Institute — 2-UC
PO BOX 148029 37214 — 889-8700
John A. Gupton College — 1-CC
1616 CHURCH ST 37203 — 327-3927
Meharry Medical College — 3-UC
1005 DR DB TODD JR BLVD 37208 — 327-6111
Metropolitan Nashville General Hospital — HSP
72 HERMITAGE AVE 37210 — 259-5775
Montgomery Bell Academy — 3-00011
4001 HARDING RD 37205 — 298-5514
Douglas Paschall, prin.
Nashville Auto-Diesel College — 4-CC
1524 GALLATIN RD 37206 — 226-3990
Nashville Christian S — 2-11111
7555 SAWYER BROWN RD 37221 — 356-5600
Donnie Keeton, prin.
Nashville State Technical Institute — 5-CC
120 WHITE BRIDGE RD 37209 — 353-3233
Peabody College of Vanderbilt University — 4-UC
PO BOX 327 37202 — 322-8410
St. Cecilia Academy — 2-00011
4210 HARDING RD 37205 — 298-4525
Mary Sallese, prin.
St. Thomas Hospital — HSP
PO BOX 380 37202 — 386-2111
Seminary Ext. Independent Study Inst. — 2-HMS
901 COMMERCE ST STE 500 37203
— 242-2453
Southeastern Inst. Paralegal Education — 1-CS
2416 21ST AVE S STE 300 37212
— 800-336-4457
State Area Vocational-Technical School — 2-CS
100 WHITE BRIDGE RD 37209 — 741-1241
Tennessee State University — 6-UC
3500 JOHN A MERRITT BLVD 37209 — 320-3420
Trevecca Nazarene College — 4-UC
333 MURFREESBORO RD 37210 — 248-1200
University of Tennessee — 2-UC
1720 W END AVE 37203 — 329-1212
University S of Nashville — 3-11111
2000 EDGEHILL AVE 37212 — 327-8158
Edward Costello, prin.
Vanderbilt University — 6-UC
W END AVE 37240 — 322-7311
Watkins Institute, 601 CHURCH ST 37219 — 2-00011
Don Mobley, prin. — 242-1851
Watkins Institute-School Interior Design — 2-CC
601 CHURCH ST 37219 — 242-1851

Newbern, AC 901, PC 5, Dyer
Dyer County SD
Supt. — See Dyersburg
Dyer County HS — 3-00011
LANESFERRY ROAD 38059 — 627-2229
John Snider, prin.

State Area Vocational-Technical School — 2-CS
340 WASHINGTON ST 38059 — 627-2511

Newport, AC 615, PC 6, Cocke
Cocke County SD — 5-11111
224 MURRAY DR 37821 — 623-7821
Larry Blazer, supt.
Cocke County HS — 4-00011
216 HEADRICK DR 37821 — 623-8718
Jack Reynolds, prin.
Hooper Vo HS, 210 HEADRICK DR 37821 — Vo Tech
Donald Frazier, prin. — 623-6072
Other Schools — See Cosby

Norris, AC 615, PC 4, Anderson
Anderson County SD
Supt. — See Clinton

Norris MS, GENERAL DELIVERY 37828 — 2-00100
Rebecca Stewart, prin. — 494-7171

Oakdale, AC 615, PC 2, Morgan
Morgan County SD
Supt. — See Wartburg
S, RR 1 37829 — 2-11111
Paul Scarbrough, prin. — 369-3885

Oak Ridge, AC 615, PC 8, Anderson
Oak Ridge CSD, PO BOX 6588 37831 — 5-11111
Robert Smallridge, supt. — 482-6320
SHS, 127 PROVIDENCE RD 37830 — 4-00001
William Hodgers, prin. — 482-8508
Jefferson JHS, 200 FAIRBANKS RD 37830 — 3-00110
Rob Moss, prin. — 482-8540
Robertsville JHS — 3-00110
245 ROBERTSVILLE RD 37830 — 482-8536
Tom Hayes, prin.

Old Hickory, AC 615, PC see Nashville
Davidson County SD
Supt. — See Nashville
Dupont MS, 2001 HADLEY AVE 37138 — 2-00100
Ray Hogan, prin. — 847-7300

Oliver Springs, AC 615, PC 5, Anderson
Anderson County SD
Supt. — See Clinton
Norwood MS — 2-00100
655 TRI COUNTY BLVD E 37840 — 435-7749
Harold Heath, prin.

Roane County SD
Supt. — See Kingston
HS, PO BOX 309 37840 — 2-00011
Ken Bailey, prin. — 435-7216

Oneida, AC 615, PC 5, Scott
Oneida CSD, PO BOX 4819 37841 — 4-11111
L. Mayfield Brown, supt. — 569-8912
HS, PO BOX 4549 37841 — 2-00011
William Smith, prin. — 569-8818
MS, PO BOX 5029 37841 — 2-00100
Cheryl Butler, prin. — 569-2475

State Area Vocational-Technical School — 2-CS
120 ELI LN 37841 — 569-8338

Ooltewah, AC 615, PC 5, Hamilton
Hamilton County SD
Supt. — See Chattanooga
HS, 6112 SNOWHILL RD 37363 — 4-00011
Theresa Harvey, prin. — 238-5221
Harrison Bay Vo HS — Vo Tech
9050 CAREER LN 37363 — 344-1433
Charles Gates, prin.
MS — 4-00100
5100 OOLTEWAH RINGGOLD RD 37363 — 238-5732
Steven McClure, prin.

Palmersville, AC 901, PC 2, Weakley
Weakley County SD
Supt. — See Dresden
S, ZION RD 38241 — 2-11111
Robert Montgomery, prin. — 822-4325

Paris, AC 901, PC 6, Henry
Henry County SD — 5-11111
217 GROVE BLVD 38242 — 642-9733
William Atchison, supt.
Henry County HS, S WILSON ST 38242 — 4-00011
John Hinson, prin. — 642-5232
Grove MS, 900 GROVE ST 38242 — 2-00100
Thomas Rushing, prin. — 642-4586

State Area Vocational-Technical School — 2-CS
312 S WILSON ST 38242

Parsons, AC 901, PC 4, Decatur
Decatur County SD
Supt. — See Decaturville
Riverside HS 38363 — 3-00011
Larry Barrett, prin. — 847-3941
JHS, 303 HILL ST 38363 — 2-01100
Grafton Dodd, prin. — 847-6510

Pigeon Forge, AC 615, PC 5, Sevier
Sevier County SD
Supt. — See Sevierville
MS, 310 WEARS VALLEY RD 37863 — 3-01100
Jerry Wear, prin. — 453-2401

Pikeville, AC 615, PC 4, Bledsoe
Bledsoe County SD — 4-11111
PO BOX 369 37367 — 447-2914
Thad Colvard, supt.
Bledsoe County HS — 2-00011
1051 S MAIN ST 37367 — 447-6851
Sanford Quay, prin.
Other Schools — See Dunlap

Pleasant View, AC 615, PC 2, Cheatham
Cheatham County SD
Supt. — See Ashland City
Sycamore MS — 3-00100
1025 OLD CLARKSVILLE PIKE 37146 — 746-5013
Norma Shearon, prin.

Portland, AC 615, PC 6, Sumner
Sumner County SD
Supt. — See Gallatin
HS, 604 N BROADWAY 37148 — 3-00011
John Meece, prin. — 325-9201
Sumner County North Vo Ctr — Vo Tech
HIGHWAY 109 S 37148 — 325-9204
Thomas Utley, prin.

MS, 922 S BROADWAY 37148   3-00100
Bob Little, prin.   325-4146

Highland Academy   2-00011
21100 HIGHLAND CIR 37148   325-2036
James Ingersol, prin.

Powell, AC 615, PC 6, Knox
Knox County SD
Supt. — See Knoxville
HS, 2136 EMORY RD W 37849   4-00011
Vicki Dunaway, prin.   938-2171
MS, 5329 EMORY RD W 37849   3-00100
Benton Stewart, prin.   938-9008

Pulaski, AC 615, PC 6, Giles
Giles County SD   5-11111
720 W FLOWER ST 38478   363-4558
Sam Collins, supt.
Giles County HS   3-00011
200 SHEILA FROST DR 38478   363-6532
Leslie Parker, prin.
Bridgeforth MS   2-01100
1051 BRIDGEFORTH CIR 38478   363-7526
J. B. Smith, prin.
Other Schools – See Lynnville

Martin Methodist College   2-CC
433 W MADISON ST 38478   800-727-1273
State Area Vocational-Technical School 2-CS
PO BOX 614 38478   363-1588

Red Boiling Springs, AC 615, PC 3, Macon
Clay County SD
Supt. — See Celina
Hermitage Springs S 37150   2-11111
Ron Roberts, prin.   699-2414
Tri-County Vo Ctr   Vo Tech
PO BOX 214 37150   699-2224
Jerry Spivey, prin.

Macon County SD
Supt. — See Lafayette
S, HILLCREST DR 37150   2-11111
Mike Emberton, prin.   699-3125

Ripley, AC 901, PC 6, Lauderdale
Lauderdale County SD   6-11111
PO BOX 350 38063   635-2941
Bobby Webb, supt.
HS, 254 S JEFFERSON ST 38063   3-00011
Jon Pavletic, prin.   635-2642
Lauderdale MS, 230 GRIGGS AVE 38063 4-01100
Jim Douglass, prin.   635-1391
Other Schools – See Halls

State Area Vocational-Technical School 1-CS
SOUTH INDUSTRIAL PARK 38063   635-3368

Roan Mountain, AC 615, PC 4, Carter
Carter County SD
Supt. — See Elizabethton
Cloudland JSHS, RR 3 37687   2-00111
Richard Winters, prin.   772-5300

Rockwood, AC 615, PC 6, Roane
Roane County SD
Supt. — See Kingston
HS, 512 W ROCKWOOD ST 37854   2-00011
James Wilson, prin.   354-0882
JHS, 434 W ROCKWOOD ST 37854   2-00100
William Thompson, prin.   354-0931

Rogersville, AC 615, PC 5, Hawkins
Hawkins County SD   6-11111
200 N DEPOT ST 37857   272-7629
James Dykes, supt.
Cherokee HS, RR 7 BOX 280 37857   4-00011
Daffin Anderson, prin.   272-6507
MS, 950 E MCKINNEY AVE 37857   3-01100
Joe Davis, prin.   272-7603
Other Schools – See Church Hill, Eidson,
Surgoinsville

Russellville, AC 615, PC 4, Hamblen
Hamblen County SD
Supt. — See Morristown
East Ridge MS   3-00100
5273 E ANDREW JOHNSON HWY 37860
Glen Kanipe, prin.   581-3041

Rutledge, AC 615, PC 3, Grainger
Grainger County SD   5-11111
PO BOX 38 37861   828-3611
Earl Coffey, supt.
HS, RR 4 BOX 51 37861   3-00011
Ron Cabbage, prin.   828-5291
Other Schools – See Washburn

Saint Andrews, AC 615, PC 2, Franklin

St. Andrew's-Sewanee S   2-00111
GENERAL DELIVERY 37372   598-5651
William Wade, prin.

Sale Creek, AC 615, PC 4, Hamilton
Hamilton County SD
Supt. — See Chattanooga
S, 211 PATTERSON RD 37373   2-11111
John Crane, prin.   332-8819

Santa Fe, AC 615, PC 2, Maury
Maury County SD
Supt. — See Columbia
S, NEW HIGHWAY 7 38482   2-11111
Ken Jackson, prin.   682-2172

Savannah, AC 901, PC 6, Hardin
Hardin County SD   5-11111
116 N GUINN ST 38372   925-3943
Bob Cromwell, supt.
Hardin County HS   4-00011
915 S PICKWICK RD 38372   925-3976
J. Smith, prin.
Hardin County MS   3-00100
RR 7 BOX 174 38372   925-9037
Jim Vernon, prin.

Scotts Hill, AC 901, PC 3, Henderson
Decatur County SD
Supt. — See Decaturville
S 38374   2-11111
Dale Crews, prin.   549-3411

Henderson County SD
Supt. — See Lexington
S 38374   3-11111
Dale Crews, prin.   549-3145

Selmer, AC 901, PC 5, McNairy
McNairy County SD   5-11111
COURTHOUSE 38375   645-3267
Billy Joe Glover, supt.
McNairy Central HS   3-00011
RR 2 BOX 350 38375   645-3226
Martha Glover, prin.
MS, 635 POPLAR AVE 38375   2-01100
Freddie Moore, prin.   645-7977
Other Schools – See Adamsville

Sevierville, AC 615, PC 6, Sevier
Sevier County SD, 226 CEDAR ST 37862 7-11111
Jack Parton, supt.   453-4671
Sevier County HS   4-00011
1200 DOLLY PARTON PKY 37862   453-5525
Gary Reach, prin.
MS, 550 HIGH ST 37862   3-00100
William Love, prin.   453-0311
Other Schools – See Gatlinburg, Pigeon Forge,
Seymour

Sewanee, AC 615, PC 4, Franklin

University of the South   4-UC
735 UNIVERSITY AVE 37375   598-1238

Seymour, AC 615, PC 7, Sevier
Sevier County SD
Supt. — See Sevierville
HS, 732 BOYDS CREEK HWY 37865   3-00011
Bruce Wilson, prin.   577-7040
MS, 212 N PITNER RD 37865   3-01100
John Wade, prin.   573-9320

Kings Academy   2-00111
202 SMOTHERS RD 37865   573-8321
John Grubb, prin.

Sharon, AC 901, PC 4, Weakley
Weakley County SD
Supt. — See Dresden
S, N WOODLAWN DR 38255   2-11111
Don Capps, prin.   456-2672

Shelbyville, AC 615, PC 7, Bedford
Bedford County SD   6-11111
500 MADISON ST 37160   684-3284
James Shemwell, supt.
Central HS, 401 EAGLE BLVD 37160 4-00011
Mike Bone, prin.   684-5672
Bedford County Vo Ctr   Vo Tech
1407 MADISON ST 37160   684-1889
James Helton, prin.
Harris MS, 400 ELM ST 37160   3-00100
Terry Saylor, prin.   684-5195
Other Schools – See Unionville, Wartrace

State Area Vocational-Technical School 2-CS
1405 MADISON ST 37160   685-5013

Signal Mountain, AC 615, PC 6, Hamilton
Hamilton County SD
Supt. — See Chattanooga
MS, 315 AULT RD 37377   2-00100
Sheila Young, prin.   886-0876

Smithville, AC 615, PC 5, De Kalb
DeKalb County SD, 198 S 3RD ST 37166 5-11111
Aubrey Turner, supt.   597-4084
DeKalb County HS   3-00011
1130 W BROAD ST 37166   597-4094
Charles Collier, prin.
DeKalb County MS   3-01100
1132 W BROAD ST 37166   597-7987
Tucker Hendrix, prin.

Smyrna, AC 615, PC 7, Rutherford
Rutherford County SD
Supt. — See Murfreesboro
HS, 100 BULLDOG RD 37167   4-00011
Rob Raikes, prin.   459-6872
MS, 712 HAZELWOOD DR 37167   3-00100
Donald Jernigan, prin.   459-8934

Sneedville, AC 615, PC 4, Hancock
Hancock County SD   4-11111
PO BOX 629 37869   733-2591
Kenneth Givens, supt.
Hancock County JSHS   2-00111
PO BOX 659 37869   733-2252
Dennis Greene, prin.

Soddy-Daisy, AC 615, PC 6, Hamilton
Hamilton County SD
Supt. — See Chattanooga
HS, 618 SEQUOYAH RD 37379   4-00011
Robert Smith, prin.   332-8828
Sequoya Vo Ctr   Vo Tech
9517 RIDGE TRAIL RD 37379   843-4707
Paul Smith, prin.
MS, 200 TURNER RD 37379   3-00100
Freddie Schmid, prin.   332-8800

Somerville, AC 901, PC 4, Fayette
Fayette County SD, PO BOX 10 38068 5-11111
Dale Summitt, supt.   465-5260
Fayette-Ware HS, PO BOX 409 38068 4-00011
Myles Wilson, prin.   466-9838

Fayette Academy, PO BOX 130 38068 2-00011
Tom Gunn, prin.   465-3241

South Fulton, AC 901, PC 5, Obion
Obion County SD
Supt. — See Union City
JSHS, 202 W SMITH ST 38257   2-00111
Don Braswell, prin.   479-1441

South Pittsburg, AC 615, PC 5, Marion
Marion County SD
Supt. — See Jasper
JSHS, 717 ELM AVE 37380   2-00111
Harl Miller, prin.   837-7561

Sparta, AC 615, PC 5, White
White County SD, 136 BAKER ST 38583 5-11111
Don Haley, supt.   836-2229
White County HS, 229 ALLEN DR 38583 3-00011
Charles Dycus, prin.   836-3214
White County MS   3-00100
136 HIGH SCHOOL ST 38583   836-3376
Barry Roberts, prin.

Speedwell, AC 615, PC 1, Claiborne
Claiborne County SD
Supt. — See Tazewell
Powell Valley HS, RR 1 BOX 275A 37870 2-00011
Larry Anderson, prin.   869-4275

Spencer, AC 615, PC 4, Van Buren
Van Buren County SD   3-11111
PO BOX 98 38585   946-2242
Larry Yates, supt.
Van Buren County JSHS 38585   2-00111
Neal O'Neal, prin.   946-2442

Springfield, AC 615, PC 7, Robertson
Robertson County SD   6-11111
2121 WOODLAND ST 37172   384-5588
Jerome Ellis, supt.
HS, 5240 HIGHWAY 76 E 37172   3-00011
Clayton Sykes, prin.   384-3516
Robertson County Vo Ctr   Vo Tech
5326 HIGHWAY 76 E 37172   384-2491
Clyde Delk, prin.
MS, 715 5TH AVE W 37172   3-00100
Dick Stewart, prin.   384-4821
Other Schools – See Cedar Hill, Cross Plains,
Greenbrier

Strawberry Plains, AC 615, PC 3, Jefferson
Knox County SD
Supt. — See Knoxville
Carter HS   3-00011
210 N CARTER SCHOOL RD 37871   933-3434
Bob Pollard, prin.
Carter MS   3-00100
204 N CARTER SCHOOL RD 37871   933-3426
Sandra Clift, prin.

Summertown, AC 615, PC 3, Lawrence
Lawrence County SD
Supt. — See Lawrenceburg
JSHS, PO BOX 88 38483   2-00111
Ken Hay, prin.   964-3539

Sunbright, AC 615, PC 3, Morgan
Morgan County SD
Supt. — See Wartburg
S, PO BOX 129 37872   3-11111
James Jones, prin.   628-2128

Surgoinsville, AC 615, PC 4, Hawkins
Hawkins County SD
Supt. — See Rogersville
MS, PO BOX 9 37873   2-01100
Kirby Gillenwater, prin.   345-2252

Sweetwater, AC 615, PC 6, Monroe
Monroe County SD
Supt. — See Madisonville
HS, S HIGH STREET 37874   3-00011
Kevin Smith, prin.   337-7881

Sweetwater CSD, PO BOX 231 37874 4-11100
S. Hickey, supt.   337-7051
JHS, CANNON AVE 37874   2-00100
W. Stein, prin.   337-7336

Tazewell, AC 615, PC 4, Claiborne
Claiborne County SD   5-11111
PO BOX 179 37879   626-3543
Ray Norris, supt.
Claiborne County HS, RR 1 37879   3-00011
Linda Gibson, prin.   626-3532
Claiborne County Vo Ctr, RR 1 37879 Vo Tech
Jim Welch, prin.   626-5984

Soldiers Memorial MS   3-01100
RR 1 BOX 55 37879   626-3531
Lynn Barnard, prin.
Other Schools — See Harrogate, Speedwell

Tellico Plains, AC 615, PC 3, Monroe
Monroe County SD
Supt. — See Madisonville
HS, RR 4 37385   2-00011
Alice Fouts, prin.   253-2530
JHS, RR 4 37385   2-00100
J. E. Staier, prin.   253-2250

Tiptonville, AC 901, PC 4, Lake
Lake County SD, PO BOX 397 38079   4-11111
Roland Pope, supt.   253-6601
Lake County HS   2-00011
300 COCHRAN ST 38079   253-7733
Howard Todd, prin.

Tracy City, AC 615, PC 4, Grundy
Grundy County SD
Supt. — See Altamont
Grundy County HS   3-00011
PO BOX 1239 37387   592-2481
Ted Ladd, prin.

Trenton, AC 901, PC 5, Gibson
Trenton CSD, 201 W 10TH ST 38382   4-11111
Larry Ridings, supt.   855-1191
Peabody HS   2-00011
1269 US HIGHWAY 45 BYP N 38382   855-2601
Sam Miles, prin.
MS, 421 E 2ND ST 38382   2-01100
Juanita Johnson, prin.   855-2422

Trezevant, AC 901, PC 3, Carroll
West Carroll SD, PO BOX 279 38258   4-11111
Fred Martin, supt.   669-5005
West Carroll MS, PO BOX 278 38258   2-01100
Claudia Argo, prin.   669-3851
Other Schools — See Atwood

Troy, AC 901, PC 4, Obion
Obion County SD
Supt. — See Union City
Obion County Central HS, RR 1 38260   3-00011
Bill Hampton, prin.   536-4688

Tullahoma, AC 615, PC 7, Coffee
Tullahoma CSD   5-11111
510 S JACKSON ST 37388   454-2600
Donald Embry, supt.
HS, 1001 N JACKSON ST 37388   4-00011
Mel Covington, prin.   454-2620
East MS, 900 COUNTRY CLUB DR 37388   2-00100
Rob Osteen, prin.   454-2632
West MS, 301 W DECHERD ST 37388   2-00100
John Wilson, prin.   454-2605

Motlow State Community College   4-CC
PO BOX 88100 37388   455-8511

Union City, AC 901, PC 7, Obion
Obion County SD, PO BOX 747 38281   5-11111
Vinson Thompson, supt.   885-9743
Obion-Lake Vo Ctr, 1700 N 5TH ST 38261   Vo Tech
Bill Dean, prin.   885-7171
Other Schools — See South Fulton, Troy

Union City CSD, PO BOX 749 38281   4-11111
Baxter Wheatley, supt.   885-3922
HS, 1305 HIGH SCHOOL DR 38261   3-00011
James Towater, prin.   885-2373
MS, 1111 HIGH SCHOOL DR 38261   2-00100
Bill Dowell, prin.   885-2901

Unionville, AC 615, PC 2, Bedford
Bedford County SD
Supt. — See Shelbyville
Community S   3-11111
3470 HIGHWAY 41A N 37180   294-5125
Mike Landis, prin.

Vonore, AC 615, PC 3, Monroe
Monroe County SD
Supt. — See Madisonville
JSHS, PO BOX 219 37885   2-00011
Mike Lowry, prin.   884-6384

Walland, AC 615, PC 3, Blount
Blount County SD
Supt. — See Maryville
MS, 247 E MILLERS COVE RD 37886   2-00100
William Miller, prin.   983-2801

Wartburg, AC 615, PC 3, Morgan
Morgan County SD   5-11111
PO BOX 348 37887   346-6214
Allan Nance, supt.
Central HS, PO BOX 303 37887   2-00011
Edward Diden, prin.   346-6616
Morgan County Vo Ctr   Vo Tech
PO BOX 40 37887   346-6285
David Hennessee, prin.
Other Schools — See Coalfield, Oakdale, Sunbright

Wartrace, AC 615, PC 2, Bedford
Bedford County SD
Supt. — See Shelbyville
Cascade S   3-11111
1165 BELL BUCKLE WRTRACE RD 37183
Hal Skelton, prin.   389-9389

Washburn, AC 615, PC 2, Grainger
Grainger County SD
Supt. — See Rutledge
JSHS, PO BOX 69 37888   2-00111
John Jones, prin.   497-2557

Watertown, AC 615, PC 4, Wilson
Wilson County SD
Supt. — See Lebanon
JSHS, PO BOX 67 37184   2-00111
John Johnson, prin.   237-3434

Waverly, AC 615, PC 5, Humphreys
Humphreys County SD   5-11111
103 S CHURCH ST 37185   296-2568
James Long, supt.
Waverly Central HS   3-00011
PO BOX 1325 37185   296-3911
Gene Trotter, prin.
Humphreys County Vo HS   Vo Tech
RR 1 BOX 55 37185   296-7867
Wilbur McCashland, prin.
JHS, E HWY 70 37185   3-01100
Robert Reid, prin.   296-4514
Other Schools — See Mc Ewen

Waynesboro, AC 615, PC 4, Wayne
Wayne County SD   5-11111
PO BOX 658 38485   722-3548
Pat Brewer, supt.
Wayne County HS, 707 S MAIN ST 38485   2-00011
Gailand Grinder, prin.   722-3238
Wayne County Vo Ctr   Vo Tech
703 S MAIN ST 38485   722-5495
Michael Price, prin.
MS, PO BOX 657 38485   2-01100
Sarah Jones, prin.   722-5545
Other Schools — See Clifton, Collinwood

Westmoreland, AC 615, PC 4, Sumner
Sumner County SD
Supt. — See Gallatin
HS, 4128 HAWKINS DR 37186   2-00011
DeWayne Oldham, prin.   644-2280
MS, 2116 OLD HIGHWAY 31 E 37186   2-00100
Ben Bills, prin.   644-3003

White Bluff, AC 615, PC 4, Dickson
Dickson County SD
Supt. — See Dickson
James JHS   2-00110
3030 TRACE CREEK RD 37187   797-3201
Louise Buchanan, prin.

White House, AC 615, PC 5, Sumner
Sumner County SD
Supt. — See Gallatin
HS, 508 TYREE SPRINGS RD S 37188   3-00011
Bob Langford, prin.   672-3761
MS, 111 MEADOWS RD 37188   3-01100
Carl Fussell, prin.   672-4379

Whites Creek, AC 615, PC see Nashville
Davidson County SD
Supt. — See Nashville
HS, 7277 OLD HICKORY BLVD 37189   4-00011
Bruce Bowers, prin.   876-5132

Whiteville, AC 901, PC 4, Hardeman

State Area Vocational-Technical School   2-CS
PO BOX 489 38075   254-8521

Whitwell, AC 615, PC 4, Marion
Marion County SD
Supt. — See Jasper
JSHS, RR 4 BOX 220 37397   3-00111
John Shelley, prin.   658-5141

Winchester, AC 615, PC 6, Franklin
Franklin County SD   6-11111
PO BOX 129 37398   967-0626
Patty Priest, supt.
Franklin County SHS   4-00001
925 DINAH SHORE BLVD 37398   967-2821
Joe Guess, prin.
North JHS, 2990 DECHERD BLVD 37398   3-00110
John Butler, prin.   967-5323
Other Schools — See Cowan, Huntland

Woodbury, AC 615, PC 4, Cannon
Cannon County SD   4-11111
301 W MAIN ST 37190   563-5752
Nell Smith, supt.
Cannon County HS, 1 LION DR 37190   3-00011
Robert Pitts, prin.   563-2144

TEXAS

TEXAS EDUCATION AGENCY
William B. Travis Building
1701 N. Congress Ave., Austin 78701
(512) 463-9734

Commissioner of Education   Lionel Meno

Executive Associate Commissioner Field Services   Gene Davenport

Executive Deputy Commissioner Curriculum & Assessment   Linda Cimusz

Executive Deputy Commissioner Accountability   Ruben Olivarez

Executive Deputy Commissioner Special Programs   Jay Cummings

STATE BOARD OF EDUCATION
1701 N. Congress Ave., Austin 78701

Chairperson   Carolyn Crawford

PUBLIC, PRIVATE AND CATHOLIC SECONDARY SCHOOLS

Abbott, AC 817, PC 2, Hill
Abbott ISD, PO BOX 226 76621 — 2-11111
  Harley Johnson, supt. — 582-9442
S, PO BOX 226 76621 — 2-11111
  Terry Timmons, prin. — 582-3011

Abernathy, AC 806, PC 5, Hale
Abernathy ISD, 505 7TH ST 79311 — 3-11111
  Charles Floyd, supt. — 298-2563
HS, 505 7TH ST 79311 — 2-00011
  Larry McBee, prin. — 298-2563
MS, 505 7TH ST 79311 — 2-01100
  Steve Burleson, prin. — 298-2563

Abilene, AC 915, PC 9, Taylor
Abilene ISD, PO BOX 981 79604 — 7-11111
  Charles Hundley, supt. — 677-1444
HS, 2800 N 6TH ST 79603 — 4-00011
  Royce Curtis, prin. — 677-1731
Cooper HS, 3639 SAYLES BLVD 79605 — 4-00011
  Jeri Pfeifer, prin. — 691-1000
Woodson Skill Ctr — Vo Tech
  342 COCKERELL DR 79601 — 676-7177
  Elizabeth Dolton, prin.
Clack MS, 1610 CORSICANA AVE 79605 — 3-00100
  Robert Starr, prin. — 692-1961
Franklin MS, 1200 MERCHANT ST 79603 — 3-00100
  Kay Taylor, prin. — 677-3791
Jefferson MS, 1741 S 14TH ST 79602 — 3-00100
  Hubert Pickett, prin. — 677-3505
Lincoln MS, 1699 S 1ST ST 79602 — 3-00100
  Jim Short, prin. — 672-3279
Madison MS, 3145 BARROW ST 79605 — 3-00100
  Mac Hurley, prin. — 692-5661
Mann MS, 2545 MIMOSA DR 79603 — 3-00100
  Idas Petty, prin. — 672-8493

Wylie ISD — 4-11111
  7049 BUFFALO GAP RD 79606 — 692-4353
  Cecil Davis, supt.
Wylie HS, 4010 BELTWAY S 79606 — 3-00011
  Larry Shackelford, prin. — 695-1910
Wylie MS, 3158 BELTWAY S 79606 — 2-00100
  Joseph Light, prin. — 695-6870

Abilene Christian S — 2-11111
  2550 N JUDGE ELY BLVD 79601 — 672-9200
  Gene Sheets, prin.
Abilene Christian University — 5-UC
  ACU STATION # 6000 79699 — 800-888-0228
American Commercial College — 2-CS
  402 BUTTERNUT ST 79602 — 672-8495
Hardin-Simmons University — 4-UC
  2200 HICKORY ST 79698 — 670-1206
Hendrick Medical Center — HSP
  1242 N 19TH ST 79601 — 670-2201
McMurry University — 4-UC
  14TH AND SAYLES 79697 — 691-6200

Ackerly, AC 915, PC 2, Dawson
Sands ISD, PO BOX 218 79713 — 2-11111
  Donald Bryan, supt. — 353-4888
Sands S, PO BOX 218 79713 — 2-11111
  B. Keyes, prin. — 353-4888

Addison, AC 214, PC 6, Dallas

Trinity Christian Academy — 2-00011
  17001 ADDISON RD 75248 — 931-8325
  Ed Aronson, prin.

Adrian, AC 806, PC 2, Oldham
Adrian ISD, PO BOX 189 79001 — 2-11111
  Albert Blankenship, supt. — 538-6203
S, PO BOX 189 79001 — 2-11111
  Russ Chisum, prin. — 538-6203

Afton, AC 806, PC 2, Dickens
Patton Springs ISD, PO BOX 32 79220 — 2-11111
  Lee Clanton, supt. — 689-2229
Patton Springs JSHS — 1-00111
  PO BOX 32 79220 — 689-2220
  Lee Clanton, prin.

Agua Dulce, AC 512, PC 3, Nueces
Agua Dulce ISD, PO BOX 250 78330 — 2-11111
  Charles Thompson, supt. — 998-2542
JSHS, PO BOX 250 78330 — 2-00111
  Donald Hise, prin. — 998-2214

Alamo, AC 210, PC 6, Hidalgo
Pharr-San Juan-Alamo ISD
  Supt. — See Pharr
MS, 1819 W US HIGHWAY 83 78516 — 3-00100
  Rene Ramilaz, prin. — 783-1212

Valley Christ Heritage S — 2-11111
  RR 1 BOX 3E 78516 – Mary Rydl, prin. — 787-9743

Alba, AC 903, PC 2, Wood
Alba-Golden ISD, RR 2 BOX 212H 75410 — 3-11111
  Lacy Hogue, supt. — 768-2472
Alba-Golden JSHS — 2-00111
  RR 2 BOX 212 75410 — 768-2301
  Cary Ellis, prin.

Albany, AC 915, PC 4, Shackelford
Albany ISD, PO BOX 188 76430 — 3-11111
  Ron Kincaid, supt. — 762-3974
JSHS, PO BOX 188 76430 — 2-00111
  David Penn, prin. — 762-3974

Aledo, AC 817, PC 4, Parker
Aledo ISD, 412 FM 1187 S 76008 — 4-11111
  Willard Stuard, supt. — 441-8327
HS, 412 FM 1187 S 76008 — 3-00011
  Lynn Boger-McKinney, prin. — 441-8711
MS, 412 FM 1187 S 76008 — 2-00100
  Alicia Massingill, prin. — 441-8347

Alice, AC 512, PC 7, Jim Wells
Alice ISD, 1801 E MAIN ST 78332 — 6-11111
  Henry Herrera, supt. — 664-0981
SHS, 1800 COYOTE TRL 78332 — 4-00001
  Rebecca Palacios, prin. — 664-0126
Adams JHS, 901 E 3RD ST 78332 — 3-00110
  Amando Soto, prin. — 664-9561

Alief, AC 713, PC see Houston
Alief ISD, PO BOX 68 77411 — 8-11111
  M. Willhelm, supt. — 498-8110
Elsik HS, 12601 HIGH STAR 77411 — 5-00011
  Charles Cothran, prin. — 498-8110
Hastings HS, 12301 HIGH STAR 77411 — 5-00011
  Elsie Keeling, prin. — 498-8110
MS, 4415 COOK RD 77411 — 4-00100
  Joe Dombrowski, prin. — 983-8422
Other Schools – See Houston

Allen, AC 214, PC 7, Collin
Allen ISD, PO BOX 13 75002 — 6-11111
  Gene Davenport, supt. — 727-0511
HS, 601 E MAIN ST 75002 — 4-00011
  Patti Barrett, prin. — 727-0400
Ford MS, 630 PARK PLACE DR 75002 — 3-00100
  Ellen Brock, prin. — 727-0590

Allison, AC 806, PC 2, Wheeler
Allison ISD, PO BOX 50 79003 — 1-11111
  Jim Copeland, supt. — 375-2381
S, PO BOX 50 79003 — 1-11111
  Jim Copeland, prin. — 375-2433

Alpine, AC 915, PC 6, Brewster
Alpine ISD, 302 N 6TH ST 79830 — 4-11111
  Kenneth Milligan, supt. — 837-3476
HS, 300 HENDRYX DR 79830 — 2-00011
  Conrado Arriola, prin. — 837-3474
JHS, 704 E SUL ROSS AVE 79830 — 2-00100
  Manuel Jimenez, prin. — 837-2534

Sul Ross State University 79832 — 4-UC
— 837-8052

Altair, AC 409, PC 2, Colorado
Rice Consolidated ISD — 4-11111
  PO BOX 338 77412 — 234-3531
  M. McGaughey, supt.
Rice HS, PO BOX 338 77412 — 2-00011
  Barbara Williams, prin. — 234-3535
Eagle Lake MS, PO BOX 338 77412 — 2-01100
  Jose Rodriguez, prin. — 234-3501

Alto, AC 409, PC 4, Cherokee
Alto ISD, RR 1 BOX 1000 75925 — 3-11111
  Leland Edge, supt. — 858-4391
JSHS, RR 1 BOX 1000 75925 — 2-00111
  Carol Boyd, prin. — 858-3355

Alvarado, AC 817, PC 5, Johnson
Alvarado ISD, PO BOX 387 76009 — 4-11111
  Cleburne Colwell, supt. — 783-2202
HS, PO BOX 387 76009 — 3-00011
  Clarence Phillips, prin. — 783-6840
MS, PO BOX 387 76009 — 3-00100
  Jerald McCanlies, prin. — 783-6825

Alvin, AC 713, PC 7, Brazoria
Alvin ISD, 301 E HOUSE ST 77511 — 6-11111
  William Hasse, supt. — 388-1130
HS, 301 E HOUSE ST 77511 — 5-00011
  Dana Drew, prin. — 331-8151
JHS, 301 E HOUSE ST 77511 — 3-00100
  Linda Robinson, prin. — 585-8491
Harby JHS, 301 E HOUSE ST 77511 — 3-00100
  Cliff Whitlock, prin. — 585-6626
Other Schools – See Manvel

Alvin Community College — 5-CC
  3110 MUSTANG RD 77511 — 388-4636
Living Stones Christian S — 2-11111
  1407 VICTORY LN 77511 — 331-0086
  Bruce Hunter, prin.

Alvord, AC 817, PC 3, Wise
Alvord ISD, PO BOX 70 76225 — 2-11111
  Ray Lea, supt. — 427-5975
HS, PO BOX 70 76225 — 2-00011
  Terry Antoine, prin. — 427-5511
JHS, PO BOX 70 76225 — 2-00100
  Terry Antoine, prin. — 427-5975

Amarillo, AC 806, PC 9, Potter
Amarillo ISD — 8-11111
  7200 W INTERSTATE 40 79106 — 354-4200
  John Wilson, supt.
HS, 4225 DANBURY ST 79109 — 4-00011
  (—), prin. — 354-4400
Caprock HS, 3001 E 34TH AVE 79103 — 4-00011
  Rebecca Harrison, prin. — 371-5500
Palo Duro HS, 1400 N GRANT ST 79107 — 4-00011
  Donald Plumlee, prin. — 381-7100
Tascosa HS, 3921 WESTLAWN ST 79102 — 4-00011
  Calvin Boyer, prin. — 354-4500

Austin MS, 1808 WIMBERLY RD 79109 — 3-00100
  Fred Rutherford, prin. — 354-4450
Bonham MS, 5600 W 49TH AVE 79109 — 3-00100
  Pat Williams, prin. — 354-4550
Bowie MS, 3001 E 12TH AVE 79104 — 4-00100
  Richard La Favers, prin. — 371-5580
Crockett MS, 4720 FLOYD AVE 79106 — 3-00100
  Jan Bowser, prin. — 354-4470
Fannin MS, 4627 S RUSK ST 79110 — 3-00100
  Helen Vinyard, prin. — 354-4570
Houston MS — 3-00100
  815 S INDEPENDENCE ST 79106 — 371-5560
  Brenda Price, prin.
Mann MS, 610 N BUCHANAN ST 79107 — 3-00100
  Cindy Greever, prin. — 371-5600
Travis MS, 2815 MARTIN RD 79107 — 3-00100
  Charles Ritchie, prin. — 381-7200

Canyon ISD
  Supt. — See Canyon
Randall HS, 5800 ATTEBURY DR 79118 — 3-00011
  Stacy Barela, prin. — 358-3888
Valleyview JHS — 3-00100
  9000 VALLEYVIEW DR 79118 — 358-7551
  Steve West, prin.

Highland Park ISD — 3-11111
  PO BOX 30430 79120 — 335-2823
  Michael Salvato, supt.
Highland Park JSHS — 2-00111
  PO BOX 30430 79120 — 335-2821
  Fred Wagner, prin.

River Road ISD, RR 9 BOX 1 79108 — 4-11111
  Marian Fikac, supt. — 383-9578
River Road JSHS, RR 9 BOX 1 79108 — 3-00111
  Glenn Hudgins, prin. — 383-8867

Alamo Catholic HS — 1-00011
  4114 S BONHAM ST 79110 — 355-9637
  Sr. Patricia Connolly, prin.
Amarillo Affiliated School/Medical Tech. — 2-CS
  PO BOX 1110 79175 — 354-1756
Amarillo Catholic MS — 1-00100
  4110 S BONHAM ST 79110 — 356-0550
  Sr. Patricia Connolly, prin.
Amarillo College — 5-CC
  PO BOX 447 79178 — 371-5000
Metro Business Academy — 2-CS
  PO BOX 7609 79114 — 354-0581
San Jacinto Academy — 2-11111
  501 S MISSISSIPPI ST 79106 — 372-2285
  Harry Litle, prin.
Texas State Technical Institute — 3-CC
  PO BOX 11197 79111 — 335-2316

Amherst, AC 806, PC 3, Lamb
Amherst ISD, PO BOX 248 79312 — 2-11111
  Kermit Sorrells, supt. — 246-3501
S, PO BOX 248 79312 — 2-11111
  Byron Shelley, prin. — 246-3221

Anahuac, AC 409, PC 4, Chambers
Anahuac ISD, PO BOX 369 77514 — 4-11111
  Robert Barrett, supt. — 267-3600
HS, PO BOX 369 77514 — 2-00011
  Paul Rice, prin. — 267-6491
JHS, PO BOX 849 77514 — 2-00100
  Robert Perry, prin. — 267-3421

Anderson, AC 409, PC 3, Grimes
Anderson-Shiro Consolidated ISD — 2-11111
  PO BOX 289 77830 — 873-2802
  Michael Morrow, supt.
JSHS, PO BOX 289 77830 — 2-00111
  John Spencer, prin. — 873-2061

Andrews, AC 915, PC 7, Andrews
Andrews ISD, 405 NW 3RD ST 79714 — 5-11111
  Ervin Huddleston, supt. — 523-3640
HS, 405 NW 3RD ST 79714 — 3-00011
  Michael Fetner, prin. — 523-3640
MS, 405 NW 3RD ST 79714 — 3-00100
  Gary Petross, prin. — 523-3640

Angleton, AC 409, PC 7, Brazoria
Angleton ISD — 6-11111
  1900 N DOWNING RD 77515 — 849-8594
  James Smith, supt.
HS, 1201 W HENDERSON RD 77515 — 4-00011
  James Hejl, prin. — 849-8206
Northside S — 3-11111
  1000 RIDGECREST ST 77515 — 849-6189
  Walton Hood, prin.
Angleton MS East — 4-00100
  1800 N DOWNING RD 77515 — 849-4318
  Mark Comneck, prin.
Angleton MS West — 3-00100
  1001 W MULBERRY ST 77515 — 848-8990
  Lorenzo Garcia, prin.

Anna, AC 214, PC 3, Collin
Anna ISD, PO BOX 128 75409 — 3-11111
  A. Mosby, supt. — 924-3955
HS, PO BOX 128 75409 — 2-00011
  Edwin Jones, prin. — 924-3261
MS, PO BOX 128 75409 — 2-00100
  Christy Benedict, prin. — 924-2380

Anson, AC 915, PC 5, Jones
Anson ISD   3-11111
   1509 COMMERCIAL AVE   79501   823-3671
   Bill Huber, supt.
   HS, 1509 COMMERCIAL AVE   79501   2-00011
   Michael Brown, prin.   823-2404
   MS, 1120 AVENUE M   79501   2-00100
   Marvin Ansley, prin.   823-2771

Anthony, AC 915, PC 5, El Paso
Anthony ISD, PO BOX B   79951   3-11111
   Gert Peck, supt.   886-3622
   JSHS, PO BOX B   79951   2-00111
   Joe Varro, prin.   886-6131

Anton, AC 806, PC 4, Hockley
Anton ISD, PO BOX 309   79313   2-11111
   Max Washington, supt.   997-2301
   JSHS, 100 ELLWOOD BLVD   79313   2-00011
   Harvey Chenault, prin.   997-5211

Apple Springs, AC 409, PC 2, Trinity
Apple Springs ISD   2-11111
   PO BOX 125   75926   831-3344
   Martin Earley, supt.
   JSHS, PO BOX 125   75926   1-00011
   Leroy Spencer, prin.   831-3344

Aquilla, AC 817, PC 2, Hill
Aquilla ISD, RR 1 BOX 8A   76622   2-11111
   Elroy Otte, supt.   694-3770
   S, RR 1 BOX 8A   76622   2-11111
   (—), prin.   694-3770

Aransas Pass, AC 512, PC 6, San Patricio
Aransas Pass ISD   4-11111
   244 W HARRISON BLVD   78336   758-3466
   Bob Smith, supt.
   HS, 450 S AVENUE A   78336   3-00011
   Dewey Smith, prin.   758-3248
   Blunt MS, 2103 DEMORY LN   78336   2-00100
   Mary Vickery, prin.   758-2711

Archer City, AC 817, PC 4, Archer
Archer City ISD, PO BOX 926   76351   3-11111
   Donald Shearmire, supt.   574-4536
   JSHS, PO BOX 926   76351   2-00111
   Charles Winkles, prin.   574-4713

Arlington, AC 817, PC 10, Tarrant
Arlington ISD   8-11111
   1203 W PIONEER PKY   76013   460-4611
   Mary Hale, supt.
   SHS, 818 W PARK ROW DR   76013   4-00001
   James Adams, prin.   459-8100
   Houston SHS   4-00001
   2000 SAM HOUSTON DR   76014   460-6282
   Jerry Griffen, prin.
   Lamar SHS, 1400 W LAMAR BLVD   76012   4-00001
   Weldon English, prin.   460-4721
   Martin SHS   4-00001
   4501 W PLEASANT RIDGE RD   76016   483-0400
   John Jacoby, prin.
   Bowie HS, 2101 HIGHBANK DR   76018   4-00011
   Jean Richerson, prin.   468-9370
   Bailey JHS, 2411 WINEWOOD ST   76013   4-00110
   John Moore, prin.   460-3933
   Barnett JHS, 2101 HARWOOD RD   76018   3-00110
   Rebecca Henley, prin.   468-1952
   Boles JHS   4-00110
   3900 SW GREEN OAKS BLVD   76017   483-5216
   (—), prin.
   Carter JHS, 701 THARP ST   76010   4-00110
   Grace Alaman, prin.   460-3242
   Gunn JHS, 3000 S FIELDER RD   76015   3-00110
   Martha Partlow, prin.   465-6381
   Hutcheson JHS   4-00110
   2101 BROWNING DR   76010   460-6572
   Anita Buttram, prin.
   Nichols JHS   4-00110
   2201 ASCENSION BLVD   76006   460-7161
   Linda Denson, prin.
   Shackelford JHS   3-00110
   2000 N FIELDER RD   76012   460-7631
   Tom Dabbert, prin.
   Workman JHS   4-00110
   701 E ARBROOK BLVD   76014   465-4741
   Dave Jones, prin.
   Young JHS, 3200 WOODSIDE DR   76016   4-00110
   B. Burdette, prin.   457-7300

Mansfield ISD
   Supt. — See Mansfield
Howard MS, 7501 CALENDER RD   76017   3-00100
   Sam Bean, prin.   473-5600

Arlington Baptist College   2-UC
   3001 W DIVISION ST   76012   461-8741
Arlington Court Reporting College   3-CS
   1201 N WATSON RD STE 270   76006
   640-8852
Bauder Fashion College   2-CC
   508 S CENTER ST   76010   261-7586
Bryan Institute   2-CS
   1719 W PIONEER PKY   76013   265-5588
Burton Adventist Academy   2-11111
   4611 KELLY ELLIOTT RD   76017   572-0081
   John Hopps, prin.
International Aviation & Travel Academy   2-CS
   300 W ARBROOK BLVD   76014
ITT Technical Institute   2-CC
   2201 ARLINGTON DOWNS RD   76011   640-7100
Oakridge S, 5900 W PIONEER PKY   76013   3-11111
   Andy Broadus, prin.   451-4994

Texas Christian Academy   2-11111
   915 WEB ST   76011   274-5201
   Nolan Lebeaux, prin.
University of Texas   7-UC
   UTA # 19125   76019   273-2011

Arp, AC 903, PC 3, Smith
Arp ISD, PO BOX 70   75750   3-11111
   M. Cosby, supt.   859-8482
   HS, PO BOX 70   75750   2-00011
   Fred Gamble, prin.   859-4917
   JHS, PO BOX 70   75750   2-00100
   Lindsay Marshall, prin.   859-4936

Asherton, AC 210, PC 4, Dimmit
Asherton ISD, PO BOX 398   78827   2-11111
   (—), supt.   468-3323
   JSHS, PO BOX 398   78827   2-00111
   Onesimo Marti, prin.   468-3877

Aspermont, AC 817, PC 4, Stonewall
Aspermont ISD, PO BOX 549   79502   2-11111
   Max Schwarz, supt.   989-3355
   HS, PO BOX 549   79502   1-00011
   Tom Hancock, prin.   989-2707
   JHS, PO BOX 549   79502   1-00100
   Alex Long, prin.   989-3307

Athens, AC 903, PC 7, Henderson
Athens ISD, 104 HAWN ST   75751   5-11111
   E. Martin, supt.   677-6900
   HS, 708 E COLLEGE ST   75751   3-00011
   Tom Whitman, prin.   677-6920
   MS, 610 E COLLEGE ST   75751   3-00100
   Ted Hull, prin.   677-6940

Trinity Valley Community College   5-CC
   500 N PRAIRIEVILLE ST   75751   675-6211

Atlanta, AC 903, PC 6, Cass
Atlanta ISD, 315 N BUCKNER ST   75551   4-11111
   J. Cox, supt.   796-4194
   HS, 705 RABBIT BLVD   75551   3-00011
   Donald Brown, prin.   796-4411
   JHS, 600 HIGH SCHOOL LN   75551   3-00100
   Lewis Lincoln, prin.   796-7928

Aubrey, AC 817, PC 4, Denton
Aubrey ISD, 415 TISDELL LN   76227   3-11111
   James Monaco, supt.   365-2721
   JSHS, 415 TISDELL LN   76227   2-00111
   Marvin Beaty, prin.   365-2433

Austin, AC 512, PC 10, Travis
Austin ISD, 1111 W 6TH ST   78703   8-11111
   Terry Bishop, supt.   499-1700
   Anderson HS, 8403 MESA DR   78759   4-00011
   Darrel Baker, prin.   345-5020
   HS, 1715 W CESAR CHAVEZ ST   78703   4-00011
   Joe Kopec, prin.   474-5951
   Bowie HS   4-00011
   4103 SLAUGHTER LN W   78749   280-5247
   Gregory Ewing, prin.
   Crockett HS   4-00011
   5601 MANCHACA RD   78745   444-5737
   David Kernwein, prin.
   Johnson HS   4-00011
   7309 LAZY CREEK DR   78724   926-9900
   Ed Orum, prin.
   Johnston HS   4-00011
   1112 ARTHUR STILES RD   78721   369-6500
   Hector Montenegro, prin.
   Lanier HS, 1201 PEYTON GIN RD   78758   4-00011
   Ruth Kane, prin.   836-2340
   McCallum HS   4-00011
   5600 SUNSHINE DR   78756   453-2849
   Penny Miller, prin.
   Reagan HS, 7104 BERKMAN DR   78752   4-00011
   Glenn Nolley, prin.   452-9922
   Robbins HS, 3908 AVENUE B   78751   2-00011
   Wanda Flowers, prin.   453-2929
   Travis HS, 1211 E OLTORF ST   78704   4-00011
   Elena Vela, prin.   440-5001
   Bailey MS   3-00100
   4020 LOST OASIS HOLW   78739   292-0480
   Marsha Lyons-Gray, prin.
   Bedichek MS   4-00100
   6800 BILL HUGHES RD   78745   444-2676
   Shelly Pittman, prin.
   Burnet MS, 8401 HATHAWAY DR   78757   3-00100
   James Wilson, prin.   452-6581
   Covington MS   4-00100
   3700 CONVICT HILL RD   78749   892-1643
   Bergeron Harris, prin.
   Dobie MS, 1200 E RUNDBERG LN   78753   4-00100
   Mary Robinson, prin.   836-9301
   Fulmore MS, 200 E MARY ST   78704   3-00100
   Vicky Baldwin, prin.   442-6411
   Kealing JHS   3-00100
   1607 PENNSYLVANIA AVE   78702   478-1797
   Sam Watson, prin.
   Lamar MS, 6201 WYNONA AVE   78757   3-00100
   Darlene Westbrook, prin.   459-6822
   Martin JHS, 1601 HASKELL ST   78702   3-00100
   Martin Bera, prin.   477-9961
   Mendez MS   4-00100
   5106 VILLAGE SQUARE DR   78744   462-3933
   Miguel Perez, prin.
   Murchison MS, 3700 N HILLS DR   78731   4-00100
   Leroy Davis, prin.   345-0674
   O'Henry MS, 2610 W 10TH ST   78703   3-00100
   Pam Hall, prin.   477-2511

   Pearce MS, 6401 N HAMPTON DR   78723   3-00100
   Jane Spencer, prin.   926-7048
   Porter MS, 2206 PRATHER LN   78704   4-00100
   Frances Bush, prin.   442-7073
   Webb MS   2-00100
   601 E SAINT JOHNS AVE   78752   452-7516
   Ernestina Juarez, prin.

Eanes ISD, 601 CAMP CRAFT RD   78746   6-11111
   John Phillips, supt.   329-3626
   Westlake HS   4-00011
   4100 WESTBANK DR   78746   328-4100
   John Matysek, prin.
   Hill Country MS   3-00100
   1300 WALSH TARLTON LN   78746   327-3771
   Richard Bentley, prin.
   West Ridge MS   3-00100
   9201 SCENIC BLUFF DR   78733   263-3144
   Carol McKenzie, prin.

Lake Travis ISD   4-11111
   3322 RANCH RD 620 S   78734   263-4400
   Gloria Berry, supt.
   Lake Travis HS   2-00011
   3322 RANCH RD 620 S   78734   263-4444
   Jeff Kuntzman, prin.
   Lake Travis MS   2-00100
   3322 RANCH RD 620 S   78734   263-4500
   Bill Wakefield, prin.

Pflugerville ISD
   Supt. — See Pflugerville
Westview MS, 1805 SCOFIELD LN   78727   3-00100
   Bonifacio Duran, prin.   837-7795

Round Rock ISD
   Supt. — See Round Rock
Westwood HS   4-00011
   12400 MELLOW MEADOW DR   78750   250-1051
   Linda Watkins, prin.
Canyon Vista MS   3-00100
   8455 SPICEWOOD SPRINGS RD   78759   331-1666
   Don Dishon, prin.
Deerpark MS   3-00100
   8849 ANDERSON MILL RD   78729   335-5196
   Jeff Rhodes, prin.
Grisham MS   3-00100
   10805 SCHOOL HOUSE LN   78750   258-6667
   Helen Herrington, prin.
McNeil JHS, 5720 MCNEIL DR   78729   3-00010
   Alan Veach, prin.   258-3199

Allied Health Careers   2-CS
   5424 W HIGHWAY 290 STE 105   78735
   892-5210
Austin Community College   7-CC
   5930 MIDDLE FISKVILLE RD   78752   483-7000
Austin Presbyterian Theological Seminary   2-UC
   100 E 27TH ST   78705   472-6736
Austin State Hospital   HSP
   4110 GUADALUPE ST   78751   452-0381
Brentwood Christian S   2-11111
   11908 N LAMAR BLVD   78753   835-5983
   Marquita Moss, prin.
Capitol City Careers   2-CS
   4630 WESTGATE BLVD   78745   892-4270
Capitol City Trade and Technical School   1-CS
   205 E RIVERSIDE DR   78704   444-3257
Concordia Lutheran College   3-UC
   3400 N I H 35   78705   800-735-3232
Episcopal Theological Seminary   1-UC
   PO BOX 2247   78768   472-4133
Great Hills Christian S   2-11111
   10500 JOLLYVILLE RD   78759   343-6167
   David Culpepper, prin.
Huston-Tillotson College   3-UC
   1820 E 8TH ST   78702   476-7421
Hyde Park Baptist S   3-11111
   3901 SPEEDWAY   78751   465-8331
   Eugene Johnson, prin.
Institute for Christian Studies   1-UC
   1909 UNIVERSITY AVE   78705   476-2772
ITT Technical Institute   3-CC
   1821 RUTHERFORD LN   78754   339-8200
Kirby Hall S, 306 W 29TH ST   78705   2-11111
   Beverly Rase, prin.   474-1771
Nell Executive Secretary School   2-CS
   2101 S I H 35 STE 300   78741   447-9415
Phillips Sch. of Business and Technology   2-CS
   119 W 8TH ST   78701   478-3446
St. Edward's University   4-UC
   3001 S CONGRESS AVE   78704   448-8500
St. Michaels Academy   2-00011
   3000 BARTON CREEK BLVD   78735   328-2323
   Joel Konzen, prin.
St. Stephens Episcopal S   2-00111
   PO BOX 1868   78767   327-1213
   Frederick Weissbach, prin.
Shivers Cancer Center   HSP
   2600 E MARTIN LUTHER KING J   78702
   478-9681
Southwest School of Electronics   2-CS
   5424 W HIGHWAY 290 STE 200   78735
   892-2640
University of Texas at Austin   8-UC
   0 THE UNIV OF TEXAS   78712   471-7601

Avalon, AC 214, PC 2, Ellis
Avalon ISD, PO BOX 455   76623   2-11111
   Pepper Wells, supt.   627-3251
   S, PO BOX 455   76623   2-11111
   Mark Chesley, prin.   627-3251

Avery, AC 903, PC 2, Red River
Avery ISD, PO BOX 97 75554 2-11111
  Cecil Davis, supt. 684-3460
JSHS, PO BOX 97 75554 2-00111
  Marcus Weaver, prin. 684-3431

Avinger, AC 903, PC 2, Cass
Avinger ISD, RR 2 BOX 22 75630 2-11111
  Charles Traylor, supt. 562-0111
JSHS, RR 2 BOX 22 75630 2-00111
  Doug Carter, prin. 562-1355

Avoca, AC 915, PC 2, Jones
Lueders-Avoca ISD
  Supt. — See Lueders
HS 79503 1-00011
  (—), prin. 773-2938

Axtell, AC 817, PC 2, McLennan
Axtell ISD, PO BOX 429 76624 3-11111
  Stanley Harris, supt. 863-5301
JSHS, PO BOX 429 76624 2-00111
  Dale Monsey, prin. 863-5301

Azle, AC 817, PC 6, Tarrant
Azle ISD, 300 ROE ST 76020 6-11111
  William Ortego, supt. 444-3235
HS, 1200 BOYD RD 76020 4-00011
  Rouel Rothenberger, prin. 444-5555
JHS, 201 SCHOOL ST 76020 3-00100
  D. Hufstedler, prin. 444-2564

Baird, AC 915, PC 4, Callahan
Baird ISD, PO BOX 1147 79504 2-11111
  Steve Maikell, supt. 854-1400
JSHS, PO BOX 1147 79504 2-00111
  James Rector, prin. 854-1334

Ballinger, AC 915, PC 5, Runnels
Ballinger ISD, PO BOX 231 76821 4-11111
  Rodney Gordon, supt. 365-3588
HS, PO BOX 231 76821 2-00011
  Larry Howe, prin. 365-3547
JHS, PO BOX 231 76821 2-00100
  Jim Stubblefield, prin. 365-3537

Balmorhea, AC 915, PC 3, Reeves
Balmorhea ISD, PO BOX 368 79718 2-11111
  Robert Clanton, supt. 375-2223
S, PO BOX 368 79718 2-11111
  Elizabeth Cook, prin. 375-2223

Bandera, AC 210, PC 3, Bandera
Bandera ISD, PO BOX 727 78003 4-11111
  James Stewart, supt. 796-3313
HS, PO BOX 727 78003 2-00011
  Richard Delamain, prin. 796-3753
JHS, PO BOX 727 78003 2-00100
  Robert Weyman, prin. 796-3753

Bangs, AC 915, PC 4, Brown
Bangs ISD, PO BOX 969 76823 3-11111
  Bill Rankin, supt. 752-6612
HS, PO BOX 969 76823 2-00011
  Ronald Beard, prin. 752-6822
JHS, PO BOX 969 76823 2-00100
  Phil Mitchell, prin. 752-6088

Banquete, AC 512, PC 3, Nueces
Banquete ISD, PO BOX 369 78339 3-11111
  Roberto Garcia, supt. 387-2551
HS, PO BOX 369 78339 2-00011
  Paul Smith, prin. 387-8588
JHS, PO BOX 369 78339 2-00100
  Edwin Stuart, prin. 387-6504

Barksdale, AC 210, PC 2, Edwards
Nueces Canyon Consolidated ISD 2-11111
  PO BOX 118 78828 234-3514
  Bob Hatley, supt.
Nueces Canyon HS 2-00011
  PO BOX 118 78828 234-3524
  Warren Colwell, prin.

Bartlett, AC 817, PC 4, Bell
Bartlett ISD, PO BOX 170 76511 2-11111
  William Stidham, supt. 527-4247
JSHS, PO BOX 170 76511 1-00011
  James Crews, prin. 527-3338

Bastrop, AC 512, PC 5, Bastrop
Bastrop ISD, 105 LOOP 150 W 78602 5-11111
  Paul Fleming, supt. 321-2292
HS, 105 LOOP 150 W STE J 78602 4-00011
  (—), prin. 321-1151
MS, 105 LOOP 150 W STE J 78602 4-00100
  Ron Swafford, prin. 321-3911

Bay City, AC 409, PC 7, Matagorda
Bay City ISD, PO BOX 631 77404 5-11111
  David Damerall, supt. 245-5766
HS, 1507 SYCAMORE AVE 77414 4-00011
  Gary Adams, prin. 245-5771
JHS, 2417 16TH ST 77414 3-00100
  James Bowles, prin. 245-6345
McAllister JHS 3-00100
  HIRAM BRANDON DR 77414 245-5591
  John Keys, prin.

Baytown, AC 713, PC 8, Harris
Goose Creek ISD, PO BOX 30 77522 7-11111
  Harry Griffith, supt. 420-4800
Lee HS, PO BOX 30 77522 4-00011
  David Hall, prin. 420-4535
Sterling HS, PO BOX 30 77522 4-00011
  Jim Creel, prin. 420-4500

JHS, PO BOX 30 77522 3-00100
  Charles Polk, prin. 420-4560
Cedar Bayou JHS, PO BOX 30 77522 4-00100
  Mark Stafford, prin. 420-4570
Gentry JHS, PO BOX 30 77522 3-00100
  Rebecca Kaatz, prin. 420-4590
Mann JHS, PO BOX 30 77522 3-00100
  Frank Hutchins, prin. 420-4585
Other Schools – See Highlands

Lee College 5-CC
  511 S WHITING ST 77520 427-5611

Beaumont, AC 409, PC 9, Jefferson
Beaumont ISD 7-11111
  3395 HARRISON AVE 77706 899-9972
  Gerald Mallett, supt.
Central HS, 88 ROYAL PURPLE DR 77702 4-00011
  Sybil Comeaux, prin. 832-2501
West Brook HS 4-00011
  8750 PHELAN BLVD 77706 866-1476
  Terry Ingram, prin.
Austin MS, 3410 AUSTIN ST 77706 4-00100
  Tom Amons, prin. 892-0193
Bowie MS, 3525 CLEVELAND ST 77703 2-00100
  Levoris Roy, prin. 832-4431
Central JHS, 4415 CONCORD RD 77703 3-00010
  Calvin Williams, prin. 892-3811
Crockett MS, 1400 ROYAL ST 77701 3-00100
  Clifford Hardeman, prin. 833-3521
Marshall MS, 6455 GLADYS AVE 77706 3-00100
  Marilyn Busceme, prin. 866-4174
Odom MS, 2550 W VIRGINIA ST 77705 4-00100
  John Nickelbur, prin. 842-3217
South Park MS 3-00100
  4500 HIGHLAND AVE 77705 838-3941
  J. Allardyce, prin.
Westbrook 9th Grade Center 3-00010
  3443 FANNETT RD 77705 842-3841
  David Dunivant, prin.
Hamshire-Fannett ISD
  Supt. — See Hamshire
Hamshire-Fannett MS 2-00100
  RR 8 BOX 1500 77705 794-1502
  Mike Mason, prin.

Baptist Hospital of Southeast Texas HSP
  PO BOX 1591 77704 839-5351
Chenier Business School 2-CS
  4320 CALDER AVE 77706 899-1862
Delta Career Institute 2-CS
  1310 PENNSYLVANIA ST 77701 833-6161
Lamar University 6-UC
  PO BOX 10009 77710 880-8888
Monsignor Kelly HS 3-00011
  5950 KELLY DR 77707 866-2351
  Mary Gagne, prin.
St. Elizabeth Hospital HSP
  2830 CALDER ST 77702 892-7171
Wilson HS 2-00111
  8001 OLD VOTH ROAD 77708 899-4615
  Ron Miller, prin.

Beckville, AC 903, PC 3, Panola
Beckville ISD, PO BOX 37 75631 3-11111
  James Dunlap, supt. 678-3311
HS, PO BOX 37 75631 2-00011
  Donald Fallin, prin. 678-3591
MS, PO BOX 37 75631 2-00100
  Charles Bledsoe, prin. 678-3851

Bedford, AC 817, PC 8, Tarrant
Hurst-Euless-Bedford ISD 7-11111
  1849 CENTRAL DR 76022 283-4461
  Ronald Caloss, supt.
Tech Ed Ctr 76022 Vo Tech
  George Leigh, prin. 354-3542
JHS, 325 CAROLYN DR 76021 3-00110
  Carl Mathews, prin. 285-3284
Harwood JHS, 3000 MARTIN DR 76021 3-00110
  Sam Whitley, prin. 354-3360
Other Schools – See Euless, Hurst

Beeville, AC 512, PC 7, Bee
Beeville ISD 5-11111
  2400 N SAINT MARYS ST 78102 358-7111
  Larry Moehnke, supt.
Jones HS, 1900 N ADAMS ST 78102 4-00011
  Bill Doughty, prin. 358-5935
Moreno JHS 3-00100
  301 N MINNESOTA ST 78102 358-6262
  Albert McGuill, prin.

Bee County College 4-CC
  3800 CHARCO RD 78102 358-3130

Bellaire, AC 713, PC 7, Harris
Houston ISD
  Supt. — See Houston
HS, 5100 MAPLE ST 77401 5-00011
  Vivian Dailey, prin. 295-3704

Episcopal HS 2-00011
  4621 FOURNACE PL 77401 660-7840
  Rev. Borg, prin.

Bellevue, AC 817, PC 2, Clay
Bellevue ISD, PO BOX 38 76228 2-11111
  Benjamin Daws, supt. 928-2505
S, PO BOX 38 76228 2-11111
  G. Chasteen, prin. 928-2104

Bells, AC 903, PC 3, Grayson
Bells ISD, PO BOX 7 75414 3-11111
  Joe Stubblefield, supt. 965-7721
HS, PO BOX 7 75414 2-00111
  Joe Moore, prin. 965-7315
MS, PO BOX 7 75414 2-00100
  (—), prin. 965-4835

Bellville, AC 409, PC 5, Austin
Bellville ISD, 404 E MAIN ST 77418 4-11111
  Bill Shaver, supt. 865-3133
HS, 404 E MAIN ST 77418 2-00011
  Wayne Alexander, prin. 865-3681
JHS, 404 E MAIN ST 77418 2-00100
  John Conley, prin. 865-5966

Belton, AC 817, PC 7, Bell
Belton ISD, PO BOX 269 76513 6-11111
  J. Pirtle, supt. 939-1881
HS, PO BOX 300 76513 4-00011
  Robert Hughes, prin. 939-5884
Career Ctr 76513 Vo Tech
  Ken Von Gonten, prin. 939-5872
JHS, PO BOX 360 76513 4-00100
  Joe Brooks, prin. 939-3535

University of Mary Hardin-Baylor 4-UC
  UMHB STATION BOX 8001 76513
  800-727-8642

Benavides, AC 512, PC 4, Duval
Benavides ISD, PO BOX P 78341 3-11111
  Ramon Tanguma, supt. 256-3333
HS, FM 2295 W 78341 2-00011
  Trinidad Perez, prin. 256-3311
JHS, SCHOOL ST 78341 2-01100
  Victoriano Leal, prin. 256-3372

Ben Bolt, AC 512, PC 2, Jim Wells
Ben Bolt-Palito Blanco ISD 2-11111
  PO BOX 547 78342 664-9822
  David Deaver, supt.
Ben Bolt-Palito Blanco HS 2-00011
  PO BOX 547 78342 664-9822
  Susan Warner, prin.
MS, PO BOX 547 78342 2-01100
  Reynaldo Moreno, prin. 664-9568

Benjamin, AC 817, PC 2, Knox
Benjamin ISD, PO BOX 166 79505 1-11111
  John Koepf, supt. 454-2231
S, PO BOX 166 79505 1-11111
  Louis Baty, prin. 454-2231

Ben Wheeler, AC 903, PC 3, Van Zandt
Martins Mill ISD 2-11111
  RR 2 BOX 280 75754 479-3234
  Seth Adams, supt.
Martins Mills S, RR 2 BOX 280 75754 2-11111
  Guy Furr, prin. 479-3706

Big Lake, AC 915, PC 5, Reagan
Reagan County ISD 4-11111
  1111 E 12TH ST 76932 884-3705
  Robert Carruthers, supt.
Reagan HS, 1111 E 12TH ST 76932 2-00011
  Richard McReavy, prin. 884-3714
Reagan MS 2-00100
  500 N PENNSYLVANIA AVE 76932 884-3728
  John Walts, prin.

Big Sandy, AC 903, PC 4, Upshur
Big Sandy ISD, PO BOX 598 75755 3-11111
  Richard Gott, supt. 636-4455
JSHS, PO BOX 598 75755 2-00111
  William Smith, prin. 636-5287

Big Spring, AC 915, PC 7, Howard
Big Spring ISD, 708 E 11TH PL 79720 5-11111
  William McQueary, supt. 264-3600
HS, PO BOX 590 79721 4-00011
  Robert Bowermon, prin. 264-3641
Runnels JHS, PO BOX 590 79721 2-00100
  Royce Cox, prin. 264-4135

Howard College 4-CC
  1001 BIRDWELL LN 79720 264-5000
Howard College 4-CC
  AVE C BIG SPRING INDST PARK 79720
  267-6311
Scenic Mountain Medical Center HSP
  1601 W 11TH PL 79720 263-1211

Bishop, AC 512, PC 5, Nueces
Bishop Consolidated ISD 4-11111
  719 E 6TH ST 78343 584-3591
  Nathan Lee, supt.
HS, 717 E 6TH ST 78343 2-00011
  Charles Schooley, prin. 584-2547
Luehrs JHS, 701 E 6TH ST 78343 2-00100
  John Parker, prin. 584-3576

Blackwell, AC 915, PC 2, Nolan
Blackwell Consolidated ISD 2-11111
  PO BOX 505 79506 282-2311
  Richard Wood, supt.
HS, PO BOX 505 79506 1-00011
  Jack Vining, prin. 282-2311

Blanco, AC 210, PC 4, Blanco
Blanco ISD, PO BOX 340 78606 3-11111
  Gerald Atkins, supt. 833-4414
HS, PO BOX 340 78606 2-00011
  Don Boyd, prin. 893-4337

MS, PO BOX 340 78606 — 2-00100
Tom Bibb, prin. — 833-5570

Blanket, AC 915, PC 2, Brown
Blanket ISD, PO BOX 1138 76432 — 2-11111
Michael Turner, supt. — 748-5311
HS, PO BOX 1138 76432 — 1-00011
David Ingram, prin. — 748-3341

Bloomburg, AC 903, PC 2, Cass
Bloomburg ISD, PO BOX 156 75556 — 2-11111
Ron Surratt, supt. — 728-5216
JSHS, PO BOX 156 75556 — 2-00011
Bill Frost, prin. — 728-5216

Blooming Grove, AC 903, PC 3, Navarro
Blooming Grove ISD
PO BOX 258 76626 — 3-11111
Robert Clanton, supt. — 695-2541
JSHS, PO BOX 258 76626 — 2-00011
Hugh Ellis, prin. — 695-2536

Bloomington, AC 512, PC 4, Victoria
Bloomington ISD, PO BOX 158 77951 — 3-11111
Michael Nelms, supt. — 897-1323
JSHS, PO BOX 158 77951 — 2-00011
Eddie Rendon, prin. — 897-1551

Blue Ridge, AC 214, PC 3, Collin
Blue Ridge ISD
425 N CHURCH ST 75424 — 2-11111
Mark Weisner, supt. — 752-5554
HS, 425 N CHURCH ST 75424 — 2-00011
Lyndall Pittman, prin. — 752-5707

Blum, AC 817, PC 2, Hill
Blum ISD, PO BOX 548 76627 — 2-11111
Randolph Garner, supt. — 874-5231
JSHS, PO BOX 548 76627 — 2-00011
Jerry Kirby, prin. — 874-5231

Boerne, AC 210, PC 5, Kendall
Boerne ISD, 123 JOHNS RD 78006 — 5-11111
Joseph Doenges, supt. — 249-2567
HS, 1 GREYHOUND LN 78006 — 3-00011
Samuel Champion, prin. — 249-2591
MS, 240 JOHNS RD 78006 — 3-00100
Sandra Radtke, prin. — 249-2528

Bogata, AC 903, PC 4, Red River
Talco-Bogata Consolidated ISD
PO BOX 130 75417 — 3-11111
Fred Wade, supt. — 632-5205
Rivercrest HS, PO BOX 130 75417 — 2-00011
Lenard Miller, prin. — 632-5204

Boling, AC 409, PC 3, Wharton
Boling ISD, PO BOX 278 77420 — 3-11111
Charles Butcher, supt. — 657-2770
HS, PO BOX 428 77420 — 2-00011
Jack Moss, prin. — 657-2816
Iago JHS, PO BOX 158 77420 — 2-00100
Ron Luco, prin. — 657-2826

Bonham, AC 903, PC 6, Fannin
Bonham ISD, PO BOX 490 75418 — 4-11111
W. McEachern, supt. — 583-5526
HS, PO BOX 490 75418 — 2-00011
Mike Reece, prin. — 583-5567
Rather JHS, PO BOX 490 75418 — 2-00100
Delores Babers, prin. — 583-7474

Booker, AC 806, PC 4, Lipscomb
Booker ISD, PO BOX 288 79005 — 2-11111
Larry Darbison, supt. — 658-4501
HS, PO BOX 288 79005 — 2-00011
Jim Hoyle, prin. — 658-4521
JHS, PO BOX 288 79005 — 2-01100
Jim Hoyle, prin. — 658-4521

Borger, AC 806, PC 7, Hutchinson
Borger ISD, 200 E 9TH ST 79007 — 5-11111
Larry Coffman, supt. — 273-6481
HS, 600 W 1ST ST 79007 — 3-00011
George Hanna, prin. — 273-1029
MS, 1200 S FLORIDA ST 79007 — 4-01100
Thomas Rogers, prin. — 273-1037

Frank Phillips College — 2-CC
PO BOX 5118 79008 — 274-5311

Bovina, AC 806, PC 4, Parmer
Bovina ISD, PO BOX 70 79009 — 3-11111
Thomas Cathey, supt. — 238-1336
JSHS, PO BOX 70 79009 — 2-00111
Glenda Nuttall, prin. — 238-1317
JHS, PO BOX 70 79009 — 2-00100
Brenda Wilson, prin. — 238-1317

Bowie, AC 817, PC 5, Montague
Bowie ISD, PO BOX 1168 76230 — 4-11111
Joe Vassar, supt. — 872-1151
HS, 800 N MILL ST 76230 — 3-00011
John Hodge, prin. — 872-1154
JHS, 421 E TARRANT ST 76230 — 2-00100
Thomas McMurray, prin. — 872-1152

Gold Burg ISD, RR 1 76230 — 2-11111
Tom Stillwell, supt. — 872-3562
Stone Burg JSHS, RR 1 76230 — 1-00111
Carroll Magee, prin. — 872-3562

Boyd, AC 817, PC 4, Wise
Boyd ISD, PO BOX 608 76023 — 4-11111
Larry Enis, supt. — 433-2327

SHS, PO BOX 608 76023 — 2-00001
Jerry Howard, prin. — 433-2327
MS, PO BOX 608 76023 — 2-00110
William Bishop, prin. — 433-2327

Boys Ranch, AC 806, PC 3, Oldham
Boys Ranch ISD, PO BOX 219 79092 — 2-11111
Hayden Willhite, supt. — 534-2221
HS, PO BOX 219 79092 — 2-00011
Ken Sawin, prin. — 534-2221
Blakemore MS, PO BOX 219 79092 — 2-00100
Frederick Wagner, prin. — 534-2221

Brackettville, AC 210, PC 4, Kinney
Brackett ISD, PO BOX 586 78832 — 3-11111
Grady Mills, supt. — 563-2491
JSHS, PO BOX 586 78832 — 2-00111
Don Sims, prin. — 563-2491

Brady, AC 915, PC 6, McCulloch
Brady ISD, 1000 S WALL ST 76825 — 4-11111
Douglas Moore, supt. — 597-2301
HS, 1000 S WALL ST 76825 — 2-00011
Jerry Dyes, prin. — 597-2491
JHS, 1000 S WALL ST 76825 — 2-00100
David Siler, prin. — 597-8522

Breckenridge, AC 817, PC 6, Stephens
Breckenridge ISD
PO BOX 1738 76424 — 4-11111
Marshall McMillan, supt. — 559-2278
HS, 500 W LINDSEY ST 76424 — 2-00011
Robert Parks, prin. — 559-2231
JHS, 500 W LINDSEY ST 76424 — 2-00100
William Ash, prin. — 559-6581

Bremond, AC 817, PC 4, Robertson
Bremond ISD, PO BOX 190 76629 — 2-11111
James Johnson, supt. — 746-7145
HS, PO BOX 190 76629 — 2-00011
Debbi Doan, prin. — 746-7061
MS, PO BOX 190 76629 — 1-00100
Anthony Miller, prin. — 746-5022

Brenham, AC 409, PC 7, Washington
Brenham ISD, PO BOX 1147 77834 — 5-11111
Darrell Garrison, supt. — 836-5672
HS, 1200 CARLEE DR 77833 — 4-00011
Steven Murray, prin. — 836-5611
MS, 1600 S HORTON ST 77833 — 4-00100
Ben Seeker, prin. — 836-6122

Blinn College — 6-CC
902 COLLEGE AVE 77833 — 830-4140

Bridge City, AC 409, PC 6, Orange
Bridge City ISD, PO BOX 847 77611 — 5-11111
Harold Ramm, supt. — 735-5459
HS, PO BOX 847 77611 — 3-00011
James Aarons, prin. — 735-5516
JHS, PO BOX 697 77611 — 3-00100
Randy Codsy, prin. — 735-5313

Bridgeport, AC 817, PC 5, Wise
Bridgeport ISD, 2107 15TH ST 76426 — 4-11111
John Brooks, supt. — 683-5124
HS, 702 17TH ST 76426 — 2-00011
Robert Sivley, prin. — 683-4064
MS, 1400 HIGHWAY 380 76426 — 3-00100
Jack Burns, prin. — 683-2273

Briscoe, AC 806, PC 1, Wheeler
Fort Elliott CISD, PO BOX 138 79011 — 1-11111
Fred Downs, supt. — 375-2454
Other Schools – See Mobeetie

Broaddus, AC 409, PC 2, San Augustine
Broaddus ISD, PO BOX 58 75929 — 2-11111
Hershell Gore, supt. — 872-3041
JSHS, PO BOX 58 75929 — 2-00111
Virgil Pate, prin. — 872-3610

Bronte, AC 915, PC 3, Coke
Bronte ISD, PO BOX 670 76933 — 2-11111
Michael Hartman, supt. — 473-2511
JSHS, PO BOX 670 76933 — 2-00111
John Turner, prin. — 473-2511

Brookeland, AC 409, PC 2, Sabine
Brookeland ISD, PO BOX 8 75931 — 2-11111
John Lynch, supt. — 698-2677
JSHS, PO BOX 8 75931 — 1-00111
Donald Powell, prin. — 698-2413

Brookesmith, AC 915, PC 1, Brown
Brookesmith ISD, PO BOX 706 76827 — 2-11111
Tom Hall, supt. — 643-3023
HS, PO BOX 706 76827 — 1-00011
Tom Hall, prin. — 646-3791

Brookshire, AC 713, PC 5, Waller
Royal ISD
Supt. — See Pattison
Royal MS, PO BOX 577 77423 — 2-00100
Robert Reeves, prin. — 934-2241

Brownfield, AC 806, PC 6, Terry
Brownfield ISD, 601 TAHOKA RD 79316 — 5-11111
John Dosher, supt. — 637-2591
HS, 701 N FIR ST 79316 — 3-00011
Carey White, prin. — 637-4523
MS, 1001 E BROADWAY ST 79316 — 3-00100
Lowell Strike, prin. — 637-7521

Union ISD, HC 5 BOX 61 79316 — 1-11111
(—), supt. — 755-2721
Union S, HC 5 BOX 61 79316 — 1-11111
James Adkins, prin. — 755-2724

Brownsboro, AC 903, PC 3, Henderson
Brownsboro ISD, PO BOX 465 75756 — 4-11111
Elton Caldwell, supt. — 852-3701
HS, PO BOX 465 75756 — 3-00011
Bob Teague, prin. — 852-2321
JHS, PO BOX 465 75756 — 2-00100
Tony Volentine, prin. — 852-6931

Brownsville, AC 210, PC 9, Cameron
Brownsville ISD, 1900 PRICE RD 78521 — 8-11111
Esperanza Zendejas, supt. — 548-8000
Hanna HS, 2615 E PRICE RD 78521 — 5-00011
Sylvia Perez, prin. — 548-7600
Lopez HS, 3205 S DAKOTA AVE 78521 — 3-00011
Lovella Ervin, prin. — 542-4918
Pace HS — 4-00011
314 W LOS EBANOS BLVD 78520 — 548-7700
Timothy Coyle, prin.
Porter HS — 5-00011
3500 INTERNATIONAL BLVD 78521 — 548-7800
Brenda Fernandez, prin.
Rivera HS, 6955 FM 802 78521 — 4-00011
Daniel Salinas, prin. — 831-8700
Central IS, 708 PALM BLVD 78520 — 4-00100
Alfredo Garcia, prin. — 548-8600
Cummings IS — 3-00100
1800 CUMMINGS PL 78520 — 548-8630
Estela Aguirre, prin.
Faulk IS, 2200 ROOSEVELT ST 78521 — 3-00100
William Gutierrez, prin. — 548-8500
Oliveira IS — 4-00100
444 LAND O LAKES DR 78521 — 548-8530
Carlos Garza, prin.
Perkins IS, 4750 AUSTIN RD 78521 — 4-00100
Hector Hernandez, prin. — 831-8770
Stell IS — 3-00100
1105 E LOS EBANOS BLVD 78520 — 548-8560
Raquel Ayala, prin.
Vela IS, 4905 PAREDES LINE RD 78521 — 3-00100
John Pineda, prin. — 548-7770

St. Joseph Academy — 3-00111
101 SAINT JOSEPH DR 78520 — 542-3581
Br. Garza, prin.
South Texas Vocational-Technical Inst. — 2-CS
2255 N CORIA ST 78520
Texas Southmost College — 6-CC
80 FORT BROWN ST 78520 — 544-8200
University of Texas-Pan American — 3-UC
1614 RIDGELY RD 78520 — 542-6882

Brownwood, AC 915, PC 7, Brown
Brownwood ISD, PO BOX 730 76804 — 5-11111
Don Martin, supt. — 643-5644
HS, 2100 SLAYDEN ST 76801 — 3-00011
Tony Swafford, prin. — 646-9549
JHS — 3-00100
STEPHEN AUSTIN AND CALVERT 76801 — 646-9547
Roland Graves, prin.

Central Texas Commercial College — 2-CS
PO BOX 1324 76804 — 646-0521
Howard Payne University — 4-UC
1000 FISK AVE 76801 — 646-2502

Bruni, AC 512, PC 2, Webb
Webb Consolidated ISD — 2-11111
PO BOX 206 78344 — 747-5415
David Jones, supt.
HS, PO BOX 206 78344 — 1-00011
David Jones, prin. — 747-5323
MS, PO BOX 206 78344 — 1-01100
David Jones, prin. — 747-5261

Bryan, AC 409, PC 8, Brazos
Bryan ISD, 101 N TEXAS AVE 77803 — 7-11111
Sarah Ashburn, supt. — 361-5200
SHS, 3401 E 29TH ST 77802 — 4-00001
Jerry Ellis, prin. — 361-5400
Austin MS, 801 S ENNIS ST 77803 — 3-00100
John Moehlman, prin. — 361-9700
Bryan JHS At Lamar — 3-00010
1901 VILLA MARIA 77803 — 361-9770
Gradyne Sennette, prin.
Long MS, 449 S FM 2818 77803 — 3-00100
David Garinger, prin. — 361-9500
Rayburn MS — 3-00100
1449 S EAST BYPASS 77802 — 361-9600
Harry Crenshaw, prin.

Allen Academy, PO BOX 953 77806 — 2-11111
Lynred Hoepfner, prin. — 776-0731
Blinn College — 2-CC
1905 TEXAS AVE 77590 — 822-5278
St. Michael's Academy — 2-11111
2505 S COLLEGE AVE 77801 — 822-2715
Lynred Hoepfner, prin.

Bryson, AC 817, PC 3, Jack
Bryson ISD, PO BOX 309 76427 — 2-11111
Bill Wood, supt. — 392-3281
JSHS, PO BOX 309 76427 — 2-00111
Tom Tomlin, prin. — 392-2601

Buckholts, AC 817, PC 2, Milam
Buckholts ISD, PO BOX 248 76518 — 2-11111
J. Hauk, supt. — 593-3011

S, PO BOX 248 76518 — 2-11111
Thomas Rector, prin. — 593-2744

Buffalo, AC 903, PC 4, Leon
Buffalo ISD, PO BOX C 75831 — 3-11111
Harvey Compton, supt. — 322-3765
HS, CEDAR CREEK RD 75831 — 2-00011
Harvey Compton, prin. — 322-4243
MS, PO BOX C 75831 — 3-01100
Dudley Dickens, prin. — 322-4340

Bullard, AC 903, PC 3, Smith
Bullard ISD, PO BOX 250 75757 — 3-11111
James Tollett, supt. — 894-6639
HS, PO BOX 250 75757 — 2-00011
Curtis Miles, prin. — 894-6591
MS, PO BOX 250 75757 — 2-01100
Richard Tedder, prin. — 894-6533

Buna, AC 409, PC 4, Jasper
Buna ISD, PO BOX 1087 77612 — 4-11111
Leland Williams, supt. — 994-5102
HS, PO BOX 1087 77612 — 2-00011
David Hicks, prin. — 994-3311
JHS, PO BOX 1087 77612 — 3-01100
Thomas Saunders, prin. — 994-3838

Burkburnett, AC 817, PC 7, Wichita
Burkburnett ISD — 5-11111
416 GLENDALE ST 76354 — 569-3326
Danny Taylor, supt.
HS, 109 E KRAMER RD 76354 — 3-00011
Bill Darland, prin. — 569-1411
JHS, 102 S AVENUE D 76354 — 3-00100
J. Phillips, prin. — 569-3381

Burkeville, AC 409, PC 3, Newton
Burkeville ISD, PO BOX 218 75932 — 2-11111
James Holt, supt. — 565-2201
JSHS, PO BOX 218 75932 — 2-00111
William Turner, prin. — 565-4338

Burleson, AC 817, PC 7, Johnson
Burleson ISD — 6-11111
1160 SW WILSHIRE BLVD 76028 — 447-5730
Wallace Cockerham, supt.
HS, 517 SW JOHNSON AVE 76028 — 4-00011
Terry Ford, prin. — 447-5700
MS, 316 SW THOMAS ST 76028 — 4-00100
Susan Shaha, prin. — 447-5750

Burnet, AC 512, PC 5, Burnet
Burnet Consolidated ISD — 4-11111
308 E BRIER LN 78611 — T. Scott, supt. — 756-2124
HS, 1401 N MAIN ST 78611 — 3-00011
Mike Cargill, prin. — 756-6193
MS, 308 E BRIER LN 78611 — 2-00100
Elvin Simmons, prin. — 756-6182

Burton, AC 409, PC 2, Washington
Burton ISD, PO BOX 37 77835 — 2-11111
Gary Herbert, supt. — 289-3131
JSHS, PO BOX 37 77835 — 2-00111
B. Hauerland, prin. — 289-3830

Byers, AC 817, PC 3, Clay
Byers ISD, PO BOX 286 76357 — 2-11111
J. Priddy, supt. — 529-6102
S, PO BOX 286 76357 — 2-11111
Joseph Turner, prin. — 529-6101

Bynum, AC 817, PC 2, Hill
Bynum ISD, PO BOX 68 76631 — 2-11111
Polly Boyd, supt. — 623-4251
S, PO BOX 68 76631 — 2-11111
Amy Feller, prin. — 623-4251

Caddo Mills, AC 903, PC 4, Hunt
Caddo Mills ISD, PO BOX 160 75135 — 3-11111
Jerry Hollon, supt. — 527-3164
HS, PO BOX 160 75135 — 2-00011
Anthony Mulkey, prin. — 527-3164
MS, PO BOX 160 75135 — 2-00100
H. Rickerson, prin. — 527-3161

Caldwell, AC 409, PC 5, Burleson
Caldwell ISD, 203 N GRAY ST 77836 — 4-11111
Larry Nichols, supt. — 567-9559
HS, 203 N GRAY ST 77836 — 2-00011
Ed Presley, prin. — 567-9506
MS, 203 N GRAY ST 77836 — 2-00100
Richard Taylor, prin. — 567-3282

Calvert, AC 409, PC 4, Robertson
Calvert ISD, PO BOX 7 77837 — 2-11111
Hugh Norwood, supt. — 364-2824
JSHS, PO BOX 7 77837 — 2-00111
James Gwaltney, prin. — 364-2845

Cameron, AC 817, PC 6, Milam
Cameron ISD, PO BOX 712 76520 — 4-11111
B. Dulin, supt. — 697-3512
Yoe HS, 400 E 10TH ST 76520 — 2-00011
Luther Flinn, prin. — 697-3902
Thomas JHS, 1400 W 6TH ST 76520 — 2-00100
John Matlock, prin. — 697-2131

Campbell, AC 903, PC 3, Hunt
Campbell ISD, PO BOX 157 75422 — 2-11111
James Calvert, supt. — 862-3250
JSHS, PO BOX 157 75422 — 2-00111
James Hudson, prin. — 862-3250

Canadian, AC 806, PC 4, Hemphill
Canadian ISD, 800 HILLSIDE AVE 79014 — 3-11111
Marlin Marcum, supt. — 323-5393

HS, 800 HILLSIDE AVE 79014 — 2-00011
David Jackson, prin. — 323-5373
MS, 800 HILLSIDE AVE 79014 — 2-00100
Larry Dyess, prin. — 323-5351

Canton, AC 903, PC 5, Van Zandt
Canton ISD, 225 W ELM ST 75103 — 4-11111
Monte Geren, supt. — 567-4179
HS, 1100 N HIGHWAY 243 75103 — 2-00011
Kelvin Hesse, prin. — 567-6561
MS, 1115 S BUFFALO ST 75103 — 2-00100
Richard Callahan, prin. — 567-4329

Canutillo, AC 915, PC 5, El Paso
Canutillo ISD, PO BOX 100 79835 — 5-11111
John Brooks, supt. — 877-3726
HS, PO BOX 100 79835 — 3-00011
Lionel Rubio, prin. — 877-2511
MS, PO BOX 100 79835 — 3-00100
Ronald Haugen, prin. — 877-2551

Canyon, AC 806, PC 7, Randall
Canyon ISD, PO BOX 899 79015 — 6-11111
Francis King, supt. — 655-1081
HS, 100 9TH AVE 79015 — 3-00011
Duane Chapman, prin. — 655-2168
JHS, 606 8TH ST 79015 — 3-00100
Robert Daniel, prin. — 655-2108
Other Schools – See Amarillo

West Texas State University — 6-UC
2501 4TH AVE 79016 — 656-2020

Carmine, AC 409, PC 2, Fayette
Round Top-Carmine ISD — 2-11111
PO BOX 385 78932 — 278-3252
Jack Flinn, supt.
JSHS, PO BOX 385 78932 — 1-00111
Alvis Mueller, prin. — 278-3252

Carrizo Springs, AC 210, PC 6, Dimmit
Carrizo Springs Consolidated ISD — 4-11111
102 N 5TH ST 78834 — 876-3503
Dorothy Carter, supt.
HS, FM ROAD 1556 78834 — 3-00011
Manuel Saldana, prin. — 876-5237
JHS, 102 N 5TH ST 78834 — 3-00100
Gustavo Marinez, prin. — 876-2496

Carrollton, AC 214, PC 8, Dallas
Carrollton-Farmers Branch ISD — 7-11111
PO BOX 115186 75011 — 323-5700
Monte Sriver, supt.
Smith HS, 2335 N JOSEY LN 75006 — 4-00011
Kathy Alvoid, prin. — 323-5800
Turner HS, 1600 S JOSEY LN 75006 — 4-00011
Sheila Maher, prin. — 323-5900
Blalack JHS — 3-00100
1706 E PETERS COLONY RD 75007 — 323-6480
Lora Folsom, prin.
Perry JHS, 1709 E BELT LINE RD 75006 — 3-00100
Bob Burns, prin. — 323-6625
Other Schools – See Dallas, Farmers Branch

Carrollton Christian Academy — 3-11111
1820 PEARL ST 75006 — 242-6688
Emerald Cummings, prin.

Carthage, AC 903, PC 6, Panola
Carthage ISD, 1 BULLDOG DR 75633 — 5-11111
Jesse Wheat, supt. — 693-3806
HS, 1 BULLDOG DR 75633 — 3-00011
Wallace Bird, prin. — 693-2552
JHS, 1 BULLDOG DR 75633 — 3-00100
Russell Porter, prin. — 693-2751

Panola College — 4-CC
1109 W PANOLA ST 75633 — 800-776-8153

Castroville, AC 210, PC 4, Medina
Medina Valley ISD, 8449 FM 471 S 78009 — 4-11111
Dana Marable, supt. — 538-2243
Medina Valley HS, 8395 FM 471 S 78009 — 2-00011
Paul Holzhaus, prin. — 538-2514
Medina Valley JHS, 8557 FM 471 S 78009 — 2-00100
William Harmon, prin. — 538-2770

Cayuga, AC 903, PC 2, Anderson
Cayuga ISD, PO BOX 427 75832 — 3-11111
Tom Sanders, supt. — 928-2102
JSHS, PO BOX 427 75832 — 2-00111
(—), prin. — 928-2294

Cedar Hill, AC 214, PC 7, Dallas
Cedar Hill ISD — 5-11111
270 S HIGHWAY 67 75104 — 291-1581
(—), supt.
HS, PO BOX 248 75106 — 4-00011
John Rich, prin. — 291-4273
Permenter MS, PO BOX 248 75106 — 3-00100
John Ringhauser, prin. — 291-5270

Northwood University — 4-UC
PO BOX 58 75106 — 800-927-9663
Trinity Christian S — 3-11111
PO BOX 949 75106 — 291-2501
Kathy Watts, prin.

Cedar Park, AC 512, PC 6, Williamson

Hilltop Baptist Academy — 2-00111
1150 S BELL BLVD 78613 — 258-0089
Jim Clarke, prin.

Celeste, AC 903, PC 3, Hunt
Celeste ISD, PO BOX 67 75423 — 2-11111
Cecil Lafavers, supt. — 568-4721
HS, PO BOX 67 75423 — 2-00011
Don Williams, prin. — 568-4721
MS, PO BOX 67 75423 — 1-00100
Susan Morton, prin. — 568-4612

Celina, AC 214, PC 4, Collin
Celina ISD, PO BOX 188 75009 — 3-11111
Don Newsom, supt. — 382-2751
HS, PO BOX 188 75009 — 2-00011
Eddie Burkett, prin. — 382-2303
MS, PO BOX 188 75009 — 2-01100
Jerry Moore, prin. — 382-2373

Center, AC 409, PC 5, Shelby
Center ISD, 404 MOSBY ST 75935 — 4-11111
H. Halvorson, supt. — 598-5642
HS, 302 KENNEDY ST 75935 — 3-00011
Charlene Crocker, prin. — 598-6173
JHS, 624 MALONE DR 75935 — 2-00100
Lyndon Jobe, prin. — 598-5619

Center Point, AC 210, PC 3, Kerr
Center Point ISD, PO BOX 377 78010 — 2-11111
Donald Madden, supt. — 634-2171
JSHS, PO BOX 377 78010 — 2-00111
Steve Freeman, prin. — 634-2244

Centerville, AC 903, PC 3, Leon
Centerville ISD, PO BOX 218 75833 — 3-11111
Bob Hardee, supt. — 536-2935
JSHS, PO BOX 218 75833 — 2-00111
B. Hardee, prin. — 536-2625

Channelview, AC 713, PC 8, Harris
Channelview ISD — 6-11111
1403 SHELDON RD 77530 — 452-8008
Larry Curry, supt.
HS, 828 SHELDON RD 77530 — 4-00011
W. Bigott, prin. — 457-7300
Johnson JHS, 15500 PROCTOR ST 77530 — 3-00100
James Barker, prin. — 452-8030

Channing, AC 806, PC 2, Hartley
Channing ISD, PO BOX A 79018 — 2-11111
James Davis, supt. — 235-3432
S, PO BOX A 79018 — 2-11111
Don Johnson, prin. — 235-3719

Charlotte, AC 210, PC 4, Atascosa
Charlotte ISD, PO BOX 489 78011 — 3-11111
R. Sinks, supt. — 277-1431
HS, PO BOX 489 78011 — 2-00011
Don Morrow, prin. — 277-1432
JHS, PO BOX 489 78011 — 2-00100
Margaret McCloskey, prin. — 277-1646

Cherokee, AC 915, PC 2, San Saba
Cherokee ISD, PO BOX 100 76832 — 2-11111
James Ball, supt. — 622-4298
JSHS, PO BOX 100 76832 — 1-00111
Kenneth Johanson, prin. — 622-4298

Chester, AC 409, PC 2, Tyler
Chester ISD, PO BOX 28 75936 — 2-11111
Gary Gazaway, supt. — 969-2211
JSHS, PO BOX 28 75936 — 2-00111
James Clements, prin. — 969-2211

Chico, AC 817, PC 3, Wise
Chico ISD, PO BOX 95 76431 — 3-11111
Bill Kingston, supt. — 644-2228
HS, PO BOX 95 76431 — 2-00011
Brian Deady, prin. — 644-5783
MS, PO BOX 95 76431 — 1-00100
Kit Mason, prin. — 644-2228

Childress, AC 817, PC 6, Childress
Childress ISD, PO BOX 179 79201 — 4-11111
James Apple, supt. — 937-2501
HS, PO BOX 179 79201 — 2-00011
Bill Clifton, prin. — 937-6131
JHS, PO BOX 179 79201 — 2-00100
Tom Morris, prin. — 937-3641

Chillicothe, AC 817, PC 3, Hardeman
Chillicothe ISD, PO BOX 418 79225 — 2-11111
Jerry Baird, supt. — 852-5391
JSHS, PO BOX 550 79225 — 2-00111
Greg Stone, prin. — 852-5322

Chilton, AC 817, PC 3, Falls
Chilton ISD, PO BOX 488 76632 — 2-11111
Jack Davis, supt. — 546-3101
S, PO BOX 488 76632 — 2-11111
Ann McGruder, prin. — 546-3101

China, AC 409, PC 4, Jefferson
Hardin-Jefferson ISD
Supt. — See Sour Lake
Henderson JHS, PO BOX 278 77613 — 2-00100
Ronnie Sims, prin. — 752-2141

China Spring, AC 817, PC 3, McLennan
China Spring ISD, PO BOX 250 76633 — 4-11111
Susan Holley, supt. — 836-1115
HS, PO BOX 250 76633 — 2-00011
Sherry Hungate, prin. — 836-4611
MS, PO BOX 250 76633 — 2-00100
David McClellan, prin. — 836-4611

Chireno, AC 409, PC 2, Nacogdoches
Chireno ISD, PO BOX 85 75937 — 2-11111
Harold Hagle, supt. — 362-2132

HS, PO BOX 85 75937 — 1-00011
Jamie Parmer, prin. — 362-2132

Christoval, AC 915, PC 3, Tom Green
Christoval ISD, PO BOX 162 76935 — 2-11111
John Reeves, supt. — 896-2520
JSHS, PO BOX 162 76935 — 2-00111
Brad Bressie, prin. — 896-2355

Cisco, AC 817, PC 5, Eastland
Cisco ISD, PO BOX 1645 76437 — 3-11111
C. Saunders, supt. — 442-3056
HS, PO BOX 1645 76437 — 2-00011
Randy Simmans, prin. — 442-3051
JHS, PO BOX 1645 76437 — 2-00100
Mary Schustereit, prin. — 442-3004

Cisco Junior College — 4-CC
RR 3 BOX 3 76437 — 442-2567

Clarendon, AC 806, PC 4, Donley
Clarendon ISD, PO BOX 610 79226 — 2-11111
James Barefield, supt. — 874-2062
HS, PO BOX 610 79226 — 2-00011
Elvin Hargis, prin. — 874-2181

Clarendon College — 3-CC
PO BOX 968 79226 — 874-3571

Clarksville, AC 903, PC 5, Red River
Clarksville ISD, PO BOX 1016 75426 — 4-11111
William Wilkens, supt. — 427-3891
HS, PO BOX 1016 75426 — 2-00011
Dharlene Jones, prin. — 427-3891
Cheatham MS, PO BOX 1016 75426 — 2-00100
Robert Williams, prin. — 427-3891

Claude, AC 806, PC 4, Armstrong
Claude ISD, PO BOX 209 79019 — 2-11111
J. Collier, supt. — 226-7331
HS, PO BOX 209 79019 — 2-00011
Virgie Montgomery, prin. — 226-2191

Cleburne, AC 817, PC 7, Johnson
Cleburne ISD, 103 S WALNUT ST 76031 — 6-11111
James Grunert, supt. — 645-4373
HS, 1501 HARLIN DR 76031 — 4-00011
Joe Ripple, prin. — 641-6641
JHS, 801 N COLONIAL DR 76031 — 3-00100
Lonnie Borden, prin. — 645-4318

Cleveland, AC 713, PC 6, Liberty
Cleveland ISD, 103 LEGION AVE 77327 — 5-11111
Linden Parrish, supt. — 592-8717
HS, 2000 E HOUSTON ST 77327 — 3-00011
Lubbie Whitmire, prin. — 592-8752
JHS, 1600 E HOUSTON ST 77327 — 3-00100
Curtis Brinkley, prin. — 593-1148

Tarkington ISD, RR 6 BOX 130 77327 — 4-11111
Ken Miller, supt. — 592-8781
Tarkington HS, RR 6 BOX 130 77327 — 2-00011
Joel Lawson, prin. — 592-7739
Tarkington JHS, RR 6 BOX 130 77327 — 2-00100
George Daniel, prin. — 592-7737

Heritage Christian Academy — 2-11111
510 RIVER ST 77327 — 592-6430
Jennifer Cooper, prin.

Clifton, AC 817, PC 5, Bosque
Clifton ISD, 1102 N AVENUE N 76634 — 4-11111
Marlene Zipperlen, supt. — 675-8606
HS, 1102 N AVENUE N 76634 — 2-00011
Ron Massey, prin. — 675-8606
MS, 411 S AVENUE H 76634 — 2-00100
Ronnie Prueitt, prin. — 675-6544

Clint, AC 915, PC 4, El Paso
Clint ISD, PO BOX 779 79836 — 5-11111
Carroll Welch, supt. — 851-3368
HS, PO BOX 779 79836 — 2-00011
Herman Hudson, prin. — 851-2344
Mountain View HS — 3-00011
PO BOX 779 79836 — 857-1011
Richard Burton, prin.
JHS, PO BOX 779 79836 — 2-00100
Carlos Lopez, prin. — 851-2261
East Montana MS, PO BOX 779 79836 — 2-01100
Higinio Pena, prin. — 855-6840

Clute, AC 409, PC 6, Brazoria
Brazosport ISD
Supt. — See Freeport
Brazoswood HS — 4-00011
302 W BRAZOSWOOD DR 77531 — 265-6161
Elizabeth Allen, prin.
Clute IS, 421 E MAIN ST 77531 — 3-00100
Larry Meche, prin. — 265-2531

Clyde, AC 915, PC 5, Callahan
Clyde Consolidated ISD — 4-11111
PO BOX 479 79510 — 893-4222
Tony Reed, supt.
HS, PO BOX 660 79510 — 2-00011
Jim Parker, prin. — 893-2161
JHS, PO BOX 776 79510 — 2-00100
Randy Berryhill, prin. — 893-5788

Eula ISD, RR 1 BOX 229A 79510 — 2-11111
Teddy Bedwell, supt. — 529-3186
Eula HS, RR 1 BOX 229A 79510 — 2-00011
Bill Acorn, prin. — 529-3605

Eula MS, RR 1 BOX 229A 79510 — 2-00100
Bill Acorn, prin. — 529-3287

Coahoma, AC 915, PC 4, Howard
Coahoma ISD, PO BOX 110 79511 — 3-11111
L. Monroe, supt. — 394-4290
HS, PO BOX 110 79511 — 2-00011
Larry Hudson, prin. — 394-4535
JHS, PO BOX 110 79511 — 2-00100
Thomas Alvis, prin. — 394-4615

Coldspring, AC 409, PC 3, San Jacinto
Coldspring-Oakhurst Consolidated ISD — 4-11111
PO BOX 39 77331 — 653-4638
Larry Bennett, supt.
Jones HS, PO BOX 39 77331 — 2-00011
James Marsh, prin. — 653-2367
Lincoln JHS, PO BOX 39 77331 — 2-00100
Frank Dawson, prin. — 653-2397

Coleman, AC 915, PC 6, Coleman
Coleman ISD, PO BOX 900 76834 — 4-11111
Arthur Casey, supt. — 625-3575
HS, 201 W 15TH ST 76834 — 2-00011
Royce Young, prin. — 625-2156
JHS, 301 W 15TH ST 76834 — 2-00100
Tim Parrott, prin. — 625-3593

College Station, AC 409, PC 8, Brazos
College Station ISD — 6-11111
1812 WELSH AVE 77840 — 764-5400
Raymond Chancellor, supt.
A & M Cons. HS, 701 WEST LOOP 77840 — 4-00011
William Currey, prin. — 764-5500
JHS, 900 ROCK PRAIRIE RD 77845 — 3-00100
Thomas Stolt, prin. — 764-5545

Texas A & M University — 8-UC
0 TEXAS A AND M UNIV 77843 — 845-1031

Colleyville, AC 817, PC 7, Tarrant
Grapevine-Colleyville ISD
Supt. — See Grapevine
MS, 1100 BOGART ST 76034 — 3-00100
Gilbert Jennings, prin. — 498-3371
Heritage MS, 5300 HERITAGE AVE 76034 — 4-00100
Leslie Evan, prin. — 488-9588

Collinsville, AC 903, PC 4, Grayson
Collinsville ISD, PO BOX 49 76233 — 2-11111
John Henry, supt. — 429-6112
JSHS, PO BOX 49 76233 — 2-00111
Walton Vincent, prin. — 429-6272

Colmesneil, AC 409, PC 3, Tyler
Colmesneil ISD, PO BOX 37 75938 — 2-11111
Larry Stenson, supt. — 837-5757
HS, PO BOX 37 75938 — 2-00011
Ben Stewart, prin. — 837-2225
MS, PO BOX 37 75938 — 2-01100
Walter McAlpin, prin. — 837-5757

Colorado City, AC 915, PC 5, Mitchell
Colorado ISD, PO BOX 1268 79512 — 4-11111
Don Nimmo, supt. — 728-3721
Colorado HS, PO BOX 1268 79512 — 2-00011
Russell Merket, prin. — 728-3424
Colorado MS, 312 E 12TH ST 79512 — 2-00100
Mark Merrell, prin. — 728-2673

Columbus, AC 409, PC 5, Colorado
Columbus ISD — 4-11111
105 HIGHWAY FM 806 78934 — 732-5704
W. Clore, supt.
HS, 105 HIGHWAY FM 806 78934 — 2-00011
James Story, prin. — 732-5746
JHS, 702 RAMPART ST 78934 — 2-00100
Michael Payne, prin. — 732-2891

Comanche, AC 915, PC 5, Comanche
Comanche ISD, 405 N LANE ST 76442 — 4-11111
Gene Williams, supt. — 356-2727
HS, N HIGHWAY 16 76442 — 2-00011
Jerome Hall, prin. — 356-2581
Jeffries JHS, VALLEY FORGE DR 76442 — 2-00100
Bernard Pope, prin. — 356-5467

Comfort, AC 210, PC 4, Kendall
Comfort ISD, PO BOX 398 78013 — 3-11111
George Derr, supt. — 995-3664
HS, PO BOX 280 78013 — 2-00011
Douglas Coleman, prin. — 995-3533
MS, PO BOX 280 78013 — 2-01100
Larry Stanley, prin. — 995-3533

Commerce, AC 903, PC 6, Hunt
Commerce ISD, PO BOX 1251 75429 — 4-11111
Patricia Pope, supt. — 886-3755
HS, PO BOX 1251 75429 — 2-00011
Jon Whittemore, prin. — 886-3756
MS, PO BOX 1251 75429 — 2-00100
Lonnie Beadles, prin. — 886-3795

East Texas State University — 6-UC
ETSU STATION 75429 — 886-5081

Como, AC 903, PC 3, Hopkins
Como-Pickton ISD, PO BOX 18 75431 — 3-11111
Lewis Teer, supt. — 488-3600
Como-Pickton S, PO BOX 18 75431 — 3-11111
Sandra Billodeau, prin. — 488-3671

Comstock, AC 915, PC 2, Val Verde
Comstock ISD, PO BOX 905 78837 — 2-11111
David Nelson, supt. — 292-4444

S, PO BOX 905 78837 — 2-11111
Elvia Vielma, prin. — 292-4444

Conroe, AC 409, PC 8, Montgomery
Conroe ISD, 702 N THOMPSON ST 77301 — 7-11111
David Lusk, supt. — 756-7751
HS, 3200 W DAVIS ST 77304 — 5-00011
David Graham, prin. — 756-4416
Oak Ridge HS — 4-00011
27330 OAK RIDGE SCHOOL RD 77385 — 292-9800
John Burke, prin.
Area Vo S 77301 — Vo Tech
David Graham, prin. — 760-6660
Travis JHS — 3-00100
1100 N THOMPSON ST 77301 — 756-2621
Chris Kattner, prin.
Washington JHS, 507 AVENUE K 77301 — 3-00100
Rosalyn Bratcher, prin. — 756-3023
York JHS — 3-00100
27300 OAK RIDGE SCHOOL RD 77385 — 367-6753
Hartwell Brown, prin.
Other Schools – See The Woodlands

Lifestyle Christian S — 2-11111
1201 HILLCREST DR 77301 — 756-9383
Steve Grysells, prin.

Converse, AC 512, PC 6, Bexar
Judson ISD, PO BOX 249 78109 — 7-11111
G. Elolf, supt. — 659-9600
Judson HS, 9142 FM 78 78109 — 5-00011
Thomas Parsley, prin. — 658-6251
Other Schools – See San Antonio, Universal City

Coolidge, AC 817, PC 3, Limestone
Coolidge ISD, PO BOX 70 76635 — 2-11111
James Smith, supt. — 786-4822
S, PO BOX 70 76635 — 2-11111
Danny Baker, prin. — 786-4822

Cooper, AC 903, PC 4, Delta
Cooper ISD, PO BOX 478 75432 — 3-11111
F. Wilkerson, supt. — 395-2112
HS, PO BOX 478 75432 — 2-00011
Jerry Stout, prin. — 395-2111
JHS, PO BOX 478 75432 — 2-00100
Gary McCain, prin. — 395-2111

Coppell, AC 214, PC 7, Dallas
Coppell ISD — 5-11111
200 S DENTON TAP RD 75019 — 471-1111
Wilburn Echols, supt.
HS, 185 W PARKWAY BLVD 75019 — 3-00011
Mary King, prin. — 471-2002
MS East, 400 MOCKINGBIRD LN 75019 — 3-00100
Judy Denman, prin. — 393-3131
MS West, 1301 WRANGLER DR 75019 — 3-00100
Vernon Edin, prin. — 462-1200

Copperas Cove, AC 817, PC 7, Coryell
Copperas Cove ISD — 6-11111
PO BOX 580 76522 — 547-7076
Richard Kirkpatrick, supt.
HS, PO BOX 580 76522 — 4-00011
W. Sanders, prin. — 547-2535
JHS, PO BOX 580 76522 — 3-00100
Stacey Schulze, prin. — 547-6959

Corpus Christi, AC 512, PC 10, Nueces
Calallen ISD, 4205 WILDCAT DR 78410 — 5-11111
Arturo Almendarez, supt. — 241-9321
Calallen HS, 4001 WILDCAT DR 78410 — 4-00011
Michael Sandroussi, prin. — 241-4841
Calallen MS, 4602 CORNETT DR 78410 — 4-00100
Donna Magee, prin. — 241-2302

Corpus Christi ISD — 8-11111
PO BOX 110 78403 — 886-9200
Abelardo Saavedra, supt.
Carroll HS, 5301 WEBER RD 78411 — 4-00011
Scott Owings, prin. — 853-0151
King HS, 5225 GOLLIHAR RD 78412 — 4-00011
Sherry Blackett, prin. — 992-0130
Miller HS, 1 BATTLIN BUC BLVD 78408 — 4-00011
Conrado Garcia, prin. — 884-4963
Moody HS, 1818 TROJAN DR 78416 — 4-00011
Ricardo Almendarez, prin. — 854-3261
Ray HS, 1002 TEXAN TRL 78411 — 4-00011
Bill Hamrick, prin. — 855-7361
Baker MS, 3445 PECAN ST 78411 — 4-00100
Raymond Davis, prin. — 878-1420
Browne MS — 4-00100
4301 SCHANEN BLVD 78413 — 878-1426
Jan Powers, prin.
Cullen MS, 5225 GREELY DR 78412 — 3-00100
Sid Garner, prin. — 994-3630
Cunningham MS — 3-00100
4321 PRESCOTT ST 78416 — 878-1432
Raul Prezas, prin.
Driscoll MS, 261 DRISCOLL DR 78408 — 3-00100
Marvin Spears, prin. — 886-9365
Haas MS, 6630 MCARDLE RD 78412 — 3-00100
Adolfo Garza, prin. — 994-3636
Hamlin MS, 3900 HAMLIN DR 78411 — 3-00100
Nancy Benson, prin. — 878-1438
Kaffie MS — 4-00100
5922 BROCKHAMPTON ST 78414 — 994-3600
Arnold Saavedra, prin.
Martin MS — 3-00100
3502 GREENWOOD DR 78416 — 878-1400
Maggie Ramirez, prin.
Seale MS, 1707 AYERS ST 78404 — 3-00100
Richard Harbin, prin. — 886-9359

South Park MS   3-00100
3001 MCARDLE RD   78415   878-1446
O. Garcia, prin.

Flour Bluff ISD   6-11111
2505 WALDRON RD   78418   937-2681
Ronald Rowell, supt.

Flour Bluff HS   4-00011
2505 WALDRON RD   78418   937-2635
Nancy Horton, prin.

Flour Bluff JHS   3-00100
2505 WALDRON RD   78418   937-3135
Ralph Gowens, prin.

Tuloso-Midway ISD   5-11111
PO BOX 10900   78460   241-3286
Suzanne Nelson, supt.

Tuloso-Midway HS   3-00011
PO BOX 10900   78460   241-4253
Rodney Sumner, prin.

Tuloso-Midway JHS   3-00100
PO BOX 10900   78460   241-2396
Melodie McClarren, prin.

West Oso ISD   4-11111
5050 ROCKFORD DR   78416   855-3321
Arthur Gregory, supt.

West Oso HS, 5202 BEAR LN   78405   2-00011
Daniel Noyola, prin.   289-5214

West Oso JHS   2-00100
1115 BLOOMINGTON ST   78416   855-0221
Elvira Garcia, prin.

Archbishop Romero JHS   2-00100
2121 MARY ST   78405   882-1601
Mary Sayre, prin.

Bishop Garriga JHS   2-00100
3114 SARATOGA BLVD   78415   851-0853
Barbara Heater, prin.

Corpus Christi Academy   2-00011
3036 SARATOGA BLVD   78415   853-6227
Thomas Hart, prin.

Corpus Christi State University   5-UC
6300 OCEAN DR   78412   994-2624

Del Mar College   6-CC
101 BALDWIN BLVD   78404   886-1398

Incarnate Word Academy   2-00011
2910 S ALAMEDA ST   78404   883-0857
George Potter, prin.

Incarnate Word JHS   2-00100
2917 AUSTIN ST   78404   883-0857
Sr. Barbara Netek, prin.

Southern Careers Institute   2-CS
5333 EVERHART RD   78411   857-5700

Corrigan, AC 409, PC 4, Polk
Corrigan-Camden ISD   4-11111
PO BOX 01060   75939   398-4040
Jacob Sherman, supt.

Corrigan-Camden HS   2-00011
S HOME ST #01060   75939   398-2543
Sam McDonald, prin.

Corrigan-Camden JHS   2-00100
S HOME ST #01060   75939   398-2962
Allen Norton, prin.

Corsicana, AC 903, PC 7, Navarro
Corsicana ISD, 601 N 13TH ST   75110   5-11111
James Dickson, supt.   874-7441

SHS, 3701 W HIGHWAY 22   75110   3-00100
Alexander Williams, prin.   874-8211

Collins JHS, 1500 DOBBINS RD   75110   3-00110
Gilbert Hall, prin.   872-3979

Mildred ISD, RR 6 BOX 113   75110   2-11111
Douglas Lane, supt.   872-6505

Mildred JSHS, RR 6 BOX 113   75110   2-00111
Ray Goodman, prin.   872-6505

Navarro College   5-CC
3200 W 7TH AVE   75110   874-6501

Cotton Center, AC 806, PC 2, Hale
Cotton Center ISD   2-11111
PO BOX 350   79021   879-2160
Keith Gast, supt.

S, PO BOX 350   79021   2-11111
Jeffrey McClure, prin.   879-2176

Cotulla, AC 210, PC 5, La Salle
Cotulla ISD, PO BOX 699   78014   4-11111
Ernesto Tijerina, supt.   879-3073

HS, PO BOX 699   78014   2-00011
(—), prin.   879-2374

JHS, PO BOX 699   78014   2-00100
Jesus Jaimes, prin.   879-3031

Covington, AC 817, PC 2, Hill
Covington ISD, PO BOX 67   76636   2-11111
Charles Moore, supt.   854-2215

S, PO BOX 67   76636   2-11111
Henry Strauch, prin.   854-2215

Crandall, AC 214, PC 4, Kaufman
Crandall ISD, PO BOX 128   75114   4-11111
Ben Brandenburg, supt.   287-5346

HS, PO BOX 520   75114   2-00011
Sarah Wright, prin.   472-3910

Raynes MS, PO BOX 490   75114   2-01100
Dorothy Wasunyk, prin.   472-3644

Crane, AC 915, PC 5, Crane
Crane ISD, 511 W 8TH ST   79731   4-11111
Joe Allen, supt.   558-2292

HS, 511 W 8TH ST   79731   2-00011
James Crews, prin.   558-3573

JHS, 511 W 8TH ST   79731   2-00100
Jesse McWhorter, prin.   558-3701

Cranfills Gap, AC 817, PC 2, Bosque
Cranfills Gap ISD, PO BOX 67   76637   2-11111
John Bryant, supt.   597-2505

S, PO BOX 67   76637   2-11111
Charles McGehee, prin.   597-2225

Crawford, AC 817, PC 3, McLennan
Crawford ISD, PO BOX 120   76638   2-11111
Kenneth Judy, supt.   486-2381

JSHS, PO BOX 120   76638   2-00111
Edwin Harris, prin.   486-2381

Crockett, AC 409, PC 6, Houston
Crockett ISD   4-11111
704 E BURNETT AVE   75835   544-2125
Dorman Jackson, supt.

HS, 704 E BURNETT AVE   75835   2-00011
William Miller, prin.   544-2193

JHS, 704 E BURNETT AVE   75835   2-00100
Roy Tucker, prin.   544-2149

Crosby, AC 713, PC 4, Harris
Crosby ISD, PO BOX 2009   77532   5-11111
Don Hendrix, supt.   328-9200

HS, 14703 FM 2100 RD   77532   3-00100
Jerri Bone, prin.   328-9237

MS, 14705 FM 2100 RD   77532   3-00100
Roy Gilbert, prin.   328-9264

Crosbyton, AC 806, PC 4, Crosby
Crosbyton ISD   3-11111
204 S HARRISON ST   79322   675-2611
Jerry Scott, supt.

HS, 204 S HARRISON ST   79322   2-00011
Edred Robinson, prin.   675-2201

JHS, 204 S HARRISON ST   79322   2-00100
Doris Scoggin, prin.   675-2032

Cross Plains, AC 817, PC 4, Callahan
Cross Plains ISD, PO BOX 669   76443   2-11111
Marion Thompson, supt.   725-6121

HS, PO BOX 669   76443   2-00011
Jerry Boyd, prin.   725-6121

Crowell, AC 817, PC 4, Foard
Crowell ISD, PO BOX 239   79227   2-11111
L. Wall, supt.   684-1331

JSHS, PO BOX 239   79227   2-00111
Don Ballard, prin.   684-1331

Crowley, AC 817, PC 6, Tarrant
Crowley ISD, PO BOX 688   76036   6-11111
S. Poynter, supt.   297-5800

HS, 1005 W MAIN ST   76036   4-00011
Michael Leach, prin.   297-5810

Stevens MS   3-00100
1016 HIGHWAY 1187   76036   297-5840
Richard Allie, prin.

Other Schools – See Fort Worth

Crystal City, AC 210, PC 6, Zavala
Crystal City ISD   4-11111
805 E CROCKETT ST   78839   374-2367
Rodolfo Espinosa, supt.

HS, 1111 N 11TH AVE   78839   3-00011
Mercedes Casarez, prin.   374-2341

Fly JHS, 715 E CROCKETT ST   78839   2-00100
Manuel Espinosa, prin.   374-2371

Cuero, AC 512, PC 6, De Witt
Cuero ISD   4-11111
405 PARK HEIGHTS DR   77954   275-3832
Dwight Winkler, supt.

HS, 401 PARK HEIGHTS DR   77954   3-00011
Aubrey Kelley, prin.   275-6157

JHS, 502 PARK HEIGHTS DR   77954   2-00100
Kenneth Bright, prin.   275-2222

Cumby, AC 903, PC 3, Hopkins
Cumby ISD, RR 2 BOX 25H   75433   2-11111
Ron Stanley, supt.   994-2261

JSHS, RR 2 BOX 25H   75433   1-00111
Robert Fairchild, prin.   994-2260

Miller Grove ISD   2-11111
RR 2 BOX 101   75433   459-3288
Tommy Turner, supt.

Miller Grove S, RR 2 BOX 101   75433   2-11111
Alan Simpson, prin.   459-3288

Cushing, AC 409, PC 3, Nacogdoches
Cushing ISD, PO BOX 337   75760   2-11111
Albert Tidwell, supt.   326-4890

S, PO BOX 337   75760   2-11111
Lynn Moore, prin.   326-4271

Daingerfield, AC 903, PC 5, Morris
Daingerfield-Lone Star ISD   4-11111
200 TIGER DR   75638   645-2239
Bobby Brown, supt.

HS, 202 TIGER DR   75638   3-00011
Robert Caskey, prin.   645-3968

JHS, 200 TEXAS ST   75638   2-00100
Jim Davis, prin.   645-2261

Daisetta, AC 409, PC 3, Liberty
Hull-Daisetta ISD, PO BOX 477   77533   3-11111
Curtis Barnett, supt.   536-6321

Hull-Daisetta HS, PO BOX 477   77533   2-00011
Larry Boyette, prin.   536-6307

Hull-Daisetta JHS, PO BOX 477   77533   2-00100
Richard Oakes, prin.   587-4366

Dalhart, AC 806, PC 6, Dallam
Dalhart ISD   4-11111
315 ROCK ISLAND AVE   79022   249-2256
Ned Burns, supt.

HS, 1802 E 16TH ST   79022   2-00011
Cecil Marshall, prin.   249-8626

JHS, 801 OAK AVE   79022   2-00100
Jack Boston, prin.   249-2551

Dallas, AC 214, PC 12, Dallas
Carrollton-Farmers Branch ISD
Supt. — See Carrollton

Long JHS, 2525 FRANKFORD RD   75287   3-00100
Kathy McWhorter, prin.   323-5941

Dallas ISD, 3700 ROSS AVE   75204   9-11111
Chad Woolery, supt.   824-1620

Adams HS, 2101 MILLMAR DR   75228   4-00011
Larry Smith, prin.   319-0140

Adamson HS, 201 E 9TH ST   75203   4-00011
Martin Riojas, prin.   944-3800

Business Management HS   3-00011
2218 BRYAN ST   75201   953-1123
Thelma Benavides, prin.

Carter HS   4-00011
1819 W WHEATLAND RD   75232   224-3584
Joseph Brew, prin.

Health Profession Magnet HS   3-00011
4515 ROSS AVE   75204   841-5120
Betty Stapp, prin.

Hillcrest HS, 9924 HILLCREST RD   75230   4-00011
Linda Isaacks, prin.   987-8412

Jefferson HS   4-00011
4001 WALNUT HILL LN   75229   904-1000
Margaret Steere, prin.

Kimball HS   4-00011
3606 S WESTMORELAND RD   75233   331-7700
Roosevelt Vaughn, prin.

Law & Public Administration Magnet HS   2-00011
912 S ERVAY ST   75201   746-2600
Robert Giesler, prin.

Lincoln HS, 2826 HATCHER ST   75215   4-00011
Napoleon Lewis, prin.   421-7121

Madison HS   3-00011
3000 MRTN LTHR KING JR BLVD   75215   565-6510
Ora Watson, prin.

North Dallas HS   4-00011
3120 N HASKELL AVE   75204   559-1900
Oscar Rodriguez, prin.

Pinkston HS, 2200 DENNISON ST   75212   3-00011
Charles Fisher, prin.   689-1603

Roosevelt HS   4-00011
525 BONNIE VIEW RD   75203   944-3540
Melvin Traylor, prin.

Samuell HS, 8928 PALISADE DR   75217   4-00011
Bill Poteet, prin.   309-7040

Seagoville HS   3-00011
15920 SEAGOVILLE RD   75253   557-6300
(—), prin.

Skyline HS, 7777 FORNEY RD   75227   5-00011
Robert Payton, prin.   388-5731

Smith HS, 3030 STAG RD   75241   3-00011
Thurman Stephens, prin.   302-2030

South Oak Cliff HS   4-00011
3601 S MARSALIS AVE   75216   371-4391
Waylon Wallace, prin.

Spruce HS   4-00011
9733 OLD SEAGOVILLE RD   75217   286-0330
Cele Rodriguez, prin.

Sunset HS   4-00011
2120 W JEFFERSON BLVD   75208   944-3640
Michael Stiles, prin.

Washington HS, 2501 FLORA ST   75201   3-00011
Robert Watkins, prin.   720-7300

White HS, 4505 RIDGESIDE DR   75244   4-00011
Thomas Ward, prin.   308-8900

Wilson HS, 100 S GLASGOW DR   75214   4-00011
Eduardo Torres, prin.   841-5100

Metropolitan HS   2-00111
1403 CORINTH ST   75215   565-6447
Donna Johnson, prin.

Multiple Careers Magnet HS   Vo Tech
4528 RUSK AVE   75204   841-5220
Norwood King, prin.

Skyline Career Development Ctr   Vo Tech
7777 FORNEY RD   75227   388-5731
Robert Payton, prin.

Anderson MS, 3400 GARDEN LN   75215   4-00100
Wilber Williams, prin.   565-6400

Atwell MS   3-00100
1303 REYNOLDSTON LN   75232   302-2150
Robert Craft, prin.

Browne MS, 3333 SPRAGUE DR   75233   4-00100
Reginald Walker, prin.   331-7944

Cary MS, 3978 KILLION DR   75229   3-00100
Joy Barnhart, prin.   904-1120

Comstock MS, 7044 HODDE ST   75217   3-00100
John Washington, prin.   309-7115

Edison Environmental Science Academy   3-00100
2940 SINGLETON BLVD   75212   689-1649
Joseph Lopez, prin.

Florence MS   3-00100
1625 N MASTERS DR   75217   216-3000
Willie Sanders, prin.

Franklin MS, 6920 MEADOW RD   75230   3-00100
Vickie Miller, prin.   987-8450

Gaston MS, 9565 MERCER DR   75228   3-00100
Karen Ramos, prin.   319-0240

Greiner MS | 4-00100
625 S EDGEFIELD AVE 75208 | 944-3420
Linda Kimm, prin.
Hill MS, 505 EASTON RD 75218 | 3-00100
Michael Paschall, prin. | 553-4400
Holmes MS, 2001 E KIEST BLVD 75216 | 4-00100
Ronald Peace, prin. | 302-2380
Hood MS, 7625 HUME DR 75227 | 3-00100
Arthur Gillum, prin. | 381-8700
Hulcy MS, 9339 S POLK ST 75232 | 3-00100
Eugene Young, prin. | 228-7530
Long MS, 6116 REIGER AVE 75214 | 3-00100
Alan Harris, prin. | 841-5270
Longfellow MS, 5314 BOAZ ST 75209 | 2-00100
Carrie Coy, prin. | 904-1190
Marsh MS | 3-00100
3838 CROWN SHORE DR 75244 | 888-3100
John Riddles, prin.
Rusk MS, 2929 INWOOD RD 75235 | 3-00100
Robert Munoz, prin. | 904-1050
Spence MS, 4001 CAPITOL AVE 75204 | 3-00100
Claudia Lozano, prin. | 841-5200
Stockard MS, 2300 S RAVINIA DR 75211 | 3-00100
Alberto Miranda, prin. | 331-7800
Stone MS, 4747 VETERANS DR 75216 | 2-00100
Myrtle Walker, prin. | 302-2180
Storey MS, 3000 MARYLAND AVE 75216 | 3-00100
Clyde Stokes, prin. | 302-2240
Zumwalt MS | 3-00100
2445 E LEDBETTER DR 75216 | 302-2200
Claudis Allen, prin.
Other Schools – See Seagoville

Duncanville ISD
Supt. — See Duncanville
Duncanville 9th Grade S | 3-00010
7101 W WHEATLAND RD 75249 | 298-5436
Mike Chrietzberg, prin.

Highland Park ISD | 5-11111
7015 WESTCHESTER DR 75205 | 523-1600
John Connolly, supt.
Highland Park HS | 4-00011
4220 EMERSON AVE 75205 | 523-1700
(—), prin.
McCulloch MS | 3-00100
3520 NORMANDY AVE 75205 | 523-1900
Robert Dyer, prin.

Richardson ISD
Supt. — See Richardson
Lake Highlands SHS | 4-00001
9449 CHURCH RD 75238 | 553-4200
Ron Mathews, prin.
Forest Meadow JHS | 4-00110
9373 WHITEHURST DR 75243 | 341-1550
Jeff Kane, prin.
Lake Highlands JHS | 3-00110
10301 KINGSLEY RD 75238 | 348-0313
Randall Reid, prin.
Liberty JHS, 10330 LAWLER RD 75243 | 3-00110
Olen Pyles, prin. | 690-3191
Parkhill JHS | 3-00110
16500 SHADYBANK DR 75248 | 931-8304
Lynda Mayberry, prin.
Westwood JHS | 3-00110
7630 ARAPAHO RD 75248 | 233-7751
Selma Russell, prin.

Wilmer-Hutchins ISD | 5-11111
3820 E ILLINOIS AVE 75216 | 376-7311
Charles Matthews, supt.
Kennedy-Curry JHS | 3-00100
6605 SEBRING DR 75241 | 225-4264
Walter Houston, prin.
Other Schools – See Hutchins

Advance Career Training | 2-CS
8800 N CENTRAL EXPY STE 120 75231 | 692-5400
American Institute of Commerce | 2-CS
9930 LBJ FWY STE 350 75243 | 690-1978
American Trades Institute | 1-CS
6627 MAPLE AVE 75235 | 352-2222
Art Institute of Dallas | 2-CC
8080 PARK LN 75231 | 692-8080
ATI Career Training School | 2-CS
2351 W NORTHWEST HWY # 1301 75220 | 902-8191
ATI Graphic Arts Institute | 2-CS
11034 SHADY TRL 75229 | 353-9056
ATI Health Education Center | 2-CS
8150 BROOKRIVER DR FL 5 75247 | 263-0512
Baylor College of Dentistry | 2-UC
3302 GASTON AVE 75246 | 828-8230
Baylor University Medical Center | 3-UC
3500 GASTON AVE 75246
Bishop Dunne HS | 2-00011
3900 RUGGED DR 75224 | 339-6561
Michael Satarino, prin.
Central Texas Commercial College | 2-CS
9400 N CENTRAL EXPY STE 200 75231 | 368-3680
Court Reporting Institute of Dallas | 2-CS
8585 N STEMMONS FWY # 200 75247 | 350-9722
Criswell College | 2-UC
4010 GASTON AVE 75246 | 800-899-0012
Dalfort Aircraft Technology | 2-CS
7701 LEMMON AVE 75209 | 358-7820
Dallas Baptist University | 4-UC
7777 W KIEST BLVD 75211 | 333-5360

Dallas Christian College | 2-UC
2700 CHRISTIAN PKY 75234 | 241-3371
Dallas Christian S | 2-00011
PO BOX 28295 75228 | 270-5495
Kenneth Farris, prin.
Dallas Institute of Funeral Service | 2-CS
3909 S BUCKNER BLVD 75227 | 800-235-5444
Dallas Theological Seminary | 4-UC
3909 SWISS AVE 75204 | 824-3994
El Centro College | 8-CC
801 MAIN ST 75202 | 746-2311
Episcopal S of Dallas | 2-01111
4100 MERRELL RD 75229 | 358-4368
Rebecca Royall, prin.
Executive Secretarial School | 3-CS
4849 GREENVILLE AVE STE 200 75206 | 369-9009
Fairhill S, 16150 PRESTON RD 75248 | 2-11111
Jane Sego, prin. | 233-1026
First Baptist Academy | 2-00111
PO BOX 868 75221 | 969-2475
Suzette Estes, prin.
Gospel Lighthouse Christian Academy | 2-11111
5525 W ILLINOIS AVE 75211 | 339-2207
David Pruett, prin.
Greenhill S, 14255 MIDWAY RD 75244 | 4-11111
Michael York, prin. | 661-1211
Hockaday S, 11600 WELCH RD 75229 | 3-11111
Raymond Doerge, prin. | 363-6311
Interactive Learning Systems | 2-CS
8585 N STEMMONS FWY STE M50 75247 | 637-3377
Jesuit College Prep S | 3-00011
12345 INWOOD RD 75244 | 387-8700
Fr. Deutsch, prin.
KD Studio | 2-CS
2600 N STEMMONS FWY STE 117 75207 | 638-0484
Lakehill Prep S | 2-11111
2720 HILLSIDE DR 75214 | 826-2931
Diane Harris, prin.
Lakemont Academy | 2-11111
3993 W NORTHWEST HWY 75220 | 351-6404
Edward Fidellow, prin.
Lexington Academy | 2-11111
2427 CARRICK ST 75234 | 620-0073
Larry Lindsay, prin.
Lobias Murray Christian Academy | 2-11111
330 E ANN ARBOR AVE 75216 | 372-6466
Raymond Robinson, prin.
Lutheran JSHS, 8494 STULTS RD 75243 | 2-00111
Patricia Klekamp, prin. | 349-8912
Miss Wade's Fashion Merchandising Coll. | 2-CC
PO BOX 586343 75258 | 637-3530
Mountain View College | 5-CC
4849 W ILLINOIS AVE 75211 | 333-8603
NEC-National Institute of Technology | 3-CC
10945 ESTATE LN 75238 | 800-242-6995
Parker College of Chiropractic | 3-UC
2540 WALNUT HILL LN 75229 | 438-6932
Parkland Memorial Hospital | HSP
5201 HARRY HINES BLVD 75235 | 590-8076
Paul Quinn College | 2-UC
3837 SIMPSON STUART RD 75241 | 753-6415
PCI Health Training Center | 2-CS
8101 JOHN W CARPENTER FWY 75247 | 630-0568
Richland College | 6-CC
12800 ABRAMS RD 75243 | 238-6100
St. Marks S, 10600 PRESTON RD 75230 | 3-11111
Frank Jones, prin. | 363-6491
Southeastern Inst. Paralegal Education | 1-CS
5440 HRVEST HILL RD STE 200 75230
Southern Methodist University | 6-UC
HILLCREST AT UNIV 75275 | 800-323-0672
Texas Aero Tech | 3-CS
6911 LEMMON AVE 75209 | 358-7295
Tyler Street Christian Academy | 2-00011
927 W 10TH ST 75208 | 941-9717
Karen Egger, prin.
University of Texas S.W. Medical Center | 4-UC
5323 HARRY HINES BLVD 75235 | 688-3606
Ursuline Academy | 3-00011
4900 WALNUT HILL LN 75229 | 363-6551
Jean Placke, prin.
Winston S, 5707 ROYAL LN 75229 | 2-11111
Walter Sorenson, prin. | 691-6950

Danbury, AC 409, PC 4, Brazoria
Danbury ISD, PO BOX 378 77534 | 3-11111
Ronald Heilmann, supt. | 922-1218
HS, PO BOX 377 77534 | 2-00011
Robert Rosier, prin. | 922-1226
MS, PO BOX 586 77534 | 2-00100
Patrick Callahan, prin. | 922-8403

Darrouzett, AC 806, PC 2, Lipscomb
Darrouzett ISD, PO BOX 98 79024 | 1-11111
Rex Peeples, supt. | 624-2221
S, PO BOX 98 79024 | 1-11111
Rex Peeples, prin. | 624-3001

Dawson, AC 817, PC 3, Navarro
Dawson ISD, PO BOX 278 76639 | 2-11111
William Brown, supt. | 578-1031
JSHS, PO BOX 278 76639 | 2-00111
Carl Rogers, prin. | 578-1031

Dayton, AC 409, PC 6, Liberty
Dayton ISD, PO BOX 248 77535 | 5-11111
Will Moore, supt. | 258-2667

HS, PO BOX 248 77535 | 3-00011
Frank Davis, prin. | 258-2510
Wilson JHS, PO BOX 248 77535 | 3-00100
Larry Wadzeck, prin. | 258-2309

Decatur, AC 817, PC 5, Wise
Decatur ISD, 309 S CATES ST 76234 | 4-11111
Kenneth McKay, supt. | 627-3215
HS, 1201 W THOMPSON ST 76234 | 2-00011
John White, prin. | 627-2155
MS, 1200 W EAGLE DR 76234 | 2-00100
David Mosley, prin. | 627-2384

Deer Park, AC 713, PC 8, Harris
Deer Park ISD, 203 IVY AVE 77536 | 7-11111
David Hicks, supt. | 930-4600
HS, 710 W SAN AUGUSTINE ST 77536 | 5-00011
Gary Berry, prin. | 930-4851
Bonnette JHS | 3-00100
5010 W PASADENA BLVD 77536 | 930-4731
David Switzer, prin.
JHS, 410 E 9TH ST 77536 | 3-00100
Arnold Adair, prin. | 930-4701
Other Schools – See Pasadena

De Kalb, AC 903, PC 4, Bowie
De Kalb ISD, 152 SW MAPLE ST 75559 | 4-11111
Anne Farris, supt. | 667-2566
HS, 152 SW MAPLE ST 75559 | 2-00011
James Brewer, prin. | 667-2422
JHS, 152 SW MAPLE ST 75559 | 2-01100
Lonnie Mahone, prin. | 667-2834

De Leon, AC 817, PC 4, Comanche
DeLeon ISD, PO BOX 256 76444 | 3-11111
E. Bills, supt. | 893-6222
HS, PO BOX 256 76444 | 2-00011
Linda Reaves, prin. | 893-6222
MS, PO BOX 256 76444 | 2-00100
Nelda Priddy, prin. | 893-6222

Dell City, AC 915, PC 3, Hudspeth
Dell City ISD, PO BOX 37 79837 | 2-11111
Kay Karr, supt. | 964-2663
S, 110 N MAIN 79837 | 2-11111
(—), prin. | 964-2495

Del Rio, AC 210, PC 8, Val Verde
San Felipe-Del Rio Consolidated ISD | 6-11111
PO BOX 420128 78842 | 774-9200
Walter Williams, supt.
HS, PO BOX 420128 78842 | 4-00011
Charles Dugan, prin. | 774-9316
Del Rio Freshman HS | 3-00010
PO BOX 420128 78842 | 774-9361
Robert Chavira, prin.
Del Rio MS, PO BOX 420128 78842 | 3-00100
Samuel Lopez, prin. | 774-9391

Del Valle, AC 512, PC 4, Travis
Del Valle ISD, 2407 SHAPARD LN 78617 | 6-11111
Edward Neal, supt. | 385-0890
HS, 2407 SHAPARD LN 78617 | 4-00011
Gordon Perez, prin. | 385-0120
JHS, 2407 SHAPARD LN 78617 | 3-00100
Susan Oglesbee, prin. | 247-2222

Denison, AC 903, PC 7, Grayson
Denison ISD, 1201 S RUSK AVE 75020 | 5-11111
William Scott, supt. | 465-4244
HS, 1901 S MIRICK AVE 75020 | 4-00011
Robert Mears, prin. | 465-2488
McDaniel MS, 400 S LILLIS LN 75020 | 4-00100
Bill Parker, prin. | 465-1255

Grayson County College | 5-CC
6101 HIGHWAY 691 75020 | 465-6030

Denton, AC 817, PC 8, Denton
Denton ISD, PO BOX 2387 76202 | 7-11111
Albert Thomas, supt. | 387-6151
Denton-Ryan SHS | 4-00001
5101 E MCKINNEY ST 76208 | 566-7926
Kenneth Dinges, prin.
Calhoun MS | 4-00100
709 W CONGRESS ST 76201 | 387-8566
Gayla Blair, prin.
Denton JHS West | 2-00010
1007 FULTON ST 76201 | 382-9611
Milton Wallace, prin.
Strickland MS | 4-00100
324 E WINDSOR DR 76201 | 383-1621
Barbara Fischer, prin.

Business Skills Training Center | 2-CS
616 FORT WORTH DR STE B 76201 | 382-7922
International Business School | 3-CS
3801 N INTRSTATE 35 STE 138 76207 | 382-5126
Liberty Christian S | 2-00011
1500 S BONNIE BRAE ST 76207 | 565-0466
Dwight Gailey, prin.
Texas Women's University | 6-UC
PO BOX 23925 76204 | 898-3000
University of North Texas | 7-UC
PO BOX 13797 76203 | 565-2681

Denver City, AC 806, PC 6, Yoakum
Denver City ISD | 4-11111
501 MUSTANG DR 79323 | 592-2500
Lynn Pollard, supt.
HS, 601 MUSTANG DR 79323 | 3-00011
Dag Azam, prin. | 592-2933

JHS, 419 MUSTANG DR 79323 — 2-00100
William Gravitt, prin. — 592-2446

De Soto, AC 214, PC 8, Dallas
De Soto ISD, 200 E BELT LINE RD 75115 — 6-11111
John Moore, supt. — 223-6666
HS, 600 EAGLE DR 75115 — 4-00011
Judy Moss, prin. — 230-0726
De Soto East JHS — 3-00100
601 E BELT LINE RD 75115 — 223-0690
William Richardson, prin.
De Soto West JHS — 2-00100
800 N WESTMORELAND RD 75115 — 230-1820
David Robbins, prin.

Detroit, AC 903, PC 3, Red River
Detroit ISD, RR 2 BOX 105 75436 — 2-11111
Don Fry, supt. — 674-2646
JSHS, RR 2 BOX 105 75436 — 2-00111
Roy Pieper, prin. — 674-2646

Devine, AC 210, PC 5, Medina
Devine ISD, PO BOX I 78016 — 4-11111
Anthony Kneupper, supt. — 663-3611
HS, 1225 W HONDO AVE 78016 — 3-00011
Bob Bendele, prin. — 663-2864
MS, 400 CARDINAL DR 78016 — 2-00100
Don Sessions, prin. — 663-3677

Deweyville, AC 409, PC 4, Newton
Deweyville ISD, PO BOX 408 77614 — 3-11111
Paul Czerwinski, supt. — 746-2731
HS, PO BOX 259 77614 — 2-00011
Larry Williams, prin. — 746-3173
MS, PO BOX 159 77614 — 2-00100
Karen Laughlin, prin. — 746-2924

D'Hanis, AC 210, PC 3, Medina
D'Hanis ISD, PO BOX 307 78850 — 2-11111
Donald Krumrey, supt. — 363-7216
S, PO BOX 307 78850 — 2-11111
Amos Finger, prin. — 363-7216

Diana, AC 903, PC 2, Upshur
New Diana ISD, PO BOX 26 75640 — 3-11111
Norton Lovell, supt. — 663-1812
New Diana HS, PO BOX 26 75640 — 2-00011
Don Gross, prin. — 663-1170
New Diana JHS, PO BOX 26 75640 — 2-00100
Linda Wilson, prin. — 663-6340

Diboll, AC 409, PC 5, Angelina
Diboll ISD, PO BOX 550 75941 — 4-11111
Bill Ward, supt. — 829-4718
HS, 1000 HARRIS ST 75941 — 3-00011
Gary Campbell, prin. — 829-5626
JHS, 403 DENNIS ST 75941 — 2-00100
Robert Anderson, prin. — 829-5225

Dickinson, AC 713, PC 6, Galveston
Dickinson ISD, PO BOX Z 77539 — 6-11111
Bill Borgers, supt. — 534-3581
HS, 3800 BAKER DR 77539 — 4-00011
Ronald Ahlhorn, prin. — 534-6800
McAdams JHS, 4007 VIDEO ST 77539 — 3-00100
Linda Hanson, prin. — 534-6880

Dilley, AC 210, PC 5, Frio
Dilley ISD, PO BOX 18040 78017 — 4-11111
Jack Seals, supt. — 965-1912
HS, PO BOX 18040 78017 — 2-00011
James Tatsch, prin. — 965-1814
Harper MS, PO BOX 18040 78017 — 2-00100
Oscar Martinez, prin. — 965-2195

Dime Box, AC 409, PC 2, Lee
Dime Box ISD, PO BOX 157 77853 — 2-11111
Larry Pennington, supt. — 884-2324
S, PO BOX 157 77853 — 2-11111
Byron Welch, prin. — 884-3366

Dimmitt, AC 806, PC 5, Castro
Dimmitt ISD, 608 W HALSELL ST 79027 — 4-11111
Charles Miller, supt. — 647-3101
HS, 1505 WESTERN CIR 79027 — 2-00011
R. Stockstill, prin. — 647-3105
MS, 805 W JONES ST 79027 — 3-01100
George Rasor, prin. — 647-3108

Dodd City, AC 903, PC 2, Fannin
Dodd City ISD, RR 1 BOX 2 75438 — 2-11111
B. Matthews, supt. — 583-7585
S, RR 1 BOX 2 75438 — 2-11111
Craig Reed, prin. — 583-7585

Donna, AC 210, PC 7, Hidalgo
Donna ISD, 116 N 10TH ST 78537 — 6-11111
Israel Rodriguez, supt. — 464-4461
HS, 116 N 10TH ST 78537 — 4-00011
Francisco Gonzales, prin. — 464-6003
Todd JHS, 116 N 10TH ST 78537 — 3-00100
Ludivina Perez, prin. — 464-1800

Douglass, AC 409, PC 2, Nacogdoches
Douglass ISD, PO BOX 38 75943 — 2-11111
Lowell McCuistion, supt. — 569-9804
S, PO BOX 38 75943 — 2-11111
Robert Baker, prin. — 569-9804

Dripping Springs, AC 512, PC 4, Hays
Dripping Springs ISD — 4-11111
PO BOX 479 78620 — 858-4905
Mary Kosub, supt.
HS, PO BOX 280 78620 — 2-00011
Don Forrester, prin. — 858-4612

MS, 510 MERCER ST 78620 — 2-00100
(—), prin. — 858-4902

Dublin, AC 817, PC 5, Erath
Dublin ISD, PO BOX D 76446 — 4-11111
Roy Neff, supt. — 445-3341
HS, PO BOX D 76446 — 2-00011
Stacy Rhodes, prin. — 445-2555
JHS, PO BOX D 76446 — 2-00100
John Grimland, prin. — 445-2618

Dumas, AC 806, PC 7, Moore
Dumas ISD, PO BOX 615 79029 — 5-11111
Larry Appel, supt. — 935-6461
SHS, PO BOX 615 79029 — 3-00001
Bob Callahan, prin. — 935-4151
JHS, PO BOX 615 79029 — 3-00110
Mark Stroebel, prin. — 935-4155

Duncanville, AC 214, PC 8, Dallas
Duncanville ISD, 802 S MAIN ST 75137 — 7-11111
Carol Griffin, supt. — 296-4761
SHS, 900 W CAMP WISDOM RD 75116 — 4-00001
Lynn Dobbins, prin. — 298-6136
Byrd JHS — 3-00100
1040 W WHEATLAND RD 75116 — 298-6106
Ron Golden, prin.
Reed JHS, 530 E FREEMAN ST 75116 — 3-00100
Mel Morris, prin. — 709-2900
Other Schools – See Dallas

Eagle Pass, AC 210, PC 7, Maverick
Eagle Pass ISD, PO BOX 1409 78853 — 7-11111
Leonel Galaviz, supt. — 773-5181
SHS, PO BOX 1409 78853 — 4-00001
Jose Guerra, prin. — 773-2381
JHS, PO BOX 1409 78853 — 4-00110
Maria Sotto, prin. — 773-9478
Memorial JHS, PO BOX 1409 78853 — 4-00110
Ana Gonzalez, prin. — 773-8838

Early, AC 915, PC 4, Brown
Early ISD, PO BOX 3315 76803 — 4-11111
John King, supt. — 646-7934
HS, PO BOX 3315 76803 — 2-00011
Dean Blair, prin. — 643-4593
MS, PO BOX 3315 76803 — 2-00100
Ruth Marsh, prin. — 643-5665

Earth, AC 806, PC 4, Lamb
Springlake-Earth ISD — 3-11111
PO BOX 130 79031 — 257-3310
Robert Conkin, supt.
Springlake HS, PO BOX 130 79031 — 2-00011
Robert Bolton, prin. — 257-3819
Springlake JHS, PO BOX 130 79031 — 2-00100
Walter Baker, prin. — 257-3813

East Bernard, AC 409, PC 4, Wharton
East Bernard ISD, PO BOX Z 77435 — 3-11111
Nancy McNeal, supt. — 335-7519
HS, PO BOX Z 77435 — 2-00011
Jim Bruce, prin. — 335-7519
JHS, PO BOX Z 77435 — 2-01100
Emmett Tugwell, prin. — 335-4896

Eastland, AC 817, PC 5, Eastland
Eastland ISD, PO BOX 31 76448 — 4-11111
Dale Watkins, supt. — 629-8221
HS, PO BOX 31 76448 — 2-00011
Gary Upchurch, prin. — 629-8384
JHS, PO BOX 31 76448 — 2-00100
Rickie Pack, prin. — 629-1422

Ector, AC 903, PC 2, Fannin
Ector ISD, PO BOX 128 75439 — 2-11111
Frederick Schubert, supt. — 961-2355
S, PO BOX 128 75439 — 2-11111
Roger Morris, prin. — 961-2355

Edcouch, AC 210, PC 5, Hidalgo
Edcouch-Elsa ISD, PO BOX 127 78538 — 5-11111
Daniel Hernandez, supt. — 262-2136
Edcouch-Elsa HS, PO BOX 127 78538 — 4-00011
Guadalupe Castillo, prin. — 262-4731
Edcouch-Elsa JHS — 3-00100
PO BOX 127 78538 — 262-4735
Jose Martinez, prin.

Eddy, AC 817, PC 4, McLennan
Bruceville-Eddy ISD — 3-11111
PO BOX 99 76524 – J. Payne, supt. — 859-5832
Bruceville-Eddy JSHS — 2-00111
PO BOX 99 76524 — 859-5848
Vonn Murray, prin.

Eden, AC 915, PC 4, Concho
Eden Consolidated ISD, PO BOX X 76837 — 2-11111
J. Chant, supt. — 869-4121
JSHS, PO BOX X 76837 — 2-00111
Roger Walker, prin. — 869-5180

Edgewood, AC 903, PC 4, Van Zandt
Edgewood ISD, PO BOX 6 75117 — 3-11111
Ellis Carroll, supt. — 896-4332
HS, PO BOX 6 75117 — 2-00011
Steve Steadham, prin. — 896-4856
MS, PO BOX 6 75117 — 2-00100
Carolyn James, prin. — 896-1530

Edinburg, AC 210, PC 8, Hidalgo
Edinburg ISD, PO BOX 990 78540 — 7-11111
Miguel De Los Santos, supt. — 383-0731
HS, 801 E CANTON AVE 78539 — 4-00011
Luis Ramos, prin. — 381-0931

Edinburg North HS — 4-00011
3101 N US HIGHWAY 281 78539 — 318-3647
(—), prin.
Edinburg North JHS — 4-00100
411 N 8TH AVE 78539 — 383-4916
J. Salinas, prin.
Edinburg South JHS — 4-00100
601 W FREDDY GONZALEZ DR 78539 — 383-4941
Randy Palmatier, prin.

Rio Grande Bible Institute — 2-UC
4300 S US HIGHWAY 281 78539 — 380-8100
University of Texas-Pan American — 6-UC
1201 W UNIVERSITY DR 78539 — 381-2206

Edna, AC 512, PC 6, Jackson
Edna ISD, PO BOX D 77957 — 4-11111
Charlott Baker, supt. — 782-3573
HS, PO BOX D 77957 — 2-00011
Eugene Kana, prin. — 782-5255
JHS, PO BOX D 77957 — 2-00100
Gary Ott, prin. — 782-2351

El Campo, AC 409, PC 7, Wharton
El Campo ISD, 700 W NORRIS ST 77437 — 5-11111
Guy Gorden, supt. — 543-6771
HS, 600 W NORRIS ST 77437 — 3-00011
William Carpenter, prin. — 543-6341
MS, 1401 MCCLURE ST 77437 — 3-00100
Thomas Rowland, prin. — 543-6362

Eldorado, AC 915, PC 4, Schleicher
Schleicher ISD, PO BOX W 76936 — 3-11111
Robert Barton, supt. — 853-2514
HS, PO BOX W 76936 — 2-00011
Ken Newman, prin. — 853-2549
MS, PO BOX W 76936 — 2-01100
Steve Peters, prin. — 853-3028

Electra, AC 817, PC 5, Wichita
Electra ISD, 621 N WAGGONER ST 76360 — 3-11111
D. Windham, supt. — 495-3683
HS, 400 E ROOSEVELT AVE 76360 — 2-00011
Dan Clack, prin. — 495-2218
JHS, 621 S BAILEY ST 76360 — 2-01100
Olan Bourland, prin. — 495-2533

Elgin, AC 512, PC 5, Bastrop
Elgin ISD, PO BOX 351 78621 — 4-11111
(—), supt. — 285-3434
HS, 902 W 2ND ST 78621 — 3-00011
Janie Simmons, prin. — 285-3438
MS, 510 S AVENUE F 78621 — 3-00100
Nancy Frazier, prin. — 285-3382

Elkhart, AC 903, PC 4, Anderson
Elkhart ISD, RR 1 BOX 1001 75839 — 3-11111
John Booth, supt. — 764-2952
JSHS, RR 1 BOX 1001 75839 — 2-00111
Wilburn Mcdaniel, prin. — 764-5161

Slocum ISD, RR 2 BOX 2334 75839 — 2-11111
Sandra Lowery, supt. — 478-3624
Slocum S, RR 2 BOX 2334 75839 — 2-11111
Thomas Naismith, prin. — 478-3624

Elmaton, AC 512, PC 2, Matagorda
Tidehaven ISD, PO BOX B 77440 — 3-11111
Allen Dusek, supt. — 588-6321
Tidehaven HS, PO BOX B 77440 — 2-00011
Robert Dwight, prin. — 588-6810
Tidehaven IS, PO BOX A 77440 — 2-00100
Debra Taska, prin. — 588-6600

El Paso, AC 915, PC 11, El Paso
El Paso ISD, PO BOX 20100 79998 — 8-11111
Estanislad Y Paz, supt. — 779-3781
Andress HS — 4-00011
5400 SUN VALLEY DR 79924 — 751-8841
Pete Ramos, prin.
Austin HS, 3500 MEMPHIS AVE 79930 — 4-00011
Efren Yturralde, prin. — 562-7611
Bowie HS — 4-00011
801 S SAN MARCIAL ST 79905 — 544-8130
Paul Strelzin, prin.
Burges HS — 4-00011
7800 EDGEMERE BLVD 79925 — 772-7451
Nicasio Cobos, prin.
Coronado HS — 4-00011
100 CHAMPIONS PL 79912 — 584-9441
Burl Whatley, prin.
El Paso HS, 800 E SCHUSTER AVE 79902 — 4-00011
Luis Sanchez, prin. — 533-6851
Franklin HS, 825 E REDD RD 79912 — 4-00011
John Doran, prin. — 585-1668
Irvin HS, 9465 ROANOKE DR 79924 — 4-00011
Benny Lesley, prin. — 755-7687
Jefferson HS — 4-00011
4700 ALAMEDA AVE 79905 — 532-4963
Manuel Aguirre, prin.
El Paso Tech Ctr — Vo Tech
2231 ARIZONA AVE 79930 — 545-5900
Celia Grant, prin.
Bassett MS, 4400 ELM ST 79930 — 4-00100
Rodolfo Hernandez, prin. — 565-9938
Canyon Hills JHS — 3-00100
8930 ECLIPSE ST 79904 — 751-1253
James Stephens, prin.
Charles MS, 4909 TROJAN DR 79924 — 3-00100
Beverly Stevens, prin. — 821-2850
Guillen IS, 900 S COTTON ST 79901 — 3-00100
Salvador Pena, prin. — 533-5566
Henderson MS — 4-00100
5505 ROBERT ALVA AVE 79905 — 778-4401
Ralph Chavez, prin.

Lincoln MS, 500 MULBERRY AVE 79932   4-00100
Janet Lumpee, prin.   584-9404
Magoffin MS   3-00100
4931 HERCULES AVE 79904   755-7695
Arturo Delgado, prin.
Morehead MS, 5625 CONFETTI DR 79912   4-00100
Robert Bransford, prin.   584-3481
Ross MS, 6101 HUGHEY CIR 79925   3-00100
Mary Lou Martinez, prin.   778-4261
Terrace Hills MS   3-00100
4835 BLOSSOM AVE 79924   751-2367
Dianne Jones, prin.
Wiggs MS, 1300 CIRCLE DR 79902   4-00100
Carmen Stearns, prin.   544-6768

Socorro ISD, PO BOX 27400 79926   7-11111
R. Jerry Barber, supt.   860-3400
Montwood HS   4-00011
12000 MONTWOOD DR 79936   857-4400
Art Shaw, prin.
Socorro HS   5-00011
10150 ALAMEDA AVE 79927   860-3500
Michael Quatrini, prin.
Sanchez MS, 321 N RIO VISTA RD 79927   3-00100
Edward Gabaldon, prin.   860-3650
Slider MS, 11700 SCHOOL LN 79936   4-00100
Charles Vass, prin.   857-4450
Socorro MS, 321 BOVEE RD 79927   3-00100
Armando Bustamante, prin.   860-3550

Ysleta ISD, 9600 SIMS DR 79925   8-11111
Anthony Trujillo, supt.   595-5500
Bel Air HS   4-00011
731 N YARBROUGH DR 79915   598-3437
Noe Ramirez, prin.
Del Valle HS, 950 BORDEAUX DR 79907   4-00011
Lionel Nava, prin.   858-6980
Eastwood HS, 2430 MCRAE BLVD 79925   4-00011
Barbara Matthews, prin.   598-3481
Hanks HS   5-00011
2001 N LEE TREVINO DR 79936   593-7335
Vernon Butler, prin.
Parkland HS, 5932 QUAIL AVE 79924   3-00011
Edward Endlich, prin.   751-6411
Riverside HS, 301 MIDWAY DR 79915   4-00011
Ralph Ornelas, prin.   778-5491
Ysleta HS, 8600 ALAMEDA AVE 79907   4-00011
Rudy Murillo, prin.   859-7982
Academy of Science/Tech   Vo Tech
300 VOCATIONAL DR 79915   778-5208
Tom Stokes, prin.
Camino Real MS   3-00100
9393 ALAMEDA AVE 79907   858-1013
Bob Beauford, prin.
Desert View MS   3-00100
1641 BILLIE MARIE DR 79936   594-1026
Maynard Pike, prin.
Eastwood MS   3-00100
2612 CHASWOOD ST 79935   598-3443
(—), prin.
Hillcrest MS, 800 HILTON AVE 79907   3-00100
Felipe Candelaria, prin.   592-4181
Indian Ridge MS   3-00100
11201 PEBBLE HILLS BLVD 79936   592-7787
Jana Penney, prin.
Parkland MS, 6045 NOVA WAY 79924   3-00100
(—), prin.   751-2389
Ranchland Hills MS   2-00100
7615 YUMA DR 79915   598-4923
Leo Pleasants, prin.
Riverside MS, 7615 MIMOSA AVE 79915   3-00100
James Mesta, prin.   778-4474
Valley View MS, 8674 N LOOP DR 79907   3-00100
(—), prin.   859-2111
Yselta MS   3-00100
8691 INDEPENDENCE DR 79907   859-1613
Judy Johnson, prin.

Agape Christian S   3-11111
8960 ESCOBAR DR 79907   594-3305
Sandra Carranza, prin.
Career Centers of Texas   2-CS
8375 BURNHAM RD 79907   595-1935
Cathedral HS   3-00011
1309 N STANTON ST 79902   532-3238
Br. Hayden, prin.
Computer Career Center   2-CS
6101 MONTANA AVE 79925   779-8031
David Carrasco Job Corps Center   2-CS
11155 GATEWAY BLVD W 79935   594-0022
El Paso Community College   8-CC
PO BOX 20500 79998   594-2580
Father Yermo HS   2-00011
250 WASHINGTON ST 79905   533-3185
Maria Tirres, prin.
International Business College   4-CS
4121 MONTANA AVE 79903   566-8644
Jesus Chapel S   2-11111
10555 EDGEMERE BLVD 79925   593-1153
Jack Hon, prin.
Loretto Academy   3-00011
1300 HARDAWAY ST 79903   566-9372
Sam Forsythe, prin.
Loretto MS, 1300 HARDAWAY ST 79903   2-00100
Sr. Patricia Williams, prin.   566-5453
Lydia Patterson Institute HS   2-00011
PO BOX 11 79999   533-8286
David Rodriguez, prin.
Radford S, 2001 RADFORD ST 79903   2-11111
Yolanda Ahner, prin.   565-2737

St. Michaels Tutorial English S   2-00110
616 S VIRGINIA ST 79901   542-1253
Sr. Rose Mendez, prin.
Southwest Inst. Merchandising & Design   2-CC
9611 ACER AVE 79925   593-7328
University of Texas at El Paso   7-UC
500 W UNIVERSITY AVE 79968   747-5576
Western Technical Institute   3-CC
1000 TEXAS AVE 79901   532-3737
Western Technical Institute   2-CC
4710 ALABAMA ST 79930   566-9621

Elysian Fields, AC 903, PC 2, Harrison
Elysian Fields ISD   3-11111
PO BOX 120 75642   633-2420
Brian Nichols, supt.
HS, PO BOX 120 75642   2-00011
Guy Yarborough, prin.   633-2455
JHS, PO BOX 120 75642   2-00100
Maynard Chapman, prin.   633-2218

Emory, AC 903, PC 3, Rains
Rains ISD, PO BOX 247 75440   4-11111
Guy Harrison, supt.   473-2648
Rains HS, PO BOX 247 75440   2-00011
James Clopton, prin.   473-2222
Rains JHS, PO BOX 247 75440   2-00100
Maybeth McMahan, prin.   473-2223

Ennis, AC 214, PC 7, Ellis
Ennis ISD, PO BOX 1420 75120   5-11111
David Cochran, supt.   875-9027
HS, 1405 W LAKE BARDWELL DR 75119   3-00011
Bill Chapman, prin.   875-9011
JHS, 501 N GAINES ST 75119   4-00100
Floyd Tolston, prin.   875-3779

St. John JSHS, 701 S PARIS ST 75119   2-00111
David Del Bosque, prin.   875-2226

Era, AC 817, PC 2, Cooke
Era ISD, PO BOX 98 76238   2-11111
Randel Beaver, supt.   665-5961
S, PO BOX 98 76238   2-11111
Sharon Durham, prin.   665-5961

Euless, AC 817, PC 8, Tarrant
Hurst-Euless-Bedford ISD
Supt. — See Bedford
Trinity SHS   4-00011
500 N INDUSTRIAL BLVD 76039   571-0271
William Shatford, prin.
Central JHS, 3191 W PIPELINE RD 76040   3-00110
Jack Ingle, prin.   354-3350
JHS, 306 AIRPORT FWY 76039   3-00110
Linda Densman, prin.   354-3340

Mid-Cities Learning Center   2-11111
RURAL ROUTE 01 BOX 257 76040   283-1771
Christine Kallstrom, prin.

Eustace, AC 903, PC 3, Henderson
Eustace ISD, PO BOX 188 75124   4-11111
Robert Bethea, supt.   425-7131
HS, PO BOX 188 75124   2-00011
E. Kirk, prin.   425-7901
IS, PO BOX 188 75124   2-01100
Phil Ward, prin.   425-2381

Evadale, AC 409, PC 4, Jasper
Evadale ISD, PO BOX 497 77615   2-11111
James Cook, supt.   276-1337
HS, PO BOX 497 77615   2-00011
Norman Plemons, prin.   276-1939

Evant, AC 817, PC 2, Coryell
Evant ISD, PO BOX 339 76525   2-11111
J. Williams, supt.   471-3160
HS, PO BOX 339 76525   1-00011
Bill Brister, prin.   471-3160
JHS, PO BOX 339 76525   1-00100
Bill Brister, prin.   471-3160

Everman, AC 817, PC 6, Tarrant
Everman ISD, 608 TOWNLEY DR 76140   5-11111
Joe Bean, supt.   568-3500
HS, 1000 S RACE ST 76140   3-00011
James Melton, prin.   568-3550
JHS, 8901 OAK GROVE RD 76140   3-00100
A. O'Connor, prin.   568-3530

Fabens, AC 915, PC 6, El Paso
Fabens ISD, PO BOX 697 79838   4-11111
Jesus Gandara, supt.   764-2025
HS, PO BOX 697 79838   3-00011
(—), prin.   764-2246
JHS, PO BOX 697 79838   3-00100
Ramiro Esparza, prin.   764-2712

Fairfield, AC 903, PC 5, Freestone
Fairfield ISD, 615 POST OAK RD 75840   4-11111
Don Posey, supt.   389-2532
HS, 631 POST OAK RD 75840   2-00011
Von Wade, prin.   389-4177
JHS, 701 POST OAK RD 75840   3-01100
David Price, prin.   389-4210

Falfurrias, AC 512, PC 6, Brooks
Brooks ISD, PO BOX 589 78355   4-11111
A. Byington, supt.   325-5681
HS, PO BOX 589 78355   3-00011
Claudio Salinas, prin.   325-5681
MS, PO BOX 589 78355   2-00100
Daniel Yzaguirre, prin.   325-5681

Falls City, AC 210, PC 2, Karnes
Falls City ISD, PO BOX 399 78113   2-11111
Luther Thomas, supt.   254-3551
JSHS, PO BOX 399 78113   2-00111
R. Stadler, prin.   254-3551

Farmers Branch, AC 214, PC 8, Dallas
Carrollton-Farmers Branch ISD
Supt. — See Carrollton
Field JHS, 13551 DENNIS LN 75234   3-00100
Conan Reinken, prin.   247-7197

Brookhaven College   6-CC
3939 VALLEY VIEW LN 75244   620-4700

Farmersville, AC 214, PC 5, Collin
Farmersville ISD, PO BOX 472 75442   3-11111
Vickie Kivell, supt.   782-6601
HS, PO BOX 472 75442   2-00011
James Hemby, prin.   782-7757
MS, 807 N MAIN ST 75442   2-00100
Marvin Schkade, prin.   782-6202

Farwell, AC 806, PC 4, Parmer
Farwell ISD, PO BOX F 79325   3-11111
Richard Boothby, supt.   481-3371
HS, PO BOX F 79325   2-00011
Larry Gregory, prin.   481-3351
JHS, PO BOX F 79325   2-00100
Jerry Owen, prin.   481-9260

Fayetteville, AC 409, PC 2, Fayette
Fayetteville ISD, PO BOX 129 78940   2-11111
Robert French, supt.   378-4242
JSHS, PO BOX 129 78940   1-00111
Jon Forsythe, prin.   378-4242

Ferris, AC 214, PC 4, Ellis
Ferris ISD, PO BOX 459 75125   4-11111
James Harrison, supt.   544-3858
HS, PO BOX 461 75125   2-00011
Dan Gibson, prin.   544-3737
MS, PO BOX 459 75125   2-00100
Robbin Wall, prin.   544-2279

Flatonia, AC 512, PC 4, Fayette
Flatonia ISD, PO BOX 189 78941   2-11111
James Schroeder, supt.   865-2941
HS, PO BOX 189 78941   2-00011
Richard Steinhauser, prin.   865-2944

Florence, AC 817, PC 3, Williamson
Florence ISD, PO BOX 489 76527   3-11111
Larry Jones, supt.   793-2850
HS, PO BOX 488 76527   2-00011
Douglas Thorp, prin.   793-2504
MS, PO BOX 489 76527   2-00100
Steven Ray, prin.   793-2540

Floresville, AC 210, PC 6, Wilson
Floresville ISD, 1103 4TH ST 78114   5-11111
Joe Robinson, supt.   393-3147
HS, 1000 10TH ST 78114   3-00011
Hugh Jones, prin.   393-5370
MS, 1813 TIGER LN 78114   3-01100
Hurvey Elliot, prin.   393-5350

Flower Mound, AC 214, PC 7, Denton
Lewisville ISD
Supt. — See Lewisville
Marcus HS, 5707 MORRISS RD 75028   4-00011
Larry Sigler, prin.   539-1591
Forestwood MS   2-00100
2810 MORRISS RD 75028   420-0144
Gary Goldsmith, prin.
Lamar MS   4-00100
4000 TIMBER CREEK RD 75028   539-0886
Brant Buck, prin.

Floydada, AC 806, PC 5, Floyd
Floydada ISD   4-11111
226 W CALIFORNIA ST 79235   983-3498
Jerry Cannon, supt.
HS, 618 S TREE ST 79235   2-00011
Joe Christian, prin.   983-3256
JHS, 910 N 5TH ST 79235   2-00100
Bruce Bramlet, prin.   983-2161

Follett, AC 806, PC 2, Lipscomb
Follett ISD, PO BOX 28 79034   2-11111
Bill Goodwin, supt.   653-2301
S, PO BOX 28 79034   2-11111
Gerald Danley, prin.   653-4241

Forestburg, AC 817, PC 2, Montague
Forestburg ISD, PO BOX 415 76239   2-11111
Jackie Barton, supt.   964-2323
S, PO BOX 415 76239   2-11111
David Bellile, prin.   964-2323

Forney, AC 214, PC 5, Kaufman
Forney ISD, 811 S BOIS D ARC ST 75126   4-11111
Chester St. Clair, supt.   552-3902
HS, 811 S BOIS D ARC ST 75126   2-00011
Jim Luther, prin.   552-3890
MS, 800 FM 741 S 75126   2-00100
Dana Chambliess, prin.   552-3967

Forsan, AC 915, PC 2, Howard
Forsan ISD, PO BOX A 79733   3-11111
George White, supt.   457-2223
JSHS, PO BOX A 79733   2-00111
John Parker, prin.   457-2223

Fort Davis, AC 915, PC 4, Jeff Davis
Ft. Davis ISD, PO BOX 1339 79734   2-11111
Ernesto Martinez, supt.   426-3220

JSHS, PO BOX 1339 79734   2-00111
(—), prin.   426-3229
High Frontier JSHS   1-00111
  PO BOX 1339 79734   364-2450
  Ann Fitzgerald, prin.

Fort Hancock, AC 915, PC 3, Hudspeth
Ft. Hancock ISD, PO BOX 98 79839   2-11111
  Bill Franklin, supt.   769-3867
S, PO BOX 98 79839   2-11111
  Jim Liner, prin.   769-3867

Fort Hood, AC 817, PC 8, Bell
Killeen ISD
  Supt. — See Killeen
Smith MS   3-00100
  51000 COPPERAS COVE RD 76544   532-1250
  Jerry Lewis, prin.

Fort Stockton, AC 915, PC 6, Pecos
Fort Stockton ISD   5-11111
  101 W DIVISION ST 79735   336-8517
  Luis Gonzalez, supt.
HS, 1200 W 17TH ST 79735   3-00011
  Paul Pasqua, prin.   336-5201
MS, 2500 W 5TH ST 79735   3-00100
  Manuel Espino, prin.   336-5241

Fort Worth, AC 817, PC 10, Tarrant
Birdville ISD, 6125 E BELKNAP ST 76117   7-11111
  Bob Griggs, supt.   831-5700
Haltom HS, 5501 HALTOM RD 76137   4-00011
  Jo Ann Kelley, prin.   581-5300
Richland HS, 5201 HOLIDAY LN 76180   4-00011
  Annette Keller, prin.   581-5400
Haltom MS, 5000 DANA DR 76117   3-00100
  Jack Atkins, prin.   831-5841
North Richland MS   3-00100
  4800 RUFE SNOW DR 76180   581-5342
  Ray Thompson, prin.
North Ridge MS   3-00100
  7332 DOUGLAS LN 76180   581-5447
  Charlotte Fritz, prin.
North Oaks MS   2-00100
  4800 JORDAN PARK DR 76117   581-5344
  Wanda Strong, prin.
Richland MS   2-00100
  7400 HOVENKAMP AVE 76118   595-5143
  Dale Hensarling, prin.
Smithfield MS, 8400 MAIN ST 76180   3-00100
  Doris Tipps, prin.   581-5446
Watauga MS, 6300 MAURIE DR 76148   3-00100
  Deborah Tribble, prin.   581-5345

Castleberry ISD   5-11111
  315 CHURCHILL RD 76114   737-7235
  Jerry Cook, supt.
Castleberry HS   3-00011
  315 CHURCHILL RD 76114   732-4455
  Fred Barney, prin.
Marsh MS, 415 HAGG DR 76114   3-00100
  Carroll Gilbreath, prin.   738-2129

Crowley ISD
  Supt. — See Crowley
Crowley MS   3-00100
  3800 W RISINGER RD 76123   370-5650
  David Walker, prin.

Eagle Mtn.-Saginaw ISD   5-11111
  PO BOX 79160 76179   232-0880
  William Anderson, supt.
Boswell HS, PO BOX 79160 76179   4-00011
  James Hafley, prin.   237-3315
Wayside MS, PO BOX 79160 76179   3-00100
  Dan Jordan, prin.   232-0541

Fort Worth ISD   8-11111
  100 N UNIVERSITY DR 76107   871-2455
  Don Roberts, supt.
Arlington Heights HS   4-00011
  4501 W ROSEDALE ST 76107   377-7200
  Winnie Taylor, prin.
Carter-Riverside HS   3-00011
  3301 YUCCA AVE 76111   838-1500
  Sam Peterson, prin.
Diamond Hill-Jarvis HS   3-00011
  1411 MAYDELL ST 76106   740-5400
  Joe Martinez, prin.
Dunbar HS, 5700 RAMEY AVE 76112   4-00011
  Shirley Benton, prin.   496-7400
Eastern Hills HS   4-00011
  5701 SHELTON ST 76112   496-7600
  John Largent, prin.
North Side HS   4-00011
  2211 MCKINLEY AVE 76106   740-5300
  James Torres, prin.
Paschal HS   4-00011
  3001 FOREST PARK BLVD 76110   922-6600
  Anita Whiteside, prin.
Polytechnic HS   3-00011
  1300 CONNER AVE 76105   531-6200
  Pat Dungy, prin.
Southwest HS   4-00011
  4100 ALTAMESA BLVD 76133   370-5800
  Dan Powell, prin.
Trimble Technical HS   4-00011
  1003 W CANNON ST 76104   871-3400
  Paul Galvan, prin.
Western Hills HS   4-00011
  3600 BOSTON AVE 76116   560-5600
  William Roper, prin.
Wyatt HS, 2400 E SEMINARY DR 76119   4-00011
  Walter Dansby, prin.   531-6300

Metro Opportunity S   Vo Tech
  215 NE 14TH ST 76106   740-5550
  Gladys Pettid, prin.
Pope Adolescent Training Ctr   Vo Tech
  4701 W ROSEDALE ST 76107   731-8681
  Carolyn Jones, prin.
Daggett MS, 1108 CARLOCK ST 76110   3-00100
  Gary Vaught, prin.   922-6550
Dunbar MS, 2501 STALCUP RD 76119   3-00100
  Helen Curtis, prin.   496-7430
Elder MS, 709 NW 21ST ST 76106   3-00100
  Mary Jara Wright, prin.   740-5450
Forest Oak MS, 3221 PECOS ST 76119   3-00100
  Larry Stacy, prin.   531-6330
Handley MS, 2801 PATINO RD 76112   3-00100
  David Ponder, prin.   496-7450
Horizon MS, 2749 PUTNAM ST 76112   3-00100
  William Gay, prin.   496-7461
James MS, 1101 NASHVILLE AVE 76105   4-00100
  George Thompson, prin.   531-6230
Kirkpatrick MS   2-00100
  3201 REFUGIO AVE 76106   740-5350
  Jorge Mendoza, prin.
Leonard MS, 8900 CHAPIN RD 76116   3-00100
  Betty Hanebutt, prin.   560-5630
McLean MS, 3816 STADIUM DR 76109   3-00100
  Mary Cockerell, prin.   927-6830
Meacham MS, 3600 WEBER ST 76106   3-00100
  Hector Beltram, prin.   740-5330
Meadowbrook MS   3-00100
  2001 EDERVILLE RD S 76103   531-6250
  Mildred Sims, prin.
Monnig MS, 3136 BIGHAM BLVD 76116   3-00100
  Jannis Dillworth, prin.   377-7250
Morningside MS   3-00100
  2751 MISSISSIPPI AVE 76104   922-6680
  Odessa Ravin, prin.
Riverside MS, 1600 BOLTON ST 76111   3-00100
  Rodney Stanaland, prin.   838-1530
Rosemont MS   4-00100
  1501 W SEMINARY DR 76115   922-6650
  Hervey Gomez, prin.
Stripling MS, 2100 CLOVER LN 76107   3-00100
  Richard Galindo, prin.   377-7230
Wedgewood MS   4-00100
  3909 WILKIE WAY 76133   370-5830
  Billie Younger, prin.

Keller ISD
  Supt. — See Keller
Fossil Hill MS   3-00100
  3821 STAGHORN CIR S 76137   847-1046
  Mark White, prin.

Masonic Home ISD   2-11111
  PO BOX 15040 76119   531-9300
  J. Stewart, supt.
Masonic Home S   2-11111
  PO BOX 15040 76119   531-9350
  Bill Holt, prin.

All Saints' Episcopal Hospital   HSP
  PO BOX 31 76101   927-6298
All Saints Episcopal S   3-11111
  8200 TUMBLEWEED TRL 76108   246-2413
  Al Shaw, prin.
American Trades Institute   1-CS
  1200 SUMMIT AVE STE 200 76102   429-1045
Avalon Vocational Technical Institute   1-CS
  1407 TEXAS ST 76102
Calvary Academy, 1600 W 5TH ST 76102   2-11111
  Sue Tidwell, prin.   332-3315
Cassata Learning Center   2-00011
  1400 HEMPHILL ST 76104   926-1745
  Dollie Blevins, prin.
Fort Worth Christian S   3-11111
  7517 BOGART DR 76180   281-6504
  Wayne McReynolds, prin.
Fort Worth Country S   3-11111
  4200 COUNTRY DAY LN 76109   732-7718
  Geoffrey Butler, prin.
General Dynamics Logistics Training Ctr.   2-CS
  PO BOX 748 76101   763-6800
Harris Hospital   HSP
  1300 W CANNON ST 76104   878-2106
Hill S, 4817 ODESSA AVE 76133   2-01100
  Lucille Helton, prin.   923-9482
Key S, 4113 WARNOCK CT 76109   2-11111
  Mary Key, prin.   921-3737
Lake Country Christian S   2-11111
  7050 LAKE COUNTRY DR 76179   236-8703
  Stacy Key, prin.
Meadowbrook Christian S   2-11111
  6801 MEADOWBROOK DR 76112   457-2345
  Michael Jackson, prin.
Moncrief Radiation Center   1-CS
  1450 8TH AVE 76104   923-7393
NEC-Fort Worth Campus   2-CC
  300 E LOOP 820 76112   451-0017
Nolan S, 4501 BRIDGE ST 76103   4-00111
  Fr. Paul, prin.   457-2920
Office Careers Centre   1-CS
  7001 GRAPEVINE HWY STE 202 76180
   -284-8107
Southwest Christian S   2-11111
  4600B ALTAMESA BLVD 76133   294-0350
  Pam Womack, prin.
Southwestern Baptist Theological Sem.   5-UC
  2001 W SEMINARY DR 76122   923-1921
Tarrant County Junior College   7-CC
  1500 HOUSTON ST 76102   336-7851

Tarrant County Junior College   4-CC
  4801 MARINE CREEK PKY 76179
Tarrant County Junior College   4-CC
  5301 CAMPUS DR 76119
Temple Christian S   2-01111
  PO BOX 8499 76124   457-0770
  Truett Linehan, prin.
Texas Christian University   6-UC
  2800 S UNIVERSITY DR 76129   800-828-8777
Texas Wesleyan University   4-UC
  1201 WESLEYAN ST 76105   800-580-8980
Trinity Valley S   3-11111
  6101 MCCART AVE 76133   292-6060
  Dennis Fleming, prin.
University of N Texas Health Science Ctr   2-UC
  3500 CAMP BOWIE BLVD 76107   735-2000

Franklin, AC 409, PC 4, Robertson
Franklin ISD, PO BOX 369 77856   3-11111
  Thomas Phillips, supt.   828-3236
HS, PO BOX 369 77856   2-00011
  Robert Hailey, prin.   828-3236
JHS, PO BOX 367 77856   2-01100
  Tom Jackson, prin.   828-5434

Frankston, AC 903, PC 4, Anderson
Frankston ISD, PO BOX 428 75763   3-11111
  Ronald Nelms, supt.   876-2556
HS, PO BOX 428 75763   2-00011
  Terry Lapic, prin.   876-2215
MS, PO BOX 428 75763   2-00100
  C. J. O'Neal, prin.   876-2215

Fredericksburg, AC 210, PC 6, Gillespie
Fredericksburg ISD   4-11111
  300B W MAIN ST 78624   997-9551
  John Walch, supt.
HS, 1107 HIGHWAY 16 S 78624   3-00011
  John Clawson, prin.   997-7551
MS, 110 W TRAVIS ST 78624   3-00100
  Lawrence Pesek, prin.   997-7657

Freeport, AC 409, PC 7, Brazoria
Brazosport ISD, PO BOX Z 77541   7-11111
  Gerald Anderson, supt.   265-6181
Brazosport HS, 1800 W 2ND ST 77541   3-00011
  Leon Rodgers, prin.   233-0151
IS, 311 W 4TH ST 77541   3-00100
  Herminia Uresti, prin.   233-7285
Other Schools – See Clute, Lake Jackson

Freer, AC 512, PC 5, Duval
Freer ISD, PO BOX 240 78357   4-11111
  Carlos Lopez, supt.   394-6025
HS, PO BOX 240 78357   2-00011
  Saul Hinojosa, prin.   394-6717
JHS, PO BOX 240 78357   2-00100
  Doug Harvey, prin.   394-7102

Friendswood, AC 713, PC 7, Galveston
Clear Creek ISD
  Supt. — See League City
Clear Brook HS, 4607 FM 2351 RD 77546   4-00011
  Sandra Mossman, prin.   996-5446

Friendswood ISD, 302 LAUREL DR 77546   5-11111
  Gary Clay, supt.   482-1267
HS, 702 GREENBRIAR AVE 77546   4-00011
  Curtis Wilson, prin.   482-3413
JHS, 402 LAUREL DR 77546   3-00100
  Margaret Trlica, prin.   482-7818

Microcomputer Technology Institute   2-CC
  17164 BLACKHAWK BLVD 77546   996-8180

Friona, AC 806, PC 5, Parmer
Friona ISD, 909 E 11TH ST 79035   4-11111
  Hal Ratcliff, supt.   247-2747
HS, 909 E 11TH ST 79035   2-00011
  Clifton Stephens, prin.   247-3951
JHS, 909 E 11TH ST 79035   2-00100
  Kevin Wiseman, prin.   247-2788

Frisco, AC 214, PC 6, Collin
Frisco ISD, PO BOX 910 75034   4-11111
  J. Wakeland, supt.   335-4500
HS, PO BOX 910 75034   2-00011
  Rick Burnett, prin.   335-4144
MS, PO BOX 910 75034   2-00100
  Doug Zambiasi, prin.   335-3883

Fritch, AC 806, PC 4, Hutchinson
Sanford ISD, PO BOX 1290 79036   4-11111
  Alton Fields, supt.   857-3122
Sanford-Fritch HS   3-00011
  PO BOX 1290 79036   857-3121
  Ken Hayes, prin.
Sanford-Fritch MS   2-00100
  PO BOX 1290 79036   857-9268
  Jesse Thornton, prin.

Frost, AC 903, PC 3, Navarro
Frost ISD, PO BOX K 76641   2-11111
  Jim Revill, supt.   682-2711
JSHS, PO BOX K 76641   2-00111
  Gordon Lockett, prin.   682-2541

Fruitvale, AC 903, PC 2, Van Zandt
Fruitvale ISD, PO BOX 77 75127   2-11111
  Don Travis, supt.   896-1191
JSHS, PO BOX 77 75127   2-00111
  Stan Surratt, prin.   896-4363

Gail, AC 806, PC 2, Borden
Borden County ISD 2-11111
  PO BOX 95 79738 756-4313
  Jim Thomas, supt.
Borden S, PO BOX 95 79738 2-11111
  Mickey McMeans, prin. 756-4314

Gainesville, AC 817, PC 7, Cooke
Callisburg ISD, RR 2 BOX 259 76240 3-11111
  Mac Hewlett, supt. 665-0540
Callisburg HS, RR 2 BOX 259 76240 2-00011
  Larry Smith, prin. 665-0961
Callisburg JHS, RR 2 BOX 259 76240 2-00100
  Larry Smith, prin. 665-0961
Gainesville ISD 5-11111
  1201 S LINDSAY ST 76240 665-4362
  Thomas Myers, supt.
HS, 1201 S LINDSAY ST 76240 3-00011
  Eddie Morris, prin. 665-5528
MS, 421 N DENTON ST 76240 3-00100
  Welton Stocker, prin. 665-4062

North Central Texas College 5-CC
  1525 W CALIFORNIA ST 76240 668-7731

Galena Park, AC 713, PC 7, Harris
Galena Park ISD, PO BOX 565 77547 7-11111
  Don Hooper, supt. 672-7491
HS, 1000 KEENE ST 77547 4-00011
  (—), prin. 672-6331
JSHS, 1700 3RD ST 77547 3-00011
  David Hopkins, prin. 672-2486
Other Schools – See Houston

Galveston, AC 409, PC 8, Galveston
Galveston ISD, PO BOX 660 77553 7-11111
  Richard Toledo, supt. 765-9366
Ball HS, 4115 AVENUE O 77550 4-00011
  (—), prin. 766-5715
Central MS, 3014 SEALY ST 77550 4-00100
  Jack Stork, prin. 765-6637

Galveston College 4-CC
  4015 AVENUE Q 77550 763-6551
O'Connell HS, 1320 TREMONT ST 77550 2-00011
  Sr. Mary Heins, prin. 765-5534
Texas A & M at Galveston 4-UC
  PO BOX 1675 77553 740-4422
University of Texas Medical Branch 4-UC
  77555 761-1215

Ganado, AC 512, PC 4, Jackson
Ganado ISD, PO BOX D 77962 3-11111
  Reuben Cosby, supt. 771-3482
JSHS, PO BOX D 77962 2-00011
  Leland Moore, prin. 771-3430

Garden City, AC 915, PC 2, Glasscock
Glasscock ISD, PO BOX 9 79739 2-11111
  Charles Zachry, supt. 354-2230
Glasscock JSHS, PO BOX 9 79739 2-00111
  Scott King, prin. 354-2244

Garland, AC 214, PC 9, Dallas
Garland ISD, 720 STADIUM DR 75040 8-11111
  Jill Shugart, supt. 494-8201
Forest HS 4-00011
  4843 NAAMAN FOREST BLVD 75040 494-8670
  George Lyons, prin.
Garland HS, 310 S GARLAND AVE 75040 4-00011
  Bob Price, prin. 494-8492
Lakeview HS, 3505 HAYMAN DR 75043 4-00011
  Andy Coleman, prin. 494-8592
North Garland HS 4-00011
  2109 W BUCKINGHAM RD 75042 494-8451
  Linda Richey, prin.
South Garland HS 4-00011
  600 COLONEL DR 75043 494-8424
  Tom Poore, prin.
Austin Academy for Excellence MS 3-00100
  1125 BEVERLY DR 75040 494-8331
  Ann Poore, prin.
Brandenburg MS 3-00100
  626 NICKENS RD 75043 494-8305
  Mike Richey, prin.
Bussey MS, 1204 TRAVIS ST 75040 3-00100
  Lemuel Nichols, prin. 494-8391
Houston MS, 2232 SUSSEX DR 75041 3-00100
  B. Willis, prin. 494-8344
Hudson MS, 4405 HUDSON PARK 75048 2-00100
  Sara Johnson, prin. 494-8201
Jackson MS, 1310 BOBBIE LN 75042 3-00100
  Henry Brackett, prin. 494-8362
Lyles MS 4-00100
  4655 S COUNTRY CLUB RD 75043 494-8648
  Marlene Carter, prin.
Memorial MS, 2825 S 1ST ST 75041 2-00100
  Larry Rhodes, prin. 494-8357
O'Banion MS 3-00100
  700 BIRCHWOOD DR 75043 279-6103
  David Chapasko, prin.
Sellers MS, 1009 MARS DR 75040 3-00100
  Steve Baker, prin. 494-8337
Webb MS 3-00100
  1610 SPRING CREEK DR 75040 494-8313
  Jim Lewis, prin.
Other Schools – See Rowlett

Alpha Christian Academy 2-11111
  701 W STATE ST 75040 272-8521
  James Black, prin.

Amber University 4-UC
  1700 EASTGATE DR 75041 279-6511
Garland Christian Academy 3-11111
  1522 LAVON DR 75040 487-0043
  John McCartt, prin.
ITT Technical Institute 2-CC
  1640 EASTGATE DR # 100 75041 279-0500

Garrison, AC 409, PC 3, Nacogdoches
Garrison ISD, PO BOX 510 75946 3-11111
  James Bogue, supt. 347-2940
JSHS, PO BOX 510 75946 2-00111
  Robert Marshall, prin. 347-2271

Gary, AC 903, PC 2, Panola
Gary ISD, PO BOX 189 75643 2-11111
  Stanley Yarbrough, supt. 685-2291
S, PO BOX 189 75643 2-11111
  (—), prin. 685-2291

Gatesville, AC 817, PC 7, Coryell
Gatesville ISD, 311 S LOVERS LN 76528 4-11111
  Tracy Barnes, supt. 865-7251
HS, 311 S LOVERS LN 76528 3-00011
  Roland Lambert, prin. 865-8281
JHS, 311 S LOVERS LN 76528 2-00100
  Marion Hines, prin. 865-8271

Georgetown, AC 512, PC 7, Williamson
Georgetown ISD 6-11111
  603 LAKEWAY DR 78628 863-6595
  Jim Gunn, supt.
HS, 1701 N AUSTIN AVE 78626 4-00011
  Gary Crowell, prin. 863-6593
JHS, 1601 LEANDER RD 78628 3-00100
  Carlos Cantu, prin. 863-3802

Southwestern University 4-UC
  UNIVERSITY AVE AT MAPLE ST 78626
  800-252-5788

George West, AC 512, PC 5, Live Oak
George West ISD, PO BOX G 78022 4-11111
  Charles Williams, supt. 449-1914
HS, PO BOX G 78022 2-00011
  Steve Lackey, prin. 449-1741
JHS, PO BOX G 78022 2-00100
  Collin Stanton, prin. 449-1814

Geronimo, AC 210, PC 2, Guadalupe
Navarro ISD, PO BOX 10 78115 3-11111
  Clarence Frase, supt. 372-1930
Navarro JSHS, PO BOX 10 78115 2-00111
  Emma Jean Becker, prin. 372-1931

Giddings, AC 409, PC 5, Lee
Giddings ISD, PO BOX 389 78942 4-11111
  Gene Burton, supt. 542-2854
HS, PO BOX 389 78942 2-00011
  Leroy Lorenz, prin. 542-3351
MS, PO BOX 389 78942 2-00100
  Thomas Campbell, prin. 542-2057

Gilmer, AC 903, PC 5, Upshur
Gilmer ISD, PO BOX 40 75644 4-11111
  Joe Bob Smith, supt. 843-2525
HS, PO BOX 40 75644 3-00011
  Don Ogg, prin. 843-3021
JHS, PO BOX 40 75644 3-00100
  Hayden Mayfield, prin. 843-3051

Harmony ISD, RR 4 BOX 652 75644 3-11111
  Jack Thompson, supt. 725-5492
Harmony HS, RR 4 BOX 652 75644 2-00011
  James Westbrook, prin. 725-5495
Harmony MS, RR 4 BOX 652 75644 2-01100
  William Humphrey, prin. 725-5485

Union Hill ISD, PO BOX 370 75644 2-11111
  Richard Woods, supt. 762-2138
Union Hill JSHS, PO BOX 370 75644 2-00111
  Herbert Blackstone, prin. 762-2138

Gladewater, AC 903, PC 6, Gregg
Gladewater ISD 4-11111
  700 W MELBA AVE # A 75647 845-6991
  David Sharp, supt.
HS, 2201 W GAY AVE 75647 3-00011
  Link Fuller, prin. 845-5591
MS, 700 W MELBA AVE 75647 3-00100
  Peggy Mitchell, prin. 845-2243

Sabine ISD, RR 1 BOX 189 75647 4-11111
  Jerry Welty, supt. 984-8564
Sabine HS, RR 1 BOX 189 75647 2-00011
  Jerry Wallace, prin. 984-8587
Sabine JHS, RR 1 BOX 189 75647 2-00100
  Bobby Fortson, prin. 984-4767

Union Grove ISD 3-11111
  PO BOX 1447 75647 845-5509
  Dan Rose, supt.
Union Grove JSHS 2-00111
  PO BOX 1447 75647 845-5506
  Gilbert Kalinec, prin.

Glen Rose, AC 817, PC 4, Somervell
Glen Rose ISD, PO BOX 2129 76043 4-11111
  Marion Czaja, supt. 897-2517
HS, PO BOX 2129 76043 2-00011
  David Craft, prin. 897-4383
MS, PO BOX 2129 76043 2-00100
  Gary Kaseberg, prin. 897-4442

Godley, AC 817, PC 3, Johnson
Godley ISD, PO BOX 128 76044 3-11111
  Kenneth Bateman, supt. 389-2536
HS, PO BOX 128 76044 2-00011
  Gary Dugger, prin. 389-2265
MS, PO BOX 128 76044 2-00100
  Murrell Loflin, prin. 389-2121

Goldthwaite, AC 915, PC 4, Mills
Goldthwaite ISD, PO BOX 608 76844 3-11111
  Harry Wetzel, supt. 648-3531
JSHS, PO BOX 608 76844 2-00111
  Alan Hildebrand, prin. 648-2718

Goliad, AC 512, PC 4, Goliad
Goliad ISD, PO BOX 830 77963 4-11111
  James Young, supt. 645-3259
HS, PO BOX 830 77963 2-00011
  Bradford Barnes, prin. 645-3257
MS, PO BOX 830 77963 2-00100
  Jim Najvar, prin. 645-3146

Gonzales, AC 210, PC 6, Gonzales
Gonzales ISD, PO BOX 157 78629 5-11111
  Erwin Ckodre, supt. 672-9551
HS, PO BOX M 78629 3-00011
  Jack Morgan, prin. 672-7535
JHS, PO BOX N 78629 3-00100
  Mary Menking, prin. 672-8641

Goodrich, AC 409, PC 2, Polk
Goodrich ISD, PO BOX 193 77335 2-11111
  Ed Burleson, supt. 365-2247
JSHS, PO BOX 193 77335 2-00111
  Thalia Chaney, prin. 365-2747

Gordon, AC 817, PC 2, Palo Pinto
Gordon ISD, PO BOX 47 76453 2-11111
  Randy Savage, supt. 693-5582
S, PO BOX 47 76453 2-11111
  Nelson Campbell, prin. 693-5342

Goree, AC 817, PC 2, Knox
Goree ISD, PO BOX 156 76363 1-11111
  E. Hosea, supt. 422-5233
S, PO BOX 156 76363 1-11111
  George Cotton, prin. 422-5218

Gorman, AC 817, PC 4, Eastland
Gorman ISD, PO BOX 8 76454 2-11111
  Gene Shackleford, supt. 734-3171
JSHS, PO BOX 8 76454 2-00011
  Bill Sandlin, prin. 734-2614

Graford, AC 817, PC 3, Palo Pinto
Graford ISD, RR 1 BOX 1 76449 2-11111
  Eddie Scheer, supt. 664-3101
JSHS, RR 1 BOX 1 76449 2-00011
  Connie Wilson, prin. 664-3161

Graham, AC 817, PC 6, Young
Graham ISD, 1000 KENTUCKY ST 76450 5-11111
  Bob Parker, supt. 549-0595
HS, 1000 KENTUCKY ST 76450 3-00011
  Dee Didriksen, prin. 549-4030
JHS, 1000 KENTUCKY ST 76450 3-00100
  Alan Hardin, prin. 549-6801

Granbury, AC 817, PC 5, Hood
Granbury ISD, 600 W PEARL ST 76048 6-11111
  Gwyn Boyter, supt. 579-2200
HS, 2000 W PEARL ST 76048 4-00011
  Troy Green, prin. 579-2230
MS, 217 N JONES ST 76048 3-00100
  Marsha Grissom, prin. 579-2250
Meadows MS 3-00100
  1021 S MEADOW DR 76048 579-2260
  Bill Henderson, prin.

Happy Hill Farm Academy 1-11111
  HC BOX 56 76048 897-4822
  Jo Ellen Rickard, prin.

Grandfalls, AC 915, PC 3, Ward
Grandfalls-Royalty ISD 2-11111
  PO BOX 10 79742 – J. Stocks, supt. 547-2266
Grandfalls-Royalty HS 1-00011
  PO BOX 10 79742 547-2244
  Jim Yancey, prin.
Grandfalls-Royalty JHS 1-00100
  PO BOX 10 79742 547-2821
  Jim Yancey, prin.

Grand Prairie, AC 214, PC 9, Dallas
Grand Prairie ISD 7-11111
  PO BOX 531170 75053 264-6141
  Marvin Crawford, supt.
HS, 101 HIGHSCHOOL DR 75050 4-00011
  Alwyn Berry, prin. 264-5711
South Grand Prairie HS 4-00011
  301 W WARRIOR TRL 75052 264-4731
  Vern Alexander, prin.
Adams MS, 833 W TARRANT RD 75050 3-00100
  Michael Brinkley, prin. 262-1934
Jackson MS, 305 W WARRIOR TRL 75052 3-00100
  Gary Gilbreath, prin. 264-2704
Kennedy MS, 2205 SE 4TH ST 75051 3-00100
  Sally Bingham, prin. 264-8651
Lee MS 2-00100
  401 E GRAND PRAIRIE RD 75051 262-6785
  Antonio Lawrence, prin.
Truman MS 3-00100
  1501 COFFEYVILLE TRL 75052 641-7676
  Dennis Hale, prin.

Evangel Temple Christian S — 2-11111
302 W HIGHWAY 303 75051 — 264-1303
Carol Lohman, prin.
Lincoln Technical Institute — 3-CS
2501 ARKANSAS LN 75052 — 660-5701

Grand Saline, AC 903, PC 5, Van Zandt
Grand Saline ISD — 3-11111
400 STADIUM DR 75140 — 962-7546
Gerald Gilbert, supt.
HS, 400 STADIUM DR 75140 — 2-00011
J. Witt, prin. — 962-7533
MS, 300 STADIUM DR 75140 — 2-00100
Richard Montgomery, prin. — 962-5596

Grandview, AC 817, PC 4, Johnson
Grandview ISD, PO BOX 310 76050 — 3-11111
Harold Pinkerton, supt. — 866-2450
HS, PO BOX 310 76050 — 2-00011
Larry Smith, prin. — 866-3320
JHS, PO BOX 310 76050 — 2-00100
Alan Neff, prin. — 866-2492

Granger, AC 512, PC 4, Williamson
Granger ISD, PO BOX 578 76530 — 2-11111
Raymond Etheridge, supt. — 859-2613
S, PO BOX 578 76530 — 2-11111
Jimmie Lange, prin. — 859-2173

Grapeland, AC 409, PC 4, Houston
Grapeland ISD, PO BOX 249 75844 — 3-11111
James Caveness, supt. — 687-4619
HS, PO BOX 249 75844 — 2-00011
Ralph Barnett, prin. — 687-4661
JHS, PO BOX 249 75844 — 2-00100
Larry Hughes, prin. — 687-2351

Grapevine, AC 817, PC 8, Tarrant
Grapevine-Colleyville ISD — 6-11111
3051 W HIGHWAY 26 76051 — 488-9588
James Thompson, supt.
SHS, 3223 MUSTANG DR 76051 — 4-00001
Jennifer Killian, prin. — 488-9596
JHS, 2301 POOL RD 76051 — 4-00010
Jennifer Killian, prin. — 488-6941
MS, 730 E WORTH ST 76051 — 3-00100
Juneria Berges, prin. — 488-9592
Other Schools – See Colleyville

Greenville, AC 903, PC 7, Hunt
Greenville ISD, PO BOX 1022 75403 — 6-11111
Gilbert Weaver, supt. — 457-2500
HS, 3515 LIONS LAIR RD 75402 — 4-00011
James Fuller, prin. — 457-2550
MS, 3611 TEXAS ST 75401 — 3-00100
George Vaughn, prin. — 457-2621

Greenville Christian S — 2-11111
8420 JACK FINNEY BLVD 75402 — 454-1111
Glenn Slater, prin.

Gregory, AC 512, PC 4, San Patricio
Gregory-Portland ISD — 5-11111
PO BOX 338 78359 — 643-6566
Bob Jameson, supt.
Other Schools – See Portland

Groesbeck, AC 817, PC 5, Limestone
Groesbeck ISD, PO BOX 559 76642 — 4-11111
Larry Butler, supt. — 729-3808
HS, 1202 N ELLIS ST 76642 — 2-00011
Robert Windham, prin. — 729-5933
JHS, 502 ELWOOD ENGE DR 76642 — 2-00100
Gary Caudle, prin. — 729-3435

Groom, AC 806, PC 3, Carson
Groom ISD, PO BOX 598 79039 — 2-11111
Kenneth Sweatt, supt. — 248-7557
S, PO BOX 598 79039 — 2-11111
Judy Babcock, prin. — 248-7474

Groves, AC 409, PC 7, Jefferson
Port Neches ISD
Supt. — See Port Neches
MS, 5201 WILSON ST 77619 — 3-00100
Sam LaRue, prin. — 962-0225

Groveton, AC 409, PC 4, Trinity
Centerville ISD, RR 1 BOX 146 75845 — 2-11111
James Davis, supt. — 642-1597
Centerville JSHS — 1-00111
RR 1 BOX 146 75845 — 642-1597
Colleen Moore, prin.

Groveton ISD, PO BOX 728 75845 — 3-11111
John Reynolds, supt. — 642-1473
JSHS, PO BOX 700 75845 — 2-00111
James Wise, prin. — 642-1128

Grulla, AC 210, PC 4, Starr
Rio Grande City ISD
Supt. — See Rio Grande City
JHS, GENERAL DELIVERY 78548 — 2-00100
Merardo Bando, prin. — 487-5558

Gruver, AC 806, PC 4, Hansford
Gruver ISD, PO BOX 650 79040 — 3-11111
Barry Haenisch, supt. — 733-2001
HS, PO BOX 747 79040 — 2-00011
Lloyd Looper, prin. — 733-2477
JHS, PO BOX 709 79040 — 2-01100
Laura Blassingame, prin. — 733-2081

Gunter, AC 903, PC 3, Grayson
Gunter ISD, PO BOX 109 75058 — 2-11111
R. Cohagan, supt. — 433-4750

JSHS, PO BOX 109 75058 — 2-00111
Gayle Banner, prin. — 433-1543

Gustine, AC 915, PC 2, Comanche
Gustine ISD, PO BOX 169 76455 — 2-11111
Walter Richards, supt. — 667-7981
S, PO BOX 169 76455 — 2-11111
Ron Johnson, prin. — 667-7303

Guthrie, AC 806, PC 2, King
Guthrie Common SD — 1-11111
PO BOX 70 79236 — 596-4466
Keith Richardson, supt.
S, PO BOX 70 79236 — 1-11111
Harvey Wellman, prin. — 596-4466

Hale Center, AC 806, PC 4, Hale
Hale Center ISD, PO BOX M 79041 — 3-11111
Wilbur Crabbs, supt. — 839-2451
HS, PO BOX M 79041 — 2-00011
Walter Cox, prin. — 839-2452
JHS, PO BOX M 79041 — 2-01100
Linda Gossett, prin. — 839-2141

Hallettsville, AC 512, PC 5, Lavaca
Hallettsville ISD, PO BOX 368 77964 — 4-11111
Robert Haas, supt. — 798-2242
HS, 200 N RIDGE ST 77964 — 2-00011
David Kalich, prin. — 798-3241
JHS, 410 S RUSSELL ST 77964 — 2-01100
Stephen Hunter, prin. — 798-2591

Sacred Heart S, 313 S TEXANA ST 77964 — 2-11111
David Smolik, prin. — 798-4251

Hallsville, AC 903, PC 4, Harrison
Hallsville ISD, PO BOX 810 75650 — 5-11111
Bob Browning, supt. — 660-4473
HS, PO BOX 810 75650 — 3-00011
Roy Knight, prin. — 668-3312
JHS, PO BOX 810 75650 — 2-00100
Charles McGough, prin. — 668-2397

Hamilton, AC 817, PC 5, Hamilton
Hamilton ISD, PO BOX 392 76531 — 3-11111
James Whitehead, supt. — 386-3149
HS, PO BOX 392 76531 — 2-00011
Eddie Sneed, prin. — 386-3140

Hamlin, AC 915, PC 5, Jones
Hamlin ISD, PO BOX 338 79520 — 3-11111
Curtis Parsons, supt. — 576-2722
HS, 450 SW AVENUE F 79520 — 2-00011
Terry Kinard, prin. — 576-3625
MS, 250 SW AVENUE F 79520 — 2-00100
Andy Brown, prin. — 576-2933

Hamshire, AC 409, PC 3, Jefferson
Hamshire-Fannett ISD — 4-11111
PO BOX 223 77622 — 243-2133
Eddy Zachary, supt.
Hamshire-Fannett HS — 2-00011
PO BOX 223 77622 — 243-2131
James Bass, prin.
Other Schools – See Beaumont

Happy, AC 806, PC 3, Swisher
Happy ISD, PO BOX 458 79042 — 2-11111
Bill Mayfield, supt. — 558-5331
JSHS, PO BOX 458 79042 — 2-00111
Ken Plumlee, prin. — 558-5311

Hardin, AC 409, PC 3, Liberty
Hardin ISD, PO BOX 330 77561 — 4-11111
F. Sheffield, supt. — 298-2112
HS, PO BOX 330 77561 — 2-00011
Alan Tidwell, prin. — 298-2118
JHS, PO BOX 330 77561 — 2-00100
Monty Upton, prin. — 298-2054

Harker Heights, AC 817, PC 7, Bell
Killeen ISD
Supt. — See Killeen
Eastern Hills MS, 300 INDIAN TRL 76543 — 3-00100
Edward Lusk, prin. — 680-2226

Harleton, AC 903, PC 2, Harrison
Harleton ISD, PO BOX 710 75651 — 3-11111
Pamela McGill, supt. — 777-8601
HS, PO BOX 710 75651 — 2-00011
Bill Traylor, prin. — 777-2711
JHS, PO BOX 710 75651 — 1-00100
Bill Traylor, prin. — 777-3010

Harlingen, AC 210, PC 8, Cameron
Harlingen Consolidated ISD — 7-11111
1409 E HARRISON ST 78550 — 430-4400
James Smith, supt.
HS, 1201 MARSHALL ST 78550 — 4-00011
Verna Young, prin. — 427-3600
Harlingen HS South — 4-00011
1701 DIXIELAND RD 78552 — 427-3800
Guadalupe Nava, prin.
Coakley JHS, 1401 S 6TH ST 78550 — 3-00100
William Pietro, prin. — 427-3000
Memorial JHS, 13TH & MADISON 78550 — 3-00100
Guillermo Rodriguez, prin. — 427-3020
Vernon JHS, 125 W 13TH ST 78550 — 3-00100
Noe Salinas, prin. — 427-3040

Marine Military Academy — 2-00111
320 IWO JIMA BLVD 78550 — 423-6006
John Arick, prin.
National Career Institute — 2-CS
1209 N 7TH ST 78550 — 425-4183

Texas State Technical Institute — 4-CC
78550 — 800-852-8784
Valley Baptist Academy — 2-00111
3700 E HARRISON ST 78550 — 423-0632
Robert Tidwell, prin.

Harper, AC 210, PC 2, Gillespie
Harper ISD, PO BOX 68 78631 — 2-11111
James Ward, supt. — 864-4044
JSHS, PO BOX 68 78631 — 2-00111
Alan Richey, prin. — 864-4044

Harrold, AC 817, PC 2, Wilbarger
Harrold ISD, PO BOX 400 76364 — 2-11111
Don Fritsche, supt. — 886-2213
S, PO BOX 400 76364 — 2-11111
Ronald Brandon, prin. — 886-2213

Hart, AC 806, PC 4, Castro
Hart ISD, PO BOX 490 79043 — 3-11111
Michael Smith, supt. — 938-2143
JSHS, PO BOX 490 79043 — 2-00111
Wallace Elam, prin. — 938-2141

Hartley, AC 806, PC 2, Hartley
Hartley ISD, PO BOX 56 79044 — 2-11111
Dan Cochran, supt. — 365-4458
S, PO BOX 56 79044 — 2-11111
Dan Cochran, prin. — 365-4459

Haskell, AC 817, PC 5, Haskell
Haskell ISD, PO BOX 937 79521 — 3-11111
William Stewart, supt. — 864-2602
JSHS, PO BOX 937 79521 — 2-00111
Greg Melton, prin. — 864-2848

Paint Creek ISD, RR 2 BOX 190 79521 — 2-11111
Jerry Morgan, supt. — 864-2471
Paint Creek S, RR 2 BOX 190 79521 — 2-11111
Max Calk, prin. — 864-2471

Hawkins, AC 903, PC 4, Wood
Hawkins ISD, PO BOX L 75765 — 3-11111
Robert Pool, supt. — 769-2181
HS, PO BOX L 75765 — 2-00011
Wiley Vonner, prin. — 769-2141
MS, PO BOX L 75765 — 2-00100
Tommy Riggs, prin. — 769-3504

Jarvis Christian College — 3-UC
PO BOX G 75765 — 769-2174

Hawley, AC 915, PC 3, Jones
Hawley ISD, PO BOX D 79525 — 3-11111
Ed Womack, supt. — 537-2214
JSHS, PO BOX D 79525 — 2-00111
Robert Shipley, prin. — 537-2722

Hearne, AC 409, PC 6, Robertson
Hearne ISD, 900 WHEELOCK ST 77859 — 4-11111
H. Bonorden, supt. — 279-3200
HS, 1210 HACKBERRY ST 77859 — 2-00011
Debra Lamb, prin. — 279-2332
JHS, 401 WHEELOCK ST 77859 — 2-00100
Bill Humphries, prin. — 279-2449

Hebbronville, AC 512, PC 5, Jim Hogg
Jim Hogg County ISD — 4-11111
PO BOX 880 78361 — 527-3203
Mona Hopkins, supt.
HS, PO BOX 880 78361 — 2-00011
Humberto Gonzalez, prin. — 527-5751
JHS, PO BOX 880 78361 — 2-00100
Joe Solis, prin. — 527-4815

Hedley, AC 806, PC 2, Donley
Hedley ISD, PO BOX 69 79237 — 2-11111
Thomas Robertson, supt. — 856-5323
S, PO BOX 69 79237 — 2-11111
Bryan Hill, prin. — 856-5323

Hemphill, AC 409, PC 4, Sabine
Hemphill ISD, PO BOX 1950 75948 — 3-11111
Douglas Butler, supt. — 787-3371
JSHS, PO BOX 1950 75948 — 2-00111
Robert Lane, prin. — 787-3371

Hempstead, AC 409, PC 5, Waller
Hempstead ISD, PO BOX 1007 77445 — 4-11111
Robert Roy, supt. — 826-3304
HS, PO BOX 1007 77445 — 2-00011
Kenneth Johnson, prin. — 826-3331
JHS, PO BOX 1007 77445 — 2-00100
James Palmer, prin. — 826-2530

Henderson, AC 903, PC 7, Rusk
Henderson ISD, PO BOX 728 75653 — 5-11111
Jerry Christian, supt. — 657-8511
HS, PO BOX 728 75653 — 4-00011
Joel Hale, prin. — 657-8511
MS, PO BOX 728 75653 — 3-00100
George Kale, prin. — 657-8511

Henrietta, AC 817, PC 5, Clay
Henrietta ISD — 3-11111
1801 E CRAFTON ST 76365 — 538-4581
Rondall Preston, supt.
HS, 1700 E CRAFTON ST 76365 — 2-00011
Clarence Gilstrap, prin. — 538-4397
JHS, 308 E GILBERT ST 76365 — 2-00100
Jim Crump, prin. — 538-5121

Midway ISD, RR 2 BOX 179 76365 — 2-11111
Hollis Adams, supt. — 476-2222
Midway S, RR 2 BOX 179 76365 — 2-11111
Hollis Adams, prin. — 476-2215

Hereford, AC 806, PC 7, Deaf Smith
Hereford ISD, 136 AVENUE F 79045 5-11111
Charles Greenawalt, supt. 364-0606
HS, 200 AVENUE F 79045 4-00011
Terry Russell, prin. 363-7620
JHS, 704 LA PLATA ST 79045 3-00100
Marilyn Leasure, prin. 363-7630

Hermleigh, AC 915, PC 2, Scurry
Hermleigh ISD, PO BOX 195 79526 2-11111
Jerry Church, supt. 863-2772
S, PO BOX 195 79526 2-11111
Clarence Spieker, prin. 863-2451

Hico, AC 817, PC 4, Hamilton
Hico ISD, PO BOX 218 76457 3-11111
Gary Bottoms, supt. 796-2181
JSHS, PO BOX 218 76457 2-00111
Jim Everitt, prin. 796-2184

Hidalgo, AC 210, PC 5, Hidalgo
Hidalgo ISD, PO BOX D 78557 5-11111
Alejo Salinas, supt. 843-8401
HS, PO BOX D 78557 3-00011
Daniel King, prin. 843-3160
Diaz JHS, PO BOX D 78557 3-00100
Juan Alvarez, prin. 843-3140

Higgins, AC 806, PC 2, Lipscomb
Higgins ISD, PO BOX 238 79046 2-11111
Harold Whipkey, supt. 852-2171
S, PO BOX 238 79046 2-11111
Harold Whipkey, prin. 852-2631

High Island, AC 409, PC 3, Galveston
High Island ISD, PO BOX 246 77623 2-11111
Jeffery Campbell, supt. 286-5314
JSHS, PO BOX 246 77623 2-00111
Jim Shurtleff, prin. 286-5313

Highlands, AC 713, PC 6, Harris
Goose Creek ISD
Supt. — See Baytown
JHS, 1212 E WALLISVILLE RD 77562 3-00100
Carol Fontenot, prin. 420-4695

Hillsboro, AC 817, PC 6, Hill
Hillsboro ISD, PO BOX 459 76645 4-11111
Leon Murdoch, supt. 582-3171
HS, PO BOX 1076 76645 2-00011
Joe Westmoreland, prin. 582-3612
Harris Career Ctr, PO BOX 371 76645 Vo Tech
Karen Kleine, prin. 582-5631
JHS, PO BOX 977 76645 2-00100
Dennis Smith, prin. 582-3311

Hill College 4-CC
PO BOX 619 76645 582-2555

Hitchcock, AC 409, PC 6, Galveston
Hitchcock ISD 4-11111
8117 HIGHWAY 6 77563 986-5514
William Banks, supt.
HS, 7801 NEVILLE AVE 77563 2-00011
Robert Tomlinson, prin. 986-5581
Crosby JHS, 7805 NEVILLE AVE 77563 2-00100
Bobby Smith, prin. 986-5528

Holland, AC 817, PC 4, Bell
Holland ISD, PO BOX 217 76534 2-11111
Michael Roasa, supt. 657-2224
JSHS, PO BOX 217 76534 2-00111
Reggie Whalen, prin. 657-2523

Holliday, AC 817, PC 4, Archer
Holliday ISD, PO BOX 689 76366 3-11111
Richard Owen, supt. 586-1281
HS, PO BOX 947 76366 2-00011
Bill Lee, prin. 586-1624
MS, PO BOX 977 76366 2-00100
Jake Cottrell, prin. 586-1314

Hondo, AC 210, PC 6, Medina
Hondo ISD, PO BOX 308 78861 4-11111
Newell Woolls, supt. 426-3027
HS, 2603 AVENUE H 78861 2-00011
James Keath, prin. 426-3341
McDowell JHS, 1602 27TH ST S 78861 3-01100
Vicente Arcos, prin. 426-2261

Honey Grove, AC 903, PC 4, Fannin
Honey Grove ISD, 400 6TH ST 75446 3-11111
Harvey Milton, supt. 378-2264
HS, 400 6TH ST 75446 2-00011
(—), prin. 378-2263
MS, 400 6TH ST 75446 2-00100
Robert Milton, prin. 378-7142

Hooks, AC 903, PC 5, Bowie
Hooks ISD, PO BOX 39 75561 4-11111
James Wilcox, supt. 547-6077
HS, PO BOX 1447 75561 2-00011
Dwight Duncan, prin. 547-2215
JHS, PO BOX 249 75561 2-01100
Herman Hanes, prin. 547-2568

Houston, AC 713, PC 12, Harris
Aldine ISD 8-11111
14910 ALDINE WESTFIELD RD 77032 449-1011
M. Donaldson, supt.
Aldine HS, 11101 AIRLINE DR 77037 5-00011
Ralph Norman, prin. 448-5231
Eisenhower HS 5-00011
7922 ANTOINE DR 77088 448-8401
Fred Richardson, prin.

MacArthur HS 5-00011
4400 ALDINE MAIL RD 77039 442-2511
Wilbert Johnson, prin.
Nimitz HS 4-00011
2005 W W THORNE BLVD 77073 443-7480
John Amshoff, prin.
Aldine MS 4-00100
14910 ALDINE WESTFIELD RD 77032 442-8458
Barbara Glass, prin.
Drew MS 2-00100
1910 W LITTLE YORK RD 77091 447-6321
Pat Nash, prin.
Grantham MS 4-00100
13300 CHRISMAN RD 77039 987-2038
Ramiro Galindo, prin.
Hambrick MS 4-00100
4600 ALDINE MAIL RD 77039 442-8433
Ralph Ramirez, prin.
Hoffman MS 4-00100
6101 W LITTLE YORK RD 77091 683-0338
James Royster, prin.
Shotwell MS 4-00100
6515 TRAIL VALLEY WAY 77086 931-7765
James Murrell, prin.
Stovall HS, 11201 AIRLINE DR 77037 4-00011
Dixie King, prin. 448-5283
Other Schools — See Humble

Alief ISD
Supt. — See Alief
Kerr HS 3-00011
8150 SUGAR LAND HOLLOW 77083 498-8110
(—), prin.
Albright MS 4-00100
6315 WINKLEMAN RD 77083 983-8411
Dennis Paul, prin.
Holub MS 4-00100
9515 S DAIRY ASHFORD ST 77099 983-8433
Linda Sheehan, prin.
Killough MS, 7600 SYNOTT RD 77083 4-00100
Dave Stokan, prin. 983-8444
O'Donnell MS, PO BOX 68 77001 3-00100
Vickie Schoppe, prin. 495-6000
Olle MS, 9200 BOONE RD 77099 4-00100
Patricia Paquin, prin. 983-8455

Clear Creek ISD
Supt. — See League City
Clear Lake HS 5-00011
2929 BAY AREA BLVD 77058 488-6670
Edgar Taylor, prin.
Clear Lake IS 4-00100
15545 EL CAMINO REAL 77062 488-1296
Alan Schultz, prin.
Space Center IS 3-00100
2903 FALCON PASS 77062 488-6670
Jim Stephens, prin.

Cypress-Fairbanks ISD 8-11111
PO BOX 692003 77269 897-4000
Richard Berry, supt.
Cy-Fair HS 5-00011
22602 HEMPSTEAD RD 77040 897-4600
Jodie Smith, prin.
Cypress Creek HS 5-00011
9815 GRANT RD 77070 897-4200
Jan Aragon, prin.
Cypress Falls HS 4-00011
9811 HUFFMEISTER RD 77095 856-1000
George Hopper, prin.
Jersey Village HS 5-00011
7600 SOLOMON ST 77040 896-3400
Leon Meek, prin.
Langham Creek HS 4-00011
17610 FM 529 RD 77095 463-5400
Leonard Brautigam, prin.
Carlton Pre-Vo Ctr Vo Tech
22602 HEMPSTEAD RD 77040 897-4750
Timothy LaCourt, prin.
Arnold JHS, 11111 TELGE RD 77040 4-00100
Phyllis Hamilton, prin. 897-4700
Bleyl JHS, 10800 MILLS RD 77070 4-00100
Nadine Fidler, prin. 897-4340
Campbell JHS, 11415 BOBCAT RD 77064 4-00100
Margie Pope, prin. 897-4300
Cook JHS, 9111 WHEATLAND DR 77064 4-00100
Ray Housley, prin. 897-4400
Labay JHS 4-00100
15435 WILLOW RIVER DR 77095 463-5800
Bob Warner, prin.
Truitt JHS 4-00100
6600 ADDICKS SATSUMA RD 77084 856-1100
Titika Liollio, prin.
Watkins JHS 4-00100
4800 CAIRNVILLAGE ST 77084 463-5850
Sherrill Fisk, prin.
Other Schools — See Katy

Galena Park ISD
Supt. — See Galena Park
North Shore HS 4-00011
13501 HOLLYPARK DR 77015 453-7183
Malcomb Dennis, prin.
Cunningham MS 4-00100
14110 WALLISVILLE RD 77049 453-0196
Corliss Rogers, prin.
North Shore MS 4-00100
13801 HOLLYPARK DR 77015 453-3501
Raymond Kilgo, prin.
Woodland Acres MS 3-00100
12947 MYRTLE LN 77015 455-1615
Dale Moore, prin.

Houston ISD 9-11111
3830 RICHMOND AVE 77027 892-6000
Frank Petruzielo, supt.
Austin HS, 1700 DUMBLE ST 77023 5-00011
Jose Trevino, prin. 923-7751
Contemporary Learning Center HS 2-00011
1906 CLEBURNE ST 77004 526-3629
Naurita Daniels, prin.
Davis HS, 1101 QUITMAN ST 77009 4-00011
Emily Cole, prin. 226-4900
Furr HS, 520 MERCURY DR 77013 4-00011
Julie Shannon, prin. 675-1118
Health Professions HS 3-00011
3100 SHENANDOAH ST 77021 741-2410
Charlesetta Collins, prin.
HS, 9400 IRVINGTON BLVD 77076 5-00011
Paul Campbell, prin. 696-8970
HS/Law Enforcement/Criminology 3-00011
4701 DICKSON ST 77007 861-5100
Norma Morris, prin.
Jones HS, 7414 SAINT LO RD 77033 4-00011
Arthur Pace, prin. 733-1111
Jordan HS, 5800 EASTEX FWY 77026 4-00011
Ellis Douglas, prin. 631-8363
Kashmere HS 4-00011
6900 WILEYVALE RD 77028 636-6400
David Alexander, prin.
Lamar HS, 3325 WESTHEIMER RD 77098 5-00011
Walter Day, prin. 522-5960
Lee HS, 6529 BEVERLYHILL ST 77057 4-00011
James Claypool, prin. 782-7310
Madison HS 4-00011
13719 WHITE HEATHER DR 77045 433-9801
Warner Erwin, prin.
Milby HS, 1601 BROADWAY ST 77012 5-00011
Richard Vasquez, prin. 928-7401
Performing & Visual Arts HS 3-00011
4001 STANFORD ST 77006 522-7811
Rosa Watson, prin.
Reagan HS, 413 E 13TH ST 77008 4-00011
James Lavois, prin. 861-5694
Scarborough HS 3-00011
4141 COSTA RICA RD 77092 681-3679
Vivian Dailey, prin.
Sharpstown HS 4-00011
7504 BISSONNET ST 77074 771-7215
Arnold Ramirez, prin.
Sterling HS 4-00011
11625 MARTINDALE RD 77048 991-0510
Daisy Maura, prin.
Waltrip HS, 1900 W 34TH ST 77018 4-00011
Glen Prenzler, prin. 688-1361
Washington HS, 119 E 39TH ST 77018 4-00011
Ira Wesley, prin. 692-5947
Westbury HS, 5575 GASMER DR 77035 4-00011
Shirley Johnson, prin. 723-6015
Wheatley HS, 4900 MARKET ST 77020 4-00011
Harold Crawford, prin. 671-3900
Worthing HS, 9215 SCOTT ST 77051 4-00011
Larry Alexander, prin. 733-3433
Yates HS, 3703 SAMPSON ST 77004 4-00011
Ronald Johnson, prin. 748-5400
Marshall JSHS, 1115 NOBLE ST 77009 4-00111
Roberto Gonzalez, prin. 227-1761
Rogers JSHS, 5840 SAN FELIPE ST 77057 2-00111
Meredith Wedin, prin. 783-6220
Carter HS, 1700 GREGG ST 77020 Vo Tech
Mildred Nicks, prin. 223-0147
Attucks MS, 4330 BELLFORT ST 77051 3-00100
Frank Thomas, prin. 733-9253
Black MS, 1575 CHANTILLY LN 77018 3-00100
William Meagher, prin. 613-2505
Burbank MS, 315 BERRY RD 77022 4-00100
Glenda Alvarez, prin. 694-2813
Clifton MS 4-00100
6001 GOLDEN FOREST DR 77092 613-2516
Mira Baptiste, prin.
Contemporary Learning Center MS 2-00100
1906 CLEBURNE ST 77004 – (—), prin. 526-3629
Cullen MS, 6900 SCOTT ST 77021 3-00100
Nobleton Jones, prin. 747-1255
Deady MS, 2500 BROADWAY ST 77012 4-00100
Georgia McGlasson, prin. 845-7411
Dowling MS 4-00100
14000 STANCLIFF ST 77045 433-5132
Dianne Shakesnider, prin.
Edison MS, 6901 AVENUE I 77011 4-00100
Rogelio Torres, prin. 921-1400
Fleming MS 3-00100
4910 COLLINGSWORTH ST 77026 674-3415
Chester Smith, prin.
Fondren MS 4-00100
6333 S BRAESWOOD BLVD 77096 771-1134
Frances Lavois, prin.
Fonville MS 3-00100
725 E LITTLE YORK RD 77076 692-2210
James Waites, prin.
Gregory-Lincoln MS 3-00100
1101 TAFT ST 77019 522-4219
Margaret Kilgo, prin.
Hamilton MS, 139 E 20TH ST 77008 4-00100
Diana Mulet, prin. 861-0913
Hartman MS, 7111 WESTOVER ST 77087 4-00100
Nabor Cortez, prin. 845-7434
Henry MS, 10702 E HARDY RD 77093 4-00100
Maureen Tobola, prin. 692-0161
Hogg MS, 1100 MERRILL ST 77009 4-00100
Armando Alaniz, prin. 861-5691
Holland MS, 1600 GELLHORN DR 77029 4-00100
Adele Rogers, prin. 675-3538

Jackson MS, 5100 POLK ST 77023 — 4-00100
Lupita Cerna, prin. — 921-0918
Johnston MS — 4-00100
10410 MANHATTAN DR 77096 — 726-3616
David Haller, prin.
Key MS, 4000 KELLEY ST 77026 — 3-00100
Charles Henderson, prin. — 635-2353
Lanier MS, 2600 WOODHEAD ST 77098 — 4-00100
Brenda Lanclos, prin. — 529-5451
Long MS, 6501 BELLAIRE BLVD 77074 — 4-00100
Robert Farquharson, prin. — 774-6620
McReynolds MS — 3-00100
5910 MARKET ST 77020 — 674-6544
Elodia Hough, prin.
Pershing MS, 7000 BRAES BLVD 77025 — 4-00100
Patsy Finch, prin. — 295-5240
Revere MS — 4-00100
10502 BRIAR FOREST DR 77042 — 782-1132
Dorothea Smith, prin.
Ryan MS, 2610 ELGIN ST 77004 — 4-00100
Anita Ellis, prin. — 528-0922
Sharpstown MS, 8330 TRIOLA LN 77036 — 4-00100
Margaret Beltran, prin. — 771-8995
Smith MS, 1701 BRINGHURST ST 77020 — 2-00100
Glyn Johnson, prin. — 222-6077
Stevenson MS, 9595 WINKLER DR 77017 — 3-00100
Margaret Acosta, prin. — 892-6000
Terrell MS — 2-00100
4610 E CROSSTIMBERS ST 77016 — 631-1753
William Kerfoot, prin.
Thomas MS, 5655 SELINSKY RD 77048 — 3-00100
Fred Lewis, prin. — 734-2864
Welch MS, 11544 S GESSNER DR 77071 — 4-00100
Deborah Singleton, prin. — 995-1100
Williams MS, 6100 KNOX ST 77091 — 3-00100
Ross Cahee, prin. — 691-2033
Woodson MS — 3-00100
10720 SOUTHVIEW ST 77047 — 733-2345
Richard Gardner, prin.
Other Schools – See Bellaire

Katy ISD
Supt. — See Katy
Mayde Creek HS — 4-00011
19202 GROESCHKE RD 77084 — 492-1651
Ronald Jetton, prin.
Mayde Creek JHS — 4-00100
2700 GREENHOUSE RD 77084 — 492-8039
Linda Menius, prin.

Klein ISD
Supt. — See Klein
Klein Forest HS — 5-00011
11400 MISTY VALLEY DR 77066 — 586-4550
Don Black, prin.
Klein IS — 3-00100
4710 W MOUNT HOUSTON RD 77088 — 999-9917
Don Rather, prin.
Wunderlich IS — 4-00100
11800 MISTY VALLEY DR 77066 — 586-3500
Karen Dawdy, prin.

North Forest ISD — 7-11111
PO BOX 23278 77228 — 633-1600
Carrol Thomas, supt.
Forest Brook HS — 4-00100
7525 TIDWELL RD 77016 — 631-7720
Dennis Flim, prin.
Smiley HS, 10725 MESA DR 77078 — 4-00011
Lemmie Watson, prin. — 636-4300
Elmore MS, 8200 TATE ST 77028 — 2-00100
Leslie Berry, prin. — 672-7466
Kirby MS, 9709 MESA DR 77078 — 4-00100
Adley Richard, prin. — 633-7640
Northwood MS — 3-00100
10750 HOMESTEAD RD 77016 — 633-4000
Marshal Dupas, prin.
Oak Village MS — 3-00100
6602 WINFIELD RD 77050 — 449-6561
Lillian Parker, prin.

Pasadena ISD
Supt. — See Pasadena
Dobie HS, 11111 BEAMER RD 77089 — 4-00011
Jerry Speer, prin. — 481-3000
Beverly Hills IS, 10415 FUQUA ST 77089 — 4-00100
Stephanie Wright, prin. — 946-5561
Thompson IS — 3-00100
11309 SAGEDOWNE LN 77089 — 481-4953
Vicki Thomas, prin.

Sheldon ISD, 8540 C E KING PKY 77044 — 5-11111
Bobby Wood, supt. — 459-7301
King HS, 8540 C E KING PKY 77044 — 4-00011
Rick Harvey, prin. — 459-7356
King JHS, 8530 C E KING PKY 77044 — 3-00100
Miriam Martin, prin. — 459-7433

Spring Branch ISD — 8-11111
955 CAMPBELL RD 77024 — 464-1511
Harold Guthrie, supt.
Memorial HS, 935 ECHO LN 77024 — 4-00100
Virginia Leiker, prin. — 468-7721
Northbrook HS, 9650 ALCOTT DR 77080 — 4-00011
Harriett Brittenham, prin. — 461-0527
Spring Woods HS — 4-00011
2045 GESSNER DR 77080 — 465-3486
Lorenzo Garcia, prin.
Stratford HS, 14555 FERN DR 77079 — 4-00011
Frazer Dealy, prin. — 496-9200
Landrum JHS — 3-00100
2200 RIDGECREST DR 77055 — 468-2693
Nabor Cortez, prin.

Memorial JHS, 12550 VINDON DR 77024 — 3-00100
M. Eldridge, prin. — 468-7613
Northbrook MS — 3-00100
3030 ROSEFIELD DR 77080 — 497-3333
Susan Wolf, prin.
Spring Branch JHS — 3-00100
1000 PINEY POINT RD 77024 — 468-1791
Tom Byrd, prin.
Spring Forest JHS — 3-00100
14240 MEMORIAL DR 77079 — 497-3066
Vicki Mathews, prin.
Spring Oaks MS — 3-00100
2150 SHADOWDALE DR 77043 — 464-2766
James Reap, prin.
Spring Woods JHS — 3-00100
9810 NEUENS RD 77080 — 468-5434
Gracie Clouse, prin.

Spring ISD, 16717 ELLA BLVD 77090 — 7-11111
Gordon Anderson, supt. — 586-1100
Westfield HS, 16713 ELLA BLVD 77090 — 5-00011
Kenneth McKinney, prin. — 586-1300
Bammel MS, 1500 S RIDGE RD 77090 — 4-00100
John Riddile, prin. — 444-6062
Wells MS, 4033 GLADERIDGE DR 77068 — 4-00100
Daniel Twardowski, prin. — 444-7070
Other Schools – See Spring

Alfred G. Glassell School of Art — 2-CS
5101 MONTROSE BLVD 77006 — 639-7500
Art Institute of Houston — 4-CC
1900 YORKTOWN ST 77056 — 800-275-4244
Awty International S — 3-11111
7455 AWTY SCHOOL LN 77055 — 686-4850
Norbert Milochevitch, prin.
Baylor College of Medicine — 3-UC
1 BAYLOR PLZ 77030 — 798-4951
Ben Taub Hospital — HSP
1502 TAUB LOOP 77030 — 751-1200
Bradford School of Business — 2-CS
4669 SOUTHWEST FWY STE 350 77027 — 629-8940
Briarwood S — 2-11111
12207 WHITTINGTON DR 77077 — 493-1070
Barbara Bellati, prin.
Broadway Baptist S — 2-11111
1020 CORAL ST 77012 — 926-2631
Joanne Crowell, prin.
Center for Advanced Legal Studies — 2-CS
3015 RICHMOND AVE 77098 — 529-2778
Chenier Business School — 2-CS
6300 RICHMOND AVE STE 300 77057
Commonwealth Institute / Funeral Service — 1-CC
415 BARREN SPRINGS DR 77090 — 873-0262
Duchesne Academy — 3-11111
10202 MEMORIAL DR 77024 — 468-8211
Deborah Cate, prin.
Hebrew Academy — 2-11111
5435 S BRAESWOOD BLVD 77096 — 723-7170
Esther Friedman, prin.
Houston Baptist University — 4-UC
7502 FONDREN RD 77074 — 800-969-3210
Houston Community College — 7-CC
PO BOX 7849 77270 — 868-0763
Houston Graduate School of Theology — 1-UC
6910 FANNIN ST STE 207 77030 — 791-9505
Houston Learning Academy — 2-00111
7000 REGENCY SQUARE BLVD 77036 — 789-9197
Spyros Catechis, prin.
Houston Training School — 2-CS
709 SHOTWELL ST 77020
Incarnate Word Academy — 2-00011
609 CRAWFORD ST 77002 — 227-3637
Sr. Brigid Cummins, prin.
International Career School — 2-CS
7647 BELLFORT ST 77061 — 649-0067
ITT Technical Institute — 2-CC
15621 BLUE ASH DR STE 160 77090 — 873-0512
ITT Technical Institute — 3-CC
9421 W SAM HOUSTON PKY S 77099 — 270-1634
Kinkaid S — 4-11111
201 KINKAID SCHOOL DR 77024 — 782-1640
Timothy McIntire, prin.
Lutheran HS North — 2-00011
1130 W 34TH ST 77018 — 880-3131
Bruce Schaller, prin.
Lutheran HS South — 2-00111
7703 S LOOP E 77012 — 645-4178
Wayne Kramer, prin.
M&M Word Processing Institute — 2-CS
5050 WESTHEIMER RD STE 300 77056 — 961-0500
Memorial Hall S — 2-11111
3721 DACOMA ST 77092 — 688-5566
Carl Bradley, prin.
Memorial Hospital System — HSP
7600 BEECHNUT ST 77074 — 776-5100
Methodist Hospital — HSP
6565 FANNIN ST 77030 — 790-3366
Microcomputer Technology Institute — 4-CC
7277 REGENCY SQUARE BLVD 77036 — 974-7181
Mt. Carmel HS — 2-00011
6700 MOUNT CARMEL ST 77087 — 649-2745
Anthony Durso, prin.
NEC-Bryman Campus — 4-CC
9724 BEECHNUT ST STE 300 77036 — 776-3656
NEC-Bryman Campus — 3-CC
16416 NORTHCHASE DR STE 300 77060 — 447-6656

North Harris County College — 7-CC
2700 W W THORNE BLVD 77073 — 443-5400
Northland Christian S — 2-11111
4363 SYLVANFIELD DR 77014 — 440-1060
Robert Kraner, prin.
Northwest Academy — 3-11111
4211 WATONGA BLVD 77092 — 688-0391
Jane Johndrow, prin.
Ocean Corporation, The — 2-CS
10840 ROCKLEY RD 77099 — 530-0202
Polytechnic Institute — 2-CS
4625 NORTH FWY STE 109 77022 — 694-6027
Prairie View A&M University — 5-UC
6436 FANNIN ST STE 916 77030
Rice Aviation — 2-CS
205 BRISBANE ST 77061 — 644-7777
Rice Aviation — 2-CS
7811 N SHEPHERD DR STE 100 77088 — 820-9470
Rice Aviation Main Office — 4-CS
8880 TELEPHONE RD 77061 — 644-6616
Rice University — 5-UC
PO BOX 1892 77251 — 800-527-6957
R/S Institute — 1-CS
7122 LAWNDALE ST 77023 — 923-6968
St. Agnes Academy — 3-00011
9000 BELLAIRE BLVD 77036 — 771-8392
Sr. Jane Meyer, prin.
St. John's S — 4-11111
2401 CLAREMONT ST 77019 — 850-0222
Dwight Raulston, prin.
St. Luke's Episcopal Hospital — HSP
6720 BERTNER ST 77030 — 791-2070
St. Peter the Apostle MS — 2-01100
6220 LA SALETTE ST 77021 — 747-9484
Lucius Guillory, prin.
St. Pius X HS — 3-00011
811 W DONOVAN ST 77091 — 692-3581
Sr. Donna Pollard, prin.
St. Thomas HS — 3-00011
4500 MEMORIAL DR 77007 — 864-6348
Fr. Gaelens, prin.
Sanchez S, 6001 GULF FWY 77023 — 2-00011
Patricia Flores, prin. — 926-1112
School of Automotive Machinists — 2-CS
1911 ANTOINE DR 77055 — 683-3817
Second Baptist S — 4-11111
6410 WOODWAY DR 77057 — 468-8339
Jake Walters, prin.
Seton Catholic JHS — 2-00100
801 ROSELANE ST 77037 — 447-2132
Jane Fucheck, prin.
South Texas College of Law — 3-UC
1303 SAN JACINTO ST 77002 — 659-8040
Strake Jesuit College Prep — 3-00011
8900 BELLAIRE BLVD 77036 — 774-7651
Richard Nevle, prin.
Sweetwater Christian S — 3-11111
8600 SWEETWATER LN 77037 — 447-0391
Jack Hightower, prin.
Texas Dental Technology School — 2-CS
2414 BROADWAY ST 77012 — 645-1612
Texas School of Business — 3-CS
711 AIR TEX DR 77073 — 876-2888
Texas School of Business — 3-CS
10250 BISSONNET ST STE 100 77036 — 771-7177
Texas Southern University — 6-UC
3100 CLEBURNE ST 77004 — 527-7070
Universal Technical Institute — 4-CC
721 LOCKHAVEN DR 77073 — 443-6262
University of Houston — 8-UC
4800 CALHOUN RD 77204 — 749-2321
University of Houston-Clear Lake — 4-UC
2700 BAY AREA BLVD 77058 — 283-2500
University of Houston-Downtown — 6-UC
1 MAIN ST 77002 — 221-8533
University of St. Thomas — 4-UC
3812 MONTROSE BLVD 77006 — 522-7911
University of Texas Anderson Cancer Ctr. — HSP
1515 HOLCOMBE BLVD 77030 — 792-6000
University of Texas Health Science Ctr. — 5-UC
PO BOX 20036 77225 — 792-7444
University of Texas-Houston — 2-UC
1100 HOLCOMBE BLVD 77030 — 792-7873
Weiner Jewish S — 2-00100
12583 S GESSNER DR 77071 — 981-0993
Nancy Epstein, prin.
Westbury Christian S — 3-11111
10420 HILLCROFT ST 77096 — 551-8100
Harold Wade, prin.

Howe, AC 903, PC 4, Grayson
Howe ISD, PO BOX 187 75459 — 3-11111
Edward King, supt. — 532-5518
HS, PO BOX 576 75459 — 2-00011
Deborah Tidwell, prin. — 532-5222
MS, PO BOX 367 75459 — 2-01100
Tom Skipworth, prin. — 532-6013

Hubbard, AC 817, PC 4, Hill
Hubbard ISD, PO BOX 218 76648 — 3-11111
Les Farmer, supt. — 576-2066
HS, PO BOX 218 76648 — 2-00011
Ken Hutchison, prin. — 576-2549
MS, PO BOX 218 76648 — 2-00100
Sam Sexton, prin. — 576-2758

Huffman, AC 713, PC 4, Harris
Huffman ISD — 4-11111
24403 E LAKE HOUSTON PKY 77336 — 324-1871
Norman Hall, supt.

Hargrave HS 3-00011
3407 HUFFMAN EASTGATE RD 77336 324-1845
Glenn Lemke, prin.
MS 2-00100
24403 E LAKE HOUSTON PKY 77336 324-1871
Richard Crosby, prin.

Hughes Springs, AC 903, PC 4, Cass
Hughes Springs ISD 3-11111
PO BOX 398 75656 639-2501
Leland Cockrill, supt.
HS, PO BOX 399 75656 2-00011
Michael Price, prin. 639-2891
JHS, PO BOX 1389 75656 2-00100
Bob Stewart, prin. 639-2671

Humble, AC 713, PC 7, Harris
Aldine ISD
Supt. — See Houston
Teague MS, 21700 RAYFORD RD 77338 4-00100
Sue Wooten, prin. 443-0730

Humble ISD, PO BOX 2000 77347 7-11111
Michael Say, supt. 540-5000
HS, 1700 WILSON RD 77338 5-00011
David Bishop, prin. 540-5400
Atascocita MS 4-00100
18810 W LAKE HOUSTON PKY 77346 540-5690
Ron Westerfeld, prin.
MS, 11207 WILL CLAYTON PKY 77346 4-00100
Karon Rilling, prin. 540-5600
Other Schools – See Kingwood

Huntington, AC 409, PC 4, Angelina
Huntington ISD, PO BOX 328 75949 4-11111
Klaus Driessen, supt. 876-4287
HS, PO BOX 328 75949 2-00011
Michael Nesbit, prin. 876-4150
JHS, PO BOX 328 75949 2-00100
Butch Felkner, prin. 876-4722

Huntsville, AC 409, PC 8, Walker
Huntsville ISD, 441 FM 2821 RD E 77340 6-11111
Ernest Dixon, supt. 295-3421
HS, 441 FM 2821 RD E 77340 4-00011
Phyllis Froelich, prin. 293-2626
JHS, 441 FM 2821 RD E 77340 3-00100
Karen Henderson, prin. 293-2717
Mance Park JHS 3-00100
441 FM 2821 RD E 77340 293-2755
Lucy Larrison, prin.

Sam Houston State University 7-UC
SAM HOUSTON UNIVERSITY 77341 294-1056
Sebring Career School 2-CS
2212 AVENUE I 77340

Hurst, AC 817, PC 8, Tarrant
Hurst-Euless-Bedford ISD
Supt. — See Bedford
Bell SHS, 1601 BROWN TRL 76054 4-00001
E. Don Brown, prin. 282-2551
JHS, 200 W REDBUD DR 76053 3-00110
Steve Griffin, prin. 285-3220

American Trades Institute 2-CS
235 NE LOOP 820 STE 110 76053 284-1141
Tarrant County Junior College 4-CC
828 W HARWOOD RD 76054

Hutchins, AC 214, PC 5, Dallas
Wilmer-Hutchins ISD
Supt. — See Dallas
Wilmer-Hutchins HS 3-00011
2620 LANGDON RD 75141 255-6143
Clyde Stokes, prin.

Hutto, AC 512, PC 3, Williamson
Hutto ISD, PO BOX 430 78634 3-11111
Ernest Laurence, supt. 846-3134
JSHS, PO BOX 430 78634 2-00111
Bobby West, prin. 846-4800

Idalou, AC 806, PC 4, Lubbock
Idalou ISD, PO BOX 1338 79329 3-11111
Stephen Davidson, supt. 892-2552
HS, PO BOX 1558 79329 2-00011
Jeri Bush, prin. 892-2123
JHS, PO BOX 1338 79329 2-00100
Richard Belt, prin. 892-2133

Imperial, AC 915, PC 3, Pecos
Buena Vista ISD, PO BOX 370 79743 2-11111
Joe Boyd, supt. 536-2336
Buena Vista S, PO BOX 370 79743 1-11111
John Coats, prin. 536-2263

Ingleside, AC 512, PC 6, San Patricio
Ingleside ISD, PO BOX HH 78362 4-11111
G. Mircovich, supt. 776-7631
HS, PO BOX HH 78362 2-00011
David Lyons, prin. 776-2712
Taylor JHS, PO BOX HH 78362 2-00100
Gene Schreiber, prin. 776-2232

Ingram, AC 210, PC 4, Kerr
Ingram ISD, 700 HIGHWAY 39 78025 4-11111
Mary Ward, supt. 367-5517
Ingram-Tom Moore JSHS 2-00111
700 HIGHWAY 39 78025 367-4111
Edward Hall, prin.

Iola, AC 409, PC 2, Grimes
Iola ISD, PO BOX 159 77861 2-11111
Morris Ogden, supt. 394-2361
JSHS, PO BOX 159 77861 2-00111
Larry White, prin. 394-2361

Iowa Park, AC 817, PC 6, Wichita
Iowa Park Consolidated ISD 4-11111
PO BOX 898 76367 592-4193
Glen Mitchell, supt.
HS, 1513 US HIGHWAY 287 E 76367 3-00011
Richard Davis, prin. 592-2144
JHS, 412 E CASH ST 76367 2-00100
Randall Lovelady, prin. 592-2196

Ira, AC 915, PC 2, Scurry
Ira ISD, PO BOX 240 79527 2-11111
Richard Howard, supt. 573-2629
S, PO BOX 240 79527 2-11111
Thelma Matlock, prin. 573-2628

Iraan, AC 915, PC 4, Pecos
Iraan-Sheffield ISD 3-11111
PO BOX 486 79744 639-2512
Bob McCall, supt.
HS, PO BOX 486 79744 2-00011
Bob King, prin. 639-2722
JHS, PO BOX 486 79744 2-00100
Don Malone, prin. 639-2867

Iredell, AC 817, PC 2, Bosque
Iredell ISD, PO BOX 39 76649 2-11111
M. McClure, supt. 364-2411
S, PO BOX 39 76649 2-11111
Bob Andrews, prin. 364-2437

Irving, AC 214, PC 9, Dallas
Irving ISD, PO BOX 152637 75015 7-11111
Jack Singley, supt. 259-4575
HS, 900 N O CONNOR RD 75061 4-00011
William Althoff, prin. 254-1525
MacArthur HS 4-00011
3700 N MACARTHUR BLVD 75062 255-2171
Herman Ladewig, prin.
Nimitz HS, 100 W OAKDALE RD 75060 4-00011
William Morgan, prin. 259-3621
Austin JHS 3-00100
825 E UNION BOWER RD 75061 438-7880
Kenneth Tillman, prin.
Bowie JHS, 600 E 6TH ST 75060 3-00100
James Puryear, prin. 579-7022
Crockett JHS, 2431 HANCOCK ST 75061 3-00100
Victor Rucker, prin. 790-2505
Houston JHS 3-00100
3033 COUNTRY CLUB DR W 75038 258-1224
Linda Ivins, prin.
Lamar JHS, 219 CRANDALL RD 75060 3-00100
William McAlister, prin. 986-9155
Travis JHS, 1600 FINLEY RD 75062 3-00100
Jim Simmons, prin. 255-7161

Cistercian Prep HS 2-01111
1 CISTERCIAN RD 75039 438-4956
Fr. Marton, prin.
DeVry Institute of Technology 4-UC
4801 REGENT BLVD 75063 800-243-3879
Highlands S 2-11111
1451 E NORTHGATE DR 75062 554-1980
David Dean, prin.
North Lake College 5-CC
5001 N MACARTHUR BLVD 75038 659-5225
University of Dallas 5-UC
1845 E NORTHGATE DR 75062 800-628-6999

Italy, AC 214, PC 4, Ellis
Italy ISD, PO BOX 909 76651 3-11111
Elton Freeman, supt. 483-7411
JSHS, PO BOX 909 76651 2-00111
Don Rinehart, prin. 483-7411

Itasca, AC 817, PC 4, Hill
Itasca ISD, 123 N COLLEGE ST 76055 3-11111
Randall Smith, supt. 687-2057
HS, 123 N COLLEGE ST 76055 2-00011
Philo Waters, prin. 687-2651
JHS, 123 N COLLEGE ST 76055 1-00100
William Daniel, prin. 687-2400

Ivanhoe, AC 903, PC 2, Fannin
Sam Rayburn ISD 2-11111
RR 1 BOX 127 75447 664-2255
Jim Smith, supt.
Rayburn JSHS, RR 1 BOX 127 75447 2-00111
R. Morris, prin. 664-2165

Jacksboro, AC 817, PC 5, Jack
Jacksboro ISD 3-11111
812 W BELKNAP ST 76458 567-5544
Ray Crass, supt.
HS, 812 W BELKNAP ST 76458 2-00011
Delmar Day, prin. 567-5732
Lowrance MS, 117 N 4TH ST 76458 2-00100
Larry Johnson, prin. 567-2613

Jacksonville, AC 903, PC 7, Cherokee
Jacksonville ISD, PO BOX 631 75766 5-11111
Walter Harris, supt. 586-6511
HS, 1602 MASON DR 75766 4-00011
David Simmons, prin. 586-3661
MS, PO BOX 631 75766 4-00100
Gary Mooring, prin. 586-3686

Baptist Missionary Theological Seminary 1-UC
1530 E PINE ST 75766 586-2501
Jacksonville College 2-CC
105 B J ALBRITTON DR 75766 586-2518
Lon Morris College 2-CC
822 COLLEGE AVE 75766 800-594-2201

Jarrell, AC 512, PC 3, Williamson
Jarrell ISD, PO BOX 429 76537 2-11111
Larry Hausenfluke, supt. 746-2124
JSHS, PO BOX 429 76537 2-00111
Curtis Locklear, prin. 746-2124

Jasper, AC 409, PC 6, Jasper
Jasper ISD, 128 PARK LN 75951 5-11111
Arthur Kees, supt. 384-2401
HS, SPRINGHILL ROAD 75951 3-00011
Travis Summerlin, prin. 384-3242
MS, 128 PARK LN 75951 3-00100
Billy Burt, prin. 384-3585

Jayton, AC 806, PC 3, Kent
Jayton-Girard ISD, PO BOX 168 79528 2-11111
Gary Harrell, supt. 237-2991
JSHS, PO BOX 168 79528 1-00111
John Richey, prin. 237-2991

Jefferson, AC 903, PC 4, Marion
Jefferson ISD, 510 S LINE ST 75657 4-11111
Carol Harrell, supt. 665-2461
HS, PO BOX 645 75657 2-00011
Ronald Bowman, prin. 665-3916
MS, 411 E HARRISON ST 75657 3-01100
Robert Clark, prin. 665-2451

Jewett, AC 903, PC 3, Leon
Leon ISD, PO BOX 157 75846 3-11111
E. McAdams, supt. 626-4532
Leon HS, PO BOX 157 75846 2-00011
Jay Winn, prin. 626-4444
Leon JHS, PO BOX 157 75846 1-00100
Jay Winn, prin. 626-4937

Joaquin, AC 409, PC 3, Shelby
Joaquin ISD, PO BOX 338 75954 3-11111
John Rinehart, supt. 269-3128
JSHS, PO BOX 338 75954 2-00111
Charlie Thomas, prin. 269-3127

Johnson City, AC 210, PC 3, Blanco
Johnson City ISD, PO BOX 498 78636 3-11111
John Lands, supt. 868-7410
JSHS, PO BOX 498 78636 2-00111
(—), prin. 868-4025

Jonesboro, AC 817, PC 2, Coryell
Jonesboro ISD, PO BOX 125 76538 2-11111
Dale Smiley, supt. 463-2111
S, PO BOX 125 76538 2-11111
Tom Rhea, prin. 463-2111

Joshua, AC 817, PC 5, Johnson
Joshua ISD, PO BOX 40 76058 5-11111
Glenn Acker, supt. 558-3703
HS, 909 S BROADWAY ST 76058 3-00011
Kenneth Leverett, prin. 558-4703
MS, 520 STADIUM DR 76058 3-00100
R. Loflin, prin. 558-4503

Jourdanton, AC 210, PC 5, Atascosa
Jourdanton ISD 4-11111
200 ZANDERSON AVE 78026 769-3548
Milam Jones, supt.
HS, 200 ZANDERSON AVE 78026 2-00011
Elizabeth Crabb, prin. 769-2350
JHS, 200 ZANDERSON AVE 78026 2-00100
Robert Rutkowski, prin. 769-2234

Junction, AC 915, PC 5, Kimble
Junction ISD, 1700 COLLEGE ST 76849 3-11111
Earl Luce, supt. 446-3510
HS, 1700 COLLEGE ST 76849 2-00011
Jack Moss, prin. 446-3326
MS, 1700 COLLEGE ST 76849 2-00100
Archie Elmore, prin. 446-2464

Justin, AC 817, PC 4, Denton
Northwest ISD, RR 2 BOX 39A 76247 5-11111
William Wolston, supt. 648-2611
Northwest HS, RR 2 BOX 42 76247 3-00011
Ron Andres, prin. 648-2211
Northwest MS, RR 2 BOX 40 76247 3-00100
Sharon Price, prin. 648-3201

Karnack, AC 903, PC 3, Harrison
Karnack ISD, PO BOX 259 75661 2-11111
John Ferguson, supt. 679-3117
JSHS, PO BOX 259 75661 2-00111
Luther Cockerham, prin. 679-3113

Karnes City, AC 210, PC 5, Karnes
Karnes City ISD, PO BOX 38 78118 4-11111
William Gary, supt. 780-2321
HS, 400 E HIGHWAY 123 78118 2-00011
Earl Luce, prin. 780-2437
JHS, 410 E HIGHWAY 123 78118 2-00100
Elaine Richardson, prin. 780-2417

Katy, AC 713, PC 6, Harris
Cypress-Fairbanks ISD
Supt. — See Houston
Thornton JHS 4-00100
19802 KIETH HARROW BLVD 77449 856-1500
James Wells, prin.

Katy ISD, PO BOX 159 77492 7-11111
Hugh Hayes, supt. 391-2184
HS, 6331 HIGHWAY BLVD 77494 4-00011
Bill Haskett, prin. 391-8138

Taylor HS
20700 KINGSLAND BLVD 77450   4-00011
James McDonald, prin.   492-7000
Opportunity Awareness Ctr   Vo Tech
1732 KATYLAND DR 77493   391-6858
Peter Dempsey, prin.
JHS, 6501 HIGHWAY BLVD 77494   3-00100
Rosemary Gambino, prin.   391-9731
McDonald JHS   4-00100
3635 LAKES OF BRDGEWATER DR 77449
Danny Bryan, prin.   578-9410
Memorial Parkway JHS   4-00100
21203 HIGHLAND KNOLLS DR 77450   492-3421
Malcolm Smith, prin.
West Memorial JHS   3-00100
22311 PROVINCIAL BLVD 77450   392-7096
James Tays, prin.
Other Schools – See Houston

Kaufman, AC 214, PC 6, Kaufman
Kaufman ISD   5-11111
1000 S HOUSTON ST 75142   932-2622
Wayne Pierce, supt.
HS, 1000 S HOUSTON ST 75142   3-00011
Ron Eubanks, prin.   932-2811
Norman JHS   2-01110
1000 S HOUSTON ST 75142   932-2410
Ed Crouch, prin.

Trinity Valley Community College   2-CC
800 W HIGHWAY 243 75142   932-4309

Keene, AC 817, PC 5, Johnson
Keene ISD, PO BOX 656 76059   3-11111
Wanda Smith, supt.   556-9082
HS, PO BOX 656 76059   2-00011
Stan Rhone, prin.   641-4843
JHS, PO BOX 656 76059   1-00100
Keith Scharnhorst, prin.   641-2931

Chisholm Trail Academy   2-00011
PO BOX 717 76059   641-6626
Mervin Kesler, prin.
Southwestern Adventist College   3-UC
PO BOX 567 76059   800-433-2240

Keller, AC 817, PC 7, Tarrant
Keller ISD, 328 LORINE ST 76248   6-11111
(—), supt.   431-1555
HS, 101 INDIAN TRL 76248   4-00011
Sharon Mayes, prin.   431-1555
MS, 301 LORINE ST 76248   3-00100
Randy Baker, prin.   431-1555
Other Schools – See Fort Worth

Kemp, AC 903, PC 4, Kaufman
Kemp ISD, 202 W 17TH ST 75143   4-11111
William Harlan, supt.   498-4121
HS, RR 9 BOX 14 75143   2-00011
David McKee, prin.   498-7271
MS, RR 9 BOX 14 75143   2-00100
Letcher Tindall, prin.   498-2861

Kendleton, AC 409, PC 2, Fort Bend

Bay Ridge Christian College   1-UC
PO BOX 726 77451   532-3982

Kenedy, AC 210, PC 5, Karnes
Kenedy ISD, 401 FM 719 78119   4-11111
William Chapman, supt.   583-3651
HS, 401 FM 719 78119   2-00011
Larry Kiesling, prin.   583-3494
JHS, 501 FM 719 78119   2-00100
George Dumont, prin.   583-3454

Kennard, AC 409, PC 2, Houston
Kennard ISD, PO BOX 38 75847   2-11111
Gene Glover, supt.   655-2161
JSHS, PO BOX 38 75847   2-00111
Joe Roach, prin.   655-2121

Kennedale, AC 817, PC 5, Tarrant
Kennedale ISD, PO BOX 467 76060   4-11111
G. Cockerham, supt.   478-1166
HS, PO BOX 1208 76060   2-00011
Rickie Larkin, prin.   478-1143
JHS, PO BOX 489 76060   2-00100
Edward Farmer, prin.   478-6171

Kerens, AC 903, PC 4, Navarro
Kerens ISD, PO BOX 310 75144   3-11111
Fred McFarland, supt.   396-2924
S, PO BOX 310 75144   3-11111
William Foster, prin.   396-2931

Kermit, AC 915, PC 6, Winkler
Kermit ISD, 601 S POPLAR ST 79745   4-11111
Charles Helmer, supt.   586-3381
HS, 601 S POPLAR ST 79745   2-00011
Gillespie Baker, prin.   586-6487
JHS, 601 S POPLAR ST 79745   2-00100
Lee Lentz, prin.   586-6502

Kerrville, AC 210, PC 7, Kerr
Kerrville ISD, 1009 BARNETT ST 78028   5-11111
Allen Brown, supt.   257-2201
Tivy HS, 1607 SIDNEY BAKER ST 78028   4-00011
Bill Reed, prin.   257-2211
Peterson JHS, 605 TIVY ST 78028   3-00100
G. Miears, prin.   257-2204

Schreiner College   3-UC
2100 MEMORIAL BLVD 78028   800-343-4919

Kilgore, AC 903, PC 7, Gregg
Kilgore ISD, 711 N LONGVIEW ST 75662   5-11111
Jerry Roberts, supt.   984-2073
HS, 711 N LONGVIEW ST 75662   3-00011
Jerry Roberts, prin.   984-5591
Laird MS, 711 N LONGVIEW ST 75662   3-00100
Zane Vaughan, prin.   984-5072

Kilgore College   5-CC
1100 BROADWAY BLVD 75662   983-8209

Killeen, AC 817, PC 8, Bell
Killeen ISD, PO BOX 967 76540   7-11111
Charles Patterson, supt.   520-1309
Ellison HS, 909 E ELMS RD 76542   4-00011
Marvin Rainwater, prin.   520-1815
HS, 500 N 38TH ST 76543   4-00011
Corbett Lawler, prin.   680-2303
Killeen Area Vo HS   Vo Tech
500 N 38TH ST 76543 – (—), prin.   680-2200
Fairway MS, 701 WHITLOW DR 76541   3-00100
Joe Maines, prin.   520-1646
Manor MS   3-00100
1700 S W S YOUNG DR 76543   680-2141
Sandra Brown, prin.
Nolan MS, 505 E JASPER DR 76541   3-00100
Kathleen Moore, prin.   520-1600
Rancier MS, 3301 HILLIARD AVE 76543   3-00100
A. Powell, prin.   680-2454
Other Schools – See Fort Hood, Harker Heights

Central Texas College   6-CC
PO BOX 1800 76540   526-1104
University of Central Texas   2-UC
PO BOX 1416 76540   526-8262

Kingsville, AC 512, PC 7, Kleberg
Kingsville ISD, PO BOX 871 78364   6-11111
Raul Rosales, supt.   592-3387
King HS, PO BOX 871 78364   4-00011
Rodolfo Calderon, prin.   592-6401
Gillett MS, PO BOX 871 78364   3-00100
Oscar Acosta, prin.   592-3309
Memorial MS, PO BOX 871 78364   3-00100
Manuel Cano, prin.   592-5771

Presbyterian Pan-American S   1-00011
PO BOX 1578 78364   592-4307
Everett McAulay, prin.
Texas A & I University   6-UC
CAMPUS BOX 101 78363   595-3907

Kingwood, AC 713, PC 8, Harris
Humble ISD
Supt. – See Humble
HS, 2701 KINGWOOD DR 77339   5-00011
Andrew Wells, prin.   540-5300
Creekwood MS   3-00100
3603 LAKE HOUSTON PKY 77339   540-5280
Charlotte Bilderback, prin.
MS, 3000 WOODLAND HILLS DR 77339   4-00100
Richard Barrett, prin.   540-5270
Riverwood MS   3-00100
2910 HIGH VALLEY DR 77345   540-5750
Paul Roser, prin.

Kirbyville, AC 409, PC 4, Jasper
Kirbyville ISD, 206 E MAIN ST 75956   4-11111
Merlin Tilley, supt.   423-2284
HS, 109 E PINE ST 75956   2-00011
Bill Godwin, prin.   423-4668
JHS, 2200 S MARGARET AVE 75956   2-00100
Robert Corley, prin.   423-2761

Klein, AC 713, PC 7, Harris
Klein ISD   8-11111
7200 SPRING CYPRESS RD 77379   376-4180
D. Collins, supt.
HS   5-00011
16715 STUEBNER AIRLINE RD 77379   320-4400
James Laminack, prin.
Doerre IS   4-00100
18218 THEISS MAIL ROUTE RD 77379   320-4130
Larry Whitehead, prin.
Kleb IS, 7425 LOUETTA RD 77379   3-00100
Lawrence Fricke, prin.   320-4310
Strack IS   4-00100
18027S KUYKENDAHL RD 77379   320-4000
Gary Jones, prin.
Other Schools – See Houston, Spring

Knippa, AC 210, PC 2, Uvalde
Knippa ISD, PO BOX 99 78870   2-11111
Dan Bielfeldt, supt.   934-2176
S, PO BOX 99 78870   2-11111
Dan Bielfeldt, prin.   934-2177

Knox City, AC 817, PC 4, Knox
Knox City-O'Brien ISD   2-11111
PO BOX 638 79529   658-3521
Charles Reed, supt.
HS, PO BOX 638 79529   2-00011
Will Steger, prin.   658-3565
O'Brien MS, PO BOX 638 79529   2-01100
Joel Haragan, prin.   658-3731

Kopperl, AC 817, PC 2, Bosque
Kopperl ISD, PO BOX 67 76652   2-11111
Carl Foster, supt.   889-3506
S, PO BOX 67 76652   2-11111
Michael Cunningham, prin.   889-3506

Kountze, AC 409, PC 4, Hardin
Kountze ISD, PO BOX 460 77625   4-11111
Ann Parker, supt.   246-3352
HS, PO BOX 460 77625   2-00011
Fred Williams, prin.   246-3474
JHS, PO BOX 460 77625   2-00100
John Ferguson, prin.   246-3551

Kress, AC 806, PC 3, Swisher
Kress ISD, PO BOX 970 79052   2-11111
Frank Muir, supt.   684-2652
JSHS, PO BOX 970 79052   2-00111
Mike Brown, prin.   684-2651

Krum, AC 817, PC 4, Denton
Krum ISD, PO BOX 158 76249   3-11111
James Bible, supt.   482-3794
HS, PO BOX 158 76249   2-00011
Gale Marshall, prin.   482-3204
MS, PO BOX 158 76249   2-00100
Mike Pierson, prin.   482-6162

Kyle, AC 512, PC 4, Hays
Hays Consolidated ISD   5-11111
215100 N IH 35 78640   268-2141
Joddie Witte, supt.
Hays HS, 215100 N IH 35 78640   4-00011
Bob Presley, prin.   268-2911
Barton JHS, 215100 IH 35 78640   2-00100
Joseph Murphy, prin.   268-1472

Ladonia, AC 903, PC 3, Fannin
Fannindel ISD, 601 W MAIN ST 75449   2-11111
Alfred Conley, supt.   367-7251
Fannindel HS, 601 W MAIN ST 75449   2-00111
Larry Braley, prin.   367-7251

Lago Vista, AC 512, PC 4, Travis
Lago Vista ISD, PO BOX 4929 78645   2-11111
Virginia Collier, supt.   267-8300
JSHS, PO BOX 4929 78645   2-00111
Michael Riggs, prin.   267-8315

La Feria, AC 210, PC 5, Cameron
La Feria ISD, PO BOX 1157 78559   4-11111
Joseph Wenke, supt.   797-2612
HS, 500 N CANAL ST 78559   3-00011
Richard Renaud, prin.   797-1353
Vail MS, 500 S MAIN ST 78559   3-00100
Carlos Verduzco, prin.   797-1512

La Grange, AC 409, PC 5, Fayette
La Grange ISD, PO BOX 100 78945   4-11111
Fred Weaver, supt.   968-6433
HS, 187 S JACKSON ST 78945   2-00011
William Wagner, prin.   968-8378
MS 78945   3-01100
L. Calley, prin.   968-8376

La Joya, AC 512, PC 5, Hidalgo
La Joya ISD, PO BOX J 78560   6-11111
Jerry Doyle, supt.   585-9781
HS, PO BOX J 78560   5-00011
Leonel Barrera, prin.   585-9710
MS, PO BOX J 78560   3-00100
Maria Leo, prin.   580-5241
Schunior JHS, PO BOX J 78560   3-00100
Juan Salinas, prin.   580-5230

Lake Dallas, AC 817, PC 5, Denton
Lake Dallas ISD, PO BOX 548 75065   4-11111
Thomas Davenport, supt.   497-4039
HS, PO BOX 548 75065   2-00011
Ralph Funk, prin.   497-4032
MS, PO BOX 548 75065   2-00100
Rodney Southard, prin.   497-4037

Lake Jackson, AC 409, PC 7, Brazoria
Brazosport ISD
Supt. — See Freeport
IS, 500 CIRCLE WAY ST 77566   4-00100
Melvin Blair, prin.   297-3021

Brazosport College   4-CC
500 COLLEGE DR 77566   265-6131

Lakeview, AC 806, PC 2, Hall
Lakeview ISD, PO BOX 70 79239   1-11111
R. Meadows, supt.   867-2871
S, PO BOX 70 79239   1-11111
Rollen Meadows, prin.   867-2871

Lake Worth, AC 817, PC 5, Tarrant
Lake Worth ISD   4-11111
6800 TELEPHONE RD 76135   237-1491
Dale Pitts, supt.
HS, 4210 BOAT CLUB RD 76135   2-00011
Tom Prisoc, prin.   237-3387
Hodgkins S, 6800 TELEPHONE RD 76135   2-11111
Lisa Avery, prin.   237-2081
Howry MS, 6800 TELEPHONE RD 76135   2-00100
Dewayne Kennemore, prin.   237-3625

La Marque, AC 409, PC 7, Galveston
La Marque ISD, PO BOX 7 77568   6-11111
Paul Arnold, supt.   938-4251
HS, 300 VAUTHIER ST 77568   4-00011
Caryl Robinson, prin.   938-4261
JHS, 1711 MAGNOLIA DR 77568   4-00100
Tommye Boyd, prin.   938-4286

Lamesa, AC 806, PC 7, Dawson
Klondike ISD, RR 1 BOX 276A 79331   2-11111
Mike Cope, supt.   462-7334
Klondike JSHS, RR 1 BOX 276A 79331   2-00111
Kenneth Brown, prin.   462-7332

Lamesa ISD, PO BOX 261 79331 5-11111
  Neal Chastain, supt. 872-5461
  HS, 600 N 14TH ST 79331 3-00011
    Randy Moczygemba, prin. 872-8385
  MS, BRYAN 79331 3-00100
    John Thomas, prin. 872-8301

Lampasas, AC 512, PC 6, Lampasas
  Lampasas ISD, 207 W 8TH ST 76550 4-11111
    Dick Parker, supt. 556-6224
  HS, 902 S BROAD ST 76550 3-00011
    Robert Parks, prin. 556-3614
  MS, 207 E AVENUE A 76550 3-00100
    Rex Daniels, prin. 556-3101

Lancaster, AC 214, PC 7, Dallas
  Lancaster ISD, PO BOX 400 75146 5-11111
    Jerry Toon, supt. 227-4141
  Lancaster HS 4-00011
    822 W PLEASANT RUN RD 75146 227-2418
    Robert Payne, prin.
  JHS, 1109 W MAIN ST 75146 3-00100
    James Berry, prin. 227-4804

Cedar Valley College 4-CC
  3030 N DALLAS AVE 75134 372-8200

Laneville, AC 903, PC 2, Rusk
  Laneville ISD, PO BOX 127 75667 2-11111
    Ken Manning, supt. 863-5353
  S, PO BOX 127 75667 2-11111
    Dexter Lovett, prin. 863-5354

La Porte, AC 713, PC 8, Harris
  La Porte ISD 6-11111
    301 E FAIRMONT PKY 77571 842-2550
    Richard Hays, supt.
  HS, 301 E FAIRMONT PKY 77571 4-00011
    Jerry Dennis, prin. 842-2120
  JHS, 301 E FAIRMONT PKY 77571 3-00100
    Britton Phillips, prin. 842-2700
  Lomax JHS 3-00100
    301 E FAIRMONT PKY 77571 842-2900
    Pamela Newman, prin.

La Pryor, AC 210, PC 4, Zavala
  La Pryor ISD, PO BOX 519 78872 3-11111
    Rudolph Lopez, supt. 365-4427
  JSHS, PO BOX 519 78872 2-00111
    Ed Ramirez, prin. 365-4467

Laredo, AC 210, PC 9, Webb
  Laredo ISD, 1702 HOUSTON ST 78040 7-11111
    V. Trevino, supt. 727-4401
  Cigarroa HS 4-00011
    2600 ZACATECAS ST 78043 722-4693
    Pedro Lara, prin.
  Martin HS 4-00011
    2002 SAN BERNARDO AVE 78040 723-5572
    R. Flores, prin.
  Nixon HS, 2000 E PLUM ST 78043 5-00011
    Viola Moore, prin. 722-9911
  Cigarroa MS 4-00100
    2600 PALO BLANCO ST 78043 722-8175
    Romeo Rodriguez, prin.
  Christen MS 4-00100
    2001 SANTA MARIA AVE 78040 723-2012
    Cecilia Moreno, prin.
  Lamar MS, 2502 GALVESTON ST 78043 4-00100
    Alfonso Ornelas, prin. 723-5501
  Memorial MS 3-00100
    2002 MARCELLA AVE 78040 722-9901
    Samuel Moreno, prin.

United ISD 7-11111
  201 LINDENWOOD DR 78041 722-3938
  David Barbosa, supt.
United HS 4-00011
  8800 MCPHERSON AVE 78041 726-4700
  Jose Trevino, prin.
United South HS 4-00011
  4001 LOS PRESIDENTES AVE 78043 721-5600
  Eduardo Perales, prin.
United IS-8th Grade 3-00100
  700 E DEL MAR BLVD 78041 723-0052
  Raul Trevino, prin.
United South JHS 3-00100
  3707 LOS PRESIDENTES AVE 78043 721-5650
  Fernando Sanchez, prin.

Laredo Junior College 6-CC
  1 W END WASHINGTON ST 78040 721-5109
St. Augustine JSHS 2-00111
  1300 GALVESTON ST 78040 724-8131
  Sr. Antoinette Billeaud, prin.
South Texas Vocational-Technical Inst. 1-CS
  605 CALLE DE NORTE 78041
Texas A & M International University 3-UC
  1 W END WASHINGTON ST 78040 722-8001

Larue, AC 903, PC 2, Henderson
  La Poynor ISD, RR 2 BOX 108 75770 2-11111
    Douglas Steger, supt. 876-4057
  La Poynor JSHS, RR 2 BOX 108 75770 2-00111
    Rudy Waters, prin. 876-2373

Latexo, AC 409, PC 2, Houston
  Latexo ISD, PO BOX 975 75849 2-11111
    Clifford Price, supt. 544-5664
  JSHS, PO BOX 975 75849 2-00111
    James Applewhite, prin. 544-5638

La Vernia, AC 210, PC 3, Wilson
  La Vernia ISD, PO BOX 309 78121 4-11111
    Jay Martin, supt. 779-2181
  HS, PO BOX 309 78121 2-00011
    Ronald Haug, prin. 779-5611
  JHS, PO BOX 309 78121 2-00100
    Paul Kalkwarf, prin. 779-3102

La Villa, AC 210, PC 4, Hidalgo
  La Villa ISD, PO BOX 9 78562 3-11111
    Eduardo Gonzalez, supt. 262-4755
  HS, PO BOX 9 78562 2-00011
    Ruben Escamilla, prin. 262-4715
  MS, PO BOX 9 78562 2-00100
    Hector Elizondo, prin. 262-4760

Lazbuddie, AC 806, PC 2, Parmer
  Lazbuddie ISD, PO BOX A 79053 2-11111
    James Warren, supt. 965-2156
  S, PO BOX A 79053 2-11111
    R Copp, prin. 965-2152

League City, AC 713, PC 8, Galveston
  Clear Creek ISD, PO BOX 799 77574 7-11111
    Ronald McLeod, supt. 332-2828
  Clear Creek HS, 2305 E MAIN ST 77573 4-00011
    Ralph Parr, prin. 338-5600
  Creekside IS, 4320 W MAIN ST 77573 3-00100
    Douglas Reed, prin. 332-8494
  IS, 2451 E MAIN ST 77573 4-00100
    Joe Wiseman, prin. 338-7000
  Other Schools – See Friendswood, Houston,
    Seabrook, Webster

Bay Area Christian S 2-11111
  4800 W MAIN ST 77573 332-4814
  Freddie Cullins, prin.
Devereux Hospital and Institute of Texas 2-HND
  1150 DEVEREUX DR 77573 332-0011

Leakey, AC 210, PC 2, Real
  Leakey ISD, PO BOX 808 78873 2-11111
    Ken Wimberley, supt. 232-6122
  S, PO BOX 808 78873 2-11111
    Larry Lee, prin. 232-5595

Leander, AC 512, PC 5, Williamson
  Leander ISD, PO BOX 218 78646 6-11111
    Tom Glenn, supt. 259-1113
  HS, 3301 S BAGDAD RD 78641 4-00011
    Charles Rouse, prin. 259-1198
  JHS, 501 S HIGHWAY 183 78641 3-00100
    Ronald Lafevers, prin. 259-0041

Lefors, AC 806, PC 3, Gray
  Lefors ISD, PO BOX 390 79054 2-11111
    A. Roper, supt. 835-2533
  S, PO BOX 390 79054 2-11111
    A. Roper, prin. 835-2533

Leggett, AC 409, PC 2, Polk
  Leggett ISD, PO BOX 68 77350 2-11111
    Bennett Geeslin, supt. 398-2804
  JSHS, PO BOX 68 77350 1-00111
    Walter McAlpin, prin. 398-2412

Lenorah, AC 915, PC 2, Martin
  Grady ISD, HC 72 BOX 4 79749 2-11111
    Thomas Walker, supt. 459-2444
  Grady S, HC 72 BOX 4 79749 2-11111
    Richard Gibson, prin. 459-2445

Leonard, AC 903, PC 4, Fannin
  Leonard ISD, PO BOX G 75452 3-11111
    James Tucker, supt. 587-2318
  HS, PO BOX G 75452 2-00011
    Raymond Marshall, prin. 587-3556
  JHS, PO BOX G 75452 2-00100
    Gary McDonald, prin. 587-2315

Levelland, AC 806, PC 7, Hockley
  Levelland ISD, 704 11TH ST 79336 5-11111
    Kyle Wargo, supt. 894-9628
  SHS, 704 11TH ST 79336 3-00001
    Kelly Baggett, prin. 894-8515
  JHS, 704 11TH ST 79336 3-00110
    Guy Miles, prin. 894-7086

South Plains College 5-CC
  1401 COLLEGE AVE 79336 894-9611

Lewisville, AC 214, PC 8, Denton
  Lewisville ISD, PO BOX 217 75067 7-11111
    Clayton Downing, supt. 539-1551
  HS, 1098 W MAIN ST 75067 4-00011
    Charles Killough, prin. 221-3535
  Jackson Career Ctr Vo Tech
    1597 S EDMONDS LN 75067 221-0909
    Joanne Smith, prin.
  Delay MS, 136 W PURNELL RD 75057 3-00100
    David Fields, prin. 436-6525
  Hedrick MS, 1526 BELLAIRE LN 75067 3-00100
    Marsha Medcalf, prin. 436-4536
  Milliken MS, 2103 SAVAGE LN 75057 3-00100
    Barbara Stagner, prin. 436-7581
  Other Schools – See Flower Mound, The Colony

Lexington, AC 409, PC 3, Lee
  Lexington ISD, PO BOX 248 78947 3-11111
    Donald Garrett, supt. 773-2254
  Lexington HS, PO BOX 248 78947 2-00011
    (—), prin. 773-2255
  MS, PO BOX 248 78947 2-00100
    Archie Elmore, prin. 773-2255

Liberty, AC 409, PC 6, Liberty
  Liberty ISD, 1600 GRAND AVE 77575 4-11111
    Joe Crane, supt. 336-7215
  HS, 2615 JEFFERSON DR 77575 3-00011
    Don Lorenz, prin. 336-6483
  MS, 1629 GRAND AVE 77575 3-00100
    William Thornton, prin. 336-3582

Liberty Hill, AC 512, PC 3, Williamson
  Liberty Hill ISD, PO BOX 68 78642 3-11111
    Paul Curtis, supt. 515-6088
  HS, PO BOX 68 78642 2-00011
    Dalton West, prin. 515-6357
  MS, PO BOX 68 78642 2-01100
    Richard Hastings, prin. 515-5121

Lindale, AC 903, PC 4, Smith
  Lindale ISD, PO BOX 370 75771 4-11111
    George Williford, supt. 882-6157
  HS, PO BOX 370 75771 3-00011
    Jim Bernard, prin. 882-6138
  JHS, PO BOX 370 75771 3-00100
    Jane Holbrook, prin. 882-4655

Linden, AC 903, PC 4, Cass
  Linden-Kildare Consolidated ISD 4-11111
    PO BOX 840 75563 756-5027
    Michael Jansen, supt.
  Linden-Kildare HS 2-00011
    PO BOX 840 75563 756-7026
    Vance Rucker, prin.
  Linden-Kildare JHS 2-00100
    PO BOX 840 75563 756-5381
    Mark Smith, prin.

Lindsay, AC 817, PC 3, Cooke
  Lindsay ISD, PO BOX 145 76250 2-11111
    Gilbert Hermes, supt. 668-8923
  HS, PO BOX 145 76250 2-00011
    Jim Anderson, prin. 668-8923

Lingleville, AC 817, PC 2, Erath
  Lingleville ISD, PO BOX 134 76461 2-11111
    Dannah Proctor, supt. 968-2596
  S, PO BOX 134 76461 2-11111
    Jerry Brock, prin. 968-4598

Lipan, AC 817, PC 2, Hood
  Lipan ISD, PO BOX 188 76462 2-11111
    Nelson Eichman, supt. 646-2266
  S, PO BOX 188 76462 2-11111
    Melissa Scott, prin. 646-2266

Little Elm, AC 214, PC 4, Denton
  Little Elm ISD, PO BOX 9 75068 3-11111
    Dennis Brent, supt. 292-1847
  HS, PO BOX 9 75068 2-00011
    Bob Scallan, prin. 292-1840
  MS, PO BOX 9 75068 2-00100
    Linda Blase, prin. 292-3200

Littlefield, AC 806, PC 6, Lamb
  Littlefield ISD 4-11111
    1500 E DELANO AVE 79339 385-3844
    Jerry Blakely, supt.
  HS, 1500 E DELANO AVE 79339 2-00011
    Charles Driskell, prin. 385-5683
  JHS, 1500 E DELANO AVE 79339 2-00100
    C. Rogers, prin. 385-3922

Little River, AC 817, PC 4, Bell
  Academy ISD, 704 E MAIN ST 76554 3-11111
    J. Holland, supt. 982-4304
  Academy HS, PO BOX 548 76554 2-00011
    Larry Simpson, prin. 982-4201
  Academy JHS 2-01100
    205 N HIGHWAY 95 76554 982-4620
    Joann Hopper, prin.

Livingston, AC 409, PC 6, Polk
  Big Sandy ISD, RR 3 BOX 422 77351 2-11111
    Vernis Rogers, supt. 563-2371
  Big Sandy S, RR 3 BOX 422 77351 2-11111
    Robert Fountain, prin. 563-4679
  Livingston ISD, PO BOX 1297 77351 5-11111
    Glenn Pearson, supt. 327-4351
  HS, 1500 E CHURCH ST 77351 3-00011
    Dell Brown, prin. 327-3731
  JHS, 819 W CHURCH ST 77351 3-00100
    Bobbie Fagan, prin. 327-4294

Llano, AC 915, PC 5, Llano
  Llano ISD, 1402 OATMAN ST 78643 4-11111
    Dorman Moore, supt. 247-4747
  HS, 400 E HIGHWAY 71 78643 2-00011
    Dennis Hill, prin. 247-4187
  JHS, 1400 OATMAN ST 78643 2-00100
    Tom Henderson, prin. 247-4659

Lockhart, AC 512, PC 6, Caldwell
  Lockhart ISD, PO BOX 120 78644 5-11111
    Tony Jones, supt. 398-2371
  HS, 906 CENTER ST 78644 3-00011
    (—), prin. 398-2335
  JHS, 419 BOIS DARC ST 78644 3-00100
    Herbert Schulze, prin. 398-5278

Lockney, AC 806, PC 4, Floyd
  Lockney ISD, PO BOX 428 79241 3-11111
    Raymond Lusk, supt. 652-2115
  HS, PO BOX 1058 79241 2-00011
    James Poole, prin. 652-3325
  JHS, PO BOX 550 79241 2-00100
    Terry Ellison, prin. 652-2236

Lohn, AC 915, PC 2, McCulloch
Lohn ISD, PO BOX 277 76852 — 2-11111 — 344-5749
  Marlene Shelton, supt.
S, PO BOX 277 76852 — 2-11111 — 344-5755
  John Freeman, prin.

Lolita, AC 512, PC 3, Jackson
Industrial ISD
  Supt. — See Vanderbilt
Industrial JHS, PO BOX 208 77971 — 2-00100 — 874-4343
  Dennis O'Connell, prin.

Lometa, AC 512, PC 3, Lampasas
Lometa ISD, PO BOX 250 76853 — 2-11111 — 752-3384
  Richard Stockman, supt.
S, PO BOX 250 76853 — 2-11111 — 752-3384
  Charles Fields, prin.

Lone Oak, AC 903, PC 3, Hunt
Lone Oak ISD, PO BOX 38 75453 — 3-11111 — 662-5427
  Bob Fannin, supt.
HS, PO BOX 38 75453 — 2-00011 — 662-5227
  Jesse Marshall, prin.
JHS, PO BOX 38 75453 — 2-00100 — 662-5121
  John Stahmer, prin.

Longview, AC 903, PC 8, Gregg
Longview ISD, PO BOX 3268 75606 — 6-11111 — 753-0206
  R. McMichael, supt.
HS, PO BOX 3268 75606 — 4-00011 — 663-1301
  Robert McMinn, prin.
Forest Park MS, PO BOX 3268 75606 — 3-00100 — 758-9971
  Mary Schmitz, prin.
Foster MS, PO BOX 3268 75606 — 3-00100 — 753-1692
  Doris Waits, prin.
Judson MS, PO BOX 3268 75606 — 3-00100 — 663-0206
  Gary Whitwell, prin.

Pine Tree ISD, PO BOX 5878 75608 — 5-11111 — 295-5000
  Marc Williamson, supt.
Pine Tree SHS, PO BOX 5878 75608 — 3-00001 — 295-5031
  Raymond Schroeder, prin.
Pine Tree JHS, PO BOX 5878 75608 — 3-00110 — 295-5081
  Royce Shipp, prin.

Spring Hill ISD — 4-11111 — 759-4404
  3101 SPRING HILL RD 75605
  D. Michael Crossland, supt.
Spring Hill HS — 2-00011 — 759-4404
  3101 SPRING HILL RD 75605
  Gene King, prin.
Spring Hill JHS — 2-00100 — 759-4404
  3101 SPRING HILL RD 75605
  Bob Moore, prin.

Bish Mathis Institute — 2-CS — 758-7300
  2521 JUDSON RD 75605
LeTourneau College — 3-UC — 800-759-8811
  PO BOX 7001 75607
Trinity S of Texas, 906 PADON ST 75601 — 2-11111 — 753-0612
  Julia Wall, prin.

Loop, AC 806, PC 3, Gaines
Loop ISD, PO BOX 917 79342 — 2-11111 — 487-6411
  Richard Roberts, supt.
S, PO BOX 917 79342 — 2-11111 — 487-6411
  Richard Roberts, prin.

Loraine, AC 915, PC 3, Mitchell
Loraine ISD, PO BOX 457 79532 — 2-11111 — 737-2225
  Gary Buckingham, supt.
S, PO BOX 457 79532 — 2-11111 — 737-2225
  Kenneth Kendall, prin.

Lorena, AC 817, PC 4, McLennan
Lorena ISD, PO BOX 97 76655 — 4-11111 — 857-3239
  K. Riley, supt.
HS, PO BOX 97 76655 — 2-00011 — 857-4604
  Woodrow Brewton, prin.
MS, PO BOX 97 76655 — 2-00100 — 857-4621
  Herman Roessler, prin.

Lorenzo, AC 806, PC 4, Crosby
Lorenzo ISD, PO BOX 520 79343 — 3-11111 — 634-5591
  Jim Norris, supt.
JSHS, PO BOX 520 79343 — 2-00111 — 634-5592
  Van Cypert, prin.

Los Fresnos, AC 210, PC 4, Cameron
Los Fresnos Consolidated ISD — 5-11111 — 233-4407
  PO BOX 309 78566
  Martin Pena, supt.
HS, PO BOX 309 78566 — 4-00011 — 233-3300
  Rey Farias, prin.
JHS, PO BOX 309 78566 — 3-00100 — 233-4427
  Faustino Rivas, prin.

Louise, AC 409, PC 3, Wharton
Louise ISD, PO BOX 97 77455 — 2-11111 — 648-2982
  Lloyd Nelson, supt.
JSHS, PO BOX 97 77455 — 2-00111 — 648-2202
  Rodney Hutto, prin.

Lovelady, AC 409, PC 3, Houston
Lovelady ISD, PO BOX 250 75851 — 2-11111 — 636-7616
  Paul Dobbs, supt.
HS, PO BOX 250 75851 — 2-00011 — 636-7636
  Narvel Parker, prin.

Lubbock, AC 806, PC 9, Lubbock
Lubbock-Cooper ISD — 4-11111 — 863-2282
  RR 6 BOX 400 79423
  Michael Caplinger, supt.
Cooper HS, RR 6 BOX 400 79423 — 2-00011 — 863-3160
  Pat Henderson, prin.

Cooper JHS, RR 6 BOX 400 79423 — 2-00100 — 863-2282
  Oliver Thompson, prin.

Lubbock ISD, 1628 19TH ST 79401 — 8-11111 — 766-1000
  Mike Moses, supt.
Coronado SHS — 4-00001 — 766-0600
  3301 VICKSBURG AVE 79410
  Jackie Booe, prin.
Dunbar SHS, 2010 E 26TH ST 79404 — 3-00001 — 766-1300
  Virgil Johnson, prin.
Estacado SHS, 1504 E ITASCA ST 79403 — 3-00001 — 766-1400
  Ken Wallace, prin.
SHS, 2004 19TH ST 79401 — 4-00001 — 766-1444
  Rose Mediano, prin.
Monterey SHS, 3211 47TH ST 79413 — 4-00001 — 766-0700
  Richard Bennett, prin.
Alderson JHS, 219 WALNUT AVE 79403 — 2-00110 — 766-1500
  Stanley Chatman, prin.
Atkins JHS, 5401 AVENUE U 79412 — 3-00110 — 766-1522
  Eric McKnight, prin.
Cavazos JHS — 3-00110 — 766-6600
  210 N UNIVERSITY AVE 79415
  Enrique Galindo, prin.
Evans JHS, 4211 58TH ST 79413 — 3-00110 — 766-0722
  G. Nell, prin.
Hutchinson JHS — 3-00110 — 766-0755
  3102 CANTON AVE 79410
  Neal Logan, prin.
Irons JHS, 5214 79TH ST 79424 — 4-00110 — 766-2044
  Gaylord Carter, prin.
Mackenzie JHS, 5402 12TH ST 79416 — 2-00110 — 766-0777
  Beth Fischenich, prin.
Slaton JHS, 1602 32ND ST 79405 — 3-00110 — 766-1555
  Larry Christian, prin.
Wilson JHS, 4402 31ST ST 79410 — 3-00110 — 766-0799
  Ronald Dingle, prin.

Roosevelt ISD, RR 1 BOX 402 79401 — 4-11111 — 842-3282
  D. Taylor, supt.
Roosevelt JSHS, RR 1 BOX 402 79401 — 3-00111 — 842-3283
  James Rose, prin.

American Commercial College — 3-CS — 747-4339
  2007 34TH ST 79411
International Business College — 3-CS — 797-1933
  4630 50TH ST STE 100 79414
Lubbock Christian S — 2-11111 — 796-8700
  2604 DOVER AVE 79407
  Russell Beene, prin.
Lubbock Christian University — 3-UC — 792-3221
  5601 19TH ST 79407
Methodist Hospital — HSP — 797-0955
  3615 19TH ST 79410
Texas Tech University — 7-UC — 742-1480
  1 TEXAS TECH UNIVERSITY 79409

Lueders, AC 915, PC 2, Jones
Lueders-Avoca ISD — 2-11111 — 228-4211
  PO BOX 68 79533
  Tom Alvis, supt.
Other Schools – See Avoca

Lufkin, AC 409, PC 8, Angelina
Hudson ISD, RR 5 BOX 3420 75904 — 4-11111 — 875-3351
  Joe Smith, supt.
Hudson HS, RR 5 BOX 3420 75904 — 2-00011 — 875-3351
  Judy Black, prin.
Hudson JHS, RR 5 BOX 3420 75904 — 2-00100 — 875-3351
  Michael Patrick, prin.

Lufkin ISD, PO BOX 1407 75902 — 6-11111 — 634-6696
  Frances Sicola, supt.
SHS, 900 E DENMAN AVE 75901 — 4-00001 — 632-7721
  James Bowie, prin.
Lufkin East JHS — 3-00110 — 633-7120
  309 S MEDFORD DR 75901
  Robert Toney, prin.
Lufkin West JHS — 3-00110 — 632-6679
  602 S RAGUET ST 75904
  Helen Strohschein, prin.

Angelina College — 4-CC — 639-1301
  PO BOX 1768 75902

Luling, AC 210, PC 5, Caldwell
Luling ISD, 216 E BOWIE ST 78648 — 4-11111 — 875-3191
  George Bujnoch, supt.
HS, 218 E TRAVIS ST 78648 — 2-00011 — 875-2458
  Robert Kosub, prin.
JHS, 214 E BOWIE ST 78648 — 2-00100 — 875-2121
  Gilbert Gerdes, prin.

Lumberton, AC 409, PC 6, Hardin
Lumberton ISD, PO BOX 8123 77711 — 5-11111 — 755-4943
  Fred Morgan, supt.
HS, PO BOX 8123 77711 — 3-00011 — 755-4974
  William Higgins, prin.
MS, PO BOX 8123 77711 — 3-00100 — 755-4911
  Lonnie Roberts, prin.

Lyford, AC 210, PC 4, Willacy
Lyford ISD, PO BOX 220 78569 — 4-11111 — 347-3521
  Jose Flores, supt.
HS, PO BOX 220 78569 — 2-00011 — 347-3521
  Michael Hammond, prin.
JHS, PO BOX 220 78569 — 2-00100 — 347-3521
  Julio Saldana, prin.

Lytle, AC 210, PC 4, Atascosa
Lytle ISD, PO BOX 745 78052 — 4-11111 — 772-4701
  James Bullion, supt.
HS, PO BOX 190 78052 — 2-00011 — 772-4741
  Robert Woosley, prin.

JHS, PO BOX 190 78052 — 2-00100 — 772-4741
  Henry Siller, prin.

Mabank, AC 903, PC 4, Kaufman
Mabank ISD, 124 E MARKET ST 75147 — 5-11111 — 887-9311
  Larry Hawkins, supt.
HS, 124 E MARKET ST 75147 — 3-00011 — 887-9333
  (—), prin.
JHS, 124 E MARKET ST 75147 — 2-00100 — 887-9360
  Stanley Rice, prin.

Mc Allen, AC 210, PC 8, Hidalgo
McAllen ISD, 2000 N 23RD ST 78501 — 7-11111 — 686-0515
  Jose Lopez, supt.
HS, 2021 LA VISTA AVE 78501 — 5-00011 — 632-3100
  David Guel, prin.
McAllen Memorial HS — 4-00011 — 632-5201
  101 E HACKBERRY AVE 78501
  Nicolas Gonzalez, prin.
Rowe HS, 2101 N WARE RD 78501 — 4-00011 — 632-5100
  William Parry, prin.
Brown JHS, 2700 S WARE RD 78503 — 4-00100 — 632-8700
  George Padilla, prin.
De Leon JHS, 4201 N 29TH ST 78504 — 3-00100 — 632-8800
  Delia Longoria, prin.
Lamar JHS, 1009 N 10TH ST 78501 — 3-00100 — 682-1581
  Priscila Martinez, prin.
Lincoln JHS, 1601 N 27TH ST 78501 — 3-00100 — 971-4200
  Rosalinda Martinez, prin.
Morris JHS, 1400 TRENTON RD 78504 — 3-00100 — 618-7300
  Jose Perez, prin.
Travis JHS, 600 E HOUSTON AVE 78501 — 3-00100 — 971-4242
  Mary Correa, prin.

San Antonio College Medical Dental Asst. — 2-CS — 630-1499
  3900 N 23RD ST 78501
South Texas Vocational-Technical Inst. — 2-CS — 631-1107
  2901 N 23RD ST # B 78501

Mc Camey, AC 915, PC 4, Upton
McCamey ISD, PO BOX 1069 79752 — 3-11111 — 652-3666
  Joe Neill, supt.
HS, PO BOX 1069 79752 — 2-00011 — 652-8603
  Jerry Stinson, prin.
MS, PO BOX 1069 79752 — 2-01100 — 652-3391
  Jim Witcher, prin.

Mc Gregor, AC 817, PC 5, McLennan
McGregor ISD, PO BOX 356 76657 — 4-11111 — 840-2828
  J. Keltner, supt.
HS, PO BOX 356 76657 — 2-00011 — 840-2853
  Sherman Fruge, prin.
Isbill JHS, PO BOX 356 76657 — 2-01100 — 840-3251
  William Zacharias, prin.

Mc Kinney, AC 214, PC 7, Collin
McKinney ISD, 1 DUVALL ST 75069 — 6-11111 — 569-6400
  Jack Cockrill, supt.
HS, 1400 WILSON CREEK PKY 75069 — 4-00011 — 569-6100
  Carol Hunter, prin.
Faubion MS — 3-00100 — 569-6168
  2000 DOE ROLLINS ST 75069
  Jim Randolph, prin.
Slaughter MS, 2706 WOLFORD ST 75070 — 3-00100 — 569-6157
  Beverly Rodgers, prin.

Collin County Community College — 6-CC — 548-6742
  2200 W UNIVERSITY DR 75070

Mclean, AC 806, PC 3, Gray
Mclean ISD, PO BOX 90 79057 — 2-11111 — 779-2301
  Lauren Lamb, supt.
S, PO BOX 69 79057 — 2-11111 — 779-2491
  John Griffin, prin.

Mc Leod, AC 903, PC 2, Cass
Mc Leod ISD, PO BOX 350 75565 — 2-11111 — 796-7181
  Gary Watson, supt.
S, PO BOX 350 75565 — 2-11111 — 796-7181
  Gary McCasland, prin.

Madisonville, AC 409, PC 5, Madison
Madisonville Consolidated ISD — 4-11111 — 348-2797
  PO BOX 879 77864
  C. Walker, supt.
HS, PO BOX 879 77864 — 2-00011 — 348-2721
  William Parten, prin.
JHS, PO BOX 819 77864 — 2-00100 — 348-3587
  (—), prin.

Magnolia, AC 713, PC 3, Montgomery
Magnolia ISD, PO BOX 88 77355 — 5-11111 — 356-3570
  Derrith Welch, supt.
HS, PO BOX 428 77355 — 3-00011 — 356-3572
  Patricia Yarbrough, prin.
JHS, PO BOX 476 77355 — 3-00100 — 356-1327
  Robert Peters, prin.

Malakoff, AC 903, PC 4, Henderson
Cross Roads ISD — 3-11111 — 489-2001
  RR 1 BOX 1265 75148
  D. McKinnerney, supt.
Cross Roads HS — 2-00011 — 489-1275
  RR 1 BOX 1265 75148
  Don Lewis, prin.
Cross Roads JHS — 2-00100 — 489-1275
  RR 1 BOX 1265 75148
  Glenda Wisenbaker, prin.

Malakoff ISD, 107 JACKSON ST 75148 — 4-11111 — 489-1152
  Don Reynolds, supt.
HS, 107 JACKSON ST 75148 — 2-00011 — 489-1527
  Larry Scoggin, prin.

JHS, 107 JACKSON ST 75148   2-00100
John Brown, prin.   489-0264

Manor, AC 512, PC 4, Travis
Manor ISD, PO BOX L 78653   4-11111
Noel Jett, supt.   272-5591
HS, PO BOX 679 78653   2-00100
James Savage, prin.   272-5541
JHS, PO BOX 388 78653   3-00100
Brenda Boardman, prin.   272-5579

Mansfield, AC 817, PC 7, Tarrant
Mansfield ISD, 605 E BROAD ST 76063   6-11111
Larry Blair, supt.   473-5600
HS, 1520 N WALNUT CREEK DR 76063   4-00011
Jerry Kirby, prin.   473-5660
Worley MS   4-00100
500 PLEASANT RIDGE DR 76063   473-5668
Robert White, prin.
Other Schools – See Arlington

Manvel, AC 713, PC 5, Brazoria
Alvin ISD
Supt. — See Alvin
JHS, PO BOX 158 77578   2-00100
Bill Knapick, prin.   489-8257

Maple, AC 806, PC 2, Bailey
Three Way ISD, PO BOX 60 79344   2-11111
Don Parker, supt.   927-5531
Three Way S, PO BOX 60 79344   2-11111
William Hood, prin.   927-5315

Marathon, AC 915, PC 3, Brewster
Marathon ISD, PO BOX 416 79842   2-11111
Travis Slaton, supt.   386-4431
S, PO BOX 416 79842   1-11111
Travis Slaton, prin.   386-4431

Marble Falls, AC 210, PC 5, Burnet
Marble Falls ISD   4-11111
2001 BROADWAY ST 78654   693-4357
Phil Barnett, supt.
HS, 2101 MUSTANG DR 78654   3-00011
Jeffery Ford, prin.   693-4375
MS, 1511 PONY DR 78654   3-00100
Andrew Shell, prin.   693-4439

Marfa, AC 915, PC 4, Presidio
Marfa ISD, PO BOX T 79843   3-11111
Judy Ledbetter, supt.   729-4252
HS, 300 N HILL 79843   2-00011
Sam Robinson, prin.   729-4861

Marion, AC 210, PC 3, Guadalupe
Marion ISD, PO BOX 127 78124   3-11111
Thomas Stockstill, supt.   420-2311
HS, PO BOX 127 78124   2-00011
Dennis Dreyer, prin.   420-2613
MS, PO BOX 127 78124   2-00100
Albert Abel, prin.   420-2366

Marlin, AC 817, PC 6, Falls
Marlin ISD, 130 COLEMAN ST 76661   4-11111
Raymond Morris, supt.   883-3585
HS, 130 COLEMAN ST 76661   2-00011
Glynn Lindsey, prin.   883-2394
MS, 130 COLEMAN ST 76661   2-01100
Murray Wise, prin.   883-9241

Marshall, AC 903, PC 7, Harrison
Marshall ISD, PO BOX 879 75671   6-11111
Patsy Smith-Gasperson, supt.   935-3914
HS, 1900 MAVERICK DR 75670   4-00011
Robert Lane, prin.   938-3311
JHS, 201 S COLLEGE ST 75670   4-00100
Ora Johnson, prin.   935-7402

East Texas Baptist University   3-UC
1200 N GROVE ST 75670   935-7963
Wiley College   3-UC
711 WILEY AVE 75670   938-8341

Mart, AC 817, PC 4, McLennan
Mart ISD, PO BOX 120 76664   3-11111
John Bass, supt.   876-2523
HS, PO BOX 120 76664   2-00011
Mark Stretcher, prin.   876-2574
IS, PO BOX 120 76664   2-01100
Steve Huffman, prin.   876-2762

Martinsville, AC 409, PC 2, Nacogdoches
Martinsville ISD, PO BOX 100 75958   2-11111
L. Worsham, supt.   564-3455
S, PO BOX 100 75958   2-11111
Richard Hawthorne, prin.   564-3455

Mason, AC 915, PC 4, Mason
Mason ISD, PO BOX 410 76856   3-11111
Ted Kerr, supt.   347-5557
HS, PO BOX 410 76856   2-00011
Oscar Graham, prin.   347-5921

Matador, AC 806, PC 3, Motley
Motley County ISD
PO BOX 310 79244   2-11111
George Blanch, supt.   347-2677
Motley S, PO BOX 310 79244   2-11111
Albert Van Hoose, prin.   347-2676

Mathis, AC 512, PC 6, San Patricio
Mathis ISD, PO BOX 1177 78368   4-11111
Jim Weeks, supt.   547-3378
HS, PO BOX 1177 78368   3-00011
Paul Vranish, prin.   547-3322

McCraw JHS, PO BOX 1177 78368   2-00100
Donald Shelton, prin.   547-2381

Maud, AC 903, PC 4, Bowie
Maud ISD, PO BOX 1001 75567   2-11111
Robert Stinnett, supt.   585-2219
S, PO BOX 1001 75567   2-11111
Ronald Stewart, prin.   585-2219

May, AC 817, PC 2, Brown
May ISD, PO BOX 38 76857   2-11111
Donald Rhodes, supt.   259-2091
HS, PO BOX 38 76857   1-00011
Ron Watkins, prin.   259-2131

Maypearl, AC 214, PC 3, Ellis
Maypearl ISD, PO BOX 40 76064   3-11111
Wilburn Roesler, supt.   435-2116
HS, PANTHER LN 76064   2-00011
Jim Fowler, prin.   435-2581
MS, PANTHER LN 76064   2-00100
Lynn Whitaker, prin.   435-2170

Meadow, AC 806, PC 3, Terry
Meadow ISD, RR 1 BOX 1A 79345   2-11111
David Rice, supt.   539-2246
S, RR 1 BOX 1A 79345   2-11111
Joe Ward, prin.   539-2527

Medina, AC 210, PC 2, Bandera
Medina ISD, PO BOX 1470 78055   2-11111
Thomas Morris, supt.   589-2852
S, PO BOX 1470 78055   2-11111
Dale Naumann, prin.   589-2851

Megargel, AC 817, PC 2, Archer
Megargel ISD, PO BOX 39 76370   1-11111
Tom Loftin, supt.   563-2431
JSHS, PO BOX 39 76370   1-00111
C. D. Knobloch, prin.   563-2431

Melissa, AC 214, PC 3, Collin
Melissa ISD, PO BOX 127 75454   2-11100
Don Hankey, supt.   837-2291
MS, PO BOX 127 75454   1-00100
Pamela Parmley, prin.   837-2291

Memphis, AC 806, PC 4, Hall
Memphis ISD, PO BOX 460 79245   3-11111
L. Neal Hindman, supt.   259-2443
HS, 1501 HIGH ST 79245   2-00011
Edgar Bailey, prin.   259-2525
JHS, 1110 N 16TH ST 79245   1-00100
Johnnie Myers, prin.   259-3400

Menard, AC 915, PC 4, Menard
Menard ISD, PO BOX 729 76859   2-11111
Andrew Patton, supt.   396-2404
HS, PO BOX 729 76859   2-00111
Leonard Wilson, prin.   396-2513

Mercedes, AC 210, PC 7, Hidalgo
Mercedes ISD, PO BOX 419 78570   5-11111
Monte Churchill, supt.   565-2655
HS, 1200 FLORIDA ST 78570   4-00011
Salvador Garcia, prin.   565-3111
JHS, 839 S OHIO ST 78570   3-00100
Mauro Vasquez, prin.   565-2681

South Texas ISD   4-00011
100 MED HIGH DR 78570   565-2454
Ron Schraer, supt.
South Texas HS-Health   3-00011
700 MED HIGH DR 78570   565-2454
Daniel Menchaca, prin.
Other Schools – See San Benito

Meridian, AC 817, PC 4, Bosque
Meridian ISD, PO BOX 349 76665   2-11111
Johnnie Hauerland, supt.   435-2081
S, PO BOX 349 76665   2-11111
Brooks Symank, prin.   435-2723

Merit, AC 903, PC 2, Hunt
Bland ISD, PO BOX 216 75458   2-11111
Larry Johnson, supt.   776-2239
Bland JSHS, PO BOX 216 75458   2-00111
Bryan Clark, prin.   776-2161

Merkel, AC 915, PC 4, Taylor
Merkel ISD, PO BOX 430 79536   4-11111
James Logan, supt.   928-5813
HS, PO BOX 430 79536   2-00011
Gaylon Brnovak, prin.   928-5511
MS, PO BOX 430 79536   2-00100
Paul Lippe, prin.   928-5521

Mertzon, AC 915, PC 3, Irion
Irion County ISD, PO BOX 469 76941   2-11111
Arvel Rotan, supt.   835-6111
Irion JSHS, PO BOX 469 76941   2-00111
Jerry Johnson, prin.   835-2881

Mesquite, AC 214, PC 9, Dallas
Mesquite ISD, 405 E DAVIS ST 75149   8-11111
John Horn, supt.   288-6411
HS, 300 E DAVIS ST 75149   4-00011
Howard Hall, prin.   285-8861
North Mesquite HS   4-00011
18240 LYNDON B JOHNSON FWY 75150
Ronnie Pardun, prin.   279-6721
Poteet HS, 3300 POTEET DR 75150   4-00011
Lannie Frasier, prin.   270-8737
West Mesquite HS   4-00011
2500 MEMORIAL BLVD 75149   288-5431
Sidney Hudson, prin.

Agnew MS, 729 WILKINSON DR 75149   3-00100
Bill Porter, prin.   285-6371
Kimbrough MS   3-00100
3900 N GALLOWAY AVE 75150   681-5097
Lena Malone, prin.
McDonald MS   4-00100
2930 N TOWN EAST BLVD 75150   270-6596
Gary Fortenberry, prin.
New MS, 3700 N BELT LINE RD 75182   3-00100
Jim Williams, prin.   557-5585
Vanston MS, 3230 KARLA DR 75150   3-00100
Kevin Woolley, prin.   279-3646
Wilkinson MS   3-00100
2100 CREST PARK DR 75149   285-5222
Glenda Heil, prin.

Eastfield College   7-CC
3737 MOTLEY DR 75150   324-7100

Mexia, AC 817, PC 6, Limestone
Mexia ISD, PO BOX 2000 76667   4-11111
Howard Andrews, supt.   562-2888
HS, PO BOX 2000 76667   3-00011
Larry Devitt, prin.   562-2831
JHS, PO BOX 2000 76667   3-00100
T. Wilkins, prin.   562-2666

Miami, AC 806, PC 3, Roberts
Miami ISD, PO BOX 368 79059   2-11111
Allan Dinsmore, supt.   868-3971
S, PO BOX 368 79059   2-11111
Larry Neighbors, prin.   868-3971

Midland, AC 915, PC 8, Midland
Greenwood ISD, 2700 FM 1379 79706   4-11111
Quentin Burnett, supt.   685-7800
Greenwood JSHS   3-00111
2700 FM 1379 79706   685-7805
Faye Welch, prin.
Midland ISD   7-11111
615 W MISSOURI AVE 79701   689-1000
Joseph Baressi, supt.
Lee HS, 3500 NEELY AVE 79707   4-00001
George Cooper, prin.   689-1600
SHS, 906 W ILLINOIS AVE 79701   4-00001
Jane Carrens, prin.   689-1100
Coleman JSHS   2-00111
500 E NOBLES AVE 79701   689-1591
Helen Lackey, prin.
Alamo JHS, 3800 STOREY AVE 79703   4-00100
David Dennis, prin.   689-1700
Goddard JHS, 2500 HAYNES DR 79705   4-00100
Karen Wentworth, prin.   689-1300
Lee Freshman HS   3-00010
1400 E OAK AVE 79705   689-1250
Dan Green, prin.
Midland Freshman HS   3-00010
100 E GIST AVE 79701   689-1200
Neil Richmond, prin.
San Jacinto JHS, 1400 N N ST 79701   3-00100
Jack Ratcliff, prin.   689-1350

Midland Christian S   2-11111
2001 CULVER DR 79705   694-1661
James Blake, prin.
Midland Co. Hospital District   HSP
2200 W ILLINOIS AVE 79701   685-1533
Midland College   5-CC
3600 N GARFIELD ST 79705   685-4500
Trinity S of Midland   2-11111
3500 W WADLEY AVE 79707   697-3281
William Fleischmann, prin.

Midlothian, AC 214, PC 6, Ellis
Midlothian ISD, 925 S 9TH ST 76065   5-11111
Jim Carpenter, supt.   775-8296
HS, 925 S 9TH ST 76065   3-00011
David Goodman, prin.   775-8226
MS, 925 S 9TH ST 76065   3-00100
Bill Barrett, prin.   775-6145

Milano, AC 512, PC 2, Milam
Milano ISD, PO BOX 145 76556   2-11111
James Hubert, supt.   455-2533
JSHS, PO BOX 145 76556   2-00111
William Spivey, prin.   455-6701

Miles, AC 915, PC 3, Runnels
Miles ISD, PO BOX 308 76861   2-11111
Wesley Hayes, supt.   468-2861
JSHS, PO BOX 308 76861   2-00111
Robert McCarson, prin.   468-2131

Milford, AC 214, PC 3, Ellis
Milford ISD, PO BOX 545 76670   2-11111
Bill Bates, supt.   493-2911
S, PO BOX 545 76670   2-11111
Neal Harrison, prin.   493-2921

Millsap, AC 817, PC 2, Parker
Millsap ISD, 305 PINE ST 76066   3-11111
Robert Simmons, supt.   682-7365
JSHS, 305 PINE ST 76066   2-00111
David Wolf, prin.   682-7365

Mineola, AC 903, PC 5, Wood
Mineola ISD   4-11111
1000 W LOOP 564 75773   569-2448
John Abbott, supt.
HS, 900 W PATTEN ST 75773   2-00011
Edwin Hebron, prin.   569-3000
MS, 1000 W LOOP 564 75773   2-00100
Jerry Cloud, prin.   569-5338

Mineral Wells, AC 817, PC 7, Palo Pinto
Mineral Wells ISD   5-11111
906 SW 5TH AVE 76067   325-6404
Robert Munday, supt.
HS, 3801 RAM BLVD 76067   3-00011
Clarence Holliman, prin.   325-4408
JHS, 1200 SE 14TH AVE 76067   3-00100
Barbara Qualls, prin.   325-0711

Mirando City, AC 512, PC 2, Webb
Mirando City ISD, PO BOX 130 78369   2-11111
Humberto Gonzalez, supt.   586-4667
JSHS, PO BOX 130 78369   1-00111
Zulema Gutierrez, prin.   586-4667

Mission, AC 210, PC 8, Hidalgo
Mission Consolidated ISD   7-11111
1201 BRYCE DR 78572   580-5500
Rafael Cantu, supt.
HS, 1201 BRYCE DR 78572   5-00011
Gustavo Zapata, prin.   580-5700
JHS, 1201 BRYCE DR 78572   3-00100
Fidel Cantu, prin.   580-5680
White JHS, 1201 BRYCE DR 78572   3-00100
Linda Alaniz, prin.   580-5690

Sharyland ISD, 1106 N SHARY RD 78572   5-11111
James McDaniel, supt.   585-6701
Sharyland HS, 1106 N SHARY RD 78572   3-00011
Hector Madrigal, prin.   585-1381
Sharyland/Gray JHS   3-00100
1106 N SHARY RD 78572   585-8329
Alfonso Solis, prin.

Mobeetie, AC 806, PC 2, Wheeler
Fort Elliott CISD
Supt. — See Briscoe
Fort Elliott S, PO BOX 177 79061   1-11111
David Johnson, prin.   375-2454

Monahans, AC 915, PC 6, Ward
Monahans-Wickett-Pyote ISD   5-11111
606 S BETTY ST 79756   943-6711
Jerry Larned, supt.
HS, 808 S BETTY ST 79756   3-00011
Dick McClanahan, prin.   943-2519
Walker JHS, 800 S FAYE ST 79756   2-00100
Elmo Freeman, prin.   943-4622

Mont Belvieu, AC 713, PC 4, Chambers
Barbers Hill ISD, PO BOX 1108 77580   4-11111
Al Dennis, supt.   576-2221
Barbers Hill HS, 9600 EAGLE DR 77580   3-00011
Richard Bethell, prin.   576-2221
Barbers Hill MS, 9600 EAGLE DR 77580   2-00100
Dan Grimes, prin.   576-2221

Montgomery, AC 409, PC 2, Montgomery
Montgomery ISD   4-11111
PO BOX 1475 77356   597-6462
Susan Brooks, supt.
HS, PO BOX 1475 77356   3-00011
Leon Combs, prin.   597-6401
JHS, PO BOX 1475 77356   3-00100
Rick Cowan, prin.   597-6466

Moody, AC 817, PC 4, McLennan
Moody ISD, PO BOX 448 76557   3-11111
Marcus Anderson, supt.   853-2172
HS, PO BOX 448 76557   2-00011
Marvin Agnew, prin.   853-2181
MS, PO BOX 448 76557   2-00100
Clayton Brantley, prin.   853-3622

Moran, AC 915, PC 2, Shackelford
Moran ISD, PO BOX 98 76464   2-11111
H. Hooper, supt.   945-3101
S, PO BOX 98 76464   2-11111
Jack Thomason, prin.   945-3101

Morgan, AC 817, PC 2, Bosque
Morgan ISD, PO BOX 300 76671   2-11111
John Bryant, supt.   635-2311
S, PO BOX 300 76671   2-11111
George Shackelford, prin.   635-2311

Morton, AC 806, PC 5, Cochran
Morton ISD, 500 CHAMPION DR 79346   3-11111
Charles Skeen, supt.   266-5505
HS, 500 CHAMPION DR 79346   2-00011
Thomas Phelps, prin.   266-5524
JHS, 500 CHAMPION DR 79346   2-00100
Richard Houston, prin.   266-8856

Moulton, AC 512, PC 3, Lavaca
Moulton ISD, PO BOX C 77975   2-11111
Edward Pustka, supt.   596-4609
JSHS, PO BOX C 77975   2-00111
Gene Harrison, prin.   596-4691

Mount Enterprise, AC 903, PC 3, Rusk
Mt. Enterprise ISD   2-11111
PO BOX 130 75681   822-3575
Arthur Clemons, supt.
JSHS, PO BOX 130 75681   2-00111
Bob Lee, prin.   822-3721

Mount Pleasant, AC 903, PC 7, Titus
Mount Pleasant ISD   5-11111
PO BOX 1117 75456   572-6686
David Anthony, supt.
HS, PO BOX 1117 75456   4-00011
Dave Dubose, prin.   572-1891
Wallace JHS, DUNN ST 75456   3-00100
Jason Watkins, prin.   572-1873

Northeast Texas Community College   4-CC
PO BOX 1307 75456   572-1911

Mount Vernon, AC 903, PC 4, Franklin
Mt. Vernon ISD, PO BOX 98 75457   4-11111
Richard Harper, supt.   537-2546
HS, PO BOX 1139 75457   2-00011
Bill Travis, prin.   537-2266
JHS, PO BOX 1139 75457   2-00100
Robert Robinson, prin.   537-2266

Muenster, AC 817, PC 4, Cooke
Muenster ISD, PO BOX 608 76252   2-11111
Steven Cooper, supt.   759-2281
JSHS, PO BOX 608 76252   2-00111
Ed Green, prin.   759-2282

Sacred Heart S, PO BOX 588 76252   2-11111
Jack Murdock, prin.   759-4121

Muleshoe, AC 806, PC 5, Bailey
Muleshoe ISD, 514 W AVENUE G 79347   4-11111
William Moore, supt.   272-3389
HS, 514 W AVENUE G 79347   2-00011
Albert Bishop, prin.   272-7571
Watson JHS, 514 W AVENUE G 79347   2-00100
Bob Graves, prin.   272-7521

Mullin, AC 915, PC 2, Mills
Mullin ISD, PO BOX 128 76864   2-11111
Gayland Carson, supt.   985-3374
S, PO BOX 128 76864   2-11111
Linda Buffe, prin.   985-3374

Munday, AC 817, PC 4, Knox
Munday ISD, PO BOX 300 76371   2-11111
Roy Lowrance, supt.   422-4241
JSHS, PO BOX 300 76371   2-00111
Phil Hall, prin.   422-4321

Nacogdoches, AC 409, PC 8, Nacogdoches
Central Heights ISD   2-11111
RR 13 BOX 2390 75961   564-2681
Gene Isabell, supt.
Central Heights S   2-11111
RR 13 BOX 2390 75961   564-0177
Clara Skinner, prin.

Nacogdoches ISD   6-11111
PO BOX 631521 75963   569-5000
James Partin, supt.
HS, PO BOX 631521 75963   4-00011
John Walker, prin.   564-2466
Rusk MS, PO BOX 631521 75963   3-00100
Steve Green, prin.   569-3100

Massey Business College   2-CS
PO BOX 630444 75963   564-3788
Stephen F. Austin State University   7-UC
PO BOX 6078 75962   568-2504

Natalia, AC 512, PC 4, Medina
Natalia ISD, PO BOX 548 78059   3-11111
J. Barta, supt.   663-4416
HS, PO BOX 548 78059   2-00011
(—), prin.   663-4417
JHS, PO BOX 548 78059   2-00100
Amy Schacht, prin.   663-4027

Navasota, AC 409, PC 6, Grimes
Navasota ISD, PO BOX 511 77868   5-11111
Elizabeth Abernethy, supt.   825-4200
HS, PO BOX 511 77868   3-00011
Don Lightfoot, prin.   825-4250
JHS, PO BOX 511 77868   3-01100
William Hood, prin.   825-4225

Nazareth, AC 806, PC 2, Castro
Nazareth ISD, PO BOX 189 79063   2-11111
N. Johnson, supt.   945-2231
S, PO BOX 189 79063   2-11111
D. Wood, prin.   945-2231

Neches, AC 903, PC 2, Anderson
Neches ISD, PO BOX 310 75779   2-11111
Philip Wood, supt.   584-3311
JSHS, PO BOX 310 75779   2-00111
Joe Ellis, prin.   584-3443

Nederland, AC 409, PC 7, Jefferson
Nederland ISD, 220 N 17TH ST 77627   6-11111
Lee Robinson, supt.   724-2391
HS, 220 N 17TH ST 77627   4-00011
Stephen Fleming, prin.   727-2741
Central MS, 220 N 17TH ST 77627   3-01100
Beverly Krohn, prin.   727-5765
Wilson MS, 220 N 17TH ST 77627   3-01100
Gary Tiner, prin.   727-6224

Needville, AC 409, PC 4, Fort Bend
Needville ISD, PO BOX 412 77461   4-11111
Gary Sage, supt.   793-4308
HS, PO BOX 412 77461   3-00011
Albert Freberg, prin.   793-4158
MS, PO BOX 412 77461   3-00100
Charles Roehling, prin.   793-3027

Nevada, AC 214, PC 2, Collin
Community ISD, PO BOX 400 75173   3-11111
David McClendon, supt.   853-2474
Community HS, PO BOX 400 75173   2-00011
John Roderick, prin.   853-2192
Community MS, PO BOX 400 75173   2-01100
Collin Clark, prin.   853-2141

New Boston, AC 903, PC 6, Bowie
New Boston ISD   4-11111
600 N MCCOY BLVD 75570   628-2521
James Westfall, supt.
HS, 115 W COUNTY ST 75570   2-00011
Jerry May, prin.   628-6551
JHS, RR 2 BOX 362 75570   2-00100
John Dempsey, prin.   628-6588

New Braunfels, AC 512, PC 8, Comal
Comal ISD   6-11111
1421 N US HIGHWAY 81 78130   625-8081
Gerald Major, supt.
Canyon HS, 1510 N IH 35 78130   3-00011
Will Krieg, prin.   625-6251
Canyon MS, RR 14 BOX 521P 78130   3-00100
Robert Brockman, prin.   625-7355
Other Schools – See Spring Branch

New Braunfels ISD   6-11111
PO BOX 311688 78131   620-6200
Charles Bradberry, supt.
HS, 2551 LOOP 337 78130   4-00011
John Turman, prin.   625-6271
MS, 656 S GUENTHER AVE 78130   3-00100
Peggy Simpson, prin.   625-7728

New Caney, AC 713, PC 5, Montgomery
New Caney ISD, RR 4 BOX 89 77357   6-11111
Jerry Hall, supt.   354-1166
HS, RR 4 BOX 90 77357   4-00011
Randy Burchfield, prin.   354-3505
Other Schools – See Porter

Newcastle, AC 817, PC 3, Young
Newcastle ISD, PO BOX 129 76372   2-11111
Solomon Kepley, supt.   846-3531
JSHS, PO BOX 129 76372   1-00111
Deborah Queen, prin.   846-3531

New Deal, AC 806, PC 3, Lubbock
New Deal ISD, PO BOX 280 79350   3-11111
Allan Gamblin, supt.   746-5833
HS, PO BOX 250 79350   2-00011
David Willis, prin.   746-5933
MS, PO BOX 308 79350   2-01100
William Montgomery, prin.   746-6633

New Home, AC 806, PC 2, Lynn
New Home ISD, PO BOX 248 79383   2-11111
Tom Templeton, supt.   924-7542
JSHS, PO BOX 248 79383   1-00111
Robert Brown, prin.   924-7543

New London, AC 903, PC 3, Rusk
West Rusk ISD, PO BOX 168 75682   4-11111
Gerald Lancaster, supt.   895-4503
West Rusk HS, PO BOX 168 75682   2-00111
Glenn Barber, prin.   895-4428
West Rusk JHS, PO BOX 168 75682   2-00100
Janis Underwood, prin.   657-3436

New Summerfield, AC 903, PC 3, Cherokee
New Summerfield ISD   2-11111
PO BOX 6 75780   726-3306
Bill Hooper, supt.
S, PO BOX 6 75780   2-11111
Kelly Pickle, prin.   726-3306

Newton, AC 409, PC 4, Newton
Newton ISD, PO BOX 448 75966   4-11111
Gerald Rosebure, supt.   379-3291
HS, PO BOX 448 75966   2-00011
Golda Davis, prin.   379-4731
MS, PO BOX 448 75966   2-00100
(—), prin.   379-8324

New Waverly, AC 409, PC 3, Walker
New Waverly ISD, PO BOX 38 77358   3-11111
Alvin Davis, supt.   344-6751
HS, PO BOX 38 77358   2-00011
Truman Goodwin, prin.   344-6451
Gulf Coast Trades Ctr   Vo Tech
PO BOX 38 77358   344-6677
W. Warner, prin.
MS, PO BOX 38 77358   2-00100
James Youngblood, prin.   344-2246

Gulf Coast Trades Center   2-CS
PO BOX 515 77358

Nixon, AC 210, PC 4, Gonzales
Nixon-Smiley Consolidated ISD   3-11111
PO BOX 400 78140   582-1536
Richard Faulkner, supt.
Nixon-Smiley HS, PO BOX 400 78140   2-00011
William Fennell, prin.   582-1013
Nixon-Smiley MS   2-00100
PO BOX 400 78140   587-6401
Melanie Musgraves, prin.

Nocona, AC 817, PC 5, Montague
Nocona ISD, PO BOX 210 76255   3-11111
David Brewer, supt.   825-3267
HS, PO BOX 210 76255   2-00011
Harold Reynolds, prin.   825-3264
MS, PO BOX 210 76255   2-00100
Ronnal Bell, prin.   825-3121

Prairie Valley ISD   2-11111
RR 3 BOX 550 76255   825-4425
James Braiser, supt.
Prairie Valley JSHS   1-00111
RR 3 BOX 550 76255   825-3695
Terry Dunlap, prin.

Nordheim, AC 512, PC 2, De Witt
Nordheim ISD, PO BOX 8 78141   2-11111
  Vance Frosch, supt.   938-5211
S, PO BOX 8 78141   2-11111
  Michaelroy Stern, prin.   938-5211

Normangee, AC 409, PC 3, Leon
Normangee ISD, PO BOX 219 77871   2-11111
  Roddy McIver, supt.   396-3111
JSHS, PO BOX 219 77871   2-00110
  Danny Denton, prin.   396-6111

North Zulch, AC 409, PC 3, Madison
North Zulch ISD, PO BOX 158 77872   2-11111
  Glenn Connor, supt.   399-5222
HS, PO BOX 158 77872   1-00011
  James Vinson, prin.   399-2821

Novice, AC 915, PC 2, Coleman
Novice ISD, PO BOX 205 79538   2-11111
  Roland Bell, supt.   625-4069
S, PO BOX 205 79538   2-11111
  Tom Norrell, prin.   625-4500

Oakwood, AC 903, PC 3, Leon
Oakwood ISD, 802 HOLLY ST 75855   2-11111
  Ronnie Durham, supt.   545-2666
JSHS, 802 HOLLY ST 75855   2-00110
  Howard Powers, prin.   545-2808

Odem, AC 512, PC 4, San Patricio
Odem-Edroy ISD, PO BOX 727 78370   4-11111
  Douglas Koebernick, supt.   368-2561
HS, PO BOX 1050 78370   2-00011
  Manuel Lunoff, prin.   368-3401
JHS, PO BOX 1407 78370   2-00100
  Alberto Aleman, prin.   368-8661

Odessa, AC 915, PC 8, Ector
Ector County ISD   8-11111
  PO BOX 3912 79760   332-9151
  Gene Buinger, supt.
HS, 1301 DOTSY AVE 79763   4-00011
  Raymond Starnes, prin.   337-6655
Permian HS, 1800 E 42ND ST 79762   4-00011
  Steve Chapman, prin.   366-3652
Ector JSHS, 809 W CLEMENTS ST 79763   4-00111
  Robert Brown, prin.   337-8693
Hood JSHS, 600 E 38TH ST 79762   3-00110
  Gilbert Vasquez, prin.   362-2371
Bonham JHS, 2201 E 21ST ST 79761   4-00110
  Olen Grady, prin.   366-2811
Bowie JHS, 500 W 21ST ST 79761   3-00110
  Paul Hooper, prin.   337-8361
Crockett JHS, 2301 CONOVER AVE 79763   3-00110
  Alma Guerrero, prin.   332-1451
Nimitz JHS, 4900 MAPLE AVE 79762   3-00110
  Robert McCarley, prin.   366-2891

American Commercial College   2-CS
  2115 E 8TH ST 79761   332-0768
Avalon Vocational Technical Institute   4-CS
  4241 TANGLEWOOD LN 79762   367-2622
Odessa College   5-CC
  201 W UNIVERSITY BLVD 79764   335-6575
University of Texas of the Permian Basin   4-UC
  4901 E UNIVERSITY BLVD 79762

Odonnell, AC 806, PC 4, Lynn
Odonnell ISD, PO BOX 487 79351   2-11111
  Homer Read, supt.   428-3241
HS, PO BOX 487 79351   2-00011
  Ira Hopkins, prin.   428-3247
JHS, PO BOX 487 79351   2-00100
  Ira Hopkins, prin.   428-3248

Oglesby, AC 817, PC 2, Coryell
Oglesby ISD, PO BOX 158 76561   2-11111
  James Brown, supt.   456-2271
S, PO BOX 158 76561   2-11111
  Kerry Hansen, prin.   456-2242

Olney, AC 817, PC 5, Young
Olney ISD, PO BOX 548 76374   3-11111
  Charles Thompson, supt.   564-3519
HS, PO BOX 548 76374   2-00011
  Theria Berry, prin.   564-5637
JHS, PO BOX 548 76374   2-00100
  Bill Cranfill, prin.   564-3517

Olton, AC 806, PC 4, Lamb
Olton ISD, PO BOX 388 79064   3-11111
  Monte Vern Lee, supt.   285-2641
HS, PO BOX 667 79064   2-00011
  Mike Wallace, prin.   285-2691
JHS, PO BOX 509 79064   2-00100
  Larry Morgan, prin.   285-2681

Omaha, AC 903, PC 3, Morris
Pewitt ISD, PO BOX 1106 75571   3-11111
  Richard Kitchens, supt.   884-2804
Pewitt HS, PO BOX 1106 75571   2-00011
  Rex Ranes, prin.   884-2293
Pewitt JHS, PO BOX 1106 75571   2-00100
  Tammy Crockett, prin.   884-2505

Onalaska, AC 409, PC 3, Polk
Onalaska ISD, PO BOX 1000 77360   2-11100
  John Leonard, supt.   646-4058
MS, PO BOX 1000 77360   2-00100
  Gladys Ray, prin.   646-5203

Orange, AC 409, PC 7, Orange
Little Cypress-Mauriceville ISD   5-11111
  7293 16TH ST 77632 – H. Hebert, supt.   883-2232

Little Cypress-Mauriceville HS   3-00011
  7293 16TH ST 77632 – Roy Dunn, prin.   886-5821
Little Cypress JHS   3-00100
  RR 8 BOX 1065 77632   883-2317
  Keith Lindsey, prin.
Mauriceville MS   2-01100
  5200 W FM 1130 RD 77632   745-1958
  Robert Finch, prin.

West Orange-Cove Consolidated ISD   5-11111
  PO BOX 1107 77631   882-5500
  L. Neswick, supt.
West Orange-Stark HS   3-00011
  1400 NEWTON ST 77630   882-5570
  Andrew Hayes, prin.
Career Ctr 77631   Vo Tech
  Andrew Hayes, prin.   882-5412
West Orange MS, 500 13TH ST 77630   3-00100
  James Maher, prin.   882-5520

Baptist Hospital   HSP
  PO BOX 37 77631   883-9361
Community Christian S   2-11111
  1911 16TH ST 77630   883-4531
  Catherine Stewart, prin.
Lamar University   3-CC
  410 W FRONT ST 77630   883-7750

Orangefield, AC 409, PC 3, Orange
Orangefield ISD, PO BOX 228 77639   4-11111
  Robert Montagne, supt.   735-5337
HS, PO BOX 228 77639   2-00011
  Charles Donnaud, prin.   735-3851
JHS, PO BOX 228 77639   2-01100
  Raylin Johnston, prin.   735-6737

Orange Grove, AC 512, PC 4, Jim Wells
Orange Grove ISD   4-11111
  PO BOX 534 78372   384-2495
  Joe Brown, supt.
HS, PO BOX 534 78372   2-00011
  Frederick Brand, prin.   384-2330
MS, PO BOX 534 78372   2-00100
  Jesus Maldonado, prin.   384-2323

Orchard, AC 409, PC 2, Fort Bend
Wallis-Orchard ISD
  Supt. — See Wallis
Brazos JHS, PO BOX 69 77464   2-00100
  Jackie Ellis, prin.   478-6411

Ore City, AC 903, PC 3, Upshur
Ore City ISD, PO BOX 100 75683   3-11111
  T. Ferguson, supt.   968-3300
HS, PO BOX 100 75683   2-00011
  Tom Barnett, prin.   968-3300
JHS, PO BOX 100 75683   2-00100
  Carolyn Coleman, prin.   968-3300

Overton, AC 903, PC 4, Rusk
Overton ISD, PO BOX 130 75684   2-11111
  Joel Johnston, supt.   834-6145
JSHS, PO BOX 130 75684   2-00111
  Harold Stanger, prin.   834-6143

Ozona, AC 915, PC 5, Crockett
Crockett Co. Consolidated SD   3-11111
  PO BOX 400 76943   392-5501
  James Payne, supt.
Ozona HS, PO BOX 400 76943   2-00011
  John Curry, prin.   392-5501
JHS, PO BOX 400 76943   2-00100
  Tom Humber, prin.   392-5501

Paducah, AC 806, PC 4, Cottle
Paducah ISD, PO BOX P 79248   2-11111
  John Brinson, supt.   492-3524
HS, 810 GOODWIN 79248   2-00011
  Randall Ryan, prin.   492-2009

Paint Rock, AC 915, PC 2, Concho
Paint Rock ISD, PO BOX 277 76866   2-11111
  Harold Miller, supt.   732-4314
S, PO BOX 277 76866   2-11111
  Charles Van Winkle, prin.   732-4384

Palacios, AC 512, PC 5, Matagorda
Palacios ISD, 1209 12TH ST 77465   4-11111
  Rudy Okruhlik, supt.   972-5491
HS, 100 SHARK DR 77465   2-00011
  Robert Crager, prin.   972-2571
JHS, 200 SHARK DR 77465   2-00100
  Bob McMahan, prin.   972-2417

Palestine, AC 903, PC 7, Anderson
Palestine ISD   5-11111
  1600 S LOOP 256 75801   731-8000
  Robert Caster, supt.
HS, 1600 S LOOP 256 75801   3-00011
  Bill Lawson, prin.   731-8005
MS, 233 BEN MILAM DR 75801   3-00100
  Jerry Mayo, prin.   731-8008

Westwood ISD, PO BOX 260 75802   4-11111
  Marvin Thompson, supt.   729-1776
Westwood HS, 1820 CHISM DR 75801   2-00011
  Jack Cherry, prin.   729-1773
Westwood JHS, 1801 CHISM DR 75801   2-00100
  Dan Bell, prin.   723-0423

Palmer, AC 214, PC 4, Ellis
Palmer ISD, PO BOX 790 75152   3-11111
  B. Earl Richardson, supt.   449-3389
JSHS, PO BOX 790 75152   2-00111
  Michael Reel, prin.   449-3319

Pampa, AC 806, PC 7, Gray
Pampa ISD, 321 W ALBERT ST 79065   5-11111
  Dawson Orr, supt.   669-4700
HS, 111 E HARVESTER AVE 79065   4-00011
  John Coward, prin.   669-4800
MS, 2401 CHARLES ST 79065   3-00100
  Jerome Stewart, prin.   669-4901

Panhandle, AC 806, PC 4, Carson
Panhandle ISD, PO BOX 1030 79068   3-11111
  Ronnie Teichelman, supt.   537-3568
HS, PO BOX 1030 79068   2-00011
  Ronnie Wood, prin.   537-3851
JHS, PO BOX 1030 79068   2-00100
  C. Gill, prin.   537-3541

Paradise, AC 817, PC 2, Wise
Paradise ISD, RR 2 BOX 646 76073   3-11111
  E. Todd, supt.   969-2501
JSHS, RR 2 BOX 646 76073   2-00111
  John Seerey, prin.   969-2821

Paris, AC 903, PC 7, Lamar
Chisum ISD, 3250 S CHURCH ST 75462   3-11111
  Harvey Hohenberger, supt.   737-2830
Chisum JSHS, 3250 S CHURCH ST 75462   2-00111
  Lynn Patterson, prin.   737-2800
Chisum MS, 3250 S CHURCH ST 75462   2-00100
  James Erwin, prin.   737-2806

North Lamar ISD, 3201 LEWIS LN 75462   5-11111
  James Dawson, supt.   737-2000
North Lamar HS, 3201 LEWIS LN 75462   3-00011
  Philip Trice, prin.   737-2011
Bailey MS, 3201 LEWIS LN 75462   3-00100
  C. Bolton, prin.   737-2041

Paris ISD, 1920 CLARKSVILLE ST 75460   5-11111
  Elaine Ballard, supt.   737-7473
HS, 2400 JEFFERSON RD 75460   3-00011
  Robert High, prin.   737-7400
Travis MS, 3270 GRAHAM ST 75460   2-00100
  Sandra Lassiter, prin.   737-7434

Paris Junior College   4-CC
  2400 CLARKSVILLE ST 75460   800-232-5804

Pasadena, AC 713, PC 9, Harris
Deer Park ISD
  Supt. — See Deer Park
Deepwater JHS   3-00100
  501 GLENMORE DR 77503   475-6101
  Jim Davis, prin.

Pasadena ISD, PO BOX 1799 77501   8-11111
  Frederick Schneider, supt.   920-6800
HS, 206 SHAVER ST 77506   4-00011
  Thomas Hancock, prin.   477-1501
Rayburn HS   4-00011
  2121 CHERRYBROOK LN 77502   477-3601
  Barbara Crowson, prin.
Bondy MS, 5101 KEITH AVE 77505   3-00100
  Thomas Baccaro, prin.   487-7548
Challenger IS, 3212 LAFFERTY RD 77504   3-00100
  Maria Moreno, prin.   920-4601
Jackson IS, 100 JACKSON AVE 77506   3-00100
  Graciela Kavulla, prin.   472-1285
Miller IS, 1002 FAIRMONT PKY 77504   4-00100
  James Smith, prin.   944-0770
Park View IS, 3003 DABNEY DR 77502   4-00100
  Merlin Mohr, prin.   944-0734
Queens IS, 1112 QUEENS RD 77502   3-00100
  Robert Tyler, prin.   473-7675
San Jacinto IS   3-00100
  3102 SAN AUGUSTINE AVE 77503   473-8158
  David Post, prin.
Southmore IS   4-00100
  1200 HOUSTON AVE 77502   473-9456
  Cary Partin, prin.
Other Schools – See Houston, South Houston

Faith Christian Academy   2-11111
  3519 BURKE RD 77504   941-4416
  Brett Hurst, prin.
San Jacinto College   7-CC
  4624 FAIRMONT PKY 77504   998-6100
Texas Chiropractic College   2-UC
  5912 SPENCER HWY 77505   487-1170

Pattison, AC 713, PC 2, Waller
Royal ISD, PO BOX 489 77466   4-11111
  James Kemp, supt.   934-2248
Royal HS, PO BOX 469 77466   2-00011
  J. Davis, prin.   934-2215
Other Schools – See Brookshire

Pattonville, AC 903, PC 2, Lamar
Prairiland ISD, RR 1 BOX 200 75468   3-11111
  L. Stout, supt.   652-6476
Prairiland HS, RR 1 BOX 200 75468   2-00011
  Gary Ballard, prin.   652-5681

Pearland, AC 713, PC 7, Brazoria
Pearland ISD, PO BOX 7 77588   6-11111
  James Schleider, supt.   485-3203
HS, 3775 S MAIN ST 77581   4-00011
  Gregory Smith, prin.   997-7445
Pearland East JHS, PO BOX 7 77588   4-00100
  Jacqueline Cobbin, prin.   485-2481
Pearland West JHS   3-00100
  2337 GALVESTON AVE 77581   485-3203
  Sonia Serrano, prin.

Pearsall, AC 210, PC 6, Frio
Pearsall ISD, 522 E FLORIDA ST 78061 — 5-11111
John Kelly, supt. — 334-8001
HS, 1990 MAVERICK DR 78061 — 3-00011
Hank Nannen, prin. — 334-8011
JHS, 614 N PECAN ST 78061 — 3-00100
Esther Barrientos, prin. — 334-8021

Peaster, AC 817, PC 2, Parker
Peaster ISD, PO BOX 129 76485 — 2-11111
Philip Bledsoe, supt. — 594-3434
S, PO BOX 129 76485 — 2-11111
Timothy Lewelling, prin. — 594-3700

Pecos, AC 915, PC 7, Reeves
Pecos-Barstow-Toyah ISD — 5-11111
PO BOX 869 79772 — 447-7201
Mario Sotelo, supt.
HS, PO BOX 869 79772 — 3-00011
Alice Duerksen, prin. — 447-7222
Crockett MS-8th, PO BOX 869 79772 — 2-00100
Beatrice Jenkins, prin. — 447-7251

Penelope, AC 817, PC 2, Hill
Penelope ISD, PO BOX 68 76676 — 2-11111
Bill Sparks, supt. — 533-2215
S, PO BOX 68 76676 — 2-11111
Bill Sparks, prin. — 533-2215

Perrin, AC 817, PC 2, Jack
Perrin-Whitt Consolidated ISD — 2-11111
PO BOX 39 76486 — 798-3718
Charles Scott, supt.
JSHS, PO BOX 39 76486 — 2-00111
Ray King, prin. — 798-3845

Perryton, AC 806, PC 6, Ochiltree
Perryton ISD, PO BOX 1048 79070 — 4-11111
K. Leifeste, supt. — 435-5478
HS, PO BOX 1048 79070 — 2-00011
Joe Gibson, prin. — 435-3633
JHS, PO BOX 1048 79070 — 2-00100
Charles McLarty, prin. — 435-3601

Petersburg, AC 806, PC 4, Hale
Petersburg ISD, PO BOX 160 79250 — 2-11111
William Grimes, supt. — 667-3585
JSHS, PO BOX 160 79250 — 2-00111
Gary Sherman, prin. — 667-3991

Petrolia, AC 817, PC 3, Clay
Petrolia ISD, PO BOX 176 76377 — 2-11111
Edward Gilliland, supt. — 524-3555
S, PO BOX 176 76377 — 2-11111
Gene Gee, prin. — 524-3264

Pettus, AC 512, PC 3, Bee
Pettus ISD, PO BOX D 78146 — 2-11111
Dennis Harrod, supt. — 375-2296
JSHS, PO BOX D 78146 — 2-00111
Ramon Rodriguez, prin. — 375-2484

Pflugerville, AC 512, PC 5, Travis
Pflugerville ISD — 6-11111
1401 W PECAN ST 78660 — 251-4159
Robert Spoonemore, supt.
HS, 1301 W PECAN ST 78660 — 4-00011
L. Bradley, prin. — 251-2238
MS, 1600 SETTLERS VALLEY DR 78660 — 3-00100
Fred Fasel, prin. — 251-4123
Other Schools – See Austin

Pharr, AC 210, PC 8, Hidalgo
Pharr-San Juan-Alamo ISD — 7-11111
PO BOX Y 78577 — 787-5551
Ernesto Alvarado, supt.
Pharr-San Juan-Alamo North HS — 4-00011
500 NOLANA RD 78577 — 783-3300
Jose Farias, prin.
Pharr-San Juan-Alamo HS — 5-00011
1229 S I RD 78577 — 783-2200
Esteban Garcia, prin.
Johnson JHS, 500 E SIOUX RD 78577 — 3-00100
Jose Garza, prin. — 781-2461
Memorial MS — 4-00100
714 E US HIGHWAY 83 78577 — 787-5531
Marisela Zepeda, prin.
Other Schools – See Alamo, San Juan

Valley View ISD — 4-11111
RR 1 BOX 122 78577 — 843-8825
Leonel Galaviz, supt.
Valley View HS, RR 1 BOX 122 78577 — 2-00011
Jose Santillan, prin. — 843-9222
Valley View JHS — 2-00100
RR 1 BOX 122 78577 — 843-2452
Hugo Munoz, prin.

Texas Vocational School — 2-CS
RR 2 BOX 791 78577 — 631-6181

Pilot Point, AC 817, PC 5, Denton
Pilot Point ISD — 3-11111
829 S HARRISON ST 76258 — 686-5221
John Grigsby, supt.
Selz HS, 829 S HARRISON ST 76258 — 2-00011
John Hudson, prin. — 686-2189
Gee HS, 114 S HARRISON ST 76258 — 2-00100
Jackie McBroom, prin. — 686-2174

Pineland, AC 409, PC 3, Sabine
West Sabine ISD, PO BOX 8 75968 — 3-11111
Jackie Hilton, supt. — 584-2655
West Sabine JSHS, TIGER DR 75968 — 2-00111
Jack Leath, prin. — 584-2525

Pittsburg, AC 903, PC 5, Camp
Pittsburg ISD, PO BOX 621 75686 — 4-11111
Noel Kendall, supt. — 856-3628
HS, 300 N TEXAS ST 75686 — 3-00011
Harold Hinsley, prin. — 856-3646
MS, 313 BROACH ST 75686 — 3-00100
Don Peek, prin. — 856-6432

Plains, AC 806, PC 4, Yoakum
Plains ISD, PO BOX 479 79355 — 3-11111
Melton Simmons, supt. — 456-7401
JSHS, PO BOX 479 79355 — 2-01111
J. Wilson, prin. — 456-7498

Plainview, AC 806, PC 7, Hale
Plainview ISD, PO BOX 1540 79073 — 6-11111
Dennis Townsend, supt. — 296-6392
HS, 1501 QUINCY ST 79072 — 4-00011
Jerry George, prin. — 296-4051
Estacado JHS, 2500 W 20TH ST 79072 — 2-00100
Oliver Dunlap, prin. — 296-4165

Wayland Baptist University — 4-UC
1900 W 7TH ST 79072 — 296-5521

Plano, AC 214, PC 9, Collin
Plano ISD, 2700 W 15TH ST 75075 — 8-11111
James Surratt, supt. — 519-8100
Plano East SHS — 4-00001
3000 LOS RIOS BLVD 75074 — 423-9664
Archie McAfee, prin.
Plano SHS — 5-00001
2200 INDEPENDENCE PKY 75075 — 519-8500
Doyle Dean, prin.
Shepton Freshman HS — 4-00010
5601 W PARKER RD 75093 — 403-1425
Bob Seei, prin.
Vines Freshman HS — 4-00010
1401 HIGHEDGE DR 75075 — 596-4405
Tom Salmon, prin.
Williams Freshman HS — 4-00010
1717 17TH ST 75074 – Jeff Bailey, prin. 423-4521
Armstrong MS — 3-00100
3805 TIMBERLINE DR 75074 — 423-8330
D. Beavert, prin.
Bowman MS, 2501 JUPITER RD 75074 — 3-00100
Joe Chesney, prin. — 423-5514
Carpenter MS — 4-00100
1501 CROSS BEND RD 75023 — 424-6552
David Dooley, prin.
Clark Freshman HS — 4-00100
523 W SPRING CREEK PKY 75023 — 517-5105
Phil Saviano, prin.
Haggard MS, 2401 WESTSIDE DR 75075 — 4-00100
Ravina McKellar, prin. — 867-0430
Hendrick MS, 7400 RED RIVER DR 75025 — 3-00100
Carolyn Warterfield, prin. — 517-1831
Renner MS, 5505 W PLANO PKY 75093 — 3-01100
Mike Collinsworth, prin. — 931-0339
Schimelpfenig MS — 4-00100
2400 MAUMELLE DR 75023 — 618-6703
Tom Leyden, prin.
Wilson MS, 1001 CUSTER RD 75075 — 4-00100
Beverly Sellers, prin. — 423-1112

Pleasanton, AC 210, PC 6, Atascosa
Pleasanton ISD, 831 STADIUM DR 78064 — 5-11111
George Pool, supt. — 569-2171
HS, 831 STADIUM DR 78064 — 3-00011
Larry Brown, prin. — 569-2197
JHS, 831 STADIUM DR 78064 — 3-00100
Kenneth Whiteker, prin. — 569-2514

Pollok, AC 409, PC 2, Angelina
Central ISD, RR 1 BOX 39 75969 — 4-11111
Bob Baker, supt. — 853-2216
Central HS, RR 1 BOX 39 75969 — 2-00011
Raymond Holder, prin. — 853-2167
Central JHS, RR 1 BOX 39 75969 — 2-01100
Laura Cummings, prin. — 853-2215

Ponder, AC 817, PC 2, Denton
Ponder ISD, PO BOX 278 76259 — 2-11111
Emmett Baker, supt. — 479-2266
JSHS, PO BOX 278 76259 — 2-00111
William Moeller, prin. — 479-2245

Poolville, AC 817, PC 2, Parker
Poolville ISD, PO BOX 96 76487 — 2-11111
A. Jowitt, supt. — 594-4539
S, PO BOX 96 76487 — 2-11111
Michelle Berkey, prin. — 594-4539

Port Aransas, AC 512, PC 4, Nueces
Port Aransas ISD — 2-11111
PO BOX 1297 78373 — 749-5500
Lawrence Lane, supt.
HS, PO BOX 1297 78373 — 2-00011
Harold Lister, prin. — 749-5257
Brundrett MS, PO BOX 1297 78373 — 2-00100
Ernest Page, prin. — 749-5258

Port Arthur, AC 409, PC 8, Jefferson
Port Arthur ISD, PO BOX 1388 77641 — 7-11111
Kenneth Greene, supt. — 989-6244
Jefferson HS, 2200 JEFFERSON DR 77642 — 4-00011
Robert Bledsoe, prin. — 962-8451
Lincoln HS — 3-00011
1023 ABE LINCOLN AVE 77640 — 985-2551
Melvin Getwood, prin.
Austin JHS, 2441 61ST ST 77640 — 3-00111
Eddie Fowler, prin. — 736-1031
Stillwell Tech Ctr, 4801 9TH AVE 77642 — Vo Tech
Guy Jones, prin. — 983-3286

Edison MS, 3501 12TH ST 77642 — 4-00100
William Farris, prin. — 985-4314
Wilson MS, 1500 LAKESHORE DR 77640 — 3-00100
Sylvester Pace, prin. — 985-9347

Lamar University — 4-CC
PO BOX 310 77641 — 983-4921

Porter, AC 713, PC 6, Montgomery
New Caney ISD
Supt. — See New Caney
MS, 34801 HIGHWAY 59 N 77365 — 3-00100
Cheryle Beck, prin. — 354-4137

Port Isabel, AC 210, PC 5, Cameron
Point Isabel ISD, PO BOX AH 78578 — 4-11111
Jose Manzano, supt. — 943-7971
HS, PO BOX AH 78578 — 2-00011
Raul Villarreal, prin. — 943-6491
JHS, PO BOX AH 78578 — 3-01100
Maria Perez, prin. — 943-2652

Portland, AC 512, PC 7, San Patricio
Gregory-Portland ISD
Supt. — See Gregory
Gregory-Portland HS — 4-00011
4600 WILDCAT DR 78374 — 643-2538
Bill Lytle, prin.
Gregory-Portland JHS — 3-00100
4200 WILDCAT DR 78374 — 643-2552
William Barr, prin.

Port Lavaca, AC 512, PC 7, Calhoun
Calhoun County ISD — 5-11111
PO BOX 68 77979 — 552-9728
Michael Moehler, supt.
Calhoun HS, 0 SANDCRAB BLVD 77979 — 4-00011
Van Pryor, prin. — 552-3775
Travis MS, 705 N NUECES ST 77979 — 3-00100
Juan Rodriguez, prin. — 552-3784
Other Schools – See Seadrift

Port Neches, AC 409, PC 7, Jefferson
Port Neches ISD, PO BOX 877 77651 — 6-11111
Zach Byrd, supt. — 722-3351
Port Neches-Groves HS — 4-00011
1225 MERRIMAN ST 77651 — 722-8142
Richard Briggs, prin.
MS, 2031 LLANO ST 77651 — 3-00100
Ray McCuller, prin. — 722-8115
Other Schools – See Groves

Post, AC 806, PC 5, Garza
Post ISD, PO BOX 70 79356 — 4-11111
Bob Bain, supt. — 495-3343
HS, 200 E 6TH ST 79356 — 2-00011
Joe Giddens, prin. — 495-2770
MS, 405 W 8TH ST 79356 — 2-00100
Marita Jackson, prin. — 495-2874

Poteet, AC 210, PC 5, Atascosa
Poteet ISD, PO BOX 138 78065 — 4-11111
James Henry, supt. — 742-3567
HS, PO BOX 138 78065 — 2-00011
Andres Gutierrez, prin. — 742-3522
JHS, PO BOX 138 78065 — 2-00100
Chris Trevino, prin. — 742-3571

Poth, AC 210, PC 4, Wilson
Poth ISD, PO BOX 250 78147 — 3-11111
Michael Harris, supt. — 484-3330
HS, PO BOX 250 78147 — 2-00011
Donald Braun, prin. — 484-3322
JHS, PO BOX 250 78147 — 2-00100
Paul Tarter, prin. — 484-3323

Pottsboro, AC 903, PC 4, Grayson
Pottsboro ISD, PO BOX 555 75076 — 4-11111
Carolyn Sewell, supt. — 786-3051
HS, PO BOX 555 75076 — 2-00011
Gary Utsler, prin. — 786-2470
MS, PO BOX 555 75076 — 2-01100
Ronald Ray, prin. — 786-9702

Prairie Lea, AC 512, PC 2, Caldwell
Prairie Lea ISD, PO BOX 9 78661 — 2-11111
James Summers, supt. — 488-2310
S, PO BOX 9 78661 — 2-11111
Paula Bostick, prin. — 488-2328

Prairie View, AC 409, PC 5, Waller

Prairie View A&M University — 5-UC
PO BOX 3089 77446 — 857-2626

Premont, AC 512, PC 5, Jim Wells
Premont ISD, PO BOX 530 78375 — 3-11111
Jose Johnson, supt. — 348-3915
HS, PO BOX B 78375 — 2-00011
Salvador Chapa, prin. — 348-3587
JHS, PO BOX 769 78375 — 2-00100
Ignacio Guerra, prin. — 348-3588

Presidio, AC 915, PC 5, Presidio
Presidio ISD, PO BOX S 79845 — 4-11111
Santiago Alanis, supt. — 229-3275
HS, PO BOX 5 79845 — 2-00011
Paul Abundez, prin. — 229-3365
JHS, 100 MARKET ST 79845 — 2-00100
James Bassett, prin. — 229-3113

Price, AC 903, PC 3, Rusk
Carlisle ISD, PO BOX 187 75687 — 2-11111
Joe Woodland, supt. — 861-3801
Carlisle S, PO BOX 187 75687 — 2-11111
Walter Moon, prin. — 861-3811

Priddy, AC 915, PC 2, Mills
Priddy ISD, PO BOX 40 76870   1-11111
  Rick Davidson, supt.   966-3323
S, PO BOX 40 76870   1-11111
  Melvin Eilers, prin.   966-3323

Princeton, AC 214, PC 4, Collin
Princeton ISD, 321 PANTHER PKY 75407   4-11111
  Frank Garner, supt.   736-3503
HS, 321 PANTHER PKY 75407   2-00011
  Hubert Duncan, prin.   736-2431
Clark MS, 321 PANTHER PKY 75407   3-00100
  Larry Latham, prin.   736-3211

Progreso, AC 210, PC 4, Hidalgo
Progreso ISD, PO BOX 613 78579   4-11111
  Robert Rivera, supt.   565-6203
HS, PO BOX 613 78579   2-00011
  Adolfo Chavez, prin.   565-4142
MS, PO BOX 613 78579   2-00100
  Ludivina Livas, prin.   565-6539

Prosper, AC 214, PC 4, Collin
Prosper ISD, PO BOX 107 75078   3-11111
  William Rushing, supt.   347-2561
JSHS, 606 E 7TH ST 75078   2-00011
  Bill Sudbury, prin.   346-2455

Quanah, AC 817, PC 5, Hardeman
Quanah ISD, PO BOX 150 79252   3-11111
  Charles Jaggers, supt.   663-2281
HS, 7TH AND EARLE 79252   2-00011
  Walter Knight, prin.   663-2791
Travis MS, 7TH AND SHAW 79252   2-00100
  Terry Allen, prin.   663-2226

Queen City, AC 903, PC 4, Cass
Queen City ISD, PO BOX 128 75572   4-11111
  Chester Juroska, supt.   796-8256
HS, PO BOX 128 75572   2-00011
  Darrell Floyd, prin.   796-8259
Upchurch MS, PO BOX 128 75572   2-01100
  Douglas Devine, prin.   796-6412

Quinlan, AC 903, PC 4, Hunt
Boles ISD, RR 3 BOX 48 75474   2-11111
  Graham Sweeney, supt.   883-2161
Boles JSHS, RR 3 BOX 48 75474   2-00111
  William Long, prin.   883-2161
Quinlan ISD, PO BOX 466 75474   4-11111
  Alvis Martin, supt.   356-3293
Ford HS, RR 3 BOX 20 75474   3-00011
  Paul Shipley, prin.   356-2155
Thompson MS, RR 3 BOX 18 75474   3-00100
  Philip Anthony, prin.   356-2154

Quitman, AC 903, PC 4, Wood
Quitman ISD, 1101 E GOODE ST 75783   4-11111
  Richard Swetnam, supt.   763-4593
HS, 1101 E GOODE ST 75783   2-00011
  David Seago, prin.   763-5413
JHS, 1101 E GOODE ST 75783   2-00100
  David Seago, prin.   763-5415

Ralls, AC 806, PC 4, Crosby
Ralls ISD, PO BOX AD 79357   3-11111
  Larry Taylor, supt.   253-2509
JSHS, PO BOX AD 79357   2-00111
  Faith Ballard, prin.   253-2571

Ranger, AC 817, PC 5, Eastland
Ranger ISD, RR 3 BOX 12D 76470   3-11111
  Joe Phariss, supt.   647-1187
JSHS, RR 3 BOX 12D 76470   2-00111
  Richard McCarson, prin.   647-3216

Ranger Junior College   3-CC
  PO BOX 135 76470   647-3234

Rankin, AC 915, PC 4, Upton
Rankin ISD, PO BOX 90 79778   2-11111
  Leonard Kent, supt.   693-2461
HS, PO BOX 90 79778   2-00011
  Harold Hooker, prin.   693-2351
MS, PO BOX 90 79778   2-01100
  Harold Hooker, prin.   693-2232

Raymondville, AC 210, PC 6, Willacy
Raymondville ISD   5-11111
  1 BEARCAT BLVD 78580   689-2471
  Joe Herod, supt.
HS, 1 BEARCAT BLVD 78580   3-00011
  Jeff Hembree, prin.   689-2471
Green JHS, 1 BEARCAT BLVD 78580   3-00100
  Olga Martinez, prin.   689-2471

Red Oak, AC 214, PC 5, Ellis
Red Oak ISD, PO BOX 9000 75154   5-11111
  J. Sullivan, supt.   617-2941
HS, PO BOX 9000 75154   3-00011
  Cecil Bowman, prin.   617-3535
JHS, PO BOX 9000 75154   3-00100
  Gary Autrey, prin.   617-0066

Redwater, AC 903, PC 3, Bowie
Redwater ISD, PO BOX 347 75573   3-11111
  Joe.Lee, supt.   671-3481
HS, PO BOX 347 75573   2-00011
  Carlos McGregor, prin.   671-3421
JHS, PO BOX 347 75573   2-01100
  James Spencer, prin.   671-3412

Refugio, AC 512, PC 5, Refugio
Refugio ISD, PO BOX 190 78377   3-11111
  James Boyle, supt.   526-2325

HS, PO BOX 190 78377   2-00011
  Michael Kellner, prin.   526-2344
MS, PO BOX 190 78377   2-01100
  Janice Boyle, prin.   526-2434

Richards, AC 409, PC 2, Grimes
Richards ISD, PO BOX 308 77873   2-11111
  Charles Hall, supt.   851-2364
JSHS, PO BOX 308 77873   1-00111
  Willow Walker, prin.   851-2364

Richardson, AC 214, PC 8, Dallas
Richardson ISD   8-11111
  400 S GREENVILLE AVE 75081   301-3333
  Arzell Ball, supt.
Berkner SHS   4-00001
  1600 E SPRING VALLEY RD 75081   301-4100
  Don Skaggs, prin.
Pearce SHS, 1600 N COIT RD 75080   4-00001
  Robert London, prin.   952-8300
SHS, 1250 W BELT LINE RD 75080   4-00001
  Jerry Bishop, prin.   301-4700
Apollo JHS, 1600 APOLLO RD 75081   4-00110
  Edwin Dailey, prin.   690-6770
JHS, 450 ABRAMS RD 75081   3-00110
  Willie Fowlks, prin.   235-2323
Richardson-North JHS   3-00110
  1820 N FLOYD RD 75080   235-4593
  Lucy Long, prin.
Richardson-West JHS   3-00110
  1309 HOLLY DR 75080   235-7125
  Harold Kellogg, prin.
Other Schools – See Dallas

Alexander S   1-00111
  409 INTERNATIONAL PKY 75081   690-9210
  Andrew Cody, prin.
Professional Court Reporting School   2-CS
  1401 N CENTRAL EXPY STE 100 75080
  231-9502
University of Texas at Dallas   6-UC
  PO BOX 830688 75083   690-2296

Richland Springs, AC 915, PC 2, San Saba
Richland Springs ISD, PO BOX E 76871   2-11111
  Charles Brandenburg, supt.   452-3524
S, PO BOX E 76871   2-11111
  Bob Spikes, prin.   452-3427

Riesel, AC 817, PC 3, McLennan
Riesel ISD, PO BOX 40 76682   2-11111
  Ronald Urbantke, supt.   896-6411
S, PO BOX 40 76682   2-11111
  William Wren, prin.   896-3171

Rio Grande City, AC 210, PC 6, Starr
Rio Grande City ISD   6-11111
  1 S FORT RINGGOLD ST 78582   487-5591
  Ruben Saenz, supt.
HS, 1 S FORT RINGGOLD ST 78582   4-00011
  Roel Smith, prin.   487-5591
Ringgold JHS   3-00100
  1 S FORT RINGGOLD ST 78582   487-5591
  Miguel Villarreal, prin.
Other Schools – See Grulla

Rio Hondo, AC 210, PC 4, Cameron
Rio Hondo ISD, PO BOX 220 78583   4-11111
  Charles Bright, supt.   748-3361
HS, PO BOX 220 78583   2-00011
  Ismael Garcia, prin.   748-2332
JHS, PO BOX 220 78583   2-00100
  Roger Harms, prin.   748-2542

Rio Vista, AC 817, PC 3, Johnson
Rio Vista ISD, PO BOX 369 76093   3-11111
  Sharron Miles, supt.   373-2241
HS, PO BOX 369 76093   2-00011
  Steven Gast, prin.   373-2669
MS, PO BOX 369 76093   2-00100
  Gary Peacock, prin.   373-2009

Rising Star, AC 817, PC 3, Eastland
Rising Star ISD, PO BOX 37 76471   2-11111
  Garland Calhoun, supt.   643-2717
JSHS, PO BOX 37 76471   2-00111
  Robby Stuteville, prin.   643-3521

Riviera, AC 512, PC 3, Kleberg
Riviera ISD, RR 1 BOX 500 78379   3-11111
  Charles Zepeda, supt.   296-3101
Kaufer HS, RR 1 BOX 500 78379   2-00011
  Keith Chapman, prin.   296-3607
De La Paz MS, RR 1 BOX 500 78379   2-00100
  Mary Moore, prin.   296-3610

Robert Lee, AC 915, PC 4, Coke
Robert Lee ISD   2-11111
  HC 61 BOX 303 76945   453-2612
  William Hood, supt.
S, HC 61 BOX 303 76945   2-11111
  Lane Jackson, prin.   453-2333

Robstown, AC 512, PC 7, Nueces
Robstown ISD, 801 N 1ST ST 78380   5-11111
  Feliciano Gallegos, supt.   387-9402
HS, 1101 PICKER LN 78380   3-00011
  Adrian Oliveira, prin.   387-9402
Seale JHS, 401 E AVENUE G 78380   3-00100
  Eulogia De La Cruz, prin.   387-9402

Roby, AC 915, PC 3, Fisher
Roby Consolidated ISD   2-11111
  PO BOX 519 79543   776-2222
  George Price, supt.

HS, PO BOX 519 79543   1-00011
  David Mims, prin.   776-2223

Rochelle, AC 915, PC 2, McCulloch
Rochelle ISD, PO BOX 167 76872   2-11111
  Bob Doyal, supt.   243-5224
S, PO BOX 167 76872   2-11111
  Joe Skalak, prin.   243-5224

Rochester, AC 817, PC 2, Haskell
Rochester ISD, PO BOX 190 79544   2-11111
  Dickie Sloan, supt.   743-3441
S, PO BOX 190 79544   2-11111
  Rod Townsend, prin.   743-3260

Rockdale, AC 512, PC 6, Milam
Rockdale ISD, PO BOX 632 76567   4-11111
  Walter Pond, supt.   446-3403
HS, PO BOX 632 76567   3-00011
  Raymon Puente, prin.   446-3471
JHS, PO BOX 632 76567   2-00100
  Jim Hughes, prin.   446-2585

Rockport, AC 512, PC 5, Aransas
Aransas County ISD   5-11111
  PO BOX 907 78381   790-2210
  Karen Hall, supt.
Rockport-Fulton HS   3-00011
  PO BOX 907 78381   790-2220
  Wilburn McDonald, prin.
Rockport-Fulton JHS   3-00100
  PO BOX 907 78381   790-2230
  Preston Adams, prin.

Rocksprings, AC 210, PC 4, Edwards
Rocksprings ISD, PO BOX 157 78880   2-11111
  Norman Plemons, supt.   683-4137
HS, PO BOX 157 78880   2-00011
  Dale Ethridge, prin.   683-4136

Rockwall, AC 214, PC 7, Rockwall
Rockwall ISD   5-11111
  801 E WASHINGTON ST 75087   771-0605
  Wayne Bingham, supt.
HS, 901 YELLOW JACKET LN 75087   4-00011
  Mike Hopson, prin.   771-3361
Williams MS   3-00100
  1201 HIGH SCHOOL DR 75087   771-5281
  James Martin, prin.

Rogers, AC 817, PC 4, Bell
Rogers ISD, PO BOX A 76569   3-11111
  Glynis Rosas, supt.   642-3802
HS, PO BOX A 76569   2-00011
  Michael Holland, prin.   642-3224
JHS, PO BOX A 76569   2-00100
  Bob Peschel, prin.   642-3250

Roma, AC 210, PC 6, Starr
Roma ISD, PO BOX 187 78584   6-11111
  Eleuterio Garza, supt.   849-1377
HS, PO BOX 187 78584   4-00011
  Humberto Vasquez, prin.   849-1333
JHS, PO BOX 187 78584   4-00100
  Danelo Gonzalez, prin.   849-1434

Ropesville, AC 806, PC 2, Hockley
Ropes ISD, PO BOX 8 79358   2-11111
  John Trice, supt.   562-4031
Ropes HS, PO BOX 8 79358   1-00011
  Jackie Gaskins, prin.   562-4211
Ropes JHS, PO BOX 8 79358   2-01100
  V. Scott, prin.   562-3011

Roscoe, AC 915, PC 4, Nolan
Highland ISD, 6625 FM 608 79545   2-11111
  Edward Donahue, supt.   766-3652
Highland S, 6625 FM 608 79545   2-11111
  Janey Burke, prin.   766-3652
Roscoe ISD, PO BOX 579 79545   2-11111
  Monte Barnes, supt.   766-3629
JSHS, PO BOX 579 79545   2-00111
  Charles Carter, prin.   766-3327

Rosebud, AC 817, PC 4, Falls
Rosebud-Lott ISD, PO BOX 638 76570   3-11111
  Charley McMath, supt.   583-4510
Rosebud-Lott HS, PO BOX 638 76570   2-00011
  George Ganze, prin.   583-7967
Rosebud-Lott JHS, PO BOX 638 76570   2-00100
  George Ganze, prin.   583-7967

Rosenberg, AC 713, PC 7, Fort Bend
Lamar Consolidated ISD   7-11111
  3911 AVENUE I 77471   341-3100
  Michael Zolkoski, supt.
Lamar Consolidated HS   4-00011
  4606 MUSTANG AVE 77471   341-3434
  Lyda Dawes, prin.
Terry HS, 5500 AVENUE N 77471   4-00011
  Robert Haley, prin.   341-3500
George JHS, 4601 AIRPORT AVE 77471   3-00100
  Eugene Tomas, prin.   341-3399
Lamar JHS, 4814 MUSTANG AVE 77471   3-00100
  Michael Greenwood, prin.   341-3388

Rotan, AC 915, PC 4, Fisher
Rotan ISD, 102 N MCKINLEY AVE 79546   3-11111
  Nolan Kinsey, supt.   735-2332
HS, 102 N MCKINLEY AVE 79546   2-00011
  Mickey Early, prin.   735-3041
JHS, 102 N MCKINLEY AVE 79546   2-01100
  Jim Cain, prin.   735-3162

Round Rock, AC 512, PC 8, Williamson
Round Rock ISD — 7-11111
  1311 ROUND ROCK AVE 78681 — 255-4431
  Dan McLendon, supt.
HS, 300 N LAKE CREEK DR 78681 — 5-00011
  H. Lynn Russell, prin. — 255-2594
Chisholm Trail MS — 4-00100
  500 OAKRIDGE DR 78681 — 255-7866
  Darla Regner, prin.
Fulkes MS — 4-00100
  300 W ANDERSON AVE 78664 — 255-4471
  Tom Stokes, prin.
Other Schools – See Austin

Rowlett, AC 214, PC 7, Dallas
Garland ISD
  Supt. — See Garland
Coyle MS, 4500 SKYLINE DR 75088 — 3-00100
  Larry Butler, prin. — 475-3711

Roxton, AC 903, PC 3, Lamar
Roxton ISD, PO BOX 307 75477 — 2-11111
  James Hesson, supt. — 346-3213
JSHS, PO BOX 307 75477 — 1-00111
  Golda Humphries, prin. — 346-3213

Royse City, AC 214, PC 4, Rockwall
Royse City ISD, PO BOX 479 75189 — 4-11111
  William Fort, supt. — 635-2413
HS, PO BOX 479 75189 — 2-00011
  Norris Cherry, prin. — 635-9503
MS, PO BOX 479 75189 — 2-00100
  Ernest Smith, prin. — 635-9544

Rule, AC 817, PC 3, Haskell
Rule ISD, PO BOX 307 79547 — 2-11111
  A. Kutch, supt. — 997-2521
S, PO BOX 307 79547 — 2-11111
  Steve Long, prin. — 997-2246

Runge, AC 210, PC 4, Karnes
Runge ISD, PO BOX 158 78151 — 2-11111
  Harold King, supt. — 239-4315
JSHS, PO BOX 158 78151 — 2-00111
  Lonnie Blake, prin. — 239-4864

Rusk, AC 903, PC 5, Cherokee
Rusk ISD, 203 E 7TH ST 75785 — 4-11111
  T. Murray, supt. — 683-5592
HS, 203 E 7TH ST 75785 — 2-00011
  Dean Evans, prin. — 683-5401
JHS, 203 E 7TH ST 75785 — 2-00100
  Louis Caveness, prin. — 683-2503

Sabinal, AC 210, PC 4, Uvalde
Sabinal ISD, PO BOX 338 78881 — 2-11111
  Jim Ryan, supt. — 988-2472
JSHS, PO BOX 338 78881 — 2-00111
  Gary Oliphant, prin. — 988-2475

Sabine Pass, AC 409, PC 3, Jefferson
Sabine Pass ISD, PO BOX 1148 77655 — 2-11111
  John Villot, supt. — 971-2321
S, PO BOX 1148 77655 — 2-11111
  Bob Chumley, prin. — 971-2321

Sadler, AC 903, PC 2, Grayson
S & S Consolidated ISD — 3-11111
  PO BOX 837 76264 — 564-6051
  Jim Malone, supt.
S & S Consolidated HS — 2-00011
  PO BOX 837 76264 — 564-3768
  Joe Wardell, prin.
S & S Consolidated MS — 2-01100
  PO BOX 837 76264 — 893-7962
  John Pate, prin.

Saint Jo, AC 817, PC 4, Montague
St. Jo ISD, PO BOX L 76265 — 2-11111
  Anthony Daugherty, supt. — 995-2668
JSHS, PO BOX L 76265 — 2-00111
  L. T. Bailey, prin. — 995-2532

Salado, AC 817, PC 4, Bell
Salado ISD, PO BOX 98 76571 — 3-11111
  Steven Ervin, supt. — 947-5479
JSHS, PO BOX 98 76571 — 2-00111
  Richard Brown, prin. — 947-5429

Saltillo, AC 903, PC 2, Hopkins
Saltillo ISD, PO BOX 269 75478 — 2-11111
  Kerry Garmon, supt. — 537-2386
S, PO BOX 269 75478 — 2-11111
  Pearl Garmon, prin. — 537-2386

Samnorwood, AC 806, PC 1, Collingsworth
Samnorwood ISD, PO BOX 765 79077 — 2-11111
  John McGregor, supt. — 256-2039
S, PO BOX 765 79077 — 2-11111
  J. Brown, prin. — 256-2039

San Angelo, AC 915, PC 8, Tom Green
San Angelo ISD — 7-11111
  1621 UNIVERSITY AVE 76904 — 947-3700
  Bill Graves, supt.
Central SHS — 4-00001
  100 COTTONWOOD ST 76901 — 659-3400
  Robert Meek, prin.
Lake View HS, 900 E 43RD ST 76903 — 3-00011
  Jim Hundley, prin. — 659-3500
Edison JHS, 218 N OAKES ST 76903 — 3-00110
  Jesse Martinez, prin. — 659-3576
Glenn JHS — 4-00110
  2201 UNIVERSITY AVE 76904 — 947-3841
  Sam Cervantez, prin.

Lee JHS, 2500 SHERWOOD WAY 76901 — 3-00110
  J. Hoppe, prin. — 947-3871
Lincoln JHS, 4100 BOWIE ST 76903 — 3-00100
  Steve Van Hoozer, prin. — 659-3550

American Commercial College — 2-CS
  3177 EXECUTIVE DR 76904 — 942-6797
Angelo State University — 6-UC
  2601 W AVENUE N 76909 — 942-2041
Chenier Business School — 1-CS
  2819 LOOP 306 76904
Shannon West Texas Memorial Hospital — HSP
  9 S MAGDALEN ST 76903 — 653-6741

San Antonio, AC 210, PC 11, Bexar
Alamo Heights ISD — 5-11111
  7101 BROADWAY ST 78209 — 824-2483
  Charles Slater, supt.
Alamo Heights HS — 4-00011
  6900 BROADWAY ST 78209 — 820-8850
  Linda Foster, prin.
Alamo Heights JHS — 3-00100
  7607 N NEW BRAUNFELS AVE 78209 — 824-3231
  Jane Leizear, prin.

East Central ISD — 6-11111
  6634 NEW SULPHUR SPRINGS RD 78263
  Anthony Constanzo, supt. — 648-7861
East Central HS, 7173 FM 1628 78263 — 4-00011
  Jimmy Inman, prin. — 649-2951
Oak Crest MS — 3-00100
  9787 NEW SULPHUR SPRINGS RD 78263
  Jake Wyatt, prin. — 649-2121
Salado MS, 3602 S WW WHITE RD 78222 — 3-00100
  Charles Shobe, prin. — 648-3310

Edgewood ISD — 7-11111
  5358 W COMMERCE ST 78237 — 433-2361
  Dolores Munoz, supt.
Edgewood HS, 607 SW 34TH ST 78237 — 3-00011
  Rich Bocanegra, prin. — 433-9000
Kennedy HS — 4-00011
  1922 S GENERAL MCMULLEN DR 78226
  Ray Moncus, prin. — 433-9343
Memorial HS — 3-00011
  1227 MEMORIAL ST 78228 — 433-9434
  Thomas Levine, prin.
Brentwood MS — 3-00100
  1626 THOMPSON PL 78226 — 433-7401
  Jose Marquez, prin.
Garcia JHS, 3306 RUIZ ST 78228 — 3-00100
  Rosendo Valdez, prin. — 433-7953
Truman JHS, 1018 NW 34TH ST 78228 — 2-00100
  Joseph Orr, prin. — 433-8651
Wrenn JHS, 627 S ACME RD 78237 — 3-00100
  Lucy Hall, prin. — 433-7792

Ft. Sam Houston ISD — 4-11111
  1902 WINANS RD 78234 — 824-7539
  Thomas Mosely, supt.
Cole JSHS, 1900 WINANS RD 78234 — 3-00111
  Clinton Compton, prin. — 804-4121

Harlandale ISD — 7-11111
  102 GENEVIEVE DR 78214 — 921-4300
  Raymond Vick, supt.
Harlandale HS — 4-00011
  114 E GERALD AVE 78214 — 924-9411
  Robert Pacheco, prin.
McCollum HS — 4-00011
  500 W FORMOSA BLVD 78221 — 921-4500
  Virginia Aguilar, prin.
Harlandale MS, 300 W HUFF AVE 78214 — 4-00100
  Santiago Zamora, prin. — 921-4507
Kingsborough MS — 3-00100
  422 E ASHLEY RD 78221 — 924-5948
  Blanche Mora, prin.
Leal MS — 3-00100
  743 W SOUTHCROSS BLVD 78211 — 921-4570
  Angelo Russo, prin.
Wells MS, 422 W HUTCHINS PL 78221 — 3-00100
  Santiago Bernal, prin. — 922-6325

Judson ISD
  Supt. — See Converse
Kirby JHS, 5441 SEGUIN RD 78219 — 4-00100
  Loretta Carter, prin. — 661-4295

Lackland ISD, 2460 BONG AVE 78236 — 3-11111
  Mary Stacey, supt. — 670-4350
Lackland JSHS, 2460 BONG AVE 78236 — 2-00111
  Linda Lang, prin. — 670-4360

North East ISD — 8-11111
  10333 BROADWAY ST 78217 — 657-8600
  Richard Middleton, supt.
Churchill HS, 12049 BLANCO RD 78216 — 4-00011
  Elton Churchill, prin. — 341-5111
Lee HS — 4-00011
  1400 JACKSON KELLER RD 78213 — 341-7761
  Bill Fish, prin.
MacArthur HS — 5-00011
  2923 E BITTERS RD 78217 — 653-3920
  Anthony Petri, prin.
Madison HS, 5005 STAHL RD 78247 — 4-00011
  Bea Devlin, prin. — 637-4400
Roosevelt HS, 5110 WALZEM RD 78218 — 4-00011
  Mark Scheffler, prin. — 653-3900
Bradley MS, 14819 HEIMER RD 78232 — 4-00100
  Bill Boyd, prin. — 496-2666
Driscoll MS — 4-00100
  17150 JONES MALTSBERGER RD 78247
  Shirley Kearns, prin. — 491-6450

Eisenhower MS, 8231 BLANCO RD 78216 — 4-00100
  Judy Gamble, prin. — 342-5293
Garner MS — 4-00100
  4302 HARRY WURZBACH RD 78209 — 824-3254
  Walter Howard, prin.
Jackson MS — 4-00100
  4538 VANCE JACKSON RD 78230 — 341-1375
  Tom Defosset, prin.
Krueger MS, 438 LANARK DR 78218 — 3-00100
  D. Bird, prin. — 655-3120
Nimitz MS, 5426 BLANCO RD 78216 — 3-00100
  Joe Reasons, prin. — 344-3496
White MS, 7800 MIDCROWN DR 78218 — 4-00100
  James Washington, prin. — 653-1230
Wood MS, 14800 JUDSON RD 78233 — 4-00100
  Shirley Nichols, prin. — 657-5555

Northside ISD, 5900 EVERS RD 78238 — 8-11111
  Jack Jordan, supt. — 647-2100
Clark HS, 5150 DE ZAVALA RD 78249 — 5-00011
  Phyliss Giffin, prin. — 696-8145
Health Careers HS — 3-00011
  4646 HAMILTON WOLFE RD 78229 — 692-0022
  John Boyers, prin.
Holmes HS, 6500 INGRAM RD 78238 — 5-00011
  Gary Haass, prin. — 684-1414
Jay HS, 7611 MARBACH RD 78227 — 5-00011
  Richard Krueger, prin. — 673-1110
Marshall HS, 8000 LOBO LN 78240 — 5-00011
  William Watts, prin. — 681-3060
Taft HS, 11600 W FM 471 78253 — 4-00011
  Roger Harris, prin. — 688-9010
Hobby MS — 4-00100
  11843 VANCE JACKSON RD 78230 — 690-6300
  Jay Dubose, prin.
Jones MS, 1256 PINN RD 78227 — 4-00100
  Charles Burling, prin. — 678-2100
Jordan MS, 1725 RICHLAND HLS 78251 — 3-00100
  Kathleen Wong, prin. — 523-4850
Neff MS, 5227 EVERS RD 78238 — 4-00100
  Steve Skipper, prin. — 523-4550
Pease MS, 201 HUNT LN 78245 — 4-00100
  Sterling Christy, prin. — 673-8773
Rayburn MS — 3-00100
  1400 CEDARHURST DR 78227 — 678-2150
  David Doyle, prin.
Rudder MS, 6558 HORN BLVD 78240 — 4-00100
  Lewis Patton, prin. — 696-6366
Stevenson MS, 8403 TEZEL RD 78250 — 4-00100
  Linda Garcia, prin. — 681-0720
Stinson MS, 13200 SKYHAWK DR 78249 — 3-00100
  Debbie Sonnen, prin. — 561-3600
Sul Ross MS — 4-00100
  3630 CALLAGHAN RD 78228 — 431-6350
  John Bordano, prin.
Zachry MS, 9410 TIMBER PATH 78250 — 4-00100
  Dean Krueger, prin. — 647-5600

San Antonio ISD, 141 LAVACA ST 78210 — 8-11111
  Victor Rodriguez, supt. — 299-5500
Brackenridge HS — 4-00011
  400 EAGLELAND DR 78210 — 533-8144
  John Taylor, prin.
Burbank HS, 1002 EDWARDS 78204 — 4-00011
  Ernest Longoria, prin. — 532-4241
Edison HS, 701 SANTA MONICA 78212 — 4-00011
  Charles Munoz, prin. — 733-9147
Fox Tech HS, 637 N MAIN AVE 78205 — 4-00011
  Barbara Arnold, prin. — 226-5103
Highlands HS, 3118 ELGIN AVE 78210 — 4-00011
  William Grindle, prin. — 333-0421
Houston HS, 4635 E HOUSTON ST 78220 — 4-00011
  Betty Williams, prin. — 661-4134
Jefferson HS — 4-00011
  723 DONALDSON AVE 78201 — 736-1981
  Henry Young, prin.
Lanier HS — 4-00011
  1514 W DURANGO BLVD 78207 — 223-2926
  Roy Mendoza, prin.
Connell MS — 3-00100
  400 HOT WELLS BLVD 78223 — 534-6511
  Joanne Cockrell, prin.
Cooper MS, 1700 TAMPICO ST 78207 — 3-00100
  Ruben Flores, prin. — 223-9031
Davis MS, 4702 E HOUSTON ST 78220 — 3-00100
  Lloyd Bagwell, prin. — 662-8184
Harris MS, 325 PRUITT AVE 78204 — 3-00100
  Sylvia Sanchez, prin. — 226-4952
Irving MS, 1300 DELGADO ST 78207 — 3-00100
  Ray Bibb, prin. — 734-2937
King MS — 3-00100
  3501 MARTIN LUTHER KING DR 78220
  Donald McClure, prin. — 223-8621
Longfellow MS — 3-00100
  1130 E SUNSHINE DR 78228 — 433-0311
  Juan Hernandez, prin.
Lowell MS, 919 THOMPSON PL 78226 — 3-00100
  Tony Pedraza, prin. — 223-4741
Mann MS — 3-00100
  2123 W HUISACHE AVE 78201 — 732-4851
  Sylvia De La Pena, prin.
Page MS, 401 BERKSHIRE AVE 78210 — 3-00100
  Raul Zamora, prin. — 533-7331
Poe MS, 814 ARANSAS AVE 78210 — 3-00100
  Clyde Clack, prin. — 534-6331
Rhodes MS, 3000 TAMPICO ST 78207 — 3-00100
  Bohn Hilliard, prin. — 433-5092
Rogers MS, 314 GALWAY ST 78223 — 3-00100
  Kathy Tackett, prin. — 333-7551

Tafolla MS   4-00100
  1303 W DURANGO BLVD 78207   227-3383
  John Almaguer, prin.
Twain MS, 2411 SAN PEDRO AVE 78212   3-00100
  Nancy Harlan, prin.   732-4641
Wheatley MS, 415 GABRIEL 78202   3-00100
  Juretta Marshall, prin.   227-3921
Whittier MS, 2101 EDISON DR 78201   3-00100
  Raul Prado, prin.   735-7181

South San Antonio ISD   7-11111
  2515 SIOUX ST 78224   924-8541
  Ron Durbon, supt.
South San Antonio HS   4-00011
  2515 NAVAJO ST 78224   924-9211
  Susie Burling, prin.
South San Antonio HS West   3-00011
  5622 RAY ELLISON BLVD 78242   623-1550
  Pat West, prin.
South San Antonio Career Ed   Vo Tech
  2615 NAVAJO ST 78224   923-0436
  Henry Castillon, prin.
Kazen MS, 1520 GILLETTE BLVD 78224   3-00100
  Manuel Bejarano, prin.   924-9021
Shepard MS   3-00100
  5558 RAY ELLISON BLVD 78242   623-1311
  Harry Baker, prin.

Southside ISD   5-11111
  1610 MARTINEZ LOSOYA RD 78221   625-2561
  Thomas Brown, supt.
Southside HS   3-00011
  1610 MARTINEZ LOSOYA RD 78221   626-0550
  Joe Arriaga, prin.
Southside MS   3-00100
  1610 MARTINEZ LOSOYA RD 78221   626-0575
  Ray Conner, prin.

Southwest ISD   6-11111
  11914 DRAGON LN 78252   622-3488
  Richard Clifford, supt.
Southwest HS, 11914 DRAGON LN 78252   4-00011
  Bill Holmes, prin.   622-3401
McAuliffe MS, 11914 DRAGON LN 78252   3-00100
  Louis Cisnero, prin.   623-7700
McNair MS, 11914 DRAGON LN 78252   3-00100
  Helen Hargis, prin.   622-3494

Antonian HS, 6425 WEST AVE 78213   2-00011
  James Kittell, prin.   344-9265
Baptist Memorial Hospital System   HSP
  111 DALLAS ST 78286   222-8431
Blessed Sacrament Academy   2-00011
  1135 MISSION RD 78210   532-9161
  Mildred Truchard, prin.
Cancer Therapy and Research Center   HSP
  8122 DATAPOINT DR STE 600 78229
      616-5500
Career Point Business School   2-CS
  485 SPENCER LN 78201   732-3000
Castle Hills First Baptist S   3-11111
  2220 NW MILITARY HWY # P 78213   377-8485
  Sandy Harris, prin.
Central Catholic HS   3-00011
  1403 N SAINT MARYS ST 78215   225-6794
  Br. Grieshaber, prin.
Faith Outreach Christian Academy   2-11111
  3806 SUNSHINE RANCH RD 78228   734-5034
  Carlos Ferreyro, prin.
Hallmark Institute of Technology   2-CC
  PO BOX 780459 78278   924-8551
Hallmark Institute of Technology   3-CC
  10401 W IH 10 78230   690-9000
Healy-Murphy Center HS   2-00011
  618 LIVE OAK 78202   223-2944
  Janie Whiteley, prin.
Holy Cross JSHS   2-00011
  426 N SAN FELIPE AVE 78228   433-9395
  Br. Mullett, prin.
Incarnate Word College   4-UC
  4301 BROADWAY ST 78209   829-6005
Incarnate Word HS   3-00011
  727 E HILDEBRAND AVE 78212   829-3100
  Patricia Watkins, prin.
ITT Technical Institute   2-CC
  4242 E PIEDRAS DR STE 100 78228
      737-1881
Keystone S, 119 E CRAIG PL 78212   2-11111
  Glenn Sobey, prin.   735-4022
Laurel Ridge S   2-11111
  PO BOX 700590 78270   491-3559
Medical Center Hospital   HSP
  4502 MEDICAL DR 78229   694-2000
NEC-National Institute of Technology   2-CC
  3622 FREDERICKSBURG RD 78201   733-6000
Oblate School of Theology   2-UC
  285 OBLATE DR 78216   341-1366
Our Lady of the Lake University   4-UC
  411 SW 24TH ST 78207   434-6711
Palo Alto College   5-CC
  1400 W VILLARET BLVD 78224   921-5000
Providence S   2-00011
  1215 N SAINT MARYS ST 78215   224-6651
  Sr. Romona Bezner, prin.
St. Anthony HS   2-00011
  3200 MCCULLOUGH AVE 78212   736-4521
  Dan Higgins, prin.
St. Francis Academy   2-00011
  1807 CENTENNIAL BLVD 78211   923-1421
  Sr. Jeanne Ulica, prin.

St. Gerard HS   2-00011
  521 S NEW BRAUNFELS AVE 78203   533-8061
  Maurice Abadie, prin.
St. Mary's Hall, PO BOX 33430 78265   3-11111
  Ted Dunham, prin.   655-7721
St. Mary's University of San Antonio   5-UC
  1 CAMINO SANTA MARIA ST 78228   436-3126
St. Phillip's College   5-CC
  2111 NEVADA ST 78203   531-3200
San Antonio Art Institute   1-UC
  PO BOX 6092 78209
      800-369-7224
San Antonio Christian S   3-11111
  12 BURWOOD LN 78216   340-1864
  Walter Garland, prin.
San Antonio College   7-CC
  1300 SAN PEDRO AVE 78212   733-2300
San Antonio College Medical Dental Asst.   2-CS
  4205 SAN PEDRO AVE 78212   733-0777
San Antonio College Medical Dental Asst.   2-CS
  5280 MEDICAL DR # 100 78229   692-3829
San Antonio Trade School   2-CS
  120 PLAYMOOR ST 78210   533-9126
San Antonio Training Division   2-CS
  9350 S PRESA ST 78223   633-2893
Southwest School of Medical Assistants   2-CS
  201 W SHERIDAN 78204   224-2296
SW School of Business & Tech Careers   2-CS
  602 W SOUTHCROSS BLVD 78221
Texas Military Institute   2-00011
  20955 W TEJAS TRL 78257   698-7171
  Karlyn Hicks, prin.
Texas Vocational School   2-CS
  1913 S FLORES ST 78204   225-3253
The Winston S   2-11111
  703 TRAFALGAR RD 78216   342-5345
  Charles Karulak, prin.
Trinity University   4-UC
  715 STADIUM DR 78212   800-874-6489
University of Texas at San Antonio   7-UC
  78285   800-669-0919
University of Texas Health Science Ctr.   4-UC
  7703 FLOYD CURL DR 78284   567-2621

San Augustine, AC 409, PC 4, San Augustine
San Augustine ISD   4-11111
  702 HIGH SCHOOL DR 75972   275-2306
  Alfred Broden, supt.
HS, 702 HIGH SCHOOL DR 75972   2-00011
  Leroy Hughes, prin.   275-9603
IS, 1002 BARRETT ST 75972   2-01100
  Warren Norvell, prin.   275-2318

San Benito, AC 210, PC 7, Cameron
San Benito Consolidated ISD   6-11111
  195 W ADELE ST 78586   361-1020
  Hector Ibarra, supt.
HS, 450 S WILLIAMS RD 78586   4-00011
  Robert Tumberlinson, prin.   361-1200
Cabaza MS, 500 N DOWLING ST 78586   3-00100
  Jose Gonzalez, prin.   361-1260
Jordan MS, 700 N DOWLING ST 78586   3-00100
  Antonio Limon, prin.   361-1280

South Texas ISD
  Supt. — See Mercedes
South Texas HS   2-00011
  151 HELEN MOORE RD 78586   399-4331
  Willis Parsons, prin.

Sanderson, AC 915, PC 4, Terrell
Terrell County ISD   2-11111
  PO BOX 747 79848   345-2515
  Kenneth Norris, supt.
HS, PO BOX 747 79848   1-00011
  Philip Dodd, prin.   345-2282
JHS, PO BOX 747 79848   1-00100
  Philip Dodd, prin.   345-2601

San Diego, AC 512, PC 5, Duval
San Diego ISD, 609 W LABBE ST 78384   4-11111
  Braulio Ruelas, supt.   279-3382
HS, 609 W LABBE ST 78384   2-00011
  Alvaro Garza, prin.   279-3382
Jaime JHS, 609 W LABBE ST 78384   2-00100
  Julio Rangel, prin.   279-3373

San Elizario, AC 915, PC 5, El Paso
San Elizario ISD, PO BOX 920 79849   4-11111
  Fred Hase, supt.   851-2780
HS, PO BOX 920 79849   2-00011
  (—), prin.   851-2789
MS, PO BOX 920 79849   2-00100
  Rafaela Pitcher, prin.   851-1035

Sanger, AC 817, PC 5, Denton
Sanger ISD, PO BOX 188 76266   4-11111
  Mike Rosenberg, supt.   458-7438
HS, PO BOX 188 76266   2-00011
  Kent Crutsinger, prin.   458-7497
MS, PO BOX 188 76266   2-00100
  Larry Shuman, prin.   458-7916

San Isidro, AC 210, PC 3, Starr
San Isidro ISD, PO BOX 10 78588   2-11111
  Lisandro Ramon, supt.   481-3311
HS, PO BOX 10 78588   2-00011
  San Juanita Farias, prin.   481-3311

San Juan, AC 210, PC 7, Hidalgo
Pharr-San Juan-Alamo ISD
  Supt. — See Pharr
Austin JHS, PO BOX 1336 78589   4-00100
  Eleazar Romero, prin.   787-5975

San Marcos, AC 512, PC 8, Hays
San Marcos ISD, PO BOX 1087 78667   6-11111
  H. Fuller, supt.   353-6700
HS, 1301 HIGHWAY 123 78666   4-00011
  Nicolas Retana, prin.   396-6800
Goodnight JHS   3-00100
  607 PETER GARZA DR 78666   353-6760
  Susan Perez, prin.

Gary Job Corps Center   4-CS
  PO BOX 967 78667
San Marcos Baptist Academy   2-00111
  2801 RANCH RD 12 78666   353-2400
  Don Davidson, prin.
Southwest Texas State University   7-UC
  601 UNIVERSITY DR 78666   245-2364

San Perlita, AC 210, PC 3, Willacy
San Perlita ISD, PO BOX 37 78590   2-11111
  Jim Crow, supt.   248-5563
S, PO BOX 37 78590   2-11111
  Raul Chapa, prin.   248-5250

San Saba, AC 915, PC 5, San Saba
San Saba ISD, 607 W STOREY ST 76877   3-11111
  W. Grusendorf, supt.   372-3771
HS, 607 W STOREY ST 76877   2-00011
  Samuel Preece, prin.   372-3786
JHS, 607 W STOREY ST 76877   2-00100
  Richard Barker, prin.   372-3698

Santa Anna, AC 915, PC 4, Coleman
Santa Anna ISD, PO BOX 99 76878   2-11111
  Jim McPherson, supt.   348-3136
JSHS, PO BOX 99 76878   2-00011
  Richard Gray, prin.   348-3137

Santa Fe, AC 409, PC 6, Galveston
Santa Fe ISD, PO BOX 370 77510   5-11111
  Richard Ownby, supt.   925-3526
HS, PO BOX 370 77510   4-00011
  Gary Causey, prin.   925-3526
JHS, PO BOX 370 77510   3-00100
  Bob Brundrett, prin.   925-3526

Santa Maria, AC 512, PC 3, Cameron
Santa Maria ISD, PO BOX 448 78592   2-11111
  Homero Garcia, supt.   565-6308
HS, PO BOX 448 78592   2-00011
  Hector Gonzalez, prin.   565-9144
MS, PO BOX 448 78592   2-01100
  Rainer Clover, prin.   565-5318

Santa Rosa, AC 210, PC 4, Cameron
Santa Rosa ISD, PO BOX 368 78593   4-11111
  A. Garcia, supt.   636-1813
HS, PO BOX 368 78593   2-00011
  Andres Contreras, prin.   636-1811
MS, PO BOX 368 78593   2-00100
  Miguel Ruiz, prin.   636-1725

Santo, AC 817, PC 3, Palo Pinto
Santo ISD, PO BOX 67 76472   2-11111
  Robert Stathem, supt.   769-3215
JSHS, PO BOX 67 76472   2-00111
  Edward Munn, prin.   769-3215

Saratoga, AC 409, PC 4, Hardin
West Hardin Consolidated ISD   3-11111
  PO BOX 128 77585   274-5511
  Jay Watson, supt.
West Hardin HS, PO BOX 128 77585   2-00011
  Oscar Whitmire, prin.   274-5061
West Hardin JHS, PO BOX 128 77585   2-00100
  Albert Madsen, prin.   274-5061

Savoy, AC 903, PC 3, Fannin
Savoy ISD, PO BOX 446 75479   2-11111
  David Williams, supt.   965-5262
S, PO BOX 446 75479   2-11111
  Joan Brown, prin.   965-4024

Schertz, AC 512, PC 7, Guadalupe
Schertz-Cibolo-U. City ISD   5-11111
  1060 ELBEL RD 78154   658-3553
  Byron Steele, supt.
Clemens HS, 1001 ELBEL RD 78154   4-00011
  Jerry Mason, prin.   658-3535
Corbett JHS, 301 MAIN 78154   3-00100
  Stephen Nash, prin.   658-3141

Schulenburg, AC 409, PC 4, Fayette
Schulenburg ISD, 517 NORTH ST 78956   3-11111
  Greg Gant, supt.   743-3448
HS, 150 COLLEGE ST 78956   2-00011
  Greg Gant, prin.   743-3605
JHS, 104 LYONS AVE 78956   2-00100
  Michael Bonner, prin.   743-4864

Scurry, AC 214, PC 2, Kaufman
Scurry-Rosser ISD   3-11111
  10717 S STATE HIGHWAY 34 75158   452-8823
  Harold Johnson, supt.
Scurry-Rosser HS   2-00011
  10729 S STATE HIGHWAY 34 75158   452-3292
  Travis Stodghill, prin.
Scurry-Rosser MS   2-00100
  10717 S STATE HIGHWAY 34 75158   452-8844
  James Whitworth, prin.

Seabrook, AC 713, PC 6, Harris
Clear Creek ISD
  Supt. — See League City
Seabrook IS, 2401 MEYER RD 77586   3-00100
  (—), prin.   474-2539

Seadrift, AC 512, PC 4, Calhoun
Calhoun County ISD
 Supt. — See Port Lavaca
 Fannin MS, PO BOX 279   77983 — 2-00100
  John Woods, prin. — 785-3451

Seagoville, AC 214, PC 6, Dallas
Dallas ISD
 Supt. — See Dallas
 MS, 808 HIGH SCHOOL DR   75159 — 3-00100
  Wayne Neu, prin. — 557-6250

Seagraves, AC 806, PC 4, Gaines
Seagraves ISD, PO BOX 577   79359 — 3-11111
  M. Kinnison, supt. — 546-2035
 HS, PO BOX 1505   79359 — 2-00011
  Gary Cox, prin. — 546-2520
 JHS, PO BOX 938   79359 — 2-00100
  Warren Wallace, prin. — 546-2646

Sealy, AC 409, PC 5, Austin
Sealy ISD, 939 WEST ST   77474 — 4-11111
  Thomas Golson, supt. — 885-3516
 HS, 939 WEST ST   77474 — 2-00011
  Charles Lincecum, prin. — 885-3515
 JHS, 939 WEST ST   77474 — 3-01100
  Aubrey Stuessel, prin. — 885-3292

Seguin, AC 210, PC 7, Guadalupe
Seguin ISD, PO BOX 31   78156 — 6-11111
  Charles Holloway, supt. — 372-5770
 HS, 815 LAMAR   78155 — 4-00011
  Alfonso Lopez, prin. — 372-5770
 Briesemeister MS — 3-00100
  1616 W COURT ST   78155 — 379-0660
  John Burks, prin.
 Saegert MS, 118 N BOWIE ST   78155 — 2-00100
  John Burks, prin. — 379-4717

Texas Lutheran College — 4-UC
 1000 W COURT ST   78155 — 800-880-1107

Seminole, AC 915, PC 6, Gaines
Seminole ISD, PO BOX 900   79360 — 4-11111
  Robert Ryan, supt. — 758-3662
 HS, PO BOX 900   79360 — 3-00011
  Vernon Paul, prin. — 758-5873
 JHS, PO BOX 900   79360 — 3-00100
  Allan Bryson, prin. — 758-9431

Seymour, AC 817, PC 5, Baylor
Seymour ISD, 409 W IDAHO ST   76380 — 3-11111
  Benjamin Grill, supt. — 888-3525
 JSHS, 409 W IDAHO ST   76380 — 2-00111
  Jim Lee, prin. — 888-2947

Shallowater, AC 806, PC 4, Lubbock
Shallowater ISD, PO BOX 220   79363 — 4-11111
  C. Hohertz, supt. — 832-4531
 HS, PO BOX 220   79363 — 2-00011
  Tom Townsend, prin. — 832-4535
 MS, PO BOX 220   79363 — 2-00100
  William Garland, prin. — 832-4531

Shamrock, AC 806, PC 4, Wheeler
Shamrock ISD, 100 S ILLINOIS ST   79079 — 2-11111
  Ron Gregory, supt. — 256-3492
 S, 100 S ILLINOIS ST   79079 — 2-11111
  Quince Cogburn, prin. — 256-2241

Shelbyville, AC 409, PC 2, Shelby
Shelbyville ISD, PO BOX 325   75973 — 3-11111
  Curtis Williams, supt. — 598-2641
 S, PO BOX 325   75973 — 3-11111
  Rudy Eddington, prin. — 598-7323

Shepherd, AC 409, PC 4, San Jacinto
Shepherd ISD, PO BOX 429   77371 — 4-11111
  R. Corn, supt. — 628-3396
 HS, PO BOX 429   77371 — 2-00011
  William Shaw, prin. — 628-3371
 JHS, 28 RAILROAD AVE S   77371 — 2-01100
  Roger Williams, prin. — 628-3377

Sherman, AC 903, PC 8, Grayson
Sherman ISD, PO BOX 1176   75091 — 6-11111
  Robert Denton, supt. — 892-9115
 HS, 2201 E LAMAR ST   75090 — 4-00011
  Phillip Garrett, prin. — 893-8101
 Piner MS, 402 W PECAN ST   75090 — 3-00100
  Charles Byler, prin. — 893-4395

Austin College — 4-UC
 900 N GRAND AVE   75090 — 800-442-5363
 International Business School — 2-CS
 4107 TEXOMA PKY   75090 — 893-6604

Shiner, AC 512, PC 4, Lavaca
Shiner ISD, PO BOX 804   77984 — 3-11111
  Aubrey O'Bannion, supt. — 594-3121
 JSHS, PO BOX 804   77984 — 2-00111
  W. Zimmerman, prin. — 594-3131

St. Paul Academy — 2-11111
 424 SAINT LUDMILA ST   77984 — 594-2313
 Patricia Pesek, prin.

Sidney, AC 817, PC 1, Comanche
Sidney ISD, PO BOX 190   76474 — 2-11111
  D. Andrews, supt. — 842-5500
 S, PO BOX 190   76474 — 2-11111
  John Rodgers, prin. — 842-5500

Sierra Blanca, AC 915, PC 3, Hudspeth
Sierra Blanca ISD, PO BOX 308   79851 — 2-11111
  Henry Dyer, supt. — 369-3741
 S, PO BOX 308   79851 — 2-11111
  (—), prin. — 369-2781

Silsbee, AC 409, PC 6, Hardin
Silsbee ISD, 415 W AVENUE N   77656 — 5-11111
  Herbert Muckleroy, supt. — 385-5288
 HS, 1140 HIGHWAY 327 E   77656 — 4-00011
  Ronald Nash, prin. — 385-5574
 MS, 1005 N 7TH ST   77656 — 3-00100
  Bill Conway, prin. — 385-2291

Silverton, AC 806, PC 3, Briscoe
Silverton ISD, PO BOX 608   79257 — 2-11111
  Frank Kirchoffner, supt. — 823-2476
 S, PO BOX 608   79257 — 2-11111
  Stan Fogerson, prin. — 823-2476

Simms, AC 903, PC 2, Bowie
Simms ISD, PO BOX 8   75574 — 2-11111
  Gerald Stegall, supt. — 543-2219
 Bowie JSHS, PO BOX 8   75574 — 2-00111
  Larry Mathews, prin. — 543-2275

Sinton, AC 512, PC 6, San Patricio
Sinton ISD, PO BOX 1337   78387 — 4-11111
  Roy Pugh, supt. — 364-1190
 HS, 400 N PIRATE BLVD   78387 — 3-00011
  J. Don Jones, prin. — 364-4080
 Smith JHS — 2-00100
  900 S SAN PATRICIO ST   78387 — 364-4143
  Reynaldo Torres, prin.

Skidmore, AC 512, PC 3, Bee
Skidmore-Tynan ISD — 3-11111
 PO BOX 409   78389 — 287-3426
  Steven Tom, supt.
 Skidmore-Tynan HS — 2-00011
 PO BOX 409   78389 — 287-3427
  Michael Cogburn, prin.
 Skidmore-Tynan JHS — 2-00100
 PO BOX 409   78389 — 287-3424
  Alfredo Maldonado, prin.

Slaton, AC 806, PC 6, Lubbock
Slaton ISD, 300 S 9TH ST   79364 — 4-11111
  Jerry Hogue, supt. — 828-6591
 HS, 100 N 20TH ST   79364 — 2-00011
  James Starkey, prin. — 828-5833
 JHS, 100 W JEAN ST   79364 — 2-00100
  Ricky Tiffin, prin. — 828-6583

Slidell, AC 817, PC 2, Wise
Slidell ISD, PO BOX 69   76267 — 2-11111
  Elizabeth Treadway, supt. — 466-3118
 S, PO BOX 69   76267 — 2-11111
  Eugene Franklin, prin. — 466-3118

Smithville, AC 512, PC 5, Bastrop
Smithville ISD, PO BOX 479   78957 — 4-11111
  Larry Edwards, supt. — 237-2487
 HS, PO BOX 479   78957 — 2-00011
  John Thornell, prin. — 237-2451
 JHS, PO BOX 479   78957 — 2-00100
  Gene Sampson, prin. — 237-2407

Smyer, AC 806, PC 2, Hockley
Smyer ISD, PO BOX 206   79367 — 2-11111
  James Allison, supt. — 234-2935
 JSHS, PO BOX 206   79367 — 2-00111
  Dane Kerns, prin. — 234-3871

Snook, AC 409, PC 2, Burleson
Snook ISD, PO BOX 87   77878 — 2-11111
  Floyd Jackson, supt. — 272-8307
 S, PO BOX 87   77878 — 2-11111
  Melvin Schoeneman, prin. — 272-8307

Snyder, AC 915, PC 7, Scurry
Snyder ISD, 2901 37TH ST   79549 — 5-11111
  Dalton Moseley, supt. — 573-5401
 HS, 2901 37TH ST   79549 — 3-00011
  Larry Scott, prin. — 573-6301
 JHS, 2901 37TH ST   79549 — 3-00100
  Alfred Solis, prin. — 573-6356

Western Texas College — 4-CC
 6200 COLLEGE AVE   79549 — 573-8511

Somerset, AC 210, PC 4, Bexar
Somerset ISD, PO BOX 279   78069 — 4-11111
  Ann Dixon, supt. — 622-3462
 HS, PO BOX 279   78069 — 2-00011
  Shirleen Zacharias, prin. — 622-5671
 JHS, PO BOX 279   78069 — 2-00100
  Raymond Carmickle, prin. — 622-5673

Somerville, AC 409, PC 4, Burleson
Somerville ISD, PO BOX 997   77879 — 3-11111
  James Schroeder, supt. — 596-2153
 HS, PO BOX 997   77879 — 2-00011
  James Rosebrock, prin. — 596-1534
 JHS, PO BOX 997   77879 — 2-00100
  Ann Shumate, prin. — 596-1461

Sonora, AC 915, PC 5, Sutton
Sonora ISD, 807 S CONCHO AVE   76950 — 4-11111
  Charles Russell, supt. — 387-2220
 HS, 807 S CONCHO AVE   76950 — 2-00011
  Terrell Marrs, prin. — 387-6533
 JHS, 807 S CONCHO AVE   76950 — 2-00100
  Janet Patton, prin. — 387-3023

Sour Lake, AC 409, PC 4, Hardin
Hardin-Jefferson ISD — 4-11111
 PO BOX 490   77659 — 287-3571
  Jim Coulston, supt.
 Hardin-Jefferson HS — 3-00011
 PO BOX 639   77659 — 287-3565
  James Faulkner, prin.
 Other Schools – See China

South Houston, AC 713, PC 7, Harris
Pasadena ISD
 Supt. — See Pasadena
 HS, 3820 S SHAVER ST   77587 — 4-00011
  Doris Barnes, prin. — 944-2450
 IS, 900 COLLEGE AVE   77587 — 4-00100
  Lucas Vegas, prin. — 946-7247

Southlake, AC 817, PC 6, Tarrant
Carroll ISD — 4-11111
 1201 N CARROLL AVE   76092 — 481-5775
  William Branum, supt.
 Carroll HS — 3-00011
 1501 W SOUTHLAKE BLVD   76092 — 481-2185
  Linda Smiles, prin.
 Carroll MS, 1101 E DOVE RD   76092 — 3-00100
  Richard Wilkinson, prin. — 481-2183

Southland, AC 806, PC 2, Garza
Southland ISD, RR 2 BOX 103   79364 — 2-11111
  Terry Smith, supt. — 996-5599
 JSHS, RR 2 BOX 103   79364 — 2-00111
  Brett Koch, prin. — 996-5330

Spade, AC 806, PC 2, Lamb
Spade ISD, PO BOX 69   79369 — 2-11111
  David Case, supt. — 233-2521
 S, PO BOX 69   79369 — 2-11111
  Clint Carpenter, prin. — 233-2131

Spearman, AC 806, PC 5, Hansford
Spearman ISD, 403 E 11TH AVE   79081 — 3-11111
  Willard Murrey, supt. — 659-3233
 HS, 403 E 11TH AVE   79081 — 2-00011
  Sam Atwood, prin. — 659-2584
 JHS, 315 W 5TH AVE   79081 — 2-00100
  Larry Morris, prin. — 659-2563

Splendora, AC 713, PC 3, Montgomery
Splendora ISD, PO BOX 168   77372 — 4-11111
  Leon Cubillas, supt. — 689-3128
 HS, PO BOX 168   77372 — 3-00011
  Ken Williams, prin. — 689-3125
 JHS, PO BOX 168   77372 — 2-00100
  Dairell Hurst, prin. — 689-6343

Spring, AC 713, PC 8, Harris
Klein ISD
 Supt. — See Klein
 Klein Oak HS — 4-00011
 22603 NORTHCREST DR   77389 — 320-4450
  Byron Rushing, prin.
 Hildebrandt IS — 4-00100
 22800 HILDEBRANDT RD   77389 — 320-4200
  Laurence Liles, prin.
 Spring ISD
 Supt. — See Houston
 HS, 19428 INTERSTATE 45   77373 — 4-00011
  Gloria Marshall, prin. — 353-3465
 Wunsche S — 2-11111
 800 SPRING CYPRESS RD   77373 — 353-0120
  Denise Drexler, prin.
 Dueitt MS, 5119 TREASCHWIG RD   77373 — 3-00100
  Rosalind Keck, prin. — 350-2518
 Twin Creeks MS — 4-00100
 27100 CYPRESSWOOD DR   77373 — 353-5451
  Mike Mier, prin.

Spring Branch, AC 512, PC 1, Comal
Comal ISD
 Supt. — See New Braunfels
 Smithson Valley HS — 3-00011
 14001 STATE HIGHWAY 46 W   78070 — 885-7273
  Joe Rogers, prin.
 Smithson Valley MS — 3-00100
 6101 FM 311   78070 — 885-7000
  Patrick Hollis, prin.

Springtown, AC 817, PC 4, Parker
Springtown ISD, 101 E 2ND ST   76082 — 5-11111
  Lloyd Treadwell, supt. — 523-7243
 HS, 300 PO JO DR   76082 — 3-00011
  Clarence Culwell, prin. — 523-4816
 MS, 500 PO JO DR   76082 — 3-00100
  Michael Gilley, prin. — 523-7281

Spur, AC 806, PC 4, Dickens
Spur ISD, PO BOX 550   79370 — 2-11111
  E. Hamilton, supt. — 271-3272
 JSHS, 800 CALVERT AVE   79370 — 2-00111
  Ron Walker, prin. — 271-3385

Spurger, AC 409, PC 3, Tyler
Spurger ISD, PO BOX 38   77660 — 2-11111
  John Lewis, supt. — 429-3464
 HS, PO BOX 38   77660 — 2-00011
  James Swinney, prin. — 429-3327
 JHS, PO BOX 38   77660 — 2-00100
  James Swinney, prin. — 429-3327

Stafford, AC 713, PC 6, Fort Bend
Stafford Metro SD — 4-11111
 1625 STAFFORDSHIRE RD   77477 — 261-9200
  Gary Rotan, supt.
 HS, 1625 STAFFORDSHIRE RD   77477 — 2-00011
  Don Levinski, prin. — 261-9239

MS, 1625 STAFFORDSHIRE RD 77477   2-00100
   David Pirtle, prin.   261-9215

Stamford, AC 915, PC 5, Jones
Stamford ISD, 507 S ORIENT ST 79553   3-11111
   Robert Damron, supt.   773-2705
JSHS, 507 S ORIENT ST 79553   2-00011
   Tom Bearden, prin.   773-2701

Stanton, AC 915, PC 5, Martin
Stanton ISD, PO BOX 730 79782   3-11111
   John McGregor, supt.   756-2244
HS, PO BOX 730 79782   2-00011
   Jim White, prin.   756-3326
MS, PO BOX 730 79782   2-00100
   Bill Young, prin.   756-2544

Star, AC 915, PC 2, Mills
Star ISD, PO BOX 838 76880   1-11111
   James Ethridge, supt.   948-3661
S, PO BOX 838 76880   1-11111
   Henry Lind, prin.   948-3661

Stephenville, AC 817, PC 7, Erath
Huckabay ISD, RR 4 BOX 182 76401   2-11111
   James Stone, supt.   968-5274
S, RR 4 BOX 182 76401   2-11111
   Arley Echols, prin.   968-5274

Stephenville ISD   5-11111
   726 N CLINTON ST 76401   968-7990
   George Gilbert, supt.
HS, 2650 W OVERHILL DR 76401   3-00011
   Garry Horn, prin.   968-4141
JHS, 1067 W JONES ST 76401   2-00100
   Edmond Henderson, prin.   968-6967

Tarleton State University   6-UC
   1297 W WASHINGTON ST 76402   968-9000

Sterling City, AC 915, PC 4, Sterling
Sterling City ISD, PO BOX 786 76951   2-11111
   Wilbur Thompson, supt.   378-4781
S, PO BOX 786 76951   2-11111
   Ron Krejci, prin.   378-5821

Stinnett, AC 806, PC 4, Hutchinson
Plemons-Stinnett-Phillips ISD   3-11111
   PO BOX 3440 79083   878-2858
   Joel Lynch, supt.
West Texas HS, PO BOX Y 79083   2-00011
   Mike Horton, prin.   878-2456
West Texas MS, PO BOX Y 79083   2-00100
   Robin Adkins, prin.   878-2247

Stockdale, AC 210, PC 4, Wilson
Stockdale ISD, PO BOX 7 78160   3-11111
   Bennie Wolff, supt.   996-3551
HS, PO BOX 7 78160   2-00011
   Neal Harris, prin.   996-3103
JHS, PO BOX 7 78160   2-00100
   Glenn Thompson, prin.   996-3153

Stratford, AC 806, PC 4, Sherman
Stratford ISD, PO BOX 108 79084   2-11111
   Sam Brite, supt.   396-5571
HS, PO BOX 108 79084   2-00011
   Steve Haynes, prin.   396-2341
JHS, PO BOX 108 79084   2-01100
   James Taliaferro, prin.   396-5690

Strawn, AC 817, PC 3, Palo Pinto
Strawn ISD, PO BOX 428 76475   2-11111
   Andrew Lindsey, supt.   672-5313
S, PO BOX 428 76475   2-11111
   Bradley Bressie, prin.   672-5776

Sudan, AC 806, PC 3, Lamb
Sudan ISD, PO BOX 249 79371   2-11111
   Hollis Lowrance, supt.   227-2431
JSHS, PO BOX 249 79371   2-00111
   Roy Willingham, prin.   227-2336

Sugar Land, AC 713, PC 7, Fort Bend
Fort Bend ISD, PO BOX 1004 77487   8-11111
   Raj Chopra, supt.   980-1300
Clements HS, PO BOX 1004 77487   4-00011
   Betty Baitland, prin.   980-6899
Dulles HS, PO BOX 1004 77487   5-00011
   Charles Marshall, prin.   491-7100
Elkins HS, PO BOX 1004 77487   4-00011
   James Patterson, prin.   261-7600
Kempner HS, PO BOX 1004 77487   5-00011
   Michael Emerson, prin.   242-4100
Willowridge HS, PO BOX 1004 77487   5-00011
   Yvonne Friday, prin.   437-1988
Fort Bend Area Career S   Vo Tech
   PO BOX 1004 77487   491-7100
   Stephen Pike, prin.
Dulles JHS, PO BOX 1004 77487   4-00100
   Leland Wilhelm, prin.   491-7100
First Colony JHS   4-00100
   PO BOX 1004 77487   980-6899
   Debbie Dunlap, prin.
Hodges Bend JHS   4-00100
   PO BOX 1004 77487   242-4100
   James Gant, prin.
Lake Olympia MS   4-00100
   PO BOX 1004 77487   980-1300
   Kay Saunders, prin.
McAuliffe JHS, PO BOX 1004 77487   4-00100
   Ross Gahee, prin.   437-1988
Missouri City JHS   3-00100
   PO BOX 1004 77487   499-9537
   Harrison Hodge, prin.

Quail Valley JHS   4-00100
   PO BOX 1004 77487   499-5516
   Michael Leach, prin.
JHS, PO BOX 1004 77487   4-00100
   Vernon Madden, prin.   242-4100

Sulphur Bluff, AC 903, PC 2, Hopkins
Sulphur Bluff ISD, PO BOX 30 75481   2-11111
   Charles Fielden, supt.   945-2460
S, PO BOX 7 75481   2-11111
   James Morton, prin.   945-2460

Sulphur Springs, AC 903, PC 7, Hopkins
North Hopkins ISD   2-11111
   RR 3 BOX 486 75482   945-2192
   Tom Long, supt.
North Hopkins JSHS   2-00111
   RR 3 BOX 486 75482   945-2192
   Rick Teran, prin.

Sulphur Springs ISD   5-11111
   631 CONNALLY ST 75482   885-2153
   Paul Glover, supt.
HS, 1200 CONNALLY ST 75482   4-00011
   Judy Tipping, prin.   885-6669
MS, 800 BELL ST 75482   3-00100
   Foy Williams, prin.   885-7721

Sundown, AC 806, PC 4, Hockley
Sundown ISD, PO BOX 1110 79372   3-11111
   G. Lasater, supt.   229-3021
HS, PO BOX 1110 79372   2-00011
   Mike Motheral, prin.   229-2511
JHS, PO BOX 1110 79372   2-00100
   James Mitchell, prin.   229-4691

Sunray, AC 806, PC 4, Moore
Sunray ISD, PO BOX 240 79086   3-11111
   Richard Oller, supt.   948-4411
HS, PO BOX 240 79086   2-00011
   George Porter, prin.   948-5515

Sweeny, AC 409, PC 5, Brazoria
Sweeny ISD, 1310 N ELM ST 77480   4-11111
   Andrew Shanks, supt.   548-2731
HS, 1310 N ELM ST 77480   3-00011
   Randy Miksch, prin.   548-2157
JHS, 1310 N ELM ST 77480   3-00100
   Lester Dupler, prin.   548-3361

Sweetwater, AC 915, PC 7, Nolan
Sweetwater ISD   5-11111
   207 MUSGROVE ST 79556   235-8601
   David Welch, supt.
HS, 1205 RAGLAND ST 79556   3-00011
   Joe Marlett, prin.   235-4371
MS, 305 LAMAR ST 79556   3-00100
   Miguel Ramos, prin.   236-6303

Texas State Technical Institute   3-CC
   PO BOX 18 79556   800-592-8784

Taft, AC 512, PC 5, San Patricio
Taft ISD, 400 COLLEGE ST 78390   4-11111
   Ruben Corkill, supt.   528-2636
HS, 502 RINCON RD 78390   2-00011
   Ralph Garrett, prin.   528-3212
JHS, 727 MCINTYRE AVE 78390   2-00100
   David Tamez, prin.   528-2646

Tahoka, AC 806, PC 5, Lynn
Tahoka ISD, PO BOX 1230 79373   3-11111
   James Carter, supt.   998-4105
JSHS, PO BOX 1230 79373   2-00111
   Charles Cate, prin.   998-4538

Tatum, AC 903, PC 4, Rusk
Tatum ISD, PO BOX 808 75691   4-11111
   Jack Clemmons, supt.   947-6482
HS, PO BOX 808 75691   2-00011
   Robert Williams, prin.   947-6482
MS, PO BOX 808 75691   2-00100
   Stacey Bryce, prin.   947-6482

Taylor, AC 512, PC 7, Williamson
Taylor ISD, 602 W 12TH ST 76574   4-11111
   Herman Smith, supt.   352-6361
HS, 3101 N MAIN ST 76574   3-00011
   Carroll Ruthven, prin.   352-6326
MS, 410 W 7TH ST 76574   3-00100
   Larry Sutton, prin.   352-2815

Teague, PC 5, Freestone
Teague ISD, 800 MAIN ST 75860   4-11111
   Gary Barker, supt.   817-739-3071
HS   3-00011
   HIGHWAY 84 & LOOP 255 75860
   Bud Lowe, prin.   817-739-2532
JHS   2-00100
   HIGHWAY 84 & LOOP 255 75860
   Orvis Meggs, prin.   817-739-3011

Temple, AC 817, PC 8, Bell
Temple ISD, PO BOX 788 76503   6-11111
   Jack Reeves, supt.   778-6721
HS, 415 N 31ST ST 76504   4-00011
   Rex Lawson, prin.   778-6721
Bonham MS, 4600 MIDWAY DR 76502   3-00100
   Candance Medley, prin.   773-1501
Lamar MS, 2120 N 1ST ST 76501   3-00100
   Ron Henson, prin.   778-2746
Travis MS, 1500 S 19TH ST 76504   3-00100
   Nelda Howton, prin.   778-2781

Scott & White Memorial Hospital & Clinic   2-HSP
   2401 S 31ST ST 76508   774-2111
Temple Junior College   4-CC
   2600 S 1ST ST 76504   773-9961

Tenaha, AC 409, PC 4, Shelby
Tenaha ISD, PO BOX 318 75974   2-11111
   Melvin Kennedy, supt.   248-3311
JSHS, PO BOX 318 75974   2-00111
   (—), prin.   248-3931

Terrell, AC 214, PC 7, Kaufman
Terrell ISD, 212 W HIGH ST 75160   5-11111
   James Wood, supt.   563-7504
HS, 400 POETRY RD 75160   3-00011
   Herman Furlough, prin.   563-7525
MS, 701 TOWN DR N 75160   3-00100
   Oscar Hinchen, prin.   563-7501

Southwestern Christian College   2-UC
   PO BOX 10 75160   524-3341
Terrell Christian S   2-11111
   805 JOHNSON ST 75160   563-5291
   Martin Schumaker, prin.

Texarkana, AC 903, PC 8, Bowie
Liberty-Eylau ISD   5-11111
   2901 LEOPARD DR 75501   832-1535
   Nicholas Blain, supt.
Liberty-Eylau HS   3-00011
   2905 LEOPARD DR 75501   832-1535
   Donald Rader, prin.
Liberty-Eylau MS   3-00100
   5555 LEOPARD DR 75501   838-5555
   Bill Hastings, prin.

Pleasant Grove ISD   4-11111
   5605 COOKS LN 75503   831-4086
   Margaret Davis, supt.
Pleasant Grove HS   3-00011
   5406 MCKNIGHT RD 75501   832-8005
   Kelly Rodgers, prin.
Pleasant Grove MS   3-01100
   5605 COOKS LN 75503   831-4295
   Michael Roberts, prin.

Texarkana ISD   6-11111
   4241 SUMMERHILL RD 75503   794-3651
   Gary Collins, supt.
Texas HS, 2112 KENNEDY LN 75503   4-00011
   James McSwain, prin.   794-3891
Pine Street MS, 1915 PINE ST 75501   3-00100
   George Moore, prin.   793-5631
Westlawn MS   3-00100
   410 WESTLAWN DR 75501   838-4565
   Gwendolyn Poteet, prin.

East Texas State University   3-UC
   PO BOX 5518 75505   838-6514
Texarkana Community College   5-CC
   2500 N ROBISON RD 75501   838-4541
Wadley Hospital   HSP
   PO BOX 1878 75504   793-4511

Texas City, AC 409, PC 8, Galveston
Texas City ISD, PO BOX 1150 77592   6-11111
   Leonard Merrell, supt.   942-2713
HS, 1800 9TH AVE N 77590   4-00011
   William Martin, prin.   942-2645
Blocker MS, 500 14TH AVE N 77590   3-00100
   R. Carter, prin.   942-2756

College of the Mainland   5-CC
   1200 N AMBURN RD 77591   938-1211

Texline, AC 806, PC 2, Dallam
Texline ISD, PO BOX 60 79087   2-11111
   Dean Foshee, supt.   362-4667
S, PO BOX 60 79087   2-11111
   Allen Jackson, prin.   362-4284

The Colony, AC 214, PC 7, Denton
Lewisville ISD
   Supt. — See Lewisville
HS, 4301 BLAIR OAKS DR 75056   4-00011
   Mitchell Hall, prin.   625-9000
Griffin MS   3-00100
   5105 N COLONY BLVD 75056   625-9030
   Beverly Faries, prin.
Lakeview MS, 4300 KEYS DR 75056   3-00100
   Ben Swearingen, prin.   625-9040

The Woodlands, AC 713, PC 8, Montgomery
Conroe ISD
   Supt. — See Conroe
McCullough HS   4-00011
   3800 S PANTHER CREEK DR 77381   292-4455
   Elizabeth Gardner, prin.
Knox JHS, 12104 SAWMILL RD 77380   4-00100
   Mary Jones, prin.   367-0010

Cooper S   2-11111
   3333 COCHRANS CROSSING DR 77381
   Raymond Bailey, prin.   367-0900

Thorndale, AC 512, PC 4, Milam
Thorndale ISD, PO BOX 336 76577   2-11111
   Jerry Doherty, supt.   898-2538
JSHS, PO BOX 336 76577   2-00111
   Heather Klotz, prin.   898-2321

Thrall, AC 512, PC 3, Williamson
Thrall ISD, PO BOX 398 76578   2-11111
Thomas Bowman, supt.   898-5193
JSHS, PO BOX 398 76578   2-00011
Jack Jordan, prin.   898-5138

Three Rivers, AC 512, PC 4, Live Oak
Three Rivers ISD, PO BOX 640 78071   3-11111
Charles Arnott, supt.   786-3626
HS, PO BOX 640 78071   2-00011
Donald Kasper, prin.   786-3531
MS, PO BOX 640 78071   2-00100
Curry Newport, prin.   786-3803

Throckmorton, AC 817, PC 4, Throckmorton
Throckmorton ISD   2-11111
210 COLLEGE ST 76483   849-2411
Ward Cooksey, supt.
JSHS, 210 CCLLEGE ST 76483   2-00111
Larry Letbetter, prin.   849-2421

Tilden, AC 512, PC 2, McMullen
McMullen County ISD   2-11111
PO BOX 359 78072   274-3315
Frank Franklin, supt.
McMullen County S   2-11111
PO BOX 359 78072   274-3315
Jim Bauman, prin.

Timpson, AC 409, PC 4, Shelby
Timpson ISD, PO BOX 370 75975   3-11111
Rich Higgenbotham, supt.   254-2463
HS, PO BOX 370 75975   2-00011
Robert Cousins, prin.   254-3125

Tivoli, AC 512, PC 3, Refugio
Austwell-Tivoli ISD   2-11111
RR 1 BOX 995 77990   286-3212
B. Welkener, supt.
Austwell-Tivoli JSHS   1-00111
RR 1 BOX 995 77990   286-3582
Antonio Aguirre, prin.

Tolar, AC 817, PC 3, Hood
Tolar ISD, PO BOX 368 76476   2-11111
Dale Taylor, supt.   835-4317
S, PO BOX 368 76476   2-11111
Charles Carroll, prin.   835-4316

Tomball, AC 713, PC 6, Harris
Tomball ISD, 221 W MAIN ST 77375   5-11111
Rex Carr, supt.   357-3100
HS, 13705 SANDY LN 77375   4-00011
R. Todd, prin.   357-3220
JHS, 221 W MAIN ST 77375   3-00100
John Bailey, prin.   357-3000

Tom Bean, AC 903, PC 3, Grayson
Tom Bean ISD, PO BOX 128 75489   3-11111
Sheri Sides, supt.   546-6076
HS, PO BOX 128 75489   2-00011
A. Quinn, prin.   546-6319
MS, PO BOX 128 75489   2-00100
Richard Horner, prin.   546-6161

Tornillo, AC 915, PC 3, El Paso
Tornillo ISD, PO BOX 170 79853   2-11111
John Sutton, supt.   764-2366
S, PO BOX 170 79853   2-11111
Gloria Levins, prin.   764-2040

Trent, AC 915, PC 2, Taylor
Trent ISD, PO BOX 105 79561   2-11111
Bob Howell, supt.   862-6400
S, PO BOX 105 79561   2-11111
John Stevens, prin.   862-6125

Trenton, AC 903, PC 3, Fannin
Trenton ISD, PO BOX 5 75490   2-11111
Daniel Jones, supt.   989-2242
JSHS, PO BOX 5 75490   2-00111
Gary Bohannon, prin.   989-2242

Trinidad, AC 903, PC 4, Henderson
Trinidad ISD, PO BOX 349 75163   2-11111
John Singleton, supt.   778-2673
S, PO BOX 349 75163   2-11111
Randy Hutchins, prin.   778-2415

Trinity, AC 409, PC 5, Trinity
Trinity ISD, PO BOX 752 75862   4-11111
Robert Henderson, supt.   594-3569
HS, PO BOX 752 75862   2-00011
John Copley, prin.   594-3560
JHS, PO BOX 752 75862   2-00100
Michael Holland, prin.   594-2321

Troup, AC 903, PC 4, Smith
Troup ISD, PO BOX 578 75789   3-11111
Gene Whitsell, supt.   842-3065
HS, PO BOX 578 75789   2-00011
Cecil Brown, prin.   842-3065
MS, PO BOX 578 75789   2-00100
Michael Payne, prin.   842-3071

Troy, AC 817, PC 4, Bell
Troy ISD, PO BOX 409 76579   4-11111
John Gibler, supt.   938-2543
HS, PO BOX 409 76579   2-00011
Jerry Hargrove, prin.   938-2561
MS, PO BOX 409 76579   2-00100
Larry Hennig, prin.   938-2544

Tulia, AC 806, PC 5, Swisher
Tulia ISD, 702 NW 8TH ST 79088   4-11111
Joe Vinyard, supt.   995-4591

HS, 501 NE 4TH ST 79088   2-00011
Linda Hicks, prin.   995-2759
JHS, 401 NE 3RD ST 79088   2-00100
Don Stout, prin.   995-4842

Turkey, AC 806, PC 3, Hall
Turkey-Quitaque ISD   2-11111
PO BOX 397 79261   455-1411
Jerry Smith, supt.
Valley S, PO BOX 397 79261   2-11111
Jon Davidson, prin.   455-1411

Tuscola, AC 915, PC 3, Taylor
Jim Ned ISD, PO BOX 9 79562   3-11111
R. Kenneth Crouch, supt.   554-7500
Jim Ned HS   2-00011
9TH ST AND HIGHWAY 83 79562   554-7755
Dale Lefevre, prin.

Tyler, AC 903, PC 8, Smith
Chapel Hill ISD   5-11111
11134 COUNTY ROAD 2249 75707   566-2441
John Johnston, supt.
Chapel Hill HS   3-00011
13172 STATE HIGHWAY 64 E 75707   566-2311
Bob Watkins, prin.
Chapel Hill MS   3-01100
13174 STATE HIGHWAY 64 E 75707   566-1491
Thomasine Norris-Cleaver, prin.

Tyler ISD, PO BOX 2035 75710   7-11111
Thomas Hagler, supt.   531-3500
Lee HS   4-00011
411 E SOUTHEAST LOOP 323 75701   531-3900
Glen Milham, prin.
HS   4-00011
1120 N NORTHWEST LOOP 323 75702   531-9200
Alfred Ray, prin.
Boulter MS   3-00100
2926 GARDEN VALLEY RD 75702   531-3700
Nathan Hollis, prin.
Dogan MS, 2621 N BORDER AVE 75702   2-00100
Zeb Cantley, prin.   531-3710
Hogg MS, 920 S BROADWAY AVE 75701   2-00100
James Moyers, prin.   531-3720
Hubbard MS, 1300 HUBBARD DR 75703   4-00100
Martha Raney, prin.   531-3850
Moore MS, 1200 S TIPTON AVE 75701   3-00100
Al Harris, prin.   531-3730
Stewart MS, 2800 W SHAW ST 75701   2-00100
Gerald Barnes, prin.   531-3740

Bishop Gorman HS   2-01111
1405 E NORTHEAST LOOP 323 75708
Rosemary Henry-Caruth, prin.   561-2424
Careers Unlimited   2-CS
335 S BONNER AVE 75702   593-4424
Texas College   2-UC
2404 N GRAND AVE 75702   593-8311
Tyler Junior College   6-CC
PO BOX 9020 75711   510-2398
University of Texas at Tyler   5-UC
3900 UNIVERSITY BLVD 75799   800-888-9537

Universal City, AC 512, PC 7, Bexar
Judson ISD
Supt. — See Converse
Kitty Hawk JHS   3-00100
840 OLD CIMMARON TRL 78148   659-1928
Steve Blackmon, prin.

Randolph Field ISD   4-11111
PO BOX 2217 78148   658-3576
Barbara Maddox, supt.
Randolph HS, PO BOX 2217 78148   2-00011
Bruce Cannon, prin.   658-6391
Randolph MS, PO BOX 2217 78148   2-00100
Bruce Cannon, prin.   658-6391

Utopia, AC 210, PC 2, Uvalde
Utopia ISD, PO BOX 218 78884   2-11111
J. McFadin, supt.   966-3339
S, PO BOX 218 78884   2-11111
Alice Causey, prin.   966-3339

Uvalde, AC 210, PC 7, Uvalde
Uvalde Consolidated ISD   6-11111
PO BOX 1909 78802   278-6655
John Harrell, supt.
HS, PO BOX 1909 78802   4-00011
Noris Garcia, prin.   278-2571
JHS, PO BOX 1909 78802   3-00100
Gayle Watkins, prin.   278-4413

Southwest Texas Junior College   4-CC
2401 GARNER FIELD RD 78801   278-4401

Valentine, AC 915, PC 2, Jeff Davis
Valentine ISD, PO BOX 188 79854   1-11111
J. Lusk, supt.   467-2671
S, PO BOX 188 79854   1-11111
(—), prin.   467-2671

Valley Mills, AC 817, PC 4, Bosque
Valley Mills ISD, PO BOX 518 76689   3-11111
Gary Patterson, supt.   932-5210
JSHS, PO BOX 518 76689   2-00111
David Jacobs, prin.   932-5251

Valley View, AC 817, PC 3, Cooke
Valley View ISD, PO BOX 125 76272   3-11111
Steven Schneider, supt.   726-3522
S, PO BOX 125 76272   3-11111
Beverly Hogan, prin.   726-3522

Van, AC 903, PC 4, Van Zandt
Van ISD, PO BOX 697 75790   4-11111
Jeffrey Turner, supt.   963-8328
HS, PO BOX 697 75790   2-00011
Kenn Franklin, prin.   963-8623
JHS, PO BOX 697 75790   2-00100
David Allen, prin.   963-8321

Van Alstyne, AC 903, PC 4, Grayson
Van Alstyne ISD, PO BOX 518 75495   3-11111
Charles Williams, supt.   482-6617
HS, PO BOX 518 75495   2-00011
Michael Mitchusson, prin.   482-5346
JHS, PO BOX 699 75495   2-00100
Roger Ferguson, prin.   482-5447

Vanderbilt, AC 512, PC 3, Jackson
Industrial ISD, PO BOX 369 77991   3-11111
Bob Nicholson, supt.   284-3226
Industrial HS, PO BOX 399 77991   2-00011
Bernard Zarosky, prin.   284-3216
Other Schools – See Lolita

Van Horn, AC 915, PC 5, Culberson
Culberson County ISD   3-11111
PO BOX 899 79855   283-2245
Guadalupe Sotello, supt.
HS, PO BOX 899 79855   2-00011
Lewis Rogers, prin.   283-2245
JHS, PO BOX 899 79855   1-00100
Kaye Koehn, prin.   283-9212

Van Vleck, AC 409, PC 4, Matagorda
Van Vleck ISD, PO BOX O 77482   4-11111
Kenneth Loveless, supt.   245-8518
HS, PO BOX 649 77482   2-00011
William McGonagle, prin.   245-4664
JHS, PO BOX Q 77482   2-00100
Byron Laws, prin.   245-6401

Vega, AC 806, PC 3, Oldham
Vega ISD, PO BOX 190 79092   2-11111
Steve Hopper, supt.   267-2123
JSHS, PO BOX 190 79092   2-00111
Charles Parsley, prin.   267-2126

Venus, AC 214, PC 3, Johnson
Venus ISD, PO BOX 364 76084   3-11111
Joe Hall, supt.   366-3448
JSHS, PO BOX 364 76084   2-00111
Marvin Minor, prin.   366-3358

Vernon, AC 817, PC 7, Wilbarger
Northside ISD   2-11111
18040 US HIGHWAY 283 76384   552-2551
J. Reed, supt.
Northside S   2-11111
18040 US HIGHWAY 283 76384   552-2551
John Gore, prin.

Vernon ISD   5-11111
1713 WILBARGER ST # 203 76384   553-1900
Edwin Davis, supt.
HS, 2102 YUCCA LN 76384   3-00011
Kenny Railsback, prin.   553-3377
IS, 2201 YAMPARIKA ST 76384   3-00100
Don Coats, prin.   552-6231

Vernon Regional Junior College   4-CC
4400 COLLEGE DR 76384   552-6291

Victoria, AC 512, PC 8, Victoria
Victoria ISD, PO BOX 1759 77902   7-11111
Robert Brezina, supt.   576-3131
Stroman HS, 3002 E NORTH ST 77901   4-00011
Arvelle Scott, prin.   578-2711
HS, 1110 SAM HOUSTON DR 77901   4-00011
Melissa Porche, prin.   575-7451
Victoria Career Development S   Vo Tech
104 PROFIT DR 77901   576-3131
Tommy Haney, prin.
Crain IS, 2706 N AZALEA ST 77901   4-00100
Joe Martinez, prin.   573-7453
Howell IS, 2502 FANNIN DR 77901   4-00100
L. Middleton, prin.   578-1561
Welder IS, 1604 E NORTH ST 77901   4-00100
Rudy Duran, prin.   575-4553

Citizens Medical Center   HSP
2701 HOSPITAL DR 77901   573-9181
Devereux Psychiatric Residential Center   HND
120 DAVID WADE DR 77902   800-383-5000
St. Joseph HS   2-00011
110 E RED RIVER ST 77901   573-2446
Sr. Emilie Eilers, prin.
Texas Vocational School   2-CS
1921 E RED RIVER ST 77901   575-4768
University of Houston-Victoria   3-UC
2301 E RED RIVER ST 77901   576-3151
Victoria College   4-CC
2200 E RED RIVER ST 77901   573-3291

Vidor, AC 409, PC 7, Orange
Vidor ISD, 120 E BOLIVAR ST 77662   6-11111
Tom Mauer, supt.   769-2143
HS, 500 ORANGE ST 77662   4-00011
Robert Madding, prin.   769-5418
JHS, 945 N TRAM RD 77662   3-00100
Jerry Webb, prin.   769-2461

Voss, AC 915, PC 1, Coleman
Panther Creek Consolidated ISD   2-11111
PO BOX 32 76888   357-4449
Charles Bryant, supt.

Panther Creek JSHS | 2-00111
PO BOX 32 76888 | 357-4449
Melvin Hale, prin. |

Waco, AC 817, PC 9, McLennan
Bosqueville ISD, RR 3 BOX 470 76708 | 2-11111
Roy Trussell, supt. | 752-8513
Bosqueville S, RR 3 BOX 470 76708 | 2-11111
C. Hammond, prin. | 752-6006

Connally ISD, 715 N RITA ST 76705 | 4-11111
Byron Brown, supt. | 799-2426
Connally HS, 715 N RITA ST 76705 | 3-00011
Don Hancock, prin. | 799-5565
Connally JHS, 715 N RITA ST 76705 | 3-00100
Keith Pate, prin. | 799-2660

La Vega ISD, 3100 BELLMEAD DR 76705 | 4-11111
Tom Whitlock, supt. | 799-4963
La Vega HS, 555 N LOOP 340 76705 | 3-00011
T. Holbrook, prin. | 799-4951
Miles MS, 508 E LOOP 340 76705 | 3-00100
Bryant Adams, prin. | 799-2428

Midway ISD | 6-11111
1205 FOUNDATION DR 76712 | 666-7773
Jerry Christian, supt. |
Midway HS | 4-00011
1205 FOUNDATION DR 76712 | 666-5151
Donald Taylor, prin. |
Midway JHS | 4-00100
1205 FOUNDATION DR 76712 | 772-4412
Lee Harrington, prin. |

Robinson ISD | 4-11111
500 W LYNDALE AVE 76706 | 662-0194
James Smith, supt. |
Robinson HS | 3-00011
500 W LYNDALE AVE 76706 | 662-3840
Thomas Gerik, prin. |
Robinson JHS | 2-00100
500 W LYNDALE AVE 76706 | 662-3843
Melinda Hawkins, prin. |

Waco ISD, PO BOX 27 76703 | 7-11111
Fred Zachary, supt. | 752-8341
University HS, 2600 BAGBY AVE 76711 | 4-00011
Rudy Lopez, prin. | 756-1843
JSHS, 2020 N 42ND ST 76710 | 4-00111
Wilbur Luce, prin. | 776-1150
Lake Air MS, 4601 COBBS DR 76710 | 2-00110
Barbara Lessman, prin. | 772-1910
Tennyson MS | 3-00100
6100 TENNYSON DR 76710 | 772-1440
George Dupree, prin. |
University MS | 3-00100
1820 IRVING LEE ST 76711 | 753-1533
Fhae Lee, prin. |
Waco Ninth Grade Ctr. | 3-00110
500 N UNIVERSITY PARKS DR 76701 | 753-6486
Jan Hungate, prin. |
Wiley MS, 1030 E LIVE OAK ST 76704 | 2-00100
Sharon Shields, prin. | 752-9691

Baylor University | 7-UC
PO BOX 97008 76798 | 755-3435
Four-C College | 2-CS
PO BOX 4 76703 | 756-7201
McLennan Community College | 5-CC
1400 COLLEGE DR 76708 | 750-3622
Reicher Catholic HS | 2-00011
2102 N 23RD ST 76708 | 752-8349
Leo Baysinger, prin. |
Texas State Technical College | 5-CC
3801 CAMPUS DR 76705 | 867-3371
Vanguard JSHS | 2-00111
2517 MOUNT CARMEL DR 76710 | 772-8111
Edward Davis, prin. |
Waco Christian S, 816 N NEW RD 76710 | 2-11111
William Wyatt, prin. | 776-4321

Waelder, AC 512, PC 3, Gonzales
Waelder ISD, PO BOX 247 78959 | 2-11111
James Phipps, supt. | 665-7161
JSHS, PO BOX 247 78959 | 1-00111
John Orta, prin. | 665-7151

Wall, AC 915, PC 2, Tom Green
Wall ISD, PO BOX 259 76957 | 3-11111
R. Gibson, supt. | 653-7790
HS, PO BOX 259 76957 | 2-00011
Walter Holik, prin. | 651-7521
MS, PO BOX 259 76957 | 2-00100
Ted Hallford, prin. | 651-8556

Waller, AC 409, PC 4, Waller
Waller ISD, 1918 KEY ST 77484 | 5-11111
Robert Schumacher, supt. | 931-3685
HS, 2402 WALLER ST 77484 | 3-00011
Howard Hawkins, prin. | 372-3654
Schultz MS, 19010 STOKES RD 77484 | 3-00100
B. Miller, prin. | 931-9103

Wallis, AC 409, PC 4, Austin
Wallis-Orchard ISD | 3-11111
PO BOX 819 77485 | 478-6551
Will Jones, supt. |
Brazos HS, PO BOX 458 77485 | 2-00011
Claud Ridgway, prin. | 478-6832
Other Schools – See Orchard

Walnut Springs, AC 817, PC 3, Bosque
Walnut Springs ISD | 2-11111
PO BOX 63 76690 | 797-2191
D. Edwards, supt. |
S, PO BOX 63 76690 | 2-11111
V. Munden, prin. | 797-2191

Warren, AC 409, PC 3, Tyler
Warren ISD, PO BOX 69 77664 | 3-11111
Bettie Yates, supt. | 547-2241
HS, PO BOX 190 77664 | 2-00011
Isaac Addison, prin. | 547-2243
JHS, PO BOX 205 77664 | 2-00100
William Mitchell, prin. | 547-2246

Waskom, AC 903, PC 4, Harrison
Waskom ISD, PO BOX 748 75692 | 3-11111
Joe Gassiott, supt. | 687-3361
HS, PO BOX 748 75692 | 2-00011
James Powell, prin. | 687-3362
MS, PO BOX 748 75692 | 2-00100
Jim Cox, prin. | 687-3402

Water Valley, AC 915, PC 2, Tom Green
Water Valley ISD, PO BOX 711 76958 | 2-11111
Dan Harris, supt. | 484-2478
JSHS, PO BOX 711 76958 | 2-00111
Richard Bain, prin. | 484-2424

Waxahachie, AC 214, PC 7, Ellis
Waxahachie ISD | 5-11111
411 N GIBSON ST 75165 | 923-4631
David Montgomery, supt. |
HS, 411 N GIBSON ST 75165 | 4-00011
Joe Harrison, prin. | 923-4600
JHS, 411 N GIBSON ST 75165 | 3-00100
Carolyn McCreight, prin. | 923-4680

Southwestern Assemblies of God College | 3-UC
1200 SYCAMORE ST 75165 | 800-445-0071

Weatherford, AC 817, PC 7, Parker
Brock ISD, 100 GRINDSTONE RD 76087 | 2-11111
Clead Cheek, supt. | 594-7642
Brock JSHS, 100 GRINDSTONE RD 76087 | 2-00111
J Branch, prin. | 594-3492

Weatherford ISD, PO BOX 439 76086 | 6-11111
Joseph Tison, supt. | 598-2808
HS, 1007 S MAIN ST 76086 | 4-00011
Michael O'Shea, prin. | 598-2858
Hall MS, 902 CHARLES ST 76086 | 3-00100
Anita Ellis, prin. | 598-2822

Weatherford College | 4-CC
308 E PARK AVE 76086 | 594-5471

Webster, AC 713, PC 5, Harris
Clear Creek ISD
Supt. — See League City
IS, 400 S WALNUT ST 77598 | 4-00100
John Seidensticker, prin. | 332-2411

Weimar, AC 409, PC 4, Colorado
Weimar ISD, 506 W MAIN ST 78962 | 3-11111
Wayne Wise, supt. | 725-9504
HS, 506 W MAIN ST 78962 | 2-00011
Bob McMahan, prin. | 725-9504
JHS, 411 N EAGLE ST 78962 | 1-00100
Jerry Hudec, prin. | 725-9515

Welch, AC 806, PC 2, Dawson
Dawson ISD, PO BOX 180 79377 | 2-11111
Jim Airhart, supt. | 489-7461
Dawson JSHS, PO BOX 180 79377 | 1-00111
Bill Pierce, prin. | 489-7461

Wellington, AC 806, PC 4, Collingsworth
Wellington ISD, PO BOX 1028 79095 | 3-11111
James Collins, supt. | 447-2512
HS, 812 15TH ST 79095 | 2-00011
Carl Taylor, prin. | 447-2527
JHS, 812 15TH ST 79095 | 2-00100
Barbara Williams, prin. | 447-5726

Wellman, AC 806, PC 2, Terry
Wellman ISD, PO BOX 68 79378 | 2-11111
John Yeager, supt. | 637-4910
S, PO BOX 128 79378 | 2-11111
Thomas Fowler, prin. | 637-4619

Wells, AC 409, PC 3, Cherokee
Wells ISD, PO BOX 469 75976 | 2-11111
(—), supt. | 867-4466
JSHS, PO BOX 469 75976 | 2-00111
(—), prin. | 867-4400

Weslaco, AC 210, PC 7, Hidalgo
Weslaco ISD, PO BOX 266 78599 | 7-11111
James Lehmann, supt. | 969-6500
South Palms Garden HS | 4-00011
PO BOX 266 78599 | 969-6500
Alfonso Fernandez, prin. |
SHS, 1005 W PIKE BLVD 78596 | 5-00001
Jose Rivera, prin. | 969-6700
Central HS, 506 E 6TH ST 78596 | 4-00100
Andres Elizondo, prin. | 969-6710
Cuellar MS, 1201 S BRIDGE AVE 78596 | 3-00100
Hillary Dufner, prin. | 969-6720
Hoge Academy MS | 3-00010
2302 S INTERNATIONAL BLVD 78596 | 969-6730
Rodolfo Silva, prin. |

South Texas Vocational-Technical Inst. | 2-CS
PO BOX 629 78596 | 969-1564
Valley Grande Academy | 2-00011
PO BOX 1126 78599 | 968-0523
Andrew Leonie, prin. |

West, AC 817, PC 5, McLennan
West ISD, 801 N REAGAN ST 76691 | 4-11111
Jack Crain, supt. | 826-3728
HS, 801 N REAGAN ST 76691 | 2-00011
Hank Masur, prin. | 826-3711
MS, 801 N REAGAN ST 76691 | 2-00100
Harvey Siems, prin. | 826-3739

Westbrook, AC 915, PC 2, Mitchell
Westbrook ISD, PO BOX 99 79565 | 2-11111
Raymond Hollis, supt. | 644-2311
S, PO BOX 99 79565 | 2-11111
Robert Criswell, prin. | 644-2311

West Columbia, AC 409, PC 5, Brazoria
Columbia-Brazoria ISD | 5-11111
PO BOX 158 77486 | 345-5147
Virgil Tiemann, supt. |
Columbia HS, PO BOX 158 77486 | 3-00011
C. Alicardi, prin. | 345-5147
JHS, PO BOX 158 77486 | 3-00100
John Parker, prin. | 345-4131

Columbia Christian ES | 2-11111
725 W BRAZOS AVE 77486 | 345-2434
Linda Barnett, prin. |

Wharton, AC 409, PC 6, Wharton
Wharton ISD, 2100 N FULTON ST 77488 | 5-11111
Gary Grogan, supt. | 532-3612
HS, 1 TIGER AVE 77488 | 3-00011
Darlyn Dusek, prin. | 532-4211
JHS, 1120 N RUSK ST 77488 | 2-00100
James King, prin. | 532-3152

Wharton County Junior College | 4-CC
911 E BOLING HWY 77488 | 532-4560

Wheeler, AC 806, PC 4, Wheeler
Kelton ISD, RR 1 BOX 157 79096 | 1-11111
Bill Crockett, supt. | 826-5795
Kelton S, RR 1 BOX 157 79096 | 1-11111
Bill Crockett, prin. | 826-5708

Wheeler ISD, PO BOX 1010 79096 | 2-11111
Glyndol Holland, supt. | 826-5241
S, PO BOX 1010 79096 | 2-11111
Douglas Rives, prin. | 826-5534

White Deer, AC 806, PC 4, Carson
White Deer ISD, PO BOX 517 79097 | 2-11111
Larry Johnston, supt. | 883-2311
HS, PO BOX 248 79097 | 2-00011
Kenneth Cox, prin. | 883-6411

Whiteface, AC 806, PC 3, Cochran
Whiteface Consolidated ISD | 2-11111
PO BOX 7 79379 | 287-1154
David Foote, supt. |
JSHS, PO BOX 67 79379 | 2-00111
Tom Johnson, prin. | 287-1104

Whitehouse, AC 903, PC 5, Smith
Whitehouse ISD | 5-11111
106 WILDCAT DR 75791 | 839-5500
Thomas Neill, supt. |
HS, 108 WILDCAT DR 75791 | 3-00011
Jim Jennings, prin. | 839-5551
Holloway MS, 701 E MAIN ST 75791 | 2-00100
Greg Whitman, prin. | 839-5590

White Oak, AC 903, PC 6, Gregg
White Oak ISD | 4-11111
200 S WHITE OAK RD 75693 | 759-4492
Timothy Sonnenberg, supt. |
HS, 200 S WHITE OAK RD 75693 | 2-00011
Dan Noll, prin. | 759-4511
MS, 200 S WHITE OAK RD 75693 | 2-00100
Ronald Hughes, prin. | 759-4536

Whitesboro, AC 903, PC 5, Grayson
Whitesboro ISD, 115 4TH ST 76273 | 4-11111
Jerry Dickson, supt. | 564-3583
HS, 115 4TH ST 76273 | 2-00011
James Graham, prin. | 564-5912
JHS, 115 4TH ST 76273 | 2-00100
Kenneth Russell, prin. | 564-3461

White Settlement, AC 817, PC 7, Tarrant
White Settlement ISD | 5-11111
401 S CHERRY LN 76108 | 367-1350
Jim Welch, supt. |
Brewer HS, 1000 S CHERRY LN 76108 | 4-00011
Dale Brock, prin. | 367-1200
Brewer MS, 1000 S CHERRY LN 76108 | 3-00100
Homer Dear, prin. | 367-1267

Whitewright, AC 903, PC 4, Grayson
Whitewright ISD, PO BOX 888 75491 | 3-11111
Sandra Hill, supt. | 364-2155
HS, PO BOX 888 75491 | 2-00011
Howard Roach, prin. | 364-2535
MS, PO BOX 888 75491 | 2-00100
Howard Hodge, prin. | 364-2151

Whitharral, AC 806, PC 2, Hockley
Whitharral ISD, PO BOX H 79380 | 2-11111
Oscar Mccormack, supt. | 299-1184

S, PO BOX H 79380	2-11111
Thomas Hoskins, prin.	299-1135

Whitney, AC 817, PC 4, Hill

Whitney ISD, PO BOX 518 76692	4-11111
Marcus Kret, supt.	694-2254
HS, PO BOX 518 76692	2-00011
Gene Schatz, prin.	694-3457
JHS, PO BOX 518 76692	2-01100
John Thiele, prin.	694-3446

Wichita Falls, AC 817, PC 8, Wichita

Wichita Falls ISD	7-11111
PO BOX 2570 76307	720-3273
Leslie Carnine, supt.	
Hirschi HS, 3106 BORTON ST 76305	4-00011
Cleeland Minniear, prin.	720-3300
Rider HS, 4611 CYPRESS AVE 76310	4-00011
Lloyd Byers, prin.	720-3000
HS, 2149 AVENUE H 76309	4-00011
Herby Carr, prin.	720-3177
Barwise JHS, 3807 KEMP BLVD 76308	3-00100
Robert Mobley, prin.	720-3035
Kirby Math-Science Center	2-00100
1715 LOOP 11 76305	720-3310
Diann Taylor, prin.	
McNiel JHS, 4712 BARNETT RD 76310	3-00100
Patricia Bradley, prin.	720-3030
Zundelowitz JHS, 1706 POLK ST 76309	3-00100
Clifford O'Neal, prin.	720-3170

Midwestern State University	5-UC
3400 TAFT BLVD 76308	692-6611
Notre Dame S	2-11111
2821 LANSING BLVD 76309	692-6041
Joseph Cluley, prin.	
Wichita General Hospital	HSP
1600 8TH ST 76301	723-1461

Willis, AC 409, PC 5, Montgomery

Willis ISD, 204 W ROGERS ST 77378	5-11111
Tom Crowe, supt.	856-4571
HS, 1304 N CAMPBELL ST 77378	3-00011
George Reedy, prin.	856-4571
Hardy JHS, 701 GERALD ST 77378	3-00100
Fred Rush, prin.	856-4571

Wills Point, AC 903, PC 5, Van Zandt

Wills Point ISD, PO BOX 30 75169	4-11111
James Norman, supt.	873-3161
HS, 200 TIGER DR 75169	3-00011
Charles Curtis, prin.	873-2371
MS, 101 SCHOOL ST 75169	3-00100
Thomas Harp, prin.	873-3617

Wilson, AC 806, PC 3, Lynn

Wilson ISD, PO BOX 9 79381	2-11111
Nancy Templeton, supt.	628-6271
JSHS, PO BOX 9 79381	1-00111
Robert Williams, prin.	628-6201

Wimberley, AC 512, PC 4, Hays

Wimberley ISD, PO BOX 1809 78676	3-11111
Vernon Newsom, supt.	847-2414
Danforth JSHS, PO BOX 1808 78676	2-00111
Gordon Franzen, prin.	847-5729

Windthorst, AC 817, PC 2, Archer

Windthorst ISD, PO BOX 190 76389	2-11111
H. Neeb, supt.	423-6688
JSHS, PO BOX 190 76389	1-00111
(—), prin.	423-6680

Wink, AC 915, PC 4, Winkler

Wink-Loving ISD, PO BOX 637 79789	2-11111
Maxie Watts, supt.	527-3880
JSHS, PO BOX 637 79789	2-00111
Steven O'Quinn, prin.	527-3432

Winnie, AC 409, PC 4, Chambers

East Chambers ISD	3-11111
PO BOX 417 77665	296-4307
Roy Tully, supt.	
East Chambers HS	2-00011
PO BOX 417 77665	296-4184
Dee Hartt, prin.	
East Chambers JHS	2-00100
PO BOX 417 77665	296-4183
Donald Gaus, prin.	

Winnsboro, AC 903, PC 5, Wood

Winnsboro ISD, 207 E PINE ST 75494	4-11111
Jerry Hardy, supt.	342-3737
HS, 409 NEWSOME ST 75494	2-00011
Phil Hart, prin.	342-3641
Memorial MS	2-01100
505 S CHESTNUT ST 75494	342-5711
Jim Whittle, prin.	

Winona, AC 903, PC 2, Smith

Winona ISD, PO BOX 218 75792	3-11111
Robert Iden, supt.	877-3140
HS, PO BOX 218 75792	2-00011
Darrell Nickerson, prin.	877-3392
MS, PO BOX 218 75792	2-00100
Ron Foster, prin.	877-2127

Winters, AC 915, PC 5, Runnels

Winters ISD, PO BOX 125 79567	3-11111
T. Lancaster, supt.	754-5574
JSHS, PO BOX 125 79567	2-00111
Charles Kidwell, prin.	754-5516

Woden, AC 409, PC 2, Nacogdoches

Woden ISD, PO BOX 100 75978	3-11111
W. King, supt.	564-7903
HS, PO BOX 100 75978	2-00011
Larry Mason, prin.	564-7903
JHS, PO BOX 100 75978	2-00100
James Lowery, prin.	564-7903

Wolfe City, AC 903, PC 4, Hunt

Wolfe City ISD, PO BOX L 75496	3-11111
John Sneed, supt.	496-2283
HS, PO BOX L 75496	2-00011
Dean Whitaker, prin.	496-7333
JHS, PO BOX L 75496	1-00100
Jim Felty, prin.	496-7333

Wolfforth, AC 806, PC 4, Lubbock

Frenship ISD, PO BOX 100 79382	5-11111
Paul Whitton, supt.	866-9541
Frenship HS, FM 179 79382	3-00011
Bruce Cunningham, prin.	866-4440
Frenship JHS, 500 MAIN ST 79382	3-00100
Smythie Lawrence, prin.	866-4464

Woodsboro, AC 512, PC 4, Refugio

Woodsboro ISD, PO BOX 770 78393	3-11111
Barbara Shaver, supt.	543-4518
HS, PO BOX 770 78393	2-00011
Donald Long, prin.	543-4521
JHS, PO BOX 770 78393	2-00100
Jose Loera, prin.	543-4622

Woodson, AC 817, PC 2, Throckmorton

Woodson ISD, PO BOX 287 76491	2-11111
Dan Bellah, supt.	345-6528
S, PO BOX 287 76491	2-11111
Hugh Willis, prin.	345-6521

Woodville, AC 409, PC 5, Tyler

Woodville ISD	4-11111
505 N CHARLTON ST 75979	283-3752
Carol Moffett, supt.	
HS, 700 EAGLE DR 75979	3-00011
Tom Harvey, prin.	283-3714
MS, 500 EAGLE DR 75979	2-00100
Clifford Larson, prin.	283-7109

Wortham, AC 817, PC 4, Freestone

Wortham ISD, PO BOX 247 76693	2-11111
Edward Donahue, supt.	765-3678
JSHS, PO BOX 247 76693	2-00111
Cynthia Smith, prin.	765-3451

Wylie, AC 214, PC 6, Collin

Wylie ISD, PO BOX 490 75098	5-11111
Susan Williamson, supt.	442-5444
HS, PO BOX 490 75098	3-00011
R. Shirley, prin.	442-2218
MS, PO BOX 490 75098	3-00100
James McAdams, prin.	442-5476

Yantis, AC 903, PC 2, Wood

Yantis ISD, PO BOX 149 75497	2-11111
Jim Day, supt.	383-2463
S, PO BOX 149 75497	2-11111
Mark Panter, prin.	383-2463

Yoakum, AC 512, PC 6, De Witt

Yoakum ISD, PO BOX 737 77995	4-11111
Harvey Schneider, supt.	293-3162
HS, PO BOX 737 77995	3-00011
Robert Manning, prin.	293-3442
JHS, PO BOX 737 77995	2-00100
William Wendtland, prin.	293-3111

Yorktown, AC 512, PC 4, De Witt

Yorktown ISD, PO BOX 487 78164	3-11111
W. Stephenson, supt.	564-2252
HS, PO BOX 487 78164	2-00011
Charles Bailey, prin.	564-4225
JHS, PO BOX 487 78164	2-00100
Jim Elliott, prin.	564-4209

Zapata, AC 210, PC 6, Zapata

Zapata ISD, PO BOX 158 78076	5-11111
Arturo Gutierrez, supt.	765-6546
HS, PO BOX 158 78076	3-00011
Roberto Hein, prin.	765-6542
JHS, PO BOX 158 78076	2-00100
Eliseo Perez, prin.	765-4321

Zavalla, AC 409, PC 3, Angelina

Zavalla ISD, PO BOX 45 75980	2-11111
Michael Ford, supt.	897-2271
JSHS, PO BOX 45 75980	2-00111
Ronald Fant, prin.	897-2301

Zephyr, AC 915, PC 2, Brown

Zephyr ISD, RR 1 BOX 1 76890	2-11111
David Whisenhunt, supt.	739-5331
JSHS, PO BOX 708 76890	1-00111
Gary Bufe, prin.	739-5331

UTAH

STATE OFFICE OF EDUCATION
250 E 500 S, Salt Lake City 84111
(801) 533-7500

Superintendent of Public Instruction	Scott Bean
Deputy Superintendent	Laurie Chivers
Associate Superintendent Instructional Services	Jerry Peterson
Associate Superintendent Applied Technology Services	Bruce Griffin

STATE BOARD OF EDUCATION
250 East 5th South, Salt Lake City 84111

Chairman	C. Grant Hurst

PUBLIC, PRIVATE AND CATHOLIC SECONDARY SCHOOLS

Altamont, AC 801, PC 2, Duchesne
Duchesne SD
Supt. — See Duchesne
JSHS, PO BOX 130 84001 2-00111
Scott Bowles, prin. 454-3314

American Fork, AC 801, PC 7, Utah
Alpine SD, 575 N 100 E 84003 8-11111
Steven Baugh, supt. 756-8400
SHS, 510 N 600 E 84003 4-00001
Vernon Henshaw, prin. 756-8547
JHS, 20 W 1120 N 84003 4-00110
MacNeil Ogden, prin. 756-8543
Other Schools – See Highland, Lehi, Lindon, Orem,
Pleasant Grove

Beaver, AC 801, PC 4, Beaver
Beaver SD, PO BOX 31 84713 4-11111
Carl Holmes, supt. 438-2291
JSHS, 150 N MAIN ST 84713 2-00111
Melvyn Osborn, prin. 438-2301
Other Schools – See Milford

Bicknell, AC 801, PC 2, Wayne
Wayne SD, 79 N 100 W 84715 3-11111
Stanley Allen, supt. 425-3813
Wayne HS, 55 N CENTER ST 84715 2-00011
Mark Elmer, prin. 425-3411
Wayne MS, 265 N 400 W 84715 2-00100
Oscar Taylor, prin. 425-3421

Bingham Canyon, AC 801, Salt Lake
Jordan SD
Supt. — See Sandy
Bingham MS, 96 W STATE HWY 84006 3-00110
Al Zylstra, prin. 565-7518

Blanding, AC 801, PC 5, San Juan
San Juan SD
Supt. — See Monticello
San Juan JSHS, 311 N 100 E 84511 2-00111
James Harris, prin. 678-2291
Lyman MS, 535 N 100 E 84511 2-00100
Chris Johnson, prin. 678-2212

Bountiful, AC 801, PC 8, Davis
Davis SD
Supt. — See Farmington
SHS, 695 ORCHARD DR 84010 4-00001
Rulon Homer, prin. 299-2055
Viewmont SHS, 120 W 1000 N 84010 4-00001
Paul Waite, prin. 299-2065
JHS, 30 W 400 N 84010 3-00110
J. Wayne Baker, prin. 299-2034
Milcreek JHS, 245 E 1000 S 84010 3-00110
Andrew Odoardi, prin. 299-2042
Mueller Park JHS 3-00110
955 MUELLER PARK RD 84010 299-2046
Steven Mangel, prin.
South Davis JHS, 298 W 2600 S 84010 4-00110
Dale Rees, prin. 299-2050

Brigham City, AC 801, PC 7, Box Elder
Box Elder SD, 230 W 200 S 84302 7-11111
Steven Laing, supt. 723-5281
Box Elder HS, 380 S 600 W 84302 4-00011
Jay Stewart, prin. 723-8533
Box Elder JHS, 18 S 500 E 84302 4-00100
LaMar Bourne, prin. 723-3493
Other Schools – See Garland, Tremonton

Castle Dale, AC 801, PC 4, Emery
Emery SD
Supt. — See Huntington
Emery County SHS 3-00001
PO BOX 499 84513 381-2689
Brent Arnold, prin.

Cedar City, AC 801, PC 7, Iron
Iron SD, 75 N 300 W 84720 6-11111
Dee Stapley, supt. 586-2804
HS, 703 W 600 S 84720 4-00011
Ron Ferguson, prin. 586-2820
MS, 450 W CENTER ST 84720 3-00100
Alan Garfield, prin. 586-2830
Other Schools – See Parowan

Southern Utah University 5-UC
351 W CENTER ST 84720 586-7740

Centerville, AC 801, PC 7, Davis
Davis SD
Supt. — See Farmington
JHS, 625 S MAIN ST 84014 4-00110
Jane Muna, prin. 299-2038

Clearfield, AC 801, PC 7, Davis
Davis SD
Supt. — See Farmington
SHS, 938 S 1000 E 84015 4-00001
Tamara Lowe, prin. 774-7461
North Davis JHS, 835 STATE ST 84015 4-00110
Kent Smith, prin. 774-7430

Coalville, AC 801, PC 4, Summit
North Summit SD 3-11111
PO BOX 497 84017 336-5654
Ronald Stanfield, supt.
North Summit HS 2-00011
PO BOX 497 84017 336-5656
Earl Blonquist, prin.
North Summit MS 2-01100
PO BOX 497 84017 336-5960
Jim Brooks, prin.

Delta, AC 801, PC 5, Millard
Millard SD, PO BOX 666 84624 5-11111
Kenneth Topham, supt. 864-2764
HS, 50 W 300 N 84624 3-00011
Mitchell Myers, prin. 864-2745
Delta Tech Ctr, 305 E 200 N 84624 Vo Tech
David Taylor, prin. 864-2054
MS, 351 E 300 N 84624 3-00100
Eleanor Dalton, prin. 864-3891
Other Schools – See Fillmore

Duchesne, AC 801, PC 4, Duchesne
Duchesne SD, PO BOX 446 84021 5-11111
John Aland, supt. 738-2411
JSHS, PO BOX 330 84021 2-00111
J. Mitchell, prin. 738-2211
Other Schools – See Altamont, Myton, Roosevelt,
Tabiona

Dugway, AC 801, PC 4, Tooele
Tooele SD
Supt. — See Tooele
JSHS 84022 2-00111
George Bruce, prin. 831-4566

Eden, AC 801, PC 2, Weber
Weber SD
Supt. — See Ogden
Snowcrest JHS 2-00110
2755 N HIGHWAY 162 84310 745-2608
Carl Bruce, prin.

Enterprise, AC 801, PC 3, Washington
Washington SD
Supt. — See Saint George
JSHS, 186 S 100 E 84725 2-00111
Richard McMullin, prin. 878-2248

Ephraim, AC 801, PC 5, Sanpete
South Sanpete SD
Supt. — See Manti
MS, 555 S 100 E 84627 2-00100
James Petersen, prin. 283-4037

Snow College 4-CC
150 E 100 N 84627 283-4021

Escalante, AC 801, PC 3, Garfield
Garfield SD
Supt. — See Panguitch
JSHS, PO BOX 228 84726 2-00111
Myron Cottam, prin. 826-4205

Eureka, AC 801, PC 3, Juab
Tintic SD, GENERAL DELIVERY 84628 2-11111
Fred Openshaw, supt. 433-6363
Tintic JSHS, PO BOX 210 84628 1-00111
Gordon Grimstead, prin. 433-6939
Other Schools – See Trout Creek

Farmington, AC 801, PC 6, Davis
Davis SD, 45 E STATE ST 84025 8-11111
Richard Kendell, supt. 451-1251
JHS, 150 S 200 W 84025 4-00110
Rick Call, prin. 451-1020
Other Schools – See Bountiful, Centerville,
Clearfield, Kaysville, Layton, Sunset, Syracuse,
Woods Cross

Ferron, AC 801, PC 4, Emery
Emery SD
Supt. — See Huntington
San Rafael JHS, PO BOX 790 84523 2-00110
J. J. Grant, prin. 384-2335

Fillmore, AC 801, PC 4, Millard
Millard SD
Supt. — See Delta
Millard HS, 200 W CENTER ST 84631 2-00011
Earl Slack, prin. 743-6201
MS, 435 S 500 W 84631 2-01100
LaVoy Starley, prin. 743-5733

Garland, AC 801, PC 4, Box Elder
Box Elder SD
Supt. — See Brigham City
Bear River HS, 1450 S MAIN ST 84312 4-00011
Richard Williams, prin. 257-5431

Grantsville, AC 801, PC 5, Tooele
Tooele SD
Supt. — See Tooele
HS, 155 E CHERRY ST 84029 2-00011
Randall Houk, prin. 884-4500
MS, 318 S HALE ST 84029 3-00100
Sandra Shepard, prin. 884-4510

Green River, AC 801, PC 3, Emery
Emery SD
Supt. — See Huntington
JSHS, PO BOX 450 84525 2-00111
Larry Rowley, prin. 564-3461

Gunnison, AC 801, PC 4, Sanpete
South Sanpete SD
Supt. — See Manti
Gunnison Valley JSHS, 35 E 600 S 84634 3-00110
Donald Hill, prin. 528-7256

Heber City, AC 801, PC 5, Wasatch
Wasatch SD, 173 E 200 N 84032 5-11111
Henry Jolley, supt. 654-0280
Wasatch HS, 64 E 600 S 84032 3-00011
Brad Kendall, prin. 654-0640

Wasatch MS, 175 E 800 S 84032 3-00100
Douglas Hardy, prin. 654-0550

Helper, AC 801, PC 4, Carbon
Carbon SD
Supt. — See Price
JHS, 130 UINTAH ST 84526 2-00110
Gary Wilson, prin. 472-5441

Highland, AC 801, PC 6, Utah
Alpine SD
Supt. — See American Fork
Mountain Ridge JHS 4-00110
5500 W 10400 N 84003 763-7010
Sheldon Worthington, prin.

Huntington, AC 801, PC 4, Emery
Emery SD, 130 N MAIN 84528 5-11111
Blaine Evans, supt. 687-9846
Canyon View JHS, PO BOX 250 84528 2-00110
Gwen Callahan, prin. 687-2265
Other Schools – See Castle Dale, Ferron, Green River

Hurricane, AC 801, PC 5, Washington
Washington SD
Supt. — See Saint George
SHS, 345 W 100 S 84737 3-00001
Robert Goulding, prin. 635-2931
JHS, 395 N 200 W 84737 3-00110
Jim McKim, prin. 635-4634

Hyrum, AC 801, PC 5, Cache
Cache SD
Supt. — See Logan
Mountain Crest SHS, 255 S 800 E 84319 4-00001
Mike Salveson, prin. 245-6093
South Cache MS, 29 N 400 W 84319 3-00110
Tom Bailey, prin. 245-6433

Junction, AC 801, PC 2, Piute
Piute SD, PO BOX 69 84740 2-11111
Randy Johnson, supt. 577-2912
Piute JSHS 84740 2-00111
Kirt Robinson, prin. 577-2881

Kamas, AC 801, PC 4, Summit
South Summit SD, 375 E 300 S 84036 4-11111
Mark Littleford, supt. 783-4301
South Summit HS, 45 S 300 E 84036 2-00011
Eric Moser, prin. 783-4313
South Summit MS, 355 E 300 S 84036 2-00110
Tom Crittenden, prin. 783-4341

Kanab, AC 801, PC 5, Kane
Kane SD 4-11111
746 S CONSTITUTION DR 84741 644-2555
Nils Bayles, supt.
HS, 59 E RED SHADOW LN 84741 2-00011
Lynn McArthur, prin. 644-5821
MS, 5 S 100 E 84741 2-00100
C. Henderson, prin. 644-5800
Other Schools – See Orderville

Kaysville, AC 801, PC 7, Davis
Davis SD
Supt. — See Farmington
Davis SHS, 325 S MAIN ST 84037 4-00001
Michael Duckworth, prin. 546-7940
JHS, 100 E 350 S 84037 4-00110
John Sadler, prin. 546-7930

Kearns, AC 801, PC 8, Salt Lake
Granite SD
Supt. — See Salt Lake City
SHS, 5525 COUGAR LN 84118 4-00001
Barry Richards, prin. 964-7500
Jefferson JHS, 5850 S 5600 W 84118 4-00110
Paul Hansen, prin. 964-7970
JHS, 4400 SAMS BLVD 84118 4-00110
Parley Jacobs, prin. 964-7650

Lake Powell, AC 801, San Juan
San Juan SD
Supt. — See Monticello
Halls Crossing S 1-11111
HALLS CROSSING MARINA 84533 684-2325
Sheila Sakizzie, prin.

Laketown, AC 801, PC 2, Rich
Rich SD
Supt. — See Randolph
Rich JHS 84038 2-00100
Christine Kearl, prin. 946-3359

Layton, AC 801, PC 8, Davis
Davis SD
Supt. — See Farmington
SHS, 440 WASATCH DR 84041 4-00001
Paul Smith, prin. 546-7950
Northridge SHS 4-00001
2416 HILL FIELD RD 84041 774-7660
Ross Poore, prin.
Central Davis JHS 4-00110
663 CHURCH ST 84041 546-7923
Michael Timothy, prin.
North Layton JHS 4-00110
1100 W ANTELOPE DR 84041 774-7451
Scott Greenwell, prin.

Lehi, AC 801, PC 6, Utah
Alpine SD
Supt. — See American Fork
HS, 180 N 500 E 84043 3-00011
Russell Felt, prin. 768-7000

JHS, 700 CEDAR HOLLOW DR 84043   4-00100
   Virgil Jacobsen, prin.   768-7010

Lindon, AC 801, PC 5, Utah
Alpine SD
   Supt. — See American Fork
Oak Canyon JHS, 750 E 200 S 84042   4-00110
   Steven Steward, prin.   785-8760

Logan, AC 801, PC 8, Cache
Cache SD, 2063 N 1200 E 84321   7-11111
   Larry Jensen, supt.   752-3925
Other Schools — See Hyrum, Richmond, Smithfield

Logan CSD, 101 W CENTER ST 84321   6-11111
   Gary Carlston, supt.   755-2300
HS, 162 W 1ST S 84321   4-00011
   Rulon Olsen, prin.   755-2380
Mt. Logan MS, 875 N 2ND E 84321   4-00100
   Donald Jeppesen, prin.   755-2370

Utah State University 84322   7-UC
   750-1107

Magna, AC 801, PC 7, Salt Lake
Granite SD
   Supt. — See Salt Lake City
Cyprus SHS, 8623 W 3000 S 84044   4-00001
   William Christopulos, prin.   250-8600
Brockbank JHS, 2935 S 8560 W 84044   4-00110
   Lynn Boehme, prin.   250-8645

Manila, AC 801, PC 2, Daggett
Dagett SD, 2 N 2 W 84046   2-11111
   Gerold Erickson, supt.   784-3174
JSHS 84046   1-00111
   Stephen Garrett, prin.   784-3474

Manti, AC 801, PC 4, Sanpete
South Sanpete SD, 39 S MAIN ST 84642   5-11111
   Lewis Mullins, supt.   835-2261
HS, 100 W 500 N 84642   3-00011
   Earl Wheeler, prin.   835-2281
Other Schools — See Ephraim, Gunnison

Midvale, AC 801, PC 7, Salt Lake
Jordan SD
   Supt. — See Sandy
Hillcrest SHS, 7350 S 900 E 84047   4-00001
   Bruce Garrison, prin.   565-7566
MS, 138 PIONEER ST 84047   3-00110
   Lee Jenson, prin.   565-7530

Milford, AC 801, PC 4, Beaver
Beaver SD
   Supt. — See Beaver
JSHS, PO BOX 159 84751   2-00111
   Enoch Swain, prin.   387-2751

Moab, AC 801, PC 5, Grand
Grand SD, 264 S 400 E 84532   4-11111
   Richard Averett, supt.   259-5317
Grand HS, 439 S 100 E 84532   2-00011
   Larry Price, prin.   259-8931
Grand County MS   2-00100
   217 E CENTER ST 84532   259-7158
   Margaret Hopkin, prin.

Monroe, AC 801, PC 4, Sevier
Sevier SD
   Supt. — See Richfield
South Sevier HS, 430 W 100 S 84754   2-00011
   Allen Coryell, prin.   527-4651
South Sevier MS   2-00100
   300 E CENTER ST 84754   527-4607
   Randall Brown, prin.

Montezuma Creek, AC 801, PC 2, San Juan
San Juan SD
   Supt. — See Monticello
Whitehorse JSHS, PO BOX 660 84534   2-00111
   Ron Barlow, prin.   651-3427

Monticello, AC 801, PC 4, San Juan
San Juan SD, PO BOX 219 84535   5-11111
   Jerald Mikesell, supt.   587-2254
JSHS, PO BOX 69 84535   2-00111
   Dennis Crane, prin.   587-2465
Other Schools — See Blanding, Lake Powell,
   Montezuma Creek, Monument Valley

Monument Valley, AC 801, PC 2, San Juan
San Juan SD
   Supt. — See Monticello
JSHS, PO BOX 360008 84536   2-00111
   Patricia Seltzer, prin.   727-3204

Morgan, AC 801, PC 4, Morgan
Morgan SD, PO BOX 530 84050   4-11111
   J. Dale Christensen, supt.   829-3411
HS, 55 N 200 E 84050   3-00011
   Hugh Davis, prin.   829-3418
MS, 75 S 100 E 84050   3-01100
   Vernile Matheson, prin.   829-3467

Moroni, AC 801, PC 4, Sanpete
North Sanpete SD
   Supt. — See Mount Pleasant
North Sanpete MS, 655 N 100 S 84646   3-00100
   Phillip Johnson, prin.   436-8206

Mount Pleasant, AC 801, PC 4, Sanpete
North Sanpete SD, 41 W MAIN ST 84647   4-11111
   Dennis Mower, supt.   462-2485
North Sanpete HS, 390 E 700 S 84647   3-00011
   Courtney Syme, prin.   462-2452
Other Schools — See Moroni

Wasatch Academy, 120 S 100 W 84647   2-00011
   Joseph Loftin, prin.   462-2411

Murray, AC 801, PC 8, Salt Lake
Murray SD, 147 E 5065 S 84107   6-11111
   Ron Stephens, supt.   264-7400
SHS, 5440 S STATE ST 84107   4-00001
   Richard Tranter, prin.   264-7460
Hillcrest JHS, 126 E 5300 S 84107   3-00110
   Dee Jensen, prin.   264-7442
Riverview JHS, 751 TRIPP LN 84123   3-00110
   Al Church, prin.   264-7446

ITT Technical Institute   2-UC
   920 LEVOY DR 84123   263-3313
Mt. Vernon Academy   1-11111
   184 E VINE ST 84107   266-5521
   Lynn Evans, prin.

Myton, AC 801, PC 2, Duchesne
Duchesne SD
   Supt. — See Duchesne
Con Amore Training Center   Vo Tech
   PO BOX 88 84052   722-4629
   John Osborne, prin.

Nephi, AC 801, PC 5, Juab
Juab SD, 42 E 200 N 84648   4-11111
   Kirk Wright, supt.   623-1940
Juab HS, 555 E 750 N 84648   2-00011
   Andrew Cindrich, prin.   623-1764
Juab MS, 475 E 800 N 84648   2-00100
   Steven Olsen, prin.   623-1541

Ogden, AC 801, PC 8, Weber
Ogden SD, 2444 ADAMS AVE 84401   7-11111
   James West, supt.   625-8700
Lomond HS, 800 JACKSON AVE 84404   4-00011
   Cy Freston, prin.   625-8885
HS, 2828 HARRISON BLVD 84403   4-00011
   Larry Leatham, prin.   625-8914
Central MS, 781 25TH ST 84401   3-00100
   Charles Nelson, prin.   625-8845
Highland MS   3-00100
   325 GRAMERCY AVE 84404   625-8855
   Marshal Garrett, prin.
Mound Fort MS   3-00100
   1396 LIBERTY AVE 84404   625-8865
   Deborah Gomberg, prin.
Mt. Ogden MS   3-00100
   3260 HARRISON BLVD 84403   625-8875
   Sandy Schoch, prin.

Weber SD, 5320 ADAMS AVE 84405   8-11111
   Steven Mecham, supt.   476-7800
Bonneville SHS   4-00001
   251 E LAKER WAY 84405   476-5806
   Richard Rhees, prin.
Fremont HS, 1975 S 4700 W 84401   3-00001
   Gary Reed, prin.   626-2591
Weber SHS, 3650 N 500 W 84414   4-00001
   Earl Heninger, prin.   786-2000
Washington HS   Vo Tech
   3279 WASHINGTON BLVD 84401   625-8935
   Bruce Penland, prin.
Bell JHS, 165 W 5100 S 84405   3-00110
   Rob Stillwell, prin.   476-5829
North Ogden JHS, 575 E 2900 N 84414   4-00110
   Michael Wright, prin.   786-2015
South Ogden JHS   3-00110
   4300 MADISON AVE 84403   476-5816
   Roger Cox, prin.
Wahlquist JHS, 1033 N 1200 W 84404   4-00110
   David Vanden Bosch, prin.   626-2512
Other Schools — See Eden, Roy, West Haven

Certified Careers Institute   2-CS
   2661 WSHINGTON BLVD STE 203 84401   621-4925
McKay-Dee Hospital Center   HSP
   3939 HARRISON BLVD 84403   625-2700
St. Joseph's HS, 1790 LAKE ST 84401   2-00011
   Fr. Norman, prin.   394-1515
Stevens Henager College   2-CC
   2168 WASHINGTON BLVD 84401   394-7791
Utah Schools for the Deaf and the Blind   HND
   742 HARRISON BLVD 84404   629-4700
Weber State University   7-UC
   3750 HARRISON BLVD 84408   626-6050

Orderville, AC 801, PC 2, Kane
Kane SD
   Supt. — See Kanab
Valley HS, 150 E CENTER 84758   2-00111
   James Glover, prin.   648-2278

Orem, AC 801, PC 8, Utah
Alpine SD
   Supt. — See American Fork
SHS, 175 S 400 E 84058   4-00001
   John Childs, prin.   227-8765
Mountain View HS   4-00011
   665 W CENTER ST 84057   227-8759
   William Delaney, prin.
Canyon View JHS, 655 W 950 N 84057   4-00110
   James McCoy, prin.   227-8748
Lakeridge JHS, 951 S 400 W 84058   4-00110
   Glen Clark, prin.   227-8752
JHS, 765 N 600 W 84057   4-00110
   Pam Hallam, prin.   227-8756

Utah Valley Community College   6-CC
   1200 S 800 W 84058   222-8000

Panguitch, AC 801, PC 4, Garfield
Garfield SD, 145 E CENTER 84759   4-11111
   Philip Blais, supt.   676-8821
HS, PO BOX 362 84759   2-00011
   Ted Chidester, prin.   676-8805
MS, PO BOX 393 84759   2-00100
   Ted Chidester, prin.   676-8225
Other Schools — See Escalante, Tropic

Park City, AC 801, PC 5, Summit
Park City SD, PO BOX 680310 84068   5-11111
   Don Fielder, supt.   645-5600
HS, PO BOX 1120 84060   3-00011
   Michael Andrews, prin.   645-5650
Treasure Mountain MS   3-01100
   PO BOX 1920 84060   645-5640
   Mona Briggs, prin.

Parowan, AC 801, PC 4, Iron
Iron SD
   Supt. — See Cedar City
JSHS, 168 N MAIN ST 84761   2-00111
   John Pensis, prin.   477-3366

Payson, AC 801, PC 6, Utah
Nebo SD
   Supt. — See Spanish Fork
SHS, 1050 S MAIN ST 84651   4-00001
   Ron Hitchcock, prin.   465-6025
JHS, 1025 S HIGHWAY 6 84651   3-00110
   Lynn Jones, prin.   465-6015

Pleasant Grove, AC 801, PC 7, Utah
Alpine SD
   Supt. — See American Fork
SHS, 700 E 200 S 84062   4-00001
   Eris Waymire, prin.   785-8700
JHS, 810 N 100 E 84062   4-00100
   Kay Giles, prin.   785-8707

Price, AC 801, PC 6, Carbon
Carbon SD, PO BOX 1438 84501   6-11111
   Val Bush, supt.   637-1732
Carbon SHS, 750 E 400 N 84501   4-00001
   Boyd Bell, prin.   637-2463
Mont Harmon JHS, 60 W 400 N 84501   3-00110
   Tonita Crookston, prin.   637-0510
Other Schools — See Helper, Sunnyside

College of Eastern Utah   4-CC
   451 E 400 N 84501   637-2120

Provo, AC 801, PC 8, Utah
Provo SD, 280 W 940 N 84604   7-11111
   Kay Laursen, supt.   374-4800
HS, 1125 N UNIVERSITY AVE 84604   4-00011
   Patti Harrington, prin.   373-6550
Timpview HS   4-00011
   3570 TIMPVIEW DR 84604   221-9720
   Randall Merrill, prin.
Dixon JHS, 750 W 200 N 84601   4-00100
   Robert Gentry, prin.   374-4980
Farrer JHS, 100 N 600 E 84606   3-00110
   Robert Howard, prin.   374-4971

American Inst. of Medical-Dental Tech.   2-CS
   1675 N FREEDOM BLVD 84604   377-2900
Brigham Young University 84602   8-UC
   378-2507
Provo College   1-CS
   1450 W 820 N 84601   375-1861
Stevens Henager College   2-CC
   25 E 1700 S 84606   375-5455
Utah Valley Regional Medical Center   HSP
   1034 N 500 W 84604   373-7850

Randolph, AC 801, PC 2, Rich
Rich SD, PO BOX 67 84064   3-11111
   Daryl Nelson, supt.   793-2135
Rich HS 84064   2-00011
   Dale Lamborn, prin.   793-2365
Other Schools — See Laketown

Richfield, AC 801, PC 6, Sevier
Sevier SD, 195 E 5TH N 84701   5-11111
   Brent Thorne, supt.   896-8214
Cedar Ridge HS, 50 N 650 W 84701   1-00011
   Ray Terry, prin.   896-9464
HS, 510 W 1ST S 84701   3-00011
   Teresa Robinson, prin.   896-8247
Red Hills MS, 405 S 600 W 84701   3-00100
   Bruce Douglas, prin.   896-6421
Other Schools — See Monroe, Salina

Richmond, AC 801, PC 4, Cache
Cache SD
   Supt. — See Logan
North Cache MS   3-00110
   571 S HIGHWAY 91 84333   258-2452
   Earl Lindley, prin.

Riverton, AC 801, PC 7, Salt Lake
Jordan SD
   Supt. — See Sandy
Oquirrh Hills MS, 12949 S 2700 W 84065   4-00110
   Dennis Hansen, prin.   254-8053

Roosevelt, AC 801, PC 5, Duchesne
Duchesne SD
   Supt. — See Duchesne

Union HS
135 N UNION ST # 124-3   84066   3-00011   722-2474
Lloyd Burton, prin.
JHS, 265 N 300 W # 425-1   84066   2-00100   722-2991
Guy Coleman, prin.

Uintah SD
Supt. — See Vernal
West JHS, RR 2 BOX 2466   84066   2-00100   722-4563
John Greene, prin.

Roy, AC 801, PC 7, Weber
Weber SD
Supt. — See Ogden
SHS, 2150 W 4800 S   84067   4-00001   774-4922
Jan Parrish, prin.
JHS, 5400 S 2100 W   84067   4-00110   774-4906
Dean Oborn, prin.
Sand Ridge JHS, 2075 W 4600 S   84067   3-00110   732-6012
Noel Zabriskie, prin.

Saint George, AC 801, PC 8, Washington
Washington SD
189 W TABERNACLE ST   84770   7-11111   673-3553
Steven Peterson, supt.
Dixie SHS, 350 E 700 S   84770   4-00001   673-4682
Ross Taylor, prin.
Pineview SHS, 750 N 2850 E   84770   4-00001   628-5255
David Broadhead, prin.
Dixie JHS, 825 S 100 E   84770   3-00110   628-0441
Michael Stephenson, prin.
Pine View JHS, 2145 E 130 N   84770   3-00110   628-7915
Ray Brooks, prin.
Snow Canyon MS
1215 LAVA FLOW DR   84770   3-00110   634-9953
Dale Barlow, prin.
Other Schools — See Enterprise, Hurricane, Washington

Dixie College   4-CC
225 S 700 E   84770   673-4811

Salina, AC 801, PC 4, Sevier
Sevier SD
Supt. — See Richfield
North Sevier HS, 350 W 400 N   84654   2-00011   529-3717
Larry Shumway, prin.
North Sevier MS, 135 N 100 W   84654   2-00100   529-3841
Boyd Gurney, prin.

Salt Lake City, AC 801, PC 9, Salt Lake
Granite SD, 340 E 3545 S   84115   8-11111   263-6100
Loren Burton, supt.
Cottonwood SHS, 5715 S 1300 E   84121   4-00001   273-2100
Michael Bennett, prin.
Granite SHS, 3305 S 500 E   84106   4-00001   481-7150
Diane Hesleph, prin.
Olympus SHS, 4055 S 2300 E   84124   4-00001   273-2000
McKell Withers, prin.
Skyline SHS, 3251 E 3760 S   84109   4-00001   273-2080
Louie Long, prin.
Taylorsville SHS   4-00001
5225 S REDWOOD RD   84123   263-6153
David Gourley, prin.
Bennion JHS, 6055 S 2700 W   84118   4-00110   964-7665
David Stevens, prin.
Bonneville JHS, 5330 GURENE DR   84117   4-00110   273-2130
Susan Greenlief, prin.
Churchill JHS, 3450 OAKVIEW DR   84124   4-00110   273-2015
Annette Duzett, prin.
Eisenhower JHS   4-00110
4351 S REDWOOD RD   84123   263-6165
Ben Lems, prin.
Evergreen JHS, 3401 S 2000 E   84109   3-00110   481-7215
Dorothy Bingman, prin.
Granite Park JHS, 450 E 3700 S   84115   3-00110   263-6140
Bryce Holbrook, prin.
Olympus JHS   3-00110
2217 MURRAY HOLLADAY RD   84117   273-2120
Mary Voelker, prin.
Wasatch JHS, 3750 S 3100 E   84109   3-00110   273-2115
Karl Moody, prin.
Other Schools — See Kearns, Magna, West Valley

Jordan SD
Supt. — See Sandy
Brighton SHS   4-00001
2220 BENGAL BLVD   84121   944-2914
Ted Lovato, prin.
Butler MS, 7530 S 2700 E   84121   4-00110   944-2955
Marvin Reid, prin.

Salt Lake SD, 440 E 1ST S   84111   8-11111   578-8599
John Bennion, supt.
East HS, 840 S 1300 E   84102   4-00011   583-1661
Kay Peterson, prin.
Highland HS, 2166 S 1700 E   84106   4-00011   484-4343
Charles Shackett, prin.
West HS, 241 N 300 W   84103   4-00011   578-8500
William Boston, prin.
Bryant MS, 40 S 800 E   84102   3-00100   578-8118
Joyce Gray, prin.
Clayton MS, 1471 S 1800 E   84108   3-00100   481-4810
Cherrie Brinlee, prin.
Glendale MS, 1430 ANDREW AVE   84104   3-00100   974-8320
Larry Odom, prin.
Hillside MS, 2375 GARFIELD AVE   84108   3-00100   481-4828
Millie Fletcher, prin.
Northwest MS   3-00100
1400 GOODWIN AVE   84116   578-8547
Rosemary Baron, prin.

American Technical Center   2-CS
1144 W 3300 S   84119   975-1000
Anchor Christian Academy   2-11111
1880 E 5600 S   84121   272-9405
Wayne Musson, prin.
Bryman School   3-CS
1144 W 3300 S   84119   975-7000
Certified Careers Institute   2-CC
1455 W 2200 S # 200   84119   973-7008
Intermountain Christian S   2-11111
6515 LION LN   84121   942-8811
Robert Payne, prin.
Intermountain College of Court Reporting   2-CS
5980 FASHION BLVD   84107   268-9271
Judge Memorial Catholic HS   3-00011
650 S 1100 E   84102   363-8895
Br. Hathaway, prin.
Latter-Day Saints Hospital   HSP
325 8TH AVE   84143   321-1150
L.D.S. Business College   3-CC
411 E SOUTH TEMPLE   84111   800-999-5767
Phillips Junior College   4-CC
3098 HIGHLAND DR # 100   84106   485-0221
Realms of Inquiry S, 1140 S 900 E   84105   1-11111   467-5911
Ross Jones, prin.
Rowland Hall-St. Mark's S   2-00111
843 LINCOLN ST   84102   355-7494
Carl Sturges, prin.
Salt Lake Community College   7-CC
4600 S REDWOOD RD   84123   561-4531
Salt Lake Lutheran HS   1-00011
4020 S 900 E   84124   531-8431
Dennis Haberhern, prin.
University of Utah   7-UC
1400 E 200 S   84112   581-7281
Westminster College of Salt Lake City   4-UC
1840 S 1300 E   84105   800-748-4753

Sandy, AC 801, PC 8, Salt Lake
Jordan SD, 9361 S 300 E   84070   8-11111   567-8100
Raymond Whittenburg, supt.
Alta SHS, 11055 S 1000 E   84094   5-00001   572-7040
Linda Sandstrom, prin.
Jordan SHS, 9351 STATE ST   84070   4-00001   565-7570
Fred Ash, prin.
Valley SHS, 11020 STATE ST   84070   2-00001   572-7035
Clyde Mellberg, prin.
Jordan Tech HS, 825 E 9085 S   84094   Vo Tech   565-7582
John Taylor, prin.
Albion MS, 2755 NEWCASTLE DR   84093   4-00110   944-2946
Craig Stark, prin.
Crescent View MS, 11150 S 300 E   84070   4-00100   572-7063
Tom Hicks, prin.
Eastmont MS, 10100 S 1300 E   84094   4-00110   572-7026
N. J. Tullos, prin.
Indian Hills MS   4-00110
1180 SANDERS RD   84094   572-7012
Eduardo Alba, prin.
Mt. Jordan MS, 9360 S 300 E   84070   3-00110   565-7534
Robert Sproul, prin.
Union MS, 615 E 8000 S   84070   4-00110   565-7540
Liane Smith, prin.
Other Schools — See Bingham Canyon, Midvale, Riverton, Salt Lake City, South Jordan, West Jordan

Waterford S, 1480 E 9400 S   84093   3-11111   572-1780
Nancy Heuston, prin.

Smithfield, AC 801, PC 6, Cache
Cache SD
Supt. — See Logan
Sky View SHS, 520 S 250 E   84335   4-00001   563-6273
Myron Benson, prin.

South Jordan, AC 801, PC 7, Salt Lake
Jordan SD
Supt. — See Sandy
Bingham SHS   5-00001
2160 W SOUTH JORDAN PKY   84095   254-8005
Denny Simkins, prin.
South Jordan MS, 10245 S 2700 W   84095   4-00110   254-8034
Dennis Johnson, prin.

Spanish Fork, AC 801, PC 7, Utah
Nebo SD, 350 S MAIN ST   84660   7-11111   798-4000
Denis Poulsen, supt.
SHS, 99 N 300 W   84660   4-00001   798-4060
Robert Wadley, prin.
IS, 600 TORONTO LN   84660   4-00110   798-4075
Mark Koyle, prin.
Other Schools — See Payson, Springville

Springville, AC 801, PC 7, Utah
Nebo SD
Supt. — See Spanish Fork
SHS, 1205 E 900 S   84663   4-00001   489-2870
Lynn Patterson, prin.
JHS, 165 S 700 E   84663   3-00110   489-2880
Almon Mosher, prin.

Sunnyside, AC 801, PC 2, Carbon
Carbon SD
Supt. — See Price
East Carbon JSHS   2-00111
GENERAL DELIVERY   84539   888-4461
Doug Hintze, prin.

Sunset, AC 801, PC 6, Davis
Davis SD
Supt. — See Farmington

JHS, 1610 N 250 W   84015   4-00110   774-7440
Larry Brewer, prin.

Syracuse, AC 801, PC 5, Davis
Davis SD
Supt. — See Farmington
JHS, 1450 S 2000 W   84075   4-00110   774-7491
James Schmidt, prin.

Tabiona, AC 801, PC 2, Duchesne
Duchesne SD
Supt. — See Duchesne
JSHS, PO BOX 470   84072   1-00111   848-5635
Robert Park, prin.

Tooele, AC 801, PC 7, Tooele
Tooele SD, 66 W VINE ST   84074   6-11111   833-1900
Michael Jacobsen, supt.
HS, 240 W 100 S   84074   4-00011   833-1978
Larry Harrison, prin.
Tooele Valley HS, 240 W 100 S   84074   Vo Tech   833-1928
Larry Harrison, prin.
JHS, 412 W VINE ST   84074   3-00100   833-1921
Louis Killpack, prin.
Other Schools — See Dugway, Grantsville, Wendover

Tremonton, AC 801, PC 5, Box Elder
Box Elder SD
Supt. — See Brigham City
Bear River MS, 900 N 400 E   84337   4-00100   257-5361
Jim Baty, prin.

Tropic, AC 801, PC 2, Garfield
Garfield SD
Supt. — See Panguitch
Bryce Valley JSHS, PO BOX 70   84776   2-00111   679-8719
Scott Jackson, prin.

Trout Creek, AC 801, Juab
Tintic SD
Supt. — See Eureka
West Desert HS   84083   1-00011   693-3112
Edgar Alder, prin.

Vernal, AC 801, PC 6, Uintah
Uintah SD, 635 W 200 S   84078   6-11111   781-3100
Grant Drollinger, supt.
Uintah SHS, 1880 W 500 N   84078   4-00001   781-3110
Ted Taylor, prin.
Ashley Valley HS   Vo Tech
650 N VERNAL AVE   84078   781-3125
A. J. Pease, prin.
JHS, 161 N 1000 W   84078   3-00110   781-3130
Robert Vincent, prin.
MS, 721 W 100 S   84078   3-00110   781-3140
Bill Murphy, prin.
Other Schools — See Roosevelt

Washington, AC 801, PC 5, Washington
Washington SD
Supt. — See Saint George
Millcreek HS   2-00011
25 E TELEGRAPH ST   84780   628-2462
Terry Carr, prin.

Wendover, AC 801, PC 4, Tooele
Tooele SD
Supt. — See Tooele
JSHS, PO BOX 610   84083   2-00111   665-2343
Gary Brogan, prin.

West Haven, AC 801, PC 99, Weber
Weber SD
Supt. — See Ogden
Rocky Mountain HS   3-00110
4300 W 4850 S   84401   626-2590
Darwin Brimhall, prin.

West Jordan, AC 801, PC 8, Salt Lake
Jordan SD
Supt. — See Sandy
SHS, 8136 S 2700 W   84088   4-00001   565-7576
Sidney Beveridge, prin.
Jensen MS, 8105 S 3200 W   84088   4-00110   565-7528
Roger Miner, prin.
MS, 7550 REDWOOD RD   84084   4-00110   565-7542
Gary Steele, prin.

West Valley, AC 801, PC 8, Salt Lake
Granite SD
Supt. — See Salt Lake City
Granger SHS, 3690 S 3600 W   84119   4-00001   964-7600
Dan Talbot, prin.
Hunter SHS, 4200 S 5600 W   84120   4-00001   964-7585
Sheryl Benson, prin.
Hunter JHS, 6131 W 3785 S   84120   4-00110   964-7900
Tim Dyson, prin.
Kennedy JHS, 4495 S 4800 W   84120   4-00110   964-7640
Lloyd Bybee, prin.
Valley JHS, 4195 S 3200 W   84119   4-00110   964-7635
Jerrie Frank, prin.
West Lake JHS, 3400 S 3450 W   84119   4-00110   964-7630
Tom Given, prin.

Woods Cross, AC 801, PC 6, Davis
Davis SD
Supt. — See Farmington
SHS, 600 W 2200 N   84087   4-00001   299-2075
Douglas Beer, prin.

VERMONT

STATE DEPARTMENT OF EDUCATION
State Office Building
120 State St., Montpelier 05602
(802) 828-3135

Commissioner of Education	Richard Mills
Deputy Commissioner	Bruce Richardson
Manager Career & Lifelong Learning	Gerard Asselin
Manager Core Services	Vacant
Manager Family & Educational Support	Dennis Kane
Manager Financial Management	Mark O'Day
Manager School Development & Information	Bob McNamara
Manager Teaching & Learning	Douglas Walker

STATE BOARD OF EDUCATION
120 State St., Montpelier 05602

Chairperson   Sally Sugerman

PUBLIC, PRIVATE AND CATHOLIC SECONDARY SCHOOLS

Arlington, AC 802, PC 3, Bennington
Arlington Supervisory SD — 3-11111
  E ARLINGTON RD 05250 — 375-9744
  Richard Stewart, supt.
Arlington Memorial JSHS — 2-00111
  E ARLINGTON RD 05250 — 375-2589
  Sue Kardas Gee, prin.

Ascutney, AC 802, PC 2, Windsor
Windsor Southeast Supervisory Union
  Supt. — See Windsor
Weathersfield MS, PO BOX 28 05030 — 2-01100
  Marie Commoss, prin. — 674-5400

Barre, AC 802, PC 6, Washington
Barre City Supervisory SD — 4-11111
  60 WASHINGTON ST 05641 — 476-5011
  Lyman Amsden, supt.
Spaulding Union HS 41 — 3-00011
  155 AYERS ST 05641 — 476-4811
  Kay Paterson, prin.
Barre Regional AVC — Vo Tech
  155 AYERS ST 05641 — 476-6237
  Kathleen Finck, prin.
Spaulding MS — 2-00100
  60 WASHINGTON ST 05641 — 476-6541
  David Baker, prin.

Washington Central Supervisory Union — 4-11111
  RR 3 BOX 6685 05641 — 229-0553
  George Olive, supt.
Other Schools – See Montpelier

Bellows Falls, AC 802, PC 5, Windham
Windham Northeast Supervisory Union — 4-11111
  8 1/2 ATKINSON ST 05101 — 463-9958
  Hugh Haggerty, supt.
Bellows Falls Union HS 27 — 2-00011
  131 WESTMINSTER RD 05101 — 463-3944
  Ed Caron, prin.
MS, 11 SCHOOL ST 05101 — 2-01100
  Lawrence Diamond, prin. — 463-4366

Bennington, AC 802, PC 6, Bennington
Southwest Vermont Supervisory Union — 5-11111
  RR 3 BOX 3600 05201 — 447-7501
  Philip Hyjek, supt.
Mt. Anthony Union HS 14 — 4-00011
  301 PARK ST 05201 — 447-7511
  Anthony Krulikowski, prin.
Mt. Anthony MS, 640 MAIN ST 05201 — 3-00100
  H. Combs, prin. — 447-7541

Bennington College 05201 — 3-UC / 800-833-6845

Southern Vermont College — 3-UC
  MONUMENT AVE 05201 — 442-5427

Bethel, AC 802, PC 3, Windsor
Windsor Northwest Supervisory Union — 3-11111
  PO BOX 37 05032 — 234-5364
  Michael Waring, supt.
Whitcomb JSHS, ROUTE 12 05032 — 2-00111
  Steve Michlovitz, prin. — 234-9967
Other Schools – See Rochester

Bradford, AC 802, PC 3, Orange
Orange East Supervisory Union — 4-11111
  PO BOX 396 05033 — 222-5216
  Russell Collins, supt.
Oxbow Union JSHS 30 — 3-00111
  RR 1 BOX 182 05033 — 222-5214
  Duane Benage, prin.
Oxbow AVC, PO BOX 618 05033 — Vo Tech
  Russell Haviland, prin. — 222-5212

Brandon, AC 802, PC 4, Rutland
Rutland Northeast Supervisory Union — 4-11111
  2 UNION ST 05733 — 247-5757
  William Mathis, supt.
Otter Valley Union JSHS 8 — 3-00111
  RR 1 BOX 1115 05733 — 247-6833
  Nancy Crandall, prin.

Brattleboro, AC 802, PC 6, Windham
Windham Southeast Supervisory Union — 5-11111
  15 GREEN ST 05301 — 254-3731
  Raymond McNulty, supt.
Brattleboro Union HS 6 — 3-00011
  50 FAIRGROUND RD 05301 — 257-0356
  Anthony Broom, prin.
Brattleboro Area MS — 2-00100
  27 SUNNY ACRES ST 05301 — 257-0356
  Andrew Paciulli, prin.

Austine School for the Deaf — HND
  120 MAPLE ST 05301
School for International Training — 3-UC
  PO BOX 676 05302 — 257-7751

Bristol, AC 802, PC 4, Addison
Addison Northeast Supervisory Union — 4-11111
  9 AIRPORT DR 05443 — 453-3657
  James Lombardo, supt.
Mt. Abraham Union JSHS 28 — 3-00111
  7 AIRPORT DR 05443 — 453-2333
  David Royce, prin.

Burlington, AC 802, PC 8, Chittenden
Burlington Supervisory SD — 5-11111
  150 COLCHESTER AVE 05401 — 864-8461
  Paul Danyow, supt.
HS, 52 INSTITUTE RD 05401 — 3-00011
  Philip Lanoue, prin. — 864-8411
Burlington Tech Ctr — Vo Tech
  52 INSTITUTE RD 05401 — 864-8426
  Marcia Baker, prin.
Edmunds MS, 275 MAIN ST 05401 — 2-00100
  Steven Hiersche, prin. — 864-8486
Hunt MS, 1364 NORTH AVE 05401 — 2-00100
  Linda Carroll, prin. — 864-8469

Burlington College — 2-UC
  95 NORTH AVE 05401 — 862-9616
Champlain College — 4-UC
  PO BOX 670 05402 — 860-2727
Medical Center Hospital of Vermont — HSP
  111 COLCHESTER AVE 05401 — 656-5133

Shaker Mountain S — 2-00011
  PO BOX 1802 05402
Trinity College — 3-UC
  208 COLCHESTER AVE 05401 — 658-0337
University of Vermont — 6-UC
  194 S PROSPECT ST 05401 — 656-3370

Cabot, AC 802, PC 2, Washington
Washington Northeast Supervisory Union
  Supt. — See Plainfield
Cabot S, MAIN ST 05647 — 2-11111
  Marge DesGroseilliers, prin. — 563-2289

Canaan, AC 802, PC 2, Essex
Essex North Supervisory Union — 2-11111
  PO BOX 100 05903 — 266-3330
  Wayne Murray, supt.
S, PO BOX 69 05903 — 2-11111
  James Bibbo, prin. — 266-7068

Castleton, AC 802, PC 3, Rutland

Castleton State College 05735 — 4-UC / 468-5611

Chelsea, AC 802, PC 3, Orange
Orange-Windsor Supervisory Union
  Supt. — See South Royalton
S, RR 1 BOX 24E 05038 — 2-11111
  Phillip Van Orman, prin. — 685-4551

Chester, AC 802, PC 3, Windsor
Windsor Southwest Supervisory Union — 4-11111
  RR 1 BOX 4 05143 — 875-3365
  Dale Lanphear, supt.
Green Mountain Union JSHS 35 — 2-00111
  RR 3 BOX 72A 05143 — 875-2146
  Andrew Hatt, prin.

Colchester, AC 802, PC 2, Chittenden
Colchester Supervisory SD — 4-11111
  PO BOX 27 05446 — 658-4047
  Roger Bourassa, supt.
HS, PO BOX 31 05446 — 3-00011
  John Willard, prin. — 658-1570
MS, PO BOX 30 05446 — 3-01100
  B. Fitzgerald, prin. — 655-1772

New England Culinary Institute — 2-CS
  1700 TROY AVE # 1 05446 — 655-0808
St. Michael's College — 4-UC
  WINOOSKI PARK 05439 — 654-2000

Concord, AC 802, PC 2, Essex
Essex-Caledonia Supervisory SD — 3-11111
  MAIN ST 05824 – David Elwood, supt. — 695-3373
S 05824 — 2-11111
  Bruce Lynch, prin. — 695-2550

Craftsbury Common, AC 802, PC 2, Orleans
Orleans Southwest Supervisory Union
  Supt. — See Hardwick
Craftsbury S 05827 — 2-11111
  Richard Shanley, prin. — 586-2541

Sterling College 05827   2-CC 586-7711

Danville, AC 802, PC 2, Caledonia
Caledonia Central Supervisory Union   3-11111
PO BOX 216 05828   684-3801
Robert Dikon, supt.
Danville S, PO BOX 176 05828   2-11111
George Sincerbeaux, prin.   684-3651

Derby, AC 802, PC 3, Orleans
Orleans-Essex North Supervisory Union   5-11111
RR 1 BOX 126 05829   766-2251
Paul Moccia, supt.
North Country JHS   2-00100
RR 1 BOX 125 05829   766-2276
Elizabeth LeRoy, prin.
Other Schools – See Newport

Dorset, AC 802, PC 3, Bennington

Long Trail S, RR 2 BOX 1556 05251   1-00111
David Wilson, prin.   867-5717

East Burke, AC 802, PC 99, Caledonia

Burke Mountain Academy   1-00111
PO BOX 78 05832   626-5607
Finn Gunderson, prin.

Enosburg Falls, AC 802, PC 4, Franklin
Franklin Northeast Supervisory Union
Supt. — See Richford
SHS, PO BOX 417 05450   2-00001
Ronald Stahley, prin.   933-7777
Enosburg AVC, PO BOX 278 05450   Vo Tech
George Ambrose, supt.   933-4003
JHS, PO BOX 417 05450   2-00110
Scott Lang, prin.   933-7777

Essex Junction, AC 802, PC 6, Chittenden
Chittenden Central Supervisory Union   4-11111
7 MEADOW TER 05452   879-5576
Robert Harrison, supt.
HS, 2 EDUCATIONAL DR 05452   4-00011
Paul Henry, prin.   879-7121
Essex Junction Regional Tech Ctr   Vo Tech
2 EDUCATIONAL DR 05452   879-5560
Richard Flies, prin.
Lawton MS, 104 MAPLE ST 05452   2-01100
John Bossange, prin.   878-1388

Essex Supervisory SD   4-11100
PO BOX 440 05453   878-8168
Raymond Proulx, supt.
Essex MS, 40 FOSTER RD 05452   2-00100
Howard Magnant, prin.   879-7173

Fairfax, AC 802, PC 2, Franklin
Franklin West Supervisory Union   4-11111
PO BOX 152 05454   849-2283
Donald Collins, supt.
Bellows Free Academy   3-11111
PO BOX 68 05454   849-6711
Richard Brown, prin.
Other Schools – See Saint Albans

Fair Haven, AC 802, PC 5, Rutland
Addison-Rutland Supervisory Union   4-11111
3 N PARK PL 05743   265-4905
Raymond Pentkowski, supt.
Fair Haven Union HS 16   3-00011
3 MECHANIC ST 05743   265-4966
Bruce Gee, prin.

Hardwick, AC 802, PC 4, Caledonia
Orleans Southwest Supervisory Union   4-11111
PO BOX 338 05843   472-6532
Lyonel Tracy, supt.
Hazen Union JSHS 26   2-00111
PO BOX 368 05843   472-6511
James Frail, prin.
Other Schools – See Craftsbury Common

Hinesburg, AC 802, PC 2, Chittenden
Chittenden South Supervisory Union   5-11111
RR 2 BOX 161 05461   482-3885
William Crocoll, supt.
Champlain Valley Union HS 15   3-00011
RR 2 BOX 160 05461   482-2101
Valerie Gardner, prin.
Other Schools – See Shelburne

Hyde Park, AC 802, PC 2, Lamoille
Lamoille North Supervisory Union   4-11111
PO BOX 4133 05655   888-3142
Gayle Utley, supt.
Lamoille Union JSHS 18   3-00111
PO BOX 304 05655   888-4261
Nancy Guyette, prin.
Lamoille AVC, PO BOX 304 05655   Vo Tech
Richard Cross, prin.   888-4447

Jacksonville, AC 802, PC 2, Windham
Windham Southwest Supervisory Union   3-11111
PO BOX 589 05342   368-7712
M. Wright, supt.
Whitingham S, PO BOX 199 05342   2-11111
John Doty, prin.   368-2880
Other Schools – See Wilmington

Jericho, AC 802, PC 4, Chittenden
Chittendon East Supervisory Union
Supt. — See Richmond

Mt. Mansfield Union HS 17   3-00011
RR 2 BOX 120 05465   899-4690
Robert Stevens, prin.

Johnson, AC 802, PC 4, Lamoille

Johnson State College 05656   4-UC 635-2356

Ludlow, AC 802, PC 4, Windsor
Rutland-Windsor Supervisory Union   3-11111
92 MAIN ST # A 05149   228-4771
Lanning Nicoloff, supt.
Black River JSHS 39, 43 MAIN ST 05149   2-00111
Wilfred Cunningham, prin.   228-4721

Lyndon Center, AC 802, PC 2, Caledonia

Lyndon Institute 05850   3-00111
Dwight Davis, prin.   626-3357

Lyndonville, AC 802, PC 4, Caledonia

Lyndon State College 05851   3-UC 800-225-1998

Manchester, AC 802, PC 3, Bennington

Burr and Burton Seminary   2-00011
GENERAL DELIVERY 05254   362-1775
Robert Kennedy, prin.

Marlboro, AC 802, PC 2, Windham

Marlboro College   2-UC
GENERAL DELIVERY 05344   257-4333

Middlebury, AC 802, PC 6, Addison
Addison Central Supervisory Union   4-11111
3 CHARLES AVE 05753   388-2971
Alan Myers, supt.
Middlebury Union HS 3   3-00011
1 CHARLES AVE 05753   388-3111
Ilene Levitt, prin.
Addison County AVC   Vo Tech
CHARLES AVE 05753   388-3115
Robert Morse, prin.
JHS, CHARLES AVE 05753   2-00100
Raymond Pelligrini, prin.   388-3114

Middlebury College 05753   4-UC 388-3711

Milton, AC 802, PC 4, Chittenden
Milton Supervisory SD   4-11111
PO BOX 21 05468   893-3210
A. Keith Ober, supt.
JSHS, 17 LOCUST DR 05468   3-00111
Bill Cofiero, prin.   893-3230

Montpelier, AC 802, PC 6, Washington
Montpelier Supervisory SD   4-11111
58 BARRE ST 05602   223-9796
Edwin Jacobs, supt.
HS, 5 HIGH SCHOOL DR 05602   2-00011
Peter Clarke, prin.   223-6366
Main Street MS, 170 MAIN ST 05602   2-01100
Rebecca Tarrant, prin.   223-3404

Washington Central Supervisory Union
Supt. — See Barre
Union 32 JSHS   3-00111
RR 2 BOX 3315 05602   229-0321
John Coolidge, prin.

New England Culinary Institute   2-UC
250 MAIN ST 05602   223-6324
Norwich University Vermont College   3-UC
05602   223-8780
Woodbury College   1-CS
660 ELM ST 05602   229-0516

Moretown, AC 802, PC 2, Washington
Washington West Supervisory Union   4-11111
PO BOX 1065 05660   244-8877
Thomas Meagher, supt.
Harwood Union JSHS 19   3-00111
RR 1 BOX 790 05660   244-5186
Glenn Frank, prin.

Morrisville, AC 802, PC 4, Lamoille
Lamoille South Supervisory Union   4-11111
PO BOX 340 05661   888-4541
Alice Angney, supt.
Peoples Academy   2-00111
RR 3 BOX 40 05661   888-4600
Michael Mahoney, prin.
Other Schools – See Stowe

Newfane, AC 802, PC 2, Windham
Windham Central Supervisory Union   4-11111
PO BOX 186 05345   365-7651
Thomas Lewis, supt.
Other Schools – See Townshend

Newport, AC 802, PC 5, Orleans
Orleans-Essex North Supervisory Union
Supt. — See Derby
North Country HS #22   4-00011
VETERANS 05855   334-7921
Susan Ginnett, prin.

North Clarendon, AC 802, PC 3, Rutland
Rutland South Supervisory Union   4-11111
PO BOX 87 05759   775-3264
Henry Burnham, supt.

Mill River Union JSHS 40   3-00111
PO BOX 6 05759   775-3451
John Fillioe, prin.

Northfield, AC 802, PC 4, Washington
Washington South Supervisory Union   4-11111
19 MAPLE AVE 05663   485-7755
Ron Paquette, supt.
JSHS, 31 VINE ST 05663   2-00111
Daniel DiLena, prin.   485-5751

Norwich University   4-UC
65 S MAIN ST 05663   800-468-6679

Orleans, AC 802, PC 3, Orleans
Orleans Central Supervisory Union   4-11111
PO BOX 207 05860   754-6945
Larry Ross, supt.
Lake Region Union HS 24   2-00011
RR 1 BOX 76 05860   754-6521
Richard Aubuchon, prin.

Plainfield, AC 802, PC 3, Washington
Washington Northeast Supervisory Union   3-11111
RR 1 BOX 1130 05667   426-3245
William Erickson, supt.
Twinfield S #33   3-11111
RR 1 BOX 1020 05667   426-3213
John Wells, prin.
Other Schools – See Cabot

Goddard College   2-UC
PO BOX G 05667   454-8311

Poultney, AC 802, PC 4, Rutland
Rutland Southwest Supervisory Union   3-11111
PO BOX 238 05764   287-5286
Robert Jarvis, supt.
JSHS, 16 E MAIN ST 05764   2-00111
Darlene Hill, prin.   287-5861

Green Mountain College   3-UC
16 COLLEGE ST 05764   800-776-6675

Proctor, AC 802, PC 4, Rutland
Rutland Central Supervisory Union
Supt. — See Rutland
JSHS, 4 PARK ST 05765   2-00111
Marilyn Grunewald, prin.   459-3353

Putney, AC 802, PC 4, Windham

Landmark College 05346   1-CC 387-4767
Putney S, ELM LEA FARM 05346   2-00111
Sven Huseby, prin.   387-5566

Randolph, AC 802, PC 4, Orange
Orange Southwest Supervisory Union   4-11111
PO BOX 250 05060   728-5052
Edgar Sims, supt.
Randolph Union JSHS 2   3-00111
15 FOREST ST 05060   728-3397
Albert Miller, prin.
Randolph AVC, FOREST ST 05060   Vo Tech
Brian Wrigley, prin.   728-9595

Randolph Center, AC 802, PC 2, Orange

Vermont Technical College 05061   3-CC 728-3391

Richford, AC 802, PC 4, Franklin
Franklin Northeast Supervisory Union   4-11111
PO BOX 130 05476   848-7661
Michael Deweese, supt.
JSHS, 1 CORLISS HTS 05476   2-00111
Kathryn Crockett, prin.   848-7416
Other Schools – See Enosburg Falls

Richmond, AC 802, PC 3, Chittenden
Chittendon East Supervisory Union   5-11111
PO BOX 282 05477   434-2128
Harold Boyden, supt.
Camels Hump MS, RR 1 05477   2-01100
Robert Goudreau, prin.   434-2188
Other Schools – See Jericho, Underhill

Rochester, AC 802, PC 3, Windsor
Windsor Northwest Supervisory Union
Supt. — See Bethel
JSHS, RR 1 BOX 100 05767   2-00111
E. Ann Bonney, prin.   767-3161

Rutland, AC 802, PC 7, Rutland
Rutland Central Supervisory Union   4-11111
PO BOX 440 05702   775-4342
Paul Tracy, supt.
Other Schools – See Proctor, West Rutland

Rutland City Supervisory SD   4-11111
6 CHURCH ST 05701   773-1900
Richard Brothers, supt.
HS, 67 LIBRARY AVE 05701   3-00011
John Poljacik, prin.   773-1955
Stafford Tech Ctr, STRATTON RD 05701   Vo Tech
Sharon Crowley, prin.   773-1990
JHS, 65 LIBRARY AVE 05701   2-00100
Sanford Bassett, prin.   773-1960

College of Saint Joseph   2-UC
71 CLEMENT RD 05701   773-5905
Mt. St. Joseph Academy   2-00011
132 CONVENT AVE 05701   775-0151
Sr. Shirley Davis, prin.

Rutland Regional Medical Center	HSP	
160 ALLEN ST 05701	775-7111	

Saint Albans, AC 802, PC 6, Franklin
Franklin Central Supervisory Union	4-11100	
40 KINGMAN ST 05478	524-2600	
James Aitchison, supt.		
St. Albans Town Central MS	2-01100	
165 S MAIN ST 05478	527-7191	
Terence Keating, prin.		

Franklin West Supervisory Union
Supt. — See Fairfax
Georgia MS, RR 2 BOX 311 05478	2-01100	
Bonnie Poe, prin.	524-6106	

Bellows Free Academy	3-00011	
71 S MAIN ST 05478		

Saint Johnsbury, AC 802, PC 6, Caledonia
St. Johnsbury Supervisory SD	3-11100	
26 WESTERN AVE 05819	748-4744	
Joseph Kasprzak, supt.		
MS, 24 WESTERN AVE 05819	2-00100	
Charles King, prin.	748-8912	

St. Johnsbury Academy	3-00011	
7 MAIN ST 05819 – Bernier Mago, prin.	748-8171	

Saxtons River, AC 802, PC 3, Windham
Vermont Academy	2-00011	
PO BOX 500 05154	869-2121	
Robert Long, prin.		

Shelburne, AC 802, PC 2, Chittenden
Chittendon South Supervisory Union
Supt. — See Hinesburg
MS, 40 HARBOR RD 05482	2-01100	
Carol Spencer, prin.	985-3331	

South Barre, AC 802, PC 4, Washington
Orange North Supervisory Union	3-11111	
PO BOX 397 05670	479-1011	
David Bisson, supt.		
Other Schools – See Williamstown		

South Burlington, AC 802, PC 7, Chittenden
South Burlington Supervisory SD	4-11111	
550 DORSET ST 05403	658-9050	
Fred Tuttle, supt.		
HS, 550 DORSET ST 05403	3-00011	
Bruce Ladeau, prin.	658-9001	
Tuttle MS, 500 DORSET ST 05403	2-00100	
David Ford, prin.	658-9080	

Rice Memorial HS	2-00011	
99 PROCTOR AVE 05403	862-6521	
Br. Lemoyne, prin.		

South Royalton, AC 802, PC 3, Windsor
Orange-Windsor Supervisory Union	4-11111	
PO BOX 240 05068	763-8840	
David Savidge, supt.		
S, RR 2 BOX 11 05068	2-11111	
Shaun Pickett, prin.	763-8844	
Other Schools – See Chelsea		

Vermont Law School	2-UC	
PO BOX 96 05068	763-8303	

Springfield, AC 802, PC 5, Windsor
Springfield Supervisory SD	4-11111	
60 PARK ST 05156	885-5141	
David MacDonald, supt.		
Springfield HS, 303 SOUTH ST 05156	3-00011	
Wayne Ogden, prin.	885-8482	
Technical Ctr at Springfield	Vo Tech	
303 SOUTH ST 05156	885-8484	
Scott Davis, prin.		
Riverside MS	2-00100	
13 FAIRGROUND RD 05156	885-8490	
Rodney Tulonen, prin.		

Stowe, AC 802, PC 2, Lamoille
Lamoille South Supervisory Union
Supt. — See Morrisville
JSHS, 413 BARROWS RD 05672	2-00111	
Martin Giuffre, prin.	253-7229	

Stratton Mountain, AC 802, PC 99, Windham
Stratton Mountain S 05155	1-00111	
Robert Campbell, prin.	297-1886	

Swanton, AC 802, PC 4, Franklin
Franklin Northwest Supervisory Union	5-11111	
PO BOX 130 05488	868-4967	
Douglas Harris, supt.		
Missisquoi Valley Union JSHS 7	4-00111	
RR 2 BOX 268 05488	868-7311	
John Pierce, prin.		

Thetford, AC 802, PC 2, Orange
Thetford Academy	1-00111	
PO BOX 165 05074	785-4805	
Robert Brigham, prin.		

Townshend, AC 802, PC 2, Windham
Windham Central Supervisory Union
Supt. — See Newfane
Leland-Gray Union JSHS 34	2-00111	
PO BOX 128 05353 – (—), prin.	365-7355	

Underhill, AC 802, PC 2, Chittenden
Chittendon East Supervisory Union
Supt. — See Richmond
Browns River MS	2-01100	
RR 1 BOX 3345 05489	899-3711	
Paul Corologos, prin.		

Vergennes, AC 802, PC 5, Addison
Addison Northwest Supervisory Union	4-11111	
185 MAIN ST 05491 – W. Botka, supt.	877-3332	
Vergennes Union JSHS 5	3-00111	
50 MONKTON RD 05491	877-2938	
John Connolly, prin.		

Waitsfield, AC 802, PC 2, Washington
Green Mount Valley S	1-00011	
RR 1 BOX 166 05673	496-2150	
David Gavett, prin.		

Waterbury, AC 802, PC 4, Washington
Community College of Vermont	4-CC	
PO BOX 120 05676	241-3535	

Wells River, AC 802, PC 2, Orange
Blue Mountain Supervisory SD	3-11111	
RR 1 BOX 50A 05081	757-2766	
Albert DePetrillo, supt.		
Blue Mountain Union S 21	3-11111	
RR 1 BOX 50A 05081	757-2711	
James Bonnell, prin.		

West Rutland, AC 802, PC 4, Rutland
Rutland Central Supervisory Union
Supt. — See Rutland
S, RR 2 BOX 05777	2-11111	
Charles Memoe, prin.	438-2288	

White River Junction, AC 802, PC 5, Windsor
Hartford Supervisory SD	4-11111	
2 TAFT AVE 05001 – Carl Mock, supt.	295-8600	
Hartford HS, 28 HIGHLAND AVE 05001	3-00011	
Phillip DuTremble, prin.	295-8610	
Hartford AVC, SAUNDERS AVE 05001	Vo Tech	
Michael Redington, prin.	295-8631	
Hartford Memorial MS	2-01100	
30 HIGHLAND AVE 05001	295-8640	
John Bacon, prin.		

Williamstown, AC 802, PC 3, Orange
Orange North Supervisory Union
Supt. — See South Barre
HS, PO BOX 507 05679	2-00011	
John Desrochers, prin.	433-5359	
MS, PO BOX 507 05679	2-00100	
John Eklund, prin.	433-1036	

Williston, AC 802, PC 2, Chittenden
Pine Ridge S, 1075 WILLISTON RD 05495	1-00011	
Mary Thielen, prin.	434-2161	

Wilmington, AC 802, PC 3, Windham
Windham Southwest Supervisory Union
Supt. — See Jacksonville
JSHS, PO BOX 397 05363	2-00111	
Frank Spencer, prin.	464-5255	

Windsor, AC 802, PC 5, Windsor
Windsor Southeast Supervisory Union	4-11111	
21 RIVER ST 05089	674-2144	
Charles Knisley, supt.		
JSHS, 29 UNION ST 05089	2-00111	
Joe Silver, prin.	674-6344	
Other Schools – See Ascutney		

Winooski, AC 802, PC 6, Chittenden
Winooski Supervisory SD	3-11111	
60 NORMAND ST 05404	655-0485	
George Cross, supt.		
JSHS, 80 NORMAND ST 05404	2-00111	
Sandra Tanquay, prin.	655-3530	

Woodstock, AC 802, PC 4, Windsor
Windsor Central Supervisory Union	4-11111	
MOUNT TOM 05091	457-1213	
Leo Corriveau, supt.		
HS, 29 W WOODSTOCK 05091	2-00011	
Larry Lattanzi, prin.	457-1317	
Woodstock Union MS, RR 4 05091	2-00100	
Johanna Harpster, prin.	457-1317	

VIRGINIA

STATE DEPARTMENT OF EDUCATION
James Monroe Building
P.O. Box 2120, Richmond 23216
(804) 225-3820

Superintendent of Public Instruction	Joseph Spagnolo
Deputy Superintendent Legislative Coordination	Edward Carr
Deputy Superintendent Research, Policy & Information Systems	Doris Redfield
Deputy Superintendent Student Services	Ida Hill

STATE BOARD OF EDUCATION
P.O. Box 2120, Richmond 23216

President	James Jones

PUBLIC, PRIVATE AND CATHOLIC SECONDARY SCHOOLS

Abingdon, AC 703, PC 6, Washington
Washington County SD ... 6-11111
  812 THOMPSON DR 24210 ... 628-1826
  George Stainback, supt.
HS, 705 THOMPSON DR 24210 ... 3-00011
  Berkley Clear, prin. ... 628-1850
Neff Vo-Tech, 255 STANLEY ST 24210 ... Vo Tech
  Norma Keesee, prin. ... 628-1870
Washington Vo-Tech ... Vo Tech
  850 THOMPSON DR 24210 ... 628-1880
  Carl McMurray, prin.
Stanley MS, 297 STANLEY ST 24210 ... 3-00100
  Curtis Burkett, prin. ... 628-1875
Other Schools – See Bristol, Damascus, Glade Spring

Virginia Highlands Community College ... 4-CC
PO BOX 828 24212 ... 628-6094
Washington County Adult Skill Center ... 1-CS
  848 THOMPSON DR 24210

Accomac, AC 804, PC 2, Accomack
Accomack County SD ... 6-11111
  PO BOX 330 23301 ... 787-5754
  Robert DeRonda, supt.
Smith MS, PO BOX 120 23301 ... 2-00100
  Edward Smith, prin. ... 787-3444
Other Schools – See Chincoteague, Oak Hall, Onley,
  Painter, Parksley, Tangier

Alberta, AC 804, PC 2, Brunswick

Southside Virginia Community College ... 4-CC
RR 1 BOX 60 23821 ... 949-7111

Alexandria, AC 703, PC 9, (Indep. City)
Alexandria CSD ... 6-11111
  2000 N BEAUREGARD ST 22311 ... 824-6610
  Paul Masem, supt.
Williams SHS, 3330 KING ST 22302 ... 4-00001
  John Porter, prin. ... 824-6800
Secondary Training Education Program ... Vo Tech
  3330 KING ST 22302 ... 824-6631
  Louise Nickens, prin.
Hammond MS ... 4-00100
  4646 SEMINARY RD 22304 ... 461-4100
  Andre Assalian, prin.
Howard JHS ... 3-00010
  3801 W BRADDOCK RD 22302 ... 824-6750
  Margaret Walsh, prin.
Washington MS ... 4-00100
  1005 MOUNT VERNON AVE 22301 ... 706-4500
  Lawrence Jointer, prin.

Fairfax County SD
  Supt. — See Fairfax
Edison HS, 5801 FRANCONIA RD 22310 ... 4-00011
  Luther Fennell, prin. ... 971-6850
Jefferson Science & Tech HS ... 4-00011
  6560 BRADDOCK RD 22312 ... 750-8300
  Geoffrey Jones, prin.
Mt. Vernon HS ... 4-00011
  8515 OLD MOUNT VERNON RD 22309 ... 360-5900
  Calanthia Tucker, prin.
West Potomac HS ... 4-00011
  6500 QUANDER RD 22307 ... 768-2121
  Teressa Caldwell, prin.
Hayfield JSHS ... 5-00111
  7630 TELEGRAPH RD 22310 ... 922-5020
  J. Victor Lutz, prin.
Glasgow MS, 4101 FAIRFAX PKY 22312 ... 3-00100
  David Smith, prin. ... 813-8700
Holmes MS, 6525 MONTROSE ST 22312 ... 3-00100
  Vera Blake, prin. ... 658-5900
Sandburg MS ... 3-00100
  8428 FORT HUNT RD 22308 ... 799-6100
  Linda Whitfield, prin.
Twain MS, 4700 FRANCONIA RD 22310 ... 3-00100
  (—), prin. ... 313-3700
Whitman MS, 2500 PARKERS LN 22306 ... 3-00100
  Eugene Jordan, prin. ... 660-2400

Regional Academic Governors School Dist
  Supt. — See Richmond
Jefferson HS for Science and Technology ... 4-00011
  6560 BRADDOCK RD 22312 ... 750-8300
  Geoffrey Jones, prin.

Bishop Ireton HS ... 3-00011
  210 CAMBRIDGE RD 22314 ... 751-7606
  Fr. Metzger, prin.
Computer Learning Center of Washington ... 2-CS
  6295 EDSALL RD # 210 22312 ... 823-0300
Episcopal HS, 1200 N QUAKER LN 22302 ... 2-00111
  Lee Ainslie, prin. ... 379-6530
Northern Virginia Community College ... 4-CC
  3001 N BEAUREGARD ST 22311 ... 845-6200
Notre Dame Apostolic Catechetical Inst ... 2-UC
  4407 SANO ST 22312 ... 658-4304
Protestant Episcopal Theologcl. Seminary ... 2-UC
  3737 SEMINARY RD 22304 ... 370-6600
St. Stephens/St. Agnes S ... 3-11111
  1000 SAINT STEPHENS RD 22304 ... 751-2700
  Joan Holden, prin.
TESST Electronic School ... 2-CS
  1400 DUKE ST 22314 ... 548-4800

Altavista, AC 804, PC 5, Campbell
Campbell County SD
  Supt. — See Rustburg

JSHS, 900 BEDFORD AVE 24517 ... 3-00111
  Scott Worner, prin. ... 369-4768

Amelia Court House, AC 804, PC 3, Amelia
Amelia County SD ... 4-11111
  16410 DUNN ST 23002 ... 561-2621
  Charles Shell, supt.
Amelia JSHS ... 3-00111
  8500 OTTERBURN RD 23002 ... 561-2101
  Susan Roberts, prin.

Amherst, AC 804, PC 4, Amherst
Amherst County SD ... 5-11111
  PO BOX 1257 24521 ... 946-9386
  John Daniels, supt.
HS, PO BOX 410 24521 ... 4-00011
  Karl Carter, prin. ... 946-9391
MS, PO BOX 450 24521 ... 2-00100
  Jenny Lambdin, prin. ... 946-9394
Other Schools – See Madison Heights

Annandale, AC 703, PC 8, Fairfax
Fairfax County SD
  Supt. — See Fairfax
HS, 4700 MEDFORD DR 22003 ... 4-00011
  George Watson, prin. ... 256-4600
Poe MS, 7000 CINDY LN 22003 ... 3-00100
  Barbara Nissen, prin. ... 813-3800

Northern Virginia Community College ... 7-CC
  8333 LITTLE RIVER TPKE 22003 ... 323-3000

Appalachia, AC 703, PC 4, Wise
Wise County SD
  Supt. — See Wise
JSHS, 205 LEE ST 24216 ... 2-00111
  R. Nash, prin. ... 565-0214

Appomattox, AC 804, PC 4, Appomattox
Appomattox County SD ... 4-11111
  PO BOX 548 24522 ... 352-8251
  Jack Thomas, supt.
HS, ROUTE 727 24522 ... 3-00111
  Shirley Eye, prin. ... 352-7146
MS, 300 N CHURCH ST 24522 ... 2-00100
  Leverne Marshall, prin. ... 352-8257

Arlington, AC 703, PC 9, Arlington
Arlington County SD ... 7-11111
  1426 N QUINCY ST 22207 ... 358-6010
  Arthur Gosling, supt.
Wakefield HS ... 4-00011
  4901 S CHESTERFIELD RD 22206 ... 358-6700
  Dr. Marie Shiels-Djouadi, prin.
Washington-Lee HS ... 4-00011
  1300 N QUINCY ST 22201 ... 358-6200
  Dr. William Sharbaugh, prin.
Yorktown HS, 5201 28TH ST N 22207 ... 4-00011
  Michael Durso, prin. ... 358-5400
Tech Ed & Career Ctr ... Vo Tech
  816 S WALTER REED DR 22204 ... 358-5800
  THOMAS SMOLINSKI, prin.
Jefferson MS ... 4-00100
  125 S OLD GLEBE RD 22204 ... 358-5900
  Lawrence Grove, prin.
Kenmore MS ... 3-00100
  200 S CARLIN SPRINGS RD 22204 ... 358-6800
  Carlton Lampkins, prin.
Swanson MS ... 3-00100
  5800 WASHINGTON BLVD 22205 ... 358-5500
  Marion Spraggins, prin.
Williamsburg MS ... 3-00100
  3600 N HARRISON ST 22207 ... 358-5450
  Margaret McCourt-Dirner, prin.

Denis J. O'Connell HS ... 4-00011
  6600 LITTLE FALLS RD 22213 ... 237-1400
  Alward Burch, prin.
Marymount University ... 4-UC
  2807 N GLEBE RD 22207 ... 800-548-7638

Arrington, AC 804, PC 2, Nelson
Nelson County SD
  Supt. — See Lovingston
Nelson MS, RR 1 BOX 262 22922 ... 2-00100
  Jesse Taylor, prin. ... 263-4801

Ashburn, AC 703, PC 5, Loudoun
Loudoun County SD
  Supt. — See Leesburg
Broad Run HS, PO BOX 200 22011 ... 4-00011
  E. Wayne Griffith, prin. ... 771-6620

Ashland, AC 804, PC 6, Hanover
Hanover County SD ... 7-11111
  200 BERKLEY ST 23005 ... 752-6000
  Stephen Baker, supt.
Henry HS, RR 3 BOX 2700 23005 ... 4-00011
  Lloyd Jones, prin. ... 752-6023
Liberty MS, RR 3 BOX 2500 23005 ... 4-00100
  Cheryl Magill, prin. ... 752-6020
Other Schools – See Mechanicsville

Randolph-Macon College ... 4-UC
  200 HENRY ST 23005 ... 752-7345

Axton, AC 703, PC 2, Henry
Henry County SD
  Supt. — See Collinsville
Axton MS, PO BOX 426 24054 ... 2-00100
  Charles Craddock, prin. ... 650-1193

Bassett, AC 703, PC 4, Henry
Henry County SD
  Supt. — See Collinsville
HS, RR 4 BOX 546 24055 ... 3-00011
  Robert Gunter, prin. ... 629-1731
MS, RR 7 BOX 890 24055 ... 3-00100
  Stephen Burton, prin. ... 629-2587

Bealeton, AC 703, PC 1, Fauquier
Fauquier County SD
  Supt. — See Warrenton
Cedar-Lee JHS, PO BOX 97 22712 ... 3-00110
  John Harrison, prin. ... 439-3207

Bedford, AC 703, PC 6, (Indep. City)
Bedford County SD ... 6-11111
  310 S BRIDGE ST 24523 ... 586-1045
  Dr. John Kent, supt.
Liberty HS, 100 MINUTE MAN DR 24523 ... 3-00011
  F Dewitt House, prin. ... 586-2541
Bedford Vo-Tech ... Vo Tech
  600 EDMUND ST 24523 ... 586-3933
  Patrick Sherman, prin.
MS, 503 LONGWOOD AVE 24523 ... 2-00100
  Faye Craghead, prin. ... 586-7735
Other Schools – See Forest, Moneta

Ben Hur, AC 703, PC 2, Lee
Lee County SD
  Supt. — See Jonesville
Lee Vo-Tech, PO BOX 100 24218 ... Vo Tech
  Charles Ledger, prin. ... 346-1960

Berryville, AC 703, PC 5, Clarke
Clarke County SD ... 4-11111
  309 W MAIN ST 22611 ... 955-6100
  Dennis Kellison, supt.
Clarke County HS ... 2-00111
  RR 3 BOX 5578 22611 ... 955-6130
  John English, prin.
Johnson-Williams MS ... 2-00100
  200 SWAN AVE 22611 ... 955-6125
  Mary Anne Biggs, prin.

Grafton School ... HND
  PO BOX 112 22611 ... 955-2400

Big Stone Gap, AC 703, PC 5, Wise
Wise County SD
  Supt. — See Wise
Powell Valley HS, PO BOX P 24219 ... 3-00011
  David Dowdy, prin. ... 523-1290
Powell Valley MS ... 3-01100
  PO BOX 280 24219 ... 523-0195
  George Collins, prin.

Mountain Empire Community College ... 4-CC
  PO BOX 700 24219 ... 800-262-7323

Blacksburg, AC 703, PC 8, Montgomery
Montgomery County SD
  Supt. — See Christiansburg
HS, 550 PATRICK HENRY DR 24060 ... 3-00011
  (—), prin. ... 951-4455
MS, 501 S MAIN ST 24060 ... 3-00100
  Gary McCoy, prin. ... 552-2401

Virginia Polytechnic Institute & State U ... 7-UC
  24061 ... 231-6267

Blairs, AC 804, PC 2, Pittsylvania
Pittsylvania SD
  Supt. — See Chatham
JHS, RR 2 BOX 31 24527 ... 2-00100
  Jeremiah Hemingway, prin. ... 836-2540

Bland, AC 703, PC 3, Bland
Bland County SD, PO BOX 339 24315 ... 4-11111
  Morris Witten, supt. ... 688-3361
JSHS, RR 14 24315 ... 2-00111
  Roger Thompson, prin. ... 688-3621
Other Schools – See Rocky Gap

Bluefield, AC 703, PC 6, Tazewell
Tazewell County SD
  Supt. — See Tazewell
Graham HS, RR 4 BOX 308G 24605 ... 3-00011
  Charles Grindstaff, prin. ... 326-1235
Graham MS 24605 ... 3-00100
  Jerry Cromer, prin. ... 326-1101

Bluefield College ... 2-UC
  3000 COLLEGE DR 24605 ... 800-872-0175
National Business College ... 2-CC
  100 LOGAN ST 24605 ... 326-3621

Bowling Green, AC 804, PC 3, Caroline
Caroline County SD, RR 1 BOX 2J 22427 ... 5-11111
  Richard Glancy, supt. ... 633-5088
Other Schools – See Milford

Boydton, AC 804, PC 2, Mecklenburg
Mecklenburg County SD ... 6-11111
  PO BOX 190 23917 ... 738-6111
  William Chapman, supt.
Other Schools – See Skipwith, South Hill

Bridgewater, AC 703, PC 5, Rockingham
Rockingham County SD
  Supt. — See Harrisonburg
Ashby HS, 800 N MAIN ST 22812 ... 3-00011
  Michael Loso, prin. ... 828-2008

Bridgewater College   3-UC
   402 E COLLEGE ST 22812   828-2501

Bristol, AC 703, PC 7, (Indep. City)
Bristol CSD, 222 OAK ST 24201   5-11111
   David Lenker, supt.   669-8181
Virginia HS   3-00011
   1200 LONG CRESCENT DR 24201   669-2136
   Albert Outlaw, prin.
Virginia Vo-Tech S   Vo Tech
   1200 LONG CRESCENT DR 24201   466-8118
   Donald Wright, prin.
Virginia MS, 501 PIEDMONT AVE 24201   2-00100
   Donald Davis, prin.   669-2042

Washington County SD
   Supt. — See Abingdon
Battle HS, 21264 BATTLE HILL DR 24202   3-00011
   William Brannon, prin.   645-2300
Wallace MS   2-00100
   13077 WALLACE PIKE 24202   645-2370
   Gary Catron, prin.

Graham Bible College   2-UC
   PO BOX 1630 24203   968-4201
National Business College   2-CC
   300A PIEDMONT AVE 24201   669-5333
Virginia Intermont College   3-UC
   1013 MOORE ST 24201   800-451-1842

Broadway, AC 703, PC 4, Rockingham
Rockingham County SD
   Supt. — See Harrisonburg
HS, GOBBLER DR 22815   3-00011
   Delmer Botkin, prin.   896-7081
Myers MS, PO BOX 517 22815   3-00100
   Ronald Smith, prin.   896-8961

Buchanan, AC 703, PC 4, Botetourt
Botetourt County SD
   Supt. — See Fincastle
James River HS, RR 1 BOX 317AA 24066   2-00011
   Lawrence Journell, prin.   254-1121

Buckingham, AC 804, PC 2, Buckingham
Buckingham County SD   4-11111
   PO BOX 24 23921 – D. Gold, supt.   969-4212
SHS, HC 2 BOX 376 23921   3-00001
   Lawrence Lenz, prin.   969-4280
Other Schools – See Dillwyn

Buena Vista, AC 703, PC 6, (Indep. City)
Buena Vista CSD, PO BOX 110 24416   4-11111
   James Bradford, supt.   261-2129
McCluer HS   2-00011
   2329 CHESTNUT AVE 24416   261-2128
   Wayne Flint, prin.
McCluer MS   2-00100
   2329 CHESTNUT AVE 24416   261-7340
   Robert Williams, prin.

Southern Virginia College for Women   2-CC
   1 COLLEGE HILL DR 24416   800-229-8420

Burke, AC 703, PC 8, Fairfax
Fairfax County SD
   Supt. — See Fairfax
Lake Braddock JSHS   5-00111
   9200 BURKE LAKE RD 22015   323-9000
   Jack Dorminey, prin.

Carson, AC 804, PC 2, Dinwiddie
Jointly Operated Vo Tech SD
   Supt. — See Richmond
Rowanty Vo-Tech Ctr   Vo Tech
   20000 ROWANTY RD 23830   732-4950
   Charles Friedl, prin.

Castlewood, AC 703, PC 4, Russell
Russell County SD
   Supt. — See Lebanon
JSHS, RR 3 24224   2-00111
   Roger Glovier, prin.   762-9449

Centreville, AC 703, PC 8, Fairfax
Fairfax County SD
   Supt. — See Fairfax
Stone MS, 5500 SULLY PARK DR 22020   3-00100
   Susan DeCorpo, prin.   631-5500

Chantilly, AC 703, PC 8, Fairfax
Fairfax County SD
   Supt. — See Fairfax
HS, 13120 POPLAR TREE RD 22033   4-00011
   Stephen Wareham, prin.   222-8100
Franklin MS   4-00100
   3300 LEES CORNER RD 22021   904-5100
   Johnnie Hamilton, prin.
Rocky Run MS   4-00100
   4400 STRINGFELLOW RD 22021   378-4100
   Richard Lavine, prin.

Charles City, AC 804, PC 1, Charles City
Charles City County SD   4-11111
   10910 COURTHOUSE RD 23030   829-2401
   Willie Townes, supt.
Charles City Co. JSHS   2-00111
   10039 COURTHOUSE RD 23030   829-9223
   (—), prin.

Charlotte Court House, AC 804, PC 3, Charlotte
Charlotte County SD   4-11111
   PO BOX 790 23923   542-5151
   Paul Stapleton, supt.

Randolph-Henry HS   3-00011
   PO BOX 668 23923   542-4111
   Judy Lacks, prin.
Central MS, PO BOX 748 23923   2-00100
   Albert Randolph, prin.   542-5149

Charlottesville, AC 804, PC 8, (Indep. City)
Albermarle County SD   7-11111
   401 MCINTIRE RD 22902   296-5826
   Robert Paskel, supt.
Albermarle HS   4-00011
   2775 HYDRAULIC RD 22901   973-5351
   William Raines, prin.
Burley MS, 901 ROSE HILL DR 22903   3-00100
   Thomas Zimorski, prin.   295-5101
Jouett MS, 2065 LAMBS RD 22901   3-00100
   James Helvin, prin.   973-5374
Walton MS, RR 1 BOX 200 22903   3-00100
   Paul Tiscornia, prin.   977-5615
Other Schools – See Crozet

Charlottesville CSD   5-11111
   1562 DAIRY RD 22903   979-9250
   Joseph McGeehan, supt.
HS, 1400 MELBOURNE RD 22901   4-00011
   Robert Thompson, prin.   296-5131
Buford MS, 617 9TH ST SW 22903   3-00100
   David Rogers, prin.   296-5571

Jointly Operated Vo Tech SD
   Supt. — See Richmond
Charlottsville-Albemarle Vo-Tech Ctr   Vo Tech
   1000 E RIO RD 22901   973-4461
   Vicki Behr, prin.

Institute of Textile Technology   1-UC
   2551 IVY RD 22903   296-5511
Lafayette Academy   HND
   1023 MILLMONT ST 22903
Miller S of Albemarle 22901   2-01111
   James Warren, prin.   823-4805
National Business College   2-CC
   1819 EMMET ST N 22901   295-0136
Piedmont Virginia Community College   4-CC
   RR 6 BOX 1A 22902   977-3900
St. Anne's Belfield S, 2132 IVY RD 22903   3-11111
   Rev. Conway, prin.   296-5106
University of Virginia   7-UC
   PO BOX 9017 22906   924-7751
University of Virginia Medical Center   4-HSP
   22908

Chatham, AC 804, PC 4, Pittsylvania
Pittsylvania SD, PO BOX 232 24531   6-11111
   John Reece, supt.   432-2761
JSHS, RR 2 BOX 112A 24531   3-00011
   Ruth Still, prin.   432-8305
Pittsylvania Vo-Tech   Vo Tech
   RR 2 BOX 102K 24531   432-9416
   Ralph Cypress, prin.
Other Schools – See Blairs, Dry Fork, Gretna,
Ringgold

Chatham Hall S, 1 PRUDEN AVE 24531   2-00011
   Jerry VanVoorhis, prin.   432-2941
Hargrave Military Academy   2-00111
   RR 5 24531 – Ronald Sykes, prin.   432-2481

Chesapeake, AC 804, PC 9, (Indep. City)
Chesapeake CSD   8-11111
   PO BOX 15204 23328   547-4114
   C. Fred Bateman, supt.
Great Bridge SHS   4-00001
   301 HANBURY RD W 23320   482-5191
   Robert Robinson, prin.
Deep Creek HS   4-00011
   2900 MARGARET BOOKER DR 23323   494-7520
   Nathan Hardee, prin.
Indian River HS   4-00011
   2301 DUNBARTON DR 23325   494-7510
   James Frye, prin.
Smith HS, 2500 RODGERS ST 23324   4-00011
   Glen Koonce, prin.   494-7500
Western Branch HS   4-00011
   4222 TERRY DR 23321   494-7530
   Arthur Brandriff, prin.
Chesapeake Science & Tech   Vo Tech
   1617 CEDAR RD 23320   547-0134
   Janet Garner, prin.
Crestwood JHS   3-00100
   1420 GREAT BRIDGE BLVD 23320   494-7560
   Linda Byrd, prin.
Deep Creek JHS, 1955 DEAL DR 23323   3-00100
   Clyde Sheely, prin.   494-7570
Great Bridge JHS   4-00110
   441 BATTLEFIELD BLVD S 23320   482-5128
   Clifton Randolph, prin.
Indian River JHS   4-00100
   2300 OLD GREENBRIER RD 23325   494-7580
   Robert Glisson, prin.
Truitt MS, 1100 HOLLY AVE 23324   3-00100
   Charlie Jubilee, prin.   494-7590
Western Branch MS   4-00100
   4201 HAWKSLEY DR 23321   494-7540
   Craig Jones, prin.

Rice Aviation   2-CS
   5202 W MILITARY HWY 23321   465-2813
Tidewater Community College   3-CC
   1428 CEDAR RD 23320   547-9271
Tidewater Tech   2-CS
   1417 BATTLEFIELD BLVD N 23320   548-2828

Chester, AC 804, PC 7, Chesterfield
Chesterfield County SD
   Supt. — See Chesterfield
Dale HS, 3626 W HUNDRED RD 23831   4-00011
   Aubrey Lindsey, prin.   768-6245
Carver MS   3-00100
   12400 BRANDERS BRIDGE RD 23831   768-6130
   T. Tilley, prin.
MS, 3900 W HUNDRED RD 23831   3-00100
   Wayne Wawner, prin.   768-6145

John Tyler Community College   5-CC
   13101 JEFFERSON DAVIS HWY 23831
     800-522-3490

Chesterfield, AC 804, PC 3, Chesterfield
Chesterfield County SD   8-11111
   PO BOX 10 23832   748-1411
   Thomas Fulghum, supt.
Bird HS, 10301 COURTHOUSE RD 23832   4-00011
   John Baskerville, prin.   768-6110
Chesterfield Vo-Tech   Vo Tech
   10101 COURTHOUSE RD 23832   768-6145
   JEFF BAUGHMAN, prin.
Other Schools – See Chester, Ettrick, Matoaca,
Midlothian, Richmond

Chilhowie, AC 703, PC 4, Smyth
Smyth County SD
   Supt. — See Marion
JSHS, PO BOX Z 24319   3-00111
   Carlisle Hostetter, prin.   646-8967

Chincoteague, AC 804, PC 5, Accomack
Accomack County SD
   Supt. — See Accomac
JSHS, N MAIN STREET 23336   2-00111
   Mark Flynn, prin.   336-6166

Christchurch, AC 804, PC 1, Middlesex

Christchurch S 23031   2-00011
   Rev. Phipps, prin.   758-2306

Christiansburg, AC 703, PC 7, Montgomery
Montgomery County SD   6-11111
   200 JUNKIN ST 24073   382-5100
   Herman Bartlett, supt.
HS, 1200 INDEPENDENCE BLVD 24073   3-00011
   George Porterfield, prin.   382-5178
MS, 208 COLLEGE ST 24073   3-00100
   William Fletcher, prin.   382-5168
Other Schools – See Blacksburg, Riner, Shawsville

Clifton, AC 703, PC 2, Fairfax
Fairfax County SD
   Supt. — See Fairfax
Centreville HS   4-00011
   6001 UNION MILL RD 22024   968-7444
   William Trussell, prin.

Clifton Forge, AC 703, PC 5, (Indep. City)
Alleghany Highlands CSD
   Supt. — See Covington
Clifton MS, COMMERCIAL ST 24422   2-00100
   L. Carter, prin.   863-1726

Dabney S. Lancaster Community College   3-CC
   PO BOX 1000 24422   862-4246

Clinchco, AC 703, PC 3, Dickenson
Dickenson County SD
   Supt. — See Clintwood
Dickenson Vo-Tech 24226   Vo Tech
   DON MULLINS, prin.   835-9384

Clinchport, AC 703, PC 1, Scott
Scott County SD
   Supt. — See Gate City
Rye Cove JSHS, RR 4 24244   2-00111
   Michael Brickey, prin.   940-2701

Clintwood, AC 703, PC 4, Dickenson
Dickenson County SD   5-11111
   PO BOX 1127 24228   926-4643
   Gerald Triplett, supt.
JSHS, PO BOX 577 24228   3-00111
   Douglas Mullins, prin.   926-8400
Other Schools – See Clinchco, Haysi, Nora

Coeburn, AC 703, PC 4, Wise
Wise County SD
   Supt. — See Wise
JSHS, PO BOX 2036 24230   3-00111
   Danny Greear, prin.   395-3389

Flatwoods Conservation Center   2-CS
   RR 1 BOX 211 24230

Collinsville, AC 703, PC 6, Henry
Henry County SD   6-11111
   PO BOX 8958 24078   638-5321
   Virgil Poore, supt.
Fieldale-Collinsville HS   3-00011
   415 MILES RD 24078   647-3841
   R. Brent Vann, prin.
Other Schools – See Axton, Bassett, Fieldale,
Martinsville, Ridgeway

Colonial Beach, AC 804, PC 5, Westmoreland
Colonial Beach CSD   3-11111
   16 IRVING AVE N 22443   224-0906
   Donald Warner, supt.
Colonial Beach S, 100 1ST ST 22443   3-11111
   Lee Stevenson, prin.   224-7166

Colonial Heights, AC 804, PC 7, (Indep. City)
Colonial Heights CSD — 5-11111
512 BOULEVARD 23834 — 526-0811
James Ruffa, supt.
HS, 3600 CONDUIT RD 23834 — 3-00011
Robert Goulder, prin. — 526-0922
MS, 500 CONDUIT RD 23834 — 3-00100
Ann Williams, prin. — 526-7790

Courtland, AC 804, PC 3, Southampton
Southhampton County SD — 5-11111
PO BOX 26 23837 — 653-2692
Howard Wainwright, supt.
Southampton HS — 3-00011
23450 SOUTHAMPTON PKY 23837 — 653-2751
Bill Wright, prin.
Southampton MS — 3-00100
23116 MEHERRIN RD 23837 — 653-9250
James Ricks, prin.

Southampton Academy — 2-11111
26495 OLD PLANK RD 23837 — 653-2512
Russell Glenn, prin.

Covington, AC 703, PC 6, (Indep. City)
Alleghany Highlands CSD — 5-11111
110 ROSEDALE AVE 24426 — 965-1800
Martin Loughlin, supt.
Alleghany HS, RR 2 24426 — 3-00011
Phillip Douglas, prin. — 863-1700
Other Schools – See Clifton Forge

Covington CSD — 3-11111
340 E WALNUT ST 24426 — 965-1400
Tom Robertson, supt.
JSHS, 530 S LEXINGTON AVE 24426 — 2-00111
John Clemmer, prin. — 962-1410

Jointly Operated Vo Tech SD
Supt. — See Richmond
Jackson River Vo-Tech Ctr — Vo Tech
105 E COUNTRY CLUB LN 24426 — 862-1308
W Graham, prin.

Crewe, AC 804, PC 4, Nottoway
Nottoway County SD
Supt. — See Nottoway
Southside Vo-Tech — Vo Tech
PO BOX 258 23930 — 645-7471
GARY GRONEWEG, prin.

Southside Training Skill Center — 1-CS
PO BOX 258 23930 — 645-7471

Crozet, AC 804, PC 4, Albemarle
Albermarle County SD
Supt. — See Charlottesville
Western Albermarle HS — 4-00011
RR 1 BOX 425 22932 — 823-4314
Anne Coughlin, prin.
Henley MS, RR 1 BOX 519 22932 — 3-00100
Donald Vale, prin. — 823-4393

Culpeper, AC 703, PC 6, Culpeper
Culpepper County SD — 6-11111
1051 N MAIN ST 22701 — 825-3677
Tony Stewart, supt.
Culpeper County SHS — 3-00001
475 ACHIEVEMENT DR 22701 — 825-8310
Walter Pearson, prin.
JHS, 500 ACHIEVEMENT DR 22701 — 4-00110
R. Steven Nichols, prin. — 825-4140

Jointly Operated Vo Tech SD
Supt. — See Richmond
Piedmont Vo-Tech Ctr — Vo Tech
PO BOX 999 22701 — 825-0476
John Bodine, prin.

Cumberland, AC 804, PC 2, Cumberland
Cumberland County SD — 4-11111
PO BOX 170 23040 — 492-4212
James Irons, supt.
JSHS, PO BOX 140 23040 — 2-00011
Steven Dimmett, prin. — 492-4808
MS, PO BOX 170 23040 — 2-00100
Janice Page, prin. — 492-9627

Daleville, AC 703, PC 4, Botetourt
Botetourt County SD
Supt. — See Fincastle
Lord Botetourt HS — 3-00011
755 ROANOKE RD 24083 — 992-1261
James Sledd, prin.

Damascus, AC 703, PC 3, Washington
Washington County SD
Supt. — See Abingdon
Holston HS, 21308 MONROE RD 24236 — 2-00111
Duane Alderman, prin. — 628-1890
MS, 32101 GOVERNMENT RD 24236 — 2-01100
V. Rector, prin. — 628-1845

Danville, AC 804, PC 8, (Indep. City)
Danville CSD, PO BOX 9600 24543 — 6-11111
Mark Edwards, supt. — 799-6400
Washington SHS, 701 BROAD ST 24541 — 4-00011
Charles Lackey, prin. — 799-6410
Bonner JHS, 300 APOLLO AVE 24540 — 3-00100
Robert Haskins, prin. — 799-6446
Langston JHS — 3-00110
228 CLEVELAND ST 24541 — 799-6443
Reamous Gunn, prin.

Averett College — 4-UC
420 W MAIN ST 24541 — 791-5660
Danville Community College — 4-CC
1008 S MAIN ST 24541 — 797-3553
Memorial Hospital — HSP
142 S MAIN ST 24541 — 799-4510
National Business College — 2-CC
734 MAIN ST 24541 — 793-6822

Davenport, AC 703, PC 1, Buchanan
Buchanan County SD
Supt. — See Grundy
JSHS, PO BOX 70 24239 — 2-00111
Willie Sullivan, prin. — 859-2627

Dayton, AC 703, PC 3, Rockingham
Rockingham County SD
Supt. — See Harrisonburg
Pence MS, PO BOX 1199 22821 — 3-00100
Joann Wenger, prin. — 879-2535

Dendron, AC 804, PC 2, Surry
Surry County SD
Supt. — See Surry
Surry JSHS, RR 1 BOX 15 23839 — 3-00111
Frank Williams, prin. — 267-2211

Dillwyn, AC 804, PC 2, Buckingham
Buckingham County SD
Supt. — See Buckingham
Buckingham JHS, PO BOX 77 23936 — 2-00110
Mary Louise Jones, prin. — 983-2102

Dinwiddie, AC 804, PC 2, Dinwiddie
Dinwiddie County SD — 5-11111
PO BOX 7 23841 — 469-4517
Thomas Gaul, supt.
Dinwiddie County HS — 4-00011
PO BOX 299 23841 — 469-3711
Daniel Wells, prin.
Dinwiddie Co. MS — 3-00100
PO BOX 340 23841 – (—), prin. — 469-7028

Disputanta, AC 804, PC 2, Prince George
Prince George County SD
Supt. — See Prince George
Moore JHS — 3-00110
11033 PRINCE GEORGE DR 23842 — 733-2740
Charles Boschen, prin.

Dry Fork, AC 804, PC 2, Pittsylvania
Pittsylvania SD
Supt. — See Chatham
Tunstall JSHS, RR 1 BOX 265 24549 — 3-00111
Calvin Scarce, prin. — 724-7111

Dublin, AC 703, PC 4, Pulaski
Pulaski County SD
Supt. — See Pulaski
Pulaski HS, PO BOX 518 24084 — 4-00011
Thomas Debolt, prin. — 674-4606
MS, PO BOX 1067 24084 — 3-00100
Paul Phillips, prin. — 674-4663

Regional Academic Governors School Dist
Supt. — See Richmond
SW VA Governors S Science Math & Tech — 1-00001
PO BOX 1739 24084 — 674-1980
Margaret Duncan, prin.

New River Community College — 4-CC
PO BOX 1127 24084 — 674-3603

Dumfries, AC 703, PC 5, Prince William
Prince William County SD
Supt. — See Manassas
Potomac HS — 4-00011
16706 JEFFERSON DAVIS HWY 22026 — 221-1134
Michael Campbell, prin.

Dyke, AC 804, PC 1, Greene

Blue Ridge S 22935 — 2-00011
Edward McFarlane, prin. — 985-2811

Eastville, AC 804, PC 2, Northampton
Northampton County SD — 5-11111
PO BOX 37 23347 — 678-5151
S. Goldstine, supt.
Northampton HS — 3-00011
GENERAL DELIVERY 23347 — 678-5144
Paul Custis, prin.
Other Schools – See Machipongo

Elkton, AC 703, PC 4, Rockingham
Rockingham County SD
Supt. — See Harrisonburg
MS, 401 BLUE AND GOLD DR 22827 — 2-00100
Joseph Dudash, prin. — 298-1228

Emory, AC 703, PC 4, Washington

Emory & Henry College — 3-UC
GENERAL DELIVERY 24327 — 944-3121

Emporia, AC 804, PC 6, (Indep. City)
Greensville County SD — 5-11111
PO BOX 1156 23847 — 634-3748
Dorothea Shannon, supt.
Greensville HS, 403 HARDING ST 23847 — 3-00011
Paul Britt, prin. — 634-2195
Wyatt MS, 206 SLAGLES LAKE RD 23847 — 2-00100
William Hawkins, prin. — 634-5159

Ettrick, AC 804, PC 6, Chesterfield
Chesterfield County SD
Supt. — See Chesterfield

Matoaca HS, 6001 HICKORY RD 23803 — 3-00011
James Ballard, prin. — 590-3110

Ewing, AC 703, PC 3, Lee
Lee County SD
Supt. — See Jonesville
Walker JSHS, PO BOX 39 24248 — 2-00111
Ernie Chadwell, prin. — 445-4111

Exmore, AC 804, PC 4, Northampton

Broadwater Academy — 2-11111
PO BOX 546 23350 — 442-9041
John Ordeman, prin.

Fairfax, AC 703, PC 7, (Indep. City)
Fairfax County SD — 9-11111
10700 PAGE AVE 22030 — 246-2631
Robert Spillane, supt.
HS, 3500 OLD LEE HWY 22030 — 4-00011
Donald Weinheimer, prin. — 591-8350
Woodson HS, 9525 MAIN ST 22031 — 4-00011
Gary Miller, prin. — 323-1911
Robinson JSHS — 5-00111
5035 SIDEBURN RD 22032 – (—), prin. — 323-7500
Frost MS, 4101 PICKETT RD 22032 — 3-00100
Leslie Kent, prin. — 503-2600
Lanier MS, 3710 BEVAN DR 22030 — 3-00100
James Walters, prin. — 273-0790
Other Schools – See Alexandria, Annandale, Burke,
Centreville, Chantilly, Clifton, Falls Church,
Herndon, Mc Lean, Reston, Springfield, Vienna

George Mason University — 7-UC
4400 UNIVERSITY DR 22030 — 323-2100
Paul VI HS, 10675 LEE HWY 22030 — 4-00011
Fr. Mulligan, prin. — 352-0925

Fairfield, AC 703, PC 2, Rockbridge
Rockbridge County SD
Supt. — See Lexington
Rockbridge MS, PO BOX 328 24435 — 2-00100
Russell Fleshman, prin. — 348-5445

Falls Church, AC 703, PC 6, (Indep. City)
Fairfax County SD
Supt. — See Fairfax
HS, 7521 JAGUAR TRL 22042 — 4-00011
Marvin Spratley, prin. — 573-4900
Marshall HS — 4-00011
7731 LEESBURG PIKE 22043 — 893-7400
Elizabeth Goodman, prin.
Stuart HS — 4-00011
3301 PEACE VALLEY LN 22044 — 820-1114
Nancy Weisgerber, prin.
Community Base Vo Ed — Vo Tech
7423 CAMP ALGER AVE 22042 — 698-0400
Teresa Fleming, prin.
Jackson MS, 3020 GALLOWS RD 22042 — 3-00100
Michael Doran, prin. — 204-8100
Longfellow MS — 3-00100
2000 WESTMORELAND ST 22043 — 533-2600
Ann Monday, prin.

Falls Church CSD — 4-11111
301 N WASHINGTON ST 22046 — 241-7602
Stewart Roberson, supt.
Mason HS, 7124 LEESBURG PIKE 22043 — 2-00011
Robert Snee, prin. — 241-7620
Mason JHS, 7124 LEESBURG PIKE 22043 — 2-00110
Rochelle Friedman, prin. — 241-7654

ATI Career Institute — 2-CS
7777 LEESBURG PIKE # 100 22043
— 800-444-0804
Child Development Ctr. of Northern VA — HND
111 N CHERRY ST 22046
Fairfax Hospital — HSP
3300 GALLOWS RD 22042 — 698-3371

Falmouth, AC 703, PC 5, Stafford
Stafford County SD
Supt. — See Stafford
Drew MS, 501 CAMBRIDGE ST 22405 — 3-00100
Donald Dixon, prin. — 371-1415
Gayle MS, 610 GAYLE ST 22405 — 3-00100
David Ward, prin. — 373-0383

Farmville, AC 804, PC 6, Prince Edward
Prince Edward County SD — 5-11111
RR 5 BOX 680 23901 — 392-8893
James Anderson, supt.
Prince Edward HS — 3-00011
RR 5 BOX 680 23901 — 392-6167
Ervin McQuaige, prin.
Prince Edward MS — 3-01100
RR 5 BOX 680 23901 — 392-9594
Maurice Finney, prin.

Fuqua S, PO BOX 328 23901 — 3-11111
Robert Redd, prin. — 392-4131
Longwood College 23901 — 5-UC
— 395-2060

Ferrum, AC 703, PC 4, Franklin

Ferrum College 24088 — 4-UC
— 800-868-9797

Fieldale, AC 703, PC 4, Henry
Henry County SD
Supt. — See Collinsville
Carver MS, PO BOX 837 24089 — 2-00100
R Donivan Edwards, prin. — 957-2226

Fincastle, AC 703, PC 2, Botetourt
Botetourt County SD 5-11111
PO BOX 309 24090 473-8263
Dr. Clarence McClure, supt.
Botetourt Vo-Tech, PO BOX 97 24090 Vo Tech
J Jenkins, prin. 473-8216
Botetourt MS, RR 2 BOX 41 24090 3-00100
Lewis Barlow, prin. 473-8333
Other Schools – See Buchanan, Daleville

Fishersville, AC 703, PC 5, Augusta
Augusta County SD 7-11111
RR 1 BOX 252 22939 245-5100
Edward Clymore, supt.
Wilson Memorial HS 3-00011
RR 1 BOX 260 22939 886-4286
Charles Wymer, prin.
Other Schools – See Fort Defiance, Staunton, Stuarts Draft, Swoope

Jointly Operated Vo Tech SD
Supt. — See Richmond
Valley Vo-Tech Ctr Vo Tech
RR 1 BOX 265 22939 245-5002
G. Avoli, prin.

Regional Academic Governors School Dist
Supt. — See Richmond
Central Shenandoah Valley Gov S Sci/Tech 2-00001
RR 1 BOX 265 22939 245-5088
Linda Newbern Cauley, prin.

Augusta Medical Center HSP
PO BOX 1000 22939 887-2168
Wilson Rehabilitation Center 1-CS
PO BOX 81 22939 332-7166

Floyd, AC 703, PC 2, Floyd
Floyd County SD 4-11111
220 NEWTOWN RD 24091 745-9400
Terry Arbogast, supt.
JSHS, 859 BAKER ST 24091 3-00111
Norman Blanchard, prin. 745-9450

Forest, AC 804, PC 6, Bedford
Bedford County SD
Supt. — See Bedford
Forest HS, 1 CAVALIER CIR 24551 3-00011
John Walker, prin. 525-2674
Forest MS, 137 PERROWVILLE RD 24551 2-00100
John Walker, prin. 525-6630

Fork Union, AC 804, PC 2, Fluvanna
Fluvanna County SD
Supt. — See Palmyra
Fluvanna MS, RR 1 BOX 57DD 23055 3-00100
Willa Powell, prin. 842-2222

Fork Union Military Academy 3-00111
PO BOX 278 23055 842-3212
Ronnie Clark, prin.

Fort Defiance, AC 703, PC 2, Augusta
Augusta County SD
Supt. — See Fishersville
HS, PO BOX 38 24437 3-00011
Charles Huffman, prin. 248-4867
Stewart MS, PO BOX 37 24437 3-00100
Donald Curtis, prin. 248-1800

Franklin, AC 804, PC 6, (Indep. City)
Franklin CSD, 800 W 2ND AVE 23851 4-11111
Alfred Butler, supt. 569-8111
JSHS, 310 CRESCENT DR 23851 3-00111
Samuel Jones, prin. 562-5187

Paul D. Camp Community College 3-CC
PO BOX 737 23851 562-2171

Fredericksburg, AC 703, PC 7, (Indep. City)
Fredericksburg CSD 4-11111
817 PRINCESS ANNE ST 22401 372-1130
J. Garnett, supt.
Monroe JSHS 3-00111
2300 WASHINGTON AVE 22401 372-1100
Robert Burch, prin.

Spotsylvania County SD
Supt. — See Spotsylvania
Chancellor HS 4-00011
6300 HARRISON RD 22407 786-2606
John Winston, prin.
Battlefield MS 3-00100
11120 LEAVELLS RD 22407 786-4400
Dwight Frazier, prin.
Chancellor MS 4-00100
6320 HARRISON RD 22407 786-8099
Mary Spiri, prin.

Stafford County SD
Supt. — See Stafford
Stafford HS 4-00011
33 STAFFORD INDIANS LN 22405 371-7200
William Pugh, prin.

Mary Washington College 5-UC
1701 COLLEGE AVE 22401 899-4681

Fries, AC 703, PC 3, Grayson
Grayson County SD
Supt. — See Independence
MS, PO BOX 446 24330 2-00100
Reginald Gardner, prin. 744-7201

Front Royal, AC 703, PC 7, Warren
Warren County SD 5-11111
111 E CRISER RD 22630 635-2171
Samuel Cook, supt.
Warren County HS 4-00011
240 S LURAY AVE 22630 635-4144
V. Douglas Joyner, prin.
Warren County MS 4-00100
500 W 15TH ST 22630 635-2194
Edward Holler, prin.

Christendom College 2-UC
2101 SHENANDOAH SHORES RD 22630 636-2900
Randolph-Macon Academy 2-00111
201 W 3RD ST 22630 636-5200
Trevor Turner, prin.

Galax, AC 703, PC 6, (Indep. City)
Galax CSD, 223 LONG ST 24333 4-11111
Jimmy Stuart, supt. 236-2911
HS, 200 CLARK AVE 24333 2-00011
Douglas Arnold, prin. 236-2991
MS, CLARK AVE 24333 2-00100
Rebecca Cardwell, prin. 236-6124

Gate City, AC 703, PC 4, Scott
Scott County SD 5-11111
261 E JACKSON ST 24251 386-6118
Michael Basham, supt.
SHS, 127 BEECH ST 24251 2-00001
H. Clabaugh, prin. 386-7522
Scott County Vo-Tech Vo Tech
150 BROADWATER AVE 24251 386-6515
Thomas Haynes, prin.
JHS, 125 BEECH ST 24251 3-00110
Ralph Quesinberry, prin. 386-6065
Other Schools – See Clinchport, Nickelsville

Glade Spring, AC 703, PC 4, Washington
Washington County SD
Supt. — See Abingdon
Henry HS, 31437 HILLMAN HWY 24340 3-00011
David Fore, prin. 628-1895
MS, RR 1 BOX 111 24340 2-00100
Douglas Sparks, prin. 628-1846

Glen Allen, AC 804, PC 6, Henrico
Henrico County SD
Supt. — See Richmond
VA Randolph Community Vo-Tech Vo Tech
2204 MOUNTAIN RD 23060 261-5085
Martha Collier, prin.
Short Pump MS 4-00100
4701 POUNCEY TRACT RD 23060 360-0800
Lynn Thorpe, prin.

Glenns, AC 804, PC 3, Gloucester

Rappahannock Community College 3-CC
PO BOX 287 23149 758-5324

Gloucester, AC 804, PC 4, Gloucester
Gloucester County SD 6-11111
RR 5 BOX 243 23061 693-1425
J. Hoover, supt.
HS, RR 4 BOX 502 23061 4-00011
C. Gray, prin. 693-2526
Page MS, RR 4 BOX 2790 23061 3-00100
Paul Douglas, prin. 693-2540
Peasley MS, RR 5 BOX 1131 23061 3-00100
Daniel Fary, prin. 693-1499

Gloucester Point, AC 804, PC 6, Gloucester

College of William and Mary 23062 3-UC

Goochland, AC 804, PC 3, Goochland
Goochland County SD 4-11111
PO BOX 169 23063 556-5316
Harold Absher, supt.
HS, 1860 SANDY HOOK RD 23063 2-00011
(—), prin. 556-5322
MS, 2748 DOGTOWN RD 23063 2-00100
Barbara Brown, prin. 556-5320

Gretna, AC 804, PC 4, Pittsylvania
Pittsylvania SD
Supt. — See Chatham
HS, PO BOX 398 24557 2-00011
W. Scruggs, prin. 656-2246
MS, PO BOX 308 24557 2-00100
Clarke Scott, prin. 656-2217

Grundy, AC 703, PC 4, Buchanan
Buchanan County SD 6-11111
PO BOX 833 24614 935-2331
Paul Hatfield, supt.
SHS, RR 5 BOX 23 24614 3-00001
James Branham, prin. 935-2106
Buchanan Vo-Tech Vo Tech
RR 5 BOX 110 24614 935-4541
Robert Rife, prin.
JHS, PO BOX 669 24614 3-00110
Nathan Harper, prin. 935-7030
Other Schools – See Davenport, Hurley, Oakwood, Pilgrims Knob

Halifax, AC 804, PC 3, Halifax
Halifax County SD 6-11111
PO BOX 1849 24558 476-2171
Kenneth Walker, supt.
Other Schools – See South Boston

Hampden-Sydney, AC 804, PC 4, Prince Edward

Hampden-Sydney College 3-UC
PO BOX 128 23943 223-4388

Hampton, AC 804, PC 9, (Indep. City)
Hampton CSD 7-11111
1819 NICKERSON BLVD 23663 850-5225
Raymond Washington, supt.
Bethel HS, 1067 BIG BETHEL RD 23666 4-00011
W. David Pearson, prin. 825-4400
HS, 1491 W QUEEN ST 23669 4-00011
Richard Thomas, prin. 825-4430
Kecoughtan HS 4-00011
522 WOODLAND RD 23669 850-5000
Thomas Bailey, prin.
Phoebus HS, 100 IRELAND ST 23663 4-00011
Clayton Washington, prin. 727-1000
Davis MS, 1435 TODDS LN 23666 4-00100
John Pauls, prin. 825-4520
Eaton MS 3-00100
2108 CUNNINGHAM DR 23666 825-4540
Ashby Kilgore, prin.
Lindsay MS, 1636 BRIARFIELD RD 23661 3-00100
Arnold Baker, prin. 825-4560
Spratley MS, 339 WOODLAND RD 23669 4-00100
Cornelius Sherman, prin. 850-5032
Syms MS, 170 FOX HILL RD 23669 4-00100
Ivey Hawkins, prin. 850-5050

Jointly Operated Vo Tech SD
Supt. — See Richmond
New Horizons Vo-Tech Ctr Vo Tech
520 BUTLER FARM RD 23666 766-0000
Ralph Johnson, prin.

Regional Academic Governors School Dist
Supt. — See Richmond
New Horizons S Science and Technology 1-00001
520 BUTLER FARM RD 23666 766-0000
Ralph Johnson, prin.

Commonwealth College 2-CC
1120 W MERCURY BLVD 23666 838-2122
ECPI Computer Institute 2-CS
1919 COMMERCE DR 23666 838-9191
Hampton University 23668 6-UC
727-5328
Peninsula Academy HND
2244 EXECUTIVE DR 23666
Thomas Nelson Community College 5-CC
PO BOX 9407 23670 825-2800
Virginia School for the Deaf and Blind HND
700 SHELL RD 23661

Harrisonburg, AC 703, PC 8, (Indep. City)
Harrisonburg CSD, 317 S MAIN ST 22801 5-11111
C. Alan Hiner, supt. 434-9916
HS, 300 W GRACE ST 22801 3-00011
John Heubach, prin. 433-2652
Harrison MS, 1311 W MARKET ST 22801 3-00100
James Goodloe, prin. 434-1949

Jointly Operated Vo Tech SD
Supt. — See Richmond
Massanutten Vo-Tech Ctr Vo Tech
325 PLEASANT VALLEY RD 22801 434-5961
Jimmie Tickle, prin.

Rockingham County SD 6-11111
404 COUNTY OFFICE BLDG 22801 564-3200
Dr. David Andes, supt.
Other Schools – See Bridgewater, Broadway, Dayton, Elkton, Penn Laird

---

Dominion Business School 1-CS
933 RESERVOIR ST 22801 433-6977
Eastern Mennonite College 4-UC
1200 PARK RD 22801 368-2665
Eastern Mennonite HS 2-00111
801 PARKWOOD DR 22801 433-9107
David Yoder, prin.
James Madison University 22807 7-UC
568-6147
National Business College 2-CC
51B BURGESS RD 22801 432-0943
Rockingham Memorial Hospital HSP
235 CANTRELL AVE 22801 564-5407

Haysi, AC 703, PC 2, Dickenson
Dickenson County SD
Supt. — See Clintwood
JSHS 24256 3-00111
George Rasnake, prin. 865-5126

Heathsville, AC 804, PC 2, Northumberland
Northumberland County SD 4-11111
PO BOX 10 22473 – C. Suggs, supt. 529-6134
Northumberland HS 2-00011
PO BOX 40 22473 580-5192
Dale Wittler, prin.
Northumberland MS 2-00100
PO BOX 100 22473 580-5753
Robert Bailey, prin.

Herndon, AC 703, PC 7, Fairfax
Fairfax County SD
Supt. — See Fairfax
HS, 700 BENNETT ST 22070 4-00011
Dale Sander, prin. 437-6800
MS, 901 LOCUST ST 22070 4-00100
Henry Ticknor, prin. 437-1725

Highland Springs, AC 804, PC 7, Henrico
Henrico County SD
  Supt. — See Richmond
  HS, 15 S OAK AVE 23075   4-00011
    Joseph Oley, prin.   328-4000
  Highland Springs Vo-Tech   Vo Tech
    15 S OAK AVE 23075   328-4075
    ROY BILLINGSLEY, prin.

Hillsville, AC 703, PC 4, Carroll
Carroll County SD   5-11111
  PO BOX 1328 24343   728-3191
    Oliver McBride, supt.
  Carroll County SHS   3-00011
  PO BOX 1268 24343   728-2125
    Harold Golding, prin.
  JHS, 1036 N MAIN ST 24343   3-00110
    Charles Smythers, prin.   728-2382

Hollins College, PC 7, Roanoke

Hollins College   4-UC
  PO BOX 9707 24020   800-456-9595

Honaker, AC 703, PC 3, Russell
Russell County SD
  Supt. — See Lebanon
  JSHS, PO BOX 764 24260   3-00111
    Harry Steffey, prin.   873-6363

Hopewell, AC 804, PC 7, (Indep. City)
Hopewell CSD, 103 N 11TH AVE 23860   5-11111
    David Stuckwisch, supt.   541-2365
  HS, 400 S MESA DR 23860   4-00011
    Gayle Keith, prin.   541-2370
  Woodson MS   3-00100
    1000 WINSTON CHURCHILL DR 23860   541-2380
    Ernestine Wilson, prin.

Hot Springs, AC 703, PC 2, Bath
Bath County SD
  Supt. — See Warm Springs
  Bath JSHS, RR 2 BOX 575 24445   2-00111
    (—), prin.   839-2431

Hurley, AC 703, PC 2, Buchanan
Buchanan County SD
  Supt. — See Grundy
  HS, RR 1 BOX 249 24620   2-00011
    Clarence Brown, prin.   566-8334
  MS, RR 1 BOX 111 24620   2-01100
    Marvin Lewis, prin.   566-8523

Independence, AC 703, PC 3, Grayson
Grayson County SD   4-11111
  PO BOX 219 24348   773-2832
    Sidney Harvey, supt.
  Grayson County HS   3-00011
  PO BOX 190 24348   773-2131
    Mike Phipps, prin.
  Grayson Vo-Tech, PO BOX 707 24348   Vo Tech
    Jerry Cock, prin.   773-2951
  MS, PO BOX 155 24348   2-00100
    Olen Webb, prin.   773-3020
  Other Schools – See Fries, Whitetop

Isle of Wight, AC 804, PC 1, Isle of Wight
Isle of Wight County SD   5-11111
  PO BOX 78 23397   357-4393
    Jane Truelove-York, supt.
  Other Schools – See Smithfield, Windsor

Isle of Wight Academy   2-11111
  PO BOX 105 23397   357-3866
    Benjamin Vaughn, prin.

Jetersville, AC 804, PC 99, Amelia
Jointly Operated Vo Tech SD
  Supt. — See Richmond
  Amelia-Nottoway Vo-Tech Ctr   Vo Tech
  PO BOX 965 23083   645-7854
    Richard Glowinski, prin.

Jonesville, AC 703, PC 3, Lee
Lee County SD, 5 PARK ST 24263   5-11111
    Jerry Bishop, supt.   346-2107
  Lee HS, RR 2 BOX 740 24263   4-00011
    Gary Perdue, prin.   346-0173
  MS, RR 1 BOX 104H 24263   2-01100
    Jake Doss, prin.   346-1011
  Other Schools – See Ben Hur, Ewing, Pennington Gap

Keysville, AC 804, PC 3, Charlotte
Regional Academic Governors School Dist
  Supt. — See Richmond
  Southside VA Regional Governors S   2-00001
    SOUTHSIDE VA COMM COLLEGE 23947
    George Schauer, prin.   736-0616

Southside Virginia Community College   2-CC
  RR 1 BOX 15 23947

Kilmarnock, AC 804, PC 4, Lancaster
Lancaster County SD   4-11111
  PO BOX 2000 22482   435-3183
    T. Dickerson, supt.
  Lancaster MS, PO BOX 1927 22482   3-01100
    Randolph Latimore, prin.   435-1681
  Other Schools – See Lancaster

King and Queen Court House, AC 804, PC 1, King and Queen
King & Queen County SD   3-11111
  PO BOX 97 23085   785-6241
    Lloyd Hamlin, supt.

Central JSHS, PO BOX 8C 23085   2-00111
    John Whittington, prin.   785-6102

King George, AC 703, PC 2, King George
King George County SD   5-11111
  10139 JAMES MADISON PKY 22485   775-5833
    L. Bulger, supt.
  HS, 9 W DAHLGREN RD 22485   3-00011
    Richard Roberts, prin.   775-3055
  MS, 71 W DAHLGREN RD 22485   3-00100
    Emory Turner, prin.   775-2331

King William, AC 804, PC 1, King William
King William County SD   4-11111
  PO BOX 185 23086   769-3434
    Sue Burgess, supt.
  HS, RR 1 BOX 401 23086   2-00011
    Harry Rippeon, prin.   769-2708
  Hamilton-Holmes MS   3-01100
    RR 1 BOX 96 23086   769-3316
    Douglas Childers, prin.

Lancaster, AC 804, PC 1, Lancaster
Lancaster County SD
  Supt. — See Kilmarnock
  HS, PO BOX 123 22503   2-00111
    Doris Estreet, prin.   462-5177

Lawrenceville, AC 804, PC 4, Brunswick
Brunswick County SD   5-11111
  PO BOX 309 23868   848-3138
    Dale Baird, supt.
  Brunswick SHS, RR 1 BOX 15 23868   3-00011
    R. Gerald Burke, prin.   848-2716
  Russell JHS, RR 1 BOX 239 23868   3-00110
    Walden Evans, prin.   848-2132

Brunswick Academy   2-11111
  RR 1 BOX 196 23868   848-2220
    Jean Grizzard, prin.
St. Paul's College   3-UC
  406 WINDSOR AVE 23868   848-3984

Lebanon, AC 703, PC 5, Russell
Russell County SD, PO BOX 8 24266   5-11111
    Larry Massie, supt.   889-6500
  HS, PO BOX 217 24266   3-00011
    O. Sword, prin.   889-6539
  Russell Vo-Tech, PO BOX 848 24266   Vo Tech
    Charles Lowdermilk, prin.   889-6550
  MS, PO BOX 577 24266   3-01100
    Charles Duty, prin.   889-6548
  Other Schools – See Castlewood, Honaker

Leesburg, AC 703, PC 7, Loudoun
Loudoun County SD   7-11111
  102 NORTH ST NW 22075   771-6410
    Edgar Hatrick, supt.
  Loudoun HS   4-00011
  415 DRY MILL RD SW 22075   771-6580
    Edward Starzenski, prin.
  Monroe Vo-Tech   Vo Tech
  715 CHILDRENS CENTER RD SW 22075
    MICHAEL MEGEATH, prin.   771-6560
  Simpson MS, RR 1 BOX 372 22075   3-00100
    Francis Fera, prin.   771-6640
  Other Schools – See Ashburn, Purcellville, Sterling

Catholic Home Study Institute   HMS
  9 LOUDOUN ST SE 22075   800-258-2474
Morven Park Intnl Equestrian Institute   1-CS
  RR 4 BOX 43 22075   777-2890

Lexington, AC 703, PC 6, (Indep. City)
Lexington CSD, 300A WHITE ST 24450   2-11100
    Nicholas Maschal, supt.   463-7146
  Lylburn-Downing MS   2-00100
  300 DIAMOND ST 24450   463-3532
    Clyde Keen, prin.

Rockbridge County SD   5-11111
  417 MORNINGSIDE DR 24450   463-7386
    Glen Suter, supt.
Rockbridge Co. HS, RR 7 BOX 40A 24450   3-00011
    John Reynolds, prin.   463-5555
Maury River MS   2-00100
  600 WADDELL ST 24450   463-3129
    Roy Gray, prin.
Other Schools – See Fairfield

Virginia Military Institute 24450   4-UC
     464-7211
Washington & Lee University 24450   4-UC
     463-8710

Locust Grove, AC 703, PC 1, Orange

Germanna Community College   4-CC
  PO BOX 339 22508   399-1333

Lovingston, AC 804, PC 3, Nelson
Nelson County SD   4-11111
  PO BOX 276 22949   263-8311
    Ellwood Lewis, supt.
  Nelson HS, PO BOX 249 22949   3-00011
    Charles Sprinkle, prin.   263-8317
  Other Schools – See Arrington

Low Moor, AC 703, PC 3, Alleghany

Alleghany Regional Hospital   HSP
  PO BOX 7 24457   862-6011

Luray, AC 703, PC 5, Page
Page County SD, 735 W MAIN ST 22835   5-11111
    David Nagy, supt.   743-6533
  JSHS, PO BOX 422 22835   3-00111
    C. Jordan, prin.   743-3800
  Page County Technical Ctr   Vo Tech
  RR 5 BOX 154 22835   778-2281
    Philip Secrist, prin.
  Other Schools – See Shenandoah

Lynchburg, AC 804, PC 8, (Indep. City)
Campbell County SD
  Supt. — See Rustburg
  Brookville HS, 1111 LAXTON RD 24502   3-00011
    Donald Kelsey, prin.   239-2636
  Brookville MS, 1113 LAXTON RD 24502   3-01100
    Terry Hoggatt, prin.   239-9267

Lynchburg CSD, PO BOX 1599 24505   6-11111
    James McCormick, supt.   522-3700
  Glass HS, 2111 MEMORIAL AVE 24501   4-00011
    Howard Hurt, prin.   522-3712
  Heritage HS   4-00011
  3020 WARDS FERRY RD 24502   582-1147
    Roger Roberts, prin.
  Dunbar MS, 1200 POLK ST 24504   3-00100
    John Lange, prin.   522-3740
  Linkhorne MS   3-00100
  2525 LINKHORNE DR 24503   384-5150
    Charles Booker, prin.
  Sandusky MS, 805 CHINOOK PL 24502   3-00100
    Consuella Woods, prin.   582-1120

Regional Academic Governors School Dist
  Supt. — See Richmond
  Central VA Governors S Science & Tech   1-00001
  3020 WARDS FERRY RD 24502   582-1104
    Thomas Morgan, prin.

Centra Health   HSP
  TATE SPRINGS ROAD 24501   947-3000
Central Virginia Community College   4-CC
  3506 WARDS RD 24502   800-563-3060
Holy Cross S   2-11111
  2125 LANGHORNE RD 24501   847-5436
    John Jones, prin.
Liberty University   7-UC
  PO BOX 20000 24506   582-2158
Lynchburg Christian Academy   2-11111
  701 THOMAS RD 24514   239-9281
    Charles Schneider, prin.
Lynchburg College   4-UC
  1501 LAKESIDE DR 24501   522-8100
National Business College   2-CC
  104 CANDLEWOOD CT 24502   239-3500
Phillips Business College   2-CS
  PO BOX 169 24505   847-7701
Randolph-Macon Woman's College   3-UC
  2500 RIVERMONT AVE 24503   846-7392
Seven Hills S   2-00111
  2001 RIVERMONT AVE 24503   847-1013
Virginia Episcopal S   2-00011
  PO BOX 408 24505   384-6221
    Charles Zimmer, prin.

Machipongo, AC 804, PC 2, Northampton
Northampton County SD
  Supt. — See Eastville
Northampton MS 23405   3-00100
    Calvin Brickhouse, prin.   678-5383

Mc Lean, AC 703, PC 7, Fairfax
Fairfax County SD
  Supt. — See Fairfax
Langley HS   4-00011
  6520 GEORGETOWN PIKE 22101   356-1960
    Joseph Arangio, prin.
HS, 1633 DAVIDSON RD 22101   4-00011
    Elizabeth Lodal, prin.   356-0700
Cooper MS, 977 BALLS HILL RD 22101   3-00100
    Bernard Gross, prin.   442-5800

Madeira S   2-00011
  8328 GEORGETOWN PIKE 22102   556-8200
    Elisabeth Griffith, prin.
Potomac S   3-11111
  1301 POTOMAC SCHOOL RD 22101   356-4100
    Brian Wright, prin.

Madison, AC 703, PC 2, Madison
Madison County SD   4-11111
  PO BOX 647 22727   948-6836
    Thomas Campbell, supt.
  Madison County HS   3-00111
  RR 1 BOX 104M 22727   948-5271
    Colin Owens, prin.
  Wetsel MS 22727   2-00100
    John Anderson, prin.   948-4558

Madison Heights, AC 804, PC 7, Amherst
Amherst County SD
  Supt. — See Amherst
Monelison MS, 250 DANIELS DR 24572   3-00100
    H. Paris, prin.   846-1307

Manassas, AC 703, PC 8, (Indep. City)
Manassas CSD, 9000 TUDOR LN 22110   6-11111
    James Upperman, supt.   361-0166
  Osbourn SHS, 9005 TUDOR LN 22110   3-00001
    Marion Stephens, prin.   369-2121
  Metz JHS, 9700 FAIRVIEW AVE 22111   4-00110
    Ann Yeck, prin.   368-5580

Prince William County SD — 8-11111
PO BOX 389 22110 — 791-8712
Edward Kelly, supt.
Jackson HS, 8820 RIXLEW LN 22110 — 4-00011
George Thoms, prin. — 368-2107
Osbourn Park HS — 4-00011
8909 EUCLID AVE 22111 – (—), prin. — 361-1101
Marsteller MS, 8730 SUDLEY RD 22110 — 3-00100
William Perry, prin. — 368-8134
Parkside MS, 8602 MATHIS AVE 22110 — 3-00100
Eugene Kidwell, prin. — 361-3106
Saunders MS, 13557 SPRIGGS RD 22111 — 4-00100
Gary Beauchamp, prin. — 670-9188
Stonewall MS — 3-00100
10100 LOMOND DR 22110 — 361-3185
Kenneth Lawrence, prin.
Other Schools – See Dumfries, Nokesville, Triangle,
Woodbridge

Northern Virginia Community College — 4-CC
6901 SUDLEY RD 22110 — 368-0184
Strayer College — 3-UC
7000 INFNTRY RDG RD STE 202 22110 — 330-8400

Manassas Park, AC 703, PC 6, (Indep. City)
Manassas Park CSD — 4-11111
1 PARK CENTER CT # A 22111 — 335-8850
J. Martin, supt.
HS, 8200 EUCLID AVE 22111 — 2-00011
Ben Kiser, prin. — 361-9131
MS, 8200 EUCLID AVE 22111 — 2-00100
Ralph Moore, prin. — 361-1510

Marion, AC 703, PC 6, Smyth
Smyth County SD — 6-11111
PO BOX 987 24354 — 783-3791
Marvin Winters, supt.
HS, 848 STAGE ST 24354 — 3-00011
J. Rolen, prin. — 783-4731
Smyth Vo-Tech, RR 2 BOX 653 24354 — Vo Tech
MICHAEL SNAVELY, prin. — 646-8117
MS, 134 WILDEN ST 24354 — 2-00100
William Pugh, prin. — 783-4466
Other Schools – See Chilhowie, Saltville

Marshall, AC 703, PC 3, Fauquier
Fauquier County SD
Supt. — See Warrenton
JHS, PO BOX 117 22115 — 2-00110
Donald Armentrout, prin. — 364-1551

Martinsville, AC 703, PC 7, (Indep. City)
Henry County SD
Supt. — See Collinsville
Laurel Park HS, RR 8 BOX 67 24112 — 3-00011
Charles Preston, prin. — 632-7216

Martinsville CSD — 5-11111
PO BOX 5548 24115 — 632-6313
S. Lamm, supt.
HS — 3-00011
351 COMMONWEALTH BLVD E 24112 — 632-9755
Ralph Nolen, prin.
MS, 30 CLEVELAND AVE 24112 — 2-00100
Willis Via, prin. — 638-3921

Carlisle S, PO BOX 5388 24115 — 2-11111
Colin Ferguson, prin. — 632-7288
National Business College — 2-CC
10 CHURCH ST 24112 — 632-5621
Patrick Henry Community College — 4-CC
PO BOX 5311 24115 — 638-8777

Mathews, AC 804, PC 3, Mathews
Mathews County SD — 4-11111
PO BOX 369 23109 — 725-3909
Harry Ward, supt.
HS, PO BOX 38 23109 — 2-00011
John Lanford, prin. — 725-3702
Hunter MS, PO BOX 339 23109 — 3-01100
Dino Papas, prin. — 725-2434

Matoaca, AC 804, PC 4, Chesterfield
Chesterfield County SD
Supt. — See Chesterfield
MS, 20300 HALLOWAY AVE 23803 — 3-00100
Howard Warren, prin. — 590-3103

Max Meadows, AC 703, PC 3, Wythe
Wythe County SD
Supt. — See Wytheville
Ft. Chiswell JSHS — 3-00111
RR 3 BOX 255 24360 — 637-3437
Joseph Bean, prin.

Mechanicsville, AC 804, PC 7, Hanover
Hanover County SD
Supt. — See Ashland
Atlee HS — 4-00011
10301 ATLEE STATION RD 23111 — 730-3395
Thomas Shortt, prin.
Lee-Davis HS — 4-00011
6590 MECHANICSVILLE PIKE 23111 — 746-5261
Jonathon Lewis, prin.
Chickahominy MS — 4-00100
10441 ATLEE STATION RD 23111 — 730-8240
Theresa Stimpson, prin.
Jackson MS, RR 2 BOX 421 23111 — 3-00100
Wade Valentino, prin. — 730-3307

Melfa, AC 804, PC 2, Accomack

Eastern Shore Community College — 2-CC
29300 LANKFORD HWY 23410 — 787-5912

Middleburg, AC 703, PC 3, Loudoun

Foxcroft S, PO BOX 5555 22117 — 2-00011
Mary Hepheimer, prin. — 687-5555
Notre Dame Academy — 2-00011
RR 1 BOX 197 22117 — 687-5581
Sr. Cecilia Liberatore, prin.

Middletown, AC 703, PC 4, Frederick

Lord Fairfax Community College — 4-CC
PO BOX 47 22645 — 800-666-5322

Midlothian, AC 804, PC 2, Chesterfield
Chesterfield County SD
Supt. — See Chesterfield
Clover Hill HS — 4-00011
13900 HULL STREET RD 23112 — 739-6230
Jacqueline Wilson, prin.
Manchester HS — 4-00011
12601 BAILEY BRIDGE RD 23112 — 739-6275
David Jones, prin.
HS, 401 CHARTER COLONY PKY 23113 — 4-00011
Edward Witthoefft, prin. — 378-2440
Bailey Bridge MS — 4-00100
12501 BAILEY BRIDGE RD 23112 — 739-6200
William Gillespie, prin.
MS, 13501 MIDLOTHIAN TPKE 23113 — 4-00100
Larry Buchanan, prin. — 378-2460
Robious MS — 4-00100
2701 ROBIOUS CROSSING DR 23113 — 378-2510
Brenda Mayo, prin.
Swift Creek MS — 4-00100
3700 OLD HUNDRED RD 23112 — 739-6315
Joy Brown, prin.

Milford, AC 804, PC 3, Caroline
Caroline County SD
Supt. — See Bowling Green
Caroline HS, PO BOX 248 22514 — 3-00011
Bobbie Chance, prin. — 633-9886
Caroline MS, RR 1 BOX 679 22514 — 3-00100
Stanley Jones, prin. — 633-6561

Mineral, AC 703, PC 2, Louisa
Louisa County SD, PO BOX 7 23117 — 5-11111
William Thomas, supt. — 894-5115
Louisa HS, PO BOX 328 23117 — 4-00011
James Smith, prin. — 894-5436
Louisa MS, PO BOX 448 23117 — 2-00100
Lewis Stephens, prin. — 894-5457

Moneta, AC 703, PC 2, Bedford
Bedford County SD
Supt. — See Bedford
Staunton River HS — 3-00011
1 GOLDEN EAGLE DR 24121 — 297-7151
Robert Ashwell, prin.
Staunton River MS — 3-00100
RR 4 BOX 733 24121 — 297-4152
James Phares, prin.

Monterey, AC 703, PC 2, Highland
Highland County SD — 2-11111
PO BOX 250 24465 — 468-2240
Dwayne Harkleroad, supt.
Highland JSHS, PO BOX 430 24465 — 2-00111
William Fenn, prin. — 468-2129

Montross, AC 804, PC 2, Westmoreland
Westmoreland County SD — 4-11111
PO BOX 1060 22520 — 493-8018
Larry Hixson, supt.
Washington & Lee HS 22520 — 2-00011
Paul Hutnyan, prin. — 493-8015
Johnson JHS 22520 — 2-00100
James Dumminger, prin. — 493-9818

Mount Jackson, AC 703, PC 4, Shenandoah
Shenandoah County SD
Supt. — See Woodstock
Jackson HS, PO BOX 385 22842 — 2-00011
Peter Hughes, prin. — 477-2732
Triplett Vo-Tech, PO BOX 365 22842 — Vo Tech
WILLIAM MOYERS, prin. — 477-3161
North Folk MS, PO BOX 423 22842 — 2-01100
Bill Smitherman, prin. — 477-2953

Mouth of Wilson, AC 703, PC 2, Grayson

Oak Hill Academy, RR 1 24363 — 2-00111
Edward Patton, prin. — 579-2619

Narrows, AC 703, PC 4, Giles
Giles County SD
Supt. — See Pearisburg
JSHS, PO BOX 339 24124 — 3-00111
Paul Hale, prin. — 726-2384

Naruna, AC 804, PC 2, Campbell
Campbell County SD
Supt. — See Rustburg
Campbell HS — 2-00011
GENERAL DELIVERY 24576 — 376-2015
Gregory Killough, prin.
Campbell MS — 2-00100
GENERAL DELIVERY 24576 — 376-2347
Daniel Frazier, prin.

New Castle, AC 703, PC 2, Craig
Craig County SD, PO BOX 245 24127 — 3-11111
M. Helems, supt. — 864-5191
Craig County JSHS — 2-00111
PO BOX 268 24127 — 864-5185
Brian Green, prin.

New Kent, AC 804, PC 1, New Kent
New Kent County SD — 4-11111
PO BOX 110 23124 — 966-9646
R Joseph Adams, supt.
New Kent County HS — 3-00011
PO BOX 130 23124 — 966-9671
Louise Carlton, prin.
New Kent County MS — 2-00100
PO BOX 190 23124 — 966-9655
Howard Ormond, prin.

New Market, AC 703, PC 4, Shenandoah

Shenandoah Valley Academy — 2-00011
RR 3 BOX 29 22844 — 740-3161
Dean Hunt, prin.

Newport News, AC 804, PC 9, (Indep. City)
Newport News CSD — 8-11111
12465 WARWICK BLVD 23606 — 591-4545
Eric Smith, supt.
Denbigh HS, 259 DENBIGH BLVD 23602 — 4-00011
J. Hochman, prin. — 886-7700
Ferguson HS, 11 SHOE LN 23606 — 4-00011
Stanley Mayo, prin. — 591-4600
Menchville HS — 4-00011
275 MENCHVILLE RD 23602 — 886-7722
John Kilpatrick, prin.
Warwick HS, 51 COPELAND LN 23601 — 4-00011
(—), prin. — 591-4700
Dozier MS — 4-00100
432 INDUSTRIAL PARK DR 23602 — 888-3300
Stephen Chantry, prin.
Gildersleeve MS, 1 MINTON DR 23606 — 4-00100
Donna Whitmore, prin. — 591-4682
Hines MS, 561 MCLAWHORNE DR 23601 — 4-00100
Rebecca Lett, prin. — 591-4878
Huntington MS — 4-00100
3401 ORCUTT AVE 23607 — 928-6846
Carol Lambiotte, prin.
Newsome Park MS — 3-00100
4200 MARSHALL AVE 23607 — 928-6810
Willie Carrington, prin.
Reservoir MS — 3-00100
15638 WARWICK BLVD 23602 — 888-3310
Frederick Cheeks, prin.
Washington MS — 2-00100
3700 CHESTNUT AVE 23607 — 928-6860
Terry Cline, prin.

Apprentice Sch. - Newport News Shipbldg. — 3-CS
4101 WASHINGTON AVE 23607 — 380-2682
Career Development Center — 2-CS
605 THMBL SHLS BLVD STE 209 23606 — 599-4088
Christopher Newport College — 5-UC
50 SHOE LN 23606 — 594-7015
Hampton Roads Academy — 2-00111
739 OYSTER POINT RD 23602 — 249-1489
Evan Peterson, prin.
Mary Immaculate Hospital — 2-HSP
800 DENBIGH BLVD 23602 — 872-0100
NEC-Kee Business College — 3-CS
803 DILIGENCE DR 23606 — 873-1111
Peninsula Catholic HS — 2-00111
332 34TH ST 23607 — 245-4216
William Hammond, prin.
Riverside Regional Medical Center — HSP
420 J CLYDE MORRIS BLVD 23601 — 599-2700
Tidewater CS — 2-CS
616 DENBIGH BLVD 23602 — 874-2121

Nickelsville, AC 703, PC 2, Scott
Scott County SD
Supt. — See Gate City
Twin Springs JSHS, RR 1 24271 — 2-00111
Jim Williams, prin. — 479-2185

Nokesville, AC 703, PC 2, Prince William
Prince William County SD
Supt. — See Manassas
Brentsville District JSHS — 3-00111
12109 ADEN RD 22123 — 594-2161
George Clark, prin.

Nora, AC 703, PC 2, Dickenson
Dickenson County SD
Supt. — See Clintwood
Ervinton JSHS, PO BOX 406 24272 — 2-00111
Rodney Compton, prin. — 835-8604

Norfolk, AC 804, PC 10, (Indep. City)
Norfolk CSD, PO BOX 1357 23501 — 8-11111
Roy Nichols, supt. — 441-2107
Granby HS, 7101 GRANBY ST 23505 — 4-00011
Theodore Smith, prin. — 441-1265
Lake Taylor HS — 4-00011
1384 KEMPSVILLE RD 23502 — 441-5650
John Osteen, prin.
Maury HS, 322 SHIRLEY AVE 23517 — 4-00011
James Slaughter, prin. — 441-2611
Norview HS, 1 MIDDLETON PL 23513 — 4-00011
Marjorie Stealey, prin. — 441-5865
Washington HS, 1111 PARK AVE 23504 — 4-00011
Thomas Newby, prin. — 441-2443

Coronado Vo-Tech — Vo Tech
1025 WIDGEON RD 23513 — 441-5857
Vandelyn Whitehurst, prin.
Madison Career S — Vo Tech
1091 W 37TH ST 23508 — 441-5216
Bill Polley, prin.
Norfolk Vo-Tech — Vo Tech
1330 N MILITARY HWY 23502 — 441-5625
William Davis, prin.
Azalea MS — 4-00100
7721 AZALEA GARDEN RD 23518 — 441-1801
Frank Steadman, prin.
Blair MS, 730 SPOTSWOOD AVE 23517 — 4-00100
Michael Caprio, prin. — 441-2441
Lafayette-Winona MS — 4-00100
1701 ALSACE AVE 23509 — 441-2506
Stephen Peters, prin.
Lake Taylor MS — 3-00100
1380 KEMPSVILLE RD 23502 — 441-5635
Joel Wagner, prin.
Northside MS, 8720 GRANBY ST 23503 — 4-00100
Robert Hahne, prin. — 441-1825
Norview MS — 4-00100
6325 SEWELLS POINT RD 23513 — 441-5860
Jack Leslie, prin.
Rosemont MS, 1401 AUBURN AVE 23513 — 3-00100
James Jordan, prin. — 441-5880
Ruffner MS, 489 TIDEWATER DR 23504 — 3-00100
Mary Holley, prin. — 441-2614

Regional Academic Governors School Dist
Supt. — See Richmond
Governors S for the Arts — 2-00011
OLD DOMINION UNIVERSITY 23529 — 451-4711
John Allen, prin.

Commonwealth College — 2-CC
300 BOUSH ST 23510 — 625-5891
De Paul Medical Center — HSP
150 KINGSLEY LN 23505 — 489-5131
Eastern Virginia Medical School — 2-UC
23501
ITT Technical Institute — 2-CC
863 GLENROCK RD 23502 — 466-1260
Johnson & Wales University — 2-CC
2428 ALMEDA AVE STE 316 23513 — 853-3508
Medical College of Hampton Roads — 2-UC
825 FAIRFAX AVE 23507 — 446-5600
Norfolk Academy — 4-11111
1585 WESLEYAN DR 23502 — 461-6236
John Tucker, prin.
Norfolk Christian S — 3-11111
255 THOLE ST 23505 — 423-5735
Robert Miller, prin.
Norfolk Collegiate S — 3-11111
7336 GRANBY ST 23505 — 480-2885
Mary Stanek, prin.
Norfolk General Hospitals — HSP
600 GRESHAM DR 23507 — 628-4879
Norfolk Skills Center — 2-CS
922 W 21ST ST 23517 — 441-2665
Norfolk State University — 6-UC
2401 CORPREW AVE 23504 — 683-8396
Old Dominion University — 7-UC
5215 HAMPTON BLVD 23508 — 800-247-9628
Tidewater Tech — 2-CS
1760 E LITTLE CREEK RD 23518 — 588-2121
Virginia Wesleyan College — 4-UC
1584 WESLEYAN DR 23502 — 455-3208

Norton, AC 703, PC 5, (Indep. City)
Norton CSD, PO BOX 498 24273 — 3-11111
Albert Armentrout, supt. — 679-2330
Burton JSHS, 109 11TH ST SW 24273 — 2-00111
William Passan, prin. — 679-2554

Nottoway, AC 804, PC 2, Nottoway
Nottoway County SD — 4-11111
PO BOX 47 23955 — 645-9596
James Blevins, supt.
HS, GENERAL DELIVERY 23955 — 2-00011
Patricia Harris, prin. — 292-5373
MS, GENERAL DELIVERY 23955 — 2-00100
Douglas Bradley, prin. — 292-5375
Other Schools — See Crewe

Oak Hall, AC 804, PC 2, Accomack
Accomack County SD
Supt. — See Accomac
Arcadia HS, PO BOX 69 23416 — 3-00011
John Gray, prin. — 824-5613
Badger North Vo-Tech — Vo Tech
PO BOX 100 23416 — 824-6386
Alma Brim, prin.

Oakwood, AC 703, PC 2, Buchanan
Buchanan County SD
Supt. — See Grundy
Garden JSHS, PO BOX GHS 24631 — 2-00111
Janie Owens, prin. — 498-4537

Onley, AC 804, PC 3, Accomack
Accomack County SD
Supt. — See Accomac
Nandua HS, PO BOX 489 23418 — 3-00011
Larry Thomas, prin. — 787-4514
Badger South Vo-Tech — Vo Tech
PO BOX 302 23418 — 787-4522
William Griswold, prin.

Orange, AC 703, PC 5, Orange
Orange County SD — 5-11111
PO BOX 349 22960 — 672-1390
Renfro Manning, supt.

Orange County HS, 201 SELMA RD 22960 — 4-00011
Gerald Stover, prin. — 672-5564
Prospect Heights MS — 3-00100
200 CAROLINE ST 22960 — 672-2296
Robert Otto, prin.

Painter, AC 804, PC 2, Accomack
Accomack County SD
Supt. — See Accomac
Central MS, PO BOX 10 23420 — 2-00100
Emily Roberts, prin. — 442-6818

Palmyra, AC 804, PC 2, Fluvanna
Fluvanna County SD — 4-11111
PO BOX 419 22963 — 589-8208
Wayne White, supt.
Fluvanna HS, RR 1 BOX 41 22963 — 3-00011
Rita McGeehan, prin. — 589-3666
Other Schools — See Fork Union

Parksley, AC 804, PC 3, Accomack
Accomack County SD
Supt. — See Accomac
MS, PO BOX 85 23421 — 2-00100
David Elebash, prin. — 665-5051

Pearisburg, AC 703, PC 2, Giles
Giles County SD, RR 1 BOX 52 24134 — 5-11111
Robert McCracken, supt. — 921-1421
Giles JSHS, PO BOX G 24134 — 3-00111
Steven Fitch, prin. — 921-1711
Giles Vo-Tech, PO BOX 479 24134 — Vo Tech
FOREST FOWLER, prin. — 921-1166
Other Schools — See Narrows

Pennington Gap, AC 703, PC 4, Lee
Lee County SD
Supt. — See Jonesville
Pennington MS — 3-01100
307 E MORGAN AVE 24277 — 546-1453
Mary Laster, prin.

Penn Laird, AC 703, PC 2, Rockingham
Rockingham County SD
Supt. — See Harrisonburg
Spotswood HS, RR 1 22846 — 3-00011
Brownie Cummins, prin. — 289-9456
Montevideo MS 22846 — 3-00100
Robert Scott, prin. — 289-9451

Petersburg, AC 804, PC 8, (Indep. City)
Petersburg CSD, 141 E WYTHE ST 23803 — 6-11111
Germaine Fauntleroy, supt. — 732-0510
HS, 3101 JOHNSON RD 23805 — 4-00011
Cyril Hawkins, prin. — 732-0510
Blandford JSHS, 816 E BANK ST 23803 — 4-00111
Rudolph Stephenson, prin. — 732-0510
Peabody MS, 725 WESLEY ST 23803 — 3-00100
Leon Hairston, prin. — 732-0510

Richard Bland College — 3-CC
11301 JOHNSON RD 23805 — 862-6249
St. Vincent De Paul HS — 2-00111
240 WAGNER RD 23805 — 733-4305
Patricia Crisci, prin.
Southside Regional Medical Center — HSP
801 S ADAMS ST 23803 — 862-5801
Virginia State University 23803 — 5-UC
— 524-5902

Pilgrims Knob, AC 703, PC 2, Buchanan
Buchanan County SD
Supt. — See Grundy
Whitewood JSHS, PO BOX 190 24634 — 2-00111
Thomas Dye, prin. — 259-7818

Pocahontas, AC 703, PC 3, Tazewell
Tazewell County SD
Supt. — See Tazewell
JSHS, GENERAL DELIVERY 24635 — 2-00111
Roy Meadows, prin. — 945-5988

Poquoson, AC 804, PC 7, (Indep. City)
Poquoson CSD, PO BOX 2068 23662 — 4-11111
Raymond Vernall, supt. — 868-6666
HS, 51 ODD RD 23662 — 3-00111
Donald Bock, prin. — 868-7123
JHS, 985 POQUOSON AVE 23662 — 3-00100
Roger Tomlinson, prin. — 868-6031

Portsmouth, AC 804, PC 9, (Indep. City)
Portsmouth CSD, PO BOX 998 23705 — 7-11111
Richard Trumble, supt. — 393-8742
Churchland HS, 4301 CEDAR LN 23703 — 4-00011
Raymond Hale, prin. — 686-2500
Norcom HS, 2900 TURNPIKE RD 23707 — 4-00011
Dewayne Jeter, prin. — 393-8793
Wilson HS, 1401 ELMHURST LN 23701 — 4-00011
Lindell Wallace, prin. — 465-2907
Clarke Vo-Tech — Vo Tech
2801 TURNPIKE RD 23707 — 393-8527
William Saunders, prin.
Churchland MS — 4-00100
4051 RIVER SHORE RD 23703 — 686-2512
Gerard Gavin, prin.
Mapp MS, 21 ALDEN AVE 23702 — 4-00100
Patricia Fisher, prin. — 393-8788
Hunt/Mapp MS — 3-00100
3701 WILLETT DR 23707 — 393-8806
Kenneth Hopkins, prin.
Waters MS — 3-00100
600 ROOSEVELT BLVD 23701 — 558-2813
Michael Spencer, prin.

NEC-Kee Business College — 2-CS
2106 COUNTY ST 23704 — 461-2922
Tidewater Community College — 6-CC
RT 135 23703 — 484-2121

Pound, AC 703, PC 3, Wise
Wise County SD
Supt. — See Wise
JSHS, PO BOX 768 24279 — 3-00111
James Hurt, prin. — 796-4432

Powhatan, AC 804, PC 3, Powhatan
Powhatan County SD — 5-11111
2320 SKAGGS RD 23139 — 794-4913
Margaret Meara, supt.
JSHS — 3-00111
4135 OLD BUCKINGHAM RD 23139 — 598-5710
Ernest Cundiff, prin.
Powhatan Vo-Tech — Vo Tech
4125 OLD BUCKINGHAM RD 23139 — 598-5714
LAWRENCE GILL, prin.

Blessed Sacrament HS — 1-00111
PO BOX 519 23139 — 598-4729
Lou Hopewell, prin.
Huguenot Academy — 2-11111
2501 ACADEMY RD 23139 — 598-8736
Don Deaton, prin.

Prince George, AC 804, PC 2, Prince George
Prince George County SD — 6-11111
PO BOX 80 23875 — 733-2700
Thomas Nichols, supt.
HS, 7801 LAUREL SPRING RD 23875 — 4-00011
Charlotte Martin, prin. — 733-2720
Clements JHS — 3-00110
7800 PRINCE GEORGE DR 23875 — 733-2730
Gregory Hulcher, prin.
Other Schools — See Disputanta

Pulaski, AC 703, PC 6, Pulaski
Pulaski County SD, 44 3RD ST NW 24301 — 6-11111
William Asbury, supt. — 980-2237
MS, 500 PICO TER 24301 — 3-00100
Herbert Olinger, prin. — 980-8770
Other Schools — See Dublin

Purcellville, AC 703, PC 4, Loudoun
Loudoun County SD
Supt. — See Leesburg
Loudoun Valley HS — 3-00011
340 N MAPLE AVE 22132 — 338-6800
Kenneth Culbert, prin.
Blue Ridge MS, 551 E A ST 22132 — 3-00100
Joseph Mauck, prin. — 338-6820

Radford, AC 703, PC 7, (Indep. City)
Radford CSD, PO BOX 3698 24143 — 4-11111
Michael Wright, supt. — 731-3647
HS, 50 DALTON DR 24141 — 2-00011
James Martin, prin. — 731-3649
MS, 60 DALTON DR 24141 — 2-00100
Robert Young, prin. — 731-3651

Radford University — 6-UC
PO BOX 5430 24142 — 831-5371

Reston, AC 703, PC 8, Fairfax
Fairfax County SD
Supt. — See Fairfax
South Lakes HS — 4-00011
11400 S LAKES DR 22091 — 476-5270
Diane Schmelzer, prin.
Hughes MS — 4-00100
11401 RIDGE HEIGHTS RD 22091 — 715-3600
R. Edgar Thacker, prin.

Richlands, AC 703, PC 5, Tazewell
Tazewell County SD
Supt. — See Tazewell
HS, 43 FRONT ST 24641 — 4-00011
George Brown, prin. — 964-4602
MS, 45 FRONT ST 24641 — 3-00100
Karen Webb, prin. — 963-5370

Southwest Virginia Community College — 4-CC
PO BOX SVCC 24641 — 964-2555

Richmond, AC 804, PC 9, (Indep. City)
Chesterfield County SD
Supt. — See Chesterfield
Meadowbrook HS — 4-00011
4901 COGBILL RD 23234 — 743-3675
James Porach, prin.
Monacan HS — 4-00011
11501 SMOKETREE DR 23236 — 378-2480
John Titus, prin.
Falling Creek MS — 4-00100
4724 HOPKINS RD 23234 — 743-3640
Janet Keith, prin.
Manchester MS — 4-00100
7401 HULL STREET RD 23235 — 674-1385
David Dobbs, prin.
Providence MS — 3-00100
900 STARLIGHT LN 23235 — 674-1355
John Galloway, prin.
Salem Church MS — 4-00100
9700 SALEM CHURCH RD 23237 — 768-6225
Edward Leslie, prin.

Henrico County SD 8-11111
PO BOX 23120 23223 226-3717
William Bosher, supt.
Freeman HS 4-00011
8701 THREE CHOPT RD 23229 673-3700
Thomas Stavredes, prin.
Godwin HS, 2101 PUMP RD 23233 4-00011
John McGinty, prin. 750-2600
Henrico HS, 302 AZALEA AVE 23227 4-00011
Bernadine Johnson, prin. 228-2700
Hermitage HS 4-00011
8301 HUNGARY SPRING RD 23228 756-3000
N. Douglas Hunt, prin.
Tucker HS, 2910 N PARHAM RD 23294 4-00011
William Caldwell, prin. 527-4600
Varina HS, 7053 MESSER RD 23231 4-00011
Harold Lawson, prin. 226-8700
Hermitage Vo-Tech Vo Tech
8301 HUNGARY SPRING RD 23228 756-3020
W. Matthews, prin.
Brookland MS, 9200 LYDELL DR 23228 4-00100
William Hite, prin. 261-5000
Byrd MS, 9400 QUIOCCASIN RD 23233 4-00100
William Ware, prin. 750-2630
Fairfield MS, 5121 NINE MILE RD 23223 4-00100
Thomas Walls, prin. 328-4020
Moody MS, 7800 WOODMAN RD 23228 4-00100
Rebecca Grant, prin. 261-5015
Rolfe MS, 6901 MESSER RD 23231 4-00100
Paul Vecchione, prin. 226-8730
Tuckahoe MS 4-00100
9000 THREE CHOPT RD 23229 673-3720
Diana Winston, prin.
Other Schools – See Glen Allen, Highland Springs

Jointly Operated Vo Tech SD 4-00001
PO BOX 2120 23216 – (—), supt. 225-2755
Other Schools – See Carson, Charlottesville, Covington, Culpeper, Fishersville, Hampton, Harrisonburg, Jetersville, Suffolk, Warsaw, Winchester

Regional Academic Governors School Dist 4-00011
PO BOX 2120 23216 – (—), supt. 225-2755
Jefferson HS Government and Intl Studies 2-00011
4100 W GRACE ST 23230 780-6155
Steven Ballowe, prin.
Other Schools – See Alexandria, Dublin, Fishersville, Hampton, Keysville, Lynchburg, Norfolk, Roanoke

Richmond CSD, 301 N 9TH ST 23219 8-11111
Lucille Brown, supt. 780-7700
Armstrong HS, 1611 N 31ST ST 23223 3-00011
George Bowser, prin. 780-4017
Franklin Military HS 2-00011
1611 N 31ST ST 23223 780-8526
Joseph Cooper, prin.
Huguenot HS 4-00011
7945 FOREST HILL AVE 23225 320-7967
Carlton Stevens, prin.
Jefferson Center/Intnl. Government Study 3-00011
4100 W GRACE ST 23230 780-6028
Edward Pruden, prin.
Kennedy HS, 2300 COOL LN 23223 3-00011
Ethan Pitts, prin. 780-4449
Marshall HS 3-00011
4225 OLD BROOK RD 23227 780-6052
Beverly Braxton, prin.
Open HS, 600 S PINE ST 23220 2-00011
Brenda Drew, prin. 780-4661
Richmond Community HS 2-00011
5800 PATTERSON AVE 23226 285-1015
Pamela Trotter-Cornell, prin.
Wythe HS 3-00011
4314 CRUTCHFIELD ST 23225 780-5037
James Bynum, prin.
Career Development Vo Tech
119 W LEIGH ST 23220 780-4388
Jerry Browder, prin.
Richmond Career S Vo Tech
2015 WESTWOOD AVE 23230 780-6272
Roger Lacourse, prin.
Richmond Tech S Vo Tech
2020 WESTWOOD AVE 23230 780-6237
J. Brown, prin.
Binford MS, 1701 FLOYD AVE 23220 3-00100
Jacqueline Cameron, prin. 780-6231
Boushall Mid School 3-00100
3400 HOPKINS RD 23234 230-3557
Frank Butts, prin.
Chandler MS 3-00100
210 E BROOKLAND PARK BLVD 23222
Sandra Parker, prin. 780-4156
Elkhardt MS 3-00100
6300 HULL STREET RD 23224 745-3600
John Lane, prin.
Henderson MS 3-00100
4319 OLD BROOK RD 23227 780-8288
Harold Fitrer, prin.
Hill MS, 3400 PATTERSON AVE 23221 2-00100
Bradford Fellows, prin. 780-6107
Thompson MS 4-00100
7824 FOREST HILL AVE 23225 272-7554
Kenneth Geiger, prin.

Benedictine HS 2-00011
304 N SHEPPARD ST 23221 342-1300
David Bouton, prin.
Braxton School 2-CS
4917 AUGUSTA AVE 23230 353-4458
Buford Academy HND
PO BOX 26665 23261
Collegiate S 4-11111
201 N MOORELAND RD 23229 740-7077
Robertson Hershey, prin.
Commonwealth College 2-CS
8141 HULL STREET RD 23235 745-2444
ECPI Computer Institute 2-CS
4303 W BROAD ST 23230 359-3535
J. Sargeant Reynolds Community College 6-CC
PO BOX C-23040 23261
NEC-Kee Business College 3-CS
6301 MIDLOTHIAN TPKE 23225 745-5660
Presbyterian School of Christian Educ. 2-UC
1205 PALMYRA AVE 23227 359-5031
Reporting Academy of Virginia 2-CS
1001 BOULDERS PKY STE 305 23225
323-1020
Richmond Memorial Hospital HSP
1300 WESTWOOD AVE 23227 254-6293
St. Catherines S, 6001 GROVE AVE 23226 3-11111
Auguste Bannard, prin. 288-2804
St. Christophers S 2-11111
711 SAINT CHRISTOPHERS RD 23226 282-3185
George McVey, prin.
St. Gertrude HS 2-00011
3215 STUART AVE 23221 358-9114
Sr. Charlotte Lange, prin.
St. Mary's Hospital HSP
5801 BREMO RD 23226 285-2011
Trinity Episcopal HS 2-00111
3850 PITTAWAY DR 23235 272-5864
Thomas Aycock, prin.
Union Theological Seminary in Virginia 2-UC
3401 BROOK RD 23227 278-4300
University of Richmond 23173 5-UC
289-8640
Virginia Commonwealth University 7-UC
910 W FRANKLIN ST 23284 367-1222
Virginia Home for Boys HND
8716 W BROAD ST 23294
Virginia Union University 4-UC
1500 N LOMBARDY ST 23220 257-5856

Ridgeway, AC 703, PC 3, Henry
Henry County SD
Supt. — See Collinsville
Magna Vista HS 3-00011
RR 2 BOX 1170 24148 956-3147
Joseph Devault, prin.
Mason MS, RR 3 BOX 27 24148 3-00100
Robert Wingfield, prin. 956-3154

Riner, AC 703, PC 2, Montgomery
Montgomery County SD
Supt. — See Christiansburg
Auburn JSHS, 4163 RINER RD 24149 3-00111
Robert Miller, prin. 382-5160

Ringgold, AC 804, PC 2, Pittsylvania
Pittsylvania SD
Supt. — See Chatham
Dan River JSHS, RR 3 BOX 947 24586 2-00111
David Foster, prin. 822-6023

Roanoke, AC 703, PC 8, (Indep. City)
Regional Academic Governors School Dist
Supt. — See Richmond
Roanoke Valley Governors S Science/Tech 2-00001
2104 GRANDIN RD SW 24015 981-2116
Richard Shelly, prin.

Roanoke County SD
Supt. — See Salem
Cave Spring SHS 4-00001
3712 CHAPARRAL DR 24018 772-7550
Martha Cobble, prin.
Northside SHS 3-00001
6758 NRTHSDE HIGH SCHOOL RD 24019
Donna Henderson, prin. 561-8155
Cave Spring JHS 3-00110
4880 BRAMBLETON AVE 24018 772-7560
Steven Boyer, prin.
Hidden Valley JHS 3-00110
4902 HDDEN VALLEY SCHOOL RD 24018
David Blevins, prin. 772-7570
Northside JHS 3-00110
6810 NRTHSDE HIGH SCHOOL RD 24019
James Wood, prin. 561-8145

Roanoke CSD, PO BOX 13145 24031 7-11111
E Harris, supt. 981-2381
Fleming HS 4-00011
3649 FERNCLIFF AVE NW 24017 981-2781
Alyce Szathmary, prin.
Henry HS, 2102 GRANDIN RD SW 24015 4-00011
Elizabeth Lee, prin. 981-2255
Addison Aerospace Magnet MS 2-00100
1220 5TH ST NW 24016 981-2681
Beverly Burks, prin.
Breckinridge MS 2-00100
3901 WILLIAMSON RD NW 24012 981-2251
Helen Townsend, prin.
Jackson MS, 1022 9TH ST SE 24013 2-00100
Charles Kennedy, prin. 981-2881
Madison MS 3-01100
1160 OVERLAND RD SW 24015 981-2351
Philip Jepson, prin.
Ruffner MS 3-00100
3601 FERNCLIFF AVE NW 24017 981-2605
James Wilson, prin.
Wilson MS, 1813 CARTER RD SW 24015 2-00100
Katherine Duffy, prin. 981-2358

Carilion Health Systems 1-CS
PO BOX 13727 24036 981-7347
College of Health Sciences 2-CC
PO BOX 13186 24031 985-8483
Dominion Business School 2-CS
4142 MELROSE AVE NW STE 1 24017
362-7738
ECPI Computer Institute 2-CS
1030 S JEFFERSON ST 24016 342-0043
National Business College 2-HSP
PO BOX 6400 24017 986-1800
North Cross S 3-11111
4254 COLONIAL AVE 24018 989-6641
William Stacey, prin.
Roanoke Catholic S 2-11111
621 N JEFFERSON ST 24016 982-3532
Karen Mabry, prin.
Virginia Western Community College 5-CC
PO BOX 14025 24038 857-7319

Rocky Gap, AC 703, PC 2, Bland
Bland County SD
Supt. — See Bland
JSHS, PO BOX 10 24366 2-00111
Charlie Puckett, prin. 928-1100

Rocky Mount, AC 703, PC 5, Franklin
Franklin County SD 6-11111
102 BERNARD RD 24151 483-5138
Leonard Gereau, supt.
Franklin HS, 506 PELL AVE 24151 4-00011
William Gibson, prin. 483-0221
Franklin East MS, RR 1 24151 3-00100
Reginald Harris, prin. 483-5105
Franklin West MS, RR 1 24151 3-00100
Gwendolyn Adkins, prin. 483-5105

Rural Retreat, AC 703, PC 3, Wythe
Wythe County SD
Supt. — See Wytheville
JSHS, PO BOX 10 24368 2-00111
Gary Houseman, prin. 686-4143

Rustburg, AC 804, PC 3, Campbell
Campbell County SD 6-11111
PO BOX 99 24588 – G. Nolley, supt. 332-5161
HS 24588 3-00011
H. Pendleton, prin. 332-5171
Campbell Vo-Tech Vo Tech
RR 1 BOX 576 24588 821-6213
Ron Cox, prin.
MS 24588 3-01100
Charles Arthur, prin. 332-5141
Other Schools – See Altavista, Lynchburg, Naruna

Saint Paul, AC 703, PC 4, Wise
Wise County SD
Supt. — See Wise
JSHS, PO BOX G 24283 2-00111
James Short, prin. 762-5221

Salem, AC 703, PC 7, (Indep. City)
Roanoke County SD 7-11111
526 S COLLEGE AVE 24153 387-6403
Bayes Wilson, supt.
Glenvar JSHS, 4549 MALUS DR 24153 3-00111
Guy McClearn, prin. 387-6536
Burton Vo-Tech Vo Tech
1760 ROANOKE BLVD 24153 344-4643
JAMES JOHNSON, prin.
Other Schools – See Roanoke, Vinton

Salem CSD, 19 N COLLEGE AVE 24153 5-11111
N. Tripp, supt. 389-0130
HS, 400 SPARTAN DR 24153 4-00011
Caleb Hall, prin. 387-2437
Lewis MS, 616 S COLLEGE AVE 24153 3-00100
Jerome Campbell, prin. 387-2513

Minnick Educational Center HND
PO BOX 905 24153
National Business College 3-CC
1813 E MAIN ST 24153 986-1800
Roanoke College 4-UC
221 COLLEGE LN 24153 375-2270
Virginia College 2-CC
2163 APPERSON DR 24153 776-0755

Saltville, AC 703, PC 4, Smyth
Smyth County SD
Supt. — See Marion
Northwood HS, PO BOX Y 24370 2-00011
E. Barbrow, prin. 496-7751

Saluda, AC 804, PC 2, Middlesex
Middlesex County SD 4-11111
PO BOX 205 23149 758-2277
Ernest Worley, supt.
Middlesex JSHS 23149 2-00111
James Sills, prin. 758-2132

Shawsville, AC 703, PC 4, Montgomery
Montgomery County SD
Supt. — See Christiansburg
JSHS, 4179 OLDTOWN RD 24162 3-00111
Nelson Simpkins, prin. 268-2262

Shenandoah, AC 703, PC 4, Page
Page County SD
Supt. — See Luray
Page JSHS, RR 1 22849 3-00111
Morgan Phenix, prin. 652-8712

Skipwith, AC 804, PC 2, Mecklenburg
Mecklenburg County SD
Supt. — See Boydton

Bluestone HS, RR 1 BOX 96C 23968   3-00011
David Francis, prin.   372-5177
Bluestone MS, RR 1 BOX 55A 23968   3-00100
Jerome Watson, prin.   372-3266

Smithfield, AC 804, PC 5, Isle of Wight
Isle of Wight County SD
Supt. — See Isle of Wight
JSHS, 14171 TURNER DR 23430   3-00011
Eugene Blair, prin.   357-3108

South Boston, AC 804, PC 6, (Indep. City)
Halifax County SD
Supt. — See Halifax
Halifax HS, PO BOX 310 24592   4-00011
Larry Clark, prin.   572-4977
Halifax MS, PO BOX 838 24592   4-00100
Bristol Martin, prin.   572-3952

South Hill, AC 804, PC 5, Mecklenburg
Mecklenburg County SD
Supt. — See Boydton
Park View HS, RR 1 BOX 118 23970   3-00011
Bowman Burton, prin.   447-3435
Park View MS, RR 1 BOX 921 23970   3-00100
Sidney Clark, prin.   447-3761

Sperryville, AC 703, PC 2, Rappahonnock
Rappahannock County SD
PO BOX 273 22740   3-11111
David Gangel, supt.   987-8773
Rappahannock JSHS
PO BOX 295 22740   2-00111
John Toth, prin.   987-8575

Spotsylvania, AC 703, PC 2, Spotsylvania
Spotsylvania County SD   7-11111
6717 SMITH STATION RD 22553   898-6032
Alan Farley, supt.
Courtland HS   4-00011
6701 SMITH STATION RD 22553   898-4445
Thomas Noakes, prin.
HS, 8801 COURTHOUSE RD 22553   4-00011
Cary Atkins, prin.   582-6336
Spotsylvania Vo-Tech   Vo Tech
6703 SMITH STATION RD 22553   898-2655
Bernice Covert, prin.
MS, 8800 COURTHOUSE RD 22553   3-00100
Walter McWhirt, prin.   582-6341
Wright MS   3-00100
7565 COURTHOUSE RD 22553   582-6377
Mary Barton, prin.
Other Schools – See Fredericksburg

Springfield, AC 703, PC 7, Fairfax
Fairfax County SD
Supt. — See Fairfax
Lee HS, 6540 FRANCONIA RD 22150   4-00011
Thomas Engley, prin.   971-6000
West Springfield HS   4-00011
6100 ROLLING RD 22152   451-6403
Glynn Bates, prin.
Irving MS   4-00100
8100 OLD KEENE MILL RD 22152   912-4500
Edward Barker, prin.
Key MS, 6402 FRANCONIA RD 22150   3-00100
Richard Doyle, prin.   313-3900

Accotink Academy   HND
8519 TUTTLE RD 22152
Maryland Drafting Institute   1-CS
8001 FORBES PL 22151   321-9777
Reporting Academy of Virginia   2-CS
5501 BACKLICK RD STE 104 22151   658-0588

Stafford, AC 703, PC 3, Stafford
Stafford County SD   7-11111
1729 JEFFERSON DAVIS HWY 22554   659-3141
Russell Watson, supt.
North Stafford HS   4-00011
839 GARRISONVILLE RD 22554   659-4176
Robert White, prin.
Brooke Point JHS   3-00010
1700 COURTHOUSE RD 22554   720-1750
Kerrington Tillery, prin.
MS, 101 SPARTAN LN 22554   3-00100
Jerry Jenkins, prin.   659-2171
Wright MS, 100 WOOD DR 22554   4-00100
Stephen Trant, prin.   659-4114
Other Schools – See Falmouth, Fredericksburg

Stanardsville, AC 804, PC 2, Greene
Greene County SD, PO BOX 98 22973   4-11111
Raymond Dingledine, supt.   985-5254
Monroe HS, PO BOX 8 22973   3-00011
William Baggett, prin.   985-5273
Monroe MS, 3 MONROE DR 22973   3-00100
Zed French, prin.   985-5240

Staunton, AC 703, PC 7, (Indep. City)
Augusta County SD
Supt. — See Fishersville
Riverheads HS, RR 2 BOX 351 24401   2-00111
Gregory McGhee, prin.   337-1921
Beverley Manor MS   3-00100
RR 1 BOX 2 24401   886-5806
Glen Patterson, prin.

Staunton CSD, PO BOX 9000 24401   5-11111
Kenneth Frank, supt.   332-3920
Lee HS, 1100 N COALTER ST 24401   3-00111
James Peak, prin.   332-3926
Shelburne MS, 300 GRUBERT AVE 24401   2-00100
Phyllis Brown, prin.   332-3930

Dominion Business School   2-CS
825 RICHMOND AVE 24401   886-3596
Mary Baldwin College 24401   4-UC
  800-826-0154
Stuart Hall, 235 W FREDERICK ST 24401   2-00111
Rev. Fox, prin.   885-0356
Virginia School for the Deaf and Blind   HND
24401

Stephens City, AC 703, PC 4, Frederick
Frederick County SD
Supt. — See Winchester
Sherando HS, 185 S WARRIOR DR 22655   4-00011
John Frossard, prin.   869-0060
Aylor MS, 5200 AYLOR RD 22655   4-00100
Larry Mullin, prin.   869-3736

Sterling, AC 703, PC 7, Loudoun
Loudoun County SD
Supt. — See Leesburg
Park View High School   4-00011
400 W LAUREL AVE 20164   444-7500
James Person, prin.
Seneca Ridge MS   4-00100
98 SENECA RIDGE DR 20164   444-7480
Josie Stewart, prin.
MS, 201 W HOLLY AVE 20164   3-00100
Charles Haydt, prin.   444-7490

Northern Virginia Community College   4-CC
1000 HARRY FLOOD BYRD HWY 20164   323-3000

Strasburg, AC 703, PC 5, Shenandoah
Shenandoah County SD
Supt. — See Woodstock
HS, HOLIDAY ST 22657   2-00011
Pamela Hardy, prin.   465-5195
Signal Knob MS   2-01100
RR 4 BOX 784 22657   465-4557
Carol Brallier, prin.

Stuart, AC 703, PC 3, Patrick
Patrick County SD   5-11111
PO BOX 346 24171   694-3163
Dennis Witt, supt.
Patrick JSHS, RR 5 BOX 65 24171   4-00111
Bill Dillon, prin.   694-7137

Stuarts Draft, AC 703, PC 6, Augusta
Augusta County SD
Supt. — See Fishersville
HS, RR 4 BOX 108 24477   3-00011
William Schindler, prin.   949-7115
MS, RR 4 BOX 106 24477   3-00100
George Kidd, prin.   885-2542

Suffolk, AC 804, PC 8, (Indep. City)
Jointly Operated Vo Tech SD
Supt. — See Richmond
Pruden Vo-Tech Ctr   Vo Tech
4169 PRUDEN BLVD 23434   539-7407
Peggy Wade, prin.

Suffolk CSD, PO BOX 1549 23439   6-11111
Beverly Cox, supt.   925-5500
Lakeland HS, 214 KENYON RD 23434   4-00011
William Hill, prin.   925-5530
Nansemond River HS   4-00011
3301 NANSEMOND PKY 23434   538-5420
Allen Breland, prin.
Forest Glen MS   3-00100
200 FOREST GLEN DR 23434   925-5550
John Edwards, prin.
Kennedy MS   3-00100
2325 E WASHINGTON ST 23434   925-5560
Michaele Penn, prin.
Yeates MS   3-00100
4901 BENNETTS PASTURE RD 23435   538-5400
Edward Darden, prin.

Louise Obici School of Nursing   1-HSP
PO BOX 1100 23439   934-4742
Nansemond-Suffolk Academy   3-11111
PO BOX 1249 23439   539-8789
Douglas Naismith, prin.

Surry, AC 804, PC 2, Surry
Surry County SD, PO BOX 317 23883   4-11111
Clarence Penn, supt.   294-5229
Other Schools – See Dendron

Sussex, AC 804, PC 1, Sussex
Sussex County SD   4-11111
PO BOX 1368 23884   246-5511
John Hicks, supt.
Sussex Central JSHS   3-00111
GENERAL DELIVERY 23884   246-6051
Gurnery Ramsey, prin.

Sweet Briar, PC 2, Amherst

Sweet Briar College   3-UC
GENERAL DELIVERY 24595   800-537-4300

Swoope, AC 703, PC 1, Augusta
Augusta County SD
Supt. — See Fishersville
Buffalo Gap HS, RR 1 BOX 124A 24479   3-00011
William Deardorff, prin.   337-6021

Tabb, AC 804, PC 3, York
York County SD
Supt. — See Yorktown

HS, 4431 BIG BETHEL RD 23693   4-00011
Michael Tylavsky, prin.   898-0330
MS, 300 YORKTOWN RD 23693   4-00100
James Carmines, prin.   867-7420

Tangier, AC 804, PC 3, Accomack
Accomack County SD
Supt. — See Accomac
S, PO BOX 245 23440   2-11111
Dennis Crockett, prin.   891-2234

Tappahannock, AC 804, PC 4, Essex
Essex County SD, PO BOX 756 22560   4-11111
Ronald Mersky, supt.   443-4366
Essex JSHS, PO BOX 1006 22560   3-00111
Karl Leap, prin.   443-4301

St. Margarets S, PO BOX 158 22560   2-00111
Margaret Broad, prin.   443-3357

Tazewell, AC 703, PC 5, Tazewell
Tazewell County SD   6-11111
209 W FINCASTLE ST 24651   988-5511
Woodrow Mullins, supt.
HS, 627 E FINCASTLE ST 24651   3-00011
Charles Thomason, prin.   988-6502
Tazewell Vo-Tech 24651   Vo Tech
S. John Estey, prin.   988-2529
MS, 100 BULL DOG AVE 24651   3-00100
James Hammond, prin.   988-6513
Other Schools – See Bluefield, Pocahontas, Richlands

Toano, AC 804, PC 3, James City
Williamsburg-James City SD
Supt. — See Williamsburg
Toano MS, 7817 RICHMOND RD 23168   3-00100
Stephanie McConachie, prin.   566-4251

Triangle, AC 703, PC 5, Prince William
Prince William County SD
Supt. — See Manassas
Graham Park MS   3-00100
3513 GRAHAM PARK RD 22172   221-2118
Joyce Harte, prin.

Victoria, AC 804, PC 4, Lunenburg
Lunenburg County SD, PO BOX X 23974   4-11111
Richard Greig, supt.   696-2116
Central HS, RR 2 BOX 63 23974   3-00011
John Gentry, prin.   696-2137
Lunenburg MS, RR 1 23974   2-00100
Wayne Staples, prin.   696-2161

Vienna, AC 703, PC 7, Fairfax
Fairfax County SD
Supt. — See Fairfax
Madison HS   4-00011
2500 JAMES MADISON DR 22181   938-2225
Ed Ryan, prin.
Oakton HS, 2900 SUTTON RD 22181   4-00011
Brad Draeger, prin.   281-4900
Kilmer MS, 8100 WOLFTRAP RD 22182   3-00100
Donald Thurston, prin.   846-8800
Thoreau MS, 2505 CEDAR LN 22180   3-00100
Bruce Oliver, prin.   846-8000

Washington Business School/Northern VA   2-CS
1980 GALLOWS RD 22182   556-8888

Vinton, AC 703, PC 6, Roanoke
Roanoke County SD
Supt. — See Salem
Byrd HS   3-00011
2902 E WASHINGTON AVE 24179   890-3090
R. Patterson, prin.
Byrd MS   3-00100
2910 E WASHINGTON AVE 24179   890-1035
Steve Lonker, prin.

Virginia Beach, AC 804, PC 10, (Indep. City)
Virginia Beach CSD   8-11111
PO BOX 6038 23456   427-4326
Sidney Faucette, supt.
Bayside HS, 4960 HAYGOOD RD 23455   4-00011
Michael Debranski, prin.   473-5050
Cox HS, 2425 SHOREHAVEN DR 23454   4-00011
Emilie Tilley, prin.   496-6767
First Colonial HS   4-00011
1272 MILL DAM RD 23454   496-6711
Charles Atkinson, prin.
Green Run HS, 1700 DAHLIA DR 23456   4-00011
Jerry Deviney, prin.   431-4040
Kellam HS, 2323 HOLLAND RD 23456   4-00011
Albert Williams, prin.   427-3232
Kempsville HS   4-00011
574 KEMPSVILLE RD 23464   474-8400
Louis Tonelson, prin.
Princess Ann HS   4-00011
4400 VA BEACH BLVD 23462   473-5000
Nancy Jones, prin.
Salem HS   4-00011
2300 LYNNHAVEN PKY 23464   474-8484
Ramona Stenzhorn, prin.
Tallwood HS   4-00011
1668 KEMPSVILLE RD 23464   474-8555
Bernard Morgan, prin.
JSHS, 273 N WITCHDUCK RD 23462   2-00111
Arthur Scarborough, prin.   473-5058
Vo-Tech, 2925 N LANDING RD 23456   Vo Tech
WILLIAM MOOSHA, prin.   427-5300
Bayside JHS, 965 NEWTOWN RD 23462   4-00100
Donald Stowers, prin.   473-5080
Brandon JHS, 1700 POPE ST 23464   4-00100
Jonathan Harnden, prin.   366-4545

Great Neck JHS 4-00100
1848 N GREAT NECK RD 23454 496-6770
Edward Jones, prin.
Independence JHS 4-00110
1370 DUNSTAN LN 23455 460-7500
Edith Eidson, prin.
Kempsville JHS 4-00110
860 CHURCHILL DR 23464 474-8444
Frank Peele, prin.
Landstown MS 2-00100
2204 RECREATION DR 23456 430-2412
George McGovern, prin.
Larkspur MS 2-00100
4696 PRINCESS ANNE RD 23462 427-4326
(—), prin.
Lynnhaven JHS, 1250 BAYNE DR 23454 4-00110
Victor Gregor, prin. 496-6790
Plaza JHS 4-00100
3080 S LYNNHAVEN RD 23452 431-4060
James Walker, prin.
Princess Anne JHS 3-00100
2509 SEABOARD RD 23456 427-5325
Charles Perkinson, prin.
Salem JHS 4-00110
2380 LYNNHAVEN PKY 23464 474-8411
Julius Wooten, prin.
JHS, 600 25TH ST 23451 3-00110
Donald Harvey, prin. 437-4892

Atlantic Academy HND
1701 WILL O WISP DR 23454
Cape Henry Collegiate S 2-11111
1320 MILL DAM RD 23454 481-2446
Daniel Richardson, prin.
Catholic HS 2-00111
4552 PRINCESS ANNE RD 23462 467-0284
Fr. Pitt, prin.
Commonwealth College 2-CC
4160 VIRGINIA BEACH BLVD 23452 340-0222
Computer Dynamics Institute 2-CS
5361 VIRGINIA BEACH BLVD 23462 486-7300
ECPI Computer Institute 3-CS
5555 GREENWICH RD STE 300 23462
671-7171
Fischer Technical Institute 2-CS
5700 SOUTHERN BLVD 23462 490-1241
Regent University 3-UC
1000 CENTERVILLE TPKE 23464 523-7444
Reporting Academy of Virginia 2-CS
PEMBROKE ONE #600 23462 499-5447
Tidewater Community College 3-CC
1700 COLLEGE CRES 23456 468-6348
Tidewater Tech 2-CS
2697 DEAN DR # 100 23452 340-2121

Wakefield, AC 804, PC 4, Sussex

Tidewater Academy 2-00111
PO BOX 536 23888 899-5401
Frank Freudig, prin.

Warm Springs, AC 703, PC 2, Bath
Bath County SD, PO BOX 67 24484 3-11111
Michael Sams, supt. 839-2981
Other Schools – See Hot Springs

Warrenton, AC 703, PC 5, Fauquier
Fauquier County SD, 10 HOTEL ST 22186 6-11111
Anthony Lease, supt. 347-8729
Fauquier SHS 4-00001
705 WATERLOO RD 22186 – (—), prin. 347-6100
Taylor JHS, 350 E SHIRLEY AVE 22186 3-00110
John Bannister, prin. 347-6140
JHS, 244 WATERLOO ST 22186 3-00110
Charlie Rogers, prin. 347-6160
Other Schools – See Bealeton, Marshall

Warsaw, AC 804, PC 3, Richmond
Jointly Operated Vo Tech SD
Supt. — See Richmond
Northern Neck Vo-Tech Ctr Vo Tech
PO BOX 787 22572 333-4940
George Fiddler, prin.

Richmond County SD 4-11111
PO BOX 735 22572 333-3681
Karl Odell, supt.
Rappahannock HS 2-00011
PO BOX 550 22572 333-3551
George Drewry, prin.
Richmond County MS 2-00100
PO BOX 519 22572 333-3560
William Brann, prin.

Waynesboro, AC 703, PC 7, (Indep. City)
Waynesboro CSD, 301 PINE AVE 22980 5-11111
T. Lowell Lemons, supt. 946-4600
HS, 1200 W MAIN ST 22980 3-00011
Thomas Muncy, prin. 946-4616

Fishburne Military S 2-00111
PO BOX 988 22980 943-1171
Robert Miller, prin.

West Point, AC 804, PC 5, King William
West Point CSD, PO BOX T 23181 3-11111
K. Jane Massey-Wilson, supt. 843-4368
JSHS, 2700 MATTAPONI AVE 23181 2-00111
Ron Flowe, prin. 843-3630

Weyers Cave, AC 703, PC 2, Augusta

Blue Ridge Community College 4-CC
PO BOX 80 24486 234-9261

Whitetop, AC 703, PC 2, Grayson
Grayson County SD
Supt. — See Independence
Mt. Rogers S, RR 1 BOX 193 24292 1-11111
Wilma Testerman, prin. 388-3489

Williamsburg, AC 804, PC 7, (Indep. City)
Williamsburg-James City SD 6-11111
PO BOX 179 23187 253-6762
Gayden Carruth, supt.
LaFayette HS, 4460 LONGHILL RD 23188 4-00011
(—), prin. 565-0373
Berkley MS 2-00100
1118 IRONBOUND RD 23188 229-8051
Troy Maxwell, prin.
Blair MS, 117 IRONBOUND RD 23185 3-00100
Parker Land, prin. 229-1341
Other Schools – See Toano

York County SD
Supt. — See Yorktown
Bruton HS 3-00011
185 ROCHAMBEAU DR 23188 898-0384
Michael Evans, prin.
Queens Lake MS 2-00100
124 W QUEENS DR 23185 220-4080
Sewell Rowley, prin.

College of William and Mary 23185 6-UC
221-4223
Walsingham Academy 3-11111
PO BOX 8702 23187 229-6026
Sr. Virginia Kauffmann, prin.
Williamsburg Flite Center 1-CS
1 MINOR CT 23188

Winchester, AC 703, PC 7, (Indep. City)
Frederick County SD 6-11111
PO BOX 3508 22604 662-3888
R. Malcolm, supt.
Wood HS 4-00011
161 APPLE PIE RIDGE RD 22603 667-5226
Don Shirley, prin.
Frederick MS, 441 LINDEN DR 22601 4-00100
Fred Jefferson, prin. 667-4233
Wood MS, 1313 AMHERST ST 22601 3-00100
James Plaugher, prin. 667-7500
Other Schools – See Stephens City

Jointly Operated Vo Tech SD
Supt. — See Richmond
Howard Vo-Tech Ctr Vo Tech
156 DOWELL J CIR 22602 662-8997
Richard Harvey, prin.

Winchester CSD, PO BOX 551 22604 5-11111
Glenn Barbour, supt. 667-4253
Handley HS, HANDLEY BLVD 22601 3-00011
John Taylor, prin. 662-3471
Morgan MS, 48 S PURCELL AVE 22601 3-00100
Diana Carpenter, prin. 667-7171

Shenandoah University 3-UC
1460 UNIVERSITY DR 22601 665-4500
Winchester Memorial Hospital HSP
PO BOX 3340 22604 722-8000

Windsor, AC 804, PC 4, Isle of Wight
Isle of Wight County SD
Supt. — See Isle of Wight
JSHS, 20 CHURCH ST 23487 3-00111
William Worsham, prin. 242-6172

Wise, AC 703, PC 5, Wise
Wise County SD, PO BOX 1217 24293 6-11111
Jim Graham, supt. 328-9421
Kelly JSHS, PO BOX 796 24293 3-00111
Donald Alvey, prin. 328-8015
Wise County Vo-Tech Vo Tech
PO BOX 1218 24293 328-6113
Robert Raines, prin.
Other Schools – See Appalachia, Big Stone Gap,
Coeburn, Pound, Saint Paul

Clinch Valley College of the Univ. of VA 4-UC
PO BOX 16 24293 328-0100

Woodberry Forest, AC 703, PC 2, Madison

Woodberry Forest S 2-00011
PO BOX 10 22989 672-3900
John Grinalds, prin.

Woodbridge, AC 703, PC 8, Prince William
Prince William County SD
Supt. — See Manassas
Gar-Field HS 5-00011
14000 SMOKETOWN RD 22192 670-2131
Roger Dallek, prin.
Hylton HS, 14051 SPRIGGS RD 22193 4-00011
Wayne Mallard, prin. 670-5198
HS, 3001 OLD BRIDGE RD 22192 5-00011
Pamela White, prin. 494-7135
Beville MS, 4900 DALE BLVD 22193 3-00100
Allan Nixson, prin. 878-3496
Godwin MS 3-00100
14800 DARBYDALE AVE 22193 670-6166
Karen Poindexter, prin.
Lynn MS, 2451 LONGVIEW DR 22191 4-00100
Sharon Blackwell, prin. 494-5157
Lake Ridge MS 4-00100
10350 MOHICAN RD 22192 494-5154
Ron Keeler, prin.
Rippon MS 3-00100
15101 BLACKBURN RD 22191 491-2171
James Council, prin.
MS, 2201 YORK DR 22191 3-00100
Rob Stine, prin. 494-3181

Northern Virginia Community College 4-CC
15200 NEABSCO MILLS RD 22191 670-2191
Woodbridge Business Institute 2-CS
14573 JEFFERSON DAVIS HWY 22191 491-3715

Woodstock, AC 703, PC 5, Shenandoah
Shenandoah County SD 6-11111
PO BOX 488 22664 459-4091
Dr. Jerry Webb, supt.
Central HS, 1147 SUSAN AVE 22664 3-00011
Maxwell Hutton, prin. 459-2161
MS, PO BOX 465 22664 2-00100
Carolyn Garman, prin. 459-2941
Other Schools – See Mount Jackson, Strasburg

Massanutten Military Academy 2-00111
614 S MAIN ST 22664 459-2167
Robert Osterling, prin.

Wytheville, AC 703, PC 6, Wythe
Wythe County SD 5-11111
1570 W RESERVOIR ST 24382 228-5411
James Vaught, supt.
Wythe JSHS, 1500 W PINE ST 24382 3-00111
Danny McDaniel, prin. 228-3157
Wythe Vo-Tech Vo Tech
1500 W SPILLER ST 24382 228-5481
Ernestine Dalton, prin.
Other Schools – See Max Meadows, Rural Retreat

Alliance Tractor Trailer Training Center 3-CS
PO BOX 804 24382 228-6101
Wytheville Community College 4-CC
1000 W MAIN ST 24382 228-5541

Yorktown, AC 804, PC 2, York
York County SD, 302 DARE RD 23692 7-11111
Steve Staples, supt. 898-0300
York HS 4-00011
9300 GEORGE WSHNGTN MEM HWY 23692
Barry Beers, prin. 898-0354
MS 3-00100
11201 GORGE WSHNGTN MEM HWY 23690
(—), prin. 898-0360
Other Schools – See Tabb, Williamsburg

WASHINGTON

STATE DEPARTMENT OF EDUCATION
Old Capitol Building
P.O. Box 47200, Olympia 98504
(206) 753-6738

Superintendent of Public Instruction	Judith Billings
Deputy Superintendent Administrative & School Business	David Moberly
Deputy Superintendent Instructional Programs	John Pearson

STATE BOARD OF EDUCATION
P.O. Box 47200, Olympia 98504

Executive Director   Monica Schmidt

EDUCATIONAL SERVICE DISTRICTS

ESD 101
Brian Talbott   509-456-6320
1025 W INDIANA AVE
Spokane 99205
ESD 105
Michael Bernazzani   509-575-2885
33 S 2ND AVE, Yakima 98902
ESD 112
Bill Fromhold, 2500 NE 65TH AVE   206-750-7500
Vancouver 98661

ESD 113
Larry Wise, 601 MCPHEE RD SW   206-586-2933
Olympia 98502
Olympic ESD 114
Frank Deebach   206-479-0993
105 NATIONAL AVE N
Bremerton 98312
Puget Sound ESD
Terry Lindquist   206-439-3636
400 SW 152ND ST, Seattle 98166

ESD 123
Larry Sappington   509-529-3700
1705 W ROSE ST
Walla Walla 99362
North Central ESD 171
Gene Sharratt   509-663-8799
PO BOX 1847, Wenatchee 98807
Northwest ESD 189
Dennis Couch, 205 STEWART RD   206-424-9573
Mount Vernon 98273

PUBLIC, PRIVATE AND CATHOLIC SECONDARY SCHOOLS

Aberdeen, AC 206, PC 7, Grays Harbor
Aberdeen SD 5, 216 N G ST 98520   5-11111
Sonja Martin, supt.   538-2000
Weatherwax HS, 414 N I ST 98520   4-00011
Mike Brophy, prin.   538-2040
Miller JHS, 100 LINDSTROM ST 98520   3-00100
Jerry Salstrom, prin.   538-2100

Wishkah Valley SD 117   2-11111
4640 WISHKAH RD 98520   532-3128
Jim Miller, supt.
Wishkah Valley JSHS   1-00111
4640 WISHKAH RD 98520   532-3128
Dale Bowen, prin.

Grays Harbor College   5-CC
1620 EDWARD P SMITH DR 98520   532-9020

Adna, AC 206, PC 2, Lewis
Adna SD 226, PO BOX 118 98522   3-11111
Bernard Rodgers, supt.   748-0362
JSHS, PO BOX 148 98522   2-00111
Ed Rothlin, prin.   748-0315

Almira, AC 509, PC 2, Lincoln
Almira SD 17, PO BOX 217 99103   2-11100
Walter Wilson, supt.   639-2414
MS, PO BOX 217 99103   1-00100
Rick Doehle, prin.   639-2414

Amanda Park, AC 206, PC 3, Grays Harbor
Quinault Lake SD 97   2-11111
PO BOX 38 98526   288-2260
Ray Lorton, supt.
Lake Quinault HS, PO BOX 38 98526   2-00011
Al Kelling, prin.   288-2414

Amboy, AC 206, PC 2, Clark
Battle Ground SD 116
Supt. — See Battle Ground
MS, 22115 NE CHELATCHIE RD 98601   2-01100
Tom Nadal, prin.   247-5426

Anacortes, AC 206, PC 7, Skagit
Anacortes SD 103, 2200 M AVE 98221   5-11111
D. Sharon Hill, supt.   293-1200
HS, 1916 J AVE 98221   3-00011
Duane Reidenbach, prin.   293-2166
MS, 2200 M AVE 98221   2-00100
Jerry Lynch, prin.   293-1230

Arlington, AC 206, PC 5, Snohomish
Arlington SD 16, PO BOX 309 98223   5-11111
James Maw, supt.   435-2156
HS, 135 S FRENCH AVE 98223   3-00011
Herb Hower, prin.   435-2119
Post MS, 1220 E 5TH ST 98223   3-00100
Rob Pattermann, prin.   435-3458

Asotin, AC 509, PC 3, Asotin
Asotin-Anatone SD 420   3-11111
PO BOX 489 99402   243-1100
Paul Boeckman, supt.
JSHS, PO BOX 489 99402   2-00111
Rich Goodwin, prin.   243-4151

Auburn, AC 206, PC 8, King
Auburn SD 408, 915 4TH ST NE 98002   7-11111
James Fugate, supt.   931-4900
SHS, 800 4TH ST NE 98002   4-00001
Kip Herren, prin.   931-4880
Cascade JHS, 1015 24TH ST NE 98002   3-00110
Bruce Phillips, prin.   931-4998
Olympic JHS, 1825 K ST SE 98002   3-00110
Randy Taylor, prin.   931-4969
Rainier JHS, 30620 116TH AVE SE 98002   3-00110
Carol Shell, prin.   931-4843

Federal Way SD 210
Supt. — See Federal Way
Jefferson SHS, 4248 S 288TH ST 98001   4-00001
Ken Olsson, prin.   839-7490
Kilo JHS, 4400 S 308TH ST 98001   3-00110
Mark Davidson, prin.   839-8550

Auburn Adventist Academy   2-00011
5000 AUBURN WAY S 98002   939-5000
Wayne Culmore, prin.
Green River Community Colleges   6-CC
12401 SE 320TH ST 98002   833-9111
Kent View Christian JSHS   2-00111
19830 SE 328TH PL 98002   735-1413
Wes Dennison, prin.

Bainbridge Island, AC 206, PC 5, Kitsap
Bainbridge Island SD 303   5-11111
8489 MADISON AVE NE 98110   842-4714
William Bleakney, supt.
Bainbridge HS   3-00011
9330 NE HIGH SCHOOL RD 98110   842-2634
David Ellick, prin.
Bainbridge MS   3-00100
9530 NE HIGH SCHOOL RD 98110   842-4787
Jerrold McLaughlin, prin.

Battle Ground, AC 206, PC 5, Clark
Battle Ground SD 116   6-11111
204 W MAIN ST 98604   256-2628
Leo Beck, supt.
HS, 416 W MAIN ST 98604   4-00011
Velda Sutton, prin.   687-6550
Lewisville MS, 1008 W MAIN ST 98604   2-01100
Gerald Edwards, prin.   687-6545
Maple Grove MS   3-01100
12500 NE 199TH ST 98604   687-6570
Cindy Larson, prin.
Other Schools – See Amboy, Brush Prairie,
Vancouver

Columbia Adventist Academy   2-00011
11100 NE 189TH ST 98604   687-3161
Kelly Block, prin.

Belfair, AC 206, PC 3, Mason
North Mason SD 403   4-11111
PO BOX 167 98528   275-2881
Marie Pickel, supt.
North Mason HS, PO BOX 167 98528   3-00011
Tom Marrs, prin.   275-2811
Hawkins MS, PO BOX 167 98528   3-00100
Janet Johnson, prin.   275-4461

Bellevue, AC 206, PC 8, King
Bellevue SD 405   7-11111
PO BOX 90010 98009   455-6015
Don O'Neil, supt.
HS, 10416 SE KILMARNOCK ST 98004   4-00011
Kevin Wulff, prin.   455-6146
Interlake HS, 16245 NE 24TH ST 98008   3-00011
Michael Bacigalupi, prin.   455-6171
Newport HS, 4333 128TH AVE SE 98006   3-00011
Karin Cathey, prin.   455-6136
Sammamish HS   4-00011
100 140TH AVE SE 98005   455-6162
Don Haid, prin.
Chinook MS, 2001 98TH AVE NE 98004   3-00100
Shuzo Takeuchi, prin.   455-6218
Highland MS, 15027 BEL RED RD 98007   3-00100
Nancy Savory, prin.   455-6187
Odle MS, 14401 NE 8TH ST 98007   3-00100
Ian Armitage, prin.   455-6211
Olympus Northwest MS   2-00100
14401 NE 8TH ST 98007   455-6152
Jan Fluter, prin.
Tillicum MS, 16020 SE 16TH ST 98008   3-00100
Jim Hoff, prin.   455-6193
Tyee MS, 13630 SE ALLEN RD 98006   3-00100
Jan Toner, prin.   455-6230

Bellevue Christian JSHS   2-00111
1601 98TH AVE NE 98004   454-4028
Bill Safstrom, prin.
Bellevue Community College   7-CC
3000 LANDERHOLM CIR SE 98007   641-0111
City University   5-UC
16661 NORTHUP WAY 98008   800-422-4898
Eastside Catholic HS   3-00011
11650 SE 60TH ST 98006   644-7737
James Dean, prin.
Forest Ridge JSHS   2-01111
4800 139TH AVE SE 98006   641-0700
Sr. Suzanne Cooke, prin.

Bellingham, AC 206, PC 8, Whatcom
Bellingham SD 501   6-11111
PO BOX 878 98227   676-6400
Dale Kinsley, supt.

480

HS, 2020 CORNWALL AVE 98225   4-00011 676-6471
  Robert Jones, prin.
Sehome HS   4-00011 676-6481
  2700 BILL MCDONALD PKY 98225
  Larry Brown, prin.
Fairhaven MS   3-00100 676-6450
  110 PARKRIDGE RD 98225
  Gail Aarstal, prin.
Shuksan MS   3-00100 676-6454
  2713 ALDERWOOD AVE 98225
  Michael Copland, prin.
Whatcom MS, 810 HALLECK ST 98225   3-00100 676-6460
  William Fox, prin.

Meridian SD 505   4-11111 398-7111
  214 W LAUREL RD 98226
  Donald Bauthues, supt.
Meridian HS, 194 W LAUREL RD 98226   2-00011 398-8111
  James Kistner, prin.
Other Schools – See Lynden

Bellingham Vocational Technical School   1-CS 676-6490
  3028 LINDBERG AVE 98225
Northwest Indian College 98226   3-CC 676-2772

Western Washington University   7-UC 676-3000
  516 HIGH ST 98225
Whatcom Community College   5-CC 676-2170
  237 W KELLOGG RD 98226

Benton City, AC 509, PC 4, Benton
Kiona-Benton City SD 52   4-11111 588-3717
  PO BOX 488 99320
  Gary Henderson, supt.
Kiona-Benton City JSHS   2-00111 588-3310
  PO BOX 488 99320
  Mark Muxen, prin.

Bickleton, AC 509, PC 2, Klickitat
Bickleton SD 203, PO BOX 10 99322   1-11111 896-5473
  Donald Newhall, supt.
HS, PO BOX 10 99322   1-00011 896-5473
  Donald Newhall, prin.

Blaine, AC 206, PC 4, Whatcom
Blaine SD 503, PO BOX 3489 98231   4-11111 332-5881
  Gordon Dolman, supt.
HS, PO BOX 3489 98231   2-00011 332-6045
  Dan Newell, prin.
MS, PO BOX 3489 98231   2-01100 332-8226
  William Kelly, prin.

Bothell, AC 206, PC 7, King
Northshore SD 417   7-11111 489-6000
  18315 BOTHELL WAY NE 98011
  Dennis Ray, supt.
HS, 18125 92ND AVE NE 98011   4-00001 489-6100
  Allen Haynes, prin.
Inglemoor SHS   4-00001 489-6500
  15400 SIMONDS RD NE 98011
  Vicki Sherwood, prin.
Canyon Park JHS   3-00110 489-6476
  23723 23RD AVE SE 98021
  Stephanie Haskins, prin.
Kenmore JHS   3-00110 489-6211
  20323 66TH AVE NE 98011
  June Anderson, prin.
Northshore JHS   3-00110 489-6411
  12101 NE 160TH ST 98011
  Bill Killien, prin.
Skyview JHS, 21404 35TH AVE SE 98021   3-00110 489-6040
  Holly Call, prin.
Other Schools – See Woodinville

ITT Technical Institute   2-CS 485-0303
  2525 223RD ST SE 98021

Bremerton, AC 206, PC 8, Kitsap
Bremerton SD 100-C   6-11111 478-5151
  300 N MONTGOMERY AVE 98312
  DeWayne Boyd, supt.
HS, 1500 13TH ST 98337   4-00011 478-0753
  Marilee Hanson, prin.
Kitsap Peninsula Vo HS   Vo Tech 478-5083
  101 NATIONAL AVE N 98312
  Mourine Anduiza, prin.
MS, 1300 E 30TH ST 98310   4-00100 478-5025
  Judith Mackey, prin.
Mountain View MS   3-00100 478-5130
  2400 PERRY AVE 98310
  Flint Walpole, prin.

Central Kitsap SD 401
  Supt. — See Silverdale
Olympic SHS   4-00001 692-3180
  7070 STAMPEDE BLVD NW 98311
  Emma Walker, prin.
Fairview JHS   3-00110 692-3129
  8107 CENTRAL VALLEY RD NW 98311
  Karen Hansen, prin.

Kings West S   2-11111 377-7700
  4012 CHICO WAY NW 98312
  Joanna Schoenknecht, prin.
Olympic College   6-CC 478-4504
  1600 CHESTER AVE 98337

Brewster, AC 509, PC 4, Okanogan
Brewster SD 111, PO BOX 97 98812   3-11111 689-3418
  Mark Jacobson, supt.
HS, PO BOX 97 98812   2-00011 689-3449
  Randy Phillips, prin.

Bridgeport, AC 509, PC 4, Douglas
Bridgeport SD 75   3-11111 686-9501
  PO BOX 1060 98813
  Robert Allen, supt.
HS, PO BOX 1090 98813   2-00011 686-8770
  Steve Warren, prin.
MS, PO BOX 1060 98813   2-00100 686-9501
  Robert Allen, prin.

Brush Prairie, AC 206, PC 5, Clark
Battle Ground SD 116
  Supt. — See Battle Ground
Prairie HS, 11500 NE 117TH AVE 98606   4-00011 254-5777
  Charles Elliot, prin.
Hockinson SD 98   4-11100 256-5270
  15916 NE 182ND AVE 98606
  Roger Bieber, supt.
Hockinson MS   2-00100 892-4953
  15916 NE 182ND AVE 98606
  Nancy Faaren, prin.

Buckley, AC 206, PC 5, Pierce
White River SD 416, PO BOX G 98321   5-11111 829-0600
  Dale Almlie, supt.
White River HS, PO BOX G 98321   3-00011 829-0600
  Keith Banks, prin.
White River MS, PO BOX G 98321   3-00100 829-0600
  Patricia Cullen, prin.

Rainier School   HND
  PO BOX 600 98321

Burbank, AC 509, PC 4, Walla Walla
Columbia SD 400, PO BOX 548 99323   3-11111 547-2136
  Don Anderson, supt.
Columbia HS   2-00011 545-8573
  GENERAL DELIVERY 99323
  Star Christman, prin.
Columbia MS   2-00100 545-8571
  GENERAL DELIVERY 99323
  Bob Nolan, prin.

Burlington, AC 206, PC 5, Skagit
Burlington-Edison SD 100   5-11111 757-3311
  927 E FAIRHAVEN AVE 98233
  Paul Chaplik, supt.
Burlington-Edison HS   3-00011 757-4074
  301 N BURLINGTON BLVD 98233
  Harry Warren, prin.

Camas, AC 206, PC 6, Clark
Camas SD 117, 2041 NE IONE ST 98607   4-11111 834-2811
  Milt Dennison, supt.
HS, 1612 NE GARFIELD ST 98607   3-00011 834-8806
  Harvey Keene, prin.
Zellerbach MS, 841 NE 22ND AVE 98607   3-00100 834-8807
  Patricia Boles, prin.

Carnation, AC 206, PC 4, King
Riverview SD 407   5-11111 333-4115
  32240 NE 50TH ST 98014
  J. Clifton Ernst, supt.
Tolt MS, 3740 TOLT AVE 98014   3-00100 333-4191
  Kathie McMahon, prin.
Other Schools – See Duvall

Cashmere, AC 509, PC 5, Chelan
Cashmere SD 222   4-11111 782-3355
  210 S DIVISION ST 98815
  Richard Langum, supt.
HS, 329 TIGNER RD 98815   2-00011 782-2914
  Sam Willsey, prin.
MS, 300 TIGNER RD 98815   2-01100 782-2001
  Ed Tuggle, prin.

Castle Rock, AC 206, PC 4, Cowlitz
Castle Rock SD 401   4-11111 274-8311
  PO BOX 220 98611
  Bennet Acker, supt.
HS, PO BOX 130 98611   2-00011 274-6634
  Gary Udd, prin.
MS, PO BOX 100 98611   2-00100 274-8232
  Tom Byrne, prin.

Cathlamet, AC 206, PC 3, Wahkiakum
Wahkiakum SD 200   2-11111 795-3971
  PO BOX 398 98612
  John Thomas, supt.
Wahkiakum HS, PO BOX 398 98612   2-00011 795-3271
  Michael Messenger, prin.

Centralia, AC 206, PC 7, Lewis
Centralia SD 401, PO BOX 610 98531   5-11111 736-9387
  Bruce Blain, supt.
HS, 813 ESHOM RD 98531   4-00011 736-9303
  Ethel Clarke, prin.
MS, 901 JOHNSON RD 98531   3-00100 736-9382
  Neal Kirby, prin.

Centralia College   5-CC 736-9391
  600 W LOCUST ST 98531

Chattaroy, AC 509, PC 2, Spokane
Riverside SD 416   4-11111 292-0201
  34515 N NEWPORT HWY 99003
  Jerry Wilson, supt.
Riverside HS   3-00011 292-0210
  4120 E DEER PARK MILAN RD 99003
  Mark Gorman, prin.
Riverside MS   3-01100 292-0220
  3814 E DEER PARK MILAN RD 99003
  Sheila Whisler, prin.

Chehalis, AC 206, PC 6, Lewis
Chehalis SD 302, 310 SW 16TH ST 98532   4-11111 748-8681
  Mike Boring, supt.
West HS, 342 SW 16TH ST 98532   3-00011 748-0273
  Linda Smith, prin.
MS, 1060 SW 20TH ST 98532   3-00100 748-1330
  Gerald Pierson, prin.

Chelan, AC 509, PC 5, Chelan
Lake Chelan SD 129   4-11111 682-3515
  PO BOX 369 98816
  Tom Reese, supt.
HS, PO BOX 369 98816   2-00011 682-4061
  Larry Bowers, prin.
MS, PO BOX 369 98816   2-00100 682-4073
  Karen Walters, prin.

Cheney, AC 509, PC 6, Spokane
Cheney SD 360, 520 4TH ST 99004   5-11111 235-6205
  Phil Snowden, supt.
SHS, 460 N 6TH ST 99004   3-00001 235-9510
  Jerry Knott, prin.
JHS, 2716 N 6TH ST 99004   3-00110 235-9526
  Ronald VanHorn, prin.

Eastern Washington University 99004   6-UC 359-2397

Chewelah, AC 509, PC 4, Stevens
Chewelah SD 36, PO BOX 47 99109   4-11111 935-8671
  Glenn Frizzell, supt.
Jenkins HS, PO BOX 47 99109   2-00011 935-8533
  Lorren Hagen, prin.
Jenkins MS, PO BOX 47 99109   2-00100 935-8544
  Douglas Asbjornsen, prin.

Chimacum, AC 206, PC 3, Jefferson
Chimacum SD 49, PO BOX 278 98325   4-11111 385-3922
  Marcia Harris, supt.
HS, PO BOX 278 98325   2-00011 732-4481
  Wayne Johnson, prin.
JHS, PO BOX 278 98325   2-00100 732-4219
  Cathy Wales, prin.

Clarkston, AC 509, PC 6, Asotin
Clarkston SD J 250-185   5-11111 758-2532
  PO BOX 70 99403
  James Keene, supt.
Adams HS, PO BOX 370 99403   3-00011 758-5591
  Jim Poindexter, prin.
Lincoln MS, 1945 4TH AVE 99403   2-00100 758-5506
  Jack Adams, prin.

Cle Elum, AC 509, PC 4, Kittitas
Cle Elum-Roslyn SD 404   3-11111 649-2393
  HC 60 BOX 5010 98922
  H. Walker, supt.
HS, HC 60 BOX 5011 98922   2-00011 649-2291
  Jim Stephenson, prin.
Other Schools – See Roslyn

Colfax, AC 509, PC 5, Whitman
Colfax SD 300   3-11111 397-3042
  1110 N MORTON ST 99111
  Donald Cox, supt.
HS, 1110 N MORTON ST 99111   2-00011 397-4368
  Rich Hilty, prin.

College Place, AC 509, PC 6, Walla Walla
College Place SD 250   3-11100 525-4827
  1755 S COLLEGE AVE 99324
  C. Murphy, supt.
Sager MS, 1755 S COLLEGE AVE 99324   2-00100 525-5300
  Bruce Wildfang, prin.

Walla Walla College   4-UC 800-541-8900
  204 S COLLEGE AVE 99324
Walla Walla Valley Academy   2-00011 525-1050
  PO BOX 457 99324
  John Deming, prin.

Colton, AC 509, PC 2, Whitman
Colton SD 306, PO BOX 109 99113   2-11111 229-3385
  C. Foley, supt.
JSHS, PO BOX 109 99113   1-00111 229-3386
  Wynn Van Ausdle, prin.

Colville, AC 509, PC 5, Stevens
Colville SD 115   5-11111 684-2536
  430 E HAWTHORNE AVE 99114
  Richard Cole, supt.
HS, 154 HIGHWAY 20 E 99114   3-00011 684-7800
  James Monasmith, prin.
JHS, 990 S CEDAR ST 99114   2-00100 684-4546
  Tom Flugel, prin.

Concrete, AC 206, PC 3, Skagit
Concrete SD 11, PO BOX 386 98237   3-11111 853-8141
  Gordon Wallace, supt.
HS, PO BOX 999 98237   2-00011 853-8143
  Rick Hinds, prin.
MS, PO BOX 999 98237   2-00100 853-8141
  Ryle Kiser, prin.

Connell, AC 509, PC 4, Franklin
North Franklin SD J 51-162   4-11111 234-2031
  PO BOX 829 99326
  Darell Cain, supt.
HS 99326   2-00011 234-2911
  Duane Gottschalk, prin.
Olds JHS 99326   2-00100 234-3931
  John Sebastian, prin.

Cosmopolis, AC 206, PC 4, Grays Harbor
North River SD 200 1-11111
HC 77 BOX 395 98537 532-3079
J. Sorensen, supt.
North River JSHS 1-00111
HC 77 BOX 395 98537 532-3079
J. Sorensen, prin.

Coulee City, AC 509, PC 3, Grant
Coulee-Hartline SD 151 2-11111
PO BOX 428 99115 632-5231
Walter Wilson, supt.
MS, PO BOX 548 99115 1-00100
Anna Parsons, prin. 632-5312
Other Schools – See Hartline

Coulee Dam, AC 509, PC 4, Grant
Grand Coulee Dam SD 301J 3-11111
110 STEVENS AVE 99116 633-2143
Dennis Przychodzin, supt.
Lake Roosevelt HS 2-00011
500 CIVIC WAY 99116 633-1442
Jim Parker, prin.
Other Schools – See Grand Coulee

Coupeville, AC 206, PC 4, Island
Coupeville SD 204, 2 S MAIN ST 98239 3-11111
Ernie Bartelson, supt. 678-4522
JSHS, 501 S MAIN ST 98239 3-00111
Rock White, prin. 678-4409

Cowiche, AC 509, PC 2, Yakima
Highland SD 203, PO BOX 38 98923 3-11111
George Asan, supt. 678-4173
Highland HS, PO BOX 38 98923 2-00011
Rick Slater, prin. 678-4161
Other Schools – See Tieton

Creston, AC 509, PC 2, Lincoln
Creston SD 73, PO BOX 17 99117 2-11111
Michael Crowell, supt. 636-2721
JSHS, PO BOX 17 99117 1-00111
Wayne Kannberg, prin. 636-2721

Curlew, AC 509, PC 2, Ferry
Curlew SD 50, PO BOX 370 99118 2-11111
John Magers, supt. 779-4931
S, PO BOX 370 99118 2-11111
Steve Tedrow, prin. 779-4931

Cusick, AC 509, PC 2, Pend Oreille
Cusick SD 59, PO BOX 270 99119 2-11111
Charles Crickman, supt. 445-1125
JSHS, PO BOX 270 99119 2-00111
Allen Robinson, prin. 445-1125

Darrington, AC 206, PC 4, Snohomish
Darrington SD 330, PO BOX 27 98241 3-11111
William Edwards, supt. 436-1323
JSHS, PO BOX 27 98241 2-00111
Dan Smith, prin. 436-1140

Davenport, AC 509, PC 4, Lincoln
Davenport SD 207, PO BOX 8 99122 2-11111
Dave Iverson, supt. 725-1481
JSHS, PO BOX 8 99122 2-00111
Harold Patterson, prin. 725-4021

Dayton, AC 509, PC 4, Columbia
Dayton SD 2, 609 S 2ND ST 99328 3-11111
Steve Chestnut, supt. 382-2544
JSHS, 614 S 3RD ST 99328 2-00111
Van Cummings, prin. 382-4775

Deer Park, AC 509, PC 4, Spokane
Deer Park SD 414, PO BOX 490 99006 4-11111
Glenys Hill, supt. 276-5051
HS, PO BOX 550 99006 2-00011
Jean Chandler, prin. 276-2959
JHS, PO BOX 882 99006 2-00100
David Feldhusen, prin. 276-8861

Deming, AC 206, PC 2, Whatcom
Mt. Baker SD 507, PO BOX 95 98244 4-11111
Gerald Hunter, supt. 592-5153
Mt. Baker JSHS, PO BOX 95 98244 3-00111
Kennett Robinson, prin. 592-5151

Des Moines, AC 206, PC 7, King
Highline SD 401
Supt. — See Seattle
Mount Rainier HS 4-00011
22450 19TH AVE S 98198 433-2441
Tom O'Keeffe, prin.
Pacific MS, 22705 24TH AVE S 98198 3-00100
Lamar Strain, prin. 433-2581

Commercial Training Services 2-CS
24325 PACIFIC HWY S 98198 824-3970
Highline Community College 98198 6-CC
878-3710

Duvall, AC 206, PC 5, King
Riverview SD 407
Supt. — See Carnation
Cedarcrest HS 3-00011
29000 NE 150TH ST 98019 788-7116
Harry Vanikiotis, prin.

Easton, AC 509, PC 2, Kittitas
Easton SD 28, PO BOX 8 98925 1-11111
George Park, supt. 656-2317
S, PO BOX 8 98925 1-11111
George Park, prin. 656-2317

Eastsound, AC 206, PC 4, San Juan
Orcas Island SD 137 2-11111
PO BOX 167 98245 376-2284
Barry Acker, supt.
Orcas Island HS, PO BOX 167 98245 2-00011
Barb Kline, prin. 376-2287
Orcas Island MS, PO BOX 167 98245 1-00100
Barb Kline, prin. 376-2286

East Wenatchee, AC 509, PC 5, Douglas
Eastmont SD 206, 460 9TH ST NE 98802 5-11111
Walt Bigby, supt. 884-7169
Eastmont SHS, 955 3RD ST NE 98802 3-00001
Rich Boon, prin. 884-6665
Eastmont JHS, 270 9TH ST NE 98802 3-00110
Mark Spurgeon, prin. 884-2407

Eatonville, AC 206, PC 4, Pierce
Eatonville SD 404 4-11111
PO BOX 698 98328 832-4766
William Lahmann, supt.
HS, PO BOX 699 98328 2-00011
Wally Lis, prin. 832-3302
Vo Services, PO BOX 699 98328 Vo Tech
Michael Thompson, prin. 832-3302
MS, PO BOX 910 98328 2-00100
Howard King, prin. 832-6261

Edmonds, AC 206, PC 8, Snohomish
Edmonds SD 15
Supt. — See Lynnwood
Edmonds-Woodway HS 4-00011
23200 100TH AVE W 98020 670-7977
Rainer Houser, prin.

Puget Sound Christian College 1-UC
410 4TH AVE N 98020 775-8686
Sno-King Lutheran JSHS 2-00111
410 4TH AVE N 98020 774-3916
Jack Kniseley, prin.

Edwall, AC 509, PC 2, Lincoln

Christian Heritage S 2-11111
PO BOX 118 99008 236-2224
Jess Kennison, prin.

Ellensburg, AC 509, PC 7, Kittitas
Ellensburg SD 401 4-11111
506 N SPRAGUE ST 98926 925-0848
Keith Tolzin, supt.
HS, 1300 E 3RD AVE 98926 3-00011
Dave Hall, prin. 925-6185
Morgan MS, 400 E 1ST AVE 98926 3-00100
Donald Price, prin. 962-9878

Central Washington University 98926 6-UC
963-1211

Elma, AC 206, PC 5, Grays Harbor
Elma SD 68 4-11111
1235 ELMA MONTE RD 98541 482-2822
Gregory Johnson, supt.
HS, 1235 ELMA MONTE RD 98541 3-00011
Paul Ganalon, prin. 482-3121
MS, 1235 ELMA MONTE RD 98541 2-00100
Tami Hickle, prin. 482-2237

Mary M. Knight SD 311 2-11111
2987 W MATLOCK BRADY RD 98541 426-6767
Fred Yancey, supt.
Knight JSHS 2-00111
2987 W MATLOCK BRADY RD 98541 426-6767
Fred Yancey, prin.

Endicott, AC 509, PC 2, Whitman
Endicott SD 308, PO BOX 327 99125 2-11100
Tim McCarthy, supt. 657-3523
Endicott-St. John MS 1-00100
PO BOX 327 99125 657-3524
Suzanne Schmick, prin.

Entiat, AC 509, PC 2, Chelan
Entiat SD 127, 2650 ENTIAT WAY 98822 2-11111
Thomas Jentges, supt. 784-1800
JSHS, 2650 ENTIAT WAY 98822 2-00111
Loren Gilson, prin. 784-1911

Enumclaw, AC 206, PC 6, King
Enumclaw SD 216 5-11111
2929 MCDOUGALL AVE 98022 825-2588
James Barchek, supt.
HS, 226 SEMANSKI ST 98022 4-00011
Terry Parker, prin. 825-2585
JHS, 550 SEMANSKI ST 98022 3-00100
Lea Anna Portmann, prin. 825-2581

Ephrata, AC 509, PC 6, Grant
Ephrata SD 165, PO BOX 788 98823 4-11111
Larry MacGuffie, supt. 754-2474
HS, 333 4TH AVE NW 98823 3-00011
Gary Carlton, prin. 754-2043
MS, 384 A ST SE 98823 3-00100
Pat Flannery, prin. 754-4659

Everett, AC 206, PC 8, Snohomish
Everett SD 2, PO BOX 2098 98203 7-11111
Jane Hammond, supt. 339-4200
Cascade HS, 801 CASINO RD 98203 4-00011
Gary Axtell, prin. 356-4500
HS, 2416 COLBY AVE 98201 4-00011
Lee VanWinkle, prin. 339-4400
Eisenhower MS 4-00100
10200 25TH AVE SE 98208 338-5110
Judy Heidman, prin.
Evergreen MS, 7621 BEVERLY LN 98203 3-00100
Carole Bowers, prin. 356-4550
North MS, 2514 RAINIER AVE 98201 3-00100
Charles Lisk, prin. 339-4370
Other Schools – See Mill Creek

Lake Stevens SD 4
Supt. — See Lake Stevens
Lake Stevens MS 3-00100
1031 91ST AVE SE 98205 335-1544
Sue Galletti, prin.

Mukilteo SD 6, 9401 SHARON DR 98204 7-11111
James Shoemake, supt. 356-1220
Mariner HS, 200 120TH ST SW 98204 4-00011
Cheryl Boze, prin. 356-1700
Sno-Isle Vo Skills Ctr Vo Tech
9001 AIRPORT RD 98204 353-8810
Claudia Buxton, prin.
Explorer MS, 9600 SHARON DR 98204 3-00100
Marilyn McGuire, prin. 356-1240
Voyager MS, 11711 4TH AVE W 98204 3-00100
John Logan, prin. 356-1730
Other Schools – See Mukilteo

Eton Technical Institute 2-CS
209 E CASINO RD 98208 353-4888
Everett Community College 6-CC
801 WETMORE AVE 98201 259-7151
Holy Cross HS, 2617 CEDAR ST 98201 2-00011
Kristine Smith, prin. 252-6203

Fall City, AC 206, PC 4, King
Snoqualmie Valley SD 410
Supt. — See Snoqualmie
Chief Kanim MS, PO BOX 639 98024 2-00100
Barbara Gibson, prin. 222-6686

Federal Way, AC 206, PC 8, King
Federal Way SD 210 7-11111
31405 18TH AVE S 98003 941-0100
G. Harris, supt.
Decatur SHS, 2800 SW 320TH ST 98023 4-00001
Gerald Millett, prin. 927-5861
SHS, 30611 16TH AVE S 98003 4-00001
Tim Sherry, prin. 839-0523
Illahee JHS, 36001 1ST AVE S 98003 4-00110
Joe Pope, prin. 927-3073
Lakota JHS, 1415 SW 314TH ST 98023 3-00110
Karin Stevens, prin. 927-7981
Sacajawea JHS 3-00110
1101 S DASH POINT RD 98003 839-7650
Judith Seiwerath, prin.
Saghalie JHS, 36001 1ST AVE S 98003 3-00110
Duane Hammil, prin. 925-5223
Other Schools – See Auburn, Kent

Eton Technical Institute 2-CS
31919 6TH AVE S 98003 941-5800

Ferndale, AC 206, PC 6, Whatcom
Ferndale SD 502, PO BOX 698 98248 5-11111
Roger Lehnert, supt. 384-9200
HS, PO BOX 428 98248 4-00011
Elvis Dellinger, prin. 384-9211
Vista MS, PO BOX 1328 98248 3-00100
James Kowalkowski, prin. 384-9240

Forks, AC 206, PC 5, Clallam
Quillayute Valley SD 402 4-11111
PO BOX 60 98331 374-6262
John Jones, supt.
JSHS, PO BOX 60 98331 2-00111
James Bennett, prin. 374-6116

Friday Harbor, AC 206, PC 4, San Juan
San Juan Island SD 149 3-11111
PO BOX 458 98250 378-4133
Gretta Merwin, supt.
JSHS, PO BOX 458 98250 2-00111
Jeff Davis, prin. 378-5215

Garfield, AC 509, PC 3, Whitman
Garfield SD 302, PO BOX 398 99130 2-11100
Bill Thurston, supt. 635-1331
Garfield/Palouse MS 1-00100
PO BOX 398 99130 635-1331
Beverly Fox, prin.

Gig Harbor, AC 206, PC 5, Pierce
Peninsula SD 401 6-11111
14015 62ND AVE NW 98332 857-6171
Tom Hulst, supt.
HS, 5101 ROSEDALE ST 98335 4-00011
Jan Reeder, prin. 851-6131
Peninsula HS 4-00011
14105 PURDY DR NW 98332 857-3530
Jon Kellett, prin.
Goodman MS 3-00100
3701 38TH AVE NW 98335 858-5500
Rod Mitchell, prin.
Harbor Ridge MS 2-00100
9010 PRENTICE AVE 98332 858-5530
Rob Lang, prin.
Kopachuck MS 3-00100
10414 56TH ST NW 98335 265-3392
Craig Shurick, prin.
Other Schools – See Lakebay

Glenwood, AC 509, PC 2, Klickitat
Glenwood SD 401, PO BOX 12 98619 2-11111
James Sikes, supt. 364-3595
S, PO BOX 12 98619 2-11111
(—), prin. 364-3565

Goldendale, AC 509, PC 5, Klickitat
Goldendale SD 404 — 4-11111
603 S ROOSEVELT AVE 98620 — 773-5177
Ian Grabenhorst, supt.
HS, 525 E SIMCOE DR 98620 — 2-00011
Jim Thrasher, prin. — 773-5846
MS, 520 E COLLINS ST 98620 — 2-01100
Mike Lindhe, prin. — 773-4323

Graham, AC 206, PC 2, Pierce
Bethel SD 403
Supt. — See Spanaway
Frontier JHS, 22110 108TH AVE E 98338 — 3-00110
Mary Dickey, prin. — 846-8544

Grand Coulee, AC 509, PC 3, Grant
Grand Coulee Dam SD 301J
Supt. — See Coulee Dam
Grand Coulee Dam MS, PO BOX J 99133 — 2-01100
Ralph Hocking, prin. — 633-1520

Grandview, AC 509, PC 6, Yakima
Grandview SD 116-200 — 5-11111
913 W 2ND ST 98930 — 882-2271
Michael Palanuk, supt.
HS, 1601 W 5TH ST 98930 — 3-00011
Gary Sansom, prin. — 882-3223
MS, 1401 W 2ND ST 98930 — 3-00100
Arthur Smith, prin. — 882-2398

Granger, AC 509, PC 4, Yakima
Granger SD 204, PO BOX 400 98932 — 4-11111
Jerry House, supt. — 854-1515
JSHS, PO BOX 400 98932 — 2-00111
Dave Uggetti, prin. — 854-1115

Granite Falls, AC 206, PC 4, Snohomish
Granite Falls SD 332 — 4-11111
PO BOX 9 98252 — 691-7717
Bob Gilden, supt.
HS 98252 — 2-00011
Peter Finch, prin. — 691-7713
MS 98252 — 2-01100
Sallie Hartman, prin. — 691-7710

Greenacres, AC 509, PC 5, Spokane
Central Valley SD 356 — 6-11111
19307 E CATALDO AVE 99016 — 922-6700
Richard Sovde, supt.
JHS, 17409 E SPRAGUE AVE 99016 — 3-00110
Sharon Jayne, prin. — 922-6730
Other Schools – See Spokane, Veradale

Harrington, AC 509, PC 2, Lincoln
Harrington SD 204 — 2-11111
PO BOX 204 99134 — 253-4331
Mitchell Denning, supt.
HS, PO BOX 204 99134 — 1-00011
Kurt Hoffman, prin. — 253-4331

Hartline, AC 509, PC 2, Grant
Coulee-Hartline SD 151
Supt. — See Coulee City
Almira/Coulee-Hartline HS — 2-00011
PO BOX 98 99135 — 639-2611
Rick Doehle, prin.

Hoquiam, AC 206, PC 6, Grays Harbor
Hoquiam SD 28 — 4-11111
312 SIMPSON AVE 98550 — 532-6543
Stanley Pinnick, supt.
HS, 501 W EMERSON AVE 98550 — 3-00011
Bob Miller, prin. — 532-3760
MS, 203 W EKLUND AVE 98550 — 2-00100
Loran Northcutt, prin. — 532-7361

Hunters, AC 509, PC 2, Stevens
Columbia SD 206, PO BOX 7 99137 — 2-11111
Roy Graffis, supt. — 722-3871
Columbia S, PO BOX 7 99137 — 2-11111
Fred Pflugrath, prin. — 722-3311

Ilwaco, AC 206, PC 3, Pacific
Ocean Beach SD 101 — 4-11111
PO BOX 860 98624 — 642-3739
Gilbert Johnson, supt.
JSHS, PO BOX F 98624 — 2-00111
Bruce Slama, prin. — 642-3731

Inchelium, AC 509, PC 2, Ferry
Inchelium SD 70, PO BOX 285 99138 — 2-11111
Jim Sutton, supt. — 722-6181
S, PO BOX 285 99138 — 2-11111
Peato Ena, prin. — 722-6181

Ione, AC 509, PC 3, Pend Oreille
Selkirk SD 70
Supt. — See Metaline Falls
Selkirk JSHS, HC 2 BOX 595 99139 — 2-00111
Kim Carlson, prin. — 446-3505

Issaquah, AC 206, PC 6, King
Issaquah SD 411 — 7-11111
565 NW HOLLY ST 98027 — 557-7000
William Stewart, supt.
HS, 700 2ND AVE SE 98027 — 4-00011
Ed Marcoe, prin. — 557-6000
MS, 400 1ST AVE SE 98027 — 3-00100
Marilyn Luckman, prin. — 557-6800
Pine Lake MS — 3-00100
3200 228TH AVE SE 98027 — 557-5700
Bette De Salvo, prin.
Other Schools – See Renton

Lutheran Bible Institute of Seattle — 2-UC
4221 228TH AVE SE 98027 — 800-843-5659

Joyce, AC 206, PC 2, Clallam
Crescent SD 313, PO BOX 20 98343 — 2-11111
Richard Wilson, supt. — 928-3311
Crescent JSHS, PO BOX 20 98343 — 2-00111
Doug Kubalek, prin. — 928-3311

Kahlotus, AC 509, PC 2, Franklin
Kahlotus SD 56, PO BOX 69 99335 — 1-11111
Robert Weller, supt. — 282-3338
JSHS, PO BOX 69 99335 — 1-00111
Robert Weller, prin. — 282-3338

Kalama, AC 206, PC 4, Cowlitz
Kalama SD 402 — 3-11111
548 CHINA GARDEN RD 98625 — 673-5225
Charles Anderson, supt.
JSHS, 548 CHINA GARDEN RD 98625 — 2-00111
Randy Brown, prin. — 673-5225

Kelso, AC 206, PC 7, Cowlitz
Kelso SD 458, 601 CRAWFORD ST 98626 — 6-11111
Gay Selby, supt. — 577-2400
SHS, 1904 ALLEN ST 98626 — 4-00001
Paula Radich, prin. — 577-2422
Coweeman JHS, 2000 ALLEN ST 98626 — 3-00110
Jay DeVries, prin. — 577-2435
Huntington JHS, 500 REDPATH ST 98626 — 3-00110
Mark Hottowe, prin. — 577-2427

Kennewick, AC 509, PC 8, Benton
Finley SD 53, RR 2 BOX 2685 99337 — 4-11111
Don Fekete, supt. — 586-3217
River View HS, RR 2 BOX 2670 99337 — 2-00011
Robin Emmingham, prin. — 582-2158
Finley MS, RR 2 BOX 2681 99337 — 2-00100
Robin Emmingham, prin. — 586-7561

Kennewick SD 17 — 7-11111
200 S DAYTON ST 99336 — 736-2100
Gary Fields, supt.
Kamiakin HS, 600 N ARTHUR ST 99336 — 4-00011
Robert McMullen, prin. — 736-2200
HS, 500 S DAYTON ST 99336 — 4-00011
Neal Powell, prin. — 736-2600
Tri-City Area Vo Skill Ctr — Vo Tech
5929 W METALINE AVE 99336 — 736-2500
Richard Hare, prin.
Desert Hills MS — 3-00100
6011 W 10TH AVE 99336 — 736-2240
Larry Gregory, prin.
Highlands MS, 425 S TWEEDT ST 99336 — 3-00100
Robert Bonner, prin. — 736-2260
Horse Heaven Hills MS — 3-00100
3500 S VANCOUVER ST 99337 — 736-2100
Jim Verhulp, prin.
Park MS, 1011 W 10TH AVE 99336 — 3-00100
Mike Hepworth, prin. — 736-2180

Trend College — 2-CS
3311 W CLEARWATER AVE #1201 99336 — 735-8515

Kent, AC 206, PC 8, King
Federal Way SD 210
Supt. — See Federal Way
Totem JHS, 26630 40TH AVE S 98032 — 3-00110
Mel McDonald, prin. — 852-5100

Kent SD 415, 12033 SE 256TH ST 98031 — 7-11111
James Hager, supt. — 813-9550
Kent-Meridian SHS — 4-00001
10020 SE 256TH ST 98031 — 813-7405
Ben Dillard, prin.
Kentridge SHS — 4-00001
12430 SE 208TH ST 98031 — 813-7345
Robert Davidson, prin.
Kentwood SHS — 4-00001
25800 164TH AVE SE 98042 — 813-7680
Rich Knuth, prin.
Cedar Heights JHS — 4-00110
19640 SE 272ND ST 98042 — 813-7620
Janice Bechtel, prin.
JHS, 620 CENTRAL AVE N 98032 — 3-00110
Doug Boushey, prin. — 813-7447
Mattson JHS, 16400 SE 251ST ST 98042 — 3-00110
Calvin Kam, prin. — 813-7368
Meridian JHS — 3-00110
23480 120TH AVE SE 98031 — 813-7387
Mike Davidson, prin.
Sequoia JHS, 11000 SE 264TH ST 98031 — 3-00110
Paul Cooper, prin. — 813-7542
Other Schools – See Renton

Tahoma SD 409
Supt. — See Maple Valley
Tahoma HS, 18200 SE 240TH ST 98042 — 4-00011
Catherine Davidson, prin. — 432-4484

St. Christopher Academy — 2-11111
318 3RD AVE S 98032 — 852-1515
Darlene Jevne, prin.

Kettle Falls, AC 509, PC 4, Stevens
Kettle Falls SD 212 99141 — 3-11111
John Mathis, supt. — 738-6625
HS 99141 — 2-00011
Marie Phillips, prin. — 738-6388
MS 99141 — 2-01100
Ricke Swaim, prin. — 738-6014

Kingston, AC 206, PC 4, Kitsap
North Kitsap SD 400
Supt. — See Poulsbo

JHS — 3-00110
9000 NE WEST KINGSTON RD 98346 — 297-7070
Cindy Simonsen, prin.

Kirkland, AC 206, PC 8, King
Lake Washington SD 414 — 7-11111
PO BOX 2909 98083 — 828-3200
L. Scarr, supt.
Juanita SHS, 10601 NE 132ND ST 98034 — 4-00001
Sue Cohn, prin. — 823-7600
Lake Washington SHS — 4-00001
12033 NE 80TH ST 98033 — 828-3371
Paul Gentle, prin.
Finn Hill JHS, 8040 NE 132ND ST 98034 — 3-00110
Barb Connor, prin. — 821-6544
Kamiakin JHS — 3-00110
14111 132ND AVE NE 98034 — 823-6750
Steve Mezich, prin.
JHS, 430 18TH AVE 98033 — 3-00110
Dennis Lis-Sette, prin. — 822-6224
Other Schools – See Redmond

Cogswell Polytechnical College — 2-UC
10626 NE 37TH CIR 98033 — 822-3137
Lake Washington Vocational Tech. Inst. — 4-CS
11605 132ND AVE NE 98034 — 828-5627
Northwest College Assemblies of God — 3-UC
PO BOX 579 98083 — 822-8266

Kittitas, AC 509, PC 3, Kittitas
Kittitas SD 403, PO BOX 599 98934 — 3-11111
Jerry Harding, supt. — 968-3014
HS, PO BOX 599 98934 — 2-00011
Lee Day, prin. — 968-3902

Klickitat, AC 509, PC 3, Klickitat
Klickitat SD 402, PO BOX 37 98628 — 2-11111
Roger Mortensen, supt. — 369-4145
HS, PO BOX 37 98628 — 1-00011
Roger Mortensen, prin. — 369-4145

La Center, AC 206, PC 2, Clark
La Center SD 101, PO BOX 168 98629 — 3-11111
Clifford Campbell, supt. — 263-2131
HS, PO BOX 5001 98629 — 2-00011
Warren Hopkins, prin. — 263-1700
IS, PO BOX 168 98629 — 2-01100
Ferrin Kilby, prin. — 263-2136

La Conner, AC 206, PC 3, Skagit
La Conner SD 311, PO BOX D 98257 — 2-11111
Tim Bruce, supt. — 466-3171
HS, PO BOX D 98257 — 2-00011
Ken Winkes, prin. — 466-3173
MS, PO BOX D 98257 — 2-00100
Maureen Harlan, prin. — 466-4113

Lacey, AC 206, PC 7, Thurston
North Thurston SD 3 — 7-11111
305 COLLEGE ST NE 98516 — 493-9002
David Steele, supt.
North Thurston HS — 4-00011
600 SLEATER KINNEY RD NE 98506 — 493-2900
Karen Eitreim, prin.
Timberline HS — 4-00011
6120 MULLEN RD SE 98503 — 493-2938
Bernie Josefsburg, prin.
Chinook MS, 4301 6TH AVE NE 98516 — 3-00100
James Stuart, prin. — 493-2720
Komachin MS — 3-00100
3650 COLLEGE ST SE 98503 — 438-8800
Norm Bykerk, prin.
Nisqually MS — 3-00100
8100 STEILACOOM RD SE 98503 — 493-2743
Michele Hendrickson, prin.
Other Schools – See Olympia

St. Martin's College — 4-UC
700 COLLEGE ST NE 98516 — 438-4330

Lacrosse, AC 509, PC 2, Whitman
Lacrosse SD 126 99143 — 2-11111
Monte Swenson, supt. — 549-3591
HS 99143 — 1-00011
Jim Hill, prin. — 549-3592

Lakebay, AC 206, PC 3, Pierce
Peninsula SD 401
Supt. — See Gig Harbor
Key Penninsula MS — 3-00100
5510 KEY PENINSULA HWY N 98349 — 884-4800
Judi Cleghorn, prin.

Lake Stevens, AC 206, PC 5, Snohomish
Lake Stevens SD 4 — 5-11111
2202A 123RD AVE NE 98258 — 335-1500
Joseph Ghaffari, supt.
HS, 2908 113TH AVE NE 98258 — 4-00011
Robert Estes, prin. — 335-1515
North Lake MS — 3-00100
2202B 123RD AVE NE 98258 — 335-1530
Fran Ennis, prin.
Other Schools – See Everett

Lakewood, AC 206, PC 3, Snohomish
Lakewood SD 306 — 4-11111
PO BOX 220 98259 — 652-7519
Wayne Robertson, supt.
JSHS, PO BOX 10 98259 — 3-00111
Kris McDuffy, prin. — 652-7511

Lamont, AC 509, PC 1, Whitman
Lamont SD 264, RR 2 BOX 50 99017 — 1-00100
Richard Hattrup, supt. — 257-2463

MS, RR 2 BOX 50 99017 — 1-00100
Joseph Whipple, prin. — 257-2463

Langley, AC 206, PC 3, Island
South Whidbey SD 206 — 4-11111
PO BOX 346 98260 — 221-6100
Arthur Jarvis, supt.
South Whidbey HS — 3-00011
PO BOX 390 98260 — 221-4300
Guy Pitzer, prin.
MS, PO BOX 370 98260 — 3-00100
Greg Willis, prin. — 221-5100

Leavenworth, AC 509, PC 4, Chelan
Cascade SD 228, 330 EVANS ST 98826 — 4-11111
Marilynn Baker, supt. — 548-5885
Cascade HS — 2-00011
10190 CHUMSTICK CANYON RD 98826
Bill Keim, prin. — 548-5277
Icicle River MS, 10195 TITUS RD 98826 — 2-01100
Mike Franza, prin. — 548-4042

Lind, AC 509, PC 2, Adams
Lind SD 158, PO BOX 340 99341 — 2-11111
Robert Beath, supt. — 677-3481
JSHS, PO BOX 340 99341 — 1-00111
David Balcom, prin. — 677-3408

Longview, AC 206, PC 8, Cowlitz
Longview SD 122, 2715 LILAC ST 98632 — 6-11111
Nicholas Seaver, supt. — 577-2700
Long HS, 2903 NICHOLS BLVD 98632 — 3-00011
Rolland Johnson, prin. — 577-2731
Morris HS — 3-00011
1602 MARK MORRIS CT 98632 — 577-2751
Gary Kipp, prin.
Cascade MS, 2821 PARKVIEW DR 98632 — 3-00100
Bruce Holway, prin. — 577-2770
Monticello MS — 3-00100
2800 HEMLOCK ST 98632 — 577-2760
Dean Yohe, prin.

Columbia Heights Christian Academy — 2-11111
3609 COLUMBIA HEIGHTS RD 98632 — 425-1251
Paul Dehmert, prin.
Lower Columbia College — 5-CC
PO BOX 3010 98632 — 577-3400
St. John's Medical Center — HSP
PO BOX 3002 98632 — 423-1530
Trend College — 2-CS
1260 COMMERCE AVE 98632 — 425-4790

Lopez, AC 206, PC 3, San Juan
Lopez SD 144, RR 1 BOX 1270 98261 — 2-11111
Daniel Levine, supt. — 468-2219
JSHS, RR 1 BOX 1270 98261 — 2-00111
Robert Spiering, prin. — 468-2219

Lyle, AC 509, PC 3, Klickitat
Lyle SD 406, PO BOX 368 98635 — 2-11111
Bob Garrett, supt. — 365-2191
HS 98635 — 1-00011
Stu Evans, prin. — 365-2211
MS 98635 — 1-00100
Stu Evans, prin. — 365-2211

Lynden, AC 206, PC 6, Whatcom
Lynden SD 504 — 4-11111
1203 BRADLEY RD 98264 — 354-4443
Howard Heppner, supt.
HS 98264 — 3-00011
Ken Axelson, prin. — 354-4401
MS, 516 MAIN ST 98264 — 3-01100
Mike Kirby, prin. — 354-2952

Meridian SD 505
Supt. — See Bellingham
Meridian MS, 861 TEN MILE RD 98264 — 2-00100
Bruce Taubenheim, prin. — 398-2291

Lynden Christian HS — 4-11111
515 DRAYTON ST 98264 — 354-3221
Ronald Polinder, prin.

Lynnwood, AC 206, PC 8, Snohomish
Edmonds SD 15 — 7-11111
20420 68TH AVE W 98036 — 670-7000
Brian Benzel, supt.
HS, 3001 184TH ST SW 98037 — 4-00011
Steve Anderson, prin. — 670-7520
Meadowdale HS — 4-00011
6002 168TH ST SW 98037 — 670-7650
Rod Waddell, prin.
Scriber Lake HS — 2-00011
19400 56TH AVE W 98036 — 670-7270
Karol Gadwa, prin.
Alderwood MS — 3-00100
20000 28TH AVE W 98036 — 670-7579
Jeanine Casper, prin.
Brier Terrace MS, 22200 BRIER RD 98036 — 3-00100
Barbara Marsh, prin. — 670-7834
College Place MS — 3-00100
7501 208TH ST SW 98036 — 670-7451
Ann Foley, prin.
Meadowdale MS — 3-00100
6500 168TH ST SW 98037 — 670-7707
Alicia Musgrave, prin.
Other Schools – See Edmonds, Mountlake Terrace

Edmonds Community College — 6-CC
20000 68TH AVE W 98036 — 771-1500

Mabton, AC 509, PC 4, Yakima
Mabton SD 120, PO BOX 37 98935 — 3-11111
S. Knott, supt. — 894-4852
JSHS, PO BOX 38 98935 — 2-00111
Keith Morris, prin. — 894-4951

Mansfield, AC 509, PC 2, Douglas
Mansfield SD 207 — 2-11111
PO BOX 188 98830 — 683-1012
Bill Thornton, supt.
JSHS, PO BOX 188 98830 — 1-00111
Bill Thornton, supt. — 683-1012

Manson, AC 509, PC 3, Chelan
Manson SD 19, PO BOX A 98831 — 3-11111
Daniel Farrell, supt. — 687-3140
JSHS 98831 — 2-00111
Marsha Hanson, prin. — 687-9585

Maple Valley, AC 206, PC 4, King
Tahoma SD 409 — 5-11111
25720 MPL VLLY BLCK D RD SE 98038 — 432-4481
Mike Maryanski, supt.
HS, 23015 SE 216TH WAY 98038 — 1-00011
Gary Morris, prin. — 432-5702
Tahoma JHS, 24425 SE 216TH ST 98038 — 3-00100
Bruce Zahradnik, prin. — 432-4442
Other Schools – See Kent

Marysville, AC 206, PC 7, Snohomish
Marysville SD 25 — 6-11111
4220 80TH ST NE 98270 — 653-7058
Ronald Barnes, supt.
Marysville-Pilchuck SHS — 4-00001
5611 108TH ST NE 98271 — 653-0600
Darrel DeGross, prin.
Cedarcrest JHS, 6400 88TH ST NE 98270 — 3-00110
Harlean Mailloux, prin. — 653-0850
JHS, 1605 7TH ST 98270 — 3-00110
Robert Foster, prin. — 653-0610

Grace Academy — 2-11111
8521 67TH AVE NE 98270 — 659-8517
Thomas Williams, prin.
Masters Touch Christian S — 2-11111
9610 48TH DR NE 98270 — 653-8976

Mattawa, AC 509, PC 3, Grant
Wahluke SD 73, PO BOX 907 99344 — 3-11111
William Miller, supt. — 932-4565
Wahluke HS, PO BOX 907 99344 — 2-00011
John Cordell, prin. — 932-4477
Schott MS, PO BOX 907 99344 — 2-00100
Mike Holland, prin. — 932-4455

Mead, AC 509, PC 4, Spokane
Mead SD 354, 12508 N FREYA ST 99021 — 6-11111
William Mester, supt. — 468-3000
JHS, 12509 N MARKET ST 99021 — 3-00110
Ralph Sharp, prin. — 468-3077
Other Schools – See Spokane

Medical Lake, AC 509, PC 5, Spokane
Medical Lake SD 326 — 4-11111
PO BOX 128 99022 — 299-3156
Terry Munther, supt.
HS, PO BOX 128 99022 — 3-00011
Russell Brown, prin. — 299-3167
MS, PO BOX 128 99022 — 2-00100
Richard Cerenzia, prin. — 299-5176

Lakeland Village School — HND
PO BOX 200 99022

Menlo, AC 206, PC 2, Pacific
Willapa Valley SD 160 — 2-11111
GENERAL DELIVERY 98561 — 942-5855
Ronald Erickson, supt.
Willapa Valley HS — 2-00011
GENERAL DELIVERY 98561 — 942-2006
Judith Friedlander, prin.
MS, GENERAL DELIVERY 98561 — 1-00100
Judith Friedlander, prin. — 942-2006

Mercer Island, AC 206, PC 7, King
Mercer Island SD 400 — 5-11111
4160 86TH AVE SE 98040 — 236-3300
Richard Giger, supt.
HS, 9100 SE 42ND ST 98040 — 4-00011
Judy Smith, prin. — 236-3345
Islander MS, 8225 SE 72ND ST 98040 — 3-00100
Wayne Hashiguchi, prin. — 236-3400

Northwest Yeshiva HS — 1-00011
5017 90TH ST SE 98040 — 232-5272
Rabbi Fox, prin.

Metaline Falls, AC 509, PC 2, Pend Oreille
Selkirk SD 70, PO BOX 129 99153 — 2-11111
Robert Fromm, supt. — 446-2951
Other Schools – See Ione

Mill Creek, AC 206, PC 6, Snohomish
Everett SD 2
Supt. — See Everett
Heatherwood MS — 3-00100
1419 TRILLIUM BLVD SE 98012 — 338-5000
Virginia Marriott, prin.

Milton, AC 206, PC 5, Pierce
Fife SD 417
Supt. — See Tacoma
Surprise Lake MS — 2-00100
2001 MILTON WAY 98354 — 922-6695
Deborah Brewer, prin.

Monroe, AC 206, PC 5, Snohomish
Monroe SD 103, PO BOX 687 98272 — 5-11111
Bill Prenevost, supt. — 794-7777
HS, 1408 W MAIN ST 98272 — 4-00011
Nancy Martin, prin. — 794-3010
MS, 351 SHORT COLUMBIA ST 98272 — 3-00100
Mike Weatherbie, prin. — 794-3020
Wagner MS, 639 W MAIN ST 98272 — 2-00100
John Strong-Cvetich, prin. — 794-3017

Montesano, AC 206, PC 5, Grays Harbor
Montesano SD 66 — 4-11111
302 CHURCH ST N 98563 — 249-3942
Jack Adams, supt.
JSHS, 303 CHURCH ST N 98563 — 3-00111
Ron Bennett, prin. — 249-4041

Morton, AC 206, PC 4, Lewis
Morton SD 214, PO BOX H 98356 — 3-11111
Richard Morton, supt. — 496-5300
JSHS, PO BOX F 98356 — 2-00111
Richard Conley, prin. — 496-5137

Moses Lake, AC 509, PC 7, Grant
Moses Lake SD 161 — 6-11111
1318 W IVY AVE 98837 — 766-2650
Ben Edlund, supt.
SHS, 803 SHARON AVE E 98837 — 4-00001
Larry Smith, prin. — 766-2666
Chief Moses JHS — 3-00110
1517 S PIONEER WAY 98837 — 766-2661
Peter Erickson, prin.
Frontier JHS, 517 W 3RD AVE 98837 — 3-00110
Lisa Hanson, prin. — 766-2662

Big Bend Community College — 5-CC
7662 CHANUTE ST NE 98837 — 762-6226
Moses Lake Christian S — 2-11111
1001 N GRAPE DR 98837 — 765-9704
Larry Joecks, prin.

Mossyrock, AC 206, PC 2, Lewis
Mossyrock SD 206 — 3-11111
PO BOX 478 98564 — 753-4535
John Stencil, supt.
HS, PO BOX 454 98564 — 2-00011
Tom Manke, prin. — 983-3183
MS, PO BOX 455 98564 — 2-00100
Gary Haslett, prin. — 983-3184

Mountlake Terrace, AC 206, PC 7, Snohomish
Edmonds SD 15
Supt. — See Lynnwood
HS, 21801 44TH AVE W 98043 — 4-00011
Elaine Klein, prin. — 670-7776

Mount Vernon, AC 206, PC 7, Skagit
Mount Vernon SD 320 — 6-11111
124 E LAWRENCE ST 98273 — 428-6110
Dolores Gibbons, supt.
HS, 314 N 9TH ST 98273 — 4-00011
Martin Chorba, prin. — 428-6100
LaVenture MS — 3-00100
1200 N LAVENTURE RD 98273 — 428-6116
John Clark, prin.

Mt. Vernon Christian S — 2-11111
820 W BLACKBURN RD 98273 — 424-9157
Jerry Van Vliet, prin.
Skagit Valley College — 6-CC
2405 E COLLEGE WAY 98273 — 428-1261
Viewcrest Christian S — 2-11111
830 N 16TH ST 98273 — 428-3043
Clarisann Crabtree, prin.

Mukilteo, AC 206, PC 6, Snohomish
Mukilteo SD 6
Supt. — See Everett
Kamiak HS — 4-00011
10801 HARBOUR POINTE BLVD 98275 — 356-6620
William Sarvis, prin.
Harbour Pointe MS — 3-00100
5000 HARBOUR POINTE BLVD 98275 — 356-6658
Alan Bulger, prin.
Olympic View MS — 3-00100
PO BOX 665 98275 — 356-1308
Mark Flotlin, prin.

Naches, AC 509, PC 3, Yakima
Naches Valley SD JT3 — 4-11111
PO BOX 99 98937 — 653-2220
Nick Eddy, supt.
Naches Valley HS — 2-00011
PO BOX 159 98937 — 653-2342
Robert Ames, prin.
Naches Valley MS, PO BOX 39 98937 — 2-00100
James Seamons, prin. — 653-2725

Napavine, AC 206, PC 3, Lewis
Napavine SD 14 — 3-11111
GENERAL DELIVERY 98565 — 262-3303
George Crawford, prin.
JSHS, GENERAL DELIVERY 98565 — 2-00111
Douglas Skinner, prin. — 262-3301

Naselle, AC 206, PC 4, Pacific
Naselle-Grays River Valley SD 155 — 2-11111
HC 78 BOX 471S 98638 — 484-7123
Richard Johnson, supt.
Naselle-Grays River JSHS — 2-00111
HC 78 BOX 471S 98638 — 484-7121
Thomas Alsbury, prin.

Neah Bay, AC 206, PC 3, Clallam
Cape Flattery SD 401
Supt. — See Sekiu
JSHS, PO BOX 86 98357   2-00111
Grover Garvin, prin.   645-2221

Newman Lake, AC 509, PC 3, Spokane
East Valley SD 361
Supt. — See Spokane
Mountain View MS   3-00100
6011 N CHASE RD 99025   226-1379
Kenneth Woolf, prin.

Newport, AC 509, PC 4, Pend Oreille
Newport SD 56-415   4-11111
PO BOX 70 99156   447-3167
Rich McBride, supt.
HS, PO BOX 70 99156   2-00011
Louis Musso, prin.   447-2481
JHS, PO BOX 70 99156   2-00100
Scott Hudson, prin.   447-2482

Nine Mile Falls, AC 509, PC 2, Spokane
Nine Mile Falls SD 325   4-11111
10103 W CHARLES RD 99026   466-5512
Shirley Holloway, supt.
Lakeside HS   3-00011
5909 HIGHWAY 291 99026   466-1369
Jim McConnell, prin.
Lakeside MS   2-00100
5909 HIGHWAY 291 99026   466-1369
Larry Guenther, prin.

Nooksack, AC 206, PC 3, Whatcom
Nooksack Valley SD 506   4-11111
PO BOX 4307 98276   988-4754
Mark Johnson, supt.
Nooksack Valley JSHS   3-00111
PO BOX 4307 98276   988-2641
Kenneth Crawford, prin.

Northport, AC 509, PC 2, Stevens
Northport SD 211 99157   2-11111
Dennis Hauff, supt.   732-4251
JSHS, PO BOX 180 99157   1-00111
Karlene Hayward, prin.   732-4430

Oakesdale, AC 509, PC 2, Whitman
Oakesdale SD 324   2-11111
PO BOX 228 99158   285-5296
Melvin Louk, supt.
JSHS, PO BOX 228 99158   1-00111
Buddy Gibson, prin.   285-5281

Oak Harbor, AC 206, PC 7, Island
Oak Harbor SD 201   6-11111
1250 MIDWAY BLVD 98277   679-5800
Rick Schulte, supt.
HS, 8616 800TH AVE W 98277   4-00011
Richard Devlin, prin.   679-5806
North Whidbey MS   3-00100
8115 800TH AVE W 98277   679-5807
Frank Atkinson, prin.
MS, 5400 500TH AVE W 98277   3-00100
Kathleen Vohland, prin.   679-5808

Oakville, AC 206, PC 2, Grays Harbor
Oakville SD 400, PO BOX H 98568   2-11111
(—), supt.   273-8229
JSHS, PO BOX H 98568   2-00111
Leo Eliason, prin.   273-5947

Ocean Shores, AC 206, PC 4, Grays Harbor
North Beach SD 64   3-11111
PO BOX 159 98569   289-2447
Robert Kochis, supt.
North Beach JSHS   2-00111
PO BOX 969 98569   289-3888
Ann Marchbank, prin.

Odessa, AC 509, PC 3, Lincoln
Odessa SD 105-157-166 J   2-11111
PO BOX 248 99159   982-2668
Steven Smedley, supt.
HS, PO BOX 248 99159   1-00011
Gordon Neale, prin.   982-2111

Okanogan, AC 509, PC 4, Okanogan
Okanogan SD 105   3-11111
PO BOX 592 98840   422-3629
Richard Johnson, supt.
JSHS, PO BOX 592 98840   2-00111
Robert Shacklett, prin.   422-3770

Olympia, AC 206, PC 8, Thurston
North Thurston SD 3
Supt. — See Lacey
River Ridge JHS   3-00010
8929 MARTIN WAY E 98516   493-9000
(—), prin.

Olympia SD 111   6-11111
1113 LEGION WAY SE 98501   753-8850
Albert Cohen, supt.
Capital HS   4-00011
2707 CONGER AVE NW 98502   753-8847
Doug Heay, prin.
Olympia HS, 1302 NORTH ST SE 98501   4-00011
Dale Herron, prin.   753-8921
Jefferson MS   3-00100
2200 CONGER AVE NW 98502   753-8985
Kevin Evoy, prin.
Reeves MS, 2200 QUINCE ST NE 98506   2-00100
Martha Kriss, prin.   753-8975
Washington MS, 3100 CAIN RD SE 98501   3-00100
Norman Josephson, prin.   753-8979

West Side MS   2-00100
3939 20TH AVE NW 98502   753-0106
Kevin Evoy, prin.

Evergreen State College   5-UC
2700 EVERGREEN PKY NW 98505   866-6000
South Puget Sound Community College   5-CC
2011 MOTTMAN RD SW 98512   754-7711

Omak, AC 509, PC 5, Okanogan
Omak SD 19, PO BOX 833 98841   4-11111
Barry McCombs, supt.   826-0320
HS, PO BOX 833 98841   3-00011
Roy Abshire, prin.   826-5150
MS, PO BOX 833 98841   3-00100
Ted Pearson, prin.   826-2320

Onalaska, AC 206, PC 3, Lewis
Onalaska SD 300   3-11111
540 CARLISLE AVE 98570   978-4111
Robert Kraig, supt.
HS, 540 CARLISLE AVE 98570   2-00011
Larry Peterson, prin.   978-4113

Oroville, AC 509, PC 4, Okanogan
Oroville SD 410   3-11111
10TH & IRONWOOD 98844   476-2281
James Gilman, supt.
JSHS, RR 1 BOX 100 98844   2-00111
Vic Elmore, prin.   476-3612

Orting, AC 206, PC 4, Pierce
Orting SD 344, PO BOX 460 98360   4-11111
Lee Thoren, supt.   893-6500
HS, PO BOX 460 98360   2-00011
Gary Walkup, prin.   893-2246
MS, PO BOX 460 98360   2-00100
Gary Benedetti, prin.   893-3565

Othello, AC 509, PC 5, Adams
Othello SD 147-163-55   5-11111
PO BOX 588 99344   488-2659
Dennis Carter, supt.
HS, 340 S 7TH AVE 99344   3-00011
Mert Barth, prin.   488-3351
McFarland JHS, 790 S 10TH AVE 99344   2-00100
Curtis Squires, prin.   488-3326

Palouse, AC 509, PC 3, Whitman
Palouse SD 301, RR 1 BOX 100 99161   2-11111
Bill Thurston, supt.   878-1921
Garfield-Palouse HS   1-00011
RR 1 BOX 100 99161   878-1921
Norm Hoffman, prin.

Pasco, AC 509, PC 7, Franklin
Pasco SD 1, 1004 N 16TH AVE 99301   6-11111
George Murdock, supt.   547-9531
SHS, 1108 N 10TH AVE 99301   4-00001
Ray Reynolds, prin.   547-5581
McLaughlin JHS   4-00110
2803 N ROAD 88 99301   547-4542
C. Domingos, prin.
Stevens JHS, 1120 N 22ND AVE 99301   3-00110
Clarence Alford, prin.   547-9703

Columbia Basin College   6-CC
2600 N 20TH AVE 99301   547-0511
Faith Christian Academy   2-11111
PO BOX 3848 99302   547-6498
Margaret Jacobson, prin.

Pateros, AC 509, PC 3, Okanogan
Pateros SD 122, PO BOX 98 98846   2-11111
Gary Patterson, supt.   923-2751
JSHS, PO BOX 98 98846   2-00111
Joseph Worsham, prin.   923-2343

Pe Ell, AC 206, PC 3, Lewis
Pe Ell SD 301, PO BOX 368 98572   2-11111
Thomas Wood, supt.   291-3244
JSHS 98572   2-00111
Patrick Meehan, prin.   291-3244

Pomeroy, AC 509, PC 4, Garfield
Pomeroy SD 110, PO BOX 950 99347   2-11111
Rick Anthony, supt.   843-3393
JSHS 99347   2-00111
Tim Burt, prin.   843-1331

Port Angeles, AC 206, PC 7, Clallam
Port Angeles SD 121   6-11111
216 E 4TH ST 98362 – John Pope, supt.   457-8575
HS, 304 E PARK AVE 98362   4-00011
Steve Rogers, prin.   452-7602
Roosevelt MS, 106 MONROE RD 98362   3-00100
Tom Anderson, prin.   452-8973
Stevens MS, 1139 W 14TH ST 98362   3-00100
Jim Widsteen, prin.   452-5590

Peninsula College   5-CC
1502 E LAURIDSEN BLVD 98362   452-9277

Port Orchard, AC 206, PC 5, Kitsap
South Kitsap SD 402   7-11111
1962 HOOVER AVE SE 98366   876-7300
DeWayne Gower, supt.
South Kitsap SHS   4-00001
425 MITCHELL AVE 98366   876-7318
Keith Canton, prin.
Cedar Heights JHS   3-00110
2220 POTTERY AVE 98366   876-7323
James Whitford, prin.

Sedgewick JHS   3-00110
8995 SEDGWICK RD SE 98366   876-7376
Bill Wyant, prin.
Whitman JHS   4-00110
1887 MADRONA DR SE 98366   876-7326
Rich Basnaw, prin.

Eton Technical Institute   2-CS
3649 W FRONTAGE RD 98366   479-3866

Port Townsend, AC 206, PC 6, Jefferson
Port Townsend SD 50, 450 FIR ST 98368   4-11111
Eugene Medina, supt.   385-3614
JSHS, 1610 BLAINE ST 98368   3-00111
Arcella Hall, prin.   385-2121

Northwest School of Wooden Boatbuilding   2-CS
251 OTTO ST 98368   385-5089

Poulsbo, AC 206, PC 5, Kitsap
North Kitsap SD 400   6-11111
18360 CALDART AVE NE 98370   779-8704
Robert Ellsperman, supt.
North Kitsap SHS   4-00001
1780 NE HOSTMARK ST 98370   779-4408
David Andersen, prin.
JHS, 2003 NE HOSTMARK ST 98370   3-00110
Gregg Epperson, prin.   779-4453
Other Schools – See Kingston

Northwest College of Art   2-UC
16464 STATE HIGHWAY 305 NE 98370   779-9993

Prescott, AC 509, PC 2, Walla Walla
Prescott SD 402-37, PO BOX 65 99348   2-11111
Scott Harris, supt.   849-2216
JSHS, PO BOX 65 99348   2-00111
Scott Harris, prin.   849-2215

Prosser, AC 509, PC 5, Benton
Prosser SD 116, 823 PARK AVE 99350   5-11111
Ray Tolcacher, supt.   786-3323
HS, 1203 PROSSER AVE 99350   3-00011
Donald Young, prin.   786-1224
Housel MS, 2001 HIGHLAND DR 99350   3-00100
Steven Ellis, prin.   786-1732

Pullman, AC 509, PC 7, Whitman
Pullman SD 267   4-11111
115 NW STATE ST 99163   332-3581
Doug Nelson, supt.
HS, LARRY & HALL DRIVE 99163   3-00011
Lynn Baker, prin.   332-1551
Lincoln MS   2-00100
315 SE CRESTVIEW ST 99163   334-3411
Phyllis Vettrus, prin.

Washington State University 99164   7-UC
   335-5586

Puyallup, AC 206, PC 7, Pierce
Puyallup SD 3, PO BOX 370 98371   7-11111
Herbert Berg, supt.   841-1301
Puyallup SHS, 105 7TH ST SW 98371   4-00001
Linda Quinn, prin.   841-8711
Rogers SHS, 12801 86TH AVE E 98373   4-00001
Paul Stilnovich, prin.   841-8717
Aylen JHS, 101 15TH ST SW 98371   3-00110
Richard Slater, prin.   841-8723
Ballou JHS, 9916 136TH ST E 98373   3-00110
Sue Lobland, prin.   841-8725
Edgemont JHS, 10909 24TH ST E 98372   2-00110
Mike Deal, prin.   841-8727
Ferrucci JHS   3-00110
3213 WILDWOOD PARK DR 98374   841-8756
Don Malloy, prin.
Kalles JHS, 515 3RD ST SE 98372   3-00110
John Bustad, prin.   841-8729
Stahl JHS, 9610 168TH ST E 98373   3-00110
Mike Warr, prin.   840-8881

Pierce College   2-CC
1601 39TH AVE SE 98374   840-8400

Quilcene, AC 206, PC 4, Jefferson
Quilcene SD 48, PO BOX 40 98376   2-11111
Marshall Jeffries, supt.   765-3363
S, PO BOX 40 98376   2-11111
James Reynolds, prin.   765-3363

Quincy, AC 509, PC 5, Grant
Quincy SD 144-101, 119 J ST SW 98848   4-11111
Tom Pickett, supt.   787-4571
HS, 16 6TH AVE SE 98848   2-00011
Jim Spence, prin.   787-3501
JHS, 417 C ST SE 98848   2-00100
Rick Thompson, prin.   787-4435

Rainier, AC 206, PC 3, Thurston
Rainier SD 307 98576   3-11111
Bob Golphenee, supt.   446-2207
HS 98576   2-00011
John Dekker, prin.   446-2205
JHS 98576   2-00100
John Dekker, prin.   446-2205

Randle, AC 206, PC 3, Lewis
White Pass SD 303 98377   3-11111
Gene Schmidt, supt.   497-3791
White Pass JSHS   2-00111
516 SILVERBROOK RD 98377   497-5816
Gretchen Caulfield, prin.

Raymond, AC 206, PC 5, Pacific
Raymond SD 116   3-11111
  1016 COMMERCIAL ST   98577   942-3415
  Roy Williams, supt.
  JSHS, 1016 COMMERCIAL ST   98577   2-00111
  Paul Furchert, prin.   942-2474

Reardan, AC 509, PC 2, Lincoln
Reardan-Edwall SD 9   3-11111
  PO BOX 225   99029   796-2721
  Thomas Crowley, supt.
  HS   99029   2-00011
  David Cain, prin.   796-2701

Redmond, AC 206, PC 8, King
Lake Washington SD 414
  Supt. — See Kirkland
  SHS, 17272 NE 104TH ST   98052   4-00001
  Al Kovats, prin.   881-4330
  Evergreen JHS   3-00110
   6900 208TH AVE NE   98053   868-8220
  Linda Whitehead, prin.
  Inglewood JHS, 24120 NE 8TH ST   98053   3-00110
  Tim Stonich, prin.   868-2300
  JHS, 10055 166TH AVE NE   98052   3-00110
  Billie Arneson, prin.   885-7034
  Rose Hill JHS, 13505 NE 75TH ST   98052   3-00110
  Paul Spoor, prin.   881-2079

Overlake School   2-01111
  20301 NE 108TH ST   98053   868-1000
  Jerry Millhon, prin.

Renton, AC 206, PC 8, King
Issaquah SD 411
  Supt. — See Issaquah
  Liberty HS, 16655 SE 136TH ST   98059   3-00011
  Bill Buell, prin.   557-4800
  Maywood MS   3-00100
   14490 168TH AVE SE   98059   557-6900
  Bill Sebring, prin.

Kent SD 415
  Supt. — See Kent
  Meeker JHS, 12600 SE 192ND ST   98058   4-00110
  Steve Beck, prin.   813-7284

Renton SD 403, 435 MAIN AVE S   98055   7-11111
  Gary Kohlwes, supt.   235-2200
  Hazen HS   4-00011
   1101 HOQUIAM AVE NE   98059   235-2220
  Louis Pappas, prin.
  Lindbergh HS   4-00011
   16426 128TH AVE SE   98058   235-2460
  David Kurth, prin.
  HS, 400 S 2ND ST   98055   3-00011
  Kay Hermann, prin.   235-2255
  McKnight MS, 2600 NE 12TH ST   98056   3-00100
  Patricia Blix, prin.   235-2266
  Nelson MS, 2403 JONES AVE S   98055   3-00100
  Willke Lew, prin.   235-2276

Renton Technical College   7-CS
  3000 NE 4TH ST   98056   235-2352

Republic, AC 509, PC 3, Ferry
Republic SD 309   3-11111
  915 HIGHWAY 20 E   99166   775-3173
  Lynn Lupfer, supt.
  JSHS, 915 HIGHWAY 20 E   99166   2-00111
  Randy Behrens, prin.   775-3171

Richland, AC 509, PC 8, Benton
Richland SD 400, 615 SNOW AVE   99352   6-11111
  Marge Chow, supt.   946-6106
  HS, 930 LONG AVE   99352   4-00011
  Yvonne Ryans, prin.   946-5121
  Hanford JSHS, 450 HANFORD ST   99352   4-00111
  Ken Surby, prin.   375-9671
  Carmichael JHS, 620 THAYER DR   99352   3-00100
  Nancy Kyle, prin.   946-5145

Ridgefield, AC 206, PC 4, Clark
Ridgefield SD 122   4-11111
  2724 HILLHURST RD   98642   887-0200
  John Simpson, supt.
  HS, 2630 S HILLHURST RD   98642   2-00011
  Chris Thompson, prin.   887-0220
  View Ridge MS   2-00100
   510 PIONEER AVE   98642   887-0225
  Tom Rockefeller, prin.

Ritzville, AC 509, PC 4, Adams
Ritzville SD 160-67   2-11111
  10 E WELLSANDT RD   99169   659-1660
  John McGregor, supt.
  HS, 10 E WELLSANDT RD   99169   2-00011
  Robert Hammann, prin.   659-1720

Rochester, AC 206, PC 4, Thurston
Rochester SD 401, PO BOX 457   98579   4-11111
  Gilbert Holt, supt.   273-5536
  HS, 19800 CARPER RD SW   98579   2-00011
  Dean Naffziger, prin.   273-5534
  MS, PO BOX 398   98579   2-00100
  Dale Munson, prin.   273-5958

Rockford, AC 509, PC 2, Spokane
Freeman SD 358   3-11111
  15001 S JACKSON RD   99030   291-3695
  Harry Amend, supt.
  Freeman HS   2-00011
   15001 S JACKSON RD   99030   291-3721
  Dennis Schuerman, prin.

Rosalia, AC 509, PC 3, Whitman
Rosalia SD 320, PO BOX 128   99170   2-11111
  Jerry Simon, supt.   523-3061
  HS, PO BOX 128   99170   1-00011
  Michael Williams, prin.   523-3061

Roslyn, AC 509, PC 3, Kittitas
Cle Elum-Roslyn SD 404
  Supt. — See Cle Elum
  Strom JHS, PO BOX 91   98941   2-00100
  Leon Maras, prin.   649-3560

Royal City, AC 509, PC 4, Grant
Royal SD 160, PO BOX 486   99357   3-11111
  David James, supt.   346-2222
  Royal HS, PO BOX 486   99357   2-00011
  Jack Hill, prin.   346-2256
  Royal MS, PO BOX 486   99357   2-00100
  P. Andersen, prin.   346-2268

Saint John, AC 509, PC 2, Whitman
St. John SD 322, PO BOX 58   99171   2-11111
  Tim McCarthy, supt.   648-3336
  St. John-Endicott HS   1-00011
   PO BOX 58   99171   648-3336
  Dick Behrens, prin.

Seattle, AC 206, PC 11, King
Highline SD 401   7-11111
  PO BOX 66100   98166   433-0111
  Marvin Evans, supt.
  Evergreen HS, 830 SW 116TH ST   98146   4-00011
  Ernie Olson, prin.   433-2311
  Highline HS, 225 S 152ND ST   98148   4-00011
  Tom Sawyer, prin.   433-2511
  Tyee HS, 4424 S 188TH ST   98188   3-00011
  Jean Shumate, prin.   433-2341
  Sea Tac Occupational Skills Ctr   Vo Tech
   18010 8TH AVE S   98148   433-2524
  Reba Gilman, prin.
  Cascade MS, 11212 10TH AVE SW   98146   3-00100
  Larry Reynolds, prin.   433-2551
  Chinook MS, 18650 42ND AVE S   98188   3-00100
  Roy Adler, prin.   433-2231
  Sylvester MS   3-00100
   16222 SYLVESTER RD SW   98166   433-2401
  Patty Spangler, prin.
  Other Schools – See Des Moines

Seattle SD 1, 815 4TH AVE N   98109   8-11111
  William Kendrick, supt.   298-7000
  Ballard HS, 1418 NW 65TH ST   98117   4-00011
  Chuck Chinn, prin.   281-6010
  Cleveland HS, 5511 15TH AVE S   98108   4-00011
  Ted Howard, prin.   281-6020
  Franklin HS   4-00011
   3013 S MOUNT BAKER BLVD   98144   281-6030
  Sharon Green, prin.
  Garfield HS, 400 23RD AVE   98122   4-00011
  Perry Wilkins, prin.   281-6040
  Hale HS, 10750 30TH AVE NE   98125   4-00011
  Eric Benson, prin.   281-6920
  Ingraham HS, 1819 N 135TH ST   98133   4-00011
  Gloria Izard-Baldwin, prin.   281-6080
  Rainier Beach HS   4-00011
   8815 SEWARD PARK AVE S   98118   281-6090
  Marta Cano-Hinz, prin.
  Roosevelt HS, 1410 NE 66TH ST   98115   4-00011
  Marilyn Day, prin.   281-6050
  Sealth HS, 2600 SW THISTLE ST   98126   4-00011
  Joan Butterworth, prin.   281-6060
  West Seattle HS   3-00011
   4075 SW STEVENS ST   98116   281-6070
  Jim McConnell, prin.
  Vocational Education Program   Vo Tech
   315 22ND AVE S   98144   281-6282
  Malver Haynes, prin.
  Denny MS, 8402 30TH AVE SW   98126   3-00100
  Pat Batiste-Brown, prin.   281-6110
  Eckstein MS, 3003 NE 75TH ST   98115   4-00100
  Lynn Caldwell, prin.   281-6120
  Hamilton MS, 1610 N 41ST ST   98103   3-00100
  Allen Nakano, prin.   281-6130
  Madison MS, 3429 45TH AVE SW   98116   3-00100
  Marella Griffin, prin.   281-6140
  McClure MS, 1915 1ST AVE W   98119   3-00100
  Beatrice Cox, prin.   281-6150
  Meany MS, 301 21ST AVE E   98112   3-00100
  Carol Huff-Flagg, prin.   281-6160
  Mercer MS   3-00100
   1600 S COLUMBIAN WAY   98108   281-6170
  Dean Sanders, prin.
  South Shore MS   3-00100
   8825 RAINIER AVE S   98118   281-6180
  John German, prin.
  Washington MS   3-00100
   2101 S JACKSON ST   98144   281-6190
  Bruce Hunter, prin.
  Whitman MS, 9201 15TH AVE NW   98117   3-00100
  Bi Hoa Caldwell, prin.   281-6930

Shoreline SD 412   6-11111
  18560 1ST AVE NE   98155   367-6111
  Mary Kendall-Mitchell, supt.
  Shorecrest HS   4-00011
   15343 25TH AVE NE   98155   361-4286
  Susan Derse, prin.
  Shorewood HS   4-00011
   17300 FREMONT AVE N   98133   361-4372
  Rick Robbins, prin.
  Einstein MS, 19343 3RD AVE NW   98177   3-00100
  Robert Kogane, prin.   368-4730

Kellogg MS, 16045 25TH AVE NE   98155   3-00100
  Michael Malan, prin.   368-4783

Antioch University   2-UC
  2607 2ND AVE   98121   441-5352
Art Institute of Seattle   3-CC
  2323 ELLIOTT AVE   98121   800-275-2471
Bastyr College   2-UC
  144 NE 54TH ST   98105   523-9585
Blanchet HS   3-00011
  8200 WALLINGFORD AVE N   98103   527-7711
  Joseph Haggerty, prin.
Bush S, 405 36TH AVE E   98112   3-11111
  Fred Dust, prin.   322-7978
Children's Hospital & Medical Center   HSP
  PO BOX 5371   98105   526-2000
Christian Faith S   3-11111
  PO BOX 98800   98198   878-6036
  Dana Larson, prin.
Cornish College of the Arts   3-UC
  710 E ROY ST   98102   800-726-2787
Court Reporting Institute   2-CS
  929 N 130TH ST STE 2   98133   363-8300
Divers Institute of Technology   2-CS
  PO BOX 70667   98107   800-634-8377
Harborview Medical Center   HSP
  325 9TH AVE   98104   223-3036
Holy Names Academy   2-00011
  728 21ST AVE E   98112   323-4272
  Sr. Mary Tracy, prin.
ITT Technical Institute   3-UC
  12720 GATEWAY DR STE 100   98168   244-3300
John F. Kennedy Memorial HS   3-00011
  140 S 140TH ST   98168   246-0500
  John Schuster, prin.
King's JSHS   3-00111
  19303 FREMONT AVE N   98133   546-7241
  Linda Montgomery, prin.
Laboratory of Pathology   CS
  PO BOX 14950   98114   386-2730
Lakeside HS, 13510 1ST AVE NE   98125   2-01100
  Frank Magusin, prin.   368-3630
Lakeside Upper S   3-00111
  14050 1ST AVE NE   98125   368-3600
  Terry Macaluso, prin.
North Seattle Christian S   2-11111
  12345 8TH AVE NE   98125   365-2720
  Harold Drake, prin.
North Seattle Community College   6-CC
  9600 COLLEGE WAY N   98103   527-3600
Northwest S, 1415 SUMMIT AVE   98122   2-00111
  Ellen Taussig, prin.   682-7309
O'Dea HS, 802 TERRY AVE   98104   2-00011
  Br. Murray, prin.   622-6596
Pima Medical Institute   2-CS
  1627 EASTLAKE AVE E   98102   322-6100
Resource Center for the Handicapped   CC
  20150 45TH AVE NE   98155   362-2273
Seattle Academy of Arts & Sciences   2-00111
  1432 15TH AVE   98122   323-6600
  Jean Orvis, prin.
Seattle Central Community College   6-CC
  1701 BROADWAY   98122   587-3800
Seattle Christian S   3-11111
  19639 28TH AVE S   98188   824-1310
  Judy Jennings, prin.
Seattle Lutheran HS   2-00011
  4141 41ST AVE SW   98116   937-7722
  Robert Christian, prin.
Seattle Pacific University   7-UC
  3307 3RD AVE W   98119   281-2000
Seattle Preparatory S   3-00011
  2400 11TH AVE E   98102   324-0400
  Christopher Conroy, prin.
Seattle University   5-UC
  BROADWAY AVE & MADISON   98122   296-6000
Shoreline Community College   6-CC
  16101 GREENWOOD AVE N   98133   546-4101
South Seattle Community College   6-CC
  6000 16TH AVE SW   98106   764-5300
University of Washington   98195   8-UC
     543-2100
University Prep Academy   2-00111
  8000 25TH AVE NE   98115   525-2714
  Roger Bass, prin.
Watson Groen Christian S   2-11111
  2400 NE 147TH ST   98155   364-7777
  Timothy Visser, prin.

Sedro Woolley, AC 206, PC 6, Skagit
Sedro Woolley SD 101   5-11111
  2079 COOK RD   98284   856-0831
  Pamela Carnahan, supt.
  HS, 1235 3RD ST   98284   3-00011
  Robert Penny, prin.   855-1231
  Cascade MS, 201 N TOWNSHIP ST   98284   3-00100
  Virginia Beck, prin.   856-1126

Sekiu, AC 206, PC 3, Clallam
Cape Flattery SD 401   3-11111
  PO BOX 109   98381   963-2329
  Gene Laes, supt.
  Clallam Bay S, PO BOX 109   98381   2-11111
  Gregg Saunders, prin.   963-2324
  Other Schools – See Neah Bay

Selah, AC 509, PC 6, Yakima
Selah SD 119   5-11111
  105 W BARTLETT AVE   98942   697-7243
  Jerry Jenkins, supt.

HS, 801 N 1ST ST 98942 — 3-00011 — 697-0770
Anton Pasckvale, prin.
MS, 411 N 1ST ST 98942 — 3-00100 — 697-0750
Burlan Johnson, prin.

Sequim, AC 206, PC 5, Clallam
Sequim SD 323 — 4-11111
503 N SEQUIM AVE 98382 — 683-3336
Lew Moormann, supt.
HS, 601 N SEQUIM AVE 98382 — 3-00011 — 683-4136
James Bumgarner, prin.
MS, 220 W ALDER ST 98382 — 3-00100 — 683-7961
Tim Madden, prin.

Shelton, AC 206, PC 6, Mason
Hood Canal SD 404 — 2-11100
111 N STATE ROUTE 106 98584 — 877-9700
William Lanning, supt.
Hood Canal JHS — 2-00100
111 N STATE ROUTE 106 98584 — 877-5463
Kjell-Jon Rye, prin.

Pioneer SD 402, 611 E AGATE RD 98584 — 3-11100 — 426-9115
Richard Sirokman, supt.
Pioneer MS, 611 E AGATE RD 98584 — 2-00100 — 426-8291
Peg Stock, prin.

Shelton SD 309, 207 N 9TH ST 98584 — 5-11111 — 426-1687
H. Hansen, supt.
HS — 4-00011
3737 N SHELTON SPRINGS RD 98584 — 426-4471
William Moulton, prin.
MS — 3-00100
3301 N SHELTON SPRINGS RD 98584 — 426-7991
Linda Farrimond, prin.

Silverdale, AC 206, PC 6, Kitsap
Central Kitsap SD 401 — 7-11111
PO BOX 8 98383 — 692-3111
Janet Barry, supt.
Central Kitsap SHS, PO BOX 8 98383 — 4-00001 — 692-3120
Janell Newman, prin.
Central Kitsap JHS, PO BOX 8 98383 — 3-00110 — 692-3126
Cheryl Boatman, prin.
Ridgetop JHS — 3-00110
10600 RIDGETOP BLVD NW 98383 — 692-3250
Priscilla Orcutt, prin.
Other Schools – See Bremerton

Trident Training Facility 98315 — 6-CS

Skykomish, AC 206, PC 2, King
Skykomish SD 404 — 2-11111
GENERAL DELIVERY 98288 — 677-2623
William Tipton, supt.
JSHS, GENERAL DELIVERY 98288 — 1-00111 — 677-2623
William Tipton, prin.

Snohomish, AC 206, PC 6, Snohomish
Snohomish SD 201 — 6-11111
1601 AVENUE D 98290 – (—), supt. — 568-3151
SHS, 1316 5TH ST 98290 — 4-00001 — 568-0636
Raymond Johnson, prin.
Centennial MS — 3-00100
3000 S MACHIAS RD 98290 — 568-2500
Larry Aalbu, prin.
Snohomish Freshman Campus — 3-00010
601 GLEN AVE 98290 — 568-0661
Jerry Simicich, prin.
Valley View MS — 3-00100
14308 BROADWAY AVE 98290 — 568-0671
Ken Knautz, prin.

Snoqualmie, AC 206, PC 4, King
Snoqualmie Valley SD 410 — 5-11111
PO BOX 400 98065 — 888-2334
Richard McCullough, supt.
Mount Si HS — 3-00011
619 MEADOWBROOK WAY SE 98065 — 888-1921
David Humphrey, prin.
MS — 2-00100
39500 SE SNOQUALMIE NORTH B 98065 — 888-1102
Jack McCullough, prin.
Other Schools – See Fall City

Soap Lake, AC 509, PC 4, Grant
Soap Lake SD 156 — 2-11111
PO BOX 158 98851 — 246-1822
Linda Creech, supt.
JSHS, PO BOX 878 98851 — 2-00111 — 246-1201
Randy Hill, prin.

South Bend, AC 206, PC 4, Pacific
South Bend SD 118 — 2-11111
PO BOX 437 98586 — 875-6041
Virgie Fryrear, supt.
JSHS 98586 — 2-00111 — 875-5707
Donald Lorentsen, prin.

Spanaway, AC 206, PC 7, Pierce
Bethel, SD 403, 516 176TH ST E 98387 — 7-11111 — 536-7272
Donald Berger, supt.
Spanaway Lake SHS — 3-00100 — 535-2972
1305 168TH ST E 98387
Grant Hosford, prin.
Bethel HS, 22215 38TH AVE E 98387 — 4-00011 — 846-9710
David Rich, prin.
Bethel JHS, 22201 38TH AVE E 98387 — 3-00100 — 846-9720
Robert Duke, prin.
Cedarcrest JHS — 3-00110 — 847-6485
19120 13TH AVE E 98387
Deborah Lucker-Davis, prin.
Other Schools – See Graham, Tacoma

Spangle, AC 509, PC 2, Spokane
Liberty SD 362 — 3-11111
29818 S NORTH PINE CREEK RD 99031 — 245-3223
Armin Vogt, supt.
Liberty HS — 2-00011
6404 E SPANGLE WAVERLY RD 99031 — 245-3229
Tom Ashenbrenner, prin.

Upper Columbia Academy — 2-00011
2525 E SPANGLE WAVERLY RD 99031 — 245-3600
Larry Marsh, prin.

Spokane, AC 509, PC 9, Spokane
Central Valley SD 356
Supt. — See Greenacres
University SHS, 10212 E 9TH AVE 99206 — 4-00001 — 922-6710
Dennis Hill, prin.
Bowdish JHS — 3-00110
2109 S SKIPWORTH RD 99206 — 922-6880
(—), prin.
Horizon JHS, 3915 S PINES RD 99206 — 3-00110 — 922-6966
Glenna Smith, prin.
North Pines JHS, 701 N PINES RD 99206 — 2-00110 — 922-6910
Dave Bouge, prin.

East Valley SD 361 — 5-11111
3415 N PINES RD 99206 — 924-1830
Charles Stocker, supt.
East Valley HS — 4-00011
15711 E WELLESLEY AVE 99216 — 927-3200
Donald Kartevold, prin.
East Valley MS — 3-00100
4920 N PROGRESS RD 99216 — 924-9383
Susan Kincaid, prin.
Other Schools – See Newman Lake

Mead SD 354
Supt. – See Mead
Mead SHS, 302 W HASTINGS RD 99218 — 4-00001 — 468-3050
Steve Hogue, prin.
Northwood JHS — 3-00110
13120 N PITTSBURG ST 99208 — 468-3086
JoAnne Rehberg, prin.

Spokane SD 81 — 8-11111
200 N BERNARD ST 99201 — 353-5242
Gary Livingston, supt.
Ferris HS, 3020 E 37TH AVE 99223 — 4-00011 — 353-4400
Johnathan Bentz, prin.
Lewis & Clark HS, 521 W 4TH AVE 99204 — 4-00011 — 353-4520
Michael Howson, prin.
North Central HS — 4-00011
1600 N HOWARD ST 99205 — 353-5220
H. Fink, prin.
Rogers HS — 4-00011
1622 E WELLESLEY AVE 99207 — 353-4540
Wallace Williams, prin.
Shadle Park HS, 4327 N ASH ST 99205 — 4-00011 — 353-4531
Michael Dunn, prin.
Spokane Area Vo Skills Ctr — Vo Tech
4141 N REGAL ST 99207 — 353-3304
Ruth Bragg, prin.
Garry MS, 725 E JOSEPH AVE 99207 — 3-00100 — 353-5271
Don Miller, prin.
Glover MS — 3-00100
2404 W LONGFELLOW AVE 99205 — 353-4484
Alison Olzendam, prin.
Libby MS, 2900 E 1ST AVE 99202 — 3-00100 — 353-4461
Rodger Lake, prin.
Sacajawea MS, 401 E 33RD AVE 99203 — 4-00100 — 353-4470
Herbert Rotchford, prin.
Salk MS, 6411 N ALBERTA ST 99208 — 3-00100 — 353-4450
Mary Haugen, prin.
Shaw MS, 4106 N COOK ST 99207 — 3-00100 — 353-4505
Pete Lewis, prin.

West Valley SD 363 — 5-11111
PO BOX 11739 99211 — 924-2150
David Smith, supt.
Spokane Valley HS — 2-00011
8920 E VALLEY WAY 99212 — 922-5475
Doug Grace, prin.
West Valley HS — 3-00100
8301 E BUCKEYE AVE 99212 — 922-5488
Cleve Penberthy, prin.
Centennial MS, 915 N ELLA RD 99212 — 3-00100 — 922-5482
Amy Bragdon, prin.

Deaconess Medical Center — HSP
800 W 5TH AVE 99204 — 458-7003
Gonzaga Prep S — 3-00011
1224 E EUCLID AVE 99207 — 483-8511
John Traynor, prin.
Gonzaga University — 4-UC
502 E BOONE AVE 99258 — 800-523-9712
Gonzaga University — 3-UC
PO BOX 3528 99220 — 328-4220
Holy Family Hospital — HSP
5633 N LIDGERWOOD ST 99207 — 482-2450
Intercollegiate Center/Nursing Education — 2-UC
2917 W FORT GORGE WRIGHT DR 99204
ITT Technical Institute — 1-CC
1050 N ARGONNE RD 99212 — 800-777-8324
Northwest Christian S — 2-11111
1412 W CENTRAL AVE 99205 — 328-4400
Lewis Button, prin.
Phillips Junior College of Spokane — 2-CC
1101 N FANCHER RD 99212 — 535-7771
Sacred Heart Medical Center — HSP
101 W 8TH AVE 99204 — 455-3040

St. George's S — 2-11111
2929 W WAIKIKI RD 99208 — 466-1636
George Swope, prin.
Spokane Community College — 6-CC
1810 N GREENE ST 99207 — 536-7001
Spokane Falls Community College — 6-CC
3410 W FORT GORGE WRIGHT DR 99204 — 459-3512
Trend College — 4-CS
214 N WALL ST 99201 — 838-3521
Valley Christian S — 2-11111
2303 S BOWDISH RD 99206 — 924-9131
Wes Evans, prin.
Whitworth College — 4-UC
300 W HAWTHORNE RD 99251 — 800-533-4668

Sprague, AC 509, PC 2, Lincoln
Sprague SD 8, PO BOX 305 99032 — 2-11011 — 257-2591
Richard Hattrup, supt.
HS, PO BOX 305 99032 — 1-00011 — 257-2511
Patrick Whipple, prin.

Springdale, AC 509, PC 2, Stevens
Mary Walker SD — 2-11111
PO BOX 159 99173 — 258-4534
Michael Sowder, supt.
Walker HS 99173 — 2-00011 — 258-4533
Gary Coe, prin.
MS 99173 — 2-00100 — 258-7357
Lynn Rowse, prin.

Stanwood, AC 206, PC 4, Snohomish
Stanwood SD 401 — 5-11111
PO BOX 430 98292 — 629-9575
Raymond Reid, supt.
HS, 7400 272ND ST NW 98292 — 3-00011 — 629-2167
Ted Jansen, prin.
MS, PO BOX 879 98292 — 3-00100 — 629-6510
Ron Hendricks, prin.

Steilacoom, AC 206, PC 6, Pierce
Steilacoom Historical SD 1 — 4-11111
510 CHAMBERS ST 98388 — 588-1772
Steve Wilson, supt.
HS, 54 SENTINEL DR 98388 — 2-00011 — 588-1885
Gordy Hansen, prin.
Pioneer MS, 511 CHAMBERS ST 98388 — 2-00100 — 582-8300
Gary Simon, prin.

Stevenson, AC 509, PC 4, Skamania
Stevenson-Carson SD 303 — 4-11111
PO BOX 850 98648 — 427-5674
Bill Bentley, supt.
HS, PO BOX 850 98648 — 2-00011 — 427-5631
James Saltness, prin.
Wind River MS, PO BOX 850 98648 — 2-00100 — 427-8952
Kathleen Browning, prin.

Sultan, AC 206, PC 4, Snohomish
Sultan SD 311, PO BOX 399 98294 — 4-11111 — 793-9800
James Turner, supt.
HS, PO BOX 1480 98294 — 2-00011 — 793-9860
Jann Siegert, prin.
MS, PO BOX 309 98294 — 2-00100 — 793-9850
Jann Siegert, prin.

Sumner, AC 206, PC 6, Pierce
Dieringer SD 343 — 3-11100
1320 178TH AVE E 98390 — 862-2537
Gary Newbill, supt.
North Tapps MS, 20029 12TH ST E 98390 — 2-00100 — 862-2776
John Keaton, prin.

Sumner SD 320, 1202 WOOD AVE 98390 — 6-11111 — 863-2201
Donald Eismann, supt.
SHS, 1707 MAIN ST 98390 — 4-00001 — 863-8181
Sue Hall, prin.
Lakeridge JHS, 5909 MYERS RD 98390 — 3-00110 — 863-8164
Marilouise Petersen, prin.
JHS, 1508 WILLOW ST 98390 — 3-00110 — 863-4438
Terry Beckstead, prin.

Sunnyside, AC 509, PC 7, Yakima
Sunnyside SD 201, 1110 S 6TH ST 98944 — 5-11111 — 837-5851
James Chambers, supt.
HS, 16TH & EDISON 98944 — 4-00011 — 837-2601
William Gant, prin.
Harrison MS, 1110 S 6TH ST 98944 — 4-00100 — 837-3601
Dennis Birr, prin.

Sunnyside Christian S — 2-00011
1820 SHELLER RD 98944 — 837-3044
Terry Kok, prin.

Tacoma, AC 206, PC 9, Pierce
Bethel SD 403
Supt. — See Spanaway
Spanaway JHS, 15701 B ST E 98445 — 3-00110 — 531-8666
Sterling Thurston, prin.

Clover Park SD 400 — 7-11111
10903 GRAVELLY LAKE DR SW 98499 — 589-7500
Karen Forys, supt.
Clover Park SHS — 4-00001
11023 GRAVELLY LAKE DR SW 98499 — 589-7600
Donald Larsen, prin.
Lakes SHS — 3-00001
10320 FARWEST DR SW 98498 — 589-7700
Brenda Bias, prin.
Hudtloff JHS — 3-00110
7702 PHILLIPS RD SW 98498 — 589-7655
Don McPherson, prin.
Lochburn JHS — 3-00110
5431 STEILACOOM BLVD SW 98499 — 589-7665
Georgia Dewhurst, prin.

Mann JHS, 11509 HOLDEN RD SW 98498 3-00110
Dennis Madison, prin. 589-7670
Woodbrook JHS 3-00110
14920 SPRING ST SW 98439 589-7680
Robin Blankers, prin.

Fife SD 417, 5602 20TH ST E 98424 4-11111
Patrick Hoban, supt. 922-6697
Fife HS, 5616 20TH ST E 98424 3-00011
C. Silvernail, prin. 922-8751
Other Schools – See Milton

Franklin Pierce SD 402 6-11111
315 129TH ST S 98444 537-0211
Steve Rasmussen, supt.
Pierce HS, 11002 18TH AVE E 98445 3-00011
Frank Hewins, prin. 535-9880
Washington HS 3-00011
12420 AINSWORTH AVE S 98444 535-9881
James Mancuso, prin.
Ford MS, 1602 104TH ST E 98445 3-00100
Gary Benson, prin. 535-9883
Keithley MS, 12324 12TH AVE S 98444 3-00100
John Jackson, prin. 535-9884

Tacoma SD 10, PO BOX 1357 98401 8-11111
Rudolf Crew, supt. 596-1000
Foss HS, 2112 S TYLER ST 98405 4-00011
Ethelda Burke, prin. 596-2300
Lincoln HS, 701 S 37TH ST 98408 4-00011
Charlie Walker, prin. 596-2000
Mount Tahoma HS 4-00011
6229 S TYLER ST 98409 596-1800
Lois Bishop, prin.
Stadium HS, 111 N E ST 98403 4-00011
Marvin Shain, prin. 596-1325
Wilson HS, 1202 N ORCHARD ST 98406 4-00011
Paul Apostle, prin. 596-2200
Baker MS, 8320 S I ST 98408 3-00100
Ronald Urquhart, prin. 596-2100
Gault MS, 1115 E DIVISION LN 98404 2-00100
Cherry Goudeau, prin. 596-1405
Gray MS, 3109 S 60TH ST 98409 3-00100
Terry Bouck, prin. 596-1860
Hunt MS, 6501 S 10TH ST 98465 3-00100
Terry Meisenburg, prin. 596-2335
Lee MS, 602 N SPRAGUE AVE 98403 3-00100
Charlotte Carr, prin. 596-1395
Mason MS, 2812 N MADISON ST 98407 3-00100
Gaile McLaurin, prin. 596-2256
McIlvaigh MS, 1801 E 56TH ST 98404 3-00100
Jay Stricherz, prin. 596-2080
Meeker MS 3-00100
4402 NASSAU AVE NE 98422 596-1377
Judy Yoshida, prin.
Stewart MS, 5010 PACIFIC AVE 98408 3-00100
William Rossman, prin. 596-2085
Truman MS, 6501 N 23RD ST 98406 3-00100
Dick Hopkins, prin. 596-2245

University Place SD 83 5-11111
8805 40TH ST W 98466 566-5600
Donald Krag, supt.
Curtis SHS, 8425 40TH ST W 98466 4-00001
Vicki Bickle, prin. 566-5710
Curtis JHS, 8901 40TH ST W 98466 3-00110
Mary Reeves, prin. 566-5670

Annie Wright S 2-11111
827 TACOMA AVE N 98403 272-2216
Robert Klarsch, prin.
Bates Technical College 8-CS
1101 S YAKIMA AVE 98405 596-1500
Bellarmine Prep S 3-00011
2300 S WASHINGTON ST 98405 752-7701
Christopher Gavin, prin.
Capitol Business College 2-CS
5005 PACIFIC HWY E STE 11 98424
926-2382
Cascade Christian ES 2-11111
1819 E 72ND ST 98404 473-0590
Frank Washburn, prin.
Charles Wright Academy 3-11111
7723 CHAMBERS CREEK RD W 98467 546-2171
Robert Minnerly, prin.
Clover Park Technical College 1-CS
4500 STEILACOOM BLVD SW 98499 589-5843
Crown Academy 2-CS
8739 S HOSMER ST 98444 531-3123
Northwest Baptist Seminary 1-UC
4301 N STEVENS ST 98407 759-6104
Pacific Lutheran University 5-UC
12180 PARK AVE S 98447 800-225-1843
Pierce College 7-CC
9401 FARWEST DR SW 98498 964-6501
Tacoma Baptist HS 2-11111
2052 S 64TH ST 98409 475-7226
Douglas Bond, prin.
Tacoma Community College 6-CC
5900 S 12TH ST 98465 566-5000
University of Puget Sound 5-UC
1500 N WARNER ST 98416 756-3211
University of Puget Sound 3-UC
950 BROADWAY 98402

Taholah, AC 206, PC 3, Grays Harbor
Taholah SD 77, PO BOX 249 98587 2-11111
Mary Hall, supt. 276-4729
S, PO BOX 249 98587 2-11111
(—), prin. 276-4514

Tekoa, AC 509, PC 3, Whitman
Tekoa SD 265, PO BOX 869 99033 2-11111
Jim Menzies, supt. 284-3401
JSHS 99033 1-00111
John Jaegar, prin. 284-3281

Tenino, AC 206, PC 4, Thurston
Tenino SD 402 98589 4-11111
Jack Jutte, supt. 264-4123
HS 98589 2-00111
Ray Cooper, prin. 264-2230
MS 98589 2-00100
Mike Duffy, prin. 264-2663

Thorp, AC 509, PC 2, Kittitas
Thorp SD 400, PO BOX 150 98946 2-11111
Calvin McRae, supt. 964-2107
HS, PO BOX 150 98946 1-00011
Calvin McRae, prin. 964-2107

Tieton, AC 509, PC 3, Yakima
Highland SD 203
Supt. — See Cowiche
MS, PO BOX 6 98947 2-01100
Mark Hummel, prin. 673-3141

Toledo, AC 206, PC 3, Lewis
Toledo SD 237, PO BOX 469 98591 3-11111
Robert Donaldson, supt. 864-6325
HS 98591 2-00111
Dennis Clark, prin. 864-2391
MS 98591 2-01100
Dave Filla, prin. 864-2395

Tonasket, AC 509, PC 3, Okanogan
Tonasket SD 404, PO BOX 745 98855 4-11111
Randall Hauff, supt. 486-2126
HS, PO BOX 468 98855 2-00011
Gary Jorgenson, prin. 486-2161
MS, PO BOX 448 98855 2-00100
Steve Pile, prin. 486-4933

Toppenish, AC 509, PC 6, Yakima
Toppenish SD 202 5-11111
106 FRANKLIN AVE 98948 865-4455
Eileen Beiersdorf, prin.
HS, 141 WARD RD 98948 3-00011
Steve Myers, prin. 865-3370
MS, 104 GOLDENDALE AVE 98948 3-00100
John Karas, prin. 865-2730

Heritage College 2-UC
3240 FORT RD 98948 865-2244

Touchet, AC 509, PC 2, Walla Walla
Touchet SD 300, PO BOX 1135 99360 2-11111
Samuel Gerla, supt. 394-2352
JSHS, PO BOX 1135 99360 2-00111
Robert Milliken, prin. 394-2352

Toutle, AC 206, PC 2, Cowlitz
Toutle Lake SD 130 3-11111
5050 SPIRIT LAKE HWY 98649 274-6182
Carl Maw, supt.
Toutle Lake JSHS 2-00111
5050 SPIRIT LAKE HWY 98649 274-6132
Gerald Black, prin.

Trout Lake, AC 509, PC 3, Klickitat
Trout Lake SD R-400 2-11111
PO BOX 310 98650 395-2571
Dee Michaels, supt.
JSHS, 31 LITTLE MOUNTAIN RD 98650 1-00111
Dee Michaels, prin. 395-2571

Tukwila, AC 206, PC 7, King
South Central SD 406 4-11111
4640 S 144TH ST 98168 248-7565
Michael Silver, supt.
Foster HS, 4242 S 144TH ST 98168 2-00011
Horst Momber, prin. 248-7570
Showalter MS, 4628 S 144TH ST 98168 2-00100
Lee Allen, prin. 248-7540

Tumwater, AC 206, PC 6, Thurston
Tumwater SD 33 6-11111
419 LINWOOD AVE SW 98512 586-9300
Norman Wisner, supt.
HS, 700 ISRAEL RD SW 98501 4-00011
Terry Pullen, prin. 586-9359
New Market Vocational Skills Center Vo Tech
7299 NEW MARKET ST SW 98501 586-9375
James Taylor, prin.
MS, 6335 LITTLEROCK RD SW 98512 3-00100
Susan Haskin, prin. 586-9353

Twisp, AC 509, PC 3, Okanogan
Methow Valley SD 350 3-11111
PO BOX 126 98856 996-9205
Suellen White, supt.
Liberty Bell JSHS, PO BOX 126 98856 2-00111
Dennis Young, prin. 996-2215

Valley, AC 509, PC 2, Stevens
Valley SD 070, PO BOX 157 99181 2-11100
Donald Munson, supt. 937-2791
JHS 99181 1-00100
Gerald Ely, prin. 937-2413

Vancouver, AC 206, PC 8, Clark
Battle Ground SD 116
Supt. — See Battle Ground
Laurin MS, 13601 NE 97TH AVE 98662 2-01100
Bert Brumbaugh, prin. 896-4400
Pleasant Valley MS 3-01100
14320 NE 50TH AVE 98686 896-4422
Bob Legato, prin.

Evergreen SD 114 7-11111
PO BOX 8910 98668 260-4000
K. Schmauder, supt.
Evergreen SHS, 14300 NE 18TH ST 98684 4-00001
Nancy Lange, prin. 256-6034
Mountain View SHS 4-00001
1500 SE BLAIRMONT DR 98684 253-2500
Jerry Piland, prin.
Clark County Skills Ctr Vo Tech
12200 NE 28TH ST 98682 256-6079
Dennis Kampe, prin.
Cascade JHS, 13900 NE 18TH ST 98684 3-00110
Vonne Williams, prin. 256-6052
Covington JHS 3-00110
11200 NE ROSEWOOD AVE 98662 256-6065
Samara Gilroy-Hicks, prin.
Pacific JHS, 2017 NE 172ND AVE 98684 4-00110
Reinhard Brunsch, prin. 254-7326
Wy' East JHS, 1112 SE 136TH AVE 98684 4-00110
Gary Tichenor, prin. 256-6014

Vancouver SD 37 7-11111
PO BOX 8937 98668 696-7000
James Parsley, supt.
Columbia River HS 4-00011
800 NW 99TH ST 98665 696-7171
Patricia Friauf, prin.
Ft. Vancouver HS, 5700 E 18TH ST 98661 4-00011
Ralph Riden, prin. 696-7111
Hudson's Bay HS 4-00011
1206 E RESERVE ST 98661 696-7221
Doug Goodlett, prin.
Alki MS, 1800 NW BLISS RD 98685 3-00100
Bill Doenecke, prin. 737-7348
Gaiser MS, 3000 NE 99TH ST 98665 3-00100
Ed Little, prin. 696-7177
Lee MS, 8500 NW 9TH AVE 98665 3-00100
Brad Fritts, prin. 696-7131
McLoughlin MS 4-00100
5802 MACARTHUR BLVD 98661 696-7291
Scott Williams, prin.
Shumway MS, 3101 MAIN ST 98663 3-00100
Terry Nelson, prin. 696-7101

Clark College 6-CC
1800 E MCLOUGHLIN BLVD 98663 699-0392
Fries Piano Hospital & Training Center 2-CS
2510 E EVERGREEN BLVD 98661 693-1511
International Air Academy 4-CS
2901 E MILL PLAIN BLVD 98661 695-2500
Vocational Training Institute 2-CS
6400 NE HIGHWAY 99 98665 695-5186
Washington State School for the Blind HND
2214 E 13TH ST 98661
Washington State School for the Deaf HND
611 GRAND BLVD 98661
Western Business College 2-CS
6625 E MILL PLAIN BLVD 98661 694-3225

Vashon, AC 206, PC 4, King
Vashon Island SD 402 4-11111
20414 VASHON HWY SW 98070 463-2121
Richard Semler, supt.
Vashon Island HS 2-00011
20120 VASHON HWY SW 98070 463-9171
John McGean, prin.
McMurray IS 2-00100
9329 SW CEMETERY RD 98070 463-9168
Michael Kirk, prin.

Veradale, AC 509, PC 6, Spokane
Central Valley SD 356
Supt. — See Greenacres
Central Valley SHS 4-00001
821 S SULLIVAN RD 99037 922-6750
Larry Parsons, prin.
Evergreen JHS, 14221 E 16TH AVE 99037 3-00110
Lance Erie, prin. 922-6890

Waitsburg, AC 509, PC 3, Walla Walla
Waitsburg SD 401-100 2-11111
PO BOX 217 99361 337-6301
Burton Dickerson, supt.
HS, PO BOX 217 99361 2-00011
Dan Butler, prin. 337-6351
MS, PO BOX 217 99361 1-00100
Dan Butler, prin. 337-6351

Walla Walla, AC 509, PC 8, Walla Walla
Walla Walla SD 140 6-11111
364 S PARK ST 99362 527-3000
Ellen Wolf, supt.
HS, 800 ABBOTT RD 99362 4-00011
Albert Roberts, prin. 527-3020
Garrison MS, 906 CHASE ST 99362 3-00100
James Howard, prin. 527-3040
Pioneer MS, 450 BRIDGE ST 99362 3-00100
Ron Wilkinson, prin. 527-3050

DeSales HS, 919 E SUMACH ST 99362 2-00111
Robert Wehde, prin. 525-3030
Walla Walla Community College 6-CC
500 TAUSICK WAY 99362 527-4283
Whitman College 4-UC
345 BOYER AVE 99362 527-5176

Wapato, AC 509, PC 5, Yakima
Wapato SD 207, PO BOX 38 98951 5-11111
Pete Vander Wegen, supt. 877-4181
HS, PO BOX 38 98951 3-00011
Leroy Werkhoven, prin. 877-3138

JHS, PO BOX 38 98951
Scott Dolquist, prin.
3-00100
877-2173

Warden, AC 509, PC 4, Grant
Warden SD 146-161
PO BOX 308 98857
Dennis Brandon, supt.
3-11111
349-2366
HS, PO BOX 308 98857
Russ Davis, prin.
2-00011
349-2581
MS, PO BOX 308 98857
Russ Davis, prin.
2-00100
349-2902

Washougal, AC 206, PC 5, Clark
Washougal SD 112-6, 2349 B ST 98671
Brent Garrett, supt.
4-11111
835-2191
HS, 1201 39TH ST 98671
Edward Fitts, prin.
3-00011
835-2155
Jemtegaard MS
35300 SE EVERGREEN BLVD 98671
Claire Schozman, prin.
3-00100
835-8763

Washtucna, AC 509, PC 2, Adams
Washtucna SD 109-43
PO BOX 688 99371
Dale Clark, supt.
2-11111
646-3237
JSHS 99371
Larry Thomas, prin.
1-00111
646-3401

Waterville, AC 509, PC 3, Douglas
Waterville SD 209
PO BOX 490 98858
Lafe Bretthauer, supt.
2-11111
745-8584
JSHS, PO BOX 490 98858
Steven Boosinger, prin.
2-00111
745-8583

Wellpinit, AC 509, PC 2, Stevens
Wellpinit SD 49, PO BOX 390 99040
Reid Riedlinger, supt.
2-11111
258-4535
JSHS, PO BOX 390 99040
Nakonia Hayes, prin.
1-00111
258-4535

Wenatchee, AC 509, PC 7, Chelan
Wenatchee SD 246
PO BOX 1767 98807
Robert Lehman, supt.
6-11111
663-8161
HS, 1101 MILLERDALE AVE 98801
Joan Wright, prin.
4-00011
663-8117
Foothills MS, 1410 MAPLE ST 98801
Gary Callison, prin.
2-00100
664-8961
Orchard MS, 1024 ORCHARD ST 98801
Kevin Pearl, prin.
2-00100
662-7745
Pioneer MS, 1620 RUSSELL ST 98801
Jay Brahe, prin.
3-00100
663-7171

Cascade Christian Academy
600 WESTERN AVE N 98801
Edward Tillotson, prin.
2-11111
662-2723
Trend College
230 GRANT RD 98802
2-CS
884-1587
Wenatchee Valley College
1300 5TH ST 98801
5-CC
664-2533

Westport, AC 206, PC 4, Grays Harbor
Ocosta SD 172
2580 S MONTESANO ST 98595
Richard Jones, supt.
3-11111
268-9125

Ocosta JSHS
2580 S MONTESANO ST 98595
William Parks, prin.
2-00111
268-9123

White Salmon, AC 509, PC 4, Klickitat
White Salmon Valley SD 405-17
PO BOX 157 98672
Richard Carter, supt.
4-11111
493-1500
Columbia HS
1455 NW BRUIN COUNTRY RD 98672
Lee Davis, prin.
2-00011
493-1970
Henkle MS, 480 NW LOOP RD 98672
Douglas Miller, prin.
3-01100
493-1502

White Swan, AC 509, PC 5, Yakima
Mount Adams SD 209
PO BOX 578 98952
R. Hoptowit, supt.
4-11111
874-2611
HS, PO BOX 578 98952
Gary Fendell, prin.
2-00011
874-2324
MS, PO BOX 578 98952
Furman Wheeler, prin.
2-00100
874-2324

Wilbur, AC 509, PC 3, Lincoln
Wilbur SD 200, PO BOX 1090 99185
Lester Portner, supt.
2-11111
647-2221
JSHS, PO BOX 1090 99185
Dennis Bolz, prin.
2-00111
647-5602

Wilson Creek, AC 509, PC 2, Grant
Wilson Creek SD 167-202
PO BOX 46 98860
Bob Periman, supt.
2-11111
345-2541
JSHS, GENERAL DELIVERY 98860
A. Wilson, prin.
1-00111
345-2541

Winlock, AC 206, PC 4, Lewis
Winlock SD 232, 311 NW FIR ST 98596
Larry Hearst, supt.
3-11111
785-3582
HS, 241 N MILITARY RD 98596
John Stemkoski, prin.
2-00011
785-3537
MS, 241 N MILITARY RD 98596
John Stemkoski, prin.
2-00100
785-3046

Wishram, AC 509, PC 3, Klickitat
Wishram SD 94, PO BOX 268 98673
Dave Holmer, supt.
1-11111
748-2551
S, PO BOX 268 98673
Dave Holmer, prin.
1-11111
748-2551

Woodinville, AC 206, PC 7, King
Northshore SD 417
Supt. — See Bothell
SHS, 19819 136TH AVE NE 98072
David Jones, prin.
4-00001
489-6700
Leota MS, 19301 168TH AVE NE 98072
Chris Kuhnly, prin.
3-00110
489-6391

Chrysalis S
14241 NE WDNVILLE DUVALL RD 98072
Karen Fogle, prin.
2-11111
481-2228

Woodland, AC 206, PC 5, Cowlitz
Woodland SD 404
PO BOX 370 98674
W. Bohrnsen, supt.
4-11111
225-9451
HS, PO BOX 370 98674
Lee Knight, prin.
2-00011
225-8201

MS, PO BOX 370 98674
Terry Gatz, prin.
2-00100
225-9416

Yakima, AC 509, PC 8, Yakima
East Valley SD 90
2002 BEAURY RD 98901
Ronald Whittaker, supt.
4-11111
248-7757
East Valley HS
1900 BEAURY RD 98901
Mark Lyons, prin.
3-00011
248-3211
East Valley Central MS
2010 BEAURY RD 98901
Patty Page, prin.
3-00100
248-7300

West Valley SD 208, 8902 ZIER RD 98908
Peter Ansingh, supt.
5-11111
965-2000
West Valley SHS, 9206 ZIER RD 98908
Jerry Craig, prin.
3-00001
965-2040
West Valley JHS, 7505 ZIER RD 98908
Steve Smith, prin.
4-00110
965-2012

Yakima SD 7, 104 N 4TH AVE 98902
Larry Petry, supt.
7-11111
575-3230
Davis HS, 212 S 6TH AVE 98902
Karen Garrison, prin.
4-00011
575-3308
Eisenhower HS, 702 S 40TH AVE 98908
David Betzing, prin.
4-00011
575-3270
Yakima Valley Vocational Skills Center
1116 S 15TH AVE 98902
John Schieche, prin.
Vo Tech
575-3436
Franklin MS, 410 S 19TH AVE 98902
Wes Crago, prin.
3-00100
575-3405
Lewis & Clark MS
1114 W PIERCE ST 98902
Guy Kaplicky, prin.
3-00100
575-3411
Washington MS, 501 S 7TH ST 98901
Mickie Clise, prin.
3-00100
575-3344
Wilson MS, 902 S 44TH AVE 98908
Janeen Grimes, prin.
3-00100
575-3325

Perry Technical Institute
2011 W WASHINGTON AVE 98903
2-CS
453-0374
Trend College
112 N PIERCE AVE 98902
3-CS
248-4806
West Side Christian S
6901 SUMMITVIEW AVE 98908
Glenn Kessinger, prin.
2-11111
965-2602
Yakima Valley Community College
16TH AVE & NOB HILL BLVD 98902
6-CC
575-2373

Yelm, AC 206, PC 4, Thurston
Yelm SD 2, PO BOX 476 98597
Charles Hall, supt.
5-11111
458-1900
HS, PO BOX 476 98597
Gary Martin, prin.
3-00011
458-7777
MS, PO BOX 476 98597
Drew Braun, prin.
3-00100
458-3600

Zillah, AC 509, PC 4, Yakima
Zillah SD 205, PO BOX 225 98953
Jim Busey, supt.
4-11111
829-5911
HS, PO BOX 777 98953
Jim Busey, prin.
2-00011
829-5565
MS, PO BOX 225 98953
Sue Torres, prin.
2-00100
829-5511

WEST VIRGINIA

STATE DEPARTMENT OF EDUCATION
State Capitol Complex
1900 Kanawha St., Charleston 25305
(304) 348-2681

State Superintendent of Schools Henry Marockie

Assistant Superintendent Administrative Services Carolyn Arrington

Assistant Superintendent Technical & Adult Education Adam Sponaugle

Division Chief Instructional & Student Services Keith Smith

STATE BOARD OF EDUCATION
1900 Kanawha St., Charleston 25305

President Michael Greer

PUBLIC, PRIVATE AND CATHOLIC SECONDARY SCHOOLS

Ansted, AC 304, PC 4, Fayette
Fayette County SD
Supt. — See Fayetteville
MS, PO BOX 766 25812 — 2-01100
John Eades, prin. — 658-5170

Ashton, AC 304, PC 2, Mason
Mason County SD
Supt. — See Point Pleasant
Hannan JSHS — 2-00111
6770 ASHTON UPLAND RD 25503 — 576-2571
Richard Haycraft, prin.

Athens, AC 304, PC 3, Mercer
Mercer County SD
Supt. — See Princeton
JSHS, PO BOX 608 24712 — 2-00111
Daniel Zirkle, prin. — 384-9888

Concord College 24712 — 4-UC
384-3115

Baker, AC 304, PC 1, Hardy
Hardy County SD
Supt. — See Moorefield
East Hardy HS, PO BOX 120 26801 — 2-00011
Steven Wilson, prin. — 897-5948

Barboursville, AC 304, PC 5, Cabell
Cabell County SD
Supt. — See Huntington
MS, 641 MAIN ST 25504 — 3-00100
Orman Hall, prin. — 733-3012

Beaver, AC 304, PC 4, Raleigh
Raleigh County SD
Supt. — See Beckley
Shady Spring JHS — 3-00110
PO BOX 248 25813 — 256-4570
Charles Meadows, prin.

Beckley, AC 304, PC 7, Raleigh
Raleigh County SD, 105 ADAIR ST 25801 — 7-11111
Dwight Dials, supt. — 256-4500
Wilson SHS, 410 STANAFORD RD 25801 — 4-00001
Miller Hall, prin. — 256-4646
Raleigh County Vo-Tech Ctr — Vo Tech
410 1/2 STANAFORD RD 25801 — 256-4615
Mary Vaught, prin.
JHS, 320 S KANAWHA ST 25801 — 3-00110
Ronald Cantley, prin. — 256-4616
Park JHS, 212 PARK AVE 25801 — 3-00110
Richard Davis, prin. — 256-4586
Stratton JHS, 1129 S FAYETTE ST 25801 — 2-00110
Malvin Ross, prin. — 256-4580
Other Schools – See Beaver, Coal City, Glen Daniel, Naoma, Shady Spring, Sophia, Sundial, Surveyor

Beckley College — 4-CC
PO BOX AG 25802 — 253-7351
Veterans Administration Hospital — HSP
200 VETERANS AVE 25801 — 255-2121

Belington, AC 304, PC 4, Barbour
Barbour County SD
Supt. — See Philippi
MS, PO BOX 927 26250 — 2-00100
Norma Harris, prin. — 823-1281

Belle, AC 304, PC 4, Kanawha
Kanawha County SD
Supt. — See Charleston
Dupont SHS, 301 W 34TH ST 25015 — 3-00001
James Law, prin. — 348-1978
Dupont JHS, 201 W MAIN ST 25015 — 3-00110
Forest Mann, prin. — 348-1977

Belmont, AC 304, PC 3, Pleasants
Pleasants County SD
Supt. — See Saint Mary's
Pleasants County MS — 2-01100
PO BOX 469 26134 — 665-2415
Donna Barksdale, prin.

Benwood, AC 304, PC 4, Marshall
Marshall County SD
Supt. — See Moundsville
Union JHS, 1690 MARSHALL ST S 26031 — 2-00110
David Takach, prin. — 232-7190

Berkeley Springs, AC 304, PC 3, Morgan
Morgan County SD — 4-11111
903 S WASHINGTON ST 25411 — 258-2430
Jerry Jones, supt.
JSHS, 836 CONCORD AVE 25411 — 3-00111
Kenneth Whittington, prin. — 258-2871
Other Schools – See Paw Paw

Bethany, AC 304, PC 4, Brooke

Bethany College 26031 — 3-UC
829-7111

Blacksville, AC 304, PC 2, Monongalia
Monongalia County SD
Supt. — See Morgantown
Clay-Battelle JSHS — 2-00111
PO BOX 154 26521 — 432-8208
Gary Smith, prin.

Bluefield, AC 304, PC 7, Mercer
Mercer County SD
Supt. — See Princeton
SHS, 535 W CUMBERLAND RD 24701 — 3-00001
John Disibbio, prin. — 325-9116

JHS, 2002 STADIUM DR 24701 — 3-00110
Mack Barber, prin. — 325-2481

Bluefield Regional Medical Center — HSP
500 CHERRY ST 24701 — 327-1701
Bluefield State College — 4-UC
219 ROCK ST 24701 — 327-4030

Bradley, AC 304, PC 4, Raleigh

Appalachian Bible College — 2-UC
PO BOX ABC 25818 — 877-6428

Branchland, AC 304, PC 3, Lincoln
Lincoln County SD
Supt. — See Hamlin
Guyan Valley JSHS — 3-00111
700 STATE ROUTE 10 25506 — 824-3235
Paul Winter, prin.

Brenton, AC 304, PC 3, Wyoming
Wyoming County SD
Supt. — See Pineville
Baileysville HS, PO BOX 214 24818 — 3-00011
Deborah Marsh, prin. — 732-7254

Bridgeport, AC 304, PC 6, Harrison
Harrison County SD
Supt. — See Clarksburg
HS, 515 JOHNSON AVE 26330 — 3-00011
Lindy Bennett, prin. — 842-3693
JHS, 225 NEWTON AVE 26330 — 3-00100
William Fahey, prin. — 842-5251

Buckeye, AC 304, PC 2, Pocahontas
Pocahontas County SD
Supt. — See Marlinton
Marlinton MS, RR 2 BOX 52S 24924 — 2-01100
Thomas Sanders, prin. — 799-6773

Buckhannon, AC 304, PC 6, Upshur
Upshur County SD — 5-11111
PO BOX 580 26201 — 472-5480
Lynn Westfall, supt.
Buckhannon-Upshur HS — 4-00011
50 BUCKHANNON UPSHUR DR 26201 — 472-3720
Hal McComas, prin.
Eberle Tech Ctr, RR 5 BOX 2 26201 — Vo Tech
Kenneth Davidson, prin. — 472-1259
Buckhannon-Upshur MS — 4-00100
PO BOX 250 26201 — 472-1520
Steven Paine, prin.

West Virginia Wesleyan College — 4-UC
59 COLLEGE AVE 26201 — 800-722-9933

Buffalo, AC 304, PC 3, Putnam
Putnam County SD
Supt. — See Winfield
HS, PO BOX 40 25033 — 2-00011
Vernon Goff, prin. — 937-2661

Bunker Hill, AC 304, PC 3, Berkeley
Berkeley County SD
Supt. — See Martinsburg
Musselman HS, RR 2 BOX 122 25413 — 3-00011
John Cole, prin. — 229-5815
Musselman MS, RR 2 BOX 119 25413 — 3-00100
Willard Aikens, prin. — 229-0022

Cameron, AC 304, PC 4, Marshall
Marshall County SD
Supt. — See Moundsville
JSHS, 61 MAPLE AVE 26033 — 2-00111
David Hall, prin. — 686-3336

Capon Bridge, AC 304, PC 2, Hampshire
Hampshire County SD
Supt. — See Romney
JHS, PO BOX 45 26711 — 2-00110
Ronald Stephans, prin. — 856-2534

Ceredo, AC 304, PC 4, Wayne
Wayne County SD
Supt. — See Wayne
Ceredo-Kenova MS — 2-00100
PO BOX 705 25507 — 453-3588
Emma Lou Akers, prin.

Chapmanville, AC 304, PC 4, Logan
Logan County SD
Supt. — See Logan
SHS, PO BOX 4580 25508 — 2-00001
Ernest Amburgey, prin. — 855-4522
JHS, PO BOX 309 25508 — 3-00110
Ed Napier, prin. — 855-9186

Charleston, AC 304, PC 8, Kanawha
Kanawha County SD — 8-11111
200 ELIZABETH ST 25311 — 348-7770
Jorea Marple, supt.
Capital SHS — 4-00001
1500 GREENBRIER ST 25311 — 348-6500
John Clendenen, prin.
Washington SHS — 3-00000
1522 TENNIS CLUB RD 25314 — 348-7729
Larry Lohan, prin.
Sissonville HS — 3-00011
6100 SISSONVILLE DR 25312 — 348-1954
Calvin McKinney, prin.
Carver Career & Tech Ed Ctr — Vo Tech
4799 MIDLAND DR 25306 — 348-1965
Norma Miller, prin.

Adams JHS — 3-00110
2002 PRESIDENTIAL DR 25314 — 348-6652
Thomas Kidd, prin.
Jackson JHS, 812 PARK AVE 25302 — 3-00110
Charles Maxwell, prin. — 348-6123
Jackson JHS, 5445 BIG TYLER RD 25313 — 3-00110
Melanie Vickers, prin. — 776-3310
Mann JHS — 2-00110
4302 MACCORKLE AVE SE 25304 — 348-1971
Lewis Gargarella, prin.
Roosevelt JHS, 502 RUFFNER AVE 25311 — 3-00110
David Miller, prin. — 348-6101
Other Schools – See Belle, Clendenin, Dunbar, East Bank, Elkview, Nitro, Saint Albans, Sissonville, South Charleston

Charleston Area Medical Center — HSP
3200 MACCORKLE AVE SE 25304 — 348-5570
Charleston Catholic HS — 2-00111
1033 VIRGINIA ST E 25301 — 342-8415
Debra Sullivan, prin.
Cross Lanes Christian S — 2-11111
5330 FLORADALE DR 25313 — 776-4471
Richard Corbin, prin.
Fairhaven Christian S — 2-11111
689 FAIRHAVEN DR 25306 — 925-5954
David Kilburn, prin.
University of Charleston — 4-UC
2300 MACCORKLE AVE SE 25304 — 800-995-4682
West Virginia Career College — 2-CC
1000 VIRGINIA ST E 25301 — 345-2820

Charles Town, AC 304, PC 5, Jefferson
Jefferson County SD — 6-11111
110 MORDINGTON AVE 25414 — 725-9741
Frederick Colvard, supt.
JHS, 817 HIGH ST 25414 — 3-00110
Densil Nibert, prin. — 725-7821
Other Schools – See Harpers Ferry, Shenandoah Junction, Shepherdstown

Charmco, AC 304, PC 3, Greenbrier
Greenbrier County SD
Supt. — See Lewisburg
Greenbrier West SHS — 2-00001
PO BOX 325 25958 — 438-6191
David Smith, prin.

Chester, AC 304, PC 5, Hancock
Hancock County SD
Supt. — See New Cumberland
Oak Glen MS, 601 6TH ST 26034 — 2-00100
Don Licker, prin. — 387-2363

Circleville, AC 304, PC 2, Pendleton
Pendleton County SD
Supt. — See Franklin
S, PO BOX 9 26804 — 2-11111
Calvin Thompson, prin. — 567-2515

Clarksburg, AC 304, PC 7, Harrison
Harrison County SD — 7-11111
408 WATER ST 26301 — 624-3300
Robert Kittle, supt.
Irving HS, 443 LEE AVE 26301 — 3-00011
Leon Pilewski, prin. — 624-3271
Liberty HS, RR 3 BOX 800 26301 — 3-00011
David Book, prin. — 624-3264
United Technical Ctr — Vo Tech
RR 3 BOX 43C 26301 — 624-3280
Joan Smith, prin.
Gore JHS, RR 3 BOX 43B 26301 — 1-00110
William Montgomery, prin. — 624-3260
Roosevelt-Wilson JHS — 1-00110
116 PENNSYLVANIA AVE 26301 — 624-3248
Richard Drummond, prin.
Other Schools – See Bridgeport, Lost Creek, Lumberport, Salem, Shinnston

Notre Dame HS, 127 E PIKE ST 26301 — 2-00111
Sr. Mary Homan, prin. — 623-1026
Salem College-Clarksburg — 2-CC
112 N 6TH ST 26301
United Hospital Center — HSP
PO BOX 2308 26302 — 624-2332
West Virginia Business College — 2-CS
215 W MAIN ST 26301 — 624-7695

Clay, AC 304, PC 3, Clay
Clay County SD, 242 CHURCH ST 25043 — 4-11111
James Dawson, supt. — 587-4266
Clay County HS, 1 PANTHER DR 25043 — 3-00011
Kenneth Tanner, prin. — 587-4226
MS, PO BOX 489 25043 — 3-00100
Larry Gillespie, prin. — 587-2343

Clendenin, AC 304, PC 4, Kanawha
Kanawha County SD
Supt. — See Charleston
Hoover HS, 275 ELK RIVER RD S 25045 — 4-00011
Charles Burford, prin. — 965-3394
JHS, PO BOX 480 25045 — 2-00110
Michael Cunningham, prin. — 965-5221

Coal City, AC 304, PC 4, Raleigh
Raleigh County SD
Supt. — See Beckley
Independence SHS, PO BOX AA 25823 — 3-00001
Wayne Peters, prin. — 683-3228
Stoco JHS, PO BOX W 25823 — 2-00110
John Kerzic, prin. — 683-5141

Craigsville, AC 304, PC 4, Nicholas
Nicholas County SD
　Supt. — See Summersville
Nicholas County Career and Technical Ctr　Vo Tech
　PO BOX 406 26205　742-5416
　Harlan Hardway, prin.

Cross Lanes, AC 304, PC 7, Kanawha

NEC-National Institute of Technology　2-CC
　5514 BIG TYLER RD 25313　776-6290

Crum, AC 304, PC 2, Wayne
Wayne County SD
　Supt. — See Wayne
MS, PO BOX 9 25669　2-00100
　William Brubeck, prin.　393-3200

Danville, AC 304, PC 3, Boone
Boone County SD
　Supt. — See Madison
Boone County Career & Tech Ctr　Vo Tech
　HC BOX 50 B 25053　369-4585
　Jimmy Dolan, prin.

Boone County Career Center　1-CS
　PO BOX 50 25053　369-4585

Delbarton, AC 304, PC 3, Mingo
Mingo County SD
　Supt. — See Williamson
Burch SHS, RR 2 BOX 52 25670　2-00001
　Jim Fletcher, prin.　475-5106
Mingo County Vo-Tech Ctr　Vo Tech
　RR 2 BOX 52A 25670　475-3347
　James Chafin, prin.
Burch JHS, PO BOX 240 25670　2-00110
　Thomas Slone, prin.　475-2141

Dunbar, AC 304, PC 6, Kanawha
Kanawha County SD
　Supt. — See Charleston
Franklin Vocational Ctr　Vo Tech
　500 28TH ST 25064　766-0369
　Alvin Brown, prin.
JHS, 325 27TH ST 25064　3-00110
　Lynda Gilkeson, prin.　766-0363

Dunmore, AC 304, PC 1, Pocahontas
Pocahontas County SD
　Supt. — See Marlinton
Pocahontas County HS　2-00011
　RR 1 BOX 133A 24934　799-6565
　Kenneth Vance, prin.

East Bank, AC 304, PC 3, Kanawha
Kanawha County SD
　Supt. — See Charleston
SHS, PO BOX 499 25067　3-00001
　Richard Clendenin, prin.　949-2482
JHS, PO BOX 897 25067　3-00110
　Garnes Reed, prin.　949-6566

Eleanor, AC 304, PC 4, Putnam
Putnam County SD
　Supt. — See Winfield
Putnam Vo-Tech S　Vo Tech
　PO BOX 640 25070　586-3494
　Ron Peters, prin.
Washington MS, PO BOX 660 25070　2-00100
　Jeff Wymer, prin.　586-2875

Elizabeth, AC 304, PC 3, Wirt
Wirt County SD, PO BOX 189 26143　4-11111
　Larry Williams, supt.　275-4279
Wirt County HS, PO BOX 219 26143　2-00011
　Stephen Simonton, prin.　275-4241
Wirt Co MS, PO BOX 699 26143　2-01100
　Daniel Metz, prin.　275-3977

Elk Garden, AC 304, PC 2, Mineral
Mineral County SD
　Supt. — See Keyser
S, PO BOX 10 26717　2-11111
　John Haines, prin.　446-5141

Elkins, AC 304, PC 6, Randolph
Randolph County SD, 40 11TH ST 26241　5-11111
　Tony Marchio, supt.　636-9150
Forest Hills HS, 100 KENNEDY DR 26241　1-00011
　Thomas Pritt, prin.　636-9170
Randolph County Vo-Tech Ctr　Vo Tech
　RR 3 BOX 246 26241　636-9195
　Glen Karlen, prin.
JHS, 303 ROBERT E LEE AVE 26241　3-00100
　David Roth, prin.　636-9176
Other Schools — See Harman, Mill Creek, Pickens

Davis & Elkins College　3-UC
　100 CAMPUS DR 26241　636-1900

Elkview, AC 304, PC 4, Kanawha
Kanawha County SD
　Supt. — See Charleston
JHS, 5090 ELK RIVER RD 25071　3-00110
　Jerry Morrison, prin.　348-1947

Elk Valley Christian S　2-11111
　PO BOX 625 25071　965-7062
　Ron Barnes, prin.

Fairmont, AC 304, PC 7, Marion
Marion County SD　6-11111
　200 GASTON AVE 26554　367-2100
　Jane Reynolds, supt.

East Fairmont HS　3-00011
　1993 AIRPORT RD 26554　367-2140
　Tom Dragich, prin.
HS, 1 LOOP PARK DR 26554　4-00011
　William Furgason, prin.　367-2150
East Fairmont JHS, 1 ORION LN 26554　1-00100
　David Madigan, prin.　367-2100
Miller JHS　2-00100
　2 PENNSYLVANIA AVE 26554　366-3821
　Stephen Higgins, prin.
Other Schools — See Fairview, Farmington,
　Mannington, Monongah

Calvary Christian S　2-11111
　RR 3 BOX 342 26554　363-8008
　Ron Blackburn, prin.
Computer Tech　2-CS
　MIDDLTWN MALL I-79 & RT 250 26554
　363-5100
Fairmont State College　6-UC
　1201 LOCUST AVE 26554　367-4151
Webster College　2-CC
　412 FAIRMONT AVE 26554　363-8824

Fairview, AC 304, PC 3, Marion
Marion County SD
　Supt. — See Fairmont
MS, PO BOX 300 26570　2-01100
　Judith Robinson, prin.　449-1312

Farmington, AC 304, PC 2, Marion
Marion County SD
　Supt. — See Fairmont
North Marion HS　4-00011
　RR 1 BOX 100 26571　986-3063
　Paul Donato, prin.
Marion Vo-Tech Ctr　Vo Tech
　RR 1 BOX 100A 26571　986-3590
　Roger Perdue, prin.

Fayetteville, AC 304, PC 4, Fayette
Fayette County SD　6-11111
　111 FAYETTE AVE 25840　574-1176
　Rick Powell, supt.
HS, 515 W MAPLE AVE 25840　2-00011
　Ben Argento, prin.　574-0560
MS, 135 HIGH ST 25840　2-00100
　Peggy Freeman, prin.　574-2449
Other Schools — See Ansted, Gauley Bridge, Hico,
　Lookout, Meadow Bridge, Montgomery, Mount
　Hope, Oak Hill, Smithers

Follansbee, AC 304, PC 5, Brook
Brooke County SD
　Supt. — See Wellsburg
MS, 1400 MAIN ST 26037　3-01100
　Joseph Martray, prin.　527-1942

Fort Gay, AC 304, PC 3, Wayne
Wayne County SD
　Supt. — See Wayne
Tolsia HS, 1 REBEL DR 25514　3-00011
　Gary Adkins, prin.　648-5566
MS, PO BOX 460 25514　2-00100
　Michael Ferguson, prin.　648-5404

Franklin, AC 304, PC 3, Pendleton
Pendleton County SD　4-11111
　PO BOX 888 26807　358-2207
　Charles Smith, supt.
JSHS, PO BOX 216 26807　2-00111
　O. Hoover, prin.　358-2573
Other Schools — See Circleville

Gauley Bridge, AC 304, PC 3, Fayette
Fayette County SD
　Supt. — See Fayetteville
HS, PO BOX 579 25085　2-00011
　Sam Snead, prin.　632-2511
MS, PO BOX 827 25085　2-01100
　Harry Carelli, prin.　632-1022

Gilbert, AC 304, PC 2, Mingo
Mingo County SD
　Supt. — See Williamson
SHS, PO BOX 366 25621　2-00001
　Jim May, prin.　664-8197
JHS, PO BOX 948 25621　2-00110
　Burma Hatfield, prin.　664-3330

Glen Dale, AC 304, PC 4, Marshall
Marshall County SD
　Supt. — See Moundsville
Marshall SHS　4-00001
　1300 WHEELING AVE 26038　843-4444
　Sam Barberio, prin.

Glen Daniel, AC 304, PC 3, Raleigh
Raleigh County SD
　Supt. — See Beckley
Liberty HS, PO BOX 265 25844　3-00011
　Connie Giammerino, prin.　934-5307

Glenville, AC 304, PC 4, Gilmer
Gilmer County SD　4-11111
　201 N COURT ST 26351　462-7386
　Charles McCann, supt.
Gilmer County JSHS, 300 PINE ST 26351　3-00111
　John Barton, prin.　462-7960

Glenville State College　4-UC
　200 HIGH ST 26351　462-7361

Grafton, AC 304, PC 6, Taylor
Taylor County SD, 306 BEECH ST 26354　5-11111
　Wendell Teets, supt.　265-2497

HS, 400 RIVERSIDE DR 26354　3-00011
　Gregory Cartwright, prin.　265-3046
Taylor County Vo Ctr　Vo Tech
　115 LUBY ST 26354　265-1050
　Robert Brown, prin.
Taylor County MS　3-01100
　RR 2 BOX 148A 26354　265-0722
　William Whitescarver, prin.

Grantsville, AC 304, PC 3, Calhoun
Calhoun County SD, HIGH ST 26147　4-11111
　John Hager, supt.　354-7011
Calhoun County JSHS　3-00111
　PO BOX 898 26147　354-6148
　R. Daquilante, prin.
Calhoun Gilmer Career Ctr　Vo Tech
　RR 1 BOX 542A 26147　354-6151
　Elizabeth Parmer, prin.

Griffithsville, AC 304, PC 2, Lincoln
Lincoln County SD
　Supt. — See Hamlin
Duval JSHS, PO BOX 67 25521　3-00111
　David Bell, prin.　524-2101

Hambleton, AC 304, PC 2, Tucker
Tucker County SD
　Supt. — See Parsons
Tucker County HS　2-00011
　RR 1 BOX 153 26269　478-2651
　Howard Moore, prin.
Tucker County Career Ctr　Vo Tech
　RR 1 BOX 152 26269　478-3111
　Howard Moore, prin.

Hamlin, AC 304, PC 4, Lincoln
Lincoln County SD, 238 MAIN ST 25523　5-11111
　Dallas Kelley, supt.　824-3033
JSHS, GENERAL DELIVERY 25523　2-00111
　Francis McComas, prin.　824-3036
Lincoln Vo-Tech Center　Vo Tech
　10 MARLAND AVE 25523　824-5449
　Daryl Elkins, prin.
Other Schools — See Branchland, Griffithsville, Harts

Harman, AC 304, PC 2, Randolph
Randolph County SD
　Supt. — See Elkins
S, PO BOX 135 26270　2-11111
　Wayne Kennedy, prin.　227-4114

Harpers Ferry, AC 304, PC 2, Jefferson
Jefferson County SD
　Supt. — See Charles Town
JHS, RR 3 BOX 93 25425　2-00110
　Joseph Spurgas, prin.　535-6357

Harrisville, AC 304, PC 4, Ritchie
Ritchie County SD　4-11111
　217 W MAIN ST 26362　643-2991
　David Meador, supt.
Ritchie County HS　3-00110
　135 S PENN AVE 26362　643-2230
　Thomas Cowan, prin.
Cokely Ctr, 134 S PENN AVE 26362　Vo Tech
　(—), prin.　643-4120

Harts, AC 304, PC 2, Lincoln
Lincoln County SD
　Supt. — See Hamlin
JSHS, RR 1 BOX 60A 25524　2-00111
　David Lucas, prin.　855-4881

Hedgesville, AC 304, PC 2, Berkeley
Berkeley County SD
　Supt. — See Martinsburg
HS, RR 1 BOX 89 25427　4-00011
　Frank Allveto, prin.　754-3354
MS, 101 POPLAR ST 25427　3-00100
　Gary Greenfield, prin.　754-3313

Hico, AC 304, PC 3, Fayette
Fayette County SD
　Supt. — See Fayetteville
Midland Trail HS, PO BOX 89 25854　2-00011
　Chris Perkins, prin.　658-5184

Hinton, AC 304, PC 5, Summers
Summers County SD　4-11111
　116 MAIN ST 25951　466-6000
　Charles Rodes, supt.
JSHS, 400 TEMPLE ST 25951　3-00111
　Garnette Crowder, prin.　466-6030
Summers County Career Ctr　Vo Tech
　ROUTE 20 BOX 11A 25951　466-6021
　Harry Keaton, prin.

Hundred, AC 304, PC 2, Wetzel
Wetzel County SD
　Supt. — See New Martinsville
HS, PO BOX 830 26575　2-00011
　J. Shriver, prin.　775-5221

Huntington, AC 304, PC 8, Cabell
Cabell County SD, 620 20TH ST 25703　7-11111
　Robert Brewster, supt.　528-5000
Huntington East HS　4-00011
　2850 5TH AVE 25702　528-5134
　James Wyatt, prin.
HS, 900 8TH ST 25701　3-00011
　Charles Buell, prin.　528-5147
Cabell County Vo-Tech Ctr　Vo Tech
　1035 NORWAY AVE 25705　528-5106
　Albert Tenney, prin.
Beverly Hills MS　3-00100
　2901 SALTWELL RD 25705　528-5102
　David Roach, prin.

Cammack MS, 200 10TH AVE 25701   3-00100
  Ralph Rood, prin.   528-5116
Enslow MS, 2613 COLLIS AVE 25702   2-00100
  Larry Jordan, prin.   528-5121
West MS, 1001 JEFFERSON AVE 25704   2-00100
  Brenda Tanner, prin.   528-5180
Other Schools – See Barboursville, Lesage, Ona

Wayne County SD
  Supt. — See Wayne
Vinson HS, 3851 PIEDMONT RD 25704   2-00011
  John Mullens, prin.   429-1641
Wayne County Northern Vo-Tech Ctr   Vo Tech
  1640 SPRING VALLEY DR 25704   429-7176
  Gary Adkins, prin.
Westmoreland MS   2-00100
  3609 HUGHES ST 25704   429-5621
  Jesse Jones, prin.

Cabell Huntington Hospital   HSP
  1340 16TH ST 25701   526-2111
Grace Christian S   2-11111
  1111 ADAMS AVE 25704   525-1532
  Mike Reynolds, prin.
Huntington Junior College of Business   3-CC
  900 5TH AVE 25701   697-7550
Marshall University   6-UC
  400 HAL GREER BLVD 25755   696-2300
St. Joseph Central HS   2-00111
  600 13TH ST 25701   525-5096
  Sr. Lillian Jordan, prin.
St. Mary's Hospital   HSP
  2900 1ST AVE 25702   526-1415

Hurricane, AC 304, PC 5, Putnam
Putnam County SD
  Supt. — See Winfield
HS, 3350 TEAYS VALLEY RD 25526   3-00011
  Bill Sanders, prin.   562-3991
MS, 518 MIDLAND TRL 25526   3-00100
  Ernest Messinger, prin.   562-9271

Calvary Baptist Academy   2-11111
  3655 TEAYS VALLEY RD 25526   757-6768
  Milton Thompson, prin.

Iaeger, AC 304, PC 3, McDowell
McDowell County SD
  Supt. — See Welch
HS, PO BOX 779 24844   3-00011
  Jerry Horne, prin.   938-2431
IS, PO BOX 300 24844   1-00100
  Joseph Hatfield, prin.   938-2211

Institute, AC 304, PC 4, Kanawha

University of West Virginia   3-UC
  PO BOX 1003 25112   766-1989
West Virginia State College   5-UC
  PO BOX 1000 25112   766-3221

Kenova, AC 304, PC 5, Wayne
Wayne County SD
  Supt. — See Wayne
Buffalo HS, RR 1 25530   3-00011
  Dennis Bradley, prin.   429-4071
Ceredo-Kenova HS, 800 BEECH ST 25530   2-00011
  John Hussell, prin.   453-2231
Buffalo MS, RR 1 25530   2-00100
  Glenna Plymale, prin.   429-6062

Kermit, AC 304, PC 2, Mingo
Mingo County SD
  Supt. — See Williamson
JHS, PO BOX 168 25674   2-00110
  Ron Hatfield, prin.   393-3151

Keyser, AC 304, PC 6, Mineral
Mineral County SD, 1 BAKER PL 26726   5-11111
  Charles Kalbaugh, supt.   788-4200
HS, PO BOX 788 26726   3-00011
  Robert Hutcheson, prin.   788-4230
Mineral County Vo-Tech S   Vo Tech
  600 S WATER ST 26726   788-4240
  Terry Cannon, prin.
Other Schools – See Elk Garden, Ridgeley

Potomac State College of West Virginia U   4-CC
  26726   788-3011

Kingwood, AC 304, PC 5, Preston
Preston County SD, 121 E HIGH ST 26537   6-11111
  Elmer Pritt, supt.   329-0580
Preston SHS, 400 PRESTON DR 26537   4-00001
  Gary Livengood, prin.   329-0400
Central Preston JHS   2-00110
  100 E HIGH ST 26537   329-0033
  David Friend, prin.
Other Schools – See Masontown, Tunnelton

Lenore, AC 304, PC 2, Mingo
Mingo County SD
  Supt. — See Williamson
JHS, GENERAL DELIVERY 25676   2-00110
  Talmadge Harper, prin.   475-2411

Mingo Christian S   2-11111
  GENERAL DELIVERY 25676   475-3070
  Glenn Prichard, prin.

Le Roy, AC 304, PC 1, Jackson
Jackson County SD
  Supt. — See Ripley

Roane-Jackson Tech Ctr   Vo Tech
  4800 SPENCER RD 25252   372-7335
  Oscar Harris, prin.

Lesage, AC 304, PC 3, Cabell
Cabell County SD
  Supt. — See Huntington
Cox Landing MS, 6363 COX LN 25537   2-00100
  Charles Campbell, prin.   733-3021

Lewisburg, AC 304, PC 5, Greenbrier
Greenbrier County SD   6-11111
  202 CHESTNUT ST 24901   647-6470
  Stephen Baldwin, supt.
Greenbrier East SHS   4-00001
  RR 2 BOX 163 24901   647-6464
  Charles Carney, prin.
Other Schools – See Charmco, Ronceverte

West Virginia Sch./Osteopathic Medicine   2-UC
  400 N LEE ST 24901   645-6270

Lindside, AC 304, PC 2, Monroe
Monroe County SD
  Supt. — See Union
Monroe County Vo-Tech Ctr   Vo Tech
  RR 1 BOX 97 24951   832-6724
  James Higginbotham, prin.

Logan, AC 304, PC 4, Logan
Logan County SD   6-11111
  506 HOLLY AVE 25601   752-1550
  John Myers, supt.
SHS, 100 MIDDLEBURG IS 25601   4-00001
  Robert Lonker, prin.   752-6606
Willis Vo-Tech S, PO BOX 477 25601   Vo Tech
  Sandra Carroll, prin.   752-4687
Logan Central JHS   2-00110
  300 KANADA ST 25601   752-8501
  Wilma Zigmond, prin.
JHS, 500 UNIVERSITY AVE 25601   3-00110
  Robert Adkins, prin.   752-2510
Other Schools – See Chapmanville, Man

Southern West Virginia Community College   4-CC
  PO BOX 2900 25601   752-4300

Lookout, AC 304, PC 2, Fayette
Fayette County SD
  Supt. — See Fayetteville
Nuttall MS, PO BOX 130 25868   2-01100
  Donald Lockett, prin.   574-0429

Lost Creek, AC 304, PC 2, Harrison
Harrison County SD
  Supt. — See Clarksburg
South Harrison JHS   3-00110
  RR 1 BOX 57 26385   745-3315
  Gary Fain, prin.

Lumberport, AC 304, PC 4, Harrison
Harrison County SD
  Supt. — See Clarksburg
MS, PO BOX 328 26386   3-00100
  R. Nile Goff, prin.   584-4090

Mc Mechen, AC 304, PC 4, Marshall

Bishop Donahue HS   2-00011
  325 LOGAN ST 26040   233-3850
  Alan Jafrate, prin.

Madison, AC 304, PC 5, Boone
Boone County SD, 69 AVENUE B 25130   6-11111
  Manuel Arvon, supt.   369-3131
Scott HS, 1 SKYHAWK PL 25130   3-00011
  Mary Carter, prin.   369-3011
MS, 404 RIVERSIDE DR W 25130   3-00100
  Keith Phipps, prin.   369-4464
Other Schools – See Danville, Seth, Van, Whitesville

Man, AC 304, PC 3, Logan
Logan County SD
  Supt. — See Logan
SHS, 800 E MCDONALD AVE 25635   3-00001
  James Mankin, prin.   583-6521
JHS, 600 MAIN ST 25635   3-00110
  Thomas Keffer, prin.   583-7441

Mannington, AC 304, PC 4, Marion
Marion County SD
  Supt. — See Fairmont
MS, 113 CLARKSBURG ST 26582   2-01100
  Concetta Pulice, prin.   986-1050

Marlinton, AC 304, PC 4, Pocahontas
Pocahontas County SD   4-11111
  926 5TH AVE 24954   799-4505
  Thomas Long, supt.
Other Schools – See Buckeye, Dunmore

Martinsburg, AC 304, PC 7, Berkeley
Berkeley County SD   7-11111
  401 S QUEEN ST 25401   267-3500
  James Bennett, supt.
HS, 701 S QUEEN ST 25401   4-00011
  Richard Deuell, prin.   267-3530
Pikeside Pre-Vo Ctr   Vo Tech
  2140 WINCHESTER PIKE 25401   267-3555
  A. Edwards, prin.
Rumsey Vo-Tech S   Vo Tech
  RR 6 BOX 268 25401   754-7925
  James Spears, prin.
Martinsburg North MS   3-00100
  105 EAST RD 25401   267-3540
  Wendell Christopher, prin.

Martinsburg South MS   3-00100
  400 BUXTON ST 25401   267-3545
  Manny Arvon, prin.
Other Schools – See Bunker Hill, Hedgesville

Martinsburg Christian Academy   2-11111
  PO BOX 1356 25401   267-6368
  Joanne Smith, prin.

Mason, AC 304, PC 4, Mason
Mason County SD
  Supt. — See Point Pleasant
Wahama JSHS, PO BOX 348 25260   3-00111
  James Reymond, prin.   773-5539

Masontown, AC 304, PC 3, Preston
Preston County SD
  Supt. — See Kingwood
West Preston JHS, PO BOX 70 26542   2-00110
  Michael Teets, prin.   874-5221

Matewan, AC 304, PC 3, Mingo
Mingo County SD
  Supt. — See Williamson
SHS, ROUTE 49 25678   2-00001
  Thomas Hoffman, prin.   426-6555
JHS, PO BOX 535 25678   2-00110
  Noble Harper, prin.   426-4480

Matoaka, AC 304, PC 2, Mercer
Mercer County SD
  Supt. — See Princeton
JSHS, PO BOX 408 24736   2-00111
  Albert Clark, prin.   467-8282

Meadow Bridge, AC 304, PC 2, Fayette
Fayette County SD
  Supt. — See Fayetteville
JSHS, PO BOX 10 25976   2-00111
  Gary McClung, prin.   484-7917

Middlebourne, AC 304, PC 3, Tyler
Tyler County SD, PO BOX 25 26149   4-11111
  Sandy Weese, supt.   758-2145
Other Schools – See Sistersville

Mill Creek, AC 304, PC 3, Randolph
Randolph County SD
  Supt. — See Elkins
Tygarts Valley JSHS   2-00111
  PO BOX 68 26280   335-4575
  Wilbert Smith, prin.

Monongah, AC 304, PC 4, Marion
Marion County SD
  Supt. — See Fairmont
MS, 1 CAMDEN RD 26554   2-01100
  James Pulice, prin.   367-2164

Montcalm, AC 304, PC 4, Mercer
Mercer County SD
  Supt. — See Princeton
JSHS, PO BOX 330 24737   2-00111
  B. Lee, prin.   589-3719

Montgomery, AC 304, PC 4, Fayette
Fayette County SD
  Supt. — See Fayetteville
MS, 514 5TH AVE 25136   2-00100
  J. O'Donnell, prin.   442-4132

West Virginia Institute of Technology   5-UC
  405 FAYETTE PIKE 25136   442-3146

Moorefield, AC 304, PC 4, Hardy
Hardy County SD, 510 ASHBY ST 26836   4-11111
  John Miller, supt.   538-2348
JSHS, 401 N MAIN ST 26836   3-00111
  Douglas Hines, prin.   538-6034
Other Schools – See Baker

Morgantown, AC 304, PC 8, Monongalia
Monongalia County SD   7-11111
  13 S HIGH ST 26505   291-9200
  Jack Dulaney, supt.
SHS, 109 WILSON AVE 26505   4-00001
  Thomas Hart, prin.   291-9260
University HS, N PRICE ST 26505   3-00011
  William Wilson, prin.   291-9270
Monongalia County Tech Ed Ctr   Vo Tech
  1000 MISSISSIPPI ST 26505   291-9240
  Marlene Lawrence, prin.
Cheat Lake JHS, RR 7 BOX 153 26505   1-01100
  J. Kenneth Walls, prin.   594-1165
South JHS, 500 E PARKWAY DR 26505   3-00110
  Daniel Berry, prin.   291-9340
Suncrest Flatts JHS   2-00110
  360 BALDWIN ST 26505   291-9335
  W. Ryan, prin.
Other Schools – See Blacksville, Westover

West Virginia Career College   2-CC
  148 WILLEY ST 26505   296-8282
West Virginia University   7-UC
  PO BOX 6001 26506   293-0111
West Virginia University Hospital   HSP
  PO BOX 6401 26506   293-7075

Moundsville, AC 304, PC 7, Marshall
Marshall County SD, 2700 4TH ST 26041   6-11111
  Nick Zervos, supt.   843-4400
JHS, 401 TOMLINSON AVE 26041   3-00110
  Thomas Wood, prin.   843-4440
Other Schools – See Benwood, Cameron, Glen Dale,
  Wheeling

Mount Hope, AC 304, PC 4, Fayette
Fayette County SD
  Supt. — See Fayetteville
  HS, 110 HIGH SCHOOL DR 25880   2-00011
    Raymond Domingues, prin.   877-2121
  MS, 510 MAIN ST 25880   2-00100
    Gary Hough, prin.   877-6641

Mount Storm, AC 304, PC 2, Grant
Grant County SD
  Supt. — See Petersburg
  Union JSHS, HC 76 BOX 750 26739   2-00111
    Mark Nicol, prin.   693-7612

Mullens, AC 304, PC 4, Wyoming
Wyoming County SD
  Supt. — See Pineville
  HS, 801 MORAN AVE 25882   2-00011
    Don Nuckols, prin.   294-5131
  MS, PO BOX 1025 25882   2-01100
    Stephen Kirby, prin.   294-5757

Naoma, AC 304, PC 99, Raleigh
Raleigh County SD
  Supt. — See Beckley
  Marsh Fork HS, PO BOX 307 25140   2-00011
    Gary Rumberg, prin.   854-1151

Naugatuck, AC 304, PC 2, Mingo
Mingo County SD
  Supt. — See Williamson
  Tug Valley SHS, PO BOX 218 25685   3-00001
    James Spence, prin.   235-2266

New Cumberland, AC 304, PC 4, Hancock
Hancock County SD   6-11111
  104 N COURT ST 26047   564-3411
    Daniel Curry, supt.
  Oak Glen HS, RR 1 BOX 422A 26047   3-00011
    Thomas Salvati, prin.   564-3500
  Hancock Vo-Tech Ctr   Vo Tech
    RR 2 BOX 138A 26047   564-3337
    Danny Kaser, prin.
  Other Schools — See Chester, Weirton

New Martinsville, AC 304, PC 6, Wetzel
Wetzel County SD   5-11111
  333 FOUNDRY ST 26155   455-2441
    Martha Dean, supt.
  Magnolia HS, 601 MAPLE AVE 26155   3-00011
    Keith Herrick, prin.   455-1990
  Wetzel County Technology Ctr   Vo Tech
    RR 2 BOX 107 26155   455-5150
    Gerald Bissett, prin.
  Other Schools — See Hundred, Paden City, Pine Grove

Nitro, AC 304, PC 6, Kanawha
Kanawha County SD
  Supt. — See Charleston
  HS, 1301 PARK AVE 25143   3-00011
    Paul McClanahan, prin.   755-4321

Northfork, AC 304, PC 3, McDowell
McDowell County SD
  Supt. — See Welch
  JHS, PO BOX J 24868   1-00100
    Jeff Nash, prin.   862-3331

Oak Hill, AC 304, PC 6, Fayette
Fayette County SD
  Supt. — See Fayetteville
  HS, W OYLER AVE 25901   3-00011
    Paul Nichols, prin.   469-3551
  Fayette Plateau Vo Ctr   Vo Tech
    300 OYLER AVE 25901   469-2911
    Jerry Sizemore, prin.
  Collins MS, 601 JONES AVE 25901   3-01100
    David Perry, prin.   469-3711

Oakvale, AC 304, PC 2, Mercer
Mercer County SD
  Supt. — See Princeton
  JSHS, OLD ROUTE 460 24739   2-00111
    Steve Akers, prin.   898-2541

Oceana, AC 304, PC 4, Wyoming
Wyoming County SD
  Supt. — See Pineville
  HS, PO BOX 310 24870   3-00011
    Mike Brenick, prin.   682-6259
  MS, PO BOX 520 24870   2-01100
    Richard Cook, prin.   682-6296

Ona, AC 304, PC 3, Cabell
Cabell County SD
  Supt. — See Huntington
  Cabell Midland HS   3-00011
    US ROUTE 60 25545   743-7320
    Richard Fillmore, prin.
  MS, 2300 ROUTE 60 25545   3-00100
    Dennis Miller, prin.   743-7320

Paden City, AC 304, PC 5, Wetzel
Wetzel County SD
  Supt. — See New Martinsville
  HS, 201 N 4TH AVE 26159   2-00011
    Warren Grace, prin.   337-2266

Parkersburg, AC 304, PC 8, Wood
Wood County SD, 1210 13TH ST 26101   7-11111
    William Staats, supt.   420-9663
  Parkersburg South SHS   4-00001
    1511 BLIZZARD DR 26101   420-9610
    Timothy Swarr, prin.
  SHS, 2101 DUDLEY AVE 26101   4-00001
    Steven Summers, prin.   420-9595

Wood County Technical Ctr   Vo Tech
    1511 BLIZZARD DR 26101   420-9501
    William Butler, prin.
Blennerhassett JHS   3-00110
    RR 4 BOX 475A 26101   863-3356
    William Miday, prin.
Edison JHS, 1201 HILLCREST ST 26101   3-00110
    John Farley, prin.   420-9525
Hamilton JHS, 3501 CADILLAC DR 26104 3-00110
    James Strader, prin.   420-9547
Vandevender JHS, 918 31ST ST 26104   3-00110
    Gary Kiger, prin.   420-9645
Other Schools — See Vienna, Williamstown

Camden Clark Memorial Hospital   HSP
  717 ANN ST 26101   424-2200
Mountain State College   2-CS
  1508 SPRING ST 26101   485-5487
Ohio Valley College   2-UC
  4501 COLLEGE PKY 26101   800-678-6780
Parkersburg Catholic JSHS   2-00111
  3201 FAIRVIEW AVE 26104   485-6341
    Robert Hattman, prin.
Parkersburg Christian S   2-11111
  1093 CORE RD 26104   485-6654
    Ralph Tisdale, prin.
West Virginia University at Parkersburg 4-CC
  RR 5 BOX 167A 26101   424-8200

Parsons, AC 304, PC 4, Tucker
Tucker County SD   4-11111
  PO BOX 369 26287   478-2771
    Mary Klein, supt.
  Other Schools — See Hambleton

Paw Paw, AC 304, PC 3, Morgan
Morgan County SD
  Supt. — See Berkeley Springs
  JSHS, PO BOX 40 25434   2-00111
    Dennis Beyer, prin.   947-7425

Petersburg, AC 304, PC 4, Grant
Grant County SD   4-11111
  204 JEFFERSON AVE 26847   257-1011
    Raymond Woolsey, supt.
  JSHS, 207 JEFFERSON AVE 26847   3-00110
    David Cooper, prin.   257-1444
  South Branch Vo Ctr   Vo Tech
    401 PIERPONT ST 26847   257-1331
    Robert Sisk, prin.
  Other Schools — See Mount Storm

Peterstown, AC 304, PC 3, Monroe
Monroe County SD
  Supt. — See Union
  JSHS, RR 1 BOX 546 24963   2-00111
    James Gore, prin.   753-4322

Philippi, AC 304, PC 5, Barbour
Barbour County SD   5-11111
  105 S RAILROAD ST 26416   457-3030
    William Phillips, supt.
  Barbour HS, RR 2 BOX 268A 26416   3-00011
    Douglas Schiefelbein, prin.   457-1360
  Barbour County Vo S   Vo Tech
    RR 2 BOX 268 26416   457-4807
    Edward Larry, prin.
  MS, RR 3 26416   2-00100
    Dana Stemple, prin.   457-2999
  Other Schools — See Belington

Alderson-Broaddus College 26416   3-UC
                                     457-1700

Pickens, AC 304, PC 2, Randolph
Randolph County SD
  Supt. — See Elkins
  S, ROUTE 45 26230   1-11111
    James Biggs, prin.   924-5525

Pine Grove, AC 304, PC 3, Wetzel
Wetzel County SD
  Supt. — See New Martinsville
  Valley HS, PO BOX 337 26419   2-00011
    Clarence Groves, prin.   889-3151

Pineville, AC 304, PC 3, Wyoming
Wyoming County SD   6-11111
  PO BOX 69 24874   732-6262
    Frank Blackwell, supt.
  SHS, PO BOX 219 24874   2-00001
    Raymond Rose, prin.   732-6744
  Wyoming County Vo Ctr   Vo Tech
    PO BOX 609 24874   732-8050
    Paul McNair, prin.
  MS, PO BOX 470 24874   2-00110
    Ronnie Ellison, prin.   732-6442
  Other Schools — See Brenton, Mullens, Oceana

Poca, AC 304, PC 4, Putnam
Putnam County SD
  Supt. — See Winfield
  HS, RR 1 BOX 5B 25159   3-00011
    John Cunningham, prin.   755-5001
  MS, PO BOX 647 25159   2-00100
    David Wall, prin.   755-7343

Point Pleasant, AC 304, PC 5, Mason
Mason County SD, 307 8TH ST 25550   5-11111
    Michael Whalen, supt.   675-4540
  SHS, 2312 JACKSON AVE 25550   3-00001
    Rick Northrup, prin.   675-1350
  Mason County Vo S, RR 1 BOX 4A 25550 Vo Tech
    Ed Sommer, prin.   675-3039
  Other Schools — See Ashton, Mason

Princeton, AC 304, PC 6, Mercer
Mercer County SD   7-11111
  1420 HONAKER AVE 24740   487-1551
    Deborah Akers, supt.
  SHS, 1321 STAFFORD DR 24740   3-00001
    Edward Gillespie, prin.   425-8101
  Mercer County Technical Education Ctr Vo Tech
    1397 STAFFORD DR 24740   425-9551
    Janice Terry, prin.
  Glenwood JHS, RR 1 BOX 460 24740   2-00110
    Edward Clark, prin.   425-5970
  JHS, 300 N JOHNSTON ST 24740   3-00110
    (—), prin.   425-7517
  Other Schools — See Athens, Bluefield, Matoaka,
    Montcalm, Oakvale, Spanishburg

Mercer Christian Academy   2-11111
  314 OAKVALE RD 24740   425-5671
    Larry Deeds, prin.

Prosperity, AC 304, PC 4, Raleigh

Greater Beckley Christian S   2-11111
  PO BOX 670 25909   255-1571
    Don Patton, prin.

Rainelle, AC 304, PC 4, Greenbrier

Rainelle Christian Academy   2-11111
  PO BOX 784 25962   438-8874
    Cheryl Altizer, prin.

Ravenswood, AC 304, PC 5, Jackson
Jackson County SD
  Supt. — See Ripley
  HS, 100 PLAZA DR 26164   3-00011
    Fred Aldridge, prin.   273-9301
  MS, 409 SYCAMORE ST 26164   2-00100
    Dan Hunter, prin.   273-5480

Richwood, AC 304, PC 5, Nicholas
Nicholas County SD
  Supt. — See Summersville
  SHS, 1 VALLEY AVE 26261   3-00001
    Dennis Bennett, prin.   846-2591
  JHS, 2 VALLEY AVE 26261   3-00110
    C. Lester, prin.   846-2638

Ridgeley, AC 304, PC 3, Mineral
Mineral County SD
  Supt. — See Keyser
  Frankfort HS, RR 3 BOX 169 26753   3-00011
    Robert Woy, prin.   726-4767
  Frankfort MS, RR 3 BOX 170 26753   3-01100
    Clarence Golden, prin.   726-4339

Ripley, AC 304, PC 5, Jackson
Jackson County SD   6-11111
  PO BOX 770 25271   372-7300
    Carroll Staats, supt.
  HS, CHARLESTON RD 25271   3-00011
    Jack Wiseman, prin.   372-7355
  MS, RR 2 BOX 75A 25271   3-00100
    John Ray, prin.   372-7350
  Other Schools — See Le Roy, Ravenswood

Romney, AC 304, PC 4, Hampshire
Hampshire County SD   5-11111
  46 S HIGH ST 26757   822-3528
    Gerald Mathias, supt.
  Hampshire SHS   3-00011
    HC 74 BOX 87 26757   822-5016
    Richard Hicks, prin.
  JHS, 101 SCHOOL ST 26757   2-00110
    Janet Keister, prin.   822-5014
  Other Schools — See Capon Bridge

West Virginia Schools/Deaf and Blind   HND
  26757

Ronceverte, AC 304, PC 4, Greenbrier
Greenbrier County SD
  Supt. — See Lewisburg
  East Greenbrier JHS   4-00110
    RR 1 BOX 150 24970   647-6498
    Glen McClung, prin.

Saint Albans, AC 304, PC 7, Kanawha
Kanawha County SD
  Supt. — See Charleston
  SHS, 2100 KANAWHA TER 25177   4-00001
    Alvin Anderson, prin.   722-0212
  Hayes JHS, 830 STRAWBERRY RD 25177 3-00110
    Sam Lee, prin.   722-0222
  McKinley JHS   2-00110
    3000 KANAWHA TER 25177   722-0218
    David Gillespie, prin.

Saint Mary's, AC 304, PC 4, Pleasants
Pleasants County SD   4-11111
  202 FAIRVIEW AVE 26170   684-2215
    Harold Carl, supt.
  HS, 1002 2ND ST 26170   2-00011
    Glen DeHaven, prin.   684-2421
  P R T Vo-Tech Ctr, PO BOX 29 26170 Vo Tech
    James Ankrom, prin.   684-2464
  Other Schools — See Belmont

Salem, AC 304, PC 4, Harrison
Harrison County SD
  Supt. — See Clarksburg
  JHS, PO BOX 312 26426   1-00110
    Thomas Connor, prin.   782-1131

Salem-Teikyo University 26426 — 3-UC
782-5011

Scott Depot, AC 304, PC 3, Putnam

Teays Christian S, PO BOX 168 25560 — 2-11111
Tony Etris, prin. — 757-9550

Seth, AC 304, PC 3, Boone
Boone County SD
Supt. — See Madison
Sherman HS, PO BOX AB 25181 — 3-00011
Marc Arvon, prin. — 837-3301
Sherman JHS, PO BOX AA 25181 — 2-00100
John Hudson, prin. — 837-3694

Shady Spring, AC 304, PC 4, Raleigh
Raleigh County SD
Supt. — See Beckley
SHS, PO BOX A 25918 — 3-00001
James Richmond, prin. — 256-4647

Shenandoah Junction, AC 304, PC 2, Jefferson
Jefferson County SD
Supt. — See Charles Town
Jefferson SHS, RR 1 BOX 83 25442 — 4-00001
Jim Carpenter, prin. — 725-8491

Shepherdstown, AC 304, PC 4, Jefferson
Jefferson County SD
Supt. — See Charles Town
JHS, PO BOX 70 25443 — 2-00110
Michael Kessinger, prin. — 876-6120

Shepherd College 25443 — 5-UC
876-2511

Shinnston, AC 304, PC 5, Harrison
Harrison County SD
Supt. — See Clarksburg
Lincoln HS, RR 1 BOX 300 26431 — 3-00011
Jerry Toth, prin. — 592-2248

Sissonville, AC 304, PC 5, Kanawha
Kanawha County SD
Supt. — See Charleston
JHS, 8316 OLD MILL RD 25320 — 3-00110
David Tidquist, prin. — 348-1993

Sistersville, AC 304, PC 4, Tyler
Tyler County SD
Supt. — See Middlebourne
Tyler County HS — 1-00011
1993 SILVER KNIGHT DR 26175 — 758-9000
Charles Heinlein, prin.
Tyler County MS — 1-00100
1993 SILVER KNIGHT DR 26175 — 758-4100
Norris Stombock, prin.

Smithers, AC 304, PC 4, Fayette
Fayette County SD
Supt. — See Fayetteville
Valley HS, PO BOX 457 25186 — 2-00011
James McCune, prin. — 442-8284

Sophia, AC 304, PC 4, Raleigh
Raleigh County SD
Supt. — See Beckley
JHS, PO BOX 338 25921 — 2-00110
Terry Poe, prin. — 683-4392

South Charleston, AC 304, PC 7, Kanawha
Kanawha County SD
Supt. — See Charleston
SHS, 1 EAGLE WAY 25309 — 4-00001
Patricia Petty, prin. — 766-0352
JHS, 400 3RD AVE SW 25303 — 3-00110
Jim Compton, prin. — 348-1918

Spanishburg, AC 304, PC 2, Mercer
Mercer County SD
Supt. — See Princeton
JSHS, PO BOX 7 25922 — 2-00111
Carl Bandy, prin. — 425-7261

Spencer, AC 304, PC 4, Roane
Roane County SD — 5-11111
108 CHAPMAN AVE 25276 — 927-6400
Joe Evans, supt.
Roane County HS — 1-00011
702 CHARLESTON RD 25276 — 927-6420
Ed Westfall, prin.
MS, 102 CHAPMAN AVE 25276 — 3-01100
Stephen Goffreda, prin. — 927-6415
Other Schools — See Walton

Summersville, AC 304, PC 5, Nicholas
Nicholas County SD — 6-11111
400 OLD MAIN DR 26651 — 872-3611
William Grizzell, supt.
Nicholas County SHS — 3-00001
RR 1 BOX 1978 26651 — 872-2141
Harold Brooks, prin.
JHS, 40 GRIZZLEY LN 26651 — 3-00110
Gus Penix, prin. — 872-5092
Other Schools — See Craigsville, Richwood

Sundial, AC 304, PC 2, Raleigh
Raleigh County SD
Supt. — See Beckley
Marsh Fork MS — 2-00100
8801 COAL RIVER RD 25189 — 854-1951
Donald Jarrell, prin.

Surveyor, AC 304, PC 2, Raleigh
Raleigh County SD
Supt. — See Beckley
Trap Hill MS, PO BOX 229 25932 — 2-00100
Tom Harmon, prin. — 934-5392

Sutton, AC 304, PC 3, Braxton
Braxton County SD, 400 4TH ST 26601 — 5-11111
Kenna Seal, supt. — 765-7101
Braxton County HS — 3-00011
200 JERRY BURTON DR 26601 — 765-7331
Ramsey White, prin.
Braxton Co MS — 3-01100
100 CARTER BRAXTON DR 26601 — 765-2644
Virginia Chapman, prin.

Tunnelton, AC 304, PC 2, Preston
Preston County SD
Supt. — See Kingwood
South Preston JHS — 2-00110
PO BOX 400 26444 — 568-2331
Randal Zinn, prin.

Union, AC 304, PC 3, Monroe
Monroe County SD — 4-11111
PO BOX 330 24983 — 772-3094
Lyn Guy, supt.
SHS, SCHOOL ST 24983 — 2-00001
Randall McCutcheon, prin. — 772-3078
Other Schools — See Lindside, Peterstown

Upperglade, AC 304, PC 2, Webster
Webster County SD
Supt. — See Webster Springs
Webster County HS — 3-00011
1 HIGHLAND DR 26266 — 226-5772
D. Bean, prin.

Van, AC 304, PC 3, Boone
Boone County SD
Supt. — See Madison
JSHS, PO BOX 100 25206 — 2-00110
Bennie Pauley, prin. — 245-8237

Vienna, AC 304, PC 7, Wood
Wood County SD
Supt. — See Parkersburg
Jackson JHS, 1601 34TH ST 26105 — 3-00110
Stephen Smith, prin. — 420-9551

Walton, AC 304, PC 2, Roane
Roane County SD
Supt. — See Spencer
MS, PO BOX 8 25286 — 1-01100
Dennis Carpenter, prin. — 577-6734

War, AC 304, PC 4, McDowell
McDowell County SD
Supt. — See Welch
Big Creek HS, PO BOX 278 24892 — 2-00011
Fred Bailey, prin. — 875-2287

Wayne, AC 304, PC 4, Wayne
Wayne County SD, PO BOX 70 25570 — 6-11111
William Carman, supt. — 272-5116
HS, PO BOX 940 25570 — 3-00011
Ferrell Mills, prin. — 272-5639
MS, PO BOX 458 25570 — 3-00100
Nancy Adkins, prin. — 272-3227
Other Schools — See Ceredo, Crum, Fort Gay,
Huntington, Kenova

Webster Springs, AC 304, PC 3, Webster
Webster County SD — 4-11111
315 S MAIN ST 26288 — 847-5638
Ronald Williams, supt.
Other Schools — See Upperglade

Weirton, AC 304, PC 7, Hancock
Hancock County SD
Supt. — See New Cumberland
Weir HS, SINCLAIR AVE 26062 — 3-00011
George Kohelis, prin. — 748-7600
Weir MS, 125 SINCLAIR AVE 26062 — 3-00100
Larry Fernandez, prin. — 748-6080

Madonna HS, 150 MICHAEL AVE 26062 — 2-00011
Robert Gill, prin. — 723-0545
West Virginia Northern Community College — 3-CC
150 PARK AVE 26062

Welch, AC 304, PC 5, McDowell
McDowell County SD — 6-11111
30 CENTRAL AVE 24801 — 436-8441
J. Kenneth Roberts, supt.
Mount View HS, PO BOX 609 24801 — 4-00011
Barbara Hairston, prin. — 436-2939
McDowell County Vo S, PO BOX V 24801 — Vo Tech
Ron Estep, prin. — 436-3488
Welch JHS, 225 MAPLE AVE 24801 — 1-00100
William Slade, prin. — 436-3222
Other Schools — See Iaeger, Northfork, War

Wellsburg, AC 304, PC 5, Brooke
Brooke County SD — 5-11111
1201 PLEASANT AVE 26070 — 737-3481
William Harvey, supt.
Brooke HS, RR 3 BOX 610 26070 — 4-00011
Carl Walker, prin. — 527-1410
MS, 1447 MAIN ST 26070 — 3-01100
Curtis Tarr, prin. — 737-2922
Other Schools — See Follansbee

West Liberty, AC 304, PC 4, Ohio

West Liberty State College — 4-UC
GENERAL DELIVERY 26074 — 336-8000

Weston, AC 304, PC 5, Lewis
Lewis County SD, 322 E 3RD ST 26452 — 5-11111
Joseph Mace, supt. — 269-8300
Lewis County HS — 3-00011
358 COURT AVE 26452 — 269-8315
Thomas King, prin.
Bland MS, 250 COURT AVE 26452 — 3-00100
Marcella Linger, prin. — 269-8325

Westover, AC 304, PC 5, Monongalia
Monongalia County SD
Supt. — See Morgantown
JHS, 200 W PARK AVE 26505 — 2-00100
Jerry Edens, prin. — 291-9300

West Union, AC 304, PC 3, Doddridge
Doddridge County SD — 4-11111
104 SISTERSVILLE PIKE 26456 — 873-2300
Ronald Nichols, prin.
Doddridge County HS — 2-00011
200 STUART ST 26456 — 873-2521
Edward Cumpston, prin.
Doddridge Co MS, RR 2 BOX 35C 26456 — 2-01100
Janice Michaels, prin. — 873-2332

Wheeling, AC 304, PC 8, Ohio
Marshall County SD
Supt. — See Moundsville
Sherrard JHS — 2-00110
1000 FAIRMONT PIKE 26003 — 233-3331
Michael Burk, prin.

Ohio County SD — 6-11111
2203 NATIONAL RD 26003 — 243-0300
H. Jones, supt.
Wheeling Park HS, RR 4 26003 — 4-00011
George Krelis, prin. — 243-0400
Bridge Street MS, 19 JUNIOR AVE 26003 — 2-00100
Raymond Chenoweth, prin. — 243-0381
Triadelphia MS — 2-00100
1636 NATIONAL RD 26003 — 243-0387
Frank Blake, prin.
Warwood MS — 2-00100
1610 WARWOOD AVE 26003 — 243-0394
James Monderine, prin.
MS, 3500 CHAPLINE ST 26003 — 2-00100
Tom Innocenti, prin. — 243-0425

Central Catholic HS, 75 14TH ST 26003 — 2-00011
Joseph Viglietta, prin. — 233-1660
Linsly Institute, 60 KNOX LN 26003 — 2-01111
Reno Diorio, prin. — 233-3260
Mt. De Chantal Vistation Academy — 2-11111
410 WASHINGTON AVE 26003 — 233-3771
George Claffey, prin.
Ohio Valley Medical Center — HSP
2000 EOFF ST 26003 — 234-8294
West Virginia Business College — 2-CS
1052 MAIN ST 26003 — 232-0361
West Virginia Northern Community College — 4-CC
COLLEGE SQ 26003 — 233-5900
Wheeling Hospital — HSP
1 MEDICAL PARK 26003 — 243-3000
Wheeling Jesuit College — 4-UC
316 WASHINGTON AVE 26003 — 243-2233

Whitesville, AC 304, PC 2, Boone
Boone County SD
Supt. — See Madison
JHS, PO BOX 476 25209 — 2-01110
Georgia Price, prin. — 854-1301

Williamson, AC 304, PC 5, Mingo
Mingo County SD — 6-11111
815 ALDERSON ST 25661 — 235-3333
Everett Conn, supt.
SHS, 801 ALDERSON ST 25661 — 2-00001
James Williamson, prin. — 235-2518
JHS, 801 ALDERSON ST 25661 — 2-00110
Don Gillman, prin. — 235-3430
Other Schools — See Delbarton, Gilbert, Kermit,
Lenore, Matewan, Naugatuck

Southern West Virginia Community College — 3-CC
25661

Williamstown, AC 304, PC 5, Wood
Wood County SD
Supt. — See Parkersburg
JSHS, 219 W 5TH ST 26187 — 3-00111
Raymond Davidson, prin. — 464-4000

Winfield, AC 304, PC 4, Putnam
Putnam County SD — 6-11111
PO BOX 47 25213 — 586-0500
Sam Sentelle, supt.
HS, PO BOX 88 25213 — 3-00011
Virgil Rice, prin. — 586-3279
MS, PO BOX 118 25213 — 3-00100
Eugene Anderson, prin. — 586-3072
Other Schools — See Buffalo, Eleanor, Hurricane, Poca

WISCONSIN

STATE DEPARTMENT OF PUBLIC INSTRUCTION
P.O. Box 7841, Madison 53707
(608) 266-1771

Superintendent of Public Instruction	John Benson
Deputy Superintendent	Robert Gomoll
Administrator Handicapped Children & Pupil Services	Juanita Pawlisch
Administrator Instructional Services	Pauline Nikolay
Administrator Management & Budget	Steve Dold
Administrator Financial Resources & Management Services	Bambi Statz

PUBLIC, PRIVATE AND CATHOLIC SECONDARY SCHOOLS

Abbotsford, AC 715, PC 4, Clark
Abbotsford SD, 307 N 4TH AVE 54405 3-11111 223-2387
 Bradley Gillaspie, supt.
HS, 307 N 4TH AVE 54405 2-00011 223-2386
 P. Cassata, prin.
JHS, 307 N 4TH AVE 54405 2-00100 223-2386
 P. Cassata, prin.

Adams, AC 608, PC 4, Adams
Adams-Friendship Area SD 4-11111 339-3213
 PO BOX 346 53910
 Robert Beaver, supt.
Adams-Friendship HS 3-00011 339-3921
 PO BOX 346 53910
 Paul Ochtrup, prin.
Adams-Friendship MS 2-00100 339-4064
 PO BOX 346 53910
 Tom Beversdorf, prin.

Albany, AC 608, PC 4, Green
Albany SD, PO BOX 349 53502 2-11111 862-3225
 Ron Bentley, supt.
HS, PO BOX 349 53502 2-00011 862-3135
 David Botz, prin.
MS, PO BOX 349 53502 1-00100 862-3135
 David Botz, prin.

Algoma, AC 414, PC 5, Kewaunee
Algoma SD, 1715 DIVISION ST 54201 3-11111 487-7001
 Dale Larson, supt.
HS, 1715 DIVISION ST 54201 2-00011 487-7001
 John Kasten, prin.

Alma, AC 608, PC 3, Buffalo
Alma SD 2-11111 685-4416
 S1618 STATE ROAD 35 54610
 Steven Sedlmayr, supt.
JSHS, S1618 STATE ROAD 35 54610 2-00011 685-4416
 Bert Plucker, prin.

Alma Center, AC 715, PC 2, Jackson
Alma Center SD, PO BOX 38 54611 3-11111 964-8271
 Randall Stanley, supt.
Lincoln HS, PO BOX 38 54611 2-00011 964-5311
 Craig McIntosh, prin.
Lincoln JHS, PO BOX 38 54611 1-00100 964-5311
 Craig McIntosh, prin.

Almond, AC 715, PC 2, Portage
Almond-Bancroft SD 2-11111 366-7331
 PO BOX 130 54909
 Ed Poock, supt.
HS, PO BOX 130 54909 2-00011 366-2941
 Corinn Solsrud, prin.

Altoona, AC 715, PC 6, Eau Claire
Altoona SD, 1903 BARTLETT AVE 54720 4-11111 839-6032
 A. Adair, supt.
HS, 711 7TH ST W 54720 2-00011 839-6031
 Barry Remmel, prin.
MS, 1903 BARTLETT AVE 54720 2-01100 839-6030
 Joyce Simmons, prin.

Amery, AC 715, PC 5, Polk
Amery SD, 115 BIRCH TER N 54001 4-11111 268-9771
 Raymond Norsted, supt.
HS, 555 MINNEAPOLIS AVE S 54001 2-00011 268-9771
 John Wyatt, prin.
MS, 501 MINNEAPOLIS AVE S 54001 2-00100 268-9771
 Patricia Graves, prin.

Amherst, AC 715, PC 3, Portage
Tomorrow River SD 3-11111 824-5521
 357 N MAIN ST 54406
 Joseph Reed, supt.
HS, 357 N MAIN ST 54406 2-00011 824-5522
 Robert Lane, prin.
JHS, 357 N MAIN ST 54406 2-00100 824-5522
 Robert Lane, prin.

Antigo, AC 715, PC 6, Langlade
Antigo SD, 120 S DORR ST 54409 5-11111 627-4355
 Wayne Haasl, supt.
SHS, 815 7TH AVE 54409 3-00001 623-7611
 Ken Ogi, prin.
JHS, 815 7TH AVE 54409 3-00110 623-4173
 Jiles Cole, prin.

Appleton, AC 414, PC 8, Outagamie
Appleton Area SD 7-11111 832-6126
 PO BOX 2019 54913
 Jerry Patterson, supt.
Appleton East SHS 4-00001 832-6200
 2121 E EMMERS DR 54915
 Daryl Herrick, prin.
Appleton West SHS 4-00001 832-4100
 610 N BADGER AVE 54914
 Keith Fuchs, prin.
Einstein JHS, 324 E FLORIDA AVE 54911 3-00110 832-6240
 Gail Bowers, prin.
Madison JHS 3-00110 832-6276
 2020 S CARPENTER ST 54915
 Robert Simon, prin.
Roosevelt JHS 3-00110 832-6294
 318 E BREWSTER ST 54911
 Terrence Werner, prin.
Wilson JHS, 225 N BADGER AVE 54914 3-00110 832-6226
 Patrick O'Reilly, prin.

Fox Valley Lutheran HS 3-00011 739-4441
 2626 N ONEIDA ST 54911
 Rev. Plitzuweit, prin.
Fox Valley Technical College 5-CC 735-5731
 PO BOX 2277 54913
Lawrence University 4-UC 739-3681
 PO BOX 599 54912
St. Elizabeth Hospital HSP 738-2015
 1506 S ONEIDA ST 54915
St. Joseph MS 2-00100 730-8849
 323 W LAWRENCE ST 54911
 Anthony Abts, prin.
Xavier HS 2-00011 733-6632
 1600 W PROSPECT AVE 54914
 Matt Reynebeau, prin.

Arcadia, AC 608, PC 4, Trempealeau
Arcadia SD, 308 E MAIN ST 54612 3-11111 323-3315
 Howard Sims, supt.
HS, 308 E MAIN ST 54612 2-00011 323-3334
 Paul Vine, prin.

Argyle, AC 608, PC 3, Lafayette
Argyle SD, PO BOX 1 53504 2-11111 543-3318
 Thomas Tuttle, supt.
JSHS, PO BOX 1 53504 2-00011 543-3314
 Verla Schumacher, prin.

Arkansaw, AC 715, PC 2, Pepin
Durand SD
 Supt. — See Durand
MS, RR 2 BOX EEE 54721 2-00100 285-5315
 Eugene Koci, prin.

Ashland, AC 715, PC 6, Ashland
Ashland SD, 120 MAIN ST E 54806 4-11111 682-7080
 Stephen Kelly, supt.
HS, 1900 BEASER AVE 54806 3-00011 682-7089
 William Davis, prin.
MS, 203 11TH ST E 54806 2-00100 682-7087
 Mary Podlesny, prin.

Northland College 3-UC 682-4531
 1411 ELLIS AVE 54806

Athens, AC 715, PC 3, Marathon
Athens SD, PO BOX F 54411 3-11111 257-7511
 Robert Clinton, supt.
HS, PO BOX F 54411 2-00011 257-7511
 Lance Alwin, prin.

MS, PO BOX F 54411 1-00100 257-7511
 Lance Alwin, prin.

Auburndale, AC 715, PC 3, Wood
Auburndale SD, PO BOX 190 54412 3-11111 652-2117
 Gary Rooney, supt.
HS, PO BOX 190 54412 2-00011 652-2115
 Bill Slough, prin.

Augusta, AC 715, PC 4, Eau Claire
Augusta SD, RR 2 54722 3-11111 286-2236
 Frederick Brown, supt.
HS, RR 2 BOX 67 54722 2-00011 286-2291
 Ken Stahl, prin.

Baldwin, AC 715, PC 4, St. Croix
Baldwin-Woodville Area SD 4-11111 684-3411
 780 MAIN ST #2 54002
 Duane Lones, supt.
Baldwin-Woodville HS 2-00011 684-3321
 1000 13TH AVE 54002
 Howard Ott, prin.
Other Schools – See Woodville

Balsam Lake, AC 715, PC 3, Polk
Unity SD, PO BOX 307 54810 4-11111 825-3515
 Glen Schimke, supt.
Unity HS, PO BOX 307 54810 2-00011 825-2131
 William Alleva, prin.
Unity MS, PO BOX 307 54810 2-00100 825-2101
 Thomas Witasek, prin.

Bangor, AC 608, PC 4, La Crosse
Bangor SD, PO BOX 99 54614 3-11111 486-2332
 Steve Lang, supt.
JSHS, 401 14TH AVE S 54614 2-00111 486-2331
 Roger Foegen, prin.

Baraboo, AC 608, PC 6, Sauck
Baraboo SD, 101 2ND AVE 53913 4-11111 355-3950
 Anthony Kujawa, supt.
SHS, 1201 DRAPER ST 53913 3-00001 355-3940
 John Young, prin.
JHS, 1531 DRAPER ST 53913 3-00110 355-3930
 Gwynne Peterson, prin.

University of Wisconsin Center 2-UC 356-8351
 1006 CONNIE RD 53913

Barneveld, AC 608, PC 3, Iowa
Barneveld SD, PO BOX 98 53507 2-11111 924-4711
 Gwen O'Cull, supt.
HS, PO BOX 98 53507 1-00011 924-4711
 (—), prin.

Barron, AC 715, PC 5, Barron
Barron Area SD 4-11111 537-5612
 100 W RIVER AVE 54812
 Gerald Christianson, supt.
HS, 1050 E WOODLAND AVE 54812 2-00011 537-5627
 Kirk Haugestuen, prin.
Riverview MS, 135 W RIVER AVE 54812 2-01100 537-5641
 Ron Berg, prin.

Bayfield, AC 715, PC 3, Bayfield
Bayfield SD, PO BOX 5001 54814 2-11111 779-3201
 Guy Habeck, supt.
HS 54814 2-00011 779-5666
 Terrence Bauer, prin.
MS 54814 2-00100 779-5851
 Mary Peterson, prin.

Beaver Dam, AC 414, PC 7, Dodge
Beaver Dam SD 5-11111 887-7131
 705 MCKINLEY ST 53916
 Richard Fitzpatrick, supt.
SHS, 500 GOULD ST 53916 3-00001 885-7324
 Kim Hussli, prin.
JHS, 108 4TH ST 53916 3-00110 885-7365
 Barbara Link, prin.

495

Moraine Park Technical College — 3-CC
700 GOULD ST 53916 — 887-1101
Wayland Academy — 2-00111
101 N UNIVERSITY AVE 53916 — 885-3373
William Ellis, prin.

Belleville, AC 608, PC 4, Dane
Belleville SD, 101 S GRANT ST 53508 — 3-11111
Darrell Fitch, supt. — 424-3315
JSHS, 101 S GRANT ST 53508 — 2-00111
Rodger Moe, prin. — 424-3371

Belmont, AC 608, PC 3, Lafayette
Belmont Community SD — 2-11111
PO BOX 348 53510 — 762-5131
Johannus Benkers, supt.
HS, PO BOX 348 53510 — 2-00011
Eugene Hawkinson, prin. — 762-5131

Beloit, AC 608, PC 8, Rock
Beloit-Turner SD — 4-11111
1231 INMAN PKY 53511 — 364-6372
Charles Melvin, supt.
Turner HS, 1231 INMAN PKY 53511 — 2-00011
Elizabeth Cabanowski, prin. — 364-6370
Turner MS, 1237 INMAN PKY 53511 — 2-00100
Andrew Toutloff, prin. — 364-6367

Beloit SD, 1633 KEELER AVE 53511 — 6-11111
Rosa Smith, supt. — 364-6000
Memorial SHS, 1225 4TH ST 53511 — 4-00001
James Fitzpatrick, prin. — 364-6140
Aldrich JHS — 3-00110
1859 NORTHGATE DR 53511 — 364-6120
William Henning, prin.
McNeel JHS, 1524 FREDERICK ST 53511 — 3-00110
Virgil Wenger, prin. — 364-6130

Beloit Catholic HS — 2-00011
1221 HENRY AVE 53511 — 362-8931
William Gifford, prin.
Beloit College — 4-UC
700 COLLEGE ST 53511 — 363-2201
Beloit Memorial Hospital — HSP
1969 W HART RD 53511 — 364-5011

Benton, AC 608, PC 3, Lafayette
Benton SD, PO BOX 7 53803 — 2-11111
Fred Sams, supt. — 759-3581
JSHS, PO BOX 7 53803 — 2-00011
James Sebanc, prin. — 759-4002

Berlin, AC 414, PC 6, Green Lake
Berlin Area SD — 4-11111
295 E MARQUETTE ST 54923 — 361-2004
William Anderson, supt.
HS, 289 E HURON ST 54923 — 3-00011
Kenneth Keenlance, prin. — 361-2000
Clay MS, 259 E MARQUETTE ST 54923 — 2-00100
Diane Toraason, prin. — 361-2441

Birchwood, AC 715, PC 2, Washburn
Birchwood SD, 300 S WILSON ST 54817 — 2-11111
James Connell, supt. — 354-3471
HS, 300 S WILSON ST 54817 — 1-00011
John Osterloth, prin. — 354-3471

Black River Falls, AC 715, PC 5, Jackson
Black River Falls SD — 4-11111
301 N 4TH ST 54615 — 284-4357
Dennis Richards, supt.
Black River Falls HS — 2-00011
1200 PIERCE ST 54615 — 284-4324
Roger Sands, prin.
Black River Falls MS — 2-00100
1202 PIERCE ST 54615 — 284-5315
Warren Rosin, prin.

Blair, AC 608, PC 4, Trempealeau
Blair-Taylor SD, 219 S MAIN ST 54616 — 3-11111
Guy Leavitt, supt. — 989-2881
Blair-Taylor HS, 219 S MAIN ST 54616 — 2-00011
Donald Annis, prin. — 989-2525
Other Schools – See Taylor

Blanchardville, AC 608, PC 3, Lafayette
Pecatonica SD, PO BOX 117 53516 — 2-11111
Nancy Hendrickson, supt. — 523-4248
Pecatonica JSHS, PO BOX 117 53516 — 2-01111
Jerry Casselberry, prin. — 523-4285

Bloomer, AC 715, PC 5, Chippewa
Bloomer SD, 1310 17TH AVE 54724 — 4-11111
Pauline Roll, supt. — 568-2800
HS, 1310 17TH AVE 54724 — 2-00011
Vernon Verkuilen, prin. — 568-5300
MS, 1325 15TH AVE 54724 — 2-00100
Douglas Martin, prin. — 568-1025

Bloomington, AC 608, PC 3, Grant
Bloomington SD, 545 MILL ST 53804 — 2-11111
John Cooper, supt. — 994-2711
HS, 545 MILL ST 53804 — 2-00011
John Cooper, prin. — 994-2711

Blue River, AC 608, PC 2, Grant
Riverdale SD
Supt. — See Muscoda
Riverdale MS, PO BOX 66 53518 — 2-00100
Marsha Spees, prin. — 537-2468

Bonduel, AC 715, PC 4, Shawano
Bonduel SD, 400 E GREEN BAY ST 54107 — 3-11111
Peter Behnke, supt. — 758-2148

HS, 400 E GREEN BAY ST 54107 — 2-00011
Wayne Carroll, prin. — 758-2148
MS, 400 E GREEN BAY ST 54107 — 2-00100
Connie Rutledge, prin. — 758-2148

Boscobel, AC 608, PC 5, Grant
Boscobel SD — 4-11111
903 WISCONSIN AVE 53805 — 375-4164
(—), supt.
HS, 300 BRINDLEY ST 53805 — 2-00011
Patricia Roseliep, prin. — 375-4161
MS, 300 BRINDLEY ST 53805 — 2-00100
Patricia Roseliep, prin. — 375-4161

Bowler, AC 715, PC 2, Shawano
Bowler SD, PO BOX 8 54416 — 3-11111
William Trautt, supt. — 793-4101
JSHS, PO BOX 8 54416 — 2-00111
Curtis Brend, prin. — 793-4101

Boyceville, AC 715, PC 3, Dunn
Boyceville Community SD — 3-11111
RR 2 BOX 500 54725 — 643-4311
Delsea Boley, supt.
JSHS, RR 2 BOX 500 54725 — 2-00111
Alan Hackbarth, prin. — 643-4321

Brandon, AC 414, PC 3, Fond du Lac
Rosendale-Brandon SD
Supt. — See Rosendale
MS, 200 W BOWEN 53919 — 2-00100
Joseph Cramer, prin. — 346-2915

Brillion, AC 414, PC 5, Calumet
Brillion SD, 315 S MAIN ST 54110 — 3-11111
Jack Lewis, supt. — 756-2368
HS, 315 S MAIN ST 54110 — 2-00011
Jacqueline Ackerman, prin. — 756-2166
MS, 315 S MAIN ST 54110 — 1-00100
Carol Lamp, prin. — 756-2166

Brodhead, AC 608, PC 5, Green
Brodhead SD, PO BOX 258 53520 — 4-11111
Steven Ashmore, supt. — 897-2141
HS, PO BOX 258 53520 — 2-00011
Jerry Rosso, prin. — 897-2155
MS, PO BOX 258 53520 — 2-01100
Heidi Lyght-Smith, prin. — 897-2184

Brookfield, AC 414, PC 8, Waukesha
Elmbrook SD, 13780 HOPE ST 53005 — 6-11111
David Cronin, supt. — 781-3030
Central HS, 16900 GEBHARDT RD 53005 — 4-00011
Margaret Janssen, prin. — 785-3910
East HS, 3305 LILLY RD 53005 — 3-00011
Theodore Carlsen, prin. — 781-3500
Center HS, 13780 HOPE ST 53005 — Vo Tech
(—), prin. — 781-3030
Other Schools – See Elm Grove

Brookfield Academy — 2-11111
3460 N BROOKFIELD RD 53045 — 783-3200
Robert Solsrud, prin.

Brown Deer, AC 414, PC 7, Milwaukee
Brown Deer SD, 8200 N 60TH ST 53223 — 4-11111
Kenneth Moe, supt. — 354-9437
HS, 8060 N 60TH ST 53223 — 3-00011
Charles Hayes, prin. — 354-4180
MS, 5757 W DEAN RD 53223 — 3-01100
Charles Radtke, prin. — 354-7878

Bruce, AC 715, PC 3, Rusk
Bruce SD, PO BOX 308 54819 — 3-11111
Lee Paul, supt. — 868-2533
HS, PO BOX 308 54819 — 2-00011
William Abeng, prin. — 868-2585

Brussels, AC 414, PC 2, Door
Southern Door SD — 4-11111
8240 STATE HIGHWAY 57 54204 — 825-7311
Joseph Innis, supt.
Southern Door HS — 2-00011
8240 STATE HIGHWAY 57 54204 — 825-7333
Lois Mahaffey, prin.
Southern Door MS — 2-01100
8240 STATE HIGHWAY 57 54204 — 825-7321
Dyan Pasono, prin.

Catholic Central HS — 2-00011
148 MCHENRY ST 53105 — 763-1510
Janice Matulis, prin.

Butternut, AC 715, PC 2, Ashland
Butternut SD, PO BOX 247 54514 — 2-11111
Larry Swanson, supt. — 769-3434
HS, PO BOX 247 54514 — 2-00011
(—), prin. — 769-3434

Cadott, AC 715, PC 4, Chippewa
Cadott Community SD — 4-11111
PO BOX 310 54727 — 839-2880
Robert Butterfield, supt.
HS, PO BOX 310 54727 — 2-00011
Martin Schultz, prin. — 839-6027

JHS, PO BOX 310 54727 — 2-00100
Martin Schultz, prin. — 839-6027

Cambria, AC 414, PC 3, Columbia
Cambria-Friesland SD — 3-11111
410 E EDGEWATER ST 53923 — 348-5548
Jeff Walker, supt.
Cambria-Friesland HS — 2-00011
410 E EDGEWATER ST 53923 — 348-5135
Karen Kritz, prin.
Cambria-Friesland MS — 2-01100
410 E EDGEWATER ST 53923 — 348-5135
Karen Kritz, prin.

Cambridge, AC 608, PC 3, Dane
Cambridge SD, PO BOX 27 53523 — 3-11111
Monte Hottmann, supt. — 423-4345
HS, PO BOX 27 53523 — 2-00011
James Lumb, prin. — 423-3262
Nikolay MS, PO BOX 27 53523 — 2-00100
James Lumb, prin. — 423-3262

Cameron, AC 715, PC 4, Barron
Cameron SD, PO BOX 378 54822 — 3-11111
Howard Hanson, supt. — 458-4560
HS, SOUTH ST 54822 — 2-00011
Michael Schoch, prin. — 458-4510

Campbellsport, AC 414, PC 4, Fond du Lac
Campbellsport SD — 4-11111
114 SHEBOYGAN ST 53010 — 533-8381
Joseph Bertone, supt.
HS, 114 SHEBOYGAN ST 53010 — 2-00011
David LaBorde, prin. — 533-4811

Casco, AC 414, PC 3, Kewaunee
Luxemburg-Casco SD
Supt. — See Luxemburg
Luxemburg-Casco JHS — 2-00110
619 CHURCH AVE 54205 — 837-2205
John LeClair, prin.

Cashton, AC 608, PC 3, Monroe
Cashton SD, PO BOX 129 54619 — 3-11111
M. Healy, supt. — 654-5131
JSHS, PO BOX 129 54619 — 2-00111
Norbert Resheske, prin. — 654-5131

Cassville, AC 608, PC 4, Grant
Cassville SD, PO BOX 660 53806 — 2-11111
Robert Klauer, supt. — 725-5116
JSHS, PO BOX 660 53806 — 2-00111
Jim Reed, prin. — 725-5116

Catawba, AC 715, PC 2, Price
Phillips SD
Supt. — See Phillips
MS, 102 GRUBER ST 54515 — 1-01100
Diane Willett, prin. — 474-3368

Cazenovia, AC 608, PC 2, Richland
Weston SD, E2511 COUNTY RD S 53924 — 2-11111
Harold Justman, supt. — 986-2151
Weston HS, E2511 COUNTY RD S 53924 — 2-00011
Jack Drew, prin. — 986-2151
Weston MS, E2511 COUNTY RD S 53924 — 1-01100
Jack Drew, prin. — 986-2151

Cedarburg, AC 414, PC 6, Ozaukee
Cedarburg SD — 4-11111
W68N611 EVERGREEN BLVD 53012 — 375-5208
Gary Compton, supt.
HS, W68N611 EVERGREEN BLVD 53012 — 3-00011
Jay Grieger, prin. — 375-5200
Webster MS — 3-01100
W75N624 WAUWATOSA RD 53012 — 375-5255
Suzanne Rapp, prin.

Cedar Grove, AC 414, PC 4, Sheboygan
Cedar Grove-Belgium SD — 3-11111
50 W UNION AVE 53013 — 668-8518
Roger Klumb, supt.
JSHS, 50 W UNION AVE 53013 — 2-00111
Ron Sternard, prin. — 668-8518

Chetek, AC 715, PC 4, Barron
Chetek SD, 1201 6TH ST 54728 — 4-11111
Robert Rykal, supt. — 924-3136
HS, 1001 KNAPP ST 54728 — 2-00011
Duane Fjelstad, prin. — 924-3136
MS, 1001 KNAPP ST 54728 — 2-00100
Leo Eckerman, prin. — 924-3136

Chilton, AC 414, PC 5, Calumet
Chilton SD, 509 SCHOOL CT 53014 — 4-11111
W. Demaster, supt. — 849-2358
HS, 509 SCHOOL CT 53014 — 2-00011
Timothy Schaid, prin. — 849-2358
MS, 421 COURT ST 53014 — 2-00100
Robert Knadle, prin. — 849-9152

Chippewa Falls, AC 715, PC 7, Chippewa
Chippewa Falls Area SD — 5-11111
1130 MILES ST 54729 — 726-2417
Larry Annett, supt.
SHS, 735 TERRILL ST 54729 — 3-00011
Thomas Schmelzle, prin. — 726-2406
JHS, 750 TROPICANA BLVD 54729 — 4-00110
Thomas Welch, prin. — 726-2400

McDonnell Central HS — 2-00011
1316 BEL AIR BLVD 54729 — 723-9126
Michael Sullivan, prin.
Notre Dame MS, 22 S PRAIRIE ST 54729 — 2-00100
Nancy Klein, prin. — 723-4777

Clayton, AC 715, PC 2, Polk
Clayton SD, PO BOX A 54004 — 2-11111
Maurice Veilleux, supt. — 948-2165
HS, PO BOX A 54004 — 1-00011
John Haugen, prin. — 948-2163

Clear Lake, AC 715, PC 3, Polk
Clear Lake SD, PO BOX 428 54005 — 3-11111
Ray Smith, supt. — 263-2114
HS, PO BOX 428 54005 — 2-00011
Scott Clifton, prin. — 263-2113
MS, PO BOX 428 54005 — 2-00100
Scott Clifton, prin. — 263-2113

Cleveland, AC 414, PC 4, Manitowoc

Lakeshore Technical College — 3-CC
1290 NORTH AVE 53015 — 458-4183

Clinton, AC 608, PC 4, Rock
Clinton Community SD — 4-11111
PO BOX 566 53525 — 676-2223
Robert Jensen, supt.
HS, PO BOX 566 53525 — 2-00011
Stephan Cass, prin. — 676-2223
MS, PO BOX 559 53525 — 2-01100
Rebecca Nodorft, prin. — 676-2275

Clintonville, AC 715, PC 5, Waupaca
Clintonville SD, 26 9TH ST 54929 — 4-11111
Jerald Schoenike, supt. — 823-7200
SHS, 255 N MAIN ST 54929 — 2-00001
Robert Tomczyk, prin. — 823-7215
JHS, 26 9TH ST 54929 — 2-00110
Richard King, prin. — 823-7245

Colby, AC 715, PC 4, Clark
Colby SD, PO BOX 139 54421 — 4-11111
Mel Lightner, supt. — 223-2301
JSHS, PO BOX 110 54421 — 2-00111
John Hocking, prin. — 223-2338

Coleman, AC 414, PC 3, Marinette
Coleman SD, PO BOX 259 54112 — 4-11111
Leslie Larmour, supt. — 897-4011
HS, PO BOX 259 54112 — 2-00011
Theodore Verges, prin. — 897-2291

Colfax, AC 715, PC 4, Dunn
Colfax SD, 601 UNIVERSITY AVE 54730 — 3-11111
Lee Bjurquist, supt. — 962-3773
HS, 601 UNIVERSITY AVE 54730 — 2-00011
Ronald Fandry, prin. — 962-3155

Columbus, AC 414, PC 5, Columbia
Columbus SD, 200 W SCHOOL ST 53925 — 4-10111
Timothy Gavigan, supt. — 623-5950
HS, 1164 FARNHAM ST 53925 — 2-00011
Tom Antioho, prin. — 623-5956
MS, 400 S DICKASON BLVD 53925 — 2-00100
Wayne Bobholz, prin. — 623-5954

Wisconsin Academy — 2-00011
N2355 DU BORG RD 53925 — 623-3300
Steve Brown, prin.

Cornell, AC 715, PC 4, Chippewa
Cornell SD, PO BOX 517 54732 — 3-11111
Thomas Wilkins, supt. — 239-6463
JSHS, PO BOX 517 54732 — 2-00111
Vita Sherry, prin. — 239-6464

Crandon, AC 715, PC 4, Forest
Crandon SD, PO BOX 310 54520 — 3-11111
Robert Jaeger, supt. — 478-3339
HS, PO BOX 310 54520 — 2-00011
Erhardt Van Duser, prin. — 478-3713
JHS, PO BOX 310 54520 — 2-00100
John Gruber, prin. — 478-3713

Crivitz, AC 715, PC 3, Marinette
Crivitz SD, PO BOX 130 54114 — 3-11111
Al Brown, supt. — 854-2721
HS, 802 HALL HAY ST 54114 — 2-00011
Nicholas Lakari, prin. — 854-7492
MS, 802 HALL HAY ST 54114 — 2-00100
Eugene Chapman, prin. — 854-7491

Cuba City, AC 608, PC 4, Grant
Cuba City SD, 101 N SCHOOL ST 53807 — 3-11111
Jack Landes, supt. — 744-2847
HS, 101 N SCHOOL ST 53807 — 2-00011
John Doyle, prin. — 744-8888

Cudahy, AC 414, PC 7, Milwaukee
Cudahy SD, 2915 E RAMSEY AVE 53110 — 5-11111
John Watson, supt. — 769-2300
HS, 4950 S LAKE DR 53110 — 3-00011
Peter Derubeis, prin. — 769-2321
MS, 5530 S BARLAND AVE 53110 — 3-00100
Neil Mitchel, prin. — 769-2356

Cumberland, AC 715, PC 4, Barron
Cumberland SD, PO BOX 67 54829 — 4-11111
Merwin Moen, supt. — 822-4611
HS, PO BOX 67 54829 — 2-00011
Robert Nugent, prin. — 822-2251
MS, PO BOX 67 54829 — 2-00100
Elizabeth Rhyner, prin. — 822-2251

Darlington, AC 608, PC 4, Lafayette
Darlington Community SD — 3-11111
11838 CENTER HILL RD 53530 — 776-4001
Dennis Pratt, supt.
HS, 11838 CENTER HILL RD 53530 — 2-00011
Dave Chellevold, prin. — 776-4001

Deerfield, AC 608, PC 4, Dane
Deerfield Community SD — 3-11111
300 SIMONSON BLVD 53531 — 764-8261
Edward Van Ravenstein, supt.
HS, 300 SIMONSON BLVD 53531 — 2-00011
Linda Duncan, prin. — 764-5431
MS, 300 SIMONSON BLVD 53531 — 2-00100
Linda Duncan, prin. — 764-5431

De Forest, AC 608, PC 5, Dane
De Forest Area SD — 4-11111
520 E HOLUM ST 53532 — 846-6500
Jim Stillman, supt.
HS, 815 JEFFERSON ST 53532 — 3-00011
Gary Einerson, supt. — 846-6600
MS, PO BOX 496 53532 — 3-00100
Margaret Reinert, prin. — 846-6560

Delafield, AC 414, PC 6, Waukesha

St. Johns Military Academy — 2-00111
1101 N GENESEE ST 53018 — 646-3311
David Williams, prin.

Delavan, AC 414, PC 6, Walworth
Delavan-Darien SD — 4-11111
324 BELOIT ST 53115 — 728-2642
James Ticknor, supt.
Delavan-Darien HS — 3-00011
150 CUMMING ST 53115 — 728-3451
Ronald Miller, prin.
Phoenix MS, 414 BELOIT ST 53115 — 3-01100
Michael Nummerdor, prin. — 728-6366

Wisconsin School for the Deaf — HND
309 W WALWORTH AVE 53115

Denmark, AC 414, PC 4, Brown
Denmark SD, 450 N WALL ST 54208 — 4-11111
David Ewald, supt. — 863-2176
HS, 450 N WALL ST 54208 — 2-00011
Leroy Meles, prin. — 863-2176
JHS, 450 N WALL ST 54208 — 2-00100
James Mostek, prin. — 863-8611

De Pere, AC 414, PC 7, Brown
De Pere SD, 1700 CHICAGO ST 54115 — 4-11111
Richard Yenchesky, supt. — 337-1020
HS, 1700 CHICAGO ST 54115 — 3-00011
Donald Pierce, prin. — 337-1020
MS, 615 S BROADWAY 54115 — 3-01100
William Howes, prin. — 337-1024

West De Pere SD — 4-11111
1155 WESTWOOD DR 54115 — 337-1090
Randy Freese, supt.
West De Pere HS, 665 GRANT ST 54115 — 3-00011
Mark Sheedy, prin. — 337-1080
West De Pere JHS, 1177 S 9TH ST 54115 — 2-00100
Kathy Brockdorf, prin. — 337-1090

St. Norbert College — 4-UC
100 GRANT ST 54115 — 800-236-4878

De Soto, AC 608, PC 2, Crawford
De Soto Area SD, PO BOX 7 54624 — 3-11111
Charles Oberstar, supt. — 648-3620
HS, PO BOX 7 54624 — 2-00011
Martin Kirchhof, prin. — 648-3311
JHS, PO BOX 7 54624 — 1-00100
Jay Joppa, prin. — 648-3311

Dodgeville, AC 608, PC 5, Iowa
Dodgeville SD — 4-11111
400 N JOHNSON ST 53533 — 935-3910
David Westhoff, supt.
HS, 912 W CHAPEL ST 53533 — 2-00011
Jeff Athey, prin. — 935-3307
MS, 325 W CHAPEL ST 53533 — 2-00100
Bruce Rundle, prin. — 935-3388

Dousman, AC 414, PC 4, Waukesha
Kettle Moraine SD
Supt. — See Wales
Kettle Moraine MS — 3-00100
301 E OTTAWA AVE 53118 — 965-6500
Charlotte Hall, prin.

Drummond, AC 715, PC 2, Bayfield
Drummond SD, PO BOX 40 54832 — 2-11111
Tom McMullen, supt. — 739-6231
HS, PO BOX 40 54832 — 2-00011
Daniel Vernetti, prin. — 739-6231
JHS, PO BOX 40 54832 — 1-00100
Daniel Vernetti, prin. — 739-6231

Durand, AC 715, PC 4, Pepin
Durand SD, 604 7TH AVE E 54736 — 4-11111
Terry Olson, supt. — 672-8919
HS, 604 7TH AVE E 54736 — 2-00011
Stephen Schiell, prin. — 672-8917
Other Schools – See Arkansaw

Eagle River, AC 715, PC 4, Vilas
Northland Pines SD — 4-11111
PO BOX 847 54521 — 479-6487
Jann Peterson, supt.
Northland Pines HS — 2-00011
PO BOX 1269 54521 — 479-4473
Robert Rickard, prin.
Northland Pines MS — 2-00100
PO BOX 1028 54521 — 479-6479
Thomas Thielke, prin.

East Troy, AC 414, PC 5, Walworth
East Troy Community SD — 4-11111
PO BOX 915 53120 — 642-6710
Don Kangas, supt.
HS, PO BOX 137 53120 — 3-00011
Susan Alexander, prin. — 642-6761
MS, PO BOX 587 53120 — 2-00100
L. Patrick Showalter, prin. — 642-6740

Eau Claire, AC 715, PC 8, Eau Claire
Eau Claire Area SD, 500 MAIN ST 54701 — 7-11111
Lee Hansen, supt. — 833-3465
Memorial SHS, 2225 KEITH ST 54701 — 4-00001
Brenda Finn, prin. — 834-8191
North SHS, 2700 MERCURY AVE 54703 — 4-00001
John Bowman, prin. — 834-2071
Delong JHS, 2000 VINE ST 54703 — 4-00110
Gregg Butler, prin. — 834-5376
South MS, 2115 MITSCHER AVE 54701 — 4-00100
Bruce Emberson, prin. — 832-8484

Chippewa Valley Technical College — 4-CC
620 W CLAIREMONT AVE 54701 — 833-6200
Eau Claire Academy — 2-01111
PO BOX 1168 54702 — 834-6681
Dave Hoban, prin.
Luther Hospital — HSP
310 CHESTNUT ST 54703 — 839-3323
Regis HS, 2100 FENWICK AVE 54701 — 2-00011
Fr. Stoetzel, prin. — 835-5141
Sacred Heart Hospital — HSP
900 W CLAIREMONT AVE 54701 — 839-4131
St. Patrick S, 322 FULTON ST 54703 — 1-00100
Robert Fortener, prin. — 835-8931
University of Wisconsin 54701 — 6-UC
836-2326

Edgar, AC 715, PC 4, Marathon
Edgar SD, PO BOX 196 54426 — 3-11111
Barkley Anderson, supt. — 352-2351
HS, PO BOX 196 54426 — 2-00011
Mark Lacke, prin. — 352-2352
MS, PO BOX 198 54426 — 2-00100
Robert Christianson, prin. — 352-2727

Edgerton, AC 608, PC 5, Rock
Edgerton SD, 200 ELM HIGH DR 53534 — 4-11111
Norman Fjelstad, supt. — 884-9402
HS, 200 ELM HIGH DR 53534 — 3-00011
Jeffrey Gibson, prin. — 884-9402
MS, 300 ELM HIGH DR 53534 — 2-00100
Larry Miller, prin. — 884-9402

Oaklawn Academy — 2-01100
432 LIQUORI RD 53534 — 884-3428
Fr. Moylan, prin.

Elcho, AC 715, PC 3, Langlade
Elcho SD, PO BOX 800 54428 — 2-11111
Joseph Whitcomb, supt. — 275-3205
HS 54428 — 2-00011
Charles Kellstrom, prin. — 275-3225

Elkhart Lake, AC 414, PC 4, Sheboygan
Elkhart Lake-Glenbeulah SD — 3-11111
201 N LINCOLN 53020 — 876-3381
David Magar, supt.
HS, PO BOX K 53020 — 2-00011
Richard Anderson, prin. — 876-3381

Elkhorn, AC 414, PC 6, Walworth
Elkhorn Area SD — 4-11111
3 N JACKSON ST 53121 — 723-3160
Tony Serpe, supt.
Elkhorn Area HS — 2-00011
482 E GENEVA ST 53121 — 723-4920
Keith Rodda, prin.
Elkhorn Area MS — 2-00100
3 N JACKSON ST 53121 — 723-6800
Gary Baumann, prin.

Gateway Technical College — 3-CC
400 COUNTY ROAD H 53121 — 723-5390

Elk Mound, AC 715, PC 3, Dunn
Elk Mound Area SD — 3-11111
405 UNIVERSITY AVE 54739 — 879-5066
William Vincent, supt.
HS, 405 UNIVERSITY AVE 54739 — 2-00011
Jay Silvernail, prin. — 879-5521
MS, 302 UNIVERSITY AVE 54739 — 2-00100
Delphine Rogalla, prin. — 879-5502

Ellsworth, AC 715, PC 5, Pierce
Ellsworth Community SD — 4-11111
349 N GRANT ST 54011 — 273-3900
Eugene Swanson, supt.
SHS, 333 W HILLCREST ST 54011 — 2-00001
Charles Buckel, prin. — 273-3904
JHS, 254 S CHESTNUT 54011 — 2-00110
Steve Broton, prin. — 273-3908

Elm Grove, AC 414, PC 6, Waukesha
Elmbrook SD
Supt. — See Brookfield
Elmbrook MS, 1500 PILGRIM PKY 53122 — 3-00100
Donald Van Buskirk, prin. — 785-3920

Elmwood, AC 715, PC 3, Pierce
Elmwood SD, 103 WILSON AVE W 54740 — 2-11111
Frederic Schmit, supt. — 639-2711
HS, 103 WILSON AVE W 54740 — 2-00011
Arland Lien, prin. — 639-2721

Elroy, AC 608, PC 4, Juneau
Elroy-Kendall-Wilton SD 4-11111
PO BOX A 53929 462-8241
Charles Twork, supt.
Royall HS, PO BOX A 53929 2-00011
William Bush, prin. 462-8231

Evansville, AC 608, PC 5, Rock
Evansville Community SD 4-11111
420 S 4TH ST 53536 882-5224
Thomas Benzinger, supt.
HS, 420 S 4TH ST 53536 2-00011
(—), prin. 882-4600
MS, 307 S 1ST ST 53536 2-01100
Vincent Maloney, prin. 882-4780

Fall Creek, AC 715, PC 4, Eau Claire
Fall Creek SD 3-11111
336 E HOOVER AVE 54742 877-2123
Patrick Saunders, supt.
HS, 336 E HOOVER AVE 54742 2-00011
Gerald Berseth, prin. 877-2809
MS, 142 E WASHINGTON AVE 54742 2-00100
James Sutherland, prin. 877-2511

Fall River, AC 414, PC 3, Columbia
Fall River SD, 150 BRADLEY ST 53932 2-11111
Steven Rubert, supt. 484-3327
HS, 150 BRADLEY ST 53932 1-00011
Bradley Johnsrud, prin. 484-3326

Fennimore, AC 608, PC 4, Grant
Fennimore Community SD 3-11111
1397 9TH ST 53809 822-3243
Edgar Ryun, supt.
JSHS, 510 7TH ST 53809 2-00111
Douglas Collister, prin. 822-3245

Southwest Wisconsin Technical College 3-CC
BRONSON BLVD 53809 822-3262

Fish Creek, AC 414, PC 2, Door
Gibralter Area SD, PO BOX 205G 54212 3-11111
Robert Dahlstrom, supt. 868-3284
Gibraltar HS, PO BOX 205G 54212 2-00011
Jack Whaley, prin. 868-3284

Florence, AC 715, PC 3, Florence
Florence SD, PO BOX 440 54121 3-11111
Gerald Gerard, supt. 528-3217
HS, PO BOX 440 54121 2-00011
John Kriegl, prin. 528-3215
JHS, PO BOX 440 54121 1-00100
John Kriegl, prin. 528-3215

Fond du Lac, AC 414, PC 8, Fond du Lac
Fond Du Lac SD 6-11111
72 S PORTLAND ST 54935 929-2760
Michael Homes, supt.
Goodrich SHS, 382 LINDEN ST 54935 4-00001
Jon Kaiser, prin. 929-2707
Sabish JHS, 100 N PETERS AVE 54935 3-00110
Delbert Schultz, prin. 929-2800
Theisen JHS, 525 E PIONEER RD 54935 3-00110
Richard Bestor, prin. 929-2850

Marian College of Fond du Lac 4-UC
45 S NATIONAL AVE 54935 923-7600
Moraine Park Technical College 4-CC
PO BOX 1940 54936 922-8611
St. Mary S, 63 E MERRILL AVE 54935 2-00100
Carol Makolm, prin. 921-9610
St. Mary's Springs HS 2-00011
255 COUNTY ROAD K 54935 921-4870
Thomas Borek, prin.
University of Wisconsin Center 54935 3-CC
929-3606
Winnebago Lutheran Academy HS 2-00011
475 E MERRILL AVE 54935 921-4930
Randall Westphal, prin.

Fort Atkinson, AC 414, PC 7, Jefferson
Fort Atkinson SD, 317 S HIGH ST 53538 4-11111
Gerald McGowen, supt. 563-7807
Fort Atkinson HS, 310 S 4TH ST E 53538 3-00011
Paul Pelnar, prin. 563-7811
Luther MS, 201 PARK ST 53538 3-00100
Joseph Slaney, prin. 563-7833

Fountain City, AC 608, PC 3, Buffalo
Cochrane-Fountain City SD 3-11111
PO BOX 517 54629 687-7771
Gene Wellman, supt.
Cochrane-Fountain City JSHS 2-00111
PO BOX 517 54629 687-4391
Kenneth Jackson, prin.

Franklin, AC 414, PC 7, Milwaukee
Franklin SD 5-11111
7380 S NORTH CAPE RD 53132 529-8220
Gerald Freitag, supt.
HS, 8222 S 51ST ST 53132 3-00011
R. Scott Pierce, prin. 423-4640
Forest Park MS 2-00100
8225 W FOREST HILL AVE 53132 529-8250
Denise Bowens, prin.

Frederic, AC 715, PC 4, Polk
Frederic SD, PO BOX 790 54837 3-11111
Reginald Gobin, supt. 327-5630
HS, PO BOX 790 54837 2-00011
Robert Berquist, prin. 327-4223

Fredonia, AC 414, PC 4, Ozaukee
Northern Ozaukee SD 3-11111
401 HIGHLAND DR 53021 692-2489
Frank Parsons, supt.
Ozaukee HS, 401 HIGHLAND DR 53021 2-00011
Gerald Malueg, prin. 692-2453
Ozaukee MS, 401 HIGHLAND DR 53021 2-01100
Thomas Maurer, prin. 692-2463

Freedom, AC 414, PC 2, Outagamie
Freedom Area SD 4-11111
PO BOX 1008 54131 788-7944
Gary Scheuerell, supt.
HS, PO BOX 1008 54131 2-00011
Richard Lovett, prin. 788-7940
MS, PO BOX 1008 54131 2-00100
James Harke, prin. 788-7945

Galesville, AC 608, PC 4, Trempealeau
Galesville-Ettrick-Trempealeau SD 4-11111
1007 N MAIN ST 54630 582-2291
Wayne Edwards, supt.
Gale-Ettr-Tremp HS 2-00011
PO BOX 4000 54630 582-2291
Gerald Eichman, prin.
Other Schools – See Trempealeau

Gays Mills, AC 608, PC 3, Crawford
North Crawford SD 3-11111
PO BOX 68 54631 735-4318
Michael Cox, supt.
North Crawford JSHS 2-00111
PO BOX 68 54631 735-4311
Henry Lamkin, prin.

Germantown, AC 414, PC 7, Washington
Germantown SD 5-11111
N104W13840 DONGES BAY RD 53022 253-3904
Louis Birchbauer, supt.
HS, W180N11501 RIVER LN 53022 3-00011
Bruce Seastrand, prin. 253-3400
Kennedy MS 3-00100
W160N11836 CRUSADER CT 53022 253-3450
Alan Spiegel, prin.

Gillett, AC 414, PC 4, Oconto
Gillett SD, 208 W MAIN ST 54124 3-11111
Orland Mccollum, supt. 855-2138
HS, 208 W MAIN ST 54124 2-00011
Henry Dupuis, prin. 855-2138
JHS, 208 W MAIN ST 54124 2-00100
Henry Dupuis, prin. 855-2138

Gilman, AC 715, PC 2, Taylor
Gilman SD, PO BOX 188 54433 3-11111
David Welter, supt. 447-8216
JSHS, FIFTH AVE 54433 2-00111
Alan Arnold, prin. 447-8211

Gilmanton, AC 715, PC 2, Buffalo
Gilmanton SD, PO BOX 28 54743 2-11111
Clark Sheerar, supt. 946-3158
JSHS, PO BOX 28 54743 2-00111
Peter Klas, prin. 946-3158

Glendale, AC 414, PC 7, Milwaukee
Nicolet UNHSD 4-00011
6701 N JEAN NICOLET RD 53217 351-7525
Elliott Moser, supt.
Nicolet Union HS 4-00011
6701 N JEAN NICOLET RD 53217 351-7525
Elliott Moser, prin.

Glenwood City, AC 715, PC 4, St. Croix
Glenwood City SD, 859 320TH ST 54013 3-11111
Michael Weber, supt. 265-4757
HS, HWY 170 54013 2-00011
Julian Bender, prin. 265-4266
MS, HWY 170 54013 2-00100
Julian Bender, prin. 265-4266

Glidden, AC 715, PC 3, Ashland
Glidden SD, PO BOX 96 54527 2-11111
James Dohm, supt. 264-2021
HS, PO BOX 96 54527 1-00011
James Dohm, prin. 264-2141

Goodman, AC 715, PC 2, Marinette
Goodman-Armstrong SD 2-11111
PO BOX 160 54125 336-2575
Steven Hutchens, supt.
JSHS, PO BOX 160 54125 1-00111
Steven Hutchens, prin. 336-2575

Grafton, AC 414, PC 6, Ozaukee
Grafton SD 4-11111
1900 WASHINGTON ST 53024 377-6103
Edward Eckhardt, supt.
HS, 1950 WASHINGTON ST 53024 3-00011
Edward Schmidt, prin. 377-6100
Long MS, 700 HICKORY ST 53024 2-00100
Richard Gonzalez, prin. 377-7791

Granton, AC 715, PC 2, Clark
Granton Area SD, PO BOX 78 54436 2-11111
James Friesen, supt. 238-7292
HS, PO BOX 78 54436 1-00011
Gordon Port, prin. 238-7175

Grantsburg, AC 715, PC 4, Burnett
Grantsburg SD, 480 E JAMES AVE 54840 3-11111
John Sauerberg, supt. 463-2531
HS, 480 E JAMES AVE 54840 2-00011
Robert Werner, prin. 463-2531
MS, 480 E JAMES AVE 54840 2-00100
William Stapp, prin. 463-2455

Gratiot, AC 608, PC 2, Lafayette
Black Hawk SD
Supt. — See South Wayne
Black Hawk MS, MAIN ST 53541 1-00100
Jerry Mortimer, prin. 922-6457

Green Bay, AC 414, PC 8, Brown
Ashwaubenon SD 5-11111
1055 GRIFFITHS LN 54304 492-2902
Richard Slaven, supt.
Ashwaubenon HS 3-00011
2391 S RIDGE RD 54304 492-2950
Donald Maslinski, prin.
Parkview MS, 955 WILLARD DR 54304 3-00100
Paul Kane, prin. 492-2940

Green Bay Area SD 7-11111
PO BOX 23387 54305 448-2101
Thomas Joynt, supt.
East HS, 1415 E WALNUT ST 54301 4-00011
Joseph Seroogy, prin. 448-2090
Preble HS, 241 S DANZ AVE 54302 4-00011
Duane Hoerning, prin. 391-2400
Southwest HS 4-00011
1330 PACKERLAND DR 54304 492-2650
Don Lundin, prin.
West HS, 966 SHAWANO AVE 54303 4-00011
Hollister Jansen, prin. 492-2600
Edison MS, 442 ALPINE DR 54302 3-00100
Michael Hermans, prin. 391-2450
Franklin MS, 1234 W MASON ST 54303 3-00100
Keith Cauwenbergh, prin. 492-2670
Lombardi MS, 1520 S POINT RD 54313 3-00100
Nancy Croy, prin. 492-2625
Washington MS, 314 S BAIRD ST 54301 3-00100
Jack Washington, prin. 448-2095

Howard-Suamico SD 5-11111
2700 LINEVILLE RD 54313 434-4018
Fredric Stieg, supt.
Bay Port HS, 1217 CARDINAL LN 54313 3-00011
Larry Dunning, prin. 434-4006
Bay View MS, 2700 LINEVILLE RD 54313 3-00100
Kris Servais, prin. 434-4010

Bellin College of Nursing 2-UC
PO BOX 23400 54305 433-5803
Bellin Hospital HSP
PO BOX 23400 54305 433-3673
Northeast Wisconsin Technical College 4-CC
PO BOX 19042 54307 498-5411
Notre Dame High S 3-00011
610 MARYHILL DR 54303 498-6464
Fr. Radecki, prin.
St. Thomas Moore MS 2-01100
1420 HARVEY ST 54302 437-3382
Jeanne Pischke, prin.
St. Vincent Hospital HSP
PO BOX 13508 54307 433-8155
University of Wisconsin 5-UC
2420 NICOLET DR 54311 465-2207

Greendale, AC 414, PC 7, Milwaukee
Greendale SD, 5900 S 51ST ST 53129 4-11111
Donald Tuler, supt. 423-2702
HS, 6801 SOUTHWAY 53129 3-00011
Raymond Petitpren, prin. 423-0110
MS, 6800 SCHOOLWAY 53129 2-00100
Charles Herman, prin. 423-2800

Martin Luther HS, 5201 S 76TH ST 53129 2-00011
Carl Eisman, prin. 421-4000

Greenfield, AC 414, PC 8, Milwaukee
Greenfield SD 5-11111
8500 W CHAPMAN AVE 53228 529-9090
William Larkin, supt.
HS, 4800 S 60TH ST 53220 4-00011
Robert Laabs, prin. 281-6200
MS, 3200 W BARNARD AVE 53221 3-00100
Clifford Sheldon, prin. 282-4700

Whitnall SD, 5000 S 116TH ST 53228 4-11111
William Hittman, supt. 425-4000
Whitnall HS, 5000 S 116TH ST 53228 3-00011
(—), prin. 425-4004
Whitnall MS, 5025 S 116TH ST 53228 3-01100
Brian McCormack, prin. 425-4002

Green Lake, AC 414, PC 4, Green Lake
Green Lake SD, PO BOX 369 54941 2-11111
Thomas Roy, supt. 294-6441
HS, PO BOX 369 54941 2-00011
(—), prin. 294-6411

Greenwood, AC 715, PC 3, Clark
Greenwood SD 3-11111
209 S HENDREN AVE 54437 267-6103
John Kammerud, supt.
JSHS, 209 S HENDREN AVE 54437 2-00111
Knute Wallin, prin. 267-6101

Gresham, AC 715, PC 3, Shawano
Shawano-Gresham SD
Supt. — See Shawano
HS, 501 SCHABOW ST 54128 1-00011
Robert Klopke, prin. 787-3211

Hales Corners, AC 414, PC 6, Milwaukee

Sacred Heart School of Theology 2-UC
PO BOX 429 53130 425-8300

Hammond, AC 715, PC 4, St. Croix
St. Croix Central SD — 3-11111
  PO BOX 118 54015 — 796-2256
  Dan Woll, supt.
St. Croix HS, PO BOX 118 54015 — 2-00011
  Gary Reineck, prin. — 796-2256
St. Croix JHS, PO BOX 118 54015 — 2-00100
  Gary Reineck, prin. — 796-2256

Hartford, AC 414, PC 6, Washington
Hartford J1 SD — 4-11100
  600 HIGHLAND AVE 53027 — 673-3155
  Greg McElwee, supt.
Central MS, 1100 CEDAR ST 53027 — 2-00100
  Phillip May, prin. — 673-8040

Hartford UNHSD, 805 CEDAR ST 53027 — 4-00011
  Richard Zimmerman, supt. — 673-8950
HS, 805 CEDAR ST 53027 — 4-00011
  Richard Zimmerman, prin. — 673-8950

Hartland, AC 414, PC 6, Waukesha
Arrowhead UNHSD — 4-00011
  700 NORTH AVE 53029 — 367-3611
  David Lodes, supt.
Arrowhead Union HS — 4-00011
  700 NORTH AVE 53029 — 367-3611
  Bonnie Laugerman, prin.

University Lake S — 2-11111
  4024 NAGAWICKA RD 53029 — 367-6011
  Edward Wucker, prin.

Hayward, AC 715, PC 4, Sawyer
Hayward Community SD — 4-11111
  PO BOX 860 54843 — 634-2619
  Donald Reinicke, supt.
HS, PO BOX 860 54843 — 3-00011
  Robert Schmidt, prin. — 634-2616
MS, PO BOX 860 54843 — 3-01100
  Douglas Beck, prin. — 634-8414

Lac Courte Oreilles Ojibwa Comm College — 2-CC
  RR 2 BOX 2357 54843 — 634-4790

Hazel Green, AC 608, PC 4, Grant
Southwestern Wisconsin SD — 3-11111
  PO BOX 368 53811 — 854-2261
  Neil Winchell, supt.
Southwestern Wisconsin HS — 2-00011
  PO BOX 368 53811 — 854-2124
  Darryl Bartz, prin.

Highland, AC 608, PC 3, Iowa
Highland SD, PO BOX 2850 53543 — 2-11111
  James Siedenburg, supt. — 929-4525
HS, PO BOX 2850 53543 — 1-00011
  Rick Cardey, prin. — 929-4525

Hilbert, AC 414, PC 4, Calumet
Hilbert SD — 3-11111
  11TH AND MILWAUKEE ST 54129 — 853-3558
  F. Holewinski, supt.
JSHS, 11TH & MILWAUKEE 54129 — 2-00111
  Terry Fondow, prin. — 853-3558

Hillsboro, AC 608, PC 4, Vernon
Hillsboro SD, PO BOX 526 54634 — 3-11111
  Bruce Lemery, supt. — 489-2221
JSHS, PO BOX 526 54634 — 2-00011
  Wayne Stahlkopf, prin. — 489-2221

Holcombe, AC 715, PC 2, Chippewa
Lake Holcombe SD, PO BOX 40 54745 — 3-11111
  William Stimeling, supt. — 595-4241
HS, PO BOX 40 54745 — 2-00011
  Don Lapp, prin. — 595-4241

Holmen, AC 608, PC 5, La Crosse
Holmen SD — 4-11111
  500 N HOLMEN DR STE 508 54636 — 526-6610
  Fred Frick, supt.
HS, 502 N MAIN ST 54636 — 3-00011
  Trygve Mathison, prin. — 526-3372
MS, 511 4TH AVE E 54636 — 3-01100
  Dan Koch, prin. — 526-3391

Horicon, AC 414, PC 5, Dodge
Horicon SD, 611 MILL ST 53032 — 4-11111
  Larry Ballwahn, supt. — 485-2898
HS, 841 GRAY ST 53032 — 2-00011
  David Kotewa, prin. — 485-4441
MS, 611 MILL ST 53032 — 2-00100
  Elizabeth Fritz, prin. — 485-4423

Hortonville, AC 414, PC 4, Outagamie
Hortonville SD, PO BOX 70 54944 — 4-11111
  Gregory Joseph, supt. — 779-4172
HS, PO BOX 220 54944 — 3-00011
  Ronald Conradt, prin. — 779-4684
MS, 246 N OLK ST 54944 — 2-00100
  Eugene Conger, prin. — 779-4043

Howards Grove, AC 414, PC 4, Sheboygan
Howards Grove SD — 3-11111
  437 N WISCONSIN DR 53083 — 565-4454
  Ronald E. Albert, supt.
HS, 506 KENNEDY AVE 53083 — 2-00011
  Chris Ligocki, prin. — 565-4450
Other Schools – See Sheboygan

Hubertus, AC 414, PC 2, Washington
Richfield J11 SD — 2-01100
  1750 COUNTY ROAD J 53033 — 628-2380
  Mark Flynn, supt.

Friess Lake MS — 1-01100
  1750 COUNTY ROAD J 53033 — 628-2380
  Mark Flynn, prin.

Hudson, AC 715, PC 6, St. Croix
Hudson SD, 416 SAINT CROIX ST 54016 — 5-11111
  Ronnie Bernth, supt. — 386-4220
SHS, 1501 VINE ST 54016 — 3-00001
  Robert Laney, prin. — 386-4226
JHS, 1401 VINE ST 54016 — 3-00110
  Jerome Dunaski, prin. — 386-4229

Hurley, AC 715, PC 4, Iron
Hurley SD — 3-11111
  1S517 RANGE VIEW DR 54534 — 561-4900
  Roger Myren, supt.
JSHS, 1S517 RANGE VIEW DR 54534 — 2-00111
  Robert Lambert, prin. — 561-3340

Hustisford, AC 414, PC 3, Dodge
Hustisford SD, PO BOX 326 53034 — 2-11111
  David Elliot, supt. — 349-3261
JSHS, PO BOX 326 53034 — 2-00111
  Thomas Hercules, prin. — 349-3261

Independence, AC 715, PC 4, Trempealeau
Independence SD, 108 S 6TH ST 54747 — 2-11111
  William Jeske, supt. — 985-2144
HS, 108 S 6TH ST 54747 — 2-00011
  Kevin Larson, prin. — 985-3172

Iola, AC 715, PC 4, Waupaca
Iola-Scandinavia SD — 3-11111
  450 DIVISION ST 54945 — 445-2411
  Chester Fraley, supt.
Iola-Scandinavia HS — 2-00011
  540 S JACKSON ST 54945 — 445-2411
  Tom Heimerl, prin.

Jackson, AC 414, PC 4, Washington

Kettle Moraine Lutheran HS — 2-00011
  3399 DIVISION RD 53037 — 677-4051
  Wayne Baxmann, prin.

Janesville, AC 608, PC 8, Rock
Janesville SD, 527 S FRANKLIN ST 53545 — 6-11111
  Donald Mrdjenovich, supt. — 758-6400
Craig HS, 401 S RANDALL AVE 53545 — 4-00011
  Thomas Evert, prin. — 758-6300
Parker HS — 4-00011
  3125 MINERAL POINT AVE 53545 — 758-6304
  William Reis, prin.
Edison MS, 1649 S CHATHAM ST 53546 — 3-00100
  Donald Tyriver, prin. — 758-6306
Franklin MS, 450 N CROSBY AVE 53545 — 3-00100
  Kim Ehrhardt, prin. — 758-6307
Marshall MS, 408 S MAIN ST 53545 — 3-00100
  Roger Kussmann, prin. — 758-6308

Blackhawk Technical College — 3-CC
  PO BOX 5009 53547 — 757-7769
University of Wisconsin Center — 3-CC
  2909 KELLOGG AVE 53546 — 755-2823
Wisconsin School/Visually Handicapped — HND
  1700 W STATE ST 53546

Jefferson, AC 414, PC 6, Jefferson
Jefferson SD, 206 S TAFT AVE 53549 — 4-11111
  Hollister De Motts, supt. — 674-7040
HS, 700 W MILWAUKEE ST 53549 — 3-00011
  Joseph Houston, prin. — 674-7044
MS, 201 S COPELAND AVE 53549 — 2-00100
  Allan Peters, prin. — 674-7048

St. Coletta School — HND
  RR 1 BOX 43 53549

Johnson Creek, AC 414, PC 4, Jefferson
Johnson Creek SD, 111 SOUTH ST 53038 — 3-11111
  Allan Schaefer, supt. — 699-2811
JSHS, 111 SOUTH ST 53038 — 2-00111
  Steve Patz, prin. — 699-3481

Juda, AC 608, PC 2, Green
Juda SD, N2385 SPRING ST 53550 — 2-11111
  Don Budde, supt. — 934-5251
HS, N2385 SPRING ST 53550 — 1-00011
  Don Budde, prin. — 934-5251

Juneau, AC 414, PC 4, Dodge
Dodgeland SD, 302 S MAIN ST 53039 — 3-11111
  Carl Munson, supt. — 386-4404
Dodgeland HS, 302 S MAIN ST 53039 — 2-00011
  Ronald Douglas, prin. — 386-2601
Other Schools – See Reeseville

Kaukauna, AC 414, PC 7, Outagamie
Kaukauna Area SD — 5-11111
  112 MAIN AVE 54130 — 766-6100
  Lee Siudzinski, supt.
HS, 101 OAK ST 54130 — 3-00011
  Franz Zillner, prin. — 766-6113
Quinney MS — 3-00100
  2601 SULLIVAN AVE 54130 — 766-6116
  Jack Pautz, prin.

Kenosha, AC 414, PC 8, Kenosha
Kenosha SD, PO BOX 340 53141 — 7-11111
  Anthony Bisciglia, supt. — 653-6323
Bradford SHS — 4-00011
  3700 WASHINGTON RD 53144 — 653-6200
  Joseph Mangi, prin.
Tremper SHS, 8560 26TH AVE 53143 — 4-00001
  Chester Pulaski, prin. — 942-2200

Hillcrest HS, 4616 24TH ST 53144 — Vo Tech
  Stephen Frank, prin. — 653-6118
Bullen Jr High School — 3-00100
  2804 39TH AVE 53144 — 597-4460
  Sandon Kohlhepp, prin.
Lance JHS, 4515 80TH ST 53142 — 3-00110
  Ronald Soulek, prin. — 942-2240
Lincoln JHS, 6729 18TH AVE 53143 — 3-00110
  Joseph Gassert, prin. — 653-6295
McKinley JHS, 5710 32ND AVE 53144 — 3-00110
  Robert Crist, prin. — 653-6367
Reuther JHS, 913 57TH ST 53140 — 2-00010
  Rochelle Henning, prin. — 653-6160
Washington JHS — 3-00110
  811 WASHINGTON RD 53140 — 653-6291
  George Zimmer, prin.

Carthage College — 4-UC
  2001 ALFORD DR 53140 — 551-8500
Christian Life S, 10700 75TH ST 53142 — 2-11111
  Paul Blount, prin. — 652-1685
Gateway Technical College — 4-CC
  3520 30TH AVE 53144 — 656-6916
St. Catherine's Hospital — HSP
  3556 7TH AVE 53140 — 656-3312
St. Joseph HS, 2401 69TH ST 53143 — 2-00111
  Lawrence Pesch, prin. — 654-8651
University of Wisconsin — 5-UC
  PO BOX 2000 53141 — 553-2211

Keshena, AC 715, PC 3, Menominee
Menominee Indian SD — 3-11111
  PO BOX 399 54135 — 799-3824
  John Rothlisberg, supt.
Menominee Indian HS — 2-00011
  PO BOX 850 54135 — 799-3846
  Mark Fry, prin.
Menominee MS, PO BOX 50 54135 — 2-00100
  Marilyn Meisenheimer, prin. — 799-3846

Kewaskum, AC 414, PC 5, Washington
Kewaskum SD, PO BOX 37 53040 — 4-11111
  David Heather, supt. — 626-8427
HS, 1510 BILGO LANE 53040 — 3-00011
  Charles Heidner, prin. — 626-2166
MS, 1676 REIGLE DR 53040 — 2-00100
  David Jones, prin. — 626-2178

Kewaunee, AC 414, PC 5, Kewaunee
Kewaunee SD, 911 3RD ST 54216 — 4-11111
  Roy Stone, supt. — 388-3230
HS, 911 3RD ST 54216 — 2-00011
  Jack Stronstad, prin. — 388-2951
Marquette MS, 317 DORELLE ST 54216 — 2-01100
  Robert Ratzburg, prin. — 388-2458

Kiel, AC 414, PC 5, Calumet
Kiel Area SD, PO BOX 201 53042 — 4-11111
  Don Mattox, supt. — 894-2266
HS, 210 RAIDER HTS 53042 — 2-00011
  Glen Miller, prin. — 894-2263
MS, 502 PAINE ST 53042 — 2-01100
  David Slosser, prin. — 894-2264

Kimberly, AC 414, PC 6, Outagamie
Kimberly Area SD — 4-11111
  217 E KIMBERLY AVE 54136 — 788-7900
  Edward Wulgaert, supt.
HS, 545 S JOHN ST 54136 — 3-00011
  Michael Rietveld, prin. — 788-7905
Gerrits MS, 125 E KIMBERLY AVE 54136 — 2-00100
  Lisa Gies, prin. — 788-7910

Kohler, AC 414, PC 4, Sheboygan
Kohler SD, 230 SCHOOL ST 53044 — 2-11111
  John Egan, supt. — 459-2920
JSHS, 230 SCHOOL ST 53044 — 2-00111
  Mary Gadzinski, prin. — 459-2921

La Crosse, AC 608, PC 8, La Crosse
La Crosse SD, 807 EAST AVE S 54601 — 6-11111
  Richard Swantz, supt. — 789-7600
Central HS, 1801 LOSEY BLVD S 54601 — 4-00011
  Thomas Barth, prin. — 789-7900
Logan HS, 1500 RANGER DR 54603 — 3-00011
  Kenneth Bates, prin. — 789-7700
Lincoln MS, 510 9TH ST S 54601 — 2-00100
  Alan Bassuener, prin. — 789-7780
Logan MS, 1450 AVON ST 54603 — 3-00100
  Roger Fish, prin. — 789-7740
Longfellow MS, 1900 DENTON ST 54601 — 3-00100
  Melvin Jenkins, prin. — 789-7670

Aquinas HS, 315 11TH ST S 54601 — 2-00111
  James Vail, prin. — 784-0414
University of Wisconsin — 6-UC
  1725 STATE ST 54601 — 785-8000
Viterbo College — 3-UC
  815 9TH ST S 54601 — 784-0040
Western Wisconsin Technical College — 5-CS
  PO BOX 908 54602 — 785-9101

Ladysmith, AC 715, PC 5, Rusk
Ladysmith-Hawkins SD — 4-11111
  1700 EDGEWOOD AVE E 54848 — 532-5277
  C Riter, supt.
HS, 1700 EDGEWOOD AVE E 54848 — 2-00011
  Donald Rubow, prin. — 532-5531
MS, 115 E 6TH ST S 54848 — 2-00100
  David Wall, prin. — 532-5252

Mt. Senario College   3-UC
1500 COLLEGE AVE W   54848   532-5511

La Farge, AC 608, PC 3, Vernon
La Farge SD, PO BOX 898   54639   2-11111
Paul Jacobson, supt.   625-2400
HS, PO BOX 898   54639   1-00011
Barbara Whyte, prin.   625-2400

Lake Geneva, AC 414, PC 6, Walworth
Lake Geneva-Genoa City SD   3-00011
208 E SOUTH ST   53147   248-9177
Harry Van Dyke, supt.
Badger HS, 220 E SOUTH ST   53147   3-00011
A. Dean Dare, prin.   248-6243

Lake Geneva J1 SD   4-11100
208 E SOUTH ST   53147   248-9177
Harry Van Dyke, supt.
Denison MS, 900 WISCONSIN ST   53147   2-00100
Erwin Roth, prin.   248-6215

Northwestern Military & Naval Academy   2-00111
W4598 S LAKESHORE DR   53147   248-4465
Col. Grieshaber, prin.

Lake Mills, AC 414, PC 5, Jefferson
Lake Mills Area SD   4-11111
318 COLLEGE ST   53551   648-2215
Sandra Ludeman, supt.
HS, 615 CATLIN DR   53551   2-00011
Boyd Forest, prin.   648-2355
MS, 318 COLLEGE ST   53551   2-00100
Doris Thompson, prin.   648-2358

Lakeside Lutheran HS   2-00011
231 WOODLAND BEACH RD   53551   648-2321
Jason Nelson, prin.

Lancaster, AC 608, PC 5, Grant
Lancaster Community SD   4-11111
925 W MAPLE ST   53813   723-2175
Dan Dahlgren, supt.
HS, 806 E ELM ST   53813   2-00011
Gary Swanstrom, prin.   723-2173
MS, 802 E ELM ST   53813   2-01100
Ron Meissner, prin.   723-6425

Laona, AC 715, PC 3, Forest
Laona SD, PO BOX 57   54541   2-11111
Storm Carroll, supt.   674-2143
JSHS, PO BOX 57   54541   2-00111
(—), prin.   674-2143

Lena, AC 414, PC 3, Oconto
Lena SD, PO BOX 48   54139   2-11111
Ray Artz, supt.   829-5244
HS, PO BOX 48   54139   2-00011
Dennis Barry, prin.   829-5244
MS, PO BOX 48   54139   2-01100
Dennis Barry, prin.   829-5244

Little Chute, AC 414, PC 6, Outagamie
Little Chute Area SD   4-11111
PO BOX 268   54140 – (—), supt.   788-7605
HS, 1402 FREEDOM RD   54140   2-00011
William Fitzpatrick, prin.   788-7600
MS, 329 GRAND AVE   54140   2-01100
Donald Bangert, prin.   788-7607

Livingston, AC 608, PC 3, Grant
Iowa-Grant SD, 462 COUNTY I-G   53554   3-11111
J. Bruce Bradley, supt.   943-6311
Iowa-Grant HS, RR 1   53554   2-00011
Gary Guerin, prin.   943-6312

Lodi, AC 608, PC 4, Columbia
Lodi SD, PO BOX 166   53555   4-11111
Charles Pursell, supt.   592-3851
HS, 101 SCHOOL ST   53555   2-00011
Greg Anderson, prin.   592-3851
MS, 101 SCHOOL ST   53555   2-00100
Karen Mathis, prin.   592-3851

Lomira, AC 414, PC 4, Dodge
Lomira SD, 1030 4TH ST   53048   3-11111
John Mason, supt.   269-4396
HS, 1030 4TH ST   53048   2-00011
Patrick Sackett, prin.   269-4396
JHS, 1030 4TH ST   53048   2-00100
Dennis Anderson, prin.   269-4396

Loyal, AC 715, PC 4, Clark
Loyal SD, PO BOX 10   54446   3-11111
David Miskulin, supt.   255-8552
HS, PO BOX 10   54446   2-00011
Steven Shaw, prin.   255-8511
JHS, PO BOX 10   54446   1-00100
Steven Shaw, prin.   255-8511

Luck, AC 715, PC 4, Polk
Luck SD, 710 E BUTTERNUT AVE   54853   3-11111
Allen Ormson, supt.   472-2151
JSHS, 710 E BUTTERNUT AVE   54853   2-00111
William Grelle, prin.   472-2152

Luxemburg, AC 414, PC 4, Kewaunee
Luxemburg-Casco SD   4-11111
PO BOX 10   54217   845-2391
Raymond Thillman, supt.
Luxemburg-Casco SHS, PO BOX A   54217   2-00001
Steve Okoniewski, prin.   845-2336
Other Schools – See Casco

Madison, AC 608, PC 9, Dane
Madison Metro SD   7-11111
545 W DAYTON ST   53703   266-6235
Cheryl Wilhoyte, supt.
East HS   4-00011
2222 E WASHINGTON AVE   53704   246-4403
Milton McPike, prin.
LaFollette HS, 702 PFLAUM RD   53716   4-00011
Michael Meissen, prin.   221-6681
Memorial HS, 201 S GAMMON RD   53717   4-00011
Carolyn Taylor, prin.   829-4000
Shabazz-City HS   2-00011
1601 N SHERMAN AVE   53704   246-5040
Steve Hartley, prin.
West HS, 30 ASH ST   53705   4-00011
Elizabeth Burmaster, prin.   267-7014
Sapar Program HS   Vo Tech
210 S BROOKS ST   53715   266-6459
Mary Gulbrandsen, prin.
Work and Learning HS   Vo Tech
210 S BROOKS ST # 212   53715   266-6549
Penny Fitzgerald, prin.
Black Hawk MS   3-00100
1402 WYOMING WAY   53704   246-5005
Michael Owens, prin.
Cherokee Heights MS   3-00100
4301 CHEROKEE DR   53711   267-2043
Mary Ramberg, prin.
Hamilton MS   3-00100
4801 WAUKESHA ST   53705   267-4289
Marvin Meissen, prin.
Jefferson MS, 101 S GAMMON RD   53717   2-00100
Jack Horton, prin.   829-4111
Madison 2000 MS   2-00100
3802 REGENT ST   53705   267-1144
Offie Hobbs, prin.
O'Keeffe MS   3-00100
510 S THORNTON AVE   53703   267-4246
Thomas Vandervest, prin.
Sennett MS, 502 PFLAUM RD   53716   3-00100
Jan Dowden, prin.   221-6600
Sherman MS, 1610 RUSKIN ST   53704   3-00100
John Daly, prin.   246-4746
Toki MS, 5602 RUSSETT RD   53711   3-00100
Gary Sisler, prin.   273-5910
Whitehorse MS, 230 SCHENK ST   53714   2-00100
Robert Pellegrino, prin.   246-4476

Abundant Life Christian S   2-11111
4909 E BUCKEYE RD   53716   221-1520
David Wagner, prin.
Edgewood College   3-UC
855 WOODROW ST   53711   257-4861
Edgewood HS, 2219 MONROE ST   53711   3-00011
Lawrence Black, prin.   257-1023
Holy Name Seminary   2-00011
3577 HIGH POINT RD   53719   833-1010
Fr. Flanagan, prin.
Madison Area Technical College   6-CC
3550 ANDERSON ST   53704   246-6676
Madison Junior College of Business   3-CC
1110 SPRING HARBOR DR   53705   238-4266
State Laboratory of Hygiene   3-UC
465 HENRY MALL   53706   262-1293
Trans American School of Broadcasting   2-CS
1 POINT PL STE 1   53719   829-2728
University of Wisconsin   8-UC
500 LINCOLN DR   53706   262-9946
Wisconsin School of Electronics   2-CC
1227 N SHERMAN AVE   53704   249-6611

Manawa, AC 414, PC 4, Waupaca
Manawa SD, PO BOX 400   54949   3-11111
Douglas Smith, supt.   596-2525
Little Wolf HS, PO BOX 400   54949   2-00011
Floyd Gerl, prin.   596-2524
MS, PO BOX 400   54949   2-01100
John Fossum, prin.   596-2551

Manitowoc, AC 414, PC 8, Manitowoc
Manitowoc SD, PO BOX 1657   54221   5-11111
John Crubaugh, supt.   683-4777
Lincoln SHS, 1433 S 8TH ST   54220   4-00001
James McCartney, prin.   683-4833
Washington JHS   3-00110
2101 DIVISION ST   54220   683-4803
Robert Schneider, prin.
Wilson JHS, 1201 N 11TH ST   54220   3-00110
Donald Cooley, prin.   683-4813

Acme Institute of Technology   1-CS
102 REVERE DR   54220   682-6144
Manitowoc Lutheran HS   2-00011
4045 LANCER CIR   54220   682-0215
George Lagrow, prin.
Roncalli HS, 2000 MIRRO DR   54220   2-00011
Sr. Adrianna Schouten, prin.   682-8801
St. Francis Cabrini MS   2-00100
2109 MARSHALL ST   54220   683-6884
James Clark, prin.
Silver Lake College   3-UC
2406 S ALVERNO RD   54220   684-6691
University of Wisconsin Center   2-CC
705 VIEBAHN ST   54220   683-4707

Maple, AC 715, PC 2, Douglas
Maple SD, PO BOX 188   54854   4-11111
L. G. Kavajecz, supt.   363-2431
Northwestern HS, PO BOX 188   54854   2-00011
Thomas Henning, prin.   363-2434
Other Schools – See Poplar

Marathon, AC 715, PC 4, Marathon
Marathon City SD, 204 EAST ST   54448   3-11111
Robert Burmester, supt.   443-2227
HS, PO BOX 37   54448   2-00011
Dennis Erstad, prin.   443-2226

Marinette, AC 715, PC 7, Marinette
Marinette SD, 1010 MAIN ST   54143   5-11111
Robert Froelich, supt.   732-7905
HS, 2135 PIERCE AVE   54143   3-00011
James Kranpitz, prin.   732-7920
MS, 1010 MAIN ST   54143   3-00100
Robert Picard, prin.   732-7900

Marinette Catholic Central HS   2-00011
1200 MAIN ST   54143   735-7481
Gary Burley, prin.
Northeast Wisconsin Technical College   3-CC
1601 UNIVERSITY DR   54143   863-7208
University of Wisconsin Center   2-CC
750 W BAY SHORE ST   54143   735-7470

Marion, AC 715, PC 4, Waupaca
Marion SD, 1001 N MAIN ST   54950   3-11111
Jerry Smith, supt.   754-2511
HS, 105 SCHOOL ST   54950   2-00011
John Justman, prin.   754-5273

Markesan, AC 414, PC 4, Green Lake
Markesan SD, 100 W VISTA BLVD   53946   4-11111
Lyle Plagenz, supt.   398-2373
HS, 100 W VISTA BLVD   53946   2-00011
Louis Mullin, prin.   398-2373
MS, 100 W VISTA BLVD   53946   3-01100
Lester Schruck, prin.   398-2373

Marshall, AC 608, PC 4, Dane
Marshall SD, PO BOX 76   53559   3-11111
Wayne Sherry, supt.   655-3466
HS, PO BOX 76   53559   2-00011
Robert Thompson, prin.   655-3466
MS, PO BOX 106   53559   2-00100
Robert Seyffer, prin.   655-3466

Marshfield, AC 715, PC 7, Wood
Marshfield SD, 1010 E 4TH ST   54449   5-11111
Kenneth Krahn, supt.   387-1101
SHS, 1401 E BECKER RD   54449   3-00001
Dennis Myers, prin.   387-8464
JHS, 900 E 4TH ST   54449   3-00110
Richard Welton, prin.   387-1249

Columbus HS   2-00011
710 S COLUMBUS AVE   54449   387-1177
Fr. Lauzon, prin.
Marshfield Medical Center Laboratory   CS
1000 N OAK AVE   54449   387-5123
Mid-State Technical College   3-CC
2600 W 5TH ST   54449
St. Joseph Hospital   HSP
611 SAINT JOSEPH AVE   54449   387-1713
University of Wisconsin Center   2-CC
PO BOX 150   54449   389-6530

Mauston, AC 608, PC 5, Juneau
Mauston SD, 508 GRAYSIDE AVE   53948   4-11111
Jay Mitchell, supt.   847-5451
HS, 508 GRAYSIDE AVE   53948   2-00011
William Bomber, prin.   847-4410
Olson MS, 508 GRAYSIDE AVE   53948   2-01100
William Shaw, prin.   847-6603

Mayville, AC 414, PC 5, Dodge
Mayville SD, 500 N CLARK ST   53050   4-11111
Stephen Bushke, supt.   387-7963
HS, 500 N CLARK ST   53050   2-00011
Robert Reinke, prin.   387-7960
MS, 200 DAYTON ST   53050   2-01100
Richard Weber, prin.   387-7970

Mazomanie, AC 608, PC 4, Dane
Wisconsin Heights SD   3-11111
PO BOX 520   53560   767-2595
Tom Simonson, supt.
Wisconsin Hts. HS   2-00011
PO BOX 520   53560   767-2586
Cindy Rockow, prin.

Mc Farland, AC 608, PC 6, Dane
Mc Farland SD   4-11111
5101 FARWELL ST   53558   838-3169
Lee Olsen, supt.
HS, 5101 FARWELL ST   53558   2-00011
James Hickey, prin.   838-3166
Indian Mound MS   2-01100
6330 EXCHANGE ST   53558   838-8980
Jerry Adrian, prin.

Medford, AC 715, PC 5, Taylor
Medford Area SD   4-11111
124 W STATE ST   54451   748-4620
Paul Schoenberger, supt.
HS, 1015 W BROADWAY AVE   54451   3-00011
Steven Russ, prin.   748-5951
MS, 509 CLARK ST   54451   2-00100
John Penn, prin.   748-2516

Mellen, AC 715, PC 3, Ashland
Mellen SD, 420 S MAIN STREET   54546   2-11111
Richard Stokes, supt.   274-3601
HS, 420 S MAIN ST   54546   2-00011
(—), prin.   274-3601

Melrose, AC 608, PC 3, Jackson
Melrose-Mindoro SD ... 3-11111
  RR 2 BOX 300 54642 ... 488-2201
  Stephen Frederick, supt.
Melrose-Mindoro HS ... 2-00011
  RR 2 BOX 300 54642 ... 488-2201
  Ron Perry, prin.

Menasha, AC 414, PC 7, Winnebago
Menasha SD, PO BOX 360 54952 ... 5-11111
  William Decker, supt. ... 751-5070
HS, 420 7TH ST 54952 ... 3-00011
  Dale Watt, prin. ... 751-5010
Maplewood MS ... 3-00100
  1600 MIDWAY RD 54952 ... 832-5780
  Bernard Mitchell, prin.

St. Mary HS, 528 2ND ST 54952 ... 2-00011
  Richard Doty, prin. ... 722-7796
Seton Catholic MS ... 2-00100
  312 NICOLET BLVD 54952 ... 727-0279
  Monica Bausom, prin.
University of Wisconsin Center 54952 ... 3-CC
  ... 832-2620

Menomonee Falls, AC 414, PC 8, Waukesha
Menomonee Falls SD ... 5-11111
  N84W16579 MENOMONEE AVE 53051 ... 255-8440
  James Shaw, supt.
HS, W142N8101 MERRIMAC DR 53051 ... 4-00011
  Richard Woosencraft, prin. ... 255-8444
North MS ... 3-00100
  N87W16750 GARFIELD DR 53051 ... 255-8450
  Sidney Truckenbrod, prin.

Calvary Baptist School ... 2-11111
  N84W16971 MENOMONEE AVE 53051 ... 251-0320
  Neil Doese, prin.
Falls Baptist Academy ... 2-11111
  PO BOX 164 53052 ... 251-7051
  Charles Welner, prin.

Menomonie, AC 715, PC 7, Dunn
Menomonie Area SD ... 4-11111
  718 BROADWAY ST N 54751 ... 232-1642
  David Smette, supt.
HS, 1715 5TH ST W 54751 ... 3-00011
  Lee Benish, prin. ... 232-2606
MS, 1715 5TH ST W 54751 ... 2-00100
  Robert Klimpke, prin. ... 232-1673

University of Wisconsin ... 6-UC
  200 BROADWAY ST S 54751 ... 232-2441

Mequon, AC 414, PC 7, Ozaukee
Mequon-Thiensville SD ... 5-11111
  5000 W MEQUON RD 53092 ... 242-2412
  Karl Hertz, supt.
Homestead HS ... 4-00011
  5000 W MEQUON RD 53092 ... 242-2400
  Mark Roherty, prin.
Lake Shore MS ... 2-00100
  11036 N RANGE LINE RD 53092 ... 242-1880
  Michael Dietz, prin.
Steffen MS, 6633 W STEFFEN DR 53092 ... 2-00100
  William Hughes, prin. ... 242-3201

Concordia University ... 4-UC
  12800 N LAKE SHORE DR 53097 ... 243-5700
Milwaukee Area Technical College ... 4-CC
  5555 W HIGHLAND RD 53092 ... 931-1200

Mercer, AC 715, PC 4, Iron
Mercer SD, PO BOX 567 54547 ... 2-11111
  Jack English, supt. ... 476-2154
HS, PO BOX 567 54547 ... 1-00011
  Jack English, prin. ... 476-2154

Merrill, AC 715, PC 6, Lincoln
Merrill Area SD, 1111 N SALES ST 54452 ... 5-11111
  Ralph Neale, supt. ... 536-4581
SHS, 100 N POLK ST 54452 ... 3-00011
  Lanny Tibaldo, prin. ... 536-4594
JHS, 1201 N SALES ST 54452 ... 3-00110
  Strand Wedul, prin. ... 536-9593

Middleton, AC 608, PC 7, Dane
Middleton-Cross Plains SD ... 5-11111
  7106 SOUTH AVE 53562 ... 828-1600
  Gene Thieleke, supt.
HS, 7400 NORTH AVE 53562 ... 4-00011
  Mary Herrmann, prin. ... 828-1620
Kromrey MS, 7009 DONNA DR 53562 ... 3-00100
  Michael Harris, prin. ... 828-1640

Milton, AC 608, PC 5, Rock
Milton SD, 430 E HIGH ST # 2 53563 ... 4-11111
  Jon Platts, supt. ... 868-9204
HS, 114 W HIGH ST 53563 ... 3-00011
  Thomas Kemppainen, prin. ... 868-9300
MS, 20 E MADISON AVE 53563 ... 3-00100
  Allan Smejkal, prin. ... 868-9350

Milwaukee, AC 414, PC 11, Milwaukee
Fox Point J2 SD ... 3-11100
  7300 N LOMBARDY RD 53217 ... 351-7483
  Janice Sodos, supt.
Bayside MS ... 2-01100
  601 E ELLSWORTH LN 53217 ... 351-7486
  Jill Wiedmann, prin.

Glendale-River Hills SD ... 4-11100
  2600 W MILL RD 53209 ... 351-7170
  Robert Kattman, supt.
Glen Hills MS, 2600 W MILL RD 53209 ... 2-00100
  Donald Behrens, prin. ... 351-7160

Maple Dale-Indian Hill SD ... 3-11100
  2600 W MILL RD 53209 ... 351-7170
  Robert Kattman, supt.
Maple Dale MS ... 2-01100
  8377 N PORT WASHINGTON RD 53217
  Yvonne Frink, prin. ... 351-7380

Milwaukee SD, PO BOX 10K 53201 ... 8-11111
  Howard Fuller, supt. ... 475-8393
Bay View HS, 2751 S LENOX ST 53207 ... 4-00011
  Robert Kraiss, prin. ... 744-9840
Custer HS ... 4-00011
  5075 N SHERMAN BLVD 53209 ... 461-6600
  Robert Peters, prin.
Hamilton HS ... 4-00011
  6215 W WARNIMONT AVE 53220 ... 541-7720
  Clark Lovell, prin.
Juneau HS ... 3-00011
  6415 W MOUNT VERNON AVE 53213 ... 476-5480
  Ezell Conner, prin.
King HS, 1801 W OLIVE ST 53209 ... 4-00011
  Thomas Balistreri, prin. ... 374-5450
Madison HS ... 4-00011
  8135 W FLORIST AVE 53218 ... 466-8450
  Willie Jude, prin.
Marshall HS, 4141 N 64TH ST 53216 ... 4-00011
  Ann Griffiths, prin. ... 461-8830
Milwaukee Arts HS ... 3-00011
  2300 W HIGHLAND AVE 53233 ... 933-1500
  Jo Alice Bender, prin.
Milwaukee Technical HS ... 4-00011
  319 W VIRGINIA ST 53204 ... 271-1708
  Janie Hatton, prin.
North Division HS ... 4-00011
  1011 W CENTER ST 53206 ... 265-1110
  Archie Ivy, prin.
Pleasant View HS ... 2-00011
  4920 W CAPITOL DR 53216 ... 464-2772
  Rosalie Greco, prin.
Pulaski HS ... 4-00011
  2500 W OKLAHOMA AVE 53215 ... 671-4000
  Michael Sonnenberg, prin.
Riverside HS, 1615 E LOCUST ST 53211 ... 4-00011
  Robert DiDonato, prin. ... 964-5900
South Division HS ... 4-00011
  1515 W LAPHAM BLVD 53204 ... 384-9900
  Efrain Vila, prin.
Vincent HS ... 4-00011
  7501 N GRANVILLE RD 53224 ... 354-4144
  Gloria Erkins, prin.
Washington HS ... 4-00011
  2525 N SHERMAN BLVD 53210 ... 444-9760
  Robert Nelson, prin.
Audubon MS, 3300 S 39TH ST 53215 ... 4-00100
  Suzanne Lundin, prin. ... 647-0300
Bell MS ... 3-00100
  6506 W WARNIMONT AVE 53220 ... 327-4720
  Donald Krueger, prin.
Burroughs MS, 6700 N 80TH ST 53223 ... 3-00100
  Victor Brazil, prin. ... 353-3220
Edison MS, 5372 N 37TH ST 53209 ... 3-00100
  Roy Robertson, prin. ... 461-3750
Fritsche MS, 2969 S HOWELL AVE 53207 ... 3-00100
  William Andrekopoulos, prin. ... 481-6720
Grand Ave MS ... 3-00100
  2430 W WISCONSIN AVE 53233 ... 993-9900
  Thomas McGinnity, prin.
Kosciuszko MS ... 3-00100
  971 W WINDLAKE AVE 53204 ... 383-3750
  John Valdes, prin.
Lincoln MS of the Arts ... 3-00100
  820 E KNAPP ST 53202 ... 272-6060
  Hector Perez-Laboy, prin.
Malcolm X Academy ... 3-00100
  2760 N 1ST ST 53212 – Ken Holt, prin. ... 264-0160
Morse MS, 4601 N 84TH ST 53225 ... 3-00100
  Rogers Onick, prin. ... 466-9920
Muir MS, 5496 N 72ND ST 53218 ... 3-00100
  Theadoll Taylor, prin. ... 464-6701
Parkman MS, 3620 N 18TH ST 53206 ... 3-00100
  Lafayette Golden, prin. ... 445-9930
Robinson MS, 3245 N 37TH ST 53216 ... 2-00100
  Alvin Spearman, prin. ... 445-7384
Roosevelt MS, 800 W WALNUT ST 53205 ... 3-00100
  Michael Hickey, prin. ... 263-2555
Scott MS, 1017 N 12TH ST 53233 ... 3-00100
  James Towns, prin. ... 344-6200
Sholes MS, 4965 S 20TH ST 53221 ... 3-00100
  Daniel Donder, prin. ... 281-5900
Steuben MS, 2360 N 52ND ST 53210 ... 3-00100
  William Stroud, prin. ... 449-0395
Walker MS, 1712 S 32ND ST 53215 ... 3-00100
  Marie Campos, prin. ... 647-1360
Webster MS, 6850 N 53RD ST 53223 ... 3-00100
  Saul Reeves, prin. ... 353-2680
Wright MS, 8400 W BURLEIGH ST 53222 ... 3-00100
  Susan Ratka, prin. ... 461-0150

Acme Institute of Technology ... 1-CS
  819 S 60TH ST 53214 ... 257-1011
Alverno College ... 4-UC
  PO BOX 343922 53234 ... 382-6064
Aurora Health Care ... 2-CS
  3000 W MONTANA ST 53215 ... 647-3000

Cardinal Stritch College ... 5-UC
  6801 N YATES RD 53217 ... 352-5400
Columbia College of Nursing ... 2-UC
  2121 E NEWPORT AVE 53211 ... 961-3890
Columbia Hospital ... HSP
  2025 E NEWPORT AVE 53211 ... 961-4202
Divine Savior-Holy Angles HS ... 3-00011
  4257 N 100TH ST 53222 ... 466-3706
  Angela Pienkos, prin.
Franciscan Shared Laboratory ... CS
  5000 W CHAMBERS ST 53210 ... 447-2355
Franciscan Shared Laboratory ... CS
  2400 W VILLARD AVE 53209 ... 527-8122
ITT Technical Institute ... 2-CC
  6300 W LAYTON AVE 53220 ... 282-9494
Marquette University ... 7-UC
  1217 W WISCONSIN AVE 53233 ... 800-222-6544
Marquette University HS ... 3-00011
  3401 N WISCONSIN AVE 53208 ... 933-7220
  Gordon Sharafinski, prin.
MBTI Business Training Institute ... 4-CS
  606 W WISCONSIN AVE 53203 ... 272-2192
Medical College of Wisconsin ... 3-UC
  8701 W WATERTOWN PLANK RD 53226 ... 257-8225
Messmer HS, 742 W CAPITOL DR 53206 ... 2-00011
  Br. Robert Smith, prin. ... 264-5440
Milwaukee Area Technical College ... 7-CC
  700 W STATE ST 53233 ... 278-6320
Milwaukee Institute of Art & Design ... 2-UC
  273 E ERIE ST 53202 ... 276-7889
Milwaukee Lutheran HS ... 3-00011
  9700 W GRANTOSA DR 53222 ... 461-6000
  Paul Bahr, prin.
Milwaukee School of Engineering ... 4-UC
  1025 N BROADWAY 53202 ... 277-7200
Mt. Mary College ... 4-UC
  2900 N MENOMONEE RIVER PKY 53222 ... 258-4810
Pius XI HS, 135 N 76TH ST 53213 ... 4-00011
  John Halupka, prin. ... 258-0532
St. Francis Hospital ... HSP
  3237 S 16TH ST 53215 ... 647-5106
St. Francis Seminary ... 1-UC
  3257 S LAKE DR 53235 ... 747-6400
St. Joan Antida HS ... 2-00011
  1341 N CASS ST 53202 ... 272-8423
  Sr. Monica Fumo, prin.
St. Luke's Medical Center ... HSP
  2900 W OKLAHOMA AVE 53215 ... 649-7500
Stratton College ... 3-CC
  1300 N JACKSON ST 53202 ... 276-5200
Thomas More HS ... 3-00011
  2601 E MORGAN AVE 53207 ... 481-8370
  Thomas Knitter, prin.
University of Wisconsin ... 7-UC
  PO BOX 413 53201 ... 229-4331
University S ... 3-11111
  2100 W FAIRY CHASM RD 53217 ... 352-6000
  Carol Krueger, prin.
Wisconsin Conservatory of Music ... 2-CS
  1584 N PROSPECT AVE 53202 ... 276-5760
Wisconsin Lutheran College ... 2-UC
  8830 W BLUEMOUND RD 53226 ... 774-8620
Wisconsin Lutheran HS ... 3-00011
  330 N GLENVIEW AVE 53213 ... 453-4567
  Ned Goede, prin.
Wisconsin School/Professional Psychology ... 1-UC
  9120 W HAMPTON AVE STE 212 53225 ... 281-3580
Zablocki VA Medical Center ... HSP
  5000 W NATIONAL AVE 53295 ... 384-2000

Mineral Point, AC 608, PC 4, Iowa
Mineral Point SD, 530 MAIDEN ST 53565 ... 3-11111
  Jeffrey Gruber, supt. ... 987-2371
HS, 706 RIDGE ST 53565 ... 2-00011
  Gary Adams, prin. ... 987-2321
MS, 530 MAIDEN ST 53565 ... 2-01100
  Katherine Martin, prin. ... 987-2371

Minocqua, AC 715, PC 4, Oneida
Lakeland UNHSD ... 3-00011
  8669 OLD HIGHWAY 70 54548 ... 356-5252
  Scott Peterson, supt.
Lakeland Union HS ... 3-00011
  8669 OLD HIGHWAY 70 54548 ... 356-5252
  Bruce Larose, prin.

Minong, AC 715, PC 3, Washburn
Northwood SD, PO BOX 10 54859 ... 2-11111
  Donald Danielson, supt. ... 466-2297
Northwood JSHS, PO BOX 10 54859 ... 2-00111
  Lee Block, prin. ... 466-2297

Mishicot, AC 414, PC 4, Manitowoc
Mishicot SD, PO BOX 93 54228 ... 3-11111
  (—), supt. ... 755-4633
JSHS, 660 WASHINGTON ST 54228 ... 2-00111
  Terry Vanhimbergen, prin. ... 755-2041

Mondovi, AC 715, PC 4, Buffalo
Mondovi SD, 337 N JACKSON ST 54755 ... 4-11111
  Glen Denk, supt. ... 926-3684
JSHS, 337 N JACKSON ST 54755 ... 2-00111
  Dean Anderson, prin. ... 926-3656

Monona, AC 608, PC 6, Dane
Monona Grove SD ... 4-11111
  5301 MONONA DR 53716 ... 221-7660
  John Box, supt.

Monona Grove HS
4400 MONONA DR 53716   3-00011
Gordon McChesney, prin.   221-7666
Winnequah MS   2-00100
800 GREENWAY RD 53716   221-7676
Jeffrey Klaisner, prin.

Monroe, AC 608, PC 7, Green
Monroe SD, 1220 16TH AVE 53566   5-11111
James Munro, supt.   328-9147
HS, 1600 26TH ST 53566   3-00011
Maurice Sathoff, prin.   328-9117
MS, 1510 13TH ST 53566   2-00100
Vincent Barnes, prin.   328-9120

Montello, AC 608, PC 4, Marquette
Montello SD, 222 FOREST LN 53949   3-11111
Roger Klug, supt.   297-7617
HS, 222 FOREST LN 53949   2-00011
Richard Natynski, prin.   297-2126

Monticello, AC 608, PC 4, Green
Monticello SD, PO BOX 67 53570   2-11111
James Egan, supt.   938-4194
JSHS, PO BOX 67 53570   2-00111
Joel Espe, prin.   938-4194

Mosinee, AC 715, PC 5, Marathon
Mosinee SD
591 W STATE HIGHWAY 153 54455   4-11111
Dennis Rislove, supt.   693-2530
HS, 1000 HIGH ST 54455   3-00011
James Debroux, prin.   693-2550
MS, 700 HIGH ST 54455   3-01100
James Kammerzelt, prin.   693-3660

Mount Calvary, AC 414, PC 3, Fond du Lac

St. Lawrence Seminary HS   2-00011
301 CHURCH ST 53057   753-3911
Fr. Clark, prin.

Mount Horeb, AC 608, PC 5, Dane
Mt. Horeb Area SD, PO BOX 87 53572   4-11111
Raymond Waier, supt.   437-5595
HS, 305 S 8TH ST 53572   2-00011
Richard Feutz, prin.   437-5516
MS, 207 ACADEMY ST 53572   2-00100
(—), prin.   437-3031

Mukwonago, AC 414, PC 5, Waukesha
Mukwonago SD, 423 DIVISION ST 53149   5-11111
Paul Strobel, supt.   363-6304
HS, 605 W SCHOOL RD 53149   4-00011
Dale Henry, prin.   363-6200
Park View MS   3-00100
930 N ROCHESTER ST 53149   363-6292
David Petersen, prin.

Norris SD   1-00111
W247S10395 CENTER RD 53149   662-3336
Roger Ellsworth, supt.
Norris JSHS   1-00111
W247S10395 CENTER RD 53149   662-3336
(—), prin.

Muscoda, AC 608, PC 4, Grant
Riverdale SD, PO BOX 66 53573   3-11111
Thomas Yager, supt.   739-3832
Riverdale HS, PO BOX 66 53573   2-00011
David McHenry, prin.   739-3116
Other Schools – See Blue River

Muskego, AC 414, PC 7, Waukesha
Muskego-Norway SD   5-11111
PO BOX 900 53150   422-1000
Richard Wasson, supt.
HS, PO BOX 901 53150   4-00011
Robert Rammer, prin.   679-2300
Bay Lane MS, PO BOX 902 53150   3-00100
Thomas Brown, prin.   422-0430

Nashotah, AC 414, PC 3, Waukesha
Lake Country SD   2-11100
W329N4476 LAKELAND DR 53058   367-3606
Melinda Waggoner, supt.
MS, W329N4476 LAKELAND DR 53058   2-01100
Bernard Stankewicz, prin.   367-3606

Nashotah House   1-UC
2777 MISSION RD 53058   646-3371

Necedah, AC 608, PC 3, Juneau
Necedah Area SD, 200 W 6TH ST 54646   3-11111
David Tymus, supt.   565-7045
HS, 200 W 6TH ST 54646   2-00011
Charlie Krupa, prin.   565-2256

Neenah, AC 414, PC 7, Winnebago
Neenah SD   6-11111
410 S COMMERCIAL ST 54956   751-6808
Richard Carlson, supt.
SHS, 1275 TULLAR RD 54956   4-00001
Larry Lewis, prin.   751-6905
Shattuck JHS, 600 ELM ST 54956   4-00110
Keith Ryskoski, prin.   751-6854

Queen of the Holy Rosary S   2-11111
W5606 SHRINE RD 54646   565-2341
Joan McNally, prin.
Theda Clark Regional Medical Center   HSP
130 2ND ST 54956   729-2004

Neillsville, AC 715, PC 5, Clark
Neillsville SD, 614 E 5TH ST 54456   4-11111
Richard Quast, supt.   743-3323
HS, 401 CENTER ST 54456   2-00011
John Gaier, prin.   743-3323
MS, 504 E 5TH ST 54456   2-00100
Duane Arndt, prin.   743-3323

Nekoosa, AC 715, PC 5, Wood
Nekoosa SD, 600 S SECTION ST 54457   4-11111
Richard Millenbah, supt.   886-8000
HS, 500 CEDAR ST 54457   2-00011
Boyd Campbell, prin.   886-8060
Alexander MS, 310 1ST ST 54457   2-01100
Peter Pavloski, prin.   886-8040

New Auburn, AC 715, PC 2, Chippewa
New Auburn SD, PO BOX 110 54757   2-11111
Daniel Hickey, supt.   237-2202
HS, PO BOX 110 54757   2-00011
Charles Zielin, prin.   237-2505

New Berlin, AC 414, PC 8, Waukesha
New Berlin SD   5-11111
4333 S SUNNYSLOPE RD 53151   786-6220
James Benfield, supt.
Eisenhower HS   3-00011
4333 S SUNNYSLOPE RD 53151   789-6300
Ted Oertel, prin.
HS, 18695 W CLEVELAND AVE 53146   3-00011
Douglas Straus, prin.   789-6400
Eisenhower MS   2-00100
4333 S SUNNYSLOPE RD 53151   789-6300
Paul Holweck, prin.
MS, 18695 W CLEVELAND AVE 53146   2-00100
John Harder, prin.   789-6470

New Glarus, AC 608, PC 4, Green
New Glarus SD, PO BOX 37 53574   3-11111
Peter Etter, supt.   527-2810
JSHS, PO BOX 7 53574   2-00011
Duane Schober, prin.   527-2410

New Holstein, AC 414, PC 5, Calumet
New Holstein SD   4-11111
1715 PLYMOUTH ST 53061   898-5115
Charles Basting, supt.
HS, 1715 PLYMOUTH ST 53061   3-00011
George Brandenstein, prin.   898-4256

New Lisbon, AC 608, PC 4, Juneau
New Lisbon SD, PO BOX 205 53950   3-11111
Roger Derrickson, supt.   562-3700
HS, 500 S FOREST ST 53950   2-00011
Kenneth Adams, prin.   562-3700

New London, AC 414, PC 6, Waupaca
New London SD   4-11111
901 W WASHINGTON ST 54961   982-8530
Kenneth Renning, supt.
SHS, 1000 W WASHINGTON ST 54961   3-00001
John Partenheimer, prin.   982-8532
Washington JHS   3-00110
500 W WASHINGTON ST 54961   982-8536
Carol Bitar, prin.

New Richmond, AC 715, PC 6, St. Croix
New Richmond SD, 152 E 4TH ST 54017   4-11111
Thomas Kleppe, supt.   243-7411
HS, 152 E 4TH ST 54017   3-00011
Steven Wojan, prin.   243-7451
MS, 152 E 4TH ST 54017   3-01100
James Johnson, prin.   243-7471

Wisconsin Indianhead Technical College   2-CS
1019 S KNOWLES AVE 54017   246-6561

Niagara, AC 715, PC 4, Marinette
Niagara SD, 700 JEFFERSON AVE 54151   3-11111
Frederick Aronson, supt.   251-1330
JSHS, 1200 RIVER ST 54151   2-00011
Kerry Grippen, prin.   251-4541

North Fond du Lac, AC 414, PC 5, Fond du Lac
North Fond Du Lac SD   4-11111
225 MCKINLEY ST 54937   929-3750
Donald Kellogg, supt.
Mann High School   2-00011
225 MCKINLEY ST 54937   929-3740
Bradley Hintze, prin.
Allen MS, 923 MINNESOTA AVE 54937   2-01100
Steven Sontag, prin.   929-3754

Oak Creek, AC 414, PC 7, Milwaukee
Oak Creek-Franklin SD   5-11111
7630 S 10TH ST 53154   768-5886
Lawrence Pekoe, supt.
HS, 340 E PUETZ RD 53154   4-00011
Irwin Smith, prin.   768-6210
Oak Creek East MS   3-00100
9330 S SHEPARD AVE 53154   768-6260
Paul Sigler, prin.
Oak Creek West MS   3-00100
8401 S 13TH ST 53154   768-6260
Carol Hansis, prin.

Milwaukee Area Technical College   4-CC
6665 S HOWELL AVE 53154   762-2500
Parkway Christian Academy   2-11111
10940 S NICHOLSON RD 53154   764-4130
Frank Tamel, prin.

Oakfield, AC 414, PC 4, Fond du Lac
Oakfield SD, PO BOX 99 53065   3-11111
Joseph Heinzelman, supt.   583-3146

HS, PO BOX 39 53065   2-00011
Paul Dix, prin.   583-3141
MS, PO BOX 69 53065   2-00100
Paul Dix, prin.   583-4117

Oconomowoc, AC 414, PC 7, Waukesha
Oconomowoc Area SD   5-11111
W360N7077 BROWN ST 53066   567-6633
John Graves, supt.
HS, 641 E FOREST ST 53066   4-00011
Frank Rosengren, prin.   567-1505
MS, 623 SUMMIT AVE 53066   3-00100
Keith Hicklin, prin.   567-1617

Oconto, AC 414, PC 5, Oconto
Oconto SD, 1717 SUPERIOR AVE 54153   4-11111
Jerome Sommer, supt.   834-7800
HS, 1717 SUPERIOR AVE 54153   2-00011
Larry Elliott, prin.   834-7800
Washington JHS   2-00100
400 MICHIGAN AVE 54153   834-7806
Beatrice Elsworth, prin.

Oconto Falls, AC 414, PC 5, Oconto
Oconto Falls SD, 200 FARM ROAD 54154   4-11111
David Polashek, supt.   846-4471
HS, 408 CEDAR AVE 54154   3-00011
William Lachapell, prin.   846-4467
Washington MS   2-00100
102 S WASHINGTON ST 54154   846-4463
K Makuck, prin.

Omro, AC 414, PC 5, Winnebago
Omro SD, 455 LEACH ST 54963   4-11111
Oren Barker, supt.   685-5666
HS, 455 LEACH ST 54963   2-00011
Edward Goss, prin.   685-5668
MS, 455 LEACH ST 54963   2-00100
Terrance Taylor, prin.   685-5603

Onalaska, AC 608, PC 7, La Crosse
Onalaska SD, PO BOX 429 54650   4-11111
Robert Weber, supt.   781-9700
HS, 700 HILLTOPPER PL 54650   3-00011
Paul Neman, prin.   783-4561
MS, 711 QUINCY ST 54650   3-01100
Francis Finco, prin.   783-5366

Luther HS, PO BOX 129 54650   2-00011
James Raabe, prin.   783-5435

Ontario, AC 608, PC 2, Vernon
Norwalk-Ontario SD   2-11111
RR 1 BOX 130 54651   337-4403
Al Szepi, supt.
Brookwood JSHS   2-00111
RR 1 BOX 130 54651   337-4401
Robert Keller, prin.

Oostburg, AC 414, PC 4, Sheboygan
Oostburg SD, 410 NEW YORK AVE 53070   3-11111
Marvin Hopland, supt.   564-2346
HS, 410 NEW YORK AVE 53070   2-00011
Michael Donnelly, prin.   564-2346
MS, 408 NEW YORK AVE 53070   2-00100
John Lacke, prin.   564-2367

Oregon, AC 608, PC 5, Dane
Oregon SD, 200 N MAIN ST 53575   4-11111
Linda Barrows, supt.   835-3161
HS, 456 N PERRY PKY 53575   3-00011
Gilman Voss, prin.   835-3161
JHS, 601 PLEASANT OAK DR 53575   2-00100
Steven Staton, prin.   835-3161

Orfordville, AC 608, PC 4, Rock
Parkview SD, PO BOX 250 53576   4-11111
David Romstad, supt.   876-6227
Parkview HS, PO BOX 247 53576   2-00011
Donald Albright, prin.   879-2994
Parkview JHS, PO BOX 247 53576   2-00100
Greg Fahrman, prin.   879-2994

Osceola, AC 715, PC 4, Polk
Osceola SD, PO BOX 128 54020   4-11111
Michael Williams, supt.   294-4140
HS, PO BOX 128 54020   2-00011
James Martell, prin.   294-2127
MS, PO BOX 128 54020   2-01100
Roger Kumlien, prin.   294-4180

Oshkosh, AC 414, PC 8, Winnebago
Oshkosh Area SD   6-11111
PO BOX 3048 54903   424-0160
James Henderson, supt.
North HS, 1100 W SMITH AVE 54901   4-00011
Robert Kellerman, prin.   233-7000
West HS, 375 N EAGLE ST 54901   4-00011
John Sheehy, prin.   424-4090
Merrill MS   2-00100
108 W NEW YORK AVE 54901   424-0177
Donald Dutton, prin.
South Park MS   2-00100
1551 DELAWARE ST 54901   424-0431
William Holm, prin.
Stanley MS, 915 HAZEL ST 54901   2-00100
(—), prin.   424-0442
Tipler MS, 325 S EAGLE ST 54901   2-00100
James Hoffman, prin.   424-0320

Lourdes Academy   2-00011
110 N SAWYER ST 54901   235-5670
Carol Staszkiewicz, prin.

Mercy Medical Center ... HSP
  631 HAZEL ST 54901 ... 233-5110
Oshkosh Christian S ... 2-11111
  808 N MAIN ST 54901 ... 231-9704
    Larry Detmers, prin.
St. John Neumann S ... 2-00100
  449 HIGH AVE 54901 ... 235-6155
    Sr. Carol Peterson, prin.
University of Wisconsin ... 6-UC
  800 ALGOMA BLVD 54901 ... 424-0200
Wyldewood Christian S ... 2-11111
  3030 E COUNTY RD E 54904 ... 235-5400
    Randall King, prin.

Osseo, AC 715, PC 4, Trempealeau
Osseo-Fairchild SD ... 3-11111
  PO BOX 130 54758 ... 597-3141
    Gerald Nelson, supt.
Osseo-Fairchild HS ... 2-00011
  PO BOX 130 54758 ... 597-3141
    Dean Sanders, prin.
JHS, PO BOX 130 54758 ... 2-00100
    Robert Gamache, prin. ... 597-3141

Owen, AC 715, PC 3, Clark
Owen-Withee SD, PO BOX 417 54460 ... 3-11111
    Gary Marine, supt. ... 229-2151
Owen-Withee HS ... 2-00011
  PO BOX 417 54460 ... 229-2151
    Charles Deery, prin.
Owen-Withee JHS ... 2-00100
  PO BOX 417 54460 ... 229-2151
    Charles Deery, prin.

Palmyra, AC 414, PC 4, Jefferson
Palmyra-Eagle Area SD ... 4-11111
  709 MAPLE ST 53156 ... 495-7100
    Carolyn Stoner, supt.
Palmyra-Eagle HS ... 2-00011
  123 BURR OAK ST 53156 ... 495-7101
    Jeff Tortomasi, prin.
JHS, 701 MAPLE ST 53156 ... 2-00100
    Mary Topp, prin. ... 495-7102

Pardeeville, AC 608, PC 4, Columbia
Pardeeville Area SD ... 3-11111
  120 S OAK ST 53954 ... 429-2153
    Arthur Keenan, supt.
HS, 120 S OAK ST 53954 ... 2-00011
    Cynthia Bomber, prin. ... 429-2153
JHS, 120 S OAK ST 53954 ... 2-00110
    Cynthia Bomber, prin. ... 429-2153

Park Falls, AC 715, PC 5, Price
Park Falls SD, 420 2ND AVE N 54552 ... 3-11111
    Michael Peterson, supt. ... 762-4343
HS, 400 9TH ST N 54552 ... 2-00011
    Anthony Burant, prin. ... 762-2474
Lincoln MS, 420 2ND AVE N 54552 ... 2-00100
    Richard Ross, prin. ... 762-3815

Patch Grove, AC 608, PC 2, Grant
West Grant SD, PO BOX 78 53817 ... 2-11111
    Kenneth Ochalla, supt. ... 994-2718
West Grant HS, PO BOX 78 53817 ... 2-00011
    Kenneth Ochalla, prin. ... 994-2718
West Grant MS, PO BOX 78 53817 ... 1-00100
    Kenneth Ochalla, prin. ... 994-2718

Pembine, AC 715, PC 3, Marinette
Beecher-Dunbar-Pembine SD ... 2-11111
  PO BOX 247 54156 ... 324-5314
    Cornelis Vander Zeyden, supt.
HS, PO BOX 247 54156 ... 2-00011
    Dan Nylund, prin. ... 324-5314

Pepin, AC 715, PC 3, Pepin
Pepin Area SD, PO BOX 128 54759 ... 2-11111
    Rick Palmer, supt. ... 442-2391
HS, PO BOX 128 54759 ... 2-00011
    Greg Danke, prin. ... 442-3151

Peshtigo, AC 715, PC 5, Marinette
Peshtigo SD, 341 N EMERY AVE 54157 ... 3-11111
    George Fox, supt. ... 582-3677
JSHS, 380 GREEN ST 54157 ... 2-00111
    Richard McDougal, prin. ... 582-3711

Pewaukee, AC 414, PC 5, Waukesha
Pewaukee SD, 510 LAKE ST 53072 ... 4-11111
    Lee Wille, supt. ... 691-2100
HS, 510 LAKE ST 53072 ... 2-00011
    Hollis Herrell, prin. ... 691-2100
MS, 510 LAKE ST 53072 ... 2-00100
    Ronald Feuerstein, prin. ... 691-2100

Waukesha County Technical College ... 4-CC
  800 MAIN ST 53072 ... 691-5201

Phelps, AC 715, PC 3, Vilas
Phelps SD, PO BOX 6 54554 ... 2-11111
    Tom Strick, supt. ... 545-2724
HS, PO BOX 6 54554 ... 1-00011
    Tom Strick, prin. ... 545-2724

Phillips, AC 715, PC 4, Price
Phillips SD, PO BOX 70 54555 ... 4-11111
    Frank Harrington, supt. ... 339-2141
HS, PO BOX 70 54555 ... 2-00011
    Scott Johnson, prin. ... 339-2141
MS, PO BOX 70 54555 ... 2-01100
    Randal Braun, prin. ... 339-3393
Other Schools – See Catawba

Pittsville, AC 715, PC 3, Wood
Pittsville SD, PO BOX 6 54466 ... 3-11111
    Milo Fossen, supt. ... 884-6694
HS, PO BOX 6 54466 ... 2-00011
    Richard Adams, prin. ... 884-6412

Plainfield, AC 715, PC 3, Waushara
Tri-County Area SD ... 3-11111
  PO BOX 67 54966 ... 335-6391
    James Erdman, supt.
Tri-County HS, PO BOX 67 54966 ... 2-00011
    Dennis Ferriter, prin. ... 335-6366
Tri-County MS, PO BOX 67 54966 ... 2-01100
    James Miller, prin. ... 335-4654

Platteville, AC 608, PC 6, Grant
Platteville SD, 780 N 2ND ST 53818 ... 4-11111
    Dean Isaacson, supt. ... 342-4400
HS, 710 E MADISON ST 53818 ... 3-00011
    Robert Trickel, prin. ... 342-4420
MS, 40 E MADISON ST 53818 ... 3-01100
    Alan Eveland, prin. ... 342-4480

University of Wisconsin ... 6-UC
  1 UNIVERSITY PLZ 53818 ... 342-1125

Plum City, AC 715, PC 3, Pierce
Plum City SD, 907 MAIN ST 54761 ... 2-11111
    Tom Casey, supt. ... 647-2591
HS, 907 MAIN ST 54761 ... 2-00011
    Michael Crowley, prin. ... 647-2591

Plymouth, AC 414, PC 6, Sheboygan
Plymouth SD ... 4-11111
  106 S HIGHLAND AVE 53073 ... 892-2661
    Paul Brandl, supt.
HS, 125 S HIGHLAND AVE 53073 ... 3-00011
    Jeff Jacobson, prin. ... 893-6911
Riverview MS ... 2-00100
  300 RIVERVIEW CIR 53073 ... 892-4353
    Russell Groblewski, prin.

Poplar, AC 715, PC 3, Douglas
Maple SD
  Supt. — See Maple
Northwestern MS, PO BOX 46 54864 ... 2-00100
    Norb Philipsek, prin. ... 364-2218

Portage, AC 608, PC 6, Columbia
Portage Community SD ... 4-11111
  904 DE WITT ST 53901 ... 742-4879
    Daniel Pulsfus, supt.
SHS, 2505 NEW PINERY RD 53901 ... 3-00001
    Stephen Willson, prin. ... 742-8545
JHS, 117 W FRANKLIN ST 53901 ... 2-00110
    Wayne Bartels, prin. ... 742-2165

Port Edwards, AC 715, PC 4, Wood
Port Edwards SD, 801 2ND ST 54469 ... 2-11111
    Steve Mieden, supt. ... 887-3150
Edwards HS, 801 2ND ST 54469 ... 2-00011
    Pat Swartz, prin. ... 887-3150

Port Washington, AC 414, PC 6, Ozaukee
Port Washington-Saukville SD ... 5-11111
  100 W MONROE ST 53074 ... 284-7700
    James Badertscher, supt.
HS, 427 W JACKSON ST 53074 ... 3-00011
    James Gottinger, prin. ... 284-7712
Jefferson MS, 1403 N HOLDEN ST 53074 ... 3-01100
    Arlan Galarowicz, prin. ... 284-7731

Port Wing, AC 715, PC 2, Bayfield
South Shore SD, PO BOX 40 54865 ... 2-11111
    Paul Prevenas, supt. ... 774-3500
South Shore JSHS ... 2-00111
  PO BOX 105 54865 ... 774-3361
    Russell McGillivray, prin.

Potosi, AC 608, PC 3, Grant
Potosi SD, PO BOX 193 53820 ... 2-11111
    Eric Briehl, supt. ... 763-2163
HS, PO BOX 193 53820 ... 2-00011
    Steve Lozeau, prin. ... 763-2161

Poynette, AC 608, PC 4, Columbia
Poynette SD, PO BOX 10 53955 ... 4-11111
    John Sarnow, supt. ... 635-4347
HS, 108 N CLEVELAND 53955 ... 2-00011
    Craig McCallum, prin. ... 635-4345
MS, 108 N CLEVELAND 53955 ... 2-00100
    James Carelli, prin. ... 635-4341

Prairie Du Chien, AC 608, PC 6, Crawford
Prairie Du Chien Area SD ... 4-11111
  800 E CRAWFORD ST 53821 ... 326-8437
    John Foster, supt.
HS, 800 E CRAWFORD ST 53821 ... 2-00011
    Duane Bark, prin. ... 326-8437
MS, 400 S WACOUTA AVE 53821 ... 2-00100
    Merle Frommelt, prin. ... 326-8451

Martin Luther Prep S ... 2-00011
  405 E CAMPION BLVD 53821 ... 326-8480
    Rev. Olsen, prin.
St. John Nepomucene ES ... 2-00100
  720 S WACOUTA AVE 53821 ... 326-4400
    Lee Kaschinska, prin.

Prairie Du Sac, AC 608, PC 4, Sauk
Sauk Prairie SD
  Supt. — See Sauk City
Sauk Prairie HS, 105 9TH ST 53578 ... 3-00011
    Thomas Andres, prin. ... 643-3336

Prairie Farm, AC 715, PC 2, Barron
Prairie Farm SD, 630 RIVER AVE 54762 ... 2-11111
    John Banks, supt. ... 455-1683
JSHS, 630 RIVER AVE 54762 ... 2-00111
    Brad Pettit, prin. ... 455-1861

Prentice, AC 715, PC 3, Price
Prentice SD, PO BOX 110 54556 ... 3-11111
    Gregory Krause, supt. ... 428-2813
HS, PO BOX 110 54556 ... 2-00011
    Richard Meneau, prin. ... 428-2811

Prescott, AC 715, PC 5, Pierce
Prescott SD ... 4-11111
  1220 SAINT CROIX ST 54021 ... 262-5782
    Carroll Lehman, supt.
HS, 1220 SAINT CROIX ST 54021 ... 2-00011
    Daniel Bodette, prin. ... 262-5010
MS, 125 ELM ST N 54021 ... 2-00100
    R. W. Hoffmann, prin. ... 262-5052

Princeton, AC 414, PC 4, Green Lake
Princeton SD, PO BOX 147 54968 ... 2-11111
    Marvin Groskreutz, supt. ... 295-6571
HS, PO BOX 147 54968 ... 2-00011
    Troy Gunderson, prin. ... 295-6571

Pulaski, AC 414, PC 4, Brown
Pulaski Community SD ... 5-11111
  PO BOX 36 54162 ... 822-4200
    Steven Koch, supt.
HS, N911 SAINT AUGUSTINE ST 54162 ... 3-00011
    Guy David, prin. ... 822-4223

Racine, AC 414, PC 8, Racine
Racine SD ... 7-11111
  2220 NORTHWESTERN AVE 53404 ... 631-7064
    Major Armstead, supt.
Case HS ... 4-00011
  7374 WASHINGTON AVE 53406 ... 886-2716
    Joseph Mitchell, prin.
Horlick HS, 2119 RAPIDS DR 53404 ... 4-00011
    Nola Starling-Ratliff, prin. ... 631-7008
Park HS, 1901 12TH ST 53403 ... 4-00011
    Peter Alvino, prin. ... 631-7222
Gilmore MS, 2201 HIGH ST 53404 ... 4-00100
    Patricia Stephens-Rogers, prin. ... 632-1657
Jerstad-Agerholm MS ... 3-00100
  3601 LA SALLE ST 53402 ... 639-5600
    Tom Siefert, prin.
McKinley MS, 2326 MOHR AVE 53405 ... 3-00100
    John Pelej, prin. ... 631-7210
Mitchell MS, 2701 DREXEL AVE 53403 ... 4-00100
    Ralph Montgomery, prin. ... 633-2491
Starbuck MS, 1516 OHIO ST 53405 ... 3-00100
    Judith Mortell, prin. ... 637-8801

Gateway Technical College ... 3-CC
  1001 S MAIN ST 53403 ... 637-9881
Lutheran HS, 251 LUEDTKE AVE 53405 ... 2-00011
    Raymond Hauer, prin. ... 637-6538
Prairie S, 4050 LIGHTHOUSE DR 53402 ... 2-11111
    Mark Murphy, prin. ... 631-3845
St. Catherines HS, 1200 PARK AVE 53403 ... 3-00011
    Joseph Peschges, prin. ... 632-2785
St. Luke's Memorial Hospital ... HSP
  1320 WISCONSIN AVE 53403 ... 636-2218
St. Mary's Medical Center ... HSP
  3801 SPRING ST 53405 ... 636-4285

Randolph, AC 414, PC 4, Columbia
Randolph SD ... 2-11111
  110 MEADOWOOD DR 53956 ... 326-3141
    Albert Holmquist, supt.
HS, 110 MEADOWOOD DR 53956 ... 2-00011
    Christopher Nelson, prin. ... 326-3141

Random Lake, AC 414, PC 4, Sheboygan
Random Lake SD ... 4-11111
  605 RANDOM LAKE RD 53075 ... 994-4342
    Francis Murphy, supt.
HS, 605 RANDOM LAKE RD 53075 ... 2-00011
    Kenneth Jakubowski, prin. ... 994-9193
MS, 605 RANDOM LAKE RD 53075 ... 2-00100
    David Farnham, prin. ... 994-2498

Reedsburg, AC 608, PC 6, Sauk
Reedsburg SD, 710 N WEBB AVE 53959 ... 4-11111
    Robert Allen, supt. ... 524-2401
Webb HS, 707 N WEBB AVE 53959 ... 3-00011
    Randy Kuhnau, prin. ... 524-4327
MS, 1121 8TH ST 53959 ... 2-01100
    James Wieczorek, prin. ... 524-2328

Reedsville, AC 414, PC 4, Manitowoc
Reedsville SD, PO BOX 82 54230 ... 3-11111
    Jerome Runice, supt. ... 754-4341
HS, PO BOX 82 54230 ... 2-00011
    William Dietz, prin. ... 754-4341
JHS, PO BOX 82 54230 ... 1-00100
    William Dietz, prin. ... 754-4341

Reeseville, AC 414, PC 3, Dodge
Dodgeland SD
  Supt. — See Juneau
Dodgeland JHS, PO BOX 8 53579 ... 2-00100
    Robert Peterson, prin. ... 927-3831

Rhinelander, AC 715, PC 6, Oneida
Rhinelander SD ... 5-11111
  315 S ONEIDA AVE 54501 ... 362-3465
    Robert Hanson, supt.
HS, 665 COOLIDGE AVE 54501 ... 3-00011
    James Gehrke, prin. ... 365-9506

Williams MS, 915 ACACIA LN 54501 — 3-00100 — 369-1315
Robert Fabich, prin.

Nicolet Area Technical College — 2-CC — 369-4410
PO BOX 518 54501

Rib Lake, AC 715, PC 3, Taylor
Rib Lake SD, PO BOX 278 54470 — 3-11111 — 427-3222
Ramon Parks, supt.
HS, PO BOX 278 54470 — 2-00011 — 427-3220
Paul Peterson, prin.
MS, PO BOX 278 54470 — 2-00100 — 427-5446
Dan Boxx, prin.

Rice Lake, AC 715, PC 6, Barron
Rice Lake Area SD — 5-11111 — 234-9007
700 AUGUSTA ST 54868
Robert Foster, supt.
HS, 30 S WISCONSIN AVE 54868 — 3-00011 — 234-2182
Robert Fisher, prin.
MS, 204 CAMERON RD 54868 — 3-00100 — 234-8157
Thomas Hickox, prin.

University of Wisconsin Center — 2-CC — 234-8176
1800 COLLEGE DR 54868

Richland Center, AC 608, PC 6, Richland
Ithaca SD, RR 2 53581 — 2-11111 — 585-2512
Stephen Pearson, supt.
Ithaca HS, RR 2 53581 — 1-00011 — 585-2311
Ernest Modjeski, prin.
Ithaca JHS, RR 2 53581 — 1-00100 — 585-2311
Ernest Modjeski, prin.

Richland SD — 4-11111 — 647-6106
125 S CENTRAL AVE 53581
Edwin Meyer, supt.
HS, 649 N PARK ST 53581 — 3-00011 — 647-6131
Daniel Davies, prin.
Richland MS, RR 4 53581 — 2-00100 — 647-6381
David Siefkes, prin.

University of Wisconsin Center 53581 — 2-CC — 647-6186

Rio, AC 414, PC 3, Columbia
Rio Community SD — 3-11111 — 992-3141
PO BOX 275 53960
Terry Milfred, supt.
HS, PO BOX 275 53960 — 2-00011 — 992-3141
Douglas Shippert, prin.

Ripon, AC 414, PC 6, Fond du Lac
Ripon SD, PO BOX 991 54971 — 4-11111 — 748-5151
Michael Heckman, supt.
HS, PO BOX 991 54971 — 3-00011 — 748-4616
Roland Alger, prin.
MS, PO BOX 991 54971 — 2-00100 — 748-4638
Leland Nelson, prin.

Ripon College — 3-UC — 748-8118
PO BOX 248 54971

River Falls, AC 715, PC 7, Pierce
River Falls SD, 852 E DIVISION ST 54022 — 5-11111 — 425-1800
Dennis Kraft, supt.
HS, 230 N 9TH ST 54022 — 3-00011 — 425-1810
G. R. Hanson, prin.
MS, 211 N FREEMONT ST 54022 — 3-00100 — 425-1820
G. Schramm, prin.

University of Wisconsin 54022 — 5-UC — 425-3500

Rosendale, AC 414, PC 3, Fond du Lac
Rosendale-Brandon SD — 4-11111 — 872-2151
PO BOX 1000 54974
Ronald Milton, supt.
Laconia HS, PO BOX 147 54974 — 2-00011 — 872-2161
Gary Hanson, prin.
MS, PO BOX 545 54974 — 2-00100 — 872-2126
(—), prin.
Other Schools – See Brandon

Rosholt, AC 715, PC 3, Portage
Rosholt SD, PO BOX 310 54473 — 3-11111 — 677-4542
Kathleen Martinsen, supt.
JSHS, 346 W RANDOLPH ST 54473 — 2-00111 — 677-4541
James Krems, prin.

Saint Croix Falls, AC 715, PC 4, Polk
St. Croix Falls SD, PO BOX 130 54024 — 3-11111 — 483-9823
Fred Johnson, supt.
HS, PO BOX 130 54024 — 2-00011 — 483-9826
Monte Fay, prin.
Sorensen MS, PO BOX 130 54024 — 2-00100 — 483-9823
Kathleen Willow, prin.

Saint Francis, AC 414, PC 6, Milwaukee
St. Francis SD, 4225 S LAKE DR 53235 — 4-11111 — 483-7636
David Ross, supt.
HS, 4225 S LAKE DR 53235 — 2-00011 — 481-2840
J. P. Campion, prin.

Salem, AC 414, PC 4, Kenosha
Central-Westosha UNHSD — 3-00011 — 843-2321
PO BOX 38 53168
Gerald Sorenson, supt.
Central HS, PO BOX 38 53168 — 3-00011 — 843-2321
Sigmund Koland, prin.

Sauk City, AC 608, PC 5, Sauk
Sauk Prairie SD, 213 MAPLE ST 53583 — 4-11111 — 643-3336
Richard Magnuson, supt.

Sauk Prairie MS, 207 MAPLE ST 53583 — 2-00100 — 643-3336
Ellen Paul, prin.
Other Schools – See Prairie Du Sac

Schofield, AC 715, PC 4, Marathon
D. C. Everest Area SD — 5-11111 — 359-4221
6300 ALDERSON ST 54476
Gerald Makie, supt.
D C Everest SHS — 4-00001 — 359-6561
6500 ALDERSON ST 54476
Roger Dodd, prin.
D C Everest JHS — 4-00110 — 359-0511
1000 MACHMUELLER ST 54476
Robert Knaack, prin.

Seneca, AC 608, PC 2, Crawford
Seneca SD, PO BOX 34 54654 — 2-11111 — 734-3411
Sara Croney, supt.
HS, PO BOX 34 54654 — 2-00011 — 734-3411
Ronald Boettcher, prin.
JHS, PO BOX 34 54654 — 1-00100 — 734-3411
Ronald Boettcher, prin.

Seymour, AC 414, PC 5, Outagamie
Seymour Community SD — 4-11111 — 833-2304
10 CIRCLE DR 54165
William Loasching, supt.
HS, 10 CIRCLE DR 54165 — 3-00011 — 833-2306
John Peterson, prin.
Seymour MS, 10 CIRCLE DR 54165 — 2-00100 — 833-7199
Robert Battisti, prin.

Shawano, AC 715, PC 6, Shawano
Shawano-Gresham SD — 4-11111 — 526-3194
210 S FRANKLIN ST 54166
Frederick Davel, supt.
HS, 1050 S UNION ST 54166 — 3-00011 — 526-2175
James Lehto, prin.
Franklin MS, 210 S FRANKLIN ST 54166 — 2-00100 — 526-2192
James Yeakey, prin.
Other Schools – See Gresham

Sheboygan, AC 414, PC 8, Sheboygan
Howards Grove SD
Supt. — See Howards Grove
Northview MS, 902 TYLER RD 53083 — 2-01100 — 565-4457
Diane Weiland, prin.

Sheboygan Area SD — 6-11111 — 459-3511
830 VIRGINIA AVE 53081
George Longo, supt.
North HS, 1042 SCHOOL AVE 53083 — 4-00011 — 459-3603
Robert Ericson, prin.
South HS, 3128 S 12TH ST 53081 — 4-00011 — 459-3634
Thomas Edson, prin.
Farnsworth MS, 1017 UNION AVE 53081 — 3-00100 — 459-3655
Allan Calabresa, prin.
Mann MS, 2820 UNION AVE 53081 — 3-00100 — 459-3666
Warren Brewer, prin.
Urban MS, 1226 NORTH AVE 53083 — 3-00100 — 459-3677
James Lowell, prin.

Lakeland College — 4-UC — 565-1201
PO BOX 359 53082
Lutheran HS — 2-00011 — 452-3323
3323 UNIVERSITY DR 53081
Robert Kasten, prin.
Sheboygan County Christian HS — 2-00011 — 458-9981
929 GREENFIELD AVE 53081
Merl Alons, prin.
University of Wisconsin Center — 2-CC — 459-3733
1 UNIVERSITY DR 53081

Sheboygan Falls, AC 414, PC 6, Sheboygan
Sheboygan Falls SD — 4-11111 — 467-7893
220 AMHERST AVE 53085
Norman Frakes, supt.
HS, 220 AMHERST AVE 53085 — 3-00011 — 467-7890
Thomas Grams, prin.
MS, SCHOOL STREET 53085 — 2-00100 — 467-7880
Brian Hanes, prin.

Shell Lake, AC 715, PC 4, Washburn
Shell Lake SD, RR 1 BOX 267 54871 — 3-11111 — 468-7816
Roger Hulne, supt.
HS, RR 1 BOX 267 54871 — 2-00011 — 468-7814
Terry Reynolds, prin.
MS, RR 1 BOX 267 54871 — 2-00100 — 468-7814
Terry Reynolds, prin.

Wisconsin Indianhead Technical College — 4-CC — 468-2815
HC 69 BOX 10B 54871

Shiocton, AC 414, PC 3, Outagamie
Shiocton SD, PO BOX 68 54170 — 3-11111 — 986-3351
Robert McCoy, supt.
HS, PO BOX 68 54170 — 2-00011 — 986-3351
Jim Quinn, prin.

Shorewood, AC 414, PC 7, Milwaukee
Shorewood SD — 4-11111 — 963-6901
1701 E CAPITOL DR 53211
John Linehan, supt.
HS, 1701 E CAPITOL DR 53211 — 3-00011 — 963-6921
John Linehan, prin.
JHS, 3830 N MORRIS BLVD 53211 — 2-00100 — 963-6951
Roxanne Hanney, prin.

Shullsburg, AC 608, PC 4, Lafayette
Shullsburg SD — 2-11111 — 965-4427
444 N JUDGEMENT ST 53586
John Timmerman, supt.
HS, 444 N JUDGEMENT ST 53586 — 2-00011 — 965-4427
David Klein, prin.

JHS, 444 N JUDGEMENT ST 53586 — 1-00100 — 965-4427
David Klein, prin.

Siren, AC 715, PC 3, Burnett
Siren SD, PO BOX 29 54872 — 2-11111 — 349-2290
Gerald Mikunda, supt.
HS, PO BOX 29 54872 — 2-00011 — 349-2277
James Bucher, prin.

Slinger, AC 414, PC 4, Washington
Slinger SD — 4-11111 — 644-9615
207 E WASHINGTON ST 53086
Mark Heyerdahl, supt.
SHS, 209 E WASHINGTON ST 53086 — 2-00001 — 644-5261
Joseph Wikrent, prin.
JHS, 205 E WASHINGTON ST 53086 — 3-00110 — 644-5226
Kevin Bacon, prin.

Solon Springs, AC 715, PC 3, Douglas
Solon Springs SD — 2-11111 — 378-2263
RR 1 BOX 571 54873
Bruce Anderson, supt.
St. Croix JSHS, RR 1 BOX 571 54873 — 2-00011 — 378-2263
S. Berger, prin.

Somers, AC 414, PC 3, Kenosha

Shoreland Lutheran HS — 2-00011 — 859-2595
PO BOX 295 53171
Neil Scriver, prin.

Somerset, AC 715, PC 4, St. Croix
Somerset SD, PO BOX 100 54025 — 3-11111 — 247-3313
Dianne Beeler, supt.
JSHS, PO BOX 100 54025 — 2-00111 — 247-3355
Randy Rosburg, prin.

South Milwaukee, AC 414, PC 7, Milwaukee
South Milwaukee SD — 5-11111 — 768-6307
1225 MEMORIAL DR 53172
Robert Luckett, supt.
HS, 1001 15TH AVE 53172 — 4-00011 — 768-6322
Howard Kallio, prin.
MS, 1225 MEMORIAL DR 53172 — 2-00100 — 768-6353
Daniel Bowe, prin.

South Wayne, AC 608, PC 2, Lafayette
Black Hawk SD, PO BOX D 53587 — 3-11111 — 439-5400
Ann Jerdee, supt.
Black Hawk HS, PO BOX D 53587 — 2-00011 — 439-5371
Rick McCaffry, prin.
Other Schools – See Gratiot

Sparta, AC 608, PC 6, Monroe
Sparta Area SD — 5-11111 — 269-3151
506 N BLACK RIVER ST 54656
Richard Newkirk, supt.
SHS, 506 N BLACK RIVER ST 54656 — 3-00011 — 269-2107
David Pera, prin.
JHS, 201 E FRANKLIN ST 54656 — 3-00110 — 269-2185
Rex McNown, prin.

Spencer, AC 715, PC 4, Marathon
Spencer SD, 300 SCHOOL ST 54479 — 3-11111 — 659-5347
Larry Stordahl, supt.
HS, 300 SCHOOL ST 54479 — 2-00011 — 659-4211
John Olig, prin.

Spooner, AC 715, PC 4, Washburn
Spooner SD, 500 COLLEGE ST 54801 — 4-11111 — 635-2171
James Kling, supt.
HS, 500 COLLEGE ST 54801 — 2-00011 — 635-2172
Donald Hauck, prin.
MS, 500 COLLEGE ST 54801 — 2-01100 — 635-2173
Roger Noe, prin.

Spring Green, AC 608, PC 4, Sauk
River Valley SD, PO BOX 729 53588 — 4-11111 — 588-2551
Michael Manning, supt.
River Valley SHS, PO BOX 729 53588 — 2-00001 — 588-2556
Kaaren Larson, prin.
River Valley JHS, PO BOX 729 53588 — 2-00110 — 588-2554
(—), prin.

Spring Valley, AC 715, PC 4, Pierce
Spring Valley SD, PO BOX 427 54767 — 3-11111 — 778-5551
Gene Roland, supt.
JSHS, PO BOX 427 54767 — 2-00111 — 778-5554
Daniel Tuinstra, prin.

Stanley, AC 715, PC 4, Chippewa
Stanley-Boyd Area SD, E 4TH AVE 54768 — 4-11111 — 644-5357
Charles Poulter, supt.
Stanley-Boyd HS, 507 E 1ST AVE 54768 — 2-00011 — 644-5534
Robert Hauser, prin.
Stanley-Boyd MS, 509 E 1ST AVE 54768 — 2-01100 — 644-5715
Robert Hauser, prin.

Stevens Point, AC 715, PC 7, Portage
Stevens Point Area SD — 6-11111 — 345-5444
1900 POLK ST 54481
Richard Eisenhauer, supt.
SHS, 1201 N POINT DR 54481 — 4-00001 — 345-5400
Ed Von Feldt, prin.
Franklin JHS, 2000 POLK ST 54481 — 3-00110 — 345-5413
Marc Pecha, prin.
Jacobs JHS, 2400 MAIN ST 54481 — 3-00110 — 345-5422
O. Philip Idsvoog, prin.

Mid-State Technical College — 3-CC — 344-3063
933 MICHIGAN AVE 54481
Pacelli HS, 1301 MARIA DR 54481 — 2-00011 — 341-2442
Br. Vietoris, prin.
St. Peter MS, 708 1ST ST 54481 — 2-00100 — 344-1890
Dewayne Byrnes, prin.

University of Wisconsin 54481 — 6-UC — 346-2123

Stockbridge, AC 414, PC 3, Calumet
Stockbridge SD, PO BOX 188 53088 — 2-11111 — 439-1159
　Terry Wiseman, supt.
HS, PO BOX 188 53088 — 2-00011 — 439-1159
　Terry Wiseman, prin.

Stoughton, AC 608, PC 6, Dane
Stoughton Area SD — 5-11111
　PO BOX 189 53589 — 873-2660
　Matthew Gibson, supt.
HS, PO BOX 189 53589 — 3-00011 — 873-2711
　Olin Harried, prin.
MS, PO BOX 189 53589 — 3-00100 — 873-2684
　Mark Mulholland, prin.

Stratford, AC 715, PC 4, Marathon
Stratford SD, PO BOX 7 54484 — 3-11111 — 687-3130
　Jeffrey Dickert, supt.
HS, PO BOX 7 54484 — 2-00011 — 687-4311
　Michael Young, prin.
MS, PO BOX 7 54484 — 2-00100 — 687-4311
　Michael Young, prin.

Strum, AC 715, PC 3, Trempealeau
Eleva-Strum SD, RR 1 BOX 500 54770 — 3-11111 — 695-2696
　Paul Zavada, supt.
Eleva-Strum JSHS — 2-00111
　RR 1 BOX 500 54770 — 695-2696
　James Tocko, prin.

Sturgeon Bay, AC 414, PC 6, Door
Sevastopol SD — 3-11111
　4550 STATE HIGHWAY 57 54235 — 743-6282
　Joseph McMahon, supt.
Sevastopol HS — 2-00011
　4550 STATE HIGHWAY 57 54235 — 743-6283
　Lee Kotyza, prin.
Sturgeon Bay SD — 4-11111
　1230 MICHIGAN ST 54235 — 746-2801
　Jerome Kain, supt.
HS, 1230 MICHIGAN ST 54235 — 2-00011 — 746-2802
　Robert Grimmer, prin.
Walker MS, 19 N 14TH AVE 54235 — 2-00100 — 746-2803
　Robert White, prin.

Northeast Wisconsin Technical College — 3-CC
229 N 14TH AVE 54235 — 743-2207

Sun Prairie, AC 608, PC 7, Dane
Sun Prairie SD — 5-11111
　509 COMMERCIAL AVE 53590 — 837-2541
　Allen Rosenthal, supt.
HS, 220 KRONCKE DR 53590 — 4-00011 — 837-2547
　Gerald Hopfensperger, prin.
MS, 160 SOUTH ST 53590 — 3-00100 — 837-2544
　Terrence Ludkey, prin.

Diesel Truck Driver Training School — 3-CS
PO BOX 47 53590 — 837-7800

Superior, AC 715, PC 8, Douglas
Superior SD, 3025 TOWER AVE 54880 — 6-11111 — 394-8700
　Benjamin Kanninen, supt.
SHS, 2600 CATLIN AVE 54880 — 4-00001 — 394-8720
　Ray Mickolajak, prin.
Central JHS, 1015 BELKNAP ST 54880 — 3-00110 — 394-8740
　John Blankush, prin.
East JHS, 1814 E 5TH ST 54880 — 2-00110 — 398-3405
　Dean Neumann, prin.

Maranatha Academy — 2-11111
RR 2 BOX 569 54880 — 399-8757
　Patricia Malloy, prin.
University of Wisconsin — 4-UC
1800 GRAND AVE 54880 — 394-8223

Suring, AC 414, PC 3, Oconto
Suring SD, PO BOX 158 54174 — 3-11111 — 842-2181
　William Kean, supt.
HS, PO BOX 158 54174 — 2-00011 — 842-2181
　Jeff Reeder, prin.

Sussex, AC 414, PC 6, Waukesha
Hamilton SD — 5-11111
　W220N6151 TOWNLINE RD 53089 — 246-6471
　Kathleen Cooke, supt.
Hamilton HS — 3-00011
　W220N6151 TOWNLINE RD 53089 — 246-6471
　(—), prin.
Templeton MS — 3-01100
　N59W22490 SILVER SPRING DR 53089 — 246-6471
　Gary Amoroso, prin.

Taylor, AC 715, PC 2, Jackson
Blair-Taylor SD
　Supt. — See Blair
Blair-Taylor MS, 141 PEARL ST 54659 — 2-00100 — 662-2311
　Robert Eckles, prin.

Thorp, AC 715, PC 4, Clark
Thorp SD, PO BOX 449 54771 — 3-11111 — 669-5401
　Don Schneider, supt.
HS, PO BOX 449 54771 — 2-00011 — 669-5401
　Dale Haymann, prin.

Three Lakes, AC 715, PC 3, Oneida
Three Lakes SD, PO BOX 280 54562 — 3-11111 — 546-3321
　George Karling, supt.
HS, PO BOX 280 54562 — 2-00011 — 546-3321
　Richard Parks, prin.

JHS, PO BOX 280 54562 — 1-00100 — 546-3321
　Richard Parks, prin.

Tigerton, AC 715, PC 3, Shawano
Tigerton SD, PO BOX 10 54486 — 2-11111 — 535-2122
　Walter Barker, supt.
JSHS, PO BOX 40 54486 — 2-00111 — 535-2185
　Tim Hodkiewicz, prin.

Tomah, AC 608, PC 6, Monroe
Tomah Area SD — 5-11111
　129 W CLIFTON ST 54660 — 374-7210
　Anthony Hinden, supt.
SHS, 901 LINCOLN AVE 54660 — 3-00001 — 374-7240
　Alan Chittick, prin.
JHS, 611 CLARK ST 54660 — 3-00110 — 374-7248
　Tom Hill, prin.

Tomahawk, AC 715, PC 5, Lincoln
Tomahawk SD — 4-11111
　18 E WASHINGTON AVE 54487 — 453-5551
　Curtis Powell, supt.
HS, 1048 E KING RD 54487 — 2-00011 — 453-2106
　John Stahmer, prin.
MS, 1048 E KING RD 54487 — 2-00100 — 453-5371
　Tom Freude, prin.

Tony, AC 715, PC 2, Rusk
Flambeau SD, PO BOX 86 54563 — 3-11111 — 532-3183
　John Schomisch, supt.
Flambeau HS, PO BOX 86 54563 — 2-00011 — 532-5559
　(—), prin.
Flambeau JHS, PO BOX 86 54563 — 1-00100 — 532-5559
　(—), prin.

Trempealeau, AC 608, PC 4, Trempealeau
Galesville-Ettrick-Trempealeau SD
　Supt. — See Galesville
Gale-Ettr-Tremp MS — 2-00100
　4TH & GROVE ST 54661 — 534-6391
　Craig Gerlach, prin.

Turtle Lake, AC 715, PC 3, Barron
Turtle Lake SD, PO BOX 1000 54889 — 3-11111 — 986-2597
　Mark Collins, supt.
HS, PO BOX 1000 54889 — 2-00011 — 986-4470
　Michael Kenner, prin.

Two Rivers, AC 414, PC 7, Manitowoc
Two Rivers SD, 1500 27TH ST 54241 — 4-11111 — 793-4560
　Keith Martin, supt.
Washington HS, 1500 27TH ST 54241 — 3-00001 — 793-2291
　Ridgley Schott, prin.
Clarke MS, 4608 BELLEVUE PL 54241 — 2-00100 — 794-1614
　Randy Fredrikson, prin.

Union Grove, AC 414, PC 5, Racine
Union Grove J1 SD, 810 14TH AVE 53182 — 3-11100 — 878-2015
　Giles Williams, supt.
Union Grove MS — 2-01100
　1745 MILLDRUM ST 53182 — 878-3465
　Donald Voss, prin.
Union Grove UNHSD — 3-00011
　3433 S COLONY AVE 53182 — 878-4427
　Russell Draeger, supt.
Union Grove HS — 3-00011
　3433 S COLONY AVE 53182 — 878-2434
　Aaron Trummer, prin.

Union Grove Christian S — 2-11111
417 15TH AVE 53182 — 878-1265
　George Schlagel, prin.

Valders, AC 414, PC 3, Manitowoc
Valders SD, 138 JEFFERSON ST 54245 — 4-11111 — 775-9500
　Thomas Fabian, supt.
HS, 138 WILSON ST 54245 — 2-00011 — 775-9530
　Robert Ganka, prin.
MS, 201 W WILSON ST 54245 — 2-01100 — 775-9520
　Derrick Krey, prin.

Verona, AC 608, PC 6, Dane
Verona Area SD, 700 N MAIN ST 53593 — 5-11111 — 845-6451
　Robert Gilpatrick, supt.
Verona Area HS, 300 RICHARD ST 53593 — 3-00011 — 845-6453
　Terry Downen, prin.
Verona Area MS, 740 N MAIN ST 53593 — 3-00100 — 845-6454
　John Berge, prin.

Viola, AC 608, PC 3, Richland
Kickapoo Area SD — 3-11111
　RR 2 BOX 63 54664 — 627-1494
　Jeaneta Kirkpatrick, supt.
Kickapoo JSHS, RR 2 BOX 63 54664 — 2-00111 — 627-1494
　David Quick, prin.

Viroqua, AC 608, PC 5, Vernon
Viroqua Area SD — 4-11111
　100 BLACKHAWK DR 54665 — 637-7962
　Jim Waller, supt.
HS, 100 BLACKHAWK DR 54665 — 2-00011 — 637-3191
　James Sciacca, prin.
MS, 100 BLACKHAWK DR 54665 — 2-01100 — 637-3171
　Jim McGrath, prin.

Wabeno, AC 715, PC 3, Forest
Wabeno Area SD, PO BOX 60 54566 — 3-11111 — 473-2592
　Ronald Lahnala, supt.
JSHS, PO BOX 60 54566 — 2-00111 — 473-5122
　Marah Nelson, prin.

Wales, AC 414, PC 4, Waukesha
Kettle Moraine SD — 5-11111
　PO BOX 901 53183 — 968-6300
　Sarah Jerome, supt.

Kettle Moraine HS — 4-00011
　PO BOX 902 53183 — 968-6201
　Richard Ohm, prin.
　Other Schools – See Dousman

Walworth, AC 414, PC 4, Walworth
Big Foot UNHSD, PO BOX 99 53184 — 2-00011 — 275-2116
　Paul Weber, supt.
Big Foot Union HS, PO BOX 99 53184 — 2-00011 — 275-2116
　Robert Schultz, prin.

Washburn, AC 715, PC 4, Bayfield
Washburn SD, 305 W 4TH ST 54891 — 3-11111 — 373-6187
　Fred Schlichting, supt.
HS, 309 W 4TH ST 54891 — 2-00011 — 373-6188
　Kenneth Kasinski, prin.
Dupont MS, 305 W 4TH ST 54891 — 2-00100 — 373-6188
　Kenneth Kasinski, prin.

Washington Island, AC 414, PC 2, Door
Washington SD, RR 1 BOX 2 54246 — 1-11111 — 847-2507
　Terence Crowley, supt.
HS, RR 1 BOX 2 54246 — 1-00011 — 847-2507
　Terence Crowley, prin.

Waterford, AC 414, PC 4, Racine
Washington-Caldwell SD — 2-11100
　8937 BIG BEND RD 53185 — 662-3466
　Howard Leafblad, supt.
Washington MS — 1-01100
　8937 BIG BEND RD 53185 — 662-3466
　Howard Leafblad, prin.

Waterford J1 SD, 819 W MAIN ST 53185 — 4-11100 — 534-5065
　Richard Marta, supt.
Fox River MS, 921 W MAIN ST 53185 — 2-01100 — 534-3146
　Carl Breitlow, prin.
Waterford UNHSD — 3-00011
　110 S CENTER ST 53185 — 534-3189
　David Richmond, supt.
HS, 110 S CENTER ST 53185 — 3-00011 — 534-3189
　Peter Hassemer, prin.

Waterloo, AC 414, PC 5, Jefferson
Waterloo SD, 813 N MONROE ST 53594 — 3-11111 — 478-3633
　Ronald Ertner, supt.
JSHS, 865 N MONROE ST 53594 — 2-00111 — 478-2171
　John Pare, prin.

Watertown, AC 414, PC 7, Jefferson
Watertown SD, 111 DODGE ST 53094 — 5-11111 — 262-1460
　Suzanne Hotter, supt.
HS, 505 S 8TH ST 53094 — 4-00011 — 262-1470
　Kathleen Wagner, prin.
Riverside MS, 131 HALL ST 53094 — 3-00100 — 262-1480
　Lawrence Madsen, prin.

Madison Area Technical College — 4-CC
1300 W MAIN ST 53098
Maranatha Baptist Bible College — 2-UC
　PO BOX 438 53094 — 261-9300
Northwestern College — 2-UC
1300 WESTERN AVE 53094 — 261-4352
Northwestern Prep S — 2-00011
　1300 WESTERN AVE 53094 — 261-4352
　Rev. Schroeder, prin.

Waukesha, AC 414, PC 8, Waukesha
Waukesha SD, 222 MAPLE AVE 53186 — 7-11111 — 521-8864
　David Kampschroer, supt.
North SHS, 2222 MICHIGAN AVE 53188 — 4-00001 — 521-8777
　Ryan Champeau, prin.
South SHS, 401 E ROBERTA AVE 53186 — 4-00001 — 521-8920
　Robert Gruell, prin.
West SHS, 3243 SAYLESVILLE RD 53188 — 4-00001 — 524-6700
　Ted Bear, prin.
Butler JHS, 310 N HINE AVE 53188 — 3-00110 — 521-8710
　Heidi Laabs, prin.
Central JHS, 400 N GRAND AVE 53186 — 4-00110 — 521-8914
　John Schliecker, prin.
Horning JHS, 2000 WOLF RD 53186 — 3-00110 — 521-8971
　Harvey Stowe, prin.

Carroll College — 4-UC
100 N EAST AVE 53186 — 547-1211
Catholic Memorial HS — 3-00011
　601 E COLLEGE AVE 53186 — 542-7101
　Paul Stauffacher, prin.
MBTI Business Training Institute — 2-CS
237 SOUTH ST 53186 — 527-3221
St. Joseph MS, 818 N EAST AVE 53186 — 2-00100 — 896-2930
　Maureen Rossiter, prin.
University of Wisconsin Center — 4-CC
1500 N UNIVERSITY DR 53188 — 521-5210
Waukesha Christian Academy — 2-11111
　PO BOX 31 53187 — 542-7766
　Glen Teasdale, prin.

Waunakee, AC 608, PC 6, Dane
Waunakee Community SD — 4-11111
　101 SCHOOL DR 53597 — 849-2000
　Eugene Hamele, supt.
HS, 100 SCHOOL DR 53597 — 3-00011 — 849-2100
　Brian Kersten, prin.
MS, 1001 SOUTH ST 53597 — 2-00100 — 849-2060
　Shelly Weiss, prin.

Waupaca, AC 715, PC 5, Waupaca
Waupaca SD, 515 SCHOOL ST 54981 — 4-11111 — 258-4121
　David Poeschl, supt.
HS, 1149 SHOEMAKER RD 54981 — 3-00011 — 258-4131
　Bruce Gunderson, prin.

MS, 1515 SHOEMAKER RD 54981 — 2-00100
Joseph McClone, prin. — 258-4140

Waupun, AC 414, PC 6, Fond du Lac
Waupun SD, 950 WILCOX ST 53963 — 4-11111
William Bobbe, supt. — 324-9341
HS, 451 E SPRING ST 53963 — 3-00011
James La Valley, prin. — 324-5591
MS, 450 E FRANKLIN ST 53963 — 2-00100
Richard Steinbach, prin. — 324-9322

Wausau, AC 715, PC 8, Marathon
Wausau SD, 415 SEYMOUR ST 54403 — 6-11111
Penelope Kleinhans, supt. — 848-2934
East HS, 708 FULTON ST 54403 — 4-00011
Thomas Beattie, prin. — 845-7252
West HS, 1200 W WAUSAU AVE 54401 — 4-00011
(—), prin. — 675-3351
Life Skills Center HS — Vo Tech
120 S 14TH AVE 54401
Marion Sells, prin. — 842-5797
Mann MS, 3101 N 13TH ST 54403 — 3-00100
Joy Trollop, prin. — 845-9500
Muir MS, 1400 STEWART AVE 54401 — 4-00100
Charles Morrill, prin. — 845-2191

Newman High S — 2-00011
1130 W BRIDGE ST 54401 — 845-8274
Donald Sisler, prin.
Northcentral Technical College — 3-CC
1000 W CAMPUS DR 54401 — 675-3331
St. Matthew MS, 225 S 28TH AVE 54401 — 2-00100
Devery Quandt, prin. — 842-4857
University of Wisconsin Center — 4-CC
518 S 7TH AVE 54401 — 845-9602
Wausau Hospital Center — HSP
333 PINE RIDGE BLVD 54401 — 847-2117

Wausaukee, AC 715, PC 3, Marinette
Wausaukee SD, PO BOX 258 54177 — 3-11111
Cleland Methner, supt. — 856-5153
HS, PO BOX 258 54177 — 2-00111
Peter Ninnemann, prin. — 856-5151
JHS, PO BOX 258 54177 — 2-00100
Peter Ninnemann, prin. — 856-5151

Wautoma, AC 414, PC 4, Washara
Wautoma Area SD — 4-11111
PO BOX 870 54982 — 787-7112
Clifford Hudson, supt.
HS, PO BOX 870 54982 — 2-00011
Allan Prosser, prin. — 787-3354

Wauwatosa, AC 414, PC 8, Milwaukee
Wauwatosa SD — 6-11111
12121 W NORTH AVE 53226 — 259-4495
George Goens, supt.
East HS, 7500 MILWAUKEE AVE 53213 — 4-00011
John Hays, prin. — 778-6565
Plank Road HS — 2-00011
9508 W WATERTOWN PLANK RD 53226
Stephen King, prin. — 257-7128
West HS, 11400 W CENTER ST 53222 — 3-00011
Audrey Evers, prin. — 778-6550
Longfellow MS — 3-00100
7600 W NORTH AVE 53213
Gerald Mullins, prin. — 778-6540
Whitman MS — 2-00100
11100 W CENTER ST 53222
Jeff Keranen, prin. — 778-6530

Franciscan Shared Laboratory-Central Lab — CS
11020 W PLANK CT # 100 53226 — 476-3400

Wauzeka, AC 608, PC 3, Crawford
Wauzeka-Steuben SD — 2-11111
PO BOX 347 53826 — 875-5792
Jerome Fiene, supt.
HS, PO BOX 347 53826 — 2-00011
Michael French, prin. — 875-5792

Webster, AC 715, PC 3, Burnett
Webster SD, PO BOX 9 54893 — 3-11111
Orlin Anderson, supt. — 866-4391
HS, PO BOX 9 54893 — 2-00011
(—), prin. — 866-4281
JHS, PO BOX 9 54893 — 2-00100
Paul Amundson, prin. — 866-4281

West Allis, AC 414, PC 8, Milwaukee
West Allis SD — 6-11111
9333 W LINCOLN AVE 53227 — 546-5550
Harold Sloan, supt.
Central HS, 8516 W LINCOLN AVE 53227 — 4-00011
Ronald Bieri, prin. — 546-5580
Hale HS, 11601 W LINCOLN AVE 53227 — 3-00011
Gerald Braun, prin. — 546-5590

Mann MS, 6213 W LAPHAM ST 53214 — 2-00100
Richard Minga, prin. — 546-5607
Wright MS — 3-00100
9501 W CLEVELAND AVE 53227 — 546-5612
Kate Hardiman-Frank, prin.

Heritage Christian S — 3-11111
1300 S 109TH ST 53214 — 259-1231
Thomas Wittkamper, prin.
Milwaukee Area Technical College — 4-CC
1200 S 71ST ST 53214 — 476-3040
Milwaukee County Medical Complex — HSP
1304 S 70TH ST 53214 — 257-6747

West Bend, AC 414, PC 7, Washington
West Bend SD, 697 S 5TH AVE 53095 — 6-11111
Michael Wiziards, supt. — 335-5435
East HS, 1305 E DECORAH RD 53095 — 4-00011
Mary Skalecki, prin. — 335-5532
West HS, 1305 E DECORAH RD 53095 — 4-00011
Memoree Vander Heyden, prin. — 335-5587
Badger MS, 710 S MAIN ST 53095 — 3-00100
Michael Murphy, prin. — 335-5456
Silverbrook MS — 3-01100
120 N SILVERBROOK DR 53095 — 335-5499
Ted Distefano, prin.

Moraine Park Technical College — 3-CC
2151 N MAIN ST 53095 — 334-3413
University of Wisconsin Center — 3-CC
400 S UNIVERSITY DR 53095 — 335-5201

Westby, AC 608, PC 4, Vernon
Westby Area SD, 206 WEST AVE S 54667 — 4-11111
Roy Green, supt. — 634-3101
HS, 206 WEST AVE S 54667 — 2-00011
Jeff Jordan, prin. — 634-3101

Westfield, AC 608, PC 4, Marquette
Westfield SD, PO BOX 356 53964 — 4-11111
Larry Shay, supt. — 296-3408
HS, 303 THOMAS ST 53964 — 2-00011
Jon Swenson, prin. — 296-2141

West Salem, AC 608, PC 5, La Crosse
West Salem SD, 405 E HAMLIN ST 54669 — 4-11111
Eugene Ertz, supt. — 786-0700
HS, 405 E HAMLIN ST 54669 — 2-00011
Gerald Trochinski, prin. — 786-1220
MS, 450 N MARK ST 54669 — 2-01100
James Burger, prin. — 786-2090

Weyauwega, AC 414, PC 4, Waupaca
Weyauwega-Fremont SD — 3-11111
PO BOX 580 54983 — 867-2148
Robert Hecht, supt.
HS, PO BOX 580 54983 — 2-00011
David Schlegel, prin. — 867-2171
MS, PO BOX 580 54983 — 2-00100
Frank Zaboj, prin. — 867-3138

Weyerhaeuser, AC 715, PC 2, Rusk
Weyerhaeuser Area SD — 2-11111
PO BOX 1000 54895 — 353-2254
Marcia Hochhalter, supt.
HS, PO BOX 1000 54895 — 1-00011
Marcia Hochhalter, prin. — 353-2254

Whitefish Bay, AC 414, PC 7, Milwaukee
Whitefish Bay SD — 4-11111
1200 E FAIRMOUNT AVE 53217 — 963-3921
Bradford Allison, supt.
HS, 1200 E FAIRMOUNT AVE 53217 — 3-00011
Stephen Seyfer, prin. — 963-3928
MS, 1144 E HENRY CLAY ST 53217 — 2-00100
Joann Truss, prin. — 963-6800

Dominican HS — 2-00011
120 E SILVER SPRING DR 53217 — 332-1170
Sr. Suzanne Lorentz, prin.

Whitehall, AC 715, PC 4, Trempealeau
Whitehall SD, PO BOX 37 54773 — 3-11111
Gerald Freimark, supt. — 538-4374
HS, PO BOX 37 54773 — 2-00011
Bruce Ausderau, prin. — 538-4364
JHS, PO BOX 37 54773 — 1-00100
Bruce Ausderau, prin. — 538-4364

White Lake, AC 715, PC 2, Langlade
White Lake SD, PO BOX 67 54491 — 2-11111
Harold Brennan, supt. — 882-8421
HS, PO BOX 67 54491 — 2-00011
Harold Brennan, prin. — 882-2361

Whitewater, AC 414, PC 7, Walworth
Whitewater SD — 4-11111
401 S ELIZABETH ST 53190 — 472-4887
John Negley, supt.

HS, 401 S ELIZABETH ST 53190 — 3-00011
Patrick Brooks, prin. — 472-4834
MS, 118 S SUMMIT ST 53190 — 2-00100
James Jacobson, prin. — 472-4803

University of Wisconsin — 6-UC
800 W MAIN ST 53190 — 472-1918

Wild Rose, AC 414, PC 3, Waushara
Wild Rose SD, PO BOX 276 54984 — 3-11111
William Thompson, supt. — 622-4203
JSHS, PO BOX 276 54984 — 2-00111
Charles Schuessler, prin. — 622-4201

Williams Bay, AC 414, PC 4, Walworth
Williams Bay SD, PO BOX 259 53191 — 2-11111
Peter Geissal, supt. — 245-5571
JSHS, PO BOX 259 53191 — 2-00111
Dan Bice, prin. — 245-6224

Faith Christian S — 2-11111
PO BOX 1230 53191 — 245-9404
Scott Brown, prin.

Wilmot, AC 414, PC 3, Kenosha
Wilmot UNHSD — 3-00011
11112 308TH AVE 53192 — 862-2884
Jack Roller, supt.
HS, 11112 308TH AVE 53192 — 3-00011
Larry Berg, prin. — 862-2351

Winneconne, AC 414, PC 4, Winnebago
Winneconne Community SD — 4-11111
233 S 3RD AVE 54986 — 582-5802
Alan Johnson, supt.
HS, 233 S 3RD AVE 54986 — 2-00011
Michael Schweie, prin. — 582-5810
MS, 233 S 3RD AVE 54986 — 2-00100
Frederick Gierke, prin. — 582-5800

Winter, AC 715, PC 2, Sawyer
Winter SD, PO BOX 7 54896 — 3-11111
James Schuchardt, supt. — 266-3301
HS, PO BOX 7 54896 — 2-00011
Edward Sheridan, prin. — 266-3301
MS, PO BOX 7 54896 — 2-00100
Robert Langham, prin. — 266-6701

Wisconsin Dells, AC 608, PC 4, Columbia
Wisconsin Dells SD — 4-11111
811 COUNTY ROAD H 53965 — 254-7769
Robert Stirn, supt.
HS, 520 RACE ST 53965 — 2-00011
(—), prin. — 253-1461

Wisconsin Rapids, AC 715, PC 7, Wood
Wisconsin Rapids SD — 6-11111
510 PEACH ST 54494 — 422-6003
Timothy Laatsch, supt.
Lincoln SHS, 1801 16TH ST S 54494 — 4-00011
Thomas Mancuso, prin. — 423-1520
East JHS, 311 LINCOLN ST 54494 — 3-00110
David Johnson, prin. — 422-6116
West JHS, 1921 27TH AVE S 54495 — 3-00110
Gilbert Hamre, prin. — 422-6181

Assumption HS — 2-00011
445 CHESTNUT ST 54494 — 423-2920
James Dyer, prin.
Mid-State Technical College — 4-CC
500 32ND ST N 54494 — 423-5650

Wittenberg, AC 715, PC 4, Shawano
Wittenberg-Birnamwood SD — 4-11111
PO BOX 269 54499 — 253-2213
Richard Roth, supt.
Wittenberg-Birnamwood HS — 2-00011
PO BOX 269 54499 — 253-2211
David Bardo, prin.

Wonewoc, AC 608, PC 3, Juneau
Wonewoc-Union Center SD — 2-11111
PO BOX 368 53968 — 464-3165
Kent Nelson, supt.
JSHS, PO BOX 368 53968 — 2-00111
(—), prin. — 464-3165

Woodville, AC 715, PC 3, St. Croix
Baldwin-Woodville Area SD
Supt. — See Baldwin
Viking MS, 116 ELDER ST 54028 — 2-01100
George Streeck, prin. — 698-2456

Wrightstown, AC 414, PC 4, Brown
Wrightstown Community SD — 3-11111
PO BOX 128 54180 — 532-5551
Larry Lark, supt.
JSHS, PO BOX 128 54180 — 2-00111
Greg Peyer, prin. — 532-5553

WYOMING

STATE DEPARTMENT OF EDUCATION
Hathaway Building
2300 Capitol Ave., Cheyenne 82002
(307) 777-7673

Superintendent of Public Instruction   Diana Ohman

Deputy Superintendent   Patricia O'Brien

STATE BOARD OF EDUCATION
2300 Capitol Ave., Cheyenne 82002

Chairperson   Elizabeth Field

PUBLIC, PRIVATE AND CATHOLIC SECONDARY SCHOOLS

Afton, AC 307, PC 4, Lincoln
Lincoln County SD 2 83110   5-11111
Dr. J. Allen Lowe, supt.   886-3811
Star Valley HS, 235 E 4TH 83110   3-00011
Kirk Brower, prin.   886-3019
Star Valley JHS 83110   2-00100
Alan Lindford, prin.   886-5208
Other Schools – See Cokeville

Albin, AC 307, PC 2, Laramie
Laramie County SD 2
Supt. — See Pine Bluffs
S, PO BOX 32 82050   2-11111
Richard Goodschmidt, prin.   246-3362

Baggs, AC 307, PC 2, Carbon
Carbon County SD 1
Supt. — See Rawlins
Little Snake River Valley HS   1-00011
PO BOX 9 82321   383-2185
Bill Wisenhunt, prin.

Basin, AC 307, PC 4, Big Horn
Big Horn County SD 4   2-11111
PO BOX 151 82410   568-2684
W. T. Weatherill, supt.
Riverside HS, PO BOX 151 82410   2-00011
Jim Keef, prin.   568-2416
Other Schools – See Manderson

Big Horn, AC 307, PC 2, Sheridan
Sheridan County SD 1
Supt. — See Ranchester
HS, PO BOX 490 82833   1-00011
Joel Dvorak, prin.   674-8190
MS, PO BOX 490 82833   1-00100
Joel Dvorak, prin.   672-8190

Big Piney, AC 307, PC 2, Sublette
Sublette County SD 9   3-11111
FINE ARTS CENTER 83113   276-3322
E. Lon Luty, supt.
HS, 650 PINEY DRIVE 83113   2-00011
Richard Costello, prin.   276-3324
MS, 510 NICHOLS ST S 83113   2-00100
Gerald Wilson, prin.   276-3315

Buffalo, AC 307, PC 5, Johnson
Johnson County SD 1   4-11111
601 W LOTT ST 82834   684-9571
Von Dahl, supt.
HS, 326 S BURRITT AVE 82834   2-00011
Ricki Newton, prin.   684-2269
Clear Creek MS, 58 N ADAMS AVE 82834   2-01100
Donald Tavegie, prin.   684-5594
Other Schools – See Kaycee

Burlington, AC 307, PC 2, Big Horn
Big Horn County SD 1
Supt. — See Cowley
S, 109 NORTH ST 82411   2-11111
Larry Johnson, prin.   762-3334

Burns, AC 307, PC 2, Laramie
Laramie County SD 2
Supt. — See Pine Bluffs
JSHS, PO BOX 160 82053   2-00111
James Benoit, prin.   547-3511

Byron, AC 307, PC 2, Big Horn
Big Horn County SD 1
Supt. — See Cowley
Rocky Mountain HS   2-00011
PO BOX 176 82412   548-2723
Joe Davis, prin.

Casper, AC 307, PC 8, Natrona
Natrona County SD 1   7-11111
970 N GLENN RD 82601   577-0200
Chip Zullinger, supt.

Natrona County SHS   4-00001
930 S ELM ST 82601   577-0330
Byron Moore, prin.
Walsh SHS, 3500 E 12TH ST 82609   4-00001
Joe Simpson, prin.   577-4640
Centennial JHS   3-00110
1421 WATERFORD ST 82609   577-4600
Del Dittburner, prin.
Cy JHS, 2211 ESSEX AVE 82604   3-00110
Dean Braughton, prin.   577-4474
East JHS, 900 S BEVERLY ST 82609   3-00110
Sheila Rulli, prin.   577-4400
Morgan JHS, 1440 S ELM ST 82601   3-00110
Craig Sorenson, prin.   577-4440
Other Schools – See Midwest

Calvary Baptist Christian S   2-00011
1800 S CONWELL ST 82601
Casper College   5-CC
125 COLLEGE DR 82601   268-2548
Wyoming School for the Deaf   HND
539 PAYNE AVE 82609

Cheyenne, AC 307, PC 8, Laramie
Laramie County SD 1   7-11111
2810 HOUSE AVE 82001   771-2100
Jack Iversen, supt.
Central SHS   4-00001
5500 EDUCATION DR 82009   771-2680
Edward Achziger, prin.
East SHS, 2800 E PERSHING BLVD 82001   4-00001
Melanie Jensen, prin.   771-2663
Carey JHS   3-00110
1780 E PERSHING BLVD 82001   771-2580
Larry Furtney, prin.
Johnson JHS, 1236 W ALLISON RD 82007   3-00110
David Orr, prin.   771-2640
McCormick JHS   4-00110
6000 EDUCATION DR 82009   771-2650
James Schumacher, prin.

Cheyenne Aero Tech   3-CS
1204 AIRPORT PKY 82001   800-366-2376
Laramie County Community College   5-CC
1400 E COLLEGE DR 82007   778-5222

Chugwater, AC 307, PC 2, Platte
Platte County SD 1
Supt. — See Wheatland
S, PO BOX 68 82210   1-11111
Larry Yost, prin.   422-3501

Clearmont, AC 307, PC 2, Sheridan
Sheridan County SD 3 82835   2-11111
William Raduenz, supt.   758-4412
Arvada-Clearmont JSHS 82835   1-00111
William Raduenz, prin.   758-4412

Cody, AC 307, PC 6, Park
Park County SD 6, 919 CODY AVE 82414   5-11111
Alan Hafer, supt.   587-4253
HS, 1225 10TH ST 82414   3-00011
Terry Statton, prin.   587-4251
JHS, 920 BECK AVE 82414   3-00100
Tom Cook, prin.   587-4273

Grace Baptist S   2-00011
4 SOUTHFORK RD 82414
West Park Hospital   HSP
707 SHERIDAN AVE 82414   527-7501

Cokeville, AC 307, PC 2, Lincoln
Lincoln County SD 2
Supt. — See Afton
JSHS 83114   2-00011
Dale Lamborn, prin.   279-3273

Cowley, AC 307, PC 2, Big Horn
Big Horn County SD 1   3-11111
PO BOX 688 82420   548-2254
Grant Sanders, supt.
Other Schools – See Burlington, Byron, Deaver

Dayton, AC 307, PC 3, Sheridan
Sheridan County SD 1
Supt. — See Ranchester
Tongue River HS, PO BOX 408 82836   2-00011
Robert C. Edwards, prin.   655-2236

Deaver, AC 307, PC 2, Big Horn
Big Horn County SD 1
Supt. — See Cowley
Rocky Mountain MS   2-00100
PO BOX 185 82421   664-2252
Billie Bymers, prin.

Diamondville, AC 307, PC 3, Lincoln
Lincoln County SD 1   4-11111
PO BOX 335 83116   877-9095
Ronald Maughan, supt.
Other Schools – See Kemmerer

Douglas, AC 307, PC 6, Converse
Converse County SD 1   4-11111
615 HAMILTON ST 82633   358-2942
Jeff Jacobson, supt.
HS, 615 HAMILTON ST 82633   3-00011
Gale Lane, prin.   358-2940
MS, 615 HAMILTON ST 82633   2-00100
Jenne Twiford, prin.   358-9771

Calvary Christian Academy   2-00011
PO BOX 1020 82633

Dubois, AC 307, PC 3, Fremont
Fremont County SD 2   2-11111
PO BOX 188 82513   455-2323
James Robinson, supt.
JSHS, PO BOX 188 82513   2-00111
James Robinson, prin.   455-2529

Encampment, AC 307, PC 2, Carbon
Carbon County SD 2
Supt. — See Saratoga
S, PO BOX 277 82325   2-11111
Gary White, prin.   327-5442

Ethete, AC 307, PC 1, Fremont
Fremont County SD 14   3-11111
636 BLUE SKY HWY 82520   332-3904
Raymond Streeter, supt.
Wyoming Indian HS   2-00011
636 BLUE SKY HWY 82520   332-9765
Lonny Hoffman, prin.
Wyoming Indian JHS   1-00100
636 BLUE SKY HWY 82520   332-2992
Ray Streeter, prin.

Evanston, AC 307, PC 7, Uinta
Uinta County SD 1   5-11111
PO BOX 6002 82931   789-7571
Norman Gaines, supt.
HS, 701 W CHEYENNE DR 82930   2-00011
Larry Stick, prin.   789-0757
Davis MS, 845 10TH ST 82930   2-00100
Doris Woodbury, prin.   789-8096
Evanston MS, 341 SUMMIT ST 82930   2-00100
Fred Ball, prin.   789-5499

Farson, AC 307, PC 2, Sweetwater
Sweetwater County SD 1
Supt. — See Rock Springs
Farson-Eden S, PO BOX A 82932   2-11111
Gregory Lasley, prin.   273-9301

Fort Laramie, AC 307, PC 2, Goshen
Goshen County SD 1
Supt. — See Torrington

MS, PO BOX 126 82212 — 1-00100
  Mike Durfee, prin. — 837-2283

Gillette, AC 307, PC 7, Campbell
Campbell County SD 1 — 6-11111
  PO BOX 3033 82717 — 682-5171
  Mark Higdon, supt.
Campbell County SHS — 4-00001
  1000 CAMEL DR 82716 — 682-7247
  John Riley, prin.
Sage Valley JHS — 3-00110
  1000 W LAKEWAY RD 82718 — 682-2225
  Daniel Espeland, prin.
Twin Spruce JHS — 3-00110
  701 S GILLETTE AVE 82716 — 682-3144
  Dave Foreman, prin.
Other Schools – See Wright

Bible Baptist Academy — 2-00011
  1170 COUNTRY CLUB RD 82718
Northern Wyoming Community College — 2-CC
  720 W 8TH ST # 1 82716 — 686-1358

Glendo, AC 307, PC 2, Platte
Platte County SD 1
  Supt. — See Wheatland
S, 305 PAIGE ST 82213 — 1-11111
  Stanetta Twiford, prin. — 735-4471

Glenrock, AC 307, PC 4, Converse
Converse County SD 2 — 3-11111
  PO BOX 1300 82637 — 436-5331
  David Swantek, supt.
HS, PO BOX 1300 82637 — 2-00011
  Claude Christian, prin. — 436-9201
MS, PO BOX 1300 82637 — 2-01100
  Kirk Hughes, prin. — 436-9258

Green River, AC 307, PC 7, Sweetwater
Sweetwater County SD 2 — 5-11111
  400 N 1ST EAST ST 82935 — 872-5500
  Gene Carmody, supt.
HS, 300 MONROE AVE 82935 — 4-00011
  Craig Butler, prin. — 872-5555
Lincoln MS — 2-00100
  600 W 3RD NORTH ST 82935 — 872-5525
  John Grenevitch, prin.
Monroe MS, 250 MONROE AVE 82935 — 2-00100
  Monte Silk, prin. — 872-5535

Greybull, AC 307, PC 4, Big Horn
Big Horn County SD 3 — 3-11111
  636 14TH AVE N 82426 — 765-4756
  J. Franklin Houk, supt.
HS, 600 N 6TH ST 82426 — 2-00011
  Bill Gerrard, prin. — 765-2537
MS, 640 8TH AVE N 82426 — 2-00100
  Gary Lehnhoff, prin. — 765-4492

Guernsey, AC 307, PC 4, Platte
Platte County SD 2 — 2-11111
  PO BOX 189 82214 – H. Ebert, supt. — 836-2735
Guernsey-Sunrise JSHS — 2-00111
  172 W BURLINGTON 82214 — 836-2745
  Ken Griffith, prin.

Hanna, AC 307, PC 4, Carbon
Carbon County SD 1
  Supt. — See Saratoga
Hanna-Elk Mountain JSHS — 2-00111
  PO BOX 810 82327 — 325-6545
  Jackson Hilstad, prin.

Hulett, AC 307, PC 2, Crook
Crook County SD 1
  Supt. — See Sundance
S, PO BOX 127 82720 — 2-11111
  John Balber, prin. — 467-5231

Jackson, AC 307, PC 5, Teton
Teton County SD 1 — 4-11111
  PO BOX 568 83001 — 733-2704
  Thomas Nelson, supt.
Jackson Hole HS — 3-00011
  1855 W HIGH SCHOOL LANE 83001 — 733-7475
  Albert Storrs, prin.
Western Wyoming HS — 1-00011
  220 S GLENWOOD 83001 — 733-9116
  Len Geiger, prin.
Jackson Hole MS, 1230 S PARK RD 83001 — 2-00100
  Terry Roice, prin. — 733-4234

Jeffrey City, AC 307, PC 2, Fremont
Fremont County SD 9 — 1-11111
  PO BOX 130 82310 — 544-2253
  W. Beaver, supt.
S, PO BOX 130 82310 — 1-11111
  W. Beaver, prin. — 544-2253

Kaycee, AC 307, PC 2, Johnson
Johnson County SD 1
  Supt. — See Buffalo
JSHS, PO BOX 6 82639 — 1-00111
  James Doyle, prin. — 738-2323

Kemmerer, AC 307, PC 5, Lincoln
Lincoln County SD 1
  Supt. — See Diamondville
JSHS, 3RD AND ANTELOPE 83101 — 3-00111
  Marlow Viehweg, prin. — 877-6991

Kinnear, AC 307, PC 2, Fremont
Fremont County SD 6 — 2-11111
  11162 HIGHWAY 26 82516 — 856-7970
  Duane Roehrick, supt.

Wind River HS — 2-00011
  11162 HIGHWAY 26 82516 — 856-4248
  Kent Cook, prin.

Lander, AC 307, PC 6, Fremont
Fremont County SD 1 — 4-11111
  32 BALDWIN CREEK RD 82520 — 332-4711
  Wayne King, supt.
Lander Valley HS — 3-00011
  1000 W MAIN ST 82520 — 332-4433
  Craig Loper, prin.
Starrett JHS — 2-00100
  863 SWEETWATER ST 82520 — 332-4040
  Jim Chumley, prin.

Wyoming State Training School — HND
  82520

Laramie, AC 307, PC 8, Albany
Albany County SD 1 — 5-11111
  1948 E GRAND AVE 82070 — 721-4400
  Charles Head, supt.
SHS, 1275 N 11TH ST 82070 — 3-00001
  Bob Bryant, prin. — 721-4420
JHS, 1355 N 22ND ST 82070 — 3-00110
  William Teegerstrom, prin. — 721-4430
Other Schools – See Rock River

Cathedral Home HS — 2-00011
  PO BOX E 82070
University of Wyoming — 7-UC
  PO BOX 3434 82071 — 766-4121
Wyoming Technical Institute — 3-CC
  4373 N 3RD ST 82070 — 742-3776

Lingle, AC 307, PC 2, Goshen
Goshen County SD 1
  Supt. — See Torrington
Lingle-Ft. Laramie HS 82223 — 1-00011
  Mike Durfee, prin. — 837-2296

Lovell, AC 307, PC 4, Big Horn
Big Horn County SD 2 — 3-11111
  502 HAMPSHIRE AVE 82431 — 548-2259
  Don Bartling, supt.
HS, 502 HAMPSHIRE AVE 82431 — 2-00011
  Ralph Winland, prin. — 548-2256
MS, 325 W 9TH ST 82431 — 2-00100
  Norman Opp, prin. — 548-6553

Lusk, AC 307, PC 4, Niobrara
Niobrara County SD 1 — 2-11111
  PO BOX 629 82225 — 334-3793
  Richard Claycomb, supt.
Niobrara County HS — 2-00011
  PO BOX 1050 82225 — 334-3320
  Richard Luchsinger, prin.

Lyman, AC 307, PC 4, Uinta
Uinta County SD 6 — 4-11111
  PO BOX 1090 82937 — 787-6333
  Randy Hillstead, supt.
HS, PO BOX 1090 82937 — 2-00011
  Mike Hicks, prin. — 787-6197
MS, PO BOX 1090 82937 — 2-00100
  Kevin Carney, prin. — 786-4608

Manderson, AC 307, PC 1, Big Horn
Big Horn County SD 4
  Supt. — See Basin
Cloud Peak MS 82432 — 1-00100
  Robert Nicholson, prin. — 568-2846

Medicine Bow, AC 307, PC 2, Carbon
Carbon County SD 2
  Supt. — See Saratoga
S, PO BOX 185 82329 — 2-11111
  Larry Mowry, prin. — 379-2345

Meeteetse, AC 307, PC 2, Park
Park County SD 16 — 2-11111
  PO BOX 218 82433 — 868-2501
  Glenn Schimke, supt.
S, 2107 IDAHO ST 82433 — 2-11111
  John Block, prin. — 868-2501

Midwest, AC 307, PC 2, Natrona
Natrona County SD 1
  Supt. — See Casper
S 82643 — 2-11111
  Ron Watson, prin. — 437-6545

Moorcroft, AC 307, PC 3, Crook
Crook County SD 1
  Supt. — See Sundance
JSHS, PO BOX 129 82721 — 2-00111
  Richard Freudenberg, prin. — 756-3446

Mountain View, AC 307, PC 4, Uinta
Uinta County SD 4 — 4-11111
  PO BOX 130 82939 — 782-3377
  Allen Knapp, supt.
HS, PO BOX 130 82939 — 2-00011
  Terri Wenzlaff, prin. — 782-6340
MS, PO BOX 130 82939 — 2-00100
  Jack Cozort, prin. — 782-6338

Newcastle, AC 307, PC 5, Weston
Weston County SD 1 — 4-11111
  116 CASPER AVE 82701 — 746-4451
  Ray Partridge, supt.
HS, 15 STAMPEDE ST 82701 — 2-00011
  Gerald Anderson, prin. — 746-2713
MS, 116 CASPER AVE 82701 — 2-00100
  Ross Farber, prin. — 746-2746

Pine Bluffs, AC 307, PC 4, Laramie
Laramie County SD 2 — 3-11111
  PO BOX 368 82082 — 245-3738
  Dr. Ronald White, supt.
HS, 7TH & ELM 82082 — 2-00011
  Gary Datus, prin. — 245-3682
JHS, 6TH & ELM 82082 — 1-00100
  Gary Datus, prin. — 245-3682
Other Schools – See Albin, Burns

Pinedale, AC 307, PC 4, Sublette
Sublette County SD 1 — 3-11111
  PO BOX 549 82941 — 367-2139
  Donald Wright, supt.
HS, PO BOX 549 82941 — 2-00011
  David Holmer, prin. — 367-2137
MS, PO BOX 549 82941 — 2-00100
  Kyle Walker, prin. — 367-2821

Powell, AC 307, PC 6, Park
Park County SD 1 — 4-11111
  160 N EVARTS ST 82435 — 754-2215
  Rich Gregory, supt.
HS, 160 N EVARTS ST 82435 — 2-00011
  Steve Sexton, prin. — 754-2287
MS, 160 N EVARTS ST 82435 — 2-00100
  Merton Rustad, prin. — 754-5716

Northwest College — 4-CC
  231 W 6TH ST 82435 — 754-6200

Ranchester, AC 307, PC 3, Sheridan
Sheridan County SD 1 — 3-11111
  PO BOX 819 82839 — 655-9541
  Bob Mcleod, supt.
Tongue River MS, PO BOX 879 82839 — 2-01100
  Suzanne Elliott, prin. — 655-9533
Other Schools – See Big Horn, Dayton

Rawlins, AC 307, PC 6, Carbon
Carbon County SD 1 — 4-11111
  PO BOX 160 82301 — 328-9200
  Jon Fisher, supt.
HS, 801 E BROOKS ST 82301 — 3-00011
  Robert McGrew, prin. — 328-9280
MS, 801 E BROOKS ST 82301 — 3-00100
  Harvey Soulek, prin. — 328-9205
Other Schools – See Baggs

Rawlins Baptist S, 613 1ST ST 82301 — 2-00011

Riverton, AC 307, PC 6, Fremont
Fremont County SD 25 — 5-11111
  121 N 5TH ST W 82501 — 856-9407
  B. Weldon Shelley, supt.
HS, 2001 W SUNSET DR 82501 — 3-00011
  Stephen Roberts, prin. — 856-9491
Career Center HS — Vo Tech
  851 COLLEGE VIEW DR 82501 — 856-6557
  Kip Hanich, prin.
MS, 413 N 4TH ST W 82501 — 3-00100
  Steve Hoff, prin. — 856-9443

Central Wyoming College — 4-CC
  2660 PECK ST 82501 — 856-9291

Rock River, AC 307, PC 2, Albany
Albany County SD 1
  Supt. — See Laramie
S 82083 — 1-11111
  Bob Jahns, prin. — 378-2271

Rock Springs, AC 307, PC 7, Sweetwater
Sweetwater County SD 1 — 6-11111
  PO BOX 1089 82902 — 382-2474
  Don Baumberger, supt.
SHS, 1375 JAMES DR 82901 — 4-00001
  Robert Plant, prin. — 382-8590
Rock Springs East JHS, GOBEL ST 82901 — 3-00110
  Jim Forrest, prin. — 362-3783
White Mountain JHS — 3-00110
  FOOTHILL BLVD 82901 — 382-4160
  John Norris, prin.
Other Schools – See Farson

Western Wyoming Community College — 4-CC
  2500 COLLEGE DR 82901 — 382-1600

Saratoga, AC 307, PC 4, Carbon
Carbon County SD 2 — 4-11111
  PO BOX 1530 82331 — 326-5271
  Neal Carrol, supt.
HS, PO BOX 1710 82331 — 2-00011
  Robin Devine, prin. — 326-5246
MS, PO BOX 1710 82331 — 2-00100
  Jeffrey Degenhart, prin. — 326-8351
Other Schools – See Encampment, Hanna, Medicine Bow

Sheridan, AC 307, PC 7, Sheridan
Sheridan County SD 2 — 5-11111
  PO BOX 919 82801 — 674-7405
  Russell Carlson, supt.
SHS, 1056 LONG DR 82801 — 3-00001
  Woodrow Jensen, prin. — 672-2495
JHS, 620 ADAIR AVE 82801 — 3-00110
  David Treick, prin. — 672-9745

Red Grade Christian Academy — 2-00011
  4351 BIG HORN AVE 82801
Sheridan Christian S — 2-00011
  118 W 5TH ST 82801

Sheridan College   4-CC
  PO BOX 1500   82801   674-6446

Shoshoni, AC 307, PC 2, Fremont
  Fremont County SD 24   2-11111
    PO BOX 327   82649   876-2583
    John Meeks, supt.
  JSHS, PO BOX 327   82649   2-00111
    Larry Bowman, prin.   876-2576

Sundance, AC 307, PC 4, Crook
  Crook County SD 1   4-11111
    PO BOX 830   82729   283-2299
    Jeffrey Carrier, supt.
  JSHS, PO BOX 850   82729   2-00111
    Randy Ludeman, prin.   283-1007
  Other Schools – See Hulett, Moorcroft

Ten Sleep, AC 307, PC 2, Washakie
  Washakie County SD 2   2-11111
    PO BOX 105   82442   366-2223
    Leslie Stencel, supt.
  S   82442   2-11111
    Linda Anderson, prin.   366-2233

Thermopolis, AC 307, PC 5, Hot Springs
  Hot Springs County SD 1   3-11111
    415 SPRINGVIEW ST   82443   864-2331
    Douglas Cobb, supt.

Hot Springs County HS   2-00011
  331 PARK ST   82443   864-2144
  Lyle Brownlee, prin.
MS, 315 SPRINGVIEW ST   82443   2-01100
  Marilynn Tanner, prin.   864-2202

Torrington, AC 307, PC 6, Goshen
  Goshen County SD 1, 2602 W E ST   82240   4-11111
    Paul Novak, supt.   532-2171
  HS, 24TH & WEST C ST   82240   3-00011
    John Binning, prin.   532-7101
  MS, 25TH & WEST E ST   82240   2-00100
    Marvin Haimen, prin.   532-7014
  Other Schools – See Fort Laramie, Lingle, Yoder

Eastern Wyoming College   4-CC
  3200 W C ST   82240   800-658-3195

Upton, AC 307, PC 3, Weston
  Weston County SD 7   2-11111
    PO BOX 470   82730   468-2461
    Lloyd Bailey, supt.
  JSHS, PO BOX 470   82730   2-00111
    Mark Mitchell, prin.   468-2361

Wheatland, AC 307, PC 5, Platte
  Platte County SD 1, 1350 OAK ST   82201   4-11111
    Don Bryngelson, supt.   322-2434

HS, 13TH AT OAK   82201   2-00011
  Merle Smith, prin.   322-2075
JHS, 1150 PINE ST   82201   2-00100
  Mark Knickerbocker, prin.   322-2433
Other Schools – See Chugwater, Glendo

Worland, AC 307, PC 6, Washakie
  Washakie County SD 1   4-11111
    1900 HOWELL AVE   82401   347-9286
    Jerry Maurer, supt.
  HS, 17TH & WASHAKIE   82401   2-00011
    Mike Hejtmanek, prin.   347-2412
  MS, 1200 CULBERTSON AVE   82401   2-00100
    Paul Soriano, prin.   347-3233

Wright, AC 307, PC 4, Campbell
  Campbell County SD 1
    Supt. — See Gillette
  Wright SHS, PO BOX 490   82732   2-00001
    Robert Watson, prin.   939-1384
  JHS, PO BOX 490   82732   2-00110
    Robert Watson, prin.   939-1384

Yoder, AC 307, PC 2, Goshen
  Goshen County SD 1
    Supt. — See Torrington
  Southeast JSHS   82244   2-00111
    Brian Grasmick, prin.   532-7176

AMERICAN SAMOA

DEPARTMENT OF EDUCATION
Pago Pago 96799
(684) 633-5159

Director of Education   Lealofi Uiagalelei

PUBLIC, PRIVATE AND CATHOLIC SECONDARY SCHOOLS

Pago Pago, AC 684

American Samoa Schools 96799		6-00011
(—), supt.		633-5159
Fagaituna HS 96799		2-00011
(—), prin.		622-7550

Leone HS 96799		2-00011
(—), prin.		688-7688
Manua HS 96799		2-00011
(—), prin.		677-3512
Samoana HS 96799		2-00011
(—), prin.		633-4579

Tafuna HS 96799		2-00011
(—), prin.		699-1303
American Samoa Community College		4-CC
PO BOX 2609 96799		699-9155

GUAM

DEPARTMENT OF EDUCATION
P. O. Box DE, Agana 96910
(671) 472-8901

Director of Education   J. A. Quitugua

PUBLIC, PRIVATE AND CATHOLIC SECONDARY SCHOOLS

Agana, AC 671, PC 9

Department Of Education		4-11111
PO BOX DE 96910		472-8901
Anita Sukola, supt.		
Inarajan HS, PO BOX DE 96910		2-00011
Joaquin Guzman, prin.		828-8671
Kennedy HS, PO BOX DE 96910		2-00011
Gayle Hendricks, prin.		646-8615
Oceanview HS, PO BOX DE 96910		2-00011
Ken Chargualaf, prin.		565-2961
Sanchez HS, PO BOX DE 96910		2-00011
Karolyn Duponcheel, prin.		653-2313
Washington HS, PO BOX DE 96910		2-00011
Liz Manibusan, prin.		734-2011
Dededo MS, PO BOX DE 96910		2-00100
Joe Quitugua, prin.		632-5647

Guerrero MS, PO BOX DE 96910		2-00100
Judith Pat-Borja, prin.		653-2080
Inarajan MS, PO BOX DE 96910		2-00100
Salvador Avilla, prin.		828-8631
Johnston MS, PO BOX DE 96910		2-00100
James Denight, prin.		472-6785
Piti MS, PO BOX DE 96910		2-00100
Eleuterio Mesa, prin.		477-9377
Untalan MS, PO BOX DE 96910		2-00100
Joe Manibusan, prin.		734-3961

Academy Of Our Lady Of Guam		2-00011
233 ARCHBISHOP FLEIXBERTO S 96910		
Sr. Francis Jerome, prin.		477-8203

Baumgartner JHS		2-00100
281 CALLE ANGEL FLORES 96926		472-6670
Sr. Orlean Pereda, prin.		
Father Duenas Mem School		2-00011
PO BOX FD 96910		734-2261
William Roth, prin.		
Guam Adventist Academy		2-00011
1200 AGUILAR RD 96914		
Guam Community College		5-CC
PO BOX 23069 96921		734-4311
International Business College of Guam		CS
PO BOX 3783 96910		646-6901
Notre Dame HS, SAN MIGUEL ST 96914		2-00011
Sr. Mary Comacho, prin.		789-1676
University of Guam		4-UC
UOG STATION 96923		734-9450

MARIANA ISLANDS

DEPARTMENT OF EDUCATION
P.O. Box 1370 CK, Siapan 95950
(670) 332-6451

Superintendent of Education   William Torres

PUBLIC, PRIVATE AND CATHOLIC SECONDARY SCHOOLS

Saipan, AC 670

Northern Mariana Islands School System		6-11111
PO BOX 1370 96950		332-3194
Elizabeth Diaz Rechebei, supt.		

Marianas SHS 96950		3-00001
Herman Sablan, prin.		332-3194
Hopwood JHS 96950		3-00110
Thomas Pangelinan, prin.		332-3194

Rota JHS 96950		2-00110
Oscar Quitugua, prin.		332-3194

PUERTO RICO

DEPARTMENT OF EDUCATION
P.O. Box 190759, San Juan 00919
(809) 758-4949

Secretary of Education   Jose Arsenio Torres

PUBLIC, PRIVATE AND CATHOLIC SECONDARY SCHOOLS

Adjuntas, AC 809, PC 6, Adjuntas Municipio
Adjuntas SD   5-11111
   18 CALLE RODULFO GONZALEZ   00601
   Edgar Reyes, supt.   829-2140
Lugo HS   3-00001
   75 CALLE FRANCISCO PIETRI   00601   829-0408
   Jose Altieri, prin.
Jimenez JHS   00601   3-00110
   Elba Velez, prin.   829-3890
Rivera JHS, BO YAHUECAS   00601   2-01110
   Angel Velez, prin.   829-3030

Aguada, AC 809, PC 5, Aguada Municipio
Aguada SD, PO BOX 519   00602   6-11111
   Ramon Cruz, supt.   868-5910
Gonzalez SHS   3-00001
   BARRIO GUANIQUILLA   00602   868-3280
   Miguel Patino, prin.
Lopez JSHS, GUANABANO ST   00602   4-00111
   Jose Aviles, prin.   868-2161
Martinez JHS   00602   3-00110
   Abraham Gonzalez, prin.   868-2260

Colegio Tecnologico y Comercial   2-CS
   CALLE PAZ 165 ALTOS   00602   868-2688

Aguadilla, AC 809, PC 6, Aguadilla Municipio
Aguadilla SD   6-11111
   CENTRO GUBERNAMENTAL   00603   891-0455
   Hernan Morell, supt.
Cerezo SHS, BO BORINQUEN   00603   3-00001
   Marisol Moure, prin.   891-5000
Fuentes HS   00603   2-00001
   Melba Gonzalez, prin.   890-2935
Jose De Diego HS   3-00011
   CALLE LORENCITA ARELLANO   00603   891-2220
   Gilberto Cubero, prin.
Badillo JHS, BO MONTANA   00610   3-00110
   Maria Hernandez, prin.   890-3360
Del Valle JHS   2-00110
   CALLE AGUSTIN STAHL   00603   891-0620
   Agustin Maltes, prin.
Rivera JHS, COMASEYES ST   00603   3-00110
   Julio Muniz, prin.   890-2418
Stahl JHS   00603   2-00110
   Hector Mendez, prin.   891-1000

Colegio San Carlos   3-11111
   PO BOX 1009   00605   891-1445
   Nydia Nieves, prin.
Inter American University   5-UC
   CALL BOX 2000   00603   891-0925
University of Puerto Rico   4-CC
   PO BOX 160   00604   890-2681

Aguas Buenas, AC 809, PC 5, Aguas Buenas Municipio
Aguas Buenas SD   6-11111
   CALLE RAFAEL LASA FINAL   00607   732-3156
   Jose Alicea, supt.
Pastrana SHS, PIO RECHANI ST   00607   3-00001
   Josefina Arroyo, prin.   732-3601
Marin JHS   3-00110
   SECTOR ARANA BO SUMIDERO   00607
   Heriberto Del Valle, prin.   732-3521

Aguirre, AC 809, Guayama Municipio

Professional Electrical School   2-CS
   PO BOX 1797   00704   854-4776

Aibonito, AC 809, PC 6, Aibonito Municipio
Aibonito SD, 52 BALDORITY ST   00609   6-11111
   Noemi Aguirre, supt.   735-4181
Gandara SHS, SAN JOSE ST   00609   4-00001
   Miriam Oyola, prin.   735-7290
Sanchez JHS, 119 SAN JOSE ST   00609   3-00110
   Victor Sanchez, prin.   735-4631

Anasco, AC 809, PC 5, Anasco Municipio
Anasco SD   6-11111
   CALLE NICOLAS SOTO   00610   826-2659
   Angel Hernandez, supt.
Marin SHS, BO MARIOS   00610   3-00001
   Mario Feliciano, prin.   826-1476
Figueroa JHS   00610   3-00110
   Aurea Muniz, prin.   826-2195
Suarez JHS   00610   3-00110
   Carmen Velez, prin.   826-2575

Arecibo, AC 809, PC 7, Arecibo Municipio
Arecibo SD 1   00612   6-11111
   Joaquin De La Cruz, supt.   878-1068

Martinez SHS   4-00001
   ESTEBAN PADILLA AVE   00612   878-3480
   Ivonne Lajara, prin.
Jefferson JHS, DE DIEGO AVE   00612   3-00110
   Victor Torano, prin.   878-3332
Marin JHS, BO HATO ABAJO   00612   3-00110
   Emilio Saavedra, prin.   880-0757

Arecibo SD 2   6-11111
   152 AVE JUAN ROSADO   00612   878-8860
   Carmen Arroyo, supt.
Luchetti HS   3-00001
   10 AVE JUAN ROSADO   00612   878-3130
   Carmen Torres Coll, prin.

Arecibo SD 3   6-11111
   JOSE DE DIEGO AVE   00616   878-2535
   Rosendo Mercado, supt.
Padilla De Sanz HS   3-00001
   653 VILLA LOS SANTOS   00612   878-1365
   Nivia Gonzalez, prin.
Otero HS   00612   2-00001
   Haydee Morales, prin.   879-2614
Varona MS, TANAMA ST   00612   1-00110
   (—), prin.   878-5366

Catholic University of Puerto Rico   4-UC
   PO BOX 495   00613   881-1212
Colegio La Milagrosa   2-11111
   AVE COTTO 987   00612   878-0341
   Maria Vicens, prin.
Colegio San Felipe   3-11111
   PO BOX 673   00613   878-3532
   Sr. Veronica Oravec, prin.
Institute of Multiple Technology   2-CS
   PO BOX 707   00613   878-6844
Interamerican Business College   2-CS
   CALLE BETANCES ESQ PALMAS   00612
   384-4481
Inter American University of Puerto Rico   5-UC
   CALL BOX UI   00612   878-5475
National College/Business & Technology   2-CS
   AVENUE GONZALO MARIN #109   00612
   879-5044
University of Puerto Rico   5-UC
   P O BOX A-1806   00613   878-2830

Arroyo, AC 809, PC 6, Arroyo Municipio
Arroyo SD   00714   5-11111
   Wilfredo Rodriguez, supt.   839-3130
Huyke SHS, ISIDRO CORA NORTE   00615   4-00001
   Juanita Morrabal, prin.   839-2655
Choudens JHS, 113 CALLE MORSE   00714   3-00110
   Gilberto Burgos, prin.   839-5390
Cora IS, BO PITAHAYA   00615   3-01110
   Ricardo Reyes, prin.   839-4030

Colegio Mayor de Technologia   2-CS
   CALLE MORSE #151   00714   839-5266

Barceloneta, AC 809, PC 2, Barceloneta Municipio
Barceloneta SD, APDO 338   00617   5-11111
   Angel Otero, supt.   846-3110
Chaves HS   00617   2-00011
   Carmen Colon, prin.   846-6750
Balseiro JHS, 1 GEORGETTI ST   00617   3-00110
   Juan Guzman, prin.   846-2460

Barranquitas, AC 809, PC 5, Barranquitas Municipio
Barranquitas SD   6-11111
   EDIFICIO MOLINA   00618   857-0242
   Carlos Marrero, supt.
Berdecia SHS   3-00001
   156 AVE ANTONIO BARCELO   00618   857-2897
   Carlos Bernardi, prin.
Marin SHS, SECTOR NUEVO   00618   3-00001
   Tomasita Rivera, prin.   857-3714
Berdecia JHS   2-00110
   MELITON PERELEZ ST   00618   857-2305
   Hector Ramirez, prin.
Laboy JHS, BO QUEBRADILLAS   00618   2-00110
   Rafael Ortiz, prin.   857-2845

Benedict School of Languages & Commerce   2-CS
   CARR 719 AVENIDA VILLA #15   00794
Inter American University of Puerto Rico   4-UC
   PO BOX 517   00794   857-4040

Bayamon, AC 809, Bayamon Municipio
Bayamon SD 2
   Supt. — See San Juan

Papa Juan JSHS   00959   4-00111
   Militza Mendez, prin.   785-3449

Bayamon SD 3   00957   6-11111
   Miguel Fernandez, supt.   786-3010
Other Schools – See San Juan

Bayamon SD 4
   Supt. – See San Juan
Rodriguez JHS   00959   2-00110
   Elizabeth Valentin, prin.   798-4970

Academia Santo Tomas   4-11111
   PO BOX 1557   00960   785-8600
   Sr. Carmen Martinez, prin.
Allied Schools of Puerto Rico   2-CS
   PO BOX 98   00960   780-1612
American Educational College   2-CS
   PO BOX 62   00960   798-1199
American University of Puerto Rico   5-UC
   PO BOX 2037   00960   798-2022
Bayamon Central University   5-UC
   PO BOX 1725   00960   786-3030
Bayamon Technical & Commercial Institute   2-CS
   PO BOX 6007   00619   787-8805
Caribbean University   4-UC
   PO BOX 493   00960   780-0070
Colegio De La Salle   3-01111
   APARTADO 518   00621   785-7150
   Yolanda Lopez, prin.
Colegio Santa Rosa   3-00111
   APARTADO 6032   00619   785-1195
   Luz Valentin, prin.
Escuela Superior Catolica   3-00011
   PO BOX 4225   00958   798-5260
   Sr. Maria Marxuach, prin.
Fashion Design College   2-CS
   CALLE DEGETAU #5 ESQ BETANC   00961
   785-2388
Fashion Merchandising and Technical Inst   2-CS
   PO BOX 2206   00960   798-8870
Inter American University of Puerto Rico   5-UC
   RD 174 MINILLAS IND PARK   00959   780-4040
Merlix Professional and Technical Inst   2-CS
   PO BOX 6241   00914   786-7035
National College/Business & Technology   2-CS
   PO BOX 2036   00960   780-5134
Professional Technical Institute   2-CS
   AVENID BETANCES #73 STE 491   00959
   740-6810
Puerto Rico Professional College   2-CS
   CALLE DR VEVE #51 ESQ DEGET   00960
   798-8718
Universidad Central Del Caribe   2-UC
   PO BOX 60327   00960   798-3001
University of Puerto Rico   00959   5-UC
   786-2885

Cabo Rojo, AC 809, PC 6, Cabo Rojo Municipio
Cabo Rojo SD   6-11111
   CALLE JOSE DE DIEGO   00623   851-1035
   Gregorio Velez, supt.
Leon De Irizarry SHS   2-00001
   BO BOQUERON   00623   254-2288
   Marilyn Aguilar, prin.
Marin SHS   3-00001
   CALLE BARBOSA NORTE   00623   851-5037
   Ermes Morales, prin.
Colberg JHS, PUEBLO NUEVO ST   00623   3-00110
   Milton Bracero, prin.   851-1470
Marin JHS, PUEBLO NUEVA   00623   2-00110
   Ana Rodriguez, prin.   851-1601

Colegio San Agustin   3-11111
   PO BOX 926   00623   851-1950
   Gloria De Delgado, prin.

Caguas, AC 809, PC 7, Caguas Municipio
Caguas SD 1   6-11111
   CENTRO JUDICIAL BVO PISO   00625   743-4605
   Yolanda Caballero, supt.
Pascual SHS   00725   3-00001
   Norma Cruz, prin.   746-5506
Morice SHS   4-00001
   CALLE 5 CAGUAS NORTE   00625   743-9310
   Angel Mendez, prin.
Aldea JHS   3-00110
   13 CALLE RAFAEL CORDERO   00725   743-5065
   Francisco Flores, prin.
Vidal JHS, CALLE 31 FINAL   00625   2-00110
   Magaly Rivera, prin.   744-5666

Centeno JHS 3-00110
CALLE 1 URB SANTA JUANA 00625 746-5660
Luis Lozada, prin.
Nieves JHS, BO RIO CANAS 00625 3-00110
Jose Perez, prin. 747-2026

Caguas SD 2, 52 BETANCES ST 00625 6-11111
Zoraida Miranda, supt. 743-4328
Benitez SHS 00725 4-00001
Luisa Delgado, prin. 743-4211
Costa Rica SHS 3-00001
39 CALLE HECTOR BUNKER 00625 743-4113
Valentin Rivera, prin.
Gonzalez JHS 3-00110
GAUTIER BENITEZ ST 00625 743-2311
Sara Lopez, prin.
Sola JHS, MERCURIO ST 00625 3-00110
(—), prin. 743-3276

Caguas SD 3, 2 CALLE PADIAL 00725 6-11111
Virginia Santos, supt. 746-2011
Pedreira SHS 2-00001
CALLE 4 URB VILLA DEL CARME 00625
Anabel Quilez, prin. 743-4868
Kennedy JHS 00725 2-00110
Naniel Diaz, prin. 743-6916
Caraballo JHS 00725 3-00110
Maria Miranda, prin. 744-4575
Osuna 2 JHS 00725 2-00110
Ana Adorno, prin. 743-4868

Academia Cristo De Los Milagros 4-11111
PO BOX 7618 00726 743-4855
Epifania Parrilla, prin.
Arts and Business College of Puerto Rico 2-CS
PO BOX 1269 00725 744-5493
Colegio Catolico Notre Dame 4-00111
PO BOX 541 00726 743-3693
Sr. Jose Grillo, prin.
Colegio San Jose Superior 2-00111
PO BOX 1101 00726 744-8993
Brenda Soler, prin.
Columbia College 3-CC
PO BOX 8517 00726 743-4041
Huertas Junior College 4-CC
PO BOX 8429 00726 743-2156
Instituto Vocacional y Comercial EDIC 2-CS
PO BOX 9120 00726 743-4346
International College of Business & Tech 2-CS
PLAZA SAN ALFONSO 2ND FLOOR 00627
746-3777
Liceo De Arte Y Disenos 2-CS
PO BOX 1889 00626 743-7447

Camuy, AC 809, PC 5, Camuy Municipio
Camuy SD, AMADOR ST 00627 6-11111
Miguel Cardona, supt. 898-2180
Gonzalez SHS 00627 3-00001
Marcial Lopez, prin. 898-3770
Palmer S, CARR 486 KM 1.6 00627 4-11111
Ruben Marcial, prin. 898-7976
Acosta JHS, MUNOZ RIVERA AVE 00627 3-00110
Jorge Martinez, prin. 898-3790

Canovanas, AC 809, PC 7, Canovanas Municipio
Canovanas SD 00729 6-11111
Santiago Velazquez, supt. 876-3195
Carrillo SHS, CARR 185 KM 7 00629 2-00001
William Rivera, prin. 886-2200
Veronne SHS 00729 4-00001
Martha Delgado, prin. 876-2395
Cubuy JSHS, BO CUBUY 00629 2-00111
Elba Castro, prin. 876-7807
Barcelio JHS 00729 3-00110
Dionisio Delgado, prin. 876-4055
Quinones JHS 3-00110
21 CALLE JARDINES DE PALMAR 00629
Carmen Delgado, prin. 876-4493

Carolina, AC 809, PC 7, Carolina Municipio
Carolina SD 1 6-11111
5 IGNACIO ARZUAGA ST 00630 769-4102
Luz Rodriguez, supt.
Bohena JSHS 00979 4-00111
Pilar Birriel, prin. 769-0386
Vizcarrondo SHS 3-00001
8 CALLE QUINONES 00630 769-0870
Margarita Robles, prin.
Bueso JHS 2-00110
30 CALLE SAN RAFAEL 00630 769-8350
Ada Salgado, prin.

Carolina SD 2 6-11111
FIDALGO DIAZ AVE 00630 768-2020
Jorge Torres, supt.
Calderon SHS, 18 CENTRAL BLVD 00985 3-00001
Marta Rosa, prin. 768-4044
Gracia SHS 3-00001
SANCHEZ OSORIO AVE 00630 768-2216
Iris Calero, prin.
Rodriguez JSHS 00985 3-00111
Miguel Ortiz, prin. 752-1410
Bultron JHS 00985 2-00110
Lydia Marcial, prin. 752-3131
Cabrera JHS, CENTRAL BLVD 00985 3-00110
Wanda Hernandez, prin. 752-3465
Gonzalez JHS 00983 3-00110
Celia Perez, prin. 768-3031
Rodriguez JHS 00979 3-00110
Irma Figueroa, prin. 752-0225

Carolina SD 3, A-18 GALICIA AVE 00630 6-11111
Luz Castro, supt. 769-0365
Lazaro SHS 4-00001
EL COMANDANTE AVE 00630 769-3638
Alma Mundo, prin.
Gonzalez JHS 00979 2-00110
Jorge Diaz, prin. 757-3890
Marques JHS 00983 3-00110
Emilse Rivera, prin. 757-2760
Saldana JHS 00983 2-00110
Carmen Santiago, prin. 769-3753
Vigo JHS 00630 2-00110
Jose Rodriguez, prin. 769-3255

Colegio Maria Auxiliadora 4-11111
PO BOX 797 00986 768-6924
Lelis Iglesias, prin.
Instituto de Educacion Universal 2-CS
APTDO 209 00986 757-5000
Instituto Del Arte Moderno 2-CS
AVENIDA MONSERRATE FR-5 00983

University of Puerto Rico 768-2532
PO BOX 4800 00984 4-CC
257-0000

Cayey, AC 809, PC 7, Cayey Municipio
Cayey SD 6-11111
AVE ANTONIO R BARCELO 00633 738-3251
Miguel Alvelo, supt.
Harrison SHS, 249 JOSE DE DIEGO 00633 3-00001
Miguel Ortiz, prin. 738-2616
Munoz SHS, BARCELO AVE 00633 4-00001
Angel Marrero, prin. 738-3078
Betances JHS, BARCELO AVE 00633 3-00110
Ismael Gonzalez, prin. 738-3745
Garcia JHS 00736 3-00110
Elba Collazo, prin. 738-2626
Leon JHS 2-00110
LUIS MUNOZ MORALES ST 00633 738-2440
(—), prin.

DMart Institute 2-CS
PO BOX 2337 00737 738-5474
Instituto de Banca y Comercio 2-CS
PO BOX K 00737 738-5555
University of Puerto Rico 5-UC
ANTONIO BARCELO AVE 00736 738-2161

Ceiba, AC 809, PC 5, Ceiba Municipio
Ceiba SD 4-11111
CENTRO GUBERNAMENTAL 00635 885-2460
Luz Carrion, supt.
Pantin SHS 2-00001
CALLE FRANCISCO GAUTHIER 00635 885-3200
Felix Torres, prin.
Nueva JHS, CALLE BARCELONA 00635 3-00110
David Castro, prin. 885-3170

Ciales, AC 809, PC 5, Ciales Municipio
Ciales SD, 48 CALLE PALMER 00638 4-11111
Elba Martorell, supt. 871-2135
Serpa SHS, CORCHADO EXT ST 00638 3-00001
Carmen Marrero, prin. 871-3225
Valderas JHS, CORCHADO EXT ST 00638 3-00110
Francisco Lugo, prin. 871-3165

Cidra, AC 809, PC 5, Cidra Municipio
Cidra SD, 40 CALLE BALDORIOTY 00739 6-11111
Jose Berrios, supt. 739-3021
Candelas SHS, SALIDA DE CAYEY 00639 3-00001
Alda Cruz, prin. 739-8070
Iglesias SHS 00739 3-00001
Angel Colon, prin. 739-3011
Pinero JHS 3-00100
CALLE MIGUEL PLANELLAS 00739 739-2481
Bernaldina Concepcion, prin.
Pinero Anexos JHS 00739 2-00010
Milagros Perez, prin. 739-5623

Coamo, AC 809, PC 7, Coamo Municipio
Coamo SD 00640 6-11111
Ernesto Santiago, supt. 825-1686
Davila HS 00769 3-00001
Agustin Rivera, prin. 825-1247
Zayas HS, CALLE 19 00769 2-00001
Hilsa Fernandez, prin. 825-5911
Franklin JHS 3-00110
82 CALLE JOSE I QUINTON 00769 825-1284
Irma Bermudez, prin.
Santiago JHS 3-00110
116 CALLE JOSE I QUINTON 00769 825-1575
Ida Collazo, prin.

Colegio De Valvanera 2-11111
PO BOX 1903 00769 825-1145
Sr. Ida Zayas, prin.

Comerio, AC 809, PC 6, Comerio Municipio
Comerio SD 5-11111
53 CALLE GEORGETTI 00782 875-3245
Delma Santiago, supt.
Colon SHS, 8TH ST 00642 3-00001
Modesto Quiles, prin. 875-2130
Marin JHS, BO PINAS 00642 3-00110
Fidencio Alicea, prin. 875-3390

Corozal, AC 809, PC 6, Corozal Municipio
Corozal SD 6-11111
CARR 159 BOX 709 00643 859-2130
Miguel Nieves, supt.
Delgado JHS, CARR 159 00643 4-00001
Jesus Sanchez, prin. 859-2037
Garcia SHS, BO CUCHILLAS 00643 2-00001
Carmen Rojas, prin. 859-0288

Gali JHS 00783 3-00110
Jose Albino, prin. 859-2270

Colegio Sagrada Familia 3-11111
PO BOX 769 00783 859-2420
Maria Salvador, prin.

Culebra, AC 809, Culebra Municipio
Vieques SD
Supt. — See Vieques
Barcelo JSHS, CALLE SALISBURY 00645 2-00111
Ana Garcia, prin. 742-3583

Dorado, AC 809, PC 7, Dorado Municipio
Dorado SD, CALLE NORTE 200 00646 6-11111
Max Otero, supt. 796-1750
Alegria SHS 4-00001
CALLE ESPANA FINAL 00646 796-1520
Hernan Burgos, prin.
Laracuente JHS 3-00110
CALLE LUIS MUNOZ RIVERA 00646 796-1222
Hedrian Ponce, prin.
Maguayo JHS, BO MAGUAYO 00646 2-00110
(—), prin. 796-2761

Fajardo, AC 809, PC 7, Fajardo Municipio
Fajardo SD 6-11111
CENTRO GUBERNAMENTAL 00648 863-1450
Felix Rosello, supt.
Calzada SHS 4-00001
GENERAL VALERO ST 00648 863-0125
Norma Gomez, prin.
Bernabe JHS 4-00110
GENERAL VALERO ST 00648 863-0024
Ana Flores, prin.
Ferrero JHS, CALLE A ESQUINA B 00648 3-00110
Horacio Rivera, prin. 863-6770

Colegio Santiago Apostol 3-11111
PO BOX 907 00738 863-0524
Sr. Luis Matta, prin.
Humacao Community College 2-CS
PO BOX 1185 00738 863-5210
Instituto de Banca y Comercio 2-CS
MUNOZ RIVERA 205 00738 860-6262
Inter American University of Puerto Rico 4-UC
PO BOX 1029 00738 863-2390
National Computer College 2-CS
PO BOX 1009 00738 863-0593

Florida, AC 809, PC 7, Florida Municipio
Florida SD 00650 4-11111
Carmen de Leon, supt. 822-2030
Ponce De Leon SHS, TORRES ST 00650 3-00001
Angel Mendoza, prin. 822-2050
Morales MS 00650 3-00110
Felipe Morales, prin. 822-2263

Guanica, AC 809, PC 6, Guanica Municipio
Guanica SD 00653 5-11111
Carmen Martinez, supt. 821-2010
Claudio SHS, 133 CARR OCHOA 00653 3-00001
Hector Zapata, prin. 821-2800
Roosevelt S 3-00001
50 CALLE 13 DE MARZO 00653 821-2010
Hector Zapata, prin.
Seda JHS 3-00110
45 CALLE 13 DE MARZO 00653 821-2570
Lavinia Lopez, prin.
Siurano JHS, 36 LAJAS RD 00653 2-00110
Zaida Portalatin, prin. 821-2300

Guayama, AC 809, PC 7, Guayama Municipio
Guayama SD 00784 6-11111
Ada Cora, supt. 864-0952
Landron SHS, URB VIVES 00784 3-00001
Victor Burgos, prin. 864-4366
Boyrie JSHS 00784 3-00111
Elisa Rolon, prin. 864-3879
Mendoza JSHS 3-00111
CARR 3 KM 143.8 00654 864-7700
Demetrio Acevedo, prin.
Madera JHS, CALLE MCARTHUR 00784 3-00110
Esther Quinones, prin. 864-0768
Rivera JHS, CALLE MCARTHUR 00784 2-00110
Lydia Rodriguez, prin. 864-0968

Catholic University of Puerto Rico 4-UC
PO BOX 10785 864-0550
Instituto de Banca y Comercio 2-CS
PO BOX 6092 00654 864-3220
Inter American University of Puerto Rico 4-CC
APDO 1559 00785 864-2222

Guayanilla, AC 809, PC 6, Guayanilla Municipio
Guayanilla SD 5-11111
CALLE LUIS MUNOZ RIVERA 00656 835-2580
Nancy Lugo, supt.
Sala HS, BO QUEBRADAS 00656 3-00001
Santiago Gonzales, prin. 835-2030
Quiros JHS 4-00110
CALLE LUIS MUNOZ RIVERA 00656 835-2985
Rafael Rodriguez, prin.

Guaynabo, AC 809, PC 8, Guaynabo Municipio
Guaynabo SD 00657 7-11111
Jose Torres, supt. 720-5374
Barcelo SHS 00965 3-00001
Lupicinia Rodriguez, prin. 790-6482
Martinez JSHS, CALLE ROSALINA 00657 3-00111
Providencia Jorge, prin. 783-8385
Palacios SHS 00657 4-00001
Sara Rodriguez, prin. 720-2427
Miranda JHS, FRAILES ST 00657 3-00110
Isabel Diaz, prin. 790-8198

Nadal JHS, CALLE MORGA 00965   3-00110
  Vilma Maldonado, prin.   720-3356

Academia San Jose, 2M-215 00657   4-11111
  Sr. Catherine Ortiz, prin.   792-7489
American Military Academy   3-00111
  PO BOX 7884 00970   720-6801
  Julio Hedesa, prin.
Atlantic College   2-CS
  PO BOX 1774 00970   720-1022
Colegio Marista   4-11111
  CALLE MARCELINO CHAMPAGNAT 00969
  Felipe Vegas, prin.   720-2186
Colegio Sagrados Corazones   3-11111
  AVENIDA A URB PONCE DE LEON 00657
  Ana Arce De Marrero, prin.   720-2585
Colegio San Pedro Martir   3-11111
  APARTADO 2560 00651   720-2219
  Aurea Fuentes, prin.

Gurabo, AC 809, PC 6, Gurabo Municipio
Gurabo SD   6-11111
  CALLE EUGENIO SANCHEZ LOPEZ 00658
  Eduardo Melendez, supt.   737-2151
Cuevas SHS   3-00001
  CARR 30 RAMAL 944 00778   737-2700
  Marta Lopez, prin.
Garcia JHS 00778   3-00110
  Margarita Viera, prin.   737-2056

Universidad Del Turabo   6-UC
  PO BOX 3030 00778   743-7979

Hatillo, AC 809, PC 6, Hatillo Municipio
Hatillo SD, PO BOX 7 00659   6-11111
  Irma Munoz Cortes, supt.   898-3960
Gandia SHS, LACOMBA ST 00659   3-00001
  Israel Rodriguez, prin.   898-4300
Rodriguez S, NARANJITO ST 00659   4-11111
  Julio Colon, prin.   898-9497
Casey JHS, LACOMBA ST 00659   3-00110
  Juan Monrouzeau, prin.   898-4170
Delgado JHS, BO BUENA VISTA 00659   3-00110
  Delia Nieves, prin.   898-9566

Colegio Nuestra Del Carmen   3-11111
  APARTADO 937 00659   898-2800
  Angelica Peguero, prin.

Hato Rey, AC 809, PC 99, San Juan Municipio
Rio Piedras SD 1
  Supt. — See San Juan
Canales MS 00928   2-01110
  Sebastian Ramos, prin.   781-1773

Rio Piedras SD 2   6-11111
  374 BARBOSA AVE 00917   764-3485
  Carlos Romero, supt.
Other Schools – See San Juan

Benedict School of Languages & Commerce   2-CS
  45 MUNOZ RIVERA AVE 00918   754-1199
Centro de Estudios Multidisciplinarios   2-CS
  BARBOSA AVE #602 2ND FLOOR 00917
    765-4210
Colegio Espiritu Santo   3-11111
  PO BOX 1715 00919   754-0490
  E. Santos, prin.
Colegio Lourdes, PO BOX 847 00919   3-11111
  HNA Aivarez, prin.   767-6106
Electronic Data Processing College   2-CS
  PO BOX 192303 00918   765-3560
Instituto de Educacion Universal   2-CS
  404 AVE BARBOSA 00917   767-2000
Interamerican Business College   2-CS
  PO BOX 202 00902   753-1500
Puerto Rico Technical Jr College   2-CS
  AVE PONCE DE LEON #703 00917   751-0133

Hormigueros, AC 809, PC 6, Hormigueros Municipio
Hormigueros SD 00660   5-11111
  Juan Irizarry, supt.   849-2790
Belvis HS 00660   3-00011
  Juan Gonzalez, prin.   849-2610
Rodriguez JHS, CALLE COMERCIO 00660   3-00110
  Nydia Santiago, prin.   849-4270

Humacao, AC 809, PC 7, Humacao Municipio
Humacao SD 00791   7-11111
  Diani Rivera, supt.   852-1434
Mercado SHS, BO TEJAS 00661   3-00001
  Maria Santana, prin.   852-7780
Roque SHS, DR VIDAL ST 00661   4-00001
  Luis Cintron, prin.   852-1115
Ponce De Leon JHS   2-00110
  CALLE DR VIDAL 00661   852-6800
  Nelson Rivera, prin.
Ufret JHS, 80 ROOSEVELT AVE 00661   4-00110
  William Torres, prin.   852-1865

Centro de Estudios Multidisciplinarios   2-CS
  6 DR VIDAL ST 00791   852-5530
Colegio Nuestra Senora   3-11111
  PO BOX 910 00792   852-0845
  Mercedes Arroyo, prin.
Colegio San Antonio Abad   2-00111
  PO BOX 729 00792   852-1616
  Rev. Rodriguez, prin.
Humacao Community College   2-CS
  PO BOX 8948 00792   852-1430
Interamerican Business College   2-CS
  PO BOX 823 00792   852-6444

International College of Business & Tech   2-CS
  FONT MARTELO ST 00971   850-0055
University of Puerto Rico   5-UC
  CUH STATION RD 908 BO TEJAS 00791
    850-9346

Isabela, AC 809, PC 7, Isabela Municipio
Isabela SD, FERROCARRIL AVE 00662   6-11111
  Julio Acevedo, supt.   872-2695
Domenech SHS   2-00001
  CARR 2 BO MORA 00662   872-2915
  Gabriel Corchado, prin.
Mendoza SHS 00662   3-00001
  Josefa Carrero, prin.   872-2275
Munoz JHS, FERROCARRIL AVE 00662   3-00110
  Alice Badillo, prin.   872-4070
Rivera JHS, 60 BARBOSA ST 00662   3-00110
  Gloria Martinez, prin.   872-2388
Rosario JHS   3-00110
  CARR 112 KM 2 HM 1 00662   830-2025
  Alessay Arroyo, prin.

Benedict School of Languages & Commerce   2-CS
  112 STREET KM 6 BARRIO MORA 00662
Colegio San Antonio   2-11111
  PO BOX 897 00662   872-2406
  Sr. Ida Negron, prin.
Escuela de Peritos Electricitas   2-CS
  PO BOX 457 00662   872-1747

Jayuya, AC 809, PC 5, Jayuya Municipio
Jayuya SD 00664   5-11111
  Cristina Cancel, supt.   828-6080
Zayas HS, CARR 144 00664   3-00001
  Jose Figueroa, prin.   828-5700
Torrado JHS   3-00110
  GUILLERMO ESTEVES ST 00664   828-3625
  Luis Lopez, prin.

Juana Diaz, AC 809, PC 6, Juana Diaz Municipio
Juana Diaz SD 00665   7-11111
  Nora Algarin, supt.   837-2463
Marin JSHS, BO PASTILLO 00665   3-00111
  Fernando Torres, prin.   837-8151
Torres HS 00795   3-00001
  Maria Leon, prin.   837-2670
Veiga HS 00795   3-00001
  Carmen Rosario, prin.   837-2435
Campos MS, CALLE 30 00795   2-00100
  Hector Rivera, prin.   837-2463
Diaz JHS 00795   4-00110
  Israel Martinez, prin.   837-2365

San Juan City College   2-CS
  PO BOX 1821 00795   837-5050

Juncos, AC 809, PC 6, Juncos Municipio
Juncos SD   6-11111
  4 CALLE BASILIO VELAZQUE 00777   734-2241
  Jorge Galarza, supt.
Colon SHS   3-00001
  BO CEIBA NORTE JUNCOS 00666   734-4345
  Jose Cuadrado, prin.
Flores SHS, CEIBÁ NORTE 00666   3-00001
  Magdaleno Flores, prin.   734-6816
Castro JHS   2-00110
  CALLE ALGARIN FINAL 00666   734-4544
  Jose Carrasquillo, prin.
Lebron JHS   3-00110
  CALLE 31 SALIDA JUNCOS 00666   734-6705
  Maria Charboniere, prin.

Lajas, AC 809, PC 6, Lajas Municipio
Lajas SD, 15 CALLE SAN BLAS 00667   5-11111
  Ruth Landron, supt.   899-1500
Rodriguez SHS   3-00001
  20 CALLE SANTA ROSA 00667   899-1695
  Felix Acevedo, prin.
Rivera JHS   3-00110
  65 CALLE INFANTERIA 00667   899-1452
  Victor Mendez, prin.

Academia San Luis   2-10111
  28 CALLE SAN BLAS 00667   899-4080
  Sr. Teresita Alicea, prin.

Lares, AC 809, PC 6, Lares Municipio
Lares SD, 48 CALLE COMERCIO 00669   6-11111
  Sonia Fuster, supt.   897-2530
Collazo SHS   4-00001
  CALLE RAMON DE JESUS 00669   897-2408
  Hector Colon, prin.
Mistral JSHS, BO CASTANER 00669   2-00111
  Osvaldo Pagan, prin.   897-2530
Linares JHS   2-01110
  SECTOR PALMER LLANOS 00669   897-4070
  Herminio Marrero, prin.
Pagan JHS, CARR 454 KM 1 00669   2-01110
  Carmen Jesurun, prin.   897-2530
Sierra JHS 00669   3-00110
  Carmen Velez, prin.   897-2590

Las Marias, AC 809, PC 5, Las Marias Municipio
Las Marias SD   5-11111
  CALLE SAN BENITO 00670   827-2150
  Juan Velazquez, supt.
Custodio SHS, CALLE COMERIO 00670   2-00001
  Emilia Quilas, prin.   827-4115
Hostos JHS 00670   2-00110
  Alberto Rivera, prin.   827-2100

Las Piedras, AC 809, PC 5, Las Piedras Municipio
Las Piedras SD   6-11111
  CALLE JESUS T PINERO 00671   733-2151
  Amparo Alejandro, supt.

Giralt HS, CALLE JESUS T PINERO 00671   4-00001
  Ana Cintron, prin.   733-2561
Torres JHS, BO TEJAS 00671   3-00110
  Ana Mojica, prin.   733-8081

Loiza, AC 809, PC 5, Loiza Municipio
Loiza SD   6-11111
  CALLE GARCIA DE LA NOCEDA 00672
  Jose Munoz, supt.   876-2295
Lopez SHS 00772   3-00001
  Angelina De Jesus, prin.   876-2060
Zequeira JHS   3-00110
  205 CALLE SAN PATRICIO 00672   256-3060
  Norma Rodriguez, prin.
Vizcarrondo JHS   3-00110
  BO MEDIANIA ALTA 00672   876-1377
  Amparo Fontanez, prin.

Luquillo, AC 809, PC 5, Luquillo Municipio
Luquillo SD   5-11111
  EDIFICIO GUBERNAMENTAL 00673   889-4255
  Migdalia Pacheco, supt.
Sanchez SHS   3-00001
  CALLE FERNANDO GARCIA 00673   889-3243
  Wilfredo Saldana, prin.
Coca JHS   3-00110
  1 CALLE FERNANDEZ GARCIA 00773   889-2180
  Evelyn Carrion, prin.

Manati, AC 809, PC 7, Manati Municipio
Manati SD, BALDORIOTY ST 00701   6-11111
  Layda Ocasio, supt.   854-2035
Callejo SHS 00674   4-00001
  Ada Mercado, prin.   854-2629
Pinero JHS 00674   3-00110
  Victor Perez, prin.   854-2259
Quinones JHS, ROSAS AVE 00701   3-00110
  Daisy Figueroa, prin.   854-2264

Colegio La Inmaculada Concepcion   3-11111
  PO BOX 3400 00674   854-2079
  Luz Arzuaga, prin.
Colegio Marista, PO BOX 462 00674   3-11111
  Salvador Garcia, prin.   854-1075
Instituto de Banca y Comercio   2-CS
  CARR #2 KM 49.4 00701   854-6709

Maricao, AC 809, PC 4, Maricao Municipio
Maricao SD   4-11111
  1 CALLE BALDORIOTY 00606   838-2360
  Miriam Estrada, supt.
Ibarra JSHS, CALLE LUCHETTI 00706   3-00111
  Mildred Bonilla, prin.   838-2150
Vicenty JHS, BUCARABONES 00706   2-01110
  Irma Velez, prin.   838-2360

Maunabo, AC 809, PC 5, Maunabo Municipio
Maunabo SD   5-11111
  CENTRO GUBERNAMETAL 00707   861-2290
  Eugenio Brito, supt.
Martinez SHS   3-00001
  AVE CALIMANO EXT 00707   861-2300
  Ana Perez, prin.
Martinez JHS   2-00110
  AVE CALIMANO EXT 00707   861-3500
  Eugenio Sanchez, prin.

Mayaguez, AC 809, PC 8, Mayaguez Municipio
Mayaguez SD 1   6-11111
  255 CALLE ADUANA 00680   832-1786
  Franklin Ramirez, supt.
Fajardo SHS   4-00001
  LLORENS TORRES ST 00708   833-0865
  Gladys Hernandez, prin.
Hostos SHS 00680   4-00001
  Benjamin Albino, prin.   834-0600
Barreto JHS 00680   3-00110
  Felix Garcia, prin.   832-3046
Benitez JHS, BALBOA ST 00708   3-00110
  Sonia Agostini, prin.   834-0900
La Soledad JHS   2-00110
  PARCELAS SOLEDAD 00708   831-6200
  Roman Jimenez, prin.

Mayaguez SD 2 00680   6-11111
  Ana Melloves, supt.   834-6700
Diego HS, CALLE POST SUR 00708   3-00110
  Edwin Cordero, prin.   833-4818
Faria JHS   2-00110
  AVE JOSE C GONZALEZ 00708   834-9289
  Edwin Hernandez, prin.
Rivera JHS 00680   3-00110
  Guillermo Sanchez, prin.   833-5560

Academia Immac Concepcion   3-00111
  PO BOX 1749 00681   834-7824
  Haydee Carrau, prin.
Catholic University of Puerto Rico   3-UC
  PO BOX 1326 00681   834-5151
Colegio La Milagrosa   2-11111
  CALLE POST 8 NORTE 00708   834-0345
  Cecilia Serrano, prin.
Colegio San Benito   2-11111
  CARR 348 BUZON 400 00708   832-9626
  Padre Paulino Mazuelas, prin.
Institucion Chaviano de Mayaguez   2-CS
  CALLE RAMOS ANTONINI #116 00680
    833-2474
Institute of Multiple Technology   2-CS
  PO BOX 209 00681   833-6305
Instituto de Banca y Comercio   2-CS
  CALLE POST #154 NORTE 00708   833-4647
Universidad Adventista de las Antillas   3-UC
  PO BOX 118 00681   834-9595
University of Puerto Rico   6-UC
  PO BOX 5000 00681   832-4040

Moca, AC 809, PC 5, Moca Municipio
Moca SD, PO BOX 166 00676 — 6-11111
  Pedro Bras, supt. — 877-2380
Hidalgo SHS — 4-00001
  CALLE MONSENOR JOSE TORRES 00716
  Wilfredo Soto, prin. — 877-5575
Roman JSHS, BO VOLADORA 00717 — 3-00111
  Bienvenido Bosques, prin. — 877-2324
Pedreira JHS, CALLE ANASCO 00716 — 4-00110
  Aracelia Perez, prin. — 877-2830

Morovis, AC 809, PC 5, Morovis Municipio
Morovis SD — 6-11111
  AVE BUENA VISTA 5 00717 — 862-2480
  Sylvia Marrero, supt.
Collazo Del Rio SHS — 3-00001
  AVE COROZAL 00717 — 862-2300
  Rene Marrero, prin.
Claudio JHS, MOROVIS PUEBLO 00687 — 3-00110
  Hiram Soto, prin. — 862-4985

Naguabo, AC 809, PC 5, Naguabo Municipio
Naguabo SD, CELIS AGUILERA ST 00718 — 5-11111
  Eduardo Lopez Ayala, supt. — 874-3350
Rocca SHS — 3-00001
  7 CALLE ANTONIO RIOS 00718 — 874-2155
  Hilda Morales, prin.
Mariana MS, MARIANA ST 00718 — 1-01110
  Elizabeth Alvira, prin. — 874-0080
Urbana JHS — 3-00110
  7 CALLE ANTONIO RIOS 00718 — 874-3315
  Ana Figueroa, prin.

Naranjito, AC 809, PC 5, Naranjito Municipio
Naranjito SD, CALLE GEORGETTI 00719 — 6-11111
  Jose Rivera, supt. — 869-2670
Morales SHS — 4-00001
  CARR 164 KM 6 HM 0 00719 — 869-3160
  Jose Rosado, prin.
Rosado JHS, CALLE GEORGETTI 00719 — 3-00110
  Elsa Lopez, prin. — 869-3130
Vazquez JHS, BO ACHIOTE 00719 — 3-00110
  Hilda Cruz, prin. — 869-1309

Academia Santa Teresita — 2-11111
  PO BOX 244 00719 — 869-5101
  Lilia Rivera, prin.

Orocovis, AC 809, PC 5, Orocovis Municipio
Orocovis SD, PO BOX 2115 00720 — 6-11111
  Cervulo Aponte, supt. — 867-3545
Cortes SHS, HOSPITAL ST 00720 — 3-00001
  Hector Colon, prin. — 867-2630
Gato 1 MS, BO GATO 00720 — 2-00110
  Carlos Hernandez, prin. — 867-2410
Torres JHS — 3-00110
  CARR 155 KM 26 SALIDA COAMO 00720
  Eranio Ocasio, prin. — 867-3936

Patillas, AC 809, PC 5, Patillas Municipio
Patillas SD 00723 — 5-11111
  Onvaldo Cora, supt. — 839-3490
Ramos SHS — 3-00001
  CALLE PRINCIPAL FINAL 00723 — 839-2275
  Carmela Ramos, prin.
Munoz JHS — 3-00110
  CARR 181 SALIDA SAN LORENZO 00723
  Antonia Lopez, prin. — 839-3630

Penuelas, AC 809, PC 5, Penuelas Municipio
Penuelas SD — 6-11111
  CALLE PEDRO VELAZQUEZ 00724 — 836-1120
  Kermit Perez, supt.
Rivera HS — 3-00001
  CALLE LUIS MUNOZ RIVERA 00724 — 836-1005
  Aida Caliz, prin.
Irizarry JHS — 3-00110
  CALLE PEDRO ALVARADO 00724 — 836-1177
  Angel Montalvo, prin.

Ponce, AC 809, PC 9, Ponce Municipio
Ponce SD 1, GLENVIEW GARDENS 00731 — 6-11111
  Elba Echevarria, supt. — 844-5285
Ponce SHS — 3-00001
  URB JARDINES DE PONCE 00730 — 840-7785
  Carmen Moreu, prin.
Serralles SHS — 2-00001
  BO COTTO LAUREL 00730 — 848-2005
  Marilyn Ramos, prin.
Pato JHS 00731 — 3-00110
  Cristina Martinez, prin. — 843-7175
Jardines De Ponce JHS — 3-00110
  URB JARDINES DE PONCE 00730 — 844-3400
  Regina Zayas, prin.
Pujals JHS, CALLE LOLITA TIZOL 00731 — 2-00110
  Priscilla Figueroa, prin. — 840-4600
Serralles JHS 00731 — 3-00110
  Milagros Echevarria, prin. — 848-2005

Ponce SD 2, HOSTOS AVE 00731 — 6-11111
  Norma Colon, supt. — 843-5185
Aguayo SHS, HOSTOS AVE 00731 — 3-00001
  Lourdes Perez, prin. — 843-8245
Bernard SHS, AVE JUAN RAMON 00731 — 3-00001
  Dora Vives, prin. — 842-7091
Albizu Campos JHS — 3-00110
  CARR 2 KM 22 HM 1 00730 — 841-2548
  Pedro Guevara, prin.
Colon JHS 00731 — 3-00110
  Dilia Besosa, prin. — 840-3500
Degetau MS, 145 CALLE REINA 00731 — 2-01110
  Enid Muniz, prin. — 842-6178
Gonzalez JHS, HOSTOS AVE 00731 — 3-00110
  Ramon Maldonado, prin. — 842-5028

Ponce SD 3 00731 — 5-11111
  (—), supt. — 844-7770
Toro SHS 00731 — 2-00001
  Israel Acevedo, prin. — 844-3388
Antonini JHS 00731 — 3-00110
  Edwin Caraballo, prin. — 843-2336
Paoli JHS 00731 — 2-00110
  Maria De La Rosa, prin. — 844-0615

Ponce SD 4, HOSTOS AVE 00731 — 6-11111
  Nilda Domenech, supt. — 842-8226
Ponce SHS 00731 — 4-00001
  Lidia Quinones, prin. — 842-4156
Maldonado JHS, BO SAN ANTON 00731 — 3-00110
  Maria Manzano, prin. — 843-2135
Del Carmen JHS — 2-00110
  AVE CONSTANCIA 00731 — 840-6075
  Francisco Aviles, prin.

Ponce SD 5, HOSTOS AVE 00731 — 6-11111
  Myrtelina Martinez, supt. — 844-2166
Delicias SHS 00731 — 3-00001
  Irma Perez, prin. — 840-1080
Pila SHS — 3-00001
  CARR PONCE A GUAYANILLA 00731 — 840-4800
  Migdonia Serrano, prin.
Las Delicias JHS — 3-00110
  2 AVE LORENCITA FERRE 00730 — 840-1080
  Elba Colon, prin.
Gandia JHS, CIVIL ST 00731 — 3-00110
  Nilda Ortiz, prin. — 840-0112

Academia Cristo Rey — 2-11111
  AVE A C-5 LA RAMBLA 00731 — 843-0766
  Luz David, prin.
Academia Santa Maria — 3-11111
  APARTADO 225 ESTACION 6 00732
  Aida Carde De Reyes, prin. — 842-1164
Academia Singer Dealer Autorizado — 2-CS
  101 COMERCIO ST 00731 — 848-4949
Catholic University of Puerto Rico — 6-UC
  LAS AMERICAS AVE 00732 — 841-2000
Centro San Francisco 00731 — 2-11111
  Sr. Anita Moseley, prin. — 844-2434
Colegio La Milagrosa — 2-11111
  GUADALUPE #9 00731 — 842-6349
  Sr. Anibal Rivera, prin.
Colegio Ponceno — 3-11111
  HC 6 BOX 4701 00780 — 848-2525
  Jose Basols, prin.
Colegio Sagrada Familia — 3-11111
  AVE HOSTOS #7 00731 — 842-3208
  Elena Cintron, prin.
Colegio Sagrado Corazon — 3-11111
  OBISPADO FINAL LA ALHAMBRA 00731
  Martha Bernier, prin. — 843-4718
Colegio San Conrado — 3-11111
  AVE ROOSEVELT ESO CARR 7111 00732
  Sr. Nildred Rodriguez, prin. — 843-1405
Instituto de Banca y Comercio — 2-CS
  PO BOX 7623 00732 — 840-6119
Inter American University — 5-UC
  MERCEDITA STATION 00715 — 840-9090
Metro College — 2-CS
  VILLA 144 00731 — 259-7272
Ponce Paramedical College — 2-CS
  L-15 ACACIA ST 00731 — 259-0169
Ponce School of Medicine 00731 — 2-UC
   — 840-2575
Ponce Technical School — 2-CS
  16 SALUD ST 00731 — 844-7940
University of Puerto Rico — 4-UC
  PO BOX 7186 00732 — 844-8181

Puerto Nuevo, AC 809, PC 99, San Juan Municipio

Colegio Tecnico de Electricidad — 2-CS
  1251 FRANKLIN ROOSEVELT AVE 00920
   — 782-5126

Quebradillas, AC 809, PC 5, Quebradillas Municipio
Quebradillas SD 00678 — 5-11111
  Samuel Alvarez, supt. — 895-2760
Arizmendi HS, AVILA ST 00742 — 3-00001
  Migdalia Marichal, prin. — 895-2180
Campos JHS, CALLE LINARES 00742 — 3-00110
  Juan Soto, prin. — 895-2780

Rincon, AC 809, PC 4, Rincon Municipio
Rincon SD 00677 — 5-11111
  Carlos Morales, supt. — 823-2395
Pedroza SHS 00677 — 2-00001
  Lydia Beltran, prin. — 823-2400
Crespo JHS 00677 — 3-00110
  Daisy Ramos, prin. — 823-2087

Rio Grande, AC 809, PC 7, Rio Grande Municipio
Rio Grande SD — 6-11111
  25 CALLE SAN JOSE 00745 — 887-2380
  Carmen Carreras, supt.
Cepeda SHS, CIENAGA ALTA 00745 — 2-00001
  Luz Fuente, prin. — 887-5295
Falu SHS 00745 — 4-00001
  Narcisa Navarro, prin. — 887-2778
Castro JHS — 3-00110
  2 CALLE JUAN R GONZALEZ 00745 — 887-2730
  Hector Calderon, prin.
Cepeda JHS, BO CIENAGA ALTA 00745 — 3-00110
  Myrna Feliciano, prin. — 887-4410
Millan JHS, GUZMAN ST 00745 — 3-00110
  Oscar Jimenez, prin. — 887-4574

Columbia College — 2-CS
  SAN JOSE ST 00745 — 887-3352

Rio Piedras, AC 809

Academia Maria Reina — 2-00111
  AVENIDA GLASGOW Y PADUA 00921 — 764-0690
  Sr. Maria De Sales, prin.
Academia Nuestra De La Providencia — 3-11111
  1733 SANTA AGUEDA 00926 — 767-6552
  Maria Lee De Cobo, prin.
Colegio Angeles Custodios — 2-11111
  13 CALLE SICILIA 00923 — 763-3829
  Sr. Luis Cepeda, prin.
Colegio Buen Pastor — 2-11111
  CAMINO ALEJANDRINO 00927 — 720-4988
  M. Martinez, prin.
Colegio Calasanz — 3-11111
  PO BOX 29067 00929 — 750-2500
  Fr. P. Torralba, prin.
Colegio De La Milagrosa — 2-11111
  107 CALLE DE DIEGO 00925 — 765-6114
  Maria Flores, prin.
Colegio Nuestra Altagracia — 2-11111
  APARTADO 29493 00929 — 763-7755
  Carmen Espiet, prin.
Colegio Nuestra Del Carmen — 3-11111
  RR 2 BUZON 15 00928 — 761-8010
  Maria de Barnardo, prin.
Colegio Nuestra De Lourdes — 3-11111
  PO BOX 29193 00929 — 769-6284
  Mary de Iglesias, prin.
Colegio Nuestra Del Pilar — 3-00111
  RR 3 BOX 3120 00928 — 767-6962
  SRA Cruz, prin.
Colegio San Antonio — 4-11111
  APARTADO 21350 00928 — 763-2366
  Sr. Miguel Rosa, prin.
Colegio San Ignacio De Loyola — 3-00111
  1940 CALLE SAUCO FINAL 00927 — 765-3814
  Fr. P. Feely, prin.
Colegio San Jose — 3-00111
  APARTADO 21300 00928 — 751-8177
  Fr. P. Suarez, prin.
Fashion Design College — 2-CS
  210 ARZUAGE ST 00925 — 765-0001
Instituto de Banca y Comercio — 2-CS
  996 MUNOZ RIVERA AVE 00926 — 765-8687
International Technical College — 2-CS
  1302 CENTRAL AVE 00921 — 792-5620
Metro College — 2-CS
  1126 PONCE DE LEON AVE 00928 — 754-7120

Sabana Grande, AC 809, PC 6, Sabana Grande Municipio
Sabana Grande SD 00637 — 5-11111
  Carlos Vega, supt. — 873-2770
Malaret HS, CALLE FELIX TIO 00637 — 4-00001
  Carlos Rivera, prin. — 873-3980
Castillo JHS, 1 CALLE FELIX TIO 00747 — 3-00110
  Magda Velez, prin. — 873-3120

Sabana Seca, AC 809, PC 99, Toa Baja Municipio

Instituto de Educacion Universal — 2-CS
  PO BOX 1027 00952 — 798-8606

Saint Just, AC 809, PC 99, Trujillo Alto Municipio

Colegio Biblico Pentecostal De PR — 2-UC
  PO BOX 901 00978 — 761-0640

Salinas, AC 809, PC 6, Salinas Municipio
Salinas SD 00751 — 6-11111
  Elsa Rivera, supt. — 824-2150
Marquez JHS — 4-00010
  CALLE UNION SALINAS 00751 — 824-3357
  Maria Vega, prin.
Olimpico JHS — 2-00110
  ALBARGUE OLIMPICO 00751 — 824-1534
  Madeline Rosario, prin.
Rivera JHS 00751 — 3-00110
  Roberto Mercado, prin. — 824-2470

San German, AC 809, PC 7, San German Municipio
San German SD, PO BOX 65 00683 — 6-11111
  Efren Rodriguez, supt. — 892-1355
De Tio SHS, AVE DR VEVE 00753 — 4-00001
  Milagros Agrait, prin. — 892-1320
Mercado S — 3-11111
  CALLE NESTOR TORRES BALLEST 00753
  Esther Rivera, prin. — 832-4155
Rosado S — 3-11111
  PARCELAS SABANA ENEAS 00683 — 892-1335
  Amilda Cordero, prin.
Guzman JHS, DR HARRIS ST 00753 — 3-00110
  Wilfredo Vazquez, prin. — 892-1168

Colegio San Jose, PO BOX 87 00683 — 3-11111
  Sr. Maria Martin, prin. — 892-1009
Inter American University of Puerto Rico — 5-UC
  HARRIS DR CALL BOX 5100 00683 — 892-1095

San Juan, AC 809, PC 10, San Juan Municipio
Bayamon SD 1 — 5-11111
  80 BETANCES AVE 00619 — 780-1152
  Evaristo Rosado, supt.
Agueybana SHS 00926 — 3-00001
  Carmen Landron, prin. — 780-9709
Agueybana JHS, CALLE 60 00619 — 3-00110
  Marixa Acevedo, prin. — 780-9906
Jimenez JHS — 3-00110
  CARR 864 HATO TEJAS 00619 — 798-5428
  Ediberto Torres, prin.

Bayamon SD 2 — 6-11111
20 CALLE BETANCES 00917 — 785-6545
Ibis Concepcion, supt.
Casals JHS — 3-00110
CALLE C ESQ CALLE D 00619 — 797-1215
Roberto Sanchez, prin.
Other Schools – See Bayamon

Bayamon SD 3
Supt. — See Bayamon
Munoz JSHS, 3 CALLE A 00619 — 4-00111
Haydee Nunez, prin. — 797-7300
Rexville SHS, 41 CALLE IBIZA 00926 — 4-00001
Nancy Scheffler, prin. — 797-1850
Umpierre JSHS — 3-00111
CARR 167 KM 8 00619 — 797-5360
Cesar Casta, prin.
Rexville JHS, 41 ST 00619 — 3-00110
Militza Mendez, prin. — 797-3340

Bayamon SD 4, CALLE 20 V-1 00619 — 6-11111
Victor Torres, supt. — 786-4619
Stahl SHS, PARQUE ST 00619 — 4-00001
Eva Morales, prin. — 785-3469
Davila JHS — 3-00110
SALIDA BAYAMON A COMERIO 00619 — 785-2292
Carmen Rosario, prin.
Erazo JHS, ABAD ST 00619 — 3-00110
Emma Morales, prin. — 787-4831
Other Schools – See Bayamon

Bayamon SD 5 — 6-11111
AVE MAGNOLIA ESQ CALLE 16 00619 — 785-6817
Candido Rivera, supt.
Casablanca SHS — 4-00001
CALLE 21 JARDINES DE CAPARR 00619 — 782-1562
Carmen Pereida, prin.
Matos JSHS, CALLE 11 00619 — 3-00110
Carlos Perales, prin. — 786-4275
Ongay SHS, MINILLAS AVE 00619 — 3-00001
Maria De Jesus, prin. — 785-3414
Saavedra SHS — 4-00001
CARR 831 LOMAS VERDES 00619 — 785-4065
Damaris Alvarez, prin.
Balseiro JHS — 2-00110
CARR ESTATAL 831 LOMAS VERD 00619 — 785-9185
Milagros Rivera, prin.
Ponce JHS — 2-00110
COLECTORA CENTRAL AVE 00962 — 780-3119
Efrain Hernandez, prin.

Catano SD, PROGRESO ST 00632 — 6-11111
Apolinar Rivera, supt. — 788-0150
Oller SHS, LAS NEREIDAS AVE 00632 — 3-00001
Magdalena Soto, prin. — 788-1696
Colorado JHS — 3-00110
FLOR DEL VALLE AVE 00632 — 788-4025
Encarnacion Bachiller, prin.
Carballeira JHS — 3-00110
LAS NEREIDAS AVE 00632 — 784-8975
Luis Diaz, prin.

Rio Piedras SD 1, CALLE 16 00928 — 6-11111
Aracelias Alcala, supt. — 767-3174
Mistral SHS, PINERO ST 00920 — 3-00001
Angel Perez, prin. — 782-4208
Musica JSHS, JOSE OLIVER ST 00917 — 3-00111
Luis Boria, prin. — 754-1335
Osuna JSHS 00918 — 2-00111
Felipe Valentin, prin. — 763-7178
Las Americas JHS 00920 — 2-00110
Francisco Diaz, prin. — 782-0070
Other Schools – See Hato Rey

Rio Piedras SD 2
Supt. — See Hato Rey
Ponce De Leon SHS — 3-00001
357 BARBOSA AVE 00912 — 765-3485
Milagros Nieves, prin.
Gandara JHS 00923 — 2-00110
Elmy Bonilla, prin. — 763-0950
Jimenez JHS 00923 — 2-00110
Rosa Montijo, prin. — 767-9463
Marin JHS 00917 — 2-00100
Norberto Rodriguez, prin. — 753-9304
Tio JHS 00917 — 2-00010
Noelia Torres, prin. — 753-7635

Rio Piedras SD 3 — 6-11111
1058 LUIS MUNOZ RIVERA AVE 00924
Jose Rodriguez, supt. — 763-8210
Colombia SHS — 3-00001
CALLE MAXIMO ALOMAR 00923 — 764-4910
Angel Rivera, prin.
Mayo SHS, CALLE BRUMBAUGH 00925 — 2-00011
Myrna Rodriguez, prin. — 765-5320
Such SHS, BARBOSA AVE 00912 — 3-00001
Irida Villanueva, prin. — 751-3780
Barbosa JHS, 42 CALLE ROBLES 00925 — 2-00110
Arturo Albo, prin. — 751-6250
Granada JHS 00923 — 2-00110
Julio Rivera, prin. — 751-5934
Venus Gardens JHS 00926 — 3-00110
Laura Rondon, prin. — 755-3120

Rio Piedras SD 4 — 6-11111
65 AVE INFANTERIA 00924 — 768-7010
Luis Arce, supt.
Berwin SHS 00924 — 3-00001
Antonia Perez, prin. — 752-9720
Egozcue JHS 00924 — 3-00110
Cruz Rodriguez, prin. — 769-7415
Nieves JHS 00924 — 2-00110
Dora Perez, prin. — 751-6280
Berwind JHS 00917 — 2-00110
Gilberto Mejias, prin. — 752-0055

Llana JHS 00924 — 2-00110
Eglantina La Placa, prin. — 767-2438

Rio Piedras SD 5 00926 — 6-11111
Maria Arana, supt. — 767-1132
Marin JSHS 00926 — 4-00111
Paula Burgos, prin. — 763-5218

Rio Piedras SD 6 — 6-11111
1002 OLIMPO PLAZA 00928 — 764-0030
Jose Ramos, supt.
University Gardens SHS — 3-00001
NOTRE DAME AVE 00927 — 764-2503
Maria Jurado, prin.
Boyce JHS 00924 — 2-00110
Carmen Hernandez, prin. — 792-4931
Figueroa JHS, PALMA REAL ST 00927 — 3-00110
Edna Del Valle, prin. — 765-8132
Huyke JHS 00926 — 2-00110
(—), prin. — 782-6144
Mejico JHS, CALLE 50 00921 — 2-00110
Jeanette Gonzalez, prin. — 782-2979

San Juan SD 1 — 6-11111
25 FERNANDEZ JUNCOS AVE 00907 — 726-4690
Myrna Ayala, supt.
Barbosa JSHS — 2-00111
PONCE DE LEON AVE 00918 — 722-5340
Juana Barbosa, prin.
Blanco JSHS — 2-01111
CALLE MARTIN TRAVISSO 00901 — 726-9021
Milagros Garcia, prin.
Central JSHS — 3-00111
PONCE DE LEON AVE 00917 — 722-4328
Carmen Martinez, prin.
Cordero SHS 00907 — 2-00001
Gabriel Cruz, prin. — 722-2974
Giralt SHS 00911 — 2-00001
Jose Rivera, prin. — 727-4830
Luchetti SHS, 70 CONDADO AVE 00907 — 2-00001
Luis Pizarro, prin. — 723-4072
Rufo JSHS — 2-00111
236 CALLE DEL PARQUE 00912 — 723-4930
Ana Ramos, prin.
Acosta JHS, PONCE DE LEON AVE 00917 — 2-00110
Pablo Borges, prin. — 722-1253
Labra JHS, PONCE DE LEON AVE 00917 — 2-00110
Lilia Rodriguez, prin. — 722-1443
Peru JHS 00911 — 2-00110
Nilda Soto, prin. — 726-1432

San Juan SD 2 00915 — 2-11111
Rosa Ayala, supt. — 727-7805
Einstein SHS 00915 — 2-00001
Fernando Litchfield, prin. — 727-5525
Antonini JHS, BORINQUEN AVE 00915 — 3-00110
Emma Rodriguez, prin. — 726-4480
Asenjo JHS, BORINQUEN AVE 00915 — 2-00100
Lucy Roig, prin. — 724-4605
Bacener JHS 00915 — 2-00110
Narciso Calderon, prin. — 726-4865
Buesco JHS, DEL VALLE ST 00915 — 3-00110
Jesus Arroyo, prin. — 727-4578
Vizcarrondo JHS 00926 — 2-00110
Carlos Raymundi, prin. — 726-0125

Trujillo Alto SD — 6-11111
28 MUNOZ RIVERA ST 00760 — 761-0410
Jose Ramos, supt.
Cordero JHS 00976 — 2-00110
(—), prin. — 761-0340
Hostos JHS, CUEVAS 00760 — 2-00110
Brizeida Velille, prin. — 761-0860
Valcarcel JHS — 3-00110
CALLE ANDRES VALCARCEL 00760 — 761-1060
(—), prin.
Other Schools – See Trujillo Alto

Academia Del Perpetuo Socorro 00917 — 4-11111
Sr. Marie Ayala, prin. — 724-1447
Antilles Military Academy — 3-00011
PO BOX 666 00902 — 761-1710
Antilles School of Technical Careers — 2-CS
APARTADO 1536 00919 — 764-7576
Caribbean Center for Advanced Studies — 2-UC
APARTADO 3711 00904 — 725-6500
Carribbean Consolidated School — 2-00111
PO BOX 70177 00936 — 765-4411
Angie Amador, prin.
Centro De Estudios Avanzados — 2-UC
DEL CRISTO ST #52 BOX S4467 00904
— 723-4481
Colegio Madre Cabrini — 2-11111
1564 CALLE ENCARNACION 00920 — 792-6180
Mayra Mendez, prin.
Colegio Nuestra De La Guadalupe — 3-11111
PO BOX 4125 00902 — 782-0330
Dora De Emmanuelli, prin.
Colegio Nuestra De La Merced — 3-11111
PO BOX 4048 00936 — 765-7342
Rita De Bravo, prin.
Colegio Nuestra De La Providencia — 4-11111
PO BOX 11610 00922 — 782-6344
Clara Castillo, prin.
Colegio Nuestra Denora De Belen — 4-11111
PO BOX 10845 00922 — 792-3115
L. Cintron, prin.
Conservatory of Music — 2-UC
PO BOX 41227 00940 — 751-0160
Escuela De Artes Plasticas — 2-UC
APARTADO 4184 00905 — 725-8120
Evangelical Seminary of Puerto Rico — 2-UC
776 PONCE DE LEON AVE 00925 — 763-6084

Instituto Comercial de Puerto Rico — 2-CC
558 MUNOZ RIVERA AVE #304 00918
— 763-1010
Inter American University of Puerto Rico — 3-UC
PO BOX 191293 00919 — 727-1930
Inter American University of Puerto Rico — 7-UC
PO BOX 1293 00902 — 758-8000
Inter American University of Puerto Rico — 7-UC
PO BOX 1293 00902 — 250-1912
International College of Business & Tech — 2-CS
PO BOX 8245 00910 — 725-8718
Liceo de Arte Y Tecnologia — 2-CS
PO BOX 2346 00902 — 759-9800
Polytechnic University — 4-UC
PO BOX 2017 00902 — 754-8000
Puerto Rico Hotel School — 2-CS
PO BOX 4435 00902 — 791-6210
Puerto Rico Junior College — 5-CC
PO BOX 21373 00928 — 758-7171
Ramirez College of Business Technology — 4-CC
PO BOX 8074 00910 — 763-3120
Technological College of San Juan — 3-CC
JOSE OLIVER FINAL BOX 70179 00918
— 250-7111
Universidad Metropolitana — 6-UC
PO BOX 21150 00928 — 766-1717
University of Puerto Rico — 4-UC
PO BOX 5067 00906 — 758-2525
University of Puerto Rico — 7-UC
PO BOX 23300 00931 — 764-0000
University of the Sacred Heart — 6-UC
PO BOX 12383 00914 — 728-1515
York College — 2-CS
PO BOX 5183 00906 — 722-2000

San Lorenzo, AC 809, PC 6, San Lorenzo Municipio
San Lorenzo SD — 6-11111
CALLE LUIS MUNOZ RIVERA 00754 — 736-8784
Gloria Aponte, supt.
Campeche SHS 00754 — 4-00001
Victor Quinones, prin. — 736-2701
Rultrago JSHS, BO ESPINO 00754 — 3-00111
Antonio Hernandez, prin. — 736-9272
Munoz JHS, CARR 181 00754 — 4-00110
Luis Velazquez, prin. — 736-6658

San Sebastian, AC 809, PC 7, San Sebastian Municipio
San Sebastian SD — 6-11111
29 CALLE HOSTOS 00685 — 896-1250
Enrique Carretero, supt.
Liciaga HS 00685 — 3-00001
Edith Ramirez, prin. — 896-1380
Ramirez SHS 00685 — 3-00001
Ida Rodriguez, prin. — 896-3970
Rodriguez JSHS — 3-00111
CARR 447 BO HOYAMALA 00755 — 896-4142
Guillermo Tirado, prin.
Cabrera IS 00685 — 3-00100
Elba Serrano, prin. — 896-1164
Mendez JSHS — 3-00110
CARR 111 KM 17 00755 — 896-1745
Madeline Rosa, prin.

Electronic Data Processing College — 2-CS
PO BOX 1674 00685 — 896-2137

Santa Isabel, AC 809, PC 6, Santa Isabel Municipio
Santa Isabel SD 00757 — 5-11111
Olga Molina, supt. — 845-2220
Kennedy SHS — 3-00001
CALLE BALDORIOTY DE CASTRO 00757 — 845-2560
Hiram Vega, prin.
Monserrate JHS — 3-00110
3 CALLE BALDORIOTY DE CASTR 00757 — 845-3160
Noami Torres, prin.

Santurce, AC 809

Academia Del Sagrado Corazon — 3-11111
PO BOX 11368 00910 — 721-3300
C. Mercado, prin.
Academia San Jorge — 3-11111
CALLE COLON ESQ SAN JORGE 00911 — 722-3182
Maria Ambruso, prin.
Academia Santa Monica — 3-11111
PO BOX 13726 00908 — 723-2573
Eva Torres, prin.
Academia Santa Teresita — 3-11111
CALLE LOIZA 2059 00911 — 727-4358
Flor Caraballo, prin.
Colegio De La Inmaculada — 3-11111
AVE PONCE DE LEON #1711 00909 — 727-6673
E. Aceuedo, prin.
Colegio La Piedad — 3-11111
PO BOX 6277 00914 — 727-2460
Sr. Sheila O'Brien, prin.
Colegio Maria Auxiliadora — 2-11111
CALLE EDUARDO CONDE 2273 00915 — 726-8288
M. Zubocco, prin.
Colegio San Juan Bosco — 2-01111
PO BOX 14367 00916 — 726-1995
P. Robbs, prin.
Colegio San Vicente De Paul — 2-11111
PO BOX 8699 00910 — 727-4274
Carmen Camacho, prin.
MBTI Business Training Institute — 4-CS
1256 PONCE DE LEON AVE 00908 — 723-9402
San Juan City College — 2-CS
PO BOX 9300 00908 — 724-5050

Toa Alta, AC 809, PC 5, Toa Alta Municipio
Toa Alta SD 00953 — 6-11111
Lilliam Nater, supt. — 870-2290

Sevilla SHS, 1ST ST   00758   4-00001
   Adonis Alamo, prin.   870-2570
Gonzalez JHS   2-00110
   CARR 159 BO QUEBRADA ARENAS   00758
   Maria Rivas, prin.   870-2500
Morales JHS, CALLE BARCELO   00758   3-00110
   Reymond De Jesus, prin.   870-2135
Pinas JHS, BO PINAS   00953   3-00110
   Luis Hernandez, prin.   797-0315

Toa Baja, AC 809, PC 4, Toa Baja Municipio
Toa Baja SD 1, PO BOX 2477   00951   6-11111
   Maria Medina, supt.   794-1714
Puig SHS   3-00001
   CALLE LUIS M RIVERA FINAL   00759   794-2018
   William Hernandez, prin.
Landron JHS   4-00110
   7 MUNOZ RIVERA ST   00759   794-1465
   Felix Perez, prin.

Toa Baja SD 2   6-11111
   AVE AMALIA PAOLI   00759   795-0660
   Fuaristo Luna, supt.
Campo SHS, AVE BOULEVARD   00759   4-00001
   Francisco Oliver, prin.   784-4605
Pineiro SHS   2-00001
   CALLE MARQUEZ FINAL   00759   784-4140
   Julio Rivera, prin.
Gomez MS, PASEO AZALEA 1   00949   2-01110
   Mariam Colon, prin.   784-0125
Hernandez JHS   3-00110
   AVE DE DIEGO #1   00759   795-6570
   Carmen Rivera, prin.

Academia Espiritu Santo   3-11111
   PO BOX 51540   00949   784-0905
   Rosa Perez, prin.

Trujillo Alto, AC 809, PC 99, San Juan Municipio
Trujillo Alto SD
   Supt. — See San Juan
Carazo SHS   00976   3-00001
   Petra Ortiz, prin.   761-1954

Colegio Santa Cruz   3-11111
   APARTADO 1809   00760   761-1100
   Ana De Matos, prin.

Utuado, AC 809, PC 7, Utuado Municipio
Utuado SD   6-11111
   CENTRO GUBERNAMENTAL   00761   894-2645
   Angel Cruz, supt.
Rivera SHS   00641   3-00001
   Bruno Ramos, prin.   894-2670
Angeles S   3-11111
   CARR 607 KM 1 BO LOS ANGELE   00761
   Daisy Gonzalez, prin.   894-7702
Ramos JHS, DR CUETO ST   00761   3-00110
   Nora Pons, prin.   894-2470
Vivas JHS   2-00010
   AVE NUEVA CARR 111   00761   894-3446
   Harold Hernandez, prin.

Colegio San Miguel   2-11111
   PO BOX 10   00641   894-2187
   Esther Negron, prin.
University of Puerto Rico   3-CC
   P O BOX 2500   00641   894-2828

Vega Alta, AC 809, PC 7, Vega Alta Municipio
Vega Alta SD   00692   6-11111
   Ramon Gonzalez, supt.   883-3990
Martinez SHS   4-00001
   MUNOZ RIVERA ST   00762   883-5105
   Maria Arroyo, prin.
San Antonio JHS   4-00110
   MUNOZ RIVERA ST   00762   883-3130
   Alfredo Sierra, prin.

Vega Baja, AC 809, PC 7, Vega Baja Municipio
Vega Baja SD, PO BOX 4396   00694   7-11111
   Sigfredo Alvira, supt.   858-2140
Morell SHS, CALLE Q FINAL   00693   3-00001
   Nilda Santiago, prin.   858-0859
Rivera SHS, TULIO OTERO ST   00763   4-00001
   John Vega, prin.   858-2110
Martinez JHS   4-00110
   4 CALLE TULIO OTERO   00693   858-2120
   Jorge Adrover, prin.

Colegio Nuestra Senora   3-11111
   PO BOX 1457   00694   858-4111
   Fr. P. Rodriguez, prin.

Vieques, AC 809, PC 4, Vieques Municipio
Vieques SD, MUNOZ RIVERA ST   00765   4-11111
   Luis Casillas, supt.   741-2896

Rieckehoff SHS, CARR 993   00765   2-00001
   Inocencia Davila, prin.   741-8340
Escuela JHS   00765   2-00110
   Nilo Colon, prin.   741-3091
Serrano JHS, PUERTO REAL   00765   1-00110
   Ruben Bonano, prin.   741-8692
Other Schools – See Culebra

Villalba, AC 809, PC 6, Villalba Municipio
Villalba SD   00766   6-11111
   Luis Colon, supt.   847-2130
Santana SHS   4-00001
   CARR 150 KM 0 HM 1   00766   847-2110
   Gilberto David, prin.
Urbana JHS   3-00110
   CARR 153 KM 0 HM 0   00766   847-9090
   William Ramirez, prin.

Yabucoa, AC 809, PC 6, Yabucoa Municipio
Yabucoa SD   6-11111
   CALLE JOSE F CINTRON   00767   893-2480
   Gilberto Pagan, supt.
Marin SHS   00767   2-00001
   Mercedes Torres, prin.   893-2880
Mora SHS   4-00001
   CARRETERA CEMENTERIO   00767   893-2216
   Julia Alverio, prin.
Rivera JHS   00767   3-00110
   Mercedes Davila, prin.   893-3390

Yauco, AC 809, PC 7, Yauco Municipio
Yauco SD   00768   7-11111
   Nidia Estrada, supt.   856-1395
Marin SHS   4-00001
   CARR 128 KM 0 HM 2   00698   856-2144
   Ana Torres, prin.
Antonini JHS   00768   3-00110
   Ana Torres, prin.   856-1325
Fermoso JHS   3-00110
   CARR 128 KM 1 HM 9   00698   856-2143
   Antonio Pietri, prin.
Vicente JHS, 48 BARBOSA AVE   00768   3-00110
   Jannette Morales, prin.   856-1394

Colegio Santisimo Rosario   3-11111
   CALLE COMERCIO APARTADO 26   00698
   Judith Negron, prin.   856-1001
Columbia College   2-CS
   PO BOX 3062   00698   856-0845

VIRGIN ISLANDS

DEPARTMENT OF EDUCATION
44-46 Kongens Gade, Charlotte Amalie 00802
(809) 774-2810

Commissioner of Education   Linda Creque

PUBLIC, PRIVATE AND CATHOLIC SECONDARY SCHOOLS

Charlotte Amali, AC 809, PC 8, .
St. Thomas/St. John SD
   PO BOX 6640   00801 – (—), supt.   4-11111
     776-6238
Charlotte Amalie HS   2-00011
   GENERAL DELIVERY   00801   774-0780
   (—), prin.
Kean JSHS, GENERAL DELIVERY   00801   2-00111
   (—), prin.   775-6208
Boschulte JHS   2-00100
   GENERAL DELIVERY   00801   775-4222
   (—), prin.
Cancryn JHS   00801   2-00100
   (—), prin.   774-4540

SS. Peter & Paul HS   2-00011
   PO BOX 1706   00803   774-2199
   David Corey, prin.

University of the Virgin Islands   00802   4-UC
     776-9200

Christiansted, AC 809, PC 7
St. Croix SD, PO BOX I   00820   4-11111
   (—), supt.   773-1095
Christian JHS   2-00100
   GENERAL DELIVERY   00820   773-4445
   (—), prin.
Other Schools – See Frederiksted, Kingshill

Frederiksted, AC 809, PC 7
St. Croix SD
   Supt. — See Christiansted
Richards JHS   00840   2-00110
   (—), prin.   772-1500
Woodson JHS   00840   2-00110
   (—), prin.   773-4445

St. Joseph HS   2-00011
   3 E MOUNT PLEASANT   00840   772-0455

Kingshill, AC 809
St. Croix SD
   Supt. — See Christiansted
St Croix Central HS   2-00011
   GENERAL DELIVERY   00851   778-0123
   (—), prin.

University of the Virgin Islands   2-UC
   00802

ARCHDIOCESAN AND DIOCESAN CATHOLIC SCHOOL SUPERINTENDENTS

ALABAMA

Birmingham — 205-838-8303
Brice A. Hendrick, supt.
PO BOX 186, Birmingham 35201

Mobile — 205-438-4611
Gwen Byrd, supt.
PO BOX 129, Mobile 36601

ALASKA

Anchorage — 907-486-3513
Sr. Diane Bardol, supt.
2932 MILL BAY RD, Kodiak 99615

Fairbanks — 907-456-7970
Nancy Cook, supt.
615 MONROE ST, Fairbanks 99701

Juneau — 907-225-7400
Paul Hepler, supt.
433 JACKSON ST
Ketchikan 99901

ARIZONA

Phoenix — 602-257-5578
Marybeth Mueller, supt.
400 E MONROE ST, Phoenix 85004

Tucson — 602-886-5204
Ronald Starcher, supt.
8800 E 22ND ST, Tucson 85710

ARKANSAS

Little Rock — 501-664-0340
Michael Rockers, supt.
PO BOX 7565, Little Rock 72217

CALIFORNIA

Fresno — 209-488-7420
Richard Sexton, supt.
1510 N FRESNO ST, Fresno 93703

Los Angeles — 213-251-3300
Jerome Porath, supt.
1520 W 9TH ST
Los Angeles 90015

Monterey — 408-373-1608
Agnes Leonardich, supt.
PO BOX 350, Monterey 93942

Oakland — 510-893-4711
Sr. Rose Hennessy, supt.
2910 LAKESHORE AVE
Oakland 94610

Orange — 714-282-3000
Br. Carriere, supt.
2811 E VILLA REAL DR
Orange 92667

Sacramento — 916-441-4891
James Adams, supt.
1121 K ST, Sacramento 95814

San Bernardino — 909-384-8261
Thomas Heding, supt.
1739 N D ST
San Bernardino 92405

San Diego — 619-574-6326
Sr. Claire Fitzgerald, supt.
PO BOX 85728, San Diego 92186

San Francisco — 415-565-3660
Sr. Glenn McPhee, supt.
443 CHURCH ST
San Francisco 94114

San Jose — 408-983-0185
Sr. Mary Power, supt.
900 LAFAYETTE ST # 3
Santa Clara 95050

Santa Rosa — 707-525-9525
Sr. Ann O'Connor, supt.
PO BOX 6654, Santa Rosa 95406

Stockton — 209-464-3775
Sr. Maureen O'Brien, supt.
PO BOX 4237, Stockton 95204

COLORADO

Colorado Springs — 719-636-2345
Sr. Joseph Kasel, supt.
29 W KIOWA ST
Colorado Springs 80903

Denver — 303-388-4411
Sr. Patricia Beckman, supt.
200 JOSEPHINE ST, Denver 80206

Pueblo — 719-544-9861
Sr. Andrea Vasquez, supt.
1001 N GRAND AVE
Pueblo 81003

CONNECTICUT

Bridgeport — 203-372-4301
Bernard Helfrich, supt.
238 JEWETT AVE
Bridgeport 06606

Hartford — 203-242-4362
Fr. Kriss, supt.
467 BLOOMFIELD AVE
Bloomfield 06002

Norwich — 203-887-4086
Howard Bennett, supt.
43 PERKINS AVE, Norwich 06360

DELAWARE

Wilmington — 302-573-3133
Sr. Marie Vanston, supt.
1626 N UNION ST
Wilmington 19806

DISTRICT OF COLUMBIA

Washington DC — 202-853-4518
Lawrence Callahan, supt.
PO BOX 29260, Washington 20017

FLORIDA

Miami — 305-757-6241
Sr. Noreen Werner, supt.
9401 BISCAYNE BLVD
Miami Shores 33138

Orlando — 407-246-4905
Maureen Huntington, supt.
PO BOX 1800, Orlando 32802

Palm Beach — 407-775-9547
Sr. Joan Dawson, supt.
9995 N MILITARY TRL
West Palm Beach 33410

Pensacola/Tallahassee — 904-432-1515
Sr. R. Cianciolo, supt.
PO BOX 17329, Pensacola 32522

St. Augustine — 904-262-3200
Patricia Tierney, supt.
PO BOX 24000, Jacksonville 32241

St Petersburg — 813-345-3338
Fr. Kroll, supt.
PO BOX 43022
Saint Petersburg 33743

Venice — 813-484-9543
Sr. Marlene Weidenborner, supt.
PO BOX 2006, Venice 34284

GEORGIA

Atlanta — 404-888-7833
Maureen Kane, supt.
680 W PEACHTREE ST NW
Atlanta 30308

Savannah — 912-238-2344
Sr. Mary Sobczak, supt.
601 E LIBERTY ST
Savannah 31401

HAWAII

Honolulu — 808-263-8844
Fr. Dever, supt.
6301 PALI HWY, Kaneohe 96744

IDAHO

Boise — 208-342-1311
Bob Fontaine, supt.
303 FEDERAL WAY, Boise 83705

ILLINOIS

Belleville — 618-235-9601
Thomas Posnanski, supt.
2620 LEBANON AVE
Belleville 62221

Chicago — 312-751-5200
Elaine Schuster, supt.
PO BOX 1979, Chicago 60690

Joliet — 815-727-4674
Sr. Jeanette Zielinski, supt.
425 SUMMIT ST, Joliet 60435

Peoria — 309-671-1550
Joseph Benning, supt.
412 NE MADISON AVE
Peoria 61603

Rockford — 815-962-7791
Sr. Joella Miller, supt.
1260 N CHURCH ST
Rockford 61103

Springfield — 217-698-8282
Sr. Marilyn Runkel, supt.
PO BOX 3187, Springfield 62708

INDIANA

Evansville — 812-424-5536
Phyllis Beshears, supt.
PO BOX 4169, Evansville 47724

Fort Wayne/South Bend — 219-422-4611
Jeanette Kam, supt.
PO BOX 390, Fort Wayne 46801

Gary — 219-769-9292
John Sheilds, supt.
9292 BROADWAY, Gary 46410

Indianapolis — 317-236-1430
Daniel Elsener, supt.
PO BOX 1410, Indianapolis 46206

Lafayette — 317-474-6644
Sr. Marilyn Winter, supt.
2300 S 9TH ST, Lafayette 47905

IOWA

Davenport — 319-324-1911
Msgr. W. R. Schmidt, supt.
2706 N GAINES ST
Davenport 52804

Des Moines — 515-235-5013
Sr. Jude Fitzpatrick, supt.
PO BOX 1816, Des Moines 50306

Dubuque — 319-556-2580
Fr. Toale, supt.
PO BOX 479, Dubuque 52004

Sioux City — 712-255-7933
Fr. Patrick O'Kane, supt.
PO BOX 3379, Sioux City 51102

KANSAS

Dodge City — 316-227-1500
Sr. Sylvana Schulte, supt.
PO BOX 137, Dodge City 67801

Kansas City — 913-721-1570
Sr. Michelle Faltus, supt.
12615 PARALLEL AVE
Kansas City 66109

Salina — 913-827-8746
Sr. Clarissa Tenbrink, supt.
PO BOX 825, Salina 67402

Wichita — 316-269-3950
Bob Voboril, supt.
424 N BROADWAY ST
Wichita 67202

KENTUCKY

Covington — 606-283-6230
Lawrence Bowman, supt.
PO BOX 18548, Covington 41018

Lexington — 606-253-1993
Sr. Mary Bankemper, supt.
PO BOX 12350, Lexington 40582

Louisville — 502-626-0296
Sr. Amelia Stenger, supt.
1200 S SHELBY ST
Louisville 40203

Owensboro — 502-683-1545
Joseph O'Brien, supt.
600 LOCUST ST
Owensboro 42301

LOUISIANA

Alexandria — 318-445-2401
Sr. Marice Elvekrog, supt.
PO BOX 7417, Alexandria 71306

Baton Rouge — 504-387-0561
Sr. M. Michaeline, supt.
PO BOX 2028, Baton Rouge 70821

Houma/Thibodaux — 504-868-7720
Sr. Immaculata Paisant, supt.
PO BOX 9077, Houma 70361

Lafayette — 318-261-5529
Richard Meaux, supt.
1408 CARMEL AVE
Lafayette 70501

Lake Charles — 318-439-7418
Sr. Gloria Cain, supt.
4029 AVENUE G
Lake Charles 70601

New Orleans — 504-861-6220
Howard Jenkins, supt.
7887 WALMSLEY AVE
New Orleans 70125

Shreveport — 318-222-2006
Robert Mizia, supt.
2500 LINE AVE, Shreveport 71104

MAINE

Portland — 207-773-6471
Sr. Rosemary Donohoe, supt.
PO BOX 11559, Portland 04104

MARYLAND

Baltimore — 410-547-5384
Ronald Valenti, supt.
320 CATHEDRAL ST
Baltimore 21201

MASSACHUSETTS

Boston — 617-298-6555
Sr. Ann Roach, supt.
468 BEACON ST, Boston 02115

Fall River — 508-678-2828
Fr. Richard Beaulieu, supt.
423 HIGHLAND AVE
Fall River 02720

Springfield — 413-732-3175
Sr. Bette Gould, supt.
625 CAREW ST, Springfield 01104

Worcester — 508-791-7171
Charles McManus, supt.
49 ELM ST, Worcester 01609

517

MICHIGAN

Detroit   313-237-5925
Sr. Christine Mihelcic, supt.
305 MICHIGAN AVE
Detroit 48226

Gaylord   517-732-5147
Rev. McCracken, supt.
1665 W M 32, Gaylord 49735

Grand Rapids   616-243-0491
Michael Gross, supt.
600 BURTON ST SE
Grand Rapids 49507

Kalamazoo   616-349-6427
Frank Wippel, supt.
PO BOX 50951, Kalamazoo 49005

Lansing   517-342-2482
Sr. Dorita Wotiska, supt.
228 N WALNUT ST
Lansing 48933

Marquette   906-226-3515
Clifford Luft, supt.
PO BOX 280, Marquette 49855

Saginaw   517-799-7910
Marian Mikolaizyk, supt.
5800 WEISS ST, Saginaw 48603

MINNESOTA

Crookston   218-281-4533
Sr. Pat Murphy, supt.
1200 MEMORIAL DR
Crookston 56716

Duluth   218-727-9111
Daniel Corbett, supt.
2830 E 4TH ST, Duluth 55812

New Ulm   507-359-2966
Sr. Betty Larson, supt.
1400 6TH ST N, New Ulm 56073

Saint Cloud   612-251-0111
Sr. Catherine Kallhoff, supt.
305 7TH AVE N STE 201
Saint Cloud 56303

Saint Paul/Minneapolis   612-291-4500
Sr. Nathalie Meyer, supt.
328 KELLOGG BLVD W
Saint Paul 55102

Winona   507-454-4643
Dr. Luvern Gubbles, supt.
PO BOX 588, Winona 55987

MISSISSIPPI

Biloxi   601-374-0440
Sr. Joanne Cozzi, supt.
PO BOX 1189, Biloxi 39533

Jackson   601-969-1880
Fr. Cullen, supt.
PO BOX 2248, Jackson 39225

MISSOURI

Jefferson City   314-635-9127
Sr. Ann Bonvie, supt.
PO BOX 417, Jefferson City 65102

Kansas City-Saint Joseph   816-756-1850
Sr. Vickie Perkins, supt.
PO BOX 419037
Kansas City 64141

Saint Louis   314-371-4980
Sr. Mary Eckhoff, supt.
4140 LINDELL BLVD
Saint Louis 63108

Springfield/Cape Girardeau   417-866-0841
Sr. Lucille Kalinoski, supt.
601 S JEFFERSON AVE
Springfield 65806

MONTANA

Great Falls/Billings   406-252-0997
Sr. Katherine Franchett, supt.
PO BOX 31158, Billings 59107

Helena   406-442-5820
James Tucker, supt.
PO BOX 1729, Helena 59624

NEBRASKA

Grand Island   308-382-6565
Fr. Thomas Ryan, supt.
PO BOX 996, Grand Island 68802

Lincoln   402-488-0921
Fr. John Perkinton, supt.
PO BOX 80328, Lincoln 68501

Omaha   402-554-8493
Sr. Patricia Mulcahey, supt.
3212 N 60TH ST, Omaha 68104

NEVADA

Reno/Las Vegas   702-329-9274
Br. Cunningham, supt.
PO BOX 1211, Reno 89504

NEW HAMPSHIRE

Manchester   603-669-3100
William Garland, supt.
PO BOX 310, Manchester 03105

NEW JERSEY

Camden   609-756-7900
David Coghlan, supt.
1845 HADDON AVE
Camden 08103

Metuchen   908-826-6616
Leonard Defiore, supt.
103 CENTER ST
Perth Amboy 08861

Newark   201-596-4260
Sr. Dominica Rocchio, supt.
100 LINDEN AVE, Irvington 07111

Paterson   201-777-8818
Frank Petrucelli, supt.
777 VALLEY RD, Clifton 07013

Trenton   609-771-0141
Sr. Loretta Hogan, supt.
1018 WHITEHEAD ROAD EXT
Trenton 08638

NEW MEXICO

Gallup   505-863-3563
Fr. Maikowski, supt.
PO BOX 1028, Farmington 87499

Las Cruces   505-523-7577
Sr. Joan Berninger, supt.
1280 MED PARK DR
Las Cruces 88005

Santa Fe   505-831-8173
Sr. Michelle Micek, supt.
4000 SAINT JOSEPHS PL NW
Albuquerque 87120

NEW YORK

Albany   518-453-6666
Sr. Ann McCarthy, supt.
40 N MAIN AVE, Albany 12203

Brooklyn   718-492-1800
Msgr. Breen, supt.
6025 6TH AVE, Brooklyn 11220

Buffalo   716-847-5501
Ronald Cook, supt.
795 MAIN ST, Buffalo 14203

New York City   212-371-1000
Catherine Hickey, supt.
1011 1ST AVE, New York 10022

Ogdensburg   315-393-2921
Fr. Lawrence Deno, supt.
PO BOX 369, Ogdensburg 13669

Rochester   716-328-3210
Timothy Dwyer, supt.
1150 BUFFALO RD
Rochester 14624

Rockville Center   516-678-5800
Sr. Joanne Callahan, supt.
50 N PARK AVE
Rockville Centre 11570

Syracuse   315-470-1450
Sr. Mary Heenan, supt.
240 E ONONDAGA ST
Syracuse 13202

NORTH CAROLINA

Charlotte   704-377-6871
Michael Skube, supt.
1524 E MOREHEAD ST
Charlotte 28207

Raleigh   919-821-9748
Sr. Lois Meyer, supt.
300 CARDINAL GIBBONS DR
Raleigh 27606

NORTH DAKOTA

Bismarck   701-222-3035
Morris Martin, supt.
PO BOX 1137, Bismarck 58502

Fargo   701-235-6429
Michael Nygaard, supt.
1310 BROADWAY, Fargo 58102

OHIO

Cincinnati   513-421-3131
Sr. Kathryn Connelly, supt.
100 E 8TH ST, Cincinnati 45202

Cleveland   216-696-6525
Sr. Carol Smith, supt.
1031 SUPERIOR AVE E
Cleveland 44114

Columbus   614-221-5829
Fr. Noble, supt.
197 E GAY ST, Columbus 43215

Steubenville   614-282-9706
Sr. Mary Corr, supt.
PO BOX 1196, Steubenville 43952

Toledo   419-244-6711
Sr. Janet Doyle, supt.
PO BOX 985, Toledo 43697

Youngstown   216-744-8451
Nicholas Wolsonovich, supt.
144 W WOOD ST
Youngstown 44503

OKLAHOMA

Oklahoma City   405-721-4202
Sr. Anne Leonard, supt.
PO BOX 32184
Oklahoma City 73123

Tulsa   918-587-3115
Arden Glenn, supt.
PO BOX 2009, Tulsa 74101

OREGON

Baker   503-388-4004
Allen Christel, supt.
PO BOX 5999, Bend 97708

Portland   503-234-5334
Larry Thompson, supt.
2838 E BURNSIDE ST
Portland 97214

PENNSYLVANIA

Allentown   215-866-0581
James Cusimano, supt.
PO BOX 2607, Lehigh Valley 18001

Altoona/Johnstown   814-695-5579
Sr. Charmaine Grilliot, supt.
PO BOX 126, Hollidaysburg 16648

Erie   814-824-1111
Sr. Mary Tann, supt.
PO BOX 10397, Erie 16514

Greensburg   412-836-1281
Philip Boggio, supt.
723 E PITTSBURGH ST
Greensburg 15601

Harrisburg   717-657-4804
Sr. Marilou MacDonald, supt.
PO BOX 3553, Harrisburg 17105

Philadelphia   215-587-3700
Richard McCarron, supt.
222 N 17TH ST
Philadelphia 19103

Pittsburgh   412-456-3090
Sr Elizabeth Meegan, supt.
111 BLVD OF THE ALLIES
Pittsburgh 15222

Scranton   717-346-8940
Fr. John Jordan, supt.
300 WYOMING AVE
Scranton 18503

RHODE ISLAND

Providence   401-278-4550
Br. Casey, supt.
1 CATHEDRAL SQ
Providence 02903

SOUTH CAROLINA

Charleston   803-769-2160
Sr. Jane Hosch, supt.
1662 INGRAM RD
Charleston 29407

SOUTH DAKOTA

Rapid City   605-343-3541
Richard Thompson, supt.
PO BOX 678, Rapid City 57709

Sioux Falls   605-333-3366
Fr. Carroll, supt.
3000 W 41ST ST
Sioux Falls 57105

TENNESSEE

Knoxville   615-383-6393
Aurelia Montgomery, supt.
417 ERIN DR, Knoxville 37919

Memphis   901-722-4719
Carol Kulpa, supt.
PO BOX 41679, Memphis 38174

Nashville   615-383-6393
Steve Hammond, supt.
2400 21ST AVE S, Nashville 37212

TEXAS

Amarillo   806-383-2243
Sr. Cornella Knezek, supt.
PO BOX 5644, Amarillo 79117

Austin   512-873-7771
Sr. Thecla Cain, supt.
8000 CENTRE PARK DR STE 160
Austin 78754

Beaumont   409-838-0451
Br. Dygert, supt.
PO BOX 3948, Beaumont 77704

Brownsville   210-542-2501
Sr. Mary Doyle, supt.
PO BOX 2279, Brownsville 78522

Corpus Christi   512-289-6501
Rosemarie Kamke, supt.
1200 LANTANA ST
Corpus Christi 78407

Dallas   214-528-2360
Fr. Callahan, supt.
PO BOX 190507, Dallas 75219

El Paso   915-595-5026
Sr. Lucia Daluz, supt.
499 SAINT MATTHEWS ST
El Paso 79907

Fort Worth   817-560-3300
Edward Doherty, supt.
800 W LOOP 820 S
Fort Worth 76108

Galveston/Houston   713-741-8704
Sr. Colleen Hennessey, supt.
2401 HOLCOMBE BLVD
Houston 77021

Lubbock   806-792-3943
Roberta Meyer, supt.
PO BOX 98700, Lubbock 79499

San Angelo   915-651-7500
  Sr. Joan Markus, supt.
  804 FORD ST, San Angelo 76905
San Antonio   210-734-2620
  Br. Pontolillo, supt.
  PO BOX 28410, San Antonio 78228
Tyler   409-838-0451
  Br. Dygert, supt.
  PO BOX 3948, Beaumont 77704
Victoria   210-573-0828
  Br. Pontolillo, supt.
  PO BOX 28410, San Antonio 78228

UTAH

Salt Lake City   801-328-8641
  Sr. Genevra Rolf, supt.
  27 C ST, Salt Lake City 84103

VERMONT

Burlington   802-658-6110
  Sr. Marianne Read, supt.
  351 NORTH AVE
  Burlington 05401

VIRGINIA

Arlington   703-841-2519
  Marie Powell, supt.
  200 N GLEBE RD, Arlington 22203
Richmond   804-359-5661
  Diane Bialkowski, supt.
  811 CATHEDRAL PL # A
  Richmond 23220

WASHINGTON

Seattle   206-382-4861
  Mary Sontgerath, supt.
  910 MARION ST, Seattle 98104
Spokane   509-456-7130
  Duane Schafer, supt.
  PO BOX 1453, Spokane 99210
Yakima   509-965-7110
  Cathy Colver, supt.
  5301B TIETON DR, Yakima 98908

WEST VIRGINIA

Wheeling/Charleston   304-233-0880
  Judith Minear, supt.
  PO BOX 230, Wheeling 26003

WISCONSIN

Green Bay   414-437-7531
  Sr. Leland Nagel, supt.
  PO BOX 23825, Green Bay 54305
La Crosse   608-788-7707
  Donald Novotney, supt.
  PO BOX 4004, La Crosse 54602
Madison   608-256-0872
  James Silver, supt.
  142 W JOHNSON ST
  Madison 53703
Milwaukee   414-769-3300
  John Norris, supt.
  PO BOX 07912, Milwaukee 53207
Superior   715-392-1042
  Phyllis Schlagel, supt.
  PO BOX 969, Superior 54880

WYOMING

Cheyenne   307-237-2723
  Ed McCarthy, supt.
  623 S WOLCOTT ST, Casper 82601

GUAM

Agana   671-472-6116
  Rev. Apuron, supt.
  196B CUESTA SAN RAMON
  Agana 96910

PUERTO RICO

Arecibo   809-878-1095
  Lydia Hernandez, supt.
  PO BOX 1683, Arecibo 00613
Caguas   809-743-1171
  Fr. Victor Ortiz, supt.
  PO BOX 8699, Caguas 00726
Mayaguez   809-833-6087
  Sr. Vivina Sepulveda, supt.
  PO BOX 2272, Mayaguez 00681
Ponce   809-842-2102
  Sr. Maria Una Garcia RAD, supt.
  P O BOX 557 STATION 6
  Ponce 00731
San Juan   809-268-6700
  Raphael Morales, supt.
  PUMARADA 1708, Santurce 00916

VIRGIN ISLANDS

Diocese of St. Thomas   809-774-3166
  Diana Parker, supt.
  PO BOX 1825, Saint Thomas 00803

LUTHERAN SCHOOL SUPERINTENDENTS

LUTHERAN CHURCH MISSOURI SYNOD
Board of Parish Education
1333 S KIRKWOOD RD
Saint Louis, MO 63122
314-965-9000

Atlantic   914-337-5700
  Rev. D. Mau
  171 WHITE PLAINS RD
  Bronxville, NY 10708
California-Nevada-Hawaii   415-468-2336
  Joel Koerschen
  465 WOOLSEY ST
  San Francisco, CA 94134
Central Illinois   217-793-1802
  David Bernhardt
  PO BOX 7003, Springfield, IL 62791
Eastern   716-634-5111
  William Cochran
  5111 MAIN ST, Williamsville, NY 14221
English   313-478-3662
  Ervin Henkelmann
  23001 GRAND RIVER AVE
  Detroit, MI 48219
Florida-Georgia   408-857-5556
  Mark Brink
  7207 MONETARY DR, Orlando, FL 32809
Indiana   219-423-1511
  Eugene Brunow
  1145 BARR ST, Fort Wayne, IN 46802
Iowa East   319-393-9010
  Lawrence Schmidt
  4403 1ST AVE SE
  Cedar Rapids, IA 52402
Iowa West   515-576-7666
  Rev. Larry Reinhardt
  PO BOX 1155, Fort Dodge, IA 50501
Kansas   913-357-4441
  Alan Gunderman
  2318 SW 10TH AVE, Topeka, KS 66604
Michigan   313-665-3791
  Don Kell
  3773 GEDDES RD, Ann Arbor, MI 48105
Mid-South   901-767-9270
  Rev. Andrew Brondos
  1580 W MASSEY RD
  Memphis, TN 38120

Minnesota North   218-829-1781
  Paul Brill
  PO BOX 604, Brainerd, MN 56401
Minnesota South   612-435-2550
  David Roth
  14301 GRAND AVE
  Burnsville, MN 55306
Missouri   314-268-1500
  Duane Hingst
  3558 S JEFFERSON AVE
  Saint Louis, MO 63118
Montana   406-259-2908
  Paul Blunck
  30 BROADWATER AVE
  Billings, MT 59101
Nebraska   402-643-2961
  Neil Sandfort
  PO BOX 407, Seward, NE 68434
New England   413-783-0131
  Rev. Ralph Sachschewsky
  400 WILBRAHAM RD
  Springfield, MA 01109
New Jersey   908-233-8111
  Kenneth Werring
  1168 SPRINGFIELD AVE
  Mountainside, NJ 07092
North Dakota   701-293-9001
  William Sharpe
  PO BOX 9029, Fargo, ND 58106
North Wisconsin   715-845-8241
  Gary Beyer
  3103 SEYMOUR LN, Wausau, WI 54401
Northern Illinois   708-449-3020
  Rev. William Ameiss
  2301 S WOLF RD, Hillside, IL 60162
Northwest   503-288-8383
  Arthur Linnemann
  1700 NE KNOTT ST, Portland, OR 97212
Ohio   216-235-2297
  Ewald Kane
  PO BOX 38277, Olmsted Falls, OH 44138

Oklahoma   918-272-9858
  Tom Christman
  9222 N GARNETT RD, Owasso, OK 74055
Pacific Southwest   714-854-3232
  Dean Dammann
  1540 CONCORDIA, Irvine, CA 92715
Rocky Mountain   303-695-8001
  H. Allen Herbst
  PO BOX 441395, Aurora, CO 80044
SELC   216-845-0070
  Gerald Kovac
  6800 W PLEASANT VALLEY RD
  Parma, OH 44129
South Dakota   605-361-1514
  Rev. Hartwig
  PO BOX 89110, Sioux Falls, SD 57105
South Wisconsin   414-464-8100
  Jeffery Schubert
  8100 W CAPITOL DR
  Milwaukee, WI 53222
Southeastern   703-971-9371
  Rev. Wagner
  PO BOX 10415, Alexandria, VA 22310
Southern   504-282-2632
  Jan Case
  PO BOX 8396, New Orleans, LA 70122
Southern Illinois   618-234-4767
  Daniel Roth
  2408 LEBANON AVE
  Belleville, IL 62221
Texas   512-926-4272
  Rev. Ray Schkade
  7900 E HIGHWAY 290, Austin, TX 78724
Wyoming   307-265-9000
  Rev. Brown
  2400 HICKORY ST, Casper, WY 82604

GENERAL CONFERENCE OF SEVENTH-DAY ADVENTISTS SUPERINTENDENTS

DEPARTMENT OF EDUCATION
6840 EASTERN AVE NW
Washington, DC   20012

ATLANTIC UNION
Paul Kilgore, supt.
PO BOX 1189
South Lancaster, MA   01561

Bermuda Mission
David Rogers, supt.
P O BOX 1170, Hamilton , Bermuda
Greater New York Conference
(—), supt.
PO BOX 1029, Manhasset, NY   11030
New York Conference
Beverly MacLaughlin, supt.
PO BOX 67, Syracuse, NY   13215
Northeastern Conference
Esme Bovell, supt.
11550 MERRICK BLVD
Jamaica, NY   11434
Northern New England Conference
Peggy Fisher, supt.
PO BOX 1340, Portland, ME   04104
Southern New England Conference
Gary Temple, supt.
PO BOX 1169
South Lancaster, MA   01561

MID-AMERICA UNION CONFERENCE
Melvin Northrup, supt.
PO BOX 6128, Lincoln, NE   68506

Central States Conference
Alex Bryant, supt.
5737 SWOPE PKY
Kansas City, MO   64130
Dakota Conference
Dan Kittle, supt.
PO BOX 520, Pierre, SD   57501
Iowa-Missouri Conference
Duane Barnett, supt.
PO BOX 65665
West Des Moines, IA   50265
Kansas-Nebraska Conference
Daniel Peters, supt.
3440 SW URISH RD, Topeka, KS   66614
Minnesota Conference
Beverly Lamon, supt.
7384 KIRKWOOD CT
Maple Grove, MN   55369
Rocky Mountain Conference
Gary Sudds, supt.
2520 S DOWNING ST, Denver, CO   80210

COLUMBIA UNION CONFERENCE
Richard Osborn, supt.
5427 TWIN KNOLLS RD
Columbia, MD   21045

Allegheny East Conference
Lolethia Morgan, supt.
PO BOX 266, Pine Forge, PA   19548
Allegheny West Conference
Harcourt King, supt.
1339 E BROAD ST, Columbus, OH   43205
Chesapeake Conference
Lon Gruesbeck, supt.
6600 MARTIN RD, Columbia, MD   21044
Mountain View Conference
Kingsley Whitsett, supt.
1400 LIBERTY ST
Parkersburg, WV   26101

New Jersey Conference
Ron Patterson, supt.
2160 BRUNSWICK AVE
Trenton, NJ   08648
Ohio Conference
Robert Skeggs, supt.
PO BOX 1230, Mount Vernon, OH   43050
Pennsylvania Conference
David Cadavero, supt.
720 MUSEUM RD, Reading, PA   19611
Potomac Conference
Violet Weiss, supt.
PO BOX 1208, Staunton, VA   24402

LAKE UNION CONFERENCE
F. R. Stephan, supt.
PO BOX C, Berrien Springs, MI   49103

Illinois Conference
Lou Ann Howard, supt.
3721 PRAIRIE AVE, Brookfield, IL   60513
Indiana Conference
Archie Moore, supt.
PO BOX 1950, Carmel, IN   46032
Lake Region Conference
Ivan Van Lange, supt.
8517 S STATE ST, Chicago, IL   60619
Michigan Conference
Duane Roush, supt.
PO BOX 19009, Lansing, MI   48901
Wisconsin Conference
Herbert Wrate, supt.
PO BOX 7310, Madison, WI   53707

NORTH PACIFIC UNION CONFERENCE
Don Keele, supt.
PO BOX 16677, Portland, OR   97216

Alaska Mission
William Hinman, supt.
6100 OMALLEY RD
Anchorage, AK   99516
Idaho Conference
Morian Perry, supt.
PO BOX 4878, Boise, ID   83711
Montana Conference
Larry Unterseher, supt.
PO BOX 743, Bozeman, MT   59771
Oregon Conference
C. E. Boyatt, supt.
13400 SE 97TH AVE
Clackamas, OR   97015
Upper Columbia Conference
Ron Scott, supt.
PO BOX 19039, Spokane, WA   99219
Washington Conference
David Escobar, supt.
20015 BOTHELL WAY SE
Bothell, WA   98012

PACIFIC UNION CONFERENCE
G. E. Thompson, supt.
PO BOX 5005, Thousand Oaks, CA   91359

Arizona Conference
Irma Hadley, supt.
PO BOX 12340, Scottsdale, AZ   85267
Central California Conference
William Wright, supt.
PO BOX 770, Clovis, CA   93613

Hawaiian Conference
(—), supt.
2728 PALI HWY, Honolulu, HI   96817
Nevada-Utah Conference
Derral Reeve, supt.
PO BOX 10730, Reno, NV   89510
Northern California Conference
K. W. Hutchins, supt.
PO BOX 23165, Pleasant Hill, CA   94523
Southeastern California Conference
Charles McKinstry, supt.
PO BOX 8050, Riverside, CA   92515
Southern California Conference
James Clizbe, supt.
PO BOX 969, Glendale, CA   91209

SOUTHERN UNION CONFERENCE
K. J. Epperson, supt.
PO BOX 849, Decatur, GA   30031

Carolina Conference
Gordon Klocko, supt.
PO BOX 25848, Charlotte, NC   28229
Florida Conference
Gerald Kovalski, supt.
PO BOX 1313, Orlando, FL   32802
Georgia-Cumberland Conference
Hamlet Canosa, supt.
PO BOX 12000, Calhoun, GA   30703
Gulf States Conference
Barry Mahorney, supt.
PO BOX 17100, Montgomery, AL   36193
Kentucky-Tennessee Conference
Devern Biloff, supt.
PO BOX 459, Madison, TN   37116
South Atlantic Conference
Conrad Gill, supt.
PO BOX 92447, Atlanta, GA   30314
South Central Conference
Nathaniel Higgs, supt.
PO BOX 24936, Nashville, TN   37202
Southeastern Conference
Oster Paul, supt.
PO BOX 160067
Altamonte Springs, FL   32716

SOUTHWESTERN UNION CONFERENCE
Doug Walker, supt.
PO BOX 4000, Burleson, TX   76097

Arkansas-Louisiana Conference
Alvin Astrup, supt.
PO BOX 3100, Shreveport, LA   71133
Oklahoma Conference
Jerry Beem, supt.
PO BOX 32098
Oklahoma City, OK   73123
Southwest Region Conference
(—), supt.
PO BOX 226289, Dallas, TX   75222
Texas Conference
Lyle Hansen, supt.
PO BOX 800, Alvarado, TX   76009
Texico Conference
George Lloyd, supt.
PO BOX 7770, Amarillo, TX   79114

EDUCATIONAL ASSOCIATIONS AND SOCIETIES

Of exceeding importance to the work stream of education in the United States and the hundreds of associations, societies and other groups representing the various interests and disciplines of the educational community.

ACCREDITATION

Accreditation serves as an assurance that an institution has gone through a self-study and a peer review and has been judged to be "accreditable" in terms of it's own statement of scope and mission and in comparison to similar institutions.

NATIONAL INSTITUTIONAL ACCREDITING ASSOCIATIONS

Accrediting Commission of Career Schools\Colleges of Technology
750 1ST ST NE # 905
Washington, DC 20002

Accrediting Council for Independent Colleges and Schools
750 1ST ST NE
Washington, DC 20002

American Association of Bible Colleges
PO BOX 1523
Fayetteville, AR 72702

Association of Advanced Rabbinical & Talmudic Schools
175 5TH AVE # 711
New York, NY 10010

Association of Theological Schools in the USA & Canada
10 SUMMIT PARK DR
Pittsburgh, PA 15275

Distance Education and Training Council
1601 18TH ST NW
Washington, DC 20009

REGIONAL ACCREDITING ASSOCIATIONS

Middle States Association of Colleges & Schools
3624 MARKET ST
Philadelphia, PA 19104

New England Association of Schools & Colleges
15 HIGH ST
Winchester, MA 01890

North Central Association of Colleges & Schools
159 N DEARBORN ST
Chicago, IL 60601

Northwest Association of Schools & Colleges
1910 UNIVERSITY DR
Boise, ID 83725

Southern Association of Colleges & Schools
1866 SOUTHERN LN
Decatur, GA 30033

Western Association of Schools & Colleges
3060 VALENCIA AVE
Aptos, CA 95003

SPECIALIZED ACCREDITING ASSOCIATIONS

Accreditation Board for Engineering & Technology
345 E 47TH ST
New York, NY 10017

Accrediting Bureau of Health Education Schools
29089 US 20 W
Elkhart, IN 46514

Accrediting Commission on Education for Health Services Administration
1911 FORT MYER DR # 503
Arlington, VA 22209

Accrediting Council on Education in Journalism & Mass Communication
STAUFFER-FLINT HALL UNIV KS
Lawrence, KS 66045

American Assembly of Collegiate Schools of Business
605 OLD BALLAS RD STE 220
Saint Louis, MO 63141

American Association for Counseling & Development
5999 STEVENSON AVE
Alexandria, VA 22304

American Bar Association
550 S WORTH AVE
Indianapolis, IN 46241

American Board of Funeral Service Education
14 CRESTWOOD RD
Cumberland Center, ME 04021

American Council for Construction Education
901 HUDSON LN
Monroe, LA 71201

American Council on Pharmaceutical Education
311 W SUPERIOR ST # 512
Chicago, IL 60610

American Dental Association
211 E CHICAGO AVE
Chicago, IL 60611

American Dietetic Association
216 W JACKSON BLVD
Chicago, IL 60606

American Home Economics Association
1555 KING ST
Alexandria, VA 22314

American Library Association
50 E HURON ST
Chicago, IL 60611

American Medical Association
535 N DEARBORN ST
Chicago, IL 60610

American Medical Association Committee on Allied Health Education
515 N STATE ST
Chicago, IL 60610

American Optometric Association
243 N LINDBERGH BLVD
Saint Louis, MO 63141

American Osteopathic Association
142 E ONTARIO ST
Chicago, IL 60611

American Physical Therapy Association
1111 N FAIRFAX ST
Alexandria, VA 22314

American Podiatric Medical Association
9312 OLD GEORGETOWN RD
Bethesda, MD 20814

American Psychological Association
1200 17TH ST NW
Washington, DC 20036

American Society of Landscape Architects
4401 CONNECTICUT AVE NW
Washington, DC 20008

American Speech-Language-Hearing Association
10801 ROCKVILLE PIKE
Rockville, MD 20852

American Veterinary Medical Association
1931 N MEACHAM RD STE 100
Schaumburg, IL 60173

Association of American Law Schools
1201 CONNECTICUT AVE NW
Washington, DC 20036

Computer Science Accreditation Commission
345 E 47TH ST
New York, NY 10017

Council on Chiropractic Education
4401 WESTLAWN PKY #120
West Des Moines, IA 50265

Council on Education for Public Health
1015 15TH ST NW # 403
Washington, DC 20005

Council on Rehabilitation Education
PO BOX 1860
Champaign, IL 61824

Council on Social Work Education
1600 DUKE ST # 300
Alexandria, VA 22314

Foundation for Interior Design Education Research
60 MONROE CENTER ST NW
Grand Rapids, MI 49503

National Accred Comm./Schools & Colleges of Acupuncture & Oriental Medicine
14 16TH ST NW #501
Washington, DC 20036

National Architectural Accrediting Board
1735 NEW YORK AVE NW
Washington, DC 20006

National Association of Schools of Art & Design
11250 ROGER BACON DR # 21
Reston, VA 22090

National Association of Schools of Music
11250 ROGER BACON DR # 21
Reston, VA 22090

National Association of Schools of Public Affairs & Administration
1120 G ST NW # 520
Washington, DC 20005

National Council for Accreditation of Teacher Education
2029 K ST NW # 500
Washington, DC 20006

National League for Nursing
350 HUDSON ST
New York, NY 10014

National Recreation & Park Association
3101 PARK CENTER DR
Alexandria, VA 22302

Planning Accreditation Board
1776 MASSACHUSETTS AVE NW
Washington, DC 20036

Society of American Foresters
5400 GROSVENOR LN
Bethesda, MD 20814

NATIONAL PROFESSIONAL ASSOCIATIONS FOR EDUCATIONAL ADMINISTRATORS AND EDUCATORS

Academy of Osteopathic Directors of Medical Education
50 N PERRY ST
Pontiac, MI 48342

Academy of Security Educators and Trainers
RR 2 BOX 3644
Berryville, VA 22611

Aerospace Department Chairmens Association
TEXAS A & M UNIV
College Station, TX 77843

American Academy of Teachers of Singing
75 BANK ST
New York, NY 10014

American Association of Chairmen of Departments of Psychiatry
Hanover, NH 03756

American Association of Collegiate Registrars and Admissions Officers
1 DUPONT CIR NW # 330
Washington, DC 20036

American Association of Diabetes Educators
500 N MICHIGAN AVE STE 1400
Chicago, IL 60611

American Association of Early Childhood Educators
5105 BACKLICK RD
Annandale, VA 22003

American Association of Housing Educators
TEXAS A & M UNIV
College Station, TX 77843

American Association of Philosophy Teachers
PO BOX 26901
Oklahoma City, OK 73190

American Association of Physics Teachers
5112 BERWYN RD
College Park, MD 20740

American Association of Presidents of Independent Colleges & Universities
13800 BIOLA AVE
La Mirada, CA 90639

American Association of Professors of Yiddish
QUEENS COLLEGE
Flushing, NY 11367

American Association of School Administrators
1801 N MOORE ST
Arlington, VA 22209

American Association of School Librarians
50 E HURON ST
Chicago, IL 60611

American Association of School Personnel Administrators
2330 ALHAMBRA BLVD STE 157
Sacramento, CA 95817

American Association of Sex Educators, Counselors and Therapists
435 N MICHIGAN AVE STE 1717
Chicago, IL 60611

American Association of Teacher Educators in Agriculture
UNIVERSITY OF MISSOURI
Columbia, MO 65211

American Association of Teachers of Arabic
BRIGHAM YOUNG UNIV
Provo, UT 84602

American Association of Teachers of French
57 E ARMORY AVE
Champaign, IL 61820

American Association of Teachers of German
112 HADDONTOWNE CT STE 104
Cherry Hill, NJ 08034

American Association of Teachers of Italian
WAYNE STATE UNIV
Detroit, MI 48202

American Association of Teachers of Slavic & East European Languages
NORTHERN ILLINOIS UNIV
De Kalb, IL 60115

American Association of Teachers of Spanish & Portuguese
MISSISSIPPI STATE UNIV
Mississippi State, MS 39762

American Association of University Administrators
2121 I ST NW
Washington, DC 20052

American Association of University Professors
1012 14TH ST NW STE 500
Washington, DC 20005

American College Personnel Association
5999 STEVENSON AVE
Alexandria, VA 22304

American Conference of Academic Deans
1818 R ST NW
Washington, DC 20009

American Council of Teachers of Russian
1619 MASSACHUSETTS AVE NW
Washington, DC 20036

American Council on the Teaching of Foreign Languages
PO BOX 1077
Yonkers, NY 10701

American Federation of School Administrators
853 BROADWAY # 2109
New York, NY 10003

American Federation of Teachers
555 NEW JERSEY AVE NW
Washington, DC 20001

American School Counselor Association
5999 STEVENSON AVE
Alexandria, VA 22304

American Society of Educators
1429 WALNUT ST
Philadelphia, PA 19102

American String Teachers Association
7368 QUAILHOLLOW RD
Cincinnati, OH 45243

Association for Counselor Education and Supervision
5999 STEVENSON AVE
Alexandria, VA 22304

Association for School, College and University Staffing
1600 DODGE AVE # S-350
Evanston, IL 60201

Association for Supervision & Curriculum Development
1250 N PITT ST
Alexandria, VA 22314

Association for the Education of Teachers of Science
AUBURN UNIV
Auburn, AL 36849

Association of Chairman of Departments of Mechanics
OHIO STATE UNIVERSITY
Columbus, OH 43210

Association of College & University Telecommunications Administrators
LEXINGTON FINANCIAL CTR
Lexington, KY 40507

Association of College and University Auditors
PO BOX 7202
Raleigh, NC 27695

Association of College and University Housing Officers
101 CURL DR # 140
Columbus, OH 43210

Association of Community College Trustees
1740 N ST NW
Washington, DC 20036

Association of Governing Boards of Universities & Colleges
1 DUPONT CIR NW STE 400
Washington, DC 20036

Association of Lutheran College Faculties
PACIFIC LUTHERAN UNIV
Tacoma, WA 98447

Association of Optometric Educators
424 BEACON ST
Boston, MA 02115

Association of Overseas Educators
INDIANA UNIVERSITY OF PA
Indiana, PA 15705

Association of Physical Plant Administrators of Universities & Colleges
1466 DUKE ST
Alexandria, VA 22314

Association of Professors & Researchers in Religious Education
1100 E 55TH ST
Chicago, IL 60615

Association of Professors of Medicine
1101 CONNECTICUT AVE NW
Washington, DC 20036

Association of Professors of Mission
FULLER THEOLOGICAL SMN
Pasadena, CA 91182

Association of Program Directors in Internal Medicine
700 13TH ST NW # 250
Washington, DC 20005

Association of School Business Officials
11401 N SHORE DR
Reston, VA 22090

Association of Seventh-day Adventists Educators
12501 OLD COLUMBIA PIKE
Silver Spring, MD 20904

Association of Teacher Educators
1900 ASSOCIATION DR # ATE
Reston, VA 22091

Association of Teachers of Japanese
MIDDLEBURY COLL
Middlebury, VT 05753

Association of Teachers of Latin American Studies
252 63RD AVE
Flushing, NY 11362

Association of Teachers of Preventive Medicine
1030 15TH ST NW # 410
Washington, DC 20005

Association of Teachers of Technical Writing
UNIV OF CENT FLORIDA
Orlando, FL 32816

CAUSE
4840 PEARL EAST CIR # 302
Boulder, CO 80301

Chinese Language Teachers Association
3545 W LAURELHURST DR NE
Seattle, WA 98105

College and University Personnel Association
1233 20TH ST NW # 503
Washington, DC 20036

College Media Advisers
MEMPHIS STATE UNIV
Memphis, TN 38152

College Placement Council
62 HIGHLAND AVE
Bethlehem, PA 18017

Convention of American Instructors of the Deaf
PO BOX 2025
Austin, TX 78768

Council on Library-Media Technicians
2900 COMMUNITY COLLEGE AVE
Cleveland, OH 44115

Country Day School Headmasters Association of the US
1440 CARMEL RD
Charlotte, NC 28226

Dance Educators of America
PO BOX 509
Oceanside, NY 11572

Headmasters Association
22 E 91ST ST
New York, NY 10128

Independent Scholars of Asia
2321 RUSSELL ST APT 3A
Berkeley, CA 94705

International Association of Jazz Educators
PO BOX 724
Manhattan, KS 66502

International Association of Pupil Personnel Workers
2025 JUNEWAY DR
Michigan City, IN 46360

International Porcelain Art Teachers Association
706 E 3RD ST
Flint, MI 48503

International Reading Association
PO BOX 8139
Newark, DE 19714

Jewish Teachers Association-Morim
45 E 33RD ST # 604
New York, NY 10016

Music Educators National Conference
1902 ASSOCIATION DR
Reston, VA 22091

Music Teachers National Association
617 VINE ST STE 1432
Cincinnati, OH 45202

National Alliance of Black School Educators
2816 GEORGIA AVE NW
Washington, DC 20001

National Association of Biology Teachers
11250 ROGERS BACON DR #19
Reston, VA 22090

National Association of Business Education State Supervisors
1535 W JEFFERSON ST
Phoenix, AZ 85007

National Association of Classroom Education in Business Education
Cambridge City, IN 47327

National Association of College Admissions Counselors
1800 DIAGONAL RD # 430
Alexandria, VA 22314

National Association of College and University Business Officers
1 DUPONT CIR NW # 500
Washington, DC 20036

National Association of College Deans, Registrars & Admissions Officers
917 DORSETT AVE
Albany, GA 31701

National Association of College Wind and Percussion Instructors
NE MISSOURI STATE UNIV
Kirksville, MO 63501

National Association of Colleges & Teachers of Agriculture
UNIV OF ILLINOIS
Urbana, IL 61801

National Association of Collegiate Directors of Athletics
PO BOX 16428
Cleveland, OH 44116

National Association of Educational Office Personnel
7223 LEE HWY # 301
Falls Church, VA 22046

National Association of Elementary School Principals
1615 DUKE ST
Alexandria, VA 22314

National Association of Federal Education Program Administrators
1801 N MOORE ST
Alexandria, VA 22209

National Association of Flight Instructors
PO BOX 793
Dublin, OH 43017

National Association of Geology Teachers
PO BOX 5443
Bellingham, WA 98227

National Association of Hebrew Day School Administrators
1114 AVENUE J
Brooklyn, NY 11230

National Association of Industrial & Technical Teacher Educators
FERRIS STATE UNIV
Big Rapids, MI 49307

National Association of Principals of Schools for Girls
4050 LITTLE RIVER RD
Hendersonville, NC 28739

National Assoc. of Professors of Hebrew in American Inst of Higher Learning
UNIV OF WISCONSIN
Madison, WI 53706

National Association of Pupil Services Administrators
660 CHAFFIN RDG
Columbus, OH 43214

National Association of School Nurses
PO BOX 1300
Scarborough, ME 04070

National Association of Secondary School Principals
1904 ASSOCIATION DR
Reston, VA 22091

National Assoc. of State Administrators & Supervisors of Private Schools
32 E WASHINGTON ST STE 804
Indianapolis, IN 46204

National Association of State Directors of Migrant Education
PO BOX 94064
Baton Rouge, LA 70804

National Association of State Directors of Special Education
2021 K ST NW # 315
Washington, DC 20006

National Association of State Directors of Vocational-Technical Education
1420 16TH ST NW # 301
Washington, DC 20036

National Association of State Directors/Teacher Education & Certification
3600 WHITMAN AVE N APT 105
Seattle, WA 98103

National Association of State Supervisors of Music
229 STATE HOUSE
Indianapolis, IN 46204

National Association of State Supervisors of Trade & Industrial Education
1500 W 7TH AVE
Stillwater, OK 74074

National Association of State Supervisors/Directors of Secondary Education
700 GOVERNORS DR
Pierre, SD 57501

National Association of Student Activity Advisers
1904 ASSOCIATION DR
Reston, VA 22091

National Association of Student Financial Aid Administrators
1920 L ST NW # 200
Washington, DC 20036

National Association of Student Personnel Administrators
1700 18TH ST NW # 301
Washington, DC 20009

National Association of Substance Abuse Trainers and Educators
6400 PRESS DR
New Orleans, LA 70126

National Association of Supervisors of Business Education
15955 NEW HALLS FERRY RD
Florissant, MO 63031

National Association of Teachers of Singing
2800 UNIVERSITY BLVD N
Jacksonville, FL 32211

National Association of Temple Educators
707 SUMMERLY DR
Nashville, TN 37209

National Association of Trade & Industrial Instructors
6605 E US HIGHWAY 66 ST
El Reno, OK 73036

National Association of Veteran Program Administrators
UNIV OF CENTRAL FLORIDA
Orlando, FL 32816

National Association of Vocational Home Economics Teachers
RR 2 BOX 62
Hackleburg, AL 35564

National Association of Womens Deans, Administrators and Counselors
1325 18TH ST NW APT 210
Washington, DC 20036

National Conference of Yeshiva Principals
160 BROADWAY
New York, NY 10038

National Council of Local Admin. of Vocational Education & Practical Arts
66 RUGBY RD
Brooklyn, NY 11226

National Council of State Directors of Community Junior Colleges
319 7TH AVE
Olympia, WA 98501

National Council of State Supervisors of Foreign Languages
STATE HOUSE #229
Indianapolis, IN 46204

National Council of Teachers of English
1111 W KENYON RD
Urbana, IL 61801

National Council of Teachers of Mathematics
1906 ASSOCIATION DR
Reston, VA 22091

National Council of Writing Program Administrators
MIAMI UNIV
Oxford, OH 45056

National Federation of Modern Language Teachers Association
659 N 57TH AVE
Omaha, NE 68132

National Guild of Piano Teachers
808 RIO GRANDE ST
Austin, TX 78701

National Marine Educators Association
PO BOX 51215
Pacific Grove, CA 93950

National Organization for Hearing Education
RR 1 BOX 460
Falconer, NY 14733

National School Public Relations Association
1501 LEE HWY # 201
Arlington, VA 22209

National Science Supervisors Association
PO BOX AL
Amagansett, NY 11930

National Science Teachers Association
1742 CONNECTICUT AVE NW
Washington, DC 20009

National Vocational Agricultural Teachers Association
PO BOX 15440
Alexandria, VA 22309

Performing Arts Education Association
1224 POPLAR ST
Greensburg, PA 15601

Professional Dance Teachers Association
PO BOX 38
Waldwick, NJ 07463

Society for Music Teacher Education
1902 ASSOCIATION DR
Reston, VA 22091

Society of Professors of Education
UNIV OF TENNESSEE
Knoxville, TN 37996

Society of Teachers of Family Medicine
PO BOX 8729
Kansas City, MO 64114

State Higher Education Executive Officers
707 17TH ST STE 2700
Denver, CO 80202

University Council for Educational Administration
116 FARMER BLDG
Tempe, AZ 85287

Patterson's
SCHOOLS CLASSIFIED

Part II

POST-SECONDARY SCHOOLS

HOW TO USE PATTERSON'S SCHOOLS CLASSIFIED

Patterson's SCHOOLS CLASSIFIED contains the broadest assortment of post-secondary schools available in any single directory. More than 7,000 post-secondary schools, accredited by the organizations shown below, are classified by school type and academic discipline.

The basic listing for both School and Academic Classifications contains the school name, mailing address and contact person needed for supplementary information or registration details. Many of the listings are in larger type or contain additional descriptive material supplied by the school. The student should interpret the added emphasis as an indication of the school's desire to attract qualified students. Listings are arranged alphabetically within each classification, first by state and then by school name.

In addition to our regular editorial work, each school has been contacted within the past twelve months to verify names, addresses, academic subjects covered and degrees offered. The contributions of the responding schools is sincerely appreciated.

11 Institutional Accrediting Organizations

Accrediting Commission of Career Schools/Colleges of Technology
Accrediting Council for Independent Colleges and Schools
American Association of Bible Colleges
Association of Advanced Rabbinical & Talmudic Schools
Association of Theological Schools in the USA & Canada
Middle States Association of Colleges & Schools
New England Association of Schools & Colleges
North Central Association of Colleges & Schools
Northwest Association of Schools & Colleges
Southern Association of Colleges & Schools
Western Association of Schools & Colleges

39 Professional and Specialized Accrediting Organizations

Accreditation Board for Engineering & Technology
Accrediting Bureau of Health Education Schools
Accrediting Commission on Education for Health Services Administration
Accrediting Council on Education in Journalism & Mass Communication
American Assembly of Collegiate Schools of Business
American Association for Counseling & Development
American Board of Funeral Service Education
American Council for Construction Education
American Council on Pharmaceutical Education
American Dental Association
American Dietetic Association
American Home Economics Association
American Library Association
American Medical Association
American Medical Association Committee on Allied Health Education
American Optometric Association
American Osteopathic Association
American Physical Therapy Association
American Podiatric Medical Association
American Psychological Association
American Society of Landscape Architects
American Speech-Language-Hearing Association
American Veterinary Medical Association
Association of American Law Schools
Computer Science Accreditation Commission
Council on Chiropractic Education
Council on Education for Public Health
Council on Rehabilitation Education
Council on Social Work Education
Foundation for Interior Design Education Research
National Architectural Accrediting Board
National Association of Schools of Art & Design
National Association of Schools of Music
National Association of Schools of Public Affairs & Administration
National Council for Accreditation of Teacher Education
National League for Nursing
National Recreation & Park Association
Planning Accreditation Board
Society of American Foresters

SCHOOL CLASSIFICATIONS

If you are looking for a particular school by name and you know whether it is a University, Community or Junior College, Career School or Hospital go to the first page of the appropriate section of the index where you will find an explanation of how the index works.

If unsure, go to the first page of the index (page 819).

If you are interested in a particular type of school, such as a **Career School** or a **Community** or **Junior College**, go directly to that classification and you will find a listing of accredited schools.

ACADEMIC CLASSIFICATIONS

Academic Classifications cover the major areas of study selected by more than 90% of secondary students. Once the student has selected a major, reference to that classification will direct him to an appropriate selection of schools.

Academic Classifications offered by a relatively small number of schools, such as **Architecture**, **Forestry** and **Theology** are intended to be complete at the Baccalaureate level. However, to list every school under every possible classification would make the directory so large as to be a disservice to the student. **Music**, for example, is taught in one form or another by virtually every school. **Music** listings include all schools approved by the National Association of Schools of Music. They do not, however, include all of the schools that offer degrees in music. The reader should recognize that the omission of a school from such disciplines as **Music**, **Liberal Arts and Sciences** or **Business and Management** is not a failure in editorial content but, an effort to reduce redundancy.

Inclusion in Academic Classifications of schools below the Baccalaureate Degree is progressively more selective. For a broader selection, the student may choose to contact schools from a School Classification.

COMMINGLED SCHOOLS IN ACADEMIC CLASSIFICATIONS

A special feature of this book is the commingling of colleges, community and junior colleges and career schools in Academic Classifications. The student considering further education is exposed to a wide range of educational opportunities without the need for multiple directories. In all cases listings for schools which offer less than a Baccalaureate Degree are identified by a symbol to the left of the school name to help the reader quickly identify the highest degree, diploma or certificate offered. See page 528.

INSTITUTIONAL AND PROFESSIONAL ACCREDITATION

In thirty-one classifications a second symbol (†) to the left of the school name identifies schools meeting the requirements of a particular professional accrediting group. A paragraph at the beginning of the classification identifies the accrediting group.

The accreditation symbol is not intended as an indication of merit, but does establish that the classification contains all of the core schools that have sought and attained specialized accreditation. For example, in the classification **Allied Health Science** every school accredited by the AMA Committee on Allied Health Education and Accreditation (†) or the Accrediting Bureau of Health Education Schools (‡) is shown with a symbol. Other schools offering associate, baccalaureate or even advanced degrees in Allied Health Science may or may not have sought the particular professional accreditation. All of the schools listed under **Allied Health Science** are either institutionally or professionally accredited.

GUIDE TO EDITORIAL STYLE

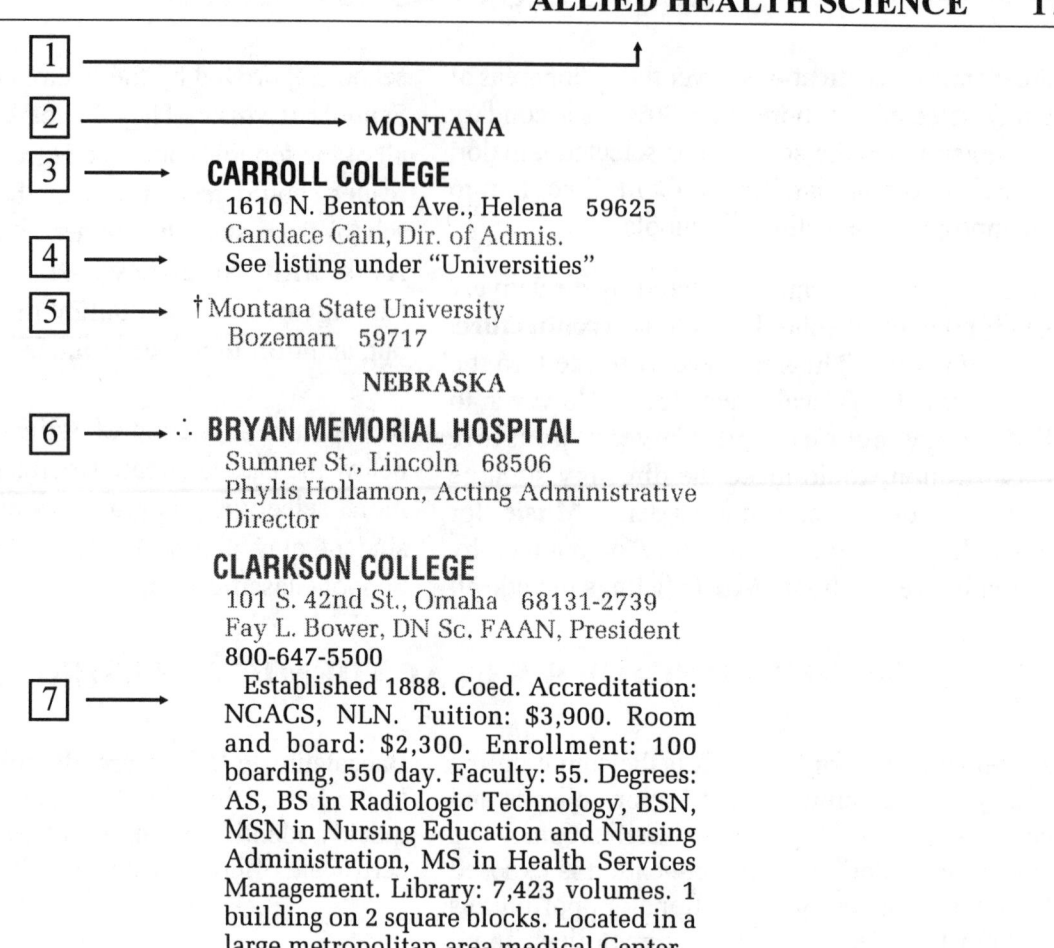

1. __Classification and page number.__

2. __State__ (in alphabetical sequence within each classification).

3. __School name and address__ (in alphabetical sequence within each state).

4. __Cross reference line__ (to direct the reader's attention to a school's larger listing in a different classification).

5. __Accreditation symbol__ (a paragraph at the beginning of thirty-one classifications identifies the accrediting body for that classification).

Allied Health Science	Funeral Service Education	Pharmacy
Architecture	Home Economics	Podiatric Medicine
Art	Interior Design	Psychology
Biblical Studies	Landscape Architecture	Public Health
Business and Management	Law	Rabbinical Studies
Chiropractic Colleges	Library Science	Speech And Drama
Communications	Medicine	Teacher Education
Computer and Information Science	Music	Theology
Dentistry	Nursing	Veterinary Medicine
Engineering	Optometry	
Forestry	Osteopathic Medicine	

6. __School type code__ (identifies school type if below the baccalaureate degree in academic classifications).

∴	Community and Junior Colleges	∷	Preparatory Schools
⫶	Career Schools	⫶∶	Handicapped Schools
∵	Teaching Hospitals	⸪	Home Study Schools

7. __Supplemental information provided by the school.__

CLASSIFICATIONS

Aeronautics, Aviation and Space

Agriculture

Allied Health Science

Architecture

Art

Biblical Studies

Biological Science

Business and Management

Career Schools

Chiropractic Colleges

Communications

Community and Junior Colleges

Computer and Information Science

Dentistry

Engineering

Ethnic Studies

Fashion Art

Forestry

Funeral Service Education

Graduate Schools

Handicapped, Schools for the

Home Economics

Home Study and Correspondence

Interior Design

Landscape Architecture

Law

Liberal Arts and Sciences

Library Science

Master of Business Administration

Mathematics

Medicine

Men's Colleges

Military Science

Mines and Metallurgy

Music

Nursing

Oceanography

Optometry

Osteopathic Medicine

Pharmacy

Photography

Physical Education

Physical Science

Podiatric Medicine

Preparatory Schools for Boys

Preparatory Schools - Coeducational

Preparatory Schools for Girls

Psychology

Public Health

Rabbinical Studies

Secretarial Science

Social Science

Speech and Drama

Study Abroad

Summer Sessions

Teacher Education

Theology

Universities and Colleges - Coeducational

Veterinary Medicine

Women's Colleges

Women's Studies

AERONAUTICS, AVIATION AND SPACE

ALABAMA

ALABAMA AVIATION & TECHNICAL COLLEGE
Highway 231 S., Ozark 36360
800-624-3468
Off-Campus Center in Mobile
205-438-2816
The only public two-year college in the Southeastern US with the primary mission of preparing technicians for the aviation industry. Certificate and associate degree programs in Aviation Maintenance, Airframe, Powerplant, Avionics, Flight (Airplane and Helicopter). Accreditation: SACS. Enrollment: 450. Per quarter tuition/fees (based on 15 credit hours): $327 (resident), $549 (out-of-state). Campus housing. FAA certified. VA Approved.

Auburn University, Auburn 36849

· Community College of the Air Force
130 W. Maxwell Blvd., Montgomery 36112

University of Alabama at Birmingham
University Station, Birmingham 35294

· Wallace State Community College
P.O. Box 2000, Hanceville 35077

ARIZONA

Arizona State University, Tempe 85287

· Cochise College, Douglas
Rural Route 01 Box 100, 85607
Andrew S. Moreland, Pres.

Embry-Riddle Aeronautical University
3200 Willow Creek Rd., Prescott 86301
800-442-ERAU

:: Rice Aviation-Southwest Regional Campus
3201 E. Broadway Rd., Phoenix 85040
800-736-7014

University of Arizona, Tucson 85721
Loyd Bell, Director of Admissions

ARKANSAS

Henderson State University
1100 Henderson St., Arkadelphia 71999

· Southern Arkansas University
P.O. Box 3048, East Camden 71701

CALIFORNIA

· Antelope Valley College
3041 W. Avenue K, Lancaster 93534

:: Aris Helicopters, Ltd.
1138 Coleman Ave., San Jose 95110
408-998-3266

California Institute of Technology
1201 E. California Blvd., Pasedena 91125
Carole L. Snow, Dir. of Admis.

California Polytechnic State University
San Luis Obispo 93407
Helen Linstrum, Dir. of Admis.

· Cerritos College
11110 E. Alondra Blvd., Norwalk 90650

· Chaffey College
5885 Haven Ave., Rancho Cucamonga 91737
JoAnne Edmison, Director of Admissions

· City College of San Francisco
33 Gough St., San Francisco 94103
Chui Tsang, Dean
415-241-2306

· College of the Redwoods
7351 Tompkins Hill Rd., Eureka 95501

· Cypress College
9200 Valley View St., Cypress 90630

· Foothill College
12345 El Monte Ave., Los Altos Hills 94022

· Gavilan Community College
5055 Santa Teresa Blvd., Gilroy 95020

· Glendale Community College
1500 N. Verdugo Rd., Glendale 91208

· Grossmont College
8800 Grossmont College Dr., El Cajon 92020

· Kings River Community College
955 N. Reed Ave., Reedley 93654
Abel Sykes, President

· Los Angeles Mission College
13356 Eldridge Ave., Sylmar 91342

· Mira Costa College
1 Barnard Dr., Oceanside 92056

· Mt. San Antonio College
1100 N. Grand Ave., Walnut 91789

· Navajo Aviation
145 John Glenn Dr., Concord 94520
Flight Training Center
510-685-1150

· Northrop-Rice Aviation Institute of Technology
8911 Aviation Blvd., Inglewood 90301
310-337-4444

· Ohlone College
P.O. Box 3909, Fremont 94539

ORANGE COAST COLLEGE
P.O. Box 5005, Costa Mesa 92628
See listing under "Community and Junior Colleges"

· Palomar Community College
1140 W. Mission Rd., San Marcos 92069

· San Bernardino Valley College
701 S. Mt. Vernon Ave., San Bernardino 92410

· San Diego Miramar College
10440 Black Mountain Rd., San Diego 92126

San Diego State University
5300 Campanile Dr., San Diego 92115

· Shasta College
1065 N. Old Oregon Tr., Redding 96003

· Sierra Academy of Aeronautics
P.O. Box 2429, Oakland 94614

· Solano Community College
P.O. Box 246, Suisun City 94585

University of California, Davis
376 Mrak Hall, Davis 95616

West Coast University
440 Shatto Pl., Los Angeles 90020

· West Los Angeles College
4800 Freshman Dr., Culver City 90230

COLORADO

· Aims Community College
P.O. Box 69, Greeley 80632
William Green, Registrar

· Colorado Aero Tech
10851 W. 120th Ave., Broomfield 80021-3465
John Walker, Executive Director

· Colorado Northwestern Community College
500 Kennedy Dr., Rangely 81648
Pat Kalahar, Dir. Marketing/Recruitment
800-562-1105

· Emery Aviation College
1245 A Aviation Way, Colorado Springs 80916
719-591-9488

Metropolitan State College of Denver
P.O. Box 173362, Campus Box 16
Denver 80217-3362

Otero Junior College
1802 Colorado Ave., La Junta 81050
Joe Treece, Dir. of Admissions

· Pikes Peak Community College
5675 S. Academy Blvd.
Colorado Springs 80906-5498
Roberta Erickson, Dir. of Admis.
See listing under "Community and Junior Colleges"

United States Air Force Academy
Colorado Springs 80840

University of Colorado at Boulder
Boulder 80309
William A. Douglas, Dean of Admis.

CONNECTICUT

· Quinebaug Valley Community College
P.O. Box 59, Danielson 06239

· Thames Valley State Technical College
574 New London Trnpk., Norwich 06360

DELAWARE

: Dawn Training Institute
120 Old Churchmans Rd., New Castle 19720
Cheryl Zapata, Dir. of Admis.

DISTRICT OF COLUMBIA

University of the District of Columbia
Georgia Ave.-Harvard St. Campus
1100 Harvard St., N.W., Washington 20009

University of the District of Columbia
Van Ness Campus
4200 Connecticut Ave., N.W., Washington 20008

FLORIDA

· Broward Community College
225 E. Las Olas Blvd., Ft. Lauderdale 33301

· Broward Community College
225 E. Las Olas Blvd., Ft. Lauderdale 33301

Embry-Riddle Aeronautical University
600 S. Clyde Morris Blvd.
Daytona Beach 32114-3900
800-222-ERAU

: Engine Technical Institute
P.O. Box 109600, West Palm Beach 33410

: FAA Center for Management Development
4500 Palm Coast Pky., S.E., Palm Coast 32137

· F.I.T. Aviation, Inc.
640 Harry Sutton Rd., Melbourne 32901
Michael F. Wilson, President

: FlightSafety International
P.O. Box 2708, Vero Beach 32961
Jeffrey Krell, Marketing Supervisor

:: FLORIDA AIR ACADEMY
1950 South Academy Dr., Melbourne 32901
Major James Dwight, President

Florida Institute of Technology
150 W. University Blvd., Melbourne 32901
Louis T. Levy, Dean of Admissions
800-888-4348

· Gulf Coast Community College
5230 Hwy. 98, W., Panama City 32401
Roy Smith, Dir. of Admis. and Records

: Huffman Aviation International
400 E. Airport Ave., Venice 34285
Greg Huffman, Dir. of Admis.

· Manatee Community College
5840 26th St., W., Bradenton 34207

· National Aviation Academy
5770 Roosevelt Blvd. Ste. 105
Clearwater 34620
813-531-2080 or 800-659-2080

· Palm Beach Community College
4200 S. Congress Ave., Lake Worth 33461

· Phoenix College of Aeronautics
P.O. Box 11706, Daytona Beach 32120
T. Voyt, Registrar
See listing under "Community and Junior Colleges"

· Phoenix East Aviation
561 Pearl Harbor Dr., Daytona Beach 32114
Andre Maye, Dir. of Admissions
See listing under "Career Schools"

· St. Petersburg Junior College
P.O. Box 1284, Terpon Springs 34688

: S & S Aircraft Flight Academy
P.O. Box 1196, Plant City 33564
Charles Aybar, President

University of Florida
226 Tigert Hall, Gainesville 32611

GEORGIA

Clayton State College
P.O. Box 285, Morrow 30260

: Houston Aeronautical College
R.R. 3 Box 250, Sandersville 31082

SOUTHEASTERN SCHOOL OF AERONAUTICS
Herbert Smart Airport, Macon 31201
Patrick Murphy, President
800-423-7510 or 912-745-0964
Established 1980. Private. Coed. Accreditation: SACS. Enrollment: 50 full-time, 30 part-time. Faculty: 25. Student-faculty ratio: 3:1. Programs: Flight Training (private through ATP); Airplane and Helicopter; Turbo-Prop and B737 type rating; Aviation Mechanic Training(Airframe and Powerplant). Library: 1,000 volumes. 14 buildings on 296 acres. On airport location. Housing at airport. 12 month mechanic program. 6 month pilot program. Metro area population: 250,000. Only 80 miles south of Atlanta. Monthly enrollment.

IDAHO

AERO TECHNICIANS
P.O. Box 7, Rexburg 83440
Julina Hart, Director of Admissions
208-356-4446 or 208-356-4447
Established 1946. Private. Coed. Accreditation: ACCET, FAA, Idaho Department of Education. Tuition: $8,160. Room and board: $3,000. Fees: $350. Tools: $1,200. Enrollment: 25 full-time, 35 part-time. Faculty: 4. Student-faculty ratio: 6:1. Licenses: FAA Airframe and Powerplant Mechanic, Avionics, Professional Pilot. Library: 1,000 volumes. 1 building 28,000 square feet. FAR part 141 school for Professional Pilot, fixed wing aircraft and helicopters. Ideal location for all pilot training. Fleet of 12 airplanes and helicopters. Aviation has excellent growth potential. Placement help available. Federal financial aid for US citizens if you qualify.

ILLINOIS

· Belleville Area College
2500 Carlyle Rd., Belleville 62221

· Carl Sandburg College
2232 S. Lake Storey Rd., Galesburg 61401

LEWIS UNIVERSITY
Rt. 53, Romeoville 60441
Irish O'Reilly, Director of Admissions
See listing under "Universities"

Parks College of St. Louis University
500 Falling Springs Rd., Cahokia 62206
John Wilbur, Dir. of Admis.

· Rock Valley College
3301 N. Mulford Rd., Rockford 61114

· South Suburban College of Cook County
15800 State St., South Holland 60473

University of Illinois
506 S. Wright St., Urbana 61801

INDIANA

:: Culver Military Academy and Summer Camps
1300 Academy Rd., Culver 46511
Richard Edwards, Dir. of Admis.

Purdue University
Schleman Hall, West Lafayette 47907

Tri-State University, Angola 46703
Director of Admission
800-347-4878

University of Notre Dame
Notre Dame 46556
Kevin M. Rooney, Dir. of Admis.

· Vincennes University
1002 N. 1st St., Vincennes 47591

IOWA

· Hawkeye Community College
1501 E. Orange Rd., Waterloo 50701
319-296-2320 Ext. 4000

· Indian Hills Community College
525 Grandview, Ottumwa 52501
515-683-5111

· Iowa Lakes Community College
300 S. 18th St., Estherville 51334
John Nelson, Dir. of Admis.
712-362-2604

Iowa State University, Ames 50011
Karsten Smedal, Dir. of Admis.

· Iowa Western Community College
2700 College Rd., Council Bluffs 51503
Thomas Dutch, Dir. of Admis.

KANSAS

· Aviation Education Center
2021 S. Eisenhower St., Wichita 67209
316-833-3595

Central College
1200 S. Main St., McPherson 67460
Greg Gossell, Dir. of Admis.

· Hesston College
P.O. Box 3000, Hesston 67062

· Hutchinson Community College
1300 N. Plum St., Hutchinson 67501
Duane Halpain, Dir. of Admis.

· Kansas State University
College of Technology
2409 Scanlan Ave., Salina 67401

University of Kansas, Lawrence 66045

Wichita State University
1845 Fairmount, Wichita 67260
800-362-2594
See listing under "Universities"

KENTUCKY

Embry Riddle Aeronautical University
P.O. Box 130, Fort Knox 40121

LOUISIANA

Tulane University
6823 Saint Charles Ave.
New Orleans 70118

MARYLAND

· Frederick Community College
7932 Opossumtown Pike, Frederick 21702
Gerard Blake, Director

: Rice Aviation-Martin State Airport Campus
701 Wilson Point Rd., Baltimore 21220

University of Maryland, College Park 20742

University of Maryland Eastern Shore
11868 Academic Oval, Princess Anne 21853
Dr. Rochell Peoples, Dir. of Admis.
410-651-6410

MASSACHUSETTS

Boston University
685 Commonwealth Ave., Boston 02215

: East Coast Aero Tech School
Division of Wentworth Technical Schools
696 Virginia Rd., Concord 01742
Mark Holzwarth, Dir. of Admis.
508-371-9977

Massachusetts Institute of Technology
77 Massachusetts Ave., Cambridge 02139

· North Shore Community College
1 Ferncroft Rd., Danvers 01923

MICHIGAN

· Alpena Community College
666 Johnson St., Alpena 49707

: AMR COMBS FLIGHT TRAINING ACADEMY

Kent County International Airport
P.O. Box 888380, Grand Rapids 49588
Carlton G. Francis, Director of Training
800-262-4953 or 616-956-1646
Established 1953. Coed. Accreditation: MI Dept. of Education, MI Dept. of Aeronautics, Federal Aviation Administration. Fees: $3,000 - $23,000. Enrollment: 20 full-time, 70 part-time. Faculty: 10. Student-faculty ratio: 9:1. Certificates: Private Pilot through Airline Transport Pilot. AMR Combs is a division of AMR Corp - parent company to American Airlines, and has

11 locations around the US. Our Grand Rapids location is one of the largest flight training facilities within the great lakes region. We are an FAA approved school offering professional pilot training programs, we have 13 training & rental aircraft available and one of the most sophisticated Multi-engine, Visual Flight Simulators available for initial training. Government guaranteed student loans are available to eligible students. The Academy is also approved by the US Dept. of Justice to accept international students for F-1 Visas.

Baker College of Flint
1050 W. Bristol Rd., Flint 48507
Mark Heaton, Dir. of Admis.

Baker College of Muskegon
141 Hartford Ave., Muskegon 49442
Kathy Jacobson, Dir. of Admis.

Baker College of Owosso
1020 S. Washington St., Owosso 48867
Bruce A. Lundeen, Dir. of Admis.

· Jackson Community College
2111 Emmons Rd., Jackson 49201
Mark Ulseth, Dir. Enrollment Services

· Kirtland Community College
10775 St. Helen Rd. F-97, Roscommon 48653

· Lansing Community College
521 Washington Square N., Lansing 48933

· Macomb Community College
14500 E. 12 Mile Rd., Warren 48093

· Michigan Institute of Aeronautics
47884 D St., Belleville 48111

· Montcalm Community College
2800 College Dr., Sidney 48885

· Northwestern Michigan College
Career Pilot Program
1701 E. Front St., Traverse City 49686
Bob Buttleman, Director
800-748-0566

· Southwestern Michigan College
58900 Cherry Grove Rd., Dowagiac 49047
David Schultz, VP for Student Services
616-782-5113

University of Michigan-Ann Arbor
815 S. University Ave., Ann Arbor 48109

· Wayne County Community College
801 Fort St., W., Detroit 48226

Western Michigan University, Kalamazoo 49008
Stanley Henderson, Dir. of Enrl. Mgt. & Admis.
616-387-2000

MINNESOTA

ACADEMY OF AVIATION

3050 Metro Dr. #200, Minneapolis 55425
Gary McNulty, Director of Admissions
612-851-0066

· Aviation Training Academy
3050 Metro Dr. #200, Minneapolis 55425

· NEI COLLEGE OF TECHNOLOGY

825 41st Ave. N.E., Minneapolis 55421
Richard Thomson, Dir. of Admis.
Call 800-777-7NEI for Info.
See listing under "Career Schools"

St. Cloud State University
740 4th Ave., S., St. Cloud 56301
Sherwood Reid, Dir. of Admis.
800-369-4260

: Thunderbird Aviation
14091 Pioneer Trail, Eden Prairie 55347
612-941-1212

University of Minnesota, Twin Cities
Minneapolis 55455

MISSISSIPPI

· Hinds Community College, Raymond 39154

MISSOURI

Central Missouri State University
Warrensburg 64093
Delores Hudson, Dir. of Admis.

· Maple Woods Community College
2601 N.E. Barry Rd., Kansas City 64156

· St. Louis Community College at Meramec
11333 Big Bend Rd., Kirkwood 63122

St. Louis University
221 N. Grand Blvd., St. Louis 63103
Louis A. Menard, Dean of Admissions

University of Missouri, Rolla
102 Parker Hall, Rolla 65401
David J. Allen, Dir. of Admis. & Financial Aid
800-522-0938

MONTANA

Rocky Mountain College
1511 Poly Dr., Billings 59102
David Heringer, Dir. of Admis.
See listing under "Universities"

NEBRASKA

Grace College of the Bible
Ninth and William, Omaha 68108
Jeffrey A. Edgar, Director of Admissions
800-383-1422

· Western Nebraska Community College
Sidney 69162
Jim Copley, Admissions

NEW HAMPSHIRE

Daniel Webster College
New England Aeronautical Institute
20 University Dr, Nashua 03063

· NEW HAMPSHIRE TECHNICAL COLLEGE

505 Amherst St., Nashua 03063
John T. Fischer, Dean of Student Affairs
603-882-6923
Established 1970. Public. Coed. Accreditation: NEASC. Tuition: In-State: $2,296; New England Regional: $3,300; Out-of-state: $5,230. Enrollment: 425 full-time, 99 part-time. Faculty: 54. Degree offered: AAS in Aviation (FAA Cert. #NSUTO25K), Business, Computer Networking, Electronic/Mechanical Technology, Opticianry, Telecommunications, Electrical Engineering and Computer Engineering (ABET). Suburban campus one hour from Boston.

NEW JERSEY

· Mercer County Community College
West Windsor Campus
1200 Old Trenton Rd., Trenton 08690
Joe Blazenstein, Coordinator
See listing under "Community and Junior Colleges"

Princeton University, Princeton 08544

: Raritan Valley Flying School
Princeton Airport
Route 206, Princeton 08540
Naomi Nierenberg, President

: Teterboro School of Aeronautics
80 Moonachie Ave., Teterboro 07608-1083
Edward Chudzik, Director
201-288-6300 FAX 201-288-5609

NEW MEXICO

· Eastern New Mexico University-Roswell Campus
P.O. Box 6000, Roswell 88202
Tim Raftery, Director of Admissions and Records

NEW YORK

COLLEGE OF AERONAUTICS

La Guardia Airport, Flushing 11371
Dr. Richard B. Goetze, Jr., President
Donald J Whitman, Dir. of Admis.
800-776-2376
Established 1932. Private. Independent. Coed. Accreditation: MSACS. Tuition: $5,820. Estimated total yearly expenses: $1,000. Enrollment: 1,200 students. Faculty: 65. Degrees: AAS, AOS, BT. Library: 60,000 volumes. 3 buildings on 6 acres. Located in New York City. Fully computerized engine test cells, hangar, engine labs, avionic labs, computer labs, and airline training center. Financial aid, grants, scholarships, and loans available.

Cornell University
410 Thurston Ave., Ithaca 14853

Manhattan College
4513 Manhattan College Pky., Riverdale 10471
Dr. John Patterson, Dean of Engineering

Polytechnic University
333 Jay St., Brooklyn 11201

Rensselaer Polytechnic Institute, Troy 12180
Conrad Sharrow, Dean of Admissions

Rochester Institute of Technology
1 Lomb Memorial Dr., Rochester 14623
716-475-6631
See listing under "Universities"

Syracuse University, Syracuse 13244

U.S. Military Academy, West Point 10996

NORTH CAROLINA

· Guilford Technical Community College
P.O. Box 309, Jamestown 27282

· Lenoir Community College
P.O. Box 188, Kinston 28502

· Wayne Community College
Caller Box 8002, Goldsboro 27533
Bill Bennett, Public Information Officer
919-735-5151

NORTH DAKOTA

: DAKOTA AERO TECH, INC.

1801 23rd Ave., N. #111, Fargo 58102
Gordon Person, Dir. of Admis.
701-237-5305 or 800-435-4147
Established 1966. Private. Coed. Accreditation: non-accredited, approved by the FAA and the ND State Approving Agency, ND Board of Vocational Education, Veteran's Administration, ND & MN Job Service. Tuition: $6,900. Enrollment: 200 full-time. Faculty: 11. Student-faculty ratio: 17:1. Degrees: Airframe and Powerplant License in one year or a four year option in Aero-Manufacturing Engineering Technology in association with NDSU. 4 buildings. A & P Mechanic School in conjunction with an FAA approved repair station, which creates an ideal atmosphere to learn, by working on or observing the maintenance of aircraft.

OHIO

Case Western Reserve University
2040 Adelbert Rd., Cleveland 44106

· Columbus State Community College
550 E. Spring St., Columbus 43215
Mary Jo Deerwester, Dir. of Admis.

· Cuyahoga Community College, Western Campus
11000 W. Pleasant Valley Rd.
Parma Heights 44130

· **DAVIS JUNIOR COLLEGE**
4747 Monroe St., Toledo 43623
Diane Brunner, President
Keven Creek, Chairperson
Established 1858. Private. Coed. Accreditation:
AICS, AAMA, NCACS. Tuition: $5,600. Fees: $25
application fee. Enrollment: 350 full-time, 100 part-
time. Faculty: 35. Student-faculty ratio: 15:1. Degree:
associate. Specialized library. 2 buildings including
an airport. Admissions test (CPAT) & specialized.
High school graduate or GED. Enroll each quarter.
90% placement overall. Unique professional pilot
program.

Franklin University
201 S. Grant Ave., Columbus 43215

Kent State University
P.O. Box 5190, Kent 44242
Bruce Riddle, Dir. of Admis.

Ohio State University
190 N. Oval Mall, Columbus 43210

University of Cincinnati
2700 Clifton Ave., Cincinnati 45221

University of Dayton
300 College Park Ave., Dayton 45469-0210
Toll-free 800-837-7433
See listing under "Universities"

OKLAHOMA

· National Education Center-Spartan School of
Aeronautics
8820 E. Pine St. #51133, Tulsa 74115
800-331-1204

Oklahoma State University, Stillwater 74078
Kenneth E. Wiggins, Dept. Head

Southeastern Oklahoma State University
Station A, Durant 74701

University of Oklahoma at Norman
660 Parrington Oval, Norman 73019

OREGON

· Portland Community College
P.O. Box 19000, Portland 97280

PENNSYLVANIA

· Community College of Allegheny County
North Campus
111 Pines Plaza, Pittsburgh 15237

Pennsylvania State University
201 Shields Bldg., University Park 16802

· Pittsburgh Institute of Aeronautics
P.O. Box 10897, Pittsburgh 15236

University of Pittsburgh at Bradford
300 Campus Dr., Bradford 16701

SOUTH CAROLINA

· Florence Darlington Technical College
P.O. Box 8000, Florence 29501

TENNESSEE

· Hiwassee College, Madisonville 37354

Knoxville College
901 College St., N.W., Knoxville 37921

Middle Tennessee State University
Murfreesboro 37132
Roger D. Sims, Dir. of Admis.

· Motlow State Community College
P.O. Box 88100, Tullahoma 37388

TEXAS

· Central Texas College
P.O. Box 1800, Killeen 76540

· Hallmark Institute of Technology
South Campus-Aviation Technology
P.O. Box 780459, San Antonio 78278
Richard Fessler, President
Bill Buss, Campus Director
210-924-8551

· Houston Community College
P.O. Box 7849, Houston 77270

· Mountain View College
4849 W. Illinois Ave., Dallas 75211

· Rice Aviation-Hobby Airport Campus
205 Brisbane St., Houston 77061
713-644-7777

· Rice Aviation-North Houston Campus
7811 N. Shepherd #100, Houston 77088
713-820-9470

: Rice Aviation, Main Office
8880 Telephone Rd., Houston 77061
713-644-6616

Rice University
P.O. Box 1892, Houston 77251

· Texarkana Community College
2500 N. Robison Rd., Texarkana 75501

Texas A & M University
College Station 77843

: Texas Aero Tech
6911 Lemmon Ave., Dallas 75209
800-856-2376

· Texas State Technical College Waco/Marshall
3801 Campus Dr., Waco 76705
817-867-3371

University of Texas at Arlington
UTA Box 19125, Arlington 76019
R. Zack Prince, Dir. of Admis.

University of Texas at Austin
0 the University of Texas, Austin 78712

UTAH

Utah State University, Logan 84322-1600
Rod Clark, Director of Admissions
801-750-1107

VIRGINIA

Averett College
420 W. Main St., Danville 24541
Gary Sherman, Dean of Enrollment Mgmt.

:: Randolph-Macon Academy
201 W. 3rd St., Front Royal 22630
Col. Trevor Turner, USA Ret, President

: Rice Aviation-Virginia Campus
5202 W. Military Hwy., Chesapeake 23321
804-465-2813

University of Virginia
P.O. Box 9017, Charlottesville 22906

Virginia Polytechnic Institute & State University
Blacksburg 24061
David Bousquet, Dir. of Undergraduate Admis.

: Williamsburg Flite Center
1 Minor Ct., Williamsburg 23188

WASHINGTON

· Big Bend Community College
7662 Chanute St. N.E.
Moses Lake 98837

· Everett Community College
801 Wetmore Ave., Everett 98201
206-388-9534

· Green River Community Colleges
12401 S.E. 320th St., Auburn 98002

· South Seattle Community College
6000 16th Ave., S.W., Seattle 98106

· Spokane Community College
1810 N. Greene St., Spokane 99207

University of Washington, Seattle 98195

WEST VIRGINIA

West Virginia University
P.O. Box 6001, Morgantown 26506

WEST VIRGINIA WESLEYAN COLLEGE
59 College Ave., Buckhannon 26201
Robert Skinner, Director of Admission
See listing under "Universities"

WISCONSIN

· Gateway Technical College
4940 88th Ave, Kenosha 53144

AGRICULTURE

ALABAMA

Alabama A & M University
P.O. Box 1087, Normal 35762
Dr. James Shuford, Dean
See listing under "Universities"

Auburn University, Auburn 36849

· Gadsden State Community College
P.O. Box 227, Gadsden 35902
W. Bryan Stone, Dir. of Admis.

Tuskegee University
Tuskegee Institute 36088

ALASKA

Sheldon Jackson College
801 Lincoln St., Sitka 99835
Dennis Trotter, Dir. of Admis.
907-747-5221

University of Alaska Fairbanks
Fairbanks 99775

ARIZONA

· Arizona Western College
P.O. Box 929, Yuma 85366-0929
Bob Davis, Dir. of Admis.

University of Arizona, Tucson 85721
Loyd Bell, Director of Admissions

ARKANSAS

Arkansas State University
P.O. Box 1080, State University 72467

Arkansas Tech University
215 W. O St., Russellville 72801

University of Arkansas at Fayetteville
Fayetteville 72701

University of Arkansas at Monticello
P.O. Box 3596, Monticello 71656

University of Arkansas at Pine Bluff
1200 University Dr., Pine Bluff 71601-2799

CALIFORNIA

· Bakersfield College
1801 Panorama Dr., Bakersfield 93305
Robert M. Bruker, Dir. of Admis.

California Polytechnic State University
San Luis Obispo 93407
Helen Linstrum, Dir. of Admis.

California State University, Chico
Chico 95929-0440
Dr. Thomas Dickinson, Dean

California State University, Fresno
Shaw & Cedar Ave., Fresno 93710

· College of the Desert
43-500 Monterey Ave., Palm Desert 92260

· College of the Sequoias
915 S. Mooney Blvd., Visalia 93277

· Imperial Valley College
P.O. Box 158, Imperial 92251

· Kings River Community College
955 N. Reed Ave., Reedley 93654
Abel Sykes, President

· Lassen College
P.O. Box 3000, Susanville 96130

· Los Angeles Pierce College
6201 Winnetka Ave., Woodland Hills 91371
See listing under "Community and Junior
Colleges"

· Merced College
3600 M St., Merced 95348

· Mt. San Antonio College
1100 N. Grand Ave., Walnut 91789

· San Bernardino Valley College
701 S. Mt. Vernon Ave., San Bernardino 92410

· San Joaquin Delta College
5151 Pacific Ave., Stockton 95207

· Shasta College
1065 N. Old Oregon Tr., Redding 96003

· Sierra College
5000 Rocklin Rd., Rocklin 95677

University of California, Davis
376 Mrak Hall, Davis 95616

University of California, Riverside
P.O. Box 112, Riverside 92521

· Ventura College
4667 Telegraph Rd., Ventura 93003

· West Hills College
300 Cherry Lane, Coalinga 93210

COLORADO

Colorado State University
102 Administration Building, Fort Collins 80523
Mary Ontireros, Dir. of Admissions

Mesa State College
P.O. Box 2647, Grand Junction 81502
Sherri Pe'a, Dir. of Admis.

CONNECTICUT

· Mattatuck Community College
750 Chase Parkway, Waterbury 06708
Dr. Richard Sanders, President

University of Connecticut, Storrs 06268
Hugo John, Dean

DELAWARE

Delaware State College
1200 N. DuPont Hwy., Dover 19901
Jethro C. Williams, Dir. of Admis.

University of Delaware, Newark 19711

DISTRICT OF COLUMBIA

University of the District of Columbia
Van Ness Campus
4200 Connecticut Ave., N.W., Washington 20008

FLORIDA

Florida A & M University, Tallahassee 32307

University of Florida
226 Tigert Hall, Gainesville 32611

GEORGIA

· Abraham Baldwin Agriculture College
P.O. Box 1, Tifton 31793

University of Georgia, Athens 30602
Dr. William P. Flatt, Dean

HAWAII

University of Hawaii at Manoa
2500 Campus Rd., Honolulu 96822

IDAHO

· Ricks College, Rexburg 83460
Steven Bennion, President

University of Idaho, Moscow 83843
Peter Brown, Dir. of Admis.

ILLINOIS

· Black Hawk College, East Campus
P.O. Box 489, Kewanee 61443

· John Wood Community College
150 S. 48th St., Quincy 62301

· Parkland College
2400 W. Bradley Ave., Champaign 61821-1899
217-351-2208 or 800-346-8089

Southern Illinois University at Carbondale
Carbondale 62901

University of Illinois
506 S. Wright St., Urbana 61801

INDIANA

Purdue University
Schleman Hall, West Lafayette 47907

IOWA

Dordt College
498 4th Ave., N.E., Sioux Center 51250
Quentin Van Essen, Dir. of Admissions
800-343-6738

· Hawkeye Community College
1501 E. Orange Rd., Waterloo 50701
319-296-2320 Ext. 4000

· Iowa Lakes Community College
3200 College Dr., Emmetsburg 50536
John Nelson, Dir. of Admis.
712-852-3554

Iowa State University, Ames 50011
Karsten Smedal, Dir. of Admis.

· Iowa Western Community College
2700 College Rd., Council Bluffs 51503
Thomas Dutch, Dir. of Admis.

· Kirkwood Community College
P.O. Box 2068, Cedar Rapids 52406
Jim Miller, Dir. of Admis.
319-398-5517

Morningside College, Sioux City 51106
Lora Vanderzwaag, Dir. of Admis.

· Southeastern Community College
P.O. Box F., West Burlington 52655
Edward Schieffer, Director

Upper Iowa University
P.O. Box 1857, Fayette 52142

KANSAS

COLBY COMMUNITY COLLEGE
1255 S. Range Ave., Colby 67701
Theron Johnson, Dir. of Admis.

· Dodge City Community College
2501 N. 14th Ave., Dodge City 67801
Debbie Lloyd, Director of Admissions
800-FOR-DCCC

Fort Hays State University
600 Park St., Hays 67601-4099
Dr. Mike Gould, Chrpsn.

· Hutchinson Community College
1300 N. Plum St., Hutchinson 67501
Duane Halpain, Dir. of Admis.

Kansas State University
Anderson Hall 110, Manhattan 66506
Ellsworth M. Gerritz, Admis. & Records

McPherson College
1600 E. Euclid St., McPherson 67460

Mid-America Nazarene College
P.O. Box 1776, Olathe 66051

KENTUCKY

Midway College
512 E. Stephens St., Midway 40347
Carl P. Rollins II, Dir. of Admis.

Morehead State University, Morehead 40351
Charles Myers, Director of Admissions
606-783-2000

Murray State University, Murray 42071
Phil Bryan, Director of Admissions
800-272-4MSU

LOUISIANA

Louisiana State University and A & M College
Baton Rouge 70803

Southeastern Louisiana University
P.O. Box 784, Hammond 70404

University of Southwestern Louisiana
P.O. Box 44492, Lafayette 70504
318-231-6967

MAINE

UNITY COLLEGE
Quaker Hill Rd., Unity 04988
207-948-3131
Wilson G. Hess, President
John Craig, Dean for Admissions
    Established 1965. Private. Coed. Accreditation:
NEASC. Tuition: $9,750. Room and board: $4,750.
Enrollment: 475. Faculty: 34. Degrees: AAA, AAS,
BA, BS. Majors: environmental science (forestry,
wildlife, ecology, aquaculture, fisheries, conservation
law enforcement, arboriculture), social sciences (land
use planning, park management, environmental education, environmental policy), outdoor recreation and
pre-law. These programs blend a strong liberal arts
core with solid career preparation through hands-on
experience and internships. Excellent support services in academic tutoring, career planning, and placement.

University of Maine, Orono 04469

MARYLAND

University of Maryland, College Park 20742

University of Maryland Eastern Shore
11868 Academic Oval, Princess Anne 21853
Dr. Carolyn Brucks, Chrpsn.

MASSACHUSETTS

Hampshire College, Amherst 01002
Audrey Y. Smith, Dir. of Admissions
413-582-5471

University of Massachusetts, Amherst 01003
Arlene Wesley Cash, Dir. of Admis.

MICHIGAN

Andrews University, Berrien Springs 49104
Jack Mentges, Dir. of Admis.

Michigan State University, East Lansing 48824
Dr. James H. Anderson, Dean

MINNESOTA

Southwest State University, Marshall 56258

University of Minnesota, Twin Cities
Minneapolis 55455

UNIVERSITY OF MINNESOTA-CROOKSTON
2900 University Ave., Crookston 56716
Dr. James McBee, Chrpsn.
800-232-6466
See listing under "Universities"

WORTHINGTON COMMUNITY COLLEGE
1450 College Way, Worthington 56187
Conrad Burchill, President
507-372-2107

MISSISSIPPI

Alcorn State University
P.O. Box 359, Lorman 39096
D. W. Wilburn, Registrar

MISSOURI

Central Missouri State University
Warrensburg 64093
Delores Hudson, Dir. of Admis.

College of the Ozarks, Point Lookout 65726
Dr. Kenton Olson, Dean of the College

· North Central Missouri College
1301 Main St., Trenton 64683
Bill Hinkebein, Department Head
816-359-3948 ext. 314 or 800-880-6180

Northeast Missouri State University
Kirksville 63501

Southeast Missouri State University
1 University Plz., Cape Girardeau 63701
New Student Relations 314-651-2590
See listing under "Universities"

Southwest Missouri State University
901 S. National Ave., Springfield 65804
Dr. Anson Elliott, Department Head
417-836-5638

MONTANA

Montana State University, Bozeman 59717

NEBRASKA

Chadron State College
1000 Main St., Chadron 69337
Dale Williamson, Dir. of Admis.

· Northeast Community College
P.O. Box 469, Norfolk 68702
Eugene Hart, Dir. of Admis.

UNIVERSITY OF NEBRASKA
NEBRASKA COLLEGE OF TECHNICAL
AGRICULTURE
Operated by the University of Nebraska-Lincoln
Institute of Agriculture and Natural Resources
P.O. Box 69, Curtis 69025
Bill Siminoe, Associate Dean
Gerald Huntwork, Assistant Dean & Director of
    Academic Affairs
Delroy Hemsath, Director of Student Affairs
Gerald Sundquist, Information and Placement
Wats 1-800-3CURTIS, 308-367-4124
    Two year. Public. Accreditation: NCACS, Nebraska
Department of Education, Veterans Administration
approved courses, animal technology programs by
AVMA. Tuition: $616 per semester, resident, $1,232
per semester, non-resident. Room & board: $1,275 per
semester. 1 summer session. Enrollment: 95 men, 80
women, 20 faculty.
    Degrees: AA in Agriculture, majors in animal health
technology, production systems, business and management, environmental and natural resources, horticulture, power and equipment. Transfer program to
University of Nebraska-Lincoln is possible.
    Admissions: High School diploma, ACT required.
Applications for admissions taken until third week in
August or first week in January for spring semester.
    Complete financial aid program. (PELL Grants,
NDSL, CWSP, SEOG, PLUS) and limited scholarships.
    There are 2 dormitories, 1 cafeteria and 1 fraternity
on the 70 acre campus, and off-campus housing. A 400
acre farm serves as a field lab; 172,000 square feet of
instructional classroom and lab space are utilized in
the education program. 45 minutes from the nearest
city. Students enjoy a relaxed, small town atmosphere
in a rural setting.

University of Nebraska at Lincoln
AgH 103, Lincoln 68583
D. M. Edwards, Dean

· Western Nebraska Community College
1601 E. 27th St., Scottsbluff 69361
Roger Hovey, Admissions

NEW MEXICO

Eastern New Mexico University
Portales 88130
Larry Fuqua, Dir. of Admis.

NEW YORK

Cornell University
410 Thurston Ave., Ithaca 14853

Friends World Program, Long Island University
Montauk Hwy., Southampton 11968
Carol Gilbert, Dir. of Admis.

SUNY College of Agriculture & Technology
Cobleskill 12043
John Devney, Jr., Dir. of Admis.

· SUNY College of Agriculture and Technology
Morrisville 13408
Dennis Nostrand, Dir. of Admis.

· SUNY College of Technology, Alfred 14802
Deborah J. Goodrich, Dir. of Admis.
607-587-4215

SUNY College of Technology at Delhi
2 Main St., Delhi 13753

NORTH CAROLINA

· James Sprunt Community College
P.O. Box 398, Kenansville 28349
Rita Brown, Registrar
910-296-2500

North Carolina A&T State University
1601 E. Market St., Greensboro 27411

North Carolina State University
P.O. Box 7001, Raleigh 27695
George Dixon, Dir. of Admis.

OHIO

· Hocking College
3301 Hocking Pky., Nelsonville 45764
Candace Vancko, VP for Enrollment
800-282-4163

Ohio State University
190 N. Oval Mall, Columbus 43210

· Ohio State University-Agricultural Technical Institute
1328 Dover Rd., Wooster 44691

Wilmington College
P.O. Box 1185, Wilmington 45177
Rhonda Inderhees, Dir. of Admis.

OKLAHOMA

Cameron University
2800 W. Gore Blvd., Lawton 73505
Louise Brown, Dir. of Admis.

· Eastern Oklahoma State College
1301 W. Main St., Wilburton 74578
Jerry Smith, Registrar

Langston University
P.O. Box 907, Langston 73050

· Northeastern Oklahoma A & M College
200 I St. N.E., Miami 74354
K. Dale Patterson, Dean of Admissions

· Oklahoma Horseshoeing School
3000 N. Interstate 35, Oklahoma City 73111

Oklahoma Panhandle State University
P.O. Box 430, Goodwell 73939

Oklahoma State University, Stillwater 74078
Charles Browning, Dean

OREGON

Oregon State University, Corvallis 97333
Wallace Gibbs, Dir. of Admis.

· Treasure Valley Community College
650 College Blvd., Ontario 97914
Ron Kulm, Dir. of Admis.

PENNSYLVANIA

Delaware Valley College of Science & Agriculture
Doylestown 18901
Stephen Zenko, Dir. of Admis.

Pennsylvania State University
201 Shields Bldg., University Park 16802

RHODE ISLAND

University of Rhode Island, Kingston 02881
Robert Miller, Dean

SOUTH DAKOTA

South Dakota State University
P.O. Box 2207, Brookings 57007
Dr. David Bryant, Dean
605-688-4148
See listing under "Universities"

: Western Dakota Technical Institute
1600 Sedivy Ln., Rapid City 57701
See listing under "Career Schools"

TENNESSEE

Austin Peay State University
601 College St., Clarksville 37044

Tennessee Technological University
P.O. Box 5006, Cookeville 38505

University of Tennessee at Martin
Martin 38238
Paul Kelley, Director of Admissions
See listing under "Universities"

University of Tennessee, Knoxville
527 Andy Holt Tower, Knoxville 37996
Dr. Gordon Stanley, Dir. of Admis.

TEXAS

· North Central Texas College
1525 W. California, Gainesville 76240
Doug Willis, Dir. of Admis.

Prairie View A & M University
P.O. Box 3089, Prairie View 77446-3089
Linda S. Berry, Dir. of Admis.

Stephen F. Austin State University
P.O. Box 6078. Nacogdoches 75962

Sul Ross State University, Alpine 79832

Tarleton State University
1297 W. Washington St., Stephenville 76402

Texas A & I University
Campus Box 101, Kingsville 78363

Texas A & M University
College Station 77843

Texas Tech University, Lubbock 79409

West Texas State University
2501 4th Ave., Canyon 79016
Lila Vars, Dir. of Admis.

UTAH

Southern Utah University
351 W. Center St., Cedar City 84720
Dr. Al Tait, Dean
801-586-7921

Utah State University, Logan 84322-1600
Rod Clark, Director of Admissions
801-750-1107

VERMONT

University of Vermont
194 S. Prospect St., Burlington 05401
802-656-3370

· Vermont Technical College
Randolph Center 05061
Robert Clarke, President

VIRGINIA

Ferrum College, Ferrum 24088
Bob Bailey, Dir. of Admis.

Virginia Polytechnic Institute & State University
Blacksburg 24061
David Bousquet, Dir. of Undergraduate Admis.

Virginia State University, Petersburg 23803
Mable C. Mountcastle, Dir. of Recording

WASHINGTON

· Skagit Valley College
2405 E. College Way, Mt. Vernon 98273

· Walla Walla Community College
500 Tausick Way, Walla Walla 99362
Jerry Kjack, Director
509-527-4283
See listing under "Community and Junior Colleges"

Washington State University, Pullman 99164
Stan Berry, Dir. of Admis.

WEST VIRGINIA

West Virginia University
P.O. Box 6001, Morgantown 26506

WISCONSIN

· Chippewa Valley Technical College
620 Clairemont Ave., W., Eau Claire 54701

· Fox Valley Technical College
P.O. Box 2277, Appleton 54913

· Madison Area Technical College
3550 Anderson Rd., Madison 53704
Beverly Simone, District Director

University of Wisconsin, Madison
500 Lincoln Dr., Madison 53706

University of Wisconsin
1 University Plaza, Platteville 53818
Richard Schumacher, Dean of Admissions

University of Wisconsin, River Falls
River Falls 54022
Alan Tuchtenhagen, Dir. of Admis.

: Western Wisconsin Technical College
304 N. 6th St., La Crosse 54602

WYOMING

University of Wyoming
P.O. Box 3434, Laramie 82071
Richard Davis, Dir. of Admis.

GUAM

University of Guam
UOG Station, Mangilao 96923
Kathleen Owings, Dir. of Admis.

PUERTO RICO

University of Puerto Rico, Mayaguez Campus
P.O. Box 5000, Mayaguez 00681
Neysa Lopez, Dir. of Admis.

ALLIED HEALTH SCIENCE

This classification contains schools accredited by the American Medical Association Committee on Allied Health Education and Accreditation (†), the Accrediting Bureau of Health Education Schools (‡) and a selection of programs from institutionally accredited schools. Colleges and Universities (no dot code) generally offer four-year or advanced programs; Community and Junior Colleges (·) generally offer associate degrees; Career Schools (:) and Hospital Schools (··) generally offer diplomas. As there are over 30 disciplines in allied health, ranging from diagnostic and treatment services to medical office and laboratory technologies, the individual schools should be contacted for specifics on their program.

ALABAMA

† Auburn University at Montgomery
7300 University Dr., Montgomery 36117
H. H. Funderburk, VP

··† Baptist Medical Center
School of Medical Technology
2105 E. South Blvd., Montgomery 36116

··† Baptist Medical Centers
School of Medical Technology
P.O. Box 830605, Birmingham 35283

· Bishop State Community College
351 N. Broad St., Mobile 36603-5898
Yvonne Kennedy, President
205-690-6801

: ‡ CAPPS College
3100 Cottage Hill Rd. #500, Mobile 36606

··† Carraway Methodist Medical Center
1615 25th St., N. Birmingham 35234

··† Druid City Hospital
809 University Blvd., E., Tuscaloosa 35401

· † Gadsden State Community College
P.O. Box 227, Gadsden 35902
W. Bryan Stone, Dir. of Admis.

··† Humana Hospital
301 S. Ripley St., Montgomery 36104

··† Huntsville Hospital
School for Radiologic Technologists
101 Sivley Rd., Huntsville 35801

· † Jefferson State Community College
2601 Carson Rd., Birmingham 35215
Jim Blackburn, Dir. of Admis.

··† Mobile Infirmary Medical Center
P.O. Box 2144, Mobile 36652

Samford University
800 Lakeshore Dr., Birmingham 35229
Jim Fisk, Professor, Chemistry

: † Trenholm State Technical College
1225 Air Base Blvd., Montgomery 36108

Troy State University, Troy 36082
Brenda Riley, Dean

† Tuskegee University
Tuskegee Institute 36088

† University of Alabama
P.O. Box 870132, Tuscaloosa 35487-0132
Roy Smith, Dir. of Admis.

† University of Alabama at Birmingham
University Station, Birmingham 35294

··† University of Alabama Hospital
619 S. 19th St., Birmingham 35233

† University of Alabama in Huntsville
P.O. Box 1247, Huntsville 35899
Ron R. Koger Ed.D., Dir. of Admis.

† University of South Alabama
307 University Blvd. N., Mobile 36688

· Walker College
1411 Indiana Ave., Jasper 35501
James West, Dir. of Admis.

· † Wallace College - Dothan
Route 6, Box 62, Dothan 36303
Larry Beaty, President
205-983-3521

· † Wallace State Community College
P.O. Box 2000, Hanceville 35077

ALASKA

University of Alaska Anchorage
3211 Providence Dr., Anchorage 99508
907-786-1480

ARIZONA

: ‡ Apollo College
3870 N. Oracle Rd., Tucson 85705

· † Apollo College
8503 N. 27th Ave., Phoenix 85051

: ‡ Apollo College
630 W. Southern Ave., Mesa 85210

: ‡ Apollo College
7502 W. Thomas Rd #6, Phoenix 85033

: ‡ Arizona Academy of Medical and Dental Assistants
2575 E. Seventh Ave., Flagstaff 86004

: Arizona Academy of Medical and Dental Assistants
1020 Sandretto Dr. # A, Prescott 86301

† Arizona State University, Tempe 85287

· Arizona Western College
P.O. Box 929, Yuma 85366-0929
Bob Davis, Dir. of Admis.

: † Bryman School
4343 N. 16th St., Phoenix 85016

· † Gateway Community College
108 N. 40th St., Phoenix 85034
Bill Harris, Dean of Student Services

: Institute of Business-Medical Technology
20 E. Main St. #600, Mesa 85201
602-833-0470

: † Long Medical Institute
4126 N. Black Canyon Hwy., Phoenix 85017
Galyn Smock, Director

Northern Arizona University
P.O. Box 4092, Flagstaff 86011
Dr. Margaret Cibik, Dir. of Admis.

· † Phoenix College
1202 W. Thomas Rd., Phoenix 85013
Cheryl Axtell, Allied Health Admis.

· † Pima Community College
2202 W. Anklam Rd., Tucson 85709
Dr. Denis F. Viri, Registrar

: † Pima Medical Institute
3350 E. Grant Rd., Tucson 85716

: † Pima Medical Institute
2300 E. Broadway Rd., Tempe 85282

∴† St. Joseph's Hospital & Medical Center
350 W. Thomas Rd., Phoenix 85013
T. Abner Huff, Exec. Dir.

∴† St. Mary's Hospital
1601 W. St. Mary's Rd., Tucson 85745

: ‡ Tucson College of Business
7310 E. 22nd St., Tucson 85710
Daniel Waterman, Dir. of Admis.

† University of Arizona, Tucson 85721
Loyd Bell, Director of Admissions

University of Arizona Medical Center
1501 N. Campbell Ave., Tucson 85724

ARKANSAS

† Arkansas College
2300 Highland Rd., Batesville 72501
Jonathan M. Stroud, Dean of Admissions
800-423-2542

† Arkansas State University
P.O. Box 69, State University 72467

† Arkansas Tech University
215 W. O St., Russellville 72801

: † Arkansas Valley Vocational Technical School
P.O. Box 506, Ozark 72949

∴† **BAPTIST SCHOOLS OF ALLIED HEALTH**
11900 Colonel Glenn Rd. #10
Little Rock 72210-2820
501-223-7415
School of Coding Technology
School of Histotechnology
School of Medical Technology
School of Medical Transcription
School of Nuclear Medicine Technology
School of Radiography

: † Black River Vocational Techical School
P.O. Box 468, Pocahontas 72455

: † CARTI School of Radiation Therapy Technology
P.O. Box 5210, Little Rock 72215

: ‡ Eastern College of Health Vocations
6423 Forbing Rd., Little Rock 72209

· † Garland Co. Community College
1 College Dr., Hot Springs 71913

∴† Jefferson Regional Medical Center
1515 W. 42nd Ave., Pine Bluff 71603

John Brown University
2000 W. University, Siloam Springs 72761
Don Crandall, Director of Enrollment Management

· † Phillips County Community College
P.O. Box 785, Helena 72342
Dr. Steven Jones, President
James R. Brasel, Dean of Admissions

: † Pulaski Vocational Technical School
3000 W. Scenic Rd., North Little Rock 72118

∴† St. Edward Mercy Medical Center
School of Radiography
7301 Rogers Ave., Fort Smith 72917
Sr. Judith Marie Keith, RSM, Admin.

∴† St. Vincent Infirmary Medical Center
2 St. Vincent Circle, Little Rock 72205

· † Southern Arkansas University, El Dorado Branch
300 South West Ave., El Dorado 71730
Dr. Kermit Parks, Acad. Dean

∴† Sparks Regional Medical Center
Schools of Medical & Radiologic Tech.
1311 S. I St., Fort Smith 72901

∴† University of Arkansas & VA Medical Center
4300 W. Seventh St., Little Rock 72205

† University of Arkansas for Medical Sciences
4301 W. Markham St., Little Rock 72205

† University of Central Arkansas
201 Donaghey Ave., Conway 72035

· † Westark Community College
P.O. Box 3649, Ft. Smith 72913
Joel Stubblefield, President

CALIFORNIA

: ‡ **AMERICAN CAREER COLLEGE**
4021 Rosewood Ave., Los Angeles 90004
Ginny White, Director of Admissions
800-956-7832
Established 1978. Private. Coed. Accreditation:
ACCSCT. Enrollment: 370. Faculty: 15. Tuition: varies per program. Registration: $75. Diploma programs.
Teaching optical dispensing, pharmacy technician,
medical assisting, medical bills/health claims examiner and vocational nursing. Excellent job placement.
Short programs. Financial aid available to qualified
students.

· † American River College
4700 College Oak Ave., Sacramento 95841

: ‡ Andon College at Modesto
1314 H St., Modesto 95354

: ‡ Andon College at Stockton
1201 N. El Dorado St., Stockton 95202

· Antelope Valley College
3041 W. Avenue K, Lancaster 93534

· † Bakersfield College
1801 Panorama Dr., Bakersfield 93305
Robert M. Bruker, Dir. of Admis.

· † Butte College
3536 Butte Campus Dr., Oroville 95965
Romeo E. Morin, Dir. Admis.

· † Cabrillo College
6500 Soquel Dr., Aptos 95003

† California College for Health Sciences
222 W. 24th St., National City 91950
619-477-4800

: † California Paramedical & Technical College
3745 N. Long Beach Blvd., Long Beach 90807
310-595-6638

: ‡ California Paramedical & Technical College
4550 La Sierra Ave., Riverside 92505
800-247-1011 or 714-687-9006

† California State University, Dominguez Hills
1000 E. Victoria St., Carson 90747

California State University, Fresno
Shaw & Cedar Ave., Fresno 93710

† California State University, Northridge
18111 Nordhoff St., Northridge 91330
Ned C. Reynolds, Dir. of Admis.

† California State University-Bakersfield
9001 Stockdale Hwy., Bakersfield 93311
Dr. Homer S. Montalvo, Dir. of Admis.

· † Canada College
4200 Farm Hill Blvd., Redwood City 94061
Lois S. Chanslor, Dir. of Admissions

: † **CANCER FOUNDATION OF SANTA BARBARA**
Schools of Radiation Therapy & Nuclear Medicine
Technologies
P.O. Box 837, Santa Barbara 93102
Lindsay H. Blount, MD, Medical Director
Sofiann Langhorne, RT (T)(R), Director of Education
805-682-7300

∴† Cedars-Sinai Medical Center
8700 Beverly Blvd., Los Angeles 90048
Richard J. Plasse, Program Director

· Cerritos College
11110 E. Alondra Blvd., Norwalk 90650

· † Chabot College
25555 Hesperian Blvd., Hayward 94545

· † Chaffey College
5885 Haven Ave., Rancho Cucamonga 91737
JoAnne Edmison, Director of Admissions

∴† Children's Hospital of Los Angeles
4650 Sunset Blvd., Los Angeles 90027
Henry B. Dunlap, Exec. Director

∴† Children's Hospital of San Francisco
School of Medical Technology
3700 California St., San Francisco 94118

· Citrus College
1000 W. Foothill Blvd., Glendora 91741
Dan Angel, President

· † City College of San Francisco
1860 Hayes St., San Francisco 94117
Natalie Berg, Dean
415-561-1908

∴† City of Hope Medical Center
1500 E. Duarte Rd., Duarte 91010

· College of Alameda
School for Medical Assistants
555 Atlantic Ave., Alameda 94501

· College of Marin
835 College Ave., Kentfield 94904

† College of Osteopathic Medicine of the Pacific
309 Pomona Mall East, Pomona 91766

· College of San Mateo
Dental Assisting Program
1700 W. Hillsdale Blvd., San Mateo 94402

· † College of the Desert
43-500 Monterey Ave., Palm Desert 92260

· Compton Community College
1111 E. Artesia Blvd., Compton 90221

: † ConCorde Career Institute/Valley College
4150 Lankershim Blvd., North Hollywood 91602

: † ConCorde Career Institute
1717 S. Brookhurst, Anaheim 92804
H. Tom Smith, Director

: ‡ Concorde Career Institute
6850 Van Nuys Blvd., Van Nuys 91405

· Contra Costa College
2600 Mission Bell Dr., San Pablo 94806

· † Cosumnes River College
8401 Center Parkway, Sacramento 95823

· † Crafton Hills College
11711 Sand Canyon Rd., Yucaipa 92399
Luis S. Gomez, President
909-794-2161

· † Cypress College
9200 Valley View St., Cypress 90630

∴† Daniel Freeman Memorial Hospital
333 N. Prairie Ave., Inglewood 90301

· † DeAnza College
21250 Stevens Creek Blvd., Cupertino 95014

· Diablo Valley College
321 Golf Club Rd., Pleasant Hill 94523

∴† Drew Medical Center
1621 E. 120th St., Los Angeles 90059

· † East Los Angeles College
1301 Avenida Cesar Chavez
Monterey Park 91754

· Edutek Professional Colleges
Allied Health Division
5952 El Cajon Blvd., San Diego 92115
Carol Ruiz, Executive Director

∴† Eisenhower Medical Center
39000 Bob Hope Dr., Rancho Mirage 92270

· † El Camino College
16007 Crenshaw Blvd., Torrance 90506

∴† El Camino Hospital
2500 Grant Rd., Mountain View 94040

∴† Enloe Hospital
1531 Esplanade, Chico 95926

: † Fairgrove Adult School
15540 Fairgrove Ave., La Puente 91744

Fielding Institute
2112 Santa Barbara St., Santa Barbara 93105
Sylvia Williams, Dir. of Admis.

· † Foothill College
12345 El Monte Ave., Los Altos Hills 94022

· † Fresno City College
1101 E. University Ave., Fresno 93741
Brice Harris, President
209-442-4600

∴† Fresno Community Hospital & Medical Center
P.O. Box 1232, Fresno 93715

: ‡ Glendale Career College
1021 Grandview Ave., Glendale 91201

· † Grossmont College
8800 Grossmont College Dr., El Cajon 92020

∴† Grossmont District Hospital
5555 Grossmont Ctr. Dr., La Mesa 91942

: ‡ Health Staff Training Institute
1505 E. 17th St. #122, Santa Ana 92701

∴† Huntington Memorial Hospital
Schools of Medical & Radiologic Technology
100 Congress St., Pasadena 91105

· Institute of Business & Medical Technology
75110 St. Charles Pl. #10
Palm Desert 92211

La Sierra University
4700 Pierce St., Riverside 92505
800-874-5587

† Loma Linda University, Loma Linda 92350
Tony Valenzuela, EdD, Chrpsn.
800-422-4LLU

· † Long Beach City College
4901 E. Carson St., Long Beach 90808
J. Dawdy, Dean of Admissions & Records

· † Los Angeles City College
855 N. Vermont Ave., Los Angeles 90029
Dr. Stelle Feuers, President

∴† Los Angeles Co. Harbor-UCLA Medical Center
1000 W. Carson St., Torrance 90502

∴† Los Angeles County USC Medical Center
1200 N. State St., Los Angeles 90033

· † Los Angeles Valley College
5800 Fulton Avenue, Van Nuys 91401

: ‡ Maric College
7202 Princess View Dr., San Diego 92120

: ‡ Maric College of Medical Careers
1300 Rancheros Dr., San Marcos 92069

: ‡ Maric College of Medical Careers
1593C E. Vista Way, Vista 92084

· † Merced College
3600 M St., Merced 95348

· † Merritt College
12500 Campus Dr., Oakland 94619
Larry Gurley, Assistant Dean

· † Modesto Junior College
435 College Ave., Modesto 95397

· Monterey Peninsula College
980 Fremont Ave., Monterey 93940
David Hopkins, President

· † Mt. San Antonio College
1100 N. Grand Ave., Walnut 91789
Mental Health Technology
Radiologic Technology
Respiratory Technology
Emergency Medical Technology
Karen Meyers, Division Dean, Health Sciences

· † Napa Valley College
2277 Napa-Vallejo Hwy., Napa 94558
Delores Smith, Asst. Dean of Admissions
707-253-3000

: † **NATIONAL EDUCATION CENTER-BRYMAN CAMPUS**
For Medical & Dental Assistants
5350 Atlantic Ave., Long Beach 90805
Roger Gugelmeyer, Director
310-422-6007

: ‡ National Education Center-Bryman Campus
20835 Sherman Way, Winnetka 91306
Don Hyde, Director

: † National Education Center-Bryman Campus
3505 N. Hart Ave., Rosemead 91770

: † National Education Center-Bryman Campus
731 Market St., San Francisco 94103

: † National Education Center-Bryman Campus
4212 W. Artesia Blvd., Torrance 90504

: † National Education Center-Bryman Campus
2015 Naglee Ave., San Jose 95128

: † National Education Center-Bryman Campus
1732 Reynolds St., Irvine 92714

· † Ohlone College
P.O. Box 3909, Fremont 94539

· † **ORANGE COAST COLLEGE**
P.O. Box 5005, Costa Mesa 92628
See listing under "Community and Junior Colleges"

· Palomar Community College
1140 W. Mission Rd., San Marcos 92069

· † Pasadena City College
1570 E. Colorado Blvd., Pasadena 91106

·.† Peninsula Hospital
1783 El Camino Real, Burlingame 94010

·.† Radio Association of Sacramento Medical Group
1800 I St., Sacramento 95814

· Rio Hondo College
3600 Workman Mill Rd., Whittier 90601

· Sacramento City College
3835 Freeport Blvd., Sacramento 95822

·.† Sacramento Medical Foundation Blood Bank
1625 Stockton Blvd., Sacramento 95816

·.† St. John's Hospital
333 N. F Street, Oxnard 93030

·.† St. John's Hospital & Health Center
1328 22nd St., Santa Monica 90404

·.† St. Joseph Hospital
1100 W. Stewart Dr., Orange 92668

·.† St. Mary Medical Center
1050 Linden Ave., Long Beach 90813

·.† San Bernardino County Medical Center
School of Radiologic Technology
24600 Arrowhead Springs Rd.
San Bernardino 92414

· † San Diego Mesa College
7250 Mesa College Dr., San Diego 92111

† San Francisco State University
1600 Holloway Ave., San Francisco 94132
Corwin Bjonerud, Dir. of Admis.

·.† San Joaquin General Hospital
Schools of Medical & Radiologic Technology
P.O. Box 1020, Stockton 95201
Michael N. Smith, Director

· ‡ San Joaquin Valley College
201 New Stine Rd., Bakersfield 93309

· ‡ San Joaquin Valley College
3333 N. Bond, Fresno 93726

· ‡ San Joaquin Valley College
8400 W. Mineral King Ave., Visalia 93291
Robert Perry, President

·.† San Jose Medical Center
School of Medical Technology
675 E. Santa Clara St., San Jose 95112
P. Vincent, MD, Director

† San Jose State University
1 Washington Sq., San Jose 95192

· † Santa Barbara City College
721 Cliff Dr., Santa Barbara 93109
805-965-0581

·.† Santa Barbara Cottage & General Hospital
P.O. Box 689, Santa Barbara 93102

· † Santa Monica College
School for Respiratory Therapists
1900 Pico Blvd., Santa Monica 90405
Mel Welch, Director
See listing under "Community and Junior Colleges"

· Santa Rosa Junior College
1501 Mendocino Ave., Santa Rosa 95401
Joe Hagerty, Coordinator

·.† Scripps Clinic & Research Foundation
10666 N. Torrey Pines Rd., La Jolla 92037

·.† Scripps Memorial Hospital
9888 Genesee Ave., La Jolla 92037

·.† Sharp Memorial Hospital
7901 Frost St., San Diego 92123

· † Simi Valley Adult Education
3192 Los Angeles Ave., Simi Valley 93065

· † Skyline College, 3300 College Dr., San Bruno 94066
James C. Wyatt, President

† Stanford University, Stanford 94305

·.† Sutter Community Hospitals
2820 L Street, Sacramento 95816

: ‡ Technical Health Careers School
11603 S. Western Ave., Los Angeles 90047

: United Health Careers Institute
570 W. 4th St. #907, San Bernardino 92401
Paula Hermann, Dir. of Admis.
714-884-8891

† University of California, Davis
376 Mrak Hall, Davis 95616

† University of California, San Francisco
Parnassus & 3rd Ave., San Francisco 94143

† University of California-Davis
2315 Stockton Blvd., Sacramento 95817
Baldwin G. Lamson, M.D., Act'g. Dir.

† UCLA Center for the Health Sciences
10833 Le Conte Ave., Los Angeles 90024

University of California-Irvine Med. Ctr.
101 City Blvd., W., Orange 92668

† University of Southern California
Health Science Campus, Los Angeles 90033
Stephen Ryan, Interim Dean

·.† Valley Childrens Hospital
3151 N. Millbrook Ave., Fresno 93703

·.† VA Medical Center
150 Muir Rd., Martinez 94553

·.† Veterans Administration Medical Center
5901 E. Seventh St., Long Beach 90822

·.† Veterans Administration Medical Center
16111 Plummer St, Sepulveda 91343

· † Victor Valley College
18422 Bear Valley Rd., Victorville 92392-9699

: ‡ Western Career College
8909 Folsom Blvd., Sacramento 95826
916-361-1660

: ‡ Western Career College
170 Bayfair Mall, San Leandro 94578
510-276-3888

·.† West Los Angeles VA Medical Center
Wilshire & Sawtelle Blvds., Los Angeles 90073

· † West Valley College
14000 Fruitvale Ave., Saratoga 95070

Whittier College
13406 Philadelphia St., Whittier 90601
310-907-4238

· † Yuba College
2088 N. Beale Rd., Marysville 95901
Susan Singhas, Dean of Admissions,
Counseling and Records

COLORADO

Adams State College, Alamosa 81102
Cheryl Billingsley, Dir. of Admis.
800-824-6494

· † Aims Community College
P.O. Box 69, Greeley 80632
William Green, Registrar

· † Arapahoe Community College
P.O. Box 9002, Littleton 80160
James F. Weber, President

· **BEL-REA INSTITUTE OF ANIMAL TECHNOLOGY**
1681 S. Dayton, Denver 80231
303-751-8700 or 800-950-8001
See listing under "Career Schools"

: † Boulder Valley Area Vocational Technical Center
6600 E. Arapahoe, Boulder 80303

·.† Colorado Association of Paramedical Education
9191 Grant St., Thornton 80229

Colorado College
14 E. Cache La Poudre, Colorado Springs 80903
Terry Swenson, Dir. of Admis.

· Colorado Northwestern Community College
Dental Hygiene
500 Kennedy Dr., Rangely 81648
Pat Kalahar, Dir. Marketing/Recruitment
800-562-1105

† Colorado State University
102 Administration Building, Fort Collins 80523
Mary Ontireros, Dir. of Admissions

· † Community College of Denver
1111 W. Colfax Ave., Denver 80204

· ‡ Denver Technical College
225 S. Union Blvd., Colorado Springs 80910
Oscar Adams, Dir. of Admis.

· ‡ Denver Technical College
925 S. Niagara St., Denver 80224
Oscar Adams, Dir. of Admis.

: † Emily Griffith Opportunity School
1250 Welton St., Denver 80204-2197
Dr. Mary Ann Parthum, Principal
303-572-8218
See listing under "Career Schools"

· † Front Range Community College
Dental Assisting Program
3645 W. 112th Ave., Westminster 80030

· Heritage College of Health Careers
12 Lakeside Ln., Denver 80212
Larry Camack, Director

·.† Lutheran Medical Center
8300 W. 38th Ave., Wheat Ridge 80033

: ‡ Medical Careers Training Center
4020 S. College Ave., Fort Collins 80525
Richard Laub, President

·.† Memorial Hospital
School of Medical & Radiologic Technology
1400 E. Boulder St., Colorado Springs 80909
Marshall Petring, Executive Director

† Mesa State College
P.O. Box 2647, Grand Junction 81502
Sherri Pe'a, Dir. of Admis.

· Morgan Community College
17800 Road 20, Fort Morgan 80701
Kurtis Armstrong, Dir. of Admis.

·.† North Colorado Medical Center
School of Medical Technology
1801 16th St., Greeley 80631

· Parks College
9065 Grant St., Denver 80229
Randall C. Ricks, Dir. of Admis.
303-457-2757

·.† Parkview Episcopal Hospital
400 W. 16th St., Pueblo 81003

·.† Penrose Hospital
2215 N. Cascade Ave., Colorado Springs 80907

: † Pickens Technical Center
500 Buckley Rd., Aurora 80011

· Pikes Peak Community College
5675 S. Academy Blvd.
Colorado Springs 80906-5498
Roberta Erickson, Dir. of Admis.
See listing under "Community and Junior Colleges"

: ‡ Pima Medical Institute
7290 Samuel Dr. #200, Denver 80221
Sue Anderson, Director

: ‡ PPI Health Careers School
2345 N. Academy Blvd., Colorado Springs 80909
719-596-7400

·.† Presbyterian St. Luke's Center
for Health Sciences Education
601 E. 19th Ave., Denver 80203

·.† Presbyterian/Saint Lukes Center
for Health Science Education
School of Medical Technology
1719 E. 19th Ave., Denver 80218
Karen Myers, Program Director
303-839-6485

: Pueblo College of Business & Technology
330 Lake Ave., Pueblo 81004
719-545-3100

· † Pueblo Community College
900 W. Orman Ave., Pueblo 81004
Victor Tenorio, Dir. of Admis.

† Regis University
3333 Regis Blvd., Denver 80221
Robert Blust, Director of Admissions

·.† St. Anthony Hospital Systems
4231 W. 16th Ave., Denver 80204

·.† Swedish Medical Center
501 E. Hampden Ave., Englewood 80110

† University of Colorado Health Sciences Center
4200 E. 9th Ave., Denver 80262
Richard D. Krugman, MD, Dean

University of Northern Colorado, Greeley 80639
Vincent Scalia, Dean
303-351-2877

University of Southern Colorado
2200 Bonforte Blvd., Pueblo 81001

CONNECTICUT

·.† American Red Cross Blood Services
209 Farmington Ave., Farmington 06032

· Briarwood College
2279 Mt. Vernon Rd., Southington 06489
Debra La Roche, Dir. of Admis.

·.† Bridgeport Hospital
267 Grant St., Bridgeport 06610
Frank Crane, Pres.

·.† **DANBURY HOSPITAL**
see our ad page 537

·.† Hartford Hospital
P.O. Box 5037, Hartford 06102
Angela Callahan, Dir. of Admis.

· † Housatonic Community College
510 Barnum Ave., Bridgeport 06608
Stephen Serman, Dir. of Admissions

·.† Lawrence & Memorial Hospitals
365 Montauk Ave., New London 06320

· † Manchester Community College
P.O. Box 1046, Manchester 06045
William E. Vincent, President

·.† Manchester Memorial Hospital
School for Radiologic Technology
71 Haynes St., Manchester 06040
Frances Dressler, AS, RTR, Program Director

· † Mattatuck Community College
750 Chase Parkway, Waterbury 06708
Dr. Richard Sanders, President

· † Middlesex Community College
100 Training Hill Rd., Middletown 06457
Robert A. Chapman, President

∴† Morse School of Business
275 Asylum St., Hartford 06103
Michael S. Taub, President

∴† Mt. Sinai Hospital
School for Radiologic Technologists
500 Blue Hills Ave., Harford 06112
H. Moskowitz, MD, Program Director

∴† New Britain General Hospital
100 Grand St., New Britain 06052

∴† Norwalk Hospital
24 Stevens St., Norwalk 06850

† **QUINNIPIAC COLLEGE**
275 Mount Carmel Ave., Hamden 06518
John Lahey, President
Joan Isaac Mohr, VP and Dean of Admissions
Established 1929. Private. Coed. Accreditation:
NEASC. Tuition: $11,250. Room and board: $5,790.
Enrollment: 2,583 boarding, 3,444 day. Faculty 333.
Degrees: BA, BS, MAT, MBA, MHS, MPS. Library:
290,000 volumes. 30 buildings on 170 acres. Gym.
Suburban location at the base of Sleeping Giant State
Park, close to New Haven and Yale University. Con-
venient to New York City, Boston, and Upper New
England. Building a new $7 million School of Busi-
ness Center.

† Sacred Heart University
5151 Park Ave., Fairfield 06432-1000
Dr. Anthony J. Cernera, President

∴† St. Vincent's Medical Center
2800 Main St., Bridgeport 06606

· † South Central Community College
60 Sargent Dr., New Haven 06511
Dr. Antonio Perez, President

∴† **STAMFORD HOSPITAL**
School of Radiologic Technology
P.O. Box 9317, Stamford 06904
Dorothy Saia, BS, RT, Program Director

University of Bridgeport
126 Park Ave., Bridgeport 06601
Andrew G. Nelson, Dean Admis./Financial Aid
203-576-4552
See listing under "Universities"

University of Connecticut, Storrs 06268
Glenda Price, Dean

† University of Connecticut Health Center
Farmington 06032

† University of Hartford
200 Bloomfield Ave., West Hartford 06117
Richard Zeiser, Dir. of Admis.
See listing under "Universities"

∴† **VETERAN'S MEMORIAL MEDICAL CENTER
SCHOOL OF RADIOGRAPHY**
P.O. Box 1009, Meriden 06450
Linda E. Gejda, RT(R), Program Director
203-238-8270

∴† Waterbury Hospital
School of Medical Technology
64 Robbins St., Waterbury 06708
Susan O'Brien, MS, MT (ASCP), Program Director

∴† Windham Community Memorial Hospital
112 Mansfield Ave., Willimantic 06226

† Yale University
60 College St., New Haven 06519

DELAWARE

· † Delaware Technical & Community College
School for Medical Laboratory Technicians
P.O. Box 610, Georgetown 19947

· † Delaware Technical & Community College
333 Shipley St., Wilmington 19801
William Faucett, Director

∴† St. Francis Hospital
701 N. Clayton St., Wilmington 19805

† University of Delaware, Newark 19711

DISTRICT OF COLUMBIA

† Catholic University of America
620 Michigan Ave. N.E., Washington 20064
Robert J. Talbot, Dir. of Admis. & Fin. Aid.

† Georgetown University
37th and O Sts., N.W., Washington 20057
Dr. Joseph A. Chalmers, Dean of Admis. & Rec.

† George Washington University
Washington 20052

† Howard University
2400 6th St., N.W., Washington 20059
James E. Cheek, President

: ‡ National Education Center-Capitol Hill Campus
810 First St., N.E., Washington 20002

† University of the District of Columbia
Georgia Ave.-Harvard St. Campus
1100 Harvard St., N.W., Washington 20009

University of the District of Columbia
Van Ness Campus
4200 Connecticut Ave., N.W., Washington 20008

∴† Walter Reed Medical Center
6825 16th St., N.W., Washington 20307

∴· Washington Hospital Center
School of Medical Technology
110 Irving St., N.W., Washington 20010
Dunlop Ecker, Chief Exec. Officer

FLORIDA

: ‡ American Medical Training Institute
7360 SW 167th St., Miami 33157
James Brodie, Administrator

∴† Baptist Medical Centers
800 Prudential Dr., Jacksonville 32207

Barry University
11300 N.E. 2nd Ave., Miami Shores 33161
Robin Ray Roberts, Dean of Admissions

∴† Bayfront Medical Center
School of Medical Technology
701 6th St., S., St. Petersburg 33701

: ‡ Beacon Career Institute
2900 N.W. 183rd St., Opa Locka 33056

∴† Bethesda-Kennedy Hospital
School for Medical Lab Technology
2815 S. Seacrest Blvd., Boynton Beach 33425

† Bethune-Cookman College
640 Mary McLeod Bethune Blvd.
Daytona Beach 32114

· † Brevard Community College
1519 Clearlake Rd., Cocoa 32922
Maxwell C. King, President

· † Broward Community College
225 E. Las Olas Blvd., Ft. Lauderdale 33301

· † Broward Community College
225 E. Las Olas Blvd., Ft. Lauderdale 33301

∴· † Central Florida Blood Bank
SBB Program Master of Health
32 W. Gore St., Orlando 32806

· † Central Florida Community College
P.O. Box 1388, Ocala 34478
Casius Pealer, Dir. of Admis.

· † Daytona Beach Community College
P.O. Box 2811, Daytona Beach 32120

· † Edison Community College
8099 College Pky., Fort Myers 33919
Mailing address: P.O. Box 60210
Fort Myers 33906-6210
Sandra Fahey, Dir. of Admis. and Records

· † Erwin Vocational Technical Center
2010 E. Hillsborough Ave., Tampa 33610

† Florida A & M University, Tallahassee 32307

· † Florida Community College
501 State St., W., Jacksonville 32202
E. Guy Kerby, Dir. of Admis. and Student Aid

· Florida Community College at Jacksonville
North Campus
4501 Capper Rd., Jacksonville 32218

∴· † Florida Hospital Medical Center
601 E. Rollins, Orlando 32803

: ‡ Florida Institute of Ultrasound
8800 University Pky., Ste. 4A, Pensacola 32514

† Florida International University
Tamiami Trail, Miami 33199

· † Gulf Coast Community College
5230 Hwy. 98, W., Panama City 32401
Roy Smith, Dir. of Admis. and Records

∴· † Halifax Medical Center
P.O Box 2830, Daytona Beach 32120
Richard W. Dodd, M.D., Director

· † Hillsborough Community College
P.O. Box 31127, Tampa 33631

· † Indian River Community College
School for Radiologic Technologists
3209 Virginia Ave., Fort Pierce 34981

∴· † Jackson Memorial Medical Center
1611 N.W. 12th Ave., Miami 33136

Jones College
5353 Arlington Expy., Jacksonville 32211
Dorothy D. Jones, Chief Executive Officer

· ‡ Keiser College of Technology
1500 N.W. 49th St.,
Fort Lauderdale 33309

· ‡ Keiser College of Technology
701 S. Babcock St., Melbourne 32901

· † Lake City Community College
R.R. 3, Box 7, Lake City 32055

: ‡ Lake County Area Vocational-Technical Center
2001 Kurt St., Eustis 32726

∴· † Lakeland Regional Medical Center
1400 Lakeland Hills Blvd., Lakeland 33805

∴· † Lee Memorial Hospital
School of Radiologic Technology
School of Diagnostic Medical Sonography
2776 Cleveland Ave., Fort Myers 33901
Lynda David, Education Coordinator

· † Lindsey Hopkins Technical Education Center
750 N.W. 20th St., Miami 33127

: † Manatee Area Vocational-Technical Center
5603 34th St., Bradenton 34210

· † Manatee Community College
Radiologic Technology / Respiratory Care
5840 26th St., W., Bradenton 34207

· † Marion County School of Radiologic Technology
438 S.W. 3rd St., Ocala 34474

: † **MEDICAL ARTS TRAINING CENTER**
441 S. State Road 7 #4, Margate 33068
800-334-6282

· · Miami-Dade Community College
11011 S.W. 104 St., Miami 33176

∴· † Mt. Sinai Medical Center
4300 Alton Rd., Miami Beach 33140

: ‡ National School of Technology
4355 W. 16th Ave., Hialeah 33012

: ‡ National School of Technology, Inc.
Two locations:
16150 N.E. 17th Ave., North Miami Beach 33162
4355 W. 16th Ave., Hialeah 33012

Orlando College - North
5500 Diplomat Circle, Orlando 32810

∴· † Orlando Regional Medical Center
1414 S. Kuhl Ave., Orlando 32806

· † Palm Beach Community College
Dental Assisting Program
4200 S. Congress Ave., Lake Worth 33461

· † Pasco-Hernando Community College
2401 State Hwy. 41, No., Dade City 33525
Milton O. Jones, President

· † Pensacola Junior College
1000 College Blvd., Pensacola 32504
Horace E. Hartsell, President

: † Pinellas Technical Education Center
901 34th St., S., St. Petersburg 33711

· † Polk Community College
999 Ave. H, N.E., Winter Haven 33881
Marly Vanleer Peck, President

· † Radiation Therapy Regional Centers
7341 Gladiolus Dr., Fort Myers 33908

: ‡ Ross Technical Institute
1490 S. Military Tr. #11, West Palm Beach 33415

DANBURY HOSPITAL
24 Hospital Avenue
Danbury 06810

ALLIED HEALTH PROGRAMS

DEPARTMENT OF EDUCATION & RESEARCH
(203)731-8609

DIAGNOSTIC ULTRASOUND TECHNOLOGY
Mena Moreira, Program Director
(203)797-7179

MEDICAL CODING
Gary Goetz, Program Director
(203)797-7693

MEDICAL TECHNOLOGY
Carol Tully, Program Director
(203)797-7522

MEDICAL TRANSCRIPTION
Gary Goetz, Program Director
(203)797-7693

NUCLEAR MEDICINE TECHNOLOGY
John Cannaverde, Program Director
(203)797-7428

RADIATION THERAPY
Suzanne McLean, Program Director
(203)797-7528

RADIOLOGIC TECHNOLOGY
Kris Johnston, Program Director
(203)797-7182

SURGICAL TECHNOLOGY
Mary Janell, Program Director
(203)797-7724

∴† St. Augustine Technical Center
2980 Collins Ave., Saint Augustine   32095

∴† St. Joseph's Hospital
P.O. Box 4227, Tampa   33677

∴† St. Mary's Hospital
901 45th St., West Palm Beach   33407

· † St. Petersburg Junior College
P.O. Box 13489, St. Petersburg   33733
Dr. Carl M. Kuttler, Jr., President

∴† St. Vincent's Medical Center
2708 Saint Johns Ave., Jacksonville   32205

· † Santa Fe Community College
3000 N.W. 83rd St., Gainesville   32606
Lawrence W. Tyree, President

: † Sarasota County Vocational Technical Center
4748 Beneva Rd., Sarasota   34233

· † Seminole Community College
100 Weldon Blvd., Sanford   32773

: † Sheridan Vocational-Technical Center
5400 Sheridan St., Hollywood   33021
305-985-3220

· † South College
1760 N. Congress Ave., West Palm Beach   33409

∴† Southwest Florida Blood Bank
P.O. Box 2125, Tampa   33601

Stetson University
401 N. Woodland Blvd., De Land   32720
Gary A. Meadows, Dean of Admis.

· † Tallahassee Community College
444 Appleyard Dr., Tallahassee   32304
Dr. Fred W. Turner, President

∴† Tallahassee Memorial Hospital,
School of Medical Technology
1300 Miccosukee Rd., Tallahassee   32308
M. J. Mustian, Executive Director

Tampa College
3319 W. Hillsborough Ave., Tampa   33614
David Zorn, President

Tampa College - Pinellas
15064 U.S. Hwy. 19 N., Clearwater   34624
Mark A. Page, President
813-530-9495

∴† Tampa General Hospital
School of Medical Technology
P.O. Box 1289, Tampa   33601
Laura Ferguson, BSMT (ASCP), Program Director

: ‡ Ultrasound Diagnostic School
2760 E. Atlantic Blvd., Pompano Beach   33062

: ‡ Ultrasound Diagnostic School
5804 E. Breckenridge Pky., Tampa   33610

∴† University Medical Center of Jacksonville
655 W. 8th St., Jacksonville   32209

† University of Central Florida
P.O. Box 25000, Orlando   32816

† University of Florida
226 Tigert Hall, Gainesville   32611

† University of Miami
P.O. Box 248006, Coral Gables   33124

† University of West Florida
11000 University Pky., Pensacola   32514

· † Valencia Community College, West Campus
P.O. Box 3028, Orlando   32802
Charles H. Drosin, Registrar

∴† West Boca Medical Center
21644 State Rd. 7, Boca Raton   33428

: † Winter Park Adult Vocational Center
901 Webster Ave., Winter Park   32789
Dr. Kaye Chastain, Director

GEORGIA

: † Albany Technical Institute
1021 Lowe Rd., Albany   31701

∴† American Red Cross Blood Services
1925 Monroe Dr., N.E., Atlanta   30324

† Armstrong State College
11935 Abercorn St., Savannah   31419
Kim West, Director of Admissions

· † Athens Area Technical Institute
U.S. Hwy. 29, N., Athens   30601

: † Atlanta Area Technical Institute
1560 Stewart Ave., S.W., Atlanta   30310
Sandra S. Puckett, Dept. Chairperson

: † Atlanta College of Medical and Dental Careers
1400 W. Peachtree St., N.W., Atlanta   30309
Gary Vance, Dir. of Admis.

· † Augusta Technical Institute
3116 Dean Bridge Rd., Augusta   30906

· † Brunswick College
3700 Altama Ave., Brunswick   31520-3644
Dorothy L. Lord, President

† Clark Atlanta University
240 James Brawley Dr., S.W., Atlanta   30314
Thomas W. Cole, President

† Columbus College
3600 Algonquin Dr., Columbus   31907

· † Columbus Technical Institute
928 45th St., Columbus   31904

∴† Crawford Long Hospital of Emory University
550 Peachtree St. N.E., Atlanta   30308

· † Dalton College
213 College Dr., Dalton   30720
Dr. Derrell Roberts, President

· † Darton College
2400 Gillionville Rd., Albany   31707

∴† De Kalb Medical Center
2701 N. Decatur Rd., Decatur   30033

: † DeKalb Technical Institute
495 N. Indian Creek Dr., Clarkston   30021
Velon Gray, Dir. of Admissions

† Emory University
1462 Clifton Rd., Atlanta   30322

† Emory University Hospital
1364 Clifton Rd., N.E., Atlanta   30322
R. D. Woodruff, M.D., Program Director

∴† Floyd Medical Center
P.O. Box 233, Rome   30162

· Gainesville College
P.O. Box 1358, Gainesville   30503
Carol S. Nobles, Dir. of Admis.
404-535-6241

∴† Georgia Baptist Medical Center
300 Blvd., N.E., Atlanta   30312
Robert E. DeLashmutt, M.D., Director

Georgia College
231 W. Hancock St., Milledgeville   31061
912-453-5004

: ‡ Georgia Medical Institute
40 Marietta St. N.W. #1333, Atlanta   30303
404-525-3272

† Georgia State University
University Plaza, Atlanta   30303
Ernest Beals, Dean of Admissions

∴† Grady Memorial Hospital
80 Butler St., S.E., Atlanta   30303

: ‡ Griffin Institute
501 Varsity Rd., Griffin   30223

: † Gwinnett Technical Institute
P.O. Box 1505, Lawrenceville   30246

∴† Kennestone Regional Medical Center
737 Church St., Marietta   30060

: † Lanier Technical Institute
P.O. Box 58, Oakwood   30566

: † Macon Technical Institute
3300 Macon Tech. Dr., Macon   31206

∴† Medical Center
710 Center St., Columbus   31901

∴† Medical Center of Central Georgia
School of Radiologic Technology
777 Hemlock St., Macon   31201
Barbara Wright, RT (ARRT), Program Director

† Medical College of Georgia
1120 15th St., Augusta   30901
Elizabeth Griffin, Dir. of Undergraduate Admis.

: ‡ NEC Bryman Campus
40 Marietta St. N.W. Ste. 8, Atlanta   30303

: † North Georgia Technical Institute
P.O. Box 65, Clarkesville   30523

: † Okefenokee Technical Institute
1701 Carswell Ave., Waycross   31503

∴† St. Joseph's Hospital
5665 Peachtree-Dunwoody Rd., Atlanta   30342
D. F. Truesdell, Prog. Dir.

· † Savannah Technical Institute
5717 White Bluff Rd., Savannah   31405

· † South College
709 Mall Blvd., Savannah   31406

: † Thomas Technical Institute
P.O. Box 1578, Thomasville   31799

: ‡ Ultrasound Diagnostic School
13 Corporate Square Office Park, Atlanta   30329

∴† University Hospital
1350 Walton Way, Augusta   30901

: † Valdosta Technical Institute
4089 Val Tech Rd., Valdosta   31602
James Bridges, President

: † West Georgia Technical Institute
303 Fort Dr., La Grange   30240

HAWAII

· † Kapiolani Community College
4303 Diamond Head Rd., Honolulu   96816

: ‡ Medical Assisting School of Hawaii
1149 Bethel St. #606, Honolulu   96813

∴† St. Francis Hospital
2230 Liliha St., Honolulu   96817

† University of Hawaii at Manoa
2500 Campus Rd., Honolulu   96822

IDAHO

: ‡ American Institute of Health Technology
6600 Emerald, Boise   83704

† Boise State University
1910 University Dr., Boise   83725

: Eastern Idaho Technical College
Dental Assisting Program
2299 E. 17th St., Idaho Falls   83404
Mary Mueller, Instructor

† Idaho State University
P.O. Box 8270, Pocatello   83209

∴† St. Alphonsus Regional Medical Center
School of Medical Technology
1055 N. Curtis Rd., Boise   83706
Sandra Perotto, Program Director

∴† St. Luke's Hospital
130 W. Bannock St., Boise   83702
E. E. Gilbertson, Admin.

ILLINOIS

Aurora University
347 S. Gladstone Ave., Aurora   60506
Peter Pitts, Dir. of Admis.

· † Belleville Area College
2500 Carlyle Rd., Belleville   62221

· † Black Hawk College, Quad Cities Campus
6600 34th Ave., Moline   61265
Barton Schiermeyer, Dir. of Admis.

∴† Blessing Hospital
1005 Broadway St., Quincy   62301
Lawrence L. Swearingen, Admin.

∴† **BLOOMINGTON-NORMAL SCHOOL OF RADIOGRAPHY**
900 Franklin Ave., Normal   61761
Beth Kuhfuss, MS, RT (R) ARRT, Program Director
309-452-2834

· † Carl Sandburg College
2232 S. Lake Storey Rd., Galesburg   61401

∴† Central Du Page Hospital
0N025 Winfield Rd., Winfield   60190
Diane Fleming, Program Director

· † Chicago City-Wide College
226 W. Jackson Blvd., Chicago   60606

† Chicago State University
9501 S. King Dr., Chicago   60628

∴† Christ Hospital
4440 95th St., Oak Lawn   60453

· † College of Du Page
Health & Public Services Division
425 22nd St., Glen Ellyn   60137
Betsy Cabitit-Segal, Assoc. Dean

· † College of Lake County
19351 W. Washington St., Grayslake   60030
John O. Hunter, President

: Commonwealth Business College
1527 47th Ave., Moline   61265
Don Watson, Director
309-762-2100

∴† Cook County Hospital
School of Radiologic Technology
1825 W. Harrison St., Chicago   60612
John Robinson, Director Education

∴† Decatur Memorial Hospital
School of Radiologic Technology
2300 N. Edward St., Decatur   62526
217-876-8121 ext. 2331

De Paul University
1 E. Jackson Blvd., Chicago   60604
Thomas D. Abrahamson, Dean of Admissions
See listing under "Universities"

Eastern Illinois University, Charleston   61920
Robert Bates, Chrpsn.
See listing under "Universities"

∴† Edward Hines, Jr., VA Hospital
5th Ave. & Roosevelt Rd., Hines   60141

∴† Foster G. McGaw Hospital, Loyola University
School of Medical Technology
2160 S. 1st Ave., Maywood   60153
Jackie Streid, MEd, MT(ASCP), Program Director
708-216-8939

∴† Franciscan Medical Center
School of Radiologic Technology
2701 17th St., Rock Island   61201
Elaine Foht, Program Director

· ‡ Gem City College
700 State St., Quincy   62301
R. Hagenah, President

† Governors State University
1 University Pky., University Park   60466
Richard Pride, Dir. of Admis.

· † Harry S. Truman College
1145 W. Wilson Ave., Chicago   60640
Dr. Wallace B. Appelson, President

∴† Hinsdale Sanitarium & Hospital
120 N. Oak St., Hinsdale   60521

∴† Holy Cross Hospital
2701 W. 68th St., Chicago   60629

Illinois Benedictine College
5700 College Rd., Lisle   60532

· † Illinois Central College
One College Dr., East Peoria   61635
Dr. Thomas K. Thomas, President

: Illinois Medical Training Center
162 N. State St., Chicago   60601

† Illinois State University
  212 N. School St., Normal 61761

· Illinois Valley Community College
  R.R. 1, Oglesby 61348
  Dr. Alfred Wisgoski, President

·† John A. Logan College
  R.R. 2, Carterville 62918
  Dr. Ray Hancock, President

·† Kankakee Community College
  P.O. Box 888, Kankakee 60901
  Lilburn H. Horton, Jr., President

·† **KASKASKIA COLLEGE**
  27210 College Rd., Centralia 62801
  618-532-1981 or 800-642-0859 (Illinois)
  Raymond D. Woods, President
  Marilyn Brookman, PhD, College Dean
  Constance Stohlman, Director of Admissions,
  Public Relations, and Resource Development
    Kaskaskia College is situated on a beautifully
  wooded tract of land consisting of 190 acres. Its brick
  and frame buildings provide 228,830 square feet of
  space for college facilities. Kaskaskia College is fully
  accredited by NCACS, ADA, AMA, NLN, IBE, ICCB,
  and IBHE. The College is recognized and approved by
  the bureau of Veterans Affairs and is authorized under
  Federal law to enroll non-immigrant alien students.
  In district tuition and fees are $33.75 per semester
  credit hour. Degrees: AA, AS, AAS, and AGS. University
  transfer programs, pre-professional, liberal arts,
  courses offered days, evenings, and weekends. Training
  in career fields. State and Federal financial aid
  programs available.

·† Kishwaukee College
  21193 Malta Rd., Malta 60150
  Dr. Walter Lamar Fly, President

· Lake Land College
  Dental Assisting & Hygiene Programs
  5001 Lake Land Blvd., Mattoon 61938

·† Lewis & Clark Community College
  5800 Godfrey Rd., Godfrey 62035
  J. Neil Admire, President

LEWIS UNIVERSITY
  Rt. 53, Romeoville 60441
  Irish O'Reilly, Director of Admissions
  See listing under "Universities"

·† LifeSource
  1255 N. Greenview Ave., Chicago 60622

·† Lincoln Land Community College
  Shepherd Rd., Springfield 62794-9256
  Ron Gregoire, Dir. of Admis.
  Information: 800-727-4161

·† Louis A. Weiss Memorial Hospital
  School of Medical & Radiologic Technology
  4646 N. Marine Dr., Chicago 60640
  James Champer, Dir. of Admis.

Loyola University
  Dental Assisting Education Program
  2160 S. 1st Ave., Maywood 60153

·† McDonough District Hospital
  School of Radiologic Technology
  525 E. Grant St., Macomb 61455
  Richard Hart, Program Director

·† Malcolm X College
  1900 W. Van Buren St., Chicago 60612
  Clifford Fields, Dean, Career Programs

:‡ Medical Careers Institute
  116 S. Michigan Ave., Chicago 60603

·† Methodist Medical Center of Illinois
  School of Medical Technology
  221 N.E. Glen Oak Ave., Peoria 61603
  J. Sutherland, M.A., M.T. (ASCP), Program Director

·† Michael Reese Hospital & Medical Center
  Lakeshore Dr. at 31st St., Chicago 60616

·† Midstate College
  244 S.W. Jefferson St., Peoria 61602
  R. Dale Bunch, President
  309-673-6365

· Montay College
  3750 W. Peterson Ave., Chicago 60659
  Scott Dalhouse, Dir. of Admis.

·† Moraine Valley Community College
  10900 S. 88th Ave., Palos Hills 60465
  Dr. Vernon Crawley, President

· Morton College
  3801 S. Central Ave., Cicero 60650
  Charles P. Ferro, President

† National-Louis University
  2840 Sheridan Ave., Evanston 60201

Northern Illinois University, De Kalb 60115

·† Northwest Community Hospital
  School of Radiologic Technology
  800 W. Central Rd., Arlington Heights 60005
  G. Awad, Program Director

Northwestern University
  303 E. Chicago Ave., Chicago 60611

·† Oakton Community College
  1600 E. Golf Rd., Des Plaines 60016
  Constance Churchill, Dean

·† Olney Central College
  305 Northwest St., Olney 62450
  Dr. Charles R. Novak, President

·† Parkland College
  2400 W. Bradley Ave., Champaign 61821-1899
  217-351-2208 or 800-346-8089

· Prairie State College
  Dental Assisting Program
  P.O. Box 487, Chicago Heights 60411
  Beverly McKeown, Coordinator

Quincy College
  1800 College Ave., Quincy 62301
  Fr. Michael Lanning, O.F.M., Dir. of Admis.

·:† **RAVENSWOOD HOSPITAL MEDICAL CENTER
SCHOOL OF RADIOLOGIC TECHNOLOGY**
  4550 N. Winchester Ave., Chicago 60640
  Philis George, Program Director

† Robert Morris College
  180 N. La Salle St., Chicago 60601

·:† Rockford Memorial Hospital
  School of Radiography
  2400 N. Rockton Ave., Rockford 61103

·† Rock Valley College
  3301 N. Mulford Rd., Rockford 61114

ROOSEVELT UNIVERSITY
  430 S. Michigan Ave., Chicago 60605
  William Smyser, Director of Admissions
  See listing under "Universities"

·:† Rush Presbyterian St. Luke's Medical Center
  1753 W. Congress Pky., Chicago 60612

·:† St. Anthony Medical Center
  5666 E. State St., Rockford 61108
  Kevin Schoeplein, Administrator

·:† St. Elizabeth Hospital
  School of Medical Technology
  211 S. 3rd St., Belleville 62220
  P. J. Soto, Jr., MD, Medical Director
  Jo Ann B. Denaro, Program Director
  618-234-2120 Ext. 1380

·:† St. Francis Hospital
  School of Radiologic Technology
  355 Ridge Ave., Evanston 60202
  Marianne Rhodes, RT (R), Program Director

·:† Saint Francis Medical Center
  School of Radiologic Technology
  530 N.E. Glen Oak Ave., Peoria 61637
  Sr. M. Canisia, OSF, Administrator

·:† St. John's Hospital
  800 E. Carpenter, Springfield 62769
  Sr. Agnes McDougall, Asst. Admin.

·:† St. Joseph Hospital
  77 N. Airlite St., Elgin 60123
  John T. Hoyt, Admin.

·:† St. Mary Hospital
  School of Medical Technology
  1415 Vermont St., Quincy 62301
  A. M. Bernzen, Prgm. Dir.

† Sangamon State University
  Shepherd Rd., Springfield 62794-9243
  Admissions and Records, 217-786-6626

·† Sauk Valley Community College
  R. R. 1, Dixon 61021
  W. Harold Garner, President

·:† South Chicago Community Hospital
  2320 E. 93rd St., Chicago 60617
  M. J. Dywan, Program Director

† Southern Illinois University at Carbondale
  Carbondale 62901

·† South Suburban College of Cook County
  School of Radiologic Technology
  15800 State St., South Holland 60473
  Wm. E. Piland, Dean, Career Education

·:† Swedish-American Hospital
  1400 Charles St., Rockford 61104
  Lorinda Schiller, MT, MEd, Program Director

Trinity Christian College
  6601 W. College Dr., Palos Heights 60463
  Kenneth Bootsma, President

·† Triton College
  2000 N. 5th Ave., River Grove 60171
  Gail Fuller, Dir. of Admission & Records
  See listing under "Community and Junior Colleges"

·:† United Medical Center
  501 10th Ave., Moline 61265

·:† United Samaritans Medical Center
  School of Radiologic Technology
  812 N. Logan Ave., Danville 61832
  Robert Verkler, Director

† University of Chicago
  5801 S. Ellis Ave., Chicago 60637

† University of Health Sciences
  The Chicago Medical School
  3333 Green Bay Rd., North Chicago 60064

† University of Illinois at Chicago
  P.O. Box 5220, Chicago 60680
  Dr. David Broski, Dean

·† Wilbur Wright College North
  4300 N. Narragansett Ave., Chicago 60634
  312-794-3100

·† William Rainey Harper College
  1200 W. Algonquin Rd., Palatine 60067

INDIANA

: Aristotle College of Medical and Dental Technology
  P.O. Box 8, Greenwood 46142

:‡ Aristotle College/Medical & Dental Tech.
  5245 South US 31, Indianapolis 46227

:‡ Aristotle College of Medical and Dental Technology
  5255 Hohman Ave., Hammond 46320

·:† Ball Memorial Hospital
  2401 W. University Ave., Muncie 47303

† Ball State University
  2000 W. University Ave., Muncie 47306
  Ruth Vedvik, Dir. of Admis.

: Commonwealth Business College
  8995 N. State Rd. 39, La Porte 46350
  Faye Mercer, Director
  219-362-3338

:‡ Commonwealth Business College
  4200 W. Lincoln Hwy., Merrillville 46410
  Al Conaway, Director
  219-769-3321

·:† Community Hospital of Indianapolis
  1500 N. Ritter Ave., Indianapolis 46219
  G. J. Kurlander, M.D., Program Director

·‡ Davenport College of Business
  7121 Grape Rd., Granger 46530

·‡ Davenport College of Business
  8200 Georgia St., Merrillville 46410

Franklin College
  501 E. Monroe, Franklin 46131
  B. Stephen Richards, VP Enrollment

·:† Good Samaritan Hospital
  Allied Health Sciences
  520 S. 7th St., Vincennes 47591

·:† Hancock Memorial Hospital
  School of Radiologic Technology
  801 N. State St., Greenfield 46140
  Susan Thompson, Prgm. Dir.

Huntington College
  2303 College Ave., Huntington 46750
  Paul Breininger, Dir. of Admis. Services

† Indiana State University
  217 N. 6th St., Terre Haute 47809

† Indiana University Northwest
  3400 N. Broadway, Gary 46408

† Indiana University-Purdue University
  355 N. Lansing, Indianapolis 46202

· Indiana Vocational Technical College (IVY)
  P.O. Box 1763, Indianapolis 46206

† Indiana Wesleyan University
  4201 S. Washington St., Marion 46953
  800-332-6901

· International Business College
  3811 Illinois Rd., Fort Wayne 46804

· International Business College
  7205 Shadeland Station, Indianapolis 46256

· Ivy Tech Central
  1 W. 26th St., Indianapolis 46208
  Meredith Carter, V.P., Dean

· Ivy Tech Columbus
  4475 Central Ave., Columbus 47203
  Homer Smith, V.P., Dean

· Ivy Tech East Central
  P.O. Box 3100, Muncie 47307
  Richard L. Davidson, V.P., Dean

· Ivy Tech Kokomo
  1815 E. Morgan St., Kokomo 46901
  Charles Hefley, V.P., Dean

· Ivy Tech Lafayette
  P.O. Box 6299, Lafayette 47903
  Thomas Reckerd, V.P., Dean

· Ivy Tech Northcentral
  1534 W. Sample St., South Bend 46619
  Carl Lutz, V.P., Dean

· Ivy Tech Northeast
  3800 N. Anthony Blvd., Fort Wayne 46805
  Jon Rupright, V.P., Dean

· Ivy Tech Northwest
  1440 E. 35th Ave., Gary 46409
  Mearle Donica, Dean

· Ivy Tech SouthCentral
  8204 W. Hwy. 31, Sellersburg 47172
  Jonothan Thomas, V.P., Dean

· Ivy Tech Southeast
  Highway 62 & Ivy Tech Drive, Madison 47250
  Gregory Flood, V.P., Dean

· Ivy Tech Southwest
  3501 1st Ave., Evansville 47710
  H. Victor Baldi, V.P., Dean

· Ivy Tech Valparaiso
  2401 Valley Dr., Valparaiso 46383

· Ivy Tech Wabash Valley
  7377 S. Dixie Bee Rd., Terre Haute 47802
  Samuel Borden, V.P., Dean

· Ivy Tech Whitewater
  2325 Chester Blvd., Richmond 47374
  Judith Redwine, V.P., Dean

·:† King's Daughter's Hospital
  P.O. Box 447, Madison 47250

: † **LAKESHORE MEDICAL LABORATORY TRAINING PROGRAMS**
402 Franklin St., Michigan City 46360
Toni Schlichtenmyer, MT (ASCP), Program Director

† Lutheran College of Health Professions
535 Home Ave., Fort Wayne 46807

Manchester College
604 College Ave., North Manchester 46962
Dr. Edward Miller, Professor

† Marian College
3200 Cold Spring Rd., Indianapolis 46222
Don French, Dir. of Admis.

.·† Memorial Hospital
School of Radiologic Technology
615 N. Michigan St., South Bend 46601
James Field, MD, Medical Director

.·† Methodist Hospital of Indiana
Connelly Allied Health Education Center
P.O. Box 1367, Indianapolis 46206

· † Michiana College
1030 E. Jefferson Blvd., South Bend 46617
Philip Heine, Director
800-743-2447

· Michiana College
4807 Illinois Rd., Fort Wayne 46804
Anthony Conti, Director
800-743-2447

.·† Parkview Memorial Hospital
2200 Randallia Dr., Fort Wayne 46805

.·† Porter Memorial Hospital
School of Radiologic Technology
814 La Porte Ave., Valparaiso 46383
Bridget Burge, BSRT, Program Director

: † Professional Careers Institute
2611 Waterfront Pky., Indianapolis 46214

† Purdue University
1401 S. U.S. Hwy. 421, Westville 46391

.·† Reid Memorial Hospital
1401 Chester Blvd., Richmond 47374
J. C. Spellmeyer, M.D., Program Director

.·† St. Francis Hospital Center
1600 Albany St., Beech Grove 46107

.·† **ST. JOSEPH HOSPITAL & HEALTH CENTER**
1907 W. Sycamore St., Kokomo 46901
Sr. M. M. McEntee, President
317-456-5308

.·† St. Joseph Medical Center
Fort Wayne School of Radiography
700 Broadway, Fort Wayne 46802

ST. JOSEPH'S COLLEGE
P.O. Box 890, Rensselaer 47978
Louis Levy, Dean of Admissions
800-447-8781

.·† St. Margaret Hospital
Medical Technology Program
5454 Hohman Ave., Hammond 46320
G. Shipplett, Program Director

.·† St. Mary Medical Center
1500 S. Lake Park Ave., Hobart 46342

.·† St. Mary's Medical Center
3700 Washington Ave., Evansville 47750

.·† St. Vincent Hospital
School of Radiologic Technology
2001 W. 86th St., Indianapolis 46260

: ‡ **SAWYER COLLEGE**
6040 Hohman Ave., Hammond 46320
Mary Jo Dixon, Director
800-964-0208

: ‡ **SAWYER COLLEGE**
3803 E. Lincoln Hwy., Merrillville 46410
Mary Jo Dixon, Director
800-964-0218

† University of Indianapolis
1400 E. Hanna Ave., Indianapolis 46227

† University of Southern Indiana
8600 University Blvd., Evansville 47712

· † Vincennes University
1002 N. 1st St., Vincennes 47591

.·† Welborn Baptist Hospital
401 S.E. 6th St., Evansville 47713

IOWA

.·† Allen Memorial Hospital
1825 Logan Ave., Waterloo 50703

Clarke College
1550 Clarke Dr., Dubuque 52001
Clyde Killian, PhD, Chair/Physical Therapy Dept.
800-383-2345

.·† Covenant Medical Center
3421 W. 9th St., Waterloo 50702

· † Des Moines Area Community College
2006 S. Ankeny Blvd., Ankeny 50021
James Frazee, Dir. of Admissions

Graceland College, Lamoni 50140
800-638-0053, Outside Iowa 800-346-9208
Bonita Booth, Dean of Admissions
See listing under "Universities"

· † Hawkeye Community College
1501 E. Orange Rd., Waterloo 50701
319-296-2320 Ext. 4000

· † Indian Hills Community College
525 Grandview, Ottumwa 52501
515-683-5111

· † Iowa Central Community College
330 Avenue M, Fort Dodge 50501
Dale Daggy, Dir. of Admis.

.·† Iowa Methodist Medical Center
1200 Pleasant St., Des Moines 50309
Margaret Page, MS., RTR., Program Director

· † Iowa Western Community College
2700 College Rd., Council Bluffs 51503
Thomas Dutch, Dir. of Admis.

.·† Jennie Edmundson Memorial Hospital
933 E. Pierce St., Council Bluffs 51503
R. G. McDonald, M.D., Program Director

· † Kirkwood Community College
P.O. Box 2068, Cedar Rapids 52406
Jim Miller, Dir. of Admis.
319-398-5517

Luther College
700 College Dr., Decorah 52101
David Sallee, Dean for Enrollment

.·† Marion Health Center
624 Jones St., Sioux City 51105

· † Marshalltown Community College
Dental Assisting Program
P.O. Box 536, Marshalltown 50158

.·† Mercy Hospital
400 University Ave., Des Moines 50314
Suzanne Mains, Director

Morningside College, Sioux City 51106
Lora Vanderzwaag, Dir. of Admis.

· † Northeast Iowa Technical Institute
R.R. 1, Peosta 52068
Donald Roby, Ass't. Supt.

.·† St. Joseph Mercy Hospital
84 Beaumont Dr., Mason City 50401

.·† St. Luke's Hospital
1026 A Ave., N.E., Cedar Rapids 52402

.·† St. Luke's Regional Medical Center
Medical Technology Program
2720 Stone Park Blvd., Sioux City 51104
J. S. Pennepacker, M.D., Program Director

· † **SCOTT COMMUNITY COLLEGE**
500 Belmont Rd., Bettendorf 52722
Kris Barkdoll, Assoc. Dean Enrollment Management

· † Southeastern Community College
P.O. Box F., West Burlington 52655
Edward Schieffer, Director

: Spencer College
217 W. 5th St., Spencer 51301
Harvey Work, Director
See listing under "Career Schools"

† University of Iowa, Iowa City 52242

† University of Osteopathic Medicine & Health Sciences
3200 Grand Ave., Des Moines 50312
Dennis Bates, PhD, Dir. of Admis.
515-271-1450

· † Western Iowa Technical Community College
P.O. Box 265, Sioux City 51102
R. H. Kiser, Supt.

KANSAS

· † Barton County Community College
R.R. 3, Box 136Z, Great Bend 67530
Dr. Jim Downing, President

.·† Bethany Medical Center
51 N. 12th St., Kansas City 66102
John L. Millard, President

: ‡ Bryan Institute
1004 S. Oliver St., Wichita 67218

· **COLBY COMMUNITY COLLEGE**
1255 S. Range Ave., Colby 67701
Theron Johnson, Dir. of Admis.

· † Dodge City Community College
2501 N. 14th Ave., Dodge City 67801
Debbie Lloyd, Director of Admissions
800-FOR-DCCC

† Fort Hays State University
600 Park St., Hays 67601-4099
Dr. Virgil Howe, Dean, College of Health & Life Sciences
MEDICAL TECHNOLOGY (Cooperative Program)
Dr. Judith Vogt, Coordinator
ASSOCIATE OF SCIENCE (Radiologic Technology, X-Ray)
Dr. Michael Madden, Advisor

· Haskell Indian Junior College
155 Indian Ave. #1305, Lawrence 66046
Gerald Gipp, President

.·† HCA Wesley Medical Center
550 N. Hillside St., Wichita 67214
Kathy Riedel, Director

· † Hutchinson Community College
1300 N. Plum St., Hutchinson 67501
Duane Halpain, Dir. of Admis.

· † Johnson County Community College
12345 College Blvd., Overland Park 66210
Pat Long, Dir. of Admis.

· † Labette Community College
200 S. 14th St., Parsons 67357
Dr. Bob C. Burns, Dean of Instr.

McPherson College
1600 E. Euclid St., McPherson 67460

.·† St. Francis Regional Medical Center
929 N. St. Francis Ave., Wichita 67214

.·† St. Joseph Medical Center
3600 E. Harry, Wichita 67218
W. J. Reals, M.D.

· † Seward County Community College
P.O. Box 1137, Liberal 67905

SOUTHWESTERN COLLEGE
100 College St., Winfield 67156
800-846-1543

: † Topeka School of Medical Technology
1915 S.W. 6th Ave. #207, Topeka 66606

† University of Kansas Medical Center
3901 Rainbow Blvd., Kansas City 66160
Dr. James Cooney, Dean

† Washburn University of Topeka
1700 S.W. College Ave., Topeka 66621
John E. Triggs, Dir. of Admissions

: † Wichita Area Vocational Technical School
217 N. Water, Wichita 67202

† Wichita State University
1845 Fairmount, Wichita 67260
800-362-2594
See listing under "Universities"

KENTUCKY

.·† Brown Cancer Center
529 S. Jackson St., Louisville 40202

† Eastern Kentucky University
521 Lancaster Ave., Richmond 40475

· Fugazzi College
406 Lafayette Ave., Lexington 40502
606-266-0401

· † Henderson Community College
2660 S. Green St., Henderson 42420
Marshall Arnold, Director

· † Jefferson Community College
109 E. Broadway, Louisville 40202
Margaret Miller, Chrpsn.

: † Kentucky Tech Bowling Green Vocational Technical School
P.O. Box 1868, Bowling Green 42102

: † Kentucky Tech Central KY State Vocational Technical School
150 Vo Tech Rd., Lexington 40510

: † Kentucky Tech Laurel Co State Vocational Technical School
1711 N. Main St., London 40741

: † Kentucky Tech Madisonville State Vocational Technical School
100 School St., Madisonville 42431

: † Kentucky Tech Rowan State Vocational Technical School
P.O. Box 1098, Morehead 40351

: † Kentucky Tech West KY State Vocational Technical School
P.O. Box 7769, Paducah 42002

.·† King's Daughter's Hospital
School of Radiologic Technology
P.O. Box 151, Ashland 41105
T. L. Dobbins, R.T., Program Director

· Lexington Community College
Oswald Bldg., Cooper Dr., Lexington 40506
Dr. Sharon Jaggard, Director

.·† Lourdes Hospital
1530 Lone Oak Rd., Paducah 42003

· † Madisonville Community College
2000 College Dr., Madisonville 42431
Arthur D. Stumpf, Director

.·† Methodist Hospital of Kentucky
911 S. Bypass Rd., Pikeville 41501

† Morehead State University, Morehead 40351
Charles Myers, Director of Admissions
606-783-2000

† Murray State University, Murray 42071
Phil Bryan, Director of Admissions
800-272-4MSU

† Northern Kentucky University
Louie B. Nunn Dr., Highland Heights 41076

.·† Owensboro-Daviess Co. Hospital
P.O. Box 570, Owensboro 42302

: † Pathology and Cytology Laboratories
290 Big Run Rd., Lexington 40503

Pikeville College
214 Sycamore St., Pikeville 41501
Dr. John W. Sanders, Dean of Admissions

.·† St. Anthony Medical Center
1313 St. Anthony Pl., Louisville 40204

∴† St. Elizabeth Medical Center
  School of Medical Technology
  1 Medical Village Dr., Edgewood   41017
  Christopher Barczak, Program Director

∴† St. Joseph's Hospital
  1400 Harrodsburg Rd., Lexington   40504

· † Somerset Community College
  808 Montecello St., Somerset   42501
  R. C. Kelley, Director

· Southeast Community College
  300 College Rd., Cumberland   40823
  J. Bruce Wilson, Director

: ‡ Southwestern College of Business
  2929 S. Dixie Hwy., Covington   41017

  Spalding University
  851 S. 4th St., Louisville   40203
  Dorothy G. Allen, Dir. of Admis.

: † Spencerian College
  P.O. Box 16418, Louisville   40256
  Harold Stice, Executive Director

† University of Kentucky, Lexington   40506

† University of Louisville
  2301 S. 3rd St., Louisville   40292
  Robert Parrent, Dir. of Admis.

† Western Kentucky University
  1526 Russellville Rd., Bowling Green   42101

LOUISIANA

∴† Baton Rouge General Medical Center
  P.O. Box 2511, Baton Rouge   70821

· † Bossier Parish Community College
  2719 Airline Dr., Bossier City   71111
  Mrs. Faye Powell, Registrar

∴† Charity Hospital of Louisiana
  1532 Tulane Ave., New Orleans   70112

· † Delgado Community College
  501 City Park Ave., New Orleans   70119
  Dr. Carmen Smith, Director of Admissions

: ‡ Domestic Health Care Institute
  4826 Jamestown Ave., Baton Rouge   70808

∴† Earl K. Long Memorial Hospital
  5825 Airline Hwy., Baton Rouge   70805

: ‡ Eastern College of Health Vocations
  3540 I-10 Service Rd., S., Metairie   70001

∴† Lafayette General Medical Center
  P.O. Box 52009, Lafayette   70505

: † Lafayette Regional Vocational-Technical School
  P.O. Box 4909, Lafayette   70502

∴† Lake Charles Memorial Hospital
  School of Medical Technology
  1701 Oak Park Blvd., Lake Charles   70601
  A. Cook, MD, Program Director
  318-494-2481

  Louisiana College
  College Station, Pineville   71359
  Byron McGee, Dir. of Admis.
  318-487-7386
  See listing under "Liberal Arts"

† Louisiana State University
  8515 Youree Dr., Shreveport   71115

† Louisiana State University Medical Center
  433 Bolivar St., New Orleans   70112

· † Louisiana State University at Eunice
  P.O. Box 1129, Eunice   70535

† Lousiana Technical University
  P.O. Box 3168, Ruston   71272

  Loyola University
  6363 St. Charles Ave., New Orleans   70118

† McNeese State University
  4100 Ryan St., Lake Charles   70605

† Nicholls State University
  LA Hwy. 1, Thibodaux   70301

† Northeast Louisiana University
  700 University Ave., Monroe   71209

† Northwestern State University
  Natchitoches   71497

: † Ochsner School of Allied Health Sciences
  880 W. Commerce Rd., New Orleans   70123
  Edward D. Frohlich, MD, VP Academic Affairs
  504-842-3267

∴† Our Lady of the Lake Medical Center
  School of Medical Technology
  5000 Hennessy Blvd., Baton Rouge   70808
  R. Nunnally, M.D., Program Director

∴† Overton Brooks VA Medical Center
  510 E. Stoner Ave., Shreveport   71101

· † Phillips Junior College
  822 S. Clearview Pky., New Orleans   70123
  Jerry Adams, Director

∴† Rapides General Hospital
  P.O. Box 30101, Alexandria   71301

∴† St. Francis Medical Center
  309 Jackson St., Monroe   71201

∴† St. Patrick's Hospital
  524 S. Ryan St., Lake Charles   70601

∴† Schumpert Medical Center
  P.O. Box 21976, Shreveport   71120

∴† Seventh Ward General Hospital
  Hwy. 51 S., Hammond   70401

† Southeastern Louisiana University
  P.O. Box 784, Hammond   70404

· † Southern University
  Shreveport-Bossier City Campus
  3050 M. L. King Dr., Shreveport   71107
  Clifton Jones, Registrar

∴† Touro Infirmary
  School of Medical Technology
  1401 Foucher St., New Orleans   70115
  L. Weymann, Program Director

∴† University Medical Center
  P.O. Box 4016, Lafayette   70502

† University of Southwestern Louisiana
  P.O. Box 42490, Lafayette   70504
  318-231-6808

: † West Jefferson Technical Institute
  475 Manhattan Blvd., Harvey   70058

MAINE

· † Beal College, 629 Main St., Bangor   04401

· † Central Maine Medical Center
  300 Main St., Lewiston   04240
  Laird P. Covey, VP of Medical Affairs

∴† Eastern Maine Medical Center
  489 State St., Bangor   04401

· † Eastern Maine Vocational Technical Institute
  School of Radiography Technology
  354 Hogan Rd., Bangor   04401

· † Kennebec Valley Technical College
  92 Western Ave., Fairfield   04937
  Barbara Woodlee, Director

· † Maine Medical Center
  School of Surgical Technology
  22 Bramhall St., Portland   04102
  Diane Dussault, RN, Program Director

∴† Mercy Hospital
  144 State St., Portland   04101

∴† Mid-Maine Medical Center-Seton Unit
  30 Chase Ave., Waterville   04901

· † Southern Maine Technical College
  2 Fort Rd., South Portland   04106
  See listing under "Career Schools"

† University of Maine
  University Hts., Augusta   04330

† University of Maine, Orono   04469

† University of Maine
  181 Main St., Presque Isle   04769

† University of New England
  11 Hills Beach Rd., Biddeford   04005
  Patricia Cribby, Dir. of Admis.

  Westbrook College
  716 Stevens Ave., Portland   04103
  207-797-7261

MARYLAND

· † Allegany Community College
  12401 Willowbrook Rd., Cumberland   21502
  W. Ardell Haines, President

· † Chesapeake College
  P.O. Box 8, Wye Mills   21679

† Columbia Union College
  7600 Flower Ave., Takoma Park   20912

· † Community College of Baltimore
  2901 Liberty Heights Ave., Baltimore   21215
  Joseph Stein, Director of Admissions

· † Essex Community College
  7201 Rossville Blvd., Baltimore   21237
  Diane Lane, Dir. of Admis.

∴† Greater Baltimore Medical Center
  6701 N. Charles St., Baltimore   21204

· † Hagerstown Junior College
  11400 Robinwood Dr., Hagerstown   21742
  Atlee C. Kepler, President

∴† Harbor Hospital Center
  School of Radiologic Technology
  3001 S. Hanover St., Baltimore   21225
  Linda Caplis, RT, Program Director

· † Harford Community College
  401 Thomas Run Rd., Bel Air   21015
  Richard Pappas, President

∴† Holy Cross Hospital
  1500 Forest Glen Rd., Silver Spring   20910

∴† Hunter Memorial Laboratory
  8218 Wisconsin Ave. #202, Bethesda   20814

∴† Johns Hopkins Hospital
  600 N. Wolfe St., Baltimore   21205

† Johns Hopkins University
  600 N. Wolfe St., Baltimore   21205

∴† Maryland General Hospital
  827 Linden Ave., Baltimore   21201

: † Medix School
  1017 York Rd., Towson   21204
  Richard Stensing, Dir. of Admis.

∴† Mercy Hospital
  301 St. Paul Pl., Baltimore   21202
  Sr. Mary Thomas, R.S.M., President

· † Montgomery College
  Pre-Medical Technology
  51 Mannakee St., Rockville   20850
  Germantown - 301-353-7798
  Rockville - 301-279-5124
  Takoma Park - 301-650-1332

· Montgomery College
  7600 Takoma Ave., Takoma Park   20912
  301-650-1500

† Morgan State University
  Cold Spring Ln. and Hillen Rd., Baltimore   21239

† National Institute of Health
  9000 Rockville Pike Bldg. 10, Bethesda   20892

· † Prince George's Community College
  301 Largo Rd., Largo   20772
  Leon Weaver, Dir. of Admis. & Test.

† Salisbury State University
  1101 Camden Ave., Salisbury   21801

† Towson State University
  800 York Rd., Towson   21204
  Dr. Hoke Smith, President

: ‡ Ultrasound Diagnostic School
  1320 Fenwick Ln., Silver Spring   20910

∴† Union Memorial Hospital
  School of Medical Technology
  201 E. University Pkwy., Baltimore   21218
  D. K. Merenyi, M.D., Prgm. Dir.

† University of Maryland
  Baltimore Professional Schools
  522 W. Lombard St., Baltimore   21201

  University of Maryland Eastern Shore
  11868 Academic Oval, Princess Anne   21853
  Dr. Raymond Blakley, Chrpsn.

† Villa Julie College
  1525 Greenspring Valley Rd., Stevenson   21153
  Carolyn Manuszak, President

∴† Washington Adventist Hospital
  7600 Carroll Ave., Takoma Park   20912
  Ted Vanderlaan, Program Director

· † Wor-Wic Technical Community College
  30 Wesley Dr., Salisbury   21801

MASSACHUSETTS

† Anna Maria College
  2 Sunset Ln., Paxton   01612
  Dr. Bernadette Madore, SSA, President

· † Aquinas College at Milton
  303 Adams St., Milton   02186
  617-696-3100

  Atlantic Union College
  P.O. Box 1000, South Lancaster   01561
  Osa Canto, Registrar

BAY PATH COLLEGE

588 Longmeadow St., Longmeadow   01106
Paula DesRoberts, Dean of Admis.
413-567-0621 or 800-782-PATH
  Established: 1897. Private. Women. Accreditation: NEASC, Legal programs ABA approved. Tuition: $10,200. Room and board: $6,225. Enrollment: 600. Faculty: 42. Student-faculty ratio: 14:1. Degrees: AA, AS, BA, BS. Library: 38,000 volumes. 27 buildings on 30 acres. Secure, suburban campus near Springfield and Hartford. 15 Associate degree programs in business, education, fashion/design, criminal justice, paralegalism, hospitality/tourism, health, human services, occupational therapy, psychology, liberal arts. Baccalaureates in business, business/accounting, legal studies, psychology, psychology/criminal justice, psychology/early childhood education. Extensive career services. 95-98% of students obtain jobs after graduation. Transfer welcome.

· ‡ Bay State College
  122 Commonwealth Ave., Boston   02116

∴† Bay State Medical Center
  759 Chestnut St., Springfield   01199

· † Berkshire Community College
  1350 West St., Pittsfield   01201
  Adrienne A. Rulnick, Dir. of Admissions

∴† Berkshire Medical Center
  725 North St., Pittsfield   01201

† Boston University
  685 Commonwealth Ave., Boston   02215

† Boston University Medical Center
  100 E. Newton St., Boston   02118
  Maxine Peck, Director

· † Bristol Community College
  777 Elsbree St., Fall River   02720
  Frank Noble, Dir. of Admis.

· † Bunker Hill Community College
  School of Radiologic Technology
  New Rutherford Ave., Boston   02129
  Janice M. Bonanno, Dir. of Admis.

∴† Cambridge Hospital
  School of Medical Technology
  1493 Cambridge St., Cambridge   02139
  M. Zschokke, MS, Director

∴† Children's Hospital
  300 Longwood Ave., Boston   02115

  Emerson College
  148 Beacon St., Boston   02116

Emmanuel College
400 The Fenway, Boston 02115
Margaret Bonilla, Dir. of Admis.

· Endicott College
376 Hale St., Beverly 01915
Elizabeth Macomber, Dir. of Admis.

† Fitchburg State College
160 Pearl St., Fitchburg 01420
Marke Vickers, Dir. of Admis.

: **FORSYTH SCHOOL FOR DENTAL HYGIENISTS**
140 Fenway, Boston 02115
Judith Harvey, Dir. of Admis.
617-262-5200 ext. 212, 213.

· † Holyoke Community College
303 Homestead Ave., Holyoke 01040
George E. Frost, President

· † Laboure College
2120 Dorchester Ave., Boston 02124
Sr. Maureen St. Charles, President

·∴† Lawrence General Hospital
School of Medical Technology
1 General St., Lawrence 01841
Cynthia A. Freyberger, M.Ed. MT(ASCP), Dir.
508-683-4000 ext 2748

: † Life Laboratories
299 Carew St., Springfield 01104

· † Massachusetts Bay Community College
50 Oakland St., Wellesley 02181

† Massachusetts College of Pharmacy
& Allied Health Sciences
179 Longwood Ave., Boston 02115

Massachusetts General Hospital
32 Fruit St., Boston 02114

· † Massasoit Community College
1 Massasoit Blvd., Brockton 02402
Roberta Noodell, Dir. of Admis.

MGH Institute of Health Professions
101 Merrimac St., Boston 02114

· † Middlesex Community College
Springs Rd., Bedford 01730
617-280-3200

· Middlesex Community College
33 Kearney Sq., Lowell 01852
508-656-3211

·∴† Mt. Auburn Hospital
Radiography Program
330 Mt. Auburn St., Cambridge 02138
Maryann Blaine, BSRT, (R), Program Director

Mt. Ida College
777 Dedham St., Newton Center 02159
Jim Mulligan, Dean of Admis.

· † Mt. Wachusett Community College
444 Green St., Gardner 01440
Sidney Goldfader, Dir. of Admis.

· † Newbury College
129 Fisher Ave., Brookline 02146
Judy LeGraw, Dir. of Admis.

·∴† New England Deaconess Hospital
110 Francis St., Boston 02215

·∴† New England Medical Center
P.O. Box 451, Boston 02111

·∴† Newton Wellesley Hospital
School of Medical Technology
2014 Washington St., Newton Lower Falls 02162
R. H. Scott, M.D., Program Dir.

North Adams State College
375 Church St., North Adams 01247
413-664-4511 or 800-292-6632
See listing under "Universities or Graduate Schools"

† Northeastern University
360 Huntington Ave., Boston 02115
Kevin Kelly, Dean and Dir. of Undergraduate
Admis.

· † Northern Essex Community College
100 Elliott St., Haverhill 01830

· † North Shore Community College
1 Ferncroft Rd., Danvers 01923

· † Quincy Junior College
34 Coddington St., Quincy 02169
Richard Pessin, Dean of Enrollment Services

· † Quinsigamond Community College
670 W. Boylston St., Worcester 01606
Ron Smith, Dir. of Admis.

† Salem State College
352 Lafayette St., Salem 01970
David Sartwell, Dir. of Admis.

Simmons College
300 The Fenway, Boston 02115

: † Southeastern Technical Institute
250 Foundry St., South Easton 02375

· † **SPRINGFIELD TECHNICAL COMMUNITY
COLLEGE**
1 Armory Square, Springfield 01105
Dr. Patrick E. Tigue, Dir. of Admissions
413-781-7822

† Tufts University
520 Boston Ave., Medford 02155

Tufts University, Medical School
136 Harrison Ave., Boston 02111

: ‡ Ultrasound Diagnostic School
57 Providence Hwy., Norwood 02062

University of Massachusetts
100 Morrissey Blvd., Boston 02125

† University of Massachusetts Dartmouth
Old Westport Rd., North Dartmouth 02747
Raymond Barrows, Dir. of Admissions
508-999-8605

† University of Massachusetts Lowell
1 University Ave., Lowell 01854

† University of Massachusetts
Medical School
55 Lake Ave., N., Worcester 01655

·∴ Veterans Administration Hospital
150 S. Huntington Ave., Boston 02130

∴ Worcester City Hospital
455 Main St. #306, Worcester 01608

† Worcester State College
486 Chandler St., Worcester 01602

MICHIGAN

† Andrews University, Berrien Springs 49104
Jack Mentges, Dir. of Admis.

Baker College of Auburn Hills
1500 University Dr., Auburn Hills 48326
John A. Tomaszewski, Dir. of Admis.

Baker College of Cadillac
9600 E. 13th St., Cadillac 49601
Candace Baldwin, Dir. of Admis.

† Baker College of Flint
1050 W. Bristol Rd., Flint 48507
Mark Heaton, Dir. of Admis.

Baker College of Mount Clemens
34950 Little Mack Ave., Clinton Township 48035
Annette M. Wendling, Dir. of Admis.

† Baker College of Muskegon
141 Hartford Ave., Muskegon 49442
Kathy Jacobson, Dir. of Admis.

† Baker College of Owosso
1020 S. Washington St., Owosso 48867
Bruce A. Lundeen, Dir. of Admis.

Baker College of Port Huron
3403 Lapeer Rd., Port Huron 48060
David C. Hickman, Dir. of Admis.

·∴† Blodgett Memorial Medical Center
1840 Wealthy, S.E., Grand Rapids 49506

·∴† Bronson Methodist Hospital
252 E. Lovell St., Kalamazoo 49007
Peter Froyd, President

·∴† Butterworth Hospital
School of Medical Technology
100 Michigan St., N.E., Grand Rapids 49503
S. M. Tomlinson, Program Director

:· † **CARNEGIE INSTITUTE**
550 Stephenson Hwy. #100, Troy 48083
Gloria J. McEachern, President
810-589-1078

† Davenport College of Business
415 E. Fulton St., Grand Rapids 49503
Donald Maine, President

‡ Davenport College of Business
4123 W. Main St., Kalamazoo 49006

· † Delta College, University Center 48710
John Flattery, Division Chrpsn.

: † Detroit Institute Ophthalmology
15415 E. Jefferson Ave., Detroit 48230

† Eastern Michigan University, Ypsilanti 48197
Associated Health Professions
Stephen Sonnstein, Department Head
313-487-3060 or 800-GO-TO-EMU

† Ferris State University
Office of Admission
420 Oak St., Big Rapids 49307-2020

·· † Ford Community College
5101 Evergreen Rd., Dearborn 48128
Marion Gorham, Director

·∴† Garden City Hospital
6245 N. Inkster Rd., Garden City 48135

·· † Grace Hospital
18700 Meyers Rd., Detroit 48235

· † Grand Rapids Community College
School of Radiologic Technology
143 Bostwick Ave., N.E., Grand Rapids 49503
Robert S. Duffy, Dean, Occupational Education

: ‡ Grand Rapids Educational Center
1750 Woodworth St., N.E. #100
Grand Rapids 49505

: ‡ Grand Rapids Educational Center
5349 W. Main, Kalamazoo 49009

·· † Harper-Grace Hospital
3990 John R St., Detroit 48201

·· † Henry Ford Hospital
2799 W. Grand Blvd., Detroit 48202

· † Highland Park Community College
School for Respiratory Therapists
12541 2nd Ave., Highland Park 48203
Oretta Todd, PhD, Dean

·· † Hurley Medical Center
701 W. 8th Ave., Flint 48503
Richard C. Schripsema, Director

· † Jackson Community College
2111 Emmons Rd., Jackson 49201
Mark Ulseth, Dir. Enrollment Services

· † Kalamazoo Valley Community College
6767 W. O Ave., Kalamazoo 49009
Marilyn Schlack, President

· † Kellogg Community College
450 North Ave., Battle Creek 49017
Richard F. Whitmore, President

· † Lake Michigan College
2755 E. Napier, Benton Harbor 49022
Rentzell Cleaveland, Jr., Registrar

· † Lansing Community College
521 Washington Square N., Lansing 48933

· Macomb Community College
16500 Hall Rd., Clinton Twp. 48038

· Macomb Community College
14500 E. 12 Mile Rd., Warren 48093

·· † Marquette General Hospital
420 W. Magnetic St., Marquette 49855

† Marygrove College
8425 W. McNichols Rd., Detroit 48221

† Michigan State University, East Lansing 48824
Judy Schwinghamer, Preprofessional Advisor

Michigan Technological University
1400 Townsend Dr., Houghton 49931
Joseph A. Galetto, Dir. Enrollment Mgmt.
906-487-2335

· † Mid Michigan Community College
Radiography Program
1375 S. Clare Ave., Harrison 48625
Chal Bauer, Education Coordinator

· † Monroe County Community College
1555 Raisinville S., Monroe 48161
Gerald Welch, President

· † Mott Community College
1401 E. Court St., Flint 48503

·· † Munson Medical Center
Medical Technologist School
1105 6th St., Traverse City 49684

· † Muskegon Community College
221 Quarterline Rd., S., Muskegon 49442
John G. Thompson, President

· † North Central Michigan College
1515 Howard St., Petosky 49770

† Northern Michigan University
610 Cohodas Admin. Center, Marquette 49855
Nancy Rehling, Dir. of Admis.

·· † North Oakland Medical Center
461 W. Huron, Pontiac 48341

· Oakland Community College
2480 Opdyke Rd., Bloomfield Hills 48304

· † Oakland Community College
7350 Cooley Lake Rd., Union Lake 48387

· † Oakland Community College-Orchard Ridge Campus
27055 Orchard Lake Rd.
Farmington Hills 48334

·∴† Oakwood Hospital
P.O. Box 2500, Dearborn 48123
Neil McGinniss, Director

·· † Port Huron Hospital
1001 Kearney St., Port Huron 48060

·∴† Providence Hospital
Radiography Program
16001 W. 9 Mile Rd., Southfield 48075
810-424-3293

: ‡ Ross Business Institute
1285 N. Telegraph, Monroe 48161

: ‡ Ross Medical Education Center
1036 Gilbert Rd., Flint 48532

: ‡ Ross Medical Education Center
2035 28th St. S.E., #O, Grand Rapids 49508

: ‡ Ross Medical Education Center
950 W. Norton, Muskegon 49441

: Ross Medical Education Center
253 Summit Dr., Waterford 48328

: ‡ Ross Medical Education Center
913 W. Holmes #260, Lansing 48910

: ‡ Ross Medical Education Center
26417 Hoover Rd., Warren 48089

: ‡ Ross Medical Education Center
1188 West Ave., Jackson 49202

: ‡ Ross Medical Education Center
4054 Bay Rd., Saginaw 48603

: ‡ Ross Technical Institute
1553 Woodward Ave. #750, Detroit 48226

: ‡ Ross Technical Institute
20820 Greenfield Rd., Oak Park 48237

·· † St. John's Hospital
22101 Moross Rd., Detroit 48236

·· † St. Joseph Hospital
302 Kensington Ave., Flint 48503
Sr. Agnes Breitenbeck, President

∴† St. Mary's Medical Center
830 S. Jefferson Ave., Saginaw 48601

· † Schoolcraft College
18600 Haggerty Rd., Livonia 48152
Barbara A. Geil, Dir. of Admissions

∴ Southeast Michigan Red Cross Blood Center
School for Specialists in Blood Bank Technology
P.O. Box 33351, Detroit 48232
Shobha Shah, MD, Medical Director

· Suomi College
601 Quincy St., Hancock 49930
John Ruohoniemi, Dean/Enrollment Development
800-682-7604

∴† United Care, Annapolis Hospital
Radiography Program
33155 Annapolis St., Wayne 48184
Julia West, Program Director

† University of Detroit Mercy
4001 W. McNichols
PO Box 19900, Detroit 48219-0900
313-993-1245
See listing under "Universities"

† University of Michigan-Ann Arbor
815 S. University Ave., Ann Arbor 48109

∴† W. A. Foote Memorial Hospital
205 N. East Ave., Jackson 49201

· † Washtenaw Community College
4800 E. Huron River Dr., Ann Arbor 48105

· Wayne County Community College
801 Fort St., W., Detroit 48226

† Wayne State University
5980 Cass Ave., Detroit 48202
Dr. J. R. Thorderson, Dir. of Admis.

† Western Michigan University, Kalamazoo 49008
Stanley Henderson, Dir. of Enrl. Mgt. & Admis.
616-387-2000

∴† William Beaumont Hospital
3601 W. 13 Mile Rd., Royal Oak 48073

MINNESOTA

∴† Abbott-Northwestern Hospital
810 E. 27th St., Minneapolis 55407

· † Alexandria Technical College
1601 Jefferson St., Alexandria 56308

: † Anoka Technical Institute
1355 W. Main St., Anoka 55303

· **AUSTIN COMMUNITY COLLEGE**
1600 8th Ave., N. W., Austin 55912
Barbara Orcutt, Admissions
507-433-0517

Bethel College
3900 Bethel Dr., St. Paul 55112
Dr. George Brushaber, President

College of Saint Benedict
37 S. College Ave., St. Joseph 56374

† College of St. Catherine
2004 Randolph Ave., St. Paul 55105

† College of St. Scholastica
1200 Kenwood Ave., Duluth 55811
Sr. Marguerite Baxter & Dr. Cecelia Taylor,
Co-Chrpsn's.
800-447-5444
See listing under "Liberal Arts"

: Duluth Business University
412 W. Superior St., Duluth 55802
Bonnie Kupczynski, Director

: † Duluth Technical College
2101 Trinity Rd., Duluth 55811

· † Fergus Falls Community College
1414 College Way, Fergus Falls 56537
Wesley A. Waage, President

∴† Hennepin County Medical Center
701 Park Ave., Minneapolis 55415

· † Hibbing Community College
1515 E. 25th St., Hibbing 55746
Orville Olson, Provost

: † Hibbing Technical Institute
2900 E. Beltline, Hibbing 55746

: † Lakeland Medical-Dental Academy
1402 W. Lake St., Minneapolis 55408

· † Lakewood Community College
3401 Century Ave., White Bear Lake 55110
Dr. Neil Christenson, President

Mankato State University
P.O. Box 8400, Mankato 56002

† Mayo Foundation
200 1st St., N.W., Rochester 55901

: ‡ Medical Institute of Minnesota
5503 Green Valley Dr., Bloomington 55437
Phillip Miller, President

∴† Memorial Blood Center of Minneapolis
2304 Park Ave., Minneapolis 55404
Herbert Polesky, MD, Director

∴† Methodist Hospital
6500 Excelsior Blvd., St. Louis Park 55426
P. Olson, M.D., Program Director

: † Minneapolis Business College
1711 County Road B W., Roseville 55113

∴† Minneapolis VA Medical Center
1 Veterans Dr., Minneapolis 55417

· Normandale Community College
9700 France Ave., S., Bloomington 55431
Thomas Horak, President

: † Northeast Metro Technical College
3300 Century Ave., N., White Bear Lake 55110

· North Hennepin Community College
School for Respiratory Therapists
7411 85th Ave., N., Brooklyn Park 55445
Janis Weiss, Dean of Instruction

∴† North Memorial Medical Center
3220 Lowry Ave., N., Minneapolis 55422
Richard M. Amundson, R.T., Program Director

: † **NORTHWEST TECHNICAL COLLEGE - EAST GRAND FORKS**
Hwy. 220, N., East Grand Forks 56721
Dr. A. Cooley, Medical Director

: † Northwest Technical College
Dental Assisting, Medical Records
1900 28th Ave., S., Moorhead 56560
Dale White, Dir. of Admis.
218-299-6512

∴† Rice Memorial Hospital
School of Radiologic Technology
301 Becker Ave., S.W., Willmar 56201
Luther Linn, RT, Program Director
612-231-4530

: † Riverland Technical College
1926 Collegeview Rd., E., Rochester 55904
507-285-8631 or 800-247-1296

: † Riverland Technical College
1225 3rd St., S.W., Faribault 55021
507-334-3965 or 800-422-0391

· † Rochester Community College
851 30th Ave. S.E., Rochester 55904
Charles E. Hill, President

∴† St. Cloud Hospital
1406 6th Ave., N., St. Cloud 56303

St. Cloud State University
740 4th Ave., S., St. Cloud 56301
Sherwood Reid, Dir. of Admis.
800-369-4260

· St. Cloud Technical College
1540 Northway Dr., Saint Cloud 56303
612-252-0101

St. John's University
P.O. Box 7155, Collegeville 56321

· St. Mary's Campus of the College of St. Catherine
2500 6th St., S., Minneapolis 55454
Pamela Johnson, Dir. of Admis.

† St. Mary's College of Minnesota
700 Terrace Heights #2, Winona 55987
Tony Piscitiello, VP for Admission

∴† St. Paul-Ramsey Medical Center
School of Medical Technology
640 Jackson St., St. Paul 55101
Bruce E. Hyde, MD, Medical Director

· † St. Paul Technical College
235 Marshall Ave., Saint Paul 55102

Southwest State University, Marshall 56258

∴† United Hospital
333 N. Smith Ave., Saint Paul 55102

† University of Minnesota, Twin Cities
Minneapolis 55455

· Willmar Community College
P.O. Box 797, Willmar 56201
Arlen Sjervan, Director of Admissions
612-231-5199

MISSISSIPPI

· † Copiah-Lincoln Community College
P.O. Box 457, Wesson 39191
J. M. Lewis, Dir. of Admis.

∴† Hattiesburg Radiology Group
116 S. 25th Ave., Hattiesburg 39401

· † Hinds Community College, Raymond 39154

· Itawamba Community College
Hwy. 78, Fulton 38843
Carl C. Comer, Dir. of Admis.

· Meridian Community College
910 Hwy. 19, N., Meridian 39307

· † Mississippi Delta Community College
P.O. Box 668, Moorhead 38761
J. T. Hall, President

· † Mississippi Gulf Coast Community College
Perkinston Campus
P.O. Box 67, Perkinston 39573

∴† Mississippi Medical Center
1225 N. State St., Jackson 39202
Paul J. Pryor, Admin.

Mississippi University for Women
P.O. Box W-1602, Columbus 39701
Teresa Thompson, Exec. Dir. of Enrollment

· † Northeast Mississippi Community College
101 Cunningham Blvd., Booneville 38829

∴† North Mississippi Medical Center
830 S. Gloster, Tupelo 38801
Carron Sheffield, Program Director

· † Northwest Mississippi Community College
510 N. Panola, Senatobia 38668
Henry B. Koon, President

· † Pearl River Community College, Poplarville 39470
Dr. Marvin R. White, President

∴† South Central Regional Medical Center
P.O. Box 607, Laurel 39441

† University of Mississippi Medical Center
2500 N. State St., Jackson 39216

† University of Southern Mississippi
P.O. Box 5165, Hattiesburg 39406

† William Carey College
498 Tuscan Ave., Hattiesburg 39401

MISSOURI

: ‡ AL-MED Academy
10963 St. Charles Rock Rd., Saint Ann 63074

† Avila College
11901 Wornall Rd., Kansas City 64145
Maril Hauber, Director

∴† Barnes Hospital
4949 Barnes Hospital Plz., Saint Louis 63110

: ‡ Bryan Institute
12184 Natural Bridge Rd., Bridgeton 63044

: ‡ Cape Girardeau Vocational Technical School
301 N. Clark, Cape Girardeau 63701

: **CONCORDE CAREER INSTITUTE**
3239 Broadway St., Kansas City 64111
Pamela Tiemeyer, Director
816-531-5223
Established 1983. Private. Coed. Accreditation: Accrediting Commission for Career Schools and Colleges of Technology (ACCSCT). Faculty: 15. Student-faculty ratio: 25:1. Diploma offered. 1 building. Programs offered include: Respiratory Therapy Technician; Medical Assistant, Dental Assistant, Medical Office Professional; and Computerized Accounting. The institution is dedicated to training individuals for their chosen career in the shortest time practical at a reasonable cost. It is our aim to provide students with the knowledge and technical proficiency that will make them employable for entry-level positions upon graduation.

: ‡ Eastern Jackson County College of Allied Health
808 S. 15th St., Blue Springs 64015

Evangel College
1111 N. Glenstone Ave., Springfield 65802
David Schoolfield, Dir. of Enrollment

: † Hannibal Area Vocational Technical School
4550 McMasters Ave.
Hannibal 63401-2285
Harold D. Ward, Director
314-221-4430

∴† Jewish Hospital of St. Louis
216 S. Kingshighway Blvd., St. Louis 63110
M. Russell, Asst. Exec. Director

∴† Lester E. Cox Medical Center
1423 N. Jefferson Ave., Springfield 65802
Neil C. Wortley, Admin.

: † Mallinckrodt Institute of Radiology
510 S. Kingshighway Blvd., Saint Louis 63110

Maryville University of St. Louis
13550 Conway Rd., Saint Louis 63141
314-576-9300 or 800-MARYVLL

∴† Menorah Medical Center
4949 Rockhill Rd., Kansas City 64110

: ‡ Metro Business College
1732 N. Kingshighway St., Cape Giradeau 63701

: ‡ Metro Business College
1407 Southwest Blvd., Jefferson City 65109

: ‡ Metro Business College
2305 N. Bishop Ave., Rolla 65401

: ‡ Midwest Institute for Medical Assistants
112 W. Jefferson Ave., Kirkwood 63122

· Mineral Area College, Flat River 63601
Richard Caster, President

∴† Mineral Area Regional Medical Center
1212 Weber Rd., Farmington 63640

Missouri Baptist College
12542 Conway Rd., St. Louis 63141

: ‡ Missouri School for Doctors' Assistants
10121 Manchester Rd., St. Louis 63122

† Missouri Southern State College
School of Radiologic Technology
3950 Newman Rd., Joplin 64801-1595
C. Young, MD, Program Director
See listing under "Universities"

∴† North Kansas City Hospital
2800 Hospital Dr., North Kansas City 64116

· Penn Valley Community College
3201 S.W. Traffic Way, Kansas City 64111
A. K. Longfellow, Dean of Admissions

· Phillips Junior College
1010 W. Sunshine St., Springfield 65807
Barbara Loven, President
417-864-7220 or 800-475-2669

∴† Research Medical Center
Schools of Radiology & Medical Technology
2316 E. Meyer Blvd., Kansas City 64132
Wynn Presson, Executive Director

: † Rolla Area Vocational-Technical School
    1304 E. Tenth St., Rolla   65401

· † St. Charles County Community College
    4601 Mid Rivers Mall Dr.
    P.O. Box 76975, Saint Peters   63376-0975

·.·† St. John's Mercy Medical Center
    615 S. New Ballas Rd., St. Louis   63141
    Sr. Mary Roch Rocklage, President

·.·† St. John's Regional Health Center
    1235 E. Cherokee St., Springfield   65804

·.·† St. John's Regional Medical Center
    School of Medical Technology
    2727 McClelland Blvd., Joplin   64804
    Leo Dougherty, MT (ASCP), Program Director

· ‡ St. Louis College of Health Careers
    4484 W. Pine Blvd., Saint Louis   63108
    Kim Green, Admissions Coordinator
    314-652-0300

· † St. Louis Community College at Forest Park
    5600 Oakland Ave., St. Louis   63110
    Elizabeth Halpin, Registrar

·   St. Louis Community College at Meramec
    11333 Big Bend Rd., Kirkwood   63122

† St. Louis University
    221 N. Grand Blvd., St. Louis   63103
    Louis A. Menard, Dean of Admissions

· † Saint Luke's Hospital
    4400 Wornall Rd., Kansas City   64111
    816-932-2000

    Southeast Missouri State University
    1 University Plz., Cape Girardeau   63701
    New Student Relations 314-651-2590
    See listing under "Universities"

    Southwest Baptist University
    1601 S. Springfield Ave., Bolivar   65613

† Southwest Missouri State University
    901 S. National Ave., Springfield   65804
    Dr. A. Duane Addleman, Dean
    417-836-4176

· † State Fair Community College
    Respiratory Therapy Technician Program
    3201 W. 16th St., Sedalia   65301-2199
    Susan Whitcomb, Program Director

† Stephens College, Columbia   65215
    Mary Ann Sprinkle, Dir. of Admis.

· † Three Rivers Community College
    Poplar Bluff   63901
    Dr. Steve Poort, President

·.·† Trinity Lutheran Hospital
    School of Medical Technology
    31st & Wyandotte Sts., Kansas City   64108
    Sandra Claussen, MT (ASCP), Program Director

: † United Health Careers Institute
    1100 Main St., 10th Floor, Kansas City   64105

† University of Missouri, Columbia
    228 Jesse Hall, Columbia   65211

† Washington University
    4559 Scott Ave., St. Louis   63110

    William Woods College
    200 W. 12th St., Fulton   65251
    Dr. Jahnae Barnett, VP of Admis.

MONTANA

† **CARROLL COLLEGE**
    1610 N. Benton Ave., Helena   59625
    Candace Cain, Dir. of Admis.
    See listing under "Universities"

·.·† Columbus Hospital
    500 15th Ave. S., Great Falls   59405
    William Downer, Administrator

· † Great Falls Vocational Technical Center
    2100 16th Ave., S., Great Falls   59405

· † Missoula Vocational Technical Center
    909 South Ave. W, Missoula   59801
    Charles Couture, Dir. of Admis.

·.·† Montana Deaconess Medical Center
    1101 26th St., S., Great Falls   59405
    John Curtis, M.D., Chrpsn.

·.·† St. James Community Hospital
    400 S. Clark St., Butte   59701
    J. A. Newman, M.D., Program Director

·.·† St. Patrick Hospital
    Radiographer Program
    P.O. Box 4587, Missoula   59806
    Anita McMahon, RT, Program Director

·.·† St. Vincent's Hospital
    2915 12th Ave., N., Billings   59101
    J. Anderson, M.D., Program Director

NEBRASKA

·.·† Archbishop Bergan Mercy Hospital
    Medical Technology Program
    7500 Mercy Rd., Omaha   68124
    John F. Fitzgibbons, M.D., Med. Dir.

·.·† Bishop Clarkson Memorial Hospital
    4350 Dewey Ave., Omaha   68105

·   Central Community College-Hastings Campus
    P.O. Box 1024, Hastings   68902-1024

CLARKSON COLLEGE
101 S. 42nd St., Omaha   68131-2739
Fay L. Bower, DN Sc, FAAN, President
800-647-5500
    Established 1888. Coed. Accreditation: NCACS,
NLN. Tuition: $3,900. Room and board: $2,300. Enrollment: 100 boarding, 550 day. Faculty: 55. Degrees:
AS, BS in Radiologic Technology, BSN, MSN in Nursing Education and Nursing Administration, MS in
Health Services Management. Library: 7,423 volumes. 1 building on 2 square blocks. Located in a large
metropolitan area medical center with ample recreational and cultural opportunities. RN/LPN/ advanced
placement for transfer students.

† College of Saint Mary
    1901 S. 72nd St., Omaha   68124
    Sheila Haggas, Dir. of Admis.

    Concordia College
    800 N. Columbia Ave., Seward   68434
    Don Vos, Dir. of Admis.

† Creighton University
    2500 California St., Omaha   68178
    Dr. L. Kirk Benedict, Dean

    Dana College
    2848 College Dr., Blair   68008
    John Schueth, Dir. of Admis.
    800-444-3262
    See listing under "Universities"

·.·† Immanuel Medical Center
    6901 N. 72nd St., Omaha   68122
    Riley M. Green, Admin.

·.·† Mary Lanning Memorial Hospital
    715 N. St. Joseph Ave., Hastings   68901
    W. Richard, M.D., Program Director

† Methodist College of Nursing & Health
    8501 W. Dodge Rd., Omaha   68114
    Deann Clyde, Coordinator of Admissions

· † Metropolitan Community College
    30th & Fort Sts., Omaha   68111
    Roy Phillips, President

·   Mid-Plains Community College
    1101 Halligan Dr., North Platte   69101
    Angie Pacheco, Admissions
    800-658-4308

    Nebraska Wesleyan University
    5000 Saint Paul Ave., Lincoln   68504
    Ken Sieg, Dir. of Admis.

· † Omaha College of Health Careers
    10845 Harney St., Omaha   68154
    Mark A Stuckey, V.P. Acad. Affairs

·.·† Regional West Medical Center
    4021 Ave. B, Scottsbluff   69361

·.·† St. Joseph Hospital
    School of Radiologic Technology
    601 N. 30th St., Omaha   68131-2197
    Carol McCormick, Program Director
    402-449-4812

† University of Nebraska Medical Center
    600 S., 42nd & Dewey, Omaha   68198
    Alastair M. Connell, Dean

    Western Nebraska Community College
    1601 E. 27th St., Scottsbluff   69361
    Roger Hovey, Admissions

NEVADA

:   American Academy for Career Education
    3120 E. Desert Inn Rd., Las Vegas   89121

· † Community College of Southern Nevada
    Formerly Clark County Community College
    3200 E. Cheyenne Ave., North Las Vegas   89030
    Arlie J. Stops, Dir. of Enrollment Management

· † Truckee Meadows Community College
    7000 Dandini Blvd., Reno   89512
    John Gwaltney, President

† University of Nevada, Reno
    Reno   89557

† University of Nevada Las Vegas
    4505 S. Maryland Pky., Las Vegas   89154-1021
    Admissions: 702-895-3443 or 800-334-UNLV

NEW HAMPSHIRE

· † New Hampshire Technical College
    One College Dr., Claremont   03743
    Willis S. Reed, President

·   New Hampshire Technical College at Stratham
    277 R. Portsmouth Ave., Stratham   03885
    Patricia A. Shay, Dean of Students

· † New Hampshire Technical Institute
    P.O. Box 2039, Concord   03302
    Daniel M. Burke, Dean of Admissions

† University of New Hampshire, Durham   03824
    Stanwood C. Fish, Dir. of Admissions

NEW JERSEY

·.·† Atlantic City Medical Center
    1925 Pacific Ave., Atlantic City   08401
    A. J. Salzman, Dir., Medical Education

· † Atlantic Community College
    5100 Black Horse Pike, Mays Landing   08330
    Bob Royal, Director/College Recruitment

·.·† Barnert Memorial Hospital
    School of Medical Technology
    680 Broadway, Paterson   07514

· † Berdan Institute
    265 State Rt. 46, Totowa   07512
    E. Lynn Thacker, Director
    201-256-3444

· † Bergen Community College
    400 Paramus Rd., Paramus   07652
    Frederick R. Prisco, Jr., Dir. of Admis.

    Bloomfield College
    1 Park Place, Bloomfield   07003
    Warner Smith, Dean for Admissions
    201-748-9000, Ext. 230

· † Brookdale Community College
    765 Newman Springs Rd., Lincroft   07738
    Peter F. Burnham, President

·.·† Burdette Tomlin Memorial Hospital
    2 Stone Harbor Blvd., Cape May Crt. Hse.   08210
    D. Wilner, M.D., Program Director

· † Burlington County College
    County Route 530, Pemberton   08068
    Juan Harris, Dir. of Admis.

·.·† Burlington Co. Memorial Hospital
    175 Madison Ave., Mt. Holly   08060
    William D. Locke, Admin.

· † Camden County College
    P.O. Box 200, Blackwood   08012
    Dr. Robert Ramsay, President

: † Camden Co. Vocational/Technical Schools
    P.O. Box 556, Sicklerville   08081

·.·† Cooper Medical Center
    6th & Stevens Sts., Camden   08103
    W. H. Jenkins, Admin.

· † County College of Morris
    200 Center Grove Rd., Randolph   07869

· † Cumberland County College
    P.O. Box 517, Vineland   08360

·.·† Elizabeth General Medical Center
    925 E. Jersey St., Elizabeth   07201

·.·† Englewood Hospital
    350 Engle St., Englewood   07631
    J. J. Gallagher, M.D., Program Director

· † Essex County College
    303 University Ave., Newark   07102

· † Fairleigh Dickinson University
    Edw. Williams College
    150 Kotte Pl., Hackensack   07601
    Kenneth Vehrkens, Dean
    201-692-2675

    Fairleigh Dickinson University, Madison   07940
    Lissa Anderson, Dir. of Admis.
    201-593-8906

    Fairleigh Dickinson University, Teaneck   07666
    Dennis Craig, Dir. of Admis.
    201-692-2732

† **FELICIAN COLLEGE**
    262 S. Main St., Lodi   07644
    Sr. Mary Austin, OSB, Dir. of Admis.
    201-778-1029
    See listing under "Universities"

· † Gloucester County College
    R.R. 4 Box 203, Sewell   08080
    Richard Jones, President

·.·† Hackensack Medical Center
    School of Radiography
    30 Prospect Ave., Hackensack   07601

·.·† Helene Fuld Medical Center
    750 Brunswick Ave., Trenton   08638

:   Ho-Ho-Kus School of Secretarial and Medical
    Sciences
    Medical Office Assistant
    27 S. Franklin Trnpk., Ramsey   07446
    Thomas Eastwick, Director
    201-327-8877

·.·   Hospital Center at Orange
    188 S. Essex Ave., Orange   07050
    Katherine Britchford, Director

·.·† Hudson Area School of Radiologic Technology
    29 E. 29th St., Bayonne   07002
    Kenneth Lee, BS, RT, Program Director

· † Hudson County Community College
    168 Sip Ave., Jersey City   07306
    Joseph O'Halloran, Director of Admissions
    201-714-2127

    Jersey City State College
    2039 Kennedy Blvd., Jersey City   07305
    201-200-3234

·.·† Jersey Shore Medical Center
    1945 State Route 33, Neptune   07753
    J. Price, MD, Program Director

·.·† John F. Kennedy Medical Center
    65 James St., Edison   08820
    F. D. Wald, M.D., Program Director

† Kean College of New Jersey
    1000 Morris Ave., Union   07083

· † Mercer County Community College
    West Windsor Campus
    School of Radiography
    1200 Old Trenton Rd., Trenton   08690
    Sandra Kerr, Coordinator
    See listing under "Community and Junior
    Colleges"

∴ Mercer Medical Center
P.O. Box 1658, Trenton 08607

· † Middlesex County College
Schools of Dental Hygiene, Medical Lab
Technology, Nursing, Radiography
P.O. Box 3050, Edison 08818
Dr. Marilyn Keener, Dean, Health Tech. Div.

∴† Monmouth Medical Center
3rd & Pavilion Aves., Long Branch 07740

∴† Morristown Memorial Hospital
100 Madison Ave., Morristown 07960
Stephen Wang, MD, Director of Medical Education

∴† Mountainside Hospital
1 Bay Ave., Montclair 07042
Gloria Corbo, Director

∴† Muhlenberg Regional Medical Center
1200 Randolph Rd., Plainfield 07060
Bong Hak Hyun, M.D., Director

∴† Newark Beth Israel Medical Center
201 Lyons Ave., Newark 07112
K. Gal, M.D., Program Director

· † Ocean County College
0 College Dr., Toms River 08753
Arthur Knies, Dir. of Admis. & Records

: ‡ Omega Institute
Route 130 S., Cinnaminson 08077

∴† Overlook Hospital, 193 Morris Ave., Summit 07901
Robert E. Heinlein, Director

∴† Pascack Valley Hospital
School of Radiologic Technology
250 Old Hook Rd., Westwood 07675
Deborah Rossi, RT, Program Director

· † Passaic Co. Community College
170 College Blvd., Paterson 07505
Dr. Gustavo A. Mellander, President

∴† Riverview Medical Center
35 Union St., Red Bank 07701

∴† St. Barnabas Medical Center
94 Old Short Hills Rd., Livingston 07039
John D. Phillips, Director

∴† St. Francis Medical Center
601 Hamilton Ave., Trenton 08629
Sr. Catherine Lawrence Meyer, Dir.

∴† St. Joseph's Medical Center
703 Main St., Paterson 07503
Sr. Jane Frances, Admin.

∴† St. Michael's Medical Center
268 Martin Luther King Jr. Blvd., Newark 07102
R. E. Carnes, M.D.

∴† St. Peter's Medical Center
254 Easton Ave., New Brunswick 08901

∴† Somerset Medical Center
100 Rehill Ave., Somerville 08876

∴† **SOUTH JERSEY HOSPITAL SYSTEM**
School of Radiologic Technology
Magnolia & Irving Aves., Bridgeton 08302
Edith Rodriguez, RT (R), Program Director

Stockton State College, Pomona 08240
Sal Catalfamo, Dir. of Admis.

Thomas Edison State College
101 W. State St., Trenton 08608

: ‡ Ultrasound Diagnostic School
Plaza One at Gill Ln. #6B, Iselin 08830

· † Union County College
1033 Springfield Ave., Cranford 07016
George Lynes, Dir. of Admis.

† University of Medicine and Dentistry of New Jersey
30 Bergen St., Newark 07107

Upsala College
345 Prospect St., East Orange 07017
George Lynes, Dean of Admissions

∴† Valley Hospital
301 Linwood Ave., Ridgewood 07450

∴† West Jersey Hospital
1000 Atlantic Ave., Camden 08104
J. F. Centrone, M.D., Program Director

NEW MEXICO

· † Albuquerque Technical-Vocational Institute
525 Buena Vista Dr., S.E., Albuquerque 87106
Jane Campbell, Registrar
See listing under "Career Schools"

· † Clovis Community College
417 Schepps Blvd., Clovis 88101

· † Dona Ana Branch Community College
P.O. Box 3001, Las Cruces 88003

∴† Eastern New Mexico University-Medical Center
405 W. Country Club Rd., Roswell 88201
505-622-8170

Eastern New Mexico University
Portales 88130
Larry Fuqua, Dir. of Admis.

∴† Memorial Medical Center
2801 E. University Ave., Las Cruces 88001
A. W. Fayen, M.D., Program Director

· † New Mexico Junior College
5317 Lovington Hwy., Hobbs 88240
Robert Snow, Registrar

· New Mexico State University
P.O. Box 477, Alamogordo 88311
Charles Ridlinger, Dir.

· † New Mexico State University
1500 University Dr., Carlsbad 88220
Shelton Marlow, Provost

· † Northern New Mexico Community College
1002 Onate St., Espanola 87532
Dan Simundson, Dean

: † Pima Medical Institute
2201 San Pedro Dr., N.E., Albuquerque 87110

† University of New Mexico, Albuquerque 87131
Robert Weaver, Dean of Admissions

· University of New Mexico
P.O. Box 1756, Gallup 87305

NEW YORK

∴† Albany Medical Center
43 New Scotland Ave., Albany 12208
Michael Vanko, Ph.D., Pres.

† Albany Medical College
47 New Scotland Ave., Albany 12208

∴† Albany Memorial Hospital
School of Radiologic Technology
600 Northern Blvd., Albany 12204
Colleen Carnegie, Program Director

: † Albany School of Cytotechnology
432 Western Ave., Albany 12203

∴† **ARNOT-OGDEN MEDICAL CENTER**
School of Radiologic Technology
600 Roe Ave., Elmira 14905-1676
Ellen Richards, BS RT (R) Director
607-737-4289

∴† Bayley Seton Hospital
75 Vanderbilt Ave., Staten Island 10304

∴† Bellevue Hospital Center
462 1st Ave., New York 10016
A. Keegan, M.D., Program Director

∴† Brooklyn Hospital
121 DeKalb Ave., Brooklyn 11201
Robert Markowitz, Exec. Director

· † Bryant & Stratton Business Institute
1028 Main St., Buffalo 14202

· † Bryant & Stratton Business Institute
82 St. Paul St., Rochester 14604

· † Bryant & Stratton Business Institute
953 James St., Syracuse 13203

∴† Catholic Medical Center
88-25 153rd St., Jamaica 11408

∴† Central Suffolk Hospital
School of Radiologic Technology
1300 Roanoke Ave., Riverhead 11901
M. D. Mangieri, M.D., Program Director

∴† Champlain Valley Physicians Hospital
100 Beekman St., Plattsburgh 12901

† College of St. Rose
432 Western Ave., Albany 12203

† Columbia University
617 W. 168th St., New York 10032

: ‡ Continental Dental Assistant School
633 Jefferson Rd., Rochester 14623

† Cornell University Medical College
1300 York Ave., New York 10021
Thomas H. Meikle, Jr., Dean

· CUNY Borough of Manhattan Community College
199 Chambers St., New York 10007

· † CUNY Bronx Community College
181st St. & University Ave., Bronx 10453
Roscoe C. Brown, Jr., President

† CUNY City College
Convent Ave. at 138th St., New York 10031

† CUNY College of Staten Island
130 Stuyvesant Pl., Staten Island 10301

· † CUNY Hostos Community College
475 Grand Concourse, Bronx 10451
Nydia Edgecombe, Dir of Admis.
718-518-6622

CUNY Hunter College
695 Park Ave., New York 10021
Donna Shalala, President

† CUNY New York City Technical College
300 Jay St., Brooklyn 11201
Ursula C. Schwerin, President

† CUNY York College
9420 Guy R. Brewer Blvd., Jamaica 11451

† Daemen College
4380 Main St., Amherst 14226
Maria Dillard, Dir. of Admis.
in NY 800-462-7652 or 716-839-8225

† Dominican College of Blauvelt
460 N. Western Hwy., Orangeburg 10962
Louis Kern, Dir. of Admis.
914-359-7800

Elmira College
Park Pl., Elmira 14901
William S. Neal, Dean of Admissions
See listing under "Liberal Arts"

∴† **GENESEE HOSPITAL**
School of Radiologic Technology
224 Alexander St., Rochester 14607
W. Siewers, RT, MS, Director of Education
716-263-5947

∴† Glens Falls Hospital
100 Park St., Glens Falls 12801

: Institute of Allied Medical Professions
106 Central Park S. #23D, New York 10019

† Ithaca College
953 Danby Rd., Ithaca 14850

† Keuka College
P.O. Box 98, Keuka Park 14478
Robert J. Ianuzzo, Dean of Admissions

The King's College, Briarcliff Manor 10510
Frederic Rowley, Dean of Admissions

∴† Long Island College Hospital
School of Radiologic Technology
340 Henry St., Brooklyn 11201
Ellen Shyman, BA, R.T., Program Director

Long Island University-Brooklyn Campus
School of Respiratory Therapy
1 University Plaza, Brooklyn 11201
Dr. Philip McGinn, Dean

† Long Island University-C. W. Post Campus
Rt. 25A, Brookville 11548
Dr. Ellen Duffy, Associate Dean
516-299-3046

: ‡ Mandl School
254 W. 54th St., New York 10019

† Manhattan College
4513 Manhattan College Pky., Riverdale 10471
John Brennan, Dean of Admissions

· Maria College of Albany
700 New Scotland Ave., Albany 12208
Laurie Gilmore, Dir. of Admis.

† **MARIST COLLEGE**
290 North Rd., Poughkeepsie 12601
Harry W. Wood, VP Admissions
914-575-3226

: † Memorial Sloan Kettering Cancer Center
1275 York Ave., New York 10021

Mercy College
555 Broadway, Dobbs Ferry 10522
James Nesbitt, Dean of Admissions

∴† Mercy Hospital
School of Radiologic Technology
1000 Village Ave., N., Rockville Ctr. 11570
J. Magovern, MD, Program Director

∴† Methodist Hospital of Brooklyn
School of Medical Technology
506 6th St., Brooklyn 11215-9008
Lynda Dines, Program Director

∴† Millard Fillmore Hospital
3 Gates Circle, Buffalo 14209

∴† Montefiore Medical Center
111 E. 210th St., Bronx 10467

∴† New York City Health & Hospitals Corporation
Respiratory Therapy Program
346 Broadway, New York 10013
C. Riley, Program Director

∴† New York Eye & Ear Infirmary
310 E. 14th St., New York 10003
S. Shippman, Program Director

∴† New York Hospital-Cornell Medical Center
525 E. 68th St., New York 10021
David Thompson, M.D., Director

† New York Institute of Technology
Old Westbury Campus, Old Westbury 11568

: New York School for Medical & Dental Assistants
11616 Queens Blvd., Forest Hills 11375
Thomas Haggerty, Director

† New York University
70 Washington Sq., New York 10012

† New York University
550 1st Ave., New York 10016
Dr. Ivan L. Bennett, Dean

∴† Northern Westchester Hospital Center
School of Medical Technology
400 Main St., Mt. Kisco 10549
P. Wade, President

∴† Northport Veterans Administration Hospital
79 Middleville Rd., Northport 11768

∴† North Shore University Hospital
St. Andrews Lane, Glen Cove 11542

Pace University, New York Campus
1 Pace Plaza, New York 10038

∴† Peninsula Hospital Center
5115 Beach Channel Dr., Far Rockaway 11691

∴† Rochester General Hospital
1425 Portland Ave., Rochester 14621
Z. M. Tomkiewicz, M.D., Program Director

† Rochester Institute of Technology
1 Lomb Memorial Dr., Rochester 14623
716-475-6631
See listing under "Universities"

Russell Sage College
51 1st St., Troy 12180

∴† St. Elizabeth Hospital
School of Radiologic Technology
2209 Genesee St., Utica 13501
See listing under "Nursing"

∴† St. James Mercy Hospital
411 Canisteo St, Hornell 14843

∴† St. Lukes Memorial Hospital Center
School of Medical Radiography
P.O. Box 479, Utica 13503-0479
Rosemary Morin, BS, RTR, Director

∴† ST. MARY'S HOSPITAL
Medical Technology Program
89 Genesee St., Rochester 14611
Arlene Nikiel, Program Director

ST. THOMAS AQUINAS COLLEGE
Rt. 340, Sparkill 10976
Andrea Kraeft, Dir. of Admis.
800-999-STAC
See listing under "Liberal Arts"

∴† St. Vincent's Hospital
27 Christopher St., New York 10014
Sr. Miriam Phillips, Director

∴† South Nassau Communities Hospital
School of Radiologic Technology
2445 Oceanside Rd., Oceanside 11572
R. J. Hochstim, M.D., Program Director

† SUNY at Buffalo
501 Capen Hall, Amherst 14260

† SUNY Health Science Center
155 Elizabeth Blackwell St., Syracuse 13210

† SUNY at Stony Brook, Health Sciences Center
Stony Brook 11790

† SUNY Health Science Center at Brooklyn
450 Clarkson Ave., Brooklyn 11203

SUNY at Buffalo
17 Capen Hall
P.O. Box 601660, Buffalo 14260-1660
716-645-6900

· † SUNY Broome Community College
907 Upper Front St., Binghamton 13905
Donald Dellow, President

· † SUNY Clinton Community College
Bluff Point, Plattsburgh 12901

† SUNY College of Agriculture & Technology
Cobleskill 12043
John Devney, Jr., Dir. of Admis.

· † SUNY College of Technology, Alfred 14802
Deborah J. Goodrich, Dir. of Admis.
607-587-4215

· † SUNY College of Technology
34 Cornell Dr., Canton 13617
Thomas R. Fletcher, Director of Admissions
800-388-7123

· † SUNY Dutchess Community College
Poughkeepsie 12601

· † SUNY Erie Community College, City Campus
121 Ellicott St., Buffalo 14203
Dr. Louis Ricci, President

· SUNY Erie Community College, North Campus
6205 Main St., Williamsville 14221

· SUNY HUDSON VALLEY COMMUNITY COLLEGE
80 Vandenburgh Ave., Troy 12180
Joseph Bulmer, President
Linda Sweetman, Dir. of Admis.
Mary Giles, Dean, School of Health Science
518-283-1100
Established 1953. Public. Coed. Accreditation: NLN, Commission on Dental Accreditation, Council on Medical Education of the AMA, American Registry of Radiological Technologists. Tuition: $1,550 full-time. Estimated total yearly expenses: $2,500 full-time. Enrollment: 5,878 full-time, 4,498 part-time. Faculty: 240 full-time, 350 part-time. Degrees: AAS, AS. Library: 105,000 volumes. 14 buildings on 165 acres. Gym. Majors: medical lab tech., dental hygiene, funeral services, nursing, physician's assistant, radiologic tech. (x-ray), respiratory care, cooperative program with Albany Medical College. All programs lead to professional licensure, university transfer or immediate employment.

† SUNY INSTITUTE OF TECHNOLOGY AT UTICA/ROME
P.O. Box 3050, Utica 13504
Roger Sullivan, Dir. of Admis.
See listing under "Universities"

· † SUNY Jefferson Community College
1220 Coffeen St., Watertown 13601
Rosanne N. Weir, Dir. of Admis.

· † SUNY Mohawk Valley Community College
1101 Sherman Dr., Utica 13501

· † SUNY Monroe Community College
1000 E. Henrietta Rd., Rochester 14623
716-292-2000

· † SUNY Nassau Community College
1 Education Dr., Garden City 11530
Bernard Iantosca, Dir of Admis.

· † SUNY Niagara County Community College
3111 Saunders Settlement Rd., Sanborn 14132
R. J. Mirabelli, Admis. Ofc.

· † SUNY North Country Community College
School of Radiologic Technology
P.O. Box 89, Saranac Lake 12983
P. Monagan, Program Director

· † SUNY Onondaga Community College
Onondaga Rd., Syracuse 13215
Joseph Insel, Dir. of Admis.

· Suny Orange County Community College
115 South St., Middletown 10940
914-341-4030

· † SUNY Rockland Community College
Medical Lab Technology
145 College Rd., Suffern 10901
Marge Warren, Coordinator

· SUNY Suffolk County Community College
533 College Rd., Selden 11784
Robert Kreiling, President

· † SUNY Westchester Community College
75 Grasslands Rd., Valhalla 10595-1698
Alan Seidman, Dir. of Admis.

: Swedish Institute, Inc.
School of Massage Therapy
226 W. 26th St. #5, New York 10001
Patricia Eckardt, Director
212-924-5900

∴† Tompkins Community Hospital
School of Radiologic Technology
101 Dates Dr., Ithaca 14850
Tom Kleckner, Program Director

† Touro College
844 Avenue of the Americas, New York 10001

· † Trocaire College
110 Red Jacket Pky., Buffalo 14220
Mary Schinner, Dean of Health Sciences
716-826-1200

: ‡ Ultrasound Diagnostic School
2269 Saw Mill River Rd., Elmsford 10523

: ‡ Ultrasound Diagnostic School
One Old Country Rd., Carle Place 11514

: ‡ Ultrasound Diagnostic School
121 W. 27th St., New York 10001

∴† United Hospital Medical Center
406 Boston Post Rd., Port Chester 10573
Richard A. Stolnacke, President

† University of Rochester
500 Joseph C. Wilson Blvd., Rochester 14627
Wayne A. Locust, Dir. of Admis.
See listing under "Universities"

† Utica College of Syracuse University
1600 Burrstone Rd., Utica 13502

† WAGNER COLLEGE
631 Howard Ave., Staten Island 10301
Joseph Foulke, Dean Admissions and Financial Aid
See listing under "Universities"

∴† Winthrop University Hospital
259 1st St., Mineola 11501

∴† Woman's Christian Association Hospital
207 Foote Ave., Jamestown 14701
E. F. Foley, M.D., Program Director

NORTH CAROLINA

· Alamance Community College
P.O. Box 623, Haw River 27258
W. Ronald McCarter, President

· † Asheville Buncombe Technical Community College
340 Victoria Rd., Asheville 28801
Connie Buckner, Dir. of Admis.

· † Beaufort County Community College
Medical Laboratory Technology
P.O. Box 1069, Washington 27889
Gary Burbage, Dir. of Admis.

· Bladen Community College
School for Medical Lab. Technicians
P.O. Box 266, Dublin 28332
J. F. Knechtges, Program Director

· † Caldwell Community College
P.O. Box 600, Lenoir 28645
Dr. H. E. Beam, President

∴† Carolinas Medical Center
P.O. Box 32861, Charlotte 28232

· † Carteret Community College
Department of Respiratory Care & Radiologic Technology
3505 Arendell St., Morehead City 28557
Rick Hill, Susan Phillips, Counselors
919-247-4142 ext. 153

· † Catawba Valley Community College
R.R. 3, Box 283, Hickory 28602
Robert E. Paap, President

· † Central Piedmont Community College
P.O. Box 35009, Charlotte 28235
Dr. Ruth Shaw, President

∴ Charlotte Memorial Hospital & Medical Center
1000 Blythe Blvd., Charlotte 28203
H. Green, Director

· † Cleveland Community College
137 S. Post Rd., Shelby 28152

· † Coastal Carolina Community College
School for Surgical Technicians
444 Western Blvd, Jacksonville 28546

† Duke University, Durham 27706

∴† Durham County General Hospital
School of Radiologic Technology
3643 N. Roxboro Rd., Durham 27704
D. M. Monson, M.D., Program Director

· † Durham Technical Community College
School for Respiratory Therapists
1637 E. Lawson St., Durham 27703
Dr. Richard Miller, Program Director

† East Carolina University
1000 E. 5th St., Greenville 27858
Dr. Harold P. Jones, Dean

· † Edgecombe Community College
2009 Wilson St., W., Tarboro 27886
Thomas Anderson, VP of Student Services
919-823-5166

Elon College
P.O. Box 2700, Elon College 27244
Nan P. Clark, Dean of Admissions

· † Fayetteville Technical Community College
P.O. Box 35236, Fayetteville 28303

∴† Forsyth Memorial Hospital
3333 Silas Creek Pky., Winston-Salem 27103

· † Forsyth Technical Community College
2100 Silas Creek, Winston-Salem 27103
Dr. Bob Greene, President

Gardner-Webb University
General Delivery, Boiling Springs 28017
Dee Hunt, Chrpsn.
704-434-2361

· † Gaston College
201 Highway 321, S., Dallas 28034

∴† Gaston Memorial Hospital
2525 Court Dr., Gastonia 28054
L. M. Morris, M.D., Program Director

· † Guilford Technical Community College
P.O. Box 309, Jamestown 27282

· † Halifax Community College
P.O. Box 809, Weldon 27890

· † Haywood Community College
Freedlander Dr., Clyde 28721
Carol Smith, Dir. of Admis.

· James Sprunt Community College
P.O. Box 398, Kenansville 28349
Rita Brown, Registrar
910-296-2500

· † Johnston Community College
School of Radiologic Technology
P.O. Box 2350, Smithfield 27577
Joan Jones, Director of Admissions

· † King's College
322 Lamar Ave., Charlotte 28204
Debbie Remelius, Registrar

· † Lenoir Community College
P.O. Box 188, Kinston 28502

∴† Lenoir Memorial Hospital
School of Radiologic Technology
P.O. Box 1678, Kinston 28503

Mars Hill College
Main St., Mars Hill 28754
Dr. Smith Goodrum, Dean of Admis.

∴† Moses H. Cone Memorial Hospital
1200 Elm St., N., Greensboro 27401
Dr. Leonard J. Rubold, Dir., Education

∴† New Hanover Memorial Hospital
2131 17th St., S., Wilmington 28401
H. P. Singletary, M.D., Program Director

∴† North Carolina Memorial Hospital
101 Manning Dr., Chapel Hill 27514

∴‡ Northern Hospital of Surry County
P.O. Box 1101, Mount Airy 27030

· † Pitt Community College
School of Radiologic Technology
P.O. Box 7007, Greenville 27835
Sylvia S. Corey, Registrar

∴† PRESBYTERIAN HOSPITAL
P.O. Box 33549, Charlotte 28233
Michael Smith, Dir. of Admis.
704-384-4141
Established 1903. Coed. Accreditation: NLN, North Carolina State Board of Nursing. Tuition: $3,555. Room: $2,400. Fees: $370. Enrollment: 300 full-time. Faculty: 26. Student-faculty ratio: 11:1. Degrees: Diploma, qualified graduates may receive BSN in one calendar year at Queens College. Library: 8,000 volumes, 155 subscriptions. Largest hospital based nursing program in the Carolinas. 97% of graduates pass the state board exam for their registered nurse license. Students begin clinical nursing early in the second year.

· † Rowan-Cabarrus Community College
School of Radiologic Technology
P.O. Box 1595, Salisbury 28145

Salem College
P.O. Box 10548, Winston-Salem 27108
Katherine Knapp, Director of Admissions
800-32-SALEM
See listing under "Women's College"

· † Sandhills Community College
2200 Airport Rd., Pinehurst 28374
910-692-6185

· † Southwestern Community College
275 Webster Rd., Sylva 28779

· † Stanly Community College
School for Respiratory Therapy Technicians
R.R. 4, Box 55, Albemarle 28001

† University of North Carolina at Chapel Hill
Chapel Hill 27599
James C. Walters, Dir. Undergrad Admis.

· † Vance-Granville Community College
P.O. Box 917, Henderson 27536

† Wake Forest University
Bowman Gray School of Medicine
Medical Center Blvd., Winston-Salem 27157

· † Wake Technical Community College
School for Medical Laboratory Technicians
9101 Fayetteville Rd., Raleigh 27603

· Wayne Community College
Caller Box 8002, Goldsboro 27533
Bill Bennett, Public Information Officer
919-735-5151

† Western Carolina University
Cullowhee 28723
Tyree H. Kiser, Dir. of Admissions

· † Western Piedmont Community College
1001 Burkemont Ave., Morganton 28655
H. D. Moretz, Dean of College

·.† Wilkes Regional Medical Center
School of Radiologic Technology
P.O. Box 609, North Wilkesboro 28659

† Wingate College, Wingate 28174

† Winston-Salem State University
601 S. Martin Luther King Jr.
Winston-Salem 27110
Van Wilson, Dir. of Admissions

NORTH DAKOTA

· † **BISMARCK STATE COLLEGE**
1500 Edwards Ave., Bismarck 58501
Dr. Kermit Lidstrom, President
701-224-5400

: † Minot School for Allied Health
20 Burdick Expy. W. #603, Minot 58701

· North Dakota State College of Science
800 N. 6th St., Wahpeton 58075
Dr. Rodney J. Casad, Director

·.† Quain & Ramstad Clinic
221 N. 5th St., Bismarck 58501
S. K. Imes, M.D., Program Director

·.† St. Alexius Medical Center
P.O. Box 5510, Bismark 58502-5510
701-244-7070

·.† St. Joseph's Hospital
3rd St. & 4th Ave., S.E., Minot 58701

·.† St. Luke's Hospital
5th St. & Mills Ave., Fargo 58105

·.† Trinity Medical Center
3 Burdick Expy., Minot 58701

: ‡ Turtle Mt. School of Paramedical Technique
Bottineau 58318

† University of North Dakota
Box 8193 University Station, Grand Forks 58203

OHIO

·.† Akron General Medical Center
400 Wabash Ave., Akron 44307

: † Akron Medical-Dental Institute
1625 Portage Trail W., Cuyahoga Falls 44223
Elizabeth Husk, Director
216-762-9788

·.† American Red Cross Blood Services
3747 Euclid Ave., Cleveland 44115

: ‡ Aristotle Institute of Medical & Dental Technology
5900 Westerville Rd., Westerville 43081

·.† Aultman Hospital
2600 6th St., S.W., Canton 44710
Richard Pryce, President

† Bowling Green State University
Bowling Green 43403
John Martin, Dir. of Admis.

† Case Western Reserve University
2040 Adelbert Rd., Cleveland 44106

· Central Ohio Technical College
University Dr., Newark 43055
John Merrin, Coordinator of Admissions

·.† Children's Hospital Medical Center
281 Locust St., Akron 44302

: † Choffin Career Center
P.O. Box 550, Youngstown 44501

·.† Christ Hospital
2139 Auburn Ave., Cincinnati 45219

· Cincinnati Technical College
3520 Central Pkwy., Cincinnati 45223
Dr. Geraldine Kaminski, Chrpsn.

· Clark State Community College
570 E. Leffels Ln., Springfield 45505
Leigh Fisher, Admissions Specialist

: † Cleveland Clinic Foundation
9500 Euclid Ave., Cleveland 44195

: ‡ Cleveland Institute of Dental & Medical Assistants
5733 Hopkins Rd., Mentor 44060

: ‡ Cleveland Institute of Dental-Medical Assistants
5564 Mayfield Rd., Lyndhurst 44124

: ‡ Cleveland Institute of Dental and Medical Assisting
1836 Euclid Ave. #401, Cleveland 44115
Alan Steinberger, Director

· Cleveland State University
Euclid Ave. at 24th St., Cleveland 44115

† College of Mount St. Joseph
5701 Delhi Rd., Cincinnati 45233-1672
See listing under "Universities"

· Columbus State Community College
550 E. Spring St., Columbus 43215
Mary Jo Deerwester, Dir. of Admis.

·.† Community Hospital
School of Radiologic Technology
P.O. Box 1228, Springfield 45501
Bonnie Young, Education Coordinator
513-328-9354

∴ Cooperative Medical Technology Program of Akron
One Perkins Square, Akron 44308-1062
Suzanne Conner, MA, Program Director
216-379-8720

· † Cuyahoga Community College, Eastern Campus
25444 Harvard Rd., Warrensville Heights 44122

· Cuyahoga Community College, Metropolitan Campus
2900 Community College Ave., Cleveland 44115

· Cuyahoga Community College, Western Campus
11000 W. Pleasant Valley Rd.
Parma Heights 44130

· † **DAVIS JUNIOR COLLEGE**
4747 Monroe St., Toledo 43623
Diane Brunner, President
Established 1858. Private. Coed. Accreditation:
AICS, AAMA, NCACS. Tuition: $5,600. Fees: $25
application fee. Enrollment: 350 full-time, 100 part-
time. Faculty: 35. Student-faculty ratio: 15:1. Degree:
associate. Specialized library. 2 buildings including
an airport. Admissions test (CPAT) & specialized.
High school graduate or GED. Enroll each quarter.
90% placement overall. Unique professional pilot
program.

∴ Fairview General Hospital
School of Medical Technology
18101 Lorain Ave., Cleveland 44111
Harlan Peterjohn, M.D., Director

· Hocking College
3301 Hocking Pky., Nelsonville 45764
Candace Vancko, VP for Enrollment
800-282-4163

∴ Huron Road Hospital
13951 Terrace Rd., East Cleveland 44112
I. Ahmad, M.D., Program Director

: ‡ Institute of Medical & Dental Technology
375 Glenspring Dr. #201, Cincinnati 45246

: ‡ Institute of Medical & Dental Technology
4452 Eastgate Blvd. #209, Cincinnati 45245

· Jefferson Technical College
4000 Sunset Blvd., Steubenville 43952
Chuck Mascellino, Dir. of Admis.
800-456-TECH

· Kent State University
P.O. Box 5190, Kent 44242
Bruce Riddle, Dir. of Admis.

· † Kettering College of Medical Arts
3737 Southern Blvd., Kettering 45429
Curt Dolinsky, Dir. of College Relations
800-433-5262

· † Lakeland Community College
7700 Clocktower Dr., Kirtland 44094
Bill Kraus, Dir. of Admis.

· † Lima Technical College
4240 Campus Dr., Lima 45804
S. D. Bassitt, Program Director

· † Lorain County Community College
1005 Abbe Rd., N., Elyria 44035
Dr. John W. Thrash, Jr., Registrar

LOURDES COLLEGE
6832 Convent Blvd., Sylvania 43560
Mary E. Briggs, Dir. of Admis.
419-885-5291 or 800-878-3210

Malone College
515 25th St., N.W., Canton 44709
Lee Sommers, Dean of Admissions

·.† Marion General Hospital
School of Radiologic Technology
96 McKinley Park Dr., Marion 43302
Linda Rizzo, Program Director

· † Marion Technical College
1467 Mt. Vernon Ave., Marion 43302-5694
Joel Liles, Dir. of Admis.

Medical College of Ohio
P.O. Box 10008, Toledo 43699
Barry L. Richardson, PhD, Dean for Admissions

·.† Memorial Hospital
401 Matthew St., Marietta 45750

·.† Mercy Hospital
116 Dayton St., Hamilton 45011
Sr. M. C. Medosch, Admin.

·.† Mercy Hospital
School of Medical Technology
2200 Jefferson Ave., Toledo 43624
D. Hanson, MD, Program Director

·.† Meridia Euclid Hospital
School of Radiologic Technology
18901 Lake Shore Blvd., Euclid 44119

·.† Meridia Hillcrest Hospital
6780 Mayfield Rd., Cleveland 44124

·.† MetroHealth Medical Center
3395 Scranton Rd., Cleveland 44109

·.† Middletown Regional Hospital
105 McKnight Dr., Middletown 45044

·.· Mt. Carmel Medical Center
793 W. State St., Columbus 43222
William R. Hughes, Director

Mount Union College
1972 Clark Ave., Alliance 44601
Amy Tomko, Dir. of Admis.

Mt. Vernon Nazarene College
800 Martinsburg Rd., Mt. Vernon 43050
Ronald Hyson, Dir. of Admis.

: † MTI Business College
1901 E. 13th St. #310, Cleveland 44114

· Muskingum Area Technical College
1555 Newark Rd., Zanesville 43701

· North Central Technical College
P.O. Box 698, Mansfield 44901

† Ohio State University
190 N. Oval Mall, Columbus 43210

·.† Ohio State University Hospitals
410 W. 10th Ave., Columbus 43210

· † **OHIO VALLEY BUSINESS COLLEGE**
500 Maryland Ave., East Liverpool 43920
216-385-1070

·.† Ohio Valley Hospital
School of Medical Technology
1 Ross Park, Steubenville 43952
Sheila Hendricks, Program Director

· † Owens Community College
P.O. Box 10000, Toledo 43699
Jim Welling, Admissions
419-661-7225

· Owens Community College
300 Davis St., Findlay 45840
Stacy Davidson, Admissions
419-423-6827

: ‡ Professional Skills Institute
1232 Flaire Dr., Toledo 43615

·.† Providence Hospital
School of Radiologic Technology
2446 Kipling Ave., Cincinnati 45239

·.† **PROVIDENCE HOSPITAL**
School of Radiologic Technology
1912 Hayes Ave., Sandusky 44870
Cynthia Felske, Program Coordinator

·.† Richmond Heights General Hospital
27100 Chardon Rd., Richmond Heights 44143

·.† Riverside Hospital
1600 Superior St., N., Toledo 43604
D. B. Harding, Jr., M.D., Program Director

·.† Riverside Methodist Hospital
3535 Olentangy River Rd., Columbus 43214

·.† St. Charles Hospital
School of Medical Technology
2600 Navarre Ave., Oregon 43616
Barb Morman, MT(ASCP), Program Director

·.† St. Elizabeth Hospital
P.O. Box 1790, Youngstown 44501

·.† St. Elizabeth Medical Center
601 S. Edwin C. Moses Blvd., Dayton 45408
W. Abramson, M.D., Program Director

·.† St. Luke's Hospital
11311 Shaker Blvd., Cleveland 44104

·.† St. Vincent Medical Center
2201 Cherry St., Toledo 43608
Lynn Wagoner, Director

† Shawnee State University
940 2nd St., Portsmouth 45662
Rosemary K. Poston, Dir. of Admis.

· † Sinclair Community College
444 W. 3rd St., Dayton 45402-1460
Sara P. Smith, Director of Admissions
800-315-3000

· † Southern Ohio College
1055 Laidlaw Ave., Cincinnati 45237
Duane Hawkins, President

· † Southern Ohio College
2791 Mogadore Rd., Akron 44312

· † Southern Ohio College
4641 Bach Ln., Fairfield 45014

: ‡ Southwestern College of Business
225 W. 1st St., Dayton 45402

: ‡ Southwestern College of Business
9910 Princeton-Glendale Rd., Cincinnati 45246

· ‡ Southwestern College of Business
717 Race St., Cincinnati 45202

· ‡ Southwestern College of Business
631 S. Briel Blvd., Middletown 45044

·˙† Southwest General Hospital
18697 E. Bagley Rd., Middleburg Hgts. 44130

· † Stark Technical College
6200 Frank Ave., N.W., Canton 44720

· ‡ Stautzenberger College
4404 Secor Rd., Toledo 43623

·˙† Summa Health System/Akron City Hospital
525 E. Market St., Akron 44309

· Technology Education College
288 S. Hamilton Rd., Columbus 43213
Ronald Dooley, President
See listing under "Career Schools"

·˙† Timken Mercy Medical Center
1320 Timken Mercy Dr., N.W., Canton 44708

·˙† Trumbull Memorial Hospital
1350 E. Market St., Warren 44483

·˙† University Hospital of Cleveland
2065 Adelbert Rd., Cleveland 44106
David W. Clark, Admin.

† University of Akron
381 Buchtel Common, Akron 44325
Kris MacDermott, Asst. Provost Enrollment

† University of Cincinnati
2700 Clifton Ave., Cincinnati 45221

† University of Findlay
1000 N. Main St., Findlay 45840
Dan Crabtree, Dir. of Admis.

† University of Rio Grande
School for Medical Lab Technicians
General Delivery, Rio Grande 45674
Carolyn Quittner, Program Director
614-245-5353, Ext. 7301

† University of Toledo
2801 Bancroft St., W., Toledo 43606
Richard Eastop, Dir. of Admis.

· † Washington Community College
710 Collegiate Dr., Marietta 45750
Dr. Donald R. Neff, President

·˙† Western Reserve Care System
345 Oak Hill Ave., Youngstown 44502

Wittenberg University
P.O. Box 720, Springfield 45504

† Wright State University
3640 Colonel Glenn Hwy., Dayton 45435

† Xavier University
3800 Victory Pky., Cincinnati 45207

† Youngstown State University
410 Wick Ave., Youngstown 44555
Leslie H. Cochran, President

OKLAHOMA

· † Bacone College
99 Bacone Rd., Muskogee 74403-1597
David Norfolk, Dean of Enrollment Management

: ‡ Bryan Institute
2843 E. 51st St., Tulsa 74105
E. Gough, Director

Cameron University
2800 W. Gore Blvd., Lawton 73505
Louise Brown, Dir. of Admis.

·˙† Comanche County Memorial Hospital
3401 W. Gore Blvd., Lawton 73505
R. Dix, M.D., Program Director

† East Central University, Ada 74820
School for Medical Record Administrators
Lorraine Hooker, Program Director

: † Great Plains Area Vocational Technical School
4500 W. Lee Blvd., Lawton 73505

: † Indian Meridian Vocational Technical School
1312 S. Sangre St., Stillwater 74074

·˙† Mercy Health Center
4300 W. Memorial Rd., Oklahoma City 73120
Sr. Mary Coletta, President

·˙† Muskogee General Hospital
300 Rockefeller Dr., Muskogee 74401
T. S. Gafford, Jr., M.D., Program Director

· † Northeastern Oklahoma A & M College
200 I St. N.E., Miami 74354
K. Dale Patterson, Dean of Admissions

Oklahoma Panhandle State University
P.O. Box 430, Goodwell 73939

Oral Roberts University
7777 S. Lewis Ave., Tulsa 74171
Arthur E. Matzkvech, Dir. of Admis.

·˙† Presbyterian Hospital
700 N.E. 13th St., Oklahoma City 73104

· † Rose State College
6420 S.E. 15th St., Midwest City 73110
Robert Alyea, Registrar

·˙† St. Anthony Hospital
1000 N. Lee, Oklahoma City 73102
W. T. Snoddy, M.D., Program Director

·˙† St. Francis Hospital
6161 S. Yale Ave., Tulsa 74136

·˙† St. Mary's Hospital
305 5th St., S., Enid 73701
John McMilen, President

· † Seminole Junior College
P.O. Box 351, Seminole 74818

† Southwestern Oklahoma State University
100 Campus Dr., Weatherford 73096

: ‡ Southwestern Oklahoma State University
409 E. Mississippi, Sayre 73662
Don Roberts, Dean

: † Tulsa Co. Area Vocational Technical District 18
3420 S. Memorial Dr., Tulsa 74145

· † Tulsa Junior College
6111 E. Skelly Dr. #200, Tulsa 74135

: † Tuttle Vocational Technical Center
12777 N. Rockwell Ave., Oklahoma City 73142

University of Central Oklahoma
100 N. University Dr., Edmond 73034

† University of Oklahoma Health Sciences Center
P.O. Box 26901, Oklahoma City 73126
Dr. Lee Holder, Dean, College of Allied Health

·˙† Valley View Regional Hospital
430 N. Monte Vista St., Ada 74820
Cheryl Weems, MT (ASCP), Program Director

OREGON

: ‡ Apollo College of Medical and Dental Careers
2600 S.E. 98th Ave., Portland 97266

· Blue Mountain Community College
2411 N.W. Carden, Pendleton 97801

· † Central Oregon Community College
School for Medical Record Technicians
2600 N.W. College Way, Bend 97701
Christine Kerlin, Dir. of Admis.
503-383-7500

· † Chemeketa Community College
P.O. Box 14007, Salem 97309
Carol Brownlow, Director
503-399-5113

: † CollegeAmerica
921 S.W. Washington #200, Portland 97205

· † Lane Community College
4000 E. 30th Ave., Eugene 97405
Sharon K. Moore, Dir. of Admis.

Linfield College
900 S. Baker St., McMinnville 97128
Thomas Meicho, Dean of Admissions

Linfield College
2215 N.W. Northrup St., Portland 97210

· † Mt. Hood Community College
School for Respiratory Therapists
26000 S.E. Stark St., Gresham 97030
Jan Bohlmann, Coordinator

† Oregon Health Sciences University
3181 S.W. Sam Jackson Park Rd., Portland 97201
Marian Ewell, MT (ASCP) SBB

† Oregon Institute of Technology
School of Medical Technology
3201 Campus Dr., Klamath Falls 97601

·˙† Pacific NW Red Cross Blood Services
School of Blood Bank Technology
3131 N. Vancouver Ave., Portland 97227

† Pacific University
2043 College Way, Forest Grove 97116
Barbara Mergen, Dir. of Admis.

: † Paramedic Training Institute
P.O. Box 1878, Beaverton 97075

· † Portland Community College
P.O. Box 19000, Portland 97280

· † Rogue Community College
School for Respiratory Therapy Technicians
3345 Redwood Hwy., Grants Pass 97527
Ted Risser, Registrar
503-471-3501
See listing under "Community and Junior Colleges"

·˙† St. Vincent Hospital & Medical Center
9205 S.W. Barnes Rd., Portland 97225

University of Portland
5000 N. Willamette Blvd., Portland 97203

·˙† Veterans Administration Medical Center
P.O. Box 1034, Portland 97207

: ‡ Western Medical College of Allied Health
3000 Market St., N.E. #541, Salem 97301
Marcella Arnold, Director

PENNSYLVANIA

·˙† **ABINGTON MEMORIAL HOSPITAL**
1200 Old York Rd., Abington 19001
215-576-2650

: ‡ Academy of Medical Arts and Business
279 Boas St., Harrisburg 17102

·˙† **ALBERT EINSTEIN MEDICAL CENTER**
School of Radiologic Technology
5501 Old York Rd., Philadelphia 19141
Mary Susan Kane, Program Director
215-456-6234
Established 1946. Public. Coed. Accreditation: Joint Review Committee on Education in Radiologic Tech. Tuition: $1,500. Fees: $600. Enrollment: 30. Faculty: 3. Student-faculty ratio: 10:1. Degrees: Certificate in Radiologic Technology. Library: 17,000 volumes. 8 buildings.

·˙† Aliquippa Hospital
School of Radiologic Technology
2500 Hospital Dr., Aliquippa 15001
Debra Majetic, Program Director
412-857-1246

·˙† Allegheny General Hospital
320 E. North Ave., Pittsburgh 15212
H. D. Sanders, Senior VP

·˙† Allegheny Valley Hospital
1301 Carlisle St., Natrona 15065
John B. Richardson, Admin.

·˙† Allentown Hospital-Lehigh Valley Hospital Center
P.O. Box 1110, Allentown 18105

: ‡ Allied Medical Careers
P.O. Box 1648, Kingston 18704

: ‡ Allied Medical Careers
2901 Pittston Ave., Scranton 18505
Damon Young, President

·˙† Altoona Hospital
School of Medical Technology & Radiology
620 Howard Ave., Altoona 16601
Joseph Noel, MT (ASCP), Dir.
Carole Daski, RT, Dir.

: Antonelli Medical & Professional Institute
1700 Industrial Hwy., Pottstown 19464
Paula Bauer, Dir. of Admis.

·˙† Armstrong County Memorial Hospital
1 Nolte Dr., Kittanning 16201

·˙† Ashland State General Hospital
R.R. 61, Ashland 17921

Beaver College
450 S. Easton Rd., Glenside 19038-3295
Dennis Nostrand, VP for Enrollment Management
Phone: 800-776-BEAVER(2328)
Fax: 215-572-4049
See listing under "Universities"

Bloomsburg University, Bloomsburg 17815
Bernard Vinovrski, Dir. of Admis.

·˙† Bradford Regional Medical Center
School of Radiography
116 Interstate Parkway, Bradford 16701
J. Piatko, Program Director
814-362-8292

: † Bradford School
355 Fifth Ave., Pittsburgh 15222
John A. Besser, Director

·˙† Brandywine Hospital
201 Reeceville Rd., Coatesville 19320

·˙† Bryn Mawr Hospital
School of Allied Health Science
130 S. Bryn Mawr Ave., Bryn Mawr 19010

California University of Pennsylvania
3rd St., California 15419
Norman Hasbrouck, Dean for Enrollment

: † Career Training Academy
703 5th Ave., New Kensington 15068
John M. Reddy, President

·˙† Carlisle Hospital School of Radiologic Technology
P.O. Box 310, Carlisle 17013
Sandra Foster, BSRT, Program Director
717-245-5440

† Cedar Crest College
100 College Dr., Allentown 18104-6196
Cynthia Phillips, Dir. of Admissions

· † Central Pennsylvania Business School
College Hill Rd., Summerdale 17093

·˙† Chambersburg Hospital
112 N. 7th St., Chambersburg 17201
J. Kuhnert, Program Director

·˙† Clearfield Hospital
P.O. Box 992, Clearfield 16830

† College Misericordia
301 Lake St., Dallas 18612
Michael Joseph, Dir. of Enrollment Mgmt.

· † Community College of Allegheny Co.
Allegheny Campus
808 Ridge Ave., Pittsburgh 15212

· † Community College of Allegheny Co., Boyce Campus
595 Beatty Rd., Monroeville 15146

· † Community College of Allegheny Co., South Campus
1750 Clairton Rd., West Mifflin 15122

· † Community College of Beaver County
College Drive, Monaca 15061

· † Community College of Philadelphia
1700 Spring Garden St., Philadelphia 19130
Allen T. Bonnell, President

·˙† Community General Hospital
145 N. 6th St., Reading 19601
J. L. Stolz, M.D., Program Director

·˙ Community Medical Center
School of Radiologic Technology
1822 Mulberry St., Scranton 18510
Robert Schuman, MD, Program Director

·˙† Conemaugh Valley Memorial Hospital
1086 Franklin St., Johnstown 15905
Bonnie Ford, RN, MSN, Acting Director

·˙† Crozer-Chester Medical Center
Schools of Clinical Neurophysiology
401 W. 15th St., Chester 19013
Kellee Trice, Dir. of Admis.

· † Delaware County Community College
901 Media Line Rd., Media 19063

: ‡ Delaware Valley Academy of Medical & Dental Assts.
3330 Grant Ave., Philadelphia 19114
Glenn Goldsmith, Director
215-676-1200

∴† Divine Providence Hospital
1100 Grampian Blvd., Williamsport 17701
L. A. Moffatt, Program Director

∴† Doylestown Hospital
595 W. State St., Doylestown 18901
D. Parlee, MD, Program Director

· † Duffs Business Institute
110 9th St., Pittsburgh 15222

Duquesne University
600 Forbes Ave., Pittsburgh 15282
Thomas Schaefer, C.S.Sp., Dir. of Admis.

Eastern College
10 Fairview Dr., Saint Davids 19087
Ronald Keller, VP for Enrollment Management

East Stroudsburg University of Pennsylvania
East Stroudsburg 18301
Alan Chesterton, Dir. of Admis.

Edinboro University of Pennsylvania
Edinboro 16444
Admissions Office: 800-626-2203

† Elizabethtown College
1 Alpha Dr., Elizabethtown 17022

∴† Episcopal Hospital
100 E. Lehigh Ave., Philadelphia 19125

· Erie Business Center
246 W. 9th St., Erie 16501
Tony Piccirillo, Dir. of Admis.
See listing under "Career Schools"

∴† Franklin Hospital
1 Spruce St., Franklin 16323
T. A. Gardner, M.D., Program Director

† Gannon University
109 University Sq., Erie 16541

∴† Geisinger Medical Center
School of Medical Technology
N. Academy Ave., Danville 17822

∴† Germantown Hospital & Medical Center
1 Penn Blvd., Philadelphia 19144
Bonnie Benson, RT., Program Director

† GWYNEDD-MERCY COLLEGE
Sumneytown Pike, Gwynedd Valley 19437
Marjorie DeSimone, Dean of Admissions
800-DIAL-GMC
See listing under "Universities"

† Hahnemann University
230 N. Broad St., Philadelphia 19102

∴† Hamot Medical Center
201 State St., Erie 16507

· † Harcum Junior College, Bryn Mawr 19010
Mary Pontius, Dean of Admissions

· Harrisburg Area Community College
3300 N. Cameron Street Road, Harrisburg 17110

∴† Hazelton-St. Joseph Medical Center
Program of Radiologic Technology
687 N. Church St., Hazleton 18201
Sandra Breznitsky, B.S., R.T., Program Dir.

† Holy Family College
Grant & Frankford Ave., Philadelphia 19114
Dr. Mott Linn, Dir. of Admis.
215-637-3050

∴† Holy Spirit Hospital
505 N. 21st St., Camp Hill 17011
B. Kunkel, MD, Program Director

· ICM School of Business
10 Wood St., Pittsburgh 15222
800-441-5222

† Indiana University of Pennsylvania, Indiana 15705
Fred Dadak, Dean, Admissions

: ‡ James Martin Adult Health Occupations
2600 Red Lion Rd., Philadelphia 19114

Juniata College
1700 Moore St., Huntington 16652

· Keystone Junior College
P.O. Box 50, La Plume 18440
Kevin McIntyre, Dir. of Admis.

† King's College
133 N. River St., Wilkes Barre 18711

∴† Lancaster General Hospital
P.O. Box 3555, Lancaster 17604
Kathryn Trego, RN, Admissions Counselor

∴† Lankenau Hospital
120 E. Lancaster Ave., Wynnewood 19096

La Roche College
9000 Babcock Blvd., Pittsburgh 15237
Marianne Leister, Dir. of Admis.

∴† Latrobe Area Hospital
School of Medical Technology
101 W. 2nd Ave., Latrobe 15650

∴† Lee Hospital
320 Main St., Johnstown 15901
R. F. Seifert, Admin.

· † Lehigh County Community College
2370 Main St., Schnecksville 18078

· † Luzerne Co. Community College
1333 S. Prospect St., Nanticoke 18634

Lycoming College, Williamsport 17701

· ‡ McCarrie School of Health Sciences & Technology
512 S. Broad St., Philadelphia 19146

· † Manor Junior College
710 Fox Chase Rd., Jenkintown 19046
Sr. Mary Cecilia, President

† Mansfield University of Pennsylvania
Mansfield 16933

· † Median School of Allied Health Careers
125 7th St., Pittsburgh 15222
William Mosle, President

∴† Medical Center of Beaver County
1000 Dutch Ridge Rd., Beaver 15009
W. E. Conrady, M.D., Program Director

∴† Mercy Hospital, 2601 8th Ave., Altoona 16602

Mercyhurst College
501 E. 38th St., Erie 16546
Andrew Roth, Dean of Enrollment
800-825-1926

† Millersville University of Pennsylvania
Millersville 17551
Blair Treasure, Dean of Admissions

∴† Milton S. Hershey Medical Center Hospital
P.O. Box 850, Hershey 17033
G. Victor Rohrer, MD, Assoc. Dean

∴† Monsour Medical Center
70 Lincoln Hwy., E., Jeannette 15644
G. Shaw, M.D., Program Director

· † Montgomery County Community College
340 DeKalb Pike, Blue Bell 19422-0758
Dennis Murphy, Dir. of Admis.

† Mt. Aloysius College
1 College Dr., Cresson 16630
Sylvia Hirsch, Dir. of Admis.

∴† Nazareth Hospital
2601 Holme Ave., Philadelphia 19152
Sr. M. Salvatore, Admin.

· NEC-Allentown Business School Campus
1501 Lehigh St., Allentown 18103
610-791-5100

† Neumann College
Concord Rd., Aston 19014

· † Northampton Co. Area Community College
3835 Green Pond Rd., Bethlehem 18017
Janice Keim, Assoc. Dir. of Admis.

: ‡ North Hills School of Health Occupations
1500 Northway Mall, Pittsburgh 15237

∴† Ohio Valley General Hospital
School of Radiologic Technology
25 Heckel Rd., McKees Rocks 15136

· † Pennsylvania College of Technology
1 College Ave., Williamsport 17701

∴† Pennsylvania Hospital
800 Spruce St., Philadelphia 19107
M. Rondish, Program Director

· † Pennsylvania State University, Hazleton Campus
Hazleton 18201

· † Pennsylvania State University
3550 Seventh St. Rd.
New Kensington 15068

· † Pennsylvania State University, Schuylkill Campus
200 University Dr.
Schuylkill Haven 17972

Philadelphia College of Pharmacy & Science
600 S. 43rd St., Philadelphia 19104-4495
215-596-8810

∴† Point Park College-St. Francis Medical Center
400 45th St., Pittsburgh 15201

∴† Polyclinic Medical Center
2601 N. 3rd St., Harrisburg 17110
Howard Robertson, EdD, Director of Education
717-782-2136

∴† Presbyterian-University Hospital
230 Lothrop St., Pittsburgh 15213
Daniel L. Stickler, Admin.

· † Reading Area Community College
P.O. Box 1706, Reading 19603
Robin Sodomsky, Dir. of Admis.

∴† Reading Hospital & Medical Center
300 S. 6th St., Reading 19602

∴† Robert Packer Hospital
1 Guthrie Square, Sayre 18840

∴† Rolling Hill Hospital Diagnostic Center
60 Township Line Rd., Elkins Park 19117
T. G. Balbus, M.D., Program Director

∴† Sacred Heart Hospital
School of Medical Technology
421 W. Chew St., Allentown 18102
Sandra Neiman, Program Director
610-776-4745

∴† Sacred Heart Medical Center
School of Diagnostic Radiography
9th & Wilson Sts., Chester 19013
Frances Diegnan, RT, AS, Program Director

† St. Francis College
P.O. Box 600, Loretto 15940

∴† St. Francis Hospital of New Castle
School of Radiography
1000 S. Mercer St., New Castle 16101
412-656-6134

∴† St. Joseph Hospital
250 College Ave., Lancaster 17603
James Lyons, President

∴† St. Joseph's Hospital
School of Radiography
N. 12th and Walnut St., Reading 19603
Sr. Helen Martin, Director

∴† St. Vincent Health Center
232 W. 25th St., Erie 16544
Joyce Boxer, Director

: ‡ Sawyer School
717 Liberty Ave., Pittsburgh 15222
W. Nicholas Hoban, Director

· † Scranton Medical Technology Consortium
700 Quincy Ave., Scranton 18510

∴† Sewickley Valley Hospital
700 Blackburn Rd., Sewickley 15143

∴† Shadyside Hospital School of Nursing
5230 Centre Ave., Pittsburgh 15232
Dr. Margaret Dietz, Director

∴† Sharon Regional Health System
School of Radiologic Technology
740 E. State St., Sharon 16146
Sandra Robison, RTR, Program Director
412-983-3911 Ext. 4846

: Shenango Valley School of Business
500 S. Mill St., New Castle 16101
412-654-1976

: Shenango Valley School of Business
124 W. Spring St., Titusville 16354
814-827-9567

: Shenango Valley School of Business
335 Boyd Dr., Sharon 16146
412-983-0700

Slippery Rock University, Slippery Rock 16057
Director of Admissions

∴† Somerset Hospital
School of Radiography
225 S. Center Ave., Somerset 15501
814-443-5028

: ‡ SOUTH HILLS BUSINESS SCHOOL
480 Waupelani Dr., State College 16801-4516
Maralyn Mazza, Director
Admissions: 814-234-7755
Established 1970. Private. Coed. Tuition: $6,420 per
year. Enrollment: 350. Faculty: 50. Accredited by
CCA. ASB degrees in accounting, management, secretarial, computer information systems and health information technology. Diplomas in accounting,
secretarial, clerical, retail management, travel, and
microcomputers. One and two-year programs available. Financial aid, counseling and placement assistance. Housing nearby, cafeteria and day care
facilities.

† Temple University
Broad St. & Montgomery Ave.
Philadelphia 19122

† Temple University
3307 N. Broad St., Philadelphia 19140

† Thiel College
75 College Ave., Greenville 16125
Robert Weaver, Dir. of Admis.

† Thomas Jefferson University
130 S. 9th St., Suite 1620
Philadelphia 19107

: ‡ Ultrasound Diagnostic School
3511 Cottman Ave., Philadelphia 19149

∴† University Health Center
Forbes Ave. & Halket St., Pittsburgh 15213

† University of Pennsylvania
0 Levy Park, Philadelphia 19104

† University of Pittsburgh
4200 5th Ave., Pittsburgh 15260

† University of Pittsburgh at Johnstown
450 Schoolhouse Rd., Johnstown 15904

∴† Washington Hospital
155 Wilson Ave., Washington 15301
E. Strosser, President

† West Chester University of Pennsylvania
S. High St., West Chester 19380

∴† Western Pennsylvania Hospital
4800 Friendship Ave., Pittsburgh 15224

: † Western School of Health and Business Careers
411 7th Ave., Pittsburgh 15219

: ‡ Western School of Health & Business Careers
3824 Northern Pike, Monroeville 15146

∴† Westmoreland Hospital Association
532 W. Pittsburgh, Greensburg 15601
T. K. Morrow, M.D., Program Director

∴† Wilkes Barre General Hospital
575 N. River St., Wilkes Barre 18702

Wilkes University
184 S. River St., Wilkes-Barre 18766
Emory P. Guffrovich Jr., Dean of Admissions

∴† Williamsport Hospital
  777 Rural Ave., Williamsport 17701

† York College of Pennsylvania
  P.O. Box 15199, York 17405-7199
  Nancy Spataro, Dir. of Admis.
  717-849-1600
  See listing under "Universities"

∴† York Hospital
  Allied Health Schools
  1001 S. George St., York 17403
  Kathleen Valetsky, EdM, Director-Radiography
  Brenda Kile, MA, Director-Medical Technology
  Mark Simmons, MS, Director-Respiratory Therapy
  717-851-2942

RHODE ISLAND

·   Community College of Rhode Island
  Flanagan Campus
  1762 Louisquisset Pike, Lincoln 02865

· † Community College of Rhode Island
  Knight Campus
  400 East Ave., Warwick 02886

∴† Memorial Hospital of Rhode Island
  School of Medical Technology
  111 Brewster St., Pawtucket 02860
  Judith Campbell, Program Director
  401-729-2428

∴† Rhode Island Hospital
  593 Eddy St., Providence 02903

∴† Rhode Island Medical Center
  P.O. Box 8269, Cranston 02920

∴† St. Joseph's Hospital
  200 High Service Ave., North Providence 02904

  Salve Regina University
  1 Ochre Point Ave., Newport 02840
  Roselina McKillop, Dean of Admissions

:   School of Medical & Legal Secretarial Sciences
  60 S. Angell St., Providence 02906
  Norma Casale, Director

SOUTH CAROLINA

∴† Anderson Memorial Hospital
  800 N. Fant St., Anderson 29621
  D. K. Oglesby, Jr., Admin.

∴† Baptist Medical Center
  1519 Marion St., Columbia 29201

  Erskine College & Seminary
  Washington St., Due West 29639
  Dot Carter, Dir. of Admis.

· † Florence Darlington Technical College
  P.O. Box 8000, Florence 19501

· † Greenville Technical College
  P.O. Box 5616, Greenville 29606

  Lander College
  320 Stanley Ave., Greenwood 29649

∴† McLeod Regional Medical Center
  555 E. Cheves St., Florence 29501

† Medical University of South Carolina
  171 Ashley Ave., Charleston 29425
  W. Marcus Newberry, M.D., Dean

· † Midlands Technical College
  P.O. Box 2408, Columbia 29202

· † Orangeburg-Calhoun Technical College
  School of Radiologic Technology
  3250 Saint Matthews Rd. N.E., Orangeburg 29115
  Moses P. Pyatt, Dean

· † Piedmont Technical College
  School of Radiologic Technology
  P.O. Box 1467, Greenwood 29648
  J. R. Agner, Program Director

· † Spartanburg Technical College
  P.O. Box 4386, Spartanburg 29305
  Pam Hagan, Dir. Admissions & Counseling
  803-591-3800

· † Tri-County Tech College
  P.O. Box 587, Pendleton 29670

· † Trident Technical College
  P.O. Box 10367, Charleston 29411
  Charles Branch, President

  University of South Carolina, Columbia 29208
  Terry Davis, Dir. of Admis.
  803-777-7700

· † York Technical College
  452 S. Anderson Rd., Rock Hill 29730

SOUTH DAKOTA

† Dakota State University
  College for Medical Record Technicians
  & Respiratory Care
  820 N. Washington Ave., Madison 57042
  Mike Foss, Dean
  605-256-5139

  Dakota Wesleyan University
  1300 W. University Ave., Mitchell 57301

: † Lake Area Vocational-Technical Institute
  P.O. Box 730, Watertown 57201

∴† McKennan Hospital
  800 E. 21st St., Sioux Falls 57105
  Henry J. Morris, Exec. Director

· † Mitchell Vocational-Technical School
  821 N. Capital St., Mitchell 57301

† Mt. Marty College
  1105 W. 8th St., Yankton 57078
  Paula Tacke, Dir. of Admis.

† National College
  321 Kansas City St., Rapid City 57701
  Keith T. Carlyle, Dir. of Admis.

· Nettleton Junior College
  100 S. Spring Ave., Sioux Falls 57104
  Herman Whitaker, Dir. of Admissions
  800-727-1837 or 605-336-1837

† Presentation College
  1500 N. Main St., Aberdeen 57401
  Sr. Lucille Welbig, Dir. of Admis.

∴† Rapid City Regional Hospital
  353 Fairmont Blvd., Rapid City 57701
  Ellen McGovern, Director

∴† Sacred Heart Hospital
  501 Summit St., Yankton 57078

∴† St. Joseph Hospital
  5th & Foster, Mitchell 57301

∴† St. Luke's Midland Regional Medical Center
  305 S. State St., Aberdeen 57401

∴† Sioux Valley Hospital
  1123 S. Euclid Ave., Sioux Falls 57105
  Lyle Schroeder, President

TENNESSEE

·   Aquinas Junior College
  4210 Harding Rd., Nashville 37205
  Sr. Robert Ann Britton, President

† Austin Peay State University
  601 College St., Clarksville 37044

∴† Baptist Memorial Hospital
  899 Madison Ave., Memphis 38146

  Carson-Newman College
  P.O. Box 70552, Jefferson City 37760
  See listing under "Universities"

· Chattanooga State Technical Community College
  4501 Amnicola Hwy., Chattanooga 37406

† Christian Brothers College
  650 E. Parkway, S., Memphis 38104

· Cleveland State Community College
  P.O. Box 3570, Cleveland 37320

· † Columbia State Community College
  P.O. Box 1315, Columbia 38402

· † Cumberland School of Technology
  1065 E. 10th St., Cookeville 38501

  David Lipscomb University
  3901 Granny White Pike, Nashville 37204-3951
  Wade Sandrell, Dir. of Admis.
  800-333-4358

† **EAST TENNESSEE STATE UNIVERSITY**
  P.O. Box 70731, Johnson City 37614
  Dr. Nancy Dishner, Dean, Enrollment Management
  615-929-4213 or 800-462-3878

  Freed-Hardeman University
  158 E. Main St., Henderson 38340
  800-342-7837

∴† Holston Valley Hospital & Medical Center
  W. Ravine Rd., Kingsport 37660

· Jackson State Community College
  P.O. Box 2467, Jackson 38302

† Knoxville College
  901 College St., N.W., Knoxville 37921

† Lincoln Memorial University
  P.O. Box 2012, Harrogate 37752
  Conrad Daniels, Dir. of Admis.

  Meharry Medical College
  1005 Dr. D. Todd Jr. Blvd., Nashville 37208

· † Memphis AVTS
  620 Mosby Ave., Memphis 38105

∴† Methodist Hospital
  1265 Union Ave., Memphis 38104

∴† Metropolitan Nashville General Hospital
  School of Radiologic Technology
  72 Hermitage Ave., Nashville 37210
  James Wood, Education Coord.

: ‡ Nashville College
  1160 Gallatin Rd., S., Madison 37115

· † Roane State Community College
  276 Patton Ln., Harriman 37748
  Donna Pierce, Associate Dean

∴† St. Francis Hospital
  5959 Park Ave., Memphis 38119
  Catherine Jones, RN, Director

· St. Joseph Hospital
  204 Overton Ave., Memphis 38105

∴† St. Thomas Hospital
  School of Medical Technology
  P.O. Box 380, Nashville 37202
  Leigh Ann Hobbs, Director

· † Shelby State Community College
  P.O. Box 40568, Memphis 38174

† Tennessee State University
  3500 John A. Merritt Blvd., Nashville 37209

† Trevecca Nazarene College
  333 Murfreesboro Rd., Nashville 37210

  Tusculum College
  P.O. Box 5035, Greeneville 37743
  Ronald Porter, Dir. of Admis.

  University of Tennessee at Martin
  Martin 38238
  Paul Kelley, Director of Admissions
  See listing under "Universities"

† University of Tennessee, Memphis
  Health Science Center
  800 Madison Ave., Memphis 38163
  Office of Enrollment Management

: University of Tennessee Medical Center
  600 Henley St. #100, Knoxville 37902

† Vanderbilt University
  West End Ave., Nashville 37240

· Volunteer State Community College
  School for Respiratory Therapy Technicians
  1360 Nashville Pike, Gallatin 37066
  G. Constatin, Program Director

TEXAS

∴† All Saints Episcopal Hospital
  P.O. Box 31, Fort Worth 76101

· † Alvin Community College
  3110 Mustang Rd., Alvin 77511

: † Amarillo Affiliated School/Medical Technology
  P.O. Box 1110, Amarillo 79175

· † Amarillo College
  P.O. Box 447, Amarillo 79178
  Dale Hardgrove, Registrar

: ‡ American Trades Institute
  1200 Summit Ave. #200, Fort Worth 76102

· Angelina College
  P.O. Box 1768, Lufkin 75902
  Jill A. Hill, Registrar
  See listing under "Community and Junior Colleges"

: ‡ ATI Health Education Center
  8150 Brookriver Dr. 5th Floor, Dallas 75247

· † Austin Community College
  1020 Grove Blvd., Austin 78741
  Nancy Glass, Dean
  512-389-4060

∴† Austin State Hospital
  4110 Guadalupe St., Austin 78751
  Luis H. Laosa, M.D., Supt.

∴† Baptist Hospital
  P.O. Box 37, Orange 77631

∴† Baptist Hospital of Southeast Texas
  P.O. Box 1591, Beaumont 77704
  Guy H. Dalrymple, President

∴† Baptist Memorial Hospital System
  111 Dallas St., San Antonio 78286
  Peggy Brown, Administrator

† Baylor College of Medicine
  Center for Allied Health Manpower Development
  1 Baylor Plaza, Houston 77030
  Robert E. Roush, Director

† Baylor University Medical Center
  3500 Gaston Ave., Dallas 75246
  Boone Powell, Jr., Executive Director

∴† Ben Taub Hospital
  1502 Taub Loop, Houston 77030
  Michael Bullard, Admin.

: ‡ Bryan Institute
  1719 Pioneer Pkwy., Arlington 76013

∴† **CANCER THERAPY AND RESEARCH CENTER**
  8122 Datapoint Dr. Suite 600, San Antonio 78229
  SCHOOL OF RADIATION THERAPY TECHNOLOGY
  Karen Cox, RT (R) (T), Program Director
  SCHOOL OF MEDICAL DOSIMETRY
  Ray Federico, RT (R) CMD, School Administrator
  210-616-5500

: ‡ Career Centers of Texas
  8375 Burnham Dr., El Paso 79907

· † Central Texas College
  P.O. Box 1800, Killeen 76540

∴† Citizens Medical Center
  School of Radiologic Technology
  2701 Hospital Dr., Victoria 77901
  Jonnye Griffin, B.S., R.T., Program Director

† Corpus Christi State University
  6300 Ocean Dr., Corpus Christi 78412

· † Del Mar College
  101 Baldwin Blvd., Corpus Christi 78404
  Lawrence Jasman, Registrar

· † El Centro College
  801 Main St., Dallas 75202
  Queen Randall, President

· † El Paso Community College
  P.O. Box 20500, El Paso 79998
  Dr. Robert E. Shapack, President

· † Galveston College
  4015 Ave. Q, Galveston 77550
  John Pickelman, President

· † Grayson County College
  6101 Highway 691, Denison 75020
  Jim Williams, President

∴† Harris Hospital
1300 W. Cannon, Fort Worth 76104
W. P. Earngey, Admin.

∴† Hendrick Medical Center
1242 N. 19th St., Abilene 79601

· † Houston Community College
P.O. Box 7849, Houston 77270
Janet Schnautz, Chrpsn.

Howard Payne University
1000 Fisk Ave., Brownwood 76801

† Incarnate Word College
4301 Broadway St., San Antonio 78209
Sr. Sally Mitchell, Dean of Enrollment

· † Kilgore College
1100 Broadway Blvd., Kilgore 75662
Joe Cruseturner, Registrar

† Lamar University
P.O. Box 10009, Beaumont 77710
800-458-7558

· † Laredo Junior College
1 W. End Washington St., Laredo 78040
Ann Puig, Chrpsn.

· † McLennan Community College
1400 College Dr., Waco 76708
Dennis Michaelis, President

∴† Medical Center Hospital
4502 Medical Dr., San Antonio 78229

∴† Memorial Hospital System
7600 Beechnut, Houston 77074
W. Wilson Turner, President

∴† The Methodist Hospital
6565 Fannin St., M.S. STB1-20, Houston 77030
713-790-6353
SCHOOL OF MEDICAL TECHNOLOGY
Abdus Saleem, MD, Medical Director
Judy Jobe, MT (ASCP), Program Director
SCHOOL OF HISTOTECHNOLOGY
Richard Brown, MD, Medical Director
Judy Jobe, MT (ASCP), Program Director
JoEllen Atkins, HT (ASCP)
Education Coordinator

∴† Methodist Hospital
2002 Miami, Lubbock 79410
Irene Wilson, RN, Dean

· † Midland College
3600 N. Garfield St., Midland 79705
Dr. David E. Daniel, President

∴† Midland Co. Hospital District
2200 W. Illinois St., Midland 79701
M. Madsen, M.D., Program Director

† Midwestern State University
3400 Taft Blvd., Wichita Falls 76308

: † Moncrief Radiation Center
School of Radiation Therapy Technology
1450 8th Ave., Fort Worth 76104
Nancy Fagan, M.Ed., R.T. (R)(T), Dir. of Ed.
817-923-7393

· ‡ Navarro College
3200 W. 7th Ave., Corsicana 75110

· ‡ National Education Center-Bryman Campus
9724 Beechnut #300, Houston 77036

· † North Harris County College
2700 W. W. Thorne Blvd., Houston 77073

· † Odessa College
201 W. University, Odessa 79764

∴† Parkland Memorial Hospital
5201 Harry Hines Blvd., Dallas 75235
A. L. Smith, MD, Director

∴† St. Elizabeth Hospital
School of Medical Technology
2830 Calder St., Beaumont 77702
Deborah Zink, Program Director

∴† St. Luke's Episcopal Hospital
6720 Bertner Ave., Houston 77030
N. E. France, Exec. Director

· † St. Phillip's College
2111 Nevada St., San Antonio 78203
John B. Murphy, Dean

· † San Antonio College
1300 San Pedro Ave., San Antonio 78212

: ‡ San Antonio College of Medical and Dental
Assistants
4205 San Pedro Ave., San Antonio 78212
Comer Alden, President

: ‡ San Antonio College of Medical and Dental
Assistants
3900 N. 23rd St., McAllen 78501

: † San Jacinto College
4624 Fairmont Pky., Pasadena 77504
Thomas M. Spencer, President

∴† Scenic Mountain Medical Center
1601 W. 11th Pl., Big Spring 79720

∴† Scott & White Memorial Hospital & Clinic
2401 S. 31st St., Temple 76508

∴† Shannon West Texas Memorial Hospital
9 S. Magdalen, San Angelo 76903
R. F. Trotter, M.D., Program Director

∴† Shivers Cancer Center
School of Radiation Therapy Technology
2600 E. Martin Luther King Jr. Blvd.
Austin 78702
Paula F. Salvitti, Director
512-478-9681

· † South Plains College
1401 College Ave., Levelland 79336
Marvin L. Baker, President

· † Southwest Texas State University
School of Respiratory Therapy
601 University Dr., San Marcos 78666

† Tarleton State University
1297 W. Washington St., Stephenville 76402

· † Temple Junior College
2600 S. 1st St., Temple 76504

Texas Christian University
2800 S. University Dr., Ft. Worth 76129
Dr. Edward Boehm, Jr., Dean of Admissions

: Texas School of Business
711 Air Tex Dr., Houston 77073
Madeline Burillo, Director
713-846-2888

† Texas Southern University
School for Respiratory Therapists
3100 Cleburne St., Houston 77004

· † Texas Southmost College
83 Fort Brown, Brownsville 78520
Dr. Albert A. Besteiro, President

Texas State Technical College Waco/Marshall
3801 Campus Dr., Waco 76705
817-867-3371

† Texas State Technical Institute, Harlingen 78550

Texas State Technical Institute
P.O. Box 18, Sweetwater 79556

† Texas Tech University, Lubbock 79409

† Texas Women's University
P.O. Box 23925, Denton 76204

· † Trinity Valley Community College
500 N. Prairieville, Athens 75751

· † Tyler Junior College
P.O. Box 9020, Tyler 75711
Raymond Hawkins, President
See listing under "Community and Junior Colleges"

† University of Houston-Clear Lake
2700 Bay Area Blvd., Houston 77058
Darella Banks, Exec. Dir. Enrollment Services

∴† University of Texas M. D. Anderson Cancer Center
1515 Holcombe Blvd., Houston 77030
Programs in: Radiation Therapy Technology,
Histotechnology,
Cytotechnology, Medical Dosimetry, Medical
Technology

† University of Texas at El Paso
500 W. University Ave., El Paso 79968

† University of Texas at Tyler
3900 University Blvd., Tyler 75799
Martha Wheat, Dir. of Admis.

† University of Texas Health Science Center
P.O. Box 20036, Houston 77225

† University of Texas Health Science Center
7703 Floyd Curl Dr., San Antonio 78284

† The University of Texas Medical Branch at Galveston
Galveston 77555-1305

† University of Texas-Pan American
1201 W. University Dr., Edinburg 78539
Miguel Nerarez, President

† University of Texas Southwestern Medical Center
5323 Harry Hines Blvd., Dallas 75235

· † Victoria College
2200 E. Red River St., Victoria 77901
Roland E. Bing, President

∴† Wadley Hospital
P.O. Box 1878, Texarkana 75504
A. L. McElmurry, Admin.

· † Western Technical Institute
1000 Texas Ave., El Paso 79901

West Texas State University
2501 4th Ave., Canyon 79016
Lila Vars, Dir. of Admis.

· † Wharton County Junior College
911 Boling Hwy., Wharton 77488
Dr. Theodore Nicksick, Jr., President

∴† Wichita General Hospital
Medical Technology Program
1600 8th St., Wichita Falls 76301
Carol Mass, MS,MT(ASCP), Program Director

UTAH

: ‡ American Institute of Medical-Dental Technology
1675 N. Freedom Blvd., Provo 84604

† Brigham Young University, Provo 84602

: † Bryman School
1144 W. 3300 S., Salt Lake City 84119
Kenneth J. Carlson, Director of Admissions

∴† Latter-Day Saints Hospital
325 8th Ave., Salt Lake City 84143
David B. Withlin, Admin.

† L.D.S. Business College
411 E. South Temple
Salt Lake City 84111

∴† McKay-Dee Hospital Center
3939 Harrison Blvd., Ogden 84403
H. A. Totzke, M.D., Program Director

· † Salt Lake Community College
4600 S. Redwood Rd., Salt Lake City 84123

† University of Utah
1400 E. 200 S., Salt Lake City 84112
Dr. J. Stayner Landward, Dir. of Admis.

∴† Utah Valley Regional Medical Center
1034 N. 500 W., Provo 84604
L. Rutschman, R.T., Coordinator

† Weber State University
3750 Harrison Blvd., Ogden 84408

VERMONT

† Champlain College
P.O. Box 670, Burlington 05402
Josephine Churchill, Dir. of Admis.
802-860-2727
See listing under "Universities"

∴† Medical Center Hospital of Vermont
School of Cytotechnology
111 Colchester Ave., Burlington 05401
Sandra Giroux, Program Director
802-656-5133

NORWICH UNIVERSITY
65 S. Main St., Northfield 05663
Frank Griffis, Dir. of Admis.
See listing under "Universities"

∴† Rutland Regional Medical Center
School of Radiologic Technology
160 Allen St., Rutland 05701
Sandra Bechtel, Program Director

Trinity College
208 Colchester Ave., Burlington 05401

† University of Vermont
194 S. Prospect St., Burlington 05401
802-656-3370

VIRGINIA

∴† Alleghany Regional Hospital
P.O. Box 7, Low Moor 24457

∴† AUGUSTA MEDICAL CENTER
School of Clinical Laboratory Science
P.O. Box 1000, Fishersville 22939
Bernadette Bekken, Program Director
Formerly:
AHC/King's Daughters' Hospital
School of Medical Technology, Staunton, VA.

: † Carilion Health Systems
P.O. Box 13727, Roanoke 24036

· † Central Virginia Community College
3506 Wards Rd., Lynchburg 24502
Belle Wheelan, President

· † College of Health Sciences
P.O. Box 13186, Roanoke 24031
Ruth Robertson, Registrar

· Commonwealth College
300 Boush St., Norfolk 23510
Debbi Huck, Dean of Admissions

· Commonwealth College
4160 Virginia Beach Blvd., Virginia Beach 23452
Nancy Kennedy, Dean of Admissions

· Commonwealth College
1120 W. Mercury Blvd., Hampton 23666
Robyn Rickenbach, Dean of Admissions

∴† DePaul Medical Center
150 Kingsley Ln., Norfolk 23505

Eastern Mennonite College
1200 Park Rd., Harrisonburg 22801
Jerry Miller, Dir. of Admis.

∴† Fairfax Hospital
3300 Gallows Rd., Falls Church 22042
P. David Youngdahl, Admin.

George Mason University
4400 University Dr., Fairfax 22030-4444
Patricia Riordan, Dean of Admissions

· † J. Sargeant Reynolds Community College
P.O. Box C-23040, Richmond 23261

Lynchburg College
1501 Lakeside Dr., Lynchburg 24501
Ernest Chadderton, Dean of Enrollment

∴† Mary Immaculate Hospital
800 Denbigh Blvd., Newport News 23602

∴† Memorial Hospital
142 S. Main St., Danville 24541
Hunter A. Grumbles, Adminstrator

· † Mountain Empire Community College
P.O. Box 700, Big Stone Gap 24219
Victor B. Ficker, President

∴† National Business College
P.O. Box 6400, Roanoke 24017
703-986-1800

∴† Norfolk General Hospital
600 Gresham Dr., Norfolk 23507
Florence Bogush, Director

† Norfolk State University
2401 Corprew Ave., Norfolk 23504

· † Northern Virginia Community College
8333 Little River Turnpike, Annandale 22003
Dr. Barbara Guthrie-Morse, Provost

† Old Dominion University
5215 Hampton Blvd., Norfolk 23508

· † Piedmont Virginia Community College
Respiratory Therapy Program
R.R. 6, Box 1A, Charlottesville 22902
Pat Doorley, Program Head

∴ Richmond Memorial Hospital
1300 Westwood Ave., Richmond 23227
John Simpson, Executive V.P.

∴† Riverside Regional Medical Center
J. Clyde Morris Blvd., Newport News 23601

∴† ROCKINGHAM MEMORIAL HOSPITAL
School of Medical Technology
235 Cantrell Ave., Harrisonburg 22801
Randall Vandevander, Program Director
703-564-5407 or 800-543-2201

∴† St. Mary's Hospital
School of Radiologic Sciences
5801 Bremo Rd., Richmond 23226
Joyce Hawkins, Coordinator

† SHENANDOAH UNIVERSITY
1460 University Dr., Winchester 22601
Dr. Daris Small, Dean
See listing under "Universities"

∴† Southside Regional Medical Center
801 S. Adams St., Petersburg 23803

· † Southwest Virginia Community College
P.O. Box SVCC, Richland 24641
Dr. Charles R. King, President

· † Thomas Nelson Community College
P.O. Box 9407, Hampton 23670
Judy B. McMillan, Dir. of Admis.

· † Tidewater Community College, Portsmouth Campus
Rt. 135, Portsmouth 23703
Dr. Larry L. Whitworth, President

· Tidewater Community College
1700 College Crescent, Virginia Beach 23456
Dr. Larry L. Whitworth, President

∴† University of Virginia Medical Center
Charlottesville 22908
Jules I. Levine, Asst. Dean

† Virginia Commonwealth University
910 W. Franklin St., Richmond 23284

Virginia Intermont College
1013 Moore St., Bristol 24201
Lawton Blandford, Dir. of Admis.

· † Virginia Western Community College
P.O. Box 14025, Roanoke 24038
Charles L. Downs, President

∴† Winchester Memorial Hospital
P.O. Box 3340, Winchester 22604
Carl S. Napps, Admin.

· † Wytheville Community College
School for Medical Lab Techs
1000 W. Main St., Wytheville 24382
Dr. Terrance Suarez, Chrmn.

WASHINGTON

Bastyr College
144 N.E. 54th St., Seattle 98105
Dr. Ron Hobbs, Dir. of Admis.

· Bellevue Community College
3000 Landerholm Circle, S.E., Bellevue 98007

: † Bellingham Vocational Technical School
3028 Lindberg Ave., Bellingham 98225

∴† Children's Hospital and Medical Center
Clinical Laboratory Science Program
P.O. Box 5371, MS: CH-37, Seattle 98105
Kay Davis, Program Director

: † Clover Park Technical College
4500 Steilacoom Blvd., S.W., Tacoma 98499
Alson Green, Jr., President

∴† Deaconess Medical Center
School of Medical Technology
800 W. 5th Ave., Spokane 99204
Alice Berg, Program Director

· † Edmonds Community College
20000 68th Ave., W., Lynnwood 98036
Thomas Nielsen, President

: Eton Technical Institute
3649 Frontage Rd., Port Orchard 98366
Jim Martin, President
206-479-3866

∴† Harborview Medical Center
325 Ninth Ave., Seattle 98104

· † Highline Community College, Des Moines 98198

∴† Holy Family Hospital
5633 N. Lidgerwood St., Spokane 99207

: † Laboratory of Pathology
P.O. Box 14950, Seattle 98114

· North Seattle Community College
School for Medical Assistants
9600 College Way, N., Seattle 98103

: ‡ Pima Medical Institute
1627 Eastlake Ave. E., Seattle 98102
Walter Greenly, Director

: † Renton Technical College
3000 N.E. 4th St., Renton 98056
Cherl Welding, Registrar
See listing under "Career Schools"

∴† Sacred Heart Medical Center
101 W. 8th Ave., Spokane 99204

∴† St. John's Medical Center
School of Medical Technology
P.O. Box 3002, Longview 98632

· † Seattle Central Community College
1701 Broadway, Seattle 98122
Loris A. Blue, Dir. of Admis.

† Seattle University
Broadway Ave. & Madison, Seattle 98122
Lee Gerig, Dean of Admissions

· † Shoreline Community College
School for Medical Record Technicians
16101 Greenwood Ave., N., Seattle 98133
Chuck Fields, Registrar

· South Puget Sound Community College
2011 Mottman Rd., S.W., Olympia 98512

· † Spokane Community College
1810 N. Greene St., Spokane 99207

· † Tacoma Community College
5900 S. 12th St., Tacoma 98465

: † Trend College
214 N. Wall St., Spokane 99201

† University of Puget Sound
1500 N. Warner St., Tacoma 98416

† University of Washington, Seattle 98195

· † Walla Walla Community College
500 Tausick Way, Walla Walla 99362
Joseph Frostad, Dir. of Admis.
509-527-4283
See listing under "Community and Junior Colleges"

· † Wenatchee Valley College
School of Radiologic Technology
1300 5th St., Wenatchee 98801

· † Yakima Valley Community College
16th & Nob Hill Blvd., Yakima 98902

WEST VIRGINIA

† Alderson-Broaddus College
Philippi 26416
Craig W. Gould, Director of Admissions
304-457-1700

· † Beckley College
P.O. Box AG, Beckley 25802
Patricia Campbell, Dean Recruitment/Admissions

∴† Bluefield Regional Medical Center
500 Cherry St., Bluefield 24701

† Bluefield State College
219 Rock St., Bluefield 24701

: ‡ Boone Co. Career Center
P.O. Box 50-B, Danville 25053
J. Dolan, Director

∴† Cabell Huntington Hospital
1340 16th St., Huntington 25701
Kenneth W. Wood, Admin.

∴† Camden Clark Memorial Hospital
717 Ann St., Parkersburg 26101

∴† Charleston Area Medical Center
School for Cytotechnologists
3200 MacCorkle Ave., S.E., Charleston 25304
Carolyn Stevens, Program Director
304-348-5570

† Fairmont State College
1201 Locust Ave., Fairmont 26554
John Conaway, Dir. of Admis.

† Marshall University
400 Hal Greer Blvd., Huntington 25755
See listing under "Universities"

∴† Ohio Valley Medical Center
2000 Eoff St., Wheeling 26003

∴† St. Mary's Hospital
2900 1st Ave., Huntington 25702
H. W. Dransfeld, M.D., Program Director

∴† United Hospital Center
School of Radiologic Technology
P.O. Box 2308, Clarksburg 26302
Jacqueline Brumage, R.T., Program Director

† The University of Charleston
2300 MacCorkle Ave., S.E., Charleston 25304
800-995-GO UC

∴† Veterans Administration Hospital
200 Veterans Ave., Beckley 25801
C. Christie, Program Director

† West Liberty State College, West Liberty 26074

· † West Virginia Northern Community College
College Square, Wheeling 26003

† West Virginia State College
P.O. Box 1000, Institute 25112

† West Virginia University
P.O. Box 6001, Morgantown 26506

∴† West Virginia University Hospital
P.O. Box 6401, Morgantown 26506

WEST VIRGINIA WESLEYAN COLLEGE
59 College Ave., Buckhannon 26201
Robert Skinner, Director of Admission
See listing under "Universities"

∴† Wheeling Hospital
1 Medical Park, Wheeling 26003
George M. Kellas, M.D., Director

† Wheeling Jesuit College
316 Washington Ave., Wheeling 26003
Fr. Thomas Acker, SJ, President

WISCONSIN

: † Aurora Health Care
3000 W. Montana Ave., Milwaukee 53201

∴† Bellin Hospital
School of Radiologic Technology
P.O. Box 23400, Green Bay 54305-3400
Linda Joppe, Program Director

∴† Beloit Memorial Hospital
1969 W. Hart Rd., Beloit 53511

Cardinal Stritch College
6801 N. Yates Rd., Milwaukee 53217
David Wegener, Dir. of Admis.

Carthage College
2001 Alford Dr., Kenosha 53140
Brenda A. Porter, VP Enrollment

· Chippewa Valley Technical College
620 Clairemont Ave., W., Eau Claire 54701

∴† Columbia Hospital
2025 E. Newport Ave., Milwaukee 53211

Concordia University
12800 N. Lake Shore Dr., Mequon 53097
414-243-5700

· Fox Valley Technical College
P.O. Box 2277, Appleton 54913

: † Franciscan Shared Laboratory-St. Joseph's
5000 W. Chambers St., Milwaukee 53210

: † Franciscan Shared Laboratory-St. Michael
2400 W. Villard Ave., Milwaukee 53209

: † Franciscan Shared Laboratory-Central Lab
Medical Technology Program
11020 W. Plank Ct. #100, Wauwatosa 53226
J. Doellman, E. Schmeda, Program Directors

· † Gateway Technical College
3520 30th Ave., Kenosha 53144

· † Lakeshore Technical College
1290 North Ave., Cleveland 53015

∴† Luther Hospital
310 Chestnut St., Eau Claire 54703
James D. M. Russell, Admin.

· † Madison Area Technical College
3550 Anderson Rd., Madison 53704
Beverly Simone, District Director

Marquette University
1217 W. Wisconsin Ave., Milwaukee 53233
Raymond A. Brown, Dean of Admissions

: † Marshfield Medical Center Laboratory
1000 N. Oak Ave., Marshfield 54449
Virginia R. Narlock, PhD, Program Dir.

† Medical College of Wisconsin
8701 Watertown Plank Rd., Milwaukee 53226
Richard Cooper, MD, Dean/Executive VP

∴† Mercy Medical Center
631 Hazel St., Oshkosh 54901
Bernard J. Schlueter, President

· † Mid-State Technical College
2600 W. 5th, Marshfield 54449

· † Milwaukee Area Technical College
School for Respiratory Therapists
700 W. State St., Milwaukee 53233

∴† Milwaukee County Medical Complex
1304 S. 70th St., West Allis 53214
Jo Ann Dillon, RN, Admissions

† Milwaukee School of Engineering
1025 N. Broadway, Milwaukee 53202
Owen Smith, Dean of Admission
800-332-6763 or 414-277-7200 in metro Milwaukee

· Moraine Park Technical College
2151 N. Main St., West Bend 53095-1598
Maureen Josten, Campus Administrator
414-334-3413

· † Moraine Park Technical College
235 N. National Ave., Fond du Lac 54936
Dr. John Shanahan, President
414-922-8611

† Mt. Mary College
2900 N. Menomonee River Pky.
Milwaukee 53222

· † Northcentral Technical College
1000 Campus Dr., Wausau 54401
Dr. Donald Hagen, President

· † Northeast Wisconsin Technical College
School for Medical Assistants
P.O. Box 19042, Green Bay 54307

Ripon College, P.O. Box 248, Ripon 54971
James Reilly, Dean of Admis.

∴† Sacred Heart Hospital
900 W. Clairemont Ave., Eau Claire 54701
Matthew W. Hubler, Admin.

∴† St. Catherine's Hospital
3556 7th Ave., Kenosha 53140
Sr. Mary Dolorosa, Admin.

∴† St. Elizabeth Hospital
Medical Technology Program
1506 S. Oneida St., Appleton 54915
Carla Salmon, Program Director
414-738-2128

∴† St. Francis Hospital
3237 S. 16th St., Milwaukee 53215

∴† St. Joseph Hospital/Marshfield Clinic
611 St. Josephs Ave., Marshfield 54449

∴† St. Luke's Medical Center
2900 W. Oklahoma Ave., Milwaukee 53215
J. A. Palese, M.D., Dir., Medical Education

∴† St. Luke's Memorial Hospital
1320 S. Wisconsin Ave., Racine 53403

∴† St. Mary's Medical Center
Medical Technology Program
3801 Spring St., Racine 53405
M. Schuster, M.D., Director

∴† St. Vincent Hospital
P.O. Box 13508, Green Bay 54307
D. P. Skarphol, M.D., Medical Dir.

† State Laboratory of Hygiene
465 Henry Mall, Madison 53706

STRATTON COLLEGE
1300 N. Jackson St., Milwaukee 53202
Robert H. Ley, Director
414-276-5200

∴† Theda Clark Regional Medical Center
130 2nd St., Neenah 54956

University of Wisconsin, La Crosse
115 Main Hall, La Crosse 54601
608-785-8067

† University of Wisconsin, Madison
500 Lincoln Dr., Madison 53706

† University of Wisconsin
P.O. Box 413, Milwaukee 53201
V. M. Allison, Registrar

Viterbo College
815 9th St., S., La Crosse 54601
Roland W. Nelson, Dir. of Admis.

· † Waukesha County Technical College
800 Main St., Pewaukee 53072
Dr. Richard T. Anderson, Dir.

∴† Wausau Hospital Center
333 Pine Ridge Blvd., Wausau 54401

: † Western Wisconsin Technical College
304 N. 6th St., La Crosse 54602

: † Wisconsin Indianhead Technical College
1019 S. Knowles Ave., New Richmond 54017

∴† Zablocki VA Medical Center
5000 W. National Ave., Milwaukee 53295

WYOMING

· † Casper College
125 College Dr., Casper 82601
A. W. Vance, Dir. of Admis.

· Central Wyoming College
2660 Peck St., Riverton 82501
Mary Gores, Admissions Officer
307-856-9291
See listing under "Community and Junior Colleges"

· Laramie County Community College
1400 E. College Dr., Cheyenne 82007
Dr. Harlan L. Heglar, President

† University of Wyoming
P.O. Box 3434, Laramie 82071
Richard Davis, Dir. of Admis.

· † Western Wyoming Community College
2500 College Dr., Rock Springs 82901
Jackie Freeze, Dir. of Admis.
See listing under "Community and Junior Colleges"

∴† West Park Hospital
707 Sheridan Ave., Cody 82414
Deborah Martin, BSRT, Dir. of Admis.

PUERTO RICO

: ‡ Antilles School of Technical Careers
Apartado 1536, San Juan 00919
Ignacio Saenz, President

† Catholic University of Puerto Rico
School of Medical Technology
Las Americas Ave., Ponce 00732

† Inter American University of Puerto Rico
Metropolitan Campus
P.O. Box 1293, San Juan 00902

† Inter American University of Puerto Rico
San German Campus
Harris Dr. Call Box 5100, San German 00683

: ‡ Ponce Technical School
16 Salud St., Ponce 00731
Fernando Torres, President

· † Puerto Rico Junior College
School for Medical Record Technicians
P.O. Box 21373, San Juan 00928

† Universidad Central Del Caribe
P.O. Box 60327, Bayamon 00960

† Universidad Metropolitana
P.O. Box 21150, San Juan 00928

† University of Puerto Rico, Medical Sciences Campus
P.O. Box 5067, San Juan 00906

† University of the Sacred Heart
P.O. Box 12383, San Juan 00914

ARCHITECTURE

This classification contains schools offering either a Bachelor of Architecture or a Master of Architecture degree accredited by the National Architectural Accrediting Board (†) and a selection of programs from institutionally accredited schools. Colleges and Universities (no dot code) generally offer four-year or advanced programs in architecture, architectural engineering or architectural technology; Community and Junior Colleges (·) generally offer associate degrees in architectural engineering or technology; Career Schools (:) generally offer diplomas in architectural engineering technology.

ALABAMA

† Auburn University, Auburn 36849

† Tuskegee University
Tuskegee Institute 36088

ARIZONA

† Arizona State University, Tempe 85287

† University of Arizona, Tucson 85721
Loyd Bell, Director of Admissions

Wright School of Architecture
Taliesin West, Scottsdale 85261

· Yavapai College
1100 E. Sheldon St., Prescott 86301
Dr. Doreen Dailey, President
602-445-7300
See listing under "Community and Junior Colleges"

ARKANSAS

· Phillips County Community College
P.O. Box 785, Helena 72342
Dr. Steven Jones, President
James R. Brasel, Dean of Admissions

† University of Arkansas at Fayetteville
Fayetteville 72701

CALIFORNIA

California College of Arts & Crafts
San Francisco Campus
1700 17th St., San Francisco 94103
415-703-9500

† California Polytechnic State University
San Luis Obispo 93407
Helen Linstrum, Dir. of Admis.

† California State Polytechnic University
3801 W. Temple Ave., Pomona 91768

· City College of San Francisco
50 Phelan Ave. Box L133, San Francisco 94112
Nestor Regino, Dept. Chair
415-239-3264

· New School of Architecture
1249 F St., San Diego 92101
Gordon Bishop, President

OTIS COLLEGE OF ART AND DESIGN
2401 Wilshire Blvd., Los Angeles 90057
Neil Hoffman, President
See listing under "Art"

† Southern California Institute of Architecture
5454 Beethoven St., Los Angeles 90066
310-574-3625

† University of California, Los Angeles
1247 Murphy Hall, Los Angeles 90024

† University of California at Berkeley
Wurster Hall, Berkeley 94720

† University of Southern California
University Park Campus
Los Angeles 90089

Woodbury University
7500 Glenoaks Blvd., Burbank 91504
See listing under "Universities"

COLORADO

· Front Range Community College
3645 W. 112th Ave., Westminister 80030
Dr. Patricia Lammers, Dir. of Admis.

· Pikes Peak Community College
5675 S. Academy Blvd.
Colorado Springs 80906-5498
Roberta Erickson, Dir. of Admis.
See listing under "Community and Junior Colleges"

University of Colorado at Boulder
Boulder 80309
William A. Douglas, Dean of Admis.

† University of Colorado at Denver
1200 Larimer, Denver 80204

CONNECTICUT

† Yale University
1605A Yale Station, New Haven 06520

DISTRICT OF COLUMBIA

† Catholic University of America
620 Michigan Ave. N.E., Washington 20064
Robert J. Talbot, Dir. of Admis. & Fin. Aid.

† Howard University
2400 6th St., N.W., Washington 20059
James E. Cheek, President

University of the District of Columbia
Georgia Ave.-Harvard St. Campus
1100 Harvard St., N.W., Washington 20009

University of the District of Columbia
Van Ness Campus
4200 Connecticut Ave., N.W., Washington 20008

FLORIDA

† Florida A & M University, Tallahassee 32307

Florida A&M University/University of S. Florida
Cooperative M.ARCH Program
3702 Spectrum Blvd. #180, Tampa 33612

† University of Florida
226 Tigert Hall, Gainesville 32611

† University of Miami
P.O. Box 248006, Coral Gables 33124

GEORGIA

† Georgia Institute of Technology
225 North Ave. N.W., Atlanta 30332

† **SAVANNAH COLLEGE OF ART & DESIGN**
342 Bull St., Savannah 31401
Richard Rowan, President
May Poetter, VP of Admissions
Paula Rowan, Provost
Judith Van Baron, VP for Academic Affairs
912-238-2483
Established 1979. Private. Non-profit. Coed. Accreditation: Southern Association of Colleges and Schools and National Architectural Accrediting Board. Enrollment: 2,330. Faculty: 140, all hold rank of Professor. Average student-faculty ratio: 14:1. 1994-95 tuition per quarter: $3,300 full-time. Room: $3,000

- $3,500 (per academic year) varies by dormitory. The student body includes students from all 50 states and 60 foreign countries. There are no more than 20 students in any class. Summer sessions offered in Savannah, New York City & Europe.

Men's and women's dormitories available on campus. Rental apartments readily available in the area. No fraternities or sororities.

Degrees: Bachelor of Architecture, Bachelor of Fine Arts, Master of Fine Arts. BFA and MFA offered in 14 visual arts majors including art history, computer art, fashion, fiber arts, graphic design, historic preservation, interior design, painting, illustration, video, photography, furniture design, sequential art, and metals and jewelry.

Library: 30,000 volumes. 35 buildings, Urban campus. Our college has 8 gallery spaces and 11 computer laboratories. Fully equipped labs for students in fiber arts, photography, video, architecture, graphic design, historic preservation, painting, illustration, interior design, furniture design, sequential art, and metals and jewelry.

Admissions: Minimum 2.0 GPA in high school, undergraduate applicants must submit high school or college transcript, SAT or ACT scores, and letters of recommendation. Graduate applicants must submit college transcript, letters of recommendation, and portfolio and must have a personal interview. All applicants must pay a $50 application fee.

The college offers a graduated scholarship totaling $10,000 over four years to students who score over 1200 on the SAT or a composite score of 28 on the ACT, to students who are high school valedictorians, to students who attend selected Governor's Schools, and to selected students who are recognized through the ICSA program (a college-sponsored scholarship for talented artists).

The college is located within 30 minutes of the coastal beaches of Georgia and South Carolina and enjoys a mild, southern climate. The college exists for the purpose of preparing talented young people for a career in art, design, architecture, or historic preservation. The entire college is focused toward the personal, academic, and professional success of each student.

HAWAII

† University of Hawaii at Manoa
2500 Campus Rd., Honolulu 96822

IDAHO

† University of Idaho, Moscow 83843
Peter Brown, Dir. of Admis.

ILLINOIS

† Illinois Institute of Technology
3300 S. Federal St., Chicago 60616
Wendell R. Webb, Dir. of Admissions

· Morrison Institute of Technology
701 Portland Ave., Morrison 61270-2959
Dr. Dale Trimpe, Dir. of Admis.
See listing under "Career Schools"

† University of Illinois
506 S. Wright St., Urbana 61801

† University of Illinois at Chicago
P.O. Box 4348, Chicago 60680
Richard R. Whitaker, Jr., Dean

INDIANA

† Ball State University
2000 W. University Ave., Muncie 47306
Ruth Vedvik, Dir. of Admis.

† University of Notre Dame, Notre Dame 46556
Robert L. Amico, Chrmn.

IOWA

† Iowa State University, Ames 50011
Karsten Smedal, Dir. of Admis.

· Waldorf College
106 S. 6th St., Forest City 50436
Steve Lovik, Dir. of Admis.
800-292-1903

KANSAS

† Kansas State University
Anderson Hall 110, Manhattan 66506
Ellsworth M. Gerritz, Admis. & Records

† University of Kansas, Lawrence 66045

KENTUCKY

· Louisville Technical Institute
3901 Atkinson Dr., Louisville 40218
George Nunley, Dir. of Admis.

† University of Kentucky, Lexington 40506

LOUISIANA

Louisiana College
College Station, Pineville 71359
Byron McGee, Dir. of Admis.
318-487-7386
See listing under "Liberal Arts"

† Louisiana State University and A & M College
Baton Rouge 70803

† Lousiana Technical University
P.O. Box 3168, Ruston 71272

† Southern University A & M College
Baton Rouge 70813

† Tulane University
6823 Saint Charles Ave., New Orleans 70118
Richard Whiteside, Dean of Admission

† University of Southwestern Louisiana
P.O. Box 43850, Lafayette 70504
318-231-6224

MAINE

College of the Atlantic
105 Eden St., Bar Harbor 04609
Steve Thomas, Dir. of Admis.

· Northern Maine Technical College
33 Edgemont Dr., Presque Isle 04769

MARYLAND

† Morgan State University
Cold Spring Ln. and Hillen Rd., Baltimore 21239

† University of Maryland, College Park 20742

MASSACHUSETTS

† Boston Architectural Center
320 Newbury St., Boston 02115
Ellen Driscoll, Admissions

† Harvard University
Graduate School of Design
Gund Hall, Cambridge 02138

† Massachusetts Institute of Technology
77 Massachusetts Ave., Cambridge 02139

Wellesley College, Wellesley 02181
Janet A. Lavin, Dir. of Admis.

Wentworth Institute of Technology
550 Huntington Ave., Boston 02115

MICHIGAN

† Andrews University, Berrien Springs 49104
Jack Mentges, Dir. of Admis.

† Lawrence Technological University
21000 W. Ten Mile Rd., Southfield 48075
800-225-5588 ext. 3160

† University of Detroit Mercy
4001 W. McNichols
PO Box 19900, Detroit 48219-0900
313-993-1245
See listing under "Universities"

† University of Michigan-Ann Arbor
815 S. University Ave., Ann Arbor 48109

MINNESOTA

† University of Minnesota, Twin Cities
Minneapolis 55455

MISSISSIPPI

† Mississippi State University
P.O. Box J, Mississippi State University 39762

MISSOURI

† Drury College
900 N. Benton Ave., Springfield 65802
Michael G. Thomas, Dir. of Admis.

† Washington University
1 Brookings Dr., St. Louis 63130

MONTANA

† Montana State University, Bozeman 59717

NEBRASKA

† University of Nebraska at Lincoln
Arch 210, Lincoln 68588
W.C. Steward, Dean

NEVADA

· Truckee Meadows Community College
7000 Dandini Blvd., Reno 89512
John Gwaltney, President

University of Nevada Las Vegas
4505 S. Maryland Pky., Las Vegas 89154-1021
Admissions: 702-895-3443 or 800-334-UNLV

NEW JERSEY

· Mercer County Community College
West Windsor Campus
1200 Old Trenton Rd., Trenton 08690
Michael Glass, Dir. of Admis.
See listing under "Community and Junior Colleges"

† New Jersey Institute of Technology
323 Martin Luther King Jr. Blvd., Newark 07102

† Princeton University, Princeton 08544

NEW MEXICO

† University of New Mexico, Albuquerque 87131
Robert Weaver, Dean of Admissions

NEW YORK

† Columbia University
612 W. 115th St., New York 10025

† Cooper Union
41 Cooper Square, New York 10003
John Hejduk, Dean
See listing under "Universities"

† Cornell University
410 Thurston Ave., Ithaca 14853

† CUNY City College
Convent Ave. at 138th St., New York 10031

† New York Institute of Technology
Old Westbury Campus, Old Westbury 11568

Parsons School of Design
66 5th Ave., New York 10011

† Pratt Institute
200 Willoughby Ave., Brooklyn 11205

† Rensselaer Polytechnic Institute, Troy 12180
Conrad Sharrow, Dean of Admissions

† SUNY at Buffalo
17 Capen Hall
P.O. Box 601660, Buffalo 14260-1660
716-645-6900

· SUNY College of Agriculture and Technology
Morrisville 13408
Dennis Nostrand, Dir. of Admis.

SUNY College of Technology at Farmingdale
Route 110, Farmingdale 11735
Janet Snyder, Dir. of Admis.
516-420-2200

† Syracuse University, Syracuse 13244

NORTH CAROLINA

† North Carolina State University
P.O. Box 7001, Raleigh 27695
George Dixon, Dir. of Admis.

† University of North Carolina at Charlotte
Charlotte 28223
J. H. Woodward, Chancellor

NORTH DAKOTA

† North Dakota State University, Fargo 58105
Richard Shearer, Acting Dir. of Admis.

OHIO

· Columbus State Community College
550 E. Spring St., Columbus 43215
Mary Jo Deerwester, Dir. of Admis.

† Kent State University
P.O. Box 5190, Kent 44242
Bruce Riddle, Dir. of Admis.

† Miami University
E. High St., Oxford 45056

† Ohio State University
190 N. Oval Mall, Columbus 43210

· Owens Community College
P.O. Box 10000, Toledo 43699
Jim Welling, Admissions
419-661-7225

† University of Cincinnati
2700 Clifton Ave., Cincinnati 45221

OKLAHOMA

† Oklahoma State University, Stillwater 74078
James F. Knight, Dept. Head

† University of Oklahoma at Norman
660 Parrington Oval, Norman 73019

OREGON

· Treasure Valley Community College
650 College Blvd., Ontario 97914
Ron Kulm, Dir. of Admis.

† University of Oregon
1 University of Oregon, Eugene 97403

PENNSYLVANIA

† Carnegie Mellon University
5000 Forbes Ave., Pittsburgh 15213

† Drexel University
3141 Chestnut St., Philadelphia 19104
Dean of Enrollment Management

· Pennsylvania Institute of Technology
Rose Valley-Notre Dame Campus
800 Manchester Ave., Media 19063
610-565-7900

† Pennsylvania State University
201 Shields Bldg., University Park 16802

† Temple University
Broad St. & Montgomery Ave.
Philadelphia 19122

† University of Pennsylvania
0 Levy Park, Philadelphia 19104

University of the Arts
320 S. Broad St., Philadelphia 19102
Margaret Heuges, Dir. of Admis.

RHODE ISLAND

† Rhode Island School of Design
2 College St., Providence 02903

† Roger Williams College
1 Old Ferry Rd., Bristol 02809
William Dunfey, Dir. of Admis.

SOUTH CAROLINA

† Clemson University
201 Sikes Hall, Clemson 29634

TENNESSEE

† University of Tennessee, Knoxville
527 Andy Holt Tower, Knoxville 37996
Dr. Gordon Stanley, Dir. of Admis.

TEXAS

Prairie View A & M University
P.O. Box 3089, Prairie View 77446-3089
Linda S. Berry, Dir. of Admis.

† Rice University
P.O. Box 1892, Houston 77251

† Texas A & M University
College Station 77843

† Texas Tech University, Lubbock 79409

† University of Houston
4800 Calhoun Rd., Houston 77204

† University of Texas at Arlington
UTA Box 19125, Arlington 76019
R. Zack Prince, Dir. of Admis.

† University of Texas at Austin
0 the University of Texas, Austin 78712

UTAH

† University of Utah
1400 E. 200 S., Salt Lake City 84112
Dr. J. Stayner Landward, Dir. of Admis.

VERMONT

Bennington College, Bennington 05201
Karen Kristof, Dir. of Admis.
800-833-6845

NORWICH UNIVERSITY
65 S. Main St., Northfield 05663
Frank Griffis, Dir. of Admis.
See listing under "Universities"

· Vermont Technical College
Randolph Center 05061
Robert Clarke, President

VIRGINIA

† Hampton University, Hampton 23668
Ollie Bowman, Dean of Admissions

† University of Virginia
P.O. Box 9017, Charlottesville 22906

† Virginia Polytechnic Institute & State University
Blacksburg 24061
David Bousquet, Dir. of Undergraduate Admis.

WASHINGTON

† University of Washington, Seattle 98195

† Washington State University, Pullman 99164
Stan Berry, Dir. of Admis.

WISCONSIN

University of Wisconsin, Madison
500 Lincoln Dr., Madison 53706

† University of Wisconsin
P.O. Box 413, Milwaukee 53201
V. M. Allison, Registrar

PUERTO RICO

† University of Puerto Rico, Rio Piedras Campus
P.O. Box 23300, San Juan 00931
Victor Lopez, Dir. of Admis.

ART

This classification contains schools accredited by the National Association of Schools of Art and Design (†) and a selection of programs from institutionally accredited schools.

ALABAMA

Alabama A & M University
P.O. Box 455, Normal 35762
Dr. Clifton Pearson, Chrpsn.
See listing under "Universities"

† Auburn University, Auburn 36849

· Gadsden State Community College
P.O. Box 227, Gadsden 35902
W. Bryan Stone, Dir. of Admis.

Huntingdon College
1500 E. Fairview Ave., Montgomery 36106-2148
Carolyn A. Phillips, Dean of Enrollment
800-763-0313

Samford University
800 Lakeshore Dr., Birmingham 35229
Lowell Vann, Chrpsn.

Troy State University, Troy 36082
Dr. Robert Stampfli, Dean

† University of Alabama
P.O. Box 870132, Tuscaloosa 35487-0132
Roy Smith, Dir. of Admis.

UNIVERSITY OF ALABAMA IN HUNTSVILLE
P.O. Box 1247, Huntsville 35899
Ron R. Koger Ed.D., Dir. of Admis.
205-895-6070
Established 1969. Public. Coed. Accreditation: SACS, ABET, NLN, CSAB, ACS. Tuition: $2,418 resident, $4,836 non-resident. Room & Board: $3,450. Undergraduate enrollment: 2,674 full-time, 3,439 part-time. Graduate enrollment: 1,860. Faculty: 282. Student-faculty ratio: 18:1. Degrees: BS, BA, BSBA, BSE, MS, MSM, Ph.D., BSN, MSN, MA. 20 buildings on 350 acres. Comprehensive research university located in the Tennessee Valley of northern Alabama. Huntsville is the locale of major government and private research centers. Metropolitan population approaching 300,000.

UNIVERSITY OF MOBILE
P.O. Box 13220, Mobile 36663-0220
Kim Leousis, Dir. of Admissions
205-675-5990
See listing under "Universities"

† University of Montevallo, Montevallo 35115

† University of North Alabama
University Station, Florence 35632

ARIZONA

· Al Collins Graphic Design School
1140 S. Priest Dr., Tempe 85281
Chuck Collins, President/CEO

: Conservatory of Recording Arts & Sciences
1110 E. Missouri Ave. #530, Phoenix 85014
800-562-6383
See listing under "Music"

Grand Canyon University
3300 W. Camelback Rd., Phoenix 85017
Sherri Willborn, Dir. of Admis.
See listing under "Liberal Arts and Sciences"

Northern Arizona University
P.O. Box 4092, Flagstaff 86011
Dr. Margaret Cibik, Dir. of Admis.

University of Arizona, Tucson 85721
Loyd Bell, Director of Admissions

· Yavapai College
1100 E. Sheldon St., Prescott 86301
Dr. Doreen Dailey, President
602-445-7300
See listing under "Community and Junior Colleges"

ARKANSAS

† Arkansas State University
P.O. Box 1200, State University 72467

Ouachita Baptist University
410 Ouachita St., Arkadelphia 71998
Randy Garner, Dir. of Admis.
800-DIAL-OBU

University of Arkansas at Fayetteville
Fayetteville 72701

† University of Arkansas at Little Rock
2801 S. University Ave., Little Rock 72204

University of Arkansas at Pine Bluff
1200 University Dr., Pine Bluff 71601-2799

Williams Baptist College
P.O. Box 3667, Walnut Ridge 72476
Scott Wright, Dir. of Admis.

CALIFORNIA

† Academy of Art College
79 New Montgomery St., San Francisco 94105

· Advertising Arts College
10025 Mesa Rim Rd., San Diego 92121
Tracy Cantor, Dir. of Admis.

AMERICAN COLLEGE FOR THE APPLIED ARTS
1651 Westwood Blvd., Los Angeles 90024
310-470-2000
See listing under "Universities"

† American Film Institute Center
2021 N. Western Ave., Los Angeles 90027

† Art Center College of Design
1700 Lida St., Pasadena 91103
Kit Baron, V.P., Student Services
818-396-2373

† Art Institute of Southern California
2222 Laguna Canyon Rd., Laguna Beach 92651

· Bakersfield College
1801 Panorama Dr., Bakersfield 93305
Robert M. Bruker, Dir. of Admis.

† California College of Arts & Crafts
5212 Broadway, Oakland 94618
Sheri McKenzie, Dir. of Admis.
510-653-6522

† California Institute of the Arts
24700 McBean Pkwy., Valencia 91355
Kenneth Young, Dir. of Admis.

† California State University, Chico
Chico 95929-0820
Vernon Patrick, Chrpsn.

† California State University, Dominguez Hills
1000 E. Victoria St., Carson 90747

† California State University, Long Beach
1250 Bellflower Blvd., Long Beach 90840

† California State University, Los Angeles
5151 Paseo Rancho Castilla, Los Angeles 90032

† California State University, Sacramento
6000 J St., Sacramento 95819

† California State University, San Bernardino
5500 University Pky., San Bernardino 92407
909-880-5188

† California State University-Fullerton
Fullerton 92632

† California State University-Hayward
25800 Carlos Bee Blvd., Hayward 94542

† California State University-Stanislaus
801 W. Monte Vista Ave., Turlock 95382
Frances Cook, Dean Enrollment Services

Chapman University
333 N. Glassell St., Orange 92666
Michael Drummy, Dir. of Admis.

· City College of San Francisco
50 Phelan Ave. Box V32, San Francisco 94112
Mike Ruiz, Dept. Chair
415-239-3252

COGSWELL POLYTECHNICAL COLLEGE
10420 Bubb Rd., Cupertino 95014
Paul Schreivogel, Dean of Student Services
800-264-7955
Established 1887. Private. Coed. Accreditation: WASC. Tuition: $6,600. Enrollment: 100 full-time, 248 part-time. Faculty: 42. Student-faculty ratio: 9:1. Degrees: BS Engineering Technology, BS Electrical and Software Engineering. Library: 12,000 volumes. 1 building on 4 acres. Only Bachelor of Science degree in Music Engineering Technology and Bachelor of Arts degree in Computer and Video Imaging.

College of Notre Dame
1500 Ralston Ave., Belmont 94002
Greg M. Smith, PhD., Dir. of Admis.

DOMINICAN COLLEGE OF SAN RAFAEL
50 Acacia Ave., San Rafael 94901-8008
Office of Admissions
800-788-3522

· FASHION INSTITUTE OF DESIGN & MERCHANDISING
919 S. Grand Ave., Los Angeles 90015
213-624-1201 or 800-421-0127 outside California
See listing under "Community and Junior Colleges"

† Humboldt State University
1 Harps St., Arcata 95521

:: Idyllwild School of Music & the Arts
P.O. Box 38P, Idyllwild 92549
Anne Behnke, Admissions
909-659-2171, FAX 909-659-2058
See listing under "Prep-Coed"

La Sierra University
4700 Pierce St., Riverside 92505
800-874-5587

† Loyola Marymount University
Loyola Blvd. at W. 80th, Los Angeles 90045
M. L'Heureux, Dir. of Admis.

Mills College
5000 MacArthur Blvd., Oakland 94613
Genevieve Ann Flaherty, Dean of Admissions
800-87-MILLS

† OTIS COLLEGE OF ART AND DESIGN
2401 Wilshire Blvd., Los Angeles 90057
213-251-0505 or 800-527-OTIS (catalog request)
Neil Hoffman, President
Dann Grindemann, Dean
Joseph Suszynski, Director of Admissions
Established 1918. Private. Coed. Accreditation: NASAD, WASC. Tuition: $12,286 for academic year (two semesters). Approximately 70% of students receive more than $2.5 million in scholarships and financial aid. Residence housing available. Single: $4,050 (per year), double: $2,700. Enrollment: 700 full-time and 1,000 part-time students. Degrees: BFA, MFA, AFA. BFA programs in fine arts, communication art, illustration, fashion design, photography, ceramics, environmental arts, surface design. Admissions based on portfolio and academic background. No deadline for enrollment. Student exchange programs with fourteen accredited colleges across the country and abroad. Pre-college program for high school students.

Pitzer College
1050 N. Mills Ave., Claremont 91711
Katharine Leighton, Dir. of Admis.

Pomona College
333 N. College Way, Claremont 91711
Peter W. Stanley, President

· Porterville College
100 E. College Ave., Porterville 93257
John McCuen, President

† San Diego State University
5300 Campanile Dr., San Diego 92115

† San Francisco Art Institute
800 Chestnut St., San Francisco 94133

† San Francisco State University
1600 Holloway Ave., San Francisco 94132
Corwin Bjonerud, Dir. of Admis.

† San Jose State University
1 Washington Sq., San Jose 95192

Santa Barbara City College
721 Cliff Dr., Santa Barbara 93109
805-965-0581

Scripps College
1030 Columbia Ave., Claremont 91711
Leslie Miles, Dean of Admissions

† Sonoma State University
1801 E. Cotati Ave., Rohnert Park 94928

University of California, Los Angeles
1247 Murphy Hall, Los Angeles 90024

University of California at Berkeley
Kroeber Hall, Berkeley 94720

University of La Verne
1950 3rd St., La Verne 91750
Mark Bornholdt, Dir. of Admis.

University of San Diego
5998 Alcala Park, San Diego 92110
Warren Muller, Dir. of Admis.
619-260-4506

University of San Francisco
2130 Fulton St., San Francisco 94117
Bill Henley, Dir. of Admis.

† University of the Pacific
3601 Pacific Ave, Stockton 95211
Elliott J. Taylor, Dean of Admissions

Woodbury University
7500 Glenoaks Blvd., Burbank 91504
See listing under "Universities"

COLORADO

Adams State College, Alamosa 81102
Cheryl Billingsley, Dir. of Admis.
800-824-6494

Colorado College
14 E. Cache La Poudre, Colorado Springs 80903
Terry Swenson, Dir. of Admis.

Colorado Institute of Art
200 E. 9th Ave., Denver 80203
Barbara Browning, Dir. of Admis.
800-275-2420
See listing under "Career Schools"

Mesa State College
P.O. Box 2647, Grand Junction 81502
Sherri Pe'a, Dir. of Admis.

Metropolitan State College of Denver
P.O. Box 173362, Campus Box 16
Denver 80217-3362

Pikes Peak Community College
5675 S. Academy Blvd.
Colorado Springs 80906-5498
Roberta Erickson, Dir. of Admis.
See listing under "Community and Junior
Colleges"

ROCKY MOUNTAIN COLLEGE OF ART & DESIGN

6875 E. Evans Ave., Denver 80224
303-753-6046
800-888-2787
Steven Steele, President
Rex Whisman, Dir. of Admis.
Carla Morse, Finance Director
Nancy Behr, Financial Aid Director
Lisa Steele, Academic Dean
Michael Bird, Registrar
Established 1963. Private. Coed. Accreditation:
Colorado Commission on Higher Education, CCA.
Enrollment: 350. Total charge: $2,940 per trimester for
all full-time students. All programs run year-round.
Off-campus housing assistance provided.
Bachelor of Fine Arts Degree Programs (4 year):
Advertising and Graphic Design, Illustration, Interior
Design, Painting and Drawing, Sculpture and Draw-
ing, and Environmental Graphic Design. The BFA
Degrees are made up of studio art/design courses,
courses that are related directly to the professional
aspects of the field, and liberal arts courses. Graduates
from a BFA Degree program have the technical skills
to be successful in their chosen career, and also possess a well rounded education that will cultivate a
lifelong interest in learning about the world in which
we live.
Associate of Arts Degree Programs (2 year): Advertising and Graphic Design, Illustration, Interior Design, and Environmental Graphic Design. The
Associate of Arts Degree is made up of studio art/de-
sign courses, courses that are related directly to the
professional aspects of the field, and Liberal Arts
courses. Graduates are well prepared to be successful
in their chosen careers.
This intensive art and design college provides the
foundation and the skills necessary for the talented
individual who is seeking a creative career. The faculty and administration strive to inspire the spirit of
academic freedom that is necessary for creative work
as well as the self discipline required, from entering
students to the most advanced levels. The combination of professional artists and serious students who
care about learning creates an educational environment which flourishes from our unique combination

of real world experience and academic excellence.
Admission: All degree candidates must be either
high school graduates or possess a GED. All degree
applicants must submit ACT or SAT scores. Entrance
is based on portfolio review and acceptance by the
admissions committee.
Scholarships: Available to all full-time applicants
on a yearly competitive basis. Financial aid is available for those who qualify. Approved for veterans
training.

University of Denver
2199 S. University Blvd., Denver 80210

University of Northern Colorado, Greeley 80639
Richard Munson, Department Chrpsn.
303-351-2143

Western State College of Colorado
Gunnison 81231
Monica Bruning, Dir. of Admis.
See listing under "Universities"

CONNECTICUT

CONNECTICUT INSTITUTE OF ART

581 W. Putnam Ave., Greenwich 06830
August Propersi, President/Director
Linda MacDonald, Associate Director
Accreditation: Approved by the Connecticut Commissioner of Education. Accredited member of the
Career College Association. Approved for Veterans.
Authorized under Federal Law to enroll non-immigrant alien students. Federal and financial aid available. Two year program (24 months). Day & evening
sessions. Current Enrollment: 275.
Courses: The curriculum at the Institute is a progressive one, starting with foundation courses leading to
a highly diversified combination of 4 majors. In a two
year period the program includes fine arts, advertising art, illustration and graphic design. In addition,
many other subjects are covered such as computer
graphics, airbrush and photography for the artist. The
courses are structured so that the CIA graduate has
more than one option available upon graduation from
the Institute.
Professional instructors: All instructors at the Connecticut Institute of Art are practicing professional
artists teaching their specialty.
Portfolio and placement: A professional portfolio is
achieved through the development of various skills.
Graduating students undergo a portfolio evaluation
session at which time the portfolio is given final
approval. CIA offers career placement assistance
through our Placement Department. These services
include resume preparation and job referrals.
Admissions: A personal interview is required as
part of the application process. To schedule an appointment, call the Admissions Department at 203-
869-4430.

Mattatuck Community College
750 Chase Parkway, Waterbury 06708
Dr. Richard Sanders, President

† University of Bridgeport
126 Park Ave., Bridgeport 06601
Andrew G. Nelson, Dean Admis./Financial Aid
203-576-4552
See listing under "Universities"

† University of Connecticut, Storrs 06268
Jerome M. Birdman, Dean

† UNIVERSITY OF HARTFORD

200 Bloomfield Ave., West Hartford 06117
Richard Zeiser, Dir. of Admis.
See listing under "Universities"

University of New Haven
300 Orange Ave., West Haven 06516
Joseph Chepaitis, Dean
203-932-7000

Yale University
1605A Yale Station, New Haven 06520

DELAWARE

University of Delaware, Newark 19711

DISTRICT OF COLUMBIA

The American University
4400 Massachusetts Ave. N.W.
Washington 20016

† Corcoran School of Art
500 17th St., N.W., Washington 20006
Mark Sistek, Dir. of Admissions

† Howard University
2400 6th St., N.W., Washington 20059
James E. Cheek, President

University of the District of Columbia
Georgia Ave.-Harvard St. Campus
1100 Harvard St., N.W., Washington 20009

University of the District of Columbia
Van Ness Campus
4200 Connecticut Ave., N.W., Washington 20008

FLORIDA

Art Institute of Fort Lauderdale
1799 S.E. 17th St., Ft. Lauderdale 33316
Eileen Northrop, V.P./Dir. of Admis.

Barry University
11300 N.E. 2nd Ave., Miami Shores 33161
Robin Ray Roberts, Dean of Admissions

Flagler College
P.O. Box 1027, St. Augustine 32085
Marc G. Williar, Dir. of Admis.
904-829-6481

Florida Atlantic University
500 N.W. 20th St., Boca Raton 33431
Brian Levin-Stankevich, Dir. of Admis.

Florida Southern College
111 Lake Hollingsworth Dr., Lakeland 33801
William Stephens, Jr., Dir. of Admis.

■ INTERNATIONAL FINE ARTS COLLEGE

1737 N. Bayshore Dr., Miami 33132
Sir Edward Porter, President
Frayda Parnes, Dir. of Admis.
800-225-9023 or 305-373-4684
Established 1965. Independent. Accreditation:
SACS. Tuition: $8,630. Apartment: $2,640. Enrollment: 650 day. Library: 13,450 volumes. Faculty: 31.
Degree: AA. Study-travel tours to Europe. Frequent
field trips throughout south Florida. Residences are
waterfront, luxurious apartment buildings, exquisitely furnished. Houseparents, swimming pools, recreation rooms, laundry room, storage facilities.
Majors: fashion merchandising, interior design, commercial art, fashion design, computer graphics.

Jacksonville University
2800 University Blvd., N., Jacksonville 32211

LYNN UNIVERSITY

(Est. 1962 as College of Boca Raton)
3601 N. Military Trail, Boca Raton 33431
407-994-0770 or 800-544-8035
See listing under "Universities"

† Ringling School of Art & Design
2700 N. Tamiami Trl., Sarasota 34234
Dr. Arland Christ-Janer, President

St. Leo College
P.O. Box 2008, St. Leo 33574
Bonnie Black, Dir. of Admis.

SCHILLER INTERNATIONAL UNIVERSITY (FLORIDA & EUROPE)

U.S. Admissions Office
Dept. PA, 453 Edgewater Dr., Dunedin 34698-7532
800-336-4133 Fax: 813-736-6263
Dr. Walter Liebrecht, President
Karen Altieri, Associate Director of Admissions
See listing under "Universities"

Stetson University
401 N. Woodland Blvd., De Land 32720
Gary A. Meadows, Dean of Admis.

Tampa College
3319 W. Hillsborough Ave., Tampa 33614
David Zorn, President

GEORGIA

Agnes Scott College
201 E. College Ave., Decatur 30030
Teresa Lahti, Dir. of Admis.

AMERICAN COLLEGE FOR THE APPLIED ARTS

3330 Peachtree Rd., N.E., Atlanta 30326
404-231-9000
See listing under "Universities".

Art Institute of Atlanta
3376 Peachtree Rd., N.E., Atlanta 30326
J. Robert Bouchard, Dir. of Admis.

† Atlanta College of Art
Woodruff Arts Center
1280 Peachtree St., N.E., Atlanta 30309
John Farkas, Dir. of Enrollment Management

Georgia College
231 W. Hancock St., Milledgeville 31061
912-453-5004

† Georgia State University
University Plaza, Atlanta 30303
Ernest Beals, Dean of Admissions

Kennesaw State College
P.O. Box 444, Marietta 30061
Joe Head, Dir. of Admis.

La Grange College
601 Broad St., La Grange 30240
Phil Dodson, Dir. of Admis.
706-882-2911

Oglethorpe University
4484 Peachtree Rd., N.E., Atlanta 30319
Dennis Matthews, Dir. of Admis.

Piedmont College
P.O. Box 10, Demorest 30535
Penny L. Graber, Dir of Admis.
800-277-7020

Portfolio Center
125 Bennett St., N.W., Atlanta 30309
800-255-3169
See listing under "Career Schools"

SAVANNAH COLLEGE OF ART & DESIGN

342 Bull St., Savannah 31401
Richard Rowan, President
May Poetter, VP of Admissions
Paula Rowan, Provost
Judith Van Baron, VP for Academic Affairs
912-238-2483
Established 1979. Private. Non-profit. Coed. Ac-
creditation: Southern Association of Colleges and
Schools and National Architectural Accrediting
Board. Enrollment: 2,330. Faculty: 140, all hold rank

of Professor. Average student-faculty ratio: 14:1. 1994-95 tuition per quarter: $3,300 full-time. Room: $3,000 - $3,500 (per academic year) varies by dormitory. The student body includes students from all 50 states and 60 foreign countries. There are no more than 20 students in any class. Summer sessions offered in Savannah, New York City & Europe.

Men's and women's dormitories available on campus. Rental apartments readily available in the area. No fraternities or sororities.

Degrees: Bachelor of Architecture, Bachelor of Fine Arts, Master of Fine Arts. BFA and MFA offered in 14 visual arts majors including art history, computer art, fashion, fiber arts, graphic design, historic preservation, interior design, painting, illustration, video, photography, furniture design, sequential art, and metals and jewelry.

Library: 30,000 volumes. 35 buildings. Urban campus. Our college has 8 gallery spaces and 11 computer laboratories. Fully equipped labs for students in fiber arts, photography, video, architecture, graphic design, historic preservation, painting, illustration, interior design, furniture design, sequential art, and metals and jewelry.

Admissions: Minimum 2.0 GPA in high school, undergraduate applicants must submit high school or college transcript, SAT or ACT scores, and letters of recommendation. Graduate applicants must submit college transcript, letters of recommendation, and portfolio and must have a personal interview. All applicants must pay a $50 application fee.

The college offers a graduated scholarship totaling $10,000 over four years to students who score over 1200 on the SAT or a composite score of 28 on the ACT, to students who are high school valedictorians, to students who attend selected Governor's Schools, and to selected students who are recognized through the ICSA program (a college-sponsored scholarship for talented artists).

The college is located within 30 minutes of the coastal beaches of Georgia and South Carolina and enjoys a mild, southern climate. The college exists for the purpose of preparing talented young people for a career in art, design, architecture, or historic preservation. The entire college is focused toward the personal, academic, and professional success of each student.

Spelman College
350 Spelman Ln., S.W., Atlanta 30314
Aline Rivers, Dir. of Admis.

† University of Georgia, Athens 30602
Francis A. Ruzicka, Head

Valdosta State College
Patterson St., Valdosta 31698

HAWAII

Brigham Young University, Hawaii Campus
55-220 Kulanui St., Laie 96762
Clark E. Hirschi, Coordinator of Admis.

Chaminade University of Honolulu
3140 Waialae Ave., Honolulu 96816
Charles Schafer, VP Enrollment Services

IDAHO

· Ricks College, Rexburg 83460
Steven Bennion, President

University of Idaho, Moscow 83843
Peter Brown, Dir. of Admis.

ILLINOIS

· American Academy of Art
332 S. Michigan Ave. 3rd Fl.
Chicago 60604

: American College of Technology
1300 W. Washington St., Bloomington 61701
Glenn L. Plotner, Dir. of Admis.
800-593-5151

Aurora University
347 S. Gladstone Ave., Aurora 60506
Peter Pitts, Dir. of Admis.

Barat College, Lake Forest 60045
Loretta Brickman, Dir. of Admis.

† Bradley University
1501 W. Bradley Ave., Peoria 61625

Columbia College
600 S. Michigan Ave., Chicago 60605
Debra McGrath, Dir. of Admis.

† Eastern Illinois University, Charleston 61920
James Johnson, Chrpsn.
See listing under "Universities"

Governors State University
1 University Pky., University Park 60466
Richard Pride, Dir. of Admis.

Illinois Institute of Technology
3300 S. Federal St., Chicago 60616
Wendell R. Webb, Dir. of Admissions

† Illinois State University
212 N. School St., Normal 61761

ILLINOIS WESLEYAN UNIVERSITY
P.O. Box 2900, Bloomington 61702
Miles Bair, Director
309-556-3077

Knox College, Galesburg 61401
309-343-0112 or 800-678-KNOX
See listing under "Universities"

LEWIS UNIVERSITY
Rt. 53, Romeoville 60441
Irish O'Reilly, Director of Admissions
See listing under "Universities"

MacMurray College
447 E. College Ave., Jacksonville 62650
Edwin R. Hockett, Dean of Admissions

Millikin University
1184 W. Main St., Decatur 62522
Lin Stoner, Dean of Admissions
800-373-7733

· Montay College
3750 W. Peterson Ave., Chicago 60659
Scott Dalhouse, Dir. of Admis.

North Central College
30 N. Brainard St.
P.O. Box 3065, Naperville 60566-7065
Marguerite Waters, Director of Admission
708-420-3414

Northeastern Illinois University
5500 N. St. Louis Ave., Chicago 60625

† Northern Illinois University, De Kalb 60115

Olivet Nazarene University, Kankakee 60901
John Mongerson, Dir. of Admis.
815-939-5203

Parkland College
2400 W. Bradley Ave., Champaign 61821-1899
217-351-2208 or 800-346-8089

Quincy College
1800 College Ave., Quincy 62301
Fr. Michael Lanning, O.F.M., Dir. of Admis.

RAY COLLEGE OF DESIGN
AAS, BA, BFA degrees
401 N. Wabash Ave., Chicago 60611
312-280-3500
Woodfield Campus
1051 Perimeter Dr., Schaumburg 60173
708-619-3450

Rockford College
5050 E. State St., Rockford 61108
Miriam King, V.P. for Enrollment Management
See listing under "Universities"

Rosary College
7900 W. Division St., River Forest 60305
Hildegarde Schmidt, Dir. of Admis.

Sangamon State University
Shepherd Rd., Springfield 62794-9243
Admissions and Records, 217-786-6626

† School of the Art Institute of Chicago
37 S. Wabash, Chicago 60603
Ellen B. Cropp, Dir. of Admis.

† Southern Illinois University at Carbondale
Carbondale 62901

Southern Illinois University at Edwardsville
Edwardsville 62026
Eugene J. Magac, Dir. of Admissions & Records

· Springfield College in Illinois
1500 N. Fifth St., Springfield 62702
Dr. H. Brent DeLand, President

Trinity Christian College
6601 W. College Dr., Palos Heights 60463
Kenneth Bootsma, President

† University of Illinois
506 S. Wright St., Urbana 61801

† University of Illinois at Chicago
P.O. Box 4348, Chicago 60680
Martin Hurtig, Dir. of Art & Design

INDIANA

Ball State University
2000 W. University Ave., Muncie 47306
Ruth Vedvik, Dir. of Admis.

Franklin College
501 E. Monroe, Franklin 46131
B. Stephen Richards, VP Enrollment

Goshen College
1700 S. Main St., Goshen 46526
Abner Hershberger, Chairperson

Grace College
200 Seminary Dr., Winona Lake 46590
Ron Henry, Dir. of Admis.

† Indiana State University
217 N. 6th St., Terre Haute 47809

† Indiana University at Bloomington
300 N. Jordan Ave., Bloomington 47406

Indiana University-Purdue University at Fort Wayne
2101 Coliseum Blvd. E., Fort Wayne 46805

† Indiana University-Purdue University
355 N. Lansing, Indianapolis 46202

Indiana Wesleyan University
4201 S. Washington St., Marion 46953
800-332-6901

Manchester College
604 College Ave., North Manchester 46962
Gregory Miller, Dir. of Admis.

St. Mary-of-the-Woods College
Saint Mary-of-the-Woods 47876
Lynn M. Rubick, Director of Admissions
800-926-SMWC

† St. Mary's College
46 Madeliva, Notre Dame 46556
Mary Ann Rowan, Dir. of Admissions

Taylor University
500 W. Reade Ave., Upland 46989
Craig Moore, Head

University of Evansville
1800 Lincoln Ave., Evansville 47722
Les Miley, Dept. Chair
800-423-8633

University of Notre Dame, Notre Dame 46556
Frederick S. Beckman, Chrpsn.

· † Vincennes University
1002 N. 1st St., Vincennes 47591

IOWA

Clarke College
1550 Clarke Dr., Dubuque 52001
Carmelle Zserdin, BVM, MFA, Chair
800-383-2345

Coe College
1220 1st Ave., N.E., Cedar Rapids 52402
Michael White, Director of Enrollment Services

Dordt College
498 4th Ave., N.E., Sioux Center 51250
Quentin Van Essen, Dir. of Admissions
800-343-6738

† Drake University
2507 E. University Ave., Des Moines 50311
Thomas Willoughby, Dir. of Admis.

Graceland College, Lamoni 50140
800-638-0053, Outside Iowa 800-346-9208
Bonita Booth, Dean of Admissions
See listing under "Universities"

Grand View College
1200 Grandview Ave., Des Moines 50316
Lori Hanson, Dir. of Admissions
800-444-6083

Grinnell College
P.O. Box 805, Grinnell 50112

· Hawkeye Community College
1501 E. Orange Rd., Waterloo 50701
319-296-2320 Ext. 4000

· Iowa Lakes Community College
300 S. 18th St., Estherville 51334
John Nelson, Dir. of Admis.
712-362-2604

Iowa State University, Ames 50011
Karsten Smedal, Dir. of Admis.

Iowa Wesleyan College
601 N. Main St., Mt. Pleasant 52641

Luther College
700 College Dr., Decorah 52101
David Sallee, Dean for Enrollment

Maharishi International University
Route 1, Fairfield 52556
Gregory Polakow, Dir. of Admis.

Morningside College, Sioux City 51106
Lora Vanderzwaag, Dir. of Admis.

Mount Mercy College
1330 Elmhurst Dr., N.E., Cedar Rapids 52402
Carol Williamson, Dir. of Admis.

Teikyo Marycrest University
1607 W. 12th St., Davenport 52804
Tim McDonough, Dir. of Admis.
See listing under "Universities"

† University of Northern Iowa, Cedar Falls 50614

· Waldorf College
106 S. 6th St., Forest City 50436
Steve Lovik, Dir. of Admis.
800-292-1903

KANSAS

Bethany College
421 N. 1st St., Lindsborg 67456
Dennis Chaput, Dir. of Admis.

Emporia State University
1200 Commercial St., Emporia 66801
Dr. Barbara Hilgendorf, Dir. of Admissions

Fort Hays State University
600 Park St., Hays 67601-4099
Gary Coulter, Chrpsn.

McPherson College
1600 E. Euclid St., McPherson 67460

Ottawa University
1001 S. Cedar St., Ottawa 66067
Steve Koberlein, Dir. of Admis.
800-755-5200

Saint Mary College
4100 S. 4th St., Leavenworth 66048
Irene Keehan, Dir. of Admis.

† University of Kansas, Lawrence 66045

KENTUCKY

Asbury College
1 Macklem Dr., Wilmore 40390
Jonah Mitchell, Dir. of Admis.

Bellarmine College
2001 Newburg Rd., Louisville 40205
Thomas LaBaugh, Dean of Admissions

Cumberland College
6178 College Station Dr., Williamsburg 40769
See listing under "Universities"

Kentucky Wesleyan College
3000 Frederica St., Owensboro 42301
Kimble Bromley, Director

Morehead State University, Morehead 40351
Charles Myers, Director of Admissions
606-783-2000

† Murray State University, Murray 42071
Phil Bryan, Director of Admissions
800-272-4MSU

Pikeville College
214 Sycamore St., Pikeville 41501
Dr. John W. Sanders, Dean of Admissions

Spalding University
851 S. 4th St., Louisville 40203
Dorothy G. Allen, Dir. of Admis.

† Western Kentucky University
1526 Russellville Rd., Bowling Green 42101

LOUISIANA

Louisiana College
College Station, Pineville 71359
Byron McGee, Dir. of Admis.
318-487-7386
See listing under "Liberal Arts"

† Louisiana State University and A & M College
Baton Rouge 70803

† Lousiana Technical University
P.O. Box 3168, Ruston 71272

Tulane University
6823 Saint Charles Ave., New Orleans 70118
Richard Whiteside, Dean of Admission

† University of New Orleans
New Orleans 70148

MAINE

Bowdoin College, Brunswick 04011
William Mason, Dir. of Admis.

College of the Atlantic
105 Eden St., Bar Harbor 04609
Steve Thomas, Dir. of Admis.

: HEARTWOOD SCHOOL OF ART
P.O. Box 1100, Kennebunkport 04046
Berri Inoue, Director
207-967-8444

† Maine College of Art
97 Spring St., Portland 04101
Elizabeth Shea, Dir. of Admis.

† University of Maine, Orono 04469

† University of Southern Maine
96 Falmouth St., Portland 04103
Rose Marasco, Chrpsn.

MARYLAND

· Harford Community College
401 Thomas Run Rd., Bel Air 21015
Nancy Klapp, Coordinator

Loyola College
4501 N. Charles St., Baltimore 21210
William Bossemeyer III, Dir. of Admis.

· † Maryland College of Art & Design
10500 Georgia Ave., Silver Spring 20902

† Maryland Institute College of Art
1300 W. Mt. Royal Ave., Baltimore 21217
Theresa Lynch Bedoya, Dean of Admissions

· Montgomery College
51 Mannakee St., Rockville 20850
301-279-5115

Morgan State University
Cold Spring Ln. and Hillen Rd., Baltimore 21239

Towson State University
800 York Rd., Towson 21204
Dr. Hoke Smith, President

University of Maryland Eastern Shore
11868 Academic Oval, Princess Anne 21853
Dr. Gerald Johnson, Chrpsn.

Villa Julie College
1525 Greenspring Valley Rd., Stevenson 21153
Carolyn Manuszak, President

MASSACHUSETTS

Anna Maria College
2 Sunset Ln., Paxton 01612
Dr. Bernadette Madore, SSA, President

† THE ART INSTITUTE OF BOSTON
700 Beacon St., Boston 02215
Stan Trecker, President
Diana Arcadipone, Dir. of Admissions
617-262-1223 or 800-773-0494
(NY, PA, New England)
Fax 617-437-1226
Established 1912. Private. Coed. Accreditation: NASAD. Tuition: $9,450. Fees: $500 - $650. Enrollment: 350 full-time, 150 part-time. Faculty: 75. Student-faculty ratio: 12:1. Degrees: BFA, 3-year Certificate and 2-year Diploma in Fine Arts, Design, Illustration, Photography, and combined majors. Library: 10,000 volumes. 75% of faculty are working professional artists, 85% of graduates complete bac-

calaureate degrees, outstanding artist's exhibition schedule in college's gallery. Located in the heart of Boston's student center.

Atlantic Union College
P.O. Box 1000, South Lancaster 01561
Osa Canto, Registrar

Boston University
685 Commonwealth Ave., Boston 02215

Brandeis University
415 South St, Waltham 02154
David Gould, Dean of Admissions
617-736-3500

Bridgewater State College
Bridgewater 02325
James Plotner, Jr., Dir. of Admis.

: BUTERA SCHOOL OF ART
Commercial Art-Sign Painting
111 Beacon St., Boston 02116
Charles Banks, Director

Clark University
950 Main St., Worcester 01610
Richard Pierson, Dean of Admis.

Curry College
1071 Blue Hill Ave., Milton 02186
617-333-0500

DEAN COLLEGE
99 Main St, Franklin 02038
Kathleen Teehan, Dean of Admissions
508-528-9100
See listing under "Community and Junior Colleges"

ELMS COLLEGE
291 Springfield St., Chicopee 01013
800-255-ELMS

Emmanuel College
400 The Fenway, Boston 02115
Margaret Bonilla, Dir. of Admis.

· Endicott College
376 Hale St., Beverly 01915
Elizabeth Macomber, Dir. of Admis.

Hampshire College, Amherst 01002
Audrey Y. Smith, Dir. of Admissions
413-582-5471

† Massachusetts College of Art
621 Huntington Ave., Boston 02115

† MONTSERRAT COLLEGE OF ART
P.O. Box 26, Beverly 01915
Arthur Greenblatt, President
James Sawyer, Dir. of Admis.
Established 1970. North Shore Community Arts Foundation. Coed. Accreditation: NEASC, NASAD. Tuition: $8,960. Est. total yrly. exp.: $15,000. Enrollment: 300. Faculty: 37. Degrees: 4 year diploma, BFA programs. Library: 20,000 volumes. 2 buildings. Seacoast city, 20 minutes north of Boston and museums. Areas of concentration in painting, graphic design, illustration, printmaking, photography, sculpture and general fine arts. Apartment-style housing and financial aid available. Information: 508-922-8222 or Toll Free 1-800-836-0487.

Mt. Holyoke College
College St., South Hadley 01075
Anita Smith, Director of Admissions
413-538-2023

: New England School of Art & Design
28 Newbury St., Boston 02116
Anne Blevins, Dir. of Admis.

Pine Manor College
400 Heath St., Chestnut Hill 02167
Gillian Lloyd, Dir. of Admis.

† Salem State College
352 Lafayette St., Salem 01970
David Sartwell, Dir. of Admis.

† SCHOOL OF THE MUSEUM OF FINE ARTS
230 Fenway, Boston 02115
Alan Van Reed, Dean of Admissions
617-267-1218

Simmons College
300 The Fenway, Boston 02115

Suffolk University
8 Ashburton Place, Boston 02108
Barbara K. Ericson, Assoc. Dean Enrollment & Retention
617-573-8460

† University of Massachusetts Dartmouth
Old Westport Rd., North Dartmouth 02747
Raymond Barrows, Dir. of Admissions
508-999-8605

† University of Massachusetts Lowell
1 University Ave., Lowell 01854

Wellesley College, Wellesley 02181
Janet A. Lavin, Dir. of Admis.

Westfield State College
577 Western Ave., Westfield 01085
John F. Marcus, Dir. of Admis.

MICHIGAN

Adrian College
110 S. Madison St., Adrian 49221
George Wolf, Dir. of Admis.
See listing under "Universities"

Albion College
611 E. Porter, Albion 49224
800-858-6770

Aquinas College
1607 Robinson Rd., S.E., Grand Rapids 49506
Paula Meehan, Dean of Admissions
800-678-9593

† CENTER FOR CREATIVE STUDIES
COLLEGE OF ART & DESIGN
201 E. Kirby St., Detroit 48202
Frank Couzens, Interim President
Eddie Kent Tallent, Asst. Dean for Enrollment
Established 1926. Private. Coed. Accreditation: NCACS, NASAD. Tuition: $11,100. Room and board: $4,500. Enrollment: 180 boarding, 680 day. Faculty: 170. Degree: BFA. Library: 22,000 volumes. Over 136,000 square feet of studio & academic space. Campus size: 7.5 acres. CCS-CAD is one of the 10 largest private, professional colleges of art and design in the U.S. offering 17 concentrations in the visual arts in the following fields: fine arts, crafts, industrial design, graphic communications, and photography. The college is located in Detroit's University Cultural Center, approximately 4 miles north of the downtown area. College owned and operated, fully furnished housing facilities located on-campus are available.

† Cranbrook Academy of Art
P.O. Box 801, Bloomfield Hills 48303
Barbara Price, Dean

Eastern Michigan University, Ypsilanti 48197
John E. Van Haren, Head
313-487-3060 or 800-GO-TO-EMU

† Grand Valley State University
1 Campus Dr., Allendale 49401
Forrest Armstrong, Dean

HILLSDALE COLLEGE
33 E. College St., Hillsdale 49242
Professor Sam Kecht, Director
517-437-7341

† Hope College
69 E. 10th St., Holland 49423
Gordon Van Wylen, President

:: Interlochen Arts Academy
P.O. Box 199, Interlochen 49643
Tom Bewley, Dir. of Admis.

† Kendall College of Art & Design
111 N. Division Ave., Grand Rapids 49503
Charles Deihl, President
800-676-2787

Lawrence Technological University
21000 W. Ten Mile Rd., Southfield 48075
800-225-5588 ext. 3160

Michigan State University, East Lansing 48824
Prof. Irving Taran, Chrpsn.

Olivet College
300 S. Main St., Olivet 49076
Vicki Gallas, Registrar
See listing under "Universities"

† Siena Heights College
1247 E. Siena Heights Dr., Adrian 49221

· Suomi College
601 Quincy St., Hancock 49930
John Ruohoniemi, Dean/Enrollment Development
800-682-7604

† University of Michigan-Ann Arbor
815 S. University Ave., Ann Arbor 48109

† Western Michigan University, Kalamazoo 49008
Stanley Henderson, Dir. of Enrl. Mgt. & Admis.
616-387-2000

MINNESOTA

Bemidji State University
1500 Birchmont Dr., N.E., Bemidji 56601
800-475-2001

Bethel College
3900 Bethel Dr., St. Paul 55112
Dr. George Brushaber, President

Carleton College
One N. College St., Northfield 55057
Paul Thiboutot, Dir. of Admis.

COLLEGE OF ASSOCIATED ARTS
344 Summit Ave., Saint Paul 55102
Sherry Essen, Dir. of Admis.
Admissions Office, 612-224-3416

College of Saint Benedict
37 S. College Ave., St. Joseph 56374

College of St. Catherine
2004 Randolph Ave., St. Paul 55105

Concordia College
901 8th St. S., Moorhead 56562
Robert Meadows-Rogers, Chairperson
See listing under "Universities"

Concordia College-St. Paul
275 N. Syndicate, St. Paul 55104
Tim Utter, Dir. of Admis.

Gustavus Adolphus College
800 W. College Ave., St. Peter 56082
Mark Anderson, Dir. of Admis.

† Mankato State University
P.O. Box 8400, Mankato 56002

† MINNEAPOLIS COLLEGE OF ART & DESIGN
2501 Stevens Ave., S., Minneapolis 55404
Rebecca Haas, Dir. of Admis.
Admissions Office 800-874-6223

† Moorhead State University
1104 7th Ave. S., Moorhead 56560

Northwestern College
3003 Snelling Ave., N., St. Paul 55113
Ralph Anderson, Dean of Admissions
800-827-6827 or 612-631-5111

† St. Cloud State University
740 4th Ave., S., St. Cloud 56301
Sherwood Reid, Dir. of Admis.
800-369-4260

St. John's University
P.O. Box 7155, Collegeville 56321

St. Mary's College of Minnesota
700 Terrace Heights #2, Winona 55987
Tony Piscitiello, VP for Admission

St. Olaf College, Northfield 55057
Jan Shoger, Chrpsn.
507-646-3248

Southwest State University, Marshall 56258

University of Minnesota, Twin Cities
Minneapolis 55455

MISSISSIPPI

† Belhaven College
1500 Peachtree St., Jackson 39202

† Delta State University
Hwy. 8 W., Cleveland 38732

† Jackson State University
1400 Lynch St., Jackson 39203

† Mississippi State University
P.O. Box J, Mississippi State University 39762

† Mississippi University for Women
P.O. Box W-1602, Columbus 39701
Teresa Thompson, Exec. Dir. of Enrollment

† Mississippi Valley State University
14000 Hwy. 82 W., Itta Bena 38941
Maxcine B. Rush, Director of Admissions
See listing under "Universities"

† University of Mississippi, University 38677

† University of Southern Mississippi
P.O. Box 5165, Hattiesburg 39406

MISSOURI

† Central Missouri State University
Warrensburg 64093
Delores Hudson, Dir. of Admis.

Columbia College
1001 Rogers St., Columbia 65216
Ron Cronacher, Dir. of Admissions
800-231-2391

· Cottey College
1000 W. Austin St., Nevada 64772
Wendy Beckemeyer, Dir. of Admis.

Evangel College
1111 N. Glenstone Ave., Springfield 65802
David Schoolfield, Dir. of Enrollment

Fontbonne College
6800 Wydown Blvd., St. Louis 63105
Peggy Musen, Dir. of Admis.

† Kansas City Art Institute
4415 Warwick Blvd., Kansas City 64111
Charles Van Gilder, Dir. of Admis.
800-522-5224

Maryville University of St. Louis
13550 Conway Rd., Saint Louis 63141
314-576-9300 or 800-MARYVLL

Missouri Southern State College
3950 Newman Rd., Joplin 64801-1595
Jim Bray, Dept. Head
See listing under "Universities"

Missouri Valley College
500 E. College St., Marshall 65340
816-886-6924 ext. 114
See listing under "Universities"

Missouri Western State College
4525 Downs Dr., St. Joseph 64507
Howard McCauley, Dir. of Admis.

Northeast Missouri State University
Kirksville 63501

Park College, Parkville 64152
Dr. Edwin Rawn, Dean of Admis.

· † St. Louis Community College at Florissant Valley
3400 Pershall Rd., St. Louis 63135
Milton Woody, Dir. of Admis.

Southeast Missouri State University
1 University Plz., Cape Girardeau 63701
New Student Relations 314-651-2590
See listing under "Universities"

Southwest Baptist University
1601 S. Springfield Ave., Bolivar 65613

Southwest Missouri State University
901 S. National Ave., Springfield 65804
Dr. James K. Hill, Department Head
417-836-5110

Stephens College, Columbia 65215
Mary Ann Sprinkle, Dir. of Admis.

† Washington University
1 Brookings Dr., St. Louis 63130

Webster University
470 E. Lockwood Ave., St. Louis 63119
Peter Sargent, Associate Dean
See listing under "Universities"

William Woods College
200 W. 12th St., Fulton 65251
Dr. Jahnae Barnett, VP of Admis.

MONTANA

† Montana State University, Bozeman 59717

† Montana State University - Billings
1500 N. 30th St., Billings 59101
Karen Everett, Dir. of Admis.
406-657-2158

Rocky Mountain College
1511 Poly Dr., Billings 59102
David Heringer, Dir. of Admis.
See listing under "Universities"

† University of Montana, Missoula 59812
800-462-8636

NEBRASKA

Bellevue College
1000 Galvin Rd. S., Bellevue 68005
Chari Leader, VP of Enrollment

College of Saint Mary
1901 S. 72nd St., Omaha 68124
Sheila Haggas, Dir. of Admis.

Concordia College
800 N. Columbia Ave., Seward 68434
Don Vos, Dir. of Admis.

Creighton University
2500 California St., Omaha 68178
Jerome Horning, Chrpsn.

Dana College
2848 College Dr., Blair 68008
John Schueth, Dir. of Admis.
800-444-3262
See listing under "Universities"

Nebraska Wesleyan University
5000 Saint Paul Ave., Lincoln 68504
Ken Sieg, Dir. of Admis.

· Northeast Community College
P.O. Box 469, Norfolk 68702
Eugene Hart, Dir. of Admis.

Peru State College, Peru 68421
Pamela J. Cosgrove, Dir. of Admis.
402-872-3815

† University of Nebraska at Lincoln
Old H 1223, Lincoln 68588
John Peters, Dean

NEVADA

Sierra Nevada College-Lake Tahoe
P.O. Box 4269, Incline Village 89450
Lane Murray, Dir. of Admissions
See listing under "Universities"

† University of Nevada Las Vegas
4505 S. Maryland Pky., Las Vegas 89154-1021
Admissions: 702-895-3443 or 800-334-UNLV

NEW HAMPSHIRE

Keene State College
229 Main St., Keene 03435
Kathryn Dodge, Dir. of Admis.

New England College
26 Bridge St., Henniker 03242
John Spaulding, Dir. of Admis.

NOTRE DAME COLLEGE
2321 Elm St., Manchester 03104
603-669-4298

Rivier College
420 S. Main St., Nashua 03060
Admissions: 800-44-RIVIER

· White Pines College
40 Chester St., Chester 03036
603-887-4401

NEW JERSEY

Caldwell College
9 Ryerson Ave., Caldwell 07006

: Du Cret School of the Arts
1030 Central Ave., Plainfield 07060
Frank Falotico, Director

FELICIAN COLLEGE
262 S. Main St., Lodi 07644
Sr. Mary Austin, OSB, Dir. of Admis.
201-778-1029
See listing under "Universities"

Georgian Court College
900 Lakewood Ave., Lakewood 08701
908-364-2200 Ext. 348

† Jersey City State College
2039 Kennedy Blvd., Jersey City 07305
201-200-3234

: Kubert School of Cartoon & Graphic Arts
37 Myrtle Ave., Dover 07801

· Mercer County Community College
West Windsor Campus
1200 Old Trenton Rd., Trenton 08690
Michael Glass, Dir. of Admis.
See listing under "Community and Junior Colleges"

† Montclair State University
1 Normal Ave., Upper Montclair 07043

Princeton University, Princeton 08544

Rowan College of New Jersey, Glassboro 08028
Marvin G. Sills, Dir. of Admis.

Rutgers, The State University of NJ
Mason Gross School of the Arts
New Brunswick 08903

Stockton State College, Pomona 08240
Sal Catalfamo, Dir. of Admis.

Thomas Edison State College
101 W. State St., Trenton 08608

Upsala College
345 Prospect St., East Orange 07017
George Lynes, Dean of Admissions

NEW MEXICO

· Art Center
2268 Wyoming Blvd. N.E., Albuquerque 87112

College of Santa Fe
1600 St. Michaels Dr., Santa Fe 87505
800-456-2673

Eastern New Mexico University
Portales 88130
Larry Fuqua, Dir. of Admis.

· † Institute of American Indian Arts
P.O. Box 20007, Santa Fe 87504
Jerry Zollars, Dir. of Admis.

New Mexico Highlands University, Las Vegas 87701
Dr. Jorge P. Thomas, VP Academic Affairs

University of New Mexico, Albuquerque 87131
Robert Weaver, Dean of Admissions

NEW YORK

Adelphi University, Garden City 11530
Dr. Elliot Pruzan, Asst. Provost & Dir. of Admis.
516-877-3050

Alfred University
Alumni Hall, Alfred 14802
Laurie Richer, Director of Admissions
800-541-9229

CAZENOVIA COLLEGE
Cazenovia 13035
Dr. James Parker, VP for Enrollment Management
See listing under "Universities"

College of New Rochelle
29 Castle Pl., New Rochelle 10805

† College of St. Rose
432 Western Ave., Albany 12203

† Cooper Union
41 Cooper Square, New York 10003
Arthur Corwin, Acting Dean
See listing under "Universities"

Daemen College
4380 Main St., Amherst 14226
Maria Dillard, Dir. of Admis.
in NY 800-462-7652 or 716-839-8225

Elmira College
Park Pl., Elmira 14901
William S. Neal, Dean of Admissions
See listing under "Liberal Arts"

: † Folk Art Institute
61 W. 62nd St., New York 10023

Fordham University
441 E. Fordham Rd., Bronx 10458
718-817-1000

Friends World Program, Long Island University
Montauk Hwy., Southampton 11968
Carol Gilbert, Dir. of Admis.

† Hartwick College, Oneonta 13820

Long Island University-C. W. Post Campus
Rt. 25A, Brookville 11548
Prof. Howard La Marca, Chrpsn.
516-299-2464

Manhattanville College
2900 Purchase St., Purchase 10577

Marymount College
100 Marymount Ave., Tarrytown 10591
Gina R. Campbell, Dir. of Admis.
800-724-4312

Marymount Manhattan College
221 E. 71st St., New York 10021
Suzanne M. Murphy, Dir. of Admis.

Mercy College
555 Broadway, Dobbs Ferry 10522
James Nesbitt, Dean of Admissions

Molloy College
1000 Hempstead Ave., Rockville Centre 11570
Wayne James, Dir. of Admis.
See listing under "Universities"

: † Munson-Williams-Proctor Institute
310 Genesee St., Utica 13502

Nazareth College of Rochester
4245 East Ave., Rochester 14618
Paul Kenyon, Dir. of Admis.

New York Institute of Technology
Old Westbury Campus, Old Westbury 11568

† New York State College of Ceramics at Alfred
University
Alfred 14802
800-541-9229

Pace University, Pleasantville/Briarcliff Campus
Bedford Rd., Pleasantville 10570

† Parsons School of Design
66 5th Ave., New York 10011

† Pratt Institute
200 Willoughby Ave., Brooklyn 11205

† Roberts Wesleyan College
2301 Westside Dr., Rochester 14624
Loren Baker, Chrpsn.
See listing under "Universities"

† Rochester Institute of Technology
1 Lomb Memorial Dr., Rochester 14623
716-475-6631
See listing under "Universities"

· † Rochester Institute of Technology (NTID)
National Technical Institute for the Deaf
1 Lomb Memorial Dr., Rochester 14623

Russell Sage College
51 1st St., Troy 12180

· † Russell Sage Junior College of Albany
140 New Scotland Ave., Albany 12208

ST. THOMAS AQUINAS COLLEGE
Rt. 340, Sparkill 10976
Andrea Kraeft, Dir. of Admis.
800-999-STAC
See listing under "Liberal Arts"

† School of Visual Arts
209 E. 23rd St., New York 10010

† Skidmore College, Saratoga Springs 12866
Kent Jones, Dir. of Admis.

: † Sotheby's Educational Studies
1334 York Ave., New York 10021

† SUNY at Buffalo
17 Capen Hall
P.O. Box 601660, Buffalo 14260-1660
716-645-6900

SUNY College at Brockport
Brockport 14420

SUNY College at Old Westbury
P.O. Box 210, Old Westbury 11568
Michael Sheehy, Dir. of Admis.

SUNY at Oswego, Oswego 13126
Dr. Joseph Grant, Jr., Dean of Admissions
315-341-2250

SUNY College at Plattsburgh, Plattsburgh 12901
Richard Mikkelson, Chrpsn.
518-564-2460

SUNY College of Technology at Farmingdale
Route 110, Farmingdale 11735
Janet Snyder, Dir. of Admis.
516-420-2200

† SUNY Fashion Institute of Technology
227 W. 27th St., New York 10001

· SUNY Nassau Community College
1 Education Dr., Garden City 11530
Bernard Iantosca, Dir of Admis.

† Syracuse University, Syracuse 13244

University of Rochester
500 Joseph C. Wilson Blvd., Rochester 14627
Wayne A. Locust, Dir. of Admis.
See listing under "Universities"

Utica College of Syracuse University
1600 Burrstone Rd., Utica 13502

· Villa Maria College of Buffalo
240 Pine Ridge Rd., Buffalo 14225
Lynn D'Auria, Dir. of Admis.

NORTH CAROLINA

· Alamance Community College
P.O. Box 623, Haw River 27258
W. Ronald McCarter, President

Barton College
College Station, Wilson 27893
Anthony Britt, Dir. of Admis.
800-345-4973/919-399-6318
See listing under "Universities"

· Brevard College
Brevard 28712
Bob McLendon, Dean of Admissions

· Chowan College
P.O. Box 1848, Murfreesboro 27855
Winslow Carter, Dir. of Admis.

· College of The Albemarle
P.O. Box 2327, Elizabeth City 27906
John M. Wells, Asst. Dean of Admissions
919-335-0821, Ext. 220

† East Carolina University
1000 E. 5th St., Greenville 27858
Michael Dorsey, Dean

Gardner-Webb University
General Delivery, Boiling Springs 28017
Ray M. Hardee, Dean of Admissions
800-253-6472

Greensboro College
815 W. Market St., Greensboro 27401

· Halifax Community College
P.O. Box 809, Weldon 27890

· Haywood Community College
Freedlander Dr., Clyde 28721
Carol Smith, Dir. of Admis.

High Point College
933 Montlieu Ave., High Point 27262
Jim Schlimmer, Dir. of Admis.

Mars Hill College
Main St., Mars Hill 28754
Dr. Smith Goodrum, Dean of Admis.

Methodist College
5400 Ramsey St., Fayetteville 28311
Fiore Bergamasco, Dir. of Admis.

Pembroke State University
P.O. Box 1510, Pembroke 28372
Anthony Locklear, Dir. of Admissions
919-521-6262

QUEENS COLLEGE
1900 Selwyn Ave., Charlotte 28274
D. Stephen Cloniger, VP for Enrollment Management
See listing under "Liberal Arts"

Salem College
P.O. Box 10548, Winston-Salem 27108
Katherine Knapp, Director of Admissions
800-32-SALEM
See listing under "Women's College"

· Sandhills Community College
2200 Airport Rd., Pinehurst 28374
910-692-6185

University of North Carolina at Chapel Hill
Chapel Hill 27599
James C. Walters, Dir. Undergrad Admis.

NORTH DAKOTA

† University of North Dakota
Box 8193 University Station, Grand Forks 58203

OHIO

ACA COLLEGE OF DESIGN
2528 Kemper Ln., Cincinnati 45206
Cyndi Mendell, Dir. of Admis.
513-751-1206
Established 1976. Two year design college. Small classes, individual instruction. Faculty: 7 (professional designers). Limited enrollment of 75. Accreditation: CCA. First year, commercial art foundation; Second year, integrates illustration, design with computers - a computer on each drawing table. Plus a 2 week illustration workshop. Associate degree or diploma offered.

· Antonelli Institute of Art & Photography
124 E. 7th St., Cincinnati 45202

† ART ACADEMY OF CINCINNATI
1125 Saint Gregory St., Cincinnati 45202
Roger Williams, Director
Douglas Dobbins, Dir. of Admis.
Established 1887. Private. Coed. Accreditation: NCACS, NASAD. Tuition: $8,990. Enrollment: 250. Faculty: 30. Degrees: AS, BFA. Library: 50,000 volumes. 2 buildings on 184 acres of park land. Major programs: communication design, fine art, art history. Part-time, night and summer classes. Children's classes on Saturdays.

· Art Advertising Academy
4343 Bridgetown Rd., Cincinnati 45211
513-574-1010
2 year Associate of Applied Business in Commercial Art, 2 year commercial art diploma program including computer art and airbrush art. Small individual classes.

† Bowling Green State University
Bowling Green 43403
John Martin, Dir. of Admis.

Capital University
2199 E. Main St., Columbus 43209
Dolphus E. Henry, Associate Provost

† Cleveland Institute of Art
11141 East Blvd., Cleveland 44106
Thomas Steffen, Dir. of Admis.
In OH 800-223-6500 other 800-223-4700

College of Mount St. Joseph
5701 Delhi Rd., Cincinnati 45233-1672
See listing under "Universities"

College of Wooster
1189 Beall Ave., Wooster 44691
Hayden Schilling, Dean of Admis.

† COLUMBUS COLLEGE OF ART & DESIGN
107 N. 9th St., Columbus 43215-1758
Joseph V. Canzani, President
Mary Kinney, VP
Thomas Green, Dir. of Admissions
614-224-9101
Founded in 1879, CCAD is one of the finest and oldest colleges of art and design in the nation. With a 17-building campus, the college is located in Downtown Columbus adjacent to the Columbus Museum of Art. Students receive professional art training with a BFA degree within the Divisions of: Advertising Design, Retail Advertising (Fashion Illustration & Fashion Design), Industrial Design, Interior Design, Illustration, Photography, and Fine Arts. Concentrated directions in package design, environmental

design, art therapy, video, computer graphics and electronic publishing may be integrated in the above majors. The newly opened Joseph V. Canzani Center has quickly become the focal point at the college; the building houses an exhibition hall, auditorium, student recreation center and a library/resource center. An on-campus dormitory houses all incoming freshman and transfer students from outside the Columbus area. Applicants to the college must be high school graduates (or have received a certificate of equivalence) with a minimum cumulative GPA of 2.0. Artwork reflecting the student's artistic ability must be submitted either in person or by sending slides. Academic transcripts from high school (and college if applicable) and letters of recommendation are also desirable. A personal on-campus interview is recommended, but not mandatory. The college is non-profit with accreditation by NASAD and NCACS. Enrollment: 1662. Tuition: $9,700 per year. Room and board: $5,400. Cafeteria available. Library: 36,000 volumes. See advertising this classification.

· Cuyahoga Community College, Eastern Campus
25444 Harvard Rd., Warrensville Heights 44122

· Cuyahoga Community College, Metropolitan Campus
2900 Community College Ave., Cleveland 44115

· Cuyahoga Community College, Western Campus
11000 W. Pleasant Valley Rd.
Parma Heights 44130

DAVIS JUNIOR COLLEGE
4747 Monroe St., Toledo 43623
Diane Brunner, President
Timothy Brunner, Chairperson
Established 1858. Private. Coed. Accreditation: AICS, AAMA, NCACS. Tuition: $5,600. Fees: $25 application fee. Enrollment: 350 full-time, 100 part-time. Faculty: 35. Student-faculty ratio: 15:1. Degree: associate. Specialized library. 2 buildings including an airport. Admissions test (CPAT) & specialized. High school graduate of GED. Enroll each quarter. 90% placement overall. Unique professional pilot program.

† Kent State University
P.O. Box 5190, Kent 44242
Bruce Riddle, Dir. of Admis.

LOURDES COLLEGE
6832 Convent Blvd., Sylvania 43560
Mary E. Briggs, Dir. of Admis.
419-885-5291 or 800-878-3210

Malone College
515 25th St., N.W., Canton 44709
Lee Sommers, Dean of Admissions

MARIETTA COLLEGE
210 5th St., Marietta 45750
Dennis R. DePerro, Dean Admis./Financial Aid
800-331-7896

† Miami University
E. High St., Oxford 45056

Mount Union College
1972 Clark Ave., Alliance 44601
Amy Tomko, Dir. of Admis.

Mt. Vernon Nazarene College
800 Martinsburg Rd., Mt. Vernon 43050
Ronald Hyson, Dir. of Admis.

Muskingum College
147 Center St., New Concord 43762

Oberlin College
135 W. Lorain St., Oberlin 44074
Susan Kane, Chrpsn.

Ohio Dominican College
1216 Sunbury Rd., Columbus 43219
800-955-OHIO

OHIO NORTHERN UNIVERSITY
525 S. Main St., Ada 45810
Bruce Chesser, Chrpsn.
412-772-2000

† Ohio State University
190 N. Oval Mall, Columbus 43210

Ohio University, Athens 45701

Ohio Wesleyan University
61 S. Sandusky St., Delaware 43015
Donald Bishop, Dean for Enrollment

† University of Akron
381 Buchtel Common, Akron 44325
Kris MacDermott, Asst. Provost Enrollment

† University of Cincinnati
2700 Clifton Ave., Cincinnati 45221

University of Dayton
300 College Park Ave., Dayton 45469-1690
Toll-free 800-837-7433
See listing under "Universities"

University of Rio Grande
General Delivery, Rio Grande 45674
Dr. James Allen, Dean
614-245-5353, Ext. 7461

Ursuline College
2550 Lander Rd., Cleveland 44124

OKLAHOMA

Cameron University
2800 W. Gore Blvd., Lawton 73505
Louise Brown, Dir. of Admis.

Oklahoma Christian University of Science and Arts
P.O. Box 11000, Oklahoma City 73136
Duane Eggleston, Vice President
800-877-5010

Oklahoma City University
2501 N. Blackwelder Ave., Oklahoma City 73106
Jack Davis, Director
See listing under "Universities"

Oklahoma State University, Stillwater 74078
Nancy B. Wilkinson, Dept. Head

Oral Roberts University
7777 S. Lewis Ave., Tulsa 74171
Arthur E. Matzkvech, Dir. of Admis.

University of Central Oklahoma
100 N. University Dr., Edmond 73034

University of Oklahoma at Norman
660 Parrington Oval, Norman 73019

University of Tulsa
600 S. College Ave., Tulsa 74104
Dr. Steve Sumner, Director

OREGON

Lewis & Clark College
0615 S.W. Palatine Hill Rd., Portland 97219
Michael Sexton, Dean of Admissions

Linfield College
900 S. Baker St., McMinnville 97128
Thomas Meicho, Dean of Admissions

Marylhurst College for Lifelong Learning
P.O. Box 261, Marylhurst 97036
Kay Slusarenko, Chrpsn.
800-634-9982

† Oregon School of Arts & Crafts
8245 S.W. Barnes Rd., Portland 97225
Jean Malarkey, Dean of Admissions
503-297-5544

† PACIFIC NORTHWEST COLLEGE OF ART
1219 S.W. Park Ave., Portland 97205
Sally Lawrence, Director
Colin Page, Dir. of Admis.
503-226-0462
    Established 1909. Private. Coed. Accreditation:
NASC, NASAD. Tuition: $7,750. Estimated total
yearly expenses: $16,250. Rolling admissions. Fac-
ulty: 42. Degree: BFA. Library: 22,500 volumes. 1
building on 1 city block. Majors in graphic design,
painting, drawing, illustration, photography, sculpture, printmaking, ceramics, and crafts. Joint degree
program with Reed College. 5 year BA/BFA. Art museum, film and video center.

Reed College
3202 S.E. Woodstock Blvd., Portland 97202

· Treasure Valley Community College
650 College Blvd., Ontario 97914
Ron Kulm, Dir. of Admis.

PENNSYLVANIA

Albright College
P.O. Box 15234, Reading 19612

Allegheny College
520 N. Main St., Meadville 16335
Gayle Pollack, Dir. of Admis.

· Antonelli Institute of Art & Photography
P.O. Box 570, Plymouth Meeting 19462
215-275-3040 or 800-722-7871

· The Art Institute of Philadelphia
1622 Chestnut St., Philadelphia 19103
215-567-7080

: ART INSTITUTE OF PITTSBURGH
526 Penn Ave., Pittsburgh 15222
Lee Colker, Dir. of Admis.
    Established 1921. Private. Coed. Accreditation:
NATTS(ACTTS). Enrollment: 2,500. Faculty: 110.
Student-faculty rato: 20:1 average. Degrees: AST and
ASB. Programs include visual communications, computer animation, fashion illustration, fashion marketing, interior design, photography, industrial design
technology and music and video business. Located in
the downtown cultural district. Housing, part-time
jobs and graduate employment assistance available.
Call 800-275-2470 for information.

† Beaver College
450 S. Easton Rd., Glenside 19038-3295
Dennis Nostrand, VP for Enrollment Management
Phone: 800-776-BEAVER(2328)
Fax: 215-572-4049
See listing under "Universities"

Bloomsburg University, Bloomsburg 17815
Bernard Vinovrski, Dir. of Admis.

· Bradley Academy for the Visual Arts
625 E. Philadelphia St., York 17403
Loren H. Kroh, Director
717-848-1447

· † Bucks County Community College
Swamp Rd., Newtown 18940

California University of Pennsylvania
3rd St., California 15419
Norman Hasbrouck, Dean for Enrollment

† Carnegie Mellon University
5000 Forbes Ave., Pittsburgh 15213

Cedar Crest College
100 College Dr., Allentown 18104-6196
Cynthia Phillips, Dir. of Admissions

Chatham College
Woodland Rd., Pittsburgh 15232
Suellen Ofe, Dean of Admis./Financial Aid
See listing under "Women's College"

Drexel University
3141 Chestnut St., Philadelphia 19104
Dean of Enrollment Management

Eastern College
10 Fairview Dr., Saint Davids 19087
Ronald Keller, VP for Enrollment Management

Edinboro University of Pennsylvania
Edinboro 16444
Admissions Office: 800-626-2203

· Harcum Junior College, Bryn Mawr 19010
Mary Pontius, Dean of Admissions

Holy Family College
Grant & Frankford Ave., Philadelphia 19114
Dr. Mott Linn, Dir. of Admis.
215-637-3050

· Hussian School of Art
1118 Market St., Philadelphia 19107
Wilbur Crawford, Director of Admissions

· Keystone Junior College
P.O. Box 50, La Plume 18440
Kevin McIntyre, Dir. of Admis.

Lafayette College, Easton 18042
G. Gary Ripple, Dir. of Admis.
610-250-5100

La Roche College
9000 Babcock Blvd., Pittsburgh 15237
Marianne Leister, Dir. of Admis.

Lycoming College, Williamsport 17701

† Marywood College
2300 Adams Ave., Scranton 18509

Mercyhurst College
501 E. 38th St., Erie 16546
Andrew Roth, Dean of Enrollment
800-825-1926

Millersville University of Pennsylvania
Millersville 17551
Blair Treasure, Dean of Admissions

· Montgomery County Community College
340 DeKalb Pike, Blue Bell 19422-0758
Dennis Murphy, Dir. of Admis.

† Moore College of Art and Design
1920 Race St., Philadelphia 19103
Claire E. Gallicano, Dir. of Admis.

: † PENNSYLVANIA ACADEMY OF THE FINE ARTS
118 N. Broad St., Philadelphia 19102
Drawing, Painting, Printmaking, Sculpture
215-972-7625

: † Pennsylvania School of Art and Design
204 N. Prince St., Lancaster 17603

† Pennsylvania State University
201 Shields Bldg., University Park 16802

Seton Hill College, Greensburg 15601
Peter Egan, Dir. of Admis.
800-826-6234 or 412-838-4255

Slippery Rock University, Slippery Rock 16057
Director of Admissions

† Temple University
Broad St. & Montgomery Ave.
Philadelphia 19122

University of Pennsylvania
0 Levy Park, Philadelphia 19104

† University of the Arts
320 S. Broad St., Philadelphia 19102
Margaret Heuges, Dir. of Admis.

Washington & Jefferson College
60 S. Lincoln St., Washington 15301
Thomas O'Connor, Dir. of Admis.

WESTMINSTER COLLEGE
New Wilmington 16172
Richard Dana Paul, Dir. of Admis.
412-946-7100

Wilkes University
184 S. River St., Wilkes-Barre 18766
Emory P. Guffrovich Jr., Dean of Admissions

RHODE ISLAND

† Rhode Island College
600 Mt. Pleasant Ave., Providence 02908

† Rhode Island School of Design
2 College St., Providence 02903

† Salve Regina University
1 Ochre Point Ave., Newport 02840
Roselina McKillop, Dean of Admissions

SOUTH CAROLINA

Converse College
580 E. Main St., Spartanburg 29302
Dr. Martha Rogers, VP Enrollment Management

Lander College
320 Stanley Ave., Greenwood 29649

North Greenville College
P.O. Box 1892, Tigerville 29688
Gary Wells, Dir. of Admis.
See listing under "Universities"

South Carolina State University
P.O. Box 7127, Orangeburg 29117-0001
803-536-7185

University of South Carolina, Columbia 29208
Terry Davis, Dir. of Admis.
803-777-7700

† Winthrop University
701 W. Oakland Ave., Rock Hill 29733
James McCammon, Jr., Dir. of Admis.

SOUTH DAKOTA

Dakota State University
820 N. Washington Ave., Madison 57042
Dr. Eric Johnson, Dean
605-256-5139

Northern State University
1200 S. Jay St., Aberdeen 57401

SIOUX FALLS COLLEGE
1501 S. Prairie Ave., Sioux Falls 57105
Susan Reese, Dir. of Admis.
800-888-1047
See listing under "Universities"

South Dakota State University
P.O. Box 2223, Brookings 57007
Dr. Norman Gambill, Department Head
605-688-4103
See listing under "Universities"

† University of South Dakota
414 E. Clark St., Vermillion 57069
Dave Lorenz, Dir. of Admis.

TENNESSEE

† Austin Peay State University
601 College St., Clarksville 37044

Carson-Newman College
P.O. Box 70552, Jefferson City 37760
See listing under "Universities"

David Lipscomb University
3901 Granny White Pike, Nashville 37204-3951
Wade Sandrell, Dir. of Admis.
800-333-4358

† EAST TENNESSEE STATE UNIVERSITY
P.O. Box 70731, Johnson City 37614
Dr. Nancy Dishner, Dean, Enrollment Management
615-929-4213 or 800-462-3878

Freed-Hardeman University
158 E. Main St., Henderson 38340
800-342-7837

† Memphis College of Art
1930 Poplar Ave., Memphis 38104
Susan Miller, Dir. of Admis.

Nossi College of Art
907 Two Mile Pky. #E6, Goodlettsville 37072
Nossi Vatandoost, Director
615-851-1088

O'MORE COLLEGE OF DESIGN
P.O. Box 908, Franklin 37065
Eloise Pitts O'More, Director
615-794-4254
See listing under "Interior Design"

Tusculum College
P.O. Box 5035, Greeneville 37743
Ronald Porter, Dir. of Admis.

† University of Memphis, Memphis 38152
Dr. John Eubank, Dean of Admissions

† University of Tennessee at Martin
Martin 38238
Paul Kelley, Director of Admissions
See listing under "Universities"

University of Tennessee, Knoxville
527 Andy Holt Tower, Knoxville 37996
Dr. Gordon Stanley, Dir. of Admis.

TEXAS

: The Alfred G. Glassell, Jr., School of Art
5101 Montrose Blvd., Houston 77006

· Art Institute of Dallas
8080 Park Ln., Dallas 75231
Lee Colker, Dir. of Admis.

· The Art Institute of Houston
1900 Yorktown St., Houston 77056
Cherie R. McNeel, Dir. of Admis.
800-275-4244

Austin College
900 N. Grand Ave., Sherman 75090
Rodney Oto, Dean of Admission
800-442-5363

Baylor University
P.O. Box 97008, Waco 76798-7008
Diana Ramey, Director of Admissions

· † Del Mar College
101 Baldwin Blvd., Corpus Christi 78404
Lawrence Jasman, Registrar

Incarnate Word College
4301 Broadway St., San Antonio 78209
Sr. Sally Mitchell, Dean of Enrollment

Lamar University
P.O. Box 10009, Beaumont 77710
800-458-7558

· North Central Texas College
1525 W. California, Gainesville 76240
Doug Willis, Dir. of Admis.

St. Edward's University
3001 S. Congress Ave., Austin 78704
John Lambert, Dir. of Admis.

† San Antonio Art Institute
P.O. Box 6092, San Antonio 78209

Schreiner College
2100 Memorial Blvd., Kerrville 78028
800-343-4919

Stephen F. Austin State University
P.O. Box 6078. Nacogdoches 75962

Texas Christian University
2800 S. University Dr., Ft. Worth 76129
Dr. Edward Boehm, Jr., Dean of Admissions

· Texas State Technical College Waco/Marshall
3801 Campus Dr., Waco 76705
817-867-3371

† Texas Tech University, Lubbock 79409

Texas Women's University
P.O. Box 23925, Denton 76204

University of Dallas
1845 E. Northgate Dr., Irving 75062
Jim Whitaker, Dir. of Admis.

University of Texas at Arlington
UTA Box 19125, Arlington 76019
R. Zack Prince, Dir. of Admis.

University of Texas at Austin
0 the University of Texas, Austin 78712

† University of Texas at San Antonio
San Antonio 78285
James Broderick, Director

West Texas State University
2501 4th Ave., Canyon 79016
Lila Vars, Dir. of Admis.

UTAH

† Brigham Young University, Provo 84602

Southern Utah University
351 W. Center St., Cedar City 84720
Mark Talbert, Chrpsn.
801-586-5427

University of Utah
1400 E. 200 S., Salt Lake City 84112
Dr. J. Stayner Landward, Dir. of Admis.

Utah State University, Logan 84322-1600
Rod Clark, Director of Admissions
801-750-1107

Westminster College of Salt Lake City
1840 S. 1300 E., Salt Lake City 84105
800-748-4753

VERMONT

Bennington College, Bennington 05201
Karen Kristof, Dir. of Admis.
800-833-6845

Burlington College
95 North Ave., Burlington 05401
Nancy Wilson, Dir. of Admis.
See listing under "Liberal Arts"

Goddard College
P.O. Box G, Plainfield 05667
Jackson Kytle, President

Saint Michael's College
Winooski Park, Colchester 05439
800-SMC-8000
See listing under "Liberal Arts"

University of Vermont
194 S. Prospect St., Burlington 05401
802-656-3370

VIRGINIA

Christopher Newport College
50 Shoe Ln., Newport News 23606

Eastern Mennonite College
1200 Park Rd., Harrisonburg 22801
Jerry Miller, Dir. of Admis.

Ferrum College, Ferrum 24088
Bob Bailey, Dir. of Admis.

George Mason University
4400 University Dr., Fairfax 22030-4444
Patricia Riordan, Dean of Admissions

† James Madison University, Harrisonburg 22807

Longwood College, Farmville 23901

Lynchburg College
1501 Lakeside Dr., Lynchburg 24501
Ernest Chadderton, Dean of Enrollment

Mary Washington College
1701 College Ave., Fredericksburg 22401
Martin Wilder, V.P. for Admissions

Radford University
P.O. Box 5430, Radford 24142

Randolph-Macon College
200 Henry St., Ashland 23005
John Conkright, Dean of Admissions

Roanoke College
221 College Ln., Salem 24153

Sweet Briar College, Sweet Briar 24595
Nancy Church, Dir. of Admis.

† Virginia Commonwealth University
910 W. Franklin St., Richmond 23284

Virginia Intermont College
1013 Moore St., Bristol 24201
Lawton Blandford, Dir. of Admis.

Virginia Polytechnic Institute & State University
Blacksburg 24061
David Bousquet, Dir. of Undergraduate Admis.

WASHINGTON

· Art Institute of Seattle
2323 Elliott Ave., Seattle 98121
Doug Worsley, Dir. of Admis.

Central Washington University, Ellensburg 98926
William Swain, Director of Admissions

Cornish College of the Arts
710 E. Roy St., Seattle 98102
Jane Buckman, Admissions
800-726-ARTS

NORTHWEST COLLEGE OF ART
16464 State Highway 305 N.E., Poulsbo 98370
206-779-9993 or 800-769-ARTS
Craig Freeman, President
Willo Huard, Program Chair
Jessica Jalbert Kempf, Registrar
Kim Perigard, Financial Aid Director
Craig Freeman, Admissions Director
Established in 1982. Private. Coed. Four year college with a maximum enrollment of 200 full time day and 100 evening students. Tuition total per academic year is $7,100. Federal and private financial aid available for qualified students. Institutional scholarships available and should be filed by March 15, July 15 and November 15 of each calendar year.
Northwest College of Art (NCA) is a tri-semester college offering three semesters per calendar year. Full time status is 15 credits per semester. Our modified full time schedule is 5 four hour long courses over 2 1/2 days (example; Mon. and Tues.- 8 am-12 class and 1-5 pm class, Wed.- 8 am-12 class). Bachelor of arts degree is completed in 32 months. Largest class size is 20 with average size about 10.
All courses are taught by active professionals holding BA, BS and/or MA degrees and teach only their individual area of expertise. Features of NCA include full placement service for all graduates, a student gallery, visiting artist gallery, library/resource available to all students and an on campus book and art supply store. Picturesque retreat campus on 46 acre estate located 2 miles from Poulsbo, WA on the Olympic Peninsula.
Recreation is plentiful with winter skiing/snowboarding two hours away by car. Seattle downtown, the hub of northwest nightlife, is just 45 minutes away. Summer activities such as hiking, fishing, hot springs, and swimming are numerous all 1-2 hours commute from the campus.
Admissions is year round and rolling with program starts in September, January and May. Students applying for freshman admission should submit an application, high school/college transcripts, two page essay outlining career goals, 6-15 slides of art work for Fine Arts or Visual Communication or 6-8 photos of room interiors, commercial design, furniture design, fabric design or sketches for the Interior Design program.
NCA recommends all students personally visit the campus and complete an interview with the Director who is our sole admissions representative. Phone interviews are possible if a campus visit cannot be arranged.

Pacific Lutheran University
12180 Park Ave. S., Tacoma 98447
John Hallam, Chrpsn.

University of Washington, Seattle 98195

WEST VIRGINIA

Marshall University
400 Hal Greer Blvd., Huntington 25755
See listing under "Universities"

The University of Charleston
2300 MacCorkle Ave., S.E., Charleston 25304
800-995-GO UC

† West Virginia University
P.O. Box 6001, Morgantown 26506

WEST VIRGINIA WESLEYAN COLLEGE
59 College Ave., Buckhannon 26201
Robert Skinner, Director of Admission
See listing under "Universities"

WISCONSIN

Alverno College
P.O. Box 343922, Milwaukee 53234
Colleen Hayes, Dir. of Admis.

Beloit College
700 College St., Beloit 53511
Michael Simon, Professor and Chair
608-363-2679

Cardinal Stritch College
6801 N. Yates Rd., Milwaukee 53217
David Wegener, Dir. of Admis.

Carroll College
100 N. East Ave., Waukesha 53186
Ken Moyer, Dir. of Admis.

Carthage College
2001 Alford Dr., Kenosha 53140
Brenda A. Porter, VP Enrollment

Lawrence University
P.O. Box 599, Appleton 54912
Steven Syverson, Dean of Admissions

† Milwaukee Institute of Art & Design
273 E. Erie St., Milwaukee 53202
Holly Grey, Dir. of Admis.

St. Norbert College
100 Grant St., De Pere 54115
Craig S. Wesley, Dean of Admission
See listing under "Universities"

Silver Lake College
2406 S. Alverno Road, Manitowoc 54220
Sandra Schwartz, Dir. of Admis.

† University of Wisconsin, Madison
500 Lincoln Dr., Madison 53706

University of Wisconsin
P.O. Box 413, Milwaukee 53201
V. M. Allison, Registrar

University of Wisconsin, Oshkosh
800 Algoma Blvd., Oshkosh 54901-8602
August Helgerson, Dir. of Admis.

University of Wisconsin
1 University Plaza, Platteville 53818
Richard Schumacher, Dean of Admissions

University of Wisconsin, River Falls
River Falls 54022
Alan Tuchtenhagen, Dir. of Admis.

† University of Wisconsin, Stevens Point 54481
Dr. John A. Larsen, Dir. of Admis.

† University of Wisconsin
200 BroadWay St. S., Menomonie 54751
Robert B. Swanson, Chancellor

University of Wisconsin
800 W. Main St., Whitewater 53190

Viterbo College
815 9th St., S., La Crosse 54601
Roland W. Nelson, Dir. of Admis.

: Western Wisconsin Technical College
304 N. 6th St., La Crosse 54602

WYOMING

· Central Wyoming College
2660 Peck St., Riverton 82501
Mary Gores, Admissions Officer
307-856-9291
See listing under "Community and Junior Colleges"

University of Wyoming
P.O. Box 3434, Laramie 82071
Richard Davis, Dir. of Admis.

BIBLICAL STUDIES

This classification contains schools accredited by the American Association of Bible Colleges (†) and a selection of programs from institutionally accredited schools.

ALABAMA

· Gadsden State Community College
P.O. Box 227, Gadsden 35902
W. Bryan Stone, Dir. of Admis.

† International Bible College
P.O. Box IBC, Florence 35630
Charles Payne, Dir. of Enrollment Services

Samford University
800 Lakeshore Dr., Birmingham 35229
Bill Leonard, Chrpsn.

† Southeastern Bible College
3001 Hwy. 280, S., Birmingham 35243
800-749-8878

UNIVERSITY OF MOBILE
P.O. Box 13220, Mobile 36663-0220
Kim Leousis, Dir. of Admissions
205-675-5990
See listing under "Universities"

ALASKA

† Alaska Bible College
P.O. Box 289, Glennallen 99588
Connie Reidman, Dir. of Admis.
800-47-TRUTH, FAX: 907-822-5027

ARIZONA

American Indian Bible College
10020 N. 15th Ave., Phoenix 85021
Pete Cordova, Dir. of Admis.
800-933-3828

† ARIZONA COLLEGE OF THE BIBLE
2045 W. Northern Ave., Phoenix 85021
Frances Scoggin, Director of Admission
800-847-2138 or 602-995-2670
Established 1970. Private. Coed. Accreditation: AABC. Tuition: $4,730. Dorm room: $1,450. Fees: $50. Enrollment: 53 full-time, 77 part-time. Faculty: 18. Student-faculty ratio: 10:1. Degrees offered: BA, AA, 3 year diploma, 1 year certificate. Library: 30,000 volumes, 185 periodicals. 7 acre campus. Non-denominational Bible college. 50% of students complete degrees.

GRAND CANYON UNIVERSITY
3300 W. Camelback Rd., Phoenix 85017
Dr. D. C. Martin, Dept. Head
See listing under "Liberal Arts and Sciences"

† SOUTHWESTERN COLLEGE
A Conservative Baptist Bible College
2625 E. Cactus Rd., Phoenix 85032
800-247-2697

ARKANSAS

† Central Baptist College
CBC Station, Conway 72032

John Brown University
2000 W. University, Siloam Springs 72761
Don Crandall, Director of Enrollment Management

Ouachita Baptist University
410 Ouachita St., Arkadelphia 71998
Randy Garner, Dir. of Admis.
800-DIAL-OBU

Williams Baptist College
P.O. Box 3667, Walnut Ridge 72476
Scott Wright, Dir. of Admis.

CALIFORNIA

† Bethany Bible College
800 Bethany Dr., Scotts Valley 95066
Randal McNally, Dir. of Admis.

Biblical Christian College and Graduate School
1601 W. Malvern Ave., Fullerton 92633
Dr. Robert S. McBirnie, President

Biola University
13800 Biola Ave., La Mirada 90639
Wayne Chute, Dean of Admissions

Christian Heritage College
2100 Greenfield Dr., El Cajon 92019
Pam Daly, Dir. of Admis.
800-676-2242

Concordia University
1530 Concordia, Irvine 92715
Stan Meyer, Dean of Admission
800-229-1200
See listing under "Universities"

Fresno Pacific College
1717 S. Chestnut Ave., Fresno 93702
209-453-2039

† L.I.F.E. Bible College
1100 W. Covina Blvd., San Dimas 91773
Dr. Ron Mehl, President
800-356-0001

Lutheran Bible Institute of California
641 S. Western Ave., Anaheim 92804
Jill Aldrich, Dir. of Admis.

Master's College
P.O. Box 221450, Newhall 91322
Don Gilmore, Dir. of Admis.

† Pacific Christian College
2500 E. Nutwood Ave., Fullerton 92631
Knofel Staton, President

PATTEN COLLEGE
2433 Coolidge Ave., Oakland 94601
Dr. Priscilla Benham, President
Sharon Barta, Associate Director of Admissions
510-533-8300
Established 1945. Affiliated with Christian Cathedral Church. Coed. Accreditation: WASC. Tuition: $4,620. Room and board: $5,135. Enrollment: full-time 131, part-time 593. Faculty: 27. Degrees: credential program, AA, BA. Library: 20,000 volumes. 10 buildings on 5 acres. Patten is located within a few minutes of a great number of recreational, athletic, cultural, & religious activities.

Point Loma Nazarene College
3900 Lomaland Dr., San Diego 92106
Bill Young, Dir. of Admis.

† San Jose Christian College
P.O. Box 1090, San Jose 95108
Michael J. Bowman, Dean

Simpson College
2211 College View Dr., Redding 96003
Joe Barth, Registrar

Southern California College
55 Fair Dr., Costa Mesa 92626
Richard Hardy, Asst. Dean for Enrollment

UNIVERSITY OF JUDAISM/LEE COLLEGE
15600 Mulholland Dr., Los Angeles 90077
Tamara Greenebaum, Dean of Admissions
See listing under "Universities"

· † West Coast Christian College
6901 N. Maple Ave., Fresno 93710

COLORADO

† Colorado Christian University
180 S. Garrison St., Lakewood 80226
Debra Seefeldt, Dir. of Admis.

† Nazarene Bible College
P.O. Box 15749, Colorado Springs 80935
Rev. Dale Miller, Dir. of Admis.
719-596-5110

FLORIDA

Clearwater Christian College
3400 Gulf-to-Bay Blvd., Clearwater 34619
Benjamin Puckett, Dir. of Admis.

FLORIDA BAPTIST THEOLOGICAL COLLEGE
5400 College Dr., Graceville 32440
O. Lavan Wilson, Dir of Admis.
904-263-3261

† FLORIDA BIBLE COLLEGE
1701 Poinciana Blvd., Kissimmee 34758
Marie Brady, Dir. of Admis.
800-869-0258 or 407-933-4500
Private. Coed. Accreditation: AABC. Tuition: $4,320. Room and board $2,200. Fees: $288. Degrees: one year Bible Certificate, AA, BA. Programs of study are: Biblical Counseling, Biblical Education, Church Education, Education, Missions, Theology, Pastoral Studies, Youth Ministry. Situated in the geographical center of Florida, the campus is ideally located for student ministry, employment and recreational opportunities. Modern dorm facilities, a swimming pool, soccer field, outdoor volleyball and basketball courts and a library are on campus.

† Florida Christian College
1011 Osceola Blvd., Kissimmee 34744
A. Wayne Lowen, President

† Hobe Sound Bible College
P.O. Box 1065, Hobe Sound 33475
Ann French, Dir. of Admis.

† Miami Christian College
P.O. Box 19674, Miami 33101

† Southeastern College of the Assemblies of God
1000 Longfellow Blvd., Lakeland 33801
James L. Hennesy, President

Spurgeon Baptist Bible College
4440 Spurgeon Dr., Mulberry 33860
R. Mark Shaw, Asst. to the President

† TRINITY COLLEGE OF FLORIDA
2430 Trinity Oaks Blvd., New Port Richey 34655
813-376-6911
Glenn C. Speed, President
Karen Board, Director of Admissions
Joel Riley, Director of Recruitment
Audrey Ahern, Financial Aid Director
Established 1932. Private. Coed. Interdenominational. Accreditation: AABC (candidate status). Enrollment: 117 undergraduate, 105 graduate. Annual tuition: $3,000. Room and board: $1,800. Fees: $260. Degrees offered: BA in Biblical Studies (with Professional Study tracks in Christian Education, Music, Pastoral Ministries, Youth Ministries, Counseling, Elementary Education, Missions), AA, AS in Secretarial Science, One-Year Bible Certificate. Evening and weekend classes available on main campus and extension campuses in Tampa and Clearwater. Graduate program to become branch of Dallas Theological Seminary in 1994.
Pell Grants and institutional scholarships available. Over 75% of students receive financial aid.
Faculty: 15. Student-faculty ratio: 8:1. All courses taught by qualified faculty with Masters degree or higher. 16 week semester. Small classes and individual attention.
5 buildings on 20 acres. Library: 36,000 volumes. Brand new campus in pristine rural area, minutes from world class beaches, close to Disney, located in greater Tampa Bay. New on-campus air-conditioned, carpeted residence halls for men and women, one bath every two rooms, refrigerator and microwave, vertical blinds in each room.
Admissions: students may enter Fall or Spring semester. Must submit application, photo, autobiographical sketch, 3 references, high school transcripts, and ACT/SAT scores. Transfer students should submit college transcripts. Foreign students submit TOEFL.

GEORGIA

† Atlanta Christian College
2605 Ben Hill Rd., East Point 30344
Paul K. Carrier, President

BEULAH HEIGHTS BIBLE COLLEGE
P.O. Box 18145, Atlanta 30316
Dr. James Keiller, Dir. of Admis.
404-627-2681

BREWTON-PARKER COLLEGE
P.O. Box 197, Mount Vernon 30445
Dr. Y. Lynn Holmes, President
912-583-2241

† Emmanuel College
P.O. Box 128, Franklin Springs 30639
Levy Moore, Dir. of Admis.

Luther Rice Seminary
3038 Evans Mills Rd., Lithonia 30038
Gene Williams, President

Mercer University
1400 Coleman Ave., Macon 31207

† Toccoa Falls College
Office of Admissions, Toccoa Falls 30598
Matthew L. King, Dir. of Admis.
800-868-3257

IDAHO

† Boise Bible College
8695 Marigold St., Boise 83714
Dr. Charles A. Crane, President

ILLINOIS

Garrett-Evangelical Theological Seminary
2121 Sheridan Rd., Evanston 60201
Contact Admissions at 800-SEMINARY

† Lincoln Christian College
100 Campus View Dr., Lincoln 62656
Mr. Lynn Laughlin, Dir. of Admis.

† Moody Bible Institute
820 N. LaSalle Dr., Chicago 60610
Carolyn Klingbeil, Administrator of Admis.

INDIANA

Associated Mennonite Biblical Seminary
3003 Benham Ave., Elkhart 46517
Steven L. Fath, Admissions Counselor

Bethel College
1001 W. McKinley Ave., Mishawaka 46545
Steve Matteson, Dir. of Admis.

Goshen College
1700 S. Main St., Goshen 46526
Don Blosser, Chairperson

Grace College
200 Seminary Dr., Winona Lake 46590
Ron Henry, Dir. of Admis.

Huntington College
2303 College Ave., Huntington 46750
Paul Breininger, Dir. of Admis. Services

Hyles-Anderson College
8400 Burr St., Crown Point 46307
Jack Hyles, Chancellor

Indiana Wesleyan University
4201 S. Washington St., Marion 46953
800-332-6901

Taylor University
500 W. Reade Ave., Upland 46989
Dr. Paul House, Head

† Taylor University - Fort Wayne Campus
1025 W. Rudisill Blvd., Fort Wayne 46807
Jan Paul Storey, Dir. of Admis.

IOWA

† Emmaus Bible College
2570 Asbury Rd., Dubuque 52001
Daniel Smith, President

† Faith Baptist Bible College & Theological Seminary
1900 N.W. 4th St., Ankeny 50021
Jeff Newman, Director of Admissions
Admissions: 800-352-0147

Luther College
700 College Dr., Decorah 52101
David Sallee, Dean for Enrollment

† Vennard College
P.O. Box 29, University Park 52595
Mark Becker, Dir. of Admis.
800-338-2407

· Waldorf College
106 S. 6th St., Forest City 50436
Steve Lovik, Dir. of Admis.
800-292-1903

KANSAS

† **BARCLAY COLLEGE**
P.O. Box 288, Haviland 67059
Lonny R. Choate, Dir. of Admis.

Central College
1200 S. Main St., McPherson 67460
Greg Gossell, Dir. of Admis.

Kansas City College & Bible School
7401 Metcalf Ave., Overland Park 66204
Ray Crooks, President

† Manhattan Christian College
1415 Anderson Ave., Manhattan 66502
John Poulson, Dir. of Admis.

KENTUCKY

† Clear Creek Baptist Bible College
300 Clear Creek Rd., Pineville 40977
Dr. Bill Whittaker, President

Cumberland College
6178 College Station Dr., Williamsburg 40769
See listing under "Universities"

† Kentucky Christian College
617 N. Carol Malone Blvd., Grayson 41143

· † Kentucky Mountain Bible College
P.O. Box 10, Vancleve 41385

Louisville Presbyterian Theological Seminary
1044 Alta Vista Rd., Louisville 40205
502-895-3411 or 800-264-1839

Union College
310 College St., Barbourville 40906
Don Hapward, Dean of Admission
See listing under "Universities"

MARYLAND

Eastern Christian College
P.O. Box 629, Bel Air 21014
Robin Underhill, President
410-879-9300

::: **HOME STUDY INTERNATIONAL**
12501 Old Columbia Pike, Silver Spring 20914
P.O. Box 4437, Silver Spring 20914-4437 (mailing)
Dr. Joseph Gurubatham, President
800-782-GROW(4769)
See listing under "Home Study and Correspondence"

Morgan State University
Cold Spring Ln. and Hillen Rd., Baltimore 21239

† Washington Bible College
6511 Princess Garden Pkwy.
Lanham-Seabrook 20706

MASSACHUSETTS

Weston School of Theology
3 Phillips Pl., Cambridge 02138
Mary Ellen Herx, Dir. of Admis.
See listing under "Theology"

MICHIGAN

Andrews University, Berrien Springs 49104
Jack Mentges, Dir. of Admis.

Concordia College
4090 Geddes Rd., Ann Arbor 48105
Mary Froelich, Dir. of Admis.

† Grace Bible College
P.O. Box 910, Grand Rapids 49509
Linda K. Siler, Dir. of Admis.

† Great Lakes Bible College
6211 W. Willow Hwy., Lansing 48917
Nancy Hooper, Dir. of Admis.

Michigan Christian College
800 W. Avon Rd., Rochester Hills 48307
Kent Hoggatt, Dir. of Admis.

† **REFORMED BIBLE COLLEGE**
3333 East Beltline N.E., Grand Rapids 49505
Dorothy Hostetter, Dir. of Admis.
616-363-2050
Established 1939. Private. Coed. Accreditation: AABC. Tuition: $6,200. Room and board: $3,200-$3,300. Fees: $165. Enrollment: 148 full-time, 48 part-time. Faculty: 11. Student-faculty ratio: 18:1. Degrees: BRE, AA, Associate of Religious Education. Library: 50,000 volumes. 7 buildings on 28 acres. RBC moved to its beautiful, award winning campus in 1990. RBC graduates enter the following careers: church staff, 24%; overseas missions, 20%; social work, 9%; semi-

nary/graduate programs, 25%; business and service, 13%. RBC welcomes transfer students and adults changing careers as well as recent high school graduates.

· Suomi College
601 Quincy St., Hancock 49930
John Ruohoniemi, Dean/Enrollment Development
800-682-7604

† William Tyndale College
35700 W. Twelve Mile Rd.
Farmington Hills 48331

MINNESOTA

· Bethany Lutheran College
734 Marsh St., Mankato 56001
Steven Jaeger, Dir. of Admis.
507-625-2977

Bethel College
3900 Bethel Dr., St. Paul 55112
Dr. George Brushaber, President

Concordia College-St. Paul
275 N. Syndicate, St. Paul 55104
Tim Utter, Dir. of Admis.

† Crown College
6425 County Rd. 30, St. Bonifacius 55375
See listing under "Universities"

† Minnesota Bible College
920 Mayowood Rd., S.W., Rochester 55902
Tay Schield, Director of Recruitment
507-288-4563

† North Central Bible College
910 Elliot Ave., Minneapolis 55404
800-289-NCBC
Dan Neary, Dir. of Admis.
See listing under "Universities"

Northwestern College
3003 Snelling Ave., N., St. Paul 55113
Ralph Anderson, Dean of Admissions
800-827-6827 or 612-631-5111

† Oak Hills Bible College
1600 Oak Hills Rd. S.W., Bemidji 56601

PILLSBURY BAPTIST BIBLE COLLEGE
315 S. Grove St., Owatonna 55060
Alan Potter, President
Larry Tindall, Director of Admissions
800-747-4557

MISSISSIPPI

† **MAGNOLIA BIBLE COLLEGE**
P.O. Box 1109, Kosciusko 39090
Cecil May, Jr., President
800-748-8655

† Southeastern Baptist College
4229 Hwy. 15, N., Laurel 39440
A. Wilson, President

† Wesley College
P.O. Box 70, Florence 39073
David Coker, President

MISSOURI

† Baptist Bible College
628 E. Kearney St., Springfield 65803

† Calvary Bible College
15800 Calvary Rd., Kansas City 64147
J. Robert Brundage, Dir. of Admis.

† Central Bible College
3000 N. Grant Ave., Springfield 65803
Elmer Kirsch, Dean
417-833-2551

† Central Christian College of the Bible
911 Urbandale Dr., Moberly 65270
Lloyd Pelfrey, President

Evangel College
1111 N. Glenstone Ave., Springfield 65802
David Schoolfield, Dir. of Enrollment

† Ozark Christian College
1111 N. Main St., Joplin 64801
Jim Marcum, Dir. of Admis.
800-299-4622

† St. Louis Christian College
1360 Grandview Dr., Florissant 63033
Roger Clark, Dean

Southwest Baptist University
1601 S. Springfield Ave., Bolivar 65613

NEBRASKA

† **GRACE COLLEGE OF THE BIBLE**
Ninth and William, Omaha 68108
Jeffrey A. Edgar, Director of Admissions
800-383-1422

† Nebraska Christian College
1800 Syracuse Ave., Norfolk 68701

NEW YORK

Hebrew Union College
Jewish Institute of Religion
1 W. 4th St., New York 10012
Rabbi Gary Zola, National Dean of Admissions

Nyack College, Nyack 10960
Miguel Sanchez, Dir. of Admis.
800-33-NYACK

† Practical Bible Training School
P.O. Box 601, Bible School Park 13737
David Murphy, Dir. of Admis.

Roberts Wesleyan College
2301 Westside Dr., Rochester 14624
Paul Livermore, Chrpsn.
See listing under "Universities"

ST. BERNARD'S INSTITUTE
1100 S. Goodman St., Rochester 14620
Georgia Crissy, Dir. of Admissions
716-271-1320

NORTH CAROLINA

† East Coast Bible College
6900 Wilkinson Blvd., Charlotte 28214
Ronald Martin, President

Gardner-Webb University
General Delivery, Boiling Springs 28017
Alice Cullinan, Chrpsn.
704-434-2361

† John Wesley College
2314 Centennial St., N., High Point 27265
Ron Cathey, Dir. of Admis.

Lees-McRae College
P.O. Box 128, Banner Elk 28604
Brenda S. Lyerly, Dean of Admissions

Montreat-Anderson College
P.O. Box 1267, Montreat 28757
David E. Walters, Dir. of Admissions
800-MAC-N-YOU
See listing under "Universities"

† Piedmont Bible College
716 Franklin St., Winston-Salem 27101

† Roanoke Bible College
714 1st St., Elizabeth City 27909
William Griffin, President

NORTH DAKOTA

:: **OAK GROVE LUTHERAN HIGH SCHOOL**
124 N. Terrace, Fargo 58102
Denise Brewster, Director of Admissions
See listing under "Preparatory Schools-Coed"

† Trinity Bible College
50 S. 6th Ave., Ellendale 58436
Janet A. Johnson, Dir. of Academic Records
701-349-3621

OHIO

Ashland University
401 College Ave., Ashland 44805

† Cincinnati Bible College
P.O. Box 04320, Cincinnati 45204
C. Barry McCarty, President

† **CIRCLEVILLE BIBLE COLLEGE**
P.O. Box 458, Circleville 43113
Michael Adkins, Dir. of Enrollment
614-477-7701

† God's Bible School and College
1810 Young St., Cincinnati 45210
Bence Miller, President

Hebrew Union College
Jewish Institute of Religion
3101 Clifton Ave., Cincinnati 45220
Rabbi Gary Zola, National Dean of Admissions

LOURDES COLLEGE
6832 Convent Blvd., Sylvania 43560
Mary E. Briggs, Dir. of Admis.
419-885-5291 or 800-878-3210

Malone College
515 25th St., N.W., Canton 44709
Lee Sommers, Dean of Admissions

United Theological Seminary
1810 Harvard Blvd., Dayton 45406
The Rev. Duane Anders, Dir. of Admis.

WINEBRENNER THEOLOGICAL SEMINARY
P.O. Box 478, Findlay 45839
Dr. David Draper, President
419-422-4824

OKLAHOMA

Hillsdale Free Will Baptist College
P.O. Box 7208, Moore 73153
Jim Shepherd, President

† Mid-America Bible College
3500 S.W. 119th St., Oklahoma City 73170
Tony O'Brien, Registrar
405-691-3800

Southwestern College of Christian Ministries
P.O. Box 340, Bethany 73008
Dr. Richard M. Waters, Dean of Academics

OREGON

CASCADE COLLEGE
BRANCH CAMPUS OF OKLAHOMA CHRISTIAN UNIVERSITY
9101 E. Burnside St., Portland 97216
Brad Fisher, Director of Admission
800-550-PORT
Established 1994. Private. Coed. Accreditation: North Central Association of Schools and Colleges. Tuition: $6,400. Room and board: $3,200. Fees: $200. Enrollment: 160 full-time, 50 part-time. Faculty: 18. Student-faculty ratio: 12:1. Degrees: Bachelor of Arts in Business Administration, Liberal Studies, Liberal Studies with Teacher Certification, Biblical Studies.

9 buildings on 10 acres. Branch campus of Oklahoma Christian University of Science and Arts. Intramural and club athletics. Near I-205 in East Portland, City of Roses. Choir. Drama.

† EUGENE BIBLE COLLEGE
2155 Bailey Hill Rd., Eugene 97405
Trent Combs, Dir. of Admis.
800-322-2638

† MULTNOMAH BIBLE COLLEGE
8435 N.E. Glisan St., Portland 97220
Joseph Aldrich, President

Northwest Christian College
828 E. 11th Ave., Eugene 97401
Randy Jones, Dir. of Admis.

† Western Baptist College, Salem 97301
800-845-3005

PENNSYLVANIA

† Baptist Bible College of Pennsylvania
538 Venard Rd., Clarks Summit 18411

Biblical Theological Seminary
200 N. Main St., Hatfield 19440
Wayne Arndt, Dean Student Services

Eastern College
10 Fairview Dr., Saint Davids 19087
Ronald Keller, VP for Enrollment Management

Gratz College
Old York Rd. and Melrose Ave.
Melrose Park 19126
Evelyn Klein, Dir. of Admissions
215-635-7300

† LANCASTER BIBLE COLLEGE
901 Eden Rd., Lancaster 17601
Dr. Gilbert Peterson, President
Joanne Roper, Dir. of Admis.
800-544-7335
Established 1933. Coed. Accreditation: AABC, MSACS. Approved by ACSI. In addition to ACSI certification, graduates of the Elementary Education program receive state certification from the Pa. Dept of Education. Tuition: $7,150. Room and board: $3,300. Enrollment: 507. Faculty: 39. Degrees: AS in Bible, AS degree in Secretarial Studies, BS in Bible, plus 2 one-year programs. Library: 54,000 volumes. 16 buildings on 36 acres. Gym. Located within 15 minutes of 4 colleges for co-op use of libraries and cultural events.

Manna Bible Institute
700 E. Church Ln., Philadelphia 19144
Greg O'Loughlin, Dir. of Admis.

· Northeastern Christian Junior College
1860 Montgomery Ave., Villanova 19085
John Hall, President

Penn View Bible Institue
P.O. Box 970, Penns Creek 17862
John Zechman, President

† Philadelphia College of Bible
BS in Bible Degree
200 Manor Ave., Langhorne 19047-2990
Wesley Willis, VP for Academic Affairs
800-366-0049

Trinity Episcopal School for Ministry
311 11th St., Ambridge 15003
Sandra Griffin, Dir. of Admis.

† Valley Forge Christian College
1401 Charlestown Rd., Phoenixville 19460
Bernard Rossier, Registrar

SOUTH CAROLINA

Central Wesleyan College
P.O. Box 1020, Central 29630
Lillian A. Robbins, Dir. of Admis.

Columbia Biblical Seminary
P.O. Box 3122, Columbia 29230
Lawrence Dabeck, Dir. of Admis.
See listing under "Biblical Studies"

† COLUMBIA INTERNATIONAL UNIVERSITY
P.O. Box 3122, Columbia 29230
Phone 800-777-CBCS (2227)
Dr. Johnny V. Miller, President
Frank J. Bedell, Dir. of Bible College Admissions
Lawrence M. Dabeck, Dir. of Seminary Admissions
Established 1923. Nondenominational. Coed. Privately supported, nonprofit. Accredited by the commission on colleges of the Southern Association of Colleges and Schools (SACS). Bible College accred-

ited by the American Association of Bible Colleges (AABC) and Seminary by the Association of Theological Schools (ATS).
Columbia Bible College: Enrollment (Fall 93) 280 men, 250 women. Tuition: $3,325 for each semester (two). $171 per credit for summer and winter short quarters. Curriculum: one year Bible Certificate, AA, BS, BA, MEd, MA Teaching for state certification, Bible/Theology, Elementary Education, Psychology, Communication, Music, Missions, Pastoral or Youth Ministry, Pre-seminary, co-operative program with Midlands Technical College. Admission: Christian testimony, SAT or ACT and HS transcripts or GED required, references, essay. Single students 23 years old or younger must live on-campus.
Columbia Biblical Seminary: Enrollment (Fall 93) 316 men, 146 women. Tuition: $3,460 for each of the two semesters, $202 per credit for summer & winter short quarters. Curriculum: one year Bible Certificate, Master of Divinity - N. American or Cross-cultural (emphases in N.T., Counseling, Church Planting, Youth Ministry, C.E. Urban Ministry & Evangelism). MA in English Bible (Old Testament or New Testament), Missions, TEFL/Intercultural Studies, Christian Education (with counseling emphasis), Evangelism, Intercultural Studies (with or without TEFL) and Old Testament Hebrew. Doctorate of Ministry (Pastoral Theology or Missions). Flexible training for college graduates, with or without Bible training, and for pastors or missionaries. Admission: Christian testimony, baccalaureate degree transcripts with 2.7 GPA or upper 50% GRE score, essay, references. Separate housing for single graduate students, on campus mobile home park for some married students. Faculty to student ratio: 1:22. No admission deadline. Located on scenic 400 acre campus, seven miles from state capital
Mission: to glorify God by assisting the church to evangelize the world in this generation, through educational programs which will help God's people grow in spiritual maturity, Bible knowledge, and ministry skills. Distinctives: Inerrancy of Scripture, Academic Excellence, Evangelical Pluralism, World Evangelization, Total Life Training - spiritual life, academics, ministry skills, and Victorious Christian Living.
Motto: To Know Him and To Make Him Known.

North Greenville College
P.O. Box 1892, Tigerville 29688
Gary Wells, Dir. of Admis.
See listing under "Universities"

Southern Methodist College
P.O. Box 1027, Orangeburg 29116
803-534-7826

SOUTH DAKOTA

† Central Indian Bible College
P.O. Box 550, Mobridge 57601

TENNESSEE

† American Baptist College
1800 World Baptist Ctr. Dr., Nashville 37207

Bryan College
Box 7000, Dayton 37321
Thomas A. Shaw, Dir. of Admis.

Carson-Newman College
P.O. Box 70552, Jefferson City 37760
See listing under "Universities"

Crichton College
6655 Winchester Rd., Memphis 38115
901-367-9800

David Lipscomb University
3901 Granny White Pike, Nashville 37204-3951
Wade Sandrell, Dir. of Admis.
800-333-4358

Freed-Hardeman University
158 E. Main St., Henderson 38340
800-342-7837

† Free Will Baptist Bible College
P.O. Box 50117, Nashville 37205

† Johnson Bible College
7900 Johnson Dr., Knoxville 37998
Larry Green, Dir. of Admis.
615-573-4517

::: Seminary Extension Independent Study Institute
901 Commerce St. #500, Nashville 37203-3631
615-242-2453

† Tennessee Temple University
1815 Union Ave., Chattanooga 37404
Dr. L. W. Nichols, President

TEXAS

† Arlington Baptist College
3001 W. Division St., Arlington 76012
Helen Sullivan, Registrar

† Bay Ridge Christian College
P.O. Box 726, Kendleton 77451

† Dallas Christian College
2700 Christian Pkwy., Dallas 75234

INSTITUTE FOR CHRISTIAN STUDIES
1909 University Ave., Austin 78705
Cindy Lippe, Dir. of Admis.
512-476-2772

† Rio Grande Bible Institute
4300 S. US Highway 281, Edinburg 78539

Schreiner College
2100 Memorial Blvd., Kerrville 78028
800-343-4919

† Southwestern Assemblies of God College
1200 Sycamore St., Waxahachie 75165
Bill Morgan, Dir. of Admis.

VIRGINIA

Eastern Mennonite College
1200 Park Rd., Harrisonburg 22801
Jerry Miller, Dir. of Admis.

Graham Bible College
P.O. Box 1630, Bristol 24203
R. Irene Brown, Registrar

LIBERTY UNIVERSITY
P.O. Box 20000, Lynchburg 24506
Jay Spencer, VP Recruitment
800-376-2800
See listing under "Universities"

SHENANDOAH UNIVERSITY
1460 University Dr., Winchester 22601
Dr. Jack Balcer, Division Chair
See listing under "Universities"

WASHINGTON

Lutheran Bible Institute of Seattle
4221 228th Ave., S.E., Issaquah 98027
Dorothy Baumgartner, Director of Admissions
800-843-5659

NORTHWEST BAPTIST SEMINARY
4301 N. Stevens St., Tacoma 98407
206-759-6104

† Northwest College of the Assemblies of God
P.O. Box 579, Kirkland 98083-0579
Bob Foster, Dir. of Public Relations

† Puget Sound Christian College
410 4th Ave., N., Edmonds 98020
Glen Basey, President

WEST VIRGINIA

Alderson-Broaddus College
Philippi 26416
Craig W. Gould, Director of Admissions
304-457-1700

† APPALACHIAN BIBLE COLLEGE
P.O. Box ABC, Bradley 25818
Dr. Daniel Anderson, President
Cathie P. Canary, Dir. of Admis.
Established 1950. Private. Coed. Accreditation: AABC, State College and University System of WV. Tuition: $3,800. Room and board $2,700. Fees: $410. Enrollment: 250. Faculty: 16. Student-faculty ratio: 15:1. Degrees: AA, BA, BTh, Bible Certificate. Library: 35,000+ volumes. 20 buildings on 120+ acres. An independent, fundamental, non-denominational school. The majority of the student body are members of independent Bible and independent Baptist churches. Call the admissions office toll-free at 800-6789-ABC.

Ohio Valley College
College Pky., Parkersburg 26101
See listing under "Universities"

WEST VIRGINIA WESLEYAN COLLEGE
59 College Ave., Buckhannon 26201
Robert Skinner, Director of Admission
See listing under "Universities"

PUERTO RICO

† Colegio Biblico Pentecostal De Puerto Rico
P.O. Box 901, Saint Just 00978
Roberto Rivera, President

BIOLOGICAL SCIENCE

ALABAMA

Alabama A & M University
P.O. Box 610, Normal 35762
Dr. Charles McMillan, Chrpsn.
See listing under "Universities"

Gadsden State Community College
P.O. Box 227, Gadsden 35902
W. Bryan Stone, Dir. of Admis.

Huntingdon College
1500 E. Fairview Ave., Montgomery 36106-2148
Carolyn A. Phillips, Dean of Enrollment
800-763-0313

Oakwood College
Oakwood Rd., N.W., Huntsville 35896

Samford University
800 Lakeshore Dr., Birmingham 35229
Ron Jenkins, Chrpsn.

Spring Hill College
4000 Dauphin St., Mobile 36608
Ben Hamd, Dir. of Admis.

STILLMAN COLLEGE
P.O. Box 1430, Tuscaloosa 35403
Barbara K. Smith, Director of Admissions
See listing under "Universities"

Talladega College
627 Battle St., W., Talladega 35160

Troy State University, Troy 36082
Dr. Charles Chapman, Dean

Troy State University at Dothan
P.O. Box 8368, Dothan 36304
Bob Willis, Dir. of Undergraduate Admissions

Tuskegee University
Tuskegee Institute 36088

University of Alabama
P.O. Box 870132, Tuscaloosa 35487-0132
Roy Smith, Dir. of Admis.

University of Alabama at Birmingham
University Station, Birmingham 35294

UNIVERSITY OF ALABAMA IN HUNTSVILLE
P.O. Box 1247, Huntsville 35899
Ron R. Koger Ed.D., Dir. of Admis.
205-895-6070
Established 1969. Public. Coed. Accreditation:
SACS, ABET, NLN, CSAB, ACS. Tuition: $2,418 resident, $4,836 non-resident. Room & Board: $3,450.
Undergraduate enrollment: 2,674 full-time, 3,439
part-time. Graduate enrollment: 1,860. Faculty: 282.
Student-faculty ratio: 18:1. Degrees: BS, BA, BSBA,
BSE, MS, MSM, Ph.D., BSN, MSN, MA. 20 buildings
on 350 acres. Comprehensive research university located in the Tennessee Valley of northern Alabama.
Huntsville is the locale of major government and
private research centers. Metropolitan population approaching 300,000.

UNIVERSITY OF MOBILE
P.O. Box 13220, Mobile 36663-0220
Kim Leousis, Dir. of Admissions
205-675-5990
See listing under "Universities"

University of Montevallo, Montevallo 35115

ALASKA

Sheldon Jackson College
801 Lincoln St., Sitka 99835
Dennis Trotter, Dir. of Admis.
907-747-5221

University of Alaska Southeast
11120 Glacier Hwy., Juneau 99801
Greg Wagner, Coordinator of Admissions

ARIZONA

Grand Canyon University
3300 W. Camelback Rd., Phoenix 85017
Sherri Willborn, Dir. of Admis.
See listing under "Liberal Arts and Sciences"

Northern Arizona University
P.O. Box 4092, Flagstaff 86011
Dr. Margaret Cibik, Dir. of Admis.

University of Arizona, Tucson 85721
Loyd Bell, Director of Admissions

Yavapai College
1100 E. Sheldon St., Prescott 86301
Dr. Doreen Dailey, President
602-445-7300
See listing under "Community and Junior
Colleges"

ARKANSAS

Arkansas State University
P.O. Box 1630, State University 72467

John Brown University
2000 W. University, Siloam Springs 72761
Don Crandall, Director of Enrollment Management

Ouachita Baptist University
410 Ouachita St., Arkadelphia 71998
Randy Garner, Dir. of Admis.
800-DIAL-OBU

University of Arkansas at Monticello
P.O. Box 3596, Monticello 71656

Williams Baptist College
P.O. Box 3667, Walnut Ridge 72476
Scott Wright, Dir. of Admis.

CALIFORNIA

Bakersfield College
1801 Panorama Dr., Bakersfield 93305
Robert M. Bruker, Dir. of Admis.

Biola University
13800 Biola Ave., La Mirada 90639
Wayne Chute, Dean of Admissions

California Baptist College
8432 Magnolia Ave., Riverside 92504
800-782-3382

California Institute of Technology
1201 E. California Blvd., Pasadena 91125
Carole L. Snow, Dir. of Admis.

California Lutheran University
60 Olsen Rd., Thousand Oaks 91360
800-252-5884

California Polytechnic State University
San Luis Obispo 93407
Helen Linstrum, Dir. of Admis.

California State University, Chico
Chico 95929-0515
Dr. William Derr, Chrpsn.

California State University-Stanislaus
801 W. Monte Vista Ave., Turlock 95382
Frances Cook, Dean Enrollment Services

Chapman University
333 N. Glassell St., Orange 92666
Michael Drummy, Dir. of Admis.

City College of San Francisco
50 Phelan Ave. Box 565, San Francisco 94112
Ed Bedecarrax, Dept. Chair
415-239-3645

Claremont McKenna College
890 Columbia Ave., Claremont 91711

College of Notre Dame
1500 Ralston Ave., Belmont 94002
Greg M. Smith, PhD., Dir. of Admis.

Concordia University
1530 Concordia, Irvine 92715
Stan Meyer, Dean of Admission
800-229-1200
See listing under "Universities"

DOMINICAN COLLEGE OF SAN RAFAEL
50 Acacia Ave., San Rafael 94901-8008
Office of Admissions
800-788-3522

Fresno Pacific College
1717 S. Chestnut Ave., Fresno 93702
209-453-2039

Holy Names College
3500 Mountain Blvd., Oakland 94619

La Sierra University
4700 Pierce St., Riverside 92505
800-874-5587

Loma Linda University, Loma Linda 92350
800-422-4LLU

Loyola Marymount University
Loyola Blvd. at W. 80th, Los Angeles 90045
M. L'Heureux, Dir. of Admis.

Master's College
P.O. Box 221450, Newhall 91322
Don Gilmore, Dir. of Admis.

Menlo College
1000 El Camino Real, Atherton 94027

Mills College
5000 MacArthur Blvd., Oakland 94613
Genevieve Ann Flaherty, Dean of Admissions
800-87-MILLS

Mt. St. Mary's College
12001 Chalon Rd., Los Angeles 90049

Pitzer College
1050 N. Mills Ave., Claremont 91711
Katharine Leighton, Dir. of Admis.

Point Loma Nazarene College
3900 Lomaland Dr., San Diego 92106
Bill Young, Dir. of Admis.

Pomona College
333 N. College Way, Claremont 91711
Peter W. Stanley, President

Porterville College
100 E. College Ave., Porterville 93257
John McCuen, President

San Francisco State University
1600 Holloway Ave., San Francisco 94132
Corwin Bjonerud, Dir. of Admis.

Santa Clara University, Santa Clara 95053

Scripps College
1030 Columbia Ave., Claremont 91711
Leslie Miles, Dean of Admissions

Sonoma State University
1801 E. Cotati Ave., Rohnert Park 94928

Southern California College
55 Fair Dr., Costa Mesa 92626
Richard Hardy, Asst. Dean for Enrollment

University of California at Berkeley
LSB, Berkeley 94720

University of California-Santa Cruz
Santa Cruz 95064
Joseph Allen, Dir. of Admis.

University of La Verne
1950 3rd St., La Verne 91750
Mark Bornholdt, Dir. of Admis.

University of Redlands
P.O. Box 3080, Redlands 92373

University of San Diego
5998 Alcala Park, San Diego 92110
Warren Muller, Dir. of Admis.
619-260-4506

University of San Francisco
2130 Fulton St., San Francisco 94117
Bill Henley, Dir. of Admis.

Whittier College
13406 Philadelphia St., Whittier 90601
310-907-4238

COLORADO

Adams State College, Alamosa 81102
Cheryl Billingsley, Dir. of Admis.
800-824-6494

Colorado Christian University
180 S. Garrison St., Lakewood 80226
Debra Seefeldt, Dir. of Admis.

Colorado College
14 E. Cache La Poudre, Colorado Springs 80903
Terry Swenson, Dir. of Admis.

Mesa State College
P.O. Box 2647, Grand Junction 81502
Sherri Pe'a, Dir. of Admis.

Metropolitan State College of Denver
P.O. Box 173362, Campus Box 16
Denver 80217-3362

Regis University
3333 Regis Blvd., Denver 80221
Robert Blust, Director of Admissions

University of Denver
2199 S. University Blvd., Denver 80210

University of Northern Colorado, Greeley 80639
Margaret Heimbrook, Department Chrpsn.
303-351-2921

University of Southern Colorado
2200 Bonforte Blvd., Pueblo 81001

Western State College of Colorado
Gunnison 81231
Monica Bruning, Dir. of Admis.
See listing under "Universities"

CONNECTICUT

Albertus Magnus College
700 Prospect St., New Haven 06511
Richard Lolatte, Dir. of Admissions
203-773-8501 or 800-578-9160

Eastern Connecticut State University
83 Windham St., Willimantic 06226
Dr. Charles Booth, Chrpsn.

QUINNIPIAC COLLEGE
275 Mount Carmel Ave., Hamden 06518
See listing under "Universities"

St. Joseph College
1678 Asylum Ave., West Hartford 06117
Mary C. Demo, Dir. of Admis.

Trinity College
300 Summit St., Hartford 06106
Dr. David Borus, Dean of Admissions

University of Bridgeport
126 Park Ave., Bridgeport 06601
Andrew G. Nelson, Dean Admis./Financial Aid
203-576-4552
See listing under "Universities"

University of Hartford
200 Bloomfield Ave., West Hartford 06117
Richard Zeiser, Dir. of Admis.
See listing under "Universities"

University of New Haven
300 Orange Ave., West Haven 06516
Joseph Chepaitis, Dean
203-932-7000

DELAWARE

University of Delaware, Newark 19711

DISTRICT OF COLUMBIA

The American University
4400 Massachusetts Ave. N.W.
Washington 20016

University of the District of Columbia
Georgia Ave.-Harvard St. Campus
1100 Harvard St., N.W., Washington 20009

University of the District of Columbia
Van Ness Campus
4200 Connecticut Ave., N.W., Washington 20008

FLORIDA

Barry University
11300 N.E. 2nd Ave., Miami Shores 33161
Robin Ray Roberts, Dean of Admissions

Bethune-Cookman College
640 Mary McLeod Bethune Blvd.
Daytona Beach 32114

Clearwater Christian College
3400 Gulf-to-Bay Blvd., Clearwater 34619
Benjamin Puckett, Dir. of Admis.

Eckerd College
P.O. Box 12560, St. Petersburg 33733
Richard Hallin, Dir. of Admis.

Florida Atlantic University
500 N.W. 20th St., Boca Raton 33431
Brian Levin-Stankevich, Dir. of Admis.

Florida Institute of Technology
150 W. University Blvd., Melbourne 32901
Louis T. Levy, Dean of Admissions
800-888-4348

Florida Southern College
111 Lake Hollingsworth Dr., Lakeland 33801
William Stephens, Jr., Dir. of Admis.

Jacksonville University
2800 University Blvd., N., Jacksonville 32211

Palm Beach Atlantic College
P.O. Box 24708, West Palm Beach 33416-4708
See listing under "Universities"

Rollins College
P.O. Box 2720, Winter Park 32790

St. Leo College
P.O. Box 2008, St. Leo 33574
Bonnie Black, Dir. of Admis.

St. Thomas University
16400 N.W. 32nd Ave., Miami 33054
John M. Letvinchuk, Dir. of Admis.

Stetson University
401 N. Woodland Blvd., De Land 32720
Gary A. Meadows, Dean of Admis.

University of Miami
P.O. Box 248006, Coral Gables 33124

GEORGIA

Agnes Scott College
201 E. College Ave., Decatur 30030
Teresa Lahti, Dir. of Admis.

BREWTON-PARKER COLLEGE

P.O. Box 197, Mount Vernon 30445
Dr. Y. Lynn Holmes, President
912-583-2241

Georgia College
231 W. Hancock St., Milledgeville 31061
912-453-5004

Kennesaw State College
P.O. Box 444, Marietta 30061
Joe Head, Dir. of Admis.

La Grange College
601 Broad St., La Grange 30240
Phil Dodson, Dir. of Admis.
706-882-2911

Mercer University
1400 Coleman Ave., Macon 31207

Oglethorpe University
4484 Peachtree Rd., N.E., Atlanta 30319
Dennis Matthews, Dir. of Admis.

Paine College
1235 15th St., Augusta 30901
Phyllis Wyatt-Woodruff, Dir. Enrollment Mgmt.

Piedmont College
P.O. Box 10, Demorest 30535
Penny L. Graber, Dir of Admis.
800-277-7020

Savannah State College
State College Branch, Savannah 31404
Robert Ray, Dir. of Admis.

Shorter College
315 Shorter Ave., Rome 30165

Spelman College
350 Spelman Ln., S.W., Atlanta 30314
Aline Rivers, Dir. of Admis.

University of Georgia, Athens 30602
Dr. Claire Swann, Dir. of Admis.

Wesleyan College
4760 Forsyth Rd., Macon 31297

West Georgia College, Carrollton 30118
C. Doyle Bickers, Dir. of Admis.

HAWAII

Brigham Young University, Hawaii Campus
55-220 Kulanui St., Laie 96762
Clark E. Hirschi, Coordinator of Admis.

Chaminade University of Honolulu
3140 Waialae Ave., Honolulu 96816
Charles Schafer, VP Enrollment Services

IDAHO

Lewis Clark State College
500 8th Ave., Lewiston 83501
800-933-5272 or 208-799-5272

University of Idaho, Moscow 83843
Peter Brown, Dir. of Admis.

ILLINOIS

Augustana College
639 38th St., Rock Island 61201
Martin R. Sauer, Director of Admission
800-798-8100

Aurora University
347 S. Gladstone Ave., Aurora 60506
Peter Pitts, Dir. of Admis.

Blackburn College
700 College Ave., Carlinville 62626
Dwight Smith, Dir. of Admis.

De Paul University
1 E. Jackson Blvd., Chicago 60604
Thomas D. Abrahamson, Dean of Admissions
See listing under "Universities"

Elmhurst College
190 Prospect Ave., Elmhurst 60126

Eureka College
300 E. College Ave., Eureka 61530

Governors State University
1 University Pky., University Park 60466
Richard Pride, Dir. of Admis.

Greenville College
315 E. College Ave., Greenville 62246
Kent Krober, Dir. of Admis.

Illinois College
1101 W. College Ave., Jacksonville 62650
Gale Vaugn, Dir. of Admis.

ILLINOIS WESLEYAN UNIVERSITY

P.O. Box 2900, Bloomington 61702
Dr. Bruce Criley, Chrpsn.
309-556-3277

Knox College, Galesburg 61401
309-343-0112 or 800-678-KNOX
See listing under "Universities"

LEWIS UNIVERSITY

Rt. 53, Romeoville 60441
Irish O'Reilly, Director of Admissions
See listing under "Universities"

Loyola University - Mundelein College
6363 N. Sheridan Rd., Chicago 60660
Judith Bobber, Dir. of Admis.

MacMurray College
447 E. College Ave., Jacksonville 62650
Edwin R. Hockett, Dean of Admissions

Millikin University
1184 W. Main St., Decatur 62522
Lin Stoner, Dean of Admissions
800-373-7733

Monmouth College
700 E. Broadway, Monmouth 61462

North Central College
30 N. Brainard St.
P.O. Box 3065, Naperville 60566-7065
Marguerite Waters, Director of Admission
708-420-3414

Northeastern Illinois University
5500 N. St. Louis Ave., Chicago 60625

Northern Illinois University, De Kalb 60115

Olivet Nazarene University, Kankakee 60901
John Mongerson, Dir. of Admis.
815-939-5203

Parkland College
2400 W. Bradley Ave., Champaign 61821-1899
217-351-2208 or 800-346-8089

Principia College, Elsah 62028

Quincy College
1800 College Ave., Quincy 62301
Fr. Michael Lanning, O.F.M., Dir. of Admis.

Rockford College
5050 E. State St., Rockford 61108
Miriam King, V.P. for Enrollment Management
See listing under "Universities"

ROOSEVELT UNIVERSITY

430 S. Michigan Ave., Chicago 60605
William Smyser, Director of Admissions
See listing under "Universities"

Rosary College
7900 W. Division St., River Forest 60305
Hildegarde Schmidt, Dir. of Admis.

St. Xavier College
3700 W. 103rd St., Chicago 60655
Mary Hendry, Dean of Admissions

Sangamon State University
Shepherd Rd., Springfield 62794-9243
Admissions and Records, 217-786-6626

Trinity Christian College
6601 W. College Dr., Palos Heights 60463
Kenneth Bootsma, President

Trinity College
2077 Half Day Rd., Deerfield 60015
Dr. Kenneth Meyer, Pres.

University of Chicago
5801 S. Ellis Ave., Chicago 60637

University of Illinois at Chicago
P.O. Box 5220, Chicago 60680
Dr. Marilyn R. Fiduccia, Dir. of Admis.

Western Illinois University
900 W. Adams St., Macomb 61455
Alan DeRoos, Registrar
309-298-1891

INDIANA

Ball State University
2000 W. University Ave., Muncie 47306
Ruth Vedvik, Dir. of Admis.

Bethel College
1001 W. McKinley Ave., Mishawaka 46545
Steve Matteson, Dir. of Admis.

Calumet College
2400 New York Ave., Whiting 46394
Sharon Sweeney, Dir. of Admis.

DePauw University
313 S. Locust St., Greencastle 46135
Dr. Eleanor Ypma, Registrar

Earlham College
801 National Rd. W., Richmond 47374
Robert deVeer, Dean of Admis.

Franklin College
501 E. Monroe, Franklin 46131
B. Stephen Richards, VP Enrollment

Goshen College
1700 S. Main St., Goshen 46526
Jim Miller, Chairperson

Grace College
200 Seminary Dr., Winona Lake 46590
Ron Henry, Dir. of Admis.

Huntington College
2303 College Ave., Huntington 46750
Paul Breininger, Dir. of Admis. Services

Indiana Wesleyan University
4201 S. Washington St., Marion 46953
800-332-6901

Manchester College
604 College Ave., North Manchester 46962
Dr. William Eberly, Chrpsn.

Marian College
3200 Cold Spring Rd., Indianapolis 46222
Don French, Dir. of Admis.

Oakland City College
143 N. Lucretia St., Oakland City 47660
Tracy Siekman, Dir. of Admis.

Purdue University
Schleman Hall, West Lafayette 47907

Purdue University, Calumet Campus
2233 171st St., Hammond 46323

ST. JOSEPH'S COLLEGE

P.O. Box 890, Rensselaer 47978
Louis Levy, Dean of Admissions
800-447-8781

St. Mary-of-the-Woods College
Saint Mary-of-the-Woods 47876
Lynn M. Rubick, Director of Admissions
800-926-SMWC

Taylor University
500 W. Reade Ave., Upland 46989
Tim Burkholder, Head

Tri-State University, Angola 46703
Director of Admission
800-347-4878

University of Evansville
1800 Lincoln Ave., Evansville 47722
Dr. Wayne Mueller, Dept. Chair
800-423-8633

University of Notre Dame
Notre Dame 46556
Kevin M. Rooney, Dir. of Admis.

Valparaiso University, Valparaiso 46383

Wabash College
301 W. Wabash Ave., Crawfordsville 47933
Greg Birk, Dir. of Admis.

IOWA

Briar Cliff College
3303 Rebecca St., Sioux City 51104
Patricia White, Dir. of Admis.

Clarke College
1550 Clarke Dr., Dubuque 52001
Mary Murphy, BVM, PhD, Chair
800-383-2345

Coe College
1220 1st Ave., N.E., Cedar Rapids 52402
Roger Johanson, Chrpsn.

Cornell College
600 1st St., W., Mt. Vernon 52314
Kevin Crockett, Dean of Admissions

Dordt College
498 4th Ave., N.E., Sioux Center 51250
Quentin Van Essen, Dir. of Admissions
800-343-6738

Drake University
2507 E. University Ave., Des Moines 50311
Thomas Willoughby, Dir. of Admis.

Graceland College, Lamoni 50140
800-638-0053, Outside Iowa 800-346-9208
Bonita Booth, Dean of Admissions
See listing under "Universities"

Grand View College
1200 Grandview Ave., Des Moines 50316
Lori Hanson, Dir. of Admissions
800-444-6083

Grinnell College
P.O. Box 805, Grinnell 50112

Iowa State University, Ames 50011
Karsten Smedal, Dir. of Admis.

Luther College
700 College Dr., Decorah 52101
David Sallee, Dean for Enrollment

Maharishi International University
Route 1, Fairfield 52556
Gregory Polakow, Dir. of Admis.

Morningside College, Sioux City 51106
Lora Vanderzwaag, Dir. of Admis.

Mount Mercy College
1330 Elmhurst Dr., N.E., Cedar Rapids 52402
Carol Williamson, Dir. of Admis.

Northwestern College
101 7th St. S.W., Orange City 51041

Teikyo Marycrest University
1607 W. 12th St., Davenport 52804
Tim McDonough, Dir. of Admis.
See listing under "Universities"

Teikyo Westmar University
1002 3rd Ave., S.E., Le Mars 51031
Dr. Jim Utesch, Dir. of Admis.

University of Iowa, Iowa City 52242

University of Northern Iowa, Cedar Falls 50614

Waldorf College
106 5th St., Forest City 50436
Steve Lovik, Dir. of Admis.
800-292-1903

KANSAS

Benedictine College
1020 N. Second St., Atchison 66002
James Hoffman, Dir. of Admis.

Bethany College
421 N. 1st St., Lindsborg 67456
Dennis Chaput, Dir. of Admis.

Coffeyville Community College
402 W. 11th St., Coffeyville 67337
Helen Ellerman, Dir. of Admis.

Fort Hays State University
600 Park St., Hays 67601-4099
Dr. Robert Nicholson, Chrpsn.

Kansas Newman College
3100 McCormick Ave., Wichita 67213
Dr. Robert Giroux, President

McPherson College
1600 E. Euclid St., McPherson 67460

Mid-America Nazarene College
P.O. Box 1776, Olathe 66051

Ottawa University
1001 S. Cedar St., Ottawa 66067
Steve Koberlein, Dir. of Admis.
800-755-5200

SOUTHWESTERN COLLEGE
100 College St., Winfield 67156
800-846-1543

Wichita State University
1845 Fairmount, Wichita 67260
800-362-2594
See listing under "Universities"

KENTUCKY

Asbury College
1 Macklem Dr., Wilmore 40390
Jonah Mitchell, Dir. of Admis.

Bellarmine College
2001 Newburg Rd., Louisville 40205
Thomas LaBaugh, Dean of Admissions

Centre College
600 W. Walnut St., Danville 40422

Cumberland College
6178 College Station Dr., Williamsburg 40769
See listing under "Universities"

Georgetown College
400 E. College St., Georgetown 40324
Garvel Kindrick, Director of Admissions
See listing under "Universities"

Kentucky Wesleyan College
3000 Frederica St., Owensboro 42301
Dr. David Oettinger, Chrpsn.

Morehead State University, Morehead 40351
Charles Myers, Director of Admissions
606-783-2000

Murray State University, Murray 42071
Phil Bryan, Director of Admissions
800-272-4MSU

Northern Kentucky University
Louie B. Nunn Dr., Highland Heights 41076

Pikeville College
214 Sycamore St., Pikeville 41501
Dr. John W. Sanders, Dean of Admissions

Spalding University
851 S. 4th St., Louisville 40203
Dorothy G. Allen, Dir. of Admis.

Transylvania University
300 Broadway St., N., Lexington 40508
Pat Bain, Dir. of Admis.

LOUISIANA

Centenary College of Louisiana
P.O. Box 41188, Shreveport 71134

Loyola University
6363 St. Charles Ave., New Orleans 70118

OUR LADY OF HOLY CROSS COLLEGE
4123 Woodland Dr., New Orleans 70131

Southeastern Louisiana University
P.O. Box 784, Hammond 70404

Tulane University
6823 Saint Charles Ave., New Orleans 70118
Richard Whiteside, Dean of Admission

MAINE

Bowdoin College, Brunswick 04011
William Mason, Dir. of Admis.

College of the Atlantic
105 Eden St., Bar Harbor 04609
Steve Thomas, Dir. of Admis.

St. Joseph's College, North Windham 04062

UNITY COLLEGE
Quaker Hill Rd., Unity 04988
207-948-3131
Wilson G. Hess, President
John Craig, Dean for Admissions
Established 1965. Private. Coed. Accreditation:
NEASC. Tuition: $9,750. Room and board: $4,750.
Enrollment: 475. Faculty: 34. Degrees: AAA, AAS,
BA, BS. Majors: environmental science (forestry,
wildlife, ecology, aquaculture, fisheries, conservation law enforcement, arboriculture), social sciences
(land use planning, park management, environmental
education, environmental policy), outdoor recreation
and pre-law. These programs blend a strong liberal
arts core with solid career preparation through hands-
on experience and internships. Excellent support
services in academic tutoring, career planning, and
placement.

University of Maine at Fort Kent
25 Pleasant St., Fort Kent 04743
Jerry Nadeau, Dir. of Admis.

University of Maine
9 O'Brien Ave., Machias 04654

University of New England
11 Hills Beach Rd., Biddeford 04005
Patricia Cribby, Dir. of Admis.

University of Southern Maine
96 Falmouth St., Portland 04103
Pat O'Mahoney-Damon, Chrpsn.

MARYLAND

Goucher College
1021 Dulaney Valley Rd., Baltimore 21204

Hood College
400 Rosemont Ave., Frederick 21701

Loyola College
4501 N. Charles St., Baltimore 21210
William Bossemeyer III, Dir. of Admis.

Morgan State University
Cold Spring Ln. and Hillen Rd., Baltimore 21239

Mt. St. Mary's College
16300 Old Emmitsburg Rd., Emmitsburg 21727
Michael D. Kennedy, Dir. of Admis.

Towson State University
800 York Rd., Towson 21204
Dr. Hoke Smith, President

University of Maryland Eastern Shore
11868 Academic Oval, Princess Anne 21853
Dr. Gian Gupta, Chrpsn.

Villa Julie College
1525 Greenspring Valley Rd., Stevenson 21153
Carolyn Manuszak, President

Washington College
Washington Ave., Chestertown 21620
Kevin Coveney, Dir. of Admis.

Western Maryland College
2 College Hill, Westminster 21157

MASSACHUSETTS

American International College
1000 State St., Springfield 01109
Peter Miller, Dean of Admissions

Amherst College, Amherst 01002
Jane E. Reynolds, Dean of Admissions

Anna Maria College
2 Sunset Ln., Paxton 01612
Dr. Bernadette Madore, SSA, President

Atlantic Union College
P.O. Box 1000, South Lancaster 01561
Osa Canto, Registrar

Boston College
140 Commonwealth Ave., Chestnut Hill 02167

Boston University
685 Commonwealth Ave., Boston 02215

Brandeis University
415 South St, Waltham 02154
David Gould, Dean of Admissions
617-736-3500

Bridgewater State College
Bridgewater 02325
James Plotner, Jr., Dir. of Admis.

Clark University
950 Main St., Worcester 01610
Richard Pierson, Dean of Admis.

Curry College
1071 Blue Hill Ave., Milton 02186
617-333-0500

ELMS COLLEGE
291 Springfield St., Chicopee 01013
800-255-ELMS

Emmanuel College
400 The Fenway, Boston 02115
Margaret Bonilla, Dir. of Admis.

Fitchburg State College
160 Pearl St., Fitchburg 01420
Marke Vickers, Dir. of Admis.

Hampshire College, Amherst 01002
Audrey Y. Smith, Dir. of Admissions
413-582-5471

Massachusetts Institute of Technology
77 Massachusetts Ave., Cambridge 02139

Mt. Holyoke College
College St., South Hadley 01075
Anita Smith, Director of Admissions
413-538-2023

Mt. Ida College
777 Dedham St., Newton Center 02159
Jim Mulligan, Dean of Admis.

North Adams State College
375 Church St., North Adams 01247
413-664-4511 or 800-292-6632
See listing under "Universities or Graduate
Schools"

Simmons College
300 The Fenway, Boston 02115

Springfield College
263 Alden St., Springfield 01109
Frederick Bartlett, Dean of Admissions

SPRINGFIELD TECHNICAL COMMUNITY COLLEGE
1 Armory Square, Springfield 01105
Dr. Patrick E. Tigue, Dir. of Admissions
413-781-7822

Suffolk University
8 Ashburton Place, Boston 02108
Barbara K. Ericson, Assoc. Dean Enrollment &
Retention
617-573-8460

University of Massachusetts
100 Morrissey Blvd., Boston 02125

University of Massachusetts Dartmouth
Old Westport Rd., North Dartmouth 02747
Raymond Barrows, Dir. of Admissions
508-999-8605

Wellesley College, Wellesley 02181
Janet A. Lavin, Dir. of Admis.

Western New England College
1215 Wilbraham Rd., Springfield 01119
800-325-1122

Westfield State College
577 Western Ave., Westfield 01085
John F. Marcus, Dir. of Admis.

Wheaton College
26 E. Main St., Norton 02766
Gail Berson, Dean/Admis. & Student Aid

Worcester Polytechnic Institute
100 Institute Rd., Worcester 01609
Kay R. Dietrich, Director of Admissions
508-831-5286

MICHIGAN

Adrian College
110 S. Madison St., Adrian 49221
George Wolf, Dir. of Admis.
See listing under "Universities"

Albion College
611 E. Porter, Albion 49224
800-858-6770

Alma College
614 W. Superior St., Alma 48801-1599
John Seveland, VP for Enrollment
800-321-ALMA
See listing under "Universities"

Andrews University, Berrien Springs 49104
Jack Mentges, Dir. of Admis.

Aquinas College
1607 Robinson Rd., S.E., Grand Rapids 49506
Paula Meehan, Dean of Admissions
800-678-9593

Calvin College
3201 Burton St., S.E., Grand Rapids 49546

Concordia College
4090 Geddes Rd., Ann Arbor 48105
Mary Froelich, Dir. of Admis.

Eastern Michigan University, Ypsilanti 48197
William L. Fennel, Head
313-487-3060 or 800-GO-TO-EMU

Grand Valley State University
1 Campus Dr., Allendale 49401
JoAnn Foerster, Dir. of Admis.

HILLSDALE COLLEGE
33 E. College St., Hillsdale 49242
Dr. Francis Steiner, Chrpsn.
517-437-7341

Lake Superior State University
1000 College Dr., Sault St. Marie 49783

Marygrove College
8425 W. McNichols Rd., Detroit 48221

Michigan State University, East Lansing 48824
Jane Smith, Student Affairs Specialist

Michigan Technological University
1400 Townsend Dr., Houghton 49931
Joseph A. Galetto, Dir. Enrollment Mgmt.
906-487-2335

Olivet College
300 S. Main St., Olivet 49076
Vicki Gallas, Registrar
See listing under "Universities"

St. Mary's College
Orchard Lake & Commerce Rd.
Orchard Lake 48324

Spring Arbor College
106 E. Main St., Spring Arbor 49283

Suomi College
601 Quincy St., Hancock 49930
John Ruohoniemi, Dean/Enrollment Development
800-682-7604

MINNESOTA

Augsburg College
731 21st Ave., S., Minneapolis 55454

Bemidji State University
1500 Birchmont Dr., N.E., Bemidji 56601
800-475-2001

Bethel College
3900 Bethel Dr., St. Paul 55112
Dr. George Brushaber, President

Carleton College
One N. College St., Northfield 55057
Paul Thiboutot, Dir. of Admis.

College of Saint Benedict
37 S. College Ave., St. Joseph 56374

College of St. Catherine
2004 Randolph Ave., St. Paul 55105

College of St. Scholastica
1200 Kenwood Ave., Duluth 55811
Sr. Donna Schroeder, Chrpsn.
800-447-5444
See listing under "Liberal Arts"

Concordia College
901 8th St. S., Moorhead 56562
Lee Johnson, Dir. of Admis.
See listing under "Universities"

Concordia College-St. Paul
275 N. Syndicate, St. Paul 55104
Tim Utter, Dir. of Admis.

Gustavus Adolphus College
800 W. College Ave., St. Peter 56082
Mark Anderson, Dir. of Admis.

Hamline University
1536 Hewitt Ave., St. Paul 55104
Scott Pratt, Dir. of Admis.

Northwestern College
3003 Snelling Ave., N., St. Paul 55113
Ralph Anderson, Dean of Admissions
800-827-6827 or 612-631-5111

PILLSBURY BAPTIST BIBLE COLLEGE
315 S. Grove St., Owatonna 55060
Alan Potter, President
Larry Tindall, Director of Admissions
800-747-4557

St. Cloud State University
740 4th Ave., S., St. Cloud 56301
Sherwood Reid, Dir. of Admis.
800-369-4260

St. John's University
P.O. Box 7155, Collegeville 56321

St. Mary's College of Minnesota
700 Terrace Heights #2, Winona 55987
Tony Piscitiello, VP for Admission

St. Olaf College, Northfield 55057
Kathleen Fishbeck, Chrpsn.
507-646-3100

Southwest State University, Marshall 56258

University of Minnesota
600 E. Fourth St., Morris 56267

Winona State University
P.O. Box 5838, Winona 55987
Dr. J. Mootz, Dir. of Admis.

MISSISSIPPI

Belhaven College
1500 Peachtree St., Jackson 39202

Millsaps College
P.O. Box 150556, Jackson 39210
Florence Hines, Dir. of Admis.

Mississippi College
P.O. Box 4086, Clinton 39058

Mississippi University for Women
P.O. Box W-1602, Columbus 39701
Teresa Thompson, Exec. Dir. of Enrollment

Tougaloo College
500 E. County Line Rd., Tougaloo 39174

MISSOURI

Avila College
11901 Wornall Rd., Kansas City 64145

Central Missouri State University
Warrensburg 64093
Delores Hudson, Dir. of Admis.

College of the Ozarks, Point Lookout 65726
Dr. Kenton Olson, Dean of the College

Cottey College
1000 W. Austin St., Nevada 64772
Wendy Beckemeyer, Dir. of Admis.

Drury College
900 N. Benton Ave., Springfield 65802
Michael G. Thomas, Dir. of Admis.

Evangel College
1111 N. Glenstone Ave., Springfield 65802
David Schoolfield, Dir. of Enrollment

Fontbonne College
6800 Wydown Blvd., St. Louis 63105
Peggy Musen, Dir. of Admis.

Maryville University of St. Louis
13550 Conway Rd., Saint Louis 63141
314-576-9300 or 800-MARYVLL

Missouri Baptist College
12542 Conway Rd., St. Louis 63141

Missouri Southern State College
3950 Newman Rd., Joplin 64801-1595
Dr. John P. Messick, Dept. Head
See listing under "Universities"

Missouri Valley College
500 E. College St., Marshall 65340
816-886-6924 ext. 114
See listing under "Universities"

Missouri Western State College
4525 Downs Dr., St. Joseph 64507
Howard McCauley, Dir. of Admis.

Northeast Missouri State University
Kirksville 63501

Northwest Missouri State University
800 University Dr., Maryville 64468

Park College, Parkville 64152
Dr. Edwin Rawn, Dean of Admis.

Southeast Missouri State University
1 University Plz., Cape Girardeau 63701
New Student Relations 314-651-2590
See listing under "Universities"

Southwest Baptist University
1601 S. Springfield Ave., Bolivar 65613

Southwest Missouri State Univerity
901 S. National Ave., Springfield 65804
Dr. Richard Myers, Department Head
417-836-5126

Stephens College, Columbia 65215
Mary Ann Sprinkle, Dir. of Admis.

University of Missouri, Rolla
102 Parker Hall, Rolla 65401
David J. Allen, Dir. of Admis. & Financial Aid
800-522-0938

University of Missouri
8001 Natural Bridge Rd., St. Louis 63121
Mimi LaMarca, Dir. of Admis.

Washington University
1 Brookings Dr., St. Louis 63130

Webster University
470 E. Lockwood Ave., St. Louis 63119
Dr. James Staley, Associate Dean
See listing under "Universities"

Westminster College
501 Westminster Ave., Fulton 65251
Gary Forney, Dean of Admis.

William Woods College
200 W. 12th St., Fulton 65251
Dr. Jahnae Barnett, VP of Admis.

MONTANA

CARROLL COLLEGE
1610 N. Benton Ave., Helena 59625
Candace Cain, Dir. of Admis.
See listing under "Universities"

College of Great Falls
1301 20th St., S., Great Falls 59405
Jean Walker, Dir. of Admis.

Montana State University, Bozeman 59717

Montana State University - Billings
1500 N. 30th St., Billings 59101
Karen Everett, Dir. of Admis.
406-657-2158

Rocky Mountain College
1511 Poly Dr., Billings 59102
David Heringer, Dir. of Admis.
See listing under "Universities"

University of Montana, Missoula 59812
800-462-8636

NEBRASKA

Chadron State College
1000 Main St., Chadron 69337
Dr. Ted Davis, Dean

College of Saint Mary
1901 S. 72nd St., Omaha 68124
Sheila Haggas, Dir. of Admis.

Concordia College
800 N. Columbia Ave., Seward 68434
Don Vos, Dir. of Admis.

Creighton University
2500 California St., Omaha 68178
Dr. Allen Schlesinger, Chrpsn.

Dana College
2848 College Dr., Blair 68008
John Schueth, Dir. of Admis.
800-444-3262
See listing under "Universities"

Midland Lutheran College
900 Clarkson St., Fremont 68025
Roland Kahnk, V.P. Admissions

Nebraska Wesleyan University
5000 Saint Paul Ave., Lincoln 68504
Ken Sieg, Dir. of Admis.

Northeast Community College
P.O. Box 469, Norfolk 68702
Eugene Hart, Dir. of Admis.

Peru State College, Peru 68421
Pamela J. Cosgrove, Dir. of Admis.
402-872-3815

Union College
3800 S. 48th St., Lincoln 68506

Wayne State College
200 E. Tenth St., Wayne 68787

NEVADA

Sierra Nevada College-Lake Tahoe
P.O. Box 4269, Incline Village 89450
Lane Murray, Dir. of Admissions
See listing under "Universities"

University of Nevada Las Vegas
4505 S. Maryland Pky., Las Vegas 89154-1021
Admissions: 702-895-3443 or 800-334-UNLV

NEW HAMPSHIRE

Colby-Sawyer College
100 Main St., New London 03257

Franklin Pierce College, Rindge 03461

Keene State College
229 Main St., Keene 03435
Kathryn Dodge, Dir. of Admis.

New England College
26 Bridge St., Henniker 03242
John Spaulding, Dir. of Admis.

NOTRE DAME COLLEGE
2321 Elm St., Manchester 03104
603-669-4298

Rivier College
420 S. Main St., Nashua 03060
Admissions: 800-44-RIVIER

Saint Anselm College
87 Saint Anselm Dr., Manchester 03102
Don Healy, Dir. of Admis.

NEW JERSEY

Bloomfield College
1 Park Place, Bloomfield 07003
Warner Smith, Dean for Admissions
201-748-9000, Ext. 230

Caldwell College
9 Ryerson Ave., Caldwell 07006

Fairleigh Dickinson University, Madison 07940
Lissa Anderson, Dir. of Admis.
201-593-8906

Fairleigh Dickinson University, Teaneck 07666
Dennis Craig, Dir. of Admis.
201-692-2553

FELICIAN COLLEGE
262 S. Main St., Lodi 07644
Sr. Mary Austin, OSB, Dir. of Admis.
201-778-1029
See listing under "Universities"

Georgian Court College
900 Lakewood Ave., Lakewood 08701
908-364-2200 Ext. 345

Jersey City State College
2039 Kennedy Blvd., Jersey City   07305
201-200-3234

Mercer County Community College
West Windsor Campus
1200 Old Trenton Rd., Trenton   08690
Michael Glass, Dir. of Admis.
See listing under "Community and Junior
Colleges"

Monmouth College
400 Cedar Ave., West Long Branch   07764
Joan Rudinski, Dir. of Admis.

Princeton University, Princeton   08544

Rider University
2083 Lawrenceville Rd., Lawrenceville   08648
Susan Christian, Dir. of Admis.

Rowan College of New Jersey, Glassboro   08028
Marvin G. Sills, Dir. of Admis.

Seton Hall University
400 S. Orange Ave., South Orange   07079
Lee Cooke, Dir. of Admis.

Stockton State College, Pomona   08240
Sal Catalfamo, Dir. of Admis.

Thomas Edison State College
101 W. State St., Trenton   08608

Upsala College
345 Prospect St., East Orange   07017
George Lynes, Dean of Admissions

NEW MEXICO

College of Santa Fe
1600 St. Michaels Dr., Santa Fe   87505
800-456-2673

College of the Southwest
6610 N. Lovington Hwy., Hobbs   88240

Eastern New Mexico University
Portales   88130
Larry Fuqua, Dir. of Admis.

New Mexico Highlands University, Las Vegas   87701
Dr. Jorge P. Thomas, VP Academic Affairs

New Mexico Institute of Mining & Technology
801 Leroy Pl., Socorro   87801

University of New Mexico, Albuquerque   87131
Robert Weaver, Dean of Admissions

NEW YORK

Adelphi University, Garden City   11530
Dr. Elliot Pruzan, Asst. Provost & Dir. of Admis.
516-877-3050

Alfred University
Alumni Hall, Alfred   14802
Laurie Richer, Director of Admissions
800-541-9229

Barnard College
3009 Broadway, New York   10027

Canisius College
2001 Main St., Buffalo   14208
Penelope Lips, Dir. of Admis.
800-843-1517

Clarkson University, Potsdam   13699
Robert Croot, Dir. of Admis.

Colgate University
13 Oak Dr., Hamilton   13346
Dean of Admissions
315-824-7401

College of St. Rose
432 Western Ave., Albany   12203

Columbia University
612 W. 115th St., New York   10025

Cornell University
410 Thurston Ave., Ithaca   14853

CUNY College of Staten Island
130 Stuyvesant Pl., Staten Island   10301

CUNY York College
9420 Guy R. Brewer Blvd., Jamaica   11451

Daemen College
4380 Main St., Amherst   14226
Maria Dillard, Dir. of Admis.
in NY 800-462-7652 or 716-839-8225

D'Youville College
320 Porter Ave., Buffalo   14201
Ronald Dannecker, Dir. of Admis.

Elmira College
Park Pl., Elmira   14901
William S. Neal, Dean of Admissions
See listing under "Liberal Arts"

Fordham University
441 E. Fordham Rd., Bronx   10458
718-817-1000

Friends World Program, Long Island University
Montauk Hwy., Southampton   11968
Carol Gilbert, Dir. of Admis.

Hartwick College, Oneonta   13820

Hobart & William Smith College
Pulteney St., Geneva   14456

Houghton College
P.O. Box 128, Houghton   14744
Tim Fuller, Dir. of Admis.

IONA COLLEGE
715 North Ave., New Rochelle   10801
800-231-IONA or 914-633-2503
See listing under "Universities"

Ithaca College
953 Danby Rd., Ithaca   14850

Keuka College
P.O. Box 98, Keuka Park   14478
Robert J. Ianuzzo, Dean of Admissions

The King's College, Briarcliff Manor   10510
Frederic Rowley, Dean of Admissions

Le Moyne College
1419 Salt Springs Rd., Syracuse   13214-1301
Edwin B. Harris, Dir. of Admis.

Long Island University-Brooklyn Campus
1 University Plaza, Brooklyn   11201
Alan Chaves, Dean of Admissions

Long Island University-C. W. Post Campus
Rt. 25A, Brookville   11548
Dr. Newton Meisenman, Chrpsn.

Long Island University-Southampton Campus
Southampton   11968
Carol Gilbert, Dir. of Admis.

Manhattan College
4513 Manhattan College Pky., Riverdale   10471
Dr. Mary Ann O'Donnell, Acting Dean of Arts

Manhattanville College
2900 Purchase St., Purchase   10577

MARIST COLLEGE
290 North Rd., Poughkeepsie   12601
Harry W. Wood, VP Admissions
914-575-3226

Marymount College
100 Marymount Ave., Tarrytown   10591
Gina R. Campbell, Dir. of Admis.
800-724-4312

Mercy College
555 Broadway, Dobbs Ferry   10522
James Nesbitt, Dean of Admissions

Molloy College
1000 Hempstead Ave., Rockville Centre   11570
Wayne James, Dir. of Admis.
See listing under "Universities"

Mt. St. Mary College
330 Powell Ave., Newburgh   12550

Nazareth College of Rochester
4245 East Ave., Rochester   14618
Paul Kenyon, Dir. of Admis.

New York Institute of Technology
Old Westbury Campus, Old Westbury   11568

Niagara University, Niagara University   14109
George Pachter, Dean of Admissions
800-462-2111
See listing under "Universities"

Pace University, New York Campus
1 Pace Plaza, New York   10038

Pace University, Pleasantville/Briarcliff Campus
Bedford Rd., Pleasantville   10570

Pace University, White Plains Campus
78 N. Broadway, White Plains   10603

Paul Smith's College, Paul Smiths   12970
Enrico Miller, Dir. of Admis.
800-421-2605

Rensselaer Polytechnic Institute, Troy   12180
Conrad Sharrow, Dean of Admissions

Roberts Wesleyan College
2301 Westside Dr., Rochester   14624
Dr. Philip Ogden, Chrpsn.
See listing under "Universities"

Rochester Institute of Technology
1 Lomb Memorial Dr., Rochester   14623
716-475-6631
See listing under "Universities"

Russell Sage College
51 1st St., Troy   12180

St. John Fisher College
3690 East Ave., Rochester   14618
Peter Lindsey, Dir. of Admis.

St. John's University
Grand Central & Utopia Parkways, Jamaica   11439

St. Joseph's College
245 Clinton Ave., Brooklyn   11205
Geraldine Foudy, Dir. of Admis.
718-636-6868

St. Joseph's College, Suffolk Campus
25 Audobon Ave., Patchogue   11772

St. Lawrence University, Canton   13617
Joel R. Wincowski, Dean of Admis. & Financial Aid

Sarah Lawrence College, Bronxville   10708

Skidmore College, Saratoga Springs   12866
Kent Jones, Dir. of Admis.

SUNY Adirondack Community College
439 Bay Rd., Queensbury   12804
Levi Brown, Dir. of Admis.
518-793-4491
See listing under "Community and Junior
Colleges"

SUNY at Buffalo
17 Capen Hall
P.O. Box 601660, Buffalo   14260-1660
716-645-6900

SUNY College at Brockport
Brockport   14420

SUNY College at Old Westbury
P.O. Box 210, Old Westbury   11568
Michael Sheehy, Dir. of Admis.

SUNY at Oswego, Oswego   13126
Dr. Joseph Grant, Jr., Dean of Admissions
315-341-2250

SUNY College at Plattsburgh, Plattsburgh   12901
Roger Heintz, Chrpsn.
518-564-3155

SUNY College at Purchase
735 Anderson Hill Rd., Purchase   10577
Gene Ann Flaherty, Dir. of Admissions

SUNY College of Environmental Science & Forestry
1 Forestry Dr., Syracuse   13210
800-7777-ESF or 315-470-6600

University of Rochester
500 Joseph C. Wilson Blvd., Rochester   14627
Wayne A. Locust, Dir. of Admis.
See listing under "Universities"

Utica College of Syracuse University
1600 Burrstone Rd., Utica   13502

Vassar College
125 Raymond Ave., Poughkeepsie   12601

NORTH CAROLINA

Barton College
College Station, Wilson   27893
Anthony Britt, Dir. of Admis.
800-345-4973/919-399-6318
See listing under "Universities"

Belmont Abbey College
1 Abbey Pl., Belmont   28012
Admissions, 800-523-2355

Bennett College
900 E. Washington St., Greensboro   27401

Catawba College
2300 W. Innes St., Salisbury   28144
Mark Stokes, Dir. of Admis.

East Carolina University
1000 E. 5th St., Greenville   27858
Dr. Charles Bland, Chair

Elon College
P.O. Box 2700, Elon College   27244
Nan P. Perkins, Dean of Admissions

Gardner-Webb University
General Delivery, Boiling Springs   28017
Les Brown, Chrpsn.
704-434-2361

Greensboro College
815 W. Market St., Greensboro   27401

Guilford College
5800 W. Friendly Ave., Greensboro   27410
Larry West, Dir. of Admis.
See listing under "Universities"

Livingstone College
701 W. Monroe St., Salisbury   28144

Mars Hill College
Main St., Mars Hill   28754
Dr. Smith Goodrum, Dean of Admis.

Methodist College
5400 Ramsey St., Fayetteville   28311
Fiore Bergamasco, Dir. of Admis.

North Carolina A&T State University
1601 E. Market St., Greensboro   27411

North Carolina State University
P.O. Box 7001, Raleigh   27695
George Dixon, Dir. of Admis.

North Carolina Wesleyan College
3400 N. Wesleyan Blvd., Rocky Mount   27804

Pembroke State University
P.O. Box 1510, Pembroke   28372
Anthony Locklear, Dir. of Admissions
919-521-6262

Pfeiffer College
General Delivery, Misenheimer   28109

QUEENS COLLEGE
1900 Selwyn Ave., Charlotte   28274
D. Stephen Cloniger, VP for Enrollment Management
See listing under "Liberal Arts"

St. Andrews Presbyterian College
1700 Dogwood Mile, Laurinburg   28352
Dale B. Montague, Dir. of Admis.

Salem College
P.O. Box 10548, Winston-Salem   27108
Katherine Knapp, Director of Admissions
800-32-SALEM
See listing under "Women's College"

Warren Wilson College
P.O. Box 9000, Asheville   28802-9000
Tom Weede, Dir. of Admis.

Wingate College, Wingate   28174

OHIO

Antioch University
795 Livermore St., Yellow Springs   45387

Baldwin-Wallace College
275 Eastland Rd., Berea 44017
Juliann K. Baker, Dir. of Admis.

Capital University
2199 E. Main St., Columbus 43209
Dolphus E. Henry, Associate Provost

Cleveland State University
Euclid Ave. at 24th St., Cleveland 44115

College of Mount St. Joseph
5701 Delhi Rd., Cincinnati 45233-1672
See listing under "Universities"

College of Wooster
1189 Beall Ave., Wooster 44691
Hayden Schilling, Dean of Admis.

Heidelberg College
310 E. Market St., Tiffin 44883
Stephen E. Eidson, Dean of Admission
800-925-9250

Hiram College
P.O. Box 96, Hiram 44234
Gary Craig, Dean of Admis.

John Carroll University
20700 N. Park Blvd., Cleveland 44118

Kent State University
P.O. Box 5190, Kent 44242
Bruce Riddle, Dir. of Admis.

Lake Erie College
391 W. Washington St., Painesville 44077

Lorain County Community College
1005 Abbe Rd., N., Elyria 44035
Dr. John W. Thrash, Jr., Registrar

LOURDES COLLEGE
6832 Convent Blvd., Sylvania 43560
Mary E. Briggs, Dir. of Admis.
419-885-5291 or 800-878-3210

Malone College
515 25th St., N.W., Canton 44709
Lee Sommers, Dean of Admissions

MARIETTA COLLEGE
210 5th St., Marietta 45750
Dennis R. DePerro, Dean Admis./Financial Aid
800-331-7896

Mount Union College
1972 Clark Ave., Alliance 44601
Amy Tomko, Dir. of Admis.

Mt. Vernon Nazarene College
800 Martinsburg Rd., Mt. Vernon 43050
Ronald Hyson, Dir. of Admis.

Oberlin College
135 W. Lorain St., Oberlin 44074
David Miller, Chrpsn.

Ohio Dominican College
1216 Sunbury Rd., Columbus 43219
800-955-OHIO

OHIO NORTHERN UNIVERSITY
525 S. Main St., Ada 45810
Terry Keiser, Chrpsn.
412-772-2000

Ohio Wesleyan University
61 S. Sandusky St., Delaware 43015
Donald Bishop, Dean for Enrollment

University of Akron
381 Buchtel Common, Akron 44325
Kris MacDermott, Asst. Provost Enrollment

University of Cincinnati
2700 Clifton Ave., Cincinnati 45221

University of Dayton
300 College Park Ave., Dayton 45469-2320
Toll-free 800-837-7433
See listing under "Universities"

University of Rio Grande
General Delivery, Rio Grande 45674
Dr. Robert Wolfe, Dean
614-245-5353, Ext. 7397

Urbana University
100 College Way, Urbana 43078
Donald Burns, Dir. of Admis.

Wilmington College
P.O. Box 1185, Wilmington 45177
Rhonda Inderhees, Dir. of Admis.

OKLAHOMA

Bartlesville Wesleyan College
2201 Silverlake Rd., Bartlesville 74006

Cameron University
2800 W. Gore Blvd., Lawton 73505
Louise Brown, Dir. of Admis.

East Central University, Ada 74820
James Peak, Dir. of Admis.

Oklahoma Christian University of Science and Arts
P.O. Box 11000, Oklahoma City 73136
Duane Eggleston, Vice President
800-877-5010

Oklahoma City University
2501 N. Blackwelder Ave., Oklahoma City 73106
Susan Barker, Director
See listing under "Universities"

Oklahoma State University, Stillwater 74078
Jerry Wilhm, Dept. Head

Oral Roberts University
7777 S. Lewis Ave., Tulsa 74171
Arthur E. Matzkvech, Dir. of Admis.

Southern Nazarene University
6729 N.W. 39th Expy., Bethany 73008

University of Tulsa
600 S. College Ave., Tulsa 74104
Dr. Glen Collier, Chrpsn.

OREGON

Central Oregon Community College
2600 N.W. College Way, Bend 97701
Christine Kerlin, Dir. of Admis.
503-383-7500

Lewis & Clark College
0615 S.W. Palatine Hill Rd., Portland 97219
Michael Sexton, Dean of Admissions

Pacific University
2043 College Way, Forest Grove 97116
Barbara Mergen, Dir. of Admis.

Reed College
3202 S.E. Woodstock Blvd., Portland 97202

University of Portland
5000 N. Willamette Blvd., Portland 97203

Warner Pacific College
2219 S.E. 68th Ave., Portland 97215
Sherry Moore, Enrollment Management Director

PENNSYLVANIA

Albright College
P.O. Box 15234, Reading 19612

Allegheny College
520 N. Main St., Meadville 16335
Gayle Pollack, Dir. of Admis.

Allentown College of St. Frances de Sales
2755 Station Ave., Center Valley 18034
George Kelley, Dir. of Admis.

Alvernia College
400 Bernardine St., Reading 19607
Lisa Grabowski, Dir. of Admis.

Beaver College
450 S. Easton Rd., Glenside 19038-3295
Dennis Nostrand, VP for Enrollment Management
Phone: 800-776-BEAVER(2328)
Fax: 215-572-4049
See listing under "Universities"

Bloomsburg University, Bloomsburg 17815
Bernard Vinovrski, Dir. of Admis.

Cabrini College
610 King of Prussia Rd., Radnor 19087

California University of Pennsylvania
3rd St., California 15419
Norman Hasbrouck, Dean for Enrollment

Carlow College
3333 5th Ave., Pittsburgh 15213

Carnegie Mellon University
5000 Forbes Ave., Pittsburgh 15213

Cedar Crest College
100 College Dr., Allentown 18104-6196
Cynthia Phillips, Dir. of Admissions

Chatham College
Woodland Rd., Pittsburgh 15232
Suellen Ofe, Dean of Admis./Financial Aid
See listing under "Women's College"

Clarion University of Pennsylvania
840 Wood St., Clarion 16214

College Misericordia
301 Lake St., Dallas 18612
Michael Joseph, Dir. of Enrollment Mgmt.

Delaware Valley College of Science & Agriculture
Doylestown 18901
Stephen Zenko, Dir. of Admis.

Drexel University
3141 Chestnut St., Philadelphia 19104
Dean of Enrollment Management

Eastern College
10 Fairview Dr., Saint Davids 19087
Ronald Keller, VP for Enrollment Management

East Stroudsburg University of Pennsylvania
East Stroudsburg 18301
Alan Chesterton, Dir. of Admis.

Edinboro University of Pennsylvania
Edinboro 16444
Admissions Office: 800-626-2203

Elizabethtown College
1 Alpha Dr., Elizabethtown 17022

Franklin & Marshall College
P.O. Box 3003, Lancaster 17604

Gannon University
109 University Sq., Erie 16541

Geneva College
3200 College Ave., Beaver Falls 15010

Grove City College
100 Campus Dr., Grove City 16127
Dr. Arnold W. Sodergren, Chrpsn.

GWYNEDD-MERCY COLLEGE
Sumneytown Pike, Gwynedd Valley 19437
Marjorie DeSimone, Dean of Admissions
800-DIAL-GMC
See listing under "Universities"

Haverford College
370 Lancaster Ave., Haverford 19041

Holy Family College
Grant & Frankford Ave., Philadelphia 19114
Dr. Mott Linn, Dir. of Admis.
215-637-3050

Immaculata College
Immaculata 19345
James P. Sullivan, Dir. of Admis.

Juniata College
1700 Moore St., Huntington 16652

Lafayette College, Easton 18042
G. Gary Ripple, Dir. of Admis.
610-250-5100

La Roche College
9000 Babcock Blvd., Pittsburgh 15237
Marianne Leister, Dir. of Admis.

La Salle University
1900 W. Olney Ave., Philadelphia 19141
Br. Gerald Fitzgerald, Dir. of Admis.
See listing under "Universities"

Lincoln University, Lincoln University 19352
Jimmy Arrington, Dir. of Admis.

Lycoming College, Williamsport 17701

Marywood College
2300 Adams Ave., Scranton 18509

Mercyhurst College
501 E. 38th St., Erie 16546
Andrew Roth, Dean of Enrollment
800-825-1926

Millersville University of Pennsylvania
Millersville 17551
Blair Treasure, Dean of Admissions

Montgomery County Community College
340 DeKalb Pike, Blue Bell 19422-0758
Dennis Murphy, Dir. of Admis.

Muhlenberg College
2400 W. Chew St., Allentown 18104
Chris Hooker-Haring, Dir. of Admis.

Neumann College
Concord Rd., Aston 19014

Pennsylvania State University
201 Shields Bldg., University Park 16802

Pennsylvania State University
Beaver Campus, Monaca 15061
Regina S. Miller, Dir. of Admis.
See listing under "Universities"

Pennsylvania State University
5091 Station Rd., Erie 16563

Philadelphia College of Pharmacy & Science
600 S. 43rd St., Philadelphia 19104-4495
215-596-8810

Point Park College
201 Wood St., Pittsburgh 15222

St. Joseph's University
5600 City Ave., Philadelphia 19131
Randy Miller, Dir. of Admis.

St. Vincent College
300 Fraser Purchase Rd., Latrobe 15650

Seton Hill College, Greensburg 15601
Peter Egan, Dir. of Admis.
800-826-6234 or 412-838-4255

Slippery Rock University, Slippery Rock 16057
Director of Admissions

Susquehanna University
514 University Ave., Selinsgrove 17870

Thiel College
75 College Ave., Greenville 16125
Robert Weaver, Dir. of Admis.

UNIVERSITY OF PITTSBURGH AT TITUSVILLE
McKinney Hall
504 E Main St., Titusville 16354
Jamie Mowat, Dir. of Admis./Financial Aid
814-827-4427

Villanova University
845 E. Lancaster Ave., Villanova 19085
Stephen R. Merritt, Dir. of Admis.

Washington & Jefferson College
60 S. Lincoln St., Washington 15301
Thomas O'Connor, Dir. of Admis.

West Chester University of Pennsylvania
S. High St., West Chester 19380

WESTMINSTER COLLEGE
New Wilmington 16172
Richard Dana Paul, Dir. of Admis.
412-946-7100

Wilkes University
184 S. River St., Wilkes-Barre 18766
Emory P. Guffrovich Jr., Dean of Admissions

York College of Pennsylvania
P.O. Box 15199, York 17405-7199
Nancy Spataro, Dir. of Admis.
717-849-1600
See listing under "Universities"

RHODE ISLAND

Brown University, Providence 02906

Rhode Island College
600 Mt. Pleasant Ave., Providence 02908

Roger Williams College
1 Old Ferry Rd., Bristol 02809
William Dunfey, Dir. of Admis.

Salve Regina University
1 Ochre Point Ave., Newport 02840
Roselina McKillop, Dean of Admissions

University of Rhode Island, Kingston 02881
David Taggart, Dean of Admissions/Financial Aid

SOUTH CAROLINA

Central Wesleyan College
P.O. Box 1020, Central 29630
Lillian A. Robbins, Dir. of Admis.

Coastal Carolina College
P.O. Box 1954, Myrtle Beach 29578
Dr. Ed Cerny, Director of Admissions

Columbia College
1301 Columbia College Dr., Columbia 29203

Converse College
580 E. Main St., Spartanburg 29302
Dr. Martha Rogers, VP Enrollment Management

Erskine College & Seminary
Washington St., Due West 29639
Dot Carter, Dir. of Admis.

Lander College
320 Stanley Ave., Greenwood 29649

Presbyterian College
503 S. Broad St., Clinton 29325
Margaret Williamson, Dean of Admis.

South Carolina State University
P.O. Box 7127, Orangeburg 29117-0001
803-536-7185

University of South Carolina, Columbia 29208
Terry Davis, Dir. of Admis.
803-777-7700

University of South Carolina at Aiken
171 University Pkwy., Aiken 29801

Voorhees College
Voorhees Rd., Denmark 29042

Winthrop University
701 W. Oakland Ave., Rock Hill 29733
James McCammon, Jr., Dir. of Admis.

Wofford College
429 N. Church St., Spartanburg 29303
Charles Gray, Dir. of Admis.

SOUTH DAKOTA

Augustana College
29th & S. Summit, Sioux Falls 57197

Dakota Wesleyan University
1300 W. University Ave., Mitchell 57301

Mt. Marty College
1105 W. 8th St., Yankton 57078
Paula Tacke, Dir. of Admis.

SIOUX FALLS COLLEGE
1501 S. Prairie Ave., Sioux Falls 57105
Susan Reese, Dir. of Admis.
800-888-1047
See listing under "Universities"

South Dakota State University
P.O. Box 2207, Brookings 57007
Dr. David Bryant, Dean
605-688-4148
See listing under "Universities"

University of South Dakota
414 E. Clark St., Vermillion 57069
Dave Lorenz, Dir. of Admis.

TENNESSEE

Austin Peay State University
601 College St., Clarksville 37044

Bryan College
Box 7000, Dayton 37321
Thomas A. Shaw, Dir. of Admis.

Carson-Newman College
P.O. Box 70552, Jefferson City 37760
See listing under "Universities"

Christian Brothers College
650 E. Parkway, S., Memphis 38104

Crichton College
6655 Winchester Rd., Memphis 38115
901-367-9800

David Lipscomb University
3901 Granny White Pike, Nashville 37204-3951
Wade Sandrell, Dir. of Admis.
800-333-4358

Freed-Hardeman University
158 E. Main St., Henderson 38340
800-342-7837

Le Moyne-Owen College
807 Walker Ave., Memphis 38126
901-942-7302 or 800-737-7778

Lincoln Memorial University
P.O. Box 2012, Harrogate 37752
Conrad Daniels, Dir. of Admis.

Maryville College
800 S. Court St., Maryville 37801
Annabelle J. Libby, Dir. of Admis.

Tennessee Temple University
1815 Union Ave., Chattanooga 37404
Dr. L. W. Nichols, President

Trevecca Nazarene College
333 Murfreesboro Rd., Nashville 37210

Tusculum College
P.O. Box 5035, Greeneville 37743
Ronald Porter, Dir. of Admis.

University of Memphis, Memphis 38152
Dr. John Eubank, Dean of Admissions

University of Tennessee at Martin
Martin 38238
Paul Kelley, Director of Admissions
See listing under "Universities"

University of Tennessee, Knoxville
527 Andy Holt Tower, Knoxville 37996
Dr. Gordon Stanley, Dir. of Admis.

Vanderbilt University
West End Ave., Nashville 37240

TEXAS

Austin College
900 N. Grand Ave., Sherman 75090
Rodney Oto, Dean of Admission
800-442-5363

Baylor University
P.O. Box 97008, Waco 76798-7008
Diana Ramey, Director of Admissions

Concordia Lutheran College
3400 N. Interstate 35, Austin 78705
Kevin Pieper, Dir. of Admis.

Dallas Baptist University
7777 W. Kiest Blvd., Dallas 75211

East Texas Baptist University
1200 N. Grove Ave., Marshall 75670

Incarnate Word College
4301 Broadway St., San Antonio 78209
Sr. Sally Mitchell, Dean of Enrollment

Lamar University
P.O. Box 10009, Beaumont 77710
800-458-7558

LeTourneau College
P.O. Box 7001, Longview 75607
Roger Kieffer, Dir. of Admis.

Midwestern State University
3400 Taft Blvd., Wichita Falls 76308

Prairie View A & M University
P.O. Box 3089, Prairie View 77446-3089
Linda S. Berry, Dir. of Admis.

Rice University
P.O. Box 1892, Houston 77251

St. Edward's University
3001 S. Congress Ave., Austin 78704
John Lambert, Dir. of Admis.

St. Mary's University of San Antonio
1 Camino Santa Maria, San Antonio 78228
Rick Castillo, Dir. of Admis.

Schreiner College
2100 Memorial Blvd., Kerrville 78028
800-343-4919

Southern Methodist University
Hillcrest at University, Dallas 75275

Texas A & I University
Campus Box 101, Kingsville 78363

Texas A & M University
College Station 77843

Texas Christian University
2800 S. University Dr., Ft. Worth 76129
Dr. Edward Boehm, Jr., Dean of Admissions

Texas Lutheran College
1000 W. Court St., Seguin 78155
Jennifer B. Ehlers, Dir. of Admis.

Texas Wesleyan University
1201 Wesleyan St., Fort Worth 76105
Kim Campbell, Dir. of Freshman Admission

Texas Women's University
P.O. Box 23925, Denton 76204

University of Dallas
1845 E. Northgate Dr., Irving 75062
Jim Whitaker, Dir. of Admis.

University of Houston-Clear Lake
2700 Bay Area Blvd., Houston 77058
Darella Banks, Exec. Dir. Enrollment Services

University of St. Thomas
3812 Montrose Blvd., Houston 77006
Elsie Biron, Dir. of Admis.

University of Texas at Arlington
UTA Box 19125, Arlington 76019
R. Zack Prince, Dir. of Admis.

University of Texas at Austin
0 the University of Texas, Austin 78712

University of Texas at San Antonio
San Antonio 78285
Dr. John H. Brown, Dir. of Admis.

West Texas State University
2501 4th Ave., Canyon 79016
Lila Vars, Dir. of Admis.

UTAH

Southern Utah University
351 W. Center St., Cedar City 84720
Dr. Al Tait, Dean
801-586-7921

University of Utah
1400 E. 200 S., Salt Lake City 84112
Dr. J. Stayner Landward, Dir. of Admis.

Utah State University, Logan 84322-1600
Rod Clark, Director of Admissions
801-750-1107

Westminster College of Salt Lake City
1840 S. 1300 E., Salt Lake City 84105
800-748-4753

VERMONT

Bennington College, Bennington 05201
Karen Kristof, Dir. of Admis.
800-833-6845

Castleton State College, Castleton 05735
Gary Fallis, Dir. of Admis.

Lyndon State College, Lyndonville 05851

Marlboro College
General Delivery, Marlboro 05344

NORWICH UNIVERSITY
65 S. Main St., Northfield 05663
Prof. Lauren Howard, Dept. Chrpsn.
See listing under "Universities"

Saint Michael's College
Winooski Park, Colchester 05439
800-SMC-8000
See listing under "Liberal Arts"

Trinity College
208 Colchester Ave., Burlington 05401

University of Vermont
194 S. Prospect St., Burlington 05401
802-656-3370

VIRGINIA

Averett College
420 W. Main St., Danville 24541
Gary Sherman, Dean of Enrollment Mgmt.

Bridgewater College
402 E College St., Bridgewater 22812

Christopher Newport College
50 Shoe Ln., Newport News 23606

Clinch Valley College of the University of Virginia
P.O. Box 16, Wise 24293
Lana Low, Dir. Enrollment Management

Eastern Mennonite College
1200 Park Rd., Harrisonburg 22801
Jerry Miller, Dir. of Admis.

Emory & Henry College
General Delivery, Emory 24327

Ferrum College, Ferrum 24088
Bob Bailey, Dir. of Admis.

George Mason University
4400 University Dr., Fairfax 22030-4444
Patricia Riordan, Dean of Admissions

LIBERTY UNIVERSITY
P.O. Box 20000, Lynchburg 24506
Jay Spencer, VP Recruitment
800-376-2800
See listing under "Universities"

Longwood College, Farmville 23901

Lynchburg College
1501 Lakeside Dr., Lynchburg 24501
Ernest Chadderton, Dean of Enrollment

Mary Baldwin College, Staunton 24401
Douglas E. Clark, Exec. Dir. of Enrollment

Marymount University
2807 N. Glebe Rd., Arlington 22207
Charles Coe, Director of Admissions
800-548-7638 or 703-284-1500
See listing under "Universities"

Mary Washington College
1701 College Ave., Fredericksburg 22401
Martin Wilder, V.P. for Admissions

Radford University
P.O. Box 5430, Radford 24142

Randolph-Macon College
200 Henry St., Ashland 23005
John Conkright, Dean of Admissions

Roanoke College
221 College Ln., Salem 24153

SHENANDOAH UNIVERSITY
1460 University Dr., Winchester 22601
Dr. John Happ, Division Chair
See listing under "Universities"

Sweet Briar College, Sweet Briar 24595
Nancy Church, Dir. of Admis.

University of Virginia
P.O. Box 9017, Charlottesville 22906

Virginia Intermont College
1013 Moore St., Bristol 24201
Lawton Blandford, Dir. of Admis.

Virginia Military Institute, Lexington 24450

Virginia Polytechnic Institute & State University
Blacksburg 24061
David Bousquet, Dir. of Undergraduate Admis.

Virginia Wesleyan College
1584 Wesleyan Dr., Norfolk 23502
W. Steve Stocks, V.P. for Admis.

WASHINGTON

Central Washington University, Ellensburg 98926
  William Swain, Director of Admissions

Pacific Lutheran University
  12180 Park Ave. S., Tacoma 98447
  Angelia Alexander, Chrpsn.

St. Martin's College
  700 College St. N.E., Lacey 98516

Skagit Valley College
  2405 E. College Way, Mt. Vernon 98273

University of Puget Sound
  1500 N. Warner St., Tacoma 98416

Washington State University, Pullman 99164
  Stan Berry, Dir. of Admis.

WEST VIRGINIA

Alderson-Broaddus College
  Philippi 26416
  Craig W. Gould, Director of Admissions
  304-457-1700

Bethany College, Bethany 26031
  John Giesman, Registrar

Concord College, Athens 24712

Davis & Elkins College
  100 Campus Dr., Elkins 26241
  Kevin D. Chenoweth, Dir. of Admis.

GLENVILLE STATE COLLEGE
  200 High St., Glenville 26351
  Mack Samples, Dean of Admissions
  See listing under "Liberal Arts"

Marshall University
  400 Hal Greer Blvd., Huntington 25755
  See listing under "Universities"

The University of Charleston
  2300 MacCorkle Ave., S.E., Charleston 25304
  800-995-GO UC

West Virginia University
  P.O. Box 6001, Morgantown 26506

WEST VIRGINIA WESLEYAN COLLEGE
  59 College Ave., Buckhannon 26201
  Robert Skinner, Director of Admission
  See listing under "Universities"

Wheeling Jesuit College
  316 Washington Ave., Wheeling 26003
  Fr. Thomas Acker, SJ, President

WISCONSIN

Beloit College
  700 College St., Beloit 53511
  John R. Jungck, Professor and Chair
  608-363-2267

Cardinal Stritch College
  6801 N. Yates Rd., Milwaukee 53217
  David Wegener, Dir. of Admis.

Carroll College
  100 N. East Ave., Waukesha 53186
  Ken Moyer, Dir. of Admis.

Carthage College
  2001 Alford Dr., Kenosha 53140
  Brenda A. Porter, VP Enrollment

Edgewood College
  855 Woodrow St., Madison 53711
  Robert Blust, Dir. of Admis.

Lakeland College
  P.O. Box 359, Sheboygan 53082

Lawrence University
  P.O. Box 599, Appleton 54912
  Steven Syverson, Dean of Admissions

Marian College of Fond du Lac
  45 S. National Ave., Fond du Lac 54935
  Carol Reichenberger, Dean of Admissions

Marquette University
  1217 W. Wisconsin Ave., Milwaukee 53233
  Raymond A. Brown, Dean of Admissions

Mt. Senario College
  1500 W. College Ave., Ladysmith 54848
  Dewey Floberg, Dean of Admissions

Northland College
  1411 Ellis Ave., Ashland 54806
  Jim Miller, Dean of Admissions

Ripon College, P.O. Box 248, Ripon 54971
  James Reilly, Dean of Admis.

St. Norbert College
  100 Grant St., De Pere 54115
  Craig S. Wesley, Dean of Admission
  See listing under "Universities"

Silver Lake College
  2406 S. Alverno Road, Manitowoc 54220
  Sandra Schwartz, Dir. of Admis.

University of Wisconsin, Eau Claire
  Eau Claire 54701

University of Wisconsin, Green Bay
  2420 Nicolet Dr., Green Bay 54311
  Dr. Robert Wenger, Chrpsn.

University of Wisconsin, La Crosse
  115 Main Hall, La Crosse 54601
  608-785-8067

University of Wisconsin, Oshkosh
  800 Algoma Blvd., Oshkosh 54901-8602
  August Helgerson, Dir. of Admis.

University of Wisconsin
  P.O. Box 2000, Kenosha 53141
  414-553-2211

University of Wisconsin
  1 University Plaza, Platteville 53818
  Richard Schumacher, Dean of Admissions

University of Wisconsin, River Falls
  River Falls 54022
  Alan Tuchtenhagen, Dir. of Admis.

Viterbo College
  815 9th St., S., La Crosse 54601
  Roland W. Nelson, Dir. of Admis.

WYOMING

Central Wyoming College
  2660 Peck St., Riverton 82501
  Mary Gores, Admissions Officer
  307-856-9291
  See listing under "Community and Junior Colleges"

GUAM

University of Guam
  UOG Station, Mangilao 96923
  Kathleen Owings, Dir. of Admis.

PUERTO RICO

Catholic University of Puerto Rico
  Las Americas Ave., Ponce 00732
  Carilin Frau, Dir. of Admis.

University of Puerto Rico
  Arecibo Technical University College
  P.O. Box A-1806, Arecibo 00613

University of Puerto Rico
  Antonio Barcelo Ave., Cayey 00736
  Antonio Rosario, Dir. of Admis.

University of Puerto Rico
  CUH Station Rd. 908 Bo Tejas, Humacao 00791

University of Puerto Rico, Mayaguez Campus
  P.O. Box 5000, Mayaguez 00681
  Neysa Lopez, Dir. of Admis.

University of Puerto Rico, Rio Piedras Campus
  P.O. Box 23300, San Juan 00931
  Victor Lopez, Dir. of Admis.

BUSINESS AND MANAGEMENT

This classification contains schools accredited by the American Assembly of Collegiate Schools of Business
(†) and a selection of programs from institutionally accredited schools.

ALABAMA

Alabama A & M University
  P.O. Box 429, Normal 35762
  Dr. Herman Mixon, Chrpsn.
  See listing under "Universities"

Alabama State University
  P.O. Box 271, Montgomery 36101

† Auburn University, Auburn 36849

† Auburn University at Montgomery
  7300 University Dr., Montgomery 36117
  H. H. Funderburk, VP

Birmingham Southern College
  900 Arkadelphia Rd., Birmingham 35254

Bishop State Community College
  351 N. Broad St., Mobile 36603-5898
  Yvonne Kennedy, President
  205-690-6801

Gadsden State Community College
  P.O. Box 227, Gadsden 35902
  W. Bryan Stone, Dir. of Admis.

Huntingdon College
  1500 E. Fairview Ave., Montgomery 36106-2148
  Carolyn A. Phillips, Dean of Enrollment
  800-763-0313

Livingston University
  Station #4, Livingston 35470
  See listing under "Universities"

Oakwood College
  Oakwood Rd., N.W., Huntsville 35896

Samford University
  800 Lakeshore Dr., Birmingham 35229
  Robert David, Dean

Spring Hill College
  4000 Dauphin St., Mobile 36608
  Ben Hamd, Dir. of Admis.

STILLMAN COLLEGE
  P.O. Box 1430, Tuscaloosa 35403
  Barbara K. Smith, Director of Admissions
  See listing under "Universities"

Talladega College
  627 Battle St., W., Talladega 35160

Troy State University, Troy 36082
  Dr. Wayne Curtis, Dean

Troy State University at Dothan
  P.O. Box 8368, Dothan 36304
  Bob Willis, Dir. of Undergraduate Admissions

Tuskegee University
  Tuskegee Institute 36088

† University of Alabama
  P.O. Box 870132, Tuscaloosa 35487-0132
  Roy Smith, Dir. of Admis.

† University of Alabama at Birmingham
  University Station, Birmingham 35294

UNIVERSITY OF ALABAMA IN HUNTSVILLE
  P.O. Box 1247, Huntsville 35899
  Ron R. Koger Ed.D., Dir. of Admis.
  205-895-6070
    Established 1969. Public. Coed. Accreditation:
  SACS, ABET, NLN, CSAB, ACS. Tuition: $2,418 resident, $4,836 non-resident. Room & Board: $3,450.
  Undergraduate enrollment: 2,674 full-time, 3,439
  part-time. Graduate enrollment: 1,860. Faculty: 282.
  Student-faculty ratio: 18:1. Degrees: BS, BA, BSBA,
  BSE, MS, MSM, Ph.D., BSN, MSN, MA. 20 buildings
  on 350 acres. Comprehensive research university located in the Tennessee Valley of northern Alabama.
  Huntsville is the locale of major government and
  private research centers. Metropolitan population approaching 300,000.

UNIVERSITY OF MOBILE
  P.O. Box 13220, Mobile 36663-0220
  Kim Leousis, Dir. of Admissions
  205-675-5990
  See listing under "Universities"

† University of Montevallo, Montevallo 35115

University of North Alabama
  University Station, Florence 35632

† University of South Alabama
  307 University Blvd. N., Mobile 36688

ALASKA

Alaska Junior College
  800 E. Dimond Blvd. # 3-350
  Anchorage 99515

Alaska Pacific University
  4101 University Dr., Anchorage 99508
  Director of Admissions
  See listing under "Universities"

Sheldon Jackson College
  801 Lincoln St., Sitka 99835
  Dennis Trotter, Dir. of Admis.
  907-747-5221

University of Alaska Anchorage
  3211 Providence Dr., Anchorage 99508
  907-786-1480

† University of Alaska Fairbanks
  Fairbanks 99775

University of Alaska Southeast
  11120 Glacier Hwy., Juneau 99801
  Greg Wagner, Coordinator of Admissions

UNIVERSITY OF ALASKA SOUTHEAST-KETCHIKAN
  2600 7th Ave., Ketchikan 99901-5798
  Dr. Frances Feinerman, Director
  William Trudeau, Student Services
    Established 1954. State. Coed. Accreditation:
  NASC. Yearly tuition: $1,670 resident, $5,500 non-resident. Est. total yrly. exp.: $8,000. Faculty: 10 full-time, 50 part-time. Degrees: AA, AAS in Business
  Office Administration, Travel Industry and Hospitality Industry. Certificates in Accounting, Business
  Tech, Office Skills, Travel Industry, Hospitality Industry and Welding. Library: 42,000 volumes. 4 buildings on 40 acres. UAS-Ketchikan is a member of the
  statewide University of Alaska system. Ketchikan is
  located on Revilla Island, on the beautiful inside
  passage of southeast Alaska.

ARIZONA

· Academy of Business College
3320 W. Cheryl Dr. #115, Phoenix 85051
See listing under "Community and Junior
Colleges"

: American Institute
3443 N. Central Ave. #1800, Phoenix 85012

: Arizona Institute of Business and Technology
6049 N. 43rd Ave., Phoenix 85019
Jeff Olson, Director

† Arizona State University, Tempe 85287

· Arizona Western College
P.O. Box 929, Yuma 85366-0929
Bob Davis, Dir. of Admis.

: Chaparral Career College
4585 E. Speedway Blvd. #204, Tucson 85712
A. Lauren Rhude, President

DeVry Institute of Technology
2149 W. Dunlap Ave., Phoenix 85021
Kim Galetti, Dir. of Admis.
602-870-9201
See Illinois listing under "Universities"

Embry-Riddle Aeronautical University
3200 Willow Creek Rd., Prescott 86301
800-442-ERAU

GRAND CANYON UNIVERSITY
3300 W. Camelback Rd., Phoenix 85017
Sherri Willborn, Dir. of Admis.
See listing under "Liberal Arts and Sciences"

· Lamson Junior College
2701 W. Bethany Home Rd., Phoenix 85017

· Lamson Junior College
1980 W. Main #250, Mesa 85201
Kirt Hamm, Dir. of Admis.

† Northern Arizona University
P.O. Box 4092, Flagstaff 86011
Dr. Margaret Cibik, Dir. of Admis.

: Tucson College of Business
7310 E. 22nd St., Tucson 85710
Daniel Waterman, Dir. of Admis.

† University of Arizona, Tucson 85721
Loyd Bell, Director of Admissions

University of Phoenix
4615 E. Elwood St., Phoenix 85040
Sue Murphy, Registrar

Western International University
10202 N. 19th Ave., Phoenix 85021

· Yavapai College
1100 E. Sheldon St., Prescott 86301
Dr. Doreen Dailey, President
602-445-7300
See listing under "Community and Junior
Colleges"

ARKANSAS

Arkansas College
2300 Highland Rd., Batesville 72501
Jonathan M. Stroud, Dean of Admissions
800-423-2542

† Arkansas State University
P.O. Box 59, State University 72467

Arkansas Tech University
215 W. O St., Russellville 72801

Henderson State University
1100 Henderson St., Arkadelphia 71999

John Brown University
2000 W. University, Siloam Springs 72761
Don Crandall, Director of Enrollment Management

Ouachita Baptist University
410 Ouachita St., Arkadelphia 71998
Randy Garner, Dir. of Admis.
800-DIAL-OBU

· Phillips County Community College
P.O. Box 785, Helena 72342
Dr. Steven Jones, President
James R. Brasel, Dean of Admissions

Southern Arkansas University
SAU Box 1402, Magnolia 71753

† University of Arkansas at Fayetteville
Fayetteville 72701

† University of Arkansas at Little Rock
2801 S. University Ave., Little Rock 72204

University of Arkansas at Monticello
P.O. Box 3596, Monticello 71656

University of Arkansas at Pine Bluff
1200 University Dr., Pine Bluff 71601-2799

† University of Central Arkansas
201 Donaghey Ave., Conway 72035

Williams Baptist College
P.O. Box 3667, Walnut Ridge 72476
Scott Wright, Dir. of Admis.

CALIFORNIA

: Academy Pacific Business & Travel College
1777 N. Vine St. #30, Hollywood 90028

AMERICAN COLLEGE FOR THE APPLIED ARTS
1651 Westwood Blvd., Los Angeles 90024
310-470-2000
See listing under "Universities"

ANTIOCH UNIVERSITY
801 Garden St. #101, Santa Barbara 93101
805-962-8179

Armstrong University
2222 Harold Way, Berkeley 94704
Rowena Ricafrentre, Dir. of Admis.
510-848-2500

Azusa Pacific University
P.O. Box 7000, Azusa 91702

· Bakersfield College
1801 Panorama Dr., Bakersfield 93305
Robert M. Bruker, Dir. of Admis.

Biola University
13800 Biola Ave., La Mirada 90639
Wayne Chute, Dean of Admissions

California Baptist College
8432 Magnolia Ave., Riverside 92504
800-782-3382

CALIFORNIA COAST UNIVERSITY
700 N. Main St., Santa Ana 92701
Admissions Office: 800-854-8768 or 714-547-9625
Thomas Neal, President
Linda B. Smith, VP Academic Affairs
William Barcroft, Dean of Admissions
Established 1973. Proprietary. Coed. Accreditation:
National Association of Private Non-Traditional
Schools & Colleges, California State Department of
Education, charter member California Association of
State Approved Colleges & Universities, member As-
sociation for Adult & Continuing Education. Tuition:
$2,200-$3,500. Enrollment: 7,500.
A private college offering off-campus independent
study programs in the traditional areas of business
administration, management, engineering, psychology, & education. Admissions: rolling trimester, requires official transcripts, letters of recommendation,
detailed curriculum vita or occupational history.
Process: evaluation of prior academic work followed by analysis of occupational history, including
participation in workshops, seminars, training programs, specialized projects for credit. Credit is demonstrated by challenge exams or specialized course
by course independent study programs.
Residency: All course work may be completed off
campus, utilizing correspondence methods. All doctoral candidates must meet with faculty advisors in
person, upon completion of doctoral dissertation.
Scholarships: Interest free loans available to students.

California Lutheran University
60 Olsen Rd., Thousand Oaks 91360
800-252-5884

† California Polytechnic State University
San Luis Obispo 93407
Helen Linstrum, Dir. of Admis.

† California State University, Chico
Chico 95929-0001
Dr. Arno Rethans, Dean

California State University, Dominguez Hills
1000 E. Victoria St., Carson 90747

† California State University, Fresno
Shaw & Cedar Ave., Fresno 93710

† California State University, Long Beach
1250 Bellflower Blvd., Long Beach 90840

† California State University, Los Angeles
5151 Paseo Rancho Castilla, Los Angeles 90032

† California State University, Northridge
18111 Nordhoff St., Northridge 91330
Ned C. Reynolds, Dir. of Admis.

† California State University, Sacramento
6000 J St., Sacramento 95819

California State University, San Bernardino
5500 University Pky., San Bernardino 92407
909-880-5188

† California State University-Bakersfield
9001 Stockdale Hwy., Bakersfield 93311
Dr. Homer S. Montalvo, Dir. of Admis.

† California State University-Fullerton
Fullerton 92632

† California State University-Hayward
25800 Carlos Bee Blvd., Hayward 94542

California State University-Stanislaus
801 W. Monte Vista Ave., Turlock 95382
Frances Cook, Dean Enrollment Services

Chapman University
333 N. Glassell St., Orange 92666
Michael Drummy, Dir. of Admis.

Christian Heritage College
2100 Greenfield Dr., El Cajon 92019
Pam Daly, Dir. of Admis.
800-676-2242

· City College of San Francisco
50 Phelan Ave. C105, San Francisco 94112
Lavaine Koffman, Dept. Chair
415-239-3203

College of Notre Dame
1500 Ralston Ave., Belmont 94002
Greg M. Smith, PhD., Dir. of Admis.

: Computer Learning Center
222 S. Harbor Blvd., Anaheim 92805

: Computer Learning Center
3130 Wilshire Blvd., Los Angeles 90010
Stephen Woody, Director

Concordia University
1530 Concordia, Irvine 92715
Stan Meyer, Dean of Admission
800-229-1200
See listing under "Universities"

DeVry Institute of Technology
901 Corporate Center Dr., Pomona 91746
Keith Paridy, Dir. of Admis.
909-622-9800
See Illinois listing under "Universities"

DOMINICAN COLLEGE OF SAN RAFAEL
50 Acacia Ave., San Rafael 94901-8008
Office of Admissions
800-788-3522

: EMPIRE COLLEGE
SCHOOL OF BUSINESS & LAW
3033 Cleveland Ave. # 107, Santa Rosa 95403
707-546-4000
Established 1961. Private. Coed. Accreditation:
ACICS/Committee of Bar Examiners. Tuition: $3,720
- $7,290. Fees: $75 - $95. Enrollment: 700 full-time,
25 part-time. Faculty: 50. Student-faculty ratio: 21:1.
Specialized Associate degree offered in Accounting
and Administrative Assistant; Juris Doctor. 1 21,000
sq. ft. building. Positive, supportive environment for
students in the business school with start dates every
six weeks; evening law classes taught by practicing
attorneys.

Fielding Institute
2112 Santa Barbara St., Santa Barbara 93105
Sylvia Williams, Dir. of Admis.

Fresno Pacific College
1717 S. Chestnut Ave., Fresno 93702
209-453-2039

· Heald Business College
684 El Paseo De Saratoga, San Jose 95130
Carol Hunter, Director

· Heald Business College
777 Southland Dr. #210, Hayward 94545
Shelli Spangler, Director

· Heald College
1000 Broadway, Oakland 94607
Marie-Louise Coppinger, Director

· Heald 4 C's College
255 W. Bullard, Fresno 93704
209-438-4222

Holy Names College
3500 Mountain Blvd., Oakland 94619

Humboldt State University
1 Harps St., Arcata 95521

: Irvine College of Business
16591 Noyes Ave., Irvine 92714
W. D. Polick, Director

KELSEY-JENNEY COLLEGE
Two locations
201 A St., San Diego 92101
7084 Miramar Rd., San Diego 92121
Robert Evans, President

La Sierra University
4700 Pierce St., Riverside 92505
800-874-5587

LINCOLN UNIVERSITY
281 Masonic Ave., San Francisco 94118
Clarence Rippel, Acting President
Accredited Member ACICS

† Loyola Marymount University
Loyola Blvd. at W. 80th, Los Angeles 90045
M. L'Heureux, Dir. of Admis.

Master's College
P.O. Box 221450, Newhall 91322
Don Gilmore, Dir. of Admis.

Menlo College
1000 El Camino Real, Atherton 94027
David Butler, Dean

Monterey Institute of International Studies
425 Van Buren St., Monterey 93940

Mt. St. Mary's College
12001 Chalon Rd., Los Angeles 90049

: MTI-Western Business College
5221 Madison Ave., Sacramento 95841
John Zimmerman, President

· Napa Valley College
2277 Napa-Vallejo Hwy., Napa 94558
Delores Smith, Asst. Dean of Admissions
707-253-3000

National University
4141 Camino del Rio, S., San Diego 92108

ORANGE COAST COLLEGE
P.O. Box 5005, Costa Mesa 92628
See listing under "Community and Junior Colleges"

Pacific Christian College
2500 E. Nutwood Ave., Fullerton 92631
Knofel Staton, President

Pacific Union College
1 Angwin Ave., Angwin 94508
Dr. Gary Gifford, Dir. of Admis.

Pepperdine University
24255 Pacific Coast Hwy., Malibu 90263
Paul Long, Dean of Admissions
310-456-4392

: Phillips College
4300 Central Ave., Riverside 92506
Judi Murakami, Director of Education

Point Loma Nazarene College
3900 Lomaland Dr., San Diego 92106
Bill Young, Dir. of Admis.

· Porterville College
100 E. College Ave., Porterville 93257
John McCuen, President

· Rancho Santiago College
1530 W. 17th St., Santa Ana 92706

† San Diego State University
5300 Campanile Dr., San Diego 92115

† San Francisco State University
1600 Holloway Ave., San Francisco 94132
Corwin Bjonerud, Dir. of Admis.

San Joaquin Valley College
8400 W. Mineral King Ave., Visalia 93291
Robert Perry, President

† San Jose State University
1 Washington Sq., San Jose 95192

· Santa Barbara City College
721 Cliff Dr., Santa Barbara 93109
805-965-0581

† Santa Clara University, Santa Clara 95053

: Sawyer College
2101 E. Gonzales Rd., Oxnard 93030
Roger Ferguson, Dir. of Education

Sonoma State University
1801 E. Cotati Ave., Rohnert Park 94928

Southern California College
55 Fair Dr., Costa Mesa 92626
Richard Hardy, Asst. Dean for Enrollment

† Stanford University, Stanford 94305

UNITED STATES INTERNATIONAL UNIVERSITY
10455 Pomerado Rd., San Diego 92131
619-693-4772
See listing under "Universities"

† University of California, Los Angeles
1247 Murphy Hall, Los Angeles 90024

† University of California at Berkeley
Barrows Hall, Berkeley 94720

† University of California, Irvine
Irvine 92715

University of California, Riverside
P.O. Box 112, Riverside 92521

University of California-Santa Cruz
Santa Cruz 95064
Joseph Allen, Dir. of Admis.

UNIVERSITY OF JUDAISM/LEE COLLEGE
15600 Mulholland Dr., Los Angeles 90077
Tamara Greenebaum, Dean of Admissions
See listing under "Universities"

University of La Verne
1950 3rd St., La Verne 91750
Mark Bornholdt, Dir. of Admis.

University of Redlands
P.O. Box 3080, Redlands 92373

† University of San Diego
5998 Alcala Park, San Diego 92110
Warren Muller, Dir. of Admis.
619-260-4506

† University of San Francisco
2130 Fulton St., San Francisco 94117
Bill Henley, Dir. of Admis.

† University of Southern California
University Park Campus
Los Angeles 90089

† University of the Pacific
3601 Pacific Ave, Stockton 95211
Elliott J. Taylor, Dean of Admissions

· Valley Commercial College
910 12th St., Modesto 95354
Greg Martin, President

West Coast University
440 Shatto Pl., Los Angeles 90020

Whittier College
13406 Philadelphia St., Whittier 90601
310-907-4238

Woodbury University
7500 Glenoaks Blvd., Burbank 91504
See listing under "Universities"

COLORADO

Adams State College, Alamosa 81102
Cheryl Billingsley, Dir. of Admis.
800-824-6494

Colorado Christian University
180 S. Garrison St., Lakewood 80226
Debra Seefeldt, Dir. of Admis.

· Colorado Northwestern Community College
500 Kennedy Dr., Rangely 81648
Pat Kalahar, Dir. Marketing/Recruitment
800-562-1105

† Colorado State University
102 Administration Building, Fort Collins 80523
Mary Ontireros, Dir. of Admissions

COLORADO TECHNICAL COLLEGE
4435 N. Chestnut St., Colorado Springs 80907
719-598-0200

The transition from high-tech education to high-tech careers is Colorado Tech's specialty! Situated in the middle of a space age community known as Silicon Mountain, the college takes pride in its mission to serve high-tech businesses and industries by providing graduates able to hit the ground running in such fields as: computer engineering, computer science, electrical engineering, electronic engineering technology, telecommunications, systems management, and logistics. Colorado Tech, accredited by NCA and ABET, offers Associate, Bachelor and Master degrees.

Bachelor of Science degrees are offered in computer science, electrical engineering, computer engineering, logistics systems management, systems management, and telecommunication electronics technology. Master of Science degrees are offered in computer science, computer engineering, electrical engineering and management. The Master of Science in management has concentrations in systems management and logistics systems management.

Colorado Tech believes students should not only learn in the classroom, but in the laboratory as well, applying their knowledge to real world problems. The professor and students work in an environment that encourages constant interaction in the learning process. Class size is limited to 40 students and labs are limited to 24 students. Colorado Tech's state of the art equipment is always available: no one waits in line.

It is no suprise that companies such as Digital, Loral, MCI, Apple, Atmel, Litton, United Technologies, Hewlett-Packard, Ford Microelectronics, GE Aerospace, Hughes Aircraft and Cray Research have chosen Colorado Springs with its USAF space center and US Space Foundation to locate facilities here. Many of these companies have representatives who sit on our advisory boards and many of our professors come from these companies.

The Colorado Springs area offers many recreational activities such as skiing, fishing, hunting, hiking, mountain climbing and four wheeling. NFL football, NBA basketball, National League baseball, the symphony and varied expressions of popular culture provide ample entertainment for every taste. Soar to meet your destiny through higher education at Colorado Tech.

· Denver Technical College
225 S. Union Blvd., Colorado Springs 80910
Oscar Adams, Dir. of Admis.

· Denver Technical College
925 S. Niagara St., Denver 80224
Oscar Adams, Dir. of Admis.

† Ft. Lewis College
1000 Rim Dr., Durango 81301

· Front Range Community College
3645 W. 112th Ave., Westminister 80030
Dr. Patricia Lammers, Dir. of Admis.

Mesa State College
P.O. Box 2647, Grand Junction 81502
Sherri Pe'a, Dir. of Admis.

· Metropolitan State College of Denver
P.O. Box 173362, Campus Box 16
Denver 80217-3362

· Morgan Community College
17800 Road 20, Fort Morgan 80701
Kurtis Armstrong, Dir. of Admis.

· Pikes Peak Community College
5675 S. Academy Blvd.
Colorado Springs 80906-5498
Roberta Erickson, Dir. of Admis.
See listing under "Community and Junior Colleges"

Regis University
3333 Regis Blvd., Denver 80221
Robert Blust, Director of Admissions

† University of Colorado at Boulder
Boulder 80309
William A. Douglas, Dean of Admis.

† University of Colorado at Colorado Springs
P.O. Box 7150, Colorado Springs 80933

† University of Colorado at Denver
1200 Larimer, Denver 80204

† University of Denver
2199 S. University Blvd., Denver 80210

University of Northern Colorado, Greeley 80639
William Duff, Jr., Dean of Business Administration
303-351-2764

University of Southern Colorado
2200 Bonforte Blvd., Pueblo 81001

Western State College of Colorado
Gunnison 81231
Monica Bruning, Dir. of Admis.
See listing under "Universities"

CONNECTICUT

Albertus Magnus College
700 Prospect St., New Haven 06511
Richard Lolatte, Dir. of Admissions
203-773-8501 or 800-578-9160

Eastern Connecticut State University
83 Windham St., Willimantic 06226
Dr. John St. Unge, Chrpsn.

Fairfield University
25 N. Benson Rd., Fairfield 06430

· Greater New Haven State Technical College
88 Bassett Rd., North Haven 06473
Chester Schnepf, Dir. of Admis.

: Huntington Institute
193 Broadway, Norwich 06360
Thomas J. Haggerty, Director

· Katharine Gibbs School
142 East Ave., Norwalk 06851
Henry Mondschein, Dir. of Admis.

· Mattatuck Community College
750 Chase Parkway, Waterbury 06708
Dr. Richard Sanders, President

QUINNIPIAC COLLEGE
275 Mount Carmel Ave., Hamden 06518
John Lahey, President
Joan Isaac Mohr, VP and Dean of Admissions
Established 1929. Private. Coed. Accreditation: NEASC. Tuition: $11,250. Room and board: $5,790. Enrollment: 2,583 boarding, 3,444 day. Faculty 333. Degrees: BA, BS, MAT, MBA, MHS, MPS. Library: 290,000 volumes. 30 buildings on 170 acres. Gym. Suburban location at the base of Sleeping Giant State Park, close to New Haven and Yale University. Convenient to New York City, Boston, and Upper New England. Building a new $7 million School of Business Center.

St. Joseph College
1678 Asylum Ave., West Hartford 06117
Mary C. Demo, Dir. of Admis.

TEIKYO POST UNIVERSITY
800 Country Club Rd.
P.O. Box 2540, Waterbury 06723-2540
800-345-2562 or 203-596-4520
Established 1890. Private. Coed. Accreditation: NEASC. Tuition: $11,960. Room and board: $5,400. Application fee: $40. Enrollment: 996 full-time, 1,488 part-time. Faculty: 29 full-time, 260 part-time. Student-faculty ratio: 15:1. Degrees: AA, AS, BA, BS. Library: 55,000 volumes. 11 buildings on 70 acres. Excellent business majors with strong liberal arts and international component. Faculty with dynamic business experience, assistance to help students succeed in a global marketplace. ESL Institute.

† University of Bridgeport
126 Park Ave., Bridgeport 06601
Andrew G. Nelson, Dean Admis./Financial Aid
203-576-4552
See listing under "Universities"

† University of Connecticut, Storrs 06268
Ronald J. Patten, Dean

UNIVERSITY OF HARTFORD
200 Bloomfield Ave., West Hartford 06117
Richard Zeiser, Dir. of Admis.
See listing under "Universities"

University of New Haven
300 Orange Ave., West Haven 06516
M. L. McLaughlin, Dean
203-932-7000

† Yale University
135 Prospect St., New Haven 06520

DELAWARE

Goldey Beacom College
4701 Limestone Rd., Wilmington 19808
Sherry Humphrey, Dean of Admissions

† University of Delaware, Newark 19711

Wilmington College
320 N. DuPont Hwy., New Castle 19720

DISTRICT OF COLUMBIA

† The American University
4400 Massachusetts Ave. N.W.
Washington 20016

Gallaudet University
800 Florida Ave., N.E., Washington 20002
See listing under "Universities"

† Georgetown University
37th and O Sts., N.W., Washington 20057
Dr. Joseph A. Chalmers, Dean of Admis. & Rec.

† George Washington University
Washington 20052

† Howard University
2400 6th St., N.W., Washington 20059
James E. Cheek, President

Southeastern University
501 I St., S.W., Washington 20024

: Strayer College
6630 Laurel St. N.W., Washington 20012
Ron K. Bailey, President

Trinity College
125 Michigan Ave., N.E., Washington 20017
Donna Quinn, Dir. of Admis.

University of the District of Columbia
Georgia Ave.-Harvard St. Campus
1100 Harvard St., N.W., Washington 20009

University of the District of Columbia
Van Ness Campus
4200 Connecticut Ave., N.W., Washington 20008

FLORIDA

Barry University
11300 N.E. 2nd Ave., Miami Shores 33161
Robin Ray Roberts, Dean of Admissions

Bethune-Cookman College
640 Mary McLeod Bethune Blvd.
Daytona Beach 32114

: Boyd Career School
2090 Palm Beach Lakes Blvd.
West Palm Beach 33409
See listing this classification in Pennsylvania

Clearwater Christian College
3400 Gulf-to-Bay Blvd., Clearwater 34619
Benjamin Puckett, Dir. of Admis.

Eckerd College
P.O. Box 12560, St. Petersburg 33733
Richard Hallin, Dir. of Admis.

· Edison Community College
8099 College Pky., Fort Myers 33919
Mailing address: P.O. Box 60210
Fort Myers 33906-6210
Sandra Fahey, Dir. of Admis. and Records

Embry-Riddle Aeronautical University
600 S. Clyde Morris Blvd.
Daytona Beach 32114-3900
800-222-ERAU

Flagler College
P.O. Box 1027, St. Augustine 32085
Marc G. Williar, Dir. of Admis.
904-829-6481

Florida A & M University, Tallahassee 32307

† Florida Atlantic University
500 N.W. 20th St., Boca Raton 33431
Brian Levin-Stankevich, Dir. of Admis.

Florida Institute of Technology
150 W. University Blvd., Melbourne 32901
Louis T. Levy, Dean of Admissions
800-888-4348

† Florida International University
Tamiami Trail, Miami 33199

Florida Southern College
111 Lake Hollingsworth Dr., Lakeland 33801
William Stephens, Jr., Dir. of Admis.

† Florida State University
600 W. College Ave., Tallahassee 32306

Fort Lauderdale College
1040 Bayview Dr., Ft. Lauderdale 33304
William P. Bedard, Director

· Gulf Coast Community College
5230 Hwy. 98, W., Panama City 32401
Roy Smith, Dir. of Admis. and Records

International Academy of Merchandising and Design
211 S. Hoover Blvd., Tampa 33609
Mike Santoro, President
813-286-8585

Jacksonville University
2800 University Blvd., N., Jacksonville 32211

Jones College
5353 Arlington Expy., Jacksonville 32211
Dorothy D. Jones, Chief Executive Officer

Jones College
5975 Sunset Dr. #100, South Miami 33143

LYNN UNIVERSITY
(Est. 1962 as College of Boca Raton)
3601 N. Military Trail, Boca Raton 33431
407-994-0770 or 800-544-8035
See listing under "Universities"

· National Education Center-Bauder Campus
4801 N. Dixie Hwy., Ft. Lauderdale 33334
Brian Woods, Dir. of Admis.
305-491-7171

Northwood University
2600 N. Military Trail, West Palm Beach 33409
Brad Sargent, Dir. of Admis.
800-458-8325

Nova Southeastern University
3301 College Ave., Ft. Lauderdale 33314

Orlando College - North
5500 Diplomat Circle, Orlando 32810

Palm Beach Atlantic College
P.O. Box 24708, West Palm Beach 33416-4708
See listing under "Universities"

· Phoenix College of Aeronautics
P.O. Box 11706, Daytona Beach 32120
T. Voyt, Registrar
See listing under "Community and Junior
Colleges"

† Rollins College
P.O. Box 2720, Winter Park 32790

St. Leo College
P.O. Box 2008, St. Leo 33574
Bonnie Black, Dir. of Admis.

St. Thomas University
16400 N.W. 32nd Ave., Miami 33054
John M. Letvinchuk, Dir. of Admis.

SCHILLER INTERNATIONAL UNIVERSITY (FLORIDA & EUROPE)
U.S. Admissions Office
Dept. PA, 453 Edgewater Dr., Dunedin 34698-7532
800-336-4133 Fax: 813-736-6263
Dr. Walter Liebrecht, President
Karen Altieri, Associate Director of Admissions
See listing under "Universities"

Stetson University
401 N. Woodland Blvd., De Land 32720
Dr. James Wright, Dean

Tampa College
3319 W. Hillsborough Ave., Tampa 33614
David Zorn, President

Tampa College - Pinellas
15064 U.S. Hwy. 19 N., Clearwater 34624
Mark A. Page, President
813-530-9495

† University of Central Florida
P.O. Box 25000, Orlando 32816

† University of Florida
226 Tigert Hall, Gainesville 32611

† University of Miami
P.O. Box 248006, Coral Gables 33124

† University of North Florida
4567 St. Johns Bluff Rd. S., Jacksonville 32224

UNIVERSITY OF SARASOTA
5250 17th St., Sarasota 34235
Linda Volz, Dir. of Enrollment Management
800-331-5995
Established 1969. Coed. Accreditation: SACS. Tuition: $235 per credit hour. Enrollment: 470. Faculty: 30. Degrees: MAEd, MBA, EdD. Year round, non-traditional calender, flexible, small seminars, much individual attention to students, performance oriented.

† University of South Florida
4202 Fowler Ave., Tampa 33620

University of West Florida
11000 University Pky., Pensacola 32514

Warner Southern College
5301 U.S. Hwy. 27, S., Lake Wales 33853
Valerie S. Rutland, Dir. Enrollment Mgmt.
800-949-7248

Webber College
P.O. Box 96, Babson Park 33827
Steve G. Wilson, Dir. of Admis.

GEORGIA

Albany State College
504 College Dr., Albany 31705

AMERICAN COLLEGE FOR THE APPLIED ARTS
3330 Peachtree Rd., N.E., Atlanta 30326
404-231-9000
See listing under "Universities".

: Asher School of Business
100 Pinnacle Way #110, Norcross 30071
Joe Voyles, President

AUGUSTA COLLEGE
2500 Walton Way, Augusta 30904-2200
Lee Young, Dir. of Admis.
706-737-1405

BREWTON-PARKER COLLEGE
P.O. Box 197, Mount Vernon 30445
Dr. Y. Lynn Holmes, President
912-583-2241

: Brown College of Court Reporting & Business
1100 Spring St. #200, Atlanta 30309
Fred Rich, President

† Clark Atlanta University
240 James Brawley Dr., S.W., Atlanta 30314
Thomas W. Cole, President

DeVry Institute of Technology
250 N. Arcadia Ave., Decatur 30030
George Ollennu, Dir. of Admis.
404-292-2645
See Illinois listing under "Universities"

† Emory University
1462 Clifton Rd., Atlanta 30322

· Gainesville College
P.O. Box 1358, Gainesville 30503
Carol S. Nobles, Dir. of Admis.
404-535-6241

Georgia College
231 W. Hancock St., Milledgeville 31061
912-453-5004

† Georgia Institute of Technology
225 North Ave. N.W., Atlanta 30332

† Georgia Southern University, Statesboro 30460

† Georgia State University
University Plaza, Atlanta 30303
Ernest Beals, Dean of Admissions

Kennesaw State College
P.O. Box 444, Marietta 30061
Joe Head, Dir. of Admis.

: Kerr Business College
P.O. Box 1986, Augusta 30903
Darryl Kerr, President

: Kerr Business College
P.O. Box 976, La Grange 30241
Douglas Davies, Director

La Grange College
601 Broad St., La Grange 30240
Phil Dodson, Dir. of Admis.
706-882-2911

Mercer University in Atlanta
3001 Mercer University Dr., Atlanta 30341

Mercer University
1400 Coleman Ave., Macon 31207

Morehouse College
830 Westview Dr., S.W., Atlanta 30310
Gary Bussey, Dir. of Admissions

Morris Brown College
643 Martin Luther King Jr. Dr. N.W.
Atlanta 30314

Oglethorpe University
4484 Peachtree Rd., N.E., Atlanta 30319
Dennis Matthews, Dir. of Admis.

Paine College
1235 15th St., Augusta 30901
Phyllis Wyatt-Woodruff, Dir. Enrollment Mgmt.

· Phillips Junior College
1400 W. Peachtree St., N.W., Atlanta 30309

Piedmont College
P.O. Box 10, Demorest 30535
Penny L. Graber, Dir of Admis.
800-277-7020

Savannah State College
State College Branch, Savannah 31404
Robert Ray, Dir. of Admis.

Shorter College
315 Shorter Ave., Rome 30165

† University of Georgia, Athens 30602
Dr. Albert Niemi, Dean

† Valdosta State College
Patterson St., Valdosta 31698

Wesleyan College
4760 Forsyth Rd., Macon 31297

† West Georgia College, Carrollton 30118
C. Doyle Bickers, Dir. of Admis.

HAWAII

Brigham Young University, Hawaii Campus
55-220 Kulanui St., Laie 96762
Clark E. Hirschi, Coordinator of Admis.

Chaminade University of Honolulu
3140 Waialae Ave., Honolulu 96816
Charles Schafer, VP Enrollment Services

: Hawaii Business College
111 N. King St., Honolulu 96817
Mitsuru Omori, Director

Hawaii Pacific University
1166 Fort Street Mall, Honolulu 96813
Don Barlow, Dir. of Admis.

Hawaii Pacific University
45-045 Kamehameha Hwy., Kaneohe 96744

· Heald Business College
1500 Kapiolani Blvd. #202, Honolulu 96814
Evelyn Schemmel, President
808-955-1500 Fax: 808-955-6964

Japan-America Institute of Management Science
6660 Hawaii Kai Dr., Honolulu 96825
Roxanne Kam, Academic Services Coordinator
808-395-2314

† University of Hawaii at Manoa
2500 Campus Rd., Honolulu 96822

IDAHO

† Boise State University
1910 University Dr., Boise 83725

† Idaho State University
P.O. Box 8270, Pocatello 83209

Lewis Clark State College
500 8th Ave., Lewiston 83501
800-933-5272 or 208-799-5272

· Ricks College, Rexburg 83460
Steven Bennion, President

University of Idaho, Moscow 83843
Peter Brown, Dir. of Admis.

ILLINOIS

Augustana College
639 38th St., Rock Island 61201
Martin R. Sauer, Director of Admission
800-798-8100

Aurora University
347 S. Gladstone Ave., Aurora 60506
Peter Pitts, Dir. of Admis.

Barat College, Lake Forest 60045
Loretta Brickman, Dir. of Admis.

Blackburn College
700 College Ave., Carlinville 62626
Dwight Smith, Dir. of Admis.

† Bradley University
1501 W. Bradley Ave., Peoria 61625

· Chicago College of Commerce
11 E. Adams St., Chicago 60603
Mae Glassbrenner, Chrpsn.

: Commonwealth Business College
1527 47th Ave., Moline 61265
Don Watson, Director
309-762-2100

† De Paul University
1 E. Jackson Blvd., Chicago 60604
Thomas D. Abrahamson, Dean of Admissions
See listing under "Universities"

DeVry Institute of Technology
3300 N. Campbell Ave., Chicago 60618
Richard Yaconis, Dir. of Admis.
312-929-6550
See Illinois listing under "Universities"

DeVry Institute of Technology
1221 N. Swift Rd., Addison 60101
Milt Kobus, Dir. of Admis.
708-953-2000
See Illinois listing under "Universities"

Eastern Illinois University, Charleston 61920
Theodore Ivarie, Dean
See listing under "Universities"

Elmhurst College
190 Prospect Ave., Elmhurst 60126

Eureka College
300 E. College Ave., Eureka 61530

FOX COLLEGE OF EXECUTIVE/LEGAL ASSISTANTS
4201 W. 93rd St., Oak Lawn 60453
Edward L. Kay, Director
See listing under "Career Schools"

Gem City College
700 State St., Quincy 62301
R. Hagenah, President

Governors State University
1 University Pky., University Park 60466
Richard Pride, Dir. of Admis.

Greenville College
315 E. College Ave., Greenville 62246
Kent Krober, Dir. of Admis.

Illinois Benedictine College
5700 College Rd., Lisle 60532

Illinois College
1101 W. College Ave., Jacksonville 62650
Gale Vaugn, Dir. of Admis.

Illinois Institute of Technology
3300 S. Federal St., Chicago 60616
Wendell R. Webb, Dir. of Admissions

† Illinois State University
212 N. School St., Normal 61761

ILLINOIS WESLEYAN UNIVERSITY
P.O. Box 2900, Bloomington 61702
Dr. Mona Gardner, Director
309-556-3171

International Academy of Merchandising & Design
1 N. State St. Suite 400, Chicago 60602
Cynthia A. Reynolds, President
312-828-0422

Judson College
1151 N. State St., Elgin 60123
Jack Powell, Dir. of Enrollment Services

KASKASKIA COLLEGE
27210 College Rd., Centralia 62801
618-532-1981 or 800-642-0859 (Illinois)
Raymond D. Woods, President
Marilyn Brookman, PhD, College Dean
Constance Stohlman, Director of Admissions,
Public Relations, and Resource Development
   Kaskaskia College is situated on a beautifully wooded tract of land consisting of 190 acres. Its brick and frame buildings provide 228,800 square feet of space for college facilities. Kaskaskia College is fully accredited by NCACS, ADA, AMA, NLN, IBE, ICCB, and IBHE. The College is recognized and approved by the bureau of Veterans Affairs and is authorized under Federal law to enroll non-immigrant alien students. In district tuition and fees are $33.75 per semester credit hour. Degrees: AA, AS, AAS, and AGS. University transfer programs, pre-professional, liberal arts, courses offered days, evenings, and weekends. Training in career fields. State and Federal financial aid programs available.

Keller Graduate School of Management
10 S. Riverside Plaza, Chicago 60606
Ronald L. Taylor, Dean

Kendall College
2408 Orrington Ave., Evanston 60201
Peter Pauletti, Dir. of Admis.

Lake Forest Graduate School of Management
Sheridan & Maplewood Rds., Lake Forest 60045
Carolyn Brune, Dir. of Admis.
708-234-5080

Lake Forest Graduate School of Management
1295 E. Algonquin Rd., Schaumburg 60196
Shawna Lanning, Dir. of Admis.
708-576-1212 Extension 24

Lake Forest Graduate School of Management
230 S. La Salle St., Chicago 60604
Meena Ariagno, Dir. of Admis.
312-435-5330

LEWIS UNIVERSITY
Rt. 53, Romeoville 60441
Irish O'Reilly, Director of Admissions
See listing under "Universities"

Loyola University-Mallinckrodt Campus
1041 Ridge Rd., Wilmette 60091
Karen Sullivan, Admissions

† Loyola University of Chicago
820 N. Michigan Ave., Chicago 60611
Allen V. Lentino, Dir. of Admis.

Loyola University - Mundelein College
6363 N. Sheridan Rd., Chicago 60660
Judith Bobber, Dir. of Admis.

MacMurray College
447 E. College Ave., Jacksonville 62650
Edwin R. Hockett, Dean of Admissions

: Marycrest College
280 E. Merchant St., Kankakee 60901
Michael Steinbach, Director

Midstate College
244 S.W. Jefferson St., Peoria 61602
R. Dale Bunch, President
309-673-6365

MILLIKIN UNIVERSITY
1184 W. Main St., Decatur 62522
Lin Stoner, Dean of Admissions
800-373-7733

Monmouth College
700 E. Broadway, Monmouth 61462

Montay College
3750 W. Peterson Ave., Chicago 60659
Scott Dalhouse, Dir. of Admis.

Moraine Valley Community College
10900 S. 88th Ave., Palos Hills 60465
Dr. Vernon Crawley, President

North Central College
30 N. Brainard St.
P.O. Box 3065, Naperville 60566-7065
Marguerite Waters, Director of Admission
708-420-3414

Northeastern Illinois University
5500 N. St. Louis Ave., Chicago 60625

† Northern Illinois University, De Kalb 60115

† Northwestern University
2001 Sheridan Rd., Evanston 60208

Olivet Nazarene University, Kankakee 60901
John Mongerson, Dir. of Admis.
815-939-5203

· Parkland College
2400 W. Bradley Ave., Champaign 61821-1899
217-351-2208 or 800-346-8089

Parks College of St. Louis University
500 Falling Springs Rd., Cahokia 62206
John Wilbur, Dir. of Admis.

Principia College, Elsah 62028

Quincy College
1800 College Ave., Quincy 62301
Fr. Michael Lanning, O.F.M., Dir. of Admis.

ROCKFORD BUSINESS COLLEGE
730 N. Church St., Rockford 61103
David Swank, President
Susan Swank, VP
815-965-8616

Rockford College
5050 E. State St., Rockford 61108
Miriam King, V.P. for Enrollment Management
See listing under "Universities"

ROOSEVELT UNIVERSITY
430 S. Michigan Ave., Chicago 60605
William Smyser, Director of Admissions
See listing under "Universities"

Rosary College
7900 W. Division St., River Forest 60305
Hildegarde Schmidt, Dir. of Admis.

St. Xavier College
3700 W. 103rd St., Chicago 60655
Mary Hendry, Dean of Admissions

Sangamon State University
Shepherd Rd., Springfield 62794-9243
Admissions and Records, 217-786-6626

† Southern Illinois University at Carbondale
Carbondale 62901

† Southern Illinois University at Edwardsville
Edwardsville 62026
Eugene J. Magac, Dir. of Admissions & Records

· Springfield College in Illinois
1500 N. Fifth St., Springfield 62702
Dr. H. Brent DeLand, President

Trinity Christian College
6601 W. College Dr., Palos Heights 60463
Kenneth Bootsma, President

Trinity College
2077 Half Day Rd., Deerfield 60015
Dr. Kenneth Meyer, Pres.

† University of Chicago
5801 S. Ellis Ave., Chicago 60637

† University of Illinois
506 S. Wright St., Urbana 61801

† University of Illinois at Chicago
P.O. Box 4348, Chicago 60680
Dr. Marcus Alexis, Dean

† Western Illinois University
900 W. Adams St., Macomb 61455
Alan DeRoos, Registrar
309-298-1891

INDIANA

† Ball State University
2000 W. University Ave., Muncie 47306
Ruth Vedvik, Dir. of Admis.

Bethel College
1001 W. McKinley Ave., Mishawaka 46545
Steve Matteson, Dir. of Admis.

Butler University
4600 Sunset Ave., Indianapolis 46208

Calumet College
2400 New York Ave., Whiting 46394
Sharon Sweeney, Dir. of Admis.

: Commonwealth Business College
8995 N. State Rd. 39, La Porte 46350
Faye Mercer, Director
219-362-3338

: Commonwealth Business College
4200 W. Lincoln Hwy., Merrillville 46410
Al Conaway, Director
219-769-3321

DePauw University
313 S. Locust St., Greencastle 46135
Dr. Eleanor Ypma, Registrar

Franklin College
501 E. Monroe, Franklin 46131
B. Stephen Richards, VP Enrollment

Goshen College
1700 S. Main St., Goshen 46526
Del Good, Chairperson

Grace College
200 Seminary Dr., Winona Lake 46590
Ron Henry, Dir. of Admis.

Huntington College
2303 College Ave., Huntington 46750
Paul Breininger, Dir. of Admis. Services

Indiana Institute of Technology
1600 E. Washington Blvd., Fort Wayne 46803

† Indiana State University
217 N. 6th St., Terre Haute 47809

† Indiana University at Bloomington
300 N. Jordan Ave., Bloomington 47406

Indiana University at Kokomo
P.O. Box 9003, Kokomo 46904

† Indiana University at South Bend
P.O. Box 7111, South Bend 46634

† Indiana University Northwest
3400 N. Broadway, Gary 46408

† Indiana University Southeast
4201 Grantline Rd., New Albany 47150

† Indiana University-Purdue University at Fort Wayne
2101 Coliseum Blvd. E., Fort Wayne 46805

Indiana University-Purdue University
355 N. Lansing, Indianapolis 46202

· Indiana Vocational Technical College (IVY)
P.O. Box 1763, Indianapolis 46206

Indiana Wesleyan University
4201 S. Washington St., Marion 46953
800-332-6901

· ITT Technical Institute
9511 Angola Ct., Indianapolis 46268

· Ivy Tech Central
1 W. 26th St., Indianapolis 46208
Meredith Carter, V.P., Dean

· Ivy Tech Columbus
4475 Central Ave., Columbus 47203
Homer Smith, V.P., Dean

· Ivy Tech East Central
P.O. Box 3100, Muncie 47307
Richard L. Davidson, V.P., Dean

· Ivy Tech Kokomo
1815 E. Morgan St., Kokomo 46901
Charles Hefley, V.P., Dean

· Ivy Tech Lafayette
P.O. Box 6299, Lafayette 47903
Thomas Reckerd, V.P., Dean

· Ivy Tech Northcentral
1534 W. Sample St., South Bend 46619
Carl Lutz, V.P., Dean

· Ivy Tech Northeast
3800 N. Anthony Blvd., Fort Wayne 46805
Jon Rupright, V.P., Dean

· Ivy Tech Northwest
1440 E. 35th Ave., Gary 46409
Mearle Donica, Dean

· Ivy Tech SouthCentral
8204 W. Hwy. 31, Sellersburg 47172
Jonothan Thomas, V.P., Dean

· Ivy Tech Southeast
Highway 62 & Ivy Tech Drive, Madison 47250
Gregory Flood, V.P., Dean

· Ivy Tech Southwest
3501 1st Ave., Evansville 47710
H. Victor Baldi, V.P., Dean

· Ivy Tech Wabash Valley
7377 S. Dixie Bee Rd., Terre Haute 47802
Samuel Borden, V.P., Dean

Ivy Tech Whitewater
2325 Chester Blvd., Richmond 47374
Judith Redwine, V.P., Dean

Manchester College
604 College Ave., North Manchester 46962
Dr. Richard Harshbarger, Chrpsn.

Marian College
3200 Cold Spring Rd., Indianapolis 46222
Don French, Dir. of Admis.

Martin University
P.O. Box 18567, Indianapolis 46218

Oakland City College
143 N. Lucretia St., Oakland City 47660
Tracy Siekman, Dir. of Admis.

† Purdue University
Schleman Hall, West Lafayette 47907

Purdue University, Calumet Campus
2233 171st St., Hammond 46323

Purdue University
1401 S. U.S. Hwy. 421, Westville 46391

ST. JOSEPH'S COLLEGE
P.O. Box 890, Rensselaer 47978
Louis Levy, Dean of Admissions
800-447-8781

St. Mary-of-the-Woods College
Saint Mary-of-the-Woods 47876
Lynn M. Rubick, Director of Admissions
800-926-SMWC

St. Mary's College
46 Madeliva, Notre Dame 46556
Mary Ann Rowan, Dir. of Admissions

: **SAWYER COLLEGE**
6040 Hohman Ave., Hammond 46320
Mary Jo Dixon, Director
800-964-0208

: **SAWYER COLLEGE**
3803 E. Lincoln Hwy., Merrillville 46410
Mary Jo Dixon, Director
800-964-0218

Taylor University
500 W. Reade Ave., Upland 46989
Robert Gortner, Head

Tri-State University, Angola 46703
Director of Admission
800-347-4878

University of Evansville
1800 Lincoln Ave., Evansville 47722
Dr. Terry Mullins, Dean
800-423-8633

University of Indianapolis
1400 E. Hanna Ave., Indianapolis 46227

† University of Notre Dame, Notre Dame 46556
Frank K. Reilly, Dean

University of Southern Indiana
8600 University Blvd., Evansville 47712

Valparaiso University, Valparaiso 46383

IOWA

American Institute of Business
2500 Fleur Dr., Des Moines 50321
Tom Shively, Dir. of Admis.

American Institute of Commerce
1801 E. Kimberly Rd., Davenport 52807
John Huston, President
319-355-3500

Briar Cliff College
3303 Rebecca St., Sioux City 51104
Patricia White, Dir. of Admis.

Buena Vista College
610 W. 4th St., Storm Lake 50588
Joanne Loonan, Director of Admissions

Clarke College
1550 Clarke Dr., Dubuque 52001
Tom Tully, MPA, Chair
800-383-2345

Coe College
1220 1st Ave., N.E., Cedar Rapids 52402
William Spellman, Chrpsn.

Dordt College
498 4th Ave., N.E., Sioux Center 51250
Quentin Van Essen, Dir. of Admissions
800-343-6738

† Drake University
2507 E. University Ave., Des Moines 50311
Thomas Willoughby, Dir. of Admis.

Graceland College, Lamoni 50140
800-638-0053, Outside Iowa 800-346-9208
Bonita Booth, Dean of Admissions
See listing under "Universities"

Grand View College
1200 Grandview Ave., Des Moines 50316
Lori Hanson, Dir. of Admissions
800-444-6083

Hawkeye Community College
1501 E. Orange Rd., Waterloo 50701
319-296-2320 Ext. 4000

Iowa Lakes Community College
3200 College Dr., Emmetsburg 50536
John Nelson, Dir. of Admis.
712-852-3554

Iowa Lakes Community College
300 S. 18th St., Estherville 51334
John Nelson, Dir. of Admis.
712-362-2604

† Iowa State University, Ames 50011
Karsten Smedal, Dir. of Admis.

Iowa Wesleyan College
601 N. Main St., Mt. Pleasant 52641

Iowa Western Community College
2700 College Rd., Council Bluffs 51503
Thomas Dutch, Dir. of Admis.

Kirkwood Community College
P.O. Box 2068, Cedar Rapids 52406
Jim Miller, Dir. of Admis.
319-398-5517

Loras College
1450 Alta Vista, Dubuque 52001
Dan Conry, Dir. of Admis.

Luther College
700 College Dr., Decorah 52101
David Sallee, Dean for Enrollment

Maharishi International University
Route 1, Fairfield 52556
Gregory Polakow, Dir. of Admis.

Morningside College, Sioux City 51106
Lora Vanderzwaag, Dir. of Admis.

Mount Mercy College
1330 Elmhurst Dr., N.E., Cedar Rapids 52402
Carol Williamson, Dir. of Admis.

Mount St. Clare College
400 N. Buff Blvd., Clinton 52732

Northwestern College
101 7th St. S.W., Orange City 51041

St. Ambrose University
518 W. Locust St., Davenport 52803

Simpson College
P.O. Box 708, Indianola 50125

: Spencer College
217 W. 5th St., Spencer 51301
Harvey Work, Director
See listing under "Career Schools"

Teikyo Marycrest University
1607 W. 12th St., Davenport 52804
Tim McDonough, Dir. of Admis.
See listing under "Universities"

Teikyo Westmar University
1002 3rd Ave., S.E., Le Mars 51031
Dr. Jim Utesch, Dir. of Admis.

† University of Iowa, Iowa City 52242

University of Northern Iowa, Cedar Falls 50614

Upper Iowa University
P.O. Box 1857, Fayette 52142

Vennard College
P.O. Box 29, University Park 52595
Mark Becker, Dir. of Admis.
800-338-2407

Waldorf College
106 S. 6th St., Forest City 50436
Steve Lovik, Dir. of Admis.
800-292-1903

Wartburg College
P.O. Box 1003, Waverly 50677

William Penn College
201 Trueblood Ave., Oskaloosa 52577
Eric Otto, Dir. of Admis.

KANSAS

Benedictine College
1020 N. Second St., Atchison 66002
James Hoffman, Dir. of Admis.

Bethany College
421 N. 1st St., Lindsborg 67456
Henry Hays, Chrpsn.

COLBY COMMUNITY COLLEGE
1255 S. Range Ave., Colby 67701
Theron Johnson, Dir. of Admis.

Emporia State University
1200 Commercial St., Emporia 66801
Dr. Barbara Hilgendorf, Dir. of Admissions

Fort Hays State University
600 Park St., Hays 67601-4099
Dr. Jack McCullick, Dean

Kansas Newman College
3100 McCormick Ave., Wichita 67213
Dr. Robert Giroux, President

† Kansas State University
Anderson Hall 110, Manhattan 66506
Ellsworth M. Gerritz, Admis. & Records

McPherson College
1600 E. Euclid St., McPherson 67460

Mid-America Nazarene College
P.O. Box 1776, Olathe 66051

Ottawa University
1001 S. Cedar St., Ottawa 66067
Steve Koberlein, Dir. of Admis.
800-755-5200

Pittsburg State University
1701 S. Broadway St., Pittsburg 66762
James E. Parker, Dir of Admis.

Saint Mary College
4100 S. 4th St., Leavenworth 66048
Irene Keehan, Dir. of Admis.

SOUTHWESTERN COLLEGE
100 College St., Winfield 67156
800-846-1543

: Topeka Technical College
1620 N.W. Gage Blvd., Topeka 66618
Vicki Johnson, Director

† University of Kansas, Lawrence 66045

Washburn University of Topeka
1700 S.W. College Ave., Topeka 66621
John E. Triggs, Dir. of Admissions

: Wichita Business College
501 E. Pawnee St. #515, Wichita 67211
See listing under "Career Schools"

† Wichita State University
1845 Fairmount, Wichita 67260
800-362-2594
See listing under "Universities"

KENTUCKY

Asbury College
1 Macklem Dr., Wilmore 40390
Jonah Mitchell, Dir. of Admis.

Bellarmine College
2001 Newburg Rd., Louisville 40205
Thomas LaBaugh, Dean of Admissions

Centre College
600 W. Walnut St., Danville 40422

Cumberland College
6178 College Station Dr., Williamsburg 40769
See listing under "Universities"

Georgetown College
400 E. College St., Georgetown 40324
Garvel Kindrick, Director of Admissions
See listing under "Universities"

Kentucky State University
400 E. Main St., Frankfort 40601

Kentucky Wesleyan College
3000 Frederica St., Owensboro 42301
Raju Chenna, Chrpsn.

Midway College
512 E. Stephens St., Midway 40347
Carl P. Rollins II, Dir. of Admis.

Morehead State University, Morehead 40351
Charles Myers, Director of Admissions
606-783-2000

† Murray State University, Murray 42071
Phil Bryan, Director of Admissions
800-272-4MSU

Northern Kentucky University
Louie B. Nunn Dr., Highland Heights 41076

Pikeville College
214 Sycamore St., Pikeville 41501
Dr. John W. Sanders, Dean of Admissions

Spalding University
851 S. 4th St., Louisville 40203
Dorothy G. Allen, Dir. of Admis.

† University of Kentucky, Lexington 40506

† University of Louisville
2301 S. 3rd St., Louisville 40292
Robert Parrent, Dir. of Admis.

† Western Kentucky University
1526 Russellville Rd., Bowling Green 42101

LOUISIANA

Centenary College of Louisiana
P.O. Box 41188, Shreveport 71134

: Delta Junior College
7290 Exchange Pl., Baton Rouge 70806
511 Westbank Expressway, Gretna 70053
3321 Hessmer Ave., Metaire 70002
Billy B. Clark, President

Grambling State University
P.O. Box 607, Grambling 71245
Dr. Harold W. Lundy, President

Louisiana College
College Station, Pineville 71359
Byron McGee, Dir. of Admis.
318-487-7386
See listing under "Liberal Arts"

† Louisiana State University and A & M College
Baton Rouge 70803

† Lousiana Technical University
P.O. Box 3168, Ruston 71272

† Loyola University
6363 St. Charles Ave., New Orleans 70118

† McNeese State University
4100 Ryan St., Lake Charles 70605

† Nicholls State University
LA Hwy. 1, Thibodaux 70301

† Northeast Louisiana University
700 University Ave., Monroe 71209

Northwestern State University
Natchitoches 71497

OUR LADY OF HOLY CROSS COLLEGE
4123 Woodland Dr., New Orleans 70131

† Southeastern Louisiana University
P.O. Box 784, Hammond 70404

† Tulane University
6823 Saint Charles Ave., New Orleans 70118
Richard Whiteside, Dean of Admission

† University of New Orleans
New Orleans 70148
John E. Altazan, Dean

University of Southwestern Louisiana
P.O. Box 44249, Lafayette 70504
318-231-6219

MAINE

HUSSON COLLEGE
One College Circle, Bangor 04401
William Beardsley, President
Jane Goodwin, Dir. of Admis.
In ME 800-4HU-SSON
Established 1898. Private. Coed. Accreditation: NEASC, NLN. Tuition: $7,800. Room and board: $4,000. Fees: $100. Enrollment: 1,033 full-time, 874 part-time. Faculty: 62. Student-faculty ratio: 21:1. Degrees: associate's, bachelor's, master's. Library: 33,000 volumes. 6 buildings on 200 acres. Gym. Pool. International Center for Language Studies (ICLS). Programs include accounting, court reporting, office management, business administration, business teacher education, management information systems.

Maine Maritime Academy
Battle Ave., Castine 04420
Dan Jones, Dir. of Admis.
207-326-2206

· Northern Maine Technical College
33 Edgemont Dr., Presque Isle 04769

St. Joseph's College, North Windham 04062

Thomas College
180 W. River Rd., Waterville 04901
Susan Potter, Dir. of Admis.
207-877-0101, ME only 800-339-7001

University of Maine
University Hts., Augusta 04330

University of Maine at Fort Kent
25 Pleasant St., Fort Kent 04743
Jerry Nadeau, Dir. of Admis.

University of Maine
9 O'Brien Ave., Machias 04654

† University of Maine, Orono 04469

University of New England
11 Hills Beach Rd., Biddeford 04005
Patricia Cribby, Dir. of Admis.

University of Southern Maine
96 Falmouth St., Portland 04103
Robert Patton, Dean

Westbrook College
716 Stevens Ave., Portland 04103
207-797-7261

MARYLAND

Capitol College
11301 Springfield Rd., Laurel 20708
Anthony G. Miller, Director of Admis.
800-950-1992

· Essex Community College
7201 Rossville Blvd., Baltimore 21237
Diane Lane, Dir. of Admis.

: Fleet Business School
2530 Riva Rd. #201, Annapolis 21401
Kenan Habetler, Dir. of Admis.

Frostburg State University, Frostburg 21532

Goucher College
1021 Dulaney Valley Rd., Baltimore 21204

HAGERSTOWN BUSINESS COLLEGE
18618 Crestwood Dr., Hagerstown 21742
Jim Gifford, President
See listing under "Community and Junior Colleges"

· Harford Community College
401 Thomas Run Rd., Bel Air 21015
Sandie Ferrita, Coordinator

::: **HOME STUDY INTERNATIONAL**
12501 Old Columbia Pike, Silver Spring 20904
P.O. Box 4437, Silver Spring 20914-4437 (mailing)
Dr. Joseph Gurubatham, President
800-782-GROW(4769)
Established 1909. Private. Coed. Accreditation: National Home Study Council. Affiliation: Columbia Union College. External degree programs, which are accredited by the Middle States Association of Colleges and Schools.
See listing under "Home Study and Correspondence"

Hood College
400 Rosemont Ave., Frederick 21701

† Loyola College
4501 N. Charles St., Baltimore 21210
William Bossemeyer III, Dir. of Admis.

· Montgomery College
51 Mannakee St., Rockville 20850
Germantown - 301-353-7731
Rockville - 301-270-5137
Takoma Park - 301-650-1453

Morgan State University
Cold Spring Ln. and Hillen Rd., Baltimore 21239

Mt. St. Mary's College
16300 Old Emmitsburg Rd., Emmitsburg 21727
Michael D. Kennedy, Dir. of Admis.

Towson State University
800 York Rd., Towson 21204
Dr. Hoke Smith, President

† University of Baltimore
1420 N. Charles St., Baltimore 21201
Clare MacDonald, Dean of Admissions

† University of Maryland, College Park 20742

University of Maryland, University College
University Blvd. & Adelphi Rd.
College Park 20742

University of Maryland Eastern Shore
11868 Academic Oval, Princess Anne 21853
Dr. Dorothy Mattison, Chrpsn.

Villa Julie College
1525 Greenspring Valley Rd., Stevenson 21153
Carolyn Manuszak, President

Western Maryland College
2 College Hill, Westminster 21157

· Woodridge Business Institute
309 E. Main St., Salisbury 21801
Phil Turk, Dir. of Admis.

MASSACHUSETTS

American International College
1000 State St., Springfield 01109
Peter Miller, Dean of Admissions

Anna Maria College
2 Sunset Ln., Paxton 01612
Dr. Bernadette Madore, SSA, President

· Aquinas College
15 Walnut Park, Newton 02158
Ellen Ronayne, Dir. of Admis.

· Aquinas College at Milton
303 Adams St., Milton 02186
617-696-3100

Arthur D. Little Management Education Institute
35 Acorn Park, Cambridge 02140

Assumption College
500 Salisbury St., Worcester 01609

Atlantic Union College
P.O. Box 1000, South Lancaster 01561
Osa Canto, Registrar

† Babson College
One College Dr., Babson Park 02157
Charles S. Nolan, Dean of Admission
800-488-3696

· **BAY PATH COLLEGE**
588 Longmeadow St., Longmeadow 01106
Paula DesRoberts, Dean of Admis.
413-567-0621 or 800-782-PATH
Established: 1897. Private. Women. Accreditation: NEASC, Legal programs ABA approved. Tuition: $10,200. Room and board: $6,225. Enrollment: 600. Faculty: 42. Student-faculty ratio: 14:1. Degrees: AA, AS, BA, BS. Library: 38,000 volumes. 27 buildings on 30 acres. Secure, suburban campus near Springfield and Hartford. 15 Associate degree programs in business, education, fashion/design, criminal justice, paralegalism, hospitality/tourism, health, human services, occupational therapy, psychology, liberal arts. Baccalaureates in business, business/accounting, legal studies, psychology, psychology/criminal justice, psychology/early childhood education. Extensive career services. 95-98% of students obtain jobs after graduation. Transfer welcome.

† Bentley College
175 Forest St., Waltham 02154
Joann McKenna, Dir. of Admis.

† Boston College
140 Commonwealth Ave., Chestnut Hill 02167
John J. Neuhauser, Dean

† Boston University
685 Commonwealth Ave., Boston 02215

Bradford College
320 S. Main St., Bradford 01835

Bridgewater State College
Bridgewater 02325
James Plotner, Jr., Dir. of Admis.

· **BURDETT SCHOOL**
745 Boylston St., Boston 02116
Maralin Manning, President
617-859-1900

† Clark University
950 Main St., Worcester 01610
Richard Pierson, Dean of Admis.

Curry College
1071 Blue Hill Ave., Milton 02186
617-333-0500

· **DEAN COLLEGE**
99 Main St, Franklin 02038
Kathleen Teehan, Dean of Admissions
508-528-9100
See listing under "Community and Junior Colleges"

ELMS COLLEGE
291 Springfield St., Chicopee 01013
800-255-ELMS

Emerson College
148 Beacon St., Boston 02116

Emmanuel College
400 The Fenway, Boston 02115
Margaret Bonilla, Dir. of Admis.

· Endicott College
376 Hale St., Beverly 01915
Elizabeth Macomber, Dir. of Admis.

Fisher College
118 Beacon St., Boston 02116
Sandra Robbins, Dir. of Admis.

Fitchburg State College
160 Pearl St., Fitchburg 01420
Marke Vickers, Dir. of Admis.

† Harvard University
Havard Business School
Dillon Hall
Soldiers Field Rd., Boston 02163

: Kinyon-Campbell Business School
59 Linden St., New Bedford 02740
David Daganhardt, Director

Lesley College
29 Everett St., Cambridge 02138-2790
Jane Raley, Dir. of Admissions

· **MARIAN COURT COLLEGE**
35 Little's Point Rd., Swampscott 01907
Jodi T. Quinn, Dir. of Admis.
617-595-6768

† Massachusetts Institute of Technology
77 Massachusetts Ave., Cambridge 02139

· Massasoit Community College
1 Massasoit Blvd., Brockton 02402
Roberta Noodell, Dir. of Admis.

· Merrimack College
315 Turnpike St., North Andover 01845
Dennis Farrell, Dean of Admissions

· Middlesex Community College
Springs Rd., Bedford 01730
617-280-3200

· Middlesex Community College
33 Kearney Sq., Lowell 01852
508-656-3211

: New England School of Business
P.O. Box 888, Watertown 02272
John Carey, Director of Education

Nichols College, Dudley 01570

North Adams State College
375 Church St., North Adams 01247
413-664-4511 or 800-292-6632
See listing under "Universities or Graduate Schools"

† Northeastern University
360 Huntington Ave., Boston 02115
Kevin Kelly, Dean and Dir. of Undergraduate Admis.

· North Shore Community College
1 Ferncroft Rd., Danvers 01923

Pine Manor College
400 Heath St., Chestnut Hill 02167
Gillian Lloyd, Dir. of Admis.

· Quincy Junior College
34 Coddington St., Quincy 02169
Richard Pessin, Dean of Enrollment Services

Quinsigamond Community College
670 W. Boylston St., Worcester 01606
Ron Smith, Dir. of Admis.

Salem State College
352 Lafayette St., Salem 01970
David Sartwell, Dir. of Admis.

Simmons College
300 The Fenway, Boston 02115

Springfield College
263 Alden St., Springfield 01109
Frederick Bartlett, Dean of Admissions

· **SPRINGFIELD TECHNICAL COMMUNITY COLLEGE**
1 Armory Square, Springfield 01105
Dr. Patrick E. Tigue, Dir. of Admissions
413-781-7822

Stonehill College
320 Washington St., North Easton 02357
508-230-1373

† Suffolk University
8 Ashburton Place, Boston 02108
Barbara K. Ericson, Assoc. Dean Enrollment & Retention
617-573-8460

† University of Massachusetts, Amherst 01003
Arlene Wesley Cash, Dir. of Admis.

University of Massachusetts
100 Morrissey Blvd., Boston 02125

University of Massachusetts Dartmouth
Old Westport Rd., North Dartmouth 02747
Raymond Barrows, Dir. of Admissions
508-999-8605

† University of Massachusetts Lowell
1 University Ave., Lowell 01854

Western New England College
1215 Wilbraham Rd., Springfield 01119
800-325-1122

Westfield State College
577 Western Ave., Westfield 01085
John F. Marcus, Dir. of Admis.

Worcester Polytechnic Institute
100 Institute Rd., Worcester 01609
Kay R. Dietrich, Director of Admissions
508-831-5286

Worcester State College
486 Chandler St., Worcester 01602

MICHIGAN

ADRIAN COLLEGE
110 S. Madison St., Adrian 49221
George Wolf, Dir. of Admis.
See listing under "Universities"

Albion College
611 E. Porter, Albion 49224
800-858-6770

Andrews University, Berrien Springs 49104
Jack Mentges, Dir. of Admis.

Aquinas College
1607 Robinson Rd., S.E., Grand Rapids 49506
Paula Meehan, Dean of Admissions
800-678-9593

Baker College of Auburn Hills
1500 University Dr., Auburn Hills 48326
John A. Tomaszewski, Dir. of Admis.

Baker College of Cadillac
9600 E. 13th St., Cadillac 49601
Candace Baldwin, Dir. of Admis.

Baker College of Flint
1050 W. Bristol Rd., Flint 48507
Mark Heaton, Dir. of Admis.

Baker College of Mount Clemens
34950 Little Mack Ave., Clinton Township 48035
Annette M. Wendling, Dir. of Admis.

Baker College of Muskegon
141 Hartford Ave., Muskegon 49442
Kathy Jacobson, Dir. of Admis.

Baker College of Owosso
1020 S. Washington St., Owosso 48867
Bruce A. Lundeen, Dir. of Admis.

Baker College of Port Huron
3403 Lapeer Rd., Port Huron 48060
David C. Hickman, Dir. of Admis.

Calvin College
3201 Burton St., S.E., Grand Rapids 49546

† Central Michigan University
100 Warriner Hall, Mt. Pleasant 48858

Cleary College - Livingston Campus
3750 Cleary College Dr., Howell 48843
Tom Sullivan, President
800-589-1979

Cleary College - Washtenaw Campus
2170 Washtenaw Ave., Ypsilanti 48197
Tom Sullivan, President
800-686-1883

Concordia College
4090 Geddes Rd., Ann Arbor 48105
Mary Froelich, Dir. of Admis.

Davenport College of Business
415 E. Fulton St., Grand Rapids 49503
Donald Maine, President

Davenport College of Business
67 Michigan Ave. W., Battle Creek 49017

Davenport College of Business
220 E. Kalamazoo St., Lansing 48933
Don Colizzi, Dean

Detroit College of Business
4801 Oakman Blvd., Dearborn 48126
James Farmer, V.P. for Admissions

Detroit College of Business-Flint
3115 Lawndale Ave., Flint 48504

Detroit College of Business-Warren
27500 Dequindre Rd., Warren 48092

† Eastern Michigan University, Ypsilanti 48197
Stewart Tubbs, Dean
313-487-3060 or 800-GO-TO-EMU

Ferris State University
Office of Admission
420 Oak St., Big Rapids 49307-2020

GMI Engineering & Management Institute
1700 W. 3rd Ave., Flint 48504
Phillip D. Lavender, Dir. of Admis.
See listing under "Engineering"

Grace Bible College
P.O. Box 910, Grand Rapids 49509
Linda K. Siler, Dir. of Admis.

Grand Valley State University
1 Campus Dr., Allendale 49401
Marvin G. DeVries, Dean

Great Lakes Junior College of Business
310 S. Washington Ave., Saginaw 48607
Angelo Guerriero, President

HILLSDALE COLLEGE
33 E. College St., Hillsdale 49242
Dr. Charles Van Eaton, Director
517-437-7341

Jordan College-Berrien County Campus
185 E. Main St., Benton Harbor 49022
Jodi Hunsicker, Dean
616-927-3333

Jordan College-Detroit Campus
15400 Grand River Ave., Detroit 48227
Mark Jackson, Dean
313-835-5100

Jordan College-Flint Campus
3488 N. Jennings Rd., Flint 48504
L. B. McCune, Dean
810-789-0520

Jordan College-Grand Rapids Campus
1925 Breton Rd., S.E., Grand Rapids 49506
Jack Kooyman, Dean
616-957-3999

Jordan College-Thumb Area Campus
6667 Main St., Cass City 48726
Jerry White, Dean
517-872-4394

Lake Superior State University
1000 College Dr., Sault St. Marie 49783

Lawrence Technological University
21000 W. Ten Mile Rd., Southfield 48075
800-225-5588 ext. 3160

· Lewis College of Business
17370 Meyers Rd., Detroit 48235
K. Frank DeShazok, Dir. of Admis.
313-862-6300

Marygrove College
8425 W. McNichols Rd., Detroit 48221

† Michigan State University, East Lansing 48824
Dr. Richard J. Lewis, Dean

Michigan Technological University
1400 Townsend Dr., Houghton 49931
Joseph A. Galetto, Dir. Enrollment Mgmt.
906-487-2335

: Northeastern School of Commerce
701 N. Madison Ave., Bay City 48708
Louis H. Bork, Director

Northern Michigan University
610 Cohodas Admin. Center, Marquette 49855
Nancy Rehling, Dir. of Admis.

· Northwestern Michigan College
1701 E. Front St., Traverse City 49686
Roberta Teahan, Dean of Occupational Studies
800-748-0566

Northwood University
3225 Cook Rd., Midland 48640
Daniel F. Toland, Dir. of Admis.
800-457-7878

† Oakland University, Rochester 48309
Larry Bartalucci, Registrar

Olivet College
300 S. Main St., Olivet 49076
Vicki Gallas, Registrar
See listing under "Universities"

Saginaw Valley State University
2250 Pierce Rd., University Center 48710

St. Mary's College
Orchard Lake & Commerce Rd.
Orchard Lake 48324

Spring Arbor College
106 E. Main St., Spring Arbor 49283

· Suomi College
601 Quincy St., Hancock 49930
John Ruohoniemi, Dean/Enrollment Development
800-682-7604

† University of Detroit Mercy
4001 W. McNichols
PO Box 19900, Detroit 48219-0900
313-993-1245
See listing under "Universities"

† University of Michigan-Ann Arbor
815 S. University Ave., Ann Arbor 48109

University of Michigan-Dearborn
4901 Evergreen Rd., Dearborn 48128
Carol S. Mack, Dir. of Admis.
313-593-5100

† University of Michigan-Flint
303 Kearsley St., Flint 48502

Walsh College of Accountancy & Business
Administration
P.O. Box 7006, Troy 48007

† Wayne State University
5980 Cass Ave., Detroit 48202
Dr. J. R. Thorderson, Dir. of Admis.

† Western Michigan University, Kalamazoo 49008
Stanley Henderson, Dir. of Enrl. Mgt. & Admis.
616-387-2000

William Tyndale College
35700 W. Twelve Mile Rd.
Farmington Hills 48331

MINNESOTA

ACADEMY OF ACCOUNTANCY
3050 Metro Dr. #200, Bloomington 55425
Gary McNulty, Director of Admissions
612-851-0066

Augsburg College
731 21st Ave., S., Minneapolis 55454

Bemidji State University
1500 Birchmont Dr., N.E., Bemidji 56601
800-475-2001

Bethel College
3900 Bethel Dr., St. Paul 55112
Dr. George Brushaber, President

College of Saint Benedict
37 S. College Ave., St. Joseph 56374

College of St. Catherine
2004 Randolph Ave., St. Paul 55105

College of St. Scholastica
1200 Kenwood Ave., Duluth 55811
Dr. Jessica Jenner, Chrpsn.
800-447-5444
See listing under "Liberal Arts"

Concordia College
901 8th St. S., Moorhead 56562
Lee Johnson, Dir. of Admis.
See listing under "Universities"

Concordia College-St. Paul
275 N. Syndicate, St. Paul 55104
Tim Utter, Dir. of Admis.

Crown College
6425 County Rd. 30, St. Bonifacius 55375
See listing under "Universities"

: Duluth Business University
412 W. Superior St., Duluth 55802
Bonnie Kupczynski, Director

Gustavus Adolphus College
800 W. College Ave., St. Peter 56082
Mark Anderson, Dir. of Admis.

Hamline University
1536 Hewitt Ave., St. Paul 55104
Scott Pratt, Dir. of Admis.

· Inver Hills Community College
8445 College Trail, E., Inver Grove Heights 55076
Cheryl Frank, Director

Mankato State University
P.O. Box 8400, Mankato 56002

· Minneapolis Community College
1501 Hennepin Ave., Minneapolis 55403-1779
Bonnie Wiger, Registrar
612-341-7000

: Minnesota School of Business
1401 W. 76th St., Richfield 55423

Moorhead State University
1104 7th Ave. S., Moorhead 56560

Northwestern College
3003 Snelling Ave., N., St. Paul 55113
Ralph Anderson, Dean of Admissions
800-827-6827 or 612-631-5111

: Northwest Technical College
1900 28th Ave., S., Moorhead 56560
Dale White, Dir. of Admis.
218-299-6512

PILLSBURY BAPTIST BIBLE COLLEGE
315 S. Grove St., Owatonna 55060
Alan Potter, President
Larry Tindall, Director of Admissions
800-747-4557

† St. Cloud State University
740 4th Ave., S., St. Cloud 56301
Sherwood Reid, Dir. of Admis.
800-369-4260

St. John's University
P.O. Box 7155, Collegeville 56321

St. Mary's College of Minnesota
700 Terrace Heights #2, Winona 55987
Tony Piscitiello, VP for Admission

St. Olaf College, Northfield 55057
William Carlson, Chrpsn.
507-646-3156

Southwest State University, Marshall 56258

University of Minnesota
600 E. Fourth St., Morris 56267

† University of Minnesota, Twin Cities
Minneapolis 55455

UNIVERSITY OF MINNESOTA-CROOKSTON
2900 University Ave., Crookston 56716
Robert Smith, Chrpsn.
800-232-6466
See listing under "Universities"

University of St. Thomas
2115 Summit Ave., St. Paul 55105

Winona State University
P.O. Box 5838, Winona 55987
Dr. J. Mootz, Dir. of Admis.

WORTHINGTON COMMUNITY COLLEGE
1450 College Way, Worthington 56187
Conrad Burchill, President
507-372-2107

MISSISSIPPI

Alcorn State University
P.O. Box 359, Lorman 39096
D. W. Wilburn, Registrar

Belhaven College
1500 Peachtree St., Jackson 39202

Delta State University
Hwy. 8 W., Cleveland 38732

† Millsaps College
P.O. Box 150556, Jackson 39210
Florence Hines, Dir. of Admis.

Mississippi College
P.O. Box 4086, Clinton 39058

† Mississippi State University
P.O. Box J, Mississippi State University 39762

Mississippi University for Women
P.O. Box W-1602, Columbus 39701
Teresa Thompson, Exec. Dir. of Enrollment

Mississippi Valley State University
14000 Hwy. 82 W., Itta Bena 38941
Maxcine B. Rush, Director of Admissions
See listing under "Universities"

Tougaloo College
500 E. County Line Rd., Tougaloo 39174

† University of Mississippi, University 38677

† University of Southern Mississippi
P.O. Box 5165, Hattiesburg 39406

William Carey College
498 Tuscan Ave., Hattiesburg 39401

MISSOURI

Avila College
11901 Wornall Rd., Kansas City 64145

Central Missouri State University
Warrensburg 64093
Delores Hudson, Dir. of Admis.

College of the Ozarks, Point Lookout 65726
Dr. Kenton Olson, Dean of the College

Columbia College
1001 Rogers St., Columbia 65216
Ron Cronacher, Dir. of Admissions
800-231-2391

DeVry Institute of Technology
11224 Holmes St., Kansas City 64131
Michael Thompson, Dir. of Admis.
816-941-2810
See Illinois listing under "Universities"

Drury College
900 N. Benton Ave., Springfield 65802
Michael G. Thomas, Dir. of Admis.

Evangel College
1111 N. Glenstone Ave., Springfield 65802
David Schoolfield, Dir. of Enrollment

Fontbonne College
6800 Wydown Blvd., St. Louis 63105
Peggy Musen, Dir. of Admis.

Harris-Stowe State College
3026 Laclede Ave., St. Louis 63103
Valerie Beeson, Dir. of Admis. and Advisement
314-340-3300

: Hickey School
940 Westport Plaza #101, St. Louis 63146
Bonnie Schulte, Dir. of Admis.

Maryville University of St. Louis
13550 Conway Rd., Saint Louis 63141
314-576-9300 or 800-MARYVLL

Missouri Baptist College
12542 Conway Rd., St. Louis 63141

Missouri Southern State College
3950 Newman Rd., Joplin 64801-1595
Jim Gray, Dean
See listing under "Universities"

Missouri Valley College
500 E. College St., Marshall 65340
816-886-6924 ext. 114
See listing under "Universities"

Missouri Western State College
4525 Downs Dr., St. Joseph 64507
Howard McCauley, Dir. of Admis.

· North Central Missouri College
1301 Main St., Trenton 64683
Julie Hefley, Department Head
816-359-3948 ext. 313 or 800-880-6180

Northeast Missouri State University
Kirksville 63501

Northwest Missouri State University
800 University Dr., Maryville 64468

Park College, Parkville 64152
Dr. Edwin Rawn, Dean of Admis.

† St. Louis University
221 N. Grand Blvd., St. Louis 63103
Louis A. Menard, Dean of Admissions

Southeast Missouri State University
1 University Plz., Cape Girardeau 63701
New Student Relations 314-651-2590
See listing under "Universities"

Southwest Baptist University
1601 S. Springfield Ave., Bolivar 65613

Southwest Missouri State University
901 S. National Ave., Springfield 65804
Dr. Ronald Bottin, Dean
417-836-5646

Stephens College, Columbia 65215
Mary Ann Sprinkle, Dir. of Admis.

† University of Missouri, Columbia
228 Jesse Hall, Columbia 65211

† University of Missouri, Kansas City
5100 Rockhill Rd., Kansas City 64110
Leo J. Sweeney, Dir. of Admis. & Registrar

† University of Missouri
8001 Natural Bridge Rd., St. Louis 63121
Mimi LaMarca, Dir. of Admis.

† Washington University
1 Brookings Dr., St. Louis 63130

Webster University
470 E. Lockwood Ave., St. Louis 63119
Dr. James Staley, Associate Dean
See listing under "Universities"

Westminister College
501 Westminster Ave., Fulton 65251
Gary Forney, Dean of Admis.

William Woods College
200 W. 12th St., Fulton 65251
Dr. Jahnae Barnett, VP of Admis.

MONTANA

CARROLL COLLEGE
1610 N. Benton Ave., Helena 59625
Candace Cain, Dir. of Admis.
See listing under "Universities"

College of Great Falls
1301 20th St., S., Great Falls 59405
Jean Walker, Dir. of Admis.

· Missoula Vocational Technical Center
909 South Ave. W, Missoula 59801
Charles Couture, Dir. of Admis.

† Montana State University, Bozeman 59717

Montana State University - Billings
1500 N. 30th St., Billings 59101
Karen Everett, Dir. of Admis.
406-657-2158

Northern Montana College
P.O. Box 7751, Havre 59501
Ralph A. Brigham, Dir. of Admis.

Rocky Mountain College
1511 Poly Dr., Billings 59102
David Heringer, Dir. of Admis.
See listing under "Universities"

† University of Montana, Missoula 59812
800-462-8636

NEBRASKA

Bellevue College
1000 Galvin Rd. S., Bellevue 68005
Chari Leader, VP of Enrollment

Chadron State College
1000 Main St., Chadron 69337
Dr. Merlyn Gramberg, Dean

College of Saint Mary
1901 S. 72nd St., Omaha 68124
Sheila Haggas, Dir. of Admis.

Concordia College
800 N. Columbia Ave., Seward 68434
Don Vos, Dir. of Admis.

† Creighton University
2500 California St., Omaha 68178
Dr. Guy Banville, Dean

Dana College
2848 College Dr., Blair 68008
John Schueth, Dir. of Admis.
800-444-3262
See listing under "Universities"

Midland Lutheran College
900 Clarkson St., Fremont 68025
Roland Kahnk, V.P. Admissions

· Nebraska College of Business
3636 California St., Omaha 68131
Pamela Boehm, Director

Nebraska Wesleyan University
5000 Saint Paul Ave., Lincoln 68504
Ken Sieg, Dir. of Admis.

· Northeast Community College
P.O. Box 469, Norfolk 68702
Eugene Hart, Dir. of Admis.

· Peru State College, Peru 68421
Pamela J. Cosgrove, Dir. of Admis.
402-872-3815

: Spencer School of Business
410 W. Second St., Grand Island 68801
Connie Collin, Dir. of Admis.

Union College
3800 S. 48th St., Lincoln 68506

University of Nebraska
905 W. 25th St., Kearney 68849

† University of Nebraska at Lincoln
CBA 240, Lincoln 68588
Gary Schwendiman, Dean

† University of Nebraska at Omaha
Omaha 68182

Wayne State College
200 E. Tenth St., Wayne 68787

· Western Nebraska Community College
1601 E. 27th St., Scottsbluff 69361
Roger Hovey, Admissions

· Western Nebraska Community College
Sidney 69162
Jim Copley, Admissions

NEVADA

Morrison College
140 Washington St., Reno 89503
Mary T. Morrison, VP Administration
702-323-4145

· Phillips Junior College
3320 E. Flamingo Rd. #30, Las Vegas 89121
Robert Ramey, Dir. of Admis.

Sierra Nevada College-Lake Tahoe
P.O. Box 4269, Incline Village 89450
Lane Murray, Dir. of Admissions
See listing under "Universities"

· Truckee Meadows Community College
7000 Dandini Blvd., Reno 89512
John Gwaltney, President

† University of Nevada, Reno
Reno 89557

† University of Nevada Las Vegas
4505 S. Maryland Pky., Las Vegas 89154-1021
Admissions: 702-895-3443 or 800-334-UNLV

NEW HAMPSHIRE

ANTIOCH NEW ENGLAND GRADUATE SCHOOL
40 Avon St., Keene 03431-3516
Gael R. Minton, Dir. of Admis.
603-357-3122
See listing under "Graduate Schools"

· Castle College
21 Searles Rd., Windham 03087
Andrea Bard, Dir. of Admis.
603-893-6111

† Dartmouth College, Hanover 03755

Franklin Pierce College, Rindge 03461

Keene State College
229 Main St., Keene 03435
Kathryn Dodge, Dir. of Admis.

New England College
26 Bridge St., Henniker 03242
John Spaulding, Dir. of Admis.

New Hampshire College
2500 North River Rd., Manchester 03106
Brad Poznanski, Dir. of Admis.
603-645-9611

· New Hampshire Technical College at Stratham
277 R. Portsmouth Ave., Stratham 03885
Patricia A. Shay, Dean of Students

NOTRE DAME COLLEGE
2321 Elm St., Manchester 03104
603-669-4298

Rivier College
420 S. Main St., Nashua 03060
Admissions: 800-44-RIVIER

Saint Anselm College
87 Saint Anselm Dr., Manchester 03102
Don Healy, Dir. of Admis.

NEW JERSEY

BERKELEY COLLEGE OF BUSINESS
44 Rifle Camp Rd., West Paterson 07424
Kevin Luing, President
800-446-5400 ext. GQ1

BERKELEY COLLEGE OF BUSINESS
430 Rahway Ave., Woodbridge 07095
Kevin Luing, President
800-446-5400 ext. GQ1

BERKELEY COLLEGE OF BUSINESS
100 W. Prospect St., Waldwick 07463
Kevin Luing, President
800-446-5400 ext. GQ1

Bloomfield College
1 Park Place, Bloomfield 07003
Warner Smith, Dean for Admissions
201-748-9000, Ext. 230

: Brick Computer Science Institute
515 Rte. 70, Brick 08723
Robert H. Forshee, Director
See listing under "Career Schools"

Caldwell College
9 Ryerson Ave., Caldwell 07006

: The Chubb Institute
P.O. Box 342, Parsippany 07054

: Dover Business College
15 E. Blackwell St., Dover 07801
David Weaver, Director

Fairleigh Dickinson University, Madison 07940
Lissa Anderson, Dir. of Admis.
201-593-8906

Fairleigh Dickinson University, Teaneck 07666
Dennis Craig, Dir. of Admis.
201-692-2732

FELICIAN COLLEGE
262 S. Main St., Lodi 07644
Sr. Mary Austin, OSB, Dir. of Admis.
201-778-1029
See listing under "Universities"

: Ho-Ho-Kus School of Secretarial and Medical
Sciences
Secretarial Word Processing
27 S. Franklin Trnpk., Ramsey 07446
Thomas Eastwick, Director
201-327-8877

· Hudson County Community College
168 Sip Ave., Jersey City 07306
Joseph O'Halloran, Director of Admissions
201-714-2127

Jersey City State College
2039 Kennedy Blvd., Jersey City 07305
201-200-3234

Kean College of New Jersey
1000 Morris Ave., Union 07083

· Mercer County Community College
West Windsor Campus
1200 Old Trenton Rd., Trenton 08690
Michael Glass, Dir. of Admis.
See listing under "Community and Junior
Colleges"

Monmouth College
400 Cedar Ave., West Long Branch 07764
Joan Rudinski, Dir. of Admis.

Montclair State College
1 Normal Ave., Upper Montclair 07043

New Jersey Institute of Technology
323 Martin Luther King Jr. Blvd., Newark 07102

Rider University
2083 Lawrenceville Rd., Lawrenceville 08648
Susan Christian, Dir. of Admis.

Rowan College of New Jersey, Glassboro 08028
Marvin G. Sills, Dir. of Admis.

† Rutgers, The State University of NJ
Rutgers College
New Brunswick 08903

† Seton Hall University
400 S. Orange Ave., South Orange 07079
Lee Cooke, Dir. of Admis.

Stockton State College, Pomona 08240
Sal Catalfamo, Dir. of Admis.

Thomas Edison State College
101 W. State St., Trenton 08608

Trenton State College
Hillwood Lakes CN 4700, Trenton 08650

Upsala College
345 Prospect St., East Orange 07017
George Lynes, Dean of Admissions

NEW MEXICO

· Albuquerque Technical-Vocational Institute
525 Buena Vista Dr., S.E., Albuquerque 87106
Jane Campbell, Registrar
See listing under "Career Schools"

College of Santa Fe
1600 St. Michaels Dr., Santa Fe 87505
800-456-2673

College of the Southwest
6610 N. Lovington Hwy., Hobbs 88240

Eastern New Mexico University
Portales 88130
Larry Fuqua, Dir. of Admis.

· Eastern New Mexico University-Roswell Campus
P.O. Box 6000, Roswell 88202
Tim Raftery, Director of Admissions and Records

New Mexico Highlands University, Las Vegas 87701
Dr. Jorge P. Thomas, VP Academic Affairs

† New Mexico State University
P.O. Box 30001, Las Cruces 88003

† University of New Mexico, Albuquerque 87131
Robert Weaver, Dean of Admissions

NEW YORK

Adelphi University, Garden City 11530
Dr. Arnold Weinstein, Dean, Schools of Business
516-877-4685

† Alfred University
Alumni Hall, Alfred 14802
Laurie Richer, Director of Admissions
800-541-9229

BERKELEY COLLEGE
40 W. Red Oak Ln., White Plains 10604
Rose Mary Healy, President
800-446-5400 ext. GQ1

BERKELEY COLLEGE
3 E. 43rd St., New York 10017
Dr. Glen Zeitzer, President
800-446-5400 ext. GQ1

· Bryant & Stratton Business Institute
1259 Central Ave., Albany 12205
Bob Flynn, Dir. of Admis.

† Canisius College
2001 Main St., Buffalo 14208
Penelope Lips, Dir. of Admis.
800-843-1517

CAZENOVIA COLLEGE
Cazenovia 13035
Dr. James Parker, VP for Enrollment Management
See listing under "Universities"

· Central City Business Institute
224 Harrison St., Syracuse 13202
Michael Greenfest, Dir. of Admissions
800-945-2224

† Clarkson University, Potsdam 13699
Robert Croot, Dir. of Admis.

College for Human Services
345 Hudson St., New York 10014

College of Insurance
101 Murray St., New York 10007
Theresa C. Marro, Director of Admissions
See listing under "Universities"

College of St. Rose
432 Western Ave., Albany 12203

† Columbia University
612 W. 115th St., New York 10025

† Cornell University
410 Thurston Ave., Ithaca 14853

† CUNY Baruch College
17 Lexington Ave., New York 10010

CUNY College of Staten Island
130 Stuyvesant Pl., Staten Island 10301

CUNY York College
9420 Guy R. Brewer Blvd., Jamaica 11451

Daemen College
4380 Main St., Amherst 14226
Maria Dillard, Dir. of Admis.
in NY 800-462-7652 or 716-839-8225

Dominican College of Blauvelt
460 N. Western Hwy., Orangeburg 10962
Louis Kern, Dir. of Admis.
914-359-7800

Dowling College,
150 Idle Hour Blvd., Oakdale 11769
Dr. Jerome Traiger, Dean

D'Youville College
320 Porter Ave., Buffalo 14201
Ronald Dannecker, Dir. of Admis.

: Elmira Business Institute
180 Clemens Center Pkwy., Elmira 14901
Brad Phillips, Director
607-733-7177

Elmira College
Park Pl., Elmira 14901
William S. Neal, Dean of Admissions
See listing under "Liberal Arts"

FIVE TOWNS COLLEGE
305 N. Service Rd., Dix Hills 11746
Jennifer Roemer, Coordinator of Admissions
516-424-7000
See listing under "Universities"

Fordham University
441 E. Fordham Rd., Bronx 10458
718-817-1000

† Fordham University
Lincoln Center Campus
113 W. 60th St., New York 10023
Edward Bristow, Dean

Friends World Program, Long Island University
Montauk Hwy., Southampton 11968
Carol Gilbert, Dir. of Admis.

Hartwick College, Oneonta 13820

† Hofstra University
1000 Fulton Ave., Hempstead 11550
Margaret Shields, Dean of Admissions

Houghton College
P.O. Box 128, Houghton 14744
Tim Fuller, Dir. of Admis.

IONA COLLEGE
715 North Ave., New Rochelle 10801
800-231-IONA or 914-633-2503
See listing under "Universities"

Ithaca College
953 Danby Rd., Ithaca 14850

· Jamestown Business College
P.O. Box 429, Jamestown 14702
David Spencer, Registrar

Keuka College
P.O. Box 98, Keuka Park 14478
Robert J. Ianuzzo, Dean of Admissions

The King's College, Briarcliff Manor 10510
Frederic Rowley, Dean of Admissions

Laboratory Institute of Merchandising
12 E. 53rd St., New York 10022
Mary Ann M. Elberfeld, Dir. of Admis.

Le Moyne College
1419 Salt Springs Rd., Syracuse 13214-1301
Edwin B. Harris, Dir. of Admis.

Long Island University-Brooklyn Campus
1 University Plaza, Brooklyn 11201
Alan Chaves, Dean of Admissions

Long Island University-C. W. Post Campus
Rt. 25A, Brookville 11548
Dr. Robert Sanator, Dean
516-299-3017

Long Island University-Southampton Campus
Southampton 11968
Carol Gilbert, Dir. of Admis.

Manhattan College 4513 Manhattan College Pky.,
Riverdale 10471
Dr. James Suarez, Dean

Manhattanville College
2900 Purchase St., Purchase 10577

· Maria College of Albany
700 New Scotland Ave., Albany 12208
Laurie Gilmore, Dir. of Admis.

MARIST COLLEGE
290 North Rd., Poughkeepsie 12601
Harry W. Wood, VP Admissions
914-575-3226

Marymount College
100 Marymount Ave., Tarrytown 10591
Gina R. Campbell, Dir. of Admis.
800-724-4312

· Mater Dei College
Riverside Dr., Ogdensburg 13669
Mark Dougherty, Dir. of Admis.

Medaille College
18 Agassiz Cir., Buffalo 14214
Jacqueline Smukeer, Dir. of Admis.

Mercy College
555 Broadway, Dobbs Ferry 10522
James Nesbitt, Dean of Admissions

Molloy College
1000 Hempstead Ave., Rockville Centre 11570
Wayne James, Dir. of Admis.
See listing under "Universities"

Mt. St. Mary College
330 Powell Ave., Newburgh 12550

Nazareth College of Rochester
4245 East Ave., Rochester 14618
Paul Kenyon, Dir. of Admis.

New York Institute of Technology
Old Westbury Campus, Old Westbury 11568

† New York University
70 Washington Sq., New York 10012

New York University
Purchase St., Purchase 10577

Niagara University, Niagara University 14109
George Pachter, Dean of Admissions
800-462-2111
See listing under "Universities"

Nyack College, Nyack 10960
Miguel Sanchez, Dir. of Admis.
800-33-NYACK

· Olean Business Institute
301 N. Union St., Olean 14760
Patrick McCarthy, Director
Jeanne Johnston, Director of Admissions
716-372-7978

::: On-Line Campus
New York Institute of Technology
P.O. Box 8000, Old Westbury 11568-8000
800-222-NYIT

Pace University, New York Campus
1 Pace Plaza, New York 10038

Pace University, Pleasantville/Briarcliff Campus
Bedford Rd., Pleasantville 10570

Pace University, White Plains Campus
78 N. Broadway, White Plains 10603

· Paul Smith's College, Paul Smiths 12970
Enrico Miller, Dir. of Admis.
800-421-2605

· Plaza Business Institute
7409 37th Ave., Jackson Heights 11372
Sally Ann Weger, Director of Admissions
718-779-1430

Polytechnic University
333 Jay St., Brooklyn 11201

REGENTS COLLEGE OF THE UNIVERSITY OF THE STATE OF NEW YORK
7 Columbia Circle, Albany 12203-5159
518-464-8500

† Rensselaer Polytechnic Institute, Troy 12180
Conrad Sharrow, Dean of Admissions

Roberts Wesleyan College
2301 Westside Dr., Rochester 14624
Daniel Barlow, Chrpsn.
See listing under "Universities"

· Rochester Business Institute
1850 Ridge Rd. E., Rochester 14622

† Rochester Institute of Technology
1 Lomb Memorial Dr., Rochester 14623
716-475-6631
See listing under "Universities"

Russell Sage College
51 1st St., Troy 12180

St. Bonaventure University, St. Bonaventure 14778
June T. Solan, Dir. of Admis.

St. John Fisher College
3690 East Ave., Rochester 14618
Peter Lindsey, Dir. of Admis.

† St. John's University
Grand Central & Utopia Parkways, Jamaica 11439

St. Joseph's College
245 Clinton Ave., Brooklyn   11205
Geraldine Foudy, Dir. of Admis.
718-636-6868

St. Joseph's College, Suffolk Campus
25 Audobon Ave., Patchogue   11772

ST. THOMAS AQUINAS COLLEGE
Rt. 340, Sparkill   10976
Andrea Kraeft, Dir. of Admis.
800-999-STAC
See listing under "Liberal Arts"

Skidmore College, Saratoga Springs   12866
Kent Jones, Dir. of Admis.

SUNY Adirondack Community College
439 Bay Rd., Queensbury   12804
Levi Brown, Dir. of Admis.
518-793-4491
See listing under "Community and Junior Colleges"

SUNY Maritime College
6 Pennyfield Ave., Bronx   10465
Peter Cooney, Dir. of Admis.

† SUNY at Albany
1400 Washington Ave., Albany   12222
Micheileen Treadwell, Dir. of
Admission/Financial Aid
518-442-5431

† SUNY at Binghamton
P.O. Box 6001, Binghamton   13902

† SUNY at Buffalo
17 Capen Hall
P.O. Box 601660, Buffalo   14260-1660
716-645-6900

SUNY College at Brockport
Brockport   14420
Dr. Joseph Mason, Chrpsn.

SUNY College at Old Westbury
P.O. Box 210, Old Westbury   11568
Michael Sheehy, Dir. of Admis.

SUNY at Oswego, Oswego   13126
Dr. Joseph Grant, Jr., Dean of Admissions
315-341-2250

SUNY College at Plattsburgh, Plattsburgh   12901
Prem Gandhi, Dean
518-564-3184

SUNY College of Agriculture and Technology
Morrisville   13408
Dennis Nostrand, Dir. of Admis.

SUNY College of Technology, Alfred   14802
Deborah J. Goodrich, Dir. of Admis.
607-587-4215

SUNY College of Technology
34 Cornell Dr., Canton   13617
Thomas R. Fletcher, Director of Admissions
800-388-7123

SUNY College of Technology at Farmingdale
Route 110, Farmingdale   11735
Janet Snyder, Dir. of Admis.
516-420-2200

SUNY INSTITUTE OF TECHNOLOGY AT UTICA/ROME
P.O. Box 3050, Utica   13504
Roger Sullivan, Dir. of Admis.
See listing under "Universities"

SUNY Monroe Community College
1000 E. Henrietta Rd., Rochester   14623
716-292-2000

SUNY Nassau Community College
1 Education Dr., Garden City   11530
Bernard Iantosca, Dir of Admis.

SUNY Schenectady County Community College
78 Washington Ave., Schenectady   12305
Robert Dinello, Dir. of Admis.
518-346-6211, ext. 166

† Syracuse University, Syracuse   13244

Union College, Schenectady   12308

† University of Rochester
500 Joseph C. Wilson Blvd., Rochester   14627
Wayne A. Locust, Dir. of Admis.
See listing under "Universities"

Utica College of Syracuse University
1600 Burrstone Rd., Utica   13502

Utica School of Commerce
201 Bleecker St., Utica   13501
Judith Kelly, Dir. of Admis.

Villa Maria College of Buffalo
240 Pine Ridge Rd., Buffalo   14225
Lynn D'Auria, Dir. of Admis.

Westchester Business Institute
325 Central Ave., White Plains   10606
Dale Smith, Dean of Admissions

Wood School
8 E. 40th St., New York   10016
Rosemary Duggan, President

NORTH CAROLINA

Alamance Community College
P.O. Box 623, Haw River   27258
W. Ronald McCarter, President

† Appalachian State University
ASU Station, Boone   28608
Joe Watts, Admissions Officer

Asheville Buncombe Technical Community College
340 Victoria Rd., Asheville   28801
Connie Buckner, Dir. of Admis.

Barton College
College Station, Wilson   27893
Anthony Britt, Dir. of Admis.
800-345-4973/919-399-6318
See listing under "Universities"

Belmont Abbey College
1 Abbey Pl., Belmont   28012
Admissions, 800-523-2355

Brevard College
Brevard   28712
Bob McLendon, Dean of Admissions

Campbell University
P.O. Box 127, Buies Creek   27506

Catawba College
2300 W. Innes St., Salisbury   28144
Mark Stokes, Dir. of Admis.

College of The Albemarle
P.O. Box 2327, Elizabeth City   27906
John M. Wells, Asst. Dean of Admissions
919-335-0821, Ext. 220

† Duke University, Durham   27706

† East Carolina University
1000 E. 5th St., Greenville   27858
Dr. Ernest B. Uhr, Dean

Elon College
Love School of Business
P.O. Box 2700, Elon College   27244
Nan P. Perkins, Dean of Admissions

Fayetteville State University
1200 Murchison Rd., Fayetteville   28301
Donald W. Lahuffman, Dir. of Admissions

Gardner-Webb University
General Delivery, Boiling Springs   28017
Keith Griggs, Chrpsn.
704-434-2361

Greensboro College
815 W. Market St., Greensboro   27401

Guilford College
5800 W. Friendly Ave., Greensboro   27410
Larry West, Dir. of Admis.
See listing under "Universities"

Halifax Community College
P.O. Box 809, Weldon   27890

High Point College
933 Montlieu Ave., High Point   27262
Jim Schlimmer, Dir. of Admis.

King's College
322 Lamar Ave., Charlotte   28204
Ed Besterfeldt, President

Livingstone College
701 W. Monroe St., Salisbury   28144

Mars Hill College
Main St., Mars Hill   28754
Dr. Smith Goodrum, Dean of Admis.

Methodist College
5400 Ramsey St., Fayetteville   28311
Fiore Bergamasco, Dir. of Admis.

Montreat-Anderson College
P.O. Box 1267, Montreat   28757
David E. Walters, Dir. of Admissions
800-MAC-N-YOU
See listing under "Universities"

† North Carolina A&T State University
1601 E. Market St., Greensboro   27411

North Carolina Central University
P.O. Box 19617, Durham   27707

North Carolina State University
P.O. Box 7001, Raleigh   27695
George Dixon, Dir. of Admis.

North Carolina Wesleyan College
3400 N. Wesleyan Blvd., Rocky Mount   27804

Pembroke State University
P.O. Box 1510, Pembroke   28372
Anthony Locklear, Dir. of Admissions
919-521-6262

Pfeiffer College
General Delivery, Misenheimer   28109

QUEENS COLLEGE
1900 Selwyn Ave., Charlotte   28274
D. Stephen Cloniger, VP for Enrollment Management
See listing under "Liberal Arts"

St. Andrews Presbyterian College
1700 Dogwood Mile, Laurinburg   28352
Dale B. Montague, Dir. of Admis.

St. Augustine's College
1315 Oakwood Ave., Raleigh   27610
I. E. Spraggins, Dir. Admissions

Salem College
P.O. Box 10548, Winston-Salem   27108
Katherine Knapp, Director of Admissions
800-32-SALEM
See listing under "Women's College"

SALISBURY BUSINESS COLLEGE
1400 Jake Alexander Blvd. W., Salisbury   28147
Bill Hensley, President
704-636-4071
Established 1917. Private. Coed. Accreditation: Accrediting Council for Independent Colleges and Schools. Tuition: $2,600. Room and board: $2,000. Fees: $100. Enrollment: 125 full-time, 15 part-time. Faculty: 13. Student-faculty: 15:1. 12,000 square foot building. Individual attention. Once a graduate under any program of study, there is no charge to refresh or retake program of study.

Sandhills Community College
2200 Airport Rd., Pinehurst   28374
910-692-6185

† University of North Carolina
1000 Spring Garden St., Greensboro   27412

University of North Carolina
601 S. College Rd., Wilmington   28403
W. H. Wagoner, Chancellor

† University of North Carolina at Chapel Hill
Chapel Hill   27599
James C. Walters, Dir. Undergrad Admis.

† University of North Carolina at Charlotte
Charlotte   28223
J. H. Woodward, Chancellor

† Wake Forest University
P.O. Box 7285, Winston-Salem   27109

Warren Wilson College
P.O. Box 9000, Asheville   28802-9000
Tom Weede, Dir. of Admis.

† Western Carolina University
Cullowhee   28723
Tyree H. Kiser, Dir. of Admissions

Wilkes Community College
P.O. Box 120, Wilkesboro   28697
Mac Warren, Dir. of Admis.

Wingate College, Wingate   28174

Winston-Salem State University
601 S. Martin Luther King Jr.
Winston-Salem   27110
Van Wilson, Dir. of Admissions

NORTH DAKOTA

MAYVILLE STATE UNIVERSITY
330 3rd St., N.E., Mayville   58257
Ronald Brown, Dir. of Admis.
See listing under "Universities"

University of Mary
7500 University Dr., Bismarck   58504
Steph Storey, Dir. of Admis.

† University of North Dakota
Box 8193 University Station, Grand Forks   58203

OHIO

Antonelli Institute of Art & Photography
124 E. 7th St., Cincinnati   45202

Baldwin-Wallace College
275 Eastland Rd., Berea   44017
Juliann K. Baker, Dir. of Admis.

Belmont Technical College
120 Fox Shannon Place, St. Clairsville   43950
Thomas Tarowsky, Asst. Dean of Student Services

Bohecker's Business College
326 E. Main St., Ravenna   44266
Douglas Kern, Director

† Bowling Green State University
Bowling Green   43403
John Martin, Dir. of Admis.

Bradford School
6170 Busch Blvd., Columbus   43229
Patrick Denton, President
614-846-9410

Capital University
2199 E. Main St., Columbus   43209
Dolphus E. Henry, Associate Provost

† Case Western Reserve University
2040 Adelbert Rd., Cleveland   44106

Central State University
1400 Brush Row Rd., Wilberforce   45384

Cincinnati School of Court Reporting & Business
600 Executive Building
35 E. 7th St., Cincinnati   45202
Adeline M. Womack, President

† Cleveland State University
Euclid Ave. at 24th St., Cleveland   44115

College of Mount St. Joseph
5701 Delhi Rd., Cincinnati   45233-1672
See listing under "Universities"

College of Wooster
1189 Beall Ave., Wooster   44691
Hayden Schilling, Dean of Admis.

Columbus State Community College
550 E. Spring St., Columbus   43215
Mary Jo Deerwester, Dir. of Admis.

Cuyahoga Community College, Eastern Campus
25444 Harvard Rd., Warrensville Heights   44122

Cuyahoga Community College, Metropolitan Campus
2900 Community College Ave., Cleveland   44115

· Cuyahoga Community College, Western Campus
11000 W. Pleasant Valley Rd.
Parma Heights 44130

DAVIS JUNIOR COLLEGE
4747 Monroe St., Toledo 43623
Diane Brunner, President
Marcia Eiser, Chairperson
Established 1858. Private. Coed. Accreditation: AICS, AAMA, NCACS. Tuition: $5,600. Fees: $25 application fee. Enrollment: 350 full-time, 100 part-time. Faculty: 35. Student-faculty ratio: 15:1. Degree: associate. Specialized library. 2 buildings including an airport. Admissions test (CPAT) & specialized. High school graduate or GED. Enroll each quarter. 90% placement overall. Unique professional pilot program.

DeVry Institute of Technology
1350 Alum Creek Dr., Columbus 43209
Richard Rodman, Dir. of Admis.
614-253-1525
See Illinois listing under "Universities"

Dyke College
112 Prospect Ave. S.E., Cleveland 44115

Franklin University
201 S. Grant Ave., Columbus 43215

Heidelberg College
310 E. Market St., Tiffin 44883
Stephen E. Eidson, Dean of Admission
800-925-9250

Hiram College
P.O. Box 96, Hiram 44234
Gary Craig, Dean of Admis.

· Hocking College
3301 Hocking Pky., Nelsonville 45764
Candace Vancko, VP for Enrollment
800-282-4163

† John Carroll University
20700 N. Park Blvd., Cleveland 44118

† Kent State University
P.O. Box 5190, Kent 44242
Bruce Riddle, Dir. of Admis.

· Kent State University-Ashtabula Campus
3325 W. 13th St., Ashtabula 44004
John Mahan, Dean

· Kent State University-East Liverpool Campus
400 E. 4th St., East Liverpool 43920
Suzanne Fitzgerald, Dean

· Kent State University-Geauga Campus
14111 Claridon-Troy Rd., Burton 44021
Larry Jones, Dean

· Kent State University-Salem Campus
2491 State Rt. 45 S., Salem 44460
Dr. James Cooney, Dean

Lake Erie College
391 W. Washington St., Painesville 44077

· Lima Technical College
4240 Campus Dr., Lima 45804
Cynthia E. Spiers, Director of Admissions

· Lorain County Community College
1005 Abbe Rd., N., Elyria 44035
Dr. John W. Thrash, Jr., Registrar

LOURDES COLLEGE
6832 Convent Blvd., Sylvania 43560
Mary E. Briggs, Dir. of Admis.
419-885-5291 or 800-878-3210

Malone College
515 25th St., N.W., Canton 44709
Lee Sommers, Dean of Admissions

MARIETTA COLLEGE
210 5th St., Marietta 45750
Dennis R. DePerro, Dean Admis./Financial Aid
800-331-7896

† Miami University
E. High St., Oxford 45056

Mount Union College
1972 Clark Ave., Alliance 44601
Amy Tomko, Dir. of Admis.

Mt. Vernon Nazarene College
800 Martinsburg Rd., Mt. Vernon 43050
Ronald Hyson, Dir. of Admis.

Ohio Dominican College
1216 Sunbury Rd., Columbus 43219
800-955-OHIO

OHIO NORTHERN UNIVERSITY
525 S. Main St., Ada 45810
Dr. Terry Maris, Dean
412-772-2000

† Ohio State University
190 N. Oval Mall, Columbus 43210

† Ohio University, Athens 45701

Ohio Wesleyan University
61 S. Sandusky St., Delaware 43015
Donald Bishop, Dean for Enrollment

· Owens Community College
P.O. Box 10000, Toledo 43699
Jim Welling, Admissions
419-661-7225

· Owens Community College
300 Davis St., Findlay 45840
Stacy Davidson, Admissions
419-423-6827

· Penn-Ohio College
3517 Market St., Youngstown 44507
William Clark, Jr., President

Shawnee State University
940 2nd St., Portsmouth 45662
Rosemary K. Poston, Dir. of Admis.

: Southeastern Business College
1907 N. Ridge Rd., Lorain 44055
Nancy Bonzar, Dir. of Admis.

: Southeastern Business College
4020 Milan Rd., Sandusky 44870

: Southeastern Business College
1855 Western Ave., Chillicothe 45601
John T. Danicki, Executive Director

: Southeastern Business College
420 E. Main St., Jackson 45640
Janet Travis, Director

: Southeastern Business College
1522 Sheridan Dr., Lancaster 43130
Alex Bosserman, Director

: Southeastern Business College
3879 Rhodes Ave., New Boston 45662
Annita Thompson, Director

: Stautzenberger College
5355 Southwyck Blvd., Toledo 43614
Jack Peeples, Dir.

Tiffin University
155 Miami St., Tiffin 44883
Kristine M. Boyle, Dir. of Admis.

† University of Akron
381 Buchtel Common, Akron 44325
Kris MacDermott, Asst. Provost Enrollment

† University of Cincinnati
2700 Clifton Ave., Cincinnati 45221

† University of Dayton
300 College Park Ave., Dayton 45469-2226
Toll-free 800-837-7433
See listing under "Universities"

University of Findlay
1000 N. Main St., Findlay 45840
Dan Crabtree, Dir. of Admis.

University of Rio Grande
General Delivery, Rio Grande 45674
Dr. Charles Palmer, Dean
614-245-5353, Ext. 7216

† University of Toledo
2801 Bancroft St., W., Toledo 43606
Richard Eastop, Dir. of Admis.

Urbana University
100 College Way, Urbana 43078
Donald Burns, Dir. of Admis.

Ursuline College
2550 Lander Rd., Cleveland 44124

Wilmington College
P.O. Box 1185, Wilmington 45177
Rhonda Inderhees, Dir. of Admis.

Wittenberg University
P.O. Box 720, Springfield 45504

† Wright State University
3640 Colonel Glenn Hwy., Dayton 45435

Xavier University
3800 Victory Pky., Cincinnati 45207

Youngstown State University
410 Wick Ave., Youngstown 44555
Leslie H. Cochran, President

OKLAHOMA

Bartlesville Wesleyan College
2201 Silverlake Rd., Bartlesville 74006

Cameron University
2800 W. Gore Blvd., Lawton 73505
Louise Brown, Dir. of Admis.

Mid-America Bible College
3500 S.W. 119th St., Oklahoma City 73170
Tony O'Brien, Registrar
405-691-3800

Northeastern State University
600 N. Grand Ave., Tahlequah 74464

Oklahoma Christian University of Science and Arts
P.O. Box 11000, Oklahoma City 73136
Duane Eggleston, Vice President
800-877-5010

Oklahoma City University
2501 N. Blackwelder Ave., Oklahoma City 73106
David Carmichael, Dean
See listing under "Universities"

Oklahoma Panhandle State University
P.O. Box 430, Goodwell 73939

† Oklahoma State University, Stillwater 74078
Robert Sandmeyer, Dean

Oral Roberts University
7777 S. Lewis Ave., Tulsa 74171
Arthur E. Matzkvech, Dir. of Admis.

Southeastern Oklahoma State University
Station A, Durant 74701

Southern Nazarene University
6729 N.W. 39th Expy., Bethany 73008

Southwestern Oklahoma State University
100 Campus Dr., Weatherford 73096

University of Central Oklahoma
100 N. University Dr., Edmond 73034

† University of Oklahoma at Norman
660 Parrington Oval, Norman 73019

† University of Tulsa
600 S. College Ave., Tulsa 74104
Dr. Markham Collins, Acting Dean

OREGON

CASCADE COLLEGE
BRANCH CAMPUS OF OKLAHOMA CHRISTIAN UNIVERSITY
9101 E. Burnside St., Portland 97216
Brad Fisher, Director of Admission
800-550-PORT
Established 1994. Private. Coed. Accreditation: North Central Association of Schools and Colleges. Tuition: $6,400. Room and board: $3,200. Fees: $200. Enrollment: 160 full-time, 50 part-time. Faculty: 18. Student-faculty ratio: 12:1. Degrees: Bachelor of Arts in Business Administration, Liberal Studies, Liberal Studies with Teacher Certification, Biblical Studies. 9 buildings on 10 acres. Branch campus of Oklahoma Christian University of Science and Arts. Intramural and club athletics. Near I-205 in East Portland, City of Roses. Choir. Drama.

· Central Oregon Community College
2600 N.W. College Way, Bend 97701
Christine Kerlin, Dir. of Admis.
503-383-7500

· Chemeketa Community College
P.O. Box 14007, Salem 97309
Barbara Cockrell, Director
503-399-5114

Lewis & Clark College
0615 S.W. Palatine Hill Rd., Portland 97219
Michael Sexton, Dean of Admissions

Marylhurst College for Lifelong Learning
P.O. Box 261, Marylhurst 97036
Tom Swenson, Chrpsn.
800-634-9984

Northwest Christian College
828 E. 11th Ave., Eugene 97401
Randy Jones, Dir. of Admis.

† Oregon State University, Corvallis 97333
Wallace Gibbs, Dir. of Admis.

Pacific University
2043 College Way, Forest Grove 97116
Barbara Mergen, Dir. of Admis.

† Portland State University
P.O. Box 751, Portland 97207

Southern Oregon State College
1250 Siskiyou Blvd., Ashland 97520

· Treasure Valley Community College
650 College Blvd., Ontario 97914
Ron Kulm, Dir. of Admis.

: Trend College
1050 Green Acres Rd., Eugene 97401
Sue Port, Director

† University of Oregon
1 University of Oregon, Eugene 97403

† University of Portland
5000 N. Willamette Blvd., Portland 97203

Warner Pacific College
2219 S.E. 68th Ave., Portland 97215
Sherry Moore, Enrollment Management Director

Western Baptist College, Salem 97301
800-845-3005

· Western Business College
425 S.W. Washington St., Portland 97204
Donald Waldbauer, President

Willamette University
900 State St. S.E., Salem 97301

PENNSYLVANIA

Albright College
P.O. Box 15234, Reading 19612

Allentown College of St. Frances de Sales
2755 Station Ave., Center Valley 18034
George Kelley, Dir. of Admis.

Alvernia College
400 Bernardine St., Reading 19607
Lisa Grabowski, Dir. of Admis.

· The Art Institute of Philadelphia
1622 Chestnut St., Philadelphia 19103
215-567-7080

Beaver College
450 S. Easton Rd., Glenside 19038-3295
Dennis Nostrand, VP for Enrollment Management
Phone: 800-776-BEAVER(2328)
Fax: 215-572-4049
See listing under "Universities"

Bloomsburg University, Bloomsburg 17815
Bernard Vinovrski, Dir. of Admis.

BOYD SCHOOL
1 Chatham Center, Pittsburgh 15219
Branch: 2090 Palm Beach Lakes Blvd.
West Palm Beach FL 33409
Ruth Delach, President

Elizabeth McKinney, Dir. of Admissions, Graduate Services, Executive VP
Established 1968. Private. Coed. With student body capacity up to 2,250 per year in both locations. Programs offered include financial aid and lifetime job placement to qualified students. Costs vary depending on length of program selected. Courses offered are airline/travel industry training (15 weeks), executive travel (9 months), secretarial, bookkeeping, administrative assistant (6 & 9 months). Programs begin three times per year in both locations. Resident housing is available at both locations. School monitored apartments adjacent to schools. Admission is through personal home interview with school's representative or school visit. High school diploma or GED is required for entrance. Strict dress code is observed in school. Accreditation: member of CCA, and licensed by individual states. Graduates number 25,000 with very active alumni association in all fifty states and many countries. Sixty percent of students are referrals from alumni. The Boyd School is in the process of requesting a certificate of approval to award an Associate in Specialized Business degree.

· Bradley Academy for the Visual Arts
   625 E. Philadelphia St., York 17403
   Loren H. Kroh, Director
   717-848-1447

Cabrini College
   610 King of Prussia Rd., Radnor 19087

California University of Pennsylvania
   3rd St., California 15419
   Norman Hasbrouck, Dean for Enrollment

Cambria-Rowe Business College
   221 Central Ave., Johnstown 15902
   William M. Coward, President

Carlow College
   3333 5th Ave., Pittsburgh 15213

† Carnegie Mellon University
   5000 Forbes Ave., Pittsburgh 15213

Cedar Crest College
   100 College Dr., Allentown 18104-6196
   Cynthia Phillips, Dir. of Admissions

· Central Pennsylvania Business School
   College Hill Rd., Summerdale 17093

Chatham College
   Woodland Rd., Pittsburgh 15232
   Suellen Ofe, Dean of Admis./Financial Aid
   See listing under "Women's College"

· Churchman Business School
   355 Spring Garden St., Easton 18042
   Charles Churchman, Jr., President

Clarion University of Pennsylvania
   840 Wood St., Clarion 16214

College Misericordia
   301 Lake St., Dallas 18612
   Michael Joseph, Dir. of Enrollment Mgmt.

Delaware Valley College of Science & Agriculture
   Doylestown 18901
   Stephen Zenko, Dir. of Admis.

† Drexel University
   3141 Chestnut St., Philadelphia 19104
   Dean of Enrollment Management

† Duquesne University
   600 Forbes Ave., Pittsburgh 15282
   Thomas Schaefer, C.S.Sp., Dir. of Admis.

Eastern College
   10 Fairview Dr., Saint Davids 19087
   Ronald Keller, VP for Enrollment Management

Edinboro University of Pennsylvania
   Edinboro 16444
   Admissions Office: 800-626-2203

Elizabethtown College
   1 Alpha Dr., Elizabethtown 17022

· Erie Business Center
   246 W. 9th St., Erie 16501
   Tony Piccirillo, Dir. of Admis.
   See listing under "Career Schools"

Franklin & Marshall College
   P.O. Box 3003, Lancaster 17604

Gannon University
   109 University Sq., Erie 16541

Geneva College
   3200 College Ave., Beaver Falls 15010

Grove City College
   100 Campus Dr., Grove City 16127
   Dr. John Sparks, Chrpsn.

GWYNEDD-MERCY COLLEGE
   Sumneytown Pike, Gwynedd Valley 19437
   Marjorie DeSimone, Dean of Admissions
   800-DIAL-GMC
   See listing under "Universities"

· Harcum Junior College, Bryn Mawr 19010
   Mary.Pontius, Dean of Admissions

Holy Family College
   Grant & Frankford Ave., Philadelphia 19114
   Dr. Mott Linn, Dir. of Admis.
   215-637-3050

Immaculata College
   Immaculata 19345
   James P. Sullivan, Dir. of Admis.

Juniata College
   1700 Moore St., Huntington 16652

· Keystone Junior College
   P.O. Box 50, La Plume 18440
   Kevin McIntyre, Dir. of Admis.

King's College
   133 N. River St., Wilkes Barre 18711

Lackawanna Junior College
   901 Prospect Ave., Scranton 18505
   Renee J. Garvey, Dir. of Admis.

Lansdale School of Business
   201 Church Rd., North Wales 19454
   Marlon Keller, Director

La Roche College
   9000 Babcock Blvd., Pittsburgh 15237
   Marianne Leister, Dir. of Admis.

La Salle University
   1900 W. Olney Ave., Philadelphia 19141
   Joseph Kane, Dean
   See listing under "Universities"

† Lehigh University
   27 Memorial Dr. W., Bethlehem 18015

Lincoln University, Lincoln University 19352
   Jimmy Arrington, Dir. of Admis.

Lycoming College, Williamsport 17701

: McCann School of Business
   47 S. Main St., Mahanoy City 17948
   John Slodysko, Director

· McCann School of Business
   Wilkes Barre Campus
   2004 Wyoming Ave., Wyoming 18644
   James Noone, Director

Marywood College
   2300 Adams Ave., Scranton 18509

Mercyhurst College
   501 E. 38th St., Erie 16546
   Andrew Roth, Dean of Enrollment
   800-825-1926

Millersville University of Pennsylvania
   Millersville 17551
   Blair Treasure, Dean of Admissions

· Montgomery County Community College
   340 DeKalb Pike, Blue Bell 19422-0758
   Dennis Murphy, Dir. of Admis.

Mt. Aloysius College
   1 College Dr., Cresson 16630
   Sylvia Hirsch, Dir. of Admis.

Muhlenberg College
   2400 W. Chew St., Allentown 18104
   Chris Hooker-Haring, Dir. of Admis.

· NEC-Allentown Business School Campus
   1501 Lehigh St., Allentown 18103
   610-791-5100

Neumann College
   Concord Rd., Aston 19014

· Peirce Junior College
   1420 Pine St., Philadelphia 19102
   David Schleicher, Dir. of Admis.

· Pennsylvania Institute of Technology
   Rose Valley-Notre Dame Campus
   800 Manchester Ave., Media 19063
   610-565-7900

† Pennsylvania State University
   201 Shields Bldg., University Park 16802

· Pennsylvania State University, Wilkes-Barre Campus
   P.O. Box PSU, Lehman 18627
   800-426-2358

Pennsylvania State University
   Rt. 230, Middletown 17057
   Mary E. Gundel, Dir. of Admis.

Philadelphia College of Textiles & Science
   4201 Henry Ave., Philadelphia 19144

Point Park College
   201 Wood St., Pittsburgh 15222

· Reading Area Community College
   P.O. Box 1706, Reading 19603
   Robin Sodomsky, Dir. of Admis.

Robert Morris College
   Narrows Run Rd., Coraopolis 15108
   James R. Welsh, Dean of Admissions
   See listing under "Universities"

Robert Morris College
   600 5th Ave., Pittsburgh 15219
   James R. Welsh, Dean of Admissions
   See listing under "Universities"

St. Francis College
   P.O. Box 600, Loretto 15940

St. Joseph's University
   5600 City Ave., Philadelphia 19131
   Randy Miller, Dir. of Admis.

St. Vincent College
   300 Fraser Purchase Rd., Latrobe 15650

Seton Hill College, Greensburg 15601
   Peter Egan, Dir. of Admis.
   800-826-6234 or 412-838-4255

: Shenango Valley School of Business
   500 S. Mill St., New Castle 16101
   412-654-1976

: Shenango Valley School of Business
   124 W. Spring St., Titusville 16354
   814-827-9567

: Shenango Valley School of Business
   335 Boyd Dr., Sharon 16146
   412-983-0700

† Shippensburg University, Shippensburg 17257

Slippery Rock University, Slippery Rock 16057
   Director of Admissions

SOUTH HILLS BUSINESS SCHOOL
   480 Waupelani Dr., State College 16801-4516
   Maralyn Mazza, Director
   Admissions: 814-234-7755
   Established 1970. Private. Coed. Tuition: $6,420 per year. Enrollment: 350. Faculty: 50. Accredited by CCA. ASB degrees in accounting, management, secretarial, computer information systems and health information technology. Diplomas in accounting, secretarial, clerical, retail management, travel, and microcomputers. One and two-year programs available. Financial aid, counseling and placement assistance. Housing nearby, cafeteria and day care facilities.

Susquehanna University
   514 University Ave., Selinsgrove 17870

† Temple University
   Broad St. & Montgomery Ave.
   Philadelphia 19122

Thiel College
   75 College Ave., Greenville 16125
   Robert Weaver, Dir. of Admis.

† University of Pennsylvania
   0 Levy Park, Philadelphia 19104

† University of Pittsburgh
   4200 5th Ave., Pittsburgh 15260

University of Pittsburgh, Greensburg Campus
   1150 Mt. Pleasant Rd., Greensburg 15601
   Larry Whatule, Dir. of Admis.
   412-836-9880

UNIVERSITY OF PITTSBURGH AT TITUSVILLE
   McKinney Hall
   504 E Main St., Titusville 16354
   Jamie Mowat, Dir. of Admis./Financial Aid
   814-827-4427

† Villanova University
   845 E. Lancaster Ave., Villanova 19085
   Stephen R. Merritt, Dir. of Admis.

Washington & Jefferson College
   60 S. Lincoln St., Washington 15301
   Thomas O'Connor, Dir. of Admis.

Waynesburg College
   51 W. College St., Waynesburg 15370
   Robin Moore, Dir. of Admis.
   800-225-7393

West Chester University of Pennsylvania
   S. High St., West Chester 19380

WESTMINSTER COLLEGE
   New Wilmington 16172
   Richard Dana Paul, Dir. of Admis.
   412-946-7100

Widener University
   700 E. 14th St., Chester 19013

Wilkes University
   184 S. River St., Wilkes-Barre 18766
   Emory P. Guffrovich Jr., Dean of Admissions

York College of Pennsylvania
   P.O. Box 15199, York 17405-7199
   Nancy Spataro, Dir. of Admis.
   717-849-1600
   See listing under "Universities"

: Yorktowne Business Institute
   0 W. 7th Ave., York 17404
   John Halpin, Admissions Representative

RHODE ISLAND

Brown University, Providence 02906

Bryant College
   1150 Douglas Pike, Smithfield 02917

Johnson & Wales University
   111 Dorrance St., Providence 02903
   Mark S. Burke, Dir. of Admis.

: Katharine Gibbs School
   178 Butler Ave., Providence 02906
   401-861-1420

: Nasson Institute
   1080 Newport Ave., Pawtucket 02861

: Ocean State Business Institute
   140 Point Judith Rd. #3A, Narragansett 02882
   Assunta Pouliot, Director
   401-789-0287

Providence College
   River Ave., Providence 02918

Rhode Island College
   600 Mt. Pleasant Ave., Providence 02908

Roger Williams College
   1 Old Ferry Rd., Bristol 02809
   William Dunfey, Dir. of Admis.

Salve Regina University
   1 Ochre Point Ave., Newport 02840
   Roselina McKillop, Dean of Admissions

: School of Medical & Legal Secretarial Sciences
60 S. Angell St., Providence 02906
Norma Casale, Director

† University of Rhode Island, Kingston 02881
Sydney Stern, Dean

SOUTH CAROLINA

Anderson College
316 S. Boulevard, Anderson 29621
Carl D. Lockman, Dir. of Admis.
800-542-3594

Central Wesleyan College
P.O. Box 1020, Central 29630
Lillian A. Robbins, Dir. of Admis.

Charleston Southern University
P.O. Box 10087, Charleston 29411
Melinda Mitchum, Dir. of Admis.

† Clemson University
201 Sikes Hall, Clemson 29634

Coastal Carolina College
P.O. Box 1954, Myrtle Beach 29578
Dr. Ed Cerny, Director of Admissions

† College of Charleston
66 George St., Charleston 29424

Columbia College
1301 Columbia College Dr., Columbia 29203

· Columbia Junior College of Business
P.O. Box 1196, Columbia 29202
Michael Gorman, President

Erskine College & Seminary
Washington St., Due West 29639
Dot Carter, Dir. of Admis.

Furman University
3300 Poinsett Hwy., Greenville 29613
Charles Brock, Dir. of Admis.

· Greenville Technical College
P.O. Box 5616, Greenville 29606

Lander College
320 Stanley Ave., Greenwood 29649

North Greenville College
P.O. Box 1892, Tigerville 29688
Gary Wells, Dir. of Admis.
See listing under "Universities"

Presbyterian College
503 S. Broad St., Clinton 29325
Margaret Williamson, Dean of Admis.

South Carolina State University
P.O. Box 7127, Orangeburg 29117-0001
803-536-7185

· Spartanburg Technical College
P.O. Box 4386, Spartanburg 29305
Pam Hagan, Dir. Admissions & Counseling
803-591-3800

† University of South Carolina, Columbia 29208
Terry Davis, Dir. of Admis.
803-777-7700

University of South Carolina at Aiken
171 University Pkwy., Aiken 29801

University of South Carolina at Union
P.O. Box 729, Union 29379
James Edwards, Dean

Voorhees College
Voorhees Rd., Denmark 29042

† Winthrop University
701 W. Oakland Ave., Rock Hill 29733
James McCammon, Jr., Dir. of Admis.

Wofford College
429 N. Church St., Spartanburg 29303
Charles Gray, Dir. of Admis.

SOUTH DAKOTA

Augustana College
29th & S. Summit, Sioux Falls 57197

Dakota State University
820 N. Washington Ave., Madison 57042
Dr. Richard Puetz, Dean
605-256-5139

Dakota Wesleyan University
1300 W. University Ave., Mitchell 57301

· Kilian Community College
224 N. Phillips Ave., Sioux Falls 57102
605-336-1711 or 800-888-1147

Mt. Marty College
1105 W. 8th St., Yankton 57078
Paula Tacke, Dir. of Admis.

National College
321 Kansas City St., Rapid City 57701
Keith T. Carlyle, Dir. of Admis.

· Nettleton Junior College
100 S. Spring Ave., Sioux Falls 57104
Herman Whitaker, Dir. of Admissions
800-727-1837 or 605-336-1837

Northern State University
1200 S. Jay St., Aberdeen 57401

Presentation College
1500 N. Main St., Aberdeen 57401
Sr. Lucille Welbig, Dir. of Admis.

SIOUX FALLS COLLEGE
1501 S. Prairie Ave., Sioux Falls 57105
Susan Reese, Dir. of Admis.
800-888-1047
See listing under "Universities"

South Dakota State University
P.O. Box 0504A, Brookings 57007
Dr. Ardelle Lundeen, Department Head
605-688-4141
See listing under "Universities"

: Stenotype Institute
705 W. Avenue N, Sioux Falls 57104
Linda Clauson, President

† University of South Dakota
414 E. Clark St., Vermillion 57069
Dave Lorenz, Dir. of Admis.

: Western Dakota Technical Institute
1600 Sedivy Ln., Rapid City 57701
See listing under "Career Schools"

TENNESSEE

Austin Peay State University
601 College St., Clarksville 37044

Bristol University
P.O. Box 4366, Bristol 37625
Dr. W. David Willis, Academic Dean
See listing under "Universities"

Bryan College
Box 7000, Dayton 37321
Thomas A. Shaw, Dir. of Admis.

Carson-Newman College
P.O. Box 70552, Jefferson City 37760
See listing under "Universities"

Christian Brothers College
650 E. Parkway, S., Memphis 38104

· Cooper Institute
724 5th Ave., N., Knoxville 37917
Judy Ferguson, Dean

Crichton College
6655 Winchester Rd., Memphis 38115
901-367-9800

David Lipscomb University
3901 Granny White Pike, Nashville 37204-3951
Wade Sandrell, Dir. of Admis.
800-333-4358

† EAST TENNESSEE STATE UNIVERSITY
P.O. Box 70731, Johnson City 37614
Dr. Nancy Dishner, Dean, Enrollment Management
615-929-4213 or 800-462-3878

Freed-Hardeman University
158 E. Main St., Henderson 38340
800-342-7837

Le Moyne-Owen College
807 Walker Ave., Memphis 38126
901-942-7302 or 800-737-7778

Lincoln Memorial University
P.O. Box 2012, Harrogate 37752
Conrad Daniels, Dir. of Admis.

Maryville College
800 S. Court St., Maryville 37801
Annabelle J. Libby, Dir. of Admis.

† Middle Tennessee State University
Murfreesboro 37132
Roger D. Sims, Dir. of Admis.

Rhodes College
2000 N. Parkway, Memphis 38112

† Tennessee Technological University
P.O. Box 5006, Cookeville 38505

Tennessee Temple University
1815 Union Ave., Chattanooga 37404
Dr. L. W. Nichols, President

Trevecca Nazarene College
333 Murfreesboro Rd., Nashville 37210

Tusculum College
P.O. Box 5035, Greeneville 37743
Ronald Porter, Dir. of Admis.

Union University
2447 US Highway 45 Bypass, Jackson 38305
Dr. Robert Wyatt, Dean
901-668-1818
See listing under "Universities"

† University of Memphis, Memphis 38152
Dr. John Eubank, Dean of Admissions

University of Tennessee at Martin
Martin 38238
Paul Kelley, Director of Admissions
See listing under "Universities"

† University of Tennessee at Chattanooga
615 McCallie Ave., Chattanooga 37403

† University of Tennessee, Knoxville
527 Andy Holt Tower, Knoxville 37996
Dr. Gordon Stanley, Dir. of Admis.

† Vanderbilt University
West End Ave., Nashville 37240

TEXAS

Abilene Christian University
ACU Station, Box 6000, Abilene 79699

Amber University
1700 Eastgate Dr., Garland 75041

: American Commercial College
402 Butternut St., Abilene 79602
Michael Otto, Director

· Art Institute of Dallas
8080 Park Ln., Dallas 75231
Lee Colker, Dir. of Admis.

Austin College
900 N. Grand Ave., Sherman 75090
Rodney Oto, Dean of Admission
800-442-5363

† Baylor University
P.O. Box 97008, Waco 76798-7008
Diana Ramey, Director of Admissions

Concordia Lutheran College
3400 N. Interstate 35, Austin 78705
Kevin Pieper, Dir. of Admis.

Corpus Christi State University
6300 Ocean Dr., Corpus Christi 78412

Dallas Baptist University
7777 W. Kiest Blvd., Dallas 75211

DeVry Institute of Technology
4801 Regent Blvd., Irving 75063
Daniel Millan, Dir. of Admis.
214-929-5777
See Illinois listing under "Universities"

East Texas Baptist University
1200 N. Grove Ave., Marshall 75670

† East Texas State University
ETSU Station, Commerce 75429

Houston Baptist University
7502 Fondren Rd., Houston 77074

Incarnate Word College
4301 Broadway St., San Antonio 78209
Sr. Sally Mitchell, Dean of Enrollment

† Lamar University
P.O. Box 10009, Beaumont 77710
800-458-7558

LeTourneau College
P.O. Box 7001, Longview 75607
Roger Kieffer, Dir. of Admis.

Midwestern State University
3400 Taft Blvd., Wichita Falls 76308
Dr. Garland Hadley, Head

· North Central Texas College
1525 W. California, Gainesville 76240
Doug Willis, Dir. of Admis.

Northwood University
P.O. Box 58, Cedar Hill 75106
Jim Hickerson, Dir. of Admis.
800-927-WOOD

Our Lady of the Lake University
411 S.W. 24th St., San Antonio 78207-4689
210-434-6711

Prairie View A & M University
P.O. Box 3089, Prairie View 77446-3089
Linda S. Berry, Dir. of Admis.

Rice University
P.O. Box 1892, Houston 77251

St. Edward's University
3001 S. Congress Ave., Austin 78704
John Lambert, Dir. of Admis.

St. Mary's University of San Antonio
1 Camino Santa Maria, San Antonio 78228
Rick Castillo, Dir. of Admis.

Sam Houston State University, Huntsville 77341

Schreiner College
2100 Memorial Blvd., Kerrville 78028
800-343-4919

† Southern Methodist University
Hillcrest at University, Dallas 75275

Southwest Texas State University
601 University Dr., San Marcos 78666

† Stephen F. Austin State University
P.O. Box 6078. Nacogdoches 75962

Texas A & I University
Campus Box 101, Kingsville 78363

† Texas A & M University
College Station 77843

† Texas Christian University
2800 S. University Dr., Ft. Worth 76129
Dr. Edward Boehm, Jr., Dean of Admissions

Texas Lutheran College
1000 W. Court St., Seguin 78155
Jennifer B. Ehlers, Dir. of Admis.

: Texas School of Business
711 Air Tex Dr., Houston 77073
Madeline Burillo, Director
713-846-2888

Texas Southern University
3100 Cleburne St., Houston 77004

† Texas Tech University, Lubbock 79409

Texas Wesleyan University
1201 Wesleyan St., Fort Worth 76105
Kim Campbell, Dir. Freshman Admission

Texas Women's University
P.O. Box 23925, Denton 76204

University of Central Texas
P.O. Box 1416, Killeen 76540
Dr. Pauline Moseley, Dean of the Faculty

University of Dallas
1845 E. Northgate Dr., Irving 75062
Jim Whitaker, Dir. of Admis.

† University of Houston
4800 Calhoun Rd., Houston 77204

† University of Houston-Clear Lake
2700 Bay Area Blvd., Houston 77058
Darella Banks, Exec. Dir. Enrollment Services

† University of North Texas
P.O. Box 13797, Denton 76203

University of St. Thomas
3812 Montrose Blvd., Houston 77006
Elsie Biron, Dir. of Admis.

† University of Texas at Arlington
UTA Box 19125, Arlington 76019
R. Zack Prince, Dir. of Admis.

† University of Texas at Austin
0 the University of Texas, Austin 78712

University of Texas at Dallas
P.O. Box 830688, Richardson 75083-0688

† University of Texas at El Paso
500 W. University Ave., El Paso 79968

† University of Texas at San Antonio
San Antonio 78285
Dr. John H. Brown, Dir. of Admis.

University of Texas at Tyler
3900 University Blvd., Tyler 75799
Dr. Robert Partain, Dean

† University of Texas-Pan American
1201 W. University Dr., Edinburg 78539
Miguel Nerarez, President

West Texas State University
2501 4th Ave., Canyon 79016
Lila Vars, Dir. of Admis.

UTAH

† Brigham Young University, Provo 84602

Southern Utah University
351 W. Center St., Cedar City 84720
Robert Salmon, Dean
801-586-5401

† University of Utah
1400 E. 200 S., Salt Lake City 84112
Dr. J. Stayner Landward, Dir. of Admis.

† Utah State University, Logan 84322-1600
Rod Clark, Director of Admissions
801-750-1107

Weber State University
3750 Harrison Blvd., Ogden 84408

Westminster College of Salt Lake City
1840 S. 1300 E., Salt Lake City 84105
800-748-4753

VERMONT

Castleton State College, Castleton 05735
Gary Fallis, Dir. of Admis.

Champlain College
P.O. Box 670, Burlington 05402
Josephine Churchill, Dir. of Admis.
802-860-2727
See listing under "Universities"

College of St. Joseph
71 Clement Rd., Rutland 05701

Goddard College
P.O. Box G, Plainfield 05667
Jackson Kytle, President

Lyndon State College, Lyndonville 05851

NORWICH UNIVERSITY
65 S. Main St., Northfield 05663
Prof. Frank Vanecek, Head
See listing under "Universities"

Saint Michael's College
Winooski Park, Colchester 05439
800-SMC-8000
See listing under "Liberal Arts"

Southern Vermont College
Monument Ave., Bennington 05201
See listing under "Universities"

Trinity College
208 Colchester Ave., Burlington 05401

† University of Vermont
194 S. Prospect St., Burlington 05401
802-656-3370

VIRGINIA

Averett College
420 W. Main St., Danville 24541
Gary Sherman, Dean of Enrollment Mgmt.

Bluefield College
3000 College Dr., Bluefield 24605
Dr. Roy Dobyns, President
See listing under "Universities"

Bridgewater College
402 E College St., Bridgewater 22812

Christopher Newport College
50 Shoe Ln., Newport News 23606

Clinch Valley College of the University of Virginia
P.O. Box 16, Wise 24293
Lana Low, Dir. Enrollment Management

† College of William and Mary, Williamsburg 23185
Jean A. Scott, Dean of Admission

· Commonwealth College
300 Boush St., Norfolk 23510
Debbi Huck, Dean of Admissions

· Commonwealth College
4160 Virginia Beach Blvd., Virginia Beach 23452
Nancy Kennedy, Dean of Admissions

· Commonwealth College
1120 W. Mercury Blvd., Hampton 23666
Robyn Rickenbach, Dean of Admissions

Eastern Mennonite College
1200 Park Rd., Harrisonburg 22801
Jerry Miller, Dir. of Admis.

Emory & Henry College
General Delivery, Emory 24327

Ferrum College, Ferrum 24088
Bob Bailey, Dir. of Admis.

† George Mason University
4400 University Dr., Fairfax 22030-4444
Patricia Riordan, Dean of Admissions

† James Madison University, Harrisonburg 22807

LIBERTY UNIVERSITY
P.O. Box 20000, Lynchburg 24506
Jay Spencer, VP Recruitment
800-376-2800
See listing under "Universities"

Longwood College, Farmville 23901

Lynchburg College
1501 Lakeside Dr., Lynchburg 24501
Ernest Chadderton, Dean of Enrollment

Mary Baldwin College, Staunton 24401
Douglas E. Clark, Exec. Dir. of Enrollment

Marymount University
2807 N. Glebe Rd., Arlington 22207
Charles Coe, Director of Admissions
800-548-7638 or 703-284-1500
See listing under "Universities"

Mary Washington College
1701 College Ave., Fredericksburg 22401
Martin Wilder, V.P. for Admissions

† Norfolk State University
2401 Corprew Ave., Norfolk 23504

† Old Dominion University
5215 Hampton Blvd., Norfolk 23508

Radford University
P.O. Box 5430, Radford 24142

Randolph-Macon College
200 Henry St., Ashland 23005
John Conkright, Dean of Admissions

Roanoke College
221 College Ln., Salem 24153

SHENANDOAH UNIVERSITY
1460 University Dr., Winchester 22601
Dr. Daniel Pavsek, Dean
See listing under "Universities"

· Southern Virginia College for Women
One College Hill Dr., Buena Vista 24416
Mark A. Camper, Assoc. Dir. of Admis.
800-229-8420
See listing under "Women's Colleges"

· Tidewater Community College, Chesapeake Campus
1428 Cedar Rd., Chesapeake 23320
Dr. Larry L. Whitworth, President

· Tidewater Community College, Portsmouth Campus
Rt. 135, Portsmouth 23703
Dr. Larry L. Whitworth, President

· Tidewater Community College
1700 College Crescent, Virginia Beach 23456
Dr. Larry L. Whitworth, President

† University of Richmond, Richmond 23173

† University of Virginia
P.O. Box 9017, Charlottesville 22906

† Virginia Commonwealth University
910 W. Franklin St., Richmond 23284

Virginia Intermont College
1013 Moore St., Bristol 24201
Lawton Blandford, Dir. of Admis.

Virginia Military Institute, Lexington 24450

† Virginia Polytechnic Institute & State University
Blacksburg 24061
David Bousquet, Dir. of Undergraduate Admis.

Virginia State University, Petersburg 23803
Mable C. Mountcastle, Dir. of Recording

Virginia Union University
1500 N. Lombardy St., Richmond 23220
Janice D. Bailey, Dir. of Admissions

Virginia Wesleyan College
1584 Wesleyan Dr., Norfolk 23502
W. Steve Stocks, V.P. for Admis.

† Washington and Lee University
Lexington 24450
William M. Hartog, Dir. of Admis.

WASHINGTON

: Capitol Business College
5005 Pacific Hwy. E., Ste. 11
Olympia 98424

Central Washington University, Ellensburg 98926
William Swain, Director of Admissions

City University
16661 Northup Way, Bellevue 98008
800-422-4898

† Eastern Washington University, Cheney 99004
Elroy McDermott, Interim Dean
See listing under "Universities"

† Gonzaga University
502 E. Boone Ave., Spokane 99258
Philip Ballinger, Dean of Admissions

Northwest College of the Assemblies of God
P.O. Box 579, Kirkland 98083-0579
Bob Foster, Dir. of Public Relations

† Pacific Lutheran University
12180 Park Ave. S., Tacoma 98447
Dr. Joseph McCann III, Dean

St. Martin's College
700 College St. N.E., Lacey 98516

Seattle Pacific University
3307 3rd Ave., W., Seattle 98119

† Seattle University
Broadway Ave. & Madison, Seattle 98122
Lee Gerig, Dean of Admissions

· Skagit Valley College
2405 E. College Way, Mt. Vernon 98273

University of Puget Sound
1500 N. Warner St., Tacoma 98416

† University of Washington, Seattle 98195

Walla Walla College
204 S. College Ave., College Place 99324

· Walla Walla Community College
500 Tausick Way, Walla Walla 99362
Dan Biagi, Director
509-527-4283
See listing under "Community and Junior Colleges"

† Washington State University, Pullman 99164
Stan Berry, Dir. of Admis.

† Western Washington University
516 High St., Bellingham 98225
Karen G. Copetas, Dir. of Admis.

WEST VIRGINIA

Alderson-Broaddus College
Philippi 26416
Craig W. Gould, Director of Admissions
304-457-1700

Concord College, Athens 24712

Davis & Elkins College
100 Campus Dr., Elkins 26241
Kevin D. Chenoweth, Dir. of Admis.

GLENVILLE STATE COLLEGE
200 High St., Glenville 26351
Dr. William Simmons, President
Mack Samples, Dean of Admissions
Established 1872. State. Coed. Accreditation:
NCACS. Annual tuition: $3,460 resident, $4,054 non-
resident. Room and board: $3,080. Enrollment: 900
boarding, 1,500 day. Faculty: 72. Degrees: AA, AS,
BA, BS. Library: 210,000 volumes. 10 buildings. Gym
& pool, golf course nearby. Beautiful rural setting, 16
miles from I-79. Popular 2 year forestry program;
special education.

Marshall University
400 Hal Greer Blvd., Huntington 25755
See listing under "Universities"

Shepherd College, Shepherdstown 25443

The University of Charleston
2300 MacCorkle Ave., S.E., Charleston 25304
800-995-GO UC

· Webster College
412 Fairmont Ave., Fairmont 26554
Sharron Stephens, Director

West Liberty State College, West Liberty 26074

West Virginia Graduate College
P.O. Box 1003, Institute 25112

West Virginia State College
P.O. Box 1000, Institute 25112

† West Virginia University
P.O. Box 6001, Morgantown 26506

WEST VIRGINIA WESLEYAN COLLEGE
59 College Ave., Buckhannon 26201
Robert Skinner, Director of Admission
See listing under "Universities"

Wheeling Jesuit College
316 Washington Ave., Wheeling 26003
Fr. Thomas Acker, SJ, President

WISCONSIN

Alverno College
P.O. Box 343922, Milwaukee 53234
Colleen Hayes, Dir. of Admis.

Beloit College
700 College St., Beloit 53511
Jeffrey L. Adams, Professor and Chair
608-363-2327

Cardinal Stritch College
6801 N. Yates Rd., Milwaukee 53217
David Wegener, Dir. of Admis.

Carroll College
100 N. East Ave., Waukesha 53186
Ken Moyer, Dir. of Admis.

Carthage College
2001 Alford Dr., Kenosha 53140
Brenda A. Porter, VP Enrollment

· Chippewa Valley Technical College
620 Clairemont Ave., W., Eau Claire 54701

Concordia University
12800 N. Lake Shore Dr., Mequon 53097
414-243-5700

Edgewood College
855 Woodrow St., Madison 53711
Robert Blust, Dir. of Admis.

Lakeland College
P.O. Box 359, Sheboygan 53082

· Madison Junior College of Business
1110 Spring Harbor Dr., Madison 53705
Jeffry S. Sears, President
608-238-4266

Marian College of Fond du Lac
45 S. National Ave., Fond du Lac 54935
Carol Reichenberger, Dean of Admissions

† Marquette University
1217 W. Wisconsin Ave., Milwaukee 53233
Raymond A. Brown, Dean of Admissions

Milwaukee School of Engineering
1025 N. Broadway, Milwaukee 53202
Owen Smith, Dean of Admission
800-332-6763 or 414-277-7200 in metro Milwaukee

Mt. Senario College
1500 W. College Ave., Ladysmith 54848
Dewey Floberg, Dean of Admissions

Ripon College, P.O. Box 248, Ripon 54971
James Reilly, Dean of Admis.

St. Norbert College
100 Grant St., De Pere 54115
Craig S. Wesley, Dean of Admission
See listing under "Universities"

Silver Lake College
2406 S. Alverno Road, Manitowoc 54220
Sandra Schwartz, Dir. of Admis.

· **STRATTON COLLEGE**
1300 N. Jackson St., Milwaukee 53202
Robert H. Ley, Director
414-276-5200

† University of Wisconsin, Eau Claire
Eau Claire 54701

† University of Wisconsin, La Crosse
115 Main Hall, La Crosse 54601
608-785-8067

† University of Wisconsin, Madison
500 Lincoln Dr., Madison 53706

† University of Wisconsin
P.O. Box 413, Milwaukee 53201
V. M. Allison, Registrar

† University of Wisconsin, Oshkosh
800 Algoma Blvd., Oshkosh 54901-8602
August Helgerson, Dir. of Admis.

University of Wisconsin
P.O. Box 2000, Kenosha 53141
414-553-2211

University of Wisconsin
1 University Plaza, Platteville 53818
Richard Schumacher, Dean of Admissions

University of Wisconsin, River Falls
River Falls 54022
Alan Tuchtenhagen, Dir. of Admis.

University of Wisconsin, Superior 54880
Richard E. Morrison, Dir. Univ. Relations

† University of Wisconsin
800 W. Main St., Whitewater 53190

Viterbo College
815 9th St., S., La Crosse 54601
Roland W. Nelson, Dir. of Admis.

: Western Wisconsin Technical College
304 N. 6th St., La Crosse 54602

WYOMING

· Central Wyoming College
2660 Peck St., Riverton 82501
Mary Gores, Admissions Officer
307-856-9291
See listing under "Community and Junior Colleges"

† University of Wyoming
P.O. Box 3434, Laramie 82071
Richard Davis, Dir. of Admis.

· Western Wyoming Community College
2500 College Dr., Rock Springs 82901
Jackie Freeze, Dir. of Admis.
See listing under "Community and Junior Colleges"

GUAM

: International Business College of Guam
P.O. Box 3783, Agana 96910
Director of Admissions

University of Guam
UOG Station, Mangilao 96923
Kathleen Owings, Dir. of Admis.

PUERTO RICO

Catholic University of Puerto Rico
Las Americas Ave., Ponce 00732
Carilin Frau, Dir. of Admis.

Universidad Adventista de las Antillas
P.O. Box 118, Mayaguez 00681
Wilma Gonzalez, Dir. of Admis.

University of Puerto Rico
Arecibo Technical University College
P.O. Box A-1806, Arecibo 00613

University of Puerto Rico
Bayamon Technical University College
Bayamon 00959

University of Puerto Rico
Antonio Barcelo Ave., Cayey 00736
Antonio Rosario, Dir. of Admis.

University of Puerto Rico
CUH Station Rd. 908 Bo Tejas, Humacao 00791

University of Puerto Rico, Mayaguez Campus
P.O. Box 5000, Mayaguez 00681
Neysa Lopez, Dir. of Admis.

University of Puerto Rico
Ponce Technological University College
P.O. Box 7186, Ponce 00732

University of Puerto Rico, Rio Piedras Campus
P.O. Box 23300, San Juan 00931
Victor Lopez, Dir. of Admis.

:CAREER SCHOOLS

ALABAMA

ALABAMA AVIATION & TECHNICAL COLLEGE
P.O. Box 1209, Ozark 36361
800-624-3468
See listing under "Aeronautics"

Atmore State Technical College
P.O. Box 1119, Atmore 36504

Ayers State Technical College
P.O. Box 1647, Anniston 36202

Bessemer State Technical College
P.O. Box 308, Bessemer 35021

Bishop State Community College
925 Dauphin Island Pky., Mobile 36605

CAPPS College
3100 Cottage Hill Rd. #500, Mobile 36606

Career Development Institute
2233 Fourth Ave., N., Birmingham 35203

Career Development Institute
505 Montgomery St., Montgomery 36104

Career Development Institute
1060 Springhill Ave., Mobile 36604

Carver State Technical College
414 Stanton Rd., Mobile 36617

Central Alabama Skills Center
P.O. Box 240369, Montgomery 36124

Coastal Training Institute
5950 S. Monticello Dr., Montgomery 36117

Diesel Driving Academy
3295 Wetumpka Hwy., Montgomery 36110

Drake State Technical College
3421 Meridian St., N., Huntsville 35811

East Alabama Skills Center
301 S. 4th St., Gadsden 35901

Faulkner Area Vocational Center
33 W. Elm, Prichard 36610

Fredd State Technical College
3401 ML King Jr. Blvd., Tuscaloosa 35401

Gadsden Business College of Anniston
P.O. Box 1575, Anniston 36202

Gadsden Business College
P.O. Box 1544, Gadsden 35902
Gene Beecham, President

· Gadsden State Community College
P.O. Box 227, Gadsden 35902
W. Bryan Stone, Dir. of Admis.

Herzing Institute
1218 20th St., S., Birmingham 35205

Ingram State Technical College
P.O. Box 209, Deatsville 36022

John Pope Eden Area Vocational Center
RR 2 Box 1855, Ashville 35953

MacArthur State Technical College
P.O. Box 649, Opp 36467

National Career College
1351 McFarland Blvd., Tuscaloosa 35404

New World College of Business
1031 Noble St., Anniston 36201

North Alabama Skills Center
P.O. Box 3269, Huntsville 35810

Opelika State Technical College
P.O. Box 2268, Opelika 36803

Patterson State Technical College
3920 Troy Hwy., Montgomery 36116

Pittard Area Vocational School
22401 AL Highway 21, Alpine 35014

Prince Institute of Professional Studies
7735 Atlanta Highway, Montgomery 36117

Reid State Technical College
P.O. Box 588, Evergreen 36401

Rice College
2116 Bessemer Rd., Birmingham 35208

South Alabama Skills Center
846 Butler Dr. #A, Mobile 36693

Southeast Alabama Skills Center
P.O. Box 6268, Dothan 36302

Southeast College of Technology
828 Downtowner Loop W., Mobile 36609

Southern Vocational College
P.O. Box 688, Tuskegee 36083
Adell Hicks, Registrar

Sparks State Technical College
P.O. Box 580, Eufaula 36072
205-687-3543

Tallapoosa-Alexander City Area Vocational Center
100 E. Junior College Dr., Alexander City 35010

Trenholm State Technical College
1225 Air Base Blvd., Montgomery 36108

Virginia College
2800A Bob Wallace Ave.
Huntsville 35805

Virginia College-Birmingham
1900 28th Ave. S., Birmingham 35209

· Wallace College - Dothan
Route 6, Box 62, Dothan 36303
Larry Beaty, President
205-983-3521

West Central Alabama Skills Center
2112 11th Ave., S. #201, Birmingham 35205

Winston County Area Vocational Center
P.O. Box 146, Double Springs 35553

ALASKA

Charter College
2221 E. Northern Lights Blvd. #120
Anchorage 99508

The Travel Academy
1415 E. Tudor Rd., Anchorage 99507
Jennifer Deitz, President

University of Alaska Anchorage
3211 Providence Dr., Anchorage 99508
907-786-1480

UNIVERSITY OF ALASKA SOUTHEAST-KETCHIKAN
2600 7th Ave., Ketchikan 99901-5798
See listing under "Community and Junior Colleges"

ARIZONA

· Academy of Business College
3320 W. Cheryl Dr. #115, Phoenix 85051
See listing under "Community and Junior Colleges"

· Al Collins Graphic Design School
1140 S. Priest Dr., Tempe 85281
Chuck Collins, President/CEO

American Institute
3443 N. Central Ave. #1800, Phoenix 85012

American Institute of Technology
440 S. 54th Ave., Phoenix 85043

American Technical Center
3116 E. Shea Blvd., Phoenix 85028

American Teller Schools
635 W. Indian School Rd. #201, Phoenix 85013
Randy Utley, Director

American Teller Schools
1819 S. Dobson Rd., Mesa 85202

American Teller Schools
4023 E. Grant Rd. #A, Tucson 85712

Apollo College
3870 N. Oracle Rd., Tucson 85705

Apollo College
630 W. Southern Ave., Mesa 85210

Arizona Academy of Medical and Dental Assistants
2575 E. Seventh Ave., Flagstaff 86004

Arizona Institute of Business and Technology
6049 N. 43rd Ave., Phoenix 85019
Lynda Angel, Executive Director

Arizona Institute of Business and Technology
4136 N. 75th Ave. #211, Phoenix 85033
Jill Humphrey, Director

Arizona Institute of Business and Technology
925 S. Gilbert Rd. #201, Mesa 85204
Sue Boyer, Director

AzTech College
941 S. Dobson Rd. Rm. 120, Mesa 85202
Francis J. Cody, President

Bryman School
4343 N. 16th St., Phoenix 85016

CAD Institute/The CAD Center
4100 E. Broadway Rd., Phoenix 85040
Dominic Pistillo, President
CAD and Virtual Reality Degree
800-658-5744

Chaparral Career College
4585 E. Speedway Blvd. #204, Tucson 85712
A. Lauren Rhude, President

Conservatory of Recording Arts & Sciences
1110 E. Missouri Ave. #530, Phoenix 85014
800-562-6383
See listing under "Music"

Denver Business College
1550 S. Alma School Rd. #100, Mesa 85210

Desert Institute of the Healing Arts
639 N. Sixth Ave., Tucson 85705
Jan Schwartz, Admissions Director
800-733-8098

Institute of Business & Medical Technology
20 E. Main St. #600, Mesa 85201

Lamson Business College
6367 E. Tanque Verde Rd. #100, Tucson 85715
Fred McDerment, Director

Long Medical Institute
4126 N. Black Canyon Hwy., Phoenix 85017
Galyn Smock, Director

Motorcycle Mechanics Institute a division
of Clinton Technical Institute
2844 W. Deer Valley Rd., Phoenix 85027
David Miller, National Director
800-528-7995

Mundus Institute
4745 N. 7th St. #100, Phoenix 85014

Northern Arizona Institute of Technology
1120 W. Kaibab Ln., Flagstaff 86001

Phoenix College
1202 W. Thomas Rd., Phoenix 85013
William Anderson, Chrpsn.

Pima Medical Institute
3350 E. Grant Rd., Tucson 85716

Pima Medical Institute
2300 E. Broadway Rd., Tempe 85282

Refrigeration School
4210 E. Washington St., Phoenix 85034
Edwin Lee Loney, Dir. of Admis.

Rice Aviation-Southwest Regional Campus
3201 E. Broadway Rd., Phoenix 85040
800-736-7014

Roberto-Venn School of Luthiery
4011 S. 16th St., Phoenix 85040

Scottsdale Culinary Institute
8100 E. Camelback Rd., Scottsdale 85251

Sterling School
801 E. Indian School Rd., Phoenix 85014

Tucson College of Business
7310 E. 22nd St., Tucson 85710
Daniel Waterman, Dir. of Admis.

Western Truck School
1835 S. Black Canyon Hwy. #1, Phoenix 85009

Yavapai College
1100 E. Sheldon St., Prescott 86301
Dr. Doreen Dailey, President
602-445-7300
See listing under "Community and Junior Colleges"

ARKANSAS

Arkansas Valley Vocational Technical School
P.O. Box 506, Ozark 72949

Black River Vocational Techical School
P.O. Box 468, Pocahontas 72455

CARTI School of Radiation Therapy Technology
P.O. Box 5210, Little Rock 72215

Eastern College of Health Vocations
6423 Forbing Rd., Little Rock 72209

Health Care Training Institute
222 N. 6th St., West Memphis 72301

ITT Technical Institute
4520 S. University Ave.
Little Rock 72204

Phillips County Community College
P.O. Box 785, Helena 72342
Dr. Steven Jones, President
James R. Brasel, Dean of Admissions

Pulaski Vocational Technical School
3000 W. Scenic Rd., North Little Rock 72118

Remington College
7601 Scott Hamilton Dr.
Little Rock 72209

Remington College
3348 N. College St.
Fayetteville 72703

St. Edward Mercy Medical Center
School of Radiography
7301 Rogers Ave., Fort Smith 72917
Sr. Judith Marie Keith, RSM, Admin.

South Central Career College
4500 W. Commercial Dr., North Little Rock 72116

South Central Career College
2311 E. Nettleton #G, Jonesboro 72401

South Central Career College
1614 Brentwood Dr., Pine Bluff 71601

CALIFORNIA

Academy Pacific Business & Travel College
1777 N. Vine St. #30, Hollywood 90028

Advance School of Driving
P.O. Box 443, Walnut 91788

Advertising Arts College
10025 Mesa Rim Rd., San Diego 92121
Tracy Cantor, Dir. of Admis.

American Academy of Dramatic Arts/West
2550 Paloma St., Pasadena 91107

AMERICAN CAREER COLLEGE
4021 Rosewood Ave., Los Angeles 90004
Ginny White, Director of Admissions
800-956-7832
   Established 1978. Private. Coed. Accreditation: ACCSCT. Enrollment: 370. Faculty: 15. Tuition: varies per program. Registration: $75. Diploma programs. Teaching optical dispensing, pharmacy technician, medical assisting, medical bills/health claims examiner and vocational nursing. Excellent job placement. Short programs. Financial aid available to qualified students.

AMERICAN NANNY COLLEGE
4650 Arrow Hwy. #A10, Montclair 91763
800-462-7711

Ameritech Colleges
6843 Lennox Ave., Van Nuys 91405

Andon College at Modesto
1314 H St., Modesto 95354

Andon College at Stockton
1201 N. El Dorado St., Stockton 95202

Associated Technical College
1670 W. Wilshire Blvd., Los Angeles 90017
Ronald Quam, Director

Associated Technical College
1475 6th Ave., San Diego 92101

Associated Technical College
395 N. E St., San Bernardino 92418

Associated Technical College
1177 N. Magnolia Ave., Anaheim 92801

BROOKS INSTITUTE OF PHOTOGRAPHY
801 Alston Rd., Santa Barbara 93108
Lynn Cederquist, Dir. of Admis.
805-966-3888 Ext. 217 or Ext. 218
See listing under "Photography"

Bryan College of Court Reporting
2511 Beverly Blvd., Los Angeles 90057
Nancy Patterson, Director
213-484-8850

Cabot Colleges
41 E. 12th St., National City 91950
Wayne A. Cox, Director

California Academy of Merchandising Art & Design
1333 Howe Ave. #208, Sacramento 95825

California Career School
392 W. Cerritos Ave., Anaheim 92805

CALIFORNIA CULINARY ACADEMY
625 Polk St., San Francisco 94102
Harvey Tsutsui, Dir. of Admis.
800-BAY-CHEF or 415-771-3536
   Established 1977. Private. Coed. Accreditation:

ACCSCT and the ACFEIAC. Tuition: $22,940. Room and board: $8,000. Fees: $1,200. Enrollment: 694. Faculty: 29. Degree: Associate of Occupational Studies in Culinary Arts. Library: 2,500 volumes. One 56,700 square foot building. 16 month program with 6 registration dates. 30 week Baking/Pastry Arts Certificate program. Financial aid, grants, and scholarships are available to those who qualify. There are three restaurants, state of the art kitchens for Garde Manger, Pastry, Baking and Butcher shop, a Culinary Theatre and three Lecture rooms. We emphasize hands-on experience in cooking and the theory/practice of restaurant management.

California Institute
4365 Atlantic Ave., Long Beach 90807

California Institute of Locksmithing (Est. 1972)
14721 Oxnard St., Van Nuys 91411
Charles Hasekian, President
818-994-7426

California Nannie College
910 Howe Ave., Sacramento 95825

California Paramedical & Technical College
3745 N. Long Beach Blvd., Long Beach 90807
310-595-6638

California Paramedical & Technical College
4550 La Sierra Ave., Riverside 92505
800-247-1011 or 714-687-9006

California School of Court Reporting
1201 N. Main St., Santa Ana 92701

California School of Court Reporting
3510 Adams St., Riverside 92504

Cancer Foundation of Santa Barbara
Schools of Radiation Therapy & Nuclear Medicine Technologies
P.O. Box 837, Santa Barbara 93102

Career West Academy
2505b Zanella Way, Chico 95928

Catherine College
8155 Van Nuys Blvd. #200, Panorama City 91402

Central California School of Continuing Education
3195 McMillan Ave. #F, San Luis Obispo 93401
Gene Appleby, Director

Century Business College
3325 Wilshire Blvd., Los Angeles 90010

City College of San Francisco
33 Gough St., San Francisco 94103
415-241-2306

CollegeAmerica - San Francisco
814 Mission St. Suite 300
San Francisco 94103

College for Recording Arts
665 Harrison St., San Francisco 94107
Leo de Gar Kulka, Dir. of Admis.

COLLEGE OF OCEANEERING
272 S. Fries Ave., Wilmington 90744
Ron Friedrich, Executive Director
Rhonda Doma, Director of Admissions
800-432-DIVE or 310-834-2501
   Established 1969. Private. Coed. Accreditation: WASC, ACDE (Association of Commercial Diving Educators). Enrollment: 261. Faculty: 17. Student-faculty ratio: 15:1. Degree: AS in Marine Technology. The College of Oceaneering has achieved worldwide recognition for its innovative approach to diver training, and was the first to offer many technical programs including Diver Medic and Underwater Inspection and Photography. We remain the only diving school in the United States with an open water, fully operational, Bell/Saturation System.

Columbia College
925 N. La Brea Ave., Los Angeles 90038
Kurt Wolfe, Dir. of Admis.

Computer Learning Center
222 S. Harbor Blvd., Anaheim 92805

Computer Learning Center
3130 Wilshire Blvd., Los Angeles 90010
Stephen Woody, Director

Computer Learning Center
661 Howard St., San Francisco 94105

Computer Learning Center
111 N. Market St. #105, San Jose 95113

ConCorde Career Institute/Valley College
4150 Lankershim Blvd., North Hollywood 91602

ConCorde Career Institute
123 Camino De La Reina, San Diego 92108
Nelson Melchior, Director
619-688-0800

ConCorde Career Institute
1290 N. 1st St., San Jose 95112

ConCorde Career Institute
1717 S. Brookhurst, Anaheim 92804
H. Tom Smith, Director

Concorde Career Institute
6850 Van Nuys Blvd., Van Nuys 91405

Consolidated Welding School
4343 E. Imperial Hwy., Lynwood 90262

Dickinson-Warren Business College
1001 S. 57th St., Richmond 94804

Dootson School of Trucking
11625 Clark St., Arcadia 91006

D. T. I. Career Institute
1937 W. Chapman Ave. #100, Orange 92668
E. Ray Poole, Director of Admissions
714-937-3989

Educorp Career College
230 E. Third St., Long Beach 90802
Kenneth Boyle, Director

Edutek Professional Colleges
Centre City Campus
1541 Broadway, San Diego 92101
Carol Ruiz, Executive Director

Edutek Professional Colleges
College Area Campus
5952 El Cajon Blvd., San Diego 92115
Carol Ruiz, Executive Director

Edutek Professional Colleges
4560 Alvarado Canyon Rd., San Diego 92120

Edutek Professional Colleges
Allied Health Division
5952 El Cajon Blvd., San Diego 92115
Carol Ruiz, Executive Director

El Dorado College
2204 S. El Camino Real #104, Oceanside 92054

El Dorado College
385 N. Escondido Blvd., Escondido 92025

Eldorado College
2255 Camino Del Rio S. #200, San Diego 92108
Jay Jarman, Director

El Dorado College
1901 Pacific Ave., West Covina 91790

EMPIRE COLLEGE

SCHOOL OF BUSINESS & LAW
3033 Cleveland Ave. # 107, Santa Rosa 95403
707-546-4000
Established 1961. Private. Coed. Accreditation:
ACICS/Committee of Bar Examiners. Tuition: $3,720
- $7,290. Fees: $75 - $95. Enrollment: 700 full-time,
25 part-time. Faculty: 50. Student-faculty ratio: 21:1.
Specialized Associate degree offered in Accounting
and Administrative Assistant; Juris Doctor. 1 21,000
sq. ft. building. Positive, supportive environment for
students in the business school with start dates every
six weeks; evening law classes taught by practicing
attornies.

Estelle Harman Actor's Workshop
522 N. La Brea Ave., Los Angeles 90036
213-931-8137

Fashion Careers of California
1923 Morena Blvd., San Diego 92110
Andrew Bisaha, Dir. of Admis.
See listing under "Fashion Art"

Fresno Institute of Technology
1545 Fulton St., Fresno 93721
Jim Hines, Director

Galen College of Medical & Dental Assistants
3746 W. Mineral King #C, Visalia 93291

Galen College of Medical & Dental Assistants
1604 Ford Ave. #10, Modesto 95350

Galen College of Medical-Dental Assistants
1325 N. Wishon Ave., Fresno 93728

GEMOLOGICAL INSTITUTE OF AMERICA

1660 Stewart St., Santa Monica 90404
Veronica Clark-Hudson, Educational Advisor
Established 1931. Non-profit. Private. Coed. Ac-
creditation: ACCS/CT. Diplomas: Graduate Gemolo-
gist, Graduate Jeweler, Graduate Jeweler Gemologist.
Programs and courses range from seven weeks to one
year. Financial aid. Classes begin year round.
Call 800-421-7250 X292 or 310-829-2991 X292, or
write the Educational Advisor at the above address.
See listing under "Home Study".

Glendale Career College
1021 Grandview Ave., Glendale 91201

Golf Academy of San Diego
P.O. Box 3050, Rancho Santa Fe 92067
800-342-SDGA

Heald Business College
777 Southland Dr. #210, Hayward 94545
Shelli Spangler, Director

Heald College
1000 Broadway, Oakland 94607
Marie-Louise Coppinger, Director

Heald Institute of Technology
2860 Howe Rd., Martinez 94553
M. K. Michaels, Director

Health Staff Training Institute
1505 E. 17th St. #122, Santa Ana 92701

High-Tech Institute
1111 Howe Ave., Sacramento 95825

Huntington College of Dental Technology
7466 Edinger Ave., Huntington Beach 92647

INSTITUTE FOR BUSINESS AND TECHNOLOGY

2550 Scott Blvd., Santa Clara 95050
800-548-8545

Institute of Business & Medical Technology
75110 St. Charles Pl. #10
Palm Desert 92211

International Air Academy
2980 Inland Empire Blvd., Ontario 91764

Irvine College of Business
16591 Noyes Ave., Irvine 92714
W. D. Polick, Director

ITT Technical Institute
26239 Executive Pl., Hayward 94545

KELSEY-JENNEY COLLEGE

Two locations
201 A St., San Diego 92101
7084 Miramar Rd., San Diego 92121
Robert Evans, President

Lederwolff Culinary Academy
3300 Stockton Blvd., Sacramento 95820

Leicester School
1106 W. Olympic Blvd., Los Angeles 90015
Daniel Turniansky, Director

Los Angeles ORT Technical Institute
635 S. Harvard Blvd. #116, Los Angeles 90005

Los Angeles ORT Technical Institute
15130 Ventura Blvd. #250, Sherman Oaks 91403

Los Angeles Pierce College
6201 Winnetka Ave., Woodland Hills 91371
See listing under "Community and Junior
Colleges"

LOUISE SALINGER ACADEMY OF FASHION

101 Jessie St., San Francisco 94105
Esther Herschelle, President
415-974-6666

Management College of San Francisco
1255 Post St. #450
San Francisco 94109

Maric College
7202 Princess View Dr., San Diego 92120

Maric College of Medical Careers
1300 Rancheros Dr., San Marcos 92069

Maric College of Medical Careers
1593C E. Vista Way, Vista 92084

Med-Help Training School
2702 Clayton Rd. #201, Concord 94519

Merit College
7101 Sepulveda Blvd., Van Nuys 91405
J. Robert Evans, President

Modern Technology School of X-Ray
6180 Laurel Canyon Blvd. #100
North Hollywood 91606

Modern Technology School X-Ray
962 S. Euclid, Anaheim 92802

MTI Business College of Stockton
6006 N. El Dorado St., Stockton 95207

MTI College
2011 W. Chapman Ave., Orange 92668

MTI College
760 Via Lata, #300, Colton 92324

MTI-Western Business College
5221 Madison Ave., Sacramento 95841
John Zimmerman, President

MUSICIANS INSTITUTE

1655 McCadden Pl., Hollywood 90028
Patrick Hicks, President
See listing under "Music"

NATIONAL CAREER EDUCATION

6060 Sunrise Vista Dr. #3000
Citrus Heights 95610
800-441-4623

Navajo Aviation
145 John Glenn Dr., Concord 94520
Flight Training Center
510-685-1150

National Education Center-Bryman Campus
1017 Wilshire Blvd., Los Angeles 90017

NATIONAL EDUCATION CENTER-BRYMAN CAMPUS

For Medical & Dental Assistants
5350 Atlantic Ave., Long Beach 90805
Roger Gugelmeyer, Director
310-422-6007

National Education Center-Bryman Campus
20835 Sherman Way, Winnetka 91306
Don Hyde, Director

National Education Center-Bryman Campus
3505 N. Hart Ave., Rosemead 91770

National Education Center-Bryman Campus
731 Market St., San Francisco 94103

National Education Center-Bryman Campus
4212 W. Artesia Blvd., Torrance 90504

National Education Center-Bryman Campus
2015 Naglee Ave., San Jose 95128

National Education Center-Bryman Campus
1600 Broadway #201, Oakland 94612

National Education Center-Bryman Campus
1732 Reynolds St., Irvine 92714

NEC-National Institute of Technology
1120 N. Brookhurst St., Anaheim 92801

NEC-San Jose Campus
1302 N. 4th St., San Jose 95112

National Education Center-Sawyer Campus
8475 Jackson Rd., Sacramento 95826
916-383-1909

National Education Center-Sawyer Campus
5500 S. Eastern Ave., City of Commerce 90040

National Education Center-Skadron College
1200 N.E. St., San Bernardino 92405

Newbridge College
700 El Camino Real, Tustin 92680
J. Villanueva, Director

North Park College
3956 30th St., San Diego 92104
619-297-3333

Northrop-Rice Aviation Institute of Technology
8911 Aviation Blvd., Inglewood 90301
310-337-4444

Northwest College of Medical & Dental Assistants
124 S. Glendale Ave., Glendale 91205

North-West College of Medical & Dental Assistants
2121 W. Garvey Ave., West Covina 91790

Northwest College of Medical & Dental Assistants
530 E. Union Ave., Pasadena 91101

Northwest College of Medical & Dental Assistants
134 W. Holt Ave., Pomona 91768

Nova Institute of Health Technology
11416 Whittier Blvd., Whittier 90601

Nova Institute of Health Technology
2400 S. Western Ave.
Los Angeles 90018

Nova Institute of Health Technology
520 N. Euclid Ave., Ontario 91762

Oakland College of Court Reporting
449 15th St. 2nd Floor, Oakland 94612

ORANGE COAST COLLEGE

P.O. Box 5005, Costa Mesa 92628
See listing under "Community and Junior Colleges"

Orange County Business College
2035 E. Ball Rd., Anaheim 92806
A. J. Pitale, President

Pacific Coast College
118 W. Fifth St., Santa Ana 92701

Pacific Coast College
1261 Third St. #B, Chula Vista 91911

Pacific Gateway College
3018 Carmel St., Los Angeles 90065

Pacific Travel School
2515 N. Main St., Santa Ana 92701
Roy Agee, Director

Phillips College
4300 Central Ave., Riverside 92506
Judi Murakami, Director of Education

PHILLIPS JUNIOR COLLEGE

Condie Campus
1 W. Campbell Ave., Campbell 95008
Marilyn McKnight, Dir. of Admis.

Platt College
6250 El Cajon Blvd., San Diego 92115

Platt College
2920 Inland Empire Blvd. #102, Ontario 91764

Platt College
10900 E. 183rd St. #290, Cerritos 90701

Platt College
7470 N. Figueroa St., Los Angeles 90041

Platt College
3901 MacArthur Blvd. #101
Newport Beach 92660

Platt College
301 Mission St., San Francisco 94105

Practical Schools
900 E. Ball Rd., Anaheim 92805
Marlyn Sheehan, President

Professional Career Centers
4041 MacArthur Blvd. #210
Newport Beach 92660

San Francisco State University
1600 Holloway Ave., San Francisco 94132
Corwin Bjonerud, Dir. of Admis.

San Joaquin Valley College of Aeronautics
4985 E. Andersen Ave., Fresno 93727

Santa Barbara Business College
5266 Hollister Ave., Santa Barbara 93111
Ellen B. Saad, Administrator

Santa Barbara Business College
211 S. Real Rd., Bakersfield 93309

Santa Barbara Business College
4333 Hansen Ave., Fremont 94536

Santa Barbara Business College
303 E. Plaza Dr., Santa Maria 93454

Santa Barbara City College
721 Cliff Dr., Santa Barbara 93109
805-965-0581

Sawyer College of Business
441 W. Trimble Rd., San Jose 95131

Sawyer College
1021 E. Holt Ave., Pomona 91767
909-629-2534

Sawyer College
2101 E. Gonzales Rd., Oxnard 93030
Roger Ferguson, Dir. of Education

School of Communication Electronics
184 2nd St., San Francisco 94105

SEQUOIA INSTITUTE
420 Whitney Pl., Fremont 94539
Lane V. Hart, Dir. of Admissions
800-248-8585

Established 1962. Private. Coed. Accreditation: ACCS/CT. Tuition: Auto $10,900, CCRT $9,600. Fees: $100 refundable security deposit and $75 reservation fee. Enrollment: 1,000. Faculty: 52. Student-faculty ratio: 40:1 in shop, 20:1 in classroom. 2 buildings on 6 acres. Sequoia Institute offers certification in the careers of Automotive and Climate Control and Refrigeration Technology. Financial aid is available for those who qualify. A high school diploma or GED and a passing score on the school's entrance test are required for enrollment. School approved housing is available. Sequoia is located 45 minutes south of San Francisco in the heart of the Bay area.

Sierra Valley Business College
4747 N 1st St. #D, Fresno 93726

Silicon Valley College
41350 Christy St., Fremont 94538
Darryl Lindsey, President

South Coast College of Court Reporting
1380 S. Sanderson Ave., Anaheim 92803
Jean Gonzalez, President
714-635-6464

Southern California College of Business & Law
595 W. Lambert Rd., Brea 92621
Cynthia Cramer, Director

Southern California College of Court Reporting
1100 S. Claudina Pl., Anaheim 92805
Debra Lee, Director

SUTECH School of Vocational/Technical Training
3427 E. Olympic Blvd., Los Angeles 90023
Oswaldo Forvo, Director

Systems Programming Development Institute
4900 Triggs St.
City of Commerce 90022

Technical Health Careers School
11603 S. Western Ave., Los Angeles 90047

TRAVEL AND TRADE CAREER INSTITUTE
3635 Atlantic Ave., Long Beach 90807
Rodger Erickson, President
David K. Hall, Director
800-777-8824

Established 1962. Private. Coed. Accreditation: ACCSCT. Tuition: $4,895-$5,750. Room and board: $1,182-$3,500. Enrollment: 375 full-time. Faculty: 18. Student-faculty ratio: 20:1. Diploma offered. Courses offered in: Travel and Tourism, Hotel Hospitality, Import/Export/International Transportation, Business Preparation/Data Entry, Computer Operations, and Medical Office Assistant. Many courses VA approved. Housing available.

TRAVEL AND TRADE CAREER INSTITUTE
12541 Brookhurst St., Garden Grove 92640
Rodger Erickson, President
Larry Paxton, Director
714-636-2611

Established 1962. Private. Coed. Accreditation: ACCSCT. Tuition: $4,895-$5,750. Room and board: $1,182-$3,500. Enrollment: 150 full-time. Faculty: 8. Student-faculty ratio: 19:1. Diploma offered. Courses offered in: Travel and Tourism, Import/Export/International Transportation, Electronic Technician, Business Preparation/Data Entry, Medical Office Assistant, and Computer Operations. Many courses VA approved. Housing available.

Travel University International
3655 Ruffin Rd. N., #225, San Diego 92123

Truck Driving Academy
5711 Florin-Perkins Rd., Sacramento 95828

Truck Driving Academy
5168 N. Blythe Ave. #102, Fresno 93722
209-276-5708

UCC Vocational Center
1322 Coronado Ave., Long Beach 90804
Than Pok, Director

United Health Careers Institute
570 W. 4th St. #907, San Bernardino 92401
Paula Hermann, Dir. of Admis.
714-884-8891

United States Truck Driving School
924 W. Rialto Ave., Rialto 92376
800-825-7364 or 714-875-8000

Valley Commercial College
910 12th St., Modesto 95354
Greg Martin, President

Watterson College
1165 E. Colorado Blvd., Pasadena 91106

Watterson College Pacific
815 N. Oxnard Blvd., Oxnard 93030

Watterson College Pacific
2030 University Dr., Vista 92083

Watterson College Pasadena
1422 S. Azusa Ave., West Covina 91791

Westech College
500 W. Mission Blvd., Pomona 91766
Barry Maleki, Director

Western Career College
8909 Folsom Blvd., Sacramento 95826
916-361-1660

Western Career College
170 Bayfair Mall, San Leandro 94578
510-276-3888

Western Truck School
P.O. Box 980040, West Sacramento 95798

Western Truck School
2849-A Whipple Rd., Union City 94587

Western Truck School
4565 N. Golden State Blvd., Fresno 93722

Western Truck School
5801 State Rd., Bakersfield 93308

Western Truck School
1002 N. Broadway Ave., Stockton 95205

Western Truck School
2425 Mar Industry Dr.
San Diego 92121

Western Truck School
2316 Nickerson Dr., Modesto 95358

Westlake Institute of Technology
31826A Village Center Rd.
Westlake Village 91361

COLORADO

Academy of Floral Design
837 Acoma, Denver 80204

AMERICAN DIESEL & AUTOMOTIVE COLLEGE
1002 S. Jason St., Denver 80223
Mel Jones, Director
Dale Jones, Registrar

Established 1976. Coed. Tuition: $7,700. Room and board: $3,600. Enrollment: 300.
FACILITIES: College has 3 buildings with 26,000 square feet for shops and classrooms.
ACCREDITATION: NATTS (CCA), approved for veterans training, approved by the State of Colorado.
CURRICULUM: 9 to 18 month programs available in "Automotive Technology" or "Automotive and Diesel Technology". Degree available in either program. The curriculum is relevant-designed to prepare students to enter the job market. The college is known for its "Committment to Excellence" and the instructors provide a broad range of professional experience in their respective fields. All courses taught by ASE certified instructors. Courses will prepare student for ASE certification tests. Average class size is 20 students. 50% "Hands-on" training. Student-faculty ratio: 20:1. Day and evening classes available.
DEGREES OFFERED: Associate of Occupational Studies
FINANCIAL AID: Federal and State financial aid is available. VA approved.
EMPLOYMENT ASSISTANCE: College will assist students in finding employment for those that want to work in addition to attending classes. Graduates have consistently enjoyed 80-90% job placement in fields related to their area of study.
STUDENT HOUSING: Off-campus housing assistance is available for single or married students.
LOCATION: Located in Denver CO. The mountains offer Colorado skiing, fishing, and hunting only one hour away. Drag strips, stock car races, four-wheeling, rodeos and music concerts are popular events in the summer.
ADMISSIONS: Classes start 8 times a year. Video explaining programs is available. For information call toll-free 800-279-8402.

Barnes Business College
150 Sheridan Blvd., Denver 80226
Shirley Lowery, Director

BEL-REA INSTITUTE OF ANIMAL TECHNOLOGY
1681 S. Dayton, Denver 80231
303-751-8700, Toll Free 800-950-8001
Mary Lynn Ritter, Administrator

Established 1971. Private. Coed. Enrollment: 230, 80% female, 20% male. Tuition: $9,500 for 18 month program. Typical yearly expenses for men and women excluding tuition are $4,000 per academic year. Total faculty: 15, 6 veterinarians. Student-faculty ratio: 10:1.

Bel-Rea offers an 18 month program to train veterinary technicians. Students are awarded an Associate of Applied Science degree upon graduation. The program is on a quarter system, with classes starting four times per year: September, January, March and June. The school offers written transfer agreements with the University of Denver & Western State College of Colorado and a joint degree program is offered leading to a BS degree in Biology with an emphasis in Animal Technology.

The Institute's programs are conducted at the school and in their veterinary hospital in Denver, offering students the advantages of a large city. Emphasis is placed on clinical training with the last three months of the program consisting of a clinical internship within the hospital.

Admissions: Applicants are admitted who have been awarded a high school diploma by an accredited high school or who have a GED. Students must have a minimum of a C average to apply. No specific courses are required to apply for admission.

Facilities: Bel-Rea has a modern laboratory and classroom facility. The building contains classrooms, a teaching laboratory, an audio-visual room, three demonstration rooms, a library, student lounge, administrative offices, and kennel area for dogs, cats, and laboratory animals. The large-animal facility adjoins the teaching facility. This area comprises a stable, tack room, surgery suite, and a corral area for large animals. The teaching hospital includes operating rooms, scrub room, radiology room, ward space, isolation facility, treatment area, ICU, laboratory, necropsy, exam room and office and consultation space.

Location: The school is located in the suburbs of Denver, along the eastern border of the city. The downtown central core of the city is approximately eight miles away. Denver is a fast growing city which offers many cultural and recreational activities. The mountains offer some of the finest skiing in the country, with many main resorts like Vail, Copper Mountain, Keystone, and Winter Park less than two hours away. Denver has its own symphony and theatre center as well as the famous Red Rocks outdoor amphitheatre with its complete pop, rock and country concert schedule during the summer months.

Accreditation: CCA, American Veterinary Medical Association. Approved and regulated by the Department of Higher Education, Division of Private Occupational Schools.

Boulder Valley Area Vocational Technical Center
6600 E. Arapahoe, Boulder 80303

CollegeAmerica
720 S. Colorado Blvd. #260
Denver 80222

Colorado Career Academy
13790 E. Rice Pl., Aurora 80015
Valos Athanasiou, Director

Colorado Career Academy
95 S. Wadsworth Blvd., Lakewood 80226
Valos Athanasiou, Director

COLORADO INSTITUTE OF ART
200 E. 9th Ave., Denver 80203
William C. Bottoms, President
Barbara Browning, Dir. of Admis.
800-275-2420

Established 1952. Private. Coed. Accreditation: CCA. Yearly tuition: Approximately $8,175. Fees: $275 general, plus $50 application. Enrollment: 1,350 full-time. Faculty: 74. Student-faculty ratio: 20:1. Degree: AAS. 5 buildings. Located in Denver, Colorado. The curriculum is relevant-designed to prepare students to enter the job market. The art institute is noted for its standard of excellence and institute instructors provide a broad range of professional experience in their respective fields.

Colorado Northwestern Community College
500 Kennedy Dr., Rangely 81648
Pat Kalahar, Dir. Marketing/Recruitment
800-562-1105

COLORADO TECHNICAL COLLEGE
4435 N. Chestnut St., Colorado Springs 80907
719-598-0200

The transition from high-tech education to high-tech careers is Colorado Tech's specialty! Situated in the middle of a space age community known as Silicon Mountain, the college takes pride in its mission to serve high-tech businesses and industries by providing graduates able to hit the ground running in such fields as: computer engineering, computer science, electrical engineering, electronic engineering technology, telecommunications, systems management, and logistics. Colorado Tech, accredited by NCA and ABET, offers Associate, Bachelor and Master degrees.

Colorado Tech's Specialized Skills Certificate Programs focus on the specific skills that are most in demand: Computer Repair, Manufacturing Processes, Telecommunications Repair, Electronics Repair. In just nine months, you'll learn the basics of electronics, digital components, computer systems, and applied science...knowledge that goes beyond theory to hands-on skills. Courses completed through the Specialized Skills Certificate Program are 100% applicable toward Technology Degrees in Electronic Engineering Technology or Telecommunications Electronics Technology. Program features a total of 6 courses, each lasting 5 1/2 weeks; classes taken one at a time for increased focus, concentration and flexibility. Taken consecutively, students can earn their certificate in nine months. Start dates on a quarterly basis.

Colorado Tech believes students should not only learn in the clasroom, but in the laboratory as well, applying their knowledge to real world problems. The teacher and students work in an environment that encourages constant interaction in the learning process. Class size is limited to 40 students and labs are limited to 18 students. Colorado Tech's state of the art equipment is always available: no one waits in line.

It is no suprise that companies such as Digital, Loral, MCI, Apple, Atmel, Litton, United Technologies, Hewlett-Packard, Ford Microelectronics, GE Aerospace, Hughes Aircraft and Cray Research have chosen Colorado Springs with its USAF space center and US Space Foundation to locate facilities here. Many of these companies have representatives who sit on our advisory boards and many of our professors come from these companies.

The Colorado Springs area offers many recreational activities such as skiing, fishing, hunting, hiking, mountain climbing and four wheeling. NFL football, NBA basketball, National League baseball, the symphony and varied expressions of popular culture provide ample entertainnment for every taste. Soar to meet your destiny through higher education at Colorado Tech.

ConCorde Career Institute
770 Grant, Denver 80203

Denver Academy of Court Reporting
7290 Samuel Dr. #200, Denver 80221
Charles W. Jarstfer, Pres.
303-427-5292

Denver Academy of Court Reporting
220 Ruskin Dr., Colorado Springs 80910
719-574-5010

DENVER AUTOMOTIVE & DIESEL COLLEGE
460 S. Lipan St., Denver 80223
Joseph R. Chalupa, College Director
800-347-3232 or 303-722-5724
Established 1963. Private. Coed. Accreditation:
CCA. Tuition: $7,000. Fees: $150 for registration. Enrollment: 400. Faculty: 30. Student-faculty ratio: 20:1.
Degrees: AOS in Automotive and Diesel Technology,
several diploma (specialized) programs. Library:
5,000 volumes. 70,000 sq. feet facilities. ASE Master
certified curriculum. College located in the mile high
city of Denver CO next to the Rocky Mountains, off
street parking, National Industry Advisory Board.
Morning, afternoon or evening classes. Lifetime job
placement assistance.

Denver Business College
7350 N. Broadway, Denver 80221

Denver Institute of Technology
The Educational Plaza
7350 N. Broadway, Denver 80221

Denver Paralegal Institute
1401 19th St., Denver 80202

Denver Paralegal Institute
105 E. Vermijo Ave., Colorado Springs 80903
Brenda Mientka, Director

Durango Air Service
1300 County Road 309, Durango 81301

Emery Aviation College
1245 A Aviation Way, Colorado Springs 80916
719-591-9488

EMILY GRIFFITH OPPORTUNITY SCHOOL
1250 Welton St., Denver 80204-2197
Dr. Mary Ann Parthum, Principal
303-572-8218
Established 1916 for "all who wish to learn". The
Denver Public Schools adult vocational complex. The
school offers low-cost, competitive prices for all Colorado residents. Certificates of completion given in
apprenticeship, business education, continuing education, health occupations, consumer and family
studies, marketing education, technical trades and
industrial education. Second Chance, a retrieval program for 17-21 year-olds who have not completed
high school. Community college credit is available.

Heritage College of Health Careers
12 Lakeside Ln., Denver 80212
Larry Camack, Director

Intermountain College
4070 Autumn Heights Dr. Unit B
Colorado Springs 80906
Peter Schlosser, Director

Intermountain College
5801 W. 44th Ave., Denver 80212
Peter Schlosser, Director

Medical Careers Training Center
4020 S. College Ave., Fort Collins 80525
Richard Laub, President

Mile Hi College
6464 W. 14th Ave., Denver 80214
David Phillips, Dir. of Admis.

NATIONAL ACADEMY OF NANNIES, INC.
1681 S. Dayton St., Denver 80231
Marc Schapiro, President
Marianna Bagge, Director
Phone: 303-333-6264, Fax 303-751-9969
or Toll Free 800-222-NANI
Established 1983. Staff: 13. For-Profit. Nonmembership. Private training school for nannies. Courses
focus on infant, toddler and childhood care, emphasizing physical, emotional, intellectual, and personal
growth and development for child and nanny. Topics
covered include infant care, preschool science, math,
reading, and language; creative play preparation, nutrition/meal planning; psychological growth and well
being; family/employment relations; special needs
children; CPR and first aid. Offers a 12-18 month
Sponsorship Program in which students attend
classes in the evenings and gain tuition sponsorship,
room and board, and $350/month spending money
from the N.A.N.I. sponsoring family. Also, offers 6
month Fast Track Program, in which a family provides a student with free room and board in exchange
for 25 hours per week of family assistance. Sponsors
seminars available for families. Awards an In-Home
Child Care Specialist certification. Placement services also available on a national level. Computerized
Services: Mailing list.

National Training
9600 E. 104th Ave., Henderson 80640

Parks Junior College
6 Abilene St., Aurora 80011
303-367-2757

Pickens Technical Center
500 Buckley Rd., Aurora 80011

Pima Medical Institute
7290 Samuel Dr. #200, Denver 80221
Sue Anderson, Director

Platt College
3100 S. Parker Rd., Aurora 80014
Jerald B. Sirbu, President

PPI Health Careers School
2345 N. Academy Blvd., Colorado Springs 80909
719-596-7400

Pueblo College of Business & Technology
330 Lake Ave., Pueblo 81004
719-545-3100

Rocky Mountain School of Meatcutting
790 W. Evans Ave., Denver 80223
Leland Osborne, Director

San Juan Basin AVTS
P.O. Box 970, Cortez 81321
303-565-8457

Technical Trades Institute
2315 E. Pikes Peak Ave., Colorado Springs 80909
719-632-7626

Technical Trades Institute
722 Horizon Dr., Grand Junction 81506
719-245-8101

United States Truck Driving School
8150 W. 48th St., Wheat Ridge 80033
800-727-7364 or 303-431-7600

United States Truck Driving School
19825 Wigwam Rd., Midway 81008
800-666-7364 or 719-382-3000

CONNECTICUT

Allstate Tractor Trailer Training School
2064 Main St., Bridgeport 06604

BARAN INSTITUTE OF TECHNOLOGY
611 Day Hill Rd., Windsor 06095
Michael Phelps, Dir. of Admissions
203-688-3353
BRANCH CAMPUS
15 Kimberly Ave., West Haven 06516
203-934-7289
Established 1980. Private. Coed. Accreditation:
ACCS/CT. Tuition: $8,900. Enrollment: 800 full-time,
120 part-time. Faculty: 50: Student-faculty ratio: 20:1.
Diploma offered. Library: 200 volumes. Housed in a
50,000 square foot building. Hands on programs in:
Automotive Technology, Auto Body Technology,
Diesel Technology, Electronic Technology, Heating,
Air-Conditioning, Refrigeration.
Housing available at both locations. 50% of students
are from out of state. Over 1000 students at both
locations. Courses emphasize 'hands on' training.
Financial aid is available for those that qualify. Scholarship program. Full-time placement dept.

Baran Institute of Technology
15 Kimberly Ave., West Haven 06516
203-934-7289
See listing under "Career Schools"

Branford Hall Career Institute
9 Business Park Dr., Branford 06405
Nelson Bernabucci, Director

Butler Business School
2710 North Ave., Bridgeport 06604
Morton S. Butler, President

Connecticut Business Institute
605 Broad St., Stratford 06497

Connecticut Business Institute
984 Chapel St., New Haven 06510

Connecticut Business Institute
809 Main St., East Hartford 06108

Connecticut Center for Massage Therapy
75 Kitts Ln., Newington 06111
Wes Sager, Admin. Director
203-667-1886

Connecticut Center for Massage Therapy
25 Sylvan Rd. S., Westport 06880
Susan Scoboria, Admin. Director
203-221-7325

Connecticut Institute of Art
581 W. Putnam Ave., Greenwich 06830
See listing under "Art"

Connecticut School of Electronics
586 Ella T. Grasso Blvd., New Haven 06519
Karen George, Director
203-624-2121

Data Institute
745 Burnside Ave., East Hartford 06108
Mark Scheinberg, Director
Lorren Lissitchuk, Dir. of Admis.
203-528-4111

Data Institute
101 Pierpont Rd., Waterbury 06705

Data Institute
109 Church St., New Haven 06512

Hartford Secretarial School
765 Asylum Ave., Hartford 06105
Patrick Fox, Director

Huntington Institute
193 Broadway, Norwich 06360
Thomas J. Haggerty, Director

Industrial Management and Training
233 Mill St., Waterbury 06706

Mattatuck Community College
750 Chase Parkway, Waterbury 06708
Dr. Richard Sanders, President

Morse School of Business
275 Asylum St., Hartford 06103
Michael S. Taub, President

New England Technical Institute
200 John Downey Dr., New Britain 06051
Marian D. Garay, Dir. of Admissions

New England Tractor Trailer Training
P.O. Box 326, Somers 06071
Arlan Greenberg, President

Porter & Chester Institute
125 Silas Deane Hwy., Wethersfield 06109

Porter and Chester Institute
138 Weymouth St., Enfield 06082
Henry Kamerzel, Director

Porter and Chester Institute
670 Lordship Blvd., Stratford 06497

Porter and Chester Institute
320 Sylvan Lake Rd., Watertown 06779

Ridley-Lowell Business and Technical Institute
P.O. Box 652, New London 06320
Louise Popp, Director

Salter School
1 Grove St., New Britain 06053

Stone Academy
1315 Dixwell Ave., Hamden 06514
Neil Zimmerman, Dir. of Admissions
203-288-7474

Swiss Hospitality Institute Cesar Ritz
101 Wykeham Rise Rd.
Washington 06793

Technical Careers Institute
11 Kimberly Ave., West Haven 06516
Michael Centers, Dir. of Admis.

Technical Careers Institute
605 Day Hill Rd., Windsor 06095
Michael L. Centers, Dir. of Admis.

UNIVERSITY OF HARTFORD
200 Bloomfield Ave., West Hartford 06117
Richard Zeiser, Dir. of Admis.
See listing under "Universities"

Waterbury State Technical College
750 Chase Pkwy., Waterbury 06708-3089

DELAWARE

Career Institute
711 Market Street Mall, Wilmington 19801

Star Technical Institute
631 W. Newport Pike, Wilmington 19804
Edward Webber, Director

DISTRICT OF COLUMBIA

Ardis School of Fashion Design
1728 Connecticut Ave., N.W., Washington 20009
Mary Simmons, Registrar
202-234-6537

Automation Academy
666 11th St., N.W. #750, Washington 20001

Barclay Career School
1511 K St. NW. #200, Washington 20005

National Conservatory of Dramatic Arts
1556 Wisconsin Ave., N.W., Washington 20007
C. Wayne Rudisill, President
202-333-2202

National Education Center-Capitol Hill Campus
810 First St., N.E., Washington 20002

PTC Career Institute
529 14th. St. N.W. Suite 350, Washington 20045
William Little, Director

Strayer College
6830 Laurel St. N.W., Washington 20012
Ron K. Bailey, President

FLORIDA

American Flyers College
5400 N.W. 21st Ter.
Fort Lauderdale 33309

American Medical Training Institute
7360 SW 167th St., Miami 33157
James Brodie, Administrator

Art Institute of Fort Lauderdale
1799 S.E. 17th St., Ft. Lauderdale 33316
Eileen Northrop, V.P./Dir. of Admis.
305-463-3000

ATI Career Training Center
3501 Powerline Rd., Oakland Park 33309

ATI Career Training Center
1 N.E. 19th St., Miami 33132

ATI Health Education Center
1395 N.W. 167th St., #200, Miami 33169
Max Sultan, Dir. of Admissions
800-938-2484
Offering Specialized Associate Degree programs in
Respiratory Therapy Technology or Medical
Assistant.

Atlantic Coast Institute
5225 W. Broward Blvd., Fort Lauderdale 33317
Ronald Dooley, Director

Atlantic Vocational-Technical Center
4700 Coconut Creek Pky., Coconut Creek 33063

Automotive Transmission School
453 E. Okeechobee Rd., Hialeah 33010

Baker Aviation School
3275 N.W. 42nd Ave., Miami 33142

Bay Area Legal Academy
3924 Coconut Palm Dr., Tampa 33619

Bay Area Vocational-Technical School
1976 Lewis Turner Blvd.
Fort Walton Beach 32547

Beacon Career Institute
2900 N.W. 183rd St., Opa Locka 33056

Boyd Career School
2090 Palm Beach Lakes Blvd.
West Palm Beach 33409
See listing this classification in Pennsylvania

Branell Institute
1700 Halstead Blvd. #2-2, Tallahassee 32308

Brewster Vocational-Technical Center
2222 N. Tampa St., Tampa 33602

Business Training Institute
1900 Evans Rd. #131, Melbourne 32904

Business Training Institute
21649 U.S. Highway 19, N. #200
Clearwater 34625

Career Center
1750 45th St. #204, West Palm Beach 33407

Career City College
1317 N.E. Fourth Ave., Fort Lauderdale 33304

Career Training Institute
2120 W. Colonial Dr., Orlando 32804

Career Training Institute
101 W. Main St., Leesburg 34748

CHAPMAN SCHOOL OF SEAMANSHIP
4343 S.E. St. Lucie Blvd., Stuart 34997
407-283-8130 or 800-225-2841
Jennifer Castle Field, President & Administrator
Gretchen Waterbury, Dir. of Admissions
   Established 1971. Coed. Named for co-founder, author of Piloting, Seamanship & Small Boat Handling. Private, not for profit. Professional mariner career course U.S. Coast Guard approved. Designated The Maritime School of Florida by state legislature. Licensed by State of Florida. Approved for veterans and alien students. Contract trainer for U.S. Navy. "HANDS ON, AT THE HELM TRAINING" CAREER PROGRAMS: Professional mariner training (12 weeks). Subjects include piloting, celestial and electronic navigation, boat & marine engine maintenance, rules of the road, marlinspike, weather, preparation for USCG license exam. Yacht and small craft surveying (6 weeks) - yacht design, construction methods and materials, onboard systems, practice condition & valuation surveys and report writing. RECREATIONAL PROGRAMS: Recreational Boating I (1 week) seamanship & safety; basic navigation; maintenance; and boathandling for new boaters. Recreational Boating II (1 week) advanced navigation; weather; rules of the road; marine electronics and boathandling. Offshore Sailing (6 days/5 nights) - for future ocean sailors. Marine Electronics (12 hours/weekend) - for boaters seeking to learn on the latest in navigation and marine communication equipment. Marine Engine Maintenance (12 hours/weekend) - for boaters who need to learn how to take better care of their boats. Power Boat Handling (16 hours/weekend) - A full weekend of at-the-helm training. American Sailing Association (A.S.A.) certification facility.
   Facilities include power/sail training fleet, student housing, 4 classrooms, library, swimming pool, limited number of boat slips at modest rates.
   Campus located 135 miles SE of Disney World 85 miles North of Ft. Lauderdale.
   For current information on class schedules, tuition, fees and student services call or write the Admissions Office.

Charlotte Vocational-Technical Center
18300 Toledo Blade Blvd., Port Charlotte 33948

Chauffeurs Training School
4101 N.W. 27th Ave., Miami 33142

ConCorde Career Institute
7960 Arlington Expressway #120
Jacksonville 32211

ConCorde Career Institute
4000 N. State Rd. 7, Lauderdale Lakes 33319

ConCorde Career Institute
4202 W. Spruce St., Tampa 33607

ConCorde Career Institute
285 NW 199th St., Miami 33169

COOPER ACADEMY OF COURT REPORTING
2247 Palm Beach Lakes Blvd. #110
West Palm Beach 33409
Margaret Williams, Director of Admissions
407-640-6999
   Established 1988. Private. Coed. Accreditation: ACICS. Tuition: $6,120. Enrollment: 200. Faculty: 8. Student-faculty ratio: 18:1. Specialized associate degree in court reporting offered. Excellent placement. Current retention 93%. Internship with affiliated court reporting firm. Recommended by court reporters in Palm Beach County. Approved by National Court Reporters Association.

Crown Business Institute
1223 S.W. Fourth St., Miami 33135

Erwin Vocational Technical Center
2010 E. Hillsborough Ave., Tampa 33610

FlightSafety International
P.O. Box 2708, Vero Beach 32961
Jeffrey Krell, Marketing Supervisor

Florida Computer and Business School
8300 Flagler St. #200, Miami 33144

Florida Institute of Ultrasound
8800 University Pky., Ste. 4A, Pensacola 32514

Florida Keys Community College
5901 College Rd., Key West 33040
Mitch Grabois, Director of Admissions
305-296-9081 Ext. 284

Florida School of Business
2990 N.W. 81st Ter., Miami 33147

Florida School of Business
4817 N. Florida Ave., Tampa 33603

Florida Technical College
1819 N. Semoran Blvd., Orlando 32807

Florida Technical College
8711 Lone Star Rd., Jacksonville 32211

Florida Technical College
4750 E. Adamo Dr., Tampa 33605

FULL SAIL CENTER FOR THE RECORDING ARTS
3300 University Blvd. #160, Winter Park 32792
407-679-0100 or 800-226-7625
Jon Phelps, Founder and President
Garry Jones, Senior Vice President
   Course/Program Title: Recording Arts Specialized Associate Degree and/or Video and Film Production Specialized Associate Degree. Programs in audio and/or video and film cover the major aspects utilizing hands-on training on current technology including Montage and CMX editors; 1", 3/4" and Beta Cam SP video formats; NEVE and SSL audio consoles; tapeless studios; Chyron, Grass Valley, Sony and Ikegami video gear; Studer, Otari and Ampex recorders. The courses of study center upon bankable skills by teaching students in the fields of recording engineering, post-production, digital audio work stations, music business, film production, video production, set designs, special effects and more. Over 2,700 contact hours are offered with more than 1,350 of them gained in hands-on labs. Both associate degree programs offer optional six-week externships. Short courses are available. Full Sail is the winner of the 1989, 1990 and 1991 TEC Awards for Best Recording School Program, the official training center for NEVE and Montage, nationally accredited by ACTTS, capable of offering financial aid to those who qualify, and is job placement oriented. Call and tell us about your career goals. We take your dreams seriously. 800-CAN-ROCK

Garces Commercial College
1301 S.W. 1st St., Miami 33135
Pelayo G. Garces, Director

George Stone Vocational Technical Center
2400 Longleaf Dr., Pensacola 32526

Golf Academy of the South
307 Daneswood Way, Casselberry 32707
800-786-0108

Haney Vocational-Technical Center
3016 Highway 77, Panama City 32405

HARRY WENDELSTEDT UMPIRE SCHOOL
88 S. Saint Andrews Dr., Ormond Beach 32174
Harry Wendelstedt, President

Hialeah Technical Center
1780 E. Fourth Ave., Hialeah 33010

Hi-Tech School of Miami
10350 W. Flagler St., Miami 33174
Eric Arencibia, President

International Technical Institute
P.O. Box 11497, Tampa 33680

Keiser College of Technology
1605 E. Plaza Dr., Tallahassee 32308
Maura Freeberg, Director

Lake County Area Vocational-Technical Center
2001 Kurt St., Eustis 32726

Lee Co. Vocational-Technical School
3800 Michigan Ave., Fort Myers 33916

Lindsey Hopkins Technical Education Center
750 N.W. 20th St., Miami 33127

Lively Area Vocational Technical School
500 N. Appleyard Dr., Tallahassee 32304

Locklin Voccational-Technical School
5330 Berryhill Rd., Milton 32570

McFatter Vocational-Technical Center
6500 Nova Dr., Davie 33317

Manatee Area Vocational-Technical Center
5603 34th St., Bradenton 34210

Marion County School of Radiologic Technology
438 S.W. 3rd St., Ocala 34474

MEDICAL ARTS TRAINING CENTER
441 S. State Road 7 #4, Margate 33068
800-334-6282

Miami Institute of Technology
1001 S.W. First St., Miami 33130

Miami Job Corps Center
660 S.W. Third St., Miami 33130

Miami Lakes Technical Education Center
5780 N.W. 158th St., Hialeah 33014

Miami Technical College
1001 N. Federal Hwy., Hallandale 33009

Miami Technical College
8672 Bird Rd., Miami 33155

Miami Technical College
7601 W. Flagler St., Miami 33144

Miami Technical College
8546 Bird Rd., Miami 33155

Miami Technical Institute
14701 N.W. 7th Ave., North Miami 33168

Mid-Florida Tech. Institute, Graphic Tech. Dept.
2900 W. Oak Ridge Rd., Orlando 32809
L. Evans, Director

Morgan Vocational-Technical Institute
18180 W. 122nd Ave., Miami 33177

Motorcycle Mechanics Institute and Marine Mechanics Institute divisions of Clinton Technical Institute
9751 Delegates Dr., Orlando 32837
David Miller, National Director
800-528-7995

National Aviation Academy
5770 Roosevelt Blvd. Ste. 105
Clearwater 34620
813-531-2080 or 800-659-2080

National Career Institute
3910 U.S. Highway 301, N., #200, Tampa 33619
Carroll Gossage, President
813-620-1446 or 800-683-5000
Careers in Airline Travel & Tourism, Hotel & Resort Management, Medical Assistant, Medical Office Management.

National School of Technology
4355 W. 16th Ave., Hialeah 33012

National School of Technology, Inc.
Two locations:
16150 N.E. 17th Ave., North Miami Beach 33162
4355 W. 16th Ave., Hialeah 33012

National Training
P.O. Box 1899, Orange Park 32067

National Training
State Rt. 209, Green Cove Springs 32043

National Education Center-Bauder Campus
4801 N. Dixie Hwy., Ft. Lauderdale 33334
Brian Woods, Dir. of Admis.
305-491-7171

North Technical Education Center
7071 Garden Rd., Riviera Beach 33404

Omni Technical School
1710 N.W. 7th St., Miami 33125
H. Ramos, Director

Orlando Vocational-Technical Center
301 W. Amelia St., Orlando 32801

Paralegal Careers
1211 N. Westshore Blvd., S. #100, Tampa 33607

PHOENIX EAST AVIATION, INC.
561 Pearl Harbor Dr., Daytona Beach 32114
Fred DeWitt, Vice President
904-258-0703 or 800-868-4359
   Established 1972. Private. Coed. Accreditation: FAA approved, FAR Part 141 and FAR part 61. Tuition, room and board vary. Enrollment fee: $50. Enrollment: 250 full-time, 50 part-time. Faculty: 55 flight instructors. Student-faculty ratio: 5:1. Degrees: FAA pilot certificates-private, commercial, instrument, multi CFI, CFII, MEI, ATP, King Air, B727. Phoenix East Aviation offers a wide variety of teaching programs from professional pilot courses to airline transport pilot. In addition, Phoenix East Aviation has developed advanced programs to enhance the training of the student and meet the needs of the industry. The reputation for quality is enhanced by its Daytona Beach location, which provides an excellent environment for the training of career pilots. Students are exposed to every facet of professional training with year-round flying conditions.

Pinellas Technical Education Center
901 34th St., S., St. Petersburg 33711

Pinellas Technical Education Center
6100 154th Ave., N., Clearwater 34620

Politechnical Institute of Florida
1405 S.W. 107th Ave. #201-C, Miami 33174
305-220-0400

Pompano Academy of Aeronautics
1006 N.E. 10th St., Pompano Beach 33060
Frank Besanceney, Director

Poynter Institute for Media Studies
801 Third St., S., Saint Petersburg 33701

Prospect Hall School of Business
2620 Hollywood Blvd., Hollywood 33020

QUALTEC Institute
11760 U.S. Hwy. 1 #500
North Palm Beach 33408

RETS Technical Centers
3501 Powerline Rd., Ft. Lauderdale 33309

Ridge Vocational-Technical Center
7700 State Rd. 544, Winter Haven 33881

Ross Technical Institute
1490 S. Military Tr. #11, West Palm Beach 33415

St. Augustine Technical Center
2980 Collins Ave., Saint Augustine 32095

Sarasota County Vocational Technical Center
4748 Beneva Rd., Sarasota 34233

SER-IBM Business Institute
42 N.W. 27th Ave. #421, Miami 33125

Sheridan Vocational-Technical Center
5400 Sheridan St., Hollywood 33021
305-985-3220

::: Southeastern Academy
P.O. Box 421768, Kissimmee 34742

Southern Technical Center
19151 S. Dixie Hwy., Miami 33157
Carlos Sangoinetti, Director

South Technical Education Center
1300 S.W. 30th Ave., Boynton Beach 33426

Southwest Florida College of Business
1685 Medical Ln. #200, Fort Myers 33907

Stenotype Institute of Jacksonville
500 9th Ave., N.
Jacksonville Beach 32250

Suncoast School of Massage Therapy
4910 W. Cypress St., Tampa 33607

Suwanee-Hamilton Area Vocational-Technical Center
415 Pinewood Dr., S.W., Live Oak 32060

Tampa College - Pinellas
15064 U.S. Hwy. 19 N., Clearwater 34624
Mark A. Page, President
813-530-9495

Traviss Vocational-Technical Center
3225 Winter Lake Rd., Lakeland 33803

Ultrasound Diagnostic School
2760 E. Atlantic Blvd., Pompano Beach 33062

Ultrasound Diagnostic School
5804 E. Breckenridge Pky., Tampa 33610

U. S. Schools
100 N. Plaza, Miami 33147

Walker Vocational-Technical Center
3702 Estey Ave., Naples 33942

WARD STONE COLLEGE KENDALL CAMPUS
9020 S.W. 137th Ave., Miami 33186
Dr. Leo Orsino, President
305-386-9900, FAX 305-388-1740

Washington Holmes Area Vocational-Technical
Center
757 Hoyt St., Chipley 32428

Westside Vocational-Technical Center
955 E. Story Rd., Winter Garden 34787

West Technical Education Center
2625 N.W. 16th St., Belle Glade 33430
Diane Wilson, Guidance

Winter Park Adult Vocational Center
901 Webster Ave., Winter Park 32789
Dr. Kaye Chastain, Director

Withlacoohee Technical Institute
1201 W. Main St., Inverness 34450

GEORGIA

Albany Technical Institute
1021 Lowe Rd., Albany 31701

· Art Institute of Atlanta
3376 Peachtree Rd., N.E., Atlanta 30326
J. Robert Bouchard, Dir. of Admis.

Asher School of Business
100 Pinnacle Way #110, Norcross 30071
Joe Voyles, President

Atlanta Area Technical Institute
1560 Stewart Ave., S.W., Atlanta 30310
Sandra S. Puckett, Dept. Chairperson

Atlanta College of Medical and Dental Careers
1400 W. Peachtree St., N.W., Atlanta 30309
Gary Vance, Dir. of Admis.

Atlanta Job Corps Center
239 W. Lake Ave., N.W., Atlanta 30314

Ben Hill Irwin Area Vocational Technical Institute
P.O. Box 1069, Fitzgerald 31750

Branell Institute
5255 Snapfinger Park Dr. #120
Decatur 30035

Branell Institute
4876 Riverdale Rd. #A, College Park 30337

Branell Institute
1000 Circle 75 Pky., N.W., #100, Atlanta 30339

Brown College of Court Reporting & Business
1100 Spring St. #200, Atlanta 30309
Fred Rich, President

Carroll Technical Institute
997 S. Highway 16, Carrollton 30116
Dr. Judy Hulsey, President
404-836-6800

Coosa Valley Technical Institute
112 Hemlock St., Rome 30161

Dalton Vocational School of Health Occupations
1221 Elkwood Dr., Dalton 30720

DeKalb County Occupational Education Center
3075 Alton Rd., Chamblee 30341

DeKalb County Occupational Education Center
1995 Womack Rd., Dunwoody 30338

DeKalb County Occupational Educational Center
3303 Pantherville Rd., Decatur 30034

Draughons College
1430 W. Peachtree St. N.W., #101
Atlanta 30309

Flint River Technical Institute
P.O. Box 1089, Thomaston 30286

Georgia Medical Institute
40 Marietta St. N.W. #1333, Atlanta 30303
404-525-3272

Griffin Institute
501 Varsity Rd., Griffin 30223

Gwinnett College of Business
4230 Lawrenceville Hwy. N.W., Lilburn 30247
Billy L. Clark, President
404-381-7200

Heart of Georgia Area Technical Institute
560 Pinehall Rd., Dublin 31021

Interactive Learning Systems
5600 Roswell Rd., N.E., Atlanta 30342

Interactive Learning Systems
200 Cleveland Rd. Ste 6, Bogart 30622

Kerr Business College
P.O. Box 1986, Augusta 30903
Darryl Kerr, President

Kerr Business College
P.O. Box 976, La Grange 30241
Douglas Davies, Director

Lanier Technical Institute
P.O. Box 58, Oakwood 30566

Macon Technical Institute
3300 Macon Tech. Dr., Macon 31206

Macon Technical Institute
940 Forsyth St., Macon 31201

Massey Institute
5299 Roswell Rd. #320, Atlanta 30342

Meadows College of Business
832 S. Slappey Blvd., Albany 31701
Fred Hawkins, Director

Medix School
2480 Windy Hill Rd., Marietta 30067

Middle Georgia Technical Institute
1311 Corder Rd., Warner Robins 31088

Moultrie Area Industrial-Technical Institute
Tift Co. School of Practical Nursing
314 E. 14th St., Tifton 31794
800-755-8316

Moultrie Area Technical Institute
P.O. Box 520, Moultrie 31776
Dr. Robert Hooks, Jr., VP Student Services
800-755-8316

National Business Institute
243 W. Ponce De Leon Ave., Decatur 30030

NEC Bryman Campus
40 Marietta St. N.W. Ste. 8, Atlanta 30303

North Georgia Technical Institute
P.O. Box 65, Clarkesville 30523

North Metro Technical Institute
5198 Ross Rd., Acworth 30102

Okefenokee Technical Institute
1701 Carswell Ave., Waycross 31503

· Phillips Junior College
1400 W. Peachtree St., N.W., Atlanta 30309

Pickens Technical Institute
100 Pickens Technical Dr.
Jasper 30143

PORTFOLIO CENTER
125 Bennett St., N.W., Atlanta 30309
John S. Hunsinger, Jr., Dir. of Admis.
800-255-3169
Established 1979. Private. Coed. Accreditation: SACS/COEI. Tuition: $10,200. Fees: $100. Enrollment: 300 full-time. Student-faculty ratio: 5:1. Library: 10,000 volumes. Considered by many to be the best advertising school in the country, Portfolio Center teams Art Directors, Copywriters, Designers, Photographers and Illustrators together on projects that meet professional standards in the creative industries. Faculty are professionals working on the fields they teach. Students come from all over the U.S. and abroad. 70% have previous degrees and 25% have some college experience. Graduates of the two year program work for the top ad agencies, design firms and photo studies in the country. Portfolio required for admission.

PTC Career Institute
44 Broad St. N.W., Atlanta 30303

Quality Plus Business School
1655 Peachtree Rd. N.E. #450, Atlanta
30309-2432

Southeastern Center for the Arts
1935 Cliff Valley Way N.E., Atlanta 30329
Fred W. Rich, Administrator

Southeastern School of Aeronautics
Herbert Smart Airport, Macon 31201
Patrick Murphy, President
800-423-7510
See listing under "Aeronautics"

South Georgia Technical Institute
728 Southerfield Rd., Americus 31709
B. J. Thomas, VP/SDS
912-928-0283

Swainsboro Technical Institute
201 Kite Rd., Swainsboro 30401
912-237-6465

Thomas Technical Institute
P.O. Box 1578, Thomasville 31799

Turner Job Corps Center
2000 Schilling Ave., Albany 31705

Ultrasound Diagnostic School
13 Corporate Square Office Park, Atlanta 30329

Valdosta Technical Institute
4089 Val Tech Rd., Valdosta 31602
James Bridges, President

Walker Technical Institute
265 Bicentennial Trail
Rock Spring 30739

West Georgia Technical Institute
303 Fort Dr., La Grange 30240

HAWAII

Brigham Young University, Hawaii Campus
55-220 Kulanui St., Laie 96762
Clark E. Hirschi, Coordinator of Admis.

Denver Business College
1916 Young St. #101, Honolulu 96826

Hawaii Business College
111 N. King St., Honolulu 96817
Sandra H. Morin, Director

· Heald Business College
1500 Kapiolani Blvd. #202, Honolulu 96814
Evelyn Schemmel, President
808-955-1500 Fax: 808-955-6964

Medical Assisting School of Hawaii
1149 Bethel St. #606, Honolulu 96813

New York Technical Institute of Hawaii
1375 Dillingham Blvd., Honolulu 96817

Travel Institute of the Pacific
1314 S. King St. #1164
Honolulu 96814

Travel University International
1441 Kapiolani Blvd. #1414
Honolulu 96814

IDAHO

AERO TECHNICIANS
P.O. Box 7, Rexburg 83440
Julina Hart, Director of Admissions
208-356-4446 or 208-356-4447
Established 1946. Private. Coed. Accreditation: AC-CET, FAA, Idaho Department of Education. Tuition: $8,160. Room and board: $3,000. Fees: $350. Tools: $1,200. Enrollment: 25 full-time, 35 part-time. Faculty: 4. Student-faculty ratio: 6:1. Licenses: FAA Airframe and Powerplant Mechanic, Avionics, Professional Pilot. Library: 1,000 volumes. 1 building 28,000 square feet. FAR part 141 school for Professional Pilot, fixed wing aircraft and helicopters. Ideal location for all pilot training. Fleet of 12 airplanes and helicopters. Aviation has excellent growth potential. Placement help available. Federal financial aid for US citizens if you qualify.

American Institute of Health Technology
6600 Emerald, Boise 83704

Eastern Idaho Technical College
2299 E. 17th St., Idaho Falls 83404

Lewis Clark State College
500 8th Ave., Lewiston 83501
800-933-5272 or 208-799-5272

· North Idaho College
1000 W. Garden Ave., Couer d'Alene 83814
Clarence Haught, Director

ILLINOIS

· American Academy of Art
332 S. Michigan Ave. 3rd Fl.
Chicago 60604

American College of Technology
1300 W. Washington St., Bloomington 61701
Glenn L. Plotner, Dir. of Admis.
800-593-5151

American Floral Art School
529 S. Wabash Ave. #600, Chicago 60605-1679
James Moretz, Director, AIFD
312-922-9328

Automotive Technical Institute
5567 N. Elston Ave., Chicago 60630

Brown's Business College
601 Burns Ln., Springfield 62702
Larry Weber, President

Cave Technical Institute
2842 S. State St., Lockport 60441

College of Office Technology
1514 W. Division #2, Chicago 60622

Commonwealth Business College
1527 47th Ave., Moline 61265
Don Watson, Director
309-762-2100

Computer Learning Center
200 S. Michigan Ave. 3rd FL, Chicago 60604
Larry Jetter, Dir. of Admis.
312-427-2700

Connecticut School of Broadcasting
200 W. 22nd St. #202, Lombard 60148

Cooking and Hospitality Institute of Chicago
361 W. Chestnut, Chicago 60610

Coyne American Institute
1235-57 W. Fullerton Ave., Chicago 60614
E. Lakickas, Director

Environmental Technical Institute
1054 E. Irving Park, Bensenville 60106

Environmental Technical Institute
13010 S. Division St., Blue Island 60406

FOX COLLEGE OF EXECUTIVE/LEGAL ASSISTANTS
4201 W. 93rd St., Oak Lawn 60453
Edward Kay, Jr., Dir. of Admis.
Established 1932. Private. Women. Accreditation: Illinois State Board of Education, AICS. Tuition: $7,440. Fees: $50. Enrollment: 150. Faculty: 8. Student-faculty ratio: 18:1. One building. One year of serious study. Recognized by the major corporations of Chicagoland for academic excellence. Only college specializing exclusively in executive and legal assistants. Students may pay tuition after career placement; 100% career placement record in 1990. Must interview to be accepted.

Gem City College
700 State St., Quincy 62301
R. Hagenah, President

Heartland School of Business
211 W. State St. Suite 204
Jacksonville 62650

Illinois Medical Training Center
162 N. State St., Chicago 60601

ITT Technical Institute
600 Holiday Plaza Dr.
Matteson 60443

KASKASKIA COLLEGE
27210 College Rd., Centralia 62801
618-532-1981 or 800-642-0859 (Illinois)
Raymond D. Woods, President
Marilyn Brookman, PhD, College Dean
Constance Stohlman, Director of Admissions, Public Relations, and Resource Development
Kaskaskia College is situated on a beautifully wooded tract of land consisting of 190 acres. Its brick and frame buildings provide 228,830 square feet of space for college facilities. Kaskaskia College is fully accredited by NCACS, ADA, AMA, NLN, IBE, ICCB, and IBHE. The College is recognized and approved by the bureau of Veterans Affairs and is authorized under Federal law to enroll non-immigrant alien students. In district tuition and fees are $33.75 per semester credit hour. Degrees: AA, AS, AAS, and AGS. University transfer programs, pre-professional, liberal arts, courses offered days, evenings, and weekends. Training in career fields. State and Federal financial aid programs available.

Lewis & Clark Community College
5800 Godfrey Rd., Godfrey 62035
J. Neil Admire, President

Lincoln Land Community College
Shepherd Rd., Springfield 62794-9256
Ron Gregoire, Dir. of Admis.
Information: 800-727-4161

LINCOLN TECHNICAL INSTITUTE
8920 S. Cicero Ave., Oak Lawn 60453
Kenneth Ruff, Director
708-423-9000
Established 1946. Coed. Accredited Member School: ACCSCT. Providing technical training in Automotive or Diesel Truck Technology. Financial aid for those who qualify. Employment assistance program.

LINCOLN TECHNICAL INSTITUTE
7320 W. Agatite Ave., Norridge 60656
James Yeaman, Director
312-625-1535
Established 1946. Coed. Accredited Member School: ACCSCT. Providing technical training in: Automotive or Diesel Truck Technology. Financial aid for those who qualify. Employment assistance program.

Marycrest College
280 E. Merchant St., Kankakee 60901
Michael Steinbach, Director

Medical Careers Institute
116 S. Michigan Ave., Chicago 60603

Moraine Valley Community College
10900 S. 88th Ave., Palos Hills 60465
Dr. Vernon Crawley, President

MORRISON INSTITUTE OF TECHNOLOGY
701 Portland Ave., Morrison 61270-2959
Dr. Richard Parkinson, President
Dr. Dale Trimpe, Dir. of Admis.
Established 1961. Private. Coed. Accreditation:

Technical Accreditation Committee - Accreditation Board for Engineering and Technology (ABET), State, Federal, Veterans. Tuition: $6,500. Room and board: $1,800. Enrollment: 170 full-time, 2 part-time. Faculty: 13. Student-faculty ratio: 18:1. Degree: Associate in Engineering Technology. Library: 5,000 volumes. 5 buildings on 17 acres. Specialized areas of study: CAD/design & drafting technology, highway engineering technology, CAD/architectural & mechanical technology. CAD/CAM specialty all areas. Strong Placement.

Music Center of the North Shore
300 Green Bay Rd., Winnetka 60093

NEC-Bryman Campus
4101 W. 95th St., Oak Lawn 60453
Doloris Reynolds, Director

NEC-Bryman Campus
17 N. State St., #1800, Chicago 60602

Parkland College
2400 W. Bradley Ave., Champaign 61821-1899
217-351-2208 or 800-346-8089

Parks College of St. Louis University
500 Falling Springs Rd., Cahokia 62206
John Wilbur, Dir. of Admis.

Pathfinder School
19 E. 21st St., Chicago 60616
Melvyn May, President

PBS Training Center
529 S. Wabash 2nd Fl., Chicago 60605
Anthony McElligott, President

PTC Career Institute
11 E. Adams St. #400, Chicago 60603

Quincy Technical Schools
501 N. 3rd St., Quincy 62301

RAY COLLEGE OF DESIGN
AAS, BA, BFA degrees
401 N. Wabash Ave., Chicago 60611
312-280-3500
Woodfield Campus
1051 Perimeter Dr., Schaumburg 60173
708-619-3450

ROCKFORD BUSINESS COLLEGE
730 N. Church St., Rockford 61103
David Swank, President
815-965-8616

Sanford-Brown Business College
3237 W. Chain of Rocks Rd., Granite City 62040

Sparks College
131 S. Morgan St., Shelbyville 62565
Roger B. Sparks, President

Taylor Business Institute
36 S. State St. #800, Chicago 60603
Janice Parker, President

Triton College
2000 N. 5th Ave., River Grove 60171
Gail Fuller, Dir. of Admission & Records
See listing under "Community and Junior Colleges"

Tyler School of Secretarial Sciences
8030 S. Kedzie Ave., Chicago 60652
312-436-5050

Universal Technical Institute
601 Regency Dr., Glendale Heights 60139
708-529-2662 or 800-441-4248

Western Illinois University
900 W. Adams St., Macomb 61455
Alan DeRoos, Registrar
309-298-1891

Woodridge Business Institute
1310 Mercantile Dr., Highland 62249

WORSHAM COLLEGE OF MORTUARY SCIENCE
495 Northgate Pky., Wheeling 60090-2646
Bruno B. Bak, President
Joan D. Tomczak, Director of Admissions
Frederick Cappetta, Chief Administrator
708-808-8444, FAX 708-808-8493
Established 1911. Private. Coed. Accreditation: American Board of Funeral Service Education. Tuition: $7,000. Enrollment: 150 full-time, four days a week for twelve months. All courses taught by qualified faculty. Enrollment held only on September and March. In a modern air-conditioned building on a two acre campus with ample parking that is a half hour from Chicago (closest large city). The registrar helps students to locate housing off campus or a job in local funeral homes with housing.

INDIANA

Aristotle College/Medical & Dental Tech.
5245 South US 31, Indianapolis 46227

Aristotle College of Medical and Dental Technology
5255 Hohman Ave., Hammond 46320

College of Court Reporting
111 W. 10th, Hobart 46342

Commonwealth Business College
8995 N. State Rd. 39, La Porte 46350
Faye Mercer, Director
219-362-3338

Commonwealth Business College
4200 W. Lincoln Hwy., Merrillville 46410
Al Conaway, Director
219-769-3321

Indiana Business College
1320 E. 53rd St. #106, Anderson 46013

Indiana Business College
P.O. Box 1906, Columbus 47202

Indiana Business College
802 N. Meridian St., Indianapolis 46204

Indiana Business College
1170 S. Creasy Lane, Lafayette 47905

Indiana Business College
830 N. Miller Ave., Marion 46952

Indiana Business College
1809 N. Walnut St., Muncie 47303

Indiana Business College
3175 S. 3rd Pl., Terre Haute 47802

Indiana Business College
4601 Theatre Dr., Evansville 47715

Indiana Business College - Medical
5460 Victory Dr. #100
Indianapolis 46203

Indiana Business College
1431 Willow St., Vincennes 47591

Indiana Vocational Technical College (IVY)
P.O. Box 1763, Indianapolis 46206

ITT Technical Institute
9511 Angola Ct., Indianapolis 46268

Ivy Tech Central
1 W. 26th St., Indianapolis 46208
Meredith Carter, V.P., Dean

Ivy Tech Columbus
4475 Central Ave., Columbus 47203
Homer Smith, V.P., Dean

Ivy Tech East Central
P.O. Box 3100, Muncie 47307
Richard L. Davidson, V.P., Dean

Ivy Tech Kokomo
1815 E. Morgan St., Kokomo 46901
Charles Hefley, V.P., Dean

Ivy Tech Lafayette
P.O. Box 6299, Lafayette 47903
Thomas Reckerd, V.P., Dean

Ivy Tech Northcentral
1534 W. Sample St., South Bend 46619
Carl Lutz, V.P., Dean

Ivy Tech Northeast
3800 N. Anthony Blvd., Fort Wayne 46805
Jon Rupright, V.P., Dean

Ivy Tech Northwest
1440 E. 35th Ave., Gary 46409
Mearle Donica, Dean

Ivy Tech SouthCentral
8204 W. Hwy. 31, Sellersburg 47172
Jonothan Thomas, V.P., Dean

Ivy Tech Southeast
Highway 62 & Ivy Tech Drive, Madison 47250
Gregory Flood, V.P., Dean

Ivy Tech Southwest
3501 1st Ave., Evansville 47710
H. Victor Baldi, V.P., Dean

Ivy Tech Wabash Valley
7377 S. Dixie Bee Rd., Terre Haute 47802
Samuel Borden, V.P., Dean

Ivy Tech Whitewater
2325 Chester Blvd., Richmond 47374
Judith Redwine, V.P., Dean

Lakeshore Medical Laboratory Training Programs
402 Franklin St., Michigan City 46360
Toni Schlichtenmyer, MT (ASCP), Program Director

LINCOLN TECHNICAL INSTITUTE
1201 Stadium Dr., Indianapolis 46202
Merlyn Cooper, Director
317-632-5553
Established 1946. Coed. Accredited Member School: ACCSCT. Providing technical training in: Automotive or Diesel Truck Technology, *Automotive or Diesel Truck Service and Management, *Architectural/Mechanical Drafting and CAD Technology. Financial aid for those who qualify. Employment assistance program. (*Associate of Applied Science Degree).

Michiana College
1030 E. Jefferson Blvd., South Bend 46617
Philip Heine, Director
800-743-2447

Michiana College
4807 Illinois Rd., Fort Wayne 46804
Anthony Conti, Director
800-743-2447

Professional Careers Institute
2611 Waterfront Pky., Indianapolis 46214

Reppert School of Auctioneering, Inc.
P.O. Box 189, Decatur 46733
Phil Neuenschwander, President
219-724-3804

SAWYER COLLEGE
6040 Hohman Ave., Hammond 46320
Mary Jo Dixon, Director
800-964-0208

SAWYER COLLEGE
3803 E. Lincoln Hwy., Merrillville 46410
Mary Jo Dixon, Director
800-964-0218

Valparaiso Technical Institute
1 Center St., Valparaiso 46383
Helen L. Green, Dir. of Admis.

IOWA

· American Institute of Commerce
1801 E. Kimberly Rd., Davenport 52807
John Huston, President
319-355-3500

American Institute of Commerce
2302 W. First St., Cedar Falls 50613
John Huston, President
319-277-0220

Hamilton Business College
100 1st St., N.W., Mason City 50401
Laurie Caspers, Director

Hamilton Business College
1924 D St., S.W., Cedar Rapids 52404

Hamilton Business College
2300 Euclid Ave., Des Moines 50310

HAMILTON TECHNICAL COLLEGE
1011 E. 53rd St., Davenport 52807
319-386-3570
Charles Hamilton, Jr., President
Maryanne Hamilton, Director
Established 1970. Coed. Accreditation: CCA. Tuition: $5,250 per year. Enrollment: 400. Staff and faculty: 35. Degrees: Diploma, Associate and Bachelor areas of study include biomedical electronics, communication technology, computer-aided-drafting, computer technology, industrial electronics, solid state and medical assisting technology. Suburban campus. Student services: personal and career advising, aptitude testing, employment service for undergraduates, placement service for graduates and facilities for handicapped.

· Hawkeye Community College
1501 E. Orange Rd., Waterloo 50701
319-296-2320 Ext. 4000

· Indian Hills Community College
525 Grandview, Ottumwa 52501
515-683-5111

· Iowa Lakes Community College
3200 College Dr., Emmetsburg 50536
John Nelson, Dir. of Admis.
712-852-3554

· Iowa Western Community College
2700 College Rd., Council Bluffs 51503
Thomas Dutch, Dir. of Admis.

KIRKWOOD COMMUNITY COLLEGE
P.O. Box 2068, Cedar Rapids 52406
Jim Miller, Dir. of Admis.
319-398-5517

Maharishi International University
Route 1, Fairfield 52556
Gregory Polakow, Dir. of Admis.

SCOTT COMMUNITY COLLEGE
500 Belmont Rd., Bettendorf 52722
Kris Barkdoll, Assoc. Dean Enrollment Management

SPENCER COLLEGE
217 W. 5th St., Spencer 51301
Harvey Work, Director
800-383-7290
Established 1968. Private. Coed. Accreditation: AICS, AMA, NCACS (candidate status). Tuition: $1,961/quarter. Room: $625/quarter. Fees: $50. Enrollment: 160 full-time, 40 part-time. Faculty: 12. Student-faculty ratio: 16:1. Diploma and AAS degrees offered. 4 buildings. Large blue water lake 15 miles north. Northwest Iowa population 13,000. Apartment style housing. Lifetime placement. High placement rate. 85% graduation rate.

World Wide College of Auctioneering
Formerly Reisch
Four Terms Per Year
P.O. Box 949, Dept. AE, Mason City 50402
Bill Addis, President
515-423-5242

KANSAS

American Institute of Baking
1213 Bakers Way, Manhattan 66502
Ken Embers, Dir. of Admissions
800-633-5137

Amtech Institute
4011 E. 31st St., S., Wichita 67210

Bryan Institute
1004 S. Oliver St., Wichita 67218

Bryan Travel College
1527 Fairlain Rd., Topeka 66604

Center for Training in Business & Industry
2211 Silicon Ave., Lawrence 66046

Climate Control Institute
3030 N. Hillside St., Wichita 67219

· Dodge City Community College
2501 N. 14th Ave., Dodge City 67801
Debbie Lloyd, Director of Admissions
800-FOR-DCCC

· Kansas State University
College of Technology
2409 Scanlan Ave., Salina 67401

LIBERAL AREA VOCATIONAL/TECHNICAL SCHOOL
P.O. Box 1599, Liberal 67905-1599
Toby Hale, Dir. of Student Services
James Sweeney, Director 316-626-3819

North Central KS Area Vocational-Technical School
P.O. Box 507, Beloit 67420

Southern Technical College
2015 S. Meridian St., Wichita 67213

Topeka School of Medical Technology
1915 S.W. 6th Ave. #207, Topeka 66606

Topeka Technical College
1620 N.W. Gage Blvd., Topeka 66618
Vicki Johnson, Director

WICHITA BUSINESS COLLEGE
501 E. Pawnee St. #515, Wichita 67211
Larry Prather, Dir. of Student Services
316-263-1261
Established 1883. Private. Coed. Accreditation: CCA - AICS. Tuition: $100 per credit hour. Fees: $60. Enrollment: 160 full-time, 80 part-time. Faculty: 15. Student-faculty ratio: 14:1. Library: 3,000 vols. Wichita Business College is located in the largest city in Kansas and is one of the oldest continuing business colleges west of the Mississippi. Our campus is in a mall which provides a campus setting and free parking. The school offers computerized training in many fields of study and is progressive in its business offerings.

Wichita Technical Institute
942 S. West St., Wichita 67213
Paul D. Moore, President

Wright Business School
9500 Marshall Dr., Lenexa 66215

KENTUCKY

Clements Job Corps Center
2302 U.S. Highway 60 E., Morganfield 42437

Computer School, The
820 Lane Allen Rd., Lexington 40504
John Weikel, President

Draughons Junior College
2424 Airway Ct., Bowling Green 42103

· Institute of Electronic Technology
509 S. 30th St., Paducah 42001
800-995-4438

ITT Technical Institute
10509 Timberwood Cir.
Louisville 40223

Kentucky Career Institue
P.O. Box 143, Florence 41022

Kentucky Tech Ashland State Vocational Technical School
4818 Roberts Dr., Ashland 41102

Kentucky Tech Bowling Green Vocational Technical School
P.O. Box 1868, Bowling Green 42102

Kentucky Tech Central KY State Vocational Technical School
150 Vo Tech Rd., Lexington 40510

Kentucky Tech Elizabethtown State Vocational Technical School
505 University Dr., Elizabethtown 42701

Kentucky Tech Hazard State Vocational Technical School
101 Vo-Tech Dr., Hazard 41701

Kentucky Tech Jefferson State Vocational Technical School
727 W. Chestnut St., Louisville 40203

Kentucky Tech Laurel Co State Vocational Technical School
1711 N. Main St., London 40741

Kentucky Tech Madisonville State Vocational Technical School
100 School St., Madisonville 42431

Kentucky Tech Mayo State Vocational Technical School
513 3rd St., Paintsville 41240

Kentucky Tech Northern Kentucky State Vocational Technical School
1025 Amsterdam Rd., Covington 41011

Kentucky Tech Owensboro Vocational Technical School
P.O. Box 1677, Owensboro 42302

Kentucky Tech Rowan State Vocational Technical School
P.O. Box 1098, Morehead 40351

Kentucky Tech Somerset Area Vocational Technical School
230 Airport Rd., Somerset 42501

Kentucky Tech West KY State Vocational Technical School
P.O. Box 7769, Paducah 42002

Lexington Electronics Institute
3340 Holwyn Rd., Lexington 40503
Joe Major, Dir. of Admis.
800-456-3253 or 606-223-3310

· Louisville Technical Institute
3901 Atkinson Dr., Louisville 40218
George Nunley, Dir. of Admis.

Perkins Job Corps Center
Box G-11 Goble Roberts Rd., Prestonsburg 41653

Southwestern College of Business
2929 S. Dixie Hwy., Covington 41017

Spencerian College
P.O. Box 16418, Louisville 40256
Harold Stice, Executive Director

LOUISIANA

Acadian Technical Institute
P.O. Box 820, Crowley 70527

Alexandria Regional Technical Institute
P.O. Box 5698, Alexandria 71307

American School of Business
702 Professional Dr. N.
Shreveport 71105

Ascension Technical Institute
P.O. Box 38, Sorrento 70778

Avoyelles Technical Institute
P.O. Box 307, Cottonport 71327

Ayers Institute
2924 Knight St. #318, Shreveport 71105
R. G. Hammett, Admin.

Bastrop Technical Institute
P.O. Box 1120, Bastrop 71221

Baton Rouge Technical Institute
3250 N. Acadian Thruway, Baton Rouge 70805

Bayou Technical Institute
P.O. Box 13128, New Orleans 70185

Camelot Career College
2618 Wooddale Blvd., Baton Rouge 70805

Cameron College
2740 Canal St., New Orleans 70119

Career Training Specialists
1611 Louisville Ave., Monroe 71201

Charles B. Coreil Technical Institute
P.O. Box 296, Ville Platte 70586

Claiborne Technical Institute
3001 Minden Rd., Homer 71040

Coastal College
5520 Industrial Dr., Bossier City 71112

Coastal College
119 Yokum Rd., Hammond 70403

Coastal College
2001 Canal St. #300, New Orleans 70112

Coastal College
2318 W. Park Ave., Houma 70364

Commercial College of Baton Rouge
5677 Florida Blvd., Suite 210, Baton Rouge 70806
William McClure, Administrator

Commercial College of Shreveport
2640 Youree Dr., Shreveport 71104
John Kelsall, President

Concordia Technical Institute
P.O. Box 152, Ferriday 71334

Culinary Arts Institute of Louisiana
427 Lafayette St., Baton Rouge 70802
Violet Harrington, President

Delta Career College
1702 Hudson Ln., Monroe 71201

Delta Career College
1900 Cameron St., Lafayette 70506

Delta College
3827 W. Main St., Houma 70360

Delta-Ouachita Technical Institute
609 Vocational Pky., West Monroe 71292

Delta Schools
4549 Johnston St., Lafayette 70503
Bernard F. Szymanski, Director

Delta Schools
413 W. Admiral Doyle St., New Iberia 70560

Diesel Driving Academy
P.O. Box 36949, Shreveport 71133

Diesel Driving Academy
8136 Airline Hwy., Baton Rouge 70815

Domestic Health Care Institute
4826 Jamestown Ave., Baton Rouge 70808

Eastern College of Health Vocations
3540 I-10 Service Rd., S., Metairie 70001

Evangeline Technical Institute
P.O. Box 68, St. Martinville 70582

Florida Parishes Technical Institute
P.O. Box 130, Greensburg 70441

Folkes Technical Institute
P.O. Box 808, Jackson 70748

Franklin College of Court Reporting
1200 S. Clearview Pky., New Orleans 70123

Gulf Area Technical Institute
P.O. Box 878, Abbeville 70511

Hammond Area Technical Institute
P.O. Box 489, Hammond 70404

Harris Technical Institute
P.O. Box 713, Opelousas 70571

Jefferson College
12 Westbank Expressway, Gretna 70053

Jefferson Davis Technical Institute
1230 N. Main St., Jennings 70546

Jefferson Technical Institute
5200 Blair Dr., Metairie 70001
504-736-7072

Lafayette Regional Vocational-Technical School
P.O. Box 4909, Lafayette 70502

Long Technical Institute
303 S. Jones St., Winnfield 71483

Louisiana Art Institute
7380 Exchange Pl., Baton Rouge 70806

Louisiana Institute of Technology
3349 Masonic Dr., Alexandria 71301

Memorial Technical Institute
P.O. Box 725, New Roads 70760

Natchitoches Technical Institute
P.O. Box 657, Natchitoches 71458

NEC-Bryman Campus
2322 Canal St., New Orleans 70119

New Orleans Regional Technical Institute
980 Navarre Ave., New Orleans 70124

North Central Area Technical Institute
P.O. Box 548, Farmerville 71241

Northeast Louisiana Technical Institute
1710 Warren St., Winnsboro 71295

Northwest Louisiana Technical Institute
P.O. Box 835, Minden 71058
Charles T. Strong, Director

Oakdale Technical Institute
P.O. Box EM, Oakdale 71463

Ochsner School of Allied Health Sciences
880 W. Commerce Rd., New Orleans 70123
Edward D. Frohlich, MD, VP Academic Affairs
504-842-3267

Randazzo Vocational Training Institute
125 Lafayette St., Gretna 70053

Remington College
303 Rue Louis XIV #8, Lafayette 70508

River Parish Technical Institute
P.O. Box AQ, Reserve 70084

Ruston Technical Institute
P.O. Box 1070, Ruston 71273

Sabine Valley Technical Institute
P.O. Box 790, Many 71449

Salter Technical Institute
Route 2 Box 25, Leesville 71446

Shreveport-Bossier Technical Institute
P.O. Box 78527, Shreveport 71137

Slidell Technical Institute
P.O. Box 827, Slidell 70459

South Louisiana Technical Institute
P.O. Box 5033, Houma 70361

Sowela Regional Technical Institute
3820 Legion St., Lake Charles 70601
Rex H. Smelser, Director

Sullivan Technical Institute
1710 Sullivan Dr., Bogalusa 70427
504-732-6640

Tallulah Technical Institute
P.O. Box 1740, Tallulah 71284

Teche Area Technical Institute
P.O. Box 11057, New Iberia 70562

Thibodaux Area Technical Institute
1425 Tiger Dr., Thibodaux 70301

West Jefferson Technical Institute
475 Manhattan Blvd., Harvey 70058

Westside Technical Institute
P.O. Box 733, Plaquemine 70765

Young Memorial Technical Institute
P.O. Box 2148, Morgan City 70381

MAINE

Air Tech
R.R. 11 Box 170, Limerick 04048

· Central Maine Technical College
1250 Turner St., Auburn 04210
Dr. William J. Hierstein, President

· Kennebec Valley Technical College
92 Western Ave., Fairfield 04937
Barbara Woodlee, Director

Landing School of Boatbuilding & Design
P.O. Box 1490, Kennebunkport 04046
207-985-7976

New England School of Broadcasting
One College Circle, Bangor 04401
207-947-6083

· Northern Maine Technical College
33 Edgemont Dr., Presque Isle 04769

SOUTHERN MAINE TECHNICAL COLLEGE
2 Fort Rd., South Portland 04106
Wayne Ross, President
Robert Weimont, Dir. of Admis.

Scott McDonald, Director of Financial Aid
207-767-9500
Established 1946. State. Coed. Tuition: in-state $1,044 per semester, out-of-state $2,286 per semester. Room and board: $3,200 per year for all students. Total enrollment: 2,200 students, (1,400 men, 800 women). Coed dormitories located on-campus. Off-campus housing available in apartments and rooms in private houses. Assistance provided in locating.
Curriculum: Associate degree and two year diploma programs in: applied marine biology & oceanography, automated office management, automotive technology, building construction, computer technology, culinary arts, dietetic technician, electrical technology, electronics technology, environmental engineering, fire science, heating & air conditioning, hotel, motel, & restaurant management, industrial electronics, industrial electricity, law enforcement, machine tool technology, marine science deck & engineering, plant and soil technology, radiation therapy, radiologic technology, respiratory therapy. One year programs in: cardiovascular technology, drafting, plant & soil technology, plumbing & heating, practical nursing, wastewater technology.
Admissions: Normally, freshman students are in the upper three-fifths of their graduating class. SAT required for Associate degree applicants. PELL, SEOG, GSBL, work study, limited scholarships, are available.
Environment: Southern Maine Technical College is located on the beautiful shore of Casco Bay in a quiet residential neighborhood just 10 minutes away from downtown Portland. Portland is Maine's largest city and enjoys a national reputation as one of the most livable small urban centers in the nation. Attractive bathing beach and a beautiful shore walkway are on or immediately adjacent to campus.
144 faculty members with a student-faculty ratio of 9:1. Graduates have regularly enjoyed 80-90% job placement in fields directly related to their area of study.

Washington County Technical College
R.R. 1 Box 22C, Calais 04619
Ronald Renaud, President
207-454-2144

MARYLAND

Abbie Business Institute
5310 Spectrum Dr. #A, Frederick 21701

All-State Career School
201 S. Arlington Ave., Baltimore 21223
Carson Burke, Director

Arundel Institute of Technology
Electronics and Drafting School
1808 Edison Hwy., Baltimore 21213
Manfred Bloch, Director

Broadcasting Institute of Maryland
7200 Harford Rd., Baltimore 21234
John Jeppi, President
800-942-9246

Diesel Institute of America
P.O. Box 69, Grantsville 21536

· Essex Community College
7201 Rossville Blvd., Baltimore 21237
Diane Lane, Dir. of Admis.

Fleet Business School
2530 Riva Rd. #201, Annapolis 21401
Kenan Habetler, Dir. of Admis.

LINCOLN TECHNICAL INSTITUTE
3200 Wilkens Ave., Baltimore 21229
Steve Buchenot, Director
410-646-5480
Established 1946. Coed. Accredited Member School: ACCSCT. Providing technical training in Automotive Technology. Financial aid for those who qualify. Employment assistance program.

LINCOLN TECHNICAL INSTITUTE
7800 Central Ave., Landover 20785
Elizabeth Wellman, Director
301-336-7250
Established 1946. Coed. Accredited Member School: ACCSCT. Providing technical training in: Automotive Technology, Air Conditioning, Refrigeration and Heating Technology. Financial aid for those who qualify. Employment assistance program.

Maryland Drafting Institute
2045 University Blvd., E., Langley Park 20783
C. B. Sawyer, Dir. Administration

Medix School
1017 York Rd., Towson 21204
Richard Stensing, Dir. of Admis.

· Montgomery College
20200 Observation Dr., Germantown 20876
301-353-7700

· Montgomery College
51 Mannakee St., Rockville 20850
301-279-5000

National Institute of Health
9000 Rockville Pike Bldg. 10, Bethesda 20892

New England Tractor Trailer Training
1410 Bush St., Baltimore 21230

PTC Career Institute
201 E. Baltimore St., Baltimore 21202

RETS TECHNICAL TRAINING CENTER
1520 S. Caton Ave., Baltimore 21227-1063
H. V. Leslie, President
410-644-6400
Established 1956. Private. Coed. Accreditation: Accrediting Commission of Career Schools and Colleges of Technology. One and two year programs in electronic engineering, computers, robotic technologies, refrigeration, air-conditioning, heating, heat pumps, solar energy technologies, and engineering drafting with C.A.D.D.

Rice Aviation-Martin State Airport Campus
701 Wilson Point Rd., Baltimore 21220

TESST Electronics and Computer Institute
5122 Baltimore Ave., Hyattsville 20781
Joseph W. Fox, Director
301-864-5750

Ultrasound Diagnostic School
1320 Fenwick Ln., Silver Spring 20910

Woodridge Business Institute
309 E. Main St., Salisbury 21801
Phil Turk, Dir. of Admis.

MASSACHUSETTS

Associated Technical Institute
345 W. Cummings Park, Woburn 01801

Bay State School of Appliances
225 Turnpike St., Canton 02021

BURDETT SCHOOL
745 Boylston St., Boston 02116
Maralin Manning, President
617-859-1900

Burdett School
100 Front St., Worcester 01608

Butera School of Art
Commercial Art-Sign Painting
111 Beacon St., Boston 02116
Charles Banks, Director

Cambridge School of Culinary Arts
2020 Massachusetts Ave., Cambridge 02140

Computer Learning Center
5 Middlesex Ave., Somerville 02145

Computer Learning Center
436 Broadway, Methuen 01844

Computer Processing Institute
615 Massachusetts Ave., Cambridge 02139

East Coast Aero Tech School
Division of Wentworth Technical Schools
696 Virginia Rd., Concord 01742
Mark Holzwarth, Dir. of Admis.
508-371-9977

Essex Agricultural & Technical Institute
Hathorne 01937

· Franklin Institute of Boston
41 Berkeley St., Boston 02116
Richard P. D'Onofrio, President
617-423-4630
See listing under "Engineering"

Hallmark Institute of Photography
P.O. Box 308, Turners Falls 01376
Bill Chenaille, Dir. of Admis.
413-863-2478

ITT Technical Institute
1671 Worcester Rd. #100, Framingham 01701

Kinyon-Campbell Business School
59 Linden St., New Bedford 02740
David Daganhardt, Director

Mildred Elley Business School
400 Columbus Ave., Pittsfield 01201

National Education Center-Bryman Campus
323 Boylston St., Brookline 02146
Robert S. Moon, Director
617-232-6035

New England Fuel Institute
P.O. Box 888, Watertown 02272
John Carey, Director of Education

New England School of Accounting
155 Ararat St., Worcester 01606
Lloyd Buckley, Educ. Dir.

New England School of Art & Design
28 Newbury St., Boston 02116
Anne Blevins, Dir. of Admis.

New England School of Business
P.O. Box 888, Watertown 02272
John Carey, Director of Education

New England School of Photography
537 Commonwealth Ave., Boston 02215
Martha Hassell, Academic Director
617-437-1868

New England Tractor Trailer Training
1093 N. Montello St., Brockton 02401

NORTH BENNET STREET SCHOOL
39 N. Bennet St., Boston 02113
Cynthia Stone, Executive Director
617-227-0155
Established 1885. Coed. Accreditation: ACCSCT. Tuition: $650-$850 per month. Enrollment: 150. Faculty: 15. Diploma offered. Cabinet and furniture making, carpentry, jewelry making and repair, locksmithing, piano tuning and restoration, violin

making and restoration, bookbinding, and preservation carpentry. Financial aid available to eligible students.

Northeast Broadcasting School
142 Berkeley St., Boston 02116
Howard Horton, President

NORTHEAST INSTITUTE OF INDUSTRIAL TECHNOLOGY
41 Phillips St., Boston 02114-3699
John Hoffman, President

Quinsigamond Community College
670 W. Boylston St., Worcester 01606
Ron Smith, Dir. of Admis.

RETS Electronic School
965 Commonwealth Ave., Boston 02215
Henry J. Renzi, Director

St. John's School of Business
P.O. Box 1190, West Springfield 01090
Kenneth Ballard, Director

Salter School
458 Bridge St., Springfield 01103

Salter School
155 Ararat St., Worcester 01606

Southeastern Technical Institute
250 Foundry St., South Easton 02375

SPRINGFIELD TECHNICAL COMMUNITY COLLEGE
1 Armory Square, Springfield 01105
Dr. Patrick E. Tigue, Dir. of Admissions
413-781-7822

TAD TECHNICAL INSTITUTE
45 Spruce St., Chelsea 02150
John Riha, Admissions Director
800-370-1589

Ultrasound Diagnostic School
57 Providence Hwy., Norwood 02062

Wentworth Technical School
191 Spring St., Lexington 02173

WORCESTER TECHNICAL INSTITUTE
251 Belmont St., Worcester 01605
Janet M. Doe, Director
John Lynch, Dean of Student Affairs
508-799-1945
  Established 1958. Public two year technical institute. Coed. Tuition: $2,000. Rolling admissions. Enrollment: 425. Programs: architecture and construction, commercial art and design, dental assistant, mechanical design/drafting, electronics technology, electric technology, HVAC/R, medical assistant, opticianary, practical nursing, surgical technology, welding technology. Financial aid available.

MICHIGAN

Academy of Court Reporting
26111 Evergreen Rd. #101, Southfield 48076

Academy of Health Careers
27301 Dequindre Rd., #200
Madison Heights 48071

American Education Centers
26075 Woodward Ave.
Huntington Woods 48070

American Education Centers
4339 Canal Ave. S.W., Grandville 49418
Rebecca Slough, Director

AMR COMBS FLIGHT TRAINING ACADEMY
P.O. Box 888380, Grand Rapids 49588
Carlton G. Francis, Director of Training
See listing under "Aeronautics"

Black Forest Hall
P.O. Box 140, Harbor Springs 49740

CARNEGIE INSTITUTE
550 Stephenson Hwy. #100, Troy 48083
Gloria J. McEachern, President
810-589-1078

Chauffeurs Training School
14601 Dequindre St., Detroit 48212

Davenport College of Business
67 Michigan Ave. W., Battle Creek 49017

Davenport College of Business
3030 Eastern Ave., S.E., Grand Rapids 49508

Detroit Business Institute
115 State St., Detroit 48226
Jeanne L. Kretschmer, President

Detroit Business Institute
19100 Fort St., Riverview 48192

Detroit Business Institute
21700 Northwestern Hwy. #515, Southfield 48075

Detroit Institute Ophthalmology
15415 E. Jefferson Ave., Detroit 48230

Dorsey Business School
15755 Northline St., Southgate 48195
Dennis Stockemer, General Manager

Dorsey Business School
31542 Gratiot Ave., Roseville 48066
William G. Stockemer, President

Dorsey Business School
30821 Barrington Ave.
Madison Heights 48071

Dorsey Business School
24901 Northwestern Hwy. #202, Southfield 48075

Dorsey Business School
34841 Veteran's Plaza, Wayne 48184

::: EDUCATIONAL INSTITUTE OF THE AMERICAN HOTEL & MOTEL ASSOCIATION
P.O. Box 1240, East Lansing 48826
E. Ray Swan, President
Phone: 800-344-3320 or 517-353-5500; Fax: 517-353-5527
  Established 1952. Accreditation: Accrediting Commission of the Distance Education and Training Council, Michigan Department of Education. A nonprofit educational foundation of the American Hotel & Motel Association. Offers 30 comprehensive courses covering every area of a hotel/motel and restaurant operation; 5-course Areas of Specialization to prepare students for departmental management; the 8-course Hospitality Operations Certificate offering operational expertise; and a 12-course Hospitality Management Diploma program that gives students the knowledge needed for upper-level management. Certificates from the AH&MA are awarded upon successful completion of each course/program.

Grand Rapids Educational Center
1750 Woodworth St., N.E. #100
Grand Rapids 49505

Grand Rapids Educational Center
5349 W. Main, Kalamazoo 49009

ITT Technical Institute
4020 Sparks Dr. S.E., Grand Rapids 49546

Jackson Business Institute
234 S. Mechanic St., Jackson 49201
Jack Bunce, President

Jackson Community College
2111 Emmons Rd., Jackson 49201
Mark Ulseth, Dir. Enrollment Services

Krainz Woods Academy of Medical Technology
4327 E. Seven Mile Rd., Detroit 48234

Lansing Computer Institute
501 N. Marshall St. #101, Lansing 48912

Lawton School
21800 Greenfield Rd., Oak Park 48237

Michigan Career Institute
Auto Mechanic Training
14520 Gratiot Ave., Detroit 48205-2395
William C. Carson, President
313-526-6600

Mo Tech Education Center
35155 Industrial Rd., Livonia 48150

NEC-Bryman Campus
4244 Oakman Blvd., Detroit 48204

NEC-National Institute of Technology
2620 Remico St., S.W., Wyoming 49509

NEC-National Institute of Technology
18000 Newburgh Rd., Livonia 48152
Norbert Opyd, Director

NEC-National Institute of Technology
15115 Deerfield, East Detroit 48021

Northeastern School of Commerce
701 N. Madison Ave., Bay City 48708
Louis H. Bork, Director

Payne-Pulliam School of Trade & Commerce
2345 Cass Ave., Detroit 48201
Betty Pulliam, President

Pontiac Business Institute
P.O. Box 459, Oxford 48371

Ross Business Institute
1285 N. Telegraph, Monroe 48161

Ross Business Institute
22293 Eureka Rd., Taylor 48180

Ross Business Institute
37065 S. Gratiot Ave., Clinton Township 48036

Ross Medical Education Center
1036 Gilbert Rd., Flint 48532

Ross Medical Education Center
15670 E. Eight Mile Rd., Detroit 48205

Ross Medical Education Center
2035 28th St. S.E., #O, Grand Rapids 49508

Ross Medical Education Center
950 W. Norton, Muskegon 49441

Ross Medical Education Center
253 Summit Dr., Waterford 48328

Ross Medical Education Center
913 W. Holmes #260, Lansing 48910

Ross Medical Education Center
26417 Hoover Rd., Warren 48089

Ross Medical Education Center
1188 West Ave., Jackson 49202

Ross Medical Education Center
4054 Bay Rd., Saginaw 48603

Ross Technical Institute
4703 Washtenaw, Ann Arbor 48108
Elizabeth Elliott, Director

Ross Technical Institute
5757 Whitmore Lake Rd., Brighton 48116

Ross Technical Institute
1553 Woodward Ave. #750, Detroit 48226

Ross Technical Institute
20820 Greenfield Rd., Oak Park 48237

Sawyer School of Business
26051 Hoover Rd., Warren 48089

SER Business and Technical Institute
9301 Michigan Ave., Detroit 48210

Southwestern Michigan College
58900 Cherry Grove Rd., Dowagiac 49047
David Schultz, VP for Student Services
616-782-5113

Specs Howard School of Broadcast Arts
16900 W. Eight Mile Rd. #115, Southfield 48075
Specs Howard, Director
810-569-0101

MINNESOTA

ACADEMY OF ACCOUNTANCY
3050 Metro Dr. #200, Bloomington 55425
Gary McNulty, Director of Admissions
612-851-0066

ACADEMY OF AVIATION
3050 Metro Dr. #200, Minneapolis 55425
Gary McNulty, Director of Admissions
612-851-0066

Alexandria Technical College
1601 Jefferson St., Alexandria 56308
Dick Greengo, Coordinator

Anoka Technical Institute
1355 W. Main St., Anoka 55303

CDI COMPUTERS - ACADEMY
3050 Metro Dr. #200, Minneapolis 55425
Gary McNulty, Director of Admissions
612-851-0066

ConCorde Career Institute
12 N. 12th St., Minneapolis 55403
Jeanne Herrmann, Dir. of Admis.

Duluth Business University
412 W. Superior St., Duluth 55802
Bonnie Kupczynski, Director

DUNWOODY INSTITUTE
818 Dunwoody Blvd., Minneapolis 55403
612-374-5800 or 800-292-GOAL
Dr. M. James Bensen, President
Bernie Morgan, Director of Admissions
  Founded in 1914. Named as one of the top ten technical schools in the country by the US Dept. of Education (two years ago). Dunwoody is a private, non-profit, endowed technical school offering 40 different courses of two years or less. Accredited by CCA, AAS Degrees in 15 programs. Tuition: $3,726. Enrollment: 900 full-time, 957 part-time. Faculty: 150. Student-faculty ratio: 13:1. 2 buildings on a 12 acre campus. Dunwoody's coeducational programs include architectural drafting and estimating, automotive collision repair and refinishing, automotive service, baking, HVAC design, HVAC systems servicing, civil technology and land surveying, computer and digital systems, electrical construction and maintenance, electronics, heating and cooling systems, machine drafting and design, machine tool technology, printing and graphics, refrigeration service, and welding.
  Dunwoody offers scholarships for outstanding students, selected women and minority students, students in selected courses, plus comprehensive financial aid.
  For further information, write or call the Admissions Office at Dunwoody.

Globe College of Business
175 5th St. E. Ste. 201
Saint Paul 55101

Hibbing Technical Institute
2900 E. Beltline, Hibbing 55746

HUTCHINSON TECHNICAL COLLEGE
A campus of Hutchinson-Willmar Regional Technical College
Hutchinson 55350
Ron Erpelding, President
George Halonen, Vice President
Garey Knudsen, Vice President
Ron Jonas, Registrar
Meg Mielke, Counselor
Fred Hanson, Placement
  Established 1967. Accreditation: NCACS. Located 60 miles west of Minneapolis in Hutchinson (pop. 11,500). Two year coed college. Tuition: $37.35/credit. Financial Aid available through scholarships, grants, loans and college work-study. Enrollment: 1,201 day, 13,000 extension. Degrees: AAS Degree or diploma.
  Hutchinson Technical College is dedicated to providing a variety of quality educational programs ranging in scope from traditional programs to those on the cutting edge of new technology. Expanding opportunities exist in many of these fields with the addition of general education courses providing the option of attaining the AAS Degree.
  Offer over 40 programs, several of which are not available elsewhere. Quality education with a technical emphasis taught by qualified faculty. National reputation. Offer 2 primary start dates in all three quarters plus a summer session.

Numerous clubs, intramural sports, open gym at the high school, Student Senate, all school activities, events and seminars.

Students may apply for admission for any term by submitting a completed application form with a transcript of past grades.

Lakeland Medical-Dental Academy
1402 W. Lake St., Minneapolis 55408

LOWTHIAN COLLEGE
825 2nd Ave. S., Minneapolis 55402
Petrena Lowthian, President
612-332-3361 or 800-777-3643
Established 1964. Coed. Private. Accreditation: ACICS. Associate of Applied Science degree programs: FASHION MERCHANDISING: Tuition $9,180, FASHION DESIGN: Tuition $12,240, INTERIOR DESIGN: Tuition 13,260. Curriculums prepare students for positions in management, product promotion, sales and consulting, clothing design and construction, and residential and commercial space planning and design. College credit transfer.

McConnell School
831 2nd Ave., S., Minneapolis 55402
William McKay, President

Medical Institute of Minnesota
5503 Green Valley Dr., Bloomington 55437
Phillip Miller, President

Minneapolis Business College
1711 County Road B W., Roseville 55113

Minneapolis Drafting School
5700 W. Broadway Ave., Minneapolis 55428
Robert Casserly, Director

Minnesota School of Business
1401 W. 76th St., Richfield 55423

Minnesota School of Business
6120 Earle Brown Dr., Brooklyn Center 55430

· National Education Center-Brown Institute Campus
2225 E. Lake St., Minneapolis 55407
Rick Simmons, Director of Admissions

· NEI COLLEGE OF TECHNOLOGY
825 41st Ave., N.E., Minneapolis 55421
Charles R. Dettmann, President
Richard Thomson, Dir. of Admis.
Call 800-777-7NEI for Info.
Established 1930. Coed. Private. Non-Profit. Accreditation: CCA. Tuition: $4,185. Room and board: $3,500. Enrollment: 500. Faculty: 39. Degree: Associate in Electronics Technology. Library: 500 volumes. 1 building on 7-1/2 acres. Gym, tennis courts on campus. Golf nearby. Majors: avionics, computer/industrial, communications/VCR, TV, compact disc, stereo. College credit transfer. Lab time approximately 40%. Average class size: 22.

Northeast Metro Technical College
3300 Century Ave., N., White Bear Lake 55110

NORTHWEST TECHNICAL COLLEGE - EAST GRAND FORKS
Hwy. 220, N., East Grand Forks 56721
Admissions Office

NORTHWEST TECHNICAL COLLEGE - WADENA
P.O. Box 566, Wadena 56482
218-631-3530

Northwest Technical College
1900 28th Ave., S., Moorhead 56560
Dale White, Dir. of Admis.
218-299-6512

Rasmussen Business College
3500 Federal Dr., Eagan 55122

Rasmussen Business College
Good Counsel Dr., Mankato 56001

Rasmussen Business College
12450 Wayzata Blvd., Minnetonka 55305

Riverland Technical College
1926 Collegeview Rd., E., Rochester 55904
507-285-8631 or 800-247-1296

Riverland Technical College
1225 3rd St., S.W., Faribault 55021
507-334-3965 or 800-422-0391

Riverland Technical College
Campuses in Austin, Faribault, & Rochester
Write: 1900 8th Ave., N.W., Austin 55912
507-433-0600 or 800-247-5039

St. Cloud Business College
245 N. 37th Ave., St. Cloud 56303
Cathy Wogen, Director

· St. Cloud Technical College
1540 Northway Dr., Saint Cloud 56303
612-252-0101

School of Communication Arts
2526 27th Ave., S., Minneapolis 55406
Rodger Klietz, President

South Central Technical College
Albert Lea Campus
2200 Tech Dr., Albert Lea 56007
800-333-2584

SOUTHWESTERN TECHNICAL COLLEGE
Pipestone Campus
P.O. Box 250, Pipestone 56164
800-658-2330

SOUTHWESTERN TECHNICAL COLLEGE
Canby Campus
1011 1st St., W., Canby 56220
800-658-2535

SOUTHWESTERN TECHNICAL COLLEGE
Jackson Campus
401 West St., Jackson 56143
800-658-2522

SOUTHWESTERN TECHNICAL COLLEGE
Granite Falls Campus
1593 11th Ave., Granite Falls 56241
800-657-3247

UNIVERSITY OF MINNESOTA-CROOKSTON
2900 University Ave., Crookston 56716
John Bywater, Dir. of Admis.
800-232-6466
See listing under "Universities"

Winona Technical College
1250 Homer Rd., Winona 55987
800-372-8164

MISSISSIPPI

Batesville Job Corps Center
R.R. 3 Box 2J, Batesville 38606

Gulfport Job Corps Center
3300 20th St., Gulfport 39501

Mississippi Job Corps Center
P.O. Box 817, Crystal Springs 39059

Moore Career College
2460 Terry Rd., Jackson 39204

Moore Career College
1500 N. 31st St., Hattiesburg 39401

Moore Career College
1500 Hwy. 19, N., Meridian 39307

Moore Career College
880 Cliff Gookin Blvd., Tupelo 38801

Rice College
2525 Robinson Rd., Jackson 39209

MISSOURI

Aero Mechanics School
200 Northwest Pky., Riverside 64150
Steven Kalina, Director

AL-MED Academy
10963 St. Charles Rock Rd., Saint Ann 63074

Bryan Institute
12184 Natural Bridge Rd., Bridgeton 63044

Bryan Travel College
520 W. University Suite B, Springfield 65807

Cape Girardeau Vocational Technical School
301 N. Clark, Cape Girardeau 63701

CONCORDE CAREER INSTITUTE
3239 Broadway St., Kansas City 64111
Pamela Tiemeyer, Director
816-531-5223
Established 1983. Private. Coed. Accreditation: Accrediting Commission for Career Schools and Colleges of Technology (ACCSCT). Faculty: 15. Student-faculty ratio: 25:1. Diploma offered. 1 building. Programs offered include: Respiratory Therapy Technician; Medical Assistant, Dental Assistant, Medical Office Professional; and Computerized Accounting. The institution is dedicated to training individuals for their chosen career in the shortest time practical at a reasonable cost. It is our aim to provide students with the knowledge and technical proficiency that will make them employable for entry-level positions upon graduation.

Dick Hill International Flight
P.O. Box 10603, Springfield 65808

Eastern Jackson County College of Allied Health
808 S. 15th St., Blue Springs 64015

Florissant Upholstery School
1420 N. Vandeventer St., Saint Louis 63113

Hannibal Area Vocational Technical School
4550 McMasters Ave.
Hannibal 63401-2285
Harold D. Ward, Director
314-221-4430

Hickey School
940 Westport Plaza #101, St. Louis 63146
Bonnie Schulte, Dir. of Admis.

Lewis & Clark Technical School
2400 Zumbehl Rd., St. Charles 63301
Midge Haas, Counselor
314-723-4829 or 314-946-7726

Linn Technical College
1 Technology Dr., Linn 65051
William Bunch, VP Administrative Services
Ron Hunziger, Financial Aid Director
314-897-3603

Linn Technical College
308 E. High St., Jefferson City 65101
Jeanne Schwaller, Director
Computer office training
314-634-7897

Mallinckrodt Institute of Radiology
510 S. Kingshighway Blvd., Saint Louis 63110

Metro Business College
1732 N. Kingshighway St., Cape Giradeau 63701

Metro Business College
1407 Southwest Blvd., Jefferson City 65109

Metro Business College
2305 N. Bishop Ave., Rolla 65401

Mid-America Paralegal Institute
8008 Carondelet Ave. Suite 211, Clayton 63105
Robert Withington, Director

Midwest Institute for Medical Assistants
112 W. Jefferson Ave., Kirkwood 63122

Missouri Auction School
1600 Genessee St., Kansas City 64102
Paul Dewees, President

Missouri Western State College
4525 Downs Dr., St. Joseph 64507
Howard McCauley, Dir. of Admis.

National Career Institute
17601 E. US Highway 40, Independence 64055

Patricia Stevens College
1000 St. Louis Union Station, St. Louis 63103
Joanne Klute, President

· Ranken Technical College
4431 Finney Ave., St. Louis 63113

Rolla Area Vocational-Technical School
1304 E. Tenth St., Rolla 65401

St. Louis College of Health Careers
4484 W. Pine Blvd., Saint Louis 63108
Kim Green, Admissions Coordinator
314-652-0300

SAINT LOUIS TECH
9741 St. Charles Rock Rd., St. Louis 63114
314-427-3600
Federal Student Aid available

Sanford-Brown Business College
355 Brookes Dr., Hazelwood 63042

Sanford-Brown Business College
3555 Franks Dr., Saint Charles 63301

Sanford-Brown Business College
3901 Blue Ridge Cut Off, Kansas City 64133
Patricia Dixon, Director

Sanford-Brown Business College
1655 Des Peres Rd. #150, Saint Louis 63131

Southwest School of Broadcasting
1031 E. Battlefield, #212B, Springfield 65807

· State Fair Community College
Court Reporting Program
3201 W. 16th St., Sedalia 65301-2199
Laura Taylor, Program Coordinator

TAD Technical Institute
7910 Troost Ave., Kansas City 64131

TRANS WORLD TECHNICAL ACADEMY
Owned and operated by TWA, Inc.
533 Mexico City Ave., Kansas City 64153
816-464-6800 or 800-TWA-TECH
Trans World Technical Academy is an airline affiliated maintenance training school prepared to offer you programs dedicated to commercial aircraft maintenance in one of four specialized areas: Aircraft Structural Repair, Aircraft Systems Repair, Powerplant Overhaul, and Avionic Systems Repair. Each of TWTA's specialty programs will provide hands-on and classroom training beginning with basic job skills, and progress through applications requiring use of today's more advanced technologies. Classes will be taught by professional instructors from the TWA maintenance training staff, providing students the opportunity to interface with some of the industry's most knowledgeable aircraft maintenance personnel. Free TWA air transportation to/from training and reduced rate housing is available to all students.

⋮⋮⋮ TRANS WORLD TRAVEL ACADEMY
Owned and operated by TWA, Inc.
11495 Natural Bridge Rd. #214, St. Louis 63044
314-895-6754 or 1-800-942-7467
Campuses: St. Louis, Los Angeles, Kansas City, and Chicago. TWTA offers computerized reservations sales training for persons interested in careers as a travel agent, corporate travel planner, ticketing agent, or reservations agent. TWA job interviews for all residency program graduates. Zero % financing plan available. Home study program available for persons who need/prefer to study at home. Home study is followed by a 2 week residency course at a TWTA campus. Free TWA transportation to/from training and reduced rate housing for all students. Customized and contract training is available to travel industry employees and employers. Accredited member of the National Home Study Council. TWTA also has a flight attendant career home study/residency program and specialty training for aircraft maintenance.

Vanderschmidt School
4625 Lindell Blvd., Saint Louis 63108
314-361-6000

Vatterott College
210 S. Main, Independence 64050
Paula Jerden, Director

Vatterott College
N. Main St., Joplin 64801
Linda Lynch, Director

Vatterott College
1258 E. Trafficway St., Springfield 65802
J. Mannion, Director

Vatterott Education Center
3854 Washington Blvd., St. Louis 63108

· Wright Business School
5528 N.E. Antioch Rd., Kansas City 64119

MONTANA

Billings Business College
2520 Fifth Ave., S., Billings 59101

Billings Vocational Technical Center
3803 Central Ave., Billings 59102

Butte Vocational-Technical Center, Butte 59701

· Helena College of Technology of the Univ. of Montana
1115 N. Roberts St., Helena 59601
Annette Walstad, Admissions Officer
406-444-6800

May Technical College
1306 Central Ave., Billings 59102
406-259-7000

May Technical College
1807 3rd St. N.W., Great Falls 59404
406-761-4000

· Missoula Vocational Technical Center
909 South Ave. W, Missoula 59801
Charles Couture, Dir. of Admis.

NEBRASKA

· Central Community College-Hastings Campus
P.O. Box 1024, Hastings 68902-1024

· Central Community College-Platte Campus
P.O. Box 1027, Columbus 68602-1027

· Central Community College-Grand Island Campus
P.O. Box 4903, Grand Island 68802-4903

Institute of Computer Science
808 S. 74th Plaza #200, Omaha 68114

Nebraska Custom Diesel Drivers Training
14243 C Cir., Omaha 68144

NORTHEAST COMMUNITY COLLEGE
P.O. Box 469, Norfolk 68702
Eugene Hart, Dir. of Admis.

Omaha College of Business
1052 Park Ave., Omaha 68105

Omaha Opportunities Industrialization Center
2724 N. 24th St., Omaha 68110

Spencer School of Business
410 W. Second St., Grand Island 68801
Connie Collin, Dir. of Admis.

Universal Technical Institute
902 Capitol Ave., Omaha 68102
Ivan Abdouch, Director

UNIVERSITY OF NEBRASKA
NEBRASKA COLLEGE OF TECHNICAL
AGRICULTURE
P.O. Box 69, Curtis 69025
See listing under "Agriculture"

NEVADA

American Academy for Career Education
3120 E. Desert Inn Rd., Las Vegas 89121

Century Schools
3075 E. Flamingo Ave. #114
Las Vegas 89121

::: Columbia School of Broadcasting
2840 E. Flamingo Rd. #F, Las Vegas 89121
Marcia Brock-Gandy, President

Education Dynamics Institute
953 E. Sahara Ave. #102, Las Vegas 89104

Interior Design Institute
4225 S. Eastern Ave. Suite 4, Las Vegas 89119
Nancy Wolff, President

International Dealers School
503 Fremont St., Las Vegas 89101
Toni Taylor, Director
702-385-7665

International Dealers School
1055 S. Virginia St., Reno 89502
Dennis Robinson, Director
702-322-8330

Las Vegas Gaming & Technical School
3030 S. Highland Dr., Las Vegas 89109

National Academy for Casino Dealers
557 E. Sahara Ave. Suite 108, Las Vegas 89104
Al Rodrigues, President

PCI Dealers School
920 S. Valley View Blvd., Las Vegas 89107
Joel Lauer, President

PROFESSIONAL CAREERS
3305 Spring Mountain Rd., Las Vegas 89102
Beau Allan, Director of Admissions
702-368-2338
Established 1990. Private. Coed. Accreditation: Accrediting Commission of Career Schools/Colleges of Technology. Enrollment: 350. Faculty: 7. Student-faculty ratio: 12:1. Travel and Tourism; Medical Assistant; Medical Secretary; Veterinary Office Assistant. Job placement assistance. Financial aid for qualified applicants.

Vegas Career School
1110 E. Charleston Blvd., Las Vegas 89104
John Rosich, Director

Western Truck School
39 Glen Carren Circle, Sparks 89431

NEW HAMPSHIRE

· New Hampshire Technical College at Stratham
277 R. Portsmouth Ave., Stratham 03885
Patricia A. Shay, Dean of Students

Northeast Career Schools
749 E. Industrial Park Dr., Manchester 03109

NEW JERSEY

Academy of Professional Development
98 Mayfield Ave., Edison 08837

Academy of Professional Development
934 Parkway Ave., Ewing 08618

American Business Academy
66 Moore St., Hackensack 07601
Jack Kanter, Dir.

Aviation Career Academy
Fostertown Rd., Medford 08055
Fred Trepper, President

Berdan Institute
265 State Rt. 46, Totowa 07512
E. Lynn Thacker, Director
201-256-3444

Bilingual Institute
685 Broad St., Newark 07102

Bilingual Institute
2 W. Broadway, Paterson 07505

Boardwalk & Marina Casino Dealers School
2709 Atlantic Ave., Atlantic City 08401
Arnold Hasson, President

BRICK COMPUTER SCIENCE INSTITUTE
515 Rte. 70, Brick 08723
Robert H. Forshee, Director
Fred Feldman, Dir. of Admis.
800-585-3523 or 908-477-0975
Established 1971. Coed. Accreditation: CCA. Enrollment: 250 day. Faculty: 20. Diploma offered. Campus on 5 acres. Authorized Autocadd training center; Authorized Novell education center. Programs in computer aided drafting and design, office information systems, programming, computer repair, robotics, laser, fiber optic technology. Scholarships, work study programs, financial aid, housing assistance, full & half-time classes, transferability of credits, job placement assistance. 10 miles from Atlantic Ocean, centrally located between New York, Philadelphia and Atlantic City.

Business Training Institute
4 Forest Ave., Paramus 07652

The Chubb Institute
P.O. Box 342, Parsippany 07054

Chubb Institute
40 Journal Square, Jersey City 07306

THE CITTONE INSTITUTE
1697 Oak Tree Rd., Edison 08820
Jacqueline Shalhoub, Director
908-548-8798
Established 1967. Coed. Accredited Member School: ACICS. Providing training in: Court Reporting, Legal Office Specialist, Office Automation, Computerized Accounting, Computer Programming, Electronics and Computer Technology. Financial aid for those who qualify. Employment assistance program.

THE CITTONE INSTITUTE
523 Fellowship Rd., Mount Laurel 08054
Walter Whalen, Director
609-722-9333
Established 1967. Coed. Accredited Member School: ACICS. Providing training in: Court Reporting, Legal Office Specialist, Office Automation, Computerized Accounting, Medical Secretary. Financial aid for those who qualify. Employment assistance program.

THE CITTONE INSTITUTE
100 Canal Pointe Blvd., Princeton 08540
Rita Harris, Director
609-520-8798
Established 1967. Coed. Accredited Member School: ACICS. Providing training in: Court Reporting, Legal Office Specialist, Office Automation, Computerized Accounting. Financial aid for those who qualify. Employment assistance program.

Computer Learning Center
160 E. Route 4, Paramus 07652

Divers Academy of the Eastern Seaboard
2500 S. Broadway, Camden 08104
William Brown, President
800-238-3483

Dover Business College
15 E. Blackwell St., Dover 07801
David Weaver, Director

Dover Business College
E-81 Route 4, W., Paramus 07652

Drake College of Business
9 Caldwell Pl., Elizabeth 07201

Drake College of Business
60 Evergreen Pl., East Orange 07018
Catherine Palmer, Director

Du Cret School of the Arts
1030 Central Ave., Plainfield 07060
Frank Falotico, Director

Empire Technical Schools of New Jersey
576 Central Ave., East Orange 07018
Timothy Rodgers, Director

Engine City Technical Institute
2365 Route 22 W., Union 07083
Larry L. Berlin, Director

General Technical Institute
1118 Baltimore Ave., Linden 07036
G. G. Sytch, Jr., President-Director

HARRIS SCHOOL OF BUSINESS
654 Longwood Ave., Cherry Hill 08002
Alan S. Harris, Director

Ho-Ho-Kus School of Secretarial and Medical
Sciences
27 S. Franklin Trnpk., Ramsey 07446
Thomas Eastwick, Director
201-327-8877

Kane Business Institute
206 Haddonfield Rd., Cherry Hill 08002

Katherine Gibbs School
80 Kingsbridge Rd., Piscataway 08854

Kubert School of Cartoon & Graphic Arts
37 Myrtle Ave., Dover 07801

LINCOLN TECHNICAL INSTITUTE
Haddonfield Rd at Route 130 N., Pennsauken 08110
Deborah Ramentol, Director
609-665-3010
Established 1946. Coed. Accredited Member School: ACCSCT. Providing technical training in: Electronics Servicing or Computer Repair, Air Conditioning, Refrigeration & Heating Technology, Architectural/Mechanical Drafting and CAD Technology. Financial aid for those who qualify. Employment assistance program.

LINCOLN TECHNICAL INSTITUTE
2299 Vauxhall Rd., Union 07083
Brad Jones, Director
908-964-7800
Established 1946. Coed. Accredited Member School: ACCSCT. Providing technical training in: Automotive or Diesel Truck Technology, Air Conditioning, Heating & Refrigeration Technology, Architectural/Mechanical Drafting & CAD Technology. Financial aid for those who qualify. Employment Assistance Program.

LINCOLN TECHNICAL INSTITUTE
70 McKee Dr., Mahwah 07430
Fred Parcells, Director
201-529-1414
Established 1946. Coed. Accredited Member School: ACCSCT. Providing technical training in: Automotive Technology, Mechanical Drafting, Architectural Drafting, Computer-Aided Drafting Technology, Air Conditioning, Heating and Refrigeration Technology. Financial aid for those who qualify. Employment assistance program.

Metropolitan Technical Institute
11 Daniel Rd., Fairfield 07004
Frank Gergelyi, Director

National Education Center-RETS Campus
103 Park Ave., Nutley 07110
Martin Klangasky, Director
201-661-0600

Omega Institute
Route 130 S., Cinnaminson 08077

Pennco Tech
P.O. Box 1427, Blackwood 08012

Plaza School of Technology
Bergen Mall, Paramus 07652
Mark Ricciardi, Director
201-843-0344

PTC Career Institute
200 Washington St., Newark 07102

SCS Business & Technical Institute
756 Broad St., Newark 07102

SCS Business & Technical Institute
516 Main St., East Orange 07018

SCS Business & Technical Institute
2200 Bergenline Ave., Union City 07087

Star Technical Institute
2105 Hwy 35, Ocean 07712

Star Technical Institute
1255 Highway 70 #12N, Lakewood 08701

Star Technical Institute
2 White Horse Rd., Somerdale 08083

Star Technical Institute
2224 Route 130, Beverly 08010

Star Technical Institute
1386 S. Delsea Dr., Vineland 08360

Stuart School of Business Administration
2400 Belmar Blvd., Wall 07719

Teterboro School of Aeronautics
80 Moonachie Ave., Teterboro 07608-1083
Edward Chudzik, Director
201-288-6300 FAX 201-288-5609

Titan Helicopter Academy
Bldg. #90 Easterwood St., Millville 08332
Peter Amico, President

Ultrasound Diagnostic School
Plaza One at Gill Ln. #6B, Iselin 08830

NEW MEXICO

ALBUQUERQUE T-VI : A COMMUNITY COLLEGE
525 Buena Vista Dr., S.E., Albuquerque 87106
Dr. Alex A. Sanchez, President
Jane Campbell, Registrar
Established 1965. State. Accreditation: NCACS. Tuition: occupational programs are free to New Mexico residents, $885 per term for non-residents. Liberal arts courses: $26.50 per credit hour for residents, $73.75 per credit hour for non-residents. Enrollment: 19,000. Degrees: AA, AAS, AS. Programs: 25 associate degrees, 31 certificate majors in business, health, technologies and trades occupations, plus college prep and college transfer. No campus housing.

AzTech College
2201 San Pedro Dr. N.E. Bldg. 3, Albuquerque 87110
Rebecca Koontz, Director

International Business College
650 E. Montana Ave. #F, Las Cruces 88001

International Business College-Alamogordo
3200 N. White Sands Blvd., Alamogordo 88310
Fran Hveem, Dir. of Admis.

Metropolitan College of Court Reporting
2201 San Pedro N.E., Bldg. 1 #1300
Albuquerque 87110

New Mexico Junior College
5317 Lovington Hwy., Hobbs 88240
Robert Snow, Registrar

Northern Arizona Institute of Technology
11300 Lomas Blvd. N.E., Albuquerque 87112

Pima Medical Institute
2201 San Pedro Dr., N.E., Albuquerque 87110

Southwestern Indian Polytechnic Institute
P.O. Box 10146, Albuquerque 87184

NEW YORK

Academy for Career Education
5505 Myrtle Ave., Ridgewood 11385

Advanced Software Analysis
151 Lawrence St. 2nd Fl., Brooklyn 11201

Advanced Software Analysis
5 Beekman St. #700, New York 10038

Albany School of Cytotechnology
432 Western Ave., Albany 12203

Allen School for Physicians Aides
188 Montague St., Brooklyn 11201

American Academy of Dramatic Arts
120 Madison Ave., New York 10016

American Business Institute
1657 Broadway, New York 10019
Charles Gross, Director

Apex Technical School
635 Avenue of the Americas, New York 10011
John Cann, Pres.

Berk Trade School
311 W 35th St., New York 10001

Blake Business School
20 Cooper Sq., New York 10003

Business Informatics Center
134 S. Central Ave., Valley Stream 11580

Career Institute
500 8th Ave. 4th Floor, New York 10018
Harry Lokos, President

Cashier Training Institute
500 8th Ave., New York 10018

Chauffers' Training School
12 Railroad Ave., Albany 12205
Stephen Schneeweiss, Pres.

COLLEGE OF AERONAUTICS
La Guardia Airport, Flushing 11371
Dr. Richard B. Goetze, Jr., President
Donald J Whitman, Dir. of Admis.
800-776-2376
Established 1932. Private. Independent. Coed. Accreditation: MSACS. Tuition: $5,820. Estimated total yearly expenses: $1,000. Enrollment: 1,200 students. Faculty: 65. Degrees: AAS, AOS, BT. Library: 60,000 volumes. 3 buildings on 6 acres. Located in New York City. Fully computerized engine test cells, hangar, engine labs, avionic labs, computer labs, and airline training center. Financial aid, grants, scholarships, and loans available.

Commercial Driver Training School
600 Patton Ave., West Babylon 11704

Computer Career Center
474 Fulton Ave., Hempstead 11550

Continental Dental Assistant School
633 Jefferson Rd., Rochester 14623

Cope Institute
84 William St. #4, New York 10038

The Culinary Institute of America
651 S. Albany Post Rd., Hyde Park 12538-1499
Cathy Grande, Dir. of Admis.

Drake Business School
3609 Main St. 6th Fl., Flushing 11354
Barbara Reisfeld, Director

Drake Business School
225 Broadway #2, New York 10007
Diane Scappaticci, Administrator

Drake Business School
25 Victory Blvd., Staten Island 10301
Virginia Long-Karlsson, Dir.

Drake Business School
2488 Grand Concourse, Bronx 10458

Elmira Business Institute
180 Clemens Center Pkwy., Elmira 14901
Brad Phillips, Director
607-733-7177

FEGS Trades & Business School
17 Battery Place, New York 10004

FEGS Trades & Business School
199 Jay St., Brooklyn 11201
James Leggio, Director

Fell's School of Business
2541 Military Rd., Niagara Falls 14304

Folk Art Institute
61 W. 62nd St., New York 10023

French Culinary Institute
462 Broadway, New York 10013

Global Business Institute
1931 Mott Ave., Far Rockaway 11691

Global Business Institute
209 Dr. Martin Luther King Jr. Blvd.,
New York 10027

Hunter Business School
3601 Hempstead Tpke, Levittown 11756

Institute of Allied Medical Professions
106 Central Park St. #23D, New York 10019

INSTITUTE OF AUDIO RESEARCH
64 University Pl., New York 10003
Mark L. Kahn, Director of Admissions
800-544-2501 or 212-777-8550 (NY,NJ,CT)
Established 1969. Private. Coed. Accreditation: Accrediting Commission for Career Schools and Colleges of Technology (ACCSCT). Tuition: $7,988. Fees: $100. Faculty: 26. Student-faculty ratio: 15:1. Degrees: Diploma in Recording Engineering and Production. Diploma in Video Technology. 13,000 sq. ft. facility with analog and digital studios and state-of-the-art equipment. IAR offers 9 month career training in audio and video. Uniquely situated in the heart of NYC, the recording capital of the world and home of all major TV networks. IAR graduates find employment in recording studios, television stations, live concert sound, audio and video production houses, theater sound, radio, satellite and cable companies, jingle houses, post-production for film and television and more.

Interfaith Medical Center, School of Nursing
567 Prospect Pl., Brooklyn 11238
Carmen Fedrik, Admissions/Finance Officer
718-935-7901
Associate in Applied Science (AAS - Nursing) program
Coed, biannual enrollment (Fall and Spring).

Island Drafting and Technical Institute
128 Broadway, Amityville 11701
516-691-8733

Joseph Bulova School
4024 62nd St., Woodside 11377

Katharine Gibbs School
535 Brood Hollow Rd., Melville 11747
516-293-2460

KRISSLER BUSINESS INSTITUTE
166 Mansion St., Poughkeepsie 12601
Established 1936. Modern office technologies
914-471-0330

LONG ISLAND BUSINESS INSTITUTE
6500 Jericho Turnpike, Commack 11725
516-499-7100
Genevieve Baron, President
Established 1968. Private. Coed. Accreditation: Accrediting Council for Independent Colleges and Schools. Registered by the New York State Education Department. Our Court Reporting program is approved by the National Court Reporters Association. We are one of only five schools in NY State with this Recognition. Majors in court reporting, secretarial science, word processing and computer applications. Federal and State financial aid available. Enrollment: 150 full-time, 200 part-time. At the same location for 26 years.

Mandl School
254 W. 54th St., New York 10019

Mildred Elley Business School
2 Computer Dr. S., Albany 12205
David G. Sampson, Director of Admissions

Modern Welding School
1740 Broadway, Schenectady 12306
Dana J. Gillenwalters, Director

Monroe College
2501 Jerome Ave., Bronx 10468

Monroe College
434 Main St., New Rochelle 10801

Munson-Williams-Proctor Institute
310 Genesee St., Utica 13502

National Tractor Trailer School
P.O. Box 208, Liverpool 13088

National Tractor Trailer School
175 Katherine St., Buffalo 14210

New School of Contemporary Radio
50 Colvin Ave., Albany 12206
Charles Mertz, Dir. of Admis.

New York Business School
269 W. 40th St., New York 10018
Gary Kay, Exec. Dir.

New York Food & Hotel Management School
154 W. 14th St., New York 10011
Helen S. Doneger, Director

New York Institute of Business Technology
401 Park Ave., S., 2nd Fl., New York 10016

New York School for Medical & Dental Assistants
11616 Queens Blvd., Forest Hills 11375
Thomas Haggerty, Director

Northeast Institute
2643 Main St., Buffalo 14214

Olean Business Institute
301 N. Union St., Olean 14760
Patrick McCarthy, Director
Jeanne Johnston, Director of Admissions
716-372-7978

Pace Business School
164 Ashburton Ave., Yonkers 10701
Richard Pfundstein, Dir.

Pace Business School
210 E. 188th St., Bronx 10458

Paul Smith's College, Paul Smiths 12970
Enrico Miller, Dir. of Admis.
800-421-2605

Printing Trades School
233 Park Ave. S., New York 10003
Elizabeth Jenkins, President

Professional Business Institute
125 Canal St., New York 10002

Ridley-Lowell Business and Technical Institute
116 Front St., Binghamton 13905
Cindy McCue, Director

SCS Business & Tech. Institute
25 W. 17th St., New York 10011
Kamal Alsultany, Pres.

SCS Business & Technical Institute
884 Flatbush Ave., Brooklyn 11226

SCS Business & Technical Institute
2467 Jerome Ave., Bronx 10468

SCS Business & Technical Institute
16302 Jamaica Ave., Jamaica 11432

SCS Business & Technical Institute
394 Bridge St., Brooklyn 11201

Simmons Institute of Funeral Service
1828 South Ave., Syracuse 13207
Maurice C. Wightman, CEO
315-475-5142

Simmons School
190 E. Post Rd., White Plains 10601

Spanish-American Institute
215 W. 43rd St., New York 10036

Spencer Business Institute
200 State St., Schenectady 12305
518-374-7619

STENOTOPIA, THE WORLD OF COURT REPORTING, INC.
45 S. Service Rd., Plainview 11803
516-777-1117

Stenotype Academy
15 Park Row, New York 10038
Melvin Eisner, Pres.

Stuart School of Diamond Cutting
1420 Kings Hwy., Brooklyn 11229

Suburban Technical School
2650 Sunrise Hwy., East Islip 11730
516-224-5001

Suburban Technical School
175 Fulton Ave., Hempstead 11550
516-481-6660

SUNY Adirondack Community College
439 Bay Rd., Queensbury 12804
Levi Brown, Dir. of Admis.
518-793-4491
See listing under "Community and Junior Colleges"

SUNY College of Agriculture & Technology
Cobleskill 12043
John Devney, Jr., Dir. of Admis.

SUNY College of Agriculture and Technology
Morrisville 13408
Dennis Nostrand, Dir. of Admis.

SUNY College of Technology, Alfred 14802
Deborah J. Goodrich, Dir. of Admis.
607-587-4215

SUNY HUDSON VALLEY COMMUNITY COLLEGE
80 Vandenburgh Ave., Troy   12180
Joseph Bulmer, President
Linda Sweetman, Dir. of Admis.
Charles Zipprich, Dean, School of
Engineering Technologies
518-283-1100
  Established 1953. Public. Coed. Accreditation:
MSACS, Accreditation Board of Engineering & Technology. Tuition: $1,550 full-time. Estimated total
yearly expenses: $2,500 full-time. Housing adjacent
to campus. Enrollment: 5,878 full-time, 4,498 part-
time. Faculty: 240 full-time, 350 part-time. Degrees:
AS, AAS, AOS. Library: 105,000 volumes. 14 buildings on 165 acres. Gym. Extensive state-of-the-art
laboratory facilities, laser electro-optics and tele-
munications laboratories, advanced manufacturing
training facility, complete drafting facilities, latest
automotive diagnostic equipment, cooperative education program available.

· SUNY Schenectady County Community College
  78 Washington Ave., Schenectady   12305
  Robert Dinello, Dir. of Admis.
  518-346-6211, ext. 166

· SUNY Sullivan County Community College
  P.O. Box 4002, Loch Sheldrake   12759-4002
  Steve Pochard, Dean of Enrollment

Superior Career Institute
116 W. 14th St., New York   10011

Swedish Institute, Inc.
  School of Massage Therapy
  226 W. 26th St. #5, New York   10001
  Patricia Eckardt, Director
  212-924-5900

SYRIT Computer School Systems
1760 53rd St., Brooklyn   11204

Techno-Dental Training Center
101 W. 31st St. 4th Fl., New York   10001

· Tobe-Coburn School for Fashion Careers
  8 E. 40th St., New York   10016
  Patricia Nieml, President

Travel Institute
15 Park Row #617, New York   10038

Ultrasound Diagnostic School
2269 Saw Mill River Rd., Elmsford   10523

Ultrasound Diagnostic School
One Old Country Rd., Carle Place   11514

Ultrasound Diagnostic School
121 W. 27th St., New York   10001

Union Settlement Association Training School
174 E. 104th St., New York   10029

UNIVERSAL BUSINESS AND MEDIA SCHOOL
220 E. 106th St., New York   10029
212-360-1210

· Utica School of Commerce
  201 Bleecker St., Utica   13501
  Judith Kelly, Dir. of Admis.

Westchester Conservatory of Music
20 Soundview Ave., White Plains   10606

NORTH CAROLINA

· Alamance Community College
  P.O. Box 623, Haw River   27258
  W. Ronald McCarter, President

Alliance Tractor Trailer Training Center
P.O. Box 579, Benson   27504

Alliance Tractor Trailer Training Center
P.O. Box 883, Arden   28704

AMERICAN BUSINESS AND FASHION INSTITUTE
1515 Mockingbird Ln. #600, Charlotte   28209
Ellen Sheppard, Director of Admissions
704-523-3738
  Established 1973. Private. Coed. Accreditation:
ACICS. Tuition: $4,980. Room and board: $2,790.
Enrollment: 250 full-time, 10 part-time. Faculty: 14.
Student-faculty ratio: 14:1. Degrees: Diplomas and
Certificates. Small classes and programs which focus
strictly on the skills employers are looking for. Annual fashion show extravaganza. Showroom at the
Charlotte Apparel Mart allows participation in ladies'
apparel marts. Lifetime employment assistance for
graduates. Over 90% of graduates who wish to work
are placed within a few months of graduation. Spa-
cious, modern student apartments with pools and
exercise facilities. Financial assistance and VA benefits.

· Anson Community College
  P.O. Box 126, Polkton   28135
  Dr. Edwin Chapman, President
  704-272-7635 or 800-766-0319

· Asheville Buncombe Technical Community College
  340 Victoria Rd., Asheville   28801
  Connie Buckner, Dir. of Admis.

Brookstone College of Business
7815 National Service Rd., Greensboro   27409

Brookstone College of Business
8307 Univ. Exec. Park Dr. #240, Charlotte   28262

· Carteret Community College
  3505 Arendell St., Morehead City   28557
  Don Thompson, Dir. of Student Services
  919-247-4142 ext. 149

Charlotte Diesel Driving School
6000 N. Tryon St., Charlotte   28213

· Chowan College
  P.O. Box 1848, Murfreesboro   27855
  Winslow Carter, Dir. of Admis.

College of The Albemarle
  P.O. Box 2327, Elizabeth City   27906
  John M. Wells, Asst. Dean of Admissions
  919-335-0821, Ext. 220

ECPI COMPUTER INSTITUTE
7015G Albert Pick Rd., Greensboro   27409
919-665-1400

ECPI COMPUTER INSTITUTE
1121 Wood Ridge Center Dr. #150, Charlotte   28217
704-357-0077

ECPI COMPUTER INSTITUTE
4509 Creedmoor Rd., Raleigh   27612
919-571-0057

· Edgecombe Community College
  2009 Wilson St., W., Tarboro   27886
  Thomas Anderson, VP of Student Services
  919-823-5166

· Haywood Community College
  Freedlander Dr., Clyde   28721
  Carol Smith, Dir. of Admis.

· King's College
  322 Lamar Ave., Charlotte   28204
  Debbie Remelius, Registrar

Lyndon B. Johnson Conservation Center
466 Job Corps Dr., Franklin   28734

· McDowell Technical Community College
  R.R. 1, Box 170, Marion   28752
  Jim Biddix, Dean of Students

Miller-Motte Business College
606 S. College Rd., Wilmington   28403

Oconaluftee Job Corps Conservation Center
200 Park Circle, Cherokee   28719

SALISBURY BUSINESS COLLEGE
1400 Jake Alexander Blvd. W., Salisbury   28147
Bill Hensley, President
704-636-4071
  Established 1917. Private. Coed. Accreditation: Accrediting Council for Independent Colleges and
Schools. Tuition: $2,600. Room and board: $2,000.
Fees: $100. Enrollment: 125 full-time, 15 part-time.
Faculty: 13. Student-faculty: 15:1. 12,000 square foot
building. Individual attention. Once a graduate under
any program of study, there is no charge to refresh or
retake program of study.

· Sandhills Community College
  2200 Airport Rd., Pinehurst   28374
  910-692-6185

Schenck Civilian Conservation Center
98 Schenck Dr., Pisgah Forest   28768

· Wilkes Community College
  P.O. Box 120, Wilkesboro   28697
  Mac Warren, Dir. of Admis.

· Wilson Technical Community College
  P.O. Box 4305, Wilson   27893
  Dr. Frank Eagles, President

NORTH DAKOTA

Aaker's Business College
P.O. Box 876, Grand Forks   58206
R. C. Hadlich, President

Interstate Business College
520 Main Ave., E., Bismarck   58501
Rod Wentz, Director
701-255-0779

Interstate Business College
2720 32nd Ave., S.W., Fargo   58103
Tony Grindberg, Director
701-232-2477

Meyer Voc-Tech School
P.O. Box 2126, Minot   58702

Turtle Mt. School of Paramedical Technique
Bottineau   58318

UNITED TRIBES TECHNICAL COLLEGE
3315 University Dr., Bismarck   58504
Admissions Office 701-255-3285 Ext. 216 or 334

OHIO

· ACA College of Design
  2528 Kemper Ln., Cincinnati   45206
  Marion Allman, President
  See listing under "Art"

Academy of Court Reporting
614 W. Superior Ave., Cleveland   44113

Academy of Court Reporting
2930 W. Market St., Akron   44333

Academy of Court Reporting
630 E. Broad St., Columbus   43215

Akron Machining Institute
2959 Barber Rd., Barberton   44203

Akron Medical-Dental Institute
1625 Portage Trail W., Cuyahoga Falls   44223
Elizabeth Husk, Director
216-762-9788

American School of Technology
2100 Morse Rd., #4599, Columbus   43229

Antonelli Institute of Art & Photography
124 E. 7th St., Cincinnati   45202

Aristotle Institute of Medical & Dental Technology
5900 Westerville Rd., Westerville   43081

Art Advertising Academy
4343 Bridgetown Rd., Cincinnati   45211
513-574-1010
2 year Associate of Applied Business in
Commercial Art, 2 year commercial art
diploma program including computer art
and airbrush art. Small individual classes.

Belmont Technical College
120 Fox Shannon Place, St. Clairsville   43950
Thomas Tarowsky, Asst. Dean of Student Services

Bohecker's Business College
326 E. Main St., Ravenna   44266
Douglas Kern, Director

Bradford School
6170 Busch Blvd., Columbus   43229
Patrick Denton, President
614-846-9410

Bryant & Stratton Business Institute
12955 Snow Rd., Cleveland   44130
Elliott B. Jones, Director

Bryant & Stratton Business Institute
691 Richmond Rd., Richmond Heights   44143

Cincinnati School of Court Reporting & Business
600 Executive Building
35 E. 7th St., Cincinnati   45202
Adeline M. Womack, President

Cleveland Institute of Dental & Medical Assistants
5733 Hopkins Rd., Mentor   44060

Cleveland Institute of Dental-Medical Assistants
5564 Mayfield Rd., Lyndhurst   44124

Cleveland Institute of Dental and Medical Assisting
1836 Euclid Ave. #401, Cleveland   44115
Alan Steinberger, Director

· Cleveland Institute of Electronics
  1776 E. 17th St., Cleveland   44114
  800-243-6446

Cleveland Machining Institute
2500 Brookpark Rd., Cleveland   44134

Columbus Para-Professional Institute
1077 Lexington Ave., Columbus   43201

· Columbus State Community College
  550 E. Spring St., Columbus   43215
  Mary Jo Deerwester, Dir. of Admis.

Connecticut School of Broadcasting
4790 Red Bank Rd. #102, Cincinnati   45227
Robert Mills, President

Connecticut School of Broadcasting
6701 Rockside Rd. Suite 204
Independence   44131

ENGLISH NANNY AND GOVERNESS SCHOOL
30 S. Franklin St., Chagrin Falls   44022
Sheilagh Roth, Executive Director
800-733-1984

ESI Career Center
25301 Euclid Ave., Euclid   44117
Tim Duffy & James Arcaro, Directors

ESI Career Center
1985 N. Ridge Rd., Lorain   44055
216-277-8832

Hammel College
885 E. Buchtel Ave., Akron   44305

Hamrick Truck Driving School
1156 Medina Rd., Medina   44256

HOBART INSTITUTE OF WELDING TECHNOLOGY
400 Trade Square East, Troy   45373
David Manning, President
Ruth Ogletree, Registrar
Phone: 800-332-9448, Fax: 513-332-5200
  Established 1930. Private. Coed. Accreditation:
NATTS(ACCS/CT). Tuition: $300 to $775 per course;
$2,425 to $6,775 for complete programs. Room and
board not available at school, but a housing list is
provided. Individual courses provide skill training in
all major welding processes - range from 1 to 4 weeks
in length - and may be combined into complete welding programs. Entry, advanced and pipe levels offered. Equipped with 144 individual welding
stations. Student-faculty ratio: 10:1. Library: 4,000
welding books, 100 welding periodicals, and data-
base searching service. Visitors welcome.

· Hocking College
  3301 Hocking Pky., Nelsonville   45764
  Candace Vancko, VP for Enrollment
  800-282-4163

Institute of Medical & Dental Technology
375 Glenspring Dr. #201, Cincinnati   45246

Institute of Medical & Dental Technology
4452 Eastgate Blvd. #209, Cincinnati   45245

International College of Broadcasting
6 S. Smithville Rd., Dayton 45431
Michael A. Lemaster, President
513-258-8251

Kent State University
P.O. Box 5190, Kent 44242
Bruce Riddle, Dir. of Admis.

Kent State University, Tuscarawas Campus
University Dr., N.E., New Philadelphia 44663
Harold D. Shade, Dean

Kent State University-Geauga Campus
14111 Claridon-Troy Rd., Burton 44021
Larry Jones, Dean

Kent State University-Salem Campus
2491 State Rt. 45 S., Salem 44460
Dr. James Cooney, Dean

Kent State University-Stark Campus
6000 Frank Ave. N.W., Canton 44720
Dr. William Bittle, Dean

Kent State University-Trumbull Campus
4314 Mahoning Ave. N.W., Warren 44483
Dr. John Cable, Dean

McKim Technical Institute
1791 S. Jacoby Rd., Akron 44321

Marion Technical College
1467 Mt. Vernon Ave., Marion 43302-5694
Joel Liles, Dir. of Admis.

MTI Business College
1901 E. 13th St. #310, Cleveland 44114

NEC-National Education Center
14445 Broadway Ave., Cleveland 44125

NEC-National Institute of Technology
1225 Orlen Ave., Cuyahoga Falls 44221
Victor C. Richard, Director

Northshore Technical Institute
8815 Broadway Ave., Cleveland 44105

Northwest State Community College
22600 State Route 34, Archbold 43502
Dennis Gable, Admissions Coordinator

Ohio Auto/Diesel Technical Institute
1421 E. 49th St., Cleveland 44103
Marc Brenner, President
216-881-1700

OHIO INSTITUTE OF PHOTOGRAPHY & TECHNOLOGY
2029 Edgefield Rd., Dayton 45439
Cecil W. Johnston, Executive Director
513-294-6155 or 800-932-9698

OHIO VALLEY BUSINESS COLLEGE
500 Maryland Ave., East Liverpool 48920
216-385-1070

Penn-Ohio College
3517 Market St., Youngstown 44507
William Clark, Jr., President

Professional Skills Institute
1232 Flaire Dr., Toledo 43615

PTC Career Institute
1140 Euclid Ave., Cleveland 44115

Raedel College & Industrial Welding School
137 6th St., N.E., Canton 44702

Sawyer College of Business
3150 Mayfield Rd., Cleveland Hts. 44118-1721
George W. King, President
216-932-0911

School of Advertising Art
2900 Acosta St., Kettering 45420

Southeastern Business College
1907 N. Ridge Rd., Lorain 44055
Nancy Bonzar, Dir. of Admis.

Southeastern Business College
4020 Milan Rd., Sandusky 44870

Southeastern Business College
1855 Western Ave., Chillicothe 45601
John T. Danicki, Executive Director

Southeastern Business College
1176 Jackson Pike #312
Gallipolis 45631

Southeastern Business College
420 E. Main St., Jackson 45640
Janet Travis, Director

Southeastern Business College
1522 Sheridan Dr., Lancaster 43130
Alex Bosserman, Director

Southeastern Business College
3879 Rhodes Ave., New Boston 45662
Annita Thompson, Director

Southern Ohio College
1055 Laidlaw Ave., Cincinnati 45237
Duane Hawkins, President

Stautzenberger College
5355 Southwyck Blvd., Toledo 43614
Jack Peeples, Dir.

Stautzenberger College
4404 Secor Rd., Toledo 43623

Stautzenberger College
5405 Southwyck Blvd., Toledo 43614

Stautzenberger College
1637 Tiffin Ave., Findlay 45840

TECHNOLOGY EDUCATION COLLEGE
288 S. Hamilton Rd., Columbus 43213
Ronald Dooley, President
Thomas D. Greenhouse, Director
Established 1967. Private. Coed. Accreditation: CCA. Tuition: $5,400. Room and board: $3,400. Enrollment: 200 full-time, 25 part-time. Faculty: 21. Student-faculty ratio: 10:1. Degree offered: Associate in engineering drafting/CAD, electronics, accounting, and computer information systems. Library: 4,500 volumes. 1 building on a 2 acre campus.

Total Technical Institute
6500 Pearl Rd. #45, Parma Heights 44130

Truck Driver Development Service
1688 N. Pricetown Rd., Diamond 44412

Trumbull Business College
3200 Ridge Ave., S.E., Warren 44484
Dennis R. Griffith, President

University of Akron-Wayne College
1901 Smucker Rd., Orrville 44667

UNIVERSITY OF CINCINNATI OMI COLLEGE OF APPLIED SCIENCE
2220 Victory Pky., Cincinnati 45206
Frederick Kryman, Dean
513-556-6564

OKLAHOMA

Bryan Institute
2843 E. 51st St., Tulsa 74105
E. Gough, Director

Career Point Business School
3138 S Garnett Rd., Tulsa 74146

City College
1370 N. Interstate Dr., Norman 73072
Thorpe A. Mayes, Director

Climate Control Institute
708 S. Sheridan Rd., Tulsa 74112

Great Plains Area Vocational Technical School
4500 W. Lee Blvd., Lawton 73505

Indian Meridian Vocational Technical School
1312 S. Sangre St., Stillwater 74074

Metropolitan College of Court Reporting
2525 Northwest Expressway St.
Oklahoma City 73112

Metropolitan College of Legal Studies
2865 E. Skelly Dr., Tulsa 74105
David Stephenson, President

Mid-Del College
3420 S. Sunnylane Rd., Del City 73115
Sidney Carey, Director

Oklahoma Farriers College, Inc.
R.R. 2, Box 88, Sperry 74073
Bud Beaston, President
918-288-7221 or 800-331-4061

Oklahoma Horseshoeing School
3000 N. Interstate 35, Oklahoma City 73111

Oklahoma State Horseshoeing School
R.R. 1, Box 28b, Ardmore 73401

Platt College
3737 N. Portland Ave., Oklahoma City 73112
Mike Pugliese, Director

Platt College
4821 S. 72nd E. Ave., Tulsa 74145
George Gillard, President

Southwestern College of Meat Cutters
1301 S. May Ave., Oklahoma City 73108
Bill Marr, President
405-681-2633

TULSA WELDING SCHOOL
3038 Southwest Blvd., Tulsa 74107-3818
David Morgan, Director of Admissions
800-331-2934
Established 1949. Private. Coed. Accreditation: ACTTS. Enrollment: 300. Classes start every 3 weeks. Tuition and fees: $6,990-Master Welder (30 credit hours), $5,480-Combination Welder (21 credit hours). Graduates qualify for entry positions in pipe, tube, boilermaker, aircraft, and pipeline welding. Instructors all certified welders. Student-faculty ratio: 20:1.

Tuttle Vocational Technical Center
12777 N. Rockwell Ave., Oklahoma City 73142

United States Truck Driving School
7500 New Sapulpa Rd., Tulsa 74131
800-234-7364 or 918-227-4100

Wright Business School
2219 S.W. 74th St. #122, Oklahoma City 73159

OREGON

Airman Proficiency Center
3565 N.E. Cornell Rd., Hillsboro 97124
John Larson, Dir. of Admis.

Apollo College of Medical and Dental Careers
2600 S.E. 98th Ave., Portland 97266

Broadcast Professionals
11507 S.W. Pacific Hwy. #D, Tigard 97223

Central Oregon Community College
2600 N.W. College Way, Bend 97701
Christine Kerlin, Dir. of Admis.
503-383-7500

Chemeketa Community College
P.O. Box 14007, Salem 97309
Rick Levine, Vice President
503-399-5144

CollegeAmerica
921 S.W. Washington #200, Portland 97205

College of Legal Arts
527 S.W. Hall St. #308, Portland 97201

Commercial Training Services
2416 N. Marine Dr., Portland 97217

ConCorde Career Institute
1827 N.E. 44th, Portland 97213

Diesel Truck Driver Training School
90801 Hwy. 99 N., Eugene 97402

ITT Technical Institute
6035 N.E. 78th Ct., Portland 97218
James Horner, Director

La Grande College of Business
703 Washington Ave., La Grande 97850

Paramedic Training Institute
P.O. Box 1878, Beaverton 97075

Trend College
1050 Green Acres Rd., Eugene 97401
Sue Port, Director

Trend College
210 Liberty St., S.E., Salem 97301
Greg H. Otter, Director

Trend College
400 Earhart, Medford 97501

Trend College
1950 S.W. Sixth Ave., Portland 97201
Joyce Neuman, Director

WEST COAST TRAINING
2525 S.E. Stubb St., Milwaukie 97222
Russell L. Norton, School Director
800-755-5477
Established 1959. Private. Coed. Accreditation: Career College Association. Offers three Vocational Training courses in Heating, Ventilation, Air Conditioning, Cost Management, Sheet Metal: 280 Clock Hour, 14 week, Cost Management-Sheet Metal program. Tuition: $1,595. Tools: $275. Books: $110. 640 Clock Hour, 16 week Heating, Ventilation, Air Conditioning and Refrigeration: Tuition: $4,795. Tools $375. Books $145. Combination of the two above courses: 920 Clock Hours, 30 week H.V.A.C.R. - Cost Management - Sheet Metal: Tuition: $6,390. Tools: $650. Books: $255. Monday - Friday. Classes start monthly on all courses. We also offer an 8 week program in Heavy Equipment Operation. Students are taught Backhoes, Bulldozers, Graders, Scrapers, Etc. The curriculum also includes basic survey work and how to read and check grades. Tuition: $3,995. Tools and Books: $130. Financial aid available to qualified applicants. Both campuses within 2 miles of downtown Portland, Oregon.

West Coast Training
11919 N. Jensen Ave. #292
Portland 97217
See listing in Oregon this classification

Western Business College
425 S.W. Washington St., Portland 97204
Donald Waldbauer, President

Western Culinary Institute
1316 S.W. 13th Ave., Portland, 97201
Henry Deutsch, Executive Chef

Western Medical College of Allied Health
3000 Market St., N.E. #541, Salem 97301
Marcella Arnold, Director

Western Truck School
P.O. Box 826, Tualatin 97062

PENNSYLVANIA

Academy of Medical Arts and Business
279 Boas St., Harrisburg 17102

Allegheny Business Institute
339 Blvd. of the Allies, Pittsburgh 15222

Allied Medical Careers
P.O. Box 1648, Kingston 18704

Allied Medical Careers
2901 Pittston Ave., Scranton 18505
Damon Young, President

All-State Career School
501 Seminole St., Lester 19029

Altoona School of Commerce
508 58th St., Altoona 16602
Robert A. Halloran, President

American Institute of Design
1616 Orthodox St., Philadelphia 19124
Dorothy Miller, Dir. of Admis.

Antonelli Medical & Professional Institute
1700 Industrial Hwy., Pottstown 19464
Paula Bauer, Dir. of Admis.

Art Institute of Pittsburgh
526 Penn Ave., Pittsburgh 15222
Lee Colker, Dir. of Admis.
800-275-2470
See listing under "Art"

AUTOMOTIVE TRAINING CENTER
114 Pickering Way, Exton 19341
Steven C. Hiscox, Director
610-363-6716

BERKS TECHNICAL INSTITUTE
4 Park Plz., Wyomissing 19610
Kenneth Snyder, Director of Admissions
215-372-1722 or 800-821-4662
Established 1974. Private. Coed. Accreditation: ACCS/CT, CAHEA. Tuition: $8,784. Fees: $150-$300. Enrollment: 225 full-time, 100 Part-time. Faculty: 15. Student-faculty ratio: 15:1. Degrees: ASB, AST. Library: 1,200 volumes. Offers programs in Medical Assistant, Electronics, Drafting, Computer Programming, Personal Computers, Medical Secretary, Executive Secretary, Paralegal/Legal Secretary, Administrative Assistant.

Bidwell Training Center
1815 Metropolitan St, Pittsburgh 15233

BOYD SCHOOL
1 Chatham Center, Pittsburgh 15219
Branch: 2090 Palm Beach Lakes Blvd.
West Palm Beach FL 33409
Ruth Delach, President
Elizabeth McKinney, Dir. of Admissions, Graduate Services, Executive VP
Established 1968. Private. Coed. With student body capacity up to 2,250 per year in both locations. Programs offered include financial aid and lifetime job placement to qualified students. Costs vary depending on length of program selected. Courses offered are airline/travel industry training (15 weeks), executive travel (9 months), secretarial, bookkeeping, administrative assistant (6 & 9 months). Programs begin three times per year in both locations. Resident housing is available at both locations. School monitored apartments adjacent to schools. Admission is through personal home interview with school's representative or school visit. High school diploma or GED is required for entrance. Strict dress code is observed in school. Accreditation: member of CCA, and licensed by individual states. Graduates number 25,000 with very active alumni association in all fifty states and many countries. Sixty percent of students are referrals from alumni. The Boyd School is in the process of requesting a certificate of approval to award an Associate in Specialized Business degree.

Bradford School
355 Fifth Ave., Pittsburgh 15222
John A. Besser, Director

Bradley Academy for the Visual Arts
625 E. Philadelphia St., York 17403
Loren H. Kroh, Director
717-848-1447

Cambria-Rowe Business College
422 S. 13th St., Indiana 15701
Julie Crimarki, Director

Career Institute
1825 Kennedy Blvd., Philadelphia 19103

Career Training Academy
244 Center Rd. Suite 101, Monroeville 15146
M. Luczak, Director

Career Training Academy
703 5th Ave., New Kensington 15068
John M. Reddy, President

Computer Learning Center
3600 Market St., Philadelphia 19104

Computer Learning Network
2900 Fairway Dr., Altoona 16602

Computer Learning Network
1110 Fernwood Ave., Camp Hill 17011

Computer Tech
107 Sixth St. #8, Pittsburgh 15222

Consolidated School of Business
1605 Clugston Rd., York 17404

Consolidated School of Business
1817 Olde Homestead Ln. #J, Lancaster 17601

The Court Reporting Institute
1845 Walnut St. 7th Floor, Philadelphia 19103

Dean Institute of Technology
1501 W. Liberty Ave., Pittsburgh 15226
W. Nichie, Dir. of Admis.
412-531-4433, FAX: 412-531-4435

Delaware County Institute of Training
615 Avenue of the States, Chester 19013

Delaware Valley Academy of Medical & Dental Assts.
3330 Grant Ave., Philadelphia 19114
Glenn Goldsmith, Director
215-676-1200

Douglas School of Business
130 7th St., Monessen 15062
Andrew H. Solan, President

Electronic Institutes
4634 Browns Hill Rd., Pittsburgh 15217
Philip Chosky, President

ERIE BUSINESS CENTER, MAIN
246 W. 9th St., Erie 16501
Hope McGeary, Executive Director
Tony Piccirillo, Director of Admissions
800-392-3743
Established 1884. Private. Coed. Accreditation: ACICS. Tuition: $6,600 2 semesters. Room and board: $1,575. Degrees offered: ASB. Enrollment: 350. Faculty: full-time 10, part-time 12. 2 year Business Institution with 13 programs. Business Administration: Marketing/Sales, Accounting. Equine Studies. Travel/Tourism. Computer Programming and Computer Information Specialist. Medical Assistant. Legal Assistant. Secretarial Science: Executive Administrative Assistant, Legal Secretary, Medical Secretary, Medical Transcriptionist, Travel Tourism.

Erie Business Center South
700 Moravia St., New Castle 16101
Irene Marburger, Director
800-722-6227
See Main campus listing

Erie Institute of Technology
2221 Peninsula Dr., Erie 16506
Clinton Oviatt, Jr., Director

Franklin Academy
324 N. Centre St., Pottsville 17901
Franklin Schoeneman, President
717-622-8370

Garfield Business Institute
709 3rd Ave., New Brighton 15066
C. F. Buterbaugh, Director

Gateway Technical Institute
100 7th St., Pittsburgh 15222
Wayne Smith, Director

Gleim Technical Institute
200 S. Spring Garden St., Carlisle 17013
George Sauers, Director

Greensburg Institute of Technology
302 W. Otterman St., Greensburg 15601
Donna Chalfant, Director

Hussian School of Art
1118 Market St., Philadelphia 19107
Wilbur Crawford, Director of Admissions

ITT Technical Institute
8 Parkway Center, Pittsburgh 15220

JOHNSON TECHNICAL INSTITUTE
3427 N. Main Ave., Scranton 18508
Thomas Krause, President
Harry Dickinson, V.P. Institute Advancement
717-342-6404
Established 1912. Coed. Accreditation: ACCSCT. Tuition: $5,236. Enrollment: 350 day, 15 evening. Faculty: 25. Degree: AST. Library: 3,000 volumes. 6 buildings. Gym. Housing. Courses in automotive technology, building construction, carpentry and cabinetmaking, biomedical equipment technology, architectural and mechanical drafting and design technology, electronic and fluidic technology, machine tr., tool and die technology, and welding and metal fabrication technology.

Johnson Technical Institute
200 Shadylane Dr., Philipsburg 16866
William Knight, Director
814-342-5680

Lansdale School of Business
201 Church Rd., North Wales 19454
Marlon Keller, Director

Laurel Business Institute
11-15 E. Penn St., Uniontown 15401

Liberty Academy of Business
511 N. Broad St. #2000
Philadelphia 19123

LINCOLN TECHNICAL INSTITUTE
5151 W. Tilghman St., Allentown 18104
Robert Milot, Director
610-398-5300
Established 1946. Coed. Accredited Member School: ACCSCT. Providing technical training in: *Electronics Technology, Electronics Servicing, Computer Technician, *Architectural/Mechanical Drafting and CAD Technology. Financial aid for those who qualify. Employment assistance program. (*Associate in Specialized Technology Degree.)

LINCOLN TECHNICAL INSTITUTE
9191 Torresdale Ave. Philadelphia 19136
Douglas Johnson, Director
215-335-0800
Established 1946. Coed. Accredited Member School: ACCSCT. Providing technical training in: Automotive or Diesel Truck Technology, *Automotive or Diesel Truck Service and Management, *Architectural/Mechanical Drafting and CAD Technology. Financial aid for those who qualify. Employment assistance program. (*Associate in Specialized Technology Degree.)

McCann School of Business
47 S. Main St., Mahanoy City 17948
John Slodysko, Director

Median School of Allied Health Careers
125 7th St., Pittsburgh 15222
William Mosle, President

NEC-Allentown Business School Campus
1501 Lehigh St., Allentown 18103
610-791-5100

New England Tractor Trailer Training
3715 E. Thompson St., Philadelphia 19137

Northeast Institute of Education
P.O. Box 470, Scranton 18501

Northeast Institute of Education
P.O. Box 574, Bartonsville 18321

North Hills School of Health Occupations
1500 Northway Mall, Pittsburgh 15237

Oakbridge Academy of the Arts
401 9th St., New Kensington 15068

Orleans Technical Institute
1330 Rhawn St., Philadelphia 19111

Pace Institute
606 Court St., Reading 19601

Pennco Tech, 3815 Otter St., Bristol 19007

PENNSYLVANIA ACADEMY OF THE FINE ARTS
118 N. Broad St., Philadelphia 19102
Drawing, Painting, Printmaking, Sculpture
215-972-7625

Pennsylvania Business Institute
81 Robinson St., Pottstown 19464

Pennsylvania Business Institute
1 Angelini Ave., Nesquehoning 18240
Richard Miller, Director

Pennsylvania Gunsmith School
812 Ohio River Blvd., Pittsburgh 15202
George Thacker, Director
412-766-1812

Pennsylvania Institute of Technology
Rose Valley-Notre Dame Campus
800 Manchester Ave., Media 19063
610-565-7900

Pennsylvania School of Art and Design
204 N. Prince St., Lancaster 17603

Pittsburgh Institute of Mortuary Science
5808 Baum Blvd., Pittsburgh 15206
Jeanette G. Matthews, Registrar
412-362-8500

PJA School
7900 West Chester Pike, Upper Darby 19082
David Hudiak, Director

PTC Career Institute
40 N. 2nd St., Philadelphia 19106

THE RESTAURANT SCHOOL
4207 Walnut St., Philadelphia 19104
Deborah A. Dunn, Admissions Director
215-222-4200

Rosedale Technical Institute
4634 Browns Hill Rd., Pittsburgh 15217
John Binotto, Director

Sawyer School
717 Liberty Ave., Pittsburgh 15222
W. Nicholas Hoban, Director

Schuylkill Business Institute
2400 West End Ave., Pottsville 17901
Gregory Walker, Director

Scranton Medical Technology Consortium
700 Quincy Ave., Scranton 18510

SCS Business and Technical Institute
714 Market St., Philadelphia 19106

Shenango Valley School of Business
500 S. Mill St., New Castle 16101
412-654-1976

Shenango Valley School of Business
124 W. Spring St., Titusville 16354
814-827-9567

Shenango Valley School of Business
335 Boyd Dr., Sharon 16146
412-983-0700

SOUTH HILLS BUSINESS SCHOOL
480 Waupelani Dr., State College 16801-4516
Maralyn Mazza, Director
Admissions: 814-234-7755
Established 1970. Private. Coed. Tuition: $6,420 per year. Enrollment: 350. Faculty: 50. Accredited by CCA. ASB degrees in accounting, management, secretarial, computer information systems and health information technology. Diplomas in accounting, secretarial, clerical, retail management, travel, and microcomputers. One and two-year programs available. Financial aid, counseling and placement assistance. Housing nearby, cafeteria and day care facilities.

Star Technical Institute
1600 Nay Aug Ave., Scranton 18509

Star Technical Institute
212 Wyoming Ave, Kingston 18704

Star Technical Institute
1541 Alta Dr. Suite 1, Whitehall 18052

Swanson's Driving Schools
9915 Frankstown Rd., Pittsburgh 15235

Thompson's Academies
2908 State St., Erie 16508

Triangle Tech
P.O. Box 551, Du Bois 15801

Triangle Tech
2000 Liberty St., Erie 16502

Triangle Tech
222 E. Pittsburgh St.
Greensburg 15601

Triangle Tech
1940 Perrysville Ave., Pittsburgh 15214

Tri-State Business Institute
5757 W. 26th St., Erie 16506

Ultrasound Diagnostic School
3511 Cottman Ave., Philadelphia 19149

Washington Institute of Technology
82 S. Main St., Washington 15301
Stanley Bazant, Dir.

Welder Training and Testing Institute
100 Pennsylvania Ave., Selinsgrove   17870
Thomas H. Miller, Director
717-743-5500

Western School of Health and Business Careers
411 7th Ave., Pittsburgh   15219

Western School of Health & Business Careers
3824 Northern Pike, Monroeville   15146

West Virginia Career College
200 College Dr., Lemont Furnace   15456

Williamson Free School of Trades and Technology
106 S. New Middletown Rd., Media   19063
K. I. Horton, Dir. of Admis.
610-566-1776

Philadelphia Wireless Technical Institute
1533 Pine St., Philadelphia   19102
Harry A. Raske, President

York Technical Institute
3351 Whiteford Rd., York   17402
Harold L. Maley, President

Yorktowne Business Institute
0 W. 7th Ave., York   17404
Heather Venne, Admissions Representative

RHODE ISLAND

Hall Institute of Tech
P.O. Box 773, North Scituate   02857
Charles K. Rogers, President

Katharine Gibbs School
178 Butler Ave., Providence   02906
401-861-1420

Nasson Institute
1080 Newport Ave., Pawtucket   02861

Nasson Institute
1276 Bald Hill Rd., Warwick   02886

Nasson Institute
191 Social St., Woonsocket   02895

National Education Center-Rhode Island Trades Shop
School
106 Access Rd., Warwick   02886

New England Institute of Technology
2500 Post Rd., Warwick   02886
Michael K. Diehl, Dir. of Admis.
800-736-7744

New England Tractor Trailer Training
10 Dunnell Lane, Pawtucket   02860

Ocean State Business Institute
140 Point Judith Rd. #3A, Narragansett   02882
Assunta Pouliot, Director
401-789-0287

RHODE ISLAND SCHOOL OF PHOTOGRAPHY
241 Webster Ave., Providence   02909-3891
Donald Folgo, President
Call "toll free" 800-433-7477, or 401-943-7722
    Established 1944. Coed. Accreditation: Accrediting
Commission of Career Schools and Colleges of Technology. Approved for veterans education and foreign
students. Diploma for each program: Comprehensive
Photographic Program, Advanced Photographic Program. Specializing in several areas of Professional
Photography. Full-time days only (Monday-Thursday). Rolling Admissions. Two entrance dates per
year , January and September, for beginning or transfer students. Dormitories. Financial aid for those who
qualify. Student body from many states and foreign
countries.

Sawyer School
1 Cumberland St., Woonsocket   02895
John Teixeira, Director

Sawyer School
101 Main St., Pawtucket   02860
Thomas W. Kirkpatrick, President

Sawyer School
550 Hartford Ave., Providence   02909

Sawyer School
P.O. Box 4288, Middletown   02842

Sawyer School
P.O. Box 733, Westerly   02891

Sawyer School
1109 Warwick Ave., Warwick   02888

School of Medical & Legal Secretarial Sciences
60 S. Angell St., Providence   02906
Norma Casale, Director

SOUTH CAROLINA

Central Carolina Technical College
506 N. Guignard Dr., Sumter   29150
Dr. Herbert Robbins, President
803-778-6640

Chris Logan Career College
505 7th Ave. N., Myrtle Beach   29577

Forrest Junior College
601 E. River St., Anderson   29624
G. M. Forrest, President

ITT Technical Institute
1 Marcus Dr., Suite 402, Greenville   29615

Midlands Technical College
P.O. Box 2408, Columbia   29202

North American Institute of Aviation
P.O. Box 680, Conway   29526

SOUTH DAKOTA

Lake Area Vocational-Technical Institute
P.O. Box 730, Watertown   57201

Mitchell Vocational-Technical School
821 N. Capital St., Mitchell   57301

NETTLETON ACADEMY OF HAIR DESIGN
400 W. 9th St., Sioux Falls   57104
Herman Whitaker, Dir. of Admissions
800-727-1837 or 605-336-1837

NETTLETON JUNIOR COLLEGE
100 S. Spring Ave., Sioux Falls   57104
Roger Hunt, Director
800-727-1837 or 605-336-1837

Southeast Vocational-Technical Institute
2301 N. Career Pl., Sioux Falls   57107

Stenotype Institute
705 W. Avenue N, Sioux Falls   57104
Linda Clauson, President

WESTERN DAKOTA TECHNICAL INSTITUTE
1600 Sedivy Ln., Rapid City   57701
Nancy Richter, Dir. of Admis.
605-394-4034
    Established 1969. Public. Coed. Accreditation:
NCACS. Est. Tuition: $1,450. Room and board: $3,250
(9 months independent student). Fees: $732. Enroll-
ment: 700 full-time, 100 part-time. Faculty: 50. Student-faculty ratio: 15:1. Degree: AAS in 9 areas.
Library: 1,000 volumes. 2 buildings on 5 acres. Skill
training in 24 areas including business, mechanics,
construction trades, electronics, agriculture, nursing,
law enforcement, paralegal, and secretarial. Internship options available. Excellent job placement history.

TENNESSEE

Alliance Corporation Tractor Trailer Center
P.O. Box 950, Lebanon   37088

Branell Institute
786 Two Mile Pky., Goodlettsville   37072

Branell Institute
182 Eastgate Center, Chattanooga   37411

CCI Travel Careers Division
568 Colonial Rd. #102, Memphis   38117

ConCorde Career Institute
5100 Poplar Ave. #132, Memphis   38137
William Richardson, Dir. of Admis.
901-761-9494

Court Reporting Institute of Tennessee
51 Century Blvd. #350, Nashville   37214

Davidson Technical College
212 Pavilion Blvd., Nashville   37217

Health Care Training Institute
430 N. Cleveland Ave., Memphis   38104

Knoxville Job Corps Center
621 Dale Ave., Knoxville   37921

Memphis AVTS
620 Mosby Ave., Memphis   38105

Miller Hawkins Business College
1399 Madison Ave., Memphis   38104
L. E. Patrick, Director

Miller-Motte Business College
1820 Business Park Dr., Clarksville   37040

Moore School of Technology
1200 Poplar Ave., Memphis   38104

NASHVILLE AUTO-DIESEL COLLEGE
1524 Gallatin Rd., Nashville   37206
Peggie Robertson, Dir. of Admis.
615-367-1236
    Established 1919. Private. Coed. Accreditation:
CCA, Ryder. Enrollment: 800-1,000. Faculty: 36. Student-faculty ratio: 25:1. Diploma and academic associate degrees in auto-diesel and auto body repair
offered. 11 acre campus with on campus dormitories
and cafeteria. 99% graduate placement rate based on
a 70% response rate. Text books in technical courses
written and published by school included in tuition.
Tools provided for students while in school.

Nashville College
1160 Gallatin Rd., S., Madison   37115

Pellissippi State Technical Community College
P.O. Box 22990, Knoxville   37933

Rice College
2485 Union Ave. Ext., Memphis   38112

Rice College
1515 Magnolia Ave., N.E., Knoxville   37917

Southeastern Institute for Paralegal Education
2416 21st Ave. S. #300, Nashville   37212
Bruce Mallard, President
800-336-4457

State Area Vocational-Technical School
1100 Liberty St., Knoxville   37919

State Area Vocational-Technical School
P.O. Box 848, Athens   37371

State Area Vocational-Technical School
P.O. Box 249, Covington   38019

State Area Vocational-Technical School
P.O. Box 2959, Crossville   38557

State Area Vocational-Technical School
740 Hwy. 46 S., Dickson   37055

State Area Vocational-Technical School
P.O. Box 789, Elizabethton   37644
Kelly Yates, Director

State Area Vocational-Technical School
P.O. Box 1109, Harriman   37748

State Area Vocational-Technical School
716 McMurry Blvd., Hartsville   37074

State Area Vocational-Technical School
813 W. Main St., Hohenwald   38462

State Area Vocational-Technical School
P.O. Box 419, Jacksboro   37757

State Area Vocational-Technical School
McKeller-Sipes Field, Jackson   38301

State Area Vocational-Technical School
P.O. Box 219, Livingston   38570

State Area Vocational-Technical School
P.O. Box 427, Mc Kenzie   38201

State Area Vocational-Technical School
1507 Vo-Tech Dr., Mc Minnville   37110

State Area Vocational-Technical School
620 Mosby Ave., Memphis   38105

State Area Vocational-Technical School
P. O. Box 130, Morristown   37815

State Area Vocational-Technical School
1303 Old Fort Pky., Murfreesboro   37129

State Area Vocational-Technical School
100 White Bridge Rd., Nashville   37209

State Area Vocational-Technical School
340 Washington, Newbern   38059

State Area Vocational-Technical School
120 Eli Ln., Oneida   37841

State Area Vocational-Technical School
312 S. Wilson St., Paris   38242

State Area Vocational-Technical School
P.O. Box 614, Pulaski   38478

State Area Vocational-Technical School
South Industrial Park, Ripley   38063

State Area Vocational-Technical School
P.O. Box 89, Crump   38327

State Area Vocational-Technical School
1405 Madison St., Shelbyville   37160

State Area Vocational-Technical School
P.O. Box 489, Whiteville   38075

West Tennessee Business College
P.O. Box 1668, Jackson   38302
Barbara Forsyth, President

TEXAS

Advance Career Training
8800 N. Central Expy. #120, Dallas   75231

Allied Health Careers
5424 Highway 290, W. #105, Austin   78735

American Commercial College
402 Butternut St., Abilene   79602
Michael Otto, Director

American Commercial College
2115 E. Eighth St., Odessa   79761
Keith Sewell, Director

American Commercial College
3177 Executive Dr., San Angelo   76904
B. A. Reed, Director

American Commercial College
2007 34th St., Lubbock   79411

American Institute of Commerce
9930 Lyndon B. Johnson Fwy #350
Dallas   75243

American Trades Institute
6627 Maple, Dallas   75235
Joe Mehlmann, President

American Trades Institute
1200 Summit Ave. #200, Fort Worth   76102

American Trades Institute
235 Loop 820 #110, Hurst   76053

Arlington Court Report College
1201 N. Watson Rd. #270, Arlington   76006

The Art Institute of Houston
1900 Yorktown St., Houston   77056
Cherie R. McNeel, Dir. of Admis.
800-275-4244

ATI Career Training School
2351 W. Northwest Hwy. #1301, Dallas   75220

ATI Graphic Arts Institute
11034 Shady Tr., Dallas   75229

ATI Health Education Center
8150 Brookriver Dr. 5th Floor, Dallas   75247

Avalon Vocational Technical Institute
4241 Tanglewood, Odessa   79762

Avalon Vocational Technical Institute
1407 Texas St, Fort Worth   76102

Bish Mathis Institute
2521 Judson Rd., Longview   75605

Bradford School of Business
4669 Southwest Fwy., Suite 350, Houston   77027
Thomas Langford, President

Bryan Institute
1719 Pioneer Pkwy., Arlington   76013

Business Skills Training Center
616 Fort Worth Dr. Ste. B, Denton 76201
Jane Hadley, President

Capitol City Careers
4630 Westgate Blvd., Austin 78745

Capitol City Trade & Tech. School
205 E. Riverside Dr., Austin 78704

Career Centers of Texas
8375 Burnham Dr., El Paso 79907

Career Point Business School
485 Spencer Ln., San Antonio 78201

Careers Unlimited
335 S. Bonner St., Tyler 75702

Center for Advanced Legal Studies
3015 Richmond Ave., Houston 77098
713-529-2778

Central Texas Commercial College
P.O. Box 1324, Brownwood 76804
Martha Day, Administrator

Central Texas Commercial College
9400 N. Central Expy. #200, Dallas 75231

Chenier Business School
4320 Calder, Beaumont 77706

Chenier Business School
6300 Richmond Ave. #300, Houston 77057

Chenier Business School
2819 Loop 306, San Angelo 76904

Computer Career Center
6101 Montana Ave., El Paso 79925
Alex R. Talamantes, Director

Court Reporting Institute of Dallas
8585 N. Stemmons Freeway, Suite 200 North
Dallas 75247
Debra E. Smith, Dir. of Admis.
214-350-9722

Dalfort Aircraft Technology
7701 Lemmon Ave., Dallas 75209

David Carrasco Job Corps Center
11155 Gateway West, El Paso 79935

Delta Career Institute
1310 Pennsylvania Ave., Beaumont 77701

Executive Secretarial School
4849 Greenville Ave. #200, Dallas 75206
Jan V. Friedheim, Director
214-369-9009 or 800-441-3932

Four-C College
P.O. Box 4, Waco 76703
William J. Stanley, Director

Gary Job Corps Center
P.O. Box 967, San Marcos 78667

General Dynamics Logistics Training Center
P.O. Box 748, Fort Worth 76101

Gulf Coast Trades Center
P.O. Box 515, New Waverly 77358

Hallmark Institute of Technology
South Campus-Aviation Technology
P.O. Box 780459, San Antonio 78278
Richard Fessler, President
Bill Buss, Campus Director
210-924-8551

Hallmark Institute of Technology
North Campus-Electronics Technology
& Business Courses
10401 W. IH 10, San Antonio 78230
Richard Fessler, President
Jeanne Martin, Campus Director
210-690-9000

Houston Community College
P.O. Box 7849, Houston 77270
Calvin Smith, Dean

Houston Training School
709 Shotwell, Houston 77020

Interactive Learning Systems
8585 N. Stemmons Fwy. #M50, Dallas 75247

International Aviation & Travel Academy
300 W. Arbrook Blvd., Arlington 76014

International Business College
4121 Montana, El Paso 79903
Jerry R. Lawson, Dir. of Admissions

International Business College
4630 50th St. #100, Lubbock 79414
806-797-1933

International Business School
4107 Texoma Pky., Sherman 75090
903-893-6604

International Business School
3801 I-35N #138, Denton 76207
817-382-5126

International Career School
7647 Belfort, Houston 77061

KD Studio
2600 N. Stemmons Freeway #117, Dallas 75207
Nicholas S. Dalley, Director of Education
Contact Admissions Department: 214-638-0484

LINCOLN TECHNICAL INSTITUTE
2501 E. Arkansas Ln., Grand Prairie 75052
Paul McGuirk, Director
214-660-5701
Established 1946. Coed. Accredited Member

School: ACCSCT. Providing technical training in:
Automotive or Diesel Truck Technology, Air Conditioning and Refrigeration Service. Financial aid for
those who qualify. Employment assistance program.

M&M Word Processing Institute
5050 Westheimer Rd. #300, Houston 77056

Massey Business College
P.O. Box 630444, Nacogdoches 75963

Metro Business Academy
P.O. Box 7609, Amarillo 79114

Moncrief Radiation Center
School of Radiation Therapy Technology
1450 8th Ave., Fort Worth 76104
Nancy Fagan, M.Ed., R.T. (R)(T), Dir. of Ed.
817-923-7393

National Career Institute
1209 N. Seventh St., Harlingen 78550

Jacki Nell Executive Secretary School
2101 S. Interstate 35 #300, Austin 78741
Nelda Brock, Executive Director

North Central Texas College
1525 W. California, Gainesville 76240
Doug Willis, Dir. of Admis.

The Ocean Corporation
10840 Rockley Rd., Houston 77099
Les Joiner, President

Office Careers Centre
7001 Grapevine Hwy. Suite 202
Fort Worth 76180

Panola College
1109 W. Panola St., Carthage 75633
Gary McDaniel, President

PCI Health Training Center
8101 John Carpenter Fwy., Dallas 75247

Phillips School of Business and Technology
119 W. 8th St., Austin 78701

Polytechnic Institute
4625 North Fwy. #109, Houston 77022
713-694-6027

Professional Court Reporting School
1401 N. Central Expy. Suite 100
Richardson 75080
Ardith Spies, President

Rice Aviation-Hobby Airport Campus
205 Brisbane St., Houston 77061
713-644-7777

Rice Aviation-North Houston Campus
7811 N. Shepherd #100, Houston 77088
713-820-9470

Rice Aviation, Main Office
8880 Telephone Rd., Houston 77061
713-644-6616

R/S Institute
7122 Lawndale Ave., Houston 77023

San Antonio College of Medical and Dental Assistants
4205 San Pedro Ave., San Antonio 78212
Comer Alden, President

San Antonio College of Medical and Dental Assistants
3900 N. 23rd St., McAllen 78501

San Antonio College of Medical and Dental Assistants
5280 Medical Dr. #100, San Antonio 78229

San Antonio Trade School
120 Playmoor, San Antonio 78210

San Antonio Training Division
9350 S. Presa, San Antonio 78223

School of Automotive Machinists
1911 Antoine Dr., Houston 77055
Linda Massingill, Director

Sebring Career School
2212 Avenue I, Huntsville 77340

Southeastern Institute for Paralegal Education
5440 Harvest Hill Rd. #200, Dallas 75230

Southern Careers Institute
5333 Everhart Rd., Corpus Christi 78411

South Texas Vocational-Technical Institute
2255 N. Coria, Brownsville 78520

South Texas Vocational-Technical Institute
2901 N. 23rd St. #B, Mc Allen 78501

South Texas Vocational-Technical Institute
605 Calle De Norte, Laredo 78041

South Texas Vocational-Technical Institute
P.O. Box 629, Weslaco 78599

S.W. School of Business & Technical Careers
602 W. Southcross, San Antonio 78221

Southwest School of Electronics
5424 W Hwy. 290 #200, Austin 78735
Joan Uribe, Director

Southwest School of Medical Assistants
201 W. Sheridan, San Antonio 78204

Texas Dental Technology School
2414 Broadway, Houston 77012

Texas School of Business
711 Air Tex Dr., Houston 77073
Madeline Burillo, Director
713-846-2888

Texas School of Business
10250 Bissonnet St., #100
Houston 77036
713-771-7177

Texas Vocational School
1913 S. Flores St., San Antonio 78204

Texas Vocational School
Route 2 Box 791, Pharr 78577

Texas Vocational School
1921 E. Red River, Victoria 77901

UTAH

American Institute of Medical-Dental Technology
1675 N. Freedom Blvd., Provo 84604

American Technical Center
1144 W. 3300 S., Salt Lake City 84119

Bryman School
1144 W. 3300 S., Salt Lake City 84119
Kenneth J. Carlson, Director of Admissions

Certified Careers Institute
2661 Washington Blvd. #203, Ogden 84401

Intermountain College of Court Reporting
5980 S. Fashion Blvd., Salt Lake City 84107

L.D.S. Business College
411 E. South Temple
Salt Lake City 84111

Phillips Junior College
3098 Highland Dr. #100, Salt Lake City 84106
Wayne Wilson, President
801-485-0221

Provo College
1450 W. 820 N., Provo 84601

VERMONT

NEW ENGLAND CULINARY INSTITUTE
250 Main St., Montpelier 05602
Mary Beth Rowe, Associate Dir. of Admis.
802-223-6324
Established:1980. Private. Coed. Accreditation:
ACCS/CT. Tuition & Fees: $15,095. Room and board:
$2,655. Enrollment: 400. Faculty: 40. Student-faculty
ratio: 7:1. Degrees: Associate of Occupational Studies
in the Culinary Arts, and Bachelor's in Service and
Management. Library: 1,800 volumes. 8 buildings.
Hands on training in 5 foodservice operations on 2
campuses. Advanced placement program is available.
Financial aid available for qualified students.

New England Culinary Institute
1700 Troy Ave. #1, Colchester 05446

WOODBURY COLLEGE
660 Elm St., Montpelier 05602
Daniel Hecht, Director of Admissions
802-229-0516
Established 1975. Private. Coed. Accreditation:
New England Association of Schools and Colleges.
Tuition: $8,020. Enrollment: 125 full-time, 50 part-
time. Faculty: 25. Student-faculty ratio: 7:1. Degrees:
Certificates; Associate of Science. Woodbury College
specializes in training adult students. Its informal,
supportive environment is attractive to adults starting
college or those returning to school after pursuing
other interests. All programs combine theoretical and
practical learning, and offer hands-on training at law
offices, courts, state agencies, and community organizations. Programs in Mediation, Paralegal Studies,
Counseling/Human Relations, Essential Skills, and
Prevention/Community Development. The Mediation Program is the foremost such program in the U.S.;
the Prevention Program is the country's first college-
level program in the field.

VIRGINIA

Alliance Tractor Trailer Training Center
P.O. Box 804, Wytheville 24382

Apprentice School - Newport News Shipbuilding
4101 Washington Ave., Newport News 23607

ATI CAREER INSTITUTE
7777 Leesburg Pike #100 S., Falls Church 22043
Mary Ann Shurtz, Executive Director
703-821-8570 or 800-444-0804
Established 1976. Coed. Accreditation: SACS &
American Council on Continuing Education and
Training. Tuition: $3,500 - $7,500. Books, supplies &
fees: $200 - $1,000 depending on program. Enrollment: 250. Student-faculty ratio: 24:1. Diplomas offered in travel & tourism, culinary arts, hotel &
restaurant management, computer business applications & office technology. Requirements: Must be a
high school graduate or pass the GED. Courses 7-10
months in length. Placement assistance. Financial aid
available. Approved for training of Veterans.

Braxton School Inc.
4917 Augusta Ave., Richmond 23230
O. Warren Long, Director

Career Development Center
605 Thimble Shoals Blvd. #209
Newport News 23606

Commonwealth College
8141 Hull Street Rd., Richmond 23235

Computer Dynamics Institute
5361 Virginia Beach Blvd., Virginia Beach 23462
804-486-7300

Computer Learning Center of Washington
Plaza 500 Bldg., 6295 Edsall Rd. #210
Alexandria 22312
Dave Dahlke, Dir. of Admis.

Dominion Business School
4142 Melrose Ave., N.W. #1, Roanoke 24017

Dominion Business School
933 Reservoir St., Harrisonburg 22801

Dominion Business School
825 Richmond Rd., Staunton 24401

ECPI COMPUTER INSTITUTE
1919 Commerce Dr., Hampton 23666
804-838-9191

ECPI COMPUTER INSTITUTE
1030 S. Jefferson St., Roanoke 24016
703-342-0043

ECPI COMPUTER INSTITUTE
4303 W. Broad St., Richmond 23230
804-359-3535

ECPI COMPUTER INSTITUTE
5555 Greenwich Rd. #300, Virginia Beach 23462
804-671-7171

Fischer Technical Institute
5700 Southern Blvd., Virginia Beach 23462

Flatwoods Conservation Center
R.R. 1 Box 211, Coeburn 24230

Maryland Drafting Institute
8001 Forbes Pl., Springfield 22151

Morven Park International Equestrian Institute
R.R. 4, Box 43, Leesburg 22075
Maureen McDonald Kirmse, Dir. of Admis.

National Education Center-Kee Business College
803 Diligence Ct., Newport News 23606
Gail P. McLeod, Director

National Education Center-Kee Business College
2106 County St., Portsmouth 23704

National Education Center-Kee Business College
6301 Midlothian Tpke., Richmond 23225

Norfolk Skills Center
922 W. 21st St., Norfolk 23517

Phillips Business College
P.O. Box 169, Lynchburg 24505

Reporting Academy of Virginia
Pembroke One #600, Virginia Beach 23462

Reporting Academy of Virginia
1001 Boulders Pky. #305, Richmond 23225

Reporting Academy of Virginia
5501 Backlick Rd. #104, Springfield 22151
Trudi Terry, Director
703-658-0588

Rice Aviation-Virginia Campus
5202 W. Military Hwy., Chesapeake 23321
804-465-2813

Southside Training Skill Center
P.O. Box 258, Crewe 23930
Gary C. Groneweg, Director

Southside Virginia Community College
R.R. 1, Box 60, Alberta 23821
Dr. John Sykes, Jr., Dir. of Admis.

Southside Virginia Community College
John Daniel Campus
R.R. 1, Box 15, Keysville 23947
Dr. John Sykes, Jr., Dir. of Admis.

TESST Electronic School
1400 Duke St., Alexandria 22314

Tidewater Community College, Portsmouth Campus
Rt. 135, Portsmouth 23703
Dr. Larry L. Whitworth, President

Tidewater Tech
2697 Dean Dr. #100, Virginia Beach 23452

Tidewater Tech.
1760 E., Little Creek Rd., Norfolk 23518

Tidewater Tech
616 Denbigh Blvd., Newport News 23602

Tidewater Tech
1417 Battlefield Blvd. N. #310
Chesapeake 23320

Washington Business School of Northern Virginia
1980 Gallows Rd., Vienna 22182
Albert Coppola, Director

Washington County Adult Skill Center
848 Thompson Dr., Abingdon 24210

Wilson Rehabilitation Center
P.O. Box 81, Fishersville 22939

Woodbridge Business Institute
14573 Jefferson Davis Hwy., Woodbridge 22191

WASHINGTON

Art Institute of Seattle
2323 Elliott Ave., Seattle 98121
Doug Worsley, Dir. of Admis.

Bates Technical College
1101 S. Yakima Ave., Tacoma 98405
William Mohler, President
208-596-1500

Bellingham Vocational Technical School
3028 Lindberg Ave., Bellingham 98225

Capitol Business College
5005 Pacific Hwy. E., Ste. 11
Olympia 98424

Clover Park Technical College
4500 Steilacoom Blvd., S.W., Tacoma 98499
Alson Green, Jr., President

Columbia Basin College
2600 N. 20th Ave., Pasco 99301

Commercial Training Services
24325 Pacific Hwy. S., Des Moines 98198

Court Reporting Institute
929 N. 130th St. #2, Seattle 98133

Crown Academy
8739 S. Hosmer St., Tacoma 98444

DIVERS INSTITUTE OF TECHNOLOGY
P.O. Box 70667, Seattle 98107
John Ritter, President
800-634-8377

Eton Technical Institute
3649 Frontage Rd., Port Orchard 98366
Jim Martin, President
206-479-3866

Eton Technical Institute
209 E. Casino Rd., Everett 98208
206-353-4888

Eton Technical Institute
31919 Sixth Ave., S., Federal Way 98003
206-941-5800

Fries Piano Hospital and Training Center
2510 E. Evergreen Blvd.
Vancouver 98661

International Air Academy
2901 E. Mill Plain Blvd., Vancouver 98661

ITT TECHNICAL INSTITUTE
1050 N. Argonne Rd., Spokane 99212
Ralph E. Oscarson, Director
800-772-8324

ITT Technical Institute
2525 223rd St. S.E., Bothell 98021

Lake Washington Vocational Technical Institute
11605 132nd Ave., N.E., Kirkland 98034

Northwest School of Wooden Boatbuilding
251 Otto St., Port Townsend 98368

Perry Technical Institute
2011 W. Washington Ave., Yakima 98903
Fred Iraola, Director

Phillips Junior College of Spokane
1101 N. Fancher Rd., Spokane 99212

Pima Medical Institute
1627 Eastlake Ave. E., Seattle 98102
Walter Greenly, Director

RENTON TECHNICAL COLLEGE
3000 N.E. 4th St., Renton 98056
Dr. Robert Roberts, Director
Cherl Welding, Registrar
206-235-2352
Established 1942. Coed. Accreditation: NASC. Tuition: $1,275 per year. Enrollment: 2,520 (day). Faculty: 95. Degree: Associate's, Certificates of completion. 18 buildings on 30 acre main campus with 125 satellite locations. Day, evening and night training, retraining and upgrading in cooperation with industry for 13,159 total registrants.

Skagit Valley College
2405 E. College Way, Mt. Vernon 98273

Trend College
214 N. Wall St., Spokane 99201

Trend College
1260 Commerce, Longview 98632

Trend College
230 Grant Rd., Wenatchee 98802

Trend College
112 Pierce Ave., Yakima 98902

Trend College
3311 W. Clearwater Ave. #1201
Kennewick 99336

Trident Training Facility, Silverdale 98315

Vocational Training Institute
6400 N.E. Highway 99, Vancouver 98665
Charles Kroninger, President

Western Business College
6625 E. Mill Plain Blvd., Vancouver 98661

WEST VIRGINIA

Boone Co. Career Center
P.O. Box 50-B, Danville 25053
J. Dolan, Director

Computer Tech
Middltown Mall I-79 & Rt. 250, Fairmont 26554

Mountain State College
1508 Spring St., Parkersburg 26101
Judith Sutton, Director

West Virginia Business College
1052 Main St., Wheeling 26003

West Virginia Business College
215 W. Main St., Clarksburg 26301

WISCONSIN

Acme Institute of Technology
819 S. 60th St., Milwaukee 53214
William Warren, President

Acme Institute of Technology
102 Revere Dr., Manitowoc 54220
William Warren, President

Blackhawk Technical College
P.O. Box 5009, Janesville 53547

Diesel Truck Driver Training School
P.O. Box 47, Sun Prairie 53590

Lakeshore Technical College
1290 North Ave., Cleveland 53015

MBTI Business Training Institute
606 W. Wisconsin Ave., Milwaukee 53203
Nancy J. Bush, Senior VP

MBTI Business Training Institute
237 South St., Waukesha 53186

STRATTON COLLEGE
1300 N. Jackson St., Milwaukee 53202
Robert H. Ley, Director
414-276-5200

TRANS AMERICAN SCHOOL OF BROADCASTING
One Point Place #1, Madison 53719
Chris Hutchings, Dir. of Admis.
800-236-4997

Western Wisconsin Technical College
304 N. 6th St., La Crosse 54602

Wisconsin School of Electronics
1227 N. Sherman Ave., Madison 53704
Donald Madlung, Director

WYOMING

Cheyenne Aero Tech
1204 Airport Pky., Cheyenne 82001

EASTERN WYOMING COLLEGE
3200 West C St., Torrington 82240
Dr. Chuck Engbretson, President
Diana Ford, Dir. of Admis.
800-658-3195
Established 1948. Public. Coed. Accreditation: NCACS. Tuition: $2,316. Room and board: $2,500. Enrollment: 168 boarding, 480 day. Faculty: 48. Degrees: AA, AS, AAS. Library: 23,000 volumes. 10 buildings on 45 acres. Gym. Special areas of study include air conditioning/refrigeration, agribusiness, secretarial science, cosmetology, criminal justice, nanny training, veterinary technology, transport refrigeration, and welding. Relaxed western area near rivers & mountains, yet near large metropolitan areas.

Western Wyoming Community College
2500 College Dr., Rock Springs 82901
Jackie Freeze, Dir. of Admis.
See listing under "Community and Junior Colleges"

GUAM

International Business College of Guam
P.O. Box 3783, Agana 96910
Director of Admissions

PUERTO RICO

Academia Singer Dealer Autorizado
101 Comercio St., Ponce 00731

Allied Schools of Puerto Rico
P.O. Box 98, Bayamon 00960

American Educational College
P.O. Box 62, Bayamon 00960

Antilles School of Technical Careers
Apartado 1536, San Juan 00919
Ignacio Saenz, President

Arts and Business College of Puerto Rico
P.O. Box 1269, Caguas 00725

Atlantic College
P.O. Box 1774, Guaynabo 00970

Bayamon Technical & Commercial Institute
P.O. Box 6007, Bayamon 00619

Benedict School of Languages & Commerce
Carr 719 Avenida Villa #15
Barranquitas 00794

Benedict School of Languages & Commerce
45 Munoz Rivera Ave., Hato Rey 00918

Benedict School of Languages & Commerce
112 Street Km. 6 Barrio Mora
Isabela 00662

Centro de Estudios Multidisciplinarios
6 Dr. Vidal St., Humacao 00791

Centro de Estudios Multidisciplinarios
Barbosa Ave. #602 2nd Floor
Hato Rey 00917

Colegio Mayor de Technologia
Calle Morse #151, Arroyo 00714

Colegio Tecnico de Electricidad
1251 Franklin D. Roosevelt Ave.
Puerto Nuevo 00920

Colegio Tecnologico y Comercial
Calle Paz 165 Altos, Aguada 00602

Columbia College
San Jose St., Rio Grande 00745

Columbia College
P.O. Box 3062, Yauco 00698

D'Mart Institute
P.O. Box 2337, Cayey 00737

Electronic Data Processing College
P.O. Box 192303, Hato Rey 00919

Electronic Data Processing College
P.O. Box 1674, San Sebastian 00685

Escuela de Peritos Electricitas
P.O. Box 457, Isabela 00662

Fashion Design College
Calle Degetau #5 Esq. Betances
Bayamon 00961

Fashion Design College
210 Arzuage St., Rio Piedras 00925

Fashion Merchandising and Technical Institute
P.O. Box 2206, Bayamon 00960

Humacao Community College
P.O. Box 1185, Fajardo 00738

Humacao Community College
P.O. Box 8948, Humacao 00792

Institucion Chaviano de Mayaguez
Calle Ramos Antonini #116 Este
Mayaguez 00680

Institute of Multiple Technology
P.O. Box 707, Arecibo 00613

Institute of Multiple Technology
P.O. Box 209, Mayaguez 00681

Instituto de Banca y Comercio
996 Munoz Rivera Ave.
Rio Piedras 00926

Instituto de Banca y Comercio
P.O. Box 7623, Ponce 00732

Instituto de Banca y Comercio
P.O. Box K, Cayey 00737

Instituto de Banca y Comercio
Munoz Rivera 205, Fajardo 00738

Instituto de Banca y Comercio
P.O. Box 6092, Guayama 00654

Instituto de Banca y Comercio
Carr #2, Km. 49.4, Manati 00701

Instituto de Banca y Comercio
Calle Post #154 Norte, Mayaguez 00708

Instituto de Educacion Universal
APTDO 209, Carolina 00986

Instituto de Educacion Universal
P.O. Box 1027, Sabana Seca 00952

Instituto de Educacion Universal
404 Ave. Barbosa, Hato Rey 00917

Instituto Del Arte Moderno
Avenida Monserrate FR-5
Carolina 00983

Instituto Vocational y Comercial EDIC
P.O. Box 9120, Caguas 00726

Interamerican Business College
Calle Betances Esq. Palmas
Arecibo 00612

Interamerican Business College
P.O. Box 202, Hato Rey 00902

Interamerican Business College
P.O. Box 823, Humacao 00792

International College of Business & Tech
Plaza San Alfonso, 2nd Floor
Caguas 00627

International College of Business & Tech
Font Martelo St., Humacao 00971

International College of Business & Tech
P.O. Box 8245, San Juan 00910

International Technical College
1302 Central Ave., Rio Piedras 00921

Liceo De Arte Y Disenos
P.O. Box 1889, Caguas 00626

Liceo de Arte Y Tecnologia
P.O. Box 2346, San Juan 00902

MBTI Business Training Institute
1257 Ponce de Leon Ave., Santurce 00908
Carlos Vega Lebron, Director

Merlix Professional and Technical Institute
P.O. Box 6241, Bayamon 00914

Metro College
Villa 144, Ponce 00731

Metro College
1126 Ponce de Leon Ave.
Rio Piedras 00928

National College/Business & Technology
Avenue Gonzalo Marin #109
Arecibo 00612

National College/Business & Technology
P.O. Box 2036, Bayamon 00960

National Computer College
P.O. Box 1009, Fajardo 00738

Ponce Paramedical College
L-15 Acacia St., Ponce 00731

Ponce Technical School
16 Salud St., Ponce 00731
Fernando Torres, President

Professional Electrical School
P.O. Box 1797, Aguirre 00704

Professional Technical Institute
Avenida Betances #73 Ste 491
Bayamon 00959

Puerto Rico Hotel School
P.O. Box 4435, San Juan 00902

Puerto Rico Professional College
Calle Dr. Veve #51 Esq. Degetau
Bayamon 00960

San Juan City College
P.O. Box 1821, Juana Diaz 00795

San Juan City College
P.O. Box 9300, Santurce 00908

York College
P.O. Box 5183, San Juan 00906

CHIROPRACTIC COLLEGES

This classification contains schools offering the Doctor of Chiropractic degree accredited by the Council on Chiropractic Education (†) and a selection of programs from institutionally accredited schools.

CALIFORNIA

† Cleveland Chiropractic College of Los Angeles
590 N. Vermont Ave., Los Angeles 90004
A. Paul Forgetta, Dir. of Admis.
800-466-CCLA(2252)

† LIFE CHIROPRACTIC COLLEGE WEST

2005 Via Barrett, San Lorenzo 94580-1368
Gerard W. Clum, DC, President
Suzanne Smith, Admissions Director
510-276-9013 or 800-788-4476
Established 1976. Private. Coed. Accreditation: CCE. Tuition: $10,050. Enrollment: 700 day. Faculty: 86. Degree: DC Chiropractic. Library: 11,000 volumes. 6 buildings. In the beautiful San Francisco Bay area, Life West provides superb preparation for a chiropractic profession.

† Los Angeles College of Chiropractic
16200 E. Amber Valley Dr., Whittier 90604
Charlene Frontiera, PhD, Dir. of Admis.
800-221-5222

† Palmer College of Chiropractic-West
90 E. Tasman Dr., San Jose 95134

Southern California College of Chiropractic
8420 Beverly Rd., Pico Rivera 90660
Dr. Vivian Makiyama, Dean of Admis.
800-452-4476

CONNECTICUT

QUINNIPIAC COLLEGE

275 Mount Carmel Ave., Hamden 06518
See listing under "Universities"

University of Bridgeport
126 Park Ave., Bridgeport 06601
Dr. Frank Zolli, Dean
203-576-4552
See listing under "Universities"

GEORGIA

† Life College
1269 Barclay Circle, Marietta 30060
Dr. Sid Williams, President

ILLINOIS

† National College of Chiropractic
200 E. Roosevelt Rd., Lombard 60148
Dr. James Winterstein, President
708-629-2000

IOWA

† PALMER COLLEGE OF CHIROPRACTIC

1000 Brady St., Davenport 52803
Donald P. Kern, President
800-722-2586 or 319-326-9656

MINNESOTA

† NORTHWESTERN COLLEGE OF CHIROPRACTIC

2501 W. 84th St., Minneapolis 55431
Dr. John Allenburg, President
Susan Pitts, Coord. of New Student Advising
Established 1941. Private. Coed. Accredited by the Council on Chiropractic Education (CCE) and the North Central Association of Colleges and Schools (NCACS). Tuition for the 1993-94 school year is approximately $4,000 per trimester excluding books, activity fees and lab fees. Northwestern College of Chiropractic (NWCC) admits about 200 students each year distributed over three entering classes in September, January and April. The college maintains a total enrollment of about 600 students. Approximately 35 percent are women.

NWCC offers a ten-trimester (three terms per year) program leading to the Doctor of Chiropractic (DC) degree. A Bachelor of Science degree in Human Biology is available for students interested in pursuing both degrees concomitantly. The chiropractic curriculum is divided into the following three parts: basic sciences, chiropractic methods, and clinical (intern) experience at one of the College's five out-patient clinics in the Twin Cities area. NWCC prepares students to be skilled diagnosticians who serve as primary-care physicians. The Chiropractic Physicians Associate Program provides further in-depth clinical experience by allowing students to spend their last academic term as associates in private practices of participating doctors of chiropractic throughout the United States. Students are required to pass parts I and II of the national boards prior to graduation. More than 95 percent of all Northwestern graduates are successfully practicing chiropractic throughout the United States, Canada, and Europe. At the College's research facility, the Wolfe-Harris Center for Clinical Studies, primary research is conducted in the area of outcomes of chiropractic versus non-chiropractic care. Students are strongly encouraged to become involved in research.

Financial aid is available through programs that include Federal Pell Grants, Federal Supplemental Educational Opportunity Grants, Minnesota State Grants, Federal Perkins Loans, Stafford Student Loans, as well as Federal Work-Study and institutional work programs, including teaching assistantships. Many state and private scholarships are awarded to the college's students each year on a competetive basis.

The campus consists of 25 acres. The building complex is complete with laboratories, lecture halls, classrooms, a library, an auditorium, a cafeteria, a gymnasium, an indoor swimming pool, and a fitness center.

The Minneapolis/St. Paul metropolitan area is a progressive community with a population of 2.5 million, combines the advantages of a big city with those of a small community. The Twin Cities provide more public parks than any other large city in the nation. The area is noted for its many lakes and rivers. Many cultural and recreational facilities are located within or near the metropolitan area, including the Guthrie Theater, the Minneapolis Institute of Art, two zoos, and two professional sports teams. Educational facilities are also quite diverse; they include the University of Minnesota, eleven private colleges, and eight junior and community colleges, all located within the Twin Cities. The climate presents four distinct seasons.

The college maintains no on-campus housing, but the admissions department offers information about housing for both new and continuing students. Adequate accommodations are readily available near the campus and throughout the Twin Cities area. Generally single, independent students can expect costs of $450 per month for room and $225 per month for board; corresponding figures for married students are $470 and $375. APPLYING: Applicants should write to the Director of Admissions for application materials. Applicants must have a minimum grade point average of 2.5 and 60 semester credits (or 90 quarter credits) of undergraduate studies, including courses in biology, general and organic chemistry, physics, psychology, and English or communication skills. Students should write to the college for a preadmissions requirements brochure. Applications are accepted for three starting dates: September, January, and April.

For more information about NWCC and/or the prerequisites write or call:
Admissions Office
Northwestern College of Chiropractic
2501 W. 84th St.
Minneapolis, MN 55431-1599
612-888-4777 or 800-888-4777 (toll-free)

MISSOURI

† Cleveland Chiropractic College of Kansas City
6401 Rockhill Rd., Kansas City 64131
Brenda Holland, Director of Admissions
Phone: 800-467-CCKC(2252)

† Logan College of Chiropractic
P.O. Box 1065, Chesterfield 63006
Robyn Wilkerson, Dir. of Admis.

NEW JERSEY

Bloomfield College
1 Park Place, Bloomfield 07003
Warner Smith, Dean for Admissions
201-748-9000, Ext. 230

NEW YORK

† NEW YORK CHIROPRACTIC COLLEGE
P.O. Box 800, Seneca Falls 13148-0800
Dr. Kenneth Padgett, President
John Pecchia, VP for Business Affairs & Treasurer
Dr. John DeCicco, Dean of Academic Affairs
Stephen Faust, Dean of Student Affairs
Dr. Richard Kroe, Dean of Postgraduate & Continuing Education
Dr. Beth Donohue, Dean of Institutional Analysis
Glenn Fried, Registrar
800-234-6922 or 315-568-3040
Established 1919. Private. Coed. Total enrollment: 850. Tuition: $4,170 per trimester. Five year equivalent (10 trimesters, 3-1/3 yrs.) Professional school offering Doctor of Chiropractic degree program, full-time only, and continuing education programs for chiropractors. The college prepares students to enter the chiropractic profession and qualifies them for licensure in 50 states and most foreign countries. 286 acre campus 270 miles northeast of NYC, 40 miles west of Syracuse. 24,000 volume library. Most modern anatomical dissection labs in the profession. Housing and sports facilities on campus. Single residence hall suite, $1,435 per trimester, double suite $700 per trimester. 3 different meal plans available, $850 - $1,000. Athletic center has indoor 25 meter pool, 4 basketball courts, free weight room, universal weight room, 1/8 mile running track, indoor/outdoor tennis courts, 2 racquetball courts, student lounge and deli. Three outpatient clinics.
Admissions: Applicants must have completed 2 or more years of college (75 credits) in an accredited degree-granting institution, including 2 semesters each of English, general physics, general chemistry, organic chemistry, and general biology or zoology, and one semester each of psychology and social sciences/humanities BA/BS preferred. Recommendations, interview also required. Selection by Admissions Committee.
Accreditation: Council on Chiropractic Education, Middle States Association of Colleges & Schools, Chartered by the Board of Regents of the University of the State of New York.
Scholarships, grants available on a limited basis; Stafford Student Loans and Supplemental Loans to students available; college work study available.
Summer semester not optional; part of regular trimester academic year.

OREGON

† Western States Chiropractic College
2900 N.E. 132nd Ave., Portland 97230
800-641-5641

PENNSYLVANIA

Pennsylvania College of Straight Chiropractic
200 Tournament Dr. #100, Horsham 19044
215-957-6080 or 800-833-6080

SOUTH CAROLINA

Sherman College of Straight Chiropractic
P.O. Box 1452, Spartanburg 29304
Susan Newlin, Dir. of Admis.
800-849-8771 or 803-578-8770

TEXAS

† Parker College of Chiropractic
2540 Walnut Hill Ln., Dallas 75229

† Texas Chiropractic College
5912 Spencer Hwy., Pasadena 77505
Robert Cooper, Dir. of Admis.

WISCONSIN

Viterbo College
815 9th St., S., La Crosse 54601
Roland W. Nelson, Dir. of Admis.

COMMUNICATIONS

This Classification contains schools accredited by the Accrediting Council on Education in Journalism and Mass Communications (†) and a selection of programs from institutionally accredited schools.

ALABAMA

Auburn University, Auburn 36849

Huntingdon College
1500 E. Fairview Ave., Montgomery 36106-2148
Carolyn A. Phillips, Dean of Enrollment
800-763-0313

Samford University
800 Lakeshore Dr., Birmingham 35229
Jon Clemmensen, Chrpsn.

STILLMAN COLLEGE
P.O. Box 1430, Tuscaloosa 35403
Barbara K. Smith, Director of Admissions
See listing under "Universities"

Troy State University, Troy 36082
Merrill Bankester, Dean

† University of Alabama
P.O. Box 870132, Tuscaloosa 35487-0132
Roy Smith, Dir. of Admis.

UNIVERSITY OF ALABAMA IN HUNTSVILLE
P.O. Box 1247, Huntsville 35899
Ron R. Koger Ed.D., Dir. of Admis.
205-895-6070
Established 1969. Public. Coed. Accreditation: SACS, ABET, NLN, CSAB, ACS. Tuition: $2,418 resident, $4,836 non-resident. Room & Board: $3,450. Undergraduate enrollment: 2,674 full-time, 3,439 part-time. Graduate enrollment: 1,860. Faculty: 282. Student-faculty ratio: 18:1. Degrees: BS, BA, BSBA, BSE, MS, MSM, Ph.D., BSN, MSN, MA. 20 buildings on 350 acres. Comprehensive research university located in the Tennessee Valley of northern Alabama. Huntsville is the locale of major government and private research centers. Metropolitan population approaching 300,000.

UNIVERSITY OF MOBILE
P.O. Box 13220, Mobile 36663-0220
Kim Leousis, Dir. of Admissions
205-675-5990
See listing under "Universities"

ALASKA

† University of Alaska Anchorage
3211 Providence Dr., Anchorage 99508
907-786-1480

† University of Alaska Fairbanks
Fairbanks 99775

ARIZONA

† Arizona State University, Tempe 85287

· Arizona Western College
P.O. Box 929, Yuma 85366-0929
Bob Davis, Dir. of Admis.

GRAND CANYON UNIVERSITY
3300 W. Camelback Rd., Phoenix 85017
Sherri Willborn, Dir. of Admis.
See listing under "Liberal Arts and Sciences"

Northern Arizona University
P.O. Box 4092, Flagstaff 86011
Dr. Margaret Cibik, Dir. of Admis.

† University of Arizona, Tucson 85721
Loyd Bell, Director of Admissions

ARKANSAS

† Arkansas State University
P.O. Box 1930, State University 72467

Henderson State University
1100 Henderson St., Arkadelphia 71999

John Brown University
2000 W. University, Siloam Springs 72761
Don Crandall, Director of Enrollment Management

Ouachita Baptist University
410 Ouachita St., Arkadelphia 71998
Randy Garner, Dir. of Admis.
800-DIAL-OBU

† University of Arkansas at Fayetteville
Fayetteville 72701

† University of Arkansas at Little Rock
2801 S. University Ave., Little Rock 72204

University of Central Arkansas
201 Donaghey Ave., Conway 72035

CALIFORNIA

· Bakersfield College
1801 Panorama Dr., Bakersfield 93305
Robert M. Bruker, Dir. of Admis.

California Polytechnic State University
San Luis Obispo 93407
Helen Linstrum, Dir. of Admis.

California State University, Chico
Chico 95929-0145
Dr. Stephen King, Dean

† California State University, Fresno
Shaw & Cedar Ave., Fresno 93710

† California State University, Long Beach
1250 Bellflower Blvd., Long Beach 90840

California State University, Los Angeles
5151 Paseo Rancho Castilla, Los Angeles 90032

† California State University, Northridge
18111 Nordhoff St., Northridge 91330
Ned C. Reynolds, Dir. of Admis.

† California State University-Fullerton
Fullerton 92632

California State University-Hayward
25800 Carlos Bee Blvd., Hayward 94542

Chapman University
333 N. Glassell St., Orange 92666
Michael Drummy, Dir. of Admis.

· City College of San Francisco
50 Phelan Ave. Box A6, San Francisco 94112
Francine Podenski, Dept. Chair
415-239-3351

College of Notre Dame
1500 Ralston Ave., Belmont 94002
Greg M. Smith, PhD., Dir. of Admis.

· Columbia College
925 N. La Brea Ave., Los Angeles 90038
Kurt Wolfe, Dir. of Admis.

† Humboldt State University
1 Harps St., Arcata 95521

La Sierra University
4700 Pierce St., Riverside 92505
800-874-5587

Master's College
P.O. Box 221450, Newhall 91322
Don Gilmore, Dir. of Admis.

· ORANGE COAST COLLEGE
P.O. Box 5005, Costa Mesa 92628
See listing under "Community and Junior Colleges"

Pacific Union College
1 Angwin Ave., Angwin 94508
Dr. Gary Gifford, Dir. of Admis.

Pepperdine University
24255 Pacific Coast Hwy., Malibu 90263
Paul Long, Dean of Admissions
310-456-4392

† San Diego State University
5300 Campanile Dr., San Diego 92115

† San Francisco State University
1600 Holloway Ave., San Francisco 94132
Corwin Bjonerud, Dir. of Admis.

† San Jose State University
1 Washington Sq., San Jose 95192

· Santa Barbara City College
721 Cliff Dr., Santa Barbara 93109
805-965-0581

Southern California College
55 Fair Dr., Costa Mesa 92626
Richard Hardy, Asst. Dean for Enrollment

Stanford University, Stanford 94305

† University of California at Berkeley
Sproul Hall, Berkeley 94720

University of La Verne
1950 3rd St., La Verne 91750
Mark Bornholdt, Dir. of Admis.

University of San Diego
5998 Alcala Park, San Diego 92110
Warren Muller, Dir. of Admis.
619-260-4506

University of San Francisco
2130 Fulton St., San Francisco 94117
Bill Henley, Dir. of Admis.

† University of Southern California
University Park Campus
Los Angeles 90089

COLORADO

Adams State College, Alamosa 81102
Cheryl Billingsley, Dir. of Admis.
800-824-6494

Colorado Christian University
180 S. Garrison St., Lakewood 80226
Debra Seefeldt, Dir. of Admis.

† Colorado State University
102 Administration Building, Fort Collins 80523
Mary Ontireros, Dir. of Admissions

Metropolitan State College of Denver
P.O. Box 173362, Campus Box 16
Denver 80217-3362

· Pikes Peak Community College
5675 S. Academy Blvd.
Colorado Springs 80906-5498
Roberta Erickson, Dir. of Admis.
See listing under "Community and Junior Colleges"

Regis University
3333 Regis Blvd., Denver 80221
Robert Blust, Director of Admissions

† University of Colorado at Boulder
Boulder 80309
William A. Douglas, Dean of Admis.

University of Denver
2199 S. University Blvd., Denver 80210

University of Northern Colorado, Greeley 80639
Dennis Warnemunde, Department Chrpsn.
303-351-2045

University of Southern Colorado
2200 Bonforte Blvd., Pueblo 81001

Western State College of Colorado
Gunnison 81231
Monica Bruning, Dir. of Admis.
See listing under "Universities"

CONNECTICUT

Albertus Magnus College
700 Prospect St., New Haven 06511
Richard Lolatte, Dir. of Admissions
203-773-8501 or 800-578-9160

: Connecticut School of Electronics
586 Ella T. Grasso Blvd., New Haven 06519
Karen George, Director
203-624-2121

QUINNIPIAC COLLEGE
275 Mount Carmel Ave., Hamden 06518
John Lahey, President
Joan Isaac Mohr, VP and Dean of Admissions
Established 1929. Private. Coed. Accreditation:
NEASC. Tuition: $11,250. Room and board: $5,790.
Enrollment: 2,583 boarding, 3,444 day. Faculty 333.
Degrees: BA, BS, MAT, MBA, MHS, MPS. Library:
290,000 volumes. 30 buildings on 170 acres. Gym.
Suburban location at the base of Sleeping Giant State
Park, close to New Haven and Yale University. Con-
venient to New York City, Boston, and Upper New
England. Building a new $7 million School of Busi-
ness Center.

Southern Connecticut State University
501 Crescent St., New Haven 06515

University of Bridgeport
126 Park Ave., Bridgeport 06601
Andrew G. Nelson, Dean Admis./Financial Aid
203-576-4552
See listing under "Universities"

University of Connecticut, Storrs 06268
Maureen Croteau, Head

University of Hartford
200 Bloomfield Ave., West Hartford 06117
Richard Zeiser, Dir. of Admis.
See listing under "Universities"

University of New Haven
300 Orange Ave., West Haven 06516
M. L. McLaughlin, Dean
203-932-7000

DELAWARE

University of Delaware, Newark 19711

DISTRICT OF COLUMBIA

The American University
4400 Massachusetts Ave. N.W.
Washington 20016

† Howard University
2400 6th St., N.W., Washington 20059
James E. Cheek, President

Mt. Vernon College
2100 Foxhall Rd., N.W., Washington 20007
202-625-4682 or 800-682-4636, FAX: 202-338-1089

University of the District of Columbia
Georgia Ave.-Harvard St. Campus
1100 Harvard St., N.W., Washington 20009

University of the District of Columbia
Van Ness Campus
4200 Connecticut Ave., N.W., Washington 20008

FLORIDA

· Art Institute of Fort Lauderdale
1799 S.E. 17th St., Ft. Lauderdale 33316
Eileen Northrop, V.P./Dir. of Admis.

Barry University
11300 N.E. 2nd Ave., Miami Shores 33161
Robin Ray Roberts, Dean of Admissions

Flagler College
P.O. Box 1027, St. Augustine 32085
Marc G. Williar, Dir. of Admis.
904-829-6481

† Florida A & M University, Tallahassee 32307

Florida Atlantic University
500 N.W. 20th St., Boca Raton 33431
Brian Levin-Stankevich, Dir. of Admis.

Florida Institute of Technology
150 W. University Blvd., Melbourne 32901
Louis T. Levy, Dean of Admissions
800-888-4348

† Florida International University
Biscayne Blvd. and 151st St., North Miami 33181

Florida Southern College
111 Lake Hollingsworth Dr., Lakeland 33801
William Stephens, Jr., Dir. of Admis.

· Full Sail Center for the Recording Arts
3300 University Blvd. #160, Winter Park 32792
407-679-0100 or 800-CAN-ROCK
See listing under "Career Schools"

Jacksonville University
2800 University Blvd., N., Jacksonville 32211

LYNN UNIVERSITY
(Est. 1962 as College of Boca Raton)
3601 N. Military Trail, Boca Raton 33431
407-994-0770 or 800-544-8035
See listing under "Universities"

· National Education Center-Bauder Campus
4801 N. Dixie Hwy., Ft. Lauderdale 33334
Brian Woods, Dir. of Admis.
305-491-7171

St. Thomas University
16400 N.W. 32nd Ave., Miami 33054
John M. Letvinchuk, Dir. of Admis.

† University of Florida
226 Tigert Hall, Gainesville 32611

University of Miami
P.O. Box 248006, Coral Gables 33124

† University of South Florida
4202 Fowler Ave., Tampa 33620

† University of West Florida
11000 University Pky., Pensacola 32514

Warner Southern College
5301 U.S. Hwy. 27, S., Lake Wales 33853
Valerie S. Rutland, Dir. Enrollment Mgmt.
800-949-7248

GEORGIA

AUGUSTA COLLEGE
2500 Walton Way, Augusta 30904-2200
Lee Young, Dir. of Admis.
706-737-1405

Clark Atlanta University
240 James Brawley Dr., S.W., Atlanta 30314
Thomas W. Cole, President

Georgia College
231 W. Hancock St., Milledgeville 31061
912-453-5004

Georgia Southern University, Statesboro 30460

Georgia State University
University Plaza, Atlanta 30303
Ernest Beals, Dean of Admissions

Kennesaw State College
P.O. Box 444, Marietta 30061
Joe Head, Dir. of Admis.

Oglethorpe University
4484 Peachtree Rd., N.E., Atlanta 30319
Dennis Matthews, Dir. of Admis.

Savannah State College
State College Branch, Savannah 31404
Robert Ray, Dir. of Admis.

Toccoa Falls College
Office of Admissions, Toccoa Falls 30598
Matthew L. King, Dir. of Admis.
800-868-3257

† University of Georgia, Athens 30602
Dr. Thomas Russell, Dean

HAWAII

Chaminade University of Honolulu
3140 Waialae Ave., Honolulu 96816
Charles Schafer, VP Enrollment Services

† University of Hawaii at Manoa
2500 Campus Rd., Honolulu 96822

IDAHO

Boise State University
1910 University Dr., Boise 83725

Idaho State University
P.O. Box 8270, Pocatello 83209

Lewis Clark State College
500 8th Ave., Lewiston 83501
800-933-5272 or 208-799-5272

University of Idaho, Moscow 83843
Peter Brown, Dir. of Admis.

ILLINOIS

Aurora University
347 S. Gladstone Ave., Aurora 60506
Peter Pitts, Dir. of Admis.

Bradley University
1501 W. Bradley Ave., Peoria 61625

Columbia College
600 S. Michigan Ave., Chicago 60605
Debra McGrath, Dir. of Admis.

† Eastern Illinois University, Charleston 61920
John Reed, Dean
See listing under "Universities"

Governors State University
1 University Pky., University Park 60466
Richard Pride, Dir. of Admis.

Illinois State University
212 N. School St., Normal 61761

LEWIS UNIVERSITY
Rt. 53, Romeoville 60441
Irish O'Reilly, Director of Admissions
See listing under "Universities"

Loyola University of Chicago
820 N. Michigan Ave., Chicago 60611
Allen V. Lentino, Dir. of Admis.

Millikin University
1184 W. Main St., Decatur 62522
Lin Stoner, Dean of Admissions
800-373-7733

North Central College
30 N. Brainard St.
P.O. Box 3065, Naperville 60566-7065
Marguerite Waters, Director of Admission
708-420-3414

† Northern Illinois University, De Kalb 60115

North Park College & Theological Seminary
3225 W. Foster, Chicago 60625
312-509-2330

† Northwestern University
Annie May Swift Hall
1905 Sheridan Rd., Evanston 60208

· Parkland College
2400 W. Bradley Ave., Champaign 61821-1899
217-351-2208 or 800-346-8089

ROOSEVELT UNIVERSITY
430 S. Michigan Ave., Chicago 60605
William Smyser, Director of Admissions
See listing under "Universities"

Rosary College
7900 W. Division St., River Forest 60305
Hildegarde Schmidt, Dir. of Admis.

Sangamon State University
Shepherd Rd., Springfield 62794-9243
Admissions and Records, 217-786-6626

† Southern Illinois University at Carbondale
Carbondale 62901

Southern Illinois University at Edwardsville
Edwardsville 62026
Eugene J. Magac, Dir. of Admissions & Records

† University of Illinois
506 S. Wright St., Urbana 61801

Western Illinois University
900 W. Adams St., Macomb 61455
Alan DeRoos, Registrar
309-298-1891

INDIANA

† Ball State University
2000 W. University Ave., Muncie 47306
Ruth Vedvik, Dir. of Admis.

Butler University
4600 Sunset Ave., Indianapolis 46208

Calumet College
2400 New York Ave., Whiting 46394
Sharon Sweeney, Dir. of Admis.

Franklin College
501 E. Monroe, Franklin 46131
B. Stephen Richards, VP Enrollment

Indiana State University
217 N. 6th St., Terre Haute 47809

† Indiana University at Bloomington
300 N. Jordan Ave., Bloomington 47406

Indiana Wesleyan University
4201 S. Washington St., Marion 46953
800-332-6901

Manchester College
604 College Ave., North Manchester 46962
Dr. Scott Strode, Chrpsn.

Purdue University
Schleman Hall, West Lafayette 47907

St. Mary-of-the-Woods College
Saint Mary-of-the-Woods 47876
Lynn M. Rubick, Director of Admissions
800-926-SMWC

Taylor University
500 W. Reade Ave., Upland 46989
Dale Jackson, Head

University of Evansville
1800 Lincoln Ave., Evansville 47722
Dr. Dean Thomlison, Dept. Chair
800-423-8633

University of Notre Dame, Notre Dame 46556
Donald P. Costello, Chrpsn.

Valparaiso University, Valparaiso 46383

IOWA

Dordt College
498 4th Ave., N.E., Sioux Center 51250
Quentin Van Essen, Dir. of Admissions
800-343-6738

† Drake University
2507 E. University Ave., Des Moines 50311
Dr. Michael Cheney, Dean

Graceland College, Lamoni 50140
800-638-0053, Outside Iowa 800-346-9208
Bonita Booth, Dean of Admissions
See listing under "Universities"

Grand View College
1200 Grandview Ave., Des Moines 50316
Lori Hanson, Dir. of Admissions
800-444-6083

Iowa Lakes Community College
300 S. 18th St., Estherville 51334
John Nelson, Dir. of Admis.
712-362-2604

† Iowa State University, Ames 50011
Karsten Smedal, Dir. of Admis.

Iowa Wesleyan College
601 N. Main St., Mt. Pleasant 52641

Luther College
700 College Dr., Decorah 52101
David Sallee, Dean for Enrollment

Teikyo Marycrest University
1607 W. 12th St., Davenport 52804
Tim McDonough, Dir. of Admis.
See listing under "Universities"

† University of Iowa, Iowa City 52242

Waldorf College
106 S. 6th St., Forest City 50436
Steve Lovik, Dir. of Admis.
800-292-1903

KANSAS

Dodge City Community College
2501 N. 14th Ave., Dodge City 67801
Debbie Lloyd, Director of Admissions
800-FOR-DCCC

Fort Hays State University
600 Park St., Hays 67601-4099
Dr. Willis Watt, Chrpsn.

† Kansas State University
Anderson Hall 110, Manhattan 66506
Ellsworth M. Gerritz, Admis. & Records

McPherson College
1600 E. Euclid St., McPherson 67460

Ottawa University
1001 S. Cedar St., Ottawa 66067
Steve Koberlein, Dir. of Admis.
800-755-5200

SOUTHWESTERN COLLEGE
100 College St., Winfield 67156
800-846-1543

† University of Kansas, Lawrence 66045

Wichita State University
1845 Fairmount, Wichita 67260
800-362-2594
See listing under "Universities"

KENTUCKY

Georgetown College
400 E. College St., Georgetown 40324
Garvel Kindrick, Director of Admissions
See listing under "Universities"

Kentucky Wesleyan College
3000 Frederica St., Owensboro 42301
Pamela Gray, Director

Midway College
512 E. Stephens St., Midway 40347
Carl P. Rollins II, Dir. of Admis.

Morehead State University, Morehead 40351
Charles Myers, Director of Admissions
606-783-2000

† Murray State University, Murray 42071
Phil Bryan, Director of Admissions
800-272-4MSU

Northern Kentucky University
Louie B. Nunn Dr., Highland Heights 41076

Spalding University
851 S. 4th St., Louisville 40203
Dorothy G. Allen, Dir. of Admis.

Sue Bennett College
101 College St., London 40741
Don A. Gorbandt, Dir. of Admis.

† University of Kentucky, Lexington 40506

† Western Kentucky University
1526 Russellville Rd., Bowling Green 42101

LOUISIANA

Grambling State University
P.O. Box 607, Grambling 71245
Dr. Harold W. Lundy, President

Louisiana College
College Station, Pineville 71359
Byron McGee, Dir. of Admis.
318-487-7386
See listing under "Liberal Arts"

† Louisiana State University and A & M College
Baton Rouge 70803

Loyola University
6363 St. Charles Ave., New Orleans 70118

Northwestern State University
Natchitoches 71497

MAINE

University of Maine, Orono 04469

University of Southern Maine
96 Falmouth St., Portland 04103
Kathryn Lasky, Chrpsn.

MARYLAND

Bowie State University
14000 Jericho Park Rd., Bowie 20715

Loyola College
4501 N. Charles St., Baltimore 21210
William Bossemeyer III, Dir. of Admis.

Montgomery College
51 Mannakee St., Rockville 20850
301-279-5256

Morgan State University
Cold Spring Ln. and Hillen Rd., Baltimore 21239

TESST Electronics and Computer Institute
5122 Baltimore Ave., Hyattsville 20781
Joseph W. Fox, Director
301-864-5750

† University of Maryland, College Park 20742

Villa Julie College
1525 Greenspring Valley Rd., Stevenson 21153
Carolyn Manuszak, President

MASSACHUSETTS

American International College
1000 State St., Springfield 01109
Peter Miller, Dean of Admissions

Boston University
685 Commonwealth Ave., Boston 02215

Bridgewater State College
Bridgewater 02325
James Plotner, Jr., Dir. of Admis.

Curry College
1071 Blue Hill Ave., Milton 02186
617-333-0500

DEAN COLLEGE
99 Main St, Franklin 02038
Kathleen Teehan, Dean of Admissions
508-528-9100
See listing under "Community and Junior Colleges"

Emerson College
148 Beacon St., Boston 02116

Endicott College
376 Hale St., Beverly 01915
Elizabeth Macomber, Dir. of Admis.

Fitchburg State College
160 Pearl St., Fitchburg 01420
Marke Vickers, Dir. of Admis.

Hampshire College, Amherst 01002
Audrey Y. Smith, Dir. of Admissions
413-582-5471

Middlesex Community College
Springs Rd., Bedford 01730
617-280-3200

North Adams State College
375 Church St., North Adams 01247
413-664-4511 or 800-292-6632
See listing under "Universities or Graduate Schools"

Pine Manor College
400 Heath St., Chestnut Hill 02167
Gillian Lloyd, Dir. of Admis.

Simmons College
300 The Fenway, Boston 02115

SPRINGFIELD TECHNICAL COMMUNITY COLLEGE
1 Armory Square, Springfield 01105
Dr. Patrick E. Tigue, Dir. of Admissions
413-781-7822

Suffolk University
8 Ashburton Place, Boston 02108
Barbara K. Ericson, Assoc. Dean Enrollment & Retention
617-573-8460

University of Massachusetts Dartmouth
Old Westport Rd., North Dartmouth 02747
Raymond Barrows, Dir. of Admissions
508-999-8605

Western New England College
1215 Wilbraham Rd., Springfield 01119
800-325-1122

Westfield State College
577 Western Ave., Westfield 01085
John F. Marcus, Dir. of Admis.

MICHIGAN

Adrian College
110 S. Madison St., Adrian 49221
George Wolf, Dir. of Admis.
See listing under "Universities"

Aquinas College
1607 Robinson Rd., S.E., Grand Rapids 49506
Paula Meehan, Dean of Admissions
800-678-9593

Central Michigan University
100 Warriner Hall, Mt. Pleasant 48858

Eastern Michigan University, Ypsilanti 48197
Dennis M. Beagen, Head
313-487-3060 or 800-GO-TO-EMU

† Michigan State University, East Lansing 48824
Dr. Stan Soffin, Chrpsn.

Michigan Technological University
1400 Townsend Dr., Houghton 49931
Joseph A. Galetto, Dir. Enrollment Mgmt.
906-487-2335

Olivet College
300 S. Main St., Olivet 49076
Vicki Gallas, Registrar
See listing under "Universities"

Specs Howard School of Broadcast Arts
16900 W. Eight Mile Rd. #115, Southfield 48075
Specs Howard, Director
810-569-0101

University of Michigan-Ann Arbor
815 S. University Ave., Ann Arbor 48109

Wayne State University
5980 Cass Ave., Detroit 48202
Dr. J. R. Thorderson, Dir. of Admis.

Western Michigan University, Kalamazoo 49008
Stanley Henderson, Dir. of Enrl. Mgt. & Admis.
616-387-2000

MINNESOTA

Bemidji State University
1500 Birchmont Dr., N.E., Bemidji 56601
800-475-2001

Bethel College
3900 Bethel Dr., St. Paul 55112
Dr. George Brushaber, President

College of Saint Benedict
37 S. College Ave., St. Joseph 56374

College of St. Scholastica
1200 Kenwood Ave., Duluth 55811
Dr. Tammy Ostrander, Chrpsn.
800-447-5444
See listing under "Liberal Arts"

Concordia College
901 8th St. S., Moorhead 56562
Henry Tkachuk, Chairperson
See listing under "Universities"

Concordia College-St. Paul
275 N. Syndicate, St. Paul 55104
Tim Utter, Dir. of Admis.

Gustavus Adolphus College
800 W. College Ave., St. Peter 56082
Mark Anderson, Dir. of Admis.

Mankato State University
P.O. Box 8400, Mankato 56002

Moorhead State University
1104 7th Ave. S., Moorhead 56560

North Central Bible College
910 Elliot Ave., Minneapolis 55404
800-289-NCBC
Dan Neary, Dir. of Admis.
See listing under "Universities"

Northwestern College
3003 Snelling Ave., N., St. Paul 55113
Ralph Anderson, Dean of Admissions
800-827-6827 or 612-631-5111

PILLSBURY BAPTIST BIBLE COLLEGE
315 S. Grove St., Owatonna 55060
Alan Potter, President
Larry Tindall, Director of Admissions
800-747-4557

† St. Cloud State University
740 4th Ave., S., St. Cloud 56301
Sherwood Reid, Dir. of Admis.
800-369-4260

St. John's University
P.O. Box 7155, Collegeville 56321

St. Mary's College of Minnesota
700 Terrace Heights #2, Winona 55987
Tony Piscitiello, VP for Admission

Southwest State University, Marshall 56258

† University of Minnesota, Twin Cities
Minneapolis 55455

MISSISSIPPI

† Jackson State University
1400 Lynch St., Jackson 39203

Mississippi University for Women
P.O. Box W-1602, Columbus 39701
Teresa Thompson, Exec. Dir. of Enrollment

Tougaloo College
500 E. County Line Rd., Tougaloo 39174

† University of Mississippi, University 38677

† University of Southern Mississippi
P.O. Box 5165, Hattiesburg 39406

MISSOURI

Central Methodist College
411 CMC Square, Fayette 65248
See listing under "Universities"

Central Missouri State University
Warrensburg 64093
Delores Hudson, Dir. of Admis.

Evangel College
1111 N. Glenstone Ave., Springfield 65802
David Schoolfield, Dir. of Enrollment

Maryville University of St. Louis
13550 Conway Rd., Saint Louis 63141
314-576-9300 or 800-MARYVLL

Missouri Southern State College
3950 Newman Rd., Joplin 64801-1595
Richard Massa, Dept. Head
See listing under "Universities"

Missouri Valley College
500 E. College St., Marshall   65340
816-886-6924 ext. 114
See listing under "Universities"

Northwest Missouri State University
800 University Dr., Maryville   64468

Park College, Parkville   64152
Dr. Edwin Rawn, Dean of Admis.

Southeast Missouri State University
1 University Plz., Cape Girardeau   63701
New Student Relations 314-651-2590
See listing under "Universities"

Southwest Baptist University
1601 S. Springfield Ave., Bolivar   65613

Southwest Missouri State University
901 S. National Ave., Springfield   65804
Dr. John Sisco, Department Head
417-836-5218

Stephens College, Columbia   65215
Mary Ann Sprinkle, Dir. of Admis.

† University of Missouri, Columbia
228 Jesse Hall, Columbia   65211

WEBSTER UNIVERSITY
470 E. Lockwood Ave., Saint Louis   63119
Niel DeVasto, Director of Admissions
800-753-6765
Established 1915. Private. Coed. Accreditation: NCACS. Tuition: $9,160. Room and board: $4,340. Enrollment: 1300 full-time, 1500 part-time. Faculty: 110. Student-faculty ratio: 13:1. Degrees: BA, BFA, BM, BMEd, BS, BSN, MA, MBA, MAT, DMGT. Library: 230,000 volumes. 22 buildings on 45 acres. Nationally recognized programs in the performing arts and communications. Students from 35 states and 30 countries. Beautiful suburban campus in a wooded community of 20,000. Average class size of 15. New $5.5 million Student Center. Campuses in four European countries.

William Woods College
200 W. 12th St., Fulton   65251
Dr. Jahnae Barnett, VP of Admis.

MONTANA

CARROLL COLLEGE
1610 N. Benton Ave., Helena   59625
Candace Cain, Dir. of Admis.
See listing under "Universities"

Montana State University - Billings
1500 N. 30th St., Billings   59101
Karen Everett, Dir. of Admis.
406-657-2158

† University of Montana, Missoula   59812
800-462-8636

NEBRASKA

Bellevue College
1000 Galvin Rd. S., Bellevue   68005
Chari Leader, VP of Enrollment

Creighton University
2500 California St., Omaha   68178
Dr. David Haberman, Chrpsn.

Dana College
2848 College Dr., Blair   68008
John Schueth, Dir. of Admis.
800-444-3262
See listing under "Universities"

University of Nebraska
905 W. 25th St., Kearney   68849

† University of Nebraska at Lincoln
AvH 206, Lincoln   68588
Will Norton, Jr., Dean

University of Nebraska at Omaha
Omaha   68182

NEVADA

::: Columbia School of Broadcasting
2840 E. Flamingo Rd. #F, Las Vegas   89121
Marcia Brock-Gandy, President

† University of Nevada, Reno
Reno   89557

NEW HAMPSHIRE

Keene State College
229 Main St., Keene   03435
Kathryn Dodge, Dir. of Admis.

New England College
26 Bridge St., Henniker   03242
John Spaulding, Dir. of Admis.

New Hampshire College
2500 North River Rd., Manchester   03106
Brad Poznanski, Dir. of Admis.
603-645-9611

NOTRE DAME COLLEGE
2321 Elm St., Manchester   03104
603-669-4298

Rivier College
420 S. Main St., Nashua   03060
Admissions: 800-44-RIVIER

· White Pines College
40 Chester St., Chester   03036
603-887-4401

NEW JERSEY

FELICIAN COLLEGE
262 S. Main St., Lodi   07644
Sr. Mary Austin, OSB, Dir. of Admis.
201-778-1029
See listing under "Universities"

Jersey City State College
2039 Kennedy Blvd., Jersey City   07305
201-200-3234

Rider University
2083 Lawrenceville Rd., Lawrenceville   08648
Susan Christian, Dir. of Admis.

Rowan College of New Jersey, Glassboro   08028
Marvin G. Sills, Dir. of Admis.

Seton Hall University
400 S. Orange Ave., South Orange   07079
Lee Cooke, Dir. of Admis.

Stockton State College, Pomona   08240
Sal Catalfamo, Dir. of Admis.

Upsala College
345 Prospect St., East Orange   07017
George Lynes, Dean of Admissions

NEW MEXICO

Eastern New Mexico University
Portales   88130
Larry Fuqua, Dir. of Admis.

New Mexico Highlands University, Las Vegas   87701
Dr. Jorge P. Thomas, VP Academic Affairs

† University of New Mexico, Albuquerque   87131
Robert Weaver, Dean of Admissions

NEW YORK

Adelphi University, Garden City   11530
Dr. Elliot Pruzan, Asst. Provost & Dir. of Admis.
516-877-3050

Canisius College
2001 Main St., Buffalo   14208
Penelope Lips, Dir. of Admis.
800-843-1517

† Columbia University
612 W. 115th St., New York   10025

Cornell University
410 Thurston Ave., Ithaca   14853

Fordham University
441 E. Fordham Rd., Bronx   10458
718-817-1000

Friends World Program, Long Island University
Montauk Hwy., Southampton   11968
Carol Gilbert, Dir. of Admis.

IONA COLLEGE
715 North Ave., New Rochelle   10801
800-231-IONA or 914-633-2503
See listing under "Universities"

Long Island University-Brooklyn Campus
1 University Plaza, Brooklyn   11201
Alan Chaves, Dean of Admissions

Long Island University-C. W. Post Campus
Rt. 25A, Brookville   11548
Prof. Barbara Fowles, Chrpsn.
516-299-2382

Manhattan College
4513 Manhattan College Pky., Riverdale   10471
John Brennan, Dean of Admissions

MARIST COLLEGE
290 North Rd., Poughkeepsie   12601
Harry W. Wood, VP Admissions
914-575-3226

Marymount College
100 Marymount Ave., Tarrytown   10591
Gina R. Campbell, Dir. of Admis.
800-724-4312

Marymount Manhattan College
221 E. 71st St., New York   10021
Suzanne M. Murphy, Dir. of Admis.

Medaille College
18 Agassiz Cir., Buffalo   14214
Jacqueline Smukeer, Dir. of Admis.

Mercy College
555 Broadway, Dobbs Ferry   10522
James Nesbitt, Dean of Admissions

New York Institute of Technology
Old Westbury Campus, Old Westbury   11568

† New York University
70 Washington Sq., New York   10012

Niagara University, Niagara University   14109
George Pachter, Dean of Admissions
800-462-2111
See listing under "Universities"

Nyack College, Nyack   10960
Miguel Sanchez, Dir. of Admis.
800-33-NYACK

Pace University, White Plains Campus
78 N. Broadway, White Plains   10603

· Paul Smith's College, Paul Smiths   12970
Enrico Miller, Dir. of Admis.
800-421-2605

Rensselaer Polytechnic Institute, Troy   12180
Conrad Sharrow, Dean of Admissions

Roberts Wesleyan College
2301 Westside Dr., Rochester   14624
Dr. Elvera Berry, Chrpsn.
See listing under "Universities"

Rochester Institute of Technology
1 Lomb Memorial Dr., Rochester   14623
716-475-6631
See listing under "Universities"

St. Bonaventure University, St. Bonaventure   14778
June T. Solan, Dir. of Admis.

St. John Fisher College
3690 East Ave., Rochester   14618
Peter Lindsey, Dir. of Admis.

St. John's University
Grand Central & Utopia Parkways, Jamaica   11439

ST. THOMAS AQUINAS COLLEGE
Rt. 340, Sparkill   10976
Andrea Kraeft, Dir. of Admis.
800-999-STAC
See listing under "Liberal Arts"

· SUNY Adirondack Community College
439 Bay Rd., Queensbury   12804
Levi Brown, Dir. of Admis.
518-793-4491
See listing under "Community and Junior Colleges"

SUNY at Buffalo
17 Capen Hall
P.O. Box 601660, Buffalo   14260-1660
716-645-6900

SUNY College at Brockport
Brockport   14420

SUNY College at Buffalo
1300 Elmwood Ave., Buffalo   14222
Deborah K. Renzi, Dir. of Admis.

SUNY College at Old Westbury
P.O. Box 210, Old Westbury   11568
Michael Sheehy, Dir. of Admis.

SUNY at Oswego, Oswego   13126
Dr. Joseph Grant, Jr., Dean of Admissions
315-341-2250

SUNY College at Plattsburgh, Plattsburgh   12901
Albert Montanaro, Chrpsn.
518-564-2285

· SUNY College of Agriculture and Technology
Morrisville   13408
Dennis Nostrand, Dir. of Admis.

· SUNY Nassau Community College
1 Education Dr., Garden City   11530
Bernard Iantosca, Dir. of Admis.

· SUNY Ulster County Community College
Stone Ridge   12484
Thomas Maiello, Dir. of Admis.

† Syracuse University, Syracuse   13244

Utica College of Syracuse University
1600 Burrstone Rd., Utica   13502

NORTH CAROLINA

Barton College
College Station, Wilson   27893
Anthony Britt, Dir. of Admis.
800-345-4973/919-399-6318
See listing under "Universities"

East Carolina University
1000 E. 5th St., Greenville   27858
Dr. T. Harrell Allen, Chair

Elon College
P.O. Box 2700, Elon College   27244
Nan P. Perkins, Dean of Admissions

Gardner-Webb University
General Delivery, Boiling Springs   28017
Bill Stowe, Chrpsn.
704-434-2361

High Point College
933 Montlieu Ave., High Point   27262
Jim Schlimmer, Dir. of Admis.

Methodist College
5400 Ramsey St., Fayetteville   28311
Fiore Bergamasco, Dir. of Admis.

Pembroke State University
P.O. Box 1510, Pembroke   28372
Anthony Locklear, Dir. of Admissions
919-521-6262

QUEENS COLLEGE
1900 Selwyn Ave., Charlotte   28274
D. Stephen Cloniger, VP for Enrollment Management
See listing under "Liberal Arts"

Salem College
P.O. Box 10548, Winston-Salem   27108
Katherine Knapp, Director of Admissions
800-32-SALEM
See listing under "Women's College"

† University of North Carolina at Chapel Hill
Chapel Hill   27599
James C. Walters, Dir. Undergrad Admis.

· Wilkes Community College
P.O. Box 120, Wilkesboro   28697
Mac Warren, Dir. of Admis.

NORTH DAKOTA

† University of North Dakota
Box 8193 University Station, Grand Forks   58203

OHIO

† Bowling Green State University
Bowling Green 43403
John Martin, Dir. of Admis.

Capital University
2199 E. Main St., Columbus 43209
Dolphus E. Henry, Associate Provost

Cincinnati Bible College
P.O. Box 04320, Cincinnati 45204
C. Barry McCarty, President

Cleveland State University
Euclid Ave. at 24th St., Cleveland 44115

College of Mount St. Joseph
5701 Delhi Rd., Cincinnati 45233-1672
See listing under "Universities"

Heidelberg College
310 E. Market St., Tiffin 44883
Stephen E. Eidson, Dean of Admission
800-925-9250

: International College of Broadcasting
6 S. Smithville Rd., Dayton 45431
Michael A. Lemaster, President

† Kent State University
P.O. Box 5190, Kent 44242
Bruce Riddle, Dir. of Admis.

Malone College
515 25th St., N.W., Canton 44709
Lee Sommers, Dean of Admissions

MARIETTA COLLEGE
210 5th St., Marietta 45750
Dennis R. DePerro, Dean Admis./Financial Aid
800-331-7896

Mount Union College
1972 Clark Ave., Alliance 44601
Amy Tomko, Dir. of Admis.

Mt. Vernon Nazarene College
800 Martinsburg Rd., Mt. Vernon 43050
Ronald Hyson, Dir. of Admis.

Ohio Dominican College
1216 Sunbury Rd., Columbus 43219
800-955-OHIO

† Ohio State University
190 N. Oval Mall, Columbus 43210

† Ohio University, Athens 45701

Ohio Wesleyan University
61 S. Sandusky St., Delaware 43015
Donald Bishop, Dean for Enrollment

United Theological Seminary
1810 Harvard Blvd., Dayton 45406
The Rev. Duane Anders, Dir. of Admis.

University of Dayton
300 College Park Ave., Dayton 45469-1410
Toll-free 800-837-7433
See listing under "Universities"

University of Findlay
1000 N. Main St., Findlay 45840
Dan Crabtree, Dir. of Admis.

University of Toledo
2801 Bancroft St., W., Toledo 43606
Richard Eastop, Dir. of Admis.

Wilmington College
P.O. Box 1185, Wilmington 45177
Rhonda Inderhees, Dir. of Admis.

OKLAHOMA

Cameron University
2800 W. Gore Blvd., Lawton 73505
Louise Brown, Dir. of Admis.

Northeastern State University
600 N. Grand Ave., Tahlequah 74464

Oklahoma Baptist University
500 W. University St., Shawnee 74801

Oklahoma Christian University of Science and Arts
P.O. Box 11000, Oklahoma City 73136
Duane Eggleston, Vice President
800-877-5010

Oklahoma City University
2501 N. Blackwelder Ave., Oklahoma City 73106
Sandra Martin, Director
See listing under "Universities"

† Oklahoma State University, Stillwater 74078
Paul Harper, Dept. Head

University of Central Oklahoma
100 N. University Dr., Edmond 73034

† University of Oklahoma at Norman
660 Parrington Oval, Norman 73019

University of Tulsa
600 S. College Ave., Tulsa 74104
Dr. Steven Jones, Acting Chrpsn.

OREGON

Lewis & Clark College
0615 S.W. Palatine Hill Rd., Portland 97219
Michael Sexton, Dean of Admissions

Northwest Christian College
828 E. 11th Ave., Eugene 97401
Randy Jones, Dir. of Admis.

Oregon State University, Corvallis 97333
Wallace Gibbs, Dir. of Admis.

† University of Oregon
1 University of Oregon, Eugene 97403

PENNSYLVANIA

Allegheny College
520 N. Main St., Meadville 16335
Gayle Pollack, Dir. of Admis.

Allentown College of St. Frances de Sales
2755 Station Ave., Center Valley 18034
George Kelley, Dir. of Admis.

: Art Institute of Pittsburgh
526 Penn Ave., Pittsburgh 15222
Lee Colker, Dir. of Admis.
800-275-2470
See listing under "Art"

Beaver College
450 S. Easton Rd., Glenside 19038-3295
Dennis Nostrand, VP for Enrollment Management
Phone: 800-776-BEAVER(2328)
Fax: 215-572-4049
See listing under "Universities"

Bloomsburg University, Bloomsburg 17815
Bernard Vinovrski, Dir. of Admis.

California University of Pennsylvania
3rd St., California 15419
Norman Hasbrouck, Dean for Enrollment

Carnegie Mellon University
5000 Forbes Ave., Pittsburgh 15213

Chatham College
Woodland Rd., Pittsburgh 15232
Suellen Ofe, Dean of Admis./Financial Aid
See listing under "Women's College"

Drexel University
3141 Chestnut St., Philadelphia 19104
Dean of Enrollment Management

Duquesne University
600 Forbes Ave., Pittsburgh 15282
Thomas Schaefer, C.S.Sp., Dir. of Admis.

Eastern College
10 Fairview Dr., Saint Davids 19087
Ronald Keller, VP for Enrollment Management

Edinboro University of Pennsylvania
Edinboro 16444
Admissions Office: 800-626-2203

Elizabethtown College
1 Alpha Dr., Elizabethtown 17022

Gannon University
109 University Sq., Erie 16541

Indiana University of Pennsylvania, Indiana 15705
Fred Dadak, Dean, Admissions

Juniata College
1700 Moore St., Huntingdon 16652

· Keystone Junior College
P.O. Box 50, La Plume 18440
Kevin McIntyre, Dir. of Admis.

La Salle University
1900 W. Olney Ave., Philadelphia 19141
Br. Gerald Fitzgerald, Dir. of Admis.
See listing under "Universities"

Mercyhurst College
501 E. 38th St., Erie 16546
Andrew Roth, Dean of Enrollment
800-825-1926

· Montgomery County Community College
340 DeKalb Pike, Blue Bell 19422-0758
Dennis Murphy, Dir. of Admis.

Muhlenberg College
2400 W. Chew St., Allentown 18104
Chris Hooker-Haring, Dir. of Admis.

† Pennsylvania State University
201 Shields Bldg., University Park 16802

Pennsylvania State University
5091 Station Rd., Erie 16563

Point Park College
201 Wood St., Pittsburgh 15222
Dr. David Jones, Chrpsn.

Robert Morris College
Narrows Run Rd., Coraopolis 15108
James R. Welsh, Dean of Admissions
See listing under "Universities"

Robert Morris College
600 5th Ave., Pittsburgh 15219
James R. Welsh, Dean of Admissions
See listing under "Universities"

Seton Hill College, Greensburg 15601
Peter Egan, Dir. of Admis.
800-826-6234 or 412-838-4255

Shippensburg University, Shippensburg 17257

Slippery Rock University, Slippery Rock 16057
Director of Admissions

† Temple University
Broad St. & Montgomery Ave.
Philadelphia 19122

WESTMINSTER COLLEGE
New Wilmington 16172
Richard Dana Paul, Dir. of Admis.
412-946-7100

Wilkes University
184 S. River St., Wilkes-Barre 18766
Emory P. Guffrovich Jr., Dean of Admissions

RHODE ISLAND

Roger Williams College
1 Old Ferry Rd., Bristol 02809
William Dunfey, Dir. of Admis.

University of Rhode Island, Kingston 02881
Barbara Luebke, Chrpsn.

SOUTH CAROLINA

Anderson College
316 S. Boulevard, Anderson 29621
Carl D. Lockman, Dir. of Admis.
800-542-3594

Benedict College
1600 Harden St., Columbia 29204
Virginia McKee, Dir. of Admis.

Columbia International University
P.O. Box 3122, Columbia 29230
Frank Bedell, Dir. of Admis.
See listing under "Biblical Studies"

North Greenville College
P.O. Box 1892, Tigerville 29688
Gary Wells, Dir. of Admis.
See listing under "Universities"

† University of South Carolina, Columbia 29208
Terry Davis, Dir. of Admis.
803-777-7700

Winthrop University
701 W. Oakland Ave., Rock Hill 29733
James McCammon, Jr., Dir. of Admis.

SOUTH DAKOTA

Black Hills State University
1200 University St., Spearfish 57799
April Meeker, Dir. of Admis.

Mt. Marty College
1105 W. 8th St., Yankton 57078
Paula Tacke, Dir. of Admis.

SIOUX FALLS COLLEGE
1501 S. Prairie Ave., Sioux Falls 57105
Susan Reese, Dir. of Admis.
800-888-1047
See listing under "Universities"

† South Dakota State University
P.O. Box 2235, Brookings 57007
Dr. Richard Lee, Department Head
605-688-4171
See listing under "Universities"

University of South Dakota
414 E. Clark St., Vermillion 57069
Dave Lorenz, Dir. of Admis.

TENNESSEE

Bryan College
Box 7000, Dayton 37321
Thomas A. Shaw, Dir. of Admis.

Carson-Newman College
P.O. Box 70552, Jefferson City 37760
See listing under "Universities"

Christian Brothers University
650 E. Parkway, S., Memphis 38104

† EAST TENNESSEE STATE UNIVERSITY
P.O. Box 70731, Johnson City 37614
Dr. Nancy Dishner, Dean, Enrollment Management
615-929-4213 or 800-462-3878

† Middle Tennessee State University
Murfreesboro 37132
Roger D. Sims, Dir. of Admis.

Tennessee Technological University
P.O. Box 5006, Cookeville 38505

† University of Memphis, Memphis 38152
Dr. John Eubank, Dean of Admissions

University of Tennessee at Martin
Martin 38238
Paul Kelley, Director of Admissions
See listing under "Universities"

† University of Tennessee, Knoxville
527 Andy Holt Tower, Knoxville 37996
Dr. Gordon Stanley, Dir. of Admis.

TEXAS

Abilene Christian University
ACU Station, Box 6000, Abilene 79699

Angelo State University
2601 W. Ave., N., San Angelo 76909

Baylor University
P.O. Box 97008, Waco 76798-7008
Diana Ramey, Director of Admissions

Concordia Lutheran College
3400 N. Interstate 35, Austin 78705
Kevin Pieper, Dir. of Admis.

East Texas State University
ETSU Station, Commerce 75429

Incarnate Word College
4301 Broadway St., San Antonio 78209
Sr. Sally Mitchell, Dean of Enrollment

Prairie View A & M University
P.O. Box 3089, Prairie View 77446-3089
Linda S. Berry, Dir. of Admis.

Sam Houston State University, Huntsville 77341

Southern Methodist University
Hillcrest at University, Dallas 75275

Southwest Texas State University
601 University Dr., San Marcos 78666

Stephen F. Austin State University
P.O. Box 6078. Nacogdoches 75962

Texas A & I University
Campus Box 101, Kingsville 78363

† Texas A & M University
College Station 77843

† Texas Christian University
2800 S. University Dr., Ft. Worth 76129
Dr. Edward Boehm, Jr., Dean of Admissions

· Texas State Technical College Waco/Marshall
3801 Campus Dr., Waco 76705
817-867-3371

† Texas Tech University, Lubbock 79409

Texas Women's University
P.O. Box 23925, Denton 76204

Trinity University
715 Stadium Dr., San Antonio 78212

† University of North Texas
P.O. Box 13797, Denton 76203

University of St. Thomas
3812 Montrose Blvd., Houston 77006
Elsie Biron, Dir. of Admis.

University of Texas at Arlington
UTA Box 19125, Arlington 76019
R. Zack Prince, Dir. of Admis.

† University of Texas at Austin
0 the University of Texas, Austin 78712

University of Texas of the Permian Basin
4901 E. University Blvd., Odessa 79762

University of Texas-Pan American
1201 W. University Dr., Edinburg 78539
Miguel Nerarez, President

West Texas State University
2501 4th Ave., Canyon 79016
Lila Vars, Dir. of Admis.

UTAH

† Brigham Young University, Provo 84602

Southern Utah University
351 W. Center St., Cedar City 84720
D. Mark Barton, Asst. VP Student Services
801-586-7740

† University of Utah
1400 E. 200 S., Salt Lake City 84112
Dr. J. Stayner Landward, Dir. of Admis.

Utah State University, Logan 84322-1600
Rod Clark, Director of Admissions
801-750-1107

Westminster College of Salt Lake City
1840 S. 1300 E., Salt Lake City 84105
800-748-4753

VERMONT

Champlain College
P.O. Box 670, Burlington 05402
Josephine Churchill, Dir. of Admis.
802-860-2727
See listing under "Universities"

NORWICH UNIVERSITY
65 S. Main St., Northfield 05663
Prof. Scott Fields, Dept. Chrpsn.
See listing under "Universities"

Saint Michael's College
Winooski Park, Colchester 05439
800-SMC-8000
See listing under "Liberal Arts"

Southern Vermont College
Monument Ave., Bennington 05201
See listing under "Universities"

VIRGINIA

Averett College
420 W. Main St., Danville 24541
Gary Sherman, Dean of Enrollment Mgmt.

Christopher Newport College
50 Shoe Ln., Newport News 23606

James Madison University, Harrisonburg 22807

LIBERTY UNIVERSITY
P.O. Box 20000, Lynchburg 24506
Jay Spencer, VP Recruitment
800-376-2800
See listing under "Universities"

Lynchburg College
1501 Lakeside Dr., Lynchburg 24501
Ernest Chadderton, Dean of Enrollment

Marymount University
2807 N. Glebe Rd., Arlington 22207
Charles Coe, Director of Admissions
800-548-7638 or 703-284-1500
See listing under "Universities"

Radford University
P.O. Box 5430, Radford 24142

SHENANDOAH UNIVERSITY
1460 University Dr., Winchester 22601
Liz Colton, Coordinator
See listing under "Universities"

† Virginia Commonwealth University
910 W. Franklin St., Richmond 23284

Virginia Polytechnic Institute & State University
Blacksburg 24061
David Bousquet, Dir. of Undergraduate Admis.

Virginia Union University
1500 N. Lombardy St., Richmond 23220
Janice D. Bailey, Dir. of Admissions

† Washington and Lee University
Lexington 24450
William M. Hartog, Dir. of Admis.

WASHINGTON

Central Washington University, Ellensburg 98926
William Swain, Director of Admissions

Pacific Lutheran University
12180 Park Ave. S., Tacoma 98447
Michael Bartanen, Chrpsn.

Seattle University
Broadway Ave. & Madison, Seattle 98122
Lee Gerig, Dean of Admissions

· Skagit Valley College
2405 E. College Way, Mt. Vernon 98273

† University of Washington, Seattle 98195

Washington State University, Pullman 99164
Stan Berry, Dir. of Admis.

WEST VIRGINIA

Alderson-Broaddus College
Philippi 26416
Craig W. Gould, Director of Admissions
304-457-1700

† Marshall University
400 Hal Greer Blvd., Huntington 25755
See listing under "Universities"

The University of Charleston
2300 MacCorkle Ave., S.E., Charleston 25304
800-995-GO UC

† West Virginia University
P.O. Box 6001, Morgantown 26506

WEST VIRGINIA WESLEYAN COLLEGE
59 College Ave., Buckhannon 26201
Robert Skinner, Director of Admission
See listing under "Universities"

WISCONSIN

Beloit College
700 College St., Beloit 53511
Carl Balson, Professor of Theatre Arts
608-363-2366

Carroll College
100 N. East Ave., Waukesha 53186
Ken Moyer, Dir. of Admis.

† Marquette University
1217 W. Wisconsin Ave., Milwaukee 53233
Raymond A. Brown, Dean of Admissions

St. Norbert College
100 Grant St., De Pere 54115
Craig S. Wesley, Dean of Admission
See listing under "Universities"

**TRANS AMERICAN SCHOOL OF
BROADCASTING**
One Point Place #1, Madison 53719
Chris Hutchings, Dir. of Admis.
800-236-4997

† University of Wisconsin, Eau Claire
Eau Claire 54701

University of Wisconsin, La Crosse
115 Main Hall, La Crosse 54601
608-785-8067

† University of Wisconsin, Madison
500 Lincoln Dr., Madison 53706

University of Wisconsin
P.O. Box 413, Milwaukee 53201
V. M. Allison, Registrar

† University of Wisconsin, Oshkosh
800 Algoma Blvd., Oshkosh 54901-8602
August Helgerson, Dir. of Admis.

University of Wisconsin
1 University Plaza, Platteville 53818
Richard Schumacher, Dean of Admissions

† University of Wisconsin, River Falls
River Falls 54022
Alan Tuchtenhagen, Dir. of Admis.

University of Wisconsin, Stevens Point 54481
Dr. John A. Larsen, Dir. of Admis.

University of Wisconsin
800 W. Main St., Whitewater 53190

WYOMING

University of Wyoming
P.O. Box 3434, Laramie 82071
Richard Davis, Dir. of Admis.

GUAM

University of Guam
UOG Station, Mangilao 96923
Kathleen Owings, Dir. of Admis.

PUERTO RICO

University of Puerto Rico, Rio Piedras Campus
P.O. Box 23300, San Juan 00931
Victor Lopez, Dir. of Admis.

·COMMUNITY AND JUNIOR COLLEGES

And Career Schools offering an Associate Degree

ALABAMA

Alabama Southern Community College
P.O. Box 2000, Monroeville 36461

: Bevill State Community College
P.O. Box 800, Sumiton 35148

Bevill State Community College
P.O. Box 9, Hamilton 35570

Bishop State Community College
351 N. Broad St., Mobile 36603-5898
Yvonne Kennedy, President
205-690-6801

Brewer State Junior College
2631 Temple Ave., N., Fayette 35555
Nelda Oswalt, Registrar

Central Alabama Community College
P.O. Box 699, Alexander City 35010

Chattahoochee Valley State Community College
2602 College Dr., Phenix City 36869
Dr. Richard Federinko, President

Community College of the Air Force
130 W. Maxwell Blvd., Montgomery 36112

Concordia College
P.O. Box 1329, Selma 36702

Draughons Junior College
122 Commerce St., Montgomery 36104

Enterprise State Junior College
P.O. Box 1300, Enterprise 36331

Gadsden State Community College
P.O. Box 227, Gadsden 35902
W. Bryan Stone, Dir. of Admis.

James H. Faulkner State Junior College
1900 Highway 59 S., Bay Minette 36507

Jefferson Davis State Junior College
220 Alco Dr., Brewton 36426

Jefferson State Community College
2601 Carson Rd., Birmingham 35215
Jim Blackburn, Dir. of Admis.

John C. Calhoun State Community College
P.O. Box 2216, Decatur 35602-2216
Wayne Tosh, Registrar
205-306-2500

Lawson State Community College
3060 Wilson Rd., S.W., Birmingham 35221
Alfred Evans, Dean of Students

Lurleen B. Wallace State Junior College
P.O. Box 1418, Andalusia 36420
Dr. James Krudop, Dean

Marion Military Institute
1101 Washington St., Marion 36756
800-MMI-1842

Northeast Alabama State Junior College
P.O. Box 159, Rainsville 35986
E. R. Knox, Pres.

Northwest Alabama Community College
Rural Route 3, Box 77, Phil Campbell 35581
Charles Britnell, President

Phillips Junior College
3446 Demetropolis Rd., Mobile 36693

Phillips Junior College
4900 Corporate Dr. N.W. Ste. E
Huntsville 35805

Phillips Junior College/Southern Institute
115 Office Park Dr., Birmingham 35223
205-879-5100

Shelton State Community College
202 Skyland Blvd., Tuscaloosa 35405

Shoals State Technical College
P.O. Box 2545, Muscle Shoals 35662

Snead State Junior College
200 N. Walnut St., Boaz 35957
William H. Osborn, President

Southern Union State Junior College
P.O. Box 1000, Wadley 36276

Walker College
1411 Indiana Ave., Jasper 35501
James West, Dir. of Admis.

Wallace College - Dothan
Route 6, Box 62, Dothan 36303
Larry Beaty, President
205-983-3521

Wallace State Community College
P.O. Box 2000, Hanceville 35077

Wallace State Community College
P.O. Box 1049, Selma 36702

ALASKA

Alaska Junior College
800 E. Dimond Blvd. # 3-350
Anchorage 99515

Kenai Peninsula Community College
34820 College Dr., Soldotna 99669

Kodiak Community College
P.O. Box 946, Kodiak 99615

Kuskokwim Community College
P.O. Box 368, Bethel 99559

Northwest Community College
P.O. Box 400, Nome 99762

Prince William Sound Community College
P.O. Box 97, Valdez 99686

University of Alaska S.E. Sitka Campus
1332 Seward Ave., Sitka 99835

UNIVERSITY OF ALASKA SOUTHEAST-KETCHIKAN

2600 7th Ave., Ketchikan 99901-5798
Dr. Frances Feinerman, Director
William Trudeau, Student Services
Established 1954. State. Coed. Accreditation: NASC. Yearly tuition: $1,670 resident, $5,500 non-resident. Est. total yrly. exp.: $8,000. Faculty: 10 full-time, 50 part-time. Degrees: AA, AAS in Business Office Administration, Travel Industry and Hospitality Industry. Certificates in Accounting, Business Tech, Office Skills, Travel Industry, Hospitality Industry and Welding. Library: 42,000 volumes. 4 buildings on 40 acres. UAS-Ketchikan is a member of the statewide University of Alaska system. Ketchikan is located on Revilla Island, on the beautiful inside passage of southeast Alaska.

ARIZONA

ABC Technical and Trade Schools
3761 E. Technical Dr., Tucson 85713
E. B. Kessler, President

ACADEMY OF BUSINESS COLLEGE

3320 W. Cheryl Dr., Suite 115, Phoenix 85051
Toby D. Jalowsky, President
Melissa A. Gross, Executive Director
John Pechota, Admissions Director
602-942-4141
Established 1981. Private. Coed. Accreditation: ACICS; Candidate for accreditation with the Commission on Institutions of Higher Education of the North Central Association of Colleges and Schools. Tuition: $2,680 to $7,900. Certificate, Diploma and Associate of Applied Science Degree. Legal Secretary, Executive Secretary, Word Processing, Computerized Accounting, Business Administration, Paralegal, Medical Secretary, Medical Transcriptionist. Intern program enables students to be working part-time while attending classes. Student-faculty ratio: 17:1. Off campus housing available. Financial aid available to qualified students.

Apollo College
8503 N. 27th Ave., Phoenix 85051

Apollo College
7502 W. Thomas Rd #6, Phoenix 85033

Arizona Western College
P.O. Box 929, Yuma 85366-0929
Bob Davis, Dir. of Admis.

Central Arizona College
273 E. U.S. Hwy. 60, Apache Junction 85219
602-982-7261

Central Arizona College, Signal Peak Campus
8470 N. Overfield Rd., Coolidge 85228
Dr. John Klein, President
602-426-4265

Cochise College, Douglas
Rural Route 01 Box 100, 85607
Andrew S. Moreland, Pres.

: Conservatory of Recording Arts & Sciences
1110 E. Missouri Ave. #530, Phoenix 85014
800-562-6383
See listing under "Music"

Eastern Arizona College
3714 W. Church St., Thatcher 85552-0769
Gherald L. Hoopes, Jr., President
602-428-8322

Gateway Community College
108 N. 40th St., Phoenix 85034
Bill Harris, Dean of Student Services

Glendale Community College
6000 W. Olive Ave., Glendale 85302
Dr. John Waltrip, President
602-435-3000

High-Tech Institute
1515 E. Indian School Rd., Phoenix 85014

ITT Technical Institute
4837 E. McDowell Rd., Phoenix 85008
Michael Henry, School Director

ITT Technical Institute
1840 E. Benson Hwy., Tucson 85714

Lamson Junior College
2701 W. Bethany Home Rd., Phoenix 85017

Lamson Junior College
1980 W. Main #250, Mesa 85201
Kirt Hamm, Dir. of Admis.

Mesa Community College
1833 W. Southern Ave., Mesa 85202

Metropolitan College of Court Reporting
4640 E. Elwood St. #12, Phoenix 85040
David Stephenson, President

Mohave Community College
1971 Jagerson Ave., Kingman 86401
Keith A. West, President

Navajo Community College, Tsaile 86556
MacArthur Norton, Dir. Rec. & Admis.

NEC-Arizona Automotive Institute
6829 N. 46th Ave., Glendale 85301
P. A. Sandblom, President

Northland Pioneer College
P.O. Box 610, Holbrook 86025
A. Simper, Registrar

Paradise Valley Community College
18401 N. 32nd St., Phoenix 85032

Parks College
6992 E. Broadway, Tucson 85710

Phoenix College
1202 W. Thomas Rd., Phoenix 85013
Martha Cary, Dir. of Admis.

Pima Community College
2202 W. Anklam Rd., Tucson 85709
Dr. Denis F. Viri, Registrar

Rio Salado Community College
640 N. 1st Ave., Phoenix 85003

Scottsdale Community College
9000 E. Chaparral Rd., Scottsdale 85250
Dr. Art Decabooter, President

South Mountain Community College
7050 S. 24th St., Phoenix 85040

Universal Technical Institute
3121 W. Weldon Ave., Phoenix 85017
Robert Hartman, President

YAVAPAI COLLEGE

1100 E. Sheldon St., Prescott 86301
Mary Anne Bamrick, Interim President
Dr. Richard M. Boone, Dir. of Admis.
602-445-7300
Established 1966. Public. Coed. Accreditation: NCACS. Tuition: $4,350 (out-of-state only). Room and board: $2,640. Fees: $652 (in state). Enrollment: 1,376 full-time, 4,334 part-time. Faculty: 80 full-time, 180 part-time. Student-faculty ratio: 19:1. Degrees: AA, AAS. 14 buildings on 100 acres. Located in the beautiful mile high city of Prescott, AZ. Strong nationally acclaimed athletic programs for both men and women. Very nice residence halls and strong student activity programs. State of the art in the technologies and offers 25 occupation programs as well as a highly recognized transfer degree program.

ARKANSAS

Arkansas State University, Beebe Branch
P.O. Box H, Beebe 72012
William H. Owen, Jr., Dean

CROWLEY'S RIDGE COLLEGE

100 College Dr., Paragould 72450
Larry Bills, President
Paul McFadden, Dir. of Admissions
800-264-1096

East Arkansas Community College
Forrest City 72335
Steve Murray, Dir. of Admissions

Garland Co. Community College
1 College Dr., Hot Springs 71913

Mississippi County Community College
P.O. Box 1109, Blytheville 72316

NEC Arkansas College of Technology
9720 Rodney Parham Rd., Little Rock 72207
Lewis Prather, Registrar

North Arkansas Community College
420 Pioneer Ridge Dr., Harrison 72601
Leon Blackwood, Registrar

North Arkansas Community College
P.O. Box 2404, Batesville 72503

Phillips County Community College
P.O. Box 785, Helena 72342
Dr. Steven Jones, President
James R. Brasel, Dean of Admissions

Rich Mountain Community College
601 Bush St., Mena 71953

Shorter College
604 Locust St., North Little Rock 72114
Delores Voliber, Registrar

Southern Arkansas University
P.O. Box 3048, East Camden 71701

Southern Arkansas University, El Dorado Branch
300 South West Ave., El Dorado 71730
Dr. Kermit Parks, Acad. Dean

Westark Community College
P.O. Box 3649, Ft. Smith 72913
Joel Stubblefield, President

CALIFORNIA

Allan Hancock College
800 S. College Drive, Santa Maria 93454
Gary R. Edelbrock, President

American Academy of Dramatic Arts/West
2550 Paloma St., Pasadena 91107

American River College
4700 College Oak Ave., Sacramento 95841

American Technical College of Career Training
191 S. E St., San Bernardino 92401

Antelope Valley College
3041 W. Avenue K, Lancaster 93534

Bakersfield College
1801 Panorama Dr., Bakersfield 93305
Robert M. Bruker, Dir. of Admis.

Bakersfield College
1942 Randolph St., Delano 93215

Barstow College
2700 Barstow Rd., Barstow 92311

Brooks College
4825 E. Pacific Coast Hwy., Long Beach 90804
Chelena Adkins, Dir. of Admis.
800-421-3775

Butte College
3536 Butte Campus Dr., Oroville 95965
Romeo E. Morin, Dir. Admis.

Butte College
119 N. Butte St., Willows 95988

Cabrillo College
6500 Soquel Dr., Aptos 95003

California Culinary Academy
625 Polk St., San Francisco 94102
Harvey Tsutsui, Dir. of Admis.
See listing under "Career Schools"

Canada College
4200 Farm Hill Blvd., Redwood City 94061
Lois S. Chanslor, Dir. of Admissions

Century Schools
2665 5th Ave., San Diego 92103

Cerritos College
11110 E. Alondra Blvd., Norwalk 90650

Cerro Coso Community College
3000 College Heights Blvd., Ridgecrest 93555
Dr. Don Mourton, Dean of Student Services
619-375-5001

Chabot College
25555 Hesperian Blvd., Hayward 94545

Chabot College-Valley Campus
3033 Collier Canyon Rd., Livermore 94550

Chaffey College
5885 Haven Ave., Rancho Cucamonga 91737
JoAnne Edmison, Director of Admissions

Citrus College
1000 W. Foothill Blvd., Glendora 91741
Dan Angel, President

City College of San Francisco
50 Phelan Ave. Box E201, San Francisco 94112
Evan Dobelle, Chancellor
415-239-3000

Coastline Community College
11460 Warner Ave., Fountain Valley 92708

College of Alameda
555 Atlantic Ave., Alameda 94501

College of Marin
835 College Ave., Kentfield 94904

College of Marin
1800 Ignacio Blvd., Novato 94949

COLLEGE OF OCEANEERING

272 S. Fries Ave., Wilmington 90744
Ron Friedrich, Executive Director
Rhonda Doma, Director of Admissions
800-432-DIVE or 310-834-2501
Established 1969. Private. Coed. Accreditation:

WASC, ACDE (Association of Commercial Diving Educators). Enrollment: 261. Faculty: 17. Student-faculty ratio: 15:1. Degree: AS in Marine Technology. The College of Oceaneering has achieved worldwide recognition for its innovative approach to diver training, and was the first to offer many technical programs including Diver Medic and Underwater Inspection and Photography. We remain the only diving school in the United States with an open water, fully operational, Bell/Saturation System.

College of San Mateo
1700 W. Hillsdale Blvd., San Mateo 94402

College of the Canyons
26455 Rockwell Canyon Rd., Valencia 91355

College of the Desert
43-500 Monterey Ave., Palm Desert 92260

College of the Desert-Copper Mountain Campus
P.O. Box 1398, Joshua Tree 92252

College of the Redwoods
7351 Tompkins Hill Rd., Eureka 95501

College of the Sequoias
915 S. Mooney Blvd., Visalia 93277

College of the Siskiyous
800 College Ave., Weed 96094
E. Schumacher, President

Columbia College, P.O. Box 1849, Columbia 95310

Compton Community College
1111 E. Artesia Blvd., Compton 90221

Contra Costa College
2600 Mission Bell Dr., San Pablo 94806

Cosumnes River College
8401 Center Parkway, Sacramento 95823

Cosumnes River College-Placerville Center
106 Placerville Dr., Placerville 95667

Crafton Hills College
11711 Sand Canyon Rd., Yucaipa 92399
Luis S. Gomez, President
909-794-2161

Cuesta College, P.O. Box J, San Luis Obispo 93406
Dr. Frank R. Martinez, Pres.

Cuyamaca College
2950 Jamacha Rd., El Cajon 92019
Jeanne Hyde, Dir. of Admis.

Cypress College
9200 Valley View St., Cypress 90630

DeAnza College
21250 Stevens Creek Blvd., Cupertino 95014

Deep Springs College
Deep Springs, CA
Mailing Address, HC 72, Box 45001
Dyer, NV 89010-9803

Diablo Valley College
321 Golf Club Rd., Pleasant Hill 94523

Don Bosco Technical Institute
1151 San Gabriel Blvd., Rosemead 91770

D-Q University
P.O. Box 409, Davis 95617
Karen J. Bohay, Registrar

East Los Angeles College
1301 Avenida Cesar Chavez
Monterey Park 91754

El Camino College
16007 Crenshaw Blvd., Torrance 90506

Evergreen Valley College
3095 Yerba Buena Rd., San Jose 95135

FASHION INSTITUTE OF DESIGN & MERCHANDISING (FIDM)
919 S. Grand Ave., Los Angeles 90015
Three other locations in California (see below)
Tonian Hohberg, President
Established 1969. Private. Coed. Admission open to high school graduates, GED, and some Ability-to-Benefit students. Accreditation: WASC and FIDER. Total enrollment 3,000 at four modern campuses located in cosmopolitan West Coast cities. Day, evening and weekend classes. State, Federal and institutional financial aid available. Scholarships.
The college offers Associate Degrees and AA Professional Designation programs in Fashion Design, Merchandise Marketing, Interior Design, Visual Presentation/Space Design, Cosmetics and Fragrance Merchandising, Textile Design, Theatre Costume, and Apparel Manufacturing Management. Collegiate level general studies and ESL access programs available.
Courses are taught by a faculty of over 200 industry professionals complemented by an active advisory board of internationally known executives. Unique features of the Institute include specialized libraries and workrooms, large costume and textile collections, tutoring centers and job placement assistance for part-time and graduate positions. Internships and complimentary portfolio evaluation are available.
The Student Housing Office provides resources and referrals for housing needs, roommate assistance, transportation and community resources. Student activities include clubs for each major, International Student Club and special parties, dances and social events.
New programs begin every 12 weeks. A Foreign Student Advisor is available. Admissions Advisors assist with required personal interviews (out-of-state by telephone) and requesting high school transcripts,

college records (if applicable), portfolio guidelines (for some majors) and references.
Tours/interviews:
Los Angeles   213-624-1201 or 800-421-0127
San Francisco 415-433-6691 or 800-422-3436
Costa Mesa   714-546-0930
San Diego   619-235-4515 or 800-243-3436

Fashion Institute of Design & Merchandising
1010 2nd Ave., San Diego 92101
619-235-4515 or 800-243-3436 outside California
See listing under "Community and Junior Colleges"

Fashion Institute of Design & Merchandising
55 Stockton St., San Francisco 94108
415-433-6691 or 800-422-3436
See listing under "Community and Junior Colleges"

Fashion Institute of Design & Merchandising
3420 Bristol St., Costa Mesa 92626
714-546-0930 or 800-421-0127 outside California
See listing under "Community and Junior Colleges"

Feather River Community College
P.O. Box 11110, Quincy 95971

Foothill College
12345 El Monte Ave., Los Altos Hills 94022

Fresno City College
1101 E. University Ave., Fresno 93741
Brice Harris, President
209-442-4600

Fullerton College
321 E. Chapman Ave., Fullerton 92632

Gavilan Community College
5055 Santa Teresa Blvd., Gilroy 95020

Glendale Community College
1500 N. Verdugo Rd., Glendale 91208

Golden West College
15744 Goldenwest St., Huntington Beach 92647
Judith Valles, President

Grossmont College
8800 Grossmont College Dr., El Cajon 92020

Hartnell College
156 Homestead Ave., Salinas 93901

Heald Business College
1453 Mission St., San Francisco 94103
Arthur J. Katz, PhD., Dir.

Heald Business College
P.O. Box 3167, Salinas 93912

Heald Business College
684 El Paseo De Saratoga, San Jose 95130
Carol Hunter, Director

Heald Business College
777 Southland Dr. #210, Hayward 94545
Shelli Spangler, Director

Heald Business College-Rohnert Park
2425 Mendocino Ave., Santa Rosa 95403
Bruce A. Hindrichs, Dir. of Admis.

Heald Business College-Stockton
1776 W. March Ln. #330, Stockton 95207

Heald College
1000 Broadway, Oakland 94607
Marie-Louise Coppinger, Director

Heald Business College
2910 Prospect Park Dr., Rancho Cordova 95670

Heald College
2150 John Glenn Dr. #100, Concord 94520
Sherwood Burgess, V.P.

Heald 4 C's College
255 W. Bullard, Fresno 93704
209-438-4222

Heald Institute of Technology
250 Executive Park Blvd., San Francisco 94134

Heald Institute of Technology
2860 Howe Rd., Martinez 94553
M. K. Michaels, Director

Heald Institute of Technology-Hayward
24309 Southland Dr., Hayward 94545

Heald Institute of Technology-Sacramento
3737 Marconi Ave., Sacramento 95821

Heald Institute of Technology-San Jose
684 El Paseo de Saratoga #A, San Jose 95130

Imperial Valley College
P.O. Box 158, Imperial 92251

Institute of Computer Technology
3200 Wilshire Blvd. #400, Los Angeles 90010

Irvine Valley College
5500 Irvine Center Dr., Irvine 92720

ITT Technical Institute
7100 Knott Ave., Buena Park 90620

ITT Technical Institute
9680 Granite Ridge Dr., San Diego 92123

ITT Technical Institute
9700 Goethe Rd., Sacramento 95827

ITT Technical Institute
630 E. Brier Dr. #150, San Bernardino 92408
Sharon Turley, Director

ITT Technical Institute
6723 Van Nuys Blvd., Van Nuys 91405

ITT Technical Institute
1530 W. Cameron Ave., West Covina 91790

ITT Technical Institute
2035 E. 223rd St., Carson 90810

Kings River Community College
955 N. Reed Ave., Reedley 93654
Abel Sykes, President

Lake Tahoe Community College
P.O. Box 14445, South Lake Tahoe 96151

Laney College, 900 Fallon St., Oakland 94607
Glen Onizuka, Dean

Lassen College
P.O. Box 3000, Susanville 96130

Long Beach City College
4901 E. Carson St., Long Beach 90808
J. Dawdy, Dean of Admissions & Records

Los Angeles Business College
11012 Ventura Blvd. #369, Studio City 91604
Don Martin, President

Los Angeles City College
855 N. Vermont Ave., Los Angeles 90029
Dr. Stelle Feuers, President

Los Angeles Harbor College
1111 Figueroa Place, Wilmington 90744

Los Angeles Mission College
13356 Eldridge Ave., Sylmar 91342

LOS ANGELES PIERCE COLLEGE
6201 Winnetka Ave., Woodland Hills 91371
818-347-0551
Founded 1947; one of nine colleges of the Los Angeles Community College District. Accredited by the Western Association of Schools and Colleges. Total enrollment: 18,000. Two 20 week semesters beginning in August and January and a six week summer session. The enrollment fees are $10 per unit. Students with bachelors degrees pay $50 per unit. No tuition to California residents; nonresidents of California are charged $123 per unit (subject to change). Financial aid is available.
College provides a complete lower division program preparing students to transfer as juniors to four-year universities. Pierce College has one of the highest successful transfer rates in state. Also awards an associate degree in general education. The associate degree and certificates are awarded in many vocational fields including agriculture, automotive service technology, business administration, computer programming, computer technology, construction technology, drafting, electronic technology, industrial technology, interpreter for the deaf, journalism, machine shop technology, numerical control, nursing (RN), office administration, quality control, technical illustration, tooling and welding technologies.
Pierce College is situated on 425 acres in the western San Fernando Valley, a suburb of the city of Los Angeles. To the west and north of the college lies a major business and industrial complex with many electronics and computer firms. Founded originally as an agricultural college, the college maintains an operational farm program. Popular agriculture programs include animal and dairy science, animal health technology, horticulture, greenhouse management, horse science, and floral design. The Natural Resources Management Program utilize Canyon de Lana, a nature preserve located on campus.
The Pierce faculty consists of 350 full-time and 225 part-time members. Many of the part-time faculty are recruited from business and industry and provide students with the most advanced training possible. The full-time faculty are noted for its innovations and excellence of teaching.
Pierce College provides a number of support services for its students including an Honors Program, Associated Student Organization, intercollegiate athletics including a football and a rodeo team, award winning campus newspaper, career center, transfer center, child care, non-credit courses, handicapped services, and library.
Pierce College practices an open admissions policy and admits all qualified applicants. Admission is open to all high school graduates and all non-high school graduates over 18 years of age. Special programs exist for students under 18 without a high school diploma or equivalent and for students concurrently enrolled in high school.
For further information call the college at 818-347-0551.

Los Angeles Southwest College
1600 W. Imperial Hwy., Los Angeles 90047
Jess Craig, Coord., Admis.

Los Angeles Trade-Technical College
400 W. Washington Blvd., Los Angeles 90015

Los Angeles Valley College
5800 Fulton Avenue, Van Nuys 91401

Los Medanos College
2700 E. Leland Rd., Pittsburg 94565
Gail Newman, Dir. of Admis.

Marymount College
30800 Palos Verdes Dr. E.
Rancho Palos Verdes 90274
Dr. Thomas McFadden, President

Masters Institute
50 Airport Pky. #8, San Jose 95110

Mendocino College
P.O. Box 3000, Ukiah 95482
Leroy R. Lowery, President

Merced College
3600 M St., Merced 95348

Merced College-Los Banos Campus
16570 S. Mercey Springs Rd., Los Banos 93635

Merritt College
12500 Campus Dr., Oakland 94619
510-531-4911

Mira Costa College
1 Barnard Dr., Oceanside 92056

Mission College
3000 Mission College Blvd., Santa Clara 95054

Modesto Junior College
435 College Ave., Modesto 95397

Monterey Peninsula College
980 Fremont Ave., Monterey 93940
David Hopkins, President

Moorpark College
7075 Campus Rd., Moorpark 93021

Mt. San Antonio College
1100 N. Grand Ave., Walnut 91789

Mt. San Jacinto College
1499 N. State St., San Jacinto 92583
Elida Gonzales, Dir. of Admis.

Napa Valley College
2277 Napa-Vallejo Hwy., Napa 94558
Delores Smith, Asst. Dean of Admissions
707-253-3000

National Hispanic University
135 E. Gish Rd. #201, San Jose 95112

Ohlone College
P.O. Box 3909, Fremont 94539

ORANGE COAST COLLEGE
P.O. Box 5005, Costa Mesa 92628
President: David A. Grant
VP, Student Services: Sharon K. Donoff
VP, Instruction: James Fitzgerald, Acting
VP of Administrative Services: James McIlwain
Administrative Dean of Admissions and Records:
Susan Brown
Founded in 1947 on a 202 acre site which was granted to the college by the federal government. The college is part of the Coast Community College District which includes three public community college: Orange Coast College, Golden West College and Coastline Community College.

Accredited by the Western Association of Schools and Colleges. The college and its instructional programs are also approved by the board of Governors of the California Community Colleges and by the State Department of Education for training veterans.

In addition, the college offers programs which are accredited or approved by recognized accrediting agencies: The American Dental Association Commission on Dental Accreditation, The American Dietetic Association, the American Medical Association Committee on Allied Health and Accreditation, the California State Department of Health, and the Federal Aviation Agency.

Student body is coeducational consisting of approximately 27,000 students, of whom approximately 20,000 are part time students and 7,000 are full time students.

Grants the Associate in Arts Degree and Certificates of Achievement and Completion in numerous technical programs.

All courses are taught by qualified faculty, many of whom have earned Doctorate Degrees. The calender includes two 18 week semesters and a summer session. California residents pay an enrollment fee of $5.00 per unit up to a maximum of $50.00 each semester. Non-resident students pay the same enrollment fee plus an additional $102.00 per unit. Students also pay a Student Health Fee of $7.50, a College Service Charge of $10.00, miscellaneous material fees and parking fees.

OCC fields athletic teams for men and women in crew, sailing, basketball, cross country, soccer, swimming and diving, tennis, track and field and volleyball. Teams for men include football and baseball. The women also play softball. Athletic teams have won more State championships than any other community college in the State.

The OCC Speech and Debate Team has a strong history recently winning the 1990 National Speech and Debate championships.

Student services include: Counseling, Transfer Center, Adaptive Fitness Program, Assessment Center, Job Placement Center, Disabled Students Center, Learning Center, Speech and Language Center, Tutorial Center, Extended Opportunities Programs and Services (EOPS), Library Services, Consumer Resource Center, Children's Center, Financial Aid, Recycling Center and Student Health Services.

OCC has a strong student leadership program offering many opportunities for students to develop leadership skills. There is a wide assortment of social, service and professional clubs; choral and musical ensembles; theatre productions; guest lecturers and concerts.

The college also welcomes International Students from all countries. After meeting basic entry requirements, including a TOEFL of 500, the college issues an I-20 for study. International students are required to pay the same fees as all non-resident students.

Statistically, OCC transfers more students to the California State Colleges and Universities than any other community or junior college in the State. Guar-

anteed transfer programs are currently in place for the University of California at Irvine, California State University at Fullerton, and Chapman College.

Oxnard College, 4000 S. Rose Ave., Oxnard 93033
Dr. John Woolley, Dir. of Admis.

Palomar Community College
1140 W. Mission Rd., San Marcos 92069

Palo Verde College
811 W. Chanslor Way, Blythe 92225

Pasadena City College
1570 E. Colorado Blvd., Pasadena 91106

Phillips Junior College
8520 Balboa Blvd., Northridge 91325
Tom Azim, Director
818-895-2220

Phillips Junior College
1 Civic Plaza Dr. #110, Carson 90745

PHILLIPS JUNIOR COLLEGE
Fresno Campus
2048 N. Fine Ave., Fresno 93727

PHILLIPS JUNIOR COLLEGE
Condie Campus
1 W. Campbell Ave., Campbell 95008
Marilyn McKnight, Dir. of Admis.

Porterville College
100 E. College Ave., Porterville 93257
John McCuen, President

Queen of the Holy Rosary
P.O. Box 3908, Mission San Jose 94539

Rancho Santiago College
1530 W. 17th St., Santa Ana 92706

Rio Hondo College
3600 Workman Mill Rd., Whittier 90601

Riverside City College
4800 Magnolia Ave., Riverside 92506

Sacramento City College
3835 Freeport Blvd., Sacramento 95822

Saddleback Community College
28000 Marguerite Pkwy., Mission Viejo 92692

San Bernardino Valley College
701 S. Mt. Vernon Ave., San Bernardino 92410
Dr. Manuel Rivera, President

San Diego City College
1313 12th Ave., San Diego 92101

San Diego Mesa College
7250 Mesa College Dr., San Diego 92111

San Diego Miramar College
10440 Black Mountain Rd., San Diego 92126

San Francisco College of Mortuary Science
1598 Dolores St., San Francisco 94110
Jacquelyn S. Taylor, President
415-824-1313

San Joaquin Delta College
5151 Pacific Ave., Stockton 95207

San Joaquin Valley College
201 New Stine Rd., Bakersfield 93309

San Joaquin Valley College
3333 N. Bond, Fresno 93726

San Joaquin Valley College
8400 W. Mineral King Ave., Visalia 93291
Robert Perry, Registrar

San Jose City College
2100 Moorpark Ave., San Jose 95128

Santa Barbara City College
721 Cliff Dr., Santa Barbara 93109
805-965-0581

SANTA MONICA COLLEGE
1900 Pico Blvd., Santa Monica 90405
Richard Moore, Superintendent/President
Gordon Newman, Dean of Admis./Records
Established in 1929. Public, state-controlled. Accreditation: WASC. Enrollment fee: $13/unit resident, $50/unit resident for students who have a Bachelors degree, $117/unit non-resident tuition, $120/unit for students who are citizens and residents of a foreign country. Enrollment: 23,203. Scholarships, loans, grants, and awards are available - contact Financial Aid Office. Student housing not available.

College of Letters and Science, College of Fine Arts offer Associate in Arts degree in 78 majors. A general education curriculum offers a prescribed core of general education in various fields. Students desiring to transfer to a four year institution may take a curriculum of academic courses to meet lower division requirements in liberal arts and pre-professional fields. The vocational curriculum prepares students for immediate employment or occupational upgrading.

Semester System: Fall and spring comprise regular academic year. Optional summer and winter sessions available. Evening programs also available during regular academic year and summer session.

Admissions: 18 years of age or have a high school diploma. Students may apply for entrance into any term. Students applying for freshman status must submit application and high school transcripts. Transfer students must submit application and official copy of transfer work. Students should take English and math assessment exams. Foreign students wishing to enter on an F1 visa must apply through the International Student Center. To be accepted, an international student must be a high school graduate; be

able to pass the TOEFL with score of 450 or better, and have health insurance. Contact the International Student Center for more information.

All courses are taught by qualified faculty: 230 full-time instructors.

The library contains more than 100,000 books in its collection and about 5,000 reference titles, about 30 newspapers, and 800 periodicals from around the world. SMC is situated on a 44-acre campus that includes: gym, swimming pool, tennis courts, baseball and softball fields, football field, and track. Many student services, social and professional clubs, concert choir, theatre arts productions, publications, associated student government, intercollegiate competition.

Mild climate, two miles from the beach; next door to Los Angeles. Easy accessibility to recreational areas such as the beach, amusement parks, etc. Close to four year educational institutions such as UCLA, Pepperdine, Loyola Marymount.

Job placement program; cooperative work experience.

Santa Rosa Junior College
1501 Mendocino Ave., Santa Rosa 95401
Joe Hagerty, Coordinator

Santa Rosa Junior College-Petaluma Center
20 Knoss Concourse, Petaluma 94952

Shasta College
1065 N. Old Oregon Tr., Redding 96003

Sierra College
5000 Rocklin Rd., Rocklin 95677

Skyline College, 3300 College Dr., San Bruno 94066
James C. Wyatt, President

Solano Community College
P.O. Box 246, Suisun City 94585

Southwestern College
900 Otay Lakes Rd., Chula Vista 91910

Taft College, 29 Emmons Park Dr., Taft 93268
Dr. Wendell L. Reeder, President

Ventura College
4667 Telegraph Rd., Ventura 93003

Victor Valley College
18422 Bear Valley Rd., Victorville 92392-9699

Vista Community College
2020 Milvia St., Berkeley 94704
Dr. Barbara A. Beno, President

West Coast Christian College
6901 N. Maple Ave., Fresno 93710

West Hills College
300 Cherry Lane, Coalinga 93210

West Los Angeles College
4800 Freshman Dr., Culver City 90230

West Los Angeles College
9700 S. Sepulveda Blvd., Los Angeles 90045

West Valley College
14000 Fruitvale Ave., Saratoga 95070

Yuba College
2088 N. Beale Rd., Marysville 95901
Susan Singhas, Dean of Admissions,
Counseling and Records

COLORADO

Aims Community College
P.O. Box 69, Greeley 80632
William Green, Registrar

Arapahoe Community College
P.O. Box 9002, Littleton 80160
James F. Weber, President

BEL-REA INSTITUTE OF ANIMAL TECHNOLOGY
1681 S. Dayton, Denver 80231
303-751-8700 or 800-950-8001
See listing under "Career Schools"

Blair Junior College
828 Wooten Rd., Colorado Springs 80915
Darryl Armstrong, Director
719-574-1082

Colorado Aero Tech
10851 W. 120th Ave., Broomfield 80021-3465
John Walker, Executive Director

Colorado Institute of Art
200 E. 9th Ave., Denver 80203
Barbara Browning, Dir. of Admis.
800-275-2420
See listing under "Career Schools"

Colorado Mountain College
P.O. Box 10001, Glenwood Springs 81602
Barbara Edwards, Dir. of Admis.

Colorado Mountain College
901 US Highway 24, Leadville 80461

Colorado Mountain College
P.O. Box 775288, Steamboat Springs 80477

Colorado Northwestern Community College
500 Kennedy Dr., Rangely 81648
Pat Kalahar, Dir. Marketing/Recruitment
800-562-1105

Colorado School of Trades
1575 Hoyt St., Lakewood 80215
Robert Martin, Director

Community College of Aurora
16000 E. Centretech Pky., Aurora 80011

Community College of Denver
1111 W. Colfax Ave., Denver 80204

Denver Institute of Technology
The Educational Plaza
7350 N. Broadway, Denver 80221

Emery Aviation College
1245 A Aviation Way, Colorado Springs 80916
719-591-9488

Front Range Community College
3645 W. 112th Ave., Westminister 80030
Dr. Patricia Lammers, Dir. of Admis.

Front Range Community College
4616 S. Shields St., Fort Collins 80526

ITT Technical Institute
2121 S. Blackhawk St., Aurora 80014

Johnson & Wales University
616 W. Lionshead Cir., Vail 81657

LAMAR COMMUNITY COLLEGE
2401 S. Main St., Lamar 81052
719-336-2248

Lamar Colorado is located on the high plains of Colorado and has a population of 8,500.

President: Dr. Marvin Lane
Vice President of Instruction: Lauren Grasmick
Vice President of Business Services: Ron Dorn
Registrar: Dottie Matthew
Admissions Counselor: Beverly Carkhuff

Lamar Community College was established in 1937 and is a State of Colorado supported institution. Regionally accredited by North Central Association of Colleges and Schools. Coed educational with 50% men and 50% women students. 160 resident students in two residence halls. Tuition, Board and Room per semester for out of state students is approximately $4,756, and is subject to change. Typical total yearly expenses for out of state students will average $10,000. Colorado residents tuition averages $1,000 per semester. Two residence halls and dining hall provide living arrangements for nearly 160 students. Associate of Arts, Associate of Science and Associate of General Studies to transfer to four year colleges as well as numerous vocational programs for those wishing to enter the workplace after 1-2 years of study.

Admissions are open but students must be 16 years old with a high school diploma or GED certificate. Applications accepted up to twelfth day of each semester. Financial aid available only to US residents.

Small class size with a student/teacher ratio of 15:1, with great personal attention. Free tutoring lab available to all students.

Morgan Community College
17800 Road 20, Fort Morgan 80701
Kurtis Armstrong, Dir. of Admis.

Northeastern Junior College
100 College Ave., Sterling 80751
Dr. Henry Milander, President
Garnie Johnson, Director of Enrollment
Management

Otero Junior College
1802 Colorado Ave., La Junta 81050
Joe Treece, Dir. of Admissions

Parks College
9065 Grant St., Denver 80229
Randall C. Ricks, Dir. of Admis.
303-457-2757

PIKES PEAK COMMUNITY COLLEGE
5675 S. Academy Blvd.
Colorado Springs 80906-5498
Dr. Marijane Axtell Paulsen, President
Roberta Erickson, Dir. of Admis./Counseling
Established 1969. State funded & governed by State Board for Community Colleges and Occupational Education. Accreditation: NCACS.

Student body: 2,761 men, 4,069 women. Commuter campus with no boarding. Tuition and fees (actual 93-94): $628.50 per semester in-state, $2,488.50 per semester out-of-state.

Degrees: Associate degree, certificates awarded in more than 70 different areas through communications & humanities, mathematics & science, social sciences & education, business & office occupations, industrial & service occupations, and technical & health occupations. Classes are offered 6 days a week, day & night.

Open door policy admits all high school graduates & other persons with comparable qualifications as regular students. Other individuals who are at least 16 years old may also apply. Authorized under federal law to admit international & nonimmigrant alien students.

Scholarships: A variety of financial aid assistance plans are available to students in the form of scholarships, grants-in-aid, loans, and employment.

Faculty: 122 full-time, 304 part-time. Student-faculty ratio 19:1. Average class size: 17. Facilities: 212 acre campus with 3 buildings housing 82 classrooms & labs, learning resources center containing 36,000 volumes, a theatre, gym, day care center, eating facilities, bookstore, and a student center.

Environment: Located where the High Plains meet the Rocky Mountains at an altitude of 6,035 feet, Colorado Springs is a city with a climate that is semi-arid. Population of city: 281,000. Closest large city is Denver, Colorado.

Because of the city's proximity to the mountains, tourism plays an important part in its economy, but

Colorado Springs is increasingly shaped by high-technology industry and by the military. In or near the city are located Fort Carson, the U.S. Air Force Academy, Peterson Air Force Base, and the North American Aerospace Defense Command.

The United States Olympic Training Center is located near downtown Colorado Springs. Also, the Colorado Springs Fine Arts Center offers students numerous cultural opportunities. In addition, the acclaimed Pikes Peak Center Theater is located in downtown Colorado Springs and is home to the Colorado Springs Symphony Orchestra and the Music Theater of the Rockies. Major ski resorts are only two or three hours away by car.

Platt College
3100 S. Parker Rd., Aurora 80014
Jerald B. Sirbu, President

Pueblo Community College
900 W. Orman Ave., Pueblo 81004
Victor Tenorio, Dir. of Admis.

Red Rocks Community College
12600 W. 6th Ave., Golden 80401

Technical Trades Institute
2315 E. Pikes Peak Ave., Colorado Springs 80909
719-632-7626

Technical Trades Institute
722 Horizon Dr., Grand Junction 81506
719-245-8101

TRINIDAD STATE JUNIOR COLLEGE
600 Prospect St., Trinidad 81082
John Giron, Dir. of Admis.
719-846-5622
Established 1925. Public. Coed. Accreditation: NCACS, Colorado State Department of Education, NLN. Tuition: $1,164. Room and board: $3,598. Fees: $142.60. Enrollment: 1700. Faculty: 53. Student-faculty ratio: 20:1. Degrees: Certificate, AA, AAS, AGS, AS. Library: 65,000 volumes. 16 buildings on 17 acres. AAS in Gunsmithing, Certificate of Completion in Gun Repair.

CONNECTICUT

ASNUNTUCK COMMUNITY COLLEGE
170 Elm St., Enfield 06082
Vincent Fulginiti, Director of Admissions
203-253-3010

Briarwood College
2279 Mt. Vernon Rd., Southington 06489
Debra La Roche, Dir. of Admis.

Capital Community - Technical College
401 Flatbush Ave., Hartford 06106
Conrad L. Mallett, President

Greater Hartford Community College
61 Woodland St., Hartford 06105

Greater New Haven State Technical College
88 Bassett Rd., North Haven 06473
Chester Schnepf, Dir. of Admis.

Hartford College for Women
1265 Asylum Ave., Hartford 06105

Housatonic Community College
510 Barnum Ave., Bridgeport 06608
Stephen Serman, Dir. of Admissions

Katharine Gibbs School
142 East Ave., Norwalk 06851
Henry Mondschein, Dir. of Admis.

Manchester Community College
P.O. Box 1046, Manchester 06045
William E. Vincent, President

Mattatuck Community College
750 Chase Parkway, Waterbury 06708
Dr. Richard Sanders, President

Middlesex Community College
100 Training Hill Rd., Middletown 06457
Robert A. Chapman, President

Mitchell College
437 Pequot Ave., New London 06320
Kathleen Crowley, Dir. of Admis.

Mohegan Community College
21 Mahan Dr., Norwich 06360
Roland W. Wright, Act'g. Pres.

Mt. Sacred Heart College
265 Benham St., Hamden 06514
Sister M. Ursula, Dean

Northwestern Connecticut Community College
2 Park Pl., Winsted 06098
Dr. Regina M. Duffy, President

Norwalk Community College
188 Richards Ave., Norwalk 06854
William Schwab, President

Norwalk State Technical College
181 Richards Ave., Norwalk 06854
Vincent Grillo, Admissions Officer

Quinebaug Valley Community College
P.O. Box 59, Danielson 06239

South Central Community College
60 Sargent Dr., New Haven 06511
Dr. Antonio Perez, President

Thames Valley State Technical College
574 New London Trnpk., Norwich 06360

Tunxis Community College, Farmington 06032
Allen H. Premo, Dir., Admissions

University of Connecticut at Avery Point
Groton 06340

University of Connecticut at Hartford
1800 Asylum Ave., West Hartford 06117

University of Connecticut at Stamford
641 Scofieldtown Rd., Stamford 06903

University of Connecticut at Waterbury
32 Hillside Ave., Waterbury 06710

Waterbury State Technical College
750 Chase Pkwy., Waterbury 06708-3089

DELAWARE

Delaware Technical & Community College
1832 N. DuPont Hwy., Dover 19901
Dr. Linda Jolly, Campus Director

Delaware Technical & Community College
P.O. Box 610, Rt. 18, Georgetown 19947
Dr. John R. Kotula, President

Delaware Technical & Community College
400 Christiana Stanton Rd., Newark 19702
William Faucett, Director

Delaware Technical & Community College
333 Shipley St., Wilmington 19801
William Faucett, Director

FLORIDA

ATI Career Training Center
2880 W. Cypress Creek Rd., Fort Lauderdale 33309

Brevard Community College
1519 Clearlake Rd., Cocoa 32922
Maxwell C. King, President

Broward Community College
225 E. Las Olas Blvd., Ft. Lauderdale 33301

Broward Community College
225 E. Las Olas Blvd., Ft. Lauderdale 33301

Broward Community College-North Campus
1000 Coconut Creek Blvd., Coconut Creek 33066

Broward Community College-South Campus
7200 Pines Blvd.
Pembroke Pines 33024

Career City College
2400 S.W. 13th St., Gainesville 32608

Central Florida Community College
P.O. Box 1388, Ocala 34478
Casius Pealer, Dir. of Admis.

Chipola Junior College, Marianna 32446
Raymond M. Deming, President

Daytona Beach Community College
P.O. Box 2811, Daytona Beach 32120

Edison Community College
8099 College Pky., Fort Myers 33919
Mailing address: P.O. Box 60210
Fort Myers 33906-6210
Sandra Fahey, Dir. of Admis. and Records

Flagler Career Institute
3225 University Blvd., S., Jacksonville 32216

Florida College
119 N. Glen Arven Ave., Temple Terrace 33617
James R. Cope, President

Florida Community College at Jacksonville
Kent Campus
3939 Roosevelt Blvd., Jacksonville 32205

Florida Community College
501 State St., W., Jacksonville 32202
E. Guy Kerby, Dir. of Admis. and Student Aid

Florida Community College at Jacksonville
Downtown Campus
101 W. State St., Jacksonville 32202

Florida Community College at Jacksonville
North Campus
4501 Capper Rd., Jacksonville 32218

Florida Community College at Jacksonville
South Campus
11901 Beach Blvd., Jacksonville 32246

Florida Keys Community College
5901 College Rd., Key West 33040
Mitch Grabois, Director of Admissions
305-296-9081 Ext. 284

FLORIDA NATIONAL COLLEGE
4206 W. 12th Ave., Hialeah 33012
Belinda M. Gonzalez, Admissions Representative
305-821-3333
Established 1983. Private. Coed. Accreditation: SACS. Tuition: $4,950. Fees: $50. Enrollment: 1,000 full-time, 25 part-time. Faculty: 107. Student-faculty ratio: 10:1. Degrees: AS, Certificates, Diplomas. Library: 1,167 volumes. 3 buildings on 30,000 square foot campus. Three campuses (Miami, Hialeah, Coral Gables). Monday - Thursday classes only, 8:30 - 12:30 AM and 6:00 - 10:00 PM.

Full Sail Center for the Recording Arts
3300 University Blvd. #160, Winter Park 32792
407-679-0100 or 800-CAN-ROCK
See listing under "Career Schools"

Gulf Coast Community College
5230 Hwy. 98, W., Panama City 32401
Roy Smith, Dir. of Admis. and Records

Hillsborough Community College
1206 N. Park Rd., Plant City 33566

Hillsborough Community College at Brandon
1404 Tech Blvd., Tampa 33619

Hillsborough Community College
P.O. Box 30030, Tampa 33630

Hillsborough Community College
P.O. Box 31127, Tampa 33631
Andreas Paloumpls, President

Indian River Community College
3209 Virginia Ave., Fort Pierce 34981
Dr. Herman A. Heise, President

International Academy of Merchandising and Design
211 S. Hoover Blvd., Tampa 33609
Mike Santoro, President
813-286-8585

International Fine Arts College
1737 N. Bayshore Dr., Miami 33132
Frayda Parnes, Dir. of Admis.
800-225-9023 or 305-373-4684
See listing under "Art"

ITT Technical Institute
3401 S. University Dr.
Fort Lauderdale 33328

ITT Technical Institute
6600 Youngerman Circle Suite 10
Jacksonville 32244

ITT Technical Institute
4809 Memorial Hwy., Tampa 33634

ITT Technical Institute
2600 Lake Lucien Dr., #140, Maitland 32751

Johnson & Wales University
1701 N.E. 127th St.
North Miami 33181

Keiser College of Technology
1500 N.W. 49th St.,
Fort Lauderdale 33309

Keiser College of Technology
1605 E. Plaza Dr., Tallahassee 32308
Maura Freeberg, Director

Keiser College of Technology
701 S. Babcock St., Melbourne 32901

Lake City Community College
R.R. 3, Box 7, Lake City 32055

Lake-Sumter Community College
9501 S. Hwy. 441, Leesburg 34788

Manatee Community College
5840 26th St., W., Bradenton 34207

Martin College
1901 N.W. Seventh St., Miami 33125

Miami-Dade Community College
11380 N.W. 27th Ave., Miami 33167

Miami-Dade Community College
11011 S.W. 104 St., Miami 33176

Miami-Dade Community College
Medical Center Campus
950 N.W. 20th St., Miami 33127

National Education Center-Bauder Campus
7955 N.W. 12th St. #300, Miami 33126

National Education Center-Bauder Campus
4801 N. Dixie Hwy., Ft. Lauderdale 33334
Brian Woods, Dir. of Admis.
305-491-7171

National Education Center-Tampa Technical Institute
2410 E. Busch Blvd., Tampa 33612

New England Institute of Technology
1126 53rd Ct., West Palm Beach 33407

North Florida Junior College
1002 Turner Davis Dr., Madison 32340
Mildred Bruner, Dir. of Admis.

Okaloosa-Walton Community College
100 College Blvd., E., Niceville 32578
George Castle, Dir. of Admis.

Palm Beach Community College
4200 S. Congress Ave., Lake Worth 33461

Pasco-Hernando Community College
2401 State Hwy. 41, No., Dade City 33525
Milton O. Jones, President

Pasco-Hernando Community College
10239 Ridge Rd, New Port Richey 34654

Pensacola Junior College
1000 College Blvd., Pensacola 32504
Horace E. Hartsell, President

Phillips Junior College
2401 N. Harbor City Blvd., Melbourne 32935

Phillips Junior College
1491 S. Nova Rd., Daytona Beach 32114

PHOENIX COLLEGE OF AERONAUTICS
P.O. Box 11706, Daytona Beach 32120
Nino Ciancetta, Chairman
Steve Daun, President
Fred DeWitt, Vice President
William Olsen, Dean of Academics
904-253-4624
Coed. Enrollment: 250. Immigration Visa available. College offers four majors. AS degrees in aviation management, aviation maintenance management, air transport science, professional aeronautics. All courses taught by qualified faculty - no graduate students or teaching assistants. Calendar - quarter system, 11 weeks each. Average class size of 15. Classes geared toward realism and practical application. Aircraft include 12-C152'S, 12-C172'S, 6-Piper Warriors, 4-Single Engine Complex, 3-Piper Seminoles, 1-Piper Seneca, 1-Decathlon, 2-Single Engine Simulators, 2-Multi Engine Simulators, Turbo Prop Simulator, Boeing 727 Simulator.

Polk Community College
999 Ave. H, N.E., Winter Haven 33881
Marly Vanleer Peck, President

St. Johns River Community College
5001 St. Johns Ave., Palatka 32177
O'Neal Williams, Dean of Student Services

St. Petersburg Junior College
P.O. Box 13489, St. Petersburg 33733
Dr. Carl M. Kuttler, Jr., President

St. Petersburg Junior College
P.O. Box 1284, Terpon Springs 34688

Santa Fe Community College
3000 N.W. 83rd St., Gainesville 32606
Lawrence W. Tyree, President

Seminole Community College
100 Weldon Blvd., Sanford 32773

South College
1760 N. Congress Ave., West Palm Beach 33409

Southern College
5600 Lake Underhill Rd., Orlando 32807
Daniel F. Moore, President

South Florida Community College
600 W. College Dr., Avon Park 33825
William A. Stallard, President

Tallahassee Community College
444 Appleyard Dr., Tallahassee 32304
Dr. Fred W. Turner, President

Valencia Community College, West Campus
P.O. Box 3028, Orlando 32802
Charles H. Drosin, Registrar

Valencia Community College East Campus
701 N. Econlockhatchee Trl., Orlando 32825
Charles H. Drosin, Registrar

Van Dyck Institute of Tourism
1301 66th St. N., Saint Petersburg 33710
Claus Van Dyck, President

WARD STONE COLLEGE KENDALL CAMPUS
9020 S.W. 137th Ave., Miami 33186
Dr. Leo Orsino, President
305-386-9900, FAX 305-388-1740

Webster College
2002 N.W. 13th St., Gainesville 32609

Webster College
1530 S.W. 3rd Ave., Ocala 34474

Webster College
5623 U.S. Highway 19 #300
New Port Richey 34652

Webster College
2192 N. U.S. Highway 1, Fort Pierce 34946

West Virginia Career College
1104 Beville Rd. #J, Daytona Beach 32114

GEORGIA

Abraham Baldwin Agriculture College
P.O. Box 1, Tifton 31793

Andrew College, Cuthbert 31740
Ronald Devalinger, Dean of Admissions

Art Institute of Atlanta
3376 Peachtree Rd., N.E., Atlanta 30326
J. Robert Bouchard, Dir. of Admis.

Athens Area Technical Institute
U.S. Hwy. 29, N., Athens 30601

Atlanta Metro College
1630 Stewart Ave., S.W., Atlanta 30310
Edwin Thompson, President

Augusta Technical Institute
3116 Dean Bridge Rd., Augusta 30906

Bainbridge College
Hwy. 84, E., Bainbridge 31717
Edward D. Mobley, President

Bauder Fashion College
3500 Peachtree Rd., N.E., Atlanta 30326
404-237-7573 or 800-241-3797 (National)

Brunswick College
3700 Altama Ave., Brunswick 31520-3644
Dorothy L. Lord, President

Chattahoochee Technical Institute
980 S. Cobb Dr., Marietta 30060

Columbus Technical Institute
928 45th St., Columbus 31904

Dalton College
213 College Dr., Dalton 30720
Dr. Derrell Roberts, President

Darton College
2400 Gillionville Rd., Albany 31707

DeKalb College
3251 Panthersville Rd., Decatur 30034
Dr. Marvin Cole, President

DeKalb Technical Institute
495 N. Indian Creek Dr., Clarkston 30021
Velon Gray, Dir. of Admissions

East Georgia College
237 Thigpen Dr., Swainsboro 30401

Floyd College
P.O. Box 1864, Rome 30162
David B. McCorkle, President

GAINESVILLE COLLEGE
P.O. Box 1358, Gainesville 30503
Carol S. Nobles, Dir. of Admis.
404-535-6241

Georgia Military College
201 E. Green St., Milledgeville 31061
Major General Peter Boylan, President

Gordon College
419 College Dr., Barnesville 30204
Dr. M. Simmons, Director of Enrollment Services
404-358-5021, in GA 800-282-6504

Gupton-Jones College of Funeral Service
5141 Snapfinger Woods Dr., Decatur 30035-4022
Daniel Buchanan, President

Gwinnett Technical Institute
P.O. Box 1505, Lawrenceville 30246

Macon College
College Station Dr., Macon 31298
William W. Wright, President

Massey Business College
120 Ralph McGill Blvd., N.E., Atlanta 30308

Meadows College of Business
1170 Brown Ave., Columbus 31906

MIDDLE GEORGIA COLLEGE
Cochran 31014
Dr. Joe Welch, President
George Hinton, Dir. of Admis., Registrar
912-934-3103
Established 1884. Two-year unit of the University System of Georgia. Coed. Total enrollment: 2,024. Total charge boarding students: $1,246-$1,421 per quarter; out-of-state tuition $661 extra. Two-year college offering associate degree transfer and career programs. Transfer programs leading to degrees in liberal arts and sciences, engineering, mathematics, engineering technology, business administration, computer science, architecture, social sciences, education, home economics, journalism, music, agriculture and forestry. Preprofessional areas in law, medicine, veterinary medicine, pharmacy, dentistry, and allied health sciences. One-year and two-year career programs in fashion merchandising, criminal justice, business administration, data processing, public administration, nursing, library technology, and drafting and surveying.
Campus has 25 buildings on 160 acres; full intramural program plus intercollegiate teams in men's baseball, basketball, football and women's softball and tennis.
Admission: Based on high school grades and scores on SAT or ACT; early admission for exceptional students; developmental studies program available. Students admitted all quarters, including summer. Accredited by Southern Association of Colleges and Schools.
Financial aid includes grants, loans, scholarships, and work-study. Cooperative education program for engineering students.

Oxford College of Emory University
Oxford 30267

Phillips Junior College
1400 W. Peachtree St., N.W., Atlanta 30309

Reinhardt College
P.O. Box 128, Waleska 30183
C. Ray Tatum, Dir. of Admis.

Savannah Technical Institute
5717 White Bluff Rd., Savannah 31405

South College
709 Mall Blvd., Savannah 31406

South College
1015 Whitaker St., Savannah 31401

South Georgia College, Douglas 31533
John Wahl, Dir. of Admis.

Truett McConnell College, Cleveland 30528
Edna Holcomb, Registrar

Waycross College
2001 Francis St., Waycross 31503
Stephen Condon, Director/Student Services

Young Harris College
P.O. Box 98, Young Harris 30582
Thomas Yow, President
800-241-3754

HAWAII

Hawaii Community College
1175 Manono St., Hilo 96720

Heald Business College
1500 Kapiolani Blvd. #202, Honolulu 96814
Evelyn Schemmel, President
808-955-1500 Fax: 808-955-6964

Honolulu Community College
874 Dillingham Blvd., Honolulu 96817

Kansai Gaidai Hawaii College
5257 Kalanianaole Hwy., Honolulu 96821

Kapiolani Community College
4303 Diamond Head Rd., Honolulu 96816

Kauai Community College
3-1901 Kaumualii Hwy., Lihue 96766
Philip K. Palama, Admis. Ofc. & Reg.

Leeward Community College
96-045 Ala Ike, Pearl City 96782

Maui Community College
310 W. Kaahumanu Ave., Kahului 96732
Alma K. Cooper, Provost

Windward Community College
45-720 Keaahala Rd., Kaneohe 96744

IDAHO

College of Southern Idaho
P.O. Box 1238, Twin Falls 83303
Dr. John S. Martin, Dir. of Admis.

ITT Technical Institute
950 Lusk St., Boise 83706

North Idaho College
1000 W. Garden Ave., Coeur d'Alene 83814
M. Kirk Koenig, Dir. of Admis.

Ricks College, Rexburg 83460
Steven Bennion, President

ILLINOIS

American Academy of Art
332 S. Michigan Ave. 3rd Fl.
Chicago 60604

Belleville Area College
2500 Carlyle Rd., Belleville 62221

Black Hawk College, East Campus
P.O. Box 489, Kewanee 61443

Black Hawk College, Quad Cities Campus
6600 34th Ave., Moline 61265
Barton Schiermeyer, Dir. of Admis.

Carl Sandburg College
2232 S. Lake Storey Rd., Galesburg 61401

Chicago City-Wide College
226 W. Jackson Blvd., Chicago 60606

Chicago College of Commerce
11 E. Adams St., Chicago 60603

College of DuPage
425 22nd St., Glen Ellyn 60137
Harold D. McAninch, Dir. of Admis.

College of Lake County
19351 W. Washington St., Grayslake 60030
John O. Hunter, President

Danville Area Community College
2000 E. Main St., Danville 61832

Elgin Community College
1700 Spartan Dr., Elgin 60123

Frontier Community College
R.R. 1, Fairfield 62837

Gem City College
700 State St., Quincy 62301
R. Hagenah, President

Harold Washington College
30 E. Lake St., Chicago 60601
Salvatore G. Rotella, President

Harry S. Truman College
1145 W. Wilson Ave., Chicago 60640
Dr. Wallace B. Appelson, President

HIGHLAND COMMUNITY COLLEGE
2998 W. Pearl City Rd., Freeport 61032
Dr. Ruth Mercedes Smith, President
Karl J. Richards, Dir. of Admis.
815-235-6121
Established 1962. State. Coed. Accreditation: NCACS. Tuition: $1,050 resident, $3,990 non-resident. Enrollment: 930 day. Faculty: 44. Degrees: AA, AAS, AS, ABA, AGS. Library: 40,000 volumes. 11 buildings on 240 acres. Gym. Pool. Golf course nearby. One hour to 3 ski areas. 110 miles west of Chicago. Learning assistance center.

Illinois Central College
One College Dr., East Peoria 61635
Dr. Thomas K. Thomas, President

Illinois Valley Community College
R.R. 1, Oglesby 61348
Dr. Alfred Wisgoski, President

International Academy of Merchandising & Design
1 N. State St. Suite 400, Chicago 60602
Cynthia A. Reynolds, President
312-828-0422

ITT Technical Institute
375 W. Higgins Rd., Hoffman Estates 60195

John A. Logan College
R.R. 2, Carterville 62918
Dr. Ray Hancock, President

John Wood Community College
150 S. 48th St., Quincy 62301

Joliet Junior College
1216 Houbolt Dr., Joliet 60436
Dir. of Admis.

Kankakee Community College
P.O. Box 888, Kankakee 60901
Lilburn H. Horton, Jr., President

KASKASKIA COLLEGE
27210 College Rd., Centralia 62801
618-532-1981 or 800-642-0859 (Illinois)
Raymond D. Woods, President

Marilyn Brookman, PhD, College Dean
Constance Stohlman, Director of Admissions, Public Relations, and Resource Development
Kaskaskia College is situated on a beautifully wooded tract of land consisting of 190 acres. Its brick and frame buildings provide 228,830 square feet of space for college facilities. Kaskaskia College is fully accredited by NCACS, ADA, AMA, NLN, IBE, ICCB, and IBHE. The College is recognized and approved by the bureau of Veterans Affairs and is authorized under Federal law to enroll non-immigrant alien students. In district tuition and fees are $33.75 per semester credit hour. Degrees: AA, AS, AAS, and AGS. University transfer programs, pre-professional, liberal arts, courses offered days, evenings, and weekends. Training in career fields. State and Federal financial aid programs available.

Kennedy-King College
6800 S. Wentworth Ave., Chicago 60621
Ewen M. Aiken, President

Kishwaukee College
21193 Malta Rd., Malta 60150
Dr. Walter Lamar Fly, President

Lake Land College
5001 Lake Land Blvd., Mattoon 61938
Dr. David Schultz, President

Lewis & Clark Community College
5800 Godfrey Rd., Godfrey 62035
J. Neil Admire, President

Lexington Institute of Hostpitality Careers
10840 S. Western Ave., Chicago 60643

Lincoln College
300 Keokuk St., Lincoln 62656
Jack Nutt, President

Lincoln Land Community College
Shepherd Rd., Springfield 62794-9256
Ron Gregoire, Dir. of Admis.
Information: 800-727-4161

Lincoln Trail College
R.R. 3, Robinson 62454
Richard Sanders, President

MacCormac Junior College
506 S. Wabash Ave., Chicago 60605
John H. Allen, President

McHenry County College
6200 Northwest Hwy., Rm. 415
Crystal Lake 60014

Malcolm X College
1900 W. Van Buren St., Chicago 60612
Samuel Huffman, President

Midstate College
244 S.W. Jefferson St., Peoria 61602
R. Dale Bunch, President
309-673-6365

Montay College
3750 W. Peterson Ave., Chicago 60659
Scott Dalhouse, Dir. of Admis.

Moraine Valley Community College
10900 S. 88th Ave., Palos Hills 60465
Dr. Vernon Crawley, President

Morrison Institute of Technology
701 Portland Ave., Morrison 61270-2959
Dr. Dale Trimpe, Dir. of Admis.
See listing under "Career Schools"

Morton College
3801 S. Central Ave., Cicero 60650
Charles P. Ferro, President

Northwestern Business College
4829 N. Lipps, Chicago 60630

Northwestern Business College/Southwestern Campus
8020 W. 87th St., Hickory Hills 60457

Oakton Community College
1600 E. Golf Rd., Des Plaines 60016
Dr. Thomas TenHoeve, President

Olive-Harvey College
10001 S. Woodlawn Ave., Chicago 60628
James W. Moore, Dir. of Adm. & Rec.

Olney Central College
305 Northwest St., Olney 62450
Dr. Charles R. Novak, President

Parkland College
2400 W. Bradley Ave., Champaign 61821-1899
217-351-2208 or 800-346-8089

Prairie State College
P.O. Box 487, Chicago Heights 60411
Dr. Richard C. Creal, President

RAY COLLEGE OF DESIGN
AAS, BA, BFA degrees
401 N. Wabash Ave., Chicago 60611
312-280-3500
Woodfield Campus
1051 Perimeter Dr., Schaumburg 60173
708-619-3450

Rend Lake College, R.R. #1, Ina 62846
Dr. Harry Braun, President

Richard J. Daley College
7500 S. Pulaski Rd., Chicago 60652
William Conway, President

Richland Community College
One College Park, Decatur 62521
Dr. Charles Novak, President

Robert Morris College
43 Orland Square Dr., Orland Park 60462

Robert Morris College
3101 Montvale Dr., Springfield 62704

Rock Valley College
3301 N. Mulford Rd., Rockford 61114

St. Augustine College
1333 W. Argyle St., Chicago 60640

Sauk Valley Community College
R. R. 1, Dixon 61021
W. Harold Garner, President

Shawnee Community College
Shawnee College Rd., Ullin 62992
Pam Hodges, Dir. of Admis.

Southeastern Illinois College
R.R. 4 Box 510, Harrisburg 62946
Harry Abell, President

South Suburban College of Cook County
15800 State St., South Holland 60473

Spoon River College, R.R. 1, Canton 61520
Dr. Paul C. Gianini, President

Springfield College in Illinois
1500 N. Fifth St., Springfield 62702
Dr. H. Brent DeLand, President

State Community College of East St. Louis
601 James R. Thompson Rd., East St. Louis 62201
Dr. Rosetta Wheadon, President

TRITON COLLEGE
2000 N. 5th Ave., River Grove 60171
Gail Fuller, Director of Admission & Records
Established 1964. Coed. Tuition: $36.50 per semester hour. Est. total yrly. exp.: $1,282 for in district students. Enrollment: 18,000. Faculty: 1,500. Degrees: AA, AAS, AS. Library: 80,000 volumes. 18 buildings on 100+ acres. Training offered in over 84 career fields. University transfer program, pre-professional, liberal arts courses offered day and evening. State and federal financial programs available. Strong athletic program with excellent facilities. Rolling admissions.

Wabash Valley College
2222 College Dr., Mt. Carmel 62863

Waubonsee Community College
R.R. 47, Sugar Grove 60554
John Swalec, President

Wilbur Wright College North
4300 N. Narragansett Ave., Chicago 60634
312-794-3100

William Rainey Harper College
1200 W. Algonquin Rd., Palatine 60067

INDIANA

Ancilla Domini College, Donaldson 46513
Kathryn Castle, Dir. of Admis.
Judy Tulchinsky, Asst. Dir. of Admis.

Davenport College of Business
7121 Grape Rd., Granger 46530

Davenport College of Business
8200 Georgia St., Merrillville 46410

HOLY CROSS COLLEGE
P.O. Box 308, Notre Dame 46556
Vincent M. Duke, Director of Admissions
219-233-6813

Indiana Vocational Technical College (IVY)
P.O. Box 1763, Indianapolis 46206

International Business College
3811 Illinois Rd., Fort Wayne 46804

International Business College
7205 Shadeland Station, Indianapolis 46256

ITT Technical Institute
5115 Oak Grove Rd., Evansville 47715

ITT Technical Institute, Inc.
4919 Coldwater Rd., Fort Wayne 46825

ITT Technical Institute
9511 Angola Ct., Indianapolis 46268

Ivy Tech Central
1 W. 26th St., Indianapolis 46208
Meredith Carter, V.P., Dean

Ivy Tech Columbus
4475 Central Ave., Columbus 47203
Homer Smith, V.P., Dean

Ivy Tech East Central
P.O. Box 3100, Muncie 47307
Richard L. Davidson, V.P., Dean

Ivy Tech Kokomo
1815 E. Morgan St., Kokomo 46901
Charles Hefley, V.P., Dean

Ivy Tech Lafayette
P.O. Box 6299, Lafayette 47903
Thomas Reckerd, V.P., Dean

Ivy Tech Northcentral
1534 W. Sample St., South Bend 46619
Carl Lutz, V.P., Dean

Ivy Tech Northeast
3800 N. Anthony Blvd., Fort Wayne 46805
Jon Rupright, V.P., Dean

Ivy Tech Northwest
1440 E. 35th Ave., Gary 46409
Mearle Donica, Dean

Ivy Tech SouthCentral
8204 W. Hwy. 31, Sellersburg 47172
Jonothan Thomas, V.P., Dean

Ivy Tech Southeast
Highway 62 & Ivy Tech Drive, Madison 47250
Gregory Flood, V.P., Dean

Ivy Tech Southwest
3501 1st Ave., Evansville 47710
H. Victor Baldi, V.P., Dean

Ivy Tech Valparaiso
2401 Valley Dr., Valparaiso 46383

Ivy Tech Wabash Valley
7377 S. Dixie Bee Rd., Terre Haute 47802
Samuel Borden, V.P., Dean

Ivy Tech Whitewater
2325 Chester Blvd., Richmond 47374
Judith Redwine, V.P., Dean

LINCOLN TECHNICAL INSTITUTE
1201 Stadium Dr., Indianapolis 46202
Merlyn Cooper, Director
317-632-5553
Established 1946. Coed. Accredited Member School: ACCSCT. Providing technical training in: Automotive or Diesel Truck Technology, *Automotive or Diesel Truck Service and Management, *Architectural/Mechanical Drafting and CAD Technology. Financial aid for those who qualify. Employment assistance program. (*Associate of Applied Science Degree).

Michiana College
1030 E. Jefferson Blvd., South Bend 46617
Philip Heine, Director
800-743-2447

Michiana College
4807 Illinois Rd., Fort Wayne 46804
Anthony Conti, Director
800-743-2447

Mid-America College of Funeral Service
3111 Hamburg Pike, Jeffersonville 47130
Pauline R. Cooper, Registrar

Vincennes University
1002 N. 1st St., Vincennes 47591

IOWA

American Institute of Business
2500 Fleur Dr., Des Moines 50321
Tom Shively, Dir. of Admis.

American Institute of Commerce
1801 E. Kimberly Rd., Davenport 52807
John Huston, President
319-355-3500

Clinton Community College
1000 Lincoln Blvd., Clinton 52732
Dr. Desna Wallin, President

Des Moines Area Community College
2006 S. Ankeny Blvd., Ankeny 50021
James Frazee, Dir. of Admissions

Des Moines Area Community College-Carroll Campus
906 N. Grant Rd., Carroll 51401

Des Moines Area Community College
1125 Hancock Dr., Boone 50036
Byron Hamilton, Dean

Des Moines Area Community College
1107 7th St., Des Moines 50314
Zack Hamlett, Dean

Ellsworth Community College
1100 College Ave., Iowa Falls 50126
Duane Lloyd, Dean
800-322-9235

Hamilton Technical College
1011 E. 53rd St., Davenport 52807
Maryanne Hamilton, Director
See listing under "Career Schools"

Hawkeye Community College
1501 E. Orange Rd., Waterloo 50701
319-296-2320 Ext. 4000

Indian Hills Community College
721 N. 1st St., Centerville 52544
515-856-2143

Indian Hills Community College
525 Grandview, Ottumwa 52501
515-683-5111

Iowa Central Community College
316 N.W. 3rd St., Eagle Grove 50533

Iowa Central Community College
330 Avenue M, Fort Dodge 50501
Dale Daggy, Dir. of Admis.

Iowa Central Community College
916 Russell St., Storm Lake 50588

Iowa Central Community College
1725 Beach St., Webster City 50595

Iowa Lakes Community College
3200 College Dr., Emmetsburg 50536
John Nelson, Dir. of Admis.
712-852-3554

Iowa Lakes Community College
300 S. 18th St., Estherville 51334
John Nelson, Dir. of Admis.
712-362-2604

Iowa Western Community College
923 E. Washington St., Clarinda 51632
712-542-5117 or in IA 800-521-2073

Iowa Western Community College
2700 College Rd., Council Bluffs 51503
Thomas Dutch, Dir. of Admis.

KIRKWOOD COMMUNITY COLLEGE
P.O. Box 2068, Cedar Rapids 52406
Jim Miller, Dir. of Admis.
319-398-5517

Marshalltown Community College
P.O. Box 536, Marshalltown 50158

Muscatine Community College
152 Colorado St., Muscatine 52761

NEC-National Institute of Technology
1119 5th St., West Des Moines 50265

Northeast Iowa Technical Institute
P.O. Box 400, Calmar 52132
Clyde Kramer, Superintendent

Northeast Iowa Technical Institute
R.R. 1, Peosta 52068
Donald Roby, Ass't. Supt.

North Iowa Area Community College
500 College Dr., Mason City 50401
Tom Dunn, Enrollment Specialist

Northwest Iowa Community College
603 W. Park St., Sheldon 51201
712-324-5061

SCOTT COMMUNITY COLLEGE
500 Belmont Rd., Bettendorf 52722
Kris Barkdoll, Assoc. Dean Enrollment Management

Southeastern Community College
P.O. Box 27, Keokuk 52632
John Adkins, Director

Southeastern Community College
P.O. Box F., West Burlington 52655
Edward Schieffer, Director

Southwestern Community College
1501 W. Townline St., Creston 50801
Dr. Richard Byerly, Superintendent
515-782-7081

Waldorf College
106 S. 6th St., Forest City 50436
Steve Lovik, Dir. of Admis.
800-292-1903

Western Iowa Technical Community College
724 N. 1st St., Cherokee 51012

Western Iowa Technical Community College
P.O. Box 265, Sioux City 51102
R. H. Kiser, Supt.

KANSAS

Allen County Community College
1801 N. Cottonwood St., Iola 66749
Dr. Bill R. Spencer, President

Barton County Community College
R.R. 3, Box 136Z, Great Bend 67530
Dr. Jim Downing, President

Barton County Community College
P.O. Box 223, Junction City 66441

Barton County Community College
2210 Canterbury Dr., Hays 67601

Brown-Mackie College
126 S. Santa Fe, Salina 67401

Butler County Community College
901 S. Haverhill Rd., El Dorado 67042
Dr. Carl Heinrich, President

Central College
1200 S. Main St., McPherson 67460
Greg Gossell, Dir. of Admis.

Cloud County Community College
P.O. Box 1002, Concordia 66901
James P. Ihrig, President

Coffeyville Community College
402 W. 11th St., Coffeyville 67337
Helen Ellerman, Dir. of Admis.

COLBY COMMUNITY COLLEGE
1255 S. Range Ave., Colby 67701
Theron Johnson, Dir. of Admis.

Cowley County Community College
P.O. Box 1147, Arkansas City 67005
Maggie Picking, Dir. of Admis.

Dodge City Community College
2501 N. 14th Ave., Dodge City 67801
Debbie Lloyd, Director of Admissions
800-FOR-DCCC

Donnelly College
608 N. 18th St., Kansas City 66102
Sandra Brown, Dir. of Admis.

Ft. Scott Community College
2108 S. Horton St., Fort Scott 66701
Robert Hood, Adm. & Records

Garden City Community College
801 Campus Dr., Garden City 67846
Beth Tedrow, Dir. of Admis.

Haskell Indian Junior College
155 Indian Ave. #1305, Lawrence 66046
Gerald Gipp, President

Hesston College
P.O. Box 3000, Hesston 67062

Highland Community College
P.O. Box 68, Highland 66035
Dr. Eric Priest, President

Hutchinson Community College
1300 N. Plum St., Hutchinson 67501
Duane Halpain, Dir. of Admis.

Independence Community College
P.O. Box 708, Independence 67301
Don Schoening, President

Johnson County Community College
12345 College Blvd., Overland Park 66210
Pat Long, Dir. of Admis.

Kansas City Kansas Community College
7250 State Ave., Kansas City 66112
Don Stump, Dir. of Admis.

Kansas State University
College of Technology
2409 Scanlan Ave., Salina 67401

Labette Community College
200 S. 14th St., Parsons 67357
Dr. Bob C. Burns, Dean of Instr.

Neosho County Community College
1000 S. Allen Ave., Chanute 66720
Dr. George VanAllen, President

Pratt Community College
Hwy. 61, Pratt 67124
Ray O. McKinney, Dir. Admis.

Seward County Community College
P.O. Box 1137, Liberal 67905
316-624-1951

KENTUCKY

Ashland Community College
1400 College Dr., Ashland 41101
R. L. Goodpaster, Dir.

CareerCom Junior College of Business
1102 S. Virginia, Hopkinsville 42240

College of Merchandising Design
3901 Atkinson Dr., Louisville 40218

Elizabethtown Community College
600 College Street Rd., Elizabethtown 42701

Fugazzi College
406 Lafayette Ave., Lexington 40502
606-266-0401

Hazard Community College
1 Community College Dr., Hazard 41701
J. Marvin Jolly, Director

Henderson Community College
2660 S. Green St., Henderson 42420
Marshall Arnold, Director

Hopkinsville Community College
P.O. Box 2100, Hopkinsville 42241
Thomas L. Riley, Director

Institute of Electronic Technology
509 S. 30th St., Paducah 42001
800-995-4438

Jefferson Community College
109 E. Broadway, Louisville 40202
Ronald Horvath, Director

Kentucky College of Business
7627 Tanners Ln., Florence 41042
606-525-6510

Kentucky College of Business
628 E. Main St., Lexington 40508
606-253-0621

Kentucky College of Business
198 S. Mayo Trl., Pikeville 41501
606-432-5477

Kentucky College of Business
115 E. Lexington Ave., Danville 40422
606-236-6991

Kentucky College of Business
139 S. Killarney Ln., Richmond 40475
606-623-8956

Kentucky College of Business
3950 Dixie Hwy., Louisville 40216
502-447-7634

Kentucky Mountain Bible College
P.O. Box 10, Vancleve 41385

Lees College
601 Jefferson Ave., Jackson 41339
Troy R. Eslinger, President

Lexington Community College
Oswald Bldg., Cooper Dr., Lexington 40506
Dr. Sharon Jaggard, Director

Louisville Technical Institute
3901 Atkinson Dr., Louisville 40218
George Nunley, Dir. of Admis.

Madisonville Community College
2000 College Dr., Madisonville 42431
Arthur D. Stumpf, Director

Maysville Community College, Maysville 41056
James Shires, President

National Education Center-Kentucky College
Technical Campus
300 High Rise Dr., Louisville 40213

Owensboro Community College
4800 New Hartford Rd., Owensboro 42303

Owensboro Junior College of Business
1515 E. 18th St., Owensboro 42303
W. Shane Wilson, Dir. of Admis.

Paducah Community College
P.O. Box 7380, Paducah 42002
Dr. Donald J. Clemens, Dir.

Prestonsburg Community College
1 Bert T. Combs Dr., Prestonsburg 41653
Henry A. Campbell, Jr., Director

RETS Electronics Institute
4146 Outer Loop, Louisville 40219

St. Catharine College
Hwy. 150, St. Catharine 40061
Frank Sallee, Dir. of Admis.

Somerset Community College
808 Montecello St., Somerset 42501
R. C. Kelley, Director

Southeast Community College
300 College Rd., Cumberland 40823
J. Bruce Wilson, Director

Southern Ohio College
309 Buttermilk Pike, Fort Mitchell 41017

Sue Bennett College
101 College St., London 40741
Don A. Gorbandt, Dir. of Admis.

Sullivan College
N. Iroquois, Bldg. 6683, Fort Knox 40121

LOUISIANA

Baton Rouge School of Computers
9255 Interline Ave., Baton Rouge 70809

Bossier Parish Community College
2719 Airline Dr., Bossier City 71111
Mrs. Faye Powell, Registrar

Delgado Community College
501 City Park Ave., New Orleans 70119
Dr. Carmen Smith, Director of Admissions

Delta Junior College
7290 Exchange Pl., Baton Rouge 70806
511 Westbank Expressway, Gretna 70053
3321 Hessmer Ave., Metairie 70002
Billy B. Clark, President

Delta Junior College
100 Covington Centre Suite 30
Covington 70433

Delta School of Business and Technology
517 Broad St., Lake Charles 70601
Gary Holt, President

International Technical Institute
13944 Airline Hwy., Baton Rouge 70817

Louisiana State University at Alexandria
8100 Hwy. 71, Alexandria 71302
Dr. Fred Beckerdite, Acting Chancellor

Louisiana State University at Eunice
P.O. Box 1129, Eunice 70535

Nunez Community College
3700 La Fontaine St., Chalmette 70043

Phillips Junior College
822 S. Clearview Pky., New Orleans 70123
Jerry Adams, Director

RETS Training Center
3321 Hessmer Ave. #301, Metairie 70002

St. Bernard Parish Community College
2500 Palmisano Blvd., Chalmette 70043
Harold J. Clavier, Director

Southern University
Shreveport-Bossier City Campus
3050 M. L. King Dr., Shreveport 71107
Clifton Jones, Registrar

MAINE

Andover College
901 Washington Ave., Portland 04103
Sheri H. Leavitt, Dir. of Admis.
207-774-6126

Beal College, 629 Main St., Bangor 04401

Casco Bay College, 477 Congress St., Portland 04101

Central Maine Technical College
1250 Turner St., Auburn 04210
Dr. William J. Hierstein, President

Eastern Maine Technical College
354 Hogan Rd., Bangor 04401

Kennebec Valley Technical College
92 Western Ave., Fairfield 04937
Barbara Woodlee, Director

Mid-State College
88 Hardscrabble Rd., Auburn 04210
Robinson Whitney, President

Mid-State College
218 Water St., Augusta 04330

Northern Maine Technical College
33 Edgemont Dr., Presque Isle 04769

Southern Maine Technical College
2 Fort Rd., South Portland 04106
See listing under "Career Schools"

Washington County Technical College
R.R. 1 Box 22C, Calais 04619
Ronald Renaud, President
207-454-2144

MARYLAND

Allegany Community College
12401 Willowbrook Rd., Cumberland 21502
W. Ardell Haines, President

Anne Arundel Community College
101 College Pky., Arnold 21012
Herbert Curkin, Dir. of Admis.

Baltimore International Culinary College
17 Commerce St., Baltimore 21202

Carroll Community College
1601 Washington Rd., Westminister 21157
410-876-9600

Catonsville Community College
800 S. Rolling Rd., Catonsville 21228
Frederick J. Walsh, President

Cecil Community College
1000 North East Rd., North East 21901

Charles County Community College
P.O. Box 910, La Plata 20646

Chesapeake College
P.O. Box 8, Wye Mills 21679

Community College of Baltimore
2901 Liberty Heights Ave., Baltimore 21215
Joseph Stein, Director of Admissions

Community College of Baltimore
600 E. Lombard St., Baltimore 21202

Dundalk Community College
7200 Sollers Point Rd., Baltimore 21222
Karen McKenney, Dir. of Admis.

Essex Community College
7201 Rossville Blvd., Baltimore 21237
Diane Lane, Dir. of Admis.

Frederick Community College
7932 Opossumtown Pike, Frederick 21702
James Holton, Dir. of Admis. & Records

Garrett Community College
Mosser Rd., McHenry 21541

HAGERSTOWN BUSINESS COLLEGE

18618 Crestwood Dr., Hagerstown 21742
Jim Gifford, President
Teresa Adams, Dir. of Admis.
800-HBC-2670
Established 1938. Coed. Accreditation: ACICS, Maryland State Board of Higher Education. Tuition: $3,840. Room: $1,900. Enrollment: 24 boarding, 487 day. Faculty: 35. Degrees: certificates, AAS. Library: 3,475 volumes. 2 buildings on 7-1/2 acres. Special emphasis on business administration and secretarial science programs including office technologies, court reporting, and specialization in the fields of medicine and law. Equidistant (65 miles) from Washington, DC and Baltimore, Maryland.

Hagerstown Junior College
11400 Robinwood Dr., Hagerstown 21742
Atlee C. Kepler, President

Harford Community College
401 Thomas Run Rd., Bel Air 21015
Richard Pappas, President

Howard Community College
10901 Little Patuxent Pky., Columbia 21044
Dwight Burrill, President
410-992-4800

Maryland College of Art & Design
10500 Georgia Ave., Silver Spring 20902

Montgomery College
20200 Observation Dr., Germantown 20876
301-353-7700

Montgomery College
51 Mannakee St., Rockville 20850
301-279-5000

Montgomery College
7600 Takoma Ave., Takoma Park 20912
301-650-1500

Prince George's Community College
301 Largo Rd., Largo 20772
Leon Weaver, Dir. of Admis. & Test.

RETS Tech Training Center
1520 S. Caton Ave., Baltimore 21227-1063
H. V. Leslie, President
See listing under "Career Schools"

Wor-Wic Technical Community College
30 Wesley Dr., Salisbury 21801

MASSACHUSETTS

Allstate Institute of Technology
165 Front St., Door D, 5th Flr
Chicopee 01013

Aquinas College
15 Walnut Park, Newton 02158
Ellen Ronayne, Dir. of Admis.

Aquinas College at Milton
303 Adams St., Milton 02186
617-696-3100

Bay State College
122 Commonwealth Ave., Boston 02116

Becker College
3 Paxton St., Leicester 01524
Thomas Redman, Dean of Admis.

Becker College
61 Sever St., Worcester 01609
Arnold Weccer, Jr., President

Berkshire Community College
1350 West St., Pittsfield 01201
Adrienne A. Rulnick, Dir. of Admissions

Bristol Community College
777 Elsbree St., Fall River 02720
Frank Noble, Dir. of Admis.

Bunker Hill Community College
New Rutherford Ave., Boston 02129
Janice M. Bonanno, Dir. of Admis.

Cape Cod Community College
2240 Rt. 132, West Barnstable 02668
Philip Day, President

DEAN COLLEGE

99 Main St., Franklin 02038
Kathleen Teehan, Dean of Admissions
508-528-9100
Established 1865. Private. Coed. Accreditation: NEASC. Tuition: $10,455. Room and board: $6,000. Enrollment: 800 boarding, 200 day. Faculty: 45. Degrees: AA, AS. Library: 55,000 volumes. 36 buildings on 100 acres. 2 gyms. Pool.

Endicott College
376 Hale St., Beverly 01915
Elizabeth Macomber, Dir. of Admis.

Fisher College
118 Beacon St., Boston 02116
Sandra Robbins, Dir. of Admis.

Franklin Institute of Boston
41 Berkeley St., Boston 02116
Richard P. D'Onofrio, President
617-423-4630
See listing under "Engineering"

Greenfield Community College
1 College Dr., Greenfield 01301
Donald Brown, Dir. of Admis.

Hickox School, 200 Tremont St., Boston 02116
S. Arthur Verenis, President

Holyoke Community College
303 Homestead Ave., Holyoke 01040
George E. Frost, President

Katharine Gibbs School
126 Newbury St., Boston 02116

Laboure College
2120 Dorchester Ave., Boston 02124
Lianne Sullivan, Dir. of Admis.

Lasell College
1844 Commonwealth Ave., Newton 02166

MARIAN COURT COLLEGE

35 Little's Point Rd., Swampscott 01907
Jodi T. Quinn, Dir. of Admis.
617-595-6768

Massachusetts Bay Community College
50 Oakland St., Wellesley 02181

Massasoit Community College
1 Massasoit Blvd., Brockton 02402
Roberta Noodell, Dir. of Admis.

Middlesex Community College
Springs Rd., Bedford 01730
617-280-3200

Middlesex Community College
33 Kearney Sq., Lowell 01852
508-656-3211

Mt. Wachusett Community College
444 Green St., Gardner 01440
Sidney Goldfader, Dir. of Admis.

Newbury College
129 Fisher Ave., Brookline 02146
Judy LeGraw, Dir. of Admis.

New England Banking Institute
89 South St., Boston 02111

Northern Essex Community College
100 Elliott St., Haverhill 01830

North Shore Community College
1 Ferncroft Rd., Danvers 01923

Quincy Junior College
34 Coddington St., Quincy 02169
Richard Pessin, Dean of Enrollment Services

Quinsigamond Community College
670 W. Boylston St., Worcester 01606
Ron Smith, Dir. of Admis.

ROXBURY COMMUNITY COLLEGE

1234 Columbus Ave., Roxbury Crossin 02120
Michael Rice, Dir. of Admissions
617-541-5310
Established 1973. Public. Coed. Accreditation: NEASC. Tuition: $480 in state, $2,256 out of state. Fees: $950. Application fee: $10 in state, $35 out of state. Enrollment: 2,500. Faculty: 165. Student-faculty ratio: 14:1. Degrees offered: AA, AS. 4 buildings on 12.3 acre urban campus.
Member NJCAA, Women's basketball, track and field, men's basketball, track and field, soccer. Support services available, ESL coursework, GED preparatory courses and testing.

SPRINGFIELD TECHNICAL COMMUNITY COLLEGE

1 Armory Square, Springfield 01105
Dr. Patrick E. Tigue, Dir. of Admissions
413-781-7822

MICHIGAN

Alpena Community College
666 Johnson St., Alpena 49707

Bay de Noc Community College
2001 N. Lincoln Rd., Escanaba 49829
Dr. Richard L. Rinehart, President

Delta College, University Center 48710
Robert Cabello, VP of Student Services

Ford Community College
5101 Evergreen Rd., Dearborn 48128
James O. McCann, President

Glen Oaks Community College
62249 Shimmel Rd., Centreville 49032
Philip G. Ward, President

Gogebic Community College
E4946 Jackson Rd, Ironwood 49938
Steven Wesselhoft, Dean of Students

Grand Rapids Community College
143 Bostwick Ave., N.E., Grand Rapids 49503
Dr. Madalyn Binger, Provost

Great Lakes Junior College of Business
310 S. Washington Ave., Saginaw 48607
Angelo Guerriero, President

Great Lakes Junior College of Business
3930 Traxler Ct., Bay City 48706

Great Lakes Junior College of Business
1231 Cleavor Rd., Caro 48723

Great Lakes Junior College of Business
150 Nugent Rd., Bad Axe 48413

Great Lakes Junior College of Business
3555 E. Patrick Rd., Midland 48642

Highland Park Community College
12541 2nd Ave., Highland Park 48203
Ameenah Omar, Dean of Student Services

ITT TECHNICAL INSTITUTE
1225 E. Big Beaver Rd., Troy 48083
Robert Martin, Director
810-524-1800

Jackson Community College
2111 Emmons Rd., Jackson 49201
Mark Ulseth, Dir. Enrollment Services

Kalamazoo Valley Community College
6767 W. O Ave., Kalamazoo 49009
Marilyn Schlack, President

Kellogg Community College
450 North Ave., Battle Creek 49017
Richard F. Whitmore, President

Kirtland Community College
10775 St. Helen Rd. F-97, Roscommon 48653

Lake Michigan College
2755 E. Napier, Benton Harbor 49022
Rentzell Cleaveland, Jr., Registrar

Lansing Community College
521 Washington Square N., Lansing 48933

Lewis College of Business
17370 Meyers Rd., Detroit 48235
K. Frank DeShazok, Dir. of Admis.
313-862-6300

Macomb Community College
16500 Hall Rd., Clinton Twp. 48038

Macomb Community College
14500 E. 12 Mile Rd., Warren 48093

Mid Michigan Community College
1375 S. Clare Ave., Harrison 48625
Eugene Schorzmann, President

Monroe County Community College
1555 Raisinville S., Monroe 48161
Gerald Welch, President

Montcalm Community College
2800 College Dr., Sidney 48885

Mott Community College
1401 E. Court St., Flint 48503
Earl L. Mahoney, Dir. of Admissions

Muskegon Community College
221 Quarterline Rd., S., Muskegon 49442
John G. Thompson, President

North Central Michigan College
1515 Howard St., Petosky 49770

Northwestern Michigan College
1701 E. Front St., Traverse City 49686
Robert Warner, Dir Admis./Financial Aid
800-748-0566

Oakland Community College, Auburn Hills Campus
2900 Featherstone Rd., Auburn Hills 48326

Oakland Community College
2480 Opdyke Rd., Bloomfield Hills 48304

Oakland Community College, Southeast Campus
Royal Oak 48073

Oakland Community College
7350 Cooley Lake Rd., Union Lake 48387

Oakland Community College-Orchard Ridge Campus
27055 Orchard Lake Rd.
Farmington Hills 48334

St. Clair County Community College
323 Erie Street, Port Huron 48060
Earle Richardson, Dir. Admissions

Schoolcraft College
18600 Haggerty Rd., Livonia 48152
Barbara A. Geil, Dir. of Admissions

Southwestern Michigan College
58900 Cherry Grove Rd., Dowagiac 49047
David Schultz, VP for Student Services
616-782-5113

Suomi College
A two year Private College
601 Quincy St., Hancock 49930
John Ruohoniemi, Dean/Enrollment Development
800-682-7604

Washtenaw Community College
4800 E. Huron River Dr., Ann Arbor 48105

Wayne County Community College
801 Fort St., W., Detroit 48226

West Shore Community College
P.O. Box 277, Scottville 49454
Gregory J. Hartzog, Dir. of Admis.

MINNESOTA

ACADEMY OF ACCOUNTANCY
3050 Metro Dr. #200, Bloomington 55425
Gary McNulty, Director of Admissions
612-851-0066

ACADEMY OF AVIATION
3050 Metro Dr. #200, Minneapolis 55425
Gary McNulty, Director of Admissions
612-851-0066

Alexandria Technical College
1601 Jefferson St., Alexandria 56308

Anoka-Ramsey Community College
11200 Mississippi Blvd., N.W.
Coon Rapids 55433
Irene Campanaro, Dir. Student Services
612-427-2600

Anoka-Ramsey Community College
W. Highway 95, Cambridge 55008
Carlyle Davidsen, Dean of College
612-422-3456

Austin Community College
1600 8th Ave., N.W., Austin 55912
Barbara Orcutt, Admissions
507-433-0517

Aviation Training Academy
3050 Metro Dr. #200, Minneapolis 55425

Bethany Lutheran College
734 Marsh St., Mankato 56001
Steven Jaeger, Dir. of Admis.
507-625-2977

Brainerd Community College
501 W College Dr., Brainerd 56401
Sally Ihne, President

CDI COMPUTERS - ACADEMY
3050 Metro Dr. #200, Minneapolis 55425
Gary McNulty, Director of Admissions
612-851-0066

Dakota County Technical College
1300 E. 145th St., Rosemount 55068

Dunwoody Institute
818 Dunwoody Blvd., Minneapolis 55403
Bernie Morgan, Director of Admissions
See listing under "Career Schools"

Fergus Falls Community College
1414 College Way, Fergus Falls 56537
Wesley A. Waage, President

Hibbing Community College
1515 E. 25th St., Hibbing 55746
Orville Olson, Provost

Inver Hills Community College
8445 College Trail, E., Inver Grove Heights 55076
Cheryl Frank, Director

ITASCA COMMUNITY COLLEGE
1851 E. Highway 169, Grand Rapids 55744
218-327-4460

Lakewood Community College
3401 Century Ave., White Bear Lake 55110
Dr. Neil Christenson, President

Mesabi Community College
210 N. 9th Ave., Virginia 55792
Richard Kohlhase, Provost
218-749-7700

Minneapolis Community College
1501 Hennepin Ave., Minneapolis 55403-1779
Bonnie Wiger, Registrar
612-341-7000

National Education Center-Brown Institute Campus
2225 E. Lake St., Minneapolis 55407
Rick Simmons, Director of Admissions

NEI COLLEGE OF TECHNOLOGY
825 41st Ave. N.E., Minneapolis 55421
Richard Thomson, Dir. of Admis.
Call 800-777-7NEI for Info.
See listing under "Career Schools"

Normandale Community College
9700 France Ave., S., Bloomington 55431
Thomas Horak, President

North Hennepin Community College
7411 85th Ave., N., Brooklyn Park 55445
Dr. John Helling, President

Northland Community College
Hwy. 1, E., Thief River Falls 56701
Dennis Bendickson, Registrar
800-628-9918

Northwest Technical Institute
11995 Singletree Ln., Eden Prairie 55344
Norris Nelson, President
800-443-4223

Rainy River Community College
International Falls 56649

Rochester Community College
851 30th Ave. S.E., Rochester 55904
Charles E. Hill, President

St. Cloud Technical College
1540 Northway Dr., Saint Cloud 56303
612-252-0101

St. Mary's Campus of the College of St. Catherine
2500 6th St., S., Minneapolis 55454
Pamela Johnson, Dir. of Admis.

St. Paul Technical College
235 Marshall Ave., Saint Paul 55102

UNIVERSITY OF MINNESOTA-CROOKSTON
2900 University Ave., Crookston 56716
Donald Sargeant, Chancellor
800-232-6466
See listing under "Universities"

Vermilion Community College
1900 E. Camp., Ely 55731

Willmar Community College
P.O. Box 797, Willmar 56201
Arlen Sjervan, Director of Admissions
612-231-5199

Willmar Technical Institute
P.O. Box 1097, Willmar 56201

WORTHINGTON COMMUNITY COLLEGE
1450 College Way, Worthington 56187
Conrad Burchill, President
507-372-2107

MISSISSIPPI

Coahoma Community College
Rt. 1, Box 616, Clarksdale 38614
James E. Miller, President

Copiah-Lincoln Community College
P.O. Box 457, Wesson 39191
J. M. Lewis, Dir. of Admis.

East Central Community College
P.O. Box 129, Decatur 39327
Ed Smith, President

East Mississippi Community College
P.O. Box 158, Scooba 39358

Hinds Community College, Raymond 39154

Hinds Community College
1750 Chadwick Dr., Jackson 39204

Hinds Community College
755 Highway 27, Vicksburg 39180
Joseph L. Loviza, Director

Holmes Community College
P.O. Box 369, Goodman 39079
William H. Burch, Jr., Registrar

Itawamba Community College
Hwy. 78, Fulton 38843
Carl C. Comer, Dir. of Admis.

Jones County Junior College, Ellisville 39437
Jimmy Temple, Registrar

Mary Holmes College
P.O. Box 1257, West Point 39773
Joseph A. Gore, President

Meridian Community College
910 Hwy. 19, N., Meridian 39307

Mississippi Delta Community College
P.O. Box 668, Moorhead 38761
J. T. Hall, President

Mississippi Gulf Coast Community College
Perkinston Campus
P.O. Box 67, Perkinston 39573

Mississippi Gulf Coast Community College
Gulfport 39507

Mississippi Gulf Coast Community College
Gautier 39553

Northeast Mississippi Community College
101 Cunningham Blvd., Booneville 38829

Northwest Mississippi Community College
510 N. Panola, Senatobia 38668
Henry B. Koon, President

Northwest Mississippi Community College
Desoto Center, Southaven 38671

Pearl River Community College, Poplarville 39470
Dr. Marvin R. White, President

Phillips Junior College
2680 Insurance Center Dr., Jackson 39216
Dan Holder, Dir. of Admis.

Southwest Mississippi Community College
Summit 39666
Charles Breeland, Registrar

Wood College
P.O. Box 289, Mathiston 39752

MISSOURI

Basic Institute of Technology
4455 Chippewa St., St. Louis 63116

Cottey College
1000 W. Austin St., Nevada 64772
Wendy Beckemeyer, Dir. of Admis.

CROWDER COLLEGE
601 Laclede, Neosho 64850
Dr. Kent Farnsworth, President
Cecilia Morris, Dean of Students
417-451-3223
Established 1963. Public. Coed. Accreditation: NCACS, Missouri State Board of Education. Enrollment: 240 boarding, 1,850 day. Faculty: 100. Degrees: 1 year certificates, AA, AS, AAS. Library: 32,000 volumes. 8 buildings on 600 acres. Gym. Programs in the arts, sciences, and vocational-technical are available. Special programs: water/wastewater, truck driver, hazardous materials, and alternative energy technology. Nationally ranked athletic teams.

East Central College
P.O. Box 529, Union 63084
Dale Gibson, President

Electronic Institutes
15329 Kensington Ave., Kansas City 64147

ITT Technical Institute
13505 Lakefront Dr., Earth City 63045

Jefferson College
1000 Viking Dr., Hillsboro 63050
Dr. Gery Hochanadel, President

Kemper Military School & College
701 3rd St., Boonville 65233
Dr. C.W. Stewart, President
800-530-5600

Longview Community College
500 Longview Rd., Lee's Summit 64081
Aldo Leker, President
816-672-2000

Maple Woods Community College
2601 N.E. Barry Rd., Kansas City 64156

Mineral Area College, Flat River 63601
Richard Caster, President

Missouri School for Doctors' Assistants
10121 Manchester Rd., St. Louis 63122

Missouri Technical School
1167 Corporate Lake Dr., Saint Louis 63132

Moberly Area Community College
College and Rollins St., Moberly 65270
Dr. Andrew Komar, President

North Central Missouri College
1301 Main St., Trenton 64683
James Selby, President
816-359-3948 or 800-880-6180

Northwest Missouri Community College
4315 Pickett Rd., Saint Joseph 64503

Penn Valley Community College
3201 S.W. Traffic Way, Kansas City 64111
A. K. Longfellow, Dean of Admissions

Phillips Junior College
1010 W. Sunshine St., Springfield 65807
Barbara Loven, President
417-864-7220 or 800-475-2669

Ranken Technical College
4431 Finney Ave., St. Louis 63113

St. Charles County Community College
4601 Mid Rivers Mall Dr.
P.O. Box 76975, Saint Peters 63376-0975

St. Louis Community College at Florissant Valley
3400 Pershall Rd., St. Louis 63135
Milton Woody, Dir. of Admis.

St. Louis Community College at Forest Park
5600 Oakland Ave., St. Louis 63110
Elizabeth Halpin, Registrar

St. Louis Community College at Meramec
11333 Big Bend Rd., Kirkwood 63122

State Fair Community College
3201 W. 16th St., Sedalia 65301-2199
Marvin Fielding, President

Three Rivers Community College
Poplar Bluff 63901
Dr. Steve Poort, President

Vatterott College
3925 Industrial Dr., St. Ann 63074

Wentworth Military Academy
1880 Washington Ave., Lexington 64067
Brig. Gen. Gerald Childress, Superintendent

Wright Business School
5528 N.E. Antioch Rd., Kansas City 64119

MONTANA

Blackfeet Community College
P.O. Box 819, Browning 59417
Carol Murray, Registrar

Dawson Community College
P.O. Box 421, Glendive 59330
Jolene Myers, Dir. of Admis.

Dull Knife Memorial College, Lame Deer 59043

Flathead Valley Community College
777 Grandview Dr., Kalispell 59901
406-756-3846

Fort Belknap College, Harlem 59526

Fort Peck Community College, Poplar 59255

Great Falls Vocational Technical Center
2100 16th Ave., S., Great Falls 59405

Helena College of Technology of the Univ. of Montana
1115 N. Roberts St., Helena 59601
Annette Walstad, Admissions Officer
406-444-6800

Little Big Horn College, Crow Agency 59022

MILES COMMUNITY COLLEGE
2715 Dickinson St., Miles City 59301
Jud Flower, President
800-541-9281

Missoula Vocational Technical Center
909 South Ave. W, Missoula 59801
Charles Couture, Dir. of Admis.

Salish Kootenai College
P.O. Box 117, Pablo 59855
Doug Morigeau, Dir. of Student Services

Stone Child College, Box Elder 59521

NEBRASKA

Central Community College-Hastings Campus
P.O. Box 1024, Hastings 68902-1024

Central Community College-Platte Campus
P.O. Box 1027, Columbus 68602-1027

Central Community College-Grand Island Campus
P.O. Box 4903, Grand Island 68802-4903

Gateway Electronics Institute
4862 S. 96th St., Omaha 68127
Susan Burman, Director of Admissions

Gateway Electronics Institute
1033 O St. # 130, Lincoln 68508
Melanie Priess, Director of Admissions

ITT Technical Institute
9814 M St., Omaha 68127
Roger Orensteen, Director

Lincoln School of Commerce
P.O. Box 8286, Lincoln 68501

McCook Community College
1205 E. 3rd St., McCook 69001
Glenn Haney, Admissions
800-658-4348

Metropolitan Community College
P.O. Box 3777, Omaha 68103
J. Richard Gilliland, President

Metropolitan Community College
30th & Fort Sts., Omaha 68111
Roy Phillips, President

Metropolitan Community College
204th & Dodge St., Omaha 68022

Mid-Plains Community College
Vocational-Technical School
Interstate 80 & Highway 83, North Platte 69101
Angie Pacheco, Admissions
800-658-4308

Mid-Plains Community College
1101 Halligan Dr., North Platte 69101
Angie Pacheco, Admissions
800-658-4308

Nebraska College of Business
3636 California St., Omaha 68131
Pamela Boehm, Director

Nebraska Indian Community College
P.O. Box 752, Winnebago 68071

NORTHEAST COMMUNITY COLLEGE
P.O. Box 469, Norfolk 68702
Eugene Hart, Dir. of Admis.

Omaha College of Health Careers
10845 Harney St., Omaha 68154
Mark A Stuckey, V.P. Acad. Affairs

Southeast Community College, Beatrice
R.R. 2, Box 35A, Beatrice 68310

Southeast Community College, Lincoln
8800 "O" St., Lincoln 68520

Southeast Community College, Milford
R.R. 2, Box D, Milford 68405
Thomas Stone, Campus Director

Western Nebraska Community College
1601 E. 27th St., Scottsbluff 69361
Roger Hovey, Admissions

Western Nebraska Community College
Sidney 69162
Jim Copley, Admissions

NEVADA

Career College of Northern Nevada
1195-A Corporate Blvd., Reno 89502

Community College of Southern Nevada
Formerly Clark County Community College
3200 E. Cheyenne Ave., North Las Vegas 89030
Arlie J. Stops, Dir. of Enrollment Management

Education Dynamics Institute
2635 N. Decatur Blvd., Las Vegas 89108
Larry Pauciello, Dir. of Admis.

Northern Nevada Community College
901 Elm St., Elko 89801

Phillips Junior College
3320 E. Flamingo Rd. #30, Las Vegas 89121
Robert Ramey, Dir. of Admis.

Truckee Meadows Community College
7000 Dandini Blvd., Reno 89512
John Gwaltney, President

Western Nevada Community College
2201 W. Nye Lane, Carson City 89703

NEW HAMPSHIRE

Castle College
21 Searles Rd., Windham 03087
Andrea Bard, Dir. of Admis.
603-893-6111

HESSER COLLEGE
3 Sundial Ave., Manchester 03103
David Boisvert, Senior VP of Enrollment
603-668-6660 or 800-526-9231
Established 1900. Private. Coed. Accreditation: AICS, NEASC. Tuition: $6,500. Room and board: $3,660. Fees: $350. Enrollment: 800 full-time, 250 part-time. Faculty 70. Student-faculty ratio: 25:1. Degrees: Associate. Library: 46,000 volumes. Urban campus in small city, 50 miles from Boston. Evening courses available at centers in Nashua, Portsmouth, and Salem NH. Majors in accounting, business administration, business science, graphic arts, marketing, retail management, small business management, hotel/restaurant management, travel & tourism, court reporting, criminal justice, fashion design, fashion merchandising, interior design, paralegal, management information systems, computer science, administrative assistant, corporate travel assistant, executive secretary, legal secretary, medical assistant, communications, human services, liberal studies, and early childhood education.
Academic programs: Double major, independent study, internships. Learning center, reduced course load, tutoring. Placement/credit examinations: CLEP general and subject; 30 credit hours maximum for associate degree
Academic regulations: Freshmen must earn minimum 2.0 to continue in good standing. 72% of freshmen complete year in good standing. 67% return for sophomore year. Graduation requirements: 60 hours for associate. Most students required to take courses in English, humanities, mathematics.
Freshmen admissions: School achievement record is most important basis for selection. Admission granted to applicants in top 50% of graduating class with 2.0 school grade average. References and interview considered for all others.
Fall-term applications: $10 fee, may be waived for applicants with need, no closing date; applicants notified on a rolling basis; must reply within 4 weeks. Interview recommended. Deferred and early admissions available.
Student life: 48% live in college housing, 52% commute, 1% have minority backgrounds, 1% foreign students. Average age is 18.5. Postgraduate studies: 35% of graduates enter 4-year programs. Housing: dormitories (men,women,coed).
Student activities: student government, student newspaper, yearbook, special interest organizations relating to data processing, secretarial, accounting, business, travel, retailing and commuter clubs.
Athletics: Intercollegiate NJCAA Div. 2: basketball M, basketball W, soccer M, soccer W, softball W, volleyball W, volleyball M. Intramural: volleyball.
Student services: Career counseling, employment service for undergraduates, personal counseling, placement service for graduates.
Financial aid: 70% of freshmen, 60% of continuing students receive some form of aid. Scholarships are available.
Financial aid applications: Free Application for Federal Student Aid (FAFSA) and an institutional scholarship and financial aid application. Awards are made on a rolling basis and preference of consideration is given to those who demonstrate financial need.

Lebanon College
1 Court St., Lebanon 03766
Jan Chapman, President
603-448-2445

McIntosh College, 23 Cataract Ave., Dover 03820
George J. Kay, President

NEW HAMPSHIRE TECHNICAL COLLEGE
505 Amherst St., Nashua 03063
John T. Fischer, Dean of Student Affairs
603-882-6923
Established 1970. Public. Coed. Accreditation: NEASC. Tuition: In-State: $2,296; New England Regional: $3,300; Out-of-state: $5,230. Enrollment: 425 full-time, 99 part-time. Faculty: 54. Degree offered: AAS in Aviation (FAA Cert. # NSUTO25K), Business, Computer Networking, Electronic/Mechanical Technology, Opticianry, Telecommunications, Electrical Engineering and Computer Engineering (ABET). Suburban campus one hour from Boston.

New Hampshire Technical College
One College Dr., Claremont 03743
Willis S. Reed, President

New Hampshire Technical College
1066 Front St., Manchester 03102
603-668-6706 Ext. 208

New Hampshire Technical College at Stratham
277 R. Portsmouth Ave., Stratham 03885
Patricia A. Shay, Dean of Students

New Hampshire Vocational Technical College
2020 Riverside Dr., Berlin 03570

New Hampshire Vocational Technical College
Prescott Hill, Laconia 03246

New Hampshire Technical Institute
P.O. Box 2039, Concord 03302
Daniel M. Burke, Dean of Admissions

White Pines College
40 Chester St., Chester 03036
603-887-4401

NEW JERSEY

Assumption College for Sisters
Mallinckrodt Convent, Mendham 07945

Atlantic Community College
5100 Black Horse Pike, Mays Landing 08330
Bob Royal, Director/College Recruitment

Bergen Community College
400 Paramus Rd., Paramus 07652
Frederick R. Prisco, Jr., Dir. of Admis.

BERKELEY COLLEGE OF BUSINESS
44 Rifle Camp Rd., West Paterson 07424
Kevin Luing, President
800-446-5400 ext. GQ1

BERKELEY COLLEGE OF BUSINESS
430 Rahway Ave., Woodbridge 07095
Kevin Luing, President
800-446-5400 ext. GQ1

BERKELEY COLLEGE OF BUSINESS
100 W. Prospect St., Waldwick 07463
Kevin Luing, President
800-446-5400 ext. GQ1

Brookdale Community College
765 Newman Springs Rd., Lincroft 07738
Peter F. Burnham, President

Burlington County College
County Route 530, Pemberton 08068
Juan Harris, Dir. of Admis.

Camden County College
P.O. Box 200, Blackwood 08012
Dr. Robert Ramsay, President

County College of Morris
200 Center Grove Rd., Randolph 07869

Cumberland County College
P.O. Box 517, Vineland 08360

Essex County College
303 University Ave., Newark 07102
201-877-3100

Essex County College
730 Bloomfield Ave., West Caldwell 07006
201-228-3968

Fairleigh Dickinson University
Edw. Williams College
150 Kotte Pl., Hackensack 07601
Kenneth Vehrkens, Dean
201-692-2675

Gloucester County College
R.R. 4 Box 203, Sewell 08080
Richard Jones, President

Hudson County Community College
168 Sip Ave., Jersey City 07306
Joseph O'Halloran, Director of Admissions
201-714-2127

Katharine Gibbs School
33 Plymouth St., Montclair 07042

MERCER COUNTY COMMUNITY COLLEGE
WEST WINDSOR CAMPUS
1200 Old Trenton Rd., Trenton 08690
609-586-0505 or 800-392-MCCC
JAMES KERNEY CAMPUS
N. Broad & Academy Sts., Trenton 08608
Thomas D. Sepe, President
Eric M. Perkins, Vice President
Beverly Richardson, Provost, JKC
Michael Glass, Director, Admissions
Reginald Page, Director, Financial Aid
Donald Beach, Registrar and Assistant Dean
    Established: 1966. Public. Coed. Accreditation:
MSACS. Faculty: 344. Student-faculty ratio: 26:1. Library: 79,000 volumes.
    Mercer is a publicly supported, two-year college
with an open admissions policy offering 24 Associate
in Arts and Associate in Science degree programs that
lead to transfer to four-year colleges. The college also
offers Associate in Appied Science degrees in 37
career areas, some of which lead to transfer, as well
as certificates of proficiency in 17 career specializations.
    Mercer enrolls over 9,000 students (2,800 full-time
and 6,200 part-time) in both day and evening classes
at the lowest possible cost. Tuition for in-county
residents is $51.50 per credit; for out-of-county, New
Jersey residents it is $97 per credit; and for out-of-state
and foreign students it is $162 per credit. State,
federal and private financial aid programs are available. There is no on-campus housing, but an off-campus housing list is maintained.
    Mercer offers a wide array of cultural, recreational
and non-credit community service opportunities and
has a long tradition of excellence in sports. The West
Windsor campus is a beautiful, 292 acre suburban
campus which consists of 12 air-conditioned buildings as well as athletic facilities, greenhouses and
all-weather tennis courts. The James Kerney campus,
located in downtown Trenton, is a large modern facility with similar state of the art equipment and class-

rooms. For information about any of Mercer's programs, contact the Admissions Office at 609-586-0505.

Mercer County Community College
James Kerney Campus
N. Broad & Academy Sts., Trenton 08608
See listing under "Community and Junior Colleges"

Middlesex County College
P.O. Box 3050, Edison 08818
Dr. Flora Mancuso Edwards, President

Ocean County College
0 College Dr., Toms River 08753
Arthur Knies, Dir. of Admis. & Records

Passaic Co. Community College
170 College Blvd., Paterson 07505
Dr. Gustavo A. Mellander, President

Raritan Valley Community College
P.O. Box 3300, Somerville 08876

Salem Community College
460 Hollywood Ave., Carneys Point 08069
Dr. Linda C. Jolly, President

Sussex County Community College
College Hill, Newton 07860

Union County College
1033 Springfield Ave., Cranford 07016
George Lynes, Dir. of Admis.

Union County College, Elizabeth 07206

Union County College, Scotch Plains 07076

Warren County Community College
Route 57 W., Box 55A, Washington 07882
908-689-1090

NEW MEXICO

Albuquerque Technical-Vocational Institute
525 Buena Vista Dr., S.E., Albuquerque 87106
Jane Campbell, Registrar
See listing under "Career Schools"

Clovis Community College
417 Schepps Blvd., Clovis 88101

Dona Ana Branch Community College
P.O. Box 3001, Las Cruces 88003

Eastern New Mexico University
P.O. Box 6000, Roswell 88202
Tim Raftery, Director of Admissions and Records
505-624-7000

Institute of American Indian Arts
P.O. Box 20007, Santa Fe 87504
Jerry Zollars, Dir. of Admis.

ITT Technical Institute
5100 Masthead St. N.E., Albuquerque 87109

Luna Vocational Technical Institute
P.O. Box K, Las Vegas 87701
Sam Vigil, President

New Mexico Junior College
5317 Lovington Hwy., Hobbs 88240
Robert Snow, Registrar

NEW MEXICO MILITARY INSTITUTE
101 W. College Ave., Roswell 88201
LTG Winfield W. Scott, Jr., USAF(Ret.), Supt.
COL James H. Matchin, Dir. of Admis.
Toll-free 800-421-5376
    Established 1891. Public. Coed. Accreditation:
NCACS, New Mexico Department of Education. Estimated costs for 1993-94 school year, out-of-state student: $7,500, in-state student: $5,700. Enrollment:
950. Faculty: 68. Student-faculty ratio: 19:1. Degree:
AA. Library: 68,000 volumes. 19 buildings on 40 acre
main campus. Additional acreage includes an 18-hole
championship golf course and facilities for the equestrian programs. Only land grant military high school
and junior college in the United States. Prep school
for all service academies. 87% of high school graduates receive their four year college degrees. 90% of
junior college graduates receive their baccalaureate
degrees. Quality education at a fair price.

New Mexico State University
P.O. Box 477, Alamogordo 88311
Charles Ridlinger, Dir.

New Mexico State University
1500 University Dr., Carlsbad 88220
Shelton Marlow, Provost

New Mexico State University
P.O. Box 906, Grants 87020
Donaciano E. Gonzalez, Director

Northern New Mexico Community College
1002 Onate St., Espanola 87532
Dan Simundson, Dean

Parks College
1023 Tijeras, N.W., Albuquerque 87102

San Juan College
4601 College Blvd., Farmington 87402

Santa Fe Community College
P.O. Box 4187, Santa Fe 87502

University of New Mexico
P.O. Box 1756, Gallup 87305

NEW YORK

American Academy McAllister Institute
of Funeral Service
450 W. 56th St. #2, New York 10019
Patrick O'Connor, President

American Academy of Dramatic Arts
120 Madison Ave., New York 10016

BERKELEY COLLEGE
40 W. Red Oak Ln., White Plains 10604
Rose Mary Healy, President
800-446-5400 ext. GQ1

BERKELEY COLLEGE
3 E. 43rd St., New York 10017
Dr. Glen Zeitzer, President
800-446-5400 ext. GQ1

Briarcliffe School
250 Crossways Park Dr., Woodbury 11797
516-364-2055

Briarcliffe School
10 Peninsula Blvd., Lynbrook 11563
516-596-1313

Briarcliffe School
10 Lake St., Patchogue 11772
516-654-5300

Bryant & Stratton Business Institute
1214 Abbott Rd., Lackawanna 14218

Bryant & Stratton Business Institute
1028 Main St., Buffalo 14202

Bryant & Stratton Business Institute
200 Bryant & Stratton Way, Williamsville 14221

Bryant & Stratton Business Institute
82 St. Paul St., Rochester 14604

Bryant & Stratton Business Institute
953 James St., Syracuse 13203

Bryant & Stratton Business Institute
1225 Jefferson Rd., Rochester 14623

Bryant & Stratton Business Institute
5775 S. Bay Rd., Cicero 13039

Bryant & Stratton Business Institute
1259 Central Ave., Albany 12205
Bob Flynn, Dir. of Admis.

CAZENOVIA COLLEGE
Cazenovia 13035
Dr. James Parker, VP for Enrollment Management
See listing under "Universities"

Central City Business Institute
224 Harrison St., Syracuse 13202
Michael Greenfest, Dir. of Admissions
800-945-2224

The Culinary Institute of America
651 S. Albany Post Rd., Hyde Park 12538-1499
Cathy Grande, Dir. of Admis.

CUNY BOROUGH OF MANHATTAN COMMUNITY COLLEGE
199 Chambers St., New York 10007

CUNY Bronx Community College
181st St. & University Ave., Bronx 10453
Roscoe C. Brown, Jr., President

CUNY Hostos Community College
475 Grand Concourse, Bronx 10451
Nydia Edgecombe, Dir of Admis.
718-518-6622

CUNY Kingsborough Community College
2001 Oriental Blvd., Brooklyn 11235
Alan Wittes, Director of Admissions

CUNY LaGuardia Community College
31-10 Thompson Ave., Long Island City 11101
Robert O'Pray, Registrar

CUNY QUEENSBOROUGH COMMUNITY COLLEGE
22205 56th Ave., Bayside 11364
Dr. Kurt R. Schmeller, President
Mary Bryce, Dir. of Admis.
    Established 1960. Public. Coed. Accreditation:
MSACS. Tuition: $2,100. Fees: $100 per year. Enrollment: 6,000 full-time, 6,000 part-time. Faculty: 600.
Student-faculty ratio: 25:1. Degrees: AA, AAS, AS. 12
buildings on 34 acres. Degree programs in liberal arts
& sciences, business administration, marketing, management, computer information systems, office technology. Technology: Electrical, computer,
mechanical, design drafting, laser & fiber optics, music electronic technology, nursing, Medical lab technology, environmental health, fine & performing arts,
pre-engineering.

FIVE TOWNS COLLEGE
305 N. Service Rd., Dix Hills 11746
Jennifer Roemer, Coordinator of Admissions
516-424-7000
See listing under "Universities"

Fuld School of Nursing Joint Diseases
1919 Madison Ave., New York 10035

Hilbert College
5200 S. Park Ave., Hamburg 14075
George Binner, Dir. of Admis.

Interboro Institute
450 W. 56th St., New York 10019

Jamestown Business College
P.O. Box 429, Jamestown 14702
David Spencer, Registrar

Katharine Gibbs School
535 Brood Hollow Rd., Melville 11747
516-293-2460

Katharine Gibbs School
200 Park Ave., New York 10166

Laboratory Institute of Merchandising
12 E. 53rd St., New York 10022
Mary Ann M. Elberfeld, Dir. of Admis.

Maria College of Albany
700 New Scotland Ave., Albany 12208
Laurie Gilmore, Dir. of Admis.

Mater Dei College
Riverside Dr., Ogdensburg 13669
Mark Dougherty, Dir. of Admis.

Olean Business Institute
301 N. Union St., Olean 14760
Patrick McCarthy, Director
Jeanne Johnston, Director of Admissions
716-372-7978

Paul Smith's College, Paul Smiths 12970
Enrico Miller, Dir. of Admis.
800-421-2605

PLAZA BUSINESS INSTITUTE
7409 37th Ave., Jackson Heights 11372
Sally Ann Weger, Director of Admissions
718-779-1430

Rochester Business Institute
1850 Ridge Rd. E., Rochester 14622

Rochester Institute of Technology (NTID)
National Technical Institute for the Deaf
1 Lomb Memorial Dr., Rochester 14623

Russell Sage Junior College of Albany
140 New Scotland Ave., Albany 12208

SUNY ADIRONDACK COMMUNITY COLLEGE
439 Bay Rd., Queensbury 12804
Levi Brown, Dir. of Admis.
518-793-4491
Established 1961. Public. Coed. Accreditation: MSACS. Tuition: $1,900. Room and board: $4,200. Fees: $150. Enrollment: 1,800 full-time, 1,700 part-time. Faculty: 110. Student-faculty ratio: 19:1. Degrees: AA, AAS, AS. Library: 50,000 volumes. 8 buildings on 141 acres. Located in the Lake George-Saratoga Springs resort area of Northern New York. Dorm style housing located adjacent to the main campus. Honors program, learning center-tutoring program. Most popular programs include business, criminal justice, liberal arts, nursing, and travel & tourism.

SUNY Broome Community College
907 Upper Front St., Binghamton 13905
Donald Dellow, President

SUNY Cayuga County Community College
197 Franklin St., Auburn 13021
Patricia Powers-Burdick, Dir. of Admis.

SUNY Clinton Community College
Bluff Point, Plattsburgh 12901

SUNY College of Agriculture and Technology
Morrisville 13408
Frederick W. Woodward, President

SUNY College of Technology, Alfred 14802
Deborah J. Goodrich, Dir. of Admis.
607-587-4215

SUNY College of Technology
34 Cornell Dr., Canton 13617
Thomas R. Fletcher, Director of Admissions
800-388-7123

SUNY College of Technology, Wellsville 14895

SUNY College of Technology at Delhi
2 Main St., Delhi 13753

SUNY Columbia Greene Community College
P.O. Box 1000, Hudson 12534
Barbara A. Rupp, Admissions

SUNY Community College of the Finger Lakes
Lincoln Hill Rd., Canandaigua 14424
John M. Meuser, Dir. of Admis.

SUNY Corning Community College
Spencer Hill Rd., Corning 14830
Donald H. Hangen, Pres.

SUNY Dutchess Community College
Poughkeepsie 12601

SUNY Erie Community College, City Campus
121 Ellicott St., Buffalo 14203
Dr. Louis Ricci, President

SUNY Erie Community College, North Campus
6205 Main St., Williamsville 14221

SUNY Erie Community College, South Campus
4140 Southwestern Blvd., Orchard Park 14127

SUNY Fulton-Montgomery Community College
Alumni Building 67, Johnstown 12095

SUNY Genesee Community College
1 College Rd., Batavia 14020
Malcolm T. Wormley, Dir. of Admis.

SUNY Herkimer County Community College
Reservoir Rd., Herkimer 13350
John H. Thayer, Dir. of Admis.

SUNY HUDSON VALLEY COMMUNITY COLLEGE
80 Vandenburgh Ave., Troy 12180
Linda Sweetman, Dir. of Admis.
See listing under "Career Schools"

SUNY Jamestown Community College
525 Falconer St., Jamestown 14701
Paul A. Benke, President

SUNY Jamestown Community College, Olean 14760

SUNY Jefferson Community College
1220 Coffeen St., Watertown 13601
Rosanne N. Weir, Dir. of Admis.

SUNY Mohawk Valley Community College
1101 Sherman Dr., Utica 13501

SUNY Monroe Community College
1000 E. Henrietta Rd., Rochester 14623
716-292-2000

SUNY Nassau Community College
1 Education Dr., Garden City 11530
Bernard Iantosca, Dir of Admis.

SUNY Niagara County Community College
3111 Saunders Settlement Rd., Sanborn 14132
R. J. Mirabelli, Admis. Ofc.

SUNY North Country Community College
P.O. Box 89, Saranac Lake 12983

SUNY North Country Community College
Malone 12953

SUNY North Country Community College, Ticonderoga 12858

SUNY Onondaga Community College
Onondaga Rd., Syracuse 13215
Joseph Insel, Dir. of Admis.

Suny Orange County Community College
115 South St., Middletown 10940
914-341-4030

SUNY Rockland Community College
145 College Rd., Suffern 10901
Larry Gurney, Asst. Dean of Students

SUNY Rockland Community College
36 Main St., Haverstraw 10927

SUNY Rockland Community College
766 N. Main St., Spring Valley 10977

SUNY Rockland Community College
21 N. Broadway, Nyack 10960

SUNY Rockland Community College
185 N. Main St., Spring Valley 10977

SUNY Schenectady County Community College
78 Washington Ave., Schenectady 12305
Robert Dinello, Dir. of Admis.
518-346-6211, ext. 166

SUNY Suffolk County Community College
Crooked Hill Rd., Brentwood 11717

SUNY Suffolk County Community College
2 Speonk-Riverhead Rd. Riverhead 11901

SUNY Suffolk County Community College
533 College Rd., Selden 11784
Robert Kreiling, President

SUNY Sullivan County Community College
P.O. Box 4002, Loch Sheldrake 12759-4002
Steve Pochard, Dean of Enrollment

SUNY Tompkins Cortland Community College
P.O. Box 139, Dryden 13053
Jack Hewett, Dir. of Admis.

SUNY Ulster County Community College
Stone Ridge 12484
Thomas Maiello, Dir. of Admis.

SUNY Westchester Community College
75 Grasslands Rd., Valhalla 10595-1698
Alan Seidman, Dir. of Admis.

Taylor Business Institute
1 Penn Plaza, New York 10119

T.C.I. THE COLLEGE FOR TECHNOLOGY
320 W. 31st St., New York 10001
Henry Moss, President
Henry Ford, Director of Admissions
212-594-4001 or 800-878-TCI-NOW
Established 1909. Private. Coed. Accreditation: N.Y. State Board of Regents and TAC/ABET. Tuition: $1850/semester. Fees: $74. Enrollment: 4,000 full-time, 150 part-time. Faculty: 200. Student-faculty ratio: 20:1. Degrees: AAS, Electronics, Engineering Technology and AOS, Air-Conditioning/Heating and Refrigeration, Industrial Electronics, Office Technology. Library: 6,555 volumes. 2 buildings. Hands on training with heavy emphasis on laboratories.

Tobe-Coburn School for Fashion Careers
8 E. 40th St., New York 10016
Patricia Nieml, President

Trocaire College
110 Red Jacket Pky., Buffalo 14220
Sr. Barbara Ciarico, President
716-826-1200

Utica School of Commerce
201 Bleecker St., Utica 13501
Judith Kelly, Dir. of Admis.

Villa Maria College of Buffalo
240 Pine Ridge Rd., Buffalo 14225
Lynn D'Auria, Dir. of Admis.

Westchester Business Institute
325 Central Ave., White Plains 10606
Dale Smith, Dean of Admissions

Wood School
8 E. 40th St., New York 10016
Rosemary Duggan, President

NORTH CAROLINA

Alamance Community College
P.O. Box 623, Haw River 27258
W. Ronald McCarter, President

Anson Community College
P.O. Box 126, Polkton 28135
Dr. Edwin Chapman, President
704-272-7635 or 800-766-0319

Asheville Buncombe Technical Community College
340 Victoria Rd., Asheville 28801
Connie Buckner, Dir. of Admis.

Beaufort County Community College
P.O. Box 1069, Washington 27889
Gary Burbage, Dir. of Admis.

Bladen Community College
P.O. Box 266, Dublin 28332

Blue Ridge Community College
R.R. 2 Box 133A, Flat Rock 28731

Brevard College
Brevard 28712
Bob McLendon, Dean of Admissions

Brunswick Community College
P.O. Box 30, Supply 28462

Caldwell Community College
P.O. Box 600, Lenoir 28645
Dr. H. E. Beam, President

Cape Fear Community College
411 Front St., N., Wilmington 28401
Dr. E. Thomas Satterfield, President

Carteret Community College
3505 Arendell St., Morehead City 28557
Dan Krautheim, Dean of the College
919-247-3058 ext. 143

Catawba Valley Community College
R.R. 3, Box 283, Hickory 28602
Robert E. Paap, President

CECIL'S COLLEGE
P.O. Box 6407, Asheville 28816
John South, President
704-252-2486

Central Carolina Community College
1105 Kelly Dr., Sanford 27330
Marvin Joyner, President

Central Piedmont Community College
P.O. Box 35009, Charlotte 28235
Dr. Ruth Shaw, President

Chowan College
P.O. Box 1848, Murfreesboro 27855
Winslow Carter, Dir. of Admis.

Cleveland Community College
137 S. Post Rd., Shelby 28152

Coastal Carolina Community College
444 Western Blvd., Jacksonville 28546
Ronald K. Lingle, President

College of The Albemarle
P.O. Box 2327, Elizabeth City 27906
John M. Wells, Asst. Dean of Admissions
919-335-0821, Ext. 220

Craven Community College
P.O. Box 885, New Bern 28563
Debbie Hunter, Dir. of Admis.

Davidson County Community College
P.O. Box 1287, Lexington 27293
J. Bryan Brooks, President

Durham Technical Community College
1637 E. Lawson St., Durham 27703
Phail Wynn, Jr., President

Edgecombe Community College
2009 Wilson St., W., Tarboro 27886
Thomas Anderson, VP of Student Services
919-823-5166

Fayetteville Technical Community College
P.O. Box 35236, Fayetteville 28303

Forsyth Technical Community College
2100 Silas Creek, Winston-Salem 27103
Dr. Bob Greene, President

Gaston College
201 Highway 321, S., Dallas 28034

Guilford Technical Community College
P.O. Box 309, Jamestown 27282

Halifax Community College
P.O. Box 809, Weldon 27890

Haywood Community College
Freedlander Dr., Clyde 28721
Carol Smith, Dir. of Admis.

Isothermal Community College
P.O. Box 804, Spindale 28160
Willard Lewis, President

James Sprunt Community College
P.O. Box 398, Kenansville 28349
Rita Brown, Registrar
910-296-2500

Johnston Community College
P.O. Box 2350, Smithfield 27577
Joan Jones, Dir. of Admissions

King's College
322 Lamar Ave., Charlotte 28204
Debbie Remelius, Registrar

Lenoir Community College
P.O. Box 188, Kinston 28502

LOUISBURG COLLEGE
501 N. Main St., Louisburg 27549
Rick Lowe, Dir. of Admis.
919-496-2521 or 800-775-0208
Established 1787. Private. Coed. Accreditation: SACS. Tuition: $5,800. Room and board: $3,035. Fees: $449. Enrollment: 612 full-time, 68 part-time. Faculty: 45. Student-faculty ratio: 15:1. Degrees: AA, AS. Library: 60,000 volumes. 20 buildings on 75 acres. 90% of LC graduates transfer to 4-year colleges and universities. Transferable engineering program available. Offer writing center, math lab, and peer tutoring to students needing assistance.

McDowell Technical Community College
R.R. 1, Box 170, Marion 28752
Jim Biddix, Dean of Students

Martin Community College
Kehukee Park Rd., Williamston 27892
Carolyn Mills, Registrar

Mayland Community College
P.O. Box 547, Spruce Pine 28777

Mitchell Community College
500 W. Broad St., Statesville 28677

Montgomery Community College
P.O. Box 787, Troy 27371
Marvin G. Miles, President

Nash Community College
P.O. Box 7488, Rocky Mount 27804

Pamlico Community College
P.O. Box 185, Grantsboro 28529
E. Douglas Kearney, President

Peace College
15 E. Peace St., Raleigh 27604
Dr. Garrett Briggs, President
919-832-2881, Fax: 919-834-6755

Piedmont Community College
P.O. Box 1197, Roxboro 27573
Dr. Edward W. Cox, President

Pitt Community College
P.O. Box 7007, Greenville 27835
Dr. Wm. E. Fulford, Jr., President

Randolph Community College
P.O. Box 1009, Asheboro 27204-1009
L. K. Linker, President

Richmond Community College
P.O. Box 1189, Hamlet 28345
Teri Jacobs, Registrar/Dir. of Admis.

Roanoke-Chowan Community College
R.R. 2, Box 46A, Ahoskie 27910

Robeson Community College
P.O. Box 1420, Lumberton 28359

Rockingham Community College
P.O. Box 38, Wentworth 27375

Rowan-Cabarrus Community College
P.O. Box 1595, Salisbury 28145
Dr. Richard Brownell, President

Saint Mary's College
900 Hillsborough St., Raleigh 27603
Dr. Clauston Jenkins, President

Sampson Community College
P.O. Box 318, Clinton 28328

Sandhills Community College
2200 Airport Rd., Pinehurst 28374
910-692-6185

Southeastern Community College
P.O. Box 151, Whiteville 28472
Mary Miller, Dir. of Admis.

Southwestern Community College
275 Webster Rd., Sylva 28779

Stanly Community College
R.R. 4, Box 55, Albemarle 28001

Surry Community College
P.O. Box 304, Dobson 27017
Dr. Swanson Richards, President

Tri-County Community College
P.O. Box 40, Murphy 28906
Vincent W. Crisp, President

Vance-Granville Community College
P.O. Box 917, Henderson 27536

Wake Technical Community College
9101 Fayetteville Rd., Raleigh 27603

Wayne Community College
Caller Box 8002, Goldsboro 27533
Bill Bennett, Public Information Officer
919-735-5151

Western Piedmont Community College
1001 Burkemont Ave., Morganton 28655
H. D. Moretz, Dean of College

Wilkes Community College
P.O. Box 120, Wilkesboro 28697
Mac Warren, Dir. of Admis.

Wilson Technical Community College
P.O. Box 4305, Wilson 27893
Dr. Frank Eagles, President

NORTH DAKOTA

BISMARCK STATE COLLEGE
1500 Edwards Ave., Bismarck 58501
Dr. Kermit Lidstrom, President
701-224-5400

Ft. Berthold Community College
P.O. Box 490, New Town 58763
701-627-4738

Little Hoop Community College
P.O. Box 269, Fort Totten 58335

North Dakota State College of Science
800 N. 6th St., Wahpeton 58075

North Dakota State University-Bottineau
1st & Simrall Blvd., Bottineau 58318
Kenneth Grosz, Registrar

Standing Rock College
HC 01 Box 4, Fort Yates 58538

Turtle Mountain Community College
P.O. Box 340, Belcourt 58316
Admissions Office
701-477-5605

UNITED TRIBES TECHNICAL COLLEGE
3315 University Dr., Bismarck 58504
Admissions Office 701-255-3285 Ext. 216 or 334

University of North Dakota, Williston Center
P.O. Box 1326, Williston 58802
Galvin L. Stevens, Dean

University of North Dakota-Lake Region
Devils Lake 58301
Sharon Etemad, Executive Dean

OHIO

ACA College of Design
2528 Kemper Ln., Cincinnati 45206
Marion Allman, President
See listing under "Art"

Antonelli Institute of Art & Photography
124 E. 7th St., Cincinnati 45202

Art Advertising Academy
4343 Bridgetown Rd., Cincinnati 45211
513-574-1010
2 year Associate of Applied Business in Commercial Art, 2 year commercial art diploma program including computer art and airbrush art. Small individual classes.

Belmont Technical College
120 Fox Shannon Place, St. Clairsville 43950
Thomas Tarowsky, Asst. Dean of Student Services

Bowling Green State University, Firelands Campus
901 Rye Beach Rd., Huron 44839

Bradford School
6170 Busch Blvd., Columbus 43229
Patrick Denton, President
614-846-9410

Central Ohio Technical College
University Dr., Newark 43055
John Merrin, Coordinator of Admissions

Chatfield College
20918 State Rte. 251, St. Martin 45118
Sr. Xavier Ladrigan, Dean

Cincinnati Technical College
3520 Central Pkwy., Cincinnati 45223

Clark State Community College
570 E. Leffels Ln., Springfield 45505
Leigh Fisher, Admissions Specialist

Cleveland Institute of Electronics
1776 E. 17th St., Cleveland 44114
800-243-6446

Columbus State Community College
550 E. Spring St., Columbus 43215
Mary Jo Deerwester, Dir. of Admis.

Cuyahoga Community College, Eastern Campus
25444 Harvard Rd., Warrensville Heights 44122

Cuyahoga Community College, Metropolitan Campus
2900 Community College Ave., Cleveland 44115

Cuyahoga Community College, Western Campus
11000 W. Pleasant Valley Rd.
Parma Heights 44130

Davis Junior College
4747 Monroe St., Toledo 43623
Diane Brunner, President
800-477-7021 or 419-473-2700

Edison State Community College
1973 Edison Dr., Piqua 45356
Dotty Muir, Dean of Student Development

ETI Technical College
4300 Euclid Ave., Cleveland 44103

ETI Technical College
1320 W. Maple St., North Canton 44720
216-494-1214

ETI Technical College
2076-86 Youngstown-Warren Rd., Niles 44446

Hocking College
3301 Hocking Pky., Nelsonville 45764
Candace Vancko, VP for Enrollment
800-282-4163

ITT Technical Institute
3325 Stop Eight Rd., Dayton 45414

ITT Technical Institute
P.O. Box 779, Youngstown 44501

Jefferson Technical College
4000 Sunset Blvd., Steubenville 43952
Chuck Mascellino, Dir. of Admis.
800-456-TECH

Kent State University, Tuscarawas Campus
University Dr., N.E., New Philadelphia 44663
Harold D. Shade, Dean

Kent State University-Ashtabula Campus
3325 W. 13th St., Ashtabula 44004
John Mahan, Dean

Kent State University-East Liverpool Campus
400 E. 4th St., East Liverpool 43920
Suzanne Fitzgerald, Dean

Kent State University-Geauga Campus
14111 Claridon-Troy Rd., Burton 44021
Larry Jones, Dean

Kent State University-Salem Campus
2491 State Rt. 45 S., Salem 44460
Dr. James Cooney, Dean

Kent State University-Stark Campus
6000 Frank Ave. N.W., Canton 44720
Dr. William Bittle, Dean

Kent State University-Trumbull Campus
4314 Mahoning Ave. N.W., Warren 44483
Dr. John Cable, Dean

Kettering College of Medical Arts
3737 Southern Blvd., Kettering 45429
Curt Dolinsky, Dir. of College Relations
800-433-5262

Lakeland Community College
7700 Clocktower Dr., Kirtland 44094
Bill Kraus, Dir. of Admis.

Lima Technical College
4240 Campus Dr., Lima 45804
Cynthia E. Spiers, Director of Admissions

Lorain County Community College
1005 Abbe Rd., N., Elyria 44035
Dr. John W. Thrash, Jr., Registrar

Marion Technical College
1467 Mt. Vernon Ave., Marion 43302-5694
Joel Liles, Dir. of Admis.

Marti College of Fashion
P.O. Box 580, Cleveland 44107

Miami-Jacobs Junior College of Business
P.O. Box 1433, Dayton 45401
Charles Campbell, President

Miami University-Hamilton Campus
1601 Peck Blvd., Hamilton 45011

Miami University-Middletown Campus
4200 E. University Blvd., Middletown 45042

Muskingum Area Technical College
1555 Newark Rd., Zanesville 43701

North Central Technical College
P.O. Box 698, Mansfield 44901

Northwestern College
1441 N. Cable Rd., Lima 45805

Northwest State Community College
22600 State Route 34, Archbold 43502
Dennis Gable, Admissions Coordinator

OHIO INSTITUTE OF PHOTOGRAPHY & TECHNOLOGY
2029 Edgefield Rd., Dayton 45439
Cecil W. Johnston, Executive Director
513-294-6155 or 800-932-9698

Ohio State University-Agricultural Technical Institute
1328 Dover Rd., Wooster 44691

Owens Community College
P.O. Box 10000, Toledo 43699
Jim Welling, Admissions
419-661-7225

Owens Community College
300 Davis St., Findlay 45840
Stacy Davidson, Admissions
419-423-6827

RETS Institute of Technology
1606 Laskey Rd., W., Toledo 43612

RETS Technical Center
P.O. Box 130, Centerville 45459

Sawyer College of Business
13027 Lorain Ave., Cleveland 44111

Sinclair Community College
444 W. 3rd St., Dayton 45402-1460
Sara P. Smith, Director of Admissions
800-315-3000

Southern Ohio College
1055 Laidlaw Ave., Cincinnati 45237
Duane Hawkins, President

Southern Ohio College
2791 Mogadore Rd., Akron 44312

Southern Ohio College
4641 Bach Ln., Fairfield 45014

Southern State Community College
200 Hobart Dr., Hillsboro 45133
Dr. Lewis C. Miller, President

Southern State Community College
12681 U.S. Route 62, Sardinia 45171

Southern State Community College
2698 Old State Route 73, Wilmington 45177

Southwestern College of Business
225 W. 1st St., Dayton 45402

Southwestern College of Business
9910 Princeton-Glendale Rd., Cincinnati 45246

Southwestern College of Business
717 Race St., Cincinnati 45202

Southwestern College of Business
631 S. Briel Blvd., Middletown 45044

Stark Technical College
6200 Frank Ave., N.W., Canton 44720

Technology Education College
288 S. Hamilton Rd., Columbus 43213
Ronald Dooley, President
See listing under "Career Schools"

Terra Technical College
2830 Napoleon Rd., Fremont 43420

University of Akron-Wayne College
1901 Smucker Rd., Orrville 44667

University of Cincinnati
Clermont College
725 College Dr., Batavia 45103
Dr. Roger Barry, Dean

University of Cincinnati
Raymond Walters General & Technical College
9555 Plainfield Rd., Cincinnati 45236
Ernest G. Muntz, Dean

Washington Community College
710 Collegiate Dr., Marietta 45750
Dr. Donald R. Neff, President

West Side Institute of Technology
9801 Walford Ave., Cleveland 44102

Wright State University, Western Ohio Branch
7600 State Rt. 703, Celina 45822
Dr. Donald Carlson, Dean

OKLAHOMA

Bacone College
99 Bacone Rd., Muskogee 74403-1597
David Norfolk, Dean of Enrollment Management

Carl Albert State College
P.O. Box 606, Poteau 74953
Dr. Joe White, President

Connors State College
Route 1 Box 1000, Warner 74469
Dr. Carl O. Westbrook, President

Eastern Oklahoma State College
1301 W. Main St., Wilburton 74578
Jerry Smith, Registrar

El Reno Junior College
P.O. Box 370, El Reno 73036
George C. Roper, Dir. of Admis. & Records

Murray State College, Tishomingo 73460
Dr. Clyde R. Kindell, President

National Education Center-Spartan School of
Aeronautics
8820 E. Pine St. #51133, Tulsa 74115
800-331-1204

Northeastern Oklahoma A & M College
200 I St. N.E., Miami 74354
K. Dale Patterson, Dean of Admissions

Northern Oklahoma College
1220 E. Grand Ave., Tonkawa 74653

Oklahoma City Community College
7777 S. May Ave., Oklahoma City 73159
Dr. Dale L. Gibson, President

Oklahoma Junior College
3232 N.W. 65th, Oklahoma City 73116

Oklahoma State University-Technical Branch
1801 E. 4th St., Okmulgee 74447
800-722-4471 or 918-756-6211

Oklahoma State University-Technical Branch
900 N. Portland Ave., Oklahoma City 73107

ROGERS STATE COLLEGE
1701 W. Will Rogers Blvd., Claremore 74017
Dr. Richard Mosier, President
918-341-7510 Ext. 319

Rose State College
6420 S.E. 15th St., Midwest City 73110
Robert Alyea, Registrar

St. Gregory's College
1900 W. MacArthur St., Shawnee 74801
Tracy Brotherton, Dir. of Admis.

Seminole Junior College
P.O. Box 351, Seminole 74818

Southwestern Oklahoma State University
409 E. Mississippi, Sayre 73662
Don Roberts, Dean

Tulsa Junior College
6111 E. Skelly Dr. #200, Tulsa 74135

Western Oklahoma State College
2801 N. Main St., Altus 73521
Larry Paxton, Dir. of Admis. & Registrar
405-477-2000

OREGON

Blue Mountain Community College
2411 N.W. Carden, Pendleton 97801

Central Oregon Community College
2600 N.W. College Way, Bend 97701
Christine Kerlin, Dir. of Admis.
503-383-7500

Chemeketa Community College
P.O. Box 14007, Salem 97309
Dean Pielstick, Dir. of Admis.
503-399-5006

Clackamas Community College
19600 Molalla Ave., Oregon City 97045

Clatsop Community College
1653 Jerome Ave., Astoria 97103
Doreen Dailey, President

Lane Community College
4000 E. 30th Ave., Eugene 97405
Sharon K. Moore, Dir. of Admis.

Linn-Benton Community College
6500 Pacific Blvd., S.W., Albany 97321
Diane Watson, Dir. of Admis.

Mt. Hood Community College
26000 S.E. Stark St., Gresham 97030
Dr. Paul Kreider, President
503-667-7211

Oregon Denturist College
19001 S.E. McLaughlin Blvd., Milwaukie 97267

Oregon Polytechnic Institute
900 S.E. Sandy Blvd., Portland 97214

Portland Community College
P.O. Box 19000, Portland 97280

ROGUE COMMUNITY COLLEGE
3345 Redwood Hwy., Grants Pass 97527
Dr. Harvey Bennett, President
Ted Risser, Registrar
503-471-3501
Established 1970. Public. Coed. Accreditation:
NASC. Tuition: $1,044. Fees: $32. Enrollment: 1,300
full-time, 1,600 part-time. Faculty: 65 full-time, 300
part-time. Degrees offered: AA, AAS, and AGS. Programs in: Business administration, office technology,
nursing, respiratory therapy, electronics, human services, fire science, manufacturing, automotive/diesel,
computer science, criminal justice, humanities, art,
social science, and science/math. Library: 33,000 volumes. 30 buildings on a 92 acre campus. Campus is
located in scenic Rogue River valley 3 miles from
Grants Pass.

Southwestern Oregon Community College
1988 Newmark Ave., Coos Bay 97420
Jean Von Schweinitz, Registrar

Treasure Valley Community College
650 College Blvd., Ontario 97914
Ron Kulm, Dir. of Admis.

Umpqua Community College
P.O. Box 967, Roseburg 97470

PENNSYLVANIA

: American Institute of Design
1616 Orthodox St., Philadelphia 19124
Dorothy Miller, Dir. of Admis.

Antonelli Institute of Art & Photography
P.O. Box 570, Plymouth Meeting 19462
215-275-3040 or 800-722-7871

: Antonelli Medical & Professional Institute
1700 Industrial Hwy., Pottstown 19464
Paula Bauer, Dir. of Admis.

The Art Institute of Philadelphia
1622 Chestnut St., Philadelphia 19103
215-567-7080

: Art Institute of Pittsburgh
526 Penn Ave., Pittsburgh 15222
Lee Colker, Dir. of Admis.
800-275-2470
See listing under "Art"

Berean Institute
1901 W. Girard Ave., Philadelphia 19130

Bradley Academy for the Visual Arts
625 E. Philadelphia St., York 17403
Loren H. Kroh, Director
717-848-1447

Bucks County Community College
Swamp Rd., Newtown 18940

Business Careers Institute
33 W. Otterman St., Greensburg 15601
Andrew Ogrodnik, Director

Butler County Community College
P.O. Box 1203, Oak Hill, Butler 16003
William Miller, Dir. of Admis.

Cambria-Rowe Business College
221 Central Ave., Johnstown 15902
William M. Coward, President

Central Pennsylvania Business School
College Hill Rd., Summerdale 17093

CHI Institute
520 Street Rd., Southampton 18966
K. Quinn, Dir. of Admis.

Chubb Institute-Keystone School
965 Baltimore Pike, Springfield 19064

Churchman Business School
355 Spring Garden St., Easton 18042
Charles Churchman, Jr., President

Clarissa School of Fashion Design, Inc.
322 5th Ave., Pittsburgh 15222
Penelope Smith, Director

Community College of Allegheny Co.
Allegheny Campus
808 Ridge Ave., Pittsburgh 15212

Community College of Allegheny Co., Boyce Campus
595 Beatty Rd., Monroeville 15146

Community College of Allegheny Co., South Campus
1750 Clairton Rd., West Mifflin 15122

Community College of Allegheny County
North Campus
111 Pines Plaza, Pittsburgh 15237

Community College of Allegheny County
701 N. Homewood Ave., Pittsburgh 15208

Community College of Beaver County
College Drive, Monaca 15061

Community College of Philadelphia
1700 Spring Garden St., Philadelphia 19130
Allen T. Bonnell, President

Computer Systems Institute
900 Penn Ave., Pittsburgh 15222

Craft Institute
9 S. 12th St., Philadelphia 19107

Dean Institute of Technology
1501 W. Liberty Ave., Pittsburgh 15226
W. Nichie, Dir. of Admis.
412-531-4433, FAX: 412-531-4435

Delaware County Community College
901 Media Line Rd., Media 19063

Du Bois Business College
1 Beaver Dr., Du Bois 15801

Duffs Business Institute
110 9th St., Pittsburgh 15222

Electronic Institutes
19 Jamesway Plaza, Middletown 17057

Electronic Institutes
4634 Browns Hill Rd., Pittsburgh 15217
Philip Chosky, President

Erie Business Center
246 W. 9th St., Erie 16501
Tony Piccirillo, Dir. of Admis.
See listing under "Career Schools"

Erie Institute of Technology
2221 Peninsula Dr., Erie 16506
Clinton Oviatt, Jr., Director

Harcum Junior College, Bryn Mawr 19010
Mary Pontius, Dean of Admissions

Harrisburg Area Community College
3300 N. Cameron Street Road, Harrisburg 17110

Hiram G. Andrews Center
727 Goucher St., Johnstown 15905

Hussian School of Art
1118 Market St., Philadelphia 19107
Wilbur Crawford, Director of Admissions

ICM School of Business
10 Wood St., Pittsburgh 15222
800-441-5222

Information Computer Systems Institute
2201 Hangar Pl., Allentown 18103

Johnson Technical Institute
3427 N. Main Ave., Scranton 18508
Harry Dickinson, V.P. Institute Advancement
See listing under "Career Schools"

Keystone Junior College
P.O. Box 50, La Plume 18440
Kevin McIntyre, Dir. of Admis.

Lackawanna Junior College
901 Prospect Ave., Scranton 18505
Renee J. Garvey, Dir. of Admis.

Lehigh County Community College
2370 Main St., Schnecksville 18078

LINCOLN TECHNICAL INSTITUTE
5151 W. Tilghman St., Allentown 18104
Robert Milot, Director
610-398-5300
Established 1946. Coed. Accredited Member
School: ACCSCT. Providing technical training in:
*Electronics Technology, Electronics Servicing,
Computer Technician, *Architectural/Mechanical
Drafting and CAD Technology. Financial aid for those
who qualify. Employment assistance program. (*As-
sociate in Specialized Technology Degree).

LINCOLN TECHNICAL INSTITUTE
9191 Torresdale Ave. Philadelphia 19136
Douglas Johnson, Director
215-335-0800
Established 1946. Coed. Accredited Member
School: ACCSCT. Providing technical training in:
Automotive or Diesel Truck Technology, *Automotive or Diesel Truck Service and Management, *Ar-
chitectural/Mechanical Drafting and CAD
Technology. Financial aid for those who qualify. Employment assistance program. (*Associate in Specialized Technology Degree).

Lock Haven University-Clearfield Campus
119 Byers St., Clearfield 16830

Luzerne Co. Community College
1333 S. Prospect St., Nanticoke 18634

McCann School of Business
Wilkes Barre Campus
2004 Wyoming Ave., Wyoming 18644
James Noone, Director

McCarrie School of Health Sciences & Technology
512 S. Broad St., Philadelphia 19146

Manor Junior College
710 Fox Chase Rd., Jenkintown 19046
Sr. Mary Cecilia, President

Median School of Allied Health Careers
125 7th St., Pittsburgh 15222
William Mosle, President

Monroeville School of Business
105 Mall Blvd. 3rd Fl., Monroeville 15146
Edward McNutt, President

Montgomery County Community College
340 DeKalb Pike, Blue Bell 19422-0758
Dennis Murphy, Dir. of Admis.

NEC-Allentown Business School Campus
1501 Lehigh St., Allentown 18103
610-791-5100

National Education Center-Thompson Institute
3440 Market St., Philadelphia 19104

National Education Center-Thompson Institute
5650 Derry St., Harrisburg 17111

National Education Center-Vale Technical Institute
135 W. Market St., Blairsville 15717

New Castle School of Trades
R.R. 1, Pulaski 16143
Tony Mezatasta, Dir.

New Kensington Commercial School
945 Greensburg Rd., New Kensington 15068
Arthur Mullen, Dir. of Admis.

Northampton Co. Area Community College
3835 Green Pond Rd., Bethlehem 18017
Janice Keim, Assoc. Dir. of Admis.

Northeastern Christian Junior College
1860 Montgomery Ave., Villanova 19085
John Hall, President

Peirce Junior College
1420 Pine St., Philadelphia 19102
David Schleicher, Dir. of Admis.

Penn Commercial College
82 S. Main St., Washington 15301
Stanley Bazant, Dir.

Pennco Tech, 3815 Otter St., Bristol 19007

Pennsylvania College of Technology
1 College Ave., Williamsport 17701

Pennsylvania College of Technology
Mansfield Rd., Wellsboro 16901

Pennsylvania Institute of Culinary Arts
717 Liberty Ave., Pittsburgh 15222

Pennsylvania Institute of Technology
Rose Valley-Notre Dame Campus
800 Manchester Ave., Media 19063
610-565-7900

Pennsylvania State University, Altoona Campus
3000 Ivyside Park, Altoona 16601
Carson W. Veach, Director

Pennsylvania State University, Allentown Center
Fogelsville 18051

PENNSYLVANIA STATE UNIVERSITY
Beaver Campus, Monaca 15061
David Otto, Campus Executive Officer
412-773-3800
See listing under "Universities"

Pennsylvania State University, Berks Campus
P.O. Box 7009, Reading 19610

Pennsylvania State University, Delaware Campus
25 Yearsley Mill Rd., Media 19063

Pennsylvania State University, DuBois Campus
College Place, DuBois 15801
Thomas Hewitt, Dir. of Admis.

Pennsylvania State University, Fayette Campus
P.O. Box 519, Uniontown 15401
Hugh M. Barclay, Director

Pennsylvania State University, Hazleton Campus
Hazleton 18201

Pennsylvania State University
0 University Dr., Mc Keesport 15132
Cash Kawalski, Director

Pennsylvania State University, Mont Alto Campus
Mont Alto 17237

Pennsylvania State University
3550 Seventh St. Rd.
New Kensington 15068

Pennsylvania State University, Ogontz Campus
1600 Woodland Rd., Abington 19001

Pennsylvania State University, Schuylkill Campus
200 University Dr.
Schuylkill Haven 17972

Pennsylvania State University
147 Shenango Valley Ave.
Sharon 16146

Pennsylvania State University, Wilkes-Barre Campus
P.O. Box PSU, Lehman 18627
800-426-2358

Pennsylvania State University
Worthington Scranton Campus
120 Ridgeview Dr., Dunmore 18512

Pennsylvania State University
1031 Edgecombe Ave., York 17403

Penn Technical Institute
110 9th St., Pittsburgh 15222
Louis Dimasi, Director

Pittsburgh Institute of Aeronautics
P.O. Box 10897, Pittsburgh 15236

Pittsburgh Technical Institute
635 Smithfield St., Pittsburgh 15222
Cathy Gost, VP of Admissions

Reading Area Community College
P.O. Box 1706, Reading 19603
Robin Sodomsky, Dir. of Admis.

Restaurant School
4207 Walnut St., Philadelphia 19104
Deborah A. Dunn, Admissions Director

RETS Education Center
2641 West Chester Pike, Broomall 19008

Thaddeus Stevens State School of Technology
Lancaster 17602

Triangle Tech
P.O. Box 551, Du Bois 15801

Triangle Tech
2000 Liberty St., Erie 16502

Triangle Tech
222 E. Pittsburgh St.
Greensburg 15601

Triangle Tech
1940 Perrysville Ave., Pittsburgh 15214

VALLEY FORGE MILITARY ACADEMY & COLLEGE
1001 Eagle Rd., Wayne 19087
Rear Adm. Virgil Hill, USN (Ret.), President
800-234-VFMA

Welder Training and Testing Institute
100 Pennsylvania Ave., Selinsgrove 17870
Thomas H. Miller, Director
717-743-5500

Welder Training Institute
729 E. Highland St., Allentown 18103
John D. Groblewski, Director

Westmoreland County Community College
400 Armbrust Rd., Youngwood 15697

Williamsport School of Commerce
941 W. Third St., Williamsport 17701

RHODE ISLAND

Community College of Rhode Island
Flanagan Campus
1762 Louisquisset Pike, Lincoln 02865

Community College of Rhode Island
Providence Campus
1 Hilton St., Providence 02905

Community College of Rhode Island
Knight Campus
400 East Ave., Warwick 02886

New England Institute of Technology
2500 Post Rd., Warwick 02886
Michael K. Diehl, Dir. of Admis.
800-736-7744

SOUTH CAROLINA

Aiken Technical College
P.O. Box 696, Aiken 29802

Central Carolina Technical College
506 N. Guignard Dr., Sumter 29150
Dr. Herbert Robbins, President
803-778-6640

Chesterfield-Marlboro Technical College
P.O. Box 1007, Cheraw 29520

Columbia Junior College of Business
P.O. Box 1196, Columbia 29202
Michael Gorman, President

Denmark Technical College
P.O. Box 327, Denmark 29042
Joann R.G. Boyd, Ph.D., President
803-793-3301

Florence Darlington Technical College
P.O. Box 8000, Florence 29501

Greenville Technical College
P.O. Box 5616, Greenville 29606

Horry-Georgetown Technical College
P.O. Box 1966, Conway 29526

Johnson & Wales University
701 E. Bay St., Charleston 29403

Midlands Technical College
P.O. Box 2408, Columbia 29202

Nielsen Electronics Institute
1600 Meeting St., Charleston 29405
803-722-2344

Orangeburg-Calhoun Technical College
3250 Saint Matthews Rd. N.E., Orangeburg 29115

Piedmont Technical College
P.O. Box 1467, Greenwood 29648

Spartanburg Methodist College
1200 Textile Rd., Spartanburg 29301
George Fields, President

Spartanburg Technical College
P.O. Box 4386, Spartanburg 29305
Pam Hagan, Dir. Admissions & Counseling
803-591-3800

Technical College of the Lowcountry
100 S. Ribaut Rd., Beaufort 29901

Tri-County Tech College
P.O. Box 587, Pendleton 29670

Trident Technical College
P.O. Box 10367, Charleston 29411
Charles Branch, President

University of South Carolina at Beaufort
801 Carteret St., Beaufort 29902
Dr. Chris P. Plyler, Dean

University of South Carolina
P.O. Box 889, Lancaster 29721
John R. Arnold, Dean

University of South Carolina - Salkehatchie Campus
P.O. Box 617, Allendale 29810
Dr. Carl Clayton, Dean

University of South Carolina at Sumter
200 Miller Rd., Sumter 29150
J. C. Anderson, Dean

University of South Carolina at Union
P.O. Box 729, Union 29379
James Edwards, Dean

Williamsburg Technical College
601 Lane Rd., Kingstree 29556

York Technical College
452 S. Anderson Rd., Rock Hill 29730

SOUTH DAKOTA

Kilian Community College
224 N. Phillips Ave., Sioux Falls 57102
605-336-1711 or 800-888-1147

NETTLETON ACADEMY OF HAIR DESIGN
400 W. 9th St., Sioux Falls 57104
Herman Whitaker, Dir. of Admissions
800-727-1837 or 605-336-1837

NETTLETON JUNIOR COLLEGE
100 S. Spring Ave., Sioux Falls 57104
Roger Hunt, Director
800-727-1837 or 605-336-1837

Oglala Lakota Community College
PO Box 861, Pine Ridge 57770

Presentation College
1500 N. Main St., Aberdeen 57401
Sr. Lucille Welbig, Dir. of Admis.

Sisseton Wahpeton Community College
P.O. Box 689, Sisseton 57262

TENNESSEE

Aquinas Junior College
4210 Harding Rd., Nashville 37205
Sr. Robert Ann Britton, President

Chattanooga State Technical Community College
4501 Amnicola Hwy., Chattanooga 37406

Cleveland State Community College
P.O. Box 3570, Cleveland 37320

Columbia State Community College
P.O. Box 1315, Columbia 38402

Cooper Institute
724 5th Ave., N., Knoxville 37917
Judy Ferguson, Dean

Cumberland School of Technology
1065 E. 10th St., Cookeville 38501

Draughons Junior College
1860 Wilma Rudolph Blvd.
Clarksville 37040

Draughon's Junior College
3200 Elvis Presley Blvd., Memphis 38116

Draughon's Junior College
Plus Park at Pavilion Blvd., Nashville 37217

Dyersburg State Community College
P.O. Box 648, Dyersburg 38025
Carl C. Andersen, President

Electronic Computer Programming Institute
3805 Brainerd Rd., Chattanooga 37411

Fugazzi College
5042 Linbar Dr., Nashville 37211
615-333-3344

Hiwassee College, Madisonville 37354

ITT Technical Institute
P.O. Box 148029, Nashville 37214
Nathan L. Blaede, Director

ITT Technical Institute
1637 Downtown West Blvd. #22, Knoxville 37919

Jackson State Community College
P.O. Box 2467, Jackson 38302

John A. Gupton College
1616 Church St., Nashville 37203
John Gupton, President

Knoxville Business College
720 5th Ave., N., Knoxville 37917

Martin Methodist College
433 W. Madison St., Pulaski 38478
Bill Rutherford, Dean of Admissions

Morristown College
417 James St., N., Morristown 37814
Dr. Charles Wade, President

Motlow State Community College
P.O. Box 88100, Tullahoma 37388

Nashville Auto-Diesel College
1524 Gallatin Rd., Nashville 37206
Peggie Robertson, Dir. of Admis.
See listing under "Career Schools"

Nashville State Technical Institute
120 White Bridge Rd., Nashville 37209
Ed Pawlawski, Dir. of Admis.

Northeast State Technical Community College
P.O. Box 246, Blountville 37617

Nossi College of Art
907 Two Mile Pky. #E6, Goodlettsville 37072
Nossi Vatandoost, Director
615-851-1088

Pellissippi State Technical Community College
P.O. Box 22990, Knoxville 37933

ROANE STATE COMMUNITY COLLEGE
276 Patton Ln., Harriman 37748
Dr. Sherry Hoppe, President

Shelby State Community College
P.O. Box 40568, Memphis 38174

Southeast College of Technology
2731 Nonconnah Blvd., Memphis 38132

State Technical Institute
5983 Macon Cove, Memphis 38134
Charles O. Whitehead, President

Tennessee Institute of Electronics
3203 Tazewell Pk., Knoxville 37918

Volunteer State Community College
1360 Nashville Pike, Gallatin 37066
Hal Ramer, President

Walters State Community College
500 S. Davy Crockett Pky., Morristown 37813

Watkins Institute School of Interior Design
601 Church St., Nashville 37219
Wanda Palus, Director
615-242-1851

TEXAS

Alvin Community College
3110 Mustang Rd., Alvin 77511

Amarillo College
P.O. Box 447, Amarillo 79178
Dale Hardgrove, Registrar

ANGELINA COLLEGE
P.O. Box 1768, Lufkin 75902
Dr. Larry M. Phillips, President
Jill A. Hill, Registrar
409-639-1301
Established 1968. Public. Coed. Accreditation: SACS. Tuition: $550. Room and board: $2,100. Enrollment: 112 boarding, 4,000 day. Faculty: 70. Degrees: Occupational Certificate, AA, AS. Library: 40,000 volumes. 15 buildings on 140 acres. Gym. Located between Houston & Dallas, 10 miles from Lake Sam Rayburn (largest lake in Texas). State of the art computer laboratories for business science & technical majors. Academic and needs based Scholarships available.

Art Institute of Dallas
8080 Park Ln., Dallas 75231
Lee Colker, Dir. of Admis.

The Art Institute of Houston
1900 Yorktown St., Houston 77056
Cherie R. McNeel, Dir. of Admis.
800-275-4244

Austin Community College
5930 Middle Fiskville Rd., Austin 78752
Clifton Van Dyke, Dir. of Admis.
512-483-7000

Bauder Fashion College
508 S. Center St., Arlington 76010
Charm Kettle, Dir. of Admis.

Bee County College, 3800 Charco Rd., Beeville 78102
Dr. Norman Wallace, Pres.

Blinn College
902 College Ave., Brenham 77833
Waldo F. Burt, Registrar

Blinn College
1905 Texas Ave., Bryan 77590

Brazosport College
500 College Dr., Lake Jackson 77566
James Barta, Dir. of Admis.

Brookhaven College
3939 Valley View, Farmers Branch 75244
Fred Gracia, Dir. of Admissions

Cedar Valley College
3030 N. Dallas Ave., Lancaster 75134
John W. Williamson, Dir. of Admissions

Central Texas College
P.O. Box 1800, Killeen 76540

Cisco Junior College
R.R. 3, Box 3, Cisco 76437

Clarendon College, P.O. Box 968, Clarendon 79226
Kenneth D. Vaughan, Pres.

College of the Mainland
1200 Auburn Rd., Texas City 77591
Dr. Robert Johnston, Dir. of Admis.

Collin County Community College
2200 W. University, Mc Kinney 75070

Commonwealth Institute of Funeral Service
415 Barren Springs Dr., Houston 77090

Del Mar College
101 Baldwin Blvd., Corpus Christi 78404
Lawrence Jasman, Registrar

Eastfield College, 3737 Motley Dr., Mesquite 75150
Bobbie Trout, Admis. Ofc.

El Centro College
801 Main St., Dallas 75202
Queen Randall, President

El Paso Community College
P.O. Box 20500, El Paso 79998
Dr. Robert E. Shapack, President

Frank Phillips College
P.O. Box 5118, Borger 79008

Galveston College
4015 Ave. Q, Galveston 77550
John Pickelman, President

Grayson County College
6101 Highway 691, Denison 75020
Jim Williams, President

Hallmark Institute of Technology
South Campus-Aviation Technology
P.O. Box 780459, San Antonio 78278
Richard Fessler, President
Bill Buss, Campus Director
210-924-8551

Hallmark Institute of Technology
North Campus-Electronics Technology
& Business Courses
10401 W. IH 10, San Antonio 78230
Richard Fessler, President
Jeanne Martin, Campus Director
210-690-9000

Hill College
P.O. Box 619, Hillsboro 76645
W. R. Auvenshine, President

Houston Community College
P.O. Box 7849, Houston 77270
Pat Davis, Registrar

Howard College
1001 Birdwell Ln., Big Spring 79720
Linda Conway, Dir. of Admis.

Howard College
Southwest Collegiate Institute for the Deaf
Ave. C, Big Spring Industrial Park
Big Spring 79720

ITT Technical Institute
2201 Arlington Downs Rd., Arlington 76011

ITT Technical Institute
1821 Rutherford Ln., Austin 78754

ITT Technical Institute
15621 Blue Ash Dr. #160, Houston 77090

ITT Technical Institute
9421 W. Sam Houston Pky., Houston 77099

ITT Technical Institute
1640 Eastgate Dr. #100, Garland 75041

ITT Technical Institute
4242 E. Piedras Dr. #100
San Antonio 78228

JACKSONVILLE COLLEGE
105 B. J. Albritton Dr.
Jacksonville 75766
903-586-2518
Don B. Nelson, Academic Dean
Established 1899. Private. Coed. Accreditation: SACS. Tuition: $2,400. Room and board: $2,496. Fees: $370. Enrollment: 300 full-time, 75 part-time. Faculty: 18. Student-faculty ratio: 18:1. Degrees: AA, AS, Junior College Diploma. Library: 23,000 volumes. 11 buildings on 18 acres. Quality education in a Christian environment. Outstanding music department with traveling choir, vocal and wind ensembles. International student office. AJCAA men's basketball and women's volleyball action.

Kilgore College
1100 Broadway Blvd., Kilgore 75662
Joe Cruseturner, Registrar

Lamar University-Port Arthur
P.O. Box 310, Port Arthur 77641
409-727-0886

Lamar University-Orange
410 W. Front St., Orange 77630
409-883-7750

Laredo Junior College
1 W. End Washington St., Laredo 78040
Elpha Lee West, Dir. of Admis.

Lee College
511 S. Whiting, Baytown 77520
Dr. Vivian Blevins, President

Lon Morris College
822 College Ave., Jacksonville 75766
Faulk Landrum, President

McLennan Community College
1400 College Dr., Waco 76708
Dennis Michaelis, President

Microcomputer Technology Institute
7277 Regency Square Blvd., Houston 77036

Microcomputer Technology Institute
17164 Blackhawk Blvd., Friendswood 77546

Midland College
3600 N. Garfield St., Midland 79705
Dr. David E. Daniel, President

MISS WADE'S FASHION MERCHANDISING COLLEGE
Dallas Market Center, Suite M5120
The International Apparel Mart
P.O. Box 586343, Dallas 75258
800-624-4850
Frank Tortoriello, President
Suzun Wade, Executive Director
Charles Restivo, Admissions Vice President
Dr. Doris Kennedy, Academic Dean
Established 1965. Coed. Private. Accreditation: SACS Commission on Colleges. Tuition: $4,610. Room and board: $1,870. Fees: $125. Enrollment: 350. Faculty: 20. Student - faculty ratio: 15:1. Degrees: AA in Merchandising and Design. Library: 10,000 volumes. 7 buildings on 200 acres. Located in the world's largest wholesale merchandising complex - the Dallas Market Center, Located also in the world's Premier Fashion Showcase - the International Apparel Mart.

Mountain View College
4849 W. Illinois Ave., Dallas 75211

Navarro College
3200 W. 7th Ave., Corsicana 75110

National Education Center-Bryman Campus
9724 Beechnut #300, Houston 77036

National Education Center-Bryman Campus
16416 Northchase Dr. #300, Houston 77060

NEC-Fort Worth Campus
300 E. Loop 820, Fort Worth 76112

NEC-National Institute of Technology
10945 Estates Ln., Dallas 75238
L. Kent Langum, President
800-242-6995

NEC-National Institute of Technology
3622 Fredricksburg Rd.
San Antonio 78201

North Central Texas College
1525 W. California, Gainesville 76240
Doug Willis, Dir. of Admis.

NORTHEAST TEXAS COMMUNITY COLLEGE
P.O. Box 1307, Mount Pleasant 75456
903-572-1911

North Harris County College
2700 W. W. Thorne Blvd., Houston 77073

North Lake College
5001 N. MacArthur Blvd., Irving 75038

Odessa College
201 W. University, Odessa 79762
915-335-6575

Palo Alto College
1400 W. Villaret, San Antonio 78224

Panola College
1109 W. Panola St., Carthage 75633
Gary McDaniel, President

Paris Junior College
2400 Clarksville St., Paris 75460

Ranger Junior College
P.O. Box 135, Ranger 76470
Jim Cockburn, Registrar

Richland College, 12800 Abrams Rd., Dallas 75243
Dana Goodrich, Registrar

St. Phillip's College
2111 Nevada St., San Antonio 78203
John B. Murphy, Dean

San Antonio College
1300 San Pedro Ave., San Antonio 78212

San Jacinto College
4624 Fairmont Pky., Pasadena 77504
Thomas M. Spencer, President

South Plains College
1401 College Ave., Levelland 79336
Marvin L. Baker, President

Southwest Institute of Merchandising & Design
9611 Acer Ave., El Paso 79925
Mary Simon, President

Southwest Texas Junior College
2401 Garner Field Rd., Uvalde 78801
Wayne Matthews, President

Tarrant County Junior College
1500 Houston St., Ft. Worth 76102
C. A. Roberson, President

Tarrant County Junior College-N.E. Campus
828 Harwood Rd., Hurst 76054
Dr. Herman Crow, President

Tarrant County Junior College-N.W. Campus
4801 Marine Creek Pkwy., Ft. Worth 76179
Dr. Michael Saenz, President

Tarrant County Junior College-South Campus
5301 Campus Dr., Ft. Worth 76119
Dr. Jim Worden, President

Temple Junior College
2600 S. 1st St., Temple 76504

Texarkana Community College
2500 N. Robison Rd., Texarkana 75501

Texas Southmost College
83 Fort Brown, Brownsville 78520
Dr. Albert A. Besteiro, President

Texas State Technical College Waco/Marshall
3801 Campus Dr., Waco 76705
817-867-3371

Texas State Technical Institute, Amarillo Campus
Box 11197, Amarillo 79111
Dr. James Bird, Gen. Manager

Texas State Technical Institute, Harlingen 78550

Texas State Technical Institute
P.O. Box 18, Sweetwater 79556

Trinity Valley Community College
500 N. Prairieville, Athens 75751

Trinity Valley Community College
800 Hwy. 243 W., Kaufman 75142

TYLER JUNIOR COLLEGE
P.O. Box 9020, Tyler 75711
Kenneth D. Lewis, Dean of Admissions
903-510-2398
Established 1926. Public. Coed. Accreditation: SACS. Tuition: $580. Room and board: $2,100. Enrollment: 4,000 full-time, 4,200 part-time. Faculty: 300. Student-faculty ratio: 20-25:1. Degrees offered: AA, AAS, Certificate. 30 buildings on 73 acres. Strong Liberal Arts - College Transfer. 35 Vocational Technical Programs. Strong Allied Health program. Outstanding Music-Drama department. Excellent Science, Mathematics program. Athletic programs: football, baseball, mens & womens basketball, tennis, and soccer. Residential Life: 600 spaces available and Support Services available.

Universal Technical Institute
721 Lockhaven Dr., Houston 77073
In TX 713-443-6262 or 800-392-5319
Outside TX 800-325-0354

Vernon Regional Junior College
4400 College Dr., Vernon 76384
Roy Wiederanders, Dean of Admissions

Victoria College
2200 E. Red River St., Victoria 77901
Roland E. Bing, President

Weatherford College
308 E. Park Ave., Weatherford 76086
Dr. Jim Boyd, President
817-594-5471

Western Technical Institute
1000 Texas Ave., El Paso 79901

Western Technical Institute
4710 Alabama St., El Paso 79930

WESTERN TEXAS COLLEGE
6200 S. College Ave., Snyder 79549
Dr. Harry Krenek, President
Dr. Duane Hood, Dean of Student Services
915-573-8511
Established 1971. Public. Coed. Accreditation: SACS. Tuition: $600. Room and board: $2,000. Enrollment: 228 boarding, 1,300 day. Faculty: 60. Degrees: AA, AAS, AGE. Library: 25,000 volumes. 20 buildings on 165 acres. Gym. Pool. Racquetball courts. Golf course. Museum. Majors in all liberal arts and preprofessional programs, plus cosmetology, diesel mechanics, golf and landscape technology, law enforcement, management, secretarial, vocational nursing, welding, and word processing. Sports: basketball, rodeo, golf.

Wharton County Junior College
911 Boling Hwy., Wharton 77488
Dr. Theodore Nicksick, Jr., President

UTAH

Certified Careers Institute
1455 W. 2200 S. #200, Salt Lake City 84119

College of Eastern Utah
451 E. 400 N., Price 84501

Dixie College
225 S. 700 E., St. George 84770

ITT Technical Institute
920 LeVoy Dr., Murray 84123

L.D.S. Business College
411 E. South Temple
Salt Lake City 84111

Phillips Junior College
3098 Highland Dr. #100, Salt Lake City 84106
Wayne Wilson, President
801-485-0221

Salt Lake Community College
4600 S. Redwood Rd., Salt Lake City 84123

Snow College
150 E. 100 N., Ephraim 84627
Ross Findlay, Director, Admissions

Stevens Henager College
2168 Washington Blvd., Ogden 84401

Stevens Henager College
25 E. 1700 S., Provo 84606

Utah Valley Community College
1200 S. 800 W., Orem 84058

VERMONT

Community College of Vermont
P.O. Box 120, Waterbury 05676
Nancy Severance, Registrar

Landmark College, Putney 05346
802-387-4767

Sterling College, Craftsbury Common 05827
Sarabelle Hitchner, Dir. of Admis.

Vermont Technical College
Randolph Center 05061
Robert Clarke, President

VIRGINIA

Blue Ridge Community College
P.O. Box 80, Weyers Cave 24486
James R. Perkins, President

Central Virginia Community College
3506 Wards Rd., Lynchburg 24502
Belle Wheelan, President

College of Health Sciences
P.O. Box 13186, Roanoke 24031
Ruth Robertson, Registrar

Commonwealth College
300 Boush St., Norfolk 23510
Debbi Huck, Dean of Admissions

Commonwealth College
4160 Virginia Beach Blvd., Virginia Beach 23452
Nancy Kennedy, Dean of Admissions

Commonwealth College
1120 W. Mercury Blvd., Hampton 23666
Robyn Rickenbach, Dean of Admissions

Dabney S. Lancaster Community College
P.O. Box 1000, Clifton Forge 24422
John F. Backels, President

Danville Community College
1009 Bonner Ave., Danville 24541
Dr. John Backels, President

Eastern Shore Community College
29300 Lankford Hwy., Melfa 23410
John C. Fiege, President

Germanna Community College
P.O. Box 339, Locust Grove 22508
Linda Crooker, Registrar

ITT Technical Institute
863 Glenrock Rd., Norfolk 23502

Johnson & Wales University
2430 Almedea Ave., Norfolk 23513

John Tyler Community College
13101 Jefferson Davis Hwy., Chester 23831
Dr. Freddie W. Nicholas, Jr., Pres.

J. Sargeant Reynolds Community College
P.O. Box C-23040, Richmond 23261

Lord Fairfax Community College
P.O. Box 47, Middletown 22645
Dr. Marilyn Beck, President

Mountain Empire Community College
P.O. Box 700, Big Stone Gap 24219
Victor B. Ficker, President

National Business College
100 Logan St., Bluefield 24605
703-326-3621

National Business College
1819 Emmet St., Charlottesville 22901
804-295-0136

National Business College
734 Main St., Danville 24541
804-793-6822

National Business College
1813 E. Main St., Salem 24153
Frank Longaker, Chrpsn.
703-986-1800

National Business College
10 Church St., Martinsville 24112
703-632-5621

National Business College
300A Piedmont Ave., Bristol 24201
703-669-5333

National Business College
104 Candlewood Ct., Lynchburg 24502
804-239-3500

National Business College
51B Burgess Rd., Harrisonburg 22801
703-432-0943

New River Community College
P.O. Box 1127, Dublin 24084
Margaret McConnell, Coord. of Admissions

Northern Virginia Community College
3001 N. Beauregard St., Alexandria 22311
Dr. Jean Netherton, Provost

Northern Virginia Community College
8333 Little River Turnpike, Annandale 22003
Dr. Barbara Guthrie-Morse, Provost

Northern Virginia Community College
6901 Sudley Rd., Manassas 22110
Dr. Gail B. Kettelwell, Provost

Northern Virginia Community College
1000 Harry Flood Byrd Hwy., Sterling 20164
Dr. R. Neil Reynolds, Provost

Northern Virginia Community College
15200 Neabsco Mills Rd., Woodbridge 22191
Dr. Lionel B. Sylvas, Provost

Patrick Henry Community College
P.O. Box 5311, Martinsville 24115
Dr. Max Wingett, President

Paul D. Camp Community College
P.O. Box 737, Franklin 23851
Edwin Barnes, President

Piedmont Virginia Community College
R.R. 6, Box 1A, Charlottesville 22902

Rappahannock Community College
P.O. Box 287, Glenns 23149
Dr. John Upton, President

Richard Bland College of the College of William & Mary
11301 Johnson Rd., Petersburg 23805
Roger Gill, Dir. of Enrollment Services

SOUTHERN VIRGINIA COLLEGE FOR WOMEN
One College Hill Dr., Buena Vista 24416
Mark A. Camper, Assoc. Dir. of Admis.
800-229-8420
See listing under "Women's Colleges"

Southside Virginia Community College
R.R. 1, Box 60, Alberta 23821
Dr. John Sykes, Jr., Dir. of Admis.

Southside Virginia Community College
John Daniel Campus
R.R. 1, Box 15, Keysville 23947
Dr. John Sykes, Jr., Dir. of Admis.

Southwest Virginia Community College
P.O. Box SVCC, Richland 24641
Dr. Charles R. King, President

Thomas Nelson Community College
P.O. Box 9407, Hampton 23670
Judy B. McMillan, Dir. of Admis.

Tidewater Community College, Chesapeake Campus
1428 Cedar Rd., Chesapeake 23320
Dr. Larry L. Whitworth, President

Tidewater Community College, Portsmouth Campus
Rt. 135, Portsmouth 23703
Dr. Larry L. Whitworth, President

Tidewater Community College
1700 College Crescent, Virginia Beach 23456
Dr. Larry L. Whitworth, President

Virginia College
2163 Apperson Dr., Salem 24153

Virginia Highlands Community College
P.O. Box 828, Abingdon 24212
Dr. Emma W. Schulken, President

Virginia Western Community College
P.O. Box 14025, Roanoke 24038
Charles L. Downs, President

Wytheville Community College
1000 W. Main St., Wytheville 24382
Admissions Office

WASHINGTON

Art Institute of Seattle
2323 Elliott Ave., Seattle 98121
Doug Worsley, Dir. of Admis.

Bellevue Community College
3000 Landerholm Circle, S.E., Bellevue 98007

Big Bend Community College
7662 Chanute St. N.E.
Moses Lake 98837

Centralia College
600 W. Locust St., Centralia 98531
Neena Stoskopf, Dir. of Admis./Records

Clark College
1800 E. McLoughlin Blvd., Vancouver 98663

Columbia Basin College
2600 N. 20th Ave., Pasco 99301

Edmonds Community College
20000 68th Ave., W., Lynnwood 98036
Thomas Nielsen, President

Everett Community College
801 Wetmore Ave., Everett 98201
206-388-9100

Grays Harbor College
1620 Edward P. Smith Dr., Aberdeen 98520

Green River Community Colleges
12401 S.E. 320th St., Auburn 98002

Highline Community College, Des Moines 98198

ITT Technical Institute
1050 N. Argonne Rd., Spokane 99212
Ralph E. Oscarson, Director

ITT Technical Institute
12720 Gateway Dr. S. #100, Seattle 98168
Thomas M. Hauser, Director

Lower Columbia College
P.O. Box 3010, Longview 98632

North Seattle Community College
9600 College Way, N., Seattle 98103

Northwest Indian College, Bellingham 98226

Olympic College
1600 Chester Ave., Bremerton 98337
Wallace Simpson, President

Peninsula College
1502 E. Lauridsen Blvd., Port Angeles 98362
Joyce M. Helens, President

PHILLIPS JUNIOR COLLEGE OF SPOKANE
1101 N. Fancher Rd., Spokane 99212
509-535-7771

Pierce College
9401 Farwest Dr., S.W., Tacoma 98498
206-964-6501

Pierce College
1601 39th Ave. S.E., Puyallup 98374
206-840-8400

Resource Center for the Handicapped
20150 45th Ave., N.E., Seattle 98155

Seattle Central Community College
1701 Broadway, Seattle 98122
Loris A. Blue, Dir. of Admis.

Shoreline Community College
16101 Greenwood Ave., N., Seattle 98133
Chuck Fields, Registrar

Skagit Valley College
2405 E. College Way, Mt. Vernon 98273

South Puget Sound Community College
2011 Mottman Rd., S.W., Olympia 98512

South Seattle Community College
6000 16th Ave., S.W., Seattle 98106

Spokane Community College
1810 N. Greene St., Spokane 99207

Spokane Falls Community College
3410 W. Ft. George Wright Dr., Spokane 99204

Tacoma Community College
5900 S. 12th St., Tacoma 98465

WALLA WALLA COMMUNITY COLLEGE
500 Tausick Way, Walla Walla 99362
Dr. Steven VanAusdle, President
Joseph Frostad, Dir. of Admis.
509-527-4283
Established 1967. Public. State. Accreditation: NASC, SBCTC. Tuition: $1,326 resident, $5,124 non-resident. Faculty: 105. Library: over 36,000 volumes. Degree: AA or AS; Associate's degree for transfer & certified vocational programs such as farrier, cosmetology, business & commerce, mechanical & technical, and health science.

Wenatchee Valley College
1300 5th St., Wenatchee 98801
509-664-2533

Whatcom Community College
237 W. Kellogg Rd., Bellingham 98226
Laine Johnston, Coordinator of Admissions
206-676-2170

Yakima Valley Community College
16th & Nob Hill Blvd., Yakima 98902

WEST VIRGINIA

Beckley College
P.O. Box AG, Beckley 25802
Patricia Campbell, Dean Recruitment/Admissions

Huntington Junior College of Business
900 5th Ave., Huntington 25701

NEC-National Institute of Technology
5514 Big Tyler Rd., Cross Lanes 25313

Potomac State College of West Virginia University
Keyser 26726

Salem College-Clarksburg
112 N. 6th St., Clarksburg 26301

Southern West Virginia Community College
P.O. Box 2900, Logan 25601

Southern West Virginia Community College
Williamson 25661
Dr. William E. Barrett, Provost

Webster College
412 Fairmont Ave., Fairmont 26554
Sharron Stephens, Director

West Virginia Career College at Charleston
1000 Virginia St., E., Charleston 25301

West Virginia Career College at Morgantown
148 Willey St., Morgantown 26505

West Virginia Northern Community College
150 Park Ave., Weirton 26062

West Virginia Northern Community College
College Square, Wheeling 26003

West Virginia University at Parkersburg
R.R. 5, Box 167-A, Parkersburg 26101
R. Copeland, Registrar

WISCONSIN

Blackhawk Technical College
P.O. Box 5009, Janesville 53547

Chippewa Valley Technical College
620 Clairemont Ave., W., Eau Claire 54701

Fox Valley Technical College
P.O. Box 2277, Appleton 54913

Gateway Technical College
400 S. County Rd. H, Elkhorn 53121

Gateway Technical College
3520 30th Ave., Kenosha 53144

Gateway Technical College
1001 S. Main St., Racine 53403

ITT Technical Institute
6300 W. Layton Ave., Milwaukee 53220

Lac Courte Oreilles Ojibwa Community College
R.R. 2 Box 2357, Hayward 54843

Lakeshore Technical College
1290 North Ave., Cleveland 53015

Madison Area Technical College
3550 Anderson Rd., Madison 53704
Beverly Simone, District Director

Madison Area Technical College
1300 W. Main St., Watertown 53098

Madison Junior College of Business
1110 Spring Harbor Dr., Madison 53705
Jeffry S. Sears, President
608-238-4266

Mid-State Technical College
500 32nd St., N., Wisconsin Rapids 54494

Mid-State Technical College
2600 W. 5th, Marshfield 54449

Mid-State Technical College
933 Michigan Ave., Stevens Point 54481

Milwaukee Area Technical College
700 W. State St., Milwaukee 53233

Milwaukee Area Technical College
6665 S. Howell Ave., Oak Creek 53154

Milwaukee Area Technical College
West Allis 53214

Milwaukee Area Technical College-North
5555 W. Highland Rd., Mequon 53092

Moraine Park Technical College
2151 N. Main St., West Bend 53095-1598
Maureen Josten, Campus Administrator
414-334-3413

Moraine Park Technical College
235 N. National Ave., Fond du Lac 54936
Dr. John Shanahan, President
414-922-8611

Moraine Park Technical College
700 Gould St., Beaver Dam 53916-1994
Ron Thompson, Campus Administrator
414-887-1101

Nicolet Area Technical College
P.O. Box 518, Rhinelander 54501
Richard J. Brown, Director

Northcentral Technical College
1000 Campus Dr., Wausau 54401
Dr. Donald Hagen, President

Northeast Wisconsin Technical College
P.O. Box 19042, Green Bay 54307

Northeast Wisconsin Technical College
1601 University Dr., Marinette 54143

Northeast Wisconsin Technical College
229 N. 14th Ave., Sturgeon Bay 54235

Southwest Wisconsin Technical College
Fennimore 53809

STRATTON COLLEGE
1300 N. Jackson St., Milwaukee 53202
Robert H. Ley, Director
414-276-5200

University of Wisconsin Center, Manitowoc Co.
705 Viebahn St., Manitowoc 54220
Chester Natunewicz, Dean

University of Wisconsin Center, Marinette Co.
Bay Shore, Marinette 54143
William Schmidtke, Dean

University of Wisconsin Center
P.O. Box 150, Marshfield 54449
Norbert E. Koopman, Dean

University of Wisconsin Center, Fox Valley
Menasha 54952
Rue Johnson, Campus Dean

University of Wisconsin Center, Rock County
2909 Kellogg Ave., Janesville 53546
Jane Crisler, Dean
608-758-6565

University of Wisconsin Center, Richland
Richland Center 53581
Donald R. Gray, Dean

University of Wisconsin Center, Sheboygan County
1 University Dr., Sheboygan 53081
Kenneth M. Bailey, Dean

University of Wisconsin Center, Waukesha County
1500 N. University Dr., Waukesha 53188
Mary Knudten, Dean

University of Wisconsin Center, Marathon County
518 S. 7th Ave., Wausau 54401
Dr. Stephen R. Prtch, Dean

University of Wisconsin Center, Washington County
400 University Dr., West Bend 53095
Robert O. Thompson, Dean

University of Wisconsin Center-Fond du Lac
Fond du Lac 54935
Willard Henken, Dean

University of Wisconsin Center - Barron County
1800 College Dr., Rice Lake 54868
Dr. Mary H. Somers, Dean
715-234-8176

Waukesha County Technical College
800 Main St., Pewaukee 53072
Dr. Richard T. Anderson, Dir.

Wisconsin Indianhead Technical College
HCR 69, Box 10-B, Shell Lake 54871

Wisconsin School of Electronics
1227 N. Sherman Ave., Madison 53704
Donald Madlung, Director

WYOMING

Casper College
125 College Dr., Casper 82601
A. W. Vance, Dir. of Admis.

CENTRAL WYOMING COLLEGE
2660 Peck St., Riverton 82501
Mary Gores, Admissions Officer
307-856-9291
Established 1966. Public. Coed. Accreditation: NCACS. Tuition: $700 in state, $2,100 out of state. Room and board: $2,800. Fees: $138 per semester. Enrollment: 700 full-time, 850 part-time. Faculty: 46 full-time, 222 part-time and off campus. Student-faculty ratio: 16:1. Degrees offered: AA, AS, AAA, AAS, Certificate, Diploma. Library: 40,000 volumes. 13 buildings on 109 acres. Offers more than 50 degrees, diploma and certificate programs, including art, music, theatre, nursing, surgical technology, human development services, business, computer science, biology, physical science, agriculture, horse management, auto technology and welding. Outstanding music-drama department, rodeo team and livestock judging team. Individual help for students.

EASTERN WYOMING COLLEGE
3200 West C St., Torrington 82240
Dr. Chuck Engbretson, President
Diana Ford, Dir. of Admis.
800-658-3195
Established 1948. Public. Coed. Accreditation: NCACS. Tuition: $2,316. Room and board: $2,500. Enrollment: 168 boarding, 480 day. Faculty: 48. Degrees: AA, AS, AAS. Library: 23,000 volumes. 10 buildings on 45 acres. Gym. Special areas of study include air conditioning/refrigeration, agribusiness, secretarial science, cosmetology, criminal justice, nanny training, veterinary technology, transport refrigeration, and welding. Relaxed western area near rivers & mountains, yet near large metropolitan areas.

Laramie County Community College
1400 E. College Dr., Cheyenne 82007
Dr. Harlan L. Heglar, President

Northern Wyoming Community College
720 W. 8th St., #1, Gillette 82716

Northwest College
231 W. 6th St., Powell 82435
Steve Sims, Dir. of Admissions

Sheridan College
P.O. Box 1500, Sheridan 82801
Bruce Gifford, Dir. of Admis.

WESTERN WYOMING COMMUNITY COLLEGE
2500 College Dr., Rock Springs 82901
Dr. Tex Boggs, President
Marty Kelsex, Dean of Administration
Jackie Freeze, Dir. of Admis.
Established 1959. Accreditation: NCACS. Tuition: $416 per semester resident, $1,116 per semester non-resident. Estimated annual expense: $4,500. Enrollment: approximately 4,000 students, consisting of 980 full-time students and the balance part-time commuters. On-campus housing for approximately 280 full-time students. Residence halls are apartment and suite style dwellings, and are very popular. Apply for housing early; a $100 deposit is needed to hold a room.
WWCC has a open door admission policy - all applicants are accepted after meeting the basic requirements. Admission application, official copies of high school and any previous college transcripts or GED scores must be submitted prior to acceptance. 75% of the full-time students have some financial aid. Federal programs are honored and various institutional aids are available.
The transfer AA degree is offered in: anthropology, art, biology, business & management, chemistry, engineering, English, foreign language, geology, history, journalism, math, music, photography, physical education, political science, pre-law, pre-medicine, psychology, respiratory therapy, sociology and speech & theatre. The terminal AAS degree is offered in: building trades, electric/electronics, home management, industrial technology, mine maintenance, office information systems, radiology, and welding. A variety of technical certificate programs are also available.
WWCC participates in collegiate women's and men's basketball. A full intramural program is available to all students and staff.
WWCC welcomes students from all backgrounds and we do our very best to see that each student succeeds in his or her chosen endeavor. We feel that the community college provides the necessary two-years of background for a transfer student as well as adequate skills for those who wish to go directly into the working world after their two-year technical program.

Wyoming Technical Institute
4373 N. 3rd St., Laramie 82070

GUAM

American Samoa Community College
P.O. Box 2609, Pago Pago 96799

Guam Community College
P.O. Box 23069, Agana 96921

PUERTO RICO

Columbia College
P.O. Box 8517, Caguas 00726

Huertas Junior College
P.O. Box 8429, Caguas 00726

Instituto Comercial de Puerto Rico Junior College
558 Munoz Rivera Ave. #304, San Juan 00918
Pedro Sobrino, Dir. of Admissions

Inter American University of Puerto Rico
APDO 1559 Guayama 00785
Joaquin Rodriguez, Registrar

Puerto Rico Junior College
P.O. Box 21373, San Juan 00928
Rosalia Astacio, Dir. of Admissions

Puerto Rico Technical Jr College
Ave. Ponce De Leon #703
Hato Rey 00917

Ramirez College of Business Technology
P.O. Box 8074, Santurce 00910

Technological College of San Juan
Jose Oliver, Final Box 70179, San Juan 00918

University of Puerto Rico
Aguadilla Regional College
P.O. Box 160, Aguadilla 00604

University of Puerto Rico
Carolina Regional College
P.O. Box 4800, Carolina 00984

University of Puerto Rico
La Montana Regional College
P.O. Box 1449, Utuado 00641

COMPUTER AND INFORMATION SCIENCE

This classification contains schools accredited by the Computer Science Accreditation Commission (†) and a selection of programs from institutionally accredited schools.

ALABAMA

† Auburn University, Auburn 36849

· Gadsden State Community College
P.O. Box 227, Gadsden 35902
W. Bryan Stone, Dir. of Admis.

Huntingdon College
1500 E. Fairview Ave., Montgomery 36106-2148
Carolyn A. Phillips, Dean of Enrollment
800-763-0313

Samford University
800 Lakeshore Dr., Birmingham 35229
W. D. Peeples, Chrpsn.

STILLMAN COLLEGE
P.O. Box 1430, Tuscaloosa 35403
Barbara K. Smith, Director of Admissions
See listing under "Universities"

† University of Alabama
P.O. Box 870132, Tuscaloosa 35487-0132
Roy Smith, Dir. of Admis.

† University of Alabama at Birmingham
University Station, Birmingham 35294

† UNIVERSITY OF ALABAMA IN HUNTSVILLE
P.O. Box 1247, Huntsville 35899
Ron R. Koger Ed.D., Dir. of Admis.
205-895-6070
Established 1969. Public. Coed. Accreditation: SACS, ABET, NLN, CSAB, ACS. Tuition: $2,418 resident, $4,836 non-resident. Room & Board: $3,450. Undergraduate enrollment: 2,674 full-time, 3,439 part-time. Graduate enrollment: 1,860. Faculty: 282. Student-faculty ratio: 18:1. Degrees: BS, BA, BSBA, BSE, MS, MSM, Ph.D., BSN, MSN, MA. 20 buildings on 350 acres. Comprehensive research university located in the Tennessee Valley of northern Alabama. Huntsville is the locale of major government and private research centers. Metropolitan population approaching 300,000.

UNIVERSITY OF MOBILE
P.O. Box 13220, Mobile 36663-0220
Kim Leousis, Dir. of Admissions
205-675-5990
See listing under "Universities"

† University of South Alabama
307 University Blvd. N., Mobile 36688

ALASKA

† University of Alaska Fairbanks
Fairbanks 99775

ARIZONA

· Arizona Western College
P.O. Box 929, Yuma 85366-0929
Bob Davis, Dir. of Admis.

: CAD Institute/The CAD Center
4100 E. Broadway Rd., Phoenix 85040
Dominic Pistillo, President
CAD and Virtual Reality Degree
800-658-5744

DeVry Institute of Technology
2149 W. Dunlap Ave., Phoenix 85021
Kim Galetti, Dir. of Admis.
602-870-9201
See Illinois listing under "Universities"

Northern Arizona University
P.O. Box 4092, Flagstaff 86011
Dr. Margaret Cibik, Dir. of Admis.

University of Arizona, Tucson 85721
Loyd Bell, Director of Admissions

Yavapai College
1100 E. Sheldon St., Prescott 86301
Dr. Doreen Dailey, President
602-445-7300
See listing under "Community and Junior Colleges"

ARKANSAS

Arkansas State University
P.O. Box 2771, State University 72467

Ouachita Baptist University
410 Ouachita St., Arkadelphia 71998
Randy Garner, Dir. of Admis.
800-DIAL-OBU

· Phillips County Community College
P.O. Box 785, Helena 72342
Dr. Steven Jones, President
James R. Brasel, Dean of Admissions

† University of Arkansas at Little Rock
2801 S. University Ave., Little Rock 72204

CALIFORNIA

· Bakersfield College
1801 Panorama Dr., Bakersfield 93305
Robert M. Bruker, Dir. of Admis.

Biola University
13800 Biola Ave., La Mirada 90639
Wayne Chute, Dean of Admissions

† California Polytechnic State University
San Luis Obispo 93407
Helen Linstrum, Dir. of Admis.

† California State University, Chico
Chico 95929-0720
Dr. Kenneth Edson, Dir. of Admis.

† California State University, Northridge
18111 Nordhoff St., Northridge 91330
Ned C. Reynolds, Dir. of Admis.

† California State University, Sacramento
6000 J St., Sacramento 95819

† California State University, San Bernardino
5500 University Pky., San Bernardino 92407
909-880-5188

† California State University-Fullerton
Fullerton 92632

† California State University-Stanislaus
801 W. Monte Vista Ave., Turlock 95382
Frances Cook, Dean Enrollment Services

Chapman University
333 N. Glassell St., Orange 92666
Michael Drummy, Dir. of Admis.

· City College of San Francisco
50 Phelan Ave. Box L245, San Francisco 94112
Ron Cerutti, Dept. Chair
415-239-3655

College of Notre Dame
1500 Ralston Ave., Belmont 94002
Greg M. Smith, PhD., Dir. of Admis.

DeVry Institute of Technology
901 Corporate Center Dr., Pomona 91746
Keith Paridy, Dir. of Admis.
909-622-9800
See Illinois listing under "Universities"

: D. T. I. Career Institute
1937 W. Chapman Ave. #100, Orange 92668
E. Ray Poole, Director of Admissions
714-937-3989

Fresno Pacific College
1717 S. Chestnut Ave., Fresno 93702
209-453-2039

La Sierra University
4700 Pierce St., Riverside 92505
800-874-5587

Master's College
P.O. Box 221450, Newhall 91322
Don Gilmore, Dir. of Admis.

· Napa Valley College
2277 Napa-Vallejo Hwy., Napa 94558
Delores Smith, Asst. Dean of Admissions
707-253-3000

National University
4141 Camino del Rio, S., San Diego 92108
Dr. Carol Blomstrom, Dept. Head

· ORANGE COAST COLLEGE
P.O. Box 5005, Costa Mesa 92628
See listing under "Community and Junior Colleges"

Pacific Union College
1 Angwin Ave., Angwin 94508
Dr. Gary Gifford, Dir. of Admis.

· Santa Barbara City College
721 Cliff Dr., Santa Barbara 93109
805-965-0581

† University of California, San Diego
9450 Gilman Dr., La Jolla 92092

† University of California, Santa Barbara
Santa Barbara 93106

University of California-Santa Cruz
Santa Cruz 95064
Joseph Allen, Dir. of Admis.

† University of San Francisco
2130 Fulton St., San Francisco 94117
Bill Henley, Dir. of Admis.

† University of Southern California
University Park Campus
Los Angeles 90089

† University of the Pacific
3601 Pacific Ave, Stockton 95211
Elliott J. Taylor, Dean of Admissions

Woodbury University
7500 Glenoaks Blvd., Burbank 91504
See listing under "Universities"

COLORADO

COLORADO TECHNICAL COLLEGE
4435 N. Chestnut St., Colorado Springs 80907
719-598-0200
The transition from high-tech education to high-tech careers is Colorado Tech's specialty! Situated in the middle of a space age community known as Silicon Mountain, the college takes pride in its mission to serve high-tech businesses and industries by providing graduates able to hit the ground running in such fields as: computer engineering, computer science, electrical engineering, electronic engineering technology, telecommunications, systems management, and logistics. Colorado Tech, accredited by NCA and ABET, offers Associate, Bachelor and Master degrees.
Bachelor of Science degrees are offered in computer science, electrical engineering, computer engineering, logistics systems management, systems management, and telecommunication electronics technology. Master of Science degrees are offered in computer science, computer engineering, electrical engineering and management. The Master of Science in computer science has concentrations in software engineering, computer systems engineering, and systems engineering. The Carnegie Mellon University Software Engineering Institute model curriculum is offered by Colorado Tech in the software engineering concentration.
Colorado Tech believes students should not only learn in the classroom, but in the laboratory as well, applying their knowledge to real world problems. The professor and students work in an environment that encourages constant interaction in the learning process. Class size is limited to 40 students and labs are limited to 24 students. Colorado Tech's state of the art equipment is always available: no one waits in line.
It is no surprise that companies such as Digital, Loral, MCI, Apple, Atmel, Litton, United Technologies, Hewlett-Packard, Ford Microelectronics, GE Aerospace, Hughes Aircraft and Cray Research have chosen Colorado Springs with its USAF space center and US Space Foundation to locate facilities here. Many of these companies have representatives who sit on our advisory boards and many of our professors come from these companies.
The Colorado Springs area offers many recreational activities such as skiing, fishing, hunting, hiking, mountain climbing and four wheeling. NFL football, NBA basketball, National League baseball, the symphony and varied expressions of popular culture provide ample entertainment for every taste. Soar to meet your destiny through higher education at Colorado Tech.

Metropolitan State College of Denver
P.O. Box 173362, Campus Box 16
Denver 80217-3362

Regis University
3333 Regis Blvd., Denver 80221
Robert Blust, Director of Admissions

† United States Air Force Academy
Colorado Springs 80840

† University of Colorado at Colorado Springs
P.O. Box 7150, Colorado Springs 80933

University of Northern Colorado, Greeley 80639
Steve Teglovic, Department Chrpsn.
303-351-2089

CONNECTICUT

† Central Connecticut State University
1615 Stanley St., New Britain 06053

: Connecticut School of Electronics
586 Ella T. Grasso Blvd., New Haven 06519
Karen George, Director
203-624-2121

· Mattatuck Community College
750 Chase Parkway, Waterbury 06708
Dr. Richard Sanders, President

QUINNIPIAC COLLEGE
275 Mount Carmel Ave., Hamden 06518
See listing under "Universities"

University of Bridgeport
126 Park Ave., Bridgeport 06601
Andrew G. Nelson, Dean Admis./Financial Aid
203-576-4552
See listing under "Universities"

DELAWARE

University of Delaware, Newark 19711

DISTRICT OF COLUMBIA

† The American University
4400 Massachusetts Ave. N.W.
Washington 20016

† George Washington University
Washington 20052

† Howard University
2400 6th St., N.W., Washington 20059
James E. Cheek, President

Mt. Vernon College
2100 Foxhall Rd., N.W., Washington 20007
202-625-4682 or 800-682-4636, FAX: 202-338-1089

Southeastern University
501 I St., S.W., Washington 20024

FLORIDA

· Edison Community College
8099 College Pky., Fort Myers 33919
Mailing address: P.O. Box 60210
Fort Myers 33906-6210
Sandra Fahey, Dir. of Admis. and Records

Embry-Riddle Aeronautical University
600 S. Clyde Morris Blvd.
Daytona Beach 32114-3900
800-222-ERAU

† Florida Atlantic University
500 N.W. 20th St., Boca Raton 33431
Brian Levin-Stankevich, Dir. of Admis.

Florida Institute of Technology
150 W. University Blvd., Melbourne 32901
Louis T. Levy, Dean of Admissions
800-888-4348

† Florida State University
600 W. College Ave., Tallahassee 32306

· International Fine Arts College
1737 N. Bayshore Dr., Miami 33132
Frayda Parnes, Dir. of Admis.
800-225-9023 or 305-373-4684
See listing under "Art"

Jacksonville University
2800 University Blvd., N., Jacksonville 32211

Jones College
5353 Arlington Expy., Jacksonville 32211
Dorothy D. Jones, Chief Executive Officer

Orlando College - North
5500 Diplomat Circle, Orlando 32810

Palm Beach Atlantic College
P.O. Box 24708, West Palm Beach 33416-4708
See listing under "Universities"

SCHILLER INTERNATIONAL UNIVERSITY (FLORIDA & EUROPE)
U.S. Admissions Office
Dept. PA, 453 Edgewater Dr., Dunedin 34698-7532
800-336-4133 Fax: 813-736-6263
Dr. Walter Liebrecht, President
Karen Altieri, Associate Director of Admissions
See listing under "Universities"

Tampa College
3319 W. Hillsborough Ave., Tampa 33614
David Zorn, President

Tampa College - Pinellas
15064 U.S. Hwy. 19 N., Clearwater 34624
Mark A. Page, President
813-530-9495

† University of Central Florida
P.O. Box 25000, Orlando 32816

University of Miami
P.O. Box 248006, Coral Gables 33124

† University of North Florida
4567 St. Johns Bluff Rd. S., Jacksonville 32224

† University of South Florida
4202 Fowler Ave., Tampa 33620

GEORGIA

† Armstrong State College
11935 Abercorn St., Savannah 31419
Kim West, Director of Admissions

AUGUSTA COLLEGE
2500 Walton Way, Augusta 30904-2200
Lee Young, Dir. of Admis.
706-737-1405

DeVry Institute of Technology
250 N. Arcadia Ave., Decatur 30030
George Ollennu, Dir. of Admis.
404-292-2645
See Illinois listing under "Universities"

Georgia College
231 W. Hancock St., Milledgeville 31061
912-453-5004

† Georgia Institute of Technology
225 North Ave. N.W., Atlanta 30332

Kennesaw State College
P.O. Box 444, Marietta 30061
Joe Head, Dir. of Admis.

La Grange College
601 Broad St., La Grange 30240
Phil Dodson, Dir. of Admis.
706-882-2911

Oglethorpe University
4484 Peachtree Rd., N.E., Atlanta 30319
Dennis Matthews, Dir. of Admis.

· Phillips Junior College
1400 W. Peachtree St., N.W., Atlanta 30309

Savannah State College
State College Branch, Savannah 31404
Robert Ray, Dir. of Admis.

IDAHO

· Ricks College, Rexburg 83460
Steven Bennion, President

ILLINOIS

: Commonwealth Business College
1527 47th Ave., Moline 61265
Don Watson, Director
309-762-2100

De Paul University
1 E. Jackson Blvd., Chicago 60604
Thomas D. Abrahamson, Dean of Admissions
See listing under "Universities"

DeVry Institute of Technology
3300 N. Campbell Ave., Chicago 60618
Richard Yaconis, Dir. of Admis.
312-929-6550
See Illinois listing under "Universities"

DeVry Institute of Technology
1221 N. Swift Rd., Addison 60101
Milt Kobus, Dir. of Admis.
708-953-2000
See Illinois listing under "Universities"

† Illinois Benedictine College
5700 College Rd., Lisle 60532

ILLINOIS WESLEYAN UNIVERSITY
P.O. Box 2900, Bloomington 61702
Dr. Susan Anderson-Freed, Chrpsn.
309-556-3186

KASKASKIA COLLEGE
27210 College Rd., Centralia 62801
618-532-1981 or 800-642-0859 (Illinois)
Raymond D. Woods, President
Marilyn Brookman, PhD, College Dean
Constance Stohlman, Director of Admissions,
Public Relations, and Resource Development
Kaskaskia College is situated on a beautifully
wooded tract of land consisting of 190 acres. Its brick
and frame buildings provide 228,830 square feet of
space for college facilities. Kaskaskia College is fully
accredited by NCACS, ADA, AMA, NLN, IBE, ICCB,
and IBHE. The College is recognized and approved by
the bureau of Veterans Affairs and is authorized under Federal law to enroll non-immigrant alien students. In district tuition and fees are $33.75 per
semester credit hour. Degrees: AA, AS, AAS, and
AGS. University transfer programs, pre-professional,
liberal arts, courses offered days, evenings, and weekends. Training in career fields. State and Federal
financial aid programs available.

KNOWLEDGE SYSTEMS INSTITUTE
3420 Main St., Skokie 60076
Dr. Shi-Kuo Chang, President
Judy Chang, Director of Admissions
708-679-3135, FAX: 708-679-3166
Founded in 1978, Knowledge Systems Institute is a
small, private, coeducational institution offering
graduate level instruction in the Computer and Information Sciences and Management Information Systems. The Institute provides a unique curriculum
designed to train both students and professionals
through classroom and laboratory instruction and
field work in the student's chosen specialty. Most
classes are offered on weekday evenings and on weekends to accomodate the schedules of working professionals. The Institute's Certificate program introduces
students with no previous backround to the computer
and information sciences. The Master's Degree program in computer information sciences also offers a
concentration in management information systems,
so that students with an interest in business management can specialize in that area. Institute classes are
kept small, allowing each student the individual attention necessary to succeed. In addition to learning
advanced theories and concepts of computer information sciences, students learn to translate theory into
practical applications by conducting research projects under the guidance of faculty advisors. Knowledge Systems Institute is located in the community of
Skokie, Illinois. Facilities include the campus library;
Instructional Computer Laboratory; Advanced Automation Laboratory; Multi-Media Systems Laboratory;
Digital Systems Laboratory; and Center for Chinese
Language Computing. Knowledge Systems Institute
offers dormitory space within close proximity to the
campus. Degrees: M.S. in Computer and Information
Sciences, M.S. in Management Information Systems.
Tuition: $6,000. Room and board: $600/month. Fees:
$40. Student-faculty ratio: 3:1.

LEWIS UNIVERSITY
Rt. 53, Romeoville 60441
Irish O'Reilly, Director of Admissions
See listing under "Universities"

Millikin University
1184 W. Main St., Decatur 62522
Lin Stoner, Dean of Admissions
800-373-7733

· Moraine Valley Community College
10900 S. 88th Ave., Palos Hills 60465
Dr. Vernon Crawley, President

North Central College
30 N. Brainard St.
P.O. Box 3065, Naperville 60566-7065
Marguerite Waters, Director of Admission
708-420-3414

Northeastern Illinois University
5500 N. St. Louis Ave., Chicago 60625

· Parkland College
2400 W. Bradley Ave., Champaign 61821-1899
217-351-2208 or 800-346-8089

Rockford College
5050 E. State St., Rockford 61108
Miriam King, V.P. for Enrollment Management
See listing under "Universities"

ROOSEVELT UNIVERSITY
430 S. Michigan Ave., Chicago 60605
William Smyser, Director of Admissions
See listing under "Universities"

University of Illinois at Chicago
P.O. Box 4348, Chicago 60680
Dr. Robert Abrams, Head

INDIANA

† Ball State University
2000 W. University Ave., Muncie 47306
Ruth Vedvik, Dir. of Admis.

Calumet College
2400 New York Ave., Whiting 46394
Sharon Sweeney, Dir. of Admis.

: Commonwealth Business College
8995 N. State Rd. 39, La Porte 46350
Faye Mercer, Director
219-362-3338

: Commonwealth Business College
4200 W. Lincoln Hwy., Merrillville 46410
Al Conaway, Director
219-769-3321

Franklin College
501 E. Monroe, Franklin 46131
B. Stephen Richards, VP Enrollment

Indiana Wesleyan University
4201 S. Washington St., Marion 46953
800-332-6901

Martin University
P.O. Box 18567, Indianapolis 46218

Purdue University
Schleman Hall, West Lafayette 47907

SAWYER COLLEGE
6040 Hohman Ave., Hammond 46320
Mary Jo Dixon, Director
800-964-0208

SAWYER COLLEGE
3803 E. Lincoln Hwy., Merrillville 46410
Mary Jo Dixon, Director
800-964-0218

Taylor University
500 W. Reade Ave., Upland 46989
Wally Roth, Head

Tri-State University, Angola 46703
Director of Admission
800-347-4878

Valparaiso University, Valparaiso 46383

IOWA

· American Institute of Business
2500 Fleur Dr., Des Moines 50321
Tom Shively, Dir. of Admis.

Clarke College
1550 Clarke Dr., Dubuque 52001
Shiela Castaneda, Chair
800-383-2345

Dordt College
498 4th Ave., N.E., Sioux Center 51250
Quentin Van Essen, Dir. of Admissions
800-343-6738

Drake University
2507 E. University Ave., Des Moines 50311
Thomas Willoughby, Dir. of Admis.

Graceland College, Lamoni 50140
800-638-0053, Outside Iowa 800-346-9208
Bonita Booth, Dean of Admissions
See listing under "Universities"

Grand View College
1200 Grandview Ave., Des Moines 50316
Lori Hanson, Dir. of Admissions
800-444-6083

† Iowa State University, Ames 50011
Karsten Smedal, Dir. of Admis.

Morningside College, Sioux City 51106
Lora Vanderzwaag, Dir. of Admis.

Teikyo Marycrest University
1607 W. 12th St., Davenport 52804
Tim McDonough, Dir. of Admis.
See listing under "Universities"

KANSAS

· Kansas State University
College of Technology
2409 Scanlan Ave., Salina 67401

Ottawa University
1001 S. Cedar St., Ottawa 66067
Steve Koberlein, Dir. of Admis.
800-755-5200

SOUTHWESTERN COLLEGE
100 College St., Winfield 67156
800-846-1543

KENTUCKY

Cumberland College
6178 College Station Dr., Williamsburg 40769
See listing under "Universities"

† Eastern Kentucky University
521 Lancaster Ave., Richmond 40475

Georgetown College
400 E. College St., Georgetown 40324
Garvel Kindrick, Director of Admissions
See listing under "Universities"

Kentucky Wesleyan College
3000 Frederica St., Owensboro 42301

· Louisville Technical Institute
3901 Atkinson Dr., Louisville 40218
George Nunley, Dir. of Admis.

Morehead State University, Morehead 40351
Charles Myers, Director of Admissions
606-783-2000

Murray State University, Murray 42071
Phil Bryan, Director of Admissions
800-272-4MSU

LOUISIANA

† Louisiana State University
8515 Youree Dr., Shreveport 71115

† Lousiana Technical University
P.O. Box 3168, Ruston 71272

Loyola University
6363 St. Charles Ave., New Orleans 70118

† Northeast Louisiana University
700 University Ave., Monroe 71209

† Southern University A & M College
Baton Rouge 70813

† Tulane University
6823 Saint Charles Ave., New Orleans 70118
Richard Whiteside, Dean of Admission

† University of New Orleans
New Orleans 70148

† University of Southwestern Louisiana
P.O. Box 44548, Lafayette 70504
318-231-6553

MAINE

· Northern Maine Technical College
33 Edgemont Dr., Presque Isle 04769

Thomas College
180 W. River Rd., Waterville 04901
Susan Potter, Dir. of Admis.
207-877-0101, ME only 800-339-7001

University of Maine at Fort Kent
25 Pleasant St., Fort Kent 04743
Jerry Nadeau, Dir. of Admis.

University of Southern Maine
96 Falmouth St., Portland 04103
Susan Roberts, Director of Admissions

MARYLAND

· Harford Community College
401 Thomas Run Rd., Bel Air 21015
Charles Deisroth, Coordinator

† Loyola College
4501 N. Charles St., Baltimore 21210
William Bossemeyer III, Dir. of Admis.

Montgomery College
51 Mannakee St., Rockville 20850
Germantown - 301-353-7805
Rockville - 301-279-5184

Morgan State University
Cold Spring Ln. and Hillen Rd., Baltimore 21239

: TESST Electronics and Computer Institute
5122 Baltimore Ave., Hyattsville 20781
Joseph W. Fox, Director
301-864-5750

† United States Naval Academy
117 Decatur Rd., Annapolis 21402

Villa Julie College
1525 Greenspring Valley Rd., Stevenson 21153
Carolyn Manuszak, President

MASSACHUSETTS

American International College
1000 State St., Springfield 01109
Peter Miller, Dean of Admissions

Atlantic Union College
P.O. Box 1000, South Lancaster 01561
Osa Canto, Registrar

Babson College
One College Dr., Babson Park 02157
Charles S. Nolan, Dean of Admission
800-488-3696

Bentley College
175 Forest St., Waltham 02154
Joann McKenna, Dir. of Admis.

Boston University
685 Commonwealth Ave., Boston 02215

† Brandeis University
415 South St, Waltham 02154
David Gould, Dean of Admissions
617-736-3500

DEAN COLLEGE
99 Main St, Franklin 02038
Kathleen Teehan, Dean of Admissions
508-528-9100
See listing under "Community and Junior Colleges"

Fitchburg State College
160 Pearl St., Fitchburg 01420
Marke Vickers, Dir. of Admis.

Hampshire College, Amherst 01002
Audrey Y. Smith, Dir. of Admissions
413-582-5471

Massachusetts Institute of Technology
77 Massachusetts Ave., Cambridge 02139

Nichols College, Dudley 01570

† Northeastern University
360 Huntington Ave., Boston 02115
Kevin Kelly, Dean and Dir. of Undergraduate
Admis.

· North Shore Community College
1 Ferncroft Rd., Danvers 01923

· Quinsigamond Community College
670 W. Boylston St., Worcester 01606
Ron Smith, Dir. of Admis.

SPRINGFIELD TECHNICAL COMMUNITY COLLEGE
1 Armory Square, Springfield 01105
Dr. Patrick E. Tigue, Dir. of Admissions
413-781-7822

Suffolk University
8 Ashburton Place, Boston 02108
Barbara K. Ericson, Assoc. Dean Enrollment &
Retention
617-573-8460

† University of Massachusetts Dartmouth
Old Westport Rd., North Dartmouth 02747
Raymond Barrows, Dir. of Admissions
508-999-8605

† University of Massachusetts Lowell
1 University Ave., Lowell 01854

Western New England College
1215 Wilbraham Rd., Springfield 01119
800-325-1122

† Worcester Polytechnic Institute
100 Institute Rd., Worcester 01609
Kay R. Dietrich, Director of Admissions
508-831-5286

MICHIGAN

Adrian College
110 S. Madison St., Adrian 49221
George Wolf, Dir. of Admis.
See listing under "Universities"

Andrews University, Berrien Springs 49104
Jack Mentges, Dir. of Admis.

Aquinas College
1607 Robinson Rd., S.E., Grand Rapids 49506
Paula Meehan, Dean of Admissions
800-678-9593

Cleary College - Livingston Campus
3750 Cleary College Dr., Howell 48843
Tom Sullivan, President
800-589-1979

Cleary College - Washtenaw Campus
2170 Washtenaw Ave., Ypsilanti 48197
Tom Sullivan, President
800-686-1883

Eastern Michigan University, Ypsilanti 48197
V. M. Rao Tummala, Head
313-487-3060 or 800-GO-TO-EMU

Ferris State University
Office of Admission
420 Oak St., Big Rapids 49307-2020

GMI Engineering & Management Institute
1700 W. 3rd Ave., Flint 48504
Phillip D. Lavender, Dir. of Admis.
See listing under "Engineering"

Michigan State University, East Lansing 48824
Dr. Anthony Wojcik, Chrpsn.

Michigan Technological University
1400 Townsend Dr., Houghton 49931
Joseph A. Galetto, Dir. Enrollment Mgmt.
906-487-2335

: Northeastern School of Commerce
701 N. Madison Ave., Bay City 48708
Louis H. Bork, Director

Northwood University
3225 Cook Rd., Midland 48640
Daniel F. Toland, Dir. of Admis.
800-457-7878

† Oakland University, Rochester 48309
Larry Bartalucci, Registrar

† Western Michigan University, Kalamazoo 49008
Stanley Henderson, Dir. of Enrl. Mgt. & Admis.
616-387-2000

MINNESOTA

Bemidji State University
1500 Birchmont Dr., N.E., Bemidji 56601
800-475-2001

CDI COMPUTERS - ACADEMY
3050 Metro Dr. #200, Minneapolis 55425
Gary McNulty, Director of Admissions
612-851-0066

College of St. Scholastica
1200 Kenwood Ave., Duluth 55811
Dr. Michael Robinson, Chrpsn.
800-447-5444
See listing under "Liberal Arts"

Northwestern College
3003 Snelling Ave., N., St. Paul 55113
Ralph Anderson, Dean of Admissions
800-827-6827 or 612-631-5111

PILLSBURY BAPTIST BIBLE COLLEGE
315 S. Grove St., Owatonna 55060
Alan Potter, President
Larry Tindall, Director of Admissions
800-747-4557

† St. Cloud State University
740 4th Ave., S., St. Cloud 56301
Sherwood Reid, Dir. of Admis.
800-369-4260

† University of Minnesota
2400 Oakland Ave., Duluth 55812
Robert L. Heller, Provost

Winona State University
P.O. Box 5838, Winona 55987
Dr. J. Mootz, Dir. of Admis.

MISSISSIPPI

† Jackson State University
1400 Lynch St., Jackson 39203

† Mississippi State University
P.O. Box J, Mississippi State University 39762

† University of Mississippi, University 38677

† University of Southern Mississippi
P.O. Box 5165, Hattiesburg 39406

MISSOURI

Avila College
11901 Wornall Rd., Kansas City 64145

Central Methodist College
411 CMC Square, Fayette 65248
See listing under "Universities"

Central Missouri State University
Warrensburg 64093
Delores Hudson, Dir. of Admis.

Columbia College
1001 Rogers St., Columbia 65216
Ron Cronacher, Dir. of Admissions
800-231-2391

DeVry Institute of Technology
11224 Holmes St., Kansas City 64131
Michael Thompson, Dir. of Admis.
816-941-2810
See Illinois listing under "Universities"

Maryville University of St. Louis
13550 Conway Rd., Saint Louis 63141
314-576-9300 or 800-MARYVLL

Missouri Southern State College
3950 Newman Rd., Joplin 64801-1595
Steve Earney, Dept. Head
See listing under "Universities"

Missouri Valley College
500 E. College St., Marshall 65340
816-886-6924 ext. 114
See listing under "Universities"

† Southwest Missouri State University
901 S. National Ave., Springfield 65804
Dr. Douglas Durand, Department Head
417-836-4131

† University of Missouri, Rolla
102 Parker Hall, Rolla 65401
David J. Allen, Dir. of Admis. & Financial Aid
800-522-0938

Webster University
470 E. Lockwood Ave., St. Louis 63119
Dr. William Duggan, President
See listing under "Universities"

MONTANA

CARROLL COLLEGE
1610 N. Benton Ave., Helena 59625
Candace Cain, Dir. of Admis.
See listing under "Universities"

· Missoula Vocational Technical Center
909 South Ave. W, Missoula 59801
Charles Couture, Dir. of Admis.

Montana Tech
(formerly Montana College of Mineral
Science and Technology)
1300 W. Park St., Butte 59701-8997
800-445-TECH
See listing under "Engineering"

Rocky Mountain College
1511 Poly Dr., Billings 59102
David Heringer, Dir. of Admis.
See listing under "Universities"

NEBRASKA

Creighton University
2500 California St., Omaha 68178
Dr. John Mordeson, Chrpsn.

Peru State College, Peru 68421
Pamela J. Cosgrove, Dir. of Admis.
402-872-3815

NEVADA

::: Columbia School of Broadcasting
2840 E. Flamingo Rd. #F, Las Vegas 89121
Marcia Brock-Gandy, President

· Phillips Junior College
3320 E. Flamingo Rd. #30, Las Vegas 89121
Robert Ramey, Dir. of Admis.

University of Nevada Las Vegas
4505 S. Maryland Pky., Las Vegas 89154-1021
Admissions: 702-895-3443 or 800-334-UNLV

NEW HAMPSHIRE

New Hampshire College
2500 North River Rd., Manchester 03106
Brad Poznanski, Dir. of Admis.
603-645-9611

Rivier College
420 S. Main St., Nashua 03060
Admissions: 800-44-RIVIER

† University of New Hampshire, Durham 03824
Stanwood C. Fish, Dir. of Admissions

NEW JERSEY

: DeVry Technical Institute
479 Green St., Woodbridge 07095
Danielle Di Napoli, Dir. of Admis.
908-634-9510
See Illinois listing under "Universities"

† Fairleigh Dickinson University, Teaneck 07666
Dennis Craig, Dir. of Admis.
201-692-2553

FELICIAN COLLEGE
262 S. Main St., Lodi 07644
Sr. Mary Austin, OSB, Dir. of Admis.
201-778-1029
See listing under "Universities"

· Hudson County Community College
168 Sip Ave., Jersey City 07306
Joseph O'Halloran, Director of Admissions
201-714-2127

Jersey City State College
2039 Kennedy Blvd., Jersey City 07305
201-200-3234

· Mercer County Community College
West Windsor Campus
1200 Old Trenton Rd., Trenton 08690
Michael Glass, Dir. of Admis.
See listing under "Community and Junior
Colleges"

† New Jersey Institute of Technology
323 Martin Luther King Jr. Blvd., Newark 07102

Rider University
2083 Lawrenceville Rd., Lawrenceville 08648
Susan Christian, Dir. of Admis.

Rowan College of New Jersey, Glassboro 08028
Marvin G. Sills, Dir. of Admis.

† Stevens Institute of Technology, Hoboken 07030

Stockton State College, Pomona 08240
Sal Catalfamo, Dir. of Admis.

Upsala College
345 Prospect St., East Orange 07017
George Lynes, Dean of Admissions

NEW MEXICO

Eastern New Mexico University
Portales 88130
Larry Fuqua, Dir. of Admis.

† New Mexico State University
P.O. Box 30001, Las Cruces 88003

† University of New Mexico, Albuquerque 87131
Robert Weaver, Dean of Admissions

NEW YORK

† Canisius College
2001 Main St., Buffalo 14208
Penelope Lips, Dir. of Admis.
800-843-1517

Clarkson University, Potsdam 13699
Robert Croot, Dir. of Admis.

Colgate University
13 Oak Dr., Hamilton 13346
Dean of Admissions
315-824-7401

† CUNY College of Staten Island
715 Ocean Terr., Staten Island 10301

D'Youville College
320 Porter Ave., Buffalo 14201
Ronald Dannecker, Dir. of Admis.

Elmira College
Park Pl., Elmira 14901
William S. Neal, Dean of Admissions
See listing under "Liberal Arts"

IONA COLLEGE
715 North Ave., New Rochelle 10801
800-231-IONA or 914-633-2503
See listing under "Universities"

: Long Island Business Institute
6500 Jericho Turnpike, Commack 11725
Genevieve Baron, Director
516-499-7100
See listing under "Career Schools"

Long Island University-C. W. Post Campus
Rt. 25A, Brookville 11548
Prof. Susan Dorchak, Chrpsn.
516-299-2293

Manhattan College
4513 Manhattan College Pky., Riverdale 10471
Dr. Edward Brown, Acting Dean of Science

MARIST COLLEGE
290 North Rd., Poughkeepsie 12601
Harry W. Wood, VP Admissions
914-575-3226

Marymount College
100 Marymount Ave., Tarrytown 10591
Gina R. Campbell, Dir. of Admis.
800-724-4312

Medaille College
18 Agassiz Cir., Buffalo 14214
Jacqueline Smukeer, Dir. of Admis.

Mercy College
555 Broadway, Dobbs Ferry 10522
James Nesbitt, Dean of Admissions

New York Institute of Technology
Old Westbury Campus, Old Westbury 11568

Niagara University, Niagara University 14109
George Pachter, Dean of Admissions
800-462-2111
See listing under "Universities"

· Olean Business Institute
301 N. Union St., Olean 14760
Patrick McCarthy, Director
Jeanne Johnston, Director of Admissions
716-372-7978

† Pace University, New York Campus
1 Pace Plaza, New York 10038

† Pace University, Pleasantville/Briarcliff Campus
Bedford Rd., Pleasantville 10570

Pace University, White Plains Campus
78 N. Broadway, White Plains 10603

PLAZA BUSINESS INSTITUTE
7409 37th Ave., Jackson Heights 11372
Sally Ann Weger, Director of Admissions
718-779-1430

† Polytechnic University
333 Jay St., Brooklyn 11201

† Polytechnic University
901 Rt. 110, Farmingdale 11735

· Rochester Business Institute
1850 Ridge Rd. E., Rochester 14622

† Rochester Institute of Technology
1 Lomb Memorial Dr., Rochester 14623
716-475-6631
See listing under "Universities"

· SUNY Adirondack Community College
439 Bay Rd., Queensbury 12804
Levi Brown, Dir. of Admis.
518-793-4491
See listing under "Community and Junior
Colleges"

† SUNY at Albany
1400 Washington Ave., Albany 12222
Micheileen Treadwell, Dir. of
Admission/Financial Aid
518-442-5431

† SUNY at Binghamton
P.O. Box 6001, Binghamton 13902

† SUNY College at New Paltz
75 Manheim Blvd., New Paltz 12561

SUNY College at Old Westbury
P.O. Box 210, Old Westbury 11568
Michael Sheehy, Dir. of Admis.

SUNY at Oswego, Oswego 13126
Dr. Joseph Grant, Jr., Dean of Admissions
315-341-2250

† SUNY College at Plattsburgh, Plattsburgh 12901
Julius Archibald, Jr., Chrpsn.
518-564-2788

· SUNY College of Agriculture and Technology
Morrisville 13408
Dennis Nostrand, Dir. of Admis.

SUNY College of Technology at Farmingdale
Route 110, Farmingdale 11735
Janet Snyder, Dir. of Admis.
516-420-2200

SUNY Institute of Technology at Utica/Rome
P.O. Box 3050, Utica 13504
Roger Sullivan, Dir. of Admis.
See listing under "Universities"

· SUNY Monroe Community College
1000 E. Henrietta Rd., Rochester 14623
716-292-2000

· SUNY Nassau Community College
1 Education Dr., Garden City 11530
Bernard Iantosca, Dir of Admis.

University of Rochester
500 Joseph C. Wilson Blvd., Rochester 14627
Wayne A. Locust, Dir. of Admis.
See listing under "Universities"

NORTH CAROLINA

· Alamance Community College
P.O. Box 623, Haw River 27258
W. Ronald McCarter, President

† Appalachian State University
ASU Station, Boone 28608
Joe Watts, Admissions Officer

· College of The Albemarle
P.O. Box 2327, Elizabeth City 27906
John M. Wells, Asst. Dean of Admissions
919-335-0821, Ext. 220

East Carolina University
1000 E. 5th St., Greenville 27858
Dr. William R. Spickerman, Coord.

Gardner-Webb University
General Delivery, Boiling Springs 28017
Ray M. Hardee, Dean of Admissions
800-253-6472

Mars Hill College
Main St., Mars Hill 28754
Dr. Smith Goodrum, Dean of Admis.

† North Carolina State University
P.O. Box 7001, Raleigh 27695
George Dixon, Dir. of Admis.

· Sandhills Community College
2200 Airport Rd., Pinehurst 28374
910-692-6185

NORTH DAKOTA

MAYVILLE STATE UNIVERSITY
330 3rd St., N.E., Mayville 58257
Ronald Brown, Dir. of Admis.
See listing under "Universities"

† North Dakota State University, Fargo 58105
Richard Shearer, Acting Dir. of Admis.

† University of North Dakota
Box 8193 University Station, Grand Forks 58203

OHIO

: Akron Medical-Dental Institute
1625 Portage Trail W., Cuyahoga Falls 44223
Elizabeth Husk, Director
216-762-9788

· Cuyahoga Community College, Eastern Campus
25444 Harvard Rd., Warrensville Heights 44122

· Cuyahoga Community College, Metropolitan Campus
2900 Community College Ave., Cleveland 44115

· Cuyahoga Community College, Western Campus
11000 W. Pleasant Valley Rd.
Parma Heights 44130

DeVry Institute of Technology
1350 Alum Creek Dr., Columbus 43209
Richard Rodman, Dir. of Admis.
614-253-1525
See Illinois listing under "Universities"

Heidelberg College
310 E. Market St., Tiffin 44883
Stephen E. Eidson, Dean of Admission
800-925-9250

· Kent State University-East Liverpool Campus
400 E. 4th St., East Liverpool 43920
Suzanne Fitzgerald, Dean

Lorain County Community College
1005 Abbe Rd., N., Elyria 44035
Dr. John W. Thrash, Jr., Registrar

† **MARIETTA COLLEGE**
210 5th St., Marietta 45750
Dennis R. DePerro, Dean Admis./Financial Aid
800-331-7896

Mt. Vernon Nazarene College
800 Martinsburg Rd., Mt. Vernon 43050
Ronald Hyson, Dir. of Admis.

Ohio Dominican College
1216 Sunbury Rd., Columbus 43219
800-955-OHIO

Tiffin University
155 Miami St., Tiffin 44883
Kristine M. Boyle, Dir. of Admis.

University of Cincinnati
2700 Clifton Ave., Cincinnati 45221

† University of Dayton
300 College Park Ave., Dayton 45469-0228
Toll-free 800-837-7433
See listing under "Universities"

† University of Toledo
2801 Bancroft St., W., Toledo 43606
Richard Eastop, Dir. of Admis.

† Wright State University
3640 Colonel Glenn Hwy., Dayton 45435

OKLAHOMA

Oklahoma City University
2501 N. Blackwelder Ave., Oklahoma City 73106
Keith Hackett, Dean of Admissions
See listing under "Universities"

Oklahoma State University, Stillwater 74078
G. E. Hedrick, Dept. Head

† University of Tulsa
600 S. College Ave., Tulsa 74104
Dr. Roger Wainwright, Associate Chrpsn.

OREGON

Lewis & Clark College
0615 S.W. Palatine Hill Rd., Portland 97219
Michael Sexton, Dean of Admissions

PENNSYLVANIA

† Allegheny College
520 N. Main St., Meadville 16335
Gayle Pollack, Dir. of Admis.

Beaver College
450 S. Easton Rd., Glenside 19038-3295
Dennis Nostrand, VP for Enrollment Management
Phone: 800-776-BEAVER(2328)
Fax: 215-572-4049
See listing under "Universities"

† Bucknell University, Lewisburg 17837

Carnegie Mellon University
5000 Forbes Ave., Pittsburgh 15213

Chatham College
Woodland Rd., Pittsburgh 15232
Suellen Ofe, Dean of Admis./Financial Aid
See listing under "Women's College"

Clarion University of Pennsylvania
840 Wood St., Clarion 16214

† Drexel University
3141 Chestnut St., Philadelphia 19104
Dean of Enrollment Management

Edinboro University of Pennsylvania
Edinboro 16444
Admissions Office: 800-626-2203

Erie Business Center
246 W. 9th St., Erie 16501
Tony Piccirillo, Dir. of Admis.
See listing under "Career Schools"

Gannon University
109 University Sq., Erie 16541

Geneva College
3200 College Ave., Beaver Falls 15010

GWYNEDD-MERCY COLLEGE
Sumneytown Pike, Gwynedd Valley 19437
Marjorie DeSimone, Dean of Admissions
800-DIAL-GMC
See listing under "Universities"

Harcum Junior College, Bryn Mawr 19010
Mary Pontius, Dean of Admissions

Immaculata College
Immaculata 19345
James P. Sullivan, Dir. of Admis.

Juniata College
1700 Moore St., Huntington 16652

La Salle University
1900 W. Olney Ave., Philadelphia 19141
Br. Gerald Fitzgerald, Dir. of Admis.
See listing under "Universities"

† Lehigh University
27 Memorial Dr. W., Bethlehem 18015

McCann School of Business
47 S. Main St., Mahanoy City 17948
John Slodysko, Director

McCann School of Business
Wilkes Barre Campus
2004 Wyoming Ave., Wyoming 18644
James Noone, Director

Marywood College
2300 Adams Ave., Scranton 18509

Mercyhurst College
501 E. 38th St., Erie 16546
Andrew Roth, Dean of Enrollment
800-825-1926

Montgomery County Community College
340 DeKalb Pike, Blue Bell 19422-0758
Dennis Murphy, Dir. of Admis.

NEC-Allentown Business School Campus
1501 Lehigh St., Allentown 18103
610-791-5100

Robert Morris College
Narrows Run Rd., Coraopolis 15108
James R. Welsh, Dean of Admissions
See listing under "Universities"

Robert Morris College
600 5th Ave., Pittsburgh 15219
James R. Welsh, Dean of Admissions
See listing under "Universities"

St. Joseph's University
5600 City Ave., Philadelphia 19131
Randy Miller, Dir. of Admis.

Slippery Rock University, Slippery Rock 16057
Director of Admissions

Susquehanna University
514 University Ave., Selinsgrove 17870

University of Pittsburgh
4200 5th Ave., Pittsburgh 15260

University of Pittsburgh, Greensburg Campus
1150 Mt. Pleasant Rd., Greensburg 15601
Larry Whatule, Dir. of Admis.
412-836-9880

UNIVERSITY OF PITTSBURGH AT TITUSVILLE
McKinney Hall
504 E Main St., Titusville 16354
Jamie Mowat, Dir. of Admis./Financial Aid
814-827-4427

† University of Scranton
800 Linden St., Scranton 18510

† Villanova University
845 E. Lancaster Ave., Villanova 19085
Stephen R. Merritt, Dir. of Admis.

WESTMINSTER COLLEGE
New Wilmington 16172
Richard Dana Paul, Dir. of Admis.
412-946-7100

Wilkes University
184 S. River St., Wilkes-Barre 18766
Emory P. Guffrovich Jr., Dean of Admissions

RHODE ISLAND

Brown University, Providence 02906

Community College of Rhode Island
Knight Campus
400 East Ave., Warwick 02886

Johnson & Wales University
111 Dorrance St., Providence 02903
Mark S. Burke, Dir. of Admis.

Salve Regina University
1 Ochre Point Ave., Newport 02840
Roselina McKillop, Dean of Admissions

SOUTH CAROLINA

† Clemson University
201 Sikes Hall, Clemson 29634

† Coastal Carolina College
P.O. Box 1954, Myrtle Beach 29578
Dr. Ed Cerny, Director of Admissions

Spartanburg Technical College
P.O. Box 4386, Spartanburg 29305
Pam Hagan, Dir. Admissions & Counseling
803-591-3800

† University of South Carolina, Columbia 29208
Terry Davis, Dir. of Admis.
803-777-7700

† University of South Carolina, Spartanburg 29303

† Winthrop University
701 W. Oakland Ave., Rock Hill 29733
James McCammon, Jr., Dir. of Admis.

SOUTH DAKOTA

Dakota State University
820 N. Washington Ave., Madison 57042
Dr. Richard Puetz, Dean
605-256-5139

Nettleton Junior College
100 S. Spring Ave., Sioux Falls 57104
Herman Whitaker, Dir. of Admissions
800-727-1837 or 605-336-1837

SIOUX FALLS COLLEGE
1501 S. Prairie Ave., Sioux Falls 57105
Susan Reese, Dir. of Admis.
800-888-1047
See listing under "Universities"

TENNESSEE

Austin Peay State University
601 College St., Clarksville 37044

Carson-Newman College
P.O. Box 70552, Jefferson City 37760
See listing under "Universities"

David Lipscomb University
3901 Granny White Pike, Nashville 37204-3951
Wade Sandrell, Dir. of Admis.
800-333-4358

University of Memphis, Memphis 38152
Dr. John Eubank, Dean of Admissions

University of Tennessee at Martin
Martin 38238
Paul Kelley, Director of Admissions
See listing under "Universities"

TEXAS

† Baylor University
P.O. Box 97008, Waco 76798-7008
Diana Ramey, Director of Admissions

DeVry Institute of Technology
4801 Regent Blvd., Irving 75063
Daniel Millan, Dir. of Admis.
214-929-5777
See Illinois listing under "Universities"

Incarnate Word College
4301 Broadway St., San Antonio 78209
Sr. Sally Mitchell, Dean of Enrollment

Our Lady of the Lake University
411 S.W. 24th St., San Antonio 78207-4689
210-434-6711

† Texas Christian University
2800 S. University Dr., Ft. Worth 76129
Dr. Edward Boehm, Jr., Dean of Admissions

Texas State Technical College Waco/Marshall
3801 Campus Dr., Waco 76705
817-867-3371

University of Central Texas
P.O. Box 1416, Killeen 76540
Dr. Pauline Moseley, Dean of the Faculty

† University of Houston
4800 Calhoun Rd., Houston 77204

University of Houston-Clear Lake
2700 Bay Area Blvd., Houston 77058
Darella Banks, Exec. Dir. Enrollment Services

† University of North Texas
P.O. Box 13797, Denton 76203

University of Texas at Austin
0 the University of Texas, Austin 78712

† University of Texas at El Paso
500 W. University Ave., El Paso 79968

UTAH

† Brigham Young University, Provo 84602

Southern Utah University
351 W. Center St., Cedar City 84720
D. Mark Barton, Asst. VP Student Services
801-586-7740

† University of Utah
1400 E. 200 S., Salt Lake City 84112
Dr. J. Stayner Landward, Dir. of Admis.

Utah State University, Logan 84322-1600
Rod Clark, Director of Admissions
801-750-1107

Westminster College of Salt Lake City
1840 S. 1300 E., Salt Lake City 84105
800-748-4753

VERMONT

Champlain College
P.O. Box 670, Burlington 05402
Josephine Churchill, Dir. of Admis.
802-860-2727
See listing under "Universities"

NORWICH UNIVERSITY
65 S. Main St., Northfield 05663
Prof. Frank Vanecek, Head
See listing under "Universities"

Saint Michael's College
Winooski Park, Colchester 05439
800-SMC-8000
See listing under "Liberal Arts"

University of Vermont
194 S. Prospect St., Burlington 05401
802-656-3370

VIRGINIA

Averett College
420 W. Main St., Danville 24541
Gary Sherman, Dean of Enrollment Mgmt.

Christopher Newport College
50 Shoe Ln., Newport News 23606

Clinch Valley College of the University of Virginia
P.O. Box 16, Wise 24293
Lana Low, Dir. Enrollment Management

Commonwealth College
300 Boush St., Norfolk 23510
Debbi Huck, Dean of Admissions

Commonwealth College
4160 Virginia Beach Blvd., Virginia Beach 23452
Nancy Kennedy, Dean of Admissions

· Commonwealth College
    1120 W. Mercury Blvd., Hampton 23666
    Robyn Rickenbach, Dean of Admissions

: Computer Learning Center of Washington
    Plaza 500 Bldg., 6295 Edsall Rd. #210
    Alexandria 22312
    Dave Dahlke, Dir. of Admis.

Ferrum College, Ferrum 24088
    Bob Bailey, Dir. of Admis.

George Mason University
    4400 University Dr., Fairfax 22030-4444
    Patricia Riordan, Dean of Admissions

† Hampton University, Hampton 23668
    Ollie Bowman, Dean of Admissions

LIBERTY UNIVERSITY
    P.O. Box 20000, Lynchburg 24506
    Jay Spencer, VP Recruitment
    800-376-2800
    See listing under "Universities"

Marymount University
    2807 N. Glebe Rd., Arlington 22207
    Charles Coe, Director of Admissions
    800-548-7638 or 703-284-1500
    See listing under "Universities"

† Norfolk State University
    2401 Corprew Ave., Norfolk 23504

† Old Dominion University
    5215 Hampton Blvd., Norfolk 23508

SHENANDOAH UNIVERSITY
    1460 University Dr., Winchester 22601
    Dr. John Happ, Division Chair
    See listing under "Universities"

· Tidewater Community College, Chesapeake Campus
    1428 Cedar Rd., Chesapeake 23320
    Dr. Larry L. Whitworth, President

· Tidewater Community College, Portsmouth Campus
    Rt. 135, Portsmouth 23703
    Dr. Larry L. Whitworth, President

· Tidewater Community College
    1700 College Crescent, Virginia Beach 23456
    Dr. Larry L. Whitworth, President

† Virginia Commonwealth University
    910 W. Franklin St., Richmond 23284

Virginia Military Institute, Lexington 24450

WASHINGTON

: Capitol Business College
    5005 Pacific Hwy. E., Ste. 11
    Olympia 98424

† Eastern Washington University, Cheney 99004
    Roger L. Pugh, Asst. VP, Enrollment Mgmt.
    See listing under "Universities"

† Pacific Lutheran University
    12180 Park Ave. S., Tacoma 98447
    Larry Edison, Chrpsn.

· Skagit Valley College
    2405 E. College Way, Mt. Vernon 98273

† Western Washington University
    516 High St., Bellingham 98225
    Karen G. Copetas, Dir. of Admis.

WEST VIRGINIA

Alderson-Broaddus College
    Philippi 26416
    Craig W. Gould, Director of Admissions
    304-457-1700

Marshall University
    400 Hal Greer Blvd., Huntington 25755
    See listing under "Universities"

The University of Charleston
    2300 MacCorkle Ave., S.E., Charleston 25304
    800-995-GO UC

WEST VIRGINIA WESLEYAN COLLEGE
    59 College Ave., Buckhannon 26201
    Robert Skinner, Director of Admission
    See listing under "Universities"

WISCONSIN

Beloit College
    700 College St., Beloit 53511
    Georgia Duerst-Lahti, Assoc. Professor
    Gov't.; Assoc Dean/College, Computer Services
    608-363-2333

· Madison Junior College of Business
    1110 Spring Harbor Dr., Madison 53705
    Jeffry S. Sears, President
    608-238-4266

Marquette University
    1217 W. Wisconsin Ave., Milwaukee 53233
    Raymond A. Brown, Dean of Admissions

Milwaukee School of Engineering
    1025 N. Broadway, Milwaukee 53202
    Owen Smith, Dean of Admission
    800-332-6763 or 414-277-7200 in metro Milwaukee

St. Norbert College
    100 Grant St., De Pere 54115
    Craig S. Wesley, Dean of Admission
    See listing under "Universities"

· **STRATTON COLLEGE**
    1300 N. Jackson St., Milwaukee 53202
    Robert H. Ley, Director
    414-276-5200

University of Wisconsin, Eau Claire
    Eau Claire 54701

University of Wisconsin
    1 University Plaza, Platteville 53818
    Richard Schumacher, Dean of Admissions

Viterbo College
    815 9th St., S., La Crosse 54601
    Roland W. Nelson, Dir. of Admis.

GUAM

University of Guam
    UOG Station, Mangilao 96923
    Kathleen Owings, Dir. of Admis.

DENTISTRY

This classification contains schools offering a first professional degree accredited by the American Dental Association (†) and a selection of programs from institutionally accredited schools. Colleges and Universities (no dot code) generally offer four-year programs in dentistry or pre-dentistry; Community and Junior Colleges (·) generally offer associate degrees in dental assisting, hygiene and laboratory technology; Career Schools (:) generally offer diplomas in dental assisting, hygiene and laboratory technology.

ALABAMA

· Bishop State Community College
    351 N. Broad St., Mobile 36603-5898
    Yvonne Kennedy, President
    205-690-6801

Huntingdon College
    1500 E. Fairview Ave., Montgomery 36106-2148
    Carolyn A. Phillips, Dean of Enrollment
    800-763-0313

† University of Alabama at Birmingham
    University Station, Birmingham 35294

ALASKA

University of Alaska Anchorage
    3211 Providence Dr., Anchorage 99508
    907-786-1480

ARIZONA

Northern Arizona University
    P.O. Box 4092, Flagstaff 86011
    Dr. Margaret Cibik, Dir. of Admis.

CALIFORNIA

· Bakersfield College
    1801 Panorama Dr., Bakersfield 93305
    Robert M. Bruker, Dir. of Admis.

Chapman University
    333 N. Glassell St., Orange 92666
    Michael Drummy, Dir. of Admis.

La Sierra University
    4700 Pierce St., Riverside 92505
    800-874-5587

† Loma Linda University, Loma Linda 92350
    Sylvia Davis, Chrpsn.
    800-422-4LLU

Pacific Union College
    1 Angwin Ave., Angwin 94508
    Dr. Gary Gifford, Dir. of Admis.

† University of California, Los Angeles
    1247 Murphy Hall, Los Angeles 90024

† University of California, San Francisco
    Parnassus & 3rd Ave., San Francisco 94143

† University of Southern California
    University Park Campus
    Los Angeles 90089

† University of the Pacific
    2155 Webster St., San Francisco 94115
    Dr. Arthur Dugoni, Dean

COLORADO

· Pikes Peak Community College
    5675 S. Academy Blvd.
    Colorado Springs 80906-5498
    Roberta Erickson, Dir. of Admis.
    See listing under "Community and Junior
    Colleges"

Regis University
    3333 Regis Blvd., Denver 80221
    Robert Blust, Director of Admissions

† University of Colorado Health Sciences Center
    4200 E. 9th Ave., Denver 80262
    Robert E. Averbach, DDS, Dean

CONNECTICUT

QUINNIPIAC COLLEGE
    275 Mount Carmel Ave., Hamden 06518
    See listing under "Universities"

† University of Connecticut Health Center
    School of Dental Medicine
    Farmington 06032
    James E. Kennedy, DDS, Dean

DELAWARE

University of Delaware, Newark 19711

DISTRICT OF COLUMBIA

Georgetown University
    37th and O Sts., N.W., Washington 20057
    Dr. Joseph A. Chalmers, Dean of Admis. & Rec.

† Howard University
    2400 6th St., N.W., Washington 20059
    James E. Cheek, President

FLORIDA

Nova Southeastern University
    3301 College Ave., Ft. Lauderdale 33314

· Santa Fe Community College
    3000 N.W. 83rd St., Gainesville 32606
    Lawrence W. Tyree, President

† University of Florida
    226 Tigert Hall, Gainesville 32611

GEORGIA

: Atlanta College of Medical and Dental Careers
    1400 W. Peachtree St., N.W., Atlanta 30309
    Gary Vance, Dir. of Admis.

Georgia College
    231 W. Hancock St., Milledgeville 31061
    912-453-5004

Georgia Southern University, Statesboro 30460

† Medical College of Georgia
    1120 15th St., Augusta 30901
    Dr. Mike Miller, Chrpsn.

HAWAII

Hawaii Pacific University
    45-045 Kamehameha Hwy., Kaneohe 96744

IDAHO

Idaho State University
    P.O. Box 8270, Pocatello 83209

ILLINOIS

Aurora University
    347 S. Gladstone Ave., Aurora 60506
    Peter Pitts, Dir. of Admis.

† Loyola University
    Chicago College of Dental Surgery
    University Medical Center, Maywood 60153

† Northwestern University
    303 E. Chicago Ave., Chicago 60611

ROOSEVELT UNIVERSITY
    430 S. Michigan Ave., Chicago 60605
    William Smyser, Director of Admissions
    See listing under "Universities"

† Southern Illinois University at Edwardsville
    Edwardsville 62026
    Eugene J. Magac, Dir. of Admissions & Records

† University of Illinois at Chicago
    P.O. Box 5220, Chicago 60680
    Dr. Allen Anderson, Dean

INDIANA

† Indiana University-Purdue University
    355 N. Lansing, Indianapolis 46202

· Vincennes University
    1002 N. 1st St., Vincennes 47591

IOWA

† University of Iowa, Iowa City 52242

KANSAS

· Barton County Community College
    R.R. 3, Box 136Z, Great Bend 67530
    Dr. Jim Downing, President

COLBY COMMUNITY COLLEGE
1255 S. Range Ave., Colby 67701
Theron Johnson, Dir. of Admis.

- Kansas City Kansas Community College
7250 State Ave., Kansas City 66112
Don Stump, Dir. of Admis.

McPherson College
1600 E. Euclid St., McPherson 67460

KENTUCKY

Kentucky Wesleyan College
Pre-Dentistry program
3000 Frederica St., Owensboro 42301

- Maysville Community College, Maysville 41056
James Shires, President

Spalding University
851 S. 4th St., Louisville 40203
Dorothy G. Allen, Dir. of Admis.

† University of Kentucky, Lexington 40506

† University of Louisville
2301 S. 3rd St., Louisville 40292
Robert Parrent, Dir. of Admis.

LOUISIANA

† Louisiana State University Medical Center
433 Bolivar St., New Orleans 70112

MAINE

St. Joseph's College, North Windham 04062

MARYLAND

- Essex Community College
7201 Rossville Blvd., Baltimore 21237
Diane Lane, Dir. of Admis.

Goucher College
1021 Dulaney Valley Rd., Baltimore 21204

- Montgomery College
51 Mannakee St., Rockville 20850
Germantown - 301-353-7798
Rockville - 301-279-5124
Takoma Park - 301-650-1332

† University of Maryland
Baltimore Professional Schools
522 W. Lombard St., Baltimore 21201

MASSACHUSETTS

† Boston University Medical Center
100 E. Newton St., Boston 02118
Maxine Peck, Director

- Bristol Community College
777 Elsbree St., Fall River 02720
Frank Noble, Dir. of Admis.

Emmanuel College
400 The Fenway, Boston 02115
Margaret Bonilla, Dir. of Admis.

FORSYTH SCHOOL FOR DENTAL HYGIENISTS
140 Fenway, Boston 02115
Judith Harvey, Dir. of Admis.
617-262-5200 ext. 212, 213.

† Harvard University
Harvard Medical School
25 Shattuck St., Boston 02115

- Massasoit Community College
1 Massasoit Blvd., Brockton 02402
Roberta Noodell, Dir. of Admis.

Quinsigamond Community College
670 W. Boylston St., Worcester 01606
Ron Smith, Dir. of Admis.

† Tufts University, Medical School
136 Harrison Ave., Boston 02111

MICHIGAN

University of Detroit Mercy
2985 E. Jefferson Ave., Detroit 48207
313-446-1859
See listing under "Universities"

† University of Michigan-Ann Arbor
815 S. University Ave., Ann Arbor 48109

MINNESOTA

Mayo Foundation
200 1st St., N.W., Rochester 55901

St. John's University
P.O. Box 7155, Collegeville 56321

† University of Minnesota, Twin Cities
Minneapolis 55455

MISSISSIPPI

- Northeast Mississippi Community College
101 Cunningham Blvd., Booneville 38829

University of Mississippi, University 38677

† University of Mississippi Medical Center
2500 N. State St., Jackson 39216

MISSOURI

Central Methodist College
411 CMC Square, Fayette 65248
See listing under "Universities"

Culver-Stockton College, Canton 63435
Betty Smith, Dean of Admissions
800-537-1883

Evangel College
1111 N. Glenstone Ave., Springfield 65802
David Schoolfield, Dir. of Enrollment

- St. Louis Community College at Forest Park
5600 Oakland Ave., St. Louis 63110
Elizabeth Halpin, Registrar

St. Louis University
221 N. Grand Blvd., St. Louis 63103
Louis A. Menard, Dean of Admissions

† University of Missouri, Kansas City
5100 Rockhill Rd., Kansas City 64110
Leo J. Sweeney, Dir. of Admis. & Registrar

Washington University
4559 Scott Ave., St. Louis 63110

MONTANA

Rocky Mountain College
1511 Poly Dr., Billings 59102
David Heringer, Dir. of Admis.
See listing under "Universities"

NEBRASKA

† Creighton University
2500 California St., Omaha 68178
Dr. Gerald Brundo, Dean

† University of Nebraska at Lincoln
40th & Holdrege, Lincoln 68583
Stephen Leeper, Dean

University of Nebraska Medical Center
600 S., 42nd & Dewey, Omaha 68198
Alastair M. Connell, Dean

NEW HAMPSHIRE

Saint Anselm College
87 Saint Anselm Dr., Manchester 03102
Don Healy, Dir. of Admis.

NEW JERSEY

- Camden County College
P.O. Box 200, Blackwood 08012
Dr. Robert Ramsay, President

Jersey City State College
2039 Kennedy Blvd., Jersey City 07305
201-200-3234

Stockton State College, Pomona 08240
Sal Catalfamo, Dir. of Admis.

† University of Medicine and Dentistry of New Jersey
30 Bergen St., Newark 07107

NEW MEXICO

Eastern New Mexico University
Portales 88130
Larry Fuqua, Dir. of Admis.

- New Mexico Junior College
5317 Lovington Hwy., Hobbs 88240
Robert Snow, Registrar

NEW YORK

Canisius College
2001 Main St., Buffalo 14208
Penelope Lips, Dir. of Admis.
800-843-1517

Columbia University
612 W. 115th St., New York 10025

† New York University
70 Washington Sq., New York 10012

Roberts Wesleyan College
2301 Westside Dr., Rochester 14624
Linda Kurtz, Dir. of Admis.
See listing under "Universities"

SUNY at Stony Brook, Health Sciences Center
Stony Brook 11790

† SUNY at Buffalo
Squire Hall
3435 Main St., Buffalo 14214

† SUNY at Stony Brook
Stony Brook 11794

SUNY HUDSON VALLEY COMMUNITY COLLEGE
80 Vandenburgh Ave., Troy 12180
Linda Sweetman, Dir. of Admis.
See listing under "Career Schools"

University of Rochester
500 Joseph C. Wilson Blvd., Rochester 14627
Marshall Lichtman, MD, Dean
See listing under "Universities"

NORTH CAROLINA

- Alamance Community College
P.O. Box 623, Haw River 27258
W. Ronald McCarter, President

Barton College
College Station, Wilson 27893
Anthony Britt, Dir. of Admis.
800-345-4973/919-399-6318
See listing under "Universities"

- Fayetteville Technical Community College
P.O. Box 35236, Fayetteville 28303

Gardner-Webb University
General Delivery, Boiling Springs 28017
Ray M. Hardee, Dean of Admissions
800-253-6472

St. Andrews Presbyterian College
1700 Dogwood Mile, Laurinburg 28352
Dale B. Montague, Dir. of Admis.

† University of North Carolina at Chapel Hill
Chapel Hill 27599
Ken May, Dir. of Admis.

NORTH DAKOTA

Jamestown College, Jamestown 58405

- North Dakota State College of Science
800 N. 6th St., Wahpeton 58075

OHIO

Bowling Green State University
Bowling Green 43403
John Martin, Dir. of Admis.

† Case Western Reserve University
2040 Adelbert Rd., Cleveland 44106

Malone College
515 25th St., N.W., Canton 44709
Lee Sommers, Dean of Admissions

† Ohio State University
190 N. Oval Mall, Columbus 43210

OHIO VALLEY BUSINESS COLLEGE
500 Maryland Ave., East Liverpool 43920
216-385-1070

- Owens Community College
P.O. Box 10000, Toledo 43699
Jim Welling, Admissions
419-661-7225

OKLAHOMA

Oklahoma City University
2501 N. Blackwelder Ave., Oklahoma City 73106
Dr. Robert Fink, Chair
See listing under "Universities"

Oral Roberts University
7777 S. Lewis Ave., Tulsa 74171
Arthur E. Matzkvech, Dir. of Admis.

University of Oklahoma at Norman
660 Parrington Oval, Norman 73019

† University of Oklahoma Health Science Center
P.O. Box 26901, Oklahoma City 73126
Dr. William E. Brown, Dean

University of Tulsa
600 S. College Ave., Tulsa 74104
Mary Tolar, Asst. to the Dean

OREGON

Linfield College
900 S. Baker St., McMinnville 97128
Thomas Meicho, Dean of Admissions

† Oregon Health Sciences University
3181 S.W. Sam Jackson Pk. Rd., Portland 97201
Dr. Henry VanHassel, Dean

PENNSYLVANIA

Gannon University
109 University Sq., Erie 16541

Grove City College
100 Campus Dr., Grove City 16127
Jeffrey C. Mincey, Dir. of Admis.

Lycoming College, Williamsport 17701

† Temple University
3307 N. Broad St., Philadelphia 19140

† University of Pennsylvania
0 Levy Park, Philadelphia 19104

† University of Pittsburgh
4200 5th Ave., Pittsburgh 15260

WESTMINSTER COLLEGE
New Wilmington 16172
Richard Dana Paul, Dir. of Admis.
412-946-7100

RHODE ISLAND

- Community College of Rhode Island
Flanagan Campus
1762 Louisquisset Pike, Lincoln 02865

SOUTH CAROLINA

Lander College
320 Stanley Ave., Greenwood 29649

† Medical University of South Carolina
171 Ashley Ave., Charleston 29425
W. Marcus Newberry, M.D., Dean

TENNESSEE

Christian Brothers College
Preprofessional Program
650 E. Parkway, S., Memphis 38104

† Meharry Medical College
1005 Dr. D. Todd Jr. Blvd., Nashville 37208

Middle Tennessee State University
Murfreesboro 37132
Roger D. Sims, Dir. of Admis.

University of Tennessee at Martin
Martin 38238
Paul Kelley, Director of Admissions
See listing under "Universities"

† University of Tennessee, Memphis
Health Science Center
800 Madison Ave., Memphis 38163
Office of Enrollment Management

- Volunteer State Community College
1360 Nashville Pike, Gallatin 37066
Hal Ramer, President

TEXAS

† Baylor College of Dentistry
3302 Gaston Ave., Dallas 75246
Dominick DePaola, President & Dean

Baylor University
P.O. Box 97008, Waco 76798-7008
Diana Ramey, Director of Admissions

Hardin-Simmons University
2200 Hickory St., Abilene 79698
Laura Moore, Dir. of Admis.
See listing under "Universities"

· Houston Community College
P.O. Box 7849, Houston 77270
Pat Davis, Registrar

Stephen F. Austin State University
P.O. Box 6078. Nacogdoches 75962

† University of Texas Health Science Center
P.O. Box 20036, Houston 77225

† University of Texas Health Science Center
7703 Floyd Curl Dr., San Antonio 78284

West Texas State University
2501 4th Ave., Canyon 79016
Lila Vars, Dir. of Admis.

UTAH

Weber State University
3750 Harrison Blvd., Ogden 84408

VIRGINIA

Randolph-Macon College
200 Henry St., Ashland 23005
John Conkright, Dean of Admissions

† Virginia Commonwealth University
910 W. Franklin St., Richmond 23284

WASHINGTON

· Tacoma Community College
5900 S. 12th St., Tacoma 98465

† University of Washington, Seattle 98195

WEST VIRGINIA

† West Virginia University
P.O. Box 6001, Morgantown 26506

WEST VIRGINIA WESLEYAN COLLEGE
59 College Ave., Buckhannon 26201
Robert Skinner, Director of Admission
See listing under "Universities"

Wheeling Jesuit College
316 Washington Ave., Wheeling 26003
Fr. Thomas Acker, SJ, President

WISCONSIN

· Blackhawk Technical College
P.O. Box 5009, Janesville 53547

Carthage College
2001 Alford Dr., Kenosha 53140
Brenda A. Porter, VP Enrollment

· Lakeshore Technical College
1290 North Ave., Cleveland 53015

† Marquette University
604 N. 16th St., Milwaukee 53233
Arlene Wroblewski, Director of Admissions

St. Norbert College
100 Grant St., De Pere 54115
Craig S. Wesley, Dean of Admission
See listing under "Universities"

Viterbo College
815 9th St., S., La Crosse 54601
Roland W. Nelson, Dir. of Admis.

WYOMING

· Western Wyoming Community College
2500 College Dr., Rock Springs 82901
Jackie Freeze, Dir. of Admis.
See listing under "Community and Junior Colleges"

PUERTO RICO

† University of Puerto Rico, Medical Sciences Campus
P.O. Box 5067, San Juan 00906

ENGINEERING

This classification contains schools accredited by the Accreditation Board for Engineering and Technology (†) and a selection of programs from institutionally accredited schools. Colleges and Universities (no dot code) generally offer four-year or advanced programs in Engineering; Community and Junior Colleges (·) generally offer associate degrees in Engineering Technology; Career Schools (:) generally offer a diploma in Engineering Technology.

ALABAMA

† Alabama A & M University
P.O. Box 1148, Normal 35762
Dr. Arthur J. Bonds, Dean
See listing under "Universities"

† Auburn University, Auburn 36849

· Gadsden State Community College
P.O. Box 227, Gadsden 35902
W. Bryan Stone, Dir. of Admis.

· Jefferson State Community College
2601 Carson Rd., Birmingham 35215
Jim Blackburn, Dir. of Admis.

Samford University
800 Lakeshore Dr., Birmingham 35229
John Tarvin, Chrpsn.

† Tuskegee University
Tuskegee Institute 36088

† University of Alabama
P.O. Box 870132, Tuscaloosa 35487-0132
Roy Smith, Dir. of Admis.

† University of Alabama at Birmingham
University Station, Birmingham 35294

† UNIVERSITY OF ALABAMA IN HUNTSVILLE
P.O. Box 1247, Huntsville 35899
Ron R. Koger Ed.D., Dir. of Admis.
205-895-6070
Established 1969. Public. Coed. Accreditation: SACS, ABET, NLN, CSAB, ACS. Tuition: $2,418 resident, $4,836 non-resident. Room & Board: $3,450. Undergraduate enrollment: 2,674 full-time, 3,439 part-time. Graduate enrollment: 1,860. Faculty: 282. Student-faculty ratio: 18:1. Degrees: BS, BA, BSBA, BSE, MS, MSM, Ph.D., BSN, MSN, MA. 20 buildings on 350 acres. Comprehensive research university located in the Tennessee Valley of northern Alabama. Huntsville is the locale of major government and private research centers. Metropolitan population approaching 300,000.

† University of South Alabama
307 University Blvd. N., Mobile 36688

ALASKA

† University of Alaska Anchorage
3211 Providence Dr., Anchorage 99508
907-786-1480

† University of Alaska Fairbanks
Fairbanks 99775

ARIZONA

† Arizona State University, Tempe 85287

† DeVry Institute of Technology
2149 W. Dunlap Ave., Phoenix 85021
Kim Galetti, Dir. of Admis.
602-870-9201
See Illinois listing under "Universities"

† Embry-Riddle Aeronautical University
3200 Willow Creek Rd., Prescott 86301
800-442-ERAU

· † Glendale Community College
6000 W. Olive Ave., Glendale 85302
Dr. John Waltrip, President

† Northern Arizona University
P.O. Box 4092, Flagstaff 86011
Dr. Margaret Cibik, Dir. of Admis.

† University of Arizona, Tucson 85721
Loyd Bell, Director of Admissions

· Yavapai College
1100 E. Sheldon St., Prescott 86301
Dr. Doreen Dailey, President
602-445-7300
See listing under "Community and Junior Colleges"

ARKANSAS

† Arkansas State University
P.O. Box 1740, State University 72467

† Arkansas Tech University
215 W. O St., Russellville 72801

John Brown University
2000 W. University, Siloam Springs 72761
Don Crandall, Director of Enrollment Management

· Phillips County Community College
P.O. Box 785, Helena 72342
Dr. Steven Jones, President
James R. Brasel, Dean of Admissions

† University of Arkansas at Fayetteville
Fayetteville 72701

† University of Arkansas at Little Rock
2801 S. University Ave., Little Rock 72204

CALIFORNIA

CALIFORNIA COAST UNIVERSITY
700 N. Main St., Santa Ana 92701
Admissions Office: 800-854-8768 or 714-547-9625
Thomas Neal, President
Linda B. Smith, VP Academic Affairs
William Barcroft, Dean of Admissions
Established 1973. Proprietary. Coed. Accreditation: National Association of Private Non-Traditional Schools & Colleges, California State Department of Education, charter member California Association of State Approved Colleges & Universities, member Association for Adult & Continuing Education. Tuition: $2,200-$3,500. Enrollment: 7,500.
A private college offering off-campus independent study programs in the traditional areas of business administration, management, engineering, psychology, & education. Admissions: rolling trimester, requires official transcripts, letters of recommendation, detailed curriculum vita or occupational history.
Process: evaluation of prior academic work followed by analysis of occupational history, including participation in workshops, seminars, training programs, specialized projects for credit. Credit is demonstrated by challenge exams or specialized course by course independent study programs.
Residency: All course work may be completed off campus, utilizing correspondence methods. All doctoral candidates must meet with faculty advisors in person, upon completion of doctoral dissertation. Scholarships: Interest free loans available to students.

† California Institute of Technology
1201 E. California Blvd., Pasedena 91125
Carole L. Snow, Dir. of Admis.

† California Maritime Academy
P.O. Box 1392, Vallejo 94590

† California Polytechnic State University
San Luis Obispo 93407
Helen Linstrum, Dir. of Admis.

† California State Polytechnic University
3801 W. Temple Ave., Pomona 91768

† California State University, Chico
Chico 95929-0003
Dr. Michael G. Ward, Dean

† California State University, Fresno
Shaw & Cedar Ave., Fresno 93710

† California State University, Long Beach
1250 Bellflower Blvd., Long Beach 90840

† California State University, Los Angeles
5151 Paseo Rancho Castilla, Los Angeles 90032

† California State University, Northridge
18111 Nordhoff St., Northridge 91330
Ned C. Reynolds, Dir. of Admis.

† California State University, Sacramento
6000 J St., Sacramento 95819

† California State University-Fullerton
Fullerton 92633

· † City College of San Francisco
50 Phelan Ave. Box 519, San Francisco 94112
Fabio Saniee, Dept. Chair
415-239-3505

† COGSWELL POLYTECHNICAL COLLEGE
10420 Bubb Rd., Cupertino 95014
Paul Schreivogel, Dean of Student Services
800-264-7955
Established 1887. Private. Coed. Accreditation: WASC. Tuition: $6,600. Enrollment: 100 full-time, 248 part-time. Faculty: 42. Student-faculty ratio: 9:1. Degrees: BS Engineering Technology, BS Electrical and Software Engineering. Library: 12,000 volumes. 1 building on 4 acres. Only Bachelor of Science degree in Music Engineering Technology and Bachelor of Arts degree in Computer and Video Imaging.

College of Notre Dame
1500 Ralston Ave., Belmont 94002
Greg M. Smith, PhD., Dir. of Admis.

† DeVry Institute of Technology
901 Corporate Center Dr., Pomona 91746
Keith Paridy, Dir. of Admis.
909-622-9800
See Illinois listing under "Universities"

† Harvey Mudd College, Claremont 91711

† Humboldt State University
1 Harps St., Arcata 95521

† Loyola Marymount University
Loyola Blvd. at W. 80th, Los Angeles 90045
M. L'Heureux, Dir. of Admis.

Point Loma Nazarene College
3900 Lomaland Dr., San Diego   92106
Bill Young, Dir. of Admis.

† San Diego State University
5300 Campanile Dr., San Diego   92115

† San Francisco State University
1600 Holloway Ave., San Francisco   94132
Corwin Bjonerud, Dir. of Admis.

† San Jose State University
1 Washington Sq., San Jose   95192

† Santa Clara University, Santa Clara   95053

† Stanford University, Stanford   94305

† University of California, Los Angeles
1247 Murphy Hall, Los Angeles   90024

† University of California at Berkeley
McLaughlin Hall, Berkeley   94720

† University of California, Davis
376 Mrak Hall, Davis   95616

† University of California, Irvine
Irvine   92715

† University of California, San Diego
9450 Gilman Dr., La Jolla   92092

† University of California, Santa Barbara
Santa Barbara   93106

† University of California-Santa Cruz
Santa Cruz   95064
Joseph Allen, Dir. of Admis.

University of La Verne
1950 3rd St., La Verne   91750
Mark Bornholdt, Dir. of Admis.

University of Redlands
P.O. Box 3080, Redlands   92373

University of San Diego
5998 Alcala Park, San Diego   92110
Warren Muller, Dir. of Admis.
619-260-4506

† University of Southern California
University Park Campus
Los Angeles   90089

† University of the Pacific
3601 Pacific Ave, Stockton   95211
Elliott J. Taylor, Dean of Admissions

COLORADO

† Colorado School of Mines
Weaver Towers-1811 Elm St.
Golden   80401-1873
Bill Young, Dir. of Enrollment Mgmt.
303-273-3220

† Colorado State University
102 Administration Building, Fort Collins   80523
Mary Ontireros, Dir. of Admissions

† COLORADO TECHNICAL COLLEGE
4435 N. Chestnut St., Colorado Springs   80907
719-598-0200
The transition from high-tech education to high-tech careers is Colorado Tech's specialty! Situated in the middle of a space age community known as Silicon Mountain, the college takes pride in its mission to serve high-tech businesses and industries by providing graduates able to hit the ground running in such fields as: computer engineering, computer science, electrical engineering, electronic engineering technology, telecommunications, systems management, and logistics. Colorado Tech, accredited by NCA and ABET, offers Associate, Bachelor and Master degrees.
Bachelor of Science degrees are offered in computer science, electrical engineering, computer engineering, logistics systems management, systems management, and telecommunication electronics technology. Master of Science degrees are offered in computer science, computer engineering, electrical engineering and management. The Master of Science in electrical engineering has concentrations in electronic systems and communication systems.
Colorado Tech believes students should not only learn in the classroom, but in the laboratory as well, applying their knowledge to real world problems. The professor and students work in an environment that encourages constant interaction in the learning process. Class size is limited to 40 students and labs are limited to 24 students. Colorado Tech's state of the art equipment is always available: no one waits in line.
It is no suprise that companies such as Digital, Loral, MCI, Apple, Atmel, Litton, United Technologies, Hewlett-Packard, Ford Microelectronics, GE Aerospace, Hughes Aircraft and Cray Research have chosen Colorado Springs with its USAF space center and US Space Foundation to locate facilities here. Many of these companies have representatives who sit on our advisory boards and many of our professors come from these companies.
The Colorado Springs area offers many recreational activities such as skiing, fishing, hunting, hiking, mountain climbing and four wheeling. NFL football, NBA basketball, National League baseball, the symphony and varied expressions of popular culture provide ample entertainment for every taste. Soar to meet your destiny through higher education at Colorado Tech.

Mesa State College
P.O. Box 2647, Grand Junction   81502
Sherri Pe'a, Dir. of Admis.

† Metropolitan State College of Denver
P.O. Box 173362, Campus Box 16
Denver   80217-3362

Pikes Peak Community College
5675 S. Academy Blvd.
Colorado Springs   80906-5498
Roberta Erickson, Dir. of Admis.
See listing under "Community and Junior Colleges"

† United States Air Force Academy
Colorado Springs   80840

† University of Colorado at Boulder
Boulder   80309
William A. Douglas, Dean of Admis.

† University of Colorado at Colorado Springs
P.O. Box 7150, Colorado Springs   80933

† University of Colorado at Denver
1200 Larimer, Denver   80204

† University of Denver
2199 S. University Blvd., Denver   80210

† University of Southern Colorado
2200 Bonforte Blvd., Pueblo   81001

CONNECTICUT

BRIDGEPORT ENGINEERING INSTITUTE
785 Unquowa Rd., Fairfield   06430
William M. Krummel, PhD, President
Bruce Hunter, Dean of Student Services
Established 1924. Private. Coed. Accreditation: NEASC, Connecticut Department of Higher Education. Degrees: AS Engineering, BS Mechanical Engineering, BS Electrical Engineering, BS Manufacturing Engineering, BS Information Systems Engineering. Tuition: $270/credit hour for 1993-94. BEI is an evening college of engineering. Students are fully employed adults participating in part-time undergraduate programs. Faculty are mostly full-time practicing professionals, part-time teachers. Three semesters. Students may apply for admission any semester. State, federal and BEI financial aid available.

· † Capital Community - Technical College
401 Flatbush Ave., Hartford   06106
Conrad L. Mallett, President

† Central Connecticut State University
1615 Stanley St., New Britain   06053

· † Greater New Haven State Technical College
88 Bassett Rd., North Haven   06473
Chester Schnepf, Dir. of Admis.

· Mattatuck Community College
750 Chase Parkway, Waterbury   06708
Dr. Richard Sanders, President

· † Norwalk State Technical College
181 Richards Ave., Norwalk   06854
Vincent Grillo, Admissions Officer

· † Thames Valley State Technical College
574 New London Trnpk., Norwich   06360

Trinity College
300 Summit St., Hartford   06106
Dr. David Borus, Dean of Admissions

† United States Coast Guard Academy
New London   06320
Brian Wright, Admissions

† University of Bridgeport
126 Park Ave., Bridgeport   06601
Andrew E. Nelson, Dean Admis./Financial Aid
203-576-4552
See listing under "Universities"

† University of Connecticut, Storrs   06268
Wesley Harris, Dean

† UNIVERSITY OF HARTFORD
200 Bloomfield Ave., West Hartford   06117
Richard Zeiser, Dir. of Admis.
See listing under "Universities"

† University of New Haven
300 Orange Ave., West Haven   06516
M. Jerry Kenig, Dean
203-932-7000

· † Waterbury State Technical College
750 Chase Pkwy., Waterbury   06708-3089

† Yale University
2157 Yale Station, New Haven   06520

DELAWARE

· † Delaware Technical & Community College
400 Christiana Stanton Rd., Newark   19702
William Faucett, Director

† University of Delaware, Newark   19711

DISTRICT OF COLUMBIA

† Catholic University of America
620 Michigan Ave. N.E., Washington   20064
Robert J. Talbot, Dir. of Admis. & Fin. Aid.

† George Washington University
Washington   20052

† Howard University
2400 6th St., N.W., Washington   20059
James E. Cheek, President

University of the District of Columbia
Georgia Ave.-Harvard St. Campus
1100 Harvard St., N.W., Washington   20009

† University of the District of Columbia
Van Ness Campus
4200 Connecticut Ave., N.W., Washington   20008

FLORIDA

· † Broward Community College
225 E. Las Olas Blvd., Ft. Lauderdale   33301

· † Broward Community College
225 E. Las Olas Blvd., Ft. Lauderdale   33301

· Edison Community College
8099 College Pky., Fort Myers   33919
Mailing address: P.O. Box 60210
Fort Myers   33906-6210
Sandra Fahey, Dir. of Admis. and Records

† Embry-Riddle Aeronautical University
600 S. Clyde Morris Blvd.
Daytona Beach   32114-3900
800-222-ERAU

† Florida A & M University, Tallahassee   32307

† Florida Atlantic University
500 N.W. 20th St., Boca Raton   33431
Brian Levin-Stankevich, Dir. of Admis.

† Florida Institute of Technology
150 W. University Blvd., Melbourne   32901
Louis T. Levy, Dean of Admissions
800-888-4348

† Florida International University
Tamiami Trail, Miami   33199

† Florida State University
600 W. College Ave., Tallahassee   32306

· Gulf Coast Community College
5230 Hwy. 98, W., Panama City   32401
Roy Smith, Dir. of Admis. and Records

Jacksonville University
2800 University Blvd., N., Jacksonville   32211

· † St. Petersburg Junior College
P.O. Box 13489, St. Petersburg   33733
Dr. Carl M. Kuttler, Jr., President

· † Santa Fe Community College
3000 N.W. 83rd St., Gainesville   32606
Lawrence W. Tyree, President

SCHILLER INTERNATIONAL UNIVERSITY (FLORIDA & EUROPE)
U.S. Admissions Office
Dept. PA, 453 Edgewater Dr., Dunedin   34698-7532
800-336-4133 Fax: 813-736-6263
Dr. Walter Liebrecht, President
Karen Altieri, Associate Director of Admissions
See listing under "Universities"

† University of Central Florida
P.O. Box 25000, Orlando   32816

† University of Florida
226 Tigert Hall, Gainesville   32611

† University of Miami
P.O. Box 248006, Coral Gables   33124

† University of South Florida
4202 Fowler Ave., Tampa   33620

† University of West Florida
11000 University Pky., Pensacola   32514

GEORGIA

· † Athens Area Technical Institute
U.S. Hwy. 29, N., Athens   30601

· † Augusta Technical Institute
3116 Dean Bridge Rd., Augusta   30906

· † Chattahoochee Technical Institute
980 S. Cobb Dr., Marietta   30060

· † DeKalb Technical Institute
495 N. Indian Creek Dr., Clarkston   30021
Velon Gray, Dir. of Admissions

† DeVry Institute of Technology
250 N. Arcadia Ave., Decatur   30030
George Ollennu, Dir. of Admis.
404-292-2645
See Illinois listing under "Universities"

† Fort Valley State College
1005 State College Dr., Fort Valley   31030

Georgia College
231 W. Hancock St., Milledgeville   31061
912-453-5004

† Georgia Institute of Technology
225 North Ave. N.W., Atlanta   30332

† Georgia Southern University, Statesboro   30460

† Mercer University
1400 Coleman Ave., Macon   31207

† Savannah State College
State College Branch, Savannah   31404
Robert Ray, Dir. of Admis.

· † Savannah Technical Institute
5717 White Bluff Rd., Savannah   31405

† Southern College of Technology
1100 S. Marietta Pky., Marietta   30060

Spelman College
350 Spelman Ln., S.W., Atlanta   30314
Aline Rivers, Dir. of Admis.

† University of Georgia, Athens   30602
Dr. Claire Swann, Dir. of Admis.

HAWAII

† University of Hawaii at Manoa
2500 Campus Rd., Honolulu   96822

IDAHO

† Idaho State University
P.O. Box 8270, Pocatello 83209

· † Ricks College, Rexburg 83460
Steven Bennion, President

† University of Idaho, Moscow 83843
Peter Brown, Dir. of Admis.

ILLINOIS

Augustana College
639 38th St., Rock Island 61201
Martin R. Sauer, Director of Admission
800-798-8100

Aurora University
347 S. Gladstone Ave., Aurora 60506
Peter Pitts, Dir. of Admis.

† Bradley University
1501 W. Bradley Ave., Peoria 61625

† DeVry Institute of Technology
3300 N. Campbell Ave., Chicago 60618
Richard Yaconis, Dir. of Admis.
312-929-6550
See Illinois listing under "Universities"

† DeVry Institute of Technology
1221 N. Swift Rd., Addison 60101
Milt Kobus, Dir. of Admis.
708-953-2000
See Illinois listing under "Universities"

† Illinois Institute of Technology
3300 S. Federal St., Chicago 60616
Wendell R. Webb, Dir. of Admissions

· **KASKASKIA COLLEGE**
27210 College Rd., Centralia 62801
618-532-1981 or 800-642-0859 (Illinois)
Raymond D. Woods, President
Marilyn Brookman, PhD, College Dean
Constance Stohlman, Director of Admissions,
Public Relations, and Resource Development
Kaskaskia College is situated on a beautifully
wooded tract of land consisting of 190 acres. Its brick
and frame buildings provide 228,830 square feet of
space for college facilities. Kaskaskia College is fully
accredited by NCACS, ADA, AMA, NLN, IBE, ICCB,
and IBHE. The College is recognized and approved by
the bureau of Veterans Affairs and is authorized under Federal law to enroll non-immigrant alien students. In district tuition and fees are $33.75 per
semester credit hour. Degrees: AA, AS, AAS, and
AGS. University transfer programs, pre-professional,
liberal arts, courses offered days, evenings, and weekends. Training in career fields. State and Federal
financial aid programs available.

Midwest College of Engineering
600 S. Lambert Rd., Glen Ellyn 60137

· † Morrison Institute of Technology
701 Portland Ave., Morrison 61270-2959
Dr. Dale Trimpe, Dir. of Admis.
See listing under "Career Schools"

† Northern Illinois University, De Kalb 60115

† Northwestern University
2145 Sheridan Rd., Evanston 60208

Olivet Nazarene University, Kankakee 60901
John Mongerson, Dir. of Admis.
815-939-5203

· † Parkland College
2400 W. Bradley Ave., Champaign 61821-1899
217-351-2208 or 800-346-8089

† Parks College of St. Louis University
500 Falling Springs Rd., Cahokia 62206
John Wilbur, Dir. of Admis.

Rockford College
5050 E. State St., Rockford 61108
Miriam King, V.P. for Enrollment Management
See listing under "Universities"

† Southern Illinois University at Carbondale
Carbondale 62901

† Southern Illinois University at Edwardsville
Edwardsville 62026
Eugene J. Magac, Dir. of Admissions & Records

· † Triton College
2000 N. 5th Ave., River Grove 60171
Gail Fuller, Dir. of Admission & Records
See listing under "Community and Junior
Colleges"

† University of Illinois
506 S. Wright St., Urbana 61801

† University of Illinois at Chicago
P.O. Box 4348, Chicago 60680
Dr. Paul Chung, Dean

INDIANA

Bethel College
1001 W. McKinley Ave., Mishawaka 46545
Steve Matteson, Dir. of Admis.

Indiana Institute of Technology
1600 E. Washington Blvd., Fort Wayne 46803

† Indiana University-Purdue University at Fort Wayne
2101 Coliseum Blvd. E., Fort Wayne 46805

† Indiana University-Purdue University
355 N. Lansing, Indianapolis 46202

Manchester College
604 College Ave., North Manchester 46962
Gregory Miller, Dir. of Admis.

† Purdue University
Schleman Hall, West Lafayette 47907

† Purdue University, Calumet Campus
2233 171st St., Hammond 46323

† Purdue University
1401 S. U.S. Hwy. 421, Westville 46391

† Rose-Hulman Institute of Technology
5500 Wabash Ave., Terre Haute 47803
Duane Bruley, Dean

† Tri-State University, Angola 46703
Director of Admission
800-347-4878

† University of Evansville
1800 Lincoln Ave., Evansville 47722
Dr. John Tooley, Dean
800-423-8633

† University of Notre Dame, Notre Dame 46556
Roger A. Schmitz, Dean

† University of Southern Indiana
8600 University Blvd., Evansville 47712

† Valparaiso University, Valparaiso 46383

IOWA

† Dordt College
498 4th Ave., N.E., Sioux Center 51250
Quentin Van Essen, Dir. of Admissions
800-343-6738

· † Hawkeye Community College
1501 E. Orange Rd., Waterloo 50701
319-296-2320 Ext. 4000

† Iowa State University, Ames 50011
Karsten Smedal, Dir. of Admis.

· † Iowa Western Community College
2700 College Rd., Council Bluffs 51503
Thomas Dutch, Dir. of Admis.

Maharishi International University
Route 1, Fairfield 52556
Gregory Polakow, Dir. of Admis.

Teikyo Westmar University
1002 3rd Ave., S.E., Le Mars 51031
Dr. Jim Utesch, Dir. of Admis.

† University of Iowa, Iowa City 52242

· Waldorf College
106 S. 6th St., Forest City 50436
Steve Lovik, Dir. of Admis.
800-292-1903

KANSAS

· Coffeyville Community College
402 W. 11th St., Coffeyville 67337
Helen Ellerman, Dir. of Admis.

† Kansas State University
Anderson Hall 110, Manhattan 66506
Ellsworth M. Gerritz, Admis. & Records

† Kansas State University
College of Technology
2409 Scanlan Ave., Salina 67401

† Pittsburg State University
1701 S. Broadway St., Pittsburg 66762
James E. Parker, Dir of Admis.

† University of Kansas, Lawrence 66045

† Wichita State University
1845 Fairmount, Wichita 67260
800-362-2594
See listing under "Universities"

KENTUCKY

Cumberland College
6178 College Station Dr., Williamsburg 40769
See listing under "Universities"

Georgetown College
400 E. College St., Georgetown 40324
Garvel Kindrick, Director of Admissions
See listing under "Universities"

Kentucky Wesleyan College
Pre-Engineering program
3000 Frederica St., Owensboro 42301

Louisville Technical Institute
3901 Atkinson Dr., Louisville 40218
George Nunley, Dir. of Admis.

Morehead State University, Morehead 40351
Charles Myers, Director of Admissions
606-783-2000

† Murray State University, Murray 42071
Phil Bryan, Director of Admissions
800-272-4MSU

† University of Kentucky, Lexington 40506

† University of Louisville
2301 S. 3rd St., Louisville 40292
Robert Parrent, Dir. of Admis.

† Western Kentucky University
1526 Russellville Rd., Bowling Green 42101

LOUISIANA

Centenary College of Louisiana
P.O. Box 41188, Shreveport 71134

† Louisiana State University and A & M College
Baton Rouge 70803

† Lousiana Technical University
P.O. Box 3168, Ruston 71272

Loyola University
6363 St. Charles Ave., New Orleans 70118

† McNeese State University
4100 Ryan St., Lake Charles 70605

† Southern University A & M College
Baton Rouge 70813

† Tulane University
6823 Saint Charles Ave., New Orleans 70118
Richard Whiteside, Dean of Admission

† University of New Orleans
New Orleans 70148

† University of Southwestern Louisiana
P.O. Box 42251, Lafayette 70504
318-231-6685

MAINE

· † Central Maine Technical College
1250 Turner St., Auburn 04210
Dr. William J. Hierstein, President

† Maine Maritime Academy
Battle Ave., Castine 04420
Dan Jones, Dir. of Admis.
207-326-2206

† University of Maine, Orono 04469

University of Southern Maine
96 Falmouth St., Portland 04103
Brian Hodgkin, Dean

MARYLAND

† Capitol College
11301 Springfield Rd., Laurel 20708
Anthony G. Miller, Director of Admis.
800-950-1992

· Harford Community College
401 Thomas Run Rd., Bel Air 21015
Yussef Noorisa, Coordinator

† Johns Hopkins University
3400 N. 34th St., Baltimore 21218

† Loyola College
4501 N. Charles St., Baltimore 21210
William Bossemeyer III, Dir. of Admis.

· Montgomery College
20200 Observation Dr., Germantown 20876
301-353-7773

· † Montgomery College
51 Mannakee St., Rockville 20850
Germantown - 301-353-7804
Rockville - 301-279-5230
Takoma Park - 301-650-1332

· Montgomery College
7600 Takoma Ave., Takoma Park 20912
301-650-1500

† Morgan State University
Cold Spring Ln. and Hillen Rd., Baltimore 21239

· † Prince George's Community College
301 Largo Rd., Largo 20772
Leon Weaver, Dir. of Admis. & Test.

† United States Naval Academy
117 Decatur Rd., Annapolis 21402

† University of Maryland, College Park 20742

MASSACHUSETTS

† Boston University
685 Commonwealth Ave., Boston 02215

· † **FRANKLIN INSTITUTE OF BOSTON**
41 Berkeley St., Boston 02116
Richard P. D'Onofrio, President
Leah Kendall, Dir. of Admis.
617-423-4630
Established 1908. Private. Coed. Accreditation:
NEASC, ABET. Tuition: $8,090. Room and board:
$6,500. Fees: $200. Enrollment: 312 full-time, 30 part-
time. Student-faculty ratio: 10:1. Degrees offered: AS,
Associate in Engineering, Certificate of Proficiency. 2
buildings on a 2 city block campus. Unique curricula
provides hands-on approach with academic studies
to fully develop skills. Average class size of 15 students. Location in downtown Boston offers immediate access to all the city events and resources.

† Harvard University
Graduate School of Arts and Sciences
Byerly Hall, 2nd Floor
8 Garden St, Cambridge 02138

† Massachusetts Institute of Technology
77 Massachusetts Ave., Cambridge 02139

MASSACHUSETTS MARITIME ACADEMY
Cape Cod
101 Academy Dr., Buzzards Bay 02532
CDR. Keith D. Rabine, Dean of Enrollment Services
800-544-3411 or 508-830-5000

· Massasoit Community College
1 Massasoit Blvd., Brockton 02402
Roberta Noodell, Dir. of Admis.

† Merrimack College
315 Turnpike St., North Andover 01845
Dennis Farrell, Dean of Admissions

† Northeastern University
360 Huntington Ave., Boston 02115
Kevin Kelly, Dean and Dir. of Undergraduate
Admis.

· North Shore Community College
1 Ferncroft Rd., Danvers 01923

· Quinsigamond Community College
670 W. Boylston St., Worcester 01606
Ron Smith, Dir. of Admis.

Simmons College
300 The Fenway, Boston 02115

SPRINGFIELD TECHNICAL COMMUNITY COLLEGE
1 Armory Square, Springfield 01105
Dr. Patrick E. Tigue, Dir. of Admissions
413-781-7822

Suffolk University
8 Ashburton Place, Boston 02108
Barbara K. Ericson, Assoc. Dean Enrollment & Retention
617-573-8460

† Tufts University
520 Boston Ave., Medford 02155

† University of Massachusetts, Amherst 01003
Arlene Wesley Cash, Dir. of Admis.

University of Massachusetts
100 Morrissey Blvd., Boston 02125

† University of Massachusetts Dartmouth
Old Westport Rd., North Dartmouth 02747
Raymond Barrows, Dir. of Admissions
508-999-8605

† University of Massachusetts Lowell
1 University Ave., Lowell 01854

Wellesley College, Wellesley 02181
Janet A. Lavin, Dir. of Admis.

† Wentworth Institute of Technology
550 Huntington Ave., Boston 02115

† Western New England College
1215 Wilbraham Rd., Springfield 01119
800-325-1122

† Worcester Polytechnic Institute
100 Institute Rd., Worcester 01609
Kay R. Dietrich, Director of Admissions
508-831-5286

MICHIGAN

Andrews University, Berrien Springs 49104
Jack Mentges, Dir. of Admis.

† Calvin College
3201 Burton St., S.E., Grand Rapids 49546

· † Delta College, University Center 48710
Robert Cabello, VP of Student Services

† Ferris State University
Office of Admission
420 Oak St., Big Rapids 49307-2020

† GMI ENGINEERING & MANAGEMENT INSTITUTE
1700 W. 3rd Ave., Flint 48504
James John, President
Phillip D. Lavender, Dir. of Admis.
800-955-4464
Established 1919. Private. Coed. Accreditation: NCACS, ABET. Tuition: $10,910 per year. Enrollment: 2,506 students. Degrees: BS - Applied Mathematics; Computer; Electrical, Industrial Manufacturing Systems; Mechanical Engineering; Management (Business); MS - Engineering; Manufacturing Management. Library: 75,000 volumes. Five-year 100% cooperative education programs. First 9 semesters on cooperative plan. Cooperative earnings average $56,000 over the five year program. Tenth semester full-time job and project study.

† Grand Valley State University
1 Campus Dr., Allendale 49401
JoAnn Foerster, Dir. of Admis.

Jordan Energy Institute
155 Seven Mile Rd. N.W., Comstock Park 49321
Daniel Paulson, Dean
800-968-3955

† Lake Superior State University
1000 College Dr., Sault St. Marie 49783

† Lawrence Technological University
21000 W. Ten Mile Rd., Southfield 48075
800-225-5588 ext. 3160

† Michigan State University, East Lansing 48824
Dr. Lawrence Vontersch, Dean

† Michigan Technological University
1400 Townsend Dr., Houghton 49931
Joseph A. Galetto, Dir. Enrollment Mgmt.
906-487-2335

· North Central Michigan College
1515 Howard St., Petosky 49770

† Oakland University, Rochester 48309
Larry Bartalucci, Registrar

† Saginaw Valley State University
2250 Pierce Rd., University Center 48710

† University of Detroit Mercy
4001 W. McNichols
PO Box 19900, Detroit 48219-0900
313-993-1245
See listing under "Universities"

† University of Michigan-Ann Arbor
815 S. University Ave., Ann Arbor 48109

† University of Michigan-Dearborn
4901 Evergreen Rd., Dearborn 48128
Carol S. Mack, Dir. of Admis.
313-593-5100

† Wayne State University
5980 Cass Ave., Detroit 48202
Dr. J. R. Thorderson, Dir. of Admis.

† Western Michigan University, Kalamazoo 49008
Stanley Henderson, Dir. of Enrl. Mgt. & Admis.
616-387-2000

MINNESOTA

· Inver Hills Community College
8445 College Trail E., Inver Grove 55076
Keith Dunham, Director

† Mankato State University
P.O. Box 8400, Mankato 56002

NEI COLLEGE OF TECHNOLOGY
825 41st Ave. N.E., Minneapolis 55421
Richard Thomson, Dir. of Admis.
Call 800-777-7NEI for Info.
See listing under "Career Schools"

· † Rochester Community College
851 30th Ave. S.E., Rochester 55904
Charles E. Hill, President

† St. Cloud State University
740 4th Ave., S., St. Cloud 56301
Sherwood Reid, Dir. of Admis.
800-369-4260

St. Olaf College, Northfield 55057
David Dahl, Chrpsn.
507-646-3123

Southwest State University, Marshall 56258

† University of Minnesota
2400 Oakland Ave., Duluth 55812
Robert L. Heller, Provost

† University of Minnesota, Twin Cities
Minneapolis 55455

† University of St. Thomas
2115 Summit Ave., St. Paul 55105

WORTHINGTON COMMUNITY COLLEGE
1450 College Way, Worthington 56187
Conrad Burchill, President
507-372-2107

MISSISSIPPI

† Mississippi State University
P.O. Box J, Mississippi State University 39762

† University of Mississippi, University 38677

† University of Southern Mississippi
P.O. Box 5165, Hattiesburg 39406

University of Southern Mississippi
Gulf Park Campus
East Beach Blvd., Long Beach 39560

MISSOURI

† DeVry Institute of Technology
11224 Holmes St., Kansas City 64131
Michael Thompson, Dir. of Admis.
816-941-2810
See Illinois listing under "Universities"

Maryville University of St. Louis
13550 Conway Rd., Saint Louis 63141
314-576-9300 or 800-MARYVLL

· † St. Louis Community College at Florissant Valley
3400 Pershall Rd., St. Louis 63135
Milton Woody, Dir. of Admis.

† University of Missouri, Columbia
228 Jesse Hall, Columbia 65211

† University of Missouri, Rolla
102 Parker Hall, Rolla 65401
David J. Allen, Dir. of Admis. & Financial Aid
800-522-0938

† Washington University
1 Brookings Dr., St. Louis 63130

MONTANA

CARROLL COLLEGE
1610 N. Benton Ave., Helena 59625
Candace Cain, Dir. of Admis.
See listing under "Universities"

† Montana State University, Bozeman 59717

† MONTANA TECH
(formerly Montana College of Mineral Science and Technology)
1300 W. Park St., Butte 59701-8997
Ed Johnson, Director of Admissions
406-496-4178
Established 1896. Public. Coed. Accreditation: Northwest Association of Schools and Colleges, Accreditation Board for Engineering and Technology, American Chemical Society. Tuition: $5,552. Room and board: $3,360. Fees: $521. Enrollment: 1,515 full-time, 477 part-time. Faculty: 139. Student-faculty ratio: 16:1. Degrees: Associate, BS in Computer Science, Technology and Business Development, Chemistry, Business Information Systems, Society and Technology. BS/MS in Engineering, Occupational Safety and Health. 48,538 volumes in Library. 16 buildings on 56 acres. Located in Butte, Montana and surrounded by the Rocky Mountains, Montana Tech is the only college in North America offering a full comprehensive array of degree programs in the areas of minerals,

energy, safety, and environment. Montana Tech graduates get jobs because they are technically trained with management skills; they have a strong math and science foundation; and they reflect a problem-solver attitude.

NEBRASKA

† University of Nebraska at Lincoln
NH W181, Lincoln 68588
Stanley Liberty, Dean

† University of Nebraska at Omaha
Omaha 68182

NEVADA

† University of Nevada, Reno
Reno 89557

† University of Nevada Las Vegas
4505 S. Maryland Pky., Las Vegas 89154-1021
Admissions: 702-895-3443 or 800-334-UNLV

NEW HAMPSHIRE

Daniel Webster College
20 University Dr., Nashua 03063

† Dartmouth College, Hanover 03755

† New England College
26 Bridge St., Henniker 03242
John Spaulding, Dir. of Admis.

NEW HAMPSHIRE TECHNICAL COLLEGE
505 Amherst St., Nashua 03063
John T. Fischer, Dean of Student Affairs
603-882-6923
Established 1970. Public. Coed. Accreditation: NEASC. Tuition: In-State: $2,296; New England Regional: $3,300; Out-of-state: $5,230. Enrollment: 425 full-time, 99 part-time. Faculty: 54. Degree offered: AAS in Aviation (FAA Cert. #NSUTO25K), Business, Computer Networking, Electronic/Mechanical Technology, Opticianry, Telecommunications, Electrical Engineering and Computer Engineering (ABET). Suburban campus one hour from Boston.

· † New Hampshire Technical Institute
P.O. Box 2039, Concord 03302
Daniel M. Burke, Dean of Admissions

† University of New Hampshire, Durham 03824
Stanwood C. Fish, Dir. of Admissions

NEW JERSEY

· † Atlantic Community College
5100 Black Horse Pike, Mays Landing 08330
Bob Royal, Director/College Recruitment

· † Burlington County College
County Route 530, Pemberton 08068
Juan Harris, Dir. of Admis.

· † County College of Morris
200 Center Grove Rd., Randolph 07869

: † DeVry Technical Institute
479 Green St., Woodbridge 07095
Danielle Di Napoli, Dir. of Admis.
908-634-9510
See Illinois listing under "Universities"

† Fairleigh Dickinson University, Teaneck 07666
Dennis Craig, Dir. of Admis.
201-692-2553

· † Hudson County Community College
168 Sip Ave., Jersey City 07306
Joseph O'Halloran, Director of Admissions
201-714-2127

Jersey City State College
2039 Kennedy Blvd., Jersey City 07305
201-200-3234

· † Mercer County Community College
West Windsor Campus
1200 Old Trenton Rd., Trenton 08690
Michael Glass, Dir. of Admis.
See listing under "Community and Junior Colleges"

· † Middlesex County College
Schools of Dental Hygiene, Medical Lab Technology, Nursing, Radiography
P.O. Box 3050, Edison 08818
Dr. Marilyn Keener, Dean, Health Tech. Div.

† Monmouth College
400 Cedar Ave., West Long Branch 07764
Harris Drucker, Chrpsn.

† New Jersey Institute of Technology
323 Martin Luther King Jr. Blvd., Newark 07102

· † Ocean County College
0 College Dr., Toms River 08753
Arthur Knies, Dir. of Admis. & Records

† Princeton University, Princeton 08544

† Rutgers, The State University of NJ
College of Engineering
New Brunswick 08903

† Stevens Institute of Technology, Hoboken 07030

Stockton State College, Pomona 08240
Sal Catalfamo, Dir. of Admis.

† Trenton State College
Hillwood Lakes CN 4700, Trenton 08650

NEW MEXICO

· † Albuquerque Technical-Vocational Institute
525 Buena Vista Dr., S.E., Albuquerque 87106
Jane Campbell, Registrar
See listing under "Career Schools"

† New Mexico Highlands University, Las Vegas
87701
Dr. Jorge P. Thomas, VP Academic Affairs

† New Mexico Institute of Mining & Technology
801 Leroy Pl., Socorro 87801

† New Mexico State University
P.O. Box 30001, Las Cruces 88003

· † San Juan College
4601 College Blvd., Farmington 87402

† University of New Mexico, Albuquerque 87131
Robert Weaver, Dean of Admissions

NEW YORK

Alfred University
Alumni Hall, Alfred 14802
Laurie Richer, Director of Admissions
800-541-9229

Canisius College
2001 Main St., Buffalo 14208
Penelope Lips, Dir. of Admis.
800-843-1517

† Clarkson University, Potsdam 13699
Robert Croot, Dir. of Admis.

† COLLEGE OF AERONAUTICS
La Guardia Airport, Flushing 11371
Dr. Richard B. Goetze, Jr., President
Donald J Whitman, Dir. of Admis.
800-776-2376
    Established 1932. Private. Independent. Coed. Accreditation: MSACS. Tuition: $5,820. Estimated total yearly expenses: $1,000. Enrollment: 1,200 students. Faculty: 65. Degrees: AAS, AOS, BT. Library: 60,000 volumes. 3 buildings on 6 acres. Located in New York City. Fully computerized engine test cells, hangar, engine labs, avionic labs, computer labs, and airline training center. Financial aid, grants, scholarships, and loans available.

† Columbia University
612 W. 115th St., New York 10025

† Cooper Union
41 Cooper Square, New York 10003
Eleanor Baum, Dean
See listing under "Universities"

† Cornell University
410 Thurston Ave., Ithaca 14853

· † CUNY Bronx Community College
181st St. & University Ave., Bronx 10453
Roscoe C. Brown, Jr., President

† CUNY City College
Convent Ave. at 138th St., New York 10031

† CUNY College of Staten Island
130 Stuyvesant Pl., Staten Island 10301

† CUNY New York City Technical College
300 Jay St., Brooklyn 11201
Ursula C. Schwerin, President

· † CUNY Queensborough Community College
22205 56th Ave., Bayside 11364
Dr. Kurt R. Schmeller, President
See listing under "Community and Junior Colleges"

† Hofstra University
1000 Fulton Ave., Hempstead 11550
Margaret Shields, Dean of Admissions

† Manhattan College
4513 Manhattan College Pky., Riverdale 10471
Dr. John Patterson, Dean of Engineering

† New York Institute of Technology
Metropolitan Center
1855 Broadway, New York 10023

† New York Institute of Technology
Old Westbury Campus, Old Westbury 11568

† New York State College of Ceramics at Alfred
University
Alfred 14802
800-541-9229

Pace University, Pleasantville/Briarcliff Campus
Bedford Rd., Pleasantville 10570

Pace University, White Plains Campus
78 N. Broadway, White Plains 10603

† Polytechnic University
333 Jay St., Brooklyn 11201

† Polytechnic University
901 Rt. 110, Farmingdale 11735

† Pratt Institute
200 Willoughby Ave., Brooklyn 11205

† Rensselaer Polytechnic Institute, Troy 12180
Conrad Sharrow, Dean of Admissions

Roberts Wesleyan College
2301 Westside Dr., Rochester 14624
Dr. Philip Ogden, Chrpsn.
See listing under "Universities"

† Rochester Institute of Technology
1 Lomb Memorial Dr., Rochester 14623
716-475-6631
See listing under "Universities"

ST. THOMAS AQUINAS COLLEGE
Rt. 340, Sparkill 10976
Andrea Kraeft, Dir. of Admis.
800-999-STAC
See listing under "Liberal Arts"

· SUNY Adirondack Community College
439 Bay Rd., Queensbury 12804
Levi Brown, Dir. of Admis.
518-793-4491
See listing under "Community and Junior Colleges"

† SUNY Maritime College
6 Pennyfield Ave., Bronx 10465
Peter Cooney, Dir. of Admis.

† SUNY at Binghamton
P.O. Box 6001, Binghamton 13902

† SUNY at Buffalo
17 Capen Hall
P.O. Box 601660, Buffalo 14260-1660
716-645-6900

† SUNY at Stony Brook
Stony Brook 11794

· † SUNY Broome Community College
907 Upper Front St., Binghamton 13905
Donald Dellow, President

† SUNY College at New Paltz
75 Manheim Blvd., New Paltz 12561

SUNY College at Plattsburgh, Plattsburgh 12901
Richard Higgins, Dir. of Admis.
518-564-2040

† SUNY College of Agriculture and Technology
Morrisville 13408
Dennis Nostrand, Dir. of Admis.

† SUNY College of Environmental Science & Forestry
1 Forestry Dr., Syracuse 13210
800-7777-ESF or 315-470-6600

· † SUNY College of Technology, Alfred 14802
Deborah J. Goodrich, Dir. of Admis.
607-587-4215

· † SUNY College of Technology
34 Cornell Dr., Canton 13617
Thomas R. Fletcher, Director of Admissions
800-388-7123

† SUNY College of Technology at Farmingdale
Route 110, Farmingdale 11735
Janet Snyder, Dir. of Admis.
516-420-2200

· † SUNY Erie Community College, North Campus
6205 Main St., Williamsville 14221

· † SUNY HUDSON VALLEY COMMUNITY
COLLEGE
80 Vandenburgh Ave., Troy 12180
Linda Sweetman, Dir. of Admis.
See listing under "Career Schools"

† SUNY INSTITUTE OF TECHNOLOGY AT
UTICA/ROME
P.O. Box 3050, Utica 13504
Roger Sullivan, Dir. of Admis.
See listing under "Universities"

· † SUNY Mohawk Valley Community College
1101 Sherman Dr., Utica 13501

· † SUNY Monroe Community College
1000 E. Henrietta Rd., Rochester 14623
716-292-2000

· † SUNY Nassau Community College
1 Education Dr., Garden City 11530
Bernard Iantosca, Dir of Admis.

· † SUNY Niagara County Community College
3111 Saunders Settlement Rd., Sanborn 14132
R. J. Mirabelli, Admis. Ofc.

· † SUNY Onondaga Community College
Onondaga Rd., Syracuse 13215
Joseph Insel, Dir. of Admis.

· † Suny Orange County Community College
115 South St., Middletown 10940
914-341-4030

· SUNY Ulster County Community College
Stone Ridge 12484
Thomas Maiello, Dir. of Admis.

† Syracuse University, Syracuse 13244

· † T.C.I. THE COLLEGE FOR TECHNOLOGY
320 W. 31st St., New York 10001
Henry Moss, President
Henry Ford, Director of Admissions
212-594-4001 or 800-878-TCI-NOW
    Established 1909. Private. Coed. Accreditation: N.Y. State Board of Regents and TAC/ABET. Tuition: $1850/semester. Fees: $74. Enrollment: 4,000 full-time, 150 part-time. Faculty: 200. Student-faculty ratio: 20:1. Degrees: AAS, Electronics, Engineering Technology and AOS, Air-Conditioning/Heating and Refrigeration, Industrial Electronics, Office Technology. Library: 6,555 volumes. 2 buildings. Hands on training with heavy emphasis on laboratories.

† Union College, Schenectady 12308

† U.S. Merchant Marine Academy, Kings Point 11024

† U.S. Military Academy, West Point 10996

† University of Rochester
500 Joseph C. Wilson Blvd., Rochester 14627
Bruce Arden, Dean
See listing under "Universities"

† Webb Institute of Naval Architecture
200 Crescent Beach Rd., Glen Cove 11542
Dr. James J. Conti, President
William Murray, Dir. of Admis.

NORTH CAROLINA

· † Alamance Community College
P.O. Box 623, Haw River 27258
W. Ronald McCarter, President

· † Catawba Valley Community College
R.R. 3, Box 283, Hickory 28602
Robert E. Paap, President

· † Central Piedmont Community College
P.O. Box 35009, Charlotte 28235
Dr. Ruth Shaw, President

· College of The Albemarle
P.O. Box 2327, Elizabeth City 27906
John M. Wells, Asst. Dean of Admissions
919-335-0821, Ext. 220

· † Davidson County Community College
P.O. Box 1287, Lexington 27293
J. Bryan Brooks, President

† Duke University, Durham 27706

· † Fayetteville Technical Community College
P.O. Box 35236, Fayetteville 28303

· † Forsyth Technical Community College
2100 Silas Creek, Winston-Salem 27103
Dr. Bob Greene, President

Gardner-Webb University
General Delivery, Boiling Springs 28017
Ray M. Hardee, Dean of Admissions
800-253-6472

· † Gaston College
201 Highway 321, S., Dallas 28034

· † Guilford Technical Community College
P.O. Box 309, Jamestown 27282

· LOUISBURG COLLEGE
501 N. Main St., Louisburg 27549
Rick Lowe, Dir. of Admis.
919-496-2521 or 800-775-0208
See listing under "Community and Junior Colleges"

† North Carolina A&T State University
1601 E. Market St., Greensboro 27411

† North Carolina State University
P.O. Box 7001, Raleigh 27695
George Dixon, Dir. of Admis.

· Sandhills Community College
2200 Airport Rd., Pinehurst 28374
910-692-6185

† University of North Carolina at Chapel Hill
Chapel Hill 27599
James C. Walters, Dir. Undergrad Admis.

† University of North Carolina at Charlotte
Charlotte 28223
J. H. Woodward, Chancellor

· † Wake Technical Community College
9101 Fayetteville Rd., Raleigh 27603

† Western Carolina University
Cullowhee 28723
Tyree H. Kiser, Dir. of Admissions

NORTH DAKOTA

† North Dakota State University, Fargo 58105
Richard Shearer, Acting Dir. of Admis.

† University of North Dakota
Box 8193 University Station, Grand Forks 58203

OHIO

† Case Western Reserve University
2040 Adelbert Rd., Cleveland 44106

† Central State University
1400 Brush Row Rd., Wilberforce 45384

· † Cincinnati Technical College
3520 Central Pkwy., Cincinnati 45223

· † Clark State Community College
570 E. Leffels Ln., Springfield 45505
Leigh Fisher, Admissions Specialist

· Cleveland Institute of Electronics
1776 E. 17th St., Cleveland 44114
800-243-6446

† Cleveland State University
Euclid Ave. at 24th St., Cleveland 44115

· † Columbus State Community College
550 E. Spring St., Columbus 43215
Mary Jo Deerwester, Dir. of Admis.

† DeVry Institute of Technology
1350 Alum Creek Dr., Columbus 43209
Richard Rodman, Dir. of Admis.
614-253-1525
See Illinois listing under "Universities"

† Franklin University
201 S. Grant Ave., Columbus 43215

· † Hocking College
3301 Hocking Pky., Nelsonville 45764
Candace Vancko, VP for Enrollment
800-282-4163

† Kent State University, Tuscarawas Campus
University Dr., N.E., New Philadelphia 44663
Harold D. Shade, Dean

· Kent State University-Ashtabula Campus
   3325 W. 13th St., Ashtabula 44004
   John Mahan, Dean

· Kent State University-Trumbull Campus
   4314 Mahoning Ave. N.W., Warren 44483
   Dr. John Cable, Dean

· Lima Technical College
   Engineering Technologies Program
   4240 Campus Dr, Lima 45804

· Lorain County Community College
   1005 Abbe Rd., N., Elyria 44035
   Dr. John W. Thrash, Jr., Registrar

† **MARIETTA COLLEGE**
   210 5th St., Marietta 45750
   Dr. Robert Chase, Chrpsn.
   800-331-7896

† Miami University
   E. High St., Oxford 45056

· † Muskingum Area Technical College
   1555 Newark Rd., Zanesville 43701

· † Northwest State Community College
   22600 State Route 34, Archbold 43502
   Dennis Gable, Admissions Coordinator

† **OHIO NORTHERN UNIVERSITY**
   525 S. Main St., Ada 45810
   Dr. Bruce Burton, Dean
   412-772-2000

† Ohio State University
   190 N. Oval Mall, Columbus 43210

† Ohio University, Athens 45701

Ohio Wesleyan University
   61 S. Sandusky St., Delaware 43015
   Donald Bishop, Dean for Enrollment

· † Owens Community College
   P.O. Box 10000, Toledo 43699
   Jim Welling, Admissions
   419-661-7225

· Owens Community College
   300 Davis St., Findlay 45840
   Stacy Davidson, Admissions
   419-423-6827

· † Sinclair Community College
   444 W. 3rd St., Dayton 45402-1460
   Sara P. Smith, Director of Admissions
   800-315-3000

· † Stark Technical College
   6200 Frank Ave., N.W., Canton 44720

† University of Akron
   381 Buchtel Common, Akron 44325
   Kris MacDermott, Asst. Provost Enrollment

† University of Cincinnati
   2700 Clifton Ave., Cincinnati 45221

† **UNIVERSITY OF CINCINNATI
OMI COLLEGE OF APPLIED SCIENCE**
   2220 Victory Pky., Cincinnati 45206
   Frederick Kryman, Dean
   513-556-6564

† University of Dayton
   300 College Park Ave., Dayton 45469-0228
   Toll-free 800-837-7433
   See listing under "Universities"

University of Findlay
   1000 N. Main St., Findlay 45840
   Dan Crabtree, Dir. of Admis.

† University of Toledo
   2801 Bancroft St., W., Toledo 43606
   Richard Eastop, Dir. of Admis.

† Wright State University
   3640 Colonel Glenn Hwy., Dayton 45435

† Youngstown State University
   410 Wick Ave., Youngstown 44555
   Leslie H. Cochran, President

OKLAHOMA

† Oklahoma Christian University of Science and Arts
   P.O. Box 11000, Oklahoma City 73136
   Duane Eggleston, Vice President
   800-877-5010

† Oklahoma State University, Stillwater 74078
   Karl Reid, Dean

Oral Roberts University
   7777 S. Lewis Ave., Tulsa 74171
   Arthur E. Matzkvech, Dir. of Admis.

† University of Oklahoma at Norman
   660 Parrington Oval, Norman 73019

† University of Tulsa
   600 S. College Ave., Tulsa 74104
   Dr. Lewis Duncan, Dean

OREGON

· † Blue Mountain Community College
   2411 N.W. Carden, Pendleton 97801

· Central Oregon Community College
   2600 N.W. College Way, Bend 97701
   Christine Kerlin, Dir. of Admis.
   503-383-7500

Lewis & Clark College
   0615 S.W. Palatine Hill Rd., Portland 97219
   Michael Sexton, Dean of Admissions

† Oregon Institute of Technology
   3201 Campus Dr., Klamath Falls 97601
   Jesse R. Welch, Director of Enrollment

† Oregon State University, Corvallis 97333
   Wallace Gibbs, Dir. of Admis.

· † Portland Community College
   P.O. Box 19000, Portland 97280

† Portland State University
   P.O. Box 751, Portland 97207

† University of Portland
   5000 N. Willamette Blvd., Portland 97203

PENNSYLVANIA

Beaver College
   450 S. Easton Rd., Glenside 19038-3295
   Dennis Nostrand, VP for Enrollment Management
   Phone: 800-776-BEAVER(2328)
   Fax: 215-572-4049
   See listing under "Universities"

† Bucknell University, Lewisburg 17837

California University of Pennsylvania
   3rd St., California 15419
   Norman Hasbrouck, Dean for Enrollment

† Carnegie Mellon University
   5000 Forbes Ave., Pittsburgh 15213

Cedar Crest College
   100 College Dr., Allentown 18104-6196
   Cynthia Phillips, Dir. of Admissions

Chatham College
   Woodland Rd., Pittsburgh 15232
   Suellen Ofe, Dean of Admis./Financial Aid
   See listing under "Women's College"

Clarion University of Pennsylvania
   840 Wood St., Clarion 16214

† Drexel University
   3141 Chestnut St., Philadelphia 19104
   Dean of Enrollment Management

Edinboro University of Pennsylvania
   Edinboro 16444
   Admissions Office: 800-626-2203

Elizabethtown College
   1 Alpha Dr., Elizabethtown 17022

† Gannon University
   109 University Sq., Erie 16541

Geneva College
   3200 College Ave., Beaver Falls 15010

† Grove City College
   100 Campus Dr., Grove City 16127
   Joseph Goncz, Chrpsn.

· † Harrisburg Area Community College
   3300 N. Cameron Street Road, Harrisburg 17110

Juniata College
   1700 Moore St., Huntington 16652

· Keystone Junior College
   P.O. Box 50, La Plume 18440
   Kevin McIntyre, Dir. of Admis.

† Lafayette College, Easton 18042
   G. Gary Ripple, Dir. of Admis.
   610-250-5100

† Lehigh University
   27 Memorial Dr. W., Bethlehem 18015

Lincoln University, Lincoln University 19352
   Jimmy Arrington, Dir. of Admis.

Mercyhurst College
   501 E. 38th St., Erie 16546
   Andrew Roth, Dean of Enrollment
   800-825-1926

· Montgomery County Community College
   340 DeKalb Pike, Blue Bell 19422-0758
   Dennis Murphy, Dir. of Admis.

· † Pennsylvania College of Technology
   1 College Ave., Williamsport 17701

· Pennsylvania Institute of Technology
   Rose Valley-Notre Dame Campus
   800 Manchester Ave., Media 19063
   610-565-7900

· † Pennsylvania State University, Altoona Campus
   3000 Ivyside Park, Altoona 16601
   Carson W. Veach, Director

† Pennsylvania State University
   201 Shields Bldg., University Park 16802

† Pennsylvania State University
   Beaver Campus, Monaca 15061
   Regina S. Miller, Dir. of Admis.
   See listing under "Universities"

† Pennsylvania State University
   5091 Station Rd., Erie 16563

· † Pennsylvania State University, Berks Campus
   P.O. Box 7009, Reading 19610

· † Pennsylvania State University, Delaware Campus
   25 Yearsley Mill Rd., Media 19063

· † Pennsylvania State University, DuBois Campus
   College Place, DuBois 15801
   Thomas Hewitt, Dir. of Admis.

· † Pennsylvania State University, Fayette Campus
   P.O. Box 519, Uniontown 15401
   Hugh M. Barclay, Director

· † Pennsylvania State University, Hazleton Campus
   Hazleton 18201

· † Pennsylvania State University
   0 University Dr., Mc Keesport 15132
   Cash Kawalski, Director

· † Pennsylvania State University
   3550 Seventh St. Rd.
   New Kensington 15068

· † Pennsylvania State University, Ogontz Campus
   1600 Woodland Rd., Abington 19001

· † Pennsylvania State University, Schuylkill Campus
   200 University Dr.
   Schuylkill Haven 17972

· † Pennsylvania State University
   147 Shenango Valley Ave.
   Sharon 16146

· † Pennsylvania State University, Wilkes-Barre Campus
   P.O. Box PSU, Lehman 18627
   800-426-2358

· † Pennsylvania State University
   Worthington Scranton Campus
   120 Ridgeview Dr., Dunmore 18512

· † Pennsylvania State University
   1031 Edgecombe Ave., York 17403

† Pennsylvania State University
   Rt. 230, Middletown 17057
   Mary E. Gundel, Dir. of Admis.

† Point Park College
   201 Wood St., Pittsburgh 15222

† Swarthmore College
   500 College Ave., Swarthmore 19081
   Carl Wartenburg, Dean of Admissions

† Temple University
   Broad St. & Montgomery Ave.
   Philadelphia 19122

Thiel College
   75 College Ave., Greenville 16125
   Robert Weaver, Dir. of Admis.

† University of Pennsylvania
   0 Levy Park, Philadelphia 19104

† University of Pittsburgh
   4200 5th Ave., Pittsburgh 15260

† University of Pittsburgh at Johnstown
   450 Schoolhouse Rd., Johnstown 15904

· **VALLEY FORGE MILITARY ACADEMY &
COLLEGE**
   1001 Eagle Rd., Wayne 19087
   Rear Adm. Virgil Hill, USN (Ret.), President
   800-234-VFMA

† Villanova University
   845 E. Lancaster Ave., Villanova 19085
   Stephen R. Merritt, Dir. of Admis.

WESTMINSTER COLLEGE
   New Wilmington 16172
   Richard Dana Paul, Dir. of Admis.
   412-946-7100

† Widener University
   700 E. 14th St., Chester 19013

† Wilkes University
   184 S. River St., Wilkes-Barre 18766
   Emory P. Guffrovich Jr., Dean of Admissions

RHODE ISLAND

† Brown University, Providence 02906

† Roger Williams College
   1 Old Ferry Rd., Bristol 02809
   William Dunfey, Dir. of Admis.

† University of Rhode Island, Kingston 02881
   Herman Viets, Dean

SOUTH CAROLINA

· † Central Carolina Technical College
   506 N. Guignard Dr., Sumter 29150
   Dr. Herbert Robbins, President
   803-778-6640

† The Citadel
   171 Moultrie St., Charleston 29409

† Clemson University
   201 Sikes Hall, Clemson 29634

· † Florence Darlington Technical College
   P.O. Box 8000, Florence 29501

· † Greenville Technical College
   P.O. Box 5616, Greenville 29606

· † Horry-Georgetown Technical College
   P.O. Box 1966, Conway 29526

· † Midlands Technical College
   P.O. Box 2408, Columbia 29202

· † Piedmont Technical College
   P.O. Box 1467, Greenwood 29648

† South Carolina State University
   P.O. Box 7127, Orangeburg 29117-0001
   803-536-7185

· † Spartanburg Technical College
   P.O. Box 4386, Spartanburg 29305
   Pam Hagan, Dir. Admissions & Counseling
   803-591-3800

· † Tri-County Tech College
   P.O. Box 587, Pendleton 29670

· † Trident Technical College
P.O. Box 10367, Charleston 29411
Charles Branch, President

† University of South Carolina, Columbia 29208
Terry Davis, Dir. of Admis.
803-777-7700

· † York Technical College
452 S. Anderson Rd., Rock Hill 29730

SOUTH DAKOTA

† South Dakota School of Mines and Technology
501 E. St. Joseph St., Rapid City 57701
Gary Bjordal, Dir. of Admis.

† South Dakota State University
P.O. Box 2219, Brookings 57007
Dr. Duane Sander, Dean
605-688-4161
See listing under "Universities"

TENNESSEE

† American Technical Institute
8760 Baylor Rd., Brunswick 38014

Bryan College, Dayton 37321
2 year degree

· † Chattanooga State Technical Community College
4501 Amnicola Hwy., Chattanooga 37406

† Christian Brothers College
650 E. Parkway, S., Memphis 38104

David Lipscomb University
3901 Granny White Pike, Nashville 37204-3951
Wade Sandrell, Dir. of Admis.
800-333-4358

† EAST TENNESSEE STATE UNIVERSITY
P.O. Box 70731, Johnson City 37614
Dr. Nancy Dishner, Dean, Enrollment Management
615-929-4213 or 800-462-3878

· † Nashville State Technical Institute
120 White Bridge Rd., Nashville 37209
Ed Pawlawski, Dir. of Admis.

· † Northeast State Technical Community College
P.O. Box 246, Blountville 37617

· † Pellissippi State Technical Community College
P.O. Box 22990, Knoxville 37933

· † State Technical Institute
5983 Macon Cove, Memphis 38134
Charles O. Whitehead, President

† Tennessee State University
3500 John A. Merritt Blvd., Nashville 37209

† Tennessee Technological University
P.O. Box 5006, Cookeville 38505

† University of Memphis, Memphis 38152
Dr. John Eubank, Dean of Admissions

† University of Tennessee at Martin
Martin 38238
Paul Kelley, Director of Admissions
See listing under "Universities"

† University of Tennessee at Chattanooga
615 McCallie Ave., Chattanooga 37403

† University of Tennessee, Knoxville
527 Andy Holt Tower, Knoxville 37996
Dr. Gordon Stanley, Dir. of Admis.

† Vanderbilt University
West End Ave., Nashville 37240

TEXAS

· † Amarillo College
P.O. Box 447, Amarillo 79178
Dale Hardgrove, Registrar

† Baylor University
P.O. Box 97008, Waco 76798-7008
Diana Ramey, Director of Admissions

· † Del Mar College
101 Baldwin Blvd., Corpus Christi 78404
Lawrence Jasman, Registrar

† DeVry Institute of Technology
4801 Regent Blvd., Irving 75063
Daniel Millan, Dir. of Admis.
214-929-5777
See Illinois listing under "Universities"

· Hallmark Institute of Technology
North Campus-Electronics Technology
& Business Courses
10401 W. IH 10, San Antonio 78230
Richard Fessler, President
Jeanne Martin, Campus Director
210-690-9000

· † Houston Community College
P.O. Box 7849, Houston 77270
Pat Davis, Registrar

† Lamar University
P.O. Box 10009, Beaumont 77710
800-458-7558

† LeTourneau College
P.O. Box 7001, Longview 75607
Roger Kieffer, Dir. of Admis.

† Midwestern State University
3400 Taft Blvd., Wichita Falls 76308

· North Central Texas College
1525 W. California, Gainesville 76240
Doug Willis, Dir. of Admis.

† Prairie View A & M University
P.O. Box 3089, Prairie View 77446-3089
Linda S. Berry, Dir. of Admis.

† Rice University
P.O. Box 1892, Houston 77251

† St. Mary's University of San Antonio
1 Camino Santa Maria, San Antonio 78228
Rick Castillo, Dir. of Admis.

† Southern Methodist University
Hillcrest at University, Dallas 75275

† Texas A & I University
Campus Box 101, Kingsville 78363

† Texas A & M at Galveston
P.O. Box 1675, Galveston 77553
Dr. William H. Clayton, President

† Texas A & M University
College Station 77843

· Texas State Technical College Waco/Marshall
3801 Campus Dr., Waco 76705
817-867-3371

† Texas Tech University, Lubbock 79409

† Trinity University
715 Stadium Dr., San Antonio 78212

† University of Houston
4800 Calhoun Rd., Houston 77204

† University of Houston-Downtown
1 Main St., Houston 77002

† University of Texas at Arlington
UTA Box 19125, Arlington 76019
R. Zack Prince, Dir. of Admis.

† University of Texas at Austin
0 the University of Texas, Austin 78712

† University of Texas at Dallas
P.O. Box 830688, Richardson 75083-0688

† University of Texas at El Paso
500 W. University Ave., El Paso 79968

† University of Texas at San Antonio
San Antonio 78285
Dr. John H. Brown, Dir. of Admis.

UTAH

† Brigham Young University, Provo 84602

† University of Utah
1400 E. 200 S., Salt Lake City 84112
Dr. J. Stayner Landward, Dir. of Admis.

† Utah State University, Logan 84322-1600
Rod Clark, Director of Admissions
801-750-1107

· † Utah Valley Community College
1200 S. 800 W., Orem 84058

† Weber State University
3750 Harrison Blvd., Ogden 84408

VERMONT

† NORWICH UNIVERSITY
65 S. Main St., Northfield 05663
Eugene Anthony Sevi, Head
See listing under "Universities"

† University of Vermont
194 S. Prospect St., Burlington 05401
802-656-3370

· † Vermont Technical College
Randolph Center 05061
Robert Clarke, President

VIRGINIA

† George Mason University
4400 University Dr., Fairfax 22030-4444
Patricia Riordan, Dean of Admissions

· John Tyler Community College
13101 Jefferson Davis Hwy., Chester 23831
Dr. Freddie W. Nicholas, Jr., Pres.

Longwood College, Farmville 23901

Lynchburg College
1501 Lakeside Dr., Lynchburg 24501
Ernest Chadderton, Dean of Enrollment

· Old Dominion University
5215 Hampton Blvd., Norfolk 23508

† University of Virginia
P.O. Box 9017, Charlottesville 22906

† Virginia Military Institute, Lexington 24450

† Virginia Polytechnic Institute & State University
Blacksburg 24061
David Bousquet, Dir. of Undergraduate Admis.

† Virginia State University, Petersburg 23803
Mable C. Mountcastle, Dir. of Recording

· † Virginia Western Community College
P.O. Box 14025, Roanoke 24038
Charles L. Downs, President

WASHINGTON

† Central Washington University, Ellensburg 98926
William Swain, Director of Admissions

† Cogswell Polytechnical College-North Campus
10626 N.E. 37th Circle, Kirkland 98033

† Gonzaga University
502 E. Boone Ave., Spokane 99258
Philip Ballinger, Dean of Admissions

† St. Martin's College
700 College St. N.E., Lacey 98516

† Seattle Pacific University
3307 3rd Ave., W., Seattle 98119

† Seattle University
Broadway Ave. & Madison, Seattle 98122
Lee Gerig, Dean of Admissions

· Skagit Valley College
2405 E. College Way, Mt. Vernon 98273

University of Puget Sound
1500 N. Warner St., Tacoma 98416

† University of Washington, Seattle 98195

† Walla Walla College
204 S. College Ave., College Place 99324

· Walla Walla Community College
500 Tausick Way, Walla Walla 99362
Joe Small, Director
509-527-4684
See listing under "Community and Junior Colleges"

† Washington State University, Pullman 99164
Stan Berry, Dir. of Admis.

† Western Washington University
516 High St., Bellingham 98225
Karen G. Copetas, Dir. of Admis.

WEST VIRGINIA

† Bluefield State College
219 Rock St., Bluefield 24701

† Fairmont State College
1201 Locust Ave., Fairmont 26554
John Conaway, Dir. of Admis.

West Virginia Graduate College
P.O. Box 1003, Institute 25112

† West Virginia Institute of Technology
405 Fayette Pike, Montgomery 25136

† West Virginia State College
P.O. Box 1000, Institute 25112

† West Virginia University
P.O. Box 6001, Morgantown 26506

WEST VIRGINIA WESLEYAN COLLEGE
59 College Ave., Buckhannon 26201
Robert Skinner, Director of Admission
See listing under "Universities"

WISCONSIN

Alverno College
P.O. Box 343922, Milwaukee 53234
Colleen Hayes, Dir. of Admis.

· Lakeshore Technical College
1290 North Ave., Cleveland 53015

† Marquette University
1217 W. Wisconsin Ave., Milwaukee 53233
Raymond A. Brown, Dean of Admissions

† Milwaukee School of Engineering
1025 N. Broadway, Milwaukee 53202
Owen Smith, Dean of Admission
800-332-6763 or 414-277-7200 in metro Milwaukee

Mt. Senario College
1500 W. College Ave., Ladysmith 54848
Dewey Floberg, Dean of Admissions

St. Norbert College
100 Grant St., De Pere 54115
Craig S. Wesley, Dean of Admission
See listing under "Universities"

† University of Wisconsin, Madison
500 Lincoln Dr., Madison 53706

† University of Wisconsin
P.O. Box 413, Milwaukee 53201
V. M. Allison, Registrar

University of Wisconsin
P.O. Box 2000, Kenosha 53141
414-553-2211

† University of Wisconsin
1 University Plaza, Platteville 53818
Richard Schumacher, Dean of Admissions

WYOMING

† University of Wyoming
P.O. Box 3434, Laramie 82071
Richard Davis, Dir. of Admis.

PUERTO RICO

Polytechnic University of Puerto Rico
P.O. Box 2017, Hato Rey 00902
Teresa Cardona, Dir. of Admis.

† University of Puerto Rico, Mayaguez Campus
P.O. Box 5000, Mayaguez 00681
Neysa Lopez, Dir. of Admis.

ETHNIC STUDIES

ALABAMA

Tuskegee University
  Tuskegee Institute 36088

ARIZONA

Prescott College
  220 Grove Ave., Prescott 86301
  Shari Sterling, Asst. Dir. of Admis.

CALIFORNIA

California State University, Chico
  Chico 95929-0420
  Dr. Hassan Sisay, Chrpsn.

California State University, San Bernardino
  5500 University Pky., San Bernardino 92407
  909-880-5188

· City College of San Francisco
  50 Phelan Ave. Box A208, San Francisco 94112
  Sandra Handler, Dean
  415-239-3174

· DeAnza College
  21250 Stevens Creek Blvd., Cupertino 95014

· Fresno City College
  1101 E. University Ave., Fresno 93741
  Brice Harris, President
  209-442-4600

Hebrew Union College
  Jewish Institute of Religion
  3077 University Ave., Los Angeles 90007
  Rabbi Lee Bycel, Dean

Loyola Marymount University
  Loyola Blvd. at W. 80th, Los Angeles 90045
  M. L'Heureux, Dir. of Admis.

Mills College
  5000 MacArthur Blvd., Oakland 94613
  Genevieve Ann Flaherty, Dean of Admissions
  800-87-MILLS

Pomona College
  333 N. College Way, Claremont 91711
  Peter W. Stanley, President

San Francisco State University
  1600 Holloway Ave., San Francisco 94132
  Corwin Bjonerud, Dir. of Admis.

· Santa Barbara City College
  721 Cliff Dr., Santa Barbara 93109
  805-965-0581

· Santa Monica College
  1900 Pico Blvd., Santa Monica 90405
  Gloria Lopez, Assistant Dean
  See listing under "Community and Junior Colleges"

Scripps College
  1030 Columbia Ave., Claremont 91711
  Leslie Miles, Dean of Admissions

University of California at Berkeley
  Dwinelle Hall, Berkeley 94720

University of California, Davis
  376 Mrak Hall, Davis 95616

University of California, Riverside
  P.O. Box 112, Riverside 92521

UNIVERSITY OF JUDAISM/LEE COLLEGE
  15600 Mulholland Dr., Los Angeles 90077
  Tamara Greenebaum, Dean of Admissions
  See listing under "Universities"

COLORADO

Adams State College, Alamosa 81102
  Cheryl Billingsley, Dir. of Admis.
  800-824-6494

Metropolitan State College of Denver
  P.O. Box 173362, Campus Box 16
  Denver 80217-3362

University of Northern Colorado, Greeley 80639
  Roger Kovar, Dean of Arts and Sciences
  303-351-2707

CONNECTICUT

University of Hartford
  200 Bloomfield Ave., West Hartford 06117
  Richard Zeiser, Dir. of Admis.
  See listing under "Universities"

Yale University
  149 Elm St., New Haven 06520

FLORIDA

University of Miami
  P.O. Box 248006, Coral Gables 33124

GEORGIA

Clark Atlanta University
  240 James Brawley Dr., S.W., Atlanta 30314
  Thomas W. Cole, President

University of Georgia, Athens 30602
  Dr. Claire Swann, Dir. of Admis.

ILLINOIS

Augustana College
  639 38th St., Rock Island 61201
  Martin R. Sauer, Director of Admission
  800-798-8100

De Paul University
  1 E. Jackson Blvd., Chicago 60604
  Thomas D. Abrahamson, Dean of Admissions
  See listing under "Universities"

Eastern Illinois University, Charleston 61920
  William Colvin, Chrpsn.
  See listing under "Universities"

Knox College, Galesburg 61401
  309-343-0112 or 800-678-KNOX
  See listing under "Universities"

North Park College & Theological Seminary
  3225 W. Foster, Chicago 60625
  312-509-2330

Northwestern University
  2001 Sheridan Rd., Evanston 60208

· Richland Community College
  One College Park, Decatur 62521
  Dr. Charles Novak, President

ROOSEVELT UNIVERSITY
  430 S. Michigan Ave., Chicago 60605
  William Smyser, Director of Admissions
  See listing under "Universities"

University of Illinois at Chicago
  P.O. Box 4348, Chicago 60680
  Dr. Lansine Kaba, Director

INDIANA

Purdue University
  Schleman Hall, West Lafayette 47907

University of Notre Dame
  Notre Dame 46556
  Kevin M. Rooney, Dir. of Admis.

IOWA

Coe College
  1220 1st Ave., N.E., Cedar Rapids 52402
  James Randall, Chrpsn.

Grinnell College
  P.O. Box 805, Grinnell 50112

Luther College
  700 College Dr., Decorah 52101
  David Sallee, Dean for Enrollment

University of Iowa, Iowa City 52242

KANSAS

Wichita State University
  1845 Fairmount, Wichita 67260
  800-362-2594
  See listing under "Universities"

LOUISIANA

Grambling State University
  P.O. Box 607, Grambling 71245
  Dr. Harold W. Lundy, President

MAINE

Bowdoin College, Brunswick 04011
  William Mason, Dir. of Admis.

MARYLAND

Towson State University
  800 York Rd., Towson 21204
  Dr. Hoke Smith, President

MASSACHUSETTS

Amherst College, Amherst 01002
  Jane E. Reynolds, Dean of Admissions

Boston University
  685 Commonwealth Ave., Boston 02215

Brandeis University
  415 South St, Waltham 02154
  David Gould, Dean of Admissions
  617-736-3500

Hampshire College, Amherst 01002
  Audrey Y. Smith, Dir. of Admissions
  413-582-5471

Mt. Holyoke College
  College St., South Hadley 01075
  Anita Smith, Director of Admissions
  413-538-2023

Simmons College
  300 The Fenway, Boston 02115

University of Massachusetts
  100 Morrissey Blvd., Boston 02125

Wellesley College, Wellesley 02181
  Janet A. Lavin, Dir. of Admis.

MICHIGAN

University of Michigan-Dearborn
  4901 Evergreen Rd., Dearborn 48128
  Carol S. Mack, Dir. of Admis.
  313-593-5100

William Tyndale College
  35700 W. Twelve Mile Rd.
  Farmington Hills 48331

MINNESOTA

Bemidji State University
  1500 Birchmont Dr., N.E., Bemidji 56601
  800-475-2001

Carleton College
  One N. College St., Northfield 55057
  Paul Thiboutot, Dir. of Admis.

St. Olaf College, Northfield 55057
  John Barbour, Director
  507-646-3083

MISSISSIPPI

Tougaloo College
  500 E. County Line Rd., Tougaloo 39174

NEW JERSEY

Bloomfield College
  1 Park Place, Bloomfield 07003
  Warner Smith, Dean for Admissions
  201-748-9000, Ext. 230

Jersey City State College
  2039 Kennedy Blvd., Jersey City 07305
  201-200-3234

Princeton University, Princeton 08544

Stockton State College, Pomona 08240
  Sal Catalfamo, Dir. of Admis.

Upsala College
  345 Prospect St., East Orange 07017
  George Lynes, Dean of Admissions

NEW YORK

Colgate University
  13 Oak Dr., Hamilton 13346
  Dean of Admissions
  315-824-7401

Cornell University
  410 Thurston Ave., Ithaca 14853

CUNY York College
  9420 Guy R. Brewer Blvd., Jamaica 11451

Fordham University
  441 E. Fordham Rd., Bronx 10458
  718-817-1000

Fordham University
  Lincoln Center Campus
  113 W. 60th St., New York 10023
  Edward Bristow, Dean

Friends World Program, Long Island University
  Montauk Hwy., Southampton 11968
  Carol Gilbert, Dir. of Admis.

Hofstra University
  1000 Fulton Ave., Hempstead 11550
  Margaret Shields, Dean of Admissions

SUNY at Buffalo
  17 Capen Hall
  P.O. Box 601660, Buffalo 14260-1660
  716-645-6900

SUNY College at Brockport
  Brockport 14420

Vassar College
  125 Raymond Ave., Poughkeepsie 12601

WAGNER COLLEGE
  631 Howard Ave., Staten Island 10301
  Joseph Foulke, Dean Admissions and Financial Aid
  See listing under "Universities"

NORTH CAROLINA

Pembroke State University
  P.O. Box 1510, Pembroke 28372
  Anthony Locklear, Dir. of Admissions
  919-521-6262

OHIO

Bowling Green State University
  Bowling Green 43403
  John Martin, Dir. of Admis.

College of Wooster
  1189 Beall Ave., Wooster 44691
  Hayden Schilling, Dean of Admis.

Kent State University
  P.O. Box 5190, Kent 44242
  Bruce Riddle, Dir. of Admis.

Miami University
  E. High St., Oxford 45056

Oberlin College
  135 W. Lorain St., Oberlin 44074
  Adrienne Jones, Chrpsn.

United Theological Seminary
  1810 Harvard Blvd., Dayton 45406
  The Rev. Duane Anders, Dir. of Admis.

PENNSYLVANIA

Edinboro University of Pennsylvania
Edinboro 16444
Admissions Office: 800-626-2203

RHODE ISLAND

Brown University, Providence 02906

Rhode Island College
600 Mt. Pleasant Ave., Providence 02908

SOUTH CAROLINA

University of South Carolina, Columbia 29208
Terry Davis, Dir. of Admis.
803-777-7700

TEXAS

Southern Methodist University
Hillcrest at University, Dallas 75275

VERMONT

Goddard College
P.O. Box G, Plainfield 05667
Jackson Kytle, President

FASHION ART

ALABAMA

Auburn University, Auburn 36849

Samford University
800 Lakeshore Dr., Birmingham 35229
Ruth Ash, Dean

University of North Alabama
University Station, Florence 35632

ARKANSAS

University of Arkansas at Pine Bluff
1200 University Dr., Pine Bluff 71601-2799

CALIFORNIA

AMERICAN COLLEGE FOR THE APPLIED ARTS
1651 Westwood Blvd., Los Angeles 90024
310-470-2000
See listing under "Universities"

Brooks College
4825 E. Pacific Coast Hwy., Long Beach 90804
Chelena Adkins, Dir. of Admis.
800-421-3775

FASHION CAREERS OF CALIFORNIA
1923 Morena Blvd., San Diego 92110
Andrew Bisaha, Dir. of Admis.
619-275-4700, Fax 619-275-0635
Established 1979. Private. Coed. Accreditation: ACICS. Tuition: $6,900 per year for daytime fashion design or fashion merchandising program, $5,900 per year for evening program. Fees: $75. Enrollment: 100 full-time, 20 part-time. Faculty: 15. Student-faculty ratio: 25:1. Diploma and Degree programs. Library: 650 volumes. Theoretical and practical training gives students a relevant and comprehensive education in fashion merchandising and design. Placement assistance and internships available.

FASHION INSTITUTE OF DESIGN & MERCHANDISING
919 S. Grand Ave., Los Angeles 90015
213-624-1201 or 800-421-0127 outside California
See listing under "Community and Junior Colleges"

Fashion Institute of Design & Merchandising
1010 2nd Ave., San Diego 92101
619-235-4515 or 800-243-3436 outside California
See listing under "Community and Junior Colleges"

Fashion Institute of Design & Merchandising
55 Stockton St., San Francisco 94108
415-433-6691 or 800-422-3436
See listing under "Community and Junior Colleges"

Fashion Institute of Design & Merchandising
3420 Bristol St., Costa Mesa 92626
714-546-0930 or 800-421-0127 outside California
See listing under "Community and Junior Colleges"

LOUISE SALINGER ACADEMY OF FASHION
101 Jessie St., San Francisco 94105
Esther Herschelle, President
415-974-6666

OTIS COLLEGE OF ART AND DESIGN
2401 Wilshire Blvd., Los Angeles 90057
Neil Hoffman, President
See listing under "Art"

Woodbury University
7500 Glenoaks Blvd., Burbank 91504
See listing under "Universities"

COLORADO

Colorado Institute of Art
200 E. 9th Ave., Denver 80203
Barbara Browning, Dir. of Admis.
800-275-2420
See listing under "Career Schools"

CONNECTICUT

Teikyo Post University
800 Country Club Rd.
P.O. Box 2540, Waterbury 06723-2540
800-345-2562 or 203-596-4520
See listing under "Universities"

DISTRICT OF COLUMBIA

Ardis School of Fashion Design
1728 Connecticut Ave., N.W., Washington 20009
Mary Simmons, Registrar
202-234-6537

University of the District of Columbia
Georgia Ave.-Harvard St. Campus
1100 Harvard St., N.W., Washington 20009

University of the District of Columbia
Van Ness Campus
4200 Connecticut Ave., N.W., Washington 20008

FLORIDA

Art Institute of Fort Lauderdale
1799 S.E. 17th St., Ft. Lauderdale 33316
Eileen Northrop, V.P./Dir. of Admis.

International Academy of Merchandising and Design
211 S. Hoover Blvd., Tampa 33609
Mike Santoro, President
813-286-8585

INTERNATIONAL FINE ARTS COLLEGE
1737 N. Bayshore Dr., Miami 33132
Sir Edward Porter, President
Frayda Parnes, Dir. of Admis.
800-225-9023 or 305-373-4684
Established 1965. Independent. Accreditation: SACS. Tuition: $8,630. Apartment: $2,640. Enrollment: 650 day. Library: 13,450 volumes. Faculty: 31. Degree: AA. Study-travel tours to Europe. Frequent field trips throughout south Florida. Residences are waterfront, luxurious apartment buildings, exquisitely furnished. Houseparents, swimming pools, recreation rooms, laundry room, storage facilities. Majors: fashion merchandising, interior design, commercial art, fashion design, computer graphics.

LYNN UNIVERSITY
(Est. 1962 as College of Boca Raton)
3601 N. Military Trail, Boca Raton 33431
407-994-0770 or 800-544-8035
See listing under "Universities"

National Education Center-Bauder Campus
4801 N. Dixie Hwy., Ft. Lauderdale 33334
Brian Woods, Dir. of Admis.
305-491-7171

GEORGIA

AMERICAN COLLEGE FOR THE APPLIED ARTS
3330 Peachtree Rd., N.E., Atlanta 30326
404-231-9000
See listing under "Universities".

Bauder Fashion College
3500 Peachtree Rd., N.E., Atlanta 30326
404-237-7573 or 800-241-3797 (National)

Brenau College
204 Boulevard, Gainesville 30501

SAVANNAH COLLEGE OF ART & DESIGN
342 Bull St., Savannah 31401
May Poetter, VP of Admissions
See listing under "Art"

ILLINOIS

Columbia College
600 S. Michigan Ave., Chicago 60605
Debra McGrath, Dir. of Admis.

International Academy of Merchandising & Design
1 N. State St. Suite 400, Chicago 60602
Cynthia A. Reynolds, President
312-828-0422

Loyola University - Mundelein College
6363 N. Sheridan Rd., Chicago 60660
Judith Bobber, Dir. of Admis.

Midstate College
244 S.W. Jefferson St., Peoria 61602
R. Dale Bunch, President
309-673-6365

RAY COLLEGE OF DESIGN
AAS, BA, BFA degrees
401 N. Wabash Ave., Chicago 60611
312-280-3500
Woodfield Campus
1051 Perimeter Dr., Schaumburg 60173
Fashion Design, Fashion Illustration, Fashion, Merchandising, Window Display, Computer Graphics.
708-619-3450

Rosary College
7900 W. Division St., River Forest 60305
Hildegarde Schmidt, Dir. of Admis.

School of the Art Institute of Chicago
37 S. Wabash, Chicago 60603
Ellen B. Cropp, Dir. of Admis.

IOWA

Hawkeye Community College
1501 E. Orange Rd., Waterloo 50701
319-296-2320 Ext. 4000

Spencer College
217 W. 5th St., Spencer 51301
Harvey Work, Director
See listing under "Career Schools"

LOUISIANA

Louisiana State University and A & M College
Baton Rouge 70803

MASSACHUSETTS

BAY PATH COLLEGE
588 Longmeadow St., Longmeadow 01106
Paula DesRoberts, Dean of Admis.
413-567-0621 or 800-782-PATH
Established: 1897. Private. Women. Accreditation: NEASC. Legal programs ABA approved. Tuition: $10,200. Room and board: $6,225. Enrollment: 600. Faculty: 42. Student-faculty ratio: 14:1. Degrees: AA, AS, BA, BS. Library: 38,000 volumes. 27 buildings on 30 acres. Secure, suburban campus near Springfield and Hartford. 15 Associate degree programs in business, education, fashion/design, criminal justice, paralegalism, occupational therapy, psychology, liberal arts. Baccalaureates in business, business/accounting, legal studies, psychology, psychology/criminal justice, psychology/early childhood education. Extensive career services. 95-98% of students obtain jobs after graduation. Transfer welcome.

BURDETT SCHOOL
745 Boylston St., Boston 02116
Maralin Manning, President
617-859-1900

Endicott College
376 Hale St., Beverly 01915
Elizabeth Macomber, Dir. of Admis.

Fisher College
118 Beacon St., Boston 02116
Sandra Robbins, Dir. of Admis.

MICHIGAN

Adrian College
110 S. Madison St., Adrian 49221
George Wolf, Dir. of Admis.
See listing under "Universities"

Eastern Michigan University, Ypsilanti 48197
E. A. Rhodes, Head
313-487-3060 or 800-GO-TO-EMU

MINNESOTA

LOWTHIAN COLLEGE
825 2nd Ave. S., Minneapolis 55402
Petrena Lowthian, President
612-332-3361 or 800-777-3643
Established 1964. Coed. Private. Accreditation: ACICS. Associate of Applied Science degree programs: FASHION MERCHANDISING: Tuition $9,180, FASHION DESIGN: Tuition $12,240, INTERIOR DESIGN: Tuition 13,260. Curriculums prepare students for positions in management, product promotion, sales and consulting, clothing design and construction, and residential and commercial space planning and design. College credit transfer.

University of Minnesota, Twin Cities
Minneapolis 55455

MISSOURI

Columbia College
1001 Rogers St., Columbia 65216
Ron Cronacher, Dir. of Admissions
800-231-2391

Lincoln University
820 Chestnut St., Jefferson City 65101

Park College, Parkville 64152
Dr. Edwin Rawn, Dean of Admis.

Stephens College, Columbia 65215
Mary Ann Sprinkle, Dir. of Admis.

William Woods College
200 W. 12th St., Fulton 65251
Dr. Jahnae Barnett, VP of Admis.

NEW JERSEY

Jersey City State College
2039 Kennedy Blvd., Jersey City 07305
201-200-3234

NEW YORK

BERKELEY COLLEGE
40 W. Red Oak Ln., White Plains 10604
Rose Mary Healy, President
800-446-5400 ext. GQ1

BERKELEY COLLEGE
3 E. 43rd St., New York 10017
Dr. Glen Zeitzer, President
800-446-5400 ext. GQ1
Diploma in Fashion Merchandising
AAS in Fashion Marketing and Management

CAZENOVIA COLLEGE
Cazenovia 13035
Dr. James Parker, VP for Enrollment Management
See listing under "Universities"

Laboratory Institute of Merchandising
12 E. 53rd St., New York 10022
Mary Ann M. Elberfeld, Dir. of Admis.

MARIST COLLEGE
290 North Rd., Poughkeepsie 12601
Harry W. Wood, VP Admissions
914-575-3226

Marymount College
100 Marymount Ave., Tarrytown 10591
Gina R. Campbell, Dir. of Admis.
800-724-4312

Pratt Institute
200 Willoughby Ave., Brooklyn 11205

SUNY Fashion Institute of Technology
227 W. 27th St., New York 10001

SUNY Nassau Community College
1 Education Dr., Garden City 11530
Bernard Iantosca, Dir of Admis.

Tobe-Coburn School for Fashion Careers
8 E. 40th St., New York 10016
Patricia Nieml, President

NORTH CAROLINA

East Carolina University
1000 E. 5th St., Greenville 27858
Dr. Marjorie Inman, Chair

Mars Hill College
Main St., Mars Hill 28754
Dr. Smith Goodrum, Dean of Admis.

Southwestern Community College
275 Webster Rd., Sylva 28779

OHIO

Antonelli Institute of Art & Photography
124 E. 7th St., Cincinnati 45202

COLUMBUS COLLEGE OF ART & DESIGN
107 N. 9th St., Columbus 43215-1758
Thomas Green, Dir. of Admis.
614-224-9101
See listing under "Art"

University of Cincinnati
2700 Clifton Ave., Cincinnati 45221

Ursuline College
2550 Lander Rd., Cleveland 44124

PENNSYLVANIA

The Art Institute of Philadelphia
1622 Chestnut St., Philadelphia 19103
215-567-7080

Art Institute of Pittsburgh
526 Penn Ave., Pittsburgh 15222
Lee Colker, Dir. of Admis.
800-275-2470
See listing under "Art"

Bradley Academy for the Visual Arts
625 E. Philadelphia St., York 17403
Loren H. Kroh, Director
717-848-1447

Clarissa School of Fashion Design, Inc.
322 5th Ave., Pittsburgh 15222
Penelope Smith, Director

Drexel University
3141 Chestnut St., Philadelphia 19104
Dean of Enrollment Management

Harcum Junior College, Bryn Mawr 19010
Mary Pontius, Dean of Admissions

Mercyhurst College
501 E. 38th St., Erie 16546
Andrew Roth, Dean of Enrollment
800-825-1926

Moore College of Art and Design
1920 Race St., Philadelphia 19103
Claire E. Gallicano, Dir. of Admis.

NEC-Allentown Business School Campus
1501 Lehigh St., Allentown 18103
610-791-5100

RHODE ISLAND

Johnson & Wales University
111 Dorrance St., Providence 02903
Mark S. Burke, Dir. of Admis.

SOUTH CAROLINA

Winthrop University
701 W. Oakland Ave., Rock Hill 29733
James McCammon, Jr., Dir. of Admis.

SOUTH DAKOTA

Nettleton Junior College
100 S. Spring Ave., Sioux Falls 57104
Herman Whitaker, Dir. of Admissions
800-727-1837 or 605-336-1837

TENNESSEE

Lambuth College
705 Lambuth Blvd., Jackson 38301

O'MORE COLLEGE OF DESIGN
P.O. Box 908, Franklin 37065
Eloise Pitts O'More, Director
615-794-4254
See listing under "Interior Design"

TEXAS

Abilene Christian University
ACU Station, Box 6000, Abilene 79699

Art Institute of Dallas
8080 Park Ln., Dallas 75231
Lee Colker, Dir. of Admis.

The Art Institute of Houston
1900 Yorktown St., Houston 77056
Cherie R. McNeel, Dir. of Admis.
800-275-4244

Bauder Fashion College
508 S. Center St., Arlington 76010
Charm Kettle, Dir. of Admis.

Incarnate Word College
4301 Broadway St., San Antonio 78209
Sr. Sally Mitchell, Dean of Enrollment

Miss Wade's Fashion Merchandising College
Dallas Market Center, Suite M5120
The International Apparel Mart
P.O. Box 586343, Dallas 75258
See listing under "Community and Junior Colleges"

Southwest Institute of Merchandising & Design
9611 Acer Ave., El Paso 79925
Mary Simon, President

VIRGINIA

Marymount University
2807 N. Glebe Rd., Arlington 22207
Charles Coe, Director of Admissions
800-548-7638 or 703-284-1500
See listing under "Universities"

WASHINGTON

Central Washington University, Ellensburg 98926
William Swain, Director of Admissions

WEST VIRGINIA

Shepherd College, Shepherdstown 25443

WISCONSIN

University of Wisconsin, Madison
500 Lincoln Dr., Madison 53706

FORESTRY

This classification contains schools offering a first professional degree accredited by the Society of American Foresters (†) and a selection of programs from institutionally accredited schools.

ALABAMA

Alabama A & M University
P.O. Box 1208, Normal 35762
Dr. George Brown, Asst. Professor
See listing under "Universities"

† Auburn University, Auburn 36849

Samford University
800 Lakeshore Dr., Birmingham 35229
Ron Jenkins, Chrpsn.

ALASKA

Sheldon Jackson College
801 Lincoln St., Sitka 99835
Dennis Trotter, Dir. of Admis.
907-747-5221

ARIZONA

† Northern Arizona University
P.O. Box 4092, Flagstaff 86011
Dr. Margaret Cibik, Dir. of Admis.

Yavapai College
1100 E. Sheldon St., Prescott 86301
Dr. Doreen Dailey, President
602-445-7300
See listing under "Community and Junior Colleges"

ARKANSAS

† University of Arkansas at Monticello
P.O. Box 3596, Monticello 71656

CALIFORNIA

† California Polytechnic State University
San Luis Obispo 93407
Helen Linstrum, Dir. of Admis.

† Humboldt State University
1 Harps St., Arcata 95521

† University of California at Berkeley
Mulford Hall, Berkeley 94720

COLORADO

† Colorado State University
102 Administration Building, Fort Collins 80523
Mary Ontireros, Dir. of Admissions

CONNECTICUT

† Yale University
20 Sage Hall, New Haven 06520

FLORIDA

Lake City Community College
R.R. 3, Box 7, Lake City 32055

Stetson University
401 N. Woodland Blvd., De Land 32720
Gary A. Meadows, Dean of Admis.

† University of Florida
226 Tigert Hall, Gainesville 32611

GEORGIA

Georgia College
231 W. Hancock St., Milledgeville 31061
912-453-5004

† University of Georgia, Athens 30602
Dr. Leon A. Hargreaves, Dean

IDAHO

† University of Idaho, Moscow 83843
Peter Brown, Dir. of Admis.

ILLINOIS

Southeastern Illinois College
R.R. 4 Box 510, Harrisburg 62946
Harry Abell, President

† Southern Illinois University at Carbondale
Carbondale 62901

† University of Illinois
506 S. Wright St., Urbana 61801

INDIANA

† Purdue University
Schleman Hall, West Lafayette 47907

IOWA

† Iowa State University, Ames 50011
Karsten Smedal, Dir. of Admis.

Iowa Wesleyan College
601 N. Main St., Mt. Pleasant 52641

KANSAS

Baker University
8th & Grove St., Baldwin City 66006

Pittsburg State University
1701 S. Broadway St., Pittsburg 66762
James E. Parker, Dir of Admis.

KENTUCKY

† University of Kentucky, Lexington 40506

LOUISIANA

† Louisiana State University and A & M College
Baton Rouge 70803

† Lousiana Technical University
P.O. Box 3168, Ruston 71272

McNeese State University
4100 Ryan St., Lake Charles 70605

MAINE

UNITY COLLEGE
Quaker Hill Rd., Unity 04988
207-948-3131
Wilson G. Hess, President
John Craig, Dean for Admissions
  Established 1965. Private. Coed. Accreditation: NEASC. Tuition: $9,750. Room and board: $4,750. Enrollment: 475. Faculty: 34. Degrees: AAA, AAS, BA, BS. Majors: environmental science (forestry, wildlife, ecology, aquaculture, fisheries, conservation law enforcement, arboriculture), social sciences (land use planning, park management, environmental education, environmental policy), outdoor recreation and pre-law. These programs blend a strong liberal arts core with solid career preparation through hands-on experience and internships. Excellent support services in academic tutoring, career planning, and placement.

University of Maine at Fort Kent
  25 Pleasant St., Fort Kent 04743
  Jerry Nadeau, Dir. of Admis.

† University of Maine, Orono 04469

MASSACHUSETTS

Harvard University
  Graduate School of Arts and Sciences
  Byerly Hall, 2nd Floor
  8 Garden St, Cambridge 02138

† University of Massachusetts, Amherst 01003
  Arlene Wesley Cash, Dir. of Admis.

MICHIGAN

Eastern Michigan University, Ypsilanti 48197
  William L. Fennel, Head
  313-487-3060 or 800-GO-TO-EMU

Lake Superior State University
  1000 College Dr., Sault St. Marie 49783

† Michigan State University, East Lansing 48824
  Dr. Larry M. Tombaugh, Chrpsn.

† Michigan Technological University
  1400 Townsend Dr., Houghton 49931
  Joseph A. Galetto, Dir. Enrollment Mgmt.
  906-487-2335

† University of Michigan-Ann Arbor
  815 S. University Ave., Ann Arbor 48109

MINNESOTA

† University of Minnesota, Twin Cities
  Minneapolis 55455

UNIVERSITY OF MINNESOTA-CROOKSTON
2900 University Ave., Crookston 56716
John Bywater, Dir. of Admis.
800-232-6466
See listing under "Universities"

MISSISSIPPI

† Mississippi State University
  P.O. Box J, Mississippi State University 39762

MISSOURI

† University of Missouri, Columbia
  228 Jesse Hall, Columbia 65211

MONTANA

† University of Montana, Missoula 59812
  800-462-8636

NEW HAMPSHIRE

† University of New Hampshire, Durham 03824
  Stanwood C. Fish, Dir. of Admissions

NEW MEXICO

Western New Mexico University
  College Ave, Silver City 88062
  Michael Aleckson, Dir. of Admis.
  800-222-9668
  See listing under "Universities"

NEW YORK

Canisius College
  2001 Main St., Buffalo 14208
  Penelope Lips, Dir. of Admis.
  800-843-1517

· Paul Smith's College, Paul Smiths 12970
  Enrico Miller, Dir. of Admis.
  800-421-2605

· SUNY Adirondack Community College
  439 Bay Rd., Queensbury 12804
  Levi Brown, Dir. of Admis.
  518-793-4491
  See listing under "Community and Junior Colleges"

· SUNY College of Agriculture and Technology
  Morrisville 13408
  Dennis Nostrand, Dir. of Admis.

† SUNY College of Environmental Science & Forestry
  1 Forestry Dr., Syracuse 13210
  800-7777-ESF or 315-470-6600

· SUNY Nassau Community College
  1 Education Dr., Garden City 11530
  Bernard Iantosca, Dir of Admis.

NORTH CAROLINA

† Duke University, Durham 27706

· Haywood Community College
  Freedlander Dr., Clyde 28721
  Carol Smith, Dir. of Admis.

High Point College
  933 Montlieu Ave., High Point 27262
  Jim Schlimmer, Dir. of Admis.

† North Carolina State University
  P.O. Box 7001, Raleigh 27695
  George Dixon, Dir. of Admis.

OHIO

· Hocking College
  3301 Hocking Pky., Nelsonville 45764
  Candace Vancko, VP for Enrollment
  800-282-4163

Miami University
  E. High St., Oxford 45056

Ohio State University
  190 N. Oval Mall, Columbus 43210

· Ohio State University-Agricultural Technical Institute
  1328 Dover Rd., Wooster 44691

Walsh College
  2020 Easton St., N.W., Canton 44720
  Fran Kehoe, Dean of Admis.

OKLAHOMA

† Oklahoma State University, Stillwater 74078
  Edwin L. Miller, Dept. Head

OREGON

· Central Oregon Community College
  2600 N.W. College Way, Bend 97701
  Christine Kerlin, Dir. of Admis.
  503-383-7500

· Chemeketa Community College
  P.O. Box 14007, Salem 97309
  Ron Jantzi, Director
  503-399-5210

† Oregon State University, Corvallis 97333
  Wallace Gibbs, Dir. of Admis.

· Treasure Valley Community College
  650 College Blvd., Ontario 97914
  Ron Kulm, Dir. of Admis.

PENNSYLVANIA

Elizabethtown College
  1 Alpha Dr., Elizabethtown 17022

Juniata College
  1700 Moore St., Huntington 16652

· Keystone Junior College
  P.O. Box 50, La Plume 18440
  Kevin McIntyre, Dir. of Admis.

† Pennsylvania State University
  201 Shields Bldg., University Park 16802

SOUTH CAROLINA

† Clemson University
  201 Sikes Hall, Clemson 29634

TENNESSEE

University of Tennessee at Martin
  Martin 38238
  Paul Kelley, Director of Admissions
  See listing under "Universities"

† University of Tennessee, Knoxville
  527 Andy Holt Tower, Knoxville 37996
  Dr. Gordon Stanley, Dir. of Admis.

University of the South
  735 University Ave., Sewanee 37375

TEXAS

· Panola College
  1109 W. Panola St., Carthage 75633
  Gary McDaniel, President

† Stephen F. Austin State University
  P.O. Box 6078. Nacogdoches 75962

† Texas A & M University
  College Station 77843

UTAH

† Utah State University, Logan 84322-1600
  Rod Clark, Director of Admissions
  801-750-1107

VERMONT

Johnson State College, Johnson 05656
  802-635-2356 ext. 219

† University of Vermont
  194 S. Prospect St., Burlington 05401
  802-656-3370

VIRGINIA

Christopher Newport College
  50 Shoe Ln., Newport News 23606

† Virginia Polytechnic Institute & State University
  Blacksburg 24061
  David Bousquet, Dir. of Undergraduate Admis.

WASHINGTON

† University of Washington, Seattle 98195

† Washington State University, Pullman 99164
  Stan Berry, Dir. of Admis.

WEST VIRGINIA

GLENVILLE STATE COLLEGE
200 High St., Glenville 26351
Dr. William Simmons, President
Mack Samples, Dean of Admissions
  Established 1872. State. Coed. Accreditation: NCACS. Annual tuition: $3,460 resident, $4,054 non-resident. Room and board: $3,080. Enrollment: 900 boarding, 1,500 day. Faculty: 72. Degrees: AA, AS, BA, BS. Library: 210,000 volumes. 10 buildings. Gym & pool, golf course nearby. Beautiful rural setting, 16 miles from I-79. Popular 2 year forestry program; special education.

† West Virginia University
  P.O. Box 6001, Morgantown 26506

WEST VIRGINIA WESLEYAN COLLEGE
59 College Ave., Buckhannon 26201
Robert Skinner, Director of Admission
See listing under "Universities"

WISCONSIN

Northland College
  1411 Ellis Ave., Ashland 54806
  Jim Miller, Dean of Admissions

† University of Wisconsin, Madison
  500 Lincoln Dr., Madison 53706

† University of Wisconsin, Stevens Point 54481
  Dr. John A. Larsen, Dir. of Admis.

FUNERAL SERVICE EDUCATION

This classification contains schools accredited by the American Board of Funeral Service Education (†) and a selection of programs from institutionally accredited schools.

ALABAMA

· † Bishop State Community College
  351 N. Broad St., Mobile 36603-5898
  Yvonne Kennedy, President
  205-690-6801

· † Jefferson State Community College
  2601 Carson Rd., Birmingham 35215
  Jim Blackburn, Dir. of Admis.

CALIFORNIA

· † Cypress College
  9200 Valley View St., Cypress 90630

· † San Francisco College of Mortuary Science
  1598 Dolores St., San Francisco 94110
  Jacquelyn S. Taylor, President
  415-824-1313

DISTRICT OF COLUMBIA

University of the District of Columbia
  Georgia Ave.-Harvard St. Campus
  1100 Harvard St., N.W., Washington 20009

† University of the District of Columbia
  Van Ness Campus
  4200 Connecticut Ave., N.W., Washington 20008

FLORIDA

† **LYNN UNIVERSITY**
  (Est. 1962 as College of Boca Raton)
  3601 N. Military Trail, Boca Raton 33431
  407-994-0770 or 800-544-8035
  See listing under "Universities"

· Miami-Dade Community College
  11380 N.W. 27th Ave., Miami 33167

GEORGIA

· † **GUPTON-JONES COLLEGE OF FUNERAL SERVICE**
5141 Snapfinger Woods Dr., Decatur 30035-4022
Daniel Buchanan, President
404-593-2257

ILLINOIS

· † Chicago City-Wide College
226 W. Jackson Blvd., Chicago 60606

† Southern Illinois University at Carbondale
Carbondale 62901

: † **WORSHAM COLLEGE OF MORTUARY SCIENCE**
495 Northgate Pky., Wheeling 60090-2646
Bruno B. Bak, President
Joan D. Tomczak, Director of Admissions
Frederick Cappetta, Chief Administrator
708-808-8444, FAX 708-808-8493
Established 1911. Private. Coed. Accreditation: American Board of Funeral Service Education. Tuition: $7,000. Enrollment: 150 full-time, four days a week for twelve months. All courses taught by qualified faculty. Enrollment held only on September and March. In a modern air-conditioned building on a two acre campus with ample parking that is a half hour from Chicago (closest large city). The registrar helps students to locate housing off campus or a job in local funeral homes with housing.

INDIANA

· † Mid-America College of Funeral Service
3111 Hamburg Pike, Jeffersonville 47130
Pauline R. Cooper, Registrar

· † Vincennes University
1002 N. 1st St., Vincennes 47591
Marvin E. Grant, Coordinator

IOWA

· Waldorf College
106 S. 6th St., Forest City 50436
Steve Lovik, Dir. of Admis.
800-292-1903

KANSAS

· † Kansas City Kansas Community College
7250 State Ave., Kansas City 66112
Don Stump, Dir. of Admis.

LOUISIANA

· † Delgado Community College
501 City Park Ave., New Orleans 70119
Dr. Carmen Smith, Director of Admissions

McNeese State University
4100 Ryan St., Lake Charles 70605

MARYLAND

· † Catonsville Community College
800 S. Rolling Rd., Catonsville 21228
Frederick J. Walsh, President

MASSACHUSETTS

† New England Institute of Applied Arts
and Sciences at Mt. Ida College
777 Dedham St, Newton Center 02159

MICHIGAN

† Wayne State University
5980 Cass Ave., Detroit 48202
Dr. J. R. Thorderson, Dir. of Admis.

MINNESOTA

† University of Minnesota, Twin Cities
Minneapolis 55455

MISSISSIPPI

· † East Mississippi Community College
P.O. Box 158, Scooba 39358

· † Northwest Mississippi Community College
Desoto Center, Southaven 38671

MISSOURI

· † St. Louis Community College at Forest Park
5600 Oakland Ave., St. Louis 63110
Elizabeth Halpin, Registrar

NEW JERSEY

· † Mercer County Community College
West Windsor Campus
1200 Old Trenton Rd., Trenton 08690
Robert Smith, Coordinator
See listing under "Community and Junior Colleges"

NEW YORK

· † American Academy McAllister Institute
of Funeral Service
450 W. 56th St. #2, New York 10019
Patrick O'Connor, President

: † Simmons Institute of Funeral Service
1828 South Ave., Syracuse 13207
Maurice C. Wightman, CEO
315-475-5142

· † SUNY College of Technology
34 Cornell Dr., Canton 13617
Thomas R. Fletcher, Director of Admissions
800-388-7123

· † **SUNY HUDSON VALLEY COMMUNITY COLLEGE**
80 Vandenburgh Ave., Troy 12180
Joseph Bulmer, President
Linda Sweetman, Dir. of Admis.
Elaine Reinhard, Department Chairperson
518-283-1100
Established 1953. Public. Coed. Accreditation: MSACS, American Board of Funeral Service Education, NY State Dept. of Health. Tuition: $1,550 full-time. Estimated total yearly expenses: $2,500 full-time. Housing adjacent to campus. Enrollment: 5,875 full-time, 4,498 part-time. Faculty: 240 full-time, 350 part-time. Degrees: AAS, AA, AS, AOS. Library: 105,000 volumes. 14 buildings on 165 acres. Gym. Cooperative program with Albany Medical Col-

lege. Students must be available to participate in the embalming practicum during assigned periods in summer. Extensive on-campus laboratory facilities. Albany Airport & Amtrack Train connections are convenient and close.

· † SUNY Nassau Community College
1 Education Dr., Garden City 11530
Bernard Iantosca, Dir of Admis.

NORTH CAROLINA

· † Fayetteville Technical Community College
P.O. Box 35236, Fayetteville 28303

OHIO

† Cincinnati College of Mortuary Science
3860 Pacific Ave., Cincinnati 45207-1033
Dr. Dan Flory, President

OKLAHOMA

† University of Central Oklahoma
100 N. University Dr., Edmond 73034

OREGON

· † Mt. Hood Community College
26000 S.E. Stark St., Gresham 97030
Garth Nelson, Director

PENNSYLVANIA

· † Northampton Co. Area Community College
3835 Green Pond Rd., Bethlehem 18017
Janice Keim, Assoc. Dir. of Admis.

: † Pittsburgh Institute of Mortuary Science
5808 Baum Blvd., Pittsburgh 15206
Jeanette G. Matthews, Registrar
412-362-8500

TENNESSEE

· † John A. Gupton College
1616 Church St., Nashville 37203
John Gupton, President

TEXAS

· † Commonwealth Institute of Funeral Service
415 Barren Springs Dr., Houston 77090

: **DALLAS INSTITUTE OF FUNERAL SERVICE**
3909 S. Buckner Blvd., Dallas 75227
800-235-5444 or 214-388-5466

· † San Antonio College
1300 San Pedro Ave., San Antonio 78212

VIRGINIA

· † John Tyler Community College
13101 Jefferson Davis Hwy., Chester 23831
Dr. Freddie W. Nicholas, Jr., Pres.

WISCONSIN

· † Milwaukee Area Technical College
700 W. State St., Milwaukee 53233

GRADUATE SCHOOLS

ALABAMA

Alabama A & M University
P.O. Box 998, Normal 35762
Dr. Robert Lehman, Dean
See listing under "Universities"

Auburn University at Montgomery
7300 University Dr., Montgomery 36117
H. H. Funderburk, VP

Samford University
800 Lakeshore Dr., Birmingham 35229
Martha Ann Cox, Dean of Academic Services

Troy State University, Troy 36082
Teresa Rodgers, Dir. of Graduate Admissions

Troy State University
P.O. Box 8368, Dothan 36304
Reta Cordell, Dir. of Admis.

Tuskegee University
Tuskegee Institute 36088

United States Sports Academy
1 Academy Dr., Daphne 36526
Dr. Glenn Snyder, Dean of Student Services
800-626-3303

University of Alabama
P.O. Box 870132, Tuscaloosa 35487-0132
Roy Smith, Dir. of Admis.

UNIVERSITY OF ALABAMA IN HUNTSVILLE
P.O. Box 1247, Huntsville 35899
Ron R. Koger Ed.D., Dir. of Admis.
205-895-6070
Established 1969. Public. Coed. Accreditation: SACS, ABET, NLN, CSAB, ACS. Tuition: $2,418 resident, $4,836 non-resident. Room & Board: $3,450. Undergraduate enrollment: 2,674 full-time, 3,439 part-time. Graduate enrollment: 1,860. Faculty: 282.

Student-faculty ratio: 18:1. Degrees: BS, BA, BSBA, BSE, MS, MSM, Ph.D., BSN, MSN, MA. 20 buildings on 350 acres. Comprehensive research university located in the Tennessee Valley of northern Alabama. Huntsville is the locale of major government and private research centers. Metropolitan population approaching 300,000.

UNIVERSITY OF MOBILE
P.O. Box 13220, Mobile 36663-0220
Dr. Audrey Eubanks, Academic Dean
205-675-5990
See listing under "Universities"

ALASKA

ALASKA PACIFIC UNIVERSITY
4101 University Dr., Anchorage 99508
Director of Admissions
Established 1959. Private. Coed. Accreditation: NASC. Tuition: $7,560. Room and board: $4,010. Fees: $130. Enrollment: 347 full-time, 336 part-time. Faculty: 90. Student-faculty ratio: 12:1. Degrees offered: AA, BA, Masters. Library: 384,698 volumes. 6 buildings on a 300 acre campus. Consortium library shared with state university.

University of Alaska Southeast
11120 Glacier Hwy., Juneau 99801
Greg Wagner, Coordinator of Admissions

ARIZONA

American Graduate School of International
Management
15249 N. 59th Ave., Glendale 85306
Brian Bates, Dean of Admissions
800-848-9084

Northern Arizona University
P.O. Box 4092, Flagstaff 86011
Dr. Margaret Cibik, Dir. of Admis.

University of Arizona, Tucson 85721
Patricia Van Metre, Interim Dean

University of Arizona Medical Center
1501 N. Campbell Ave., Tucson 85724
Dr. James E. Dahlen, Dean

ARKANSAS

University of Arkansas at Fayetteville
Fayetteville 72701

CALIFORNIA

ANTIOCH UNIVERSITY
801 Garden St. #101, Santa Barbara 93101
805-962-8179

Armstrong University
2222 Harold Way, Berkeley 94704
Rowena Ricafrentre, Dir. of Admis.
510-848-2500

Biblical Christian College and Graduate School
1601 W. Malvern Ave., Fullerton 92633
Dr. Robert S. McBirnie, President

Biola University
13800 Biola Ave., La Mirada 90639
Wayne Chute, Dean of Admissions

BROOKS INSTITUTE OF PHOTOGRAPHY
801 Alston Rd., Santa Barbara 93108
Lynn Cederquist, Dir. of Admis.
805-966-3888 Ext. 217 or Ext. 218
See listing under "Photography"

CALIFORNIA COAST UNIVERSITY
700 N. Main St., Santa Ana 92701
Admissions Office: 800-854-8768 or 714-547-9625
Thomas Neal, President
Linda B. Smith, VP Academic Affairs
William Barcroft, Dean of Admissions
Established 1973. Proprietary. Coed. Accreditation: National Association of Private Non-Traditional Schools & Colleges, California State Department of Education, charter member California Association of State Approved Colleges & Universities, member Association for Adult & Continuing Education. Tuition: $2,200-$3,500. Enrollment: 7,500.
A private college offering off-campus independent study programs in the traditional areas of business administration, management, engineering, psychology, & education. Admissions: rolling trimester, requires official transcripts, letters of recommendation, detailed curriculum vita or occupational history.
Process: evaluation of prior academic work followed by analysis of occupational history, including participation in workshops, seminars, training programs, specialized projects for credit. Credit is demonstrated by challenge exams or specialized course by course independent study programs.
Residency: All course work may be completed off campus, utilizing correspondence methods. All doctoral candidates must meet with faculty advisors in person, upon completion of doctoral dissertation. Scholarships: Interest free loans available to students.

California College for Health Sciences
222 W. 24th St., National City 91950
619-477-4800

California College of Arts & Crafts
5212 Broadway, Oakland 94618
Sheri McKenzie, Dir. of Admis.
510-653-6522

CALIFORNIA FAMILY STUDY CENTER
5433 Laurel Canyon Blvd., North Hollywood 91607
818-509-5959
Established 1971. Private. Coed. Accreditation: WASC. Non-residential. Enrollment: 250. Faculty: full-time 13, part-time 20. Student-faculty ratio: 12:1. Degree program: MA, Marriage, Family and Child Therapy only. Library: 6,000 Volumes. Adjacent to Los Angeles. Assistance with placement in training agencies. Direct observation in case conference setting.

California Institute of Integral Studies
765 Ashbury St., San Francisco 94117
Diane Gribben, Dir. of Admis.

California Institute of Technology
1201 E. California Blvd., Pasedena 91125
Arden Albee, Dean
818-356-6346

California Institute of the Arts
24700 McBean Pkwy., Valencia 91355
Kenneth Young, Dir. of Admis.

California Lutheran University
60 Olsen Rd., Thousand Oaks 91360
805-493-3125

California Polytechnic State University
San Luis Obispo 93407
Helen Linstrum, Dir. of Admis.

CALIFORNIA SCHOOL OF PROFESSIONAL PSYCHOLOGY
2749 Hyde St., San Francisco 94109
415-346-4500
John O'Neil, President
Patty Mullen, VP Marketing & Enrollment
CAMPUSES:
CSPP-Berkeley/Alameda (B)
1005 Atlantic Ave., Alameda 94501
CSPP-Fresno (F)
1350 M St., Fresno 93721
CSPP-Los Angeles (LA)
1000 S. Fremont Ave., Alhambra 91803-1360
CSPP-San Diego (SD)
6212 Ferris Square, San Diego 92121
Established 1969. Coed. Graduate professional school offering PsyD and PhD in Clinical Psychology, PhD in Organizational Psychology (B,LA), PhD in Industrial/Organizational Psychology (SD), MS in Organizational Behavior (F), and Doctoral Respecialization Program (B,F,SD).
Systemwide enrollment: 2,200. Tuition for entering students: $14,700. Clinical PsyD is a 4 year program, clinical PhD a 5 year program, and industrial and organizational PhD a 4 year program. Clinical doctoral areas of specialization: CSPP-B - health psychology, family/child psychology, psychodynamic psychology, and multicultural education, research, intervention, and training (MERIT). CSPP-F - ecosystemic clinical child psychology, ethnocultural mental health, and general clinical psychology with optional emphasis in health psychology or neuropsychology. CSPP-LA - health psychology, individual and family clinical psychology, and multicultural and community clinical psychology. CSPP-SD - health psychology, family/child psychology, cultural psychology, and organizational behavior.
Clinical Program Admission Requirements: applicants must hold a BA from an accredited institution prior to entry, have a minimum psychology and cumulative GPA of 3.0, and must demonstrate academic preparation in one of the following three ways: BA/BS in Psychology OR a score in the 80th percentile or above on the GRE Advanced Psychology subtest OR coursework in these 4 areas: A) statistics, B) tests and measurements or differential psychology, C) abnor-

mal psychology or psychopathology, D) experimental psychology or physiological bases of behavior or learning theory. While the applicant may not have completed the degree or required course prior to application, s/he must complete them prior to entry.
Applicants may receive credit for previous graduate work leading to the PsyD in 3-4 years or the PhD in 4-5 years; to receive credit applicants must hold a MA in psychology or closely related field (B,F,SD) with minimum GPA of 3.0. Courses that may be waived or challenged vary by campus. Doctoral Respecialization Program offered for holders of doctorates in psychology who wish to specialize in professional psychology (B,F,SD).
Financial Assistance: Need based only, need is determined by GAPSFAS Financial Statement. CSPP administered aid is usually in the package form of CSPP scholarship, Perkins loan, and College-Work Study award. Also available are CSPP Minority Fellowships, Patricia Roberts Harris Program, Health Education Assistance Loans, Stafford Loans, Supplemental Loans for Students, paid assistantships and field placements.
Accreditation: WASC (all campuses). American Psychological Association (clinical PhD programs at B,F,& LA fully accredited; SD currently on probationary status. Clinical PsyD program APA accredited at LA).

California State University, Chico
Chico 95929-0875
Dr. Elaine Wangberg, Dean

Chapman University
333 N. Glassell St., Orange 92666
Michael Drummy, Dir. of Admis.

Claremont Graduate School
170 E. Tenth St., Claremont 91711
Diane J. Guido, Associate Dean
909-621-8069

College of Notre Dame
1500 Ralston Ave., Belmont 94002
Greg M. Smith, PhD., Dir. of Admis.

Concordia University
1530 Concordia, Irvine 92715
Stan Meyer, Dean of Admission
800-229-1200
See listing under "Universities"

DOMINICAN COLLEGE OF SAN RAFAEL
50 Acacia Ave., San Rafael 94901-8008
800-788-3522

Dominican School of Philosophy & Theology
2401 Ridge Rd., Berkeley 94709
Ingrid Honore, C.S.J., Dir. of Admis.
510-849-2030

Fielding Institute
2112 Santa Barbara St., Santa Barbara 93105
Sylvia Williams, Dir. of Admis.

FRANCISCAN SCHOOL OF THEOLOGY
1712 Euclid Ave., Berkeley 94709
William M. Cieslak, OFM Cap., President
Paschal Hocum, Dir. of Admis.
510-848-5232
Established 1968. Private. Coed. Accreditation: WASC, ATS. Tuition: $5,650. Fees: $40. Enrollment: 64 full-time, 23 part-time. Faculty: 12. Student-faculty ratio: 7:1. Degrees: MA, MDiv, MTS, or one year Certificate in Theological Studies. Library: The Graduate Theological Union has over 500,000 Theological holdings. The Franciscan School of Theology is a member school of the Graduate Theological Union, the largest consortium of graduate Theological schools on the West Coast which allows choices of over 250 courses each semester. 50% lay students, 50% women. Some tuition reduction available.

FULLER THEOLOGICAL SEMINARY
135 N. Oakland Ave., Pasadena 91182
Attn: Director of Admissions
Accreditation: WASC, ATS
818-584-5400 or 800-235-2222 ext. 5400

Graduate Theological Union
2400 Ridge Rd., Berkeley 94709

Hebrew Union College
Jewish Institute of Religion
3077 University Ave., Los Angeles 90007
Rabbi Lee Bycel, Dean

JESUIT SCHOOL OF THEOLOGY AT BERKELEY
1735 LeRoy Ave., Berkeley 94709
Rev. Thomas Gleeson, SJ, President
Annette Moran, CSJ, Dir. of Admis.
800-824-0122
Established 1934. Private. Coed. Accreditation: ATS, WASC. Tuition: $7,400. Fees: $100. Enrollment: 240. Faculty: 27. Student-faculty ratio: 9:1. Degrees: MDiv, MTS, MA, one year certificates in Spirituality, Advanced Masters. Library: The Graduate Theological Union library has over 500,000 theological holdings. 4 buildings. The Jesuit School of Theology is a member school of the Graduate Theological Union, the largest consortium of theological graduate schools on the West Coast. Choose from over 250 courses each semester. Lay students welcome. Scholarships available. High quality Jesuit education.

LIFE CHIROPRACTIC COLLEGE WEST
2005 Via Barrett, San Lorenzo 94580-1368
Gerard W. Clum, DC, President
Suzanne Smith, Admissions Director
510-276-9013 or 800-788-4476
Established 1976. Private. Coed. Accreditation:

CCE. Tuition: $10,050. Enrollment: 700 day. Faculty: 86. Degree: DC Chiropractic. Library: 11,000 volumes. 6 buildings. In the beautiful San Francisco Bay area, Life West provides superb preparation for a chiropractic profession.

LINCOLN UNIVERSITY
281 Masonic Ave., San Francisco 94118
Clarence Rippel, Acting President
Accredited Member ACICS

Loma Linda University, Loma Linda 92350
800-422-4LLU

Los Angeles College of Chiropractic
16200 E. Amber Valley Dr., Whittier 90604
Charlene Frontiera, PhD, Dir. of Admis.
800-221-5222

Loyola Marymount University
Loyola Blvd. at W. 80th, Los Angeles 90045
M. L'Heureux, Dir. of Admis.

Mennonite Brethren Biblical Seminary
4824 E. Butler Ave., Fresno 93727
Larry Martens, President

Monterey Institute of International Studies
425 Van Buren St., Monterey 93940

National University
4141 Camino del Rio, S., San Diego 92108
Dr. Harold C. Wells, Dean

New College for Advanced Christian Studies
2600 Dwight Way, Berkeley 94704

OTIS COLLEGE OF ART AND DESIGN
2401 Wilshire Blvd., Los Angeles 90057
Neil Hoffman, President
See listing under "Art"

PACIFIC GRADUATE SCHOOL OF PSYCHOLOGY
935 E. Meadow Dr., Palo Alto 94303
Rick Kaplowitz, Vice President
415-494-7477

Pacific Lutheran Theological Seminary
2770 Marin Ave., Berkeley 94708
Dr. Walter Stuhr, President

Pacific Oaks College
5 Westmoreland Pl., Pasadena 91103
Katherine Gabel, President

PACIFIC SCHOOL OF RELIGION
1798 Scenic Ave., Berkeley 94709
Ronald Parker, Dir. of Admis.
800-999-0528 or 510-848-0528
Established 1866. Private. Coed. Accreditation: ATS, WASC. Tuition: $5,800. Room and board: $8,260. Enrollment: 200. Faculty: 13. Degrees: MDiv, MA, DMin, 4 certificate programs. Library: 617,535 volumes. 5 buildings plus residential property on 3 acres. Member, Graduate Theological Union. Oldest Protestant seminary in the West.

Point Loma Nazarene College
3900 Lomaland Dr., San Diego 92106
Bill Young, Dir. of Admis.

RAND GRADUATE SCHOOL
P.O. Box 2138, Santa Monica 90407
Charles Wolf, Jr., Dean
310-393-0411 ext. 7690

San Francisco State University
1600 Holloway Ave., San Francisco 94132
Corwin Bjonerud, Dir. of Admis.

Santa Clara University, Santa Clara 95053

SAYBROOK INSTITUTE
450 Pacific Ave., Third Floor
San Francisco 94133
J. Bruce Francis, President
See listing under "Psychology"

Simpson College
2211 College View Dr., Redding 96003
Clinton Sparks, Dean

Southern California College
55 Fair Dr., Costa Mesa 92626
Roger Heuser, Director

Southern California Institute of Architecture
5454 Beethoven St., Los Angeles 90066
310-574-3625

UNITED STATES INTERNATIONAL UNIVERSITY
10455 Pomerado Rd., San Diego 92131
619-693-4772
See listing under "Universities"

University of California, Los Angeles
1247 Murphy Hall, Los Angeles 90024

University of California at Berkeley
Sproul Hall, Berkeley 94720

University of California, Davis
376 Mrak Hall, Davis 95616

University of California, Riverside
P.O. Box 112, Riverside 92521

University of California, San Diego
9450 Gilman Dr., La Jolla 92092

University of California-Santa Cruz
Santa Cruz 95064
John M. Ellis, Dean

University of California, San Francisco
Parnassus & 3rd Ave., San Francisco 94143

UNIVERSITY OF JUDAISM/LEE COLLEGE

15600 Mulholland Dr., Los Angeles 90077
Tamara Greenebaum, Dean of Admissions
See listing under "Universities"

University of La Verne
1950 3rd St., La Verne 91750
Mark Bornholdt, Dir. of Admis.

University of Redlands
P.O. Box 3080, Redlands 92373

University of San Diego
5998 Alcala Park, San Diego 92110
Maureen Phalen, Dir. Graduate Admissions
619-260-4524

University of San Francisco
2130 Fulton St., San Francisco 94117
Bill Henley, Dir. of Admis.

University of the Pacific
School of Dentistry
2155 Webster St., San Francisco 94115

Woodbury University
7500 Glenoaks Blvd., Burbank 91504
See listing under "Universities"

COLORADO

Adams State College, Alamosa 81102
Mark Clark, Asst. VP for Academic Affairs
800-824-6494

Colorado Christian University
180 S. Garrison St., Lakewood 80226
Dr. Richard Beal, Dir. of Admis.

COLORADO TECHNICAL COLLEGE

4435 N. Chestnut St., Colorado Springs 80907
719-598-0200
The transition from high-tech education to high-tech careers is Colorado Tech's specialty! Situated in the middle of a space age community known as Silicon Mountain, the college takes pride in its mission to serve high-tech businesses and industries by providing graduates able to hit the ground running in such fields as: computer engineering, computer science, electrical engineering, electronic engineering technology, telecommunications, systems management, and logistics. Colorado Tech, accredited by NCA and ABET, offers Associate, Bachelor and Master degrees.
Master of Science degrees are offered in computer science, computer engineering, electrical engineering and management. The Master of Science in electrical engineering has concentrations in electronic systems and communications systems. The Master of Science in management has concentrations in systems management and logistics systems management. The Master of Science in computer science has concentrations in software engineering, computer systems engineering, and systems engineering. The Carnegie Mellon University Software Engineering Institute model curriculum is offered by Colorado Tech in the software engineering concentration.
Colorado Tech believes students should not only learn in the classroom, but in the laboratory as well, applying their knowledge to real world problems. The professor and students work in an environment that encourages constant interaction in the learning process. Class size is limited to 40 students and labs are limited to 24 students. Colorado Tech's state of the art equipment is always available: no one waits in line.
It is no surprise that companies such as Digital, Texas Instruments, Loral, MCI, Apple, Atmel, Litton, United Technologies, Hewlett-Packard, Ford Microelectronics, GE Aerospace, Hughes Aircraft and Cray Research have chosen Colorado Springs with its USAF space center and US Space Foundation to locate facilities here. Many of these companies have representatives who sit on our advisory boards and many of our professors come from these companies.
The Colorado Springs area offers many recreational activities such as skiing, fishing, hunting, hiking, mountain climbing and four wheeling. NFL football, NBA basketball, National League baseball, the symphony and varied expressions of popular culture provide ample entertainment for every taste. Soar to meet your destiny through higher education at Colorado Tech.

DENVER SEMINARY

Denver Conservative Baptist Seminary
MDiv, MA, DMIN.
P.O. Box 10000, Denver 80250
Charles Sprinkle, Dir. of Admis.
1-800-922-3040

ILIFF SCHOOL OF THEOLOGY

2201 S. University Blvd., Denver 80210
Susan Mitchell, Dir. of Admis.
800-678-3360

Naropa Institute
2130 Arapahoe Ave., Boulder 80302
Dr. Jana Lynn, Director of Admissions
303-546-3572

National Technological University
700 Centre Ave., Fort Collins 80526
Eileen Moree, Dir. of Admis. and Records

NATIONAL THEATRE CONSERVATORY

1050 13th St., Denver 80204
Eduardo Ortega, Administrator
Tony Church, Dean
303-893-4000 ext. 4854

Established 1984.

Private.
Coed.
Accreditation: NCACS (fully accredited).
Full tuition waiver - Stipend paid in all three years.
Enrollment: 24.
Faculty: 14, 4 full-time.
Student-faculty ratio: 3:1.
Degrees: Master of Fine Arts in Acting, Certificate of Completion in Acting. Two buildings.
The National Theatre Conservatory offers an intensive three year training program for actors. The first two years of the actor-training program are spent on classroom and project work, and internship in the production and administrative departments of The Denver Center Theatre Company. The third year is spent in membership of the acting company, with full Equity eligibility obtained. The National Theatre Conservatory is a department of the Denver Center Theatre Company, itself a division of the Denver Center for the Performing Arts, with its Media Studios and the W. J. Gould Voice Research Center.

University of Colorado Health Sciences Center
4200 E. 9th Ave., Denver 80262
Lawrence H. Meskin, DDS, PhD, Dean

University of Denver
2199 S. University Blvd., Denver 80210

University of Denver - University College
2211 S. Josephine St., Denver 80208

University of Northern Colorado, Greeley 80639
Kyle Carter, Dean
303-351-2831

CONNECTICUT

Hartford Graduate Center
275 Windsor St., Hartford 06120

Quinnipiac College
275 Mount Carmel Ave., Hamden 06518
See listing under "Universities"

St. Joseph College
1678 Asylum Ave., West Hartford 06117
Mary C. Demo, Dir. of Admis.

University of Bridgeport
126 Park Ave., Bridgeport 06601
Andrew G. Nelson, Dean Admis./Financial Aid
203-576-4552
See listing under "Universities"

University of Connecticut, Storrs 06268
Thomas Giolas, Interim Dean

University of Hartford
200 Bloomfield Ave., West Hartford 06117
Richard Zeiser, Dir. of Admis.
See listing under "Universities"

University of New Haven
300 Orange Ave., West Haven 06516
William Gere, Dean
203-932-7133

Yale University
1504A Yale Station, New Haven 06520

DISTRICT OF COLUMBIA

The American University
4400 Massachusetts Ave. N.W.
Washington 20016

DISTRICT OF COLUMBIA SCHOOL OF LAW

719 13th St., N.W., Washington 20005
Vivian Canty, Dir. of Admis.
202-727-5232

Johns Hopkins University
School of Advanced International Studies
1740 Massachusetts Ave., N.W.
Washington 20036

University of the District of Columbia
Georgia Ave.-Harvard St. Campus
1100 Harvard St., N.W., Washington 20009

FLORIDA

Barry University
11300 N.E. 2nd Ave., Miami Shores 33161
Robin Ray Roberts, Dean of Admis.

Caribbean Center for Advanced Studies
Miami Institute of Psychology
8180 N.W. 36th St. 2nd Floor, Miami 33166
See listing under "Psychology"

Florida Atlantic University
500 N.W. 20th St., Boca Raton 33431
Brian Levin-Stankevich, Dir. of Admis.

Florida Institute of Technology
150 W. University Blvd., Melbourne 32901
Louis T. Levy, Dean of Admissions
800-888-4348

Fort Lauderdale College
1040 Bayview Dr., Ft. Lauderdale 33304
William P. Bedard, Director

Jacksonville University
2800 University Blvd., N., Jacksonville 32211

LYNN UNIVERSITY

(Est. 1962 as College of Boca Raton)
3601 N. Military Trail, Boca Raton 33431
407-994-0770 or 800-544-8035
See listing under "Universities"

Nova Southeastern University
3301 College Ave., Ft. Lauderdale 33314

Orlando College - North
5500 Diplomat Circle, Orlando 32810

St. Thomas University
16400 N.W. 32nd Ave., Miami 33054
Mary R. Conway, Dir. of Graduate Admissions

SCHILLER INTERNATIONAL UNIVERSITY (EUROPE)

U.S. Admissions Office
Dept. PA, 453 Edgewater Dr., Dunedin 34698
800-336-4133 or 813-736-5082 Fax: 813-736-6263
Dr. Walter Leibrecht, President
Karen Altieri, Associate Director of Admissions
Established 1964. Coed. Accreditation: ACICS. Tuition: $11,300. Room and board: $5,800. Est. total yrly. expense: $21,500. Enrollment in graduate programs: 327. Degrees: MA, MIM, MBA, MBA Prep. program. Programs in International Business, International Tourism and Hospitality Management, & International Relations & Diplomacy. Programs offered in London, Paris, Madrid, Berlin, Heidelberg, Strasbourg, and Leysin. Classes are in English. International curriculum. Multicultural faculty and student body.
See listing under "Universities"

Stetson University
401 N. Woodland Blvd., De Land 32720
Gary A. Meadows, Dean of Admis.

Tampa College - Pinellas
15064 U.S. Hwy. 19 N., Clearwater 34624
Mark A. Page, President
813-530-9495

University of Miami
P.O. Box 248006, Coral Gables 33124

UNIVERSITY OF SARASOTA

5250 17th St., Sarasota 34235
Linda Volz, Dir. of Enrollment Management
800-331-5995
Established 1969. Coed. Accreditation: SACS. Tuition: $265 per credit hour. Enrollment: 470. Faculty: 30. Degrees: MAEd, MBA, EdD. Year round, non-traditional calendar, flexible, small seminars, much individual attention to students, performance oriented.

GEORGIA

Clark Atlanta University
240 James Brawley Dr., S.W., Atlanta 30314
Thomas W. Cole, President

Columbia Theological Seminary
701 S. Columbia Dr., Decatur 30030
James Hudnut-Beumler, Academic Dean

Georgia College
231 W. Hancock St., Milledgeville 31061
912-453-5004

INSTITUTE OF PAPER SCIENCE & TECHNOLOGY

500 10th St. N.W., Atlanta 30318
404-853-9556
Private graduate school; multi-disciplinary program in chemistry, physics, mathematics, biology, and engineering leading to M.S. and Ph.D. US, Canadian and Mexican residents granted fellowships ($3,750 per quarter, M.S.; $4,250 per quarter, Ph.D.) plus tuition scholarships ($5,000 per quarter). Admission geared to B.S. majors in science and engineering. Abundant opportunities for lucrative careers in pulp and paper industry.

Kennesaw State College
P.O. Box 444, Marietta 30061
Joe Head, Dir. of Admis.

La Grange College
601 Broad St., La Grange 30240
Phil Dodson, Dir. of Admis.
706-882-2911

Medical College of Georgia
1120 15th St., Augusta 30901
Dr. Lowell M. Greenbaum, VP for Research

Mercer University
1400 Coleman Ave., Macon 31207

SAVANNAH COLLEGE OF ART & DESIGN

342 Bull St., Savannah 31401
May Poetter, VP of Admissions
912-238-2424
See listing under "Art"

University of Georgia, Athens 30602
Dr. John Dowling, Dean

West Georgia College, Carrollton 30118
C. Doyle Bickers, Dir. of Admis.

HAWAII

Chaminade University of Honolulu
3140 Waialae Ave., Honolulu 96816
Charles Schafer, VP Enrollment Services

Hawaii Pacific University
1166 Fort Street Mall, Honolulu 96813
Don Barlow, Dir. of Admis.

Japan-America Institute of Management Science
6660 Hawaii Kai Dr., Honolulu 96825
Roxanne Kam, Academic Services Coordinator
808-395-2314

IDAHO

University of Idaho, Moscow 83843
Peter Brown, Dir. of Admis.

ILLINOIS

Adler School of Professional Psychology
65 E. Wacker Pl., Chicago 60601-7203
Suzann Lebda, Director of Admissions
312-201-5900

THE AMERICAN CONSERVATORY OF MUSIC
16 N. Wabash Ave., Suite 1850, Chicago 60602
312-263-4161
Established 1886. Private. Coed. Conservatory of
Music. Accreditation: NASM. Degrees: Bachelor of
Music, Master of Music, Doctor of Musical Arts.
World renowned Robert R. McCormick Reference Li-
brary. Numerous Pulitzer Prize winners. Location:
Downtown Chicago, near to the Art Institute, Orches-
tra Hall, Newberry Library, the Lyric Opera. Tuition:
Estimated at $9,800 dependent on private study op-
tions. Room, board, books, and supplies: Estimated at
$8,900.

Aurora University
347 S. Gladstone Ave., Aurora 60506
Peter Pitts, Dir. of Admis.

Chicago School of Professional Psychology
806 S. Plymouth Ct., Chicago 60605
Dr. William Bruinsma, Admissions Dept.
312-786-9443

CHICAGO THEOLOGICAL SEMINARY
5757 S. University Ave., Chicago 60637
Delois Shepard, Dir. of Admissions
312-752-5757 Ext. 229

De Paul University
1 E. Jackson Blvd., Chicago 60604
Thomas D. Abrahamson, Dean of Admissions
See listing under "Universities"

Eastern Illinois University, Charleston 61920
Larry Williams, Dean
See listing under "Universities"

Garrett-Evangelical Theological Seminary
2121 Sheridan Rd., Evanston 60201
Contact Admissions at 800-SEMINARY

Governors State University
1 University Pky., University Park 60466
Richard Pride, Dir. of Admis.

Knowledge Systems Institute
3420 Main St., Skokie 60076
708-679-3135, FAX: 708-679-3166
See listing under "Computer and Info Science"

Lake Forest Graduate School of Management
Sheridan & Maplewood Rds., Lake Forest 60045
Carolyn Brune, Dir. of Admis.
708-234-5080

Lake Forest Graduate School of Management
1295 E. Algonquin Rd., Schaumburg 60196
Shawna Lanning, Dir. of Admis.
708-576-1212 Extension 24

Lake Forest Graduate School of Management
230 S. La Salle St., Chicago 60604
Meena Ariagno, Dir. of Admis.
312-435-5330

LEWIS UNIVERSITY
Rt. 53, Romeoville 60441
Irish O'Reilly, Director of Admissions
See listing under "Universities"

Lutheran School of Theology at Chicago
1100 E. 55th St., Chicago 60615
Wesley Fuerst, Dir. of Graduate Studies
312-753-0700

Midwest College of Engineering
600 S. Lambert Rd., Glen Ellyn 60137

National College of Chiropractic
200 E. Roosevelt Rd., Lombard 60148
Dr. James Winterstein, President
708-629-2000

National-Louis University
2840 Sheridan Ave., Evanston 60201

Northeastern Illinois University
5500 N. St. Louis Ave., Chicago 60625

Northern Illinois University, De Kalb 60115

Northwestern University
Crown I-502, Evanston 60208

Olivet Nazarene University, Kankakee 60901
Dr. Henry Smith, Dean

Rockford College
5050 E. State St., Rockford 61108
Winston A. McKean, Dean
See listing under "Universities"

ROOSEVELT UNIVERSITY
430 S. Michigan Ave., Chicago 60605
William Smyser, Director of Admissions
See listing under "Universities"

Rosary College
7900 W. Division St., River Forest 60305
Hildegarde Schmidt, Dir. of Admis.

St. Xavier College
3700 W. 103rd St., Chicago 60655
Mary Hendry, Dean of Admissions

Sangamon State University
Shepherd Rd., Springfield 62794-9243
Admissions and Records, 217-786-6626

School of the Art Institute of Chicago
37 S. Wabash, Chicago 60603
Ellen B. Cropp, Dir. of Admis.

Spertus College of Judaica
618 S. Michigan Ave., Chicago 60605
Sharon Fishman, Student Services Coordinator

Telshe Yeshiva-Chicago
3535 W. Foster Ave., Chicago 60625

University of Chicago
5801 S. Ellis Ave., Chicago 60637

University of Health Sciences
The Chicago Medical School
3333 Green Bay Rd., North Chicago 60064

University of Illinois at Chicago
P.O. Box 4348, Chicago 60680
Dr. Karen Hitchcock, Dean

VanderCook College of Music
3209 S. Michigan Ave., Chicago 60616
Ward Durrett, Dir of Admis.

Western Illinois University
900 W. Adams St., Macomb 61455
Alan DeRoos, Registrar
309-298-1891

Wheaton College, Wheaton 60187
James Stamoolis, Dean
800-888-0141

INDIANA

Grace Theological Seminary
Winona Lake 46590
Dr. Gary Meadors, Dir. of Admis.

Indiana University-Purdue University
355 N. Lansing, Indianapolis 46202

Indiana Wesleyan University
4201 S. Washington St., Marion 46953
800-332-6901

University of Notre Dame, Notre Dame 46556
Robert E. Gordon, V.P. for Adv. Study

IOWA

Drake University
2507 E. University Ave., Des Moines 50311
Thomas Willoughby, Dir. of Admis.

Faith Baptist Bible College & Theological Seminary
1900 N.W. 4th St., Ankeny 50021
Jeff Newman, Director of Admissions
Admissions: 800-352-0147

Iowa State University, Ames 50011
Karsten Smedal, Dir. of Admis.

Maharishi International University
Route 1, Fairfield 52556
Gregory Polakow, Dir. of Admis.

PALMER COLLEGE OF CHIROPRACTIC
1000 Brady St., Davenport 52803
Donald P. Kern, President
800-722-2586 or 319-326-9656

Teikyo Marycrest University
1607 W. 12th St., Davenport 52804
Tim McDonough, Dir. of Admis.
See listing under "Universities"

University of Iowa, Iowa City 52242

University of Northern Iowa, Cedar Falls 50614

KANSAS

CENTRAL BAPTIST THEOLOGICAL SEMINARY
741 N. 31st, Kansas City 66102-3964
800-677-CBTS (2287) or 913-371-5313
Dr. Thomas Clifton, President
Nancy J. Snyder, Director of Admissions
Established 1901. Private. Coed. Accreditation:
NCACS, ATS. Tuition: $150/hr. Room: $144/mo.(sin-
gle) Fees: $100. Enrollment: 90. Degrees: Diploma,
Master of Divinity, Master of Arts in Religious Stud-
ies. January and June sessions. Creative field educa-
tion program complements academic work. Native
American Studies. CPE (Clinical Pastoral Education)
Urban setting.

Fort Hays State University
600 Park St., Hays 67601-4099
Dr. James Forsythe, Dean

SOUTHWESTERN COLLEGE
100 College St., Winfield 67156
800-846-1543

WICHITA STATE UNIVERSITY
1845 Fairmount St., Wichita 67260
Toll-free, 800-362-2594
Established 1895. Public. Coed. Accreditation:
NCACS. Tuition: $997 resident, $3,250 non-resident,
$1,201 graduate resident, $3,430 graduate non-resident. Room and board: $1,503. Fees: $13 per semester.
Enrollment: 7,525 full-time, 7,595 part-time. Faculty:
474 full-time, 248 part-time. Student-faculty ratio:
18:1. Degrees: AA, AS, BA, BAEd, BBA, BFA, BGS,
BHS, BMus, BMusEd, BS, BSAE, BSEE, BSIE, BSME,
BSN, MEd, MAC, MAJ, MBA, MCS, MFA, MHS, Mas-
ter of Health Science, MM, MMEd, MPA, Master of
Professional Accountancy, MPT, MS, MSN, EdS,
EdD, PhD. Library: 903,000 volumes, 4,115 periodicals, 874,658 microform, computerized card catalog and 8-index LAN. 60 buildings on 330 acres.
National Institute for Aviation Research. Several
wind tunnels, 1 research quality flow-visualization

water tunnel. Ulrich Museum of Art. WSU cable 13
TV station, KMUW FM radio station. Comprehensive
fitness, physical education, and recreation center.

KENTUCKY

GEORGETOWN COLLEGE
400 E. College St., Georgetown 40324
Dr. Ben Oldham, Dean
See listing under "Universities"

Lexington Theological Seminary
631 Limestone St., S., Lexington 40508
William Paulsell, President

Louisville Presbyterian Theological Seminary
1044 Alta Vista Rd., Louisville 40205
502-895-3411 or 800-264-1839

Northern Kentucky University
Louie B. Nunn Dr., Highland Heights 41076

Spalding University
851 S. 4th St., Louisville 40203
Dorothy G. Allen, Dir. of Admis.

LOUISIANA

Grambling State University
P.O. Box 607, Grambling 71245
Dr. Harold W. Lundy, President

Loyola University
6363 St. Charles Ave., New Orleans 70118

Southeastern Louisiana University
P.O. Box 784, Hammond 70404

Tulane University
324 Gibson Hall, New Orleans 70118

University of Southwestern Louisiana
P.O. Box 44610, Lafayette 70504
318-231-6965

MAINE

HUSSON COLLEGE
One College Circle, Bangor 04401
Robert Smith, Dean of Graduate Studies
800-477-4723
See listing under "Business and Management"

University of New England
11 Hills Beach Rd., Biddeford 04005
Patricia Cribby, Dir. of Admis.

University of Southern Maine
96 Falmouth St., Portland 04103
Richard Maiman, Director

MARYLAND

Baltimore Hebrew University
5800 Park Heights Ave., Baltimore 21215
Dr. Robert O. Freedman, Dean

Loyola College
4501 N. Charles St., Baltimore 21210
Thomas Bednarsky, Graduate Admissions

Peabody Institute of The Johns Hopkins Univ.
Peabody Conservatory of Music
1 E. Mt. Vernon Place, Baltimore 21202
David Lane, Dir. of Admis.

Towson State University
800 York Rd., Towson 21204
Dr. Hoke Smith, President

Western Maryland College
2 College Hill, Westminster 21157

MASSACHUSETTS

American International College
1000 State St., Springfield 01109
Peter Miller, Dean of Admissions

Anna Maria College
2 Sunset Ln., Paxton 01612
Dr. Bernadette Madore, SSA, President

Arthur D. Little Management Education Institute
35 Acorn Park, Cambridge 02140

Bentley College
175 Forest St., Waltham 02154
Joann McKenna, Dir. of Admis.

Boston College
140 Commonwealth Ave., Chestnut Hill 02167
Donald White, Dean

Boston Conservatory
8 The Fenway, Boston 02215

Boston University Graduate School of Management
685 Commonwealth Ave., Boston 02215
Nancy Traccarella, Dir. of Admis.

Brandeis University
415 South St., Waltham 02154
617-736-3410

Bridgewater State College
Bridgewater 02325
Dr. Marilyn Barry, Dean

Cambridge College
Graduate Programs for Working Adults
1000 Massachusetts Ave., Cambridge 02138
Degrees: MEd and MMD
Bruce Grigsby, Dir. of Enrollment Services
800-877-GRAD or 617-868-1000

Clark University
950 Main St., Worcester 01610
Richard Pierson, Dean of Admis.

Conway School of Landscape Design
Delabarre Ave., Conway 01341

Curry College
1071 Blue Hill Ave., Milton 02186
617-333-0500

Emmanuel College
400 The Fenway, Boston 02115
Margaret Bonilla, Dir. of Admis.

Fitchburg State College
160 Pearl St., Fitchburg 01420
Marke Vickers, Dir. of Admis.

Harvard University
Graduate School of Arts and Sciences
Byerly Hall, 2nd Floor
8 Garden St, Cambridge 02138

Hebrew College, 43 Hawes St., Brookline 02146

Hellenic College
Holy Cross School of Theology
50 Goddard Ave., Brookline 02146
Fr. Al Demos, Director of Admission
617-731-3500

Massachusetts Institute of Technology
77 Massachusetts Ave., Cambridge 02139

NORTH ADAMS STATE COLLEGE
375 Church St., North Adams 01247
Denise Richardello, Director of Admissions
413-664-4511 or 800-292-6632
Established 1894. Public. Coed. Accreditation: New England Association of Schools and Colleges. Tuition: $1,408 in state, 5,542 out of state. Room and board: $4,212. Fees: $2,085. Enrollment: 1,394 full-time, 593 part-time. Faculty: 121. Student-faculty ratio: 17:1. Degrees: BA, BS, MEd. Library: 175,000 volumes, 510 Periodicals. 16 buildings on 80 acres. Average class size: 24. 2 1/2 hours from Boston. 2 hours from Hartford, CT. 3 1/2 hours from New York City. 100 Academic advisors on campus to assist students, 45 clubs, 8 intercollegiate programs offered on campus. Internships available in each academic area.

SCHOOL OF THE MUSEUM OF FINE ARTS
230 Fenway, Boston 02115
Alan Van Reed, Dean of Admissions
617-267-1218

Simmons College
300 The Fenway, Boston 02115

Springfield College
263 Alden St., Springfield 01109
Frederick Bartlett, Dean of Admissions

University of Massachusetts, Amherst 01003
Arlene Wesley Cash, Dir. of Admis.

University of Massachusetts
100 Morrissey Blvd., Boston 02125

University of Massachusetts Dartmouth
Old Westport Rd., North Dartmouth 02747
Dr. Richard Panofsky, Vice Chancellor Academic Affairs
508-999-8000

Western New England College
1215 Wilbraham Rd., Springfield 01119
800-325-1122

Wheelock College
200 Riverway, Boston 02215
Joan Wexler, Dean of Admis. & Financial Aid

Woods Hole Oceanographic Institution
Woods Hole 02543
J. W. Farrington, Dean of Graduate Studies

MICHIGAN

Andrews University, Berrien Springs 49104
Jack Mentges, Dir. of Admis.

Center for Humanistic Studies
40 E. Ferry Ave., Detroit 48202

Eastern Michigan University, Ypsilanti 48197
Ronald E. Goldenberg, Dean
313-487-3400 or 800-GO-TO-EMU

GMI Engineering & Management Institute
1700 W. 3rd Ave., Flint 48504
Phillip D. Lavender, Dir. of Admis.
See listing under "Engineering"

Marygrove College
8425 W. McNichols Rd., Detroit 48221

Michigan State University, East Lansing 48824

Michigan Technological University
1400 Townsend Dr., Houghton 49931
Dr. Sung M. Lee, Dean
906-487-2327

SS Cyril and Methodius Seminary
3535 Indian Trl., Orchard Lake 48324
Francis B. Koper, Rector
810-683-0311

Western Michigan University, Kalamazoo 49008
Stanley Henderson, Dir. of Enrl. Mgt. & Admis.
616-387-2000

MINNESOTA

Bemidji State University
1500 Birchmont Dr., N.E., Bemidji 56601
800-475-2001

Bethel Theological Seminary
3949 Bethel Dr., St. Paul 55112
Dr. Fred Prinzing, Exec VP, Dean

College of St. Scholastica
1200 Kenwood Ave., Duluth 55811
Dr. Chandra Mehrotra, Chrpsn.
800-447-5444
See listing under "Liberal Arts"

Luther Northwestern Theological Seminary
2481 Como Ave., St. Paul 55108
Dr. David Tiede, President

Metropolitan State University
700 7th St. E., St. Paul 55106
David Crockett, PhD, Dean

NORTHWESTERN COLLEGE OF CHIROPRACTIC
2501 W. 84th St., Minneapolis 55431
Susan Pitts, Coord. of New Student Advising
See listing under "Chiropractic Colleges"

St. Cloud State University
740 4th Ave., S., St. Cloud 56301
Sherwood Reid, Dir. of Admis.
800-369-4260

St. John's University
P.O. Box 7155, Collegeville 56321

St. Mary's College of Minnesota
2510 Park Ave., Minneapolis 55404
Suzanne James, VP

University of St. Thomas
2115 Summit Ave., St. Paul 55105

Walden University
155 5th Ave. S. #200, Minneapolis 55401

MISSISSIPPI

Mississippi University for Women
P.O. Box W-1602, Columbus 39701
Teresa Thompson, Exec. Dir. of Enrollment

MISSISSIPPI VALLEY STATE UNIVERSITY
14000 Hwy. 82 W., Itta Bena 38941
Maxcine B. Rush, Director of Admissions
601-254-9041
Established 1946. Public. Coed. Accreditation: SACS, NCATE, NASAD, and other accrediting agencies. Tuition: $2,171 (out of state fee $959). Room and board $2,025. Enrollment: 2,329 full-time, 199 part-time, 12 graduate. Faculty: 96. Student-faculty ratio: 20:1. Degrees: BS, BA, BSW, MS. Library: 120,740 volumes. 45 buildings on 450 acres. The university seeks to meet the academic, cultural and vocational needs of students. MVSU is unlimited in its potential to provide avenues for students to explore their special talents and interest. MVSU has a competitive academic scholarship program, cooperative placement/assistance program, social and academic programs.

MISSOURI

Aquinas Institute of Theology
3642 Lindell Blvd., Saint Louis 63108
Charles Bouchard, OP, President

Avila College
11901 Wornall Rd., Kansas City 64145

Calvary Graduate School of Theology
15800 Calvary Rd., Kansas City 64147
J. Robert Brundage, Dir. of Admis.

Central Missouri State University
Warrensburg 64093
Kathleen Easter, Dean of Graduate Studies

CONCORDIA SEMINARY
School for Graduate Studies
801 De Mun Ave., Saint Louis 63105
Wayne Schmidt, Director
314-721-5934

Covenant Theological Seminary
12330 Conway Rd., St. Louis 63141
Dr. Paul Kooistra, President
800-264-8064

Eden Theological Seminary
475 E. Lockwood Ave., Webster Groves 63119
Clifton Kerr, Dir. of Admis.
800-969-3627, Ext. 338

Fontbonne College
6800 Wydown Blvd., St. Louis 63105
Peggy Musen, Dir. of Admis.

FOREST INSTITUTE OF PROFESSIONAL PSYCHOLOGY
1322 S. Campbell Ave., Springfield 65807-1445
417-831-7902 or 800-424-PSYD
Richard H. Cox, Ph.D., A.B.P.P., President
Degrees: Doctor of Psychology (Psy.D.) in Clinical Psychology, Master of Arts (M.A.) in Psychology. The Psy.D. program consists of 3 years of academic courses including 6 clinical practica, plus a 1-year internship. The M.A. program consists of 5 trimesters of academic coursework, including 2 clinical practica. In addition to the coursework, both programs include a contemporary issues sequence and skill training seminars in which emphasis is placed on the student as an individual.
The primary objective of Forest Institute of Professional Psychology is to educate and train through a practitioner model doctoral level applied psychologists. Forest Institute's faculty is a highly qualified and diverse group who help to provide an innovative and practical experience for a career in psychology. There are over 150 students ranging in age from 24 to 65 years with a variety of personal and professional backgrounds. They come from all areas of the United States, including a variety of foreign countries.

Maryville University of St. Louis
13550 Conway Rd., Saint Louis 63141
314-542-4644 or 800-MARYVLL

Northwest Missouri State University
800 University Dr., Maryville 64468

SOUTHEAST MISSOURI STATE UNIVERSITY
1 University Plz., Cape Girardeau 63701
Juan Crites, Director of Admissions
314-651-2590
Established 1873. Public. Coed. Tuition: $2,364. Room and board: $3,400. Fees: $50. Enrollment: 7,300 full-time, 1,000 part-time. Faculty: 400. Student-faculty ratio: 17:1. Degrees: BA, BS, MA. Library: over 600,000 volumes. 70 buildings on 200 acres. Scenic campus with a historic look. Good variety of academic programs with a nationally recognized Teacher Education program.

Southwest Missouri State University
901 S. National Ave., Springfield 65804
Dr. Frank Einhellig, Associate VP
417-836-5335

University of Missouri, Rolla
102 Parker Hall, Rolla 65401
David J. Allen, Dir. of Admis. & Financial Aid
800-522-0938

University of Missouri
8001 Natural Bridge Rd., St. Louis 63121
Mimi LaMarca, Dir. of Admis.

Washington University
1 Brookings Dr., St. Louis 63130

Webster University
470 E. Lockwood Ave., St. Louis 63119
Dr. Neil George, V.P. Academic Affairs
See listing under "Universities"

MONTANA

College of Great Falls
1301 20th St., S., Great Falls 59405
Jean Walker, Dir. of Admis.

Montana State University, Bozeman 59717

Montana State University - Billings
1500 N. 30th St., Billings 59101
Karen Everett, Dir. of Admis.
406-657-2158

Montana Tech
(formerly Montana College of Mineral Science and Technology)
1300 W. Park St., Butte 59701-8997
800-445-TECH
See listing under "Engineering"

Northern Montana College
P.O. Box 7751, Havre 59501
Ralph A. Brigham, Dir. of Admis.

University of Montana, Missoula 59812
800-462-8636

NEBRASKA

Chadron State College
1000 Main St., Chadron 69337
Dr. James Wright, Dean

CLARKSON COLLEGE
101 S. 42nd St., Omaha 68131-2739
Fay L. Bower, DN Sc, FAAN, President
800-647-5500
Established 1888. Coed. Accreditation: NCACS, NLN. Tuition: $3,900. Room and board: $2,300. Enrollment: 100 boarding, 550 day. Faculty: 55. Degrees: AS, BS in Radiologic Technology, BSN, MSN in Nursing Education and Nursing Administration, MS in Health Services Management. Library: 7,423 volumes. 1 building on 2 square blocks. Located in a large metropolitan area medical center with ample recreational and cultural opportunities. RN/LPN/ advanced placement for transfer students.

Concordia College
800 N. Columbia Ave., Seward 68434
Don Vos, Dir. of Admis.

Creighton University
2500 California St., Omaha 68178
Dr. Michael Lawler, Dean

Peru State College, Peru 68421
Pamela J. Cosgrove, Dir. of Admis.
402-872-3815

Wayne State College
200 E. Tenth St., Wayne 68787

NEVADA

University of Nevada Las Vegas
4505 S. Maryland Pky., Las Vegas 89154-1017
Graduate Admissions
702-895-3320 or 800-334-UNLV

NEW HAMPSHIRE

ANTIOCH NEW ENGLAND GRADUATE SCHOOL
40 Avon St., Keene 03431-3516
603-357-3122
James H. Craiglow, Provost
Gael R. Minton, Dir. of Admis.
Coed. Accreditation: NCACS. Degrees: Doctor of Psychology, PsyD degree in clinical psychology. Masters degrees in: education, Waldorf Teacher Training, science and environmental education, environmental studies, resource management and administration, management, human services administration, educational supervision and administration, counseling psychology, substance abuse/addictions counseling,

marriage and family therapy, and dance/movement therapy. 1300 students. Non-residential graduate school. Practitioner-oriented programs designed for adult learners. Classes generally held one day a week permit students to study while continuing to work. Integrates practica and internships with academic work.

Keene State College, Keene 03435
    Ann Waling, Dean of Graduate Studies

New Hampshire College
    Graduate School of Business
    2500 North River Rd., Manchester 03106
    Dr. Jacqueline Mara, Dean of GSB
    603-644-3102

NOTRE DAME COLLEGE
2321 Elm St., Manchester 03104
603-669-4298

Rivier College
    420 S. Main St., Nashua 03060
    Michael Quigley, Dean of Graduate Studies
    800-44-RIVIER

NEW JERSEY

Georgian Court College
    900 Lakewood Ave., Lakewood 08701
    908-367-1717

Jersey City State College
    2039 Kennedy Blvd., Jersey City 07305
    201-200-3409

New Jersey Institute of Technology
    323 Martin Luther King Jr. Blvd., Newark 07102

Princeton University, Princeton 08544

Rider University
    2083 Lawrenceville Rd., Lawrenceville 08648
    Susan Christian, Dir. of Admis.

Rowan College of New Jersey, Glassboro 08028
    Thomas Monahan, Dir. of Admis.

Seton Hall University
    400 S. Orange Ave., South Orange 07079
    Dr. Anthony Polisi, Dean

Upsala College
    345 Prospect St., East Orange 07017
    George Lynes, Dean of Admissions

WESTMINSTER CHOIR COLLEGE OF RIDER UNIVERSITY
101 Walnut Ln., Princeton 08540-3899
800-96-CHOIR or 609-921-7100, FAX: 609-921-8829
See listing under "Music"

NEW MEXICO

Eastern New Mexico University
    Portales 88130
    Dr. Renee Neely, Dean

New Mexico Highlands University, Las Vegas 87701
    Dr. Jorge P. Thomas, VP Academic Affairs

New Mexico Institute of Mining & Technology
    801 Leroy Pl., Socorro 87801

University of New Mexico, Albuquerque 87131
    Robert Weaver, Dean of Admissions

NEW YORK

Adelphi University, Garden City 11530
    Marilyn Nissensohn, Dir. of Graduate Admis.
    516-877-3020

Alfred University
    Alumni Hall, Alfred 14802
    Laurie Richer, Director of Admissions
    607-871-2141

Bank Street College of Education
    610 W. 112th St., New York 10025
    Joseph Shenker, President
    212-875-4404
    See listing under "Teacher Education"

Bexley Hall School
    1100 Goodman St. S., Rochester 14620

Brooklyn Law School
    250 Joralemon St., Brooklyn 11201
    David Trager, Dean

Canisius College
    2001 Main St., Buffalo 14208
    James M. McDonnell, Dean
    716-888-2547

Clarkson University, Potsdam 13699
    R. Mukundan, Dean

Colgate University
    13 Oak Dr., Hamilton 13346
    Dean of Admissions
    315-824-7401

College of St. Rose
    432 Western Ave., Albany 12203

Cornell University
    410 Thurston Ave., Ithaca 14853

Cornell University Medical College
    1300 York Ave., New York 10021
    Thomas H. Meikle, Jr., Dean

CUNY Graduate School & University Center
    33 W. 42nd St., New York 10036
    Dr. Norma Rees, Graduate Dean

CUNY John Jay College of Criminal Justice
    445 W. 59th St., New York 10019

Fordham University
    441 E. Fordham Rd., Bronx 10458
    718-817-1000

Fordham University
    Lincoln Center Campus
    113 W. 60th St., New York 10023
    Edward Bristow, Dean

IONA COLLEGE
715 North Ave., New Rochelle 10801
800-231-IONA or 914-633-2503
See listing under "Universities"

Ithaca College
    953 Danby Rd., Ithaca 14850

Jewish Theological Seminary of America
    3080 Broadway, New York 10027
    Dr. Ismar Schorsch, Chancellor

Lamont-Doherty Earth Observatory of Columbia University
    Palisades 10964
    Gordon Eaton, Director

Long Island University-Brooklyn Campus
    1 University Plaza, Brooklyn 11201
    Alan Chaves, Dean of Admissions

Long Island University-C. W. Post Campus
    Rt. 25A, Brookville 11548
    Christine Natali, Dir. of Admis.
    516-299-2417

Manhattan College
    4513 Manhattan College Pky., Riverdale 10471
    John Brennan, Dean of Admissions

Manhattan School of Music
    120 Claremont Ave., New York 10027
    James Gandre, Dir. of Admis.

MARIST COLLEGE
290 North Rd., Poughkeepsie 12601
Harry W. Wood, VP Admissions
914-575-3226

Mercy College
    555 Broadway, Dobbs Ferry 10522
    James Nesbitt, Dean of Admissions

Nazareth College of Rochester
    4245 East Ave., Rochester 14618
    Paul Kenyon, Dir. of Admis.

NEW YORK CHIROPRACTIC COLLEGE
P.O. Box 800, Seneca Falls 13148-0800
Dr. Kenneth Padgett, President
John Pecchia, VP for Business Affairs & Treasurer
Dr. John DeCicco, Dean of Academic Affairs
Stephen Faust, Dean of Student Affairs
Dr. Richard Kroe, Dean of Postgraduate & Continuing Education
Dr. Beth Donohue, Dean of Institutional Analysis
Glenn Fried, Registrar
800-234-6922 or 315-568-3040
    Established 1919. Private. Coed. Total enrollment: 850. Tuition: $4,170 per trimester. Five year equivalent (10 trimesters, 3-1/3 yrs.) Professional school offering Doctor of Chiropractic degree program, full-time only, and continuing education programs for chiropractors. The college prepares students to enter the chiropractic profession and qualifies them for licensure in 50 states and most foreign countries. 286 acre campus 270 miles northeast of NYC, 40 miles west of Syracuse. 24,000 volume library. Most modern anatomical dissection labs in the profession. Housing and sports facilities on campus. Single residence hall suite, $1,435 per trimester, double suite $700 per trimester, 3 different meal plans available, $850 - $1,000. Athletic center has indoor 25 meter pool, 4 basketball courts, free weight room, universal weight room, 1/8 mile running track, indoor/outdoor tennis courts, 2 racquetball courts, student lounge and deli. Three outpatient clinics.
    Admissions: Applicants must have completed 2 or more years of college (75 credits) in an accredited degree-granting institution, including 2 semesters each of English, general physics, general chemistry, organic chemistry, and general biology or zoology, and one semester each of psychology and social sciences/humanities BA/BS preferred. Recommendations, interview also required. Selection by Admissions Committee.
    Accreditation: Council on Chiropractic Education, Middle States Association of Colleges & Schools, Chartered by the Board of Regents of the University of the State of New York.
    Scholarships, grants available on a limited basis; Stafford Student Loans and Supplemental Loans to students available; college work study available.
    Summer semester not optional; part of regular trimester academic year.

New York Institute of Technology
    Central Islip Campus
    Central Islip 11722

New York Institute of Technology
    Metropolitan Center
    1855 Broadway, New York 10023

New York Institute of Technology
    Old Westbury Campus, Old Westbury 11568

New York State College of Ceramics at Alfred University
    Alfred 14802
    800-541-9229

Niagara University, Niagara University 14109
    Dr. Gary Praetzel, Dir. of MBA Program
    Rev. Daniel O'Leary, OMI, Dir. Grad. Ed.
    Dr. Jay Albanese, Dir. Criminal Justice
    716-285-1212
    See listing under "Universities"

Pace University, New York Campus
    1 Pace Plaza, New York 10038

Pace University, Pleasantville/Briarcliff Campus
    Bedford Rd., Pleasantville 10570

Pace University, White Plains Campus
    78 N. Broadway, White Plains 10603

Polytechnic University
    36 Saw Mill River Rd., Hawthorne 10532

Rensselaer Polytechnic Institute, Troy 12180
    Conrad Sharrow, Dean of Admissions

Roberts Wesleyan College
    2301 Westside Dr., Rochester 14624
    Burton Jones, Dean Adult & Graduate Ed.
    See listing under "Universities"

Rochester Institute of Technology
    1 Lomb Memorial Dr., Rochester 14623
    716-475-6631
    See listing under "Universities"

Russell Sage College
    51 1st St., Troy 12180

ST. BERNARD'S INSTITUTE
1100 S. Goodman St., Rochester 14620
Georgia Crissy, Dir. of Admissions
716-271-1320

ST. THOMAS AQUINAS COLLEGE
Rt. 340, Sparkill 10976
Andrea Kraeft, Dir. of Admis.
800-999-STAC
See listing under "Liberal Arts"

SUNY at Buffalo
    Capen Hall, Amherst 14260

SUNY Health Science Center at Brooklyn
    450 Clarkson Ave., Brooklyn 11203

SUNY College at Brockport
    Brockport 14420

SUNY at Oswego, Oswego 13126
    Dr. C. Thomas Gooding, Dean
    315-341-3152

SUNY College at Plattsburgh, Plattsburgh 12901
    Richard Higgins, Dir. of Admis.
    518-564-2040

SUNY INSTITUTE OF TECHNOLOGY AT UTICA/ROME
P.O. Box 3050, Utica 13504
Roger Sullivan, Dir. of Admis.
See listing under "Universities"

Teachers College of Columbia University
    525 W. 120th St., New York 10027

Union College Poughkeepsie Center
    249 Hooker Ave., Poughkeepsie 12603

University of Rochester
    500 Joseph C. Wilson Blvd., Rochester 14627
    David W. Beach, Dean
    See listing under "Universities"

NORTH CAROLINA

East Carolina University
    1000 E. 5th St., Greenville 27858
    Dr. Diane Jacobs, Dean

North Carolina A&T State University
    1601 E. Market St., Greensboro 27411

North Carolina State University
    P.O. Box 7001, Raleigh 27695
    George Dixon, Dir. of Admis.

Pembroke State University
    P.O. Box 1510, Pembroke 28372
    Anthony Locklear, Dir. of Admissions
    919-521-6262

QUEENS COLLEGE
1900 Selwyn Ave., Charlotte 28274
Katie Wireman, Dir. of Admis.
See listing under "Liberal Arts"

Wake Forest University
    P.O. Box 7487, Winston-Salem 27109

NORTH DAKOTA

Tri-College University, Fargo 58105

OHIO

Cleveland State University
    Euclid Ave. at 24th St., Cleveland 44115

COLLEGE OF MOUNT SAINT JOSEPH
5701 Delhi Rd., Cincinnati 45233-1670
513-244-4200 or 800-654-9314
    Established 1920. Private. Coed. Accreditation: NCACS, Ohio Board of Regents, Ohio Department of Education. Tuition: $9,180 ($239/per credit hour 1-11 or over 18). Room and board: $4,242. Enrollment: 1,113 full-time under graduate, 33 full-time graduate. 1,307 part-time under graduate, 141 part-time graduate. Faculty: 98 full-time, 120 part-time. Student-faculty ratio: 15:1. Degrees: AA, AS, BA, BFA, BS, BSN, MA available in education and pastoral family studies. Library: 90,000 volumes. 6 buildings on 75 acres. The Mount's liberal arts core curriculum insures a

broad range of knowledge and competence for students in all majors. Classes foster skills in critical thinking, problem-solving, decision-making and communication — skills that are highly sought by employers in today's business and professional world.

Students choose from over 35 majors ranging from social sciences to business administration to nursing to fine arts. Cooperative education, internship or research opportunities are available to students in all majors, providing valuable career experience before graduation. Some majors even have the option for study or co-op experience abroad.

Hebrew Union College
Jewish Institute of Religion
3101 Clifton Ave., Cincinnati 45220
Rabbi Gary Zola, National Dean of Admissions

John Carroll University
20700 N. Park Blvd., Cleveland 44118

Kent State University
P.O. Box 5190, Kent 44242
216-672-3000

Medical College of Ohio
P.O. Box 10008, Toledo 43699
Barry L. Richardson, PhD, Dean for Admissions

Miami University
E. High St., Oxford 45056

Ohio College of Podiatric Medicine
10515 Carnegie Ave., Cleveland 44106
John E. Andrews, Dean/Student Affairs & Admission
In OH 800-821-6562 others 800-238-7903

United Theological Seminary
1810 Harvard Blvd., Dayton 45406
The Rev. Duane Anders, Dir. of Admis.

University of Akron
381 Buchtel Common, Akron 44325
Kris MacDermott, Asst. Provost Enrollment

University of Cincinnati
2700 Clifton Ave., Cincinnati 45221

WINEBRENNER THEOLOGICAL SEMINARY
P.O. Box 478, Findlay 45839
Dr. David Draper, President
419-422-4824

OKLAHOMA

Cameron University
2800 W. Gore Blvd., Lawton 73505
Louise Brown, Dir. of Admis.

Oklahoma City University
2501 N. Blackwelder Ave., Oklahoma City 73106
Laura Mitchell, Director
See listing under "Universities"

Oklahoma State University, Stillwater 74078
Thomas C. Collins, Dean

Oral Roberts University
7777 S. Lewis Ave., Tulsa 74171
Arthur E. Matzkvech, Dir. of Admis.

Southern Nazarene University
6729 N.W. 39th Expy., Bethany 73008

University of Central Oklahoma
100 N. University Dr., Edmond 73034

University of Tulsa
600 S. College Ave., Tulsa 74104
Dr. Dale Johnson, Acting Dean

OREGON

Marylhurst College for Lifelong Learning
P.O. Box 261, Marylhurst 97036
Keith Protonentis, Registrar
800-634-9982

Mt. Angel Seminary
General Delivery, St. Benedict 97373
Very Rev. J. Terrence Fitzgerald, Pres.-Rector

MULTNOMAH BIBLICAL SEMINARY
8435 N.E. Glisan St., Portland 97220
Joseph Aldrich, President

Oregon Graduate Institute of Science & Technology
19600 N.W. Von Neumann Dr., Beaverton 97006

University of Portland
5000 N. Willamette Blvd., Portland 97203

Western Conservative Baptist Seminary
5511 S.E. Hawthorne Blvd., Portland 97215
Dr. Russell Shive, Interim President

Western Evangelical Seminary
12753 S.W. 68th Ave., Portland 97223
David C. Le Shana, President
Todd M. McCollum, Dir. of Enrollment
503-639-0559

Western Oregon State College
345 Monmouth Ave., N., Monmouth 97361
Craig A. Kolins, Dir. of Admis.
503-838-8211

PENNSYLVANIA

American College
270 S. Bryn Mawr Ave., Bryn Mawr 19010

Beaver College
450 S. Easton Rd., Glenside 19038-3295
A. Richard Polis, Dean of Graduate Studies
Phone: 215-572-2925, Fax: 215-572-2126
See listing under "Universities"

Biblical Theological Seminary
200 N. Main St., Hatfield 19440
Wayne Arndt, Dean Student Services

Bloomsburg University, Bloomsburg 17815
Bernard Vinovrski, Dir. of Admis.

Bryn Mawr College
101 N. Merion Ave., Bryn Mawr 19010
Elizabeth Vermey, Dir. of Admis.

California University of Pennsylvania
3rd St., California 15419
Norman Hasbrouck, Dean for Enrollment

Carnegie Mellon University
5000 Forbes Ave., Pittsburgh 15213

Clarion University of Pennsylvania
840 Wood St., Clarion 16214

College Misericordia
301 Lake St., Dallas 18612
Michael Joseph, Dir. of Enrollment Mgmt.

Drexel University
3141 Chestnut St., Philadelphia 19104
Dean of Enrollment Management

Duquesne University
600 Forbes Ave., Pittsburgh 15282
Thomas Schaefer, C.S.Sp., Dir. of Admis.

Eastern College
10 Fairview Dr., Saint Davids 19087
Ronald Keller, VP for Enrollment Management

Edinboro University of Pennsylvania
Edinboro 16444
Admissions Office: 800-626-2203

Evangelical School of Theology
121 S. College St., Myerstown 17067
Dr. Kirby Keller, VP Academic Affairs

Gannon University
109 University Sq., Erie 16541

Gratz College
Old York Rd. and Melrose Ave.
Melrose Park 19126
Evelyn Klein, Dir. of Admissions
215-635-7300

GWYNEDD-MERCY COLLEGE
Sumneytown Pike, Gwynedd Valley 19437
Marjorie DeSimone, Dean of Admissions
800-DIAL-GMC
See listing under "Universities"

Immaculata College
Immaculata 19345
James P. Sullivan, Dir. of Admis.

Lancaster Theological Seminary of the United Church of Christ
555 W. James St., Lancaster 17603
Rev. Dr. Ann Schoup, Dir. of Admis.

La Roche College
9000 Babcock Blvd., Pittsburgh 15237
Marianne Leister, Dir. of Admis.

La Salle University
1900 W. Olney Ave., Philadelphia 19141
Br. Gerald Fitzgerald, Dir. of Admis.
See listing under "Universities"

Millersville University of Pennsylvania
Millersville 17551
Blair Treasure, Dean of Admissions

Pennsylvania State University
201 Shields Bldg., University Park 16802

Philadelphia College of Osteopathic Medicine
4170 City Ave., Philadelphia 19131
Carol Fox, Assistant Dean of Admissions
215-871-2700 or 800-999-6998

Philadelphia Theological Seminary
7372 Henry Ave., Philadelphia 19128
Danae L. Smith, Registrar
215-483-2480

ROBERT MORRIS COLLEGE
Narrows Run Rd., Coraopolis 15108
James R. Welsh, Dean of Admissions
800-762-0097 or 412-262-8200
   Established 1921. Private. Coed. Accreditation: MSACS. Tuition: $244 per credit. Enrollment: 918. Faculty: 348. Student-faculty ratio: 21:1. Degrees: MBA, MS Business Administration 4 majors, MS Business Education, MS Taxation. Library: 120,832 volumes. 26 buildings on 230 acres. Fully equipped television studio, print and graphics media, over 350 computer terminals.

Robert Morris College
600 5th Ave., Pittsburgh 15219
James R. Welsh, Dean of Admissions
See listing under "Universities"

St. Francis College
P.O. Box 600, Loretto 15940

Slippery Rock University, Slippery Rock 16057
Director of Admissions

Trinity Episcopal School for Ministry
311 11th St., Ambridge 15003
Sandra Griffin, Dir. of Admis.

Villanova University
845 E. Lancaster Ave., Villanova 19085
Stephen R. Merritt, Dir. of Admis.

West Chester University of Pennsylvania
S. High St., West Chester 19380

WESTMINSTER COLLEGE
New Wilmington 16172
Richard Dana Paul, Dir. of Admis.
412-946-7100

Wilkes University
184 S. River St., Wilkes-Barre 18766
Emory P. Guffrovich Jr., Dean of Admissions

RHODE ISLAND

Brown University, Providence 02906

Providence College
River Ave., Providence 02918

Rhode Island College
600 Mt. Pleasant Ave., Providence 02908

Salve Regina University
1 Ochre Point Ave., Newport 02840
Roselina McKillop, Dean of Admissions

University of Rhode Island, Kingston 02881
Kent Morrison, Dean

SOUTH CAROLINA

Bob Jones University, Greenville 29614
David Christ, Dir. of Admis.
See listing under "Universities"

Columbia Biblical Seminary
P.O. Box 3122, Columbia 29230
Lawrence Dabeck, Dir. of Admis.
See listing under "Biblical Studies"

Columbia International University
P.O. Box 3122, Columbia 29230
Frank Bedell, Dir. of Admis.
See listing under "Biblical Studies"

Lander College
320 Stanley Ave., Greenwood 29649

SOUTH CAROLINA STATE UNIVERSITY
P.O. Box 7127, Orangeburg 29117-0001
803-536-7064

University of South Carolina, Columbia 29208
Ose Henderson, Acting Dean-Graduate School
803-777-2443

Winthrop University
701 W. Oakland Ave., Rock Hill 29733
James McCammon, Jr., Dir. of Admis.

SOUTH DAKOTA

NORTH AMERICAN BAPTIST SEMINARY
1525 S. Grange Ave., Sioux Falls 57105
Randy Reese, Dir. of Admis.
800-440-NABS (6227)

SIOUX FALLS COLLEGE
1501 S. Prairie Ave., Sioux Falls 57105
Susan Reese, Dir. of Admis.
800-888-1047
See listing under "Universities"

South Dakota School of Mines and Technology
501 E. St. Joseph St., Rapid City 57701
Gary Bjordal, Dir. of Admis.

South Dakota State University
P.O. Box 2201, Brookings 57007
Dr. Christopher Sword, Dean
605-688-4181
See listing under "Universities"

University of South Dakota
414 E. Clark St., Vermillion 57069
Charles Kaufman, Dean

TENNESSEE

Austin Peay State University
601 College St., Clarksville 37044

Bristol University
P.O. Box 4366, Bristol 37625
Dr. W. David Willis, Academic Dean
See listing under "Universities"

David Lipscomb University
3901 Granny White Pike, Nashville 37204-3951
Wade Sandrell, Dir. of Admis.
800-333-4358

Harding University Graduate School of Religion
1000 Cherry Rd., Memphis 38117
Robert Brady, Dir. of Admis.
800-680-0809

Johnson Bible College
7900 Johnson Dr., Knoxville 37998
Richard Beam, Dir. of Graduate Studies
615-573-4517

PEABODY COLLEGE OF VANDERBILT UNIVERSITY
P.O. Box 327, Nashville 37202
Barbara Johnston, Dir. of Admis.
615-322-8410

University of Memphis, Memphis 38152
Dr. John Eubank, Dean of Admissions

University of Tennessee at Martin
Martin 38238
Paul Kelley, Director of Admissions
See listing under "Universities"

University of Tennessee, Memphis
Graduate Health Sciences
800 Madison Ave., Memphis 38163
Office of Enrollment Management

Vanderbilt University
West End Ave., Nashville 37240

TEXAS

Austin Presbyterian Theological Seminary
100 E. 27th St., Austin 78705
The Rev. Eleanor Cherryholmes, Dir. Vocations &
Admis.
512-472-6736

Baylor University
P.O. Box 97008, Waco 76798-7008
Diana Ramey, Director of Admissions

Episcopal Theological Seminary of the Southwest
P.O. Box 2247, Austin 78768
Durstan McDonald, Dean

Incarnate Word College
4301 Broadway St., San Antonio 78209
Ms. Wynette Hadnott, Director

Lamar University
P.O. Box 10009, Beaumont 77710
800-458-7558

Midwestern State University
3400 Taft Blvd., Wichita Falls 76308

Prairie View A & M University
P.O. Box 3089, Prairie View 77446-3089
Linda S. Berry, Dir. of Admis.

Rice University
P.O. Box 1892, Houston 77251

St. Mary's University of San Antonio
1 Camino Santa Maria, San Antonio 78228
Rick Castillo, Dir. of Admis.

Texas A & I University
Campus Box 101, Kingsville 78363

Texas A & M University
College Station 77843

Texas Christian University
2800 S. University Dr., Ft. Worth 76129
Dr. Edward Boehm, Jr., Dean of Admissions

University of Central Texas
P.O. Box 1416, Killeen 76540
Dr. Pauline Moseley, Dean of the Faculty

University of Dallas
1845 E. Northgate Dr., Irving 75062
Jim Whitaker, Dir. of Admis.

University of Houston-Clear Lake
2700 Bay Area Blvd., Houston 77058
Darella Banks, Exec. Dir. Enrollment Services

University of St. Thomas
3812 Montrose Blvd., Houston 77006
Elsie Biron, Dir. of Admis.

University of Texas at Arlington
UTA Box 19125, Arlington 76019
R. Zack Prince, Dir. of Admis.

University of Texas at Austin
0 the University of Texas, Austin 78712

The University of Texas Medical Branch at Galveston
Galveston 77555-1305

University of Texas Southwestern Medical Center
5323 Harry Hines Blvd., Dallas 75235
John Perkins, Dean

West Texas State University
2501 4th Ave., Canyon 79016
Lila Vars, Dir. of Admis.

UTAH

Southern Utah University
351 W. Center St., Cedar City 84720
D. Mark Barton, Asst. VP Student Services
Education and Accounting
801-586-7740

University of Utah
1400 E. 200 S., Salt Lake City 84112
Dr. J. Stayner Landward, Dir. of Admis.

Utah State University, Logan 84322-1600
Rod Clark, Director of Admissions
801-750-1107

Westminster College of Salt Lake City
1840 S. 1300 E., Salt Lake City 84105
800-748-4753

VERMONT

Bennington College, Bennington 05201
Karen Kristof, Dir. of Admis.
800-833-6845

**NORWICH UNIVERSITY VERMONT COLLEGE
CAMPUS**
Montpelier 05602
Dr. Richard Hansen, Head
See listing under "Universities"

School for International Training
World Learning Inc.
Kipling Rd., P.O. Box 676
Brattleboro 05302-0676
Marshall Brewer, Dir of Enrollment Management
800-451-4465 or 802-257-7751

University of Vermont
194 S. Prospect St., Burlington 05401
802-656-3370

VIRGINIA

George Mason University
4400 University Dr., Fairfax 22030-4444
Patricia Riordan, Dean of Admissions

Hollins College
P.O. Box 9707, Hollins College 24020
800-456-9595

Institute of Textile Technology
2551 Ivy Rd., Charlottesville 22903-4614
William M. Fornadel, Dean
804-296-5511

LIBERTY UNIVERSITY
P.O. Box 20000, Lynchburg 24506
Jay Spencer, VP Recruitment
800-376-2800
See listing under "Universities"

Lynchburg College
1501 Lakeside Dr., Lynchburg 24501
Ernest Chadderton, Dean of Enrollment

Marymount University
2807 N. Glebe Rd., Arlington 22207
Charles Coe, Director of Admissions
800-548-7638 or 703-284-1500
See listing under "Universities"

Medical College of Hampton Roads
825 Fairfax Ave., Norfolk 23507

Radford University
P.O. Box 5430, Radford 24142

Regent University
1000 Centerville Trpk., Virginia Beach 23464
804-523-7444

SHENANDOAH UNIVERSITY
1460 University Dr., Winchester 22601
Dr. Sandra Lemoine, Coordinator
See listing under "Universities"

University of Virginia
Graduate School of Arts and Sciences
437 Cabell Hall, Charlottesville 22903

Virginia Polytechnic Institute & State University
Blacksburg 24061
Gary Hooper, Dean

WASHINGTON

Bastyr College
144 N.E. 54th St., Seattle 98105
Dr. Ron Hobbs, Dir. of Admis.

Central Washington University, Ellensburg 98926
William Swain, Director of Admissions

City University
16661 Northup Way, Bellevue 98008
800-422-4898

Heritage College
3240 Fort Rd., Toppenish 98948
Dr. Robert Plumb, Dir. of Graduate Program
509-865-2244

Pacific Lutheran University
12180 Park Ave. S., Tacoma 98447
J. Robert Wills, Dean

St. Martin's College
700 College St. N.E., Lacey 98516

Washington State University, Pullman 99164
Stan Berry, Dir. of Admis.

Western Washington University
516 High St., Bellingham 98225
Karen G. Copetas, Dir. of Admis.

WEST VIRGINIA

Marshall University
400 Hal Greer Blvd., Huntington 25755
See listing under "Universities"

The University of Charleston
2300 MacCorkle Ave., S.E., Charleston 25304
800-995-GO UC

West Virginia Graduate College
P.O. Box 1003, Institute 25112

West Virginia University
P.O. Box 6001, Morgantown 26506

WEST VIRGINIA WESLEYAN COLLEGE
59 College Ave., Buckhannon 26201
Robert Skinner, Director of Admission
See listing under "Universities"

WISCONSIN

Cardinal Stritch College
6801 N. Yates Rd., Milwaukee 53217
David Wegener, Dir. of Admis.

Carthage College
2001 Alford Dr., Kenosha 53140
Brenda A. Porter, VP Enrollment

Marian College of Fond du Lac
45 S. National Ave., Fond du Lac 54935
Carol Reichenberger, Dean of Admissions

Marquette University
1217 W. Wisconsin Ave., Milwaukee 53233
Rev. Thaddeus J. Burch, S.J., Dean

Milwaukee School of Engineering
1025 N. Broadway, Milwaukee 53202
Steve Bialek, Director

St. Francis Seminary
3257 S. Lake Dr., Milwaukee 53235
Rev. Andrew Nelson, Dean

University of Wisconsin, Eau Claire
Eau Claire 54701

University of Wisconsin, Oshkosh
800 Algoma Blvd., Oshkosh 54901-8602
August Helgerson, Dir. of Admis.

University of Wisconsin
1 University Plaza, Platteville 53818
Richard Schumacher, Dean of Admissions

University of Wisconsin, River Falls
River Falls 54022
Alan Tuchtenhagen, Dir. of Admis.

GUAM

University of Guam
UOG Station, Mangilao 96923
Kathleen Owings, Dir. of Admis.

PUERTO RICO

Caribbean Center for Advanced Studies
San Juan Campus
Apartado 3711, San Juan 00904

Centro De Estudios Avanzados
Del Cristo St. #52 Box S4467, San Juan 00904

**UNIVERSITY OF PUERTO RICO, MAYAGUEZ
CAMPUS**
P.O. Box 5000, Mayaguez 00681
Neysa Lopez, Dir. of Admis.

University of Puerto Rico, Medical Sciences Campus
P.O. Box 5067, San Juan 00906

University of Puerto Rico, Rio Piedras Campus
P.O. Box 23300, San Juan 00931
Victor Lopez, Dir. of Admis.

VIRGIN ISLANDS

University of the Virgin Islands
Charlotte Amalie, St. Thomas 00802
Judith Edwin, Dir. of Admis.

∴HANDICAPPED, SCHOOLS FOR THE

ALABAMA

Alabama Institute for the Deaf and Blind
P.O. Box 698, Talladega 35160
Dr. Jack Hawkins, Jr., President

Samford University
800 Lakeshore Dr., Birmingham 35229
Richard Franklin, Dean of Students

ARIZONA

Arizona State Schools for the Deaf and the Blind
P.O. Box 5545, Tucson 85703
Ralph E. Bartley, Superintendent

DEVEREUX CENTER IN ARIZONA
6436 E. Sweetwater Ave., Scottsdale 85254
Judy Sindlinger, Admissions Director
602-998-2920

ARKANSAS

Arkansas School for the Blind
P.O. Box 668, Little Rock 72203
Hugh Pace, Supt.

Arkansas School for the Deaf
P.O. Box 3811, Little Rock 72203
Travis Higginbotham, Supt.

CALIFORNIA

Brea School of Exceptional Children
875 N. Brea Blvd., Brea 92621
Jim Powell, Director

California School for the Blind
500 Walnut Ave., Fremont 94536
Jeanne M. Vlachos, Supt.

California School for the Deaf, Northern California
39350 Gallaudet Dr., Fremont 94538
Henry Klopping, Supt.

DEVEREUX CENTER IN CALIFORNIA

P.O. Box 1079, Santa Barbara 93102
Ann McNiff & Craig Olson, Admissions Directors
800-359-7979 or 805-968-2525

Morning Sky Residential School (4-12)
Bdg; PA, PAph, PM, ED, LD,
P.O. Box 408, Mountain Center 92561

Navajo Aviation
145 John Glenn Dr., Concord 94520
Flight Training Center
510-685-1150

COLORADO

Colorado School for the Deaf and Blind
Kiowa and Institute Sts., Colorado Springs 80903
Dr. Marilyn Jaitly, Supt.

Denver Academy
1125 S. Race St., Denver 80210
Paul Knott, Director

CONNECTICUT

American School for the Deaf
139 N. Main St., West Hartford 06107

Connecticut Institute for the Blind
120 Holcomb St., Hartford 06112
Lars Guldager, Ph.D., Supt.

Connecticut Junior Republic
P.O. Box 161, Litchfield 06759

DEVEREUX CENTER IN CONNECTICUT

81 Sabbaday Ln., Washington 06793
Kathi Fitzherbert, Admissions Director
203-868-7377

Institute of Living Schools
400 Washington St., Hartford 06106
Rosemary Baggish, Director

Lake Grove School, Durham, CT
459R Wallingford Rd., Durham 06422-1116
Admissions Coordinator
203-349-3467

DISTRICT OF COLUMBIA

DEVEREUX CHILDRENS CENTER OF WASHINGTON D.C.

3050 R St. N.W., Washington 20007
Marilyn Benoit, M.D., Executive/Medical Director
202-282-1200

Model Secondary School for the Deaf
Gallaudet College, Kendall Green
Washington 20002

FLORIDA

DEVEREUX HOSPITAL & CHILDRENS CENTER IN FLORIDA

8000 Devereux Dr., Melbourne 32940
Linda Brooks, Admissions Director
407-242-9100

DEVEREUX ORLANDO CENTER

6131 Christian Way, Orlando 32808
Nancy Gallello, Admissions Director
407-296-5300

Florida School for the Deaf and Blind
207 San Marco Ave., St. Augustine 32084
William J. McClure, President

HOPE CENTER

P.O. Box 10789, Miami 33101
Dr. Judy Holland, Chief Executive Officer
Established 1955. Private. Coed. Enrollment: 120.
Private, non-profit residential and day training program for all levels of developmentally disabled individuals. No upper age limit. Training includes survival and vocational education and supported employment. A full range of residential programs are available including dormitories and apartment living emphasizing independence. Tuition based on a sliding scale. Licensed by the State of Florida.

GEORGIA

Atlanta Area School for the Deaf
890 Indian Creek Drive, Clarkston 30021
Mona McCubbin, Supt.

DEVEREUX CENTER IN GEORGIA

1291 Stanley Rd., Kennesaw 30144
Carolyn Moffitt, Admissions Officer
800-342-3357 or 404-427-0147

Georgia Academy for the Blind
2895 Vineville Ave. Macon 31204
Dr. Richard Hyer, Jr. Supt.

Georgia School for the Deaf
P.O. Box 99, Cave Spring 30124
Michael Elliott

HAWAII

Hawaii School for the Deaf and the Blind
3440 Leahi Ave., Honolulu 96815

IDAHO

Idaho State School for the Deaf and Blind
202 14th Avenue E, Gooding 83330
Keith W. Tolzin, Supt.

ILLINOIS

Grove School
40 E. Old Mill Rd., Lake Forest 60045

Hadley School for the Blind
700 Elm St., Winnetka 60093

Illinois School for the Deaf
125 S. Webster St., Jacksonville 62650

Illinois School for the Visually Impaired
658 E. State St., Jacksonville 62650
Richard Umsted, Superintendent

Jack Mabley Development Center
1120 Washington, Dixon 61021
Christian Simonson, Director

St. Mary of Providence School
4200 N. Austin Ave., Chicago 60634
Sr. Patricia McCafferty, Principal

INDIANA

Indiana School for the Deaf
1200 East 42nd St., Indianapolis 46205
Rachel Stone, Asst. Supt. of Education

Indiana State School for the Blind
7725 N. College Ave., Indianapolis 46240
Moe Harrison, Principal

IOWA

Iowa Braille and Sight Saving School
Vinton 52349
Richard M. DeMott, Supt.

Iowa School for the Deaf
Council Bluffs 51501
C. Joseph Giangreco, Supt.

Powell School and Home for the Mentally Handicapped
1005 N. 7th St., Red Oak 51566
Riley C. Nelson, F.A.A.M.D., Director

KANSAS

Kansas School for the Deaf
450 E. Park St., Olathe 66061
Gerald Johnson, Supt.

Kansas State School for the Visually Hdcpd.
1100 State Ave., Kansas City 66102
Ralph E. Bartley, Supt.

KENTUCKY

Kentucky School for the Blind
1867 Frankford Ave., Louisville 40206
Will D. Evans, Supt.

Kentucky School for the Deaf
S. 2nd St., Danville 40422
John Hudson, Supt.

LOUISIANA

Louisiana School for the Visually Impaired
P.O. Box 4328, Baton Rouge 70821
Dr. Richard Day, Supt.

Louisiana State School for the Deaf
P.O. Box 3074, Baton Rouge 70821
Dr. John E. Radvany, Supt.

MAINE

Baxter State School for the Deaf
P.O. Box 799, Portland 04104
Pamela Tetley, Act'g. Supt.

MARYLAND

Maryland School for the Blind
3501 Taylor Ave., Baltimore 21236
Louis M. Tutt, Supt.

Maryland School for the Deaf
P.O. Box 250, Frederick 21705
Frederick Ignatius Bjorlee, Head

MASSACHUSETTS

Desisto School
General Delivery, Stockbridge 01262

DEVEREUX CENTER IN MASSACHUSETTS

60 Miles Rd., Rutland 01543-0197
Kenneth Ayers, Admissions Director
508-886-4746

Lake Grove School, Wendell, MA
P.O. Box 767, Wendell 01379-9998
Admissions Coordinator
508-544-6913

PERKINS SCHOOL FOR THE BLIND

175 N. Beacon St., Watertown 02172
Christopher Underwood, Admissions
617-924-3434

Western New England College
1215 Wilbraham Rd., Springfield 01119
800-325-1122

MICHIGAN

Kambly School for Developmentally Impaired
1003 North Ave., Battle Creek 49017
Jeanne McDaniel, Dir. of Admissions

Lutheran School for the Deaf
6661 Nevada St., E., Detroit 48234
Rev. Rodney R. Rynearson, Ed.M., Exec. Dir.

Michigan School for the Blind
715 W. Willow St., Lansing 48913
Nancy J. Bryant, Supt.

MINNESOTA

Laura Baker School
Mentally Handicapped, ages 4 and up
P.O. Box 611, Northfield 55057
Gary Gleason, Administrator

Minnesota School for the Deaf
P.O. Box 308, Faribault 55021
Howard M. Quigley, Superintendent

The Wilson Center
Emotionally ill, ages 12-22
P.O. Box 917, Faribault 55021
William Kirk, Chief, Medical Staff

MISSISSIPPI

Mississippi School for the Blind
1252 Eastover Drive, Jackson 39211
R. C. Benton, Supt.

Mississippi School for the Deaf
1252 Eastover Drive, Jackson 39211
Dr. Alma Alexander, Supt.

MISSOURI

Missouri School for the Blind
3815 Magnolia Ave., St. Louis 63110
Louis Tutt, Supt.

Missouri School for the Deaf, Fulton 65251
Peter H. Ripley, Supt.

St. Josephs Institute for the Deaf
1483 82nd Blvd., St. Louis 63132
Sister Julie Guillot, Director

MONTANA

Montana School for the Deaf and the Blind
3800 Second Ave., N., Great Falls 59405
Floyd J. McDowell, Supt.

NEBRASKA

Nebraska School for the Deaf
3223 N. 45th St., Omaha 68104
Michael Burke, Principal

Nebraska School for the Visually Handicapped
10th St. & 10th Ave., Nebraska City 68410
Jerry Regler, Superintendent

NEW JERSEY

DEVEREUX CENTER IN NEW JERSEY

230 Pottersville Rd., P.O. Box 520, Chester 07930
Kristy Hartman, Admissions Director
908-879-4500

Marie Katzenbach School for the Deaf
320 Sullivan Way CN535
West Trenton 08628-0535

Milburn School for the Hearing Handicapped
Spring & Willow Sts., Millburn 07041

St. John of God Community Services
532 Delsea Dr., Westville 08093
Brother Edward McDonald, Director
609-848-4700

NEW MEXICO

Brush Ranch School
P.O. Box 2450, Santa Fe 87504
Jo Marie Williams, Director
Ages 10-18
505-757-6114, Fax: 505-757-6118

New Mexico School for the Deaf
1060 Cerrillos Rd., Santa Fe 87501
James Little, Supt.

New Mexico School for the Visually Handicapped
1900 N. White Sands Ave., Alamogordo 88310
Jerry Watkins, Superintendent

NEW YORK

DEVEREUX CENTER IN NEW YORK

Rt. 9 N., P.O. Box 40, Red Hook 12571
Mary Carey, Admissions Director
914-758-1899

Joseph Bulova School
4024 62nd St., Woodside 11377

Lake Grove School, Lake Grove, NY
P.O. Box 712, Lake Grove 11755-0712
Director of Admissions
516-585-8776

Lavelle School for the Blind and Visually Impaired
E. 221st St. & Paulding Ave., Bronx 10469
Sister M. Floretta, OP, Superintendent

Mercy College
555 Broadway, Dobbs Ferry 10522
James Nesbitt, Dean of Admissions

Mill Neck Lutheran School
Frost Mill Rd. B12, Mill Neck 11765
Eunice Weidner, Dir.

New York Institute for Special Education
999 Pelham Parkway, Bronx 10469
Robert Guarino, PhD, Executive Director

New York School for the Deaf
555 Knollwood Rd., White Plains 10603
David A. Spidal, Supt.

New York State School for the Blind
Richmond Ave., Batavia 14020
Glenn E. Thompson, Supt.

New York State School for the Deaf
401 Turin St., Rome 13440
Philip E. Cronlund, Supt.

· Rochester Institute of Technology (NTID)
National Technical Institute for the Deaf
1 Lomb Memorial Dr., Rochester 14623

Rochester School for the Deaf
1545 St. Paul St., Rochester 14621
Harold Mowl, Jr., PhD, Superintendent

St. Mary's School for the Deaf
2253 Main St., Buffalo 14214
Sr. Nora LeTourneau, Supt.

School for the Deaf
225 E. 23rd St., New York 10010
Joan O'Shea, Prin.

NORTH CAROLINA

Central North Carolina School for the Deaf
P.O. Box 14670, Greensboro 27415
Ronald Wilson, Superintendent

Eastern North Carolina Sch. for the Deaf
P.O. Box 2768, Wilson 27894
Frank Bryan, Supt.

North Carolina School for the Deaf
517 W. Fleming Dr. Morganton 28655
William M. Simpson, Superintendent

NORTH DAKOTA

North Dakota School for the Blind
500 Stanford Rd., Grand Forks 58203
Charles R. Borchert, Supt.

North Dakota School for the Deaf
Devils Lake 58301
Allen J. Hayek, Supt.

OHIO

Gallipolis State Institute, Gallipolis 45631
Robert Zimmerman, Program Dir.

Ohio School for the Deaf
500 Morse Rd., Columbus 43214
Edward R. Abernathy, Supt.

Ohio State School for the Blind
5220 N. High St., Columbus 43214
D. W. Overbeay, Supt.

St. Rita School for the Deaf
1720 Glendale-Milford Rd.
Cincinnati 45215-1258
Mary Ann Stansfield, Principal
513-771-7600

Woodrow Wilson School
Ohio Veterans' Children's Home
690 Home Ave., Xenia 45385
E. M. Freakley, Supt.

OKLAHOMA

Oklahoma School for the Deaf, Sulphur 73086
David F. Kamphaus, Supt.

Oral Roberts University
7777 S. Lewis Ave., Tulsa 74171
Arthur E. Matzkvech, Dir. of Admis.

Parkview School
Oklahoma School for the Blind
Muskogee 74401
R. M. Casey, Supt.

OREGON

Oregon State School for the Blind
700 Church St., S.E., Salem 97301

Oregon State School for the Deaf
999 Locust St., N.E., Salem 97303
B. J. Peck, Director

PENNSYLVANIA

College Misericordia
301 Lake St., Dallas 18612
Michael Joseph, Dir. of Enrollment Mgmt.

DEVEREUX-BRANDYWINE CENTER IN PENNSYLVANIA
Devereux Rd., Glenmoore 19343
Kathleen Deeming, Admissions Director
215-942-5968

DEVEREUX-EDWARD L. FRENCH CENTER IN PENNSYLVANIA
119 Old Lancaster Ave., Devon 19333
Bonnie Elliott, Admissions Director
610-964-3269

THE DEVEREUX FOUNDATION
P.O. Box 400, Devon 19333
National Referral Assistance
Michele Petti
800-345-1292 x 3045 or 610-964-3045

DEVEREUX-LEO KANNER CENTER IN PENNSYLVANIA
390 Boot Rd., West Chester 19380
Carl Villarini, Admissions Director
610-431-8174

DEVEREUX-MAPLETON CENTER IN PENNSYLVANIA
655 Sugartown Rd., Malvern 19355
Chris Barrett, Admissions Officer
610-296-6975

D. T. Watson Home for Crippled Children
95 Campmeeting Rd., Sewickley 15143
Steven Mozolak, Administrator

Edinboro University of Pennsylvania
Edinboro 16444
Admissions Office: 800-626-2203

Home for Crippled Children
1426 Denniston Ave., Pittsburgh 15217
Charles H. Bisdee, Admin.

Martha Lloyd School, Inc.
W. Main St., Troy 16947
717-297-2185

Overbrook School for the Blind
64th St. & Malvern Ave., Philadelphia 19151
Dr. Joseph Kerr, Director

PATHWAY SCHOOL
162 Egypt Rd., Jeffersonville 19403
Ted Enoch, Ed.S., Dir of Admissions
215-277-0660
    Established 1961. Coed. Accreditation: Pennsylvania Bureau of Special Education. Tuition: $15,950. Room and board: $37,800. Fees: $56,750. Enrollment: 130. Faculty: 20. Student-faculty ratio: 6:1. 12 buildings on 13 acres. The Pathway School provides services for individuals, ages 5-21, with learning, developmental, neurological and behavioral disorders using a multidisciplinary team approach. All students have individualized educational and treatment plans.

Pennsylvania School for the Deaf
100 School House Ln., Philadelphia 19144
Joseph P. Finnegan, Head

Pressley Ridge School
530 Marshall Ave., Pittsburgh 15214
Wm. Clark Luster, Exec. Dir.

Royer-Greaves School for Blind
118 South Valley Rd., Paoli 19301

Scranton State School for the Deaf
1800 N. Washington Ave., Scranton 18509
Dr. George Severns, Superintendent

Western Pennsylvania School for the Blind
Bayard at Bellefield, Pittsburgh 15213
Alton G. Kloss, Supt.

Western Pennsylvania School for the Deaf
300 E. Swissvale Ave., Pittsburgh 15218
Sam B. Craig, Supt.

Woods Schools, Langhorne 19047
A residential/habilitative facility
Robert Griffith, Ed. D., President

SOUTH CAROLINA

South Carolina School for the Deaf and the Blind
Spartanburg 29302
A. Baron Holmes IV, Pres.

SOUTH DAKOTA

South Dakota School for the Deaf
1800 E. 10th St., Sioux Falls 57103
Gordon Kaufman, Supt.

South Dakota School for the Visually Handicapped
423 S.E. 17th Ave., Aberdeen 57401
Dean North, Supt.

TENNESSEE

DEVEREUX GENESIS LEARNING CENTERS
430 B Allied Dr., Nashville 37211
Terence W. Adams, State Director
615-832-4222

Tennessee School for the Blind
115 Stewarts Ferry Pike, Donelson 37214
Garland Cross, Prin.

Tennessee School for the Deaf
2725 Island Home Park, Knoxville 37920

University of Memphis, Memphis 38152
Dr. John Eubank, Dean of Admissions

TEXAS

DEVEREUX HOSPITAL AND NEUROBEHAVIORAL INSTITUTE OF TEXAS
1150 Devereux Dr., League City 77573
Colette Sink, Admissions Director
713-332-0011

DEVEREUX PSYCHIATRIC RESIDENTIAL CENTER OF TEXAS
120 David Wade Dr., Victoria 77902-2666
Pat Franke, Admissions Director
800-383-5000 or 512-575-8271

· Howard College
Southwest Collegiate Institute for the Deaf
Ave. C, Big Spring Industrial Park
Big Spring 79720

UTAH

Utah Schools for the Deaf and the Blind
742 Harrison Blvd., Ogden 84404
Wayne Glaus, Superintendent

VERMONT

Austine School for the Deaf
120 Maple St., Brattleboro 05301
Susan Sien, Executive Director

VIRGINIA

Accotink Academy
8519 Tuttle Rd., Springfield 22152
Elaine McConnell, Director

Atlantic Academy
1701 Will-O-Wisp Dr., Virginia Beach 23454
Louis Schlain, Dir.

Buford Academy
P.O. Box 26665, Richmond 23261

Child Development Ctr. of Northern Virginia
111 N. Cherry St., Falls Church 22046
Elaine Payne, Dir.

GRAFTON SCHOOL
P.O. Box 112, Berryville 22611
Robert Stieg, Jr., Headmaster
703-955-2400
    Grafton provides individualized educational and residential services and in-community supports for individuals with severe emotional disturbance, learning disabilities, mental retardation, autistic disorders, behavioral disorders, amd other complex challenges, including physical disabilities. Offerings include an accredited high school, elementary and middle school graded classrooms, ungraded classrooms, vocational training, and participation in public school.

Lafayette Academy
1023 Millmont St., Charlottesville 22903
William Keyser II, Dir.

Minnick Educational Center
P.O. Box 905, Salem 24153
Ronald Herring, Dir.

Peninsula Academy
2244 Executive Dr., Hampton 23666
Maureen Reiman, Dir.

Virginia Home for Boys
8716 W. Broad St., Richmond 23294
Marlin Balsbaugh, Director

Virginia School for the Deaf and Blind
700 Shell Rd., Hampton 23661
Phillip Bellefleur, PhD, Superintendent

Virginia School for the Deaf and the Blind
Staunton 24401
Sheldon D. Melton, Supt.

WASHINGTON

Lakeland Village School
P.O. Box 200, Medical Lake 99022

Rainier School
P.O. Box 600, Buckley 98321

Washington State School for the Blind
2214 E. 13th St., Vancouver 98661

Washington State School for the Deaf
611 Grand Blvd., Vancouver 98661

WEST VIRGINIA

West Virginia Schools for the Deaf and Blind
Romney 26757

WISCONSIN

St. Coletta School
W4955 Hwy. 18, Jefferson 53549
Sister Elaine Weber, MS, Administrator

Wisconsin School for the Deaf
309 W. Walworth Ave., Delavan 53115
John Shipman, Supt.

Wisconsin School for Visually Handicapped
1700 W. State St., Janesville 53545
Andrew S. Papineau, Supt.

WYOMING

Wyoming School for the Deaf
539 Payne Ave., Casper 82609
Norman Anderson, Director

Wyoming State Training School, Lander 82520
Fred W. Heryford, Ed.D., Supt.

HOME ECONOMICS

This classification contains schools accredited by the American Home Economics Association (†) and the American Dietetic Association (‡) and a selection of programs from institutionally accredited schools.

ALABAMA

† Alabama A & M University
P.O. Box 639, Normal 35762
Dr. Bernice Richardson, Assoc. Dean
See listing under "Universities"

† Auburn University, Auburn 36849

· Gadsden State Community College
P.O. Box 227, Gadsden 35902
W. Bryan Stone, Dir. of Admis.

† Jacksonville State University
700 Pelham Rd. N., Jacksonville 36265

† Judson College
P O Box 120, Marion 36756

† Oakwood College
Oakwood Rd., N.W., Huntsville 35896

† Samford University
800 Lakeshore Dr., Birmingham 35229
Ruth Ash, Dean

† Tuskegee University
Tuskegee Institute 36088

† University of Alabama
P.O. Box 870132, Tuscaloosa 35487-0132
Roy Smith, Dir. of Admis.

University of Alabama at Birmingham
University Station, Birmingham 35294

† University of Montevallo, Montevallo 35115

† University of North Alabama
University Station, Florence 35632

ARIZONA

† Arizona State University, Tempe 85287

· Arizona Western College
P.O. Box 929, Yuma 85366-0929
Bob Davis, Dir. of Admis.

· ‡ Central Arizona College, Signal Peak Campus
8470 N. Overfield Rd., Coolidge 85228
Dr. John Klein, President
602-426-4265

† Northern Arizona University
P.O. Box 4092, Flagstaff 86011
Dr. Margaret Cibik, Dir. of Admis.

† University of Arizona, Tucson 85721
Loyd Bell, Director of Admissions

ARKANSAS

† Harding University
900 E. Center Ave., Searcy 72149

† Henderson State University
1100 Henderson St., Arkadelphia 71999

† Ouachita Baptist University
410 Ouachita St., Arkadelphia 71998
Randy Garner, Dir. of Admis.
800-DIAL-OBU

† Philander Smith College
812 W. 13th St., Little Rock 72202

† University of Arkansas at Fayetteville
Fayetteville 72701

† University of Arkansas at Little Rock
2801 S. University Ave., Little Rock 72204

† University of Arkansas at Pine Bluff
1200 University Dr., Pine Bluff 71601-2799

† University of Central Arkansas
201 Donaghey Ave., Conway 72035

CALIFORNIA

† California Polytechnic State University
San Luis Obispo 93407
Helen Linstrum, Dir. of Admis.

† California State Polytechnic University
3801 W. Temple Ave., Pomona 91768

† California State University, Fresno
Shaw & Cedar Ave., Fresno 93710

† California State University, Long Beach
1250 Bellflower Blvd., Long Beach 90840

† California State University, Los Angeles
5151 Paseo Rancho Castilla, Los Angeles 90032

† California State University, Northridge
18111 Nordhoff St., Northridge 91330
Ned C. Reynolds, Dir. of Admis.

† California State University, Sacramento
6000 J St., Sacramento 95819

‡ California State University, San Bernardino
5500 University Pky., San Bernardino 92407
909-880-5188

† Christian Heritage College
2100 Greenfield Dr., El Cajon 92019
Pam Daly, Dir. of Admis.
800-676-2242

‡ Drew University
1621 E. 120th St., Los Angeles 90059

· ‡ Grossmont College
8800 Grossmont College Dr., El Cajon 92020

† Humboldt State University
1 Harps St., Arcata 95521

† Loma Linda University, Loma Linda 92350
800-422-4LLU

· ‡ Long Beach City College
4901 E. Carson St., Long Beach 90808
J. Dawdy, Dean of Admissions & Records

· Los Angeles City College
855 N. Vermont Ave., Los Angeles 90029
Dr. Stelle Feuers, President

† Master's College
P.O. Box 221450, Newhall 91322
Don Gilmore, Dir. of Admis.

· Mt. San Antonio College
1100 N. Grand Ave., Walnut 91789

· ‡ **ORANGE COAST COLLEGE**
P.O. Box 5005, Costa Mesa 92628
See listing under "Community and Junior Colleges"

† Pacific Union College
1 Angwin Ave., Angwin 94508
Dr. Gary Gifford, Dir. of Admis.

‡ Pepperdine University
24255 Pacific Coast Hwy., Malibu 90263
Paul Long, Dean of Admissions
310-456-4392

† Point Loma Nazarene College
3900 Lomaland Dr., San Diego 92106
Bill Young, Dir. of Admis.

† San Diego State University
5300 Campanile Dr., San Diego 92115

† San Francisco State University
1600 Holloway Ave., San Francisco 94132
Corwin Bjonerud, Dir. of Admis.

† San Jose State University
1 Washington Sq., San Jose 95192

‡ University of California at Berkeley
Sproul Hall, Berkeley 94720

‡ University of California, Davis
376 Mrak Hall, Davis 95616

COLORADO

† Colorado State University
102 Administration Building, Fort Collins 80523
Mary Ontireros, Dir. of Admissions

· ‡ Front Range Community College
3645 W. 112th Ave., Westminister 80030
Dr. Patricia Lammers, Dir. of Admis.

‡ University of Northern Colorado, Greeley 80639
Vincent Scalia, Dean
303-351-2877

CONNECTICUT

· ‡ Briarwood College
2279 Mt. Vernon Rd., Southington 06489
Debra La Roche, Dir. of Admis.

‡ St. Joseph College
1678 Asylum Ave., West Hartford 06117
Mary C. Demo, Dir. of Admis.

· ‡ South Central Community College
60 Sargent Dr., New Haven 06511
Dr. Antonio Perez, President

‡ University of Connecticut, Storrs 06268
Robert G. Ryder, Dean

‡ University of New Haven
300 Orange Ave., West Haven 06516
Joseph Chepaitis, Dean
203-932-7000

DELAWARE

† Delaware State College
1200 N. DuPont Hwy., Dover 19901
Jethro C. Williams, Dir. of Admis.

† University of Delaware, Newark 19711

DISTRICT OF COLUMBIA

† Gallaudet University
800 Florida Ave., N.E., Washington 20002
See listing under "Universities"

† Howard University
2400 6th St., N.W., Washington 20059
James E. Cheek, President

University of the District of Columbia
Georgia Ave.-Harvard St. Campus
1100 Harvard St., N.W., Washington 20009

† University of the District of Columbia
Van Ness Campus
4200 Connecticut Ave., N.W., Washington 20008

FLORIDA

· ‡ Broward Community College
225 E. Las Olas Blvd., Ft. Lauderdale 33301

Florida A & M University, Tallahassee 32307

· ‡ Florida Community College at Jacksonville
North Campus
4501 Capper Rd., Jacksonville 32218

‡ Florida International University
Tamiami Trail, Miami 33199

† Florida State University
600 W. College Ave., Tallahassee 32306

· ‡ Miami-Dade Community College
Medical Center Campus
950 N.W. 20th St., Miami 33127

· ‡ Orlando Vocational-Technical Center
301 W. Amelia St., Orlando 32801

· ‡ Palm Beach Community College
4200 S. Congress Ave., Lake Worth 33461

· ‡ Pensacola Junior College
1000 College Blvd., Pensacola 32504
Horace E. Hartsell, President

† University of Florida
226 Tigert Hall, Gainesville 32611

‡ University of North Florida
4567 St. Johns Bluff Rd. S., Jacksonville 32224

† University of West Florida
11000 University Pky., Pensacola 32514

GEORGIA

† Berry College
2277 Martha Berry Hwy. N.W., Mt. Berry 30165

† Brenau College
204 Boulevard, Gainesville 30501

‡ Clark Atlanta University
240 James Brawley Dr., S.W., Atlanta 30314
Thomas W. Cole, President

† Fort Valley State College
1005 State College Dr., Fort Valley 31030

† Georgia College
231 W. Hancock St., Milledgeville 31061
912-453-5004

† Georgia Southern University, Statesboro 30460

‡ Georgia State University
University Plaza, Atlanta 30303
Ernest Beals, Dean of Admissions

Morris Brown College
643 Martin Luther King Jr. Dr. N.W.
Atlanta 30314

† Savannah State College
State College Branch, Savannah 31404
Robert Ray, Dir. of Admis.

† University of Georgia, Athens 30602
Dr. Emily Pou, Dean

HAWAII

† University of Hawaii at Manoa
2500 Campus Rd., Honolulu 96822

IDAHO

† Idaho State University
P.O. Box 8270, Pocatello 83209

† Northwest Nazarene College
623 Holly St., Nampa 83686
Bruce D. Webb, Dir. of Admis.

· Ricks College, Rexburg 83460
Steven Bennion, President

† University of Idaho, Moscow 83843
Peter Brown, Dir. of Admis.

ILLINOIS

† Bradley University
1501 W. Bradley Ave., Peoria 61625

‡ Chicago State University
9501 S. King Dr., Chicago 60628

† Eastern Illinois University, Charleston 61920
Joyce Crouse, Chrpsn.
See listing under "Universities"

Illinois Benedictine College
5700 College Rd., Lisle 60532

† Illinois State University
212 N. School St., Normal 61761

† Loyola University - Mundelein College
6363 N. Sheridan Rd., Chicago 60660
Judith Bobber, Dir. of Admis.

· ‡ Malcolm X College
1900 W. Van Buren St., Chicago 60612
Clifford Fields, Dean, Career Programs

‡ Northern Illinois University, De Kalb 60115

† Olivet Nazarene University, Kankakee 60901
John Mongerson, Dir. of Admis.
815-939-5203

† Rosary College
7900 W. Division St., River Forest 60305
Hildegarde Schmidt, Dir. of Admis.

† Southern Illinois University at Carbondale
Carbondale 62901

† University of Illinois
506 S. Wright St., Urbana 61801

‡ University of Illinois at Chicago
P.O. Box 5220, Chicago 60680
Dr. Marilyn R. Fiduccia, Dir. of Admis.

† Western Illinois University
900 W. Adams St., Macomb 61455
Alan DeRoos, Registrar
309-298-1891

· ‡ William Rainey Harper College
1200 W. Algonquin Rd., Palatine 60067

INDIANA

† Ball State University
2000 W. University Ave., Muncie 47306
Ruth Vedvik, Dir. of Admis.

‡ Goshen College
1700 S. Main St., Goshen 46526
Marty Lehman Hooley, Dir. of Admis.

† Indiana State University
217 N. 6th St., Terre Haute 47809

† Indiana University at Bloomington
300 N. Jordan Ave., Bloomington 47406

† Manchester College
604 E. College Ave., North Manchester 46962
Dr. Brenda Faye Sands, Chrpsn.

‡ Marian College
3200 Cold Spring Rd., Indianapolis 46222
Don French, Dir. of Admis.

† Purdue University
Schleman Hall, West Lafayette 47907

‡ Purdue University, Calumet Campus
2233 171st St., Hammond 46323

† Valparaiso University, Valparaiso 46383

IOWA

· Hawkeye Community College
1501 E. Orange Rd., Waterloo 50701
319-296-2320 Ext. 4000

‡ Iowa State University, Ames 50011
Karsten Smedal, Dir. of Admis.

Iowa Wesleyan College
601 N. Main St., Mt. Pleasant 52641

† Teikyo Marycrest University
1607 W. 12th St., Davenport 52804
Tim McDonough, Dir. of Admis.
See listing under "Universities"

† University of Northern Iowa, Cedar Falls 50614

† William Penn College
201 Trueblood Ave., Oskaloosa 52577
Eric Otto, Dir. of Admis.

KANSAS

† Benedictine College
1020 N. Second St., Atchison 66002
James Hoffman, Dir. of Admis.

† Bethel College
300 E. 27th St., North Newton 67117

† Emporia State University
1200 Commercial St., Emporia 66801
Dr. Barbara Hilgendorf, Dir. of Admissions

† Fort Hays State University
600 Park St., Hays 67601-4099
Dr. Merlene Lyman, Chrpsn.

· Hutchinson Community College
1300 N. Plum St., Hutchinson 67501
Duane Halpain, Dir. of Admis.

† Kansas State University
Anderson Hall 110, Manhattan 66506
Ellsworth M. Gerritz, Admis. & Records

† Pittsburg State University
1701 S. Broadway St., Pittsburg 66762
James E. Parker, Dir of Admis.

† Sterling College, Sterling 67579
Robert Reed, Dir. of Admis. & Records

† Washburn University of Topeka
1700 S.W. College Ave., Topeka 66621
John E. Triggs, Dir. of Admissions

KENTUCKY

† Berea College, Berea 40404
John S. Cook, Dir. of Admis.

† Eastern Kentucky University
521 Lancaster Ave., Richmond 40475

† Georgetown College
400 E. College St., Georgetown 40324
Garvel Kindrick, Director of Admissions
See listing under "Universities"

† Kentucky State University
400 E. Main St., Frankfort 40601

† Morehead State University, Morehead 40351
Charles Myers, Director of Admissions
606-783-2000

† Murray State University, Murray 42071
Phil Bryan, Director of Admissions
800-272-4MSU

‡ Spalding University
851 S. 4th St., Louisville 40203
Dorothy G. Allen, Dir. of Admis.

† University of Kentucky, Lexington 40506

‡ University of Louisville
2301 S. 3rd St., Louisville 40292
Robert Parrent, Dir. of Admis.

† Western Kentucky University
1526 Russellville Rd., Bowling Green 42101

LOUISIANA

† Grambling State University
P.O. Box 607, Grambling 71245
Dr. Harold W. Lundy, President

† Louisiana State University and A & M College
Baton Rouge 70803

† Lousiana Technical University
P.O. Box 3168, Ruston 71272

† McNeese State University
4100 Ryan St., Lake Charles 70605

† Nicholls State University
LA Hwy. 1, Thibodaux 70301

† Northeast Louisiana University
700 University Ave., Monroe 71209

† Northwestern State University
Natchitoches 71497

† Southeastern Louisiana University
P.O. Box 784, Hammond 70404

† Southern University A & M College
Baton Rouge 70813

† University of Southwestern Louisiana
P.O. Box 40400, Lafayette 70504

MAINE

· ‡ Southern Maine Technical College
2 Fort Rd., South Portland 04106
See listing under "Career Schools"

† University of Maine
102 Main St., Farmington 04938

† University of Maine, Orono 04469

MARYLAND

· ‡ Community College of Baltimore
2901 Liberty Heights Ave., Baltimore 21215
Joseph Stein, Director of Admissions

† Hood College
400 Rosemont Ave., Frederick 21701

† Morgan State University
Cold Spring Ln. and Hillen Rd., Baltimore 21239

† University of Maryland, College Park 20742

‡ University of Maryland, University College
University Blvd. & Adelphi Rd.
College Park 20742

† University of Maryland Eastern Shore
11868 Academic Oval, Princess Anne 21853
Dr. Retia Walker, Chrpsn.

MASSACHUSETTS

Atlantic Union College
P.O. Box 1000, South Lancaster 01561
Osa Canto, Registrar

† Framingham State College
100 State St., Framingham 01701
E. Joseph Lee, Director

· ‡ Holyoke Community College
303 Homestead Ave., Holyoke 01040
George E. Frost, President

· ‡ Laboure College
2120 Dorchester Ave., Boston 02124
Sr. Maureen St. Charles, President

‡ Simmons College
300 The Fenway, Boston 02115

† University of Massachusetts, Amherst 01003
Arlene Wesley Cash, Dir. of Admis.

MICHIGAN

† Adrian College
110 S. Madison St., Adrian 49221
George Wolf, Dir. of Admis.
See listing under "Universities"

† Andrews University, Berrien Springs 49104
Jack Mentges, Dir. of Admis.

† Central Michigan University
100 Warriner Hall, Mt. Pleasant 48858

† Eastern Michigan University, Ypsilanti 48197
E. A. Rhodes, Head
313-487-3060 or 800-GO-TO-EMU

† Madonna University
36600 Schoolcraft St., Livonia 48150

† Marygrove College
8425 W. McNichols Rd., Detroit 48221

† Michigan State University, East Lansing 48824
Dr. Julia Miller, Dean

† Northern Michigan University
610 Cohodas Admin. Center, Marquette 49855
Nancy Rehling, Dir. of Admis.

† Siena Heights College
1247 E. Siena Heights Dr., Adrian 49221

‡ University of Michigan-Ann Arbor
815 S. University Ave., Ann Arbor 48109

· ‡ Wayne County Community College
801 Fort St., W., Detroit 48226

‡ Wayne State University
5980 Cass Ave., Detroit 48202
Dr. J. R. Thorderson, Dir. of Admis.

† Western Michigan University, Kalamazoo 49008
Stanley Henderson, Dir. of Enrl. Mgt. & Admis.
616-387-2000

MINNESOTA

‡ College of Saint Benedict
37 S. College Ave., St. Joseph 56374

† College of St. Catherine
2004 Randolph Ave., St. Paul 55105

† College of St. Scholastica
1200 Kenwood Ave., Duluth 55811
Susan Bodin, Chrpsn.
800-447-5444
See listing under "Liberal Arts"

† Concordia College
901 8th St. S., Moorhead 56562
Lee Johnson, Dir. of Admis.
See listing under "Universities"

· ‡ Lakewood Community College
3401 Century Ave., White Bear Lake 55110
Dr. Neil Christenson, President

† Mankato State University
P.O. Box 8400, Mankato 56002

· ‡ Normandale Community College
9700 France Ave., S., Bloomington 55431
Thomas Horak, President

PILLSBURY BAPTIST BIBLE COLLEGE
315 S. Grove St., Owatonna 55060
Alan Potter, President
Larry Tindall, Director of Admissions
800-747-4557

† St. Olaf College, Northfield 55057
George Holt, Chrpsn.
507-646-3130

† University of Minnesota
2400 Oakland Ave., Duluth 55812
Robert L. Heller, Provost

† University of Minnesota, Twin Cities
Minneapolis 55455

‡ UNIVERSITY OF MINNESOTA-CROOKSTON
2900 University Ave., Crookston 56716
John Bywater, Dir. of Admis.
800-232-6466
See listing under "Universities"

University of St. Thomas
2115 Summit Ave., St. Paul 55105

MISSISSIPPI

† Alcorn State University
P.O. Box 359, Lorman 39096
D. W. Wilburn, Registrar

† Blue Mountain College
P.O. Box 338, Blue Mountain 38610

† Delta State University
Hwy. 8 W., Cleveland 38732

† Mississippi College
P.O. Box 4086, Clinton 39058

† Mississippi State University
P.O. Box J, Mississippi State University 39762

† Mississippi University for Women
P.O. Box W-1602, Columbus 39701
Teresa Thompson, Exec. Dir. of Enrollment

† University of Mississippi, University 38677

† University of Southern Mississippi
P.O. Box 5165, Hattiesburg 39406

William Carey College
498 Tuscan Ave., Hattiesburg 39401

MISSOURI

† Central Missouri State University
Warrensburg 64093
Delores Hudson, Dir. of Admis.

† College of the Ozarks, Point Lookout 65726
Dr. Kenton Olson, Dean of the College

† Fontbonne College
6800 Wydown Blvd., St. Louis 63105
Peggy Musen, Dir. of Admis.

† Lincoln University
820 Chestnut St., Jefferson City 65101

† Northeast Missouri State University
Kirksville 63501

† Northwest Missouri State University
800 University Dr., Maryville 64468

· ‡ St. Louis Community College at Florissant Valley
3400 Pershall Rd., St. Louis 63135
Milton Woody, Dir. of Admis.

† Southeast Missouri State University
1 University Plz., Cape Girardeau 63701
New Student Relations 314-651-2590
See listing under "Universities"

‡ Southwest Baptist University
1601 S. Springfield Ave., Bolivar 65613

† Southwest Missouri State University
901 S. National Ave., Springfield 65804
Dr. George Wise, Department Head
417-836-5136

† University of Missouri, Columbia
228 Jesse Hall, Columbia 65211

† William Woods College
200 W. 12th St., Fulton 65251
Dr. Jahnae Barnett, VP of Admis.

MONTANA

† Montana State University, Bozeman 59717

NEBRASKA

· ‡ Central Community College-Hastings Campus
P.O. Box 1024, Hastings 68902-1024

† Chadron State College
1000 Main St., Chadron 69337
Dr. Merlyn Gramberg, Dean

· ‡ Southeast Community College, Lincoln
8800 "O" St., Lincoln 68520

† University of Nebraska
905 W. 25th St., Kearney 68849

† University of Nebraska at Lincoln
HE 105, Lincoln 68583
Karen Craig, Dean

University of Nebraska at Omaha
Omaha 68182

† Wayne State College
200 E. Tenth St., Wayne 68787

NEVADA

† University of Nevada, Reno
Reno 89557

NEW HAMPSHIRE

† Keene State College
229 Main St., Keene 03435
Kathryn Dodge, Dir. of Admis.

† University of New Hampshire, Durham 03824
Stanwood C. Fish, Dir. of Admissions

NEW JERSEY

· ‡ Camden County College
P.O. Box 200, Blackwood 08012
Dr. Robert Ramsay, President

‡ College of Saint Elizabeth
Convent Station 07961
Sr. Jacqueline Burns, President

· ‡ Middlesex County College
Schools of Dental Hygiene, Medical Lab
Technology, Nursing, Radiography
P.O. Box 3050, Edison 08818
Dr. Marilyn Keener, Dean, Health Tech. Div.

‡ Montclair State College
1 Normal Ave., Upper Montclair 07043

NEW MEXICO

† Eastern New Mexico University
Portales 88130
Larry Fuqua, Dir. of Admis.

New Mexico Highlands University, Las Vegas 87701
Dr. Jorge P. Thomas, VP Academic Affairs

† New Mexico State University
P.O. Box 30001, Las Cruces 88003

† University of New Mexico, Albuquerque 87131
Robert Weaver, Dean of Admissions

† Western New Mexico University
College Ave, Silver City 88062
Michael Aleckson, Dir. of Admis.
800-222-9668
See listing under "Universities"

NEW YORK

† Cornell University
410 Thurston Ave., Ithaca 14853

‡ CUNY Brooklyn College
2900 Bedford Ave., Brooklyn 11210
Justin Dunn, Dir. of Admis.

† CUNY Hunter College
695 Park Ave., New York 10021
Donna Shalala, President

· ‡ CUNY LaGuardia Community College
31-10 Thompson Ave., Long Island City 11101
Robert O'Pray, Registrar

‡ CUNY Lehman College
250 Bedford Park Blvd. W., Bronx 10468
Jane Herbert, Dir. of Enrollment Management

† CUNY, Queens College
6530 Kissena Blvd., Flushing 11367

‡ D'Youville College
320 Porter Ave., Buffalo 14201
Ronald Dannecker, Dir. of Admis.

Friends World Program, Long Island University
Montauk Hwy., Southampton 11968
Carol Gilbert, Dir. of Admis.

‡ Long Island University-C. W. Post Campus
Rt. 25A, Brookville 11548
Dr. Ellen Duffy, Associate Dean
516-299-3046

† Marymount College
100 Marymount Ave., Tarrytown 10591
Gina R. Campbell, Dir. of Admis.
800-724-4312

† New York University
70 Washington Sq., New York 10012

† Pratt Institute
200 Willoughby Ave., Brooklyn 11205

‡ Rochester Institute of Technology
1 Lomb Memorial Dr., Rochester 14623
716-475-6631
See listing under "Universities"

‡ Russell Sage College
51 1st St., Troy 12180

† SUNY College at Buffalo
1300 Elmwood Ave., Buffalo 14222
Deborah K. Renzi, Dir. of Admis.

† SUNY College at Oneonta, Oneonta 13820
Clifford McVinney, Dir. of Admis.

† SUNY College at Plattsburgh, Plattsburgh 12901
Richard Higgins, Dir. of Admis.
518-564-2040

· ‡ SUNY College of Agriculture and Technology
Morrisville 13408
Dennis Nostrand, Dir. of Admis.

· ‡ SUNY Dutchess Community College
Poughkeepsie 12601

· ‡ SUNY Erie Community College, North Campus
6205 Main St., Williamsville 14221

· ‡ SUNY Rockland Community College
Medical Lab Technology
145 College Rd., Suffern 10901
Marge Warren, Coordinator

· ‡ SUNY Suffolk County Community College
2 Speonk-Riverhead Rd. Riverhead 11901

· ‡ SUNY Westchester Community College
75 Grasslands Rd., Valhalla 10595-1698
Alan Seidman, Dir. of Admis.

† Syracuse University, Syracuse 13244

NORTH CAROLINA

† Appalachian State University
ASU Station, Boone 28608
Joe Watts, Admissions Officer

† Bennett College
900 E. Washington St., Greensboro 27401

† Campbell University
P.O. Box 127, Buies Creek 27506

† East Carolina University
1000 E. 5th St., Greenville 27858
Human Environmental Sciences
Dr. Helen Grove, Dean

† Mars Hill College
Main St., Mars Hill 28754
Dr. Smith Goodrum, Dean of Admis.

† Meredith College
3800 Hillsborough St., Raleigh 27607

† North Carolina A&T State University
1601 E. Market St., Greensboro 27411

† North Carolina Central University
P.O. Box 19617, Durham 27707

† University of North Carolina
1000 Spring Garden St., Greensboro 27412

‡ University of North Carolina at Chapel Hill
Chapel Hill 27599
James C. Walters, Dir. Undergrad Admis.

† Western Carolina University
Cullowhee 28723
Tyree H. Kiser, Dir. of Admissions

NORTH DAKOTA

† North Dakota State University, Fargo 58105
Richard Shearer, Acting Dir. of Admis.

† University of North Dakota
Box 8193 University Station, Grand Forks 58203

OHIO

† Ashland University
401 College Ave., Ashland 44805

† Baldwin-Wallace College
275 Eastland Rd., Berea 44017
Juliann K. Baker, Dir. of Admis.

† Bluffton College
College Ave., Bluffton 45817

† Bowling Green State University
Bowling Green 43403
John Martin, Dir. of Admis.

† Case Western Reserve University
2040 Adelbert Rd., Cleveland 44106

· ‡ Cincinnati Technical College
3520 Central Pkwy., Cincinnati 45223

· ‡ Columbus State Community College
550 E. Spring St., Columbus 43215
Mary Jo Deerwester, Dir. of Admis.

· ‡ Cuyahoga Community College, Metropolitan Campus
2900 Community College Ave., Cleveland 44115

· ‡ Hocking College
3301 Hocking Pky., Nelsonville 45764
Candace Vancko, VP for Enrollment
800-282-4163

† Kent State University
P.O. Box 5190, Kent 44242
Bruce Riddle, Dir. of Admis.

· ‡ Lima Technical College
4240 Campus Dr., Lima 45804
Cynthia E. Spiers, Director of Admissions

† Miami University
E. High St., Oxford 45056

Mt. Vernon Nazarene College
800 Martinsburg Rd., Mt. Vernon 43050
Ronald Hyson, Dir. of Admis.

† Notre Dame College
4545 College Rd., Cleveland 44121
Sr. Mary Luke, S.N.D., President

† Ohio State University
190 N. Oval Mall, Columbus 43210

† Ohio University, Athens 45701

† Otterbein College, Westerville 43081

· ‡ Owens Community College
P.O. Box 10000, Toledo 43699
Jim Welling, Admissions
419-661-7225

· ‡ Sinclair Community College
444 W. 3rd St., Dayton 45402-1460
Sara P. Smith, Director of Admissions
800-315-3000

† University of Akron
381 Buchtel Common, Akron 44325
Kris MacDermott, Asst. Provost Enrollment

‡ University of Cincinnati
2700 Clifton Ave., Cincinnati 45221

† University of Dayton
300 College Park Ave., Dayton 45469-2335
Toll-free 800-837-7433
See listing under "Universities"

† Ursuline College
2550 Lander Rd., Cleveland 44124

† Youngstown State University
410 Wick Ave., Youngstown 44555
Leslie H. Cochran, President

OKLAHOMA

† Cameron University
2800 W. Gore Blvd., Lawton 73505
Louise Brown, Dir. of Admis.

† East Central University, Ada 74820
James Peak, Dir. of Admis.

† Langston University
P.O. Box 907, Langston 73050

† Northeastern State University
600 N. Grand Ave., Tahlequah 74464

† Northwestern Oklahoma State University
705 Oklahoma Blvd., Alva 73717

Oklahoma Baptist University
500 W. University St., Shawnee 74801

† Oklahoma Panhandle State University
P.O. Box 430, Goodwell 73939

† Oklahoma State University, Stillwater 74078
Patricia Knaub, Dean

· ‡ Oklahoma State University-Technical Branch
1801 E. 4th St., Okmulgee 74447
800-722-4471 or 918-756-6211

† Southeastern Oklahoma State University
Station A, Durant 74701

† Southern Nazarene University
6729 N.W. 39th Expy., Bethany 73008

† Southwestern Oklahoma State University
100 Campus Dr., Weatherford 73096

† University of Central Oklahoma
100 N. University Dr., Edmond 73034

‡ University of Oklahoma at Norman
660 Parrington Oval, Norman 73019

‡ University of Oklahoma Health Sciences Center
P.O. Box 26901, Oklahoma City 73126
Dr. Lee Holder, Dean, College of Allied Health

† University of Sciences & Arts of Oklahoma
P.O. Box 82345, Chickasha 73018

OREGON

† George Fox College
414 N. Meridian St., Newberg 97132

† Linfield College
900 S. Baker St., McMinnville 97128
Thomas Meicho, Dean of Admissions

† Oregon State University, Corvallis 97333
Wallace Gibbs, Dir. of Admis.

· ‡ Portland Community College
P.O. Box 19000, Portland 97280

PENNSYLVANIA

† Albright College
P.O. Box 15234, Reading 19612

· ‡ Bucks County Community College
Swamp Rd., Newtown 18940

† Cheyney University of Pennsylvania
P.O. Box 200, Cheyney 19319

· ‡ Community College of Allegheny Co.
Allegheny Campus
808 Ridge Ave., Pittsburgh 15212

· ‡ Community College of Philadelphia
1700 Spring Garden St., Philadelphia 19130
Allen T. Bonnell, President

† Drexel University
3141 Chestnut St., Philadelphia 19104
Dean of Enrollment Management

‡ Edinboro University of Pennsylvania
Edinboro 16444
Admissions Office: 800-626-2203

‡ Gannon University
109 University Sq., Erie 16541

† Immaculata College
Immaculata 19345
James P. Sullivan, Dir. of Admis.

† Indiana University of Pennsylvania, Indiana 15705
Fred Dadak, Dean, Admissions

· ‡ Luzerne Co. Community College
1333 S. Prospect St., Nanticoke 18634

† Mansfield University of Pennsylvania
Mansfield 16933

† Marywood College
2300 Adams Ave., Scranton 18509

† Mercyhurst College
501 E. 38th St., Erie 16546
Andrew Roth, Dean of Enrollment
800-825-1926

† Messiah College
General Delivery, Grantham 17027
Ron Long, Dir. of Admis.

† Pennsylvania State University
201 Shields Bldg., University Park 16802

St. Vincent College
300 Fraser Purchase Rd., Latrobe 15650

† Seton Hill College, Greensburg 15601
Peter Egan, Dir. of Admis.
800-826-6234 or 412-838-4255

‡ University of Pittsburgh
4200 5th Ave., Pittsburgh 15260

· ‡ Westmoreland County Community College
400 Armbrust Rd., Youngwood 15697

RHODE ISLAND

† University of Rhode Island, Kingston 02881
Barbara E. Brittingham, Dean

SOUTH CAROLINA

† Clemson University
201 Sikes Hall, Clemson 29634

† South Carolina State University
P.O. Box 7127, Orangeburg 29117-0001
803-536-7185

† Winthrop University
701 W. Oakland Ave., Rock Hill 29733
James McCammon, Jr., Dir. of Admis.

SOUTH DAKOTA

† Mt. Marty College
1105 W. 8th St., Yankton 57078
Paula Tacke, Dir. of Admis.

† South Dakota State University
P.O. Box 2275A, Brookings 57007
Gail Dobbs Tideman, Dean
605-688-6181
See listing under "Universities"

TENNESSEE

† Carson-Newman College
P.O. Box 70552, Jefferson City 37760
See listing under "Universities"

† David Lipscomb University
3901 Granny White Pike, Nashville 37204-3951
Wade Sandrell, Dir. of Admis.
800-333-4358

† EAST TENNESSEE STATE UNIVERSITY
P.O. Box 70731, Johnson City 37614
Dr. Nancy Dishner, Dean, Enrollment Management
615-929-4213 or 800-462-3878

† Freed-Hardeman University
158 E. Main St., Henderson 38340
800-342-7837

† Lambuth College
705 Lambuth Blvd., Jackson 38301

† Middle Tennessee State University
Murfreesboro 37132
Roger D. Sims, Dir. of Admis.

· ‡ Shelby State Community College
P.O. Box 40568, Memphis 38174

Southern Missionary College
P.O. Box 370, Collegedale 37315

† Tennessee State University
3500 John A. Merritt Blvd., Nashville 37209

† Tennessee Technological University
P.O. Box 5006, Cookeville 38505

† University of Memphis, Memphis 38152
Dr. John Eubank, Dean of Admissions

† University of Tennessee at Martin
Martin 38238
Paul Kelley, Director of Admissions
See listing under "Universities"

† University of Tennessee at Chattanooga
615 McCallie Ave., Chattanooga 37403

† University of Tennessee, Knoxville
527 Andy Holt Tower, Knoxville 37996
Dr. Gordon Stanley, Dir. of Admis.

TEXAS

† Abilene Christian University
ACU Station, Box 6000, Abilene 79699

† Baylor University
P.O. Box 97008, Waco 76798-7008
Diana Ramey, Director of Admissions

† East Texas State University
ETSU Station, Commerce 75429

· ‡ El Paso Community College
P.O. Box 20500, El Paso 79998
Dr. Robert E. Shapack, President

† Incarnate Word College
4301 Broadway St., San Antonio 78209
Sr. Sally Mitchell, Dean of Enrollment

† Lamar University
P.O. Box 10009, Beaumont 77710
800-458-7558

† Lubbock Christian University
5601 W. 19th, Lubbock 79407

† Prairie View A & M University
P.O. Box 3089, Prairie View 77446-3089
Linda S. Berry, Dir. of Admis.

· ‡ St. Phillip's College
2111 Nevada St., San Antonio 78203
John B. Murphy, Dean

† Sam Houston State University, Huntsville 77341

· ‡ San Jacinto College
4624 Fairmont Pky., Pasadena 77504
Thomas M. Spencer, President

† Southwest Texas State University
601 University Dr., San Marcos 78666

† Stephen F. Austin State University
P.O. Box 6078. Nacogdoches 75962

† Tarleton State University
1297 W. Washington St., Stephenville 76402

· ‡ Tarrant County Junior College
1500 Houston St., Ft. Worth 76102
C. A. Roberson, President

† Texas A & I University
Campus Box 101, Kingsville 78363

‡ Texas A & M University
College Station 77843

‡ Texas Christian University
2800 S. University Dr., Ft. Worth 76129
Dr. Edward Boehm, Jr., Dean of Admissions

† Texas College
2404 N. Grand St., Tyler 75702
Dr. William H. Ammons, II, Dir. of Admis.

† Texas Southern University
3100 Cleburne St., Houston 77004

† Texas Tech University, Lubbock 79409

† Texas Women's University
P.O. Box 23925, Denton 76204

† University of Houston
4800 Calhoun Rd., Houston 77204

† University of North Texas
P.O. Box 13797, Denton 76203

† University of Texas at Austin
0 the University of Texas, Austin 78712

‡ University of Texas Health Science Center
P.O. Box 20036, Houston 77225

‡ University of Texas-Pan American
1201 W. University Dr., Edinburg 78539
Miguel Nerarez, President

‡ University of Texas Southwestern Medical Center
5323 Harry Hines Blvd., Dallas 75235

UTAH

† Brigham Young University, Provo 84602

Southern Utah University
351 W. Center St., Cedar City 84720
D. Mark Barton, Asst. VP Student Services
801-586-7740

† University of Utah
1400 E. 200 S., Salt Lake City 84112
Dr. J. Stayner Landward, Dir. of Admis.

† Utah State University, Logan 84322-1600
Rod Clark, Director of Admissions
801-750-1107

VERMONT

‡ University of Vermont
194 S. Prospect St., Burlington 05401
802-656-3370

VIRGINIA

† Bridgewater College
402 E College St., Bridgewater 22812

‡ Eastern Mennonite College
1200 Park Rd., Harrisonburg 22801
Jerry Miller, Dir. of Admis.

† Hampton University, Hampton 23668
Ollie Bowman, Dean of Admissions

‡ James Madison University, Harrisonburg 22807

· ‡ J. Sargeant Reynolds Community College
P.O. Box C-23040, Richmond 23261

† LIBERTY UNIVERSITY
P.O. Box 20000, Lynchburg 24506
Jay Spencer, VP Recruitment
800-376-2800
See listing under "Universities"

† Norfolk State University
2401 Corprew Ave., Norfolk 23504

· ‡ Northern Virginia Community College
8333 Little River Turnpike, Annandale 22003
Dr. Barbara Guthrie-Morse, Provost

† Radford University
P.O. Box 5430, Radford 24142

· ‡ Tidewater Community College
1700 College Crescent, Virginia Beach 23456
Dr. Larry L. Whitworth, President

† Virginia Polytechnic Institute & State University
Blacksburg 24061
David Bousquet, Dir. of Undergraduate Admis.

† Virginia State University, Petersburg 23803
Mable C. Mountcastle, Dir. of Recording

WASHINGTON

† Central Washington University, Ellensburg 98926
William Swain, Director of Admissions

† Seattle Pacific University
3307 3rd Ave., W., Seattle 98119

· ‡ Shoreline Community College
16101 Greenwood Ave., N., Seattle 98133
Chuck Fields, Registrar

· ‡ Spokane Community College
1810 N. Greene St., Spokane 99207

‡ University of Washington, Seattle 98195

† Walla Walla College
204 S. College Ave., College Place 99324

† Washington State University, Pullman 99164
Stan Berry, Dir. of Admis.

† Western Washington University
516 High St., Bellingham 98225
Karen G. Copetas, Dir. of Admis.

· ‡ Yakima Valley Community College
16th & Nob Hill Blvd., Yakima 98902

WEST VIRGINIA

† Fairmont State College
1201 Locust Ave., Fairmont 26554
John Conaway, Dir. of Admis.

† Marshall University
400 Hal Greer Blvd., Huntington 25755
See listing under "Universities"

† Shepherd College, Shepherdstown 25443

† West Liberty State College, West Liberty 26074

† West Virginia University
P.O. Box 6001, Morgantown 26506

† WEST VIRGINIA WESLEYAN COLLEGE
59 College Ave., Buckhannon 26201
Robert Skinner, Director of Admission
See listing under "Universities"

WISCONSIN

Cardinal Stritch College
6801 N. Yates Rd., Milwaukee 53217
David Wegener, Dir. of Admis.

· ‡ Madison Area Technical College
3550 Anderson Rd., Madison 53704
Beverly Simone, District Director

· ‡ Milwaukee Area Technical College
700 W. State St., Milwaukee 53233

† Mt. Mary College
2900 N. Menomonee River Pky.
Milwaukee 53222

† Silver Lake College
2406 S. Alverno Road, Manitowoc 54220
Sandra Schwartz, Dir. of Admis.

‡ University of Wisconsin, Green Bay
2420 Nicolet Dr., Green Bay 54311
Myron Van de Ven, Dir. of Admis.

† University of Wisconsin, Madison
500 Lincoln Dr., Madison 53706

University of Wisconsin
P.O. Box 413, Milwaukee 53201
V. M. Allison, Registrar

† University of Wisconsin, Stevens Point 54481
Dr. John A. Larsen, Dir. of Admis.

‡ University of Wisconsin
200 BroadWay St. S., Menomonie 54751
Robert B. Swanson, Chancellor

: Western Wisconsin Technical College
304 N. 6th St., La Crosse 54602

WYOMING

† University of Wyoming
P.O. Box 3434, Laramie 82071
Richard Davis, Dir. of Admis.

GUAM

† University of Guam
UOG Station, Mangilao 96923
Kathleen Owings, Dir. of Admis.

PUERTO RICO

† Catholic University of Puerto Rico
Las Americas Ave., Ponce   00732
Carilin Frau, Dir. of Admis.

Inter American University of Puerto Rico
San German Campus
Harris Dr. Call Box 5100, San German   00683

† University of Puerto Rico, Rio Piedras Campus
P.O. Box 23300, San Juan   00931
Victor Lopez, Dir. of Admis.

VIRGIN ISLANDS

University of the Virgin Islands
Kingshill, St. Croix   00802

: : :HOME STUDY AND CORRESPONDENCE

ARIZONA

Laurel School
P.O. Box 5338, Phoenix   85010

Modern Schools of America, Inc.
5301 N. 37th Place, Paradise Valley   85253

TPI SCHOOLS PARALEGAL INSTITUTE
PO Box 11408, Phoenix   85061
John Morrison, President 602-272-1855, FAX 602-269-0793

CALIFORNIA

CALIFORNIA COAST UNIVERSITY
700 N. Main St., Santa Ana   92701
Admissions Office: 800-854-8768 or 714-547-9625
Thomas Neal, President
Linda B. Smith, VP Academic Affairs
William Barcroft, Dean of Admissions
   Established 1973. Proprietary. Coed. Accreditation: National Association of Private Non-Traditional Schools & Colleges, California State Department of Education, charter member California Association of State Approved Colleges & Universities, member Association for Adult & Continuing Education. Tuition: $2,200-$3,500. Enrollment: 7,500.
   A private college offering off-campus independent study programs in the traditional areas of business administration, management, engineering, psychology, & education. Admissions: rolling trimester, requires official transcripts, letters of recommendation, detailed curriculum vita or occupational history.
   Process: evaluation of prior academic work followed by analysis of occupational history, including participation in workshops, seminars, training programs, specialized projects for credit. Credit is demonstrated by challenge exams or specialized course by course independent study programs.
   Residency: All course work may be completed off campus, utilizing correspondence methods. All doctoral candidates must meet with faculty advisors in person, upon completion of doctoral dissertation. Scholarships: Interest free loans available to students.

California College for Health Sciences
222 W. 24th St., National City   91950
619-477-4800

Columbia Pacific University
North Campus
148 Wilson Hill Rd., Petaluma   94952
Dr. Richard Crews, President

Columbia Pacific University
South Campus
1415 3rd St., San Rafael   94901
Dr. Richard Crews, President

Futures in Education
1249 F St., San Diego   92101

GEMOLOGICAL INSTITUTE OF AMERICA
1660 Stewart St., Santa Monica   90404
Veronica Clark-Hudson, Educational Advisor
   Established 1931. Non-profit. Private. Accreditation: National Home Study Council. Diploma: Gemologist, Graduate Gemologist, Jewelry Sales Graduate. Courses: diamonds, diamond grading, colored stones, gem identification, colored stone grading, pearls, jewelry display, fine jewelry sales, advanced jewelry sales, pearl and bead stringing, counter sketching, gold and precious metals. Courses are available individually or as a program. For information call 800-421-7250 X292 or 310-829-2991 X292, or write the Educational Advisor at the above address. See listing under "Career Schools".

Halix Institute
1543 W. Olyic Blvd. #226, Los Angeles   90015

Hemphill Schools
510 S. Alvarado St., Los Angeles   90057
Ralph Hemphill, Director

Hollywood Scriptwriting Institute
1605 N. Cahuenga Blvd. #216, Hollywood   90028

John Tracy Clinic
806 West Adams Blvd., Los Angeles   90007
Edgar L. Lowell, Director

National Education Corporation
18400 Von Karman Ave., Irvine   92715

Niles Bryant School
3631 Stockton Blvd., Sacramento   95820
Piano tuning, electronic organ servicing

Truck Marketing Institute
P.O. Box 5000, Carpinteria   93014

United Training Institute
P.O. Box 715, Spring Valley   91976

CONNECTICUT

Charter Oak State College
66 Cedar St., Newington   06111-2646
Paul Morganti, Director of Admissions

Institute of Children's Literature
93 Long Ridge Rd., West Redding   06896-0811
Judith Brunstad, Dir. of Admis.
800-243-9645

Long Ridge Writers Group
West Redding   06896-0801
Fran Saunders, Dir. of Admis.
800-624-1476

Westlawn School of Yacht Design
733 Summer St., Stamford   06901

DELAWARE

USA Training Academy
17 Haines St., Newark   19711

DISTRICT OF COLUMBIA

McGraw-Hill Continuing Education Center
4401 Connecticut Ave., N.W., Washington   20008

FLORIDA

Southeastern Academy
P.O. Box 421768, Kissimmee   34742

Southern Career Institute
P.O. Box 2158, Boca Raton   33427

: Stenotype Institute of Jacksonville
500 9th Ave., N.
Jacksonville Beach   32250

GEORGIA

: Alliance Tractor Trailer Training Center
P.O. Box 1008, Mc Donough   30253

ILLINOIS

American Medical Record Association
919 N. Michigan Ave. #1400, Chicago   60611
Margret Amatayakul, Director

AMERICAN SCHOOL
850 E. 58th St., Chicago   60637
William H. Hunding, President
312-947-3300
   Established 1897. Accreditation: North Central Association of Colleges and Schools and the National Home Study Council. Complete high school course by correspondence study. Diploma awarded. More than 80 high school subjects. Also, make up credits, acceleration, and summer school program for resident high schools by independent study. Reasonable fees.

Governors State University
1 University Pky., University Park   60466
Richard Pride, Dir. of Admis.

Napoleon Hill Foundation
1440 Paddock Dr., Northbrook   60062

National Safety Council, Safety Trng. Inst.
1121 Spring Lake Dr #558, Itasca   60143

LOUISIANA

Grantham College of Engineering
34641 Grantham College Dr.
Slidell   70460
Donald J. Grantham, President
800-955-2527

Insurance Achievement
7330 Highland Rd., Baton Rouge   70808

MARYLAND

Emergency Management Institute
16825 S. Seton Ave., Emmitsburg   21727

HOME STUDY INTERNATIONAL
Home Study High School & Griggs University
12501 Old Columbia Pike, Silver Spring   20904
P.O. Box 4437, Silver Spring   20904-4437 (mailing)
Dr. Joseph Gurubatham, President
Dr. Alayne Thorpe, VP for Education
Mrs. Dorothy Bascom, Registrar
301-680-6570 or 800-782-GROW(4769)
FAX 301-680-6577
   Established 1909. Private. Coed. An academic correspondence school offering pre-school, kindergarten, elementary, secondary and college level courses and three degree programs. Home Study International is one of two correspondence schools in the United States offering elementary courses accredited by the Accrediting Commission of the National Home Study

Council. HSI also offers NHSC accredited and state approved high school diploma programs. NHSC accredited college course are available, as well as degree correspondence programs (AA in Personal Ministries, BA in Religion and BA in Theological Studies) through the collegiate division, Griggs University. Home Study International is affiliated with Columbia Union College, which is accredited by the Middle States Association of Colleges and Schools.

MICHIGAN

EDUCATIONAL INSTITUTE OF THE AMERICAN HOTEL & MOTEL ASSOCIATION
P.O. Box 1240, East Lansing   48826
E. Ray Swan, President
Phone: 800-344-3320 or 517-353-5500; Fax: 517-353-5527
   Established 1952. Accreditation: Accrediting Commission of the Distance Education and Training Council, Michigan Department of Education. A non-profit educational foundation of the American Hotel & Motel Association. Offers 30 comprehensive courses covering every area of a hotel/motel and restaurant operation; 5-course Areas of Specialization to prepare students for departmental management; the 8-course Hospitality Operations Certificate offering operational expertise; and a 12-course Hospitality Management Diploma program that gives students the knowledge needed for upper-level management. Certificates from the AH&MA are awarded upon successful completion of each course/program.

Heathkit Educational Systems, Benton Harbor   49022
Douglas M. Bonham, Director
800-44-HEATH (free catalog)
Electronic fundamentals, microprocessors, computer programming

MINNESOTA

Art Instruction Schools
500 S. 4th St., Minneapolis   55415
J. C. Buckbee, Jr., President

MISSOURI

Berean College
1445 Boonville Ave., Springfield   65802

Diamond Council of America
9140 Ward Pkwy., Kansas City   64114

Farmland Industries, Inc.
P.O. Box 7305, Kansas City   64116
Grant Riles, Coordinator

TRANS WORLD TRAVEL ACADEMY
Owned and operated by TWA, Inc.
11495 Natural Bridge Rd. #214, St. Louis   63044
314-895-6754 or 1-800-942-7467
   Campuses: St. Louis, Los Angeles, Kansas City, and Chicago. TWTA offers computerized business sales training for persons interested in careers as a travel agent, corporate travel planner, ticketing agent, or reservations agent. TWA job interviews for all residency program graduates. Zero % financing plan available to those qualified. Home study program available for persons who need/prefer to study at home. Home study is followed by a 2 week residency course at a TWTA campus. Free TWA transportation to/from training and reduced rate housing for all students. Customized and contract training is available to travel industry employees and employers. Accredited member of the National Home Study Council. TWTA also has a flight attendant career home study/residency program and specialty training for aircraft maintenance.

MONTANA

College of Great Falls
1301 20th St., S., Great Falls   59405
Jean Walker, Dir. of Admis.

NEVADA

Columbia School of Broadcasting
2840 E. Flamingo Rd. #F, Las Vegas   89121
Marcia Brock-Gandy, President

NEW YORK

American Institute of Music
P.O. Box 1706, Niagara Falls   14302

National Tax Training School
P.O. Box 382, Monsey   10952

On-Line Campus
New York Institute of Technology
P.O. Box 8000, Old Westbury   11568-8000
800-222-NYIT

REGENTS COLLEGE OF THE UNIVERSITY OF THE STATE OF NEW YORK
7 Columbia Circle, Albany 12203-5159
518-464-8500

OHIO

· Cleveland Institute of Electronics
1776 E. 17th St., Cleveland 44114
800-243-6446

: Hospitality Training Center
220 N. Main St., Hudson 44236

NHAW Home Study Institute
North American Heating & Airconditioning
Wholesalers Association
P.O. Box 16790, Columbus 43216

OKLAHOMA

Oral Roberts University
7777 S. Lewis Ave., Tulsa 74171
Arthur E. Matzkvech, Dir. of Admis.

PENNSYLVANIA

ICS Center for Degree Studies
Oak & Pawnee Sts., Scranton 18508
James M. Lytle, Vice President, Education

Learning and Evaluation Center
P.O. Box 616, Bloomsburg 17815

National Education Center-International
Correspondence Schools
925 Oak St., Scranton 18508

SOUTH CAROLINA

University of South Carolina, Columbia 29208
Susan Bridwell, Distance Education
803-777-7210

TENNESSEE

SEMINARY EXT. INDEPENDENT STUDY INST.
901 Commerce St. #500, Nashville 37203-3631
615-242-2453

VERMONT

NORWICH UNIVERSITY VERMONT COLLEGE CAMPUS
Montpelier 05602
Roger Cranse, Head
See listing under "Universities"

VIRGINIA

CATHOLIC HOME STUDY INSTITUTE
9 Loudoun St., S.E., Leesburg 22075-3012
800-258-2474

INTERIOR DESIGN

This classification contains schools accredited by the Foundation for Interior Design Education Research (†) and a selection of programs from institutionally accredited schools.

ALABAMA

† Auburn University, Auburn 36849

Samford University
800 Lakeshore Dr., Birmingham 35229
Lowell Vann, Chrpsn.

† University of Alabama
P.O. Box 870132, Tuscaloosa 35487-0132
Roy Smith, Dir. of Admis.

ARIZONA

† Arizona State University, Tempe 85287

Northern Arizona University
P.O. Box 4092, Flagstaff 86011
Dr. Margaret Cibik, Dir. of Admis.

· Phoenix College
1202 W. Thomas Rd., Phoenix 85013
Martha Cary, Dir. of Admis.

ARKANSAS

† University of Arkansas at Fayetteville
Fayetteville 72701

CALIFORNIA

† Academy of Art College
79 New Montgomery St., San Francisco 94105

AMERICAN COLLEGE FOR THE APPLIED ARTS
1651 Westwood Blvd., Los Angeles 90024
310-470-2000
See listing under "Universities"

Art Center College of Design
1700 Lida St., Pasadena 91103
Kit Baron, V.P., Student Services
818-396-2373

· Brooks College
4825 E. Pacific Coast Hwy., Long Beach 90804
Chelena Adkins, Dir. of Admis.
800-421-3775

† California College of Arts & Crafts
5212 Broadway, Oakland 94618
Sheri McKenzie, Dir. of Admis.
510-653-6522

† California Polytechnic State University
San Luis Obispo 93407
Helen Linstrum, Dir. of Admis.

† California State University, Fresno
Shaw & Cedar Ave., Fresno 93710

† California State University, Long Beach
1250 Bellflower Blvd., Long Beach 90840

† California State University, Sacramento
6000 J St., Sacramento 95819

Chapman University
333 N. Glassell St., Orange 92666
Michael Drummy, Dir. of Admis.

College of Notre Dame
1500 Ralston Ave., Belmont 94002
Greg M. Smith, PhD., Dir. of Admis.

† Design Institute of San Diego
8555 Commerce Ave., San Diego 92121
MaryJo Kalamon, Director

· † **FASHION INSTITUTE OF DESIGN & MERCHANDISING**
919 S. Grand Ave., Los Angeles 90015
213-624-1201 or 800-421-0127 outside California
See listing under "Community and Junior Colleges"

· Fashion Institute of Design & Merchandising
55 Stockton St., San Francisco 94108
415-433-6691 or 800-422-3436
See listing under "Community and Junior Colleges"

· † Interior Designers Institute
1061 Camelback St., Newport Beach 92660

OTIS COLLEGE OF ART AND DESIGN
2401 Wilshire Blvd., Los Angeles 90057
Neil Hoffman, President
See listing under "Art"

† San Diego State University
5300 Campanile Dr., San Diego 92115

San Jose State University
1 Washington Sq., San Jose 95192

† University of California, Los Angeles
1247 Murphy Hall, Los Angeles 90024

University of San Francisco
2130 Fulton St., San Francisco 94117
Bill Henley, Dir. of Admis.

· † West Valley College
14000 Fruitvale Ave., Saratoga 95070

† Woodbury University
7500 Glenoaks Blvd., Burbank 91504
See listing under "Universities"

COLORADO

· Colorado Institute of Art
200 E. 9th Ave., Denver 80203
Barbara Browning, Dir. of Admis.
800-275-2420
See listing under "Career Schools"

† Colorado State University
102 Administration Building, Fort Collins 80523
Mary Ontireros, Dir. of Admissions

ROCKY MOUNTAIN COLLEGE OF ART & DESIGN
6875 E. Evans Ave., Denver 80224
303-753-6046 or 800-888-2787
See listing under "Art"

· Technical Trades Institute
2315 E. Pikes Peak Ave., Colorado Springs 80909
719-632-7626

CONNECTICUT

Teikyo Post University
800 Country Club Rd.
P.O. Box 2540, Waterbury 06723-2540
800-345-2562 or 203-596-4520
See listing under "Universities"

University of Bridgeport
126 Park Ave., Bridgeport 06601
Andrew G. Nelson, Dean Admis./Financial Aid
203-576-4552
See listing under "Universities"

University of New Haven
300 Orange Ave., West Haven 06516
Joseph Chepaitis, Dean
203-932-7000

DISTRICT OF COLUMBIA

† Mt. Vernon College
2100 Foxhall Rd., N.W., Washington 20007
202-625-4682 or 800-682-4636, FAX: 202-338-1089

FLORIDA

· Art Institute of Fort Lauderdale
1799 S.E. 17th St., Ft. Lauderdale 33316
Eileen Northrop, V.P./Dir. of Admis.

† Florida State University
600 W. College Ave., Tallahassee 32306

· † International Academy of Merchandising and Design
211 S. Hoover Blvd., Tampa 33609
Mike Santoro, President
813-286-8585

· **INTERNATIONAL FINE ARTS COLLEGE**
1737 N. Bayshore Dr., Miami 33132
Sir Edward Porter, President
Frayda Parnes, Dir. of Admis.
800-225-9023 or 305-373-4684
Established 1965. Independent. Accreditation: SACS. Tuition: $8,630. Apartment: $2,640. Enrollment: 650 day. Library: 13,450 volumes. Faculty: 31. Degree: AA. Study-travel tours to Europe. Frequent field trips throughout south Florida. Residences are waterfront, luxurious apartment buildings, exquisitely furnished. Houseparents, swimming pools, recreation rooms, laundry room, storage facilities. Majors: fashion merchandising, interior design, commercial art, fashion design, computer graphics.

LYNN UNIVERSITY
(Est. 1962 as College of Boca Raton)
3601 N. Military Trail, Boca Raton 33431
407-994-0770 or 800-544-8035
See listing under "Universities"

· National Education Center-Bauder Campus
4801 N. Dixie Hwy., Ft. Lauderdale 33334
Brian Woods, Dir. of Admis.
305-491-7171

† Ringling School of Art & Design
2700 N. Tamiami Trl., Sarasota 34234
Dr. Arland Christ-Janer, President

· † Seminole Community College
100 Weldon Blvd., Sanford 32773

† University of Florida
226 Tigert Hall, Gainesville 32611

GEORGIA

AMERICAN COLLEGE FOR THE APPLIED ARTS
3330 Peachtree Rd., N.E., Atlanta 30326
404-231-9000
See listing under "Universities".

· Art Institute of Atlanta
3376 Peachtree Rd., N.E., Atlanta 30326
J. Robert Bouchard, Dir. of Admis.

Atlanta College of Art
Woodruff Arts Center
1280 Peachtree St., N.E., Atlanta 30309
John Farkas, Dir. of Enrollment Management

SAVANNAH COLLEGE OF ART & DESIGN
342 Bull St., Savannah 31401
May Poetter, VP of Admissions
See listing under "Art"

† University of Georgia, Athens 30602
John A. Huff, Coordinator

HAWAII

Chaminade University of Honolulu
3140 Waialae Ave., Honolulu 96816
Charles Schafer, VP Enrollment Services

IDAHO

· † Ricks College, Rexburg 83460
Steven Bennion, President

University of Idaho, Moscow 83843
Peter Brown, Dir. of Admis.

ILLINOIS

Columbia College
600 S. Michigan Ave., Chicago 60605
Debra McGrath, Dir. of Admis.

† **HARRINGTON INSTITUTE OF INTERIOR DESIGN**
410 S. Michigan Ave., Chicago 60605
Robert Marks, Dean
AAS, BA Degrees
312-939-4975

International Academy of Merchandising & Design
1 N. State St. Suite 400, Chicago 60602
Cynthia A. Reynolds, President
312-828-0422

Loyola University - Mundelein College
6363 N. Sheridan Rd., Chicago 60660
Judith Bobber, Dir. of Admis.

RAY COLLEGE OF DESIGN
AAS, BA, BFA degrees
401 N. Wabash Ave., Chicago 60611
312-280-3500
Woodfield Campus
1051 Perimeter Dr., Schaumburg 60173
708-619-3450

Ray College of Design
1051 Perimeter Dr., Schaumburg 60173

ROOSEVELT UNIVERSITY
430 S. Michigan Ave., Chicago 60605
William Smyser, Director of Admissions
See listing under "Universities"

School of the Art Institute of Chicago
37 S. Wabash, Chicago 60603
Ellen B. Cropp, Dir. of Admis.

† Southern Illinois University at Carbondale
Carbondale 62901

University of Illinois
506 S. Wright St., Urbana 61801

INDIANA

Ball State University
2000 W. University Ave., Muncie 47306
Ruth Vedvik, Dir. of Admis.

Indiana State University
217 N. 6th St., Terre Haute 47809

† Indiana University at Bloomington
300 N. Jordan Ave., Bloomington 47406

Purdue University
Schleman Hall, West Lafayette 47907

IOWA

Drake University
2507 E. University Ave., Des Moines 50311
Thomas Willoughby, Dir. of Admis.

Hawkeye Community College
1501 E. Orange Rd., Waterloo 50701
319-296-2320 Ext. 4000

† Iowa State University, Ames 50011
Karsten Smedal, Dir. of Admis.

William Penn College
201 Trueblood Ave., Oskaloosa 52577
Eric Otto, Dir. of Admis.

KANSAS

† Kansas State University
Anderson Hall 110, Manhattan 66506
Ellsworth M. Gerritz, Admis. & Records

McPherson College
1600 E. Euclid St., McPherson 67460

KENTUCKY

Louisville Technical Institute
3901 Atkinson Dr., Louisville 40218
George Nunley, Dir. of Admis.

Morehead State University, Morehead 40351
Charles Myers, Director of Admissions
606-783-2000

Murray State University, Murray 42071
Phil Bryan, Director of Admissions
800-272-4MSU

† University of Kentucky, Lexington 40506

LOUISIANA

† Louisiana State University and A & M College
Baton Rouge 70803

† Lousiana Technical University
P.O. Box 3168, Ruston 71272

† University of Southwestern Louisiana
P.O. Box 40449, Lafayette 70504
318-231-6829

MARYLAND

Harford Community College
401 Thomas Run Rd., Bel Air 21015
Margaret Wylie, Coordinator

Maryland Institute College of Art
1300 W. Mt. Royal Ave., Baltimore 21217
Theresa Lynch Bedoya, Dean of Admissions

Montgomery College
51 Mannakee St., Rockville 20850
301-279-5142

University of Maryland, College Park 20742

MASSACHUSETTS

Atlantic Union College
P.O. Box 1000, South Lancaster 01561
Osa Canto, Registrar

BAY PATH COLLEGE
588 Longmeadow St., Longmeadow 01106
Paula DesRoberts, Dean of Admis.
413-567-0621 or 800-782-PATH
  Established: 1897. Private. Women. Accreditation:
NEASC, Legal programs ABA approved. Tuition:
$10,200. Room and board: $6,225. Enrollment: 600.

Faculty: 42. Student-faculty ratio: 14:1. Degrees: AA,
AS, BA, BS. Library: 38,000 volumes. 27 buildings on
30 acres. Secure, suburban campus near Springfield
and Hartford. 15 Associate degree programs in business, education, fashion/design, criminal justice,
paralegalism, hospitality/tourism, health, human
services, occupational therapy, psychology, liberal
arts. Baccalaureates in business, business/account-
ing, legal studies, psychology, psychology/criminal
justice, psychology/early childhood education. Extensive career services. 95-98% of students obtain
jobs after graduation. Transfer welcome.

Boston Architectural Center
320 Newbury St., Boston 02115
Ellen Driscoll, Admissions

Endicott College
376 Hale St., Beverly 01915
Elizabeth Macomber, Dir. of Admis.

: † New England School of Art & Design
28 Newbury St., Boston 02116
Anne Blevins, Dir. of Admis.

Pine Manor College
400 Heath St., Chestnut Hill 02167
Gillian Lloyd, Dir. of Admis.

Suffolk University
8 Ashburton Place, Boston 02108
Barbara K. Ericson, Assoc. Dean Enrollment &
Retention
617-573-8460

† University of Massachusetts, Amherst 01003
Arlene Wesley Cash, Dir. of Admis.

† Wentworth Institute of Technology
550 Huntington Ave., Boston 02115

MICHIGAN

Adrian College
110 S. Madison St., Adrian 49221
George Wolf, Dir. of Admis.
See listing under "Universities"

Baker College of Flint
1050 W. Bristol Rd., Flint 48507
Mark Heaton, Dir. of Admis.

Baker College of Muskegon
141 Hartford Ave., Muskegon 49442
Kathy Jacobson, Dir. of Admis.

Baker College of Owosso
1020 S. Washington St., Owosso 48867
Bruce A. Lundeen, Dir. of Admis.

Center for Creative Studies-College of Art & Design
201 E. Kirby St., Detroit 48202
Frank Couzens, Interim President
See listing under "Art"

† Eastern Michigan University, Ypsilanti 48197
E. A. Rhodes, Head
313-487-3060 or 800-GO-TO-EMU

† Kendall College of Art & Design
111 N. Division Ave., Grand Rapids 49503
Charles Deihl, President
800-676-2787

† Lawrence Technological University
21000 W. Ten Mile Rd., Southfield 48075
800-225-5588 ext. 3160

† Michigan State University, East Lansing 48824
Dr. Jane Stolper, Chrpsn.

University of Michigan-Ann Arbor
815 S. University Ave., Ann Arbor 48109

Western Michigan University, Kalamazoo 49008
Stanley Henderson, Dir. of Enrl. Mgt. & Admis.
616-387-2000

MINNESOTA

· † Alexandria Technical College
1601 Jefferson St., Alexandria 56308
Candace Johnson, Coordinator

· † Dakota County Technical College
1300 E. 145th St., Rosemount 55068

LOWTHIAN COLLEGE
825 2nd Ave. S., Minneapolis 55402
Petrena Lowthian, President
612-332-3361 or 800-777-3643
  Established 1964. Coed. Private. Accreditation:
ACICS. Associate of Applied Science degree programs: FASHION MERCHANDISING: Tuition $9,180,
FASHION DESIGN: Tuition $12,240, INTERIOR DE-
SIGN: Tuition 13,260. Curriculums prepare students
for positions in management, product promotion,
sales and consulting, clothing design and construction, and residential and commercial space planning
and design. College credit transfer.

† University of Minnesota, Twin Cities
Minneapolis 55455

MISSISSIPPI

Mississippi University for Women
P.O. Box W-1602, Columbus 39701
Teresa Thompson, Exec. Dir. of Enrollment

† University of Southern Mississippi
P.O. Box 5165, Hattiesburg 39406

MISSOURI

Central Missouri State University
Warrensburg 64093
Delores Hudson, Dir. of Admis.

† Maryville University of St. Louis
13550 Conway Rd., Saint Louis 63141
314-576-9300 or 800-MARYVLL

Park College, Parkville 64152
Dr. Edwin Rawn, Dean of Admis.

Southwest Missouri State University
901 S. National Ave., Springfield 65804
Dr. George Wise, Department Head
417-836-5136

† University of Missouri, Columbia
228 Jesse Hall, Columbia 65211

William Woods College
200 W. 12th St., Fulton 65251
Dr. Jahnae Barnett, VP of Admis.

NEBRASKA

† University of Nebraska at Lincoln
16 Administration Bldg., Lincoln 68588
John Beacon, Dir. of Admissions

NEW JERSEY

BERKELEY COLLEGE OF BUSINESS
100 W. Prospect St., Waldwick 07463
Kevin Luing, President
800-446-5400 ext. GQ1

: Plaza School of Technology
Bergen Mall, Paramus 07652
Mark Ricciardi, Director
201-843-0344

† Trenton State College
Hillwood Lakes CN 4700, Trenton 08650

NEW YORK

CAZENOVIA COLLEGE
Cazenovia 13035
Dr. James Parker, VP for Enrollment Management
See listing under "Universities"

† Cornell University
410 Thurston Ave., Ithaca 14853

Marymount College
100 Marymount Ave., Tarrytown 10591
Gina R. Campbell, Dir. of Admis.
800-724-4312

† New York Institute of Technology
Old Westbury Campus, Old Westbury 11568

† NEW YORK SCHOOL OF INTERIOR DESIGN
170 E. 70th St., New York 10021
June Soyka, Director of Admissions
800-336-9743
  Established 1916. Private. Coed. Accreditation: FI-
DER. Tuition: $10,560. Fees: $50. Enrollment: 122
full-time, 483 part-time. Faculty: 101. Student-faculty
ratio: 18:1. Degrees offered: AAS, BFA, Design Diploma (3 year degree). Library: 5,661 volumes. Located in NY's upper east side at the center of the
interior design center. Single major college dedicated
solely to interior design. Faculty consists of designers,
architects, decorators, and artists.

† Pratt Institute
200 Willoughby Ave., Brooklyn 11205

Rochester Institute of Technology
1 Lomb Memorial Dr., Rochester 14623
716-475-6631
See listing under "Universities"

† SUNY Fashion Institute of Technology
227 W. 27th St., New York 10001

† Syracuse University, Syracuse 13244

· Villa Maria College of Buffalo
240 Pine Ridge Rd., Buffalo 14225
Lynn D'Auria, Dir. of Admis.

NORTH CAROLINA

East Carolina University
1000 E. 5th St., Greenville 27858
Dr. Marjorie Inman, Chair

Salem College
P.O. Box 10548, Winston-Salem 27108
Katherine Knapp, Director of Admissions
800-32-SALEM
See listing under "Women's College"

NORTH DAKOTA

† North Dakota State University, Fargo 58105
Richard Shearer, Acting Dir. of Admis.

OHIO

Antonelli Institute of Art & Photography
124 E. 7th St., Cincinnati 45202

College of Mount St. Joseph
5701 Delhi Rd., Cincinnati 45233-1672
See listing under "Universities"

COLUMBUS COLLEGE OF ART & DESIGN
107 N. 9th St., Columbus 43215-1758
Thomas Green, Dir. of Admis.
614-224-9101
See listing under "Art"

DAVIS JUNIOR COLLEGE
4747 Monroe St., Toledo 43623
Diane Brunner, President
Timothy Brunner, Chairperson
  Established 1858. Private. Coed. Accreditation:
AICS, AAMA, NCACS. Tuition: $5,600. Fees: $25
application fee. Enrollment: 350 full-time, 100 part-
time. Faculty: 35. Student-faculty ratio: 15:1. Degree:

associate. Specialized library. 2 buildings including an airport. Admissions test (CPAT) & specialized. High school graduate of GED. Enroll each quarter. 90% placement overall. Unique professional pilot program.

† Kent State University
  P.O. Box 5190, Kent 44242
  Bruce Riddle, Dir. of Admis.

† Miami University
  E. High St., Oxford 45056

† Ohio State University
  190 N. Oval Mall, Columbus 43210

† University of Cincinnati
  2700 Clifton Ave., Cincinnati 45221

Ursuline College
  2550 Lander Rd., Cleveland 44124

OKLAHOMA

† Oklahoma State University, Stillwater 74078
  Donna Branson, Dept. Head

† University of Oklahoma at Norman
  660 Parrington Oval, Norman 73019

OREGON

Bassist College
  2000 S.W. 5th Ave., Portland 97201
  Donald Bassist, President

Marylhurst College for Lifelong Learning
  P.O. Box 261, Marylhurst 97036
  Kay Slusarenko, Chrpsn.
  800-634-9982

† University of Oregon
  1 University of Oregon, Eugene 97403

PENNSYLVANIA

: American Institute of Design
  1616 Orthodox St., Philadelphia 19124
  Dorothy Miller, Dir. of Admis.

· Antonelli Institute of Art & Photography
  P.O. Box 570, Plymouth Meeting 19462
  215-275-3040 or 800-722-7871

· The Art Institute of Philadelphia
  1622 Chestnut St., Philadelphia 19103
  215-567-7080

: Art Institute of Pittsburgh
  526 Penn Ave., Pittsburgh 15222
  Lee Colker, Dir. of Admis.
  800-275-2470
  See listing under "Art"

Beaver College
  450 S. Easton Rd., Glenside 19038-3295
  Dennis Nostrand, VP for Enrollment Management
  Phone: 800-776-BEAVER(2328)
  Fax: 215-572-4049
  See listing under "Universities"

· Bradley Academy for the Visual Arts
  625 E. Philadelphia St., York 17403
  Loren H. Kroh, Director
  717-848-1447

† Drexel University
  3141 Chestnut St., Philadelphia 19104
  Dean of Enrollment Management

· Harcum Junior College, Bryn Mawr 19010
  Mary Pontius, Dean of Admissions

† La Roche College
  9000 Babcock Blvd., Pittsburgh 15237
  Marianne Leister, Dir. of Admis.

Mercyhurst College
  501 E. 38th St., Erie 16546
  Andrew Roth, Dean of Enrollment
  800-825-1926

† Moore College of Art and Design
  1920 Race St., Philadelphia 19103
  Claire E. Gallicano, Dir. of Admis.

RHODE ISLAND

† Rhode Island School of Design
  2 College St., Providence 02903

SOUTH CAROLINA

Anderson College
  316 S. Boulevard, Anderson 29621
  Carl D. Lockman, Dir. of Admis.
  800-542-3594

† Converse College
  580 E. Main St., Spartanburg 29302
  Dr. Martha Rogers, VP Enrollment Management

† Winthrop University
  701 W. Oakland Ave., Rock Hill 29733
  James McCammon, Jr., Dir. of Admis.

SOUTH DAKOTA

South Dakota State University
  P.O. Box 2275A, Brookings 57007
  Gail Dobbs Tideman, Dean
  605-688-6181
  See listing under "Universities"

TENNESSEE

† O'MORE COLLEGE OF DESIGN
  P.O. Box 908, Franklin 37065
  Tom Campbell, Director of Admission
  615-794-4254
    Also degree programs in fashion, historic preservation, advertising and graphic design. Established 1970. Private. Coed. Accreditation: FIDER. Tuition: $6,900. Enrollment: 105 full-time, 40 part-time. Faculty: 40. Degrees: Bachelor of Design. Located in historic Franklin TN (15 miles from Nashville). Campus includes the beautiful Abbey Leix Mansion.

University of Memphis, Memphis 38152
  Dr. John Eubank, Dean of Admissions

University of Tennessee at Martin
  Martin 38238
  Paul Kelley, Director of Admissions
  See listing under "Universities"

† University of Tennessee, Knoxville
  527 Andy Holt Tower, Knoxville 37996
  Dr. Gordon Stanley, Dir. of Admis.

· † Watkins Institute School of Interior Design
  601 Church St., Nashville 37219
  Wanda Palus, Director
  615-242-1851

TEXAS

· Art Institute of Dallas
  8080 Park Ln., Dallas 75231
  Lee Colker, Dir. of Admis.

· The Art Institute of Houston
  1900 Yorktown St., Houston 77056
  Cherie R. McNeel, Dir. of Admis.
  800-275-4244

· Bauder Fashion College
  508 S. Center St., Arlington 76010
  Charm Kettle, Dir. of Admis.

Baylor University
  P.O. Box 97008, Waco 76798-7008
  Diana Ramey, Director of Admissions

· El Centro College
  801 Main St., Dallas 75202
  Queen Randall, President

Incarnate Word College
  4301 Broadway St., San Antonio 78209
  Sr. Sally Mitchell, Dean of Enrollment

· Miss Wade's Fashion Merchandising College
  Dallas Market Center, Suite M5120
  The International Apparel Mart
  P.O. Box 586343, Dallas 75258
  See listing under "Community and Junior Colleges"

† Southwest Texas State University
  601 University Dr., San Marcos 78666

† Stephen F. Austin State University
  P.O. Box 6078, Nacogdoches 75962

† Texas Christian University
  2800 S. University Dr., Ft. Worth 76129
  Dr. Edward Boehm, Jr., Dean of Admissions

· † Texas State Technical Institute, Amarillo Campus
  Box 11197, Amarillo 79111
  Dr. James Bird, Gen. Manager

† Texas Tech University, Lubbock 79409

† University of North Texas
  P.O. Box 13797, Denton 76203

† University of Texas at Arlington
  UTA Box 19125, Arlington 76019
  R. Zack Prince, Dir. of Admis.

† University of Texas at Austin
  0 the University of Texas, Austin 78712

UTAH

† Utah State University, Logan 84322-1600
  Rod Clark, Director of Admissions
  801-750-1107

VIRGINIA

† Marymount University
  2807 N. Glebe Rd., Arlington 22207
  Charles Coe, Director of Admissions
  800-548-7638 or 703-284-1500
  See listing under "Universities"

· Southern Virginia College for Women
  One College Hill Dr., Buena Vista 24416
  Mark A. Camper, Assoc. Dir. of Admis.
  800-229-8420
  See listing under "Women's Colleges"

† Virginia Commonwealth University
  910 W. Franklin St., Richmond 23284

† Virginia Polytechnic Institute & State University
  Blacksburg 24061
  David Bousquet, Dir. of Undergraduate Admis.

WASHINGTON

· Art Institute of Seattle
  2323 Elliott Ave., Seattle 98121
  Doug Worsley, Dir. of Admis.

Cornish College of the Arts
  710 E. Roy St., Seattle 98102
  Jane Buckman, Admissions
  800-726-ARTS

· Spokane Falls Community College
  3410 W. Fort George Wright Dr., Spokane 99204
  Sharon Wilkins, Chrpsn.

† Washington State University, Pullman 99164
  Stan Berry, Dir. of Admis.

WEST VIRGINIA

The University of Charleston
  2300 MacCorkle Ave., S.E., Charleston 25304
  800-995-GO UC

WISCONSIN

Milwaukee Institute of Art & Design
  273 E. Erie St., Milwaukee 53202
  Holly Grey, Dir. of Admis.

† Mt. Mary College
  2900 N. Menomonee River Pky.
  Milwaukee 53222

† University of Wisconsin, Madison
  500 Lincoln Dr., Madison 53706

: Western Wisconsin Technical College
  304 N. 6th St., La Crosse 54602

LANDSCAPE ARCHITECTURE

This classification contains schools accredited by the American Society of Landscape Architects (†) and a selection of programs from institutionally accredited schools.

ALABAMA

† Auburn University, Auburn 36849

ARIZONA

† University of Arizona, Tucson 85721
  Loyd Bell, Director of Admissions

ARKANSAS

† University of Arkansas at Fayetteville
  Fayetteville 72701

CALIFORNIA

† California Polytechnic State University
  San Luis Obispo 93407
  Helen Linstrum, Dir. of Admis.

† California State Polytechnic University
  3801 W. Temple Ave., Pomona 91768

† University of California at Berkeley
  Wurster Hall, Berkeley 94720

† University of California, Davis
  376 Mrak Hall, Davis 95616

COLORADO

† Colorado State University
  102 Administration Building, Fort Collins 80523
  Mary Ontireros, Dir. of Admissions

† University of Colorado at Denver
  1200 Larimer St., Denver 80204

CONNECTICUT

· Mattatuck Community College
  750 Chase Parkway, Waterbury 06708
  Dr. Richard Sanders, President

FLORIDA

† University of Florida
  226 Tigert Hall, Gainesville 32611

GEORGIA

† University of Georgia, Athens 30602
  Dr. Darrel Morrison, Dean

HAWAII

University of Hawaii at Hilo
  523 W. Lanikaula, Hilo 96720

IDAHO

† University of Idaho, Moscow 83843
  Peter Brown, Dir. of Admis.

ILLINOIS

† University of Illinois
506 S. Wright St., Urbana 61801

INDIANA

† Ball State University
2000 W. University Ave., Muncie 47306
Ruth Vedvik, Dir. of Admis.

† Purdue University
Schleman Hall, West Lafayette 47907

IOWA

· Hawkeye Community College
1501 E. Orange Rd., Waterloo 50701
319-296-2320 Ext. 4000

† Iowa State University, Ames 50011
Karsten Smedal, Dir. of Admis.

KANSAS

† Kansas State University
Anderson Hall 110, Manhattan 66506
Ellsworth M. Gerritz, Admis. & Records

KENTUCKY

† University of Kentucky, Lexington 40506

LOUISIANA

† Louisiana State University and A & M College
Baton Rouge 70803

MAINE

College of the Atlantic
105 Eden St., Bar Harbor 04609
Steve Thomas, Dir. of Admis.

MARYLAND

· Montgomery College
20200 Observation Dr., Germantown 20876
301-353-7898

MASSACHUSETTS

† Harvard University
Graduate School of Design
Gund Hall, Cambridge 02138

SPRINGFIELD TECHNICAL COMMUNITY COLLEGE
1 Armory Square, Springfield 01105
Dr. Patrick E. Tigue, Dir. of Admissions
413-781-7822

† University of Massachusetts, Amherst 01003
Arlene Wesley Cash, Dir. of Admis.

MICHIGAN

† Michigan State University, East Lansing 48824
Anthony Bauer, Associate Director

† University of Michigan-Ann Arbor
815 S. University Ave., Ann Arbor 48109

MINNESOTA

† University of Minnesota, Twin Cities
Minneapolis 55455

MISSISSIPPI

† Mississippi State University
P.O. Box J, Mississippi State University 39762

NEW JERSEY

· Mercer County Community College
West Windsor Campus
1200 Old Trenton Rd., Trenton 08690
Michael Glass, Dir. of Admis.
See listing under "Community and Junior Colleges"

NEW YORK

† Cornell University
410 Thurston Ave., Ithaca 14853

† CUNY City College
Convent Ave. at 138th St., New York 10031

· Paul Smith's College, Paul Smiths 12970
Enrico Miller, Dir. of Admis.
800-421-2605

† SUNY College of Environmental Science & Forestry
1 Forestry Dr., Syracuse 13210
800-7777-ESF or 315-470-6600

NORTH CAROLINA

† North Carolina State University
P.O. Box 7001, Raleigh 27695
George Dixon, Dir. of Admis.

NORTH DAKOTA

† North Dakota State University, Fargo 58105
Richard Shearer, Acting Dir. of Admis.

OHIO

† Ohio State University
190 N. Oval Mall, Columbus 43210

· Ohio State University-Agricultural Technical Institute
1328 Dover Rd., Wooster 44691

OKLAHOMA

† Oklahoma State University, Stillwater 74078
Dale Maronek, Dept. Head

OREGON

† University of Oregon
1 University of Oregon, Eugene 97403

PENNSYLVANIA

Delaware Valley College of Science & Agriculture
Doylestown 18901
Stephen Zenko, Dir. of Admis.

† Pennsylvania State University
201 Shields Bldg., University Park 16802

† Temple University, Ambler Campus Center
Ambler 19002

† University of Pennsylvania
0 Levy Park, Philadelphia 19104

RHODE ISLAND

† Rhode Island School of Design
2 College St., Providence 02903

† University of Rhode Island, Kingston 02881
David Taggart, Dean of Admissions/Financial Aid

SOUTH DAKOTA

South Dakota State University
P.O. Box 2207, Brookings 57007
Dr. David Bryant, Dean
605-688-4148
See listing under "Universities"

TEXAS

† Texas A & M University
College Station 77843

† Texas Tech University, Lubbock 79409

University of Texas at Arlington
UTA Box 19125, Arlington 76019
R. Zack Prince, Dir. of Admis.

UTAH

† Utah State University, Logan 84322-1600
Rod Clark, Director of Admissions
801-750-1107

VIRGINIA

† University of Virginia
P.O. Box 9017, Charlottesville 22906

† Virginia Polytechnic Institute & State University
Blacksburg 24061
David Bousquet, Dir. of Undergraduate Admis.

WASHINGTON

† University of Washington, Seattle 98195

† Washington State University, Pullman 99164
Stan Berry, Dir. of Admis.

WEST VIRGINIA

† West Virginia University
P.O. Box 6001, Morgantown 26506

WISCONSIN

† University of Wisconsin, Madison
500 Lincoln Dr., Madison 53706

LAW

This classification contains schools offering a first professional degree accredited by the Association of American Law Schools (†) and a selection of programs from institutionally accredited schools. Colleges and Universities (no dot code) generally offer four-year or advanced programs in law or pre-law; Community and Junior Colleges (·) generally offer associate degrees in pre-law, legal assistant/paralegal, and legal secretary; Career Schools (:) generally offer a diploma as a legal assistant/paralegal or legal secretary.

ALABAMA

· Gadsden State Community College
Preprofessional Program
1001 George Wallace Dr., Gadsden 35999

† Samford University
800 Lakeshore Dr., Birmingham 35229
Parham Williams, Dean

† University of Alabama
P.O. Box 870132, Tuscaloosa 35487-0132
Roy Smith, Dir. of Admis.

ALASKA

· Alaska Junior College
800 E. Dimond Blvd. # 3-350
Anchorage 99515

ARIZONA

· Academy of Business College
3320 W. Cheryl Dr. #115, Phoenix 85051
See listing under "Community and Junior Colleges"

: American Institute
3443 N. Central Ave. #1800, Phoenix 85012

† Arizona State University, Tempe 85287

† University of Arizona, Tucson 85721
E. Thomas Sullivan, Dean

ARKANSAS

Arkansas College
2300 Highland Rd., Batesville 72501
Jonathan M. Stroud, Dean of Admissions
800-423-2542

† University of Arkansas at Fayetteville
Fayetteville 72701

† University of Arkansas at Little Rock
2801 S. University Ave., Little Rock 72204

Williams Baptist College
P.O. Box 3667, Walnut Ridge 72476
Scott Wright, Dir. of Admis.

CALIFORNIA

† California Western School of Law
350 Cedar St., San Diego 92101

: EMPIRE COLLEGE
SCHOOL OF BUSINESS & LAW
3033 Cleveland Ave. # 107, Santa Rosa 95403
707-546-4000
Established 1961. Private. Coed. Accreditation: ACICS/Committee of Bar Examiners. Tuition: $3,720 - $7,290. Fees: $75 - $95. Enrollment: 700 full-time, 25 part-time. Faculty: 50. Student-faculty ratio: 21:1. Specialized Associate degree offered in Accounting and Administrative Assistant; Juris Doctor. 1 21,000 sq. ft. building. Positive, supportive environment for students in the business school with start dates every six weeks; evening law classes taught by practicing attornies.

Fresno Pacific College
1717 S. Chestnut Ave., Fresno 93702
209-453-2039

† Golden Gate University
536 Mission St., San Francisco 94105

John F. Kennedy University
12 Altarinda Rd., Orinda 94563

† Loyola Marymount University
P.O. Box 15019, Los Angeles 90015
Arthur Frakt, Dean

National University
3580 Aero Ct., San Diego 92123
Dr. Howard Ovenstein, Dean

† Pepperdine University
24255 Pacific Coast Hwy., Malibu 90263
Jill Baradarson, Director of Admissions
310-456-4611

San Joaquin College of Law
3385 E. Shields Ave., Fresno 93726
Jacqueline Chavanu, Dir. of Admis.
209-225-4953

† Santa Clara University, Santa Clara 95053

† Southwestern University School of Law
675 S. Westmoreland, Los Angeles 90005
Leigh Taylor, Dean

† Stanford University, Stanford 94305

† University of California, Los Angeles
1247 Murphy Hall, Los Angeles 90024

† University of California at Berkeley
Boalt Hall, Berkeley 94720

† University of California, Davis
376 Mrak Hall, Davis 95616

† University of California, Hastings College of Law
198 McAllister St., San Francisco 94102

University of La Verne
1950 3rd St., La Verne 91750
Mark Bornholdt, Dir. of Admis.

† University of San Diego
5998 Alcala Park, San Diego 92110
Carl Eging, Dir. Law School Admissions
619-260-4528

† University of San Francisco
2130 Fulton St., San Francisco 94117
Ken Lloyd, Asst. Dean, School of Law

† University of Southern California
University Park Campus
Los Angeles 90089

† University of the Pacific
McGeorge School of Law
3200 5th Ave., Sacramento 95817
Admissions 916-739-7105

University of West Los Angeles, School of Law
1155 W. Arbor Vitae St., Inglewood 90301
Kathi Cervi, Dir. of Admis.

Western State University College of Law
1111 N. State College Blvd., Fullerton 92631
John Monks, President

Western State University College of Law
16485 Laguna Canyon Rd., Irvine 92718
John Monks, President

Western State University College of Law of San Diego
2121 San Diego Ave., San Diego 92110
John Monks, President

† Whittier College, School of Law
5353 W. Third St., Los Angeles 90020
John Fitz Randolph, Dean
213-938-3621

COLORADO

Mesa State College
P.O. Box 2647, Grand Junction 81502
Sherri Pe'a, Dir. of Admis.

: Mile Hi College
6464 W. 14th Ave., Denver 80214
David Phillips, Dir. of Admis.

† University of Colorado at Boulder
Boulder 80309
William A. Douglas, Dean of Admis.

† University of Denver
2199 S. University Blvd., Denver 80210

CONNECTICUT

QUINNIPIAC COLLEGE
275 Mount Carmel Ave., Hamden 06518
See listing under "Universities"

† University of Connecticut, Storrs 06268
John Vlandis, Dir. of Admis.

† Yale University
401A Yale Station, New Haven 06520

DELAWARE

† Widener University School of Law
P.O. Box 7474, Wilmington 19803

DISTRICT OF COLUMBIA

† The American University
4400 Massachusetts Ave. N.W.
Washington 20016

† Catholic University of America
620 Michigan Ave. N.E., Washington 20064
Robert J. Talbot, Dir. of Admis. & Fin. Aid.

DISTRICT OF COLUMBIA SCHOOL OF LAW
719 13th St., N.W., Washington 20005
Vivian Canty, Dir. of Admis.
202-727-5232

† Georgetown University
37th and O Sts., N.W., Washington 20057
Dr. Joseph A. Chalmers, Dean of Admis. & Rec.

† George Washington University
Washington 20052

† Howard University
2400 6th St., N.W., Washington 20059
James E. Cheek, President

FLORIDA

Clearwater Christian College
3400 Gulf-to-Bay Blvd., Clearwater 34619
Benjamin Puckett, Dir. of Admis.

Flagler College
P.O. Box 1027, St. Augustine 32085
Marc G. Williar, Dir. of Admis.
904-829-6481

† Florida State University
600 W. College Ave., Tallahassee 32306

† Nova Southeastern University
3301 College Ave., Ft. Lauderdale 33314

St. Thomas University
16400 N.W. 32nd Ave., Miami 33054
Veronica McKendry, Asst. Dean of Admissions

**SCHILLER INTERNATIONAL UNIVERSITY
(FLORIDA & EUROPE)**
U.S. Admissions Office
Dept. PA, 453 Edgewater Dr., Dunedin 34698-7532
800-336-4133 Fax: 813-736-6263
Dr. Walter Liebrecht, President
Karen Altieri, Associate Director of Admissions
See listing under "Universities"

† Stetson University
1401 61st St., S., St. Petersburg 33707
Dr. Bruce Jacob, Dean

† University of Florida
226 Tigert Hall, Gainesville 32611

† University of Miami
P.O. Box 248006, Coral Gables 33124

GEORGIA

† Emory University
1462 Clifton Rd., Atlanta 30322

Georgia College
231 W. Hancock St., Milledgeville 31061
912-453-5004

Georgia State University
University Plaza, Atlanta 30303
Ernest Beals, Dean of Admissions

† Mercer University, Walter F. George School of Law
1400 Coleman Ave., Macon 31207

† University of Georgia, Athens 30602
Dr. J. Ralph Beaird, Dean

HAWAII

† University of Hawaii at Manoa
2500 Campus Rd., Honolulu 96822

IDAHO

† University of Idaho, Moscow 83843
Peter Brown, Dir. of Admis.

ILLINOIS

† De Paul University
1 E. Jackson Blvd., Chicago 60604
Dennis Shea, Director of Admissions
See listing under "Universities"

**FOX COLLEGE OF EXECUTIVE/LEGAL
ASSISTANTS**
4201 W. 93rd St., Oak Lawn 60453
Edward L. Kay, Director
See listing under "Career Schools"

† Illinois Institute of Technology
Chicago-Kent College of Law
77 S. Wacker Dr., Chicago 60606
Lewis M. Collens, Dean

† John Marshall Law School
315 S. Plymouth Ct., Chicago 60604
Howard T. Markey, Dean

Loyola University-Mallinckrodt Campus
1041 Ridge Rd., Wilmette 60091
Karen Sullivan, Admissions

† Loyola University of Chicago
820 N. Michigan Ave., Chicago 60611
Allen V. Lentino, Dir. of Admis.

† Northern Illinois University, De Kalb 60115

North Park College & Theological Seminary
3225 W. Foster, Chicago 60625
312-509-2330

† Northwestern University
303 E. Chicago Ave., Chicago 60611

Rockford College
5050 E. State St., Rockford 61108
Miriam King, V.P. for Enrollment Management
See listing under "Universities"

† Southern Illinois University at Carbondale
Carbondale 62901

† University of Chicago
5801 S. Ellis Ave., Chicago 60637

† University of Illinois
506 S. Wright St., Urbana 61801

INDIANA

† Indiana University at Bloomington
300 N. Jordan Ave., Bloomington 47406

† Indiana University-Purdue University
355 N. Lansing, Indianapolis 46202

Indiana Wesleyan University
4201 S. Washington St., Marion 46953
800-332-6901

SAWYER COLLEGE
6040 Hohman Ave., Hammond 46320
Mary Jo Dixon, Director
800-964-0208

SAWYER COLLEGE
3803 E. Lincoln Hwy., Merrillville 46410
Mary Jo Dixon, Director
800-964-0218

Taylor University
500 W. Reade Ave., Upland 46989
Herb Frye, Dean of Enrollment Management

† University of Notre Dame, Notre Dame 46556
David T. Link, Dean

† Valparaiso University, Valparaiso 46383

IOWA

† Drake University
2507 E. University Ave., Des Moines 50311
David Walker, Dean

† University of Iowa, Iowa City 52242

KANSAS

† University of Kansas, Lawrence 66045

† Washburn University of Topeka
1700 S.W. College Ave., Topeka 66621
John E. Triggs, Dir. of Admissions

KENTUCKY

Kentucky Wesleyan College
Pre-Law program
3000 Frederica St., Owensboro 42301

† Northern Kentucky University
Louie B. Nunn Dr., Highland Heights 41076

Spalding University
851 S. 4th St., Louisville 40203
Dorothy G. Allen, Dir. of Admis.

† University of Kentucky, Lexington 40506

† University of Louisville
2301 S. 3rd St., Louisville 40292
Robert Parrent, Dir. of Admis.

LOUISIANA

† Louisiana State University and A & M College
Baton Rouge 70803

† Loyola University
6363 St. Charles Ave., New Orleans 70118

† Tulane University
School of Law
Joseph M. Jones Hall, New Orleans 70118

MAINE

† University of Maine, Orono 04469

University of Southern Maine
96 Falmouth St., Portland 04103
Donald Zillman, Dean

MARYLAND

· Montgomery College
Paralegal Studies
20200 Observation Dr., Germantown 20876
301-353-7731

· Montgomery College
7600 Takoma Ave., Takoma Park 20912
301-650-1453

† University of Baltimore
1420 N. Charles St., Baltimore 21201
Laurence Katz, Dean

† University of Maryland
Baltimore Professional Schools
522 W. Lombard St., Baltimore 21201

Villa Julie College
1525 Greenspring Valley Rd., Stevenson 21153
Carolyn Manuszak, President

MASSACHUSETTS

· **BAY PATH COLLEGE**
588 Longmeadow St., Longmeadow 01106
Paula DesRoberts, Dean of Admis.
413-567-0621 or 800-782-PATH
Established: 1897. Private. Women. Accreditation:
NEASC, Legal programs ABA approved. Tuition:
$10,200. Room and board: $6,225. Enrollment: 600.
Faculty: 42. Student-faculty ratio: 14:1. Degrees: AA,
AS, BA, BS. Library: 38,000 volumes. 27 buildings on
30 acres. Secure, suburban campus near Springfield
and Hartford. 15 Associate degree programs in business, education, fashion/design, criminal justice,
paralegalism, hospitality/tourism, health, human
services, occupational therapy, psychology, liberal
arts. Baccalaureates in business, business/account-
ing, legal studies, psychology, psychology/criminal
justice, psychology/early childhood education. Extensive career services. 95-98% of students obtain
jobs after graduation. Transfer welcome.

† Boston College, School of Law
885 Centre St., Newton 02159
Daniel Coquillette, JD, Dean

† Boston University
685 Commonwealth Ave., Boston 02215

ELMS COLLEGE
291 Springfield St., Chicopee 01013
800-255-ELMS

· Fisher College
118 Beacon St., Boston 02116
Sandra Robbins, Dir. of Admis.

† Harvard University
Harvard Law School
Pound Hall, Massachusetts Ave.
Cambridge 02138

New England School of Law
154 Stuart St., Boston 02116
Timothy J. Cronin, Dean

† Northeastern University
360 Huntington Ave., Boston 02115
David Hall, Dean

† Suffolk University
8 Ashburton Place, Boston 02108
John Deliso, Director of Admission
617-573-8144

University of Massachusetts
100 Morrissey Blvd., Boston 02125

† Western New England College
1215 Wilbraham Rd., Springfield 01119
800-325-1122

MICHIGAN

Albion College
611 E. Porter, Albion 49224
800-858-6770

† **DETROIT COLLEGE OF LAW**
130 E. Elizabeth St., Detroit 48201
313-226-0100 / 313-226-0169
David S. Favre, Interim Dean
Iris Wasielewski, Dir. of Admis.
Established 1891. Private. Accreditation: ABA,

AALS. Admission: bachelor's degree and Law School Admission Test (LSAT) score required. Day & evening classes admitted in August & January. Tuition: $12,000 full-time, $9,000 part-time. Financial aid: Stafford Loan, Michigan Tuition Grant (need based), Law Access Loan Program, Law Loans and a limited number of academic scholarships and awards. Special areas of concentration in Taxation and International Law. Summer programs in Montreal and Ottawa. Degree: Juris Doctor (JD). Enrollment: 756. Faculty: 29 full-time, 35 part-time. Library: 200,000 volumes. Urban, co-educational college located in central business district, across the river from Windsor, Ontario, Canada.

Thomas M. Cooley Law School
P.O. Box 13038, Lansing 48901
Stephanie Gregg, Dir. of Admis.
517-371-5140

† University of Detroit Mercy
651 E. Jefferson Ave., Detroit 48226
313-596-0264
See listing under "Universities"

† University of Michigan-Ann Arbor
815 S. University Ave., Ann Arbor 48109

† Wayne State University
5980 Cass Ave., Detroit 48202
Dr. J. R. Thorderson, Dir. of Admis.

MINNESOTA

† Hamline University
1536 Hewitt Ave., St. Paul 55104
Scott Pratt, Dir. of Admis.

† University of Minnesota, Twin Cities
Minneapolis 55455

† William Mitchell College of Law
875 Summit Ave., St. Paul 55105
James Hogg, President

MISSISSIPPI

† Mississippi College, School of Law
151 E. Griffith St., Jackson 39201
Alton H. Harvey, Dean

† University of Mississippi, University 38677

MISSOURI

† St. Louis University
221 N. Grand Blvd., St. Louis 63103
Louis A. Menard, Dean of Admissions

† University of Missouri, Columbia
228 Jesse Hall, Columbia 65211

† University of Missouri, Kansas City
5100 Rockhill Rd., Kansas City 64110
Leo J. Sweeney, Dir. of Admis. & Registrar

† Washington University
1 Brookings Dr., St. Louis 63130

MONTANA

· Missoula Vocational Technical Center
909 South Ave. W, Missoula 59801
Charles Couture, Dir. of Admis.

† University of Montana, Missoula 59812
800-462-8636

NEBRASKA

† Creighton University
2500 California St., Omaha 68178
Lawrence Raful, Dean

† University of Nebraska at Lincoln
Law 103, Lincoln 68583
Harvey Perlman, Dean

NEVADA

· Phillips Junior College
3320 E. Flamingo Rd. #30, Las Vegas 89121
Robert Ramey, Dir. of Admis.

NEW HAMPSHIRE

Franklin Pierce Law Center
2 White St., Concord 03301
Lisa Deane, Dir. of Admis.

Rivier College
Paralegal Program
420 S. Main St., Nashua 03060
Admissions: 800-44-RIVIER

NEW JERSEY

Jersey City State College
2039 Kennedy Blvd., Jersey City 07305
201-200-3234

Rowan College of New Jersey, Glassboro 08028
Marvin G. Sills, Dir. of Admis.

† Seton Hall University, School of Law
1095 Raymond Blvd., Newark 07102
Rev. Daniel Degnan, Assoc. Dean

Stockton State College, Pomona 08240
Sal Catalfamo, Dir. of Admis.

NEW MEXICO

† University of New Mexico, Albuquerque 87131
Robert Weaver, Dean of Admissions

NEW YORK

† Albany Law School of Union University
80 New Scotland Ave., Albany 12208
Martin H. Belsky, Dean

† Brooklyn Law School
250 Joralemon St., Brooklyn 11201
David Trager, Dean

Canisius College
2001 Main St., Buffalo 14208
Penelope Lips, Dir. of Admis.
800-843-1517

† Columbia University
612 W. 115th St., New York 10025

† Cornell University
410 Thurston Ave., Ithaca 14853

CUNY, Queens College
6530 Kissena Blvd., Flushing 11367

† Fordham University
Lincoln Center Campus
113 W. 60th St., New York 10023
Edward Bristow, Dean

† Hofstra University
1000 Fulton Ave., Hempstead 11550

† New York Law School
57 Worth St., New York 10013
E. Donald Shapiro, Dean

† New York University
70 Washington Sq., New York 10012

† Pace University, White Plains Campus
78 N. Broadway, White Plains 10603

Roberts Wesleyan College
2301 Westside Dr., Rochester 14624
Scott Caton, Chrpsn.
Ron Hallman, Chrpsn.
See listing under "Universities"

† St. John's University
Grand Central & Utopia Parkways, Jamaica 11439

† SUNY at Buffalo
O'Brian Hall, Amherst 14260

† Syracuse University, Syracuse 13244

Touro College
Jacob D. Fuchsberg Law Center
300 Nassau Rd., Huntington 11743

† Yeshiva Univ., Benjamin N. Cardozo Sch. of Law
55 Fifth Ave., New York 10003
Monroe Price, Dean

NORTH CAROLINA

Campbell University
P.O. Box 127, Buies Creek 27506

† Duke University, Durham 27706

Gardner-Webb University
General Delivery, Boiling Springs 28017
Ray M. Hardee, Dean of Admissions
800-253-6472

North Carolina Central University
P.O. Box 19617, Durham 27707

† University of North Carolina at Chapel Hill
Chapel Hill 27599
Judith W. Wagner, Dean

† Wake Forest University
P.O. Box 7206, Winston-Salem 27109

NORTH DAKOTA

† University of North Dakota
Box 8193 University Station, Grand Forks 58203

OHIO

† Capital University Law School
665 S. High St., Columbus 43215
Linda Mihely, Dir. of Admis.

† Case Western Reserve University
2040 Adelbert Rd., Cleveland 44106

† Cleveland State University
Euclid Ave. at 24th St., Cleveland 44115

† OHIO NORTHERN UNIVERSITY
525 S. Main St., Ada 45810
Dr. Albert Quick, Dean
412-772-2000

† Ohio State University
190 N. Oval Mall, Columbus 43210

OHIO VALLEY BUSINESS COLLEGE
500 Maryland Ave., East Liverpool 43920
216-385-1070

† University of Akron
381 Buchtel Common, Akron 44325
Kris MacDermott, Asst. Provost Enrollment

† University of Cincinnati
2700 Clifton Ave., Cincinnati 45221

† University of Dayton
300 College Park Ave., Dayton 45469-1320
Toll-free 800-837-7433
See listing under "Universities"

† University of Toledo
2801 Bancroft St., W., Toledo 43606
Richard Eastop, Dir. of Admis.

OKLAHOMA

Oklahoma City University
2501 N. Blackwelder Ave., Oklahoma City 73106
Gary Mercer, Director of Law Admissions
See listing under "Universities"

† University of Oklahoma at Norman
660 Parrington Oval, Norman 73019

† University of Tulsa
600 S. College Ave., Tulsa 74104
John Makdisi, Dean

OREGON

† Lewis & Clark College
0615 S.W. Palatine Hill Rd., Portland 97219
Michael Sexton, Dean of Admissions

† University of Oregon
1 University of Oregon, Eugene 97403

† Willamette University
900 State St. S.E., Salem 97301

PENNSYLVANIA

Chatham College
Woodland Rd., Pittsburgh 15232
Suellen Ofe, Dean of Admis./Financial Aid
See listing under "Women's College"

† Dickinson School of Law
150 S. College St., Carlisle 17013
John Maher, Acting Dean

† Duquesne University
600 Forbes Ave., Pittsburgh 15282
Thomas Schaefer, C.S.Sp., Dir. of Admis.

· Erie Business Center
246 W. 9th St., Erie 16501
Tony Piccirillo, Dir. of Admis.
See listing under "Career Schools"

† Temple University
Broad St. & Montgomery Ave.
Philadelphia 19122

† University of Pennsylvania
0 Levy Park, Philadelphia 19104

† University of Pittsburgh
4200 5th Ave., Pittsburgh 15260

† Villanova University
845 E. Lancaster Ave., Villanova 19085
Stephen R. Merritt, Dir. of Admis.

WESTMINSTER COLLEGE
New Wilmington 16172
Richard Dana Paul, Dir. of Admis.
412-946-7100

RHODE ISLAND

: Katharine Gibbs School
178 Butler Ave., Providence 02906
401-861-1420

SOUTH CAROLINA

† University of South Carolina, Columbia 29208
John Benfield, Dir. Law School Admissions
803-777-6605

SOUTH DAKOTA

National College
321 Kansas City St., Rapid City 57701
Keith T. Carlyle, Dir. of Admis.

· Nettleton Junior College
100 S. Spring Ave., Sioux Falls 57104
Herman Whitaker, Dir. of Admissions
800-727-1837 or 605-336-1837

† University of South Dakota
414 E. Clark St., Vermillion 57069
Barry Vickrey, Dean

TENNESSEE

Christian Brothers College
Preprofessional Program
650 E. Parkway, S., Memphis 38104

: Southeastern Institute for Paralegal Education
2416 21st Ave. S. #300, Nashville 37212
Bruce Mallard, President
800-336-4457

University of Memphis, Memphis 38152
Dr. John Eubank, Dean of Admissions

University of Tennessee at Martin
Martin 38238
Paul Kelley, Director of Admissions
See listing under "Universities"

† University of Tennessee, Knoxville
527 Andy Holt Tower, Knoxville 37996
Dr. Gordon Stanley, Dir. of Admis.

† Vanderbilt University
West End Ave., Nashville 37240

TEXAS

† Baylor University
P.O. Box 97008, Waco 76798-7008
Diana Ramey, Director of Admissions

† St. Mary's University of San Antonio
1 Camino Santa Maria, San Antonio 78228
Rick Castillo, Dir. of Admis.

: Southeastern Institute for Paralegal Education
5440 Harvest Hill Rd. #200, Dallas 75230

† Southern Methodist University
Hillcrest at University, Dallas 75275

South Texas College of Law
1303 San Jacinto St., Houston 77002
Deborah Dykes, Dir. of Admis.

: Texas School of Business
711 Air Tex Dr., Houston 77073
Madeline Burillo, Director
713-846-2888

Texas Southern University
Thurgood Marshall School of Law
3100 Cleburne St., Houston 77004

† Texas Tech University, Lubbock 79409

† University of Houston
4800 Calhoun Rd., Houston 77204

† University of Texas at Austin
0 the University of Texas, Austin 78712

UTAH

† Brigham Young University, Provo 84602

† University of Utah
1400 E. 200 S., Salt Lake City 84112
Dr. J. Stayner Landward, Dir. of Admis.

VERMONT

† Vermont Law School
P.O. Box 96, South Royalton 05068
Maximilian Kempner, Dean

VIRGINIA

† College of William and Mary, Williamsburg 23185
Jean A. Scott, Dean of Admission

† George Mason University
4400 University Dr., Fairfax 22030-4444
Patricia Riordan, Dean of Admissions

† University of Richmond, Richmond 23173

† University of Virginia
School of Law
North Grounds, Charlottesville 22901

† Washington and Lee University
Lexington 24450
William M. Hartog, Dir. of Admis.

WASHINGTON

† Gonzaga University
P.O. Box 3528, Spokane 99220
John E. Clute, Dean

† University of Puget Sound, Sch. of Law
950 Broadway Plaza, Tacoma 98402
Fredric C. Tausend, Dean

† University of Washington, Seattle 98195

WEST VIRGINIA

† West Virginia University
P.O. Box 6001, Morgantown 26506

WEST VIRGINIA WESLEYAN COLLEGE
59 College Ave., Buckhannon 26201
Robert Skinner, Director of Admission
See listing under "Universities"

WISCONSIN

† Marquette University
1103 W. Wisconsin Ave., Milwaukee 53233
Geraldine Klausen, Director of Admissions

St. Norbert College
100 Grant St., De Pere 54115
Craig S. Wesley, Dean of Admission
See listing under "Universities"

† University of Wisconsin, Madison
500 Lincoln Dr., Madison 53706

Viterbo College
815 9th St., S., La Crosse 54601
Roland W. Nelson, Dir. of Admis.

WYOMING

† University of Wyoming
P.O. Box 3434, Laramie 82071
Richard Davis, Dir. of Admis.

PUERTO RICO

Catholic University of Puerto Rico
Las Americas Ave., Ponce 00732
Carilin Frau, Dir. of Admis.

Inter American University of Puerto Rico
School of Law
P.O. Box 8897, San Juan 00910

† University of Puerto Rico, Rio Piedras Campus
P.O. Box 23300, San Juan 00931
Victor Lopez, Dir. of Admis.

LIBERAL ARTS AND SCIENCES

ALABAMA

Athens State College
300 N. Beaty St., Athens 35611
Larry McCoy, Dir. of Admissions

Auburn University, Auburn 36849

Auburn University at Montgomery
7300 University Dr., Montgomery 36117
H. H. Funderburk, VP

· Bishop State Community College
351 N. Broad St., Mobile 36603-5898
Yvonne Kennedy, President
205-690-6801

Faulkner University
5345 Atlanta Hwy., Montgomery 36109

· Gadsden State Community College
P.O. Box 227, Gadsden 35902
W. Bryan Stone, Dir. of Admis.

Huntingdon College
1500 E. Fairview Ave., Montgomery 36106-2148
Carolyn A. Phillips, Dean of Enrollment
800-763-0313

Livingston University
Station #4, Livingston 35470
David Taylor, Dean
See listing under "Universities"

Oakwood College
Oakwood Rd., N.W., Huntsville 35896

Samford University
800 Lakeshore Dr., Birmingham 35229
Hugh Floyd, Chrpsn.

Spring Hill College
4000 Dauphin St., Mobile 36608
Ben Hamd, Dir. of Admis.

STILLMAN COLLEGE
P.O. Box 1430, Tuscaloosa 35403
Barbara K. Smith, Director of Admissions
See listing under "Universities"

Troy State University, Troy 36082
Dr. Phil Rosen, Dean

Troy State University at Dothan
P.O. Box 8368, Dothan 36304
Bob Willis, Dir. of Undergraduate Admissions

Troy State University at Montgomery
P.O. Box 4419, Montgomery 36103

University of Alabama
P.O. Box 870132, Tuscaloosa 35487-0132
Roy Smith, Dir. of Admis.

University of Alabama at Birmingham
University Station, Birmingham 35294

UNIVERSITY OF ALABAMA IN HUNTSVILLE
P.O. Box 1247, Huntsville 35899
Ron R. Koger Ed.D., Dir. of Admis.
205-895-6070
Established 1969. Public. Coed. Accreditation: SACS, ABET, NLN, CSAB, ACS. Tuition: $2,418 resident, $4,836 non-resident. Room & Board: $3,450. Undergraduate enrollment: 2,674 full-time, 3,439 part-time. Graduate enrollment: 1,860. Faculty: 282. Student-faculty ratio: 18:1. Degrees: BS, BA, BSBA, BSE, MS, MSM, Ph.D., BSN, MSN, MA. 20 buildings on 350 acres. Comprehensive research university located in the Tennessee Valley of northern Alabama.

Huntsville is the locale of major government and private research centers. Metropolitan population approaching 300,000.

UNIVERSITY OF MOBILE
P.O. Box 13220, Mobile 36663-0220
Kim Leousis, Dir. of Admissions
205-675-5990
See listing under "Universities"

University of Montevallo, Montevallo 35115

· Walker College
1411 Indiana Ave., Jasper 35501
James West, Dir. of Admis.

ALASKA

Alaska Pacific University
4101 University Dr., Anchorage 99508
Director of Admissions
See listing under "Universities"

Sheldon Jackson College
801 Lincoln St., Sitka 99835
Dennis Trotter, Dir. of Admis.
907-747-5221

University of Alaska Southeast
11120 Glacier Hwy., Juneau 99801
Greg Wagner, Coordinator of Admissions

UNIVERSITY OF ALASKA SOUTHEAST-KETCHIKAN
2600 7th Ave., Ketchikan 99901-5798
Dr. Frances Feinerman, Director
William Trudeau, Student Services
Established 1954. State. Coed. Accreditation: NASC. Yearly tuition: $1,670 resident, $5,500 non-resident. Est. total yrly. exp.: $8,000. Faculty: 10 full-time, 50 part-time. Degrees: AA, AAS in Business Office Administration, Travel Industry and Hospitality Industry. Certificates in Accounting, Business Tech, Office Skills, Travel Industry, Hospitality Industry and Welding. Library: 42,000 volumes. 4 buildings on 40 acres. UAS-Ketchikan is a member of the statewide University of Alaska system. Ketchikan is located on Revilla Island, on the beautiful inside passage of southeast Alaska.

ARIZONA

· Arizona Western College
P.O. Box 929, Yuma 85366-0929
Bob Davis, Dir. of Admis.

· Gateway Community College
108 N. 40th St., Phoenix 85034
Bill Harris, Dean of Student Services

GRAND CANYON UNIVERSITY
3300 W. Camelback Rd., Phoenix 85017
Dr. Bill Williams, President
Sherri Willborn, Dir. of Admissions
602-249-3300
Established 1949. Southern Baptist. Coed. Accreditation: NCACS, NLN. Tuition: $7,328. Room and board: $3,100. Enrollment: 1,700 full-time, 211 part-time, 70 graduate. Faculty: 140. Degrees: BA, BS, BSN, MA, MBA, MEd. Library: 95,000 volumes. 70 acre campus with 28 buildings including Ethington Memorial Theatre, Tell Energy Science Building, apartment style housing (married and upperclassmen), dorms, gym, swimming pool. Divisions: College of Education, Samaritan College of Nursing, College of Business, Christian studies, health and exercise sci-

ence, history, humanities, math, natural sciences, College of Communications and Fine Arts, psychology, social sciences.

Prescott College
220 Grove Ave., Prescott 86301
Shari Sterling, Asst. Dir. of Admis.

University of Arizona, Tucson 85721
Loyd Bell, Director of Admissions

· Yavapai College
1100 E. Sheldon St., Prescott 86301
Dr. Doreen Dailey, President
602-445-7300
See listing under "Community and Junior Colleges"

ARKANSAS

Arkansas Baptist College
1600 High St., Little Rock 72202

Arkansas College
2300 Highland Rd., Batesville 72501
Jonathan M. Stroud, Dean of Admissions
800-423-2542

Arkansas State University
P.O. Box 1030, State University 72467

Arkansas Tech University
215 W. O St., Russellville 72801

Hendrix College
1601 Harkrider St., Conway 72032

John Brown University
2000 W. University, Siloam Springs 72761
Don Crandall, Director of Enrollment Management

Ouachita Baptist University
410 Ouachita St., Arkadelphia 71998
Randy Garner, Dir. of Admis.
800-DIAL-OBU

Philander Smith College
812 W. 13th St., Little Rock 72202

· Phillips County Community College
P.O. Box 785, Helena 72342
Dr. Steven Jones, President
James R. Brasel, Dean of Admissions

University of Arkansas at Monticello
P.O. Box 3596, Monticello 71656

University of the Ozarks
415 College Ave., Clarksville 72830

Williams Baptist College
P.O. Box 3667, Walnut Ridge 72476
Scott Wright, Dir. of Admis.

CALIFORNIA

ANTIOCH UNIVERSITY
801 Garden St. #101, Santa Barbara 93101
805-962-8179

Azusa Pacific University
P.O. Box 7000, Azusa 91702

· Bakersfield College
1801 Panorama Dr., Bakersfield 93305
Robert M. Bruker, Dir. of Admis.

Biola University
13800 Biola Ave., La Mirada 90639
Wayne Chute, Dean of Admissions

California Baptist College
8432 Magnolia Ave., Riverside 92504
800-782-3382

California Institute of Integral Studies
765 Ashbury St., San Francisco 94117
Diane Gribben, Dir. of Admis.

California Lutheran University
60 Olsen Rd., Thousand Oaks 91360
800-252-5884

California State University, Dominguez Hills
1000 E. Victoria St., Carson 90747

California State University, Los Angeles
5151 Paseo Rancho Castilla, Los Angeles 90032

California State University-Bakersfield
9001 Stockdale Hwy., Bakersfield 93311
Dr. Homer S. Montalvo, Dir. of Admis.

Chapman University
333 N. Glassell St., Orange 92666
Michael Drummy, Dir. of Admis.

Christian Heritage College
2100 Greenfield Dr., El Cajon 92019
Pam Daly, Dir. of Admis.
800-676-2242

City College of San Francisco
50 Phelan Ave. Box A208, San Francisco 94112
Paul Lorch, Dean
415-239-3127

Claremont McKenna College
890 Columbia Ave., Claremont 91711

College of Notre Dame
1500 Ralston Ave., Belmont 94002
Greg M. Smith, PhD., Dir. of Admis.

Concordia University
1530 Concordia, Irvine 92715
Stan Meyer, Dean of Admission
800-229-1200
See listing under "Universities"

Deep Springs College
Deep Springs, CA
Mailing Address, HC 72, Box 45001
Dyer, NV 89010-9803

DOMINICAN COLLEGE OF SAN RAFAEL
50 Acacia Ave., San Rafael 94901-8008
Office of Admissions
800-788-3522

Fresno Pacific College
1717 S. Chestnut Ave., Fresno 93702
209-453-2039

Holy Names College
3500 Mountain Blvd., Oakland 94619

:: Idyllwild School of Music & the Arts
P.O. Box 38P, Idyllwild 92549
Anne Behnke, Admissions
909-659-2171, FAX 909-659-2058
See listing under "Prep-Coed"

John F. Kennedy University
12 Altarinda Rd., Orinda 94563

La Sierra University
4700 Pierce St., Riverside 92505
800-874-5587

LINCOLN UNIVERSITY
281 Masonic Ave., San Francisco 94118
Clarence Rippel, Acting President
Accredited Member ACICS

Loyola Marymount University
Loyola Blvd. at W. 80th, Los Angeles 90045
M. L'Heureux, Dir. of Admis.

Master's College
P.O. Box 221450, Newhall 91322
Don Gilmore, Dir. of Admis.

Menlo College
1000 El Camino Real, Atherton 94027
Joseph Zikmund, Dean

Mills College
5000 MacArthur Blvd., Oakland 94613
Genevieve Ann Flaherty, Dean of Admissions
800-87-MILLS

Mt. St. Mary's College
12001 Chalon Rd., Los Angeles 90049

Pacific Union College
1 Angwin Ave., Angwin 94508
Dr. Gary Gifford, Dir. of Admis.

Pitzer College
1050 N. Mills Ave., Claremont 91711
Katharine Leighton, Dir. of Admis.

Point Loma Nazarene College
3900 Lomaland Dr., San Diego 92106
Bill Young, Dir. of Admis.

Pomona College
333 N. College Way, Claremont 91711
Peter W. Stanley, President

St. Mary's College of California
P.O. Box 4267, Moraga 94575

Santa Barbara City College
721 Cliff Dr., Santa Barbara 93109
805-965-0581

Scripps College
1030 Columbia Ave., Claremont 91711
Leslie Miles, Dean of Admissions

Southern California College
55 Fair Dr., Costa Mesa 92626
Richard Hardy, Asst. Dean for Enrollment

Thomas Aquinas College
1000 N. Ojai Rd., Santa Paula 93060

UNITED STATES INTERNATIONAL UNIVERSITY
10455 Pomerado Rd., San Diego 92131
619-693-4772
See listing under "Universities"

University of California, Davis
376 Mrak Hall, Davis 95616

University of California-Santa Cruz
Santa Cruz 95064
Joseph Allen, Dir. of Admis.

UNIVERSITY OF JUDAISM/LEE COLLEGE
15600 Mulholland Dr., Los Angeles 90077
Tamara Greenebaum, Dean of Admissions
See listing under "Universities"

University of La Verne
1950 3rd St., La Verne 91750
Mark Bornholdt, Dir. of Admis.

University of Redlands
P.O. Box 3080, Redlands 92373

University of San Diego
5998 Alcala Park, San Diego 92110
Warren Muller, Dir. of Admis.
619-260-4506

University of San Francisco
2130 Fulton St., San Francisco 94117
Bill Henley, Dir. of Admis.

Whittier College
13406 Philadelphia St., Whittier 90601
310-907-4238

Woodbury University
7500 Glenoaks Blvd., Burbank 91504
See listing under "Universities"

World College West
P.O. Box 481, Petaluma 94953
Dr. Richard M. Gray, President

COLORADO

Adams State College, Alamosa 81102
Cheryl Billingsley, Dir. of Admis.
800-824-6494

Colorado Christian University
180 S. Garrison St., Lakewood 80226
Debra Seefeldt, Dir. of Admis.

Colorado College
14 E. Cache La Poudre, Colorado Springs 80903
Terry Swenson, Dir. of Admis.

Colorado Northwestern Community College
500 Kennedy Dr., Rangely 81648
Pat Kalahar, Dir. Marketing/Recruitment
800-562-1105

Ft. Lewis College
1000 Rim Dr., Durango 81301

Front Range Community College
3645 W. 112th Ave., Westminister 80030
Dr. Patricia Lammers, Dir. of Admis.

Mesa State College
P.O. Box 2647, Grand Junction 81502
Sherri Pe'a, Dir. of Admis.

Metropolitan State College of Denver
P.O. Box 173362, Campus Box 16
Denver 80217-3362

Morgan Community College
17800 Road 20, Fort Morgan 80701
Kurtis Armstrong, Dir. of Admis.

Naropa Institute
2130 Arapahoe Ave., Boulder 80302
Dr. Jana Lynn, Director of Admissions
303-546-3572

Pikes Peak Community College
5675 S. Academy Blvd.
Colorado Springs 80906-5498
Roberta Erickson, Dir. of Admis.
See listing under "Community and Junior Colleges"

Regis University
3333 Regis Blvd., Denver 80221
Robert Blust, Director of Admissions

University of Colorado at Boulder
Boulder 80309
William A. Douglas, Dean of Admis.

University of Denver
2199 S. University Blvd., Denver 80210

University of Northern Colorado, Greeley 80639
Roger Kovar, Dean of Arts and Sciences
303-351-2707

University of Southern Colorado
2200 Bonforte Blvd., Pueblo 81001

Western State College of Colorado
Gunnison 81231
Monica Bruning, Dir. of Admis.
See listing under "Universities"

CONNECTICUT

Albertus Magnus College
700 Prospect St., New Haven 06511
Richard Lolatte, Dir. of Admissions
203-773-8501 or 800-578-9160

Charter Oak State College
66 Cedar St., Newington 06111-2646
Paul Morganti, Director of Admissions

Connecticut College
270 Mohegan Ave., New London 06320

Eastern Connecticut State University
83 Windham St., Willimantic 06226
Dr. Carmen Cid, Dean

Hartford College for Women
1265 Asylum Ave., Hartford 06105

Mattatuck Community College
750 Chase Parkway, Waterbury 06708
Dr. Richard Sanders, President

QUINNIPIAC COLLEGE
275 Mount Carmel Ave., Hamden 06518
John Lahey, President
Joan Isaac Mohr, VP and Dean of Admissions
Established 1929. Private. Coed. Accreditation: NEASC. Tuition: $11,250. Room and board: $5,790. Enrollment: 2,583 boarding, 3,444 day. Faculty 333. Degrees: BA, BS, MAT, MBA, MHS, MPS. Library: 290,000 volumes. 30 buildings on 170 acres. Gym. Suburban location at the base of Sleeping Giant State Park, close to New Haven and Yale University. Convenient to New York City, Boston, and Upper New England. Building a new $7 million School of Business Center.

TEIKYO POST UNIVERSITY
800 Country Club Rd.
P.O. Box 2540, Waterbury 06723-2540
800-345-2562 or 203-596-4520
Established 1890. Private. Coed. Accreditation: NEASC. Tuition: $11,960. Room and board: $5,400. Application fee: $40. Enrollment: 996 full-time, 1,488 part-time. Faculty: 29 full-time, 260 part-time. Student-faculty ratio: 15:1. Degrees: AA, AS, BA, BS. Library: 55,000 volumes. 11 buildings on 70 acres. Excellent business majors with strong liberal arts and international component. Faculty with dynamic business experience, assistance to help students succeed in a global marketplace. ESL Institute.

Trinity College
300 Summit St., Hartford 06106
Dr. David Borus, Dean of Admissions

University of Bridgeport
126 Park Ave., Bridgeport 06601
Andrew G. Nelson, Dean Admis./Financial Aid
203-576-4552
See listing under "Universities"

University of Connecticut, Storrs 06268
Frank Vasington, Interim Dean

UNIVERSITY OF HARTFORD
200 Bloomfield Ave., West Hartford 06117
Richard Zeiser, Dir. of Admis.
See listing under "Universities"

University of New Haven
300 Orange Ave., West Haven 06516
Joseph Chepaitis, Dean
203-932-7000

Wesleyan University, Middletown 06459
Karl Furstenberg, Dean of Admissions

Western Connecticut State University
181 White St., Danbury 06810

DELAWARE

Wesley College
120 N. State St., Dover 19901

DISTRICT OF COLUMBIA

The American University
4400 Massachusetts Ave. N.W.
Washington 20016

Catholic University of America
620 Michigan Ave. N.E., Washington 20064
Robert J. Talbot, Dir. of Admis. & Fin. Aid

Mt. Vernon College
2100 Foxhall Rd., N.W., Washington 20007
202-625-4682 or 800-682-4636, FAX: 202-338-1089

Trinity College
125 Michigan Ave., N.E., Washington 20017
Donna Quinn, Dir. of Admis.

University of the District of Columbia
Georgia Ave.-Harvard St. Campus
1100 Harvard St., N.W., Washington 20009

University of the District of Columbia
Van Ness Campus
4200 Connecticut Ave., N.W., Washington 20008

FLORIDA

Barry University
11300 N.E. 2nd Ave., Miami Shores 33161
Robin Ray Roberts, Dean of Admissions

Clearwater Christian College
3400 Gulf-to-Bay Blvd., Clearwater 34619
Benjamin Puckett, Dir. of Admis.

Eckerd College
P.O. Box 12560, St. Petersburg 33733
Richard Hallin, Dir. of Admis.

Edison Community College
8099 College Pky., Fort Myers 33919
Mailing address: P.O. Box 60210
Fort Myers 33906-6210
Sandra Fahey, Dir. of Admis. and Records

Edward Waters College
1658 Kings Rd., Jacksonville 32209

Flagler College
P.O. Box 1027, St. Augustine 32085
Marc G. Williar, Dir. of Admis.
904-829-6481

Florida Atlantic University
500 N.W. 20th St., Boca Raton 33431
Brian Levin-Stankevich, Dir. of Admis.

Florida International University
Tamiami Trail, Miami 33199

Florida Memorial College
15800 N.W. 42nd Ave., Opa-Locka 33054
Roberto Darragan, Jr., Dir., Admissions

Florida Southern College
111 Lake Hollingsworth Dr., Lakeland 33801
William Stephens, Jr., Dir. of Admis.

Jacksonville University
2800 University Blvd., N., Jacksonville 32211

LYNN UNIVERSITY
(Est. 1962 as College of Boca Raton)
3601 N. Military Trail, Boca Raton 33431
407-994-0770 or 800-544-8035
See listing under "Universities"

Miami Christian College
P.O. Box 19674, Miami 33101

Palm Beach Atlantic College
P.O. Box 24708, West Palm Beach 33416-4708
See listing under "Universities"

St. John Vianney College Seminary
2900 S.W. 87th Ave., Miami 33165
Rev. George Garcia, President/Rector

St. Leo College
P.O. Box 2008, St. Leo 33574
Bonnie Black, Dir. of Admis.

St. Thomas University
16400 N.W. 32nd Ave., Miami 33054
John M. Letvinchuk, Dir. of Admis.

SCHILLER INTERNATIONAL UNIVERSITY (FLORIDA & EUROPE)
U.S. Admissions Office
Dept. PA, 453 Edgewater Dr., Dunedin 34698-7532
800-336-4133 Fax: 813-736-6263
Dr. Walter Liebrecht, President
Karen Altieri, Associate Director of Admissions
See listing under "Universities"

Stetson University
401 N. Woodland Blvd., De Land 32720
Gary A. Meadows, Dean of Admis.

University of Florida
226 Tigert Hall, Gainesville 32611

University of Miami
P.O. Box 248006, Coral Gables 33124

University of Tampa
401 W. Kennedy Blvd., Tampa 33606
Robert W. Cook, Dir. of Admis.

Warner Southern College
5301 U.S. Hwy. 27, S., Lake Wales 33853
Valerie S. Rutland, Dir. Enrollment Mgmt.
800-949-7248

Webber College
P.O. Box 96, Babson Park 33827
Steve G. Wilson, Dir. of Admis.

GEORGIA

Agnes Scott College
201 E. College Ave., Decatur 30030
Teresa Lahti, Dir. of Admis.

Armstrong State College
11935 Abercorn St., Savannah 31419
Kim West, Director of Admissions

Berry College
2277 Martha Berry Hwy. N.W., Mt. Berry 30165

Clark Atlanta University
240 James Brawley Dr., S.W., Atlanta 30314
Thomas W. Cole, President

Georgia College
231 W. Hancock St., Milledgeville 31061
912-453-5004

Georgia Military College
201 E. Green St., Milledgeville 31061
Major General Peter Boylan, President

Georgia Southern University, Statesboro 30460

Georgia Southwestern College
800 Wheatley St., Americus 31709

Georgia State University
University Plaza, Atlanta 30303
Ernest Beals, Dean of Admissions

Gordon College
419 College Dr., Barnesville 30204
Dr. M. Simmons, Director of Enrollment Services
404-358-5021, in GA 800-282-6504

Kennesaw State College
P.O. Box 444, Marietta 30061
Joe Head, Dir. of Admis.

La Grange College
601 Broad St., La Grange 30240
Phil Dodson, Dir. of Admis.
706-882-2911

Mercer University
1400 Coleman Ave., Macon 31207

North Georgia College, Dahlonega 30597
Gary R. Steffey, Dir. of Admis.

Oglethorpe University
4484 Peachtree Rd., N.E., Atlanta 30319
Dennis Matthews, Dir. of Admis.

Paine College
1235 15th St., Augusta 30901
Phyllis Wyatt-Woodruff, Dir. Enrollment Mgmt.

Piedmont College
P.O. Box 10, Demorest 30535
Penny L. Graber, Dir of Admis.
800-277-7020

Shorter College
315 Shorter Ave., Rome 30165

University of Georgia, Athens 30602
Dr. William J. Payne, Dean

Valdosta State College
Patterson St., Valdosta 31698

West Georgia College, Carrollton 30118
C. Doyle Bickers, Dir. of Admis.

HAWAII

Brigham Young University, Hawaii Campus
55-220 Kulanui St., Laie 96762
Clark E. Hirschi, Coordinator of Admis.

Chaminade University of Honolulu
3140 Waialae Ave., Honolulu 96816
Charles Schafer, VP Enrollment Services

Hawaii Pacific University
1166 Fort Street Mall, Honolulu 96813
Don Barlow, Dir. of Admis.

Hawaii Pacific University
45-045 Kamehameha Hwy., Kaneohe 96744

University of Hawaii, West Oahu College
96-043 Ala Ike, Pearl City 96782

University of Hawaii at Hilo
523 W. Lanikaula, Hilo 96720

IDAHO

Boise State University
1910 University Dr., Boise 83725

College of Idaho, Caldwell 83605

Idaho State University
P.O. Box 8270, Pocatello 83209

Lewis Clark State College
500 8th Ave., Lewiston 83501
800-933-5272 or 208-799-5272

North Idaho College
1000 W. Garden Ave., Coeur d'Alene 83814
Dennis Conners, Dean of Academic Affairs

University of Idaho, Moscow 83843
Peter Brown, Dir. of Admis.

ILLINOIS

Augustana College
639 38th St., Rock Island 61201
Martin R. Sauer, Director of Admission
800-798-8100

Aurora University
347 S. Gladstone Ave., Aurora 60506
Peter Pitts, Dir. of Admis.

Barat College, Lake Forest 60045
Loretta Brickman, Dir. of Admis.

Blackburn College
700 College Ave., Carlinville 62626
Dwight Smith, Dir. of Admis.

College of St. Francis
500 Wilcox St., Joliet 60435

Elmhurst College
190 Prospect Ave., Elmhurst 60126

Governors State University
1 University Pky., University Park 60466
Richard Pride, Dir. of Admis.

Illinois College
1101 W. College Ave., Jacksonville 62650
Gale Vaugn, Dir. of Admis.

Judson College
1151 N. State St., Elgin 60123
Jack Powell, Dir. of Enrollment Services

KASKASKIA COLLEGE
27210 College Rd., Centralia 62801
618-532-1981 or 800-642-0859 (Illinois)
Raymond D. Woods, President
Marilyn Brookman, PhD, College Dean
Constance Stohlman, Director of Admissions, Public Relations, and Resource Development
Kaskaskia College is situated on a beautifully wooded tract of land consisting of 190 acres. Its brick and frame buildings provide 228,830 square feet of space for college facilities. Kaskaskia College is fully accredited by NCACS, ADA, AMA, NLN, IBE, ICCB, and IBHE. The College is recognized and approved by the bureau of Veterans Affairs and is authorized under Federal law to enroll non-immigrant alien students. In district tuition and fees are $33.75 per semester credit hour. Degrees: AA, AS, AAS, and AGS. University transfer programs, pre-professional, liberal arts, courses offered days, evenings, and weekends. Training in career fields. State and Federal financial aid programs available.

Kendall College
2408 Orrington Ave., Evanston 60201
Peter Pauletti, Dir. of Admis.

Knox College, Galesburg 61401
309-343-0112 or 800-678-KNOX
See listing under "Universities"

Lake Forest College
555 N. Sheridan Rd., Lake Forest 60045

LEWIS UNIVERSITY
Rt. 53, Romeoville 60441
Irish O'Reilly, Director of Admissions
See listing under "Universities"

Lincoln College
300 Keokuk St., Lincoln 62656
Jack Nutt, President

Loyola University-Mallinckrodt Campus
1041 Ridge Rd., Wilmette 60091
Karen Sullivan, Admissions

McKendree College
701 College Rd., Lebanon 62254
Stephen E. Jackson, Director of Admissions

MacMurray College
447 E. College Ave., Jacksonville 62650
Edwin R. Hockett, Dean of Admissions

MILLIKIN UNIVERSITY
1184 W. Main St., Decatur 62522
Lin Stoner, Dean of Admissions
800-373-7733

Monmouth College
700 E. Broadway, Monmouth 61462

Montay College
3750 W. Peterson Ave., Chicago 60659
Scott Dalhouse, Dir. of Admis.

Moraine Valley Community College
10900 S. 88th Ave., Palos Hills 60465
Dr. Vernon Crawley, President

North Central College
30 N. Brainard St.
P.O. Box 3065, Naperville 60566-7065
Marguerite Waters, Director of Admission
708-420-3414

Northeastern Illinois University
5500 N. St. Louis Ave., Chicago 60625

Northwestern University
1918 Sheridan Rd., Evanston 60208

Parkland College
2400 W. Bradley Ave., Champaign 61821-1899
217-351-2208 or 800-346-8089

Principia College, Elsah 62028

Quincy College
1800 College Ave., Quincy 62301
Fr. Michael Lanning, O.F.M., Dir. of Admis.

Rockford College
5050 E. State St., Rockford 61108
Miriam King, V.P. for Enrollment Management
See listing under "Universities"

ROOSEVELT UNIVERSITY
430 S. Michigan Ave., Chicago 60605
William Smyser, Director of Admissions
See listing under "Universities"

Rosary College
7900 W. Division St., River Forest 60305
Hildegarde Schmidt, Dir. of Admis.

Sangamon State University
Shepherd Rd., Springfield 62794-9243
Admissions and Records, 217-786-6626

Shimer College
438 N. Sheridan Rd., P.O. Box A500
Waukegan 60079
David B. Buchanan, Dir. of Admis.
708-623-8400

Southern Illinois University at Carbondale
Carbondale 62901

Springfield College in Illinois
1500 N. Fifth St., Springfield 62702
Dr. H. Brent DeLand, President

Trinity Christian College
6601 W. College Dr., Palos Heights 60463
Kenneth Bootsma, President

Trinity College
2077 Half Day Rd., Deerfield 60015
Dr. Kenneth Meyer, Pres.

University of Illinois
506 S. Wright St., Urbana 61801

University of Illinois at Chicago
P.O. Box 4348, Chicago 60680
Dr. Jay Levine, Dean

Western Illinois University
900 W. Adams St., Macomb 61455
Alan DeRoos, Registrar
309-298-1891

Wheaton College, Wheaton 60187
Daniel Crabtree, Director of Admissions
800-222-2419

INDIANA

Bethel College
1001 W. McKinley Ave., Mishawaka 46545
Steve Matteson, Dir. of Admis.

Calumet College
2400 New York Ave., Whiting 46394
Sharon Sweeney, Dir. of Admis.

DePauw University
313 S. Locust St., Greencastle 46135
Dr. Eleanor Ypma, Registrar

Earlham College
801 National Rd. W., Richmond 47374
Robert deVeer, Dean of Admis.

Franklin College
501 E. Monroe, Franklin 46131
B. Stephen Richards, VP Enrollment

Goshen College
1700 S. Main St., Goshen 46526
Marty Lehman Hooley, Dir. of Admis.

Grace College
200 Seminary Dr., Winona Lake 46590
Ron Henry, Dir. of Admis.

Hanover College, Hanover 47243
Eugene McLemore, Dir., Admis.

HOLY CROSS COLLEGE
P.O. Box 308, Notre Dame 46556
Vincent M. Duke, Director of Admissions
219-233-6613

Indiana Wesleyan University
4201 S. Washington St., Marion 46953
800-332-6901

Manchester College
604 College Ave., North Manchester 46962
Dr. James Pitts, Academic Dean

Marian College
3200 Cold Spring Rd., Indianapolis 46222
Don French, Dir. of Admis.

Martin University
P.O. Box 18567, Indianapolis 46218

St. Francis College
2701 Spring St., Ft. Wayne 46808

ST. JOSEPH'S COLLEGE
P.O. Box 890, Rensselaer 47978
Louis Levy, Dean of Admissions
800-447-8781

St. Mary-of-the-Woods College
Saint Mary-of-the-Woods 47876
Lynn M. Rubick, Director of Admissions
800-926-SMWC

St. Meinrad College
Archabbey, St. Meinrad 47577
Rev. Eugene Hensell, Provost

Taylor University
500 W. Reade Ave., Upland 46989
Dr. Robert Pitts, VP for Academic Affairs

Taylor University - Fort Wayne Campus
1025 W. Rudisill Blvd., Fort Wayne 46807
Jan Paul Storey, Dir. of Admis.

Tri-State University, Angola 46703
Director of Admission
800-347-4878

University of Evansville
1800 Lincoln Ave., Evansville 47722
Dr. Erik Nielson, Dean
800-423-8633

University of Indianapolis
1400 E. Hanna Ave., Indianapolis 46227

University of Notre Dame
Notre Dame 46556
Kevin M. Rooney, Dir. of Admis.

Wabash College
301 W. Wabash Ave., Crawfordsville 47933
Greg Birk, Dir. of Admis.

IOWA

Briar Cliff College
3303 Rebecca St., Sioux City 51104
Patricia White, Dir. of Admis.

Buena Vista College
610 W. 4th St., Storm Lake 50588
Joanne Loonan, Director of Admissions

Central College
812 University St., Pella 50219
Eric Sickler, Dir. of Admis.

Cornell College
600 1st St., W., Mt. Vernon 52314
Kevin Crockett, Dean of Admissions

Divine Word College Seminary
1 S. Center Ave., Epworth 52045
Fr. Bob Kelly, SVD, Dir. of Admis.

Dordt College
498 4th Ave., N.E., Sioux Center 51250
Quentin Van Essen, Dir. of Admissions
800-343-6738

Drake University
2507 E. University Ave., Des Moines 50311
Thomas Willoughby, Dir. of Admis.

GRACELAND COLLEGE
Lamoni 50140
800-638-0053, Outside Iowa 800-346-9208
Bonita Booth, Dean of Admissions
Established 1895. Private. Coed. Accreditation: NCACS, NLN, NCATE. Tuition: $8,585. Room and board: $2,920. Fees: $95. Enrollment: 996 full-time,

2,283 part-time. Faculty: 70. Student-faculty ratio: 14.7:1. Degrees: BA, BS, BSN. Library: 110,559 volumes. 20 buildings on 167 acres. Honors Program, CHANCE Program for remediation of students with learning disfunctions. Outreach Program for non-traditional off-campus nursing students leading to BSN. Outreach Addiction Studies major leading to BS. Field house, indoor track, pool, computerized music lab and publication design program. Internship opportunities. Academic, athletic, fine arts, and leadership grants available.

Grand View College
1200 Grandview Ave., Des Moines 50316
Lori Hanson, Dir. of Admissions
800-444-6083

Grinnell College
P.O. Box 805, Grinnell 50112

· Hawkeye Community College
1501 E. Orange Rd., Waterloo 50701
319-296-2320 Ext. 4000

· Indian Hills Community College
525 Grandview, Ottumwa 52501
515-683-5111

· Iowa Lakes Community College
3200 College Dr., Emmetsburg 50536
John Nelson, Dir. of Admis.
712-852-3554

· Iowa Lakes Community College
300 S. 18th St., Estherville 51334
John Nelson, Dir. of Admis.
712-362-2604

Iowa State University, Ames 50011
Karsten Smedal, Dir. of Admis.

Iowa Wesleyan College
601 N. Main St., Mt. Pleasant 52641

· Kirkwood Community College
P.O. Box 2068, Cedar Rapids 52406
Jim Miller, Dir. of Admis.
319-398-5517

Loras College
1450 Alta Vista, Dubuque 52001
Dan Conry, Dir. of Admis.

Luther College
700 College Dr., Decorah 52101
David Sallee, Dean for Enrollment

Maharishi International University
Route 1, Fairfield 52556
Gregory Polakow, Dir. of Admis.

Morningside College, Sioux City 51106
Lora Vanderzwaag, Dir. of Admis.

Mount Mercy College
1330 Elmhurst Dr., N.E., Cedar Rapids 52402
Carol Williamson, Dir. of Admis.

Northwestern College
101 7th St. S.W., Orange City 51041

St. Ambrose University
518 W. Locust St., Davenport 52803

SCOTT COMMUNITY COLLEGE
500 Belmont Rd., Bettendorf 52722
Kris Barkdoll, Assoc. Dean Enrollment Management

Simpson College
P.O. Box 708, Indianola 50125

· Southeastern Community College
P.O. Box 27, Keokuk 52632
John Adkins, Director

· Southeastern Community College
P.O. Box F., West Burlington 52655
Edward Schieffer, Director

Teikyo Marycrest University
1607 W. 12th St., Davenport 52804
Tim McDonough, Dir. of Admis.
See listing under "Universities"

Teikyo Westmar University
1002 3rd Ave., S.E., Le Mars 51031
Dr. Jim Utesch, Dir. of Admis.

University of Dubuque
2000 University Ave., Dubuque 52001

· Waldorf College
106 S. 6th St., Forest City 50436
Steve Lovik, Dir. of Admis.
800-292-1903

Wartburg College
P.O. Box 1003, Waverly 50677

William Penn College
201 Trueblood Ave., Oskaloosa 52577
Eric Otto, Dir. of Admis.

KANSAS

Baker University
8th & Grove St., Baldwin City 66006

Benedictine College
1020 N. Second St., Atchison 66002
James Hoffman, Dir. of Admis.

Bethel College
300 E. 27th St., North Newton 67117

· Dodge City Community College
2501 N. 14th Ave., Dodge City 67801
Debbie Lloyd, Director of Admissions
800-FOR-DCCC

Fort Hays State University
600 Park St., Hays 67601-4099
Dr. Lawrence Gould, Dean

Friends University
2100 University St., Wichita 67213

Kansas Newman College
3100 McCormick Ave., Wichita 67213
Dr. Robert Giroux, President

Kansas State University
Anderson Hall 110, Manhattan 66506
Ellsworth M. Gerritz, Admis. & Records

Kansas Wesleyan University
100 E. Claflin, Salina 67401
Dr. Daniel Bratton, President

McPherson College
1600 E. Euclid St., McPherson 67460

Mid-America Nazarene College
P.O. Box 1776, Olathe 66051

Ottawa University
1001 S. Cedar St., Ottawa 66067
Steve Koberlein, Dir. of Admis.
800-755-5200

Pittsburg State University
1701 S. Broadway St., Pittsburg 66762
James E. Parker, Dir of Admis.

Saint Mary College
4100 S. 4th St., Leavenworth 66048
Irene Keehan, Dir. of Admis.

SOUTHWESTERN COLLEGE
100 College St., Winfield 67156
800-846-1543

Sterling College, Sterling 67579
Robert Reed, Dir. of Admis. & Records

TABOR COLLEGE
400 S. Jefferson St., Hillsboro 67063
Glenn Lygrisse, VP for Enrollment Management
800-TABOR-99
Established 1908. Private. Coed. Accreditation: North Central Association of Colleges and Schools, National Association of Schools of Music. Tuition: $8,200. Room and board: $3,520. Fees: $200. Enrollment: 396 full-time, 38 part-time. Faculty: 14. Student-faculty ratio: 13:1. Degrees: Bachelor of Arts, Associate of Arts. Library: 65,000 volumes. 19 buildings on 26 acres. Evangelical Christian environment. Student and faculty lifestyle expectations. On-campus living requirement for students.

Washburn University of Topeka
1700 S.W. College Ave., Topeka 66621
John E. Triggs, Dir. of Admissions

Wichita State University
1845 Fairmount, Wichita 67260
800-362-2594
See listing under "Universities"

KENTUCKY

Alice Lloyd College
Purpose Rd., Pippa Passes 41844

Bellarmine College
2001 Newburg Rd., Louisville 40205
Thomas LaBaugh, Dean of Admissions

Brescia College
717 Frederica St., Owensboro 42301
Thomas C. Greer, Director of Admission
800-264-1234

Campbellsville College
200 College St., Campbellsville 42718
Dr. W. R. Davenport, President

Cumberland College
6178 College Station Dr., Williamsburg 40769
See listing under "Universities"

GEORGETOWN COLLEGE
400 E. College St., Georgetown 40324
Garvel Kindrick, Director of Admissions
See listing under "Universities"

Kentucky State University
400 E. Main St., Frankfort 40601

Midway College
512 E. Stephens St., Midway 40347
Carl P. Rollins II, Dir. of Admis.

Morehead State University, Morehead 40351
Charles Myers, Director of Admissions
606-783-2000

Northern Kentucky University
Louie B. Nunn Dr., Highland Heights 41076

Spalding University
851 S. 4th St., Louisville 40203
Dorothy G. Allen, Dir. of Admis.

University of Louisville
2301 S. 3rd St., Louisville 40292
Robert Parrent, Dir. of Admis.

LOUISIANA

Centenary College of Louisiana
P.O. Box 41188, Shreveport 71134

LOUISIANA COLLEGE
P.O. Box 560, Pineville 71359
Dr. Robert Lynn, President
Byron McGee, Dir. of Admis.
318-487-7386
Established 1906. Louisiana Baptist Convention.

Accredited by the Southern Association of Colleges and Schools (SACS). Coed. Total enrollment: 1,013 (367 men, 646 women). 1993-94 tuition: $159 per credit hour. Room and board: $1,492 per semester. Typical yearly expense for boarding students: $8,300, for day students: $5,300. State, federal and institutional financial aid available. LA "One App" Family Financial Statement (FFS) should be filed no later than April 1.

Fifteen academic departments offer 33 majors in art, biology, business, chemistry, communication art, education, English, history, journalism, languages, mathematics, music, nursing, philosophy, physical education, psychology, religion and sociology. Pre-professional programs are pre-law, pre-medical, and pre-veterinary.

All courses are taught by the full faculty - no graduate students or teaching assistants. 75% of faculty hold highest degree in their field. Faculty of 93 with 29 full professors, 17 assistant professors and 14 associate professors. Average class size: 18. Traditional semester calendar with two 5 week summer sessions.

The college is located on an 81 acre campus. Seven modern academic buildings. Library holds more than 125,000 volumes. Three residence halls, housing approximately 500 students. All campus buildings feature modern climate control. Athletic facilities include basketball and tennis courts, baseball and intramural fields, swimming pool and fitness course. Students also have use of a local golf course.

Student life includes 4 fraternities, 4 sororities. Wide assortment of social, service and professional clubs, choral and musical ensembles, theatre productions, guest lecturers and concerts, Student Government Association. Member of the NAIA and the Gulf Coast Athletic Conference. Men participate in basketball, baseball and cross-country. Women's sports include basketball and cross-country. Excellent intramural athletic program provides a wide range of activities.

Admissions: Students may apply for entrance into any term. No fee. Students applying for freshman admissions should submit application, high school transcript and results of ACT or SAT. Transfer students should submit application and official transcripts from all colleges previously attended. Candidates normally notified of decision within two weeks after admissions file completed.

Loyola University
6363 St. Charles Ave., New Orleans 70118

Northwestern State University
Natchitoches 71497

OUR LADY OF HOLY CROSS COLLEGE
4123 Woodland Dr., New Orleans 70131

St. Joseph Seminary College
St. Benedict 70457
V. Rev. Scott J. Underwood, OSB, President-Rector
504-892-1800

Tulane University
6823 Saint Charles Ave., New Orleans 70118
Richard Whiteside, Dean of Admission

MAINE

Bowdoin College, Brunswick 04011
William Mason, Dir. of Admis.

Colby College
150 Mayflower Hill Dr., Waterville 04901
Wm. R. Cotter, President

College of the Atlantic
105 Eden St., Bar Harbor 04609
Steve Thomas, Dir. of Admis.

St. Joseph's College, North Windham 04062

UNITY COLLEGE
Quaker Hill Rd., Unity 04988
207-948-3131
Wilson G. Hess, President
John Craig, Dean for Admissions
Established 1965. Private. Coed. Accreditation: NEASC. Tuition: $9,750. Room and board: $4,750. Enrollment: 475. Faculty: 34. Degrees: AAA, AAS, BA, BS. Small college located in central Maine. Offers liberal arts based bachelor degrees in environmental and social sciences, outdoor recreation, pre-law and interdisciplinary studies (a self-designed major). Two year degrees in liberal arts, sciences, and fine arts. Excellent support services in academic tutoring, career planning, and placement.

University of Maine
University Hts., Augusta 04330

University of Maine at Fort Kent
25 Pleasant St., Fort Kent 04743
Jerry Nadeau, Dir. of Admis.

University of Maine, Orono 04469

University of New England
11 Hills Beach Rd., Biddeford 04005
Patricia Cribby, Dir. of Admis.

University of Southern Maine
96 Falmouth St., Portland 04103
Richard Stebbins, Dean

Westbrook College
716 Stevens Ave., Portland 04103
207-797-7261

MARYLAND

Bowie State University
14000 Jericho Park Rd., Bowie 20715

College of Notre Dame of Maryland
4701 N. Charles St., Baltimore 21210

Columbia Union College
7600 Flower Ave., Takoma Park 20912

Coppin State College
2500 W. North Ave., Baltimore 21216

Essex Community College
7201 Rossville Blvd., Baltimore 21237
Diane Lane, Dir. of Admis.

Goucher College
1021 Dulaney Valley Rd., Baltimore 21204

::: HOME STUDY INTERNATIONAL
12501 Old Columbia Pike, Silver Spring 20904
P.O. Box 4437, Silver Spring 20914-4437 (mailing)
Dr. Joseph Gurubatham, President
800-782-GROW(4769)
Established 1909. Private. Coed. Accreditation: National Home Study Council. Affiliation: Columbia Union College, External degree programs, which are accredited by the Middle States Association of Colleges and Schools.
See listing under "Home Study and Correspondence"

Hood College
400 Rosemont Ave., Frederick 21701

Johns Hopkins University
3400 N. 34th St., Baltimore 21218

Loyola College
4501 N. Charles St., Baltimore 21210
William Bossemeyer III, Dir. of Admis.

Montgomery College
51 Mannakee St., Rockville 20850
Germantown - 301-353-7773
Rockville - 301-279-5147
Takoma Park - 301-650-1480

Morgan State University
Cold Spring Ln. and Hillen Rd., Baltimore 21239

Mt. St. Mary's College
16300 Old Emmitsburg Rd., Emmitsburg 21727
Michael D. Kennedy, Dir. of Admis.

St. Mary's College of Maryland
St. Mary's City 20686

Salisbury State University
1101 Camden Ave., Salisbury 21801

Sojourner-Douglass College
500 N. Caroline St., Baltimore 21205
Robin P. Quarles, Dir. of Admissions

Towson State University
800 York Rd., Towson 21204
Dr. Hoke Smith, President

University of Baltimore
1420 N. Charles St., Baltimore 21201
Clare MacDonald, Dean of Admissions

Villa Julie College
1525 Greenspring Valley Rd., Stevenson 21153
Carolyn Manuszak, President

Washington College
Washington Ave., Chestertown 21620
Kevin Coveney, Dir. of Admis.

Western Maryland College
2 College Hill, Westminster 21157

MASSACHUSETTS

American International College
1000 State St., Springfield 01109
Peter Miller, Dean of Admissions

Amherst College, Amherst 01002
Jane E. Reynolds, Dean of Admissions

Anna Maria College
2 Sunset Ln., Paxton 01612
Dr. Bernadette Madore, SSA, President

Aquinas College
15 Walnut Park, Newton 02158
Ellen Ronayne, Dir. of Admis.

Aquinas College at Milton
303 Adams St., Milton 02186
617-696-3100

Assumption College
500 Salisbury St., Worcester 01609

Atlantic Union College
P.O. Box 1000, South Lancaster 01561
Osa Canto, Registrar

BAY PATH COLLEGE
588 Longmeadow St., Longmeadow 01106
Paula DesRoberts, Dean of Admis.
413-567-0621 or 800-782-PATH
Established: 1897. Private. Women. Accreditation: NEASC, Legal programs ABA approved. Tuition: $10,200. Room and board: $6,225. Enrollment: 600. Faculty: 42. Student-faculty ratio: 14:1. Degrees: AA, AS, BA, BS. Library: 38,000 volumes. 27 buildings on 30 acres. Secure, suburban campus near Springfield and Hartford. 15 Associate degree programs in business, education, fashion/design, criminal justice, paralegalism, hospitality/tourism, health, human services, occupational therapy, psychology, liberal arts. Baccalaureates in business, business/accounting, legal studies, psychology, psychology/criminal justice, psychology/early childhood education. Extensive career services. 95-98% of students obtain jobs after graduation. Transfer welcome.

Bentley College
175 Forest St., Waltham 02154
Joann McKenna, Dir. of Admis.

Boston University
685 Commonwealth Ave., Boston 02215

Bradford College
320 S. Main St., Bradford 01835

Brandeis University
415 South St, Waltham 02154
David Gould, Dean of Admissions
617-736-3500

Bridgewater State College
Bridgewater 02325
James Plotner, Jr., Dir. of Admis.

Clark University
950 Main St., Worcester 01610
Richard Pierson, Dean of Admis.

College of the Holy Cross
1 College St., Worcester 01610
William R. Mason, Dir. of Admis.

Curry College
1071 Blue Hill Ave., Milton 02186
617-333-0500

DEAN COLLEGE
99 Main St, Franklin 02038
Kathleen Teehan, Dean of Admissions
508-528-9100
See listing under "Community and Junior Colleges"

ELMS COLLEGE
291 Springfield St., Chicopee 01013
800-255-ELMS

Emerson College
148 Beacon St., Boston 02116

Emmanuel College
400 The Fenway, Boston 02115
Margaret Bonilla, Dir. of Admis.

Endicott College
376 Hale St., Beverly 01915
Elizabeth Macomber, Dir. of Admis.

Fisher College
118 Beacon St., Boston 02116
Sandra Robbins, Dir. of Admis.

Gordon College
255 Grapevine Rd., Wenham 01984

Hampshire College, Amherst 01002
Audrey Y. Smith, Dir. of Admissions
413-582-5471

Hellenic College
50 Goddard Ave., Brookline 02146
Fr. Al Demos, Director of Admission
617-731-3500

Massachusetts Institute of Technology
77 Massachusetts Ave., Cambridge 02139

Massasoit Community College
1 Massasoit Blvd., Brockton 02402
Roberta Noodell, Dir. of Admis.

Merrimack College
315 Turnpike St., North Andover 01845
Dennis Farrell, Dean of Admissions

Middlesex Community College
33 Kearney Sq., Lowell 01852
508-656-3211

Nichols College, Dudley 01570

North Adams State College
375 Church St., North Adams 01247
413-664-4511 or 800-292-6632
See listing under "Universities or Graduate Schools"

North Shore Community College
1 Ferncroft Rd., Danvers 01923

Pine Manor College
400 Heath St., Chestnut Hill 02167
Gillian Lloyd, Dir. of Admis.

Quincy Junior College
34 Coddington St., Quincy 02169
Richard Pessin, Dean of Enrollment Services

Quinsigamond Community College
670 W. Boylston St., Worcester 01606
Ron Smith, Dir. of Admis.

REGIS COLLEGE
235 Wellesley St., Weston 02193
Valerie L. Brown, Director of Admission
800-456-1820

St. Hyacinth College and Seminary
66 School St., Granby 01033
Rev. Richard Forcier, Dir. of Admis.
See listing under "Men's Colleges"

Simmons College
300 The Fenway, Boston 02115

Simon's Rock of Bard College
80 Alford Rd., Great Barrington 01230

Smith College
Northampton 01063

SPRINGFIELD TECHNICAL COMMUNITY COLLEGE
1 Armory Square, Springfield 01105
Dr. Patrick E. Tigue, Dir. of Admissions
413-781-7822

Stonehill College
320 Washington St., North Easton 02357
508-230-1373

Suffolk University
8 Ashburton Place, Boston 02108
Barbara K. Ericson, Assoc. Dean Enrollment & Retention
617-573-8460

Tufts University
520 Boston Ave., Medford 02155

University of Massachusetts, Amherst 01003
Arlene Wesley Cash, Dir. of Admis.

University of Massachusetts
100 Morrissey Blvd., Boston 02125

University of Massachusetts Dartmouth
Old Westport Rd., North Dartmouth 02747
Raymond Barrows, Dir. of Admissions
508-999-8605

Wellesley College, Wellesley 02181
Janet A. Lavin, Dir. of Admis.

Western New England College
1215 Wilbraham Rd., Springfield 01119
800-325-1122

Westfield State College
577 Western Ave., Westfield 01085
John F. Marcus, Dir. of Admis.

Williams College, Williamstown 01267

Worcester State College
486 Chandler St., Worcester 01602

MICHIGAN

Adrian College
110 S. Madison St., Adrian 49221
George Wolf, Dir. of Admis.
See listing under "Universities"

Albion College
611 E. Porter, Albion 49224
800-858-6770

Alma College
614 W. Superior St., Alma 48801-1599
John Seveland, VP for Enrollment
800-321-ALMA
See listing under "Universities"

Aquinas College
1607 Robinson Rd., S.E., Grand Rapids 49506
R. Paul Nelson, President
Paula Meehan, Dean of Admissions
800-678-9593

Concordia College
4090 Geddes Rd., Ann Arbor 48105
Mary Froelich, Dir. of Admis.

Eastern Michigan University, Ypsilanti 48197
Barry Fish, Dean
313-487-3060 or 800-GO-TO-EMU

Grand Rapids Baptist College & Seminary
1001 East Beltline Ave., N.E.
Grand Rapids 49505

HILLSDALE COLLEGE
33 E. College St., Hillsdale 49242
Dr. Thomas Burke, Chrpsn.
517-437-7341

Hope College
69 E. 10th St., Holland 49423
Gordon Van Wylen, President

Kalamazoo College
1200 Academy St., Kalamazoo 49006

Lake Superior State University
1000 College Dr., Sault St. Marie 49783

Lawrence Technological University
21000 W. Ten Mile Rd., Southfield 48075
800-225-5588 ext. 3160

Madonna University
36600 Schoolcraft St., Livonia 48150

Marygrove College
8425 W. McNichols Rd., Detroit 48221

Michigan State University, East Lansing 48824
Dr. John W. Eadie, Dean

Michigan Technological University
1400 Townsend Dr., Houghton 49931
Joseph A. Galetto, Dir. Enrollment Mgmt.
906-487-2335

Northwestern Michigan College
1701 E. Front St., Traverse City 49686
Diane Emling, Dean
800-748-0566

Olivet College
300 S. Main St., Olivet 49076
Vicki Gallas, Registrar
See listing under "Universities"

Saginaw Valley State University
2250 Pierce Rd., University Center 48710

St. Mary's College
Orchard Lake & Commerce Rd.
Orchard Lake 48324

Siena Heights College
1247 E. Siena Heights Dr., Adrian 49221

Spring Arbor College
106 E. Main St., Spring Arbor 49283

Suomi College
601 Quincy St., Hancock 49930
John Ruohoniemi, Dean/Enrollment Development
800-682-7604

University of Detroit Mercy
4001 W. McNichols
PO Box 19900, Detroit 48219-0900
313-993-1245
See listing under "Universities"

University of Michigan-Ann Arbor
815 S. University Ave., Ann Arbor 48109

Western Michigan University, Kalamazoo 49008
Stanley Henderson, Dir. of Enrl. Mgt. & Admis.
616-387-2000

William Tyndale College
35700 W. Twelve Mile Rd.
Farmington Hills 48331

MINNESOTA

Anoka-Ramsey Community College
11200 Mississippi Blvd., N.W.
Coon Rapids 55433
Irene Campanaro, Dir. Student Services
612-427-2600

Bemidji State University
1500 Birchmont Dr., N.E., Bemidji 56601
800-475-2001

Bethany Lutheran College
734 Marsh St., Mankato 56001
Steven Jaeger, Dir. of Admis.
507-625-2977

Bethel College
3900 Bethel Dr., St. Paul 55112
Dr. George Brushaber, President

Carleton College
One N. College St., Northfield 55057
Paul Thiboutot, Dir. of Admis.

College of Saint Benedict
37 S. College Ave., St. Joseph 56374

College of St. Catherine
2004 Randolph Ave., St. Paul 55105

COLLEGE OF ST. SCHOLASTICA
1200 Kenwood Ave., Duluth 55811
Dr. Daniel Pilon, President
Becky Urbanski-Junkert, VP for Admissions & Student Financial Planning
800-447-5444
Established 1924. Roman Catholic. Coed. Accreditation: NCACS. Tuition: $11,205. Room and board: $3,588. Enrollment: 1,900. Faculty: 150 full-time. Degrees: BA, MEd, MA nursing, psychology of aging, management, occupational therapy, and physical therapy. Library: 150,000 volumes. 10 buildings on 160 acres. Gym. Situated at the head of Lake Superior, international seaport, 4-season recreational facilities, cultural center for northeast Minnesota, study center in Ireland, Russia and Costa Rica.

Concordia College
901 8th St. S., Moorhead 56562
Dr. Walter Prausnitz, Director
See listing under "Universities"

Concordia College-St. Paul
275 N. Syndicate, St. Paul 55104
Tim Utter, Dir. of Admis.

Hamline University
1536 Hewitt Ave., St. Paul 55104
Scott Pratt, Dir. of Admis.

Inver Hills Community College
8445 College Trail, E., Inver Grove Heights 55076
Cheryl Frank, Director

MacAlester College
1600 Grand Ave., St. Paul 55105

Mankato State University
P.O. Box 8400, Mankato 56002

Metropolitan State University
700 7th St. E., St. Paul 55106
Beverly Ferguson, PhD, Interim Dean

Minneapolis Community College
1501 Hennepin Ave., Minneapolis 55403-1779
Bonnie Wiger, Registrar
612-341-7000

Moorhead State University
1104 7th Ave. S., Moorhead 56560

St. Cloud State University
740 4th Ave., S., St. Cloud 56301
Sherwood Reid, Dir. of Admis.
800-369-4260

St. John's University
P.O. Box 7155, Collegeville 56321

St. Mary's College of Minnesota
700 Terrace Heights #2, Winona 55987
Tony Piscitiello, VP for Admission

ST. OLAF COLLEGE
Northfield 55057
Melvin George, President
John Ruohoniemi, Dir. of Admis.
507-646-3025

Southwest State University, Marshall 56258

University of Minnesota
600 E. Fourth St., Morris 56267

University of Minnesota, Twin Cities
Minneapolis 55455

University of St. Thomas
2115 Summit Ave., St. Paul 55105

Winona State University
P.O. Box 5838, Winona 55987
Dr. J. Mootz, Dir. of Admis.

WORTHINGTON COMMUNITY COLLEGE
1450 College Way, Worthington 56187
Conrad Burchill, President
507-372-2107

MISSISSIPPI

Blue Mountain College
P.O. Box 338, Blue Mountain 38610

Millsaps College
P.O. Box 150556, Jackson 39210
Florence Hines, Dir. of Admis.

MISSOURI

Avila College
11901 Wornall Rd., Kansas City 64145

Central Methodist College
411 CMC Square, Fayette 65248
See listing under "Universities"

Central Missouri State University
Warrensburg 64093
Delores Hudson, Dir. of Admis.

College of the Ozarks, Point Lookout 65726
Dr. Kenton Olson, Dean of the College

Columbia College
1001 Rogers St., Columbia 65216
Ron Cronacher, Dir. of Admissions
800-231-2391

Conception Seminary College, Conception 64433
Rev. Albert Bruecken, Dir. of Admis.

Cottey College
1000 W. Austin St., Nevada 64772
Wendy Beckemeyer, Dir. of Admis.

Culver-Stockton College, Canton 63435
Betty Smith, Dean of Admissions
800-537-1883

Drury College
900 N. Benton Ave., Springfield 65802
Michael G. Thomas, Dir. of Admis.

Evangel College
1111 N. Glenstone Ave., Springfield 65802
David Schoolfield, Dir. of Enrollment

Fontbonne College
6800 Wydown Blvd., St. Louis 63105
Peggy Musen, Dir. of Admis.

Hannibal-LaGrange College, Hannibal 63401

Kemper Military School & College
701 3rd St., Boonville 65233
Dr. C.W. Stewart, President
800-530-5600

Maryville University of St. Louis
13550 Conway Rd., Saint Louis 63141
314-576-9300 or 800-MARYVLL

Missouri Baptist College
12542 Conway Rd., St. Louis 63141

Missouri Southern State College
3950 Newman Rd., Joplin 64801-1595
Dr. Ray Malzahn, Dean
See listing under "Universities"

Missouri Valley College
500 E. College St., Marshall 65340
816-886-6924 ext. 114
See listing under "Universities"

Missouri Western State College
4525 Downs Dr., St. Joseph 64507
Howard McCauley, Dir. of Admis.

Park College, Parkville 64152
Dr. Edwin Rawn, Dean of Admis.

Rockhurst College
1100 Rockhurst Rd., Kansas City 64110
Barbara O'Connell, Dir. of Enrollment Services

St. Louis University
221 N. Grand Blvd., St. Louis 63103
Louis A. Menard, Dean of Admissions

Southeast Missouri State University
1 University Plz., Cape Girardeau 63701
New Student Relations 314-651-2590
See listing under "Universities"

Southwest Baptist University
1601 S. Springfield Ave., Bolivar 65613

Stephens College, Columbia 65215
Mary Ann Sprinkle, Dir. of Admis.

University of Missouri, Rolla
102 Parker Hall, Rolla 65401
David J. Allen, Dir. of Admis. & Financial Aid
800-522-0938

Washington University
1 Brookings Dr., St. Louis 63130

Webster University
470 E. Lockwood Ave., St. Louis 63119
Dr. James Staley, Associate Dean
See listing under "Universities"

Westminster College
501 Westminster Ave., Fulton 65251
J. Harvey Saunders, President

William Jewell College, Liberty 64068
T. Edwin Norris, Dir of Admis.
800-753-7009

William Woods College
200 W. 12th St., Fulton 65251
Dr. Jahnae Barnett, VP of Admis.

MONTANA

CARROLL COLLEGE
1610 N. Benton Ave., Helena 59625
Candace Cain, Dir. of Admis.
See listing under "Universities"

College of Great Falls
1301 20th St., S., Great Falls 59405
Jean Walker, Dir. of Admis.

Montana State University - Billings
1500 N. 30th St., Billings 59101
Karen Everett, Dir. of Admis.
406-657-2158

Rocky Mountain College
1511 Poly Dr., Billings 59102
David Heringer, Dir. of Admis.
See listing under "Universities"

University of Montana, Missoula 59812
800-462-8636

Western Montana College
710 S. Atlantic St., Dillon 59725

NEBRASKA

Bellevue College
1000 Galvin Rd. S., Bellevue 68005
Chari Leader, VP of Enrollment

Chadron State College
1000 Main St., Chadron 69337
Dr. Donald Green, Dean

College of Saint Mary
1901 S. 72nd St., Omaha 68124
Sheila Haggas, Dir. of Admis.

Concordia College
800 N. Columbia Ave., Seward 68434
Don Vos, Dir. of Admis.

Creighton University
2500 California St., Omaha 68178
Rev. Michael Proterra, SJ, Dean

Dana College
2848 College Dr., Blair 68008
John Schueth, Dir. of Admis.
800-444-3262
See listing under "Universities"

Doane College
1014 Boswell Ave., Crete 68333
Pappy Khouri, Dir. of Admissions

Hastings College
P.O. Box 269, Hastings 68902
Thomas Reeves, President

Nebraska Wesleyan University
5000 Saint Paul Ave., Lincoln 68504
Ken Sieg, Dir. of Admis.

Northeast Community College
P.O. Box 469, Norfolk 68702
Eugene Hart, Dir. of Admis.

Peru State College, Peru 68421
Pamela J. Cosgrove, Dir. of Admis.
402-872-3815

University of Nebraska at Lincoln
Old H 1223, Lincoln 68588
John Peters, Dean

University of Nebraska at Omaha
Omaha 68182

NEVADA

SIERRA NEVADA COLLEGE-LAKE TAHOE
P.O. Box 4269, Incline Village 89450
Mark Hurtubise, President
Lane Murray, Dir. of Admissions
Established 1969. Coed. Accreditation: NWASC.
Tuition: $9,000. Room: $2,700 to $3,000. Enrollment:
120 boarding, 500 day. Faculty: 50. Degrees: BA, BS,
BFA. Library: 20,000 volumes. 6 buildings on 19
acres. Golf course nearby. Majors in environmental
science, science, hotel, restaurant and resort management, ski business and resort management, performing arts, Humanities, and teacher education. 2 miles
from Lake Tahoe; stunning alpine environment. 22
ski resorts within 1/2 hour drive, 45 minutes from
Reno, Nevada, 4 hours from San Francisco.

University of Nevada Las Vegas
4505 S. Maryland Pky., Las Vegas 89154-1021
Admissions: 702-895-3443 or 800-334-UNLV

NEW HAMPSHIRE

Colby-Sawyer College
100 Main St., New London 03257
Kay Dethlefsen, Dir. of Admis.

Keene State College
229 Main St., Keene 03435
Kathryn Dodge, Dir. of Admis.

New England College
26 Bridge St., Henniker 03242
John Spaulding, Dir. of Admis.

New Hampshire College
2500 North River Rd., Manchester 03106
Brad Poznanski, Dir. of Admis.
603-645-9611

NOTRE DAME COLLEGE
2321 Elm St., Manchester 03104
603-669-4298

Rivier College
420 S. Main St., Nashua 03060
Admissions: 800-44-RIVIER

Saint Anselm College
87 Saint Anselm Dr., Manchester 03102
Don Healy, Dir. of Admis.

White Pines College
40 Chester St., Chester 03036
603-887-4401

NEW JERSEY

Bloomfield College
1 Park Place, Bloomfield 07003
Warner Smith, Dean for Admissions
201-748-9000, Ext. 230

Caldwell College
9 Ryerson Ave., Caldwell 07006

College of Saint Elizabeth
Convent Station 07961
Sr. Jacqueline Burns, President

Fairleigh Dickinson University
Edw. Williams College
150 Kotte Pl., Hackensack 07601
Kenneth Vehrkens, Dean
201-692-2675

Fairleigh Dickinson University, Madison 07940
Lissa Anderson, Dir. of Admis.
201-593-8906

Fairleigh Dickinson University, Teaneck 07666
Dennis Craig, Dir. of Admis.
201-692-2553

FELICIAN COLLEGE
262 S. Main St., Lodi 07644
Sr. Mary Austin, OSB, Dir. of Admis.
201-778-1029
See listing under "Universities"

Hudson County Community College
168 Sip Ave., Jersey City 07306
Joseph O'Halloran, Director of Admissions
201-714-2127

Jersey City State College
2039 Kennedy Blvd., Jersey City 07305
201-200-3234

Kean College of New Jersey
1000 Morris Ave., Union 07083

Mercer County Community College
West Windsor Campus
1200 Old Trenton Rd., Trenton 08690
Michael Glass, Dir. of Admis.
See listing under "Community and Junior
Colleges"

Monmouth College
400 Cedar Ave., West Long Branch 07764
Joan Rudinski, Dir. of Admis.

Ramapo College of New Jersey
505 Ramapo Valley Rd., Mahwah 07430
Robert Scott, President
201-529-7600

Rider University
2083 Lawrenceville Rd., Lawrenceville 08648
Susan Christian, Dir. of Admis.

Rowan College of New Jersey, Glassboro 08028
Marvin G. Sills, Dir. of Admis.

St. Peter's College
2641 John F. Kennedy Blvd.
Jersey City 07306
Mary Beth Carey, Director of Admissions
201-915-9213

Seton Hall University
400 S. Orange Ave., South Orange 07079
Lee Cooke, Dir. of Admis.

Stockton State College, Pomona 08240
Sal Catalfamo, Dir. of Admis.

Thomas Edison State College
101 W. State St., Trenton 08608

Upsala College
345 Prospect St., East Orange 07017
George Lynes, Dean of Admissions

NEW MEXICO

Albuquerque Technical-Vocational Institute
525 Buena Vista Dr., S.E., Albuquerque 87106
Jane Campbell, Registrar
See listing under "Career Schools"

College of Santa Fe
1600 St. Michaels Dr., Santa Fe 87505
800-456-2673

Eastern New Mexico University
Portales 88130
Larry Fuqua, Dir. of Admis.

Eastern New Mexico University-Roswell Campus
P.O. Box 6000, Roswell 88202
Tim Raftery, Director of Admissions and Records

St. John's College
1160 Camino de Cruz Blanca, Santa Fe 87501
Marsha Drennon, Dir. of Admis.

University of New Mexico, Albuquerque 87131
Robert Weaver, Dean of Admissions

NEW YORK

Adelphi University, Garden City 11530
Dr. William Eidson, Dean, Coll. of Arts & Sciences
516-877-4120

Alfred University
Alumni Hall, Alfred 14802
Laurie Richer, Director of Admissions
800-541-9229

AMERICAN UNIVERSITY OF PARIS
80 E. 11th St. #434, New York 10003
Thelma Bullock, Dir. of U.S. Office
See listing under "Universities"

Barnard College
3009 Broadway, New York 10027

Canisius College
2001 Main St., Buffalo 14208
Penelope Lips, Dir. of Admis.
800-843-1517

Cathedral College of the Immaculate Conception
7200 Douglaston Pkwy., Douglaston 11362
Rev. Martin Geraghty, Academic Dean

CAZENOVIA COLLEGE
Cazenovia 13035
Dr. James Parker, VP for Enrollment Management
See listing under "Universities"

Clarkson University, Potsdam 13699
Robert Croot, Dir. of Admis.

Colgate University
13 Oak Dr., Hamilton 13346
Dean of Admissions
315-824-7401

College of Mount St. Vincent
6301 Riverdale Ave., Riverdale 10471

College of St. Rose
432 Western Ave., Albany 12203

Concordia College
171 White Plains Rd., Bronxville 10708

CUNY, Queens College
6530 Kissena Blvd., Flushing 11367

Daemen College
4380 Main St., Amherst 14226
Maria Dillard, Dir. of Admis.
in NY 800-462-7652 or 716-839-8225

Dominican College of Blauvelt
460 N. Western Hwy., Orangeburg 10962
Louis Kern, Dir. of Admis.
914-359-7800

Dowling College,
150 Idle Hour Blvd., Oakdale 11769
Dr. Jerome Traiger, Dean

D'Youville College
320 Porter Ave., Buffalo 14201
Ronald Dannecker, Dir. of Admis.

ELMIRA COLLEGE
Park Place, Elmira 14901
607-735-1800
Dr. Thomas Meier, President
William S. Neal, Dean of Admissions
Established 1855. Independent. Coed. Accreditation: MSACS, NLN. Tuition: $14,990. Room and
board: $4,980. Enrollment: 1,100 day. Faculty: 65
full-time. Degrees: BA, BS, MSEd. Library: 369,000
volumes. 28 buildings on 40 acres. 2 gyms. Pool.
Optional 3 year graduation plan. Special courses -
speech clinic on campus, special spring term for
work, travel, and independent study. Field experience required in most majors.

FIVE TOWNS COLLEGE
305 N. Service Rd., Dix Hills 11746
Jennifer Roemer, Coordinator of Admissions
516-424-7000
See listing under "Universities"

Friends World Program, Long Island University
Montauk Hwy., Southampton 11968
Carol Gilbert, Dir. of Admis.

Hofstra University
1000 Fulton Ave., Hempstead 11550
Margaret Shields, Dean of Admissions

Houghton College
P.O. Box 128, Houghton 14744
Tim Fuller, Dir. of Admis.

IONA COLLEGE
715 North Ave., New Rochelle 10801
800-231-IONA or 914-633-2503
See listing under "Universities"

Ithaca College
953 Danby Rd., Ithaca 14850

Keuka College
P.O. Box 98, Keuka Park 14478
Robert J. Ianuzzo, Dean of Admissions

The King's College, Briarcliff Manor 10510
Frederic Rowley, Dean of Admissions

Le Moyne College
1419 Salt Springs Rd., Syracuse 13214-1301
Edwin B. Harris, Dir. of Admis.

Long Island University-Brooklyn Campus
1 University Plaza, Brooklyn 11201
Alan Chaves, Dean of Admissions

Long Island University-C. W. Post Campus
Rt. 25A, Brookville 11548
Dr. Maithili Schmidt, Chrpsn.
516-299-2233

Long Island University-Southampton Campus
Southampton 11968
Carol Gilbert, Dir. of Admis.

Manhattan College
4513 Manhattan College Pky., Riverdale 10471
Dr. Mary Ann O'Donnell, Acting Dean of Arts

Manhattanville College
2900 Purchase St., Purchase 10577

· Maria College of Albany
700 New Scotland Ave., Albany 12208
Laurie Gilmore, Dir. of Admis.

Marymount College
100 Marymount Ave., Tarrytown 10591
Gina R. Campbell, Dir. of Admis.
800-724-4312

· Mater Dei College
Riverside Dr., Ogdensburg 13669
Mark Dougherty, Dir. of Admis.

Medaille College
18 Agassiz Cir., Buffalo 14214
Jacqueline Smukeer, Dir. of Admis.

Mercy College
555 Broadway, Dobbs Ferry 10522
James Nesbitt, Dean of Admissions

Molloy College
1000 Hempstead Ave., Rockville Centre 11570
Wayne James, Dir. of Admis.
See listing under "Universities"

Mt. St. Mary College
330 Powell Ave., Newburgh 12550

Nazareth College of Rochester
4245 East Ave., Rochester 14618
Paul Kenyon, Dir. of Admis.

New York Institute of Technology
Old Westbury Campus, Old Westbury 11568

Niagara University, Niagara University 14109
George Pachter, Dean of Admissions
800-462-2111
See listing under "Universities"

Nyack College, Nyack 10960
Miguel Sanchez, Dir. of Admis.
800-33-NYACK

::: On-Line Campus
New York Institute of Technology
P.O. Box 8000, Old Westbury 11568-8000
800-222-NYIT

Pace University, New York Campus
1 Pace Plaza, New York 10038

Pace University, Pleasantville/Briarcliff Campus
Bedford Rd., Pleasantville 10570

Pace University, White Plains Campus
78 N. Broadway, White Plains 10603

· Paul Smith's College, Paul Smiths 12970
Enrico Miller, Dir. of Admis.
800-421-2605

Polytechnic University
333 Jay St., Brooklyn 11201

REGENTS COLLEGE OF THE UNIVERSITY OF THE STATE OF NEW YORK
7 Columbia Circle, Albany 12203-5159
518-464-8500

Roberts Wesleyan College
2301 Westside Dr., Rochester 14624
Linda Kurtz, Dir. of Admis.
See listing under "Universities"

Rochester Institute of Technology
1 Lomb Memorial Dr., Rochester 14623
716-475-6631
See listing under "Universities"

Russell Sage College
51 1st St., Troy 12180

St. Francis College
180 Remsen St., Brooklyn 11201

St. John Fisher College
3690 East Ave., Rochester 14618
Peter Lindsey, Dir. of Admis.

St. John's University
Grand Central & Utopia Parkways, Jamaica 11439

ST. JOHN'S UNIVERSITY
300 Howard Ave., Staten Island 10301

St. Joseph's College
245 Clinton Ave., Brooklyn 11205
Geraldine Foudy, Dir. of Admis.
718-636-6868

St. Joseph's College, Suffolk Campus
25 Audobon Ave., Patchogue 11772

St. Lawrence University, Canton 13617
Joel R. Wincowski, Dean of Admis. & Financial Aid

ST. THOMAS AQUINAS COLLEGE
Rt. 340, Sparkill 10976
Dr. Donald McNelis, President
Andrea Kraeft, Dir. of Admis.
800-999-STAC
Established 1952. Private. Coed. Accreditation:

MSACS, New York State Board of Regents. Tuition: $8,000. Enrollment: 300 boarding, 1,800 day. Faculty: 75. Degrees: AA, AS, BA, BS, BSEd, MSEd. Library: 100,000 vols. 13 bldgs. on 43 acres. Gym. 15 miles north of NYC; adjacent to Bergen County, NJ. Neighboring historical districts Nyack, Tappan and Piermont. Special programs in art therapy, gerontology (BS), communications, engineering and special education. Total 31 majors.

Sarah Lawrence College, Bronxville 10708

Siena College, Loudonville 12211
Harry Wood, Director, Admissions

Skidmore College, Saratoga Springs 12866
Kent Jones, Dir. of Admis.

· SUNY Adirondack Community College
439 Bay Rd., Queensbury 12804
Levi Brown, Dir. of Admis.
518-793-4491
See listing under "Community and Junior Colleges"

SUNY at Buffalo
17 Capen Hall
P.O. Box 601660, Buffalo 14260-1660
716-645-6900

SUNY at Stony Brook
Stony Brook 11794

SUNY College at Brockport
Brockport 14420

SUNY College at Cortland
P.O. Box 2000, Cortland 13045

SUNY College at Old Westbury
P.O. Box 210, Old Westbury 11568
Michael Sheehy, Dir. of Admis.

SUNY College at Plattsburgh, Plattsburgh 12901
Richard Higgins, Dir. of Admis.
518-564-2040

· SUNY College of Agriculture and Technology
Morrisville 13408
Dennis Nostrand, Dir. of Admis.

· SUNY College of Technology, Alfred 14802
Deborah J. Goodrich, Dir. of Admis.
607-587-4215

SUNY College of Technology at Farmingdale
Route 110, Farmingdale 11735
Janet Snyder, Dir. of Admis.
516-420-2200

SUNY Empire State College
1 Union Ave., Saratoga Springs 12866
Marvin Thorsland, Dir. of Admis.

· SUNY Monroe Community College
1000 E. Henrietta Rd., Rochester 14623
716-292-2000

· SUNY Nassau Community College
1 Education Dr., Garden City 11530
Bernard Iantosca, Dir of Admis.

· SUNY Onondaga Community College
Onondaga Rd., Syracuse 13215
Joseph Insel, Dir. of Admis.

· SUNY Schenectady County Community College
78 Washington Ave., Schenectady 12305
Robert Dinello, Dir. of Admis.
518-346-6211, ext. 166

Syracuse University, Syracuse 13244

· Trocaire College
110 Red Jacket Pky., Buffalo 14220
Dr. Dorothy Smith, Dean of Liberal Arts
716-826-1200

Union College, Schenectady 12308

University of Rochester
500 Joseph C. Wilson Blvd., Rochester 14627
Wayne A. Locust, Dir. of Admis.
See listing under "Universities"

Utica College of Syracuse University
1600 Burrstone Rd., Utica 13502

Vassar College
125 Raymond Ave., Poughkeepsie 12601

· Villa Maria College of Buffalo
240 Pine Ridge Rd., Buffalo 14225
Lynn D'Auria, Dir. of Admis.

WAGNER COLLEGE
631 Howard Ave., Staten Island 10301
Joseph Foulke, Dean Admissions and Financial Aid
See listing under "Universities"

Wells College, Aurora 13026
Susan Raith, Director of Admissions
315-364-3264

NORTH CAROLINA

· Alamance Community College
P.O. Box 623, Haw River 27258
W. Ronald McCarter, President

Barber-Scotia College
145 Cabarrus Ave., W., Concord 28025

Barton College
College Station, Wilson 27893
Anthony Britt, Dir. of Admis.
800-345-4973/919-399-6318
See listing under "Universities"

Belmont Abbey College
1 Abbey Pl., Belmont 28012
Admissions, 800-523-2355

· Brevard College
Brevard 28712
Bob McLendon, Dean of Admissions

Catawba College
2300 W. Innes St., Salisbury 28144
Mark Stokes, Dir. of Admis.

· College of The Albemarle
P.O. Box 2327, Elizabeth City 27906
John M. Wells, Asst. Dean of Admissions
919-335-0821, Ext. 220

Davidson College
P.O. Box 1737, Davidson 28036

Duke University, Durham 27706

Elon College
P.O. Box 2700, Elon College 27244
Nan P. Perkins, Dean of Admissions

Gardner-Webb University
General Delivery, Boiling Springs 28017
Robert E. Morgan, Chrpsn.
704-434-2361

Greensboro College
815 W. Market St., Greensboro 27401

· Halifax Community College
P.O. Box 809, Weldon 27890

High Point College
933 Montlieu Ave., High Point 27262
Jim Schlimmer, Dir. of Admis.

Mars Hill College
Main St., Mars Hill 28754
Dr. Smith Goodrum, Dean of Admis.

Methodist College
5400 Ramsey St., Fayetteville 28311
Fiore Bergamasco, Dir. of Admis.

Montreat-Anderson College
P.O. Box 1267, Montreat 28757
David E. Walters, Dir. of Admissions
800-MAC-N-YOU
See listing under "Universities"

North Carolina State University
P.O. Box 7001, Raleigh 27695
George Dixon, Dir. of Admis.

North Carolina Wesleyan College
3400 N. Wesleyan Blvd., Rocky Mount 27804

· Peace College
15 E. Peace St., Raleigh 27604
Dr. Garrett Briggs, President
919-832-2881, Fax: 919-834-6755

Pfeiffer College
General Delivery, Misenheimer 28109

QUEENS COLLEGE
1900 Selwyn Ave., Charlotte 28274
Dr. Billy O. Wireman, President
D. Stephen Cloniger, VP for Enrollment Management
704-337-2212 or 800-849-0202
Established 1857. Coed. Presbyterian, 4 year liberal arts college offering the BA, BS, BM, and BSFN degrees. Master's degrees are offered in business administration, and education. Bachelor's degrees are offered in the traditional areas of arts and sciences, and also in business, communications, health sciences, music therapy, and education. Pre-professional programs in law and medicine. Other special programs include: international experience at no extra cost to full-time students, Harvard Model UN, Washington semester, exploratory internships, leadership programs, junior year abroad, and double majors.
Accreditation: SACS, NASM, NLN, National Association for Music Therapy, North Carolina Board of Nursing, NCATE, and North Carolina Department of Public Instruction.
All courses taught by qualified faculty - no graduate or teaching assistants. 73% of tenured faculty hold PhD's. Student-faculty ratio is 12:1. Average class size: 15. Library contains 116,500 volumes, more than 6,000 microtexts, and subscribes to 650 periodicals. DEC VAX 11/750 computer with terminals in residence halls, library and computer center.
25 acre campus located in beautiful residential neighborhood. 28 buildings. Athletic facilities include lighted tennis courts, swimming pool, weight room, dance studios, regulation basketball courts, and soccer field. Intercollegiate (NCAA II) basketball, golf, soccer, tennis, softball, and volleyball teams.
Student life includes 5 national sororities , 1 national and 1 local fraternities. Wide assortment of social, service, and professional clubs; choral and music ensembles; theatre productions; guest lecturers and concerts; Student Government Association. Students may keep cars on campus.
Students applying for admission should submit application, high school transcripts, recommendation forms, and results of SAT or ACT scores. Transfer students must include the above plus all college transcripts. Solid college prep background with 4 years English, 3 years math, 2 years social science, 2 years foreign language, and 1 year laboratory science recommended. Students may apply for admission into any term. Rolling admissions (students applying will be notified of status approximately four weeks after receipt of a completed application).
Resident student comprehensive fee: $14,950 for 1993-94; commuting student comprehensive fee: $10,400. State, federal, and institutional financial aid available. Financial Aid Form (FAF) should be filed no later than March 1st. 72% of students receive financial aid. Scholarships available.

St. Andrews Presbyterian College
1700 Dogwood Mile, Laurinburg 28352
Dale B. Montague, Dir. of Admis.

St. Augustine's College
1315 Oakwood Ave., Raleigh 27610
I. E. Spraggins, Dir. Admissions

Salem College
P.O. Box 10548, Winston-Salem 27108
Katherine Knapp, Director of Admissions
800-32-SALEM
See listing under "Women's College"

Sandhills Community College
2200 Airport Rd., Pinehurst 28374
910-692-6185

Warren Wilson College
P.O. Box 9000, Asheville 28802-9000
Tom Weede, Dir. of Admis.

Western Carolina University
Cullowhee 28723
Tyree H. Kiser, Dir. of Admissions

Wingate College, Wingate 28174

Winston-Salem State University
601 S. Martin Luther King Jr.
Winston-Salem 27110
Van Wilson, Dir. of Admissions

NORTH DAKOTA

Jamestown College, Jamestown 58405

University of Mary
7500 University Dr., Bismarck 58504
Steph Storey, Dir. of Admis.

Valley City State University
101 S.W. College St., Valley City 58072
Monte Johnson, Dir. of Admis.

OHIO

Ashland University
401 College Ave., Ashland 44805

Baldwin-Wallace College
275 Eastland Rd., Berea 44017
Juliann K. Baker, Dir. of Admis.

Bluffton College
College Ave., Bluffton 45817

Capital University
2199 E. Main St., Columbus 43209
Dolphus E. Henry, Associate Provost

Case Western Reserve University
2040 Adelbert Rd., Cleveland 44106

Cleveland State University
Euclid Ave. at 24th St., Cleveland 44115

College of Mount St. Joseph
5701 Delhi Rd., Cincinnati 45233-1672
See listing under "Universities"

College of Wooster
1189 Beall Ave., Wooster 44691
Hayden Schilling, Dean of Admis.

Cuyahoga Community College, Eastern Campus
25444 Harvard Rd., Warrensville Heights 44122

Cuyahoga Community College, Metropolitan Campus
2900 Community College Ave., Cleveland 44115

Cuyahoga Community College, Western Campus
11000 W. Pleasant Valley Rd.
Parma Heights 44130

Defiance College
701 N. Clinton St., Defiance 43512
Penny D. Bell, Dir. of Admis.
419-783-2330 Collect

Heidelberg College
310 E. Market St., Tiffin 44883
Stephen E. Eidson, Dean of Admission
800-925-9250

Hiram College
P.O. Box 96, Hiram 44234
Gary Craig, Dean of Admis.

Kent State University
P.O. Box 5190, Kent 44242
Bruce Riddle, Dir. of Admis.

Kent State University-Ashtabula Campus
3325 W. 13th St., Ashtabula 44004
John Mahan, Dean

Kent State University-East Liverpool Campus
400 E. 4th St., East Liverpool 43920
Suzanne Fitzgerald, Dean

Kent State University-Geauga Campus
14111 Claridon-Troy Rd., Burton 44021
Larry Jones, Dean

Kent State University-Salem Campus
2491 State Rt. 45 S., Salem 44460
Dr. James Cooney, Dean

Kent State University-Stark Campus
6000 Frank Ave. N.W., Canton 44720
Dr. William Bittle, Dean

Lake Erie College
391 W. Washington St., Painesville 44077

Lorain County Community College
1005 Abbe Rd., N., Elyria 44035
Dr. John W. Thrash, Jr., Registrar

LOURDES COLLEGE
6832 Convent Blvd., Sylvania 43560
Mary E. Briggs, Dir. of Admis.
419-885-5291 or 800-878-3210

Malone College
515 25th St., N.W., Canton 44709
Lee Sommers, Dean of Admissions

MARIETTA COLLEGE
210 5th St., Marietta 45750
Dennis R. DePerro, Dean Admis./Financial Aid
800-331-7896

Mount Union College
1972 Clark Ave., Alliance 44601
Amy Tomko, Dir. of Admis.

Mt. Vernon Nazarene College
800 Martinsburg Rd., Mt. Vernon 43050
Ronald Hyson, Dir. of Admis.

Muskingum College
147 Center St., New Concord 43762

Notre Dame College
4545 College Rd., Cleveland 44121
Sr. Mary Luke, S.N.D., President

Ohio Dominican College
1216 Sunbury Rd., Columbus 43219
800-955-OHIO

OHIO NORTHERN UNIVERSITY
525 S. Main St., Ada 45810
Dr. Byron Hawbecker, Dean
412-772-2000

Ohio Wesleyan University
61 S. Sandusky St., Delaware 43015
Donald Bishop, Dean for Enrollment

Owens Community College
P.O. Box 10000, Toledo 43699
Jim Welling, Admissions
419-661-7225

Shawnee State University
940 2nd St., Portsmouth 45662
Rosemary K. Poston, Dir. of Admis.

University of Akron
381 Buchtel Common, Akron 44325
Kris MacDermott, Asst. Provost Enrollment

University of Cincinnati
2700 Clifton Ave., Cincinnati 45221

University of Dayton
300 College Park Ave., Dayton 45469-1549
Toll-free 800-837-7433
See listing under "Universities"

University of Findlay
1000 N. Main St., Findlay 45840
Dan Crabtree, Dir. of Admis.

University of Rio Grande
General Delivery, Rio Grande 45674
Dr. Nathaniel Daniel, Dean
614-245-5353, Ext. 7254

Urbana University
100 College Way, Urbana 43078
Donald Burns, Dir. of Admis.

Ursuline College
2550 Lander Rd., Cleveland 44124

Walsh College
2020 Easton St., N.W., Canton 44720
Fran Kehoe, Dean of Admis.

Wilmington College
P.O. Box 1185, Wilmington 45177
Rhonda Inderhees, Dir. of Admis.

Wittenberg University
P.O. Box 720, Springfield 45504

Xavier University
3800 Victory Pky., Cincinnati 45207

OKLAHOMA

Bartlesville Wesleyan College
2201 Silverlake Rd., Bartlesville 74006

Oklahoma Christian University of Science and Arts
P.O. Box 11000, Oklahoma City 73136
Duane Eggleston, Vice President
800-877-5010

Oklahoma City University
2501 N. Blackwelder Ave., Oklahoma City 73106
Dr. Leo Werneke, Dean of Arts & Sciences
See listing under "Universities"

Oklahoma State University, Stillwater 74078
Smith Holt, Dean

Oral Roberts University
7777 S. Lewis Ave., Tulsa 74171
Arthur E. Matzkvech, Dir. of Admis.

Southern Nazarene University
6729 N.W. 39th Expy., Bethany 73008

Southwestern College of Christian Ministries
P.O. Box 340, Bethany 73008
Dr. Richard M. Waters, Dean of Academics

University of Central Oklahoma
100 N. University Dr., Edmond 73034

University of Oklahoma at Norman
660 Parrington Oval, Norman 73019

University of Sciences & Arts of Oklahoma
P.O. Box 82345, Chickasha 73018

University of Tulsa
600 S. College Ave., Tulsa 74104
Dr. Kermit Hall, Dean

OREGON

CASCADE COLLEGE
BRANCH CAMPUS OF OKLAHOMA CHRISTIAN UNIVERSITY
9101 E. Burnside St., Portland 97216
Brad Fisher, Director of Admission
800-550-PORT
  Established 1994. Private. Coed. Accreditation: North Central Association of Schools and Colleges. Tuition: $6,400. Room and board: $3,200. Fees: $200. Enrollment: 160 full-time, 50 part-time. Faculty: 18. Student-faculty ratio: 12:1. Degrees: Bachelor of Arts in Business Administration, Liberal Studies, Liberal Studies with Teacher Certification, Biblical Studies. 9 buildings on 10 acres. Branch campus of Oklahoma Christian University of Science and Arts. Intramural and club athletics. Near I-205 in East Portland, City of Roses. Choir. Drama.

Central Oregon Community College
2600 N.W. College Way, Bend 97701
Christine Kerlin, Dir. of Admis.
503-383-7500

Chemeketa Community College
P.O. Box 14007, Salem 97309
Rick Levine, Vice President
503-399-5144

Concordia College
2811 N.E. Holman St., Portland 97211

George Fox College
414 N. Meridian St., Newberg 97132

Lewis & Clark College
0615 S.W. Palatine Hill Rd., Portland 97219
Michael Sexton, Dean of Admissions

Linfield College
900 S. Baker St., McMinnville 97128
Thomas Meicho, Dean of Admissions

Marylhurst College for Lifelong Learning
P.O. Box 261, Marylhurst 97036
Eilen Sawyer, Advisor
800-634-9984

Mt. Angel Seminary
General Delivery, St. Benedict 97373
Very Rev. J. Terrence Fitzgerald, Pres.-Rector

Northwest Christian College
828 E. 11th Ave., Eugene 97401
Randy Jones, Dir. of Admis.

Reed College
3202 S.E. Woodstock Blvd., Portland 97202

Treasure Valley Community College
650 College Blvd., Ontario 97914
Ron Kulm, Dir. of Admis.

University of Oregon
1 University of Oregon, Eugene 97403

University of Portland
5000 N. Willamette Blvd., Portland 97203

Warner Pacific College
2219 S.E. 68th Ave., Portland 97215
Sherry Moore, Enrollment Management Director

Western Oregon State College
345 Monmouth Ave., N., Monmouth 97361
Craig A. Kolins, Dir. of Admis.
503-838-8211

PENNSYLVANIA

Academy of the New Church College
P.O. Box 278, Bryn Athyn 19009

Albright College
P.O. Box 15234, Reading 19612

Allegheny College
520 N. Main St., Meadville 16335
Gayle Pollack, Dir. of Admis.

Allentown College of St. Frances de Sales
2755 Station Ave., Center Valley 18034
George Kelley, Dir. of Admis.

Alvernia College
400 Bernardine St., Reading 19607
Lisa Grabowski, Dir. of Admis.

Beaver College
450 S. Easton Rd., Glenside 19038-3295
Dennis Nostrand, VP for Enrollment Management
Phone: 800-776-BEAVER(2328)
Fax: 215-572-4049
See listing under "Universities"

Bloomsburg University, Bloomsburg 17815
Bernard Vinovrski, Dir. of Admis.

California University of Pennsylvania
3rd St., California 15419
Norman Hasbrouck, Dean for Enrollment

Carlow College
3333 5th Ave., Pittsburgh 15213

Carnegie Mellon University
5000 Forbes Ave., Pittsburgh 15213

CEDAR CREST COLLEGE
100 College Dr., Allentown 18104-6196
Cynthia Phillips, Dir. of Admissions

Chatham College
Woodland Rd., Pittsburgh 15232
Suellen Ofe, Dean of Admis./Financial Aid
See listing under "Women's College"

College Misericordia
301 Lake St., Dallas 18612
Michael Joseph, Dir. of Enrollment Mgmt.

Drexel University
3141 Chestnut St., Philadelphia 19104
Dean of Enrollment Management

Duquesne University
600 Forbes Ave., Pittsburgh 15282
Thomas Schaefer, C.S.Sp., Dir. of Admis.

Eastern College
10 Fairview Dr., Saint Davids 19087
Ronald Keller, VP for Enrollment Management

Edinboro University of Pennsylvania
Edinboro 16444
Admissions Office: 800-626-2203

Franklin & Marshall College
P.O. Box 3003, Lancaster 17604

Gannon University
109 University Sq., Erie 16541

Geneva College
3200 College Ave., Beaver Falls 15010

Gratz College
Old York Rd. and Melrose Ave.
Melrose Park 19126
Evelyn Klein, Dir. of Admissions
215-635-7300

Grove City College
100 Campus Dr., Grove City 16127
Jeffrey C. Mincey, Dir. of Admis.

GWYNEDD-MERCY COLLEGE
Sumneytown Pike, Gwynedd Valley 19437
Marjorie DeSimone, Dean of Admissions
800-DIAL-GMC
See listing under "Universities"

Harcum Junior College, Bryn Mawr 19010
Mary Pontius, Dean of Admissions

Haverford College
370 Lancaster Ave., Haverford 19041

Holy Family College
Grant & Frankford Ave., Philadelphia 19114
Dr. Mott Linn, Dir. of Admis.
215-637-3050

Immaculata College
Immaculata 19345
James P. Sullivan, Dir. of Admis.

Juniata College
1700 Moore St., Huntington 16652

Keystone Junior College
P.O. Box 50, La Plume 18440
Kevin McIntyre, Dir. of Admis.

King of Prussia Graduate Center
30 E. Swedesford Rd., Malvern 19355

King's College
133 N. River St., Wilkes Barre 18711

Lafayette College, Easton 18042
G. Gary Ripple, Dir. of Admis.
610-250-5100

La Roche College
9000 Babcock Blvd., Pittsburgh 15237
Marianne Leister, Dir. of Admis.

La Salle University
1900 W. Olney Ave., Philadelphia 19141
Br. Gerald Fitzgerald, Dir. of Admis.
See listing under "Universities"

Lebanon Valley College
101 N. College Ave., Annville 17003

Lycoming College, Williamsport 17701

Mansfield University of Pennsylvania
Mansfield 16933

Mercyhurst College
501 E. 38th St., Erie 16546
Andrew Roth, Dean of Enrollment
800-825-1926

Millersville University of Pennsylvania
Millersville 17551
Blair Treasure, Dean of Admissions

Montgomery County Community College
340 DeKalb Pike, Blue Bell 19422-0758
Dennis Murphy, Dir. of Admis.

Moravian College
1200 Main St., Bethlehem 18018

Muhlenberg College
2400 W. Chew St., Allentown 18104
Chris Hooker-Haring, Dir. of Admis.

Neumann College
Concord Rd., Aston 19014

Pennsylvania State University
5091 Station Rd., Erie 16563

Pennsylvania State University, Ogontz Campus
1600 Woodland Rd., Abington 19001

Pennsylvania State University, Wilkes-Barre Campus
P.O. Box PSU, Lehman 18627
800-426-2358

Point Park College
201 Wood St., Pittsburgh 15222
Dr. J. Matthew Simon, President

Reading Area Community College
P.O. Box 1706, Reading 19603
Robin Sodomsky, Dir. of Admis.

Robert Morris College
Narrows Run Rd., Coraopolis 15108
James R. Welsh, Dean of Admissions
See listing under "Universities"

Robert Morris College
600 5th Ave., Pittsburgh 15219
James R. Welsh, Dean of Admissions
See listing under "Universities"

Rosemont College
1400 Montgomery Ave., Rosemont 19010
Dean Enyart, Dean of Enrollment Mgmt.
See listing under "Women's Colleges"

St. Francis College
P.O. Box 600, Loretto 15940

St. Joseph's University
5600 City Ave., Philadelphia 19131
Randy Miller, Dir. of Admis.

Seton Hill College, Greensburg 15601
Peter Egan, Dir. of Admis.
800-826-6234 or 412-838-4255

Slippery Rock University, Slippery Rock 16057
Director of Admissions

Susquehanna University
514 University Ave., Selinsgrove 17870

Temple University
Broad St. & Montgomery Ave.
Philadelphia 19122

Thiel College
75 College Ave., Greenville 16125
Robert Weaver, Dir. of Admis.

University of Pittsburgh
4200 5th Ave., Pittsburgh 15260

University of Pittsburgh, Greensburg Campus
1150 Mt. Pleasant Rd., Greensburg 15601
Larry Whatule, Dir. of Admis.
412-836-9880

University of Pittsburgh at Bradford
300 Campus Dr., Bradford 16701

University of Pittsburgh at Johnstown
450 Schoolhouse Rd., Johnstown 15904

UNIVERSITY OF PITTSBURGH AT TITUSVILLE
McKinney Hall
504 E Main St., Titusville 16354
Jamie Mowat, Dir. of Admis./Financial Aid
814-827-4427

VALLEY FORGE MILITARY ACADEMY & COLLEGE
1001 Eagle Rd., Wayne 19087
Rear Adm. Virgil Hill, USN (Ret.), President
800-234-VFMA

Villanova University
845 E. Lancaster Ave., Villanova 19085
Stephen R. Merritt, Dir. of Admis.

Washington & Jefferson College
60 S. Lincoln St., Washington 15301
Thomas O'Connor, Dir. of Admis.

Waynesburg College
51 W. College St., Waynesburg 15370
Robin Moore, Dir. of Admis.
800-225-7393

WESTMINSTER COLLEGE
New Wilmington 16172
Richard Dana Paul, Dir. of Admis.
412-946-7100

Widener University
700 E. 14th St., Chester 19013

Wilkes University
184 S. River St., Wilkes-Barre 18766
Emory P. Guffrovich Jr., Dean of Admissions

RHODE ISLAND

Providence College
River Ave., Providence 02918

Rhode Island College
600 Mt. Pleasant Ave., Providence 02908

Roger Williams College
1 Old Ferry Rd., Bristol 02809
William Dunfey, Dir. of Admis.

Roger Williams College
612 Academy Ave., Providence 02908

Salve Regina University
1 Ochre Point Ave., Newport 02840
Roselina McKillop, Dean of Admissions

University of Rhode Island, Kingston 02881
John Grandin, Acting Dean

SOUTH CAROLINA

Anderson College
316 S. Boulevard, Anderson 29621
Carl D. Lockman, Dir. of Admis.
800-542-3594

Central Wesleyan College
P.O. Box 1020, Central 29630
Lillian A. Robbins, Dir. of Admis.

Charleston Southern University
P.O. Box 10087, Charleston 29411
Melinda Mitchum, Dir. of Admis.

Coastal Carolina College
P.O. Box 1954, Myrtle Beach 29578
Dr. Ed Cerny, Director of Admissions

Coker College
300 E. College Ave., Hartsville 29550

Converse College
580 E. Main St., Spartanburg 29302
Dr. Martha Rogers, VP Enrollment Management

Francis Marion College
P.O. Box 100547, Florence 29501
Marvin Lynch, Dir. of Admis.

Lander College
320 Stanley Ave., Greenwood 29649

Limestone College
1115 College Dr., Gaffney 29340
Peter Wood, Dir. of Admis.

North Greenville College
P.O. Box 1892, Tigerville 29688
Gary Wells, Dir. of Admis.
See listing under "Universities"

South Carolina State University
P.O. Box 7127, Orangeburg 29117-0001
803-536-7185

Spartanburg Technical College
P.O. Box 4386, Spartanburg 29305
Pam Hagan, Dir. Admissions & Counseling
803-591-3800

University of South Carolina, Columbia 29208
Terry Davis, Dir. of Admis.
803-777-7700

University of South Carolina at Union
P.O. Box 729, Union 29379
James Edwards, Dean

Voorhees College
Voorhees Rd., Denmark 29042

Winthrop University
701 W. Oakland Ave., Rock Hill 29733
James McCammon, Jr., Dir. of Admis.

Wofford College
429 N. Church St., Spartanburg 29303
Charles Gray, Dir. of Admis.

SOUTH DAKOTA

Augustana College
29th & S. Summit, Sioux Falls 57197

Black Hills State University
1200 University St., Spearfish 57799
April Meeker, Dir. of Admis.

Dakota State University
820 N. Washington Ave., Madison 57042
Dr. Eric Johnson, Dean
605-256-5139

Dakota Wesleyan University
1300 W. University Ave., Mitchell 57301

Huron University
333 Ninth St. S.W., Huron 57350

Mt. Marty College
1105 W. 8th St., Yankton 57078
Paula Tacke, Dir. of Admis.

Northern State University
1200 S. Jay St., Aberdeen 57401

Sinte Gleska College
P.O. Box 490, Rosebud 57570
Sherry Red Owl, Registrar

SIOUX FALLS COLLEGE
1501 S. Prairie Ave., Sioux Falls 57105
Susan Reese, Dir. of Admis.
800-888-1047
See listing under "Universities"

University of South Dakota
414 E. Clark St., Vermillion 57069
Dave Lorenz, Dir. of Admis.

TENNESSEE

Belmont College
1900 Belmont Blvd., Nashville 37212

Bethel College
Cherry St., Mc Kenzie 38201

Bristol University
P.O. Box 4366, Bristol 37625
Dr. W. David Willis, Academic Dean
See listing under "Universities"

Bryan College
Box 7000, Dayton 37321
Thomas A. Shaw, Dir. of Admis.

Carson-Newman College
P.O. Box 70552, Jefferson City 37760
See listing under "Universities"

Christian Brothers College
650 E. Parkway, S., Memphis 38104

Crichton College
6655 Winchester Rd., Memphis 38115
901-367-9800

David Lipscomb University
3901 Granny White Pike, Nashville 37204-3951
Wade Sandrell, Dir. of Admis.
800-333-4358

Freed-Hardeman University
158 E. Main St., Henderson 38340
800-342-7837

King College
1350 King College Rd., Bristol 37620

Lambuth College
705 Lambuth Blvd., Jackson 38301

Lee College
P.O. Box 3450, Cleveland 37320

Lincoln Memorial University
P.O. Box 2012, Harrogate 37752
Conrad Daniels, Dir. of Admis.

Maryville College
800 S. Court St., Maryville 37801
Annabelle J. Libby, Dir. of Admis.

Southern Missionary College
P.O. Box 370, Collegedale 37315

Tennessee Temple University
1815 Union Ave., Chattanooga 37404
Dr. L. W. Nichols, President

Tennessee Wesleyan College
P.O. Box 40, Athens 37371

Trevecca Nazarene College
333 Murfreesboro Rd., Nashville 37210

Tusculum College
P.O. Box 5035, Greeneville 37743
Ronald Porter, Dir. of Admis.

Union University
2447 US Highway 45 Bypass, Jackson 38305
Dr. James Baggett, Dean
901-668-1818
See listing under "Universities"

University of Memphis, Memphis 38152
Dr. John Eubank, Dean of Admissions

University of Tennessee at Martin
Martin 38238
Paul Kelley, Director of Admissions
See listing under "Universities"

University of Tennessee, Knoxville
527 Andy Holt Tower, Knoxville 37996
Dr. Gordon Stanley, Dir. of Admis.

University of the South
735 University Ave., Sewanee 37375

TEXAS

Angelo State University
2601 W. Ave., N., San Angelo 76909

Austin College
900 N. Grand Ave., Sherman 75090
Rodney Oto, Dean of Admission
800-442-5363

Concordia Lutheran College
3400 N. Interstate 35, Austin 78705
Kevin Pieper, Dir. of Admis.

Corpus Christi State University
6300 Ocean Dr., Corpus Christi 78412

Dallas Baptist University
7777 W. Kiest Blvd., Dallas 75211

East Texas Baptist University
1200 N. Grove Ave., Marshall 75670

East Texas State University
ETSU Station, Commerce 75429

Houston Baptist University
7502 Fondren Rd., Houston 77074

Howard Payne University
1000 Fisk Ave., Brownwood 76801

Huston-Tillotson College
1820 E. 8th St., Austin 78702

Incarnate Word College
4301 Broadway St., San Antonio 78209
Sr. Sally Mitchell, Dean of Enrollment

Jarvis Christian College
P.O. Box G, Hawkins 75765

Lamar University
P.O. Box 10009, Beaumont 77710
800-458-7558

· Laredo Junior College
1 W. End Washington St., Laredo 78040
Elpha Lee West, Dir. of Admis.

Lubbock Christian University
5601 W. 19th, Lubbock 79407

· North Central Texas College
1525 W. California, Gainesville 76240
Doug Willis, Dir. of Admis.

Our Lady of the Lake University
411 S.W. 24th St., San Antonio 78207-4689
210-434-6711

Paul Quinn College
3837 Simpson Stuart Rd., Dallas 75241

Prairie View A & M University
P.O. Box 3089, Prairie View 77446-3089
Linda S. Berry, Dir. of Admis.

Rice University
P.O. Box 1892, Houston 77251

St. Mary's University of San Antonio
1 Camino Santa Maria, San Antonio 78228
Rick Castillo, Dir. of Admis.

Sam Houston State University, Huntsville 77341

· Schreiner College
2100 Memorial Blvd., Kerrville 78028
800-343-4919

Southwestern Adventist College
P.O. Box 567, Keene 76059

Southwestern University
University Ave. at Maple St., Georgetown 78626

Stephen F. Austin State University
P.O. Box 6078. Nacogdoches 75962

Sul Ross State University, Alpine 79832

Texas A & I University
Campus Box 101, Kingsville 78363

Texas A & M International University
1 West End Washington St., Laredo 78040

Texas A & M University
College Station 77843

Texas Christian University
2800 S. University Dr., Ft. Worth 76129
Dr. Edward Boehm, Jr., Dean of Admissions

Texas College
2404 N. Grand St., Tyler 75702
Dr. William H. Ammons, II, Dir. of Admis.

Texas Lutheran College
1000 W. Court St., Seguin 78155
Jennifer B. Ehlers, Dir. of Admis.

Texas Southern University
3100 Cleburne St., Houston 77004

Texas Wesleyan University
1201 Wesleyan St., Fort Worth 76105
Kim Campbell, Dir. Freshman Admission

Trinity University
715 Stadium Dr., San Antonio 78212

University of Dallas
1845 E. Northgate Dr., Irving 75062
Jim Whitaker, Dir. of Admis.

University of Houston-Clear Lake
2700 Bay Area Blvd., Houston 77058
Darella Banks, Exec. Dir. Enrollment Services

University of Houston-Downtown
1 Main St., Houston 77002

University of Houston-Victoria
2302-C E. Red River St., Victoria 77901

University of Mary Hardin-Baylor
UMHB Station, Box 8001, Belton 76513
800-727-8642 or 817-939-4520

University of St. Thomas
3812 Montrose Blvd., Houston 77006
Elsie Biron, Dir. of Admis.

University of Texas at Arlington
UTA Box 19125, Arlington 76019
R. Zack Prince, Dir. of Admis.

University of Texas at Tyler
3900 University Blvd., Tyler 75799
Dr. F. Lannom Smith, Dean

University of Texas-Pan American
1201 W. University Dr., Edinburg 78539
Miguel Nerarez, President

Wiley College
711 Wiley Ave., Marshall 75670

UTAH

Utah State University, Logan 84322-1600
Rod Clark, Director of Admissions
801-750-1107

Westminster College of Salt Lake City
1840 S. 1300 E., Salt Lake City 84105
800-748-4753

VERMONT

Bennington College, Bennington 05201
Karen Kristof, Dir. of Admis.
800-833-6845

BURLINGTON COLLEGE
95 North Ave., Burlington 05401
Nancy Wilson, Dir. of Admis.
Phone 802-862-9616
  Small, nontraditional liberal arts program, geared towards needs of adult learners. Established in 1972, this private, coed college offers AA and BA programs in transpersonal psychology, feminist studies, humanities, and human services, among others; independent degree program also offered. Tuition & fees total $7,800 per year. 66 faculty, 220 students — all live off campus. Library has 50,000 books, 350 periodicals. Emphasis on small classes, flexible learning options, personalized support. Fully accredited.

Champlain College
P.O. Box 670, Burlington 05402
Josephine Churchill, Dir. of Admis.
802-860-2727
See listing under "Universities"

Goddard College
P.O. Box G, Plainfield 05667
Jackson Kytle, President

Green Mountain College
16 College St., Poultney 05764

Johnson State College, Johnson 05656
802-635-2356 ext. 219

Lyndon State College, Lyndonville 05851

Marlboro College
General Delivery, Marlboro 05344

NORWICH UNIVERSITY
65 S. Main St., Northfield 05663
Frank Griffis, Dir. of Admis.
See listing under "Universities"

SAINT MICHAEL'S COLLEGE
Winooski Park, Colchester 05439
Dr. Paul Reiss, President
Jerry Flanagan, Dean of Admission
Admission only: 800-SMC-8000, other: 802-654-2000
  Established 1904. Catholic. Coed. Accreditation: NEASC. Tuition: $12,300. Room and board: $5,600. Enrollment: 1,640. Faculty: 121. Degrees: BA, BS, MA, MEd, MSA. Library: 180,500 volumes. 30 buildings on 400 acres. Gym. Pool. Located in suburban Burlington, cultural center of Vermont. Many cultural and social opportunities, also in the heart of ski country.

Southern Vermont College
Monument Ave., Bennington 05201
See listing under "Universities"

Trinity College
208 Colchester Ave., Burlington 05401

University of Vermont
194 S. Prospect St., Burlington 05401
802-656-3370

VIRGINIA

Averett College
420 W. Main St., Danville 24541
Gary Sherman, Dean of Enrollment Mgmt.

Bluefield College
3000 College Dr., Bluefield 24605
Dr. Roy Dobyns, President
See listing under "Universities"

Christendom College
2101 Shenandoah Shores Rd., Front Royal 22630

Christopher Newport College
50 Shoe Ln., Newport News 23606

Clinch Valley College of the University of Virginia
P.O. Box 16, Wise 24293
Lana Low, Dir. Enrollment Management

Eastern Mennonite College
1200 Park Rd., Harrisonburg 22801
Jerry Miller, Dir. of Admis.

Ferrum College, Ferrum 24088
Bob Bailey, Dir. of Admis.

George Mason University
4400 University Dr., Fairfax 22030-4444
Patricia Riordan, Dean of Admissions

Hampden-Sydney College
P.O. Box 128, Hampden-Sydney 23943
Robert H. Jones, Dean of Admis.

James Madison University, Harrisonburg 22807

LIBERTY UNIVERSITY
P.O. Box 20000, Lynchburg 24506
Jay Spencer, VP Recruitment
800-376-2800
See listing under "Universities"

Longwood College, Farmville 23901

Lynchburg College
1501 Lakeside Dr., Lynchburg 24501
Ernest Chadderton, Dean of Enrollment

Marymount University
2807 N. Glebe Rd., Arlington 22207
Charles Coe, Director of Admissions
800-548-7638 or 703-284-1500
See listing under "Universities"

Mary Washington College
1701 College Ave., Fredericksburg 22401
Martin Wilder, V.P. for Admissions

Randolph-Macon College
200 Henry St., Ashland 23005
John Conkright, Dean of Admissions

Randolph-Macon Woman's College
2500 Rivermont Ave., Lynchburg 24503

· Richard Bland College of the College of William & Mary
11301 Johnson Rd., Petersburg 23805
Roger Gill, Dir. of Enrollment Services

St. Paul's College
406 Windsor Ave., Lawrenceville 23868

SHENANDOAH UNIVERSITY
1460 University Dr., Winchester 22601
Dr. Catherine Tisinger, Dean
See listing under "Universities"

Southern Virginia College for Women
One College Hill Dr., Buena Vista 24416
Mark A. Camper, Assoc. Dir. of Admis.
800-229-8420
See listing under "Women's Colleges"

Sweet Briar College, Sweet Briar 24595
Nancy Church, Dir. of Admis.

· Tidewater Community College, Chesapeake Campus
1428 Cedar Rd., Chesapeake 23320
Dr. Larry L. Whitworth, President

· Tidewater Community College, Portsmouth Campus
Rt. 135, Portsmouth 23703
Dr. Larry L. Whitworth, President

Tidewater Community College
1700 College Crescent, Virginia Beach 23456
Dr. Larry L. Whitworth, President

Virginia Intermont College
1013 Moore St., Bristol 24201
Lawton Blandford, Dir. of Admis.

Virginia Military Institute, Lexington 24450

Virginia Polytechnic Institute & State University
Blacksburg 24061
David Bousquet, Dir. of Undergraduate Admis.

WASHINGTON

Central Washington University, Ellensburg 98926
William Swain, Director of Admissions

City University
16661 Northup Way, Bellevue 98008
800-422-4898

Eastern Washington University, Cheney 99004
Roger L. Pugh, Asst. VP, Enrollment Mgmt.
See listing under "Universities"

Evergreen State College
2700 Evergreen Pky. N.W., Olympia 98505

Heritage College
3240 Fort Rd., Toppenish 98948
Dr. Michael Keenan, Chrpsn.
509-865-2244

Northwest College of the Assemblies of God
P.O. Box 579, Kirkland 98083-0579
Bob Foster, Dir. of Public Relations

Pacific Lutheran University
12180 Park Ave. S., Tacoma 98447
J. Robert Wills, Provost

St. Martin's College
700 College St. N.E., Lacey 98516

Skagit Valley College
2405 E. College Way, Mt. Vernon 98273

Walla Walla College
204 S. College Ave., College Place 99324

Walla Walla Community College
500 Tausick Way, Walla Walla 99362
George Fuhr, Director
509-527-4283
See listing under "Community and Junior Colleges"

Whitworth College
300 W. Hawthorne Rd., Spokane 99251
Kenneth P. Moyer, Dir. of Admis.

WEST VIRGINIA

Alderson-Broaddus College
Philippi 26416
Craig W. Gould, Director of Admissions
304-457-1700

Bluefield State College
219 Rock St., Bluefield 24701

Davis & Elkins College
100 Campus Dr., Elkins 26241
Kevin D. Chenoweth, Dir. of Admis.

GLENVILLE STATE COLLEGE
200 High St., Glenville 26351
Dr. William Simmons, President
Mack Samples, Dean of Admissions
   Established 1872. State. Coed. Accreditation: NCACS. Annual tuition: $3,460 resident, $4,054 non-resident. Room and board: $3,080. Enrollment: 900 boarding, 1,500 day. Faculty: 72. Degrees: AA, AS, BA, BS. Library: 210,000 volumes. 10 buildings. Gym & pool, golf course nearby. Beautiful rural setting, 16 miles from I-79. Popular 2 year forestry program; special education.

Shepherd College, Shepherdstown 25443

The University of Charleston
2300 MacCorkle Ave., S.E., Charleston 25304
800-995-GO UC

West Virginia State College
P.O. Box 1000, Institute 25112

WEST VIRGINIA WESLEYAN COLLEGE
59 College Ave., Buckhannon 26201
Robert Skinner, Director of Admission
See listing under "Universities"

Wheeling Jesuit College
316 Washington Ave., Wheeling 26003
Fr. Thomas Acker, SJ, President

WISCONSIN

Alverno College
P.O. Box 343922, Milwaukee 53234
Colleen Hayes, Dir. of Admis.

Beloit College
700 College St., Beloit 53511
Nancy A. McDowell, Dean
608-363-2668

Cardinal Stritch College
6801 N. Yates Rd., Milwaukee 53217
David Wegener, Dir. of Admis.

Carroll College
100 N. East Ave., Waukesha 53186
Ken Moyer, Dir. of Admis.

Carthage College
2001 Alford Dr., Kenosha 53140
Brenda A. Porter, VP Enrollment

Concordia University
12800 N. Lake Shore Dr., Mequon 53097
414-243-5700

Edgewood College
855 Woodrow St., Madison 53711
Robert Blust, Dir. of Admis.

Lakeland College
P.O. Box 359, Sheboygan 53082

Lawrence University
P.O. Box 599, Appleton 54912
Steven Syverson, Dean of Admissions

Marian College of Fond du Lac
45 S. National Ave., Fond du Lac 54935
Carol Reichenberger, Dean of Admissions

Marquette University
1217 W. Wisconsin Ave., Milwaukee 53233
Raymond A. Brown, Dean of Admissions

Mt. Senario College
1500 W. College Ave., Ladysmith 54848
Dewey Floberg, Dean of Admissions

Northland College
1411 Ellis Ave., Ashland 54806
Jim Miller, Dean of Admissions

NORTHWESTERN COLLEGE
1300 Western Ave., Watertown 53094
John A. Braun, President
Philip Hirsch, Dir. of Admis.
414-261-4352 FAX: 414-262-8118
   Established 1865. Private. Men's college. Accreditation: NCACS. Tuition: $3,350. Room and board: $1,880. Fees: $250. Enrollment: 187. Faculty: 23. Degree: BA. Library: 50,000 volumes. 8 buildings on 38 acres. NWC has a single preseminary (pretheological) course of study. 92% of graduates enroll at Wisconsin Lutheran Seminary of Mequon. NWC is owned and operated by the Wisconsin Evangelical Lutheran Synod for the sole purpose of providing the undergraduate training for its clergy.

Ripon College, P.O. Box 248, Ripon 54971
James Reilly, Dean of Admis.

St. Norbert College
100 Grant St., De Pere 54115
Craig S. Wesley, Dean of Admission
See listing under "Universities"

University of Wisconsin, Green Bay
2420 Nicolet Dr., Green Bay 54311
Myron Van de Ven, Dir. of Admis.

University of Wisconsin, Madison
500 Lincoln Dr., Madison 53706

University of Wisconsin
P.O. Box 413, Milwaukee 53201
V. M. Allison, Registrar

University of Wisconsin, Oshkosh
800 Algoma Blvd., Oshkosh 54901-8602
August Helgerson, Dir. of Admis.

University of Wisconsin
P.O. Box 2000, Kenosha 53141
414-553-2211

University of Wisconsin
1 University Plaza, Platteville 53818
Richard Schumacher, Dean of Admissions

University of Wisconsin, River Falls
River Falls 54022
Alan Tuchtenhagen, Dir. of Admis.

University of Wisconsin, Stevens Point 54481
Dr. John A. Larsen, Dir. of Admis.

University of Wisconsin
800 W. Main St., Whitewater 53190

University of Wisconsin Center, Baraboo/Sauk Co.
1006 Connie Rd., Baraboo 53913
Aural Umhoefer, Dean
Office of Student Services, 608-356-8724

Viterbo College
815 9th St., S., La Crosse 54601
Roland W. Nelson, Dir. of Admis.

Wisconsin Lutheran College
8830 W. Bluemound Rd., Milwaukee 53226
Michael W. Butterfield, Dir. of Admis.

WYOMING

University of Wyoming
P.O. Box 3434, Laramie 82071
Richard Davis, Dir. of Admis.

Western Wyoming Community College
2500 College Dr., Rock Springs 82901
Jackie Freeze, Dir. of Admis.
See listing under "Community and Junior Colleges"

GUAM

University of Guam
UOG Station, Mangilao 96923
Kathleen Owings, Dir. of Admis.

PUERTO RICO

Bayamon Central University
P.O. Box 1725, Bayamon 00960-1725
Christine Hernandez, Dir. of Admis.

Caribbean University
P.O. Box 493, Bayamon 00960

Inter American University of Puerto Rico
San German Campus
Harris Dr. Call Box 5100, San German 00683

Universidad Adventista de las Antillas
P.O. Box 118, Mayaguez 00681
Wilma Gonzalez, Dir. of Admis.

University of Puerto Rico
Antonio Barcelo Ave., Cayey 00736
Antonio Rosario, Dir. of Admis.

University of Puerto Rico, Mayaguez Campus
P.O. Box 5000, Mayaguez 00681
Neysa Lopez, Dir. of Admis.

University of Puerto Rico, Rio Piedras Campus
P.O. Box 23300, San Juan 00931
Victor Lopez, Dir. of Admis.

University of the Sacred Heart
P.O. Box 12383, San Juan 00914

VIRGIN ISLANDS

University of the Virgin Islands
Charlotte Amalie, St. Thomas 00802
Judith Edwin, Dir. of Admis.

LIBRARY SCIENCE

This classification contains schools offering a graduate degree accredited by the American Library Association (†) and a selection of programs from institutionally accredited schools.

ALABAMA

Alabama State University
P.O. Box 271, Montgomery 36101

Jacksonville State University
700 Pelham Rd. N., Jacksonville 36265

† University of Alabama
P.O. Box 870132, Tuscaloosa 35487-0132
Roy Smith, Dir. of Admis.

University of North Alabama
University Station, Florence 35632

University of South Alabama
307 University Blvd. N., Mobile 36688

ARIZONA

Arizona State University, Tempe 85287

† University of Arizona, Tucson 85721
Carla J. Stoffle, Dean

ARKANSAS

University of Arkansas at Little Rock
2801 S. University Ave., Little Rock 72204

University of Central Arkansas
201 Donaghey Ave., Conway 72035

CALIFORNIA

California State University, Los Angeles
5151 Paseo Rancho Castilla, Los Angeles 90032

† San Jose State University
1 Washington Sq., San Jose 95192

† University of California, Los Angeles
1247 Murphy Hall, Los Angeles 90024

† University of California at Berkeley
South Hall, Berkeley 94720

COLORADO

University of Colorado at Denver
1200 Larimer, Denver 80204

University of Denver
2199 S. University Blvd., Denver 80210

CONNECTICUT

† Southern Connecticut State University
501 Crescent St., New Haven 06515

Western Connecticut State University
181 White St., Danbury 06810

DISTRICT OF COLUMBIA

† Catholic University of America
620 Michigan Ave. N.E., Washington 20064
Robert J. Talbot, Dir. of Admis. & Fin. Aid.

University of the District of Columbia
Georgia Ave.-Harvard St. Campus
1100 Harvard St., N.W., Washington 20009

University of the District of Columbia
Van Ness Campus
4200 Connecticut Ave., N.W., Washington 20008

FLORIDA

† Florida State University
600 W. College Ave., Tallahassee 32306

University of Miami
P.O. Box 248006, Coral Gables 33124

† University of South Florida
4202 Fowler Ave., Tampa 33620

GEORGIA

† Clark Atlanta University
240 James Brawley Dr., S.W., Atlanta 30314
Thomas W. Cole, President

Emory University
1462 Clifton Rd., Atlanta 30322

Georgia Southern University, Statesboro 30460

HAWAII

† University of Hawaii at Manoa
2500 Campus Rd., Honolulu 96822

ILLINOIS

Illinois State University
212 N. School St., Normal 61761

† Northern Illinois University, De Kalb 60115

† Rosary College
7900 W. Division St., River Forest 60305
Hildegarde Schmidt, Dir. of Admis.

University of Chicago
5801 S. Ellis Ave., Chicago 60637

† University of Illinois
506 S. Wright St., Urbana 61801

INDIANA

Ball State University
2000 W. University Ave., Muncie 47306
Ruth Vedvik, Dir. of Admis.

Butler University
4600 Sunset Ave., Indianapolis 46208

Indiana State University
217 N. 6th St., Terre Haute 47809

† Indiana University at Bloomington
300 N. Jordan Ave., Bloomington 47406

Indiana University-Purdue University at Fort Wayne
2101 Coliseum Blvd. E., Fort Wayne 46805

IOWA

Northwestern College
101 7th St. S.W., Orange City 51041

† University of Iowa, Iowa City 52242

University of Northern Iowa, Cedar Falls 50614

KANSAS

† Emporia State University
1200 Commercial St., Emporia 66801
Dr. Barbara Hilgendorf, Dir. of Admissions

KENTUCKY

Spalding University
851 S. 4th St., Louisville 40203
Dorothy G. Allen, Dir. of Admis.

† University of Kentucky, Lexington 40506

Western Kentucky University
1526 Russellville Rd., Bowling Green 42101

LOUISIANA

† Louisiana State University and A & M College
Baton Rouge 70803

Northwestern State University
Natchitoches 71497

MARYLAND

† University of Maryland, College Park 20742

MASSACHUSETTS

Boston University
685 Commonwealth Ave., Boston 02215

† Simmons College
300 The Fenway, Boston 02115

MICHIGAN

Central Michigan University
100 Warriner Hall, Mt. Pleasant 48858

† University of Michigan-Ann Arbor
815 S. University Ave., Ann Arbor 48109

† Wayne State University
5980 Cass Ave., Detroit 48202
Dr. J. R. Thorderson, Dir. of Admis.

MINNESOTA

College of St. Catherine
2004 Randolph Ave., St. Paul 55105

Mankato State University
P.O. Box 8400, Mankato 56002

University of Minnesota, Twin Cities
Minneapolis 55455

University of St. Thomas
2115 Summit Ave., St. Paul 55105

MISSISSIPPI

Blue Mountain College
P.O. Box 338, Blue Mountain 38610

Delta State University
Hwy. 8 W., Cleveland 38732

† University of Southern Mississippi
P.O. Box 5165, Hattiesburg 39406

MISSOURI

Central Missouri State University
Warrensburg 64093
Delores Hudson, Dir. of Admis.

Northwest Missouri State University
800 University Dr., Maryville 64468

† University of Missouri, Columbia
228 Jesse Hall, Columbia 65211

NEBRASKA

Chadron State College
1000 Main St., Chadron 69337
Dr. Thomas P. Colgate, Dean

Nebraska Wesleyan University
5000 Saint Paul Ave., Lincoln 68504
Ken Sieg, Dir. of Admis.

University of Nebraska at Omaha
Omaha 68182

NEW JERSEY

Rutgers, The State University of NJ
Livingston College
New Brunswick 08903

† Rutgers, The State University of NJ
Douglass College
New Brunswick 08903

William Paterson College
300 Pompton Rd., Wayne 07470

NEW YORK

† CUNY, Queens College
6530 Kissena Blvd., Flushing 11367

Long Island University-C.W. Post Campus
Rt. 25 A, Brookville 11548
Dr. Anne Woodsworth, Dean
516-299-2866

† Pratt Institute
200 Willoughby Ave., Brooklyn 11205

† St. John's University
Grand Central & Utopia Parkways, Jamaica 11439

† SUNY at Buffalo
Baldy Hall, Amherst 14260

† SUNY at Albany
1400 Washington Ave., Albany 12222
Micheileen Treadwell, Dir. of
Admission/Financial Aid
518-442-5431

SUNY College at Geneseo
1 College Cir., Geneseo 14454
William L. Caren, Dir. of Admissions

† Syracuse University, Syracuse 13244

NORTH CAROLINA

East Carolina University
1000 E. 5th St., Greenville 27858
Dr. Lawrence W. S. Auld, Chair

† North Carolina Central University
P.O. Box 19617, Durham 27707

† University of North Carolina
1000 Spring Garden St., Greensboro 27412

† University of North Carolina at Chapel Hill
Chapel Hill 27599
Barbara B. Moran, Dean

OHIO

† Kent State University
P.O. Box 5190, Kent 44242
Bruce Riddle, Dir. of Admis.

Ohio Dominican College
1216 Sunbury Rd., Columbus 43219
800-955-OHIO

Owens Community College
P.O. Box 10000, Toledo 43699
Jim Welling, Admissions
419-661-7225

OKLAHOMA

Northwestern Oklahoma State University
705 Oklahoma Blvd., Alva 73717

Southwestern Oklahoma State University
100 Campus Dr., Weatherford 73096

† University of Oklahoma at Norman
660 Parrington Oval, Norman 73019

PENNSYLVANIA

† Clarion University of Pennsylvania
840 Wood St., Clarion 16214

† Drexel University
3141 Chestnut St., Philadelphia 19104
Dean of Enrollment Management

Kutztown University of Pennsylvania
Kutztown 19530

Millersville University of Pennsylvania
Millersville 17551
Blair Treasure, Dean of Admissions

Pennsylvania State University
Beaver Campus, Monaca 15061
Regina S. Miller, Dir. of Admis.
See listing under "Universities"

Shippensburg University, Shippensburg 17257

† University of Pittsburgh
4200 5th Ave., Pittsburgh 15260

Villanova University
845 E. Lancaster Ave., Villanova 19085
Stephen R. Merritt, Dir. of Admis.

RHODE ISLAND

† University of Rhode Island
74 Lower College Rd., Kingston 02881
Dr. Elizabeth Futas, Director

SOUTH CAROLINA

† University of South Carolina, Columbia 29208
Ose Henderson, Acting Dean-Graduate School
803-777-4243

SOUTH DAKOTA

Augustana College
29th & S. Summit, Sioux Falls 57197

TENNESSEE

Belmont College
1900 Belmont Blvd., Nashville 37212

Tennessee Technological University
P.O. Box 5006, Cookeville 38505

University of Tennessee at Martin
Martin 38238
Paul Kelley, Director of Admissions
See listing under "Universities"

† University of Tennessee, Knoxville
527 Andy Holt Tower, Knoxville 37996
Dr. Gordon Stanley, Dir. of Admis.

TEXAS

East Texas State University
ETSU Station, Commerce 75429

Our Lady of the Lake University
411 S.W. 24th St., San Antonio 78207-4689
210-434-6711

Sam Houston State University, Huntsville 77341

† Texas Women's University
P.O. Box 23925, Denton 76204

† University of North Texas
P.O. Box 13797, Denton 76203

† University of Texas at Austin
0 the University of Texas, Austin 78712

UTAH

† Brigham Young University, Provo 84602

VIRGINIA

James Madison University, Harrisonburg 22807

WASHINGTON

† University of Washington, Seattle 98195

WEST VIRGINIA

Concord College, Athens 24712

Marshall University
400 Hal Greer Blvd., Huntington 25755
See listing under "Universities"

Shepherd College, Shepherdstown 25443

WISCONSIN

† University of Wisconsin, Madison
500 Lincoln Dr., Madison 53706

† University of Wisconsin
P.O. Box 413, Milwaukee 53201
V. M. Allison, Registrar

PUERTO RICO

† University of Puerto Rico, Rio Piedras Campus
P.O. Box 23300, San Juan 00931
Victor Lopez, Dir. of Admis.

MASTER OF BUSINESS ADMINISTRATION

ALABAMA

Alabama A & M University
P.O. Box 429, Normal 35762
Dr. Marsha Griffin, Director
See listing under "Universities"

Samford University
800 Lakeshore Dr., Birmingham 35229
Robert David, Dean

University of Alabama
P.O. Box 870132, Tuscaloosa 35487-0132
Roy Smith, Dir. of Admis.

UNIVERSITY OF MOBILE
P.O. Box 13220, Mobile 36663-0220
Kim Leousis, Dir. of Admissions
205-675-5990
See listing under "Universities"

ALASKA

University of Alaska Southeast
11120 Glacier Hwy., Juneau 99801
Greg Wagner, Coordinator of Admissions

ARIZONA

Northern Arizona University
P.O. Box 4092, Flagstaff 86011
Dr. Margaret Cibik, Dir. of Admis.

University of Arizona, Tucson 85721
Kenneth R. Smith, Dean

University of Phoenix
4615 E. Elwood St., Phoenix 85040
Sue Murphy, Registrar

ARKANSAS

Arkansas State University
P.O. Box 59, State University 72467

University of Arkansas at Fayetteville
Fayetteville 72701

CALIFORNIA

Armstrong University
2222 Harold Way, Berkeley 94704
Rowena Ricafrentre, Dir. of Admis.
510-848-2500

CALIFORNIA COAST UNIVERSITY
700 N. Main St., Santa Ana 92701
Admissions Office: 800-854-8768 or 714-547-9625
Thomas Neal, President
Linda B. Smith, VP Academic Affairs
William Barcroft, Dean of Admissions
  Established 1973. Proprietary. Coed. Accreditation: National Association of Private Non-Traditional Schools & Colleges, California State Department of Education, charter member California Association of State Approved Colleges & Universities, member Association for Adult & Continuing Education. Tuition: $2,200-$3,500. Enrollment: 7,500.
  A private college offering off-campus independent study programs in the traditional areas of business administration, management, engineering, psychology, & education. Admissions: rolling trimester, requires official transcripts, letters of recommendation, detailed curriculum vita or occupational history.
  Process: evaluation of prior academic work followed by analysis of occupational history, including participation in workshops, seminars, training programs, specialized projects for credit. Credit is demonstrated by challenge exams or specialized course by course independent study programs.
  Residency: All course work may be completed off campus, utilizing correspondence methods. All doctoral candidates must meet with faculty advisors in person, upon completion of doctoral dissertation. Scholarships: Interest free loans available to students.

California Lutheran University
60 Olsen Rd., Thousand Oaks 91360
805-493-3125

California Polytechnic State University
San Luis Obispo 93407
Helen Linstrum, Dir. of Admis.

Chapman University
333 N. Glassell St., Orange 92666
Michael Drummy, Dir. of Admis.

College of Notre Dame
1500 Ralston Ave., Belmont 94002
Greg M. Smith, PhD., Dir. of Admis.

La Sierra University
4700 Pierce St., Riverside 92505
800-874-5587

LINCOLN UNIVERSITY
281 Masonic Ave., San Francisco 94118
Clarence Rippel, Acting President
Accredited Member ACICS

Loyola Marymount University
Loyola Blvd. at W. 80th, Los Angeles 90045
M. L'Heureux, Dir. of Admis.

National University
4141 Camino del Rio, S., San Diego 92108
Dr. Donald Carver, Dean

Pepperdine University
400 Corporate Pointe, Culver City 90230
310-568-5541

San Francisco State University
1600 Holloway Ave., San Francisco 94132
Corwin Bjonerud, Dir. of Admis.

Santa Clara University, Santa Clara 95053

Sonoma State University
1801 E. Cotati Ave., Rohnert Park 94928

Stanford University, Stanford 94305

UNITED STATES INTERNATIONAL UNIVERSITY
10455 Pomerado Rd., San Diego 92131
619-693-4772
See listing under "Universities"

University of California, Los Angeles
1247 Murphy Hall, Los Angeles 90024

University of California at Berkeley
Barrows Hall, Berkeley 94720

University of California, Davis
376 Mrak Hall, Davis 95616

University of California, Irvine
Irvine 92715

UNIVERSITY OF JUDAISM/LEE COLLEGE
15600 Mulholland Dr., Los Angeles 90077
Tamara Greenebaum, Dean of Admissions
See listing under "Universities"

University of La Verne
1950 3rd St., La Verne 91750
Mark Bornholdt, Dir. of Admis.

University of San Diego
5998 Alcala Park, San Diego 92110
Maureen Phalen, Dir. Graduate Admissions
619-260-4524

University of San Francisco
2130 Fulton St., San Francisco 94117
Bill Henley, Dir. of Admis.

Woodbury University
7500 Glenoaks Blvd., Burbank 91504
See listing under "Universities"

COLORADO

Regis University
3333 Regis Blvd., Denver 80221
Robert Blust, Director of Admissions

University of Denver
2199 S. University Blvd., Denver 80210

CONNECTICUT

QUINNIPIAC COLLEGE
275 Mount Carmel Ave., Hamden 06518
Building a new $7 million Business Center
See listing under "Universities"

University of Bridgeport
126 Park Ave., Bridgeport 06601
Andrew G. Nelson, Dean Admis./Financial Aid
203-576-4552
See listing under "Universities"

University of Hartford
200 Bloomfield Ave., West Hartford 06117
Richard Zeiser, Dir. of Admis.
See listing under "Universities"

University of New Haven
300 Orange Ave., West Haven 06516
M. L. McLaughlin, Dean
203-932-7000

DELAWARE

Wilmington College
320 N. DuPont Hwy., New Castle 19720

DISTRICT OF COLUMBIA

The American University
4400 Massachusetts Ave. N.W.
Washington 20016

University of the District of Columbia
Georgia Ave.-Harvard St. Campus
1100 Harvard St., N.W., Washington 20009

University of the District of Columbia
Van Ness Campus
4200 Connecticut Ave., N.W., Washington 20008

FLORIDA

Barry University
11300 N.E. 2nd Ave., Miami Shores 33161
Robin Ray Roberts, Dean of Admissions

Embry-Riddle Aeronautical University
600 S. Clyde Morris Blvd.
Daytona Beach 32114-3900
800-222-ERAU

Florida Atlantic University
500 N.W. 20th St., Boca Raton 33431
Brian Levin-Stankevich, Dir. of Admis.

Florida Southern College
111 Lake Hollingsworth Dr., Lakeland 33801
William Stephens, Jr., Dir. of Admis.

Jacksonville University
2800 University Blvd., N., Jacksonville 32211

Rollins College
P.O. Box 2720, Winter Park 32790

St. Thomas University
16400 N.W. 32nd Ave., Miami 33054
Mary R. Conway, Dir. of Graduate Admissions

SCHILLER INTERNATIONAL UNIVERSITY (EUROPE)
U.S. Admissions Office
Dept. PA, 453 Edgewater Dr., Dunedin 34698-7532
800-336-4133 Fax: 813-736-6263
Dr. Walter Leibrecht, President
Karen Altieri, Associate Director of Admissions
See listing under "Graduate Schools"

Stetson University
401 N. Woodland Blvd., De Land 32720
Dr. James Wright, Dean

Tampa College
3319 W. Hillsborough Ave., Tampa 33614
David Zorn, President

Tampa College - Pinellas
15064 U.S. Hwy. 19 N., Clearwater 34624
Mark A. Page, President
813-530-9495

University of Miami
P.O. Box 248006, Coral Gables 33124

UNIVERSITY OF SARASOTA
5250 17th St., Sarasota 34235
Linda Volz, Dir. of Enrollment Management
800-331-5995
  Established 1969. Coed. Accreditation: SACS. Tuition: $235 per credit hour. Enrollment: 470. Faculty: 30. Degrees: MAEd, MBA, EdD. Year round, non-traditional calender, flexible, small seminars, much individual attention to students, performance oriented.

GEORGIA

Georgia College
231 W. Hancock St., Milledgeville 31061
912-453-5004

Kennesaw State College
P.O. Box 444, Marietta 30061
Joe Head, Dir. of Admis.

La Grange College
601 Broad St., La Grange 30240
Phil Dodson, Dir. of Admis.
706-882-2911

Mercer University in Atlanta
3001 Mercer University Dr., Atlanta 30341

Mercer University
1400 Coleman Ave., Macon 31207

Savannah State College
State College Branch, Savannah 31404
Robert Ray, Dir. of Admis.

University of Georgia, Athens 30602
Dr. Albert Niemi, Dean

HAWAII

Chaminade University of Honolulu
3140 Waialae Ave., Honolulu 96816
Charles Schafer, VP Enrollment Services

Hawaii Pacific University
1166 Fort Street Mall, Honolulu 96813
Don Barlow, Dir. of Admis.

ILLINOIS

Aurora University
347 S. Gladstone Ave., Aurora 60506
Peter Pitts, Dir. of Admis.

De Paul University
1 E. Jackson Blvd., Chicago 60604
Karen Stark, Assistant Dean and Director
See listing under "Universities"

Eastern Illinois University, Charleston 61920
Larry Williams, Dean
See listing under "Universities"

Governors State University
1 University Pky., University Park 60466
Richard Pride, Dir. of Admis.

LEWIS UNIVERSITY
Rt. 53, Romeoville 60441
Suzanne Benson, Director
See listing under "Universities"

North Central College
30 N. Brainard St.
P.O. Box 3065, Naperville 60566-7065
Marguerite Waters, Director of Admission
708-420-3414

Northeastern Illinois University
5500 N. St. Louis Ave., Chicago 60625

Northern Illinois University, De Kalb 60115

Northwestern University
2001 Sheridan Rd., Evanston 60208

Rockford College
    5050 E. State St., Rockford 61108
    Miriam King, V.P. for Enrollment Management
    See listing under "Universities"

ROOSEVELT UNIVERSITY

430 S. Michigan Ave., Chicago 60605
William Smyser, Director of Admissions
See listing under "Universities"

Sangamon State University
    Shepherd Rd., Springfield 62794-9243
    Admissions and Records, 217-786-6626

University of Chicago
    5801 S. Ellis Ave., Chicago 60637

University of Illinois
    506 S. Wright St., Urbana 61801

University of Illinois at Chicago
    P.O. Box 4348, Chicago 60680
    Dr. Shari Holmer-Lewis, Director

INDIANA

Ball State University
    2000 W. University Ave., Muncie 47306
    Ruth Vedvik, Dir. of Admis.

Indiana Wesleyan University
    4201 S. Washington St., Marion 46953
    800-332-6901

Purdue University
    Young Graduate House, West Lafayette 47907

Purdue University, Calumet Campus
    2233 171st St., Hammond 46323

University of Notre Dame
    Notre Dame 46556
    Kevin M. Rooney, Dir. of Admis.

IOWA

Drake University
    2507 E. University Ave., Des Moines 50311
    Thomas Pursel, Dir. of Graduate Programs

Iowa State University, Ames 50011
    Karsten Smedal, Dir. of Admis.

University of Iowa, Iowa City 52242

University of Northern Iowa, Cedar Falls 50614

KANSAS

Fort Hays State University
    600 Park St., Hays 67601-4099
    Dr. Robert Masters, Chrpsn.

Wichita State University
    1845 Fairmount, Wichita 67260
    316-689-3095
    See listing under "Universities"

KENTUCKY

Bellarmine College
    2001 Newburg Rd., Louisville 40205
    Thomas LaBaugh, Dean of Admissions

LOUISIANA

Grambling State University
    P.O. Box 607, Grambling 71245
    Dr. Harold W. Lundy, President

Loyola University
    6363 St. Charles Ave., New Orleans 70118

Tulane University
    A. B. Freeman School of Business
    Goldring/Woldenberg Hall
    New Orleans 70118

MAINE

Thomas College
    180 W. River Rd., Waterville 04901
    Susan Potter, Dir. of Admis.
    207-877-0101, ME only 800-339-7001

University of Southern Maine
    96 Falmouth St., Portland 04103
    Susan Roberts, Director of Admissions

MARYLAND

Hood College
    400 Rosemont Ave., Frederick 21701

Loyola College
    4501 N. Charles St., Baltimore 21210
    Thomas Bednarsky, Graduate Admissions

Mt. St. Mary's College
    16300 Old Emmitsburg Rd., Emmitsburg 21727
    Michael D. Kennedy, Dir. of Admis.

MASSACHUSETTS

American International College
    1000 State St., Springfield 01109
    Peter Miller, Dean of Admissions

Anna Maria College
    2 Sunset Ln., Paxton 01612
    Dr. Bernadette Madore, SSA, President

Babson College
    One College Dr., Babson Park 02157
    William Makris, Dir. of Graduate Admis.
    617-239-5078

Boston University
    685 Commonwealth Ave., Boston 02215

Clark University
    950 Main St., Worcester 01610
    Richard Pierson, Dean of Admis.

Harvard University
    Havard Business School
    Dillon Hall
    Soldiers Field Rd., Boston 02163

Massachusetts Institute of Technology
    77 Massachusetts Ave., Cambridge 02139

Nichols College, Dudley 01570

Simmons College
    300 The Fenway, Boston 02115

Suffolk University
    8 Ashburton Place, Boston 02108
    Barbara K. Ericson, Assoc. Dean Enrollment &
    Retention
    617-573-8460

University of Massachusetts, Amherst 01003
    Arlene Wesley Cash, Dir. of Admis.

Western New England College
    1215 Wilbraham Rd., Springfield 01119
    800-325-1122

MICHIGAN

Andrews University, Berrien Springs 49104
    Jack Mentges, Dir. of Admis.

Aquinas College
    1607 Robinson Rd., S.E., Grand Rapids 49506
    Dr. Jack Dezek, Dean of Graduate Studies
    800-678-9593

Eastern Michigan University, Ypsilanti 48197
    Stewart Tubbs, Dean
    313-487-3060 or 800-GO-TO-EMU

Lawrence Technological University
    21000 W. Ten Mile Rd., Southfield 48075
    800-225-5588 ext. 3160

Michigan State University, East Lansing 48824
    Dr. William Turner, Dir. of Admis.

University of Detroit Mercy
    4001 W. McNichols
    PO Box 19900, Detroit 48219-0900
    313-993-1202
    See listing under "Universities"

University of Michigan-Ann Arbor
    815 S. University Ave., Ann Arbor 48109

MINNESOTA

St. Cloud State University
    740 4th Ave., S., St. Cloud 56301
    Sherwood Reid, Dir. of Admis.
    800-369-4260

University of St. Thomas
    2115 Summit Ave., St. Paul 55105

Winona State University
    P.O. Box 5838, Winona 55987
    Dr. J. Mootz, Dir. of Admis.

MISSISSIPPI

Millsaps College
    P.O. Box 150556, Jackson 39210
    Florence Hines, Dir. of Admis.

MISSOURI

Avila College
    11901 Wornall Rd., Kansas City 64145

Central Missouri State University
    Warrensburg 64093
    Kathleen Easter, Dean of Graduate Studies

Drury College
    900 N. Benton Ave., Springfield 65802
    Michael G. Thomas, Dir. of Admis.

Maryville University of St. Louis
    13550 Conway Rd., Saint Louis 63141
    314-576-9300 or 800-MARYVLL

Southwest Missouri State University
    901 S. National Ave., Springfield 65804
    Dr. James Pettijohn, Director of MBA Program
    417-836-5646

Washington University
    1 Brookings Dr., St. Louis 63130

Webster University
    470 E. Lockwood Ave., St. Louis 63119
    Dr. James Staley, Associate Dean
    See listing under "Universities"

MONTANA

University of Montana, Missoula 59812
    800-462-8636

NEBRASKA

Creighton University
    2500 California St., Omaha 68178
    Dr. Guy Banville, Dean

NEW HAMPSHIRE

New Hampshire College
    Graduate School of Business
    2500 North River Rd., Manchester 03106
    Dr. Jacqueline Mara, Dean of GSB
    603-644-3102

Rivier College
    420 S. Main St., Nashua 03060
    Michael Quigley, Dean of Graduate Studies
    800-44-RIVIER

NEW JERSEY

Fairleigh Dickinson University, Madison 07940
    Lissa Anderson, Dir. of Admis.
    201-593-8906

Fairleigh Dickinson University, Teaneck 07666
    Dennis Craig, Dir. of Admis.
    201-692-2553

Monmouth College
    400 Cedar Ave., West Long Branch 07764
    Elizabeth Martin, Dir. of Graduate Admis.

Rowan College of New Jersey, Glassboro 08028
    Marvin G. Sills, Dir. of Admis.

St. Peter's College
    2641 John F. Kennedy Blvd.
    Jersey City 07306
    Dr. Alessandro C. Calianese, Dir. of MBA/MIS
    Program
    201-915-9377

Stockton State College, Pomona 08240
    Sal Catalfamo, Dir. of Admis.

NEW MEXICO

Eastern New Mexico University
    Portales 88130
    Dr. Renee Neely, Dean

New Mexico Highlands University, Las Vegas 87701
    Dr. Jorge P. Thomas, VP Academic Affairs

NEW YORK

Adelphi University, Garden City 11530
    Dr. Arnold Weinstein, Dean, Schools of Business
    516-877-4685

Canisius College
    2001 Main St., Buffalo 14208
    Daniel Walker Sullivan, Associate Dean
    716-888-2140

Clarkson University, Potsdam 13699
    Suzanne Liberty, Director

College of Insurance
    101 Murray St., New York 10007
    Mary Alice Landis, Exec. Dir., Graduate Programs
    See listing under "Universities"

College of St. Rose
    432 Western Ave., Albany 12203

Cornell University
    410 Thurston Ave., Ithaca 14853

Fordham University
    Lincoln Center Campus
    113 W. 60th St., New York 10023
    Edward Bristow, Dean

Hofstra University
    1000 Fulton Ave., Hempstead 11550

IONA COLLEGE

715 North Ave., New Rochelle 10801
800-231-IONA or 914-633-2503
See listing under "Universities"

Long Island University-Brooklyn Campus
    1 University Plaza, Brooklyn 11201
    Alan Chaves, Dean of Admissions

Long Island University-C. W. Post Campus
    Rt. 25A, Brookville 11548
    Dr. Robert Sanator, Dean
    516-299-3017

Manhattan College
    4513 Manhattan College Pky., Riverdale 10471
    Dr. Faraj Abdulahad, Asst. Provost

New York Institute of Technology
    Old Westbury Campus, Old Westbury 11568

New York University
    70 Washington Sq., New York 10012

Niagara University, Niagara University 14109
    Dr. Gary Praetzel, Director
    716-286-8051
    See listing under "Universities"

Pace University, New York Campus
    1 Pace Plaza, New York 10038

Pace University, White Plains Campus
    78 N. Broadway, White Plains 10603

Rensselaer Polytechnic Institute, Troy 12180
    Conrad Sharrow, Dean of Admissions

Russell Sage College
    51 1st St., Troy 12180

St. John Fisher College
    3690 East Ave., Rochester 14618
    Peter Lindsey, Dir. of Admis.

University of Rochester
    William Simon Graduate School of Business
    Admin.
    500 Joseph C. Wilson Blvd., Rochester 14627
    See listing under "Universities"

NORTH CAROLINA

East Carolina University
    1000 E. 5th St., Greenville 27858
    Dr. Ernest B. Uhr, Dean

QUEENS COLLEGE

1900 Selwyn Ave., Charlotte 28274
Katie Wireman, Dir. of Admis.
See listing under "Liberal Arts"

University of North Carolina at Chapel Hill
    Chapel Hill 27599
    Joe Bylinski, Director

Wake Forest University
    Babcock Graduate School of Management
    P.O. Box 7659, Winston-Salem 27109

OHIO

Cleveland State University
E uclid Ave. at 24th St., Cleveland   44115

Kent State University
P.O. Box 5190, Kent   44242
Bruce Riddle, Dir. of Admis.

Lake Erie College
391 W. Washington St., Painesville   44077

Miami University
E. High St., Oxford   45056

University of Akron
381 Buchtel Common, Akron   44325
Kris MacDermott, Asst. Provost Enrollment

University of Cincinnati
2700 Clifton Ave., Cincinnati   45221

OKLAHOMA

Oklahoma City University
2501 N. Blackwelder Ave., Oklahoma City   73106
Keith Hackett, Dean of Admissions
See listing under "Universities"

Oklahoma State University, Stillwater   74078
Cynthia Gray, Program Director

Oral Roberts University
7777 S. Lewis Ave., Tulsa   74171
Arthur E. Matzkvech, Dir. of Admis.

Southern Nazarene University
6729 N.W. 39th Expy., Bethany   73008

University of Central Oklahoma
100 N. University Dr., Edmond   73034

University of Tulsa
600 S. College Ave., Tulsa   74104
Dr. Joe Goetz, Dir. Graduate Studies

OREGON

Marylhurst College for Lifelong Learning
P.O. Box 261, Marylhurst   97036
Sherman Severin, Chrpsn.
800-634-9982

PENNSYLVANIA

Bloomsburg University, Bloomsburg   17815
Bernard Vinovrski, Dir. of Admis.

California University of Pennsylvania
3rd St., California   15419
Norman Hasbrouck, Dean for Enrollment

Carnegie Mellon University
5000 Forbes Ave., Pittsburgh   15213

Clarion University of Pennsylvania
840 Wood St., Clarion   16214

Drexel University
3141 Chestnut St., Philadelphia   19104
Dean of Enrollment Management

Duquesne University
600 Forbes Ave., Pittsburgh   15282
Thomas Schaefer, C.S.Sp., Dir. of Admis.

Eastern College
10 Fairview Dr., Saint Davids   19087
Mark Seymour, Admissions Counselor

Gannon University
109 University Sq., Erie   16541

La Salle University
1900 W. Olney Ave., Philadelphia   19141
Br. Gerald Fitzgerald, Dir. of Admis.
See listing under "Universities"

Marywood College
2300 Adams Ave., Scranton   18509

Pennsylvania State University
201 Shields Bldg., University Park   16802

Pennsylvania State University
5091 Station Rd., Erie   16563

Philadelphia College of Textiles & Science
4201 Henry Ave., Philadelphia   19144
Dr. Jeffrey Berlin, Dir. of Graduate Admissions

Robert Morris College
Narrows Run Rd., Coraopolis   15108
James R. Welsh, Dean of Admissions
See listing under "Universities"

Robert Morris College
600 5th Ave., Pittsburgh   15219
James R. Welsh, Dean of Admissions
See listing under "Universities"

St. Joseph's University
5600 City Ave., Philadelphia   19131
Randy Miller, Dir. of Admis.

University of Pennsylvania
0 Levy Park, Philadelphia   19104

University of Pittsburgh
4200 5th Ave., Pittsburgh   15260

Wilkes University
184 S. River St., Wilkes-Barre   18766
Emory P. Guffrovich Jr., Dean of Admissions

RHODE ISLAND

Providence College
River Ave., Providence   02918

Salve Regina University
1 Ochre Point Ave., Newport   02840
Roselina McKillop, Dean of Admissions

SOUTH CAROLINA

Winthrop University
701 W. Oakland Ave., Rock Hill   29733
James McCammon, Jr., Dir. of Admis.

SOUTH DAKOTA

University of South Dakota
414 E. Clark St., Vermillion   57069
Thomas Davies, Coordinator

TENNESSEE

Austin Peay State University
601 College St., Clarksville   37044

Bristol University
P.O. Box 4366, Bristol   37625
Dr. W. David Willis, Academic Dean
See listing under "Universities"

University of Memphis, Memphis   38152
Dr. John Eubank, Dean of Admissions

University of Tennessee at Martin
Martin   38238
Paul Kelley, Director of Admissions
See listing under "Universities"

University of Tennessee, Knoxville
527 Andy Holt Tower, Knoxville   37996
Dr. Gordon Stanley, Dir. of Admis.

Vanderbilt University
West End Ave., Nashville   37240

TEXAS

Baylor University
P.O. Box 97008, Waco   76798-7008
Diana Ramey, Director of Admissions

Corpus Christi State University
6300 Ocean Dr., Corpus Christi   78412

Dallas Baptist University
7777 W. Kiest Blvd., Dallas   75211

Incarnate Word College
4301 Broadway St., San Antonio   78209
Sr. Sally Mitchell, Dean of Enrollment

St. Mary's University of San Antonio
1 Camino Santa Maria, San Antonio   78228
Rick Castillo, Dir. of Admis.

Southern Methodist University
Hillcrest at University, Dallas   75275

Texas A & I University
Campus Box 101, Kingsville   78363

Texas A & M University
College Station   77843

Texas Christian University
2800 S. University Dr., Ft. Worth   76129
Dr. Edward Boehm, Jr., Dean of Admissions

University of Dallas
1845 E. Northgate Dr., Irving   75062
Jim Whitaker, Dir. of Admis.

University of Houston-Clear Lake
2700 Bay Area Blvd., Houston   77058
Darella Banks, Exec. Dir. Enrollment Services

University of St. Thomas
3812 Montrose Blvd., Houston   77006
Elsie Biron, Dir. of Admis.

University of Texas at Austin
0 the University of Texas, Austin   78712

University of Texas at Dallas
P.O. Box 830688, Richardson   75083-0688

West Texas State University
2501 4th Ave., Canyon   79016
Lila Vars, Dir. of Admis.

UTAH

University of Utah
1400 E. 200 S., Salt Lake City   84112
Dr. J. Stayner Landward, Dir. of Admis.

Utah State University, Logan   84322-1600
Rod Clark, Director of Admissions
801-750-1107

Westminster College of Salt Lake City
1840 S. 1300 E., Salt Lake City   84105
800-748-4753

VERMONT

University of Vermont
194 S. Prospect St., Burlington   05401
802-656-3370

VIRGINIA

George Mason University
4400 University Dr., Fairfax   22030-4444
Ms. Sandy Mitchell, Dir. Graduate Admis.

Lynchburg College
1501 Lakeside Dr., Lynchburg   24501
Ernest Chadderton, Dean of Enrollment

Marymount University
2807 N. Glebe Rd., Arlington   22207
Charles Coe, Director of Admissions
800-548-7638 or 703-284-1500
See listing under "Universities"

Radford University
P.O. Box 5430, Radford   24142

SHENANDOAH UNIVERSITY
1460 University Dr., Winchester   22601
Dr. Daniel Pavsek, Dean
See listing under "Universities"

University of Virginia
Darden School
PO Box 6550, Charlottesville   22906

Virginia Polytechnic Institute & State University
Blacksburg   24061
David Bousquet, Dir. of Undergraduate Admis.

WASHINGTON

City University
16661 Northup Way, Bellevue   98008
800-422-4898

Pacific Lutheran University
12180 Park Ave. S., Tacoma   98447
Dr. Joseph McCann III, Dean

University of Puget Sound
1500 N. Warner St., Tacoma   98416

University of Washington, Seattle   98195

WEST VIRGINIA

The University of Charleston
2300 MacCorkle Ave., S.E., Charleston   25304
800-995-GO UC

West Virginia University
P.O. Box 6001, Morgantown   26506

WEST VIRGINIA WESLEYAN COLLEGE
59 College Ave., Buckhannon   26201
Robert Skinner, Director of Admission
See listing under "Universities"

Wheeling Jesuit College
316 Washington Ave., Wheeling   26003
Fr. Thomas Acker, SJ, President

WISCONSIN

Marquette University
606 N. 13th St., Milwaukee   53233
Joseph Fox, Dir. of Graduate Programs (Business)

University of Wisconsin, Eau Claire
Eau Claire   54701

University of Wisconsin, Oshkosh
800 Algoma Blvd., Oshkosh   54901-8602
August Helgerson, Dir. of Admis.

GUAM

University of Guam
UOG Station, Mangilao   96923
Kathleen Owings, Dir. of Admis.

PUERTO RICO

University of Puerto Rico, Mayaguez Campus
P.O. Box 5000, Mayaguez   00681
Neysa Lopez, Dir. of Admis.

University of Puerto Rico, Rio Piedras Campus
P.O. Box 23300, San Juan   00931
Victor Lopez, Dir. of Admis.

MATHEMATICS

ALABAMA

Alabama A & M University
P.O. Box 326, Normal 35762
Dr. Jerry Shipman, Chrpsn.
See listing under "Universities"

Gadsden State Community College
P.O. Box 227, Gadsden 35902
W. Bryan Stone, Dir. of Admis.

Huntingdon College
1500 E. Fairview Ave., Montgomery 36106-2148
Carolyn A. Phillips, Dean of Enrollment
800-763-0313

Judson College
P O Box 120, Marion 36756

Oakwood College
Oakwood Rd., N.W., Huntsville 35896

Samford University
800 Lakeshore Dr., Birmingham 35229
W. D. Peeples, Chrpsn.

Spring Hill College
4000 Dauphin St., Mobile 36608
Ben Hamd, Dir. of Admis.

STILLMAN COLLEGE
P.O. Box 1430, Tuscaloosa 35403
Barbara K. Smith, Director of Admissions
See listing under "Universities"

Talladega College
627 Battle St., W., Talladega 35160

Troy State University, Troy 36082
Dr. Jan Elrod, Dean

Troy State University at Dothan
P.O. Box 8368, Dothan 36304
Bob Willis, Dir. of Undergraduate Admissions

Tuskegee University
Tuskegee Institute 36088

University of Alabama
P.O. Box 870132, Tuscaloosa 35487-0132
Roy Smith, Dir. of Admis.

University of Alabama at Birmingham
University Station, Birmingham 35294

UNIVERSITY OF ALABAMA IN HUNTSVILLE
P.O. Box 1247, Huntsville 35899
Ron R. Koger Ed.D., Dir. of Admis.
205-895-6070
Established 1969. Public. Coed. Accreditation: SACS, ABET, NLN, CSAB, ACS. Tuition: $2,418 resident, $4,836 non-resident. Room & Board: $3,450. Undergraduate enrollment: 2,674 full-time, 3,439 part-time. Graduate enrollment: 1,860. Faculty: 282. Student-faculty ratio: 18:1. Degrees: BS, BA, BSBA, BSE, MS, MSM, Ph.D., BSN, MSN, MA. 20 buildings on 350 acres. Comprehensive research university located in the Tennessee Valley of northern Alabama. Huntsville is the locale of major government and private research centers. Metropolitan population approaching 300,000.

UNIVERSITY OF MOBILE
P.O. Box 13220, Mobile 36663-0220
Kim Leousis, Dir. of Admissions
205-675-5990
See listing under "Universities"

University of Montevallo, Montevallo 35115

ARIZONA

GRAND CANYON UNIVERSITY
3300 W. Camelback Rd., Phoenix 85017
Sherri Willborn, Dir. of Admis.
See listing under "Liberal Arts and Sciences"

Northern Arizona University
P.O. Box 4092, Flagstaff 86011
Dr. Margaret Cibik, Dir. of Admis.

University of Arizona, Tucson 85721
Loyd Bell, Director of Admissions

Yavapai College
1100 E. Sheldon St., Prescott 86301
Dr. Doreen Dailey, President
602-445-7300
See listing under "Community and Junior Colleges"

ARKANSAS

Arkansas State University
P.O. Box 70, State University 72467

John Brown University
2000 W. University, Siloam Springs 72761
Don Crandall, Director of Enrollment Management

Ouachita Baptist University
410 Ouachita St., Arkadelphia 71998
Randy Garner, Dir. of Admis.
800-DIAL-OBU

University of Arkansas at Fayetteville
Fayetteville 72701

University of Arkansas at Monticello
P.O. Box 3596, Monticello 71656

CALIFORNIA

Biola University
13800 Biola Ave., La Mirada 90639
Wayne Chute, Dean of Admissions

California Institute of Technology
1201 E. California Blvd., Pasadena 91125
Carole L. Snow, Dir. of Admis.

California Polytechnic State University
San Luis Obispo 93407
Helen Linstrum, Dir. of Admis.

California State University, Chico
Chico 95929-0525
Everett C. Riggle, Chrpsn.

California State University-Stanislaus
801 W. Monte Vista Ave., Turlock 95382
Frances Cook, Dean Enrollment Services

Chapman University
333 N. Glassell St., Orange 92666
Michael Drummy, Dir. of Admis.

Claremont McKenna College
890 Columbia Ave., Claremont 91711

College of Notre Dame
1500 Ralston Ave., Belmont 94002
Greg M. Smith, PhD., Dir. of Admis.

Concordia University
1530 Concordia, Irvine 92715
Stan Meyer, Dean of Admission
800-229-1200
See listing under "Universities"

DOMINICAN COLLEGE OF SAN RAFAEL
50 Acacia Ave., San Rafael 94901-8008
Office of Admissions
800-788-3522

Fresno Pacific College
1717 S. Chestnut Ave., Fresno 93702
209-453-2039

Harvey Mudd College, Claremont 91711

Holy Names College
3500 Mountain Blvd., Oakland 94619

∷ Idyllwild School of Music & the Arts
P.O. Box 38P, Idyllwild 92549
Anne Behnke, Admissions
909-659-2171, FAX 909-659-2058
See listing under "Prep-Coed"

La Sierra University
4700 Pierce St., Riverside 92505
800-874-5587

Loyola Marymount University
Loyola Blvd. at W. 80th, Los Angeles 90045
M. L'Heureux, Dir. of Admis.

Master's College
P.O. Box 221450, Newhall 91322
Don Gilmore, Dir. of Admis.

Mills College
5000 MacArthur Blvd., Oakland 94613
Genevieve Ann Flaherty, Dean of Admissions
800-87-MILLS

Mt. St. Mary's College
12001 Chalon Rd., Los Angeles 90049

National University
4141 Camino del Rio, S., San Diego 92108

Pitzer College
1050 N. Mills Ave., Claremont 91711
Katharine Leighton, Dir. of Admis.

Point Loma Nazarene College
3900 Lomaland Dr., San Diego 92106
Bill Young, Dir. of Admis.

Pomona College
333 N. College Way, Claremont 91711
Peter W. Stanley, President

San Francisco State University
1600 Holloway Ave., San Francisco 94132
Corwin Bjonerud, Dir. of Admis.

Santa Barbara City College
721 Cliff Dr., Santa Barbara 93109
805-965-0581

Santa Clara University, Santa Clara 95053

Sonoma State University
1801 E. Cotati Ave., Rohnert Park 94928

Southern California College
55 Fair Dr., Costa Mesa 92626
Richard Hardy, Asst. Dean for Enrollment

University of California at Berkeley
Evans Hall, Berkeley 94720

University of California-Santa Cruz
Santa Cruz 95064
Joseph Allen, Dir. of Admis.

University of La Verne
1950 3rd St., La Verne 91750
Mark Bornholdt, Dir. of Admis.

University of Redlands
P.O. Box 3080, Redlands 92373

University of San Diego
5998 Alcala Park, San Diego 92110
Warren Muller, Dir. of Admis.
619-260-4506

University of San Francisco
2130 Fulton St., San Francisco 94117
Bill Henley, Dir. of Admis.

Whittier College
13406 Philadelphia St., Whittier 90601
310-907-4238

COLORADO

Adams State College, Alamosa 81102
Cheryl Billingsley, Dir. of Admis.
800-824-6494

Colorado College
14 E. Cache La Poudre, Colorado Springs 80903
Terry Swenson, Dir. of Admis.

Mesa State College
P.O. Box 2647, Grand Junction 81502
Sherri Pe'a, Dir. of Admis.

Metropolitan State College of Denver
P.O. Box 173362, Campus Box 16
Denver 80217-3362

Regis University
3333 Regis Blvd., Denver 80221
Robert Blust, Director of Admissions

University of Denver
2199 S. University Blvd., Denver 80210

University of Northern Colorado, Greeley 80639
Richard Grassl, Department Chrpsn.
303-351-2820

University of Southern Colorado
2200 Bonforte Blvd., Pueblo 81001

Western State College of Colorado
Gunnison 81231
Monica Bruning, Dir. of Admis.
See listing under "Universities"

CONNECTICUT

Albertus Magnus College
700 Prospect St., New Haven 06511
Richard Lolatte, Dir. of Admissions
203-773-8501 or 800-578-9160

Eastern Connecticut State University
83 Windham St., Willimantic 06226
Dr. Stephen Kenton, Chrpsn.

Mattatuck Community College
750 Chase Parkway, Waterbury 06708
Dr. Richard Sanders, President

QUINNIPIAC COLLEGE
275 Mount Carmel Ave., Hamden 06518
See listing under "Universities"

St. Joseph College
1678 Asylum Ave., West Hartford 06117
Mary C. Demo, Dir. of Admis.

Trinity College
300 Summit St., Hartford 06106
Dr. David Borus, Dean of Admissions

University of Bridgeport
126 Park Ave., Bridgeport 06601
Andrew G. Nelson, Dean Admis./Financial Aid
203-576-4552
See listing under "Universities"

University of Hartford
200 Bloomfield Ave., West Hartford 06117
Richard Zeiser, Dir. of Admis.
See listing under "Universities"

University of New Haven
300 Orange Ave., West Haven 06516
Joseph Chepaitis, Dean
203-932-7000

DELAWARE

University of Delaware, Newark 19711

DISTRICT OF COLUMBIA

The American University
4400 Massachusetts Ave. N.W.
Washington 20016

University of the District of Columbia
Georgia Ave.-Harvard St. Campus
1100 Harvard St., N.W., Washington 20009

University of the District of Columbia
Van Ness Campus
4200 Connecticut Ave., N.W., Washington 20008

FLORIDA

Barry University
11300 N.E. 2nd Ave., Miami Shores 33161
Robin Ray Roberts, Dean of Admissions

Bethune-Cookman College
640 Mary McLeod Bethune Blvd.
Daytona Beach 32114

Clearwater Christian College
3400 Gulf-to-Bay Blvd., Clearwater 34619
Benjamin Puckett, Dir. of Admis.

Eckerd College
P.O. Box 12560, St. Petersburg 33733
Richard Hallin, Dir. of Admis.

Flagler College
P.O. Box 1027, St. Augustine 32085
Marc G. Williar, Dir. of Admis.
904-829-6481

Florida Atlantic University
500 N.W. 20th St., Boca Raton 33431
Brian Levin-Stankevich, Dir. of Admis.

Florida Institute of Technology
150 W. University Blvd., Melbourne 32901
Louis T. Levy, Dean of Admissions
800-888-4348

Florida Southern College
111 Lake Hollingsworth Dr., Lakeland 33801
William Stephens, Jr., Dir. of Admis.

Jacksonville University
2800 University Blvd., N., Jacksonville 32211

Palm Beach Atlantic College
P.O. Box 24708, West Palm Beach 33416-4708
See listing under "Universities"

Rollins College
P.O. Box 2720, Winter Park 32790

Stetson University
401 N. Woodland Blvd., De Land 32720
Gary A. Meadows, Dean of Admis.

University of Miami
P.O. Box 248006, Coral Gables 33124

GEORGIA

Agnes Scott College
201 E. College Ave., Decatur 30030
Teresa Lahti, Dir. of Admis.

Clark Atlanta University
240 James Brawley Dr., S.W., Atlanta 30314
Thomas W. Cole, President

Georgia College
231 W. Hancock St., Milledgeville 31061
912-453-5004

Kennesaw State College
P.O. Box 444, Marietta 30061
Joe Head, Dir. of Admis.

La Grange College
601 Broad St., La Grange 30240
Phil Dodson, Dir. of Admis.
706-882-2911

Mercer University
1400 Coleman Ave., Macon 31207

Oglethorpe University
4484 Peachtree Rd., N.E., Atlanta 30319
Dennis Matthews, Dir. of Admis.

Paine College
1235 15th St., Augusta 30901
Phyllis Wyatt-Woodruff, Dir. Enrollment Mgmt.

Piedmont College
P.O. Box 10, Demorest 30535
Penny L. Graber, Dir of Admis.
800-277-7020

Savannah State College
State College Branch, Savannah 31404
Robert Ray, Dir. of Admis.

Shorter College
315 Shorter Ave., Rome 30165

Spelman College
350 Spelman Ln., S.W., Atlanta 30314
Aline Rivers, Dir. of Admis.

University of Georgia, Athens 30602
Ray Kunze, Head

Wesleyan College
4760 Forsyth Rd., Macon 31297

West Georgia College, Carrollton 30118
C. Doyle Bickers, Dir. of Admis.

HAWAII

Brigham Young University, Hawaii Campus
55-220 Kulanui St., Laie 96762
Clark E. Hirschi, Coordinator of Admis.

Chaminade University of Honolulu
3140 Waialae Ave., Honolulu 96816
Charles Schafer, VP Enrollment Services

Hawaii Pacific University
1166 Fort Street Mall, Honolulu 96813
Don Barlow, Dir. of Admis.

Hawaii Pacific University
45-045 Kamehameha Hwy., Kaneohe 96744

IDAHO

Lewis Clark State College
500 8th Ave., Lewiston 83501
800-933-5272 or 208-799-5272

University of Idaho, Moscow 83843
Peter Brown, Dir. of Admis.

ILLINOIS

Augustana College
639 38th St., Rock Island 61201
Martin R. Sauer, Director of Admission
800-798-8100

Aurora University
347 S. Gladstone Ave., Aurora 60506
Peter Pitts, Dir. of Admis.

Blackburn College
700 College Ave., Carlinville 62626
Dwight Smith, Dir. of Admis.

De Paul University
1 E. Jackson Blvd., Chicago 60604
Thomas D. Abrahamson, Dean of Admissions
See listing under "Universities"

Eastern Illinois University, Charleston 61920
Ira Rosenholtz, Chrpsn.
See listing under "Universities"

Elmhurst College
190 Prospect Ave., Elmhurst 60126

Eureka College
300 E. College Ave., Eureka 61530

Greenville College
315 E. College Ave., Greenville 62246
Kent Krober, Dir. of Admis.

Illinois College
1101 W. College Ave., Jacksonville 62650
Gale Vaugn, Dir. of Admis.

ILLINOIS WESLEYAN UNIVERSITY
P.O. Box 2900, Bloomington 61702
Dr. Mel Jeter, Chrpsn.
309-556-3069

Judson College
1151 N. State St., Elgin 60123
Jack Powell, Dir. of Enrollment Services

Knox College, Galesburg 61401
309-343-0112 or 800-678-KNOX
See listing under "Universities"

LEWIS UNIVERSITY
Rt. 53, Romeoville 60441
Irish O'Reilly, Director of Admissions
See listing under "Universities"

Loyola University - Mundelein College
6363 N. Sheridan Rd., Chicago 60660
Judith Bobber, Dir. of Admis.

MacMurray College
447 E. College Ave., Jacksonville 62650
Edwin R. Hockett, Dean of Admissions

Millikin University
1184 W. Main St., Decatur 62522
Lin Stoner, Dean of Admissions
800-373-7733

Monmouth College
700 E. Broadway, Monmouth 61462

North Central College
30 N. Brainard St.
P.O. Box 3065, Naperville 60566-7065
Marguerite Waters, Director of Admission
708-420-3414

Northeastern Illinois University
5500 N. St. Louis Ave., Chicago 60625

Northern Illinois University, De Kalb 60115

North Park College & Theological Seminary
3225 W. Foster, Chicago 60625
312-509-2330

Olivet Nazarene University, Kankakee 60901
John Mongerson, Dir. of Admis.
815-939-5203

Parkland College
2400 W. Bradley Ave., Champaign 61821-1899
217-351-2208 or 800-346-8089

Principia College, Elsah 62028

Quincy College
1800 College Ave., Quincy 62301
Fr. Michael Lanning, O.F.M., Dir. of Admis.

Rockford College
5050 E. State St., Rockford 61108
Miriam King, V.P. for Enrollment Management
See listing under "Universities"

ROOSEVELT UNIVERSITY
430 S. Michigan Ave., Chicago 60605
William Smyser, Director of Admissions
See listing under "Universities"

Rosary College
7900 W. Division St., River Forest 60305
Hildegarde Schmidt, Dir. of Admis.

St. Xavier College
3700 W. 103rd St., Chicago 60655
Mary Hendry, Dean of Admissions

Sangamon State University
Shepherd Rd., Springfield 62794-9243
Admissions and Records, 217-786-6626

Trinity Christian College
6601 W. College Dr., Palos Heights 60463
Kenneth Bootsma, President

Trinity College
2077 Half Day Rd., Deerfield 60015
Dr. Kenneth Meyer, Pres.

University of Chicago
5801 S. Ellis Ave., Chicago 60637

University of Illinois at Chicago
P.O. Box 5220, Chicago 60680
Dr. Marilyn R. Fiduccia, Dir. of Admis.

Western Illinois University
900 W. Adams St., Macomb 61455
Alan DeRoos, Registrar
309-298-1891

INDIANA

Ball State University
2000 W. University Ave., Muncie 47306
Ruth Vedvik, Dir. of Admis.

Bethel College
1001 W. McKinley Ave., Mishawaka 46545
Steve Matteson, Dir. of Admis.

Earlham College
801 National Rd. W., Richmond 47374
Robert deVeer, Dean of Admis.

Franklin College
501 E. Monroe, Franklin 46131
B. Stephen Richards, VP Enrollment

Goshen College
1700 S. Main St., Goshen 46526
Merritt Gardner, Chairperson

Grace College
200 Seminary Dr., Winona Lake 46590
Ron Henry, Dir. of Admis.

Huntington College
2303 College Ave., Huntington 46750
Paul Breininger, Dir. of Admis. Services

Indiana Wesleyan University
4201 S. Washington St., Marion 46953
800-332-6901

Manchester College
604 College Ave., North Manchester 46962
Dr. Stanley Beery, Chrpsn.

Marian College
3200 Cold Spring Rd., Indianapolis 46222
Don French, Dir. of Admis.

Martin University
P.O. Box 18567, Indianapolis 46218

Purdue University
Schleman Hall, West Lafayette 47907

Purdue University, Calumet Campus
2233 171st St., Hammond 46323

ST. JOSEPH'S COLLEGE
P.O. Box 890, Rensselaer 47978
Louis Levy, Dean of Admissions
800-447-8781

St. Mary-of-the-Woods College
Saint Mary-of-the-Woods 47876
Lynn M. Rubick, Director of Admissions
800-926-SMWC

Taylor University
500 W. Reade Ave., Upland 46989
William Klinger, Head

Tri-State University, Angola 46703
Director of Admission
800-347-4878

University of Evansville
1800 Lincoln Ave., Evansville 47722
Dr. Robert Knott, Dept. Chair
800-423-8633

University of Notre Dame
Notre Dame 46556
Kevin M. Rooney, Dir. of Admis.

Valparaiso University, Valparaiso 46383

Wabash College
301 W. Wabash Ave., Crawfordsville 47933
Greg Birk, Dir. of Admis.

IOWA

Briar Cliff College
3303 Rebecca St., Sioux City 51104
Patricia White, Dir. of Admis.

Clarke College
1550 Clarke Dr., Dubuque 52001
Carol Spiegel, BVM, PhD, Chair
800-383-2345

Coe College
1220 1st Ave., N.E., Cedar Rapids 52402
Charles Lindsay, Chrpsn.

Dordt College
498 4th Ave., N.E., Sioux Center 51250
Quentin Van Essen, Dir. of Admissions
800-343-6738

Drake University
2507 E. University Ave., Des Moines 50311
Thomas Willoughby, Dir. of Admis.

Graceland College, Lamoni 50140
800-638-0053, Outside Iowa 800-346-9208
Bonita Booth, Dean of Admissions
See listing under "Universities"

Grand View College
1200 Grandview Ave., Des Moines 50316
Lori Hanson, Dir. of Admissions
800-444-6083

Grinnell College
P.O. Box 805, Grinnell 50112

Iowa State University, Ames 50011
Karsten Smedal, Dir. of Admis.

Iowa Wesleyan College
601 N. Main St., Mt. Pleasant 52641

Luther College
700 College Dr., Decorah 52101
David Sallee, Dean for Enrollment

Maharishi International University
Route 1, Fairfield 52556
Gregory Polakow, Dir. of Admis.

Morningside College, Sioux City 51106
Lora Vanderzwaag, Dir. of Admis.

Mount Mercy College
1330 Elmhurst Dr., N.E., Cedar Rapids 52402
Carol Williamson, Dir. of Admis.

Northwestern College
101 7th St. S.W., Orange City 51041

Teikyo Marycrest University
1607 W. 12th St., Davenport 52804
Tim McDonough, Dir. of Admis.
See listing under "Universities"

Teikyo Westmar University
1002 3rd Ave., S.E., Le Mars 51031
Dr. Jim Utesch, Dir. of Admis.

University of Iowa, Iowa City 52242

University of Northern Iowa, Cedar Falls 50614

Upper Iowa University
P.O. Box 1857, Fayette 52142

Waldorf College
106 S. 6th St., Forest City 50436
Steve Lovik, Dir. of Admis.
800-292-1903

KANSAS

Bethany College
421 N. 1st St., Lindsborg 67456
Dennis Chaput, Dir. of Admis.

Fort Hays State University
600 Park St., Hays 67601-4099
Dr. Ronald Sandstrom, Chrpsn.

Kansas Newman College
3100 McCormick Ave., Wichita 67213
Dr. Robert Giroux, President

McPherson College
1600 E. Euclid St., McPherson 67460

Mid-America Nazarene College
P.O. Box 1776, Olathe 66051

Ottawa University
1001 S. Cedar St., Ottawa 66067
Steve Koberlein, Dir. of Admis.
800-755-5200

Saint Mary College
4100 S. 4th St., Leavenworth 66048
Irene Keehan, Dir. of Admis.

KENTUCKY

Asbury College
1 Macklem Dr., Wilmore 40390
Jonah Mitchell, Dir. of Admis.

Bellarmine College
2001 Newburg Rd., Louisville 40205
Thomas LaBaugh, Dean of Admissions

Centre College
600 W. Walnut St., Danville 40422

Cumberland College
6178 College Station Dr., Williamsburg 40769
See listing under "Universities"

Georgetown College
400 E. College St., Georgetown 40324
Garvel Kindrick, Director of Admissions
See listing under "Universities"

Kentucky Wesleyan College
3000 Frederica St., Owensboro 42301
Dr. Kirby Chelgren, Chrpsn.

Morehead State University, Morehead 40351
Charles Myers, Director of Admissions
606-783-2000

Murray State University, Murray 42071
Phil Bryan, Director of Admissions
800-272-4MSU

Northern Kentucky University
Louie B. Nunn Dr., Highland Heights 41076

Pikeville College
214 Sycamore St., Pikeville 41501
Dr. John W. Sanders, Dean of Admissions

Spalding University
851 S. 4th St., Louisville 40203
Dorothy G. Allen, Dir. of Admis.

Transylvania University
300 Broadway St., N., Lexington 40508
Pat Bain, Dir. of Admis.

LOUISIANA

Centenary College of Louisiana
P.O. Box 41188, Shreveport 71134

Louisiana College
College Station, Pineville 71359
Byron McGee, Dir. of Admis.
318-487-7386
See listing under "Liberal Arts"

Loyola University
6363 St. Charles Ave., New Orleans 70118

OUR LADY OF HOLY CROSS COLLEGE
4123 Woodland Dr., New Orleans 70131

Southeastern Louisiana University
P.O. Box 784, Hammond 70404

Tulane University
6823 Saint Charles Ave., New Orleans 70118
Richard Whiteside, Dean of Admission

MAINE

Bowdoin College, Brunswick 04011
William Mason, Dir. of Admis.

St. Joseph's College, North Windham 04062

University of Maine at Fort Kent
25 Pleasant St., Fort Kent 04743
Jerry Nadeau, Dir. of Admis.

University of Maine
9 O'Brien Ave., Machias 04654

University of Southern Maine
96 Falmouth St., Portland 04103
Joel Irish, Chrpsn.

MARYLAND

Goucher College
1021 Dulaney Valley Rd., Baltimore 21204

Hood College
400 Rosemont Ave., Frederick 21701

Loyola College
4501 N. Charles St., Baltimore 21210
William Bossemeyer III, Dir. of Admis.

Mt. St. Mary's College
16300 Old Emmitsburg Rd., Emmitsburg 21727
Michael D. Kennedy, Dir. of Admis.

Towson State University
800 York Rd., Towson 21204
Dr. Hoke Smith, President

University of Maryland Eastern Shore
11868 Academic Oval, Princess Anne 21853
Dr. Eddie Boyd, Chrpsn.

Western Maryland College
2 College Hill, Westminster 21157

MASSACHUSETTS

American International College
1000 State St., Springfield 01109
Peter Miller, Dean of Admissions

Amherst College, Amherst 01002
Jane E. Reynolds, Dean of Admissions

Atlantic Union College
P.O. Box 1000, South Lancaster 01561
Osa Canto, Registrar

Babson College
One College Dr., Babson Park 02157
Charles S. Nolan, Dean of Admission
800-488-3696

Boston College
140 Commonwealth Ave., Chestnut Hill 02167

Boston University
685 Commonwealth Ave., Boston 02215

Brandeis University
415 South St, Waltham 02154
David Gould, Dean of Admissions
617-736-3500

Bridgewater State College
Bridgewater 02325
James Plotner, Jr., Dir. of Admis.

Clark University
950 Main St., Worcester 01610
Richard Pierson, Dean of Admis.

ELMS COLLEGE
291 Springfield St., Chicopee 01013
800-255-ELMS

Emmanuel College
400 The Fenway, Boston 02115
Margaret Bonilla, Dir. of Admis.

Fitchburg State College
160 Pearl St., Fitchburg 01420
Marke Vickers, Dir. of Admis.

Hampshire College, Amherst 01002
Audrey Y. Smith, Dir. of Admissions
413-582-5471

Harvard University
Graduate School of Arts and Sciences
Byerly Hall, 2nd Floor
8 Garden St, Cambridge 02138

Massachusetts Institute of Technology
77 Massachusetts Ave., Cambridge 02139

Mt. Holyoke College
College St., South Hadley 01075
Anita Smith, Director of Admissions
413-538-2023

North Adams State College
375 Church St., North Adams 01247
413-664-4511 or 800-292-6632
See listing under "Universities or Graduate Schools"

Simmons College
300 The Fenway, Boston 02115

Springfield College
263 Alden St., Springfield 01109
Frederick Bartlett, Dean of Admissions

SPRINGFIELD TECHNICAL COMMUNITY COLLEGE
1 Armory Square, Springfield 01105
Dr. Patrick E. Tigue, Dir. of Admissions
413-781-7822

Suffolk University
8 Ashburton Place, Boston 02108
Barbara K. Ericson, Assoc. Dean Enrollment & Retention
617-573-8460

University of Massachusetts
100 Morrissey Blvd., Boston 02125

University of Massachusetts Dartmouth
Old Westport Rd., North Dartmouth 02747
Raymond Barrows, Dir. of Admissions
508-999-8605

Wellesley College, Wellesley 02181
Janet A. Lavin, Dir. of Admis.

Western New England College
1215 Wilbraham Rd., Springfield 01119
800-325-1122

Westfield State College
577 Western Ave., Westfield 01085
John F. Marcus, Dir. of Admis.

Wheaton College
26 E. Main St., Norton 02766
Gail Berson, Dean/Admis. & Student Aid

Worcester Polytechnic Institute
100 Institute Rd., Worcester 01609
Kay R. Dietrich, Director of Admissions
508-831-5286

MICHIGAN

Adrian College
110 S. Madison St., Adrian 49221
George Wolf, Dir. of Admis.
See listing under "Universities"

Albion College
611 E. Porter, Albion 49224
800-858-6770

Andrews University, Berrien Springs 49104
Jack Mentges, Dir. of Admis.

Aquinas College
1607 Robinson Rd., S.E., Grand Rapids 49506
Paula Meehan, Dean of Admissions
800-678-9593

Calvin College
3201 Burton St., S.E., Grand Rapids 49546

Eastern Michigan University, Ypsilanti 48197
Don Raymond Lick, Head
313-487-3060 or 800-GO-TO-EMU

GMI Engineering & Management Institute
1700 W. 3rd Ave., Flint 48504
Phillip D. Lavender, Dir. of Admis.
See listing under "Engineering"

Grand Valley State University
1 Campus Dr., Allendale 49401
JoAnn Foerster, Dir. of Admis.

HILLSDALE COLLEGE
33 E. College St., Hillsdale 49242
Professor Mark Watson, Director
517-437-7341

Lake Superior State University
1000 College Dr., Sault St. Marie 49783

Lawrence Technological University
21000 W. Ten Mile Rd., Southfield 48075
800-225-5588 ext. 3160

Michigan State University, East Lansing 48824
Dr. Douglas Hall, Associate Chrpsn.

Michigan Technological University
1400 Townsend Dr., Houghton 49931
Joseph A. Galetto, Dir. Enrollment Mgmt.
906-487-2335

Olivet College
300 S. Main St., Olivet 49076
Vicki Gallas, Registrar
See listing under "Universities"

Spring Arbor College
106 E. Main St., Spring Arbor 49283

MINNESOTA

Augsburg College
731 21st Ave., S., Minneapolis 55454

Bemidji State University
1500 Birchmont Dr., N.E., Bemidji 56601
800-475-2001

Bethel College
3900 Bethel Dr., St. Paul 55112
Dr. George Brushaber, President

Carleton College
One N. College St., Northfield 55057
Paul Thiboutot, Dir. of Admis.

College of Saint Benedict
37 S. College Ave., St. Joseph 56374

College of St. Catherine
2004 Randolph Ave., St. Paul 55105

College of St. Scholastica
1200 Kenwood Ave., Duluth 55811
Alice Guckin, Chrpsn.
800-447-5444
See listing under "Liberal Arts"

Concordia College
901 8th St. S., Moorhead 56562
Lee Johnson, Dir. of Admis.
See listing under "Universities"

Gustavus Adolphus College
800 W. College Ave., St. Peter 56082
Mark Anderson, Dir. of Admis.

Hamline University
1536 Hewitt Ave., St. Paul 55104
Scott Pratt, Dir. of Admis.

Northwestern College
3003 Snelling Ave., N., St. Paul 55113
Ralph Anderson, Dean of Admissions
800-827-6827 or 612-631-5111

PILLSBURY BAPTIST BIBLE COLLEGE
315 S. Grove St., Owatonna 55060
Alan Potter, President
Larry Tindall, Director of Admissions
800-747-4557

St. Cloud State University
740 4th Ave., S., St. Cloud 56301
Sherwood Reid, Dir. of Admis.
800-369-4260

St. John's University
P.O. Box 7155, Collegeville 56321

St. Mary's College of Minnesota
700 Terrace Heights #2, Winona 55987
Tony Piscitiello, VP for Admission

St. Olaf College, Northfield 55057
Clifton Corzatt, Chrpsn.
507-646-3113

Southwest State University, Marshall 56258

University of Minnesota
600 E. Fourth St., Morris 56267

University of St. Thomas
2115 Summit Ave., St. Paul 55105

Winona State University
P.O. Box 5838, Winona 55987
Dr. J. Mootz, Dir. of Admis.

MISSISSIPPI

Belhaven College
1500 Peachtree St., Jackson 39202

Millsaps College
P.O. Box 150556, Jackson 39210
Florence Hines, Dir. of Admis.

Mississippi College
P.O. Box 4086, Clinton 39058

Mississippi University for Women
P.O. Box W-1602, Columbus 39701
Teresa Thompson, Exec. Dir. of Enrollment

Tougaloo College
500 E. County Line Rd., Tougaloo 39174

MISSOURI

Avila College
11901 Wornall Rd., Kansas City 64145

Central Missouri State University
Warrensburg 64093
Delores Hudson, Dir. of Admis.

College of the Ozarks, Point Lookout 65726
Dr. Kenton Olson, Dean of the College

Drury College
900 N. Benton Ave., Springfield 65802
Michael G. Thomas, Dir. of Admis.

Evangel College
1111 N. Glenstone Ave., Springfield 65802
David Schoolfield, Dir. of Enrollment

Fontbonne College
6800 Wydown Blvd., St. Louis 63105
Peggy Musen, Dir. of Admis.

Maryville University of St. Louis
13550 Conway Rd., Saint Louis 63141
314-576-9300 or 800-MARYVLL

Missouri Baptist College
12542 Conway Rd., St. Louis 63141

Missouri Southern State College
3950 Newman Rd., Joplin 64801-1595
Dr. J. Larry Martin, Dept. Head
See listing under "Universities"

Missouri Valley College
500 E. College St., Marshall 65340
816-886-6924 ext. 114
See listing under "Universities"

Missouri Western State College
4525 Downs Dr., St. Joseph 64507
Howard McCauley, Dir. of Admis.

Northwest Missouri State University
800 University Dr., Maryville 64468

Park College, Parkville 64152
Dr. Edwin Rawn, Dean of Admis.

Southeast Missouri State University
1 University Plz., Cape Girardeau 63701
New Student Relations 314-651-2590
See listing under "Universities"

Southwest Baptist University
1601 S. Springfield Ave., Bolivar 65613

Southwest Missouri State University
901 S. National Ave., Springfield 65804
Dr. Michael Awad, Department Head
417-836-5112

Stephens College, Columbia 65215
Mary Ann Sprinkle, Dir. of Admis.

University of Missouri, Rolla
102 Parker Hall, Rolla 65401
David J. Allen, Dir. of Admis. & Financial Aid
800-522-0938

University of Missouri
8001 Natural Bridge Rd., St. Louis 63121
Mimi LaMarca, Dir. of Admis.

Washington University
1 Brookings Dr., St. Louis 63130

Webster University
470 E. Lockwood Ave., St. Louis 63119
Dr. James Staley, Associate Dean
See listing under "Universities"

Westminister College
501 Westminster Ave., Fulton 65251
Gary Forney, Dean of Admis.

William Woods College
200 W. 12th St., Fulton 65251
Dr. Jahnae Barnett, VP of Admis.

MONTANA

CARROLL COLLEGE
1610 N. Benton Ave., Helena 59625
Candace Cain, Dir. of Admis.
See listing under "Universities"

College of Great Falls
1301 20th St., S., Great Falls 59405
Jean Walker, Dir. of Admis.

Montana State University, Bozeman 59717

Montana State University - Billings
1500 N. 30th St., Billings 59101
Karen Everett, Dir. of Admis.
406-657-2158

Montana Tech
(formerly Montana College of Mineral
Science and Technology)
1300 W. Park St., Butte 59701-8997
800-445-TECH
See listing under "Engineering"

Rocky Mountain College
1511 Poly Dr., Billings 59102
David Heringer, Dir. of Admis.
See listing under "Universities"

University of Montana, Missoula 59812
800-462-8636

NEBRASKA

Bellevue College
1000 Galvin Rd. S., Bellevue 68005
Chari Leader, VP of Enrollment

Chadron State College
1000 Main St., Chadron 69337
Dr. Ted Davis, Dean

Concordia College
800 N. Columbia Ave., Seward 68434
Don Vos, Dir. of Admis.

Creighton University
2500 California St., Omaha 68178
Dr. John Mordeson, Chrpsn.

Dana College
2848 College Dr., Blair 68008
John Schueth, Dir. of Admis.
800-444-3262
See listing under "Universities"

Midland Lutheran College
900 Clarkson St., Fremont 68025
Roland Kahnk, V.P. Admissions

Nebraska Wesleyan University
5000 Saint Paul Ave., Lincoln 68504
Ken Sieg, Dir. of Admis.

Peru State College, Peru 68421
Pamela J. Cosgrove, Dir. of Admis.
402-872-3815

Wayne State College
200 E. Tenth St., Wayne 68787

NEVADA

University of Nevada Las Vegas
4505 S. Maryland Pky., Las Vegas 89154-1021
Admissions: 702-895-3443 or 800-334-UNLV

NEW HAMPSHIRE

Keene State College
229 Main St., Keene 03435
Kathryn Dodge, Dir. of Admis.

New England College
26 Bridge St., Henniker 03242
John Spaulding, Dir. of Admis.

Rivier College
420 S. Main St., Nashua 03060
Admissions: 800-44-RIVIER

Saint Anselm College
87 Saint Anselm Dr., Manchester 03102
Don Healy, Dir. of Admis.

NEW JERSEY

Caldwell College
9 Ryerson Ave., Caldwell 07006

Fairleigh Dickinson University, Madison 07940
Lissa Anderson, Dir. of Admis.
201-593-8906

Fairleigh Dickinson University, Teaneck 07666
Dennis Craig, Dir. of Admis.
201-692-2553

FELICIAN COLLEGE
262 S. Main St., Lodi 07644
Sr. Mary Austin, OSB, Dir. of Admis.
201-778-1029
See listing under "Universities"

Georgian Court College
900 Lakewood Ave., Lakewood 08701
908-364-2200 Ext. 337

Jersey City State College
2039 Kennedy Blvd., Jersey City 07305
201-200-3234

Monmouth College
400 Cedar Ave., West Long Branch 07764
Joan Rudinski, Dir. of Admis.

Princeton University, Princeton 08544

Rider University
2083 Lawrenceville Rd., Lawrenceville 08648
Susan Christian, Dir. of Admis.

Rowan College of New Jersey, Glassboro 08028
Marvin G. Sills, Dir. of Admis.

Seton Hall University
400 S. Orange Ave., South Orange 07079
Lee Cooke, Dir. of Admis.

Stockton State College, Pomona 08240
Sal Catalfamo, Dir. of Admis.

Upsala College
345 Prospect St., East Orange 07017
George Lynes, Dean of Admissions

NEW MEXICO

College of Santa Fe
1600 St. Michaels Dr., Santa Fe 87505
800-456-2673

Eastern New Mexico University
Portales 88130
Larry Fuqua, Dir. of Admis.

New Mexico Highlands University, Las Vegas 87701
Dr. Jorge P. Thomas, VP Academic Affairs

New Mexico Institute of Mining & Technology
801 Leroy Pl., Socorro 87801

NEW YORK

Adelphi University, Garden City 11530
Dr. Elliot Pruzan, Asst. Provost & Dir. of Admis.
516-877-3050

Alfred University
Alumni Hall, Alfred 14802
Laurie Richer, Director of Admissions
800-541-9229

Barnard College
3009 Broadway, New York 10027

Canisius College
2001 Main St., Buffalo 14208
Penelope Lips, Dir. of Admis.
800-843-1517

Clarkson University, Potsdam 13699
Robert Croot, Dir. of Admis.

Colgate University
13 Oak Dr., Hamilton 13346
Dean of Admissions
315-824-7401

College of Insurance
101 Murray St., New York 10007
Theresa C. Marro, Director of Admissions
See listing under "Universities"

College of St. Rose
432 Western Ave., Albany 12203

Cornell University
410 Thurston Ave., Ithaca 14853

CUNY York College
9420 Guy R. Brewer Blvd., Jamaica 11451

Daemen College
4380 Main St., Amherst 14226
Maria Dillard, Dir. of Admis.
in NY 800-462-7652 or 716-839-8225

Dominican College of Blauvelt
460 N. Western Hwy., Orangeburg 10962
Louis Kern, Dir. of Admis.
914-359-7800

D'Youville College
320 Porter Ave., Buffalo 14201
Ronald Dannecker, Dir. of Admis.

Elmira College
Park Pl., Elmira 14901
William S. Neal, Dean of Admissions
See listing under "Liberal Arts"

Fordham University
441 E. Fordham Rd., Bronx 10458
718-817-1000

Hartwick College, Oneonta 13820

Hobart & William Smith College
Pulteney St., Geneva 14456

Houghton College
P.O. Box 128, Houghton 14744
Tim Fuller, Dir. of Admis.

IONA COLLEGE
715 North Ave., New Rochelle 10801
800-231-IONA or 914-633-2503
See listing under "Universities"

Ithaca College
953 Danby Rd., Ithaca 14850

Keuka College
P.O. Box 98, Keuka Park 14478
Robert J. Ianuzzo, Dean of Admissions

The King's College, Briarcliff Manor 10510
Frederic Rowley, Dean of Admissions

Le Moyne College
1419 Salt Springs Rd., Syracuse 13214-1301
Edwin B. Harris, Dir. of Admis.

Long Island University-C. W. Post Campus
Rt. 25A, Brookville 11548
Dr. Neo Cleopa, Chrpsn.
516-299-2448

Manhattan College
4513 Manhattan College Pky., Riverdale 10471
Dr. Edward Brown, Acting Dean of Science

Manhattanville College
2900 Purchase St., Purchase 10577

MARIST COLLEGE
290 North Rd., Poughkeepsie 12601
Harry W. Wood, VP Admissions
914-575-3226

Marymount College
100 Marymount Ave., Tarrytown 10591
Gina R. Campbell, Dir. of Admis.
800-724-4312

Mercy College
555 Broadway, Dobbs Ferry 10522
James Nesbitt, Dean of Admissions

Molloy College
1000 Hempstead Ave., Rockville Centre 11570
Wayne James, Dir. of Admis.
See listing under "Universities"

Mt. St. Mary College
330 Powell Ave., Newburgh 12550

Nazareth College of Rochester
4245 East Ave., Rochester 14618
Paul Kenyon, Dir. of Admis.

Niagara University, Niagara University 14109
George Pachter, Dean of Admissions
800-462-2111
See listing under "Universities"

Pace University, New York Campus
1 Pace Plaza, New York 10038

Pace University, Pleasantville/Briarcliff Campus
Bedford Rd., Pleasantville 10570

Pace University, White Plains Campus
78 N. Broadway, White Plains 10603

Paul Smith's College, Paul Smiths 12970
Enrico Miller, Dir. of Admis.
800-421-2605

Rensselaer Polytechnic Institute, Troy 12180
Conrad Sharrow, Dean of Admissions

Roberts Wesleyan College
2301 Westside Dr., Rochester 14624
Dr. Barbara Rose, Chrpsn.
See listing under "Universities"

Rochester Institute of Technology
1 Lomb Memorial Dr., Rochester 14623
716-475-6631
See listing under "Universities"

Russell Sage College
51 1st St., Troy 12180

St. John Fisher College
3690 East Ave., Rochester 14618
Peter Lindsey, Dir. of Admis.

St. Joseph's College
245 Clinton Ave., Brooklyn 11205
Geraldine Foudy, Dir. of Admis.
718-636-6868

St. Lawrence University, Canton 13617
Joel R. Wincowski, Dean of Admis. & Financial Aid

ST. THOMAS AQUINAS COLLEGE
Rt. 340, Sparkill 10976
Andrea Kraeft, Dir. of Admis.
800-999-STAC
See listing under "Liberal Arts"

Sarah Lawrence College, Bronxville 10708

Skidmore College, Saratoga Springs 12866
Kent Jones, Dir. of Admis.

SUNY Adirondack Community College
439 Bay Rd., Queensbury 12804
Levi Brown, Dir. of Admis.
518-793-4491
See listing under "Community and Junior Colleges"

SUNY at Buffalo
17 Capen Hall
P.O. Box 601660, Buffalo 14260-1660
716-645-6900

SUNY College at Brockport
Brockport 14420

SUNY College at Old Westbury
P.O. Box 210, Old Westbury 11568
Michael Sheehy, Dir. of Admis.

SUNY at Oswego, Oswego 13126
Dr. Joseph Grant, Jr., Dean of Admissions
315-341-2250

SUNY College at Plattsburgh, Plattsburgh 12901
David Kenoyer, Chrpsn.
518-564-3138

SUNY College at Potsdam
Potsdam 13676
Marc Davis, Dir. of Admis.

SUNY College at Purchase
735 Anderson Hill Rd., Purchase 10577
Gene Ann Flaherty, Dir. of Admissions

SUNY Schenectady County Community College
78 Washington Ave., Schenectady 12305
Robert Dinello, Dir. of Admis.
518-346-6211, ext. 166

University of Rochester
500 Joseph C. Wilson Blvd., Rochester 14627
Wayne A. Locust, Dir. of Admis.
See listing under "Universities"

Utica College of Syracuse University
1600 Burrstone Rd., Utica 13502

Vassar College
125 Raymond Ave., Poughkeepsie 12601

NORTH CAROLINA

Barton College
College Station, Wilson 27893
Anthony Britt, Dir. of Admis.
800-345-4973/919-399-6318
See listing under "Universities"

Belmont Abbey College
1 Abbey Pl., Belmont 28012
Admissions, 800-523-2355

Catawba College
2300 W. Innes St., Salisbury 28144
Mark Stokes, Dir. of Admis.

East Carolina University
1000 E. 5th St., Greenville 27858
Dr. Robert L. Bernhardt, Chair

Elon College
P.O. Box 2700, Elon College 27244
Nan P. Perkins, Dean of Admissions

Gardner-Webb University
General Delivery, Boiling Springs 28017
Paul Jolley, Chrpsn.
704-434-2361

Greensboro College
815 W. Market St., Greensboro 27401

Guilford College
5800 W. Friendly Ave., Greensboro 27410
Larry West, Dir. of Admis.
See listing under "Universities"

Mars Hill College
Main St., Mars Hill 28754
Dr. Smith Goodrum, Dean of Admis.

Methodist College
5400 Ramsey St., Fayetteville 28311
Fiore Bergamasco, Dir. of Admis.

Montreat-Anderson College
P.O. Box 1267, Montreat 28757
David E. Walters, Dir. of Admissions
800-MAC-N-YOU
See listing under "Universities"

North Carolina A&T State University
1601 E. Market St., Greensboro 27411

North Carolina State University
P.O. Box 7001, Raleigh 27695
George Dixon, Dir. of Admis.

North Carolina Wesleyan College
3400 N. Wesleyan Blvd., Rocky Mount 27804

Pembroke State University
P.O. Box 1510, Pembroke 28372
Anthony Locklear, Dir. of Admissions
919-521-6262

Pfeiffer College
General Delivery, Misenheimer 28109

QUEENS COLLEGE
1900 Selwyn Ave., Charlotte 28274
D. Stephen Cloniger, VP for Enrollment Management
See listing under "Liberal Arts"

St. Andrews Presbyterian College
1700 Dogwood Mile, Laurinburg 28352
Dale B. Montague, Dir. of Admis.

Salem College
P.O. Box 10548, Winston-Salem 27108
Katherine Knapp, Director of Admissions
800-32-SALEM
See listing under "Women's College"

Wingate College, Wingate 28174

OHIO

Capital University
2199 E. Main St., Columbus 43209
Dolphus E. Henry, Associate Provost

Cleveland State University
Euclid Ave. at 24th St., Cleveland 44115

College of Mount St. Joseph
5701 Delhi Rd., Cincinnati 45233-1672
See listing under "Universities"

College of Wooster
1189 Beall Ave., Wooster 44691
Hayden Schilling, Dean of Admis.

Heidelberg College
310 E. Market St., Tiffin 44883
Stephen E. Eidson, Dean of Admission
800-925-9250

Hiram College
P.O. Box 96, Hiram 44234
Gary Craig, Dean of Admis.

John Carroll University
20700 N. Park Blvd., Cleveland 44118

Kent State University
P.O. Box 5190, Kent 44242
Bruce Riddle, Dir. of Admis.

Lake Erie College
391 W. Washington St., Painesville 44077

Malone College
515 25th St., N.W., Canton 44709
Lee Sommers, Dean of Admissions

Miami University
E. High St., Oxford 45056

Mount Union College
1972 Clark Ave., Alliance 44601
Amy Tomko, Dir. of Admis.

Mt. Vernon Nazarene College
800 Martinsburg Rd., Mt. Vernon 43050
Ronald Hyson, Dir. of Admis.

Oberlin College
135 W. Lorain St., Oberlin 44074
Michael Henle, Chrpsn.

Ohio Dominican College
1216 Sunbury Rd., Columbus 43219
800-955-OHIO

OHIO NORTHERN UNIVERSITY
525 S. Main St., Ada 45810
Dr. Robert Hovis, Chrpsn.
412-772-2000

Ohio Wesleyan University
61 S. Sandusky St., Delaware 43015
Donald Bishop, Dean for Enrollment

University of Akron
381 Buchtel Common, Akron 44325
Kris MacDermott, Asst. Provost Enrollment

University of Cincinnati
2700 Clifton Ave., Cincinnati 45221

University of Dayton
300 College Park Ave., Dayton 45469-2316
Toll-free 800-837-7433
See listing under "Universities"

University of Findlay
1000 N. Main St., Findlay 45840
Dan Crabtree, Dir. of Admis.

University of Rio Grande
General Delivery, Rio Grande 45674
Dr. Robert Wolfe, Dean
614-245-5353, Ext. 7397

Wilmington College
P.O. Box 1185, Wilmington 45177
Rhonda Inderhees, Dir. of Admis.

OKLAHOMA

Cameron University
2800 W. Gore Blvd., Lawton 73505
Louise Brown, Dir. of Admis.

East Central University, Ada 74820
James Peak, Dir. of Admis.

Oklahoma Christian University of Science and Arts
P.O. Box 11000, Oklahoma City 73136
Duane Eggleston, Vice President
800-877-5010

Oklahoma City University
2501 N. Blackwelder Ave., Oklahoma City 73106
Keith Hackett, Dean of Admissions
See listing under "Universities"

Oklahoma Panhandle State University
P.O. Box 430, Goodwell 73939

Oklahoma State University, Stillwater 74078
Brian Conrey, Dept. Head

Oral Roberts University
7777 S. Lewis Ave., Tulsa 74171
Arthur E. Matzkvech, Dir. of Admis.

Southern Nazarene University
6729 N.W. 39th Expy., Bethany 73008

University of Central Oklahoma
100 N. University Dr., Edmond 73034

University of Tulsa
600 S. College Ave., Tulsa 74104
Dr. William Coberly, Chrpsn.

OREGON

Lewis & Clark College
0615 S.W. Palatine Hill Rd., Portland 97219
Michael Sexton, Dean of Admissions

Pacific University
2043 College Way, Forest Grove 97116
Barbara Mergen, Dir. of Admis.

Reed College
3202 S.E. Woodstock Blvd., Portland 97202

Treasure Valley Community College
650 College Blvd., Ontario 97914
Ron Kulm, Dir. of Admis.

University of Portland
5000 N. Willamette Blvd., Portland 97203

Warner Pacific College
2219 S.E. 68th Ave., Portland 97215
Sherry Moore, Enrollment Management Director

PENNSYLVANIA

Albright College
P.O. Box 15234, Reading 19612

Allegheny College
520 N. Main St., Meadville 16335
Gayle Pollack, Dir. of Admis.

Allentown College of St. Frances de Sales
2755 Station Ave., Center Valley 18034
George Kelley, Dir. of Admis.

Alvernia College
400 Bernardine St., Reading 19607
Lisa Grabowski, Dir. of Admis.

Beaver College
450 S. Easton Rd., Glenside 19038-3295
Dennis Nostrand, VP for Enrollment Management
Phone: 800-776-BEAVER(2328)
Fax: 215-572-4049
See listing under "Universities"

Bloomsburg University, Bloomsburg 17815
Bernard Vinovrski, Dir. of Admis.

Cabrini College
610 King of Prussia Rd., Radnor 19087

California University of Pennsylvania
3rd St., California 15419
Norman Hasbrouck, Dean for Enrollment

Carlow College
3333 5th Ave., Pittsburgh 15213

Carnegie Mellon University
5000 Forbes Ave., Pittsburgh 15213

Cedar Crest College
100 College Dr., Allentown 18104-6196
Cynthia Phillips, Dir. of Admissions

Chatham College
Woodland Rd., Pittsburgh 15232
Suellen Ofe, Dean of Admis./Financial Aid
See listing under "Women's College"

Clarion University of Pennsylvania
840 Wood St., Clarion 16214

College Misericordia
301 Lake St., Dallas 18612
Michael Joseph, Dir. of Enrollment Mgmt.

Delaware Valley College of Science & Agriculture
Doylestown 18901
Stephen Zenko, Dir. of Admis.

Drexel University
3141 Chestnut St., Philadelphia 19104
Dean of Enrollment Management

Eastern College
10 Fairview Dr., Saint Davids 19087
Ronald Keller, VP for Enrollment Management

East Stroudsburg University of Pennsylvania
East Stroudsburg 18301
Alan Chesterton, Dir. of Admis.

Edinboro University of Pennsylvania
Edinboro 16444
Admissions Office: 800-626-2203

Elizabethtown College
1 Alpha Dr., Elizabethtown 17022

Franklin & Marshall College
P.O. Box 3003, Lancaster 17604

Gannon University
109 University Sq., Erie 16541

Geneva College
3200 College Ave., Beaver Falls 15010

Grove City College
100 Campus Dr., Grove City 16127
Dr. John H. Ellison, Chrpsn.

GWYNEDD-MERCY COLLEGE
Sumneytown Pike, Gwynedd Valley 19437
Marjorie DeSimone, Dean of Admissions
800-DIAL-GMC
See listing under "Universities"

Haverford College
370 Lancaster Ave., Haverford 19041

Holy Family College
Grant & Frankford Ave., Philadelphia 19114
Dt. Mott Linn, Dir. of Admis.
215-637-3050

Immaculata College
Immaculata 19345
James P. Sullivan, Dir. of Admis.

Juniata College
1700 Moore St., Huntington 16652

Lafayette College, Easton 18042
G. Gary Ripple, Dir. of Admis.
610-250-5100

La Salle University
1900 W. Olney Ave., Philadelphia 19141
Br. Gerald Fitzgerald, Dir. of Admis.
See listing under "Universities"

Lincoln University, Lincoln University 19352
Jimmy Arrington, Dir. of Admis.

Lycoming College, Williamsport 17701

Marywood College
2300 Adams Ave., Scranton 18509

Mercyhurst College
501 E. 38th St., Erie 16546
Andrew Roth, Dean of Enrollment
800-825-1926

Millersville University of Pennsylvania
Millersville 17551
Blair Treasure, Dean of Admissions

Montgomery County Community College
340 DeKalb Pike, Blue Bell 19422-0758
Dennis Murphy, Dir. of Admis.

Muhlenberg College
2400 W. Chew St., Allentown 18104
Chris Hooker-Haring, Dir. of Admis.

Pennsylvania State University
201 Shields Bldg., University Park 16802

St. Francis College
P.O. Box 600, Loretto 15940

St. Joseph's University
5600 City Ave., Philadelphia 19131
Randy Miller, Dir. of Admis.

Seton Hill College, Greensburg 15601
Peter Egan, Dir. of Admis.
800-826-6234 or 412-838-4255

Slippery Rock University, Slippery Rock 16057
Director of Admissions

Susquehanna University
514 University Ave., Selinsgrove 17870

Thiel College
75 College Ave., Greenville 16125
Robert Weaver, Dir. of Admis.

University of Pittsburgh, Greensburg Campus
1150 Mt. Pleasant Rd., Greensburg 15601
Larry Whatule, Dir. of Admis.
412-836-9880

Villanova University
845 E. Lancaster Ave., Villanova 19085
Stephen R. Merritt, Dir. of Admis.

Washington & Jefferson College
60 S. Lincoln St., Washington 15301
Thomas O'Connor, Dir. of Admis.

West Chester University of Pennsylvania
S. High St., West Chester 19380

WESTMINSTER COLLEGE
New Wilmington 16172
Richard Dana Paul, Dir. of Admis.
412-946-7100

Wilkes University
184 S. River St., Wilkes-Barre 18766
Emory P. Guffrovich Jr., Dean of Admissions

RHODE ISLAND

Brown University, Providence 02906

Rhode Island College
600 Mt. Pleasant Ave., Providence 02908

Salve Regina University
1 Ochre Point Ave., Newport 02840
Roselina McKillop, Dean of Admissions

University of Rhode Island, Kingston 02881
John Montgomery, Chrpsn.

SOUTH CAROLINA

Central Wesleyan College
P.O. Box 1020, Central 29630
Lillian A. Robbins, Dir. of Admis.

Columbia College
1301 Columbia College Dr., Columbia 29203

Converse College
580 E. Main St., Spartanburg 29302
Dr. Martha Rogers, VP Enrollment Management

Erskine College & Seminary
Washington St., Due West 29639
Dot Carter, Dir. of Admis.

Lander College
320 Stanley Ave., Greenwood 29649

Presbyterian College
503 S. Broad St., Clinton 29325
Margaret Williamson, Dean of Admis.

South Carolina State University
P.O. Box 7127, Orangeburg 29117-0001
803-536-7185

University of South Carolina, Columbia 29208
Terry Davis, Dir. of Admis.
803-777-7700

University of South Carolina at Aiken
171 University Pkwy., Aiken 29801

Voorhees College
Voorhees Rd., Denmark 29042

Winthrop University
701 W. Oakland Ave., Rock Hill 29733
James McCammon, Jr., Dir. of Admis.

Wofford College
429 N. Church St., Spartanburg 29303
Charles Gray, Dir. of Admis.

SOUTH DAKOTA

Augustana College
29th & S. Summit, Sioux Falls 57197

Dakota State University
820 N. Washington Ave., Madison 57042
Mike Foss, Dean
605-256-5139

Dakota Wesleyan University
1300 W. University Ave., Mitchell 57301

Mt. Marty College
1105 W. 8th St., Yankton 57078
Paula Tacke, Dir. of Admis.

SIOUX FALLS COLLEGE
1501 S. Prairie Ave., Sioux Falls 57105
Susan Reese, Dir. of Admis.
800-888-1047
See listing under "Universities"

South Dakota School of Mines and Technology
501 E. St. Joseph St., Rapid City 57701
Gary Bjordal, Dir. of Admis.

South Dakota State University
P.O. Box 2220, Brookings 57007
Dr. Kenneth Yocom, Department Head
605-688-6196
See listing under "Universities"

University of South Dakota
414 E. Clark St., Vermillion 57069
Dave Lorenz, Dir. of Admis.

TENNESSEE

Austin Peay State University
601 College St., Clarksville 37044

Bryan College
Box 7000, Dayton 37321
Thomas A. Shaw, Dir. of Admis.

Carson-Newman College
P.O. Box 70552, Jefferson City 37760
See listing under "Universities"

Christian Brothers College
650 E. Parkway, S., Memphis 38104

David Lipscomb University
3901 Granny White Pike, Nashville 37204-3951
Wade Sandrell, Dir. of Admis.
800-333-4358

Le Moyne-Owen College
807 Walker Ave., Memphis 38126
901-942-7302 or 800-737-7778

Maryville College
800 S. Court St., Maryville 37801
Annabelle J. Libby, Dir. of Admis.

Rhodes College
2000 N. Parkway, Memphis 38112

Tennessee Temple University
1815 Union Ave., Chattanooga 37404
Dr. L. W. Nichols, President

Trevecca Nazarene College
333 Murfreesboro Rd., Nashville 37210

Tusculum College
P.O. Box 5035, Greeneville 37743
Ronald Porter, Dir. of Admis.

Union University
2447 US Highway 45 Bypass, Jackson 38305
Dr. James Baggett, Dean
901-668-1818
See listing under "Universities"

University of Memphis, Memphis 38152
Dr. John Eubank, Dean of Admissions

University of Tennessee at Martin
Martin 38238
Paul Kelley, Director of Admissions
See listing under "Universities"

University of Tennessee, Knoxville
527 Andy Holt Tower, Knoxville 37996
Dr. Gordon Stanley, Dir. of Admis.

Vanderbilt University
West End Ave., Nashville 37240

TEXAS

Austin College
900 N. Grand Ave., Sherman 75090
Rodney Oto, Dean of Admission
800-442-5363

Baylor University
P.O. Box 97008, Waco 76798-7008
Diana Ramey, Director of Admissions

Corpus Christi State University
6300 Ocean Dr., Corpus Christi 78412

Dallas Baptist University
7777 W. Kiest Blvd., Dallas 75211

East Texas Baptist University
1200 N. Grove Ave., Marshall 75670

Incarnate Word College
4301 Broadway St., San Antonio 78209
Sr. Sally Mitchell, Dean of Enrollment

Lamar University
P.O. Box 10009, Beaumont 77710
800-458-7558

LeTourneau College
P.O. Box 7001, Longview 75607
Roger Kieffer, Dir. of Admis.

Midwestern State University
3400 Taft Blvd., Wichita Falls 76308

Rice University
P.O. Box 1892, Houston 77251

St. Mary's University of San Antonio
1 Camino Santa Maria, San Antonio 78228
Rick Castillo, Dir. of Admis.

Schreiner College
2100 Memorial Blvd., Kerrville 78028
800-343-4919

Southern Methodist University
Hillcrest at University, Dallas 75275

Texas A & I University
Campus Box 101, Kingsville 78363

Texas A & M University
College Station 77843

Texas Christian University
2800 S. University Dr., Ft. Worth 76129
Dr. Edward Boehm, Jr., Dean of Admissions

Texas Lutheran College
1000 W. Court St., Seguin 78155
Jennifer B. Ehlers, Dir. of Admis.

Texas Wesleyan University
1201 Wesleyan St., Fort Worth 76105
Kim Campbell, Dir. Freshman Admission

Texas Women's University
P.O. Box 23925, Denton 76204

University of Dallas
1845 E. Northgate Dr., Irving 75062
Jim Whitaker, Dir. of Admis.

University of Houston-Clear Lake
2700 Bay Area Blvd., Houston 77058
Darella Banks, Exec. Dir. Enrollment Services

University of St. Thomas
3812 Montrose Blvd., Houston 77006
Elsie Biron, Dir. of Admis.

University of Texas at Arlington
UTA Box 19125, Arlington 76019
R. Zack Prince, Dir. of Admis.

University of Texas at Austin
0 the University of Texas, Austin 78712

University of Texas at San Antonio
San Antonio 78285
Dr. John H. Brown, Dir. of Admis.

West Texas State University
2501 4th Ave., Canyon 79016
Lila Vars, Dir. of Admis.

UTAH

Southern Utah University
351 W. Center St., Cedar City 84720
D. Mark Barton, Asst. VP Student Services
801-586-7740

University of Utah
1400 E. 200 S., Salt Lake City 84112
Dr. J. Stayner Landward, Dir. of Admis.

Utah State University, Logan 84322-1600
Rod Clark, Director of Admissions
801-750-1107

Westminster College of Salt Lake City
1840 S. 1300 E., Salt Lake City 84105
800-748-4753

VERMONT

Bennington College, Bennington 05201
Karen Kristof, Dir. of Admis.
800-833-6845

Castleton State College, Castleton 05735
Gary Fallis, Dir. of Admis.

Johnson State College, Johnson 05656
802-635-2356 ext. 219

Marlboro College
General Delivery, Marlboro 05344

NORWICH UNIVERSITY
65 S. Main St., Northfield 05663
Dr. Joseph Byrne, Dept. Chrpsn.
See listing under "Universities"

Saint Michael's College
Winooski Park, Colchester 05439
800-SMC-8000
See listing under "Liberal Arts"

Trinity College
208 Colchester Ave., Burlington 05401

University of Vermont
194 S. Prospect St., Burlington 05401
802-656-3370

VIRGINIA

Bridgewater College
402 E College St., Bridgewater 22812

Christopher Newport College
50 Shoe Ln., Newport News 23606

Clinch Valley College of the University of Virginia
P.O. Box 16, Wise 24293
Lana Low, Dir. Enrollment Management

Eastern Mennonite College
1200 Park Rd., Harrisonburg 22801
Jerry Miller, Dir. of Admis.

Emory & Henry College
General Delivery, Emory 24327

Ferrum College, Ferrum 24088
Bob Bailey, Dir. of Admis.

LIBERTY UNIVERSITY
P.O. Box 20000, Lynchburg 24506
Jay Spencer, VP Recruitment
800-376-2800
See listing under "Universities"

Longwood College, Farmville 23901

Lynchburg College
1501 Lakeside Dr., Lynchburg 24501
Ernest Chadderton, Dean of Enrollment

Marymount University
2807 N. Glebe Rd., Arlington 22207
Charles Coe, Director of Admissions
800-548-7638 or 703-284-1500
See listing under "Universities"

Mary Washington College
1701 College Ave., Fredericksburg 22401
Martin Wilder, V.P. for Admissions

Radford University
P.O. Box 5430, Radford 24142

Randolph-Macon College
200 Henry St., Ashland 23005
John Conkright, Dean of Admissions

Roanoke College
221 College Ln., Salem 24153

SHENANDOAH UNIVERSITY
1460 University Dr., Winchester 22601
Dr. John Happ, Division Chair
See listing under "Universities"

Sweet Briar College, Sweet Briar 24595
Nancy Church, Dir. of Admis.

University of Virginia
P.O. Box 9017, Charlottesville 22906

Virginia Military Institute, Lexington 24450

Virginia Polytechnic Institute & State University
Blacksburg 24061
David Bousquet, Dir. of Undergraduate Admis.

Virginia Wesleyan College
1584 Wesleyan Dr., Norfolk 23502
W. Steve Stocks, V.P. for Admis.

WASHINGTON

Central Washington University, Ellensburg 98926
William Swain, Director of Admissions

Pacific Lutheran University
12180 Park Ave. S., Tacoma 98447
Michael Dollinger, Chrpsn.

St. Martin's College
700 College St. N.E., Lacey 98516

University of Puget Sound
1500 N. Warner St., Tacoma 98416

Walla Walla College
204 S. College Ave., College Place 99324

Washington State University, Pullman 99164
Stan Berry, Dir. of Admis.

WEST VIRGINIA

Alderson-Broaddus College
Philippi 26416
Craig W. Gould, Director of Admissions
304-457-1700

Bethany College, Bethany 26031
John Giesman, Registrar

Concord College, Athens 24712

Davis & Elkins College
100 Campus Dr., Elkins 26241
Kevin D. Chenoweth, Dir. of Admis.

Marshall University
400 Hal Greer Blvd., Huntington 25755
See listing under "Universities"

The University of Charleston
2300 MacCorkle Ave., S.E., Charleston 25304
800-995-GO UC

West Virginia University
P.O. Box 6001, Morgantown 26506

WEST VIRGINIA WESLEYAN COLLEGE
59 College Ave., Buckhannon 26201
Robert Skinner, Director of Admission
See listing under "Universities"

Wheeling Jesuit College
316 Washington Ave., Wheeling 26003
Fr. Thomas Acker, SJ, President

WISCONSIN

Alverno College
P.O. Box 343922, Milwaukee 53234
Colleen Hayes, Dir. of Admis.

Beloit College
700 College St., Beloit 53511
David B. Ellis, Chair
608-363-2369

Cardinal Stritch College
6801 N. Yates Rd., Milwaukee 53217
David Wegener, Dir. of Admis.

Carroll College
100 N. East Ave., Waukesha 53186
Ken Moyer, Dir. of Admis.

Carthage College
2001 Alford Dr., Kenosha 53140
Brenda A. Porter, VP Enrollment

Edgewood College
855 Woodrow St., Madison 53711
Robert Blust, Dir. of Admis.

Lakeland College
P.O. Box 359, Sheboygan 53082

Lawrence University
P.O. Box 599, Appleton 54912
Steven Syverson, Dean of Admissions

Marian College of Fond du Lac
45 S. National Ave., Fond du Lac 54935
Carol Reichenberger, Dean of Admissions

Marquette University
1217 W. Wisconsin Ave., Milwaukee 53233
Raymond A. Brown, Dean of Admissions

Mt. Senario College
1500 W. College Ave., Ladysmith 54848
Dewey Floberg, Dean of Admissions

Ripon College, P.O. Box 248, Ripon 54971
James Reilly, Dean of Admis.

St. Norbert College
100 Grant St., De Pere 54115
Craig S. Wesley, Dean of Admission
See listing under "Universities"

Silver Lake College
2406 S. Alverno Road, Manitowoc 54220
Sandra Schwartz, Dir. of Admis.

University of Wisconsin, Eau Claire
Eau Claire 54701

University of Wisconsin, Green Bay
2420 Nicolet Dr., Green Bay 54311
Dr. Forrest Baulieu, Chrpsn.

University of Wisconsin, Oshkosh
800 Algoma Blvd., Oshkosh 54901-8602
August Helgerson, Dir. of Admis.

University of Wisconsin
1 University Plaza, Platteville 53818
Richard Schumacher, Dean of Admissions

University of Wisconsin, River Falls
River Falls 54022
Alan Tuchtenhagen, Dir. of Admis.

Viterbo College
815 9th St., S., La Crosse 54601
Roland W. Nelson, Dir. of Admis.

GUAM

University of Guam
UOG Station, Mangilao 96923
Kathleen Owings, Dir. of Admis.

PUERTO RICO

Catholic University of Puerto Rico
Las Americas Ave., Ponce 00732
Carilin Frau, Dir. of Admis.

University of Puerto Rico
Antonio Barcelo Ave., Cayey 00736
Antonio Rosario, Dir. of Admis.

University of Puerto Rico
CUH Station Rd. 908 Bo Tejas, Humacao 00791

University of Puerto Rico, Mayaguez Campus
P.O. Box 5000, Mayaguez 00681
Neysa Lopez, Dir. of Admis.

University of Puerto Rico, Rio Piedras Campus
P.O. Box 23300, San Juan 00931
Victor Lopez, Dir. of Admis.

MEDICINE

This classification contains schools offering a first professional degree accredited by the American Medical Association (†) and a selection of programs from institutionally accredited schools. Colleges and Universities (no dot code) generally offer four-year programs in pre-medicine, medicine and advanced programs in medical specialties; Community and Junior Colleges (·) generally offer associate degrees in pre-medicine.

ALABAMA

· Bishop State Community College
351 N. Broad St., Mobile 36603-5898
Yvonne Kennedy, President
205-690-6801

· Gadsden State Community College
Preprofessional Program
1001 George Wallace Dr., Gadsden 35999

Huntingdon College
1500 E. Fairview Ave., Montgomery 36106-2148
Carolyn A. Phillips, Dean of Enrollment
800-763-0313

† University of Alabama at Birmingham
University Station, Birmingham 35294

† University of South Alabama
307 University Blvd. N., Mobile 36688

ARIZONA

† University of Arizona Medical Center
1501 N. Campbell Ave., Tucson 85724
Dr. James E. Dahlen, Dean

ARKANSAS

Arkansas College
2300 Highland Rd., Batesville 72501
Jonathan M. Stroud, Dean of Admissions
800-423-2542

† University of Arkansas for Medical Sciences
4301 W. Markham St., Little Rock 72205

CALIFORNIA

Fresno Pacific College
1717 S. Chestnut Ave., Fresno 93702
209-453-2039

† Loma Linda University, Loma Linda 92350
John Thorn, EdD, Chrpsn.
800-422-4LLU

† Stanford University, Stanford 94305

† University of California, Los Angeles
1247 Murphy Hall, Los Angeles 90024

† University of California, Davis
376 Mrak Hall, Davis 95616

† University of California, Irvine
Irvine 92715

† University of California, San Diego
9450 Gilman Dr., La Jolla 92092

† University of California, San Francisco
Parnassus & 3rd Ave., San Francisco 94143

† University of Southern California
Health Science Campus, Los Angeles 90033
Stephen Ryan, Interim Dean

COLORADO

Regis University
3333 Regis Blvd., Denver 80221
Robert Blust, Director of Admissions

† University of Colorado Health Sciences Center
4200 E. 9th Ave., Denver 80262
Richard D. Krugman, MD, Dean

CONNECTICUT

QUINNIPIAC COLLEGE
275 Mount Carmel Ave., Hamden 06518
See listing under "Universities"

† University of Connecticut Health Center
School of Medicine
Farmington 06032
Eugene Sigman, MD, Dean

† Yale University
333 Cedar St., New Haven 06520
Dr. Leon Rosenberg, Dean

DISTRICT OF COLUMBIA

† Georgetown University
37th and O Sts., N.W., Washington 20057
Dr. Joseph A. Chalmers, Dean of Admis. & Rec.

† George Washington University
Washington 20052

† Howard University
2400 6th St., N.W., Washington 20059
James E. Cheek, President

FLORIDA

SCHILLER INTERNATIONAL UNIVERSITY (FLORIDA & EUROPE)
U.S. Admissions Office
Dept. PA, 453 Edgewater Dr., Dunedin 34698-7532
800-336-4133 Fax: 813-736-6263
Dr. Walter Liebrecht, President
Karen Altieri, Associate Director of Admissions
See listing under "Universities"

† University of Florida
226 Tigert Hall, Gainesville 32611

† University of Miami
P.O. Box 248006, Coral Gables 33124

† University of South Florida
4202 Fowler Ave., Tampa 33620

GEORGIA

: Atlanta College of Medical and Dental Careers
1400 W. Peachtree St., N.W., Atlanta 30309
Gary Vance, Dir. of Admis.

† Emory University
1462 Clifton Rd., Atlanta 30322

Georgia College
231 W. Hancock St., Milledgeville 31061
912-453-5004

† Medical College of Georgia
1120 15th St., Augusta 30901
Dr. Mary Ella Logan, Associate Dean

† Mercer University
1400 Coleman Ave., Macon 31207

† Morehouse School of Medicine
720 Westview Dr. S.W., Atlanta 30310

HAWAII

† University of Hawaii at Manoa
2500 Campus Rd., Honolulu 96822

ILLINOIS

† Loyola University
Stritch School of Medicine
University Medical Center, Maywood 60153

· Midstate College
244 S.W. Jefferson St., Peoria 61602
R. Dale Bunch, President
309-673-6365

North Park College & Theological Seminary
3225 W. Foster, Chicago 60625
312-509-2330

† Northwestern University
303 E. Chicago Ave., Chicago 60611

Rockford College
5050 E. State St., Rockford 61108
Miriam King, V.P. for Enrollment Management
See listing under "Universities"

† Rush University
1653 W. Congress Pky., Chicago 60612

† Southern Illinois University
School of Medicine
P.O. Box 3926, Springfield 62708

† University of Chicago
5801 S. Ellis Ave., Chicago 60637

† University of Health Sciences
The Chicago Medical School
3333 Green Bay Rd., North Chicago 60064

† University of Illinois at Chicago
P.O. Box 5220, Chicago 60680
Dr. Philip Forman, Dean

University of Illinois
Peoria School of Medicine
P.O. Box 1649, Peoria 61656

INDIANA

† Indiana University-Purdue University
355 N. Lansing, Indianapolis 46202

Indiana Wesleyan University
4201 S. Washington St., Marion 46953
800-332-6901

Taylor University
500 W. Reade Ave., Upland 46989
Herb Frye, Dean of Enrollment Management

IOWA

Cornell College
600 1st St., W., Mt. Vernon 52314
Kevin Crockett, Dean of Admissions

† University of Iowa, Iowa City 52242

· Waldorf College
106 S. 6th St., Forest City 50436
Steve Lovik, Dir. of Admis.
800-292-1903

KANSAS

† University of Kansas Medical Center
39th St. & Rainbow Blvd., Kansas City 66103
Dr. James G. Price, Dean

KENTUCKY

Kentucky Wesleyan College
Pre-Medicine program
3000 Frederica St, Owensboro 42301

Spalding University
851 S. 4th St., Louisville 40203
Dorothy G. Allen, Dir. of Admis.

† University of Kentucky, Lexington 40506

† University of Louisville
2301 S. 3rd St., Louisville 40292
Robert Parrent, Dir. of Admis.

LOUISIANA

† Louisiana State University
8515 Youree Dr., Shreveport 71115

† Louisiana State University Medical Center
433 Bolivar St., New Orleans 70112

† Tulane University
1430 Tulane Ave., New Orleans 70118

MAINE

· Central Maine Medical Center
Family Practice Residency Program
76 High St., Lewiston 04240
Dana W. Little, MD, Residency Director

MARYLAND

† Johns Hopkins University
600 N. Wolfe St., Baltimore 21205

· Montgomery College
51 Mannakee St., Rockville 20850
Germantown - 301-353-7798
Rockville - 301-279-5124
Takoma Park - 301-650-1332

† University of Maryland
Baltimore Professional Schools
522 W. Lombard St., Baltimore 21201

Villa Julie College
1525 Greenspring Valley Rd., Stevenson 21153
Carolyn Manuszak, President

MASSACHUSETTS

· Aquinas College
15 Walnut Park, Newton 02158
Ellen Ronayne, Dir. of Admis.

† Boston University Medical Center
100 E. Newton St., Boston 02118
Maxine Peck, Director

† Harvard University
Harvard Medical School
25 Shattuck St., Boston 02115

† Tufts University, Medical School
136 Harrison Ave., Boston 02111

† University of Massachusetts
Medical School
55 Lake Ave., N., Worcester 01655

Western New England College
1215 Wilbraham Rd., Springfield 01119
800-325-1122

MICHIGAN

Albion College
611 E. Porter, Albion 49224
800-858-6770

† Michigan State University, East Lansing 48824
Dr. W. Donald Weston, Dean

· Suomi College
601 Quincy St., Hancock 49930
John Ruohoniemi, Dean/Enrollment Development
800-682-7604

† University of Michigan-Ann Arbor
815 S. University Ave., Ann Arbor 48109

† Wayne State University
5980 Cass Ave., Detroit 48202
Dr. J. R. Thorderson, Dir. of Admis.

MINNESOTA

† Mayo Foundation
200 1st St., N.W., Rochester 55901

† University of Minnesota
2400 Oakland Ave., Duluth 55812
Robert L. Heller, Provost

† University of Minnesota, Twin Cities
Minneapolis 55455

MISSISSIPPI

† University of Mississippi Medical Center
2500 N. State St., Jackson 39216

MISSOURI

· Cottey College
1000 W. Austin St., Nevada 64772
Wendy Beckemeyer, Dir. of Admis.

Culver-Stockton College, Canton 63435
Betty Smith, Dean of Admissions
800-537-1883

† St. Louis University
221 N. Grand Blvd., St. Louis 63103
Louis A. Menard, Dean of Admissions

† University of Missouri, Columbia
228 Jesse Hall, Columbia 65211

† University of Missouri, Kansas City
5100 Rockhill Rd., Kansas City 64110
Leo J. Sweeney, Dir. of Admis. & Registrar

† Washington University
4559 Scott Ave., St. Louis 63110

MONTANA

Rocky Mountain College
1511 Poly Dr., Billings 59102
David Heringer, Dir. of Admis.
See listing under "Universities"

NEBRASKA

† Creighton University
2500 California St., Omaha 68178
Dr. Richard O'Brien, Dean

† University of Nebraska Medical Center
600 S., 42nd & Dewey, Omaha 68198
Alastair M. Connell, Dean

NEVADA

† University of Nevada, Reno
Reno 89557

NEW HAMPSHIRE

† Dartmouth College, Hanover 03755

NEW JERSEY

Jersey City State College
2039 Kennedy Blvd., Jersey City 07305
201-200-3234

† Johnson Medical School
P.O. Box 101, Piscataway 08855

Stockton State College, Pomona 08240
Sal Catalfamo, Dir. of Admis.

† University of Medicine and Dentistry of New Jersey
30 Bergen St., Newark 07107

NEW MEXICO

† University of New Mexico, Albuquerque 87131
Robert Weaver, Dean of Admissions

NEW YORK

† Albany Medical College
47 New Scotland Ave., Albany 12208

Canisius College
2001 Main St., Buffalo 14208
Penelope Lips, Dir. of Admis.
800-843-1517

† Columbia University
617 W. 168th St., New York 10032

† Cornell University Medical College
1300 York Ave., New York 10021
Thomas H. Meikle, Jr., Dean

† CUNY Mt. Sinai School of Medicine
1 Levy Place, New York 10029
Thomas C. Chalmers, M.D., Dean

† New York Medical College, Valhalla 10595
Samuel H. Rubin, M.D., Dean

† New York University
550 1st Ave., New York 10016
Dr. Ivan L. Bennett, Dean

Roberts Wesleyan College
2301 Westside Dr., Rochester 14624
Dr. David Roll, Chrpsn.
See listing under "Universities"

† SUNY Health Science Center
155 Elizabeth Blackwell St., Syracuse 13210

† SUNY at Stony Brook, Health Sciences Center
Stony Brook 11790

† SUNY Health Science Center at Brooklyn
450 Clarkson Ave., Brooklyn 11203

† SUNY at Buffalo
Farber Hall
3435 Main St., Buffalo 14214

† University of Rochester Medical Center
Rochester 14642
Marshall Lichtman, MD, Dean
See listing under "Universities"

† Yeshiva University
500 W. 185th St., New York 10033

NORTH CAROLINA

† Duke University, Durham 27706

† East Carolina University
1000 E. 5th St., Greenville 27858
Dr. James A. Hallock, Dean

Gardner-Webb University
General Delivery, Boiling Springs 28017
Ray M. Hardee, Dean of Admissions
800-253-6472

St. Andrews Presbyterian College
1700 Dogwood Mile, Laurinburg 28352
Dale B. Montague, Dir. of Admis.

† University of North Carolina at Chapel Hill
Chapel Hill 27599
Elizabeth S. Mann, Associate Dean

† Wake Forest University
Bowman Gray School of Medicine
Medical Center Blvd., Winston-Salem 27157

NORTH DAKOTA

† University of North Dakota
Box 8193 University Station, Grand Forks 58203

OHIO

† Case Western Reserve University
2040 Adelbert Rd., Cleveland 44106

Malone College
515 25th St., N.W., Canton 44709
Lee Sommers, Dean of Admissions

† Medical College of Ohio
P.O. Box 10008, Toledo 43699
Barry L. Richardson, PhD, Dean for Admissions

† Northeastern Ohio Universities College of Medicine
4209 State Route 44, P.O. Box 95
Rootstown 44272
Dr. Robert Blacklow, President and Dean
216-325-2511

† Ohio State University
190 N. Oval Mall, Columbus 43210

† University of Cincinnati
2700 Clifton Ave., Cincinnati 45221

Wilmington College
P.O. Box 1185, Wilmington 45177
Rhonda Inderhees, Dir. of Admis.
Pre-professional program

† Wright State University
3640 Colonel Glenn Hwy., Dayton 45435

OKLAHOMA

Oklahoma City University
2501 N. Blackwelder Ave., Oklahoma City 73106
Keith Hackett, Dean of Admissions
See listing under "Universities"

Oral Roberts University
7777 S. Lewis Ave., Tulsa 74171
Arthur E. Matzkvech, Dir. of Admis.

University of Oklahoma at Norman
660 Parrington Oval, Norman 73019

† University of Oklahoma Health Sciences Center
P.O. Box 26901, Oklahoma City 73126
Dr. Donald Kassebaum, Exec. Dean

University of Tulsa
600 S. College Ave., Tulsa 74104
Mary Tolar, Asst. to the Dean

OREGON

† Oregon Health Sciences University
3181 S.W. Sam Jackson Park Rd., Portland 97201
Dr. John Kendall, Dean

PENNSYLVANIA

Chatham College
Woodland Rd., Pittsburgh 15232
Suellen Ofe, Dean of Admis./Financial Aid
See listing under "Women's College"

† Hahnemann University
230 N. Broad St., Philadelphia 19102

† Medical College of Pennsylvania
3300 Henry Ave., Philadelphia 19129

Pennsylvania State University
201 Shields Bldg., University Park 16802

† Penn. State U., Hershey Med. Center
500 University Dr., Hershey 17033
Dr. Harry Prystowsky, Dean

† Temple University
3307 N. Broad St., Philadelphia 19140

† Thomas Jefferson University
Jefferson Medical College
1025 Walnut St., Philadelphia 19107

† University of Pennsylvania
0 Levy Park, Philadelphia 19104

† University of Pittsburgh
4200 5th Ave., Pittsburgh 15260

WESTMINSTER COLLEGE

New Wilmington 16172
Richard Dana Paul, Dir. of Admis.
412-946-7100

Wilkes University
184 S. River St., Wilkes-Barre 18766
Emory P. Guffrovich Jr., Dean of Admissions

RHODE ISLAND

† Brown University, Providence 02906

SOUTH CAROLINA

† Medical University of South Carolina
171 Ashley Ave., Charleston 29425
W. Marcus Newberry, M.D., Dean

† University of South Carolina, Columbia 29208
J. O'Neal Humphries, Dean
803-733-3325

SOUTH DAKOTA

† University of South Dakota
414 E. Clark St., Vermillion 57069
Robert C. Talley, Vice President

TENNESSEE

Christian Brothers College
Preprofessional Program
650 E. Parkway, S., Memphis 38104

† EAST TENNESSEE STATE UNIVERSITY

P.O. Box 70731, Johnson City 37614
Dr. Nancy Dishner, Dean, Enrollment Management
615-929-4213 or 800-462-3878

† Meharry Medical College
1005 Dr. D. Todd Jr. Blvd., Nashville 37208

Tennessee Wesleyan College
P.O. Box 40, Athens 37371

University of Tennessee at Martin
Martin 38238
Paul Kelley, Director of Admissions
See listing under "Universities"

† University of Tennessee, Memphis
Health Science Center
800 Madison Ave., Memphis 38163
Office of Enrollment Management

† Vanderbilt University
West End Ave., Nashville 37240

TEXAS

† Baylor College of Medicine
1 Baylor Plaza, Houston 77030
Dr. William Butler, President

† Texas A & M University
College Station 77843

† Texas Tech University, Lubbock 79409

† University of Texas Health Science Center
P.O. Box 20036, Houston 77225

† University of Texas Health Science Center
7703 Floyd Curl Dr., San Antonio 78284

† The University of Texas Medical Branch at Galveston
Galveston 77555-1305

† University of Texas Southwestern Medical Center
5323 Harry Hines Blvd., Dallas 75235
William Neaves, Dean

UTAH

† University of Utah
1400 E. 200 S., Salt Lake City 84112
Dr. J. Stayner Landward, Dir. of Admis.

VERMONT

† University of Vermont
194 S. Prospect St., Burlington 05401
802-656-3370

VIRGINIA

Eastern Virginia Medical School, Norfolk 23501

Ferrum College, Ferrum 24088
Bob Bailey, Dir. of Admis.

† University of Virginia
School of Medicine
Charlottesville 22908

† Virginia Commonwealth University
910 W. Franklin St., Richmond 23284

WASHINGTON

† University of Washington, Seattle 98195

WEST VIRGINIA

† Marshall University
400 Hal Greer Blvd., Huntington 25755
See listing under "Universities"

† West Virginia University
P.O. Box 6001, Morgantown 26506

WEST VIRGINIA WESLEYAN COLLEGE

59 College Ave., Buckhannon 26201
Robert Skinner, Director of Admission
See listing under "Universities"

WISCONSIN

† Medical College of Wisconsin
8701 Watertown Plank Rd., Milwaukee 53226
Richard Cooper, MD, Dean/Executive VP

St. Norbert College
100 Grant St., De Pere 54115
Craig S. Wesley, Dean of Admission
See listing under "Universities"

† University of Wisconsin, Madison
500 Lincoln Dr., Madison 53706

Viterbo College
815 9th St., S., La Crosse 54601
Roland W. Nelson, Dir. of Admis.

PUERTO RICO

† Ponce School of Medicine, Ponce 00731

† Universidad Central Del Caribe
P.O. Box 60327, Bayamon 00960

† University of Puerto Rico, Medical Sciences Campus
P.O. Box 5067, San Juan 00906

MEN'S COLLEGES

CALIFORNIA

Deep Springs College
Deep Springs, CA
Mailing Address, HC 72, Box 45001
Dyer, NV 89010-9803

St. John's Seminary College
5118 Seminary Rd., Camarillo 93012
Rev. Gary S. Landry, C.M., Dir. of Admis.

FLORIDA

St. John Vianney College Seminary
2900 S.W. 87th Ave., Miami 33165
Rev. George Garcia, President/Rector

St. Vincent DePaul Regional Seminary
10701 Military Trail, Boynton Beach 33436
Very Rev. Felipe J. Estevez, Rector

GEORGIA

Morehouse College
830 Westview Dr., S.W., Atlanta 30310
Gary Bussey, Dir. of Admissions

ILLINOIS

Niles College of Loyola University
7135 N. Harlem Av., Niles 60714

INDIANA

St. Meinrad College
Archabbey, St. Meinrad 47577
Rev. Eugene Hensell, Provost

Wabash College
301 W. Wabash Ave., Crawfordsville 47933
Greg Birk, Dir. of Admis.

MASSACHUSETTS

ST. HYACINTH COLLEGE AND SEMINARY

66 School St., Granby 01033
Rev. Richard Forcier, Director of Admissions
413-467-7191
  Established 1957. Private. Men's College. Accreditation: NEASC. Tuition: $3,600. Room and board: $4,500. Fees: $195-$690. Enrollment: 17 full-time, 22 part-time. Degrees: BA, AA, Pre-Theology Certificate, Lay Ministry Certificate. Library: 82,000 volumes. 5 buildings on 595 acres. A caring environment in the Franciscan tradition, where students may discern how their talents and gifts can best be utilized, in college, in a career, and in service to others.

MICHIGAN

Sacred Heart Major Seminary
2701 W. Chicago Blvd., Detroit 48206
313-883-8501

MINNESOTA

St. John's University
P.O. Box 7155, Collegeville 56321

MISSOURI

Conception Seminary College, Conception 64433
Rev. Albert Bruecken, Dir. of Admis.

NEW YORK

Cathedral College of the Immaculate Conception
7200 Douglaston Pkwy., Douglaston 11362
Rev. James Grace, President

Hobart & William Smith College
Pulteney St., Geneva 14456

Rabbinical Academy Mesivta Rabbi Chaim Berlin
1593 Coney Island Ave., Brooklyn 11230
Rabbi Aaron Schechter, President of Faculty

Wadhams Hall Seminary College
R.R. 4 Box 80, Ogdensburg 13669
Rev. Donald Robinson, Dir. of Admis.
315-393-4231

SOUTH CAROLINA

The Citadel
171 Moultrie St., Charleston 29409

VIRGINIA

Hampden-Sydney College
P.O. Box 128, Hampden-Sydney 23943
Robert H. Jones, Dean of Admis.

Virginia Military Institute, Lexington 24450

WISCONSIN

NORTHWESTERN COLLEGE

1300 Western Ave., Watertown 53094
John A. Braun, President
Philip Hirsch, Dir. of Admis.
414-261-4352 FAX: 414-262-8118
  Established 1865. Private. Men's college. Accreditation: NCACS. Tuition: $3,350. Room and board: $1,880. Fees: $250. Enrollment: 187. Faculty: 23. Degree: BA. Library: 50,000 volumes. 8 buildings on 38 acres. NWC has a single preseminary (pretheological) course of study. 92% of graduates enroll at Wisconsin Lutheran Seminary of Mequon. NWC is owned and operated by the Wisconsin Evangelical Lutheran Synod for the sole purpose of providing the undergraduate training for its clergy.

MILITARY SCIENCE

ALABAMA

Jacksonville State University
700 Pelham Rd. N., Jacksonville 36265

:: Lyman Ward Military Academy
P.O. Box 547, Camp Hill 36850
Charles Livings, Dir. of Admis.

· Marion Military Institute
1101 Washington St., Marion 36756
800-MMI-1842

ARIZONA

University of Arizona, Tucson 85721
Loyd Bell, Director of Admissions

· Yavapai College
1100 E. Sheldon St., Prescott 86301
Dr. Doreen Dailey, President
602-445-7300
See listing under "Community and Junior Colleges"

ARKANSAS

Henderson State University
1100 Henderson St., Arkadelphia 71999

CALIFORNIA

:: Army and Navy Academy
P.O. Box 3000, Carlsbad 92018
Fred W. Heinle, PhD, President
619-729-2385

California Polytechnic State University
San Luis Obispo 93407
Helen Linstrum, Dir. of Admis.

San Francisco State University
1600 Holloway Ave., San Francisco 94132
Corwin Bjonerud, Dir. of Admis.

University of San Francisco
2130 Fulton St., San Francisco 94117
Bill Henley, Dir. of Admis.

COLORADO

United States Air Force Academy
Colorado Springs 80840

CONNECTICUT

United States Coast Guard Academy
New London 06320
Brian Wright, Admissions

DISTRICT OF COLUMBIA

:: St. John's College H.S.
2607 Military Rd., N.W., Washington 20015

University of the District of Columbia
Georgia Ave.-Harvard St. Campus
1100 Harvard St., N.W., Washington 20009

University of the District of Columbia
Van Ness Campus
4200 Connecticut Ave., N.W., Washington 20008

FLORIDA

:: Admiral Farragut Academy
501 Park St., N, St. Petersburg 33710
Cpt. Michael Moriarty, Dir. of Admis.

Florida A & M University, Tallahassee 32307

FLORIDA AIR ACADEMY

1950 South Academy Dr., Melbourne 32901
Major James Dwight, President

St. Leo College
P.O. Box 2008, St. Leo 33574
Bonnie Black, Dir. of Admis.

GEORGIA

:: Benedictine Military School
6502 Seawright Drive, Savannah 31406
Rev. Conan Feigh, O.S.B., Headmaster

· Georgia Military College
201 E. Green St., Milledgeville 31061
Major General Peter Boylan, President

North Georgia College, Dahlonega 30597
Gary R. Steffey, Dir. of Admis.

:: Riverside Military Academy
1942 Riverside Dr., Gainesville 30501
Col. Billy Williams, Superintendent
404-532-6251

ILLINOIS

LEWIS UNIVERSITY

Rt. 53, Romeoville 60441
Irish O'Reilly, Director of Admissions
See listing under "Universities"

:: Marmion Military Academy
1000 Butterfield Rd., Aurora 60504
Rev. Basil Yender, OSB, Headmaster

INDIANA

:: Culver Military Academy and Summer Camps
1300 Academy Rd., Culver 46511
Richard Edwards, Dir. of Admis.

:: **HOWE MILITARY SCHOOL**
31 Academy Pl., Howe 46746
Colonel Thomas Merritt, Superintendent
Lt. Col. Reed Kimball, Headmaster
Glenn Cox, Dir. of Admis.
219-562-2131 ext. 221
  Accredited by: the North Central Association of Colleges and Schools. A member of: the North Central Association of Colleges and Schools, the Independent School Association of Central States, the Association of Military Colleges and Schools of the United States, the Council for Advancement and Support of Education, the National Association of Independent Schools, the National Association of Episcopal Schools, the College Entrance Examination Board, Cum Laude Society.
  Established 1884. Episcopal. Coed. Enrollment: 250. Total charge for a boarding student: $14,900. Financial aid available. Only military institute in Ohio, Michigan and Indiana that is a member of the US Army's JROTC program. JROTC required for all high school cadets.
  College preparatory school. Grades 5 through 12. Fully accredited faculty and staff. Individual attention given. Class size averages 10 to 12 cadets. Twenty solid units of credit are required for graduation. Seventeen and a half of them must be in English, math, history and social studies, science, foreign language, sacred studies, business and physical education and health.
  Required for admission: a desire to attend, a willingness to adhere to Howe's military discipline, be of good moral character (satisfactory references), be of average to above average intelligence (IQ test), a certificate of honorable dismissal from previous school.
  Located on 150 acres in Northeast Indiana just two miles from the Michigan border. Modern dormitories and academic facilities, library, pool, three (3) gymnasiums, athletic fields, track, canteen, 700 seat auditorium, two (2) chapels, dining hall, military department.

IOWA

Iowa State University, Ames 50011
Karsten Smedal, Dir. of Admis.

KANSAS

:: St. John's Military School
P.O. Box 827, Salina 67402
Col. Keith G. Duckers, President

KENTUCKY

:: Millersburg Military Institute
P.O. Box 278, Millersburg 40348

Morehead State University, Morehead 40351
Charles Myers, Director of Admissions
606-783-2000

LOUISIANA

Centenary College of Louisiana
P.O. Box 41188, Shreveport 71134

MAINE

Maine Maritime Academy
Battle Ave., Castine 04420
Dan Jones, Dir. of Admis.
207-326-2206

MARYLAND

Morgan State University
Cold Spring Ln. and Hillen Rd., Baltimore 21239

United States Naval Academy
117 Decatur Rd., Annapolis 21402

MASSACHUSETTS

MASSACHUSETTS MARITIME ACADEMY
Cape Cod
101 Academy Dr., Buzzards Bay 02532
CDR. Keith D. Rabine, Dean of Enrollment Services
800-544-3411 or 508-830-5000

MINNESOTA

College of Saint Benedict
37 S. College Ave., St. Joseph 56374

St. John's University
P.O. Box 7155, Collegeville 56321

:: St. Thomas Academy
949 Mendota Heights Rd., St. Paul 55120
Paul Maloney, Dir. of Admis.

MISSOURI

Central Missouri State University
Warrensburg 64093
Delores Hudson, Dir. of Admis.

· Kemper Military School & College
701 3rd St., Boonville 65233
Dr. C.W. Stewart, President
800-530-5600

:: Missouri Military Academy
204 Grand St., Mexico 65265

Missouri Southern State College
3950 Newman Rd., Joplin 64801-1595
Maj. James F. Dunn, Jr., Dept. Head
See listing under "Universities"

Southwest Baptist University
1601 S. Springfield Ave., Bolivar 65613

Southwest Missouri State University
901 S. National Ave., Springfield 65804
LTC Daniel Murphy, Department Head
417-836-5791

· Wentworth Military Academy
1880 Washington Ave., Lexington 64067
Brig. Gen. Gerald Childress, Superintendent

NEVADA

::: Columbia School of Broadcasting
2840 E. Flamingo Rd. #F, Las Vegas 89121
Marcia Brock-Gandy, President

NEW JERSEY

:: Admiral Farragut Academy
601 Riverside Dr., Pine Beach 08741
Capt. Robert W. Matthies, Jr., Headmaster

NEW MEXICO

Eastern New Mexico University
Portales 88130
Larry Fuqua, Dir. of Admis.

· ### NEW MEXICO MILITARY INSTITUTE
101 W. College Ave., Roswell 88201
LTG Winfield W. Scott, Jr., USAF(Ret.), Supt.
COL James H. Matchin, Dir. of Admis.
Toll-free 800-421-5376
Established 1891. Public. Coed. Accreditation: NCACS, New Mexico Department of Education. Estimated costs for 1993-94 school year, out-of-state student: $7,500, in-state student: $5,700. Enrollment: 950. Faculty: 68. Student-faculty ratio: 19:1. Degree: AA. Library: 68,000 volumes. 19 buildings on 40 acre main campus. Additional acreage includes an 18-hole championship golf course and facilities for the equestrian programs. Only land grant military high school and junior college in the United States. Prep school for all service academies. 87% of high school graduates receive their four year college degrees. 90% of junior college graduates receive their baccalaureate degrees. Quality education at a fair price.

NEW YORK

Canisius College
2001 Main St., Buffalo 14208
Penelope Lips, Dir. of Admis.
800-843-1517

:: Christian Brothers Academy
1 De La Salle Rd., Albany 12208

:: La Salle Center - LSMA
500 Montauk Highway, Oakdale 11769
James J. Nolan, Admissions Dir.

Manhattan College
4513 Manhattan College Pky., Riverdale 10471
Dr. Mary Ann O'Donnell, Acting Dean of Arts

:: ### NEW YORK MILITARY ACADEMY
70 Academy Ave., Cornwall-on-Hudson 12520
Col. Philip D. Riley, USA, Ret., Supt.
Peter Wicker, Dir. of Admis.
Established 1889. Coed. Accreditation: MSACS. Grades 5-12. Enrollment: 239 boarding, 10 day. Expenses: $14,400 (all inclusive) new cadet, $13,100 (all inclusive) old cadet (includes tuition, room & board). Faculty: 32. Library: 19,500 volumes. 46 buildings on 325 acres. Riding stables, gym, 3 pools, 6 tennis courts, Nautilus, gymnastics, varsity & intramural sports, horsemanship, flying, band scholarships. 1 hour north of NYC; 15 minutes from West Point. Students from 13 states, 14 foreign countries. Nondiscriminatory.

Niagara University, Niagara University 14109
George Pachter, Dean of Admissions
800-462-2111
See listing under "Universities"

SUNY Maritime College
6 Pennyfield Ave., Bronx 10465
Peter Cooney, Dir. of Admis.

U.S. Merchant Marine Academy, Kings Point 11024

U.S. Military Academy, West Point 10996

NORTH CAROLINA

Campbell University
P.O. Box 127, Buies Creek 27506

:: Oak Ridge Military Academy
P.O. Box 498, Oak Ridge 27310
F. Kennedy, President
910-643-4131

Pembroke State University
P.O. Box 1510, Pembroke 28372
Anthony Locklear, Dir. of Admissions
919-521-6262

OHIO

Central State University
1400 Brush Row Rd., Wilberforce 45384

Kent State University
P.O. Box 5190, Kent 44242
Bruce Riddle, Dir. of Admis.

OKLAHOMA

Cameron University
2800 W. Gore Blvd., Lawton 73505
Louise Brown, Dir. of Admis.

Oklahoma State University, Stillwater 74078
William McLean, Dept. Head

Southeastern Oklahoma State University
Station A, Durant 74701

University of Tulsa
600 S. College Ave., Tulsa 74104
Maj. Larry Berry, Chrpsn.

PENNSYLVANIA

California University of Pennsylvania
3rd St., California 15419
Norman Hasbrouck, Dean for Enrollment

:: Carson Long Military Institute
P.O. Box 98, New Bloomfield 17068
Col. Carson Holman, President

Drexel University
3141 Chestnut St., Philadelphia 19104
Dean of Enrollment Management

Edinboro University of Pennsylvania
Edinboro 16444
Admissions Office: 800-626-2203

Slippery Rock University, Slippery Rock 16057
Director of Admissions

· ### VALLEY FORGE MILITARY ACADEMY & COLLEGE
1001 Eagle Rd., Wayne 19087
Rear Adm. Virgil Hill, USN (Ret.), President
800-234-VFMA

SOUTH CAROLINA

· ### CAMDEN MILITARY ACADEMY
520 Highway 1, N., Camden 29020
Col. L. Risher, Headmaster
803-432-6001

The Citadel
171 Moultrie St., Charleston 29409

SOUTH DAKOTA

Black Hills State University
1200 University St., Spearfish 57799
April Meeker, Dir. of Admis.

TENNESSEE

Carson-Newman College
P.O. Box 70552, Jefferson City 37760
See listing under "Universities"

Knoxville College
901 College St., N.W., Knoxville 37921

University of Memphis, Memphis 38152
Dr. John Eubank, Dean of Admissions

University of Tennessee at Martin
Martin 38238
Paul Kelley, Director of Admissions
See listing under "Universities"

TEXAS

Baylor University
P.O. Box 97008, Waco 76798-7008
Diana Ramey, Director of Admissions

· Central Catholic High School
1403 N. St. May's St., San Antonio 78215

Lamar University
P.O. Box 10009, Beaumont 77710
800-458-7558

:: Marine Military Academy
320 Iwo Jima Blvd., Harlingen 78550
Maj. Gen. Ralph H. Spanjer, Supt.

Prairie View A & M University
P.O. Box 3089, Prairie View 77446-3089
Linda S. Berry, Dir. of Admis.

:: ### SAN MARCOS BAPTIST ACADEMY
2801 Ranch Rd. 12, San Marcos 78666-9406
Dr. Jack Byrom, President
Gerald Cessna, Dir. of Admis.
512-353-2400 FAX 512-353-7795
Established 1907. Baptist. Coed. Accreditation: SACS, ISAS, ACTABS. Tuition, room and board: $13,250 plus uniforms, books, supplies. Enrollment: 200 boarding, 102 day. Faculty: 44. Degree: diploma. Library: 17,600 volumes. 9 buildings on 200 acres. Gym. Pool. Located between Austin and San Antonio, Texas in the beautiful Hill Country about 1 hour drive from either city. The Academy accepts boarding boys in grades 6-12 and boarding girls in grades 9-12, and boys and girls as day students in grades 6-12. A 5 week summer session offered. Over 75 students from outside US. Honor School with distinction in the Jr. ROTC program. Full sports program for boys & girls. Religious emphasis program.

Texas A & M University
College Station 77843

UTAH

Utah State University, Logan 84322-1600
Rod Clark, Director of Admissions
801-750-1107

VERMONT

NORWICH UNIVERSITY
65 S. Main St., Northfield 05663
Dr. Richard Schneider, President
See listing under "Universities"

VIRGINIA

:: Benedictine Military H.S.
304 N. Sheppard St., Richmond 23221

:: ### FISHBURNE MILITARY SCHOOL
P.O. Box 988A, Waynesboro 22980
Robert Miller, Superintendent
Doris Brown, Registrar
703-943-1171, Fax: 703-943-8042
Established 1879. School for boys in grades 8-12 and PG, Army JROTC. Accreditation: SACS, VAIS. Annual fee: $11,700. Enrollment: 9 day, 172 boarding. Faculty: 22. Degree: High school diploma. Library: 18,000 volumes. 3 buildings on 10 acres. School facilities include computer center, science and photography labs, gym, indoor pool, and rifle range. Skiing, indoor tennis, and golf course nearby.

:: ### FORK UNION MILITARY ACADEMY
P.O. Box 278-N, Fork Union 23055
Col. R. L. Pulliam, Interim President
804-842-3212 or 800-462-3862

:: Hargrave Military Academy
R.R. 5, Chatham 24531
Rick Cline, Director of Admissions
804-432-2481

Marymount University
2807 N. Glebe Rd., Arlington 22207
Charles Coe, Director of Admissions
800-548-7638 or 703-284-1500
See listing under "Universities"

:: Massanutten Military Academy
614 S. Main St., Woodstock 22664

:: Miller School of Albemarle
R.R. 3, Charlottesville 22901-9328
Donaldson Tillar, Jr., Col. USA (Ret), President

:: Randolph-Macon Academy
201 W. 3rd St., Front Royal 22630
Col. Trevor Turner, USA Ret, President

Virginia Military Institute, Lexington 24450

WASHINGTON

Central Washington University, Ellensburg 98926
William Swain, Director of Admissions

WEST VIRGINIA

The University of Charleston
2300 MacCorkle Ave., S.E., Charleston 25304
800-995-GO UC

WISCONSIN

:: Northwestern Military and Naval Academy
550 S. Lake Shore Dr., Lake Geneva 53147
414-248-4465

ST. JOHN'S MILITARY ACADEMY
1101 N. Genesee St., Delafield 53018
Brigadier General David M. Williams, President
Lt. Col. Kenneth A. Clark, Director of Admissions
800-752-2338
Established in 1884. Boy's grades 7-12. Accreditation: ISACS, NAIS, AMCSUS. Tuition, room & board: $15,850. Enrollment: 300 boarding. 10 buildings on 150 acres. Gym, pool, tennis courts, golf course. College preparatory boy's boarding school. 30 minutes from Milwaukee and 90 minutes from Chicago. Extensive athletic and extracurricular offerings. JROTC honor school with distinction.

St. Norbert College
100 Grant St., De Pere 54115
Craig S. Wesley, Dean of Admission
See listing under "Universities"

University of Wisconsin, Madison
500 Lincoln Dr., Madison 53706

Viterbo College
815 9th St., S., La Crosse 54601
Roland W. Nelson, Dir. of Admis.

GUAM
University of Guam
UOG Station, Mangilao 96923
Kathleen Owings, Dir. of Admis.

PUERTO RICO
:: American Military Academy
P.O. Box 7884, Guaynabo 00970-7884
David A. Wells, Superintendent
809-720-6801

:: Antilles Military Academy
P.O. Box 666, San Juan 00902
Mrs. Genoveva Santiago, Dir. of Admissions

MINES AND METALLURGY

ALABAMA
University of Alabama
P.O. Box 870132, Tuscaloosa 35487-0132
Roy Smith, Dir. of Admis.

ALASKA
University of Alaska Fairbanks
Fairbanks 99775

ARIZONA
University of Arizona, Tucson 85721
Loyd Bell, Director of Admissions

COLORADO
Colorado School of Mines
Weaver Towers-1811 Elm St.
Golden 80401-1873
Bill Young, Dir. of Enrollment Mgmt.
303-273-3220

IDAHO
University of Idaho, Moscow 83843
Peter Brown, Dir. of Admis.

ILLINOIS
University of Illinois
506 S. Wright St., Urbana 61801

KENTUCKY
University of Kentucky, Lexington 40506

MICHIGAN
Michigan Technological University
1400 Townsend Dr., Houghton 49931
Joseph A. Galetto, Dir. Enrollment Mgmt.
906-487-2335

MISSOURI
University of Missouri, Rolla
102 Parker Hall, Rolla 65401
David J. Allen, Dir. of Admis. & Financial Aid
800-522-0938

MONTANA
Montana Tech
(formerly Montana College of Mineral Science and Technology)
1300 W. Park St., Butte 59701-8997
800-445-TECH
See listing under "Engineering"

NEW MEXICO
New Mexico Institute of Mining & Technology
801 Leroy Pl., Socorro 87801

PENNSYLVANIA
Pennsylvania State University
201 Shields Bldg., University Park 16802

SOUTH DAKOTA
South Dakota School of Mines and Technology
501 E. St. Joseph St., Rapid City 57701
Gary Bjordal, Dir. of Admis.

UTAH
University of Utah
1400 E. 200 S., Salt Lake City 84112
Dr. J. Stayner Landward, Dir. of Admis.

VIRGINIA
Virginia Polytechnic Institute & State University
Blacksburg 24061
David Bousquet, Dir. of Undergraduate Admis.

WASHINGTON
University of Washington, Seattle 98195

WEST VIRGINIA
West Virginia University
P.O. Box 6001, Morgantown 26506

WISCONSIN
University of Wisconsin, Madison
500 Lincoln Dr., Madison 53706

MUSIC

This classification contains schools accredited by the National Association of Schools of Music (†) and a selection of programs from institutionally accredited schools.

ALABAMA
Alabama A & M University
P.O. Box 295, Normal 35762
Dr. Horace Carney, Chrpsn.
See listing under "Universities"

† Alabama State University
P.O. Box 271, Montgomery 36101

† Auburn University, Auburn 36849

† Birmingham Southern College
900 Arkadelphia Rd., Birmingham 35254

· Gadsden State Community College
P.O. Box 227, Gadsden 35902
W. Bryan Stone, Dir. of Admis.

† Huntingdon College
1500 E. Fairview Ave., Montgomery 36106-2148
Carolyn A. Phillips, Dean of Enrollment
800-763-0313

† Jacksonville State University
700 Pelham Rd. N., Jacksonville 36265

† Judson College
P O Box 120, Marion 36756

† Samford University
800 Lakeshore Dr., Birmingham 35229
Milburn Price, Dean

STILLMAN COLLEGE
P.O. Box 1430, Tuscaloosa 35403
Barbara K. Smith, Director of Admissions
See listing under "Universities"

Troy State University, Troy 36082
Dr. Johnny Long, Dean

† University of Alabama
P.O. Box 870132, Tuscaloosa 35487-0132
Roy Smith, Dir. of Admis.

† University of Alabama at Birmingham
University Station, Birmingham 35294

† UNIVERSITY OF ALABAMA IN HUNTSVILLE
P.O. Box 1247, Huntsville 35899
Ron R. Koger Ed.D., Dir. of Admis.
205-895-6070
Established 1969. Public. Coed. Accreditation: SACS, ABET, NLN, CSAB, ACS. Tuition: $2,418 resident, $4,836 non-resident. Room & Board: $3,450. Undergraduate enrollment: 2,674 full-time, 3,439 part-time. Graduate enrollment: 1,860. Faculty: 282. Student-faculty ratio: 18:1. Degrees: BS, BA, BSBA, BSE, MS, MSM, Ph.D., BSN, MSN, MA. 20 buildings on 350 acres. Comprehensive research university located in the Tennessee Valley of northern Alabama. Huntsville is the locale of major government and private research centers. Metropolitan population approaching 300,000.

† UNIVERSITY OF MOBILE
P.O. Box 13220, Mobile 36663-0220
Kim Leousis, Dir. of Admissions
205-675-5990
See listing under "Universities"

† University of Montevallo, Montevallo 35115

† University of North Alabama
University Station, Florence 35632

† University of South Alabama
307 University Blvd. N., Mobile 36688

ALASKA
† University of Alaska Fairbanks
Fairbanks 99775

ARIZONA
† Arizona State University, Tempe 85287

: THE CONSERVATORY OF RECORDING ARTS & SCIENCES
1110 E. Missouri Ave. #530, Phoenix 85014
Kirt R. Hamm, Administrator
800-562-6383
Established 1987. Coed. Accreditation: ACCSCT. Enrollment: 40. Faculty: 8. Student-faculty ratio: 5:1. Diploma: Master recording program. Certificate: Audio recording & production, music business, MIDI/computer/electronic music recording, sound reinforcement, concert sound, trouble shooting maintenance. Purpose is to train highly motivated students for entry level positions in the audio recording and music industries. Through extensive hands-on training with industry standard equipment and practice with current production techniques, students gain the confidence and expertise to enter the working world as Recording Engineers.

GRAND CANYON UNIVERSITY
3300 W. Camelback Rd., Phoenix 85017
Sherri Willborn, Dir. of Admis.
See listing under "Liberal Arts and Sciences"

† Northern Arizona University
P.O. Box 4092, Flagstaff 86011
Dr. Margaret Cibik, Dir. of Admis.

SOUTHWESTERN COLLEGE
A Conservative Baptist Bible College
2625 E. Cactus Rd., Phoenix 85032
800-247-2697

† University of Arizona, Tucson 85721
Loyd Bell, Director of Admissions

· Yavapai College
1100 E. Sheldon St., Prescott 86301
Dr. Doreen Dailey, President
602-445-7300
See listing under "Community and Junior Colleges"

ARKANSAS
† Arkansas State University
P.O. Box 1200, State University 72467

† Arkansas Tech University
215 W. O St., Russellville 72801

Central Baptist College
CBC Station, Conway 72032

† Harding University
900 E. Center Ave., Searcy 72149

† Henderson State University
1100 Henderson St., Arkadelphia 71999

† Hendrix College
1601 Harkrider St., Conway 72032

John Brown University
2000 W. University, Siloam Springs 72761
Don Crandall, Director of Enrollment Management

† Ouachita Baptist University
410 Ouachita St., Arkadelphia 71998
Randy Garner, Dir. of Admis.
800-DIAL-OBU

† Southern Arkansas University
SAU Box 1402, Magnolia 71753

† University of Arkansas at Fayetteville
Fayetteville 72701

† University of Arkansas at Little Rock
2801 S. University Ave., Little Rock 72204

† University of Arkansas at Monticello
P.O. Box 3596, Monticello 71656

† University of Arkansas at Pine Bluff
1200 University Dr., Pine Bluff 71601-2799

† University of Central Arkansas
201 Donaghey Ave., Conway 72035

Williams Baptist College
P.O. Box 3667, Walnut Ridge 72476
Scott Wright, Dir. of Admis.

CALIFORNIA

Bethany Bible College
800 Bethany Dr., Scotts Valley 95066
Randal McNally, Dir. of Admis.

† Biola University
13800 Biola Ave., La Mirada 90639
Wayne Chute, Dean of Admissions

† California Baptist College
8432 Magnolia Ave., Riverside 92504
800-782-3382

† California Institute of the Arts
24700 McBean Pkwy., Valencia 91355
Kenneth Young, Dir. of Admis.

California Lutheran University
60 Olsen Rd., Thousand Oaks 91360
800-252-5884

† California State University, Chico
Chico 95929-0805
Dr. Alfred Loeffler, Chrpsn.

† California State University, Dominguez Hills
1000 E. Victoria St., Carson 90747

† California State University, Fresno
Shaw & Cedar Ave., Fresno 93710

† California State University, Long Beach
1250 Bellflower Blvd., Long Beach 90840

† California State University, Los Angeles
5151 Paseo Rancho Castilla, Los Angeles 90032

† California State University, Northridge
18111 Nordhoff St., Northridge 91330
Ned C. Reynolds, Dir. of Admis.

† California State University, Sacramento
6000 J St., Sacramento 95819

† California State University-Fullerton
Fullerton 92632

† California State University-Hayward
25800 Carlos Bee Blvd., Hayward 94542

† California State University-Stanislaus
801 W. Monte Vista Ave., Turlock 95382
Frances Cook, Dean Enrollment Services

Chapman University
333 N. Glassell St., Orange 92666
Michael Drummy, Dir. of Admis.

Christian Heritage College
2100 Greenfield Dr., El Cajon 92019
Pam Daly, Dir. of Admis.
800-676-2242

COGSWELL POLYTECHNICAL COLLEGE
10420 Bubb Rd., Cupertino 95014
Paul Schreivogel, Dean of Student Services
800-264-7955
Established 1887. Private. Coed. Accreditation: WASC. Tuition: $6,600. Enrollment: 100 full-time, 248 part-time. Faculty: 42. Student-faculty ratio: 9:1. Degrees: BS Engineering Technology, BS Electrical and Software Engineering. Library: 12,000 volumes. 1 building on 4 acres. Only Bachelor of Science degree in Music Engineering Technology and Bachelor of Arts degree in Computer and Video Imaging.

College for Recording Arts
665 Harrison St., San Francisco 94107
Leo de Gar Kulka, Dir. of Admis.

† College of Notre Dame
1500 Ralston Ave., Belmont 94002
Greg M. Smith, PhD., Dir. of Admis.

DOMINICAN COLLEGE OF SAN RAFAEL
50 Acacia Ave., San Rafael 94901-8008
Office of Admissions
800-788-3522

Eubanks Conservatory of Music & Arts
4928 Crenshaw Blvd., Los Angeles 90043
Raymond Cho, Dir. of Admis.
213-291-7821

Fresno Pacific College
1717 S. Chestnut Ave., Fresno 93702
209-453-2039

† Golden Gate Baptist Theological Seminary
Strawberry Point, Mill Valley 94941
William Crews, Jr., President

† Holy Names College
3500 Mountain Blvd., Oakland 94619

† Humboldt State University
1 Harps St., Arcata 95521

:: Idyllwild School of Music & the Arts
P.O. Box 38P, Idyllwild 92549
Anne Behnke, Admissions
909-659-2171, FAX 909-659-2058
See listing under "Prep-Coed"

La Sierra University
4700 Pierce St., Riverside 92505
800-874-5587

† Loyola Marymount University
Loyola Blvd. at W. 80th, Los Angeles 90045
M. L'Heureux, Dir. of Admis.

Master's College
P.O. Box 221450, Newhall 91322
Don Gilmore, Dir. of Admis.

Mills College
5000 MacArthur Blvd., Oakland 94613
Genevieve Ann Flaherty, Dean of Admissions
800-87-MILLS

† Mt. St. Mary's College
12001 Chalon Rd., Los Angeles 90049

: † MUSICIANS INSTITUTE
1655 McCadden Pl., Hollywood 90028
Patrick Hicks, President
213-462-1384, FAX 213-462-6978
Has five schools: guitar, bass, drums, vocal & keyboard. Emphasis on performance — all styles. Established 1976. Private. Coed. Accreditation: NASM. Tuition: Full-time programs, 1 year $7,800, 6 month $4,500. Fees: $100. 3 month, part-time program $2,000. Room and board available off campus. Enrollment: 1,000 full-time. Faculty and staff: 180. Student-faculty ratio: from 25:1 to 1:1. 60,000 square foot facility. Current audio/video library, audio/video recording facilities. Ongoing concerts and clinics by some of the most recognized performers in music. Rehearsal facilities utilizing modern learning techniques, including video and computer training. Known for graduating many outstanding players successful in all fields of music.

Napa Valley College
2277 Napa-Vallejo Hwy., Napa 94558
Delores Smith, Asst. Dean of Admissions
707-253-3000

Pacific Union College
1 Angwin Ave., Angwin 94508
Dr. Gary Gifford, Dir. of Admis.

† Pepperdine University
24255 Pacific Coast Hwy., Malibu 90263
Paul Long, Dean of Admissions
310-456-4392

Pomona College
333 N. College Way, Claremont 91711
Peter W. Stanley, President

: † R.D. Colburn School of Performing Arts
3131 S. Figueroa St., Los Angeles 90007
Joseph Thayer, Dean

† San Diego State University
5300 Campanile Dr., San Diego 92115

† San Francisco Conservatory of Music
1201 Ortega St., San Francisco 94122
Colleen Katzowitz, Dir. of Student Services

† San Francisco State University
1600 Holloway Ave., San Francisco 94132
Corwin Bjonerud, Dir. of Admis.

† San Jose State University
1 Washington Sq., San Jose 95192

Santa Barbara City College
721 Cliff Dr., Santa Barbara 93109
805-965-0581

† Santa Clara University, Santa Clara 95053

Scripps College
1030 Columbia Ave., Claremont 91711
Leslie Miles, Dean of Admissions

† Sonoma State University
1801 E. Cotati Ave., Rohnert Park 94928

Southern California College
55 Fair Dr., Costa Mesa 92626
Richard Hardy, Asst. Dean for Enrollment

University of California at Berkeley
Morrison Hall, Berkeley 94720

† University of Redlands
P.O. Box 3080, Redlands 92373

University of San Diego
5998 Alcala Park, San Diego 92110
Warren Muller, Dir. of Admis.
619-260-4506

† University of Southern California
University Park Campus
Los Angeles 90089

† University of the Pacific
3601 Pacific Ave., Stockton 95211
Elliott J. Taylor, Dean of Admissions

Whittier College
13406 Philadelphia St., Whittier 90601
310-907-4238

COLORADO

† Adams State College, Alamosa 81102
Cheryl Billingsley, Dir. of Admis.
800-824-6494

Colorado Christian University
180 S. Garrison St., Lakewood 80226
Debra Seefeldt, Dir. of Admis.

Colorado College
14 E. Cache La Poudre, Colorado Springs 80903
Terry Swenson, Dir. of Admis.

Colorado Institute of Art
200 E. 9th Ave., Denver 80203
Barbara Browning, Dir. of Admis.
800-275-2420
See listing under "Career Schools"

† Colorado State University
102 Administration Building, Fort Collins 80523
Mary Ontireros, Dir. of Admissions

† Ft. Lewis College
1000 Rim Dr., Durango 81301

Mesa State College
P.O. Box 2647, Grand Junction 81502
Sherri Pe'a, Dir. of Admis.

† Metropolitan State College of Denver
P.O. Box 173362, Campus Box 16
Denver 80217-3362

Naropa Institute
2130 Arapahoe Ave., Boulder 80302
Dr. Jana Lynn, Director of Admissions
303-546-3572

† University of Colorado at Boulder
Boulder 80309
William A. Douglas, Dean of Admis.

† University of Colorado at Denver
1200 Larimer, Denver 80204

† University of Denver
2199 S. University Blvd., Denver 80210

† University of Northern Colorado, Greeley 80639
Shirley Howell, Director
303-351-2678

† University of Southern Colorado
2200 Bonforte Blvd., Pueblo 81001

† Western State College of Colorado
Gunnison 81231
Monica Bruning, Dir. of Admis.
See listing under "Universities"

CONNECTICUT

: Hartford Camerata Conservatory
834 Asylum Ave., Hartford 06105
203-246-2588

Mattatuck Community College
750 Chase Parkway, Waterbury 06708
Dr. Richard Sanders, President

University of Bridgeport
126 Park Ave., Bridgeport 06601
Andrew G. Nelson, Dean Admis./Financial Aid
203-576-4552
See listing under "Universities"

† University of Connecticut, Storrs 06268
Dr. Dorothy Payne, Head

† UNIVERSITY OF HARTFORD
200 Bloomfield Ave., West Hartford 06117
Richard Zeiser, Dir. of Admis.
See listing under "Universities"

† Yale University
2404A Yale Station, New Haven 06520

DELAWARE

† University of Delaware, Newark 19711

DISTRICT OF COLUMBIA

† The American University
4400 Massachusetts Ave. N.W.
Washington 20016

† Catholic University of America
620 Michigan Ave. N.E., Washington 20064
Robert J. Talbot, Dir. of Admis. & Fin. Aid

† George Washington University
Washington 20052

† Howard University
2400 6th St., N.W., Washington 20059
James E. Cheek, President

: † Levine School of Music
1690 36th St. N.W., Washington 20007
Jean Kellogg, Dean
202-337-2227

University of the District of Columbia
Georgia Ave.-Harvard St. Campus
1100 Harvard St., N.W., Washington 20009

University of the District of Columbia
Van Ness Campus
4200 Connecticut Ave., N.W., Washington 20008

: † Washington Conservatory of Music
P.O. Box 5758, Washington 20016
Diana Young, Director

FLORIDA

· Art Institute of Fort Lauderdale
Music & Video Business Dept.
1799 S.E. 17th St., Ft. Lauderdale 33316
Eileen Northrop, V.P./Dir. of Admis.

Clearwater Christian College
3400 Gulf-to-Bay Blvd., Clearwater 34619
Benjamin Puckett, Dir. of Admis.

† Florida Atlantic University
500 N.W. 20th St., Boca Raton 33431
Brian Levin-Stankevich, Dir. of Admis.

Florida Southern College
111 Lake Hollingsworth Dr., Lakeland 33801
William Stephens, Jr., Dir. of Admis.

† Florida State University
600 W. College Ave., Tallahassee 32306

· Full Sail Center for the Recording Arts
3300 University Blvd. #160, Winter Park 32792
407-679-0100 or 800-CAN-ROCK
See listing under "Career Schools"

† Jacksonville University
2800 University Blvd., N., Jacksonville 32211

New College of the University of South Florida
5700 N. Taimiami Trail, Sarasota 34243

Palm Beach Atlantic College
P.O. Box 24708, West Palm Beach 33416-4708
See listing under "Universities"

† Rollins College
P.O. Box 2720, Winter Park 32790

St. Leo College
P.O. Box 2008, St. Leo 33574
Bonnie Black, Dir. of Admis.

† Stetson University
401 N. Woodland Blvd., De Land 32720
Dr. James Woodward, Dean

† University of Central Florida
P.O. Box 25000, Orlando 32816

† University of Florida
226 Tigert Hall, Gainesville 32611

† University of Miami
P.O. Box 248006, Coral Gables 33124

† University of South Florida
4202 Fowler Ave., Tampa 33620

† University of Tampa
401 W. Kennedy Blvd., Tampa 33606
Robert W. Cook, Dir. of Admis.

† University of West Florida
11000 University Pky., Pensacola 32514

Warner Southern College
5301 U.S. Hwy. 27, S., Lake Wales 33853
Valerie S. Rutland, Dir. Enrollment Mgmt.
800-949-7248

GEORGIA

Agnes Scott College
201 E. College Ave., Decatur 30030
Teresa Lahti, Dir. of Admis.

† Armstrong State College
11935 Abercorn St., Savannah 31419
Kim West, Director of Admissions

† AUGUSTA COLLEGE
2500 Walton Way, Augusta 30904-2200
Lee Young, Dir. of Admis.
706-737-1405

† Berry College
2277 Martha Berry Hwy. N.W., Mt. Berry 30165

BREWTON-PARKER COLLEGE
P.O. Box 197, Mount Vernon 30445
Dr. Y. Lynn Holmes, President
912-583-2241

† Columbus College
3600 Algonquin Dr., Columbus 31907

Emory University
1462 Clifton Rd., Atlanta 30322

† Georgia College
231 W. Hancock St., Milledgeville 31061
912-453-5004

† Georgia Southern University, Statesboro 30460

† Georgia State University
University Plaza, Atlanta 30303
Ernest Beals, Dean of Admissions

† Kennesaw State College
P.O. Box 444, Marietta 30061
Joe Head, Dir. of Admis.

† Mercer University
1400 Coleman Ave., Macon 31207

Paine College
1235 15th St., Augusta 30901
Phyllis Wyatt-Woodruff, Dir. Enrollment Mgmt.

Piedmont College
P.O. Box 10, Demorest 30535
Penny L. Graber, Dir of Admis.
800-277-7020

† Shorter College
315 Shorter Ave., Rome 30165

† Spelman College
350 Spelman Ln., S.W., Atlanta 30314
Aline Rivers, Dir. of Admis.

† Toccoa Falls College
Office of Admissions, Toccoa Falls 30598
Matthew L. King, Dir. of Admis.
800-868-3257

† University of Georgia, Athens 30602
Dr. Ralph E. Verrastro, Head

† Valdosta State College
Patterson St., Valdosta 31698

† Wesleyan College
4760 Forsyth Rd., Macon 31297

† West Georgia College, Carrollton 30118
C. Doyle Bickers, Dir. of Admis.

HAWAII

University of Hawaii at Hilo
523 W. Lanikaula, Hilo 96720

† University of Hawaii at Manoa
2500 Campus Rd., Honolulu 96822

IDAHO

† Boise State University
1910 University Dr., Boise 83725

† Idaho State University
P.O. Box 8270, Pocatello 83209

† Northwest Nazarene College
623 Holly St., Nampa 83686
Bruce D. Webb, Dir. of Admis.

· † Ricks College, Rexburg 83460
Steven Bennion, President

† University of Idaho, Moscow 83843
Peter Brown, Dir. of Admis.

ILLINOIS

† THE AMERICAN CONSERVATORY OF MUSIC
16 N. Wabash Ave., Suite 1850, Chicago 60602
312-263-4161
Established 1886. Private. Coed. Conservatory of Music. Accreditation: NASM. Degrees: Bachelor of Music, Master of Music, Doctor of Musical Arts. World renowned Robert R. McCormick Reference Library. Numerous Pulitzer Prize winners. Location: Downtown Chicago, near to the Art Institute, Orchestra Hall, Newberry Library, the Lyric Opera. Tuition: Estimated at $9,800 dependent on private study options. Room, board, books, and supplies: Estimated at $8,900.

† Augustana College
639 38th St., Rock Island 61201
Martin R. Sauer, Director of Admission
800-798-8100

† Bradley University
1501 W. Bradley Ave., Peoria 61625

Columbia College
600 S. Michigan Ave., Chicago 60605
Debra McGrath, Dir. of Admis.

† De Paul University
1 E. Jackson Blvd., Chicago 60604
Thomas D. Abrahamson, Dean of Admissions
See listing under "Universities"

† Eastern Illinois University, Charleston 61920
Herman Taylor, Chrpsn.
See listing under "Universities"

Elmhurst College
190 Prospect Ave., Elmhurst 60126

Garrett-Evangelical Theological Seminary
2121 Sheridan Rd., Evanston 60201
Contact Admissions at 800-SEMINARY

Governors State University
1 University Pky., University Park 60466
Richard Pride, Dir. of Admis.

Greenville College
315 E. College Ave., Greenville 62246
Kent Krober, Dir. of Admis.

Illinois Benedictine College
5700 College Rd., Lisle 60532

· † Illinois Central College
One College Dr., East Peoria 61635
Dr. Thomas K. Thomas, President

† Illinois State University
212 N. School St., Normal 61761

† ILLINOIS WESLEYAN UNIVERSITY
P.O. Box 2900, Bloomington 61702
Dr. Robert Kvam, Director
309-556-3061

Knox College, Galesburg 61401
309-343-0112 or 800-678-KNOX
See listing under "Universities"

LEWIS UNIVERSITY
Rt. 53, Romeoville 60441
Irish O'Reilly, Director of Admissions
See listing under "Universities"

MacMurray College
447 E. College Ave., Jacksonville 62650
Edwin R. Hockett, Dean of Admissions

† MILLIKIN UNIVERSITY
1184 W. Main St., Decatur 62522
Lin Stoner, Dean of Admissions
800-373-7733

· Montay College
3750 W. Peterson Ave., Chicago 60659
Scott Dalhouse, Dir. of Admis.

† Moody Bible Institute
820 N. LaSalle Dr., Chicago 60610
Carolyn Klingbeil, Administrator of Admis.

: † Music Center of the North Shore
300 Green Bay Rd., Winnetka 60093

North Central College
30 N. Brainard St.
P.O. Box 3065, Naperville 60566-7065
Marguerite Waters, Director of Admission
708-420-3414

Northeastern Illinois University
5500 N. St. Louis Ave., Chicago 60625

† Northern Illinois University, De Kalb 60115

† North Park College & Theological Seminary
3225 W. Foster, Chicago 60625
312-509-2330

† Northwestern University
Music Administration Bldg.
711 Elgin Rd, Evanston 60208

† Olivet Nazarene University, Kankakee 60901
John Mongerson, Dir. of Admis.
815-939-5203

· Parkland College
2400 W. Bradley Ave., Champaign 61821-1899
217-351-2208 or 800-346-8089

† Quincy College
1800 College Ave., Quincy 62301
Fr. Michael Lanning, O.F.M., Dir. of Admis.

Rockford College
5050 E. State St., Rockford 61108
Miriam King, V.P. for Enrollment Management
See listing under "Universities"

† ROOSEVELT UNIVERSITY
430 S. Michigan Ave., Chicago 60605
William Smyser, Director of Admissions
See listing under "Universities"

Rosary College
7900 W. Division St., River Forest 60305
Hildegarde Schmidt, Dir. of Admis.

† St. Xavier College
3700 W. 103rd St., Chicago 60655
Mary Hendry, Dean of Admissions

† Southern Illinois University at Carbondale
Carbondale 62901

† Southern Illinois University at Edwardsville
Edwardsville 62026
Eugene J. Magac, Dir. of Admissions & Records

· South Suburban College of Cook County
15800 State St., South Holland 60473

· Springfield College in Illinois
1500 N. Fifth St., Springfield 62702
Dr. H. Brent DeLand, President

Trinity Christian College
6601 W. College Dr., Palos Heights 60463
Kenneth Bootsma, President

Trinity College
2077 Half Day Rd., Deerfield 60015
Dr. Kenneth Meyer, Pres.

† University of Illinois
506 S. Wright St., Urbana 61801

University of Illinois at Chicago
P.O. Box 4348, Chicago 60680
William Kaplan, Head

† VanderCook College of Music
3209 S. Michigan Ave., Chicago 60616
Ward Durrett, Dir of Admis.

† Western Illinois University
900 W. Adams St., Macomb 61455
Alan DeRoos, Registrar
309-298-1891

† WHEATON COLLEGE
Wheaton Conservatory of Music
Wheaton 60187
Harold Best, Dean
Daniel Crabtree, Dir. of Admis.
800-222-2419
Established 1860. Private, interdenominational Christian college Coed. Accreditation: NCACS and NASM. Tuition: $11,480. Room and board: $4,200. Fees: $350. Enrollment: 170. Faculty: 30. Degrees: BMus, BME. Majors in music composition, education, history, literature and performance. Major choral organizations include Concert Choir, Men's Glee and Women's Chorale. Major instrumental organizations include symphony orchestra, wind ensemble and jazz ensemble. Performance studies in piano, organ, harpsichord, violin, cello, double bass, french horn, trumpet, trombone, tuba, euphonium, flute, oboe, clarinet, bassoon, sax, percussion, harp, classical guitar, and voice. Music library holds over 13,000 items. Summer program in Aspen, CO.

· † William Rainey Harper College
1200 W. Algonquin Rd., Palatine 60067

INDIANA

† Anderson University
1100 E. 5th St., Anderson 46012
Robert H. Reardon, President

† Ball State University
2000 W. University Ave., Muncie 47306
Ruth Vedvik, Dir. of Admis.

† Butler University
4600 Sunset Ave., Indianapolis 46208

† DePauw University
313 S. Locust St., Greencastle 46135
Dr. Eleanor Ypma, Registrar

Goshen College
1700 S. Main St., Goshen 46526
Doyle Preheim, Chairperson

Grace College
200 Seminary Dr., Winona Lake 46590
Ron Henry, Dir. of Admis.

† Indiana State University
217 N. 6th St., Terre Haute 47809

† Indiana University at Bloomington
300 N. Jordan Ave., Bloomington 47406

† Indiana University-Purdue University at Fort Wayne
2101 Coliseum Blvd. E., Fort Wayne 46805

Indiana Wesleyan University
4201 S. Washington St., Marion 46953
800-332-6901

Manchester College
604 College Ave., North Manchester 46962
Robert Jones, Chrpsn.

† St. Mary-of-the-Woods College
Saint Mary-of-the-Woods 47876
Lynn M. Rubick, Director of Admissions
800-926-SMWC

† St. Mary's College
46 Madeliva, Notre Dame 46556
Mary Ann Rowan, Dir. of Admissions

† Taylor University
500 W. Reade Ave., Upland 46989
Jerry Giger, Head

† University of Evansville
1800 Lincoln Ave., Evansville 47722
Dr. Alan Solomon, Dept. Chair
800-423-8633

† University of Indianapolis
1400 E. Hanna Ave., Indianapolis 46227

† University of Notre Dame, Notre Dame 46556
Calvin Bower, Chairman

† Valparaiso University, Valparaiso 46383

Wabash College
301 W. Wabash Ave., Crawfordsville 47933
Greg Birk, Dir. of Admis.

IOWA

Central College
812 University St., Pella 50219
Eric Sickler, Dir. of Admis.

† Clarke College
1550 Clarke Dr., Dubuque 52001
Kate Hendell, BVM, PhD, Chair
800-383-2345

† Coe College
1220 1st Ave., N.E., Cedar Rapids 52402
Margie Marrs, Chrpsn.

† Cornell College
600 1st St., W., Mt. Vernon 52314
Kevin Crockett, Dean of Admissions

Dordt College
498 4th Ave., N.E., Sioux Center 51250
Quentin Van Essen, Dir. of Admissions
800-343-6738

† Drake University
2507 E. University Ave., Des Moines 50311
Thomas Willoughby, Dir. of Admis.

Graceland College, Lamoni 50140
800-638-0053, Outside Iowa 800-346-9208
Bonita Booth, Dean of Admissions
See listing under "Universities"

Grinnell College
P.O. Box 805, Grinnell 50112

Iowa Lakes Community College
300 S. 18th St., Estherville 51334
John Nelson, Dir. of Admis.
712-362-2604

† Iowa State University, Ames 50011
Karsten Smedal, Dir. of Admis.

Iowa Wesleyan College
601 N. Main St., Mt. Pleasant 52641

† Luther College
700 College Dr., Decorah 52101
David Sallee, Dean for Enrollment

† Morningside College, Sioux City 51106
Lora Vanderzwaag, Dir. of Admis.

Mount Mercy College
1330 Elmhurst Dr., N.E., Cedar Rapids 52402
Carol Williamson, Dir. of Admis.

† Simpson College
P.O. Box 708, Indianola 50125

Teikyo Westmar University
1002 3rd Ave., S.E., Le Mars 51031
Dr. Jim Utesch, Dir. of Admis.

† University of Iowa, Iowa City 52242

† University of Northern Iowa, Cedar Falls 50614

Vennard College
P.O. Box 29, University Park 52595
Mark Becker, Dir. of Admis.
800-338-2407

Waldorf College
106 S. 6th St., Forest City 50436
Steve Lovik, Dir. of Admis.
800-292-1903

† Wartburg College
P.O. Box 1003, Waverly 50677

KANSAS

† Benedictine College
1020 N. Second St., Atchison 66002
James Hoffman, Dir. of Admis.

† Bethany College
421 N. 1st St., Lindsborg 67456
Elmer Copley, Chrpsn.

† Emporia State University
1200 Commercial St., Emporia 66801
Dr. Barbara Hilgendorf, Dir. of Admissions

† Fort Hays State University
600 Park St., Hays 67601-4099
Dr. James L. Murphy, Chrpsn.

† Friends University
2100 University St., Wichita 67213

† Kansas State University
Anderson Hall 110, Manhattan 66506
Ellsworth M. Gerritz, Admis. & Records

McPherson College
1600 E. Euclid St., McPherson 67460

† Mid-America Nazarene College
P.O. Box 1776, Olathe 66051

Ottawa University
1001 S. Cedar St., Ottawa 66067
Steve Koberlein, Dir. of Admis.
800-755-5200

† Pittsburg State University
1701 S. Broadway St., Pittsburg 66762
James E. Parker, Dir of Admis.

Saint Mary College
4100 S. 4th St., Leavenworth 66048
Irene Keehan, Dir. of Admis.

† **SOUTHWESTERN COLLEGE**
100 College St., Winfield 67156
800-846-1543

† Tabor College
400 S. Jefferson St., Hillsboro 67063
800-822-6799
See listing under "Liberal Arts & Sciences"

† University of Kansas, Lawrence 66045

† Washburn University of Topeka
1700 S.W. College Ave., Topeka 66621
John E. Triggs, Dir. of Admissions

† Wichita State University
1845 Fairmount, Wichita 67260
800-362-2594
See listing under "Universities"

KENTUCKY

† Asbury College
1 Macklem Dr., Wilmore 40390
Jonah Mitchell, Dir. of Admis.

Bellarmine College
2001 Newburg Rd., Louisville 40205
Thomas LaBaugh, Dean of Admissions

† Campbellsville College
200 College St., Campbellsville 42718
Dr. W. R. Davenport, President

† Cumberland College
6178 College Station Dr., Williamsburg 40769
See listing under "Universities"

† Eastern Kentucky University
521 Lancaster Ave., Richmond 40475

Georgetown College
400 E. College St., Georgetown 40324
Garvel Kindrick, Director of Admissions
See listing under "Universities"

† Kentucky State University
400 E. Main St., Frankfort 40601

Kentucky Wesleyan College
3000 Frederica St., Owensboro 42301
Dr. Diane Earle, Associate Professor

† Morehead State University, Morehead 40351
Charles Myers, Director of Admissions
606-783-2000

† Murray State University, Murray 42071
Phil Bryan, Director of Admissions
800-272-4MSU

† Northern Kentucky University
Louie B. Nunn Dr., Highland Heights 41076

† Southern Baptist Theological Seminary
2825 Lexington Rd., Louisville 40280
R. Albert Mohler, Jr., President

Sue Bennett College
101 College St., London 40741
Don A. Gorbandt, Dir. of Admis.

† University of Kentucky, Lexington 40506

† University of Louisville
2301 S. 3rd St., Louisville 40292
Robert Parrent, Dir. of Admis.

† Western Kentucky University
1526 Russellville Rd., Bowling Green 42101

LOUISIANA

† Centenary College of Louisiana
P.O. Box 41188, Shreveport 71134

Dillard University
2601 Gentilly Blvd., New Orleans 70122

† Grambling State University
P.O. Box 607, Grambling 71245
Dr. Harold W. Lundy, President

† Louisiana College
College Station, Pineville 71359
Byron McGee, Dir. of Admis.
318-487-7386
See listing under "Liberal Arts"

† Louisiana State University and A & M College
Baton Rouge 70803

† Lousiana Technical University
P.O. Box 3168, Ruston 71272

† Loyola University
6363 St. Charles Ave., New Orleans 70118

† McNeese State University
4100 Ryan St., Lake Charles 70605

† New Orleans Baptist Theological Seminary
3939 Gentilly Blvd., New Orleans 70126
Dr. Landrum P. Leavell, II, President

† Nicholls State University
LA Hwy. 1, Thibodaux 70301

† Northeast Louisiana University
700 University Ave., Monroe 71209

† Northwestern State University
Natchitoches 71497

† Southeastern Louisiana University
P.O. Box 784, Hammond 70404

† Southern University A & M College
Baton Rouge 70813

Tulane University
6823 Saint Charles Ave., New Orleans 70118
Richard Whiteside, Dean of Admission

† University of New Orleans
New Orleans 70148
Mary Ann Bulla, Chrpsn.

† University of Southwestern Louisiana
P.O. Box 40069, Lafayette 70504
318-231-6219

† Xavier University
7325 Palmetto St., New Orleans 70125

MAINE

Bowdoin College, Brunswick 04011
William Mason, Dir. of Admis.

University of Maine
University Hts., Augusta 04330

† University of Maine, Orono 04469

† University of Southern Maine
96 Falmouth St., Portland 04103
Ronald Cole, Chrpsn.

MARYLAND

· † Essex Community College
7201 Rossville Blvd., Baltimore 21237
Diane Lane, Dir. of Admis.

· † Montgomery College
51 Mannakee St., Rockville 20850
301-279-7552

† Morgan State University
Cold Spring Ln. and Hillen Rd., Baltimore 21239

† Peabody Institute of The Johns Hopkins Univ.
Peabody Conservatory of Music
1 E. Mt. Vernon Place, Baltimore 21202
David Lane, Dir. of Admis.

† St. Mary's College of Maryland
St. Mary's City 20686

† Towson State University
800 York Rd., Towson 21204
Dr. Hoke Smith, President

† University of Maryland, College Park 20742

Washington Bible College
6511 Princess Garden Pkwy.
Lanham-Seabrook 20706

MASSACHUSETTS

† Anna Maria College
2 Sunset Ln., Paxton 01612
Dr. Bernadette Madore, SSA, President

† Atlantic Union College
P.O. Box 1000, South Lancaster 01561
Osa Canto, Registrar

Berklee College of Music
1140 Boylston St., Boston 02215
Steven Lipman, Dir. of Admis.

† Boston Conservatory
8 The Fenway, Boston 02215

† Boston University
685 Commonwealth Ave., Boston 02215

Bradford College
320 S. Main St., Bradford 01835

Brandeis University
415 South St, Waltham 02154
David Gould, Dean of Admissions
617-736-3500

DEAN COLLEGE
99 Main St, Franklin 02038
Kathleen Teehan, Dean of Admissions
508-528-9100
See listing under "Community and Junior Colleges"

Emmanuel College
400 The Fenway, Boston 02115
Margaret Bonilla, Dir. of Admis.

† Gordon College
255 Grapevine Rd., Wenham 01984

Hampshire College, Amherst 01002
Audrey Y. Smith, Dir. of Admissions
413-582-5471

† LONGY SCHOOL OF MUSIC
1 Follen St., Cambridge 02138
Victor Rosenbaum, Director
617-876-0956
Established 1915. Private. Coed. Tuition: $4,100-8,950. Room and board not provided. Enrollment (full-time & part-time): 25 undergraduate, 50 graduate, 950 non-degree. Faculty: 115, including members of the Boston Symphony Orchestra and international performers and teachers. Degrees: diploma, graduate diploma, artist diploma, Master of Music, Dalcroze Eurythmics License and certificate, BM with Emerson College (Boston), Master of Creative Arts in Learning with Lesley College (Cambridge). One building in Harvard Square; acclaimed 250-seat concert hall is site of over 250 concerts yearly. Flexible, individualized study in solo performance, chamber music, theory, solfege, composition, pedagogy, new music, early music, opera.

† New England Conservatory of Music
290 Huntington Ave., Boston 02115
Robert Annis, Dean of Enrollment Services

Simmons College
300 The Fenway, Boston 02115

† University of Massachusetts, Amherst 01003
Arlene Wesley Cash, Dir. of Admis.

University of Massachusetts Dartmouth
Old Westport Rd., North Dartmouth 02747
Raymond Barrows, Dir. of Admissions
508-999-8605

† University of Massachusetts Lowell
1 University Ave., Lowell 01854

Wellesley College, Wellesley 02181
Janet A. Lavin, Dir. of Admis.

Westfield State College
577 Western Ave., Westfield 01085
John F. Marcus, Dir. of Admis.

MICHIGAN

Adrian College
110 S. Madison St., Adrian 49221
George Wolf, Dir. of Admis.
See listing under "Universities"

† Albion College
611 E. Porter, Albion 49224
800-858-6770

† Alma College
614 W. Superior St., Alma 48801-1599
John Seveland, VP for Enrollment
800-321-ALMA
See listing under "Universities"

† Andrews University, Berrien Springs 49104
Jack Mentges, Dir. of Admis.

Aquinas College
1607 Robinson Rd., S.E., Grand Rapids 49506
Paula Meehan, Dean of Admissions
800-678-9593

† Calvin College
3201 Burton St., S.E., Grand Rapids 49546

† Center for Creative Studies
Institute of Music and Dance
201 E. Kirby St., Detroit 48202

† Central Michigan University
100 Warriner Hall, Mt. Pleasant 48858

Concordia College
4090 Geddes Rd., Ann Arbor 48105
Mary Froelich, Dir. of Admis.

† Eastern Michigan University, Ypsilanti 48197
James B. Hause, EdD, Head
313-487-3060 or 800-GO-TO-EMU

Grace Bible College
P.O. Box 910, Grand Rapids 49509
Linda K. Siler, Dir. of Admis.

· † Grand Rapids Community College
143 Bostwick Ave., N.E., Grand Rapids 49503
Dr. Madalyn Binger, Provost

† Grand Valley State University
1 Campus Dr., Allendale 49401
Julianne Vanden Wyngaard, Chrpsn.

HILLSDALE COLLEGE
33 E. College St., Hillsdale 49242
Dr. Eldred Thierstein, Director
517-437-7341

† Hope College
69 E. 10th St., Holland 49423
Gordon Van Wylen, President

: :† Interlochen Arts Academy
P.O. Box 199, Interlochen 49643
Tom Bewley, Dir. of Admis.

† Michigan State University, East Lansing 48824
Kenneth Bloomquist, Chrpsn.

† Northern Michigan University
610 Cohodas Admin. Center, Marquette 49855
Nancy Rehling, Dir. of Admis.

† Olivet College
300 S. Main St., Olivet 49076
Vicki Gallas, Registrar
See listing under "Universities"

† University of Michigan-Ann Arbor
815 S. University Ave., Ann Arbor 48109

† University of Michigan-Flint
303 Kearsley St., Flint 48502

† Wayne State University
5980 Cass Ave., Detroit 48202
Dr. J. R. Thorderson, Dir. of Admis.

† Western Michigan University, Kalamazoo 49008
Stanley Henderson, Dir. of Enrl. Mgt. & Admis.
616-387-2000

William Tyndale College
35700 W. Twelve Mile Rd.
Farmington Hills 48331

MINNESOTA

† Augsburg College
731 21st Ave., S., Minneapolis 55454

† Bemidji State University
1500 Birchmont Dr., N.E., Bemidji 56601
800-475-2001

Bethel College
3900 Bethel Dr., St. Paul 55112
Dr. George Brushaber, President

College of Saint Benedict
37 S. College Ave., St. Joseph 56374

† College of St. Catherine
2004 Randolph Ave., St. Paul 55105

College of St. Scholastica
1200 Kenwood Ave., Duluth 55811
Dr. Penny Schwarze, Chrpsn.
800-447-5444
See listing under "Liberal Arts"

† Concordia College
901 8th St. S., Moorhead 56562
Dr. David Childs, Chairperson
See listing under "Universities"

Concordia College-St. Paul
275 N. Syndicate, St. Paul 55104
Tim Utter, Dir. of Admis.

Crown College
6425 County Rd. 30, St. Bonifacius 55375
See listing under "Universities"

† Gustavus Adolphus College
800 W. College Ave., St. Peter 56082
Mark Anderson, Dir. of Admis.

† Hamline University
1536 Hewitt Ave., St. Paul 55104
Scott Pratt, Dir. of Admis.

† Mankato State University
P.O. Box 8400, Mankato 56002

† Moorhead State University
1104 7th Ave. S., Moorhead 56560

: Music Tech
304 Washington Ave. N., Minneapolis 55401
Douglas Smith, Director

North Central Bible College
910 Elliot Ave., Minneapolis 55404
800-289-NCBC
Dan Neary, Dir. of Admis.
See listing under "Universities"

† Northwestern College
3003 Snelling Ave., N., St. Paul 55113
Ralph Anderson, Dean of Admissions
800-827-6827 or 612-631-5111

PILLSBURY BAPTIST BIBLE COLLEGE
315 S. Grove St., Owatonna 55060
Alan Potter, President
Larry Tindall, Director of Admissions
800-747-4557

† St. Cloud State University
740 4th Ave., S., St. Cloud 56301
Sherwood Reid, Dir. of Admis.
800-369-4260

St. John's University
P.O. Box 7155, Collegeville 56321

St. Mary's College of Minnesota
700 Terrace Heights #2, Winona 55987
Tony Piscitiello, VP for Admission

† St. Olaf College, Northfield 55057
Carolyn Jennings, Chrpsn.
507-646-3180

† Southwest State University, Marshall 56258

† University of Minnesota
2400 Oakland Ave., Duluth 55812
Robert L. Heller, Provost

† University of Minnesota, Twin Cities
Minneapolis 55455

† University of St. Thomas
2115 Summit Ave., St. Paul 55105

† Winona State University
P.O. Box 5838, Winona 55987
Dr. J. Mootz, Dir. of Admis.

MISSISSIPPI

† Alcorn State University
P.O. Box 359, Lorman 39096
D. W. Wilburn, Registrar

† Belhaven College
1500 Peachtree St., Jackson 39202

† Delta State University
Hwy. 8 W., Cleveland 38732

† Jackson State University
1400 Lynch St., Jackson 39203

† Mississippi College
P.O. Box 4086, Clinton 39058

† Mississippi State University
P.O. Box J, Mississippi State University 39762

† Mississippi University for Women
P.O. Box W-1602, Columbus 39701
Teresa Thompson, Exec. Dir. of Enrollment

† University of Mississippi, University 38677

† University of Southern Mississippi
P.O. Box 5165, Hattiesburg 39406

† William Carey College
498 Tuscan Ave., Hattiesburg 39401

MISSOURI

Avila College
11901 Wornall Rd., Kansas City 64145

Calvary Bible College
15800 Calvary Rd., Kansas City 64147
J. Robert Brundage, Dir. of Admis.

† Central Methodist College
411 CMC Square, Fayette 65248
See listing under "Universities"

† Central Missouri State University
Warrensburg 64093
Delores Hudson, Dir. of Admis.

† College of the Ozarks, Point Lookout 65726
Dr. Kenton Olson, Dean of the College

· Cottey College
1000 W. Austin St., Nevada 64772
Wendy Beckemeyer, Dir. of Admis.

† Evangel College
1111 N. Glenstone Ave., Springfield 65802
David Schoolfield, Dir. of Enrollment

Fontbonne College
6800 Wydown Blvd., St. Louis 63105
Peggy Musen, Dir. of Admis.

· Jefferson College
1000 Viking Dr., Hillsboro 63050
Dr. Gery Hochanadel, President

† Lincoln University
820 Chestnut St., Jefferson City 65101

Maryville University of St. Louis
13550 Conway Rd., Saint Louis 63141
314-576-9300 or 800-MARYVLL

Missouri Baptist College
12542 Conway Rd., St. Louis 63141

Missouri Southern State College
3950 Newman Rd., Joplin 64801-1595
Pete Havely, Dept. Head
See listing under "Universities"

† Missouri Western State College
4525 Downs Dr., St. Joseph 64507
Howard McCauley, Dir. of Admis.

† Northeast Missouri State University
Kirksville 63501

† Northwest Missouri State University
800 University Dr., Maryville 64468

Park College, Parkville 64152
Dr. Edwin Rawn, Dean of Admis.

† St. Louis Conservatory of Music
560 Trinity Ave., Saint Louis 63130
Clifford Menz, President

† Southeast Missouri State University
1 University Plz., Cape Girardeau 63701
New Student Relations 314-651-2590
See listing under "Universities"

† Southwest Baptist University
1601 S. Springfield Ave., Bolivar 65613

† Southwest Missouri State University
901 S. National Ave., Springfield 65804
Dr. Mollie Molnar, Acting Department Head
417-836-5648

Stephens College, Columbia 65215
Mary Ann Sprinkle, Dir. of Admis.

† University of Missouri, Columbia
228 Jesse Hall, Columbia 65211

† University of Missouri, Kansas City
5100 Rockhill Rd., Kansas City 64110
Leo J. Sweeney, Dir. of Admis. & Registrar

† University of Missouri
  8001 Natural Bridge Rd., St. Louis 63121
  Mimi LaMarca, Dir. of Admis.

Washington University
  1 Brookings Dr., St. Louis 63130

† WEBSTER UNIVERSITY

470 E. Lockwood Ave., Saint Louis 63119
Niel DeVasto, Director of Admissions
800-753-6765
  Established 1915. Private. Coed. Accreditation:
NCACS. Tuition: $9,160. Room and board: $4,340.
Enrollment: 1300 full-time, 1500 part-time. Faculty:
110, Student-faculty ratio: 13:1. Degrees: BA, BFA,
BM, BMEd, BS, BSN, MA, MBA, MAT, DMGT. Library: 230,000 volumes. 22 buildings on 45 acres.
Nationally recognized programs in the performing
arts and communications. Students from 35 states
and 30 countries. Beautiful suburban campus in a
wooded community of 20,000. Average class size of
15. New $5.5 million Student Center. Campuses in
four European countries.

† William Jewell College, Liberty 64068
  T. Edwin Norris, Dir of Admis.
  800-753-7009

William Woods College
  200 W. 12th St., Fulton 65251
  Dr. Jahnae Barnett, VP of Admis.

MONTANA

College of Great Falls
  1301 20th St., S., Great Falls 59405
  Jean Walker, Dir. of Admis.

† Montana State University, Bozeman 59717

† Montana State University - Billings
  1500 N. 30th St., Billings 59101
  Karen Everett, Dir. of Admis.
  406-657-2158

Rocky Mountain College
  1511 Poly Dr., Billings 59102
  David Heringer, Dir. of Admis.
  See listing under "Universities"

† University of Montana, Missoula 59812
  800-462-8636

NEBRASKA

Chadron State College
  1000 Main St., Chadron 69337
  Dr. Donald Green, Dean

Concordia College
  800 N. Columbia Ave., Seward 68434
  Don Vos, Dir. of Admis.

Dana College
  2848 College Dr., Blair 68008
  John Schueth, Dir. of Admis.
  800-444-3262
  See listing under "Universities"

† Hastings College
  P.O. Box 269, Hastings 68902
  Thomas Reeves, President

† Nebraska Wesleyan University
  5000 Saint Paul Ave., Lincoln 68504
  Ken Sieg, Dir. of Admis.

Peru State College, Peru 68421
  Pamela J. Cosgrove, Dir. of Admis.
  402-872-3815

Union College
  3800 S. 48th St., Lincoln 68506

† University of Nebraska
  905 W. 25th St., Kearney 68849

† University of Nebraska at Lincoln
  Old H 1223, Lincoln 68588
  John Peters, Dean

† University of Nebraska at Omaha
  Omaha 68182

NEVADA

Sierra Nevada College-Lake Tahoe
  P.O. Box 4269, Incline Village 89450
  Lane Murray, Dir. of Admissions
  See listing under "Universities"

† University of Nevada, Reno
  Reno 89557

† University of Nevada Las Vegas
  4505 S. Maryland Pky., Las Vegas 89154-1021
  Admissions: 702-895-3443 or 800-334-UNLV

NEW HAMPSHIRE

† Keene State College
  229 Main St., Keene 03435
  Kathryn Dodge, Dir. of Admis.

† University of New Hampshire, Durham 03824
  Stanwood C. Fish, Dir. of Admissions

NEW JERSEY

Caldwell College
  9 Ryerson Ave., Caldwell 07006

Georgian Court College
  900 Lakewood Ave., Lakewood 08701
  908-364-2200 Ext. 621

† Jersey City State College
  2039 Kennedy Blvd., Jersey City 07305
  201-200-3234

† Kean College of New Jersey
  1000 Morris Ave., Union 07083

† Montclair State College
  1 Normal Ave., Upper Montclair 07043

Princeton University, Princeton 08544

Rider University
  2083 Lawrenceville Rd., Lawrenceville 08648
  Susan Christian, Dir. of Admis.

† Rowan College of New Jersey, Glassboro 08028
  Marvin G. Sills, Dir. of Admis.

† Rutgers, The State University of NJ
  Douglass College
  New Brunswick 08903

Rutgers, The State University of NJ
  Mason Gross School of the Arts
  New Brunswick 08903

Stockton State College, Pomona 08240
  Sal Catalfamo, Dir. of Admis.

† Trenton State College
  Hillwood Lakes CN 4700, Trenton 08650

Upsala College
  345 Prospect St., East Orange 07017
  George Lynes, Dean of Admissions

† WESTMINSTER CHOIR COLLEGE OF RIDER UNIVERSITY

101 Walnut Ln., Princeton 08540-3899
Robert Annis, Dean
J. Barton Luedeke, President
Anne Farmer Meservey, Director of Admissions
800-96-CHOIR or 609-921-7100, FAX: 609-921-8829
  Westminster is an independent, coeducational college accredited by NASM, the National Association
of Schools of Music and the Middle States Association of Colleges.
  The student body is 220 undergraduates, 90 graduates and 30 special students. Tuition is $13,250. Total
cost with room, board, and other fees is $19,405. 85%
of students receive financial aid as scholarships,
grants, loans, and work study. Three modern residence halls house undergraduates. Rooms are available for unmarried graduate students.
  Westminster has a 7:1 student/faculty ratio. Faculty
teach all undergraduate and graduate courses; no
teaching assistants teach courses. The faculty are
accomplished performers, researchers, and scholars,
80% of whom have Ph.D. or other terminal degree.
  Westminster, located on a 23 acre campus in Princeton, NJ, has 4 performance halls. Instruments include
over 120 pianos and 21 pipe organs, including recital
organs by Aeolian-Skinner and Casavant. Teaching
resources include a Music Theory Computing Laboratory, a Voice Resource Center providing physiological and acoustic analysis of singing, and an academic
computing center.
  Westminster Choir College grants the Bachelor of
Music degree in Church Music, Music Education,
Organ, Piano, Voice Performance, Piano Pedagogy,
Piano Accompanying, and Theory and Composition.
The BA in Music has concentrations in voice, piano,
psychology/sociology, religion/philosophy, thea-
tre/literature, and arts administration. The Master of
Music is granted in Choral Conducting, Church Music, Composition, Music Education, Organ Performance, Piano Performance, Piano Pedagogy and
Performance, Voice Pedagogy and Performance. Piano Accompanying and Coaching.
  Westminster integrates music study with professional performance. All students sing with major
symphony orchestras. Princeton, 40 miles from New
York City and Philadelphia, offers rich culture. Students may study at Princeton University and use its
athletic and recreational facilities, as well as Rider's.
  Westminster admits students in the Fall and Spring
semesters on a rolling admissions basis. Auditions
and Basic Musicianship Evaluation are required for
Admission. Students are encouraged to come to the
campus for the audition and Basic Musicianship
Evaluation. In Addition, SAT or ACT scores, high
school transcripts, and three letters of recommendation are required. Call the Office of Admissions at
1-800-96-CHOIR for more information.

† William Paterson College
  300 Pompton Rd., Wayne 07470

NEW MEXICO

† Eastern New Mexico University
  Portales 88130
  Larry Fuqua, Dir. of Admis.

New Mexico Highlands University, Las Vegas 87701
  Dr. Jorge P. Thomas, VP Academic Affairs

† New Mexico State University
  P.O. Box 30001, Las Cruces 88003

† University of New Mexico, Albuquerque 87131
  Robert Weaver, Dean of Admissions

NEW YORK

Adelphi University, Garden City 11530
  Dr. Elliot Pruzan, Asst. Provost & Dir. of Admis.
  516-877-3050

Columbia University
  612 W. 115th St., New York 10025

: † David Hochstein Memorial Music School
  50 Plymouth Ave. N., Rochester 14614
  Margaret Quackenbush, Director

† Eastman School of Music
  26 Gibbs St., Rochester 14604
  Charles Krusenstjerna, Dir. of Admis.

· FIVE TOWNS COLLEGE

305 N. Service Rd., Dix Hills 11746
Jennifer Roemer, Coordinator of Admissions
516-424-7000
See listing under "Universities"

† Hartwick College, Oneonta 13820

Hebrew Union College
  Jewish Institute of Religion
  1 W. 4th St., New York 10012
  Rabbi Gary Zola, National Dean of Admissions

† Houghton College
  P.O. Box 128, Houghton 14744
  Tim Fuller, Dir. of Admis.

† Ithaca College
  953 Danby Rd., Ithaca 14850

Juilliard School
  60 Lincoln Center Plz., New York 10023
  Carole Everett, Dir of Admis.

The King's College, Briarcliff Manor 10510
  Frederic Rowley, Dean of Admissions

Long Island University-C. W. Post Campus
  Rt. 25A, Brookville 11548
  Prof. Walter Klauss, Chrpsn.
  516-299-2474

Manhattan School of Music
  120 Claremont Ave., New York 10027
  James Gandre, Dir. of Admis.

† Manhattanville College
  2900 Purchase St., Purchase 10577

Mannes College of Music
  150 W. 85th St., New York 10024
  Marilyn Groves, Dir. of Admis.

Mercy College
  555 Broadway, Dobbs Ferry 10522
  James Nesbitt, Dean of Admissions

Molloy College
  1000 Hempstead Ave., Rockville Centre 11570
  Wayne James, Dir. of Admis.
  See listing under "Universities"

† Nazareth College of Rochester
  4245 East Ave., Rochester 14618
  Paul Kenyon, Dir. of Admis.

New York University
  70 Washington Sq., New York 10012

† Nyack College, Nyack 10960
  Miguel Sanchez, Dir. of Admis.
  800-33-NYACK

† Roberts Wesleyan College
  2301 Westside Dr., Rochester 14624
  Dr. Robert Shewan, Chrpsn.
  See listing under "Universities"

Skidmore College, Saratoga Springs 12866
  Kent Jones, Dir. of Admis.

· SUNY Adirondack Community College
  439 Bay Rd., Queensbury 12804
  Levi Brown, Dir. of Admis.
  518-793-4491
  See listing under "Community and Junior
  Colleges"

SUNY at Buffalo
  17 Capen Hall
  P.O. Box 601660, Buffalo 14260-1660
  716-645-6900

† SUNY College at Buffalo
  1300 Elmwood Ave., Buffalo 14222
  Deborah K. Renzi, Dir. of Admis.

† SUNY College at Fredonia, Fredonia 14063
  William S. Clark, III, Dir. of Admissions

† SUNY College at New Paltz
  75 Manheim Blvd., New Paltz 12561

† SUNY at Oswego, Oswego 13126
  Dr. Joseph Grant, Jr., Dean of Admissions
  315-341-2250

† SUNY College at Potsdam
  Potsdam 13676
  Marc Davis, Dir. of Admis.

· SUNY Nassau Community College
  1 Education Dr., Garden City 11530
  Bernard Iantosca, Dir of Admis.

· SUNY Onondaga Community College
  Onondaga Rd., Syracuse 13215
  Joseph Insel, Dir. of Admis.

· SUNY Schenectady County Community College
  78 Washington Ave., Schenectady 12305
  Robert Dinello, Dir. of Admis.
  518-346-6211, ext. 166

† Syracuse University, Syracuse 13244

University of Rochester
  Eastman School of Music
  26 Gibbs St., Rochester 14604
  Robert Freeman, Director
  See listing under "Universities"

· Villa Maria College of Buffalo
  240 Pine Ridge Rd., Buffalo 14225
  Lynn D'Auria, Dir. of Admis.

: † Westchester Conservatory of Music
  20 Soundview Ave., White Plains 10606

NORTH CAROLINA

† Appalachian State University
ASU Station, Boone 28608
Joe Watts, Admissions Officer

Barton College
College Station, Wilson 27893
Anthony Britt, Dir. of Admis.
800-345-4973/919-399-6318
See listing under "Universities"

· † Brevard College
Brevard 28712
Bob McLendon, Dean of Admissions

Catawba College
2300 W. Innes St., Salisbury 28144
Mark Stokes, Dir. of Admis.

· College of The Albemarle
P.O. Box 2327, Elizabeth City 27906
John M. Wells, Asst. Dean of Admissions
919-335-0821, Ext. 220

† East Carolina University
1000 E. 5th St., Greenville 27858
Dr. Malcohn Tait, Dean

Elon College
P.O. Box 2700, Elon College 27244
Nan P. Perkins, Dean of Admissions

† Gardner-Webb University
General Delivery, Boiling Springs 28017
George Cribb, Chrpsn.
704-434-2361

Greensboro College
815 W. Market St., Greensboro 27401

† Mars Hill College
Main St., Mars Hill 28754
Dr. Smith Goodrum, Dean of Admis.

† Meredith College
3800 Hillsborough St., Raleigh 27607

Methodist College
5400 Ramsey St., Fayetteville 28311
Fiore Bergamasco, Dir. of Admis.

† North Carolina A&T State University
1601 E. Market St., Greensboro 27411

· Peace College
15 E. Peace St., Raleigh 27604
Dr. Garrett Briggs, President
919-832-2881, Fax: 919-834-6755

Pembroke State University
P.O. Box 1510, Pembroke 28372
Anthony Locklear, Dir. of Admissions
919-521-6262

† Pfeiffer College
General Delivery, Misenheimer 28109

† QUEENS COLLEGE
1900 Selwyn Ave., Charlotte 28274
D. Stephen Cloniger, VP for Enrollment Management
See listing under "Liberal Arts"

† Salem College
P.O. Box 10548, Winston-Salem 27108
Katherine Knapp, Director of Admissions
800-32-SALEM
See listing under "Women's College"

· Sandhills Community College
2200 Airport Rd., Pinehurst 28374
910-692-6185

† University of North Carolina
1000 Spring Garden St., Greensboro 27412

† University of North Carolina
601 S. College Rd., Wilmington 28403
W. H. Wagoner, Chancellor

† Western Carolina University
Cullowhee 28723
Tyree H. Kiser, Dir. of Admissions

† Wingate College, Wingate 28174

† Winston-Salem State University
601 S. Martin Luther King Jr.
Winston-Salem 27110
Van Wilson, Dir. of Admissions

NORTH DAKOTA

† Minot State University
500 University Ave. W., Minot 58701

† North Dakota State University, Fargo 58105
Richard Shearer, Acting Dir. of Admis.

:: OAK GROVE LUTHERAN HIGH SCHOOL
124 N. Terrace, Fargo 58102
Denise Brewster, Director of Admissions
See listing under "Preparatory Schools-Coed"

University of Mary
7500 University Dr., Bismarck 58504
Steph Storey, Dir. of Admis.

† University of North Dakota
Box 8193 University Station, Grand Forks 58203

OHIO

† Ashland University
401 College Ave., Ashland 44805

† Baldwin-Wallace College
275 Eastland Rd., Berea 44017
Juliann K. Baker, Dir. of Admis.

Bluffton College
College Ave., Bluffton 45817

† Bowling Green State University
Bowling Green 43403
John Martin, Dir. of Admis.

† Capital University
2199 E. Main St., Columbus 43209
Dolphus E. Henry, Associate Provost

† Case Western Reserve University
2040 Adelbert Rd., Cleveland 44106

† Central State University
1400 Brush Row Rd., Wilberforce 45384

Cincinnati Bible College
P.O. Box 04320, Cincinnati 45204
C. Barry McCarty, President

† Cleveland Institute of Music
11021 East Blvd., Cleveland 44106
William Fay, Director of Admission
216-795-3107

† Cleveland State University
Euclid Ave. at 24th St., Cleveland 44115

† College of Mount St. Joseph
5701 Delhi Rd., Cincinnati 45233-1672
See listing under "Universities"

† College of Wooster
1189 Beall Ave., Wooster 44691
Hayden Schilling, Dean of Admis.

Denison University
P.O. Box B, Granville 43023
Richard Boyden, Dir. of Admis.

† Heidelberg College
310 E. Market St., Tiffin 44883
Stephen E. Eidson, Dean of Admission
800-925-9250

† Hiram College
P.O. Box 96, Hiram 44234
Gary Craig, Dean of Admis.

† Kent State University
P.O. Box 5190, Kent 44242
Bruce Riddle, Dir. of Admis.

Malone College
515 25th St., N.W., Canton 44709
Lee Sommers, Dean of Admissions

MARIETTA COLLEGE
210 5th St., Marietta 45750
Dennis R. DePerro, Dean Admis./Financial Aid
800-331-7896

† Miami University
E. High St., Oxford 45056

† Mount Union College
1972 Clark Ave., Alliance 44601
Amy Tomko, Dir. of Admis.

Mt. Vernon Nazarene College
800 Martinsburg Rd., Mt. Vernon 43050
Ronald Hyson, Dir. of Admis.

† Muskingum College
147 Center St., New Concord 43762

† Oberlin College
135 W. Lorain St., Oberlin 44074
Karen Wolff, Dean

OHIO NORTHERN UNIVERSITY
525 S. Main St., Ada 45810
Dr. Edwin Williams, Chrpsn.
412-772-2000

† Ohio State University
190 N. Oval Mall, Columbus 43210

† Ohio University, Athens 45701

† Ohio Wesleyan University
61 S. Sandusky St., Delaware 43015
Donald Bishop, Dean for Enrollment

† Otterbein College, Westerville 43081

† University of Akron
381 Buchtel Common, Akron 44325
Kris MacDermott, Asst. Provost Enrollment

† University of Cincinnati
2700 Clifton Ave., Cincinnati 45221

† University of Dayton
300 College Park Ave., Dayton 45469-0290
Toll-free 800-837-7433
See listing under "Universities"

University of Rio Grande
General Delivery, Rio Grande 45674
Dr. Merv Murdock, Assoc. Professor
614-245-5353, Ext. 7405

† University of Toledo
2801 Bancroft St., W., Toledo 43606
Richard Eastop, Dir. of Admis.

† Wittenberg University
P.O. Box 720, Springfield 45504

† Wright State University
3640 Colonel Glenn Hwy., Dayton 45435

† Youngstown State University
410 Wick Ave., Youngstown 44555
Leslie H. Cochran, President

OKLAHOMA

† Cameron University
2800 W. Gore Blvd., Lawton 73505
Louise Brown, Dir. of Admis.

Mid-America Bible College
3500 S.W. 119th St., Oklahoma City 73170
Tony O'Brien, Registrar
405-691-3800

Northeastern State University
600 N. Grand Ave., Tahlequah 74464

† Oklahoma Baptist University
500 W. University St., Shawnee 74801

Oklahoma Christian University of Science and Arts
P.O. Box 11000, Oklahoma City 73136
Duane Eggleston, Vice President
800-877-5010

† Oklahoma City University
2501 N. Blackwelder Ave., Oklahoma City 73106
Cheryl Zrnic, Dean
See listing under "Universities"

Oklahoma Panhandle State University
P.O. Box 430, Goodwell 73939

† Oklahoma State University, Stillwater 74078
William Ballenger, Dept. Head

† Oral Roberts University
7777 S. Lewis Ave., Tulsa 74171
Arthur E. Matzkvech, Dir. of Admis.

† Phillips University
100 S University Ave., Enid 73701
Lois A. Bender, VP/Enrollment Management
800-238-1185

† Southeastern Oklahoma State University
Station A, Durant 74701

† Southwestern Oklahoma State University
100 Campus Dr., Weatherford 73096

University of Central Oklahoma
100 N. University Dr., Edmond 73034

† University of Oklahoma at Norman
660 Parrington Oval, Norman 73019

† University of Sciences & Arts of Oklahoma
P.O. Box 82345, Chickasha 73018

† University of Tulsa
600 S. College Ave., Tulsa 74104
Dr. Ron Predl, Director

OREGON

EUGENE BIBLE COLLEGE
2155 Bailey Hill Rd., Eugene 97405
Trent Combs, Dir. of Admis.
800-322-2638

† George Fox College
414 N. Meridian St., Newberg 97132

† Lewis & Clark College
0615 S.W. Palatine Hill Rd., Portland 97219
Michael Sexton, Dean of Admissions

† Linfield College
900 S. Baker St., McMinnville 97128
Thomas Meicho, Dean of Admissions

† Marylhurst College for Lifelong Learning
P.O. Box 261, Marylhurst 97036
David Deason, Chrpsn.
800-634-9984

† Oregon State University, Corvallis 97333
Wallace Gibbs, Dir. of Admis.

† Pacific University
2043 College Way, Forest Grove 97116
Barbara Mergen, Dir. of Admis.

† Portland State University
P.O. Box 751, Portland 97207

Reed College
3202 S.E. Woodstock Blvd., Portland 97202

† Southern Oregon State College
1250 Siskiyou Blvd., Ashland 97520

† University of Oregon
1 University of Oregon, Eugene 97403

Western Baptist College, Salem 97301
800-845-3005

† Western Oregon State College
345 Monmouth Ave., N., Monmouth 97361
Craig A. Kolins, Dir. of Admis.
503-838-8211

† Willamette University
900 State St. S.E., Salem 97301

PENNSYLVANIA

Allegheny College
520 N. Main St., Meadville 16335
Gayle Pollack, Dir. of Admis.

Bloomsburg University, Bloomsburg 17815
Bernard Vinovrski, Dir. of Admis.

† Bucknell University, Lewisburg 17837

· Bucks County Community College
Swamp Rd., Newtown 18940

† Carnegie Mellon University
5000 Forbes Ave., Pittsburgh 15213

Cedar Crest College
100 College Dr., Allentown 18104-6196
Cynthia Phillips, Dir. of Admissions

Chatham College
Woodland Rd., Pittsburgh 15232
Suellen Ofe, Dean of Admis./Financial Aid
See listing under "Women's College"

† Curtis Institute of Music
1726 Locust St., Philadelphia 19103
Judi Gattone, Admissions

Drexel University
3141 Chestnut St., Philadelphia 19104
Dean of Enrollment Management

† Duquesne University
600 Forbes Ave., Pittsburgh 15282
Thomas Schaefer, C.S.Sp., Dir. of Admis.

Eastern College
10 Fairview Dr., Saint Davids 19087
Ronald Keller, VP for Enrollment Management

Edinboro University of Pennsylvania
Edinboro 16444
Admissions Office: 800-626-2203

† Elizabethtown College
1 Alpha Dr., Elizabethtown 17022

Geneva College
3200 College Ave., Beaver Falls 15010

Grove City College
100 Campus Dr., Grove City 16127
Dr. Edwin Arnold, Chrpsn.

† Immaculata College
Immaculata 19345
James P. Sullivan, Dir. of Admis.

† Indiana University of Pennsylvania, Indiana 15705
Fred Dadak, Dean, Admissions

Lafayette College, Easton 18042
G. Gary Ripple, Dir. of Admis.
610-250-5100

† Lebanon Valley College
101 N. College Ave., Annville 17003

† Mansfield University of Pennsylvania
Mansfield 16933

† Marywood College
2300 Adams Ave., Scranton 18509

Mercyhurst College
501 E. 38th St., Erie 16546
Andrew Roth, Dean of Enrollment
800-825-1926

† Messiah College
General Delivery, Grantham 17027
Ron Long, Dir. of Admis.

† Millersville University of Pennsylvania
Millersville 17551
Blair Treasure, Dean of Admissions

Muhlenberg College
2400 W. Chew St., Allentown 18104
Chris Hooker-Haring, Dir. of Admis.

† Pennsylvania State University
201 Shields Bldg., University Park 16802

† Philadelphia College of Bible
BMus Degree
200 Manor Ave., Langhorne 19047-2990
Al Lunde, Chrpsn.
800-366-0049

† Seton Hill College, Greensburg 15601
Peter Egan, Dir. of Admis.
800-826-6234 or 412-838-4255

: † Settlement Music School
416 Queen St., Philadelphia 19147
Robert Capanna, Director

† Slippery Rock University, Slippery Rock 16057
Director of Admissions

† Susquehanna University
514 University Ave., Selinsgrove 17870

† Temple University
Broad St. & Montgomery Ave.
Philadelphia 19122

† University of the Arts
320 S. Broad St., Philadelphia 19102
Margaret Heuges, Dir. of Admis.

† West Chester University of Pennsylvania
S. High St., West Chester 19380

†WESTMINSTER COLLEGE
New Wilmington 16172
Richard Dana Paul, Dir. of Admis.
412-946-7100

Wilkes University
184 S. River St., Wilkes-Barre 18766
Emory P. Guffrovich Jr., Dean of Admissions

York College of Pennsylvania
P.O. Box 15199, York 17405-7199
Nancy Sparato, Dir. of Admis.
717-849-1600
See listing under "Universities"

RHODE ISLAND

† Rhode Island College
600 Mt. Pleasant Ave., Providence 02908

Salve Regina University
1 Ochre Point Ave., Newport 02840
Roselina McKillop, Dean of Admissions

† University of Rhode Island, Kingston 02881
Kenneth Keeling, Sr., Chrpsn.

SOUTH CAROLINA

† Anderson College
316 S. Boulevard, Anderson 29621
Carl D. Lockman, Dir. of Admis.
800-542-3594

† Charleston Southern University
P.O. Box 10087, Charleston 29411
Melinda Mitchum, Dir. of Admis.

† Coker College
300 E. College Ave., Hartsville 29550

† Columbia College
1301 Columbia College Dr., Columbia 29203

Columbia International University
P.O. Box 3122, Columbia 29230
Frank Bedell, Dir. of Admis.
See listing under "Biblical Studies"

† Converse College
580 E. Main St., Spartanburg 29302
Dr. Martha Rogers, VP Enrollment Management

Erskine College & Seminary
Washington St., Due West 29639
Dot Carter, Dir. of Admis.

† Furman University
3300 Poinsett Hwy., Greenville 29613
Charles Brock, Dir. of Admis.

Lander College
320 Stanley Ave., Greenwood 29649

† Limestone College
1115 College Dr., Gaffney 29340
Peter Wood, Dir. of Admis.

† Newberry College
2100 College St., Newberry 29108
Dr. John Wagner, Chrpsn.

North Greenville College
P.O. Box 1892, Tigerville 29688
Gary Wells, Dir. of Admis.
See listing under "Universities"

South Carolina State University
P.O. Box 7127, Orangeburg 29117-0001
803-536-7185

† University of South Carolina, Columbia 29208
Terry Davis, Dir. of Admis.
803-777-7700

† Winthrop University
701 W. Oakland Ave., Rock Hill 29733
James McCammon, Jr., Dir. of Admis.

SOUTH DAKOTA

† Augustana College
29th & S. Summit, Sioux Falls 57197

† Black Hills State University
1200 University St., Spearfish 57799
April Meeker, Dir. of Admis.

Dakota State University
820 N. Washington Ave., Madison 57042
Dr. Eric Johnson, Dean
605-256-5139

† Northern State University
1200 S. Jay St., Aberdeen 57401

SIOUX FALLS COLLEGE
1501 S. Prairie Ave., Sioux Falls 57105
Susan Reese, Dir. of Admis.
800-888-1047
See listing under "Universities"

† South Dakota State University
P.O. Box 2212, Brookings 57007
Dr. Corliss Johnson, Head
605-688-5215
See listing under "Universities"

† University of South Dakota
414 E. Clark St., Vermillion 57069
Dave Lorenz, Dir. of Admis.

TENNESSEE

† Austin Peay State University
601 College St., Clarksville 37044

† Belmont College
1900 Belmont Blvd., Nashville 37212

† Blair School of Music of Vanderbilt University
2400 Blakemore Ave., Nashville 37212
Assistant Dean for Admissions
615-322-7651

Bryan College
Box 7000, Dayton 37321
Thomas A. Shaw, Dir. of Admis.

† Carson-Newman College
P.O. Box 70552, Jefferson City 37760
See listing under "Universities"

David Lipscomb University
3901 Granny White Pike, Nashville 37204-3951
Wade Sandrell, Dir. of Admis.
800-333-4358

EAST TENNESSEE STATE UNIVERSITY
P.O. Box 70731, Johnson City 37614
Dr. Nancy Dishner, Dean, Enrollment Management
615-929-4213 or 800-462-3878

† Fisk University
1000 17th Ave., N., Nashville 37208

† Maryville College
800 S. Court St., Maryville 37801
Annabelle J. Libby, Dir. of Admis.

† Middle Tennessee State University
Murfreesboro 37132
Roger D. Sims, Dir. of Admis.

† Rhodes College
2000 N. Parkway, Memphis 38112

† Southern Missionary College
P.O. Box 370, Collegedale 37315

† Tennessee State University
3500 John A. Merritt Blvd., Nashville 37209

† Tennessee Technological University
P.O. Box 5006, Cookeville 38505

† Trevecca Nazarene College
333 Murfreesboro Rd., Nashville 37210

Tusculum College
P.O. Box 5035, Greeneville 37743
Ronald Porter, Dir. of Admis.

† Union University
2447 US Highway 45 Bypass, Jackson 38305
Max Pugh, Chrpsn.
901-668-1818
See listing under "Universities"

† University of Memphis, Memphis 38152
Dr. John Eubank, Dean of Admissions

† University of Tennessee at Martin
Martin 38238
Paul Kelley, Director of Admissions
See listing under "Universities"

† University of Tennessee at Chattanooga
615 McCallie Ave., Chattanooga 37403

† University of Tennessee, Knoxville
527 Andy Holt Tower, Knoxville 37996
Dr. Gordon Stanley, Dir. of Admis.

TEXAS

† Abilene Christian University
ACU Station, Box 6000, Abilene 79699

· Amarillo College
P.O. Box 447, Amarillo 79178
Dale Hardgrove, Registrar

† Angelo State University
2601 W. Ave., N., San Angelo 76909

· The Art Institute of Houston
1900 Yorktown St., Houston 77056
Cherie R. McNeel, Dir. of Admis.
800-275-4244

Austin College
900 N. Grand Ave., Sherman 75090
Rodney Oto, Dean of Admission
800-442-5363

† Baylor University
P.O. Box 97008, Waco 76798-7008
Diana Ramey, Director of Admissions

Concordia Lutheran College
3400 N. Interstate 35, Austin 78705
Kevin Pieper, Dir. of Admis.

† Corpus Christi State University
6300 Ocean Dr., Corpus Christi 78412

· Del Mar College
101 Baldwin Blvd., Corpus Christi 78404
Lawrence Jasman, Registrar

† East Texas Baptist University
1200 N. Grove Ave., Marshall 75670

† East Texas State University
ETSU Station, Commerce 75429

† Hardin-Simmons University
2200 Hickory St., Abilene 79698
Laura Moore, Dir. of Admis.
See listing under "Universities"

† Howard Payne University
1000 Fisk Ave., Brownwood 76801

Incarnate Word College
4301 Broadway St., San Antonio 78209
Sr. Sally Mitchell, Dean of Enrollment

† Lamar University
P.O. Box 10009, Beaumont 77710
800-458-7558

† Midwestern State University
3400 Taft Blvd., Wichita Falls 76308
Ronald Hough, Head

· † Odessa College
201 W. University, Odessa 79764

Rice University
P.O. Box 1892, Houston 77251

† St. Mary's University of San Antonio
1 Camino Santa Maria, San Antonio 78228
Rick Castillo, Dir. of Admis.

† Sam Houston State University, Huntsville 77341

† Southern Methodist University
Hillcrest at University, Dallas 75275

† Southwestern Baptist Theological Seminary
2001 W. Seminary Dr., Fort Worth 76122

† Southwestern University
University Ave. at Maple St., Georgetown 78626

† Southwest Texas State University
601 University Dr., San Marcos 78666

† Stephen F. Austin State University
P.O. Box 6078. Nacogdoches 75962

† Tarleton State University
1297 W. Washington St., Stephenville 76402

· † Temple Junior College
2600 S. 1st St., Temple 76504

† Texas A & I University
Campus Box 101, Kingsville 78363

† Texas Christian University
2800 S. University Dr., Ft. Worth 76129
Dr. Edward Boehm, Jr., Dean of Admissions

Texas Lutheran College
1000 W. Court St., Seguin 78155
Jennifer B. Ehlers, Dir. of Admis.

† Texas Tech University, Lubbock 79409

† Texas Wesleyan University
1201 Wesleyan St., Fort Worth 76105
Kim Campbell, Dir. Freshman Admission

† Texas Women's University
P.O. Box 23925, Denton 76204

† Trinity University
715 Stadium Dr., San Antonio 78212

† University of Houston
4800 Calhoun Rd., Houston 77204

† University of North Texas
P.O. Box 13797, Denton 76203

University of St. Thomas
3812 Montrose Blvd., Houston 77006
Elsie Biron, Dir. of Admis.

† University of Texas at Arlington
UTA Box 19125, Arlington 76019
R. Zack Prince, Dir. of Admis.

† University of Texas at Austin
0 the University of Texas, Austin 78712

† University of Texas at El Paso
500 W. University Ave., El Paso 79968

† University of Texas at San Antonio
San Antonio 78285
Donald Hodges, Acting Director

† West Texas State University
2501 4th Ave., Canyon 79016
Lila Vars, Dir. of Admis.

UTAH

† Brigham Young University, Provo 84602

† Southern Utah University
351 W. Center St., Cedar City 84720
J. Barton Shanklin, Chrpsn.
801-586-0619

† University of Utah
1400 E. 200 S., Salt Lake City 84112
Dr. J. Stayner Landward, Dir. of Admis.

† Utah State University, Logan 84322-1600
Rod Clark, Director of Admissions
801-750-1107

† Weber State University
3750 Harrison Blvd., Ogden 84408

VERMONT

Bennington College, Bennington 05201
Karen Kristof, Dir. of Admis.
800-833-6845

Goddard College
P.O. Box G, Plainfield 05667
Jackson Kytle, President

Saint Michael's College
Winooski Park, Colchester 05439
800-SMC-8000
See listing under "Liberal Arts"

† University of Vermont
194 S. Prospect St., Burlington 05401
802-656-3370

VIRGINIA

Christopher Newport College
50 Shoe Ln., Newport News 23606

Eastern Mennonite College
1200 Park Rd., Harrisonburg 22801
Jerry Miller, Dir. of Admis.

Ferrum College, Ferrum 24088
Bob Bailey, Dir. of Admis.

George Mason University
4400 University Dr., Fairfax 22030-4444
Patricia Riordan, Dean of Admissions

† Hampton University, Hampton 23668
Ollie Bowman, Dean of Admissions

† James Madison University, Harrisonburg 22807

LIBERTY UNIVERSITY
P.O. Box 20000, Lynchburg 24506
Jay Spencer, VP Recruitment
800-376-2800
See listing under "Universities"

† Longwood College, Farmville 23901

Lynchburg College
1501 Lakeside Dr., Lynchburg 24501
Ernest Chadderton, Dean of Enrollment

† Mary Washington College
1701 College Ave., Fredericksburg 22401
Martin Wilder, V.P. for Admissions

† Norfolk State University
2401 Corprew Ave., Norfolk 23504

† Old Dominion University
5215 Hampton Blvd., Norfolk 23508

† Radford University
P.O. Box 5430, Radford 24142

† SHENANDOAH UNIVERSITY
1460 University Dr., Winchester 22601
Dr. Charlotte Collins, Dean
See listing under "Universities"

Sweet Briar College, Sweet Briar 24595
Nancy Church, Dir. of Admis.

† University of Richmond, Richmond 23173

† Virginia Commonwealth University
910 W. Franklin St., Richmond 23284

Virginia Intermont College
1013 Moore St., Bristol 24201
Lawton Blandford, Dir. of Admis.

Virginia Polytechnic Institute & State University
Blacksburg 24061
David Bousquet, Dir. of Undergraduate Admis.

† Virginia State University, Petersburg 23803
Mable C. Mountcastle, Dir. of Recording

WASHINGTON

· Art Institute of Seattle
2323 Elliott Ave., Seattle 98121
Doug Worsley, Dir. of Admis.

† Central Washington University, Ellensburg 98926
William Swain, Director of Admissions

Cornish College of the Arts
710 E. Roy St., Seattle 98102
Jane Buckman, Admissions
800-726-ARTS

† Eastern Washington University, Cheney 99004
Travis Rivers, Chrpsn.
See listing under "Universities"

Northwest College of the Assemblies of God
P.O. Box 579, Kirkland 98083-0579
Bob Foster, Dir. of Public Relations

† Pacific Lutheran University
12180 Park Ave. S., Tacoma 98447
David Robbins, Chrpsn.

† Seattle Pacific University
3307 3rd Ave., W., Seattle 98119

† University of Puget Sound
1500 N. Warner St., Tacoma 98416

† University of Washington, Seattle 98195

† Walla Walla College
204 S. College Ave., College Place 99324

† Washington State University, Pullman 99164
Stan Berry, Dir. of Admis.

† Western Washington University
516 High St., Bellingham 98225
Karen G. Copetas, Dir. of Admis.

Whitman College
345 Boyer Ave., Walla Walla 99362

† Whitworth College
300 W. Hawthorne Rd., Spokane 99251
Kenneth P. Moyer, Dir. of Admis.

WEST VIRGINIA

Alderson-Broaddus College
Philippi 26416
Craig W. Gould, Director of Admissions
304-457-1700

† Marshall University
400 Hal Greer Blvd., Huntington 25755
See listing under "Universities"

The University of Charleston
2300 MacCorkle Ave., S.E., Charleston 25304
800-995-GO UC

† West Liberty State College, West Liberty 26074

† West Virginia University
P.O. Box 6001, Morgantown 26506

† WEST VIRGINIA WESLEYAN COLLEGE
59 College Ave., Buckhannon 26201
Robert Skinner, Director of Admission
See listing under "Universities"

WISCONSIN

† Alverno College
P.O. Box 343922, Milwaukee 53234
Colleen Hayes, Dir. of Admis.

Beloit College
700 College St., Beloit 53511
Kenneth Greene, Chair
608-363-2395

Carroll College
100 N. East Ave., Waukesha 53186
Ken Moyer, Dir. of Admis.

† Carthage College
2001 Alford Dr., Kenosha 53140
Dr. Ken Winkle, Chrpsn.

† Lawrence University
P.O. Box 599, Appleton 54912
Steven Syverson, Dir. of Admissions

Marian College of Fond du Lac
45 S. National Ave., Fond du Lac 54935
Carol Reichenberger, Dean of Admissions

Ripon College, P.O. Box 248, Ripon 54971
James Reilly, Dean of Admis.

St. Norbert College
100 Grant St., De Pere 54115
Craig S. Wesley, Dean of Admission
See listing under "Universities"

† Silver Lake College
2406 S. Alverno Road, Manitowoc 54220
Sandra Schwartz, Dir. of Admis.

: TRANS AMERICAN SCHOOL OF BROADCASTING
One Point Place #1, Madison 53719
Chris Hutchings, Dir. of Admis.
800-236-4997

† University of Wisconsin, Eau Claire
Eau Claire 54701

† University of Wisconsin, Green Bay
2420 Nicolet Dr., Green Bay 54311
Dr. Terence O'Grady, Chrpsn.

† University of Wisconsin, La Crosse
115 Main Hall, La Crosse 54601
608-785-8067

† University of Wisconsin, Madison
500 Lincoln Dr., Madison 53706

† University of Wisconsin
P.O. Box 413, Milwaukee 53201
V. M. Allison, Registrar

† University of Wisconsin, Oshkosh
800 Algoma Blvd., Oshkosh 54901-8602
August Helgerson, Dir. of Admis.

† University of Wisconsin
1 University Plaza, Platteville 53818
Richard Schumacher, Dean of Admissions

† University of Wisconsin, River Falls
River Falls 54022
Alan Tuchtenhagen, Dir. of Admis.

† University of Wisconsin, Stevens Point 54481
Dr. John A. Larsen, Dir. of Admis.

† University of Wisconsin, Superior 54880
Richard E. Morrison, Dir. Univ. Relations

† University of Wisconsin
800 W. Main St., Whitewater 53190

† Viterbo College
815 9th St., S., La Crosse 54601
Roland W. Nelson, Dir. of Admis.

: † Wisconsin Conservatory of Music
1584 N. Prospect Ave., Milwaukee 53202
Florence Ponzi, Director

WYOMING

· † Casper College
125 College Dr., Casper 82601
A. W. Vance, Dir. of Admis.

· Central Wyoming College
2660 Peck St., Riverton 82501
Mary Gores, Admissions Officer
307-856-9291
See listing under "Community and Junior Colleges"

† University of Wyoming
P.O. Box 3434, Laramie 82071
Richard Davis, Dir. of Admis.

PUERTO RICO

Conservatory of Music
P.O. Box 41227, Santurce 00940
Zulma Palos de Santini, Registrar

NURSING

This classification contains schools having RN preparation programs accredited by the National League for Nursing (†) and a selection of programs from institutionally or state accredited schools. Colleges and Universities (no dot code) generally offer RN, baccalaureate or graduate programs; Community and Junior Colleges (·) generally offer associate degrees in nursing; Hospitals (··) generally offer RN programs; Career Schools (:) generally offer a diploma as a nurses aid or practical nurse.

ALABAMA

† Auburn University, Auburn 36849

† Auburn University at Montgomery
7300 University Dr., Montgomery 36117
H. H. Funderburk, VP

·† Bishop State Community College
351 N. Broad St., Mobile 36603-5898
Yvonne Kennedy, President
205-690-6801

·† Chattahoochee Valley State Community College
2602 College Dr., Phenix City 36869
Dr. Richard Federinko, President

·† Gadsden State Community College
P.O. Box 227, Gadsden 35902
W. Bryan Stone, Dir. of Admis.

··† Holy Name of Jesus Hospital
Moragne Park, Gadsden 35902
Sr. Joan M. O'Neil, Director

† Jacksonville State University
700 Pelham Rd. N., Jacksonville 36265

·† Jefferson Davis State Junior College
220 Alco Dr., Brewton 36426

·† Jefferson State Community College
2601 Carson Rd., Birmingham 35215
Jim Blackburn, Dir. of Admis.

·† John C. Calhoun State Community College
P.O. Box 2216, Decatur 35602-2216
Wayne Tosh, Registrar
205-306-2500

·† Lawson State Community College
3060 Wilson Rd., S.W., Birmingham 35221
Alfred Evans, Dean of Students

† Livingston University
Station #4, Livingston 35470
Sylvia Homan, Director
See listing under "Universities"

·† Northeast Alabama State Junior College
P.O. Box 159, Rainsville 35986
E. R. Knox, Pres.

·† Northwest Alabama Community College
Rural Route 3, Box 77, Phil Campbell 35581
Charles Britnell, President

† Samford University
800 Lakeshore Dr., Birmingham 35229
Marian Baur, Dean

·† Shelton State Community College
202 Skyland Blvd., Tuscaloosa 35405

·† Southern Union State Junior College
P.O. Box 1000, Wadley 36276

··† Sylacauga Hospital
S. Mobile Ave., Sylacauga 35150
Connie L. Spradley, Dir., Sch. of Nursing

† Troy State University, Troy 36082
Dr. Sandra Greniewicki, Dean

† Tuskegee University
Tuskegee Institute 36088

† University of Alabama
P.O. Box 870132, Tuscaloosa 35487-0132
Roy Smith, Dir. of Admis.

··† University of Alabama Hospital
619 S. 19th St., Birmingham 35233

† UNIVERSITY OF ALABAMA IN HUNTSVILLE
P.O. Box 1247, Huntsville 35899
Ron R. Koger Ed.D., Dir. of Admis.
205-895-6070
Established 1969. Public. Coed. Accreditation: SACS, ABET, NLN, CSAB, ACS. Tuition: $2,418 resident, $4,836 non-resident. Room & Board: $3,450. Undergraduate enrollment: 2,674 full-time, 3,439 part-time. Graduate enrollment: 1,860. Faculty: 282. Student-faculty ratio: 18:1. Degrees: BS, BA, BSBA, BSE, MS, MSM, Ph.D., BSN, MSN, MA. 20 buildings on 350 acres. Comprehensive research university located in the Tennessee Valley of northern Alabama. Huntsville is the locale of major government and private research centers. Metropolitan population approaching 300,000.

† UNIVERSITY OF MOBILE
P.O. Box 13220, Mobile 36663-0220
Kim Leousis, Dir. of Admissions
205-675-5990
See listing under "Universities"

† University of North Alabama
University Station, Florence 35632

† University of South Alabama
307 University Blvd. N., Mobile 36688

·† Walker College
1411 Indiana Ave., Jasper 35501
James West, Dir. of Admis.

·† Wallace College - Dothan
Route 6, Box 62, Dothan 36303
Larry Beaty, President
205-983-3521

·† Wallace State Community College
P.O. Box 2000, Hanceville 35077

·† Wallace State Community College
P.O. Box 1049, Selma 36702

ALASKA

† University of Alaska Anchorage
3211 Providence Dr., Anchorage 99508
907-786-1480

ARIZONA

† Arizona State University, Tempe 85287

·† Arizona Western College
P.O. Box 929, Yuma 85366-0929
Bob Davis, Dir. of Admis.

·† Central Arizona College, Signal Peak Campus
8470 N. Overfield Rd., Coolidge 85228
Dr. John Klein, President
602-426-4265

·† Cochise College, Douglas
Rural Route 01 Box 100, 85607
Andrew S. Moreland, Pres.

·† Gateway Community College
108 N. 40th St., Phoenix 85034
Bill Harris, Dean of Student Services

·† Glendale Community College
6000 W. Olive Ave., Glendale 85302
Elaine Laeger, Director

† GRAND CANYON UNIVERSITY
3300 W. Camelback Rd., Phoenix 85017
Dr. Jennifer Wilson, Dean of Nursing
See listing under "Liberal Arts and Sciences"

·† Mesa Community College
1833 W. Southern Ave., Mesa 85202

† Northern Arizona University
P.O. Box 4092, Flagstaff 86011
Dr. Margaret Cibik, Dir. of Admis.

·† Phoenix College
1202 W. Thomas Rd., Phoenix 85013
Martha Cary, Dir. of Admis.

·† Pima Community College
2202 W. Anklam Rd., Tucson 85709
Dr. Denis F. Viri, Registrar

·† Scottsdale Community College
9000 E. Chaparral Rd., Scottsdale 85250
Dr. Art Decabooter, President

† University of Arizona Medical Center
1501 N. Campbell Ave., Tucson 85724
Dr. James E. Dahlen, Dean

† University of Phoenix
4615 E. Elwood St., Phoenix 85040
Sue Murphy, Registrar

·† Yavapai College
1100 E. Sheldon St., Prescott 86301
Dr. Doreen Dailey, President
602-445-7300
See listing under "Community and Junior Colleges"

ARKANSAS

† Arkansas State University
P.O. Box 69, State University 72467

† Arkansas Tech University
215 W. O St., Russellville 72801

··† BAPTIST SCHOOLS OF NURSING
11900 Colonel Glenn Rd.
Little Rock 72210-2820
501-223-7415
School of Nursing
School of Practical Nursing

·† Garland Co. Community College
1 College Dr., Hot Springs 71913

† Harding University
900 E. Center Ave., Searcy 72149

† Henderson State University
1100 Henderson St., Arkadelphia 71999

··† Jefferson Regional Medical Center
1515 W. 42nd Ave., Pine Bluff 71603

·† Mississippi County Community College
P.O. Box 1109, Blytheville 72316

·† North Arkansas Community College
420 Pioneer Ridge Dr., Harrison 72601
Dr. Jerry Cash, Registrar

·† Phillips County Community College
P.O. Box 785, Helena 72342
Dr. Steven Jones, President
James R. Brasel, Dean of Admissions

† Southern Arkansas University
SAU Box 1402, Magnolia 71753

† University of Arkansas at Fayetteville
Fayetteville 72701

† University of Arkansas at Little Rock
2801 S. University Ave., Little Rock 72204

† University of Arkansas at Monticello
P.O. Box 3596, Monticello 71656

† University of Arkansas at Pine Bluff
1200 University Dr., Pine Bluff 71601-2799

† University of Arkansas for Medical Sciences
4301 W. Markham St., Little Rock 72205

† University of Central Arkansas
201 Donaghey Ave., Conway 72035

·† Westark Community College
P.O. Box 3649, Ft. Smith 72913
Joel Stubblefield, President

CALIFORNIA

: American Career College
4021 Rosewood Ave., Los Angeles 90004
Ginny White, Director of Admissions
See listing under "Career Schools"

† Azusa Pacific University
P.O. Box 7000, Azusa 91702

· Bakersfield College
1801 Panorama Dr., Bakersfield 93305
Robert M. Bruker, Dir. of Admis.

† Biola University
13800 Biola Ave., La Mirada 90639
Wayne Chute, Dean of Admissions

· Cabrillo College
6500 Soquel Dr., Aptos 95003

† California State University, Chico
Chico 95929-0200
Dr. Sherry Fox, Director

† California State University, Fresno
Shaw & Cedar Ave., Fresno 93710

† California State University, Long Beach
1250 Bellflower Blvd., Long Beach 90840

† California State University, Los Angeles
5151 Paseo Rancho Castilla, Los Angeles 90032

† California State University, Sacramento
6000 J St., Sacramento 95819

† California State University, San Bernardino
5500 University Pky., San Bernardino 92407
909-880-5188

† California State University-Bakersfield
9001 Stockdale Hwy., Bakersfield 93311
Dr. Homer S. Montalvo, Dir. of Admis.

† California State University-Fullerton
Fullerton 92632

† California State University-Hayward
25800 Carlos Bee Blvd., Hayward 94542

† California State University-Stanislaus
801 W. Monte Vista Ave., Turlock 95382
Frances Cook, Dean Enrollment Services

·† Cerritos College
11110 E. Alondra Blvd., Norwalk 90650

·† Chaffey College
5885 Haven Ave., Rancho Cucamonga 91737
JoAnne Edmison, Director of Admissions

· City College of San Francisco
1860 Hayes St., San Francisco 94117
Natalie Berg, Dean
415-561-1908

·† College of Marin
835 College Ave., Kentfield 94904

· College of the Canyons
26455 Rockwell Canyon Rd., Valencia 91355
Helen C. Lusk, Coordinator

· College of the Desert
43-500 Monterey Ave., Palm Desert 92260

· Compton Community College
1111 E. Artesia Blvd., Compton 90221

· DeAnza College
21250 Stevens Creek Blvd., Cupertino 95014

† DOMINICAN COLLEGE OF SAN RAFAEL
50 Acacia Ave., San Rafael 94901-8008
Office of Admissions
800-788-3522

·† El Camino College
16007 Crenshaw Blvd., Torrance 90506

· † Evergreen Valley College
   3095 Yerba Buena Rd., San Jose 95135

· † Golden West College
   15744 Goldenwest St., Huntington Beach 92647
   Venner Farley, Director

· † Grossmont College
   8800 Grossmont College Dr., El Cajon 92020

† Holy Names College
   3500 Mountain Blvd., Oakland 94619

† Humboldt State University
   1 Harps St., Arcata 95521

· † Imperial Valley College
   P.O. Box 158, Imperial 92251

La Sierra University
   4700 Pierce St., Riverside 92505
   800-874-5587

† Loma Linda University, Loma Linda 92350
   800-422-4LLU

· † Long Beach City College
   4901 E. Carson St., Long Beach 90808
   J. Dawdy, Dean of Admissions & Records

∴† Los Angeles County USC Medical Center
   1200 N. State St., Los Angeles 90033

· † Los Angeles Pierce College
   6201 Winnetka Ave., Woodland Hills 91371
   See listing under "Community and Junior Colleges"

· † Los Angeles Valley College
   5800 Fulton Avenue, Van Nuys 91401

: Maric College
   7202 Princess View Dr., San Diego 92120

· Merritt College
   12500 Campus Dr., Oakland 94619
   Sandra Takakura, Chrpsn.

· † Monterey Peninsula College
   980 Fremont Ave., Monterey 93940
   David Hopkins, President

· Moorpark College
   7075 Campus Rd., Moorpark 93021

† Mt. St. Mary's College
   12001 Chalon Rd., Los Angeles 90049

· Mt. San Jacinto College
   1499 N. State St., San Jacinto 92583
   Elida Gonzales, Dir. of Admis.

· Ohlone College
   P.O. Box 3909, Fremont 94539

† Pacific Union College
   1 Angwin Ave., Angwin 94508
   Dr. Gary Gifford, Dir. of Admis.

· † Palomar Community College
   1140 W. Mission Rd., San Marcos 92069

· Pasadena City College
   1570 E. Colorado Blvd., Pasadena 91106

† Point Loma Nazarene College
   3900 Lomaland Dr., San Diego 92106
   Bill Young, Dir. of Admis.

· Porterville College
   100 E. College Ave., Porterville 93257
   John McCuen, President

· † Riverside City College
   4800 Magnolia Ave., Riverside 92506

· † Saddleback Community College
   28000 Marguerite Pkwy., Mission Viejo 92692

† Samuel Merritt College
   370 Hawthorne Ave., Oakland 94609
   Charisse Hughen, Dir. of Admis.

· San Bernardino Valley College
   701 S. Mt. Vernon Ave., San Bernardino 92410
   Arlene Johnson, Chrpsn.

† San Diego State University
   5300 Campanile Dr., San Diego 92115

† San Francisco State University
   1600 Holloway Ave., San Francisco 94132
   Corwin Bjonerud, Dir. of Admis.

· San Joaquin Delta College
   5151 Pacific Ave., Stockton 95207

† San Jose State University
   1 Washington Sq., San Jose 95192

· Santa Barbara City College
   721 Cliff Dr., Santa Barbara 93109
   805-965-0581

· Santa Monica College
   1900 Pico Blvd., Santa Monica 90405
   Gloria Lopez, Assistant Dean
   See listing under "Community and Junior Colleges"

· Santa Rosa Junior College
   1501 Mendocino Ave., Santa Rosa 95401
   Joe Hagerty, Coordinator

† Sonoma State University
   1801 E. Cotati Ave., Rohnert Park 94928

† University of California, San Francisco
   Parnassus & 3rd Ave., San Francisco 94143

† UCLA Center for the Health Sciences
   10833 Le Conte Ave., Los Angeles 90024

† University of San Diego
   5998 Alcala Park, San Diego 92110
   Warren Muller, Dir. of Admis.
   619-260-4506

† University of San Francisco
   2130 Fulton St., San Francisco 94117
   Bill Henley, Dir. of Admis.

† University of Southern California
   12933 Erickson Ave., Los Angeles 90242

· Victor Valley College
   18422 Bear Valley Rd., Victorville 92392-9699

COLORADO

† Beth-El College of Nursing
   2790 N. Academy, #200
   Colorado Springs 80917

· Front Range Community College
   3645 W. 112th Ave., Westminster 80030
   Alma Mueller, Coordinator

· Mesa State College
   P.O. Box 2647, Grand Junction 81502
   Sherri Pe'a, Dir. of Admis.

† Metropolitan State College of Denver
   P.O. Box 173362, Campus Box 16
   Denver 80217-3362

· Morgan Community College
   17800 Road 20, Fort Morgan 80701
   Kurtis Armstrong, Dir. of Admis.

· † Otero Junior College
   1802 Colorado Ave., La Junta 81050
   Joe Treece, Dir. of Admissions

· Pikes Peak Community College
   5675 S. Academy Blvd.
   Colorado Springs 80906-5498
   Roberta Erickson, Dir. of Admis.
   See listing under "Community and Junior Colleges"

† Regis University
   3333 Regis Blvd., Denver 80221
   Robert Blust, Director of Admissions

University of Colorado Health Sciences Center
   4200 E. 9th Ave., Denver 80262
   Clair E. Martin, PhD, RN, FAAN, Dean

† University of Northern Colorado, Greeley 80639
   Sandra Baird, Director
   303-351-2293

† University of Southern Colorado
   2200 Bonforte Blvd., Pueblo 81001

CONNECTICUT

∴† Bridgeport Hospital
   200 Mill Hill Ave., Bridgeport 06610
   Ruth Robertson, Dir., Sch. of Nursing

† Central Connecticut State University
   1615 Stanley St., New Britain 06053

† Fairfield University
   25 N. Benson Rd., Fairfield 06430

· Greater Hartford Community College
   61 Woodland St., Hartford 06105

· † Mattatuck Community College
   750 Chase Parkway, Waterbury 06708
   Dr. Richard Sanders, President

· † Mohegan Community College
   21 Mahan Dr., Norwich 06360
   Roland W. Wright, Act'g. Pres.

· † Norwalk Community College
   188 Richards Ave., Norwalk 06854
   Sylvia Schudy, Director

† QUINNIPIAC COLLEGE
School of Allied Health & Natural Sciences
   275 Mount Carmel Ave., Hamden 06518
   Joan Isaac Mohr, VP and Dean of Admissions
   See listing under "Universities"

† Sacred Heart University
   5151 Park Ave., Fairfield 06432-1000
   Dr. Anthony J. Cernera, President

∴† St. Francis Hospital
   338 Asylum St., Hartford 06103
   Sr. Dennis Marie, Dir., Sch. of Nursing

† St. Joseph College
   1678 Asylum Ave., West Hartford 06117
   Mary C. Demo, Dir. of Admis.

∴† St. Mary's Hospital School of Nursing
   41 John St., Waterbury 06708
   Sister Rose Flanagan, Director
   203-574-6445

∴† St. Vincent's Medical Center
   2800 Main St., Bridgeport 06606
   Anne T. Avallone, Director

† Southern Connecticut State University
   501 Crescent St., New Haven 06515

† University of Connecticut, Storrs 06268
   Dr. Marlene Kramer, Dean

† University of Hartford
   200 Bloomfield Ave., West Hartford 06117
   Richard Zeiser, Dir. of Admis.
   Upper Division only; RN required
   See listing under "Universities"

† Western Connecticut State University
   181 White St., Danbury 06810

∴† WILCOX COLLEGE OF NURSING
   28 Crescent St., Middletown 06457
   Susan Abbe, President
   203-344-6403

† Yale University
   855 Howard Ave., New Haven 06520
   Judith Krauss, Dean

DELAWARE

∴† BEEBE MEDICAL CENTER SCHOOL OF NURSING
   424 Savannah Rd., Lewes 19958
   Connie E. Bushey, Director
   302-645-3251

† Delaware State College
   1200 N. DuPont Hwy., Dover 19901
   Jethro C. Williams, Dir. of Admis.

· Delaware Technical & Community College
   400 Christiana Stanton Rd., Newark 19702
   William Faucett, Director

† University of Delaware, Newark 19711

† Wesley College
   120 N. State St., Dover 19901

† Wilmington College
   320 N. DuPont Hwy., New Castle 19720

DISTRICT OF COLUMBIA

† Catholic University of America
   620 Michigan Ave. N.E., Washington 20064
   Robert J. Talbot, Dir. of Admis. & Fin. Aid.

† Georgetown University
   37th and O Sts., N.W., Washington 20057
   Dr. Joseph A. Chalmers, Dean of Admis. & Rec.

† Howard University
   2400 6th St., N.W., Washington 20059
   James E. Cheek, President

† University of the District of Columbia
   Georgia Ave.-Harvard St. Campus
   1100 Harvard St., N.W., Washington 20009

† University of the District of Columbia
   Van Ness Campus
   4200 Connecticut Ave., N.W., Washington 20008

FLORIDA

† Barry University
   11300 N.E. 2nd Ave., Miami Shores 33161
   Robin Ray Roberts, Dean of Admissions

· † Broward Community College
   225 E. Las Olas Blvd., Ft. Lauderdale 33301

· † Broward Community College
   225 E. Las Olas Blvd., Ft. Lauderdale 33301

· † Broward Community College-North Campus
   1000 Coconut Creek Blvd., Coconut Creek 33066

· † Broward Community College-South Campus
   7200 Pines Blvd.
   Pembroke Pines 33024

· † Central Florida Community College
   P.O. Box 1388, Ocala 34478
   Casius Pealer, Dir. of Admis.

· † Daytona Beach Community College
   P.O. Box 2811, Daytona Beach 32120

· Edison Community College
   8099 College Pkwy., Fort Myers 33919
   Mailing address: P.O. Box 60210
   Fort Myers 33906-6210
   Dr. Shirley Ruder, Coordinator

† Florida A & M University, Tallahassee 32307

† Florida Atlantic University
   500 N.W. 20th St., Boca Raton 33431
   Brian Levin-Stankevich, Dir. of Admis.

· † Florida Community College at Jacksonville
   North Campus
   4501 Capper Rd., Jacksonville 32218

† Florida International University
   Tamiami Trail, Miami 33199

· Florida Keys Community College
   5901 College Rd., Key West 33040
   Mitch Grabois, Director of Admissions
   305-296-9081 Ext. 284

† Florida State University
   600 W. College Ave., Tallahassee 32306

· † Gulf Coast Community College
   5230 Hwy. 98, W., Panama City 32401
   Roy Smith, Dir. of Admis. and Records

· Hillsborough Community College
   P.O. Box 31127, Tampa 33631
   Andreas Paloumpls, President

· † Indian River Community College
   3209 Virginia Ave., Fort Pierce 34981
   Dr. Herman A. Heise, President

∴† Jackson Memorial Medical Center
   1611 N.W. 12th Ave., Miami 33136

† Jacksonville University
   2800 University Blvd., N., Jacksonville 32211

· Manatee Community College
   5840 26th St., W., Bradenton 34207

· † Miami-Dade Community College
   Medical Center Campus
   950 N.W. 20th St., Miami 33127

· † Polk Community College
   999 Ave. H, N.E., Winter Haven 33881
   Marly Vanleer Peck, President

· † St. Petersburg Junior College
P.O. Box 13489, St. Petersburg 33733
Dr. Carl M. Kuttler, Jr., President

· † Santa Fe Community College
3000 N.W. 83rd St., Gainesville 32606
Lawrence W. Tyree, President

· † Seminole Community College
100 Weldon Blvd., Sanford 32773

† University of Central Florida
P.O. Box 25000, Orlando 32816

† University of Florida
226 Tigert Hall, Gainesville 32611

† University of Miami
P.O. Box 248006, Coral Gables 33124

† University of North Florida
4567 St. Johns Bluff Rd. S., Jacksonville 32224

† University of South Florida
4202 Fowler Ave., Tampa 33620

† University of Tampa
401 W. Kennedy Blvd., Tampa 33606
Robert W. Cook, Dir. of Admis.

† University of West Florida
11000 University Pky., Pensacola 32514

· † Valencia Community College, West Campus
P.O. Box 3028, Orlando 32802
Charles H. Drosin, Registrar

GEORGIA

· † Abraham Baldwin Agriculture College
P.O. Box 1, Tifton 31793

† Albany State College
504 College Dr., Albany 31705

† Armstrong State College
11935 Abercorn St., Savannah 31419
Kim West, Director of Admissions

† AUGUSTA COLLEGE

2500 Walton Way, Augusta 30904-2200
Lee Young, Dir. of Admis.
706-737-1405

† Brenau College
204 Boulevard, Gainesville 30501

· † Brunswick College
3700 Altama Ave., Brunswick 31520-3644
Dorothy L. Lord, President

† Clayton State College
P.O. Box 285, Morrow 30260

† Columbus College
3600 Algonquin Dr., Columbus 31907

· † Dalton College
213 College Dr., Dalton 30720
Dr. Derrell Roberts, President

· † Darton College
2400 Gillionville Rd., Albany 31707

· † DeKalb College
3251 Panthersville Rd., Decatur 30034
Dr. Marvin Cole, President

† Emory University
1462 Clifton Rd., Atlanta 30322

· † Floyd College
P.O. Box 1864, Rome 30162
David B. McCorkle, President

∴† Georgia Baptist Medical Center
300 Blvd., N.E., Atlanta 30312
Robert E. DeLashmutt, M.D., Director

† Georgia College
231 W. Hancock St., Milledgeville 31061
912-453-5004

† Georgia Southern University, Statesboro 30460

† Georgia Southwestern College
800 Wheatley St., Americus 31709

† Georgia State University
University Plaza, Atlanta 30303
Ernest Beals, Dean of Admissions

· † Gordon College
419 College Dr., Barnesville 30204
Dr. Judith Malachowski, Nursing Chrpsn.
404-358-5085

† Kennesaw State College
P.O. Box 444, Marietta 30061
Judy Perkins, Director

† La Grange College
601 Broad St., La Grange 30240
Phil Dodson, Dir. of Admis.
706-882-2911

· † Macon College
College Station Dr., Macon 31298
William W. Wright, President

† Medical College of Georgia
1120 15th St., Augusta 30901
Elizabeth Griffin, Dir. of Undergraduate Admis.

· † MIDDLE GEORGIA COLLEGE

Cochran 31014
George Hinton, Dir. of Admis.
See listing under "Community and Junior Colleges"

† North Georgia College, Dahlonega 30597
Gary R. Steffey, Dir. of Admis.

· † South Georgia College, Douglas 31533
John Wahl, Dir. of Admis.

† Valdosta State College
Patterson St., Valdosta 31698

† West Georgia College, Carrollton 30118
C. Doyle Bickers, Dir. of Admis.

HAWAII

· † Kauai Community College
3-1901 Kaumualii Hwy., Lihue 96766
Philip K. Palama, Admis. Ofc. & Reg.

· † Maui Community College
310 W. Kaahumanu Ave., Kahului 96732
Alma K. Cooper, Provost

† University of Hawaii at Hilo
523 W. Lanikaula, Hilo 96720

† University of Hawaii at Manoa
2500 Campus Rd., Honolulu 96822

IDAHO

† Boise State University
1910 University Dr., Boise 83725

· † College of Southern Idaho
P.O. Box 1238, Twin Falls 83303
Dr. John S. Martin, Dir. of Admis.

† Idaho State University
P.O. Box 8270, Pocatello 83209

† Lewis Clark State College
500 8th Ave., Lewiston 83501
800-933-5272 or 208-799-5272

· † North Idaho College
1000 W. Garden Ave., Coeur d'Alene 83814
Joan Brogan, Director

· † Ricks College, Rexburg 83460
Steven Bennion, President

ILLINOIS

† Aurora University
347 S. Gladstone Ave., Aurora 60506
Peter Pitts, Dir. of Admis.

† Barat College, Lake Forest 60045
Loretta Brickman, Dir. of Admis.

· † Belleville Area College
2500 Carlyle Rd., Belleville 62221

· † Black Hawk College, Quad Cities Campus
6600 34th Ave., Moline 61265
Barton Schiermeyer, Dir. of Admis.

Blessing-Rieman College of Nursing
Broadway at 11th, Quincy 62301
Rita Zabor, Dean

† Bradley University
1501 W. Bradley Ave., Peoria 61625

† Chicago State University
9501 S. King Dr., Chicago 60628

· † College of DuPage
425 22nd St., Glen Ellyn 60137
Harold D. McAninch, Dir. of Admis.

† College of Lake County
19351 W. Washington St., Grayslake 60030
John O. Hunter, President

† De Paul University
1 E. Jackson Blvd., Chicago 60604
Thomas D. Abrahamson, Dean of Admissions
See listing under "Universities"

· † Elgin Community College
1700 Spartan Dr., Elgin 60123

† Elmhurst College
190 Prospect Ave., Elmhurst 60126

† Governors State University
1 University Pky., University Park 60466
Richard Pride, Dir. of Admis.

∴† Graham Hospital School of Nursing
210 W. Walnut St., Canton 61520
Jeanne Robertson, RN, Coord. of Academic Services

† Illinois Benedictine College
5700 College Rd., Lisle 60532

· † Illinois Central College
One College Dr., East Peoria 61635
Dr. Thomas K. Thomas, President

· † Illinois Valley Community College
R.R. 1, Oglesby 61348
Dr. Alfred Wisgoski, President

† ILLINOIS WESLEYAN UNIVERSITY

P.O. Box 2900, Bloomington 61702
Dr. Donna Hartweg, Director
309-556-3051

· † Joliet Junior College
1216 Houbolt Dr., Joliet 60436
Dir. of Admis.

· † Kaskaskia College
27210 College Rd., Centralia 62801
See listing under "Community and Junior Colleges"

· † Lewis & Clark Community College
5800 Godfrey Rd., Godfrey 62035
J. Neil Admire, President

† LEWIS UNIVERSITY

Rt. 53, Romeoville 60441
Irish O'Reilly, Director of Admissions
See listing under "Universities"

· † Lincoln Land Community College
Shepherd Rd., Springfield 62794-9256
Ron Gregoire, Dir. of Admis.
Information: 800-727-4161

† Loyola University of Chicago
820 N. Michigan Ave., Chicago 60611
Allen V. Lentino, Dir. of Admis.

† McKendree College
701 College Rd., Lebanon 62254
Stephen E. Jackson, Director of Admissions

† MacMurray College
447 E. College Ave., Jacksonville 62650
Edwin R. Hockett, Dean of Admissions

† Mennonite College of Nursing
804 N. East St., Bloomington 61701
Mary Ann Watkins, Dir. of Admis./Financial Aid
309-829-0718, FAX: 309-829-0765

∴† Methodist Medical Center of Illinois
221 N.E. Glen Oak Ave., Peoria 61603
Louise Guest, Director

† MILLIKIN UNIVERSITY

1184 W. Main St., Decatur 62522
Lin Stoner, Dean of Admissions
800-373-7733

· † Moraine Valley Community College
10900 S. 88th Ave., Palos Hills 60465
Dr. Vernon Crawley, President

† Northern Illinois University, De Kalb 60115

· † Oakton Community College
1600 E. Golf Rd., Des Plaines 60016
Dr. Thomas TenHoeve, President

† Olivet Nazarene University, Kankakee 60901
John Mongerson, Dir. of Admis.
815-939-5203

· † Olney Central College
305 Northwest St., Olney 62450
Dr. Charles R. Novak, President

· † Parkland College
2400 W. Bradley Ave., Champaign 61821-1899
217-351-2208 or 800-346-8089

· † Prairie State College
P.O. Box 487, Chicago Heights 60411
Dr. Richard C. Creal, President

Quincy College
1800 College Ave., Quincy 62301
Fr. Michael Lanning, O.F.M., Dir. of Admis.

∴† Ravenswood Hospital Medical Center
4550 N. Winchester Ave., Chicago 60640
Ann Mathis, Director

† Rockford College
5050 E. State St., Rockford 61108
Miriam King, V.P. for Enrollment Management
See listing under "Universities"

† Rush University
1653 W. Congress Pky., Chicago 60612

∴† St. Anthony Medical Center
5666 E. State St., Rockford 61108
Sister M. Linus, Director

∴† St. Francis Hospital
355 Ridge Ave., Evanston 60202

SAINT FRANCIS MEDICAL CENTER COLLEGE OF NURSING

211 N.E. Greenleaf St., Peoria 61603
Sr. Mary Ludgera, Dean
309-655-2596

∴† St. John's Hospital
800 E. Carpenter, Springfield 62769
Sr. Agnes McDougall, Director

St. Joseph College of Nursing
290 Springfield Ave., Joliet 60435
Alan J. Christensen, Dir. of Admis.

† St. Xavier College
3700 W. 103rd St., Chicago 60655
Mary Hendry, Dean of Admissions

† Sangamon State University
Shepherd Rd., Springfield 62794-9243
Admissions and Records, 217-786-6626

† Southern Illinois University at Edwardsville
Edwardsville 62026
Eugene J. Magac, Dir. of Admissions & Records

· † South Suburban College of Cook County
15800 State St., South Holland 60473

· Springfield College in Illinois
1500 N. Fifth St., Springfield 62702
Dr. H. Brent DeLand, President

† Trinity Christian College
6601 W. College Dr., Palos Heights 60463
Kenneth Bootsma, President

· † Triton College
2000 N. 5th Ave., River Grove 60171
Gail Fuller, Dir. of Admission & Records
See listing under "Community and Junior Colleges"

∴† United Medical Center
501 10th Ave., Moline 61265

∴ United Samaritans Medical Center
Lakeview College of Nursing
812 N. Logan Ave., Danville 61832
Irene Steward, President

† University of Illinois at Chicago
P.O. Box 5220, Chicago 60680
Dr. Mitzi Duxbury, Dean

† West Suburban College of Nursing
1 Erie Ct., Oak Park 60302

· † William Rainey Harper College
1200 W. Algonquin Rd., Palatine 60067

INDIANA

† Anderson University
1100 E. 5th St., Anderson 46012
Robert H. Reardon, President

† Ball State University
2000 W. University Ave., Muncie 47306
Ruth Vedvik, Dir. of Admis.

† Bethel College
1001 W. McKinley Ave., Mishawaka 46545
Steve Matteson, Dir. of Admis.

† DePauw University
1812 N. Capitol, Indianapolis 46202
Dr. Sherry Smith, Director

Franklin College
501 E. Monroe, Franklin 46131
B. Stephen Richards, VP Enrollment

† Goshen College
1700 S. Main St., Goshen 46526
Miriam Martin, Director

Grace College
200 Seminary Dr., Winona Lake 46590
Ron Henry, Dir. of Admis.

† Indiana State University
217 N. 6th St., Terre Haute 47809

† Indiana University at Kokomo
P.O. Box 9003, Kokomo 46904

† Indiana University at South Bend
P.O. Box 7111, South Bend 46634

† Indiana University Northwest
3400 N. Broadway, Gary 46408

† Indiana University-Purdue University at Fort Wayne
2101 Coliseum Blvd. E., Fort Wayne 46805

† Indiana University-Purdue University
355 N. Lansing, Indianapolis 46202

† Indiana Wesleyan University
4201 S. Washington St., Marion 46953
800-332-6901

· † Ivy Tech Lafayette
P.O. Box 6299, Lafayette 47903
Thomas Reckerd, V.P., Dean

· † Ivy Tech Northcentral
1534 W. Sample St., South Bend 46619
Carl Lutz, V.P., Dean

· † Ivy Tech Whitewater
2325 Chester Blvd., Richmond 47374
Judith Redwine, V.P., Dean

Marian College
3200 Cold Spring Rd., Indianapolis 46222
Don French, Dir. of Admis.

† Purdue University
Schleman Hall, West Lafayette 47907

† Purdue University, Calumet Campus
2233 171st St., Hammond 46323

† Purdue University
1401 S. U.S. Hwy. 421, Westville 46391

∴† St. Elizabeth Hospital
P.O. Box 7501, Lafayette 47903

† St. Mary's College
46 Madeliva, Notre Dame 46556
Mary Ann Rowan, Dir. of Admissions

† University of Evansville
1800 Lincoln Ave., Evansville 47722
Dr. Rita Behnke, Dept. Chair
800-423-8633

† University of Indianapolis
1400 E. Hanna Ave., Indianapolis 46227

† Valparaiso University, Valparaiso 46383

· † Vincennes University
1002 N. 1st St., Vincennes 47591

IOWA

∴† Allen Memorial Hospital
1825 Logan Ave., Waterloo 50703

† Briar Cliff College
3303 Rebecca St., Sioux City 51104
Patricia White, Dir. of Admis.

† Clarke College
1550 Clarke Dr., Dubuque 52001
Bonnie Smola, PhD, Chair
800-383-2345

† Coe College
1220 1st Ave., N.E., Cedar Rapids 52402
Evelyn Benda, Chrpsn.

· † Des Moines Area Community College
2006 S. Ankeny Blvd., Ankeny 50021
James Frazee, Dir. of Admissions

· † Des Moines Area Community College-Carroll Campus
906 N. Grant Rd., Carroll 51401

· † Des Moines Area Community College
1125 Hancock Dr., Boone 50036
Byron Hamilton, Dean

† Graceland College, Lamoni 50140
800-638-0053, Outside Iowa 800-346-9208
Bonita Booth, Dean of Admissions
See listing under "Universities"

† Grand View College
1200 Grandview Ave., Des Moines 50316
Ellen Strachota, Nursing Director
800-444-6083

· Hawkeye Community College
1501 E. Orange Rd., Waterloo 50701
319-296-2320 Ext. 4000

· Iowa Lakes Community College
3200 College Dr., Emmetsburg 50536
John Nelson, Dir. of Admis.
712-852-3554

∴† Iowa Methodist School of Nursing
1117 Pleasant St., Des Moines 50309
Pamela Bradley, Director
515-241-6333

† Iowa Wesleyan College
601 N. Main St., Mt. Pleasant 52641

∴† Jennie Edmundson Memorial Hospital
933 E. Pierce St., Council Bluffs 51503
Marjorie Matzen, Director

† Luther College
700 College Dr., Decorah 52101
David Sallee, Dean for Enrollment

∴† Mercy Hospital
400 University Ave., Des Moines 50314
Suzanne Mains, Director

† Morningside College, Sioux City 51106
Lora Vanderzwaag, Dir. of Admis.

† Mount Mercy College
1330 Elmhurst Dr., N.E., Cedar Rapids 52402
Carol Williamson, Dir. of Admis.

· North Iowa Area Community College
500 College Dr., Mason City 50401
Dick Wempen, Counselor

∴† St. Luke's Regional Medical Center
2720 Stone Park Blvd., Sioux City 51104
Ora Lee Skidmore, R.N., Director

SCOTT COMMUNITY COLLEGE
500 Belmont Rd., Bettendorf 52722
Kris Barkdoll, Assoc. Dean Enrollment Management

· Southeastern Community College
P.O. Box 27, Keokuk 52632
Marjory Leonard, Supervisor

· Southeastern Community College
P.O. Box F, West Burlington 52655
Phyllis Harrell, Supervisor

† Teikyo Marycrest University
1607 W. 12th St., Davenport 52804
Tim McDonough, Dir. of Admis.
See listing under "Universities"

† University of Dubuque
2000 University Ave., Dubuque 52001

† University of Iowa, Iowa City 52242

KANSAS

† Baker University School of Nursing
1500 W. 10th St., Topeka 66604

· † Barton County Community College
R.R. 3, Box 136Z, Great Bend 67530
Dr. Jim Downing, President

· † Barton County Community College
P.O. Box 223, Junction City 66441

† Bethel College
300 E. 27th St., North Newton 67117

· † Butler County Community College
901 S. Haverhill Rd., El Dorado 67042
Dr. Carl Heinrich, President

COLBY COMMUNITY COLLEGE
1255 S. Range Ave., Colby 67701
Theron Johnson, Dir. of Admis.

· † Dodge City Community College
2501 N. 14th Ave., Dodge City 67801
Debbie Lloyd, Director of Admissions
800-FOR-DCCC

† Fort Hays State University
600 Park St., Hays 67601-4099
Dr. Jacqueline Swanson, Chrpsn.

· † Ft. Scott Community College
2108 S. Horton St., Fort Scott 66701
Robert Hood, Adm. & Records

· † Garden City Community College
801 Campus Dr., Garden City 67846
Beth Tedrow, Dir. of Admis.

· † Hesston College
P.O. Box 3000, Hesston 67062

· † Hutchinson Community College
1300 N. Plum St., Hutchinson 67501
Duane Halpain, Dir. of Admis.

· † Johnson County Community College
12345 College Blvd., Overland Park 66210
Pat Long, Dir. of Admis.

† Kansas City Kansas Community College
7250 State Ave., Kansas City 66112
Don Stump, Dir. of Admis.

† Kansas Newman College
3100 McCormick Ave., Wichita 67213
Dr. Robert Giroux, President

† Kansas Wesleyan University
100 E. Claflin, Salina 67401
Dr. Daniel Bratton, President

· † Labette Community College
200 S. 14th St., Parsons 67357
Dr. Bob C. Burns, Dean of Instr.

† Mid-America Nazarene College
P.O. Box 1776, Olathe 66051

· † Neosho County Community College
1000 S. Allen Ave., Chanute 66720
Dr. George VanAllen, President

∴† Newman Hospital
1127 Chestnut St., Emporia 66801
Marguerite Coleman, Dir., Nursing Educ.

: North Central KS Area Vocational-Technical School
P.O. Box 507, Beloit 67420

† Pittsburg State University
1701 S. Broadway St., Pittsburg 66762
James E. Parker, Dir of Admis.

† Saint Mary College
4100 S. 4th St., Leavenworth 66048
Irene Keehan, Dir. of Admis.

· † Seward County Community College
P.O. Box 1137, Liberal 67905

†SOUTHWESTERN COLLEGE
100 College St., Winfield 67156
800-846-1543

† University of Kansas Medical Center
39th St. & Rainbow Blvd., Kansas City 66103
Dr. Eleanor Sullivan, Dean

† Washburn University of Topeka
1700 S.W. College Ave., Topeka 66621
John E. Triggs, Dir. of Admissions

† Wichita State University
1845 Fairmount, Wichita 67260
800-362-2594
See listing under "Universities"

KENTUCKY

† Bellarmine College
2001 Newburg Rd., Louisville 40205
Thomas LaBaugh, Dean of Admissions

† Berea College, Berea 40404
John S. Cook, Dir. of Admis.

† Eastern Kentucky University
521 Lancaster Ave., Richmond 40475

· Elizabethtown Community College
600 College Street Rd., Elizabethtown 42701

· † Henderson Community College
2660 S. Green St., Henderson 42420
Marshall Arnold, Director

· Jefferson Community College
109 E. Broadway, Louisville 40202
Ronald Horvath, Director

† Kentucky State University
400 E. Main St., Frankfort 40601

Kentucky Wesleyan College
3000 Frederica St., Owensboro 42301
Dr. Beth Johnson, Director

· Lexington Community College
Oswald Bldg., Cooper Dr., Lexington 40506
Dr. Sharon Jaggard, Director

· Maysville Community College, Maysville 41056
James Shires, President

† Midway College
512 E. Stephens St., Midway 40347
Carl P. Rollins II, Dir. of Admis.

Morehead State University, Morehead 40351
Charles Myers, Director of Admissions
606-783-2000

† Murray State University, Murray 42071
Phil Bryan, Director of Admissions
800-272-4MSU

† Northern Kentucky University
Louie B. Nunn Dr., Highland Heights 41076

· Paducah Community College
P.O. Box 7380, Paducah 42002
Dr. Donald J. Clemens, Dir.

Pikeville College
214 Sycamore St., Pikeville 41501
Dr. John W. Sanders, Dean of Admissions

† Spalding University
851 S. 4th St., Louisville 40203
Dorothy G. Allen, Dir. of Admis.

† Thomas More College
2771 Turkeyfoot Rd., Covington 41017
Dr. Charles Bensman, President

† University of Kentucky, Lexington 40506

† University of Louisville
2301 S. 3rd St., Louisville 40292
Robert Parrent, Dir. of Admis.

† Western Kentucky University
1526 Russellville Rd., Bowling Green 42101

LOUISIANA

·† Baton Rouge General Medical Center
P.O. Box 2511, Baton Rouge 70821

·† Charity-Delgado School of Nursing
450 S. Claiborne Ave., New Orleans 70112

† Dillard University
2601 Gentilly Blvd., New Orleans 70122

Grambling State University
P.O. Box 607, Grambling 71245
Dr. Harold W. Lundy, President

† Louisiana College
College Station, Pineville 71359
Byron McGee, Dir. of Admis.
318-487-7386
See listing under "Liberal Arts"

† Louisiana State University Medical Center
433 Bolivar St., New Orleans 70112

·† Louisiana State University at Alexandria
8100 Hwy. 71, Alexandria 71302
Dr. Fred Beckerdite, Acting Chancellor

† Lousiana Technical University
P.O. Box 3168, Ruston 71272

† Loyola University
6363 St. Charles Ave., New Orleans 70118

† McNeese State University
4100 Ryan St., Lake Charles 70605

† Nicholls State University
LA Hwy. 1, Thibodaux 70301

† Northeast Louisiana University
700 University Ave., Monroe 71209

† Northwestern State University
1800 Line Ave., Shreveport 71101
Barbara Dickerson, Head

† OUR LADY OF HOLY CROSS COLLEGE
4123 Woodland Dr., New Orleans 70131

·† Our Lady of the Lake Medical Center
5000 Hennessy Blvd., Baton Rouge 70808
Bertha Anders, Director

† Southeastern Louisiana University
P.O. Box 784, Hammond 70404

† University of Southwestern Louisiana
P.O. Box 44548, Lafayette 70504
318-231-6986

† William Carey College
2700 Napoleon Ave., New Orleans 70115

MAINE

·† Central Maine Medical Center School of Nursing
300 Main St., Lewiston 04240
Fay Ingersoll, Director

·† Central Maine Technical College
1250 Turner St., Auburn 04210
Dr. William J. Hierstein, President

† HUSSON COLLEGE
Eastern Maine Medical Center
One College Circle, Bangor 04401
Elizabeth Burns, Dean
See listing under "Business and Management"

·† Kennebec Valley Technical College
92 Western Ave., Fairfield 04937
Barbara Woodlee, Director

·† Northern Maine Technical College
33 Edgemont Dr., Presque Isle 04769

† St. Joseph's College, North Windham 04062

·† Southern Maine Technical College
2 Fort Rd., South Portland 04106
See listing under "Career Schools"

† University of Maine
University Hts., Augusta 04330

† University of Maine at Fort Kent
25 Pleasant St., Fort Kent 04743
Jerry Nadeau, Dir. of Admis.

† University of Maine, Orono 04469

† University of New England
11 Hills Beach Rd., Biddeford 04005
Patricia Cribby, Dir. of Admis.

† University of Southern Maine
96 Falmouth St., Portland 04103
Patricia Geary, Dean

† Westbrook College
716 Stevens Ave., Portland 04103
207-797-7261

MARYLAND

·† Anne Arundel Community College
101 College Pky., Arnold 21012
Herbert Curkin, Dir. of Admis.

† Bowie State University
14000 Jericho Park Rd., Bowie 20715

·† Cecil Community College
1000 North East Rd., North East 21901

·† Charles County Community College
P.O. Box 910, La Plata 20646

† College of Notre Dame of Maryland
4701 N. Charles St., Baltimore 21210

† Columbia Union College
7600 Flower Ave., Takoma Park 20912

·† Community College of Baltimore
2901 Liberty Heights Ave., Baltimore 21215
Joseph Stein, Director of Admissions

† Coppin State College
2500 W. North Ave., Baltimore 21216

·† Essex Community College
7201 Rossville Blvd., Baltimore 21237
Diane Lane, Dir. of Admis.

· Frederick Community College
7932 Opossumtown Pike, Frederick 21702
Jane Garvin, Director

·† Harbor Hospital Center
3001 S. Hanover St., Baltimore 21225

·† Harford Community College
401 Thomas Run Rd., Bel Air 21015
Judy Kupcinski, Coordinator

·† Howard Community College
10901 Little Patuxent Pky., Columbia 21044
Emily Slunt, Director

† Johns Hopkins University
600 N. Wolfe St., Baltimore 21205

·† Macqueen Gibbs Willis School of Nursing
Memorial Hospital
219 S. Washington St., Easton 21601
Joan Coccaro, Director
410-822-1000, Ext. 5895

·† Montgomery College
Pre-Nursing
7600 Takoma Ave., Takoma Park 20912
301-650-1332

·† Prince George's Community College
301 Largo Rd., Largo 20772
Leon Weaver, Dir. of Admis. & Test.

† Salisbury State University
1101 Camden Ave., Salisbury 21801

† Towson State University
800 York Rd., Towson 21204
Dr. Hoke Smith, President

·† Union Memorial Hospital
33rd and Calvert Sts., Baltimore 21218
Frances D. Tompkins, Dir. of Admis.

† University of Maryland
Baltimore Professional Schools
522 W. Lombard St., Baltimore 21201

Villa Julie College
1525 Greenspring Valley Rd., Stevenson 21153
Carolyn Manuszak, President

MASSACHUSETTS

† American International College
1000 State St., Springfield 01109
Peter Miller, Dean of Admissions

† Anna Maria College
2 Sunset Ln., Paxton 01612
Dr. Bernadette Madore, SSA, President

† Assumption College
500 Salisbury St., Worcester 01609

† Atlantic Union College
P.O. Box 1000, South Lancaster 01561
Osa Canto, Registrar

·† Bay State Medical Center
759 Chestnut St., Springfield 01199

·† Becker College
61 Sever St., Worcester 01609
Arnold Weccer, Jr., President

·† Berkshire Community College
1350 West St., Pittsfield 01201
Adrienne A. Rulnick, Dir. of Admissions

† Boston College
140 Commonwealth Ave., Chestnut Hill 02167
Dr. Mary A. Dineen, Dean

·† Bristol Community College
777 Elsbree St., Fall River 02720
Frank Noble, Dir. of Admis.

·† Brockton Hospital, 680 Centre St., Brockton 02402
Louise Pierson, Director

·† Bunker Hill Community College
New Rutherford Ave., Boston 02129
Janice M. Bonanno, Dir. of Admis.

·† Cape Cod Community College
2240 Rt. 132, West Barnstable 02668
Philip Day, President

† Curry College
1071 Blue Hill Ave., Milton 02186
617-333-0500

† ELMS COLLEGE
291 Springfield St., Chicopee 01013
800-255-ELMS

·† Emmanuel College
400 The Fenway, Boston 02115
Margaret Bonilla, Dir. of Admis.

· Endicott College
376 Hale St., Beverly 01915
Elizabeth Macomber, Dir. of Admis.

† Fitchburg State College
160 Pearl St., Fitchburg 01420
Marke Vickers, Dir. of Admis.

† Framingham State College
100 State St., Framingham 01701
E. Joseph Lee, Director

·† Framingham Union Hospital School of Nursing
85 Lincoln St., Framingham 01701

·† Greenfield Community College
1 College Dr., Greenfield 01301
Donald Brown, Dir. of Admis.

·† Holyoke Community College
303 Homestead Ave., Holyoke 01040
George E. Frost, President

·† Laboure College
2120 Dorchester Ave., Boston 02124
Roberta Pazyra, Chrpsn.

·† Lawrence Memorial Hospital
170 Governors Ave., Medford 02155
Marie McCarthy, Director
617-396-9250

† Massachusetts College of Pharmacy
& Allied Health Sciences
179 Longwood Ave., Boston 02115

·† Massasoit Community College
1 Massasoit Blvd., Brockton 02402
Roberta Noodell, Dir. of Admis.

† MGH Institute of Health Professions
101 Merrimac St., Boston 02114

·† Middlesex Community College
Springs Rd., Bedford 01730
617-280-3200

· Middlesex Community College
33 Kearney Sq., Lowell 01852
508-656-3211

·† Mt. Wachusett Community College
444 Green St., Gardner 01440
Sidney Goldfader, Dir. of Admis.

·† NEW ENGLAND BAPTIST HOSPITAL
School of Nursing
220 Fisher Ave., Boston 02120
A. Sharon Deehan, Director
617-739-5260
Established 1896. Coed. Accreditation: NLN. 2 year Professional Registered Nurse Diploma Program. Collegiate Affiliation: Emmanuel College. Number of college credits 32 (30 additional credits through ACT exams). 1993-94 costs: Residence $9,298, Commuters $6,748. Financial Assistance: Federal and state grants and loans, private scholarships and federal work-study. Transfer credits accepted. School year: August-June. Clinical experiences provided at several prominent Boston Hospitals and community agencies.

† Northeastern University
360 Huntington Ave., Boston 02115
Kevin Kelly, Dean and Dir. of Undergraduate Admis.

·† Northern Essex Community College
100 Elliott St., Haverhill 01830

· North Shore Community College
1 Ferncroft Rd., Danvers 01923

·† Quincy Junior College
34 Coddington St., Quincy 02169
Patricia Ryan, Associate Dean for Allied Health

·† Quinsigamond Community College
670 W. Boylston St., Worcester 01606
Ron Smith, Dir. of Admis.

·† REGIS COLLEGE
235 Wellesley St., Weston 02193
Amy Anderson, Dir. of Nursing Program
617-893-1820 ext. 2007

·† St. Elizabeth's Hospital School of Nursing
235 Washington St., Brighton 02135
Helen C. Fagan, Director

† Salem State College
352 Lafayette St., Salem 01970
David Sartwell, Dir. of Admis.

† Simmons College
300 The Fenway, Boston 02115

·† Somerville Hospital
125 Lowell St., Somerville 02143

·† SPRINGFIELD TECHNICAL COMMUNITY COLLEGE
1 Armory Square, Springfield 01105
Dr. Patrick E. Tigue, Dir. of Admissions
413-781-7822

† University of Massachusetts, Amherst 01003
Arlene Wesley Cash, Dir. of Admis.

† University of Massachusetts
100 Morrissey Blvd., Boston 02125

† University of Massachusetts Dartmouth
Old Westport Rd., North Dartmouth 02747
Raymond Barrows, Dir. of Admissions
508-999-8605

† University of Massachusetts Lowell
1 University Ave., Lowell 01854

·† Worcester City Hospital
School of Nursing
455 Main St. #306, Worcester 01608

† Worcester State College
486 Chandler St., Worcester 01602

MICHIGAN

† Andrews University, Berrien Springs 49104
Jack Mentges, Dir. of Admis.

∴† Bronson School of Nursing
252 E. Lovell St., Kalamazoo 49007
Jacqueline Wylie, Director

· † Delta College, University Center 48710
Louise Goodburne, Division Chrpsn.

† Eastern Michigan University, Ypsilanti 48197
Elizabeth C. King, Dean
313-487-3060 or 800-GO-TO-EMU

Ferris State University
Office of Admission
420 Oak St., Big Rapids 49307-2020

· † Ford Community College
5101 Evergreen Rd., Dearborn 48128
James O. McCann, President

· † Grand Rapids Community College
143 Bostwick Ave., N.E., Grand Rapids 49503
Dr. Madalyn Binger, Provost

† Grand Valley State University
1 Campus Dr., Allendale 49401
Mary Horan, Dir.

∴† Henry Ford Hospital
2799 W. Grand Blvd., Detroit 48202
Theresa C. Jones, Dir.

· Highland Park Community College
12541 2nd Ave., Highland Park 48203
Oretta Todd, PhD, Director of Nursing

† Hope College
69 E. 10th St., Holland 49423
Gordon Van Wylen, President

∴† Hurley Medical Center
701 W. 8th Ave., Flint 48503
May E. Werrbach, Dir.

· Jackson Community College
2111 Emmons Rd., Jackson 49201
Mark Ulseth, Dir. Enrollment Services

· † Lake Michigan College
2755 E. Napier, Benton Harbor 49022
Rentzell Cleaveland, Jr., Registrar

† Lake Superior State University
1000 College Dr., Sault St. Marie 49783

· † Lansing Community College
521 Washington Square N., Lansing 48933

· † Macomb Community College
16500 Hall Rd., Clinton Twp. 48038

† Madonna University
36600 Schoolcraft St., Livonia 48150

† Michigan State University, East Lansing 48824
Dr. Gladys A. Courtney, Dean

· Mid Michigan Community College
1375 S. Clare Ave., Harrison 48625
Eugene Schorzmann, President

· † Monroe County Community College
1555 Raisinville S., Monroe 48161
Gerald Welch, President

· † Mott Community College
1401 E. Court St., Flint 48503
Earl L. Mahoney, Dir. of Admissions

† Northern Michigan University
610 Cohodas Admin. Center, Marquette 49855
Nancy Rehling, Dir. of Admis.

· Northwestern Michigan College
1701 E. Front St., Traverse City 49686
Mary Vanderkolk, Director
800-748-0566

† Oakland University, Rochester 48309
Larry Bartalucci, Registrar

† Saginaw Valley State University
2250 Pierce Rd., University Center 48710

· Southwestern Michigan College
58900 Cherry Grove Rd., Dowagiac 49047
David Schultz, VP for Student Services
616-782-5113

· Suomi College
601 Quincy St., Hancock 49930
John Ruohoniemi, Dean/Enrollment Development
800-682-7604

† University of Detroit Mercy
4001 W. McNichols
PO Box 19900, Detroit 48219-0900
313-993-1245
See listing under "Universities"

† University of Michigan-Ann Arbor
1355 Catherine St., Ann Arbor 48104
Dr. Mary Lohr, Dean

† Wayne State University
5980 Cass Ave., Detroit 48202
Dr. J. R. Thorderson, Dir. of Admis.

MINNESOTA

· † Anoka-Ramsey Community College
11200 Mississippi Blvd., N.W.
Coon Rapids 55433
Irene Campanaro, Dir. Student Services
612-427-2600

† Augsburg College
731 21st Ave., S., Minneapolis 55454

· † Austin Community College
1600 8th Ave., N.W., Austin 55912
Barbara Orcutt, Admissions
507-433-0517

Bemidji State University
1500 Birchmont Dr., N.E., Bemidji 56601
800-475-2001

† Bethel College
3900 Bethel Dr., St. Paul 55112
Dr. George Brushaber, President

† College of Saint Benedict
37 S. College Ave., St. Joseph 56374

† College of St. Catherine
2004 Randolph Ave., St. Paul 55105

† College of St. Scholastica
1200 Kenwood Ave., Duluth 55811
Dr. Cecelia Taylor, Chrpsn.
800-447-5444
See listing under "Liberal Arts"

† Concordia College
901 8th St. S., Moorhead 56562
Dr. Lois Nelson, Chairperson
See listing under "Universities"

Gustavus Adolphus College
800 W. College Ave., St. Peter 56082
Mark Anderson, Dir. of Admis.

· † Inver Hills Community College
8445 College Trail E., Inver Grove 55076
Lee Ann Joy, Director

· † Lakewood Community College
3401 Century Ave., White Bear Lake 55110
Dr. Neil Christenson, President

† Mankato State University
P.O. Box 8400, Mankato 56002

† Metropolitan State University
700 7th St. E., St. Paul 55106
Marilyn Molen, PhD, Dean

· † Minneapolis Community College
1501 Hennepin Ave., Minneapolis 55403-1779
Bonnie Wiger, Registrar
612-341-7000

† Moorhead State University
1104 7th Ave. S., Moorhead 56560

· † Normandale Community College
9700 France Ave., S., Bloomington 55431
Thomas Horak, President

· † North Hennepin Community College
7411 85th Ave., N., Brooklyn Park 55445
Dr. John Helling, President

· † Rochester Community College
851 30th Ave. S.E., Rochester 55904
Charles E. Hill, President

St. John's University
P.O. Box 7155, Collegeville 56321

· † St. Mary's Campus of the College of St. Catherine
2500 6th St., S., Minneapolis 55454
Pamela Johnson, Dir. of Admis.

St. Olaf College, Northfield 55057
Rita Glazebrook, Chrpsn.
507-646-3265

† University of Minnesota, Twin Cities
Minneapolis 55455

· Willmar Community College
P.O. Box 797, Willmar 56201
Lynn Johnson, Director
612-231-6034

† Winona State University
P.O. Box 5838, Winona 55987
Dr. J. Mootz, Dir. of Admis.

MISSISSIPPI

† Alcorn State University
P.O. Box 359, Lorman 39096
D. W. Wilburn, Registrar

† Delta State University
Hwy. 8 W., Cleveland 38732

· † Hinds Community College
1750 Chadwick Dr., Jackson 39204

· † Itawamba Community College
Hwy. 78, Fulton 38843
Carl C. Comer, Dir. of Admis.

· † Jones County Junior College, Ellisville 39437
Jimmy Temple, Registrar

· † Meridian Community College
910 Hwy. 19, N., Meridian 39307

† Mississippi College
P.O. Box 4086, Clinton 39058

· † Mississippi Delta Community College
P.O. Box 668, Moorhead 38761
J. T. Hall, President

· † Mississippi Gulf Coast Community College
Gulfport 39507

· † Mississippi Gulf Coast Community College
Gautier 39553

† Mississippi University for Women
P.O. Box W-1602, Columbus 39701
Teresa Thompson, Exec. Dir. of Enrollment

† Mississippi University for Women-Tupelo
655 Eason Blvd., Tupelo 38801

· † Northeast Mississippi Community College
101 Cunningham Blvd., Booneville 38829

· † Northwest Mississippi Community College
510 N. Panola, Senatobia 38668
Henry B. Koon, President

· † Pearl River Community College, Poplarville 39470
Dr. Marvin R. White, President

† University of Mississippi Medical Center
2500 N. State St., Jackson 39216

† University of Southern Mississippi
P.O. Box 5165, Hattiesburg 39406

MISSOURI

† Avila College
11901 Wornall Rd., Kansas City 64145

∴† Barnes College
416 S. Kingshighway Blvd., St. Louis 63110

Central Methodist College
411 CMC Square, Fayette 65248
See listing under "Universities"

† Central Missouri State University
Warrensburg 64093
Delores Hudson, Dir. of Admis.

Culver-Stockton College, Canton 63435
Betty Smith, Dean of Admissions
800-537-1883

Deaconess College of Nursing
6150 Oakland Ave., St. Louis 63139
Martin W. Blanchard, Director

† Hannibal-LaGrange College, Hannibal 63401

∴† Jewish Hospital of St. Louis
216 S. Kingshighway Blvd., St. Louis 63110
Susan Graves, Dir.

∴† Lester E. Cox Medical Center
1423 N. Jefferson Ave., Springfield 65802
Mary Cuddy, Director

· Lincoln University
820 Chestnut St., Jefferson City 65101

∴† Lutheran Medical Center
School of Nursing
3547 S Jefferson Ave., St. Louis 63118
Jean Horrall, Dir. of Nursing Education

† Maryville University of St. Louis
13550 Conway Rd., Saint Louis 63141
314-576-9300 or 800-MARYVLL

∴† Missouri Baptist Medical Center
3015 N. Ballas Rd., Saint Louis 63131
Pamela K. Dick, Director

† Missouri Southern State College
3950 Newman Rd., Joplin 64801-1595
Dr. Barbara J. Box, Dept. Head
See listing under "Universities"

· North Central Missouri College
1301 Main St., Trenton 64683
Carol Elliot, Director
816-359-3948 ext. 316 or 800-880-6180

† Northeast Missouri State University
Kirksville 63501

· Penn Valley Community College
3201 S.W. Traffic Way, Kansas City 64111
A. K. Longfellow, Dean of Admissions

· Research College of Nursing
(in association with Rockhurst College)
2316 E. Meyer Blvd., Kansas City 64132
Dr. Nancy DeBasio, President/Dean
816-926-4100

∴† St. John's School of Nursing
4431 S. Fremont, Springfield 65804
Brenda Craven, Admissions Coordinator

· † St. Louis Community College at Florissant Valley
3400 Pershall Rd., St. Louis 63135
Milton Woody, Dir. of Admis.

· † St. Louis Community College at Forest Park
5600 Oakland Ave., St. Louis 63110
Elizabeth Halpin, Registrar

· † St. Louis Community College at Meramec
11333 Big Bend Rd., Kirkwood 63122

† St. Louis University
221 N. Grand Blvd., St. Louis 63103
Louis A. Menard, Dean of Admissions

∴† Saint Luke's College
4400 Wornall Rd., Kansas City 64111
Patricia Teager, Provost
816-932-2367

† Southeast Missouri State University
1 University Plz., Cape Girardeau 63701
New Student Relations 314-651-2590
See listing under "Universities"

Southwest Baptist University
1601 S. Springfield Ave., Bolivar 65613

† Southwest Missouri State University
901 S. National Ave., Springfield 65804
Dr. Euphemia Williams, Department Head
417-836-5310

· † Three Rivers Community College
Poplar Bluff 63901
Dr. Steve Poort, President

† University of Missouri, Columbia
228 Jesse Hall, Columbia 65211

† University of Missouri, Kansas City
5100 Rockhill Rd., Kansas City 64110
Leo J. Sweeney, Dir. of Admis. & Registrar

† University of Missouri
8001 Natural Bridge Rd., St. Louis 63121
Mimi LaMarca, Dir. of Admis.

† Webster University
470 E. Lockwood Ave., St. Louis 63119
Janice Hooper, PhD, RN, Chrpsn.
See listing under "Universities"

† William Jewell College, Liberty 64068
T. Edwin Norris, Dir of Admis.
800-753-7009

MONTANA

† **CARROLL COLLEGE**
1610 N. Benton Ave., Helena 59625
Candace Cain, Dir. of Admis.
See listing under "Universities"

· **MILES COMMUNITY COLLEGE**
2715 Dickinson St., Miles City 59301
Laura Lenau, Director
800-541-9281

· Missoula Vocational Technical Center
909 South Ave. W, Missoula 59801
Charles Couture, Dir. of Admis.

† Montana State University, Bozeman 59717

Montana State University - Billings
1500 N. 30th St., Billings 59101
Karen Everett, Dir. of Admis.
406-657-2158

NEBRASKA

·∴† **BRYAN MEMORIAL HOSPITAL**
5000 Sumner St., Lincoln 68506
Phylis Hollamon, Acting Administrative Director
402-483-3801

· † Central Community College-Grand Island Campus
P.O. Box 4903, Grand Island 68802-4903

† **CLARKSON COLLEGE**
101 S. 42nd St., Omaha 68131-2739
Fay L. Bower, DN Sc, FAAN, President
800-647-5500
Established 1888. Coed. Accreditation: NCACS, NLN. Tuition: $3,900. Room and board: $2,300. Enrollment: 100 boarding, 550 day. Faculty: 55. Degrees: AS, BS in Radiologic Technology, BSN, MSN in Nursing Education and Nursing Administration, MS in Health Services Management. Library: 7,423 volumes. 1 building on 2 square blocks. Located in a large metropolitan area medical center with ample recreational and cultural opportunities. RN/LPN/ advanced placement for transfer students.

† College of Saint Mary
1901 S. 72nd St., Omaha 68124
Sheila Haggas, Dir. of Admis.

† Creighton University
2500 California St., Omaha 68178
Dr. Shirley Dooling, Dean

Methodist College of Nursing & Health
8501 W. Dodge Rd., Omaha 68114
Deann Clyde, Coordinator of Admissions

† Midland Lutheran College
900 Clarkson St., Fremont 68025
Roland Kahnk, V.P. Admissions

† Nebraska Wesleyan University
5000 Saint Paul Ave., Lincoln 68504
Ken Sieg, Dir. of Admis.

† Union College
3800 S. 48th St., Lincoln 68506

† University of Nebraska
905 W. 25th St., Kearney 68849

† University of Nebraska at Lincoln
(UNMC) Lincoln Division, FAIR 113
Lincoln 68588
Student Services Advisor

† University of Nebraska Medical Center
600 S., 42nd & Dewey, Omaha 68198
Alastair M. Connell, Dean

· Western Nebraska Community College
1601 E. 27th St., Scottsbluff 69361
Roger Hovey, Admissions

NEVADA

· † Community College of Southern Nevada
Formerly Clark County Community College
3200 E. Cheyenne Ave., North Las Vegas 89030
Arlie J. Stops, Dir. of Enrollment Management

† University of Nevada, Reno
Reno 89557

† University of Nevada Las Vegas
4505 S. Maryland Pky., Las Vegas 89154-1021
Admissions: 702-895-3443 or 800-334-UNLV

NEW HAMPSHIRE

† Colby-Sawyer College
100 Main St., New London 03257

· † New Hampshire Technical College
One College Dr., Claremont 03743
Willis S. Reed, President

· New Hampshire Technical College at Stratham
277 R. Portsmouth Ave., Stratham 03885
Patricia A. Shay, Dean of Students

· † New Hampshire Technical Institute
P.O. Box 2039, Concord 03302
Daniel M. Burke, Dean of Admissions

† Rivier College
420 S. Main St., Nashua 03060
Admissions: 800-44-RIVIER

† Saint Anselm College
87 Saint Anselm Dr., Manchester 03102
Don Healy, Dir. of Admis.

† University of New Hampshire, Durham 03824
Stanwood C. Fish, Dir. of Admissions

NEW JERSEY

· † Atlantic Community College
5100 Black Horse Pike, Mays Landing 08330
Bob Royal, Director/College Recruitment

·∴† Bayonne Hospital
12 W. 30th St., Bayonne 07002

† Bergen Community College
400 Paramus Rd., Paramus 07652
Frederick R. Prisco, Jr., Dir. of Admis.

† Bloomfield College
1 Park Place, Bloomfield 07003
Warner Smith, Dean for Admissions
201-748-9000, Ext. 230

· Brookdale Community College
765 Newman Springs Rd., Lincroft 07738
Peter F. Burnham, President

· Burlington County College
County Route 530, Pemberton 08068
Juan Harris, Dir. of Admis.

·∴† Christ Hospital
176 Palisade Ave., Jersey City 07306

† College of Saint Elizabeth
Convent Station 07961
Sr. Jacqueline Burns, President

· County College of Morris
200 Center Grove Rd., Randolph 07869

· Cumberland County College
P.O. Box 517, Vineland 08360

·∴† Elizabeth General Medical Center
925 E. Jersey St., Elizabeth 07201

·∴† Englewood Hospital
350 Engle St., Englewood 07631
Effie Davis, Dir.

· Essex County College
303 University Ave., Newark 07102
201-877-1868

† Fairleigh Dickinson University, Teaneck 07666
Dennis Craig, Dir. of Admis.
201-692-2553

† **FELICIAN COLLEGE**
262 S. Main St., Lodi 07644
Sr. Mary Austin, OSB, Dir. of Admis.
201-778-1029
See listing under "Universities"

· † Gloucester County College
R.R. 4 Box 203, Sewell 08080
Richard Jones, President

·∴† Helene Fuld Medical Center
750 Brunswick Ave., Trenton 08638

·∴† Holy Name Hospital
690 Teaneck Rd., Teaneck 07666
Sr. M. Claire Tynan, Director

·∴† Hospital Center at Orange
188 S. Essex Ave., Orange 07050
Katherine Britchford, Director

† Jersey City State College
2039 Kennedy Blvd., Jersey City 07305
201-200-3234

·∴† Jersey Shore Medical Center
Ann May School of Nursing
1945 State Route 33, Neptune 07753
Arlene Farmer, Acting Director

† Kean College of New Jersey
1000 Morris Ave., Union 07083

· † Mercer County Community College
West Windsor Campus
1200 Old Trenton Rd., Trenton 08690
Michael Glass, Dir. of Admis.
See listing under "Community and Junior
Colleges"

·∴† Mercer Medical Center
P.O. Box 1658, Trenton 08607

· Middlesex County College
P.O. Box 3050, Edison 08818
Dr. Virginia Allen, Chrpsn.

† Monmouth College
400 Cedar Ave., West Long Branch 07764
Joan Rudinski, Dir. of Admis.

·∴† Mountainside Hospital
1 Bay Ave., Montclair 07042
Gloria Corbo, Director

·∴† Muhlenberg Regional Medical Center
1200 Randolph Rd., Plainfield 07060
Bong Hak Hyun, M.D., Director

· † Ocean County College
0 College Dr., Toms River 08753
Deborah Fuller, Chrpsn.

·∴† Our Lady of Lourdes School of Nursing
1565 Vesper Blvd., Camden 08103
Sr. Mary John Francis Coyle, Dean

· Passaic Co. Community College
170 College Blvd., Paterson 07505
Dr. Gustavo A. Mellander, President

·∴† Raritan Bay Medical Center
Gregory School of Nursing
530 New Brunswick Ave., Perth Amboy 08861

· Raritan Valley Community College
P.O. Box 3300, Somerville 08876

† Rutgers, The State University of NJ
Camden College of Arts & Sciences
Camden 08102

† Rutgers, The State University of NJ
College of Nursing
249 University Ave., Newark 07102

·∴† St. Francis Hospital
1 McWilliams Pl., Jersey City 07302
Theresa Boitano, RN, MA, Dir.

·∴† St. Francis Medical Center
601 Hamilton Ave., Trenton 08629
Sr. Catherine Lawrence Meyer, Dir.

† St. Peter's College
2641 John F. Kennedy Blvd.
Jersey City 07306
Dr. Doris L. Collins, Chair
201-915-9412

St. Peter's College
Hudson Terrace, Englewood Cliffs 07632
Barbara Pennipede, Associate Dean
201-568-7730

† Seton Hall University
400 S. Orange Ave., South Orange 07079
Lee Cooke, Dir. of Admis.

† Stockton State College, Pomona 08240
Sal Catalfamo, Dir. of Admis.

† Thomas Edison State College
101 W. State St., Trenton 08608

† Trenton State College
Hillwood Lakes CN 4700, Trenton 08650

·∴† West Jersey Hospital
1000 Atlantic Ave., Camden 08104
Regina Mastrangelo, Associate Dir.

† William Paterson College
300 Pompton Rd., Wayne 07470

NEW MEXICO

· † Albuquerque Technical-Vocational Institute
525 Buena Vista Dr., S.E., Albuquerque 87106
Jane Campbell, Registrar
See listing under "Career Schools"

· Clovis Community College
417 Schepps Blvd., Clovis 88101

·∴† Eastern New Mexico University-Medical Center
405 W. Country Club Rd., Roswell 88201
505-622-8170

New Mexico Highlands University, Las Vegas 87701
Dr. Jorge P. Thomas, VP Academic Affairs

· New Mexico Junior College
5317 Lovington Hwy., Hobbs 88240
Robert Snow, Registrar

· New Mexico State University
1500 University Dr., Carlsbad 88220
Shelton Marlow, Provost

† New Mexico State University
P.O. Box 30001, Las Cruces 88003

· San Juan College
4601 College Blvd., Farmington 87402

· Santa Fe Community College
P.O. Box 4187, Santa Fe 87502

† University of New Mexico, Albuquerque 87131
Robert Weaver, Dean of Admissions

· University of New Mexico
P.O. Box 1756, Gallup 87305

NEW YORK

† Adelphi University, Garden City 11530
Dr. Caryle Wolahan, Dean, School of Nursing
516-877-4510

·∴† Albany Memorial Hospital
600 Northern Blvd., Albany 12204

·∴† Arnot-Ogden Memorial Hospital School of Nursing
600 Roe Ave., Elmira 14905
LouNell McGrady, Director

·∴† Bellevue Hospital Center
462 1st Ave., New York 10016

† College of Mount St. Vincent
6301 Riverdale Ave., Riverdale 10471

† College of New Rochelle
29 Castle Pl., New Rochelle 10805

† Columbia University
School of Nursing
617 W. 168th St., New York 10032

⠆† CROUSE-IRVING MEMORIAL HOSPITAL SCHOOL OF NURSING
736 Irving Ave., Syracuse 13210
Mary Ann Fegert, Director
Nancy Parsons, Admissions Officer
315-470-7481
Established 1913. Private, nonprofit. Coed. Accreditation: NLN. Tuition: $4,400 per year. Room and board: $2,800. Enrollment: 250. Faculty: 35. Degrees: Approved Associate degree program. Library: 6,450 volumes. New Education Center. Close to Syracuse University and SUNY Health Science Center. Students use facilities at SUNY Health Science Center for gym, pool, tennis & squash courts. Within walking distance to downtown, Carrier Dome, Everson Museum, Civic Center. Scholarships, loans, free tuition, and college work-study positions available to eligible students.

· † CUNY Borough of Manhattan Community College
199 Chambers St., New York 10007

· † CUNY Bronx Community College
181st St. & University Ave., Bronx 10453
Roscoe C. Brown, Jr., President

† CUNY City College
Convent Ave. at 138th St., New York 10031

† CUNY College of Staten Island
130 Stuyvesant Pl., Staten Island 10301

· † CUNY Kingsborough Community College
2001 Oriental Blvd., Brooklyn 11235
Alan Wittes, Director of Admissions

· † CUNY LaGuardia Community College
31-10 Thompson Ave., Long Island City 11101
Robert O'Pray, Registrar

† CUNY Lehman College
250 Bedford Park Blvd. W., Bronx 10468
Jane Herbert, Dir. of Enrollment Management

† CUNY Medgar Evan College
1150 Carroll St., Brooklyn 11225

† CUNY New York City Technical College
300 Jay St., Brooklyn 11201
Ursula C. Schwerin, President

· CUNY Queensborough Community College
22205 56th Ave., Bayside 11364
Dr. Kurt R. Schmeller, President
See listing under "Community and Junior Colleges"

† CUNY York College
9420 Guy R. Brewer Blvd., Jamaica 11451

† Daemen College
4380 Main St., Amherst 14226
Maria Dillard, Dir. of Admis.
in NY 800-462-7652 or 716-839-8225

† Dominican College of Blauvelt
460 N. Western Hwy., Orangeburg 10962
Louis Kern, Dir. of Admis.
914-359-7800

† D'Youville College
320 Porter Ave., Buffalo 14201
Ronald Dannecker, Dir. of Admis.

⠆† Ellis Hospital, 1101 Nott St., Schenectady 12308
Ellen G. Scott, Dir. Nursing Educ.

† Elmira College
Park Pl., Elmira 14901
William S. Neal, Dean of Admissions
See listing under "Liberal Arts"

⠆† General Hospital
1919 Madison Ave., New York 10035

† Hartwick College, Oneonta 13820

⠆ Interfaith Medical Center, School of Nursing
567 Prospect Pl., Brooklyn 11238
Carmen Fedrik, Admissions/Finance Officer
718-935-7901
Associate in Applied Science (AAS - Nursing) program
Coed, biannual enrollment (Fall and Spring).

† IONA COLLEGE
715 North Ave., New Rochelle 10801
800-231-IONA or 914-633-2503
See listing under "Universities"

† Keuka College
P.O. Box 98, Keuka Park 14478
Robert J. Ianuzzo, Dean of Admissions

The King's College, Briarcliff Manor 10510
Frederic Rowley, Dean of Admissions

⠆† Long Island College Hospital
340 Henry St., Brooklyn 11201

† Long Island University-Brooklyn Campus
1 University Plaza, Brooklyn 11201
Alan Chaves, Dean of Admissions

† Long Island University-C. W. Post Campus
Rt. 25A, Brookville 11548
Dr. Theodora Grauer, Chrpsn.
516-299-2320

· † Maria College of Albany
700 New Scotland Ave., Albany 12208
Laurie Gilmore, Dir. of Admis.

† Mercy College
555 Broadway, Dobbs Ferry 10522
James Nesbitt, Dean of Admissions

⠆† Millard Fillmore Hospitals
School of Nursing
3 Gates Cir, Buffalo 14209
716-887-4860

† Molloy College
1000 Hempstead Ave., Rockville Centre 11570
Wayne James, Dir. of Admis.
See listing under "Universities"

† Mt. St. Mary College
330 Powell Ave., Newburgh 12550

⠆† Mt. Vernon Hospital
Valentine St., Mt. Vernon 10550
Mary Ahl-Heugel, R.N., Ph.D., Director

† Nazareth College of Rochester
4245 East Ave., Rochester 14618
Paul Kenyon, Dir. of Admis.

† New York University
70 Washington Sq., New York 10012

† Niagara University, Niagara University 14109
George Pachter, Dean of Admissions
800-462-2111
See listing under "Universities"

† Pace University, New York Campus
1 Pace Plaza, New York 10038

† Pace University, Pleasantville/Briarcliff Campus
Bedford Rd., Pleasantville 10570

⠆† Phillips Beth Israel School of Nursing
310 E. 22nd St., New York 10010
Dr. Cynthia Chesner, Dean
212-614-6110

† REGENTS COLLEGE OF THE UNIVERSITY OF THE STATE OF NEW YORK
7 Columbia Circle, Albany 12203-5159
518-464-8500

† Roberts Wesleyan College
2301 Westside Dr., Rochester 14624
Dr. Carol Kenyon, Chrpsn.
See listing under "Universities"

† Russell Sage College
51 1st St., Troy 12180

· † Russell Sage Junior College of Albany
140 New Scotland Ave., Albany 12208

⠆ ST. ELIZABETH HOSPITAL SCHOOL OF NURSING
2215 Genesee St., Utica 13501
Sister Walter Marie, Director
315-798-8125
Established 1904. Private. Coed. Accreditation: New York State Department of Education, New York State Board of Regents. Tuition: $5,000. Room and board: $3,500. Enrollment: 140 full-time, 78 Part-time. Faculty: 18. Student-faculty ratio: 8:1 clinical. Degree: AAS. Library: 6,000 volumes. 2 buildings. Located in a quiet residential section. Modern educational and dorm facilities with excellent security. Weekday, weekend and evening classes. Transfers accepted.

⠆† St. James Mercy Hospital, Sch. of Nursing
440 Monroe Ave., Hornell 14843
Loretta T. Haefele, Director

⠆† St. John's Riverside Hospital
967 N. Broadway, Yonkers 10701

⠆ St. Josephs Hospital & Health Center
206 Prospect Ave., Syracuse 13203

⠆† St. Vincent's Hospital
27 Christopher St., New York 10014
Sr. Miriam Phillips, Director

⠆† St. Vincent's Medical Center
2 Gridley Ave., Staten Island 10303

⠆ Samaritan Hospital
School of Nursing
2215 Burdett Ave., Troy 12180

⠆ SISTERS SCHOOL OF NURSING
Hospital-based/AAS degree conferred
2157 Main St., Buffalo 14214
Sister Margaret Ahl, Dean
716-862-2774

· SUNY Adirondack Community College
439 Bay Rd., Queensbury 12804
Levi Brown, Dir. of Admis.
518-793-4491
See listing under "Community and Junior Colleges"

† SUNY Health Science Center at Brooklyn
450 Clarkson Ave., Brooklyn 11203

† SUNY at Binghamton
P.O. Box 6001, Binghamton 13902

† SUNY at Buffalo
17 Capen Hall
P.O. Box 601660, Buffalo 14260-1660
716-645-6900

† SUNY at Stony Brook
Stony Brook 11794

· † SUNY Broome Community College
907 Upper Front St., Binghamton 13905
Donald Dellow, President

· † SUNY Cayuga County Community College
197 Franklin St., Auburn 13021
Patricia Powers-Burdick, Dir. of Admis.

· † SUNY Clinton Community College
Bluff Point, Plattsburgh 12901

† SUNY College at Brockport
Brockport 14420
Dr. Kay Wood, Chrpsn.

† SUNY College at New Paltz
75 Manheim Blvd., New Paltz 12561

† SUNY College at Plattsburgh, Plattsburgh 12901
Marilyn Morton, Chrpsn.
518-564-3124

· † SUNY College of Agriculture and Technology
Morrisville 13408
Dennis Nostrand, Dir. of Admis.

· † SUNY College of Technology, Alfred 14802
Deborah J. Goodrich, Dir. of Admis.
607-587-4215

· SUNY College of Technology
34 Cornell Dr., Canton 13617
Thomas R. Fletcher, Director of Admissions
800-388-7123

† SUNY College of Technology at Farmingdale
Route 110, Farmingdale 11735
Janet Snyder, Dir. of Admis.
516-420-2200

· SUNY Columbia Greene Community College
P.O. Box 1000, Hudson 12534
Barbara A. Rupp, Admissions

· SUNY Community College of the Finger Lakes
Lincoln Hill Rd., Canandaigua 14424
John M. Meuser, Dir. of Admis.

· SUNY Corning Community College
Spencer Hill Rd., Corning 14830
Donald H. Hangen, Pres.

· SUNY Dutchess Community College
Poughkeepsie 12601

· † SUNY Erie Community College, City Campus
121 Ellicott St., Buffalo 14203
Dr. Louis Ricci, President

· † SUNY Erie Community College, North Campus
6205 Main St., Williamsville 14221

· † SUNY Genesee Community College
1 College Rd., Batavia 14020
Malcolm T. Wormley, Dir. of Admis.

· † SUNY HUDSON VALLEY COMMUNITY COLLEGE
80 Vandenburgh Ave., Troy 12180
Linda Sweetman, Dir. of Admis.
See listing under "Career Schools"

† SUNY INSTITUTE OF TECHNOLOGY AT UTICA/ROME
P.O. Box 3050, Utica 13504
Dr. Elizabeth Kellogg-Walker, Dean
See listing under "Universities"

· SUNY Jamestown Community College
525 Falconer St., Jamestown 14701
Paul A. Benke, President

· SUNY Jefferson Community College
1220 Coffeen St., Watertown 13601
Rosanne N. Weir, Dir. of Admis.

· SUNY Mohawk Valley Community College
1101 Sherman Dr., Utica 13501

† SUNY Monroe Community College
1000 E. Henrietta Rd., Rochester 14623
716-292-2000

· SUNY Nassau Community College
1 Education Dr., Garden City 11530
Bernard Iantosca, Dir of Admis.

† SUNY Niagara County Community College
3111 Saunders Settlement Rd., Sanborn 14132
R. J. Mirabelli, Admis. Ofc.

· † SUNY Onondaga Community College
Onondaga Rd., Syracuse 13215
Joseph Insel, Dir. of Admis.

· Suny Orange County Community College
115 South St., Middletown 10940
914-341-4030

· † SUNY Rockland Community College
145 College Rd., Suffern 10901
Larry Gurney, Asst. Dean of Students

· † SUNY Suffolk County Community College
Crooked Hill Rd., Brentwood 11717

· † SUNY Suffolk County Community College
533 College Rd., Selden 11784
Robert Kreiling, President

· † SUNY Tompkins Cortland Community College
P.O. Box 139, Dryden 13053
Jack Hewett, Dir. of Admis.

† Syracuse University, Syracuse 13244

· † Trocaire College
110 Red Jacket Pky., Buffalo 14220
M. Patricia Shanks, Director
716-826-1200

† University of Rochester Medical Center
Rochester 14642
Dr. Sheila Ryan, Dean
See listing under "Universities"

† Utica College of Syracuse University
1600 Burrstone Rd., Utica 13502

† WAGNER COLLEGE
631 Howard Ave., Staten Island   10301
Joseph Foulke, Dean Admissions and Financial Aid
See listing under "Universities"

NORTH CAROLINA

· Alamance Community College
P.O. Box 623, Haw River   27258
W. Ronald McCarter, President

· Asheville Buncombe Technical Community College
340 Victoria Rd., Asheville   28801
Connie Buckner, Dir. of Admis.

† Barton College
College Station, Wilson   27893
Anthony Britt, Dir. of Admis.
800-345-4973/919-399-6318
See listing under "Universities"

·.† Louise Harkey School of Nursing
920 Church St., N., Concord   28025-2983
Anita Brown, Director
704-783-1556

· College of The Albemarle
P.O. Box 2327, Elizabeth City   27906
John M. Wells, Asst. Dean of Admissions
919-335-0821, Ext. 220

·.† Durham County General Hospital
Watts School of Nursing
3643 N. Roxboro Rd., Durham   27704

† East Carolina University
1000 E. 5th St., Greenville   27858
Dr. Phyllis Horn, Dean

· Fayetteville Technical Community College
P.O. Box 35236, Fayetteville   28303

† Gardner-Webb University
General Delivery, Boiling Springs   28017
Shirley Toney, Chrpsn.
704-434-2361

· Gaston College
201 Highway 321, S., Dallas   28034

· Halifax Community College
P.O. Box 809, Weldon   27890

· James Sprunt Community College
P.O. Box 398, Kenansville   28349
Rita Brown, Registrar
910-296-2500

· Lenoir-Rhyne College
P.O. Box 292, Hickory   28603
Steve M. Shuford, Registrar

·.† Mercy School of Nursing
1921 Vail Ave., Charlotte   28207
Dr. Kay Smith, Director
704-379-5841

† North Carolina A&T State University
1601 E. Market St., Greensboro   27411

† North Carolina Central University
P.O. Box 19617, Durham   27707

·.† PRESBYTERIAN HOSPITAL
P.O. Box 33549, Charlotte   28233
Michael Smith, Dir. of Admis.
704-384-4141
Established 1903. Coed. Accreditation: NLN, North Carolina State Board of Nursing. Tuition: $3,555. Room: $2,400. Fees: $370. Enrollment: 300 full-time. Faculty: 26. Student-faculty ratio: 11:1. Degrees: Diploma, qualified graduates may receive BSN in one calendar year at Queens College. Library: 8,000 volumes, 155 subscriptions. Largest hospital based nursing program in the Carolinas. 97% of graduates pass the state board exam for their registered nurse license. Students begin clinical nursing early in the second year.

† QUEENS COLLEGE
1900 Selwyn Ave., Charlotte   28274
D. Stephen Cloniger, VP for Enrollment Management
See listing under "Liberal Arts"

· Richmond Community College
P.O. Box 1189, Hamlet   28345
Teri Jacobs, Registrar/Dir. of Admis.

· Rowan-Cabarrus Community College
P.O. Box 1595, Salisbury   28145
Dr. Richard Brownell, President

· Sandhills Community College
2200 Airport Rd., Pinehurst   28374
910-692-6185

† University of North Carolina
1000 Spring Garden St., Greensboro   27412

† University of North Carolina
601 S. College Rd., Wilmington   28403
W. H. Wagoner, Chancellor

† University of North Carolina at Chapel Hill
Chapel Hill   27599
James C. Walters, Dir. Undergrad Admis.

† University of North Carolina at Charlotte
Charlotte   28223
J. H. Woodward, Chancellor

· Wayne Community College
Caller Box 8002, Goldsboro   27533
Bill Bennett, Public Information Officer
919-735-5151

† Western Carolina University
Cullowhee   28723
Tyree H. Kiser, Dir. of Admissions

·† Western Piedmont Community College
1001 Burkemont Ave., Morganton   28655
H. D. Moretz, Dean of College

† Wingate College, Wingate   28174

† Winston-Salem State University
601 S. Martin Luther King Jr.
Winston-Salem   27110
Van Wilson, Dir. of Admissions

NORTH DAKOTA

† Dickinson State University, Dickinson   58601
Marshall Melbye, Registrar
701-227-2331

† Jamestown College, Jamestown   58405

Medcenter One College of Nursing
512 N. Seventh St., Bismarck   58501
701-224-6271

† Minot State University
500 University Ave. W., Minot   58701

† North Dakota State University, Fargo   58105
Richard Shearer, Acting Dir. of Admis.

† University of Mary
7500 University Dr., Bismarck   58504
Steph Storey, Dir. of Admis.

† University of North Dakota
Box 8193 University Station, Grand Forks   58203

OHIO

† Ashland University
401 College Ave., Ashland   44805

·.† Aultman Hospital
2600 6th St., S.W., Canton   44710
Carolyn Watkins, Director

· Belmont Technical College
120 Fox Shannon Place, St. Clairsville   43950
Thomas Tarowsky, Asst. Dean of Student Services

† Bowling Green State University
Bowling Green   43403
John Martin, Dir. of Admis.

† Capital University
2199 E. Main St., Columbus   43209
Dolphus E. Henry, Associate Provost

† Case Western Reserve University
2040 Adelbert Rd., Cleveland   44106

† Cedarville College
P.O. Box 601, Cedarville   45314
David Ormsbee, Dir. of Admis.

· † Central Ohio Technical College
University Dr., Newark   43055
John Merrin, Coordinator of Admissions

·.† Christ Hospital
2139 Auburn Ave., Cincinnati   45219

· Clark State Community College
570 E. Leffels Ln., Springfield   45505
Carolyn Swanger, Chrpsn.

† Cleveland State University
Euclid Ave. at 24th St., Cleveland   44115

† College of Mount St. Joseph
5701 Delhi Rd., Cincinnati   45233-1672
See listing under "Universities"

· † Columbus State Community College
550 E. Spring St., Columbus   43215
Mary Jo Deerwester, Dir. of Admis.

·.† Community Hospital
School of Nursing
P.O. Box 1228, Springfield   45501
Marylin J. Theurer, RN, MSN, Director
513-328-8900

· † Cuyahoga Community College, Metropolitan Campus
2900 Community College Ave., Cleveland   44115

· Edison State Community College
1973 Edison Dr., Piqua   45356
Sharon Brown, Director of Nursing

·.† Fairview General Hospital
18101 Lorain Ave., Cleveland   44111

† Franciscan University of Steubenville
University Blvd., Steubenville   43952
Margaret Weber, Dir. of Admis.
800-783-6220 or 614-283-6226

† Franklin University
201 S. Grant Ave., Columbus   43215

·.† Good Samaritan Hospital School of Nursing
3217 Clifton Ave., Cincinnati   45220
Jacqueline Boothe, Director

·.† Hocking College
3301 Hocking Pky., Nelsonville   45764
Margaret Hubble, Director
614-753-3591

·.† Huron Road Hospital
13951 Terrace Rd., East Cleveland   44112
Mary Margaret Miller, Dir., Sch. of Nurs.

† Kent State University
P.O. Box 5190, Kent   44242
Bruce Riddle, Dir. of Admis.

· Kent State University, Tuscarawas Campus
University Dr., N.E., New Philadelphia   44663
Janet Karcagi, Director

· † Kent State University-Ashtabula Campus
3325 W. 13th St., Ashtabula   44004
John Mahan, Dean

· † Kent State University-East Liverpool Campus
400 E. 4th St., East Liverpool   43920
Suzanne Fitzgerald, Dean

· † Kettering College of Medical Arts
3737 Southern Blvd., Kettering   45429
Curt Dolinsky, Dir. of College Relations
800-433-5262

· † Lakeland Community College
7700 Clocktower Dr., Kirtland   44094
Bill Kraus, Dir. of Admis.

· † Lima Technical College
4240 Campus Dr., Lima   45804
Cynthia E. Spiers, Director of Admissions

· † Lorain County Community College
1005 Abbe Rd., N., Elyria   44035
Dr. John W. Thrash, Jr., Registrar

† LOURDES COLLEGE
6832 Convent Blvd., Sylvania   43560
Mary E. Briggs, Dir. of Admis.
419-885-5291 or 800-878-3210

Malone College
515 25th St., N.W., Canton   44709
Lee Sommers, Dean of Admissions

·.† Mansfield General Hospital School of Nursing
335 Glessner Ave., Mansfield   44903-2265
Nancy Collier, Director
419-526-8595

· † Marion Technical College
1467 Mt. Vernon Ave., Marion   43302-5694
Joel Liles, Dir. of Admis.

Medical College of Ohio
P.O. Box 10008, Toledo   43699
Barry L. Richardson, PhD, Dean for Admissions

·.† Mercy School, 2238 Jefferson Ave., Toledo   43624
Sr. Patricia Ann, Director

·.† MetroHealth Medical Center School of Nursing
1803 Valentine Ave., Cleveland   44109

† Miami University
E. High St., Oxford   45056

· Miami University-Hamilton Campus
1601 Peck Blvd., Hamilton   45011

† Miami University-Middletown Campus
4200 E. University Blvd., Middletown   45042

·.† Mount Carmel School of Nursing
127 S. Davis Ave., Columbus   43222
Eleanor S. Wilson, Director

· North Central Technical College
P.O. Box 698, Mansfield   44901

·.† Ohio State University Hospitals
410 W. 10th Ave., Columbus   43210

† Ohio University, Athens   45701

† Ohio University, Zanesville Branch
1425 Newark Rd., Zanesville   43701

·.† Ohio Valley Hospital
1 Ross Park, Steubenville   43952
Roy J. Karmosky, Director

† Otterbein College, Westerville   43081

· Owens Community College
P.O. Box 10000, Toledo   43699
Jim Welling, Admissions
419-661-7225

· Owens Community College
300 Davis St., Findlay   45840
Stacy Davidson, Admissions
419-423-6827

·.† PROVIDENCE HOSPITAL
1912 Hayes Ave., Sandusky   44870
Mary Alice Roeder, RN, Director

·.† St. Elizabeth Hospital
P.O. Box 1790, Youngstown   44501

·.† SUMMA SAINT THOMAS SCHOOL OF NURSING
41 Arch St., Akron   44304
Janice Weinhardt, RN, Director School of Nursing
Ann Johnson, RN, Coordinator Student Services
216-375-7560
Established 1928. Private. Coed. Accreditation: NLN, Ohio Board of Nursing. Tuition: $9,164. Est. total yrly. exp.: $4,582. Enrollment: 120 students. Faculty: masters prepared. Degree: Diploma in professional nursing. Library: 1,500 volumes. 1 building, 2 hospitals, 908 beds. Small classes, college credits, early clinical experience, transfer credits, financial aid. June entrance, application deadline October 1. Advanced placement opportunity.

·.† St. Vincent Medical Center
2201 Cherry St., Toledo   43608
Lynn Wagoner, Director

Shawnee State University
940 2nd St., Portsmouth   45662
Rosemary K. Poston, Dir. of Admis.

· † Sinclair Community College
444 W. 3rd St., Dayton   45402-1460
Sara P. Smith, Director of Admissions
800-315-3000

· Southern State Community College
200 Hobart Dr., Hillsboro   45133
Dr. Lewis C. Miller, President

† University of Akron
381 Buchtel Common, Akron 44325
Kris MacDermott, Asst. Provost Enrollment

† University of Cincinnati
2700 Clifton Ave., Cincinnati 45221

· † University of Cincinnati
Raymond Walters General & Technical College
9555 Plainfield Rd., Cincinnati 45236
Ernest G. Muntz, Dean

† University of Rio Grande
General Delivery, Rio Grande 45674
Janet Byers, Dean
614-245-5353, Ext. 7301

† University of Toledo
2801 Bancroft St., W., Toledo 43606
Richard Eastop, Dir. of Admis.

† Ursuline College
2550 Lander Rd., Cleveland 44124

† Walsh College
2020 Easton St., N.W., Canton 44720
Fran Kehoe, Dean of Admis.

† Wright State University
3640 Colonel Glenn Hwy., Dayton 45435

† Youngstown State University
410 Wick Ave., Youngstown 44555
Leslie H. Cochran, President

OKLAHOMA

· † Bacone College
99 Bacone Rd., Muskogee 74403-1597
David Norfolk, Dean of Enrollment Management

† Cameron University
2800 W. Gore Blvd., Lawton 73505
Louise Brown, Dir. of Admis.

· † Carl Albert State College
P.O. Box 606, Poteau 74953
Dr. Joe White, President

· † Connors State College
Route 1 Box 1000, Warner 74469
Dr. Carl O. Westbrook, President

† East Central University, Ada 74820
James Peak, Dir. of Admis.

· † Eastern Oklahoma State College
1301 W. Main St., Wilburton 74578
Marsha Green, Director

· † El Reno Junior College
P.O. Box 370, El Reno 73036
George C. Roper, Dir. of Admis. & Records

† Langston University
P.O. Box 907, Langston 73050

· † Murray State College, Tishomingo 73460
Dr. Clyde R. Kindell, President

· † Northeastern Oklahoma A & M College
200 I St. N.E., Miami 74354
K. Dale Patterson, Dean of Admissions

† Northeastern State University
600 N. Grand Ave., Tahlequah 74464

· † Northern Oklahoma College
1220 E. Grand Ave., Tonkawa 74653

† Northwestern Oklahoma State University
705 Oklahoma Blvd., Alva 73717

† Oklahoma Baptist University
500 W. University St., Shawnee 74801

· † Oklahoma City Community College
7777 S. May Ave., Oklahoma City 73159
Dr. Dale L. Gibson, President

† Oklahoma City University
2501 N. Blackwelder Ave., Oklahoma City 73106
Dr. Elaine Masters, Dean
See listing under "Universities"

· † Oklahoma State University-Technical Branch
900 N. Portland Ave., Oklahoma City 73107

† Oral Roberts University
7777 S. Lewis Ave., Tulsa 74171
Arthur E. Matzkvech, Dir. of Admis.

· † ROGERS STATE COLLEGE
1701 W. Will Rogers Blvd., Claremore 74017
Dr. Richard Mosier, President
918-341-7510 Ext. 319

· † Rose State College
6420 S.E. 15th St., Midwest City 73110
Robert Alyea, Registrar

· † Seminole Junior College
P.O. Box 351, Seminole 74818

† Southern Nazarene University
6729 N.W. 39th Expy., Bethany 73008

† Southwestern Oklahoma State University
100 Campus Dr., Weatherford 73096

· † Tulsa Junior College
6111 E. Skelly Dr. #200, Tulsa 74135

† University of Central Oklahoma
100 N. University Dr., Edmond 73034

† University of Oklahoma Health Sciences Center
P.O. Box 26901, Oklahoma City 73126
Lorraine Singer, Dean

† University of Tulsa
600 S. College Ave., Tulsa 74104
Dr. Susan Gaston, Director

· † Western Oklahoma State College
2801 N. Main St., Altus 73521
Larry Paxton, Dir. of Admis. & Registrar
405-477-2000

OREGON

· Central Oregon Community College
2600 N.W. College Way, Bend 97701
Christine Kerlin, Dir. of Admis.
503-383-7500

· † Chemeketa Community College
P.O. Box 14007, Salem 97309
Doris Williams, Director
503-399-5057

· † Clackamas Community College
19600 Molalla Ave., Oregon City 97045

· † Linfield College-Good Samaritan Hospital
School of Nursing
2255 N.W. Northrup, Portland 97210

· † Lane Community College
4000 E. 30th Ave., Eugene 97405
Sharon K. Moore, Dir. of Admis.

· † Linn-Benton Community College
6500 Pacific Blvd., S.W., Albany 97321
Diane Watson, Dir. of Admis.

· † Mt. Hood Community College
26000 S.E. Stark St., Gresham 97030
Anna Mae Tichy, Coordinator

† Oregon Health Sciences University
3181 S.W. Sam Jackson Park Rd., Portland 97201
Dr. Carol Lindeman, Dean

† Oregon Institute of Technology
3201 Campus Dr., Klamath Falls 97601
Jesse R. Welch, Director of Enrollment

· † Portland Community College
P.O. Box 19000, Portland 97280

· Rogue Community College
3345 Redwood Hwy., Grants Pass 97527
Ted Risser, Registrar
503-471-3501
See listing under "Community and Junior Colleges"

† Southern Oregon State College
1250 Siskiyou Blvd., Ashland 97520

· Southwestern Oregon Community College
1988 Newmark Ave., Coos Bay 97420
Jean Von Schweinitz, Registrar

· Treasure Valley Community College
650 College Blvd., Ontario 97914
Ron Kulm, Dir. of Admis.

· † Umpqua Comunity College
P.O. Box 967, Roseburg 97470

† University of Portland
5000 N. Willamette Blvd., Portland 97203

† Walla Walla School of Nursing
10345 S.E. Market, Portland 97216

PENNSYLVANIA

· † ABINGTON MEMORIAL HOSPITAL
1200 Old York Rd., Abington 19001
215-576-2650

† Albright College
P.O. Box 15234, Reading 19612

† Allentown College of St. Francis de Sales
2755 Station Ave., Center Valley 18034
Dr. Joan Grindley, Chrpsn.

· † Altoona Hospital, School of Nursing
620 Howard Ave., Altoona 16601
Nancy Hayes, RN, Director

† Alvernia College
400 Bernardine St., Reading 19607
Lisa Grabowski, Dir. of Admis.

: Antonelli Medical & Professional Institute
1700 Industrial Hwy., Pottstown 19464
Paula Bauer, Dir. of Admis.

† Bloomsburg University, Bloomsburg 17815
Bernard Vinovrski, Dir. of Admis.

· † Brandywine Hospital
201 Reeceville Rd., Coatesville 19320

† Bucks County Community College
Swamp Rd., Newtown 18940

· Butler County Community College
P.O. Box 1203, Oak Hill, Butler 16003
William Miller, Dir. of Admis.

† California University of Pennsylvania
3rd St., California 15419
Norman Hasbrouck, Dean for Enrollment

† Carlow College
3333 5th Ave., Pittsburgh 15213

† Cedar Crest College
100 College Dr., Allentown 18104-6196
Cynthia Phillips, Dir. of Admissions

· † Chester County Hospital School of Nursing
701 E. Marshall St., West Chester 19380
Dolores Ott, Director
610-431-5165

· † Citizens General Hospital
651 4th Ave., New Kensington 15068
Shirley Heim, C.S.J., Assistant Director

† Clarion University of Pennsylvania-Venango Campus
Oil City 16301

† College Misericordia
301 Lake St., Dallas 18612
Michael Joseph, Dir. of Enrollment Mgmt.

· † Community College of Allegheny Co.
Allegheny Campus
808 Ridge Ave., Pittsburgh 15212

· † Community College of Allegheny Co., Boyce Campus
595 Beatty Rd., Monroeville 15146

· † Community College of Allegheny Co., South Campus
1750 Clairton Rd., West Mifflin 15122

· † Community College of Allegheny County
North Campus
111 Pines Plaza, Pittsburgh 15237

· † Community College of Philadelphia
1700 Spring Garden St., Philadelphia 19130
Allen T. Bonnell, President

· † Conemaugh Valley Memorial Hospital
1086 Franklin St., Johnstown 15905
Bonnie Ford, RN, MSN, Acting Director

· † Delaware County Community College
901 Media Line Rd., Media 19063

† Duquesne University
600 Forbes Ave., Pittsburgh 15282
Thomas Schaefer, C.S.Sp., Dir. of Admis.

† Eastern College
10 Fairview Dr., Saint Davids 19087
Dr. Alan Tharpe, Dean Undergraduate Studies

† East Stroudsburg University of Pennsylvania
East Stroudsburg 18301
Alan Chesterton, Dir. of Admis.

† Edinboro University of Pennsylvania
Edinboro 16444
Admissions Office: 800-626-2203

· † Episcopal Hospital
100 E. Lehigh Ave., Philadelphia 19125
Carol E. Hamer, R.N., MSEd., Dir. Nurs. Ed.

· † Frankford Hospital
4918 Penn St., Philadelphia 19124
Mary K. Gilchrist, Director

† Gannon University
109 University Sq., Erie 16541

· † Geisinger Medical Center
N. Academy Ave., Danville 17822

· † Germantown Hospital & Medical Center
1 Penn Blvd., Philadelphia 19144
Margaret M. Gill, Director

† GWYNEDD-MERCY COLLEGE
Sumneytown Pike, Gwynedd Valley 19437
Marjorie DeSimone, Dean of Admissions
800-DIAL-GMC
See listing under "Universities"

† Hahnemann University
230 N. Broad St., Philadelphia 19102

· Harrisburg Area Community College
3300 N. Cameron Street Road, Harrisburg 17110

† Holy Family College
Grant & Frankford Ave., Philadelphia 19114
Dr. Mott Linn, Dir. of Admis.
215-637-3050

† Immaculata College
Immaculata 19345
James P. Sullivan, Dir. of Admis.

† Indiana University of Pennsylvania, Indiana 15705
Fred Dadak, Dean, Admissions

· † Jameson Memorial Hospital School of Nursing
1211 Wilmington Ave., New Castle 16105
Delores Graziani, RN, MSN, Dir. of Admis.

† Kutztown University of Pennsylvania
Kutztown 19530

· † Lancaster General Hospital
P.O. Box 3555, Lancaster 17604
Kathryn Trego, RN, Admissions Counselor

† La Roche College
9000 Babcock Blvd., Pittsburgh 15237
Marianne Leister, Dir. of Admis.

† La Salle University
1900 W. Olney Ave., Philadelphia 19141
Br. Gerald Fitzgerald, Dir. of Admis.
See listing under "Universities"

· † Louise S. McClintic School of Nursing
4631 Davison St., Pittsburgh 15201

· Luzerne Co. Community College
1333 S. Prospect St., Nanticoke 18634

† Lycoming College, Williamsport 17701

† Marywood College
2300 Adams Ave., Scranton 18509

· † Mercy Hospital
1401 Boulevard of the Allies, Pittsburgh 15219
Sr. Carolyn Schallenberger, RSM, Dean

† Mercyhurst College
501 E. 38th St., Erie 16546
Andrew Roth, Dean of Enrollment
800-825-1926

† Messiah College
General Delivery, Grantham 17027
Ron Long, Dir. of Admis.

∴† Methodist Hospital
2301 S. Broad St., Philadelphia 19148
Andree Gibson, Director

† Millersville University of Pennsylvania
Millersville 17551
Blair Treasure, Dean of Admissions

· † Montgomery County Community College
340 DeKalb Pike, Blue Bell 19422-0758
Dennis Murphy, Dir. of Admis.

† Mt. Aloysius College
1 College Dr., Cresson 16630
Nedra Farcus, Chrpsn.

† Neumann College
Concord Rd., Aston 19014

· † Northampton Co. Area Community College
3835 Green Pond Rd., Bethlehem 18017
Janice Keim, Assoc. Dir. of Admis.

∴† Northeastern Hospital
2301 E. Allegheny Ave., Philadelphia 19134
Shirley Hickman, Director

∴† Ohio Valley General Hospital
25 Heckel Rd., Mc Kees Rocks 15136

† Pennsylvania State University
201 Shields Bldg., University Park 16802

∴† Point Park College-St. Francis Medical Center
400 45th St., Pittsburgh 15201

∴† Pottsville Hospital School of Nursing
420 S. Jackson St., Pottsville 17901

· Reading Area Community College
P.O. Box 1706, Reading 19603
Robin Sodomsky, Dir. of Admis.

∴† Reading Hospital & Medical Center
300 S. 6th St., Reading 19602

∴† Roxborough Memorial Hospital
5800 Ridge Ave., Philadelphia 19128
Mary Grace Simcox, Dir. of Nursing Education
215-487-4294

† St. Francis College
P.O. Box 600, Loretto 15940

∴† **ST. FRANCIS HOSPITAL OF NEW CASTLE**
1100 S. Mercer St., New Castle 16101
Gloria Minteer, RN, Director of Nursing Education
412-656-6000

∴† St. Joseph Hospital
250 College Ave., Lancaster 17604
M. Joan Stead, Director

∴† St. Luke's Hospital
801 Ostrum St., Bethlehem 18015
Eleanor E. Carson, Director

∴† St. Vincent Health Center
232 W. 25th St., Erie 16544
Joyce Boxer, Director

∴† Sewickley Valley Hospital
700 Blackburn Rd., Sewickley 15143

∴† Shadyside Hospital School of Nursing
5230 Centre Ave., Pittsburgh 15232
Dr. Margaret Dietz, Director

∴† Sharon Regional Health System
740 E. State St., Sharon 16146
Jean Fobes, Director

† Slippery Rock University, Slippery Rock 16057
Director of Admissions

† Temple University
3307 N. Broad St., Philadelphia 19140

† Thiel College
75 College Ave., Greenville 16125
Robert Weaver, Dir. of Admis.

† Thomas Jefferson University
130 S. 9th St., Suite 1620
Philadelphia 19107

∴† Uniontown Hospital
500 W. Berkeley St., Uniontown 15401

† University of Pennsylvania
0 Levy Park, Philadelphia 19104

† University of Pittsburgh
4200 5th Ave., Pittsburgh 15260

† University of Pittsburgh at Bradford
300 Campus Dr., Bradford 16701

† University of Scranton
800 Linden St., Scranton 18510

† Villanova University
845 E. Lancaster Ave., Villanova 19085
Stephen R. Merritt, Dir. of Admis.

∴† Washington Hospital
155 Wilson Ave., Washington 15301
Anne Hast, Director

† Waynesburg College
51 W. College St., Waynesburg 15370
Robin Moore, Dir. of Admis.
800-225-7393

† West Chester University of Pennsylvania
S. High St., West Chester 19380

∴† Western Pennsylvania Hospital
4800 Friendship Ave., Pittsburgh 15224
Shirley Wilson, Director

† Widener University
700 E. 14th St., Chester 19013

† Wilkes University
184 S. River St., Wilkes-Barre 18766
Emory P. Guffrovich Jr., Dean of Admissions

† York College of Pennsylvania
P.O. Box 15199, York 17405-7199
Nancy Spataro, Dir. of Admis.
717-849-1600
See listing under "Universities"

RHODE ISLAND

· † Community College of Rhode Island
Flanagan Campus
1762 Louisquisset Pike, Lincoln 02865

· Community College of Rhode Island
Providence Campus
1 Hilton St., Providence 02905

· † Community College of Rhode Island
Knight Campus
400 East Ave., Warwick 02886

† Rhode Island College
600 Mt. Pleasant Ave., Providence 02908

∴† St. Joseph's Hospital
200 High Service Ave., North Providence 02904

† Salve Regina University
1 Ochre Point Ave., Newport 02840
Roselina McKillop, Dean of Admissions

† University of Rhode Island, Kingston 02881
Jean Miller, Dean

SOUTH CAROLINA

Bob Jones University, Greenville 29614
Kathleen Crispin, Director
See listing under "Universities"

† Clemson University
201 Sikes Hall, Clemson 29634

· † Florence Darlington Technical College
P.O. Box 8000, Florence 29501

· † Greenville Technical College
P.O. Box 5616, Greenville 29606
Jacqueline Wohn, Dean

† Lander College
320 Stanley Ave., Greenwood 29649

† Medical University of South Carolina
171 Ashley Ave., Charleston 29425
W. Marcus Newberry, M.D., Dean

· † Midlands Technical College
P.O. Box 2408, Columbia 29202

· † Orangeburg-Calhoun Technical College
3250 Saint Matthews Rd. N.E., Orangeburg 29115

South Carolina State University
P.O. Box 7127, Orangeburg 29117-0001
803-536-7185

· † Technical College of the Lowcountry
100 S. Ribaut Rd., Beaufort 29901

· † Trident Technical College
P.O. Box 10367, Charleston 29411
Charles Branch, President

† University of South Carolina, Columbia 29208
Terry Davis, Dir. of Admis.
803-777-7700

† University of South Carolina at Aiken
171 University Pkwy., Aiken 29801

† University of South Carolina, Spartanburg 29303

SOUTH DAKOTA

† Augustana College
29th & S. Summit, Sioux Falls 57197

† Dakota Wesleyan University
1300 W. University Ave., Mitchell 57301

† Huron University
333 Ninth St. S.W., Huron 57350

† Mt. Marty College
1105 W. 8th St., Yankton 57078
Paula Tacke, Dir. of Admis.

† Presentation College
1500 N. Main St., Aberdeen 57401
Sr. Lucille Welbig, Dir. of Admis.

† South Dakota State University
P.O. Box 2275, Brookings 57007
Roberta K. Olson, Acting Dean
605-688-5178
See listing under "Universities"

† University of South Dakota
414 E. Clark St., Vermillion 57069
Dave Lorenz, Dir. of Admis.

: Western Dakota Technical Institute
1600 Sedivy Ln., Rapid City 57701
See listing under "Career Schools"

TENNESSEE

· † Aquinas Junior College
4210 Harding Rd., Nashville 37205
Sr. Robert Ann Britton, President

† Austin Peay State University
601 College St., Clarksville 37044

∴† Baptist Memorial Hospital
899 Madison Ave., Memphis 38146

† Carson-Newman College
P.O. Box 70552, Jefferson City 37760
See listing under "Universities"

· † Chattanooga State Technical Community College
4501 Amnicola Hwy., Chattanooga 37406

· † Cleveland State Community College
P.O. Box 3570, Cleveland 37320
Shelby Millsaps, Director

· † Columbia State Community College
P.O. Box 1315, Columbia 38402

Crichton College
6655 Winchester Rd., Memphis 38115
Preprofessional program
901-367-9800

· † Dyersburg State Community College
P.O. Box 648, Dyersburg 38025
Carl C. Andersen, President

† **EAST TENNESSEE STATE UNIVERSITY**
P.O. Box 70731, Johnson City 37614
Dr. Nancy Dishner, Dean, Enrollment Management
615-929-4213 or 800-462-3878

∴· Ft. Sanders School of Nursing
1915 White Ave., S.W., Knoxville 37916
Barbara Lowe, Director

† Lincoln Memorial University
P.O. Box 2012, Harrogate 37752
Conrad Daniels, Dir. of Admis.

∴† Methodist Hospital
1265 Union Ave., Memphis 38104

† Middle Tennessee State University
Murfreesboro 37132
Roger D. Sims, Dir. of Admis.

· † Motlow State Community College
P.O. Box 88100, Tullahoma 37388

· † Roane State Community College
276 Patton Ln., Harriman 37748
Susan McKinney, Associate Dean

∴· St. Francis Hospital
School of Practical Nursing
5959 Park Ave., Memphis 38119
Catherine Jones, RN, Director

∴† St. Joseph Hospital
204 Overton Ave., Memphis 38105

· † Shelby State Community College
P.O. Box 40568, Memphis 38174

† Southern Missionary College
P.O. Box 370, Collegedale 37315

† Tennessee State University
3500 John A. Merritt Blvd., Nashville 37209

† Tennessee Technological University
P.O. Box 5006, Cookeville 38505

† Union University
2447 US Highway 45 Bypass, Jackson 38305
Dr. Carla Sanderson, Dean
901-668-1818
See listing under "Universities"

† University of Memphis, Memphis 38152
Dr. John Eubank, Dean of Admissions

† University of Tennessee at Martin
Martin 38238
Paul Kelley, Director of Admissions
See listing under "Universities"

† University of Tennessee at Chattanooga
615 McCallie Ave., Chattanooga 37403

† University of Tennessee, Knoxville
527 Andy Holt Tower, Knoxville 37996
Dr. Gordon Stanley, Dir. of Admis.

† University of Tennessee, Memphis
Health Science Center
800 Madison Ave., Memphis 38163
Office of Enrollment Management

† Vanderbilt University
West End Ave., Nashville 37240

· † Walters State Community College
500 S. Davy Crockett Pky., Morristown 37813

TEXAS

† Abilene Christian University
ACU Station, Box 6000, Abilene 79699

· Alvin Community College
3110 Mustang Rd., Alvin 77511

· Amarillo College
P.O. Box 447, Amarillo 79178
Dale Hardgrove, Registrar

† Angelo State University
2601 W. Ave., N., San Angelo 76909

· Austin Community College
1020 Grove Blvd., Austin 78741
Nancy Glass, Dean
512-389-4103

∴† Baptist Memorial Hospital System
111 Dallas St., San Antonio 78286
Joanna Seamans, Director

† Baylor University School of Nursing
3700 Worth St., Dallas 75246
Phyllis Karns, Dean

· Central Texas College
P.O. Box 1800, Killeen 76540

· College of the Mainland
1200 Auburn Rd., Texas City 77591
Dr. Robert Johnston, Dir. of Admis.

† Corpus Christi State University
6300 Ocean Dr., Corpus Christi   78412

† Dallas Baptist University
7777 W. Kiest Blvd., Dallas   75211

· † Del Mar College
101 Baldwin Blvd., Corpus Christi   78404
Lawrence Jasman, Registrar

· † El Centro College
801 Main St., Dallas   75202
Queen Randall, President

· † El Paso Community College
P.O. Box 20500, El Paso   79998
Dr. Robert E. Shapack, President

· † Galveston College
4015 Ave. Q, Galveston   77550
John Pickelman, President

· † Grayson County College
6101 Highway 691, Denison   75020
Jim Williams, President

† Hardin-Simmons University
2200 Hickory St., Abilene   79698
Laura Moore, Dir. of Admis.
See listing under "Universities"

† Houston Baptist University
7502 Fondren Rd., Houston   77074

· Houston Community College
P.O. Box 7849, Houston   77270
N. Jean Vandergrift, Director

· † Howard College
1001 Birdwell Ln., Big Spring   79720
Al Blount, Director

† Incarnate Word College
4301 Broadway St., San Antonio   78209
Sr. Sally Mitchell, Dean of Enrollment

· † Kilgore College
1100 Broadway Blvd., Kilgore   75662
Joe Cruseturner, Registrar

† Lamar University
P.O. Box 10009, Beaumont   77710
800-458-7558

· † Laredo Junior College
1 W. End Washington St., Laredo   78040
Vernette Carranza, Director

· † Lee College
511 S. Whiting, Baytown   77520
Dr. Vivian Blevins, President

· † McLennan Community College
1400 College Dr., Waco   76708
Dennis Michaelis, President

† McMurry University
14th and Sayles, Abilene   79697

·. † Methodist Hospital
2002 Miami, Lubbock   79410
Irene Wilson, RN, Dean

· † Midland College
3600 N. Garfield St., Midland   79705
Dr. David E. Daniel, President

· † North Central Texas College
1525 W. California, Gainesville   76240
Doug Willis, Dir. of Admis.

· † North Harris County College
2700 W. W. Thorne Blvd., Houston   77073

· † Odessa College
201 W. University, Odessa   79764

· † Paris Junior College
2400 Clarksville St., Paris   75460

† Prairie View A & M University
6436 Fannin St. #916, Houston   77030
Dr. Dorothea Webb Williams, Dean

· † San Antonio College
1300 San Pedro Ave., San Antonio   78212

· † San Jacinto College
4624 Fairmont Pky., Pasadena   77504
Thomas M. Spencer, President

· † South Plains College
1401 College Ave., Levelland   79336
Marvin L. Baker, President

† Southwestern Adventist College
P.O. Box 567, Keene   76059

† Stephen F. Austin State University
P.O. Box 6078, Nacogdoches   75962

· † Tarrant County Junior College-South Campus
5301 Campus Dr., Ft. Worth   76119
Dr. Jim Worden, President

· † Texarkana Community College
2500 N. Robison Rd., Texarkana   75501

† Texas Christian University
2800 S. University Dr., Ft. Worth   76129
Dr. Edward Boehm, Jr., Dean of Admissions

· † Texas Southmost College
83 Fort Brown, Brownsville   78520
Dr. Albert A. Besteiro, President

† Texas Tech University, Lubbock   79409

† Texas Women's University
P.O. Box 23925, Denton   76204

· † Trinity Valley Community College
800 Hwy. 243 W., Kaufman   75142

† University of Mary Hardin-Baylor
UMHB Station, Box 8001, Belton   76513
800-727-8642 or 817-939-4520

† University of Texas at Arlington
UTA Box 19125, Arlington   76019
R. Zack Prince, Dir. of Admis.

† University of Texas at Austin
0 the University of Texas, Austin   78712

† University of Texas at El Paso
500 W. University Ave., El Paso   79968

† University of Texas at Tyler
3900 University Blvd., Tyler   75799
Doris Rieman, Chrpsn.

† University of Texas Health Science Center
7703 Floyd Curl Dr., San Antonio   78284

† University of Texas-Houston School of Nursing
1100 Holcombe, Houston   77030

† The University of Texas Medical Branch at Galveston
Galveston   77555-1305

† University of Texas-Pan American
1201 W. University Dr., Edinburg   78539
Miguel Nerarez, President

· † Victoria College
2200 E. Red River St., Victoria   77901
Roland E. Bing, President

† West Texas State University
2501 4th Ave., Canyon   79016
Lila Vars, Dir. of Admis.

UTAH

† Brigham Young University, Provo   84602

Southern Utah University
351 W. Center St., Cedar City   84720
Judy Fillmore, Coordinator
Cooperative Program with Weber State College
801-586-7915

† University of Utah
1400 E. 200 S., Salt Lake City   84112
Dr. J. Stayner Landward, Dir. of Admis.

† Weber State University
3750 Harrison Blvd., Ogden   84408

† Westminster College of Salt Lake City
1840 S. 1300 E., Salt Lake City   84105
800-748-4753

VERMONT

† Castleton State College, Castleton   05735
Gary Fallis, Dir. of Admis.

† Norwich University Vermont College Campus
Montpelier   05602
Prof. Linda Ellis, Head
See listing under "Universities"

† Southern Vermont College
Monument Ave., Bennington   05201
See listing under "Universities"

† University of Vermont
194 S. Prospect St., Burlington   05401
802-656-3370

VIRGINIA

·. † Centra Health Inc.
Tate Springs Rd., Lynchburg   24501

· College of Health Sciences
P.O. Box 13186, Roanoke   24031
Ruth Robertson, Registrar

· † Dabney S. Lancaster Community College
P.O. Box 1000, Clifton Forge   24422
John F. Backels, President

·. † De Paul Medical Center
150 Kingsley Ln., Norfolk   23505

† Eastern Mennonite College
1200 Park Rd., Harrisonburg   22801
Jerry Miller, Dir. of Admis.

† George Mason University
4400 University Dr., Fairfax   22030-4444
Dr. Rita Carty, Dean

· † Germanna Community College
P.O. Box 339, Locust Grove   22508
Linda Crooker, Registrar

† Hampton University, Hampton   23668
Ollie Bowman, Dean of Admissions

† James Madison University, Harrisonburg   22807

· † John Tyler Community College
13101 Jefferson Davis Hwy., Chester   23831
Dr. Freddie W. Nicholas, Jr., Pres.

· † J. Sargeant Reynolds Community College
P.O. Box C-23040, Richmond   23261

LIBERTY UNIVERSITY
P.O. Box 20000, Lynchburg   24506
Jay Spencer, VP Recruitment
800-376-2800
See listing under "Universities"

·. † Louise Obici School of Nursing
P.O. Box 1100, Suffolk   23439

† Lynchburg College
1501 Lakeside Dr., Lynchburg   24501
Ernest Chadderton, Dean of Enrollment

† Marymount University
2807 N. Glebe Rd., Arlington   22207
Charles Coe, Director of Admissions
800-548-7638 or 703-284-1500
See listing under "Universities"

·. † Memorial Hospital
142 S. Main St., Danville   24541
Darnell Cockram, Director

·. † Norfolk General Hospital
600 Gresham Dr., Norfolk   23507
Florence Bogush, Director

† Norfolk State University
2401 Corprew Ave., Norfolk   23504

· † Northern Virginia Community College
8333 Little River Turnpike, Annandale   22003
Dr. Barbara Guthrie-Morse, Provost

† Old Dominion University
5215 Hampton Blvd., Norfolk   23508

· † Piedmont Virginia Community College
R.R. 6, Box 1A, Charlottesville   22902

† Radford University
P.O. Box 5430, Radford   24142

·. † Richmond Memorial Hospital, School of Nursing
1300 Westwood Avenue, Richmond   23227
Laura A. Murphy, Director

·. † Riverside Regional Medical Center
420 J. Clyde Morris Blvd., Newport News   23601

† SHENANDOAH UNIVERSITY
1460 University Dr., Winchester   22601
Dr. Daris Small, Dean
See listing under "Universities"

·. † Southside Regional Medical Center
801 S. Adams St., Petersburg   23803

· † Tidewater Community College, Portsmouth Campus
Rt. 135, Portsmouth   23703
Admissions Office

† University of Virginia
P.O. Box 9017, Charlottesville   22906

† Virginia Commonwealth University
910 W. Franklin St., Richmond   23284

· † Virginia Highlands Community College
P.O. Box 828, Abingdon   24212
Dr. Emma W. Schulken, President

· † Virginia Western Community College
P.O. Box 14025, Roanoke   24038
Charles L. Downs, President

· † Wytheville Community College
1000 W. Main St., Wytheville   24382
Admissions Office

WASHINGTON

· † Bellevue Community College
3000 Landerholm Circle, S.E., Bellevue   98007

· † Clark College
1800 E. McLoughlin Blvd., Vancouver   98663

· Columbia Basin College
2600 N. 20th Ave., Pasco   99301
Donna Campbell, Coordinator

· † Everett Community College
801 Wetmore Ave., Everett   98201
206-388-9463

† Gonzaga University
502 E. Boone Ave., Spokane   99258
Philip Ballinger, Dean of Admissions

† Highline Community College, Des Moines   98198

† Intercollegiate Center for Nursing Education
2917 W. Fort George Wright Dr., Spokane   99204
Dr. Thelma Cleveland, Dean

· † Lower Columbia College
P.O. Box 3010, Longview   98632

† Pacific Lutheran University
12180 Park Ave. S., Tacoma   98447
Dr. Dorothy Langen, Dean

· † St. Martin's College
700 College St. N.E., Lacey   98516

· † Seattle Central Community College
1701 Broadway, Seattle   98122
Loris A. Blue, Dir. of Admis.

· † Seattle Pacific University
3307 3rd Ave., W., Seattle   98119

† Seattle University
Broadway Ave. & Madison, Seattle   98122
Lee Gerig, Dean of Admissions

· † Shoreline Community College
16101 Greenwood Ave., N., Seattle   98133
Chuck Fields, Registrar

· † Skagit Valley College
2405 E. College Way, Mt. Vernon   98273

· † South Puget Sound Community College
2011 Mottman Rd., S.W., Olympia   98512

· † Spokane Community College
1810 N. Greene St., Spokane   99207

· † Tacoma Community College
5900 S. 12th St., Tacoma   98465

· † University of Washington, Seattle   98195

· † Walla Walla Community College
500 Tausick Way, Walla Walla　99362
Hulda Dierk, Director
509-527-4283
See listing under "Community and Junior
Colleges"

· Wenatchee Valley College
1300 5th St., Wenatchee　98801
509-664-2518

· † Yakima Valley Community College
16th & Nob Hill Blvd., Yakima　98902

WEST VIRGINIA

† Alderson-Broaddus College
Philippi　26416
Craig W. Gould, Director of Admissions
304-457-1700

† Bluefield State College
219 Rock St., Bluefield　24701

Davis & Elkins College
100 Campus Dr., Elkins　26241
Kevin D. Chenoweth, Dir. of Admis.

† Fairmont State College
1201 Locust Ave., Fairmont　26554
John Conaway, Dir. of Admis.

GLENVILLE STATE COLLEGE
200 High St., Glenville　26351
Mack Samples, Dean of Admissions
See listing under "Liberal Arts"

† Marshall University
400 Hal Greer Blvd., Huntington　25755
See listing under "Universities"

· · † St. Mary's Hospital
2900 1st Ave., Huntington　25702
Ruth B. Jones, Director

† Shepherd College, Shepherdstown　25443

· † Southern West Virginia Community College
P.O. Box 2900, Logan　25601

† The University of Charleston
2300 MacCorkle Ave., S.E., Charleston　25304
800-995-GO UC

· † West Virginia Northern Community College
College Square, Wheeling　26003

† West Virginia University
P.O. Box 6001, Morgantown　26506

· † West Virginia University at Parkersburg
R.R. 5, Box 167-A, Parkersburg　26101
R. Copeland, Registrar

† WEST VIRGINIA WESLEYAN COLLEGE
59 College Ave., Buckhannon　26201
Robert Skinner, Director of Admission
See listing under "Universities"

† Wheeling Jesuit College
316 Washington Ave., Wheeling　26003
Fr. Thomas Acker, SJ, President

WISCONSIN

† Alverno College
P.O. Box 343922, Milwaukee　53234
Colleen Hayes, Dir. of Admis.

† BELLIN COLLEGE OF NURSING
P.O. Box 23400, Green Bay　54305-3400
Teresa Halcsik, VP for Support Services
414-433-5803

· · † Bellin Hospital
P.O. Box 23400, Green Bay　54305-3400

· † Blackhawk Technical College
P.O. Box 5009, Janesville　53547

† Cardinal Stritch College
6801 N. Yates Rd., Milwaukee　53217
David Wegener, Dir. of Admis.

Carroll College
100 N. East Ave., Waukesha　53186
Ken Moyer, Dir. of Admis.

· † Chippewa Valley Technical College
620 Clairemont Ave., W., Eau Claire　54701

† Columbia College of Nursing
2121 E. Newport Ave., Milwaukee　53211

· · † Columbia Hospital
2025 E. Newport Ave., Milwaukee　53211

† Concordia University
12800 N. Lake Shore Dr., Mequon　53097
414-243-5700

† Edgewood College
855 Woodrow St., Madison　53711
Robert Blust, Dir. of Admis.

· † Fox Valley Technical College
P.O. Box 2277, Appleton　54913

· † Gateway Technical College
3520 30th Ave., Kenosha　53144

· † Lakeshore Technical College
1290 North Ave., Cleveland　53015

· † Madison Area Technical College
3550 Anderson Rd., Madison　53704
Beverly Simone, District Director

† Marian College of Fond du Lac
45 S. National Ave., Fond du Lac　54935
Carol Reichenberger, Dean of Admissions

† Marquette University
1217 W. Wisconsin Ave., Milwaukee　53233
Raymond A. Brown, Dean of Admissions

· † Milwaukee Area Technical College
700 W. State St., Milwaukee　53233

· · † Milwaukee County Medical Complex
1304 S. 70th St., West Allis　53214
Jo Ann Dillon, RN, Admissions

· † Moraine Park Technical College
2151 N. Main St., West Bend　53095-1598
Maureen Josten, Campus Administrator
414-334-3413

· † Northeast Wisconsin Technical College
P.O. Box 19042, Green Bay　54307

† Silver Lake College
2406 S. Alverno Road, Manitowoc　54220
Sandra Schwartz, Dir. of Admis.

· † Southwest Wisconsin Technical College
Fennimore　53809

† University of Wisconsin, Eau Claire
Eau Claire　54701

† University of Wisconsin, Green Bay
2420 Nicolet Dr., Green Bay　54311
Myron Van de Ven, Dir. of Admis.

† University of Wisconsin, Madison
500 Lincoln Dr., Madison　53706

† University of Wisconsin
P.O. Box 413, Milwaukee　53201
V. M. Allison, Registrar

† University of Wisconsin, Oshkosh
800 Algoma Blvd., Oshkosh　54901-8602
August Helgerson, Dir. of Admis.

† Viterbo College
815 9th St., S., La Crosse　54601
Roland W. Nelson, Dir. of Admis.

· † Waukesha County Technical College
800 Main St., Pewaukee　53072
Dr. Richard T. Anderson, Dir.

: † Western Wisconsin Technical College
304 N. 6th St., La Crosse　54602

· † Wisconsin Indianhead Technical College
HCR 69, Box 10-B, Shell Lake　54871

WYOMING

· † Casper College
125 College Dr., Casper　82601
A. W. Vance, Dir. of Admis.

· † Central Wyoming College
2660 Peck St., Riverton　82501
Mary Gores, Admissions Officer
307-856-9291
See listing under "Community and Junior
Colleges"

· † Laramie County Community College
1400 E. College Dr., Cheyenne　82007
Dr. Harlan L. Heglar, President

· † Northern Wyoming Community College
720 W. 8th St., #1, Gillette　82716

· † Sheridan College
P.O. Box 1500, Sheridan　82801
Bruce Gifford, Dir. of Admis.

† University of Wyoming
P.O. Box 3434, Laramie　82071
Richard Davis, Dir. of Admis.

GUAM

University of Guam
UOG Station, Mangilao　96923
Kathleen Owings, Dir. of Admis.

PUERTO RICO

† Catholic University of Puerto Rico
Las Americas Ave., Ponce　00732
Carilin Frau, Dir. of Admis.

† Inter American University of Puerto Rico
Metropolitan Campus
P.O. Box 1293, San Juan　00902

· † Technological College of San Juan
Jose Oliver, Final Box 70179, San Juan　00918

Universidad Adventista de las Antillas
P.O. Box 118, Mayaguez　00681
Alfredo Bonilla, Director

† Universidad Metropolitana
P.O. Box 21150, San Juan　00928

† University of Puerto Rico
Arecibo Technical University College
P.O. Box A-1806, Arecibo　00613

† University of Puerto Rico
CUH Station Rd. 908 Bo Tejas, Humacao　00791

† University of Puerto Rico, Mayaguez Campus
P.O. Box 5000, Mayaguez　00681
Neysa Lopez, Dir. of Admis.

† University of Puerto Rico, Medical Sciences Campus
P.O. Box 5067, San Juan　00906

† University of the Sacred Heart
P.O. Box 12383, San Juan　00914

OCEANOGRAPHY

ALABAMA

University of Alabama
P.O. Box 870132, Tuscaloosa　35487-0132
Roy Smith, Dir. of Admis.

ALASKA

Sheldon Jackson College
801 Lincoln St., Sitka　99835
Dennis Trotter, Dir. of Admis.
907-747-5221

University of Alaska Fairbanks
Fairbanks　99775

CALIFORNIA

California Maritime Academy
P.O. Box 1392, Vallejo　94590

California State University, Long Beach
1250 Bellflower Blvd., Long Beach　90840

Humboldt State University
1 Harps St., Arcata　95521

San Francisco State University
1600 Holloway Ave., San Francisco　94132
Corwin Bjonerud, Dir. of Admis.

· Santa Barbara City College
721 Cliff Dr., Santa Barbara　93109
805-965-0581

Stanford University
Hopkins Marine Station, Pacific Grove　93950

University of California, Irvine
Irvine　92715

University of California-Santa Cruz
Santa Cruz　95064
Wm. T. Doyle, Dir.

University of San Diego
5998 Alcala Park, San Diego　92110
Warren Muller, Dir. of Admis.
619-260-4506

CONNECTICUT

University of Connecticut, Marine Sciences Institute
Avery Point, Groton　06340
Dr. S. Y. Feng, Director

DELAWARE

University of Delaware, Newark　19711

FLORIDA

: Chapman School of Seamanship
4343 S.E. St. Lucie Blvd., Stuart　34997
See listing under "Career Schools"

Florida Institute of Technology
150 W. University Blvd., Melbourne　32901
Louis T. Levy, Dean of Admissions
800-888-4348

Nova Southeastern University
3301 College Ave., Ft. Lauderdale　33314

Palm Beach Atlantic College
P.O. Box 24708, West Palm Beach　33416-4708
See listing under "Universities"

University of Miami
Rosenstiel School of Marine and Atmospheric
Sciences
4600 Rickenbacker Cswy., Miami　33149
Dr. Warren Wisby, Assoc. Dean

University of South Florida, St. Petersburg　33701
Dr. Harold J. Humm, Chrmn., Dept. of Marine Sc.

GEORGIA

University of Georgia, Athens   30602
Dr. Claire Swann, Dir. of Admis.

HAWAII

Hawaii Pacific University
45-045 Kamehameha Hwy., Kaneohe 96744

University of Hawaii at Manoa
2500 Campus Rd., Honolulu 96822

ILLINOIS

Northeastern Illinois University
5500 N. St. Louis Ave., Chicago 60625

University of Illinois
506 S. Wright St., Urbana 61801

LOUISIANA

Louisiana State University and A & M College
Baton Rouge 70803

MAINE

College of the Atlantic
105 Eden St., Bar Harbor 04609
Steve Thomas, Dir. of Admis.

Maine Maritime Academy
Battle Ave., Castine 04420
Dan Jones, Dir. of Admis.
207-326-2206

· Southern Maine Technical College
2 Fort Rd., South Portland 04106
See listing under "Career Schools"

University of Maine, Orono 04469

University of New England
11 Hills Beach Rd., Biddeford 04005
Patricia Cribby, Dir. of Admis.

MARYLAND

Johns Hopkins University
3400 N. 34th St., Baltimore 21218

University of Maryland, College Park 20742

MASSACHUSETTS

Hampshire College, Amherst 01002
Audrey Y. Smith, Dir. of Admissions
413-582-5471

Harvard University
Graduate School of Arts and Sciences
Byerly Hall, 2nd Floor
8 Garden St, Cambridge 02138

Massachusetts Institute of Technology
77 Massachusetts Ave., Cambridge 02139

University of Massachusetts Dartmouth
Old Westport Rd., North Dartmouth 02747
Raymond Barrows, Dir. of Admissions
508-999-8605

Woods Hole Oceanographic Institution
Woods Hole 02543
Robert B. Gagosian, Acting Director

MICHIGAN

Michigan State University, East Lansing 48824
Dr. N. R. Kevern, Chrpsn.

University of Michigan-Ann Arbor
815 S. University Ave., Ann Arbor 48109

NEW JERSEY

Fairleigh Dickinson University, Teaneck 07666
Dennis Craig, Dir. of Admis.
201-692-2553

Jersey City State College
2039 Kennedy Blvd., Jersey City 07305
201-200-3234

Princeton University, Princeton 08544

Stockton State College, Pomona 08240
Sal Catalfamo, Dir. of Admis.

NEW YORK

Cornell University
410 Thurston Ave., Ithaca 14853

CUNY City College
Convent Ave. at 138th St., New York 10031

Lamont-Doherty Earth Observatory of Columbia
University
Palisades 10964
Gordon Eaton, Director

Long Island University-Southampton Campus
Southampton 11968
Carol Gilbert, Dir. of Admis.

SUNY Maritime College
6 Pennyfield Ave., Bronx 10465
Peter Cooney, Dir. of Admis.

NORTH CAROLINA

University of North Carolina
601 S. College Rd., Wilmington 28403
W. H. Wagoner, Chancellor

OHIO

Bowling Green State University
Bowling Green 43403
John Martin, Dir. of Admis.

OREGON

Oregon State University, Corvallis 97333
Wallace Gibbs, Dir. of Admis.

PENNSYLVANIA

Millersville University of Pennsylvania
Millersville 17551
Blair Treasure, Dean of Admissions

RHODE ISLAND

Brown University, Providence 02906

Roger Williams College
1 Old Ferry Rd., Bristol 02809
William Dunfey, Dir. of Admis.

SOUTH CAROLINA

Coastal Carolina College
P.O. Box 1954, Myrtle Beach 29578
Dr. Ed Cerny, Director of Admissions

University of South Carolina, Columbia 29208
Terry Davis, Dir. of Admis.
803-777-7700

TEXAS

Lamar University
P.O. Box 10009, Beaumont 77710
800-458-7558

Texas A & M at Galveston
P.O. Box 1675, Galveston 77553
Dr. William H. Clayton, President

Texas A & M University
College Station 77843

VIRGINIA

College of William and Mary
School of Marine Science
Virginia Institute of Marine Science
Gloucester Point 23062
Dennis L. Taylor, Dean/Director

WASHINGTON

Seattle Pacific University
3307 3rd Ave., W., Seattle 98119

University of Washington, Seattle 98195

OPTOMETRY

This classification contains the schools offering the Doctor of Optometry degree accredited by the American Optometric Association (†) and a selection of programs from institutionally accredited schools. Colleges and Universities (no dot code) generally offer four-year or advanced programs in optometry, pre-optometry, and optics; Community and Junior Colleges (·) generally offer associate degrees in opthalmic services; Career Schools (:) generally offer a diploma as an optometric assistant.

ALABAMA

† University of Alabama at Birmingham
University Station, Birmingham 35294

CALIFORNIA

† Southern California College of Optometry
2001 Associated Rd., Fullerton 92631

† University of California at Berkeley
Minor Hall, Berkeley 94720

GEORGIA

Georgia College
231 W. Hancock St., Milledgeville 31061
912-453-5004

ILLINOIS

† Illinois College of Optometry
3241 S. Michigan Ave., Chicago 60616
Dr. Ken Hyde, Dean of Admis.

INDIANA

† Indiana University at Bloomington
300 N. Jordan Ave., Bloomington 47406

IOWA

· Waldorf College
106 S. 6th St., Forest City 50436
Steve Lovik, Dir. of Admis.
800-292-1903

KENTUCKY

Kentucky Wesleyan College
Pre-Optometry program
3000 Frederica St., Owensboro 42301

Spalding University
851 S. 4th St., Louisville 40203
Dorothy G. Allen, Dir. of Admis.

MARYLAND

· Montgomery College
51 Mannakee St., Rockville 20850
Germantown - 301-353-7798
Rockville - 301-279-5124
Takoma Park - 301-650-1332

MASSACHUSETTS

† New England College of Optometry
424 Beacon St., Boston 02115
Hyman Kamens, O.D., Admissions

MICHIGAN

† Ferris State University
Office of Admission
420 Oak St., Big Rapids 49307-2020

MISSOURI

† University of Missouri
8001 Natural Bridge Rd., St. Louis 63121
Mimi LaMarca, Dir. of Admis.

NEW HAMPSHIRE

· **NEW HAMPSHIRE TECHNICAL COLLEGE**
505 Amherst St., Nashua 03063
John T. Fischer, Dean of Student Affairs
603-882-6923
    Established 1970. Public. Coed. Accreditation: NEASC. Tuition: In-State: $2,296; New England Regional: $3,300; Out-of-state: $5,230. Enrollment: 425 full-time, 99 part-time. Faculty: 54. Degree offered: AAS in Aviation (FAA Cert. # NSUTO25K), Business, Computer Networking, Electronic/Mechanical Technology, Opticianry, Telecommunications, Electrical Engineering and Computer Engineering (ABET). Suburban campus one hour from Boston.

NEW YORK

† SUNY College of Optometry
100 E. 24th St., New York 10010

OHIO

† Ohio State University
190 N. Oval Mall, Columbus 43210

Wittenberg University
P.O. Box 720, Springfield 45504

OKLAHOMA

† Northeastern State University
600 N. Grand Ave., Tahlequah 74464

OREGON

† Pacific University
2043 College Way, Forest Grove 97116
Barbara Mergen, Dir. of Admis.

PENNSYLVANIA

Beaver College
450 S. Easton Rd., Glenside 19038-3295
Dennis Nostrand, VP for Enrollment Management
Phone: 800-776-BEAVER(2328)
Fax: 215-572-4049
See listing under "Universities"

Gannon University
109 University Sq., Erie 16541

La Salle University
1900 W. Olney Ave., Philadelphia 19141
Br. Gerald Fitzgerald, Dir. of Admis.
See listing under "Universities"

† **PENNSYLVANIA COLLEGE OF OPTOMETRY**
1200 W. Godfrey Ave., Philadelphia 19141
Robert E. Horne, Dir. of Admis.
800-824-6262

WESTMINSTER COLLEGE
New Wilmington 16172
Richard Dana Paul, Dir. of Admis.
412-946-7100

TENNESSEE

Christian Brothers College
Preprofessional Program
650 E. Parkway, S., Memphis   38104

Lambuth College
705 Lambuth Blvd., Jackson   38301

† Southern College of Optometry
1245 Madison Ave., Memphis   38104
Robert Marchbanks, Dir. of Admis.

Tennessee Wesleyan College
P.O. Box 40, Athens   37371

University of Tennessee at Martin
Martin   38238
Paul Kelley, Director of Admissions
See listing under "Universities"

TEXAS

† University of Houston
4800 Calhoun Rd., Houston   77204

WEST VIRGINIA

WEST VIRGINIA WESLEYAN COLLEGE
59 College Ave., Buckhannon   26201
Robert Skinner, Director of Admission
See listing under "Universities"

WISCONSIN

St. Norbert College
100 Grant St., De Pere   54115
Craig S. Wesley, Dean of Admission
See listing under "Universities"

Viterbo College
815 9th St., S., La Crosse   54601
Roland W. Nelson, Dir. of Admis.

PUERTO RICO

† Inter American University of Puerto Rico
Metropolitan Campus
P.O. Box 1293, San Juan   00902

OSTEOPATHIC MEDICINE

This classification contains schools offering the Doctor of Osteopathic Medicine degree accredited by the American Osteopathic Association (†) and a selection of programs from institutionally accredited schools.

CALIFORNIA

† College of Osteopathic Medicine of the Pacific
309 Pomona Mall East, Pomona   91766

FLORIDA

† Southeastern University of the Health Sciences
1750 N.E. 168th St., North Miami Beach   33162

GEORGIA

Georgia College
231 W. Hancock St., Milledgeville   31061
912-453-5004

ILLINOIS

† Chicago College of Osteopathic Medicine
5200 S. Ellis Ave., Chicago   60615
Harold Hakes, PhD, JD, Dir. of Admis.

Chicago College of Osteopathic Medicine
555 31st St., Downers Grove   60515

IOWA

† University of Osteopathic Medicine & Health Sciences
3200 Grand Ave., Des Moines   50312
Dennis Bates, PhD, Dir. of Admis.
515-271-1450

MAINE

† University of New England
11 Hills Beach Rd., Biddeford   04005
Patricia Cribby, Dir. of Admis.

MICHIGAN

† Michigan State University, East Lansing   48824
Dr. Kay White, Director

MISSOURI

† KIRKSVILLE COLLEGE OF OSTEOPATHIC MEDICINE
800 W. Jefferson St., Kirksville   63501
Lori Haxton, Director of Admissions
In state: 800-428-3376, out of state: 800-626-5266

† University of Health Sciences
2105 Independence Ave., Kansas City   64124
William J. Robertson, Dir. of Admis./Reg.

NEW JERSEY

† School of Osteopathic Medicine
University of Medicine & Dentistry of NJ
40 E. Laurel Rd., Stratford   08084
Dr. Benjamin I. Cohen, Dean

NEW YORK

† New York Institute of Technology
Old Westbury Campus, Old Westbury   11568

OHIO

† Ohio University, Athens   45701

OKLAHOMA

† College of Osteopathic Medicine of OK State University
1111 W. 17th St., Tulsa   74107
Frank Hohengarten, M.A., Admissions Officer

PENNSYLVANIA

† Philadelphia College of Osteopathic Medicine
4170 City Ave., Philadelphia   19131
Carol Fox, Assistant Dean of Admissions
215-871-2700 or 800-999-6998

WESTMINSTER COLLEGE
New Wilmington   16172
Richard Dana Paul, Dir. of Admis.
412-946-7100

TEXAS

† University of North Texas Health Science Center
College of Osteopathic Medicine
3500 Camp Bowie Blvd., Ft. Worth   76107-2699
T. John Leppi, Ph.D., Associate Dean

WEST VIRGINIA

† West Virginia School of Osteopathic Medicine
400 N. Lee St., Lewisburg   24901
John Gorby, Dir. of Admis./Registrar

PHARMACY

This classification contains schools offering either a Baccalaureate in Pharmacy or Doctor of Pharmacy degree accredited by the American Council on Pharmaceutical Education (†) and a selection of programs from institutionally accredited schools. Colleges and Universities (no dot code) generally offer four-year or advanced programs in pharmacy, pre-pharmacy or pharmaceutical chemistry; Community and Junior Colleges (·) generally offer associate degrees in pre-pharmacy or pharmacy assistant/clerk; Career Schools (:) generally offer a diploma as a pharmacy technician.

ALABAMA

† Auburn University, Auburn   36849

† Samford University
800 Lakeshore Dr., Birmingham   35229
Joe Dean, Dean

ARIZONA

† University of Arizona, Tucson   85721
Loyd Bell, Director of Admissions

ARKANSAS

† University of Arkansas for Medical Sciences
4301 W. Markham St., Little Rock   72205

CALIFORNIA

: American Career College
4021 Rosewood Ave., Los Angeles   90004
Ginny White, Director of Admissions
See listing under "Career Schools"

† University of California, San Francisco
Parnassus & 3rd Ave., San Francisco   94143

† University of Southern California
Health Science Campus, Los Angeles   90033
Dr. John Biles, Dean

† University of the Pacific
3601 Pacific Ave, Stockton   95211
Elliott J. Taylor, Dean of Admissions

COLORADO

† University of Colorado at Boulder
Boulder   80309
William A. Douglas, Dean of Admis.

University of Colorado Health Sciences Center
4200 E. 9th Ave., Denver   80262
Louis Diamond, PhD, Dean

CONNECTICUT

† University of Connecticut, Storrs   06268
Karl A. Nieforth, Dean

DISTRICT OF COLUMBIA

Howard University
2400 6th St., N.W., Washington   20059
James E. Cheek, President

FLORIDA

† Florida A & M University, Tallahassee   32307

† Southeastern University of the Health Sciences
1750 N.E. 168th St., North Miami Beach   33162

† University of Florida
226 Tigert Hall, Gainesville   32611

GEORGIA

: Atlanta College of Medical and Dental Careers
1400 W. Peachtree St., N.W., Atlanta   30309
Gary Vance, Dir. of Admis.

Clark Atlanta University
240 James Brawley Dr., S.W., Atlanta   30314
Thomas W. Cole, President

Georgia College
231 W. Hancock St., Milledgeville   31061
912-453-5004

† Mercer University, Southern School of Pharmacy
3001 Mercer University Dr., Atlanta   30341

† University of Georgia, Athens   30602
Dr. Howard C. Ansel, Dean

IDAHO

† Idaho State University
P.O. Box 8270, Pocatello   83209

ILLINOIS

North Park College & Theological Seminary
3225 W. Foster, Chicago   60625
312-509-2330

University of Chicago
5801 S. Ellis Ave., Chicago   60637

† University of Illinois at Chicago
P.O. Box 5220, Chicago   60680
Dr. Henri Manasse, Jr., Dean

INDIANA

† Butler University
4600 Sunset Ave., Indianapolis   46208

† Purdue University
Schleman Hall, West Lafayette   47907

IOWA

† Drake University
2507 E. University Ave., Des Moines   50311
Dr. Stephen Hoag, Dean

† University of Iowa, Iowa City   52242

· Waldorf College
106 S. 6th St., Forest City   50436
Steve Lovik, Dir. of Admis.
800-292-1903

KANSAS

† University of Kansas, Lawrence   66045

KENTUCKY

Kentucky Wesleyan College
Pre-Pharmacy program
3000 Frederica St., Owensboro 42301

Spalding University
851 S. 4th St., Louisville 40203
Dorothy G. Allen, Dir. of Admis.

† University of Kentucky, Lexington 40506

LOUISIANA

† Northeast Louisiana University
700 University Ave., Monroe 71209

† Xavier University
7325 Palmetto St., New Orleans 70125

MAINE

University of New England
11 Hills Beach Rd., Biddeford 04005
Patricia Cribby, Dir. of Admis.

MARYLAND

· Montgomery College
51 Mannakee St., Rockville 20850
Germantown - 301-353-7798
Rockville - 301-279-5124
Takoma Park - 301-650-1332

† University of Maryland
Baltimore Professional Schools
522 W. Lombard St., Baltimore 21201

MASSACHUSETTS

† Massachusetts College of Pharmacy
& Allied Health Sciences
179 Longwood Ave., Boston 02115

Massachusetts Institute of Technology
77 Massachusetts Ave., Cambridge 02139

† Northeastern University
360 Huntington Ave., Boston 02115
Kevin Kelly, Dean and Dir. of Undergraduate
Admis.

Simmons College
300 The Fenway, Boston 02115

Western New England College
1215 Wilbraham Rd., Springfield 01119
800-325-1122

MICHIGAN

† Ferris State University
Office of Admission
420 Oak St., Big Rapids 49307-2020

† University of Michigan-Ann Arbor
815 S. University Ave., Ann Arbor 48109

† Wayne State University
5980 Cass Ave., Detroit 48202
Dr. J. R. Thorderson, Dir. of Admis.

MINNESOTA

† University of Minnesota, Twin Cities
Minneapolis 55455

MISSISSIPPI

† University of Mississippi, University 38677

MISSOURI

· Cottey College
1000 W. Austin St., Nevada 64772
Wendy Beckemeyer, Dir. of Admis.

Culver-Stockton College, Canton 63435
Betty Smith, Dean of Admissions
800-537-1883

† ST. LOUIS COLLEGE OF PHARMACY
4588 Parkview Pl., St. Louis 63110
Dr. Robert Smith, PharmD, Interim President
Lisa Boeschen, Director of Admissions
Established 1864. Coed. Accreditation: NCACS,
American Council on Pharmaceutical Education. Tuition: 1st yr. $7,250; 2nd-5th yr. $8,750. Room and
board: $4,150. Enrollment: 268 boarding, 760 day.
Faculty: 65. Degree: BS Pharm, PharmD, MPh Adm.
Library: 44,000 volumes. 4 buildings on 5 acres. Gym.
NAIA Division II Men's Basketball and Women's Volleyball. College located in heart of medical complex
bordering Forest Park. Scholarships & loans available
to qualified students. Admission: graduation from
accredited high school, ACT test.

† University of Missouri, Kansas City
5100 Rockhill Rd., Kansas City 64110
Leo J. Sweeney, Dir. of Admis. & Registrar

MONTANA

† University of Montana, Missoula 59812
800-462-8636

NEBRASKA

† Creighton University
2500 California St., Omaha 68178
Dr. L. Kirk Benedict, Dean

† University of Nebraska Medical Center
600 S., 42nd & Dewey, Omaha 68198
Alastair M. Connell, Dean

NEW HAMPSHIRE

NOTRE DAME COLLEGE
2321 Elm St., Manchester 03104
603-669-4298

NEW JERSEY

† Rutgers, The State University of NJ
College of Pharmacy
New Brunswick 08903

NEW MEXICO

† University of New Mexico, Albuquerque 87131
Robert Weaver, Dean of Admissions

NEW YORK

† ALBANY COLLEGE OF PHARMACY
106 New Scotland Ave., Albany 12208
Janis Fisher, Dir. of Admis.
518-445-7221

† Long Island University-Brooklyn Campus
1 University Plaza, Brooklyn 11201
Alan Chaves, Dean of Admissions

Long Island University-C. W. Post Campus
Pre-Professional Studies
Rt. 25A, Brookville 11548
Dr. Ellen Duffy, Associate Dean
516-299-3046

Mercy College
555 Broadway, Dobbs Ferry 10522
James Nesbitt, Dean of Admissions

Roberts Wesleyan College
2301 Westside Dr., Rochester 14624
Dr. Phyllis Chamberlain, Chrpsn.
See listing under "Universities"

† St. John's University
Grand Central & Utopia Parkways, Jamaica 11439

† SUNY at Buffalo
17 Capen Hall
P.O. Box 601660, Buffalo 14260-1660
716-645-6900

NORTH CAROLINA

† Campbell University
P.O. Box 127, Buies Creek 27506

Duke University, Durham 27706

† University of North Carolina at Chapel Hill
Chapel Hill 27599
James C. Walters, Dir. Undergrad Admis.

NORTH DAKOTA

† North Dakota State University, Fargo 58105
Richard Shearer, Acting Dir. of Admis.

OHIO

† OHIO NORTHERN UNIVERSITY
525 S. Main St., Ada 45810
Dr. Thomas Gossell, Dean
412-772-2000

† Ohio State University
190 N. Oval Mall, Columbus 43210

† University of Cincinnati
2700 Clifton Ave., Cincinnati 45221

† University of Toledo
2801 Bancroft St., W., Toledo 43606
Richard Eastop, Dir. of Admis.

OKLAHOMA

Oklahoma City University
2501 N. Blackwelder Ave., Oklahoma City 73106
Keith Hackett, Dean of Admissions
See listing under "Universities"

† Southwestern Oklahoma State University
100 Campus Dr., Weatherford 73096

University of Oklahoma at Norman
660 Parrington Oval, Norman 73019

† University of Oklahoma Health Science Center
P.O. Box 26901, Oklahoma City 73126
Dr. Victor Vanchick, Dean

OREGON

† Oregon State University, Corvallis 97333
Wallace Gibbs, Dir. of Admis.

PENNSYLVANIA

† Duquesne University
600 Forbes Ave., Pittsburgh 15282
Thomas Schaefer, C.S.Sp., Dir. of Admis.

Gannon University
109 University Sq., Erie 16541

Pennsylvania State University
201 Shields Bldg., University Park 16802

† PHILADELPHIA COLLEGE OF PHARMACY & SCIENCE
600 S. 43rd St., Philadelphia 19104-4495
215-596-8810

† Temple University
3307 N. Broad St., Philadelphia 19140

University of Pennsylvania
0 Levy Park, Philadelphia 19104

† University of Pittsburgh
4200 5th Ave., Pittsburgh 15260

WESTMINSTER COLLEGE
New Wilmington 16172
Richard Dana Paul, Dir. of Admis.
412-946-7100

Wilkes University
184 S. River St., Wilkes-Barre 18766
Emory P. Guffrovich Jr., Dean of Admissions

RHODE ISLAND

† University of Rhode Island, Kingston 02881
Louis Luzzi, Dean

SOUTH CAROLINA

† Medical University of South Carolina
171 Ashley Ave., Charleston 29425
W. Marcus Newberry, M.D., Dean

† University of South Carolina, Columbia 29208
Terry Davis, Dir. of Admis.
803-777-7700

SOUTH DAKOTA

† South Dakota State University
P.O. Box 2202C, Brookings 57007
Dr. Bernard Hietbrink, Dean
605-688-6197
See listing under "Universities"

TENNESSEE

Christian Brothers College
Preprofessional Program
650 E. Parkway, S., Memphis 38104

Lambuth College
705 Lambuth Blvd., Jackson 38301

Tusculum College
P.O. Box 5035, Greeneville 37743
Ronald Porter, Dir. of Admis.

University of Tennessee at Martin
Martin 38238
Paul Kelley, Director of Admissions
See listing under "Universities"

† University of Tennessee, Memphis
Health Science Center
800 Madison Ave., Memphis 38163
Office of Enrollment Management

TEXAS

† Texas Southern University
3100 Cleburne St., Houston 77004

† University of Houston
4800 Calhoun Rd., Houston 77204

† University of Texas at Austin
0 the University of Texas, Austin 78712

UTAH

† University of Utah
1400 E. 200 S., Salt Lake City 84112
Dr. J. Stayner Landward, Dir. of Admis.

VIRGINIA

Ferrum College, Ferrum 24088
Bob Bailey, Dir. of Admis.

Virginia Commonwealth University
910 W. Franklin St., Richmond 23284

WASHINGTON

† University of Washington, Seattle 98195

† Washington State University, Pullman 99164
Stan Berry, Dir. of Admis.

WEST VIRGINIA

† West Virginia University
P.O. Box 6001, Morgantown 26506

WEST VIRGINIA WESLEYAN COLLEGE
59 College Ave., Buckhannon 26201
Robert Skinner, Director of Admission
See listing under "Universities"

WISCONSIN

St. Norbert College
100 Grant St., De Pere 54115
Craig S. Wesley, Dean of Admission
See listing under "Universities"

† University of Wisconsin, Madison
500 Lincoln Dr., Madison 53706

Viterbo College
815 9th St., S., La Crosse 54601
Roland W. Nelson, Dir. of Admis.

WYOMING

† University of Wyoming
P.O. Box 3434, Laramie 82071
Richard Davis, Dir. of Admis.

PUERTO RICO

† University of Puerto Rico, Medical Sciences Campus
P.O. Box 5067, San Juan 00906

PHOTOGRAPHY

ARIZONA

Arizona State University, Tempe 85287

Northern Arizona University
P.O. Box 4092, Flagstaff 86011
Dr. Margaret Cibik, Dir. of Admis.

University of Arizona, Tucson 85721
Loyd Bell, Director of Admissions

CALIFORNIA

American Film Institute Center
2021 N. Western Ave., Los Angeles 90027

Art Center College of Design
1700 Lida St., Pasadena 91103
Kit Baron, V.P., Student Services
818-396-2373

Bakersfield College
1801 Panorama Dr., Bakersfield 93305
Robert M. Bruker, Dir. of Admis.

BROOKS INSTITUTE OF PHOTOGRAPHY
801 Alston Rd., Santa Barbara 93108
Ernest Brooks II, President
Lynn Cederquist, Dir. of Admis.
805-966-3888, Ext 217 or 218
Established 1945. Private. Coed. Accreditation:
ACICS. Tuition: $12,300. Estimated total yearly expenses: $28,600. Enrollment: 500 students. Faculty: 37. Degrees: BS, MS. Library: 6,100 volumes. The school has 3 campuses and is on the trimester system. BA: 3 years., MS: 1 year. Specialized school of professional photography and filmmaking. Prerequisite 15 college credits in general education.

California College of Arts & Crafts
5212 Broadway, Oakland 94618
Sheri McKenzie, Dir. of Admis.
510-653-6522

California Institute of the Arts
24700 McBean Pkwy., Valencia 91355
Kenneth Young, Dir. of Admis.

California State University, Long Beach
1250 Bellflower Blvd., Long Beach 90840

California State University-Fullerton
Fullerton 92632

City College of San Francisco
50 Phelan Ave. V69, San Francisco 94112
Paul Klein, Dept. Chair
415-239-3422

Columbia College
925 N. La Brea Ave., Los Angeles 90038
Kurt Wolfe, Dir. of Admis.

Idyllwild School of Music & the Arts
P.O. Box 38P, Idyllwild 92549
Anne Behnke, Admissions
909-659-2171, FAX 909-659-2058
See listing under "Prep-Coed"

ORANGE COAST COLLEGE
P.O. Box 5005, Costa Mesa 92628
See listing under "Community and Junior Colleges"

OTIS COLLEGE OF ART AND DESIGN
2401 Wilshire Blvd., Los Angeles 90057
Neil Hoffman, President
See listing under "Art"

Porterville College
100 E. College Ave., Porterville 93257
John McCuen, President

San Francisco Art Institute
800 Chestnut St., San Francisco 94133

San Francisco State University
1600 Holloway Ave., San Francisco 94132
Corwin Bjonerud, Dir. of Admis.

San Jose State University
1 Washington Sq., San Jose 95192

Santa Barbara City College
721 Cliff Dr., Santa Barbara 93109
805-965-0581

University of California, Davis
376 Mrak Hall, Davis 95616

University of California, Riverside
P.O. Box 112, Riverside 92521

University of La Verne
1950 3rd St., La Verne 91750
Mark Bornholdt, Dir. of Admis.

University of San Francisco
2130 Fulton St., San Francisco 94117
Bill Henley, Dir. of Admis.

COLORADO

Colorado Institute of Art
200 E. 9th Ave., Denver 80203
Barbara Browning, Dir. of Admis.
800-275-2420
See listing under "Career Schools"

University of Colorado at Boulder
Boulder 80309
William A. Douglas, Dean of Admis.

University of Southern Colorado
2200 Bonforte Blvd., Pueblo 81001

CONNECTICUT

Greater New Haven State Technical College
88 Bassett Rd., North Haven 06473
Chester Schnepf, Dir. of Admis.

University of Hartford
200 Bloomfield Ave., West Hartford 06117
Richard Zeiser, Dir. of Admis.
See listing under "Universities"

Wesleyan University, Middletown 06459
Karl Furstenberg, Dean of Admissions

DELAWARE

University of Delaware, Newark 19711

FLORIDA

Art Institute of Fort Lauderdale
1799 S.E. 17th St., Ft. Lauderdale 33316
Eileen Northrop, V.P./Dir. of Admis.

Barry University
11300 N.E. 2nd Ave., Miami Shores 33161
Robin Ray Roberts, Dean of Admissions

Daytona Beach Community College
P.O. Box 2811, Daytona Beach 32120

GEORGIA

Art Institute of Atlanta
3376 Peachtree Rd., N.E., Atlanta 30326
J. Robert Bouchard, Dir. of Admis.

Atlanta College of Art
Woodruff Arts Center
1280 Peachtree St., N.E., Atlanta 30309
John Farkas, Dir. of Enrollment Management

La Grange College
601 Broad St., La Grange 30240
Phil Dodson, Dir. of Admis.
706-882-2911

Portfolio Center
125 Bennett St., N.W., Atlanta 30309
800-255-3169
See listing under "Career Schools"

SAVANNAH COLLEGE OF ART & DESIGN
342 Bull St., Savannah 31401
May Poetter, VP of Admissions
See listing under "Art"

University of Georgia, Athens 30602
Wiley Sanderson, Art Dept.

HAWAII

University of Hawaii at Manoa
2500 Campus Rd., Honolulu 96822

IDAHO

University of Idaho, Moscow 83843
Peter Brown, Dir. of Admis.

ILLINOIS

Bradley University
1501 W. Bradley Ave., Peoria 61625

Columbia College
600 S. Michigan Ave., Chicago 60605
Debra McGrath, Dir. of Admis.

Governors State University
1 University Pky., University Park 60466
Richard Pride, Dir. of Admis.

Illinois Institute of Technology
3300 S. Federal St., Chicago 60616
Wendell R. Webb, Dir. of Admissions

RAY COLLEGE OF DESIGN
AAS, BA, BFA degrees
401 N. Wabash Ave., Chicago 60611
312-280-3500
Woodfield Campus
1051 Perimeter Dr., Schaumburg 60173
708-619-3450

School of the Art Institute of Chicago
37 S. Wabash, Chicago 60603
Ellen B. Cropp, Dir. of Admis.

Southern Illinois University at Carbondale
Carbondale 62901

University of Illinois at Chicago
P.O. Box 5220, Chicago 60680
Dr. Marilyn R. Fiduccia, Dir. of Admis.

INDIANA

Ball State University
2000 W. University Ave., Muncie 47306
Ruth Vedvik, Dir. of Admis.

Indiana State University
217 N. 6th St., Terre Haute 47809

Indiana University at Bloomington
300 N. Jordan Ave., Bloomington 47406

Indiana Wesleyan University
4201 S. Washington St., Marion 46953
800-332-6901

Purdue University
Schleman Hall, West Lafayette 47907

IOWA

Hawkeye Community College
1501 E. Orange Rd., Waterloo 50701
319-296-2320 Ext. 4000

University of Iowa, Iowa City 52242

University of Northern Iowa, Cedar Falls 50614

KENTUCKY

Brescia College
717 Frederica St., Owensboro 42301
Thomas C. Greer, Director of Admission
800-264-1234

MAINE

Bowdoin College, Brunswick 04011
William Mason, Dir. of Admis.

Maine College of Art
97 Spring St., Portland 04101
Elizabeth Shea, Dir. of Admis.

MARYLAND

College of Notre Dame of Maryland
4701 N. Charles St., Baltimore 21210

Loyola College
4501 N. Charles St., Baltimore 21210
William Bossemeyer III, Dir. of Admis.

Maryland Institute College of Art
1300 W. Mt. Royal Ave., Baltimore 21217
Theresa Lynch Bedoya, Dean of Admissions

Montgomery College
51 Mannakee St., Rockville 20850
301-279-5256

University of Maryland, Baltimore County
5401 Wilkens Ave., Catonsville 21228

MASSACHUSETTS

THE ART INSTITUTE OF BOSTON
700 Beacon St., Boston 02215
617-262-1223 or 800-773-0494
(NY, PA, New England)
Fax 617-437-1226
See listing under "Art"

Boston University
685 Commonwealth Ave., Boston 02215

Endicott College
376 Hale St., Beverly 01915
Elizabeth Macomber, Dir. of Admis.

Fitchburg State College
160 Pearl St., Fitchburg 01420
Marke Vickers, Dir. of Admis.

Hallmark Institute of Photography
P.O. Box 308, Turners Falls 01376
Bill Chenaille, Dir. of Admis.
413-863-2478

Hampshire College, Amherst 01002
Audrey Y. Smith, Dir. of Admissions
413-582-5471

New England School of Photography
537 Commonwealth Ave., Boston 02215
Martha Hassell, Academic Director
617-437-1868

SCHOOL OF THE MUSEUM OF FINE ARTS
230 Fenway, Boston 02115
Alan Van Reed, Dean of Admissions
617-267-1218

University of Massachusetts Dartmouth
Old Westport Rd., North Dartmouth 02747
Raymond Barrows, Dir. of Admissions
508-999-8605

MICHIGAN

Aquinas College
1607 Robinson Rd., S.E., Grand Rapids 49506
Paula Meehan, Dean of Admissions
800-678-9593

Center for Creative Studies-College of Art & Design
201 E. Kirby St., Detroit 48202
Frank Couzens, Interim President
See listing under "Art"

Central Michigan University
100 Warriner Hall, Mt. Pleasant 48858

Northern Michigan University
610 Cohodas Admin. Center, Marquette 49855
Nancy Rehling, Dir. of Admis.

University of Michigan-Ann Arbor
815 S. University Ave., Ann Arbor 48109

MINNESOTA

Mankato State University
P.O. Box 8400, Mankato 56002

MINNEAPOLIS COLLEGE OF ART & DESIGN
2501 Stevens Ave., S., Minneapolis 55404
Rebecca Haas, Dir. of Admis.
Admissions Office 800-874-6223

PILLSBURY BAPTIST BIBLE COLLEGE
315 S. Grove St., Owatonna 55060
Alan Potter, President
Larry Tindall, Director of Admissions
800-747-4557

St. Cloud State University
740 4th Ave., S., St. Cloud 56301
Sherwood Reid, Dir. of Admis.
800-369-4260

: School of Communication Arts
2526 27th Ave., S., Minneapolis 55406
Rodger Klietz, President

University of Minnesota, Twin Cities
Minneapolis 55455

MISSOURI

Kansas City Art Institute
4415 Warwick Blvd., Kansas City 64111
Charles Van Gilder, Dir. of Admis.
800-522-5224

Webster University
470 E. Lockwood Ave., St. Louis 63119
Dr. James Staley, Associate Dean
See listing under "Universities"

William Woods College
200 W. 12th St., Fulton 65251
Dr. Jahnae Barnett, VP of Admis.

MONTANA

Montana State University, Bozeman 59717

NEW HAMPSHIRE

· White Pines College
40 Chester St., Chester 03036
603-887-4401

NEW JERSEY

Jersey City State College
2039 Kennedy Blvd., Jersey City 07305
201-200-3234

· Mercer County Community College
West Windsor Campus
1200 Old Trenton Rd., Trenton 08690
Michael Glass, Dir. of Admis.
See listing under "Community and Junior Colleges"

Montclair State College
1 Normal Ave., Upper Montclair 07043

Stockton State College, Pomona 08240
Sal Catalfamo, Dir. of Admis.

NEW YORK

Alfred University
Alumni Hall, Alfred 14802
Laurie Richer, Director of Admissions
800-541-9229

Cornell University
410 Thurston Ave., Ithaca 14853

Hartwick College, Oneonta 13820

Long Island University-C. W. Post Campus
Rt. 25A, Brookville 11548
Prof. Howard La Marca, Chrpsn.
516-299-2464

New School for Social Research
66 W. 12th St., New York 10011

Pratt Institute
200 Willoughby Ave., Brooklyn 11205

Rochester Institute of Technology
1 Lomb Memorial Dr., Rochester 14623
716-475-6631
See listing under "Universities"

School of Visual Arts
209 E. 23rd St., New York 10010

SUNY at Buffalo
17 Capen Hall
P.O. Box 601660, Buffalo 14260-1660
716-645-6900

· SUNY Nassau Community College
1 Education Dr., Garden City 11530
Bernard Iantosca, Dir of Admis.

· SUNY Onondaga Community College
Onondaga Rd., Syracuse 13215
Joseph Insel, Dir. of Admis.

Syracuse University, Syracuse 13244

· Villa Maria College of Buffalo
240 Pine Ridge Rd., Buffalo 14225
Lynn D'Auria, Dir. of Admis.

NORTH CAROLINA

Barton College
College Station, Wilson 27893
Anthony Britt, Dir. of Admis.
800-345-4973/919-399-6318
See listing under "Universities"

· Chowan College
P.O. Box 1848, Murfreesboro 27855
Winslow Carter, Dir. of Admis.

· James Sprunt Community College
P.O. Box 398, Kenansville 28349
Rita Brown, Registrar
910-296-2500

OHIO

· Antonelli Institute of Art & Photography
124 E. 7th St., Cincinnati 45202

Bowling Green State University
Bowling Green 43403
John Martin, Dir. of Admis.

COLUMBUS COLLEGE OF ART & DESIGN
107 N. 9th St., Columbus 43215-1758
Thomas Green, Dir. of Admis.
614-224-9101
See listing under "Art"

Kent State University
P.O. Box 5190, Kent 44242
Bruce Riddle, Dir. of Admis.

OHIO INSTITUTE OF PHOTOGRAPHY & TECHNOLOGY
2029 Edgefield Rd., Dayton 45439
Cecil W. Johnston, Executive Director
513-294-6155 or 800-932-9698

Ohio State University
190 N. Oval Mall, Columbus 43210

Ohio University, Athens 45701

University of Akron
381 Buchtel Common, Akron 44325
Kris MacDermott, Asst. Provost Enrollment

University of Dayton
300 College Park Ave., Dayton 45469-1690
Toll-free 800-837-7433
See listing under "Universities"

PENNSYLVANIA

· Antonelli Institute of Art & Photography
P.O. Box 570, Plymouth Meeting 19462
215-275-3040 or 800-722-7871

· The Art Institute of Philadelphia
1622 Chestnut St., Philadelphia 19103
215-567-7080

: Art Institute of Pittsburgh
526 Penn Ave., Pittsburgh 15222
Lee Colker, Dir. of Admis.
800-275-2470
See listing under "Art"

Beaver College
450 S. Easton Rd., Glenside 19038-3295
Dennis Nostrand, VP for Enrollment Management
Phone: 800-776-BEAVER(2328)
Fax: 215-572-4049
See listing under "Universities"

Drexel University
3141 Chestnut St., Philadelphia 19104
Dean of Enrollment Management

Edinboro University of Pennsylvania
Edinboro 16444
Admissions Office: 800-626-2203

Moore College of Art and Design
1920 Race St., Philadelphia 19103
Claire E. Gallicano, Dir. of Admis.

Seton Hill College, Greensburg 15601
Peter Egan, Dir. of Admis.
800-826-6234 or 412-838-4255

Slippery Rock University, Slippery Rock 16057
Director of Admissions

University of the Arts
320 S. Broad St., Philadelphia 19102
Margaret Heuges, Dir. of Admis.

RHODE ISLAND

: RHODE ISLAND SCHOOL OF PHOTOGRAPHY
241 Webster Ave., Providence 02909-3891
Donald Folgo, President
Call "toll free" 800-433-7477, or 401-943-7722
Established 1944. Coed. Accreditation: Accrediting Commission of Career Schools and Colleges of Technology. Approved for veterans education and foreign students. Diploma for each program: Comprehensive Photographic Program, Advanced Photographic Program. Specializing in several areas of Professional Photography. Full-time days only (Monday-Thursday). Rolling Admissions. Two entrance dates per year, January and September, for beginning or transfer students. Dormitories. Financial aid for those who qualify. Student body from many states and foreign countries.

Salve Regina University
1 Ochre Point Ave., Newport 02840
Roselina McKillop, Dean of Admissions

SOUTH DAKOTA

University of South Dakota
414 E. Clark St., Vermillion 57069
Dave Lorenz, Dir. of Admis.

TENNESSEE

Carson-Newman College
P.O. Box 70552, Jefferson City 37760
See listing under "Universities"

TEXAS

· Art Institute of Dallas
8080 Park Ln., Dallas 75231
Lee Colker, Dir. of Admis.

· The Art Institute of Houston
1900 Yorktown St., Houston 77056
Cherie R. McNeel, Dir. of Admis.
800-275-4244

Concordia Lutheran College
3400 N. Interstate 35, Austin 78705
Kevin Pieper, Dir. of Admis.

East Texas State University
ETSU Station, Commerce 75429

Sam Houston State University, Huntsville 77341

Stephen F. Austin State University
P.O. Box 6078. Nacogdoches 75962

Texas Christian University
2800 S. University Dr., Ft. Worth 76129
Dr. Edward Boehm, Jr., Dean of Admissions

Texas Tech University, Lubbock 79409

Texas Women's University
P.O. Box 23925, Denton 76204

University of Texas at Austin
0 the University of Texas, Austin 78712

UTAH

Utah State University, Logan 84322-1600
Rod Clark, Director of Admissions
801-797-1107

Weber State University
3750 Harrison Blvd., Ogden 84408

VERMONT

Goddard College
P.O. Box G, Plainfield 05667
Jackson Kytle, President

Johnson State College, Johnson 05656
802-635-2356 ext. 219

VIRGINIA

James Madison University, Harrisonburg 22807

Virginia Intermont College
1013 Moore St., Bristol 24201
Lawton Blandford, Dir. of Admis.

WASHINGTON

· Art Institute of Seattle
2323 Elliott Ave., Seattle 98121
Doug Worsley, Dir. of Admis.

Pacific Lutheran University
12180 Park Ave. S., Tacoma 98447
Bea Geller, Director

WEST VIRGINIA

Shepherd College, Shepherdstown 25443

WISCONSIN

Milwaukee Institute of Art & Design
273 E. Erie St., Milwaukee 53202
Holly Grey, Dir. of Admis.

University of Wisconsin, Green Bay
2420 Nicolet Dr., Green Bay 54311
Dr. Jerry Dell, Chrpsn.

University of Wisconsin
P.O. Box 413, Milwaukee 53201
V. M. Allison, Registrar

University of Wisconsin, Superior 54880
Richard E. Morrison, Dir. Univ. Relations

WYOMING

· Western Wyoming Community College
2500 College Dr., Rock Springs 82901
Jackie Freeze, Dir. of Admis.
See listing under "Community and Junior Colleges"

PUERTO RICO

Bayamon Central University
P.O. Box 1725, Bayamon 00960-1725
Christine Hernandez, Dir. of Admis.

PHYSICAL EDUCATION

ALABAMA

Alabama A & M University
P.O. Box 1297, Normal 35762
Dr. Shirley Houzer, Chrpsn.
See listing under "Universities"

Gadsden State Community College
P.O. Box 227, Gadsden 35902
W. Bryan Stone, Dir. of Admis.

Huntingdon College
1500 E. Fairview Ave., Montgomery 36106-2148
Carolyn A. Phillips, Dean of Enrollment
800-763-0313

Samford University
800 Lakeshore Dr., Birmingham 35229
Jim Angel, Chrpsn.

STILLMAN COLLEGE
P.O. Box 1430, Tuscaloosa 35403
Barbara K. Smith, Director of Admissions
See listing under "Universities"

Troy State University, Troy 36082
Dr. Gene Hanson, Dean

University of Alabama
P.O. Box 870132, Tuscaloosa 35487-0132
Roy Smith, Dir. of Admis.

UNIVERSITY OF MOBILE
P.O. Box 13220, Mobile 36663-0220
Kim Leousis, Dir. of Admissions
205-675-5990
See listing under "Universities"

ARIZONA

Arizona State University, Tempe 85287

Grand Canyon University
3300 W. Camelback Rd., Phoenix 85017
Sherri Willborn, Dir. of Admis.
See listing under "Liberal Arts and Sciences"

Northern Arizona University
P.O. Box 4092, Flagstaff 86011
Dr. Margaret Cibik, Dir. of Admis.

University of Arizona, Tucson 85721
Loyd Bell, Director of Admissions

Yavapai College
1100 E. Sheldon St., Prescott 86301
Dr. Doreen Dailey, President
602-445-7300
See listing under "Community and Junior
Colleges"

ARKANSAS

Arkansas State University
P.O. Box 240, State University 72467

John Brown University
2000 W. University, Siloam Springs 72761
Don Crandall, Director of Enrollment Management

Ouachita Baptist University
410 Ouachita St., Arkadelphia 71998
Randy Garner, Dir. of Admis.
800-DIAL-OBU

University of Arkansas at Fayetteville
Fayetteville 72701

University of Arkansas at Pine Bluff
1200 University Dr., Pine Bluff 71601-2799

University of Central Arkansas
201 Donaghey Ave., Conway 72035

Williams Baptist College
P.O. Box 3667, Walnut Ridge 72476
Scott Wright, Dir. of Admis.

CALIFORNIA

Biola University
13800 Biola Ave., La Mirada 90639
Wayne Chute, Dean of Admissions

California Baptist College
8432 Magnolia Ave., Riverside 92504
800-782-3382

California Lutheran University
60 Olsen Rd., Thousand Oaks 91360
800-252-5884

California Polytechnic State University
San Luis Obispo 93407
Helen Linstrum, Dir. of Admis.

Concordia University
1530 Concordia, Irvine 92715
Stan Meyer, Dean of Admission
800-229-1200
See listing under "Universities"

Fresno Pacific College
1717 S. Chestnut Ave., Fresno 93702
209-453-2039

La Sierra University
4700 Pierce St., Riverside 92505
800-874-5587

Master's College
P.O. Box 221450, Newhall 91322
Don Gilmore, Dir. of Admis.

San Francisco State University
1600 Holloway Ave., San Francisco 94132
Corwin Bjonerud, Dir. of Admis.

Santa Barbara City College
721 Cliff Dr., Santa Barbara 93109
805-965-0581

Southern California College
55 Fair Dr., Costa Mesa 92626
Richard Hardy, Asst. Dean for Enrollment

University of California at Berkeley
Harmon Gym, Berkeley 94720

University of La Verne
1950 3rd St., La Verne 91750
Mark Bornholdt, Dir. of Admis.

University of San Francisco
2130 Fulton St., San Francisco 94117
Bill Henley, Dir. of Admis.

Whittier College
13406 Philadelphia St., Whittier 90601
310-907-4238

COLORADO

Adams State College, Alamosa 81102
Cheryl Billingsley, Dir. of Admis.
800-824-6494

Denver Technical College
225 S. Union Blvd., Colorado Springs 80910
Oscar Adams, Dir. of Admis.

Denver Technical College
925 S. Niagara St., Denver 80224
Oscar Adams, Dir. of Admis.

Mesa State College
P.O. Box 2647, Grand Junction 81502
Sherri Pe'a, Dir. of Admis.

Metropolitan State College of Denver
P.O. Box 173362, Campus Box 16
Denver 80217-3362

University of Northern Colorado, Greeley 80639
David Stotlar, Director
303-351-2565

University of Southern Colorado
2200 Bonforte Blvd., Pueblo 81001

Western State College of Colorado
Gunnison 81231
Monica Bruning, Dir. of Admis.
See listing under "Universities"

CONNECTICUT

Mattatuck Community College
750 Chase Parkway, Waterbury 06708
Dr. Richard Sanders, President

University of Connecticut, Storrs 06268
John Vlandis, Dir. of Admis.

DELAWARE

University of Delaware, Newark 19711

DISTRICT OF COLUMBIA

University of the District of Columbia
Georgia Ave.-Harvard St. Campus
1100 Harvard St., N.W., Washington 20009

University of the District of Columbia
Van Ness Campus
4200 Connecticut Ave., N.W., Washington 20008

FLORIDA

Barry University
11300 N.E. 2nd Ave., Miami Shores 33161
Robin Ray Roberts, Dean of Admissions

Clearwater Christian College
3400 Gulf-to-Bay Blvd., Clearwater 34619
Benjamin Puckett, Dir. of Admis.

Flagler College
P.O. Box 1027, St. Augustine 32085
Marc G. Williar, Dir. of Admis.
904-829-6481

Florida Southern College
111 Lake Hollingsworth Dr., Lakeland 33801
William Stephens, Jr., Dir. of Admis.

Jacksonville University
2800 University Blvd., N., Jacksonville 32211

Palm Beach Atlantic College
P.O. Box 24708, West Palm Beach 33416-4708
See listing under "Universities"

St. Leo College
P.O. Box 2008, St. Leo 33574
Bonnie Black, Dir. of Admis.

Stetson University
401 N. Woodland Blvd., De Land 32720
Gary A. Meadows, Dean of Admis.

University of Miami
P.O. Box 248006, Coral Gables 33124

Warner Southern College
5301 U.S. Hwy. 27, S., Lake Wales 33853
Valerie S. Rutland, Dir. Enrollment Mgmt.
800-949-7248

GEORGIA

AUGUSTA COLLEGE
2500 Walton Way, Augusta 30904-2200
Lee Young, Dir. of Admis.
706-737-1405

BREWTON-PARKER COLLEGE
P.O. Box 197, Mount Vernon 30445
Dr. Y. Lynn Holmes, President
912-583-2241

Georgia College
231 W. Hancock St., Milledgeville 31061
912-453-5004

Kennesaw State College
P.O. Box 444, Marietta 30061
Joe Head, Dir. of Admis.

La Grange College
601 Broad St., La Grange 30240
Phil Dodson, Dir. of Admis.
706-882-2911

University of Georgia, Athens 30602
Dr. Alphonse Buccino, Dean

Valdosta State College
Patterson St., Valdosta 31698

HAWAII

Brigham Young University, Hawaii Campus
55-220 Kulanui St., Laie 96762
Clark E. Hirschi, Coordinator of Admis.

IDAHO

University of Idaho, Moscow 83843
Peter Brown, Dir. of Admis.

ILLINOIS

Aurora University
347 S. Gladstone Ave., Aurora 60506
Peter Pitts, Dir. of Admis.

De Paul University
1 E. Jackson Blvd., Chicago 60604
Thomas D. Abrahamson, Dean of Admissions
See listing under "Universities"

Eastern Illinois University, Charleston 61920
Phoebe Church, Chrpsn.
See listing under "Universities"

Greenville College
315 E. College Ave., Greenville 62246
Kent Krober, Dir. of Admis.

LEWIS UNIVERSITY
Rt. 53, Romeoville 60441
Irish O'Reilly, Director of Admissions
See listing under "Universities"

Millikin University
1184 W. Main St., Decatur 62522
Lin Stoner, Dean of Admissions
800-373-7733

Monmouth College
700 E. Broadway, Monmouth 61462

North Central College
30 N. Brainard St.
P.O. Box 3065, Naperville 60566-7065
Marguerite Waters, Director of Admission
708-420-3414

Northeastern Illinois University
5500 N. St. Louis Ave., Chicago 60625

Northern Illinois University, De Kalb 60115

Northwestern University
2001 Sheridan Rd., Evanston 60208

Olivet Nazarene University, Kankakee 60901
John Mongerson, Dir. of Admis.
815-939-5203

Parkland College
2400 W. Bradley Ave., Champaign 61821-1899
217-351-2208 or 800-346-8089

Rockford College
5050 E. State St., Rockford 61108
Miriam King, V.P. for Enrollment Management
See listing under "Universities"

Southern Illinois University at Edwardsville
Edwardsville 62026
Eugene J. Magac, Dir. of Admissions & Records

Trinity Christian College
6601 W. College Dr., Palos Heights 60463
Kenneth Bootsma, President

University of Illinois at Chicago
P.O. Box 4348, Chicago 60680
Charles Kristufek, Dean

Western Illinois University
900 W. Adams St., Macomb 61455
Alan DeRoos, Registrar
309-298-1891

INDIANA

Ball State University
2000 W. University Ave., Muncie 47306
Ruth Vedvik, Dir. of Admis.

Franklin College
501 E. Monroe, Franklin 46131
B. Stephen Richards, VP Enrollment

Goshen College
1700 S. Main St., Goshen 46526
Sue Roth, Chairperson

Grace College
200 Seminary Dr., Winona Lake 46590
Ron Henry, Dir. of Admis.

Indiana State University
217 N. 6th St., Terre Haute 47809

Indiana University at Bloomington
300 N. Jordan Ave., Bloomington 47406

Indiana Wesleyan University
4201 S. Washington St., Marion 46953
800-332-6901

Manchester College
604 College Ave., North Manchester 46962
Lana Groombridge, Chrpsn.

Purdue University
Schleman Hall, West Lafayette 47907

Taylor University
500 W. Reade Ave., Upland 46989
Don Taylor, Head

Tri-State University, Angola 46703
Director of Admission
800-347-4878

University of Evansville
1800 Lincoln Ave., Evansville 47722
Dr. Cathy Barlow, Dean
800-423-8633

Valparaiso University, Valparaiso 46383

IOWA

Coe College
1220 1st Ave., N.E., Cedar Rapids 52402
Michael White, Director of Enrollment Services

Cornell College
600 1st St., W., Mt. Vernon 52314
Kevin Crockett, Dean of Admissions

Dordt College
498 4th Ave., N.E., Sioux Center 51250
Quentin Van Essen, Dir. of Admissions
800-343-6738

Graceland College, Lamoni 50140
800-638-0053, Outside Iowa 800-346-9208
Bonita Booth, Dean of Admissions
See listing under "Universities"

Iowa State University, Ames 50011
Karsten Smedal, Dir. of Admis.

Iowa Wesleyan College
601 N. Main St., Mt. Pleasant 52641

Luther College
700 College Dr., Decorah 52101
David Sallee, Dean for Enrollment

Morningside College, Sioux City 51106
Lora Vanderzwaag, Dir. of Admis.

Teikyo Westmar University
1002 3rd Ave., S.E., Le Mars 51031
Dr. Jim Utesch, Dir. of Admis.

Upper Iowa University
P.O. Box 1857, Fayette 52142

Waldorf College
106 S. 6th St., Forest City 50436
Steve Lovik, Dir. of Admis.
800-292-1903

William Penn College
201 Trueblood Ave., Oskaloosa 52577
Eric Otto, Dir. of Admis.

KANSAS

Emporia State University
1200 Commercial St., Emporia 66801
Dr. Barbara Hilgendorf, Dir. of Admissions

Fort Hays State University
600 Park St., Hays 67601-4099
Dr. Don Fuertges, Chrpsn.

McPherson College
1600 E. Euclid St., McPherson 67460

Ottawa University
1001 S. Cedar St., Ottawa 66067
Steve Koberlein, Dir. of Admis.
800-755-5200

Pittsburg State University
1701 S. Broadway St., Pittsburg 66762
James E. Parker, Dir of Admis.

SOUTHWESTERN COLLEGE
100 College St., Winfield 67156
800-846-1543

University of Kansas, Lawrence 66045

KENTUCKY

Asbury College
1 Macklem Dr., Wilmore 40390
Jonah Mitchell, Dir. of Admis.

Cumberland College
6178 College Station Dr., Williamsburg 40769
See listing under "Universities"

Kentucky State University
400 E. Main St., Frankfort 40601

Morehead State University, Morehead 40351
Charles Myers, Director of Admissions
606-783-2000

Murray State University, Murray 42071
Phil Bryan, Director of Admissions
800-272-4MSU

Transylvania University
300 Broadway St., N., Lexington 40508
Pat Bain, Dir. of Admis.

LOUISIANA

Centenary College of Louisiana
P.O. Box 41188, Shreveport 71134

Louisiana College
College Station, Pineville 71359
Byron McGee, Dir. of Admis.
318-487-7386
See listing under "Liberal Arts"

Northwestern State University
Natchitoches 71497

MAINE

University of Maine
181 Main St., Presque Isle 04769

MARYLAND

Montgomery College
51 Mannakee St., Rockville 20850
301-251-7575

Morgan State University
Cold Spring Ln. and Hillen Rd., Baltimore 21239

Towson State University
800 York Rd., Towson 21204
Dr. Hoke Smith, President

University of Maryland, College Park 20742

University of Maryland Eastern Shore
11868 Academic Oval, Princess Anne 21853
Dr. Hallie Gregory, Chrpsn.

MASSACHUSETTS

Atlantic Union College
P.O. Box 1000, South Lancaster 01561
Osa Canto, Registrar

Boston University
685 Commonwealth Ave., Boston 02215

Bridgewater State College
Bridgewater 02325
James Plotner, Jr., Dir. of Admis.

DEAN COLLEGE
99 Main St, Franklin 02038
Kathleen Teehan, Dean of Admissions
508-528-9100
See listing under "Community and Junior Colleges"

Endicott College
376 Hale St., Beverly 01915
Elizabeth Macomber, Dir. of Admis.

Springfield College
263 Alden St., Springfield 01109
Frederick Bartlett, Dean of Admissions

University of Massachusetts, Amherst 01003
Arlene Wesley Cash, Dir. of Admis.

Westfield State College
577 Western Ave., Westfield 01085
John F. Marcus, Dir. of Admis.

MICHIGAN

Adrian College
110 S. Madison St., Adrian 49221
George Wolf, Dir. of Admis.
See listing under "Universities"

Aquinas College
1607 Robinson Rd., S.E., Grand Rapids 49506
Paula Meehan, Dean of Admissions
800-678-9593

Eastern Michigan University, Ypsilanti 48197
Patric L. Cavanaugh, Head
313-487-3060 or 800-GO-TO-EMU

HILLSDALE COLLEGE
33 E. College St., Hillsdale 49242
Dr. Alice Hullhorst, Director
517-437-7341

Hope College
69 E. 10th St., Holland 49423
Gordon Van Wylen, President

Michigan State University, East Lansing 48824
Dr. Herbert Olson, Admissions Coordinator

Olivet College
300 S. Main St., Olivet 49076
Vicki Gallas, Registrar
See listing under "Universities"

Western Michigan University, Kalamazoo 49008
Stanley Henderson, Dir. of Enrl. Mgt. & Admis.
616-387-2000

MINNESOTA

Bemidji State University
1500 Birchmont Dr., N.E., Bemidji 56601
800-475-2001

Bethel College
3900 Bethel Dr., St. Paul 55112
Dr. George Brushaber, President

College of St. Catherine
2004 Randolph Ave., St. Paul 55105

Concordia College-St. Paul
275 N. Syndicate, St. Paul 55104
Tim Utter, Dir. of Admis.

Crown College
6425 County Rd. 30, St. Bonifacius 55375
See listing under "Universities"

Gustavus Adolphus College
800 W. College Ave., St. Peter 56082
Mark Anderson, Dir. of Admis.

Hamline University
1536 Hewitt Ave., St. Paul 55104
Scott Pratt, Dir. of Admis.

Mankato State University
P.O. Box 8400, Mankato 56002

Northwestern College
3003 Snelling Ave., N., St. Paul 55113
Ralph Anderson, Dean of Admissions
800-827-6827 or 612-631-5111

St. Olaf College, Northfield 55057
Gary Wicks, Chrpsn.
507-646-3250

Southwest State University, Marshall 56258

MISSISSIPPI

Delta State University
Hwy. 8 W., Cleveland 38732

Mississippi University for Women
P.O. Box W-1602, Columbus 39701
Teresa Thompson, Exec. Dir. of Enrollment

MISSOURI

Central Missouri State University
Warrensburg 64093
Delores Hudson, Dir. of Admis.

Drury College
900 N. Benton Ave., Springfield 65802
Michael G. Thomas, Dir. of Admis.

Evangel College
1111 N. Glenstone Ave., Springfield 65802
David Schoolfield, Dir. of Enrollment

Lincoln University
820 Chestnut St., Jefferson City 65101

Missouri Baptist College
12542 Conway Rd., St. Louis 63141

Missouri Southern State College
3950 Newman Rd., Joplin 64801-1595
Dr. Dirk J. Nelson, Dept. Head
See listing under "Universities"

Missouri Valley College
500 E. College St., Marshall 65340
816-886-6924 ext. 114
See listing under "Universities"

Missouri Western State College
4525 Downs Dr., St. Joseph 64507
Howard McCauley, Dir. of Admis.

Northwest Missouri State University
800 University Dr., Maryville 64468

Southeast Missouri State University
1 University Plz., Cape Girardeau 63701
New Student Relations 314-651-2590
See listing under "Universities"

Southwest Baptist University
1601 S. Springfield Ave., Bolivar 65613

Southwest Missouri State University
901 S. National Ave., Springfield 65804
Dr. Tom Burnett, Department Head
417-836-5370

Washington University
1 Brookings Dr., St. Louis 63130

William Woods College
200 W. 12th St., Fulton 65251
Dr. Jahnae Barnett, VP of Admis.

MONTANA

CARROLL COLLEGE
1610 N. Benton Ave., Helena 59625
Candace Cain, Dir. of Admis.
See listing under "Universities"

College of Great Falls
1301 20th St., S., Great Falls 59405
Jean Walker, Dir. of Admis.

Montana State University, Bozeman 59717

Montana State University - Billings
1500 N. 30th St., Billings 59101
Karen Everett, Dir. of Admis.
406-657-2158

Northern Montana College
P.O. Box 7751, Havre 59501
Ralph A. Brigham, Dir. of Admis.

Rocky Mountain College
1511 Poly Dr., Billings 59102
David Heringer, Dir. of Admis.
See listing under "Universities"

University of Montana, Missoula 59812
800-462-8636

NEBRASKA

Bellevue College
1000 Galvin Rd. S., Bellevue 68005
Chari Leader, VP of Enrollment

Chadron State College
1000 Main St., Chadron 69337
Dr. Thomas P. Colgate, Dean

Concordia College
800 N. Columbia Ave., Seward 68434
Don Vos, Dir. of Admis.

Creighton University
2500 California St., Omaha 68178
Dr. Thomas Baechle, Chrpsn.

Dana College
2848 College Dr., Blair 68008
John Schueth, Dir. of Admis.
800-444-3262
See listing under "Universities"

Nebraska Wesleyan University
5000 Saint Paul Ave., Lincoln 68504
Ken Sieg, Dir. of Admis.

Peru State College, Peru 68421
Pamela J. Cosgrove, Dir. of Admis.
402-872-3815

Wayne State College
200 E. Tenth St., Wayne 68787

NEVADA

University of Nevada Las Vegas
4505 S. Maryland Pky., Las Vegas 89154-1021
Admissions: 702-895-3443 or 800-334-UNLV

NEW HAMPSHIRE

Keene State College
229 Main St., Keene 03435
Kathryn Dodge, Dir. of Admis.

New England College
26 Bridge St., Henniker 03242
John Spaulding, Dir. of Admis.

NEW JERSEY

Rowan College of New Jersey, Glassboro 08028
Marvin G. Sills, Dir. of Admis.

NEW MEXICO

Eastern New Mexico University
Portales 88130
Larry Fuqua, Dir. of Admis.

New Mexico Highlands University, Las Vegas 87701
Dr. Jorge P. Thomas, VP Academic Affairs

NEW YORK

Adelphi University, Garden City 11530
Dr. Jeffrey Kane, Dean, School of Education
516-877-4100

Canisius College
2001 Main St., Buffalo 14208
Penelope Lips, Dir. of Admis.
800-843-1517

CUNY City College
Convent Ave. at 138th St., New York 10031

Hofstra University
1000 Fulton Ave., Hempstead 11550
Margaret Shields, Dean of Admissions

Ithaca College
953 Danby Rd., Ithaca 14850

The King's College, Briarcliff Manor 10510
Frederic Rowley, Dean of Admissions

Long Island University-Brooklyn Campus
1 University Plaza, Brooklyn 11201
Alan Chaves, Dean of Admissions

Long Island University-C. W. Post Campus
Rt. 25A, Brookville 11548
Dr. Mary Trotto, Chrpsn.
516-299-2671

Manhattan College
4513 Manhattan College Pky., Riverdale 10471
Dr. Beth Barnett, Dean of Education

Russell Sage College
51 1st St., Troy 12180

Skidmore College, Saratoga Springs 12866
Kent Jones, Dir. of Admis.

SUNY College at Brockport
Brockport 14420
Dr. Connie Koenig-McIntyre, Chrpsn.

SUNY Nassau Community College
1 Education Dr., Garden City 11530
Bernard Iantosca, Dir of Admis.

Syracuse University, Syracuse 13244

NORTH CAROLINA

Barton College
College Station, Wilson 27893
Anthony Britt, Dir. of Admis.
800-345-4973/919-399-6318
See listing under "Universities"

Catawba College
2300 W. Innes St., Salisbury 28144
Mark Stokes, Dir. of Admis.

East Carolina University
1000 E. 5th St., Greenville 27858
Dr. David White, Chair

Elon College
P.O. Box 2700, Elon College 27244
Nan P. Perkins, Dean of Admissions

Gardner-Webb University
General Delivery, Boiling Springs 28017
Dee Hunt, Chrpsn.
704-434-2361

High Point College
933 Montlieu Ave., High Point 27262
Jim Schlimmer, Dir. of Admis.

Johnson C. Smith University
100 Beatties Ford Rd., Charlotte 28216
Mary H. Platt, Registrar

Mars Hill College
Main St., Mars Hill 28754
Dr. Smith Goodrum, Dean of Admis.

Methodist College
5400 Ramsey St., Fayetteville 28311
Fiore Bergamasco, Dir. of Admis.

Pembroke State University
P.O. Box 1510, Pembroke 28372
Anthony Locklear, Dir. of Admissions
919-521-6262

St. Andrews Presbyterian College
1700 Dogwood Mile, Laurinburg 28352
Dale B. Montague, Dir. of Admis.

Shaw University
118 E. South St., Raleigh 27601

University of North Carolina at Chapel Hill
Chapel Hill 27599
James C. Walters, Dir. Undergrad Admis.

Western Carolina University
Cullowhee 28723
Tyree H. Kiser, Dir. of Admissions

NORTH DAKOTA

Dickinson State University, Dickinson 58601
Marshall Melbye, Registrar
701-227-2331

Minot State University
500 University Ave. W., Minot 58701

OHIO

Bowling Green State University
Bowling Green 43403
John Martin, Dir. of Admis.

Capital University
2199 E. Main St., Columbus 43209
Dolphus E. Henry, Associate Provost

College of Mount St. Joseph
5701 Delhi Rd., Cincinnati 45233-1672
See listing under "Universities"

College of Wooster
1189 Beall Ave., Wooster 44691
Hayden Schilling, Dean of Admis.

Heidelberg College
310 E. Market St., Tiffin 44883
Stephen E. Eidson, Dean of Admission
800-925-9250

Kent State University
P.O. Box 5190, Kent 44242
Bruce Riddle, Dir. of Admis.

Malone College
515 25th St., N.W., Canton 44709
Lee Sommers, Dean of Admissions

Miami University
E. High St., Oxford 45056

Mount Union College
1972 Clark Ave., Alliance 44601
Amy Tomko, Dir. of Admis.

Mt. Vernon Nazarene College
800 Martinsburg Rd., Mt. Vernon 43050
Ronald Hyson, Dir. of Admis.

Oberlin College
135 W. Lorain St., Oberlin 44074
James Foels, Director

Ohio Dominican College
1216 Sunbury Rd., Columbus 43219
800-955-OHIO

OHIO NORTHERN UNIVERSITY

525 S. Main St., Ada 45810
Gayle Lauth, Chrpsn.
412-772-2000

Ohio Wesleyan University
61 S. Sandusky St., Delaware 43015
Donald Bishop, Dean for Enrollment

University of Akron
381 Buchtel Common, Akron 44325
Kris MacDermott, Asst. Provost Enrollment

University of Dayton
300 College Park Ave., Dayton 45469-1210
Toll-free 800-837-7433
See listing under "Universities"

University of Findlay
1000 N. Main St., Findlay 45840
Dan Crabtree, Dir. of Admis.

University of Rio Grande
General Delivery, Rio Grande 45674
H. Paul Lloyd, Dean
614-245-5353, Ext. 7328

Urbana University
100 College Way, Urbana 43078
Donald Burns, Dir. of Admis.

Wilmington College
P.O. Box 1185, Wilmington 45177
Rhonda Inderhees, Dir. of Admis.

Youngstown State University
410 Wick Ave., Youngstown 44555
Leslie H. Cochran, President

OKLAHOMA

Cameron University
2800 W. Gore Blvd., Lawton 73505
Louise Brown, Dir. of Admis.

East Central University, Ada 74820
James Peak, Dir. of Admis.

Oklahoma City University
2501 N. Blackwelder Ave., Oklahoma City 73106
Keith Hackett, Dean of Admissions
See listing under "Universities"

Oklahoma Panhandle State University
P.O. Box 430, Goodwell 73939

Oklahoma State University, Stillwater 74078
Lowell Caneday, Dept. Head

Oral Roberts University
7777 S. Lewis Ave., Tulsa 74171
Arthur E. Matzkvech, Dir. of Admis.

Southwestern Oklahoma State University
100 Campus Dr., Weatherford 73096

University of Central Oklahoma
100 N. University Dr., Edmond 73034

OREGON

Oregon State University, Corvallis 97333
Wallace Gibbs, Dir. of Admis.

Treasure Valley Community College
650 College Blvd., Ontario 97914
Ron Kulm, Dir. of Admis.

University of Oregon
1 University of Oregon, Eugene 97403

Western Baptist College, Salem 97301
800-845-3005

PENNSYLVANIA

Eastern College
10 Fairview Dr., Saint Davids 19087
Ronald Keller, VP for Enrollment Management

East Stroudsburg University of Pennsylvania
East Stroudsburg 18301
Alan Chesterton, Dir. of Admis.

Edinboro University of Pennsylvania
Edinboro 16444
Admissions Office: 800-626-2203

Lock Haven University, Lock Haven 17745

Montgomery County Community College
340 DeKalb Pike, Blue Bell 19422-0758
Dennis Murphy, Dir. of Admis.

Pennsylvania State University
201 Shields Bldg., University Park 16802

Slippery Rock University, Slippery Rock 16057
Director of Admissions

Temple University
Broad St. & Montgomery Ave.
Philadelphia 19122

West Chester University of Pennsylvania
S. High St., West Chester 19380

SOUTH CAROLINA

Claflin College
700 College Ave., Orangeburg 29115
P. Palmer Worthy, Registrar

Coastal Carolina College
P.O. Box 1954, Myrtle Beach 29578
Dr. Ed Cerny, Director of Admissions

Erskine College & Seminary
Washington St., Due West 29639
Dot Carter, Dir. of Admis.

Furman University
3300 Poinsett Hwy., Greenville 29613
Charles Brock, Dir. of Admis.

Lander College
320 Stanley Ave., Greenwood 29649

South Carolina State University
P.O. Box 7127, Orangeburg 29117-0001
803-536-7185

University of South Carolina, Columbia 29208
Terry Davis, Dir. of Admis.
803-777-7700

Winthrop University
701 W. Oakland Ave., Rock Hill 29733
James McCammon, Jr., Dir. of Admis.

SOUTH DAKOTA

Augustana College
29th & S. Summit, Sioux Falls 57197

Dakota State University
820 N. Washington Ave., Madison 57042
Mark Weiss, Dir. of Admis.
605-256-5139

Mt. Marty College
1105 W. 8th St., Yankton 57078
Paula Tacke, Dir. of Admis.

Northern State University
1200 S. Jay St., Aberdeen 57401

SIOUX FALLS COLLEGE
1501 S. Prairie Ave., Sioux Falls 57105
Susan Reese, Dir. of Admis.
800-888-1047
See listing under "Universities"

South Dakota State University
P.O. Box 2820, Brookings 57007
Dr. Fred Oien, Department Head
605-688-5625
See listing under "Universities"

University of South Dakota
414 E. Clark St., Vermillion 57069
Dave Lorenz, Dir. of Admis.

TENNESSEE

Carson-Newman College
P.O. Box 70552, Jefferson City 37760
See listing under "Universities"

David Lipscomb University
3901 Granny White Pike, Nashville 37204-3951
Wade Sandrell, Dir. of Admis.
800-333-4358

Freed-Hardeman University
158 E. Main St., Henderson 38340
800-342-7837

Le Moyne-Owen College
807 Walker Ave., Memphis 38126
901-942-7302 or 800-737-7778

Maryville College
800 S. Court St., Maryville 37801
Annabelle J. Libby, Dir. of Admis.

Middle Tennessee State University
Murfreesboro 37132
Roger D. Sims, Dir. of Admis.

Tusculum College
P.O. Box 5035, Greeneville 37743
Ronald Porter, Dir. of Admis.

University of Memphis, Memphis 38152
Dr. John Eubank, Dean of Admissions

University of Tennessee at Martin
Martin 38238
Paul Kelley, Director of Admissions
See listing under "Universities"

University of Tennessee, Knoxville
527 Andy Holt Tower, Knoxville 37996
Dr. Gordon Stanley, Dir. of Admis.

TEXAS

Austin College
900 N. Grand Ave., Sherman 75090
Rodney Oto, Dean of Admission
800-442-5363

Baylor University
P.O. Box 97008, Waco 76798-7008
Diana Ramey, Director of Admissions

Frank Phillips College
P.O. Box 5118, Borger 79008

Incarnate Word College
4301 Broadway St., San Antonio 78209
Sr. Sally Mitchell, Dean of Enrollment

Lamar University
P.O. Box 10009, Beaumont 77710
800-458-7558

McMurry University
14th and Sayles, Abilene 79697

Prairie View A & M University
P.O. Box 3089, Prairie View 77446-3089
Linda S. Berry, Dir. of Admis.

Rice University
P.O. Box 1892, Houston 77251

St. Edward's University
3001 S. Congress Ave., Austin 78704
John Lambert, Dir. of Admis.

Schreiner College
2100 Memorial Blvd., Kerrville 78028
800-343-4919

Stephen F. Austin State University
P.O. Box 6078, Nacogdoches 75962

Texas A & I University
Campus Box 101, Kingsville 78363

Texas Christian University
2800 S. University Dr., Ft. Worth 76129
Dr. Edward Boehm, Jr., Dean of Admissions

University of Mary Hardin-Baylor
UMHB Station, Box 8001, Belton 76513
800-727-8642 or 817-939-4520

University of Texas at Arlington
UTA Box 19125, Arlington 76019
R. Zack Prince, Dir. of Admis.

West Texas State University
2501 4th Ave., Canyon 79016
Lila Vars, Dir. of Admis.

UTAH

Southern Utah University
351 W. Center St., Cedar City 84720
D. Mark Barton, Asst. VP Student Services
801-586-7740

University of Utah
1400 E. 200 S., Salt Lake City 84112
Dr. J. Stayner Landward, Dir. of Admis.

Utah State University, Logan 84322-1600
Rod Clark, Director of Admissions
801-750-1107

VERMONT

Castleton State College, Castleton 05735
Gary Fallis, Dir. of Admis.

NORWICH UNIVERSITY
65 S. Main St., Northfield 05663
Prof. Edward Hernandez, Dept. Chrpsn.
See listing under "Universities"

University of Vermont
194 S. Prospect St., Burlington 05401
802-656-3370

VIRGINIA

Christopher Newport College
50 Shoe Ln., Newport News 23606

College of William and Mary, Williamsburg 23185
Jean A. Scott, Dean of Admission

Eastern Mennonite College
1200 Park Rd., Harrisonburg 22801
Jerry Miller, Dir. of Admis.

Ferrum College, Ferrum 24088
Bob Bailey, Dir. of Admis.

James Madison University, Harrisonburg 22807

LIBERTY UNIVERSITY
P.O. Box 20000, Lynchburg 24506
Jay Spencer, VP Recruitment
800-376-2800
See listing under "Universities"

Longwood College, Farmville 23901

Lynchburg College
1501 Lakeside Dr., Lynchburg 24501
Ernest Chadderton, Dean of Enrollment

Radford University
P.O. Box 5430, Radford 24142

SHENANDOAH UNIVERSITY
1460 University Dr., Winchester 22601
Dr. Sandra Lemoine, Coordinator
See listing under "Universities"

Virginia Polytechnic Institute & State University
Blacksburg 24061
David Bousquet, Dir. of Undergraduate Admis.

WASHINGTON

Central Washington University, Ellensburg 98926
William Swain, Director of Admissions

Pacific Lutheran University
12180 Park Ave. S., Tacoma 98447
Dr. David Olson, Dean

Seattle Pacific University
3307 3rd Ave., W., Seattle 98119

University of Puget Sound
1500 N. Warner St., Tacoma 98416

WEST VIRGINIA

Alderson-Broaddus College
Philippi 26416
Craig W. Gould, Director of Admissions
304-457-1700

Bluefield State College
219 Rock St., Bluefield 24701

Fairmont State College
1201 Locust Ave., Fairmont 26554
John Conaway, Dir. of Admis.

Marshall University
400 Hal Greer Blvd., Huntington 25755
See listing under "Universities"

Shepherd College, Shepherdstown 25443

The University of Charleston
2300 MacCorkle Ave., S.E., Charleston 25304
800-995-GO UC

West Liberty State College, West Liberty 26074

West Virginia Institute of Technology
405 Fayette Pike, Montgomery 25136

West Virginia University
P.O. Box 6001, Morgantown 26506

WEST VIRGINIA WESLEYAN COLLEGE
59 College Ave., Buckhannon 26201
Robert Skinner, Director of Admission
See listing under "Universities"

WISCONSIN

Carroll College
100 N. East Ave., Waukesha 53186
Ken Moyer, Dir. of Admis.

Carthage College
2001 Alford Dr., Kenosha 53140
Kevin McCarthy, Athletic Director

Ripon College, P.O. Box 248, Ripon 54971
James Reilly, Dean of Admis.

University of Wisconsin, La Crosse
115 Main Hall, La Crosse 54601
608-785-8067

University of Wisconsin, Oshkosh
800 Algoma Blvd., Oshkosh 54901-8602
August Helgerson, Dir. of Admis.

University of Wisconsin
1 University Plaza, Platteville 53818
Richard Schumacher, Dean of Admissions

University of Wisconsin, River Falls
River Falls 54022
Alan Tuchtenhagen, Dir. of Admis.

WYOMING

University of Wyoming
P.O. Box 3434, Laramie 82071
Richard Davis, Dir. of Admis.

GUAM

University of Guam
UOG Station, Mangilao 96923
Kathleen Owings, Dir. of Admis.

PUERTO RICO

University of Puerto Rico, Mayaguez Campus
P.O. Box 5000, Mayaguez 00681
Neysa Lopez, Dir. of Admis.

PHYSICAL SCIENCE

ALABAMA

Gadsden State Community College
P.O. Box 227, Gadsden 35902
W. Bryan Stone, Dir. of Admis.

Samford University
800 Lakeshore Dr., Birmingham 35229
Ben Chastain, Chrpsn.

Troy State University, Troy 36082
Dr. Gene O'Masta, Dean

Troy State University at Dothan
P.O. Box 8368, Dothan 36304
Bob Willis, Dir. of Undergraduate Admissions

University of Alabama
P.O. Box 870132, Tuscaloosa 35487-0132
Roy Smith, Dir. of Admis.

UNIVERSITY OF ALABAMA IN HUNTSVILLE
P.O. Box 1247, Huntsville 35899
Ron R. Koger Ed.D., Dir. of Admis.
205-895-6070
Established 1969. Public. Coed. Accreditation: SACS, ABET, NLN, CSAB, ACS. Tuition: $2,418 resident, $4,836 non-resident. Room & Board: $3,450. Undergraduate enrollment: 2,674 full-time, 3,439 part-time. Graduate enrollment: 1,860. Faculty: 282. Student-faculty ratio: 18:1. Degrees: BS, BA, BSBA, BSE, MS, MSM, Ph.D., BSN, MSN, MA. 20 buildings on 350 acres. Comprehensive research university located in the Tennessee Valley of northern Alabama. Huntsville is the locale of major government and private research centers. Metropolitan population approaching 300,000.

ARIZONA

University of Arizona, Tucson 85721
Loyd Bell, Director of Admissions

Yavapai College
1100 E. Sheldon St., Prescott 86301
Dr. Doreen Dailey, President
602-445-7300
See listing under "Community and Junior Colleges"

ARKANSAS

Arkansas State University
P.O. Box 419, State University 72467

Ouachita Baptist University
410 Ouachita St., Arkadelphia 71998
Randy Garner, Dir. of Admis.
800-DIAL-OBU

University of Arkansas at Fayetteville
Fayetteville 72701

CALIFORNIA

Biola University
13800 Biola Ave., La Mirada 90639
Wayne Chute, Dean of Admissions

California Baptist College
8432 Magnolia Ave., Riverside 92504
800-782-3382

California Polytechnic State University
San Luis Obispo 93407
Helen Linstrum, Dir. of Admis.

California State University-Stanislaus
801 W. Monte Vista Ave., Turlock 95382
Frances Cook, Dean Enrollment Services

Chapman University
333 N. Glassell St., Orange 92666
Michael Drummy, Dir. of Admis.

College of Notre Dame
1500 Ralston Ave., Belmont 94002
Greg M. Smith, PhD., Dir. of Admis.

Fresno Pacific College
1717 S. Chestnut Ave., Fresno 93702
209-453-2039

La Sierra University
4700 Pierce St., Riverside 92505
800-874-5587

Loyola Marymount University
Loyola Blvd. at W. 80th, Los Angeles 90045
M. L'Heureux, Dir. of Admis.

Menlo College
1000 El Camino Real, Atherton 94027

Mills College
5000 MacArthur Blvd., Oakland 94613
Genevieve Ann Flaherty, Dean of Admissions
800-87-MILLS

San Francisco State University
1600 Holloway Ave., San Francisco 94132
Corwin Bjonerud, Dir. of Admis.

Santa Barbara City College
721 Cliff Dr., Santa Barbara 93109
805-965-0581

University of California at Berkeley
Campbell Hall, Berkeley 94720

University of California-Santa Cruz
Santa Cruz 95064
Joseph Allen, Dir. of Admis.

University of La Verne
1950 3rd St., La Verne 91750
Mark Bornholdt, Dir. of Admis.

COLORADO

Adams State College, Alamosa 81102
Cheryl Billingsley, Dir. of Admis.
800-824-6494

Colorado College
14 E. Cache La Poudre, Colorado Springs 80903
Terry Swenson, Dir. of Admis.

Colorado Northwestern Community College
500 Kennedy Dr., Rangely 81648
Pat Kalahar, Dir. Marketing/Recruitment
800-562-1105

Mesa State College
P.O. Box 2647, Grand Junction 81502
Sherri Pe'a, Dir. of Admis.

University of Denver
2199 S. University Blvd., Denver 80210

University of Northern Colorado, Greeley 80639
Roger Kovar, Dean of Arts and Sciences
303-351-2707

Western State College of Colorado
Gunnison 81231
Monica Bruning, Dir. of Admis.
See listing under "Universities"

CONNECTICUT

Albertus Magnus College
700 Prospect St., New Haven 06511
Richard Lolatte, Dir. of Admissions
203-773-8501 or 800-578-9160

Mattatuck Community College
750 Chase Parkway, Waterbury 06708
Dr. Richard Sanders, President

Trinity College
300 Summit St., Hartford 06106
Dr. David Borus, Dean of Admissions

DISTRICT OF COLUMBIA

The American University
4400 Massachusetts Ave. N.W.
Washington 20016

FLORIDA

Eckerd College
P.O. Box 12560, St. Petersburg 33733
Richard Hallin, Dir. of Admis.

Stetson University
401 N. Woodland Blvd., De Land 32720
Gary A. Meadows, Dean of Admis.

GEORGIA

La Grange College
601 Broad St., La Grange 30240
Phil Dodson, Dir. of Admis.
706-882-2911

Shorter College
315 Shorter Ave., Rome 30165

West Georgia College, Carrollton 30118
C. Doyle Bickers, Dir. of Admis.

HAWAII

Brigham Young University, Hawaii Campus
55-220 Kulanui St., Laie 96762
Clark E. Hirschi, Coordinator of Admis.

IDAHO

University of Idaho, Moscow 83843
Peter Brown, Dir. of Admis.

ILLINOIS

Augustana College
639 38th St., Rock Island 61201
Martin R. Sauer, Director of Admission
800-798-8100

Eastern Illinois University, Charleston 61920
Douglas Davis, Chrpsn.
See listing under "Universities"

Eureka College
300 E. College Ave., Eureka 61530

Governors State University
1 University Pky., University Park 60466
Richard Pride, Dir. of Admis.

Judson College
1151 N. State St., Elgin 60123
Jack Powell, Dir. of Enrollment Services

Knox College, Galesburg 61401
309-343-0112 or 800-678-KNOX
See listing under "Universities"

LEWIS UNIVERSITY
Rt. 53, Romeoville 60441
Irish O'Reilly, Director of Admissions
See listing under "Universities"

Loyola University - Mundelein College
6363 N. Sheridan Rd., Chicago 60660
Judith Bobber, Dir. of Admis.

Monmouth College
700 E. Broadway, Monmouth 61462

Northeastern Illinois University
5500 N. St. Louis Ave., Chicago 60625

Olivet Nazarene University, Kankakee 60901
John Mongerson, Dir. of Admis.
815-939-5203

Parkland College
2400 W. Bradley Ave., Champaign 61821-1899
217-351-2208 or 800-346-8089

Principia College, Elsah 62028

Rockford College
5050 E. State St., Rockford 61108
Miriam King, V.P. for Enrollment Management
See listing under "Universities"

University of Chicago
5801 S. Ellis Ave., Chicago 60637

University of Illinois at Chicago
P.O. Box 5220, Chicago 60680
Dr. Marilyn R. Fiduccia, Dir. of Admis.

Western Illinois University
900 W. Adams St., Macomb 61455
Alan DeRoos, Registrar
309-298-1891

INDIANA

Ball State University
2000 W. University Ave., Muncie 47306
Ruth Vedvik, Dir. of Admis.

Goshen College
1700 S. Main St., Goshen 46526
John Yordy, Chairperson

Purdue University
Schleman Hall, West Lafayette 47907

ST. JOSEPH'S COLLEGE
P.O. Box 890, Rensselaer 47978
Louis Levy, Dean of Admissions
800-447-8781

Taylor University
500 W. Reade Ave., Upland 46989
Herb Frye, Dean of Enrollment Management

Tri-State University, Angola 46703
Director of Admission
800-347-4878

University of Notre Dame
Notre Dame 46556
Kevin M. Rooney, Dir. of Admis.

Valparaiso University, Valparaiso 46383

IOWA

Clarke College
1550 Clarke Dr., Dubuque 52001
Diana Malone, BVM, PhD, Chair
800-383-2345

Dordt College
498 4th Ave., N.E., Sioux Center 51250
Quentin Van Essen, Dir. of Admissions
800-343-6738

Drake University
2507 E. University Ave., Des Moines 50311
Thomas Willoughby, Dir. of Admis.

Graceland College, Lamoni 50140
800-638-0053, Outside Iowa 800-346-9208
Bonita Booth, Dean of Admissions
See listing under "Universities"

Grinnell College
P.O. Box 805, Grinnell 50112

Iowa State University, Ames 50011
Karsten Smedal, Dir. of Admis.

Iowa Wesleyan College
601 N. Main St., Mt. Pleasant 52641

Luther College
700 College Dr., Decorah 52101
David Sallee, Dean for Enrollment

University of Northern Iowa, Cedar Falls 50614

Waldorf College
106 S. 6th St., Forest City 50436
Steve Lovik, Dir. of Admis.
800-292-1903

KANSAS

Coffeyville Community College
402 W. 11th St., Coffeyville 67337
Helen Ellerman, Dir. of Admis.

Fort Hays State University
600 Park St., Hays 67601-4099
Dr. Kwo-Sun Chu, Chrpsn.

McPherson College
1600 E. Euclid St., McPherson 67460

Ottawa University
1001 S. Cedar St., Ottawa 66067
Steve Koberlein, Dir. of Admis.
800-755-5200

SOUTHWESTERN COLLEGE
100 College St., Winfield 67156
800-846-1543

KENTUCKY

Morehead State University, Morehead 40351
Charles Myers, Director of Admissions
606-783-2000

Murray State University, Murray 42071
Phil Bryan, Director of Admissions
800-272-4MSU

Northern Kentucky University
Louie B. Nunn Dr., Highland Heights 41076

LOUISIANA

Tulane University
6823 Saint Charles Ave., New Orleans 70118
Richard Whiteside, Dean of Admission

MAINE

Bowdoin College, Brunswick 04011
William Mason, Dir. of Admis.

College of the Atlantic
105 Eden St., Bar Harbor 04609
Steve Thomas, Dir. of Admis.

St. Joseph's College, North Windham 04062

University of Maine
9 O'Brien Ave., Machias 04654

MARYLAND

Goucher College
1021 Dulaney Valley Rd., Baltimore 21204

Towson State University
800 York Rd., Towson 21204
Dr. Hoke Smith, President

MASSACHUSETTS

Boston University
685 Commonwealth Ave., Boston 02215

Brandeis University
415 South St, Waltham 02154
David Gould, Dean of Admissions
617-736-3500

Bridgewater State College
Bridgewater 02325
James Plotner, Jr., Dir. of Admis.

Clark University
950 Main St., Worcester 01610
Richard Pierson, Dean of Admis.

Hampshire College, Amherst 01002
Audrey Y. Smith, Dir. of Admissions
413-582-5471

Massachusetts Institute of Technology
77 Massachusetts Ave., Cambridge 02139

University of Massachusetts
100 Morrissey Blvd., Boston 02125

Wellesley College, Wellesley 02181
Janet A. Lavin, Dir. of Admis.

Westfield State College
577 Western Ave., Westfield 01085
John F. Marcus, Dir. of Admis.

Worcester Polytechnic Institute
100 Institute Rd., Worcester 01609
Kay R. Dietrich, Director of Admissions
508-831-5286

MICHIGAN

Adrian College
110 S. Madison St., Adrian 49221
George Wolf, Dir. of Admis.
See listing under "Universities"

Calvin College
3201 Burton St., S.E., Grand Rapids 49546

Eastern Michigan University, Ypsilanti 48197
Daniel Trochet, Head
313-487-3060 or 800-GO-TO-EMU

Grand Valley State University
1 Campus Dr., Allendale 49401
JoAnn Foerster, Dir. of Admis.

HILLSDALE COLLEGE
33 E. College St., Hillsdale 49242
Dr. Kenneth Hayes, Chrpsn.
517-437-7341

Michigan State University, East Lansing 48824
Jane Smith, Student Affairs Specialist

Michigan Technological University
1400 Townsend Dr., Houghton 49931
Joseph A. Galetto, Dir. Enrollment Mgmt.
906-487-2335

MINNESOTA

Bemidji State University
1500 Birchmont Dr., N.E., Bemidji 56601
800-475-2001

Bethel College
3900 Bethel Dr., St. Paul 55112
Dr. George Brushaber, President

College of Saint Benedict
37 S. College Ave., St. Joseph 56374

Gustavus Adolphus College
800 W. College Ave., St. Peter 56082
Mark Anderson, Dir. of Admis.

St. Cloud State University
740 4th Ave., S., St. Cloud 56301
Sherwood Reid, Dir. of Admis.
800-369-4260

St. John's University
P.O. Box 7155, Collegeville 56321

St. Mary's College of Minnesota
700 Terrace Heights #2, Winona 55987
Tony Piscitiello, VP for Admission

Southwest State University, Marshall 56258

Winona State University
P.O. Box 5838, Winona 55987
Dr. J. Mootz, Dir. of Admis.

MISSISSIPPI

Mississippi College
P.O. Box 4086, Clinton 39058

MISSOURI

Central Missouri State University
Warrensburg 64093
Delores Hudson, Dir. of Admis.

College of the Ozarks, Point Lookout 65726
Dr. Kenton Olson, Dean of the College

Cottey College
1000 W. Austin St., Nevada 64772
Wendy Beckemeyer, Dir. of Admis.

Drury College
900 N. Benton Ave., Springfield 65802
Michael G. Thomas, Dir. of Admis.

Maryville University of St. Louis
13550 Conway Rd., Saint Louis 63141
314-576-9300 or 800-MARYVLL

Missouri Baptist College
12542 Conway Rd., St. Louis 63141

Missouri Southern State College
3950 Newman Rd., Joplin 64801-1595
Dr. Vernon D. Baiamonte, Dept. Head
See listing under "Universities"

Northeast Missouri State University
Kirksville 63501

Northwest Missouri State University
800 University Dr., Maryville 64468

Southwest Baptist University
1601 S. Springfield Ave., Bolivar 65613

William Woods College
200 W. 12th St., Fulton 65251
Dr. Jahnae Barnett, VP of Admis.

MONTANA

Montana State University, Bozeman 59717

Montana State University - Billings
1500 N. 30th St., Billings 59101
Karen Everett, Dir. of Admis.
406-657-2158

NEBRASKA

Midland Lutheran College
900 Clarkson St., Fremont 68025
Roland Kahnk, V.P. Admissions

NEW HAMPSHIRE

Keene State College
229 Main St., Keene 03435
Kathryn Dodge, Dir. of Admis.

New England College
26 Bridge St., Henniker 03242
John Spaulding, Dir. of Admis.

NEW JERSEY

Caldwell College
9 Ryerson Ave., Caldwell 07006

Monmouth College
400 Cedar Ave., West Long Branch 07764
Joan Rudinski, Dir. of Admis.

Rowan College of New Jersey, Glassboro 08028
Marvin G. Sills, Dir. of Admis.

Upsala College
345 Prospect St., East Orange 07017
George Lynes, Dean of Admissions

NEW MEXICO

College of the Southwest
6610 N. Lovington Hwy., Hobbs 88240

Eastern New Mexico University
Portales 88130
Larry Fuqua, Dir. of Admis.

New Mexico Highlands University, Las Vegas 87701
Dr. Jorge P. Thomas, VP Academic Affairs

New Mexico Institute of Mining & Technology
801 Leroy Pl., Socorro 87801

NEW YORK

Adelphi University, Garden City 11530
Dr. Elliot Pruzan, Asst. Provost & Dir. of Admis.
516-877-3050

Alfred University
Alumni Hall, Alfred 14802
Laurie Richer, Director of Admissions
800-541-9229

Canisius College
2001 Main St., Buffalo 14208
Penelope Lips, Dir. of Admis.
800-843-1517

Clarkson University, Potsdam 13699
Robert Croot, Dir. of Admis.

Colgate University
13 Oak Dr., Hamilton 13346
Dean of Admissions
315-824-7401

Columbia University
612 W. 115th St., New York 10025

Houghton College
P.O. Box 128, Houghton 14744
Tim Fuller, Dir. of Admis.

Long Island University-C. W. Post Campus
Rt. 25A, Brookville 11548
Dr. Joan Shields, Chemistry Chrpsn.
516-299-2491
Dr. Robert Harrison, Geology/Geography Chrpsn.
516-299-2318
Dr. Donald Gelman, Physics Chrpsn.
516-299-2495

Manhattan College
4513 Manhattan College Pky., Riverdale 10471
Dr. Edward Brown, Acting Dean of Science

Molloy College
1000 Hempstead Ave., Rockville Centre 11570
Wayne James, Dir. of Admis.
See listing under "Universities"

Pace University, Pleasantville/Briarcliff Campus
Bedford Rd., Pleasantville 10570

Paul Smith's College, Paul Smiths 12970
Enrico Miller, Dir. of Admis.
800-421-2605

Rensselaer Polytechnic Institute, Troy 12180
Conrad Sharrow, Dean of Admissions

Rochester Institute of Technology
1 Lomb Memorial Dr., Rochester 14623
716-475-6631
See listing under "Universities"

St. Joseph's College
245 Clinton Ave., Brooklyn 11205
Geraldine Foudy, Dir. of Admis.
718-636-6868

St. Joseph's College, Suffolk Campus
25 Audobon Ave., Patchogue 11772

Sarah Lawrence College, Bronxville 10708

SUNY at Buffalo
17 Capen Hall
P.O. Box 601660, Buffalo 14260-1660
716-645-6900

SUNY College at Brockport
Brockport 14420

SUNY College at Plattsburgh, Plattsburgh 12901
Richard Higgins, Dir. of Admis.
518-564-2040

SUNY College of Environmental Science & Forestry
1 Forestry Dr., Syracuse 13210
800-7777-ESF or 315-470-6600

SUNY Nassau Community College
1 Education Dr., Garden City 11530
Bernard Iantosca, Dir of Admis.

NORTH CAROLINA

Barton College
College Station, Wilson 27893
Anthony Britt, Dir. of Admis.
800-345-4973/919-399-6318
See listing under "Universities"

Elon College
P.O. Box 2700, Elon College 27244
Nan P. Perkins, Dean of Admissions

Gardner-Webb University
General Delivery, Boiling Springs 28017
Paul Jolley, Chrpsn.
704-434-2361

Guilford College
5800 W. Friendly Ave., Greensboro 27410
Larry West, Dir. of Admis.
See listing under "Universities"

North Carolina State University
P.O. Box 7001, Raleigh 27695
George Dixon, Dir. of Admis.

Pembroke State University
P.O. Box 1510, Pembroke 28372
Anthony Locklear, Dir. of Admissions
919-521-6262

OHIO

Capital University
2199 E. Main St., Columbus 43209
Dolphus E. Henry, Associate Provost

Kent State University
P.O. Box 5190, Kent 44242
Bruce Riddle, Dir. of Admis.

Oberlin College
135 W. Lorain St., Oberlin 44074
Debra Chermonte, Dir. of Admis.

Ohio Wesleyan University
61 S. Sandusky St., Delaware 43015
Donald Bishop, Dean for Enrollment

University of Akron
381 Buchtel Common, Akron 44325
Kris MacDermott, Asst. Provost Enrollment

University of Cincinnati
2700 Clifton Ave., Cincinnati 45221

University of Dayton
300 College Park Ave., Dayton 45469-2314
Toll-free 800-837-7433
See listing under "Universities"

University of Rio Grande
General Delivery, Rio Grande 45674
Dr. Robert Wolfe, Dean
614-245-5353, Ext. 7397

Urbana University
100 College Way, Urbana 43078
Donald Burns, Dir. of Admis.

Wilmington College
P.O. Box 1185, Wilmington 45177
Rhonda Inderhees, Dir. of Admis.

OKLAHOMA

Oklahoma City University
2501 N. Blackwelder Ave., Oklahoma City 73106
Susan Barker, Director
See listing under "Universities"

Oklahoma State University, Stillwater 74078
Larry Scott, Dept. Head

Oral Roberts University
7777 S. Lewis Ave., Tulsa 74171
Arthur E. Matzkvech, Dir. of Admis.

University of Tulsa
600 S. College Ave., Tulsa 74104
Dr. Lewis Duncan, Dir. of Admis.

OREGON

Central Oregon Community College
2600 N.W. College Way, Bend 97701
Christine Kerlin, Dir. of Admis.
503-383-7500

Lewis & Clark College
0615 S.W. Palatine Hill Rd., Portland 97219
Michael Sexton, Dean of Admissions

Pacific University
2043 College Way, Forest Grove 97116
Barbara Mergen, Dir. of Admis.

PENNSYLVANIA

Beaver College
450 S. Easton Rd., Glenside 19038-3295
Dennis Nostrand, VP for Enrollment Management
Phone: 800-776-BEAVER(2328)
Fax: 215-572-4049
See listing under "Universities"

Bloomsburg University, Bloomsburg 17815
Bernard Vinovrski, Dir. of Admis.

California University of Pennsylvania
3rd St., California 15419
Norman Hasbrouck, Dean for Enrollment

Carnegie Mellon University
5000 Forbes Ave., Pittsburgh 15213

Chatham College
Woodland Rd., Pittsburgh 15232
Suellen Ofe, Dean of Admis./Financial Aid
See listing under "Women's College"

Clarion University of Pennsylvania
840 Wood St., Clarion 16214

Drexel University
3141 Chestnut St., Philadelphia 19104
Dean of Enrollment Management

East Stroudsburg University of Pennsylvania
East Stroudsburg 18301
Alan Chesterton, Dir. of Admis.

Edinboro University of Pennsylvania
Edinboro 16444
Admissions Office: 800-626-2203

Gannon University
109 University Sq., Erie 16541

Juniata College
1700 Moore St., Huntington 16652

Lafayette College, Easton 18042
G. Gary Ripple, Dir. of Admis.
610-250-5100

La Salle University
1900 W. Olney Ave., Philadelphia 19141
Br. Gerald Fitzgerald, Dir. of Admis.
See listing under "Universities"

Mercyhurst College
501 E. 38th St., Erie 16546
Andrew Roth, Dean of Enrollment
800-825-1926

Millersville University of Pennsylvania
Millersville 17551
Blair Treasure, Dean of Admissions

Montgomery County Community College
340 DeKalb Pike, Blue Bell 19422-0758
Dennis Murphy, Dir. of Admis.

Muhlenberg College
2400 W. Chew St., Allentown 18104
Chris Hooker-Haring, Dir. of Admis.

Pennsylvania State University
201 Shields Bldg., University Park 16802

Slippery Rock University, Slippery Rock 16057
Director of Admissions

Thiel College
75 College Ave., Greenville 16125
Robert Weaver, Dir. of Admis.

Villanova University
845 E. Lancaster Ave., Villanova 19085
Stephen R. Merritt, Dir. of Admis.

West Chester University of Pennsylvania
S. High St., West Chester 19380

Wilkes University
184 S. River St., Wilkes-Barre 18766
Emory P. Guffrovich Jr., Dean of Admissions

York College of Pennsylvania
P.O. Box 15199, York 17405-7199
Nancy Spararo, Dir. of Admis.
717-849-1600
See listing under "Universities"

RHODE ISLAND

Rhode Island College
600 Mt. Pleasant Ave., Providence 02908

Roger Williams College
1 Old Ferry Rd., Bristol 02809
William Dunfey, Dir. of Admis.

SOUTH DAKOTA

Augustana College
29th & S. Summit, Sioux Falls 57197

SIOUX FALLS COLLEGE
1501 S. Prairie Ave., Sioux Falls 57105
Susan Reese, Dir. of Admis.
800-888-1047
See listing under "Universities"

University of South Dakota
414 E. Clark St., Vermillion 57069
Dave Lorenz, Dir. of Admis.

TENNESSEE

Austin Peay State University
601 College St., Clarksville 37044

Carson-Newman College
P.O. Box 70552, Jefferson City 37760
See listing under "Universities"

Freed-Hardeman University
158 E. Main St., Henderson 38340
800-342-7837

University of Memphis, Memphis 38152
Dr. John Eubank, Dean of Admissions

University of Tennessee at Martin
Martin 38238
Paul Kelley, Director of Admissions
See listing under "Universities"

Vanderbilt University
West End Ave., Nashville 37240

TEXAS

Austin College
900 N. Grand Ave., Sherman 75090
Rodney Oto, Dean of Admission
800-442-5363

Concordia Lutheran College
3400 N. Interstate 35, Austin 78705
Kevin Pieper, Dir. of Admis.

St. Mary's University of San Antonio
1 Camino Santa Maria, San Antonio 78228
Rick Castillo, Dir. of Admis.

University of Texas at Austin
0 the University of Texas, Austin 78712

West Texas State University
2501 4th Ave., Canyon 79016
Lila Vars, Dir. of Admis.

UTAH

Southern Utah University
351 W. Center St., Cedar City 84720
Dr. Al Tait, Dean
801-586-7921

Utah State University, Logan 84322-1600
Rod Clark, Director of Admissions
801-750-1107

Westminster College of Salt Lake City
1840 S. 1300 E., Salt Lake City 84105
800-748-4753

VERMONT

Bennington College, Bennington 05201
Karen Kristof, Dir. of Admis.
800-833-6845

Lyndon State College, Lyndonville 05851

Marlboro College
General Delivery, Marlboro 05344

Saint Michael's College
Winooski Park, Colchester 05439
800-SMC-8000
See listing under "Liberal Arts"

University of Vermont
194 S. Prospect St., Burlington 05401
802-656-3370

VIRGINIA

Bluefield College
3000 College Dr., Bluefield 24605
Dr. Roy Dobyns, President
See listing under "Universities"

Bridgewater College
402 E College St., Bridgewater 22812

Clinch Valley College of the University of Virginia
P.O. Box 16, Wise 24293
Lana Low, Dir. Enrollment Management

Longwood College, Farmville 23901

Lynchburg College
1501 Lakeside Dr., Lynchburg 24501
Ernest Chadderton, Dean of Enrollment

Marymount University
2807 N. Glebe Rd., Arlington 22207
Charles Coe, Director of Admissions
800-548-7638 or 703-284-1500
See listing under "Universities"

Mary Washington College
1701 College Ave., Fredericksburg 22401
Martin Wilder, V.P. for Admissions

Sweet Briar College, Sweet Briar 24595
Nancy Church, Dir. of Admis.

Virginia Polytechnic Institute & State University
Blacksburg 24061
David Bousquet, Dir. of Undergraduate Admis.

Virginia Wesleyan College
1584 Wesleyan Dr., Norfolk 23502
W. Steve Stocks, V.P. for Admis.

WASHINGTON

Central Washington University, Ellensburg 98926
William Swain, Director of Admissions

Skagit Valley College
2405 E. College Way, Mt. Vernon 98273

WEST VIRGINIA

Bethany College, Bethany 26031
John Giesman, Registrar

Marshall University
400 Hal Greer Blvd., Huntington 25755
See listing under "Universities"

WEST VIRGINIA WESLEYAN COLLEGE
59 College Ave., Buckhannon 26201
Robert Skinner, Director of Admission
See listing under "Universities"

WISCONSIN

Carroll College
100 N. East Ave., Waukesha 53186
Ken Moyer, Dir. of Admis.

Edgewood College
855 Woodrow St., Madison 53711
Robert Blust, Dir. of Admis.

Lawrence University
P.O. Box 599, Appleton 54912
Steven Syverson, Dean of Admissions

Marquette University
1217 W. Wisconsin Ave., Milwaukee 53233
Raymond A. Brown, Dean of Admissions

Northland College
1411 Ellis Ave., Ashland 54806
Jim Miller, Dean of Admissions

University of Wisconsin, Eau Claire
Eau Claire 54701

University of Wisconsin, Green Bay
2420 Nicolet Dr., Green Bay 54311
Myron Van de Ven, Dir. of Admis.

University of Wisconsin, Oshkosh
800 Algoma Blvd., Oshkosh 54901-8602
August Helgerson, Dir. of Admis.

University of Wisconsin
1 University Plaza, Platteville 53818
Richard Schumacher, Dean of Admissions

University of Wisconsin, River Falls
River Falls 54022
Alan Tuchtenhagen, Dir. of Admis.

GUAM

University of Guam
UOG Station, Mangilao 96923
Kathleen Owings, Dir. of Admis.

PUERTO RICO

University of Puerto Rico, Mayaguez Campus
P.O. Box 5000, Mayaguez 00681
Neysa Lopez, Dir. of Admis.

University of Puerto Rico, Rio Piedras Campus
P.O. Box 23300, San Juan 00931
Victor Lopez, Dir. of Admis.

PODIATRIC MEDICINE

This classification contains schools offering the degree of Doctor of Podiatric Medicine accredited by the American Podiatric Medical Association (†) and a selection of programs from institutionally accredited schools.

CALIFORNIA

† California College of Podiatric Medicine
P.O. Box 7855, San Francisco 94120
Frank Jimenez, Dir. of Recruitment

CONNECTICUT

QUINNIPIAC COLLEGE
275 Mount Carmel Ave., Hamden 06518
See listing under "Universities"

FLORIDA

† Barry University
11300 N.E. 2nd Ave., Miami Shores 33161
Robin Ray Roberts, Dean of Admissions

GEORGIA

Georgia College
231 W. Hancock St., Milledgeville 31061
912-453-5004

ILLINOIS

ROOSEVELT UNIVERSITY
430 S. Michigan Ave., Chicago 60605
William Smyser, Director of Admissions
See listing under "Universities"

† Scholl College of Podiatric Medicine
1001 N. Dearborn St., Chicago 60610
Howard M. Bers, Ed.D., Assoc. Dean Student Affairs
312-280-2940 or 800-843-3059

IOWA

† University of Osteopathic Medicine & Health
Sciences
3200 Grand Ave., Des Moines 50312
For admissions contact: 515-271-1698

NEW JERSEY

Jersey City State College
2039 Kennedy Blvd., Jersey City 07305
201-200-3234

NEW YORK

† New York College of Podiatric Medicine
53 E. 124th St., New York 10035
Dr. M. J. Valletta, Assoc. Dean

OHIO

† Ohio College of Podiatric Medicine
10515 Carnegie Ave., Cleveland 44106
John E. Andrews, Dean/Student Affairs &
Admission
In OH 800-821-6562 others 800-238-7903

PENNSYLVANIA

† Pennsylvania College of Podiatric Medicine
148 N. 8th St., Philadelphia 19107
Sandra G. Mannix, VP Student Affairs

WESTMINSTER COLLEGE
New Wilmington 16172
Richard Dana Paul, Dir. of Admis.
412-946-7100

PUERTO RICO

Bayamon Central University
P.O. Box 1725, Bayamon 00960-1725
Christine Hernandez, Dir. of Admis.

::PREPARATORY SCHOOLS FOR BOYS

Primarily Boarding

ALABAMA

Lyman Ward Military Academy
P.O. Box 547, Camp Hill 36850
Charles Livings, Dir. of Admis.

ARKANSAS

Subiaco Academy
100 College Ave., Subiaco 72865
David E. Hartz, Headmaster
800-364-7824

CALIFORNIA

Army and Navy Academy
P.O. Box 3000, Carlsbad 92018
Fred W. Heinle, PhD, President
619-729-2385

Bellarmine College Preparatory
850 Elm St., San Jose 95126

Dunn School
P.O. Box 98, Los Olivos 93441

St. John Bosco High School
13640 Bellflower Blvd., Bellflower 90706
William Goodman, Principal

St. Michael's College Prep Boarding High School for
Boys
Grades 8 through 12
19292 El Toro Rd., Silverado 92676
Rev. H. Szanto, O Praem, PhD, Principal
714-858-0222

VILLANOVA PREPARATORY SCHOOL
12096 Ventura Ave., Ojai 93023-3999
Leo Molitor, Interim Headmaster
Denver Compton, Dir. of Admis.
Phone: 805-646-1464, Fax: 805-646-4430
Established 1924. Private. Catholic. Coed. Accreditation: WASC. Tuition for day students: $4,500. Tuition/room and board for 5-day boarders: $14,600, for 7-day boarders: $15,100. Enrollment: 228 (90 boarding, 138 day). Faculty: 27. Student-faculty ratio: 8:1. Average class size: 15. 9 buildings on 127 acres. 17 classrooms and labs, 2 gyms, pool, and athletic fields. 7,700 people in the community. 75 miles from Los Angeles. 100% of graduates are accepted by colleges and universities.

Webb School of California
1175 W. Baseline Rd., Claremont 91711
Nigel Taplin, Dir. of Admis.

West Coast Talmudical Seminary
7215 Waring Ave., Los Angeles 90046

CONNECTICUT

Avon Old Farms School
500 Old Farms Rd., Avon 06001
George Trautman, Headmaster

Oxford Academy
P.O. Box P, Westbrook 06498
J. A. Woodnall, Headmaster

St. Thomas More School
85 Cottage Rd., Oakdale 06370
James Hanrahan, Headmaster

Salisbury School
251 Canaan Rd., Salisbury 06068
Richard T. Flood, Jr., Headmaster

South Kent School
40 Bulls Ridge Rd., South Kent 06785
George H. Bartlett, Headmaster

Woodhall School
P.O. Box 550, Bethlehem 06751
Jonathan Woodhall, Director

DISTRICT OF COLUMBIA

St. Albans School
Mount St. Alban, Washington 20016
Rev. Mark Mullin, Headmaster
202-537-6435

St. John's College H.S.
2607 Military Rd., N.W., Washington 20015

FLORIDA

Admiral Farragut Academy
501 Park St., N, St. Petersburg 33710
Cpt. Michael Moriarty, Dir. of Admis.

Bolles School
7400 San Jose Blvd., Jacksonville 32217

FLORIDA AIR ACADEMY
1950 South Academy Dr., Melbourne 32901
Major James Dwight, President

GEORGIA

Benedictine Military School
6502 Seawright Drive, Savannah 31406
Rev. Conan Feigh, O.S.B., Headmaster

Brandon Hall School
1701 Brandon Hall Dr., Dunwoody 30350
Mary Jean Thielen, Dean

Riverside Military Academy
1942 Riverside Dr., Gainesville 30501
Col. Billy Williams, Superintendent
404-532-6251

ILLINOIS

Marmion Military Academy
1000 Butterfield Rd., Aurora 60504
Rev. Basil Yender, OSB, Headmaster

INDIANA

Culver Military Academy and Summer Camps
1300 Academy Rd., Culver 46511
Richard Edwards, Dir. of Admis.

HOWE MILITARY SCHOOL
31 Academy Pl., Howe 46746
Colonel Thomas Merritt, Superintendent
Lt. Col. Reed Kimball, Headmaster
Glenn Cox, Dir. of Admis.
219-562-2131 ext. 221
Accredited by: the North Central Association of Colleges and Schools. A member of: the North Central Association of Colleges and Schools, the Independent School Association of Central States, the Association of Military Colleges and Schools of the United States, the Council for Advancement and Support of Education, the National Association of Independent Schools, the National Association of Episcopal Schools, the College Entrance Examination Board, Cum Laude Society.
Established 1884. Episcopal. Coed. Enrollment: 250. Total charge for a boarding student: $14,900. Financial aid available. Only military institute in Ohio, Michigan and Indiana that is a member of the US Army's JROTC program. JROTC required for all high school cadets.
College preparatory school. Grades 5 through 12. Fully accredited faculty and staff. Individual attention given. Class size averages 10 to 12 cadets. Twenty solid units of credit are required for graduation. Seventeen and a half of them must be in English, math, history and social studies, science, foreign language, sacred studies, business and physical education and health.
Required for admission: a desire to attend, a willingness to adhere to Howe's military discipline, be of good moral character (satisfactory references), be of average to above average intelligence (IQ test), a certificate of honorable dismissal from previous school.
Located on 150 acres in Northeast Indiana just two miles from the Michigan border. Modern dormitories and academic facilities, library, pool, three (3) gymnasiums, athletic fields, track, canteen, 700 seat auditorium, two (2) chapels, dining hall, military department.

KANSAS

MAUR HILL PREP SCHOOL
1000 Green St., Atchison 66002
Phone 913-367-5482, Fax 913-367-5096
Rev. Edwin Watson, OSB, MA, President
Mark Watson, MA, Headmaster
Damian Ahrens, BA, Director of Admission
Established 1919. Roman Catholic. Accreditation:
NCACS, State of Kansas, National Catholic Education Association. Est. total yrly. exp.: $8,200 (five day boarding) to $11,200 (international, seven day boarding. Enrollment: 120 boarding, 80 day. Faculty: 25. High school diploma program. English as a Foreign Language program. Library: 7,000 volumes. 6 buildings on 165 acres. 2 gyms, pool, golf driving range, tennis courts, and 5 athletic fields. Benedictine College Library. Cultural events. Computer lab.

St. John's Military School
P.O. Box 827, Salina 67402

Thomas More Preparatory-Marian
1701 Hall St., Hays 67601
Sister Joanita Stelter, Dir. of Admis.

KENTUCKY

Millersburg Military Institute
P.O. Box 278, Millersburg 40348

MAINE

Bridgton Academy
P.O. Box 292, North Bridgton 04057

MARYLAND

Georgetown Preparatory School
10900 Rockville Pike, Rockville 20852
Rev. John Howard, S.J., Headmaster

MASSACHUSETTS

Belmont Hill School
350 Prospect St., Belmont 02178
Christopher Wadsworth, Headmaster

St. John's Preparatory School
72 Spring St., Danvers 01923
Bro. William Drinan, CFX, Headmaster

MICHIGAN

St. Mary's Preparatory School
3535 Orchard Lake Rd., Orchard Lake 48324
Richard Krisniski, Dir. of Admis.

MINNESOTA

Cretin Hall High School
550 Albert St. S., St. Paul 55116
Bro. Michael Walgren, FSC, Principal

St. John's Preparatory School
P.O. Box 4000, Collegeville 56321
Jerald Howard, Dir. of Admis.

St. Thomas Academy
949 Mendota Heights Rd., St. Paul 55120
Paul Maloney, Dir. of Admis.

MISSISSIPPI

St. Stanislaus College
304 S. Beach Blvd., Bay St. Louis 39520

MISSOURI

Chaminade College Preparatory School
425 S. Lindbergh Blvd.
Saint Louis 63131

Missouri Military Academy
204 Grand St., Mexico 65265

Wentworth Military Academy & Junior College
1880 Washington Ave., Lexington 64067
Brig. Gen. Gerald Childress, Superintendent
800-WMA-1880 or 816-224-1964

NEBRASKA

Mt. Michael Benedictine H.S.
22520 Mt. Michael Rd., Elkhorn 68022

NEW JERSEY

Admiral Farragut Academy
601 Riverside Dr., Pine Beach 08741
Capt. Robert W. Matthies, Jr., Headmaster

NEW YORK

Christian Brothers Academy
1 De La Salle Rd., Albany 12208

GOW SCHOOL
Emery Rd., South Wales 14139
J. William Adams, Headmaster
Robert Garcia, Director of Admissions
716-652-3450, Fax: 716-652-3457
Established 1926. Private. Mens school with coed summer program. Accreditation: NY State Association of Independent Schools. 1994-95 tuition room and board: $21,850. Fees: Approximately $1,500 for books, incidentals. Enrollment: 158. Faculty: 43. Student-faculty ratio: 3.5:1. 100% go to 4 year colleges. Library: 6,000 volumes. 20 buildings on 125 acres. The Gow School is the nations oldest college preparatory school for dyslexic/learning different young men in grades 7-12 (with a post-graduate program).

Hackley School
293 Benedict Ave., Tarrytown 10591

Kildonan School
R.R. 1, Box 294, Amenia 12501

La Salle Center
500 Montauk Highway, Oakdale 11769
James J. Nolan, Admission Dir.

St. Francis High School
4129 Lake Shore Rd., Athol Springs 14010
Rev. Xavier Nawrocki, OFM Conv., Principal

Trinity Pawling School
300 State Route 22, Pawling 12564

NORTH CAROLINA

Christ School
500 Christ School Rd., Arden 28704
Mike Knighton, Dir. of Admis.

OHIO

Grand River Academy
P.O. Box 222, Austinburg 44010
Kevin Grippi, Dir. of Admis.
216-275-2811, Fax 216-275-1825

PENNSYLVANIA

Academy of the New Church Boys' School
2815 Huntingdon Pike, Bryn Athyn 19009
The Rev. George D. McCurdy, prin.

Carson Long Military Institute
P.O. Box 98, New Bloomfield 17068
Col. Carson Holman, President

Church Farm School
P.O. Box S, Paoli 19301
John D. Kistler II, Dir. of Admis.

Hill School
717 E. High School St., Pottstown 19464
Edward Kowalchick, Dir. of Admis.

The Kiski School
1888 Brett Lane, Saltsburg 15681
Robert J. Grandizio, Dir. of Admis.
412-639-3586, Fax: 412-639-8467

Phelps School
583 Sugartown Rd., Malvern 19355
Norman T. Phelps, Headmaster

VALLEY FORGE MILITARY ACADEMY & COLLEGE
1001 Eagle Rd., Wayne 19087
Rear Adm. Virgil Hill, USN (Ret.), President
800-234-VFMA

SOUTH CAROLINA

CAMDEN MILITARY ACADEMY
520 Highway 1, N., Camden 29020
Col. L. Risher, Headmaster
803-432-6001

TENNESSEE

McCallie School
2850 McCallie Ave., Chattanooga 37404
Spencer McCallie III, Headmaster

TEXAS

Central Catholic High School
1403 N. St. May's St., San Antonio 78215

Marine Military Academy
320 iwo Jima Blvd., Harlingen 78550
Maj. Gen. Ralph H. Spanjer, Supt.

VIRGINIA

Benedictine Military H.S.
304 N. Sheppard St., Richmond 23221

Blue Ridge School, Dyke 22935
Robert J. Murphy, Dir. of Admis.
804-985-2811

CHRISTCHURCH SCHOOL
Christchurch 23031
Meade King, Dir. of Admis.
800-296-2306 or 804-758-2306

FISHBURNE MILITARY SCHOOL
P.O. Box 988A, Waynesboro 22980
Robert Miller, Superintendent
Doris Brown, Registrar
703-943-1171, Fax: 703-943-8042
Established 1879. School for boys in grades 8-12 and PG, Army JROTC. Accreditation: SACS, VAIS. Annual fee: $11,700. Enrollment: 9 day, 172 boarding. Faculty: 22. Degree: High school diploma. Library: 18,000 volumes. 3 buildings on 10 acres. School facilities include computer center, science and photography labs, gym, indoor pool, and rifle range. Skiing, indoor tennis, and golf course nearby.

FORK UNION MILITARY ACADEMY
P.O. Box 278-N, Fork Union 23055
Col. R. L. Pulliam, Interim President
804-842-3212 or 800-462-3862

Hargrave Military Academy
R.R. 5, Chatham 24531
Rick Cline, Director of Admissions
804-432-2481

Miller School of Albemarle
R.R. 3, Charlottesville 22901-9328
Donaldson Tillar, Jr., Col. USA (Ret), President

WOODBERRY FOREST SCHOOL
Woodberry Forest 22989
John S. Grinalds, Headmaster
Brendan J. O'Shea, Dir. of Admis.
703-672-6023
Established 1889. Private. All-boys boarding grades 9-12. Accreditation: NAIS, VAIS, SACS. Tuition/room and board: $15,800. Enrollment: 370. Faculty: 60. Student-faculty ratio: 7:1. Library: 50,000 volumes. 36 buildings on 1,400 acres. Strong college preparatory curriculum; electives and Advanced Placement Courses in all major disciplines. All graduates attend 4-year college or university. Foreign languages include Japanese. Honor system guides community life. Strong fine arts program. Participation in team athletics is required. 13 sports; extensive facilities including golf course, indoor and outdoor pools and tennis courts, two gyms. 6-week coed. summer session.

WEST VIRGINIA

Linsly Institute, 60 Knox Lane, Wheeling 26003
Reno DiOrio, Headmaster

WISCONSIN

Northwestern Military and Naval Academy
550 S. Lake Shore Dr., Lake Geneva 53147
414-248-4465

ST. JOHN'S MILITARY ACADEMY
1101 N. Genesee St., Delafield 53018
Brigadier General David M. Williams, President
Lt. Col. Kenneth A. Clark, Director of Admissions
800-752-2338
Established in 1884. Boy's grades 7-12. Accreditation: ISACS, NAIS, AMCSUS. Tuition, room & board: $15,850. Enrollment: 300 boarding. 10 buildings on 150 acres. Gym, pool, tennis courts, golf course. College preparatory boy's boarding school. 30 minutes from Milwaukee and 90 minutes from Chicago. Extensive athletic and extracurricular offerings. JROTC honor school with distinction.

GUAM

Father Duenas Memorial School
P.O. Box FD, Agana 96910
Joy Edwards, Registrar

::PREPARATORY SCHOOLS - COEDUCATIONAL

Primarily Boarding

ALABAMA

Indian Springs School
190 Woodward Dr., Indian Springs 35124
Charles Ellis, Dir. of Admis.

Marion Military Institute
1101 Washington St., Marion 36756
800-MMI-1842

Randolph School
1005 Drake Ave., S.E., Huntsville 35802
Christopher Hartley, Headmaster

ARIZONA

Fenster School of Southern Arizona
8500 E. Ocotillo Dr., Tucson 85715
Mary Jo Myers-Filip, Dir. of Admissions

Judson School
P.O. Box 1569, Scottsdale 85252
Allan Hilton, Dir. of Admis.

Oak Creek Ranch School
P.O. Box NN, West Sedona 86340
Jay Wick, Headmaster
602-634-5571

The Orme School
HC 63, Box 3040, Mayer 86333
James E. Smith, Director of Admissions
602-632-7601, Fax 602-632-7605

Verde Valley School
3511 Verde Valley School Rd., Sedona 86351
Roy Grimm, PhD., Headmaster
602-284-2272

ARKANSAS

Harding Academy
E. Park Ave., Searcy 72143
Randy Lambeth, Superintendent
501-268-1515

CALIFORNIA

Athenian School
P.O. Box 6000, Danville 94526
Samuel Eliot, Headmaster

Cascade School
P.O. Box 9, Whitmore 96096

Cate School
P.O. Box 5005, Carpinteria 93014-5005
Noah Hotchkiss, Dir. of Admis.

Cedu School
P.O. Box 1176, Running Springs 92382
Doug Kim-Brown, Director

Happy Valley School
P.O. Box 850, Ojai 93024
Dennis Rice, Director
805-646-4343

IDYLLWILD SCHOOL OF MUSIC AND THE ARTS, ARTS ACADEMY
P.O. Box 38P, Idyllwild 92549
909-659-2171 EXT. 223
William Lowman, Headmaster, Arts Academy
Anne Behnke, Admissions Director
Established 1986. Private. Coed. Grades: 8-12 and post-graduate program. Pre-professional training in music, dance, theatre, creative writing, and visual arts. College-preparatory academics and high school diploma offered. Accredited by WASC. Tuition: $19,750 boarding, $9,875 day. Estimated yearly expense: $1,500. Faculty: 25 (5.8 to 1 ratio).

Admission by scholastic aptitude in addition to audition or portfolio presentation. Potential for artistic development given consideration.
Campus located on 205 forested acres in San Jacinto Mountains of Southern California. Near Los Angeles and San Diego. Excellent studio, performance and exhibition facilities. Supervised dorms. Recreational activities include hiking, rock climbing and intramural athletics.
Call or write for further information.

The Linfield School
31950 Pauba Rd., Temecula 92592
Stephen Yowell, Headmaster

Lycee International De Los Angeles
4155 Russell Ave., Panorama City 91412
Monique Mickus, Dir. of Admis.

Midland School, P.O. Box 8, Los Olivos 93441
Eric Swain, Head

Monte Vista Christian School
2 School Way, Watsonville 95076
Donald Price, President

Oak Grove School
220 W. Lomita Ave., Ojai 93023

Ojai Valley School
723 El Paseo Rd., Ojai 93023

Sacred Heart Preparatory School
150 Valparaiso Ave., Menlo Park 94027

San Pasqual SDA Academy
17701 San Pasqual Valley Rd.
Escondido 92025

Southwestern Academy
2800 Monterey Rd., San Marino 91108

Squaw Valley Academy
P.O. Box 2667, Olympic Valley 96146

Stevenson School
P.O. Box 657, Pebble Beach   93953

Thacher School
5025 Thacher Rd., Ojai   93023
Willard G. Wyman, Headmaster

VILLANOVA PREPARATORY SCHOOL
12096 Ventura Ave., Ojai   93023-3999
Leo Molitor, Interim Headmaster
Denver Compton, Dir. of Admis.
Phone: 805-646-1464, Fax: 805-646-4430
Established 1924. Private. Catholic. Coed. Accreditation: WASC. Tuition for day students: $4,500. Tuition/room and board for 5-day boarders: $14,600, for 7-day boarders: $15,100. Enrollment: 228 (90 boarding, 138 day). Faculty: 27. Student-faculty ratio: 8:1. Average class size: 15. 9 buildings on 127 acres. 17 classrooms and labs, 2 gyms, pool, and athletic fields. 7,700 people in the community. 75 miles from Los Angeles. 100% of graduates are accepted by colleges and universities.

Woodside Priory School
302 Portola Rd., Portola Valley   94028
Al D. Zappelli, Dir. of Admis.
415-851-8221

Woolman School
13075 Woolman Ln., Nevada City   95959
Ted Beatty, Dir. of Admis.

COLORADO

Accelerated Schools Foundation
2160 S. Cook St., Denver   80210

ALEXANDER DAWSON SCHOOL
4801 N. 107th St., Lafayette   80026
Christopher Taylor, Headmaster
Peter Alford, Dir. of Admission
303-665-6675
Established 1970. Private. Coed. Accreditation: NCACS. Tuition, room and board: $17,500. Fees: $250. Enrollment: 240. Faculty: 28. Student-faculty ratio: 6:1. Degree: diploma. Library: 13,000 volumes. 25 buildings on 135 acres. Strong college preparatory program plus full range of athletic and arts opportunities, including ski, horsemanship, and dance programs. Located 30 miles north of Denver and 10 miles east of Boulder at the foot of the Rocky Mountains.

Aspen School
P.O. Box 2466, Aspen   81612

Colorado Academy
3800 S. Pierce St., Denver   80235
Frances Seifert, Dir. of Admis.
303-986-1501

Colorado Rocky Mountain School
1493 County Rd. 106, Box X, Carbondale   81623
Claudia Bach, Dir. of Admis.

The Colorado Springs School
21 Broadmoor Ave., Colorado Springs   80906
Betsy Robinson, Director of Admission
719-475-9747

Colorado Timberline Academy
35554 Highway 550, Durango   81301
Joseph A. Maceyak, Director

Denver Academy
1125 S. Race St., Denver   80210
Paul Knott, Director

Fountain Valley School
6155 Fountain Valley School Road
Colorado Springs   80911
Timothy Knox, Headmaster

Whiteman School
42605 County Rd. #36, Steamboat Springs   80487
Mike Whitacre, Dir. of Admis.

CONNECTICUT

CANTERBURY SCHOOL
P.O. Box 5000, New Milford   06776
Thomas J. Sheehy III, Headmaster
Patrick Finn, Dir. of Admis.
203-355-3106, Fax: 203-350-4425
Established 1915. The best of Catholic education in a traditional prep setting. Coed. Accreditation: NEASC. Tuition: $19,800 boarding, $12,300 day. Enrollment: 191 boarding, 119 day, (190 boys, 120 girls). Faculty: 53. College prep courses. Library: 20,000 volumes. 12 buildings on 150 acres. Gym, pool, enclosed ice hockey rink, 6 tennis courts, 400 seat auditorium, computer centers, AP courses.

Cheshire Academy
10 Main St., Cheshire   06410
Elliott B. Williams, Dir. of Admissions

Choate Rosemary Hall
333 Christian St., Wallingford   06492
Charles Dey, President/Principal

Forman Schools
Norfolk Rd., Litchfield   06759
Karen Lambert, Dir. of Admis.

The Gunnery School
99 Green Hill Rd., Washington Depot   06793
Elisabeth Archie, Dir. of Admis.

Hotchkiss School, Lakeville   06039
Dr. Robert Oden, Jr., Headmaster
Dr. Parnell Hagerman, Dir. of Admis.

Kent School
P.O. Box 2006, Kent   06757
Richardson Schell, Headmaster & Rector

LOOMIS CHAFFEE SCHOOL
4 Batchelder Rd., Windsor   06095
Mitchel G. Overbye, Director of Admissions
203-688-4934
Established 1911. Private. Coed. Tuition: Boarding-$20,700, Day-$14,125. Enrollment: 703. Faculty: 115. Student-faculty ratio: 7:1. Diploma offered. Library: 62,000 volumes. 300 acre campus. Boarding & Day school with students from 33 states and 13 foreign countries.

MARIANAPOLIS PREPARATORY SCHOOL
P.O. Box 368, Thompson   06277
Bro. Donald Finney, MIC, Dir. of Admis.
203-923-9565, Fax 203-923-3730
Established 1926. Private. Coed. Roman Catholic. Prep, grades 9-12 and post-graduate. Tuition: $5,750. Tuition, room and board: $12,600. Enrollment: 220. Faculty: 26. 300 acre rural campus. 22 honors/advanced placement courses. Honors or standard sections in required courses. 7 levels of English as a Second Language for foreign students. 100% college admissions.

Marvelwood School
P.O. Box 98, Cornwall   06753
H. Mark Johnson, Headmaster

Master's School
P.O. Box 143, West Simsbury   06092
Don Steele, Headmaster

MILFORD ACADEMY
150 Gulf St., Milford   06460
Dr. Dino F. Ciaburri, Headmaster
203-878-5921
Established 1916. Private. Student-faculty ratio: 9:1. 16 buildings on a 26 acre New England setting. Room and Board, Indoor Pool, Gym, and Athletic Field.

POMFRET SCHOOL
Pomfret   06258
Steven P. Danenberg, Dir. of Admis.
203-928-7969, FAX 203-963-2042
Established 1894. Private. Coed. Accreditation: NEASC. Tuition: $11,650. Room and board: $8,800. Enrollment: 302. Faculty: 47. Student-faculty ratio: 7:1. Library: 25,000 volumes. 18+ buildings on 500 acres. A traditional college preparatory school where 100% of the graduates attend 4 year, competitive colleges. Harvard, Univ. of Chicago, Univ. of Vermont, Yale, Columbia, Cornell, Amherst included. Strong arts and athletic programs. Emphasis on moral and character development.

South Kent School
40 Bulls Ridge Rd., South Kent   06785
George H. Bartlett, Headmaster

Suffield Academy
340 N. Main St., Suffield   06078
William De Salvo, Dir. of Admis.

Taft School
110 Woodbury Rd., Watertown   06795
Lance Odden, Headmaster
Phone: 203-274-2516, Fax: 203-945-3458

Westminster School
995 Hopmeadow St., Simsbury   06070
Donald Werner, Headmaster

Wooster School
Ridgebury Rd., Danbury   06810
E. John Effinger, Headmaster
203-743-6311

DELAWARE

ARCHMERE ACADEMY
3600 Philadelphia Pike, Claymont 19703
Paul J. Pomeroy Jr., Dir. of Admis.
302-798-6632 or 215-485-0373
Established 1932. Private. Coed. Accreditation: MSACS. Tuition: $9,530. Enrollment: 487. Faculty: 54. Student-faculty ratio: 9:1. Library: 13,500 volumes. 7 buildings on 36 acres, including Justin Diny Science Center and Performing Arts Center. Strong visual and performing arts programs. 14 Advanced Placement Exams offered. Quiet, scenic, college-like campus overlooking Delaware river. Computer center, writing center, campus ministry, computerized library, extensive community service club.

St. Andrew's School
350 Noxontown Rd., Middletown 19709
Jonathan O'Brien, Headmaster

FLORIDA

Hobe Sound Christian Academy
P.O. Box 1065, Hobe Sound 33475
William Marshall, Principal

Montverde Academy
P.O. Box 560097, Montverde 34756
W. L. Stephens, Jr., President

Pine Crest School
1501 N.E. 62nd St., Fort Lauderdale 33334
William J. McMillan, Headmaster

Saint Andrew's School
3900 Jog Rd., Boca Raton 33434
George E. Andrews II, Headmaster
407-483-8900

GEORGIA

Brandon Hall School
1701 Brandon Hall Dr., Dunwoody 30350
Mary Jean Thielen, Dean

Darlington School
1014 Cave Spring Rd., S.W., Rome 30161
Lisa Schlenk, Dir. of Admis.

Georgia Military College
201 E. Green St., Milledgeville 31061
Major General Peter Boylan, President

Rabun Gap-Nacoochee School
Highway 441 N., Rabun Gap 30568
Bruce Dodd, Jr., President

St. Andrew's School
P.O. Box 30639, Savannah 31410
Mary Alice Brown, Dir. of Admis.

Tallulah Falls School
P.O. Box 10, Tallulah Falls 30573

Woodward Academy
P.O. Box 87190, College Park 30337
A. Thomas Jackson, President

HAWAII

Hawaiian Mission Academy
1438 Pensacola St., Honolulu 96822
Rachel Layman, Registrar

Hawaii Preparatory Academy
P.O. Box 428, Kamuela 96743
Todd Anderson, Dir. of Admis.

Seabury Hall
480 Olinda Rd., Makawao 96768
Virginia C. Haines, Dir. of Admis.

IDAHO

Rocky Mountain Academy
R.R. 1, Bonners Ferry 83805
Ranel Hanson, Director of Admissions

ILLINOIS

Broadview Academy
P.O. Box 307, Lafox 60147
William Ruby, Principal
708-232-7441

Elgin Academy
350 Park St., Elgin 60120
Selden Edwards, Headmaster
Ann Whitney, Dir. of Admis.

LAKE FOREST ACADEMY
1500 W. Kennedy Rd., Lake Forest 60045
D. Scott Looney, Dir. of Admis.
708-615-3267 Fax 708-615-3202

LATIN SCHOOL OF CHICAGO
59 W. North Blvd., Chicago 60610
Frank Hogan, Headmaster
312-573-4500

Mississippi Valley Christian School
2009 Seminary St., Alton 62002
R. D. Johnsonbaugh, Principal

Morgan Park Academy
2153 W. 111th St., Chicago 60643
David Jones, Headmaster
312-881-6700, Fax: 312-881-8409

Routt High School, (Day)
500 E. College Ave., Jacksonville 62650
Sr. M. Simeon, Principal

INDIANA

Brebeuf Preparatory School
2801 W. 86th St., Indianapolis 46268
The Rev. M. Joseph Casey, S.J., Pres.

Concordia Lutheran High School
1601 St. Joe River Dr., Ft. Wayne 46805
Guenther Herzog, Principal

Culver Military Academy and Summer Camps
1300 Academy Rd., Culver 46511
Richard Edwards, Dir. of Admis.

HOWE MILITARY SCHOOL
31 Academy Pl., Howe 46746
Colonel Thomas Merritt, Superintendent
Lt. Col. Reed Kimball, Headmaster
Glenn Cox, Dir. of Admis.
219-562-2131 ext. 221
Accredited by: the North Central Association of Colleges and Schools. A member of: the North Central Association of Colleges and Schools, the Independent School Association of Central States, the Association of Military Colleges and Schools of the United States, the Council for Advancement and Support of Education, the National Association of Independent Schools, the National Association of Episcopal Schools, the College Entrance Examination Board, Cum Laude Society.
Established 1884. Episcopal. Coed. Enrollment: 250. Total charge for a boarding student: $14,900. Financial aid available. Only military institute in Ohio, Michigan and Indiana that is a member of the US Army's JROTC program. JROTC required for all high school cadets.
College preparatory school. Grades 5 through 12. Fully accredited faculty and staff. Individual attention given. Class size averages 10 to 12 cadets. Twenty solid units of credit are required for graduation. Seventeen and a half of them must be in English, math, history and social studies, science, foreign language, sacred studies, business and physical education and health.
Required for admission: a desire to attend, a willingness to adhere to Howe's military discipline, be of good moral character (satisfactory references), be of average to above average intelligence (IQ test), a certificate of honorable dismissal from previous school.
Located on 150 acres in Northeast Indiana just two miles from the Michigan border. Modern dormitories and academic facilities, library, pool, three (3) gymnasiums, athletic fields, track, canteen, 700 seat auditorium, two (2) chapels, dining hall, military department.

La Lumiere School
P.O. Box 5005, La Porte 46350
Joan Langley, Dir. of Admis.

IOWA

Scattergood Friends School
1951 Delta Ave., West Branch 52358
Robert Griswold, Director
319-643-7600

KANSAS

Thomas More Preparatory-Marian
1701 Hall St., Hays 67601
Sister Joanita Stelter, Dir. of Admis.

KENTUCKY

Oneida Baptist Institute
P.O. Box 67, Oneida 40972

St. Camillus Academy
709 E. Center St., Corbin 40701

MAINE

Carrabassett Valley Academy
R.R. 1, Box 2240, Kingfield 04947
Vici Robinson, Dir. of Admissions

Fryeburg Academy, 152 Main St., Fryeburg 04037
Harry M. True, Principal

Gould Academy
P.O. Box 860, Bethel 04217
William Graham, Dir. of Admis.
207-824-7777, FAX: 207-824-2926
Internet: contact gould.pvt.k12.me.us

Hebron Academy
P.O. Box 309, Hebron 04238
207-966-2100, FAX 207-966-1111

Hyde School
616 High St., Bath 04530
Malcolm Gauld, Head

Kents Hill School
P.O. Box 257, Kents Hill 04349
Rob Snow, Dir. of Admis.
207-685-4914

Lee Academy, P.O. Box 338, Lee 04455
John A. Robinson, Principal

Maine Central Institute
125 S. Main St., Pittsfield 04967
Douglas Cummings, Headmaster

MARYLAND

Bullis School
10601 Falls Rd., Potomac 20854
Lawrence Bullis, Headmaster

Friends School
5114 N. Charles St., Baltimore 21210
Dr. W. Forbush, Headmaster

Mc Donogh School
P.O. Box 380, McDonogh 21117-0380
W. Boulton Dixon, Headmaster
410-581-4720

Saint James School, St. James 21781
Drew Miller, Dir. of Admis.
301-733-9330

SANDY SPRING FRIENDS SCHOOL
16923 Norwood Rd., Sandy Spring 20860
Victoria Garner, Dir. of Admis.

West Nottingham Academy
1079 Firetower Rd., Colora 21917
Jim Smith, Dir. of Admis.

MASSACHUSETTS

Academy at Charlemont
The Mohawk Trail, Charlemont 01339
Dianne Grinnell, Dir. of Admissions

Berkshire School
245 N. Undermountain Rd., Sheffield 01257
Mei-Ling Henrickson, Dir. of Admis.

Brooks School
1160 Great Pond Rd., North Andover 01845
Marshall Moore, Dir. of Admis.

Buxton School
P.O. Box 646, Williamstown 01267

Cambridge School
45 Georgian Rd., Weston 02193
Constance May, Dir. of Admis.

Chapel Hill-Chauncy Hall School
785 Beaver St., Waltham 02154

Concord Academy, 166 Main St., Concord 01742

Cushing Academy
39 School St., Ashburnham 01430
Judith Beams, Director of Admission
508-827-5911 Fax: 508-827-6253

Deerfield Academy
Main St., Deerfield 01342
Robert E. Kaufmann, Headmaster
413-772-0241

Desisto School
General Delivery, Stockbridge 01262

Dewey Academy
389 Main St., Great Barrington 01230
Henry Radda, Director of Admissions

Falmouth Academy
7 Highfield Dr., Falmouth 02540
Elenita Muniz, Dir. of Admissions

Governor Dummer Academy
1 Elm St., Byfield 01922
John W. Ragle, Headmaster

Groton School
P.O. Box 991, Groton 01450
William Polk, Headmaster
508-448-3363

HighCroft School
P.O. Box 548, Williamstown 01267
David Wilson Milne, President

Landmark School
412 Hale St., Prides Crossing 01965

LAWRENCE ACADEMY
P.O. Box 992, Groton 01450
Steven L. Hahn, Headmaster
Robinson C. Moore, Dir. of Admis.
508-448-6535
Established 1793. Coeducational. Accreditation: NEASC. Tuition: $20,800 boarding, $14,500 day. Enrollment: 330. Faculty: 51. 36 miles northwest of Boston. College preparatory, boarding and day school for students in grades 9-12. Wide variety of courses including honors, AP innovative interdisciplinary offerings with strong emphasis on technology in the curriculum. LA II and Winterim encourage an active learning experience. Strong advisor program, athletics, and community service component enrich lives of our students. Six week, intensive ESL program for all levels available in summers for ages 14 to 18 with activity, athletic and weekend programs included. Athletic complex opened in 1993. New Arts Center planned for 1995. 20 buildings on 92 acres.

MACDUFFIE SCHOOL
3 Ames Hill Dr., Springfield 01105
Laurie Scott-Martin, Dir. of Admis.
413-734-4971
Established 1890. Private. Coed. College Preparatory: Grades 6 - 12, PG. Accreditation: NEASC. Tuition: $10,900. Room and board: $8,000. Enrollment: 155. Faculty: 26. Student-Faculty Ratio: 6:1. Library: 8,000 volumes. Outstanding academic preparation, full arts program, competitive athletics. Ames Hill Scholars Program: small boarding component for grades 9-12. Students live with faculty families in stately homes on a 12 acre residential campus.

Middlesex School
1400 Lowell Rd., Concord 01742
Sibyl Cohane, Dir. of Admis.

Milton Academy, 170 Centre St., Milton 02186

Noble and Greenough School
507 Bridge St., Dedham 02026
Rev. Edward S. Gleason, Principal

NORTHFIELD MT. HERMON SCHOOL
206 Main St., Northfield 01360
Jacqueline Smethurst, Head
Monique de Vane, Dir. of Admis.
413-498-3227
See listing under "Study Abroad"

Phillips Academy
Main St., Andover 01810-4161
Jane F. Fried, Dean of Admission
508-749-4050

St. Mark's School
  25 Marlboro Rd., Southborough 01772
  Christopher Mabley, Head

TABOR ACADEMY
226 Front St., Marion 02738
Jay Stroud, Headmaster
Virginia M. de Veer, Dir. of Admis.
508-748-2000, Fax: 508-748-0353

WILBRAHAM & MONSON ACADEMY
421 Main St., Wilbraham 01095
Richard C. Malley, Headmaster
Cameron G. Cudhea, Dir. of Admis.
413-596-6811
  Established 1804. Private. Coed. Accreditation:
NEASC. Tuition: $10,800. Room and board: $7,550.
Fees: $725 boarding, $375 day. Enrollment: 283. Faculty: 50. Student-faculty ratio: 9:1. Degree: Diploma. Library: 24,000 volumes. 10 buildings on 300 acres. Structured and supportive, ESL program, Developmental Services program. Easily accessible by public transportation, financial aid available, traditional college preparatory curriculum. Day students grades 7-postgraduate, boarding grades 8-postgraduate.

WILLISTON NORTHAMPTON SCHOOL
19 Payson Ave., Easthampton 01027
Dennis Grubbs, Headmaster
Ann Pickrell, Dir. of Admis.
413-527-1520, Fax: 413-527-9494
  Established 1841. Coed. Accreditation: NEASC, NAIS, AISNE, Art Association of New England Prep Schools. Tuition, room and board: $17,600. Fees: $775. Enrollment: 235 boarding, 185 day. Faculty: 86. Diploma offered. Grades 9-12 & post graduate. Library: 34,000 volumes. 38 buildings on 100+ acres. $37 million physical plant, $7.2 million endowment. New $5 million athletic center with pool, fitness center, training room, and squash courts. Ice rink. Stable and golf course nearby. Intersession program with intensive courses; world travel; study abroad program; strong fine & performing arts department. Located in 5 college area. 40% receive financial aid, diverse student body.

WINCHENDON SCHOOL
172 Ash St., Winchendon 01475
J. William LaBelle, Headmaster
Norman S. Jason, Dir. of Admis.
Thomas H. Covhig, Dir. of Summer School
508-297-1223 or 800-622-1119
  Established 1926. Private. Coed. Accreditation: NEASC. Tuition, room and board: $20,250. Fees: $2,000. Enrollment: 125. Faculty: 23. Student-faculty ratio: 5:1. Library: 10,000 volumes. 17 buildings on 232 acres. A traditional, coeducational, college preparatory school with an emphasis on helping the underachieving student reach his/her potential through the efforts of a highly supportive faculty and an individualized and structured program. ESL offered at three levels; beginning, intermediate and advanced.

Worcester Academy
  Providence St., Worcester 01604
  Benjamin Williams III, Headmaster

MICHIGAN

Cranbrook School
  1221 N. Woodward Ave., Bloomfield Hills 48304
  Day and Boarding School
  810-645-3610

Detroit Country Day School
  22305 W. Thirteen Mile Rd.
  Birmingham 48025

Interlochen Arts Academy
  P.O. Box 199, Interlochen 49643
  Tom Bewley, Dir. of Admis.

The Leelanau School
  1 Old Homestead Rd., Glen Arbor 49636
  Duane M. Petty, Dir. of Admis.
  616-334-3072, Fax 616-334-4315

Michigan Lutheran Seminary
  2777 Hardin St., Saginaw 48602
  William Zeiger, Acting President

MINNESOTA

St. John's Preparatory School
  P.O. Box 4000, Collegeville 56321
  Jerald Howard, Dir. of Admis.

SHATTUCK-ST. MARY'S SCHOOL
P.O. Box 218, Faribault 55021
Phillip R. Trout, Dir. of Admissions
507-332-5618
  Established 1858. Private. Coed. Accreditation: ISACS. Tuition: $17,300. Enrollment: 228. Faculty: 33. Student-faculty ratio: 7:1. Degrees: High School Diploma, Postgraduate Certificate. Library: 25,000 volumes. 25 buildings on 250 acres. Located 45 minutes south of Minneapolis/St. Paul. Grades 6-12 and postgraduate program. Students from over 30 states and 10 countries. Advanced Placement courses in every discipline. Award winning choir, orchestra and drama. Campus facilities include golf course and ice arena.

MISSISSIPPI

ALL SAINTS' EPISCOPAL SCHOOL
2730 Confederate Ave., Vicksburg 39180
The Rev. David Luckett, Rector and Headmaster
601-636-5266 or 800-748-9957
  Established 1908. Episcopal. Coed. Accreditation:

SACS. Tuition: $12,500. Enrollment: 153 boarding, 17 day. Faculty: 30. Degree: high school diploma. Library: 16,000 volumes. 8 buildings on 40 acres. Gym. Pool. Located in historic Vicksburg on the Mississippi River. An Educational Assessment Center provides information to design appropriate educational objectives for each individual student-academically, socially, and physically. College preparatory. Emphasis on community life, spiritual growth, and physical development.

Chamberlain-Hunt Academy
  124 McComb Ave., Port Gibson 39150

Piney Woods School
  P.O. Box 99, Piney Woods 39148
  Earnest Ward, Principal

MISSOURI

Kemper Military School & College
  & Kemper Girls Academy
  701 3rd St., Boonville 65233
  Michael J. Glass, Dir. of Admis.
  800-530-5600

Principia
  13201 Clayton Rd., St. Louis 63131
  William Truitt, Headmaster
  314-434-2100

ST. PAUL'S LUTHERAN HIGH SCHOOL
P.O. Box H, Concordia 64020
John C. Bobzin, Coordinator of Communications
816-463-2238, FAX 816-463-7621
  Established 1883. Private. Coed. Accreditation: NCASC. Tuition: $4,900. Room and board: $3,500. Fees: $600. Enrollment: 165. Student-faculty ratio: 17:1. College Preparatory Grades 9-12. Library: 31,000 volumes. 9 buildings on 80 acres. Full complement of athletics and activities. Beautiful campus one hour from Kansas City. College credit courses. Emphasis on care and nurturing; safe, drug free Christian environment. 110 years of continuous service to youth and families.

Thomas Jefferson School
  4100 S. Lindbergh Blvd., St. Louis 63127
  Robin U. McCoy, Headmaster

MONTANA

Lustre Christian High School
  P.O. Box 57, Frazer 59225
  Jerry Jennex, Administrator

Mt. Ellis Academy
  3641 Bozeman Trail Rd., Bozeman 59715
  Harold Grosboll, prin.

NEBRASKA

Platte Valley Academy
  R.R. 2, Shelton 68876
  Ray Davis, Principal

NEW HAMPSHIRE

Brewster Academy
  S. Main St., Wolfeboro 03894
  David Smith, Headmaster

Dublin Christian Academy
  P.O. Box 521, Dublin 03444

Dublin School, P.O. Box 77, Dublin 03444
  Michael L. Cornog, Headmaster

Hampshire Country School, Rindge 03461
  William Dickerman, Dir. of Admis.

High Mowing School-A Waldorf High School
  R.R. 2 Box 133, Wilton 03086
  David S. Mitchell, Dir. of Admis.

Holderness School, R.R. 3, Plymouth 03264
  B. W. Woodward, Jr., Headmaster
  603-536-1747

Kimball Union Academy
  Founded 1813
  P.O. Box 188, Meriden 03770
  Timothy Knox, Headmaster
  603-469-3218 or 3211 Fax 603-469-3643

Meeting School
  116 Thomas Rd., Rindge 03461
  Kate Kerman, Dir. of Admis.

New Hampton School
  P.O. Box 579, New Hampton 03256
  Scott E. Fahey, Dir of Admis.

PHILLIPS EXETER ACADEMY
20 Main St., Exeter 03833-2460
603-772-4311 Fax: 603-772-5987
Kendra Stearns O'Donnell, Principal
Thomas E. Hassan, Dir. of Admis.
  Founded 1781. Classes with 12-14 students around oval tables and a diverse student body from 46 states and 36 countries make Exeter's regular and summer sessions exciting and unique. Outstanding faculty and a selection from over 300 courses encourage students to develop independent judgement, leadership and concern for others. At the interscholastic level, Exeter offers 50 varsity and junior varsity teams in 17 sports. Off-campus programs in France, England, Germany, Japan, China, Russia, Spain and Mexico, congressional internships in Washington, and a trimester at the Milton Mountain School are available during the regular sessions. Additional programs are offered in the summer. Attrition is less than 5%, and Exeter students are admitted to many top colleges.
  Exeter accepts students in grades 9 through 12 and

post-graduates. Applicants should have a record of high achievement at their previous schools.
  The 1994-1995 fees: $18,600 for boarding students and $13,350 for day students. More than $3 million in financial aid is available.

Proctor Academy
  P.O. Box 500, Andover 03216

St. Paul's School
  325 Pleasant St., Concord 03301
  Rev. Charles Clark, Rector

Tilton School
  30 School St., Tilton 03276
  Patricia E. Spead, Dir. of Admissions

White Mountain School
  W. Farm Rd., Littleton 03561
  Nancy White, Dir. of Admis.

NEW JERSEY

Blair Academy, Blairstown 07825
  Thomas Chandler Hardwick, Headmaster

Hun School of Princeton
  176 Edgerstoune Rd., Princeton 08540
  Paul M. Feakins, Headmaster

LAWRENCEVILLE SCHOOL
P.O. Box 6008, Lawrenceville 08648
Josiah Bunting III, Headmaster
Robin Mamlet, Dean of Admis.
800-735-2030
  Established 1810. Coed. Accreditation: NAIS, NJAIS. Tuition: $20,225. Est. extra expenses: $800. Enrollment: 550 boarding, 200 day. Degree: high school diploma. Library: 34,000 vols. 30 major buildings on 500 acres. Gym. Pool. Hockey rink. Golf course. Rigorous academic. "English Plan" house system. Harkness Plan round-table teaching. Advanced placement. Near Princeton.

Peddie School
  S. Main St., Hightstown 08520
  F. Edward Potter, Jr., Headmaster

Pennington School
  112 W. Delaware Ave., Pennington 08534
  G. Donald Miller, Headmaster

NEW MEXICO

Hammer United World College
  of the American West
  P.O. Box 248, Montezuma 87731

Menaul School
  301 Menaul Blvd., N.E., Albuquerque 87107
  David Lock, Dir. of Admis.

NEW MEXICO MILITARY INSTITUTE
101 W. College Ave., Roswell 88201
LTG Winfield W. Scott, Jr. USAF(Ret.), Superintendent
COL James H. Matchin, Dir. of Admis.
Toll-free 800-421-5376
  Established 1891. Public. Coed. Accreditation: NCACS, New Mexico Department of Education. Estimated costs for 1993-94 school year, out-of-state student: $7,500, in-state student: $5,700. Enrollment: 950. Faculty: 68. Student-faculty ratio: 19:1. Degree: AA. Library: 68,000 volumes. 19 buildings on 40 acre main campus. Additional acreage includes an 18-hole championship golf course and facilities for the equestrian programs. Only land grant military high school and junior college in the United States. Prep school for all service academies. 87% of high school graduates receive their four year college degrees. 90% of junior college graduates receive their baccalaureate degrees. Quality education at a fair price.

NEW YORK

Cascadilla School
  P.O. Box 878, Ithaca 14850
  John Kendall, Headmaster

Darrow School
  Shaker Rd., New Lebanon 12125
  Diederik Van Renesse, Dir. of Admis.

Doane Stuart School
  799 S. Pearl St., Albany 12202
  Sr. Lucie Nordmann, RSCJ, Headmistress

Harvey School
  260 Jay St., Katonah 10536
  Samuel Barnett, Director of Admissions

Hoosac School
  P.O. Box 9, Hoosick 12089

Houghton Academy
  Thayer St., Houghton 14744
  Phillip Stockin, Principal

Knox School
  100 Long Beach Rd., St. James 11780
  Clifford Eriksen, Headmaster

Manlius Pebble Hill School
  5300 Jamesville Rd., De Witt 13214
  Hugh Jones, Dir. of Admis.

Millbrook School
  R.R. 1, Box 1000, Millbrook 12545
  Donald B. Abbott, Headmaster

National Sports Academy
  12 Lake Placid Club Dr.
  Lake Placid 12946

NEW YORK MILITARY ACADEMY
70 Academy Ave., Cornwall-on-Hudson 12520
Col. Philip D. Riley, USA, Ret., Supt.
Peter Wicker, Dir. of Admis.

Established 1889. Coed. Accreditation: MSACS. Grades 5-12. Enrollment: 239 boarding, 10 day. Expenses: $14,400 (all inclusive) new cadet, $13,100 (all inclusive) old cadet (includes tuition, room & board). Faculty: 32. Library: 19,500 volumes. 46 buildings on 325 acres. Riding stables, gym, 3 pools, 6 tennis courts, Nautilus, gymnastics, varsity & intramural sports, horsemanship, flying, band scholarships. 1 hour north of NYC; 15 minutes from West Point. Students from 13 states, 14 foreign countries. Nondiscriminatory.

Northwood School
P.O. Box 1070, Lake Placid   12946
W. John Friedlander, Headmaster
518-523-3357

Oakwood School
515 South Rd., Poughkeepsie   12601
Brian Fry, Dir. of Admis.

Stony Brook School
11 Cedar St., Stony Brook   11790
Robert Grinnell, Dir. of Admis.

Storm King School
314 Mountain Rd., Cornwall-on-Hudson   12520
Thad Horton, Headmaster

Union Springs Academy
R.R. 1, Union Springs   13160
R. R. Trecartin, Principal

NORTH CAROLINA

Asheville School
360 Asheville School Rd., Asheville   28806
William S. Peebles, Headmaster

Laurinburg Institute
P.O. Box 1787, Laurinburg   28353

THE MORGAN SCHOOL AT PATTERSON PRESERVE
R.R. 5, Box 170, Lenoir   28645
Judson G. Williams, Dir. of Admis.
800-367-4921
Established 1990. Private. Coed. Accreditation: SACS., State of NC. Tuition, room and board: $13,500. Fees: $1,500. Enrollment: 60. Faculty: 10. Student-faculty ratio: 6:1. High School Diploma. Library: 5,000 volumes. 11 buildings on 1,400 acres. Interdisciplined studies. Outdoor wilderness skills and character development program. Afternoon experiential learning academies that provide hands on activities which connect class with real life. Outreach program involving hospital, retirement visitation, and fund raising, big brother, big sister program, campus stewardship. Varied athletic program including traditional competitive team sports as well as non-traditional alternative sports such as karate, kayaking, rock climbing, alpine skiing. Also, learning difference specialist and learning skills programs, ESL.

Oak Ridge Military Academy
P.O. Box 498, Oak Ridge   27310
F. Kennedy, President
910-643-4131

NORTH DAKOTA

OAK GROVE LUTHERAN HIGH SCHOOL
124 N. Terrace, Fargo   58102
Pastor John Andreasen, President
Denise Brewster, Director of Admissions
701-237-0212, Fax: 701-237-4217
Established 1906. Evangelical Lutheran Church in America. Coed. Accreditation: NCACS. Tuition: 9-12; $3,250, 7-8; $1,920. Room and board: $2,980. Enrollment: 30 boarding, 141 commuting. Faculty: 22. Degree: high school diploma. 4 buildings on 8 acres. Gym. Opportunities available in sports, music, student leadership and drama. Concert Choir tours two weeks annually. Financial assistance available to families demonstrating need.

St. Mary's High School
P.O. Box 367, New England   58647

OHIO

Central Christian High School
P.O. Box 9, Kidron   44636
Bruce Kooker, Director of Admissions
216-857-7311

Gilmour Academy
34001 Cedar Rd., Gates Mills   44040-9732
Cathy Kenny, Dir. of Admis.
216-473-8050

Notre Dame Latin School
13000 Auburn Rd., Chardon   44024
Sr. Donna Paluf, SND, Principal
216-286-6226 or 216-946-3314

Olney Friends School
61830 Sandy Ridge Rd., Barnesville   43713
Barbara McLean, Admissions

Western Reserve Academy
115 College St., Hudson   44236
Timothy Trautman, Dir. of Admis.

OKLAHOMA

Cascia Hall Preparatory School
P.O. Box 52247, Tulsa   74152
Tom Stockton, Dir. of Admis.

OREGON

Delphian School and Camp
20950 S.W. Rock Creek Rd., Sheridan   97378
Donetta Phelps, Dean of Admissions
Call toll-free 800-626-6610

Oregon Episcopal School
6300 S.W. Nicol Rd., Portland   97223
Peter W. Stevens, Headmaster
503-246-7771

PENNSYLVANIA

George School, Newtown   18940
Karen S. Hallowell, Director of Admissions
215-579-6547

Girard College
Girard and Corinthian Aves.
Philadelphia   19121

Mercersburg Academy, Mercersburg   17236
Walter Burgin, Jr., Headmaster
Gordon Vink, Jr., Dir. of Admis.
717-328-2151 or 800-772-2874 Fax: 717-328-9072

MILTON HERSHEY SCHOOL
P.O. Box 830, Hershey   17033
Dr. William L. Lepley, President &
Chairman of the Board
Dr. Christine M. Miller, Dir. of Admis.
800-322-3248 or 717-534-3546
Founded 1909. Pre-K through 12. Private, residential, coeducational, nondenominational. Approved by Pennsylvania Department of Education. Accredited by MSACS (9-12), PAPAS (Pre K through 8).
Student Body: Grades Pre-K-4 approximately 200 students, grades 5-8 approximately 400 students, grades 9-12 approximately 500 students. Largest student groups from PA, NJ, MD and NY. Tuition and room/board: $0 (full cost paid by school). Additional academic fees: none. 89 student homes on campus - 11 students per student home.
Curriculum: college preparatory, business, technology courses. Courses of study include art, music, theater, English, French, German, Spanish, computers, algebra, geometry, trigonometry, health & physical education, public speaking, religion, astronomy, biology, chemistry, environmental studies, earth science, physics, social sciences, government, economics, history, technology education. Special academic programs: advanced placement courses, remedial reading, remedial math. Summer program for remediation and credit deficiencies during June-July. Interscholastic athletics include baseball/softball (boys, girls), basketball (b g), cross country (b g), diving (b g), field hockey (g), football (b), soccer (b), swimming (b g), track & field (b g), wrestling (b).
Admissions: Enrollment available to children who are at least 4 and not yet 16 years old; come from families of very limited income; have an academic record of "C" average or better and national achievement test scores of 50th percentile and above; are of good character and behavior; and must be able to fully participate in the program offered (some auxiliary aids and services might be available on request).
120 faculty members. 40 have master's degrees, 61 men, 59 women; 120 buildings on 9,000 acre campus. Facilities include Founders Hall, Senior Hall (classrooms, technology lab), Catherine Hall (classrooms, athletic, recreation facilities), Memorial Hall (classrooms), health center, supply services center and student homes. All students selected for admission receive a no-cost education which includes medical and dental services. Milton Hershey School admits boys and girls of any race, color, religion, nationality, or ethnic origin.

MMI Preparatory School
P.O. Box 89, Freeland   18224-0089
Joseph Rudawski, President
717-636-1108

MORAVIAN ACADEMY
4313 Green Pond Rd., Bethlehem   18017
Peter Sipple, Headmaster
610-691-1600

Perkiomen School
P.O. Box 130, Pennsburg   18073
Carol Dougherty, Dir. of Admis.

Shady Side Academy
423 Fox Chapel Rd., Pittsburgh   15238
Peter Kountz, PhD, President

Solebury School
P.O. Box 429, New Hope   18938
John Brown, Head

Westtown School, Westtown   19395
C. Thomas Kaesemeyer, Headmaster

Wyoming Seminary
201 N. Sprague Ave., Kingston   18704
H. Jeremy Packard, President

RHODE ISLAND

Moses Brown School
250 Lloyd Ave., Providence   02906
Dorothy Patrick, Dir. of Admis.

Portsmouth Abbey School
285 Corys Ln., Portsmouth   02871
John Wilkinson, Head

ST. ANDREW'S SCHOOL
63 Federal Rd., Barrington   02806
Everett J. Wilson, Headmaster
Andrea C.C. Martin, Director of Admissions
401-246-1230
Established 1893. Private. Coed. Accreditation:

NEASC, NAIS, State of Rhode Island. Tuition: $9,600. Room and board: $9,000. Enrollment: 141. Faculty: 28. Student-faculty ratio: 5:1. High School diploma offered. Library: 8,000 volumes. 30 buildings on 100 acres. St. Andrews School offers a college preparatory program to children of average to slightly above average ability, half of whom have learning disabilities. A state certified resource program supplements the curriculum. A strong weekend and daily activities program enhances student life.

St. George's School
Purgatory Rd., Newport   02840
George Andrews, Headmaster

SOUTH CAROLINA

Ben Lippen School
P.O. Box 3999, Columbia   29230
Les Lehman, Headmaster

Bob Jones Academy
1700 Wade Hampton Blvd., Greenville   29614
Bob Jones III, President

Hilton Head Preparatory School
8 Foxgrape Rd., Hilton Head   29928
Margaret Stupinsky, Academic Records

SOUTH DAKOTA

Sunshine Bible Academy
HC 63, Box 29, Miller   57362-9712
605-853-3071
Jack A. Jones, Superintendent
Evangelical Interdenominational Boarding School
Grades 7-12, Tuition $3,770, Foreign tuition 6,000+

TENNESSEE

Baylor School
P.O. Box 1337, Chattanooga   37401
Scott Wilson, Dir. of Admis.

Harrison Chilhowee Baptist Academy
202 Smothers Rd., Seymour   37865
Dr. William Palmer, President

Lausanne Collegiate School (7-12)
1381 W. Massey Rd., Memphis   38120
Thomas A. Eppley, Jr., Headmaster

St. Andrew's-Sewanee School
General Delivery, St. Andrews   37372

THE WEBB SCHOOL
Bell Buckle   37020
Jon Frere, Headmaster
Jon Alden, Dir. of Admis.
615-389-6003   Established 1870. Private. Coed. Accreditation: SACS. Tuition: $6,250 for day students, $15,650 for boarding students. Enrollment: 230. Faculty: 27. Student-faculty ratio: 10:1. Standard college preparatory diploma and Honors diploma. Library: 20,000 volumes. 11 buildings on 150 acres. Founded on a tradition of academic excellence with honor. Students sign honor pledges since 1870. Strong outdoor adventure activities. Very diverse student body from 14 states and 9 countries.

TEXAS

Allen Academy
P.O. Box 953, Bryan   77806
Lynred Hoepfner, Head

Presbyterian Pan American School
P.O. Box 1578, Kingsville   78363
Tom Johnson, Dir. of Admis.

SAINT MARY'S HALL
P.O. Box 33430, San Antonio   78265
Dr. Phillip Hadley, Headmaster
210-655-7721

St. Stephen's Episcopal School
P.O. Box 1868, Austin   78767

SAN MARCOS BAPTIST ACADEMY
2801 Ranch Rd. 12, San Marcos   78666-9406
Dr. Jack Byrom, President
Gerald Cessna, Dir. of Admis.
512-353-2400 FAX 512-353-7795
Established 1907. Baptist. Coed. Accreditation: SACS, ISAS, ACTABS. Tuition, room and board: $13,250 plus uniforms, books, supplies. Enrollment: 200 boarding, 102 day. Faculty: 44. Degree: diploma. Library: 17,600 volumes. 9 buildings on 200 acres. Gym. Pool. Located between Austin and San Antonio, Texas in the beautiful Hill Country about 1 hour drive from either city. The Academy accepts boarding boys in grades 6-12 and boarding girls in grades 9-12, and boys and girls as day students in grades 6-12. A 5 week summer session offered. Over 75 students from outside US. Honor School with distinction in the Jr. ROTC program. Full sports program for boys & girls. Religious emphasis program.

Selwyn School
3333 W. University Dr., Denton   76207
Diane Shannon, Dir. of Admis.

Texas Military Institute
20955 W. Tejas Trl., San Antonio   78257
Mary Jo Filip, Dir. of Admis.
210-698-7171, FAX: 210-698-0715

UTAH

Wasatch Academy
120 S. 100 W., Mt. Pleasant   84647
Jodi Tuttle, Dir. of Admis.

VERMONT

Burke Mountain Academy
P.O. Box 78, East Burke 05832
Sylvia Dodge, Administrative Coord.

Burr and Burton Seminary
Manchester 05254
Virginia Martin, Dir. of Admis.

Green Mt. Valley School
R.R. 1, Box 166, Waitsfield 05673
J. Ashley Caldwell, Head of School

Lyndon Institute
Lyndon Center 05850
Dwight A. Davis, Headmaster

Pine Ridge School
1075 Williston Rd., Williston 05495

Putney School, Elm Lea Farm, Putney 05346
Thomas A. Jones, Jr., Director

Rock Point School
Institute Rd., Burlington 05401

St. Johnsbury Academy
7 Main St., St. Johnsbury 05819
John Cummings, Dir. of Admis.

Stratton Mountain School
Stratton Mountain 05155
T. D. McCormick, Admissions Coord.

Vermont Academy, Saxtons River 05154
Robert Long, Headmaster

Vershire School
Judgement Ridge, Vershire 05079
Richard Wright, Head of School

VIRGINIA

Eastern Mennonite High School
801 Parkwood Dr., Harrisonburg 22801
Jean Fisher, Dir. of Admissions
703-433-6414

Episcopal High School
1200 N. Quaker Ln., Alexandria 22302
Lee S. Ainslie, Jr., Headmaster
John Walker, Jr., Dir. of Admis.
703-379-6530

Massanutten Military Academy
614 S. Main St., Woodstock 22664

OAK HILL ACADEMY
RR 1, Mouth of Wilson 24363
Phone: 703-579-2619, Fax: 703-579-4722
Ed Patton, President

OVER A CENTURY OF EXPERIENCE-Established 1878, affiliated with Baptist General Association of Virginia.

Coed boarding high school. Grades 8-12 Boarding facilities for 200 students—1/2 boys and 1/2 girls. Tuition, fees, room and board for nine months: $10,140.

Three boys dorms and one girls dorm; houseparents in dormitories; usually two students per room.

Academic emphasis on small classes and individual attention for grades 8-12. Student-teacher ratio 10:1, 97% admitted to college. Remedial classes in reading, writing and math. Reports to parents each nine weeks. 21 credits required for graduation. Fine Arts Program stresses all visual arts, music, and drama; computer skills class offered. Structured time schedule for classes and extra curricular activities. Required study hall from 7:30-9:00 five nights.

ADMISSIONS: Require application form, fee, medical report, school transcripts and two confidential personality evaluations. Admissions committee selects students who would most benefit from special attention. Interview preferred but not required. Limited financial aid awarded to second year students on need-ability-character criteria.

FACULTY: Full-time faculty: 9 men, 6 women plus 7 part-time instructors in Bible, business, chemistry and English. All hold baccalaureate or master's degrees.

CAMPUS: Landscaped campus of 220 acres of hills and woodlands - rural environment. Nearest airport is Tri-Cities in Blountville, TN (2-1/2 hrs. away); nearest bus is Greyhound to Marion, VA (1 hr. away). Playing field, tennis courts, riding stable, weight room, gymnasium, new visual arts lab, new academic building including library, computer lab and classrooms, main administration building, and chapel complete academic facilities. Eleven houses and apartments provide on-campus housing for faculty.

Located in Southwest Virginia near Mt. Rogers State Park and Jefferson National Forest and New River. Wide variety of recreational opportunities available. School sponsors clubs, dances, intramurals, and cultural exchange programs. Academy boasts outstanding equestrian team and prep basketball team. (ranked first in the nation by ESPN) as well as other athletic

teams for boys and girls.

ACCREDITED by SACS, SAIS, and VAIS. Approved by Virginia State Board of Education and US Government for teaching of foreign students. Non-discriminatory as to race, religion, color, handicap or national origin.

FIVE WEEK SUMMER SESSION from late June to late July. 70 boys and girls. Tuition: $2,800. May earn one new credit or two repeat credits.

Randolph-Macon Academy
201 W. 3rd St., Front Royal 22630
Col. Trevor Turner, USA Ret, President

St. Anne's-Belfield School
2132 Ivy Rd., Charlottesville 22903
Hilary Kerner, Dir. of Admis.

Shenandoah Valley Academy
R.R. 3 Box 29, New Market 22844

Tandem School
R.R. 19, Box 107, Charlottesville 22902
William Porter, Jr., Headmaster

Virginia Episcopal School
P.O. Box 408, Lynchburg 24505
Thomas Goodrich, Dir. of Admis.

WASHINGTON

Northwest School
1415 Summit Ave., Seattle 98122
Ellen Taussig, Dir. of Admis.

WISCONSIN

Wayland Academy
101 N. University Ave., Beaver Dam 53916
James R. Burnham, President

GUAM

Guam Adventist Academy
1200 Aguilar Rd., Agana 96914
David Gouge, Principal

PUERTO RICO

American Military Academy
P.O. Box 7884, Guaynabo 00970-7884
David A. Wells, Superintendent
809-720-6801

Antilles Military Academy
P.O. Box 666, San Juan 00902
Mrs. Genoveva Santiago, Dir. of Admissions

: :PREPARATORY SCHOOLS FOR GIRLS

Primarily Boarding

ARKANSAS

Mt. St. Mary Academy
3224 Kavanaugh Blvd., Little Rock 72205
Sr. Deborah Troillett, RSM, Principal

CALIFORNIA

Bishop's Schools
7607 LaJolla Blvd., LaJolla 92037

Castilleja School
1310 Bryant St., Palo Alto 94301

Flintridge Sacred Heart Academy
440 St. Katherine Dr.
La Canada Flintridge 91011
Sr. Katherine Jean, O.P., Admissions

Sacred Heart Preparatory School
150 Valparaiso Ave., Menlo Park 94027

San Domenico School
1500 Butterfield Rd., San Anselmo 94960
Amanda Mallory, Dir. of Admis.

SANTA CATALINA SCHOOL
1500 Mark Thomas Dr., Monterey 93940
Meriwether Beatty, Dir. of Admis.
408-655-9356

VILLANOVA PREPARATORY SCHOOL
12096 Ventura Ave., Ojai 93023-3999
Leo Molitor, Interim Headmaster
Denver Compton, Dir. of Admis.
Phone: 805-646-1464, Fax: 805-646-4430

Established 1924. Private. Catholic. Coed. Accreditation: WASC. Tuition for day students: $4,500. Tuition/room and board for 5-day boarders: $14,600, for 7-day boarders: $15,100. Enrollment: 228 (90 boarding, 138 day). Faculty: 27. Student-faculty ratio: 8:1. Average class size: 15. 9 buildings on 127 acres. 17 classrooms and labs, 2 gyms, pool, and athletic fields. 7,700 people in the community. 75 miles from Los Angeles. 100% of graduates are accepted by colleges and universities.

Vivian Webb School
1175 W. Baseline Rd., Claremont 91711
Nigel Taplin, Dir. of Admis.

COLORADO

St. Scholastica Academy
615 Pike Ave., Canon City 81212
Andrea Barry, Dir. of Admis.

CONNECTICUT

Academy of the Holy Family
54 W. Main St., Baltic 06330-0691
Sister Mary Patrick, SCMC, Principal
203-822-9272, Fax: 203-822-1318

Convent of the Sacred Heart
1177 King St., Greenwich 06831
Sr. Kathleen Conan, Headmistress

Ethel Walker School
230 Bushy Hill Rd., Simsbury 06070
Joanne Hoffman, Dir. of Admis.

Miss Porter's School
60 Main St., Farmington 06032
M. Burch Tracy Ford, Head
203-678-9390

Westover School
P.O. Box 847, Middlebury 06762
Joseph Molder, Headmaster
203-758-2423

FLORIDA

Bartram School
2264 Bartram Rd., Jacksonville 32207
Ruth Goin, Admis. Coordinator

Rosarian Academy
807 N. Flagler Dr., West Palm Beach 33401
Sr. Madeleine Sophie McLead, O.P., Co-Prin.
Sr. Eileen Sullivan, O.P., Co-Principal

GEORGIA

BRENAU ACADEMY
One Centennial Cir., Gainesville 30501
Frank Booth, Headmaster
Leigh Ann Doss, Dir. of Admis.
404-534-6140

Established 1928. Private. Accreditation: SACS. Comprehensive fee — boarding students: $14,200, day students: $5,800. Fees: $300 (books and supplies). Enrollment: 70. Faculty: 14. Student- faculty ratio: 8:1. Diploma awarded. Brenau Academy has a 41 acre campus including indoor pool, tennis center, ballet studios, fine arts auditorium and new 85,000 volume

library with computer lab. Associated with Brenau Women's College. Academy students can enjoy cultural programs and college courses. Interscholastic tennis, volleyball and cheerleading. Student government, clubs, and weekend activities are available. Warm, personal atmosphere.

HAWAII

St. Francis High School
2707 Pamoa Rd., Honolulu 96822
Sr. Ann Gertrude, Principal

ILLINOIS

St. Mary's Academy
P.O. Box 158, Nauvoo 62354

Woodlands Academy of the Sacred Heart
760 E. Westleigh Rd., Lake Forest 60045
Sr. Frances de La Chapelle, RSCJ, Prin.

INDIANA

Culver Military Academy and Summer Camps
1300 Academy Rd., Culver 46511
Richard Edwards, Dir. of Admis.

HOWE MILITARY SCHOOL
31 Academy Pl., Howe 46746
Colonel Thomas Merritt, Superintendent
Lt. Col. Reed Kimball, Headmaster
Glenn Cox, Dir. of Admis.
219-562-2131 ext. 221

Accredited by: the North Central Association of Colleges and Schools. A member of: the North Central Association of Colleges and Schools, the Independent School Association of Central States, the Association of Military Colleges and Schools of the United States, the Council for Advancement and Support of Education, the National Association of Independent Schools, the National Association of Episcopal Schools, the College Entrance Examination Board, Cum Laude Society.

Established 1884. Episcopal. Coed. Enrollment: 250. Total charge for a boarding student: $14,900. Financial aid available. Only military institute in Ohio, Michigan and Indiana that is a member of the US Army's JROTC program. JROTC required for all high school cadets.

College preparatory school. Grades 5 through 12. Fully accredited faculty and staff. Individual attention given. Class size averages 10 to 12 cadets. Twenty

solid units of credit are required for graduation. Seventeen and a half of them must be in English, math, history and social studies, science, foreign language, sacred studies, business and physical education and health.

Required for admission: a desire to attend, a willingness to adhere to Howe's military discipline, be of good moral character (satisfactory references), be of average to above average intelligence (IQ test), a certificate of honorable dismissal from previous school.

Located on 150 acres in Northeast Indiana just two miles from the Michigan border. Modern dormitories and academic facilities, library, pool, three (3) gymnasiums, athletic fields, track, canteen, 700 seat auditorium, two (2) chapels, dining hall, military department.

MARIAN HEIGHTS ACADEMY
812 E. 10th St., Ferdinand 47532-9240
Kathleen Kostelic, Director of Admissions
812-367-1431, Fax: 812-367-2313
Discover our world of possibilities

KANSAS

MOUNT ST. SCHOLASTICA ACADEMY
810 R St., Atchison 66002
Faye E. White, Dir. of Admis.
Phone: 913-367-1334, Fax: 913-367-5108
Established 1863. Private. Accreditation: NCACS, Kansas State Department of Education. Tuition, room and board: $7,200 - $12,500. Fees: $600. Enrollment: 114 full-time. Faculty: 13. Student-faculty ratio: 8:1. Library: 6,400 volumes. 2 buildings. Nearby Mount Conservatory of Music offers individual music/vocal lessons. Two theater productions annually. College credit courses and weighted courses offered. English as a Second Language Program available. Cooperative programs with nearby Maur Hill Prep School for Boys. Fifty miles from Kansas City, and only 35 minutes from KCI airport.

Thomas More Preparatory-Marian
1701 Hall St., Hays 67601
Sister Joanita Stelter, Dir. of Admis.

LOUISIANA

Academy of the Sacred Heart
P.O. Box 310, Grand Coteau 70541
Ann Savoy, Director of Admissions
318-662-5275

MARYLAND

Bryn Mawr School
109 W. Melrose Ave., Baltimore 21210
Ellanor Brizendine, Interim Headmistress
410-323-8800

Garrison Forest School
300 Garrison Forest Rd., Owings Mills 21117
Nancy Bets Hay, Dir. of Admis.

Gunston School
P.O. Box 200, Centreville 21617
J. Temple Blackwood, Headmaster

Oldfields School
1500 Glencoe Rd., Glencoe 21152
Hawley Rogers, Headmaster

ST. TIMOTHY'S SCHOOL
Stevenson 21153
Deborah Cook, Head of School
Jackie Casey, Director of Admissions
410-486-7400 Fax: 410-484-5910
Established 1882. Accreditation: MSACS. Member National Association of Independent Schools, Association of Independent Maryland Schools, National Association of Episcopal Schools and the Federation of American Independent Schools. All-girls, grades 9-PG. Enrollment: 83. 75% of students board, 25% are day students. Boarding tuition for 1994-95: $19,900, day tuition: $10,500. St. Tim's has one of the highest boarding/day ratios in the country. Students reside in one of two dormitories, and faculty families live in each dorm. St. Tim's focuses exclusively on a rigorous, college-preparatory program. We offer a planned, sequential liberal arts curriculum. Classes average 8 students per classroom. The curriculum provides the basic liberal arts requirements for graduation and a substantial number of choices in elective courses. A minimum of 18 academic credits is needed for a diploma. Seniors may undertake an independent study project before graduation. Advanced placement exams are available in English, biology, calculus, history of art, studio art, and foreign language. St. Tim's girls are accepted by highly selective colleges and universities both here and abroad. In 1994, graduates will enter such schools as Vassar, Tulane, Duke, Williams, and Boston University.

Girls are admitted without regard to religion, race, color, or national origin. Applications are accepted year round; however, they should be at the school before January 31 to ensure a place for the following year. In making admissions decisions, the school considers the applicant's school transcript, recommendations from principal or guidance counselor and teachers, standardized test scores, interview, applicant essay, and a personal recommendation.

Financial aid is granted on the basis of a candidate's financial need. In 1993-94, students received financial aid totaling over $336,800 including grants and loans.

In 1993-94 there are 19 full-time and 3 part-time faculty members. The faculty includes graduates of Harvard, Mt. Holyoke, Smith, and John Hopkins. 50% hold one or more advanced degrees. Student-faculty ratio: 5:1.

The Campus is located on 234 acres in Stevenson, 15 minutes from Baltimore. It has 22 buildings and includes a Performing Arts Center with a 350 seat theater, scene and costume shops, a dance studio, and music practice rooms. The library has 22,000 volumes and computerized catalog search capabilities. The Irvine Natural Science Center is located on campus. Students participate in a competitive athletic program including sports such as soccer, lacrosse, tennis, field hockey, and cross-country. St. Tim's is committed to retaining the special qualities that distinguish a boarding school from day schools, and the extracurricular program offers a full complement of weekend activities. A variety of on-campus activities allow students to pursue areas of special interest.

MASSACHUSETTS

Dana Hall School
45 Dana Rd., Wellesley 02181
Olive Long, Dir. of Admis./Financial Aid
617-235-3010

Miss Hall's School
P.O. Box 1166, Pittsfield 01202
Daniel Lee, Jr., Headmaster

Sacred Heart High School
399 Bishops Hwy, Kingston 02364

STONELEIGH-BURNHAM SCHOOL
584 Bernardston Rd., Greenfield 01301
C. Robert Wray, Headmaster
Trish Saunders, Dir. of Admis.
413-774-2711

Walnut Hill School and School of Performing Arts
12 Highland St., Natick 01760
Charles R. Nielsen, President

NEW JERSEY

Mt. St. John Academy
Mosle Rd., Gladstone 07934
Roberta Dorward, Dir. of Admis.

Mt. St. Mary Academy
1645 Hwy. 22, Plainfield 07060
Sr. M. Eloise Claire, Dir.

Purnell School, Pottersville 07979
William H. Moran, Head

Villa Walsh Academy
455 Western Ave., Morristown 07960
Sr. Doris Laventhal, M.P.F., Principal

NEW YORK

Emma Willard School
285 Pawling Ave., Troy 12180
Philip Deely, Principal

Masters School for Girls
49 Clinton Ave., Dobbs Ferry 10522
William Andres, Director of Admissions

NORTH CAROLINA

Saint Mary's College Prep
900 Hillsborough St., Raleigh 27603

SALEM ACADEMY
P.O. Box 10548, Winston-Salem 27108
David Black, Headmaster
910-721-2644

OHIO

Andrews School
38588 Mentor Ave., Willoughby 44094
Charles Marsee, Headmaster

OREGON

Valley Catholic High School
4275 S.W. 148th Ave., Beaverton 97007

PENNSYLVANIA

Academy of the New Church Girls' School
2815 Huntingdon Pike, Bryn Athyn 19009
Morna Hyatt, Principal

Grier School, (7-12) Tyrone 16686
Dr. Douglas A. Grier, Headmaster

LINDEN HALL
212 E. Main St., Lititz 17543
David J. Devey, Headmaster
717-626-8512
Established in 1746, Linden Hall is the oldest girls' boarding school in the United States and offers grades 6-12 plus a post-graduate year. Linden Hall provides a family atmosphere which nurtures young women as they live and grow and learn. Our strong academic and college preparatory curriculum is enhanced by support programs and learning strategies for the girl who might need individual specialized help. ESL courses are offered for foreign students, and support is available for girls with mild learning disabilities. With a 4:1 student-teacher ratio, resident faculty in the dorms, and faculty and staff advisors, our girls receive an abundance of attention, instruction, supervision, and affection in an environment that is challenging, supportive and exciting. Class size averages 6-12 students. Over 98% of LH graduates attend 4-year colleges.

Most students are boarders, so weekends are filled with school-sponsored activities — trips to nearby cities, including cultural activities such as plays, symphonies, and museums, as well as entertainment outings such as amusement parks, movies, shopping, and dances with nearby boys' schools. Teachers provide transportation and supervision for these activities. Day students are encouraged to participate in weekend activities.

In addition to the academic classrooms, Linden Hall has an art studio, a multi-purpose room, a photography lab and darkroom, and a modern stable and riding ring. Dance and swimming are available as after school activities. Theatre and acting courses are offered during the day. Varsity sports include teams for tennis, volleyball, basketball, softball, soccer, and riding. Girls are expected to participate in a minimum of electives.

Linden Hall's beautiful 46-acre campus is located just 2 1/2 blocks from the square in Lititz, a vibrant historic town in the heart of Pennsylvania Dutch country. Situated near Lancaster, Linden Hall is just 45 minutes from Harrisburg, 1 1/4 hours from Philadelphia, 2 1/2 hours from DC, and 3 hours from NYC. Convenient trains, planes, and buses bring girls from all over the US and around the world. Parents enjoy visiting the local chocolate and pretzel factories and the craft and gift shops when they come to campus.

The academic day consists of 8 50-minute periods scheduled, lunch, a club period, and a 30-minute academic help period. A Physical education activity is required 4 days a week after classes. Students study in their rooms from 7:30-9:30, with faculty supervision. For more information write or call: Jane E. Clark, Director of Admissions, Linden Hall, 212 E Main St., Lititz, PA 17543, 717-626-8512 or 800-258-5778.

St. Cyril Academy
580 Railroad St., Danville 17821

TEXAS

Hockaday School
11600 Welch Rd., Dallas 75229
Elizabeth M. Lee, Headmistress

VIRGINIA

Chatham Hall School
1 Pruden Ave., Chatham 24531
Jerry Van Voorhis, Rector
Andrew R.N. Walpole, Dir. of Admis.
804-432-2941, FAX: 804-432-2405

Foxcroft School, P.O. Box 5555, Middleburg 22117
Richard Wheeler, Headmaster

Madeira School
8328 Georgetown Pike, McLean 22102
Elisabeth Griffith, Headmistress

Notre Dame Academy
Rural Route 1, Box 197, Middleburg 22117
Sarah Peck, Dir. of Admis.

St. Catherine's School
6001 Grove Ave., Richmond 23226
Auguste J. Bannard, Head of the School

St. Margaret's School
P.O. Box 158, Tappahannock 22560
Viola Woolfolk, Headmistress

Stuart Hall
P.O. Box 210P, Staunton 24402
Ann Dandridge, Dean of Admissions

WASHINGTON

Annie Wright School
827 Tacoma Ave., N., Tacoma 98403
Charles R. Griffin, Dir. of Admis.
206-272-2216 or 800-847-1582

GUAM

Academy of Our Lady of Guam
233 Archbishop Fleixberto St., Agana 96910

PSYCHOLOGY

This classification contains schools offering programs in Clinical, Counseling, School and Combined Professional-Scientific Psychology accredited by the American Psychological Association (†) and a selection of programs from institutionally accredited schools.

ALABAMA

Alabama A & M University
P.O. Box 292, Normal 35762
Dr. Calvin Matthews, Chrpsn.
See listing under "Universities"

† Auburn University, Auburn 36849

· Gadsden State Community College
P.O. Box 227, Gadsden 35902
W. Bryan Stone, Dir. of Admis.

Huntingdon College
1500 E. Fairview Ave., Montgomery 36106-2148
Carolyn A. Phillips, Dean of Enrollment
800-763-0313

Judson College
P O Box 120, Marion 36756

Oakwood College
Oakwood Rd., N.W., Huntsville 35896

Samford University
800 Lakeshore Dr., Birmingham 35229
Stephen Chew, Chrpsn.

Spring Hill College
4000 Dauphin St., Mobile 36608
Ben Hamd, Dir. of Admis.

Talladega College
627 Battle St., W., Talladega 35160

Troy State University, Troy 36082
Dr. James Kimbrough, Dean

Troy State University at Dothan
P.O. Box 8368, Dothan 36304
Bob Willis, Dir. of Undergraduate Admissions

† University of Alabama
P.O. Box 870132, Tuscaloosa 35487-0132
Roy Smith, Dir. of Admis.

† University of Alabama at Birmingham
University Station, Birmingham 35294

UNIVERSITY OF ALABAMA IN HUNTSVILLE
P.O. Box 1247, Huntsville 35899
Ron R. Koger Ed.D., Dir. of Admis.
205-895-6070
Established 1969. Public. Coed. Accreditation: SACS, ABET, NLN, CSAB, ACS. Tuition: $2,418 resident, $4,836 non-resident. Room & Board: $3,450. Undergraduate enrollment: 2,674 full-time, 3,439 part-time. Graduate enrollment: 1,860. Faculty: 282. Student-faculty ratio: 18:1. Degrees: BS, BA, BSBA, BSE, MS, MSM, Ph.D., BSN, MSN, MA. 20 buildings on 350 acres. Comprehensive research university located in the Tennessee Valley of northern Alabama. Huntsville is the locale of major government and private research centers. Metropolitan population approaching 300,000.

UNIVERSITY OF MOBILE
P.O. Box 13220, Mobile 36663-0220
Kim Leousis, Dir. of Admissions
205-675-5990
See listing under "Universities"

University of Montevallo, Montevallo 35115

ALASKA

Alaska Pacific University
4101 University Dr., Anchorage 99508
Director of Admissions
See listing under "Universities"

ARIZONA

† Arizona State University, Tempe 85287

GRAND CANYON UNIVERSITY
3300 W. Camelback Rd., Phoenix 85017
Sherri Willborn, Dir. of Admis.
See listing under "Liberal Arts and Sciences"

Northern Arizona University
P.O. Box 4092, Flagstaff 86011
Dr. Margaret Cibik, Dir. of Admis.

† University of Arizona, Tucson 85721
Loyd Bell, Director of Admissions

· Yavapai College
1100 E. Sheldon St., Prescott 86301
Dr. Doreen Dailey, President
602-445-7300
See listing under "Community and Junior Colleges"

ARKANSAS

Arkansas State University
P.O. Box 940, State University 72467

John Brown University
2000 W. University, Siloam Springs 72761
Don Crandall, Director of Enrollment Management

Ouachita Baptist University
410 Ouachita St., Arkadelphia 71998
Randy Garner, Dir. of Admis.
800-DIAL-OBU

University of Arkansas at Fayetteville
Fayetteville 72701

† University of Arkansas at Monticello
P.O. Box 3596, Monticello 71656

Williams Baptist College
P.O. Box 3667, Walnut Ridge 72476
Scott Wright, Dir. of Admis.

CALIFORNIA

ANTIOCH UNIVERSITY
801 Garden St. #101, Santa Barbara 93101
805-962-8179

Bethany Bible College
800 Bethany Dr., Scotts Valley 95066
Randal McNally, Dir. of Admis.

† Biola University-Rosemead School of Psychology
13800 Biola Ave., La Mirada 90639
Wayne Chute, Dean of Admissions

California Baptist College
8432 Magnolia Ave., Riverside 92504
800-782-3382

CALIFORNIA COAST UNIVERSITY
700 N. Main St., Santa Ana 92701
Admissions Office: 800-854-8768 or 714-547-9625
Thomas Neal, President
Linda B. Smith, VP Academic Affairs
William Barcroft, Dean of Admissions
Established 1973. Proprietary. Coed. Accreditation: National Association of Private Non-Traditional Schools & Colleges, California State Department of Education, charter member California Association of State Approved Colleges & Universities, member Association for Adult & Continuing Education. Tuition: $2,200-$3,500. Enrollment: 7,500.
A private college offering off-campus independent study programs in the traditional areas of business administration, management, engineering, psychology, & education. Admissions: rolling trimester, requires official transcripts, letters of recommendation, detailed curriculum vita or occupational history.
Process: evaluation of prior academic work followed by analysis of occupational history, including participation in workshops, seminars, training programs, specialized projects for credit. Credit is demonstrated by challenge exams or specialized course by course independent study programs.
Residency: All course work may be completed off campus, utilizing correspondence methods. All doctoral candidates must meet with faculty advisors in person, upon completion of doctoral dissertation. Scholarships: Interest free loans available to students.

CALIFORNIA FAMILY STUDY CENTER
5433 Laurel Canyon Blvd., North Hollywood 91607
818-509-5959
Established 1971. Private. Coed. Accreditation: WASC. Non-residential. Enrollment: 250. Faculty: full-time 13, part-time 20. Student-faculty ratio: 12:1. Degree program: MA, Marriage, Family and Child Therapy only. Library: 6,000 Volumes. Adjacent to Los Angeles. Assistance with placement in training agencies. Direct observation in case conference setting.

California Institute of Integral Studies
765 Ashbury St., San Francisco 94117
Diane Gribben, Dir. of Admis.

California Lutheran University
60 Olsen Rd., Thousand Oaks 91360
800-252-5884

† California School of Professional Psychology
1005 Atlantic Ave., Alameda 94501
See listing under "Graduate Schools"

† California School of Professional Psychology
1350 M St., Fresno 93721
See listing under "Graduate Schools"

† California School of Professional Psychology
1000 S. Fremont Ave., Alhambra 91803-1360
See listing under "Graduate Schools"

† California School of Professional Psychology
6212 Ferris Square, San Diego 92121
See listing under "Graduate Schools"

California State University, Chico
Chico 95929-0234
Dr. Marvin Megibow, Chrpsn.

Chapman University
333 N. Glassell St., Orange 92666
Michael Drummy, Dir. of Admis.

Christian Heritage College
2100 Greenfield Dr., El Cajon 92019
Pam Daly, Dir. of Admis.
800-676-2242

Claremont McKenna College
890 Columbia Ave., Claremont 91711

College of Notre Dame
1500 Ralston Ave., Belmont 94002
Greg M. Smith, PhD., Dir. of Admis.

Concordia University
1530 Concordia, Irvine 92715
Stan Meyer, Dean of Admission
800-229-1200
See listing under "Universities"

DOMINICAN COLLEGE OF SAN RAFAEL
50 Acacia Ave., San Rafael 94901-8008
Office of Admissions
800-788-3522

Fielding Institute
2112 Santa Barbara St., Santa Barbara 93105
Sylvia Williams, Dir. of Admis.

Fresno Pacific College
1717 S. Chestnut Ave., Fresno 93702
209-453-2039

† FULLER THEOLOGICAL SEMINARY
Graduate School of Psychology
135 N. Oakland Ave., Pasadena 91182
Archibald Hart, Dean
Accreditation: APA, AAMFT, WASC
818-584-5400 or 800-235-2222

Holy Names College
3500 Mountain Blvd., Oakland 94619

La Sierra University
4700 Pierce St., Riverside 92505
800-874-5587

Loyola Marymount University
Loyola Blvd. at W. 80th, Los Angeles 90045
M. L'Heureux, Dir. of Admis.

Mills College
5000 MacArthur Blvd., Oakland 94613
Genevieve Ann Flaherty, Dean of Admissions
800-87-MILLS

Mt. St. Mary's College
12001 Chalon Rd., Los Angeles 90049

Pacific Christian College
2500 E. Nutwood Ave., Fullerton 92631
Knofel Staton, President

† Pacific Graduate School of Psychology
935 E. Meadow Dr., Palo Alto 94303
Rick Kaplowitz, Vice President
415-494-7477

Pacific Union College
1 Angwin Ave., Angwin 94508
Dr. Gary Gifford, Dir. of Admis.

† Pepperdine University
400 Corporate Pointe, Culver City 90230
310-568-5600

Pitzer College
1050 N. Mills Ave., Claremont 91711
Katharine Leighton, Dir. of Admis.

Point Loma Nazarene College
3900 Lomaland Dr., San Diego 92106
Bill Young, Dir. of Admis.

Pomona College
333 N. College Way, Claremont 91711
Peter W. Stanley, President

† San Diego State University
5300 Campanile Dr., San Diego 92115

San Francisco State University
1600 Holloway Ave., San Francisco 94132
Corwin Bjonerud, Dir. of Admis.

· Santa Barbara City College
721 Cliff Dr., Santa Barbara 93109
805-965-0581

Santa Clara University, Santa Clara 95053

SAYBROOK INSTITUTE
450 Pacific Ave., Third Floor
San Francisco 94133
J. Bruce Francis, President
415-433-9200
Established 1971. Graduate school granting master's & doctoral degrees in Psychology & Human Science. Accreditation: WASC. Tuition: $9,500 per year. Alternative, distance learning format. Interest areas within the two degree tracks: Clinical Inquiry, Consciousness Studies, Health Studies, Organizational Inquiry, Social Philosophy & Political Psychology, and Systems Inquiry.

Scripps College
1030 Columbia Ave., Claremont 91711
Leslie Miles, Dean of Admissions

Simpson College
2211 College View Dr., Redding 96003
Joe Barth, Registrar

Sonoma State University
1801 E. Cotati Ave., Rohnert Park 94928

Southern California College
55 Fair Dr., Costa Mesa 92626
Richard Hardy, Asst. Dean for Enrollment

† Stanford University, Stanford 94305

UNITED STATES INTERNATIONAL UNIVERSITY
10455 Pomerado Rd., San Diego 92131
619-693-4772
See listing under "Universities"

† University of California, Los Angeles
1247 Murphy Hall, Los Angeles 90024

† University of California at Berkeley
Tolman Hall, Berkeley 94720

† University of California, San Diego
9450 Gilman Dr., La Jolla 92092

† University of California, Santa Barbara
Santa Barbara 93106

University of California-Santa Cruz
Santa Cruz 95064
Joseph Allen, Dir. of Admis.

UNIVERSITY OF JUDAISM/LEE COLLEGE
15600 Mulholland Dr., Los Angeles 90077
Tamara Greenebaum, Dean of Admissions
See listing under "Universities"

University of La Verne
1950 3rd St., La Verne 91750
Mark Bornholdt, Dir. of Admis.

University of Redlands
P.O. Box 3080, Redlands 92373

University of San Diego
5998 Alcala Park, San Diego 92110
Warren Muller, Dir. of Admis.
619-260-4506

University of San Francisco
2130 Fulton St., San Francisco 94117
Bill Henley, Dir. of Admis.

† University of Southern California
University Park Campus
Los Angeles 90089

Whittier College
13406 Philadelphia St., Whittier 90601
310-907-4238

Woodbury University
7500 Glenoaks Blvd., Burbank 91504
See listing under "Universities"

† Wright Institute
2728 Durant Ave., Berkeley 94704

COLORADO

Adams State College, Alamosa 81102
Cheryl Billingsley, Dir. of Admis.
800-824-6494

Colorado Christian University
180 S. Garrison St., Lakewood 80226
Debra Seefeldt, Dir. of Admis.

Colorado College
14 E. Cache La Poudre, Colorado Springs 80903
Terry Swenson, Dir. of Admis.

† Colorado State University
102 Administration Building, Fort Collins 80523
Mary Ontireros, Dir. of Admissions

DENVER SEMINARY
Denver Conservative Baptist Seminary
MDiv, MA, DMIN.
P.O. Box 10000, Denver 80250
Charles Sprinkle, Dir. of Admis.
1-800-922-3040

Mesa State College
P.O. Box 2647, Grand Junction 81502
Sherri Pe'a, Dir. of Admis.

Metropolitan State College of Denver
P.O. Box 173362, Campus Box 16
Denver 80217-3362

Morgan Community College
17800 Road 20, Fort Morgan 80701
Kurtis Armstrong, Dir. of Admis.

Naropa Institute
2130 Arapahoe Ave., Boulder 80302
Dr. Jana Lynn, Director of Admissions
303-546-3572

Regis University
3333 Regis Blvd., Denver 80221
Robert Blust, Director of Admissions

† University of Colorado at Denver
1200 Larimer, Denver 80204

† University of Denver
2199 S. University Blvd., Denver 80210

† University of Northern Colorado, Greeley 80639
Charles Poston, Department Chrpsn.
303-351-2957

University of Southern Colorado
2200 Bonforte Blvd., Pueblo 81001

Western State College of Colorado
Gunnison 81231
Monica Bruning, Dir. of Admis.
See listing under "Universities"

CONNECTICUT

Albertus Magnus College
700 Prospect St., New Haven 06511
Richard Lolatte, Dir. of Admissions
203-773-8501 or 800-578-9160

Eastern Connecticut State University
83 Windham St., Willimantic 06226
Dr. Gary Sterner, Chrpsn.

QUINNIPIAC COLLEGE
275 Mount Carmel Ave., Hamden 06518
See listing under "Universities"

St. Joseph College
1678 Asylum Ave., West Hartford 06117
Mary C. Demo, Dir. of Admis.

Trinity College
300 Summit St., Hartford 06106
Dr. David Borus, Dean of Admissions

† University of Connecticut, Storrs 06268
Ann Quinley, Dir. of Admis.

† University of Hartford
200 Bloomfield Ave., West Hartford 06117
Richard Zeiser, Dir. of Admis.
See listing under "Universities"

University of New Haven
300 Orange Ave., West Haven 06516
Joseph Chepaitis, Dean
203-932-7000

† Yale University
149 Elm St., New Haven 06520

DELAWARE

† University of Delaware, Newark 19711

DISTRICT OF COLUMBIA

† The American University
4400 Massachusetts Ave. N.W.
Washington 20016

† Catholic University of America
620 Michigan Ave. N.E., Washington 20064
Robert J. Talbot, Dir. of Admis. & Fin. Aid.

† George Washington University
Washington 20052

† Howard University
2400 6th St., N.W., Washington 20059
James E. Cheek, President

University of the District of Columbia
Georgia Ave.-Harvard St. Campus
1100 Harvard St., N.W., Washington 20009

University of the District of Columbia
Van Ness Campus
4200 Connecticut Ave., N.W., Washington 20008

FLORIDA

Barry University
11300 N.E. 2nd Ave., Miami Shores 33161
Robin Ray Roberts, Dean of Admissions

Bethune-Cookman College
640 Mary McLeod Bethune Blvd.
Daytona Beach 32114

CARIBBEAN CENTER FOR ADVANCED STUDIES
MIAMI INSTITUTE OF PSYCHOLOGY
8180 N.W. 36th St. 2nd Floor, Miami 33166-6653
305-593-1223
Dr. Evelyn Diaz, Chancellor
Established 1980. Private. Coed. Accreditation: MSACS, PsyD program provisionally accredited by the American Psychological Association, effective fall 1991. Licensure: Florida State Board of Independent Colleges and Universities. Total enrollment: 418. Tuition: Undergraduate course tuition per credit: $180. Master course tuition per credit: $300. Doctoral course tuition per credit: $445. Federal and institutional financial aid available. On campus student housing not available.
The Miami Institute of Psychology of the Caribbean Center for Advanced Studies is a private, nonprofit institution offering both undergraduate and graduate programs in Psychology. Programs are designed to train professionals to work with people of diverse ethnic and cultural backgrounds.
The undergraduate program, leading to a Bachelor of Science degree in Psychology, is an upper division completion program designed for working adults holding an associate degree in arts or science (or the equivalent of either degree). The Graduate program includes a varied and comprehensive curriculum of Psychology and Mental Health studies. Graduate students participate in internship programs and clinical practicums that provide work experience to supplement academic studies. The Miami Institute of Psychology faculty works closely with students to provide personal and academic support. Students are elected to the Student Council to serve the needs and concern of the student body. The Goodman Psychological Services Center, located on campus and operated by the Institute, offers mental-health services to the surrounding community. Facilities include modern classrooms and administrative offices, the Goodman Psychological Services Center, and the Institute Library, housing a specialized collection of texts and research data base in the field of Psychology and related subjects.
BS Degree: Psychology; MS Degrees: General Psychology, Mental Health Counseling, School Counseling, Marriage & Family Therapy; PhD and PsyD Degrees: Clinical Psychology, Clinical Neuropsychology, Forensic Psychology.
Admissions: Undergraduate students: AA or AS (or equivalent of 36 semester hours) from an accredited educational institution, a maximum of 60 credits may be transferred from an associate degree or 90 credits from a four year college towards the Bachelor of Science, completed application form and $25 application fee, official transcripts from all high schools and colleges attended, minimum GPA of 2.0 or above,

curriculum vitae, two letters of recommendation and two 2x2 photographs. Graduate applicants: BA or BS from an accredited educational institution, completed application form and $50 application fee, official transcripts from all colleges and universities attended, minimum GPA of 3.0 or above, curriculum vitae, three letters of recommendation, GRE results and two 2x2 photographs.

Clearwater Christian College
3400 Gulf-to-Bay Blvd., Clearwater 34619
Benjamin Puckett, Dir. of Admis.

Eckerd College
P.O. Box 12560, St. Petersburg 33733
Richard Hallin, Dir. of Admis.

Flagler College
P.O. Box 1027, St. Augustine 32085
Marc G. Williar, Dir. of Admis.
904-829-6481

Florida Atlantic University
500 N.W. 20th St., Boca Raton 33431
Brian Levin-Stankevich, Dir. of Admis.

† Florida Institute of Technology
150 W. University Blvd., Melbourne 32901
Louis T. Levy, Dean of Admissions
800-888-4348

Florida Southern College
111 Lake Hollingsworth Dr., Lakeland 33801
William Stephens, Jr., Dir. of Admis.

† Florida State University
600 W. College Ave., Tallahassee 32306

Jacksonville University
2800 University Blvd., N., Jacksonville 32211

LYNN UNIVERSITY
(Est. 1962 as College of Boca Raton)
3601 N. Military Trail, Boca Raton 33431
407-994-0770 or 800-544-8035
See listing under "Universities"

† Nova Southeastern University
3301 College Ave., Ft. Lauderdale 33314

Palm Beach Atlantic College
P.O. Box 24708, West Palm Beach 33416-4708
See listing under "Universities"

Rollins College
P.O. Box 2720, Winter Park 32790

St. Leo College
P.O. Box 2008, St. Leo 33574
Bonnie Black, Dir. of Admis.

St. Thomas University
16400 N.W. 32nd Ave., Miami 33054
John M. Letvinchuk, Dir. of Admis.

SCHILLER INTERNATIONAL UNIVERSITY (FLORIDA & EUROPE)
U.S. Admissions Office
Dept. PA, 453 Edgewater Dr., Dunedin 34698-7532
800-336-4133 Fax: 813-736-6263
Dr. Walter Liebrecht, President
Karen Altieri, Associate Director of Admissions
See listing under "Universities"

Stetson University
401 N. Woodland Blvd., De Land 32720
Gary A. Meadows, Dean of Admis.

† University of Florida
226 Tigert Hall, Gainesville 32611

† University of Miami
P.O. Box 248006, Coral Gables 33124

† University of South Florida
4202 Fowler Ave., Tampa 33620

Warner Southern College
5301 U.S. Hwy. 27, S., Lake Wales 33853
Valerie S. Rutland, Dir. Enrollment Mgmt.
800-949-7248

GEORGIA

Agnes Scott College
201 E. College Ave., Decatur 30030
Teresa Lahti, Dir. of Admis.

BREWTON-PARKER COLLEGE
P.O. Box 197, Mount Vernon 30445
Dr. Y. Lynn Holmes, President
912-583-2241

† Emory University
1462 Clifton Rd., Atlanta 30322

Georgia College
231 W. Hancock St., Milledgeville 31061
912-453-5004

† Georgia State University
University Plaza, Atlanta 30303
Ernest Beals, Dean of Admissions

Kennesaw State College
P.O. Box 444, Marietta 30061
Joe Head, Dir. of Admis.

La Grange College
601 Broad St., La Grange 30240
Phil Dodson, Dir. of Admis.
706-882-2911

Mercer University
1400 Coleman Ave., Macon 31207

Oglethorpe University
4484 Peachtree Rd., N.E., Atlanta 30319
Dennis Matthews, Dir. of Admis.

Paine College
1235 15th St., Augusta 30901
Phyllis Wyatt-Woodruff, Dir. Enrollment Mgmt.

Piedmont College
P.O. Box 10, Demorest 30535
Penny L. Graber, Dir of Admis.
800-277-7020

Shorter College
315 Shorter Ave., Rome 30165

Spelman College
350 Spelman Ln., S.W., Atlanta 30314
Aline Rivers, Dir. of Admis.

Toccoa Falls College
Office of Admissions, Toccoa Falls 30598
Matthew L. King, Dir. of Admis.
800-868-3257

† University of Georgia, Athens 30602
Roger Thomas, Head

Wesleyan College
4760 Forsyth Rd., Macon 31297

West Georgia College, Carrollton 30118
C. Doyle Bickers, Dir. of Admis.

HAWAII

Brigham Young University, Hawaii Campus
55-220 Kulanui St., Laie 96762
Clark E. Hirschi, Coordinator of Admis.

Chaminade University of Honolulu
3140 Waialae Ave., Honolulu 96816
Charles Schafer, VP Enrollment Services

Hawaii Pacific University
1166 Fort Street Mall, Honolulu 96813
Don Barlow, Dir. of Admis.

Hawaii Pacific University
45-045 Kamehameha Hwy., Kaneohe 96744

† University of Hawaii at Hilo
523 W. Lanikaula, Hilo 96720

IDAHO

University of Idaho, Moscow 83843
Peter Brown, Dir. of Admis.

ILLINOIS

Adler School of Professional Psychology
65 E. Wacker Pl., Chicago 60601-7203
Suzann Lebda, Director of Admissions
312-201-5900

Augustana College
639 38th St., Rock Island 61201
Martin R. Sauer, Director of Admission
800-798-8100

Aurora University
347 S. Gladstone Ave., Aurora 60506
Peter Pitts, Dir. of Admis.

Barat College, Lake Forest 60045
Loretta Brickman, Dir. of Admis.

Blackburn College
700 College Ave., Carlinville 62626
Dwight Smith, Dir. of Admis.

† Chicago School of Professional Psychology
806 S. Plymouth Ct., Chicago 60605
Dr. William Bruinsma, Admissions Dept.
312-786-9443

† Concordia University
7400 Augusta St., River Forest 60305

† De Paul University
1 E. Jackson Blvd., Chicago 60604
Thomas D. Abrahamson, Dean of Admissions
See listing under "Universities"

Eastern Illinois University, Charleston 61920
Fred Jaffe, Chrpsn.
See listing under "Universities"

Elmhurst College
190 Prospect Ave., Elmhurst 60126

Eureka College
300 E. College Ave., Eureka 61530

Governors State University
1 University Pky., University Park 60466
Richard Pride, Dir. of Admis.

Greenville College
315 E. College Ave., Greenville 62246
Kent Krober, Dir. of Admis.

Illinois Benedictine College
5700 College Rd., Lisle 60532

Illinois College
1101 W. College Ave., Jacksonville 62650
Gale Vaugn, Dir. of Admis.

† Illinois Institute of Technology
3300 S. Federal St., Chicago 60616
Wendell R. Webb, Dir. of Admissions

† Illinois School of Professional Psychology
220 St. State St., Chicago 60604

ILLINOIS WESLEYAN UNIVERSITY
P.O. Box 2900, Bloomington 61702
Dr. Wayne Dornan, Chrpsn.
309-556-3006

Judson College
1151 N. State St., Elgin 60123
Jack Powell, Dir. of Enrollment Services

Knox College, Galesburg 61401
309-343-0112 or 800-678-KNOX
See listing under "Universities"

LEWIS UNIVERSITY
Rt. 53, Romeoville 60441
Irish O'Reilly, Director of Admissions
See listing under "Universities"

† Loyola University of Chicago
820 N. Michigan Ave., Chicago 60611
Allen V. Lentino, Dir. of Admis.

Loyola University - Mundelein College
6363 N. Sheridan Rd., Chicago 60660
Judith Bobber, Dir. of Admis.

MacMurray College
447 E. College Ave., Jacksonville 62650
Edwin R. Hockett, Dean of Admissions

Millikin University
1184 W. Main St., Decatur 62522
Lin Stoner, Dean of Admissions
800-373-7733

Monmouth College
700 E. Broadway, Monmouth 61462

National-Louis University
2840 Sheridan Ave., Evanston 60201

North Central College
30 N. Brainard St.
P.O. Box 3065, Naperville 60566-7065
Marguerite Waters, Director of Admission
708-420-3414

Northeastern Illinois University
5500 N. St. Louis Ave., Chicago 60625

† Northern Illinois University, De Kalb 60115

North Park College & Theological Seminary
3225 W. Foster, Chicago 60625
312-509-2330

† Northwestern University
303 E. Chicago Ave., Chicago 60611

† Northwestern University
1918 Sheridan Rd., Evanston 60208

Olivet Nazarene University, Kankakee 60901
John Mongerson, Dir. of Admis.
815-939-5203

Parkland College
2400 W. Bradley Ave., Champaign 61821-1899
217-351-2208 or 800-346-8089

Quincy College
1800 College Ave., Quincy 62301
Fr. Michael Lanning, O.F.M., Dir. of Admis.

Rockford College
5050 E. State St., Rockford 61108
Miriam King, V.P. for Enrollment Management
See listing under "Universities"

ROOSEVELT UNIVERSITY
430 S. Michigan Ave., Chicago 60605
William Smyser, Director of Admissions
See listing under "Universities"

Rosary College
7900 W. Division St., River Forest 60305
Hildegarde Schmidt, Dir. of Admis.

St. Xavier College
3700 W. 103rd St., Chicago 60655
Mary Hendry, Dean of Admissions

Sangamon State University
Shepherd Rd., Springfield 62794-9243
Admissions and Records, 217-786-6626

† Southern Illinois University at Carbondale
Carbondale 62901

Trinity Christian College
6601 W. College Dr., Palos Heights 60463
Kenneth Bootsma, President

Trinity College
2077 Half Day Rd., Deerfield 60015
Dr. Kenneth Meyer, Pres.

University of Chicago
5801 S. Ellis Ave., Chicago 60637

† University of Health Sciences
The Chicago Medical School
3333 Green Bay Rd., North Chicago 60064

† University of Illinois
506 S. Wright St., Urbana 61801

† University of Illinois at Chicago
P.O. Box 4348, Chicago 60680
Dr. L. Rowell Huesmann, Chrpsn.

Western Illinois University
900 W. Adams St., Macomb 61455
Alan DeRoos, Registrar
309-298-1891

INDIANA

† Ball State University
2000 W. University Ave., Muncie 47306
Ruth Vedvik, Dir. of Admis.

Bethel College
1001 W. McKinley Ave., Mishawaka 46545
Steve Matteson, Dir. of Admis.

Calumet College
2400 New York Ave., Whiting 46394
Sharon Sweeney, Dir. of Admis.

Earlham College
801 National Rd. W., Richmond 47374
Robert deVeer, Dean of Admis.

Franklin College
501 E. Monroe, Franklin 46131
B. Stephen Richards, VP Enrollment

Goshen College
1700 S. Main St., Goshen 46526
Duane Kauffman, Chairperson

Grace College
200 Seminary Dr., Winona Lake 46590
Ron Henry, Dir. of Admis.

Huntington College
2303 College Ave., Huntington 46750
Paul Breininger, Dir. of Admis. Services

† Indiana State University
217 N. 6th St., Terre Haute 47809

† Indiana University at Bloomington
300 N. Jordan Ave., Bloomington 47406

Indiana Wesleyan University
4201 S. Washington St., Marion 46953
800-332-6901

Manchester College
604 College Ave., North Manchester 46962
Dr. Gary Zimmerman, Chrpsn.

Marian College
3200 Cold Spring Rd., Indianapolis 46222
Don French, Dir. of Admis.

† Purdue University
Schleman Hall, West Lafayette 47907

Purdue University, Calumet Campus
2233 171st St., Hammond 46323

ST. JOSEPH'S COLLEGE
P.O. Box 890, Rensselaer 47978
Louis Levy, Dean of Admissions
800-447-8781

St. Mary-of-the-Woods College
Saint Mary-of-the-Woods 47876
Lynn M. Rubick, Director of Admissions
800-926-SMWC

Taylor University
500 W. Reade Ave., Upland 46989
Joe Lund, Head

Taylor University - Fort Wayne Campus
1025 W. Rudisill Blvd., Fort Wayne 46807
Jan Paul Storey, Dir. of Admis.

Tri-State University, Angola 46703
Director of Admission
800-347-4878

University of Evansville
1800 Lincoln Ave., Evansville 47722
Dr. Mark Kopta, Dept. Chair
800-423-8633

† University of Notre Dame
Notre Dame 46556
Kevin M. Rooney, Dir. of Admis.

Valparaiso University, Valparaiso 46383

Wabash College
301 W. Wabash Ave., Crawfordsville 47933
Greg Birk, Dir. of Admis.

IOWA

Briar Cliff College
3303 Rebecca St., Sioux City 51104
Patricia White, Dir. of Admis.

Clarke College
1550 Clarke Dr., Dubuque 52001
Henry Goldstein, Phd, Chair
800-383-2345

Coe College
1220 1st Ave., N.E., Cedar Rapids 52402
Lowry Fredrickson, Chrpsn.

Cornell College
600 1st St., W., Mt. Vernon 52314
Kevin Crockett, Dean of Admissions

Dordt College
498 4th Ave., N.E., Sioux Center 51250
Quentin Van Essen, Dir. of Admissions
800-343-6738

Drake University
2507 E. University Ave., Des Moines 50311
Thomas Willoughby, Dir. of Admis.

Graceland College, Lamoni 50140
800-638-0053, Outside Iowa 800-346-9208
Bonita Booth, Dean of Admissions
See listing under "Universities"

Grand View College
1200 Grandview Ave., Des Moines 50316
Lori Hanson, Dir. of Admissions
800-444-6083

Grinnell College
P.O. Box 805, Grinnell 50112

† Iowa State University, Ames 50011
Karsten Smedal, Dir. of Admis.

Iowa Wesleyan College
601 N. Main St., Mt. Pleasant 52641

Luther College
700 College Dr., Decorah 52101
David Sallee, Dean for Enrollment

Maharishi International University
Route 1, Fairfield 52556
Gregory Polakow, Dir. of Admis.

Morningside College, Sioux City 51106
Lora Vanderzwaag, Dir. of Admis.

Mount Mercy College
1330 Elmhurst Dr., N.E., Cedar Rapids 52402
Carol Williamson, Dir. of Admis.

Northwestern College
101 7th St. S.W., Orange City 51041

Teikyo Marycrest University
1607 W. 12th St., Davenport 52804
Tim McDonough, Dir. of Admis.
See listing under "Universities"

Teikyo Westmar University
1002 3rd Ave., S.E., Le Mars 51031
Dr. Jim Utesch, Dir. of Admis.

† University of Iowa, Iowa City 52242

University of Northern Iowa, Cedar Falls 50614

Upper Iowa University
P.O. Box 1857, Fayette 52142

Waldorf College
106 S. 6th St., Forest City 50436
Steve Lovik, Dir. of Admis.
800-292-1903

KANSAS

Benedictine College
1020 N. Second St., Atchison 66002
James Hoffman, Dir. of Admis.

Bethany College
421 N. 1st St., Lindsborg 67456
Larry Rosenkoetter, Chrpsn.

Fort Hays State University
600 Park St., Hays 67601-4099
Dr. Thomas Jackson, Chrpsn.

Kansas Newman College
3100 McCormick Ave., Wichita 67213
Dr. Robert Giroux, President

McPherson College
1600 E. Euclid St., McPherson 67460

Mid-America Nazarene College
P.O. Box 1776, Olathe 66051

Ottawa University
1001 S. Cedar St., Ottawa 66067
Steve Koberlein, Dir. of Admis.
800-755-5200

Saint Mary College
4100 S. 4th St., Leavenworth 66048
Irene Keehan, Dir. of Admis.

SOUTHWESTERN COLLEGE
100 College St., Winfield 67156
800-846-1543

† University of Kansas, Lawrence 66045

KENTUCKY

Asbury College
1 Macklem Dr., Wilmore 40390
Jonah Mitchell, Dir. of Admis.

Bellarmine College
2001 Newburg Rd., Louisville 40205
Thomas LaBaugh, Dean of Admissions

Centre College
600 W. Walnut St., Danville 40422

Cumberland College
6178 College Station Dr., Williamsburg 40769
See listing under "Universities"

Georgetown College
400 E. College St., Georgetown 40324
Garvel Kindrick, Director of Admissions
See listing under "Universities"

Kentucky Christian College
617 N. Carol Malone Blvd., Grayson 41143

Kentucky Wesleyan College
3000 Frederica St., Owensboro 42301
Dr. Michael Kagan, Chrpsn.

Louisville Presbyterian Theological Seminary
M. A. Marriage & Family Therapy
1044 Alta Vista Rd., Louisville 40205
502-895-3411 or 800-264-1839

Midway College
512 E. Stephens St., Midway 40347
Carl P. Rollins II, Dir. of Admis.

Morehead State University, Morehead 40351
Charles Myers, Director of Admissions
606-783-2000

Murray State University, Murray 42071
Phil Bryan, Director of Admissions
800-272-4MSU

Northern Kentucky University
Louie B. Nunn Dr., Highland Heights 41076

Pikeville College
214 Sycamore St., Pikeville 41501
Dr. John W. Sanders, Dean of Admissions

† Spalding University
851 S. 4th St., Louisville 40203
Dorothy G. Allen, Dir. of Admis.

Transylvania University
300 Broadway St., N., Lexington 40508
Pat Bain, Dir. of Admis.

† University of Kentucky, Lexington 40506

† University of Louisville
2301 S. 3rd St., Louisville 40292
Robert Parrent, Dir. of Admis.

LOUISIANA

Centenary College of Louisiana
P.O. Box 41188, Shreveport 71134

Louisiana College
College Station, Pineville 71359
Byron McGee, Dir. of Admis.
318-487-7386
See listing under "Liberal Arts"

† Louisiana State University
8515 Youree Dr., Shreveport 71115

Loyola University
6363 St. Charles Ave., New Orleans 70118

Southeastern Louisiana University
P.O. Box 784, Hammond 70404

† Tulane University
6823 Saint Charles Ave., New Orleans 70118
Richard Whiteside, Dean of Admission

MAINE

Bowdoin College, Brunswick 04011
William Mason, Dir. of Admis.

† University of Maine
102 Main St., Farmington 04938

University of Maine at Fort Kent
25 Pleasant St., Fort Kent 04743
Jerry Nadeau, Dir. of Admis.

University of New England
11 Hills Beach Rd., Biddeford 04005
Patricia Cribby, Dir. of Admis.

University of Southern Maine
96 Falmouth St., Portland 04103
Joseph Hearns, Chrpsn.

Westbrook College
716 Stevens Ave., Portland 04103
207-797-7261

MARYLAND

Goucher College
1021 Dulaney Valley Rd., Baltimore 21204

Hood College
400 Rosemont Ave., Frederick 21701

Loyola College
4501 N. Charles St., Baltimore 21210
William Bossemeyer III, Dir. of Admis.

Morgan State University
Cold Spring Ln. and Hillen Rd., Baltimore 21239

Mt. St. Mary's College
16300 Old Emmitsburg Rd., Emmitsburg 21727
Michael D. Kennedy, Dir. of Admis.

Towson State University
800 York Rd., Towson 21204
Dr. Hoke Smith, President

† University of Maryland
Baltimore Professional Schools
522 W. Lombard St., Baltimore 21201

† University of Maryland, Baltimore County
5401 Wilkens Ave., Catonsville 21228

Western Maryland College
2 College Hill, Westminster 21157

MASSACHUSETTS

American International College
1000 State St., Springfield 01109
Peter Miller, Dean of Admissions

Amherst College, Amherst 01002
Jane E. Reynolds, Dean of Admissions

Anna Maria College
2 Sunset Ln., Paxton 01612
Dr. Bernadette Madore, SSA, President

Atlantic Union College
P.O. Box 1000, South Lancaster 01561
Osa Canto, Registrar

BAY PATH COLLEGE
588 Longmeadow St., Longmeadow 01106
Paula DesRoberts, Dean of Admis.
413-567-0621 or 800-782-PATH
  Established: 1897. Private. Women. Accreditation: NEASC. Legal programs ABA approved. Tuition: $10,200. Room and board: $6,225. Enrollment: 600. Faculty: 42. Student-faculty ratio: 14:1. Degrees: AA, AS, BA, BS. Library: 38,000 volumes. 27 buildings on 30 acres. Secure, suburban campus near Springfield and Hartford. 15 Associate degree programs in business, education, fashion/design, criminal justice, paralegalism, hospitality/tourism, health, human services, occupational therapy, psychology, liberal arts. Baccalaureates in business, business/accounting, legal studies, psychology, psychology/criminal justice, psychology/early childhood education. Extensive career services. 95-98% of students obtain jobs after graduation. Transfer welcome.

† Boston College
140 Commonwealth Ave., Chestnut Hill 02167

† Boston University
685 Commonwealth Ave., Boston 02215

Bradford College
320 S. Main St., Bradford 01835

Brandeis University
415 South St, Waltham 02154
David Gould, Dean of Admissions
617-736-3500

Bridgewater State College
Bridgewater 02325
James Plotner, Jr., Dir. of Admis.

† Clark University
950 Main St., Worcester 01610
Richard Pierson, Dean of Admis.

Curry College
1071 Blue Hill Ave., Milton 02186
617-333-0500

ELMS COLLEGE
291 Springfield St., Chicopee 01013
800-255-ELMS

Emmanuel College
400 The Fenway, Boston 02115
Margaret Bonilla, Dir. of Admis.

Endicott College
376 Hale St., Beverly 01915
Elizabeth Macomber, Dir. of Admis.

Fitchburg State College
160 Pearl St., Fitchburg 01420
Marke Vickers, Dir. of Admis.

Hampshire College, Amherst 01002
Audrey Y. Smith, Dir. of Admissions
413-582-5471

Harvard University
Graduate School of Arts and Sciences
Byerly Hall, 2nd Floor
8 Garden St, Cambridge 02138

Lesley College
29 Everett St., Cambridge 02138-2790
Jane Raley, Dir. of Admissions

† Massachusetts School of Professional Psychology
221 Rivermoor St., Boston 02132
617-327-6777

Mt. Holyoke College
College St., South Hadley 01075
Anita Smith, Director of Admissions
413-538-2023

Nichols College, Dudley 01570

North Adams State College
375 Church St., North Adams 01247
413-664-4511 or 800-292-6632
See listing under "Universities or Graduate Schools"

Pine Manor College
400 Heath St., Chestnut Hill 02167
Gillian Lloyd, Dir. of Admis.

Simmons College
300 The Fenway, Boston 02115

Springfield College
263 Alden St., Springfield 01109
Frederick Bartlett, Dean of Admissions

SPRINGFIELD TECHNICAL COMMUNITY COLLEGE
1 Armory Square, Springfield 01105
Dr. Patrick E. Tigue, Dir. of Admissions
413-781-7822

Suffolk University
8 Ashburton Place, Boston 02108
Barbara K. Ericson, Assoc. Dean Enrollment & Retention
617-573-8460

† University of Massachusetts, Amherst 01003
Arlene Wesley Cash, Dir. of Admis.

University of Massachusetts
100 Morrissey Blvd., Boston 02125

University of Massachusetts Dartmouth
Old Westport Rd., North Dartmouth 02747
Raymond Barrows, Dir. of Admissions
508-999-8605

Wellesley College, Wellesley 02181
Janet A. Lavin, Dir. of Admis.

Western New England College
1215 Wilbraham Rd., Springfield 01119
800-325-1122

Westfield State College
577 Western Ave., Westfield 01085
John F. Marcus, Dir. of Admis.

Wheaton College
26 E. Main St., Norton 02766
Gail Berson, Dean/Admis. & Student Aid

MICHIGAN

Adrian College
110 S. Madison St., Adrian 49221
George Wolf, Dir. of Admis.
See listing under "Universities"

Albion College
611 E. Porter, Albion 49224
800-858-6770

Andrews University, Berrien Springs 49104
Jack Mentges, Dir. of Admis.

Aquinas College
1607 Robinson Rd., S.E., Grand Rapids 49506
Paula Meehan, Dean of Admissions
800-678-9593

Calvin College
3201 Burton St., S.E., Grand Rapids 49546

† Central Michigan University
100 Warriner Hall, Mt. Pleasant 48858

Eastern Michigan University, Ypsilanti 48197
Kenneth Rusiniak, Head
313-487-3060 or 800-GO-TO-EMU

Grand Valley State University
1 Campus Dr., Allendale 49401
JoAnn Foerster, Dir. of Admis.

HILLSDALE COLLEGE
33 E. College St., Hillsdale 49242
Dr. Charles Ransford, Director
517-437-7341

Lake Superior State University
1000 College Dr., Sault St. Marie 49783

Marygrove College
8425 W. McNichols Rd., Detroit 48221

† Michigan State University, East Lansing 48824
Dr. Gordon Wood, Chrpsn.

Olivet College
300 S. Main St., Olivet 49076
Vicki Gallas, Registrar
See listing under "Universities"

St. Mary's College
Orchard Lake & Commerce Rd.
Orchard Lake 48324

Spring Arbor College
106 E. Main St., Spring Arbor 49283

† University of Detroit Mercy
4001 W. McNichols
PO Box 19900, Detroit 48219-0900
313-993-1245
See listing under "Universities"

† University of Michigan-Ann Arbor
815 S. University Ave., Ann Arbor 48109

† Wayne State University
5980 Cass Ave., Detroit 48202
Dr. J. R. Thorderson, Dir. of Admis.

† Western Michigan University, Kalamazoo 49008
Stanley Henderson, Dir. of Enrl. Mgt. & Admis.
616-387-2000

William Tyndale College
35700 W. Twelve Mile Rd.
Farmington Hills 48331

MINNESOTA

Augsburg College
731 21st Ave., S., Minneapolis 55454

Bemidji State University
1500 Birchmont Dr., N.E., Bemidji 56601
800-475-2001

Bethel College
3900 Bethel Dr., St. Paul 55112
Dr. George Brushaber, President

Carleton College
One N. College St., Northfield 55057
Paul Thiboutot, Dir. of Admis.

College of Saint Benedict
37 S. College Ave., St. Joseph 56374

College of St. Catherine
2004 Randolph Ave., St. Paul 55105

College of Saint Scholastica
1200 Kenwood Ave., Duluth 55811
Dr. Darryl Dietrich, Chrpsn.
800-447-5444
See listing under "Liberal Arts"

Concordia College
901 8th St. S., Moorhead 56562
Lee Johnson, Dir. of Admis.
See listing under "Universities"

Concordia College-St. Paul
275 N. Syndicate, St. Paul 55104
Tim Utter, Dir. of Admis.

Crown College
6425 County Rd. 30, St. Bonifacius 55375
See listing under "Universities"

Gustavus Adolphus College
800 W. College Ave., St. Peter 56082
Mark Anderson, Dir. of Admis.

Hamline University
1536 Hewitt Ave., St. Paul 55104
Scott Pratt, Dir. of Admis.

North Central Bible College
910 Elliot Ave., Minneapolis 55404
800-289-NCBC
Dan Neary, Dir. of Admis.
See listing under "Universities"

Northwestern College
3003 Snelling Ave., N., St. Paul 55113
Ralph Anderson, Dean of Admissions
800-827-6827 or 612-631-5111

St. Cloud State University
740 4th Ave., S., St. Cloud 56301
Sherwood Reid, Dir. of Admis.
800-369-4260

St. John's University
P.O. Box 7155, Collegeville 56321

St. Mary's College of Minnesota
700 Terrace Heights #2, Winona 55987
Tony Piscitiello, VP for Admission

St. Olaf College, Northfield 55057
Deborah Anderson, Chrpsn.
507-646-3353

Southwest State University, Marshall 56258

University of Minnesota
600 E. Fourth St., Morris 56267

† University of Minnesota, Twin Cities
Minneapolis 55455

University of St. Thomas
2115 Summit Ave., St. Paul 55105

Winona State University
P.O. Box 5838, Winona 55987
Dr. J. Mootz, Dir. of Admis.

MISSISSIPPI

Belhaven College
1500 Peachtree St., Jackson 39202

Millsaps College
P.O. Box 150556, Jackson 39210
Florence Hines, Dir. of Admis.

Mississippi College
P.O. Box 4086, Clinton 39058

Tougaloo College
500 E. County Line Rd., Tougaloo 39174

† University of Mississippi, University 38677

† University of Southern Mississippi
P.O. Box 5165, Hattiesburg 39406

MISSOURI

Avila College
11901 Wornall Rd., Kansas City 64145

Central Missouri State University
Warrensburg 64093
Delores Hudson, Dir. of Admis.

College of the Ozarks, Point Lookout 65726
Dr. Kenton Olson, Dean of the College

Columbia College
1001 Rogers St., Columbia 65216
Ron Cronacher, Dir. of Admissions
800-231-2391

Drury College
900 N. Benton Ave., Springfield 65802
Michael G. Thomas, Dir. of Admis.

Evangel College
1111 N. Glenstone Ave., Springfield 65802
David Schoolfield, Dir. of Enrollment

Forest Institute of Professional Psychology
1322 S. Campbell Ave., Springfield 65807-1445
417-831-7902 or 800-424-PSYD
Richard H. Cox, Ph.D., A.B.P.P., President
See listing under "Graduate Schools"

Maryville University of St. Louis
13550 Conway Rd., Saint Louis 63141
314-576-9300 or 800-MARYVLL

Missouri Baptist College
12542 Conway Rd., St. Louis 63141

Missouri Southern State College
3950 Newman Rd., Joplin 64801-1595
Dr. Betsy Q. Griffen, Dept. Head
See listing under "Universities"

Missouri Valley College
500 E. College St., Marshall 65340
816-886-6924 ext. 114
See listing under "Universities"

Missouri Western State College
4525 Downs Dr., St. Joseph 64507
Howard McCauley, Dir. of Admis.

Northeast Missouri State University
Kirksville 63501

Northwest Missouri State University
800 University Dr., Maryville 64468

Park College, Parkville 64152
Dr. Edwin Rawn, Dean of Admis.

† St. Louis University
221 N. Grand Blvd., St. Louis 63103
Louis A. Menard, Dean of Admissions

Southeast Missouri State University
1 University Plz., Cape Girardeau 63701
New Student Relations 314-651-2590
See listing under "Universities"

Southwest Baptist University
1601 S. Springfield Ave., Bolivar 65613

Southwest Missouri State University
901 S. National Ave., Springfield 65804
Dr. Fred Maxwell, Department Head
417-836-5797

Stephens College, Columbia 65215
Mary Ann Sprinkle, Dir. of Admis.

† University of Missouri, Columbia
228 Jesse Hall, Columbia 65211

† University of Missouri, Kansas City
5100 Rockhill Rd., Kansas City 64110
Leo J. Sweeney, Dir. of Admis. & Registrar

University of Missouri, Rolla
102 Parker Hall, Rolla 65401
David J. Allen, Dir. of Admis. & Financial Aid
800-522-0938

† University of Missouri
8001 Natural Bridge Rd., St. Louis 63121
Mimi LaMarca, Dir. of Admis.

† Washington University
1 Brookings Dr., St. Louis 63130

Webster University
470 E. Lockwood Ave., St. Louis 63119
Dr. James Staley, Associate Dean
See listing under "Universities"

Westminister College
501 Westminster Ave., Fulton 65251
Gary Forney, Dean of Admis.

William Woods College
200 W. 12th St., Fulton 65251
Dr. Jahnae Barnett, VP of Admis.

MONTANA

CARROLL COLLEGE
1610 N. Benton Ave., Helena 59625
Candace Cain, Dir. of Admis.
See listing under "Universities"

Montana State University, Bozeman 59717

Montana State University - Billings
1500 N. 30th St., Billings 59101
Karen Everett, Dir. of Admis.
406-657-2158

Rocky Mountain College
1511 Poly Dr., Billings 59102
David Heringer, Dir. of Admis.
See listing under "Universities"

† University of Montana, Missoula 59812
800-462-8636

NEBRASKA

Bellevue College
1000 Galvin Rd. S., Bellevue 68005
Chari Leader, VP of Enrollment

Chadron State College
1000 Main St., Chadron 69337
Dr. Thomas P. Colgate, Dean

Creighton University
2500 California St., Omaha 68178
Dr. Elizabeth Dahl, Chrpsn.

Dana College
2848 College Dr., Blair 68008
John Schueth, Dir. of Admis.
800-444-3262
See listing under "Universities"

Midland Lutheran College
900 Clarkson St., Fremont 68025
Roland Kahnk, V.P. Admissions

Nebraska Wesleyan University
5000 Saint Paul Ave., Lincoln 68504
Ken Sieg, Dir. of Admis.

Peru State College, Peru 68421
Pamela J. Cosgrove, Dir. of Admis.
402-872-3815

† University of Nebraska at Lincoln
16 Administration Bldg., Lincoln 68588
John Beacon, Dir. of Admissions

NEVADA

Sierra Nevada College-Lake Tahoe
P.O. Box 4269, Incline Village 89450
Lane Murray, Dir. of Admissions
See listing under "Universities"

† University of Nevada, Reno
Reno 89557

University of Nevada Las Vegas
4505 S. Maryland Pky., Las Vegas 89154-1021
Admissions: 702-895-3443 or 800-334-UNLV

NEW HAMPSHIRE

†ANTIOCH NEW ENGLAND GRADUATE SCHOOL
40 Avon St., Keene 03431-3516
Gael R. Minton, Dir. of Admis.
603-357-3122
See listing under "Graduate Schools"

Colby-Sawyer College
100 Main St., New London 03257

Franklin Pierce College, Rindge 03461

Keene State College
229 Main St., Keene 03435
Kathryn Dodge, Dir. of Admis.

New England College
26 Bridge St., Henniker 03242
John Spaulding, Dir. of Admis.

NOTRE DAME COLLEGE
2321 Elm St., Manchester 03104
603-669-4298

Rivier College
420 S. Main St., Nashua 03060
Admissions: 800-44-RIVIER

Saint Anselm College
87 Saint Anselm Dr., Manchester 03102
Don Healy, Dir. of Admis.

NEW JERSEY

Bloomfield College
1 Park Place, Bloomfield 07003
Warner Smith, Dean for Admissions
201-748-9000, Ext. 230

Caldwell College
9 Ryerson Ave., Caldwell 07006

Fairleigh Dickinson University, Madison 07940
Lissa Anderson, Dir. of Admis.
201-593-8906

† Fairleigh Dickinson University, Teaneck 07666
Dennis Craig, Dir. of Admis.
201-692-2553

FELICIAN COLLEGE
262 S. Main St., Lodi 07644
Sr. Mary Austin, OSB, Dir. of Admis.
201-778-1029
See listing under "Universities"

Georgian Court College
900 Lakewood Ave., Lakewood 08701
908-364-2200 Ext. 635

Jersey City State College
2039 Kennedy Blvd., Jersey City 07305
201-200-3234

Monmouth College
400 Cedar Ave., West Long Branch 07764
Joan Rudinski, Dir. of Admis.

Princeton University, Princeton 08544

Rider University
2083 Lawrenceville Rd., Lawrenceville 08648
Susan Christian, Dir. of Admis.

Rowan College of New Jersey, Glassboro 08028
Marvin G. Sills, Dir. of Admis.

Seton Hall University
400 S. Orange Ave., South Orange 07079
Lee Cooke, Dir. of Admis.

Stockton State College, Pomona 08240
Sal Catalfamo, Dir. of Admis.

Thomas Edison State College
101 W. State St., Trenton 08608

Upsala College
345 Prospect St., East Orange 07017
George Lynes, Dean of Admissions

NEW MEXICO

College of Santa Fe
1600 St. Michaels Dr., Santa Fe 87505
800-456-2673

College of the Southwest
6610 N. Lovington Hwy., Hobbs 88240

Eastern New Mexico University
Portales 88130
Larry Fuqua, Dir. of Admis.

New Mexico Highlands University, Las Vegas 87701
Dr. Jorge P. Thomas, VP Academic Affairs

New Mexico Institute of Mining & Technology
801 Leroy Pl., Socorro 87801

† University of New Mexico, Albuquerque 87131
Robert Weaver, Dean of Admissions

NEW YORK

† Adelphi University, Garden City 11530
Dr. Elliot Pruzan, Asst. Provost & Dir. of Admis.
516-877-3050

Alfred University
Alumni Hall, Alfred 14802
Laurie Richer, Director of Admissions
800-541-9229

Barnard College
3009 Broadway, New York 10027

Canisius College
2001 Main St., Buffalo 14208
Penelope Lips, Dir. of Admis.
800-843-1517

Cathedral College of the Immaculate Conception
7200 Douglaston Pkwy., Douglaston 11362
Rev. James Grace, President

Colgate University
13 Oak Dr., Hamilton 13346
Dean of Admissions
315-824-7401

† Columbia University
612 W. 115th St., New York 10025

Cornell University
410 Thurston Ave., Ithaca 14853

† CUNY City College
Convent Ave. at 138th St., New York 10031

CUNY College of Staten Island
130 Stuyvesant Pl., Staten Island 10301

CUNY York College
9420 Guy R. Brewer Blvd., Jamaica 11451

Daemen College
4380 Main St., Amherst 14226
Maria Dillard, Dir. of Admis.
in NY 800-462-7652 or 716-839-8225

Dominican College of Blauvelt
460 N. Western Hwy., Orangeburg 10962
Louis Kern, Dir. of Admis.
914-359-7800

Elmira College
Park Pl., Elmira 14901
William S. Neal, Dean of Admissions
See listing under "Liberal Arts"

† Fordham University
441 E. Fordham Rd., Bronx 10458
718-817-1000

Friends World Program, Long Island University
Montauk Hwy., Southampton 11968
Carol Gilbert, Dir. of Admis.

Hartwick College, Oneonta 13820

Hobart & William Smith College
Pulteney St., Geneva 14456

† Hofstra University
1000 Fulton Ave., Hempstead 11550
Margaret Shields, Dean of Admissions

Houghton College
P.O. Box 128, Houghton 14744
Tim Fuller, Dir. of Admis.

IONA COLLEGE
715 North Ave., New Rochelle 10801
800-231-IONA or 914-633-2503
See listing under "Universities"

Ithaca College
953 Danby Rd., Ithaca 14850

Keuka College
P.O. Box 98, Keuka Park 14478
Robert J. Ianuzzo, Dean of Admissions

The King's College, Briarcliff Manor 10510
Frederic Rowley, Dean of Admissions

Le Moyne College
1419 Salt Springs Rd., Syracuse 13214-1301
Edwin B. Harris, Dir. of Admis.

Long Island University-Brooklyn Campus
1 University Plaza, Brooklyn 11201
Alan Chaves, Dean of Admissions

Long Island University-C. W. Post Campus
Rt. 25A, Brookville 11548
Dr. Sherman Tatz, Chrpsn.
516-299-2377

† Long Island University-Southampton Campus
Southampton 11968
Carol Gilbert, Dir. of Admis.

Manhattan College
4513 Manhattan College Pky., Riverdale 10471
Dr. Mary Ann O'Donnell, Acting Dean of Arts

Manhattanville College
2900 Purchase St., Purchase 10577

MARIST COLLEGE
290 North Rd., Poughkeepsie 12601
Harry W. Wood, VP Admissions
914-575-3226

Marymount College
100 Marymount Ave., Tarrytown 10591
Gina R. Campbell, Dir. of Admis.
800-724-4312

Medaille College
18 Agassiz Cir., Buffalo 14214
Jacqueline Smukeer, Dir. of Admis.

Mercy College
555 Broadway, Dobbs Ferry 10522
James Nesbitt, Dean of Admissions

Molloy College
1000 Hempstead Ave., Rockville Centre 11570
Wayne James, Dir. of Admis.
See listing under "Universities"

Mt. St. Mary College
330 Powell Ave., Newburgh 12550

Nazareth College of Rochester
4245 East Ave., Rochester 14618
Paul Kenyon, Dir. of Admis.

† New School for Social Research
66 W. 12th St., New York 10011

New York Institute of Technology
Old Westbury Campus, Old Westbury 11568

† New York University
70 Washington Sq., New York 10012

Niagara University, Niagara University 14109
George Pachter, Dean of Admissions
800-462-2111
See listing under "Universities"

Nyack College, Nyack 10960
Miguel Sanchez, Dir. of Admis.
800-33-NYACK

::: On-Line Campus
New York Institute of Technology
P.O. Box 8000, Old Westbury 11568-8000
800-222-NYIT

† Pace University, New York Campus
1 Pace Plaza, New York 10038

Pace University, Pleasantville/Briarcliff Campus
Bedford Rd., Pleasantville 10570

Pace University, White Plains Campus
78 N. Broadway, White Plains 10603

Rensselaer Polytechnic Institute, Troy 12180
Conrad Sharrow, Dean of Admissions

Roberts Wesleyan College
2301 Westside Dr., Rochester 14624
Dr. Frederick Coisman, Chrpsn.
See listing under "Universities"

Russell Sage College
51 1st St., Troy 12180

St. John Fisher College
3690 East Ave., Rochester 14618
Peter Lindsey, Dir. of Admis.

† St. John's University
Grand Central & Utopia Parkways, Jamaica 11439

St. Joseph's College
245 Clinton Ave., Brooklyn 11205
Geraldine Foudy, Dir. of Admis.
718-636-6868

St. Joseph's College, Suffolk Campus
25 Audobon Ave., Patchogue 11772

St. Lawrence University, Canton 13617
Joel R. Wincowski, Dean of Admis. & Financial Aid

ST. THOMAS AQUINAS COLLEGE
Rt. 340, Sparkill 10976
Andrea Kraeft, Dir. of Admis.
800-999-STAC
See listing under "Liberal Arts"

Sarah Lawrence College, Bronxville 10708

Skidmore College, Saratoga Springs 12866
Kent Jones, Dir. of Admis.

† SUNY at Albany
1400 Washington Ave., Albany 12222
Micheileen Treadwell, Dir. of Admission/Financial Aid
518-442-5431

† SUNY at Binghamton
P.O. Box 6001, Binghamton 13902

† SUNY at Buffalo
17 Capen Hall
P.O. Box 601660, Buffalo 14260-1660
716-645-6900

† SUNY at Stony Brook
Stony Brook 11794

SUNY College at Brockport
Brockport 14420

SUNY College at Old Westbury
P.O. Box 210, Old Westbury 11568
Michael Sheehy, Dir. of Admis.

SUNY at Oswego, Oswego 13126
Dr. Joseph Grant, Jr., Dean of Admissions
315-341-2250

SUNY College at Plattsburgh, Plattsburgh 12901
Matthew Merrens, Chrpsn.
518-564-3076

SUNY Institute of Technology at Utica/Rome
P.O. Box 3050, Utica 13504
Roger Sullivan, Dir. of Admis.
See listing under "Universities"

† Syracuse University, Syracuse 13244

† University of Rochester
500 Joseph C. Wilson Blvd., Rochester 14627
Wayne A. Locust, Dir. of Admis.
See listing under "Universities"

Utica College of Syracuse University
1600 Burrstone Rd., Utica 13502

Vassar College
125 Raymond Ave., Poughkeepsie 12601

† Yeshiva University
500 W. 185th St., New York 10033

NORTH CAROLINA

Barton College
College Station, Wilson 27893
Anthony Britt, Dir. of Admis.
800-345-4973/919-399-6318
See listing under "Universities"

Belmont Abbey College
1 Abbey Pl., Belmont 28012
Admissions, 800-523-2355

Catawba College
2300 W. Innes St., Salisbury 28144
Mark Stokes, Dir. of Admis.

† Duke University, Durham 27706

East Carolina University
1000 E. 5th St., Greenville 27858
Dr. Rand Evans, Chair

Elon College
P.O. Box 2700, Elon College 27244
Nan P. Perkins, Dean of Admissions

Gardner-Webb University
General Delivery, Boiling Springs 28017
Roger Gaddis, Chrpsn.
704-434-2361

Greensboro College
815 W. Market St., Greensboro 27401

Guilford College
5800 W. Friendly Ave., Greensboro 27410
Larry West, Dir. of Admis.
See listing under "Universities"

High Point College
933 Montlieu Ave., High Point 27262
Jim Schlimmer, Dir. of Admis.

Mars Hill College
Main St., Mars Hill 28754
Dr. Smith Goodrum, Dean of Admis.

Methodist College
5400 Ramsey St., Fayetteville 28311
Fiore Bergamasco, Dir. of Admis.

North Carolina A&T State University
1601 E. Market St., Greensboro 27411

† North Carolina State University
P.O. Box 7001, Raleigh 27695
George Dixon, Dir. of Admis.

North Carolina Wesleyan College
3400 N. Wesleyan Blvd., Rocky Mount 27804

Pembroke State University
P.O. Box 1510, Pembroke 28372
Anthony Locklear, Dir. of Admissions
919-521-6262

Pfeiffer College
General Delivery, Misenheimer 28109

QUEENS COLLEGE
1900 Selwyn Ave., Charlotte 28274
D. Stephen Cloniger, VP for Enrollment Management
See listing under "Liberal Arts"

St. Andrews Presbyterian College
1700 Dogwood Mile, Laurinburg 28352
Dale B. Montague, Dir. of Admis.

Salem College
P.O. Box 10548, Winston-Salem 27108
Katherine Knapp, Director of Admissions
800-32-SALEM
See listing under "Women's College"

† University of North Carolina
1000 Spring Garden St., Greensboro 27412

† University of North Carolina at Chapel Hill
Chapel Hill 27599
James C. Walters, Dir. Undergrad Admis.

NORTH DAKOTA

† University of North Dakota
Box 8193 University Station, Grand Forks 58203

OHIO

Baldwin-Wallace College
275 Eastland Ave., Berea 44017
Juliann K. Baker, Dir. of Admis.

† Bowling Green State University
Bowling Green 43403
John Martin, Dir. of Admis.

Capital University
2199 E. Main St., Columbus 43209
Dolphus E. Henry, Associate Provost

† Case Western Reserve University
2040 Adelbert Rd., Cleveland 44106

Cincinnati Bible College
P.O. Box 04320, Cincinnati 45204
C. Barry McCarty, President

Cleveland State University
Euclid Ave. at 24th St., Cleveland 44115

College of Wooster
1189 Beall Ave., Wooster 44691
Hayden Schilling, Dean of Admis.

· Columbus State Community College
550 E. Spring St., Columbus 43215
Mary Jo Deerwester, Dir. of Admis.

Defiance College
701 N. Clinton St., Defiance 43512
Penny D. Bell, Dir. of Admis.
419-783-2330 Collect

Heidelberg College
310 E. Market St., Tiffin 44883
Stephen E. Eidson, Dean of Admission
800-925-9250

Hiram College
P.O. Box 96, Hiram 44234
Gary Craig, Dean of Admis.

John Carroll University
20700 N. Park Blvd., Cleveland 44118

† Kent State University
P.O. Box 5190, Kent 44242
Bruce Riddle, Dir. of Admis.

Lake Erie College
391 W. Washington St., Painesville 44077

LOURDES COLLEGE
6832 Convent Blvd., Sylvania 43560
Mary E. Briggs, Dir. of Admis.
419-885-5291 or 800-878-3210

Malone College
515 25th St., N.W., Canton 44709
Lee Sommers, Dean of Admissions

† Miami University
E. High St., Oxford 45056

Mount Union College
1972 Clark Ave., Alliance 44601
Amy Tomko, Dir. of Admis.

Mt. Vernon Nazarene College
800 Martinsburg Rd., Mt. Vernon 43050
Ronald Hyson, Dir. of Admis.

Oberlin College
135 W. Lorain St., Oberlin 44074
William Friedman, Chrpsn.

Ohio Dominican College
1216 Sunbury Rd., Columbus 43219
800-955-OHIO

OHIO NORTHERN UNIVERSITY
525 S. Main St., Ada 45810
Dr. Kenneth Wildman, Chrpsn.
412-772-2000

† Ohio State University
190 N. Oval Mall, Columbus 43210

† Ohio University, Athens 45701

Ohio Wesleyan University
61 S. Sandusky St., Delaware 43015
Donald Bishop, Dean for Enrollment

† University of Akron
381 Buchtel Common, Akron 44325
Kris MacDermott, Asst. Provost Enrollment

† University of Cincinnati
2700 Clifton Ave., Cincinnati 45221

University of Dayton
300 College Park Ave., Dayton 45469-1430
Toll-free 800-837-7433
See listing under "Universities"

University of Findlay
1000 N. Main St., Findlay 45840
Dan Crabtree, Dir. of Admis.

† University of Toledo
2801 Bancroft St., W., Toledo 43606
Richard Eastop, Dir. of Admis.

Urbana University
100 College Way, Urbana 43078
Donald Burns, Dir. of Admis.

Ursuline College
2550 Lander Rd., Cleveland 44124

Wilmington College
P.O. Box 1185, Wilmington 45177
Rhonda Inderhees, Dir. of Admis.

† Wright State University
3640 Colonel Glenn Hwy., Dayton 45435

OKLAHOMA

Cameron University
2800 W. Gore Blvd., Lawton 73505
Louise Brown, Dir. of Admis.

Mid-America Bible College
3500 S.W. 119th St., Oklahoma City 73170
Tony O'Brien, Registrar
405-691-3800

Oklahoma Christian University of Science and Arts
P.O. Box 11000, Oklahoma City 73136
Duane Eggleston, Vice President
800-877-5010

Oklahoma City University
2501 N. Blackwelder Ave., Oklahoma City 73106
Keith Hackett, Dean of Admissions
See listing under "Universities"

Oklahoma Panhandle State University
P.O. Box 430, Goodwell 73939

† Oklahoma State University, Stillwater 74078
David Thomas, Dept. Head

Oral Roberts University
7777 S. Lewis Ave., Tulsa 74171
Arthur E. Matzkvech, Dir. of Admis.

Southern Nazarene University
6729 N.W. 39th Expy., Bethany 73008

University of Central Oklahoma
100 N. University Dr., Edmond 73034

† University of Oklahoma at Norman
660 Parrington Oval, Norman 73019

† University of Tulsa
600 S. College Ave., Tulsa 74104
Dr. Robert Hogan, Chrpsn.

OREGON

Lewis & Clark College
0615 S.W. Palatine Hill Rd., Portland 97219
Michael Sexton, Dean of Admissions

Northwest Christian College
828 E. 11th Ave., Eugene 97401
Randy Jones, Dir. of Admis.

† Pacific University
2043 College Way, Forest Grove 97116
Barbara Mergen, Dir. of Admis.

Reed College
3202 S.E. Woodstock Blvd., Portland 97202

† University of Oregon
1 University of Oregon, Eugene 97403

University of Portland
5000 N. Willamette Blvd., Portland 97203

Warner Pacific College
2219 S.E. 68th Ave., Portland 97215
Sherry Moore, Enrollment Management Director

Western Baptist College, Salem 97301
800-845-3005

Western Evangelical Seminary
12753 S.W. 68th Ave., Portland 97223
David C. Le Shana, President
Todd M. McCollum, Dir. of Enrollment
503-639-0559

PENNSYLVANIA

Albright College
P.O. Box 15234, Reading 19612

Allegheny College
520 N. Main St., Meadville 16335
Gayle Pollack, Dir. of Admis.

Allentown College of St. Frances de Sales
2755 Station Ave., Center Valley 18034
George Kelley, Dir. of Admis.

Alvernia College
400 Bernardine St., Reading 19607
Lisa Grabowski, Dir. of Admis.

Beaver College
450 S. Easton Rd., Glenside 19038-3295
Dennis Nostrand, VP for Enrollment Management
Phone: 800-776-BEAVER(2328)
Fax: 215-572-4049
See listing under "Universities"

Bloomsburg University, Bloomsburg 17815
Bernard Vinovrski, Dir. of Admis.

Cabrini College
610 King of Prussia Rd., Radnor 19087

California University of Pennsylvania
3rd St., California 15419
Norman Hasbrouck, Dean for Enrollment

Carlow College
3333 5th Ave., Pittsburgh 15213

Carnegie Mellon University
5000 Forbes Ave., Pittsburgh 15213

Cedar Crest College
100 College Dr., Allentown 18104-6196
Cynthia Phillips, Dir. of Admissions

Chatham College
Woodland Rd., Pittsburgh 15232
Suellen Ofe, Dean of Admis./Financial Aid
See listing under "Women's College"

Clarion University of Pennsylvania
840 Wood St., Clarion 16214

College Misericordia
301 Lake St., Dallas 18612
Michael Joseph, Dir. of Enrollment Mgmt.

Drexel University
3141 Chestnut St., Philadelphia 19104
Dean of Enrollment Management

Eastern College
10 Fairview Dr., Saint Davids 19087
Ronald Keller, VP for Enrollment Management

East Stroudsburg University of Pennsylvania
East Stroudsburg 18301
Alan Chesterton, Dir. of Admis.

Edinboro University of Pennsylvania
Edinboro 16444
Admissions Office: 800-626-2203

Elizabethtown College
1 Alpha Dr., Elizabethtown 17022

Franklin & Marshall College
P.O. Box 3003, Lancaster 17604

Gannon University
109 University Sq., Erie 16541

Geneva College
3200 College Ave., Beaver Falls 15010

Grove City College
100 Campus Dr., Grove City 16127
Dr. Peter Hill, Chrpsn.

GWYNEDD-MERCY COLLEGE
Sumneytown Pike, Gwynedd Valley 19437
Marjorie DeSimone, Dean of Admissions
800-DIAL-GMC
See listing under "Universities"

† Hahnemann University
230 N. Broad St., Philadelphia 19102

Haverford College
370 Lancaster Ave., Haverford 19041

Holy Family College
Grant & Frankford Ave., Philadelphia 19114
Dr. Mott Linn, Dir. of Admis.
215-637-3050

Immaculata College
Immaculata 19345
James P. Sullivan, Dir. of Admis.

† Indiana University of Pennsylvania, Indiana 15705
Fred Dadak, Dean, Admissions

Juniata College
1700 Moore St., Huntington 16652

· Keystone Junior College
P.O. Box 50, La Plume 18440
Kevin McIntyre, Dir. of Admis.

Lafayette College, Easton 18042
G. Gary Ripple, Dir. of Admis.
610-250-5100

La Roche College
9000 Babcock Blvd., Pittsburgh 15237
Marianne Leister, Dir. of Admis.

La Salle University
1900 W. Olney Ave., Philadelphia 19141
Br. Gerald Fitzgerald, Dir. of Admis.
See listing under "Universities"

† Lehigh University
27 Memorial Dr. W., Bethlehem 18015

Lincoln University, Lincoln University 19352
Jimmy Arrington, Dir. of Admis.

Lycoming College, Williamsport 17701

Marywood College
2300 Adams Ave., Scranton 18509

Mercyhurst College
501 E. 38th St., Erie 16546
Andrew Roth, Dean of Enrollment
800-825-1926

Millersville University of Pennsylvania
Millersville 17551
Blair Treasure, Dean of Admissions

Muhlenberg College
2400 W. Chew St., Allentown 18104
Chris Hooker-Haring, Dir. of Admis.

Neumann College
Concord Rd., Aston 19014

† Pennsylvania State University
201 Shields Bldg., University Park 16802

† Pennsylvania State University
5091 Station Rd., Erie 16563

Point Park College
201 Wood St., Pittsburgh 15222

St. Francis College
P.O. Box 600, Loretto 15940

St. Joseph's University
5600 City Ave., Philadelphia 19131
Randy Miller, Dir. of Admis.

St. Vincent College
300 Fraser Purchase Rd., Latrobe 15650

Seton Hill College, Greensburg 15601
Peter Egan, Dir. of Admis.
800-826-6234 or 412-838-4255

Slippery Rock University, Slippery Rock 16057
Director of Admissions

Susquehanna University
514 University Ave., Selinsgrove 17870

† Temple University
Broad St. & Montgomery Ave.
Philadelphia 19122

Thiel College
75 College Ave., Greenville 16125
Robert Weaver, Dir. of Admis.

† University of Pennsylvania
0 Levy Park, Philadelphia 19104

† University of Pittsburgh, Greensburg Campus
1150 Mt. Pleasant Rd., Greensburg 15601
Larry Whatule, Dir. of Admis.
412-836-9880

Villanova University
845 E. Lancaster Ave., Villanova 19085
Stephen R. Merritt, Dir. of Admis.

Washington & Jefferson College
60 S. Lincoln St., Washington 15301
Thomas O'Connor, Dir. of Admis.

West Chester University of Pennsylvania
S. High St., West Chester 19380

WESTMINSTER COLLEGE
New Wilmington 16172
Richard Dana Paul, Dir. of Admis.
412-946-7100

† Widener University
700 E. 14th St., Chester 19013

Wilkes University
184 S. River St., Wilkes-Barre 18766
Emory P. Guffrovich Jr., Dean of Admissions

York College of Pennsylvania
P.O. Box 15199, York 17405-7199
Nancy Spataro, Dir. of Admis.
717-849-1600
See listing under "Universities"

RHODE ISLAND

Brown University, Providence 02906

Rhode Island College
600 Mt. Pleasant Ave., Providence 02908

Roger Williams College
1 Old Ferry Rd., Bristol 02809
William Dunfey, Dir. of Admis.

Salve Regina University
1 Ochre Point Ave., Newport 02840
Roselina McKillop, Dean of Admissions

† University of Rhode Island, Kingston 02881
Nelson Smith, Chrpsn.

SOUTH CAROLINA

Anderson College
316 S. Boulevard, Anderson 29621
Carl D. Lockman, Dir. of Admis.
800-542-3594

Coastal Carolina College
P.O. Box 1954, Myrtle Beach 29578
Dr. Ed Cerny, Director of Admissions

Columbia College
1301 Columbia College Dr., Columbia 29203

Columbia International University
P.O. Box 3122, Columbia 29230
Frank Bedell, Dir. of Admis.
See listing under "Biblical Studies"

Converse College
580 E. Main St., Spartanburg 29302
Dr. Martha Rogers, VP Enrollment Management

Erskine College & Seminary
Washington St., Due West 29639
Dot Carter, Dir. of Admis.

Lander College
320 Stanley Ave., Greenwood 29649

Presbyterian College
503 S. Broad St., Clinton 29325
Margaret Williamson, Dean of Admis.

South Carolina State University
P.O. Box 7127, Orangeburg 29117-0001
803-536-7185

† University of South Carolina, Columbia 29208
Terry Davis, Dir. of Admis.
803-777-7700

† University of South Carolina at Aiken
171 University Pkwy., Aiken 29801

† University of South Carolina, Spartanburg 29303

Winthrop University
701 W. Oakland Ave., Rock Hill 29733
James McCammon, Jr., Dir. of Admis.

Wofford College
429 N. Church St., Spartanburg 29303
Charles Gray, Dir. of Admis.

SOUTH DAKOTA

Augustana College
29th & S. Summit, Sioux Falls 57197

Dakota Wesleyan University
1300 W. University Ave., Mitchell 57301

SIOUX FALLS COLLEGE
1501 S. Prairie Ave., Sioux Falls 57105
Susan Reese, Dir. of Admis.
800-888-1047
See listing under "Universities"

South Dakota State University
P.O. Box 0504, Brookings 57007
Dr. Allen Branum, Department Head
605-688-4322
See listing under "Universities"

† University of South Dakota
414 E. Clark St., Vermillion 57069
Dave Lorenz, Dir. of Admis.

TENNESSEE

Austin Peay State University
601 College St., Clarksville 37044

Bryan College
Box 7000, Dayton 37321
Thomas A. Shaw, Dir. of Admis.

Carson-Newman College
P.O. Box 70552, Jefferson City 37760
See listing under "Universities"

Christian Brothers College
650 E. Parkway, S., Memphis 38104

Crichton College
6655 Winchester Rd., Memphis 38115
901-367-9800

David Lipscomb University
3901 Granny White Pike, Nashville 37204-3951
Wade Sandrell, Dir. of Admis.
800-333-4358

Freed-Hardeman University
158 E. Main St., Henderson 38340
800-342-7837

Lincoln Memorial University
P.O. Box 2012, Harrogate 37752
Conrad Daniels, Dir. of Admis.

Maryville College
800 S. Court St., Maryville 37801
Annabelle J. Libby, Dir. of Admis.

† **PEABODY COLLEGE OF VANDERBILT UNIVERSITY**
P.O. Box 327, Nashville 37202
Barbara Johnston, Dir. of Admis.
615-322-8410

Rhodes College
2000 N. Parkway, Memphis 38112

Tennessee Temple University
1815 Union Ave., Chattanooga 37404
Dr. L. W. Nichols, President

Trevecca Nazarene College
333 Murfreesboro Rd., Nashville 37210

Tusculum College
P.O. Box 5035, Greeneville 37743
Ronald Porter, Dir. of Admis.

† University of Memphis, Memphis 38152
Dr. John Eubank, Dean of Admissions

† University of Tennessee at Martin
Martin 38238
Paul Kelley, Director of Admissions
See listing under "Universities"

† University of Tennessee at Chattanooga
615 McCallie Ave., Chattanooga 37403

† University of Tennessee, Knoxville
527 Andy Holt Tower, Knoxville 37996
Dr. Gordon Stanley, Dir. of Admis.

† Vanderbilt University
West End Ave., Nashville 37240

TEXAS

Austin College
900 N. Grand Ave., Sherman 75090
Rodney Oto, Dean of Admission
800-442-5363

† Baylor University
P.O. Box 97008, Waco 76798-7008
Diana Ramey, Director of Admissions

Corpus Christi State University
6300 Ocean Dr., Corpus Christi 78412

Dallas Baptist University
7777 W. Kiest Blvd., Dallas 75211

Incarnate Word College
4301 Broadway St., San Antonio 78209
Sr. Sally Mitchell, Dean of Enrollment

Lamar University
P.O. Box 10009, Beaumont 77710
800-458-7558

Midwestern State University
3400 Taft Blvd., Wichita Falls 76308

Rice University
P.O. Box 1892, Houston 77251

St. Edward's University
3001 S. Congress Ave., Austin 78704
John Lambert, Dir. of Admis.

St. Mary's University of San Antonio
1 Camino Santa Maria, San Antonio 78228
Rick Castillo, Dir. of Admis.

Schreiner College
2100 Memorial Blvd., Kerrville 78028
800-343-4919

Southern Methodist University
Hillcrest at University, Dallas 75275

Texas A & I University
Campus Box 101, Kingsville 78363

† Texas A & M University
College Station 77843

Texas Christian University
2800 S. University Dr., Ft. Worth 76129
Dr. Edward Boehm, Jr., Dean of Admissions

Texas Lutheran College
1000 W. Court St., Seguin 78155
Jennifer B. Ehlers, Dir. of Admis.

† Texas Tech University, Lubbock 79409

Texas Wesleyan University
1201 Wesleyan St., Fort Worth 76105
Kim Campbell, Dir. Freshman Admission

Texas Women's University
P.O. Box 23925, Denton 76204

University of Central Texas
P.O. Box 1416, Killeen 76540
Dr. Pauline Moseley, Dean of the Faculty

University of Dallas
1845 E. Northgate Dr., Irving 75062
Jim Whitaker, Dir. of Admis.

† University of Houston
4800 Calhoun Rd., Houston 77204

University of Houston-Clear Lake
2700 Bay Area Blvd., Houston 77058
Darella Banks, Exec. Dir. Enrollment Services

† University of North Texas
P.O. Box 13797, Denton 76203

University of St. Thomas
3812 Montrose Blvd., Houston 77006
Elsie Biron, Dir. of Admis.

University of Texas at Arlington
UTA Box 19125, Arlington 76019
R. Zack Prince, Dir. of Admis.

† University of Texas at Austin
0 the University of Texas, Austin 78712

† University of Texas Southwestern Medical Center
5323 Harry Hines Blvd., Dallas 75235
John Perkins, Dean

West Texas State University
2501 4th Ave., Canyon 79016
Lila Vars, Dir. of Admis.

UTAH

† Brigham Young University, Provo 84602

Southern Utah University
351 W. Center St., Cedar City 84720
D. Mark Barton, Asst. VP Student Services
801-586-7740

† University of Utah
1400 E. 200 S., Salt Lake City 84112
Dr. J. Stayner Landward, Dir. of Admis.

† Utah State University, Logan 84322-1600
Rod Clark, Director of Admissions
801-750-1107

Westminster College of Salt Lake City
1840 S. 1300 E., Salt Lake City 84105
800-748-4753

VERMONT

Bennington College, Bennington 05201
Karen Kristof, Dir. of Admis.
800-833-6845

Burlington College
95 North Ave., Burlington 05401
Nancy Wilson, Dir. of Admis.
See listing under "Liberal Arts"

Castleton State College, Castleton 05735
Gary Fallis, Dir. of Admis.

Goddard College
P.O. Box G, Plainfield 05667
Jackson Kytle, President

Lyndon State College, Lyndonville 05851

Marlboro College
General Delivery, Marlboro 05344

NORWICH UNIVERSITY
65 S. Main St., Northfield 05663
Prof. Johnnie Stones, Dept. Chrpsn.
See listing under "Universities"

Saint Michael's College
Winooski Park, Colchester 05439
800-SMC-8000
See listing under "Liberal Arts"

Trinity College
208 Colchester Ave., Burlington 05401

† University of Vermont
194 S. Prospect St., Burlington 05401
802-656-3370

VIRGINIA

Averett College
420 W. Main St., Danville 24541
Gary Sherman, Dean of Enrollment Mgmt.

Bluefield College
3000 College Dr., Bluefield 24605
Dr. Roy Dobyns, President
See listing under "Universities"

Bridgewater College
402 E College St., Bridgewater 22812

Christopher Newport College
50 Shoe Ln., Newport News 23606

Eastern Mennonite College
1200 Park Rd., Harrisonburg 22801
Jerry Miller, Dir. of Admis.

Emory & Henry College
General Delivery, Emory 24327

Ferrum College, Ferrum 24088
Bob Bailey, Dir. of Admis.

† George Mason University
4400 University Dr., Fairfax 22030-4444
Patricia Riordan, Dean of Admissions

LIBERTY UNIVERSITY
P.O. Box 20000, Lynchburg 24506
Jay Spencer, VP Recruitment
800-376-2800
See listing under "Universities"

Longwood College, Farmville 23901

Lynchburg College
1501 Lakeside Dr., Lynchburg 24501
Ernest Chadderton, Dean of Enrollment

Mary Baldwin College, Staunton 24401
Douglas E. Clark, Exec. Dir. of Enrollment

Marymount University
2807 N. Glebe Rd., Arlington 22207
Charles Coe, Director of Admissions
800-548-7638 or 703-284-1500
See listing under "Universities"

Mary Washington College
1701 College Ave., Fredericksburg 22401
Martin Wilder, V.P. for Admissions

Radford University
P.O. Box 5430, Radford 24142

Randolph-Macon College
200 Henry St., Ashland 23005
John Conkright, Dean of Admissions

Roanoke College
221 College Ln., Salem 24153

SHENANDOAH UNIVERSITY
1460 University Dr., Winchester 22601
Dr. Brandon Beck, Division Chair
See listing under "Universities"

Sweet Briar College, Sweet Briar 24595
Nancy Church, Dir. of Admis.

† University of Virginia
P.O. Box 9017, Charlottesville 22906

† Virginia Commonwealth University
910 W. Franklin St., Richmond 23284

† Virginia Polytechnic Institute & State University
Blacksburg 24061
David Bousquet, Dir. of Undergraduate Admis.

Virginia Wesleyan College
1584 Wesleyan Dr., Norfolk 23502
W. Steve Stocks, V.P. for Admis.

WASHINGTON

Central Washington University, Ellensburg 98926
William Swain, Director of Admissions

Northwest College of the Assemblies of God
P.O. Box 579, Kirkland 98083-0579
Bob Foster, Dir. of Public Relations

Pacific Lutheran University
12180 Park Ave. S., Tacoma 98447
Brian Baird, Chrpsn.

St. Martin's College
700 College St. N.E., Lacey 98516

Seattle University
Broadway Ave. & Madison, Seattle 98122
Lee Gerig, Dean of Admissions

Skagit Valley College
2405 E. College Way, Mt. Vernon 98273

University of Puget Sound
1500 N. Warner St., Tacoma 98416

† University of Washington, Seattle 98195

Walla Walla College
204 S. College Ave., College Place 99324

† Washington State University, Pullman 99164
Stan Berry, Dir. of Admis.

WEST VIRGINIA

Alderson-Broaddus College
Philippi 26416
Craig W. Gould, Director of Admissions
304-457-1700

Bethany College, Bethany 26031
John Giesman, Registrar

Concord College, Athens 24712

Marshall University
400 Hal Greer Blvd., Huntington 25755
See listing under "Universities"

The University of Charleston
2300 MacCorkle Ave., S.E., Charleston 25304
800-995-GO UC

† West Virginia University
P.O. Box 6001, Morgantown 26506

WEST VIRGINIA WESLEYAN COLLEGE
59 College Ave., Buckhannon 26201
Robert Skinner, Director of Admission
See listing under "Universities"

Wheeling Jesuit College
316 Washington Ave., Wheeling 26003
Fr. Thomas Acker, SJ, President

WISCONSIN

Alverno College
P.O. Box 343922, Milwaukee 53234
Colleen Hayes, Dir. of Admis.

Beloit College
700 College St., Beloit 53511
Lawrence T. White, Chair
608-363-2282

Cardinal Stritch College
6801 N. Yates Rd., Milwaukee 53217
David Wegener, Dir. of Admis.

Carroll College
100 N. East Ave., Waukesha 53186
Ken Moyer, Dir. of Admis.

Carthage College
2001 Alford Dr., Kenosha 53140
Brenda A. Porter, VP Enrollment

Edgewood College
855 Woodrow St., Madison 53711
Robert Blust, Dir. of Admis.

Lakeland College
P.O. Box 359, Sheboygan 53082

Lawrence University
P.O. Box 599, Appleton 54912
Steven Syverson, Dean of Admissions

Marian College of Fond du Lac
45 S. National Ave., Fond du Lac 54935
Carol Reichenberger, Dean of Admissions

Marquette University
1217 W. Wisconsin Ave., Milwaukee 53233
Raymond A. Brown, Dean of Admissions

Mt. Senario College
1500 W. College Ave., Ladysmith 54848
Dewey Floberg, Dean of Admissions

Ripon College, P.O. Box 248, Ripon 54971
James Reilly, Dean of Admis.

St. Norbert College
100 Grant St., De Pere 54115
Craig S. Wesley, Dean of Admission
See listing under "Universities"

University of Wisconsin, Eau Claire
Eau Claire 54701

University of Wisconsin, Green Bay
2420 Nicolet Dr., Green Bay 54311
Dr. Charles Matter, Chrpsn.

† University of Wisconsin, Madison
500 Lincoln Dr., Madison 53706

† University of Wisconsin
P.O. Box 413, Milwaukee 53201
V. M. Allison, Registrar

University of Wisconsin, Oshkosh
800 Algoma Blvd., Oshkosh 54901-8602
August Helgerson, Dir. of Admis.

University of Wisconsin
P.O. Box 2000, Kenosha 53141
414-553-2211

University of Wisconsin
1 University Plaza, Platteville 53818
Richard Schumacher, Dean of Admissions

University of Wisconsin, River Falls
River Falls 54022
Alan Tuchtenhagen, Dir. of Admis.

Viterbo College
815 9th St., S., La Crosse 54601
Roland W. Nelson, Dir. of Admis.

Wisconsin School of Professional Psychology
9120 W. Hampton Ave. #212, Milwaukee 53225

WYOMING

† University of Wyoming
P.O. Box 3434, Laramie 82071
Richard Davis, Dir. of Admis.

GUAM

University of Guam
UOG Station, Mangilao 96923
Kathleen Owings, Dir. of Admis.

PUERTO RICO

Catholic University of Puerto Rico
Las Americas Ave., Ponce 00732
Carilin Frau, Dir. of Admis.

University of Puerto Rico
Antonio Barcelo Ave., Cayey 00736
Antonio Rosario, Dir. of Admis.

University of Puerto Rico, Mayaguez Campus
P.O. Box 5000, Mayaguez 00681
Neysa Lopez, Dir. of Admis.

University of Puerto Rico, Rio Piedras Campus
P.O. Box 23300, San Juan 00931
Victor Lopez, Dir. of Admis.

PUBLIC HEALTH

This classification contains schools accredited by the Council on Education for Public Health (†) and a selection of programs from institutionally accredited schools.

ALABAMA

† University of Alabama at Birmingham
University Station, Birmingham 35294

ARIZONA

University of Arizona, Tucson 85721
Loyd Bell, Director of Admissions

CALIFORNIA

California College for Health Sciences
222 W. 24th St., National City 91950
619-477-4800

† California State University, Long Beach
1250 Bellflower Blvd., Long Beach 90840

† California State University, Northridge
18111 Nordhoff St., Northridge 91330
Ned C. Reynolds, Dir. of Admis.

Fielding Institute
2112 Santa Barbara St., Santa Barbara 93105
Sylvia Williams, Dir. of Admis.

† Loma Linda University, Loma Linda 92350
800-422-4LLU

† San Diego State University
5300 Campanile Dr., San Diego 92115

† San Jose State University
1 Washington Sq., San Jose 95192

† University of California, Los Angeles
1247 Murphy Hall, Los Angeles 90024

† University of California at Berkeley
Warren Hall, Berkeley 94720

COLORADO

† University of Colorado Health Sciences Center
4200 E. 9th Ave., Denver 80262
Phoebe Lindsey Barton, Ph.D., Director

† University of Northern Colorado, Greeley 80639
James Robinson, Department Chrpsn.
303-351-2755

CONNECTICUT

† University of Connecticut Health Center
Farmington 06032

† Yale University
149 Elm St., New Haven 06520

Yale University
60 College St., New Haven 06519

DISTRICT OF COLUMBIA

† George Washington University
Washington 20052

FLORIDA

† University of Miami
P.O. Box 248006, Coral Gables 33124

† University of South Florida
4202 Fowler Ave., Tampa 33620

GEORGIA

† Emory University
1462 Clifton Rd., Atlanta 30322

Georgia College
231 W. Hancock St., Milledgeville 31061
912-453-5004

HAWAII

† University of Hawaii at Manoa
2500 Campus Rd., Honolulu 96822

ILLINOIS

Governors State University
1 University Pky., University Park 60466
Richard Pride, Dir. of Admis.

Sangamon State University
Shepherd Rd., Springfield 62794-9243
Admissions and Records, 217-786-6626

† University of Illinois
506 S. Wright St., Urbana 61801

† University of Illinois at Chicago
P.O. Box 5220, Chicago 60680
Dr. Marilyn R. Fiduccia, Dir. of Admis.

LOUISIANA

† Tulane University
1501 Canal St., New Orleans 70118

MARYLAND

† Johns Hopkins University
600 N. Wolfe St., Baltimore 21205

Morgan State University
Cold Spring Ln. and Hillen Rd., Baltimore 21239

Towson State University
800 York Rd., Towson 21204
Dr. Hoke Smith, President

MASSACHUSETTS

† Boston University Medical Center
100 E. Newton St., Boston 02118
Maxine Peck, Director

Hampshire College, Amherst 01002
Audrey Y. Smith, Dir. of Admissions
413-582-5471

† Harvard University
8 Garden St., Cambridge 02138

† University of Massachusetts, Amherst 01003
Arlene Wesley Cash, Dir. of Admis.

MICHIGAN

Ferris State University
Office of Admission
420 Oak St., Big Rapids 49307-2020

† University of Michigan-Ann Arbor
815 S. University Ave., Ann Arbor 48109

University of Michigan-Ann Arbor
109 Observatory St., Ann Arbor 48109
Dr. Richard Remington, Dean

MINNESOTA

† University of Minnesota, Twin Cities
Minneapolis 55455

MISSOURI

† St. Louis University
221 N. Grand Blvd., St. Louis 63103
Louis A. Menard, Dean of Admissions

NEW JERSEY

† Johnson Medical School
P.O. Box 101, Piscataway 08855

Stockton State College, Pomona 08240
Sal Catalfamo, Dir. of Admis.

NEW YORK

† Columbia University
617 W. 168th St., New York 10032

Long Island University-C. W. Post Campus
Rt. 25A, Brookville 11548
Dr. Carl Figliola, Chrpsn., Public Admin.
516-299-2716

Mercy College
555 Broadway, Dobbs Ferry 10522
James Nesbitt, Dean of Admissions

† New York University
70 Washington Sq., New York 10012

SUNY College at Brockport
Brockport 14420

† University of Rochester
500 Joseph C. Wilson Blvd., Rochester 14627
Wayne A. Locust, Dir. of Admis.
See listing under "Universities"

NORTH CAROLINA

† University of North Carolina at Chapel Hill
Chapel Hill 27599
James C. Walters, Dir. Undergrad Admis.

OHIO

Kent State University
P.O. Box 5190, Kent 44242
Bruce Riddle, Dir. of Admis.

Lorain County Community College
1005 Abbe Rd., N., Elyria 44035
Dr. John W. Thrash, Jr., Registrar

† Ohio State University
190 N. Oval Mall, Columbus 43210

OKLAHOMA

† University of Oklahoma Health Sciences Center
P.O. Box 26901, Oklahoma City 73126
Dr. Charles Cameron, Dean

PENNSYLVANIA

† East Stroudsburg University of Pennsylvania
East Stroudsburg 18301
Alan Chesterton, Dir. of Admis.

† Temple University
Broad St. & Montgomery Ave.
Philadelphia 19122

† University of Pittsburgh
4200 5th Ave., Pittsburgh 15260

SOUTH CAROLINA

† University of South Carolina, Columbia 29208
Ose Henderson, Acting Dean-Graduate School
803-777-4243

TENNESSEE

† University of Tennessee, Knoxville
527 Andy Holt Tower, Knoxville 37996
Dr. Gordon Stanley, Dir. of Admis.

TEXAS

† University of Texas Health Science Center
P.O. Box 20036, Houston 77225

UTAH

† University of Utah
1400 E. 200 S., Salt Lake City 84112
Dr. J. Stayner Landward, Dir. of Admis.

Utah State University, Logan 84322-1600
Rod Clark, Director of Admissions
801-750-1107

WASHINGTON

Central Washington University, Ellensburg 98926
William Swain, Director of Admissions

† University of Washington, Seattle 98195

WISCONSIN

† Medical College of Wisconsin
8701 Watertown Plank Rd., Milwaukee 53226
Richard Cooper, MD, Dean/Executive VP

PUERTO RICO

† University of Puerto Rico, Medical Sciences Campus
P.O. Box 5067, San Juan 00906

RABBINICAL STUDIES

This classification contains schools accredited by the Association of Advanced Rabbinical and Talmudic Schools (†) and a selection of programs from institutionally accredited schools.

CALIFORNIA

Hebrew Union College
Jewish Institute of Religion
3077 University Ave., Los Angeles 90007
Rabbi Lee Bycel, Dean

UNIVERSITY OF JUDAISM/LEE COLLEGE
15600 Mulholland Dr., Los Angeles 90077
Tamara Greenebaum, Dean of Admissions
See listing under "Universities"

: :† West Coast Talmudical Seminary
7215 Waring Ave., Los Angeles 90046

COLORADO

† Yeshiva Toras Chaim Talmudic Seminary
1400 Quitman St., Denver 80204

CONNECTICUT

† Beth Benjamin Academy of Connecticut
132 Prospect St., Stamford 06901

FLORIDA

† Talmudic College of Florida
4014 Chase Ave., Miami Beach 33140
Milton Simon, Registrar

ILLINOIS

Hebrew Theological College
7135 Carpenter Rd., Skokie 60077
Dr. Jerold Isenberg, VP for Academic Affairs
312-267-9800

† Telshe Yeshiva-Chicago
3535 W. Foster Ave., Chicago 60625

MARYLAND

† Ner Israel Rabbinical College
400 Mount Wilson Ln., Baltimore 21208

MICHIGAN

† Yeshiva Beth Yehuda-Yeshiva Gedolah of Detroit
24600 Greenfield Rd., Oak Park 48237

NEW JERSEY

† Beth Medrash Govoha
617 6th St., Lakewood 08701

Rabbi Jacob Joseph School
1 Plainfield Ave., Edison 08817

† Rabbinical College of America
226 Sussex Ave., Morristown 07960

† Talmudical Academy of New Jersey
Rt. 524, Adelphia 07710

NEW YORK

Bais Medrash L'Torah Rabbinical College
118 W. Central Ave., Spring Valley 10977

† Beth HaMedrash Shaarei Yosher
4102 16th Ave. #10, Brooklyn 11204

† Beth HaTalmud Rabbinical College
2127 82nd St., Brooklyn 11214
Rabbi Chaim Wysokier, Dean

Beth Medrash Emek Halacha Rabbinical College
1763 63rd St., Brooklyn 11204
Rabbi Joseph Sorotzkin, Dean of Admissions

† Central Yeshiva Tomchei Tmimim Lubavitz
841 Ocean Pkwy., Brooklyn 11230
Avrohom Sharfstein, Registrar

† Darkei Noam Rabbinical College
2822 Avenue J, Brooklyn 11210

Hebrew Union College
Jewish Institute of Religion
1 W. 4th St., New York 10012
Rabbi Gary Zola, National Dean of Admissions

Jewish Theological Seminary of America
3080 Broadway, New York 10027
Dr. Ismar Schorsch, Chancellor

† Kehilath Yakov Rabbinical Seminary
206 Wilson St., Brooklyn 11211
Bela Sabel, Chief Exec. Officer

Kol Yaakov Torah Center
29 W. Maple Ave., Monsey 10952

Machzikei Hadath Rabbinical College
P O Box 190799, Brooklyn 11219

† Mestivta Eastern Parkway Rabbinical Seminary
510 Dahill Rd., Brooklyn 11218

† Mesivta Tifereth Jerusalem of America
145 E. Broadway, New York 10002

† Mesivta Torah Vodaath Seminary
425 E. 9th St., Brooklyn 11218

† Mirrer Yeshiva
1795 Ocean Pky., Brooklyn 11223

† Ohr HaMeir Theological Seminary
P.O. Box 2130, Peekskill 10566

† Ohr Somayach Tanenbaum
P.O. Box 334, Monsey 10952

† Rabbinical Academy Mesivta Rabbi Chaim Berlin
1593 Coney Island Ave., Brooklyn 11230
Rabbi Aaron Schechter, President of Faculty

† Rabbinical College Beth Shraga
P.O. Box 412, Monsey 10952

† Rabbinical College Bobover Yeshiva B'nei Zion
1577 48th St., Brooklyn 11219

† Rabbinical College Ch' San Sofer of New York
1876 50th St., Brooklyn 11204
Rabbi William Greenwald, Registrar

† Rabbinical College of Long Island
201 Magnolia Blvd., Long Beach 11561

† Rabbinical Seminary Adas Yereim
185 Wilson St., Brooklyn 11211

† Rabbinical Seminary M'Kor Chaim
1571 55th St., Brooklyn 11219
Rabbi Benjamin Paler, President

† Rabbinical Seminary of America
9215 69th Ave., Forest Hills 11375
Abraham Ginzberg, Asst. to the Dean

† Shor Yoshuv Rabbinical College
1526 Central Ave., Far Rockaway 11691

Talmudical Institute of Upstate New York
796 Park Ave., Rochester 14607

† Talmudical Seminary Oholei Torah
667 Eastern Pky., Brooklyn 11213

† Torah Temimah Talmudical Seminary
555 Ocean Pkwy., Brooklyn 11218

† United Talmudical Academy
82 Lee Ave., Brooklyn 11211

Yeshiva and Kolel Bais Medrash Elyon
73 Main St., Monsey 10952

Yeshiva and Kollel Harbotzas Torah
1049 E. 15th St., Brooklyn 11230

Yeshiva and Mesivta Kol Torah
4823B 48th St., Brooklyn 11224

† Yeshiva Derech Chaim
1573 39th St., Brooklyn 11218

Yeshiva Gedolah Bais Yisroel
2002 Avenue J, Brooklyn 11210

Yeshiva Gedolah Imrei Yosef D'Spinka
1460 56th St., Brooklyn 11219

† Yeshiva Karlin Stolin
1818 54th St., Brooklyn 11204

† Yeshiva of Nitra-Yeshiva Farm Settlement
194 Division Ave. Brooklyn 11211

† Yeshiva Shaar HaTorah Talmudic Research Institute
8396 117th St., Kew Gardens 11418

† Yeshivath Viznitz, P.O. Box 446, Monsey 10952

† Yeshivath Zichron Moshe
Laurel Park Rd., South Fallsburg 12779
Rabbi Abba Gorelick, Registrar

† Yeshivat Mikdash Melech
1326 Ocean Pky., Brooklyn 11230

OHIO

Hebrew Union College
Jewish Institute of Religion
3101 Clifton Ave., Cincinnati 45220
Rabbi Gary Zola, National Dean of Admissions

† Rabbinical College of Telshe
28400 Euclid Ave., Wickliffe 44092

PENNSYLVANIA

Reconstructionist Rabbinical College
Greenwood Ave. & Church Rd., Wyncote 19095

† Talmudical Yeshiva of Philadelphia
6063 Drexel Rd., Philadelphia 19131

† Yeshiva Beth Moshe
930 Hickory St., Scranton 18505
Rabbi Hershel Horowitz, Exec. Dir.

SECRETARIAL SCIENCE

ALABAMA

Alabama A & M University
P.O. Box 429, Normal 35762
Dr. Constance Dees, Interim Dean
See listing under "Universities"

· Gadsden State Community College
P.O. Box 227, Gadsden 35902
W. Bryan Stone, Dir. of Admis.

Judson College
P O Box 120, Marion 36756

Oakwood College
Oakwood Rd., N.W., Huntsville 35896

University of Alabama at Birmingham
University Station, Birmingham 35294

University of Montevallo, Montevallo 35115

· Walker College
1411 Indiana Ave., Jasper 35501
James West, Dir. of Admis.

ALASKA

· Alaska Junior College
800 E. Dimond Blvd. # 3-350
Anchorage 99515

ARIZONA

· Academy of Business College
3320 W. Cheryl Dr. #115, Phoenix 85051
See listing under "Community and Junior Colleges"

· Arizona Western College
P.O. Box 929, Yuma 85366-0929
Bob Davis, Dir. of Admis.

· Gateway Community College
108 N. 40th St., Phoenix 85034
Bill Harris, Dean of Student Services

· Lamson Junior College
1980 W. Main #250, Mesa 85201
Kirt Hamm, Dir. of Admis.

· Yavapai College
1100 E. Sheldon St., Prescott 86301
Dr. Doreen Dailey, President
602-445-7300
See listing under "Community and Junior Colleges"

ARKANSAS

Arkansas State University
P.O. Box 2771, State University 72467

John Brown University
2000 W. University, Siloam Springs 72761
Don Crandall, Director of Enrollment Management

· Phillips County Community College
P.O. Box 785, Helena 72342
Dr. Steven Jones, President
James R. Brasel, Dean of Admissions

University of Arkansas at Monticello
P.O. Box 3596, Monticello 71656

Williams Baptist College
P.O. Box 3667, Walnut Ridge 72476
Scott Wright, Dir. of Admis.

CALIFORNIA

: Bryan College of Court Reporting
2511 Beverly Blvd., Los Angeles 90057
Nancy Patterson, Director
213-484-8850

· City College of San Francisco
50 Phelan Ave. C105, San Francisco 94112
Lavaine Koffman, Dept. Chair
415-239-3203

: **EMPIRE COLLEGE**
SCHOOL OF BUSINESS & LAW
3033 Cleveland Ave. # 107, Santa Rosa 95403
707-546-4000
Established 1961. Private. Coed. Accreditation:
ACICS/Committee of Bar Examiners. Tuition: $3,720
- $7,290. Fees: $75 - $95. Enrollment: 700 full-time, 25
part-time. Faculty: 50. Student-faculty ratio: 21:1.
Specialized Associate degree offered in Accounting
and Administrative Assistant; Juris Doctor. 1 21,000
sq. ft. building. Positive, supportive environment for
students in the business school with start dates every
six weeks; evening law classes taught by practicing
attorneys.

· Heald Business College
777 Southland Dr. #210, Hayward 94545
Shelli Spangler, Director

La Sierra University
4700 Pierce St., Riverside 92505
800-874-5587

· Porterville College
100 E. College Ave., Porterville 93257
John McCuen, President

San Francisco State University
1600 Holloway Ave., San Francisco 94132
Corwin Bjonerud, Dir. of Admis.

· San Joaquin Valley College
8400 W. Mineral King Ave., Visalia 93291
Robert Perry, President

· Santa Barbara City College
721 Cliff Dr., Santa Barbara 93109
805-965-0581

: Sawyer College
2101 E. Gonzales Rd., Oxnard 93030
Roger Ferguson, Dir. of Education

COLORADO

Adams State College, Alamosa 81102
Cheryl Billingsley, Dir. of Admis.
800-824-6494

· Colorado Northwestern Community College
500 Kennedy Dr., Rangely 81648
Pat Kalahar, Dir. Marketing/Recruitment
800-562-1105

· Front Range Community College
3645 W. 112th Ave., Westminister 80030
Dr. Patricia Lammers, Dir. of Admis.

Mesa State College
P.O. Box 2647, Grand Junction 81502
Sherri Pe'a, Dir. of Admis.

· Pikes Peak Community College
5675 S. Academy Blvd.
Colorado Springs 80906-5498
Roberta Erickson, Dir. of Admis.
See listing under "Community and Junior Colleges"

CONNECTICUT

· Katharine Gibbs School
142 East Ave., Norwalk 06851
Henry Mondschein, Dir. of Admis.

· Mattatuck Community College
750 Chase Parkway, Waterbury 06708
Dr. Richard Sanders, President

DELAWARE

Goldey Beacom College
4701 Limestone Rd., Wilmington 19808
Sherry Humphrey, Dean of Admissions

DISTRICT OF COLUMBIA

University of the District of Columbia
Georgia Ave.-Harvard St. Campus
1100 Harvard St., N.W., Washington 20009

University of the District of Columbia
Van Ness Campus
4200 Connecticut Ave., N.W., Washington 20008

FLORIDA

Clearwater Christian College
3400 Gulf-to-Bay Blvd., Clearwater 34619
Benjamin Puckett, Dir. of Admis.

· Edison Community College
8099 College Pky., Fort Myers 33919
Mailing address: P.O. Box 60210
Fort Myers 33906-6210
Sandra Fahey, Dir. of Admis. and Records

· Gulf Coast Community College
5230 Hwy. 98, W., Panama City 32401
Roy Smith, Dir. of Admis. and Records

Jones College
5353 Arlington Expy., Jacksonville 32211
Dorothy D. Jones, Chief Executive Officer

Jones College
5975 Sunset Dr. #100, South Miami 33143

GEORGIA

Georgia College
231 W. Hancock St., Milledgeville 31061
912-453-5004

· Phillips Junior College
1400 W. Peachtree St., N.W., Atlanta 30309

: Quality Plus Business School
1655 Peachtree Rd. N.E. #450, Atlanta
30309-2432

Savannah State College
State College Branch, Savannah 31404
Robert Ray, Dir. of Admis.

West Georgia College, Carrollton 30118
C. Doyle Bickers, Dir. of Admis.

HAWAII

· Heald Business College
1500 Kapiolani Blvd. #202, Honolulu 96814
Evelyn Schemmel, President
808-955-1500 Fax: 808-955-6964

IDAHO

University of Idaho, Moscow 83843
Peter Brown, Dir. of Admis.

ILLINOIS

: Commonwealth Business College
1527 47th Ave., Moline 61265
Don Watson, Director
309-762-2100

Eastern Illinois University, Charleston 61920
Ted Ivarie, Business School Dean
See listing under "Universities"

: **FOX COLLEGE OF EXECUTIVE/LEGAL
ASSISTANTS**
4201 W. 93rd St., Oak Lawn 60453
Edward L. Kay, Director
See listing under "Career Schools"

Lincoln Christian College
100 Campus View Dr., Lincoln 62656
Mr. Lynn Laughlin, Dir. of Admis.

: Marycrest College
280 E. Merchant St., Kankakee 60901
Michael Steinbach, Director

· Midstate College
244 S.W. Jefferson St., Peoria 61602
R. Dale Bunch, President
309-673-6365

Northern Illinois University, De Kalb 60115

· Parkland College
2400 W. Bradley Ave., Champaign 61821-1899
217-351-2208 or 800-346-8089

: **ROCKFORD BUSINESS COLLEGE**
730 N. Church St., Rockford 61103
David Swank, President
815-965-8616

INDIANA

Ball State University
2000 W. University Ave., Muncie 47306
Ruth Vedvik, Dir. of Admis.

: Commonwealth Business College
8995 N. State Rd. 39, La Porte 46350
Faye Mercer, Director
219-362-3338

: Commonwealth Business College
4200 W. Lincoln Hwy., Merrillville 46410
Al Conaway, Director
219-769-3321

: **SAWYER COLLEGE**
6040 Hohman Ave., Hammond 46320
Mary Jo Dixon, Director
800-964-0208

: **SAWYER COLLEGE**
3803 E. Lincoln Hwy., Merrillville 46410
Mary Jo Dixon, Director
800-964-0218

IOWA

· American Institute of Business
2500 Fleur Dr., Des Moines 50321
Tom Shively, Dir. of Admis.

Dordt College
498 4th Ave., N.E., Sioux Center 51250
Quentin Van Essen, Dir. of Admissions
800-343-6738

Faith Baptist Bible College & Theological Seminary
1900 N.W. 4th St., Ankeny 50021
Jeff Newman, Director of Admissions
Admissions: 800-352-0147

· Hawkeye Community College
1501 E. Orange Rd., Waterloo 50701
319-296-2320 Ext. 4000

· Iowa Lakes Community College
3200 College Dr., Emmetsburg 50536
John Nelson, Dir. of Admis.
712-852-3554

· Southeastern Community College
P.O. Box 27, Keokuk 52632
John Adkins, Director

· Southeastern Community College
P.O. Box F., West Burlington 52655
Edward Schieffer, Director

: Spencer College
217 W. 5th St., Spencer 51301
Harvey Work, Director
See listing under "Career Schools"

University of Northern Iowa, Cedar Falls 50614

Upper Iowa University
P.O. Box 1857, Fayette 52142

KANSAS

COLBY COMMUNITY COLLEGE
1255 S. Range Ave., Colby 67701
Theron Johnson, Dir. of Admis.

· Dodge City Community College
2501 N. 14th Ave., Dodge City 67801
Debbie Lloyd, Director of Admissions
800-FOR-DCCC

Fort Hays State University
600 Park St., Hays 67601-4099
Dr. Walley Guyot, Chrpsn.

· Hutchinson Community College
1300 N. Plum St., Hutchinson 67501
Duane Halpain, Dir. of Admis.

: Wichita Business College
501 E. Pawnee St. #515, Wichita 67211
See listing under "Career Schools"

KENTUCKY

Morehead State University, Morehead 40351
Charles Myers, Director of Admissions
606-783-2000

Murray State University, Murray 42071
Phil Bryan, Director of Admissions
800-272-4MSU

· Sue Bennett College
101 College St., London 40741
Don A. Gorbandt, Dir. of Admis.

LOUISIANA

Louisiana College
College Station, Pineville 71359
Byron McGee, Dir. of Admis.
318-487-7386
See listing under "Liberal Arts"

Southeastern Louisiana University
P.O. Box 784, Hammond 70404

MAINE

HUSSON COLLEGE
Eastern Maine Medical Center
One College Circle, Bangor 04401
William Beardsley, President
800-4HU-SSON
See listing under "Business and Management"

· Northern Maine Technical College
33 Edgemont Dr., Presque Isle 04769

Thomas College
180 W. River Rd., Waterville 04901
Susan Potter, Dir. of Admis.
207-877-0101, ME only 800-339-7001

University of Maine
9 O'Brien Ave., Machias 04654

MARYLAND

: Fleet Business School
2530 Riva Rd. #201, Annapolis 21401
Kenan Habetler, Dir. of Admis.

: Medix School
1017 York Rd., Towson 21204
Richard Stensing, Dir. of Admis.

· Montgomery College
51 Mannakee St., Rockville 20850
Germantown - 301-353-7805
Rockville - 301-279-5184
Takoma Park - 301-650-1453

: TESST Electronics and Computer Institute
5122 Baltimore Ave., Hyattsville 20781
Joseph W. Fox, Director
301-864-5750

Villa Julie College
1525 Greenspring Valley Rd., Stevenson 21153
Carolyn Manuszak, President

MASSACHUSETTS

· Aquinas College
15 Walnut Park, Newton 02158
Ellen Ronayne, Dir. of Admis.

· Aquinas College at Milton
303 Adams St., Milton 02186
617-696-3100

: **BURDETT SCHOOL**
745 Boylston St., Boston 02116
Maralin Manning, President
617-859-1900

· **DEAN COLLEGE**
99 Main St, Franklin 02038
Kathleen Teehan, Dean of Admissions
508-528-9100
See listing under "Community and Junior Colleges"

· Endicott College
376 Hale St., Beverly 01915
Elizabeth Macomber, Dir. of Admis.

· Fisher College
118 Beacon St., Boston 02116
Sandra Robbins, Dir. of Admis.

: Kinyon-Campbell Business School
59 Linden St., New Bedford 02740
David Daganhardt, Director

· **MARIAN COURT COLLEGE**
35 Little's Point Rd., Swampscott 01907
Jodi T. Quinn, Dir. of Admis.
617-595-6768

· Massasoit Community College
1 Massasoit Blvd., Brockton 02402
Roberta Noodell, Dir. of Admis.

· Middlesex Community College
33 Kearney Sq., Lowell 01852
508-656-3211

· North Shore Community College
1 Ferncroft Rd., Danvers 01923

· Quinsigamond Community College
670 W. Boylston St., Worcester 01606
Ron Smith, Dir. of Admis.

· **SPRINGFIELD TECHNICAL COMMUNITY
COLLEGE**
1 Armory Square, Springfield 01105
Dr. Patrick E. Tigue, Dir. of Admissions
413-781-7822

MICHIGAN

Baker College of Auburn Hills
1500 University Dr., Auburn Hills 48326
John A. Tomaszewski, Dir. of Admis.

Baker College of Cadillac
9600 E. 13th St., Cadillac 49601
Candace Baldwin, Dir. of Admis.

Baker College of Flint
1050 W. Bristol Rd., Flint 48507
Mark Heaton, Dir. of Admis.

Baker College of Mount Clemens
34950 Little Mack Ave., Clinton Township 48035
Annette M. Wendling, Dir. of Admis.

Baker College of Muskegon
141 Hartford Ave., Muskegon 49442
Kathy Jacobson, Dir. of Admis.

Baker College of Owosso
1020 S. Washington St., Owosso 48867
Bruce A. Lundeen, Dir. of Admis.

Baker College of Port Huron
3403 Lapeer Rd., Port Huron 48060
David C. Hickman, Dir. of Admis.

Cleary College - Livingston Campus
3750 Cleary College Dr., Howell 48843
Tom Sullivan, President
800-589-1979

Cleary College - Washtenaw Campus
2170 Washtenaw Ave., Ypsilanti 48197
Tom Sullivan, President
800-686-1883

Davenport College of Business
67 Michigan Ave. W., Battle Creek 49017

Davenport College of Business
220 E. Kalamazoo St., Lansing 48933
Don Colizzi, Dean

Detroit College of Business
4801 Oakman Blvd., Dearborn 48126
James Farmer, V.P. for Admissions

Detroit College of Business-Flint
3115 Lawndale Ave., Flint 48504

Eastern Michigan University, Ypsilanti 48197
H. James Rokusek, Head
313-487-3060 or 800-GO-TO-EMU

· Jackson Community College
2111 Emmons Rd., Jackson 49201
Mark Ulseth, Dir. Enrollment Services

Lake Superior State University
1000 College Dr., Sault St. Marie 49783

Marygrove College
8425 W. McNichols Rd., Detroit 48221

: Northeastern School of Commerce
701 N. Madison Ave., Bay City   48708
Louis H. Bork, Director

MINNESOTA

: Duluth Business University
412 W. Superior St., Duluth   55802
Bonnie Kupczynski, Director

· Inver Hills Community College
8445 College Trail, E., Inver Grove Heights   55076
Cheryl Frank, Director

Northwestern College
3003 Snelling Ave., N., St. Paul   55113
Ralph Anderson, Dean of Admissions
800-827-6827 or 612-631-5111

· Northwest Technical College
1900 28th Ave., S., Moorhead   56560
Dale White, Dir. of Admis.
218-299-6512

PILLSBURY BAPTIST BIBLE COLLEGE
315 S. Grove St., Owatonna   55060
Alan Potter, President
Larry Tindall, Director of Admissions
800-747-4557

Southwest State University, Marshall   56258

UNIVERSITY OF MINNESOTA-CROOKSTON
2900 University Ave., Crookston   56716
John Bywater, Dir. of Admis.
800-232-6466
See listing under "Universities"

Winona State University
P.O. Box 5838, Winona   55987
Dr. J. Mootz, Dir. of Admis.

MISSISSIPPI

Mississippi College
P.O. Box 4086, Clinton   39058

MISSOURI

College of the Ozarks, Point Lookout   65726
Dr. Kenton Olson, Dean of the College

Evangel College
1111 N. Glenstone Ave., Springfield   65802
David Schoolfield, Dir. of Enrollment

· North Central Missouri College
1301 Main St., Trenton   64683
Carolyn Smith, Program Director
816-359-3948 ext. 323 or 800-880-6180

Southwest Baptist University
1601 S. Springfield Ave., Bolivar   65613

Southwest Missouri State University
901 S. National Ave., Springfield   65804
Dr. Arnola Ownby, Department Head
417-836-5616

MONTANA

· Missoula Vocational Technical Center
909 South Ave. W, Missoula   59801
Charles Couture, Dir. of Admis.

Montana State University - Billings
1500 N. 30th St., Billings   59101
Karen Everett, Dir. of Admis.
406-657-2158

NEBRASKA

Midland Lutheran College
900 Clarkson St., Fremont   68025
Roland Kahnk, V.P. Admissions

· Northeast Community College
P.O. Box 469, Norfolk   68702
Eugene Hart, Dir. of Admis.

University of Nebraska
905 W. 25th St., Kearney   68849

Wayne State College
200 E. Tenth St., Wayne   68787

· Western Nebraska Community College
1601 E. 27th St., Scottsbluff   69361
Roger Hovey, Admissions

· Western Nebraska Community College
Sidney   69162
Jim Copley, Admissions

NEVADA

· Phillips Junior College
3320 E. Flamingo Rd. #30, Las Vegas   89121
Robert Ramey, Dir. of Admis.

NEW HAMPSHIRE

· New Hampshire Technical College at Stratham
277 R. Portsmouth Ave., Stratham   03885
Patricia A. Shay, Dean of Students

NEW JERSEY

· **BERKELEY COLLEGE OF BUSINESS**
44 Rifle Camp Rd., West Paterson   07424
Kevin Luing, President
800-446-5400 ext. GQ1

· **BERKELEY COLLEGE OF BUSINESS**
430 Rahway Ave., Woodbridge   07095
Kevin Luing, President
800-446-5400 ext. GQ1

BERKELEY COLLEGE OF BUSINESS
100 W. Prospect St., Waldwick   07463
Kevin Luing, President
800-446-5400 ext. GQ1

· Ho-Ho-Kus School of Secretarial and Medical
Sciences
27 S. Franklin Trnpk., Ramsey   07446
Thomas Eastwick, Director
201-327-8877

: Hudson County Community College
168 Sip Ave., Jersey City   07306
Joseph O'Halloran, Director of Admissions
201-714-2127

: Plaza School of Technology
Bergen Mall, Paramus   07652
Mark Ricciardi, Director
201-843-0344

Rider University
2083 Lawrenceville Rd., Lawrenceville   08648
Susan Christian, Dir. of Admis.

NEW MEXICO

· Albuquerque Technical-Vocational Institute
525 Buena Vista Dr., S.E., Albuquerque   87106
Jane Campbell, Registrar
See listing under "Career Schools"

Eastern New Mexico University
Portales   88130
Larry Fuqua, Dir. of Admis.

· Eastern New Mexico University-Roswell Campus
P.O. Box 6000, Roswell   88202
Tim Raftery, Director of Admissions and Records

NEW YORK

· **BERKELEY COLLEGE**
40 W. Red Oak Ln., White Plains   10604
Rose Mary Healy, President
800-446-5400 ext. GQ1

· **BERKELEY COLLEGE**
3 E. 43rd St., New York   10017
Dr. Glen Zeitzer, President
800-446-5400 ext. GQ1

· Bryant & Stratton Business Institute
1259 Central Ave., Albany   12205
Bob Flynn, Dir. of Admis.

CAZENOVIA COLLEGE
Cazenovia   13035
Dr. James Parker, VP for Enrollment Management
See listing under "Universities"

· CUNY Borough of Manhattan Community College
199 Chambers St., New York   10007

: Elmira Business Institute
180 Clemens Center Pkwy., Elmira   14901
Brad Phillips, Director
607-733-7177

· **FIVE TOWNS COLLEGE**
305 N. Service Rd., Dix Hills   11746
Jennifer Roemer, Coordinator of Admissions
516-424-7000
See listing under "Universities"

· Jamestown Business College
P.O. Box 429, Jamestown   14702
David Spencer, Registrar

· Katharine Gibbs School
535 Brood Hollow Rd., Melville   11747
516-293-2460

: **KRISSLER BUSINESS INSTITUTE**
166 Mansion St., Poughkeepsie   12601
Established 1936. Modern office technologies
914-471-0330

: Long Island Business Institute
6500 Jericho Turnpike, Commack   11725
Genevieve Baron, Director
516-499-7100
See listing under "Career Schools"

· Maria College of Albany
700 New Scotland Ave., Albany   12208
Laurie Gilmore, Dir. of Admis.

· Mater Dei College
Riverside Dr., Ogdensburg   13669
Mark Dougherty, Dir. of Admis.

Nazareth College of Rochester
4245 East Ave., Rochester   14618
Paul Kenyon, Dir. of Admis.

New York Institute of Technology
Old Westbury Campus, Old Westbury   11568

· Olean Business Institute
301 N. Union St., Olean   14760
Patrick McCarthy, Director
Jeanne Johnston, Director of Admissions
716-372-7978

· **PLAZA BUSINESS INSTITUTE**
7409 37th Ave., Jackson Heights   11372
Sally Ann Weger, Director of Admissions
718-779-1430

· Rochester Business Institute
1850 Ridge Rd. E., Rochester   14622

· SUNY Adirondack Community College
439 Bay Rd., Queensbury   12804
Levi Brown, Dir. of Admis.
518-793-4491
See listing under "Community and Junior Colleges"

· SUNY College of Agriculture and Technology
Morrisville   13408
Dennis Nostrand, Dir. of Admis.

· SUNY College of Technology
34 Cornell Dr., Canton   13617
Thomas R. Fletcher, Director of Admissions
800-388-7123

· SUNY Nassau Community College
1 Education Dr., Garden City   11530
Bernard Iantosca, Dir of Admis.

· SUNY Onondaga Community College
Onondaga Rd., Syracuse   13215
Joseph Insel, Dir. of Admis.

· SUNY Schenectady County Community College
78 Washington Ave., Schenectady   12305
Robert Dinello, Dir. of Admis.
518-346-6211, ext. 166

· Trocaire College
110 Red Jacket Pky., Buffalo   14220
Irene Cuddihy, Dean of Business
716-826-1200

· Utica School of Commerce
201 Bleecker St., Utica   13501
Judith Kelly, Dir. of Admis.

· Villa Maria College of Buffalo
240 Pine Ridge Rd., Buffalo   14225
Lynn D'Auria, Dir. of Admis.

· Westchester Business Institute
325 Central Ave., White Plains   10606
Dale Smith, Dean of Admissions

· Wood School
8 E. 40th St., New York   10016
Rosemary Duggan, President

NORTH CAROLINA

· Alamance Community College
P.O. Box 623, Haw River   27258
W. Ronald McCarter, President

· College of The Albemarle
P.O. Box 2327, Elizabeth City   27906
John M. Wells, Asst. Dean of Admissions
919-335-0821, Ext. 220

· Halifax Community College
P.O. Box 809, Weldon   27890

North Carolina A&T State University
1601 E. Market St., Greensboro   27411

: **SALISBURY BUSINESS COLLEGE**
1400 Jake Alexander Blvd. W., Salisbury   28147
Bill Hensley, President
704-636-4071
Established 1917. Private. Coed. Accreditation: Accrediting Council for Independent Colleges and Schools. Tuition: $2,600. Room and board: $2,000. Fees: $100. Enrollment: 125 full-time, 15 part-time. Faculty: 13. Student-faculty: 15:1. 12,000 square foot building. Individual attention. Once a graduate under any program of study, there is no charge to refresh or retake program of study.

OHIO

· Antonelli Institute of Art & Photography
124 E. 7th St., Cincinnati   45202

· Bradford School
6170 Busch Blvd., Columbus   43229
Patrick Denton, President
614-846-9410

Cincinnati Bible College
P.O. Box 04320, Cincinnati   45204
C. Barry McCarty, President

· Columbus State Community College
550 E. Spring St., Columbus   43215
Mary Jo Deerwester, Dir. of Admis.

· Cuyahoga Community College, Eastern Campus
25444 Harvard Rd., Warrensville Heights   44122

· Cuyahoga Community College, Metropolitan Campus
2900 Community College Ave., Cleveland   44115

· Cuyahoga Community College, Western Campus
11000 W. Pleasant Valley Rd.
Parma Heights   44130

· **DAVIS JUNIOR COLLEGE**
4747 Monroe St., Toledo   43623
Diane Brunner, President
Established 1858. Private. Coed. Accreditation: AICS, AAMA, NCACS. Tuition: $5,600. Fees: $25 application fee. Enrollment: 350 full-time, 100 part-time. Faculty: 35. Student-faculty ratio: 15:1. Degree: associate. Specialized library. 2 buildings including an airport. Admissions test (CPAT) & specialized. High school graduate or GED. Enroll each quarter. 90% placement overall. Unique professional pilot program.

: ESI Career Center
25301 Euclid Ave., Euclid   44117
Tim Duffy & James Arcaro, Directors

: ESI Career Center
1985 N. Ridge Rd., Lorain   44055
216-277-8832

Hocking College
3301 Hocking Pky., Nelsonville 45764
Candace Vancko, VP for Enrollment
800-282-4163

Kent State University
P.O. Box 5190, Kent 44242
Bruce Riddle, Dir. of Admis.

Kent State University-Ashtabula Campus
3325 W. 13th St., Ashtabula 44004
John Mahan, Dean

Kent State University-East Liverpool Campus
400 E. 4th St., East Liverpool 43920
Suzanne Fitzgerald, Dean

Kent State University-Salem Campus
2491 State Rt. 45 S., Salem 44460
Dr. James Cooney, Dean

Kent State University-Trumbull Campus
4314 Mahoning Ave. N.W., Warren 44483
Dr. John Cable, Dean

Lima Technical College
4240 Campus Dr., Lima 45804
Cynthia E. Spiers, Director of Admissions

Lorain County Community College
1005 Abbe Rd., N., Elyria 44035
Dr. John W. Thrash, Jr., Registrar

Mt. Vernon Nazarene College
800 Martinsburg Rd., Mt. Vernon 43050
Ronald Hyson, Dir. of Admis.

OHIO VALLEY BUSINESS COLLEGE
500 Maryland Ave., East Liverpool 43920
216-385-1070

Owens Community College
P.O. Box 10000, Toledo 43699
Jim Welling, Admissions
419-661-7225

Owens Community College
300 Davis St., Findlay 45840
Stacy Davidson, Admissions
419-423-6827

Shawnee State University
940 2nd St., Portsmouth 45662
Rosemary K. Poston, Dir. of Admis.

Southeastern Business College
1907 N. Ridge Rd., Lorain 44055
Nancy Bonzar, Dir. of Admis.

Southeastern Business College
1855 Western Ave., Chillicothe 45601
John T. Danicki, Executive Director

Southeastern Business College
420 E. Main St., Jackson 45640
Janet Travis, Director

Southeastern Business College
1522 Sheridan Dr., Lancaster 43130
Alex Bosserman, Director

Southeastern Business College
3879 Rhodes Ave., New Boston 45662
Annita Thompson, Director

University of Rio Grande
General Delivery, Rio Grande 45674
Dr. Paul Shoemaker, Associate Professor
614-245-5353, Ext. 7301

OKLAHOMA

Oklahoma Christian University of Science and Arts
P.O. Box 11000, Oklahoma City 73136
Duane Eggleston, Vice President
800-877-5010

Oklahoma Panhandle State University
P.O. Box 430, Goodwell 73939

Southern Nazarene University
6729 N.W. 39th Expy., Bethany 73008

OREGON

Central Oregon Community College
2600 N.W. College Way, Bend 97701
Christine Kerlin, Dir. of Admis.
503-383-7500

Treasure Valley Community College
650 College Blvd., Ontario 97914
Ron Kulm, Dir. of Admis.

PENNSYLVANIA

Antonelli Medical & Professional Institute
1700 Industrial Hwy., Pottstown 19464
Paula Bauer, Dir. of Admis.

Cambria-Rowe Business College
221 Central Ave., Johnstown 15902
William M. Coward, President

Erie Business Center
246 W. 9th St., Erie 16501
Tony Piccirillo, Dir. of Admis.
See listing under "Career Schools"

Geneva College
3200 College Ave., Beaver Falls 15010

Harcum Junior College, Bryn Mawr 19010
Mary Pontius, Dean of Admissions

McCann School of Business
47 S. Main St., Mahanoy City 17948
John Slodysko, Director

McCann School of Business
Wilkes Barre Campus
2004 Wyoming Ave., Wyoming 18644
James Noone, Director

Marywood College
2300 Adams Ave., Scranton 18509

Montgomery County Community College
340 DeKalb Pike, Blue Bell 19422-0758
Dennis Murphy, Dir. of Admis.

NEC-Allentown Business School Campus
1501 Lehigh St., Allentown 18103
610-791-5100

Pennsylvania Institute of Technology
Rose Valley-Notre Dame Campus
800 Manchester Ave., Media 19063
610-565-7900

Reading Area Community College
P.O. Box 1706, Reading 19603
Robin Sodomsky, Dir. of Admis.

Robert Morris College
Narrows Run Rd., Coraopolis 15108
James R. Welsh, Dean of Admissions
See listing under "Universities"

Robert Morris College
600 5th Ave., Pittsburgh 15219
James R. Welsh, Dean of Admissions
See listing under "Universities"

Shenango Valley School of Business
500 S. Mill St., New Castle 16101
412-654-1976

Shenango Valley School of Business
124 W. Spring St., Titusville 16354
814-827-9567

Shenango Valley School of Business
335 Boyd Dr., Sharon 16146
412-983-0700

SOUTH HILLS BUSINESS SCHOOL
480 Waupelani Dr., State College 16801-4516
Maralyn Mazza, Director
Admissions: 814-234-7755
Established 1970. Private. Coed. Tuition: $6,420 per year. Enrollment: 350. Faculty: 50. Accredited by CCA. ASB degrees in accounting, management, secretarial, computer information systems and health information technology. Diplomas in accounting, secretarial, clerical, retail management, travel, and microcomputers. One and two-year programs available. Financial aid, counseling and placement assistance. Housing nearby, cafeteria and day care facilities.

Yorktowne Business Institute
0 W. 7th Ave., York 17404
John Halpin, Admissions Representative

RHODE ISLAND

Johnson & Wales University
111 Dorrance St., Providence 02903
Mark S. Burke, Dir. of Admis.

Katharine Gibbs School
178 Butler Ave., Providence 02906
401-861-1420

Nasson Institute
1080 Newport Ave., Pawtucket 02861

School of Medical & Legal Secretarial Sciences
60 S. Angell St., Providence 02906
Norma Casale, Director

SOUTH CAROLINA

Spartanburg Technical College
P.O. Box 4386, Spartanburg 29305
Pam Hagan, Dir. Admissions & Counseling
803-591-3800

University of South Carolina, Columbia 29208
Terry Davis, Dir. of Admis.
803-777-7700

SOUTH DAKOTA

Dakota State University
820 N. Washington Ave., Madison 57042
Dr. Richard Puetz, Dean
605-256-5139

Dakota Wesleyan University
1300 W. University Ave., Mitchell 57301

Kilian Community College
224 N. Phillips Ave., Sioux Falls 57102
605-336-1711 or 800-888-1147

Nettleton Junior College
100 S. Spring Ave., Sioux Falls 57104
Herman Whitaker, Dir. of Admissions
800-727-1837 or 605-336-1837

Presentation College
1500 N. Main St., Aberdeen 57401
Sr. Lucille Welbig, Dir. of Admis.

Stenotype Institute
705 W. Avenue N, Sioux Falls 57104
Linda Clauson, President

Western Dakota Technical Institute
1600 Sedivy Ln., Rapid City 57701
See listing under "Career Schools"

TENNESSEE

Austin Peay State University
601 College St., Clarksville 37044

David Lipscomb University
3901 Granny White Pike, Nashville 37204-3951
Wade Sandrell, Dir. of Admis.
800-333-4358

Freed-Hardeman University
158 E. Main St., Henderson 38340
800-342-7837

Lincoln Memorial University
P.O. Box 2012, Harrogate 37752
Conrad Daniels, Dir. of Admis.

Tennessee Temple University
1815 Union Ave., Chattanooga 37404
Dr. L. W. Nichols, President

Trevecca Nazarene College
333 Murfreesboro Rd., Nashville 37210

University of Tennessee at Martin
Martin 38238
Paul Kelley, Director of Admissions
See listing under "Universities"

TEXAS

Court Reporting Institute of Dallas
8585 N. Stemmons Freeway, Suite 200 North
Dallas 75247
Debra E. Smith, Dir. of Admis.
214-350-9722

East Texas Baptist University
1200 N. Grove Ave., Marshall 75670

Hallmark Institute of Technology
North Campus-Electronics Technology
& Business Courses
10401 W. IH 10, San Antonio 78230
Richard Fessler, President
Jeanne Martin, Campus Director
210-690-9000

Midwestern State University
3400 Taft Blvd., Wichita Falls 76308

Texas A & I University
Campus Box 101, Kingsville 78363

Texas School of Business
711 Air Tex Dr., Houston 77073
Madeline Burillo, Director
713-846-2888

Texas Women's University
P.O. Box 23925, Denton 76204

UTAH

Southern Utah University
351 W. Center St., Cedar City 84720
D. Mark Barton, Asst. VP Student Services
801-586-7740

Utah State University, Logan 84322-1600
Rod Clark, Director of Admissions
801-750-1107

VERMONT

Castleton State College, Castleton 05735
Gary Fallis, Dir. of Admis.

Champlain College
P.O. Box 670, Burlington 05402
Josephine Churchill, Dir. of Admis.
802-860-2727
See listing under "Universities"

Vermont Technical College
Randolph Center 05061
Robert Clarke, President

VIRGINIA

Commonwealth College
300 Boush St., Norfolk 23510
Debbi Huck, Dean of Admissions

Commonwealth College
4160 Virginia Beach Blvd., Virginia Beach 23452
Nancy Kennedy, Dean of Admissions

Commonwealth College
1120 W. Mercury Blvd., Hampton 23666
Robyn Rickenbach, Dean of Admissions

Tidewater Community College, Portsmouth Campus
Rt. 135, Portsmouth 23703
Dr. Larry L. Whitworth, President

Virginia Intermont College
1013 Moore St., Bristol 24201
Lawton Blandford, Dir. of Admis.

WASHINGTON

Capitol Business College
5005 Pacific Hwy. E., Ste. 11
Olympia 98424

Central Washington University, Ellensburg 98926
William Swain, Director of Admissions

Northwest College of the Assemblies of God
P.O. Box 579, Kirkland 98083-0579
Bob Foster, Dir. of Public Relations

Skagit Valley College
2405 E. College Way, Mt. Vernon 98273

Walla Walla College
204 S. College Ave., College Place 99324

Walla Walla Community College
500 Tausick Way, Walla Walla 99362
Dan Biagi, Director
509-527-4283
See listing under "Community and Junior Colleges"

WISCONSIN

· Lakeshore Technical College
    1290 North Ave., Cleveland   53015

· Madison Junior College of Business
    1110 Spring Harbor Dr., Madison   53705
    Jeffry S. Sears, President
    608-238-4266

· **STRATTON COLLEGE**
    1300 N. Jackson St., Milwaukee   53202
    Robert H. Ley, Director
    414-276-5200

University of Wisconsin, Eau Claire
    Eau Claire   54701

: Western Wisconsin Technical College
    304 N. 6th St., La Crosse   54602

WYOMING

· Western Wyoming Community College
    2500 College Dr., Rock Springs   82901
    Jackie Freeze, Dir. of Admis.
    See listing under "Community and Junior Colleges"

GUAM

: International Business College of Guam
    P.O. Box 3783, Agana   96910
    Director of Admissions

PUERTO RICO

Bayamon Central University
    P.O. Box 1725, Bayamon   00960-1725
    Christine Hernandez, Dir. of Admis.

Catholic University of Puerto Rico
    Las Americas Ave., Ponce   00732
    Carilin Frau, Dir. of Admis.

Universidad Adventista de las Antillas
    P.O. Box 118, Mayaguez   00681
    Wilma Gonzalez, Dir. of Admis.

University of Puerto Rico
    Arecibo Technical University College
    P.O. Box A-1806, Arecibo   00613

University of Puerto Rico
    Bayamon Technical University College
    Bayamon   00959

University of Puerto Rico
    CUH Station Rd. 908 Bo Tejas, Humacao   00791

University of Puerto Rico, Mayaguez Campus
    P.O. Box 5000, Mayaguez   00681
    Neysa Lopez, Dir. of Admis.

University of Puerto Rico
    Ponce Technological University College
    P.O. Box 7186, Ponce   00732

University of Puerto Rico, Rio Piedras Campus
    P.O. Box 23300, San Juan   00931
    Victor Lopez, Dir. of Admis.

SOCIAL SCIENCE

ALABAMA

Alabama A & M University
    P.O. Box 302, Normal   35762
    Shelly Wyckoff, Chrpsn.
    See listing under "Universities"

Alabama State University
    P.O. Box 271, Montgomery   36101

Auburn University, Auburn   36849

· Gadsden State Community College
    P.O. Box 227, Gadsden   35902
    W. Bryan Stone, Dir. of Admis.

Huntingdon College
    1500 E. Fairview Ave., Montgomery   36106-2148
    Carolyn A. Phillips, Dean of Enrollment
    800-763-0313

Oakwood College
    Oakwood Rd., N.W., Huntsville   35896

Samford University
    800 Lakeshore Dr., Birmingham   35229
    Hugh Floyd, Chrpsn.

Talladega College
    627 Battle St., W., Talladega   35160

Troy State University, Troy   36082
    Dr. James Kimbrough, Dean

Tuskegee University
    Tuskegee Institute   36088

University of Alabama
    P.O. Box 870132, Tuscaloosa   35487-0132
    Roy Smith, Dir. of Admis.

University of Alabama at Birmingham
    University Station, Birmingham   35294

UNIVERSITY OF ALABAMA IN HUNTSVILLE
    P.O. Box 1247, Huntsville   35899
    Ron R. Koger Ed.D., Dir. of Admis.
    205-895-6070
        Established 1969. Public. Coed. Accreditation: SACS, ABET, NLN, CSAB, ACS. Tuition: $2,418 resident, $4,836 non-resident. Room & Board: $3,450. Undergraduate enrollment: 2,674 full-time, 3,439 part-time. Graduate enrollment: 1,860. Faculty: 282. Student-faculty ratio: 18:1. Degrees: BS, BA, BSBA, BSE, MS, MSM, Ph.D., BSN, MSN, MA. 20 buildings on 350 acres. Comprehensive research university located in the Tennessee Valley of northern Alabama. Huntsville is the locale of major government and private research centers. Metropolitan population approaching 300,000.

University of Montevallo, Montevallo   35115

University of North Alabama
    University Station, Florence   35632

ALASKA

Sheldon Jackson College
    801 Lincoln St., Sitka   99835
    Dennis Trotter, Dir. of Admis.
    907-747-5221

University of Alaska Anchorage
    3211 Providence Dr., Anchorage   99508
    907-786-1480

University of Alaska Fairbanks
    Fairbanks   99775

ARIZONA

Arizona State University, Tempe   85287

Northern Arizona University
    P.O. Box 4092, Flagstaff   86011
    Dr. Margaret Cibik, Dir. of Admis.

University of Arizona, Tucson   85721
    Loyd Bell, Director of Admissions

· Yavapai College
    1100 E. Sheldon St., Prescott   86301
    Dr. Doreen Dailey, President
    602-445-7300
    See listing under "Community and Junior Colleges"

ARKANSAS

Arkansas College
    2300 Highland Rd., Batesville   72501
    Jonathan M. Stroud, Dean of Admissions
    800-423-2542

Arkansas State University
    P.O. Box 1630, State University   72467

Harding University
    900 E. Center Ave., Searcy   72149

John Brown University
    2000 W. University, Siloam Springs   72761
    Don Crandall, Director of Enrollment Management

Ouachita Baptist University
    410 Ouachita St., Arkadelphia   71998
    Randy Garner, Dir. of Admis.
    800-DIAL-OBU

University of Arkansas at Fayetteville
    Fayetteville   72701

University of Arkansas at Little Rock
    2801 S. University Ave., Little Rock   72204

University of Arkansas at Pine Bluff
    1200 University Dr., Pine Bluff   71601-2799

Williams Baptist College
    P.O. Box 3667, Walnut Ridge   72476
    Scott Wright, Dir. of Admis.

CALIFORNIA

Bethany Bible College
    800 Bethany Dr., Scotts Valley   95066
    Randal McNally, Dir. of Admis.

California Baptist College
    8432 Magnolia Ave., Riverside   92504
    800-782-3382

CALIFORNIA COAST UNIVERSITY
    700 N. Main St., Santa Ana   92701
    Admissions Office: 800-854-8768 or 714-547-9625
    Thomas Neal, President
    Linda B. Smith, VP Academic Affairs
    William Barcroft, Dean of Admissions
        Established 1973. Proprietary. Coed. Accreditation: National Association of Private Non-Traditional Schools & Colleges, California State Department of Education, charter member California Association of State Approved Colleges & Universities, member Association for Adult & Continuing Education. Tuition: $2,200-$3,500. Enrollment: 7,500.
        A private college offering off-campus independent study programs in the traditional areas of business administration, management, engineering, psychology, & education. Admissions: rolling trimester, requires official transcripts, letters of recommendation, detailed curriculum vita or occupational history.
        Process: evaluation of prior academic work followed by analysis of occupational history, including participation in workshops, seminars, training programs, specialized projects for credit. Credit is demonstrated by challenge exams or specialized course by course independent study programs.
        Residency: All course work may be completed off campus, utilizing correspondence methods. All doctoral candidates must meet with faculty advisors in person, upon completion of doctoral dissertation. Scholarships: Interest free loans available to students.

California Polytechnic State University
    San Luis Obispo   93407
    Helen Linstrum, Dir. of Admis.

California State Polytechnic University
    3801 W. Temple Ave., Pomona   91768

California State University, Chico
    Chico   95929-0450
    Dr. Rosalind Reed, Coordinator

California State University, Fresno
    Shaw & Cedar Ave., Fresno   93710

California State University, Long Beach
    1250 Bellflower Blvd., Long Beach   90840

California State University, Los Angeles
    5151 Paseo Rancho Castilla, Los Angeles   90032

California State University, Sacramento
    6000 J St., Sacramento   95819

California State University, San Bernardino
    5500 University Pky., San Bernardino   92407
    909-880-5188

Chapman University
    333 N. Glassell St., Orange   92666
    Michael Drummy, Dir. of Admis.

College of Notre Dame
    1500 Ralston Ave., Belmont   94002
    Greg M. Smith, PhD., Dir. of Admis.

Concordia University
    1530 Concordia, Irvine   92715
    Stan Meyer, Dean of Admission
    800-229-1200
    See listing under "Universities"

Fielding Institute
    2112 Santa Barbara St., Santa Barbara   93105
    Sylvia Williams, Dir. of Admis.

Fresno Pacific College
    1717 S. Chestnut Ave., Fresno   93702
    209-453-2039

Hebrew Union College
    Jewish Institute of Religion
    3077 University Ave., Los Angeles   90007
    Rabbi Lee Bycel, Dean

La Sierra University
    4700 Pierce St., Riverside   92505
    800-874-5587

Pacific Union College
    1 Angwin Ave., Angwin   94508
    Dr. Gary Gifford, Dir. of Admis.

San Diego State University
    5300 Campanile Dr., San Diego   92115

San Francisco State University
    1600 Holloway Ave., San Francisco   94132
    Corwin Bjonerud, Dir. of Admis.

San Jose State University
    1 Washington Sq., San Jose   95192

· Santa Barbara City College
    721 Cliff Dr., Santa Barbara   93109
    805-965-0581

Southern California College
    55 Fair Dr., Costa Mesa   92626
    Richard Hardy, Asst. Dean for Enrollment

University of California, Los Angeles
    1247 Murphy Hall, Los Angeles   90024

University of California at Berkeley
    Campbell Hall, Berkeley   94720

University of La Verne
    1950 3rd St., La Verne   91750
    Mark Bornholdt, Dir. of Admis.

University of Southern California
    University Park Campus
    Los Angeles   90089

Whittier College
    13406 Philadelphia St., Whittier   90601
    310-907-4238

Woodbury University
7500 Glenoaks Blvd., Burbank   91504
See listing under "Universities"

COLORADO

Colorado College
14 E. Cache La Poudre, Colorado Springs   80903
Terry Swenson, Dir. of Admis.

Colorado State University
102 Administration Building, Fort Collins   80523
Mary Ontireros, Dir. of Admissions

Mesa State College
P.O. Box 2647, Grand Junction   81502
Sherri Pe'a, Dir. of Admis.

Metropolitan State College of Denver
P.O. Box 173362, Campus Box 16
Denver   80217-3362

Regis University
3333 Regis Blvd., Denver   80221
Robert Blust, Director of Admissions

University of Denver
2199 S. University Blvd., Denver   80210

University of Northern Colorado, Greeley   80639
Roger Kovar, Dean of Arts and Sciences
303-351-2707

University of Southern Colorado
2200 Bonforte Blvd., Pueblo   81001

Western State College of Colorado
Gunnison   81231
Monica Bruning, Dir. of Admis.
See listing under "Universities"

CONNECTICUT

Albertus Magnus College
700 Prospect St., New Haven   06511
Richard Lolatte, Dir. of Admissions
203-773-8501 or 800-578-9160

Mattatuck Community College
750 Chase Parkway, Waterbury   06708
Dr. Richard Sanders, President

Quinnipiac College
275 Mount Carmel Ave., Hamden   06518
See listing under "Universities"

Sacred Heart University
5151 Park Ave., Fairfield   06432-1000
Dr. Anthony J. Cernera, President

St. Joseph College
1678 Asylum Ave., West Hartford   06117
Mary C. Demo, Dir. of Admis.

Southern Connecticut State University
501 Crescent St., New Haven   06515

University of Connecticut, Storrs   06268
Ann Quinley, Dir. of Admis.

University of Connecticut at Hartford
1800 Asylum Ave., West Hartford   06117

University of New Haven
300 Orange Ave., West Haven   06516
Joseph Chepaitis, Dean
203-932-7000

Wesleyan University, Middletown   06459
Karl Furstenberg, Dean of Admissions

Western Connecticut State University
181 White St., Danbury   06810

DELAWARE

Delaware State College
1200 N. DuPont Hwy., Dover   19901
Jethro C. Williams, Dir. of Admis.

DISTRICT OF COLUMBIA

The American University
4400 Massachusetts Ave. N.W.
Washington   20016

Catholic University of America
620 Michigan Ave. N.E., Washington   20064
Robert J. Talbot, Dir. of Admis. & Fin. Aid.

Howard University
2400 6th St., N.W., Washington   20059
James E. Cheek, President

University of the District of Columbia
Van Ness Campus
4200 Connecticut Ave., N.W., Washington   20008

FLORIDA

Barry University
11300 N.E. 2nd Ave., Miami Shores   33161
Robin Ray Roberts, Dean of Admissions

Flagler College
P.O. Box 1027, St. Augustine   32085
Marc G. Williar, Dir. of Admis.
904-829-6481

Florida A & M University, Tallahassee   32307

Florida Atlantic University
500 N.W. 20th St., Boca Raton   33431
Brian Levin-Stankevich, Dir. of Admis.

Florida International University
Tamiami Trail, Miami   33199

Florida International University
Biscayne Blvd. and 151st St., North Miami   33181

Florida Southern College
111 Lake Hollingsworth Dr., Lakeland   33801
William Stephens, Jr., Dir. of Admis.

Florida State University
600 W. College Ave., Tallahassee   32306

LYNN UNIVERSITY
(Est. 1962 as College of Boca Raton)
3601 N. Military Trail, Boca Raton   33431
407-994-0770 or 800-544-8035
See listing under "Universities"

St. Leo College
P.O. Box 2008, St. Leo   33574
Bonnie Black, Dir. of Admis.

St. Thomas University
16400 N.W. 32nd Ave., Miami   33054
John M. Letvinchuk, Dir. of Admis.

SCHILLER INTERNATIONAL UNIVERSITY (FLORIDA & EUROPE)
U.S. Admissions Office
Dept. PA, 453 Edgewater Dr., Dunedin   34698-7532
800-336-4133 Fax: 813-736-6263
Dr. Walter Liebrecht, President
Karen Altieri, Associate Director of Admissions
See listing under "Universities"

University of Central Florida
P.O. Box 25000, Orlando   32816

University of South Florida
4202 Fowler Ave., Tampa   33620

University of West Florida
11000 University Pky., Pensacola   32514

GEORGIA

Clark Atlanta University
240 James Brawley Dr., S.W., Atlanta   30314
Thomas W. Cole, President

Georgia College
231 W. Hancock St., Milledgeville   31061
912-453-5004

Georgia State University
University Plaza, Atlanta   30303
Ernest Beals, Dean of Admissions

La Grange College
601 Broad St., La Grange   30240
Phil Dodson, Dir. of Admis.
706-882-2911

Oglethorpe University
4484 Peachtree Rd., N.E., Atlanta   30319
Dennis Matthews, Dir. of Admis.

Piedmont College
P.O. Box 10, Demorest   30535
Penny L. Graber, Dir of Admis.
800-277-7020

Savannah State College
State College Branch, Savannah   31404
Robert Ray, Dir. of Admis.

University of Georgia, Athens   30602
Dr. Charles A. Stewart, Dean

HAWAII

Brigham Young University, Hawaii Campus
55-220 Kulanui St., Laie   96762
Clark E. Hirschi, Coordinator of Admis.

University of Hawaii at Hilo
523 W. Lanikaula, Hilo   96720

University of Hawaii at Manoa
2500 Campus Rd., Honolulu   96822

IDAHO

Boise State University
1910 University Dr., Boise   83725

Idaho State University
P.O. Box 8270, Pocatello   83209

Lewis Clark State College
500 8th Ave., Lewiston   83501
800-933-5272 or 208-799-5272

Northwest Nazarene College
623 Holly St., Nampa   83686
Bruce D. Webb, Dir. of Admis.

ILLINOIS

Augustana College
639 38th St., Rock Island   61201
Martin R. Sauer, Director of Admission
800-798-8100

Aurora University
347 S. Gladstone Ave., Aurora   60506
Peter Pitts, Dir. of Admis.

College of St. Francis
500 Wilcox St., Joliet   60435

Governors State University
1 University Pky., University Park   60466
Richard Pride, Dir. of Admis.

Illinois State University
212 N. School St., Normal   61761

Institute for Clinical Social Work
30 N. Michigan Ave., Chicago   60602

Kendall College
2408 Orrington Ave., Evanston   60201
Peter Pauletti, Dir. of Admis.

Knox College, Galesburg   61401
309-343-0112 or 800-678-KNOX
See listing under "Universities"

LEWIS UNIVERSITY
Rt. 53, Romeoville   60441
Irish O'Reilly, Director of Admissions
See listing under "Universities"

Loyola University of Chicago
820 N. Michigan Ave., Chicago   60611
Allen V. Lentino, Dir. of Admis.

North Central College
30 N. Brainard St.
P.O. Box 3065, Naperville   60566-7065
Marguerite Waters, Director of Admission
708-420-3414

Northeastern Illinois University
5500 N. St. Louis Ave., Chicago   60625

Olivet Nazarene University, Kankakee   60901
John Mongerson, Dir. of Admis.
815-939-5203

Parkland College
2400 W. Bradley Ave., Champaign   61821-1899
217-351-2208 or 800-346-8089

Rockford College
5050 E. State St., Rockford   61108
Miriam King, V.P. for Enrollment Management
See listing under "Universities"

ROOSEVELT UNIVERSITY
430 S. Michigan Ave., Chicago   60605
William Smyser, Director of Admissions
See listing under "Universities"

Sangamon State University
Shepherd Rd., Springfield   62794-9243
Admissions and Records, 217-786-6626

Southern Illinois University at Carbondale
Carbondale   62901

University of Chicago
5801 S. Ellis Ave., Chicago   60637

University of Illinois
506 S. Wright St., Urbana   61801

University of Illinois at Chicago
P.O. Box 5220, Chicago   60680
Dr. Marilyn R. Fiduccia, Dir. of Admis.

INDIANA

Anderson University
1100 E. 5th St., Anderson   46012
Robert H. Reardon, President

Ball State University
2000 W. University Ave., Muncie   47306
Ruth Vedvik, Dir. of Admis.

Goshen College
1700 S. Main St., Goshen   46526
Tom Meyers, Chairperson

Indiana University-Purdue University
355 N. Lansing, Indianapolis   46202

Indiana Wesleyan University
4201 S. Washington St., Marion   46953
800-332-6901

Manchester College
604 College Ave., North Manchester   46962
Dr. Leonard Williams, Professor

Purdue University
Schleman Hall, West Lafayette   47907

St. Francis College
2701 Spring St., Ft. Wayne   46808

Taylor University
500 W. Reade Ave., Upland   46989
Dr. Robert Pitts, VP for Academic Affairs

University of Evansville
1800 Lincoln Ave., Evansville   47722
Elizabeth Lyon, Associate Dir. of Admis.
800-423-8633

University of Southern Indiana
8600 University Blvd., Evansville   47712

Valparaiso University, Valparaiso   46383

IOWA

Briar Cliff College
3303 Rebecca St., Sioux City   51104
Patricia White, Dir. of Admis.

Buena Vista College
610 W. 4th St., Storm Lake   50588
Joanne Loonan, Director of Admissions

Dordt College
498 4th Ave., N.E., Sioux Center   51250
Quentin Van Essen, Dir. of Admissions
800-343-6738

Drake University
2507 E. University Ave., Des Moines   50311
Thomas Willoughby, Dir. of Admis.

Graceland College, Lamoni   50140
800-638-0053, Outside Iowa 800-346-9208
Bonita Booth, Dean of Admissions
See listing under "Universities"

Grand View College
1200 Grandview Ave., Des Moines   50316
Lori Hanson, Dir. of Admissions
800-444-6083

Iowa State University, Ames   50011
Karsten Smedal, Dir. of Admis.

Loras College
1450 Alta Vista, Dubuque   52001
Dan Conry, Dir. of Admis.

Luther College
700 College Dr., Decorah   52101
David Sallee, Dean for Enrollment

Morningside College, Sioux City   51106
Lora Vanderzwaag, Dir. of Admis.

Mount Mercy College
1330 Elmhurst Dr., N.E., Cedar Rapids   52402
Carol Williamson, Dir. of Admis.

Northwestern College
101 7th St. S.W., Orange City   51041

Teikyo Marycrest University
1607 W. 12th St., Davenport   52804
Tim McDonough, Dir. of Admis.
See listing under "Universities"

University of Dubuque
2000 University Ave., Dubuque   52001

University of Iowa, Iowa City   52242

University of Northern Iowa, Cedar Falls   50614

Waldorf College
106 S. 6th St., Forest City   50436
Steve Lovik, Dir. of Admis.
800-292-1903

Wartburg College
P.O. Box 1003, Waverly   50677

KANSAS

Bethany College
421 N. 1st St., Lindsborg   67456
David Norlin, Chrpsn.

Bethel College
300 E. 27th St., North Newton   67117

Fort Hays State University
600 Park St., Hays   67601-4099
Dr. Jean Coyle, Interim Chrpsn.

Kansas State University
Anderson Hall 110, Manhattan   66506
Ellsworth M. Gerritz, Admis. & Records

McPherson College
1600 E. Euclid St., McPherson   67460

Ottawa University
1001 S. Cedar St., Ottawa   66067
Steve Koberlein, Dir. of Admis.
800-755-5200

Pittsburg State University
1701 S. Broadway St., Pittsburg   66762
James E. Parker, Dir of Admis.

Saint Mary College
4100 S. 4th St., Leavenworth   66048
Irene Keehan, Dir. of Admis.

SOUTHWESTERN COLLEGE
100 College St., Winfield   67156
800-846-1543

Tabor College
400 S. Jefferson St., Hillsboro   67063
800-822-6799
See listing under "Liberal Arts & Sciences"

University of Kansas, Lawrence   66045

Washburn University of Topeka
1700 S.W. College Ave., Topeka   66621
John E. Triggs, Dir. of Admissions

Wichita State University
1845 Fairmount, Wichita   67260
800-362-2594
See listing under "Universities"

KENTUCKY

Asbury College
1 Macklem Dr., Wilmore   40390
Jonah Mitchell, Dir. of Admis.

Eastern Kentucky University
521 Lancaster Ave., Richmond   40475

Kentucky State University
400 E. Main St., Frankfort   40601

Kentucky Wesleyan College
3000 Frederica St., Owensboro   42301

Lindsey Wilson College
210 Lindsey Wilson St., Columbia   42728
Dr. John Begley, President

Midway College
512 E. Stephens St., Midway   40347
Carl P. Rollins II, Dir. of Admis.

Morehead State University, Morehead   40351
Charles Myers, Director of Admissions
606-783-2000

Murray State University, Murray   42071
Phil Bryan, Director of Admissions
800-272-4MSU

Northern Kentucky University
Louie B. Nunn Dr., Highland Heights   41076

Southern Baptist Theological Seminary
2825 Lexington Rd., Louisville   40280
R. Albert Mohler, Jr., President

Spalding University
851 S. 4th St., Louisville   40203
Dorothy G. Allen, Dir. of Admis.

Thomas More College
2771 Turkeyfoot Rd., Covington   41017
Dr. Charles Bensman, President

University of Kentucky, Lexington   40506

University of Louisville
2301 S. 3rd St., Louisville   40292
Robert Parrent, Dir. of Admis.

Western Kentucky University
1526 Russellville Rd., Bowling Green   42101

LOUISIANA

Grambling State University
P.O. Box 607, Grambling   71245
Dr. Harold W. Lundy, President

Louisiana College
College Station, Pineville   71359
Byron McGee, Dir. of Admis.
318-487-7386
See listing under "Liberal Arts"

Louisiana State University and A & M College
Baton Rouge   70803

Loyola University
6363 St. Charles Ave., New Orleans   70118

Northeast Louisiana University
700 University Ave., Monroe   71209

Northwestern State University
Natchitoches   71497

Southeastern Louisiana University
P.O. Box 784, Hammond   70404

Southern University A & M College
Baton Rouge   70813

Southern University in New Orleans
6400 Press Dr., New Orleans   70126
Millie M. Charles, Director

Tulane University
6823 Saint Charles Ave., New Orleans   70118
Richard Whiteside, Dean of Admission

MAINE

Bowdoin College, Brunswick   04011
William Mason, Dir. of Admis.

College of the Atlantic
105 Eden St., Bar Harbor   04609
Steve Thomas, Dir. of Admis.

University of Maine at Fort Kent
25 Pleasant St., Fort Kent   04743
Jerry Nadeau, Dir. of Admis.

University of Maine, Orono   04469

University of New England
11 Hills Beach Rd., Biddeford   04005
Patricia Cribby, Dir. of Admis.

University of Southern Maine
96 Falmouth St., Portland   04103
Eugene Schleh, Coordinator

MARYLAND

Bowie State University
14000 Jericho Park Rd., Bowie   20715

Coppin State College
2500 W. North Ave., Baltimore   21216

Hood College
400 Rosemont Ave., Frederick   21701

Loyola College
4501 N. Charles St., Baltimore   21210
William Bossemeyer III, Dir. of Admis.

Morgan State University
Cold Spring Ln. and Hillen Rd., Baltimore   21239

Salisbury State University
1101 Camden Ave., Salisbury   21801

University of Maryland
Baltimore Professional Schools
522 W. Lombard St., Baltimore   21201

University of Maryland Eastern Shore
11868 Academic Oval, Princess Anne   21853
Dr. Lamin Mbye, Chrpsn.

Western Maryland College
2 College Hill, Westminster   21157

MASSACHUSETTS

American International College
1000 State St., Springfield   01109
Peter Miller, Dean of Admissions

Anna Maria College
2 Sunset Ln., Paxton   01612
Dr. Bernadette Madore, SSA, President

Atlantic Union College
P.O. Box 1000, South Lancaster   01561
Osa Canto, Registrar

Boston College
140 Commonwealth Ave., Chestnut Hill   02167
June Gary Hopps, Dean

Boston University
685 Commonwealth Ave., Boston   02215

Bradford College
320 S. Main St., Bradford   01835

Brandeis University
415 South St, Waltham   02154
David Gould, Dean of Admissions
617-736-3500

Bridgewater State College
Bridgewater   02325
James Plotner, Jr., Dir. of Admis.

Clark University
950 Main St., Worcester   01610
Richard Pierson, Dean of Admis.

Curry College
1071 Blue Hill Ave., Milton   02186
617-333-0500

Eastern Nazarene College
23 E. Elm Ave., Quincy   02170
D. William Nichols, Dir. of Admis.

ELMS COLLEGE
291 Springfield St., Chicopee   01013
800-255-ELMS

Endicott College
376 Hale St., Beverly   01915
Elizabeth Macomber, Dir. of Admis.

Fitchburg State College
160 Pearl St., Fitchburg   01420
Marke Vickers, Dir. of Admis.

Gordon College
255 Grapevine Rd., Wenham   01984

Hampshire College, Amherst   01002
Audrey Y. Smith, Dir. of Admissions
413-582-5471

Lesley College
29 Everett St., Cambridge   02138-2790
Jane Raley, Dir. of Admissions

REGIS COLLEGE
235 Wellesley St., Weston   02193
Valerie L. Brown, Director of Admission
800-456-1820

Salem State College
352 Lafayette St., Salem   01970
David Sartwell, Dir. of Admis.

Simmons College
300 The Fenway, Boston   02115

Smith College
Northampton   01063

Suffolk University
8 Ashburton Place, Boston   02108
Barbara K. Ericson, Assoc. Dean Enrollment & Retention
617-573-8460

University of Massachusetts Dartmouth
Old Westport Rd., North Dartmouth   02747
Raymond Barrows, Dir. of Admissions
508-999-8605

Wellesley College, Wellesley   02181
Janet A. Lavin, Dir. of Admis.

Western New England College
1215 Wilbraham Rd., Springfield   01119
800-325-1122

Westfield State College
577 Western Ave., Westfield   01085
John F. Marcus, Dir. of Admis.

Wheelock College
200 Riverway, Boston   02215
Joan Wexler, Dean of Admis. & Financial Aid

MICHIGAN

Adrian College
110 S. Madison St., Adrian   49221
George Wolf, Dir. of Admis.
See listing under "Universities"

Andrews University, Berrien Springs   49104
Jack Mentges, Dir. of Admis.

Aquinas College
1607 Robinson Rd., S.E., Grand Rapids   49506
Paula Meehan, Dean of Admissions
800-678-9593

Calvin College
3201 Burton St., S.E., Grand Rapids   49546

Concordia College
4090 Geddes Rd., Ann Arbor   48105
Mary Froelich, Dir. of Admis.

Eastern Michigan University, Ypsilanti   48197
Donald Loppnow, Director
313-487-3060 or 800-GO-TO-EMU

Ferris State University
Office of Admission
420 Oak St., Big Rapids   49307-2020

Grace Bible College
P.O. Box 910, Grand Rapids   49509
Linda K. Siler, Dir. of Admis.

Grand Valley State University
1 Campus Dr., Allendale   49401
JoAnn Foerster, Dir. of Admis.

HILLSDALE COLLEGE
33 E. College St., Hillsdale   49242
Dr. Mickey Craig, Chrpsn.
517-437-7341

Madonna University
36600 Schoolcraft St., Livonia   48150

Marygrove College
8425 W. McNichols Rd., Detroit   48221

Michigan State University, East Lansing   48824
Dr. Nancy Humphreys, Director

Northern Michigan University
610 Cohodas Admin. Center, Marquette 49855
Nancy Rehling, Dir. of Admis.

Saginaw Valley State University
2250 Pierce Rd., University Center 48710

University of Detroit Mercy
4001 W. McNichols
PO Box 19900, Detroit 48219-0900
313-993-1245
See listing under "Universities"

University of Michigan-Ann Arbor
815 S. University Ave., Ann Arbor 48109

Wayne State University
5980 Cass Ave., Detroit 48202
Dr. J. R. Thorderson, Dir. of Admis.

Western Michigan University, Kalamazoo 49008
Stanley Henderson, Dir. of Enrl. Mgt. & Admis.
616-387-2000

William Tyndale College
35700 W. Twelve Mile Rd.
Farmington Hills 48331

MINNESOTA

Augsburg College
731 21st Ave., S., Minneapolis 55454

Bemidji State University
1500 Birchmont Dr., N.E., Bemidji 56601
800-475-2001

Bethel College
3900 Bethel Dr., St. Paul 55112
Dr. George Brushaber, President

College of Saint Benedict
37 S. College Ave., St. Joseph 56374

College of St. Catherine
2004 Randolph Ave., St. Paul 55105

College of St. Scholastica
1200 Kenwood Ave., Duluth 55811
David Rigoni, Chrpsn.
800-447-5444
See listing under "Liberal Arts"

Concordia College
901 8th St. S., Moorhead 56562
Lee Johnson, Dir. of Admis.
See listing under "Universities"

Concordia College-St. Paul
275 N. Syndicate, St. Paul 55104
Tim Utter, Dir. of Admis.

Gustavus Adolphus College
800 W. College Ave., St. Peter 56082
Mark Anderson, Dir. of Admis.

Mankato State University
P.O. Box 8400, Mankato 56002

Moorhead State University
1104 7th Ave. S., Moorhead 56560

Northwestern College
3003 Snelling Ave., N., St. Paul 55113
Ralph Anderson, Dean of Admissions
800-827-6827 or 612-631-5111

PILLSBURY BAPTIST BIBLE COLLEGE
315 S. Grove St., Owatonna 55060
Alan Potter, President
Larry Tindall, Director of Admissions
800-747-4557

St. Cloud State University
740 4th Ave., S., St. Cloud 56301
Sherwood Reid, Dir. of Admis.
800-369-4260

St. John's University
P.O. Box 7155, Collegeville 56321

St. Olaf College, Northfield 55057
Raymond De Vries, Chrpsn.
507-646-3351

University of Minnesota
2400 Oakland Ave., Duluth 55812
Robert L. Heller, Provost

University of Minnesota, Twin Cities
Minneapolis 55455

University of St. Thomas
2115 Summit Ave., St. Paul 55105

Winona State University
P.O. Box 5838, Winona 55987
Dr. J. Mootz, Dir. of Admis.

MISSISSIPPI

Delta State University
Hwy. 8 W., Cleveland 38732

Jackson State University
1400 Lynch St., Jackson 39203

Mississippi Valley State University
14000 Hwy. 82 W., Itta Bena 38941
Maxcine B. Rush, Director of Admissions
See listing under "Universities"

University of Mississippi, University 38677

University of Southern Mississippi
P.O. Box 5165, Hattiesburg 39406

MISSOURI

Avila College
11901 Wornall Rd., Kansas City 64145

Central Missouri State University
Warrensburg 64093
Delores Hudson, Dir. of Admis.

Columbia College
1001 Rogers St., Columbia 65216
Ron Cronacher, Dir. of Admissions
800-231-2391

Evangel College
1111 N. Glenstone Ave., Springfield 65802
David Schoolfield, Dir. of Enrollment

Fontbonne College
6800 Wydown Blvd., St. Louis 63105
Peggy Musen, Dir. of Admis.

Missouri Southern State College
3950 Newman Rd., Joplin 64801
Dr. David D. Tate, Dept. Head
See listing under "Universities"

Missouri Valley College
500 E. College St., Marshall 65340
816-886-6924 ext. 114
See listing under "Universities"

Missouri Western State College
4525 Downs Dr., St. Joseph 64507
Howard McCauley, Dir. of Admis.

Northeast Missouri State University
Kirksville 63501

Park College, Parkville 64152
Dr. Edwin Rawn, Dean of Admis.

St. Louis University
221 N. Grand Blvd., St. Louis 63103
Louis A. Menard, Dean of Admissions

Southeast Missouri State University
1 University Plz., Cape Girardeau 63701
New Student Relations 314-651-2590
See listing under "Universities"

Southwest Missouri State University
901 S. National Ave., Springfield 65804
Dr. Bernice Warren, Dean
417-836-5529

University of Missouri, Columbia
228 Jesse Hall, Columbia 65211

University of Missouri
8001 Natural Bridge Rd., St. Louis 63121
Mimi LaMarca, Dir. of Admis.

Washington University
1 Brookings Dr., St. Louis 63130

William Woods College
200 W. 12th St., Fulton 65251
Dr. Jahnae Barnett, VP of Admis.

MONTANA

CARROLL COLLEGE
1610 N. Benton Ave., Helena 59625
Candace Cain, Dir. of Admis.
See listing under "Universities"

College of Great Falls
1301 20th St., S., Great Falls 59405
Jean Walker, Dir. of Admis.

Montana State University - Billings
1500 N. 30th St., Billings 59101
Karen Everett, Dir. of Admis.
406-657-2158

Rocky Mountain College
1511 Poly Dr., Billings 59102
David Heringer, Dir. of Admis.
See listing under "Universities"

University of Montana, Missoula 59812
800-462-8636

NEBRASKA

Bellevue College
1000 Galvin Rd. S., Bellevue 68005
Chari Leader, VP of Enrollment

Chadron State College
1000 Main St., Chadron 69337
Dr. Donald Green, Dean

Concordia College
800 N. Columbia Ave., Seward 68434
Don Vos, Dir. of Admis.

Creighton University
2500 California St., Omaha 68178
Nadine Medlin, Chrpsn.

Dana College
2848 College Dr., Blair 68008
John Schueth, Dir. of Admis.
800-444-3262
See listing under "Universities"

Nebraska Wesleyan University
5000 Saint Paul Ave., Lincoln 68504
Ken Sieg, Dir. of Admis.

Peru State College, Peru 68421
Pamela J. Cosgrove, Dir. of Admis.
402-872-3815

Union College
3800 S. 48th St., Lincoln 68506

University of Nebraska
905 W. 25th St., Kearney 68849

University of Nebraska at Omaha
Omaha 68182

NEVADA

Sierra Nevada College-Lake Tahoe
P.O. Box 4269, Incline Village 89450
Lane Murray, Dir. of Admissions
See listing under "Universities"

University of Nevada, Reno
Reno 89557

University of Nevada Las Vegas
4505 S. Maryland Pky., Las Vegas 89154-1021
Admissions: 702-895-3443 or 800-334-UNLV

NEW HAMPSHIRE

ANTIOCH NEW ENGLAND GRADUATE SCHOOL
40 Avon St., Keene 03431-3516
Gael R. Minton, Dir. of Admis.
603-357-3122
See listing under "Graduate Schools"

Keene State College
229 Main St., Keene 03435
Kathryn Dodge, Dir. of Admis.

New England College
26 Bridge St., Henniker 03242
John Spaulding, Dir. of Admis.

New Hampshire College
2500 North River Rd., Manchester 03106
Brad Poznanski, Dir. of Admis.
603-645-9611

NOTRE DAME COLLEGE
2321 Elm St., Manchester 03104
603-669-4298

Rivier College
420 S. Main St., Nashua 03060
Admissions: 800-44-RIVIER

School for Lifelong Learning
Durham 03824

University of New Hampshire, Durham 03824
Stanwood C. Fish, Dir. of Admissions

NEW JERSEY

Caldwell College
9 Ryerson Ave., Caldwell 07006

Fairleigh Dickinson University, Teaneck 07666
Dennis Craig, Dir. of Admis.
201-692-2553

FELICIAN COLLEGE
262 S. Main St., Lodi 07644
Sr. Mary Austin, OSB, Dir. of Admis.
201-778-1029
See listing under "Universities"

Hudson County Community College
168 Sip Ave., Jersey City 07306
Joseph O'Halloran, Director of Admissions
201-714-2127

Jersey City State College
2039 Kennedy Blvd., Jersey City 07305
201-200-3234

Kean College of New Jersey
1000 Morris Ave., Union 07083

Monmouth College
400 Cedar Ave., West Long Branch 07764
Joan Rudinski, Dir. of Admis.

Princeton University, Princeton 08544

Ramapo College of New Jersey
505 Ramapo Valley Rd., Mahwah 07430
Robert Scott, President
201-529-7600

Rowan College of New Jersey, Glassboro 08028
Marvin G. Sills, Dir. of Admis.

Rutgers, The State University of NJ
University College - Camden
Camden 08102

Rutgers, The State University of NJ
Rutgers College
New Brunswick 08903

Seton Hall University
400 S. Orange Ave., South Orange 07079
Lee Cooke, Dir. of Admis.

Stockton State College, Pomona 08240
Sal Catalfamo, Dir. of Admis.

Upsala College
345 Prospect St., East Orange 07017
George Lynes, Dean of Admissions

William Penn College
201 Trueblood Ave., Oskaloosa 52577
Eric Otto, Dir. of Admis.

NEW MEXICO

College of Santa Fe
1600 St. Michaels Dr., Santa Fe 87505
800-456-2673

Eastern New Mexico University
Portales 88130
Larry Fuqua, Dir. of Admis.

New Mexico Highlands University, Las Vegas 87701
Dr. Jorge P. Thomas, VP Academic Affairs

New Mexico State University
P.O. Box 30001, Las Cruces 88003

NEW YORK

Adelphi University, Garden City 11530
Dr. Elliot Pruzan, Asst. Provost & Dir. of Admis.
516-877-3050

Canisius College
2001 Main St., Buffalo 14208
Penelope Lips, Dir. of Admis.
800-843-1517

CAZENOVIA COLLEGE
Cazenovia 13035
Dr. James Parker, VP for Enrollment Management
See listing under "Universities"

Colgate University
13 Oak Dr., Hamilton 13346
Dean of Admissions
315-824-7401

College of New Rochelle
29 Castle Pl., New Rochelle 10805

Columbia University
612 W. 115th St., New York 10025

Cornell University
410 Thurston Ave., Ithaca 14853

CUNY Hunter College
695 Park Ave., New York 10021
Donna Shalala, President

CUNY Lehman College
250 Bedford Park Blvd. W., Bronx 10468
Jane Herbert, Dir. of Enrollment Management

CUNY York College
9420 Guy R. Brewer Blvd., Jamaica 11451

Daemen College
4380 Main St., Amherst 14226
Maria Dillard, Dir. of Admis.
in NY 800-462-7652 or 716-839-8225

Dominican College of Blauvelt
460 N. Western Hwy., Orangeburg 10962
Louis Kern, Dir. of Admis.
914-359-7800

D'Youville College
320 Porter Ave., Buffalo 14201
Ronald Dannecker, Dir. of Admis.

Elmira College
Park Pl., Elmira 14901
William S. Neal, Dean of Admissions
See listing under "Liberal Arts"

Fordham University
441 E. Fordham Rd., Bronx 10458
718-817-1000

Fordham University
Lincoln Center Campus
113 W. 60th St., New York 10023
Edward Bristow, Dean

Friends World Program, Long Island University
Montauk Hwy., Southampton 11968
Carol Gilbert, Dir. of Admis.

Houghton College
P.O. Box 128, Houghton 14744
Tim Fuller, Dir. of Admis.

IONA COLLEGE
715 North Ave., New Rochelle 10801
800-231-IONA or 914-633-2503
See listing under "Universities"

Keuka College
P.O. Box 98, Keuka Park 14478
Robert J. Ianuzzo, Dean of Admissions

Long Island University-C. W. Post Campus
Rt. 25A, Brookville 11548
Dr. Alice Scourby, Chrpsn., Sociology and
Anthropology
516-299-2404

MARIST COLLEGE
290 North Rd., Poughkeepsie 12601
Harry W. Wood, VP Admissions
914-575-3226

Marymount College
100 Marymount Ave., Tarrytown 10591
Gina R. Campbell, Dir. of Admis.
800-724-4312

Medaille College
18 Agassiz Cir., Buffalo 14214
Jacqueline Smukeer, Dir. of Admis.

Mercy College
555 Broadway, Dobbs Ferry 10522
James Nesbitt, Dean of Admissions

Molloy College
1000 Hempstead Ave., Rockville Centre 11570
Wayne James, Dir. of Admis.
See listing under "Universities"

Nazareth College of Rochester
4245 East Ave., Rochester 14618
Paul Kenyon, Dir. of Admis.

New York Institute of Technology
Old Westbury Campus, Old Westbury 11568

New York University
70 Washington Sq., New York 10012

New York University
10 Western Hwy., Orangeburg 10962

Niagara University, Niagara University 14109
George Pachter, Dean of Admissions
800-462-2111
See listing under "Universities"

Nyack College, Nyack 10960
Miguel Sanchez, Dir. of Admis.
800-33-NYACK

∷ On-Line Campus
New York Institute of Technology
P.O. Box 8000, Old Westbury 11568-8000
800-222-NYIT

Rensselaer Polytechnic Institute, Troy 12180
Conrad Sharrow, Dean of Admissions

Roberts Wesleyan College
2301 Westside Dr., Rochester 14624
Dr. Frederick Coisman, Chrpsn.
See listing under "Universities"

Rochester Institute of Technology
1 Lomb Memorial Dr., Rochester 14623
716-475-6631
See listing under "Universities"

St. Joseph's College
245 Clinton Ave., Brooklyn 11205
Geraldine Foudy, Dir. of Admis.
718-636-6868

St. Joseph's College, Suffolk Campus
25 Audobon Ave., Patchogue 11772

Siena College, Loudonville 12211
Harry Wood, Director, Admissions

Skidmore College, Saratoga Springs 12866
Kent Jones, Dir. of Admis.

· SUNY Adirondack Community College
439 Bay Rd., Queensbury 12804
Levi Brown, Dir. of Admis.
518-793-4491
See listing under "Community and Junior Colleges"

SUNY at Albany
1400 Washington Ave., Albany 12222
Micheileen Treadwell, Dir. of
Admission/Financial Aid
518-442-5431

SUNY at Buffalo
17 Capen Hall
P.O. Box 601660, Buffalo 14260-1660
716-645-6900

SUNY at Stony Brook
Stony Brook 11794

SUNY College at Brockport
Brockport 14420
Dr. Georgianna Shepard, Chrpsn.

SUNY College at Buffalo
1300 Elmwood Ave., Buffalo 14222
Deborah K. Renzi, Dir. of Admis.

SUNY College at Plattsburgh, Plattsburgh 12901
Richard Higgins, Dir. of Admis.
518-564-2040

· SUNY Onondaga Community College
Onondaga Rd., Syracuse 13215
Joseph Insel, Dir. of Admis.

· Suny Orange County Community College
115 South St., Middletown 10940
914-341-4030

Syracuse University, Syracuse 13244

Utica College of Syracuse University
1600 Burrstone Rd., Utica 13502

Yeshiva University
500 W. 185th St., New York 10033

NORTH CAROLINA

Appalachian State University
ASU Station, Boone 28608
Joe Watts, Admissions Officer

Barton College
College Station, Wilson 27893
Anthony Britt, Dir. of Admis.
800-345-4973/919-399-6318
See listing under "Universities"

Belmont Abbey College
1 Abbey Pl., Belmont 28012
Admissions, 800-523-2355

Bennett College
900 E. Washington St., Greensboro 27401

Catawba College
2300 W. Innes St., Salisbury 28144
Mark Stokes, Dir. of Admis.

East Carolina University
1000 E. 5th St., Greenville 27858

Elon College
P.O. Box 2700, Elon College 27244
Nan P. Perkins, Dean of Admissions

Gardner-Webb University
General Delivery, Boiling Springs 28017
Tony Eastman, Chrpsn.
704-434-2361

Livingstone College
701 W. Monroe St., Salisbury 28144

Mars Hill College
Main St., Mars Hill 28754
Dr. Smith Goodrum, Dean of Admis.

Meredith College
3800 Hillsborough St., Raleigh 27607

Methodist College
5400 Ramsey St., Fayetteville 28311
Fiore Bergamasco, Dir. of Admis.

Montreat-Anderson College
P.O. Box 1267, Montreat 28757
David E. Walters, Dir. of Admissions
800-MAC-N-YOU
See listing under "Universities"

North Carolina A&T State University
1601 E. Market St., Greensboro 27411

North Carolina State University
P.O. Box 7001, Raleigh 27695
George Dixon, Dir. of Admis.

Pembroke State University
P.O. Box 1510, Pembroke 28372
Anthony Locklear, Dir. of Admissions
919-521-6262

Pfeiffer College
General Delivery, Misenheimer 28109

St. Andrews Presbyterian College
1700 Dogwood Mile, Laurinburg 28352
Dale B. Montague, Dir. of Admis.

University of North Carolina
1000 Spring Garden St., Greensboro 27412

University of North Carolina at Chapel Hill
Chapel Hill 27599
James C. Walters, Dir. Undergrad Admis.

Warren Wilson College
P.O. Box 9000, Asheville 28802-9000
Tom Weede, Dir. of Admis.

Western Carolina University
Cullowhee 28723
Tyree H. Kiser, Dir. of Admissions

NORTH DAKOTA

Minot State University
500 University Ave. W., Minot 58701

University of Mary
7500 University Dr., Bismarck 58504
Steph Storey, Dir. of Admis.

University of North Dakota
Box 8193 University Station, Grand Forks 58203

OHIO

Ashland University
401 College Ave., Ashland 44805

Bluffton College
College Ave., Bluffton 45817

Bowling Green State University
Bowling Green 43403
John Martin, Dir. of Admis.

Capital University
2199 E. Main St., Columbus 43209
Dolphus E. Henry, Associate Provost

Case Western Reserve University
2040 Adelbert Rd., Cleveland 44106

Cleveland State University
Euclid Ave. at 24th St., Cleveland 44115

College of Mount St. Joseph
5701 Delhi Rd., Cincinnati 45233-1672
See listing under "Universities"

College of Wooster
1189 Beall Ave., Wooster 44691
Hayden Schilling, Dean of Admis.

· Columbus State Community College
550 E. Spring St., Columbus 43215
Mary Jo Deerwester, Dir. of Admis.

Defiance College
701 N. Clinton St., Defiance 43512
Penny D. Bell, Dir. of Admis.
419-783-2330 Collect

Heidelberg College
310 E. Market St., Tiffin 44883
Stephen E. Eidson, Dean of Admission
800-925-9250

Kent State University
P.O. Box 5190, Kent 44242
Bruce Riddle, Dir. of Admis.

LOURDES COLLEGE
6832 Convent Blvd., Sylvania 43560
Mary E. Briggs, Dir. of Admis.
419-885-5291 or 800-878-3210

Malone College
515 25th St., N.W., Canton 44709
Lee Sommers, Dean of Admissions

Mount Union College
1972 Clark Ave., Alliance 44601
Amy Tomko, Dir. of Admis.

Oberlin College
135 W. Lorain St., Oberlin 44074
Debra Chermonte, Dir. of Admis.

Ohio Dominican College
1216 Sunbury Rd., Columbus 43219
800-955-OHIO

Ohio State University
190 N. Oval Mall, Columbus 43210

Ohio University, Athens 45701

Ohio Wesleyan University
61 S. Sandusky St., Delaware 43015
Donald Bishop, Dean for Enrollment

Shawnee State University
940 2nd St., Portsmouth 45662
Rosemary K. Poston, Dir. of Admis.

University of Akron
381 Buchtel Common, Akron 44325
Kris MacDermott, Asst. Provost Enrollment

University of Cincinnati
2700 Clifton Ave., Cincinnati 45221

University of Dayton
300 College Park Ave., Dayton 45469-1442
Toll-free 800-837-7433
See listing under "Universities"

University of Rio Grande
General Delivery, Rio Grande 45674
Dr. Nathaniel Daniel, Dean
614-245-5353, Ext. 7254

University of Toledo
2801 Bancroft St., W., Toledo 43606
Richard Eastop, Dir. of Admis.

Urbana University
100 College Way, Urbana 43078
Donald Burns, Dir. of Admis.

Wright State University
3640 Colonel Glenn Hwy., Dayton 45435

Xavier University
3800 Victory Pky., Cincinnati 45207

OKLAHOMA

East Central University, Ada 74820
James Peak, Dir. of Admis.

Oklahoma City University
2501 N. Blackwelder Ave., Oklahoma City 73106
Dr. Larry Eberhardt, Chair
See listing under "Universities"

Oral Roberts University
7777 S. Lewis Ave., Tulsa 74171
Arthur E. Matzkvech, Dir. of Admis.

University of Oklahoma at Norman
660 Parrington Oval, Norman 73019

University of Tulsa
600 S. College Ave., Tulsa 74104
Dr. Kermit Hall, Dean

OREGON

Marylhurst College for Lifelong Learning
P.O. Box 261, Marylhurst 97036
Robert Ridel, Chrpsn.
800-634-9982

Portland State University
P.O. Box 751, Portland 97207

Treasure Valley Community College
650 College Blvd., Ontario 97914
Ron Kulm, Dir. of Admis.

Western Baptist College, Salem 97301
800-845-3005

PENNSYLVANIA

Albright College
P.O. Box 15234, Reading 19612

Allegheny College
520 N. Main St., Meadville 16335
Gayle Pollack, Dir. of Admis.

Beaver College
450 S. Easton Rd., Glenside 19038-3295
Dennis Nostrand, VP for Enrollment Management
Phone: 800-776-BEAVER(2328)
Fax: 215-572-4049
See listing under "Universities"

Bloomsburg University, Bloomsburg 17815
Bernard Vinovrski, Dir. of Admis.

Bryn Mawr College
101 N. Merion Ave., Bryn Mawr 19010
Elizabeth Vermey, Dir. of Admis.

California University of Pennsylvania
3rd St., California 15419
Norman Hasbrouck, Dean for Enrollment

Carnegie Mellon University
5000 Forbes Ave., Pittsburgh 15213

Cedar Crest College
100 College Dr., Allentown 18104-6196
Cynthia Phillips, Dir. of Admissions

College Misericordia
301 Lake St., Dallas 18612
Michael Joseph, Dir. of Enrollment Mgmt.

Drexel University
3141 Chestnut St., Philadelphia 19104
Dean of Enrollment Management

Eastern College
10 Fairview Dr., Saint Davids 19087
Ronald Keller, VP for Enrollment Management

Edinboro University of Pennsylvania
Edinboro 16444
Admissions Office: 800-626-2203

Elizabethtown College
1 Alpha Dr., Elizabethtown 17022

Gannon University
109 University Sq., Erie 16541

Grove City College
100 Campus Dr., Grove City 16127
Dr. L. John Van Til, Chrpsn.

GWYNEDD-MERCY COLLEGE
Sumneytown Pike, Gwynedd Valley 19437
Marjorie DeSimone, Dean of Admissions
800-DIAL-GMC
See listing under "Universities"

Holy Family College
Grant & Frankford Ave., Philadelphia 19114
Dr. Mott Linn, Dir. of Admis.
215-637-3050

Immaculata College
Immaculata 19345
James P. Sullivan, Dir. of Admis.

Juniata College
1700 Moore St., Huntington 16652

King's College
133 N. River St., Wilkes Barre 18711

Lafayette College, Easton 18042
G. Gary Ripple, Dir. of Admis.
610-250-5100

La Salle University
1900 W. Olney Ave., Philadelphia 19141
Br. Gerald Fitzgerald, Dir. of Admis.
See listing under "Universities"

Lock Haven University, Lock Haven 17745

Mansfield University of Pennsylvania
Mansfield 16933

Marywood College
2300 Adams Ave., Scranton 18509

Mercyhurst College
501 E. 38th St., Erie 16546
Andrew Roth, Dean of Enrollment
800-825-1926

Messiah College
General Delivery, Grantham 17027
Ron Long, Dir. of Admis.

Millersville University of Pennsylvania
Millersville 17551
Blair Treasure, Dean of Admissions

Montgomery County Community College
340 DeKalb Pike, Blue Bell 19422-0758
Dennis Murphy, Dir. of Admis.

Moravian College
1200 Main St., Bethlehem 18018

Muhlenberg College
2400 W. Chew St., Allentown 18104
Chris Hooker-Haring, Dir. of Admis.

Pennsylvania State University
201 Shields Bldg., University Park 16802

Philadelphia College of Bible
BSW Degree
200 Manor Ave., Langhorne 19047-2990
William Tarr, Jr., Chrpsn.
800-366-0049

St. Francis College
P.O. Box 600, Loretto 15940

Seton Hill College, Greensburg 15601
Peter Egan, Dir. of Admis.
800-826-6234 or 412-838-4255

Shippensburg University, Shippensburg 17257

Slippery Rock University, Slippery Rock 16057
Director of Admissions

Temple University
Broad St. & Montgomery Ave.
Philadelphia 19122

University of Pennsylvania
0 Levy Park, Philadelphia 19104

University of Pittsburgh
4200 5th Ave., Pittsburgh 15260

West Chester University of Pennsylvania
S. High St., West Chester 19380

WESTMINSTER COLLEGE
New Wilmington 16172
Richard Dana Paul, Dir. of Admis.
412-946-7100

Widener University
700 E. 14th St., Chester 19013

RHODE ISLAND

Providence College
River Ave., Providence 02918

Rhode Island College
600 Mt. Pleasant Ave., Providence 02908

Salve Regina University
1 Ochre Point Ave., Newport 02840
Roselina McKillop, Dean of Admissions

SOUTH CAROLINA

Benedict College
1600 Harden St., Columbia 29204
Virginia McKee, Dir. of Admis.

Central Wesleyan College
P.O. Box 1020, Central 29630
Lillian A. Robbins, Dir. of Admis.

Columbia College
1301 Columbia College Dr., Columbia 29203

Erskine College & Seminary
Washington St., Due West 29639
Dot Carter, Dir. of Admis.

Lander College
320 Stanley Ave., Greenwood 29649

South Carolina State University
P.O. Box 7127, Orangeburg 29117-0001
803-536-7185

University of South Carolina, Columbia 29208
Terry Davis, Dir. of Admis.
803-777-7700

Winthrop University
701 W. Oakland Ave., Rock Hill 29733
James McCammon, Jr., Dir. of Admis.

Wofford College
429 N. Church St., Spartanburg 29303
Charles Gray, Dir. of Admis.

SOUTH DAKOTA

Augustana College
29th & S. Summit, Sioux Falls 57197

Dakota Wesleyan University
1300 W. University Ave., Mitchell 57301

Kilian Community College
224 N. Phillips Ave., Sioux Falls 57102
605-336-1711 or 800-888-1147

SIOUX FALLS COLLEGE
1501 S. Prairie Ave., Sioux Falls 57105
Susan Reese, Dir. of Admis.
800-888-1047
See listing under "Universities"

University of South Dakota
414 E. Clark St., Vermillion 57069
Dave Lorenz, Dir. of Admis.

TENNESSEE

Austin Peay State University
601 College St., Clarksville 37044

Carson-Newman College
P.O. Box 70552, Jefferson City 37760
See listing under "Universities"

David Lipscomb University
3901 Granny White Pike, Nashville 37204-3951
Wade Sandrell, Dir. of Admis.
800-333-4358

EAST TENNESSEE STATE UNIVERSITY
P.O. Box 70731, Johnson City 37614
Dr. Nancy Dishner, Dean, Enrollment Management
615-929-4213 or 800-462-3878

Freed-Hardeman University
158 E. Main St., Henderson 38340
800-342-7837

Le Moyne-Owen College
807 Walker Ave., Memphis 38126
901-942-7302 or 800-737-7778

Middle Tennessee State University
Murfreesboro 37132
Roger D. Sims, Dir. of Admis.

Tennessee State University
3500 John A. Merritt Blvd., Nashville 37209

University of Memphis, Memphis 38152
Dr. John Eubank, Dean of Admissions

University of Tennessee at Martin
Martin 38238
Paul Kelley, Director of Admissions
See listing under "Universities"

University of Tennessee at Chattanooga
615 McCallie Ave., Chattanooga 37403

University of Tennessee, Knoxville
527 Andy Holt Tower, Knoxville 37996
Dr. Gordon Stanley, Dir. of Admis.

University of Tennessee, Memphis
Health Science Center
800 Madison Ave., Memphis 38163
Office of Enrollment Management

University of Tennessee
1720 W. End Ave., Nashville 37202
615-329-1212

TEXAS

Abilene Christian University
ACU Station, Box 6000, Abilene 79699

Austin College
900 N. Grand Ave., Sherman 75090
Rodney Oto, Dean of Admission
800-442-5363

Baylor University
P.O. Box 97008, Waco 76798-7008
Diana Ramey, Director of Admissions

Concordia Lutheran College
3400 N. Interstate 35, Austin 78705
Kevin Pieper, Dir. of Admis.

East Texas State University
ETSU Station, Commerce 75429

Hardin-Simmons University
2200 Hickory St., Abilene 79698
Laura Moore, Dir. of Admis.
See listing under "Universities"

Houston Baptist University
7502 Fondren Rd., Houston 77074

Lamar University
P.O. Box 10009, Beaumont 77710
800-458-7558

Lubbock Christian University
5601 W. 19th, Lubbock 79407

Our Lady of the Lake University
411 S.W. 24th St., San Antonio 78207-4689
210-434-6711

Paul Quinn College
3837 Simpson Stuart Rd., Dallas 75241

Prairie View A & M University
P.O. Box 3089, Prairie View 77446-3089
Linda S. Berry, Dir. of Admis.

Rice University
P.O. Box 1892, Houston 77251

St. Edward's University
3001 S. Congress Ave., Austin 78704
John Lambert, Dir. of Admis.

Southwest Texas State University
601 University Dr., San Marcos 78666

Stephen F. Austin State University
P.O. Box 6078. Nacogdoches 75962

Tarleton State University
1297 W. Washington St., Stephenville 76402

Texas Christian University
2800 S. University Dr., Ft. Worth 76129
Dr. Edward Boehm, Jr., Dean of Admissions

Texas Southern University
3100 Cleburne St., Houston 77004

Texas Tech University, Lubbock 79409

Texas Women's University
P.O. Box 23925, Denton 76204

University of Central Texas
P.O. Box 1416, Killeen 76540
Dr. Pauline Moseley, Dean of the Faculty

University of Houston
4800 Calhoun Rd., Houston 77204

University of North Texas
P.O. Box 13797, Denton 76203

University of St. Thomas
3812 Montrose Blvd., Houston 77006
Elsie Biron, Dir. of Admis.

University of Texas at Arlington
UTA Box 19125, Arlington 76019
R. Zack Prince, Dir. of Admis.

University of Texas at Austin
0 the University of Texas, Austin 78712

University of Texas-Pan American
1201 W. University Dr., Edinburg 78539
Miguel Nerarez, President

West Texas State University
2501 4th Ave., Canyon 79016
Lila Vars, Dir. of Admis.

UTAH

Brigham Young University, Provo 84602

Southern Utah University
351 W. Center St., Cedar City 84720
Dr. Rodney Decker, Dean
801-586-7898

University of Utah
1400 E. 200 S., Salt Lake City 84112
Dr. J. Stayner Landward, Dir. of Admis.

Utah State University, Logan 84322-1600
Rod Clark, Director of Admissions
801-750-1107

Weber State University
3750 Harrison Blvd., Ogden 84408

Westminster College of Salt Lake City
1840 S. 1300 E., Salt Lake City 84105
800-748-4753

VERMONT

Bennington College, Bennington 05201
Karen Kristof, Dir. of Admis.
800-833-6845

Castleton State College, Castleton 05735
Gary Fallis, Dir. of Admis.

NORWICH UNIVERSITY
65 S. Main St., Northfield 05663
Prof. Gary Lord, Head
See listing under "Universities"

Saint Michael's College
Winooski Park, Colchester 05439
800-SMC-8000
See listing under "Liberal Arts"

Southern Vermont College
Monument Ave., Bennington 05201
See listing under "Universities"

Trinity College
208 Colchester Ave., Burlington 05401

University of Vermont
194 S. Prospect St., Burlington 05401
802-656-3370

VIRGINIA

Averett College
420 W. Main St., Danville 24541
Gary Sherman, Dean of Enrollment Mgmt.

Christopher Newport College
50 Shoe Ln., Newport News 23606

Clinch Valley College of the University of Virginia
P.O. Box 16, Wise 24293
Lana Low, Dir. Enrollment Management

Eastern Mennonite College
1200 Park Rd., Harrisonburg 22801
Jerry Miller, Dir. of Admis.

Ferrum College, Ferrum 24088
Bob Bailey, Dir. of Admis.

George Mason University
4400 University Dr., Fairfax 22030-4444
Patricia Riordan, Dean of Admissions

Hampton University, Hampton 23668
Ollie Bowman, Dean of Admissions

James Madison University, Harrisonburg 22807

LIBERTY UNIVERSITY
P.O. Box 20000, Lynchburg 24506
Jay Spencer, VP Recruitment
800-376-2800
See listing under "Universities"

Longwood College, Farmville 23901

Lynchburg College
1501 Lakeside Dr., Lynchburg 24501
Ernest Chadderton, Dean of Enrollment

Mary Washington College
1701 College Ave., Fredericksburg 22401
Martin Wilder, V.P. for Admissions

Norfolk State University
2401 Corprew Ave., Norfolk 23504

Radford University
P.O. Box 5430, Radford 24142

SHENANDOAH UNIVERSITY
1460 University Dr., Winchester 22601
Dr. Brandon Beck, Division Chair
See listing under "Universities"

Sweet Briar College, Sweet Briar 24595
Nancy Church, Dir. of Admis.

Virginia Commonwealth University
910 W. Franklin St., Richmond 23284

Virginia Intermont College
1013 Moore St., Bristol 24201
Lawton Blandford, Dir. of Admis.

Virginia Polytechnic Institute & State University
Blacksburg 24061
David Bousquet, Dir. of Undergraduate Admis.

Virginia State University, Petersburg 23803
Mable C. Mountcastle, Dir. of Recording

Virginia Union University
1500 N. Lombardy St., Richmond 23220
Janice D. Bailey, Dir. of Admissions

WASHINGTON

Eastern Washington University, Cheney 99004
Michael Frumkin, Director
See listing under "Universities"

Pacific Lutheran University
12180 Park Ave. S., Tacoma 98447
Jack Bermingham, Dean

University of Washington, Seattle 98195

Walla Walla College
204 S. College Ave., College Place 99324

WEST VIRGINIA

Alderson-Broaddus College
Philippi 26416
Craig W. Gould, Director of Admissions
304-457-1700

Concord College, Athens 24712

Marshall University
400 Hal Greer Blvd., Huntington 25755
See listing under "Universities"

Shepherd College, Shepherdstown 25443

The University of Charleston
2300 MacCorkle Ave., S.E., Charleston 25304
800-995-GO UC

West Virginia State College
P.O. Box 1000, Institute 25112

West Virginia University
P.O. Box 6001, Morgantown 26506

WEST VIRGINIA WESLEYAN COLLEGE
59 College Ave., Buckhannon 26201
Robert Skinner, Director of Admission
See listing under "Universities"

WISCONSIN

Carroll College
100 N. East Ave., Waukesha 53186
Ken Moyer, Dir. of Admis.

Carthage College
2001 Alford Dr., Kenosha 53140
Brenda A. Porter, VP Enrollment

Lawrence University
P.O. Box 599, Appleton 54912
Steven Syverson, Dean of Admissions

Marian College of Fond du Lac
45 S. National Ave., Fond du Lac 54935
Carol Reichenberger, Dean of Admissions

Marquette University
1217 W. Wisconsin Ave., Milwaukee 53233
Raymond A. Brown, Dean of Admissions

Mt. Mary College
2900 N. Menomonee River Pky.
Milwaukee 53222

Silver Lake College
2406 S. Alverno Road, Manitowoc 54220
Sandra Schwartz, Dir. of Admis.

University of Wisconsin, Eau Claire
Eau Claire 54701

University of Wisconsin, Green Bay
2420 Nicolet Dr., Green Bay 54311
Myron Van de Ven, Dir. of Admis.

University of Wisconsin, La Crosse
115 Main Hall, La Crosse 54601
608-785-8067

University of Wisconsin, Madison
500 Lincoln Dr., Madison 53706

University of Wisconsin
P.O. Box 413, Milwaukee 53201
V. M. Allison, Registrar

University of Wisconsin, Oshkosh
800 Algoma Blvd., Oshkosh 54901-8602
August Helgerson, Dir. of Admis.

University of Wisconsin
P.O. Box 2000, Kenosha 53141
414-553-2211

University of Wisconsin, River Falls
River Falls 54022
Alan Tuchtenhagen, Dir. of Admis.

University of Wisconsin, Superior 54880
Richard E. Morrison, Dir. Univ. Relations

University of Wisconsin
800 W. Main St., Whitewater 53190

Viterbo College
815 9th St., S., La Crosse 54601
Roland W. Nelson, Dir. of Admis.

WYOMING

University of Wyoming
P.O. Box 3434, Laramie 82071
Richard Davis, Dir. of Admis.

PUERTO RICO

Bayamon Central University
P.O. Box 1725, Bayamon 00960-1725
Christine Hernandez, Dir. of Admis.

Catholic University of Puerto Rico
Las Americas Ave., Ponce 00732
Carilin Frau, Dir. of Admis.

Inter American University of Puerto Rico
P.O. Box 1293, San Juan 00902

University of Puerto Rico
Antonio Barcelo Ave., Cayey 00736
Antonio Rosario, Dir. of Admis.

University of Puerto Rico
CUH Station Rd. 908 Bo Tejas, Humacao 00791

University of Puerto Rico, Mayaguez Campus
P.O. Box 5000, Mayaguez 00681
Neysa Lopez, Dir. of Admis.

University of Puerto Rico, Rio Piedras Campus
P.O. Box 23300, San Juan 00931
Victor Lopez, Dir. of Admis.

University of the Sacred Heart
P.O. Box 12383, San Juan 00914

SPEECH AND DRAMA

This classification contains schools accredited by the American Speech-Language-Hearing Association (†) and a selection of programs from institutionally accredited schools.

ALABAMA

† Auburn University, Auburn 36849

† Auburn University at Montgomery
7300 University Dr., Montgomery 36117
H. H. Funderburk, VP

Birmingham Southern College
900 Arkadelphia Rd., Birmingham 35254

· Gadsden State Community College
P.O. Box 227, Gadsden 35902
W. Bryan Stone, Dir. of Admis.

Samford University
800 Lakeshore Dr., Birmingham 35229
Harold Hunt, Chrpsn.

Troy State University, Troy 36082
Dr. David Dye, Dean

† University of Alabama
P.O. Box 870132, Tuscaloosa 35487-0132
Roy Smith, Dir. of Admis.

University of Alabama at Birmingham
University Station, Birmingham 35294

UNIVERSITY OF MOBILE
P.O. Box 13220, Mobile 36663-0220
Kim Leousis, Dir. of Admissions
205-675-5990
See listing under "Universities"

† University of Montevallo, Montevallo 35115

† University of South Alabama
307 University Blvd. N., Mobile 36688

ALASKA

University of Alaska Fairbanks
Fairbanks 99775

ARIZONA

† Arizona State University, Tempe 85287

Grand Canyon University
3300 W. Camelback Rd., Phoenix 85017
Sherri Willborn, Dir. of Admis.
See listing under "Liberal Arts and Sciences"

† Northern Arizona University
P.O. Box 4092, Flagstaff 86011
Dr. Margaret Cibik, Dir. of Admis.

· Phoenix College
1202 W. Thomas Rd., Phoenix 85013
Geoffrey Eroe, Chrpsn.

† University of Arizona, Tucson 85721
Loyd Bell, Director of Admissions

ARKANSAS

† Arkansas State University
P.O. Box 369, State University 72467

: :† Harding Academy
E. Park Ave., Searcy 72143
Randy Lambeth, Superintendent
501-268-1515

† Henderson State University
1100 Henderson St., Arkadelphia 71999

Hendrix College
1601 Harkrider St., Conway 72032

† Ouachita Baptist University
410 Ouachita St., Arkadelphia 71998
Randy Garner, Dir. of Admis.
800-DIAL-OBU

† University of Arkansas at Fayetteville
Fayetteville 72701

† University of Arkansas at Little Rock
2801 S. University Ave., Little Rock 72204

University of Arkansas at Monticello
P.O. Box 3596, Monticello 71656

University of Arkansas at Pine Bluff
1200 University Dr., Pine Bluff 71601-2799

† University of Central Arkansas
201 Donaghey Ave., Conway 72035

CALIFORNIA

· American Academy of Dramatic Arts/West
2550 Paloma St., Pasadena 91107

American Conservatory Theater
30 Grant Ave., San Francisco 94108
John Luschmann, Acting Conservatory Director
415-834-3350

† Biola University
13800 Biola Ave., La Mirada 90639
Wayne Chute, Dean of Admissions

California Baptist College
8432 Magnolia Ave., Riverside 92504
800-782-3382

California Institute of the Arts
24700 McBean Pkwy., Valencia 91355
Kenneth Young, Dir. of Admis.

† California State University, Chico
Chico 95929-0810
Dr. Randy Wonzong, Drama Chrpsn.
Dr. Stephen King, Speech Comm. Dean

† California State University, Fresno
Shaw & Cedar Ave., Fresno 93710

† California State University, Long Beach
1250 Bellflower Blvd., Long Beach 90840

† California State University, Los Angeles
5151 Paseo Rancho Castilla, Los Angeles 90032

† California State University, Northridge
18111 Nordhoff St., Northridge 91330
Ned C. Reynolds, Dir. of Admis.

† California State University-Fullerton
Fullerton 92632

California State University-Hayward
25800 Carlos Bee Blvd., Hayward 94542

Chapman University
333 N. Glassell St., Orange 92666
Michael Drummy, Dir. of Admis.

College of Notre Dame
1500 Ralston Ave., Belmont 94002
Greg M. Smith, PhD., Dir. of Admis.

Holy Names College
3500 Mountain Blvd., Oakland 94619

Humboldt State University
1 Harps St., Arcata 95521

: : Idyllwild School of Music & the Arts
P.O. Box 38P, Idyllwild 92549
Anne Behnke, Admissions
909-659-2171, FAX 909-659-2058
See listing under "Prep-Coed"

Loyola Marymount University
Loyola Blvd. at W. 80th, Los Angeles 90045
M. L'Heureux, Dir. of Admis.

Mills College
5000 MacArthur Blvd., Oakland 94613
Genevieve Ann Flaherty, Dean of Admissions
800-87-MILLS

Pitzer College
1050 N. Mills Ave., Claremont 91711
Katharine Leighton, Dir. of Admis.

Point Loma Nazarene College
3900 Lomaland Dr., San Diego 92106
Bill Young, Dir. of Admis.

Pomona College
333 N. College Way, Claremont 91711
Peter W. Stanley, President

† San Diego State University
5300 Campanile Dr., San Diego 92115

† San Francisco State University
1600 Holloway Ave., San Francisco 94132
Corwin Bjonerud, Dir. of Admis.

† San Jose State University
1 Washington Sq., San Jose 95192

Santa Clara University, Santa Clara 95053

Scripps College
1030 Columbia Ave., Claremont 91711
Leslie Miles, Dean of Admissions

Sonoma State University
1801 E. Cotati Ave., Rohnert Park 94928

Southern California College
55 Fair Dr., Costa Mesa 92626
Richard Hardy, Asst. Dean for Enrollment

University of California at Berkeley
Dwinelle Hall, Berkeley 94720

University of California, Davis
376 Mrak Hall, Davis 95616

University of California, Irvine
Irvine 92715

University of California, Riverside
P.O. Box 112, Riverside 92521

University of California-Santa Cruz
Santa Cruz 95064
Joseph Allen, Dir. of Admis.

† University of California, San Francisco
Parnassus & 3rd Ave., San Francisco 94143

University of La Verne
1950 3rd St., La Verne 91750
Mark Bornholdt, Dir. of Admis.

University of Redlands
P.O. Box 3080, Redlands 92373

University of San Francisco
2130 Fulton St., San Francisco 94117
Bill Henley, Dir. of Admis.

† University of the Pacific
3601 Pacific Ave, Stockton 95211
Elliott J. Taylor, Dean of Admissions

Whittier College
13406 Philadelphia St., Whittier 90601
310-907-4238

COLORADO

Adams State College, Alamosa 81102
Cheryl Billingsley, Dir. of Admis.
800-824-6494

Colorado College
14 E. Cache La Poudre, Colorado Springs 80903
Terry Swenson, Dir. of Admis.

† Colorado State University
102 Administration Building, Fort Collins 80523
Mary Ontireros, Dir. of Admissions

Mesa State College
P.O. Box 2647, Grand Junction 81502
Sherri Pe'a, Dir. of Admis.

† Metropolitan State College of Denver
P.O. Box 173362, Campus Box 16
Denver 80217-3362

Naropa Institute
2130 Arapahoe Ave., Boulder 80302
Dr. Jana Lynn, Director of Admissions
303-546-3572

Regis University
3333 Regis Blvd., Denver 80221
Robert Blust, Director of Admissions

† University of Colorado at Boulder
Boulder 80309
William A. Douglas, Dean of Admis.

University of Denver
2199 S. University Blvd., Denver 80210

† University of Northern Colorado, Greeley 80639
Tom McNally, Department Chrpsn.
303-351-2454

† University of Southern Colorado
2200 Bonforte Blvd., Pueblo 81001

Western State College of Colorado
Gunnison 81231
Monica Bruning, Dir. of Admis.
See listing under "Universities"

CONNECTICUT

Albertus Magnus College
700 Prospect St., New Haven 06511
Richard Lolatte, Dir. of Admissions
203-773-8501 or 800-578-9160

School of the Hartford Ballet
Hartford Courant Arts Center
224 Farmington Ave., Hartford 06105

† Southern Connecticut State University
501 Crescent St., New Haven 06515

Trinity College
300 Summit St., Hartford 06106
Dr. David Borus, Dean of Admissions

† University of Connecticut, Storrs 06268
Dr. David Kanter, Head

University of Hartford
200 Bloomfield Ave., West Hartford 06117
Richard Zeiser, Dir. of Admis.
See listing under "Universities"

Wesleyan University, Middletown 06459
Karl Furstenberg, Dean of Admissions

Yale University
1903A Yale Station, New Haven 06520

DISTRICT OF COLUMBIA

Catholic University of America
620 Michigan Ave. N.E., Washington 20064
Robert J. Talbot, Dir. of Admis. & Fin. Aid.

† Gallaudet University
800 Florida Ave., N.E., Washington 20002
See listing under "Universities"

† George Washington University
Washington 20052

† Howard University
2400 6th St., N.W., Washington 20059
James E. Cheek, President

: National Conservatory of Dramatic Arts
1556 Wisconsin Ave., N.W., Washington 20007
C. Wayne Rudisill, President
202-333-2202

† University of the District of Columbia
Van Ness Campus
4200 Connecticut Ave., N.W., Washington 20008

FLORIDA

Eckerd College
P.O. Box 12560, St. Petersburg 33733
Richard Hallin, Dir. of Admis.

Flagler College
P.O. Box 1027, St. Augustine 32085
Marc G. Williar, Dir. of Admis.
904-829-6481

Florida A & M University, Tallahassee 32307

Florida Atlantic University
500 N.W. 20th St., Boca Raton 33431
Brian Levin-Stankevich, Dir. of Admis.

Florida Southern College
111 Lake Hollingsworth Dr., Lakeland 33801
William Stephens, Jr., Dir. of Admis.

† Florida State University
600 W. College Ave., Tallahassee 32306

· Full Sail Center for the Recording Arts
3300 University Blvd. #160, Winter Park 32792
407-679-0100 or 800-CAN-ROCK
See listing under "Career Schools"

Jacksonville University
2800 University Blvd., N., Jacksonville 32211

† Nova Southeastern University
3301 College Ave., Ft. Lauderdale 33314

Palm Beach Atlantic College
P.O. Box 24708, West Palm Beach 33416-4708
See listing under "Universities"

Rollins College
P.O. Box 2720, Winter Park 32790

St. Leo College
P.O. Box 2008, St. Leo 33574
Bonnie Black, Dir. of Admis.

Stetson University
401 N. Woodland Blvd., De Land 32720
Gary A. Meadows, Dean of Admis.

† University of Central Florida
P.O. Box 25000, Orlando 32816

† University of Florida
226 Tigert Hall, Gainesville 32611

University of Miami
P.O. Box 248006, Coral Gables 33124

† University of South Florida
4202 Fowler Ave., Tampa 33620

GEORGIA

Agnes Scott College
201 E. College Ave., Decatur 30030
Teresa Lahti, Dir. of Admis.

La Grange College
601 Broad St., La Grange 30240
Phil Dodson, Dir. of Admis.
706-882-2911

Mercer University
1400 Coleman Ave., Macon 31207

Shorter College
315 Shorter Ave., Rome 30165

Spelman College
350 Spelman Ln., S.W., Atlanta 30314
Aline Rivers, Dir. of Admis.

† University of Georgia, Athens 30602
Dr. Cal Logue, Dept. Head

Valdosta State College
Patterson St., Valdosta 31698

Wesleyan College
4760 Forsyth Rd., Macon 31297

West Georgia College, Carrollton 30118
C. Doyle Bickers, Dir. of Admis.

HAWAII

Brigham Young University, Hawaii Campus
55-220 Kulanui St., Laie 96762
Clark E. Hirschi, Coordinator of Admis.

Hawaii Pacific University
45-045 Kamehameha Hwy., Kaneohe 96744

† University of Hawaii at Manoa
2500 Campus Rd., Honolulu 96822

IDAHO

† Idaho State University
P.O. Box 8270, Pocatello 83209

Lewis Clark State College
500 8th Ave., Lewiston 83501
800-933-5272 or 208-799-5272

† Northwest Nazarene College
623 Holly St., Nampa 83686
Bruce D. Webb, Dir. of Admis.

ILLINOIS

† Augustana College
639 38th St., Rock Island 61201
Martin R. Sauer, Director of Admission
800-798-8100

Aurora University
347 S. Gladstone Ave., Aurora 60506
Peter Pitts, Dir. of Admis.

Barat College, Lake Forest 60045
Loretta Brickman, Dir. of Admis.

Blackburn College
700 College Ave., Carlinville 62626
Dwight Smith, Dir. of Admis.

Bradley University
1501 W. Bradley Ave., Peoria 61625

Columbia College
600 S. Michigan Ave., Chicago 60605
Debra McGrath, Dir. of Admis.

† Eastern Illinois University, Charleston 61920
Doug Bock, Chrpsn. Speech
Ettore Guidotti, Chrpsn. Theatre Arts
See listing under "Universities"

† Elmhurst College
190 Prospect Ave., Elmhurst 60126

Eureka College
300 E. College Ave., Eureka 61530

† Governors State University
1 University Pky., University Park 60466
Richard Pride, Dir. of Admis.

Greenville College
315 E. College Ave., Greenville 62246
Kent Krober, Dir. of Admis.

Illinois College
1101 W. College Ave., Jacksonville 62650
Gale Vaugn, Dir. of Admis.

† Illinois State University
212 N. School St., Normal 61761

ILLINOIS WESLEYAN UNIVERSITY
P.O. Box 2900, Bloomington 61702
Dr. Jared Brown, Director
309-556-3011

Judson College
1151 N. State St., Elgin 60123
Jack Powell, Dir. of Enrollment Services

Knox College, Galesburg 61401
309-343-0112 or 800-678-KNOX
See listing under "Universities"

LEWIS UNIVERSITY
Rt. 53, Romeoville 60441
Irish O'Reilly, Director of Admissions
See listing under "Universities"

Loyola University of Chicago
820 N. Michigan Ave., Chicago 60611
Allen V. Lentino, Dir. of Admis.

Millikin University
1184 W. Main St., Decatur 62522
Lin Stoner, Dean of Admissions
800-373-7733

Monmouth College
700 E. Broadway, Monmouth 61462

North Central College
30 N. Brainard St.
P.O. Box 3065, Naperville 60566-7065
Marguerite Waters, Director of Admission
708-420-3414

Northeastern Illinois University
5500 N. St. Louis Ave., Chicago 60625

† Northern Illinois University, De Kalb 60115

† Northwestern University
Annie May Swift Hall
1905 Sheridan Rd., Evanston 60208

Olivet Nazarene University, Kankakee 60901
John Mongerson, Dir. of Admis.
815-939-5203

· Parkland College
2400 W. Bradley Ave., Champaign 61821-1899
217-351-2208 or 800-346-8089

Principia College, Elsah 62028

Rockford College
5050 E. State St., Rockford 61108
Miriam King, V.P. for Enrollment Management
See listing under "Universities"

ROOSEVELT UNIVERSITY
430 S. Michigan Ave., Chicago 60605
William Smyser, Director of Admissions
See listing under "Universities"

† St. Xavier College
3700 W. 103rd St., Chicago 60655
Mary Hendry, Dean of Admissions

† Southern Illinois University at Carbondale
Carbondale 62901

† Southern Illinois University at Edwardsville
Edwardsville 62026
Eugene J. Magac, Dir. of Admissions & Records

† University of Illinois
506 S. Wright St., Urbana 61801

University of Illinois at Chicago
P.O. Box 4348, Chicago 60680
Dr. R. Victor Harnack, Head

† Western Illinois University
900 W. Adams St., Macomb 61455
Alan DeRoos, Registrar
309-298-1891

INDIANA

† Ball State University
2000 W. University Ave., Muncie 47306
Ruth Vedvik, Dir. of Admis.

Calumet College
2400 New York Ave., Whiting 46394
Sharon Sweeney, Dir. of Admis.

DePauw University
313 S. Locust St., Greencastle 46135
Dr. Eleanor Ypma, Registrar

Goshen College
1700 S. Main St., Goshen 46526
Stuart Showalter, Chairperson

Grace College
200 Seminary Dr., Winona Lake 46590
Ron Henry, Dir. of Admis.

Hanover College, Hanover 47243
Eugene McLemore, Dir., Admis.

Huntington College
2303 College Ave., Huntington 46750
Paul Breininger, Dir. of Admis. Services

† Indiana State University
217 N. 6th St., Terre Haute 47809

† Indiana University at Bloomington
300 N. Jordan Ave., Bloomington 47406

† Indiana University-Purdue University at Fort Wayne
2101 Coliseum Blvd. E., Fort Wayne 46805

Indiana Wesleyan University
4201 S. Washington St., Marion 46953
800-332-6901

Manchester College
604 College Ave., North Manchester 46962
Dr. Scott Strode, Chrpsn.

Marian College
3200 Cold Spring Rd., Indianapolis 46222
Don French, Dir. of Admis.

† Purdue University
Schleman Hall, West Lafayette 47907

Purdue University, Calumet Campus
2233 171st St., Hammond 46323

ST. JOSEPH'S COLLEGE
P.O. Box 890, Rensselaer 47978
Louis Levy, Dean of Admissions
800-447-8781

St. Mary-of-the-Woods College
Saint Mary-of-the-Woods 47876
Lynn M. Rubick, Director of Admissions
800-926-SMWC

St. Mary's College
46 Madeliva, Notre Dame 46556
Mary Ann Rowan, Dir. of Admissions

Taylor University
500 W. Reade Ave., Upland 46989
Dale Jackson, Head

University of Evansville
1800 Lincoln Ave., Evansville 47722
John David Lutz, Dept. Chair
800-423-8633

University of Notre Dame
Notre Dame 46556
Kevin M. Rooney, Dir. of Admis.

Valparaiso University, Valparaiso 46383

Wabash College
301 W. Wabash Ave., Crawfordsville 47933
Greg Birk, Dir. of Admis.

IOWA

Clarke College
1550 Clarke Dr., Dubuque 52001
Carol Blitgen, BVM, PhD, Chair
800-383-2345

Coe College
1220 1st Ave., N.E., Cedar Rapids 52402
Robert Drexler, Chrpsn.

Cornell College
600 1st St., W., Mt. Vernon 52314
Kevin Crockett, Dean of Admissions

Dordt College
498 4th Ave., N.E., Sioux Center 51250
Quentin Van Essen, Dir. of Admissions
800-343-6738

Drake University
2507 E. University Ave., Des Moines 50311
Thomas Willoughby, Dir. of Admis.

Graceland College, Lamoni 50140
800-638-0053, Outside Iowa 800-346-9208
Bonita Booth, Dean of Admissions
See listing under "Universities"

Grand View College
1200 Grandview Ave., Des Moines 50316
Lori Hanson, Dir. of Admissions
800-444-6083

Grinnell College
P.O. Box 805, Grinnell 50112

Iowa State University, Ames 50011
Karsten Smedal, Dir. of Admis.

Luther College
700 College Dr., Decorah 52101
David Sallee, Dean for Enrollment

Morningside College, Sioux City 51106
Lora Vanderzwaag, Dir. of Admis.

Mount Mercy College
1330 Elmhurst Dr., N.E., Cedar Rapids 52402
Carol Williamson, Dir. of Admis.

Simpson College
P.O. Box 708, Indianola 50125

Teikyo Marycrest University
1607 W. 12th St., Davenport 52804
Tim McDonough, Dir. of Admis.
See listing under "Universities"

Teikyo Westmar University
1002 3rd Ave., S.E., Le Mars 51031
Dr. Jim Utesch, Dir. of Admis.

† University of Iowa, Iowa City 52242

† University of Northern Iowa, Cedar Falls 50614

Upper Iowa University
P.O. Box 1857, Fayette 52142

· Waldorf College
106 S. 6th St., Forest City 50436
Steve Lovik, Dir. of Admis.
800-292-1903

KANSAS

Emporia State University
1200 Commercial St., Emporia 66801
Dr. Barbara Hilgendorf, Dir. of Admissions

† Fort Hays State University
600 Park St., Hays 67601-4099
Dr. Willis Watt, Chrpsn.

† Kansas State University
Anderson Hall 110, Manhattan 66506
Ellsworth M. Gerritz, Admis. & Records

McPherson College
1600 E. Euclid St., McPherson 67460

Ottawa University
1001 S. Cedar St., Ottawa 66067
Steve Koberlein, Dir. of Admis.
800-755-5200

Pittsburg State University
1701 S. Broadway St., Pittsburg 66762
James E. Parker, Dir of Admis.

Saint Mary College
4100 S. 4th St., Leavenworth 66048
Irene Keehan, Dir. of Admis.

SOUTHWESTERN COLLEGE
100 College St., Winfield 67156
800-846-1543

† University of Kansas, Lawrence 66045

University of Kansas Medical Center
3901 Rainbow Blvd., Kansas City 66160
Dr. James Cooney, Dean

† Wichita State University
1845 Fairmount, Wichita 67260
800-362-2594
See listing under "Universities"

KENTUCKY

Asbury College
1 Macklem Dr., Wilmore 40390
Jonah Mitchell, Dir. of Admis.

† Brescia College
717 Frederica St., Owensboro 42301
Thomas C. Greer, Director of Admission
800-264-1234

Centre College
600 W. Walnut St., Danville 40422

† Eastern Kentucky University
521 Lancaster Ave., Richmond 40475

Georgetown College
400 E. College St., Georgetown 40324
Garvel Kindrick, Director of Admissions
See listing under "Universities"

Kentucky Wesleyan College
3000 Frederica St., Owensboro 42301
Todd Ellis, Director

Morehead State University, Morehead 40351
Charles Myers, Director of Admissions
606-783-2000

† Murray State University, Murray 42071
Phil Bryan, Director of Admissions
800-272-4MSU

† Spalding University
851 S. 4th St., Louisville 40203
Dorothy G. Allen, Dir. of Admis.

Transylvania University
300 Broadway St., N., Lexington 40508
Pat Bain, Dir. of Admis.

† University of Kentucky, Lexington 40506

† University of Louisville
2301 S. 3rd St., Louisville 40292
Robert Parrent, Dir. of Admis.

Western Kentucky University
1526 Russellville Rd., Bowling Green 42101

LOUISIANA

Centenary College of Louisiana
P.O. Box 41188, Shreveport 71134

Dillard University
2601 Gentilly Blvd., New Orleans 70122

† Grambling State University
P.O. Box 607, Grambling 71245
Dr. Harold W. Lundy, President

Louisiana College
College Station, Pineville 71359
Byron McGee, Dir. of Admis.
318-487-7386
See listing under "Liberal Arts"

† Louisiana State University
8515 Youree Dr., Shreveport 71115

† Louisiana State University Medical Center
433 Bolivar St., New Orleans 70112

† Louisiana State University and A & M College
Baton Rouge 70803

† Lousiana Technical University
P.O. Box 3168, Ruston 71272

Loyola University
6363 St. Charles Ave., New Orleans 70118

McNeese State University
4100 Ryan St., Lake Charles 70605

† Nicholls State University
LA Hwy. 1, Thibodaux 70301

Southeastern Louisiana University
P.O. Box 784, Hammond 70404

† Southern University in New Orleans
6400 Press Dr., New Orleans 70126
Millie M. Charles, Director

Tulane University
6823 Saint Charles Ave., New Orleans 70118
Richard Whiteside, Dean of Admission

† University of Southwestern Louisiana
P.O. Box 44548, Lafayette 70504
318-231-6553

† Xavier University
7325 Palmetto St., New Orleans 70125

MAINE

Bowdoin College, Brunswick 04011
William Mason, Dir. of Admis.

† University of Maine
102 Main St., Farmington 04938

† University of Maine, Orono 04469

University of Southern Maine
96 Falmouth St., Portland 04103
Susan Picinich, Chrpsn.

MARYLAND

Goucher College
1021 Dulaney Valley Rd., Baltimore 21204

† Loyola College
4501 N. Charles St., Baltimore 21210
William Bossemeyer III, Dir. of Admis.

· Montgomery College
51 Mannakee St., Rockville 20850
301-279-5250

Towson State University
800 York Rd., Towson 21204
Dr. Hoke Smith, President

† University of Maryland, College Park 20742

Villa Julie College
1525 Greenspring Valley Rd., Stevenson 21153
Carolyn Manuszak, President

MASSACHUSETTS

Amherst College, Amherst 01002
Jane E. Reynolds, Dean of Admissions

Boston Conservatory
8 The Fenway, Boston 02215

† Boston University
685 Commonwealth Ave., Boston 02215

Bradford College
320 S. Main St., Bradford 01835

Brandeis University
415 South St, Waltham 02154
David Gould, Dean of Admissions
617-736-3500

Bridgewater State College
Bridgewater 02325
James Plotner, Jr., Dir. of Admis.

Clark University
950 Main St., Worcester 01610
Richard Pierson, Dean of Admis.

DEAN COLLEGE
99 Main St, Franklin 02038
Kathleen Teehan, Dean of Admissions
508-528-9100
See listing under "Community and Junior Colleges"

†ELMS COLLEGE
291 Springfield St., Chicopee 01013
800-255-ELMS

† Emerson College
148 Beacon St., Boston 02116

Hampshire College, Amherst 01002
Audrey Y. Smith, Dir. of Admissions
413-582-5471

Mt. Holyoke College
College St., South Hadley 01075
Anita Smith, Director of Admissions
413-538-2023

Suffolk University
8 Ashburton Place, Boston 02108
Barbara K. Ericson, Assoc. Dean Enrollment &
Retention
617-573-8460

Tufts University
520 Boston Ave., Medford 02155

† University of Massachusetts, Amherst 01003
Arlene Wesley Cash, Dir. of Admis.

University of Massachusetts
100 Morrissey Blvd., Boston 02125

† Worcester State College
486 Chandler St., Worcester 01602

MICHIGAN

Adrian College
110 S. Madison St., Adrian 49221
George Wolf, Dir. of Admis.
See listing under "Universities"

Albion College
611 E. Porter, Albion 49224
800-858-6770

† Andrews University, Berrien Springs 49104
Jack Mentges, Dir. of Admis.

Calvin College
3201 Burton St., S.E., Grand Rapids 49546

† Central Michigan University
100 Warriner Hall, Mt. Pleasant 48858

† Eastern Michigan University, Ypsilanti 48197
Dennis Beagan, Head
313-487-3060 or 800-GO-TO-EMU

HILLSDALE COLLEGE
33 E. College St., Hillsdale 49242
Dr. Raymond Pentzell, Director
517-437-7341

Kalamazoo College
1200 Academy St., Kalamazoo 49006

Marygrove College
8425 W. McNichols Rd., Detroit 48221

† Michigan State University, East Lansing 48824
Dr. Farley Richmond, Chrpsn.

Olivet College
300 S. Main St., Olivet 49076
Vicki Gallas, Registrar
See listing under "Universities"

: Specs Howard School of Broadcast Arts
16900 W. Eight Mile Rd. #115, Southfield 48075
Specs Howard, Director
810-569-0101

University of Michigan-Ann Arbor
815 S. University Ave., Ann Arbor 48109

† Wayne State University
5980 Cass Ave., Detroit 48202
Dr. J. R. Thorderson, Dir. of Admis.

† Western Michigan University, Kalamazoo 49008
Stanley Henderson, Dir. of Enrl. Mgt. & Admis.
616-387-2000

MINNESOTA

Augsburg College
731 21st Ave., S., Minneapolis 55454

Bemidji State University
1500 Birchmont Dr., N.E., Bemidji 56601
800-475-2001

Bethel College
3900 Bethel Dr., St. Paul 55112
Dr. George Brushaber, President

College of Saint Benedict
37 S. College Ave., St. Joseph 56374

College of St. Catherine
2004 Randolph Ave., St. Paul 55105

Concordia College-St. Paul
275 N. Syndicate, St. Paul 55104
Tim Utter, Dir. of Admis.

Gustavus Adolphus College
800 W. College Ave., St. Peter 56082
Mark Anderson, Dir. of Admis.

Hamline University
1536 Hewitt Ave., St. Paul 55104
Scott Pratt, Dir. of Admis.

MacAlester College
1600 Grand Ave., St. Paul 55105

Mankato State University
P.O. Box 8400, Mankato 56002

† Moorhead State University
1104 7th Ave. S., Moorhead 56560

North Central Bible College
910 Elliot Ave., Minneapolis 55404
800-289-NCBC
Dan Neary, Dir. of Admis.
See listing under "Universities"

Northwestern College
3003 Snelling Ave., N., St. Paul 55113
Ralph Anderson, Dean of Admissions
800-827-6827 or 612-631-5111

PILLSBURY BAPTIST BIBLE COLLEGE
315 S. Grove St., Owatonna 55060
Alan Potter, President
Larry Tindall, Director of Admissions
800-747-4557

† St. Cloud State University
740 4th Ave., S., St. Cloud 56301
Sherwood Reid, Dir. of Admis.
800-369-4260

St. John's University
P.O. Box 7155, Collegeville 56321

St. Mary's College of Minnesota
700 Terrace Heights #2, Winona 55987
Tony Piscitiello, VP for Admission

St. Olaf College, Northfield 55057
Karen Peterson Wilson, Chrpsn.
507-646-3240

Southwest State University, Marshall 56258

† University of Minnesota
2400 Oakland Ave., Duluth 55812
Robert L. Heller, Provost

University of Minnesota
600 E. Fourth St., Morris 56267

† University of Minnesota, Twin Cities
Minneapolis 55455

University of St. Thomas
2115 Summit Ave., St. Paul 55105

Winona State University
P.O. Box 5838, Winona 55987
Dr. J. Mootz, Dir. of Admis.

MISSISSIPPI

† Delta State University
Hwy. 8 W., Cleveland 38732

† Jackson State University
1400 Lynch St., Jackson 39203

Millsaps College
P.O. Box 150556, Jackson 39210
Florence Hines, Dir. of Admis.

Mississippi College
P.O. Box 4086, Clinton 39058

† Mississippi University for Women
P.O. Box W-1602, Columbus 39701
Teresa Thompson, Exec. Dir. of Enrollment

† University of Mississippi, University 38677

† University of Southern Mississippi
P.O. Box 5165, Hattiesburg 39406

William Carey College
498 Tuscan Ave., Hattiesburg 39401

MISSOURI

Avila College
11901 Wornall Rd., Kansas City 64145

Central Institute for the Deaf
818 S. Euclid Ave.
Saint Louis 63110

† Central Missouri State University
Warrensburg 64093
Delores Hudson, Dir. of Admis.

College of the Ozarks, Point Lookout 65726
Dr. Kenton Olson, Dean of the College

Cottey College
1000 W. Austin St., Nevada 64772
Wendy Beckemeyer, Dir. of Admis.

Drury College
900 N. Benton Ave., Springfield 65802
Michael G. Thomas, Dir. of Admis.

Evangel College
1111 N. Glenstone Ave., Springfield 65802
David Schoolfield, Dir. of Enrollment

Fontbonne College
6800 Wydown Blvd., St. Louis 63105
Peggy Musen, Dir. of Admis.

Lincoln University
820 Chestnut St., Jefferson City 65101

Missouri Southern State College
3950 Newman Rd., Joplin 64801-1595
Dr. Jay E. Fields, Dept. Head
See listing under "Universities"

Missouri Valley College
500 E. College St., Marshall 65340
816-886-6924 ext. 114
See listing under "Universities"

Missouri Western State College
4525 Downs Dr., St. Joseph 64507
Howard McCauley, Dir. of Admis.

† Northeast Missouri State University
Kirksville 63501

Northwest Missouri State University
800 University Dr., Maryville 64468

Park College, Parkville 64152
Dr. Edwin Rawn, Dean of Admis.

† St. Louis University
221 N. Grand Blvd., St. Louis 63103
Louis A. Menard, Dean of Admissions

† Southeast Missouri State University
1 University Plz., Cape Girardeau 63701
New Student Relations 314-651-2590
See listing under "Universities"

Southwest Baptist University
1601 S. Springfield Ave., Bolivar 65613

† Southwest Missouri State University
901 S. National Ave., Springfield 65804
Dr. Robert Bradley, Head
417-836-5268

Stephens College, Columbia 65215
Mary Ann Sprinkle, Dir. of Admis.

† University of Missouri, Columbia
228 Jesse Hall, Columbia 65211

† University of Missouri, Kansas City
5100 Rockhill Rd., Kansas City 64110
Leo J. Sweeney, Dir. of Admis. & Registrar

University of Missouri
8001 Natural Bridge Rd., St. Louis 63121
Mimi LaMarca, Dir. of Admis.

Washington University
1 Brookings Dr., St. Louis 63130

Webster University
470 E. Lockwood Ave., St. Louis 63119
Peter Sargent, Associate Dean
See listing under "Universities"

Westminister College
501 Westminster Ave., Fulton 65251
Gary Forney, Dean of Admis.

William Woods College
200 W. 12th St., Fulton 65251
Dr. Jahnae Barnett, VP of Admis.

MONTANA

CARROLL COLLEGE
1610 N. Benton Ave., Helena 59625
Candace Cain, Dir. of Admis.
See listing under "Universities"

Montana State University, Bozeman 59717

Montana State University - Billings
1500 N. 30th St., Billings 59101
Karen Everett, Dir. of Admis.
406-657-2158

Rocky Mountain College
1511 Poly Dr., Billings 59102
David Heringer, Dir. of Admis.
See listing under "Universities"

University of Montana, Missoula 59812
800-462-8636

NEBRASKA

Chadron State College
1000 Main St., Chadron 69337
Dr. Donald Green, Dean

Creighton University
2500 California St., Omaha 68178
Dr. Michael Sundermeier, Chrpsn.

Dana College
2848 College Dr., Blair 68008
John Schueth, Dir. of Admis.
800-444-3262
See listing under "Universities"

Hastings College
P.O. Box 269, Hastings 68902
Thomas Reeves, President

Midland Lutheran College
900 Clarkson St., Fremont 68025
Roland Kahnk, V.P. Admissions

Nebraska Wesleyan University
5000 Saint Paul Ave., Lincoln 68504
Ken Sieg, Dir. of Admis.

Peru State College, Peru 68421
Pamela J. Cosgrove, Dir. of Admis.
402-872-3815

† University of Nebraska
905 W. 25th St., Kearney 68849

† University of Nebraska at Lincoln
16 Administration Bldg., Lincoln 68588
John Beacon, Dir. of Admissions

† University of Nebraska at Omaha
Omaha 68182

Wayne State College
200 E. Tenth St., Wayne 68787

NEVADA

† University of Nevada, Reno
Reno 89557

NEW HAMPSHIRE

Franklin Pierce College, Rindge 03461

Keene State College
229 Main St., Keene 03435
Kathryn Dodge, Dir. of Admis.

New England College
26 Bridge St., Henniker 03242
John Spaulding, Dir. of Admis.

† University of New Hampshire, Durham 03824
Stanwood C. Fish, Dir. of Admissions

NEW JERSEY

Fairleigh Dickinson University, Teaneck 07666
Dennis Craig, Dir. of Admis.
201-692-2732

Jersey City State College
2039 Kennedy Blvd., Jersey City 07305
201-200-3234

Monmouth College
400 Cedar Ave., West Long Branch 07764
Prof. Huber, Chrpsn.

† Montclair State College
1 Normal Ave., Upper Montclair 07043

Princeton University, Princeton 08544

Rider University
2083 Lawrenceville Rd., Lawrenceville 08648
Susan Christian, Dir. of Admis.

Rowan College of New Jersey, Glassboro 08028
Marvin G. Sills, Dir. of Admis.

† Stockton State College, Pomona 08240
Sal Catalfamo, Dir. of Admis.

† Trenton State College
Hillwood Lakes CN 4700, Trenton 08650

† William Paterson College
300 Pompton Rd., Wayne 07470

NEW MEXICO

College of Santa Fe
1600 St. Michaels Dr., Santa Fe 87505
800-456-2673

Eastern New Mexico University
Portales 88130
Larry Fuqua, Dir. of Admis.

† New Mexico State University
P.O. Box 30001, Las Cruces 88003

† University of New Mexico, Albuquerque 87131
Robert Weaver, Dean of Admissions

NEW YORK

† Adelphi University, Garden City 11530
Dr. Jeffrey Kane, Dean, School of Education
516-877-4100

Alfred University
Alumni Hall, Alfred 14802
Laurie Richer, Director of Admissions
800-541-9229

· American Academy of Dramatic Arts
120 Madison Ave., New York 10016

Bard College
Annandle-on-Hudson 12504

Barnard College
3009 Broadway, New York 10027

† College of New Rochelle
29 Castle Pl., New Rochelle 10805

Cornell University
410 Thurston Ave., Ithaca 14853

† CUNY Brooklyn College
2900 Bedford Ave., Brooklyn 11210
Justin Dunn, Dir. of Admis.

CUNY College of Staten Island
130 Stuyvesant Pl., Staten Island 10301

† CUNY Hunter College
695 Park Ave., New York 10021
Donna Shalala, President

† CUNY Lehman College
250 Bedford Park Blvd. W., Bronx 10468
Jane Herbert, Dir. of Enrollment Management

† CUNY, Queens College
6530 Kissena Blvd., Flushing 11367

CUNY York College
9420 Guy R. Brewer Blvd., Jamaica 11451

† CUNY Graduate School & University Center
33 W. 42nd St., New York 10036
Dr. Norma Rees, Graduate Dean

† Dominican College of Blauvelt
460 N. Western Hwy., Orangeburg 10962
Louis Kern, Dir. of Admis.
914-359-7800

† Elmira College
Park Pl., Elmira 14901
William S. Neal, Dean of Admissions
See listing under "Liberal Arts"

Fordham University
Lincoln Center Campus
113 W. 60th St., New York 10023
Edward Bristow, Dean

Friends World Program, Long Island University
Montauk Hwy., Southampton 11968
Carol Gilbert, Dir. of Admis.

Hartwick College, Oneonta 13820

† Hofstra University
1000 Fulton Ave., Hempstead 11550
Margaret Shields, Dean of Admissions

† IONA COLLEGE
715 North Ave., New Rochelle 10801
800-231-IONA or 914-633-2503
See listing under "Universities"

† Ithaca College
953 Danby Rd., Ithaca 14850

Juilliard School
60 Lincoln Center Plz., New York 10023
Carole Everett, Dir of Admis.

Long Island University-C. W. Post Campus
Rt. 25A, Brookville 11548
Prof. Cara Gargano, Chrpsn. Theatre Arts
516-299-2353
Prof. Barbara Fowles, Chrpsn. Communication
Arts
516-299-2382

Marymount College
100 Marymount Ave., Tarrytown 10591
Gina R. Campbell, Dir. of Admis.
800-724-4312

† Marymount Manhattan College
221 E. 71st St., New York 10021
Suzanne M. Murphy, Dir. of Admis.

† Mercy College
555 Broadway, Dobbs Ferry 10522
James Nesbitt, Dean of Admissions

Molloy College
1000 Hempstead Ave., Rockville Centre 11570
Wayne James, Dir. of Admis.
See listing under "Universities"

Mt. St. Mary College
330 Powell Ave., Newburgh 12550

Nazareth College of Rochester
4245 East Ave., Rochester 14618
Paul Kenyon, Dir. of Admis.

† New York University
70 Washington Sq., New York 10012

Niagara University, Niagara University 14109
George Pachter, Dean of Admissions
800-462-2111
See listing under "Universities"

Nyack College, Nyack 10960
Miguel Sanchez, Dir. of Admis.
800-33-NYACK

† Pace University, New York Campus
1 Pace Plaza, New York 10038

† St. John's University
Grand Central & Utopia Parkways, Jamaica 11439

St. Joseph's College
245 Clinton Ave., Brooklyn 11205
Geraldine Foudy, Dir. of Admis.
718-636-6868

Sarah Lawrence College, Bronxville 10708

Skidmore College, Saratoga Springs 12866
Kent Jones, Dir. of Admis.

SUNY at Albany
1400 Washington Ave., Albany 12222
Micheileen Treadwell, Dir. of
Admission/Financial Aid
518-442-5431

† SUNY at Buffalo
17 Capen Hall
P.O. Box 601660, Buffalo 14260-1660
716-645-6900

SUNY College at Brockport
Brockport 14420
Dr. Adam La Zarrc, Chrpsn.

† SUNY College at Buffalo
1300 Elmwood Ave., Buffalo 14222
Deborah K. Renzi, Dir. of Admis.

† SUNY College at Cortland
P.O. Box 2000, Cortland 13045

SUNY College at Fredonia, Fredonia 14063
William S. Clark, III, Dir. of Admissions

† SUNY College at Geneseo
1 College Cir., Geneseo 14454
William L. Caren, Dir. of Admissions

SUNY College at Old Westbury
P.O. Box 210, Old Westbury 11568
Michael Sheehy, Dir. of Admis.

† SUNY College at Oneonta, Oneonta 13820
Clifford McVinney, Dir. of Admis.

SUNY College at Plattsburgh, Plattsburgh 12901
Richard Higgins, Dir. of Admis.
518-564-2040

† Syracuse University, Syracuse 13244

† Teachers College of Columbia University
525 W. 120th St., New York 10027

Utica College of Syracuse University
1600 Burrstone Rd., Utica 13502

Vassar College
125 Raymond Ave., Poughkeepsie 12601

† Yeshiva University
500 W. 185th St., New York 10033

NORTH CAROLINA

† Appalachian State University
ASU Station, Boone 28608
Joe Watts, Admissions Officer

Catawba College
2300 W. Innes St., Salisbury 28144
Mark Stokes, Dir. of Admis.

College of The Albemarle
P.O. Box 2327, Elizabeth City 27906
John M. Wells, Asst. Dean of Admissions
919-335-0821, Ext. 220

† East Carolina University
1000 E. 5th St., Greenville 27858
John Shearin, Chair

† Elizabeth City State University
1704 Weeksville Rd., Elizabeth City 27909
William A.T. Byrd, Dir. of Admis.

Gardner-Webb University
General Delivery, Boiling Springs 28017
Ray M. Hardee, Dean of Admissions
800-253-6472

Greensboro College
815 W. Market St., Greensboro 27401

Guilford College
5800 W. Friendly Ave., Greensboro 27410
Larry West, Dir. of Admis.
See listing under "Universities"

Lenoir-Rhyne College
P.O. Box 292, Hickory 28603
Steve M. Shuford, Registrar

Mars Hill College
Main St., Mars Hill 28754
Dr. Smith Goodrum, Dean of Admis.

Methodist College
5400 Ramsey St., Fayetteville 28311
Fiore Bergamasco, Dir. of Admis.

† North Carolina A&T State University
1601 E. Market St., Greensboro 27411

North Carolina Central University
P.O. Box 19617, Durham 27707

† North Carolina State University
P.O. Box 7001, Raleigh 27695
George Dixon, Dir. of Admis.

North Carolina Wesleyan College
3400 N. Wesleyan Blvd., Rocky Mount 27804

Pfeiffer College
General Delivery, Misenheimer 28109

† Shaw University
118 E. South St., Raleigh 27601

† University of North Carolina
1000 Spring Garden St., Greensboro 27412

University of North Carolina
601 S. College Rd., Wilmington 28403
W. H. Wagoner, Chancellor

University of North Carolina at Asheville
1 University Heights, Asheville 28804
William E. Highsmith, Chancellor

† University of North Carolina at Chapel Hill
Chapel Hill 27599
James C. Walters, Dir. Undergrad Admis.

NORTH DAKOTA

Dickinson State University, Dickinson 58601
Marshall Melbye, Registrar
701-227-2331

† Minot State University
500 University Ave. W., Minot 58701

† University of North Dakota
Box 8193 University Station, Grand Forks 58203

OHIO

† Baldwin-Wallace College
275 Eastland Rd., Berea 44017
Juliann K. Baker, Dir. of Admis.

† Bowling Green State University
Bowling Green 43403
John Martin, Dir. of Admis.

Capital University
2199 E. Main St., Columbus 43209
Dolphus E. Henry, Associate Provost

† Case Western Reserve University
2040 Adelbert Rd., Cleveland 44106

† Cleveland State University
Euclid Ave. at 24th St., Cleveland 44115

† College of Wooster
1189 Beall Ave., Wooster 44691
Hayden Schilling, Dean of Admis.

Denison University
P.O. Box B, Granville 43023
Richard Boyden, Dir. of Admis.

Heidelberg College
310 E. Market St., Tiffin 44883
Stephen E. Eidson, Dean of Admission
800-925-9250

Hiram College
P.O. Box 96, Hiram 44234
Gary Craig, Dean of Admis.

† Kent State University
P.O. Box 5190, Kent 44242
Bruce Riddle, Dir. of Admis.

Kenyon College
1 Kenyon College, Gambier 43022
Philip H. Jordan, Jr., President

Lake Erie College
391 W. Washington St., Painesville 44077

Malone College
515 25th St., N.W., Canton 44709
Lee Sommers, Dean of Admissions

MARIETTA COLLEGE
210 5th St., Marietta 45750
Dennis R. DePerro, Dean Admis./Financial Aid
800-331-7896

† Miami University
E. High St., Oxford 45056

Mount Union College
1972 Clark Ave., Alliance 44601
Amy Tomko, Dir. of Admis.

Mt. Vernon Nazarene College
800 Martinsburg Rd., Mt. Vernon 43050
Ronald Hyson, Dir. of Admis.

Muskingum College
147 Center St., New Concord 43762

Notre Dame College
4545 College Rd., Cleveland 44121
Sr. Mary Luke, S.N.D., President

Oberlin College
135 W. Lorain St., Oberlin 44074
Daniel Goulding, Chrpsn.

Ohio Dominican College
1216 Sunbury Rd., Columbus 43219
800-955-OHIO

OHIO NORTHERN UNIVERSITY
525 S. Main St., Ada 45810
Nils Riess, Dept. of Comm., Chrpsn.
412-772-2000

† Ohio State University
190 N. Oval Mall, Columbus 43210

† Ohio University, Athens 45701

Ohio Wesleyan University
61 S. Sandusky St., Delaware 43015
Donald Bishop, Dean for Enrollment

† University of Akron
381 Buchtel Common, Akron 44325
Kris MacDermott, Asst. Provost Enrollment

† University of Cincinnati
2700 Clifton Ave., Cincinnati 45221

University of Findlay
1000 N. Main St., Findlay 45840
Dan Crabtree, Dir. of Admis.

University of Rio Grande
General Delivery, Rio Grande 45674
Dr. Gregory Miller, Coordinator
614-245-5353, Ext. 7364

University of Toledo
2801 Bancroft St., W., Toledo 43606
Richard Eastop, Dir. of Admis.

Wilmington College
P.O. Box 1185, Wilmington 45177
Rhonda Inderhees, Dir. of Admis.

Wittenberg University
P.O. Box 720, Springfield 45504

OKLAHOMA

Cameron University
2800 W. Gore Blvd., Lawton 73505
Louise Brown, Dir. of Admis.

Northwestern Oklahoma State University
705 Oklahoma Blvd., Alva 73717

Oklahoma City University
2501 N. Blackwelder Ave., Oklahoma City 73106
Judith Palladino, Director
See listing under "Universities"

Oklahoma Panhandle State University
P.O. Box 430, Goodwell 73939

† Oklahoma State University, Stillwater 74078
Paul Harper, Dept. Head

Oral Roberts University
7777 S. Lewis Ave., Tulsa 74171
Arthur E. Matzkvech, Dir. of Admis.

Southern Nazarene University
6729 N.W. 39th Expy., Bethany 73008

University of Central Oklahoma
100 N. University Dr., Edmond 73034

University of Oklahoma at Norman
660 Parrington Oval, Norman 73019

† University of Oklahoma Health Sciences Center
P.O. Box 26901, Oklahoma City 73126
Dr. Charles Cameron, Dean

† University of Sciences & Arts of Oklahoma
P.O. Box 82345, Chickasha 73018

† University of Tulsa
600 S. College Ave., Tulsa 74104
Dr. David Cook, Chrpsn.

OREGON

Lewis & Clark College
0615 S.W. Palatine Hill Rd., Portland 97219
Michael Sexton, Dean of Admissions

Linfield College
900 S. Baker St., McMinnville 97128
Thomas Meicho, Dean of Admissions

Oregon State University, Corvallis 97333
Wallace Gibbs, Dir. of Admis.

† Portland State University
P.O. Box 751, Portland 97207

Reed College
3202 S.E. Woodstock Blvd., Portland 97202

Southern Oregon State College
1250 Siskiyou Blvd., Ashland 97520

† University of Oregon
1 University of Oregon, Eugene 97403

University of Portland
5000 N. Willamette Blvd., Portland 97203

Warner Pacific College
2219 S.E. 68th Ave., Portland 97215
Sherry Moore, Enrollment Management Director

PENNSYLVANIA

Allegheny College
520 N. Main St., Meadville 16335
Gayle Pollack, Dir. of Admis.

Allentown College of St. Frances de Sales
2755 Station Ave., Center Valley 18034
George Kelley, Dir. of Admis.

Beaver College
450 S. Easton Rd., Glenside 19038-3295
Dennis Nostrand, VP for Enrollment Management
Phone: 800-776-BEAVER(2328)
Fax: 215-572-4049
See listing under "Universities"

Bloomsburg University, Bloomsburg 17815
Bernard Vinovrski, Dir. of Admis.

California University of Pennsylvania
3rd St., California 15419
Norman Hasbrouck, Dean for Enrollment

† Carlow College
3333 5th Ave., Pittsburgh 15213

Carnegie Mellon University
5000 Forbes Ave., Pittsburgh 15213

Cedar Crest College
100 College Dr., Allentown 18104-6196
Cynthia Phillips, Dir. of Admissions

Chatham College
Woodland Rd., Pittsburgh 15232
Suellen Ofe, Dean of Admis./Financial Aid
See listing under "Women's College"

† Clarion University of Pennsylvania
840 Wood St., Clarion 16214

† Duquesne University
600 Forbes Ave., Pittsburgh 15282
Thomas Schaefer, C.S.Sp., Dir. of Admis.

† East Stroudsburg University of Pennsylvania
East Stroudsburg 18301
Alan Chesterton, Dir. of Admis.

Edinboro University of Pennsylvania
Edinboro 16444
Admissions Office: 800-626-2203

Gannon University
109 University Sq., Erie 16541

† Geneva College
3200 College Ave., Beaver Falls 15010

Juniata College
1700 Moore St., Huntington 16652

King's College
133 N. River St., Wilkes Barre 18711

† Kutztown University of Pennsylvania
Kutztown 19530

Lycoming College, Williamsport 17701

Mansfield University of Pennsylvania
Mansfield 16933

† Marywood College
2300 Adams Ave., Scranton 18509

Muhlenberg College
2400 W. Chew St., Allentown 18104
Chris Hooker-Haring, Dir. of Admis.

† Pennsylvania State University
201 Shields Bldg., University Park 16802

Point Park College
201 Wood St., Pittsburgh 15222

St. Francis College
P.O. Box 600, Loretto 15940

Seton Hill College, Greensburg 15601
Peter Egan, Dir. of Admis.
800-826-6234 or 412-838-4255

Slippery Rock University, Slippery Rock 16057
Director of Admissions

Susquehanna University
514 University Ave., Selinsgrove 17870

† Temple University
Broad St. & Montgomery Ave.
Philadelphia 19122

† University of Pittsburgh
4200 5th Ave., Pittsburgh 15260

University of the Arts
320 S. Broad St., Philadelphia 19102
Margaret Heuges, Dir. of Admis.

Villanova University
845 E. Lancaster Ave., Villanova 19085
Stephen R. Merritt, Dir. of Admis.

West Chester University of Pennsylvania
S. High St., West Chester 19380

WESTMINSTER COLLEGE
New Wilmington 16172
Richard Dana Paul, Dir. of Admis.
412-946-7100

York College of Pennsylvania
P.O. Box 15199, York 17405-7199
Nancy Spataro, Dir. of Admis.
717-849-1600
See listing under "Universities"

RHODE ISLAND

Brown University, Providence 02906

† Rhode Island College
600 Mt. Pleasant Ave., Providence 02908

Roger Williams College
1 Old Ferry Rd., Bristol 02809
William Dunfey, Dir. of Admis.

Salve Regina University
1 Ochre Point Ave., Newport 02840
Roselina McKillop, Dean of Admissions

† University of Rhode Island, Kingston 02881
Judith Anderson, Chrpsn. Dept. of Speech Comm.

SOUTH CAROLINA

Anderson College
316 S. Boulevard, Anderson 29621
Carl D. Lockman, Dir. of Admis.
800-542-3594

Coastal Carolina College
P.O. Box 1954, Myrtle Beach 29578
Dr. Ed Cerny, Director of Admissions

† Columbia College
1301 Columbia College Dr., Columbia 29203

Converse College
580 E. Main St., Spartanburg 29302
Dr. Martha Rogers, VP Enrollment Management

Furman University
3300 Poinsett Hwy., Greenville 29613
Charles Brock, Dir. of Admis.

Lander College
320 Stanley Ave., Greenwood 29649

North Greenville College
P.O. Box 1892, Tigerville 29688
Gary Wells, Dir. of Admis.
See listing under "Universities"

South Carolina State University
P.O. Box 7127, Orangeburg 29117-0001
803-536-7185

† University of South Carolina, Columbia 29208
Terry Davis, Dir. of Admis.
803-777-7700

Winthrop University
701 W. Oakland Ave., Rock Hill 29733
James McCammon, Jr., Dir. of Admis.

SOUTH DAKOTA

Augustana College
29th & S. Summit, Sioux Falls 57197

Dakota Wesleyan University
1300 W. University Ave., Mitchell 57301

Mt. Marty College
1105 W. 8th St., Yankton 57078
Paula Tacke, Dir. of Admis.

† Northern State University
1200 S. Jay St., Aberdeen 57401

SIOUX FALLS COLLEGE
1501 S. Prairie Ave., Sioux Falls 57105
Susan Reese, Dir. of Admis.
800-888-1047
See listing under "Universities"

† South Dakota State University
P.O. Box 2218, Brookings 57007
Dr. Michael Schliessmann, Department Head
605-688-4388
See listing under "Universities"

† University of South Dakota
414 E. Clark St., Vermillion 57069
Dave Lorenz, Dir. of Admis.

TENNESSEE

Austin Peay State University
601 College St., Clarksville 37044

Carson-Newman College
P.O. Box 70552, Jefferson City 37760
See listing under "Universities"

David Lipscomb University
3901 Granny White Pike, Nashville 37204-3951
Wade Sandrell, Dir. of Admis.
800-333-4358

† EAST TENNESSEE STATE UNIVERSITY
P.O. Box 70731, Johnson City 37614
Dr. Nancy Dishner, Dean, Enrollment Management
615-929-4213 or 800-462-3878

Freed-Hardeman University
158 E. Main St., Henderson 38340
800-342-7837

† Lambuth College
705 Lambuth Blvd., Jackson 38301

Lincoln Memorial University
P.O. Box 2012, Harrogate 37752
Conrad Daniels, Dir. of Admis.

† Middle Tennessee State University
Murfreesboro 37132
Roger D. Sims, Dir. of Admis.

Rhodes College
2000 N. Parkway, Memphis 38112

Tennessee State University
3500 John A. Merritt Blvd., Nashville 37209

Tennessee Temple University
1815 Union Ave., Chattanooga 37404
Dr. L. W. Nichols, President

Trevecca Nazarene College
333 Murfreesboro Rd., Nashville 37210

Tusculum College
P.O. Box 5035, Greeneville 37743
Ronald Porter, Dir. of Admis.

† University of Memphis, Memphis 38152
Dr. John Eubank, Dean of Admissions

University of Tennessee at Martin
Martin 38238
Paul Kelley, Director of Admissions
See listing under "Universities"

† University of Tennessee, Knoxville
527 Andy Holt Tower, Knoxville 37996
Dr. Gordon Stanley, Dir. of Admis.

† Vanderbilt University
West End Ave., Nashville 37240

TEXAS

Austin College
900 N. Grand Ave., Sherman 75090
Rodney Oto, Dean of Admission
800-442-5363

† Baylor University
P.O. Box 97008, Waco 76798-7008
Diana Ramey, Director of Admissions

Dallas Baptist University
7777 W. Kiest Blvd., Dallas 75211

East Texas Baptist University
1200 N. Grove Ave., Marshall 75670

† Hardin-Simmons University
2200 Hickory St., Abilene 79698
Laura Moore, Dir. of Admis.
See listing under "Universities"

Houston Baptist University
7502 Fondren Rd., Houston 77074

Howard Payne University
1000 Fisk Ave., Brownwood 76801

Incarnate Word College
4301 Broadway St., San Antonio 78209
Sr. Sally Mitchell, Dean of Enrollment

: KD Studio
2600 N. Stemmons Freeway #117, Dallas 75207
Nicholas S. Dalley, Director of Education
Contact Admissions Department: 214-638-0484

† Lamar University
P.O. Box 10009, Beaumont 77710
800-458-7558

McMurry University
14th and Sayles, Abilene 79697

Midwestern State University
3400 Taft Blvd., Wichita Falls 76308
Dr. June Kable, Head

† Our Lady of the Lake University
411 S.W. 24th St., San Antonio 78207-4689
210-434-6711

Sam Houston State University, Huntsville 77341

Southern Methodist University
Hillcrest at University, Dallas 75275

Southwestern University
University Ave. at Maple St., Georgetown 78626

† Southwest Texas State University
601 University Dr., San Marcos 78666

Stephen F. Austin State University
P.O. Box 6078, Nacogdoches 75962

Sul Ross State University, Alpine 79832

† Texas A & I University
Campus Box 101, Kingsville 78363

Texas A & M University
College Station 77843

† Texas Christian University
2800 S. University Dr., Ft. Worth 76129
Dr. Edward Boehm, Jr., Dean of Admissions

Texas Lutheran College
1000 W. Court St., Seguin 78155
Jennifer B. Ehlers, Dir. of Admis.

† Texas Tech University, Lubbock 79409

Texas Wesleyan University
1201 Wesleyan St., Fort Worth 76105
Kim Campbell, Dir. Freshman Admission

University of Dallas
1845 E. Northgate Dr., Irving 75062
Jim Whitaker, Dir. of Admis.

† University of Houston
4800 Calhoun Rd., Houston 77204

† University of North Texas
P.O. Box 13797, Denton 76203

University of St. Thomas
3812 Montrose Blvd., Houston 77006
Elsie Biron, Dir. of Admis.

University of Texas at Arlington
UTA Box 19125, Arlington 76019
R. Zack Prince, Dir. of Admis.

† University of Texas at Austin
0 the University of Texas, Austin 78712

† University of Texas at Dallas
P.O. Box 830688, Richardson 75083-0688

West Texas State University
2501 4th Ave., Canyon 79016
Lila Vars, Dir. of Admis.

UTAH

† Brigham Young University, Provo 84602

Southern Utah University
351 W. Center St., Cedar City 84720
Gary McIntyre, Dept. of Theater Arts
801-586-5484

† University of Utah
1400 E. 200 S., Salt Lake City 84112
Dr. J. Stayner Landward, Dir. of Admis.

† Utah State University, Logan 84322-1600
Rod Clark, Director of Admissions
801-750-1107

Weber State University
3750 Harrison Blvd., Ogden 84408

Westminster College of Salt Lake City
1840 S. 1300 E., Salt Lake City   84105
800-748-4753

VERMONT

Bennington College, Bennington   05201
Karen Kristof, Dir. of Admis.
800-833-6845

Lyndon State College, Lyndonville   05851

Marlboro College
General Delivery, Marlboro   05344

Saint Michael's College
Winooski Park, Colchester   05439
800-SMC-8000
See listing under "Liberal Arts"

† University of Vermont
194 S. Prospect St., Burlington   05401
802-656-3370

VIRGINIA

Christopher Newport College
50 Shoe Ln., Newport News   23606

College of William and Mary, Williamsburg   23185
Jean A. Scott, Dean of Admission

Emory & Henry College
General Delivery, Emory   24327

George Mason University
4400 University Dr., Fairfax   22030-4444
Patricia Riordan, Dean of Admissions

† Hampton University, Hampton   23668
Ollie Bowman, Dean of Admissions

James Madison University, Harrisonburg   22807

LIBERTY UNIVERSITY
P.O. Box 20000, Lynchburg   24506
Jay Spencer, VP Recruitment
800-376-2800
See listing under "Universities"

† Longwood College, Farmville   23901

Lynchburg College
1501 Lakeside Dr., Lynchburg   24501
Ernest Chadderton, Dean of Enrollment

Mary Baldwin College, Staunton   24401
Douglas E. Clark, Exec. Dir. of Enrollment

Mary Washington College
1701 College Ave., Fredericksburg   22401
Martin Wilder, V.P. for Admissions

† Norfolk State University
2401 Corprew Ave., Norfolk   23504

† Old Dominion University
5215 Hampton Blvd., Norfolk   23508

Radford University
P.O. Box 5430, Radford   24142

Randolph-Macon College
200 Henry St., Ashland   23005
John Conkright, Dean of Admissions

Roanoke College
221 College Ln., Salem   24153

SHENANDOAH UNIVERSITY
1460 University Dr., Winchester   22601
Harold Herman, Division Chair
See listing under "Universities"

Sweet Briar College, Sweet Briar   24595
Nancy Church, Dir. of Admis.

University of Virginia
P.O. Box 9017, Charlottesville   22906

Virginia Polytechnic Institute & State University
Blacksburg   24061
David Bousquet, Dir. of Undergraduate Admis.

Virginia Wesleyan College
1584 Wesleyan Dr., Norfolk   23502
W. Steve Stocks, V.P. for Admis.

WASHINGTON

Central Washington University, Ellensburg   98926
William Swain, Director of Admissions

Cornish College of the Arts
710 E. Roy St., Seattle   98102
Jane Buckman, Admissions
800-726-ARTS

† Eastern Washington University, Cheney   99004
Robert Elton, Dean of Graduate Affairs
See listing under "Universities"

Olympic College
1600 Chester Ave., Bremerton   98337
Wallace Simpson, President

Pacific Lutheran University
12180 Park Ave. S., Tacoma   98447
Michael Bartanen, Chrpsn.

Seattle University
Broadway Ave. & Madison, Seattle   98122
Lee Gerig, Dean of Admissions

University of Puget Sound
1500 N. Warner St., Tacoma   98416

† University of Washington, Seattle   98195

Walla Walla College
204 S. College Ave., College Place   99324

† Washington State University, Pullman   99164
Stan Berry, Dir. of Admis.

† Western Washington University
516 High St., Bellingham   98225
Karen G. Copetas, Dir. of Admis.

Whitman College
345 Boyer Ave., Walla Walla   99362

WEST VIRGINIA

Alderson-Broaddus College
Philippi   26416
Craig W. Gould, Director of Admissions
304-457-1700

Concord College, Athens   24712

Marshall University
400 Hal Greer Blvd., Huntington   25755
See listing under "Universities"

Shepherd College, Shepherdstown   25443

West Virginia State College
P.O. Box 1000, Institute   25112

† West Virginia University
P.O. Box 6001, Morgantown   26506

WEST VIRGINIA WESLEYAN COLLEGE
59 College Ave., Buckhannon   26201
Robert Skinner, Director of Admission
See listing under "Universities"

WISCONSIN

Beloit College
700 College St., Beloit   53511
Rodney J. Umlas, Chair
608-363-2685

Cardinal Stritch College
6801 N. Yates Rd., Milwaukee   53217
David Wegener, Dir. of Admis.

Carroll College
100 N. East Ave., Waukesha   53186
Ken Moyer, Dir. of Admis.

Carthage College
2001 Alford Dr., Kenosha   53140
Dr. T. Holland, Chrpsn.

Lawrence University
P.O. Box 599, Appleton   54912
Steven Syverson, Dean of Admissions

† Marquette University
1217 W. Wisconsin Ave., Milwaukee   53233
Raymond A. Brown, Dean of Admissions

Ripon College, P.O. Box 248, Ripon   54971
James Reilly, Dean of Admis.

St. Norbert College
100 Grant St., De Pere   54115
Craig S. Wesley, Dean of Admission
See listing under "Universities"

† University of Wisconsin, Eau Claire
Eau Claire   54701

† University of Wisconsin, Madison
500 Lincoln Dr., Madison   53706

† University of Wisconsin
P.O. Box 413, Milwaukee   53201
V. M. Allison, Registrar

University of Wisconsin, Oshkosh
800 Algoma Blvd., Oshkosh   54901-8602
August Helgerson, Dir. of Admis.

University of Wisconsin
1 University Plaza, Platteville   53818
Richard Schumacher, Dean of Admissions

† University of Wisconsin, River Falls
River Falls   54022
Alan Tuchtenhagen, Dir. of Admis.

† University of Wisconsin, Stevens Point   54481
Dr. John A. Larsen, Dir. of Admis.

University of Wisconsin, Superior   54880
Richard E. Morrison, Dir. Univ. Relations

† University of Wisconsin
800 W. Main St., Whitewater   53190

Viterbo College
815 9th St., S., La Crosse   54601
Roland W. Nelson, Dir. of Admis.

WYOMING

† University of Wyoming
P.O. Box 3434, Laramie   82071
Richard Davis, Dir. of Admis.

PUERTO RICO

† University of Puerto Rico, Rio Piedras Campus
P.O. Box 23300, San Juan   00931
Victor Lopez, Dir. of Admis.

STUDY ABROAD

ALABAMA

Samford University
800 Lakeshore Dr., Birmingham   35229
Marlene Rikard, London Studies

University of Alabama
P.O. Box 870132, Tuscaloosa   35487-0132
Roy Smith, Dir. of Admis.

UNIVERSITY OF MOBILE
Latin American Branch Campus
San Marcos, Carazo, Nicaragua
Phone:(043) 314,312,331, Fax. (043) 336
See listing under "Universities"

ALASKA

University of Alaska Anchorage
3211 Providence Dr., Anchorage   99508
907-786-1480

ARIZONA

Northern Arizona University
P.O. Box 4092, Flagstaff   86011
Dr. Margaret Cibik, Dir. of Admis.

University of Arizona, Tucson   85721
Loyd Bell, Director of Admissions

ARKANSAS

Ouachita Baptist University
410 Ouachita St., Arkadelphia   71998
Randy Garner, Dir. of Admis.
800-DIAL-OBU

CALIFORNIA

Fresno Pacific College
1717 S. Chestnut Ave., Fresno   93702
209-453-2039

La Sierra University
4700 Pierce St., Riverside   92505
800-874-5587

Pitzer College
1050 N. Mills Ave., Claremont   91711
Katharine Leighton, Dir. of Admis.

Pomona College
333 N. College Way, Claremont   91711
Peter W. Stanley, President

Santa Barbara City College
721 Cliff Dr., Santa Barbara   93109
805-965-0581

UNITED STATES INTERNATIONAL UNIVERSITY
10455 Pomerado Rd., San Diego   92131
619-693-4772
See listing under "Universities"

University of La Verne
1950 3rd St., La Verne   91750
Mark Bornholdt, Dir. of Admis.

University of San Diego
5998 Alcala Park, San Diego   92110
Warren Muller, Dir. of Admis.
619-260-4506

University of San Francisco
2130 Fulton St., San Francisco   94117
Bill Henley, Dir. of Admis.

Whittier College
13406 Philadelphia St., Whittier   90601
310-907-4238

COLORADO

Naropa Institute
2130 Arapahoe Ave., Boulder   80302
Dr. Jana Lynn, Director of Admissions
303-546-3572

Regis University
3333 Regis Blvd., Denver   80221
Robert Blust, Director of Admissions

CONNECTICUT

Albertus Magnus College
700 Prospect St., New Haven   06511
Richard Lolatte, Dir. of Admissions
203-773-8501 or 800-578-9160

· Mattatuck Community College
750 Chase Parkway, Waterbury 06708
Dr. Richard Sanders, President

AMERICAN INSTITUTE FOR FOREIGN STUDY
102 Greenwich Ave., Greenwich 06830
800-727-AIFS

Established 1964. Summer, quarter, semester and academic year college-level programs on campuses in Australia, Austria, Czech Republic, England, France, Italy, Japan, Mexico, Spain and Russia. Courses include art, business administration, drama, economics, history, internships, languages, and political science. Fees from $4,300 per semester including one-way air transportation, tuition, housing, meal plan, insurance and support of Resident Director abroad.

DELAWARE

University of Delaware, Newark 19711

DISTRICT OF COLUMBIA

The American University
4400 Massachusetts Ave. N.W.
Washington 20016

FLORIDA

Flagler College
P.O. Box 1027, St. Augustine 32085
Marc G. Williar, Dir. of Admis.
904-829-6481

Jacksonville University
2800 University Blvd., N., Jacksonville 32211

LYNN UNIVERSITY
(Est. 1962 as College of Boca Raton)
3601 N. Military Trail, Boca Raton 33431
407-994-0770 or 800-544-8035
See listing under "Universities"

SCHILLER INTERNATIONAL UNIVERSITY (EUROPE)
U.S. Admissions Office
Dept. PA, 453 Edgewater Dr., Dunedin 34698-7532
800-336-4133 or 813-736-5082 Fax: 813-736-6263
Dr. Walter Leibrecht, President
Karen Altieri, Associate Director of Admissions

Established 1964. Coed. Accreditation: ACICS. Tuition: $11,140. Room and board: $5,800. Est. total yrly. expense: $21,000. Enrollment: 1,519. Campuses in Heidelberg, Berlin, London, Madrid, Paris, Strasbourg, and in Leysin and Engelberg, Switzerland. Degrees: AA, AAS, AS, BA, BS, BBA, BPA, MA, MIM, MBA. Classes conducted in English. U.S. transfer possibilities: 1 semester, academic year, and summer study programs. Majors in International Business, Banking, Management, Marketing, International Hotel & Tourism Management, European studies, International Relations & Diplomacy, Computer Systems Management, Commercial Art, Psychology, Engineering Management, Pre-Medicine, Economics & Foreign Languages. Also courses in history, political science, Middle Eastern studies, English, German and French literature. Also 3-8 week foreign language institutes in Germany, Spain, and Switzerland (French) for students 17 years and up. Financial aid and scholarships available. See listing under "Universities"

GEORGIA

AMERICAN COLLEGE IN LONDON
110 Marylebone High St., London W1M 3DB
US Admissions Office
3330 Peachtree Rd., N.E., Atlanta 30326
404-231-9000
Will Conard, Director of Study Abroad Programs
Private. Coed. Non-denominational. Accreditation: SACS. Study Abroad Programs in fashion design, fashion marketing, interior design, commercial art, business administration, video production and liberal arts. Student housing. Professional faculty active in the industry. Member of National Association for Foreign Student Affairs (NAFSA) and Institute of International Education (IIE). Five academic terms beginning September, January, March, May, and July. College also confers AA and BA degrees.

Mercer University
1400 Coleman Ave., Macon 31207

Oglethorpe University
4484 Peachtree Rd., N.E., Atlanta 30319
Dennis Matthews, Dir. of Admis.

University of Georgia, Athens 30602

HAWAII

Japan-America Institute of Management Science
6660 Hawaii Kai Dr., Honolulu 96825
Roxanne Kam, Academic Services Coordinator
808-395-2314

ILLINOIS

Augustana College
639 38th St., Rock Island 61201
Martin R. Sauer, Director of Admission
800-798-8100

Garrett-Evangelical Theological Seminary
2121 Sheridan Rd., Evanston 60201
Contact Admissions at 800-SEMINARY

Knox College, Galesburg 61401
309-343-0112 or 800-678-KNOX
See listing under "Universities"

North Central College
30 N. Brainard St.
P.O. Box 3065, Naperville 60566-7065
Marguerite Waters, Director of Admission
708-420-3414

Northern Illinois University, De Kalb 60115

North Park College & Theological Seminary
3225 W. Foster, Chicago 60625
312-509-2330

· Parkland College
2400 W. Bradley Ave., Champaign 61821-1899
217-351-2208 or 800-346-8089

Rockford College
5050 E. State St., Rockford 61108
Miriam King, V.P. for Enrollment Management
See listing under "Universities"

School of the Art Institute of Chicago
37 S. Wabash, Chicago 60603
Ellen B. Cropp, Dir. of Admis.

University of Illinois at Chicago
P.O. Box 5220, Chicago 60680
Dr. Marilyn R. Fiduccia, Dir. of Admis.

INDIANA

Ball State University
2000 W. University Ave., Muncie 47306
Ruth Vedvik, Dir. of Admis.

Franklin College
501 E. Monroe, Franklin 46131
B. Stephen Richards, VP Enrollment

Goshen College
1700 S. Main St., Goshen 46526
Ruth Gunden, Chairperson

Manchester College
604 College Ave., North Manchester 46962
Dr. Allen Deeter, Dir.-Brethren Colleges Abroad

Taylor University
500 W. Reade Ave., Upland 46989
Herb Frye, Dean of Enrollment Management

University of Evansville
1800 Lincoln Ave., Evansville 47722
Suzy Lantz, Associate Dir. of Admis.
800-423-8633

University of Notre Dame
Notre Dame 46556
Kevin M. Rooney, Dir. of Admis.

Wabash College
301 W. Wabash Ave., Crawfordsville 47933
Greg Birk, Dir. of Admis.

IOWA

Drake University
2507 E. University Ave., Des Moines 50311
Thomas Willoughby, Dir. of Admis.

Iowa State University, Ames 50011
Karsten Smedal, Dir. of Admis.

Luther College
700 College Dr., Decorah 52101
David Sallee, Dean for Enrollment

Teikyo Marycrest University
1607 W. 12th St., Davenport 52804
Tim McDonough, Dir. of Admis.
See listing under "Universities"

KANSAS

McPherson College
1600 E. Euclid St., McPherson 67460

LOUISIANA

Louisiana College
College Station, Pineville 71359
Byron McGee, Dir. of Admis.
318-487-7386
See listing under "Liberal Arts"

OUR LADY OF HOLY CROSS COLLEGE
4123 Woodland Dr., New Orleans 70131

MAINE

Bowdoin College, Brunswick 04011
William Mason, Dir. of Admis.

University of Southern Maine
96 Falmouth St., Portland 04103
Susan Roberts, Director of Admissions

Westbrook College
716 Stevens Ave., Portland 04103
207-797-7261

MASSACHUSETTS

Atlantic Union College
P.O. Box 1000, South Lancaster 01561
Osa Canto, Registrar

Bradford College
320 S. Main St., Bradford 01835

Bridgewater State College
Bridgewater 02325
James Plotner, Jr., Dir. of Admis.

ELMS COLLEGE
291 Springfield St., Chicopee 01013
800-255-ELMS

Hampshire College, Amherst 01002
Audrey Y. Smith, Dir. of Admissions
413-582-5471

:: **NORTHFIELD MT. HERMON SCHOOL**
Summer Abroad
France and Spain. For students entering grades 9-13. Six week programs include intensive orientation, family stay, in-country travel and field visits, study of history and culture of host country. Focus on extensive language use. Two years high school language study required for France.
Seven week China visit. Five week stay in Beijing. Travel includes Shanghai and Hong Kong. One year high school language study required. Adult leaders. Coeducational. See listing under "Summer Sessions".
International Programs Office
Northfield Mount Hermon School
Northfield 01360 413-498-3251

Simmons College
300 The Fenway, Boston 02115

Suffolk University
8 Ashburton Place, Boston 02108
Barbara K. Ericson, Assoc. Dean Enrollment & Retention
617-573-8460

Wellesley College, Wellesley 02181
Janet A. Lavin, Dir. of Admis.

Western New England College
1215 Wilbraham Rd., Springfield 01119
800-325-1122

MICHIGAN

Adrian College
110 S. Madison St., Adrian 49221
George Wolf, Dir. of Admis.
See listing under "Universities"

Aquinas College
1607 Robinson Rd., S.E., Grand Rapids 49506
Paula Meehan, Dean of Admissions
800-678-9593

HILLSDALE COLLEGE
33 E. College St., Hillsdale 49242
Dr. Ellen Justice-Templeton, Director
517-437-7341

MINNESOTA

Bemidji State University
1500 Birchmont Dr., N.E., Bemidji 56601
800-475-2001

College of Saint Benedict
37 S. College Ave., St. Joseph 56374

College of St. Scholastica
Study Center, Ireland, Russia, Costa Rica
1200 Kenwood Ave., Duluth 55811
Sr. Mary Odile Cahoon, VP, Dean of College
800-447-5444
See listing under "Liberal Arts"

Gustavus Adolphus College
800 W. College Ave., St. Peter 56082
Mark Anderson, Dir. of Admis.

Hamline University
1536 Hewitt Ave., St. Paul 55104
Scott Pratt, Dir. of Admis.

Northwestern College
3003 Snelling Ave., N., St. Paul 55113
Ralph Anderson, Dean of Admissions
800-827-6827 or 612-631-5111

St. John's University
P.O. Box 7155, Collegeville 56321

St. Mary's College of Minnesota
700 Terrace Heights #2, Winona 55987
Tony Piscitiello, VP for Admission

St. Olaf College, Northfield 55057
International Studies
Karen Jenkins, Director
507-646-3069

MISSOURI

Central Missouri State University
Warrensburg 64093
Delores Hudson, Dir. of Admis.

Culver-Stockton College, Canton 63435
Betty Smith, Dean of Admissions
800-537-1883

Maryville University of St. Louis
13550 Conway Rd., Saint Louis 63141
314-576-9300 or 800-MARYVLL

Missouri Southern State College
3950 Newman Rd., Joplin 64801-1595
Richard Humphrey, Dir. of Admis.
See listing under "Universities"

University of Missouri
8001 Natural Bridge Rd., St. Louis 63121
Mimi LaMarca, Dir. of Admis.

Webster University
470 E. Lockwood Ave., St. Louis 63119
Dr. James Groetsch, Assoc. Dean European Campuses
See listing under "Universities"

William Woods College
200 W. 12th St., Fulton 65251
Dr. Jahnae Barnett, VP of Admis.

NEBRASKA

Dana College
2848 College Dr., Blair   68008
John Schueth, Dir. of Admis.
800-444-3262
See listing under "Universities"

NEW HAMPSHIRE

Keene State College, Keene   03435
T. Durnford, Coordinator International Ed.

New England College
26 Bridge St., Henniker   03242
John Spaulding, Dir. of Admis.

NEW JERSEY

Fairleigh Dickinson University, Madison   07940
Dr. Louis Ballarin, Dir. of Overseas Program
201-593-8906

Fairleigh Dickinson University, Teaneck   07666
Dr. Louis Ballarin, Dir. of Overseas Program

Jersey City State College
2039 Kennedy Blvd., Jersey City   07305
201-200-3234

Rowan College of New Jersey, Glassboro   08028
Marvin G. Sills, Dir. of Admis.

Stockton State College, Pomona   08240
Sal Catalfamo, Dir. of Admis.

NEW YORK

Adelphi University, Garden City   11530
George DeBeir, Dir. International Student Services
516-877-4990

AFS Intercultural Programs
313 E. 43rd St., New York   10017
Dr. Beryl Levinger, President

AMERICAN UNIVERSITY OF PARIS
80 E. 11th St. #434, New York   10003
Thelma Bullock, Dir. of U.S. Office
See listing under "Universities"

BERKELEY COLLEGE
40 W. Red Oak Ln., White Plains   10604
Rose Mary Healy, President
800-446-5400 ext. GQ1

Canisius College
2001 Main St., Buffalo   14208
Penelope Lips, Dir. of Admis.
800-843-1517

CAZENOVIA COLLEGE
Cazenovia   13035
Dr. James Parker, VP for Enrollment Management
See listing under "Universities"

Colgate University
13 Oak Dr., Hamilton   13346
Dean of Admissions
315-824-7401

Elmira College
Park Pl., Elmira   14901
William S. Neal, Dean of Admissions
See listing under "Liberal Arts"

Long Island University-C. W. Post Campus
Rt. 25A, Brookville   11548
Louise Miller, Transfer Coordinator
516-299-2425

Marymount College
100 Marymount Ave., Tarrytown   10591
Sr. Rita Arthur, Dir. Study Abroad Program
914-332-8222

Molloy College
1000 Hempstead Ave., Rockville Centre   11570
Wayne James, Dir. of Admis.
See listing under "Universities"

Niagara University, Niagara University   14109
George Pachter, Dean of Admissions
800-462-2111
See listing under "Universities"

Roberts Wesleyan College
2301 Westside Dr., Rochester   14624
Linda Kurtz, Dir. of Admis.
See listing under "Universities"

St. John's University
Grand Central & Utopia Parkways, Jamaica   11439

Skidmore College, Saratoga Springs   12866
Kent Jones, Dir. of Admis.

SUNY at Buffalo
17 Capen Hall
P.O. Box 601660, Buffalo   14260-1660
716-645-6900

SUNY at Oswego, Oswego   13126
Dr. Joseph Grant, Jr., Dean of Admissions
315-341-2250

SUNY College at Plattsburgh, Plattsburgh   12901
Center for International Studies
Dodie Giltz, Coordinator
518-564-2086

NORTH CAROLINA

East Carolina University
1000 E. 5th St., Greenville   27858

Elon College
P.O. Box 2700, Elon College   27244
Nan P. Perkins, Dean of Admissions

Gardner-Webb University
General Delivery, Boiling Springs   28017
Carolyn McKinney, Dean
800-253-6472

Guilford College
5800 W. Friendly Ave., Greensboro   27410
Larry West, Dir. of Admis.
See listing under "Universities"

Mars Hill College
Main St., Mars Hill   28754
Dr. Smith Goodrum, Dean of Admis.

QUEENS COLLEGE
1900 Selwyn Ave., Charlotte   28274
D. Stephen Cloniger, VP for Enrollment Management
See listing under "Liberal Arts"

St. Andrews Presbyterian College
1700 Dogwood Mile, Laurinburg   28352
Dale B. Montague, Dir. of Admis.

Salem College
P.O. Box 10548, Winston-Salem   27108
Katherine Knapp, Director of Admissions
800-32-SALEM
See listing under "Women's College"

OHIO

College of Mount St. Joseph
5701 Delhi Rd., Cincinnati   45233-1672
See listing under "Universities"

Kent State University
P.O. Box 5190, Kent   44242
Bruce Riddle, Dir. of Admis.

Mount Union College
1972 Clark Ave., Alliance   44601
Amy Tomko, Dir. of Admis.

Ohio Dominican College
1216 Sunbury Rd., Columbus   43219
800-955-OHIO

OKLAHOMA

Oklahoma City University
2501 N. Blackwelder Ave., Oklahoma City   73106
Keith Hackett, Dean of Admissions
See listing under "Universities"

Oklahoma State University, Stillwater   74078
Brewster Fitz, Program Director

University of Tulsa
600 S. College Ave., Tulsa   74104
Mary Tolar, Asst. to the Dean

OREGON

Lewis & Clark College
0615 S.W. Palatine Hill Rd., Portland   97219
Michael Sexton, Dean of Admissions

Linfield College
900 S. Baker St., McMinnville   97128
Thomas Meicho, Dean of Admissions

PENNSYLVANIA

Allegheny College
520 N. Main St., Meadville   16335
Gayle Pollack, Dir. of Admis.

Beaver College
450 S. Easton Rd., Glenside   19038-3295
David Larsen, VP and Director
Phone: 800-776-BEAVER(2328), Fax:
215-572-4049
Semester and year-long programs in Austria,
Britain, Germany, Greece, Ireland and Mexico.
See listing under "Universities"

Chatham College
Woodland Rd., Pittsburgh   15232
Suellen Ofe, Dean of Admis./Financial Aid
See listing under "Women's College"

Drexel University
3141 Chestnut St., Philadelphia   19104
Dean of Enrollment Management

Edinboro University of Pennsylvania
Edinboro   16444
Admissions Office: 800-626-2203

Elizabethtown College
1 Alpha Dr., Elizabethtown   17022

Juniata College
1700 Moore St., Huntington   16652

Lafayette College, Easton   18042
G. Gary Ripple, Dir. of Admis.
610-250-5100

La Salle University
1900 W. Olney Ave., Philadelphia   19141
Br. Gerald Fitzgerald, Dir. of Admis.
See listing under "Universities"

Slippery Rock University, Slippery Rock   16057
Director of Admissions

University of Pittsburgh
4200 5th Ave., Pittsburgh   15260

WESTMINSTER COLLEGE
New Wilmington   16172
Richard Dana Paul, Dir. of Admis.
412-946-7100

RHODE ISLAND

Roger Williams College
1 Old Ferry Rd., Bristol   02809
William Dunfey, Dir. of Admis.

Salve Regina University
1 Ochre Point Ave., Newport   02840
Roselina McKillop, Dean of Admissions

SOUTH CAROLINA

Anderson College
316 S. Boulevard, Anderson   29621
Carl D. Lockman, Dir. of Admis.
800-542-3594

Lander College
320 Stanley Ave., Greenwood   29649

Winthrop University
701 W. Oakland Ave., Rock Hill   29733
James McCammon, Jr., Dir. of Admis.

SOUTH DAKOTA

National College
321 Kansas City St., Rapid City   57701
Keith T. Carlyle, Dir. of Admis.

TENNESSEE

University of Memphis, Memphis   38152
Dr. John Eubank, Dean of Admissions

University of Tennessee at Martin
Martin   38238
Paul Kelley, Director of Admissions
See listing under "Universities"

TEXAS

Rice University
P.O. Box 1892, Houston   77251

Schreiner College
2100 Memorial Blvd., Kerrville   78028
800-343-4919

Texas Christian University
2800 S. University Dr., Ft. Worth   76129
Dr. Edward Boehm, Jr., Dean of Admissions

University of St. Thomas
3812 Montrose Blvd., Houston   77006
Elsie Biron, Dir. of Admis.

VERMONT

Goddard College
P.O. Box G, Plainfield   05667
Jackson Kytle, President

School for International Training
World Learning Inc.
Kipling Rd., P.O. Box 676
Brattleboro   05302-0676
Marshall Brewer, Dir of Enrollment Management
800-451-4465 or 802-257-7751

Southern Vermont College
Monument Ave., Bennington   05201
See listing under "Universities"

VIRGINIA

Eastern Mennonite College
1200 Park Rd., Harrisonburg   22801
Jerry Miller, Dir. of Admis.

Hollins College
P.O. Box 9707, Hollins College   24020
800-456-9595

Lynchburg College
1501 Lakeside Dr., Lynchburg   24501
Ernest Chadderton, Dean of Enrollment

MARYMOUNT UNIVERSITY
2807 N. Glebe Rd., Arlington   22207
Charles Coe, Director of Admissions
800-548-7638 or 703-284-1500
   Established 1950. Catholic. Independent. Coed. Accreditation: SACS, NLN, FIDER, NCATE, ACBSP. Tuition: $10,804. Room and board: $5,126. Enrollment: 3,900. Faculty: 310. Student-faculty ratio: 20:1. Degrees: BA, BS, BBA, BSN, MA, MBA, MEd, MS, MSIM, MSN. Library: 125,000 volumes. 9 buildings on 21 acres. The London program, offered in fall and spring semesters to qualified juniors and seniors of all majors, includes internships in the London offices of British and American firms. Liberal Arts courses are taught by British faculty, and students live in a Marymount residence in greater London.

Randolph-Macon College
200 Henry St., Ashland   23005
John Conkright, Dean of Admissions

Sweet Briar College, Sweet Briar   24595
Nancy Church, Dir. of Admis.

Virginia Military Institute, Lexington   24450

WASHINGTON

Northwest College of the Assemblies of God
P.O. Box 579, Kirkland   98083-0579
Bob Foster, Dir. of Public Relations

Pacific Lutheran University
12180 Park Ave. S., Tacoma   98447
Ann Kelleher, Director

WEST VIRGINIA

Alderson-Broaddus College
Philippi   26416
Craig W. Gould, Director of Admissions
304-457-1700

The University of Charleston
2300 MacCorkle Ave., S.E., Charleston   25304
800-995-GO UC

WISCONSIN

Beloit College
700 College St., Beloit 53511
Terance Bigalke, World Affairs Ctr.
608-363-2380

Carthage College
2001 Alford Dr., Kenosha 53140
Brenda A. Porter, VP Enrollment

Lawrence University
P.O. Box 599, Appleton 54912
Steven Syverson, Dean of Admissions

Marquette University
Monitor Hall, Milwaukee 53233
Dawn Crowley, Programs Assistant

St. Norbert College
100 Grant St., De Pere 54115
Craig S. Wesley, Dean of Admission
See listing under "Universities"

University of Wisconsin
1 University Plaza, Platteville 53818
Richard Schumacher, Dean of Admissions

University of Wisconsin, River Falls
River Falls 54022
Alan Tuchtenhagen, Dir. of Admis.

Viterbo College
815 9th St., S., La Crosse 54601
Anita Beskar, Chair, Global Educ.

SUMMER SESSIONS

ALABAMA

Alabama A & M University
P.O. Box 908, Normal 35762
James Heyward, Dir. of Admis.
See listing under "Universities"

Samford University
800 Lakeshore Dr., Birmingham 35229
Paul Blackwell, Dean

Troy State University, Troy 36082
Jim Hutto, Dean of Enrollment Services

Tuskegee University
Tuskegee Institute 36088

University of Alabama
P.O. Box 870132, Tuscaloosa 35487-0132
Roy Smith, Dir. of Admis.

UNIVERSITY OF MOBILE
P.O. Box 13220, Mobile 36663-0220
Kim Leousis, Dir. of Admissions
205-675-5990
See listing under "Universities"

ALASKA

Alaska Junior College
800 E. Dimond Blvd. # 3-350
Anchorage 99515

Alaska Pacific University
4101 University Dr., Anchorage 99508
Director of Admissions
See listing under "Universities"

University of Alaska Anchorage
3211 Providence Dr., Anchorage 99508
907-786-1480

ARIZONA

Northern Arizona University
P.O. Box 4092, Flagstaff 86011
Dr. Margaret Cibik, Dir. of Admis.

University of Arizona, Tucson 85721
Anita McDonald, Associate Director

Yavapai College
1100 E. Sheldon St., Prescott 86301
Dr. Doreen Dailey, President
602-445-7300
See listing under "Community and Junior Colleges"

ARKANSAS

Arkansas State University
P.O. Box 1630, State University 72467

CALIFORNIA

AMERICAN COLLEGE FOR THE APPLIED ARTS
1651 Westwood Blvd., Los Angeles 90024
310-470-2000
See listing under "Universities"

Butte College
3536 Butte Campus Dr., Oroville 95965
Romeo E. Morin, Dir. Admis.

California Baptist College
8432 Magnolia Ave., Riverside 92504
800-782-3382

California State University, Chico
Chico 95929-0250
Dr. Ralph Meuter, Dean

California State University-Stanislaus
801 W. Monte Vista Ave., Turlock 95382
Frances Cook, Dean Enrollment Services

Chapman University
333 N. Glassell St., Orange 92666
Michael Drummy, Dir. of Admis.

Fresno Pacific College
1717 S. Chestnut Ave., Fresno 93702
209-453-2039

La Sierra University
4700 Pierce St., Riverside 92505
800-874-5587

Loyola Marymount University
Loyola Blvd. at W. 80th, Los Angeles 90045
M. L'Heureux, Dir. of Admis.

Menlo College
1000 El Camino Real, Atherton 94027
Fred R. Halverson, Director

Monterey Institute of International Studies
425 Van Buren St., Monterey 93940

Ohlone College
P.O. Box 3909, Fremont 94539

Pacific School of Religion
1798 Scenic Ave., Berkeley 94709
Carol Voisin, Director of Special Studies
800-999-0528
See listing under "Graduate Schools"

Point Loma Nazarene College
3900 Lomaland Dr., San Diego 92106
Bill Young, Dir. of Admis.

Porterville College
100 E. College Ave., Porterville 93257
John McCuen, President

San Francisco State University
1600 Holloway Ave., San Francisco 94132
Corwin Bjonerud, Dir. of Admis.

Santa Barbara City College
721 Cliff Dr., Santa Barbara 93109
805-965-0581

Santa Clara University, Santa Clara 95053

Sonoma State University
1801 E. Cotati Ave., Rohnert Park 94928

University of California, Los Angeles
1247 Murphy Hall, Los Angeles 90024

University of California at Berkeley
Wheeler Hall, Berkeley 94720

University of California, Davis
376 Mrak Hall, Davis 95616

University of California, Riverside
P.O. Box 112, Riverside 92521

University of California, San Diego
9450 Gilman Dr., La Jolla 92092

University of California-Santa Cruz
Santa Cruz 95064
Janice Corriden, Dean

University of San Diego
5998 Alcala Park, San Diego 92110
Warren Muller, Dir. of Admis.
619-260-4506

Woodbury University
7500 Glenoaks Blvd., Burbank 91504
See listing under "Universities"

COLORADO

Adams State College, Alamosa 81102
Mark Clark, Asst. VP for Academic Affairs
800-824-6494

Colorado College
14 E. Cache La Poudre, Colorado Springs 80903
Terry Swenson, Dir. of Admis.

COLORADO TECHNICAL COLLEGE
4435 N. Chestnut St., Colorado Springs 80907
719-598-0200
Contact: Admissions Office
See listing under "Universities"

ILIFF SCHOOL OF THEOLOGY
2201 S. University Blvd., Denver 80210
Jane Smith, Dean
800-678-3360

Metropolitan State College of Denver
P.O. Box 173362, Campus Box 16
Denver 80217-3362

Regis University
3333 Regis Blvd., Denver 80221
Robert Blust, Director of Admissions

University of Denver
2199 S. University Blvd., Denver 80210

University of Northern Colorado, Greeley 80639
Director, Summer/Evening Division
303-351-1942

University of Southern Colorado
2200 Bonforte Blvd., Pueblo 81001

Western State College of Colorado
Gunnison 81231
Monica Bruning, Dir. of Admis.
See listing under "Universities"

CONNECTICUT

Mattatuck Community College
750 Chase Parkway, Waterbury 06708
Dr. Richard Sanders, President

Mitchell College
437 Pequot Ave., New London 06320
Kathleen Crowley, Dir. of Admis.

QUINNIPIAC COLLEGE
275 Mount Carmel Ave., Hamden 06518
Rosemarie DeVivo, Office of Continuing Education
See listing under "Universities"

TEIKYO POST UNIVERSITY
800 Country Club Rd.
P.O. Box 2540, Waterbury 06723-2540
800-345-2562 or 203-596-4520
Established 1890. Private. Coed. Accreditation: NEASC. Tuition: $11,960. Room and board: $5,400. Application fee: $40. Enrollment: 996 full-time, 1,488 part-time. Faculty: 29 full-time, 260 part-time. Student-faculty ratio: 15:1. Degrees: AA, AS, BA, BS. Library: 55,000 volumes. 11 buildings on 70 acres. Excellent business majors with strong liberal arts and international component. Faculty with dynamic business experience, assistance to help students succeed in a global marketplace. ESL Institute.

University of Bridgeport
126 Park Ave., Bridgeport 06601
Andrew G. Nelson, Dean Admis./Financial Aid
203-576-4552
See listing under "Universities"

University of Hartford
200 Bloomfield Ave., West Hartford 06117
Hilda Grossman, Director
See listing under "Universities"

University of New Haven
300 Orange Ave., West Haven 06516
Dany Washington, Assoc. Dean
203-932-7231

DISTRICT OF COLUMBIA

The American University
4400 Massachusetts Ave. N.W.
Washington 20016

Southeastern University
501 I St., S.W., Washington 20024

University of the District of Columbia
Georgia Ave.-Harvard St. Campus
1100 Harvard St., N.W., Washington 20009

University of the District of Columbia
Van Ness Campus
4200 Connecticut Ave., N.W., Washington 20008

FLORIDA

Barry University
11300 N.E. 2nd Ave., Miami Shores 33161
Robin Ray Roberts, Dean of Admissions

Florida A & M University, Tallahassee 32307

FLORIDA AIR ACADEMY
1950 South Academy Dr., Melbourne 32901
Major James Dwight, President

Florida Atlantic University
500 N.W. 20th St., Boca Raton 33431
Brian Levin-Stankevich, Dir. of Admis.

Jacksonville University
2800 University Blvd., N., Jacksonville 32211

Jones College
5353 Arlington Expy., Jacksonville 32211
Dorothy D. Jones, Chief Executive Officer

Jones College
5975 Sunset Dr. #100, South Miami 33143

LYNN UNIVERSITY
(Est. 1962 as College of Boca Raton)
3601 N. Military Trail, Boca Raton 33431
407-994-0770 or 800-544-8035
See listing under "Universities"

St. Leo College
P.O. Box 2008, St. Leo 33574
Bonnie Black, Dir. of Admis.

SCHILLER INTERNATIONAL UNIVERSITY (FLORIDA & EUROPE)
U.S. Admissions Office
Dept. PA, 453 Edgewater Dr., Dunedin 34698-7532
800-336-4133 Fax: 813-736-6263
Dr. Walter Liebrecht, President
Karen Altieri, Associate Director of Admissions
See listing under "Universities"

University of Miami
P.O. Box 248006, Coral Gables 33124

UNIVERSITY OF SARASOTA
5250 17th St., Sarasota 34235
Linda Volz, Dir. of Enrollment Management
800-331-5995
Established 1969. Coed. Accreditation: SACS. Tuition: $265 per credit hour. Enrollment: 470. Faculty: 30. Degrees: MAEd, MBA, EdD. Year round, non-traditional calendar, flexible, small seminars, much individual attention to students, performance oriented.

GEORGIA

AMERICAN COLLEGE FOR THE APPLIED ARTS
3330 Peachtree Rd., N.E., Atlanta 30326
404-231-9000
See listing under "Universities".

Atlanta College of Art
Woodruff Arts Center
1280 Peachtree St., N.E., Atlanta 30309
John Farkas, Dir. of Enrollment Management

Kennesaw State College
P.O. Box 444, Marietta 30061
Joe Head, Dir. of Admis.

Mercer University
1400 Coleman Ave., Macon 31207

Oglethorpe University
4484 Peachtree Rd., N.E., Atlanta 30319
Dennis Matthews, Dir. of Admis.

South Georgia College, Douglas 31533
John Wahl, Dir. of Admis.

University of Georgia, Athens 30602
Dr. Claire Swann, Dir. of Admis.

HAWAII

Brigham Young University
55-220 Kulanui St., Laie 96762
Theresa Bigbie, Coordinator of Admis.

Chaminade University of Honolulu
3140 Waialae Ave., Honolulu 96816
Charles Schafer, VP Enrollment Services

IDAHO

University of Idaho, Moscow 83843
Peter Brown, Dir. of Admis.

ILLINOIS

Adler School of Professional Psychology
65 E. Wacker Pl., Chicago 60601-7203
Suzann Lebda, Director of Admissions
312-201-5900

American Academy of Art
332 S. Michigan Ave. 3rd Fl.
Chicago 60604

Augustana College
639 38th St., Rock Island 61201
Martin R. Sauer, Director of Admission
800-798-8100

Aurora University
347 S. Gladstone Ave., Aurora 60506
Peter Pitts, Dir. of Admis.

De Paul University
1 E. Jackson Blvd., Chicago 60604
Thomas D. Abrahamson, Dean of Admissions
See listing under "Universities"

Eastern Illinois University, Charleston 61920
Charles Colbert, Director
See listing under "Universities"

Garrett-Evangelical Theological Seminary
2121 Sheridan Rd., Evanston 60201
Contact Doris Rudy, at 800-SEMINARY

Governors State University
1 University Pky., University Park 60466
Richard Pride, Dir. of Admis.

Greenville College
315 E. College Ave., Greenville 62246
Kent Krober, Dir. of Admis.

Joliet Junior College
1216 Houbolt Dr., Joliet 60436
Dir. of Admis.

Loyola University - Mundelein College
6363 N. Sheridan Rd., Chicago 60660
Judith Bobber, Dir. of Admis.

Midstate College
244 S.W. Jefferson St., Peoria 61602
R. Dale Bunch, President
309-673-6365

Montay College
3750 W. Peterson Ave., Chicago 60659
Scott Dalhouse, Dir. of Admis.

Moraine Valley Community College
10900 S. 88th Ave., Palos Hills 60465
Dr. Vernon Crawley, President

Northeastern Illinois University
5500 N. St. Louis Ave., Chicago 60625

Northern Illinois University, De Kalb 60115

Olivet Nazarene University, Kankakee 60901
John Mongerson, Dir. of Admis.
815-939-5203

Parkland College
2400 W. Bradley Ave., Champaign 61821-1899
217-351-2208 or 800-346-8089

ROOSEVELT UNIVERSITY
430 S. Michigan Ave., Chicago 60605
William Smyser, Director of Admissions
See listing under "Universities"

Rosary College
7900 W. Division St., River Forest 60305
Hildegarde Schmidt, Dir. of Admis.

St. Xavier College
3700 W. 103rd St., Chicago 60655
Mary Hendry, Dean of Admissions

School of the Art Institute of Chicago
37 S. Wabash, Chicago 60603
Ellen B. Cropp, Dir. of Admis.

Springfield College in Illinois
1500 N. Fifth St., Springfield 62702
Dr. H. Brent DeLand, President

University of Chicago
5801 S. Ellis Ave., Chicago 60637

University of Illinois at Chicago
P.O. Box 5220, Chicago 60680
Dr. Marilyn R. Fiduccia, Dir. of Admis.

VanderCook College of Music
3209 S. Michigan Ave., Chicago 60616
Ward Durrett, Dir of Admis.

INDIANA

Ball State University
2000 W. University Ave., Muncie 47306
Ruth Vedvik, Dir. of Admis.

Culver Military Academy and Summer Camps
1300 Academy Rd., Culver 46511
Richard Edwards, Dir. of Admis.

Franklin College
501 E. Monroe, Franklin 46131
B. Stephen Richards, VP Enrollment

Grace College
200 Seminary Dr., Winona Lake 46590
Ron Henry, Dir. of Admis.

Indiana Wesleyan University
4201 S. Washington St., Marion 46953
800-332-6901

Manchester College
604 College Ave., North Manchester 46962
Dr. James Pitts, Academic Dean

Purdue University
Schleman Hall, West Lafayette 47907

University of Notre Dame, Notre Dame 46556
Robert E. Gordon, Director

Valparaiso University, Valparaiso 46383

IOWA

Briar Cliff College
3303 Rebecca St., Sioux City 51104
Patricia White, Dir. of Admis.

Drake University
2507 E. University Ave, Des Moines 50311
Thomas Westbrook, Dean

Hawkeye Community College
1501 E. Orange Rd., Waterloo 50701
319-296-2320 Ext. 4000

Iowa State University, Ames 50011
Karsten Smedal, Dir. of Admis.

Luther College
700 College Dr., Decorah 52101
David Sallee, Dean for Enrollment

Mount Mercy College
1330 Elmhurst Dr., N.E., Cedar Rapids 52402
Carol Williamson, Dir. of Admis.

Northwestern College
101 7th St. S.W., Orange City 51041

Teikyo Marycrest University
1607 W. 12th St., Davenport 52804
Tim McDonough, Dir. of Admis.
See listing under "Universities"

Teikyo Westmar University
1002 3rd Ave., S.E., Le Mars 51031
Dr. Jim Utesch, Dir. of Admis.

University of Iowa, Iowa City 52242

University of Northern Iowa, Cedar Falls 50614

KANSAS

Coffeyville Community College
402 W. 11th St., Coffeyville 67337
Helen Ellerman, Dir. of Admis.

Fort Hays State University
600 Park St., Hays 67601-4099
Dr. Rodolfo Arevalo, VP Academic Affairs

Hutchinson Community College
1300 N. Plum St., Hutchinson 67501
Duane Halpain, Dir. of Admis.

KENTUCKY

Bellarmine College
2001 Newburg Rd., Louisville 40205
Thomas LaBaugh, Dean of Admissions

LOUISIANA

Centenary College of Louisiana
P.O. Box 41188, Shreveport 71134

Loyola University
6363 St. Charles Ave., New Orleans 70118

OUR LADY OF HOLY CROSS COLLEGE
4123 Woodland Dr., New Orleans 70131

Tulane University
125 Gibson Hall, New Orleans 70118

MAINE

St. Joseph's College, North Windham 04062

University of Maine at Fort Kent
25 Pleasant St., Fort Kent 04743
Jerry Nadeau, Dir. of Admis.

University of New England
11 Hills Beach Rd., Biddeford 04005
Patricia Cribby, Dir. of Admis.

University of Southern Maine
96 Falmouth St., Portland 04103
Rosa Redonnett, Director

MARYLAND

Essex Community College
7201 Rossville Blvd., Baltimore 21237
Diane Lane, Dir. of Admis.

Hood College
400 Rosemont Ave., Frederick 21701

Loyola College
4501 N. Charles St., Baltimore 21210
Francis McGuire, Dean

MASSACHUSETTS

American International College
1000 State St., Springfield 01109
Peter Miller, Dean of Admissions

THE ART INSTITUTE OF BOSTON
700 Beacon St., Boston 02215
617-262-1223 or 800-773-0494
(NY, PA, New England)
Fax 617-437-1226
See listing under "Art"

Babson College
One College Dr., Babson Park 02157
Constance Bosse, Asst. Dean
617-239-4440

Bentley College
175 Forest St., Waltham 02154
Joann McKenna, Dir. of Admis.

Berkshire Community College
1350 West St., Pittsfield 01201
Adrienne A. Rulnick, Dir. of Admissions

Boston College
140 Commonwealth Ave., Chestnut Hill 02167
Rev. James Woods, S.J., Dean

Boston University
685 Commonwealth Ave., Boston 02215

Brandeis University
415 South St., Waltham 02154
Sanford Lottor, Director
617-736-3424

Bristol Community College
777 Elsbree St., Fall River 02720
Frank Noble, Dir. of Admis.

Chapel Hill-Chauncy Hall School
785 Beaver St., Waltham 02154

Curry College
1071 Blue Hill Ave., Milton 02186
617-333-0500

Emerson College
148 Beacon St., Boston 02116

Emmanuel College
400 The Fenway, Boston 02115
Dr. Lily Owyang, Dean of Program Support

Fitchburg State College
160 Pearl St., Fitchburg 01420
Marke Vickers, Dir. of Admis.

Harvard University
20 Garden St., Cambridge 02138

LAWRENCE ACADEMY
P.O. Box 992, Groton 01450
Steven L. Hahn, Headmaster
Robinson C. Moore, Dir. of Admis.
508-448-6535
Established 1793. Coeducational. Accreditation: NEASC. Tuition: $20,800 boarding, $14,500 day. Enrollment: 330. Faculty: 51. 36 miles northwest of Boston. College preparatory, boarding and day school for students in grades 9-12. Wide variety of courses including honors, AP innovative interdisciplinary offerings with strong emphasis on technology in the curriculum. LA II and Winterim encourage an active learning experience. Strong advisor program, athletics, and community service component enrich lives of our students. Six week, intensive ESL program for all levels available in summers for ages 14 to 18 with

activity, athletic and weekend programs included. Athletic complex opened in 1993. New Arts Center planned for 1995. 20 buildings on 92 acres.

Massachusetts Institute of Technology
77 Massachusetts Ave., Cambridge 02139

:: NORTHFIELD MT. HERMON SCHOOL
206 Main St., Northfield 01360
James B. Ward, Director
413-498-3290, FAX: 413-498-3112
Established 1961. Coed. Accreditation: NEASC. Total fees: $3,200. Enrollment: 370 boarding, 20 day. Faculty: 100. Library: 30,000 volumes. 30 buildings on 3,000 acres. Pool, gym, golf course. Enrichment courses in English, math, natural and social sciences, language and intensive Japanese and Arabic for well-motivated junior and senior high school students. See listing under "Study Abroad".

Pine Manor College
400 Heath St., Chestnut Hill 02167
Eva Kampits, Academic Dean

SCHOOL OF THE MUSEUM OF FINE ARTS
230 Fenway, Boston 02115
Don Grey, Dir. of Continuing Education
617-267-1219

Simmons College
300 The Fenway, Boston 02115

Springfield College
263 Alden St., Springfield 01109
Frederick Bartlett, Dean of Admissions

Suffolk University
8 Ashburton Place, Boston 02108
Barbara K. Ericson, Assoc. Dean Enrollment & Retention
617-573-8460

University of Massachusetts
100 Morrissey Blvd., Boston 02125

Western New England College
1215 Wilbraham Rd., Springfield 01119
800-325-1122

:: WINCHENDON SCHOOL
172 Ash St., Winchendon 01475
J. William LaBelle, Headmaster
Norman S. Jason, Dir. of Admis.
Thomas H. Covhig, Dir. of Summer School
508-297-1223 or 800-622-1119
Established 1926. Private. Coed. Accreditation: NEASC. Tuition, room and board: $20,250. Fees: $2,000. Enrollment: 125. Faculty: 23. Student-faculty ratio: 5:1. Library: 10,000 volumes. 17 buildings on 232 acres. A traditional, coeducational, college preparatory school with an emphasis on helping the underachieving student reach his/her potential through the efforts of a highly supportive faculty and an individualized and structured program. ESL offered at three levels; beginning, intermediate and advanced.

MICHIGAN

Aquinas College
1607 Robinson Rd., S.E., Grand Rapids 49506
Paula Meehan, Dean of Admissions
800-678-9593

Grace Bible College
P.O. Box 910, Grand Rapids 49509
Linda K. Siler, Dir. of Admis.

HILLSDALE COLLEGE
33 E. College St., Hillsdale 49242
Kay Cosgrove, Registrar
517-437-7341

Jackson Community College
2111 Emmons Rd., Jackson 49201
Mark Ulseth, Dir. Enrollment Services

Lawrence Technological University
21000 W. Ten Mile Rd., Southfield 48075
800-225-5588 ext. 3160

Marygrove College
8425 W. McNichols Rd., Detroit 48221

North Central Michigan College
1515 Howard St., Petosky 49770

University of Michigan-Flint
303 Kearsley St., Flint 48502

William Tyndale College
35700 W. Twelve Mile Rd.
Farmington Hills 48331

MINNESOTA

Bemidji State University
1500 Birchmont Dr., N.E., Bemidji 56601
800-475-2001

Bethel College
3900 Bethel Dr., St. Paul 55112
Dr. George Brushaber, President

College of St. Scholastica
1200 Kenwood Ave., Duluth 55811
Registrar's Office
800-447-5444
See listing under "Liberal Arts"

Concordia College-St. Paul
275 N. Syndicate, St. Paul 55104
Tim Utter, Dir. of Admis.

Gustavus Adolphus College
800 W. College Ave., St. Peter 56082
Mark Anderson, Dir. of Admis.

Hamline University
1536 Hewitt Ave., St. Paul 55104
Scott Pratt, Dir. of Admis.

Northwestern College
3003 Snelling Ave., N., St. Paul 55113
Ralph Anderson, Dean of Admissions
800-827-6827 or 612-631-5111

St. Olaf College, Northfield 55057
John Ruohoniemi, Dir. of Admis.
507-646-3025

MISSISSIPPI

Millsaps College
P.O. Box 150556, Jackson 39210
Florence Hines, Dir. of Admis.

Mississippi College
P.O. Box 4086, Clinton 39058

MISSOURI

Central Missouri State University
Warrensburg 64093
Delores Hudson, Dir. of Admis.

CONCORDIA SEMINARY
801 De Mun Ave., Saint Louis 63105
Jerrold Eickmann, Registrar
314-721-5934

Drury College
900 N. Benton Ave., Springfield 65802
Michael G. Thomas, Dir. of Admis.

Fontbonne College
6800 Wydown Blvd., St. Louis 63105
Peggy Musen, Dir. of Admis.

Maryville University of St. Louis
13550 Conway Rd., Saint Louis 63141
314-576-9300 or 800-MARYVLL

Missouri Southern State College
3950 Newman Rd., Joplin 64801-1595
Richard Humphrey, Dir. of Admis.
See listing under "Universities"

Missouri Valley College
500 E. College St., Marshall 65340
816-886-6924 ext. 114
See listing under "Universities"

Stephens College, Columbia 65215
Eugene Schmidtlein, Director

University of Missouri
8001 Natural Bridge Rd., St. Louis 63121
Mimi LaMarca, Dir. of Admis.

Washington University
1 Brookings Dr., St. Louis 63130

MONTANA

CARROLL COLLEGE
1610 N. Benton Ave., Helena 59625
Candace Cain, Dir. of Admis.
See listing under "Universities"

Montana State University, Bozeman 59717

Montana State University - Billings
1500 N. 30th St., Billings 59101
Karen Everett, Dir. of Admis.
406-657-2158

Northern Montana College
P.O. Box 7751, Havre 59501
Ralph A. Brigham, Dir. of Admis.

Rocky Mountain College
1511 Poly Dr., Billings 59102
David Heringer, Dir. of Admis.
See listing under "Universities"

NEBRASKA

Bellevue College
1000 Galvin Rd. S., Bellevue 68005
Chari Leader, VP of Enrollment

College of Saint Mary
1901 S. 72nd St., Omaha 68124
Sheila Haggas, Dir. of Admis.

Concordia College
800 N. Columbia Ave., Seward 68434
Don Vos, Dir. of Admis.

Creighton University
2500 California St., Omaha 68178
Dr. Wesley Wolfe, Dean

Midland Lutheran College
900 Clarkson St., Fremont 68025
Roland Kahnk, V.P. Admissions

Nebraska Wesleyan University
5000 Saint Paul Ave., Lincoln 68504
Ken Sieg, Dir. of Admis.

Western Nebraska Community College
1601 E. 27th St., Scottsbluff 69361
Roger Hovey, Admissions

NEVADA

Sierra Nevada College-Lake Tahoe
P.O. Box 4269, Incline Village 89450
Lane Murray, Dir. of Admissions
See listing under "Universities"

NEW HAMPSHIRE

Keene State College, Keene 03435
J. Donnelly, Dir. of Cont. Ed.

New Hampshire College
2500 North River Rd., Manchester 03106
Brad Poznanski, Dir. of Admis.
603-645-9611

New Hampshire Technical College at Stratham
277 R. Portsmouth Ave., Stratham 03885
Patricia A. Shay, Dean of Students

Rivier College
420 S. Main St., Nashua 03060
Admissions: 800-44-RIVIER

Saint Anselm College
87 Saint Anselm Dr., Manchester 03102
Don Healy, Dir. of Admis.

NEW JERSEY

Bloomfield College
1 Park Place, Bloomfield 07003
Warner Smith, Dean for Admissions
201-748-9000, Ext. 230

Caldwell College
9 Ryerson Ave., Caldwell 07006

Fairleigh Dickinson University, Madison 07940
Lissa Anderson, Dir. of Admis.
201-593-8906

Fairleigh Dickinson University, Teaneck 07666
Dennis Craig, Dir. of Admis.
201-692-2553

FELICIAN COLLEGE
262 S. Main St., Lodi 07644
Sr. Mary Austin, OSB, Dir. of Admis.
201-778-1029
See listing under "Universities"

Georgian Court College
900 Lakewood Ave., Lakewood 08701
Sr. Marie Cook, R.S.M., Acad. Dean
908-364-2200 Ext. 667

Jersey City State College
2039 Kennedy Blvd., Jersey City 07305
201-200-3234

New Jersey Institute of Technology
323 Martin Luther King Jr. Blvd., Newark 07102

Rowan College of New Jersey, Glassboro 08028
Marvin G. Sills, Dir. of Admis.

Upsala College
345 Prospect St., East Orange 07017
George Lynes, Dean of Admissions

NEW MEXICO

College of Santa Fe
1600 St. Michaels Dr., Santa Fe 87505
800-456-2673

Eastern New Mexico University
Portales 88130
Larry Fuqua, Dir. of Admis.

New Mexico Highlands University, Las Vegas 87701
Dr. Jorge P. Thomas, VP Academic Affairs

New Mexico Institute of Mining & Technology
801 Leroy Pl., Socorro 87801

St. John's College
1160 Camino de Cruz Blanca, Santa Fe 87501
Marsha Drennon, Dir. of Admis.

NEW YORK

Adelphi University, Garden City 11530
Dr. Dimitra Richardson, Dean, Summer Sessions
516-877-4982

AFS Intercultural Programs
313 E. 43rd St., New York 10017
Dr. Beryl Levinger, President

AMERICAN UNIVERSITY OF PARIS
80 E. 11th St. #434, New York 10003
Thelma Bullock, Dir. of U.S. Office
See listing under "Universities"

Canisius College
2001 Main St., Buffalo 14208
Penelope Lips, Dir. of Admis.
800-843-1517

CAZENOVIA COLLEGE
Cazenovia 13035
Dr. James Parker, VP for Enrollment Management
See listing under "Universities"

Clarkson University, Potsdam 13699
B. Williams, Director

Cornell University
410 Thurston Ave., Ithaca 14853

CUNY College of Staten Island
130 Stuyvesant Pl., Staten Island 10301

Fordham University
441 E. Fordham Rd., Bronx 10458
718-817-1000

IONA COLLEGE
715 North Ave., New Rochelle 10801
800-231-IONA or 914-633-2501
See listing under "Universities"

Ithaca College
953 Danby Rd., Ithaca 14850

The King's College, Briarcliff Manor 10510
Frederic Rowley, Dean of Admissions

Long Island University-Brooklyn Campus
1 University Plaza, Brooklyn 11201
Alan Chaves, Dean of Admissions

Long Island University-C. W. Post Campus
Rt. 25A, Brookville 11548
Dr. Nishan Najarian, Dean, University Studies
516-299-2040

Manhattan College
4513 Manhattan College Pky., Riverdale 10471
Dr. Emile Letendre, Registrar

Mercy College
555 Broadway, Dobbs Ferry 10522
James Nesbitt, Dean of Admissions

Molloy College
1000 Hempstead Ave., Rockville Centre 11570
Wayne James, Dir. of Admis.
See listing under "Universities"

New York Institute of Technology
Old Westbury Campus, Old Westbury 11568

Niagara University, Niagara University 14109
Mark LaRoach, Director
716-286-8421
See listing under "Universities"

Pace University, New York Campus
1 Pace Plaza, New York 10038

Pace University, Pleasantville/Briarcliff Campus
Bedford Rd., Pleasantville 10570

Pace University, White Plains Campus
78 N. Broadway, White Plains 10603

Rensselaer Polytechnic Institute, Troy 12180
Conrad Sharrow, Dean of Admissions

Roberts Wesleyan College
2301 Westside Dr., Rochester 14624
Linda Kurtz, Dir. of Admis.
See listing under "Universities"

St. Joseph's College, Suffolk Campus
25 Audobon Ave., Patchogue 11772

St. Lawrence University, Canton 13617
Joel R. Wincowski, Dean of Admis. & Financial Aid

Skidmore College, Saratoga Springs 12866
Kent Jones, Dir. of Admis.

SUNY College at Plattsburgh, Plattsburgh 12901
Ronald Hobson, Acting Director
518-564-2050

· SUNY Onondaga Community College
Onondaga Rd., Syracuse 13215
Joseph Insel, Dir. of Admis.

University of Rochester
500 Joseph C. Wilson Blvd., Rochester 14627
Suzanne O'Brien, Assistant Dean
See listing under "Universities"

Utica College of Syracuse University
1600 Burrstone Rd., Utica 13502

Vassar College
125 Raymond Ave., Poughkeepsie 12601

· Villa Maria College of Buffalo
240 Pine Ridge Rd., Buffalo 14225
Lynn D'Auria, Dir. of Admis.

NORTH CAROLINA

Barton College
College Station, Wilson 27893
Anthony Britt, Dir. of Admis.
800-345-4973/919-399-6318
See listing under "Universities"

East Carolina University
1000 E. 5th St., Greenville 27858
Admissions Office
919-757-6640

Gardner-Webb University
General Delivery, Boiling Springs 28017
Evan Thompson, Dean
704-434-2361 or 800-253-6473

Guilford College
5800 W. Friendly Ave., Greensboro 27410
Cathy West, Director
See listing under "Universities"

Mars Hill College
Main St., Mars Hill 28754
Dr. Smith Goodrum, Dean of Admis.

North Carolina A&T State University
1601 E. Market St., Greensboro 27411

North Carolina School of the Arts
200 Waughtown St., Winston-Salem 27127
Alex Ewing, Chancellor
910-770-3204

North Carolina State University
P.O. Box 7001, Raleigh 27695
George Dixon, Dir. of Admis.

Pfeiffer College
General Delivery, Misenheimer 28109

OHIO

ART ACADEMY OF CINCINNATI
1125 Saint Gregory St., Cincinnati 45202
Roger Williams, Director
See listing under "Art"

Cleveland State University
Euclid Ave. at 24th St., Cleveland 44115

College of Mount St. Joseph
5701 Delhi Rd., Cincinnati 45233-1672
See listing under "Universities"

COLUMBUS COLLEGE OF ART & DESIGN
107 N. 9th St., Columbus 43215-1758
Thomas Green, Dir. of Admis.
614-224-9101
See listing under "Art"

John Carroll University
20700 N. Park Blvd., Cleveland 44118

Kent State University
P.O. Box 5190, Kent 44242
Bruce Riddle, Dir. of Admis.

LOURDES COLLEGE
6832 Convent Blvd., Sylvania 43560
Mary E. Briggs, Dir. of Admis.
419-885-5291 or 800-878-3210

Miami University
E. High St., Oxford 45056

Ohio Dominican College
1216 Sunbury Rd., Columbus 43219
800-955-OHIO

OHIO NORTHERN UNIVERSITY
525 S. Main St., Ada 45810
Dr. Anne Lippert, Director
412-772-2000

Ohio Wesleyan University
61 S. Sandusky St., Delaware 43015
Donald Bishop, Dean for Enrollment

· Sinclair Community College
444 W. 3rd St., Dayton 45402-1460
Sara P. Smith, Director of Admissions
800-315-3000

University of Cincinnati
2700 Clifton Ave., Cincinnati 45221

University of Rio Grande
General Delivery, Rio Grande 45674
Mark Abell, Dir. of Admis./Enrollment Srvcs.
614-245-5353, Ext. 7206

OKLAHOMA

Oklahoma City University
2501 N. Blackwelder Ave., Oklahoma City 73106
Keith Hackett, Dean of Admissions
See listing under "Universities"

Oklahoma Panhandle State University
P.O. Box 430, Goodwell 73939

Oklahoma State University, Stillwater 74078
Robin Lacy, Registrar

University of Central Oklahoma
100 N. University Dr., Edmond 73034

University of Tulsa
600 S. College Ave., Tulsa 74104
John Corso, Dean of Admission

OREGON

· Central Oregon Community College
2600 N.W. College Way, Bend 97701
Christine Kerlin, Dir. of Admis.
503-383-7500

:: Delphian School and Camp
20950 S.W. Rock Creek Rd., Sheridan 97378
Donetta Phelps, Dean of Admissions
Call toll-free 800-626-6610

· Treasure Valley Community College
650 College Blvd., Ontario 97914
Ron Kulm, Dir. of Admis.

University of Portland
5000 N. Willamette Blvd., Portland 97203

PENNSYLVANIA

Beaver College
450 S. Easton Rd., Glenside 19038-3295
Harold W. Stewart, Registrar
Phone: 800-776-BEAVER(2328), Fax:
215-572-4049
See listing under "Universities"

Bloomsburg University, Bloomsburg 17815
Bernard Vinovrski, Dir. of Admis.

Carlow College
3333 5th Ave., Pittsburgh 15213

Carnegie Mellon University
5000 Forbes Ave., Pittsburgh 15213

Cedar Crest College
100 College Dr., Allentown 18104-6196
Cynthia Phillips, Dir. of Admissions

Chatham College
Woodland Rd., Pittsburgh 15232
Suellen Ofe, Dean of Admis./Financial Aid
See listing under "Women's College"

College Misericordia
301 Lake St., Dallas 18612
Michael Joseph, Dir. of Enrollment Mgmt.

Delaware Valley College of Science & Agriculture
Doylestown 18901
Stephen Zenko, Dir. of Admis.

Drexel University
3141 Chestnut St., Philadelphia 19104
Dean of Enrollment Management

Eastern College
10 Fairview Dr., Saint Davids 19087
Al Jepson, Exec. Dir. Continuing Education

Edinboro University of Pennsylvania
Edinboro 16444
Admissions Office: 800-626-2203

Franklin & Marshall College
P.O. Box 3003, Lancaster 17604

Gannon University
109 University Sq., Erie 16541

· Harcum Junior College, Bryn Mawr 19010
Alison Jones, Director

Juniata College
1700 Moore St., Huntington 16652

Lafayette College, Easton 18042
Director of Special Programs
610-250-5075

La Roche College
9000 Babcock Blvd., Pittsburgh 15237
Marianne Leister, Dir. of Admis.

La Salle University
1900 W. Olney Ave., Philadelphia 19141
Glenda Kuhl, Dean
See listing under "Universities"

Millersville University of Pennsylvania
Millersville 17551
Blair Treasure, Dean of Admissions

· Montgomery County Community College
340 DeKalb Pike, Blue Bell 19422-0758
Dennis Murphy, Dir. of Admis.

Muhlenberg College
2400 W. Chew St., Allentown 18104
Dr. R. Dale Lecourt, Dean

Neumann College
Concord Rd., Aston 19014

Pennsylvania State University
201 Shields Bldg., University Park 16802

St. Francis College
P.O. Box 600, Loretto 15940

St. Joseph's University
5600 City Ave., Philadelphia 19131
Randy Miller, Dir. of Admis.

Seton Hill College, Greensburg 15601
Martha Raak, Dean, Cont. Ed.
800-826-6234 or 412-838-4255

Slippery Rock University, Slippery Rock 16057
Director of Admissions

Villanova University
845 E. Lancaster Ave., Villanova 19085
Stephen R. Merritt, Dir. of Admis.

West Chester University of Pennsylvania
S. High St., West Chester 19380

WESTMINSTER COLLEGE
New Wilmington 16172
Richard Dana Paul, Dir. of Admis.
412-946-7100

RHODE ISLAND

Brown University, Providence 02906

Rhode Island College
600 Mt. Pleasant Ave., Providence 02908

Salve Regina University
1 Ochre Point Ave., Newport 02840
Roselina McKillop, Dean of Admissions

SOUTH CAROLINA

Coastal Carolina College
P.O. Box 1954, Myrtle Beach 29578
Dr. Ed Cerny, Director of Admissions

Columbia Biblical Seminary
P.O. Box 3122, Columbia 29230
Lawrence Dabeck, Dir. of Admis.
See listing under "Biblical Studies"

Columbia International University
P.O. Box 3122, Columbia 29230
Frank Bedell, Dir. of Admis.
See listing under "Biblical Studies"

South Carolina State University
P.O. Box 7127, Orangeburg 29117-0001
803-536-7185

· Spartanburg Technical College
P.O. Box 4386, Spartanburg 29305
Pam Hagan, Dir. Admissions & Counseling
803-591-3800

Wofford College
429 N. Church St., Spartanburg 29303
Charles Gray, Dir. of Admis.

SOUTH DAKOTA

Augustana College
29th & S. Summit, Sioux Falls 57197

Dakota State University
820 N. Washington Ave., Madison 57042
Kathy Callies, Registrar
605-256-5139

Dakota Wesleyan University
1300 W. University Ave., Mitchell 57301

Mt. Marty College
1105 W. 8th St., Yankton 57078
Paula Tacke, Dir. of Admis.

South Dakota State University
P.O. Box 2201, Brookings 57007
Barbara Audley, Director
See listing under "Universities"

TENNESSEE

Austin Peay State University
601 College St., Clarksville 37044

Carson-Newman College
P.O. Box 70552, Jefferson City 37760
See listing under "Universities"

David Lipscomb University
3901 Granny White Pike, Nashville 37204-3951
Wade Sandrell, Dir. of Admis.
800-333-4358

Freed-Hardeman University
158 E. Main St., Henderson 38340
800-342-7837

Lincoln Memorial University
P.O. Box 2012, Harrogate 37752
Conrad Daniels, Dir. of Admis.

PEABODY COLLEGE OF VANDERBILT UNIVERSITY
P.O. Box 327, Nashville 37202
Barbara Johnston, Dir. of Admis.
615-322-8410

University of Tennessee at Martin
Martin 38238
Paul Kelley, Director of Admissions
See listing under "Universities"

University of Tennessee at Chattanooga
615 McCallie Ave., Chattanooga 37403

Vanderbilt University
West End Ave., Nashville 37240

:: THE WEBB SCHOOL
Bell Buckle 37020
Jon Frere, Headmaster
Jon Alden, Dir. of Admis.
615-389-6003
   Established 1870. Private. Coed. Accreditation: SACS. Summer term tuition: $ 1,308 for day students, $3,360 for boarding students. Enrollment: 100. Faculty 12. Student-faculty ratio: 8:1. Library: 20,000 volumes. 11 buildings on 150 acres. Founded on a tradition of academic excellence with honor. Students sign honor pledges since 1870. Strong outdoor adventure activities. Enrichment and full credit courses in Math, English, Languages, History and Science. Also offer Study Skills, SAT Prep, ESL, and Enrichment courses.

TEXAS

Austin College
900 N. Grand Ave., Sherman 75090
Rodney Oto, Dean of Admission
800-442-5363

Schreiner College
2100 Memorial Blvd., Kerrville 78028
800-343-4919

Southern Methodist University
Hillcrest at University, Dallas 75275

Texas Christian University
2800 S. University Dr., Ft. Worth 76129
Dr. Edward Boehm, Jr., Dean of Admissions

Texas Lutheran College
1000 W. Court St., Seguin 78155
Jennifer B. Ehlers, Dir. of Admis.

:: Texas Military Institute
20955 W. Tejas Trl., San Antonio 78257
Mary Jo Filip, Dir. of Admis.
210-698-7171, FAX: 210-698-0715

Texas Wesleyan University
1201 Wesleyan St., Fort Worth 76105
Kim Campbell, Dir. Freshman Admission

University of Dallas
1845 E. Northgate Dr., Irving 75062
Jim Whitaker, Dir. of Admis.

University of St. Thomas
3812 Montrose Blvd., Houston 77006
Elsie Biron, Dir. of Admis.

UTAH

Southern Utah University
351 W. Center St., Cedar City 84720
Dr. Phil Carter, Asst. Academic VP
801-586-7850

University of Utah
1400 E. 200 S., Salt Lake City 84112
Dr. J. Stayner Landward, Dir. of Admis.

Utah State University, Logan 84322-1600
Rod Clark, Director of Admissions
801-750-1107

:: Wasatch Academy
120 S. 100 W., Mt. Pleasant 84647
Jodi Tuttle, Dir. of Admis.

Westminster College of Salt Lake City
1840 S. 1300 E., Salt Lake City 84105
800-748-4753

VERMONT

The Bennington July Program
Bennington College, Bennington 05201
Sheri Alper, Director

Burlington College
95 North Ave., Burlington 05401
Nancy Wilson, Dir. of Admis.
See listing under "Liberal Arts"

NORWICH UNIVERSITY
65 S. Main St., Northfield 05663
Ted Smith, Director
See listing under "Universities"

Saint Michael's College
Winooski Park, Colchester 05439
Jim Jackson, Summer Session
802-654-2100
See listing under "Liberal Arts"

Southern Vermont College
Monument Ave., Bennington 05201
See listing under "Universities"

VIRGINIA

:: Blue Ridge School, Dyke 22935
C. Richard Vaughan, Dir. of Admis.
804-985-2811

:: Fishburne Military School
Non-Military Summer Session
P.O. Box 988A, Waynesboro 22980
Doris Brown, Dir. of Admis.
703-943-1171, Fax: 703-943-8042
See listing under "Military Science"

George Mason University
4400 University Dr., Fairfax 22030-4444
Donna Bufundo, Dean

Longwood College, Farmville 23901

Lynchburg College
1501 Lakeside Dr., Lynchburg 24501
Ernest Chadderton, Dean of Enrollment

Marymount University
2807 N. Glebe Rd., Arlington 22207
Charles Coe, Director of Admissions
800-548-7638 or 703-284-1500
See listing under "Universities"

Mary Washington College
1701 College Ave., Fredericksburg 22401
Martin Wilder, V.P. for Admissions

:: Oak Hill Academy
RR 1, Mouth of Wilson 24363
Ed Patton, President
See listing under "Preparatory Schools - Coed"

Radford University
P.O. Box 5430, Radford 24142

:: Randolph-Macon Academy
201 W. 3rd St., Front Royal 22630
Col. Trevor Turner, USA Ret, President

SHENANDOAH UNIVERSITY
1460 University Dr., Winchester 22601
Ralph Lewis, Dir. of Continuing Education
See listing under "Universities"

Union Theological Seminary in Virginia
3401 Brook Rd., Richmond 23227
Director of Professional Development

Virginia Military Institute, Lexington 24450

WASHINGTON

Eastern Washington University, Cheney 99004
Robert Herold, Vice Provost
See listing under "Universities"

Northwest College of the Assemblies of God
P.O. Box 579, Kirkland 98083-0579
Bob Foster, Dir. of Public Relations

Pacific Lutheran University
12180 Park Ave. S., Tacoma 98447
Dr. Judith Carr, Dean

St. Martin's College
700 College St. N.E., Lacey 98516

University of Puget Sound
1500 N. Warner St., Tacoma 98416

Walla Walla College
204 S. College Ave., College Place 99324

WEST VIRGINIA

Davis & Elkins College
100 Campus Dr., Elkins 26241
Kevin D. Chenoweth, Dir. of Admis.

· Potomac State College of West Virginia University
Keyser 26726

The University of Charleston
2300 MacCorkle Ave., S.E., Charleston 25304
800-995-GO UC

WISCONSIN

Beloit College
700 College St., Beloit 53511
John Winkelmann, Director
608-363-2350

Cardinal Stritch College
6801 N. Yates Rd., Milwaukee 53217
David Wegener, Dir. of Admis.

Carroll College
100 N. East Ave., Waukesha 53186
Ken Moyer, Dir. of Admis.

Carthage College
2001 Alford Dr., Kenosha 53140
Mary Gallo, Director

Edgewood College
855 Woodrow St., Madison 53711
Robert Blust, Dir. of Admis.

Marian College of Fond du Lac
45 S. National Ave., Fond du Lac 54935
Carol Reichenberger, Dean of Admissions

Marquette University
1918 W. Wisconsin Ave., Milwaukee 53233
Dr. Robert Hasenstab, Dir. of Continuing Educ.

Milwaukee School of Engineering
1025 N. Broadway, Milwaukee 53202
Owen Smith, Dean of Admission
800-332-6763 or 414-277-7200 in metro Milwaukee

St. Norbert College
100 Grant St., De Pere 54115
Craig S. Wesley, Dean of Admission
See listing under "Universities"

University of Wisconsin, Oshkosh
800 Algoma Blvd., Oshkosh 54901-8602
August Helgerson, Dir. of Admis.

University of Wisconsin
P.O. Box 2000, Kenosha 53141
414-553-2211

University of Wisconsin
1 University Plaza, Platteville 53818
Richard Schumacher, Dean of Admissions

Viterbo College
815 9th St., S., La Crosse 54601
Michael Rancht, Cont. Summer Coord.

WYOMING

University of Wyoming
P.O. Box 3434, Laramie 82071
Richard Davis, Dir. of Admis.

GUAM

University of Guam
UOG Station, Mangilao 96923
Kathleen Owings, Dir. of Admis.

PUERTO RICO

University of Puerto Rico, Mayaguez Campus
P.O. Box 5000, Mayaguez 00681
Neysa Lopez, Dir. of Admis.

University of Puerto Rico, Rio Piedras Campus
P.O. Box 23300, San Juan 00931
Victor Lopez, Dir. of Admis.

TEACHER EDUCATION

This classification contains schools having professional education programs accredited by the National Council for Accreditation of Teacher Education (†) and a selection of programs from institutionally accredited schools. Colleges and Universities (no dot code) generally offer four-year or advanced programs in pre-elementary, elementary and secondary education; Community and Junior Colleges (·) generally offer associate degrees in teachers aide programs.

ALABAMA

Alabama A & M University
P.O. Box 262, Normal 35762
Dr. James H. Hicks, Dean
See listing under "Universities"

† Alabama State University
P.O. Box 271, Montgomery 36101

Athens State College
300 N. Beaty St., Athens 35611
Larry McCoy, Dir. of Admissions

† Auburn University, Auburn 36849

† Auburn University at Montgomery
7300 University Dr., Montgomery 36117
H. H. Funderburk, VP

† Birmingham Southern College
900 Arkadelphia Rd., Birmingham 35254

Faulkner University
5345 Atlanta Hwy., Montgomery 36109

Huntingdon College
1500 E. Fairview Ave., Montgomery 36106-2148
Carolyn A. Phillips, Dean of Enrollment
800-763-0313

† Jacksonville State University
700 Pelham Rd. N., Jacksonville 36265

Judson College
P O Box 120, Marion 36756

Livingston University
Station #4, Livingston 35470
Haywood Mayton, Dean
See listing under "Universities"

Miles College
P.O. Box 3800, Birmingham 35208

† Oakwood College
Oakwood Rd., N.W., Huntsville 35896

† Samford University
800 Lakeshore Dr., Birmingham 35229
Ruth Ash, Dean

Southeastern Bible College
3001 Hwy. 280, S., Birmingham 35243
800-749-8878

Spring Hill College
4000 Dauphin St., Mobile 36608
Ben Hamd, Dir. of Admis.

STILLMAN COLLEGE
P.O. Box 1430, Tuscaloosa 35403
Barbara K. Smith, Director of Admissions
See listing under "Universities"

† Troy State University, Troy 36082
Dr. James Kimbrough, Dean

Troy State University at Dothan
P.O. Box 8368, Dothan 36304
Bob Willis, Dir. of Undergraduate Admissions

Troy State University at Montgomery
P.O. Box 4419, Montgomery 36103

Tuskegee University
Tuskegee Institute 36088

† University of Alabama
P.O. Box 870132, Tuscaloosa 35487-0132
Roy Smith, Dir. of Admis.

† University of Alabama at Birmingham
University Station, Birmingham 35294

UNIVERSITY OF ALABAMA IN HUNTSVILLE
P.O. Box 1247, Huntsville 35899
Ron R. Koger Ed.D., Dir. of Admis.
205-895-6070
Established 1969. Public. Coed. Accreditation: SACS, ABET, NLN, CSAB, ACS. Tuition: $2,418 resident, $4,836 non-resident. Room & Board: $3,450. Undergraduate enrollment: 2,674 full-time, 3,439 part-time. Graduate enrollment: 1,860. Faculty: 282. Student-faculty ratio: 18:1. Degrees: BS, BA, BSBA, BSE, MS, MSM, Ph.D., BSN, MSN, MA. 20 buildings on 350 acres. Comprehensive research university located in the Tennessee Valley of northern Alabama. Huntsville is the locale of major government and private research centers. Metropolitan population approaching 300,000.

UNIVERSITY OF MOBILE
P.O. Box 13220, Mobile 36663-0220
Kim Leousis, Dir. of Admissions
205-675-5990
See listing under "Universities"

† University of Montevallo, Montevallo 35115

† University of North Alabama
University Station, Florence 35632

† University of South Alabama
307 University Blvd. N., Mobile 36688

ALASKA

Alaska Pacific University
4101 University Dr., Anchorage 99508
Director of Admissions
See listing under "Universities"

Sheldon Jackson College
801 Lincoln St., Sitka 99835
Dennis Trotter, Dir. of Admis.
907-747-5221

University of Alaska Anchorage
3211 Providence Dr., Anchorage 99508
907-786-1480

† University of Alaska Fairbanks
Fairbanks 99775

University of Alaska Southeast
11120 Glacier Hwy., Juneau 99801
Greg Wagner, Coordinator of Admissions

ARIZONA

Arizona State University, Tempe 85287

GRAND CANYON UNIVERSITY
3300 W. Camelback Rd., Phoenix 85017
Dr. Patty Horn, Dean
See listing under "Liberal Arts and Sciences"

Northern Arizona University
P.O. Box 4092, Flagstaff 86011
Dr. Margaret Cibik, Dir. of Admis.

SOUTHWESTERN COLLEGE
A Conservative Baptist Bible College
2625 E. Cactus Rd., Phoenix 85032
800-247-2697

† University of Arizona, Tucson 85721
Loyd Bell, Director of Admissions

ARKANSAS

† Arkansas College
2300 Highland Rd., Batesville 72501
Jonathan M. Stroud, Dean of Admissions
800-423-2542

† Arkansas State University
P.O. Box 1630, State University 72467

† Arkansas Tech University
215 W. O St., Russellville 72801

† Harding University
900 E. Center Ave., Searcy 72149

† Henderson State University
1100 Henderson St., Arkadelphia 71999

† Hendrix College
1601 Harkrider St., Conway 72032

† John Brown University
2000 W. University, Siloam Springs 72761
Don Crandall, Director of Enrollment Management

† Ouachita Baptist University
410 Ouachita St., Arkadelphia 71998
Randy Garner, Dir. of Admis.
800-DIAL-OBU

Philander Smith College
812 W. 13th St., Little Rock 72202

· Phillips County Community College
P.O. Box 785, Helena 72342
Dr. Steven Jones, President
James R. Brasel, Dean of Admissions

† Southern Arkansas University
SAU Box 1402, Magnolia 71753

† University of Arkansas at Fayetteville
Fayetteville 72701

† University of Arkansas at Little Rock
2801 S. University Ave., Little Rock 72204

† University of Arkansas at Monticello
P.O. Box 3596, Monticello 71656

† University of Arkansas at Pine Bluff
1200 University Dr., Pine Bluff 71601-2799

† University of Central Arkansas
201 Donaghey Ave., Conway 72035

† University of the Ozarks
415 College Ave., Clarksville 72830

Williams Baptist College
P.O. Box 3667, Walnut Ridge 72476
Scott Wright, Dir. of Admis.

CALIFORNIA

Azusa Pacific University
P.O. Box 7000, Azusa 91702

Bethany Bible College
800 Bethany Dr., Scotts Valley 95066
Randal McNally, Dir. of Admis.

Biola University
13800 Biola Ave., La Mirada 90639
Wayne Chute, Dean of Admissions

California Baptist College
8432 Magnolia Ave., Riverside 92504
800-782-3382

California Lutheran University
60 Olsen Rd., Thousand Oaks 91360
800-252-5884

California Polytechnic State University
San Luis Obispo 93407
Helen Linstrum, Dir. of Admis.

California State University, Chico
Chico 95929-0224
Dr. Michael Kotar, Chrpsn.

† California State University, Dominguez Hills
1000 E. Victoria St., Carson 90747

† California State University, Fresno
Shaw & Cedar Ave., Fresno 93710

California State University, Long Beach
1250 Bellflower Blvd., Long Beach 90840

† California State University, Los Angeles
5151 Paseo Rancho Castilla, Los Angeles 90032

† California State University, Northridge
18111 Nordhoff St., Northridge 91330
Ned C. Reynolds, Dir. of Admis.

California State University, San Bernardino
5500 University Pky., San Bernardino 92407
909-880-5188

† California State University-Bakersfield
9001 Stockdale Hwy., Bakersfield 93311
Dr. Homer S. Montalvo, Dir. of Admis.

† California State University-Fullerton
Fullerton 92632

† California State University-Hayward
25800 Carlos Bee Blvd., Hayward 94542

† California State University-Stanislaus
801 W. Monte Vista Ave., Turlock 95382
Frances Cook, Dean Enrollment Services

Chapman University
333 N. Glassell St., Orange 92666
Michael Drummy, Dir. of Admis.

Christian Heritage College
2100 Greenfield Dr., El Cajon 92019
Pam Daly, Dir. of Admis.
800-676-2242

College of Notre Dame
1500 Ralston Ave., Belmont 94002
Greg M. Smith, PhD., Dir. of Admis.

Concordia University
1530 Concordia, Irvine 92715
Stan Meyer, Dean of Admission
800-229-1200
See listing under "Universities"

DOMINICAN COLLEGE OF SAN RAFAEL
50 Acacia Ave., San Rafael 94901-8008
Office of Admissions
800-788-3522

Fresno Pacific College
1717 S. Chestnut Ave., Fresno 93702
209-453-2039

Hebrew Union College
Jewish Institute of Religion
3077 University Ave., Los Angeles 90007
Rabbi Lee Bycel, Dean

Holy Names College
3500 Mountain Blvd., Oakland 94619

Humboldt State University
1 Harps St., Arcata 95521

La Sierra University
4700 Pierce St., Riverside 92505
800-874-5587

Loyola Marymount University
Loyola Blvd. at W. 80th, Los Angeles 90045
M. L'Heureux, Dir. of Admis.

Master's College
P.O. Box 221450, Newhall 91322
Don Gilmore, Dir. of Admis.

Mills College
5000 MacArthur Blvd., Oakland 94613
Genevieve Ann Flaherty, Dean of Admissions
800-87-MILLS

Mt. St. Mary's College
12001 Chalon Rd., Los Angeles 90049

Occidental College
1600 Campus Rd., Los Angeles 90041

Pacific Christian College
2500 E. Nutwood Ave., Fullerton 92631
Knofel Staton, President

Pacific Oaks College
5 Westmoreland Pl., Pasadena 91103
Katherine Gabel, President

Pacific Union College
1 Angwin Ave., Angwin 94508
Dr. Gary Gifford, Dir. of Admis.

Pepperdine University
400 Corporate Pointe, Culver City 90230
310-568-5600

Point Loma Nazarene College
3900 Lomaland Dr., San Diego 92106
Bill Young, Dir. of Admis.

Porterville College
100 E. College Ave., Porterville 93257
John McCuen, President

St. Mary's College of California
P.O. Box 4267, Moraga 94575

† San Diego State University
5300 Campanile Dr., San Diego 92115

† San Francisco State University
1600 Holloway Ave., San Francisco 94132
Corwin Bjonerud, Dir. of Admis.

† San Jose State University
1 Washington Sq., San Jose 95192

Santa Barbara City College
721 Cliff Dr., Santa Barbara 93109
805-965-0581

Santa Clara University, Santa Clara 95053

Simpson College
2211 College View Dr., Redding 96003
Joe Barth, Registrar

Sonoma State University
1801 E. Cotati Ave., Rohnert Park 94928

Southern California College
55 Fair Dr., Costa Mesa 92626
Richard Hardy, Asst. Dean for Enrollment

Stanford University, Stanford 94305

UNITED STATES INTERNATIONAL UNIVERSITY
10455 Pomerado Rd., San Diego 92131
619-693-4772
See listing under "Universities"

University of California, Santa Barbara
Santa Barbara 93106

University of California-Santa Cruz
Santa Cruz 95064
Joseph Allen, Dir. of Admis.

UNIVERSITY OF JUDAISM/LEE COLLEGE
15600 Mulholland Dr., Los Angeles 90077
Tamara Greenebaum, Dean of Admissions
See listing under "Universities"

University of La Verne
1950 3rd St., La Verne 91750
Mark Bornholdt, Dir. of Admis.

University of San Diego
5998 Alcala Park, San Diego 92110
Warren Muller, Dir. of Admis.
619-260-4506

University of San Francisco
2130 Fulton St., San Francisco 94117
Bill Henley, Dir. of Admis.

† University of the Pacific
3601 Pacific Ave, Stockton 95211
Elliott J. Taylor, Dean of Admissions

COLORADO

† Adams State College, Alamosa 81102
Cheryl Billingsley, Dir. of Admis.
800-824-6494

Colorado Christian University
180 S. Garrison St., Lakewood 80226
Debra Seefeldt, Dir. of Admis.

Colorado College
14 E. Cache La Poudre, Colorado Springs 80903
Terry Swenson, Dir. of Admis.

† Colorado State University
102 Administration Building, Fort Collins 80523
Mary Ontireros, Dir. of Admissions

† Ft. Lewis College
1000 Rim Dr., Durango 81301

Mesa State College
P.O. Box 2647, Grand Junction 81502
Sherri Pe'a, Dir. of Admis.

† Metropolitan State College of Denver
P.O. Box 173362, Campus Box 16
Denver 80217-3362

Morgan Community College
17800 Road 20, Fort Morgan 80701
Kurtis Armstrong, Dir. of Admis.

Regis University
3333 Regis Blvd., Denver 80221
Robert Blust, Director of Admissions

† University of Colorado at Boulder
Boulder 80309
William A. Douglas, Dean of Admis.

† University of Colorado at Colorado Springs
P.O. Box 7150, Colorado Springs 80933

† University of Colorado at Denver
1200 Larimer, Denver 80204

University of Denver
2199 S. University Blvd., Denver 80210

† University of Northern Colorado, Greeley 80639
Gary Galluzzo, Dean
303-351-2817

University of Southern Colorado
2200 Bonforte Blvd., Pueblo 81001

† Western State College of Colorado
Gunnison 81231
Monica Bruning, Dir. of Admis.
See listing under "Universities"

CONNECTICUT

Albertus Magnus College
700 Prospect St., New Haven 06511
Richard Lolatte, Dir. of Admissions
203-773-8501 or 800-578-9160

Eastern Connecticut State University
83 Windham St., Willimantic 06226
Dr. Jeffrey Trawick-Smith, Chrpsn.

Fairfield University
25 N. Benson Rd., Fairfield 06430

QUINNIPIAC COLLEGE
275 Mount Carmel Ave., Hamden 06518
John Lahey, President
Joan Isaac Mohr, VP and Dean of Admissions
Established 1929. Private. Coed. Accreditation:
NEASC. Tuition: $11,250. Room and board: $5,790.
Enrollment: 2,583 boarding, 3,444 day. Faculty 333.
Degrees: BA, BS, MAT, MBA, MHS, MPS. Library:
290,000 volumes. 30 buildings on 170 acres. Gym.
Suburban location at the base of Sleeping Giant State
Park, close to New Haven and Yale University. Con-
venient to New York City, Boston, and Upper New
England. Building a new $7 million School of Busi-
ness Center.

Sacred Heart University
5151 Park Ave., Fairfield 06432-1000
Dr. Anthony J. Cernera, President

St. Joseph College
1678 Asylum Ave., West Hartford 06117
Mary C. Demo, Dir. of Admis.

Southern Connecticut State University
501 Crescent St., New Haven 06515

University of Bridgeport
126 Park Ave., Bridgeport 06601
Andrew G. Nelson, Dean Admis./Financial Aid
203-576-4552
See listing under "Universities"

† University of Connecticut, Storrs 06268
Dr. David Camaione, Interim Dean

† UNIVERSITY OF HARTFORD
200 Bloomfield Ave., West Hartford 06117
Richard Zeiser, Dir. of Admis.
See listing under "Universities"

Western Connecticut State University
181 White St., Danbury 06810

DELAWARE

Delaware State College
1200 N. DuPont Hwy., Dover 19901
Jethro C. Williams, Dir. of Admis.

University of Delaware, Newark 19711

DISTRICT OF COLUMBIA

† The American University
4400 Massachusetts Ave. N.W.
Washington 20016

† Catholic University of America
620 Michigan Ave. N.E., Washington 20064
Robert J. Talbot, Dir. of Admis. & Fin. Aid.

† Gallaudet University
800 Florida Ave., N.E., Washington 20002
See listing under "Universities"

† George Washington University
Washington 20052

Mt. Vernon College
2100 Foxhall Rd., N.W., Washington 20007
202-625-4682 or 800-682-4636, FAX: 202-338-1089

Trinity College
125 Michigan Ave., N.E., Washington 20017
Donna Quinn, Dir. of Admis.

University of the District of Columbia
Georgia Ave.-Harvard St. Campus
1100 Harvard St., N.W., Washington 20009

University of the District of Columbia
Van Ness Campus
4200 Connecticut Ave., N.W., Washington 20008

FLORIDA

Barry University
11300 N.E. 2nd Ave., Miami Shores 33161
Robin Ray Roberts, Dean of Admissions

† Bethune-Cookman College
640 Mary McLeod Bethune Blvd.
Daytona Beach 32114

Clearwater Christian College
3400 Gulf-to-Bay Blvd., Clearwater 34619
Benjamin Puckett, Dir. of Admis.

Eckerd College
P.O. Box 12560, St. Petersburg 33733
Richard Hallin, Dir. of Admis.

Edison Community College
8099 College Pky., Fort Myers 33919
Mailing address: P.O. Box 60210
Fort Myers 33906-6210
Sandra Fahey, Dir. of Admis. and Records

Flagler College
P.O. Box 1027, St. Augustine 32085
Marc G. Williar, Dir. of Admis.
904-829-6481

† Florida A & M University, Tallahassee 32307

† Florida Atlantic University
500 N.W. 20th St., Boca Raton 33431
Brian Levin-Stankevich, Dir. of Admis.

Florida International University
Tamiami Trail, Miami 33199

Florida Memorial College
15800 N.W. 42nd Ave., Opa-Locka 33054
Roberto Darragan, Jr., Dir., Admissions

Florida Southern College
111 Lake Hollingsworth Dr., Lakeland 33801
William Stephens, Jr., Dir. of Admis.

† Florida State University
600 W. College Ave., Tallahassee 32306

Hobe Sound Bible College
P.O. Box 1065, Hobe Sound 33475
Ann French, Dir. of Admis.

Jacksonville University
2800 University Blvd., N., Jacksonville 32211

LYNN UNIVERSITY
(Est. 1962 as College of Boca Raton)
3601 N. Military Trail, Boca Raton 33431
407-994-0770 or 800-544-8035
See listing under "Universities"

Miami Christian College
P.O. Box 19674, Miami 33101

Nova Southeastern University
3301 College Ave., Ft. Lauderdale 33314

Palm Beach Atlantic College
P.O. Box 24708, West Palm Beach 33416-4708
See listing under "Universities"

Rollins College
P.O. Box 2720, Winter Park 32790

St. Leo College
P.O. Box 2008, St. Leo 33574
Bonnie Black, Dir. of Admis.

St. Thomas University
16400 N.W. 32nd Ave., Miami 33054
John M. Letvinchuk, Dir. of Admis.

Stetson University
401 N. Woodland Blvd., De Land 32720
Dr. Donald Gill, Chrpsn.

† University of Central Florida
P.O. Box 25000, Orlando 32816

† University of Florida
226 Tigert Hall, Gainesville 32611

† University of Miami
P.O. Box 248006, Coral Gables 33124

† University of North Florida
4567 St. Johns Bluff Rd. S., Jacksonville 32224

UNIVERSITY OF SARASOTA
5250 17th St., Sarasota 34235
Linda Volz, Dir. of Enrollment Management
800-331-5995
Established 1969. Coed. Accreditation: SACS. Tuition: $265 per credit hour. Enrollment: 470. Faculty:
30. Degrees: MAEd, MBA, EdD. Year round, non-traditional calendar, flexible, small seminars, much individual attention to students, performance oriented.

† University of South Florida
4202 Fowler Ave., Tampa 33620

University of Tampa
401 W. Kennedy Blvd., Tampa 33606
Robert W. Cook, Dir. of Admis.

† University of West Florida
11000 University Pky., Pensacola 32514

Warner Southern College
5301 U.S. Hwy. 27, S., Lake Wales 33853
Valerie S. Rutland, Dir. Enrollment Mgmt.
800-949-7248

GEORGIA

† Albany State College
504 College Dr., Albany 31705

† Armstrong State College
11935 Abercorn St., Savannah 31419
Kim West, Director of Admissions

AUGUSTA COLLEGE
2500 Walton Way, Augusta 30904-2200
Lee Young, Dir. of Admis.
706-737-1405

† Berry College
2277 Martha Berry Hwy. N.W., Mt. Berry 30165

Brenau College
204 Boulevard, Gainesville 30501

BREWTON-PARKER COLLEGE
P.O. Box 197, Mount Vernon 30445
Dr. Y. Lynn Holmes, President
912-583-2241

Clark Atlanta University
240 James Brawley Dr., S.W., Atlanta 30314
Thomas W. Cole, President

† Columbus College
3600 Algonquin Dr., Columbus 31907

Emory University
1462 Clifton Rd., Atlanta 30322

† Fort Valley State College
1005 State College Dr., Fort Valley 31030

· Gainesville College
P.O. Box 1358, Gainesville 30503
Carol S. Nobles, Dir. of Admis.
404-535-6241

† Georgia College
231 W. Hancock St., Milledgeville 31061
912-453-5004

† Georgia Southern University, Statesboro 30460

† Georgia Southwestern College
800 Wheatley St., Americus 31709

† Georgia State University
University Plaza, Atlanta 30303
Ernest Beals, Dean of Admissions

† Kennesaw State College
P.O. Box 444, Marietta 30061
Joe Head, Dir. of Admis.

La Grange College
601 Broad St., La Grange 30240
Phil Dodson, Dir. of Admis.
706-882-2911

† Mercer University
1400 Coleman Ave., Macon 31207

Morehouse College
830 Westview Dr., S.W., Atlanta 30310
Gary Bussey, Dir. of Admissions

Morris Brown College
643 Martin Luther King Jr. Dr. N.W.
Atlanta 30314

† North Georgia College, Dahlonega 30597
Gary R. Steffey, Dir. of Admis.

Oglethorpe University
4484 Peachtree Rd., N.E., Atlanta 30319
Dennis Matthews, Dir. of Admis.

Paine College
1235 15th St., Augusta 30901
Phyllis Wyatt-Woodruff, Dir. Enrollment Mgmt.

Piedmont College
P.O. Box 10, Demorest 30535
Penny L. Graber, Dir of Admis.
800-277-7020

Shorter College
315 Shorter Ave., Rome 30165

† Spelman College
350 Spelman Ln., S.W., Atlanta 30314
Aline Rivers, Dir. of Admis.

Toccoa Falls College
Office of Admissions, Toccoa Falls 30598
Matthew L. King, Dir. of Admis.
800-868-3257

† University of Georgia, Athens 30602
Dr. Alphonse Buccino, Dean

† Valdosta State College
Patterson St., Valdosta 31698

Wesleyan College
4760 Forsyth Rd., Macon 31297

† West Georgia College, Carrollton 30118
C. Doyle Bickers, Dir. of Admis.

HAWAII

Brigham Young University
55-220 Kulanui St., Laie 96762
Joanne Lowe, Coordinator of Admis.

Chaminade University of Honolulu
3140 Waialae Ave., Honolulu 96816
Charles Schafer, VP Enrollment Services

University of Hawaii at Manoa
2500 Campus Rd., Honolulu 96822

IDAHO

† Boise State University
1910 University Dr., Boise 83725

College of Idaho, Caldwell 83605

† Idaho State University
P.O. Box 8270, Pocatello 83209

† Lewis Clark State College
500 8th Ave., Lewiston 83501
800-933-5272 or 208-799-5272

† Northwest Nazarene College
623 Holly St., Nampa 83686
Bruce D. Webb, Dir. of Admis.

† University of Idaho, Moscow 83843
Peter Brown, Dir. of Admis.

ILLINOIS

† Augustana College
639 38th St., Rock Island 61201
Martin R. Sauer, Director of Admission
800-798-8100

Aurora University
347 S. Gladstone Ave., Aurora 60506
Peter Pitts, Dir. of Admis.

Barat College, Lake Forest 60045
Loretta Brickman, Dir. of Admis.

Blackburn College
700 College Ave., Carlinville 62626
Dwight Smith, Dir. of Admis.

† Bradley University
1501 W. Bradley Ave., Peoria 61625

† Chicago State University
9501 S. King Dr., Chicago 60628

College of St. Francis
500 Wilcox St., Joliet 60435

† Concordia University
7400 Augusta St., River Forest 60305

† De Paul University
1 E. Jackson Blvd., Chicago 60604
Thomas D. Abrahamson, Dean of Admissions
See listing under "Universities"

† Eastern Illinois University, Charleston 61920
Charles Joley, Dean
See listing under "Universities"

† Elmhurst College
190 Prospect Ave., Elmhurst 60126

Eureka College
300 E. College Ave., Eureka 61530

Governors State University
1 University Pky., University Park 60466
Richard Pride, Dir. of Admis.

† Greenville College
315 E. College Ave., Greenville 62246
Kent Krober, Dir. of Admis.

Illinois Benedictine College
5700 College Rd., Lisle 60532

Illinois College
1101 W. College Ave., Jacksonville 62650
Gale Vaugn, Dir. of Admis.

† Illinois State University
212 N. School St., Normal 61761

Judson College
1151 N. State St., Elgin 60123
Jack Powell, Dir. of Enrollment Services

Kendall College
2408 Orrington Ave., Evanston 60201
Peter Pauletti, Dir. of Admis.

Knox College, Galesburg 61401
309-343-0112 or 800-678-KNOX
See listing under "Universities"

Lake Forest College
555 N. Sheridan Rd., Lake Forest 60045

LEWIS UNIVERSITY
Rt. 53, Romeoville 60441
Irish O'Reilly, Director of Admissions
See listing under "Universities"

Loyola University of Chicago
820 N. Michigan Ave., Chicago 60611
Allen V. Lentino, Dir. of Admis.

Loyola University - Mundelein College
6363 N. Sheridan Rd., Chicago 60660
Judith Bobber, Dir. of Admis.

McKendree College
701 College Rd., Lebanon 62254
Stephen E. Jackson, Director of Admissions

MacMurray College
447 E. College Ave., Jacksonville 62650
Edwin R. Hockett, Dean of Admissions

Millikin University
1184 W. Main St., Decatur 62522
Lin Stoner, Dean of Admissions
800-373-7733

Monmouth College
700 E. Broadway, Monmouth 61462

· Montay College
3750 W. Peterson Ave., Chicago 60659
Scott Dalhouse, Dir. of Admis.

National-Louis University
2840 Sheridan Ave., Evanston 60201

Niles College of Loyola University
7135 N. Harlem Av., Niles 60714

North Central College
30 N. Brainard St.
P.O. Box 3065, Naperville 60566-7065
Marguerite Waters, Director of Admission
708-420-3414

† Northeastern Illinois University
5500 N. St. Louis Ave., Chicago 60625

† Northern Illinois University, De Kalb 60115

North Park College & Theological Seminary
3225 W. Foster, Chicago 60625
312-509-2330

Northwestern University
School of Education
2115 N. Campus Dr., Evanston 60208

Olivet Nazarene University, Kankakee 60901
John Mongerson, Dir. of Admis.
815-939-5203

· Parkland College
2400 W. Bradley Ave., Champaign 61821-1899
217-351-2208 or 800-346-8089

Principia College, Elsah 62028

Quincy College
1800 College Ave., Quincy 62301
Fr. Michael Lanning, O.F.M., Dir. of Admis.

Rockford College
5050 E. State St., Rockford 61108
Miriam King, V.P. for Enrollment Management
See listing under "Universities"

† ROOSEVELT UNIVERSITY
430 S. Michigan Ave., Chicago 60605
William Smyser, Director of Admissions
See listing under "Universities"

St. Xavier University
3700 W. 103rd St., Chicago 60655
Mary Hendry, Dean of Admissions

Sangamon State University
Shepherd Rd., Springfield 62794-9243
Admissions and Records, 217-786-6626

School of the Art Institute of Chicago
37 S. Wabash, Chicago 60603
Ellen B. Cropp, Dir. of Admis.

† Southern Illinois University at Carbondale
Carbondale 62901

† Southern Illinois University at Edwardsville
Edwardsville 62026
Eugene J. Magac, Dir. of Admissions & Records

Trinity Christian College
6601 W. College Dr., Palos Heights 60463
Kenneth Bootsma, President

Trinity College
2077 Half Day Rd., Deerfield 60015
Dr. Kenneth Meyer, Pres.

University of Chicago
5801 S. Ellis Ave., Chicago 60637

University of Illinois
506 S. Wright St., Urbana 61801

University of Illinois at Chicago
P.O. Box 4348, Chicago 60680
Dr. Larry Braskamp, Dean

VanderCook College of Music
3209 S. Michigan Ave., Chicago 60616
Ward Durrett, Dir of Admis.

† Western Illinois University
900 W. Adams St., Macomb 61455
Alan DeRoos, Registrar
309-298-1891

INDIANA

† Anderson University
1100 E. 5th St., Anderson 46012
Robert H. Reardon, President

† Ball State University
2000 W. University Ave., Muncie 47306
Ruth Vedvik, Dir. of Admis.

Bethel College
1001 W. McKinley Ave., Mishawaka 46545
Steve Matteson, Dir. of Admis.

Butler University
4600 Sunset Ave., Indianapolis 46208

Calumet College
2400 New York Ave., Whiting 46394
Sharon Sweeney, Dir. of Admis.

† DePauw University
313 S. Locust St., Greencastle 46135
Dr. Eleanor Ypma, Registrar

Earlham College
801 National Rd. W., Richmond 47374
Robert deVeer, Dean of Admis.

Franklin College
501 E. Monroe, Franklin 46131
B. Stephen Richards, VP Enrollment

† Goshen College
1700 S. Main St., Goshen 46526
John Smith, Director

Grace College
200 Seminary Dr., Winona Lake 46590
Ron Henry, Dir. of Admis.

Hanover College, Hanover 47243
Eugene McLemore, Dir., Admis.

Huntington College
2303 College Ave., Huntington 46750
Paul Breininger, Dir. of Admis. Services

† Indiana State University
217 N. 6th St., Terre Haute 47809

† Indiana University at Bloomington
300 N. Jordan Ave., Bloomington 47406

† Indiana University at Kokomo
P.O. Box 9003, Kokomo 46904

† Indiana University at South Bend
P.O. Box 7111, South Bend 46634

† Indiana University Northwest
3400 N. Broadway, Gary 46408

† Indiana University Southeast
4201 Grantline Rd., New Albany 47150

† Indiana University-Purdue University at Fort Wayne
2101 Coliseum Blvd. E., Fort Wayne 46805

Indiana University-Purdue University
355 N. Lansing, Indianapolis 46202

† Indiana Wesleyan University
4201 S. Washington St., Marion 46953
800-332-6901

† Manchester College
604 College Ave., North Manchester 46962
Dr. Karen Doudt, Director

† Marian College
3200 Cold Spring Rd., Indianapolis 46222
Don French, Dir. of Admis.

† Oakland City College
143 N. Lucretia St., Oakland City 47660
Tracy Siekman, Dir. of Admis.

† Purdue University
Schleman Hall, West Lafayette 47907

† Purdue University, Calumet Campus
2233 171st St., Hammond 46323

Purdue University
1401 S. U.S. Hwy. 421, Westville 46391

† St. Francis College
2701 Spring St., Ft. Wayne 46808

† ST. JOSEPH'S COLLEGE
P.O. Box 890, Rensselaer 47978
Louis Levy, Dean of Admissions
800-447-8781

St. Mary-of-the-Woods College
Saint Mary-of-the-Woods 47876
Lynn M. Rubick, Director of Admissions
800-926-SMWC

† St. Mary's College
46 Madeliva, Notre Dame 46556
Mary Ann Rowan, Dir. of Admissions

† Taylor University
500 W. Reade Ave., Upland 46989
Steve Bedi, Director

Taylor University - Fort Wayne Campus
1025 W. Rudisill Blvd., Fort Wayne 46807
Jan Paul Storey, Dir. of Admis.

Tri-State University, Angola 46703
Director of Admission
800-347-4878

† University of Evansville
1800 Lincoln Ave., Evansville 47722
Dr. Cathy Barlow, Dean
800-423-8633

† University of Indianapolis
1400 E. Hanna Ave., Indianapolis 46227

† University of Southern Indiana
8600 University Blvd., Evansville 47712

† Valparaiso University, Valparaiso 46383

Wabash College
301 W. Wabash Ave., Crawfordsville 47933
Greg Birk, Dir. of Admis.

IOWA

Briar Cliff College
3303 Rebecca St., Sioux City 51104
Patricia White, Dir. of Admis.

† Buena Vista College
610 W. 4th St., Storm Lake 50588
Joanne Loonan, Director of Admissions

Clarke College
1550 Clarke Dr., Dubuque 52001
Joan Lickteig, BVM, PhD, Chair
800-383-2345

Coe College
1220 1st Ave., N.E., Cedar Rapids 52402
Roger Johanson, Chrpsn.

Cornell College
600 1st St., W., Mt. Vernon 52314
Kevin Crockett, Dean of Admissions

Dordt College
498 4th Ave., N.E., Sioux Center 51250
Quentin Van Essen, Dir. of Admissions
800-343-6738

Drake University
2507 E. University Ave., Des Moines 50311
Dr. Richard Schwab, Dean

Faith Baptist Bible College & Theological Seminary
1900 N.W. 4th St., Ankeny 50021
Jeff Newman, Director of Admissions
Admissions: 800-352-0147

† Graceland College, Lamoni 50140
800-638-0053, Outside Iowa 800-346-9208
Bonita Booth, Dean of Admissions
See listing under "Universities"

Grand View College
1200 Grandview Ave., Des Moines 50316
Lori Hanson, Dir. of Admissions
800-444-6083

Grinnell College
P.O. Box 805, Grinnell 50112

Iowa Lakes Community College
300 S. 18th St., Estherville 51334
John Nelson, Dir. of Admis.
712-362-2604

Iowa State University, Ames 50011
Karsten Smedal, Dir. of Admis.

Loras College
1450 Alta Vista, Dubuque 52001
Dan Conry, Dir. of Admis.

† Luther College
700 College Dr., Decorah 52101
David Sallee, Dean for Enrollment

Maharishi International University
Route 1, Fairfield 52556
Gregory Polakow, Dir. of Admis.

† Morningside College, Sioux City 51106
Lora Vanderzwaag, Dir. of Admis.

Mount Mercy College
1330 Elmhurst Dr., N.E., Cedar Rapids 52402
Carol Williamson, Dir. of Admis.

† Northwestern College
101 7th St. S.W., Orange City 51041

St. Ambrose University
518 W. Locust St., Davenport 52803

† Simpson College
P.O. Box 708, Indianola 50125

Teikyo Marycrest University
1607 W. 12th St., Davenport 52804
Tim McDonough, Dir. of Admis.
See listing under "Universities"

Teikyo Westmar University
1002 3rd Ave., S.E., Le Mars 51031
Dr. Jim Utesch, Dir. of Admis.

University of Dubuque
2000 University Ave., Dubuque 52001

University of Iowa, Iowa City 52242

University of Northern Iowa, Cedar Falls 50614

Upper Iowa University
P.O. Box 1857, Fayette 52142

Vennard College
P.O. Box 29, University Park 52595
Mark Becker, Dir. of Admis.
800-338-2407

Waldorf College
106 S. 6th St., Forest City 50436
Steve Lovik, Dir. of Admis.
800-292-1903

Wartburg College
P.O. Box 1003, Waverly 50677

† William Penn College
201 Trueblood Ave., Oskaloosa 52577
Eric Otto, Dir. of Admis.

KANSAS

Baker University
8th & Grove St., Baldwin City 66006

BARCLAY COLLEGE
P.O. Box 288, Haviland 67059
Lonny R. Choate, Dir. of Admis.

† Benedictine College
1020 N. Second St., Atchison 66002
James Hoffman, Dir. of Admis.

† Bethany College
421 N. 1st St., Lindsborg 67456
Sterling Benson, Chrpsn.

Bethel College
300 E. 27th St., North Newton 67117

† Emporia State University
1200 Commercial St., Emporia 66801
Dr. Barbara Hilgendorf, Dir. of Admissions

† Fort Hays State University
600 Park St., Hays 67601-4099
Dr. Mary Hoy, Dean

† Friends University
2100 University St., Wichita 67213

Kansas Newman College
3100 McCormick Ave., Wichita 67213
Dr. Robert Giroux, President

† Kansas State University
Anderson Hall 110, Manhattan 66506
Ellsworth M. Gerritz, Admis. & Records

Kansas Wesleyan University
100 E. Claflin, Salina 67401
Dr. Daniel Bratton, President

McPherson College
1600 E. Euclid St., McPherson 67460

Mid-America Nazarene College
P.O. Box 1776, Olathe 66051

Ottawa University
1001 S. Cedar St., Ottawa 66067
Steve Koberlein, Dir. of Admis.
800-755-5200

† Pittsburg State University
1701 S. Broadway St., Pittsburg 66762
James E. Parker, Dir. of Admis.

† Saint Mary College
4100 S. 4th St., Leavenworth 66048
Irene Keehan, Dir. of Admis.

SOUTHWESTERN COLLEGE
100 College St., Winfield 67156
800-846-1543

Sterling College, Sterling 67579
Robert Reed, Dir. of Admis. & Records

Tabor College
400 S. Jefferson St., Hillsboro 67063
800-822-6799
See listing under "Liberal Arts & Sciences"

† University of Kansas, Lawrence 66045

† Washburn University of Topeka
1700 S.W. College Ave., Topeka 66621
John E. Triggs, Dir. of Admissions

† Wichita State University
1845 Fairmount, Wichita 67260
800-362-2594
See listing under "Universities"

KENTUCKY

Alice Lloyd College
Purpose Rd., Pippa Passes 41844

Asbury College
1 Macklem Dr., Wilmore 40390
Jonah Mitchell, Dir. of Admis.

Bellarmine College
2001 Newburg Rd., Louisville 40205
Thomas LaBaugh, Dean of Admissions

† Berea College, Berea 40404
John S. Cook, Dir. of Admis.

Campbellsville College
200 College St., Campbellsville 42718
Dr. W. R. Davenport, President

Centre College
600 W. Walnut St., Danville 40422

Cumberland College
6178 College Station Dr., Williamsburg 40769
See listing under "Universities"

† Eastern Kentucky University
521 Lancaster Ave., Richmond 40475

GEORGETOWN COLLEGE
400 E. College St., Georgetown 40324
Garvel Kindrick, Director of Admissions
See listing under "Universities"

Kentucky Christian College
617 N. Carol Malone Blvd., Grayson 41143

† Kentucky State University
400 E. Main St., Frankfort 40601

Kentucky Wesleyan College
3000 Frederica St., Owensboro 42301
Dr. Yvonne Taylor, Director

Lindsey Wilson College
210 Lindsey Wilson St., Columbia 42728
Dr. John Begley, President

Midway College
512 E. Stephens St., Midway 40347
Carl P. Rollins II, Dir. of Admis.

† Morehead State University, Morehead 40351
Charles Myers, Director of Admissions
606-783-2000

† Murray State University, Murray 42071
Phil Bryan, Director of Admissions
800-272-4MSU

† Northern Kentucky University
Louie B. Nunn Dr., Highland Heights 41076

Pikeville College
214 Sycamore St., Pikeville 41501
Dr. John W. Sanders, Dean of Admissions

† Spalding University
851 S. 4th St., Louisville 40203
Dorothy G. Allen, Dir. of Admis.

Thomas More College
2771 Turkeyfoot Rd., Covington 41017
Dr. Charles Bensman, President

Transylvania University
300 Broadway St., N., Lexington 40508
Pat Bain, Dir. of Admis.

Union College
310 College St., Barbourville 40906
Don Hapward, Dean of Admission
See listing under "Universities"

† University of Kentucky, Lexington 40506

† University of Louisville
2301 S. 3rd St., Louisville 40292
Robert Parrent, Dir. of Admis.

† Western Kentucky University
1526 Russellville Rd., Bowling Green 42101

LOUISIANA

Centenary College of Louisiana
P.O. Box 41188, Shreveport 71134

Dillard University
2601 Gentilly Blvd., New Orleans 70122

† Grambling State University
P.O. Box 607, Grambling 71245
Dr. Harold W. Lundy, President

Louisiana College
    College Station, Pineville 71359
    Byron McGee, Dir. of Admis.
    318-487-7386
    See listing under "Liberal Arts"

† Louisiana State University
    8515 Youree Dr., Shreveport 71115

† Louisiana State University and A & M College
    Baton Rouge 70803

† Lousiana Technical University
    P.O. Box 3168, Ruston 71272

Loyola University
    6363 St. Charles Ave., New Orleans 70118

† McNeese State University
    4100 Ryan St., Lake Charles 70605

† Nicholls State University
    LA Hwy. 1, Thibodaux 70301

† Northeast Louisiana University
    700 University Ave., Monroe 71209

† Northwestern State University
    Natchitoches 71497

OUR LADY OF HOLY CROSS COLLEGE
    4123 Woodland Dr., New Orleans 70131

† Southeastern Louisiana University
    P.O. Box 784, Hammond 70404

† Southern University A & M College
    Baton Rouge 70813

Tulane University
    6823 Saint Charles Ave., New Orleans 70118
    Richard Whiteside, Dean of Admission

† University of New Orleans
    New Orleans 70148
    Milton L. Ferguson, Dean

† University of Southwestern Louisiana
    P.O. Box 44872, Lafayette 70504
    318-231-6978

Xavier University
    7325 Palmetto St., New Orleans 70125

MAINE

Bowdoin College, Brunswick 04011
    William Mason, Dir. of Admis.

College of the Atlantic
    105 Eden St., Bar Harbor 04609
    Steve Thomas, Dir. of Admis.

St. Joseph's College, North Windham 04062

Thomas College
    180 W. River Rd., Waterville 04901
    Susan Potter, Dir. of Admis.
    207-877-0101, ME only 800-339-7001

† University of Maine
    102 Main St., Farmington 04938

University of Maine at Fort Kent
    25 Pleasant St., Fort Kent 04743
    Jerry Nadeau, Dir. of Admis.

University of Maine
    9 O'Brien Ave., Machias 04654

† University of Maine, Orono 04469

University of Maine
    181 Main St., Presque Isle 04769

University of New England
    11 Hills Beach Rd., Biddeford 04005
    Patricia Cribby, Dir. of Admis.

† University of Southern Maine
    96 Falmouth St., Portland 04103
    Richard Barnes, Dean

MARYLAND

Baltimore Hebrew University
    5800 Park Heights Ave., Baltimore 21215
    Norma Furst, President

† Bowie State University
    14000 Jericho Park Rd., Bowie 20715

College of Notre Dame of Maryland
    4701 N. Charles St., Baltimore 21210

Columbia Union College
    7600 Flower Ave., Takoma Park 20912

† Coppin State College
    2500 W. North Ave., Baltimore 21216

Frostburg State University, Frostburg 21532

Goucher College
    1021 Dulaney Valley Rd., Baltimore 21204

::: HOME STUDY INTERNATIONAL
    12501 Old Columbia Pike, Silver Spring 20914
    P.O. Box 4437, Silver Spring 20914-4437 (mailing)
    Dr. Joseph Gurubatham, President
    800-782-4769
        Established 1909. Private. Coed. Accreditation: National Home Study Council. Affiliation: Columbia Union College, External degree programs. Which are accredited by the Middle States Association of Colleges and Schools. Special discounts are available to teachers for teacher certification.
    See listing under "Home Study and Correspondence"

Hood College
    400 Rosemont Ave., Frederick 21701

Loyola College
    4501 N. Charles St., Baltimore 21210
    William Bossemeyer III, Dir. of Admis.

Maryland Institute College of Art
    1300 W. Mt. Royal Ave., Baltimore 21217
    Theresa Lynch Bedoya, Dean of Admissions

· Montgomery College
    51 Mannakee St., Rockville 20850
    Germantown - 301-353-7759
    Rockville - 301-279-7465
    Takoma Park - 301-650-1400

† Morgan State University
    Cold Spring Ln. and Hillen Rd., Baltimore 21239

Mt. St. Mary's College
    16300 Old Emmitsburg Rd., Emmitsburg 21727
    Michael D. Kennedy, Dir. of Admis.

Salisbury State University
    1101 Camden Ave., Salisbury 21801

† Towson State University
    800 York Rd., Towson 21204
    Dr. Hoke Smith, President

University of Maryland, Baltimore County
    5401 Wilkens Ave., Catonsville 21228

† University of Maryland, College Park 20742

University of Maryland Eastern Shore
    11868 Academic Oval, Princess Anne 21853
    Dr. William Pender, Acting Chrpsn.

Villa Julie College
    1525 Greenspring Valley Rd., Stevenson 21153
    Carolyn Manuszak, President

Washington Bible College
    6511 Princess Garden Pkwy.
    Lanham-Seabrook 20706

Washington College
    Washington Ave., Chestertown 21620
    Kevin Coveney, Dir. of Admis.

Western Maryland College
    2 College Hill, Westminster 21157

MASSACHUSETTS

American International College
    1000 State St., Springfield 01109
    Peter Miller, Dean of Admissions

Anna Maria College
    2 Sunset Ln., Paxton 01612
    Dr. Bernadette Madore, SSA, President

· Aquinas College
    15 Walnut Park, Newton 02158
    Ellen Ronayne, Dir. of Admis.

Assumption College
    500 Salisbury St., Worcester 01609

Atlantic Union College
    P.O. Box 1000, South Lancaster 01561
    Osa Canto, Registrar

† Boston College
    140 Commonwealth Ave., Chestnut Hill 02167
    Mary D. Griffin, Dean

† Boston University
    685 Commonwealth Ave., Boston 02215

† Bridgewater State College
    Bridgewater 02325
    James Plotner, Jr., Dir. of Admis.

Clark University
    950 Main St., Worcester 01610
    Richard Pierson, Dean of Admis.

Curry College
    1071 Blue Hill Ave., Milton 02186
    617-333-0500

· DEAN COLLEGE
    99 Main St, Franklin 02038
    Kathleen Teehan, Dir. of Admissions
    508-528-9100
    See listing under "Community and Junior Colleges"

Eastern Nazarene College
    23 E. Elm Ave., Quincy 02170
    D. William Nichols, Dir. of Admis.

ELMS COLLEGE
    291 Springfield St., Chicopee 01013
    800-255-ELMS

Emmanuel College
    400 The Fenway, Boston 02115
    Dr. Rosemary Tobin, Chrpsn.

· Endicott College
    376 Hale St., Beverly 01915
    Elizabeth Macomber, Dir. of Admis.

· Fisher College
    118 Beacon St., Boston 02116
    Sandra Robbins, Dir. of Admis.

Fitchburg State College
    160 Pearl St., Fitchburg 01420
    Marke Vickers, Dir. of Admis.

Framingham State College
    100 State St., Framingham 01701
    E. Joseph Lee, Director

Hampshire College, Amherst 01002
    Audrey Y. Smith, Dir. of Admissions
    413-582-5471

Harvard University
    Harvard Graduate School of Education
    Longfellow Hall, Cambridge 02138

Lesley College
    29 Everett St., Cambridge 02138-2790
    Jane Raley, Dir. of Admissions

Merrimack College
    315 Turnpike St., North Andover 01845
    Dennis Farrell, Dean of Admissions

Mt. Holyoke College
    College St., South Hadley 01075
    Anita Smith, Director of Admissions
    413-538-2023

North Adams State College
    375 Church St., North Adams 01247
    413-664-4511 or 800-292-6632
    See listing under "Universities or Graduate Schools"

Northeastern University
    360 Huntington Ave., Boston 02115
    Kevin Kelly, Dean and Dir. of Undergraduate Admis.

Pine Manor College
    400 Heath St., Chestnut Hill 02167
    Gillian Lloyd, Dir. of Admis.

· Quinsigamond Community College
    670 W. Boylston St., Worcester 01606
    Ron Smith, Dir. of Admis.

† Salem State College
    352 Lafayette St., Salem 01970
    David Sartwell, Dir. of Admis.

SCHOOL OF THE MUSEUM OF FINE ARTS
    230 Fenway, Boston 02115
    Alan Van Reed, Dean of Admissions
    617-267-1218

Simmons College
    300 The Fenway, Boston 02115

Smith College
    Northampton 01063

Springfield College
    263 Alden St., Springfield 01109
    Frederick Bartlett, Dean of Admissions

· SPRINGFIELD TECHNICAL COMMUNITY COLLEGE
    1 Armory Square, Springfield 01105
    Dr. Patrick E. Tigue, Dir. of Admissions
    413-781-7822

† Stonehill College
    320 Washington St., North Easton 02357
    508-230-1373

Suffolk University
    8 Ashburton Place, Boston 02108
    Barbara K. Ericson, Assoc. Dean Enrollment & Retention
    617-573-8460

Tufts University
    520 Boston Ave., Medford 02155

† University of Massachusetts, Amherst 01003
    Arlene Wesley Cash, Dir. of Admis.

University of Massachusetts
    100 Morrissey Blvd., Boston 02125

† University of Massachusetts Lowell
    1 University Ave., Lowell 01854

Western New England College
    1215 Wilbraham Rd., Springfield 01119
    800-325-1122

† Westfield State College
    577 Western Ave., Westfield 01085
    John F. Marcus, Dir. of Admis.

Wheelock College
    200 Riverway, Boston 02215
    Joan Wexler, Dean of Admis. & Financial Aid

Worcester State College
    486 Chandler St., Worcester 01602

MICHIGAN

Adrian College
    110 S. Madison St., Adrian 49221
    George Wolf, Dir. of Admis.
    See listing under "Universities"

Albion College
    611 E. Porter, Albion 49224
    800-858-6770

† Andrews University, Berrien Springs 49104
    Jack Mentges, Dir. of Admis.

Aquinas College
    1607 Robinson Rd., S.E., Grand Rapids 49506
    Paula Meehan, Dean of Admissions
    800-678-9593

† Calvin College
    3201 Burton St., S.E., Grand Rapids 49506
    Leroy Stegink, Chairman

† Central Michigan University
    100 Warriner Hall, Mt. Pleasant 48858

Concordia College
    4090 Geddes Rd., Ann Arbor 48105
    Mary Froelich, Dir. of Admis.

† Eastern Michigan University, Ypsilanti 48197
    Jeanne Pietig, Head
    313-487-3060 or 800-GO-TO-EMU

Ferris State University
Office of Admission
420 Oak St., Big Rapids   49307-2020

† Grand Valley State University
1 Campus Dr., Allendale   49401
JoAnn Foerster, Dir. of Admis.

HILLSDALE COLLEGE
33 E. College St., Hillsdale   49242
Dr. Walter Lewke, Chrpsn.
517-437-7341

Hope College
69 E. 10th St., Holland   49423
Gordon Van Wylen, President

Kalamazoo College
1200 Academy St., Kalamazoo   49006

† Madonna University
36600 Schoolcraft St., Livonia   48150

† Marygrove College
8425 W. McNichols Rd., Detroit   48221

† Michigan State University, East Lansing   48824
Dr. Judith Lanier, Dean

Michigan Technological University
1400 Townsend Dr., Houghton   49931
Joseph A. Galetto, Dir. Enrollment Mgmt.
906-487-2335

† Northern Michigan University
610 Cohodas Admin. Center, Marquette   49855
Nancy Rehling, Dir. of Admis.

† Oakland University, Rochester   48309
Larry Bartalucci, Registrar

Olivet College
300 S. Main St., Olivet   49076
Vicki Gallas, Registrar
See listing under "Universities"

† Saginaw Valley State University
2250 Pierce Rd., University Center   48710

Siena Heights College
1247 E. Siena Heights Dr., Adrian   49221

† Spring Arbor College
106 E. Main St., Spring Arbor   49283

· Suomi College
601 Quincy St., Hancock   49930
John Ruohoniemi, Dean/Enrollment Development
800-682-7604

University of Detroit Mercy
4001 W. McNichols
PO Box 19900, Detroit   48219-0900
313-993-1245
See listing under "Universities"

University of Michigan-Ann Arbor
815 S. University Ave., Ann Arbor   48109

† University of Michigan-Dearborn
4901 Evergreen Rd., Dearborn   48128
Carol S. Mack, Dir. of Admis.
313-593-5100

† University of Michigan-Flint
303 Kearsley St., Flint   48502

† Wayne State University
5980 Cass Ave., Detroit   48202
Dr. J. R. Thorderson, Dir. of Admis.

† Western Michigan University, Kalamazoo   49008
Stanley Henderson, Dir. of Enrl. Mgt. & Admis.
616-387-2000

MINNESOTA

† Augsburg College
731 21st Ave., S., Minneapolis   55454

† Bemidji State University
1500 Birchmont Dr., N.E., Bemidji   56601
800-475-2001

† Bethel College
3900 Bethel Dr., St. Paul   55112
Dr. George Brushaber, President

Carleton College
One N. College St., Northfield   55057
Paul Thiboutot, Dir. of Admis.

† College of Saint Benedict
37 S. College Ave., St. Joseph   56374

† College of St. Catherine
2004 Randolph Ave., St. Paul   55105

College of St. Scholastica
1200 Kenwood Ave., Duluth   55811
David Rigoni, Chrpsn.
800-447-5444
See listing under "Liberal Arts"

† Concordia College
901 8th St. S., Moorhead   56562
Dr. Marilyn Guy, Chairperson
See listing under "Universities"

† Concordia College-St. Paul
275 N. Syndicate, St. Paul   55104
Tim Utter, Dir. of Admis.

Crown College
6425 County Rd. 30, St. Bonifacius   55375
See listing under "Universities"

Dr. Martin Luther College
1884 College Heights Dr., New Ulm   56073
Dr. John Lawrenz, President
507-354-8221, Fax: 507-354-8225

† Gustavus Adolphus College
800 W. College Ave., St. Peter   56082
Mark Anderson, Dir. of Admis.

† Hamline University
1536 Hewitt Ave., St. Paul   55104
Scott Pratt, Dir. of Admis.

† MacAlester College
1600 Grand Ave., St. Paul   55105

† Mankato State University
P.O. Box 8400, Mankato   56002

† Moorhead State University
1104 7th Ave. S., Moorhead   56560

North Central Bible College
910 Elliot Ave., Minneapolis   55404
800-289-NCBC
Dan Neary, Dir. of Admis.
See listing under "Universities"

Northwestern College
3003 Snelling Ave., N., St. Paul   55113
Ralph Anderson, Dean of Admissions
800-827-6827 or 612-631-5111

PILLSBURY BAPTIST BIBLE COLLEGE
315 S. Grove St., Owatonna   55060
Alan Potter, President
Larry Tindall, Director of Admissions
800-747-4557

† St. Cloud State University
740 4th Ave., S., St. Cloud   56301
Sherwood Reid, Dir. of Admis.
800-369-4260

† St. John's University
P.O. Box 7155, Collegeville   56321

St. Mary's College of Minnesota
700 Terrace Heights #2, Winona   55987
Tony Piscitiello, VP for Admission

† St. Olaf College, Northfield   55057
Myron Solid, Chrpsn.
507-646-3245

Southwest State University, Marshall   56258

† University of Minnesota
2400 Oakland Ave., Duluth   55812
Robert L. Heller, Provost

† University of Minnesota
600 E. Fourth St., Morris   56267

† University of Minnesota, Twin Cities
Minneapolis   55455

† University of St. Thomas
2115 Summit Ave., St. Paul   55105

† Winona State University
P.O. Box 5838, Winona   55987
Dr. J. Mootz, Dir. of Admis.

MISSISSIPPI

† Alcorn State University
P.O. Box 359, Lorman   39096
D. W. Wilburn, Registrar

Belhaven College
1500 Peachtree St., Jackson   39202

† Delta State University
Hwy. 8 W., Cleveland   38732

† Jackson State University
1400 Lynch St., Jackson   39203

† Millsaps College
P.O. Box 150556, Jackson   39210
Florence Hines, Dir. of Admis.

† Mississippi College
P.O. Box 4086, Clinton   39058

† Mississippi State University
P.O. Box J, Mississippi State University   39762

† Mississippi University for Women
P.O. Box W-1602, Columbus   39701
Teresa Thompson, Exec. Dir. of Enrollment

† Mississippi Valley State University
14000 Hwy. 82 W., Itta Bena   38941
Maxcine B. Rush, Director of Admissions
See listing under "Universities"

Rust College
150 E. Rust Ave., Holly Springs   38635

Tougaloo College
500 E. County Line Rd., Tougaloo   39174

† University of Mississippi, University   38677

† University of Southern Mississippi
P.O. Box 5165, Hattiesburg   39406

William Carey College
498 Tuscan Ave., Hattiesburg   39401

MISSOURI

Avila College
11901 Wornall Rd., Kansas City   64145

Baptist Bible College
628 E. Kearney St., Springfield   65803

Calvary Bible College
15800 Calvary Rd., Kansas City   64147
J. Robert Brundage, Dir. of Admis.

Central Methodist College
411 CMC Square, Fayette   65248
See listing under "Universities"

† Central Missouri State University
Warrensburg   64093
Delores Hudson, Dir. of Admis.

† College of the Ozarks, Point Lookout   65726
Dr. Kenton Olson, Dean of the College

Columbia College
1001 Rogers St., Columbia   65216
Ron Cronacher, Dir. of Admissions
800-231-2391

Culver-Stockton College, Canton   63435
Betty Smith, Dean of Admissions
800-537-1883

† Drury College
900 N. Benton Ave., Springfield   65802
Michael G. Thomas, Dir. of Admis.

† Evangel College
1111 N. Glenstone Ave., Springfield   65802
David Schoolfield, Dir. of Enrollment

Fontbonne College
6800 Wydown Blvd., St. Louis   63105
Peggy Musen, Dir. of Admis.

Hannibal-LaGrange College, Hannibal   63401

† Harris-Stowe State College
3026 Laclede Ave., St. Louis   63103
Valerie Beeson, Dir. of Admis. and Advisement
314-340-3300

† Lincoln University
820 Chestnut St., Jefferson City   65101

† Lindenwood College
209 S Kingshighway, Saint Charles   63301
John Guffey, Dean of Admis.

† Maryville University of St. Louis
13550 Conway Rd., Saint Louis   63141
314-576-9300 or 800-MARYVLL

Missouri Baptist College
12542 Conway Rd., St. Louis   63141

† Missouri Southern State College
3950 Newman Rd., Joplin   64801-1595
Dr. James V. Sandrin, Dept. Head
See listing under "Universities"

Missouri Valley College
500 E. College St., Marshall   65340
816-886-6924 ext. 114
See listing under "Universities"

† Missouri Western State College
4525 Downs Dr., St. Joseph   64507
Howard McCauley, Dir. of Admis.

† Northeast Missouri State University
Kirksville   63501

† Northwest Missouri State University
800 University Dr., Maryville   64468

Ozark Christian College
1111 N. Main St., Joplin   64801
Jim Marcum, Dir. of Admis.
800-299-4622

Park College, Parkville   64152
Dr. Edwin Rawn, Dean of Admis.

† St. Louis University
221 N. Grand Blvd., St. Louis   63103
Louis A. Menard, Dean of Admissions

† Southeast Missouri State University
1 University Plz., Cape Girardeau   63701
New Student Relations 314-651-2590
See listing under "Universities"

† Southwest Missouri State University
901 S. National Ave., Springfield   65804
Dr. Arthur Mallory, Dean
417-836-5255

Stephens College, Columbia   65215
Mary Ann Sprinkle, Dir. of Admis.

† University of Missouri, Columbia
228 Jesse Hall, Columbia   65211

† University of Missouri, Kansas City
5100 Rockhill Rd., Kansas City   64110
Leo J. Sweeney, Dir. of Admis. & Registrar

† University of Missouri
8001 Natural Bridge Rd., St. Louis   63121
Mimi LaMarca, Dir. of Admis.

† Washington University
1 Brookings Dr., St. Louis   63130

Webster University
470 E. Lockwood Ave., St. Louis   63119
Dr. Paul Steinmann, Associate Dean
See listing under "Universities"

Westminster College
501 Westminster Ave., Fulton   65251
J. Harvey Saunders, President

William Jewell College, Liberty   64068
T. Edwin Norris, Dir of Admis.
800-753-7009

† William Woods College
200 W. 12th St., Fulton   65251
Dr. Jahnae Barnett, VP of Admis.

MONTANA

CARROLL COLLEGE
1610 N. Benton Ave., Helena   59625
Candace Cain, Dir. of Admis.
See listing under "Universities"

College of Great Falls
    1301 20th St., S., Great Falls 59405
    Jean Walker, Dir. of Admis.

† Montana State University, Bozeman 59717

† Montana State University - Billings
    1500 N. 30th St., Billings 59101
    Karen Everett, Dir. of Admis.
    406-657-2158

Northern Montana College
    P.O. Box 7751, Havre 59501
    Ralph A. Brigham, Dir. of Admis.

Rocky Mountain College
    1511 Poly Dr., Billings 59102
    David Heringer, Dir. of Admis.
    See listing under "Universities"

† University of Montana, Missoula 59812
    800-462-8636

Western Montana College
    710 S. Atlantic St., Dillon 59725

NEBRASKA

† Chadron State College
    1000 Main St., Chadron 69337
    Dr. Thomas P. Colgate, Dean

College of Saint Mary
    1901 S. 72nd St., Omaha 68124
    Sheila Haggas, Dir. of Admis.

† Concordia College
    800 N. Columbia Ave., Seward 68434
    Don Vos, Dir. of Admis.

† Creighton University
    2500 California St., Omaha 68178
    Dr. Loren Carlson, Chrpsn.

† Dana College
    2848 College Dr., Blair 68008
    John Schueth, Dir. of Admis.
    800-444-3262
    See listing under "Universities"

† Doane College
    1014 Boswell Ave., Crete 68333
    Pappy Khouri, Dir. of Admissions

Grace College of the Bible
    Ninth and William, Omaha 68108
    Jeffrey A. Edgar, Director of Admissions
    800-383-1422

† Hastings College
    P.O. Box 269, Hastings 68902
    Thomas Reeves, President

Midland Lutheran College
    900 Clarkson St., Fremont 68025
    Roland Kahnk, V.P. Admissions

† Nebraska Wesleyan University
    5000 Saint Paul Ave., Lincoln 68504
    Ken Sieg, Dir. of Admis.

· Northeast Community College
    P.O. Box 469, Norfolk 68702
    Eugene Hart, Dir. of Admis.

† Peru State College, Peru 68421
    Pamela J. Cosgrove, Dir. of Admis.
    402-872-3815

† Union College
    3800 S. 48th St., Lincoln 68506

† University of Nebraska
    905 W. 25th St., Kearney 68849

† University of Nebraska at Lincoln
    MABL 233, Lincoln 68588
    James O'Hanlon, Dean

† University of Nebraska at Omaha
    Omaha 68182

† Wayne State College
    200 E. Tenth St., Wayne 68787

NEVADA

Sierra Nevada College-Lake Tahoe
    P.O. Box 4269, Incline Village 89450
    Lane Murray, Dir. of Admissions
    See listing under "Universities"

† University of Nevada, Reno
    Reno 89557

† University of Nevada Las Vegas
    4505 S. Maryland Pky., Las Vegas 89154-1021
    Admissions: 702-895-3443 or 800-334-UNLV

NEW HAMPSHIRE

ANTIOCH NEW ENGLAND GRADUATE SCHOOL
40 Avon St., Keene 03431-3516
Gael R. Minton, Dir. of Admis.
603-357-3122
See listing under "Graduate Schools"

Colby-Sawyer College
    100 Main St., New London 03257

Dartmouth College, Hanover 03755

Franklin Pierce College, Rindge 03461

† Keene State College
    229 Main St., Keene 03435
    Kathryn Dodge, Dir. of Admis.

New England College
    26 Bridge St., Henniker 03242
    John Spaulding, Dir. of Admis.

NOTRE DAME COLLEGE
2321 Elm St., Manchester 03104
603-669-4298

† Plymouth State College, Plymouth 03264

Rivier College
    420 S. Main St., Nashua 03060
    Admissions: 800-44-RIVIER

Saint Anselm College
    87 Saint Anselm Dr., Manchester 03102
    Don Healy, Dir. of Admis.

† University of New Hampshire, Durham 03824
    Stanwood C. Fish, Dir. of Admissions

NEW JERSEY

Caldwell College
    9 Ryerson Ave., Caldwell 07006

Centenary College
    400 Jefferson St., Hackettstown 07840
    Barbara Edler, Dir. of Admissions

College of Saint Elizabeth
    Convent Station 07961
    Sr. Jacqueline Burns, President

Fairleigh Dickinson University, Teaneck 07666
    Dennis Craig, Dir. of Admis.
    201-692-2553

FELICIAN COLLEGE
262 S. Main St., Lodi 07644
Sr. Mary Austin, OSB, Dir. of Admis.
201-778-1029
See listing under "Universities"

Georgian Court College
    900 Lakewood Ave., Lakewood 08701
    Dr. Mary Lee Batesko, Chrpsn.
    908-364-2200 Ext. 740

† Jersey City State College
    2039 Kennedy Blvd., Jersey City 07305
    201-200-3234

† Kean College of New Jersey
    1000 Morris Ave., Union 07083

Monmouth College
    400 Cedar Ave., West Long Branch 07764
    Ruth West, Chrpsn.

† Montclair State College
    1 Normal Ave., Upper Montclair 07043

† Rider University
    2083 Lawrenceville Rd., Lawrenceville 08648
    Susan Christian, Dir. of Admis.

† Rowan College of New Jersey, Glassboro 08028
    Marvin G. Sills, Dir. of Admis.

St. Peter's College
    2641 John F. Kennedy Blvd.
    Jersey City 07306
    Joseph McLaughlin, Dir. Graduate Program in
    Education
    201-915-9254

† Seton Hall University
    400 S. Orange Ave., South Orange 07079
    Lee Cooke, Dir. of Admis.

Stockton State College, Pomona 08240
    Sal Catalfamo, Dir. of Admis.

† Trenton State College
    Hillwood Lakes CN 4700, Trenton 08650

WESTMINSTER CHOIR COLLEGE OF RIDER UNIVERSITY
101 Walnut Ln., Princeton 08540-3899
800-96-CHOIR or 609-921-7100, FAX: 609-921-8829
See listing under "Music"

† William Paterson College
    300 Pompton Rd., Wayne 07470

NEW MEXICO

College of Santa Fe
    1600 St. Michaels Dr., Santa Fe 87505
    800-456-2673

College of the Southwest
    6610 N. Lovington Hwy., Hobbs 88240

† Eastern New Mexico University
    Portales 88130
    Larry Fuqua, Dir. of Admis.

New Mexico Highlands University, Las Vegas 87701
    Dr. Jorge P. Thomas, VP Academic Affairs

† New Mexico State University
    P.O. Box 30001, Las Cruces 88003

† University of New Mexico, Albuquerque 87131
    Robert Weaver, Dean of Admissions

Western New Mexico University
    College Ave, Silver City 88062
    Michael Aleckson, Dir. of Admis.
    800-222-9668
    See listing under "Universities"

NEW YORK

Adelphi University, Garden City 11530
    Dr. Jeffrey Kane, Dean, School of Education
    516-877-4100

Alfred University
    Alumni Hall, Alfred 14802
    Laurie Richer, Director of Admissions
    800-541-9229

BANK STREET COLLEGE OF EDUCATION
610 W. 112th St., New York 10025
Ann Morgan, Director of Admissions
212-875-4404
    Established 1916. Private. Coed. Accreditation: MSACS. Tuition: $12,900. Fees: $600. Enrollment: 300 full-time, 500 part-time. Faculty: 60. Student-faculty ratio: 20:1. Degrees: MS, MEd. Programs in early childhood and elementary education, early adolescence, museum education, reading, infant parent development, special education, bilingual education, educational leadership. Building also houses the Bank Street School for Children and Research Division. Nationally recognized advocate for children & families. Graduate programs combine theory & practice and include supervised field work/advisement component.

† Canisius College
    2001 Main St., Buffalo 14208
    Penelope Lips, Dir. of Admis.
    800-843-1517

Colgate University
    13 Oak Dr., Hamilton 13346
    Dean of Admissions
    315-824-7401

College of Mount St. Vincent
    6301 Riverdale Ave., Riverdale 10471

College of New Rochelle
    29 Castle Pl., New Rochelle 10805

College of St. Rose
    432 Western Ave., Albany 12203

Concordia College
    171 White Plains Rd., Bronxville 10708

CUNY Baruch College
    17 Lexington Ave., New York 10010

CUNY Brooklyn College
    2900 Bedford Ave., Brooklyn 11210
    Justin Dunn, Dir. of Admis.

† CUNY City College
    Convent Ave. at 138th St., New York 10031

CUNY College of Staten Island
    130 Stuyvesant Pl., Staten Island 10301

CUNY Hunter College
    695 Park Ave., New York 10021
    Donna Shalala, President

CUNY Medgar Evan College
    1150 Carroll St., Brooklyn 11225

CUNY, Queens College
    6530 Kissena Blvd., Flushing 11367

CUNY York College
    9420 Guy R. Brewer Blvd., Jamaica 11451

Daemen College
    4380 Main St., Amherst 14226
    Maria Dillard, Dir. of Admis.
    in NY 800-462-7652 or 716-839-8225

Dominican College of Blauvelt
    460 N. Western Hwy., Orangeburg 10962
    Louis Kern, Dir. of Admis.
    914-359-7800

Dowling College,
    150 Idle Hour Blvd., Oakdale 11769
    Dr. Jerome Traiger, Dean

D'Youville College
    320 Porter Ave., Buffalo 14201
    Ronald Dannecker, Dir. of Admis.

Elmira College
    Park Pl., Elmira 14901
    William S. Neal, Dean of Admissions
    See listing under "Liberal Arts"

FIVE TOWNS COLLEGE
305 N. Service Rd., Dix Hills 11746
Jennifer Roemer, Coordinator of Admissions
516-424-7000
See listing under "Universities"

† Fordham University
    Lincoln Center Campus
    113 W. 60th St., New York 10023
    Edward Bristow, Dean

Friends World Program, Long Island University
    Montauk Hwy., Southampton 11968
    Carol Gilbert, Dir. of Admis.

† Hofstra University
    1000 Fulton Ave., Hempstead 11550
    Margaret Shields, Dean of Admissions

Houghton College
    P.O. Box 128, Houghton 14744
    Tim Fuller, Dir. of Admis.

IONA COLLEGE
715 North Ave., New Rochelle 10801
800-231-IONA or 914-633-2503
See listing under "Universities"

Ithaca College
    953 Danby Rd., Ithaca 14850

Keuka College
    P.O. Box 98, Keuka Park 14478
    Robert J. Ianuzzo, Dean of Admissions

The King's College, Briarcliff Manor 10510
    Frederic Rowley, Dean of Admissions

Long Island University-Brooklyn Campus
1 University Plaza, Brooklyn 11201
Alan Chaves, Dean of Admissions

Long Island University-C. W. Post Campus
Rt. 25A, Brookville 11548
Dr. William Dunifon, Dean
516-299-2210

Long Island University-Southampton Campus
Southampton 11968
Carol Gilbert, Dir. of Admis.

Manhattan College
4513 Manhattan College Pky, Riverdale 10471
Dr. Beth Barnett, Dean of Education

Manhattanville College
2900 Purchase St., Purchase 10577

Maria College of Albany
700 New Scotland Ave., Albany 12208
Laurie Gilmore, Dir. of Admis.

MARIST COLLEGE
290 North Rd., Poughkeepsie 12601
Harry W. Wood, VP Admissions
914-575-3226

Marymount College
100 Marymount Ave., Tarrytown 10591
Gina R. Campbell, Dir. of Admis.
800-724-4312

Mater Dei College
Riverside Dr., Ogdensburg 13669
Mark Dougherty, Dir. of Admis.

Medaille College
18 Agassiz Cir., Buffalo 14214
Jacqueline Smukeer, Dir. of Admis.

Mercy College
555 Broadway, Dobbs Ferry 10522
James Nesbitt, Dean of Admissions

Molloy College
1000 Hempstead Ave., Rockville Centre 11570
Wayne James, Dir. of Admis.
See listing under "Universities"

Mt. St. Mary College
330 Powell Ave., Newburgh 12550

Nazareth College of Rochester
4245 East Ave., Rochester 14618
Paul Kenyon, Dir. of Admis.

New York Institute of Technology
Old Westbury Campus, Old Westbury 11568

New York University
70 Washington Sq., New York 10012

† Niagara University, Niagara University 14109
Rev. Daniel O'Leary, OMI, Dean
800-462-2111
See listing under "Universities"

Nyack College, Nyack 10960
Miguel Sanchez, Dir. of Admis.
800-33-NYACK

Pace University, Pleasantville/Briarcliff Campus
Bedford Rd., Pleasantville 10570

Pace University, White Plains Campus
78 N. Broadway, White Plains 10603

Rabbinical Academy Mesivta Rabbi Chaim Berlin
1593 Coney Island Ave., Brooklyn 11230
Rabbi Aaron Schechter, President of Faculty

Rensselaer Polytechnic Institute, Troy 12180
Conrad Sharrow, Dean of Admissions

Roberts Wesleyan College
2301 Westside Dr., Rochester 14624
Deborah Mott-Lundgren, Chrpsn.
See listing under "Universities"

Russell Sage College
51 1st St., Troy 12180

St. Bonaventure University, St. Bonaventure 14778
June T. Solan, Dir. of Admis.

St. Francis College
180 Remsen St., Brooklyn 11201

St. John Fisher College
3690 East Ave., Rochester 14618
Peter Lindsey, Dir. of Admis.

St. John's University
Grand Central & Utopia Parkways, Jamaica 11439

St. Joseph's College
245 Clinton Ave., Brooklyn 11205
Geraldine Foudy, Dir. of Admis.
718-636-6868

St. Joseph's College, Suffolk Campus
25 Audobon Ave., Patchogue 11772

St. Lawrence University, Canton 13617
Joel R. Wincowski, Dean of Admis. & Financial Aid

ST. THOMAS AQUINAS COLLEGE
Rt. 340, Sparkill 10976
Andrea Kraeft, Dir. of Admis.
800-999-STAC
See listing under "Liberal Arts"

Skidmore College, Saratoga Springs 12866
Kent Jones, Dir. of Admis.

SUNY at Albany
1400 Washington Ave., Albany 12222
Micheileen Treadwell, Dir. of
Admission/Financial Aid
518-442-5431

SUNY at Buffalo
17 Capen Hall
P.O. Box 601660, Buffalo 14260-1660
716-645-6900

SUNY College at Brockport
Brockport 14420
Dr. Jayne Vogan, Chrpsn.

† SUNY College at Buffalo
1300 Elmwood Ave., Buffalo 14222
Deborah K. Renzi, Dir. of Admis.

SUNY College at Cortland
P.O. Box 2000, Cortland 13045

SUNY College at Fredonia, Fredonia 14063
William S. Clark, III, Dir. of Admissions

SUNY College at Geneseo
1 College Cir., Geneseo 14454
William L. Caren, Dir. of Admissions

SUNY College at Old Westbury
P.O. Box 210, Old Westbury 11568
Michael Sheehy, Dir. of Admis.

SUNY College at Oneonta, Oneonta 13820
Clifford McVinney, Dir. of Admis.

SUNY at Oswego, Oswego 13126
Dr. Joseph Grant, Jr., Dean of Admissions
315-341-2250

SUNY College at Plattsburgh, Plattsburgh 12901
Dr. Raymond Domenico, Director
518-564-2122

SUNY College at Potsdam
Potsdam 13676
Marc Davis, Dir. of Admis.

SUNY College of Environmental Science & Forestry
1 Forestry Dr., Syracuse 13210
800-7777-ESF or 315-470-6600

SUNY Schenectady County Community College
78 Washington Ave., Schenectady 12305
Robert Dinello, Dir. of Admis.
518-346-6211, ext. 166

† Syracuse University, Syracuse 13244

Touro College
844 Avenue of the Americas, New York 10001

Trocaire College
110 Red Jacket Pky., Buffalo 14220
Elaine Heftka-Davis, Dir. Early Childhood Educ.
716-826-1200

University of Rochester
500 Joseph C. Wilson Blvd., Rochester 14627
Philip Wexler, Dean
See listing under "Universities"

Vassar College
125 Raymond Ave., Poughkeepsie 12601

WAGNER COLLEGE
631 Howard Ave., Staten Island 10301
Joseph Foulke, Dean Admissions and Financial Aid
See listing under "Universities"

Yeshiva University
500 W. 185th St., New York 10033

NORTH CAROLINA

Alamance Community College
P.O. Box 623, Haw River 27258
W. Ronald McCarter, President

† Appalachian State University
ASU Station, Boone 28608
Joe Watts, Admissions Officer

Barber-Scotia College
145 Cabarrus Ave., W., Concord 28025

Barton College
College Station, Wilson 27893
Anthony Britt, Dir. of Admis.
800-345-4973/919-399-6318
See listing under "Universities"

Belmont Abbey College
1 Abbey Pl., Belmont 28012
Admissions, 800-523-2355

Bennett College
900 E. Washington St., Greensboro 27401

† Campbell University
P.O. Box 127, Buies Creek 27506

† Catawba College
2300 W. Innes St., Salisbury 28144
Mark Stokes, Dir. of Admis.

Duke University, Durham 27706

† East Carolina University
1000 E. 5th St., Greenville 27858
Dr. Charles Coble, Dean

Elizabeth City State University
1704 Weeksville Rd., Elizabeth City 27909
William A.T. Byrd, Dir. of Admis.

† Elon College
P.O. Box 2700, Elon College 27244
Nan P. Perkins, Dean of Admissions

† Fayetteville State University
1200 Murchison Rd., Fayetteville 28301
Donald W. Lahuffman, Dir. of Admissions

Gardner-Webb University
General Delivery, Boiling Springs 28017
Ben Carson, Chrpsn.
704-434-2361

Greensboro College
815 W. Market St., Greensboro 27401

Guilford College
5800 W. Friendly Ave., Greensboro 27410
Larry West, Dir. of Admis.
See listing under "Universities"

Halifax Community College
P.O. Box 809, Weldon 27890

High Point College
933 Montlieu Ave., High Point 27262
Jim Schlimmer, Dir. of Admis.

Johnson C. Smith University
100 Beatties Ford Rd., Charlotte 28216
Mary H. Platt, Registrar

† Lenoir-Rhyne College
P.O. Box 292, Hickory 28603
Steve M. Shuford, Registrar

Livingstone College
701 W. Monroe St., Salisbury 28144

Mars Hill College
Main St., Mars Hill 28754
Dr. Smith Goodrum, Dean of Admis.

† Meredith College
3800 Hillsborough St., Raleigh 27607

Methodist College
5400 Ramsey St., Fayetteville 28311
Fiore Bergamasco, Dir. of Admis.

Montreat-Anderson College
P.O. Box 1267, Montreat 28757
David E. Walters, Dir. of Admissions
800-MAC-N-YOU
See listing under "Universities"

† North Carolina A&T State University
1601 E. Market St., Greensboro 27411

† North Carolina Central University
P.O. Box 19617, Durham 27707

† North Carolina State University
P.O. Box 7001, Raleigh 27695
George Dixon, Dir. of Admis.

† North Carolina Wesleyan College
3400 N. Wesleyan Blvd., Rocky Mount 27804

† Pembroke State University
P.O. Box 1510, Pembroke 28372
Anthony Locklear, Dir. of Admissions
919-521-6262

Pfeiffer College
General Delivery, Misenheimer 28109

Piedmont Bible College
716 Franklin St., Winston-Salem 27101

QUEENS COLLEGE
1900 Selwyn Ave., Charlotte 28274
D. Stephen Cloniger, VP for Enrollment Management
See listing under "Liberal Arts"

St. Andrews Presbyterian College
1700 Dogwood Mile, Laurinburg 28352
Dale B. Montague, Dir. of Admis.

St. Augustine's College
1315 Oakwood Ave., Raleigh 27610
I. E. Spraggins, Dir. Admissions

† Salem College
P.O. Box 10548, Winston-Salem 27108
Katherine Knapp, Director of Admissions
800-32-SALEM
See listing under "Women's College"

Shaw University
118 E. South St., Raleigh 27601

† University of North Carolina
1000 Spring Garden St., Greensboro 27412

† University of North Carolina
601 S. College Rd., Wilmington 28403
W. H. Wagoner, Chancellor

† University of North Carolina at Asheville
1 University Heights, Asheville 28804
William E. Highsmith, Chancellor

† University of North Carolina at Chapel Hill
Chapel Hill 27599
James C. Walters, Dir. Undergrad Admis.

† University of North Carolina at Charlotte
Charlotte 28223
J. H. Woodward, Chancellor

† Wake Forest University
P.O. Box 7305, Winston-Salem 27109

Warren Wilson College
P.O. Box 9000, Asheville 28802-9000
Tom Weede, Dir. of Admis.

† Western Carolina University
Cullowhee 28723
Tyree H. Kiser, Dir. of Admissions

Wingate College, Wingate 28174

† Winston-Salem State University
601 S. Martin Luther King Jr.
Winston-Salem 27110
Van Wilson, Dir. of Admissions

NORTH DAKOTA

Dickinson State University, Dickinson 58601
Marshall Melbye, Registrar
701-227-2331

Jamestown College, Jamestown 58405

† MAYVILLE STATE UNIVERSITY
330 3rd St., N.E., Mayville 58257
Dr. Ellen Chaffee, President
Ronald Brown, Dir. of Admis.
800-437-4104
Established 1889. State. Coed. Accreditation: NCACS, NCATE. Tuition: $1,680 in-state, $4,486 out-of-state. Room and board: $2,516. Enrollment: 291 boarding, 425 day. Faculty: 52. Degrees: AA, BA, BA General Studies, BSEd, BS Computer Information Systems. Library: 84,000 volumes. 19 buildings on 60 acres. Gym, pool, golf. "The School of Personal Service" between Fargo & Grand Forks in the Red River Valley. Special programs: development courses for entering students, learning resource center, accelerated degree, advanced standing, cooperative work-study program, summer sessions for credit, child development center, teaching & learning center.

† Minot State University
500 University Ave. W., Minot 58701

† North Dakota State University, Fargo 58105
Richard Shearer, Acting Dir. of Admis.

† Tri-College University, Fargo 58105

Trinity Bible College
50 S. 6th Ave., Ellendale 58436
Janet A. Johnson, Dir. of Academic Records
701-349-3621

University of Mary
7500 University Dr., Bismarck 58504
Steph Storey, Dir. of Admis.

† University of North Dakota
Box 8193 University Station, Grand Forks 58203

† Valley City State University
101 S.W. College St., Valley City 58072
Monte Johnson, Dir. of Admis.

OHIO

Antioch University
795 Livermore St., Yellow Springs 45387

† Ashland University
401 College Ave., Ashland 44805

† Baldwin-Wallace College
275 Eastland Rd., Berea 44017
Juliann K. Baker, Dir. of Admis.

Bluffton College
College Ave., Bluffton 45817

† Bowling Green State University
Bowling Green 43403
John Martin, Dir. of Admis.

† Capital University
2199 E. Main St., Columbus 43209
Dolphus E. Henry, Associate Provost

Cedarville College
P.O. Box 601, Cedarville 45314
David Ormsbee, Dir. of Admis.

Central State University
1400 Brush Row Rd., Wilberforce 45384

Cincinnati Bible College
P.O. Box 04320, Cincinnati 45204
C. Barry McCarty, President

Cleveland College of Jewish Studies
26500 Shaker Blvd., Beachwood 44122
Patricia Kaplan, Registrar

† Cleveland State University
Euclid Ave. at 24th St., Cleveland 44115

College of Mount St. Joseph
5701 Delhi Rd., Cincinnati 45233-1672
See listing under "Universities"

Defiance College
701 N. Clinton St., Defiance 43512
Penny D. Bell, Dir. of Admis.
419-783-2330 Collect

Denison University
P.O. Box B, Granville 43023
Richard Boyden, Dir. of Admis.

Heidelberg College
310 E. Market St., Tiffin 44883
Stephen E. Eidson, Dean of Admission
800-925-9250

† Hiram College
P.O. Box 96, Hiram 44234
Gary Craig, Dean of Admis.

† John Carroll University
20700 N. Park Blvd., Cleveland 44118

† Kent State University
P.O. Box 5190, Kent 44242
Bruce Riddle, Dir. of Admis.

Lake Erie College
391 W. Washington St., Painesville 44077

· Lorain County Community College
1005 Abbe Rd., N., Elyria 44035
Dr. John W. Thrash, Jr., Registrar

LOURDES COLLEGE
6832 Convent Blvd., Sylvania 43560
Mary E. Briggs, Dir. of Admis.
419-885-5291 or 800-878-3210

Malone College
515 25th St., N.W., Canton 44709
Lee Sommers, Dean of Admissions

MARIETTA COLLEGE
210 5th St., Marietta 45750
Dennis R. DePerro, Dean Admis./Financial Aid
800-331-7896

† Miami University
E. High St., Oxford 45056

Mount Union College
1972 Clark Ave., Alliance 44601
Amy Tomko, Dir. of Admis.

Mt. Vernon Nazarene College
800 Martinsburg Rd., Mt. Vernon 43050
Ronald Hyson, Dir. of Admis.

Muskingum College
147 Center St., New Concord 43762

Notre Dame College
4545 College Rd., Cleveland 44121
Sr. Mary Luke, S.N.D., President

Ohio Dominican College
1216 Sunbury Rd., Columbus 43219
800-955-OHIO

OHIO NORTHERN UNIVERSITY
525 S. Main St., Ada 45810
Dr. Mary Haynes, Chrpsn.
412-772-2000

† Ohio State University
190 N. Oval Mall, Columbus 43210

Ohio State University-Lima Campus
4240 Campus Dr., Lima 45804
Cynthia E. Spiers, Dir. of Admissions
419-221-1641

Ohio State University-Marion
1465 Mount Vernon Ave., Marion 43302
Becky McConnell, Dir. of Admis.

† Ohio University, Athens 45701

Ohio Wesleyan University
61 S. Sandusky St., Delaware 43015
Donald Bishop, Dean for Enrollment

† Otterbein College, Westerville 43081

Shawnee State University
940 2nd St., Portsmouth 45662
Rosemary K. Poston, Dir. of Admis.

† University of Akron
381 Buchtel Common, Akron 44325
Kris MacDermott, Asst. Provost Enrollment

† University of Cincinnati
2700 Clifton Ave., Cincinnati 45221

† University of Dayton
300 College Park Ave., Dayton 45469-0525
Toll-free 800-837-7433
See listing under "Universities"

† University of Findlay
1000 N. Main St., Findlay 45840
Dan Crabtree, Dir. of Admis.

University of Rio Grande
General Delivery, Rio Grande 45674
H. Paul Lloyd, Dean
614-245-5353, Ext. 7328

† University of Toledo
2801 Bancroft St., W., Toledo 43606
Richard Eastop, Dir. of Admis.

Urbana University
100 College Way, Urbana 43078
Donald Burns, Dir. of Admis.

Ursuline College
2550 Lander Rd., Cleveland 44124

Walsh College
2020 Easton St., N.W., Canton 44720
Fran Kehoe, Dean of Admis.

Wilmington College
P.O. Box 1185, Wilmington 45177
Rhonda Inderhees, Dir. of Admis.

Wittenberg University
P.O. Box 720, Springfield 45504

† Wright State University
3640 Colonel Glenn Hwy., Dayton 45435

Xavier University
3800 Victory Pky., Cincinnati 45207

† Youngstown State University
410 Wick Ave., Youngstown 44555
Leslie H. Cochran, President

OKLAHOMA

Bartlesville Wesleyan College
2201 Silverlake Rd., Bartlesville 74006

† Cameron University
2800 W. Gore Blvd., Lawton 73505
Louise Brown, Dir. of Admis.

† East Central University, Ada 74820
James Peak, Dir. of Admis.

† Langston University
P.O. Box 907, Langston 73050

Mid-America Bible College
3500 S.W. 119th St., Oklahoma City 73170
Tony O'Brien, Registrar
405-691-3800

† Northeastern State University
600 N. Grand Ave., Tahlequah 74464

† Northwestern Oklahoma State University
705 Oklahoma Blvd., Alva 73717

† Oklahoma Baptist University
500 W. University St., Shawnee 74801

† Oklahoma Christian University of Science and Arts
P.O. Box 11000, Oklahoma City 73136
Duane Eggleston, Vice President
800-877-5010

Oklahoma City University
2501 N. Blackwelder Ave., Oklahoma City 73106
Dr. Kathy Kass, Chair
See listing under "Universities"

Oklahoma Panhandle State University
P.O. Box 430, Goodwell 73939

Oklahoma State University, Stillwater 74078
Jo Campbell, Assoc. Dean

Oral Roberts University
7777 S. Lewis Ave., Tulsa 74171
Arthur E. Matzkvech, Dir. of Admis.

† Southeastern Oklahoma State University
Station A, Durant 74701

† Southern Nazarene University
6729 N.W. 39th Expy., Bethany 73008

† Southwestern Oklahoma State University
100 Campus Dr., Weatherford 73096

† University of Central Oklahoma
100 N. University Dr., Edmond 73034

† University of Oklahoma at Norman
660 Parrington Oval, Norman 73019

† University of Sciences & Arts of Oklahoma
P.O. Box 82345, Chickasha 73018

† University of Tulsa
600 S. College Ave., Tulsa 74104
Warren Hipsher, Chrpsn.

OREGON

CASCADE COLLEGE
BRANCH CAMPUS OF OKLAHOMA CHRISTIAN UNIVERSITY
9101 E. Burnside St., Portland 97216
Brad Fisher, Director of Admission
800-550-PORT
Established 1994. Private. Coed. Accreditation: North Central Association of Schools and Colleges. Tuition: $6,400. Room and board: $3,200. Fees: $200. Enrollment: 160 full-time, 50 part-time. Faculty: 18. Student-faculty ratio: 12:1. Degrees: Bachelor of Arts in Business Administration, Liberal Studies, Liberal Studies with Teacher Certification, Biblical Studies. 9 buildings on 10 acres. Branch campus of Oklahoma Christian University of Science and Arts. Intramural and club athletics. Near I-205 in East Portland, City of Roses. Choir. Drama.

Concordia College
2811 N.E. Holman St., Portland 97211

† Eastern Oregon State College
1410 L Ave., La Grande 97850
See listing under "Universities"

George Fox College
414 N. Meridian St., Newberg 97132

Lewis & Clark College
0615 S.W. Palatine Hill Rd., Portland 97219
Michael Sexton, Dean of Admissions

Linfield College
900 S. Baker St., McMinnville 97128
Thomas Meicho, Dean of Admissions

† Oregon State University, Corvallis 97333
Wallace Gibbs, Dir. of Admis.

Pacific University
2043 College Way, Forest Grove 97116
Barbara Mergen, Dir. of Admis.

† Portland State University
P.O. Box 751, Portland 97207

† Southern Oregon State College
1250 Siskiyou Blvd., Ashland 97520

University of Oregon
1 University of Oregon, Eugene 97403

† University of Portland
5000 N. Willamette Blvd., Portland 97203

Warner Pacific College
2219 S.E. 68th Ave., Portland 97215
Sherry Moore, Enrollment Management Director

Western Baptist College, Salem 97301
800-845-3005

† Western Oregon State College
345 Monmouth Ave., N., Monmouth 97361
Craig A. Kolins, Dir. of Admis.
503-838-8211

Willamette University
900 State St. S.E., Salem 97301

PENNSYLVANIA

Academy of the New Church College
P.O. Box 278, Bryn Athyn 19009

Albright College
P.O. Box 15234, Reading 19612

Allegheny College
520 N. Main St., Meadville 16335
Gayle Pollack, Dir. of Admis.

Alvernia College
    400 Bernardine St., Reading 19607
    Lisa Grabowski, Dir. of Admis.

Baptist Bible College of Pennsylvania
    538 Venard Rd., Clarks Summit 18411

Beaver College
    450 S. Easton Rd., Glenside 19038-3295
    Dennis Nostrand, VP for Enrollment Management
    Phone: 800-776-BEAVER(2328)
    Fax: 215-572-4049
    See listing under "Universities"

† Bloomsburg University, Bloomsburg 17815
    Bernard Vinovrski, Dir. of Admis.

Cabrini College
    610 King of Prussia Rd., Radnor 19087

† California University of Pennsylvania
    3rd St., California 15419
    Norman Hasbrouck, Dean for Enrollment

Carlow College
    3333 5th Ave., Pittsburgh 15213

Cedar Crest College
    100 College Dr., Allentown 18104-6196
    Cynthia Phillips, Dir. of Admissions

Chatham College
    Woodland Rd., Pittsburgh 15232
    Suellen Ofe, Dean of Admis./Financial Aid
    See listing under "Women's College"

Chestnut Hill College
    9601 Germantown Ave.
    Philadelphia 19118-2695
    Margaret A. Birtwistle, Dir. of Admis.

† Cheyney University of Pennsyvania
    P.O. Box 200, Cheyney 19319

† Clarion University of Pennsylvania
    840 Wood St., Clarion 16214

College Misericordia
    301 Lake St., Dallas 18612
    Michael Joseph, Dir. of Enrollment Mgmt.

Delaware Valley College of Science & Agriculture
    Doylestown 18901
    Stephen Zenko, Dir. of Admis.

Drexel University
    3141 Chestnut St., Philadelphia 19104
    Dean of Enrollment Management

Duquesne University
    600 Forbes Ave., Pittsburgh 15282
    Thomas Schaefer, C.S.Sp., Dir. of Admis.

Eastern College
    10 Fairview Dr., Saint Davids 19087
    Dr. Helen Loeb, Director

East Stroudsburg University of Pennsylvania
    East Stroudsburg 18301
    Alan Chesterton, Dir. of Admis.

† Edinboro University of Pennsylvania
    Edinboro 16444
    Admissions Office: 800-626-2203

Elizabethtown College
    1 Alpha Dr., Elizabethtown 17022

Gannon University
    109 University Sq., Erie 16541

Geneva College
    3200 College Ave., Beaver Falls 15010

Gratz College
    Old York Rd. and Melrose Ave.
    Melrose Park 19126
    Evelyn Klein, Dir. of Admissions
    215-635-7300

Grove City College
    100 Campus Dr., Grove City 16127
    Dr. William T. Shannon, Chrpsn.

GWYNEDD-MERCY COLLEGE
    Sumneytown Pike, Gwynedd Valley 19437
    Marjorie DeSimone, Dean of Admissions
    800-DIAL-GMC
    See listing under "Universities"

Harcum Junior College, Bryn Mawr 19010
    Mary Pontius, Dean of Admissions

Holy Family College
    Grant & Frankford Ave., Philadelphia 19114
    Dr. Mott Linn, Dir. of Admis.
    215-637-3050

Immaculata College
    Immaculata 19345
    James P. Sullivan, Dir. of Admis.

† Indiana University of Pennsylvania, Indiana 15705
    Fred Dadak, Dean, Admissions

Juniata College
    1700 Moore St., Huntington 16652

King of Prussia Graduate Center
    30 E. Swedesford Rd., Malvern 19355

King's College
    133 N. River St., Wilkes Barre 18711

† Kutztown University of Pennsylvania
    Kutztown 19530

Lancaster Bible College
    901 Eden Rd., Lancaster 17601
    Joanne Roper, Dir. of Admis.
    See listing under "Biblical Studies"

La Salle University
    1900 W. Olney Ave., Philadelphia 19141
    Br. Gerald Fitzgerald, Dir. of Admis.
    See listing under "Universities"

Lebanon Valley College
    101 N. College Ave., Annville 17003

† Lehigh University
    27 Memorial Dr. W., Bethlehem 18015

Lincoln University, Lincoln University 19352
    Jimmy Arrington, Dir. of Admis.

† Lock Haven University, Lock Haven 17745

Lycoming College, Williamsport 17701

† Mansfield University of Pennsylvania
    Mansfield 16933

† Marywood College
    2300 Adams Ave., Scranton 18509

Mercyhurst College
    501 E. 38th St., Erie 16546
    Andrew Roth, Dean of Enrollment
    800-825-1926

† Millersville University of Pennsylvania
    Millersville 17551
    Blair Treasure, Dean of Admissions

Montgomery County Community College
    340 DeKalb Pike, Blue Bell 19422-0758
    Dennis Murphy, Dir. of Admis.

Moravian College
    1200 Main St., Bethlehem 18018

Muhlenberg College
    2400 W. Chew St., Allentown 18104
    Chris Hooker-Haring, Dir. of Admis.

Neumann College
    Concord Rd., Aston 19014

† Pennsylvania State University
    201 Shields Bldg., University Park 16802

Philadelphia College of Bible
    BSEd Degree
    200 Manor Ave., Langhorne 19047-2990
    Martha MacCullough, Chrpsn.
    800-366-0049

Point Park College
    201 Wood St., Pittsburgh 15222

Robert Morris College
    Narrows Run Rd., Coraopolis 15108
    James R. Welsh, Dean of Admissions
    See listing under "Universities"

Robert Morris College
    600 5th Ave., Pittsburgh 15219
    James R. Welsh, Dean of Admissions
    See listing under "Universities"

St. Francis College
    P.O. Box 600, Loretto 15940

St. Joseph's University
    5600 City Ave., Philadelphia 19131
    Randy Miller, Dir. of Admis.

St. Vincent College
    300 Fraser Purchase Rd., Latrobe 15650

Seton Hill College, Greensburg 15601
    Peter Egan, Dir. of Admis.
    800-826-6234 or 412-838-4255

† Shippensburg University, Shippensburg 17257

† Slippery Rock University, Slippery Rock 16057
    Director of Admissions

Susquehanna University
    514 University Ave., Selinsgrove 17870

† Temple University
    Broad St. & Montgomery Ave.
    Philadelphia 19122

Thiel College
    75 College Ave., Greenville 16125
    Robert Weaver, Dir. of Admis.

University of Pennsylvania
    0 Levy Park, Philadelphia 19104

University of Pittsburgh
    4200 5th Ave., Pittsburgh 15260

University of Pittsburgh at Bradford
    300 Campus Dr., Bradford 16701

University of Pittsburgh at Johnstown
    450 Schoolhouse Rd., Johnstown 15904

† University of Scranton
    800 Linden St., Scranton 18510

Ursinus College
    601 E. Main St., Collegeville 19426

Villanova University
    845 E. Lancaster Ave., Villanova 19085
    Stephen R. Merritt, Dir. of Admis.

Washington & Jefferson College
    60 S. Lincoln St., Washington 15301
    Thomas O'Connor, Dir. of Admis.

Waynesburg College
    51 W. College St., Waynesburg 15370
    Robin Moore, Dir. of Admis.
    800-225-7393

† West Chester University of Pennsylvania
    S. High St., West Chester 19380

WESTMINSTER COLLEGE
    New Wilmington 16172
    Richard Dana Paul, Dir. of Admis.
    412-946-7100

Widener University
    700 E. 14th St., Chester 19013

Wilkes University
    184 S. River St., Wilkes-Barre 18766
    Emory P. Guffrovich Jr., Dean of Admissions

Wilson College
    1015 Philadelphia, Chambersburg 17201

York College of Pennsylvania
    P.O. Box 15199, York 17405-7199
    Nancy Spataro, Dir. of Admis.
    717-849-1600
    See listing under "Universities"

RHODE ISLAND

Brown University, Providence 02906

Providence College
    River Ave., Providence 02918

† Rhode Island College
    600 Mt. Pleasant Ave., Providence 02908

Roger Williams College
    1 Old Ferry Rd., Bristol 02809
    William Dunfey, Dir. of Admis.

Salve Regina University
    1 Ochre Point Ave., Newport 02840
    Roselina McKillop, Dean of Admissions

† University of Rhode Island, Kingston 02881
    Theodore Kellogg, Chrpsn.

SOUTH CAROLINA

Benedict College
    1600 Harden St., Columbia 29204
    Virginia McKee, Dir. of Admis.

Central Wesleyan College
    P.O. Box 1020, Central 29630
    Lillian A. Robbins, Dir. of Admis.

Charleston Southern University
    P.O. Box 10087, Charleston 29411
    Melinda Mitchum, Dir. of Admis.

† The Citadel
    171 Moultrie St., Charleston 29409

Claflin College
    700 College Ave., Orangeburg 29115
    P. Palmer Worthy, Registrar

† Clemson University
    201 Sikes Hall, Clemson 29634

Coastal Carolina College
    P.O. Box 1954, Myrtle Beach 29578
    Dr. Ed Cerny, Director of Admissions

Coker College
    300 E. College Ave., Hartsville 29550

College of Charleston
    66 George St., Charleston 29424

Columbia College
    1301 Columbia College Dr., Columbia 29203

Columbia International University
    P.O. Box 3122, Columbia 29230
    Frank Bedell, Dir. of Admis.
    See listing under "Biblical Studies"

Converse College
    580 E. Main St., Spartanburg 29302
    Dr. Martha Rogers, VP Enrollment Management

Erskine College & Seminary
    Washington St., Due West 29639
    Dot Carter, Dir. of Admis.

Francis Marion College
    P.O. Box 100547, Florence 29501
    Marvin Lynch, Dir. of Admis.

Furman University
    3300 Poinsett Hwy., Greenville 29613
    Charles Brock, Dir. of Admis.

Lander College
    320 Stanley Ave., Greenwood 29649

Limestone College
    1115 College Dr., Gaffney 29340
    Peter Wood, Dir. of Admis.

Morris College
    100 W. College St., Sumter 29150
    Luns C. Richardson, President

† Newberry College
    2100 College St., Newberry 29108
    Neil Clark, Dean of Admissions and Financial Aid

North Greenville College
    P.O. Box 1892, Tigerville 29688
    Gary Wells, Dir. of Admis.
    See listing under "Universities"

Presbyterian College
    503 S. Broad St., Clinton 29325
    Margaret Williamson, Dean of Admis.

† South Carolina State University
    P.O. Box 7127, Orangeburg 29117-0001
    803-536-7185

† University of South Carolina, Columbia 29208
    Terry Davis, Dir. of Admis.
    803-777-7700

University of South Carolina at Aiken
    171 University Pkwy., Aiken 29801

† Winthrop University
701 W. Oakland Ave., Rock Hill 29733
James McCammon, Jr., Dir. of Admis.

Wofford College
429 N. Church St., Spartanburg 29303
Charles Gray, Dir. of Admis.

SOUTH DAKOTA

† Augustana College
29th & S. Summit, Sioux Falls 57197

† Black Hills State University
1200 University St., Spearfish 57799
April Meeker, Dir. of Admis.

† Dakota State University
820 N. Washington Ave., Madison 57042
Dr. Patricia Whitfield, Dean
605-256-5139

Dakota Wesleyan University
1300 W. University Ave., Mitchell 57301

Mt. Marty College
1105 W. 8th St., Yankton 57078
Paula Tacke, Dir. of Admis.

† Northern State University
1200 S. Jay St., Aberdeen 57401

† **SIOUX FALLS COLLEGE**
1501 S. Prairie Ave., Sioux Falls 57105
Susan Reese, Dir. of Admis.
800-888-1047
See listing under "Universities"

† South Dakota State University
P.O. Box 0507, Brookings 57007
Dr. Darrell Jensen, Dean
605-688-4321
See listing under "Universities"

† University of South Dakota
414 E. Clark St., Vermillion 57069
Dave Lorenz, Dir. of Admis.

TENNESSEE

† Austin Peay State University
601 College St., Clarksville 37044

Belmont College
1900 Belmont Blvd., Nashville 37212

Bethel College
Cherry St., Mc Kenzie 38201

Bryan College
Box 7000, Dayton 37321
Thomas A. Shaw, Dir. of Admis.

† Carson-Newman College
P.O. Box 70552, Jefferson City 37760
See listing under "Universities"

Christian Brothers College
650 E. Parkway, S., Memphis 38104

Crichton College
6655 Winchester Rd., Memphis 38115
901-367-9800

† David Lipscomb University
3901 Granny White Pike, Nashville 37204-3951
Wade Sandrell, Dir. of Admis.
800-333-4358

† **EAST TENNESSEE STATE UNIVERSITY**
P.O. Box 70731, Johnson City 37614
Dr. Nancy Dishner, Dean, Enrollment Management
615-929-4213 or 800-462-3878

Fisk University
1000 17th Ave., N., Nashville 37208

† Freed-Hardeman University
158 E. Main St., Henderson 38340
800-342-7837

Free Will Baptist Bible College
P.O. Box 50117, Nashville 37205

Johnson Bible College
7900 Johnson Dr., Knoxville 37998
Larry Green, Dir. of Admis.
615-573-4517

King College
1350 King College Rd., Bristol 37620

Knoxville College
901 College St., N.W., Knoxville 37921

Lambuth College
705 Lambuth Blvd., Jackson 38301

Lane College
545 Lane Ave., Jackson 38301

Lee College
P.O. Box 3450, Cleveland 37320

LeMoyne-Owen College
807 Walker Ave., Memphis 38126
901-942-7335

Lincoln Memorial University
P.O. Box 2012, Harrogate 37752
Conrad Daniels, Dir. of Admis.

Maryville College
800 S. Court St., Maryville 37801
Annabelle J. Libby, Dir. of Admis.

† Middle Tennessee State University
Murfreesboro 37132
Roger D. Sims, Dir. of Admis.

† Milligan College
P.O. Box 210, Milligan College 37682

† **PEABODY COLLEGE OF VANDERBILT UNIVERSITY**
P.O. Box 327, Nashville 37202
Barbara Johnston, Dir. of Admis.
615-322-8410

Southern Missionary College
P.O. Box 370, Collegedale 37315

† Tennessee State University
3500 John A. Merritt Blvd., Nashville 37209

† Tennessee Technological University
P.O. Box 5006, Cookeville 38505

Tennessee Temple University
1815 Union Ave., Chattanooga 37404
Dr. L. W. Nichols, President

Tennessee Wesleyan College
P.O. Box 40, Athens 37371

Trevecca Nazarene College
333 Murfreesboro Rd., Nashville 37210

Tusculum College
P.O. Box 5035, Greeneville 37743
Ronald Porter, Dir. of Admis.

Union University
2447 US Highway 45 Bypass, Jackson 38305
Dr. Benny Tucker, Dean
901-668-1818
See listing under "Universities"

† University of Memphis, Memphis 38152
Dr. John Eubank, Dean of Admissions

† University of Tennessee at Martin
Martin 38238
Paul Kelley, Director of Admissions
See listing under "Universities"

† University of Tennessee at Chattanooga
615 McCallie Ave., Chattanooga 37403

† University of Tennessee, Knoxville
527 Andy Holt Tower, Knoxville 37996
Dr. Gordon Stanley, Dir. of Admis.

TEXAS

Abilene Christian University
ACU Station, Box 6000, Abilene 79699

Angelo State University
2601 W. Ave., N., San Angelo 76909

Arlington Baptist College
3001 W. Division St., Arlington 76012
Helen Sullivan, Registrar

Austin College
900 N. Grand Ave., Sherman 75090
Rodney Oto, Dean of Admission
800-442-5363

† Baylor University
P.O. Box 97008, Waco 76798-7008
Diana Ramey, Director of Admissions

Concordia Lutheran College
3400 N. Interstate 35, Austin 78705
Kevin Pieper, Dir. of Admis.

Corpus Christi State University
6300 Ocean Dr., Corpus Christi 78412

Dallas Baptist University
7777 W. Kiest Blvd., Dallas 75211

Dallas Christian College
2700 Christian Pkwy., Dallas 75234

East Texas Baptist University
1200 N. Grove Ave., Marshall 75670

† East Texas State University
ETSU Station, Commerce 75429

Houston Baptist University
7502 Fondren Rd., Houston 77074

Howard Payne University
1000 Fisk Ave., Brownwood 76801

Huston-Tillotson College
1820 E. 8th St., Austin 78702

Incarnate Word College
4301 Broadway St., San Antonio 78209
Sr. Sally Mitchell, Dean of Enrollment

Jarvis Christian College
P.O. Box G, Hawkins 75765

† Lamar University
P.O. Box 10009, Beaumont 77710
800-458-7558

Lubbock Christian University
5601 W. 19th, Lubbock 79407

McMurry University
14th and Sayles, Abilene 79697

† Midwestern State University
3400 Taft Blvd., Wichita Falls 76308
Dr. Clarence Darter, Dean

Our Lady of the Lake University
411 S.W. 24th St., San Antonio 78207-4689
210-434-6711

Paul Quinn College
3837 Simpson Stuart Rd., Dallas 75241

† Prairie View A & M University
P.O. Box 3089, Prairie View 77446-3089
Linda S. Berry, Dir. of Admis.

St. Edward's University
3001 S. Congress Ave., Austin 78704
John Lambert, Dir. of Admis.

St. Mary's University of San Antonio
1 Camino Santa Maria, San Antonio 78228
Rick Castillo, Dir. of Admis.

† Sam Houston State University, Huntsville 77341

Schreiner College
2100 Memorial Blvd., Kerrville 78028
800-343-4919

Southern Methodist University
Hillcrest at University, Dallas 75275

Southwestern Adventist College
P.O. Box 567, Keene 76059

Southwestern Assemblies of God College
1200 Sycamore St., Waxahachie 75165
Bill Morgan, Dir. of Admis.

Southwestern University
University Ave. at Maple St., Georgetown 78626

Southwest Texas State University
601 University Dr., San Marcos 78666

† Stephen F. Austin State University
P.O. Box 6078. Nacogdoches 75962

Sul Ross State University, Alpine 79832

Tarleton State University
1297 W. Washington St., Stephenville 76402

Texas A & I University
Campus Box 101, Kingsville 78363

† Texas A & M University
College Station 77843

Texas Christian University
2800 S. University Dr., Ft. Worth 76129
Dr. Edward Boehm, Jr., Dean of Admissions

Texas College
2404 N. Grand St., Tyler 75702
Dr. William H. Ammons, II, Dir. of Admis.

Texas Lutheran College
1000 W. Court St., Seguin 78155
Jennifer B. Ehlers, Dir. of Admis.

Texas Southern University
3100 Cleburne St., Houston 77004

† Texas Tech University, Lubbock 79409

Texas Wesleyan University
1201 Wesleyan St., Fort Worth 76105
Kim Campbell, Dir. Freshman Admission

Texas Women's University
P.O. Box 23925, Denton 76204

† Trinity University
715 Stadium Dr., San Antonio 78212

University of Dallas
1845 E. Northgate Dr., Irving 75062
Jim Whitaker, Dir. of Admis.

† University of Houston
4800 Calhoun Rd., Houston 77204

† University of Houston-Clear Lake
2700 Bay Area Blvd., Houston 77058
Darella Banks, Exec. Dir. Enrollment Services

University of Houston-Victoria
2302-C E. Red River St., Victoria 77901

University of Mary Hardin-Baylor
UMHB Station, Box 8001, Belton 76513
800-727-8642 or 817-939-4520

University of St. Thomas
3812 Montrose Blvd., Houston 77006
Elsie Biron, Dir. of Admis.

University of Texas at Arlington
UTA Box 19125, Arlington 76019
R. Zack Prince, Dir. of Admis.

University of Texas at Austin
0 the University of Texas, Austin 78712

University of Texas at San Antonio
San Antonio 78285
Elwood B. Traylor, Director

University of Texas at Tyler
3900 University Blvd., Tyler 75799
Dr. Robert L. Cox, Dean

University of Texas of the Permian Basin
4901 E. University Blvd., Odessa 79762

University of Texas-Pan American
1201 W. University Dr., Edinburg 78539
Miguel Nerarez, President

Wayland Baptist University
1900 W. 7th, Plainview 79072
Lorraine Nance, Registrar

West Texas State University
2501 4th Ave., Canyon 79016
Lila Vars, Dir. of Admis.

Wiley College
711 Wiley Ave., Marshall 75670

UTAH

† Brigham Young University, Provo 84602

Southern Utah University
351 W. Center St., Cedar City 84720
Dr. James Miller, Dean
801-586-7800

University of Utah
1400 E. 200 S., Salt Lake City 84112
Dr. J. Stayner Landward, Dir. of Admis.

† Utah State University, Logan 84322-1600
  Rod Clark, Director of Admissions
  801-750-1107

† Weber State University
  3750 Harrison Blvd., Ogden 84408

Westminster College of Salt Lake City
  1840 S. 1300 E., Salt Lake City 84105
  800-748-4753

VERMONT

Bennington College, Bennington 05201
  Karen Kristof, Dir. of Admis.
  800-833-6845

Castleton State College, Castleton 05735
  Gary Fallis, Dir. of Admis.

Champlain College
  P.O. Box 670, Burlington 05402
  Josephine Churchill, Dir. of Admis.
  802-860-2727
  See listing under "Universities"

College of St. Joseph
  71 Clement Rd., Rutland 05701

Goddard College
  P.O. Box G, Plainfield 05667
  Jackson Kytle, President

Green Mountain College
  16 College St., Poultney 05764

Johnson State College, Johnson 05656
  802-635-2356 ext. 219

Lyndon State College, Lyndonville 05851

Saint Michael's College
  Winooski Park, Colchester 05439
  800-SMC-8000
  See listing under "Liberal Arts"

Trinity College
  208 Colchester Ave., Burlington 05401

† University of Vermont
  194 S. Prospect St., Burlington 05401
  802-656-3370

VIRGINIA

Averett College
  420 W. Main St., Danville 24541
  Gary Sherman, Dean of Enrollment Mgmt.

Bluefield College
  3000 College Dr., Bluefield 24605
  Dr. Roy Dobyns, President
  See listing under "Universities"

Bridgewater College
  402 E College St., Bridgewater 22812

Christopher Newport College
  50 Shoe Ln., Newport News 23606

Clinch Valley College of the University of Virginia
  P.O. Box 16, Wise 24293
  Lana Low, Dir. Enrollment Management

† College of William and Mary, Williamsburg 23185
  Jean A. Scott, Dean of Admission

† Eastern Mennonite College
  1200 Park Rd., Harrisonburg 22801
  Jerry Miller, Dir. of Admis.

Emory & Henry College
  General Delivery, Emory 24327

Ferrum College, Ferrum 24088
  Bob Bailey, Dir. of Admis.

† George Mason University
  4400 University Dr., Fairfax 22030-4444
  Dr. Jack Levy, Chrpsn.

† Hampton University, Hampton 23668
  Ollie Bowman, Dean of Admissions

† James Madison University, Harrisonburg 22807

LIBERTY UNIVERSITY
  P.O. Box 20000, Lynchburg 24506
  Jay Spencer, VP Recruitment
  800-376-2800
  See listing under "Universities"

† Longwood College, Farmville 23901

Lynchburg College
  1501 Lakeside Dr., Lynchburg 24501
  Ernest Chadderton, Dean of Enrollment

Mary Baldwin College, Staunton 24401
  Douglas E. Clark, Exec. Dir. of Enrollment

† Marymount University
  2807 N. Glebe Rd., Arlington 22207
  Charles Coe, Director of Admissions
  800-548-7638 or 703-284-1500
  See listing under "Universities"

† Norfolk State University
  2401 Corprew Ave., Norfolk 23504

† Old Dominion University
  5215 Hampton Blvd., Norfolk 23508

† Radford University
  P.O. Box 5430, Radford 24142

Randolph-Macon College
  200 Henry St., Ashland 23005
  John Conkright, Dean of Admissions

Randolph-Macon Woman's College
  2500 Rivermont Ave., Lynchburg 24503

Roanoke College
  221 College Ln., Salem 24153

St. Paul's College
  406 Windsor Ave., Lawrenceville 23868

SHENANDOAH UNIVERSITY
  1460 University Dr., Winchester 22601
  Dr. Brandon Beck, Division Chair
  See listing under "Universities"

· Southern Virginia College for Women
  One College Hill Dr., Buena Vista 24416
  Mark A. Camper, Assoc. Dir. of Admis.
  800-229-8420
  See listing under "Women's Colleges"

· Tidewater Community College, Portsmouth Campus
  Rt. 135, Portsmouth 23703
  Dr. Larry L. Whitworth, President

University of Richmond, Richmond 23173

† University of Virginia
  P.O. Box 9017, Charlottesville 22906

† Virginia Commonwealth University
  910 W. Franklin St., Richmond 23284

Virginia Intermont College
  1013 Moore St., Bristol 24201
  Lawton Blandford, Dir. of Admis.

† Virginia Polytechnic Institute & State University
  Blacksburg 24061
  David Bousquet, Dir. of Undergraduate Admis.

† Virginia State University, Petersburg 23803
  Mable C. Mountcastle, Dir. of Recording

Virginia Wesleyan College
  1584 Wesleyan Dr., Norfolk 23502
  W. Steve Stocks, V.P. for Admis.

WASHINGTON

Central Washington University, Ellensburg 98926
  William Swain, Director of Admissions

City University
  16661 Northup Way, Bellevue 98008
  800-422-4898

† Eastern Washington University, Cheney 99004
  William Shreeve, Chrpsn. of Education Dept.
  See listing under "Universities"

Evergreen State College
  2700 Evergreen Pky. N.W., Olympia 98505

† Gonzaga University
  502 E. Boone Ave., Spokane 99258
  Philip Ballinger, Dean of Admissions

Northwest College of the Assemblies of God
  P.O. Box 579, Kirkland 98083-0579
  Bob Foster, Dir. of Public Relations

† Pacific Lutheran University
  12180 Park Ave. S., Tacoma 98447
  John Brickell, Acting Dean

St. Martin's College
  700 College St. N.E., Lacey 98516

† Seattle Pacific University
  3307 3rd Ave., W., Seattle 98119

† Seattle University
  Broadway Ave. & Madison, Seattle 98122
  Lee Gerig, Dean of Admissions

† University of Puget Sound
  1500 N. Warner St., Tacoma 98416

† University of Washington, Seattle 98195

Walla Walla College
  204 S. College Ave., College Place 99324

† Washington State University, Pullman 99164
  Stan Berry, Dir. of Admis.

† Western Washington University
  516 High St., Bellingham 98225
  Karen G. Copetas, Dir. of Admis.

† Whitworth College
  300 W. Hawthorne Rd., Spokane 99251
  Kenneth P. Moyer, Dir. of Admis.

WEST VIRGINIA

Alderson-Broaddus College
  Philippi 26416
  Craig W. Gould, Director of Admissions
  304-457-1700

† Bethany College, Bethany 26031
  John Giesman, Registrar

Bluefield State College
  219 Rock St., Bluefield 24701

† Concord College, Athens 24712

Davis & Elkins College
  100 Campus Dr., Elkins 26241
  Kevin D. Chenoweth, Dir. of Admis.

† Fairmont State College
  1201 Locust Ave., Fairmont 26554
  John Conaway, Dir. of Admis.

† GLENVILLE STATE COLLEGE
  200 High St., Glenville 26351
  Dr. William Simmons, President
  Mack Samples, Dean of Admissions
    Established 1872. State. Coed. Accreditation:
  NCACS. Annual tuition: $3,460 resident, $4,054 non-
  resident. Room and board: $3,080. Enrollment: 900
  boarding, 1,500 day. Faculty: 72. Degrees: AA, AS,
  BA, BS. Library: 210,000 volumes. 10 buildings. Gym
  & pool, golf course nearby. Beautiful rural setting, 16
  miles from I-79. Popular 2 year forestry program;
  special education.

† Marshall University
  400 Hal Greer Blvd., Huntington 25755
  See listing under "Universities"

Salem-Teikyo University, Salem 26426
  Frank Potter, Dir. of Admis.

† Shepherd College, Shepherdstown 25443

† The University of Charleston
  2300 MacCorkle Ave., S.E., Charleston 25304
  800-995-GO UC

West Liberty State College, West Liberty 26074

† West Virginia Graduate College
  P.O. Box 1003, Institute 25112

† West Virginia Institute of Technology
  405 Fayette Pike, Montgomery 25136

† West Virginia State College
  P.O. Box 1000, Institute 25112

† West Virginia University
  P.O. Box 6001, Morgantown 26506

WEST VIRGINIA WESLEYAN COLLEGE
  59 College Ave., Buckhannon 26201
  Robert Skinner, Director of Admission
  See listing under "Universities"

WISCONSIN

† Alverno College
  P.O. Box 343922, Milwaukee 53234
  Colleen Hayes, Dir. of Admis.

Beloit College
  700 College St., Beloit 53511
  Thomas Warren, Chrpsn.
  608-363-2336

† Cardinal Stritch College
  6801 N. Yates Rd., Milwaukee 53217
  David Wegener, Dir. of Admis.

Carroll College
  100 N. East Ave., Waukesha 53186
  Ken Moyer, Dir. of Admis.

Carthage College
  2001 Alford Dr., Kenosha 53140
  Barbara Boe, Chrpsn.

Concordia University
  12800 N. Lake Shore Dr., Mequon 53097
  414-243-5700

† Edgewood College
  855 Woodrow St., Madison 53711
  Robert Blust, Dir. of Admis.

Lakeland College
  P.O. Box 359, Sheboygan 53082

Lawrence University
  P.O. Box 599, Appleton 54912
  Steven Syverson, Dean of Admissions

† Marian College of Fond du Lac
  45 S. National Ave., Fond du Lac 54935
  Carol Reichenberger, Dean of Admissions

† Marquette University
  1217 W. Wisconsin Ave., Milwaukee 53233
  Raymond A. Brown, Dean of Admissions

† Mt. Mary College
  2900 N. Menomonee River Pky.
  Milwaukee 53222

Mt. Senario College
  1500 W. College Ave., Ladysmith 54848
  Dewey Floberg, Dean of Admissions

Northland College
  1411 Ellis Ave., Ashland 54806
  Jim Miller, Dean of Admissions

Ripon College, P.O. Box 248, Ripon 54971
  James Reilly, Dean of Admis.

St. Norbert College
  100 Grant St., De Pere 54115
  Craig S. Wesley, Dean of Admission
  See listing under "Universities"

† Silver Lake College
  2406 S. Alverno Road, Manitowoc 54220
  Sandra Schwartz, Dir. of Admis.

University of Wisconsin, Eau Claire
  Eau Claire 54701

University of Wisconsin, Green Bay
  2420 Nicolet Dr., Green Bay 54311
  Dr. Margaret Laughlin, Chrpsn.

† University of Wisconsin, La Crosse
  115 Main Hall, La Crosse 54601
  608-785-8067

University of Wisconsin, Madison
  500 Lincoln Dr., Madison 53706

University of Wisconsin
  P.O. Box 413, Milwaukee 53201
  V. M. Allison, Registrar

University of Wisconsin, Oshkosh
  800 Algoma Blvd., Oshkosh 54901-8602
  August Helgerson, Dir. of Admis.

University of Wisconsin
  P.O. Box 2000, Kenosha 53141
  414-553-2211

† University of Wisconsin
  1 University Plaza, Platteville 53818
  Richard Schumacher, Dean of Admissions

† University of Wisconsin, River Falls
  River Falls 54022
  Alan Tuchtenhagen, Dir. of Admis.

University of Wisconsin, Stevens Point 54481
  Dr. John A. Larsen, Dir. of Admis.

† University of Wisconsin
  200 BroadWay St. S., Menomonie 54751
  Robert B. Swanson, Chancellor

University of Wisconsin, Superior 54880
  Richard E. Morrison, Dir. Univ. Relations

† University of Wisconsin
  800 W. Main St., Whitewater 53190

† Viterbo College
  815 9th St., S., La Crosse 54601
  Roland W. Nelson, Dir. of Admis.

WYOMING

† University of Wyoming
  P.O. Box 3434, Laramie 82071
  Richard Davis, Dir. of Admis.

GUAM

University of Guam
  UOG Station, Mangilao 96923
  Kathleen Owings, Dir. of Admis.

PUERTO RICO

Bayamon Central University
  P.O. Box 1725, Bayamon 00960-1725
  Christine Hernandez, Dir. of Admis.

Catholic University of Puerto Rico
  Las Americas Ave., Ponce 00732
  Carilin Frau, Dir. of Admis.

Inter American University of Puerto Rico
  San German Campus
  Harris Dr. Call Box 5100, San German 00683

Universidad Adventista de las Antillas
  P.O. Box 118, Mayaguez 00681
  Wilma Gonzalez, Dir. of Admis.

University of Puerto Rico
  Arecibo Technical University College
  P.O. Box A-1806, Arecibo 00613

University of Puerto Rico
  Bayamon Technical University College
  Bayamon 00959

University of Puerto Rico
  Antonio Barcelo Ave., Cayey 00736
  Antonio Rosario, Dir. of Admis.

University of Puerto Rico
  CUH Station Rd. 908 Bo Tejas, Humacao 00791

University of Puerto Rico
  Ponce Technological University College
  P.O. Box 7186, Ponce 00732

† University of Puerto Rico, Rio Piedras Campus
  P.O. Box 23300, San Juan 00931
  Victor Lopez, Dir. of Admis.

University of the Sacred Heart
  P.O. Box 12383, San Juan 00914

THEOLOGY

This classification contains schools accredited by the Association of Theological Schools (†) and a selection of institutionally accredited schools.

ALABAMA

Huntingdon College
  1500 E. Fairview Ave., Montgomery 36106-2148
  Carolyn A. Phillips, Dean of Enrollment
  800-763-0313

Oakwood College
  Oakwood Rd., N.W., Huntsville 35896

Samford University
  800 Lakeshore Dr., Birmingham 35229
  Timothy George, Dean

Spring Hill College
  4000 Dauphin St., Mobile 36608
  Ben Hamd, Dir. of Admis.

UNIVERSITY OF MOBILE
P.O. Box 13220, Mobile 36663-0220
Kim Leousis, Dir. of Admissions
205-675-5990
See listing under "Universities"

ARIZONA

Grand Canyon University
  3300 W. Camelback Rd., Phoenix 85017
  Sherri Willborn, Dir. of Admis.
  See listing under "Liberal Arts and Sciences"

SOUTHWESTERN COLLEGE
A Conservative Baptist Bible College
2625 E. Cactus Rd., Phoenix 85032
800-247-2697

ARKANSAS

John Brown University
  2000 W. University, Siloam Springs 72761
  Don Crandall, Director of Enrollment Management

Ouachita Baptist University
  410 Ouachita St., Arkadelphia 71998
  Randy Garner, Dir. of Admis.
  800-DIAL-OBU

Williams Baptist College
  P.O. Box 3667, Walnut Ridge 72476
  Scott Wright, Dir. of Admis.

CALIFORNIA

† American Baptist Seminary of the West
  2606 Dwight Way, Berkeley 94704
  Douglas R. Sharp, Registrar

† Azusa Pacific University
  P.O. Box 7000, Azusa 91702

Bethany Bible College
  800 Bethany Dr., Scotts Valley 95066
  Randal McNally, Dir. of Admis.

Biblical Christian College and Graduate School
  1601 W. Malvern Ave., Fullerton 92633
  Dr. Robert S. McBirnie, President

† Biola University-Talbot School of Theology
  13800 Biola Ave., La Mirada 90639
  Wayne Chute, Dean of Admissions

California Baptist College
  8432 Magnolia Ave., Riverside 92504
  800-782-3382

California Institute of Integral Studies
  765 Ashbury St., San Francisco 94117
  Diane Gribben, Dir. of Admis.

† Church Divinity School of the Pacific (Epis.)
  2451 Ridge Road, Berkeley 94709
  Charles A. Perry, President, Dean

Concordia University
  1530 Concordia, Irvine 92715
  Stan Meyer, Dean of Admission
  800-229-1200
  See listing under "Universities"

† Dominican School of Philosophy & Theology
  2401 Ridge Rd., Berkeley 94709
  Ingrid Honore, C.S.J., Dir. of Admis.
  510-849-2030

† FRANCISCAN SCHOOL OF THEOLOGY
1712 Euclid Ave., Berkeley 94709
William M. Cieslak, OFM Cap., President
510-848-5232
See listing under "Graduate Schools"

† FULLER THEOLOGICAL SEMINARY
135 N. Oakland Ave., Pasadena 91182
William Dyrness, Dean
Accreditation: WASC, ATS
818-584-5400 or 800-235-2222

† Golden Gate Baptist Theological Seminary
  Strawberry Point, Mill Valley 94941
  William Crews, Jr., President

† Graduate Theological Union
  2400 Ridge Rd., Berkeley 94709

International School of Theology
  P.O. Box 5500, San Bernardino 92412
  714-886-7876

† JESUIT SCHOOL OF THEOLOGY AT BERKELEY
1735 LeRoy Ave., Berkeley 94709
Rev. Thomas Gleeson, SJ, President
See listing under "Graduate Schools"

La Sierra University
  4700 Pierce St., Riverside 92505
  800-874-5587

† Mennonite Brethren Biblical Seminary
  4824 E. Butler Ave., Fresno 93727
  Larry Martens, President

† Pacific Lutheran Theological Seminary
  2770 Marin Ave., Berkeley 94708
  Dr. Walter Stuhr, President

† Pacific School of Religion
  1798 Scenic Ave., Berkeley 94709
  800-999-0528
  See listing under "Graduate Schools"

Pacific Union College
  1 Angwin Ave., Angwin 94508
  Dr. Gary Gifford, Dir. of Admis.

St. John's Seminary
  5012 Seminary Rd., Camarillo 93012

† St. John's Seminary College
  5118 Seminary Rd., Camarillo 93012
  Rev. Gary S. Landry, C.M., Dir. of Admis.

† St. Patrick's Seminary
  320 Middlefield Rd., Menlo Park 94025

† San Francisco Theological Seminary
  2 Kensington Rd., San Anselmo 94960
  Dr. J. Randolph Taylor, President

San Jose Christian College
  P.O. Box 1090, San Jose 95108
  Michael J. Bowman, Dean

† SCHOOL OF THEOLOGY AT CLAREMONT
1325 N. College Ave., Claremont 91711
Robert W. Edgar, President
800-626-7821
  Established 1885. Accreditation: ATS, WASC, American Association of Pastoral Counselors. Multidenominational. United Methodist sponsored. Coed. Degrees: MA, M Div, D Min, PhD. Library: 140,000 volumes +1,600,000 in nearby Claremont Colleges. Research centers in Biblical manuscripts, Dead Sea Scrolls, early Christianity, process philosophy, and religion and health.

Southern California College
  55 Fair Dr., Costa Mesa 92626
  Richard Hardy, Asst. Dean for Enrollment

† Starr King School for the Ministry
  2441 Le Conte Ave., Berkeley 94709
  Rebecca Parker, President

UNIVERSITY OF JUDAISM/LEE COLLEGE
15600 Mulholland Dr., Los Angeles 90077
Tamara Greenebaum, Dean of Admissions
See listing under "Universities"

University of San Diego
  5998 Alcala Park, San Diego 92110
  Warren Muller, Dir. of Admis.
  619-260-4506

University of San Francisco
  2130 Fulton St., San Francisco 94117
  Bill Henley, Dir. of Admis.

WESTMINSTER THEOLOGICAL SEMINARY IN CALIFORNIA
Graduate School only
1725 Bear Valley Pky., Escondido 92027
619-480-8474, FAX 619-480-0252

COLORADO

† DENVER SEMINARY
Denver Conservative Baptist Seminary
MDiv, MA, DMIN.
P.O. Box 10000, Denver 80250
Charles Sprinkle, Dir. of Admis.
1-800-922-3040

† ILIFF SCHOOL OF THEOLOGY
2201 S. University Blvd., Denver 80210
Susan Mitchell, Dir. of Admis.
800-678-3360

Regis University
  3333 Regis Blvd., Denver 80221
  Robert Blust, Director of Admissions

† St. Thomas Seminary
  1300 S. Steele St., Denver 80210
  Rev. Paul L. Golden, C.M., Rector-President

CONNECTICUT

† Berkeley Divinity School
  363 St. Ronan St., New Haven 06511
  James Annand, Dean

† HARTFORD SEMINARY
77 Sherman St., Hartford 06105
Karen B. Rollins, Registrar
203-232-4451

Holy Apostles College
  33 Prospect Hill Rd., Cromwell 06416

St. Alphonsus College
  1762 Mapleton Ave., Suffield 06078

† Yale University
  Divinity School
  2024 Yale Station, New Haven 06520

DISTRICT OF COLUMBIA

† Catholic University of America
  620 Michigan Ave. N.E., Washington 20064
  Robert J. Talbot, Dir. of Admis. & Fin. Aid.

† De Sales School of Theology
  721 Lawrence St., N.E., Washington 20017
  Carol McKee, Registrar

† Dominican House of Studies/Pontifical Faculty of the Immaculate Conception
  487 Michigan Ave., N.E., Washington 20017
  Rev. Mark Heath, President

† Howard University Divinity School
　1400 Shepherd St. N.E., Washington 20017
　202-806-0500

† Oblate College
　391 Michigan Ave., N.E., Washington 20017
　Rev. Richard J. Murphy, President

† WESLEY THEOLOGICAL SEMINARY
4500 Massachusetts Ave. N.W., Washington 20016
Director of Admissions
202-885-8659 or 800-882-4987

FLORIDA

Barry University
　11300 N.E. 2nd Ave., Miami Shores 33161
　Robin Ray Roberts, Dean of Admissions

FLORIDA BAPTIST THEOLOGICAL COLLEGE
5400 College Dr., Graceville 32440
O. Lavan Wilson, Dir of Admis.
904-263-3261

Hobe Sound Bible College
　P.O. Box 1065, Hobe Sound 33475
　Ann French, Dir. of Admis.

Palm Beach Atlantic College
　P.O. Box 24708, West Palm Beach 33416-4708
　See listing under "Universities"

St. Leo College
　P.O. Box 2008, St. Leo 33574
　Bonnie Black, Dir. of Admis.

† St. Vincent DePaul Regional Seminary
　10701 Military Trail, Boynton Beach 33436
　Very Rev. Felipe J. Estevez, Rector

Warner Southern College
　5301 U.S. Hwy. 27, S., Lake Wales 33853
　Valerie S. Rutland, Dir. Enrollment Mgmt.
　800-949-7248

GEORGIA

† Columbia Theological Seminary
　701 S. Columbia Dr., Decatur 30030
　Charles Cousar, Academic Dean

† Emory University
　1462 Clifton Rd., Atlanta 30322

Georgia College
　231 W. Hancock St., Milledgeville 31061
　912-453-5004

† Interdenominational Theological Center
　671 Beckwith St., S.W., Atlanta 30314
　Dr. James H. Costen, President

La Grange College
　601 Broad St., La Grange 30240
　Phil Dodson, Dir. of Admis.
　706-882-2911

Toccoa Falls College
　Office of Admissions, Toccoa Falls 30598
　Matthew L. King, Dir. of Admis.
　800-868-3257

ILLINOIS

† Bethany Theological Seminary
　18W600 Butterfield Rd., Oak Brook 60521
　Dr. Eugene F. Roop, President
　708-620-2200

† Catholic Theological Union
　5401 S. Cornell Ave., Chicago 60615
　Ellen McClure, OSF, Dir. of Admis.

† CHICAGO THEOLOGICAL SEMINARY
5757 S. University Ave., Chicago 60637
Delois Shepard, Dir. of Admissions
312-752-5757 Ext. 229

† Garrett-Evangelical Theological Seminary
　2121 Sheridan Rd., Evanston 60201
　Contact Admissions at 800-SEMINARY

LEWIS UNIVERSITY
Rt. 53, Romeoville 60441
Irish O'Reilly, Director of Admissions
See listing under "Universities"

† Lincoln Christian College
　100 Campus View Dr., Lincoln 62656
　Mr. Lynn Laughlin, Dir. of Admis.

† Lutheran School of Theology at Chicago
　1100 E. 55th St., Chicago 60615
　Christopher Eldredge, Dir. of Admis.
　312-753-0726

† McCormick Theological Seminary
　5555 S. Woodlawn Ave., Chicago 60637
　Rev. Jan DeVries, Dir. of Admis.

† Meadville/Lombard Theological School
　5701 S. Woodlawn Ave., Chicago 60637
　Spencer Lavan, Dean

Moody Bible Institute
　820 N. LaSalle Dr., Chicago 60610
　Carolyn Klingbeil, Administrator of Admis.

North Central College
　30 N. Brainard St.
　P.O. Box 3065, Naperville 60566-7065
　Marguerite Waters, Director of Admission
　708-420-3414

† Northern Baptist Theological Seminary
　660 E. Butterfield Rd., Lombard 60148
　David Scholer, Dean of the Seminary

Olivet Nazarene University, Kankakee 60901
　John Mongerson, Dir. of Admis.
　815-939-5203

† Seabury-Western Theological Seminary (Episcopal)
　2122 Sheridan Rd., Evanston 60201
　Mark Sisk, Dean & President
　708-328-9300

Trinity Christian College
　6601 W. College Dr., Palos Heights 60463
　Kenneth Bootsma, President

† Trinity Evangelical Divinity School
　2065 Half Day Rd., Deerfield 60015
　David Reeves, Asst. Dir. of Admis.

† University of Chicago
　5801 S. Ellis Ave., Chicago 60637

† University of St. Mary of the Lake Seminary
　Mundelein 60060
　Rev. James Keleher, President

INDIANA

† Anderson University
　1100 E. 5th St., Anderson 46012
　Robert H. Reardon, President

† Associated Mennonite Biblical Seminary
　3003 Benham Ave., Elkhart 46517
　Steven L. Fath, Admissions Counselor

Calumet College
　2400 New York Ave., Whiting 46394
　Sharon Sweeney, Dir. of Admis.

† Christian Theological Seminary
　1000 W. 42nd St., Indianapolis 46208
　Richard Dickinson, Jr., President

† Concordia Theological Seminary
　6600 N. Clinton St., Ft. Wayne 46825
　Dr. David G. Schmiel, President

† Earlham College, Earlham School of Religion
　801 National Rd. W., Richmond 47374
　Tom Mullen, Dean

Grace Theological Seminary
　Winona Lake 46590
　Dr. Gary Meadors, Dir. of Admis.

Indiana Wesleyan University
　4201 S. Washington St., Marion 46953
　800-332-6901

Oakland City College
　143 N. Lucretia St., Oakland City 47660
　Dr. Presley Pendergrass, Dean

St. Francis College
　2701 Spring St., Ft. Wayne 46808

† St. Meinrad School of Theology
　St. Meinrad 47577
　Rev. Harry Hagan, Provost

Taylor University
　500 W. Reade Ave., Upland 46989
　Herb Frye, Dean of Enrollment Management

Taylor University - Fort Wayne Campus
　1025 W. Rudisill Blvd., Fort Wayne 46807
　Jan Paul Storey, Dir. of Admis.

† University of Notre Dame, Notre Dame 46556
　Rev. Richard P. McBrien, Chrpsn.

Valparaiso University, Valparaiso 46383

IOWA

Dordt College
　498 4th Ave., N.E., Sioux Center 51250
　Quentin Van Essen, Dir. of Admissions
　800-343-6738

Faith Baptist Bible College & Theological Seminary
　1900 N.W. 4th St., Ankeny 50021
　Jeff Newman, Director of Admissions
　Admissions: 800-352-0147

Grand View College
　1200 Grandview Ave., Des Moines 50316
　Lori Hanson, Dir. of Admissions
　800-444-6083

Grinnell College
　P.O. Box 805, Grinnell 50112

Luther College
　700 College Dr., Decorah 52101
　David Sallee, Dean for Enrollment

Morningside College, Sioux City 51106
　Lora Vanderzwaag, Dir. of Admis.

University of Dubuque
　2000 University Ave., Dubuque 52001

† University of Dubuque - Theological Seminary
　2000 University Ave., Dubuque 52001

Vennard College
　P.O. Box 29, University Park 52595
　Mark Becker, Dir. of Admis.
　800-338-2407

· Waldorf College
　106 S. 6th St., Forest City 50436
　Steve Lovik, Dir. of Admis.
　800-292-1903

† Wartburg Theological Seminary
　333 Wartburg Place, Dubuque 52003
　Roger Field, President

KANSAS

BARCLAY COLLEGE
P.O. Box 288, Haviland 67059
Lonny R. Choate, Dir. of Admis.

† CENTRAL BAPTIST THEOLOGICAL SEMINARY
741 N. 31st St., Kansas City 66102-3964
800-677-CBTS (2287) or 913-371-5313
Dr. Thomas Clifton, President
Nancy J. Snyder, Director of Admissions
See listing under "Graduate Schools"

McPherson College
　1600 E. Euclid St., McPherson 67460

SOUTHWESTERN COLLEGE
100 College St., Winfield 67156
800-846-1543

KENTUCKY

Asbury College
　1 Macklem Dr., Wilmore 40390
　Jonah Mitchell, Dir. of Admis.

† Asbury Theological Seminary
　204 N. Lexington Ave., Wilmore 40390
　Robert E. Jones, Dir. of Admis.
　800-227-2879

Bellarmine College
　2001 Newburg Rd., Louisville 40205
　Thomas LaBaugh, Dean of Admissions

Georgetown College
　400 E. College St., Georgetown 40324
　Garvel Kindrick, Director of Admissions
　See listing under "Universities"

Kentucky Wesleyan College
　3000 Frederica St., Owensboro 42301
　Dr. Jeff Fager, Coordinator

† Lexington Theological Seminary
　631 Limestone St., S., Lexington 40508
　William Paulsell, President

† Louisville Presbyterian Theological Seminary
　1044 Alta Vista Rd., Louisville 40205
　502-895-3411 or 800-264-1839

† Southern Baptist Theological Seminary
　2825 Lexington Rd., Louisville 40280
　R. Albert Mohler, Jr., President

LOUISIANA

† New Orleans Baptist Theological Seminary
　3939 Gentilly Blvd., New Orleans 70126
　Dr. Landrum P. Leavell, II, President

† Notre Dame Seminary
　2901 S. Carrollton Ave., New Orleans 70118

MAINE

† Bangor Theological Seminary
　300 Union St., Bangor 04401
　Malcolm Warford, EdD, President

Bowdoin College, Brunswick 04011
　William Mason, Dir. of Admis.

MARYLAND

::: Home Study International
　12501 Old Columbia Pike, Silver Spring 20904
　P.O. Box 4437, Silver Spring
　20914-4437(mailing)
　Dr. Joseph Gurubatham, President
　800-782-4769
　See listing under "Home Study and
　Correspondence"

Morgan State University
　Cold Spring Ln. and Hillen Rd., Baltimore 21239

† Mt. St. Mary's College
　16300 Old Emmitsburg Rd., Emmitsburg 21727
　Michael D. Kennedy, Dir. of Admis.

† St. Mary's Seminary (R.C.)
　5400 Roland Ave., Baltimore 21210
　Rev. Wm. J. Lee, President

† Washington Theological Union
　9001 New Hampshire Ave., Silver Spring 20903
　Rev. Vincent Cushing, President

MASSACHUSETTS

† Andover Newton Theological School
　210 Herrick Rd., Newton Center 02159
　Dr. George Peck, President

Atlantic Union College
　P.O. Box 1000, South Lancaster 01561
　Osa Canto, Registrar

† Boston University
　685 Commonwealth Ave., Boston 02215

Eastern Nazarene College
　23 E. Elm Ave., Quincy 02170
　D. William Nichols, Dir. of Admis.

Emmanuel College
　400 The Fenway, Boston 02115
　Margaret Bonilla, Dir. of Admis.

† Episcopal Divinity School
　99 Brattle St., Cambridge 02138

† Gordon-Conwell Theological Seminary
　130 Essex St., South Hamilton 01982
　Robert Cooley, President

† Harvard University
　Harvard Divinity School
　45 Francis Ave., Cambridge 02138

† Holy Cross School of Theology
50 Goddard Ave., Brookline 02146
Fr. Al Demos, Director of Admission
617-731-3500

† Pope John XXIII National Seminary
558 South Ave., Weston 02193

† St. John's Seminary
127 Lake St., Brighton 02135

SWEDENBORG SCHOOL OF RELIGION
48 Sargent St., Newton 02158
Dr. Mary Kay Klein, President

† WESTON SCHOOL OF THEOLOGY
3 Phillips Pl., Cambridge 02138
Mary Ellen Herx, Dir. of Admissions
617-492-1960
    Established 1922. Private. Coed. Accreditation: ATS. Tuition: $7,400. Fees: $100. Enrollment: 180 full-time, 25 part-time. Faculty: 16. Degrees: Master of Divinity (MDiv), Master of Theological Studies (MTS), Master of Theology (ThM). Licentiate in Sacred Theology (STL). Library: 266,000 volumes. Roman Catholic institution, sponsored by the Society of Jesus. Accepts lay people, women and men religious. Member of the Boston Theological Institute.

MICHIGAN

Adrian College
110 S. Madison St., Adrian 49221
George Wolf, Dir. of Admis.
See listing under "Universities"

† Andrews University, Berrien Springs 49104
Jack Mentges, Dir. of Admis.

† Calvin Theological Seminary
3233 Burton St., S.E., Grand Rapids 49546
James DeJong, President

Concordia College
4090 Geddes Rd., Ann Arbor 48105
Mary Froelich, Dir. of Admis.

Grace Bible College
P.O. Box 910, Grand Rapids 49509
Linda K. Siler, Dir. of Admis.

Grand Rapids Baptist College & Seminary
1001 East Beltline Ave., N.E.
Grand Rapids 49505

Reformed Bible College
3333 East Beltline N.E., Grand Rapids 49505
Dorothy Hostetter, Dir. of Admis.
616-363-2050
See listing under "Biblical Studies"

† Sacred Heart Major Seminary
2701 W. Chicago Blvd., Detroit 48206
313-883-8501

† SS Cyril and Methodius Seminary
3535 Indian Trl., Orchard Lake 48324
Francis B. Koper, Rector
810-683-0311

St. Mary's College
Orchard Lake & Commerce Rd.
Orchard Lake 48324

† Western Theological Seminary
86 E. 12th St., Holland 49423
The Rev. Marvin Hoff, President

William Tyndale College
35700 W. Twelve Mile Rd.
Farmington Hills 48331

MINNESOTA

Bethel College
3900 Bethel Dr., St. Paul 55112
Dr. George Brushaber, President

† Bethel Theological Seminary
3949 Bethel Dr., St. Paul 55112
Dr. Fred Prinzing, Exec VP, Dean

College of Saint Benedict
37 S. College Ave., St. Joseph 56374

College of St. Catherine
2004 Randolph Ave., St. Paul 55105

Concordia College-St. Paul
275 N. Syndicate, St. Paul 55104
Tim Utter, Dir. of Admis.

Crown College
6425 County Rd. 30, St. Bonifacius 55375
See listing under "Universities"

† Luther Northwestern Theological Seminary
2481 Como Ave., St. Paul 55108
Dr. David Tiede, President

Minnesota Bible College
920 Mayowood Rd., S.W., Rochester 55902
Tay Schield, Director of Recruitment
507-288-4563

North Central Bible College
910 Elliot Ave., Minneapolis 55404
800-289-NCBC
Dan Neary, Dir. of Admis.
See listing under "Universities"

Northwestern College
3003 Snelling Ave., N., St. Paul 55113
Ralph Anderson, Dean of Admissions
800-827-6827 or 612-631-5111

PILLSBURY BAPTIST BIBLE COLLEGE
315 S. Grove St., Owatonna 55060
Alan Potter, President
Larry Tindall, Director of Admissions
800-747-4557

† St. John's University
P.O. Box 7155, Collegeville 56321

St. Mary's College of Minnesota
700 Terrace Heights #2, Winona 55987
Tony Piscitiello, VP for Admission

St. Olaf College, Northfield 55057
Charles Wilson, Chrpsn.
507-646-3080

† United Theological Seminary of the Twin Cities
3000 5th St., N.W., New Brighton 55112
Admissions 800-937-1316

† St. Paul Seminary School of Divinity
of the University of Saint Thomas
2260 Summit Ave., Saint Paul 55105

MISSISSIPPI

† Reformed Theological Seminary
5422 Clinton Blvd., Jackson 39209
Luder G. Witlock, Jr., President

† Wesley Biblical Seminary
P.O. Box 9938, Jackson 39286
601-957-1314

MISSOURI

† Aquinas Institute of Theology
3642 Lindell Blvd., Saint Louis 63108
Charles Bouchard, OP, President

Assemblies of God Theological Seminary
1445 N. Boonville Ave., Springfield 65802
Del Tarr, President

Calvary Graduate School of Theology
15800 Calvary Rd., Kansas City 64147
J. Robert Brundage, Dir. of Admis.

Conception Seminary College, Conception 64433
Rev. Albert Bruecken, Dir. of Admis.

† CONCORDIA SEMINARY
801 De Mun Ave., Saint Louis 63105
John F. Johnson, President
314-721-5934

† Covenant Theological Seminary
12330 Conway Rd., St. Louis 63141
Dr. Paul Kooistra, President
800-264-8064

† Eden Theological Seminary
475 E. Lockwood Ave., Webster Groves 63119
Clifton Kerr, Dir. of Admis.
800-969-3627, Ext. 338

† Kenrick School of Theology
5200 Glennon Dr., St. Louis 63119
Rev. Ronald Ramson, President-Rector
314-644-0266, FAX: 314-644-3079

† Midwestern Baptist Theological Seminary
5001 N. Oak Trfy., Kansas City 64118
Dr. Milton Ferguson, President
816-453-4600 x 213

Missouri Baptist College
12542 Conway Rd., St. Louis 63141

† Nazarene Theological Seminary
1700 E. Meyer Blvd., Kansas City 64131
Robert Crabtree, Registrar

Ozark Christian College
1111 N. Main St., Joplin 64801
Jim Marcum, Dir. of Admis.
800-299-4622

St. Louis Christian College
1360 Grandview Dr., Florissant 63033
Roger Clark, Dean

† St. Paul School of Theology
5123 E. Truman Rd., Kansas City 64127
Lovett Weems, Jr., President

Southwest Baptist University
1601 S. Springfield Ave., Bolivar 65613

MONTANA

CARROLL COLLEGE
1610 N. Benton Ave., Helena 59625
Candace Cain, Dir. of Admis.
See listing under "Universities"

NEBRASKA

Concordia College
800 N. Columbia Ave., Seward 68434
Don Vos, Dir. of Admis.

Creighton University
2500 California St., Omaha 68178
Rev. Richard Hauser, SJ, Chrpsn.

Dana College
2848 College Dr., Blair 68008
John Schueth, Dir. of Admis.
800-444-3262
See listing under "Universities"

Grace College of the Bible
Ninth and William, Omaha 68108
Jeffrey A. Edgar, Director of Admissions
800-383-1422

NOTRE DAME COLLEGE
2321 Elm St., Manchester 03104
603-669-4298

NEW JERSEY

† Drew University
36 Madison Ave., Madison 07940
Kenneth Cole, Registrar

† Immaculate Conception Seminary
School of Theology of Seton Hall University
400 S. Orange Ave., South Orange 07079
Rev. Richard Liddy, PhD, Dean

† New Brunswick Theological Seminary
17 Seminary Pl., New Brunswick 08901
Robert White, President

† Princeton Theological Seminary
CN821, 64 Mercer St., Princeton 08540

NEW MEXICO

Eastern New Mexico University
Portales 88130
Larry Fuqua, Dir. of Admis.

NEW YORK

Bexley Hall School
1100 Goodman St. S., Rochester 14620

† Christ the King Seminary
Graduate School of Theology
P.O. Box 607, East Aurora 14052
Daniel Mc Lellan, Rector-President

† Colgate Rochester-Bexley-Crozer Seminaries
1100 Goodman St., S., Rochester 14620
Shirley Jones, President

Colgate University
13 Oak Dr., Hamilton 13346
Dean of Admissions
315-824-7401

College of New Rochelle
5 W. 29th St., New York 10001

Concordia College
171 White Plains Rd., Bronxville 10708

Fordham University
441 E. Fordham Rd., Bronx 10458
718-817-1000

† General Theological Seminary of The Episcopal Church
175 9th Ave., New York 10011
The Rt. Rev. Craig B. Anderson, President & Dean
212-243-5150

IONA COLLEGE
715 North Ave., New Rochelle 10801
800-231-IONA or 914-633-2503
See listing under "Universities"

Molloy College
1000 Hempstead Ave., Rockville Centre 11570
Wayne James, Dir. of Admis.
See listing under "Universities"

† New York Theological Seminary
5 W. 29th St., New York 10001
Keith Russell, D.Min., Pres.

† Nyack College, Nyack 10960
Miguel Sanchez, Dir. of Admis.
800-33-NYACK

† ST. BERNARD'S INSTITUTE
1100 S. Goodman St., Rochester 14620
Georgia Crissy, Dir. of Admissions
716-271-1320

† St. Joseph's Seminary
201 Seminary Ave., Yonkers 10704
Rev. John Mescall, President

† St. Vladimir's Orthodox Theological Seminary
575 Scarsdale Rd., Crestwood 10707
John Meyendorff, Dean

† Seminary of the Immaculate Conception
440 W. Neck Rd., Huntington 11743
Joan McGowan, Registrar

Unification Theological Seminary
10 Dock Rd., Barrytown 12507

† Union Theological Seminary
3041 Broadway, New York 10027
Donald W. Shriver, Jr., President

Wadhams Hall Seminary College
R.R. 4 Box 80, Ogdensburg 13669
Rev. Donald Robinson, Dir. of Admis.
315-393-4231

NORTH CAROLINA

Barton College
College Station, Wilson 27893
Anthony Britt, Dir. of Admis.
800-345-4973/919-399-6318
See listing under "Universities"

Belmont Abbey College
1 Abbey Pl., Belmont 28012
Admissions, 800-523-2355

† Duke University, Durham 27706

Gardner-Webb University
General Delivery, Boiling Springs 28017
Alice Cullinan, Chrpsn.
704-434-2361

Hood Theological Seminary
800 W. Thomas St., Salisbury 28144
704-638-5644

John Wesley College
2314 Centennial St., N., High Point 27265
Ron Cathey, Dir. of Admis.

Roanoke Bible College
714 1st St., Elizabeth City 27909
William Griffin, President

Shaw Divinity School
509 Hilltop Dr., Raleigh 27602

† Southeastern Baptist Theological Seminary
P.O. Box 1889, Wake Forest 27588
Dr. L. Paige Patterson, President

OHIO

† Ashland University
401 College Ave., Ashland 44805

† Athenaeum of Ohio
6616 Beechmont Ave., Cincinnati 45230

Cincinnati Bible College
P.O. Box 04320, Cincinnati 45204
C. Barry McCarty, President

CIRCLEVILLE BIBLE COLLEGE
P.O. Box 458, Circleville 43113
Michael Adkins, Dir. of Enrollment
614-477-7701

College of Mount St. Joseph
5701 Delhi Rd., Cincinnati 45233-1672
See listing under "Universities"

LOURDES COLLEGE
6832 Convent Blvd., Sylvania 43560
Mary E. Briggs, Dir. of Admis.
419-885-5291 or 800-878-3210

Malone College
515 25th St., N.W., Canton 44709
Lee Sommers, Dean of Admissions

† Methodist Theological School in Ohio
3081 Columbus Pike, Delaware 43015
Robert Atchley, Dir. of Admis.

Mt. Vernon Nazarene College
800 Martinsburg Rd., Mt. Vernon 43050
Ronald Hyson, Dir. of Admis.

Ohio Dominican College
1216 Sunbury Rd., Columbus 43219
800-955-OHIO

Payne Theological Seminary
P.O. Box 474, Wilberforce 45384
Dr. Louis-Charles Harvey, President
Dr. John Kampen, Academic Dean
513-376-2946

† Pontifical College Josephinum
7625 N. High St., Columbus 43235
Rev. Msgr. Dennis Sheehan, Rector

† ST. MARY SEMINARY
28700 Euclid Ave., Wickliffe 44092
Very Rev. Allan Laubenthal, President/Rector
Established 1848. Roman Catholic. Theology graduate school. Accreditation: NCACS, ATS. Tuition: $5,460. Room and board: $7,300. Estimated personal expenses: $4,000. Enrollment: 85. Faculty: 12. Degrees: MDiv, MA. Library: 55,000 volumes. 1 building on 56 acres. Gym. Located at the center for Pastoral Leadership, Diocese of Cleveland.

† Trinity Lutheran Seminary
2199 E. Main St., Columbus 43209
Dennis Anderson, President

† United Theological Seminary
1810 Harvard Blvd., Dayton 45406
The Rev. Duane Anders, Dir. of Admis.

University of Dayton
300 College Park Ave., Dayton 45469-1530
Toll-free 800-837-7433
See listing under "Universities"

† WINEBRENNER THEOLOGICAL SEMINARY
P.O. Box 478, Findlay 45839
Dr. David Draper, President
419-422-4824

OKLAHOMA

Mid-America Bible College
3500 S.W. 119th St., Oklahoma City 73170
Tony O'Brien, Registrar
405-691-3800

† Oral Roberts University
7777 S. Lewis Ave., Tulsa 74171
Arthur E. Matzkvech, Dir. of Admis.

† Phillips Graduate Seminary
102 S. University Ave., Enid 73701
405-548-2317

Southwestern College of Christian Ministries
P.O. Box 340, Bethany 73008
Dr. Richard M. Waters, Dean of Academics

OREGON

EUGENE BIBLE COLLEGE
2155 Bailey Hill Rd., Eugene 97405
Trent Combs, Dir. of Admis.
800-322-2638

† Mt. Angel Seminary
General Delivery, St. Benedict 97373
Very Rev. J. Terrence Fitzgerald, Pres.-Rector

MULTNOMAH BIBLE COLLEGE
8435 N.E. Glisan St., Portland 97220
Joseph Aldrich, President

Northwest Christian College
828 E. 11th Ave., Eugene 97401
Randy Jones, Dir. of Admis.

† Western Conservative Baptist Seminary
5511 S.E. Hawthorne Blvd., Portland 97215
Dr. Russell Shive, Interim President

† Western Evangelical Seminary
12753 S.W. 68th Ave., Portland 97223
David C. Le Shana, President
Todd M. McCollum, Dir. of Enrollment
503-639-0559

PENNSYLVANIA

Academy of the New Church College
P.O. Box 278, Bryn Athyn 19009

Allentown College of St. Frances de Sales
2755 Station Ave., Center Valley 18034
George Kelley, Dir. of Admis.

Baptist Bible College of Pennsylvania
538 Venard Rd., Clarks Summit 18411

Biblical Theological Seminary
200 N. Main St., Hatfield 19440
Wayne Arndt, Dean Student Services

† Eastern Baptist Theological Seminary
6 E. Lancaster Ave., Wynnewood 19096
Stephen Hutchison, Dir. of Admis.

Eastern College
10 Fairview Dr., Saint Davids 19087
Ronald Keller, VP for Enrollment Management

† Evangelical School of Theology
121 S. College St., Myerstown 17067
Dr. Kirby Keller, VP Academic Affairs

King's College
133 N. River St., Wilkes Barre 18711

† Lancaster Theological Seminary of the United Church of Christ
555 W. James St., Lancaster 17603
Rev. Dr. Ann Schoup, Dir. of Admis.

La Salle University
1900 W. Olney Ave., Philadelphia 19141
Br. Gerald Fitzgerald, Dir. of Admis.
See listing under "Universities"

† Lutheran Theological Seminary
61 N.W. Confederate Ave., Gettysburg 17325
Herman G. Stuempfle, Jr., President

† Lutheran Theological Seminary
7301 Germantown Ave., Philadelphia 19119
Rev. Raymond Bost, President

Moravian College
1200 Main St., Bethlehem 18018

† Moravian Theological Seminary
60 W. Locust St., Bethlehem 18018

Philadelphia Theological Seminary
7372 Henry Ave., Philadelphia 19128
Danae L. Smith, Registrar
215-483-2480

† PITTSBURGH THEOLOGICAL SEMINARY
616 N. Highland Ave., Pittsburgh 15206
412-362-5610
Director of Admissions
800-451-4194
Established 1794. Presbyterian-related. Coed. seminary. Accreditation: ATS, MSACS. Annual tuition: $5,832; other expenses vary. On-campus dorms and apts. Enrollment: 312 full-time. Faculty: 22. Day or evening study options. Library: 220,000 volumes. Degrees: Master of Divinity, MA, Master of Sacred Theology. Also joint degrees with area schools, including PhD; MDIV/MSW; MDIV/MBA; MDIV/JD; MDIV/Library Science; MDIV/Master of Health Admin.; MDIV/MS in public policy. Mission is to be a caring, ecumenical community, to nurture personal faith, corporate worship, and ministry; to promote global consciousness and service.

Reformed Presbyterian Theological Seminary
7418 Penn Ave., Pittsburgh 15208
Rev. Bruce C. Stewart, President
412-731-8690

† St. Charles Borromeo Seminary
1000 E. Wynnewood Rd., Wynnewood 19096
610-667-3394

† St. Vincent College
300 Fraser Purchase Rd., Latrobe 15650

Seton Hill College, Greensburg 15601
Peter Egan, Dir. of Admis.
800-826-6234 or 412-838-4255

Thiel College
75 College Ave., Greenville 16125
Robert Weaver, Dir. of Admis.

† Trinity Episcopal School for Ministry
311 11th St., Ambridge 15003
Sandra Griffin, Dir. of Admis.

WESTMINSTER COLLEGE
New Wilmington 16172
Richard Dana Paul, Dir. of Admis.
412-946-7100

† Westminster Theological Seminary
P.O. Box 27009, Philadelphia 19118
Dr. William S. Barker, Academic Dean

SOUTH CAROLINA

Anderson College
316 S. Boulevard, Anderson 29621
Carl D. Lockman, Dir. of Admis.
800-542-3594

Bob Jones University, Greenville 29614
David Christ, Dir. of Admis.
See listing under "Universities"

Columbia Biblical Seminary
P.O. Box 3122, Columbia 29230
Lawrence Dabeck, Dir. of Admis.
See listing under "Biblical Studies"

† Columbia International University
P.O. Box 3122, Columbia 29230
Frank Bedell, Dir. of Admis.
See listing under "Biblical Studies"

† Erskine College & Seminary
Washington St., Due West 29639
Dot Carter, Dir. of Admis.

† Lutheran Theological Southern Seminary
4201 Main St., Columbia 29203
John Largen, Dir. of Admis.

SOUTH DAKOTA

† NORTH AMERICAN BAPTIST SEMINARY
1525 S. Grange Ave., Sioux Falls 57105
Randy Reese, Dir. of Admis.
800-440-NABS (6227)

SIOUX FALLS COLLEGE
1501 S. Prairie Ave., Sioux Falls 57105
Susan Reese, Dir. of Admis.
800-888-1047
See listing under "Universities"

TENNESSEE

Carson-Newman College
P.O. Box 70552, Jefferson City 37760
See listing under "Universities"

† Church of God School of Theology
900 Walker St., N.E., Cleveland 37311

David Lipscomb University
3901 Granny White Pike, Nashville 37204-3951
Wade Sandrell, Dir. of Admis.
800-333-4358

† Emmanuel School of Religion
One Walker Dr., Johnson City 37601
David Fulks, Dir. of Admis.
800-933-3771

Harding University Graduate School of Religion
1000 Cherry Rd., Memphis 38117
Robert Brady, Dir. of Admis.
800-680-0809

† Memphis Theological Seminary
168 E. Parkway S, Memphis 38104
Dr. J. David Hester, President
901-458-8232

Mid-America Baptist Theological Seminary
1255 Poplar Ave., Memphis 38104

::: Seminary Extension Independent Study Institute
901 Commerce St. #500, Nashville 37203-3631
615-242-2453

Southern Missionary College
P.O. Box 370, Collegedale 37315

Union University
2447 US Highway 45 Bypass, Jackson 38305
Dr. James Baggett, Dean
901-668-1818
See listing under "Universities"

† University of the South
735 University Ave., Sewanee 37375

† Vanderbilt University
West End Ave., Nashville 37240

TEXAS

† Austin Presbyterian Theological Seminary
100 E. 27th St., Austin 78705
Dr. Robert Shelton, Academic Dean
512-472-6736

Baptist Missionary Association Theological Seminary
1530 E. Pine St., Jacksonville 75766
Philip Bryan, President

Concordia Lutheran College
3400 N. Interstate 35, Austin 78705
Kevin Pieper, Dir. of Admis.

Dallas Theological Seminary
3909 Swiss Ave., Dallas 75204
Eugene W. Pond, Dir. of Admis.

East Texas Baptist University
1200 N. Grove Ave., Marshall 75670

† Episcopal Theological Seminary of the Southwest
P.O. Box 2247, Austin 78768
Durstan McDonald, Dean

Houston Graduate School of Theology
6910 Fannin #207, Houston 77030

Incarnate Word College
4301 Broadway St., San Antonio 78209
Sr. Sally Mitchell, Dean of Enrollment

† Oblate School of Theology
285 Oblate Dr., San Antonio 78216-6693
Rev. Robert E. Lampert, VP Academic Affairs
210-341-1366

† Southern Methodist University
   Hillcrest at University, Dallas 75275

† Southwestern Baptist Theological Seminary
   2001 W. Seminary Dr., Fort Worth 76122

† Texas Christian University
   2800 S. University Dr., Ft. Worth 76129
   Dr. Edward Boehm, Jr., Dean of Admissions

Texas Lutheran College
   1000 W. Court St., Seguin 78155
   Jennifer B. Ehlers, Dir. of Admis.

University of Dallas
   1845 E. Northgate Dr., Irving 75062
   Jim Whitaker, Dir. of Admis.

† University of St. Thomas
   3812 Montrose Blvd., Houston 77006
   Elsie Biron, Dir. of Admis.

VIRGINIA

::: **CATHOLIC HOME STUDY INSTITUTE**
   9 Loudoun St., S.E., Leesburg 22075-3012
   800-258-2474

† Eastern Mennonite College
   1200 Park Rd., Harrisonburg 22801
   Jerry Miller, Dir. of Admis.

LIBERTY UNIVERSITY
   P.O. Box 20000, Lynchburg 24506
   Jay Spencer, VP Recruitment
   800-376-2800
   See listing under "Universities"

† Presbyterian School of Christian Education
   1205 Palmyra Ave., Richmond 23227

† Protestant Episcopal Theological Seminary in
   Virginia
   3737 Seminary Rd., Alexandria 22304

Regent University College of Theology
   1000 Centerville Tpke., Virginia Beach 23464

† Union Theological Seminary in Virginia
   3401 Brook Rd., Richmond 23227
   Director of Admissions

† Virginia Union University School of Theology
   1601 W. Leigh St., Richmond 23220

WASHINGTON

Lutheran Bible Institute of Seattle
   4221 228th Ave., S.E., Issaquah 98027
   Dorothy Baumgartner, Director of Admissions
   800-843-5659

NORTHWEST BAPTIST SEMINARY
   4301 N. Stevens St., Tacoma 98407
   206-759-6104

Northwest College of the Assemblies of God
   P.O. Box 579, Kirkland 98083-0579
   Bob Foster, Dir. of Public Relations

Seattle University
   Broadway Ave. & Madison, Seattle 98122
   Lee Gerig, Dean of Admissions

Walla Walla College
   204 S. College Ave., College Place 99324

WEST VIRGINIA

APPALACHIAN BIBLE COLLEGE
   P.O. Box ABC, Bradley 25818
   Dr. Daniel Anderson, President
   Cathie P. Canary, Dir. of Admis.
   Established 1950. Private. Coed. Accreditation:
   AABC, State College and University System of WV.
   Tuition: $3,800. Room and board $2,700. Fees: $410.
   Enrollment: 250. Faculty: 16. Student-faculty ratio:
   15:1. Degrees: AA, BA, BTh, Bible Certificate. Library:
   35,000+ volumes. 20 buildings on 120+ acres. An
   independent, fundamental, non-denominational
   school. The majority of the student body are members
   of independent Bible and independent Baptist
   churches. Call the admissions office toll-free at 800-
   6789-ABC.

WEST VIRGINIA WESLEYAN COLLEGE
   59 College Ave., Buckhannon 26201
   Robert Skinner, Director of Admission
   See listing under "Universities"

WISCONSIN

Carthage College
   2001 Alford Dr., Kenosha 53140
   Brenda A. Porter, VP Enrollment

Lakeland College
   P.O. Box 359, Sheboygan 53082

Marian College of Fond du Lac
   45 S. National Ave., Fond du Lac 54935
   Carol Reichenberger, Dean of Admissions

Marquette University
   1217 W. Wisconsin Ave., Milwaukee 53233
   Raymond A. Brown, Dean of Admissions

† Nashotah House
   2777 Mission Rd., Nashotah 53058
   The Very Rev. Gary W. Kriss, Dean
   414-646-3371

† Sacred Heart School of Theology
   P.O. Box 429, Hales Corners 53130
   Rev. Thomas Garvey, Rector

† St. Francis Seminary
   3257 S. Lake Dr., Milwaukee 53235
   Rev. Andrew Nelson, Dean

St. Norbert College
   100 Grant St., De Pere 54115
   Craig S. Wesley, Dean of Admission
   See listing under "Universities"

PUERTO RICO

Dominican Study Center of Bayamon Central
   University
   P.O. Box 1968, Bayamon 00960

† Evangelical Seminary of Puerto Rico
   776 Ponce de Leon Ave., San Juan 00925
   Rosa E. Rosado, Registrar

UNIVERSITIES AND COLLEGES - COEDUCATIONAL

ALABAMA

ALABAMA A & M UNIVERSITY
P.O. Box 908, Normal 35762
Dr. David B. Henson, President
James O. Heyward Sr., Director of Admissions
205-851-5245
   Established 1875. Public. Coed. Accreditation:
SACS, NCATE, ASDE, SIAC, ALA. Tuition: $1,550.
Room and board: $2,195. Fees: $100. Enrollment:
5,600. Student-faculty ratio: 19:1. Degrees offered: BS,
AB, MS, EdS, PhD, MBA. 2,000 acre campus. Land
grant, comprehensive university. Multicultural, 450
foreign students.

Alabama State University
   P.O. Box 271, Montgomery 36101

Athens State College
   300 N. Beaty St., Athens 35611
   Larry McCoy, Director of Admissions

Auburn University, Auburn 36849

Auburn University at Montgomery
   7300 University Dr., Montgomery 36117
   H. H. Funderburk, VP

Birmingham Southern College
   900 Arkadelphia Rd., Birmingham 35254

Faulkner University
   5345 Atlanta Hwy., Montgomery 36109

Huntingdon College
   1500 E. Fairview Ave., Montgomery 36106-2148
   Carolyn A. Phillips, Dean of Enrollment
   800-763-0313

Jacksonville State University
   700 Pelham Rd. N., Jacksonville 36265

LIVINGSTON UNIVERSITY
Station #4, Livingston 35470
Don Hines, President
Ervin L. Wood, Vice President, Student Affairs
205-652-9661
   Established 1835. Public. Accreditation: SACS.
Calender Year: Quarter. Yearly cost: Tuition: $1,740.
Room and board: $2,466. Fees: $270. Enrollment:
2,100. Student-faculty ratio: 18:1. 62% of faculty hold
doctorates. Colleges of Liberal Arts, Business and
Commerce, Education, Natural Science and Mathe-
matics. School of Nursing. Rural, 590 acre campus.
NCAA Division II Mens' sports: football, basketball,
baseball, tennis. Women's sports: softball, basketball,
volleyball, tennis. Quarterly theater productions.
Choral. Jazz programs. Marching band. Federal financial aid. Scholarships available.

Miles College
   P.O. Box 3800, Birmingham 35208

Oakwood College
   Oakwood Rd., N.W., Huntsville 35896

Samford University
   800 Lakeshore Dr., Birmingham 35229
   Martha Ann Cox, Dean of Academic Services

Selma University, 1501 Lapsley St., Selma 36701
   M. C. Cleveland, Jr., President
   Rowena P. Cleveland, Dir. of Admis.

Southern Christian University
   P.O. Box 240240, Montgomery 36124
   Mac Adkins, Dir. of Admis.

Spring Hill College
   4000 Dauphin St., Mobile 36608
   Ben Hamd, Dir. of Admis.

STILLMAN COLLEGE
P.O. Box 1430, Tuscaloosa 35403
Barbara K. Smith, Director of Admissions
205-349-4240
   Established 1876. Private. Coed. Accreditation:
SACS, Alabama State Department of Education. Tuition: $5,200. Room and board: $3,100. Enrollment:
865. Faculty: 63. Student-faculty ratio: 15:1. Degrees:
BA, BS. 17 buildings on 100 acres. Presbyterian affiliated with 16 majors and minors. Cooperative programs in Engineering, Nursing, ROTC, Social Work,
Allied Health, and Law also offered. Competitive
sports (basketball, baseball, tennis, track and field,
and volleyball). Outstanding musical department
(choir and band). School calendar: semester (fall and
spring) with seven week summer session.

Talladega College
   627 Battle St., W., Talladega 35160

Troy State University, Troy 36082
   Jim Hutto, Dean of Enrollment Services

Troy State University at Dothan
   P.O. Box 8368, Dothan 36304
   Bob Willis, Dir. of Undergraduate Admissions

Troy State University at Montgomery
   P.O. Box 4419, Montgomery 36103

Tuskegee University
   Tuskegee Institute 36088

University of Alabama
   P.O. Box 870132, Tuscaloosa 35487-0132
   Roy Smith, Dir. of Admis.

University of Alabama at Birmingham
   University Station, Birmingham 35294

UNIVERSITY OF ALABAMA IN HUNTSVILLE
P.O. Box 1247, Huntsville 35899
Ron R. Koger Ed.D., Dir. of Admis.
205-895-6070
   Established 1969. Public. Coed. Accreditation:
SACS, ABET, NLN, CSAB, ACS. Tuition: $2,418 resi-
dent, $4,836 non-resident. Room & Board: $3,450.
Undergraduate enrollment: 2,674 full-time, 3,439
part-time. Graduate enrollment: 1,860. Faculty: 282.

Student-faculty ratio: 18:1. Degrees: BS, BA, BSBA,
BSE, MS, MSM, Ph.D., BSN, MSN, MA. 20 buildings
on 350 acres. Comprehensive research university located in the Tennessee Valley of northern Alabama.
Huntsville is the locale of major government and
private research centers. Metropolitan population approaching 300,000.

UNIVERSITY OF MOBILE
P.O. Box 13220, Mobile 36663-0220
Dr. Michael Magnoli, President
H. Shoemaker, VP for Student Services
Kim Leousis, Dir. of Admissions
Barbara Smith, Registrar
205-675-5990 or 800-WIN-RAMS
   Established 1961. Baptist. Branch campus in San
Marcos, Carazo, Nicaragua. Accreditation: SACS,
NLN. Approved by US Department of Education,
Alabama Department of Education, and Veterans Administration. Tuition and fees: $6,150. Room and
board: $3,580. Enrollment: 1900+ students. Single-
sex dorms available; students required to live on
campus or with family. Federal, state and significant
institutional financial aid available. Institutional application and FAFSA required.
   Undergraduates BA, BS, BSN and ADN available in
34+ majors plus preprofessional programs in medicine, dentistry, pharmacy, veterinary medicine, law
and engineering plus dual degree programs in allied
health with the University of Alabama in Birmingham, and in engineering with Auburn University.
Army and Air Force ROTC are available. Graduate
degrees: MA in early childhood, elementary, and
secondary education, religion studies, MSN in nursing; MBA program.
   Evening courses and summer school are taught. A
special Summer Accelerated Program for exceptional
high school rising Juniors. Degree completion program for adults over 25.
   Admission requirements include application and
$30 fee, ACT scores, high school transcripts (college
transcripts for transfers). TOEFL and declaration of
finances for foreign students. Rolling application
deadlines.
   Faculty: 66 full-time, 69% with terminal degrees.
Student-faculty ratio: 15:1. 765 acre campus, forest
learning center, swimming pool, lighted tennis
courts, softball field and baseball field. Library:
128,300 volumes.
   Moderate climate, convenient to Gulf beaches.
Wide range of student activities including social and
service clubs, scholastic societies, religious organizations, special interest groups, intramural activities,
and intercollegiate athletics in golf, men's and
women's basketball, tennis, women's softball, men's
and women's soccer, men's baseball, and men's and
women's cross country.

University of Montevallo, Montevallo 35115

University of North Alabama
University Station, Florence 35632

University of South Alabama
307 University Blvd. N., Mobile 36688

ALASKA

ALASKA PACIFIC UNIVERSITY
4101 University Dr., Anchorage 99508
Director of Admissions
Established 1959. Private. Coed. Accreditation: NASC. Tuition: $7,560. Room and board: $4,010. Fees: $130. Enrollment: 347 full-time, 336 part-time. Faculty: 90. Student-faculty ratio: 12:1. Degrees offered: AA, BA, Masters. Library: 384,698 volumes. 6 buildings on a 300 acre campus. Consortium library shared with state university.

Sheldon Jackson College
801 Lincoln St., Sitka 99835
Dennis Trotter, Dir. of Admis.
907-747-5221

University of Alaska Anchorage
3211 Providence Dr., Anchorage 99508
907-786-1480

University of Alaska Fairbanks
Fairbanks 99775

University of AK-Bristol Bay Campus
P.O. Box 1070, Dillingham 99576

University of Alaska-Chuchi Campus
P.O. Box 297, Kotzebue 99752

University of Alaska/Matanuska-Susitna College
P.O. Box 2889, Palmer 99645

University of Alaska Southeast
11120 Glacier Hwy., Juneau 99801
Greg Wagner, Coordinator of Admissions

UNIVERSITY OF ALASKA SOUTHEAST-KETCHIKAN
2600 7th Ave., Ketchikan 99901-5798
Dr. Frances Feinerman, Director
William Trudeau, Student Services
Established 1954. State. Coed. Accreditation: NASC. Yearly tuition: $1,670 resident, $5,500 nonresident. Est. total yrly. exp.: $8,000. Faculty: 10 full-time, 50 part-time. Degrees: AA, AAS in Business Office Administration, Travel Industry and Hospitality Industry. Certificates in Accounting, Business Tech, Office Skills, Travel Industry, Hospitality Industry and Welding. Library: 42,000 volumes. 4 buildings on 40 acres. UAS-Ketchikan is a member of the statewide University of Alaska system. Ketchikan is located on Revilla Island, on the beautiful inside passage of southeast Alaska.

ARIZONA

Arizona College of the Bible
2045 W. Northern Ave., Phoenix 85021
800-847-2138 or 602-995-2670
See listing under "Biblical Studies"

Arizona State University, Tempe 85287

CAD Institute/The CAD Center
4100 E. Broadway Rd., Phoenix 85040
Dominic Pistillo, President
CAD and Virtual Reality Degree
800-658-5744

Conservatory of Recording Arts & Sciences
1110 E. Missouri Ave. #530, Phoenix 85014
800-562-6383
See listing under "Music"

Grand Canyon University
3300 W. Camelback Rd., Phoenix 85017
Dr. Bill Williams, President
See listing under "Liberal Arts and Sciences"

Northern Arizona University
P.O. Box 4092, Flagstaff 86011
Dr. Margaret Cibik, Dir. of Admis.

Prescott College
220 Grove Ave., Prescott 86301
Shari Sterling, Asst. Dir. of Admis.

SOUTHWESTERN COLLEGE
A Conservative Baptist Bible College
2625 E. Cactus Rd., Phoenix 85032
800-247-2697

University of Arizona, Tucson 85721
Loyd Bell, Director of Admissions

University of Arizona Medical Center
1501 N. Campbell Ave., Tucson 85724
Dr. James E. Dahlen, Dean

University of Phoenix
4615 E. Elwood St., Phoenix 85040
Sue Murphy, Registrar

ARKANSAS

Arkansas College
2300 Highland Rd., Batesville 72501
Jonathan M. Stroud, Dean of Admissions
800-423-2542

Arkansas State University
P.O. Box 1630, State University 72467

Arkansas Tech University
215 W. O St., Russellville 72801

Harding University
900 E. Center Ave., Searcy 72149

Henderson State University
1100 Henderson St., Arkadelphia 71999

Hendrix College
1601 Harkrider St., Conway 72032

John Brown University
2000 W. University, Siloam Springs 72761
Don Crandall, Director of Enrollment Management

Ouachita Baptist University
410 Ouachita St., Arkadelphia 71998
Randy Garner, Dir. of Admis.
800-DIAL-OBU

Philander Smith College
812 W. 13th St., Little Rock 72202

Southern Arkansas University
SAU Box 1402, Magnolia 71753

University of Arkansas at Fayetteville
Fayetteville 72701

University of Arkansas at Little Rock
2801 S. University Ave., Little Rock 72204

University of Arkansas at Monticello
P.O. Box 3596, Monticello 71656

University of Arkansas at Pine Bluff
1200 University Dr., Pine Bluff 71601-2799

University of Central Arkansas
201 Donaghey Ave., Conway 72035

University of the Ozarks
415 College Ave., Clarksville 72830

WILLIAMS BAPTIST COLLEGE
P.O. Box 3667, Walnut Ridge 72476
Scott Wright, Dir. of Admis.
800-722-4434
Established 1941. Private. Coed. Accreditation: NCACS. Tuition: $3,110. Room and board: $2,016. Enrollment: 447 full-time, 157 part-time. Faculty: 26. Student-faculty ratio: 17:1. Degrees: AA, AS, BA, BS. Library: 76,816 volumes. 40 buildings on 175 acres. Southerland-Mabee Center includes gymnasium, jogging track, weight room, racquetball courts. Varsity sports include: men's basketball and baseball; women's basketball and volleyball. 1993 women's basketball team was NCCAA national champions. Honors program. 2 hours from Little Rock or Memphis.

CALIFORNIA

American Armenian International College
1950 Third St., La Verne 91750
John Khanjian, Academic Dean

AMERICAN COLLEGE FOR THE APPLIED ARTS
1651 Westwood Blvd., Los Angeles 90024
310-470-2000
Kevin Martin, Dir. of Admis.
Private. Coed. Non-denominational. Degrees: AA, BFA in fashion design, fashion marketing, interior design, commercial art, and AA and BBA in business administration. Accreditation: SACS. Financial aid. Student housing. Professional faculty active in the industry, field trips, study tours, internships, placement, ESL program. Summer sessions. Study abroad and MBA programs available at The American College in London.
(See listing under "Study Abroad".)

Antioch University
4800 Lincoln Blvd., Marina Del Rey 90292

Antioch University
777 Valencia St., San Francisco 94110

ANTIOCH UNIVERSITY
801 Garden St. #101, Santa Barbara 93101
805-962-8179

Armstrong University
2222 Harold Way, Berkeley 94704
Rowena Ricafrentre, Dir. of Admis.
510-848-2500

Azusa Pacific University
P.O. Box 7000, Azusa 91702

Biola University
13800 Biola Ave., La Mirada 90639
Wayne Chute, Dean of Admissions

BROOKS INSTITUTE OF PHOTOGRAPHY
801 Alston Rd., Santa Barbara 93108
Lynn Cederquist, Dir. of Admis.
805-966-3888 Ext. 217 or Ext. 218
See listing under "Photography"

California Baptist College
8432 Magnolia Ave., Riverside 92504
800-782-3382

CALIFORNIA COAST UNIVERSITY
700 N. Main St., Santa Ana 92701
Admissions Office: 800-854-8768 or 714-547-9625
Thomas Neal, President
Linda B. Smith, VP Academic Affairs
William Barcroft, Dean of Admissions
Established 1973. Proprietary. Coed. Accreditation: National Association of Private Non-Traditional Schools & Colleges, California State Department of Education, charter member California Association of State Approved Colleges & Universities, member Association for Adult & Continuing Education. Tuition: $2,200-$3,500. Enrollment: 7,500.
A private college offering off-campus independent study programs in the traditional areas of business administration, management, engineering, psychology, & education. Admissions: rolling trimester, requires official transcripts, letters of recommendation, detailed curriculum vita or occupational history.
Process: evaluation of prior academic work followed by analysis of occupational history, including participation in workshops, seminars, training programs, specialized projects for credit. Credit is demonstrated by challenge exams or specialized course by course independent study programs.
Residency: All course work may be completed off campus, utilizing correspondence methods. All doctoral candidates must meet with faculty advisors in person, upon completion of doctoral dissertation. Scholarships: Interest free loans available to students.

California College for Health Sciences
222 W. 24th St., National City 91950
619-477-4800

California College of Arts & Crafts
5212 Broadway, Oakland 94618
Sheri McKenzie, Dir. of Admis.
510-653-6522

California Institute of Technology
1201 E. California Blvd., Pasadena 91125
Carole L. Snow, Dir. of Admis.
800-568-8324

California Lutheran University
60 Olsen Rd., Thousand Oaks 91360
800-252-5884

California Polytechnic State University
San Luis Obispo 93407
Helen Linstrum, Dir. of Admis.

California State Polytechnic University
3801 W. Temple Ave., Pomona 91768

California State University, Chico
Chico 95929-0720
Dr. Kenneth Edson, Dir. of Admis.

California State University, Dominguez Hills
1000 E. Victoria St., Carson 90747

California State University, Fresno
Shaw & Cedar Ave., Fresno 93710

California State University, Long Beach
1250 Bellflower Blvd., Long Beach 90840

California State University, Los Angeles
5151 Paseo Rancho Castilla, Los Angeles 90032

California State University, Northridge
18111 Nordhoff St., Northridge 91330
Ned C. Reynolds, Dir. of Admis.

California State University, Sacramento
6000 J St., Sacramento 95819

California State University, San Bernardino
5500 University Pky., San Bernardino 92407
909-880-5188

California State University-Bakersfield
9001 Stockdale Hwy., Bakersfield 93311
Dr. Homer S. Montalvo, Dir. of Admis.

California State University-Fullerton
Fullerton 92632

California State University-Hayward
25800 Carlos Bee Blvd., Hayward 94542

California State University
820 W. Los Vallecitos, San Marcos 92069

California State University-Stanislaus
801 W. Monte Vista Ave., Turlock 95382
Frances Cook, Dean Enrollment Services

Chapman University
333 N. Glassell St., Orange 92666
Michael Drummy, Dir. of Admis.

Christian Heritage College
2100 Greenfield Dr., El Cajon 92019
Pam Daly, Dir. of Admis.
800-676-2242

Claremont McKenna College
890 Columbia Ave., Claremont 91711

COGSWELL POLYTECHNICAL COLLEGE
10420 Bubb Rd., Cupertino 95014
Paul Schreivogel, Dean of Student Services
800-264-7955
Established 1887. Private. Coed. Accreditation: WASC. Tuition: $6,600. Enrollment: 100 full-time, 248 part-time. Faculty: 42. Student-faculty ratio: 9:1. Degrees: BS Engineering Technology, BS Electrical and Software Engineering. Library: 12,000 volumes. 1 building on 4 acres. Only Bachelor of Science degree in Music Engineering Technology and Bachelor of Arts degree in Computer and Video Imaging.

Coleman College
7380 Parkway Dr., La Mesa 91942

College of Notre Dame
1500 Ralston Ave., Belmont 94002
Greg M. Smith, PhD., Dir. of Admis.

CONCORDIA UNIVERSITY
1530 Concordia, Irvine 92715
Stan Meyer, Dean of Admission
800-229-1200
Established 1972. Private. Coed. Accreditation: WASC. Tuition: $8,895. Room and board: $3,570. Fees: $420. Enrollment: 571 full-time, 700 part-time. Faculty: 34. Student-faculty ratio: 16:1. Degrees: BA, MA. Library: 80,000 volumes. 16 buildings on 65 acres. Christ College Irvine is a liberal arts college of the Lutheran Church-Missouri Synod located in Orange County, California. CCI offers programs in teacher education, business administration, social work, natural science, and church careers. Students

may participate in theatre and music activities as well as intramural and intercollegiate sports for men and women.

Consortium of the California State University
400 Golden Shore St., Long Beach 90802

Design Institute of San Diego
8555 Commerce Ave., San Diego 92121
MaryJo Kalamon, Director

DOMINICAN COLLEGE OF SAN RAFAEL
50 Acacia Ave., San Rafael 94901-8008
Office of Admissions
800-788-3522

Dominican School of Philosophy & Theology
2401 Ridge Rd., Berkeley 94709
Ingrid Honore, C.S.J., Dir. of Admis.
510-849-2030

Drew University
1621 E. 120th St., Los Angeles 90059

Fresno Pacific College
1717 S. Chestnut Ave., Fresno 93702
209-453-2039

Golden Gate University
536 Mission St., San Francisco 94105

Harvey Mudd College, Claremont 91711

Holy Names College
3500 Mountain Blvd., Oakland 94619

Humboldt State University
1 Harps St. Arcata 95521
Margi Stevenson, Dir. of Admis.

Humphreys College
6650 Inglewood Ave., Stockton 95207
209-478-0800

John F. Kennedy University
12 Altarinda Rd., Orinda 94563

La Sierra University
4700 Pierce St., Riverside 92505
800-874-5587

LINCOLN UNIVERSITY
281 Masonic Ave., San Francisco 94118
Clarence Rippel, Acting President
Accredited Member ACICS

Loma Linda University, Loma Linda 92350
800-422-4LLU

Loyola Marymount University
Loyola Blvd. at W. 80th, Los Angeles 90045
M. L'Heureux, Dir. of Admis.

Master's College
P.O. Box 221450, Newhall 91322
Don Gilmore, Dir. of Admis.

Menlo College
1000 El Camino Real, Atherton 94027

National University
4141 Camino del Rio, S., San Diego 92108

National University
2022 University Dr., Vista 92083
Dr. Shahram Azordegan, Dean

NEW COLLEGE OF CALIFORNIA
50 Fell St., San Francisco 94102
415-241-1300

Occidental College
1600 Campus Rd., Los Angeles 90041

OTIS COLLEGE OF ART AND DESIGN
2401 Wilshire Blvd., Los Angeles 90057
Neil Hoffman, President
See listing under "Art"

Pacific Union College
1 Angwin Ave., Angwin 94508
Dr. Gary Gifford, Dir. of Admis.

PATTEN COLLEGE
2433 Coolidge Ave., Oakland 94601
Dr. Priscilla Benham, President
Sharon Barta, Associate Director of Admissions
510-533-8300
Established 1945. Affiliated with Christian Cathedral Church. Coed. Accreditation: WASC. Tuition: $4,620. Room and board: $5,135. Enrollment: full-time 131, part-time 593. Faculty: 27. Degrees: credential program, AA, BA. Library: 20,000 volumes. 10 buildings on 5 acres. Patten is located within a few minutes of a great number of recreational, athletic, cultural, & religious activities.

Pepperdine University
24255 Pacific Coast Hwy., Malibu 90263
Paul Long, Dean of Admissions
310-456-4392

Pitzer College
1050 N. Mills Ave., Claremont 91711
Katharine Leighton, Dir. of Admis.

Point Loma Nazarene College
3900 Lomaland Dr., San Diego 92106
Bill Young, Dir. of Admis.

Pomona College
333 N. College Way, Claremont 91711
Peter W. Stanley, President

St. Mary's College of California
P.O. Box 4267, Moraga 94575

San Diego State University
5300 Campanile Dr., San Diego 92115

San Francisco State University
1600 Holloway Ave., San Francisco 94132
Corwin Bjonerud, Dir. of Admis.

San Jose State University
1 Washington Sq., San Jose 95192

Santa Clara University, Santa Clara 95053

Sonoma State University
1801 E. Cotati Ave., Rohnert Park 94928

Southern California College
55 Fair Dr., Costa Mesa 92626
Richard Hardy, Asst. Dean for Enrollment

Southern California Institute of Architecture
5454 Beethoven St., Los Angeles 90066
310-574-3625

Stanford University, Stanford 94305

UNITED STATES INTERNATIONAL UNIVERSITY
10455 Pomerado Rd., San Diego 92131
619-693-4772
An international focus is an integral part of all degree programs at United States International University. The University has a 160 acre campus in San Diego and campuses in Nairobi, and Mexico City. Founded in 1952 as California Western University, USIU offers a chance to learn from an international faculty and to study with fellow students from eighty-eight countries. In its academic programs the university strives to provide students with an awareness, knowledge, and appreciation of diverse cultures and of the universality and commonality of human values. Students master a field of knowledge and its multicultural applications in an environment which encourages intellectual and scholarly development. USIU strives to foster an openness to a wide range of ideas, cultures and people, and to enhance personal growth.
USIU has an overall enrollment of 1,485; undergraduates account for 21 percent of the total student population. On each of the university's campuses students participate in a wide range of extracurricular programs including intramural sports, trips to nearby attractions, forums on topics of current interest, and student organizations, including clubs representing many cultures throughout the world. Placement, health and counseling services are available. Cars are permitted.
USIU offers graduate studies through its College of Arts and Sciences and College of Business Administration. Details on programs leading to master's degrees in various areas and doctoral degrees in business (D.B.A.) in education (Ed.D.), and in several areas of psychology (Psy.D.) are available from the Office of Admissions.

University of California, Los Angeles
1247 Murphy Hall, Los Angeles 90024

University of California at Berkeley
Sproul Hall, Berkeley 94720

University of California, Davis
376 Mrak Hall, Davis 95616

University of California, Irvine
Irvine 92715

University of California, Riverside
P.O. Box 112, Riverside 92521

University of California, San Diego
9450 Gilman Dr., La Jolla 92092

University of California, Santa Barbara
Santa Barbara 93106

University of California-Santa Cruz
Santa Cruz 95064
Joseph Allen, Dir. of Admis.

UNIVERSITY OF JUDAISM/LEE COLLEGE
15600 Mulholland Dr., Los Angeles 90077
Dr. Robert Wexler, President
Tamara Greenebaum, Dean of Admissions
310-476-0236 or 310-476-9777, Fax 310-471-1278
University established 1947; undergraduate school Lee College established 1982. Private. Jewish. Coed. Accreditation: WASC. Enrollment: 175. Library: 100,000 volumes. 8 buildings on 26 acres. Tuition: $10,560. Room and board: $6,200. Undergraduate non-need based Merit Scholarships can provide four years of free tuition and Leadership Scholarships can provide 75% of tuition.
Undergraduate majors in Business, Psychology, Literature, Judaic Studies, Political Science, Bioethics, interdisciplinary studies. Core curriculum integrates Jewish and Western civilizations. Independent study and internships are encouraged.
Master's degrees available in nonprofit Business Administration, Jewish Education, Jewish Studies, Hebrew Letters and Rabbinic Literature. Rabbinic Program is jointly offered with Jewish Theological Seminary in New York.
Faculty are recognized scholars in their fields, and outstanding teachers who enjoy working closely with students. Lee College offers a 6:1 student-faculty ratio; average class size is 15. Classes characterized by reading and discussion.
Student life includes student government, radio station, yearbook, literary magazine, Shakespeare troupe, chorus, intramural sports, and dance team. Students have access to UCLA's recreational and athletic facilities. All activities are student-run, and the administration encourages leadership. While campus affiliation is Jewish and religious life is available, observance and participation are not mandatory. Students come from all types of communities — reform, conservative, orthodox, secular and non-Jewish.

Each modern residence hall has two lounges, cable TV and hospitality rooms. Each double-occupancy room has a private bathroom, heat and air-conditioning controls, twin closets, carpeting and ample free parking.
Admissions: Lee College deadline: January 31; joint rabbinical program deadline: January 1; other graduate deadlines: March 31. Applications accepted after deadlines on a space-available basis. Freshman and transfers submit application, transcripts, SAT or ACT, two letters of recommendation. Graduate students submit application, transcripts, GRE, two letters of recommendation. $25 application fee. Candidate normally notified of decision within two weeks after admission file completed.

University of La Verne
1950 3rd St., La Verne 91750
Mark Bornholdt, Dir. of Admis.

University of Redlands
P.O. Box 3080, Redlands 92373

University of San Diego
5998 Alcala Park, San Diego 92110
Warren Muller, Dir. of Admis.
619-260-4506

University of San Francisco
2130 Fulton St., San Francisco 94117
Bill Henley, Dir. of Admis.

University of Southern California
University Park Campus
Los Angeles 90089

University of the Pacific
School of Dentistry
2155 Webster St., San Francisco 94115

University of the Pacific
3601 Pacific Ave, Stockton 95211
Elliott J. Taylor, Dean of Admissions

West Coast University
440 Shatto Pl., Los Angeles 90020

West Coast University, Orange County Center
550 S. Main St., Orange 92668

WESTMONT COLLEGE
955 La Paz Rd., Santa Barbara 93108
David Morley, Dir. of Admis.
800-777-9011
Established in 1940 as a Christian liberal arts and sciences college. Academic excellence in the liberal arts and sciences within the context of evangelical Christianity. Coed. 90% residential. Accreditation: WASC. Tuition and fees: $15,186. Room and board: $5,304. Enrollment: 1,285. Faculty: 115. Degrees: BA, BS. Library: 150,000 volumes. 133 acres in the foothills of the Santa Ynez Mountains, overlooking the Pacific Ocean. 26 majors, preprofessional programs in law, medicine, dentistry, ministry, engineering, pharmacy, physical therapy, and veterinary medicine. Independent study and honors programs available. Special programs in England, Europe, San Francisco, Washington DC, Los Angeles, East Asia and at the Institute of Holy Land Studies in Jerusalem. Cooperative programs available with 13 member consortium colleges, and Daystar University in South Africa and Costa Rica.
Student life includes Westmont College Student Association, Christian Concerns (service, mission, and outreach programs) leadership development program, honor societies, multicultural student organization, political organizations, chorale and music ensembles, theatre productions, newspaper, literary magazine, yearbook, and a radio station.
Men participate in NAIA sports in basketball, baseball, soccer, track and field, cross-country and tennis. Women participate in soccer, volleyball, tennis, track and field, and cross-country. Intramural and club sports offered. Member of Golden State Athletic Conference as well.
Admission based on high school or college transcript, SAT/ACT scores, essays, recommendations - interviews are encouraged but not required. Early Action application deadline for freshmen is December 1. Application deadline for regular decision is February 15 for freshmen and March 15 for transfers. Transfer students without 24 units of academic work are required to submit high school transcript. 80% of Westmont students receive financial aid packages in the form of grants, scholarships, loans, and on campus work. Merit aid is available. FAFSA, and FAF should be submitted no later than March 1.

Whittier College
13406 Philadelphia St., Whittier 90601
310-907-4238

WOODBURY UNIVERSITY
7500 Glenoaks Blvd., Burbank 91504
Dr. Paul E. Sago, President
Patrick N. Contrades, Director of Admission
818-767-0888
Established 1884. Private. Coed. Located 20 minutes from downtown LA on a 22 acre campus in the foothills. Enrollment: 1,106. Student-faculty ratio: 12:1. Accreditation: WASC, FIDER, granted candidacy status by NAAB. Degrees: BS in accounting, business administration, management, finance, international business, psychology and management, marketing, fashion marketing, computer information systems, history and government, graphic design, fashion design, interior design, BArch, MBA. 93-94 tuition: $12,120 (BS), $12,570 (BArch), Room and board: $5,490. 60% receive aid. 20% live in campus housing. Evening & Weekend courses available.

COLORADO

Adams State College, Alamosa 81102
Cheryl Billingsley, Dir. of Admis.
800-824-6494

College for Financial Planning
4695 S. Monaco St., Denver 80237

Colorado Christian University
180 S. Garrison St., Lakewood 80226
Debra Seefeldt, Dir. of Admis.

Colorado College
14 E. Cache La Poudre, Colorado Springs 80903
Terry Swenson, Dir. of Admis.

Colorado School of Mines
Weaver Towers-1811 Elm St.
Golden 80401-1873
Bill Young, Dir. of Enrollment Mgmt.
303-273-3220

Colorado State University
102 Administration Building, Fort Collins 80523
Mary Ontireros, Dir. of Admissions

COLORADO TECHNICAL COLLEGE

4435 N. Chestnut St., Colorado Springs 80907
719-598-0200

The transition from high-tech education to high-tech careers is Colorado Tech's specialty! Situated in the middle of a space age community known as Silicon Mountain, the college takes pride in its mission to serve high-tech businesses and industries by providing graduates able to hit the ground running in such fields as: computer engineering, computer science, electrical engineering, electronic engineering technology, telecommunications, systems management, and logistics. Colorado Tech, accredited by NCA and ABET, offers Associate, Bachelor and Master degrees.

Bachelor of Science degrees are offered in computer science, electrical engineering, computer engineering, logistics systems management, systems management, and telecommunication electronics technology. Master of Science degrees are offered in computer science, computer engineering, electrical engineering and management.

Colorado Tech believes students should not only learn in the classroom, but in the laboratory as well, applying their knowledge to real world problems. The professor and students work in an environment that encourages constant interaction in the learning process. Class size is limited to 40 students and labs are limited to 24 students. Colorado Tech's state of the art equipment is always available: no one waits in line.

It is no suprise that companies such as Digital, Loral, MCI, Apple, Atmel, Litton, United Technologies, Hewlett-Packard, Ford Microelectronics, GE Aerospace, Hughes Aircraft and Cray Research have chosen Colorado Springs with its USAF space center and US Space Foundation to locate facilities here. Many of these companies have representatives who sit on our advisory boards and many of our professors come from these companies.

The Colorado Springs area offers many recreational activities such as skiing, fishing, hunting, hiking, mountain climbing and four wheeling. NFL football, NBA basketball, National League baseball, the symphony and varied expressions of popular culture provide ample entertainment for every taste. Soar to meet your destiny through higher education at Colorado Tech.

Ft. Lewis College
1000 Rim Dr., Durango 81301

Mesa State College
P.O. Box 2647, Grand Junction 81502
Sherri Pe'a, Dir. of Admis.

Metropolitan State College of Denver
P.O. Box 173362, Campus Box 16
Denver 80217-3362

Naropa Institute
2130 Arapahoe Ave., Boulder 80302
Dr. Jana Lynn, Director of Admissions
303-546-3572

National College
2577 N. Chelton Rd., Colorado Springs 80909

National College
1325 S. Colorado Blvd. #100, Denver 80222

Nazarene Bible College
P.O. Box 15749, Colorado Springs 80935
Rev. Dale Miller, Dir. of Admis.
719-596-5110

Regis University
3333 Regis Blvd., Denver 80221
Robert Blust, Director of Admissions

ROCKY MOUNTAIN COLLEGE OF ART & DESIGN

6875 E. Evans Ave., Denver 80224
303-753-6046 or 800-888-2787
See listing under "Art"

Teikyo Loretto Heights University
3001 S. Federal Blvd., Denver 80236

United States Air Force Academy
Colorado Springs 80840

University of Colorado at Boulder
Boulder 80309
William A. Douglas, Dean of Admis.

University of Colorado at Colorado Springs
P.O. Box 7150, Colorado Springs 80933

University of Colorado at Denver
1200 Larimer, Denver 80204

University of Denver
2199 S. University Blvd., Denver 80210

University of Northern Colorado, Greeley 80639
Gary Gullickson, Dir. of Admis.
303-351-2881

University of Phoenix-Colorado Division
7800 E. Dorado Pl., Englewood 80111

University of Southern Colorado
2200 Bonforte Blvd., Pueblo 81001

WESTERN STATE COLLEGE OF COLORADO

Gunnison 81231
Dr. Kaye Howe, President
Monica Bruning, Director of Admissions
Marty Somero, Director of Financial Aid
800-876-5309 or 303-943-2119

Established 1911. Accreditation: NCACS, NCATE, AACTE, NASM, Colorado Department of Education, National Commission of Accounting, Colorado State Board of Accountancy.

Unique among college academic calendars, Western offers an innovative education characterized by problem-solving and both cooperative and experiential activities. This calendar is known as the "Western Scholars Year." Students pursue their studies choosing three of four regular terms offered throughout the year: Fall (12 weeks), Winter (8 weeks), Spring (12 weeks), and Summer (8 weeks). Weekly schedules of classes will be more intensive, and greater concentration on each subject will be focused on each subject taken in a given term. Each Wednesday will be class free. This open time offers students the opportunity for cooperative learning, study groups, field trips, special workshops, seminars, and presentations by visiting scholars and artists.

Tuition (1992-93): $1,284 per year resident, $5,054 per year non-resident. Fees: $469 per year. Room and board: $3,404 per year. Total enrollment: 2,700 students. 14 residence halls house approximately 1,300 students. Freshmen are required to live on campus. Bachelor of Arts degrees offered in 21 major fields of study plus pre-professional areas. Classes taught by 140 professional staff — 70% hold PhD's. No graduate assistants teach. The student to faculty ratio is 20:1. Savage Library holds 110,000 volumes with 825 periodical subscriptions and 750,000 microform holdings. Extensive publications available through interlibrary cooperation and an automated search service. Financial Aid is available. Submit Free Application for Federal Student Aid (FAFSA) by April 1.

Admission Requirements: Applicants to Western must have graduated from an accredited high school with a minimum of 15 units. Recommended are 4 units of English, 3 units of mathematics including Algebra I & Algebra II, 2 units of social science and 2 units of natural science. Computer science and foreign language are also strongly encouraged. Applicants will be considered for admissions on the basis of their academic performance and background, standardized tests, and personal attributes. Automatic admittance is usually granted those meeting the following criteria: 1) A grade point average of 2.5 or better and/or rank in the upper 2/3 of the class. 2) Minimum score of a 20 on the ACT or 820 on the SAT test.

Western is located on 228 acres on the Western Slope of the Continental Divide. Recreational opportunites abound year round including: rafting, sailing, windsurfing, golfing, backpacking, camping, fishing, skiing and many others.

CONNECTICUT

Albertus Magnus College
700 Prospect St., New Haven 06511
Richard Lolatte, Dir. of Admissions
203-773-8501 or 800-578-9160

BRIDGEPORT ENGINEERING INSTITUTE

785 Unquowa Rd., Fairfield 06430
William M. Krummel, PhD, President
See listing under "Engineering"

Central Connecticut State University
1615 Stanley St., New Britain 06053

Connecticut College
270 Mohegan Ave., New London 06320

Eastern Connecticut State University
83 Windham St., Willimantic 06226
Dr. Arthur Forst, Dir of Admis.

Fairfield University
25 N. Benson Rd., Fairfield 06430

Paier College of Art
20 Gorham Ave., Hamden 06514

QUINNIPIAC COLLEGE

275 Mount Carmel Ave., Hamden 06518
John Lahey, President
Joan Isaac Mohr, VP and Dean of Admissions

Established 1929. Private. Coed. Accreditation: NEASC. Tuition: $11,250. Room and board: $5,790. Enrollment: 2,583 boarding, 3,444 day. Faculty 333. Degrees: BA, BS, MAT, MBA, MHS, MPS. Library: 290,000 volumes. 30 buildings on 170 acres. Gym. Suburban location at the base of Sleeping Giant State Park, close to New Haven and Yale University. Convenient to New York City, Boston, and Upper New England. Building a new $7 million School of Business Center.

RICHMOND COLLEGE

THE AMERICAN INTERNATIONAL UNIVERSITY IN LONDON
Queens Rd. Richmond, Surrey, TW10 6JP, England
U.S. Admissions Office: 19 Bay State Rd.
Boston MA 02215
Walter McCann, President
617-954-9942

Established 1971. Private. Coed. Accreditation: MSACS. Tuition per year (2 Semesters): $16,320 (includes room and board, insurance and student activity fee). Enrollment: 1,000 from 80 countries. Fully residential. Faculty: 100. Degrees: AA, BA, MBA. Library: 55,000 volumes. 2 campuses, one in downtown Kensington for juniors and seniors, the other in a beautiful 15 acre residential site in Richmond, SW London, for freshman and sophomores. Offers programs in 14 majors: Anthropology/Sociology, Business Administration and Economics, British Studies, Computer Science, Economics, Engineering (in conjunction with the George Washington University, Washington DC), English Literature, History, History of Art, International Business, Mathematical Sciences, Political Science, Psychology, Studio Art (with concentrations in Lens Media, Drama, Painting, Ceramics and Design). International Master of Business Administration degree. Career Apprenticeship and International Internship programs. Special theater program. U.S. students may enroll as new undergraduates, or study abroad at Richmond College for a year or semester as visiting students and transfer credits to other U.S. accredited universities. International student body. Summer sessions.

Sacred Heart University
5151 Park Ave., Fairfield 06432-1000
Dr. Anthony J. Cernera, President

Southern Connecticut State University
501 Crescent St., New Haven 06515

TEIKYO POST UNIVERSITY

800 Country Club Rd.
P.O. Box 2540, Waterbury 06723-2540
800-345-2562 or 203-596-4520

Established 1890. Private. Coed. Accreditation: NEASC. Tuition: $11,960. Room and board: $5,400. Application fee: $40. Enrollment: 996 full-time, 1,488 part-time. Faculty: 29 full-time, 260 part-time. Student-faculty ratio: 15:1. Degrees: AA, AS, BA, BS. Library: 55,000 volumes. 11 buildings on 70 acres. Excellent business majors with strong liberal arts and international component. Faculty with dynamic business experience, assistance to help students succeed in a global marketplace. ESL Institute.

Trinity College
300 Summit St., Hartford 06106
Dr. David Borus, Dean of Admissions

United States Coast Guard Academy
New London 06320
Brian Wright, Admissions

UNIVERSITY OF BRIDGEPORT

126 Park Ave., Bridgeport 06601
Andrew G. Nelson, Dean of Admis. & Financial Aid
203-576-4552

Established 1927. Private. Coed. Accreditation: NEASC, AACSB, ABET, NASAD, Commission on Dental Accreditation. Tuition: $12,020. Room and board: $6,540. Fees: $405. Enrollment: 1800. Faculty: 184. Student-faculty ratio: 11:1. Degrees offered: AS, AA, BS, BA, BES, BFA, MS, MBA, 6th year, Ed.D., DC. Library: 300,000 volumes. 95 buildings on 86 acres. Diverse student body representing 30 states and 60 countries; Division II athletics; Programs in Business, Engineering, Accounting, Dental Hygiene, Computer Science, Fashion Merchandising, Art, Design, Math and Science, Liberal Arts, Education, Communications, Music, Legal Assistant, Medical Technology, English, Human Services, Pre-Chiropractic Studies, MBA. Campus located 50 miles northeast of NYC.

University of Connecticut, Storrs 06268
Dr. Ann Quinley, Director

UNIVERSITY OF HARTFORD

200 Bloomfield Ave., West Hartford 06117
Richard Zeiser, Dir. of Admis.
203-768-4296 or 800-947-4303

Established 1877. Private. Coed. Accreditation: NEASC. Tuition: $13,600. Room and board: $5,598. Enrollment: 3,768 full-time undergraduates. Degrees: AA, AS, AAS, BA, BS, BFA, BMus, BSN, BSEE, BSE, BSME, BSCE, BS CompE, BSBA, MA, MS, MBA, MM, DMA, PsyD. Over 300 acres. 9 colleges and schools on two campuses. Over 70 majors, with self-designed option. Division I varsity athletics. Cooperative education, financial aid, honors program available.

University of New Haven
300 Orange Ave., West Haven 06516
Steven T. Briggs, Dean Admis./Financial Aid
203-932-7319

Wesleyan University, Middletown 06459
Karl Furstenberg, Dean of Admissions

Western Connecticut State University
181 White St., Danbury 06810

Yale University
149 Elm St., New Haven 06520

DELAWARE

Delaware State College
1200 N. DuPont Hwy., Dover 19901
Jethro C. Williams, Dir. of Admis.

University of Delaware, Newark 19711

Wesley College
120 N. State St., Dover 19901

Wilmington College
320 N. DuPont Hwy., New Castle 19720

DISTRICT OF COLUMBIA

The American University
4400 Massachusetts Ave. N.W.
Washington 20016

Catholic University of America
620 Michigan Ave. N.E., Washington 20064
Robert J. Talbot, Dir. of Admis. & Fin. Aid.

Corcoran School of Art
500 17th St., N.W., Washington 20006
Mark Sistek, Dir. of Admissions

GALLAUDET UNIVERSITY
800 Florida Ave., N.E., Washington 20002
I. King Jordan, President
Deborah DeStefano, Dir. of Admis.
800-995-0550
Established 1864. Private. Coed. Accredited. UG for deaf and hard of hearing students only. Totally accessible communication environment. Enrollment: 2,200. Tuition, room and board: $10,100 for undergraduates. The graduate program is open to deaf, hard of hearing, and hearing students. Student-faculty ratio: 12:1. Degrees: AA, BA, MA, PhD. Honors program. Library: 195,000 volumes, 345,000 title in microform. Through ALADIN access to 7 members of Washington Research Consortium. 72% complete baccalaureate degrees.

Georgetown University
37th and O Sts., N.W., Washington 20057
Dr. Joseph A. Chalmers, Dean of Admis. & Rec.

George Washington University
Washington 20052

Howard University
2400 6th St., N.W., Washington 20059
James E. Cheek, President

Southeastern University
501 I St., S.W., Washington 20024

Strayer College
1025 15th St., N.W., Washington 20005

University of the District of Columbia
Georgia Ave.-Harvard St. Campus
1100 Harvard St., N.W., Washington 20009

University of the District of Columbia
Van Ness Campus
4200 Connecticut Ave., N.W., Washington 20008

University of the District of Columbia
800 Mt. Vernon Pl. N.W., Washington 20001

FLORIDA

Barry University
11300 N.E. 2nd Ave., Miami Shores 33161
Robin Ray Roberts, Dean of Admissions

Bethune-Cookman College
640 Mary McLeod Bethune Blvd.
Daytona Beach 32114

Clearwater Christian College
3400 Gulf-to-Bay Blvd., Clearwater 34619
Benjamin Puckett, Dir. of Admis.

Eckerd College
P.O. Box 12560, St. Petersburg 33733
Richard Hallin, Dir. of Admis.

Edward Waters College
1658 Kings Rd., Jacksonville 32209

Flagler College
P.O. Box 1027, St. Augustine 32085
Marc G. Williar, Dir. of Admis.
904-829-6481

Florida A & M University, Tallahassee 32307

Florida Atlantic University
500 N.W. 20th St., Boca Raton 33431
Brian Levin-Stankevich, Dir. of Admis.

FLORIDA BAPTIST THEOLOGICAL COLLEGE
5400 College Dr., Graceville 32440
O. Lavan Wilson, Dir of Admis.
904-263-3261

Florida Institute of Technology
150 W. University Blvd., Melbourne 32901
Louis T. Levy, Dean of Admissions
800-888-4348

Florida International University
Tamiami Trail, Miami 33199

Florida International University
Biscayne Blvd. and 151st St., North Miami 33181

Florida Memorial College
15800 N.W. 42nd Ave., Opa-Locka 33054
Roberto Darragan, Jr., Dir., Admissions

Florida Southern College
111 Lake Hollingsworth Dr., Lakeland 33801
William Stephens, Jr., Dir. of Admis.

Florida State University
600 W. College Ave., Tallahassee 32306

Fort Lauderdale College
1040 Bayview Dr., Ft. Lauderdale 33304
William P. Bedard, Director

Hobe Sound Bible College
P.O. Box 1065, Hobe Sound 33475
Ann French, Dir. of Admis.

INTERNATIONAL COLLEGE
2654 E. Tamiami Tr., Naples 33962
Nancy Rogers, Director of Admissions
800-466-8017
Established 1989. Private. Coed. Accreditation: Accrediting Council for Independent Colleges and Schools. Tuition: $6,345 (including summer term). Fees: $135/semester. Enrollment: 272 full-time, 269 part-time. Faculty: 45. Student-faculty ratio: 15:1. Degrees: Business, Management, Accounting, Computers, Paralegal, Health Information, Medical Assisting. Library: 12,362 volumes. 2 buildings. 3 miles from the Gulf of Mexico.

INTERNATIONAL COLLEGE
8695 College Pky., Fort Myers 33919
Nancy Rogers, Director of Admissions
800-466-0019
Established 1989. Private. Coed. Accreditation: Accrediting Council for Independent Colleges and Schools. Tuition: $6,345 (including summer term). Fees: $135/semester. Enrollment: 272 full-time, 269 part-time. Faculty: 45. Student-faculty ratio: 15:1. Degrees: Business, Management, Accounting, Computers, Paralegal, Health Information, Medical Assisting. Library: 12,362 volumes. 2 buildings.

Jacksonville University
2800 University Blvd., N., Jacksonville 32211

Jones College
5353 Arlington Expy., Jacksonville 32211
Dorothy D. Jones, Chief Executive Officer

Jones College
5975 Sunset Dr. #100, South Miami 33143

LYNN UNIVERSITY
(Est. 1962 as College of Boca Raton)
3601 N. Military Trail, Boca Raton 33431
Donald Ross, President
407-994-0770 or 800-544-8035
Established 1962. Coed. Accreditation: SACS. Tuition: $13,900. Room and board: $5,600. Enrollment: 750 boarding, 350 day. 40 states, and 50 countries represented. Degrees: AA, AS, BA BS, Master's in Professional Studies. Library: 85,000 volumes. 15 buildings on 125 acres. Pool, tennis courts, athletic fields. NCAA Division II men's & women's basketball, golf, soccer, and tennis, men's baseball. Guest lecturers, assortment of social clubs and service organizations. Student government organization. Lynn University offers a study abroad program in Dublin, Ireland.

New College of the University of South Florida
5700 N. Taimiami Trail, Sarasota 34243

Northwood University
2600 N. Military Trail, West Palm Beach 33409
Brad Sargent, Dir. of Admis.
800-458-8325

Nova Southeastern University
3301 College Ave., Ft. Lauderdale 33314

Orlando College - North
5500 Diplomat Circle, Orlando 32810

Orlando College - South
2411 Sand Lake Rd., Orlando 32809

PALM BEACH ATLANTIC COLLEGE
PO Box 24708, West Palm Beach 33416-4708
Dr. Paul R. Corts, President
Buck James, Dean of Admissions
800-238-3998
PBA was founded in 1968 as a unique institution of higher learning that would stress academic quality, character development, and spiritual maturity. Chartered as a Christian liberal arts college, PBA was accredited by the Southern Association of Colleges and Schools in 1972.
The cost for full-time tuition (12-18 credits per semester) is $7,900 per year. Average room and board costs are $3,400 per year. Ninety percent of the students at PBA receive some type of financial aid.
PBA is located on the Intracoastal Waterway, approximately 1 mile from the Atlantic Ocean. The college currently occupies twenty-two buildings. The E.C. Blomeyer Library contains more than 80,000 volumes and approximately 387 periodicals. The college is involved in a $100-million expansion program. Two phases of this program have already been completed.
The Bachelor of Arts is offered in art, art education, communication, drama education, economics, elementary education, English, finance/banking, history, international business, management, marketing, mathematics, music, physical education, political science, psychology, religion, secondary education, studio art, and theater arts. The Bachelor of Music degree is offered in church music and performance.
The Bachelor of Science is offered in accounting, biology, computer information systems, economics, elementary education, finance/banking, international business management, management of human resources, marketing, mathematics, music, physical education, political science, psychology, secondary education, and studio art. Pre-professional programs are offered in dentistry, legal studies, medicine, public health, and veterinary science.
Master's degree programs are offered in Master of Business Administration, Master of Science in human resource development, and Master of Education in elementary education.
PBA has an outstanding faculty of 122 full and part-time members who are dedicated to Christian education. Seventy-five percent hold doctorates.
A student may opt to get involved in college life,

including service and leadership organizations, intercollegiate and intramural sports, fine arts, religious groups, and professionally oriented organizations. All students attend weekly chapel services.
Admission decisions are made on a rolling basis as admission materials are submitted to the college.

Pensacola Christian College
P.O. Box 18000, Pensacola 32523

Rollins College
P.O. Box 2720, Winter Park 32790

St. Leo College
P.O. Box 2008, St. Leo 33574
Bonnie Black, Dir. of Admis.

St. Thomas University
16400 N.W. 32nd Ave., Miami 33054
John M. Letvinchuk, Dir. of Admis.

SCHILLER INTERNATIONAL UNIVERSITY (FLORIDA AND EUROPE)
Admissions Office, Dept PA
453 Edgewater Dr., Dunedin 34698-4964
800-336-4133 (In FL: 813-736-5082)
Fax: 813-736-6263
Dr. Walter Leibrecht, President
Karen Altieri, Associate Director of Admissions
Accredited by ACICS. Enrollment: 1,519. Student-faculty ratio: 18:1. Library: 96,000 volumes. Tuition and fees (undergrad): Florida: $10,330, Europe: $11,140. Room and board: Florida: $3,900, Europe: $5,800.
Schiller International University (SIU) is an independent, coeducational, American university with an international focus offering undergraduate and graduate degree programs and semester, summer, and full-year Study Abroad programs. Founded in 1964, with men and women from more than 100 nations currently enrolled, SIU offers students the unique opportunity to gain an American education in an international setting with English as the language of instruction at all of SIU's ten campuses in six countries: Dunedin, Florida, U.S.A.; Central and Greater London, England; Paris and Strasbourg, France; Heidelburg and Berlin, Germany; Engelberg and Leysin, Switzerland; and Madrid, Spain. The Leysin campus is the American College of Switzerland. SIU students have the unique opportunity to transfer freely among SIU's campuses without losing any credits, and while continuing their chosen program of study.
University residence halls are available in Florida, London (both campuses), Heidelberg, Strasbourg, Engelberg, and Leysin, and experienced housing staff provide assistance in securing private or host family housing at all campuses.
The largest programs are in International Business Administration (with specialty areas in management, marketing, banking, financial management), International Tourism and Hospitality Management, and International Relations and Diplomacy. Both undergraduate (BBA or BA) and graduate (MBA, MIM, or MA) degrees are available in these areas. Other undergraduate degree programs include: commercial art, computer systems management, economics, engineering management, european studies, French language and literature, German language and literature, international political studies, international studies, paralegal studies, pre-medicine, psychology, public administration.
In addition, the COLLEGIUM PALATINUM, a division of SIU, operates a series of intensive language institutes offering German (Heidelberg), Spanish (Madrid), French (Leysin), and English as a foreign language (Florida, London, Berlin, Madrid, and Leysin), in which instruction is in the respective language.
Through discussions in small classes with instructors and classmates of multicultural backgrounds, students gain firsthand knowledge of business and cultural relations among the peoples of the world. In addition, every SIU campus offers a full program of cultural and social activities, including day and weekend excursions and longer trips during mid-semester vacations. At SIU, students really do receive an education that prepares them for international careers in a rapidly changing world.

Stetson University
401 N. Woodland Blvd., De Land 32720
Gary A. Meadows, Dean of Admis.

Tampa College
3319 W. Hillsborough Ave., Tampa 33614
David Zorn, President

Tampa College
3924 Coconut Palm Dr., Tampa 33619

TAMPA COLLEGE-LAKELAND
1200 US Hwy. 98 S., Lakeland 33801
Frances J. Morris, PhD, President
Patricia Gill, EdD, Academic Dean
Terri Thomas, Adult Admissions Director
Trishia Mixon, High School Admissions Director
Linda Wagner, Student Finance Director
813-686-1444
Established 1890. Private. Coed. Accreditation: CCA-ACICS. Enrollment: 900. Degrees Offered: AS, BBA. Admissions requirements: High school diploma or GED, successful score on CPat or ACT or SAT. Student-faculty ratio: 25:1.

Tampa College - Pinellas
15064 U.S. Hwy. 19 N., Clearwater 34624
Mark A. Page, President
813-530-9495

TRINITY COLLEGE OF FLORIDA
2430 Trinity Oaks Blvd., New Port Richey 34655
813-376-6911
See listing under "Biblical Studies"

University of Central Florida
P.O. Box 25000, Orlando 32816

University of Florida
226 Tigert Hall, Gainesville 32611

University of Miami
P.O. Box 248006, Coral Gables 33124

University of North Florida
4567 St. Johns Bluff Rd. S., Jacksonville 32224

UNIVERSITY OF SARASOTA
5250 17th St., Sarasota 34235
Linda Volz, Dir. of Enrollment Management
800-331-5995
Established 1969. Coed. Accreditation: SACS. Tuition: $265 per credit hour. Enrollment: 470. Faculty: 30. Degrees: MAEd, MBA, EdD. Year round, non-traditional calendar, flexible, small seminars, much individual attention to students, performance oriented.

University of South Florida
4202 Fowler Ave., Tampa 33620

University of Tampa
401 W. Kennedy Blvd., Tampa 33606
Robert W. Cook, Dir. of Admis.

University of West Florida
11000 University Pky., Pensacola 32514

Warner Southern College
5301 U.S. Hwy. 27, S., Lake Wales 33853
Valerie S. Rutland, Dir. Enrollment Mgmt.
800-949-7248

GEORGIA

Albany State College
504 College Dr., Albany 31705

AMERICAN COLLEGE FOR THE APPLIED ARTS
3330 Peachtree Rd., N.E., Atlanta 30326
404-231-9000
Suzanne McBride, Dir. of Admis.
Private. Coed. Non-denominational. Degrees: AA and BFA in fashion design, fashion marketing, interior design, commercial art, and AA and BBA in business administration. Accreditation: SACS. Financial aid. Student housing. Professional faculty active in the industry, field trips, study tours, internships, placement, ESL program. Summer sessions. Study abroad and MBA programs available at The American College in London. (See listing under "Study Abroad".)

AMERICAN COLLEGE IN LONDON
110 Marylebone High St., London W1M 3DB
US Admissions Office
3330 Peachtree Rd., N.E., Atlanta 30326
404-231-9000
Will Conard, Director of Study Abroad Program
See listing under "Study Abroad"

Armstrong State College
11935 Abercorn St., Savannah 31419
Kim West, Director of Admissions

Atlanta College of Art
Woodruff Arts Center
1280 Peachtree St., N.E., Atlanta 30309
John Farkas, Dir. of Enrollment Management

AUGUSTA COLLEGE
2500 Walton Way, Augusta 30904-2200
Lee Young, Dir. of Admis.
706-737-1405

Berry College
2277 Martha Berry Hwy. N.W., Mt. Berry 30165

BREWTON-PARKER COLLEGE
P.O. Box 197, Mount Vernon 30445
Dr. Y. Lynn Holmes, President
912-583-2241

Clark Atlanta University
240 James Brawley Dr., S.W., Atlanta 30314
Thomas W. Cole, President

Clayton State College
P.O. Box 285, Morrow 30260

Columbus College
3600 Algonquin Dr., Columbus 31907

Covenant College
Scenic Hwy., Lookout Mountain 30750

Emmanuel College
P.O. Box 128, Franklin Springs 30639
Levy Moore, Dir. of Admis.

Emory University
1462 Clifton Rd., Atlanta 30322

Fort Valley State College
1005 State College Dr., Fort Valley 31030

Georgia College
231 W. Hancock St., Milledgeville 31061
912-453-5004

Georgia Institute of Technology
225 North Ave. N.W., Atlanta 30332

Georgia Southern University, Statesboro 30460

Georgia Southwestern College
800 Wheatley St., Americus 31709

Georgia State University
University Plaza, Atlanta 30303
Ernest Beals, Dean of Admissions

Kennesaw State College
P.O. Box 444, Marietta 30061
Joe Head, Dir. of Admis.

La Grange College
601 Broad St., La Grange 30240
Phil Dodson, Dir. of Admis.
706-882-2911

Medical College of Georgia
1120 15th St., Augusta 30901
Elizabeth Griffin, Dir. of Undergraduate Admis.

Mercer University in Atlanta
3001 Mercer University Dr., Atlanta 30341

Mercer University
1400 Coleman Ave., Macon 31207

Morris Brown College
643 Martin Luther King Jr. Dr. N.W.
Atlanta 30314

North Georgia College, Dahlonega 30597
Gary R. Steffey, Dir. of Admis.

Oglethorpe University
4484 Peachtree Rd., N.E., Atlanta 30319
Dennis Matthews, Dir. of Admis.

Paine College
1235 15th St., Augusta 30901
Phyllis Wyatt-Woodruff, Dir. Enrollment Mgmt.

Piedmont College
P.O. Box 10, Demorest 30535
Penny L. Graber, Dir of Admis.
800-277-7020

SAVANNAH COLLEGE OF ART & DESIGN
342 Bull St., Savannah 31401
May Poetter, VP of Admissions
See listing under "Art"

Savannah State College
State College Branch, Savannah 31404
Robert Ray, Dir. of Admis.

Shorter College
315 Shorter Ave., Rome 30165

Southern College of Technology
1100 S. Marietta Pky., Marietta 30060

Thomas College
1501 Millpond Rd., Thomasville 31792

Toccoa Falls College
Office of Admissions, Toccoa Falls 30598
Matthew L. King, Dir. of Admis.
800-868-3257

University of Georgia, Athens 30602
Dr. Claire Swann, Dir. of Admis.

Valdosta State University
Patterson St., Valdosta 31698

West Georgia College, Carrollton 30118
C. Doyle Bickers, Dir. of Admis.

HAWAII

Brigham Young University, Hawaii Campus
55-220 Kulanui St., Laie 96762
Clark E. Hirschi, Coordinator of Admis.

Chaminade University of Honolulu
3140 Waialae Ave., Honolulu 96816
Charles Schafer, VP Enrollment Services

Hawaii Pacific University
1166 Fort Street Mall, Honolulu 96813
Don Barlow, Dir. of Admis.

Hawaii Pacific University
45-045 Kamehameha Hwy., Kaneohe 96744

University of Hawaii at Hilo
523 W. Lanikaula, Hilo 96720

University of Hawaii at Manoa
2500 Campus Rd., Honolulu 96822

IDAHO

Boise State University
1910 University Dr., Boise 83725

College of Idaho, Caldwell 83605

Idaho State University
P.O. Box 8270, Pocatello 83209

Lewis Clark State College
500 8th Ave., Lewiston 83501
800-933-5272 or 208-799-5272

Northwest Nazarene College
623 Holly St., Nampa 83686
Bruce D. Webb, Dir. of Admis.

University of Idaho, Moscow 83843
Peter Brown, Dir. of Admis.

ILLINOIS

THE AMERICAN CONSERVATORY OF MUSIC
16 N. Wabash Ave., Suite 1850, Chicago 60602
312-263-4161
See listing under "Music or Graduate Schools"

Augustana College
639 38th St., Rock Island 61201
Martin R. Sauer, Director of Admission
800-798-8100

Aurora University
347 S. Gladstone Ave., Aurora 60506
Peter Pitts, Dir. of Admis.

Barat College, Lake Forest 60045
Loretta Brickman, Dir. of Admis.

Bradley University
1501 W. Bradley Ave., Peoria 61625

Chicago State University
9501 S. King Dr., Chicago 60628

College of St. Francis
500 Wilcox St., Joliet 60435

Columbia College
600 S. Michigan Ave., Chicago 60605
Debra McGrath, Dir. of Admis.

Concordia University
7400 Augusta St., River Forest 60305

DE PAUL UNIVERSITY
1 E. Jackson Blvd., Chicago 60604
Ms. Lucy Leusch, Dir. of Admissions
312-362-8300
Established 1898. Private. Coed. Tuition: $10,590. Enrollment: 9,107 full-time, 7,372 part-time. Faculty: 1,065. Student-faculty ratio: 17:1. Degrees: Bachelor's, Master's, Ph.D., J.D., L.L.M. Library: 932,744 volumes. 32 buildings on 32 acres. DePaul, the second largest Catholic University in the United States, is located in Chicago - a world class center for business, finance, government, law and culture. This location and the University's unique partnership with the city provides DePaul students with career-related job experiences, mentorships, service, social and cultural opportunities.

De Paul University
2323 N. Seminary Ave., Chicago 60614

DEVRY INC.
DeVry Institutes
Administrative Offices
One Tower Lane, Oakbrook Terrace 60181-4624
708-571-7700 or Toll Free 800-73-DEVRY
Nine locations:
DeVry Institute of Technology, Decatur, GA
DeVry Institute of Technology, Chicago, IL
DeVry Institute of Technology, Pomona, CA
DeVry Institute of Technology, Columbus, OH
DeVry Institute of Technology, Irving, TX
DeVry Institute of Technology, Kansas City, MO
DeVry Institute of Technology, Addison, IL
DeVry Institute of Technology, Phoenix, AZ
DeVry Technical Institute, Woodbridge, NJ
Degrees: Associate of Applied Science and Bachelor of Science awarded in all institutes except Woodbridge, NJ. Associate of Applied Science awarded at DeVry Technical Institute.
Accreditation: Commission on Institutes of Higher Education of the North Central Association of Colleges and Schools. Electronics Engineering Technology programs are accredited by the Technology Accreditation Commission of the Accreditation Board for Engineering Technology (TAC/ABET).
Majors: The Associate of Applied Science in Electronics degree is awarded upon completion of 5 semesters at all 9 schools. The Bachelor of Science degree in Electronics Engineering Technology is awarded upon completion of 9 semesters at all schools except Woodbridge, which awards an Associate of Applied Science after 5 semesters. A Bachelor of Science degree in Computer Information Systems is awarded upon completion of 9 semesters at all schools except Woodbridge, which awards an Associate of Applied Science after 5 semesters. A Bachelor of Science in Business Operations degree is awarded upon completion of 9 semesters at Decatur, Pomona, Irving, Kansas City and Phoenix, and upon completion of 8 semesters at Chicago and Addison. The Bachelor of Business Operations degree is awarded at Columbus. Telecommunications Management is offered at Addison, Kansas City, Los Angeles, and Woodbridge. A Bachelor of Science degree is awarded for Telecommunications Management after completion of 8 semesters except at Woodbridge, which awards an Associate of Applied Science after 5 semesters.
Students: 22,846 (U.S. enrolled as of fall 1993, all schools).
Tuition: $5,962 average per academic year. Application fee: $25. Tuition deposit $75 for first time enrollment (refundable if student cancels prior to start of class).
Admissions: Students must be at least 17 years of age on or before the first day of classes. Basic admission requirements are 1) possession of a high school diploma or GED certificate, and 2) satisfactory completion of the DeVry entrance examination or evidence of obtaining the following scores:
Electronics programs: Between 400-480 on the SAT math test or between 18-20 on the ACT math test.
Computer Information Systems, Business Operations, Accounting and Telecommunications Management: 440 on the SAT math test or 19 on the ACT math test.
Students who do not receive a satisfactory grade on the DeVry entrance examination will be allowed two retests before being denied admission.
For further information on academic programs, financial aid programs, scholarships and other services, write:
National Office of Admissions
DeVry Inc.
One Tower Lane
Oakbrook Terrace, IL 60181-4624

EASTERN ILLINOIS UNIVERSITY
Charleston 61920
David Jorns, President
Dale Wolf, Dir. of Admis.

217-581-2223

Established in 1895. Public. Four year university. Coed. Total enrollment: 10,400. Calendar-semester with two summer sessions and intersession. In-state tuition and fees (including textbooks): $2,532. Room and board: $2,856. Fifty-nine undergraduate majors are available through the following instructional units: the College of Arts and Sciences, the College of Business, the College of Fine Arts, the College of Health, Physical Education and Recreation, the School of Home Economics, and the School of Technology. The University is located on 325 acres and includes 41 buildings. There are 14 residence halls providing a variety of life style choices. Booth Library contains approximately 600,000 catalogued volumes, 2,880 annual periodicals and 1,193,244 microfilm units. Lantz HPER Building houses a field house, handball courts, gymnasium, rifle range, olympic swimming pool, and a new recreation center. The University participates in men's and women's intercollegiate athletics including football, basketball, cross country, track, soccer, wrestling, swimming, tennis, volleyball, baseball, and golf.

Admissions: Fall Semester - Rank in the upper half of the high school class (based on 6 or more semesters), and an enhanced ACT composite of 18 and above (SAT - 700 or higher). Transfers may be considered if they have a 2.00 (based on 4.00 grading system) as well as a 2.00 from the last institution attended (students with less than 30 semester hours must also meet beginning freshmen requirements).

Financial Aids: Awards based on demonstrated financial need with preference given to those who apply by April 15. Aid available through ISAC, PELL, SEOG, Work Study, Perkins Loan and numerous private scholarships. Use Free Federal but other forms are accepted.

Accreditation: North Central Association of Colleges and Secondary Schools, National Council of Accreditation of Teacher Education, National Association of Schools of Music, American Chemical Society, American Home Economics Association, and the American Speech and Hearing Association.

East-West University
816 S. Michigan Ave., Chicago 60605

Elmhurst College
190 Prospect Ave., Elmhurst 60126

Eureka College
300 E. College Ave., Eureka 61530

Governors State University
1 University Pky., University Park 60466
Richard Pride, Dir. of Admis.

Greenville College
315 E. College Ave., Greenville 62246
Kent Krober, Dir. of Admis.

HARRINGTON INSTITUTE OF INTERIOR DESIGN
410 S. Michigan Ave., Chicago 60605
Robert Marks, Dean
AAS, BA Degrees
312-939-4975

Illinois Benedictine College
5700 College Rd., Lisle 60532

Illinois College
1101 W. College Ave., Jacksonville 62650
Gale Vaugn, Dir. of Admis.

Illinois Institute of Technology
3300 S. Federal St., Chicago 60616
Wendell R. Webb, Dir. of Admissions

Illinois State University
212 N. School St., Normal 61761

ILLINOIS WESLEYAN UNIVERSITY
P.O. Box 2900, Bloomington 61702
James R. Ruoti, Dean of Admissions
309-556-3031 or 800-332-2498

KNOX COLLEGE
Galesburg 61401
Rick Nahm, President
John Strassburger, Dean of the College
Paul Steenis, Director of Admission
Teresa Jackson, Director of Financial Aid
309-343-0112 or 800-678-KNOX

Established 1837. Private. Independent. Coed. Residential. Total enrollment: 1,000. Comprehensive fee 1994-95: $19,995.

Knox offers the bachelors of arts degree. Over 30 academic programs as well as pre-professional advising programs in engineering, dentistry, law, medicine and veterinary medicine. Interdisciplinary concentrations in Black studies, environmental studies, religious studies and women's studies. Average class size 16. Student-faculty ratio: 11:1. All courses taught by professors, 92% of whom hold PhD or highest terminal degree. 3-3 academic calendar allows students to concentrate on three courses per term for each of three 10-week terms. Optional mini-term in December.

Facilities on the historic 70-acre campus include recently renovated Seymour Library with 250,000 volumes; a separate science library and highly equipped research facilities in the Umbeck Science and Mathematics Center; recently constructed T. Fleming Fieldhouse; and Old Main, primarily an academic and administrative building and last remaining site of the 1858 Lincoln-Douglas debates. Green Oaks, a 760-acre biological field station, lies twenty miles from campus. Students participate in twenty NCAA Division III sports: baseball (m), basketball (m/w), cross-country (m/w), football (m), golf (m/w),

soccer (m/w), softball (w), swimming (m/w), tennis (m/w), indoor and outdoor track (m/w), volleyball (w) and wrestling (m). Club sports include fencing, lacrosse and men's volleyball. Intramurals are also very popular.

Student life is enhanced by over 60 extracurricular organizations, including cultural, departmental, governmental, recreational, religious, service and social groups. About a third of students participate in Knox's five fraternities and two sororities.

Admission to Knox is competitive. Applicants for freshman admission should submit an application, essay, transcript, counselor and teacher recommendations, and ACT or SAT scores by December 1 for early action or by February 15 for regular decision. Transfer applicants are also required to submit transcripts from all colleges attended.

Lake Forest College
555 N. Sheridan Rd., Lake Forest 60045

LEWIS UNIVERSITY
Rt. 53, Romeoville 60441
Irish O'Reilly, Director of Admissions
(815,708,312) 838-0500

Established 1932. Private. Coed. Accreditation: NCACS, NLN, FAA. Tuition and fees: $10,112. Room and board: $4,200. Enrollment: 4,300. Faculty: 200. Student-faculty ratio: 20:1. Degrees offered: AS, BA, BS, BES, BSN, MA, MBA, MS, MSN, 11 aviation degree programs. Library: 200,000 volumes. 13 buildings on 600 acres. Strong aviation and nursing programs. Community theatre, NCAA Div. II athletics. Rural location 25 miles southwest of Chicago.

Loyola University
6525 N. Sheridan Rd., Chicago 60626

Loyola University-Mallinckrodt Campus
1041 Ridge Rd., Wilmette 60091
Karen Sullivan, Admissions

Loyola University of Chicago
820 N. Michigan Ave., Chicago 60611
Allen V. Lentino, Dir. of Admis.

McKendree College
701 College Rd., Lebanon 62254
Stephen E. Jackson, Director of Admissions

MacMurray College
447 E. College Ave., Jacksonville 62650
Edwin R. Hockett, Dean of Admissions

MILLIKIN UNIVERSITY
1184 W. Main St., Decatur 62522
Lin Stoner, Dean of Admissions
800-373-7733

Monmouth College
700 E. Broadway, Monmouth 61462

National-Louis University
2840 Sheridan Ave., Evanston 60201

Native American Educational Services
2838 W. Peterson Ave., Chicago 60659

NORTH CENTRAL COLLEGE
30 N. Brainard St.
P.O. Box 3065, Naperville 60566-7065
Marguerite Waters, Director of Admission
708-420-3414

Northeastern Illinois University
5500 N. St. Louis Ave., Chicago 60625

Northern Illinois University, De Kalb 60115

North Park College & Theological Seminary
3225 W. Foster, Chicago 60625
312-509-2330

Northwestern University
2001 Sheridan Rd., Evanston 60208

Olivet Nazarene University, Kankakee 60901
John Mongerson, Dir. of Admis.
815-939-5203

Principia College, Elsah 62028

Quincy College
1800 College Ave., Quincy 62301
Fr. Michael Lanning, O.F.M., Dir. of Admis.

RAY COLLEGE OF DESIGN
AAS, BA, BFA degrees
401 N. Wabash Ave., Chicago 60611
312-280-3500
Woodfield Campus
1051 Perimeter Dr., Schaumburg 60173
708-619-3450

Robert Morris College
180 N. La Salle St., Chicago 60601

ROCKFORD COLLEGE
5050 E. State St., Rockford 61108
Miriam King, V.P. for Enrollment Management
800-892-2984

Established 1847. Private. Coed. Accreditation: North Central Association of Schools and Colleges. Tuition: $11,500. Room and board: $3,800. Enrollment: 898 full-time, 712 part-time. Faculty: 80. Student-faculty ratio: 12:1. Degrees: BSN, BA, BS, BFA, MBA, MAT. Library: 165,000 volumes. 26 buildings on 130 acres. Campus is heavily wooded; park like with many wild animals, including deer. Regent's College (London, England) is accredited by Rockford College. It provides a unique cultural opportunity for students to study abroad for the same cost to attend Rockford College.

ROOSEVELT UNIVERSITY
430 S. Michigan Ave., Chicago 60605
William Smyser, Director of Admissions

Established 1945. Private. Coed. Accreditation: NCACS. Tuition: $7,410. Room and board: $4,500. Fees: $60. Enrollment: 1,320 full-time, 2,792 part-time. Faculty: 155. Student-faculty ratio: 12:1. Library: 400,000 volumes. Located in downtown Chicago, with branch campuses in Arlington Heights and Lake County, IL. Main campus located in the historic Auditorium Theatre building. Unique programs offered at Roosevelt University include Hospitality Management and Environmental Studies.

Rosary College
7900 W. Division St., River Forest 60305
Hildegarde Schmidt, Dir. of Admis.

SAINT FRANCIS MEDICAL CENTER COLLEGE OF NURSING
211 N.E. Greenleaf St., Peoria 61603
Sr. Mary Ludgera, Dean
309-655-2596

St. Xavier College
3700 W. 103rd St., Chicago 60655
Mary Hendry, Dean of Admissions

Sangamon State University
Shepherd Rd., Springfield 62794-9243
Admissions and Records, 217-786-6626

Southern Illinois University at Carbondale
Carbondale 62901

Southern Illinois University at Edwardsville
Edwardsville 62026
Eugene J. Magac, Dir. of Admissions & Records

Trinity Christian College
6601 W. College Dr., Palos Heights 60463
Kenneth Bootsma, President

Trinity College
2077 Half Day Rd., Deerfield 60015
Dr. Kenneth Meyer, Pres.

University of Chicago
5801 S. Ellis Ave., Chicago 60637

University of Illinois
506 S. Wright St., Urbana 61801

University of Illinois at Chicago
P.O. Box 5220, Chicago 60680
Dr. Marilyn R. Fiduccia, Dir. of Admis.

VanderCook College of Music
3209 S. Michigan Ave., Chicago 60616
Ward Durrett, Dir of Admis.

Western Illinois University
900 W. Adams St., Macomb 61455
Alan DeRoos, Registrar
309-298-1891

Wheaton College, Wheaton 60187
Daniel Crabtree, Director of Admissions
800-222-2419

INDIANA

Anderson University
1100 E. 5th St., Anderson 46012
Robert H. Reardon, President

Ball State University
2000 W. University Ave., Muncie 47306
Ruth Vedvik, Dir. of Admis.
800-482-4278 (IN) or 317-285-8300

Bethel College
1001 W. McKinley Ave., Mishawaka 46545
Steve Matteson, Dir. of Admis.

Bristol University
5920 Castleway West Dr. #102
Indianapolis 46250

Butler University
4600 Sunset Ave., Indianapolis 46208

Calumet College
2400 New York Ave., Whiting 46394
Sharon Sweeney, Dir. of Admis.

DePauw University
313 S. Locust St., Greencastle 46135
Dr. Eleanor Ypma, Registrar

Earlham College
801 National Rd. W., Richmond 47374
Robert deVeer, Dean of Admis.

Franklin College
501 E. Monroe, Franklin 46131
B. Stephen Richards, VP Enrollment

Goshen College
1700 S. Main St., Goshen 46526
Marty Lehman Hooley, Dir. of Admis.

Grace College
200 Seminary Dr., Winona Lake 46590
Ron Henry, Dir. of Admis.

Hanover College, Hanover 47243
Eugene McLemore, Dir., Admis.

Huntington College
2303 College Ave., Huntington 46750
Paul Breininger, Dir. of Admis. Services

Indiana State University
217 N. 6th St., Terre Haute 47809

Indiana University at Bloomington
300 N. Jordan Ave., Bloomington 47406

Indiana University at Kokomo
P.O. Box 9003, Kokomo 46904

Indiana University at South Bend
P.O. Box 7111, South Bend   46634

Indiana University East
2325 N. Chester Blvd., Richmond   47374

Indiana University Northwest
3400 N. Broadway, Gary   46408

Indiana University Southeast
4201 Grantline Rd., New Albany   47150

Indiana University-Purdue University at Fort Wayne
2101 Coliseum Blvd. E., Fort Wayne   46805

Indiana University-Purdue University
355 N. Lansing, Indianapolis   46202

Indiana Wesleyan University
4201 S. Washington St., Marion   46953
800-332-6901

Lutheran College of Health Professions
535 Home Ave., Fort Wayne   46807

Manchester College
604 College Ave., North Manchester   46962
Gregory Miller, Dir. of Admis.

Marian College
3200 Cold Spring Rd., Indianapolis   46222
Don French, Dir. of Admis.

Oakland City College
143 N. Lucretia St., Oakland City   47660
Tracy Siekman, Dir. of Admis.

Purdue University
Schleman Hall, West Lafayette   47907

Purdue University, Calumet Campus
2233 171st St., Hammond   46323

Purdue University
1401 S. U.S. Hwy. 421, Westville   46391

St. Francis College
2701 Spring St., Ft. Wayne   46808

ST. JOSEPH'S COLLEGE
P.O. Box 890, Rensselaer   47978
Louis Levy, Dean of Admissions
800-447-8781

Taylor University
500 W. Reade Ave., Upland   46989
Herb Frye, Dean of Enrollment Management

Taylor University - Fort Wayne Campus
1025 W. Rudisill Blvd., Fort Wayne   46807
Jan Paul Storey, Dir. of Admis.

Tri-State University, Angola   46703
Director of Admission
800-347-4878

University of Evansville
1800 Lincoln Ave., Evansville   47722
Elizabeth Lyon, Associate Dir. of Admis.
800-423-8633

University of Indianapolis
1400 E. Hanna Ave., Indianapolis   46227

University of Notre Dame
Notre Dame   46556
Kevin M. Rooney, Dir. of Admis.

University of Southern Indiana
8600 University Blvd., Evansville   47712

Valparaiso University, Valparaiso   46383

IOWA

Briar Cliff College
3303 Rebecca St., Sioux City   51104
Patricia White, Dir. of Admis.

Buena Vista College
610 W. 4th St., Storm Lake   50588
Joanne Loonan, Director of Admissions

Central College
812 University St., Pella   50219
Eric Sickler, Dir. of Admis.

Clarke College
1550 Clarke Dr., Dubuque   52001
Bobbe Ames, VP for Marketing/Recruitment
800-383-2345

Coe College
1220 1st Ave., N.E., Cedar Rapids   52402
Michael White, Director of Enrollment Services

Cornell College
600 1st St., W., Mt. Vernon   52314
Kevin Crockett, Dean of Admissions

Dordt College
498 4th Ave., N.E., Sioux Center   51250
Quentin Van Essen, Dir. of Admissions
800-343-6738

Drake University
2507 E. University Ave., Des Moines   50311
Thomas Willoughby, Dir. of Admis.
515-271-2191

Faith Baptist Bible College & Theological Seminary
1900 N.W. 4th St., Ankeny   50021
Jeff Newman, Director of Admissions
Admissions: 800-352-0147

GRACELAND COLLEGE
Lamoni   50140
800-638-0053, Outside Iowa 800-346-9208
Bonita Booth, Dean of Admissions
Established 1895. Private. Coed. Accreditation:
NCACS, NLN, NCATE. Tuition: $8,585. Room and
board: $2,920. Fees: $95. Enrollment: 996 full-time,

2,283 part-time. Faculty: 70. Student-faculty ratio:
14.7:1. Degrees: BA, BS, BSN. Library: 110,559 volumes. 20 buildings on 167 acres. Honors Program,
CHANCE Program for remediation of students with
learning disfunctions. Outreach Program for non-traditional off-campus nursing students leading to BSN.
Outreach Addiction Studies major leading to BS.
Field house, indoor track, pool, computerized music
lab and publication design program. Internship opportunities. Academic, athletic, fine arts, and leadership grants available.

Grand View College
1200 Grandview Ave., Des Moines   50316
Lori Hanson, Dir. of Admissions
800-444-6083

Grinnell College
P.O. Box 805, Grinnell   50112

Iowa State University, Ames   50011
Karsten Smedal, Dir. of Admis.

Iowa Wesleyan College
601 N. Main St., Mt. Pleasant   52641

Loras College
1450 Alta Vista, Dubuque   52001
Dan Conry, Dir. of Admis.

Luther College
700 College Dr., Decorah   52101
David Sallee, Dean for Enrollment

Maharishi International University
Route 1, Fairfield   52556
Gregory Polakow, Dir. of Admis.

Morningside College, Sioux City   51106
Lora Vanderzwaag, Dir. of Admis.

Mount Mercy College
1330 Elmhurst Dr., N.E., Cedar Rapids   52402
Carol Williamson, Dir. of Admis.
319-363-8213

Northwestern College
101 7th St. S.W., Orange City   51041

St. Ambrose University
518 W. Locust St., Davenport   52803

Simpson College
P.O. Box 708, Indianola   50125

TEIKYO MARYCREST UNIVERSITY
1607 W. 12th St., Davenport   52804
Dr. Joseph Olander, President
Tim McDonough, Director of Admissions
319-326-9225 or 800-728-9705
Quad City metropolitan area. Iowa/Illinois bistate
community overlooking the Mississippi River, pop.
380,000.
Established 1939. Private. Coeducational university
in the Catholic tradition welcoming people of all
faiths. Tuition: $9,980. Room and board: $3,640. State,
federal, institutional financial aid and scholarships
available. File Family Financial Statement (FFS) or
Financial Aid Form (FAF) and TMU Financial Aid
Application by April 1 for priority consideration.
More than thirty majors, featuring outstanding undergraduate programs in business, international business, art, computer graphics, biology, chemistry,
English, Food & Nutrition (dietetics), History, environmental management, communication, multi-media, global studies, education, social work, nursing,
performing arts, mathematics, and computer science.
Graduate programs in computer science (MS) and
education (MA and MAT). Pre-professional programs
in law, chiropractic, and medical fields. Study
Abroad, Cooperative Education, Weekend College,
degree completion program for R.N.'s, credit for life
experience, CLEP, daytime on campus child care center, Learning Assistance Center, Special Studies degree (design your own major) programs available.
Accreditations: North Central Association of Colleges and Schools, Council on Social Work Education
(undergraduate), National League for Nursing, Iowa
Department of Education.   1,200 students in all programs, 586, full-time day, 64% women, 36% men.
58% of full time faculty hold terminal degrees. No
graduate-level teaching assistants. Calendar: semesters with optional summer session. Student-faculty
ratio: 14:1. 30 acre campus, 11 buildings, including
three residence halls. Activities Center holds three
basketball/volleyball courts, weight/exercise room,
snack bar. Outdoor soccer/activity field.
Men participate in NAIA Division II sports in baseball, volleyball, soccer, and basketball. Intercollegiate
women's sports include soccer, basketball, volleyball,
and softball. Student life includes leadership program. Clubs and organizations in each major also
student government, International Cultures Association, Mock Trial team, Campus Ministry, voluntary
action center, Performing Arts series, Performing Arts
Company, Vocal Jazz Ensemble, TMU Chorale, guest
lecturers and performers.
Admissions: Students must submit application for
admission official transcripts from high school and
postsecondary institutions attended. ACT or SAT
scores if entering as freshman. Rolling admissions.
Accepted students normally notified within one week
of file completion.
Location offers benefits of midwestern community
in the largest metropolitan area between Chicago and
Des Moines (3 hour drive each way), and between
Minneapolis and St. Louis (4 hour drive each way).

Teikyo Westmar University
1002 3rd Ave., S.E., Le Mars   51031
Dr. Jim Utesch, Dir. of Admis.

University of Dubuque
2000 University Ave., Dubuque   52001

University of Iowa, Iowa City   52242

University of Northern Iowa, Cedar Falls   50614

Upper Iowa University
P.O. Box 1857, Fayette   52142

Wartburg College
P.O. Box 1003, Waverly   50677

William Penn College
201 Trueblood Ave., Oskaloosa   52577
Eric Otto, Dir. of Admis.

KANSAS

Baker University
8th & Grove St., Baldwin City   66006

Benedictine College
1020 N. Second St., Atchison   66002
James Hoffman, Dir. of Admis.

Bethany College
421 N. 1st St., Lindsborg   67456
Dennis Chaput, Dir. of Admis.

Bethel College
300 E. 27th St., North Newton   67117

Emporia State University
1200 Commercial St., Emporia   66801
Dr. Barbara Hilgendorf, Dir. of Admissions

Fort Hays State University
600 Park St., Hays   67601-4099
James Kellerman, Registrar

Friends University
2100 University St., Wichita   67213

Kansas Newman College
3100 McCormick Ave., Wichita   67213
Dr. Robert Giroux, President

Kansas State University
Anderson Hall 110, Manhattan   66506
Ellsworth M. Gerritz, Admis. & Records

McPherson College
1600 E. Euclid St., McPherson   67460

Mid-America Nazarene College
P.O. Box 1776, Olathe   66051

Ottawa University
1001 S. Cedar St., Ottawa   66067
Steve Koberlein, Dir. of Admis.
800-755-5200

Pittsburg State University
1701 S. Broadway St., Pittsburg   66762
James E. Parker, Dir of Admis.

Saint Mary College
4100 S. 4th St., Leavenworth   66048
Irene Keehan, Dir. of Admis.

SOUTHWESTERN COLLEGE
100 College St., Winfield   67156
800-846-1543

Sterling College, Sterling   67579
Robert Reed, Dir. of Admis. & Records

University of Kansas, Lawrence   66045

Washburn University of Topeka
1700 S.W. College Ave., Topeka   66621
John E. Triggs, Dir. of Admissions

WICHITA STATE UNIVERSITY
1845 Fairmount St., Wichita   67260
Toll-free, 800-362-2594
Established 1895. Public. Coed. Accreditation:
NCACS. Tuition: $997 resident, $3,250 non-resident,
$1,201 graduate resident, $3,430 graduate non-resident. Room and board: $1,503. Fees: $13 per semester.
Enrollment: 7,525 full-time, 7,595 part-time. Faculty:
474 full-time, 248 part-time. Student-faculty ratio:
18:1. Degrees: AA, AS, BA, BAEd, BBA, BFA, BGS,
BHS, BMus, BMusEd, BS, BSAE, BSEE, BSIE, BSME,
BSN, MEd, MAC, MAJ, MBA, MCS, MFA, MHS, Master of Health Science, MM, MMEd, MPA, Master of
Professional Accountancy, MPT, MS, MSN, EdS,
EdD, PhD. Library: 903,000 volumes, 4,115 periodicals, 874,658 microform, computerized card catalog and 8-index LAN. 60 buildings on 330 acres.
National Institute for Aviation Research. Several
wind tunnels, 1 research quality flow-visualization
water tunnel. Ulrich Museum of Art. WSU cable 13
TV station, KMUW FM radio station. Comprehensive
fitness, physical education, and recreation center.

KENTUCKY

Alice Lloyd College
Purpose Rd., Pippa Passes   41844

Asbury College
1 Macklem Dr., Wilmore   40390
Jonah Mitchell, Dir. of Admis.

Bellarmine College
2001 Newburg Rd., Louisville   40205
Thomas LaBaugh, Dean of Admissions

Berea College, Berea   40404
John S. Cook, Dir. of Admis.

Brescia College
717 Frederica St., Owensboro   42301
Thomas C. Greer, Director of Admission
800-264-1234

Campbellsville College
200 College St., Campbellsville   42718
Dr. W. R. Davenport, President

Centre College
600 W. Walnut St., Danville 40422

CUMBERLAND COLLEGE
6178 College Station Dr., Williamsburg 40769
James H. Taylor, President
Erica Harris, Senior Admissions Counselor
606-549-2200

Established 1889. Baptist. Coed. Enrollment: 1,518. Total charge boarding students: $10,156, day students: $6,630. State, Federal and institutional financial aid available. FAFSA should be filed no later than March 1 priority date. On-campus workstudy programs and local businesses offer student employment.

Undergraduate majors in liberal arts, education, business, pre-professional areas. Master's degree available in education. Accreditation: SACS.

All courses taught by qualified faculty — no graduate or teaching assistants. 100 full-time faculty. 42% of faculty hold doctoral degrees. Student faculty ratio 15:1. Average class size is 15. Library holds 145,000 volumes. 25 buildings on campus. 8 dormitories. No off-campus housing sponsored by College. No fraternities or sororities.

Athletic facilities: A basketball arena; football, track, and soccer complex; baseball field; tennis courts; field house; swimming pool; an intramural gym and field; and game room.

Men participate in NAIA Division I sports in baseball, basketball, cross country, golf, soccer, swimming, tennis, track; and NAIA Division II in football. Women participate in NAIA Division I in basketball, cross country, golf, soccer, softball, swimming, tennis, track and volleyball.

Environment: Warm summers, mild winters, four seasons. Knoxville, TN 65 miles south, Lexington, KY 100 miles north. 25 miles from scenic Cumberland Falls State Resort Park.

Student activities include Spring Fever, Madrigal Dinner, Hanging of the Green, Founder's Day, Staley Lecture Series, Palmer Lecture Series, Phi Alpha Theta Lecture Series, Siler-Jones Concert.

Although each application is considered individually, students must have fulfilled general high school requirements of 4 years of English, 3 years each of mathematics and science, and 2 years each in history and social studies. The College also recommends an interview. The GED is accepted. Two letters of recommendation from persons other than guidance counselor or relatives, recommendation from guidance counselor, ACT or SAT scores, high school transcript. Transfers must have verification from the school from which they are transferring that they are eligible to return to that school and a transcript from each previously attended school.

Eastern Kentucky University
521 Lancaster Ave., Richmond 40475

GEORGETOWN COLLEGE
400 E. College St., Georgetown 40324
502-863-8000
Dr. William H. Crouch, President
Garvel Kindrick, Director of Admissions
Established 1829. Southern Baptist. Coed. Accreditation: SACS. Tuition: $7,340. Room and board: $3,600. Enrollment: 1,100 boarding, 100 day. Faculty: 75. Degrees: BA, BS, BS Medical Technology, BME, MA. Library: 116,398 volumes. 25 buildings on 52 acres. Gym. Located in Kentucky's "bluegrass" area, 12 miles north of Lexington. Advanced placement, cooperative exchange program. Christian "climate for achievement".

Kentucky State University
400 E. Main St., Frankfort 40601

KENTUCKY WESLEYAN COLLEGE
3000 Frederica St., Owensboro 42301
Dr. Ray Purdom, Interim President
502-926-3111 Ext. 144

Lindsey Wilson College
210 Lindsey Wilson St., Columbia 42728
Dr. John Begley, President

Mid-Continent Baptist Bible College
P.O. Box 7010, Mayfield 42066

Midway College
512 E. Stephens St., Midway 40347
Carl P. Rollins II, Dir. of Admis.

Morehead State University, Morehead 40351
Charles Myers, Director of Admissions
606-783-2000

Murray State University, Murray 42071
Phil Bryan, Director of Admissions
800-272-4MSU

Northern Kentucky University
Louie B. Nunn Dr., Highland Heights 41076

Pikeville College
214 Sycamore St., Pikeville 41501
Dr. John W. Sanders, Dean of Admissions

Spalding University
851 S. 4th St., Louisville 40203
Dorothy G. Allen, Dir. of Admis.

Sullivan College
P.O. Box 33-308, Louisville 40232
James P. Crick, Director of Admissions
502-456-6504 or 800-844-1354

Sullivan College
2659 Regency Rd., Lexington 40503

Thomas More College
2771 Turkeyfoot Rd., Covington 41017
Dr. Charles Bensman, President

Transylvania University
300 Broadway St., N., Lexington 40508
Pat Bain, Dir. of Admis.

UNION COLLEGE
310 College St., Barbourville 40906
Jack C. Phillips, President
Donald Hapward, Dean of Admission
800-489-8646
Established 1879. 4 year. Private. Coed. Accreditation: SACS. Tuition: $7,800. Room and board: $2,950. Fees: $50. Enrollment: 970. Faculty: 54. Student-faculty ratio: 14:1. Degrees: AAS, BA, BS, BM, MAEd, 9 pre-professional programs. Library: 90,000 volumes. 20 buildings on 110 acre campus. 1 1/2 hours from Lexington KY and Knoxville TN. Football, basketball, baseball, softball, swimming, tennis, soccer, (m/w) cross country, (m/w) golf, volleyball. Drama, theatre, choir. Jazz and pep bands. International study available.

University of Kentucky, Lexington 40506

University of Louisville
2301 S. 3rd St., Louisville 40292
Robert Parrent, Dir. of Admis.

Western Kentucky University
1526 Russellville Rd., Bowling Green 42101

LOUISIANA

Centenary College of Louisiana
P.O. Box 41188, Shreveport 71134

Dillard University
2601 Gentilly Blvd., New Orleans 70122

Grambling State University
P.O. Box 607, Grambling 71245
Dr. Harold W. Lundy, President

Jimmy Swaggart Bible College & Seminary
P.O. Box 38000, Baton Rouge 70828

Louisiana College
College Station, Pineville 71359
Byron McGee, Dir. of Admis.
318-487-7386
See listing under "Liberal Arts"

Louisiana State University
8515 Youree Dr., Shreveport 71115

Louisiana State University and A & M College
Baton Rouge 70803

Lousiana Technical University
P.O. Box 3168, Ruston 71272

Loyola University
6363 St. Charles Ave., New Orleans 70118

McNeese State University
4100 Ryan St., Lake Charles 70605

Nicholls State University
LA Hwy. 1, Thibodaux 70301

Northeast Louisiana University
700 University Ave., Monroe 71209

Northwestern State University
Natchitoches 71497

Southeastern Louisiana University
P.O. Box 784, Hammond 70404

Southern University A & M College
Baton Rouge 70813

Southern University in New Orleans
6400 Press Dr., New Orleans 70126
Millie M. Charles, Director

Tulane University
6823 Saint Charles Ave., New Orleans 70118
Richard Whiteside, Dean of Admission

University of New Orleans
New Orleans 70148

University of Southwestern Louisiana
P.O. Box 44548, Lafayette 70504
318-231-6553

William Carey College
2700 Napoleon Ave., New Orleans 70115

Xavier University
7325 Palmetto St., New Orleans 70125

MAINE

Bates College, Lewiston 04240
William C. Hiss, Dean of Admissions

Bowdoin College, Brunswick 04011
William Mason, Dir. of Admis.

Colby College
150 Mayflower Hill Dr., Waterville 04901
Wm. R. Cotter, President

HUSSON COLLEGE
One College Circle, Bangor 04401
Jane Goodwin, Dir. of Admis.
See listing under "Business and Management"

Maine College of Art
97 Spring St., Portland 04101
Elizabeth Shea, Dir. of Admis.

Maine Maritime Academy
Battle Ave., Castine 04420
Dan Jones, Dir. of Admis.
207-326-2206

St. Joseph's College, North Windham 04062

Thomas College
180 W. River Rd., Waterville 04901
Susan Potter, Dir. of Admis.
207-877-0101, ME only 800-339-7001

University of Maine
University Hts., Augusta 04330

University of Maine
102 Main St., Farmington 04938

University of Maine at Fort Kent
25 Pleasant St., Fort Kent 04743
Jerry Nadeau, Dir. of Admis.

University of Maine
9 O'Brien Ave., Machias 04654

University of Maine, Orono 04469

University of Maine
181 Main St., Presque Isle 04769

University of New England
11 Hills Beach Rd., Biddeford 04005
Patricia Cribby, Dir. of Admis.

University of Southern Maine
96 Falmouth St, Portland 04103
Richard Pattenaude, President
Susan Roberts, Director of Admissions
207-780-5670

Westbrook College
716 Stevens Ave., Portland 04103
207-797-7261

MARYLAND

Baltimore Hebrew University
5800 Park Heights Ave., Baltimore 21215
Norma Furst, President

Bowie State University
14000 Jericho Park Rd., Bowie 20715

Capitol College
11301 Springfield Rd., Laurel 20708
Anthony G. Miller, Director of Admis.
800-950-1992

Columbia Center
6740 Alexander Bell Dr., Columbia 21046

Columbia Union College
7600 Flower Ave., Takoma Park 20912

Coppin State College
2500 W. North Ave., Baltimore 21216

Frostburg State University, Frostburg 21532

Goucher College
1021 Dulaney Valley Rd., Baltimore 21204

Johns Hopkins University
3400 N. 34th St., Baltimore 21218

Loyola College
4501 N. Charles St., Baltimore 21210
William Bossemeyer III, Dir. of Admis.

Maryland Institute College of Art
1300 W. Mt. Royal Ave., Baltimore 21217
Theresa Lynch Bedoya, Dean of Admissions

Morgan State University
Cold Spring Ln. and Hillen Rd., Baltimore 21239

Mt. St. Mary's College
16300 Old Emmitsburg Rd., Emmitsburg 21727
Michael D. Kennedy, Dir. of Admis.

St. John's College
P.O. Box 2800, Annapolis 21401
Christopher Nelson, President
John Christensen, Dir. of Admis.
800-727-9238

St. Mary's College of Maryland
St. Mary's City 20686

Salisbury State University
1101 Camden Ave., Salisbury 21801

Towson State University
800 York Rd., Towson 21204
Dr. Hoke Smith, President

United States Naval Academy
117 Decatur Rd., Annapolis 21402

University of Baltimore
1420 N. Charles St., Baltimore 21201
Clare MacDonald, Dean of Admissions

University of Maryland
Baltimore Professional Schools
522 W. Lombard St., Baltimore 21201

University of Maryland, Baltimore County
5401 Wilkens Ave., Catonsville 21228

University of Maryland, College Park 20742

University of Maryland, University College
University Blvd. & Adelphi Rd.
College Park 20742

University of Maryland Eastern Shore
11868 Academic Oval, Princess Anne 21853
Dr. Rochell Peoples, Dir. of Admis.
410-651-6410

Villa Julie College
1525 Greenspring Valley Rd., Stevenson 21153
Carolyn Manuszak, President

Washington College
Washington Ave., Chestertown 21620
Kevin Coveney, Dir. of Admis.

Western Maryland College
2 College Hill, Westminster 21157

MASSACHUSETTS

American International College
1000 State St., Springfield 01109
Peter Miller, Dean of Admissions

Amherst College, Amherst 01002
Jane E. Reynolds, Dean of Admissions

Anna Maria College
2 Sunset Ln., Paxton 01612
Dr. Bernadette Madore, SSA, President

THE ART INSTITUTE OF BOSTON
700 Beacon St., Boston 02215
617-262-1223 or 800-773-0494
(NY, PA, New England)
Fax 617-437-1226
See listing under "Art"

Assumption College
500 Salisbury St., Worcester 01609

ATLANTIC UNION COLLEGE
P.O. Box 1000, South Lancaster 01561
Osa Canto, Registrar
800-282-2030

Babson College
One College Dr., Babson Park 02157
Charles S. Nolan, Dean of Admission
800-488-3696

Bentley College
175 Forest St., Waltham 02154
Joann McKenna, Dir. of Admis.

Boston College
140 Commonwealth Ave., Chestnut Hill 02167
Rev. J. Donald Monan, S.J., President

Boston University
685 Commonwealth Ave., Boston 02215

Brandeis University
415 South St, Waltham 02154
David Gould, Dean of Admissions
617-736-3500

Bridgewater State College
Bridgewater 02325
James Plotner, Jr., Dir. of Admis.

Clark University
950 Main St., Worcester 01610
Richard Pierson, Dean of Admis.

College of the Holy Cross
1 College St., Worcester 01610
William R. Mason, Dir. of Admis.

Curry College
1071 Blue Hill Ave., Milton 02186
617-333-0500

Eastern Nazarene College
23 E. Elm Ave., Quincy 02170
D. William Nichols, Dir. of Admis.

Emerson College
148 Beacon St., Boston 02116

Emmanuel College
400 The Fenway, Boston 02115
Margaret Bonilla, Dir. of Admis.

Fitchburg State College
160 Pearl St., Fitchburg 01420
Marke Vickers, Dir. of Admis.

Framingham State College
100 State St., Framingham 01701
E. Joseph Lee, Director

Gordon College
255 Grapevine Rd., Wenham 01984

Hampshire College, Amherst 01002
Audrey Y. Smith, Dir. of Admissions
413-582-5471

Harvard University
8 Garden St., Cambridge 02138

Hellenic College
50 Goddard Ave., Brookline 02146
Fr. Al Demos, Director of Admission
617-731-3500

Massachusetts Institute of Technology
77 Massachusetts Ave., Cambridge 02139

MASSACHUSETTS MARITIME ACADEMY
Cape Cod
101 Academy Dr., Buzzards Bay 02532
CDR. Keith D. Rabine, Dean of Enrollment Services
800-544-3411 or 508-830-5000

Merrimack College
315 Turnpike St., North Andover 01845
Dennis Farrell, Dean of Admissions

Mt. Holyoke College
College St., South Hadley 01075
Anita Smith, Director of Admissions
413-538-2023

Mt. Ida College
777 Dedham St., Newton Center 02159
Jim Mulligan, Dean of Admis.

Nichols College, Dudley 01570

NORTH ADAMS STATE COLLEGE
375 Church St., North Adams 01247
Denise Richardello, Director of Admissions
413-664-4511 or 800-292-6632
Established 1894. Public. Coed. Accreditation: New England Association of Schools and Colleges. Tuition: $1,408 in state, 5,542 out of state. Room and

board: $4,212. Fees: $2,085. Enrollment: 1,394 full-time, 593 part-time. Faculty: 121. Student-faculty ratio: 17:1. Degrees: BA, BS, MEd. Library: 175,000 volumes, 510 Periodicals. 16 buildings on 80 acres. Average class size: 24. 2 1/2 hours from Boston. 2 hours from Hartford, CT. 3 1/2 hours from New York City. 100 Academic advisors on campus to assist students, 45 clubs, 8 intercollegiate programs offered on campus. Internships available in each academic area.

Northeastern University
360 Huntington Ave., Boston 02115
Kevin Kelly, Dean and Dir. of Undergraduate Admis.

Salem State College
352 Lafayette St., Salem 01970
David Sartwell, Dir. of Admis.

SCHOOL OF THE MUSEUM OF FINE ARTS
230 Fenway, Boston 02115
Alan Van Reed, Dean of Admissions
617-267-1218

Springfield College
263 Alden St., Springfield 01109
Frederick Bartlett, Dean of Admissions

Stonehill College
320 Washington St., North Easton 02357
508-230-1373

Suffolk University
8 Ashburton Place, Boston 02108
Barbara K. Ericson, Assoc. Dean Enrollment & Retention
617-573-8460

Tufts University
520 Boston Ave., Medford 02155

University of Massachusetts, Amherst 01003
413-545-0222

University of Massachusetts
100 Morrissey Blvd., Boston 02125

University of Massachusetts Dartmouth
Old Westport Rd., North Dartmouth 02747
Raymond Barrows, Dir. of Admissions
508-999-8605

University of Massachusetts Lowell
1 University Ave., Lowell 01854

Western New England College
1215 Wilbraham Rd., Springfield 01119
800-325-1122

Westfield State College
577 Western Ave., Westfield 01085
John F. Marcus, Dir. of Admis.

Wheaton College
26 E. Main St., Norton 02766
Gail Berson, Dean/Admis. & Student Aid

Wheelock College
200 Riverway, Boston 02215
Joan Wexler, Dean of Admis. & Financial Aid

Williams College, Williamstown 01267

Worcester Polytechnic Institute
100 Institute Rd., Worcester 01609
Kay R. Dietrich, Director of Admissions
508-831-5286

Worcester State College
486 Chandler St., Worcester 01602

MICHIGAN

ADRIAN COLLEGE
110 S. Madison St., Adrian 49221
Dr. Stanley Caine, President
George Wolf, Dir. of Admis.
800-877-2246
Established 1859. United Methodist. Coed. Accreditation: NCACS, NCATE, Michigan Department of Public Instruction. 1992-93 tuition and fees: $9,920. Room and board: $3,315. Enrollment: 905 boarding, 1,194 day. Faculty: 66. Degrees: AA, BA, BS, BBA, BFA, BM, BME. Library: 140,000 volumes. 31 buildings on 100 acres. Gym. Pool. Pre-professional programs: pre-medicine, pre-dentistry, pre-law, pre-engineering. 48 acre arboretum. Planetarium, observatory, greenhouse. Color TV station. FM stereo radio station. Conference center. Individually designed majors. Career advising and development center. Newman Center. Internship experience.

Albion College
611 E. Porter, Albion 49224
800-858-6770

ALMA COLLEGE
614 W. Superior St., Alma 48801-1599
John Seveland, VP for Enrollment
800-321-ALMA
Established 1886. Private. Coed. Accreditation: NCACS. Tuition: $11,926. Room and board: $4,334. Fees: $115. Enrollment: 1,306 full-time, 28 part-time. Faculty: 80. Student-faculty ratio: 15:1. Degrees: BA, BS, BFA, BM. Library: 197,000 volumes. 23 buildings on 87 acres. New Heritage Center for the Performing Arts opened fall 1993. Freshman preterm orientation precedes fall term. Generous scholarship and financial aid programs. Many international study opportunities. Phi Beta Kappa, liberal arts I institution. Affiliated with the Presbyterian Church U.S.A.

Andrews University, Berrien Springs 49104
Jack Mentges, Dir. of Admis.

Aquinas College
1607 Robinson Rd., S.E., Grand Rapids 49506
Paula Meehan, Dean of Admissions
616-732-4460 or 800-678-9593

Baker College of Auburn Hills
1500 University Dr., Auburn Hills 48326
John A. Tomaszewski, Dir. of Admis.

Baker College of Cadillac
9600 E. 13th St., Cadillac 49601
Candace Baldwin, Dir. of Admis.

Baker College of Flint
1050 W. Bristol Rd., Flint 48507
Mark Heaton, Dir. of Admis.

Baker College of Mount Clemens
34950 Little Mack Ave., Clinton Township 48035
Annette M. Wendling, Dir. of Admis.

Baker College of Muskegon
141 Hartford Ave., Muskegon 49442
Kathy Jacobson, Dir. of Admis.

Baker College of Owosso
1020 S. Washington St., Owosso 48867
Bruce A. Lundeen, Dir. of Admis.

Baker College of Port Huron
3403 Lapeer Rd., Port Huron 48060
David C. Hickman, Dir. of Admis.

Calvin College
3201 Burton St., S.E., Grand Rapids 49506
Anthony J. Diekema, President

Center for Creative Studies-College of Art & Design
201 E. Kirby St., Detroit 48202
Frank Couzens, Interim President
See listing under "Art"

Central Michigan University
100 Warriner Hall, Mt. Pleasant 48858

Cleary College - Livingston Campus
3750 Cleary College Dr., Howell 48843
Tom Sullivan, President
800-589-1979

Cleary College - Washtenaw Campus
2170 Washtenaw Ave., Ypsilanti 48197
Tom Sullivan, President
800-686-1883

Concordia College
4090 Geddes Rd., Ann Arbor 48105
Mary Froelich, Dir. of Admis.

Eastern Michigan University, Ypsilanti 48197
M. Dolan Evanovich, Director of Admissions
313-487-3060 or 800-GO-TO-EMU

Ferris State University
Office of Admission
420 Oak St., Big Rapids 49307-2020

Grand Rapids Baptist College & Seminary
1001 East Beltline Ave., N.E.
Grand Rapids 49505

Grand Valley State University
1 Campus Dr., Allendale 49401
JoAnn Foerster, Dir. of Admis.

HILLSDALE COLLEGE
33 E. College St., Hillsdale 49242
Jeffrey S. Lantis, Dir. of Admis.
517-437-7341

Hope College
69 E. 10th St., Holland 49423
Gordon Van Wylen, President

Jordan College
360 W. Pine St., Cedar Springs 49319
616-696-1180

Jordan College-Berrien County Campus
185 E. Main St., Benton Harbor 49022
Jodi Hunsicker, Dean
616-927-3333

Jordan College-Detroit Campus
15400 Grand River Ave., Detroit 48227
Mark Jackson, Dean
313-835-5100

Jordan College-Flint Campus
3488 N. Jennings Rd., Flint 48504
L. B. McCune, Dean
810-789-0520

Jordan College-Grand Rapids Campus
1925 Breton Rd., S.E., Grand Rapids 49506
Jack Kooyman, Dean
616-957-3999

Jordan College-Thumb Area Campus
6667 Main St., Cass City 48726
Jerry White, Dean
517-872-4394

Jordan Energy Institute
155 Seven Mile Rd. N.W., Comstock Park 49321
Daniel Paulson, Dean
800-968-3955

Kalamazoo College
1200 Academy St., Kalamazoo 49006

Kendall College of Art & Design
111 N. Division Ave., Grand Rapids 49503
Charles Deihl, President
800-676-2787

Lake Superior State University
1000 College Dr., Sault St. Marie 49783

Lawrence Technological University
21000 W. Ten Mile Rd., Southfield 48075
800-225-5588 ext. 3160

Lewis College of Business
17370 Meyers Rd., Detroit 48235
K. Frank DeShazok, Dir. of Admis.
313-862-6300

Madonna University
36600 Schoolcraft St., Livonia 48150

Marygrove College
8425 W. McNichols Rd., Detroit 48221

Michigan State University, East Lansing 48824
Dr. William Turner, Dir. of Admis.

Michigan Technological University
1400 Townsend Dr., Houghton 49931
Joseph A. Galetto, Dir. Enrollment Mgmt.
906-487-2335

Northern Michigan University
610 Cohodas Admin. Center, Marquette 49855
Nancy Rehling, Dir. of Admis.

Northwood University
3225 Cook Rd., Midland 48640
Daniel F. Toland, Dir. of Admis.
800-457-7878

Oakland University, Rochester 48309
Larry Bartalucci, Registrar

OLIVET COLLEGE
300 S. Main St., Olivet 49076
Durk L. Dunham, Director of Admissions
616-749-7635
Established 1844. Private. Coed. Accreditation: North Central Association of Colleges and Schools. Tuition: $11,030. Room and board: $3,680. $25 application fee. Enrollment: 627 full-time, 60 part-time. Faculty: 77. Student-faculty ratio: 9:1. Degrees: Bachelor of Arts, Bachelor of Music Education. Library: 90,000 volumes. 10 buildings on 687 acres. 150 years old, new library, personal attention, convenience of location, beautiful campus.

Saginaw Valley State University
2250 Pierce Rd., University Center 48710

Siena Heights College
1247 E. Siena Heights Dr., Adrian 49221

Spring Arbor College
106 E. Main St., Spring Arbor 49283

UNIVERSITY OF DETROIT MERCY
4001 W. McNichols, PO Box 19900
Detroit 48219-0900
Maureen A. Fay, O.P., President
Robert Johnson, Dean of Enrollment
313-993-1245
Michigan's most comprehensive Catholic university offering a quality, value-oriented education firmly rooted in the Jesuit and Mercy traditions. Private. Coed. Enrollment: 7,500. Faculty: 312. Student-faculty ratio: 16:1. Degrees: Undergraduate, graduate, and professional degrees in more than 60 fields of study. Tuition: $5,000 per term. Room and board: $1,800 per term. Scholarships and financial aid available. Nationally recognized Cooperative Education program. Six residence halls located on safe, secure campuses in residential northwest Detroit.

University of Michigan-Ann Arbor
815 S. University Ave., Ann Arbor 48109

University of Michigan-Ann Arbor
109 Observatory St., Ann Arbor 48109
Dr. Richard Remington, Dean

University of Michigan-Dearborn
4901 Evergreen Rd., Dearborn 48128
Carol S. Mack, Dir. of Admis.
313-593-5100

University of Michigan-Flint
303 Kearsley St., Flint 48502

Wayne State University
5980 Cass Ave., Detroit 48202
Dr. J. R. Thorderson, Dir. of Admis.

Western Michigan University, Kalamazoo 49008
Stanley Henderson, Dir. of Enrl. Mgt. & Admis.
616-387-2000

William Tyndale College
35700 W. Twelve Mile Rd.
Farmington Hills 48331

MINNESOTA

Alfred Adler Institute of Minnesota
1001 Hwy. 7 #344, Hopkins 55305

Augsburg College
731 21st Ave., S., Minneapolis 55454

Bemidji State University
1500 Birchmont Dr., N.E., Bemidji 56601
800-475-2001

Bethel College
3900 Bethel Dr., St. Paul 55112
Dr. George Brushaber, President

Carleton College
One N. College St., Northfield 55057
Paul Thiboutot, Dir. of Admis.

COLLEGE OF ASSOCIATED ARTS
344 Summit Ave., Saint Paul 55102
Sherry Essen, Dir. of Admis.
Admissions Office, 612-224-3416

College of St. Scholastica
1200 Kenwood Ave., Duluth 55811
Becky Urbanski-Junkert, VP for Admissions/Financial Planning
800-447-5444
See listing under "Liberal Arts"

CONCORDIA COLLEGE
901 8th St. S., Moorhead 56562
Dr. Paul Dovre, President
Lee Johnson, Dir. of Admis.
Established 1891. Evangelical Lutheran Church in America. Coed. Accreditation: NCACS. Tuition: $10,210. Room and board: $3,165. Faculty: 198 full-time, 55 part-time. Degrees: BA, BMus. More than 50 majors. Library: 282,000 volumes. 31 buildings on 120 acres. Gym, pool. Across Red River from Fargo ND, providing 165,000 combined population of Moorhead/Fargo. 2 universities in area. Tri-college, May seminars abroad, cooperative education, 2 summer school sessions.

Concordia College-St. Paul
275 N. Syndicate, St. Paul 55104
Tim Utter, Dir. of Admis.

CROWN COLLEGE
6425 County Rd. 30, St. Bonifacius 55375
Dr. Bill Lanpher, President
James D. Rightler, Dir. of Admis.
Established 1916. Private. Coed. Accreditation: AABC, NCACS. Tuition: $7,140. Room and board: $3,590. Fees: $414. Enrollment: 518. Student-faculty ratio: 13:1. Degrees: AA, BA, BS. Library: 99,000 volumes. 193 acre campus. A professional undergraduate institution that is a recognized leader in biblically-based higher education. Degrees in biblical & theological studies, business administration, Christian education, church music & ministries, English, history, linguistics, music, pastoral ministries, physical education/coaching K-12, psychology, teacher education, world mission, youth. Ethnomusicology training center. Other students undecided about a career choice enter Crown College seeking to affirm God's vocational direction for their lives through formal Bible education.

Dr. Martin Luther College
1884 College Heights Dr., New Ulm 56073
Dr. John Lawrenz, President
507-354-8221, Fax: 507-354-8225

Gustavus Adolphus College
800 W. College Ave., St. Peter 56082
Mark Anderson, Dir. of Admis.

Hamline University
1536 Hewitt Ave., St. Paul 55104
Scott Pratt, Dir. of Admis.

MacAlester College
1600 Grand Ave., St. Paul 55105

Mankato State University
P.O. Box 8400, Mankato 56002
507-389-1111

Metropolitan State University
700 7th St. E., St. Paul 55106
Richard Green, PhD, Interim President

Moorhead State University
1104 7th Ave. S., Moorhead 56560

National College
1380 Energy Ln., Saint Paul 55108

NEI COLLEGE OF TECHNOLOGY
825 41st Ave. N.E., Minneapolis 55421
Richard Thomson, Dir. of Admis.
Call 800-777-7NEI for Info.
See listing under "Career Schools"

NORTH CENTRAL BIBLE COLLEGE
910 Elliot Ave., Minneapolis 55404
800-289-NCBC
Dr. Don Argue, President
Dan Neary, Dir. of Admis.
Dr. Don Meyer, V.P. Academic Affairs
Established 1930. Private. Coed. Accreditation: NCACS. Tuition: $4,470. Room and board: $3,020. Fees: $600. Enrollment: 827 full-time, 235 part-time. Faculty: 68. Student-faculty ratio: 15:1. Degrees: BA, BS. Library: 62,100 volumes. 13 bldgs. on 6+ acres. Integrated curriculm (faith and discipline); one of 26 colleges in Minnesota to certify teachers in elementary education; location in downtown metropolitan area offers many distinct opportunities for employment and activities; enclosed campus accessible by skyways.

Northwestern College
3003 Snelling Ave., N., St. Paul 55113
Ralph Anderson, Dean of Admissions
800-827-6827 or 612-631-5111

St. Cloud State University
740 4th Ave., S., St. Cloud 56301
Sherwood Reid, Dir. of Admis.
800-369-4260

St. John's University
P.O. Box 7155, Collegeville 56321

St. Mary's College of Minnesota
700 Terrace Heights #2, Winona 55987
Tony Piscitiello, VP for Admission

St. Olaf College, Northfield 55057
John Ruohoniemi, Dir. of Admis.
507-646-3025

Southwest State University, Marshall 56258

University of Minnesota
2400 Oakland Ave., Duluth 55812
Robert L. Heller, Provost

University of Minnesota
600 E. Fourth St., Morris 56267

University of Minnesota, Twin Cities
Minneapolis 55455

UNIVERSITY OF MINNESOTA-CROOKSTON
2900 University Ave., Crookston 56716
John M. Bywater, Director of Admissions
800-232-6466
Established 1965. Public. Coed. Accreditation: NCACS. Tuition: $2,655. Room and board: $3,300. Fees: $206. Enrollment: 792 full-time, 665 part-time. Faculty: 56. Student-faculty ratio: 14:1. Degrees: Associate in Applied Science, Associate of Science, Bachelor of Science. Library: 25,000 volumes. 17 buildings on 90 acres. Polytechnic emphasis in all degrees. Bachelor degree programs began September, 1993. All full time students pay a technology fee and they are issued an IBM Laptop (notebook) computer.

University of Minnesota - Rochester Center
855 30th Ave. S.E., Rochester 55904

University of Saint Thomas
2115 Summit Ave., Saint Paul 55105
612-647-5000

Winona State University
P.O. Box 5838, Winona 55987
Dr. J. Mootz, Dir. of Admis.

MISSISSIPPI

Alcorn State University
P.O. Box 359, Lorman 39096
D. W. Wilburn, Registrar

Belhaven College
1500 Peachtree St., Jackson 39202

Delta State University
Hwy. 8 W., Cleveland 38732

Jackson State University
1400 Lynch St., Jackson 39203

MAGNOLIA BIBLE COLLEGE
P.O. Box 1109, Kosciusko 39090
Cecil May, Jr., President
800-748-8655

Millsaps College
P.O. Box 150556, Jackson 39210
Florence Hines, Dir. of Admis.

Mississippi College
P.O. Box 4086, Clinton 39058

Mississippi State University
P.O. Box J, Mississippi State University 39762

Mississippi University for Women
P.O. Box W-1602, Columbus 39701
Teresa Thompson, Exec. Dir. of Enrollment

Mississippi University for Women-Tupelo
655 Eason Blvd., Tupelo 38801

MISSISSIPPI VALLEY STATE UNIVERSITY
14000 Hwy. 82 W., Itta Bena 38941
Maxcine B. Rush, Director of Admissions
601-254-9041
Established 1946. Public. Coed. Accreditation: SACS, NCATE, NASAD, and other accrediting agencies. Tuition: $2,171 (out of state fee $959). Room and board $2,025. Enrollment: 2,329 full-time, 199 part-time, 12 graduate. Faculty: 96. Student-faculty ratio: 20:1. Degrees: BS, BA, BSW, MS. Library: 120,740 volumes. 45 buildings on 450 acres. The university seeks to meet the academic, cultural and vocational needs of students. MVSU is unlimited in its potential to provide avenues for students to explore their special talents and interest. MVSU has a competitive academic scholarship program, cooperative placement/assistance program, social and academic programs.

Rust College
150 E. Rust Ave., Holly Springs 38635

Tougaloo College
500 E. County Line Rd., Tougaloo 39174

University of Mississippi, University 38677

University of Southern Mississippi
P.O. Box 5165, Hattiesburg 39406

University of Southern Mississippi
Gulf Park Campus
East Beach Blvd., Long Beach 39560

William Carey College
498 Tuscan Ave., Hattiesburg 39401

MISSOURI

Avila College
11901 Wornall Rd., Kansas City 64145

CENTRAL METHODIST COLLEGE
411 CMC Square, Fayette 65248
Joe A. Howell, President
Anthony J. Boes, Vice President for Student Affairs
816-248-3391
Established 1854. Private. Coed. Faculty: 69. Student-faculty ratio: 12:1. Enrollment: 1,075. Accreditation: NCATE, NASM, Missouri Dept. of Education, Missouri State Board of Nursing, Univ. Senate Un. Methodist Church. Degrees: AA, AS, BA, BS, BSE, BSN, BM, BME. Over 30 areas of concentration including pre-professional areas of engineering, journalism, law, library science, medicine, dentistry,

dental hygiene, medical technology, pharmacy, O.T., P.T., nursing, ministry, religious education & social work. NAIA Division II athletics, eight sports for men and women. Centrally located in Missouri. Thirty minutes from Columbia. 36% Methodist student body.

Central Missouri State University
Warrensburg 64093
Delores Hudson, Dir. of Admis.

College of the Ozarks, Point Lookout 65726
Dr. Kenton Olson, Dean of the College

Columbia College
1001 Rogers St., Columbia 65216
Ron Cronacher, Dir. of Admissions
800-231-2391

Culver-Stockton College, Canton 63435
Betty Smith, Dean of Admissions
800-537-1883

Drury College
900 N. Benton Ave., Springfield 65802
Michael G. Thomas, Dir. of Admis.

Evangel College
1111 N. Glenstone Ave., Springfield 65802
David Schoolfield, Dir. of Enrollment
417-865-2811

Fontbonne College
6800 Wydown Blvd., St. Louis 63105
Peggy Musen, Dir. of Admis.

Hannibal-LaGrange College, Hannibal 63401

Harris-Stowe State College
3026 Laclede Ave., St. Louis 63103
Valerie Beeson, Dir. of Admis. and Advisement
314-340-3300

Lincoln University
820 Chestnut St., Jefferson City 65101

Lindenwood College
209 S Kingshighway, Saint Charles 63301
John Guffey, Dean of Admis.

Maryville University of St. Louis
13550 Conway Rd., Saint Louis 63141
314-576-9300 or 800-MARYVLL

Missouri Baptist College
12542 Conway Rd., St. Louis 63141

MISSOURI SOUTHERN STATE COLLEGE

3950 Newman Rd., Joplin 64801-1595
Richard D. Humphrey, Dir. of Admis.

Missouri Southern State College is a public, coeducational institution accredited by NCACS. The College is an undergraduate institution offering bachelor's and associate's degrees to approximately 6,000 students. The academic calendar is based on the semester system. The mission of Missouri Southern is to provide opportunities to pursue cultural and intellectual interests; prepare for a wide range of careers; pursue less than bachelor's level programs; pursue continuing education opportunities and prepare for a graduate education. An international perspective is incorporated throughout the curriculum.

Facilities:
Missouri Southern State College is located at the edge of a mid-sized city on a 334-acre campus built on the site of the former Mission Hills estate. The campus, which opened in 1967, features 25 modern buildings. The Mansion House and Barn Theatre are part of the historical legacy of the campus. Spiva Library contains 192,000 volumes, 1,300 periodicals, a 600,000 item microform collection and a federal documents depository. The library uses OCLC, DIALOG, ERIC and many other nation-wide data retrieval systems. Special collections include a federal documents depository and an archival area of tri-state mining maps, the papers of western historian Arrel Gibson and the Gene Taylor Congressional Papers. A fine arts complex houses Spiva Art Center, a 2,000 seat performing arts center and a recital hall. Athletic facilities include a football stadium seating 7,000 with artificial turf and all weather track, a basketball arena seating 2,000 and facilities for softball, soccer, tennis, swimming, racquetball, and weight training. Men's baseball facilities are located off campus. Student housing consists of one women's dorm and one men's dorm together housing 318 students, eight suite-style apartment complexes housing 320 students. Freshmen are allowed to live off campus. Opportunities for religious activity on campus are provided by the Association of Christian Athletes, the Baptist Student Center, and the Koinonia Christian Fellowship.

Curriculum:
Missouri Southern offers career education with a liberal arts background, giving graduates flexibility in adapting to rapidly changing professions as well as enriching their personal lives. A core curriculum provides a broad base of experience with required courses in English composition and communications, math, physical education, humanities and fine arts, natural science, behavioral and social sciences and international culture. Scholastic honors and projects include an honors program which encourages academic excellence by providing scholarships to students who have a 3.5+ grade point average in high school and are accepted into the program by a screening committee. A summer study program at Oxford University in England also is offered. Missouri Southern offers students opportunities to complete internships in several majors. Grading is by traditional letter grades.

Admissions Policies:
Students applying for admission to Missouri Southern must have a composite ACT score of 17 or above or rank in the upper half of their high school graduating class. Credentials required for admission include the completed application form and fee, high school transcript and ACT scores. Interviews are not required. The deadline for admission is open. Notification is on a rolling basis. The application fee is $10. A room deposit of $75 is required for on-campus housing. International students interested in attending Missouri Southern should contact the Director of Admissions.

Financial Aid:
In addition to the federal and state financial aid programs which are based on financial need, Missouri Southern offers endowed scholarships, including President's, Regent's, and Dean's scholarships and performing awards. To ensure consideration for financial assistance, complete the CSX form and submit copies of the student's and parent's income tax returns.

MISSOURI VALLEY COLLEGE

500 E. College St., Marshall 65340
Chadwick B. Freeman, VP Admissions & Fin. Aid
816-886-6924 ext. 114

Established 1889. Private. Coed. Accreditation: NCACS. Tuition: $9,000. Room and board: $4,950. Fees: $100. Enrollment: 1,054 full-time, 46 part-time. Faculty: 61. Student-faculty ratio: 18:1. Degrees: BA, BS, Associate of Arts in small business management, teacher certification. Library: 70,200+ volumes. 17 buildings on 80+ acres. 60 miles east of Kansas City. Acclaimed work/study program. Many scholarships available.

Missouri Western State College
4525 Downs Dr., St. Joseph 64507
Howard McCauley, Dir. of Admis.

Northeast Missouri State University
Kirksville 63501

Northwest Missouri State University
800 University Dr., Maryville 64468

Park College, Parkville 64152
Dr. Edwin Rawn, Dean of Admis.

Rockhurst College
1100 Rockhurst Rd., Kansas City 64110
Barbara O'Connell, Dir. of Enrollment Services

St. Louis University
221 N. Grand Blvd., St. Louis 63103
Louis A. Menard, Dean of Admissions

SOUTHEAST MISSOURI STATE UNIVERSITY

1 University Plz., Cape Girardeau 63701
Juan Crites, Director of Admissions
314-651-2590

Established 1873. Public. Coed. Tuition: $2,364. Room and board: $3,400. Fees: $50. Enrollment: 7,300 full-time, 1,000 part-time. Faculty: 400. Student-faculty ratio: 17:1. Degrees: BA, BS, MA. Library: over 600,000 volumes. 70 buildings on 200 acres. Scenic campus with a historic look. Good variety of academic programs with a nationally recognized Teacher Education program.

Southwest Baptist University
1601 S. Springfield Ave., Bolivar 65613

Southwest Missouri State University
901 S. National Ave., Springfield 65804
Don Simpson, Dir. of Admission and Records
417-836-5517 or 800-492-7900

Southwest Missouri State University
905 W. Main St., West Plains 65775
417-256-5533

University of Missouri, Columbia
228 Jesse Hall, Columbia 65211

University of Missouri, Kansas City
5100 Rockhill Rd., Kansas City 64110
Leo J. Sweeney, Dir. of Admis. & Registrar

University of Missouri, Rolla
102 Parker Hall, Rolla 65401
David J. Allen, Dir. of Admis. & Financial Aid
800-522-0938

University of Missouri
8001 Natural Bridge Rd., St. Louis 63121
Mimi LaMarca, Dir. of Admis.

Washington University
1 Brookings Dr., St. Louis 63130

WEBSTER UNIVERSITY

470 E. Lockwood Ave., Saint Louis 63119
Niel DeVasto, Director of Admissions
800-753-6765

Established 1915. Private. Coed. Accreditation: NCACS. Tuition: $9,160. Room and board: $4,340. Enrollment: 1300 full-time, 1500 part-time. Faculty: 110, Student-faculty ratio: 13:1. Degrees: BA, BFA, BM, BMEd, BS, BSN, MA, MBA, MAT, DMGT. Library: 230,000 volumes. 22 buildings on 45 acres. Nationally recognized programs in the performing arts and communications. Students from 35 states and 30 countries. Beautiful suburban campus in a wooded community of 20,000. Average class size of 15. New $5.5 million Student Center. Campuses in four European countries.

Westminister College
501 Westminster Ave., Fulton 65251
Gary Forney, Dean of Admis.

William Jewell College, Liberty 64068
T. Edwin Norris, Dir of Admis.
800-753-7009

MONTANA

CARROLL COLLEGE

1610 N. Benton Ave., Helena 59625
Dr. Matthew J. Quinn, President
Candace Cain, Dir. of Admis.

Established 1909. Catholic. Coed. Accreditation: NASC. Tuition: $7,570. Room and board: $3,650. Enrollment: 650 boarding, 750 day. Faculty: 75. Degrees: AA, BA. Library: 110,000 volumes. 8 buildings on 63 acres. Gym. Pool. 93% placement in premedicine over past 10 years. Nationally ranked debate team. National Discussion Champions, Frontier Conference Football Champions. 7 undergraduate $34,000 Truman Scholars in past 9 years.

College of Great Falls
1301 20th St., S., Great Falls 59405
Jean Walker, Dir. of Admis.

Montana State University, Bozeman 59717

Montana State University - Billings
1500 N. 30th St., Billings 59101
Karen Everett, Dir. of Admis.
406-657-2158

Montana Tech
(formerly Montana College of Mineral Science and Technology)
1300 W. Park St., Butte 59701-8997
800-445-TECH
See listing under "Engineering"

Northern Montana College
P.O. Box 7751, Havre 59501
Ralph A. Brigham, Dir. of Admis.

ROCKY MOUNTAIN COLLEGE

1511 Poly Dr., Billings 59102
David Heringer, Dir. of Admis.
800-877-6259

Established 1878. Private. Coed. Accreditation: NASC. Tuition: $9,162. Room and board: $3,502. Fees: $100. Enrollment: 612 full-time, 144 part-time. Faculty: 45 full-time, 33 part-time. Student-faculty ratio: 16:1. Degrees: AA, BA, BS. Library: 65,000 volumes. 16 buildings on 65 acre campus. Rocky Mountain College offers degrees in aviation studies, equestrian science, and environmental science. Extensive outdoor recreational opportunities available on and off campus.

University of Montana, Missoula 59812
800-462-8636

Western Montana College
710 S. Atlantic St., Dillon 59725

NEBRASKA

Bellevue College
1000 Galvin Rd. S., Bellevue 68005
Chari Leader, VP of Enrollment

Chadron State College
1000 Main St., Chadron 69337
Dale Williamson, Dir. of Admis.

Concordia College
800 N. Columbia Ave., Seward 68434
Don Vos, Dir. of Admis.

Creighton University
2500 California St., Omaha 68178
Howard Bachman, Dir. of Admis.

DANA COLLEGE

2848 College Dr., Blair 68008-1099
John Schueth, Dir. of Admis.
800-444-3262 or 402-426-7220

Established 1884. Private. Coed. Accreditation: NCACS, NCATE, CSWE. Tuition: $8,330. Room and board: $3,130. Fees: $450. Enrollment: 550 full-time, 66 part-time. Faculty: 61. Student-faculty ratio: 11:1. Degrees: BA, BS. Library: 150,000 volumes. 17 buildings on 150 acres. 45 majors with particular strength in social work, teacher education, art, biology, communications and business. NAIA athletics. Community of 7,000 and only 20 minutes from metropolitan Omaha. Activities range from theatre, choir and concert band to campus radio and TV stations. School of the ELCA, one of only two colleges in the US founded by Danish immigrants. New 6 million dollar classroom center and chapel just opened.

Doane College
1014 Boswell Ave., Crete 68333
Pappy Khouri, Dir. of Admissions

Hastings College
P.O. Box 269, Hastings 68902
Thomas Reeves, President

Midland Lutheran College
900 Clarkson St., Fremont 68025
Roland Kahnk, V.P. Admissions

Nebraska Wesleyan University
5000 Saint Paul Ave., Lincoln 68504
Ken Sieg, Dir. of Admis.

Peru State College, Peru 68421
Pamela J. Cosgrove, Dir. of Admis.
402-872-3815

Union College
3800 S. 48th St., Lincoln 68506

UNIVERSITY OF NEBRASKA NEBRASKA COLLEGE OF TECHNICAL AGRICULTURE

P.O. Box 69, Curtis 69025
See listing under "Agriculture"

University of Nebraska
905 W. 25th St., Kearney 68849

University of Nebraska at Lincoln
16 Administration Bldg., Lincoln 68588
John Beacon, Dir. of Admissions

University of Nebraska at Omaha
Omaha 68182

Wayne State College
200 E. Tenth St., Wayne 68787

YORK COLLEGE
912 Kiplinger Ave., York 68467
Larry Roberts, President
Steddon Sikes, Director of Admissions
800-927-3435
Established 1890. Private. Coed. Accreditation: NCACS. Tuition: $4,300. Room and board: $2,850. Fees: $340. Enrollment: 432 full-time, 50 part-time. Faculty: 36. Student-faculty ratio: 14:1. Degrees offered: Associates or Bachelors. 10 buildings on 15 acres. Liberal Arts college. 8,000 people in the community. 1 hour away from the state capital. Education programs. Member of NAIA.

NEVADA

Morrison College
140 Washington St., Reno 89503
Mary T. Morrison, VP Administration
702-323-4145

SIERRA NEVADA COLLEGE-LAKE TAHOE
P.O. Box 4269, Incline Village 89450
Mark Hurtubise, President
Lane Murray, Dir. of Admissions
Established 1969. Coed. Accreditation: NWASC. Tuition: $9,000. Room: $2,700 to $3,000. Enrollment: 120 boarding, 500 day. Faculty: 50. Degrees: BA, BS, BFA. Library: 20,000 volumes. 6 buildings on 19 acres. Golf course nearby. Majors in environmental science, science, hotel, restaurant and resort management, ski business and resort management, performing arts, Humanities, and teacher education. 2 miles from Lake Tahoe; stunning alpine environment. 22 ski resorts within 1/2 hour drive, 45 minutes from Reno, Nevada, 4 hours from San Francisco.

University of Nevada, Reno
Reno 89557

University of Nevada Las Vegas
4505 S. Maryland Pky., Las Vegas 89154-1021
Larry Mason, Director of Admissions
702-895-3443 or 800-334-UNLV

NEW HAMPSHIRE

Daniel Webster College
20 University Dr., Nashua 03063

Dartmouth College, Hanover 03755

Franklin Pierce College, Rindge 03461

Franklin Pierce College
130 Pembroke Rd., Concord 03301

Franklin Pierce College
43 Arch St., Keene 03431

Franklin Pierce College
P.O. Box 3060, Portsmouth 03802

Franklin Pierce College
12 Industrial Way, Salem 03079

Franklin Pierce College
20 Cotton Rd., Nashua 03063

Keene State College
229 Main St., Keene 03435
Kathryn Dodge, Dir. of Admis.

New England College
26 Bridge St., Henniker 03242
John Spaulding, Dir. of Admis.

New Hampshire College
2500 North River Rd., Manchester 03106
Brad Poznanski, Dir. of Admis.
603-645-9611

NOTRE DAME COLLEGE
2321 Elm St., Manchester 03104
603-669-4298

Plymouth State College, Plymouth 03264

Rivier College
420 S. Main St., Nashua 03060
Admissions: 800-44-RIVIER

Saint Anselm College
87 Saint Anselm Dr., Manchester 03102
Don Healy, Dir. of Admis.

University of New Hampshire, Durham 03824
Stanwood C. Fish, Dir. of Admissions

University of New Hampshire at Manchester
220 Hackett Hill Rd., Manchester 03102

NEW JERSEY

Bloomfield College
1 Park Place, Bloomfield 07003
Warner Smith, Dean for Admissions
201-748-9000, Ext. 230

Caldwell College
9 Ryerson Ave., Caldwell 07006

Drew University
36 Madison Ave., Madison 07940
Kenneth Cole, Registrar

Fairleigh Dickinson University, Madison 07940
Lissa Anderson, Dir. of Admis.
201-593-8906

Fairleigh Dickinson University, Teaneck 07666
Dale Herold, Dir. of Admis.
201-460-5194

FELICIAN COLLEGE
262 S. Main St., Lodi 07644
Sr. Mary Austin, OSB, Dir. of Admis.
201-778-1029
Established 1942. Public. Coed. Accreditation: MSACS, NLN, Committee on Allied Health Education and Accreditation (CAHEA) in cooperation with the National Accrediting Agency for Clinical Laboratory Sciences (NAACLS). Tuition: $8,000. Enrollment: 1,140. Faculty: 97. Student-faculty ratio: 15:1. Degrees: Bachelor's, Associates, Certificate Programs. 27 acre campus. Weekend college program, learning center, day care center, small classes and personal attention.

Jersey City State College
2039 Kennedy Blvd., Jersey City 07305
201-200-3234

Kean College of New Jersey
1000 Morris Ave., Union 07083

Monmouth College
400 Cedar Ave., West Long Branch 07764
Joan Rudinski, Dir. of Admis.

Montclair State College
1 Normal Ave., Upper Montclair 07043

New Jersey Institute of Technology
323 Martin Luther King Jr. Blvd., Newark 07102

Princeton University, Princeton 08544

Ramapo College of New Jersey
505 Ramapo Valley Rd., Mahwah 07430
Robert Scott, President
201-529-7600

Rider University
2083 Lawrenceville Rd., Lawrenceville 08648
Susan Christian, Dir. of Admis.

Rowan College of New Jersey
200 N. Broadway, Camden 08102

Rowan College of New Jersey, Glassboro 08028
Marvin G. Sills, Dir. of Admis.

Rutgers, The State University of NJ
University College - Camden
Camden 08102

Rutgers, The State University of NJ
Camden College of Arts & Sciences
Camden 08102

Rutgers, The State University of NJ
Cook College
New Brunswick 08901

Rutgers, The State University of NJ
Livingston College
New Brunswick 08903

Rutgers, The State University of NJ
Newark College of Arts & Sciences
249 University Ave., Newark 07102

Rutgers, The State University of NJ
Rutgers College
New Brunswick 08903

Rutgers-The State U of NJ/Univ. Coll.
249 University Ave., Newark 07102

Rutgers, The State University of NJ
University College - New Brunswick
New Brunswick 08901

ST. PETER'S COLLEGE
2641 John F. Kennedy Blvd.
Jersey City 07306
Mary Beth Carey, Director of Admissions
201-915-9213

St. Peter's College
Hudson Terrace, Englewood Cliffs 07632
Dr. Katherine M. Restaino, Dean
201-568-7730

Seton Hall University
400 S. Orange Ave., South Orange 07079
Lee Cooke, Dir. of Admis.

Stevens Institute of Technology, Hoboken 07030

Stockton State College, Pomona 08240
Sal Catalfamo, Dir. of Admis.

Thomas Edison State College
101 W. State St., Trenton 08608

Trenton State College
Hillwood Lakes CN 4700, Trenton 08650

Upsala College
345 Prospect St., East Orange 07017
George Lynes, Dean of Admissions

Upsala College
Rural Route 03 Box 138-A, Sussex 07461

WESTMINSTER CHOIR COLLEGE OF RIDER UNIVERSITY
101 Walnut Ln., Princeton 08540-3899
800-96-CHOIR or 609-921-7100, FAX: 609-921-8829
See listing under "Music"

William Paterson College
300 Pompton Rd., Wayne 07470

William Penn College
201 Trueblood Ave., Oskaloosa 52577
Eric Otto, Dir. of Admis.

NEW MEXICO

College of Santa Fe
1600 St. Michaels Dr., Santa Fe 87505
800-456-2673

College of the Southwest
6610 N. Lovington Hwy., Hobbs 88240

Eastern New Mexico University
Portales 88130
Larry Fuqua, Dir. of Admis.
505-562-2121 or 800-367-3668

National College
1202 Pennsylvania St., N.E., Albuquerque 87110

New Mexico Highlands University, Las Vegas 87701
Dr. Jorge P. Thomas, VP Academic Affairs

New Mexico Institute of Mining & Technology
801 Leroy Pl., Socorro 87801

New Mexico State University
P.O. Box 30001, Las Cruces 88003

University of New Mexico, Albuquerque 87131
Robert Weaver, Dean of Admissions

University of Phoenix-New Mexico Division
7471 Pan American Freeway N.E.
Albuquerque 87109

WESTERN NEW MEXICO UNIVERSITY
College Ave., Silver City 88062
Michael Alecksen, Dir. of Admis.
800-222-9668
Established 1893. Public. Coed. Accreditation: NCACS. Tuition: $1,190 in state, $4,352 out-of-state. Room and board: $2,030. Fees: $10 application. Enrollment: 1,390 full-time, 582 part-time. Faculty: 90. Student-faculty ratio: 18:1. Degrees: associate, bachelors, masters. Library: 140,000 volumes. 40 buildings on 80 acres. Located in the foothills of the beautiful and rugged Mogollon and Black Mountains, at the elevation of 5,900 feet. Grant County has a climate of four gentle seasons.

NEW YORK

Adelphi University, Garden City 11530
Dr. Elliot Pruzan, Asst. Provost & Dir. of Admis.
516-877-3050

Alfred University
Alumni Hall, Alfred 14802
Laurie Richer, Director of Admissions
800-541-9229

AMERICAN UNIVERSITY OF PARIS
31 Avenue Bosquet
75007 Paris, France
Telephone: (33/1) 45.55.91.73
Fax: (33/1) 47.05.34.32
Glenn W. Ferguson, President
Dr. William F. Cipolla, Dean
Thelma Bullock, Dir. of U.S. Office
The American University of Paris is an independent, four-year institution, founded in Paris more than a quarter of a century ago. It serves as a major international center of American higher education, bringing together the outstanding strengths of its American curriculum and traditions, its privileged location in Paris and Europe, and its immediate access to important cultural events and intellectual currents. The University seeks to educate its students to understand the complexities of an interdependent world.
The student body numbers 1,000: 40% American, 14% French, and 46% from 70 different countries. The American University of Paris is an urban institution, centrally located in the 7th arrondissement of Paris, on the Left Bank of the Seine, near the Eiffel Tower. Students are placed in independent lodgings or are housed with French families in central Paris.
The BA degree is awarded in the following disciplines: applied economics, art history, comparative literature, European studies, French studies, international affairs, international business administration, international economics, and modern history. The BS degree is awarded in computer science. All students are required to complete two years of French. A minimum of 120 credit hours is needed for graduation. The University operates on a semester basis; it also provides a six-week summer session and a January intersession. Transfer of credit is assumed because the University is accredited by the Middle States Association of Colleges and Schools. Extensive study/travel opportunities exist within France and Europe, and each year there are trips to other countries such as Africa, the Soviet Union and Asia. As part of its course offerings, the University sponsors an internship program which allows qualified degree candidates to gain professional experience in a wide variety of fields. Library: 100,000+ vols. on an open-stack system. Available to students is the most complete selection of English-language periodicals in Europe and numerous audio-visual materials. The University's computer laboratory offers students computer workstations which may be used for word-processing, as stand-alone computers, or as graphics terminals. These are linked to the University's extensive Harris 800 mainframe system, which provides 4.7 megabytes of physical memory, 1.6 gigabytes of online storage, and over 100 terminal connections. Tuition for 1994-1995: $13,950. Room and board and other living expenses: $12,500. Financial aid rarely exceeds three-quarters cost of tuition. Faculty: 103. The faculty are primarily American, French or Brit-

ish-educated. The majority work professionally in their fields. The American University of Paris operates on a rolling admissions policy. The final deadline for applicatons is May 1st for the Fall semester, and December 1st for the Spring semester. An applicaton for admission and further information may be obtained by contacting The American University of Paris at its US address:

The American University of Paris
80 East 11th St. #434
New York, NY 10003
Tel.: 212-677-4870
Fax: 212-475-5205

Bard College
Annandle-on-Hudson 12504

Boricua College
3755 Broadway, New York 10032

Boricua College
186 N. 6th St., Brooklyn 11211

Canisius College
2001 Main St., Buffalo 14208
Penelope Lips, Dir. of Admis.
800-843-1517

CAZENOVIA COLLEGE
Cazenovia 13035
Dr. Stephen Schneeweiss, President
Dr. Adelaide V. Titus, VP for Academic Affairs
Dr. James Parker, VP for Enrollment Management
Frank Mezzanini, VP for Business and Finance
Eileen Dullea, Dean for Student Affairs
800-654-3210
Established 1824. Private. Coed. Total enrollment: 1,075. Mostly residential. Accreditation: MSACS. Tuition: $9,384. Room: $2,420. Board: $2,420. Student-faculty ratio: 16:1. Federal, state and institutional financial aid; college meets 100 % of proven financial need.
Associate's and bachelor's degrees offered. Associate Degrees are offered in twenty one programs organized within three centers: the Center for Art & Design (advertising/graphic design, commercial illustration, commercial photography, environmental/interior design, fashion design, studio art), the Center for the Arts & Humanities (day-care services, early childhood education, individualized studies, liberal arts, special education assistant), the Center for Life Sciences (community social services, social services for children, social services for the elderly), and the Center for Management Studies (accounting, business management, computerized office management, executive secretarial studies, horsemanship, retail management, stable and farm management). Bachelor degrees are available in: Bachelor of Fine Arts in Environmental/Interior Design; Bachelor of Fine Arts in Visual Communications - Advertising/Graphic Design, Commercial Illustration; Bachelor of Professional Studies - Business Management, Retail Management; Bachelor of Science in Applied Arts & Sciences - Fine Arts, Literature & Humanities, Social Institutions, Science & Technology. Unique competency-based curriculum. Summer school, continuing education, HEOP and Title IV programs. Study abroad in England, Switzerland, Puerto Rico, Ireland. Nationally acclaimed learning resources center.
Admission: Application, SAT or ACT, transcripts, high school graduation or GED, evidence of ability to succeed academically. Transfer applicants must have a minimum overall GPA of 2.0 and 2.3 in prerequisite courses. Cazenovia has rolling admissions.
Campus has 15 acres, 21 buildings around central quadrangle. Separate 20-acre modern equine facility, newly built sports complex, college theatre, art galleries, nursery school, language laboratory, counseling services. Rapidly expanding library holds over 50,000 pieces including bound volumes and periodicals, tapes, microfilm. Outstanding food services.
Intercollegiate soccer, volleyball, tennis, basketball, softball, golf, club baseball teams. Equestrian team in stock seat and hunt seat, zone II of NIHSA.
Intimate atmosphere, friendly campus, located in picturesque lakeside village 18 miles from Syracuse. Nearby skiing, swimming, riding trails, recreational areas.

Clarkson University, Potsdam 13699
Robert Croot, Dir. of Admis.

Colgate University
13 Oak Dr., Hamilton 13346
Dean of Admissions
315-824-7401

COLLEGE OF AERONAUTICS
La Guardia Airport, Flushing 11371
Dr. Richard B. Goetze, Jr., President
Donald J Whitman, Dir. of Admis.
800-776-2376
Established 1932. Private. Independent. Coed. Accreditation: MSACS. Tuition: $5,820. Estimated total yearly expenses: $1,000. Enrollment: 1,200 students. Faculty: 65. Degrees: AAS, AOS, BT. Library: 60,000 volumes. 3 buildings on 6 acres. Located in New York City. Fully computerized engine test cells, hangar, engine labs, avionic labs, computer labs, and airline training center. Financial aid, grants, scholarships, and loans available.

COLLEGE OF INSURANCE
101 Murray St., New York 10007
Theresa C. Marro, Director of Admissions
212-815-9232 or 800-356-5146
Established 1962. Accreditation: Middle States Association of Colleges and Schools. Private. Coed. Total undergraduate enrollment: 742. Annual tuition: $10,200. Annual room and board approximately

$6,080. State, Federal, comprehensive institutional aid available.
Undergraduate degrees are a Bachelor of Business Administration (BBA) with a major in business, finance, or insurance or a Bachelor of Science (BS with a major in actuarial science). Five year Bachelor/MBA available.
Most full-time students participate in the College's highly successful Cooperative Education Program. Co-op students can alternate semester of full-time study with full-time industry work experience if sponsored by one of our Corporate Sponsors.
The Library houses, the Kathryn and Shelby Cullom Davis Library, which has the world's most comprehensive insurance collection including more than 140,000 bound volumes, subject files, pamphlets, periodicals and other pieces of informational material plus more than 10,750 microfilm items.
The College is located in the heart of New York City's financial area, three blocks from the World Trade Center. The College is housed in a ten story award winning building and has dormitory space available for both undergraduate and graduate students.
A rolling, very competitive admissions policy is employed and students are permitted to apply throughout the year. The application for admissions must be completed and a $30 non-refundable application fee is required. Official copies of secondary school and prior college transcripts and either SAT and ACT scores must be submitted. The College's SAT and ACT identification number is 2112. An admissions interview is required of all applicants. Materials should be addressed to: The Admissions Office, The College of Insurance, 101 Murray Street, New York, New York 10007, 212-815-9232 or 800-356-5146.

College of Mount St. Vincent
6301 Riverdale Ave., Riverdale 10471

College of New Rochelle
29 Castle Pl., New Rochelle 10805

College of New Rochelle
950 Baychester Ave., Bronx 10475

College of New Rochelle
125 Barclay St., New York 10007

College of New Rochelle
144 Dr. Martin Luther King Jr. Blvd.,
New York 10027

College of New Rochelle
1368 Fulton St., Brooklyn 11216

College of New Rochelle
332 E. 149th St., Bronx 10451

College of St. Rose
432 Western Ave., Albany 12203

Columbia University
612 W. 115th St., New York 10025

Concordia College
171 White Plains Rd., Bronxville 10708

COOPER UNION
41 Cooper Square, New York 10003
Richard Bory, Dean of Admissions
Established 1859. Coed. Accreditation: MSACS, NASAD, ABET, National Architectural Accrediting Board. Fees: $300. Enrollment: 1,100 students. Degrees: B Arch, BS, BE, BFA, ME. Library: 95,000 volumes. 3 building campus located in New York City. This is the only full scholarship school of its kind in the nation.

Cornell University
410 Thurston Ave., Ithaca 14853

CUNY Baruch College
17 Lexington Ave., New York 10010

CUNY Brooklyn College
2900 Bedford Ave., Brooklyn 11210
Justin Dunn, Dir. of Admis.

CUNY City College
Convent Ave. at 138th St., New York 10031

CUNY College of Staten Island
130 Stuyvesant Pl., Staten Island 10301

CUNY College of Staten Island
715 Ocean Terr., Staten Island 10301

CUNY Hunter College
695 Park Ave., New York 10021
Donna Shalala, President

CUNY Lehman College
250 Bedford Park Blvd. W., Bronx 10468
Jane Herbert, Dir. of Enrollment Management

CUNY Medgar Evan College
1150 Carroll St., Brooklyn 11225

CUNY New York City Technical College
300 Jay St., Brooklyn 11201
Ursula C. Schwerin, President

CUNY, Queens College
6530 Kissena Blvd., Flushing 11367

CUNY York College
9420 Guy R. Brewer Blvd., Jamaica 11451

Daemen College
4380 Main St., Amherst 14226
Maria Dillard, Dir. of Admis.
in NY 800-462-7652 or 716-839-8225

Dominican College of Blauvelt
460 N. Western Hwy., Orangeburg 10962
Louis Kern, Dir. of Admis.
914-359-7800

Dowling College,
150 Idle Hour Blvd., Oakdale 11769
Dr. Jerome Traiger, Dean

D'Youville College
320 Porter Ave., Buffalo 14201
Ronald Dannecker, Dir. of Admis.

Elmira College
Park Pl., Elmira 14901
William S. Neal, Dean of Admissions
See listing under "Liberal Arts"

FIVE TOWNS COLLEGE
305 N. Service Rd., Dix Hills 11746
Jennifer Roemer, Coordinator of Admissions
516-424-7000
Founded 1972. Private 2 and 4 year coed college. Accreditation: MSACS. Tuition: $7,400 per year ($310 per credit). Enrollment: 750 students. Faculty: 67. Degrees: AA, AS, AAS, BMus, BPS. Library: 40,000 volumes. 1 building on 34 acres. Rolling admissions. Majors in accounting, audio recording technology, broadcasting, business management, computer business applications, jazz/commercial music, liberal arts, marketing/retailing, music business, music composition and songwriting, music instrument technology, music performance, music teacher education, musical theatre, real estate, secretarial science, video arts. Certificate programs in basic studies, executive secretarial, music instrument repair, word processing. Financial aid and career placement assistance is available.

Fordham University
441 E. Fordham Rd., Bronx 10458
718-817-1000

Fordham University
Lincoln Center Campus
113 W. 60th St., New York 10023
Edward Bristow, Dean

Hamilton College
198 College Hill Blvd., Clinton 13323
Douglas Thompson, Dean of Admissions

Hartwick College, Oneonta 13820
607-431-4200

Hobart & William Smith College
Pulteney St., Geneva 14456

Hofstra University
1000 Fulton Ave., Hempstead 11550
Margaret Shields, Dean of Admissions

Houghton College
P.O. Box 128, Houghton 14744
Tim Fuller, Dir. of Admis.

Houghton College
910 Union Rd., West Seneca 14224

IONA COLLEGE
715 North Ave., New Rochelle 10801
800-231-IONA
Laurie Austin, Dir. of Admis., 914-633-2503
Lisa Fermicola, Dir. of Grad. Arts & Sciences Admis., 914-633-2328
Gayle Rapp, Dir. of Grad. Business Admis., 914-633-2288
Established 1940. Private. Coed. Accreditation: Middle States Association of Colleges and Secondary Schools. Tuition: $10,200. Room and board: $5,945. Enrollment: 5,350 undergraduate and 1,850 graduate students. Faculty: 428. Student-faculty ratio: 17:1. Degrees: BS, BA, BBA, MA, MS, MBA. Library: 313,000 volumes and approximately 1,250 periodicals and journals. 24 buildings on 56 acres. 500 PC terminals on campus. Easy access to New York City. 21 Div. I teams, intramural and club sports; more than 90 student clubs and activities.

IONA COLLEGE
1 Dutch Hill Rd., Orangeburg 10962
Dr. Barbara Witchel, Director
914-359-2252

Ithaca College
953 Danby Rd., Ithaca 14850

Juilliard School
60 Lincoln Center Plz., New York 10023
Carole Everett, Dir of Admis.

Keuka College
P.O. Box 98, Keuka Park 14478
Robert J. Ianuzzo, Dean of Admissions

The King's College, Briarcliff Manor 10510
Frederic Rowley, Dean of Admissions

Lamont-Doherty Earth Observatory of Columbia University
Palisades 10964
Gordon Eaton, Director

Le Moyne College
1419 Salt Springs Rd., Syracuse 13214-1301
Edwin B. Harris, Dir. of Admis.

Long Island University
Route 340, Orangeburg 10962
Dr. Joram Warmund, Provost

Long Island University
555 Broadway, Dobbs Ferry 10522
Dr. Dennis Payette, Provost

Long Island University
2nd Ave., Brentwood 11717
Dr. Dennis Payette, Provost

Long Island University-Brooklyn Campus
1 University Plaza, Brooklyn 11201
Alan Chaves, Dean of Admissions

LONG ISLAND UNIVERSITY-C. W. POST CAMPUS
Rt. 25A, Brookville 11548
Dr. David Steinberg, President
Christine Natali, Dir. of Admis.
800-LIU-PLAN or 800-548-7526
    Established 1954. Private. Coed. Accreditation: MSACS. Tuition: $10,300. Room and board: $4,980. Enrollment: 2,500 boarding, 2,300 day. Faculty: 400 full-time. Degrees: BA, BFA, BS, BPS. Library: 1,700,000 vols. 46 bldgs. on 400 acres. A 2,200 seat concert theatre attracts worlds finest orchestras & renowned concert artists to campus. 250 computer terminals are devoted to student use. College has faculties of arts and sciences, education, management, visual and performing arts, and health professions for undergraduate and graduate, and library science for graduate. Honors and merit scholarships available.

Long Island University-Southampton Campus
    Southampton 11968
    Carol Gilbert, Dir. of Admis.

Manhattan College
    4513 Manhattan College Pky., Riverdale 10471
    John Brennan, Dean of Admissions

Manhattan School of Music
    120 Claremont Ave., New York 10027
    James Gandre, Dir. of Admis.

Manhattanville College
    2900 Purchase St., Purchase 10577

MARIST COLLEGE
290 North Rd., Poughkeepsie 12601
Harry W. Wood, VP Admissions
914-575-3226

Marymount College
    100 Marymount Ave., Tarrytown 10591
    Gina R. Campbell, Dir. of Admis.
    800-724-4312

Marymount Manhattan College
    221 E. 71st St., New York 10021
    Suzanne M. Murphy, Dir. of Admis.

Medaille College
    18 Agassiz Cir., Buffalo 14214
    Jacqueline Smukeer, Dir. of Admis.

Mercy College
    555 Broadway, Dobbs Ferry 10522
    James Nesbitt, Dean of Admissions

Mercy College
    50 Antin Pl., Bronx 10462

Mercy College
    Martine Ave. & S. Broadway, White Plains 10601

Mercy College
    2651 Strang Blvd., Yorktown Heights 10598

MOLLOY COLLEGE
1000 Hempstead Ave., Rockville Centre 11570
Wayne James, Dir. of Admis.
    Established 1955. Private. Coed. Accreditation: MSACS, NLN, Board of Regents of New York, CSWE. Tuition: $8,800. Fees: $300. Enrollment: 1,306 full-time, 613 part-time. Faculty: 189. Student-faculty ratio: 11:1. Degrees: AA, AS, BA, BS, MS in Nursing. Library: 113,620 volumes. 4 buildings on 25 acres. Molloy College is proud to be the first New York college to grant a major in gerontology, and the only college in New York State to award a major in cardiorespiratory sciences.

Mt. St. Mary College
    330 Powell Ave., Newburgh 12550

Nazareth College of Rochester
    4245 East Ave., Rochester 14618
    Paul Kenyon, Dir. of Admis.

New School for Social Research
    66 W. 12th St., New York 10011

New York Institute of Technology
    Central Islip Campus
    Central Islip 11722

New York Institute of Technology
    Metropolitan Center
    1855 Broadway, New York 10023

New York Institute of Technology
    Old Westbury Campus, Old Westbury 11568

NEW YORK SCHOOL OF INTERIOR DESIGN
170 E. 70th St., New York 10021
June Soyka, Director of Admissions
800-336-9743
    Established 1916. Private. Coed. Accreditation: FIDER. Tuition: $10,560. Fees: $50. Enrollment: 122 full-time, 483 part-time. Faculty: 101. Student-faculty ratio: 18:1. Degrees offered: AAS, BFA, Design Diploma (3 year degree). Library: 5,661 volumes. Located in NY's upper east side at the center of the interior design center. Single major college dedicated solely to interior design. Faculty consists of designers, architects, decorators, and artists.

New York State College of Ceramics at Alfred University
    Alfred 14802
    800-541-9229

New York University
    70 Washington Sq., New York 10012

NIAGARA UNIVERSITY
Niagara University 14109
    Campus located on the northern limits of the city of Niagara Falls, thirty minutes from Buffalo and ninety minutes from Toronto.
The Rev. Brian J. O'Connell, CM, President
George Pachter, Dean of Admissions & Records
Maureen Salfi, Director of Financial Aid
    Niagara University, founded in 1856 by the Vincentian community, is a comprehensive, coeducational, private, independent university in the Vincentian tradition. Fully accredited by MSACS and by the National League for Nursing, Council on Social Work Education and the American Chemical Society, National Council for Accreditation of Teacher Education and Commission for Programs in Hospitality Administration. Enrollment 2,253 men and women. Faculty: 145 full-time. Student faculty ratio 16:1. Tuition: $9,660 per year (based on 15 credit hours). Room and board: $4,638 per year includes a complete meal plan (19 meals per week), $4,482 for 14 meals per week. University housing guaranteed for 4 years. Coed dormitories available for men and women.
    Degrees Offered: AA, AS, AAS, BA, BS, BBA, BFA, MEd, MBA, M in Criminal Justice. Six academic divisions; The Division of General Academic Studies, The College of Arts and Sciences, The College of Business Administration, The College of Education (elementary and secondary education), The College of Nursing and The Institute of Travel, Hotel & Restaurant Administration.
    Programs offered in accounting, biochemistry, biology, biotechnology, business, chemistry, commerce, communications, computer & information sciences, criminology & criminal justice, economics, education, English, French, general business, history, hotel management, international studies, human resources, general studies, life sciences, management, marketing, mathematics, natural sciences, nursing, philosophy, political science, psychology, religious studies, social sciences, social studies, social work, sociology, Spanish, theatre, transportation, hotel/restaurant, travel/tourism. Pre-professional programs are offered in dentistry, engineering, law and medicine. Special programs for honor students and undecided majors (EXPLORE) are also available.
    Applications are reviewed on a rolling admission basis with a candidates' reply date of May 1st. Applicants who meet admission criteria are admitted. Applicants must have been awarded a high school diploma by an accredited high school with a minimum of 16 academic units (years) in the following subjects: English 4, language 2, science 2, social studies 2, math 2 (business applicants must have 3 years of math) and academic electives 4. Candidates applying to programs in math, nursing and science must have 3 units in math and 3 units in science. Candidates without a high school diploma may be admitted on the basis of the GED test. SAT or ACT scores required. Application fee $25, non-refundable. Interviews not required but recommended.
    Financial aid is available through academic and athletic scholarships, grants, student employment and loans. Partial scholarships are offered to economically and academically disadvantaged students (HEOP). 95% of those students who apply for financial aid at Niagara University receive financial assistance. The average financial aid award is over $8,800 per year.
    Campus: Monteagle Ridge Campus: 160 acre suburban campus; 27 buildings, including the new Bailo Hall, which houses the office of admissions, the Castellani Art Museum, the Kiernan Center, a fully equipped athletic facility with large outdoor areas, the Gallagher Center, a student center, and dormitories. DeVeaux Campus: 50 acre satellite campus one mile from Monteagle Ridge Campus, suburban area, provides additional athletic facilities and administrative offices.
    Location: situated 4 miles from the world famous Niagara Falls, the University is easily accessible to every major city in eastern and mid-western US via NYS Thruway and the Buffalo International Airport. Centrally located for bus and train transportation.

Nyack College, Nyack 10960
    Miguel Sanchez, Dir. of Admis.
    800-33-NYACK

Pace University, New York Campus
    1 Pace Plaza, New York 10038

Pace University, Pleasantville/Briarcliff Campus
    Bedford Rd., Pleasantville 10570

Pace University, White Plains Campus
    78 N. Broadway, White Plains 10603

Polytechnic University
    333 Jay St., Brooklyn 11201

Polytechnic University
    901 Rt. 110, Farmingdale 11735

Pratt Institute
    200 Willoughby Ave., Brooklyn 11205

REGENTS COLLEGE OF THE UNIVERSITY OF THE STATE OF NEW YORK
7 Columbia Circle, Albany 12203-5159
518-464-8500

Rensselaer Polytechnic Institute, Troy 12180
    Conrad Sharrow, Dean of Admissions

ROBERTS WESLEYAN COLLEGE
2301 Westside Dr., Rochester 14624
Dr. William Crothers, President
Linda Kurtz, Dir. of Admis.
    Established 1866. Free Methodist. Independent.
Coed. Accreditation: MSACS, NLN, NASAD, NASM, CSWE. Tuition: $10,220. Room and board: $3,546. Enrollment: 1,115. Faculty: 110. Degrees: AS, BA, BS, MEd. Library: 99,869 volumes. 20 buildings on 75 acres. Gym. Nearby facilities include Eastman School of Music, Rochester Philharmonic Orchestra, Lake Ontario, Niagara Falls, Watkins Glen, Letchworth Park and the Finger Lakes.

ROCHESTER INSTITUTE OF TECHNOLOGY
1 Lomb Memorial Dr., Rochester 14623
Daniel Shelley, Director of Admissions
716-475-6631
    Established 1829. Private. Coed. Accreditation: MSACS. Tuition: $13,266. Room and board: $5,439. Fees: $249. Enrollment: 8,500 full-time, 4,000 part-time. Faculty: 1,076. Student-faculty ratio: 12:1. Degrees: Certificate, Diploma, AA, AAS, AOS, AS, BFA, BS, MBA, ME, MFA, MS, MST, PhD. Library: 325,000 volumes. Cooperative education work/study plan available or required in most majors. Merit based academic scholarships available. 1,300 acre campus in a suburban setting outside of New York State's third largest city. New $12 million Student Life Center opened January 1992. Housing options include residence halls, fraternities, sororoties, and campus apartments.

St. Bonaventure University, St. Bonaventure 14778
    June T. Solan, Dir. of Admis.

St. Francis College
    180 Remsen St., Brooklyn 11201

St. John Fisher College
    3690 East Ave., Rochester 14618
    Peter Lindsey, Dir. of Admis.

St. John's University
    Grand Central & Utopia Parkways, Jamaica 11439

ST. JOHN'S UNIVERSITY
300 Howard Ave., Staten Island 10301

St. Joseph's College
    245 Clinton Ave., Brooklyn 11205
    Geraldine Foudy, Dir. of Admis.
    718-636-6868

St. Joseph's College, Suffolk Campus
    25 Audobon Ave., Patchogue 11772

St. Lawrence University, Canton 13617
    Joel R. Wincowski, Dean of Admis. & Financial Aid

ST. THOMAS AQUINAS COLLEGE
Rt. 340, Sparkill 10976
Andrea Kraeft, Dir. of Admis.
800-999-STAC
See listing under "Liberal Arts"

Sarah Lawrence College, Bronxville 10708

Siena College, Loudonville 12211
    Harry Wood, Director, Admissions

Skidmore College, Saratoga Springs 12866
    Kent Jones, Dir. of Admis.

SUNY at Albany
    1400 Washington Ave., Albany 12222
    Micheileen Treadwell, Dir. of Admission/Financial Aid
    518-442-5431

SUNY at Binghamton
    P.O. Box 6001, Binghamton 13902

SUNY at Buffalo
    17 Capen Hall
    P.O. Box 601660, Buffalo 14260-1660
    716-645-6900

SUNY at Stony Brook
    Stony Brook 11794

SUNY Center for the Capital District
    845 Central Ave., Albany 12206

SUNY College at Brockport
    Brockport 14420

SUNY College at Buffalo
    1300 Elmwood Ave., Buffalo 14222
    716-878-4000

SUNY College at Cortland
    P.O. Box 2000, Cortland 13045

SUNY College at Fredonia, Fredonia 14063
    William S. Clark, III, Dir. of Admissions

SUNY College at Geneseo
    1 College Cir., Geneseo 14454
    William L. Caren, Dir. of Admissions

SUNY College at New Paltz
    75 Manheim Blvd., New Paltz 12561

SUNY College at Old Westbury
    P.O. Box 210, Old Westbury 11568
    Michael Sheehy, Dir. of Admis.

SUNY College at Oneonta, Oneonta 13820
    Clifford McVinney, Dir. of Admis.

SUNY at Oswego, Oswego 13126
    Dr. Joseph Grant, Jr., Dean of Admissions
    315-341-2250

SUNY College at Plattsburgh, Plattsburgh 12901
    Richard Higgins, Dir. of Admis.
    518-564-2040

SUNY College at Potsdam
    Potsdam 13676
    Marc Davis, Dir. of Admis.

SUNY College at Purchase
735 Anderson Hill Rd., Purchase 10577
Gene Ann Flaherty, Dir. of Admissions

SUNY College of Agriculture & Technology
Cobleskill 12043
John Devney, Jr., Dir. of Admis.

SUNY College of Environmental Science & Forestry
1 Forestry Dr., Syracuse 13210
800-7777-ESF or 315-470-6600

SUNY College of Technology at Farmingdale
Route 110, Farmingdale 11735
Janet Snyder, Dir. of Admis.
516-420-2200

SUNY Empire State College
1 Union Ave., Saratoga Springs 12866
Marvin Thorsland, Dir. of Admis.

SUNY Fashion Institute of Technology
227 W. 27th St., New York 10001

SUNY Genessee Valley Regional Center
8 Prince St., Rochester 14607

SUNY Hudson Valley Regional Center
200 N. Central Ave., Hartsdale 10530

SUNY INSTITUTE OF TECHNOLOGY AT UTICA/ROME
P.O. Box 3050, Utica 13504
Peter Cayan, President
Roger Sullivan, Dir. of Admis.
315-792-7208
Established 1966. State. Coed. Accreditation: MSACS, NY State Board of Regents. Tuition: $2,650. Room & board: $5,320. Enrollment: 2,400. Faculty: 90. Degrees: BA, BPS, BS, BT. Library: 120,000 volumes. 5 buildings on 800 acres. SUNY Tech is an upper division college designed exclusively for transfer students. Bachelor's degree programs are offered in a variety of liberal arts, technically & professionally oriented areas including: technical communication, telecommunications, engineering technology, business, computer information science, photonics, and health sciences. Also offer Master's of Science in business management, computer science, nursing administration, and nurse practitioner.

SUNY Long Island Regional Center
P.O. Box 130, Old Westbury 11568

SUNY Metropolitan Regional Center
666 Broadway, New York 10012

SUNY Niagara Frontier Regional Center
564 Franklin St., Buffalo 14202

Syracuse University, Syracuse 13244

Touro College
844 Avenue of the Americas, New York 10001

Touro College
240 E. 123rd St., New York 10035

Union College, Schenectady 12308

U.S. Merchant Marine Academy, Kings Point 11024

U.S. Military Academy, West Point 10996

UNIVERSITY OF ROCHESTER
500 Joseph C. Wilson Blvd., Rochester 14627
G. Dennis O'Brien, President
Wayne A. Locust, Dir. of Admis. - River Campus Colleges
Charles Krusenstjerna, Dir. of Admis.
Robert Freeman, Director - Eastman School of Music
Established 1850. Independent. Coed. Accreditation: MSACS, New York State Board of Regents. Tuition: $16,950 per year. Room and board: $6,286 per year. Fees: $395. Full-time undergrads 4,980, 85% live on campus. 22 dorms (ESM 1 dorm), 17 fraternities, 10 sororities.
Curriculum: Comprising 7 schools and colleges, UR offers BA, BS, BM, MA, MAT, MBA, MD, MEd, MM, MPH, MS, PhD, DMA, EdD in humanities, social sciences, natural sciences, education, music, management, engineering, medicine, & nursing. Summer and evening school courses available. Unusual undergraduate concentrations offered in optics, cognitive science, environmental studies, film studies, women's studies. Interdepartmental programs; 3/2 programs. Certificate programs in management studies, biomedical engineering, biotechnology, Asian studies, Russian studies, international relations and actuarial studies. Freshman ventures, freshman preceptorials, Perspectives, "Reach for Rochester" employment programs, University Day, REMS (Rochester Early Medical Scholars) and Rochester Plan Early Selection Programs (medical school), "Take Five," Frederick Douglass Institute for African and African-American Studies, Susan B. Anthony Center for Women's Studies, study abroad, Geology internship in marine sciences, Washington semester, British Parliamentary internship.
Admissions: 73% of incoming class in top 5th of high school class, SAT or ACT required before February of senior year, ACHV tests recommended. Score ranges for the middle 50% of all admitted students: SAT-V 490-600, SAT-M 570-680, ACT Comp. 25-30. Application deadlines: Regular January 15 (Eastman School February 20), River Campus early decision November 15. Students who select UR as their 1st choice college after November are welcome to request an early decision review in writing until February. Financial aid: Scholarships, loans and employment available. 65% of students receive University scholarships. Student-faculty ratio: 12:1.
Library contains 2,742,000 volumes also 13,849 periodical subscriptions. Student newspaper, literary magazine, AM-FM radio station, more than 90 student organizations, extensive intramural program, men's and women's intercollegiate sports, Pei-designed student union, Zornow Sports Center opened in 1982. Rochester is a founding member of the University Athletic Association, comprising nine national research universities with similar academic and athletic philosophies.
Memorial Art Gallery, Eastman Theatre, International Museum of Photography and Dryden Theatre facilities available to UR students.

Utica College of Syracuse University
1600 Burrstone Rd., Utica 13502

Vassar College
125 Raymond Ave., Poughkeepsie 12601

WAGNER COLLEGE
631 Howard Ave., Staten Island 10301
Joseph Foulke, Dean Admissions and Financial Aid
Established 1883. Private. Coed. Accreditation: MSACS. Tuition & fees: $11,250. Room and board: $5,000. Enrollment: 1,400 full-time, 100 part-time. Faculty: 155. Student-faculty ratio: 10:1. Degrees: BA, BS, MBA, EdM. Library: 276,000 volumes. 20 buildings on 86 acres. The 86 acre campus overlooks New York Harbor and the spectacular Manhattan skyline. 32 majors and concentrations. 12 Men's and Women's Division I sports, Division III football. Art gallery, renowned theater program. Honors and academic scholarships.

Yeshiva University
500 W. 185th St., New York 10033

NORTH CAROLINA

Appalachian State University
ASU Station, Boone 28608
Joe Watts, Admissions Officer

BARTON COLLEGE
College Station, Wilson 27893
James B. Hemby, Jr., President
Anthony Britt, Dir. of Admis.
800-345-4973 in Eastern U.S.
919-399-6318 nationwide
Founded 1902. Private. Coed. 4-year liberal arts college in eastern NC. 1994-95 tuition, room/board & fees: $11,190. Enrollment: 1,400 with 80% receiving financial aid. Student-faculty ratio: 13:1. Degrees: BS, BA, BFA, and BLS. 11 academic departments, 40 majors. Programs: athletics, Greek, music, theater, career planning, weekend college, college success, Global Focus international emphasis.

Belmont Abbey College
1 Abbey Pl., Belmont 28012
Admissions, 800-523-2355

Campbell University
P.O. Box 127, Buies Creek 27506

Catawba College
2300 W. Innes St., Salisbury 28144
Mark Stokes, Dir. of Admis.

Davidson College
P.O. Box 1737, Davidson 28036
704-892-2230

Duke University, Durham 27706

East Carolina University
1000 E. 5th St., Greenville 27858

Elizabeth City State University
1704 Weeksville Rd., Elizabeth City 27909
William A.T. Byrd, Dir. of Admis.

Elon College
P.O. Box 2700, Elon College 27244
Nan P. Perkins, Dean of Admissions

Fayetteville State University
1200 Murchison Rd., Fayetteville 28301
Donald W. Lahuffman, Dir. of Admissions

Gardner-Webb University
General Delivery, Boiling Springs 28017
Ray M. Hardee, Dean of Admissions
800-253-6472

Greensboro College
815 W. Market St., Greensboro 27401

GUILFORD COLLEGE
5800 W. Friendly Ave., Greensboro 27410
Larry West, Dir. of Admis.
Established 1837. Private. Coed. Accreditation: SACS. Tuition: $12,400. Room and board: $5,070. Fees: $210. Enrollment: 1,200 full-time, 45 part-time. Faculty: 91. Student-faculty ratio: 14:1. Degrees: BA, BS, BFA, BMus. Library: 227,000 volumes. 24 buildings on 300 acres. Ranked among top 10% of all liberal arts colleges. Only Quaker college in South. Has unusually diverse student body with 65% coming from out-of-state. Strong emphasis on study abroad.

High Point College
933 Montlieu Ave., High Point 27262
Jim Schlimmer, Dir. of Admis.

Johnson C. Smith University
100 Beatties Ford Rd., Charlotte 28216
Mary H. Platt, Registrar

Lees-McRae College
P.O. Box 128, Banner Elk 28604
Brenda S. Lyerly, Dean of Admissions

Lenoir-Rhyne College
P.O. Box 292, Hickory 28603
Steve M. Shuford, Registrar

Livingstone College
701 W. Monroe St., Salisbury 28144

Mars Hill College
Main St., Mars Hill 28754
Dr. Smith Goodrum, Dean of Admis.

Methodist College
5400 Ramsey St., Fayetteville 28311
Fiore Bergamasco, Dir. of Admis.

MONTREAT-ANDERSON COLLEGE
P.O. Box 1267, Montreat 28757
David E. Walters, Director of Admissions
800-MAC-N-YOU or 704-669-8011 Ext. 229
Established 1906. Private. Coed. Accreditation: SACS. Tuition: $7,600. Room and board: $3,372. Enrollment: 316 full-time, 20 part-time. Faculty: 24 full-time, 14 part-time. Student-faculty ratio: 11:1. Library: 62,000 volumes. 11 buildings on 200 acres. Located in the beautiful Blue Ridge Mountains of western North Carolina.

Mt. Olive College
209 N. Breazeale Ave., Mt. Olive 28365

North Carolina A&T State University
1601 E. Market St., Greensboro 27411

North Carolina Central University
P.O. Box 19617, Durham 27707

NORTH CAROLINA SCHOOL OF THE ARTS
200 Waughtown St., Winston-Salem 27127
Alex Ewing, Chancellor
910-770-3291

North Carolina State University
P.O. Box 7001, Raleigh 27695
George Dixon, Dir. of Admis.

North Carolina Wesleyan College
3400 N. Wesleyan Blvd., Rocky Mount 27804

Pembroke State University
P.O. Box 1510, Pembroke 28372
Anthony Locklear, Dir. of Admissions
919-521-6262

Pfeiffer College
General Delivery, Misenheimer 28109

QUEENS COLLEGE
1900 Selwyn Ave., Charlotte 28274
D. Stephen Cloniger, VP for Enrollment Management
See listing under "Liberal Arts"

St. Andrews Presbyterian College
1700 Dogwood Mile, Laurinburg 28352
Dale B. Montague, Dir. of Admis.

St. Augustine's College
1315 Oakwood Ave., Raleigh 27610
I. E. Spraggins, Dir. Admissions

Shaw University
118 E. South St., Raleigh 27601
919-546-8222

University of North Carolina
1000 Spring Garden St., Greensboro 27412

University of North Carolina
601 S. College Rd., Wilmington 28403
W. H. Wagoner, Chancellor

University of North Carolina at Asheville
1 University Heights, Asheville 28804
William E. Highsmith, Chancellor

University of North Carolina at Chapel Hill
Chapel Hill 27599
James C. Walters, Dir. Undergrad Admis.

University of North Carolina at Charlotte
Charlotte 28223
J. H. Woodward, Chancellor

Wake Forest University
P.O. Box 7305, Winston-Salem 27109

Warren Wilson College
P.O. Box 9000, Asheville 28802-9000
Tom Weede, Dir. of Admis.

Western Carolina University
Cullowhee 28723
Tyree H. Kiser, Dir. of Admissions

Wingate College, Wingate 28174

Winston-Salem State University
601 S. Martin Luther King Jr.
Winston-Salem 27110
Van Wilson, Dir. of Admissions

NORTH DAKOTA

Dickinson State University, Dickinson 58601
Marshall Melbye, Registrar
701-227-2331

Jamestown College, Jamestown 58405

MAYVILLE STATE UNIVERSITY
330 3rd St., N.E., Mayville 58257
Dr. Ellen Chaffee, President
Ronald Brown, Dir. of Admis.
800-437-4104
Established 1889. State. Coed. Accreditation: NCACS, NCATE. Tuition: $1,680 in-state, $4,486 out-of-state. Room and board: $2,516. Enrollment: 291 boarding, 425 day. Faculty: 52. Degrees: AA, BA, BA General Studies, BSEd, BS Computer Information Systems. Library: 84,000 volumes. 19 buildings on 60 acres. Gym, pool, golf. "The School of Personal Service" between Fargo & Grand Forks in the Red River Valley. Special programs: development courses for entering students, learning resource center, acceler-

ated degree, advanced standing, cooperative work-study program, summer sessions for credit, child development center, teaching & learning center.

Minot State University
500 University Ave. W., Minot 58701

North Dakota State University, Fargo 58105
Richard Shearer, Acting Dir. of Admis.

University of Mary
7500 University Dr., Bismarck 58504
Steph Storey, Dir. of Admis.

University of North Dakota
Box 8193 University Station, Grand Forks 58203

Valley City State University
101 S.W. College St., Valley City 58072
Monte Johnson, Dir. of Admis.

OHIO

Antioch University
795 Livermore St., Yellow Springs 45387

Ashland University
401 College Ave., Ashland 44805

Baldwin-Wallace College
275 Eastland Rd., Berea 44017
Juliann K. Baker, Dir. of Admis.

Bluffton College
College Ave., Bluffton 45817

Bowling Green State University
Bowling Green 43403
John Martin, Dir. of Admis.

Capital University
2199 E. Main St., Columbus 43209
Dolphus E. Henry, Associate Provost

Case Western Reserve University
2040 Adelbert Rd., Cleveland 44106

Cedarville College
P.O. Box 601, Cedarville 45314
David Ormsbee, Dir. of Admis.

Central State University
1400 Brush Row Rd., Wilberforce 45384

Cincinnati College of Mortuary Science
3860 Pacific Ave., Cincinnati 45207-1033
Dr. Dan Flory, President
513-745-3631

CIRCLEVILLE BIBLE COLLEGE
P.O. Box 458, Circleville 43113
Michael Adkins, Dir. of Enrollment
614-477-7701

Cleveland State University
Euclid Ave. at 24th St., Cleveland 44115

COLLEGE OF MOUNT SAINT JOSEPH
5701 Delhi Rd., Cincinnati 45233-1670
513-244-4531 or 800-654-9314
Edward C. Eckel, Dir. of Admis.
Established 1920. Private. Coed. Accreditation: NCACS, Ohio Board of Regents, Ohio Department of Education. Tuition: $9,180 ($239/per credit hour 1-11 or over 18). Room and board: $4,242. Enrollment: 1,113 full-time under graduate, 33 full-time graduate, 1,307 part-time under graduate, 141 part-time graduate. Faculty: 98 full-time, 120 part-time. Student-faculty ratio: 15:1. Degrees: AA, AS, BA, BFA, BS, BSN, MA available in education and pastoral family studies. Library: 90,000 volumes. 6 buildings on 75 acres.
The Mount's liberal arts core curriculum insures a broad range of knowledge and competence for students in all majors. Classes foster skills in critical thinking, problem-solving, decision-making and communication — skills that are highly sought by employers in today's business and professional world.
Students choose from over 35 majors ranging from social sciences to business administration to nursing to fine arts. Cooperative education, internship or research opportunities are available to students in all majors, providing valuable career experience before graduation. Some majors even have the option for study or co-op experience abroad.

College of Wooster
1189 Beall Ave., Wooster 44691
Hayden Schilling, Dean of Admis.

COLUMBUS COLLEGE OF ART & DESIGN
107 N. 9th St., Columbus 43215-1758
Thomas Green, Dir. of Admis.
614-224-9101
See listing under "Art"

DEFIANCE COLLEGE
701 N. Clinton St., Defiance 43512
Penny D. Bell, Dir. of Admis.
419-783-2330 Collect

Denison University
P.O. Box B, Granville 43023
Richard Boyden, Dir. of Admis.

Dyke College
112 Prospect Ave. S.E., Cleveland 44115

Franciscan University of Steubenville
University Blvd., Steubenville 43952
Margaret Weber, Dir. of Admis.
800-783-6220 or 614-283-6226

Franklin University
201 S. Grant Ave., Columbus 43215

Heidelberg College
310 E. Market St., Tiffin 44883
Stephen E. Eidson, Dean of Admission
800-925-9250

Hiram College
P.O. Box 96, Hiram 44234
Gary Craig, Dean of Admis.

John Carroll University
20700 N. Park Blvd., Cleveland 44118

Kent State University
P.O. Box 5190, Kent 44242
Bruce Riddle, Dir. of Admis.

Kenyon College
1 Kenyon College, Gambier 43022
Philip H. Jordan, Jr., President

Lake Erie College
391 W. Washington St., Painesville 44077

LOURDES COLLEGE
6832 Convent Blvd., Sylvania 43560
Mary E. Briggs, Dir. of Admis.
419-885-5291 or 800-878-3210

Malone College
515 25th St., N.W., Canton 44709
Lee Sommers, Dean of Admissions

MARIETTA COLLEGE
210 5th St., Marietta 45750
Dennis R. DePerro, Dean Admis./Financial Aid
800-331-7896

Miami University
E. High St., Oxford 45056

Mount Union College
1972 Clark Ave., Alliance 44601
Amy Tomko, Dir. of Admis.

Mt. Vernon Nazarene College
800 Martinsburg Rd., Mt. Vernon 43050
Ronald Hyson, Dir. of Admis.

Muskingum College
147 Center St., New Concord 43762

Oberlin College
135 W. Lorain St., Oberlin 44074
Debra Chermonte, Dir. of Admis.

Ohio Dominican College
1216 Sunbury Rd., Columbus 43219
800-955-OHIO

OHIO NORTHERN UNIVERSITY
525 S. Main St., Ada 45810
Dr. DeBow Freed, President
412-772-2000

Ohio State University
190 N. Oval Mall, Columbus 43210

Ohio State University-Lima Campus
4240 Campus Dr., Lima 45804
Cynthia E. Spiers, Dir. of Admissions
419-221-1641

Ohio State University-Mansfield Campus
1680 University Dr., Mansfield 44906

Ohio State University-Marion
1465 Mount Vernon Ave., Marion 43302
Becky McConnell, Dir. of Admis.

Ohio State University-Newark
1179 University Dr., Newark 43055

Ohio University, Athens 45701

Ohio University, Belmont Co. Branch
45425 National Rd. W., St. Clairsville 43950

Ohio University
Chillicothe 45601

Ohio University, Southern Campus
1804 Liberty Ave., Ironton 45638

Ohio University, Lancaster Branch
1570 Granville Pike, Lancaster 43130

Ohio University, Zanesville Branch
1425 Newark Rd., Zanesville 43701

Ohio Wesleyan University
61 S. Sandusky St., Delaware 43015
Donald Bishop, Dean for Enrollment

Otterbein College, Westerville 43081

Shawnee State University
940 2nd St., Portsmouth 45662
Rosemary K. Poston, Dir. of Admis.

Union Institute
440 E. McMillan St., Cincinnati 45206

United Theological Seminary
1810 Harvard Blvd., Dayton 45406
The Rev. Duane Anders, Dir. of Admis.

University of Akron
381 Buchtel Common, Akron 44325
Kris MacDermott, Asst. Provost Enrollment

University of Cincinnati
2700 Clifton Ave., Cincinnati 45221

UNIVERSITY OF CINCINNATI OMI COLLEGE OF APPLIED SCIENCE
2220 Victory Pky., Cincinnati 45206
Frederick Kryman, Dean
513-556-6564

UNIVERSITY OF DAYTON
300 College Park Ave., Dayton 45469-1611
Myron Achbach, Director of Admissions
513-229-4411 or 800-837-7433
Established 1850. Private. Catholic, Marianist. Coed. Accreditation: NCACS, AACSB, NCATE, ABET. Tuition: $10,670. Room and board: $4,030. Fees: $420. Enrollment: 5,889 full-time, 673 part-time. Faculty: 800. Student-faculty ratio: 15:1. Degrees: BS, BA, BFA, BM, plus various engineering bachelors degrees. Library: 1,100,000 volumes. 16 academic buildings plus various residence, fitness and dining facilities on 110 acres. Over 70 baccalaureate programs are available. Outstanding financial aid and merit scholarships. UD offers a superior level of academic and career preparation, student-faculty interaction and quality residence life.

University of Findlay
1000 N. Main St., Findlay 45840
Dan Crabtree, Dir. of Admis.

University of Rio Grande
General Delivery, Rio Grande 45674
Mark Abell, Dir. of Admis./Enrollment Srvcs.
614-245-5353, Ext. 7206

University of Toledo
2801 Bancroft St., W., Toledo 43606
Richard Eastop, Dir. of Admis.

Urbana University
100 College Way, Urbana 43078
Donald Burns, Dir. of Admis.

Walsh College
2020 Easton St., N.W., Canton 44720
Fran Kehoe, Dean of Admis.

Wilberforce University
General Delivery, Wilberforce 45384
Frank B. Heard, Registrar

Wilmington College
P.O. Box 1185, Wilmington 45177
Rhonda Inderhees, Dir. of Admis.

WINEBRENNER THEOLOGICAL SEMINARY
P.O. Box 478, Findlay 45839
Dr. David Draper, President
419-422-4824

Wittenberg University
P.O. Box 720, Springfield 45504

Wright State University
3640 Colonel Glenn Hwy., Dayton 45435

Xavier University
3800 Victory Pky., Cincinnati 45207

Youngstown State University
410 Wick Ave., Youngstown 44555
Leslie H. Cochran, President

OKLAHOMA

Cameron University
2800 W. Gore Blvd., Lawton 73505
Louise Brown, Dir. of Admis.

East Central University, Ada 74820
James Peak, Dir. of Admis.

Langston University
P.O. Box 907, Langston 73050

Mid-America Bible College
3500 S.W. 119th St., Oklahoma City 73170
Tony O'Brien, Registrar
405-691-3800

Northeastern State University
600 N. Grand Ave., Tahlequah 74464

Northwestern Oklahoma State University
705 Oklahoma Blvd., Alva 73717

Oklahoma Baptist University
500 W. University St., Shawnee 74801

Oklahoma Christian University of Science and Arts
P.O. Box 11000, Oklahoma City 73136
Duane Eggleston, Vice President
800-877-5010

OKLAHOMA CITY UNIVERSITY
2501 N. Blackwelder Ave., Oklahoma City 73106
Jerald Walker, President
Dr. Carter Blue Clark, Executive VP Mary Coffey, VP for Admin.
Keith T. Hackett, Dean of Admissions
Glen Miller, VP for University/Church Relations
Deborah Mills, VP for Finance
Cheryl Zrnic, Dean, School of Music & Performing Arts
Donald Emler, Dean, School of Religious & Church Vocations
Dr. Elaine Masters, Dean, School of Nursing
Established 1904. Independent, sponsored by United Methodist Church. Coed. Accreditation: NCACS. Tuition: $3,525 per semester. Room and board: $1,815 per semester. Enrollment: 1,633 men, 1,424 women. 5 dormitories, 3 sororities, 3 fraternities, off-campus housing at Cokesbury Court. Degrees: BA, BS, BM, BPA, BSB, MA in religion, teaching, MBA, MS in accounting, MM, MLA, MCJ, MPA, JD. Schools: arts & sciences, business science & management, musical & performing arts, religion & church vocations, nursing, law. Preprofessional courses in medicine, religion, law. Two 6 week summer school terms, evening school. Extension school: competency based degree program. Music/business, JD/MBA, business/computer degrees also offered.
Admissions: ACT or SAT required. Transfers, in good standing. Athletic, freshman academic, music,

dance, religion. Faculty: 184, 115 full-time, 69 part-time. Student-faculty ratio: 21:1. 22 buildings on 55 acres. Library: 308,000 volumes. Law library: 90,000 volumes. Gym. Residential neighborhood, mild climate. Student employment on and off-campus. Outstanding musical theatre, children's theatre, performing arts academy, religious services, and homecoming. Recreational areas include lakes and reservoirs 2 to 15 miles away.

Oklahoma Panhandle State University
P.O. Box 430, Goodwell 73939

Oklahoma State University, Stillwater 74078
Norman N. Durham, Interim Dir. of Admissions

Oral Roberts University
7777 S. Lewis Ave., Tulsa 74171
Arthur E. Matzkvech, Dir. of Admis.

Phillips University
100 S University Ave., Enid 73701
Lois A. Bender, VP/Enrollment Management
800-238-1185

Southeastern Oklahoma State University
Station A, Durant 74701

Southern Nazarene University
6729 N.W. 39th Expy., Bethany 73008

Southwestern Oklahoma State University
100 Campus Dr., Weatherford 73096

University of Central Oklahoma
100 N. University Dr., Edmond 73034

University of Oklahoma at Norman
660 Parrington Oval, Norman 73019

University of Sciences & Arts of Oklahoma
P.O. Box 82345, Chickasha 73018

University of Tulsa
600 S. College Ave., Tulsa 74104
John Corso, Dean of Admission

OREGON

Bassist College
2000 S.W. 5th Ave., Portland 97201
Donald Bassist, President

Concordia College
2811 N.E. Holman St., Portland 97211

EASTERN OREGON STATE COLLEGE
1410 L Ave., La Grande 97850
Terral Schut, Dir. of Admis.
In OR 800-452-8639 or 503-962-3393
Established 1929. Member of Oregon State System of Higher Education. Coed. Located in Northeastern Oregon in the city of La Grande (pop. 12,000). Enrollment: 2,200. EASTERN offers degrees, pre-professional and transfer programs of superior quality, close student/faculty relationships, small classes, and a beautiful mountain setting. Baccalaureate degrees in agriculture, art, biology, business, pre-dentistry, pre-law, liberal arts, mathematics, pre-medicine, music, nursing, physical education, psychology, speech and drama, teacher education, pre-veterinarian. Master's in teacher education and an associate in office administration or general studies. All undergraduate students pay resident tuition and fees.

George Fox College
414 N. Meridian St., Newberg 97132

ITT Technical Institute
6035 N.E. 78th Ct., Portland 97218
James Horner, Director

Lewis & Clark College
0615 S.W. Palatine Hill Rd., Portland 97219
Michael Sexton, Dean of Admissions

Linfield College
900 S. Baker St., McMinnville 97128
Thomas Meicho, Dean of Admissions

Marylhurst College for Lifelong Learning
P.O. Box 261, Marylhurst 97036
Keith Protonentis, Registrar
800-634-9982

Northwest Christian College
828 E. 11th Ave., Eugene 97401
Randy Jones, Dir. of Admis.

Oregon Institute of Technology
3201 Campus Dr., Klamath Falls 97601
Jesse R. Welch, Director of Enrollment

Oregon School of Arts & Crafts
8245 S.W. Barnes Rd., Portland 97225
Jean Malarkey, Dean of Admissions
503-297-5544

Oregon State University, Corvallis 97333
Wallace Gibbs, Dir. of Admis.

PACIFIC NORTHWEST COLLEGE OF ART
1219 S.W. Park Ave., Portland 97205
Sally Lawrence, Director
Colin Page, Dir. of Admis.
503-226-0462
Established 1909. Private. Coed. Accreditation: NASC, NASAD. Tuition: $7,750. Estimated total yearly expenses: $16,250. Rolling admissions. Faculty: 42. Degree: BFA. Library: 22,500 volumes. 1 building on 1 city block. Majors in graphic design, painting, drawing, illustration, photography, sculpture, printmaking, ceramics, and crafts. Joint degree program with Reed College. 5 year BA/BFA. Art museum, film and video center.

Pacific University
2043 College Way, Forest Grove 97116
Barbara Mergen, Dir. of Admis.

Portland State University
P.O. Box 751, Portland 97207

Reed College
3202 S.E. Woodstock Blvd., Portland 97202

Southern Oregon State College
1250 Siskiyou Blvd., Ashland 97520

University of Oregon
1 University of Oregon, Eugene 97403

University of Portland
5000 N. Willamette Blvd., Portland 97203

Western Baptist College, Salem 97301
800-845-3005

Western Oregon State College
345 Monmouth Ave., N., Monmouth 97361
Craig A. Kolins, Dir. of Admis.
503-838-8211

Willamette University
900 State St. S.E., Salem 97301

PENNSYLVANIA

Albright College
P.O. Box 15234, Reading 19612

Allegheny College
520 N. Main St., Meadville 16335
Gayle Pollack, Dir. of Admis.

Allentown College of St. Frances de Sales
2755 Station Ave., Center Valley 18034
George Kelley, Dir. of Admis.

Alvernia College
400 Bernardine St., Reading 19607
Lisa Grabowski, Dir. of Admis.

BEAVER COLLEGE
450 S. Easton Rd., Glenside 19038-3295
Bette E. Landman, President
Dennis Nostrand, VP for Enrollment Management
Phone: 800-776-BEAVER(2328), Fax: 215-572-4049
Established 1853. Independent. Coed. Accreditation: MSACS. Tuition: $12,250. Room and board: $5,100. Enrollment: Approx. 875 full-time undergraduate resident and commuter students; 1,050 graduate and 375 evening students. Student-faculty ratio: 13:1. Degrees: BA, BS, BFA, MA, MEd, MS (AA,AS evening program). Library: 138,000 volumes. Thirteen buildings and a new recreation and athletic center on 55 acres. Located 25 min. by train from center city Philadelphia, which offers theatre, museums, concerts, shops, sporting events and all the other diverse resources of a major metropolitan area. Also 2 hours from New York or Washington, DC or the New Jersey beaches. Special programs include: internships or co-op programs for every field of study; honors program; Distinguished Scholarships; 4 + 2 physical therapy program; student/faculty research and publication; nationally recognized study abroad program; "London Preview", a special program for freshman which features spring break in London for $150.

Biblical Theological Seminary
200 N. Main St., Hatfield 19440
Wayne Arndt, Dean Student Services

Bloomsburg University, Bloomsburg 17815
Bernard Vinovrski, Dir. of Admis.

Bucknell University, Lewisburg 17837

Cabrini College
610 King of Prussia Rd., Radnor 19087

California University of Pennsylvania
3rd St., California 15419
Norman Hasbrouck, Dean for Enrollment

Carnegie Mellon University
5000 Forbes Ave., Pittsburgh 15213

Cheyney University of Pennsylvania
P.O. Box 200, Cheyney 19319

Clarion University of Pennsylvania
840 Wood St., Clarion 16214

College Misericordia
301 Lake St., Dallas 18612
Michael Joseph, Dir. of Enrollment Mgmt.

Delaware Valley College of Science & Agriculture
Doylestown 18901
Stephen Zenko, Dir. of Admis.

Dickinson College
P.O. Box 1773, Carlisle 17013
J. Larry Mench, Dean of Admissions

Drexel University
3141 Chestnut St., Philadelphia 19104
Dean of Enrollment Management

Duquesne University
600 Forbes Ave., Pittsburgh 15282
Thomas Schaefer, C.S.Sp., Dir. of Admis.

Eastern College
10 Fairview Dr., Saint Davids 19087
Ronald Keller, VP for Enrollment Management

East Stroudsburg University of Pennsylvania
East Stroudsburg 18301
Alan Chesterton, Dir. of Admis.

Edinboro University of Pennsylvania
Edinboro 16444
Admissions Office: 800-626-2203

Elizabethtown College
1 Alpha Dr., Elizabethtown 17022

Franklin & Marshall College
P.O. Box 3003, Lancaster 17604

Gannon University
109 University Sq., Erie 16541

Geneva College
3200 College Ave., Beaver Falls 15010

Gettysburg College
300 N. Washington St., Gettysburg 17325
Delwin K. Gustafson, Dir. of Admis.

Gratz College
Old York Rd. and Melrose Ave.
Melrose Park 19126
Evelyn Klein, Dir. of Admissions
215-635-7300

Grove City College
100 Campus Dr., Grove City 16127
Jeffrey C. Mincey, Dir. of Admis.

GWYNEDD-MERCY COLLEGE
Sumneytown Pike, Gwynedd Valley 19437
Marjorie DeSimone, Dean of Admissions
800-DIAL-GMC
Established 1948. Private. Coed. Accreditation: MSACS. Tuition: $11,000. Room and board: $5,550. Enrollment: 713 full-time, 1,306 part-time. Faculty: 173. Student-faculty ratio: 11:1. Degrees: associate & bachelors. Majors in: accounting, biology, business administration, business education, cardiovascular technology, computer & information systems, gerontology, health record technology, elementary education, early childhood, English, health sciences, history, mathematics, medical technology, nursing, psychology, radiation therapy technology, respiratory care, sociology, special education. Library: 93,600 volumes. 15 buildings on 170 acres. Clinical or internship program opportunities in every major. Computer integrated classes. Courses available for athletic training certification. Graduate degree offered in nursing, reading and school counseling.

Haverford College
370 Lancaster Ave., Haverford 19041

Holy Family College
Grant & Frankford Ave., Philadelphia 19114
Dr. Mott Linn, Dir. of Admis.
215-637-3050

Indiana University of Pennsylvania, Indiana 15705
Fred Dadak, Dean, Admissions

Juniata College
1700 Moore St., Huntington 16652

King's College
133 N. River St., Wilkes Barre 18711

Kutztown University of Pennsylvania
Kutztown 19530

Lafayette College, Easton 18042
G. Gary Ripple, Dir. of Admis.
610-250-5100

La Roche College
9000 Babcock Blvd., Pittsburgh 15237
Marianne Leister, Dir. of Admis.

LA SALLE UNIVERSITY
1900 W. Olney Ave., Philadelphia 19141
Br. Joseph Burke, FSC, PhD, President
Br. Gerald Fitzgerald, FSC, MBA, Dir. of Admis.
Established 1863. Roman Catholic. Accreditation: MSACS, ACS, Pennsylvania Department of Public Instruction. Tuition: $10,970 (liberal arts & business administration students). Room and board: $5,430 (7 days). Enrollment: 1,800 boarding, 3,500 day. Faculty: 326.
Degrees: BA in Liberal Arts Sciences; BS in Business Administration; MA in Religion Education, Education, Bilingual/Bicultural Studies, Pastoral Counseling; MBA in Business Administration.
Library contains 336,000 volumes. 40 buildings on 100 acres. Gym. Pool. 36 major degree programs. La Salle in Europe. Honors and interdisciplinary programs, criminal justice and social work. Urban location. Co-op plan with Chestnut Hill College. Special education, ROTC, evening division, C.E.W. weekend.

La Salle University
675 York Rd., Warminster 18974
See listing under "Universities"

La Salle University
11101 Academy Rd., Philadelphia 19154
See listing under "Universities"

Lebanon Valley College
101 N. College Ave., Annville 17003

Lehigh University
27 Memorial Dr. W., Bethlehem 18015

Lincoln University, Lincoln University 19352
Jimmy Arrington, Dir. of Admis.

Lock Haven University, Lock Haven 17745

Lycoming College, Williamsport 17701

Mansfield University of Pennsylvania
Mansfield 16933

Mercyhurst College
501 E. 38th St., Erie 16546
Andrew Roth, Dean of Enrollment
800-825-1926

Messiah College
General Delivery, Grantham 17027
Ron Long, Dir. of Admis.

Messiah College
2026 N. Broad St., Philadelphia 19121

Millersville University of Pennsylvania
Millersville 17551
Blair Treasure, Dean of Admissions

Moravian College
1200 Main St., Bethlehem 18018

Mt. Aloysius College
1 College Dr., Cresson 16630
Sylvia Hirsch, Dir. of Admis.
814-886-4131

Muhlenberg College
2400 W. Chew St., Allentown 18104
Chris Hooker-Haring, Dir. of Admis.

Neumann College
Concord Rd., Aston 19014

Pennsylvania State University
201 Shields Bldg., University Park 16802

PENNSYLVANIA STATE UNIVERSITY
Beaver Campus, Monaca 15061
Regina S. Miller, Dir. of Admis.
412-773-3800
Established 1965. Public. Coed. Accreditation: MSACS, ABET. Tuition: In-state students, $4,404, out-of-state students, $9,574. Room and board: $3,400. Fees: $125. Enrollment: 1,000 full-time, 1,500 part-time. Faculty: 67. Student-faculty ratio: 15:1. Degrees: Over 160 baccalaureate degrees, 12 associate degrees. Library: 35,000 volumes plus access to volumes at 19 other campuses. 12 buildings on 94 acres. Students complete their freshman and sophomore years at the Beaver Campus for most baccalaureate degrees. Their junior and senior years are completed at either University Park, Behrend or Capital Campus in the Penn State system. Seven of the associate degrees can be completed at Beaver Campus. We have four intercollegiate sports: men's baseball, women's softball and volleyball and coed golf. We offer both traditional residence hall living and a townhouse option. A learning center and tutoring are available in all subject areas. Numerous scholarships and financial aid opportunities.

Pennsylvania State University
5091 Station Rd., Erie 16563

Pennsylvania State University
Rt. 230, Middletown 17057
Mary E. Gundel, Dir. of Admis.

Point Park College
201 Wood St., Pittsburgh 15222

ROBERT MORRIS COLLEGE
Narrows Run Rd., Coraopolis 15108
James R. Welsh, Dean of Admissions
800-762-0097 or 412-262-8200
Established 1921. Private. Coed. Accreditation: MSACS. Tuition: $6,000. Room and board: $4,106. Fees: $300. Enrollment: 2,621 full-time, 1,808 part-time. Faculty: 348. Student-faculty ratio: 21:1. Degrees: AA, AS, BA, BS 16 majors, MBA, MS. Library: 120,832 volumes. 26 buildings on 230 acres. Sports management, communications and health services management. Fully equipped television studio, print and graphics media, over 350 computer terminals.

Robert Morris College
600 5th Ave., Pittsburgh 15219
James R. Welsh, Dean of Admissions
See listing under "Universities"

St. Francis College
P.O. Box 600, Loretto 15940

St. Joseph's University
5600 City Ave., Philadelphia 19131
Randy Miller, Dir. of Admis.

St. Vincent College
300 Fraser Purchase Rd., Latrobe 15650

Shippensburg University, Shippensburg 17257

Slippery Rock University, Slippery Rock 16057
Director of Admissions

Susquehanna University
514 University Ave., Selinsgrove 17870

Swarthmore College
500 College Ave., Swarthmore 19081
Carl Wartenburg, Dean of Admissions

Temple University, Ambler Campus Center
Ambler 19002

Temple University
Broad St. & Montgomery Ave.
Philadelphia 19122

Temple University, City Center
1616 Walnut St., Philadelphia 19103

Thiel College
75 College Ave., Greenville 16125
Robert Weaver, Dir. of Admis.

Thomas Jefferson University
111 S. 11th St., Philadelphia 19107

University of Pennsylvania
0 Levy Park, Philadelphia 19104

University of Pittsburgh
4200 5th Ave., Pittsburgh 15260

University of Pittsburgh, Greensburg Campus
1150 Mt. Pleasant Rd., Greensburg 15601
George Chambers, President

University of Pittsburgh at Bradford
300 Campus Dr., Bradford 16701

University of Pittsburgh at Johnstown
450 Schoolhouse Rd., Johnstown 15904

UNIVERSITY OF PITTSBURGH AT TITUSVILLE
McKinney Hall
504 E Main St., Titusville 16354
Jamie Mowat, Dir. of Admis./Financial Aid
814-827-4427

University of Scranton
800 Linden St., Scranton 18510

Ursinus College
601 E. Main St., Collegeville 19426

Villanova University
845 E. Lancaster Ave., Villanova 19085
Stephen R. Merritt, Dir. of Admis.

Washington & Jefferson College
60 S. Lincoln St., Washington 15301
Thomas O'Connor, Dir. of Admis.

Waynesburg College
51 W. College St., Waynesburg 15370
Robin Moore, Dir. of Admis.
800-225-7393

West Chester University of Pennsylvania
S. High St., West Chester 19380

WESTMINSTER COLLEGE
New Wilmington 16172
Richard Dana Paul, Dir. of Admis.
412-946-7100

Widener University
700 E. 14th St., Chester 19013

Wilkes University
184 S. River St., Wilkes-Barre 18766
Emory P. Guffrovich Jr., Dean of Admissions

YORK COLLEGE OF PENNSYLVANIA
P.O. Box 15199, York 17405-7199
Nancy Spataro, Dir. of Admis.
717-849-1600
York College, selected as one of America's Best Buys in the "Barron's Best Buys in College Education" is nationally recognized for its high quality programs, friendly campus and affordable costs. Established in 1787, York is a friendly, ideal sized, private liberal arts college offering many career oriented programs of study. Emphasis is placed on outstanding teaching faculty, the majority of whom hold doctorates. Situated on a pleasant, beautifully landscaped 80 acre campus in historic southcentral Pennsylvania; convenient interstate access-one hour drive from Baltimore, two hours from Philadelphia and Washington DC, and a four hour drive from New York City and Pittsburgh. Enrollment: 3,000 full-time students from 30 states and 19 countries. Annual tuition: $4,785. Room: $1,625. Board: $1,725. Fees: $210. Competetive ranking; freshmen SAT scores surpass the national norm. Merit scholarships: Full tuition Trustees Honors Scholarships for students with a top 20% class rank and SATs over 1,100; One half tuition Presidential, Valedictorian, and Salutatorian Scholarships; or one-third tuition Dean's Scholarships for students with a top 40% class rank and SATs over 1,000 (minimum 500 math, 460 verbal).

RHODE ISLAND

Brown University, Providence 02906

Bryant College
1150 Douglas Pike, Smithfield 02917

Johnson & Wales University
111 Dorrance St., Providence 02903
Mark S. Burke, Dir. of Admis.

New England Technical College
2500 Post Rd., Warwick 02886

Providence College
River Ave., Providence 02918

Rhode Island College
600 Mt. Pleasant Ave., Providence 02908

Roger Williams College
1 Old Ferry Rd., Bristol 02809
William Dunfey, Dir. of Admis.

Roger Williams College
612 Academy Ave., Providence 02908

Salve Regina University
1 Ochre Point Ave., Newport 02840
Roselina McKillop, Dean of Admissions

University of Rhode Island, Kingston 02881
David Taggart, Dean of Admissions/Financial Aid

SOUTH CAROLINA

Allen University
1530 Harden St., Columbia 29204

Anderson College
316 S. Boulevard, Anderson 29621
Carl D. Lockman, Dir. of Admis.
800-542-3594

Benedict College
1600 Harden St., Columbia 29204
Virginia McKee, Dir. of Admis.

BOB JONES UNIVERSITY
Greenville 29614
Bob Jones III, President
David Christ, Dir. of Admis.
Established 1927. Private. Coed. Tuition: $4,140. Room and board: $3,540. Enrollment: 2,917 boarding, 1,514 day. Faculty: 350. Degrees: AAA, AAS, BA, BMus, BS, BSN, MA, MDiv, MEd, MFA, MMin, MMus, MS, DMin, PhD, EdD. Library: 222,000 volumes. 46 buildings on 185 acres. Gym. Pool. 2 & 3 year trade programs available. Internationally recognized gallery of sacred art on campus. Unusual Films produces outstanding Christian films. University Press produces Christian and educational texts.

Central Wesleyan College
P.O. Box 1020, Central 29630
Lillian A. Robbins, Dir. of Admis.

Charleston Southern University
P.O. Box 10087, Charleston 29411
Melinda Mitchum, Dir. of Admis.

Claflin College
700 College Ave., Orangeburg 29115
P. Palmer Worthy, Registrar

Clemson University
201 Sikes Hall, Clemson 29634

Coastal Carolina College
P.O. Box 1954, Myrtle Beach 29578
Dr. Ed Cerny, Director of Admissions

Coker College
300 E. College Ave., Hartsville 29550

College of Charleston
66 George St., Charleston 29424

Columbia Biblical Seminary
P.O. Box 3122, Columbia 29230
Lawrence Dabeck, Dir. of Admis.
See listing under "Biblical Studies"

Columbia International University
P.O. Box 3122, Columbia 29230
Frank Bedell, Dir. of Admis.
See listing under "Biblical Studies"

Erskine College & Seminary
Washington St., Due West 29639
Dot Carter, Dir. of Admis.

Francis Marion College
P.O. Box 100547, Florence 29501
Marvin Lynch, Dir. of Admis.

Furman University
3300 Poinsett Hwy., Greenville 29613
Charles Brock, Dir. of Admis.

Lander College
320 Stanley Ave., Greenwood 29649

Limestone College
1115 College Dr., Gaffney 29340
Peter Wood, Dir. of Admis.

Morris College
100 W. College St., Sumter 29150
Luns C. Richardson, President

Newberry College
2100 College St., Newberry 29108
Neil Clark, Dean of Admissions and Financial Aid

NORTH GREENVILLE COLLEGE
P.O. Box 1892, Tigerville 29688
Gary Wells, Dir. of Admis.
803-895-1410
Established 1892. Private. Coed. Accreditation: SACS. Tuition: $6,500. Room and board: $3,780. Fees: $15. Enrollment: 561 full-time, 38 part-time. Faculty: 34. Student-faculty ratio: 17:1. Degrees: AA, AS, Associate in Fine Arts, BA in Religion, BA in Church Music, BA in Business Administration, BA in Broadcasting/Journalism, BA in Elementary Education, BA in Early Childhood Education, BA in Music Education. Affiliated with and committed to the South Carolina Baptist Convention. Christian atmosphere. Honors program. Sports programs: 5 men, 4 women/NAIA Div. II. Located in the foothills of South Carolina.

Presbyterian College
503 S. Broad St., Clinton 29325
Margaret Williamson, Dean of Admis.

SOUTH CAROLINA STATE UNIVERSITY
P.O. Box 7127, Orangeburg 29117-0001
803-536-7185

University of South Carolina, Columbia 29208
Terry Davis, Dir. of Admis.
803-777-7700

University of South Carolina at Aiken
171 University Pkwy., Aiken 29801

University of South Carolina, Spartanburg 29303

Voorhees College
Voorhees Rd., Denmark 29042

Winthrop University
701 W. Oakland Ave., Rock Hill 29733
James McCammon, Jr., Dir. of Admis.

Wofford College
429 N. Church St., Spartanburg 29303
Charles Gray, Dir. of Admis.

SOUTH DAKOTA

Augustana College
29th & S. Summit, Sioux Falls 57197

Black Hills State University
1200 University St., Spearfish 57799
April Meeker, Dir. of Admis.

Dakota State University
820 N. Washington Ave., Madison 57042
Mark Weiss, Dir. of Admis.
605-256-5139

Dakota Wesleyan University
1300 W. University Ave., Mitchell 57301

Huron University
333 Ninth St. S.W., Huron 57350

Mt. Marty College
1105 W. 8th St., Yankton 57078
Paula Tacke, Dir. of Admis.

National College
321 Kansas City St., Rapid City 57701
Keith T. Carlyle, Dir. of Admis.

National College
3201 S. Kiwanis Ave., Sioux Falls 57105

Northern State University
1200 S. Jay St., Aberdeen 57401

Oglala Lakota Community College
P.O. Box 490, Kyle 57752

SIOUX FALLS COLLEGE
1501 S. Prairie Ave., Sioux Falls 57105
Susan Reese, Dir. of Admis.
800-888-1047
Established 1883. Private. Coed. Accreditation: NCACS, NCATE, CSWE. Tuition: $8,990. Room and board: $3,190. Enrollment: 614 full-time, 337 part-time. Faculty: 75. Student-faculty ratio: 15:1. Degrees: AA, BA, BS, MEd, 3-3 MDiv. Library: 90,000 volumes with computer library service connected to all colleges in SD. 14 buildings on 12 acres. Located in the state's largest city at the junction of Interstates 29 & 90. Serviced by 5 major airlines. New wellness/fitness center with 1/10 mile indoor track, hot tub, 4 basketball/volleyball/tennis indoor courts, 4 racquetball courts. Excellent facilities and departments of accounting, business administration, drama, elementary education, mass communications, music, pre-medicine, religion, secondary education, social work, wellness education, and wellness management.

South Dakota School of Mines and Technology
501 E. St. Joseph St., Rapid City 57701
Gary Bjordal, Dir. of Admis.

SOUTH DAKOTA STATE UNIVERSITY
P.O. Box 2201, Brookings 57007
Robert Wagner, President
Tracy Welsh, Acting Director of Admissions
605-688-4121
Established 1881. State. Coed. Accreditation: NCACS. Tuition: $2,251 resident, $2,956 Western Undergraduate Exchange (WUE) residents of AK, CO, HI, ID, MT, NV, NM, ND, OR, UT, and WY, $4,212 nonresident. Room and board: $2,080. Enrollment: 9,866. Faculty: 520. Degrees: AA, BA, BS, MS, MEd, PhD, with programs of concentration in agriculture, arts, engineering, home economics, nursing, pharmacy, science, teacher education, and pre-professional. Library: 700,000 volumes. 70 buildings on 260 acres. Gym. Pool. Agriculture Heritage Museum and Memorial Arts Center on campus. Option of general registration allows students to take classes for 1 year without declaring a major. Student receives special career counseling.

University of South Dakota
414 E. Clark St., Vermillion 57069
Dave Lorenz, Dir. of Admis.

TENNESSEE

American Technical Institute
8760 Baylor Rd., Brunswick 38014

Austin Peay State University
601 College St., Clarksville 37044

Belmont College
1900 Belmont Blvd., Nashville 37212

BRISTOL UNIVERSITY
P.O. Box 4366, Bristol 37625
Dr. W. David Willis, Academic Dean
800-366-1442
Established 1895. Private. Coed. Accreditation: AICS. Tuition: $5,900. Fees: $100. Enrollment: 590 full-time, 80 part-time. Faculty: 110 full-time and adjunct. Student-faculty ratio: 11:1. Degrees: AS, BS, MBA. Library: 50,000 volumes. 8 buildings in an Executive Park Concept. Modular teaching concept (one class at a time, one month at a time), continuous registration. Campuses in Bristol TN, Knoxville TN, Indianapolis IN. 5 concentrations in MBA, 11 concentrations in BS, accounting, human resource management, computer information management, executive management, health care administration, personnel and public relations, professional marketing and sales, real estate, recreation and fitness, administrative assistant, communication for business and professions.

Bryan College
Box 7000, Dayton 37321
Thomas A. Shaw, Dir. of Admis.

CARSON-NEWMAN COLLEGE
P.O. Box 70552, Jefferson City 37760
Sheryl M. Gray, Dir. of Admis.
615-471-3223 or 800-678-9061
Established 1851. Private. Coed. Accreditation: Southern Association of Colleges and Schools. Tui-

tion: $7,400. Room and board: $3,000. Fees: $850. Enrollment: 1,817 full-time, 309 part-time. Student-faculty ratio: 14:1. Degrees: BA, BS, BSN, BSM, MAT, MEd. Library: 190,000 volumes. New student activities center. NCAA Div. II - 15 varsity sports, Art Gallery, Appalachian Center, Bonner scholars / community service.

Christian Brothers College
650 E. Parkway, S., Memphis 38104

Cumberland University
220 S. Greenwood St., Lebanon 37087
Ernest Stockton, President

David Lipscomb University
3901 Granny White Pike, Nashville 37204-3951
Wade Sandrell, Dir. of Admis.
800-333-4358

EAST TENNESSEE STATE UNIVERSITY
P.O. Box 70731, Johnson City 37614
Dr. Nancy Dishner, Dean, Enrollment Management
615-929-4213 or 800-462-3878

Fisk University
1000 17th Ave., N., Nashville 37208

Freed-Hardeman University
158 E. Main St., Henderson 38340
800-342-7837

King College
1350 King College Rd., Bristol 37620

Knoxville College
901 College St., N.W., Knoxville 37921

Lambuth College
705 Lambuth Blvd., Jackson 38301

Lane College
545 Lane Ave., Jackson 38301

Lee College
P.O. Box 3450, Cleveland 37320

Le Moyne-Owen College
807 Walker Ave., Memphis 38126
901-942-7302 or 800-737-7778

Lincoln Memorial University
P.O. Box 2012, Harrogate 37752
Conrad Daniels, Dir. of Admis.

Maryville College
800 S. Court St., Maryville 37801
Annabelle J. Libby, Dir. of Admis.

Middle Tennessee State University
Murfreesboro 37132
Roger D. Sims, Dir. of Admis.

Milligan College
P.O. Box 210, Milligan College 37682

PEABODY COLLEGE OF VANDERBILT UNIVERSITY
P.O. Box 327, Nashville 37202
Barbara Johnston, Dir. of Admis.
615-322-8410

Rhodes College
2000 N. Parkway, Memphis 38112

Southern Missionary College
P.O. Box 370, Collegedale 37315

Tennessee State University
3500 John A. Merritt Blvd., Nashville 37209

Tennessee Technological University
P.O. Box 5006, Cookeville 38505

Tennessee Temple University
1815 Union Ave., Chattanooga 37404
Dr. L. W. Nichols, President

Tennessee Wesleyan College
P.O. Box 40, Athens 37371

Trevecca Nazarene College
333 Murfreesboro Rd., Nashville 37210

Tusculum College
P.O. Box 5035, Greeneville 37743
Ronald Porter, Dir. of Admis.

UNION UNIVERSITY
2447 US Highway 45 Bypass, Jackson 38305
Carroll Griffin, Dir. of Admis.
Admissions Office: 800-33UNION
THE COLLEGE: Union University is a private, four year, co-educational, liberal arts college. Founded in 1823. Union is the oldest college in the Southern Baptist Convention. It is fully accredited and is affiliated with the Tennessee Baptist Convention.
LOCATION: Union is situated on 230 acres of rolling terrain in Jackson, Tennessee, on the US 45 By-pass at Interstate 40. This city of 50,000 is located 80 miles east of Memphis, and 120 miles west of Nashville.
CAMPUS: Facilities include 225,000 square-feet Penrick Academic Complex and 30,000 square-feet Blasingame Academic Complex. On the grounds are men's and women's apartment villages and commons buildings as well as varsity baseball and intramural softball fields and tennis courts.
ENROLLMENT: More than 2,000 full-time men and women students are enrolled on the main campus in Jackson. More than 400 students are enrolled with our satellite program at Baptist Hospital School of Nursing in Memphis.
ACADEMICS: Union offers more than 45 fields of study in the arts, sciences, humanities, and social sciences. Union confers the Bachelor of Arts, Bachelor of Science, Bachelor of Music, Bachelor of Science in Business Administration and Bachelor of Science in Nursing degrees.

COSTS: Union University is one of the lowest priced four-year private colleges in Tennessee. The approximate total cost in 1994-95 for a full-time resident student including tuition, room and board, and books is $8,400. For winter term, summer terms, and Evening Program costs please consult our catalog.
ACCREDITATION: Union University is fully accredited by the Southern Association of Colleges and Schools, the National League for Nursing, and the National Association of Schools of Music.
ADMISSIONS: ACT/SAT scores, academic transcript, $10 application fee, and Union Application are required.
FINANCIAL AID: Financial aid includes scholarships, grants, loans, and campus work. Of our students 80% receive financial aid.
CAMPUS VISITATION: Campus Day in the Fall is designed to introduce our campus to prospective students. Join us then, or simply call and make an appointment with any of our admissions counselors at any time during the year.

University of Memphis, Memphis 38152
Dr. John Eubank, Dean of Admissions

UNIVERSITY OF TENNESSEE AT MARTIN
Martin 38238
Paul Kelley, Director of Admissions
800-829-8861
Established 1927. Public. Coed. Accreditation: SACS. Tuition: In-state $905 per semester, out-of-state $1,800 per semester. Room and board: $1,400 per semester. Enrollment: 5,500 full-time, 360 part-time. Faculty: 275. Student-faculty ratio: 19:1. Schools of: Agriculture & Home Economics, Business Administration, Engineering & Engineering Technology, Education, Arts & Sciences, and Fine and Performing Arts. Library: 400,000 volumes. 38 buildings on 500 acre campus. Situated in a rural setting. Easily accessible. No graduate assistants allowed to teach. Good value. Individual attention.

University of Tennessee at Chattanooga
615 McCallie Ave., Chattanooga 37403

University of Tennessee, Knoxville
527 Andy Holt Tower, Knoxville 37996
Dr. Gordon Stanley, Dir. of Admis.

University of the South
735 University Ave., Sewanee 37375

Vanderbilt University
West End Ave., Nashville 37240

TEXAS

Abilene Christian University
ACU Station, Box 6000, Abilene 79699

Amber University
1700 Eastgate Dr., Garland 75041

Angelo State University
2601 W. Ave., N., San Angelo 76909

Austin College
900 N. Grand Ave., Sherman 75090
Rodney Oto, Dean of Admission
800-442-5363

Baylor University
P.O. Box 97008, Waco 76798-7008
Diana Ramey, Director of Admissions

Concordia Lutheran College
3400 N. Interstate 35, Austin 78705
Kevin Pieper, Dir. of Admis.

Corpus Christi State University
6300 Ocean Dr., Corpus Christi 78412

Criswell College
4010 Gaston Ave., Dallas 75246
Leo D. Bradley, Registrar

Dallas Baptist University
7777 W. Kiest Blvd., Dallas 75211

East Texas Baptist University
1200 N. Grove Ave., Marshall 75670

East Texas State University
ETSU Station, Commerce 75429

East Texas State University
P.O. Box 5518, Texarkana 75505
John Moss, President

HARDIN-SIMMONS UNIVERSITY
2200 Hickory St. Drawer M, Abilene 79698-0002
Laura Moore, Dir. of Admis.
Established 1891. Private. Coed. Accreditation: National Association of Schools of Music, NLN, CSWE, SACS. Tuition: $200 per hour. Room and board: $2,850. Fees: $240 over 9 hours. Enrollment:1,256 full-time, 380 part-time. Faculty: 148. Student-faculty ratio: 17:1. Degrees: BA, BS, BBA, BFA, BMus, BSN. Library 350,000+ volumes 700,000+ with automation. 36 buildings on 40 acre campus. Several new buildings have been added to the campus: Frost Visual Art Center, 1987; Johnson School of Business, 1990; School of Theology, 1987; Jake Sandefer Field House, 1990.

Houston Baptist University
7502 Fondren Rd., Houston 77074

Howard Payne University
1000 Fisk Ave., Brownwood 76801

Huston-Tillotson College
1820 E. 8th St., Austin 78702

Incarnate Word College
4301 Broadway St., San Antonio 78209
Sr. Sally Mitchell, Dean of Enrollment

Jarvis Christian College
P.O. Box G, Hawkins 75765

Lamar University
P.O. Box 10009, Beaumont 77710
800-458-7558

LeTourneau College
P.O. Box 7001, Longview 75607

Lubbock Christian University
5601 W. 19th, Lubbock 79407

McMurry University
14th and Sayles, Abilene 79697

Midwestern State University
3400 Taft Blvd., Wichita Falls 76308

Northwood University
P.O. Box 58, Cedar Hill 75106
Jim Hickerson, Dir. of Admis.
800-927-WOOD

Our Lady of the Lake University
411 S.W. 24th St., San Antonio 78207-4689
210-434-6711

Prairie View A & M University
P.O. Box 3089, Prairie View 77446-3089
Linda S. Berry, Dir. of Admis.

Rice University
P.O. Box 1892, Houston 77251

St. Edward's University
3001 S. Congress Ave., Austin 78704
John Lambert, Dir. of Admis.

St. Mary's University of San Antonio
1 Camino Santa Maria, San Antonio 78228
Rick Castillo, Dir. of Admis.

Sam Houston State University, Huntsville 77341

Schreiner College
2100 Memorial Blvd., Kerrville 78028
800-343-4919

Southern Methodist University
Hillcrest at University, Dallas 75275

Southwestern Adventist College
P.O. Box 567, Keene 76059

SOUTHWESTERN CHRISTIAN COLLEGE
P.O. Box 10, Terrell 75160
John T. Edmerson, Director of Admissions
214-524-3341
Established 1949. Private. Coed. Accreditation: Southern Association of Colleges and Schools. Tuition: $1,846. Room and board: $1,337. Fees: $36. Enrollment: 250 full-time, 125 part-time. Student-faculty ratio: 13:1. Degrees: Associates in several areas, Bachelors Bible/Religious Education. 12 buildings on 2 acres. Located 30 minutes from Dallas, Texas; Intimate relationship between faculty, administration and students; historical museum on campus; a solid institution committed to your spiritual and educational development.

Southwestern University
University Ave. at Maple St., Georgetown 78626

Southwest Texas State University
601 University Dr., San Marcos 78666

Stephen F. Austin State University
P.O. Box 6078, Nacogdoches 75962

Sul Ross State University, Alpine 79832

Tarleton State University
1297 W. Washington St., Stephenville 76402

Texas A & I University
Campus Box 101, Kingsville 78363

Texas A & M International University
1 West End Washington St., Laredo 78040

Texas A & M University
College Station 77843

Texas Christian University
2800 S. University Dr., Ft. Worth 76129
Dr. Edward Boehm, Jr., Dean of Admissions

Texas College
2404 N. Grand St., Tyler 75702
Dr. William H. Ammons, II, Dir. of Admis.

Texas Lutheran College
1000 W. Court St., Seguin 78155
Jennifer B. Ehlers, Dir. of Admis.

Texas Southern University
3100 Cleburne St., Houston 77004

Texas Tech University, Lubbock 79409

Texas Wesleyan University
1201 Wesleyan St., Fort Worth 76105
Kim Campbell, Dir. Freshman Admission

Trinity University
715 Stadium Dr., San Antonio 78212

University of Central Texas
P.O. Box 1416, Killeen 76540
Dr. Pauline Moseley, Dean of the Faculty

University of Dallas
1845 E. Northgate Dr., Irving 75062
Jim Whitaker, Dir. of Admis.

University of Houston
4800 Calhoun Rd., Houston 77204

University of Houston-Clear Lake
2700 Bay Area Blvd., Houston 77058
Darella Banks, Exec. Dir. Enrollment Services

University of Houston-Downtown
1 Main St., Houston 77002

University of Houston-Victoria
2302-C E. Red River St., Victoria 77901

University of Mary Hardin-Baylor
UMHB Station, Box 8001, Belton 76513
800-727-8642 or 817-939-4520

University of North Texas
P.O. Box 13797, Denton 76203

University of St. Thomas
3812 Montrose Blvd., Houston 77006
Elsie Biron, Dir. of Admis.

University of Texas at Arlington
UTA Box 19125, Arlington 76019
R. Zack Prince, Dir. of Admis.

University of Texas at Austin
0 the University of Texas, Austin 78712

University of Texas at Dallas
P.O. Box 830688, Richardson 75083-0688

University of Texas at El Paso
500 W. University Ave., El Paso 79968

University of Texas at San Antonio
San Antonio 78285
Dr. John H. Brown, Dir. of Admis.

University of Texas at Tyler
3900 University Blvd., Tyler 75799
Martha Wheat, Dir. of Admis.

University of Texas of the Permian Basin
4901 E. University Blvd., Odessa 79762

University of Texas-Pan American
1614 Ridgeley Rd., Brownsville 78520

University of Texas-Pan American
1201 W. University Dr., Edinburg 78539
Miguel Nerarez, President

Wayland Baptist University
1900 W. 7th, Plainview 79072
Dr. Lanny Hall, President

West Texas State University
2501 4th Ave., Canyon 79016
Lila Vars, Dir. of Admis.

Wiley College
711 Wiley Ave., Marshall 75670

UTAH

Brigham Young University, Provo 84602

Southern Utah University
351 W. Center St., Cedar City 84720
D. Mark Barton, Asst. VP Student Services
801-586-7740

University of Utah
1400 E. 200 S., Salt Lake City 84112
Dr. J. Stayner Landward, Dir. of Admis.

Utah State University, Logan 84322-1600
Rod Clark, Director of Admissions
801-750-1107

Weber State University
3750 Harrison Blvd., Ogden 84408

Westminster College of Salt Lake City
1840 S. 1300 E., Salt Lake City 84105
800-748-4753

VERMONT

Bennington College, Bennington 05201
Karen Kristof, Dir. of Admis.
800-833-6845

Castleton State College, Castleton 05735
Gary Fallis, Dir. of Admis.

CHAMPLAIN COLLEGE
P.O. Box 670, Burlington 05402
Josephine Churchill, Dir. of Admis.
802-860-2727
Established 1878. Private. Coed. Accreditation: NEASC. Tuition: $7,740. Room and board: $5,550. Fees: $100. Enrollment: 1,265 full-time, 701 part-time. Faculty: 99. Student-faculty ratio: 16-1. Degrees: AS, BS. Library: 34,000 volumes. 26 buildings on 19 acres. Admitted to programs of study. Not rejected based on SAT scores. Rolling admissions. Focused programs in Business, Computers and Technology, Health, Education and Social Services, Law related careers, Office Administration and Liberal Arts.

College of St. Joseph
71 Clement Rd., Rutland 05701

Goddard College
P.O. Box G, Plainfield 05667
Jackson Kytle, President

Green Mountain College
16 College St., Poultney 05764

Johnson State College, Johnson 05656
802-635-2356 ext. 219

Lyndon State College, Lyndonville 05851

Marlboro College
General Delivery, Marlboro 05344

Middlebury College, Middlebury 05753
Geoffrey R. Smith, Dir. of Admis.

New England Culinary Institute
250 Main St., Montpelier 05602
See listing under "Career Schools"

NORWICH UNIVERSITY
65 S. Main St., Northfield 05663
Richard Schneider, President
Frank Griffis, Dir. of Admis.
802-485-2000
Established 1819. Private. Coed. Accreditation: NEASC. Tuition: $12,820. Room and board: $5,020. Enrollment: 1,550 boarding, 150 day. Faculty: 167. Degrees: AA, AS, BA, BS, MA, MAT, MEd in Physical Education. Consists of 42 bldgs. on 1,000+ acres. 300,000 volumes in libraries. University comprised of 2 student lifestyles: a Corps of Cadets, mandatory Army, Air Force or Naval ROTC, without an automatic military service obligation; and traditional students. 27 majors including architecture, business, education, engineering, criminal justice, and nursing. NCAA Division III.

NORWICH UNIVERSITY VERMONT COLLEGE CAMPUS
Montpelier 05602

Saint Michael's College
Winooski Park, Colchester 05439
800-SMC-8000
See listing under "Liberal Arts"

SOUTHERN VERMONT COLLEGE
Monument Ave., Bennington 05201
Dr. William Glasser, President
Bobbi Gabrenya, Director of Admission
802-442-5427
Established 1926. Private. Coed. Accreditation: NEASC. Tuition: $8,370. Room and board: $4,304. Enrollment: 750. Faculty: 71. Degrees: AA, AS, BA, BS. Library: 25,000 volumes. Special program for learning disabled. Bachelor Degrees: accounting, business management, child care management, communications, criminal justice, English, environmental studies, gerontology management, liberal arts, liberal arts management, nursing for RNs, private security management and social work. Associate Degrees: accounting, business, child development, criminal justice, environmental studies, gerontology, human services, liberal arts and nursing for LPNs - all emphasizing career skills with a liberal arts foundation.
SVC is housed on the former Everett Estate. The estate house is English-Norman architecture and follows the design of many 14th century great houses. The entire mansion has been converted into administrative offices, classrooms, and an expansive library. The main college building, along with five dormitories, a dining hall, a student activity center, and our newly constructed health complex are located on 371 acres on the eastern slope of Mount Anthony. The campus provides a spectacular view of the valley below.
The town of Bennington is within walking distance from the main campus. Bennington is located in southern Vermont with easy access to over fifteen ski areas and many other cultural and recreation facilities. It is a few miles from the New York and Massachusetts borders, a 1 hour drive from Albany, and a 3-1/2 hour drive from both Boston and New York City.

University of Vermont
194 S. Prospect St., Burlington 05401
802-656-3370

VIRGINIA

Averett College
420 W. Main St., Danville 24541
Gary Sherman, Dean of Enrollment Mgmt.

BLUEFIELD COLLEGE
3000 College Dr., Bluefield 24605
Pop. 18000
Dr. Roy Dobyns, President
Nina Wilburn, Vice-President for Enrollment Mgt.
703-326-4214 or 800-872-0175
Established 1922. Private. Southern Baptist. Coed. Accreditation: Southern Association of Colleges and Schools. Enrollment: 782. Tuition: $7,150. Room and board: $4,350. Federal and institutional financial aid available. Financial Aid Form (FAF) and Free Application for Federal Student Aid (FAFSA) should be filed no later than March 10.
AA, AS, BS, and BA degrees; nineteen majors and twenty-one minors. All courses taught by qualified faculty—no graduate students or teaching assistants. 57%—of faculty hold PhD's; Two semesters (15 week Fall semester and 15 week Spring semester). Summer sessions available. Average class size - 25. Student-faculty ratio: 16:1. Library: 42,000 volumes; 100 titles on microform; 210 periodical subscriptions. 85 acre campus. 5 Administrative and Academic buildings. 3 residence halls house approximately 290 students. Athletic facilities include tennis, basketball courts; baseball and softball fields.
Students participate in NAIA District 24 sports in (Men's) basketball, baseball, golf, tennis, and soccer; (Women's) basketball, softball, tennis, volleyball. Excellent intramural athletic programs also available.
Student life includes five local fraternities and three local sororities. Many social, service and professional clubs and organizations. Choral and musical ensembles (Bluefield Singers, Variations); theatre productions; guest lecturers and concerts; Student Government Association.
Admissions: students may apply for entrance into any term. Students applying for freshman admission should submit application, high school transcripts and results of SAT or ACT. Transfer students should submit application, official transcripts from all col-

leges previously attended. Rolling admissions. Candidates normally notified of decision within two weeks after admissions file completed.

Bridgewater College
402 E College St., Bridgewater 22812

Christopher Newport College
50 Shoe Ln., Newport News 23606

Clinch Valley College of the University of Virginia
P.O. Box 16, Wise 24293
Lana Low, Dir. Enrollment Management

College of William and Mary, Williamsburg 23185
Jean A. Scott, Dean of Admission

Eastern Mennonite College
1200 Park Rd., Harrisonburg 22801
703-432-4260

Eastern Virginia Medical School, Norfolk 23501

Emory & Henry College
General Delivery, Emory 24327

Ferrum College, Ferrum 24088
Bob Bailey, Dir. of Admis.

George Mason University
4400 University Dr., Fairfax 22030-4444
Patricia Riordan, Dean of Admissions

Hampton University, Hampton 23668
Ollie Bowman, Dean of Admissions

Hollins College
P.O. Box 9707, Hollins College 24020
800-456-9595

James Madison University, Harrisonburg 22807

LIBERTY UNIVERSITY
P.O. Box 20000, Lynchburg 24506
Toll Free 800-522-6225
Dr. Jerry Falwell, Chancellor
Dr. Pierre Gillerman, President
Jay Spencer, Director of Admissions
    Established 1971. Baptist. Coed. Tuition: $6,000 per year ($200 per credit hour). Room and board: $4,600 per year. State, Federal, and institutional financial aid available.
    COLLEGES: College of Arts and Science, College of General Studies, School of Business & Government, School of Communications, School of Education, School of Religion, School of Lifelong Learning, Seminary & Graduate Education.
    UNDERGRADUATE MAJORS: Accounting, Biblical Studies, Biology, Biology Education, Business (Administration, Education, Management, Management Information System, Marketing), Chemistry, Church Ministries (Music & Youth Ministries), Community Health Promotion, Computer Science, Drama (Acting and Directing, Technical Theater), Economics, Education (Early and Middle), English, Exercise Science & Fitness Programming, Finance, General Studies, Government (Administration of Justice, Politics & Public Policy, Pre-Law, Public Administration), Health Education, History, Home Economics, Human Ecology (Fashion Merchandising, General), Interdisciplinary Studies, Journalism (Advertising, Graphics, News Editorial, Public Relations), Mathematics, Missions & Cross-Cultural Studies, Modern Languages (French, Spanish), Music (Choral, Instrumental), Musical Performance (Instrumental Voice or Keyboard), Nursing, Pastoral Ministries, Philosophy, Physical Education, Psychology (Human Services/Counseling, Developmental, Clinical/Experimental), Sacred Music (Church Director), Recreation, Social Sciences, Speech Communication (Communication Disorders, Public Speaking/Oral Interpretation), Sports Management, Telecommunications (Broadcast Journalism).
    Liberty is on the early semester calendar. During the summer there are several one and two week modular classes as well as two regular sessions of four weeks each. Winter modulars are offered between semesters.
    A variety of grants, scholarships, and on-campus jobs are available at Liberty. All federally funded student financial aid programs, except the Perkins Loan Program, are available. Athletic, academic, talent, ACSI (Association of Christian Schools International), National Merit, Chancellor's and President's scholarships are also available for qualified candidates.
    All admissions materials must reach the Office of Admissions by August 15 for fall enrollment; however, applicants are encouraged to complete the application process by mid-March in order for registration to take place by mail prior to the beginning of the semester. Applicants for the spring term must complete the process by January 1, although early October is preferred.

Longwood College, Farmville 23901

Lynchburg College
1501 Lakeside Dr., Lynchburg 24501
Ernest Chadderton, Dean of Enrollment

MARYMOUNT UNIVERSITY
2807 N. Glebe Rd., Arlington 22207
Sr. Eymard Gallagher, RSHM, President
Charles Coe, Director of Admissions
800-548-7638 or 703-284-1500
    Established 1950. Catholic. Independent. Coed. Accreditation: SACS, NLN, FIDER, NCATE, ACBSP. Tuition: $10,804. Room and board: $5,126. Enrollment: 3,900. Faculty: 310. Student-faculty ratio: 20:1. Degrees: BA, BS, BBA, BSN, MA, MBA, MEd, MS, MSIM, MSN. Library: 125,000 volumes. 9 buildings on 21 acres. Gym. Pool. Exciting Washington DC area internships in corporate and government settings. Financial aid and scholarships. Clinical affiliations

with several university medical centers and prestigious research facilities. Teacher education programs use Arlington and Fairfax County public school systems for practice teaching. Excellent career placement of graduates. London Program offers juniors and seniors internships in such international and corporate settings as Mobil North Sea and European Parliament.

Mary Washington College
1701 College Ave., Fredericksburg 22401
Martin Wilder, V.P. for Admissions

Norfolk State University
2401 Corprew Ave., Norfolk 23504

Notre Dame Apostolic Catechetical Institute
4407 Sano St., Alexandria 22312

Old Dominion University
5215 Hampton Blvd., Norfolk 23508

Radford University
P.O. Box 5430, Radford 24142

Randolph-Macon College
200 Henry St., Ashland 23005
John Conkright, Dean of Admissions

Roanoke College
221 College Ln., Salem 24153

St. Paul's College
406 Windsor Ave., Lawrenceville 23868

SHENANDOAH UNIVERSITY
1460 University Dr., Winchester 22601
Dr. James Davis, President
Dr. James Kriewald, VP Enrollment Management
Patricia A. Coyle, Director of Admissions
703-665-4581 or 800-432-2266
    Established 1875. Methodist. Coed. Accreditation: SACS. Tuition: $10,700. Room and board: $4,500. Fees: All fees incorporated into tuition except: Nursing clinical, student teaching, private instructions, and private lesson fees. Enrollment: 1,037 full-time, 558 part-time. Faculty: 212. Student-faculty ratio: 9:1. Degrees: AS, BS, BA, BBA, BFA, BM, BMT, MBA, MM, MS, MME, MSOT, MPT, MSE. Library: 135,000 volumes. 15 buildings on 67 acres. Gym. Located in northern section of beautiful Shenandoah Valley, 75 miles west of Washington, DC. A major Conservatory with music theater, music therapy, dance, pedagogy, performance, and other programs, and Arts and Sciences (including communications), Business, and Health Professions (including nursing, physical and occupational therapy, and respiratory care).

Strayer College
7000 Infantry Ridge Rd. #202, Manassas 22110

University of Richmond, Richmond 23173

University of Virginia
P.O. Box 9017, Charlottesville 22906

Virginia Commonwealth University
910 W. Franklin St., Richmond 23284

Virginia Intermont College
1013 Moore St., Bristol 24201
Lawton Blandford, Dir. of Admis.

Virginia Polytechnic Institute & State University
Blacksburg 24061
David Bousquet, Dir. of Undergraduate Admis.

Virginia State University, Petersburg 23803
Mable C. Mountcastle, Dir. of Recording

Virginia Union University
1500 N. Lombardy St., Richmond 23220
804-257-5856

Virginia Wesleyan College
1584 Wesleyan Dr., Norfolk 23502
W. Steve Stocks, V.P. for Admis.

Washington and Lee University
Lexington 24450
William M. Hartog, Dir. of Admis.

WASHINGTON

Antioch University
2607 2nd Ave., Seattle 98121

Central Washington University, Ellensburg 98926
William Swain, Director of Admissions
509-963-1211

City University
16661 Northup Way, Bellevue 98008
800-422-4898

Cogswell Polytechnical College-North Campus
10626 N.E. 37th Circle, Kirkland 98033

Cornish College of the Arts
710 E. Roy St., Seattle 98102
Jane Buckman, Admissions
800-726-ARTS

EASTERN WASHINGTON UNIVERSITY
Cheney 99004
Roger L. Pugh, Asst. Vice Provost, Enrollment Mgmt.
    Established 1882. Public. Coed. Accreditation: NASC. Tuition: $1,806 resident, $6,375 undergraduate non-resident. Room and board: $3,618. Enrollment: 7,217 full-time, 1,146 part-time. Faculty: 561. Student-faculty ratio: 16:1. Degrees: BA, BAE, BFA, BAB, BS, BDH, BMU, BSN, MA, MS, MBA, MEd, MFA, MN, MURP, MPA, MSW. Library: 1,140,408 volumes. 53 buildings on a 350 acre campus. Broad selection of liberal arts offerings, with specialized programs such as business administration, computer science, physical therapy, dental hygiene, nursing, social work, biotechnology, recreation, criminal jus-

tice, health services administration, radio/TV, and others. NCAA Div. I athletics. Greek system. Programs for minorities, adults, single parents, etc.

Evergreen State College
2700 Evergreen Pky. N.W., Olympia 98505

Gonzaga University
502 E. Boone Ave., Spokane 99258
Philip Ballinger, Dean of Admissions

Lutheran Bible Institute of Seattle
4221 228th Ave., S.E., Issaquah 98027
Dorothy Baumgartner, Director of Admissions
800-843-5659

NORTHWEST BAPTIST SEMINARY
4301 N. Stevens St., Tacoma 98407
206-759-6104

Northwest College of Art
16464 State Highway 305 N.E.
Poulsbo 98370
See listing under "Art"

Pacific Lutheran University
12180 Park Ave. S., Tacoma 98447
Dr. Loren J. Anderson, President

St. Martin's College
700 College St. N.E., Lacey 98516

Seattle Pacific University
3307 3rd Ave., W., Seattle 98119

Seattle University
Broadway Ave. & Madison, Seattle 98122
206-296-6000

University of Puget Sound
1500 N. Warner St., Tacoma 98416

University of Washington, Seattle 98195

Walla Walla College
204 S. College Ave., College Place 99324

Washington State University, Pullman 99164
Stan Berry, Dir. of Admis.

Western Washington University
516 High St., Bellingham 98225
Karen G. Copetas, Dir. of Admis.

Whitman College
345 Boyer Ave., Walla Walla 99362

Whitworth College
300 W. Hawthorne Rd., Spokane 99251
Kenneth P. Moyer, Dir. of Admis.
800-533-4668

WEST VIRGINIA

Alderson-Broaddus College
Philippi 26416
Craig W. Gould, Director of Admissions
304-457-1700

Bethany College, Bethany 26031
John Giesman, Registrar

Bluefield State College
219 Rock St., Bluefield 24701

Concord College, Athens 24712

Davis & Elkins College
100 Campus Dr., Elkins 26241
Kevin D. Chenoweth, Dir. of Admis.

Fairmont State College
1201 Locust Ave., Fairmont 26554
John Conaway, Dir. of Admis.

GLENVILLE STATE COLLEGE
200 High St., Glenville 26351
Mack Samples, Dean of Admissions
See listing under "Liberal Arts"

MARSHALL UNIVERSITY
400 Hal Greer Blvd.
Huntington 25755 (Pop. 55,000)
304-696-3160 or 800-642-3463
J. Wade Gilley, President
Alan B. Gould, Vice President for Academic Affairs
Warren G. Lutz, Dean of Enrollment Management
James W. Harless, Director of Admissions
Robert Eddins, Registrar
    Established 1837; Public; Accredited by North Central Association of Colleges and Schools; Coed; Total enrollment 12,717; Tuition and fees $941/semester WV residents; $2,573/semester non-residents. Room and board $1,900/semester. Six residence halls on campus, 8 fraternities, 5 sororities. Federal and institutional financial aid available. Scholarship applications due February 1.
    Colleges of Liberal Arts, Science, Business, Fine Arts and Education; schools of Nursing and Medicine; Community and Technical College; Graduate School. Preprofessional courses in medicine, dentistry, veterinary medicine, physical therapy, pharmacy. Fall and spring semesters; two optional 5-week summer sessions.
    Admission: high school graduation; GPA 2.00 or ACT 17; transfer students accepted any term; open admission to Community and Technical College.
    Student-teacher ratio 18:1; 70% of faculty have doctoral degrees; 55-acre campus adjacent to downtown; Library holds 410,000 bound volumes, 181,000 titles on microform, 2,746 periodicals plus 15,889 records/tapes/CDs; Athletic facilities include tennis and racquetball courts, nautilus/weight rooms, human performance laboratory, Olympic size swimming pool; Computer laboratories available to students.
    Location is 140 miles from Columbus, OH; 126 miles east of Lexington, KY; served by USAir, Amtrak and Greyhound; moderate climate; good employment op-

portunities for students; within 2 hours of ski resorts; numerous cultural events including chamber orchestra, civic center events, professional hockey, minor league baseball. Student life includes many social, service and professional clubs and organizations; choral and instrumental ensembles; theatre productions; guest lectures.

Admission: Applicants must submit application, high school transcript, ACT or SAT scores. Transfer students must submit official transcripts of all previous college work. Students wishing to be considered for scholarships must be admitted by February 1.

OHIO VALLEY COLLEGE
College Pky., Parkersburg 26101
E. Keith Stotts, President
Robert W. Stephens, Jr. Executive VP
Dennis W. Cox, VP for Student Services
Daniel C. Doak, Vice President for Instruction
Dora W. Hammett, VP for Finance
Robert Crum, Director of Admissions
800-678-6780

Established 1960. Church of Christ. Coed. Total Enrollment 282. Total annual charge for boarding students $8,990, day students $6,040. State, Federal, and institutional financial aid available based on completed Financial Aid Form (FAF).

Liberal arts, offering associate degrees in selected areas with upper level offerings in business, psychology, liberal studies, elementary education (subject to final NCA action in summer 1994) and baccalaureate degrees in Bible.

All courses taught by qualified faculty - no graduate students or teaching assistants. Average class size is 15 and faculty to student ratio is 1:15. Semester system with a two-week Maymester. 125 acre campus with eight buildings. Library holdings include 25,000 volumes and 200 current periodicals. Developmental courses provided for students with academic deficiencies. Peer tutoring program, career guidance, and student computer center.

Men participate in basketball and baseball and women participate in basketball and volleyball on the intercollegiate level. Member of National Small College Athletic Association and the NAIA. Extensive intramural program involving eight intramural clubs.

Student life opportunities abound including participation in vocal and instrumental ensembles, children's theatre, theatrical productions, newspaper, yearbook, clubs, student government, special interest groups, guest lecturers and concerts.

Admission: Students may apply for entrance into any term. Students applying for freshman admission should submit application, $20 application fee, high school transcripts, personal references, and result of ACT or SAT. Transfer students should submit application, official transcripts from all colleges previously attended, personal references and SAT or ACT. Rolling Admissions. Students who apply their junior year of high school are eligible for a five percent tuition reduction their freshman year.

Salem-Teikyo University, Salem 26426
Frank Potter, Dir. of Admis.

Shepherd College, Shepherdstown 25443

The University of Charleston
2300 MacCorkle Ave., S.E., Charleston 25304
800-995-GO UC

West Liberty State College, West Liberty 26074

West Virginia Institute of Technology
405 Fayette Pike, Montgomery 25136

West Virginia State College
P.O. Box 1000, Institute 25112

West Virginia University
P.O. Box 6001, Morgantown 26506

WEST VIRGINIA WESLEYAN COLLEGE
59 College Ave., Buckhannon 26201
Robert Skinner, Director of Admissions
800-722-9933

Established 1890. Private. United Methodist related college. Coed. Accreditation: NCACS. Tuition, room and board: $16,900. Enrollment: 1,600 students from 37 states and 25 countries. Student-faculty ratio: 15:1. Degrees offered: BA, BS, BSN, BMus Ed, MBA. Library: 148,000 volumes. 23 buildings on 100 acres. 4-1-4 academic calender. 50 majors. Scenic location. Comprehensive financial aid, merit and need-based. 17 NCAA Div. II sports. Residential campus. 70 campus organizations.

Wheeling Jesuit College
316 Washington Ave., Wheeling 26003
Fr. Thomas Acker, SJ, President

WISCONSIN

Beloit College
700 College St., Beloit 53511
Alan G. McIvor, VP Enrollment Services
608-363-2380

Cardinal Stritch College
6801 N. Yates Rd., Milwaukee 53217
David Wegener, Dir. of Admis.

Carroll College
100 N. East Ave., Waukesha 53186
Ken Moyer, Dir. of Admis.

Carthage College
2001 Alford Dr., Kenosha 53140
Brenda A. Porter, VP Enrollment

Concordia University
12800 N. Lake Shore Dr., Mequon 53097
414-243-5700

Edgewood College
855 Woodrow St., Madison 53711
Robert Blust, Dir. of Admis.

Lakeland College
P.O. Box 359, Sheboygan 53082

Lawrence University
P.O. Box 599, Appleton 54912
Steven Syverson, Dean of Admissions

Maranatha Baptist Bible College
P.O. Box 438, Watertown 53094

Marian College of Fond du Lac
45 S. National Ave., Fond du Lac 54935
Carol Reichenberger, Dean of Admissions

Marquette University
1217 W. Wisconsin Ave., Milwaukee 53233
Raymond A. Brown, Dean of Admissions

Milwaukee School of Engineering
1025 N. Broadway, Milwaukee 53202
Owen Smith, Dean of Admission
800-332-6763 or 414-277-7200 in metro Milwaukee

Mt. Senario College
1500 W. College Ave., Ladysmith 54848
Dewey Floberg, Dean of Admissions

Northland College
1411 Ellis Ave., Ashland 54806
Jim Miller, Dean of Admissions

Ripon College, P.O. Box 248, Ripon 54971
James Reilly, Dean of Admis.

ST. NORBERT COLLEGE
100 Grant St., De Pere 54115
Craig S. Wesley, Dean of Admission
Established 1898. Private. Coed. Accreditation: NCACS. Tuition: $12,150. Room and board: $4,585. Fees: $75. Enrollment: 1,964 full-time, 95 part-time. Faculty: 151. Student-faculty ratio: 15:1. Degrees: BA, BMusic, BS, BBA. Library: 147,793 volumes. 27 buildings on 40 acres.

Silver Lake College
2406 S. Alverno Road, Manitowoc 54220
Sandra Schwartz, Dir. of Admis.

University of Wisconsin, Eau Claire
Eau Claire 54701

University of Wisconsin, Green Bay
2420 Nicolet Dr., Green Bay 54311
David Outcalt, Chancellor
Myron Van de Ven, Dir. of Admis.

University of Wisconsin, La Crosse
115 Main Hall, La Crosse 54601
608-785-8067

University of Wisconsin, Madison
500 Lincoln Dr., Madison 53706

University of Wisconsin
P.O. Box 413, Milwaukee 53201
V. M. Allison, Registrar

University of Wisconsin, Oshkosh
800 Algoma Blvd., Oshkosh 54901-8602
August Helgerson, Dir. of Admis.

University of Wisconsin
P.O. Box 2000, Kenosha 53141
414-553-2211

University of Wisconsin
1 University Plaza, Platteville 53818
Richard Schumacher, Dean of Admissions

University of Wisconsin, River Falls
River Falls 54022
Alan Tuchtenhagen, Dir. of Admis.

University of Wisconsin, Stevens Point 54481
Dr. John A. Larsen, Dir. of Admis.

University of Wisconsin
200 BroadWay St. S., Menomonie 54751
Robert B. Swanson, Chancellor

University of Wisconsin, Superior 54880
Richard E. Morrison, Dir. Univ. Relations

University of Wisconsin
800 W. Main St., Whitewater 53190

UNIVERSITY OF WISCONSIN CENTER, BARABOO/SAUK CO.
1006 Connie Rd., Baraboo 53913
Aural Umhoefer, Dean
Office of Student Services, 608-356-8724

Viterbo College
815 9th St., S., La Crosse 54601
Roland W. Nelson, Dir. of Admis.

WYOMING

University of Wyoming
P.O. Box 3434, Laramie 82071
Richard Davis, Dir. of Admis.

GUAM

University of Guam
UOG Station, Mangilao 96923
Kathleen Owings, Dir. of Admis.

PUERTO RICO

American University of Puerto Rico
P.O. Box 2037, Bayamon 00960

Bayamon Central University
P.O. Box 1725, Bayamon 00960-1725
Christine Hernandez, Dir. of Admis.
809-786-3030

Caribbean University
P.O. Box 493, Bayamon 00960

Catholic Univeristy of Puerto Rico, Mayaguez Center
P.O. Box 1326, Mayaguez 00681

Catholic University of Puerto Rico
Las Americas Ave., Ponce 00732
Carilin Frau, Dir. of Admis.

Catholic University of Puerto Rico, Arecibo Campus
P.O. Box 495, Arecibo 00613

Catholic University of Puerto Rico, Guayama Campus
P.O. Box 809, Guayama 00785

Escuela De Artes Plasticas
Apartado 4184, San Juan 00905

Inter American University
Call Box 2000, Aguadilla 00603
Juan Colon, Director

Inter American University
Mercedita Station, Ponce 00715
Kenneth Kalantar, Director

Inter American University of Puerto Rico
Call Box UI, Arecibo 00612
Olga Suarez, Director

Inter American University of Puerto Rico
Bayamon Campus
RD 174 Minillas Industrial Park, Bayamon 00959

Inter American University of Puerto Rico
Metropolitan Campus
P.O. Box 1293, San Juan 00902

Inter American University of Puerto Rico
P.O. Box 517 Barranquitas 00794
Jesusa A. De Rubero, Director

Inter American University of Puerto Rico
P.O. Box 1029, Fajardo 00738
Jose Martinez, Director

Inter American University of Puerto Rico
P.O. Box 1293, San Juan 00902

Inter American University of Puerto Rico
San German Campus
Harris Dr. Call Box 5100, San German 00683

Polytechnic University of Puerto Rico
P.O. Box 2017, Hato Rey 00902
Teresa Cardona, Dir. of Admis.

Universidad Adventista de las Antillas
P.O. Box 118, Mayaguez 00681
Wilma Gonzalez, Dir. of Admis.

Universidad Del Turabo
P.O. Box 3030, Gurabo 00778

Universidad Metropolitana
P.O. Box 21150, San Juan 00928

University of Puerto Rico
Arecibo Technical University College
P.O. Box A-1806, Arecibo 00613

University of Puerto Rico
Bayamon Technical University College
Bayamon 00959

University of Puerto Rico
Antonio Barcelo Ave., Cayey 00736
Antonio Rosario, Dir. of Admis.

University of Puerto Rico
CUH Station Rd. 908 Bo Tejas, Humacao 00791

UNIVERSITY OF PUERTO RICO, MAYAGUEZ CAMPUS
P.O. Box 5000, Mayaguez 00681
Neysa Lopez, Dir. of Admis.

University of Puerto Rico, Medical Sciences Campus
P.O. Box 5067, San Juan 00906

University of Puerto Rico
Ponce Technological University College
P.O. Box 7186, Ponce 00732

University of Puerto Rico, Rio Piedras Campus
P.O. Box 23300, San Juan 00931
Victor Lopez, Dir. of Admis.

University of the Sacred Heart
P.O. Box 12383, San Juan 00914

VIRGIN ISLANDS

University of the Virgin Islands
Charlotte Amalie, St. Thomas 00802
Judith Edwin, Dir. of Admis.

University of the Virgin Islands
Kingshill, St. Croix 00802

VETERINARY MEDICINE

This classification contains schools offering a degree accredited by the American Veterinary Medical Association (†) and a selection of programs from institutionally accredited schools. Colleges and Universities (no dot code) generally offer four-year programs in veterinary, pre-veterinary or animal sciences; Community and Junior Colleges (·) generally offer programs for veterinary assistant and animal technology; Career Schools (:) generally offer a diploma as a veterinary assistant.

ALABAMA

† Auburn University, Auburn 36849

† Tuskegee University
Tuskegee Institute 36088

CALIFORNIA

· Los Angeles Pierce College
6201 Winnetka Ave., Woodland Hills 91371
See listing under "Community and Junior Colleges"

† University of California, Davis
376 Mrak Hall, Davis 95616

COLORADO

· BEL-REA INSTITUTE OF ANIMAL TECHNOLOGY
1681 S. Dayton, Denver 80231
303-751-8700 or 800-950-8001
See listing under "Career Schools"

† Colorado State University
102 Administration Building, Fort Collins 80523
Mary Ontireros, Dir. of Admissions

CONNECTICUT

QUINNIPIAC COLLEGE
275 Mount Carmel Ave., Hamden 06518
See listing under "Universities"

FLORIDA

† University of Florida
226 Tigert Hall, Gainesville 32611

GEORGIA

Georgia College
231 W. Hancock St., Milledgeville 31061
912-453-5004

† University of Georgia, Athens 30602
Dr. David P. Anderson, Dean

ILLINOIS

North Park College & Theological Seminary
3225 W. Foster, Chicago 60625
312-509-2330

† University of Illinois
506 S. Wright St., Urbana 61801

INDIANA

† Purdue University
Schleman Hall, West Lafayette 47907

IOWA

† Iowa State University, Ames 50011
Karsten Smedal, Dir. of Admis.

· Waldorf College
106 S. 6th St., Forest City 50436
Steve Lovik, Dir. of Admis.
800-292-1903

KANSAS

† Kansas State University
Anderson Hall 110, Manhattan 66506
Ellsworth M. Gerritz, Admis. & Records

KENTUCKY

Kentucky Wesleyan College
Pre-Veterinary Medicine program
3000 Frederica St., Owensboro 42301

Morehead State University, Morehead 40351
Charles Myers, Director of Admissions
606-783-2000

Spalding University
851 S. 4th St., Louisville 40203
Dorothy G. Allen, Dir. of Admis.

LOUISIANA

† Louisiana State University and A & M College
Baton Rouge 70803

MASSACHUSETTS

Mt. Ida College
777 Dedham St., Newton Center 02159
Jim Mulligan, Dean of Admis.

† Tufts University, Medical School
136 Harrison Ave., Boston 02111

Worcester Polytechnic Institute
100 Institute Rd., Worcester 01609
Kay R. Dietrich, Director of Admissions
508-831-5286

MICHIGAN

† Michigan State University, East Lansing 48824
P. M. Lowrie, Asst. to the Dean

MINNESOTA

† University of Minnesota, Twin Cities
Minneapolis 55455

MISSISSIPPI

† Mississippi State University
P.O. Box J, Mississippi State University 39762

MISSOURI

Culver-Stockton College, Canton 63435
Betty Smith, Dean of Admissions
800-537-1883

· Jefferson College
1000 Viking Dr., Hillsboro 63050
Pete Ross, Dir. of Admis.

† University of Missouri, Columbia
228 Jesse Hall, Columbia 65211

MONTANA

Rocky Mountain College
1511 Poly Dr., Billings 59102
David Heringer, Dir. of Admis.
See listing under "Universities"

NEW YORK

Canisius College
2001 Main St., Buffalo 14208
Penelope Lips, Dir. of Admis.
800-843-1517

† Cornell University
410 Thurston Ave., Ithaca 14853

Medaille College
18 Agassiz Cir., Buffalo 14214
Jacqueline Smukeer, Dir. of Admis.

Mercy College
555 Broadway, Dobbs Ferry 10522
James Nesbitt, Dean of Admissions

Roberts Wesleyan College
2301 Westside Dr., Rochester 14624
Linda Kurtz, Dir. of Admis.
See listing under "Universities"

· SUNY College of Technology
34 Cornell Dr., Canton 13617
Thomas R. Fletcher, Director of Admissions
800-388-7123

NORTH CAROLINA

Gardner-Webb University
General Delivery, Boiling Springs 28017
Ray M. Hardee, Dean of Admissions
800-253-6472

† North Carolina State University
P.O. Box 7001, Raleigh 27695
George Dixon, Dir. of Admis.

OHIO

· Columbus State Community College
550 E. Spring St., Columbus 43215
Mary Jo Deerwester, Dir. of Admis.

† Ohio State University
190 N. Oval Mall, Columbus 43210

Wilmington College
P.O. Box 1185, Wilmington 45177
Rhonda Inderhees, Dir. of Admis.

OKLAHOMA

Oklahoma City University
2501 N. Blackwelder Ave., Oklahoma City 73106
Keith Hackett, Dean of Admissions
See listing under "Universities"

† Oklahoma State University, Stillwater 74078
Joseph Alexander, Dean

OREGON

† Oregon State University, Corvallis 97333
Wallace Gibbs, Dir. of Admis.

PENNSYLVANIA

Delaware Valley College of Science & Agriculture
Doylestown 18901
Stephen Zenko, Dir. of Admis.

· Harcum Junior College, Bryn Mawr 19010
Mary Pontius, Dean of Admissions

† University of Pennsylvania
0 Levy Park, Philadelphia 19104

WESTMINSTER COLLEGE
New Wilmington 16172
Richard Dana Paul, Dir. of Admis.
412-946-7100

Wilson College
1015 Philadelphia, Chambersburg 17201

SOUTH DAKOTA

National College
321 Kansas City St., Rapid City 57701
Keith T. Carlyle, Dir. of Admis.

TENNESSEE

University of Tennessee at Martin
Martin 38238
Paul Kelley, Director of Admissions
See listing under "Universities"

† University of Tennessee, Knoxville
527 Andy Holt Tower, Knoxville 37996
Dr. Gordon Stanley, Dir. of Admis.

TEXAS

† Texas A & M University
College Station 77843

UTAH

Utah State University, Logan 84322-1600
Rod Clark, Director of Admissions
801-750-1107

VIRGINIA

Ferrum College, Ferrum 24088
Bob Bailey, Dir. of Admis.

† Virginia Polytechnic Institute & State University
Blacksburg 24061
David Bousquet, Dir. of Undergraduate Admis.

WASHINGTON

† Washington State University, Pullman 99164
Stan Berry, Dir. of Admis.

WEST VIRGINIA

WEST VIRGINIA WESLEYAN COLLEGE
59 College Ave., Buckhannon 26201
Robert Skinner, Director of Admission
See listing under "Universities"

WISCONSIN

St. Norbert College
100 Grant St., De Pere 54115
Craig S. Wesley, Dean of Admission
See listing under "Universities"

† University of Wisconsin, Madison
500 Lincoln Dr., Madison 53706

University of Wisconsin, River Falls
River Falls 54022
Alan Tuchtenhagen, Dir. of Admis.

Viterbo College
815 9th St., S., La Crosse 54601
Roland W. Nelson, Dir. of Admis.

WOMEN'S COLLEGES

ALABAMA

Judson College
P O Box 120, Marion 36756

CALIFORNIA

Mills College
5000 MacArthur Blvd., Oakland 94613
Genevieve Ann Flaherty, Dean of Admissions
800-87-MILLS

Mt. St. Mary's College
12001 Chalon Rd., Los Angeles 90049

Scripps College
1030 Columbia Ave., Claremont 91711
Leslie Miles, Dean of Admissions

CONNECTICUT

Hartford College for Women
1265 Asylum Ave., Hartford 06105

St. Joseph College
1678 Asylum Ave., West Hartford 06117
Mary C. Demo, Dir. of Admis.

DISTRICT OF COLUMBIA

Mt. Vernon College
2100 Foxhall Rd., N.W., Washington 20007
202-625-4682 or 800-682-4636, FAX: 202-338-1089

Trinity College
125 Michigan Ave., N.E., Washington 20017
Donna Quinn, Dir. of Admis.

GEORGIA

Agnes Scott College
201 E. College Ave., Decatur 30030
Teresa Lahti, Dir. of Admis.

Brenau College
204 Boulevard, Gainesville 30501

Spelman College
350 Spelman Ln., S.W., Atlanta 30314
Aline Rivers, Dir. of Admis.

Wesleyan College
4760 Forsyth Rd., Macon 31297

ILLINOIS

Loyola University - Mundelein College
6363 N. Sheridan Rd., Chicago 60660
Judith Bobber, Dir. of Admis.

INDIANA

St. Mary-of-the-Woods College
Saint Mary-of-the-Woods 47876
Lynn M. Rubick, Director of Admissions
800-926-SMWC

St. Mary's College
46 Madeliva, Notre Dame 46556
Mary Ann Rowan, Dir. of Admissions

KENTUCKY

Midway College
512 E. Stephens St., Midway 40347
Carl P. Rollins II, Dir. of Admis.

LOUISIANA

Newcomb College of Tulane University
1229 Broadway St., New Orleans 70118

MARYLAND

College of Notre Dame of Maryland
4701 N. Charles St., Baltimore 21210

Hood College
400 Rosemont Ave., Frederick 21701

MASSACHUSETTS

Aquinas College
15 Walnut Park, Newton 02158
Ellen Ronayne, Dir. of Admis.

Aquinas College at Milton
303 Adams St., Milton 02186
617-696-3100

BAY PATH COLLEGE

588 Longmeadow St., Longmeadow 01106
Paula DesRoberts, Dean of Admis.
413-567-0621 or 800-782-PATH
Established: 1897. Private. Women. Accreditation: NEASC, Legal programs ABA approved. Tuition: $10,200. Room and board: $6,225. Enrollment: 600. Faculty: 42. Student-faculty ratio: 14:1. Degrees: AA, AS, BA, BS. Library: 38,000 volumes. 27 buildings on 30 acres. Secure, suburban campus near Springfield and Hartford. 15 Associate degree programs in business, education, fashion/design, criminal justice, paralegalism, hospitality/tourism, health, human services, occupational therapy, psychology, liberal arts. Baccalaureates in business, business/accounting, legal studies, psychology, psychology/criminal justice, psychology/early childhood education. Extensive career services. 95-98% of students obtain jobs after graduation. Transfer welcome.

ELMS COLLEGE

291 Springfield St., Chicopee 01013
800-255-ELMS

Emmanuel College
400 The Fenway, Boston 02115
Margaret Bonilla, Dir. of Admis.

Endicott College
376 Hale St., Beverly 01915
Elizabeth Macomber, Dir. of Admis.

Fisher College
118 Beacon St., Boston 02116
Sandra Robbins, Dir. of Admis.

Lasell College
1844 Commonwealth Ave., Newton 02166

Lesley College
29 Everett St., Cambridge 02138-2790
Jane Raley, Dir. of Admissions

Mt. Holyoke College
College St., South Hadley 01075
Anita Smith, Director of Admissions
413-538-2023

Pine Manor College
400 Heath St., Chestnut Hill 02167
Gillian Lloyd, Dir. of Admis.

REGIS COLLEGE

235 Wellesley St., Weston 02193
Valerie L. Brown, Director of Admission
800-456-1820

Simmons College
300 The Fenway, Boston 02115

Smith College
Northampton 01063

Wellesley College, Wellesley 02181
Janet A. Lavin, Dir. of Admis.

MINNESOTA

College of Saint Benedict
37 S. College Ave., St. Joseph 56374

College of St. Catherine
2004 Randolph Ave., St. Paul 55105

MISSISSIPPI

Blue Mountain College
P.O. Box 338, Blue Mountain 38610

Mississippi University for Women
P.O. Box W-1602, Columbus 39701
Teresa Thompson, Exec. Dir. of Enrollment

Mississippi University for Women-Tupelo
655 Eason Blvd., Tupelo 38801

MISSOURI

Cottey College
1000 W. Austin St., Nevada 64772
Wendy Beckemeyer, Dir. of Admis.

Stephens College, Columbia 65215
Patsy Sampson, President

William Woods College
200 W. 12th St., Fulton 65251
Dr. Jahnae Barnett, VP of Admis.

NEBRASKA

College of Saint Mary
1901 S. 72nd St., Omaha 68124
Sheila Haggas, Dir. of Admis.

NEW HAMPSHIRE

Colby-Sawyer College
100 Main St., New London 03257

NEW JERSEY

Centenary College
400 Jefferson St., Hackettstown 07840
Barbara Edler, Dir. of Admissions

College of Saint Elizabeth
Convent Station 07961
Sr. Jacqueline Burns, President

Georgian Court College
900 Lakewood Ave., Lakewood 08701
Sr. Barbara Williams, President
Sr. Cecelia Fox, Registrar
908-364-2200

Rutgers-The State University of NJ
Douglass College
New Brunswick 08903

NEW YORK

Barnard College
3009 Broadway, New York 10027

Hobart & William Smith College
Pulteney St., Geneva 14456

Marymount College
100 Marymount Ave., Tarrytown 10591
Gina R. Campbell, Dir. of Admis.
800-724-4312

Russell Sage College
51 1st St., Troy 12180

Wells College, Aurora 13026
Susan Raith, Director of Admissions
315-364-3264

Wood School
8 E. 40th St., New York 10016
Rosemary Duggan, President

NORTH CAROLINA

Bennett College
900 E. Washington St., Greensboro 27401

Meredith College
3800 Hillsborough St., Raleigh 27607

Peace College
15 E. Peace St., Raleigh 27604
Dr. Garrett Briggs, President
919-832-2881, Fax: 919-834-6755

Saint Mary's College
900 Hillsborough St., Raleigh 27603
Dr. Clauston Jenkins, President

SALEM COLLEGE

P.O. Box 10548, Winston-Salem 27108
Katherine Knapp, Director of Admissions
Established 1772. Moravian. Enrollment: 750. Comprehensive fee for boarding students: $16,775, day students: $10,425. Four year, liberal arts, residential college for women conferring Bachelor of Arts, Bachelor of Science and Bachelor of Music degrees with majors in American studies, art, arts management, biology, business administration, chemistry, communication, economics, English, foreign language management, French, German, history, interior design, international relations, mathematics, medical technology, music, philosophy, psychology, religion, sociology, and Spanish. Teacher certification is offered in early childhood, intermediate, secondary, learning disabilities, and emotionally handicapped.
Admissions: College recognizes that variations in school curricula, methods of teaching, and aptitudes of students make it difficult for any one pattern of entrance standards to be required. It is recommended that candidates present 16 academic units which include 4 in English, 2 in a foreign language, 2 in history, 3 in math, and 3 in science. SAT and/or ACT are required. Transfer students must have a 2.0 GPA. Committee on Admissions considers each application individually and bases its decision on the general excellence of the candidate's school record, test scores, extracurricular activities, and personal qualifications of the applicants. The College welcomes students of different racial, ethnic, religious, and geographic backgrounds.
Financial Aid: Salem offers both need-based financial assistance and competitive, no-need scholarships. Every effort is made to assist as many students as funds will permit. Approximately 65% receive financial aid, which consists of a combination of grant, loan and/or work. The competitive scholarships range from $2,500-$10,000 per year.
Accreditation: Southern Association of Colleges and Secondary Schools, National Association of Schools of Music, National Council for the Accreditation of Teacher Education; course in medical technology recognized by the American Medical Association and the American Society of Clinical Pathologists.

OHIO

Notre Dame College
4545 College Rd., Cleveland 44121
Sr. Mary Luke, S.N.D., President

Ursuline College
2550 Lander Rd., Cleveland 44124

PENNSYLVANIA

Bryn Mawr College
101 N. Merion Ave., Bryn Mawr 19010
Elizabeth Vermey, Dir. of Admis.

Carlow College
3333 5th Ave., Pittsburgh 15213

Cedar Crest College
100 College Dr., Allentown 18104-6196
Cynthia Phillips, Dir. of Admissions

CHATHAM COLLEGE

Woodland Rd., Pittsburgh 15232
412-365-1290 or 800-837-1290
Suellen Ofe, Dean of Admis./Financial Aid
Established 1869. Private. Women's college. Accreditation: MSACS. Tuition: $11,840. Room and board: $5,030. Fees: $150. Enrollment: 472 full-time, 158 part-time. Faculty: 65. Student-faculty ratio: 9:1. Degrees: BA, BS, MPT, MOT, MLA, MEd. Library: 126,779 volumes. 27 buildings on 32 acres. Cross registration with 9 other Pittsburgh area colleges. Junior term abroad, self-designed majors, internships, independent study, Center for Student Development, Senior Tutorial.

Chestnut Hill College
9601 Germantown Ave.
Philadelphia 19118-2695
Margaret A. Birtwistle, Dir. of Admis.

Harcum Junior College, Bryn Mawr 19010
Mary Pontius, Dean of Admissions

Immaculata College
Immaculata 19345
James P. Sullivan, Dir. of Admis.

Marywood College
2300 Adams Ave., Scranton 18509

Moore College of Art and Design
1920 Race St., Philadelphia 19103
Claire E. Gallicano, Dir. of Admis.

ROSEMONT COLLEGE
1400 Montgomery Ave., Rosemont 19010
John Enyart, Dean of Enrollment Mgmt.
215-525-6420
Established 1921. Private. Women's college. Accreditation: MSACS. Tuition: $10,700. Room and board: $5,700. Fees: $300. Enrollment: 600 full-time, 150 part-time. Faculty: 48 full-time. Student-faculty ratio: 12:1. Degrees: BA, BS, BFA, MA. Library: 150,000 volumes. 15 buildings on 56 acres. Rosemont College offers double majors, individualized majors, or interdisciplinary majors. Cross registration with area colleges. Study abroad. Joint admissions program with Hahnemann Medical School. Early child, Elementary, Secondary and Special Education offered.

Seton Hill College, Greensburg 15601
Peter Egan, Dir. of Admis.
800-826-6234 or 412-838-4255

Wilson College
1015 Philadelphia, Chambersburg 17201

SOUTH CAROLINA

Columbia College
1301 Columbia College Dr., Columbia 29203

Converse College
580 E. Main St., Spartanburg 29302
Dr. Martha Rogers, VP Enrollment Management

TEXAS

Texas Women's University
P.O. Box 23925, Denton 76204

VERMONT

Trinity College
208 Colchester Ave., Burlington 05401

VIRGINIA

Hollins College
P.O. Box 9707, Hollins College 24020
800-456-9595

Mary Baldwin College, Staunton 24401
Douglas E. Clark, Exec. Dir. of Enrollment

Randolph-Macon Woman's College
2500 Rivermont Ave., Lynchburg 24503

SOUTHERN VIRGINIA COLLEGE FOR WOMEN
One College Hill Dr., Buena Vista 24416
Mark A. Camper, Assoc. Dir. of Admis.
800-229-8420
Established 1867. Private. Two year Women's College. Accreditation: SACS. Tuition: $10,600. Room and board: $5,000. Fees: $150. Enrollment: 260 full-time, 15 part-time. Faculty: 38. Student-faculty ratio: 8:1. Degrees: AA, AS. Library: 48,000 volumes. 12 buildings on 100 acres. Equine majors with 63 stalls and 80' by 200' indoor riding arena in horsemanship center located on campus. Located in foothills of Blue Ridge Mountains in the Shenandoah Valley. Individual help for students with special needs.

Sweet Briar College, Sweet Briar 24595
Nancy Church, Dir. of Admis.

WISCONSIN

Alverno College
P.O. Box 343922, Milwaukee 53234
Colleen Hayes, Dir. of Admis.

Mt. Mary College
2900 N. Menomonee River Pky.
Milwaukee 53222

WOMEN'S STUDIES

ARIZONA
University of Arizona, Tucson 85721
Loyd Bell, Director of Admissions

CALIFORNIA
California State University, Chico
Chico 95929-0420
Dr. Hassan Sisay, Chrpsn.

Christian Heritage College
2100 Greenfield Dr., El Cajon 92019
Pam Daly, Dir. of Admis.
800-676-2242

Loyola Marymount University
Loyola Blvd. at W. 80th, Los Angeles 90045
M. L'Heureux, Dir. of Admis.

Mills College
5000 MacArthur Blvd., Oakland 94613
Genevieve Ann Flaherty, Dean of Admissions
800-87-MILLS

Pitzer College
1050 N. Mills Ave., Claremont 91711
Katharine Leighton, Dir. of Admis.

Pomona College
333 N. College Way, Claremont 91711
Peter W. Stanley, President

San Francisco State University
1600 Holloway Ave., San Francisco 94132
Corwin Bjonerud, Dir. of Admis.

Scripps College
1030 Columbia Ave., Claremont 91711
Leslie Miles, Dean of Admissions

University of California at Berkeley
Campbell Hall, Berkeley 94720

University of California, Davis
376 Mrak Hall, Davis 95616

University of California-Santa Cruz
Santa Cruz 95064
Joseph Allen, Dir. of Admis.

COLORADO
Colorado College
14 E. Cache La Poudre, Colorado Springs 80903
Terry Swenson, Dir. of Admis.

ILLINOIS
Garrett-Evangelical Theological Seminary
2121 Sheridan Rd., Evanston 60201
Contact Admissions at 800-SEMINARY

Knox College, Galesburg 61401
309-343-0112 or 800-678-KNOX
See listing under "Universities"

LEWIS UNIVERSITY
Rt. 53, Romeoville 60441
Irish O'Reilly, Director of Admissions
See listing under "Universities"

Parkland College
2400 W. Bradley Ave., Champaign 61821-1899
217-351-2208 or 800-346-8089

ROOSEVELT UNIVERSITY
430 S. Michigan Ave., Chicago 60605
William Smyser, Director of Admissions
See listing under "Universities"

Rosary College
7900 W. Division St., River Forest 60305
Hildegarde Schmidt, Dir. of Admis.

Sangamon State University
Shepherd Rd., Springfield 62794-9243
Admissions and Records, 217-786-6626

University of Illinois at Chicago
P.O. Box 4348, Chicago 60680

INDIANA
Ball State University
2000 W. University Ave., Muncie 47306
Ruth Vedvik, Dir. of Admis.

IOWA
Iowa State University, Ames 50011
Karsten Smedal, Dir. of Admis.

University of Iowa, Iowa City 52242

KANSAS
Wichita State University
1845 Fairmount, Wichita 67260
800-362-2594
See listing under "Universities"

LOUISIANA
Tulane University
6823 Saint Charles Ave., New Orleans 70118
Richard Whiteside, Dean of Admission

MAINE
Bowdoin College, Brunswick 04011
William Mason, Dir. of Admis.

University of Southern Maine
96 Falmouth St., Portland 04103
Diana Long, Director

MARYLAND
Goucher College
1021 Dulaney Valley Rd., Baltimore 21204

Towson State University
800 York Rd., Towson 21204
Dr. Hoke Smith, President

MASSACHUSETTS
Hampshire College, Amherst 01002
Audrey Y. Smith, Dir. of Admissions
413-582-5471

Massachusetts Institute of Technology
77 Massachusetts Ave., Cambridge 02139

Mt. Holyoke College
College St., South Hadley 01075
Anita Smith, Director of Admissions
413-538-2023

Simmons College
300 The Fenway, Boston 02115

Suffolk University
8 Ashburton Place, Boston 02108
Barbara K. Ericson, Assoc. Dean Enrollment & Retention
617-573-8460

Wellesley College, Wellesley 02181
Janet A. Lavin, Dir. of Admis.

MICHIGAN
Albion College
611 E. Porter, Albion 49224
800-858-6770

Aquinas College
1607 Robinson Rd., S.E., Grand Rapids 49506
Paula Meehan, Dean of Admissions
800-678-9593

MINNESOTA
Carleton College
One N. College St., Northfield 55057
Paul Thiboutot, Dir. of Admis.

St. Olaf College, Northfield 55057
Mary Cisar, Director
507-646-3231

MISSOURI
Central Missouri State University
Warrensburg 64093
Delores Hudson, Dir. of Admis.

Stephens College, Columbia 65215
Mary Ann Sprinkle, Dir. of Admis.

Washington University
1 Brookings Dr., St. Louis 63130

NEBRASKA
Bellevue College
1000 Galvin Rd. S., Bellevue 68005
Chari Leader, VP of Enrollment

NEW JERSEY
Jersey City State College
2039 Kennedy Blvd., Jersey City 07305
201-200-3234

Princeton University, Princeton 08544

Stockton State College, Pomona 08240
Sal Catalfamo, Dir. of Admis.

NEW YORK
Barnard College
3009 Broadway, New York 10027

Colgate University
13 Oak Dr., Hamilton 13346
Dean of Admissions
315-824-7401

CUNY College of Staten Island
130 Stuyvesant Pl., Staten Island 10301

Fordham University
441 E. Fordham Rd., Bronx 10458
718-817-1000

Friends World Program, Long Island University
Montauk Hwy., Southampton 11968
Carol Gilbert, Dir. of Admis.

Manhattanville College
2900 Purchase St., Purchase 10577

Marymount College
100 Marymount Ave., Tarrytown 10591
Gina R. Campbell, Dir. of Admis.
800-724-4312

Sarah Lawrence College, Bronxville 10708

SUNY at Buffalo
17 Capen Hall
P.O. Box 601660, Buffalo 14260-1660
716-645-6900

SUNY College at Brockport
Brockport 14420

SUNY College at Old Westbury
P.O. Box 210, Old Westbury 11568
Michael Sheehy, Dir. of Admis.

SUNY College at Plattsburgh, Plattsburgh 12901
Eleanor Stoller, Coordinator
518-564-3301

University of Rochester
    500 Joseph C. Wilson Blvd., Rochester 14627
    Director, Susan B. Anthony Center
    See listing under "Universities"

Vassar College
    125 Raymond Ave., Poughkeepsie 12601

NORTH CAROLINA

Salem College
    P.O. Box 10548, Winston-Salem 27108
    Katherine Knapp, Director of Admissions
    800-32-SALEM
    See listing under "Women's College"

OHIO

Antioch University
    795 Livermore St., Yellow Springs 45387

College of Mount St. Joseph
    5701 Delhi Rd., Cincinnati 45233-1672
    See listing under "Universities"

LOURDES COLLEGE
    6832 Convent Blvd., Sylvania 43560
    Mary E. Briggs, Dir. of Admis.
    419-885-5291 or 800-878-3210

Oberlin College
    135 W. Lorain St., Oberlin 44074
    Debra Chermonte, Dir. of Admis.

Ohio Wesleyan University
    61 S. Sandusky St., Delaware 43015
    Donald Bishop, Dean for Enrollment

University of Cincinnati
    2700 Clifton Ave., Cincinnati 45221

OKLAHOMA

University of Tulsa
    600 S. College Ave., Tulsa 74104
    Jane Nicholson, Co-Director

PENNSYLVANIA

Carlow College
    3333 5th Ave., Pittsburgh 15213

Chatham College
    Woodland Rd., Pittsburgh 15232
    Suellen Ofe, Dean of Admis./Financial Aid
    See listing under "Women's College"

Drexel University
    3141 Chestnut St., Philadelphia 19104
    Dean of Enrollment Management

La Salle University
    1900 W. Olney Ave., Philadelphia 19141
    Br. Gerald Fitzgerald, Dir. of Admis.
    See listing under "Universities"

RHODE ISLAND

Rhode Island College
    600 Mt. Pleasant Ave., Providence 02908

TENNESSEE

University of Memphis, Memphis 38152
    Dr. John Eubank, Dean of Admissions

Vanderbilt University
    West End Ave., Nashville 37240

TEXAS

University of Houston-Clear Lake
    2700 Bay Area Blvd., Houston 77058
    Darella Banks, Exec. Dir. Enrollment Services

UTAH

Utah State University, Logan 84322-1600
    Rod Clark, Director of Admissions
    801-750-1107

VERMONT

Burlington College
    95 North Ave., Burlington 05401
    Nancy Wilson, Dir. of Admis.
    See listing under "Liberal Arts"

Goddard College
    P.O. Box G, Plainfield 05667
    Jackson Kytle, President

VIRGINIA

Randolph-Macon College
    200 Henry St., Ashland 23005
    John Conkright, Dean of Admissions

Virginia Polytechnic Institute & State University
    Blacksburg 24061
    David Bousquet, Dir. of Undergraduate Admis.

WASHINGTON

Pacific Lutheran University
    12180 Park Ave. S., Tacoma 98447
    Elizabeth Brusco, Coordinator

WISCONSIN

Beloit College
    700 College St., Beloit 53511
    Nancy A. Krusko, Co-Chairperson
    Cheryl Kader, Co-Chairperson
    608-363-2368 or 608-363-2680

INDEX

Explanation

Schools are listed alphabetically in one of five sections. Each entry has the school name and the state where it is located.

> Universities and Colleges
> Community and Junior Colleges
> Career Schools
> Hospitals
> Preparatory Schools

If there is no three-letter code after the entry you will find the school in the classification explained in the opening paragraph to that index in the state shown. For example Abilene Christian University, TX is found in (**Universities and Colleges-Coeducational**) under Texas.

If the entry is followed by a three-letter classification code the school will be found in the indicated classification in that state. For example Academy of Art College, CA (**ART**) is found in the **ART** classification under California.

(AAT)	Aeronautics, Aviation and Space	(MNC)	Men's Colleges
(AGR)	Agriculture	(MNS)	Mines and Metallurgy
(AHS)	Allied Health Science	(MTH)	Mathematics
(ARC)	Architecture	(MUS)	Music
(ART)	Art	(NRS)	Nursing
(BBL)	Biblical Studies	(OCN)	Oceanography
(BIO)	Biological Science	(OPT)	Optometry
(BKS)	Ethnic Studies	(OST)	Osteopathic Medicine
(BUS)	Business and Management	(PBH)	Public Health
(CPC)	Chiropractic Colleges	(PED)	Physical Education
(DNT)	Dentistry	(PHR)	Pharmacy
(EGN)	Engineering	(PHS)	Physical Science
(EMB)	Funeral Service Education	(PHT)	Photography
(FRS)	Forestry	(POD)	Podiatric Medicine
(FSA)	Fashion Art	(PRB)	Preparatory Schools for Boys
(GRD)	Graduate Schools	(PRG)	Preparatory Schools for Girls
(HME)	Home Economics	(PSY)	Psychology
(HMS)	Home Study and Correspondence	(RAB)	Rabbinical Studies
(HND)	Handicapped, Schools for the	(SCT)	Secretarial Science
(IFS)	Computer and Information Science	(SCW)	Social Science
(INT)	Interior Design	(SPD)	Speech and Drama
(JRN)	Communications	(SSS)	Summer Sessions
(LAS)	Liberal Arts and Sciences	(STA)	Study Abroad
(LAW)	Law	(TED)	Teacher Education
(LBS)	Library Science	(THL)	Theology
(LND)	Landscape Architecture	(VET)	Veterinary Medicine
(MBA)	Master of Business Administration	(WMC)	Women's Colleges
(MED)	Medicine	(WMS)	Women's Studies
(MIL)	Military Science		

UNIVERSITIES AND COLLEGES - INDEX

Schools alphabetized in this section can be found in the **Universities and Colleges - Coeducational** classification unless followed by a three letter code (ART) identifying a different classification. The classifications represented by the three letter codes are shown on the first page of the index.

A

Abilene Christian University, TX
Academy of Art College, CA (ART)
Academy of the New Church College, PA (THL)
Adams State College, CO
Adelphi University, NY
Adler School of Professional Psychology, IL (GRD)
Adrian College, MI
AFS Intercultural Programs, NY (STA)
Agnes Scott College, GA (WMC)
Alabama A & M University, AL
Alabama State University, AL
Alaska Bible College, AK (BBL)
Alaska Pacific University, AK
Albany College of Pharmacy, NY (PHR)
Albany Law School of Union University, NY (LAW)
Albany Medical College, NY (MED)
Albany State College, GA
Albertus Magnus College, CT
Albion College, MI
Albright College, PA
Alcorn State University, MS
Alderson-Broaddus College, WV
Alfred Adler Institute of MN, MN
Alfred University, NY
Alice Lloyd College, KY
Allegheny College, PA
Allentown College of St. Frances de Sale, PA
Allen University, SC
Alma College, MI
Alvernia College, PA
Alverno College, WI (WMC)
Amber University, TX
American Armenian International College, CA
American Baptist College, TN (BBL)
American Baptist Seminary of the West, CA (THL)
American College, PA (GRD)
American College for the Applied Arts, CA; GA
American College in London, GA
American Conservatory of Music, The, IL
American Conservatory Theater, CA (SPD)
American Film Institute Center, CA (PHT)
American Graduate School Intrntnl. Mgmt., AZ (GRD)
American Indian Bible College, AZ (BBL)
American International College, MA
American Technical Institute, TN
American University, The, DC; NY; PR
Amherst College, MA
Anderson College, SC
Anderson University, IN
Andover Newton Theological School, MA (THL)
Andrews University, MI
Angelo State University, TX
Anna Maria College, MA
Antioch New England, NH (GRD)
Antioch University, CA; OH; WA
Appalachian Bible College, WV (BBL)
Appalachian State University, NC
Aquinas College, MI
Aquinas Institute of Theology, MO (THL)
Arizona College of the Bible, AZ
Arizona State University, AZ
Arkansas Baptist College, AR (LAS)
Arkansas College, AR
Arkansas State University, AR
Arkansas Tech University, AR
Arlington Baptist College, TX (BBL)
Armstrong State College, GA
Armstrong University, CA
Art Academy of Cincinnati, OH (ART)
Art Center College of Design, CA (ART)
Arthur D. Little Mgmt. Education Inst., MA (BUS)
Art Institute of Boston, The, MA
Art Institute of Southern California, CA (ART)
Asbury College, KY
Asbury Theological Seminary, KY (THL)
Ashland University, OH
Assemblies of God Theological Seminary, MO (THL)
Associated Mennonite Biblical Seminaries, IN (BBL)
Assumption College, MA
Athenaeum of Ohio, OH (THL)
Athens State College, AL
Atlanta Christian College, GA (BBL)
Atlanta College of Art, GA
Atlantic Union College, MA
Auburn University, AL
Augsburg College, MN
Augusta College, GA
Augustana College, IL; SD
Aurora University, IL
Austin College, TX
Austin Peay State University, TN
Austin Presbyterian Theological Seminary, TX (THL)
Averett College, VA
Avila College, MO
Azusa Pacific University, CA

B

Babson College, MA
Bais Medrash L'Torah Rabbinical College, NY (RAB)
Baker College, MI
Baker University, KS
Baker University School of Nursing, KS (NRS)
Baldwin-Wallace College, OH
Ball State University, IN
Baltimore Hebrew University, MD
Bangor Theological Seminary, ME (THL)
Bank Street College of Education, NY (TED)
Baptist Bible College, MO; PA (BBL)
Baptist Missionary Theological Seminary, TX (THL)
Barat College, IL
Barber-Scotia College, NC (LAS)
Barclay College, KS (BBL)
Bard College, NY
Barnard College, NY (WMC)
Barry University, FL
Bartlesville Wesleyan College, OK (LAS)
Barton College, NC
Bassist College, OR
Bastyr College, WA (GRD)
Bates College, ME
Bayamon Central University, PR
Baylor College of Dentistry, TX (DNT)
Baylor College of Medicine, TX (MED)
Baylor University, TX
Baylor University Medical Center, TX (NRS)
Bay Ridge Christian College, TX (BBL)
Beaver College, PA
Belhaven College, MS
Bellarmine College, KY
Bellevue College, NE
Bellin College of Nursing, WI (NRS)
Belmont Abbey College, NC
Belmont College, TN
Beloit College, WI
Bemidji State University, MN
Benedict College, SC
Benedictine College, KS
Bennett College, NC (WMC)
Bennington College, VT
Bentley College, MA
Berea College, KY
Berkeley Divinity School, CT (THL)
Berklee College of Music, MA (MUS)
Berry College, GA
Bethany Bible College, CA (BBL)
Bethany College, KS; WV
Bethany Theological Seminary, IL (THL)
Beth Benjamin Academy of Connecticut, CT (RAB)
Bethel College, IN; KS; MN
Bethel College, TN (LAS)
Beth-El College of Nursing, CO (NRS)
Bethel Theological Seminary, MN (THL)
Beth HaMedrash Shaarei Yosher, NY (RAB)
Beth HaTalmud Rabbinical College, NY (RAB)
Beth Medrash Emek Halacha Rabbncl. Coll., NY (RAB)
Beth Medrash Govoha, NJ (RAB)
Bethune-Cookman College, FL
Beulah Heights Bible College, GA (BBL)
Bexley Hall School, NY (GRD)
Biblical Christian College, CA (BBL)
Biblical Theological Seminary, PA
Biola University, CA
Birmingham Southern College, AL
Blackburn College, IL (LAS)
Black Hills State University, SD
Blair School of Music of Vanderbilt U., TN (MUS)
Blessing Hospital, IL (NRS)
Bloomfield College, NJ
Bloomsburg University, PA
Bluefield College, VA
Bluefield State College, WV
Blue Mountain College, MS (WMC)
Bluffton College, OH
Bob Jones University, SC
Boise Bible College, ID (BBL)
Boise State University, ID
Boricua College, NY
Boston Architectural Center, MA (ARC)
Boston College, MA
Boston College Law School, MA (LAW)
Boston Conservatory, MA (GRD)
Boston University, MA
Boston Univ. Graduate School of Mgmt., MA (GRD)
Boston University Medical Center, MA (MED)
Bowdoin College, ME
Bowie State University, MD
Bowling Green State University, OH
Bradford College, MA (LAS)
Bradley University, IL
Brandeis University, MA
Brenau College, GA (WMC)
Brescia College, KY
Brewton-Parker College, GA
Bridgeport Engineering Institute, CT
Bridgewater College, VA
Bridgewater State College, MA
Brigham Young University, HI; UT
Bristol University, IN; TN
Brooklyn Law School, NY (LAW)

Brooks Institute of Photography, CA
Brown University, RI
Bryan College, TN
Bryant College, RI
Bryn Mawr College, PA (WMC)
Bucknell University, PA
Buena Vista College, IA
Burlington College, VT (LAS)
Butler University, IN

C

Cabrini College, PA
Caldwell College, NJ
California Baptist College, CA
California Coast University, CA
California College of Arts & Crafts, CA (GRD)
California College of Arts & Crafts, CA (ARC)
California College of Podiatric Medicine, CA (POD)
California Family Study Center, CA (GRD)
California Institute of Integral Studies, CA (THL)
California Institute of Technology, CA
California Institute of the Arts, CA (GRD)
California Lutheran University, CA
California Maritime Academy, CA (EGN)
California Polytechnic State University, CA
California Sch. Professional Psychology, CA (PSY)
California Sch. Professional Psychology, CA (GRD)
California State Polytechnic University, CA
California State University, CA
California University of Pennsylvania, CA
California Western School of Law, CA (LAW)
Calumet College, IN
Calvary Bible College, MO (BBL)
Calvin College, MI
Calvin Theological Seminary, MI (THL)
Cambridge College, MA (GRD)
Cameron University, OK
Campbellsville College, KY
Campbell University, NC
Canisius College, NY
Capital University, OH
Capital University Law School, OH (LAW)
Capitol College, MD
Cardinal Stritch College, WI
Caribbean Center for Advanced Studies, FL; PR (GRD)
Caribbean University, PR
Carleton College, MN
Carlow College, PA (WMC)
Carnegie Mellon University, PA
Carroll College, MT; WI
Carson-Newman College, TN
Carthage College, WI
Cascade College, OR (LAS)
Case Western Reserve University, OH
Castleton State College, VT
Catawba College, NC
Cathedral College Immaculate Conception, NY (MNC)
Catholic Theological Union, IL (THL)
Catholic University of America, DC
Catholic University of Puerto Rico, PR
Cazenovia College, NY
Cedar Crest College, PA (WMC)
Cedarville College, OH
Centenary College, NJ (WMC)
Centenary College of Louisiana, LA
Center for Creative Studies, MI
Center for Humanistic Studies, MI (GRD)
Central Baptist College, AR (BBL)
Central Baptist Theological Seminary, KS (THL)
Central Bible College, MO (BBL)
Central Christian College of the Bible, MO (BBL)
Central College, KS (BBL)
Central College, IA
Central Connecticut State University, CT
Central Indian Bible College, SD (BBL)
Central Institute for the Deaf, MO (SPD)
Central Methodist College, MO
Central Michigan University, MI
Central Missouri State University, MO
Central State University, OH
Central Washington University, WA
Central Wesleyan College, SC
Central Yeshiva Tomchei Tmimim Lubavitz, NY (RAB)
Centre College, KY
Centro De Estudios Avanzados, PR (GRD)
Chadron State College, NE
Chaminade University of Honolulu, HI
Champlain College, VT
Chapman University, CA
Charleston Southern University, SC
Charter Oak State College, CT (LAS)
Chatham College, PA (WMC)
Chestnut Hill College, PA (WMC)
Cheyney University of Pennsylvania, PA
Chicago College of Osteopathic Medicine, IL (OST)
Chicago Sch. of Professional Psychology, IL (PSY)
Chicago State University, IL
Chicago Theological Seminary, IL (THL)
Christendom College, VA (LAS)
Christian Brothers College, TN
Christian Heritage College, CA
Christian Theological Seminary, IN (THL)
Christopher Newport College, VA
Christ the King Seminary, NY (THL)

Church Divinity School of the Pacific, CA (THL)
Church of God School of Theology, TN (THL)
Cincinnati Bible College, OH (BBL)
Cincinnati College of Mortuary Science, OH
Circleville Bible College, OH
Citadel, The, SC (MNC)
City University, WA
Claflin College, SC
Claremont Graduate School, CA (GRD)
Claremont McKenna College, CA
Clarion University of Pennsylvania, PA
Clarion University of Pennsylvania, PA (NRS)
Clark Atlanta University, GA
Clarke College, IA
Clarkson College, NE (GRD)
Clarkson University, NY
Clark University, MA
Clayton State College, GA
Clear Creek Baptist Bible College, KY (BBL)
Clearwater Christian College, FL
Cleary College - Livingston Campus, MI
Cleary College - Washtenaw Campus, MI
Clemson University, SC
Cleveland Chiropractic College, CA; MO (CPC)
Cleveland College of Jewish Studies, OH (TED)
Cleveland Institute of Art, OH (ART)
Cleveland Institute of Music, OH (MUS)
Cleveland State University, OH
Clinch Valley College of the Univ. of VA, VA
Coastal Carolina College, SC
Coe College, IA
Cogswell Polytechnical College, CA; WA
Coker College, SC
Colby College, ME
Colby-Sawyer College, NH (WMC)
Colegio Biblico Pentecostal De PR, PR (BBL)
Coleman College, CA
Colgate Rochestr-Bexly-Crozer Seminaries, NY (THL)
Colgate University, NY
College for Financial Planning, CO
College for Human Services, NY (BUS)
College Misericordia, PA
College of Aeronautics, NY
College of Associated Arts, MN
College of Charleston, SC
College of Great Falls, MT
College of Idaho, ID
College of Insurance, NY
College of Mount Saint Joseph, OH
College of Mount Saint Vincent, NY
College of New Rochelle, NY
College of New Rochelle, NY (THL)
College of Notre Dame, CA
College of Notre Dame of Maryland, MD (WMC)
College of Osteopathic Medicine, CA; OK (OST)
College of Saint Benedict, MN (WMC)
College of Saint Catherine, MN (WMC)
College of Saint Elizabeth, NJ (WMC)
College of Saint Francis, IL
College of Saint Joseph, VT
College of Saint Mary, NE (WMC)
College of Saint Rose, NY
College of Saint Scholastica, MN
College of Santa Fe, NM
College of the Atlantic, ME (LAS)
College of the Holy Cross, MA
College of the Ozarks, MO
College of the Southwest, NM
College of William and Mary, VA (OCN)
College of William and Mary, VA
College of Wooster, OH
Colorado Christian University, CO
Colorado College, CO
Colorado School of Mines, CO
Colorado State University, CO
Colorado Technical College, CO
Columbia Biblical Seminary, SC (BBL)
Columbia Center, MD
Columbia College, IL; MO
Columbia College, SC (WMC)
Columbia College of Nursing, WI (NRS)
Columbia International University, SC (BBL)
Columbia Theological Seminary, GA (THL)
Columbia Union College, MD
Columbia University, NY (MED)
Columbia University General Studies, NY
Columbus College, GA
Columbus College of Art & Design, OH
Conception Seminary College, MO (MNC)
Concord College, WV
Concordia College, MI; MN; NE; NY; OR
Concordia Lutheran College, TX
Concordia Seminary, MO (THL)
Concordia Theological Seminary, IN (THL)
Concordia University, CA; IL; WI
Connecticut College, CT
Conservatory of Music, PR (MUS)
Converse College, SC (WMC)
Conway School of Landscape Design, MA (GRD)
Cooper Union, NY
Coppin State College, MD
Corcoran School of Art, DC
Cornell College, IA
Cornell University, NY
Cornell University Medical College, NY (MED)
Cornish College of the Arts, WA
Corpus Christi State University, TX
Covenant College, GA
Covenant Theological Seminary, MO (THL)
Cranbrook Academy of Art, MI (ART)
Creighton University, NE
Crichton College, TN (LAS)
Criswell College, TX
Crown College, MN
Culver-Stockton College, MO
Cumberland College, KY

Cumberland University, TN
CUNY-City University of New York, NY
CUNY Graduate School University Center, NY (GRD)
CUNY John Jay College Criminal Justice, NY (GRD)
CUNY Mt. Sinai School of Medicine, NY (MED)
Curry College, MA
Curtis Institute of Music, PA (MUS)

D

Daemen College, NY
Dakota State University, SD
Dakota Wesleyan University, SD
Dallas Baptist University, TX
Dallas Christian College, TX (BBL)
Dallas Theological Seminary, TX (THL)
Dana College, NE
Daniel Webster College, NH
Darkei Noam Rabbinical College, NY (RAB)
Dartmouth College, NH
Davenport College of Business, MI (BUS)
Davenport College of Business, MI (AHS)
David Lipscomb University, TN
Davidson College, NC
Davis & Elkins College, WV
Deaconess College of Nursing, MO (NRS)
Defiance College, OH
Delaware State College, DE
Delaware Valley College, PA
Delta State University, MS
Denison University, OH
Denver Seminary, CO (THL)
De Paul University, IL
DePauw University, IN
DePauw University, IN (NRS)
De Sales School of Theology, DC (THL)
Design Institute of San Diego, CA
Detroit College of Business, MI (BUS)
Detroit College of Law, MI (LAW)
DeVry Inc., IL
DeVry Institute of Technology, AZ; CA; GA; IL; MO;
   OH; TX (BUS)
Dickinson College, PA
Dickinson School of Law, PA (LAW)
Dickinson State University, ND
Dillard University, LA
District of Columbia School of Law, DC (LAW)
Divine Word College Seminary, IA (LAS)
Doane College, NE
Dr. Martin Luther College, MN
Dominican College of Blauvelt, NY
Dominican College of San Rafael, CA
Dominican House of Studies, DC (THL)
Dominican School of Philosophy/Theology, CA
Dordt College, IA
Dowling College, NY
Drake University, IA
Drew University, CA; NJ
Drexel University, PA
Drury College, MO
Duke University, NC
Duquesne University, PA
Dyke College, OH
D'Youville College, NY

E-F

Earlham College, IN
East Carolina University, NC
East Central University, OK
East Coast Bible College, NC (BBL)
Eastern Baptist Theological Seminary, PA (THL)
Eastern Christian College, MD (BBL)
Eastern College, PA
Eastern Connecticut State University, CT
Eastern Illinois University, IL
Eastern Kentucky University, KY
Eastern Mennonite College, VA
Eastern Michigan University, MI
Eastern Nazarene College, MA
Eastern New Mexico University, NM
Eastern Oregon State College, OR
Eastern Virginia Medical School, VA
Eastern Washington University, WA
Eastman School of Music, NY (MUS)
East Stroudsburg University of PA, PA
East Tennessee State University, TN
East Texas Baptist University, TX
East Texas State University, TX
East-West University, IL
Eckerd College, FL
Eden Theological Seminary, MO (THL)
Edgewood College, WI
Edinboro University of Pennsylvania, PA
Edward Waters College, FL
Elizabeth City State University, NC
Elizabethtown College, PA
Elmhurst College, IL
Elmira College, NY
Elms College, MA (WMC)
Elon College, NC
Embry-Riddle Aeronautical University, AZ; FL; KY
   (AAT)
Emerson College, MA
Emmanuel College, GA; MA
Emmanuel School of Religion, TN (THL)
Emmaus Bible College, IA (BBL)
Emory & Henry College, VA
Emory University, GA
Emory University Hospital, GA (MED)
Emporia State University, KS
Episcopal Divinity School, MA (THL)
Episcopal Theological Seminary, TX (THL)

Erskine College & Seminary, SC
Escuela De Artes Plasticas, PR
Eubanks Conservatory of Music & Arts, CA (MUS)
Eugene Bible College, OR (BBL)
Eureka College, IL
Evangel College, MO
Evangelical School of Theology, PA (THL)
Evangelical Seminary of Puerto Rico, PR (THL)
Evergreen State College, WA
Fairfield University, CT
Fairleigh Dickinson University, NJ
Fairmont State University, WV
Faith Baptist Bible College & Seminary, IA
Faulkner University, AL
Fayetteville State University, NC
Felician College, NJ
Ferris State University, MI
Ferrum College, VA
Fielding Institute, CA (GRD)
Fisk University, TN
Fitchburg State College, MA
Flagler College, FL
Florida A&M University, FL
FL A&M University/University of South FL, FL (ARC)
Florida Atlantic University, FL
Florida Baptist Theological College, FL
Florida Bible College, FL (BBL)
Florida Christian College, FL (BBL)
Florida Institute of Technology, FL
Florida International University, FL
Florida Memorial College, FL
Florida Southern College, FL
Florida State University, FL
Fontbonne College, MO
Fordham University, NY
Forest Inst./Professional Psychology, MO (PSY)
Fort Hays State University, KS
Fort Lauderdale College, FL
Fort Lewis College, CO
Fort Valley State College, GA
Framingham State College, MA
Franciscan School of Theology, CA (THL)
Franciscan University of Steubenville, OH
Francis Marion College, SC
Franklin & Marshall College, PA
Franklin College, IN
Franklin Pierce College, NH
Franklin Pierce Law Center, NH (LAW)
Franklin University, OH
Freed-Hardeman University, TN
Free Will Baptist Bible College, TN (BBL)
Fresno Pacific College, CA
Friends University, KS
Friends World Program, NY (LAS)
Frostburg State University, MD
Fuller Theological Seminary, CA (THL)
Furman University, SC

G

Gallaudet University, DC
Gannon University, PA
Gardner-Webb University, NC
Garrett Evangelical Theological Seminary, IL (BBL)
General Theological Seminary, NY (THL)
Geneva College, PA
George Fox College, OR
George Mason University, VA
Georgetown College, KY
Georgetown University, DC
George Washington University, DC
Georgia College, GA
Georgia Institute of Technology, GA
Georgian Court College, NJ (WMC)
Georgia Southern University, GA
Georgia Southwestern College, GA
Georgia State University, GA
Gettysburg College, PA
Glenville State College, WV
GMI Engineering & Management Institute, MI (GRD)
Goddard College, VT
God's Bible School and College, OH (BBL)
Golden Gate Baptist Theological Seminary, CA (THL)
Golden Gate University, CA
Goldey Beacom College, DE (BUS)
Gonzaga University, WA
Gonzaga University, WA (LAW)
Gordon College, MA
Gordon-Conwell Theological Seminary, MA (THL)
Goshen College, IN
Goucher College, MD
Governors State University, IL
Grace Bible College, MI (BBL)
Grace College, IA
Grace College of the Bible, NE (BBL)
Graceland College, IA
Grace Theological Seminary, IN (THL)
Graduate Theological Union, CA (THL)
Graham Bible College, VA (BBL)
Grambling State University, LA
Grand Canyon University, AZ
Grand Rapids Baptist College & Seminary, MI
Grand Valley State University, MI
Grand View College, IA
Gratz College, PA
Great Lakes Bible College, MI (BBL)
Green Mountain College, VT
Greensboro College, NC
Greenville College, IL
Grinnell College, IA
Grove City College, PA
Guilford College, NC
Gustavus Adolphus College, MN
Gwynedd-Mercy College, PA

H

Hahnemann University, PA (MED)
Hamilton College, NY
Hamline University, MN
Hampden-Sydney College, VA (MNC)
Hampshire College, MA
Hampton University, VA
Hannibal-LaGrange College, MO
Hanover College, IN
Harding University, AR
Harding Univ Graduate School of Religion, TN (THL)
Hardin-Simmons University, TX
Harrington Institute of Interior Design, IL
Harris-Stowe State College, MO
Hartford Graduate Center, CT (GRD)
Hartford Seminary, CT (THL)
Hartwick College, NY
Harvard University, MA
Harvey Mudd College, CA
Hastings College, NE
Haverford College, PA
Hawaii Pacific University, HI
Hebrew College, MA (GRD)
Hebrew Theological College, IL (RAB)
Hebrew Union College, CA; NY; OH (RAB)
Heidelberg College, OH
Hellenic College, MA
Henderson State University, AR
Hendrix College, AR
Heritage College, WA (GRD)
High Point College, NC
Hillsdale College, MI
Hillsdale Free Will Baptist College, OK (BBL)
Hiram College, OH
Hobart & William Smith College, NY
Hobe Sound Bible College, FL
Hofstra University, NY
Hollins College, VA
Holy Apostles College, CT (THL)
Holy Family College, PA
Holy Names College, CA
Hood College, MD (WMC)
Hood Theological Seminary, NC (THL)
Hope College, MI
Houghton College, NY
Houston Baptist University, TX
Houston Graduate School of Theology, TX (THL)
Howard Payne University, TX
Howard University, DC
Howard University Divinity School, DC (THL)
Humboldt State University, CA
Humphreys College, CA
Huntingdon College, AL; IN
Huron University, SD
Husson College, ME
Huston-Tillotson College, TX
Hyles-Anderson College, IN (BBL)

I

Idaho State University, ID
IIT Kent College of Law, IL (LAW)
Iliff School of Theology, CO (THL)
Illinois Benedictine College, IL
Illinois College, IL
Illinois College of Optometry, IL (OPT)
Illinois Institute of Technology, IL
Illinois School/Professional Psychology, IL (PSY)
Illinois State University, IL
Illinois Wesleyan University, IL
Immaculata College, PA (BBL)
Immaculate Conception Seminary, NJ (THL)
Incarnate Word College, TX
Indiana Institute of Technology, IN (BUS)
Indiana State University, IN
Indiana University, IN; PA
Indiana U-Purdue U at Fort Wayne, IN
Indiana U-Purdue U at Indianapolis, IN
Indiana Wesleyan University, IN
Institute for Christian Studies, TX (BBL)
Institute for Clinical Social Work, IL (SCW)
Institute of Paper Science & Technology, GA (GRD)
Institute of Textile Technology, VA (GRD)
Inter American University, PR
Inter American University of Puerto Rico, PR (LAW)
Intercollegiate Center/Nursing Education, WA (NRS)
Interdenominational Theological Center, GA (THL)
International Bible College, AL (BBL)
International College, FL
International School of Theology, CA (THL)
Iona College, NY
Iowa State University, IA
Iowa Wesleyan College, IA
Ithaca College, NY
ITT Technical Institute, OR

J

Jackson State University, MS
Jacksonville State University, AL
Jacksonville University, FL
James Madison University, VA
Jamestown College, ND
Japan-America Inst./Management Science, HI (BUS)
Jarvis Christian College, TX
Jersey City State College, NJ
Jesuit School of Theology at Berkeley, CA (THL)
Jewish Theological Seminary of America, NY (RAB)
Jimmy Swaggart Bible College & Seminary, LA
John Brown University, AR
John Carroll University, OH

John F. Kennedy University, CA
John Marshall Law School, IL (LAW)
Johns Hopkins University, DC (GRD)
Johns Hopkins University, MD (MED)
Johns Hopkins University, MD
Johnson & Wales University, RI
Johnson Bible College, TN (BBL)
Johnson C. Smith University, NC
Johnson Medical School, NJ (MED)
Johnson State College, VT
John Wesley College, NC (BBL)
Jones College, FL
Jordan College, MI
Jordan Energy Institute, MI
Judson College, AL (WMC)
Judson College, IL (LAS)
Juilliard School, NY
Juniata College, PA

K

Kalamazoo College, MI
Kansas City Art Institute, MO (ART)
Kansas City College & Bible School, KS (BBL)
Kansas Newman College, KS
Kansas State University, KS
Kansas Wesleyan University, KS (LAS)
Kean College of New Jersey, NJ
Keene State College, NH
Kehilath Yakov Rabbinical Seminary, NY (RAB)
Keller Graduate School of Management, IL (BUS)
Kendall College, IL (LAS)
Kendall College of Art & Design, MI
Kennesaw State College, GA
Kenrick School of Theology, MO (THL)
Kent State University, OH
Kentucky Christian College, KY (BBL)
Kentucky State University, KY
Kentucky Wesleyan College, KY
Kenyon College, OH
Keuka College, NY
King College, TN
King of Prussia Graduate Center, PA (LAS)
King's College, The, NY; PA
Kirksville Coll. of Osteopathic Medicine, MO (OST)
Knowledge Systems Institute, IL (GRD)
Knox College, IL
Knoxville College, TN
Kol Yaakov Torah Center, NY (RAB)
Kutztown University of Pennsylvania, PA

L

Laboratory Institute of Merchandising, NY (BUS)
Lafayette College, PA
La Grange College, GA
Lake Erie College, OH
Lake Forest College, IL
Lake Forest Graduate Sch. of Management, IL (GRD)
Lakeland College, WI
Lake Superior State University, MI
Lamar University, TX
Lambuth College, TN
Lamont-Doherty Earth Observatory, NY
Lancaster Bible College, PA (BBL)
Lancaster Theological Seminary, PA (THL)
Lander College, SC
Lane College, TN
Langston University, OK
La Roche College, PA
La Salle University, PA
La Sierra University, CA
Lawrence Technological University, MI
Lawrence University, WI
Lebanon Valley College, PA
Lee College, TN
Lees-McRae College, NC
Lehigh University, PA
Le Moyne College, NY
Le Moyne-Owen College, TN
Lenoir-Rhyne College, NC
Lesley College, MA (WMC)
LeTourneau College, TX
Lewis & Clark College, OR
Lewis Clark State College, ID
Lewis University, IL
Lexington Theological Seminary, KY (THL)
Liberty University, VA
L.I.F.E. Bible College, CA (BBL)
Life Chiropractic College West, CA (GRD)
Life College, GA (CPC)
Limestone College, SC
Lincoln Christian College, IL (BBL)
Lincoln Memorial University, TN
Lincoln University, CA; MO; PA
Lindenwood College, MO
Lindsey Wilson College, KY
Linfield College, OR
Linfield College, OR (AHS)
Livingstone College, NC
Livingston University, AL
Lock Haven University, PA
Logan College of Chiropractic, MO (CPC)
Loma Linda University, CA
Long Island University, NY
Longwood College, VA
Longy School of Music, MA (MUS)
Loras College, IA
Los Angeles College of Chiropractic, CA (CPC)
Louisiana College, LA
Louisiana State University, LA
Louisiana State University, LA (MED)
Louisiana State University & A & M Coll., LA

Louisiana Technical University, LA
Louisville Presbyterian Theological Sem., KY (BBL)
Lourdes College, OH
Loyola College, MD
Loyola Marymount University, CA
Loyola Marymount University, CA (LAW)
Loyola University, IL (MED)
Loyola University, IL; LA
Loyola University - Mundelein College, IL (WMC)
Lubbock Christian University, TX
Lutheran Bible Institute of California, CA (BBL)
Lutheran Bible Institute of Seattle, WA
Lutheran College of Health Professions, IN
Lutheran School of Theology at Chicago, IL (THL)
Lutheran Theological Seminary, PA (THL)
Lutheran Theological Southern Seminary, SC (THL)
Luther College, IA
Luther Northwestern Theological Seminary, MN (THL)
Luther Rice Seminary, GA (BBL)
Lycoming College, PA
Lynchburg College, VA
Lyndon State College, VT
Lynn University, FL

M

MacAlester College, MN
McCormick Theological Seminary, IL (THL)
Machzikei Hadath Rabbinical College, NY (RAB)
McKendree College, IL
MacMurray College, IL
McMurry University, TX
McNeese State University, LA
McPherson College, KS
Madonna University, MI
Magnolia Bible College, MS
Maharishi International University, IA
Maine College of Art, ME
Maine Maritime Academy, ME
Malone College, OH
Manchester College, IN
Manhattan Christian College, KS (BBL)
Manhattan College, NY
Manhattan School of Music, NY
Manhattanville College, NY
Mankato State University, MN
Manna Bible Institute, PA (BBL)
Mannes College of Music, NY (MUS)
Mansfield University of Pennsylvania, PA
Maranatha Baptist Bible College, WI
Marian College, IN; WI
Marietta College, OH
Marist College, NY
Marlboro College, VT
Marquette University, WI
Marshall University, WV
Mars Hill College, NC
Martin University, IN (LAS)
Mary Baldwin College, VA (WMC)
Marygrove College, MI
Maryland Institute College of Art, MD
Marylhurst College for Lifelong Learning, OR
Marymount College, NY
Marymount Manhattan College, NY
Marymount University, VA
Maryville College, TN
Maryville University of St. Louis, MO
Mary Washington College, VA
Marywood College, PA (WMC)
Massachusetts College of Art, MA (ART)
MA College of Pharmacy & Allied Health, MA (NRS)
Massachusetts General Hospital, MA (AHS)
Massachusetts Institute of Technology, MA
Massachusetts Maritime Academy, MA
Massachusetts School Professional Psych., MA (PSY)
Master's College, CA
Mayo Foundation, MN (MED)
Mayville State University, ND
Meadville/Lombard Theological School, IL (THL)
Medaille College, NY
Medcenter One College of Nursing, ND (NRS)
Medical College of Georgia, GA
Medical College of Hampton Roads, VA (GRD)
Medical College of Ohio, OH (MED)
Medical College of Pennsylvania, PA (MED)
Medical College of Wisconsin, WI (MED)
Medical University of South Carolina, SC (MED)
Meharry Medical College, TN (MED)
Memphis College of Art, TN (ART)
Memphis Theological Seminary, TN (THL)
Menlo College, CA
Mennonite Brethren Biblical Seminary, CA (THL)
Mennonite College of Nursing, IL (NRS)
Mercer University in Atlanta, GA
Mercer University in Macon, GA
Mercy College, NY
Mercyhurst College, PA
Meredith College, NC (WMC)
Merrimack College, MA
Mesa State College, CO
Mesivta Eastern Parkway Rabbinical Sem., NY (RAB)
Mesivta Tifereth Jerusalem of America, NY (RAB)
Mesivta Torah Vodaath Seminary, NY (RAB)
Messiah College, PA
Methodist College, NC
Methodist College of Nursing & Health, NE (NRS)
Methodist Theological School in Ohio, OH (THL)
Metropolitan State College, CO
Metropolitan State University, MN
MGH Institute of Health Professions, MA (NRS)
Miami Christian College, FL (BBL)
Miami University, OH
Michigan Christian College, MI (BBL)
Michigan State University, MI
Michigan Technological University, MI

Mid-America Baptist Theological Seminary, TN   (THL)
Mid-America Bible College, OK
Mid-America Nazarene College, KS
Mid-Continent Baptist Bible College, KY
Middlebury College, VT
Middle Tennessee State University, TN
Midland Lutheran College, NE
Midway College, KY
Midwest College of Engineering, IL   (GRD)
Midwestern Baptist Theological Seminary, MO   (THL)
Midwestern State University, TX
Miles College, AL
Millersville University of Pennsylvania, PA
Milligan College, TN
Millikin University, IL
Millsaps College, MS
Mills College, CA   (WMC)
Milwaukee Institute of Art & Design, WI   (ART)
Milwaukee School of Engineering, WI
Minneapolis College of Art & Design, MN   (ART)
Minnesota Bible College, MN   (BBL)
Minot State University, ND
Mirrer Yeshiva, NY   (RAB)
Mississippi College, MS
Mississippi College, MS   (LAW)
Mississippi State University, MS
Mississippi University for Women, MS
Mississippi Valley State University, MS
Missouri Baptist College, MO
Missouri Southern State College, MO
Missouri Valley College, MO
Missouri Western State College, MO
Molloy College, NY
Monmouth College, IL; NJ
Montana State University, MT
Montana Tech, MT
Montclair State College, NJ
Monterey Institute of Intntnl. Studies, CA   (GRD)
Montreat-Anderson College, NC
Montserrat College of Art, MA   (ART)
Moody Bible Institute, IL   (BBL)
Moore College of Art and Design, PA   (ART)
Moorhead State University, MN
Moravian College, PA
Moravian Theological Seminary, PA   (THL)
Morehead State University, KY
Morehouse College, GA   (MNC)
Morehouse School of Medicine, GA   (MED)
Morgan State University, MD
Morningside College, IA
Morris Brown College, GA
Morris College, SC
Morrison College, NV
Mt. Aloysius College, PA
Mt. Angel Seminary, OR   (THL)
Mt. Holyoke College, MA
Mt. Ida College, MA
Mt. Marty College, SD
Mt. Mary College, WI   (WMC)
Mt. Mercy College, IA
Mt. Olive College, NC
Mt. St. Clare College, IA   (BUS)
Mt. St. Mary College, MD; NY
Mt. St. Mary's College, CA   (WMC)
Mt. Senario College, WI
Mt. Union College, OH
Mt. Vernon College, DC   (WMC)
Mt. Vernon Nazarene College, OH
Muhlenberg College, PA
Multnomah Biblical Seminary, OR   (BBL)
Murray State University, KY
Muskingum College, OH

N

Naropa Institute, CO
Nashotah House, WI   (THL)
National College, CO; MN; NM; SD
National College of Chiropractic, IL   (CPC)
National-Louis University, IL
National Technological University, CO   (GRD)
National Theatre Conservatory, CO   (GRD)
National University, CA
National University School of Law, CA   (LAW)
Native American Educational Services, IL
Nazarene Bible College, CO
Nazarene Theological Seminary, MO   (THL)
Nazareth College of Rochester, NY
Nebraska Christian College, NE   (BBL)
Nebraska Wesleyan University, NE
Ner Israel Rabbinical College, MD   (RAB)
Neumann College, PA
Newberry College, SC
New Brunswick Theological Seminary, NJ   (THL)
New College Advanced Christian Studies, CA   (GRD)
New College of California, CA
New College University of South Florida, FL
Newcomb College of Tulane University, LA   (WMC)
New England College, NH
New England College of Optometry, MA   (OPT)
New England Conservatory of Music, MA   (MUS)
New England Culinary Institute, VT
New England School of Law, MA   (LAW)
New England Technical College, RI
New Hampshire College, NH
New Jersey Institute of Technology, NJ
New Mexico Highlands University, NM
New Mexico Institute Mining & Technology, NM
New Mexico State University, NM
New Orleans Baptist Theological Seminary, LA   (THL)
New School for Social Research, NY
New York Chiropractic College, NY   (CPC)
New York College of Podiatric Medicine, NY   (POD)
New York Institute of Technology, NY
New York Law School, NY   (LAW)

New York Medical College, NY   (MED)
New York School of Interior Design, NY
NY State College Ceramics at Alfred, NY
New York Theological Seminary, NY   (THL)
New York University, NY
New York University, NY   (BUS)
New York University, NY   (SCW)
New York University Medical Center, NY   (MED)
Niagara University, NY
Nicholls State University, LA
Nichols College, MA
Niles College of Loyola University, IL   (MNC)
Norfolk State University, VA
North Adams State College, MA
North American Baptist Seminary, SD   (THL)
North Carolina A&T State University, NC
North Carolina Central University, NC
North Carolina School of the Arts, NC
North Carolina State University, NC
North Carolina Wesleyan College, NC
North Central Bible College, MN
North Central College, IL
North Dakota State University, ND
Northeastern Illinois University, IL
Northeastern Ohio Univ Coll of Medicine, OH   (MED)
Northeastern State University, OK
Northeastern University, MA
Northeast Louisiana University, LA
Northeast Missouri State University, MO
Northern Arizona University, AZ
Northern Baptist Theological Seminary, IL   (THL)
Northern Illinois University, IL
Northern Kentucky University, KY
Northern Michigan University, MI
Northern Montana College, MT
Northern State University, SD
North Georgia College, GA
North Greenville College, SC
Northland College, WI
North Park Coll. & Theological Seminary, IL
Northwest Baptist Seminary, WA
Northwest Christian College, OR
Northwest College Assemblies of God, WA   (BBL)
Northwest College of Art, WA
Northwestern College, IA; MN
Northwestern College, WI   (MNC)
Northwestern College of Chiropractic, MN   (CPC)
Northwestern State University, LA; OK
Northwestern State University, LA   (NRS)
Northwestern University, IL   (MED)
Northwestern University, IL
Northwest Missouri State University, MO
Northwest Nazarene College, ID
Northwood University, FL; MI; TX
Norwich University, VT
Norwich University Vermont College, VT
Notre Dame Apostolic Catechetical Inst, VA
Notre Dame College, NH
Notre Dame College, OH   (WMC)
Notre Dame Seminary, LA   (THL)
Nova Southeastern University, FL
Nyack College, NY

O

Oak Hills Bible College, MN   (BBL)
Oakland City College, IN
Oakland University, MI
Oakwood College, AL
Oberlin College, OH
Oblate College, DC   (THL)
Oblate School of Theology, TX   (THL)
Occidental College, CA
Oglala Lakota Community College, SD
Oglethorpe University, GA
Ohio College of Podiatric Medicine, OH   (POD)
Ohio Dominican College, OH
Ohio Northern University, OH
Ohio State University, OH
Ohio University, OH
Ohio Valley College, WV
Ohio Wesleyan University, OH
Ohr HaMeir Theological Seminary, NY   (RAB)
Ohr Somayach Tanenbaum Educational Ctr., NY   (RAB)
Oklahoma Baptist University, OK
Oklahoma Christian University, OK
Oklahoma City University, OK
Oklahoma Panhandle State University, OK
Oklahoma State University, OK
Old Dominion University, VA
Olivet College, MI
Olivet Nazarene University, IL
O'More College of Design, TN   (ART)
Oral Roberts University, OK
Oregon Graduate Institute/Science & Tech, OR   (GRD)
Oregon Health Sciences University, OR   (MED)
Oregon Institute of Technology, OR
Oregon School of Arts & Crafts, OR
Oregon State University, OR
Orlando College - North, FL
Orlando College - South, FL
Otis College of Art and Design, CA
Ottawa University, KS
Otterbein College, OH
Ouachita Baptist University, AR
Our Lady of Holy Cross College, LA   (LAS)
Our Lady of the Lake University, TX
Ozark Christian College, MO   (BBL)

P

Pace University, NY
Pacific Christian College, CA   (BBL)

Pacific Graduate School of Psychology, CA   (PSY)
Pacific Lutheran Theological Seminary, CA   (THL)
Pacific Lutheran University, WA
Pacific Northwest College of Art, OR
Pacific Oaks College, CA   (GRD)
Pacific School of Religion, CA   (THL)
Pacific Union College, CA
Pacific University, OR
Paier College of Art, CT
Paine College, GA
Palm Beach Atlantic College, FL
Palmer College of Chiropractic, CA; IA   (CPC)
Park College, MO
Parker College of Chiropractic, TX   (CPC)
Parks College of St. Louis University, IL   (BUS)
Parsons School of Design, NY   (ART)
Patten College, CA
Paul Quinn College, TX   (LAS)
Payne Theological Seminary, OH   (THL)
Peabody College of Vanderbilt University, TN
Peabody Institute Johns Hopkins Univ., MD   (GRD)
Pembroke State University, NC
Pennsylvania College of Optometry, PA   (OPT)
Pennsylvania College Podiatric Medicine, PA   (POD)
Pennsylvania Coll. Straight Chiropractic, PA   (CPC)
Pennsylvania State University, PA
Penn. State Univ. Medical College, PA   (MED)
Penn View Bible Institute, PA   (BBL)
Pensacola Christian College, FL
Pepperdine University, CA   (PSY)
Pepperdine University, CA
Peru State College, NE
Pfeiffer College, NC
Philadelphia College of Bible, PA   (BBL)
Philadelphia Coll. Osteopathic Medicine, PA   (OST)
Philadelphia Coll. of Pharmacy & Science, PA   (PHR)
Philadelphia Coll. of Textiles & Science, PA   (BUS)
Philadelphia Theological Seminary, PA   (THL)
Philander Smith College, AR
Phillips University, OK
Piedmont Bible College, NC   (BBL)
Piedmont College, GA
Pikeville College, KY
Pillsbury Baptist Bible College, MN   (BBL)
Pine Manor College, MA   (WMC)
Pittsburgh Theological Seminary, PA   (THL)
Pittsburg State University, KS
Pitzer College, CA
Plymouth State College, NH
Point Loma Nazarene College, CA
Point Park College, PA
Polytechnic University, NY; PR
Polytechnic University, NY   (GRD)
Pomona College, CA
Ponce School of Medicine, PR   (MED)
Pontifical College Josephinum, OH   (THL)
Pope John XXIII National Seminary, MA   (THL)
Portland State University, OR
Practical Bible Training School, NY   (BBL)
Prairie View A&M University, TX   (NRS)
Prairie View A&M University, TX
Pratt Institute, NY
Presbyterian College, SC
Presbyterian School of Christian Educ., VA   (THL)
Prescott College, AZ
Presentation College, SD   (NRS)
Princeton Theological Seminary, NJ   (THL)
Princeton University, NJ
Principia College, IL
Protestant Episcopal Theologcl. Seminary, VA   (THL)
Providence College, RI
Puget Sound Christian College, WA   (BBL)
Purdue University, IN

Q-R

Queens College, NC
Quincy College, IL
Quinnipiac College, CT
Rabbi Jacob Joseph School, NJ   (RAB)
Rabbinical Academy Mesivta Rabbi Chaim, NY   (MNC)
Rabbinical College Beth Shraga, NY   (RAB)
Rabbinical Coll. Bobovr Yeshiva Bnei Zn., NY   (RAB)
Rabbinical Coll. Ch' San Sofer of NY, NY   (RAB)
Rabbinical College of America, NJ   (RAB)
Rabbinical College of Long Island, NY   (RAB)
Rabbinical College of Telshe, OH   (RAB)
Rabbinical Seminary Adas Yereim, NY   (RAB)
Rabbinical Seminary M'Kor Chaim, NY   (RAB)
Rabbinical Seminary of America, NY   (RAB)
Radford University, VA
Ramapo College of New Jersey, NJ
Rand Graduate School, CA   (GRD)
Randolph-Macon College, VA
Randolph-Macon Woman's College, VA   (WMC)
Ray College of Design, IL
Reconstructionist Rabbinical College, PA   (RAB)
Reed College, OR
Reformed Bible College, MI   (BBL)
Reformed Presbyterian Theological Sem., PA   (THL)
Reformed Theological Seminary, MS   (THL)
Regents Coll of the Univ of State of NY, NY
Regent University, VA   (GRD)
Regis College, MA   (WMC)
Regis University, CO
Rensselaer Polytechnic Institute, NY
Research College of Nursing, MO   (NRS)
Rhode Island College, RI
Rhode Island School of Design, RI   (ART)
Rhodes College, TN
Rice University, TX
Richmond College, CT
Rider University, NJ
Ringling School of Art & Design, FL   (ART)
Rio Grande Bible Institute, TX   (BBL)

Ripon College, WI
Rivier College, NH
Roanoke Bible College, NC (BBL)
Roanoke College, VA
Robert Morris College, IL; PA
Roberts Wesleyan College, NY
Rochester Institute of Technology, NY
Rockford College, IL
Rockhurst College, MO
Rocky Mountain College, CO; MT
Roger Williams College, RI
Rollins College, FL
Roosevelt University, IL
Rosary College, IL
Rose-Hulman Institute of Technology, IN (EGN)
Rosemont College, PA (WMC)
Rowan College of New Jersey, NJ
Rush University, IL (MED)
Russell Sage College, NY (WMC)
Rust College, MS
Rutgers-The State U of NJ/Univ. Coll., NJ
Rutgers-The State U of NJ, NJ (EGN)
Rutgers-The State U of NJ/Douglass, NJ (WMC)
Rutgers-The State U of NJ/Mason Gross, NJ (ART)
Rutgers-The State U of NJ/Nursing, NJ (NRS)
Rutgers-The State U of NJ/Pharmacy, NJ (PHR)

S

Sacred Heart Major Seminary, MI (MNC)
Sacred Heart School of Theology, WI (THL)
Sacred Heart University, CT
Saginaw Valley State University, MI
St. Alphonsus College, CT (THL)
St. Ambrose University, IA
St. Andrews Presbyterian College, NC
St. Anselm College, NH
St. Augustine's College, NC
St. Bernard's Institute, NY (THL)
St. Bonaventure University, NY
St. Charles Borromeo Seminary, PA (THL)
St. Cloud State University, MN
SS. Cyril and Methodius Seminary, MI (GRD)
St. Edward's University, TX
St. Francis College, IN; NY; PA
St. Francis Medical Ctr. Coll of Nursing, IL
St. Francis Seminary, WI (THL)
St. Hyacinth College & Seminary, MA (MNC)
St. John Fisher College, NY
St. John's College, MD
St. John's College, NM (LAS)
St. John's Seminary, CA; MA (THL)
St. John's Seminary College, CA (MNC)
St. John's University, MN; NY
St. John Vianney College Seminary, FL (MNC)
St. Joseph College, CT (WMC)
St. Joseph College of Nursing, IL (NRS)
St. Joseph's College, IN; ME; NY
St. Joseph Seminary College, LA (LAS)
St. Joseph's Seminary, NY (THL)
St. Joseph's University, PA
St. Lawrence University, NY
St. Leo College, FL
St. Louis Christian College, MO (BBL)
St. Louis College of Pharmacy, MO (PHR)
St. Louis Conservatory of Music, MO (MUS)
St. Louis University, MO
St. Martin's College, WA
St. Mary College, KS
St. Mary-of-the-Woods College, IN (WMC)
St. Mary's College, IN (WMC)
St. Mary's College, MI (LAS)
St. Mary's College of California, CA
St. Mary's College of Maryland, MD
St. Mary's College of Minnesota, MN
St. Mary's College of Minnesota, MN (GRD)
St. Mary Seminary, OH (THL)
St. Mary's Seminary & University, MD (THL)
St. Mary's University of San Antonio, TX
St. Meinrad College, IN (MNC)
St. Meinrad School of Theology, IN (THL)
St. Michael's College, VT
St. Norbert College, WI
St. Olaf College, MN
St. Patrick's Seminary, CA (THL)
St. Paul School of Theology, MO (THL)
St. Paul's College, VA
St. Peter's College, NJ
St. Thomas Aquinas College, NY
St. Thomas Seminary, CO (THL)
St. Thomas University, FL
St. Vincent College, PA
St. Vincent DePaul Regional Seminary, FL (MNC)
St. Vladimir's Orthodox Theological Sem., NY (THL)
St. Xavier College, IL
Salem College, NC (WMC)
Salem State College, MA
Salem-Teikyo University, WV
Salisbury State University, MD
Salve Regina University, RI
Samford University, AL
Sam Houston State University, TX
Samuel Merritt College, CA (NRS)
San Antonio Art Institute, TX (ART)
San Diego State University, CA
San Francisco Art Institute, CA (ART)
San Francisco Conservatory of Music, CA (MUS)
San Francisco State University, CA
San Francisco Theological Seminary, CA (THL)
Sangamon State University, IL
San Joaquin College of Law, CA (LAW)
San Jose Christian College, CA (BBL)
San Jose State University, CA
Santa Clara University, CA
Sarah Lawrence College, NY

Savannah College of Art & Design, GA
Savannah State College, GA
Saybrook Institute, CA (PSY)
Schiller International University, FL
Scholl College of Podiatric Medicine, IL (POD)
School for International Training, VT (GRD)
School for Lifelong Learning, NH (SCW)
School of Osteopathic Medicine, NJ (OST)
School of the Art Institute of Chicago, IL (GRD)
School of the Hartford Ballet, CT (SPD)
School of the Museum of Fine Arts, MA
School of Theology at Claremont, CA (THL)
School of Visual Arts, NY (ART)
Schreiner College, TX
Scripps College, CA (WMC)
Seabury-Western Theological Seminary, IL (THL)
Seattle Pacific University, WA
Seattle University, WA
Selma University, AL
Seminary of the Immaculate Conception, NY (THL)
Seton Hall University, NJ
Seton Hall University, NJ (LAW)
Seton Hill College, PA (WMC)
Shawnee State University, OH
Shaw University, NC
Sheldon Jackson College, AK
Shenandoah University, VA
Shepherd College, WV
Sherman College of Straight Chiropractic, SC (CPC)
Shimer College, IL (LAS)
Shippensburg University, PA
Shorter College, GA
Shor Yoshuv Rabbinical College, NY (RAB)
Siena College, NY
Siena Heights College, MI
Sierra Nevada College-Lake Tahoe, NV
Silver Lake College, WI
Simmons College, MA (WMC)
Simon's Rock of Bard College, MA (LAS)
Simpson College, CA (BBL)
Simpson College, IA
Sinte Gleska College, SD (LAS)
Sioux Falls College, SD
Skidmore College, NY
Slippery Rock University, PA
Smith College, MA (WMC)
Sojourner-Douglass College, MD (LAS)
Sonoma State University, CA
South Carolina State University, SC
South Dakota School Mines and Technology, SD
South Dakota State University, SD
Southeastern Baptist College, MS (BBL)
Southeastrn Baptist Theological Seminary, NC (THL)
Southeastern Bible College, AL (BBL)
Southeastern College Assemblies of God, FL (BBL)
Southeastern Louisiana University, LA
Southeastern Oklahoma State University, OK
Southeastern University, DC
Southeastern University/Health Sciences, FL (PHR)
Southeast Missouri State University, MO
Southern Arkansas University, AR
Southern Baptist Theological Seminary, KY (THL)
Southern California College, CA
Southern California College Chiropractic, CA (CPC)
Southern California College of Optometry, CA (OPT)
Southern California Inst. Architecture, CA
Southern Christian University, AL
Southern College of Optometry, TN (OPT)
Southern College of Technology, GA
Southern Connecticut State University, CT
Southern Illinois University, IL (MED)
Southern Illinois University, IL
Southern Methodist College, SC (BBL)
Southern Methodist University, TX
Southern Missionary College, TN
Southern Nazarene University, OK
Southern Oregon State College, OR
Southern University A&M College, LA
Southern University in New Orleans, LA
Southern Utah University, UT
Southern Vermont College, VT
South Texas College of Law, TX (LAW)
Southwest Baptist University, MO
Southwestern Adventist College, TX
Southwestern Assemblies of God College, TX (BBL)
Southwestern Baptist Theological Sem., TX (THL)
Southwestern Christian College, TX
Southwestern College, AZ; KS
Southwestern Coll. Christian Ministries, OK (BBL)
Southwestern Oklahoma State University, OK
Southwestern University, TX
Southwestern University School of Law, CA (LAW)
Southwest Missouri State University, MO
Southwest State University, MN
Southwest Texas State University, TX
Spalding University, KY
Spelman College, GA (WMC)
Spertus College of Judaica, IL (GRD)
Spring Arbor College, MI
Springfield College, MA
Spring Hill College, AL
Spurgeon Baptist Bible College, FL (BBL)
Stanford University, CA (OCN)
Stanford University, CA
Starr King School for the Ministry, CA (THL)
State Laboratory of Hygiene, WI (AHS)
Stephen F. Austin State University, TX
Stephens College, MO (WMC)
Sterling College, KS
Stetson University, FL
Stetson University, FL (LAW)
Stevens Institute of Technology, NJ
Stillman College, AL
Stockton State College, NJ
Stonehill College, MA
Strayer College, DC; VA

Suffolk University, MA
Sullivan College, KY
Sul Ross State University, TX
SUNY at Buffalo, NY (GRD)
SUNY College of Optometry, NY (OPT)
SUNY Health Science Center, NY (MED)
SUNY Maritime College, NY (EGN)
SUNY State University of New York, NY
Susquehanna University, PA
Swarthmore College, PA
Swedenborg School of Religion, MA (THL)
Sweet Briar College, VA (WMC)
Syracuse University, NY

T

Tabor College, KS (LAS)
Talladega College, AL
Talmudical Academy of New Jersey, NJ (RAB)
Talmudical Institute of Upstate New York, NY (RAB)
Talmudical Seminary Oholei Torah, NY (RAB)
Talmudical Yeshiva of Philadelphia, PA (RAB)
Talmudic College of Florida, FL (RAB)
Tampa College, FL
Tarleton State University, TX
Taylor University, IN
Teachers College of Columbia University, NY (GRD)
Teikyo Loretto Heights University, CO
Teikyo Marycrest University, IA
Teikyo Post University, CT
Teikyo Westmar University, IA
Telshe Yeshiva-Chicago, IL (RAB)
Temple University, PA
Temple University, PA (MED)
Tennessee State University, TN
Tennessee Technological University, TN
Tennessee Temple University, TN
Tennessee Wesleyan College, TN
Texas A & I University, TX
Texas A & M at Galveston, TX (EGN)
Texas A & M International University, TX
Texas A & M University, TX
Texas Chiropractic College, TX (CPC)
Texas Christian University, TX
Texas College, TX
Texas Lutheran College, TX
Texas Southern University, TX
Texas Tech University, TX
Texas Wesleyan University, TX
Texas Women's University, TX (WMC)
Thiel College, PA
Thomas Aquinas College, CA (LAS)
Thomas College, GA; ME
Thomas Edison State College, NJ
Thomas Jefferson University, PA
Thomas M. Cooley Law School, MI (LAW)
Thomas More College, KY
Tiffin University, OH (BUS)
Toccoa Falls College, GA
Torah Temimah Talmudical Seminary, NY (RAB)
Tougaloo College, MS
Touro College, NY (LAW)
Touro College, NY
Towson State University, MD
Transylvania University, KY
Trenton State College, NJ
Trevecca Nazarene College, TN
Tri-College University, ND (GRD)
Trinity Bible College, ND (BBL)
Trinity Christian College, IL
Trinity College, CT; IL
Trinity College, DC; VT (WMC)
Trinity College of Florida, FL
Trinity Episcopal School for Ministry, PA (THL)
Trinity Evangelical Divinity School, IL (THL)
Trinity Lutheran Seminary, OH (THL)
Trinity University, TX
Tri-State University, IN
Troy State University, AL
Tufts University, MA
Tufts University, MA (MED)
Tulane University, LA
Tusculum College, TN
Tuskegee University, AL

U

Unification Theological Seminary, NY (THL)
Union College, KY; NE; NY
Union College Poughkeepsie Center, NY (GRD)
Union Institute, OH
Union Theological Seminary, NY; VA (THL)
Union University, TN
United States Air Force Academy, CO
United States Coast Guard Academy, CT
United States International University, CA
United States Merchant Marine Academy, NY
United States Military Academy, NY
United States Naval Academy, MD
United States Sports Academy, AL (GRD)
United Talmudical Academy, NY (RAB)
United Theological Seminary, OH
United Theological Seminary/Twin Cities, MN (THL)
Unity College, ME (LAS)
Universidad Adventista de las Antillas, PR
Universidad Central Del Caribe, PR (MED)
Universidad Del Turabo, PR
Universidad Metropolitana, PR
University of Akron, OH
University of Alabama, AL
University of Alaska, AK
University of Arizona, AZ
University of Arkansas, AR

University of Arkansas/Medical Sciences, AR (MED)
University of Baltimore, MD
University of Bridgeport, CT
University of California, CA
University of California, CA (GRD)
University of California-Davis, CA (AHS)
University of CA Hastings College of Law, CA (LAW)
UCLA Center for the Health Sciences, CA (NRS)
University of California-Irvine Med. Ctr, CA (AHS)
University of Central Arkansas, AR
University of Central Florida, FL
University of Central Oklahoma, OK
University of Central Texas, TX
University of Charleston, WV
University of Chicago, IL
University of Cincinnati, OH
University of Cincinnati/OMI College, OH
University of Colorado, CO
University of Colorado Health Sciences, CO (GRD)
University of Connecticut, CT
University of Connecticut, CT (OCN)
University of Connecticut Health Center, CT (MED)
University of Dallas, TX
University of Dayton, OH
University of Delaware, DE
University of Denver, CO
University of Denver University College, CO (GRD)
University of Detroit-Mercy, MI
University of Dubuque, IA
University of Dubuque Theological Sem., IA (THL)
University of Evansville, IN
University of Findlay, OH
University of Florida, FL
University of Georgia, GA
University of Guam, GU
University of Hartford, CT
University of Hawaii, HI (LAS)
University of Hawaii at Hilo, HI
University of Hawaii at Manoa, HI
University of Health Sciences, MO (OST)
University of Health Sciences, IL (GRD)
University of Houston, TX
University of Idaho, ID
University of Illinois, IL
University of Illinois, IL (MED)
University of Indianapolis, IN
University of Iowa, IA
University of Judaism/Lee College, CA
University of Kansas, KS
University of Kansas Medical Center, KS (MED)
University of Kentucky, KY
University of La Verne, CA
University of Louisville, KY
University of Maine, ME
University of Mary, ND
University of Mary Hardin-Baylor, TX
University of Maryland, MD
University of Massachusetts, MA
University of Massachusetts Medical S, MA (MED)
University of Medicine & Dentistry, NJ (MED)
University of Memphis, TN
University of Miami, FL
University of Miami, FL (OCN)
University of Michigan, MI
University of Minnesota, MN
University of Mississippi, MS
University of Mississippi Medical Center, MS (MED)
University of Missouri, MO
University of Mobile, AL
University of Montana, MT
University of Montevallo, AL
University of Nebraska, NE
University of Nebraska Medical Center, NE (MED)
University of Nevada, NV
University of New England, ME
University of New Hampshire, NH
University of New Haven, CT
University of New Mexico, NM
University of New Orleans, LA
University of North Alabama, AL
University of North Carolina, NC
University of North Dakota, ND
University of Northern Colorado, CO
University of Northern Iowa, IA
University of North Florida, FL
University of North Texas, TX
University of N Texas Health Science Ctr, TX (OST)
University of Notre Dame, IN
University of Oklahoma at Norman, OK
University of Oklahoma Health Sciences, OK (MED)
University of Oregon, OR
University of Osteopathic Medicine, IA (OST)
University of Pennsylvania, PA
University of Phoenix, AZ; CO; NM
University of Pittsburgh, PA
University of Portland, OR
University of Puerto Rico, PR
University of Puget Sound, WA
University of Puget Sound, WA (LAW)
University of Redlands, CA
University of Rhode Island, RI
University of Richmond, VA
University of Rio Grande, OH
University of Rochester, NY
University of Rochester Medical Center, NY (MED)
University of St. Mary of the Lake, IL (THL)
University of Saint Thomas, MN; TX
University of San Diego, CA
University of San Francisco, CA
University of Sarasota, FL
University of Sciences & Arts of OK, OK
University of Scranton, PA
University of South Alabama, AL

University of South Carolina, SC
University of South Dakota, SD
University of Southern California, CA (NRS)
University of Southern California, CA
University of Southern California, CA (MED)
University of Southern Colorado, CO
University of Southern Indiana, IN
University of Southern Maine, ME
University of Southern Mississippi, MS
University of South Florida, FL (OCN)
University of South Florida, FL
University of Southwestern Louisiana, LA
University of Tampa, FL
University of Tennessee, TN
University of Tennessee, TN (GRD)
University of Tennessee, TN (SCW)
University of Texas, TX
University of Texas Health Science Ctr., TX (MED)
University of Texas-Houston, TX (NRS)
University of Texas Medical Branch, TX (MED)
University of Texas of the Permian Basin, TX
University of Texas-Pan American, TX
University of Texas S.W. Medical Center, TX (MED)
University of the Arts, PA (ART)
University of the District of Columbia, DC
University of the Ozarks, AR
University of the Pacific, CA (LAW)
University of the Pacific, CA
University of the Sacred Heart, PR
University of the South, TN
University of the Virgin Islands, VI
University of Toledo, OH
University of Tulsa, OK
University of Utah, UT
University of Vermont, VT
University of Virginia, VA
University of Washington, WA
University of West Florida, FL
University of West Los Angeles, CA (LAW)
University of Wisconsin, WI
University of Wyoming, WY
Upper Iowa University, IA
Upsala College, NJ
Urbana University, OH
Ursinus College, PA
Ursuline College, OH (WMC)
Utah State University, UT
Utica College of Syracuse University, NY

V

Valdosta State College, GA
Valley City State University, ND
Valley Forge Christian College, PA (BBL)
Valparaiso University, IN
Vanderbilt University, TN
VanderCook College of Music, IL
Vassar College, NY
Vennard College, IA (BBL)
Vermont Law School, VT (LAW)
Villa Julie College, MD
Villanova University, PA
Virginia Commonwealth University, VA
Virginia Intermont College, VA
Virginia Military Institute, VA (MNC)
Virginia Polytechnic Institute & State U, VA
Virginia State University, VA
Virginia Union University, VA
Virginia Wesleyan College, VA
Viterbo College, WI
Voorhees College, SC

W

Wabash College, IN (LAS)
Wadhams Hall Seminary College, NY (MNC)
Wagner College, NY
Wake Forest University, NC
Wake Forest University, NC (MED)
Walden University, MN (GRD)
Walla Walla College, WA
Walla Walla School of Nursing, OR (NRS)
Walsh College, OH
Walsh Coll. Accountancy & Bus. Admin., MI (BUS)
Warner Pacific College, OR (LAS)
Warner Southern College, FL
Warren Wilson College, NC
Wartburg College, IA
Wartburg Theological Seminary, IA (THL)
Washburn University of Topeka, KS
Washington & Jefferson College, PA
Washington & Lee University, VA
Washington Bible College, MD (BBL)
Washington College, MD
Washington State University, WA
Washington Theological Union, MD (THL)
Washington University, MO
Washington University, MO (MED)
Wayland Baptist University, TX
Waynesburg College, PA
Wayne State College, NE
Wayne State University, MI
Webber College, FL (LAS)
Webb Institute of Naval Architecture, NY (EGN)
Weber State University, UT
Webster University, MO
Wellesley College, MA (WMC)
Wells College, NY (WMC)
Wentworth Institute of Technology, MA (EGN)
Wesleyan College, GA (WMC)

Wesleyan University, CT
Wesley Biblical Seminary, MS (THL)
Wesley College, DE
Wesley College, MS (BBL)
Wesley Theological Seminary, DC (THL)
Westbrook College, ME
West Chester University of Pennsylvania, PA
West Coast University, CA
Western Baptist College, OR
Western Carolina University, NC
Western Connecticut State University, CT
Western Conservative Baptist Seminary, OR (THL)
Western Evangelical Seminary, OR (THL)
Western Illinois University, IL
Western International University, AZ (BUS)
Western Kentucky University, KY
Western Maryland College, MD
Western Michigan University, MI
Western Montana College, MT
Western New England College, MA
Western New Mexico University, NM
Western Oregon State College, OR
Western State College of Colorado, CO
Western States Chiropractic College, OR (CPC)
Western State University College of Law, CA (LAW)
Western Theological Seminary, MI (THL)
Western Washington University, WA
Westfield State College, MA
West Georgia College, GA
West Liberty State College, WV
Westminster Choir College of Rider Univ., NJ (MUS)
Westminister College, MO
Westminister College, PA; UT
Westminister Theological Seminary, CA; PA (THL)
Westmont College, CA
Weston School of Theology, MA (THL)
West Suburban College of Nursing, IL (NRS)
West Texas State University, TX
West Virginia Graduate College, WV
West Virginia Institute of Technology, WV
West Virginia Sch./Osteopathic Medicine, WV (OST)
West Virginia State College, WV
West Virginia University, WV
West Virginia Wesleyan College, WV
Wheaton College, IL; MA
Wheeling Jesuit College, WV
Wheelock College, MA
Whitman College, WA
Whittier College, CA
Whittier College, CA (LAW)
Whitworth College, WA
Wichita State University, KS
Widener University, PA
Widener University School of Law, DE (LAW)
Wilberforce University, OH
Wiley College, TX
Wilkes University, PA
Willamette University, OR
William Carey College, LA; MS
William Jewell College, MO
William Mitchell College of Law, MN (LAW)
William Paterson College, NJ
William Penn College, IA
Williams Baptist College, AR
Williams College, MA
William Tyndale College, MI
William Woods College, MO (WMC)
Wilmington College, DE; OH
Wilson College, PA (WMC)
Winebrenner Theological Seminary, OH
Wingate College, NC
Winona State University, MN
Winston-Salem State University, NC
Winthrop University, SC
Wisconsin Lutheran College, WI (LAS)
Wisconsin School/Professional Psychology, WI (PSY)
Wittenberg University, OH
Wofford College, SC
Woodbury University, CA
Woods Hole Oceanographic Institution, MA (OCN)
Worcester Polytechnic Institute, MA
Worcester State College, MA
World College West, CA (LAS)
Wright Institute, CA (PSY)
Wright School of Architecture, AZ (ARC)
Wright State University, OH

X-Y-Z

Xavier University, LA; OH
Yale University, CT
Yale University, CT (MED)
Yeshiva and Kolel Bais Medrash Elyon, NY (RAB)
Yeshiva and Kollel Harbotzas Torah, NY (RAB)
Yeshiva and Mesivta Kol Torah, NY (RAB)
Yeshiva Beth Moshe, PA (RAB)
Yeshiva Beth Yehuda-Yeshiva Gedolah, MI (RAB)
Yeshiva Derech Chaim, NY (RAB)
Yeshiva Gedolah Bais Yisroel, NY (RAB)
Yeshiva Gedolah Imrei Yosef D'Spinka, NY (RAB)
Yeshiva Karlin Stolin, NY (RAB)
Yeshiva of Nitra, NY (RAB)
Yeshiva Shaar HaTorah Talmudic Research, NY (RAB)
Yeshivath Viznitz, NY (RAB)
Yeshivath Zichron Moshe, NY (RAB)
Yeshivat Mikdash Melech, NY (RAB)
Yeshiva Toras Chaim Talmudic Seminary, CO (RAB)
Yeshiva University, NY (LAW)
Yeshiva University, NY
York College, NE; PA
Youngstown State University, OH

COMMUNITY AND JUNIOR COLLEGES - INDEX

Schools alphabetized in this section can be found in the **Community and Junior Colleges** classification unless followed by a three letter code (WMC) identifying a different classification. The classifications represented by the three letter codes are shown on the first page of the index.

A

ABC Technical and Trade Schools, AZ
Abraham Baldwin Agriculture College, GA
ACA College of Design, OH
Academy of Accountancy, MN
Academy of Aviation, MN
Academy of Business College, AZ
Advertising Arts College, CA (ART)
Aiken Technical College, SC
Aims Community College, CO
Alabama Southern Community College, AL
Alamance Community College, NC
Alaska Junior College, AK
Albuquerque Technical-Vocational Inst, NM
Al Collins Graphic Design School, AZ (ART)
Alexandria Technical College, MN
Allan Hancock College, CA
Allegany Community College, MD
Allen County Community College, KS
Allstate Institute of Technology, MA
Alpena Community College, MI
Alvin Community College, TX
Amarillo College, TX
American Academy McAllister Institute, NY
American Academy of Art, IL
American Academy of Dramatic Arts, CA; NY
American Institute of Business, IA
American Institute of Commerce, IA
American River College, CA
American Samoa Community College, AS
American Technical College/Career Trng, CA
Ancilla Domini College, IN
Andover College, ME
Andrew College, GA
Angelina College, TX
Anne Arundel Community College, MD
Anoka-Ramsey Community College, MN
Anson Community College, NC
Antelope Valley College, CA
Antonelli Institute of Art & Photography, OH; PA
Apollo College, AZ
Aquinas College, MA
Aquinas Junior College, TN
Arapahoe Community College, CO
Arizona Western College, AZ
Arkansas State University, AR
Art Advertising Academy, OH
Art Center, NM (ART)
Art Institute of Atlanta, GA
Art Institute of Dallas, TX
Art Institute of Fort Lauderdale, FL (ART)
Art Institute of Houston, TX
Art Institute of Philadelphia, PA
Art Institute of Seattle, WA
Asheville Buncombe Technical Comm. Coll., NC
Ashland Community College, KY
Asnuntuck Community College, CT
Assumption College for Sisters, NJ
Athens Area Technical Institute, GA
ATI Career Training Center, FL
Atlanta Metro College, GA
Atlantic Community College, NJ
Augusta Technical Institute, GA
Austin Community College, MN; TX
Aviation Training Academy, MN

B

Bacone College, OK
Bainbridge College, GA
Bakersfield College, CA
Baltimore International Culinary College, MD
Barstow College, CA
Barton County Community College, KS
Basic Institute of Technology, MO
Baton Rouge School of Computers, LA
Bauder Fashion College, GA; TX
Bay de Noc Community College, MI
Bay Path College, MA (WMC)
Bay State College, MA
Beal College, ME
Beaufort County Community College, NC
Becker College, MA
Beckley College, WV
Bee County College, TX
Belleville Area College, IL
Bellevue Community College, WA
Belmont Technical College, OH
Bel-Rea Institute of Animal Technology, CO
Berean Institute, PA
Bergen Community College, NJ
Berkeley College, NY
Berkeley College of Business, NJ
Berkeley School, NY
Berkshire Community College, MA
Bethany Lutheran College, MN
Bevill State Community College, AL
Big Bend Community College, WA
Bishop State Community College, AL
Bismarck State College, ND
Blackfeet Community College, MT
Black Hawk College, IL
Blackhawk Technical College, WI

Bladen Community College, NC
Blair Junior College, CO
Blinn College, TX
Blue Mountain Community College, OR
Blue Ridge Community College, NC; VA
Bossier Parish Community College, LA
Bowling Green State University, OH
Bradford School, OH
Bradley Academy for the Visual Arts, PA
Brainerd Community College, MN
Brazosport College, TX
Brevard College, NC
Brevard Community College, FL
Brewer State Junior College, AL
Briarcliffe School, NY
Briarwood College, CT
Bristol Community College, MA
Brookdale Community College, NJ
Brookhaven College, TX
Brooks College, CA
Broward Community College, FL
Brown Mackie College, KS
Brunswick College, GA
Brunswick Community College, NC
Bryant & Stratton Business Institute, NY
Bucks County Community College, PA
Bunker Hill Community College, MA
Burlington County College, NJ
Business Careers Institute, PA
Butler County Community College, KS; PA
Butte College, CA

C

Cabrillo College, CA
Caldwell Community College, NC
California College for Health Sciences, CA (AHS)
California Culinary Academy, CA
Cambria-Rowe Business College, PA
Camden County College, NJ
Canada College, CA
Cape Cod Community College, MA
Cape Fear Community College, NC
Capital Community-Technical College, CT
Career City College, FL
Career College of Northern Nevada, NV
CareerCom Junior College of Business, KY
Carl Albert State College, OK
Carl Sandburg College, IL
Carroll Community College, MD
Carteret Community College, NC
Casco Bay College, ME
Casper College, WY
Castle College, NH
Catawba Valley Community College, NC
Catonsville Community College, MD
CDI Computers - Academy, MN
Cecil Community College, MD
Cecil's College, NC
Cedar Valley College, TX
Central Alabama Community College, AL
Central Arizona College, AZ
Central Carolina Community College, NC
Central Carolina Technical College, SC
Central City Business Institute, NY
Central Community College, NE
Central Florida Community College, FL
Centralia College, WA
Central Maine Medical Center, ME (AHS)
Central Maine Technical College, ME
Central Ohio Technical College, OH
Central Oregon Community College, OR
Central Pennsylvania Business School, PA
Central Piedmont Community College, NC
Central Texas College, TX
Central Virginia Community College, VA
Central Wyoming College, WY
Century Schools, CA
Cerritos College, CA
Cerro Coso Community College, CA
Certified Careers Institute, UT
Chabot College, CA
Chaffey College, CA
Charles County Community College, MD
Chatfield College, OH
Chattahoochee Technical Institute, GA
Chattahoochee Valley State Comm College, AL
Chattanooga State Tech. Comm. College, TN
Chemeketa Community College, OR
Chesapeake College, MD
Chesterfield-Marlboro Technical College, SC
Chicago City-Wide College, IL
Chicago College of Commerce, IL
CHI Institute, PA
Chipola Junior College, FL
Chippewa Valley Technical College, WI
Chowan College, NC
Chubb Institute-Keystone School, PA
Churchman Business School, PA
Cincinnati Technical College, OH
Cisco Junior College, TX
Citrus College, CA
City College of San Francisco, CA
Clackamas Community College, OR
Clarendon College, TX

Clarissa School of Fashion Design, PA
Clark College, WA
Clark State Community College, OH
Clatsop Community College, OR
Cleveland Community College, NC
Cleveland Institute of Electronics, OH
Cleveland State Community College, TN
Clinton Community College, IA
Cloud County Community College, KS
Clovis Community College, NM
Coahoma Community College, MS
Coastal Carolina Community College, NC
Coastline Community College, CA
Cochise College, AZ
Coffeyville Community College, KS
Colby Community College, KS
College of Alameda, CA
College of DuPage, IL
College of Eastern Utah, UT
College of Health Sciences, VA
College of Lake County, IL
College of Marin, CA
College of Merchandising Design, KY
College of Oceaneering, CA
College of San Mateo, CA
College of Southern Idaho, ID
College of the Albemarle, NC
College of the Canyons, CA
College of the Desert, CA
College of the Mainland, TX
College of the Redwoods, CA
College of the Sequoias, CA
College of the Siskiyous, CA
Collin County Community College, TX
Colorado Aero Tech, CO
Colorado Institute of Art, CO
Colorado Mountain College, CO
Colorado Northwestern Community College, CO
Colorado School of Trades, CO
Columbia Basin College, WA
Columbia College, CA; PR
Columbia College, CA (PHT)
Columbia Junior College of Business, SC
Columbia State Community College, OH; TN
Columbus Technical Institute, GA
Commonwealth College, VA
Commonwealth Institute / Funeral Service, TX
Community College of Allegheny County, PA
Community College of Aurora, CO
Community College of Baltimore, MD
Community College of Beaver County, PA
Community College of Denver, CO
Community College of Philadelphia, PA
Community College of Rhode Island, RI
Community College of Southern Nevada, NV
Community College of the Air Force, AL
Community College of Vermont, VT
Compton Community College, CA
Computer Systems Institute, PA
Concordia College, AL
Connors State College, OK
Contra Costa College, CA
Cooper Institute, TN
Copiah-Lincoln Community College, MS
Cosumnes River College, CA
Cottey College, MO
County College of Morris, NJ
Cowley County Community College, KS
Craft Institute, PA
Crafton Hills College, CA
Craven Community College, NC
Crowder College, MO
Crowley's Ridge College, AR
Cuesta College, CA
Culinary Institute of America, NY
Cumberland County College, NJ
Cumberland School of Technology, TN
CUNY-City University of New York, NY
Cuyahoga Community College, OH
Cuyamaca College, CA
Cypress College, CA

D-E

Dabney S. Lancaster Community College, VA
Dakota Co. Technical College, MN
Dalton College, GA
Danville Area Community College, IL
Danville Community College, VA
Darton College, GA
Davenport College of Business, IN
Davidson County Community College, NC
Davis Junior College, OH
Dawson Community College, MT
Daytona Beach Community College, FL
Dean College, MA
Dean Institute of Technology, PA
DeAnza College, CA
Deep Springs College, CA
DeKalb College, GA
DeKalb Technical Institute, GA
Delaware County Community College, PA
Delaware Technical & Community College, DE
Delgado Community College, LA
Del Mar College, TX

Delta College, MI
Delta Junior College, LA
Delta School of Business and Technology, LA
Denmark Technical College, SC
Denver Institute of Technology, CO
Denver Technical College, CO (BUS)
Des Moines Area Community College, IA
Diablo Valley College, CA
Dixie College, UT
Dodge City Community College, KS
Dona Ana Branch Community College, NM
Don Bosco Technical Institute, CA
Donnelly College, KS
D-Q University, CA
Draughons Junior College, AL; TN
Du Bois Business College, PA
Duffs Business Institute, PA
Dull Knife Memorial College, MT
Dundalk Community College, MD
Dunwoody Institute, MN
Durham Technical Community College, NC
Dyersburg State Community College, TN
East Arkansas Community College, AR
East Central College, MO
East Central Community College, MS
Eastern Arizona College, AZ
Eastern Maine Technical College, ME
Eastern New Mexico University, NM
Eastern Oklahoma State College, OK
Eastern Shore Community College, VA
Eastern Wyoming College, WY
Eastfield College, TX
East Georgia College, GA
East Los Angeles College, CA
East Mississippi Community College, MS
Edgecombe Community College, NC
Edison Community College, FL
Edison State Community College, OH
Edmonds Community College, WA
Education Dynamics Institute, NV
El Camino College, CA; TX
Electronic Computer Programming Inst., TN
Electronic Institutes, MO; PA
Elgin Community College, IL
Elizabethtown Community College, KY
Ellsworth Community College, IA
El Paso Community College, TX
El Reno Junior College, OK
Emery Aviation College, CO
Endicott College, MA
Enterprise State Junior College, AL
Erie Business Center, PA (BUS)
Erie Institute of Technology, PA
Essex Community College, MD
Essex County College, NJ
ETI Technical College, OH
Everett Community College, WA
Evergreen Valley College, CA

F

Fairleigh Dickinson University, NJ
Fashion Inst. of Design & Merchandising, CA
Fayetteville Technical Community College, NC
Feather River Community College, CA
Fergus Falls Community College, MN
Fisher College, MA
Five Towns College, NY
Flagler Career Institute, FL
Flathead Valley Community College, MT
Florence Darlington Technical College, SC
Florida College, FL
Florida Community College, FL
Florida Keys Community College, FL
Florida National College, FL
Floyd College, GA
Foothill College, CA
Ford Community College, MI
Forsyth Technical Community College, NC
Fort Belknap College, MT
Fort Bethold Community College, ND
Fort Peck Community College, MT
Fort Scott Community College, KS
Fox Valley Technical College, WI
Franklin Institute of Boston, MA
Frank Phillips College, TX
Frederick Community College, MD
Fresno City College, CA
Frontier Community College, IL
Front Range Community College, CO
Fugazzi College, KY
Fuld School of Nursing Joint Diseases, NY
Fullerton College, CA
Full Sail Center for the Recording Arts, FL

G

Gadsden State Community College, AL
Gainesville College, GA
Galveston College, TX
Garden City Community College, KS
Garland Co. Community College, AR
Garrett Community College, MD
Gaston College, NC
Gateway Community College, AZ
Gateway Electronics Institute, NE
Gateway Technical College, WI
Gavilan Community College, CA
Gem City College, IL
Georgia Military College, GA
Germanna Community College, VA
Glendale Community College, AZ; CA
Glen Oaks Community College, MI

Gloucester County College, NJ
Gogebic Community College, MI
Golden West College, CA
Gordon College, GA
Grand Rapids Community College, MI
Grays Harbor College, WA
Grayson County College, TX
Greater Hartford Community College, CT
Greater New Haven State Tech. College, CT
Great Falls Vocational Technical Center, MT
Great Lakes Junior College of Business, MI
Greenfield Community College, MA
Green River Community Colleges, WA
Greenville Technical College, SC
Grossmont College, CA
Guam Community College, GU
Guilford Technical Community College, NC
Gulf Coast Community College, FL
Gupton-Jones College of Funeral Service, GA
Gwinnett Technical Institute, GA

H

Hagerstown Business College, MD
Hagerstown Junior College, MD
Halifax Community College, NC
Hallmark Institute of Technology, TX
Hamilton Technical College, IA
Harcum Junior College, PA
Harford Community College, MD
Harold Washington College, IL
Harrisburg Area Community College, PA
Harry S. Truman College, IL
Hartford College for Women, CT
Hartnell College, CA
Haskell Indian Junior College, KS
Hawaii Community College, HI
Hawkeye Community College, IA
Haywood Community College, NC
Hazard Community College, KY
Heald Business College, CA; HI
Heald 4 C's College, CA
Heald Institute of Technology, CA
Helena College of Tech of the Univ of MT, MT
Henderson Community College, KY
Hesser College, NH
Hesston College, KS
Hibbing Community College, MN
Hickox School, MA
Highland Community College, IL; KS
Highland Park Community College, MI
Highline Community College, WA
High-Tech Institute, AZ
Hilbert College, NY
Hill College, TX
Hillsborough Community College, FL
Hinds Community College, MS
Hiram G. Andrews Center, PA
Hiwassee College, TN
Hocking College, OH
Holmes Community College, MS
Holy Cross College, IN
Holyoke Community College, MA
Honolulu Community College, HI
Hopkinsville Community College, KY
Horry-Georgetown Technical College, SC
Housatonic Community College, CT
Houston Community College, TX
Howard College, TX
Howard Community College, MD
Hudson County Community College, NJ
Huertas Junior College, PR
Huntington Junior College of Business, WV
Hussian School of Art, PA
Hutchinson Community College, KS

I

ICM School of Business, PA
Illinois Central College, IL
Illinois Valley Community College, IL
Imperial Valley College, CA
Independence Community College, KS
Indiana Vocational Technical College, IN
Indian Hills Community College, IA
Indian River Community College, FL
Information Computer Systems Institute, PA
Institute of American Indian Arts, NM
Institute of Computer Technology, CA
Institute of Electronic Technology, KY
Instituto Comercial de Puerto Rico, PR
Inter American University of Puerto Rico, PR
Interboro Institute, NY
Interior Designers Institute, CA (INT)
International Academy Merch. & Design, FL; IL
International Business College, IN
International Fine Arts College, FL
International Technical Institute, LA
Inver Hills Community College, MN
Iowa Central Community College, IA
Iowa Lakes Community College, IA
Iowa Western Community College, IA
Irvine Valley College, CA
Isothermal Community College, NC
Itasca Community College, MN
Itawamba Community College, MS
ITT Technical Institute, AZ; CA; CO; FL; ID; IL; IN; MI;
    MO; NE; NM; OH; TN; TX; UT; VA; WA; WI
IVY-Indiana Vocational Technical College, IN

J

Jackson Community College, MI
Jackson State Community College, TN
Jacksonville College, TX
James H Faulkner State Junior College, AL
James Sprunt Community College, NC
Jamestown Business College, NY
Jefferson College, MO
Jefferson Community College, KY
Jefferson Davis State Junior College, AL
Jefferson State Community College, AL
Jefferson Technical College, OH
John A. Gupton College, TN
John A. Logan College, IL
John C. Calhoun State Community College, AL
Johnson & Wales University, CO; FL; SC; VA
Johnson County Community College, KS
Johnson Technical Institute, PA
Johnston Community College, NC
John Tyler Community College, VA
John Wood Community College, IL
Joliet Junior College, IL
Jones County Junior College, MS
J. Sargeant Reynolds Community College, VA

K

Kalamazoo Valley Community College, MI
Kankakee Community College, IL
Kansai Gaidai Hawaii College, HI
Kansas City Kansas Community College, KS
Kansas State University College of Tech, KS
Kapiolani Community College, HI
Kaskaskia College, IL
Katharine Gibbs School, CT; MA; NJ; NY
Kauai Community College, HI
Keiser College of Technology, FL
Kellogg Community College, MI
Kelsey-Jenney College, CA (BUS)
Kemper Military School & College, MO
Kenai Peninsula Community College, AK
Kennebec Valley Technical College, ME
Kennedy-King College, IL
Kent State University, OH
Kentucky College of Business, KY
Kentucky Mountain Bible College, KY
Kettering College of Medical Arts, OH
Keystone Junior College, PA
Kilgore College, TX
Kilian Community College, SD
King's College, NC
Kings River Community College, CA
Kirkwood Community College, IA
Kirtland Community College, MI
Kishwaukee College, IL
Knoxville Business College, TN
Kodiak Community College, AK
Kuskokwim Community College, AK

L

Labette Community College, KS
Laboure College, MA
Lac Courte Oreilles Ojibwa Comm College, WI
Lackawanna Junior College, PA
Lake City Community College, FL
Lake Land College, IL
Lakeland Community College, OH
Lake Michigan College, MI
Lakeshore Technical College, WI
Lake-Sumter Community College, FL
Lake Tahoe Community College, CA
Lakewood Community College, MN
Lamar Community College, CO
Lamar University, TX
Lamson Junior College, AZ
Landmark College, VT
Lane Community College, OR
Laney College, CA
Lansing Community College, MI
Laramie County Community College, WY
Laredo Junior College, TX
Lasell College, MA
Lassen College, CA
Lawson State Community College, AL
L.D.S. Business College, UT
Lebanon College, NH
Lee College, TX
Lees College, KY
Leeward Community College, HI
Lehigh County Community College, PA
Lenoir Community College, NC
Lewis & Clark Community College, IL
Lewis College of Business, MI
Lexington Community College, KY
Lexington Inst. of Hostpitality Careers, IL
Lima Technical College, OH
Lincoln College, IL
Lincoln Land Community College, IL
Lincoln School of Commerce, NE
Lincoln Technical Institute, IN; PA
Lincoln Trail College, IL
Linn-Benton Community College, OR
Little Big Horn College, MT
Little Hoop Community College, ND
Lock Haven University-Clearfield Campus, PA
Long Beach City College, CA
Longview Community College, MO
Lon Morris College, TX
Lorain County Community College, OH
Lord Fairfax Community College, VA

Los Angeles Business College, CA
Los Angeles City College, CA
Los Angeles Harbor College, CA
Los Angeles Mission College, CA
Los Angeles Pierce College, CA
Los Angeles Southwest College, CA
Los Angeles Trade-Technical College, CA
Los Angeles Valley College, CA
Los Medanos College, CA
Louisburg College, NC
Louise Salinger Academy of Fashion, CA (FSA)
Louisiana State University at Alexandria, LA
Louisiana State University at Eunice, LA
Louisville Technical Institute, KY
Lower Columbia College, WA
Luna Vocational Technical Institute, NM
Lurleen B Wallace Junior College, AL
Luzerne Co. Community College, PA

M

McCann School of Business, PA (BUS)
McCarrie School Health Sciences & Tech., PA
McCook Community College, NE
MacCormac Junior College, IL
McDowell Technical Community College, NC
McHenry County College, IL
McIntosh College, NH
McLennan Community College, TX
Macomb Community College, MI
Macon College, GA
Madison Area Technical College, WI
Madison Junior College of Business, WI
Madisonville Community College, KY
Malcolm X College, IL
Manatee Community College, FL
Manchester Community College, CT
Manor Junior College, PA
Maple Woods Community College, MO
Maria College of Albany, NY
Marian Court College, MA
Marion Military Institute, AL
Marion Technical College, OH
Marshalltown Community College, IA
Marti College of Fashion, OH
Martin College, FL
Martin Community College, NC
Martin Methodist College, TN
Mary Holmes College, MS
Maryland College of Art & Design, MD
Marymount College, CA
Massachusetts Bay Community College, MA
Massasoit Community College, MA
Massey Business College, GA
Masters Institute, CA
Mater Dei College, NY
Mattatuck Community College, CT
Maui Community College, HI
Mayland Community College, NC
Maysville Community College, KY
Meadows College of Business, GA
Median School of Allied Health Careers, PA
Mendocino College, CA
Merced College, CA
Mercer County Community College, NJ
Meridian Community College, MS
Merritt College, CA
Mesabi Community College, MN
Mesa Community College, AZ
Metropolitan College of Court Reporting, AZ
Metropolitan Community College, NE
Miami-Dade Community College, FL
Miami-Jacobs Junior College of Business, OH
Miami University-Hamilton Campus, OH
Miami University-Middletown Campus, OH
Michiana College, IN
Microcomputer Technology Institute, TX
Mid-America College of Funeral Service, IN
Middle Georgia College, GA
Middlesex Community College, CT; MA
Middlesex County College, NJ
Midland College, TX
Midlands Technical College, SC
Mid-Michigan Community College, MI
Mid-Plains Community College, NE
Mid-State College, ME
Midstate College, IL
Mid-State Technical College, WI
Miles Community College, MT
Milwaukee Area Technical College, WI
Mineral Area College, MO
Minneapolis Community College, MN
Mira Costa College, CA
Mission College, CA
Mississippi County Community College, AR
Mississippi Delta Community College, MS
Mississippi Gulf Coast Community College, MS
Missoula Vocational Technical Center, MT
Missouri School for Doctors' Assistants, MO
Missouri Technical School, MO
Miss Wade's Fashion Merchandising Coll., TX
Mitchell College, CT
Mitchell Community College, NC
Moberly Area Community College, MO
Modesto Junior College, CA
Mohave Community College, AZ
Mohegan Community College, CT
Monroe County Community College, MI
Monroeville School of Business, PA
Montay College, IL
Montcalm Community College, MI
Monterey Peninsula College, CA
Montgomery College, MD
Montgomery Community College, NC
Montgomery County Community College, PA

Moorpark College, CA
Moraine Park Technical College, WI
Moraine Valley Community College, IL
Morgan Community College, CO
Morrison Institute of Technology, IL
Morristown College, TN
Morton College, IL
Motlow State Community College, TN
Mott Community College, MI
Mountain Empire Community College, VA
Mountain View College, TX
Mt. Hood Community College, OR
Mt. Sacred Heart College, CT
Mt. San Antonio College, CA
Mt. San Jacinto College, CA
Mt. Wachusett Community College, MA
Murray State College, OK
Muscatine Community College, IA
Muskegon Community College, MI
Muskingum Area Technical College, OH

N

Napa Valley College, CA
Nash Community College, NC
Nashville Auto-Diesel College, TN
Nashville State Technical Institute, TN
National Business College, VA
National Hispanic University, CA
Navajo Community College, AZ
Navarro College, TX
Nebraska College of Business, NE
Nebraska Indian Community College, NE
NEC-National Education Centers, AZ; AR; FL; IA; KY;
  MN; OK; PA; TX; WV
NEI College of Technology, MN
Neilsen Electronics Institute, SC
Neosho County Community College, KS
Nettleton Junior College, SD
Newbury College, MA
New Castle School of Trades, PA
New England Banking Institute, MA
New England Institute of Technology, FL; RI
New Hampshire Technical College, NH
New Hampshire Technical Institute, NH
New Kensington Commercial School, PA
New Mexico Junior College, NM
New Mexico Military Institute, NM
New Mexico State University, NM
New River Community College, VA
New School of Architecture, CA (ARC)
Nicolet Area Technical College, WI
Normandale Community College, MN
Northampton Co. Area Community College, PA
North Arkansas Community College, AR
North Central Michigan College, MI
North Central Missouri College, MO
North Central Technical College, OH; WI
North Central Texas College, TX
North Dakota State College of Science, ND
North Dakota State University-Bottineau, ND
Northeast Alabama State Junior College, AL
Northeast Community College, NE
Northeastern Christian Junior College, PA
Northeastern Junior College, CO
Northeastern Oklahoma A&M College, OK
Northeast Iowa Technical Institute, IA
Northeast Mississippi Community College, MS
Northeast State Tech Community College, TN
Northeast Texas Community College, TX
Northeast Wisconsin Technical College, WI
Northern Essex Community College, MA
Northern Maine Technical College, ME
Northern Nevada Community College, NV
Northern New Mexico Community College, NM
Northern Oklahoma College, OK
Northern Virginia Community College, VA
Northern Wyoming Community College, WY
North Florida Junior College, FL
North Harris County College, TX
North Hennepin Community College, MN
North Idaho College, ID
North Iowa Area Community College, IA
North Lake College, TX
Northland Community College, MN
Northland Pioneer College, AZ
North Seattle Community College, WA
North Shore Community College, MA
Northwest Alabama Community College, AL
Northwest College, WY
Northwest Community College, AK
Northwestern Business College, IL
Northwestern College, OH
Northwestern Connecticut Comm. College, CT
Northwestern Michigan College, MI
Northwest Indian College, WA
Northwest Iowa Community College, IA
Northwest Mississippi Community College, MS
Northwest Missouri Community College, MO
Northwest State Community College, OH
Northwest Technical Institute, MN
Norwalk Community College, CT
Norwalk State Technical College, CT
Nossi College of Art, TN
Nunez Community College, LA

O

Oakland Community College, MI
Oakton Community College, IL
Ocean County College, NJ
Odessa College, TX
Oglala Lakota Community College, SD

Ohio Institute of Photography & Tech, OH
Ohio State University-A & T Institute, OH
Ohlone College, CA
Okaloosa-Walton Community College, FL
Oklahoma City Community College, OK
Oklahoma Junior College, OK
Oklahoma State University, OK
Olean Business Institute, NY
Olive-Harvey College, IL
Olney Central College, IL
Olympic College, WA
Omaha College of Health Careers, NE (AHS)
Orangeburg-Calhoun Technical College, SC
Orange Coast College, CA
Oregon Denturist College, OR
Oregon Polytechnic Institute, OR
Otero Junior College, CO
Owensboro Community College, KY
Owensboro Junior College of Business, KY
Owens Community College, OH
Oxford College of Emory University, GA
Oxnard College, CA

P

Paducah Community College, KY
Palm Beach Community College, FL
Palo Alto College, TX
Palomar Community College, CA
Palo Verde College, CA
Pamlico Community College, NC
Panola College, TX
Paradise Valley Community College, AZ
Paris Junior College, TX
Parkland College, IL
Parks College, AZ; CO; NM
Pasadena City College, CA
Pasco-Hernando Community College, FL
Passaic Co. Community College, NJ
Patrick Henry Community College, VA
Paul D. Camp Community College, VA
Paul Smith's College, NY
Peace College, NC
Pearl River Community College, MS
Peirce Junior College, PA
Pellissippi State Technical Comm. Coll., TN
Peninsula College, WA
Penn Commercial College, PA
Pennco Tech, PA
Pennsylvania College of Technology, PA
Pennsylvania Institute of Culinary Arts, PA
Pennsylvania Institute of Technology, PA
Pennsylvania State University, PA
Penn Technical Institute, PA
Penn Valley Community College, MO
Pensacola Junior College, FL
Phillips County Community College, AR
Phillips Junior College, AL; CA; FL; GA; LA; MS; MO;
  NV; UT; WA
Phoenix College, AZ
Phoenix College of Aeronautics, FL
Piedmont Community College, NC
Piedmont Technical College, SC
Piedmont Virginia Community College, VA
Pierce College, WA
Pikes Peak Community College, CO
Pima Community College, AZ
Pitt Community College, NC
Pittsburgh Institute of Aeronautics, PA
Pittsburgh Technical Institute, PA
Platt College, CO
Plaza Business Institute, NY
Polk Community College, FL
Porterville College, CA
Portland Community College, OR
Potomac State College of West Virginia U, WV
Prairie State College, IL
Pratt Community College, KS
Prestonburg Community College, KY
Prince George's Community College, MD
Prince William Sound Community College, AK
Pueblo Community College, CO
Puerto Rico Junior College, PR
Puerto Rico Technical Jr College, PR

Q-R

Queen of the Holy Rosary, CA
Quincy Junior College, MA
Quinebaug Valley Community College, CT
Quinsigamond Community College, MA
Rainy River Community College, MN
Ramirez College of Business Technology, PR
Rancho Santiago College, CA
Randolph Community College, NC
Ranger Junior College, TX
Ranken Technical College, MO
Rappahannock Community College, VA
Raritan Valley Community College, NJ
Ray College of Design, IL
Reading Area Community College, PA
Red Rocks Community College, CO
Reinhardt College, GA
Rend Lake College, IL
Resource Center for the Handicapped, WA
Restaurant School, PA
RETS Education Center, KY; LA; MD; OH; PA
Richard Bland College, VA
Richard J. Daley College, IL
Richland College, TX
Richland Community College, IL; NC
Rich Mountain Community College, AR
Ricks College, ID

Rio Hondo College, CA
Rio Salado Community College, AZ
Riverside City College, CA
Roane State Community College, TN
Roanoke-Chowan Community College, NC
Robert Morris College, IL
Robeson Community College, NC
Rochester Business Institute, NY
Rochester Community College, MN
Rochester Institute of Technology (NTID), NY
Rockingham Community College, NC
Rock Valley College, IL
Rogers State College, OK
Rogue Community College, OR
Rose State College, OK
Rowan-Cabarrus Community College, NC
Roxbury Community College, MA
Russell Sage Junior College of Albany, NY

S

Sacramento City College, CA
Saddleback College, CA
St. Augustine College, IL
St. Bernard Parish Community College, LA
St. Catharine College, KY
St. Charles County Community College, MO
St. Clair County Community College, MI
St. Cloud Technical College, MN
St. Gregory's College, OK
St. Johns River Community College, FL
St. Louis Community College, MO
St. Mary's Campus Coll. of St. Catherine, MN
St. Mary's College, NC
St. Paul Technical College, MN
St. Petersburg Junior College, FL
St. Phillip's College, TX
Salem College-Clarksburg, WV
Salem Community College, NJ
Salish Kootenai College, MT
Salt Lake Community College, UT
Sampson Community College, NC
San Antonio College, TX
San Bernardino Valley College, CA
Sandhills Community College, NC
San Diego City College, CA
San Diego Mesa College, CA
San Diego Miramar College, CA
San Francisco Coll. of Mortuary Science, CA
San Jacinto College, TX
San Joaquin Delta College, CA
San Joaquin Valley College, CA
San Jose City College, CA
San Juan College, NM
Santa Barbara City College, CA
Santa Fe Community College, FL; NM
Santa Monica College, CA
Santa Rosa Junior College, CA
Sauk Valley Community College, IL
Savannah Technical Institute, GA
Sawyer College of Business, OH
Schoolcraft College, MI
Scott Community College, IA
Scottsdale Community College, AZ
Seattle Central Community College, WA
Seminole Community College, FL
Seminole Junior College, OK
Seward County Community College, KS
Shasta College, CA
Shawnee Community College, IL
Shelby State Community College, TN
Shelton State Community College, AL
Sheridan College, WY
Shoals Community College, AL
Shoreline Community College, WA
Shorter College, AR
Sierra College, CA
Sinclair Community College, OH
Sisseton Wahpeton Community College, SD
Skagit Valley College, WA
Skyline College, CA
Snead State Junior College, AL
Snow College, UT
Solano Community College, CA
Somerset Community College, KY
South Central Community College, CT
South College, FL; GA
Southeast College of Technology, TN
Southeast Community College, KY; NE
Southeastern Community College, IA; NC
Southeastern Illinois College, IL
Southern Arkansas University, AR
Southern College, FL
Southern Maine Technical College, ME
Southern Ohio College, KY; OH
Southern State Community College, OH
Southern Union State Junior College, AL
Southern University, LA
Southern Virginia College for Women, VA
Southern West Virginia Community College, WV

South Florida Community College, FL
South Georgia College, GA
South Mountain Community College, AZ
South Plains College, TX
South Puget Sound Community College, WA
South Seattle Community College, WA
Southside Virginia Community College, VA
South Suburban College of Cook County, IL
Southwestern College, CA
Southwestern College of Business, OH
Southwestern Community College, IA; NC
Southwestern Michigan College, MI
Southwestern Oklahoma State University, OK
Southwestern Oregon Community College, OR
Southwest Inst. Merchandising & Design, TX
Southwest Mississippi Community College, MS
Southwest Texas Junior College, TX
Southwest Virginia Community College, VA
Southwest Wisconsin Technical College, WI
Spartanburg Methodist College, SC
Spartanburg Technical College, SC
Spokane Community College, WA
Spokane Falls Community College, WA
Spoon River College, IL
Springfield College in Illinois, IL
Springfield Technical Community College, MA
Standing Rock College, ND
Stanly Community College, NC
Stark Technical College, OH
State Community College East St. Louis, IL
State Fair Community College, MO
State Technical Institute, TN
Sterling College, VT
Stevens Henager College, UT
Stone Child College, MT
Stratton College, WI
Sue Bennett College, KY
Sullivan College, KY
SUNY-State University of New York, NY
Suomi College, MI
Surry Community College, NC
Sussex County Community College, NJ

T

Tacoma Community College, WA
Taft College, CA
Tallahassee Community College, FL
Tarrant County Junior College, TX
Taylor Business Institute, NY
Technical Careers Institutes, NY
Technical College of the Lowcountry, SC
Technical Trades Institute, CO
Technological College of San Juan, PR
Technology Education College, OH
Temple Junior College, TX
Tennessee Institute of Electronics, TN
Terra Community College, OH
Texarkana Community College, TX
Texas Southmost College, TX
Texas State Technical College, TX
Texas State Technical Institute, TX
Thaddeus Stevens State School of Tech, PA
Thames Valley State Technical College, CT
Thomas Nelson Community College, VA
Three Rivers Community College, MO
Tidewater Community College, VA
Tobe-Coburn School for Fashion Careers, NY
Treasure Valley Community College, OR
Triangle Tech, PA
Tri-County Community College, NC
Tri-County Tech College, SC
Trident Technical College, SC
Trinidad State Junior College, CO
Trinity Valley Community College, TX
Triton College, IL
Trocaire College, NY
Truckee Meadows Community College, NV
Truett McConnell College, GA
Tulsa Junior College, OK
Tunxis Community College, CT
Turtle Mountain Community College, ND
Tyler Junior College, TX

U-V

Umpqua Comunity College, OR
Union County College, NJ
United Tribes Technical College, ND
Universal Technical Institute, AZ; TX
University of Akron-Wayne College, OH
University of Alaska SE - Sitka Campus, AK
University of Alaska Southeast-Ketchikan, AK
University of Cincinnati, OH
University of Connecticut, CT
University of New Mexico, NM
University of North Dakota, ND
University of Puerto Rico, PR
University of South Carolina, SC

University of Wisconsin Center, WI
Utah Valley Community College, UT
Utica School of Commerce, NY

V

Valencia Community College, FL
Valley Forge Military Academy & College, PA
Vance-Granville Community College, NC
Van Dyck Institute of Tourism, FL
Vatterott College, MO
Ventura College, CA
Vermilion Community College, MN
Vermont Technical College, VT
Vernon Regional Junior College, TX
Victoria College, TX
Victor Valley College, CA
Villa Maria College of Buffalo, NY
Vincennes University, IN
Virginia College, VA
Virginia Highlands Community College, VA
Virginia Western Community College, VA
Vista Community College, CA
Volunteer State Community College, TN

W-X-Y-Z

Wabash Valley College, IL
Wake Technical Community College, NC
Waldorf College, IA
Walker College, AL
Wallace College, AL
Walla Walla Community College, WA
Walters State Community College, TN
Warren County Community College, NJ
Washington Community College, OH
Washtenaw Community College, MI
Waterbury State Technical College, CT
Watkins Institute-School Interior Design, TN
Waubonsee Community College, IL
Waukesha County Technical College, WI
Waycross College, GA
Wayne Community College, NC
Wayne County Community College, MI
Weatherford College, TX
Webster College, FL; WV
Welder Training & Testing Institute, PA
Welder Training Institute, PA
Wenatchee Valley College, WA
Wentworth Military Academy, MO
Westark Community College, AR
Westchester Business Institute, NY
West Coast Christian College, CA
Western Iowa Technical Community College, IA
Western Nebraska Community College, NE
Western Nebraska Community College, NE (BUS)
Western Nevada Community College, NV
Western Oklahoma State College, OK
Western Piedmont Community College, NC
Western Technical Institute, TX
Western Texas College, TX
Western Wyoming Community College, WY
West Hills College, CA
West Los Angeles College, CA
Westmoreland County Community College, PA
West Shore Community College, MI
West Side Institute of Technology, OH
West Valley College, CA
West Virginia Career College, FL; WV
West Virginia Northern Community College, WV
West Virginia University at Parkersburg, WV
Wharton County Junior College, TX
Whatcom Community College, WA
White Pines College, NH
Wilbur Wright College North, IL
Wilkes Community College, NC
William Rainey Harper College, IL
Williamsburg Technical College, SC
Williamsport School of Commerce, PA
Willmar Community College, MN
Willmar Technical Institute, MN
Wilson Technical Community College, NC
Windward Community College, HI
Wisconsin Indianhead Technical College, WI
Wisconsin School of Electronics, WI
Wood College, MS
Wood School, NY
Worthington Community College, MN
Wor-Wic Technical Community College, MD
Wright Business School, MO
Wright State University, OH
Wyoming Technical Institute, WY
Wytheville Community College, VA
Yakima Valley Community College, WA
Yavapai College, AZ
York Technical College, SC
Young Harris College, GA
Yuba College, CA

CAREER SCHOOLS - INDEX

Schools alphabetized in this section can be found in the **Career Schools** classification unless followed by a three letter code (HMS) identifying a different classification. The classifications represented by the three letter codes are shown on the first page of the index.

A

Aaker's Business College, ND
Abbie Business Institute, MD
Academia Singer Dealer Autorizado, PR
Academy for Career Education, NY
Academy of Court Reporting, MI; OH
Academy of Floral Design, CO
Academy of Health Careers, MI
Academy of Medical Arts and Business, PA
Academy of Professional Development, NJ
Academy Pacific Business/Travel College, CA
Acadian Technical Institute, LA
Acme Institute of Technology, WI
Advance Career Training, TX
Advanced Software Analysis, NY
Advance School of Driving, CA
Aero Mechanics School, MO
Aero Technicians, ID
Airman Proficiency Center, OR
Air Tech, ME
Akron Machining Institute, OH
Akron Medical-Dental Institute, OH
Alabama Aviation & Technical College, AL
Albany School of Cytotechnology, NY
Albany Technical Institute, GA
Alexandria Regional Technical Institute, LA
Alfred G. Glassell School of Art, TX (ART)
Allegheny Business Institute, PA
Allen School for Physicians Aides, NY
Alliance Tractor Trailer Training Center, GA (HMS)
Alliance Tractor Trailer Training Center, NC; TN; VA
Allied Health Careers, TX
Allied Medical Careers, PA
Allied Schools of Puerto Rico, PR
All-State Career School, MD; PA
Allstate Tractor Trailer Training School, CT
AL-MED Academy, MO
Altoona School of Commerce, PA
Amarillo Affiliated School/Medical Tech., TX (AHS)
American Academy for Career Education, NV
American Business Academy, NJ
American Business and Fashion Institute, NC
American Business Institute, NY
American Career College, CA
American College of Technology, IL
American Commercial College, TX
American Diesel & Automotive College, CO
American Educational College, PR
American Education Centers, MI
American Floral Art School, IL
American Flyers College, FL
American Institute, AZ
American Institute of Baking, KS
American Institute of Commerce, IA; TX
American Institute of Design, PA
American Institute of Health Technology, ID
American Inst. of Medical-Dental Tech., UT
American Institute of Technology, AZ
American Medical Training Institute, FL
American Nanny College, CA
American School of Business, LA
American School of Technology, OH
American Technical Center, AZ; UT
American Teller Schools, AZ
American Trades Institute, TX
Ameritech Colleges, CA
AMR Combs Flight Training Academy, MI
Amtech Institute, KS
Andon College at Modesto, CA
Andon College at Stockton, CA
Anoka Technical Institute, MN
Antilles School of Technical Careers, PR
Antonelli Medical & Professional Inst, PA
Apex Technical School, NY
Apollo College, AZ
Apollo Coll. of Medical & Dental Careers, OR
Apprentice Sch. - Newport News Shipbldg., VA
Ardis School of Fashion Design, DC
Aris Helicopters, CA (AAT)
Aristotle College/Medical & Dental Tech., IN (AHS)
Aristotle College/Medical & Dental Tech., IN
Aristotle Institute Medical Dental Tech., OH
Arizona Academy of Medical/Dental Asst., AZ
Arizona Academy of Medical/Dental Asst., AZ (AHS)
Arizona Inst. of Business & Technology, AZ
Arkansas Valley Voc. Tech. School, AR
Arlington Court Reporting College, TX
Art Institute of Pittsburgh, PA
Arts and Business College of Puerto Rico, PR
Arundel Institute of Technology, MD
Ascension Technical Institute, LA
Asher School of Business, GA
Associated Technical College, CA
Associated Technical Institute, MA
ATI Career Institute, VA
ATI Career Training Center, FL; TX
ATI Graphic Arts Institute, TX
ATI Health Education Center, FL; TX
Atlanta Area Technical Institute, GA
Atlanta College-Medical/Dental Careers, GA
Atlanta Job Corps Center, GA
Atlantic Coast Institute, FL
Atlantic College, PR
Atlantic Vocational-Technical Center, FL

Atmore State Technical College, AL
Aurora Health Care, WI (AHS)
Automation Academy, DC
Automotive Technical Institute, IL
Automotive Training Center, PA
Automotive Transmission School, FL
Avalon Vocational Technical Institute, TX
Aviation Career Academy, NJ
Aviation Education Center, KS (AAT)
Avoyelles Technical Institute, LA
Ayers Institute, LA
Ayers State Technical College, AL
AzTech College, AZ; NM

B

Baker Aviation School, FL
Baran Institute of Technology, CT
Barclay Career School, DC
Barnes Business College, CO
Bastrop Technical Institute, LA
Bates Technical College, WA
Batesville Job Corps Center, MS
Baton Rouge Technical Institute, LA
Bayamon Technical & Commercial Institute, PR
Bay Area Legal Academy, FL
Bay Area Vocational-Technical School, FL
Bayou Technical Institute, LA
Bay State School of Appliances, MA
Beacon Career Institute, FL
Bellingham Vocational Technical School, WA
Benedict School of Languages & Commerce, PR
Ben Hill Irwin Area Voc. Tech. Institute, GA
Berdan Institute, NJ
Berks Technical Institute, PA
Berk Trade School, NY
Bessemer State Technical College, AL
Bidwell Training Center, PA
Bilingual Institute, NJ
Billings Business College, MT
Billings Vocational Technical Center, MT
Bish Mathis Institute, TX
Bishop State Community College, AL
Black Forest Hall, MI
Black River Vocational Technical School, AR
Blake Business School, NY
Boardwalk & Marina Casino Dealers School, NJ
Bohecker's Business College, OH
Boone County Career Center, WV
Boulder Valley Area Voc. Tech. Center, CO
Boyd Career School, FL; PA
Bradford School, PA; TX
Branell Institute, FL; GA; TN
Branford Hall Career Institute, CT
Braxton School, VA
Brewster Vocational-Technical Center, FL
Brick Computer Science Institute, NJ
Broadcasting Institute of Maryland, MD
Broadcast Professionals, OR
Brookstone College of Business, NC
Brown Coll. of Court Reporting & Bus., GA
Brown's Business College, IL
Bryan College of Court Reporting, CA
Bryan Institute, KS; MO; OK; TX
Bryant & Stratton Business Institute, OH
Bryan Travel College, KS; MO
Bryman School, AZ; UT
Burdett School, MA
Business Informatics Center, NY
Business Skills Training Center, TX
Business Training Institute, FL; NJ
Butera School of Art, MA
Butler Business School, CT
Butte Vocational-Technical Center, MT

C

Cabot College, CA
CAD Institute/The CAD Center, AZ
CA Academy of Merchandising Art & Design, CA
California Career Schools, CA
California Institute, CA
California Institute of Locksmithing, CA
California Nannie College, CA
California Paramedical & Tech. College, CA
California School of Court Reporting, CA
Cambria-Rowe Business College, PA
Cambridge School of Culinary Arts, MA
Camden Co. Vocational/Technical Schools, NJ (AHS)
Camelot Career College, LA
Cameron College, LA
Cancer Foundation of Santa Barbara, CA
Cape Girardeau Voc. Technical School, MO
Capitol Business College, WA
Capitol City Careers, TX
Capitol City Trade and Technical School, TX
CAPPS College, AL
Career Center, FL
Career Centers of Texas, TX
Career City College, FL
Career Development Center, VA
Career Development Institute, AL
Career Institute, DE; NY; PA
Career Point Business School, OK; TX

Careers Unlimited, TX
Career Training Academy, PA
Career Training Institute, FL
Career Training Specialists, LA
Career West Academy, CA
Carilion Health Systems, VA (AHS)
Carnegie Institute, MI
Carroll Technical Institute, GA
CARTI School of Radiation Therapy Tech, AR
Carver State Technical College, AL
Cashier Training Institute, NY
Catherine College, CA
Cave Technical Institute, IL
CCI Travel Careers Division, TN
Center for Advanced Legal Studies, TX
Center for Training in Bus. & Industry, KS
Central Alabama Skills Center, AL
Central CA School Continuing Education, CA
Central Texas Commercial College, TX
Centro de Estudios Multidisciplinarios, PR
Century Business College, CA
Century Schools, NV
Certified Careers Institute, UT
Chaparral Career College, AZ
Chapman School of Seamanship, FL
Charles B Coreil Technical Institute, LA
Charlotte Diesel Driving School, NC
Charlotte Vocational-Technical Center, FL
Charter College, AK
Chauffeurs Training School, FL; MI; NY
Chenier Business School, TX
Cheyenne Aero Tech, WY
Choffin Career Center, OH (AHS)
Chris Logan Career College, SC
Chubb Institute, NJ
Cincinnati School of Court Reporting, OH
Cittone Institute, NJ
City College, OK
Claiborne Technical Institute, LA
Clements Job Corps Center, KY
Cleveland Clinic Foundation, OH (AHS)
Cleveland Institute Dental Medical Asst., OH
Cleveland Machining Institute, OH
Climate Control Institute, KS; OK
Clover Park Technical College, WA
Coastal College, LA
Coastal Training Institute, AL
Colegio Mayor de Technologia, PR
Colegio Tecnico de Electricidad, PR
Colegio Tecnologico y Comercial, PR
CollegeAmerica, CA; CO; OR
College for Recording Arts, CA
College of Court Reporting, IN
College of Legal Arts, OR
College of Office Technology, IL
Colorado Career Academy, CO
Columbia College, PR
Columbus Para-Professional Institute, OH
Commercial College of Baton Rouge, LA
Commercial College of Shreveport, LA
Commercial Driver Training School, NY
Commercial Training Services, OR; WA
Commonwealth Business College, IL; IN
Commonwealth College, VA
Computer Career Center, NY; TX
Computer Dynamics Institute, VA
Computer Learning Center, CA; IL; MA; NJ; PA; VA
Computer Learning Network, PA
Computer Processing Institute, MA
Computer School, The, KY
Computer Tech, PA; WV
Concorde Career Institute, CA; CO; FL; MN; MO; OR; TN
Concordia Technical Institute, LA
Connecticut Business Institute, CT
Connecticut Center for Massage Therapy, CT
Connecticut Institute of Art, CT
Connecticut School of Broadcasting, IL; OH
Connecticut School of Electronics, CT
Conservatory/Recording Arts & Sciences, AZ
Consolidated School of Business, PA
Consolidated Welding School, CA
Continental Dental Assistant School, NY
Cooking & Hospitality Inst. of Chicago, IL
Cooper Academy of Court Reporting, FL
Coosa Valley Technical Institute, GA
Cope Institute, NY
Court Reporting Institute, PA; TN; TX; WA
Coyne American Institute, IL
Crown Academy, WA
Crown Business Institute, FL
Culinary Arts Institute of Louisiana, LA

D

Dakota Aero Technical, ND (AAT)
Dalfort Aircraft Technology, TX
Dallas Institute of Funeral Service, TX (EMB)
Dalton Voc. School of Health Occupations, GA
Data Institute, CT
Davenport College of Business, MI
David Carrasco Job Corps Center, TX
David Hochstein Memorial Music School, NY (MUS)
Davidson Technical College, TN
Dawn Training Institute, DE (AAT)
DeKalb Co. Occupational Education Center, GA

Delaware County Institute of Training, PA
Delaware Valley Academy-Medical & Dental, PA
Delta Career College, LA
Delta Career Institute, TX
Delta College, LA
Delta-Ouachita Technical Institute, LA
Delta Schools, LA
Denver Academy of Court Reporting, CO
Denver Automotive & Diesel College, CO
Denver Business College, AZ; CO; HI
Denver Paralegal Institute, CO
Desert Institute of the Healing Arts, AZ
Detroit Business Institute, MI
Detroit Institute Ophthalmology, MI
DeVry Technical Institute, NJ (EGN)
Dick Hill International Flight, MO
Dickinson-Warren Business College, CA
Diesel Driving Academy, AL; LA
Diesel Institute of America, MD
Diesel Truck Driver Training School, OR; WI
Divers Academy of the Eastern Seaboard, NJ
Divers Institute of Technology, WA
DMart Institute, PR
Domestic Health Care Institute, LA
Dominion Business School, VA
Dootson School of Trucking, CA
Dorsey Business School, MI
Douglas School of Business, PA
Dover Business College, NJ
Drake Business School, NY
Drake College of Business, NJ
Drake State Technical College, AL
Draughons College, GA
Draughons Junior College, KY
DTI Career Institute, CA
Du Cret School of the Arts, NJ
Duluth Business University, MN
Duluth Technical College, MN (AHS)
Durango Air Service, CO

E

East Alabama Skills Center, AL
East Coast Aero Tech School, MA
Eastern College of Health Vocations, AR; LA
Eastern Idaho Technical College, ID
Eastern Jackson Co. Coll./Allied Health, MO
ECPI Computer Institute, NC; VA
Education Dynamics Institute, NV
Educorp Career College, CA
Edutek Professional Colleges, CA
El Dorado College, CA
Electronic Data Processing College, PR
Elmira Business Institute, NY
Emily Griffith Opportunity School, CO
Empire College, CA
Empire Technical School/New Jersey, NJ
Engine City Technical Institute, NJ
Engine Technical Institute, FL (AAT)
English Nanny and Governess School, OH
Environmental Technical Institute, IL
Erie Business Center South, PA
Erwin Vocational Technical Center, FL
Escuela de Peritos Electricitas, PR
ESI Career Center, OH
Essex Agricultural & Technical Institute, MA
Estelle Harman Actor's Workshop, CA
Eton Technical Institute, WA
Evangeline Technical Institute, LA
Executive Secretarial School, TX

F

FAA Center for Management Development, FL (AAT)
Fairgrove Adult School, CA (AHS)
Fashion Careers of California, CA
Fashion Design College, PR
Fashion Merchandising and Technical Inst, PR
Faulkner Area Technical College, AL
FEGS Trades & Business School, NY
Fell's School of Business, NY
Fischer Technical Institute, VA
F.I.T. Aviation, FL (AAT)
Flatwoods Conservation Center, VA
Fleet Business School, MD
FlightSafety International, FL
Flint River Technical Institute, GA
Florida Computer and Business School, FL
Florida Institute of Ultrasound, FL
Florida Parishes Technical Institute, LA
Florida School of Business, FL
Florida Technical College, FL
Florissant Upholstery School, MO
Folk Art Institute, NY
Folkes Technical Institute, LA
Forrest Junior College, SC
Forsyth School for Dental Hygienists, MA (AHS)
Four-C College, TX
Fox College of Executive/Legal Assts., IL
Franciscan Shared Laboratory, WI (AHS)
Franklin Academy, PA
Franklin College of Court Reporting, LA
Fredd State Technical College, AL
French Culinary School, NY
Fresno Institute of Technology, CA
Fries Piano Hospital & Training Center, WA
Fugazzi College, TN (AHS)

G

Gadsden Business College, AL
Galen College Medical & Dental Assts., CA
Garces Commercial College, FL
Garfield Business Institute, PA
Gary Job Corps Center, TX
Gateway Technical Institute, PA
Gemological Institute of America, CA
General Dynamics Logistics Training Ctr., TX
General Technical Institute, NJ
George Stone Vocational Technical Center, FL
Georgia Medical Institute, GA
Gleim Technical Institute, PA
Glendale Career College, CA
Global Business Institute, NY
Globe College of Business, MN
Golf Academy of San Diego, CA
Golf Academy of the South, FL
Grand Rapids Educational Center, MI
Great Plains Area Voc. Tech. School, OK
Greensburg Institute of Technology, PA
Griffin Institute, GA
Gulf Area Technical Institute, LA
Gulf Coast Trades Center, TX
Gulfport Job Corps Center, MS
Gwinnett College of Business, GA

H

Hall Institute of Tech, RI
Hallmark Institute of Photography, MA
Hamilton Business College, IA
Hammel College, OH
Hammond Area Technical Institute, LA
Hamrick Truck Driving School, OH
Haney Vocational-Technical Center, FL
Hannibal Area Voc. Technical School, MO
Harris School of Business, NJ
Harris Technical Institute, LA
Harry Wendelstedt Umpire School, FL
Hartford Camerata Conservatory, CT (MUS)
Hartford Secretarial School, CT
Hawaii Business College, HI
Health Care Training Institute, AR; TN
Health Staff Training Institute, CA
Heartland School of Business, IL
Heart of Georgia Technical Institute, GA
Heartwood School of Art, ME (ART)
Heritage College of Health Careers, CO
Herzing Institute, AL
Hialeah Technical Center, FL
Hibbing Technical Institute, MN
Hickey School, MO
High-Tech Institute, CA
Hi-Tech School of Miami, FL
Hobart Institute of Welding Technology, OH
Ho-Ho-Kus School, NJ
Hospitality Training Center, OH (HMS)
Houston Aeronautical College, GA (AAT)
Houston Training School, TX
Huffman Aviation International, FL (AAT)
Humacao Community College, PR
Hunter Business School, NY
Huntington College of Dental Technology, CA
Huntington Institute, CT
Hutchinson Technical College, MN

I

Illinois Medical Training Center, IL
Indiana Business College, IN
Indian Meridian Vocational Tech School, OK
Industrial Management and Training, CT
Ingram State Technical Institute, AL
Institucion Chaviano de Mayaguez, PR
Institute for Business and Technology, CA
Institute of Allied Medical Professions, NY
Institute of Audio Research, NY
Institute of Business-Medical Technology, AZ; CA
Institute of Computer Science, NE
Institute of Medical & Dental Technology, OH
Institute of Multiple Technology, PR
Instituto de Banca y Comercio, PR
Instituto de Educacion Universal, PR
Instituto Del Arte Moderno, PR
Instituto Vocational y Comercial EDIC, PR
Interactive Learning Systems, GA; TX
Interamerican Business College, PR
Interior Design Institute, NV
Intermountain College, CO; UT
International Air Academy, CA; WA
International Aviation & Travel Academy, TX
International Business College, NM; TX; GU
International Business School, TX
International Career School, TX
International College of Broadcasting, OH
International College of Business & Tech, PR
International Dealers School, NV
International Technical College, PR
International Technical Institute, FL
Interstate Business College, ND
Irvine College of Business, CA
Island Drafting & Technical Institute, NY
ITT Technical Institute, AR; CA; IL; KY; MA; MI; PA;
   SC; WA

J-K

Jackson Business Institute, MI
James Martin School, PA (AHS)
Jefferson College, LA
Jefferson Davis Technical Institute, LA
Jefferson Technical Institute, LA
John Pope Eden Area Vocational Center, AL
Johnson Technical Institute, PA
Joseph Bulova School, NY
Kane Business Institute, NJ
Katharine Gibbs School, NJ; RI
KD Studio, TX
Kentucky Career Institue, KY
Kentucky Tech Ashland State Voc-Tech Sch, KY
Kentucky Tech Bowling Green Voc-Tech Sch, KY
Kentucky Tech Central KY State Voc-Tech, KY
Kentucky Tech Elizabthtwn State Voc-Tec, KY
Kentucky Tech Hazard State Voc-Tech Sch, KY
Kentucky Tech Jefferson State Voc-Tech, KY
Kentucky Tech Laurel Co State Voc-Tech, KY
Kentucky Tech Madisonville State Vo-Tech, KY
Kentucky Tech Mayo State Voc-Tech School, KY
Kentucky Tech Northern KY State Voc-Tech, KY
Kentucky Tech Owensboro Voc-Tech School, KY
Kentucky Tech Rowan State Voc-Tech Sch, KY
Kentucky Tech Somerset Area Voc-Tech Sch, KY
Kentucky Tech West KY State Voc-Tech Sch, KY
Kerr Business College, GA
Kinyon-Campbell Business School, MA
Knoxville Job Corps Center, TN
Krainz Woods Academy of Medical Tech., MI
Krissler Business Institute, NY
Kubert School of Cartoon & Graphic Arts, NJ

L

Laboratory of Pathology, WA (AHS)
Lafayette Regional Voc.-Technical School, LA
La Grande College of Business, OR
Lake Area Vocational-Technical Institute, SD
Lake County Area Vocational-Tech. Center, FL
Lakeland Medical-Dental Academy, MN
Lakeshore Medical Lab Training Programs, IN
Lake Washington Vocational Tech. Inst., WA
Lamson Business College, AZ
Landing School of Boatbuilding & Design, ME
Lanier Technical Institute, GA
Lansdale School of Business, PA
Lansing Computer Institute, MI
Las Vegas Gaming & Technical School, NV
Laurel Business Institute, PA
Lawton School, MI
Lederwolff Culinary Academy, CA
Lee Co. Vocational-Technical School, FL
Leicester School, CA
Levine School of Music, DC (MUS)
Lewis & Clark Technical School, MO
Lexington Electronics Institute, KY
Liberal Area Voc./Tech. School, KS
Liberty Academy of Business, PA
Liceo De Arte Y Disenos, PR
Liceo de Arte Y Tecnologia, PR
Life Laboratories, MA (AHS)
Lincoln Technical Institute, IL; MD; NJ; TX
Lindsey Hopkins Technical Education Ctr., FL
Linn Technical College, MO
Lively Area Vocational Technical School, FL
Locklin Vocational-Technical Center, FL
Long Island Business Institute, NY
Long Medical Institute, AZ
Long Technical Institute, LA
Los Angeles ORT Technical Institute, CA
Louisiana Art Institute, LA
Louisiana Institute of Technology, LA
Lowthian College, MN
Lyndon B Johnson Conservation Center, NC

M

MacArthur State Technical College, AL
McCann School of Business, PA
McConnell School, MN
McFatter Vocational-Technical Center, FL
McKim Technical Institute, OH
Macon Technical Institute, GA
Mallinckrodt Institute of Radiology, MO
Management College of San Francisco, CA
Manatee Area Vocational-Technical Center, FL
Mandl School, NY
M&M Word Processing Institute, TX
Maric College of Medical Careers, CA
Marion Co. School Radiologic Technology, FL
Marshfield Medical Center Laboratory, WI (AHS)
Marycrest College, IL
Maryland Drafting Institute, MD; VA
Massey Business College, TX
Massey Institute, GA
May Technical Colleges, MT
MBTI Business Training Institute, WI; PR
Meadows College of Business, GA
Med-Help Training School, CA
Medical Arts Training Center, FL
Medical Assisting School of Hawaii, HI
Medical Careers Institute, IL
Medical Careers Training Center, CO
Medical Institute of Minnesota, MN
Medix School, GA; MD
Memorial Sloan Kettering Cancer Center, NY (AHS)
Memorial Technical Institute, LA
Memphis Area Voc.-Tech. School, TN
Merit College, CA

Merlix Professional and Technical Inst, PR
Metro Business Academy, TX
Metro Business College, MO
Metro College, PR
Metropolitan College of Court Reporting, NM; OK
Metropolitan College of Legal Studies, OK
Metropolitan Technical Institute, NJ
Meyer Voc-Tech School, ND
Miami Institute of Technology, FL
Miami Job Corps Center, FL
Miami Lakes Technical Education Center, FL
Miami Technical College, FL
Miami Technical Institute, FL
Michigan Career Institute, MI
Michigan Institute of Aeronautics, MI (AAT)
Mid-America Paralegal Institute, MO
Mid-Del College, OK
Middle Georgia Technical Institute, GA
Mid-Florida Tech. Institute, FL
Midwest Institute for Medical Assistants, MO
Mildred Elley Business School, MA; NY
Mile Hi College, CO
Miller Hawkins Business College, TN
Miller-Motte Business College, NC; TN
Minneapolis Business College, MN
Minneapolis Drafting School, MN
Minnesota School of Business, MN
Minot School for Allied Health, ND (AHS)
Mississippi Job Corps Center, MS
Missouri Auction School, MO
Mitchell Vocational-Technical School, SD
Modern Technology School of X-Ray, CA
Modern Welding School, NY
Moncrief Radiation Center, TX
Monroe College, NY
Moore Career College, MS
Moore School of Technology, TN
Morgan Vocational-Technical Institute, FL
Morse School of Business, CT
Morven Park Intnl Equestrian Institute, VA
Mo Tech Education Center, MI
Motorcycle Mechanics Institute, AZ; FL
Moultrie Area Industrial-Technical Inst., GA
Mountain State College, WV
MTI Business College, CA; OH
MTI College, CA
MTI-Western Business College, CA
Mundus Institute, AZ
Munson-Williams-Proctor Institute, NY
Music Center of the North Shore, IL
Musicians Institute, CA
Music Tech, MN (MUS)

N

Nashville College, TN
Nasson Institute, RI
Natchitoches Technical Institute, LA
National Academy for Casino Dealers, NV
National Academy of Nannies, CO
National Aviation Academy, FL
National Business College, VA
National Business Institute, GA
National Career College, AL
National Career Education, CA
National Career Institute, FL; MO; TX
National College/Business & Technology, PR
National Computer College, PR
National Conservatory of Dramatic Arts, DC
National Institute of Health, MD
National School of Technology, FL
National Tractor Trailer School, NY
National Training, CO; FL
Navajo Aviation, CA
Nebraska Custom Diesel Drivers Training, NE
NEC-National Education Centers, CA; DC; GA; IL; LA;
    MA; MI; NJ; OH; RI; VA
Nell Executive Secretary School, TX
Nettleton Academy of Hair Design, SD
Newbridge College, CA
New England Culinary Institute, VT
New England Fuel Institute, MA
New England School of Accounting, MA
New England School of Art & Design, MA
New England School of Broadcasting, ME
New England School of Business, MA
New England School of Photography, MA
New England Technical Institute, CT
New England Tractor Trailer Training, CT; MD; MA;
    PA; RI
New Orleans Regional Technical Institute, LA
New School of Contemporary Radio, NY
New World College of Business, AL
New York Business School, NY
New York Food & Hotel Management School, NY
New York Inst. of Business Technology, NY
New York School for Medical Dental Asst., NY
New York Technical Institute of Hawaii, HI
Norfolk Skills Center, VA
North Alabama Skills Center, AL
North American Institute of Aviation, SC
North Bennet Street School, MA
North Central Area Technical Institute, LA
North Central KS Area Voc-Tech School, KS
Northeast Broadcasting School, MA
Northeast Career Schools, NH
Northeastern School of Commerce, MI
Northeast Institute, NY
Northeast Institute of Education, PA
Northeast Institute of Industrial Tech, MA
Northeast Louisiana Technical Institute, LA
Northeast Metro Technical College, MN
Northern Arizona Institute of Technology, AZ; NM
North Georgia Technical Institute, GA
North Hills School of Health Occupations, PA

North Metro Technical Institute, GA
North Park College, CA
Northrop-Rice Aviation Institute of Tech, CA
Northshore Technical Institute, OH
North Technical Education Center, FL
Northwest College Medical Dental Assts., CA
Northwest Louisiana Technical Institute, LA
Northwest School of Wooden Boatbuilding, WA
Northwest Technical College, MN
Nova Institute of Health Technology, CA

O

Oakbridge Academy of Arts, PA
Oakdale Technical Institute, LA
Oakland College of Court Reporting, CA
Ocean Corporation, The, TX
Ocean State Business Institute, RI
Ochsner School of Allied Health Sciences, LA
Oconaluftee Job Corps Center, NC
Office Careers Centre, TX
Ohio Auto/Diesel Technical Institute, OH
Ohio Valley Business College, OH
Okefenokee Technical Institute, GA
Oklahoma Farriers College, OK
Oklahoma Horseshoeing School, OK
Oklahoma State Horseshoeing School, OK
Omaha College of Business, NE
Omaha Opportunities Industrial Center, NE
Omega Institute, NJ
Omni Technical School, FL
Opelika State Technical College, AL
Orange County Business College, CA
Orlando Vocational-Technical Center, FL
Orleans Technical Institute, PA

P

Pace Business School, NY
Pace Institute, PA
Pacific Coast College, CA
Pacific Gateway College, CA
Pacific Travel School, CA
Paralegal Careers, FL
Paramedic Training Institute, OR
Parks Junior College, CO
Pathfinder School, IL
Pathology and Cytology Laboratories, KY (AHS)
Patricia Stevens Career College, MO
Patterson State Technical College, AL
Payne-Pulliam School of Trade & Commerce, MI
PBS Training Center, IL
PCI Dealers School, NV
PCI Health Training Center, TX
Pennco Tech, NJ
Penn-Ohio College, OH
Pennsylvania Academy of the Fine Arts, PA
Pennsylvania Business Institute, PA
Pennsylvania Gunsmith School, PA
Pennsylvania School of Art and Design, PA
Perkins Job Corps Center, KY
Perry Technical Institute, WA
Phillips Business College, VA
Phillips College, CA
Phillips Sch. of Business and Technology, TX
Phoenix East Aviation, FL
Pickens Technical Center, CO
Pickens Technical Institute, GA
Pima Medical Institute, AZ; CO; NM; WA
Pinellas Technical Education Center, FL
Pittard Area Vocational School, AL
Pittsburgh Institute of Mortuary Science, PA
PJA School, PA
Platt College, CA; OK
Plaza School of Technology, NJ
Politechnical Institute of Florida, FL
Polytechnic Institute, TX
Pompano Academy of Aeronautics, FL
Ponce Paramedical College, PR
Ponce Technical School, PR
Pontiac Business Institute, MI
Porter and Chester Institute, CT
Portfolio Center, GA
Poynter Institute for Media Studies, FL
PPI Health Careers School, CO
Practical Schools, CA
Prince Institute of Professional Studies, AL
Printing Trades School, NY
Professional Business Institute, NY
Professional Career Centers, CA
Professional Careers, NV
Professional Careers Institute, IN
Professional Court Reporting School, TX
Professional Electrical School, PR
Professional Skills Institute, OH
Professional Technical Institute, PR
Prospect Hall School of Business, FL
Provo College, UT
PTC Career Institute, DC; GA; IL; MD; NJ; OH; PA
Pueblo College of Business & Technology, CO
Puerto Rico Hotel School, PR
Puerto Rico Professional College, PR
Pulaski Vocational Technical School, AR

Q-R

Quality Plus Business School, GA
QUALTEC Institute, FL
Quincy Technical Schools, IL
Radiation Therapy Regional Centers, FL (AHS)
Raedel College & Industrial Welding Sch., OH
Randazzo Vocational Training Institute, LA
Raritan Valley Flying School, NJ (AAT)
Rasmussen Business College, MN
R.D. Colburn School of Performing Arts, CA (MUS)
Refrigeration School, AZ
Reid State Technical College, AL
Remington College, AR; LA
Renton Technical College, WA
Reporting Academy of Virginia, VA
Reppert School of Auctioneering, IN
RETS Electronic School, MA
RETS Technical Centers, FL
Rhode Island School of Photography, RI
Rice Aviation, AZ; MD; TX; VA
Rice College, AL; MS; TN
Ridge Vocational-Technical Center, FL
Ridley-Lowell Business & Technical Inst, CT; NY
Riverland Technical College, MN
River Parish Technical Institute, LA
Roberto-Venn School of Luthiery, AZ
Rockford Business College, IL
Rocky Mountain School of Meatcutting, CO
Rolla Area Vocational-Technical School, MO
Rosedale Technical Institute, PA
Ross Business Institute, MI
Ross Medical Education Center, MI
Ross Technical Institute, FL; MI
R/S Institute, TX
Ruston Technical Institute, LA

S

Sabine Valley Technical Institute, LA
St. Augustine Technical Center, FL
St. Cloud Business College, MN
St. John's School of Business, MA
St. Louis College of Health Careers, MO
St. Louis Tech, MO
Salisbury Business College, NC
Salter School, CT; MA
Salter Technical Institute, LA
San Antonio College Medical Dental Asst., TX
San Antonio Trade School, TX
San Antonio Training Division, TX
S & S Aircraft Flight Academy, FL (AAT)
Sanford-Brown Business College, IL; MO
San Joaquin Valley College of Aeronautic, CA
San Juan Basin AVTS, CO
San Juan City College, PR
Santa Barbara Business College, CA
Sarasota Co. Vocational Technical Ctr., FL
Sawyer College, CA; IN
Sawyer College of Business, OH
Sawyer School, PA; RI
Sawyer School of Business, MI
Schenck Civilian Conservation Center, NC
School of Advertising Art, OH
School of Automotive Machinists, TX
School of Communication Arts, MN
School of Communication Electronics, CA
School/Medical-Legal Secretarial Science, RI
Schuylkill Business Institute, PA
Scottsdale Culinary Institute, AZ
Scranton Medical Technology Consortium, PA
SCS Business & Technical Institute, NJ; NY; PA
Sebring Career School, TX
Sequoia Institute, CA
SER Business and Technical Institute, MI
SER-IBM Business Institute, FL
Settlement Music School, PA (MUS)
Shenango Valley School of Business, PA
Sheridan Vocational-Technical Center, FL
Shreveport-Bossier Technical Institute, LA
Sierra Academy of Aeronautics, CA (AAT)
Sierra Valley Business College, CA
Silicon Valley College, CA
Simi Valley Adult Education, CA (AHS)
Simmons Institute of Funeral Service, NY
Simmons School, NY
Slidell Technical Institute, LA
Sotheby's Educational Studies, NY (ART)
South Alabama Skills Center, AL
South Central Career College, AR
South Central Technical College, MN
South Coast College of Court Reporting, CA
Southeast Alabama Skills Center, AL
Southeast College of Technology, AL
Southeastern Business College, OH
Southeastern Center for the Arts, GA
Southeastern Inst. Paralegal Education, TN; TX
Southeastern School of Aeronautics, GA
Southeastern Technical Institute, MA
Southeast Vocational-Technical Institute, SD
Southern CA College of Business & Law, CA
Southern CA College of Court Reporting, CA
Southern Careers Institute, TX
Southern Technical Center, FL; KS
Southern Vocational College, AL
South Georgia Technical Institute, GA
South Hills Business School, PA
South Louisiana Technical Institute, LA
Southside Training Skill Center, VA
South Technical Education Center, FL
South Texas Vocational-Technical Inst., TX
Southwestern College of Business, KY
Southwestern College of Meat Cutters, OK

Southwestern Indian Polytechnic Inst., NM
Southwestern Technical College, MN
Southwest Florida College of Business, FL
Southwest School of Broadcasting, MO
SW School of Business & Tech Careers, TX
Southwest School of Electronics, TX
Southwest School of Medical Assistants, TX
Sowela Regional Technical Institute, LA
Spanish-American Institute, NY
Sparks College, IL
Sparks State Technical College, AL
Specs Howard School of Broadcast Arts, MI
Spencer Business Institute, NY
Spencer College, IA
Spencerian College, KY
Spencer School of Business, NE
Star Technical Institute, DE; NJ; PA
State Area Vocational-Technical School, TN
Stautzenberger College, OH
Stenotopia The World of Court Reporting, NY
Stenotype Academy, NY
Stenotype Institute, FL; SD
Sterling School, AZ
Stone Academy, CT
Strayer College, DC
Stuart School of Business Administration, NJ
Stuart School of Diamond Cutting, NY
Suburban Technical School, NY
Sullivan Technical Institute, LA
Suncoast School of Massage Therapy, FL
Superior Career Institute, NY
SUTECH School of Voc/Tech Training, CA
Suwanee-Hamilton Area Voc.-Tech. Center, FL
Swainsboro Technical Institute, GA
Swanson's Driving Schools, PA
Swedish Institute, NY
Swiss Hospitality Institute Cesar Ritz, CT
SYRIT Computer School Systems, NY
Systems Programming Development Inst, CA

T

TAD Technical Institute, MA; MO
Tallapoosa-Alexander City Vocational Ctr, AL
Tallulah Technical Institute, LA
Taylor Business Institute, IL
Teche Area Technical Institute, LA
Technical Careers Institute, CT
Technical Health Careers School, CA
Techno-Dental Training Center, NY
TESST Electronics and Computer Institute, MD; VA
Teterboro School of Aeronautics, NJ
Texas Aero Tech, TX (AAT)
Texas Dental Technology School, TX
Texas School of Business, TX
Texas Vocational School, TX
Thibodaux Area Technical Institute, LA
Thomas Technical Institute, GA
Thompson's Academies, PA
Thunderbird Aviation, MN (AAT)

Tidewater Tech, VA
Titan Helicopter Academy, NJ
Topeka School of Medical Technology, KS
Topeka Technical College, KS
Total Technical Institute, OH
Trans American School of Broadcasting, WI
Trans World Technical Academy, MO
Travel Academy, The, AK
Travel and Trade Career Institute, CA
Travel Institute, NY
Travel Institute of the Pacific, HI
Travel University International, CA; HI
Traviss Vocational-Technical Center, FL
Trend College, OR; WA
Trenholm State Technical College, AL
Trident Training Facility, WA
Tri-State Business Institute, PA
Truck Driver Development Service, OH
Truck Driving Academy, CA
Trumbull Business College, OH
Tucson College of Business, AZ
Tulsa Co. Area Voc Tech District 18, OK (AHS)
Tulsa Welding School, OK
Turner Job Corps Center, GA
Turtle Mt. School/Paramedical Technique, ND
Tuttle Vocational Technical Center, OK
Tyler School of Secretarial Sciences, IL

U-V

UCC Vocational Center, CA
Ultrasound Diagnostic School, FL; GA; MD; MA; NJ; NY; PA
Union Settlement Assoc. Training School, NY
United Health Careers Institute, CA
United Health Careers Institute, MO (AHS)
United States Truck Driving School, CA; CO; OK
Universal Business and Media School, NY
Universal Technical Institute, IL; NE
University of Tennessee Medical Center, TN (AHS)
U.S. Schools, FL
Valdosta Technical Institute, GA
Valley Commercial College, CA
Valparaiso Technical Institute, IN
Vanderschmidt School, MO
Vatterott College, MO
Vatterott Education Center, MO
Vegas Career School, NV
Virginia College, AL
Vocational Training Institute, WA

W-X-Y-Z

Walker Technical Institute, GA
Walker Vocational-Technical Center, FL
Ward Stone College, FL
Washington Business School/Northern VA, VA
Washington Conservatory of Music, DC (MUS)
Washington County Adult Skill Center, VA
Washington County Technical College, ME
Washington Holmes Area Voc-Technical Ctr, FL
Washington Institute of Technology, PA
Watterson College, CA
Watterson College Pacific, CA
Watterson College-Pasadena, CA
Wentworth Technical School, MA
West Central Alabama Skills Center, AL
Westchester Conservatory of Music, NY
West Coast Training, OR
Westech College, CA
Western Business College, OR; WA
Western Career College, CA
Western Culinary Institute, OR
Western Dakota Technical Institute, SD
Western Medical College of Allied Health, OR
Western School of Health & Bus. Careers, PA
Western Truck School, AZ; CA; NV; OR
Western Wisconsin Technical College, WI
West Georgia Technical Institute, GA
West Jefferson Technical Institute, LA
Westlake Institute of Technology, CA
Westside Technical Institute, LA
Westside Vocational-Technical Center, FL
West Technical Education Center, FL
West Tennessee Business College, TN
West Virginia Business College, WV
West Virginia Career College, PA
Wichita Area Vocational Technical School, KS (AHS)
Wichita Business College, KS
Wichita Technical Institute, KS
Williamsburg Flite Center, VA (AAT)
Williamson Free School/Trades and Tech, PA
Wilson Rehabilitation Center, VA
Winona Technical College, MN
Winston County Area Vocational Center, AL
Winter Park Adult Vocational Center, FL
Wireless Technical Institute, PA
Wisconsin Conservatory of Music, WI (MUS)
Wisconsin Indianhead Technical College, WI (AHS)
Withlacoohee Technical Institute, FL
Woodbridge Business Institute, VA
Woodbury College, VT
Woodridge Business Institute, IL; MD
Worcester Technical Institute, MA
World Wide College of Auctioneering, IA
Worsham College of Mortuary Science, IL
Wright Business School, KS; OK
York College, PR
York Technical Institute, PA
Yorktowne Business Institute, PA
Young Memorial Technical Institute, LA

HOSPITALS - INDEX

Schools alphabetized in this section can be found in the **Allied Health Science** classification unless followed by a (NRS) in which case the schools will be found in the **Nursing** classification.

A

Abbott-Northwestern Hospital, MN
Abington Memorial Hospital, PA
Akron General Medical Center, OH
Albany Medical Center, NY
Albany Memorial Hospital, NY
Albert Einstein Medical Center, PA
Aliquippa Hospital, PA
Alleghany Regional Hospital, VA
Allegheny General Hospital, PA
Allegheny Valley Hospital, PA
Allen Memorial Hospital, IA
Allentown-Lehigh Valley Hospital Center, PA
All Saints' Episcopal Hospital, TX
Altoona Hospital, PA
American Red Cross Blood Services, CT; GA; OH
Anderson Memorial Hospital, SC
Archbishop Bergan Mercy Hospital, NE
Armstrong County Memorial Hospital, PA
Arnot-Ogden Medical Center, NY
Arnot-Ogden Memorial Hospital, NY (NRS)
Ashland State General Hospital, PA
Atlantic City Medical Center, NJ
Augusta Medical Center, VA
Aultman Hospital, OH
Austin State Hospital, TX

B

Ball Memorial Hospital, IN
Baptist Hospital, TX
Baptist Medical Centers, AL; FL; SC
Baptist Memorial Hospital, TN; TX
Baptist Schools of Allied Health, AR
Barnert Memorial Hospital, NJ
Barnes College, MO (NRS)
Barnes Hospital, MO

Baton Rouge General Medical Center, LA
Bayfront Medical Center, FL
Bayley Seton Hospital, NY
Bayonne Hospital, NJ (NRS)
Bay State Medical Center, MA
Beebe Medical Center School of Nursing, DE (NRS)
Bellevue Hospital Center, NY
Bellin Hospital, WI
Beloit Memorial Hospital, WI
Ben Taub Hospital, TX
Berkshire Medical Center, MA
Bethany Medical Center, KS
Bethesda-Kennedy Hospital, FL
Bishop Clarkson Memorial Hospital, NE
Blessing Hospital, IL
Blodgett Memorial Medical Center, MI
Bloomington-Normal School of Radiography, IL
Bluefield Regional Medical Center, WV
Bradford Regional Medical Center, PA
Brandywine Hospital, PA
Bridgeport Hospital, CT
Bridgeport Hospital, CT (NRS)
Brockton Hospital, MA (NRS)
Bronson Methodist Hospital, MI
Brooklyn Hospital, NY
Brown Cancer Center, KY
Bryan Memorial Hospital, NE (NRS)
Bryn Mawr Hospital, PA
Burdette Tomlin Memorial Hospital, NJ
Burlington Co. Memorial Hospital, NJ
Butterworth Hospital, MI

C

Cabarrus Memorial Hospital, NC (NRS)
Cabell Huntington Hospital, WV
Cambridge Hospital, MA
Camden Clark Memorial Hospital, WV
Cancer Therapy and Research Center, TX
Carlisle Hospital, PA
Carolinas Medical Center, NC
Carraway Methodist Medical Center, AL
Catholic Medical Center, NY
Cedars-Sinai Medical Center, CA
Centra Health, VA (NRS)
Central Du Page Hospital, IL
Central Florida Blood Bank, FL
Central Suffolk Hospital, NY
Chambersburg Hospital, PA
Champlain Valley Physicians Hospital, NY
Charity-Delgado School of Nursing, LA (NRS)
Charity Hospital of Louisiana, LA
Charleston Area Medical Center, WV
Charlotte Memorial Hospital, NC
Chester County Hospital, PA (NRS)
Children's Hospital, MA
Children's Hospital & Medical Center, OH; WA
Children's Hospital of Los Angeles, CA
Children's Hospital of San Francisco, CA
Christ Hospital, NJ (NRS)
Christ Hospital, IL; OH
Citizens General Hospital, PA (NRS)
Citizens Medical Center, TX
City of Hope Medical Center, CA
Clearfield Hospital, PA
Colorado Assoc. of Paramedical Education, CO
Columbia Hospital, WI
Columbus Hospital, MT
Comanche Co. Memorial Hospital, OK
Community General Hospital, PA
Community Hospital, IN; OH
Community Medical Center, PA

Conemaugh Valley Memorial Hospital, PA
Cook County Hospital, IL
Cooperative Medical Technology Program, OH
Cooper Medical Center, NJ
Covenant Medical Center, IA
Crawford Long Hospital/Emory University, GA
Crouse-Irving Memorial Hospital, NY (NRS)
Crozer-Chester Medical Center, PA

D

Danbury Hospital, CT
Daniel Freeman Mem. Hospital, CA
Deaconess Medical Center, WA
Decatur Memorial Hospital, IL
DeKalb Medical Center, GA
De Paul Medical Center, VA
Divine Providence Hospital, PA
Doylestown Hospital, PA
Drew Medical Center, CA
Druid City Hospital, AL
Durham County General Hospital, NC

E-F-G

Earl K. Long Memorial Hospital, LA
Eastern Maine Medical Center, ME
Eastern New Mexico Medical Center, NM
Edward Hines Veterans Admin. Hospital, IL
Eisenhower Medical Center, CA
El Camino Hospital, CA
Elizabeth General Medical Center School, NJ
Ellis Hospital, NY (NRS)
Englewood Hospital, NJ
Enloe Hospital, CA
Episcopal Hospital, PA
Fairfax Hospital, VA
Fairview General Hospital, OH
Florida Hospital Medical Center, FL
Floyd Medical Center, GA
Forsyth Memorial Hospital, NC
Fort Sanders School of Nursing, TN (NRS)
Foster G. McGaw Hospital, IL
Framingham Union Hospital School/Nursing, MA
  (NRS)
Franciscan Medical Center, IL
Frankford Hospital, PA (NRS)
Franklin Hospital, PA
Fresno Community Hospital/Medical Center, CA
Garden City Hospital, MI
Gaston Memorial Hospital, NC
Geisinger Medical Center, PA
General Hospital, NY (NRS)
Genesee Hospital, NY
Georgia Baptist Medical Center, GA
Germantown Hospital & Medical Center, PA
Glens Falls Hospital, NY
Good Samaritan Hospital, IN
Good Samaritan Hospital, OH; OR (NRS)
Grace Hospital, MI
Grady Memorial Hospital, GA
Graham Hospital, IL (NRS)
Greater Baltimore Medical Center, MD
Grossmont District Hospital, CA

H

Hackensack Medical Center, NJ
Halifax Medical Center, FL
Hamot Medical Center, PA
Hancock Memorial Hospital, IN
Harbor Hospital Center, MD
Harborview Medical Center, WA
Harper-Grace Hospital, MI
Harris Hospital, TX
Hartford Hospital, CT
Hattiesburg Radiology Group, MS
Hazelton-St. Joseph Medical Center, PA
HCA Wesley Medical Center, KS
Helene Fuld Medical Center, NJ
Hendrick Medical Center, TX
Hennepin County Medical Center, MN
Henry Ford Hospital, MI
Hinsdale Sanitarium & Hospital, IL
Holston Valley Hospital & Medical Center, TN
Holy Cross Hospital, IL; MD
Holy Family Hospital, WA
Holy Name Hospital, NJ (NRS)
Holy Name of Jesus Hospital, AL (NRS)
Holy Spirit Hospital, PA
Hospital Center at Orange, NJ
Hudson Area School of Radiologic Tech., NJ
Humana Hospital, AL
Hunter Memorial Laboratory, MD
Huntington Memorial Hospital, CA
Huntsville Hospital, AL
Hurley Medical Center, MI
Huron Road Hospital, OH

I-J-K

Immanuel Medical Center, NE
Interfaith Medical Center, NY (NRS)
Iowa Methodist Medical Center, IA
Iowa Methodist School of Nursing, IA (NRS)
Jackson Memorial Hospital, FL
Jameson Memorial Hospital, PA (NRS)
Jefferson Regional Medical Center, AR
Jennie Edmundson Memorial Hospital, IA
Jersey Shore Medical Center, NJ
Jewish Hospital of St. Louis, MO

John F. Kennedy Medical Center, NJ
Johns Hopkins Hospital, MD
Kennestone Regional Medical Center, GA
King's Daughter's Hospital, IN; KY

L

Lafayette General Medical Center, LA
Lake Charles Memorial Hospital, LA
Lakeland Regional Medical Center, FL
Lancaster General Hospital, PA
Lankenau Hospital, PA
Latrobe Area Hospital, PA
Latter-Day Saints Hospital, UT
Lawrence & Memorial Hospitals, CT
Lawrence General Hospital, MA
Lawrence Memorial Hospital, MA (NRS)
Lee Hospital, PA
Lee Memorial Hospital, FL
Lenoir Memorial Hospital, NC
Lester E. Cox Medical Center, MO
LifeSource, IL
Long Island College Hospital, NY
Los Angeles Co. Harbor UCLA Medical Ctr., CA
Los Angeles County USC Medical Center, CA
Louis A. Weiss Memorial Hospital, IL
Louise Obici School of Nursing, VA (NRS)
Louise S. McClintic School of Nursing, PA (NRS)
Lourdes Hospital, KY
Lutheran Medical Center, MO (NRS)
Lutheran Medical Center, CO
Luther Hospital, WI

M

McDonough District Hospital, IL
McKay-Dee Hospital Center, UT
McKennan Hospital, SD
McLeod Regional Medical Center, SC
MacQueen Gibbs Willis School of Nursing, MD (NRS)
Maine Medical Center, ME
Manchester Memorial Hospital, CT
Mansfield General Hospital, OH (NRS)
Marion General Hospital, OH
Marion Health Center, IA
Marquette General Hospital, MI
Mary Immaculate Hospital, VA
Maryland General Hospital, MD
Mary Lanning Memorial Hospital, NE
Medical Center, GA
Medical Center Hospital, TX
Medical Center Hospital of Vermont, VT
Medical Center of Beaver County, PA
Medical Center of Central Georgia, GA
Memorial Blood Center of Minneapolis, MN
Memorial Hospital, CO; IN; OH; RI; TX; VA
Memorial Medical Center, NM
Menorah Medical Center, MO
Mercer Medical Center, NJ
Mercy Health Center, OK
Mercy Hospital, IA; ME; MD; NY; OH; PA
Mercy Hospital, PA (NRS)
Mercy Medical Center, WI
Mercy School of Nursing, NC (NRS)
Meridia Euclid Hospital, OH
Meridia Hillcrest Hospital, OH
Methodist Hospital, IN; KY; MN; NY; TN; TX
Methodist Hospital, PA (NRS)
Methodist Medical Center of Illinois, IL
MetroHealth Medical Center, OH
MetroHealth Medical Ctr. School/Nursing, OH (NRS)
Metropolitan Nashville General Hospital, TN
Michael Reese Hospital & Medical Center, IL
Middletown Regional Hospital, OH
Midland Co. Hospital District, TX
Mid-Maine Medical Center, ME
Millard Fillmore Hospital, NY
Milton S. Hershey Medical Center Hosp., PA
Milwaukee County Medical Complex, WI
Mineral Area Regional Medical Center, MO
Minneapolis VA Medical Center, MN
Mississippi Medical Center, MS
Missouri Baptist Medical Center, MO (NRS)
Mobile Infirmary Medical Center, AL
Monmouth Medical Center, NJ
Monsour Medical Center, PA
Montana Deaconess Medical Center, MT
Montefiore Medical Center, NY
Morristown Memorial Hospital, NJ
Moses H. Cone Memorial Hospital, NC
Mountainside Hospital, NJ
Mt. Auburn Hospital, MA
Mt. Carmel Medical Center, OH
Mt. Sinai Hospital, CT
Mt. Sinai Medical Center, FL
Mt. Vernon Hospital, NY (NRS)
Muhlenberg Regional Medical Center, NJ
Munson Medical Center, MI
Muskogee General Hospital, OK

N

Nazareth Hospital, PA
Newark Beth Israel Medical Center, NJ
New Britain General Hospital, CT
New England Baptist Hospital, MA (NRS)
New England Deaconess Hospital, MA
New England Medical Center, MA
New Hanover Memorial Hospital, NC
Newman Hospital, KS (NRS)
Newton-Wellesley Hospital, MA
New York City Health & Hospitals, NY

New York Eye & Ear Infirmary, NY
New York Hospital Cornell Medical Center, NY
Norfolk General Hospitals, VA
North Carolina Memorial Hospital, NC
North Colorado Medical Center, CO
Northeastern Hospital, PA (NRS)
Northern Hospital of Surry County, NC
Northern Westchester Hospital Center, NY
North Kansas City Hospital, MO
North Memorial Medical Center, MN
North Mississippi Medical Center, MS
North Oakland Medical Center, MI
Northport Veterans Administration Hosp., NY
North Shore University Hospital, NY
Northwest Community Hospital, IL
Norwalk Hospital, CT

O-P

Oakwood Hospital, MI
Ohio State University Hospitals, OH
Ohio Valley General Hospital, PA
Ohio Valley Hospital, OH
Ohio Valley Medical Center, WV
Orlando Regional Medical Center, FL
Our Lady of Lourdes School of Nursing, NJ (NRS)
Our Lady of the Lake Medical Center, LA
Overlook Hospital, NJ
Overton Brooks VA Medical Center, LA
Owensboro-Daviess Co. Hospital, KY
Pacific NW Red Cross Blood Services, OR
Parkland Memorial Hospital, TX
Parkview Episcopal Hospital, CO
Parkview Memorial Hospital, IN
Pascak Valley Hospital, NJ
Peninsula Hospital, CA; NY
Pennsylvania Hospital, PA
Penrose Hospital, CO
Phillips Beth Israel School of Nursing, NY (NRS)
Point Park College-St. Francis Med. Ctr., PA
Polyclinic Medical Center, PA
Porter Memorial Hospital, IN
Port Huron Hospital, MI
Pottsville Hospital School of Nursing, PA (NRS)
Presbyterian Hospital, NC; OK
Presbyterian Saint Luke's Center, CO
Presbyterian-University Hospital, PA
Providence Hospital, MI; OH

Q-R

Quain & Ramstad Clinic, ND
Radio Assoc. of Sacramento Medical Group, CA
Rapid City Regional Hospital, SD
Rapides General Hospital, LA
Raritan Bay Medical Center, NJ (NRS)
Ravenswood Hospital Medical Center, IL
Reading Hospital & Medical Center, PA
Regional West Medical Center, NE
Reid Memorial Hospital, IN
Research Medical Center, MO
Rhode Island Hospital, RI
Rhode Island Medical Center, RI
Rice Memorial Hospital, MN
Richmond Heights General Hospital, OH
Richmond Memorial Hospital, VA
Riverside Hospital, OH
Riverside Methodist Hospital, OH
Riverside Regional Medical Center, VA
Riverview Medical Center, NJ
Robert Packer Hospital, PA
Rochester General Hospital, NY
Rockford Memorial Hospital, IL
Rockingham Memorial Hospital, VA
Rolling Hill Hospital Diagnostic Center, PA
Roxborough Memorial Hospital, PA (NRS)
Rush Presbyterian St. Lukes Medical Ctr., IL
Rutland Regional Medical Center, VT

S

Sacramento Medical Foundation Blood Bank, CA
Sacred Heart Hospital, PA; SD; WI
Sacred Heart Medical Center, PA; WA
St. Alexius Medical Center, ND
St. Alphonsus Regional Medical Center, ID
St. Anthony Hospital, CO; OK
St. Anthony Medical Center, IL; KY
St. Barnabas Medical Center, NJ
St. Catherine's Hospital, WI
St. Charles Hospital, OH
St. Cloud Hospital, MN
St. Edward School of Radiologic Tech., AR
St. Elizabeth Hospital, IN (NRS)
St. Elizabeth Hospital, IL; NY; OH; TX; WI
St. Elizabeth Medical Center, KY; OH
St. Elizabeth's Hospital, MA (NRS)
St. Francis Hospital, CT; NJ (NRS)
St. Francis Hospital, DE; HI; IL; IN; OK; PA; TN; WI
St. Francis Medical Center, IL; LA; NJ
St. Francis Regional Medical Center, KS
St. James Community Hospital, MT
St. James Mercy Hospital, NY
St. John's Hospital, CA; IL; MI
St. John's Hospital & Health Center, CA
St. John's Medical Center, WA
St. John's Mercy Medical Center, MO
St. John's Regional Health Center, MO
St. John's Regional Medical Center, MO
St. John's Riverside Hospital, NY (NRS)
St. John's School of Nursing, MO (NRS)
St. Joseph Hospital, CA; IL; MI; NE; SD; TN; WI

05619536323543944424444444355515

St. Joseph Hospital & Health Center, IN
St. Joseph Medical Center, IN; KS
St. Joseph Mercy Hospital, IA
St. Joseph's Hospital, FL; GA; KY; ND; PA; RI
St. Josephs Hospital & Health Center, NY (NRS)
St. Joseph's Hospital & Medical Center, AZ
St. Joseph's Medical Center, NJ
St. Luke's Episcopal Hospital, TX
St. Luke's Hospital, ID; IA; MO; ND; OH
St. Luke's Hospital, PA (NRS)
St. Luke's Medical Center, WI
St. Luke's Memorial Hospital, WI
St. Lukes Memorial Hospital Center, NY
St. Luke's Midland Regional Medical Ctr., SD
St. Luke's Regional Medical Center, IA
St. Margaret Hospital, IN
St. Mary Hospital, IL
St. Mary Medical Center, CA; IN
St. Mary's Hospital, AZ; FL; NY; OK; VA; WV
St. Mary's Hospital, CT (NRS)
St. Mary's Medical Center, IN; MI; WI
St. Michael's Medical Center, NJ
St. Patrick Hospital, MT
St. Patrick's Hospital, LA
St. Paul-Ramsey Medical Center, MN
St. Peter's Medical Center, NJ
St. Thomas Hospital, TN
St. Thomas Medical Center, OH (NRS)
St. Vincent Health Center, PA
St. Vincent Hospital, IN; OR; WI
St. Vincent Infirmary Medical Center, AR
St. Vincent Medical Center, OH
St. Vincent's Hospital, MT; NY
St. Vincent's Medical Center, CT; FL
St. Vincent's Medical Center, NY (NRS)
Samaritan Hospital, NY (NRS)
San Bernardino County Medical Center, CA
San Joaquin General Hospital, CA
San Jose Medical Center, CA
Santa Barbara Cottage & Gen. Hosp., CA
Scenic Mountain Medical Center, TX
Schumpert Medical Center, LA
Scott & White Memorial Hospital & Clinic, TX
Scripps Clinic & Research Foundation, CA
Scripps Memorial Hospital, CA
Seventh Ward General Hospital, LA
Sewickley Valley Hospital, PA

Shadyside Hospital, PA
Shannon West Texas Memorial Hospital, TX
Sharon Regional Health System, PA
Sharp Memorial Hospital, CA
Shivers Cancer Center, TX
Sioux Valley Hospital, SD
Sisters School of Nursing, NY (NRS)
Somerset Community Hospital, PA
Somerset Medical Center, NJ
Somerville Hospital, MA (NRS)
South Central Regional Medical Center, MS
South Chicago Community Hospital, IL
Southeast Michigan Red Cross Blood Ctr., MI
South Jersey Hospital System, NJ
South Nassau Communities Hospital, NY
Southside Regional Medical Center, VA
Southwest Florida Blood Bank, FL
Southwest General Hospital, OH
Sparks Regional Medical Center, AR
Stamford Hospital, CT
Summa Health System/Akron City Hospital, OH
Sutter Community Hopitals, CA
Swedish-American Hospital, IL
Swedish Medical Center, CO
Sylacauga Hospital, AL (NRS)

T-U-V

Tallahassee Memorial Hospital, FL
Tampa General Hospital, FL
Theda Clark Regional Medical Center, WI
Timken Mercy Medical Center, OH
Tompkins Community Hospital, NY
Touro Infirmary, LA
Trinity Lutheran Hospital, MO
Trinity Medical Center, ND
Trumbull Memorial Hospital, OH
Union Memorial Hospital, MD
Uniontown Hospital, PA (NRS)
United Care, Annapolis Hospital, MI
United Hospital, MN; NY; WV
United Medical Center, IL
United Samaritans Medical Center, IL
University Health Center, PA
University Hospital, GA; OH
University Medical Center, FL; LA

University of Alabama Hospital, AL
University of AR & VA Medical Center, AR
University of Texas Anderson Cancer Ctr., TX
University of Virginia Medical Center, VA
Utah Valley Regional Medical Center, UT
Valley Childrens Hospital, CA
Valley Hospital, NJ
Valley View Regional Hospital, OK
VA Medical Center, CA; OR
Veterans Administration Hospital, MA; WV
Veterans Administration Medical Center, CA; OR
Veterans Memorial Medical Center, CT

W-X-Y-Z

Wadley Hospital, TX
W. A. Foote Memorial Hospital, MI
Walter Reed Medical Center, DC
Washington Adventist Hospital, MD
Washington Hospital, DC; PA
Waterbury Hospital, CT
Wausau Hospital Center, WI
Welborn Baptist Hospital, IN
West Boca Medical Center, FL
Western Pennsylvania Hospital, PA
Western Reserve Care System, OH
West Jersey Hospital, NJ
West Los Angeles VA Medical Center, CA
Westmoreland Hospital Assoc., PA
West Park Hospital, WY
West Virginia University Hospital, WV
Wheeling Hospital, WV
Wichita General Hospital, TX
Wilcox College of Nursing, CT (NRS)
Wilkes Barre General Hospital, PA
Wilkes Regional Medical Center, NC
William Beaumont Hospital, MI
Williamsport Hospital, PA
Winchester Memorial Hospital, VA
Windham Commmunity Memorial Hospital, CT
Winthrop University Hospital, NY
Woman's Christian Assoc. Hospital, NY
Worcester City Hospital, MA
York Hospital, PA
Zablocki VA Medical Center, WI

PREPARATORY SCHOOLS - INDEX

Schools alphabetized in this section can be found in the **Preparatory Schools-Coeducational** classification or **Preparatory Schools for Boys** (PRB) or **Preparatory Schools for Girls** (PRG).

A

Academy at Charlemont, MA
Academy of Our Lady of Guam, GU (PRG)
Academy of the Holy Family, CT (PRG)
Academy of the New Church, PA (PRB)
Academy of the Sacred Heart, LA (PRG)
Accelerated Schools Foundation, CO
Admiral Farragut Academy, FL; NJ (PRB)
Alexander Dawson School, CO
Allen Academy, TX
All Saints' Episcopal School, MS
American Military Academy, PR
Andrews School, OH (PRG)
Annie Wright School, WA (PRG)
Antilles Military Academy, PR
Archmere Academy, DE
Army and Navy Academy, CA (PRB)
Asheville School, NC
Aspen School, CO
Athenian School, CA
Avon Old Farms School, CT (PRB)

B

Bartram School, FL (PRG)
Baylor School, TN
Bellarmine College Preparatory, CA (PRB)
Belmont Hill School, MA (PRB)
Benedictine Military High School, VA (PRB)
Benedictine Military School, GA (PRB)
Ben Lippen School, SC
Berkshire School, MA
Bishop's Schools, CA (PRG)
Blair Academy, NJ
Blue Ridge School, VA (PRB)
Bob Jones Academy, SC
Bolles School, FL (PRB)
Brandon Hall School, GA
Brebeuf Preparatory School, IN
Brenau Academy, GA (PRG)
Brewster Academy, NH
Bridgton Academy, ME (PRB)
Broadview Academy, IL
Brooks School, MA
Bryn Mawr School, MD (PRG)
Bullis School, MD
Burke Mountain Academy, VT
Burr and Burton Seminary, VT
Buxton School, MA

C

Cambridge School, MA
Camden Military Academy, SC (PRB)
Canterbury School, CT
Carrabassett Valley Academy, ME
Carson Long Military Institute, PA (PRB)
Cascade School, CA
Cascadilla Prep School, NY
Cascia Hall Preparatory School, OK
Castilleja School for Girls, CA (PRG)
Cate School, CA
Cedu School, CA
Central Catholic High School, TX (PRB)
Central Christian High School, OH
Chamberlain-Hunt Academy, MS
Chaminade College Preparatory School, MO (PRB)
Chapel Hill-Chauncy Hall School, MA
Chatham Hall School, VA (PRG)
Cheshire Academy, CT
Choate Rosemary Hall School, CT
Christchurch School, VA (PRB)
Christian Brothers Academy, NY (PRB)
Christ School, NC (PRB)
Church Farm School, PA (PRB)
Colorado Academy, CO
Colorado Rocky Mountain School, CO
Colorado Springs School, The, CO
Colorado Timberline Academy, CO
Concord Academy, MA
Concordia Lutheran High School, IN
Convent of the Sacred Heart, CT (PRG)
Cranbrook School, MI
Cretin Hall High School, MN (PRB)
Culver Military Academy & Summer Camp, IN
Cushing Academy, MA

D-E

Dana Hall School, MA (PRG)
Darlington School, GA
Darrow School, NY
Deerfield Academy, MA
Delphian School and Camp, OR
Denver Academy, CO
Desisto School, MA
Detroit Country Day School, MI
Dewey Academy, MA
Doane Stuart School, NY
Dublin Christian Academy, NH
Dublin School, NH
Dunn School, CA (PRB)
Eastern Mennonite High School, VA

Elgin Academy, IL
Emma Willard School, NY (PRG)
Episcopal High School, VA
Ethel Walker School, CT (PRG)

F

Falmouth Academy, MA
Father Duenas Memorial School, GU (PRB)
Fenster School of Southern Arizona, AZ
Fishburne Military School, VA (PRB)
Flintridge Sacred Heart Academy, CA (PRG)
Florida Air Academy, FL (PRB)
Fork Union Military Academy, VA (PRB)
Forman School, CT
Fountain Valley School, CO
Foxcroft School, VA (PRG)
Friends School, MD
Fryeburg Academy, ME

G

Garrison Forest School, MD (PRG)
George School, PA
Georgetown Preparatory School, MD (PRB)
Gilmour Academy, OH
Girard College, PA
Gould Academy, ME
Governor Dummer Academy, MA
Gow School, NY (PRB)
Grand River Academy, OH (PRB)
Green Mount Valley School, VT
Grier School for Girls, PA (PRG)
Groton School, MA
Guam Adventist Academy, GU
Gunnery School, CT
Gunston School, MD (PRG)

H

Hackley School, NY (PRB)
Hammer United World College, NM
Hampshire Country School, NH
Happy Valley School, CA
Harding Academy, AR
Hargrave Military Academy, VA (PRB)
Harrison Chilhowee Baptist Academy, TN
Harvey School, NY
Hawaiian Mission Academy, HI
Hawaii Preparatory Academy, HI
Hebron Academy, ME
HighCroft School, MA

High Mowing School-A Waldorf High School, NH
Hill School, PA (PRB)
Hilton Head Preparatory School, SC
Hobe Sound Christian Academy, FL
Hockaday School, TX (PRG)
Holderness School, NH
Hoosac School, NY
Hotchkiss School, CT
Houghton Academy, NY
Howe Military School, IN
Hun School of Princeton, NJ
Hyde School, ME

I-J-K

Idyllwild School of Music/Arts, CA
Indian Springs School, AL
Interlochen Arts Academy, MI
Judson School, AZ
Kemper Military School & College, MO
Kent School, CT
Kents Hill School, ME
Kildonan School, NY (PRB)
Kimball Union Academy, NH
Kiski School, The, PA (PRB)
Knox School, NY

L

Lake Forest Academy, IL
La Lumiere School, IN
Landmark School, MA
La Salle Center, NY (PRB)
Latin School of Chicago, IL
Laurinburg Institute, NC
Lausanne Collegiate School, TN
Lawrence Academy, MA
Lawrenceville School, NJ
Lee Academy, ME
Leelanau School, The, MI
Linden Hall, PA (PRG)
Linfield School, The, CA
Linsly Institute, WV (PRB)
Loomis Chaffee School, CT
Lustre Christian High School, MT
Lycee International De Los Angeles, CA
Lyman Ward Military Academy, AL (PRB)
Lyndon Institute, VT

M

McCallie School, TN (PRB)
McDonogh School, MD
MacDuffie School, MA
Madeira School, VA (PRG)
Maine Central Institute, ME
Manlius Pebble Hill School, NY
Marianapolis Preparatory School, CT
Marian Heights Academy, IN (PRG)
Marine Military Academy, TX (PRB)
Marion Military Institute, AL
Marmion Military Academy, IL (PRB)
Marvelwood School, CT
Massanutten Military Academy, VA
Master's School, CT
Master's School for Girls, NY (PRG)
Maur Hill Prep School, KS (PRB)
Meeting School, NH
Menaul High School, NM
Mercersburg Academy, PA
Michigan Lutheran Seminary, MI
Middlesex School, MA
Midland School, CA
Milford Academy, CT
Millbrook School, NY
Millersburg Military Institute, KY (PRB)
Miller School of Albemarle, VA (PRB)
Milton Academy, MA
Milton Hershey School, PA
Miss Hall's School, MA (PRG)
Mississippi Valley Christian School, IL
Missouri Military Academy, MO (PRB)
Miss Porter's School, CT (PRG)
MMI Preparatory School, PA
Monte Vista Christian School, CA
Montverde Academy, FL
Moravian Academy, PA
Morgan Park Academy, IL
Morgan School at Patterson Preserve, The, NC

Moses Brown School, RI
Mt. Ellis Academy, MT
Mt. Michael Benedictine High School, NE (PRB)
Mount Saint John Academy, NJ (PRG)
Mt. St. Mary Academy, AR; NJ (PRG)
Mount St. Scholastica Academy, KS (PRG)

N-O-P

National Sports Academy, NY
New Hampton School, NH
New Mexico Military Institute, NM
New York Military Academy, NY
Noble and Greenough School, MA
Northfield Mt. Hermon School, MA
Northwestern Military and Naval Academy, WI (PRB)
Northwest School, WA
Northwood School, NY
Notre Dame Academy, VA (PRG)
Notre Dame Latin School, OH
Oak Creek Ranch School, AZ
Oak Grove Lutheran High School, ND
Oak Grove School, CA
Oak Hill Academy, VA
Oak Ridge Military Academy, NC
Oakwood School, NY
Ojai Valley School, CA
Oldfields School, MD (PRG)
Olney Friends School, OH
Oneida Baptist Institute, KY
Oregon Episcopal School, OR
Orme School, AZ
Oxford Academy, CT (PRB)
Peddie School, NJ
Pennington School, NJ
Perkiomen School, PA
Phelps School, PA (PRB)
Phillips Academy, MA
Phillips Exeter Academy, NH
Pine Crest School, FL
Pine Ridge School, VT
Piney Woods School, MS
Platte Valley SDA Academy, NE
Pomfret School, CT
Portsmouth Abbey School, RI
Presbyterian Pan-American School, TX
Principia School, MO
Proctor Academy, NH
Purnell School for Girls, NJ (PRG)
Putney School, VT

Q-R

Rabun Gap-Nacoochee School, GA
Randolph-Macon Academy, VA
Randolph School, AL
Riverside Military Academy, GA (PRB)
Rock Point School, VT
Rocky Mountain Academy, ID
Rosarian Academy, FL (PRG)
Routt High School, IL

S

Sacred Heart High School, MA (PRG)
Sacred Heart Preparatory School, CA
St. Albans School, DC (PRB)
St. Andrew's School, DE; FL; GA; RI
St. Andrew's-Sewanee School, TN
St. Anne's-Belfield School, VA
St. Camillus Academy, KY
St. Catherine's School, VA (PRG)
St. Cyril Academy, PA (PRG)
St. Francis High School, HI (PRG)
St. Francis High School, NY (PRB)
St. George's School, RI
St. James School, MD
St. John Bosco High School, CA (PRB)
St. Johnsbury Academy, VT
St. John's College High School, DC (PRB)
St. John's Military Academy, WI (PRB)
St. John's Military Academy, KS (PRB)
St. John's Preparatory School, MA (PRB)
St. John's Priory School, MN
St. Margaret's School, VA (PRG)
St. Mark's School, MA
St. Mary's Academy, IL (PRG)
St. Mary's College Prep, NC (PRG)
St. Mary's Hall, TX

St. Mary's High School, ND
St. Mary's Preparatory School, MI (PRB)
St. Michael's Prep Boarding High School, CA (PRB)
St. Paul's Lutheran High School, MO
St. Paul's School, NH
St. Scholastica Academy, CO (PRG)
St. Stanislaus College High School, MS (PRB)
St. Stephen's Episcopal School, TX
St. Thomas Academy, MN (PRB)
St. Thomas More School, CT (PRB)
St. Timothy's School, MD (PRG)
Salem Academy, NC (PRG)
Salisbury School, CT (PRB)
San Domenico School, CA (PRG)
Sandy Spring Friends School, MD
San Marcos Baptist Academy, TX
San Pasqual SDA Academy, CA
Santa Catalina School, CA (PRG)
Scattergood Friends School, IA
Seabury Hall, HI
Selwyn School, TX
Shady Side Academy, PA
Shattuck-St. Mary's School, MN
Shenandoah Valley Academy, VA
Solebury School, PA
South Kent School, CT
Southwestern Academy, CA
Squaw Valley Academy, CA
Stevenson School, CA
Stoneleigh-Burnham School, MA (PRG)
Stony Brook School, NY
Storm King School, NY
Stratton Mountain School, VT
Stuart Hall, VA (PRG)
Subiaco Academy, AR (PRB)
Suffield Academy, CT
Sunshine Bible Academy, SD

T-U-V

Tabor Academy, MA
Taft School, CT
Tallulah Falls School, GA
Tandem School, VA
Texas Military Institute, TX
Thacher School, CA
Thomas Jefferson School, MO
Thomas More Preparatory-Marian, KS
Tilton School, NH
Trinity Pawling School, NY (PRB)
Union Springs Academy, NY
Valley Catholic High School, OR (PRG)
Valley Forge Military Academy, PA (PRB)
Verde Valley School, AZ
Vermont Academy, VT
Vershire School, VT
Villanova Prep School, CA
Villa Walsh Academy, NJ (PRG)
Virginia Episcopal School, VA
Vivian Webb School, CA (PRG)

W-X-Y-Z

Walnut Hill School, MA (PRG)
Wasatch Academy, UT
Wayland Academy, WI
Webb School, The, TN
Webb School of California, CA (PRB)
Wentworth Military Academy, MO (PRB)
West Coast Talmudical School, CA (PRB)
Western Reserve Academy, OH
Westminster School, CT
West Nottingham Academy, MD
Westover School, CT (PRG)
Westtown School, PA
Whiteman School, CO
White Mountain School, NH
Wilbraham & Monson Academy, MA
Williston Northampton School, MA
Winchendon School, MA
Woodberry Forest School, VA (PRB)
Woodhall School, CT (PRB)
Woodlands Academy of the Sacred Heart, IL (PRG)
Woodside Priory School, CA
Woodward Academy, GA
Woolman School, CA
Wooster School, CT
Worcester Academy, MA
Wyoming Seminary, PA